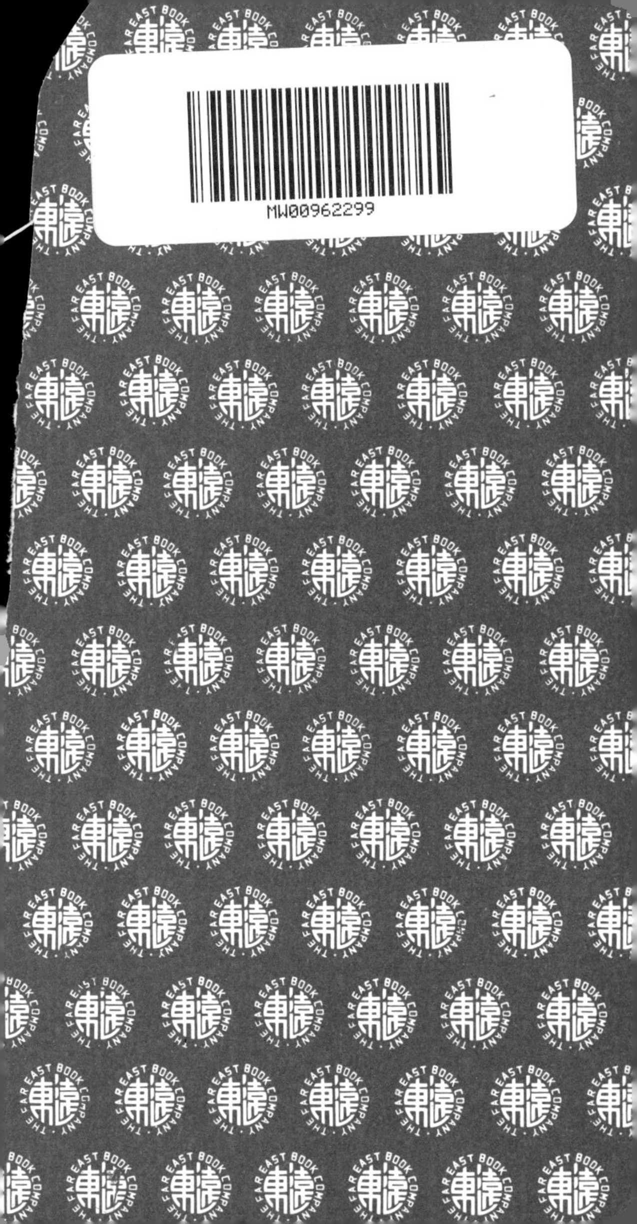
MW00962299
THE FAR EAST BOOK COMPANY
遠東

FAR EAST EVERYDAY ENGLISH-CHINESE DICTIONARY

遠東常用英漢辭典

Editor in Chief

Liang Shih-Chiu

主編　梁　實　秋

編輯者

遠東圖書公司編審委員會

遠東圖書公司印行

THE FAR EAST BOOK CO., LTD.

TAIPEI, TOKYO, HONG KONG

NEW YORK

Printed by The Far East Book Co., Ltd.

Taipei, Tokyo, Hong Kong

New York

序　言

遠東英漢大辭典，刊行於六十四年十月，因爲內容相當豐富，頗爲一般讀者所樂用。但是有一個不可克服的缺點，內容旣富，篇幅必多，體積旣大，不便取携。浦家麟先生就商於余，謂欲再編袖珍本之英漢辭典，收集單字約十萬以應另一部分讀者之需要，於是擬訂幾項原則，交由本公司編輯部同人負責編纂。

1. 以遠東英漢大辭典爲藍本。
2. 刪去部分例句。
3. 盡量保存可供日常翻檢之單字。
4. 盡量添入新字。

此項工作進行歷時將近三年，稿凡數易，以期斟酌於至當。參加工作者爲陳紹鵬、王進興、劉璉、陳銘鋭、張仲銘、張寶燕、鄭瑞玲、鄧樂然等數十位先生，而由洪傳田先生主持其事。單字之選擇，內容之增刪，頗費周章，其中艱苦不可盡述。余旣樂觀厥成，爰綴數言爲序。

梁實秋

編輯體例

1. 本辭典所收單字約十萬，新穎常用爲選字之標準。釋義，常用字力求完備，一般字則以精簡爲原則。所有單字，包括人名、地名、略字、複合字、字首、字尾，均依字母順序統一編排。

2. 常用字：特別着重者約9,000。初中程度應熟悉者約2,000，字旁標‡。高中程度應熟悉者約7,000，字旁標*。常用字酌加成語及例句。

例：**‡a·bout** 〔ə'baut; ə'baut〕 *prep.* ①關於；對於。Tell me something *about* your trip. 告訴我一些關於你旅行的情形。… —*adv.* ①將近。Supper is *about* ready. 晚飯就快預備好了。… —*adj.* ①在活動着。Few people were *about* on the streets. 街上的人很少。… ***all about*** 所有關於。We know *all about* it. 我們盡知一切。… ***what*** (or ***how***) ***about*** 關於…如何？My little dog is very clever, *what* (or *how*) *about* yours? 我的小狗甚爲聰明，你的如何？

lone·some** 〔'lonsəm; 'lounsəm〕 *adj.*, **-som·er, -som·est.** 孤單寂寞的（較 lonely 淒涼的意味更濃）。*lonesome* surroundings. 孤寂的環境。by*** (or ***on***) ***one's lonesome*** 〖俗〗單獨。She went walking *by her lonesome.* 她獨自去散步。—**ly,** *adv.* —**ness,** *n.*

3. 美英歧異：英語在若干方面，美國與英國頗有歧異。例如字的拼法（humor, humour），字的讀音（process），字的意義（elevator, lift; cracker, biscuit）等。本辭典以美國用法爲主，但亦兼顧英國習慣，必要時，且附加說明。

例：**‡lift** 〔lɪft; lift〕 *v.t.* ①舉起；…。—*n.* ①高舉；…。④〖英〗電梯。…。〖注意〗電梯 **lift** 爲英語，**elevator** 爲美語。

4. 音節及注音：本辭典單字之分音節，採用圓點，不用傳統之短橫，以免與連字符（hyphen）相混。

例：**a·ble-bod·ied** 〔'ebḷ'bɑdɪd; 'eibl'bɔdid〕 *adj.* 强健的。an *able-bodied* man. 壯丁。

單字之由二個以上之獨立字組合而成者爲複合字。組成複合字之各字於本辭典中已另列專條者，不分音節不注音。但如複合字中有部分未另列專條且讀法特殊者，則分音節並注音；至已列專條之部分，其注音則以"～"表示之。

例：**hula hoop** 呼拉圈（一種套在身上扭腰旋轉用的塑膠圈）。

ar·se·ni·ous acid 〔ɑr'sɪnɪəs～; ɑː'siːnjəs～〕 亞砒酸。

5. 字形變化：凡名詞之數（number），動詞之主要部分（principal parts），與形容詞或副詞之比較（comparison）爲不規則或在拼法上易生錯誤者，均分別標示，至規則變化者，則一概從略。

例：**au·to·bus** 〔'ɔtoˌbʌs; 'ɔːtoubʌs〕 *n.*, *pl.* **-bus·es, -bus·ses.** 〖俚〗公共汽車。

***a·bide** 〔ə'baɪd; ə'baid〕 *v.*, **a·bode** 〔ə'bod; ə'boud〕 or **a·bid·ed, a·bid·ing.** —*v.i.* ①居住；居留。—*v.t.* ①容忍；忍受。…。

‡well[1] 〔wɛl; wel〕 *adv.*, **bet·ter, best,** *adj.*, **bet·ter, best,** *n.* …。

6. 釋義：本辭典單字之釋義，如同一單字可用作二種以上詞類者，則按其詞類分別列舉。又同一詞類兼有數義者，爲便加插例句或成語，均分別以阿拉伯數字標出。

例：**‡ben·e·fit** 〔'bɛnəfɪt; 'benifit〕 *n.*, *v.*, **-fit·ed, -fit·ing.** —*n.* ①利益；裨益。This is for your *benefit.* 這是爲你的利益。②恩惠。He received *benefits* from his father-in-law. 他接受了他岳父的恩惠。③善舉；救濟金。***benefit of the doubt*** 在未證實前先假定其爲真或無罪。***for one's benefit*** 目的在使某人產生某種預期的反應。—*v.t.* 裨益；有益於。He is *benefited* by your advice. 他受惠於你的勸告。—*v.i.* 獲益。

但爲節省篇幅計，同一單字各不同詞性之釋義用語相同，或雖略有不同而不同之處可用括弧表明者，則合併之。

例：**a·glow** 〔ə'glo; ə'glou〕 *adv. & adj.* 發紅地（的）；興奮地（的）。

Is·lam·ite 〔'ɪsləmˌaɪt; 'izləmait〕 *n.*, *adj.* 回教徒（的）。

單字之釋義，有僅用於俚語、俗語，或為某種科學技藝等之專門用語者，概於各該項釋義前標明，以助理解。

例: **acid trip**〖俚〗用迷幻藥（LSD）後之神志不清的感覺。

ab·skize〔æb'skaɪz; æb'skaiz〕*v.i.*〖美俗〗逃亡；逃脫。

au·toch·tho·nous〔ɔ'tɑkθənəs; ɔː'tɔkθənəs〕*adj.* ①=**autochthonal.** ②〖醫〗本處發生的。③〖心理〗自我產生之觀念但似外來的。

access time〖電腦〗進出時間。

一單字之釋義或其某一釋義與另一單字完全相同者，為節省篇幅，逕注以該另一單字，而以等號表示之。

例: **doc·u·men·tal**〔ˌdɑkjə'mɛntḷ; ˌdɔkju'mentl〕*adj.* =**documentary.**

bi·om·e·try〔baɪ'ɑmətrɪ; bai'ɔmitri〕*n.* ①壽命測定。②=**biometrics.**

為使語義或單字之用法更臻明確，本辭典對事物之譯名常加解釋，對動詞之主語或受詞常加補足，對形容詞或副詞所修飾之對象常加說明，凡此解釋或指名之詞語，均置於括弧內。

例: **jus·sive**〔'dʒʌsɪv; 'dʒʌsiv〕*adj.*〖文法〗表示命令的。—*n.* 命令字、形態、或語態（此語態祇限於 Semitic 語言）。

i·so·bar〔'aɪsəˌbɑr; 'aisoubɑː〕*n.* ①〖氣象〗等壓線（在地圖上所畫表示氣壓相等之線）。②〖理化〗同量素。

la·gn(i)appe〔læn'jæp; læn'jæp〕*n.*〖美方〗（交易時附送給顧客之）小贈品。

ac·ti·vate〔'æktəˌvet; 'æktiveit〕*v.t.*, **-vat·ed, -vat·ing.** ①刺激；使產生活動。… ⑤灌氣於（水溝、汚物等）以使淨化。…。

7. 某單字在某釋義上常與另一字如介系詞、副詞等連用時，即在該釋義下將該字寫於〖 〗中。

例: **ab·hor·rent**〔əb'hɔrənt; əb'hɔrənt〕*adj.* ①懷憎惡之念的；嫌惡的〖of〗. I am *abhorrent* of it. 我嫌惡它。②極端相反的；悖逆的〖to〗. to be *abhorrent* to one. 與某人不投合。③性質有別的；不相容的〖from〗. ④令人憎惡或痛恨的。—**ly**, *adv.*

8. 某釋義在使用時應作單數、複數、作單數解、作複數解、加冠詞、或大小寫，即於該釋義前以 (*sing.*), (*pl.*), (作 *sing.* 解), (作 *pl.* 解), (the-) 等標示。

例: **ac·cou·ter·ment**〔ə'kutəmənt; ə'kuːtəmənt〕*n.* ①（*pl.*）衣著；服裝。②（*pl.*）（武器、軍服以外之）裝備；配備。③穿；著。（英亦作 **accoutrement**）

***e·co·nom·ics**〔ˌikə'nɑmɪks, ˌɛk-; ˌiːkə'nɔmiks, ˌek-〕*n.* ①(作 *sing.* 解) 經濟學。②(作 *pl.* 解)財務上的考慮；經濟上的要素。What are the *economics* of such a project? 這一計畫的經濟要素何在（經濟上有何利弊）?

***globe**〔glob; gloub〕*n.*, *v.*, **globed, glob·ing.** —*n.*①球；球狀物。②（常 the-）地球。…。

at·man〔'ɑtmən; 'ɑːtmən〕*n.*〖印度教〗①氣息。②生命之本源。③個人之靈魂；自我。④（A-）大我；宇宙我。⑤（A-）梵天。

Ben·e·dick〔'bɛnəˌdɪk; 'benidik〕*n.*①莎士比亞 *Much Ado About Nothing* 劇中之一獨身男子。②（b-）新婚者；有妻室者（=benedict）.

9. 括弧（ ）尚用以表示：以其中之字取代前面的字；成語及例句中可予節略而不致改變其意義的字等。

例: ***go back on*** (or ***upon***) 違背（諾言等）；背棄；食（言）。

go for a walk (***ride, swim, etc.***) 去散步（騎馬、游泳等）。

at (***the***) ***worst*** 在最壞的情形下。

10. 成語：成語（idioms）在語文中占極重要之地位，由單字結合而成之成語，常具有自身之特殊意義。本辭典對有關各單字之重要成語，均儘量蒐集，分別列於各該單字每一詞性的全部釋義及例句之後。多數成語，除解釋外更酌加例句，俾供參考。

例: **‡make**〔mek; meik〕*v.*, **made, mak·ing,** *n.* —*v.t.* ①做；…。—*v.i.* ①走動；…。***make a difference*** (***to***) 有關係；重要（= be of importance）. It doesn't *make any difference to* me. 這對我毫無關係。***make a fool of*** 愚弄。He *made a fool of* himself. 他自取愚弄（他自取嘲笑）。…。

11. 例句：辭典例句對於學者甚有幫助，可助理解，亦可爲作文造句之參考。例句宜多，尤宜精洽。本辭典例句極多，常用字更以一個定義附以一個或一個以上不同句型的例句爲原則。例句隨附於定義或成語之後，庶可得到實際用法的例證。本辭典不僅供給單字或成語之定義，並且指明某一字在某一定義下如何使用，在另一定義下又如何使用。定義或成語如無需加例句者，亦不强加。例句譯文以淺近白話爲主，有時亦用文言成語。

例：I would never *abandon* my friends. 我永遠不捨棄我的朋友。

Where there is a will there is a *way*.（諺）有志者事竟成。

例句以用完整句子爲主，有時亦只用短詞。

例：He's a very *learned* man. 他是一個很有學問的人。

a *learned* periodical. 學術性刊物。

例句以逐條列註爲原則，但爲節省篇幅計，遇有結構類似之數個例句，其共屬諸字則僅列其一，餘則置於括弧內，中文部分亦以同樣方式譯註。

例：**a·dopt·ed** 〔əˈdɑptɪd; əˈdɔptid〕 *adj.* ①收養的；過繼的。an *adopted* son (daughter). 養子（女）。…。

12. 略字一律將原字拼出，有常見之譯名者，則加列譯名。數略字相鄰，則接排以省篇幅。

例：**NBC, N.B.C.** National Broadcasting Corporation *or* Company.(美國)國家廣播公司。**NbE** north by east. **NbW** north by west. **N.C.** ① North Carolina. ②New Church. ....

13. 常見之略語，除註其原形外並加注音。

例：**we'll** 〔wil; wiːl〕 =**we shall; we will.**

14. 衍生字附於各單字後，其與該單字相同部分，原則上均以"—"代之，如省略後易於混淆者，則完全拼出。

例：***var·y** 〔ˈvɛrɪ; ˈvɛəri〕 *v.*, **var·ied, var·y·ing.** *—v.t.* ①改變；… **—var·i·er,** *n.* **—ing·ly,** *adv.*

15. 字彙中凡有闡釋必要者，如同義與反義之比較，正式與非正式之用法，標準與俚俗之差異，文法之規則與例外等，概列於該字之末，以〖注意〗或〖文法〗標明之。

例：**in·sig·ni·a** 〔ɪnˈsɪgnɪə; inˈsigniə〕 *n.* pl. of **insigne.** 徽章；勳章；標幟。〖注意〗**insignia** 雖爲複數形，但常用作單數，如 His *insignia* is a cross. 他的徽章是一個十字。有將 insignias 當 insignia 複數的用法，如 The PX sold all sorts of *insignias*. 該福利社有各種徽章出售。但嚴格說來，把 insignia 作單數用是錯的，因此，過去罕爲人用的單數形 insigne，現在其常用度又已漸增。

***noun** 〔naʊn; naun〕 *n.* 名詞。〖文法〗**noun** 爲人、動物、事物、地方等之名稱，通常分爲下列五類：**abstract noun.** 抽象名詞。**collective noun.** 集合名詞。**common noun.** 普通名詞。**material noun.** 物質名詞。**proper noun.** 專有名詞。…。

16. 外來語：英語中常用之外來語爲數甚多而來源不一。本辭典就錄入之外來語標明其來源，必要時，並舉出相當之英語，以資比較。

例：**a tem·po** 〔ɑˈtɛmpo; ɑːˈtempou〕〖義〗〖音樂〗恢復原來速度；還原速度。

ut in·fra 〔ʌtˈɪnfrə; ʌtˈinfrə〕〖拉〗如下（=as below).

音標說明

㈠ 前　言

本辭典係採"國際音標"（International Phonetic Alphabet 簡稱 IPA）注音，美英發音兼注。美國注音根據 John Samuel Kenyon 和 Thomas Albert Knott 二氏 的美國發音字典 (A Pronouncing Dictionary of American English)；英國注音根據 Daniel Jones 第十二版的英語發音字典 (Everyman's English Pronouncing Dictionary).

爲使讀者對本辭典的注音有較爲詳細的瞭解起見，對於 K.K. 音標與 Jones 音標之異同、各符號所代表的音質、外來語的音標、以及其他有關注音的種種問題，本文特爲詳細說明。茲先說明

兩點:

(一)這篇說明是給一般人看的，不是供專家研究的；是想用通俗淺易的方法，幫助一般人瞭解、鑑別、學習各種符號所代表之聲音，因此祇是在不引起字義混淆的原則下，盡量求其精確，這從語音學專家的眼光看來，當然是不够的。不過一般人學發音，祇是求“音”與“義”之間的連繫，和“音”與“音”之間的區別，聲音間之差別如果不致使字義發生混淆便够了。

(二)在說明符號所代表的聲音這一點上，我們採用的是比較方法。常聽人說，要想學好英文，必須完全拋棄本國語言的發音及思想方式，才能徹底接受英語中的語音及構思的方法。不過這對於自幼生長在中國，本國語言已根深蒂固，已變成其第二天性的一般人來說，簡直是不可能的。就拿發音來說，不但必然會受他們自己的方言或鄉音的影響，而且在不知不覺中，也必然會用他們所熟悉的語言相互參照，相互比較。這種比較往往是雜亂的，無意識的，不得要領的，但却也是無法阻止的。如果能把這兩國語音做一種淺顯的分析，告訴他們那些是相同的，那些是相近的，那些是相異的，那些是難學的，對於一般人可能不無幫助。

(二) 國 際 音 標

有些人認爲只有 Daniel Jones 所用的才是國際音標，而 Kenyon 和 Knott 兩氏所用的則不是。其實，這是一種誤解。事實上，Daniel Jones 和 Kenyon & Knott 所用的都是國際音標，不過前者所代表的是英國音，後者所代表的是美國音。由於二者都是國際音標，因此，在符號上除少數外，絕大多數仍是相同的。

國際音標係“國際語音學會”(International Phonetic Association——成立於1886年)於1888年所制定，它的主要原則是“一音一符，一符一音”。其最大的特點是全世界任何一種語言，都可以用它來注音。目前採用國際音標注音的，已有德、法、荷蘭、義大利、西班牙、葡萄牙、希臘等四十多種語言。英國語言學家 Daniel Jones 教授於1917年出版著名的“英語發音字典”(Everyman's English Pronouncing Dictionary)，係採用國際音標注出英國南部的語音，嗣後我國學術界競相採用。相習數十年，Jones 注音，已爲一般人所熟悉。

但是最近若干年來，一般學校所教授的英語，實際上是美語 (American English)，這有其學術上的理由，也有其事實上的需要，我們不擬在這裏細作分析。由於一般人學到的，聽到的，用到的，講到的，多半是美音，而不是或很少是英音，而美音與英音之間，有些地方亦頗有差異，如果字典單採 Jones 國際音標注音，則讀出來的字音僅是英國的語音，與一般人所聽的，所講的，所學的美音頗不相同。爲符合現實需要，本辭典乃兼採 Jones 音標及美國兩位語音學家，John Samuel Kenyon 氏與 Thomas Albert Knott 氏在美語發音字典 (A Pronouncing Dictionary of American English) 所用的國際音標注音。這兩位語音學家所用的音標，簡稱“K.K. 音標”。本辭典之所以把兩種注音同時並列，目的在使熟習美音者可以應用，熟習英音者也可以應用。

(三) 二種音標之比較與符號說明

下面是一張包括 K.K. 注音 (美音的國際音標) 和 Jones 注音 (英音的國際音標) 的音標對照表。

I. 元 音 (Vowels)

	K.K.	Jones	Key Words
1	i	iː	bee 〔bi; biː〕
2	ɪ	i	hit 〔hɪt; hit〕
3	ɪ(r)	(iə)	here 〔hɪr; hiə〕
4	ɛ	e	yes 〔jɛs; jes〕
5	ɛ(r)	(ɛə)	there 〔ðɛr; ðɛə〕
6	æ	æ	sat 〔sæt; sæt〕
7	a	a	參看說明 7.

8	ɑ	ɑː	palm 〔pɑm; pɑːm〕
9	ɒ		參看說明 9.
10	ɑ	ɔ	ox 〔ɑks; ɔks〕
11	ɔ	ɔː	law 〔lɔ; lɔː〕
12	(o, ə)	o(o*u*)	參看說明 12.
13	ʊ	u	book 〔bʊk; buk〕
14	u	uː	tool 〔tul; tuːl〕
15	ʌ	ʌ	cut 〔kʌt; kʌt〕
16	ɜ	əː	bird 〔bɜd; bəːd〕 (參看說明 16.)
17	ɝ	(əː)	bird 〔bɝd; bəːd〕
18	ɚ	(ə)	better 〔ˈbɛtɚ; ˈbetə〕
19	ə	ə	參看說明 19.
20	e	ei	name 〔nem; neim〕
21	o	ou	no 〔no; nou〕
22	aɪ	ai	my 〔maɪ; mai〕
23	aʊ	au	out 〔aʊt; aut〕
24	ɔɪ	ɔi	boy 〔bɔɪ; bɔi〕
25	(ɪr)	iə	參看說明 25.
26	(ɛr)	ɛə	參看說明 26.
27	(or, ɔr)	ɔə	參看說明 27.
28	(ʊr)	uə	參看說明 28.
29	ju	juː	use 〔juz; juːz〕
30	ɪu		參看說明 30.

註：㈠按國際音標之體例，列有"雙元音"（diphthong）一項，上面這張表的 Jones 音標一欄中從第20組以下皆是雙元音。但對於這點，Jones 與 K.K. 並不一致，像20, 21等組，K.K. 音標並不認爲是雙元音，故本表不將雙元音另列成一項。不過要注意，每一個雙元音祇是一個發音單位，等於一個元音（vowel)，所以像 out 〔aʊt; aut〕這種字，是單音節而不是雙音節。

㈡音標右側之〔ː〕爲"長音記號"。Jones 音標像第1、8、11、14、16等組，都有此記號，但此記號，K.K. 音標除少數字外，概不使用。

㈢上表第3、5、12、17、18、25、26、27、28等組中所加之圓括弧，係表示該種音標本無相對應之符號，不過實際發音時，等於或近於括弧內之音。

㈣下面的符號說明，其號碼與上表中所列之號碼相對應。讀者如對某一組符號發生疑難，即可參看下面說明。

符號說明

1. i, iː Jones 音標有〔ː〕記號。此記號爲長音記號，但在此及以下的第8, 11, 14, 16等組中，它不只表示"量"的延長，同時也表示"質"的變化。K.K. 音標在不致引起字義的混淆時，一律不加此記號。本組符號所代表之音，相當於國音字母中之"ㄧ"。

2. ɪ, i 注意，K.K. 是大楷體，Jones 音標是小楷體。本組符號所代表之音介於國音字母"ㄧ"與"ㄝ"之間，中國國語中無此聲音，故不易讀準，須特別練習始能分辨。

3. ɪ(r), (iə)　K.K. 音標無特別符號; Jones 音標以 iə 表示（請注意此組音標與25組音標在美音中的不同點)。

4. ɛ, e　本組符號所代表之音，相當於國音字母中之"ㄝ"。

5. ɛ(r), (ɛə)　K.K. 無特別記號; Jones 音標以 ɛə 表示之（參看說明26)。

6. æ, æ　此卽所謂 a 的短音，K.K. 與 Jones 之符號同。本組所代表的音，介於國音字母"ㄝ"與"ㄚ"之間，中國國語中無此音，故不甚易讀，須特別練習。

7. a, a　本組符號所代表之音，介於6、8組之間。在 K.K. 及 Jones 音標中除以之組成雙元音外，不單獨使用。K.K. 音標，原注此音者現已化爲 æ 或 ɑ 音，如: pass〔pæs, pɑs〕, half〔hæf, hɑf〕. 惟本辭典注外來語時，仍採用此音。

8. ɑ, ɑː　K.K. 音標無長音記號（參看說明 1)，本組符號所代表之音，相當於國音字母中之"ㄚ"。

9. ɒ　在K.K. 音標中，本符號代表之音介於第 8 組與第11 組之間，爲不穩定音，只在表示某些地方對某些字之另一種讀法時使用，如: moss〔mɔs, mɒs〕等。此音又稱爲"歷史上的短 **o** 音" (historical short **o**).

10. ɑ, ɔ　這一組音符，須說明兩點:

(a)現代美語已將此音化入第 8 組音之中，故 K. K. 音標不另造符號，逕以第 8 組之 ɑ 表示之。

(b)Jones 音標中之 ɔ 雖與 ɑ 相當，但發音却不同，仍保留 "historical short **o**" 之聲音（參看說明 9)。Jones 中之 ɔ 音，在美音中已分別化入第 8 組與第11組之中; 如: job〔dʒɑb;dʒɔb〕, cor·o·net〔ˈkɔrənɪt, ˈkɑr–; ˈkɔrənit, –rn̩it〕.

11. ɔ, ɔː　注意，K.K. 音標無長音記號（參看說明1)。本組符號所代表之音，英音與美音稍異。英音發音時，嘴唇作圓形，舌根下壓，其音與21組（除去後一音素）之音相近，美音發音時，與國音字母中之"ㄛ"雖不全同，却很類似。

12. (o, ə), o(o*u*)　卽所謂"**o**"的半長音，Jones 音標中把第21組雙元音中之後一音素略去卽得此音。K.K. 音標中無相當之符號，係化入 o 或 ə 之中。如: po·lite〔pəˈlaɪt; po*u*ˈlait〕, No·vem·ber〔noˈvɛmbɚ; no*u*ˈvembə〕, tour〔tʊr; tuə, toə〕等。

13. ʊ, u　K.K. 音標是大楷體，Jones 音標是小楷體。中國國語中無此音，須特別練習始能讀準。學時應注意不可把這一組與第14組的音相混，或誤認爲係第14組音之縮短。

14. u, uː　K.K. 音標中無長音記號（參看說明 1)，本組符號所代表之音，雖與國音字母中之"ㄨ"頗爲相似，惟不全同，讀時須將嘴唇略向後收縮。

15. ʌ, ʌ　K.K. 與 Jones 符號相同，惟目前美語中有與第19組之〔ə〕合併的趨勢。

16. ɜ, əː　這一組符號所代表的音在英音發音中重要，但在美音發音中並不重要。美音發音時將第17組中之 r 尾音去掉卽得這種聲音。K.K. 字典中只用它注某些字的另一種讀法。

17. ɝ, (əː)　美音與英音的主要區別之一，卽美音帶有 r 尾音，英音不帶 r 尾音。Jones 音標無與K.K. 音標相當之符號。əː 與 ɝ 雖接近，但無 r 尾音。本組符號相當於國音字母中之"ㄦ"。

18. ɚ, (ə)　本組符號中，美音也是帶有 r 尾音之音符，與第17組之讀法相同，不過祇用於"非重音節" (unaccented syllable) 中。Jones 音標中也無相當之符號，以 ə 表示，無 r 尾音。

19. ə, ə　本組爲"輕音符號" (schwa)，又稱 "中性元音" (neutral vowel). 本組符號所代表之音，介於國音字母的"ㄜ"與"ㄚ"之間。

20. e, ei　本組符號應注意的是 Jones 音標是雙元音，K.K. 音標不是。這卽所謂字母 **a** 的長音，但K.K. 認爲這種音雖常常是，但並非絕對是"雙元音"(diphthong)，而且卽使是 "雙元音" (從一個元音滑至另一個元音)，也不祇代表一種音，可能是 eɪ 音，也可能是 ɛɪ 或 ɛe 音，他們認爲根據語音學的原則，用一個符號 e 卽可代表這些可能的音了。本組符號所代表之音，相當於國音字母中的"ㄟ"音。

21. o, ou　本組符號 K.K. 只用一個元音表示，Jones 用雙元音符號，理由與第20組相同。本組符號所代表之音，相當於國音字母中之"ㄡ"音。

22. aɪ, ai　K.K. 與 Jones 之區別在於一個是大楷體的 ɪ，一個是小楷體的 i; 本組符號所代表之音，相當於國音字母中之"ㄞ"音。

23. aʊ, au　K.K. 與 Jones 之區別，在於一個是大楷體的 ʊ，一個是小楷體的 u; 本組符號所代表之音相當於國音字母中之"ㄠ"。國人學習英語時對此音無困難，惟須留意勿與11組之音混淆。

24. ɔɪ, ɔi　K. K. 與 Jones 之區別，一個是大楷體的 ɪ，一個是小楷體的 i；中國國語中無此音，它代表第11組加第 2 組的聲音，讀時重音在前，讀作:〔ˈɔɪ; ˈɔi〕.

25. iə　Jones 這個符號與第 3 組同。須稍加解釋: iə 當作 diphthong，卽把它看作一個發音單位時，K. K. 音標沒有與它完全相等之符號。如令與其相等，後面須附 r 音，如: mere〔mɪr; miə〕. K. K. 符號中，與它完全相當之符號，不作雙元音看待，而是兩個元音，也就是說是兩個音節，如: bac·te·ri·a〔bækˈtɪrɪə; bækˈtiəriə〕.

26. ɛə　Jones 這個符號與第 5 組同，其情形與第25組一樣，當作雙元音時，K. K. 之相當符號後面附有 r 音；如: dare〔dɛr; dɛə〕；與其完全相當之符號，皆是兩個元音之合併，而非視爲發音單位之"雙元音"。

27. ɔə　與第25組情形同，Jones 視爲雙元音，K. K. 之相當符號有 r 尾音；如: four〔fɔr; fɔə〕.

28. uə　與第25組情形同，Jones 視爲雙元音，K. K. 之相當符號有 r 尾音；如: tour〔tʊr; tuə〕.

29. ju, juː　Jones 音標有長音符號，K. K. 音標無。此非字母 **u** 本音之延長，實爲輔音加元音之混合音。本組音，因係"輔音加元音"之混合音，故以元音爲主，讀時應加重其中之〔u; uː〕音成分，前面之〔j; j〕音成分，讀時輕輕滑過卽可。

30. ɪu　K. K. 音標中此符號爲 ju 之變體，讀時讀重前面之 ɪ 音（ju 須讀重後面之 u 音）。在 K. K. 字典中，祇把它標注某些字之另一種讀法。

II. 輔　音 (Consonants)

	K. K.	Jones	Key Words
1	b	b	bob〔bɑb; bɔb〕
2	d	d	dad〔dæd; dæd〕
3	f	f	fife〔faɪf; faif〕
*4	g	g	gag〔gæg; gæg〕
5	h	h	high〔haɪ; hai〕
6	k	k	kick〔kɪk; kik〕
7	l	l	lull〔lʌl; lʌl〕
8	l̩	l̩	national〔ˈnæʃənl̩; ˈnæʃənl̩〕
9	m	m	mom〔mɑm; mɔm〕
10	m̩	m̩	參看說明 10
11	n	n	noon〔nun; nuːn〕
12	n̩	n̩	pardoner〔ˈpɑrdn̩ɚ; ˈpɑːdn̩ə〕
13	p	p	pop〔pɑp; pɔp〕
14	r	r	red〔rɛd; red〕 rare〔rɛr; rɛə〕
15	s	s	souse〔saʊs; saus〕
16	t	t	tat〔tæt; tæt〕
17	v	v	valve〔vælv; vælv〕
18	w	w	way〔we; wei〕
19	j	j	yet〔jɛt; jet〕
20	z	z	zones〔zonz; zounz〕
21	ŋ	ŋ	sing〔sɪŋ; siŋ〕
22	ʃ	ʃ	shed〔ʃɛd; ʃed〕, lash〔læʃ; læʃ〕
23	ʧ	ʧ	church〔ʧɝʧ; ʧəːʧ〕

24	ʒ	ʒ	pleasure 〔ˈplɛʒə; ˈpleʒə〕
25	dʒ	dʒ	judge 〔dʒʌdʒ; dʒʌdʒ〕
26	θ	θ	thin 〔θɪn; θin〕, path 〔pæθ; pɑːθ〕
27	ð	ð	thither 〔ˈðɪðɚ; ˈðiðə〕
28	hw	hw	why 〔hwaɪ; (h)wai〕

(帶*者表示二種音標所用之符號不同)

符號說明

1. b　二種符號相同，所代表之音近似國音字母中之"ㄅ"。
2. d　二種符號相同，所代表之音近似國音字母中之"ㄉ"。
3. f　二種符號相同，發音方法與國音字母中之"ㄈ"相同。

*4. g，ɡ　K. K. 與 Jones 符號不同，所代表之音近似國音字母中之"ㄍ"。

5. h　二種符號相同，所代表之音雖與國音字母中之"ㄏ"有相似之處，却頗不相同。ㄏ爲磨擦音，而 h 爲喉音，呼氣的成分重而無舌根與硬顎之磨擦，應多加體會與練習。
6. k　二種符號相同，發音方法與國音字母中之"ㄎ"相同。
7. l　二種符號相同，中國國語中無此音，學者應注意:
   (a)易與 r 相混淆——發 l 時舌尖在上牙齦處，發 r 時舌尖向上捲曲。
   (b)易與 n 相混淆——l 爲口腔音，n 爲鼻音。
8. l̩　二種符號相同，第8、第10、第12三組稱爲"音節性的輔音" (syllabic consonants)，須特別注意:
   (a)這三組符號稱爲"音節性的輔音"，因爲有時它們無須與元音相拼，而單獨、或與其他輔音相拼構成音節，如: national 〔ˈnæʃənl̩; ˈnæʃənl̩〕一字中之第三個音節。
   (b)這三組符號的寫法，K. K. 與 Jones 注音中，均在原字母下面加〔̩〕。
   (c)這三組符號可認爲係省去了一個"中性元音" (neutral vowel)〔ə〕，故其所代表之音與加入一個中性元音相同。如: oval 一字可作〔ˈovl̩; ˈouvl̩〕亦可作〔ˈovəl; ˈouvəl〕.
   (d)這種音節性的輔音，如在一個音節的末尾，則分辨甚易，故 Jones (不是 K. K.) 音標有將字母下面的〔̩〕取消之趨勢，如: cotton 一字 Jones 字典作〔ˈkɔtn〕(n 下無小方塊)。但不易分辨之場合仍予保留，如: cottoning 一字作〔ˈkɔtn̩iŋ〕(n 下有小方塊，故爲三個音節，此時如無小方塊，則變成兩個音節了)。
9. m　二種符號相同，所代表之音近乎國音字母中之"ㄇ"，但最後唇不張開，又極似臺語"點"之尾音。
10. m̩　二種符號相同，爲音節性的輔音，詳見說明 8；如: stop'em 〔ˈstɑpm̩; ˈstɔpm̩〕(按 stop'em 爲 stop them 之縮寫)。
11. n　二種符號相同。所代表之音，在元音之後爲國音字母中"ㄣ"音之後一半，卽舌面抵住上顎所發之鼻音。在元音之前近似國音字母中之"ㄋ"音。
12. n̩　二種符號相同，爲音節性的輔音，詳見說明 8。
13. p　二種符號相同，發音方法與國音字母中之"ㄆ"相同。
14. r　二種符號相同。在音節之末尾時，美音發國音字母中之"ㄦ"音。Jones 音標中，除注含 r 尾音之外來語外，無 r 尾音，而以 ə (schwa) 表示之。但如 r 音後接有元音，則仍保留 r 音。如order of merit 〔ˈɔːdər əv ˈmerit〕, bear up 〔ˈbɛər ˈʌp〕. 在音節之開頭時，中國國語中無此音。
15. s　二種符號相同。所代表之音近乎國音字母中之"ㄙ"。
16. t　二種符號相同。所代表之音近乎國音字母中之"ㄊ"。
17. v　二種符號相同。將第 3 組之 f 音加聲帶振動發出聲來卽成此音。
18. w　二種符號相同。這一組與下一組之音又稱爲"半元音" (semi-vowels).發音時嘴唇作圓形，舌之位置與發第13或14組元音時相同，很像國音字母中之"ㄨ"。
19. j　二種符號相同。本組亦稱爲 "半元音"。 中國國語中無此音，就一般人言，可把它讀作國音字母中之"ㄧ"，雖不精確，但亦不致發生字義上之混淆。

20. z　二種符號相同，將第15組之 s 音加聲帶振動發出聲來卽成此音。

21. ŋ　二種符號相同。此音爲國音字母"ㄥ"音之後一半，卽舌根抵住上顎所發之鼻音（可與第11組比較）。

22. ʃ　本組符號，二種相同。中國國語中無此音，讀時宜特別注意勿與"ㄕ"混淆。ㄕ以舌尖後接近硬顎，而 ʃ 則以舌面向硬顎接近，舌尖反而向下。

23. ʧ　本組符號，二種相同。中國國語中無此音，讀時宜特別注意勿與"ㄔ"混淆。ㄔ以舌尖捲回抵硬顎，而ʧ則以舌面向硬顎接近，舌尖反而向下。

24. ʒ　本組符號，二種相同。中國國語中無此音，讀時宜特別注意勿與"ㄖ"混淆。ㄖ以舌尖後接近硬顎，而 ʒ 則以舌面向硬顎接近，舌尖反而向下。

25. dʒ　本組符號，二種相同。中國國語中無此音，讀時宜特別注意勿與"ㄓ"混淆。ㄓ以舌尖捲回抵硬顎，而dʒ則以舌面向硬顎接近，舌尖反而向下。

26. θ　二種符號相同。本組符號所代表之音，中國國語中沒有，須將牙齒輕咬舌尖而發，忌與 s 相混淆。

27. ð　二種符號相同。此組發音法與第26組相同，惟爲有音收束，忌與 z 混淆。

28. hw　二種符號相同。爲 h 與 w 之合併，惟 h 單獨時爲無聲輔音，在此 hw 則爲有聲輔音。

註：K. K. 及 D. J. 兩種音標之符號雖可個別對照，但就某一單字而言，其發音却無必然對等關係，如：schedule, K. K. 讀〔ˈskɛdʒʊl〕, D. J. 則讀〔ˈʃedjuːl〕. 蓋 K. K. 所注者係美國音，D. J. 所注者係英國音。

(四) 外來語之音標及說明

很多外來語已成爲英語的一部分。外來語之發音特別令人感到困擾。本辭典對少數仍無確定英語發音的外來語，只注外來語本身的讀法。對在意義和發音方面皆已英語化的外來語，則當作標準英語處理。

就實質上說，在不同的語言中，沒有兩個音是完全相同的。譬如說，有些人用法語讀法念 envelope 這個字，成爲〔ˈɑnvəˌlop; ˈɔnvəloup〕，其結果只有〔v〕和〔p〕兩音近似法語，〔l〕音和所有的母音皆與法語大不相同，而〔n〕音並不在法語之中，其所以如此，是因說話者在模仿外來語發音時，以他自己語言中最相近的發音來代替外來語發音之故。

雖然如此，爲了實際使用方便，某些符號仍可用以標注外來語之發音。

爲使學者明瞭本辭典中之外來語讀法的全豹，茲將其一般常用之音標及其代表之聲音說明於下：

1. x　二組符號相同，用小楷體之 x 表示。其所代表之音，係將舌根抵住上顎而發國音字母之"ㄏ"音。如：Bach〔bɑx; bɑːx〕.

2. l̥　二組符號相同，在字母下面加一小圈，主用於法語中，常用在一字之末尾而其前爲一無音之輔音。其發出之音幾乎輕到聽不見。如：debacle〔deˈbɑːkl̥; deiˈbɑːkl〕. 注意：凡音標之下面加小圈，皆屬於這一類。

3. r̥　係第 2 組之同類符號，主用於法語中，詳見第 2 組之說明。如：amour-propre〔amurˈprɔ̃pr̥; ˈæmuəˈprɔpr̥〕.

4. y　本組符號主用於德語與法語中，所代表之音卽國音字母中之"ㄩ"。如：a·per·çu〔ɑpɛrˈsy; ˌæpəːˈsjuː〕.

5. ϕ　本組符號主用於德語及法語中。嘴唇作圓形好像發〔o; ou〕時的樣子，而試圖發〔e;ei〕音，卽得此音。如：mi·lieu〔miˈljϕ; miljϕ〕.

6. œ　本組符號主用於德語及法語中。o 與 e 連寫在一起。嘴唇作圓形好像發〔ɔ; ɔː〕音的樣子，而試圖發〔æ; æ〕的音，卽得此音。如：Neuchâte〔nœʃɑˈtɛl; ˌnəːʃæˈtel〕.

7. ɔ̆, (ɔ)　本組符號爲 K. K. 音標所特有，Jones 以較爲近似之 ɔ 代替。嘴唇作圓形好像發〔ɔ;ɔː〕音的樣子，而試圖發〔ʌ; ʌ〕音，卽得此音。如：bonne〔bɔ̆n; bɔn〕.

8. æ̃, ɑ̃, õ, œ̃, ɛ̃, ɔ̃, etc.　本組符號用的地方很多，K. K. 和 Jones 音標都在字母之上方加～。本組所代表之音，表示原來之符號發鼻音。如：pension〔pɑ̃ˈsjõ; ˈpɑ̃ːŋsiɔ̃ːŋ〕. 應注意者：

(a) K. K. 與 Jones 注音，有時並不完全一致，從上面例子中可以看出。

(b) æ̃與 ɛ̃ 發音很相近。

(c) 例子中之長音符"ː"，參看下面有關長音符之說明。

9. a　二組符號相同，發音見元音符號說明 7。

(五) 本辭典有關發音之一般說明及體例

1. 每一單字有兩種注音，K. K. 音標在前，Jones 音標在後。兩種音標之間，用“;”分開。如: pick 〔pɪk; pik〕.
2. 爲節省篇幅起見，一字如有兩種讀法時，其相同部分省略。省略的地方一律用連字符(hyphen)“–”表示。如: mi·nute 〔məˈnjut, maɪ–; maiˈnjuːt, mi–〕.
3. 長音符號“ː”: Jones 音標中之元音 (iː, ɑː, ɔː, uː, əː) 皆有長音符號(參看元音符號說明 1)。K. K. 音標中，一般不用此符號。但爲表示某一外來語或某一符號須有較長之音量時，則加注之。如: Moliére 〔mɔ̃ˈljɛːr〕.
4. 區分音節之符號: K. K. 與 Jones 音標中，音節與音節之間通常以重音符號區分之: 無重音者，一般不用區分音節之符號，但如二音節之發音易於混淆時，K. K. 音標則置圓點“·”於二音節之間，如: Hawaii 〔həˈwɑ·i, həˈwaɪ·i〕; Jones 音標則置短橫“–”於二音節之間。如: Wiltshire 〔ˈwilt–ʃə〕, mousetrap 〔ˈmaus–træp〕.
5. 一字有兩種或兩種以上注音時，常用的在前，不常用的在後。如: Maori 的讀法有兩種: 〔ˈmaʊrɪ, ˈmɑrɪ; ˈmauri, ˈmɑːəri〕, 前者卽較常用，後者卽較不常用。
6. 重音 (stress)
   (a)主重音 (primary stress) 兩種音標皆加在音節之前上方，K. K. 的符號爲“ˈ”, Jones 的符號爲“ˈ”; 次重音 (secondary stress) 兩種音標皆加在音節之前下方，K. K. 的符號爲“ˏ”, Jones 的符號爲“ˌ”。如: ed·u·ca·tion 〔ˏɛdʒəˈkeʃən; ˌedjuˈkeiʃən〕.
   (b)二音節以上之字通常皆注有重音符號，但外來語之人名、地名等，雖屬二音節以上之字，仍有些不注重音符號。如: tae kwon do 〔tækwondo; tækwoundou〕.

略 語 表 (I)

adj.	adjective	形容詞	*poss.*	possessive	所有格
adv.	adverb	副詞	*pp.*	past participle	過去分詞
art.	article	冠詞	*ppr.*	present participle	現在分詞
aux.	auxiliary	助動詞	*prep.*	preposition	介系詞
comp.	comparative degree	比較級	*pron.*	pronoun	代名詞
conj.	conjunction	連接詞	*pt.*	past tense	過去式
def. art.	definite article	定冠詞	*rel. pron.*	relative pronoun	關係代名詞
fem.	feminine	陰性	*sing.*	singular	單數
gen.	genitive	所有格	*sing.* or *pl.*	singular or plural	單數或複數
indef. art.	indefinite article	不定冠詞	*superl.*	superlative degree	最高級
interj.	interjection	感嘆詞	*v.*	verb	動詞
mas.	masculine	陽性	*v.i.*	intransitive verb	不及物動詞
n.	noun	名詞	*v.t.*	transitive verb	及物動詞
nom.	nominative	主格	?	uncertain	或許; 可能; 不確定
obj.	objective	受格	&	and	及
pl.	plural	複數			

略 語 表 (II)

〖解剖〗解剖學	anatomy	〖考古〗考古學	archeology
〖英印〗英印的;英印語	Anglo–Indian	〖建築〗建築學	architecture
〖人類學〗人類學(的)	anthropology, anthropological	〖算術〗算術	arithmetic
〖阿拉伯〗阿拉伯的;阿拉伯語	Arabic	〖天文〗天文學	astronomy
〖古〗古語	archaic	〖澳〗澳洲	Australia
		〖細菌〗細菌學	bacteriology
		〖生化〗生物化學	biochemistry

【生物】生物學(的)	biology, biologic, biological
【植物】植物學	botany
【英】不列顛(的)(英國;英語;英國的)	Britain, British (England, English)
【加】加拿大(的)	Canada, Canadian
【化】化學(的)	chemistry, chemical
【中】中國的;中國語	Chinese
【俗】俗語的;口語的	colloquial (informal)
【結晶學】結晶學	crystallography
【蔑】輕蔑語	derogatory (disparaging)
【方】方言	dialect
【荷】荷蘭	Dutch
【生態】生態學(的)	ecology, ecological
【經濟】經濟學	economics
【電】電的;電學	electricity, electric
【胚胎學】胚胎學	embryology
【法】法國的;法語	French
【地理】地理學(的)	geography, geographic, geographical
【地質】地質學(的)	geology, geologic, geological
【幾何】幾何學	geometry
【德】德國的;德語	German
【希臘】希臘的;希臘語	Greek
【希伯來】希伯來語;希伯來書	Hebrew, Hebrews
【史】歷史(的)	history, historical
【印歐】印歐語(的)	Indo-European
【愛】愛爾蘭的;愛爾蘭語	Irish
【義】義大利的;義大利語	Italian
【日】日本的;日本語	Japanese
【謔】戲謔語	jocular
【拉】拉丁語	Latin
【法律】法律	law
【邏輯】邏輯學	logic
【鄙】鄙俗語	low
【馬來】馬來亞	Malaya
【數學】數學	mathematics
【醫】醫學(的)	medicine, medical
【氣象】氣象學	meteorology
【軍】軍語	military
【神話】神話	mythology
【聖經】新約(舊約;聖經的)	New Testament (Old Testament, biblical)
【廢】廢語	obsolete
【古生物學】古生物學	paleontology
【藥】藥學	pharmacology
【哲】哲學	philosophy
【照相】照相術	photography
【理】物理學(的)	physics, physical
【生理】生理學	physiology
【詩】詩中用語	poetical
【葡】葡萄牙的;葡萄牙語	Portuguese
【字首】字首	prefix
【諺】諺語	proverbs
【心理】心理學	psychology
【無線電】無線電	radio
【罕】罕用語	rare
【宗教】宗教	religion
【修辭】修辭學(的)	rhetoric, rhetorical
【俄】俄國的;俄語	Russian
【梵】梵語	Sanskrit
【蘇】蘇格蘭;蘇格蘭的;蘇格蘭語	Scotland, Scottish
【俚】俚語	slang
【南非】南非共和國	South-Africa
【西班牙】西班牙的;西班牙語	Spanish
【字尾】字尾	suffix
【電訊】電訊;電報;電話	telegraph, telegram, telephone
【電視】電視	television
【神學】神學的	theological
【土】土耳其的;土耳其語	Turkish
【蘇聯】蘇聯	Union of Soviet Socialist Republics (USSR)
【美】美國	United States of America (USA)
【動物】動物學(的)	zoology, zoological

A

a·bask 〔ə'bæsk, ə'bɑsk; ə'bɑːsk〕 *adv.* (在陽光中)曝晒着;(在火邊)取暖着。

***a·bate** 〔ə'bet; ə'beit〕 *v.*, **a·bat·ed**, **abat·ing.** —*v.t.* ①減少;減輕;降低。②消除;停止。—*v.i.* 減退。—**ment,** *n.*

ab·a·t(t)is 〔'æbətɪs; 'æbətis〕 *n., pl.* **ab·a·t(t)is** 〔'æbətiz; 'æbətiːz〕 *or* **ab·a·t(t)is·es** 〔'æbətɪsɪz; 'æbətisiz〕.〖兵學〗鹿砦。

ab·at·toir 〔,æbə'twɑr; 'æbətwɑː〕 *n.* 「屠宰場;屠場。」

abb 〔æb; æb〕 *n.* (織物之)緯線。

Ab·ba 〔'æbə; 'æbə〕 *n.* 某些東正教或希臘正教對主教的稱呼;神。

ab·ba·cy 〔'æbəsɪ; 'æbəsi〕 *n., pl.* **-cies.** 男修道院院長之職務;其管區;其任期。

ab·ba·tial 〔ə'beʃəl; ə'beiʃəl〕 *adj.* 修道院院長的;修道院的。

ab·bé 〔'æbe; 'æbei〕〖法〗*n.* 修道院院長;方丈;長老;神父。

ab·bess 〔'æbɪs; 'æbis〕 *n.* 女修道院院長;「尼庵住持。」

***ab·bey** 〔'æbɪ; 'æbi〕 *n.* ①大修道院;庵堂。②一院庵之僧尼。③昔僧院或尼庵之大教堂。Westminster *Abbey.* 倫敦西敏寺大教堂。

***ab·bot** 〔'æbət; 'æbət〕 *n.* 方丈;大修道院院長。—**cy,** —**ship,** *n.*

abbr., abbrev. ①abbreviated. ②abbreviation.

ab·bre·vi·ate 〔ə'brivɪ,et; ə'briːvieit〕 *v.t.*, **-at·ed, -at·ing.** 簡縮;縮寫;縮短。

ab·bre·vi·at·ed 〔ə'brivɪ,etɪd; ə'briːvieitid〕 *adj.* ①縮短的。②短小的(衣服)。③小型的。

ab·bre·vi·a·tion 〔ə,brivɪ'eʃən; ə,briːvi'eiʃən〕 *n.* 縮短;縮寫。〖注意〗按一般規則,在縮寫字的後面均加點。但目前有一種趨勢,凡一縮寫字其最後字母卽爲原字之最後字母時,則該縮寫字後面可不加點, 如 Dr (Doctor), Mr (Mister) 等。此種趨勢在英國尤爲習見。—**ist** *n.*

ABC 〔'e'bi'si; 'eibiː'siː〕 *n., pl.* **ABC's.** ①(*pl.*) 字母。②初步; 入門; 基礎。③〖英〗按 ABC次序排列的火車時刻表。***A-B-C method*** 由淺入深循序漸進的教學法。

ABC ① American Broadcasting Company. ②Argentina, Brazil, and Chile. ③American Bowling Congress. ④Australian Broadcasting Commission.

ABC (shop) 〖英〗(Aerated Bread Company 經營之)普通咖啡店。

A.B.C. Alcoholic Beverage Control.

ABC art 基本藝術。

ABCC Atomic Bomb Casualties Commission. 核爆傷害調查委員會。

ABC Powers 阿根廷、巴西、智利三國。

ABC Warfare atomic, bacteriological, and chemical warfare. 化生放戰爭。 **ABC Weapons** atomic, bacteriological, and chemical weapons. 化生放武器。

ab·di·cant 〔'æbdəkənt; 'æbdikənt〕 *adj.* 遜位的;放棄的。—*n.*放棄者;遜位者。

ab·di·cate 〔'æbdə,ket; 'æbdikeit〕 *v.*, **-cat·ed, -cat·ing.** —*v.i.* ①棄權。②讓位;辭職。—*v.t.* ①放棄(權利)。②讓(位);辭(職)。

ab·di·ca·tion 〔,æbdə'keʃən; ,æbdi'keiʃən〕 *n.* ①放棄;棄權。②讓位;辭職;遜位。

ab·di·ca·tor 〔'æbdɪ,ketɚ; 'æbdi,keitə〕 *n.* ①放棄者;棄權者。②辭職者;遜位者。

***ab·do·men** 〔æb'domən, 'æbdəmən; 'æbdəmen, æb'doumen〕 *n., pl.* **ab·do·mens, ab·dom·i·na** 〔æb'dɑmənə; æb'dɑːmənə〕. 腹部;下腹。—**ab·dom·i·nal,** *adj.* 〖注意〗 **abdomen** 與 **belly** 同義;但 belly 較俗。在說腹部凸大時通常均用 belly.

ab·dom·i·nous 〔æb'dɑmənəs; æb'dɔminəs〕 *adj.* 肥胖的;肚皮肥滿的。

ab·du·cent 〔æb'djusənt; æb'djuːsənt〕 *adj.* 〖生理〗外旋的;外展的。

ab·duct 〔æb'dʌkt; æb'dʌkt〕 *v.t.* ①綁架;綁走;拐走。②〖生理〗使外旋。

ab·duc·tion[1] 〔æb'dʌkʃən; æb'dʌkʃən〕 *n.* ①誘拐。②〖生理〗外旋;外展。

ab·duc·tion[2] *n.* 〖邏輯〗不明推論式(大前提全正確,小前提仍有問題的三段論法)。

ab·duc·tor 〔æb'dʌktɚ; æb'dʌktə〕 *n.* ①誘拐者;拐子。②〖生理〗外展肌;外展筋。

Abd·ul·lah ibn-Hu·sein 〔əbdul-'lɑ,ibnhu'saɪn; əbdu'lɑː,ibnhu'sain〕 阿布都拉・伊本・胡笙(1882–1951, 於1946–51爲約旦國王)。

Abe 〔eb; eib〕 *n.* Abraham 之略稱。

a·beam 〔ə'bim; ə'biːm〕 *adv.* 〖航海〗與船之龍骨成直角地;橫地。

a·be·ce·dar·i·an 〔,ebɪsɪ'dɛrɪən; ,eibiː-siː'dɛəriən〕 *n.* ①學習字母者;初學者。②教授字母的人;啓蒙老師。—*adj.* ①基本的;初步的。②按字母次序的。

a·be·ce·dar·i·um 〔,ebɪsɪ'dɛrɪəm; ,ei-biːsiː'dɛəriəm〕 *n., pl.* **-dar·i·a** 〔-'dɛrɪə; -'dɛəriə〕. 教授字母所用的啓蒙讀本。

a·bed 〔ə'bɛd; ə'bed〕 *adv.* 在床上。***bring abed*** 臨蓐。

A.B.Ed. Bachelor of Arts in Education.

A·bel 〔'ebl; 'eibəl〕 *n.* 〖聖經〗亞伯(亞當「及夏娃之次子)。」

a·bele 〔ə'bil; ə'biːl〕 *n.* 〖植物〗白楊。

a·bel·mosk 〔'ebl̩,mɑsk; 'eibəl,mɔsk〕 *n.* 〖植物〗秋葵。

ab·er·rance 〔æb'ɛrəns; æ'berəns〕 *n.* 越軌;逸出。(亦作 **aberrancy**)

ab·er·rant 〔æb'ɛrənt; æ'berənt〕 *adj.* ①越乎常軌的。②〖動物〗變態的;異常的。—*n.* 行爲不正常的人。

ab·er·ra·tion 〔,æbə'reʃən; ,æbə'reiʃən〕 *n.* ①越軌。②恍惚;錯亂。③〖物理〗像差。④〖天文〗光行差。—**al,** *adj.*

a·bet 〔ə'bɛt; ə'bet〕 *v.t.*, **-bet·ted, -bet·ting.** 煽動;教唆。***aid and abet***〖法律〗教唆。—**ter,** —**tor,** —**ment,** —**tal,** *n.*

a·bey·ance 〔ə'beəns; ə'beiəns〕 *n.* ①中止;暫擱。②〖法律〗所有人未決定之狀態。—**a·bey·ant,** *adj.*

A.B.F.M. American Board of Foreign Missions.

***ab·hor** 〔əb'hɔr, æb-; əb'hɔː〕 *v.t.*, **-horred, -hor·ring.** 憎惡;痛恨。We *abhor* a traitor. 我們痛恨叛賊。—**rer,** *n.*

ab·hor·rence 〔əb'hɔrəns; əb'hɔrəns〕 *n.* ①憎恨;嫌惡。②憎惡之事物。

ab·hor·rent 〔əb'hɔrənt; əb'hɔrənt〕 *adj.* ①懷憎惡之念的;嫌惡的〖of〗. I am *abhorrent* of it. 我嫌惡它。②極端相反的;悖逆的〖to〗. to be *abhorrent* to one. 與某人不投合。③性質有別的;不相容的〖from〗. ④令人憎惡或痛恨的。—**ly,** *adv.*

a·bid·ance 〔ə'baɪdn̩s; ə'baidəns〕 *n.* ①居住。 ②固守;遵守〖by〗. *abidance* by rules. 規則之遵守。

***a·bide** 〔ə'baɪd; ə'baid〕 *v.*, **a·bode** 〔ə'bod; ə'boud〕 or **a·bid·ed, a·bid·ing.** —*v.i.* ①居住;居留。②同住。③遵守;忠於;堅持;固執〖by〗. He *abides* by his friends.

A

:A or **a** 〔*unstressed* ə; ə, *stressed* e; ei〕 *n., pl.* **A's** or **a's.** ①英文字母之第一個字母。②甲（功課的成績）。to get an *A* in English. 英文得甲。***from A to Z*** 從頭到尾。***not know from A to B*** 一無所知。—*adj.* or *indefinite article.* ①(=any)任一。*a* tree. 一棵樹。②(=one)一。*a* pound of butter. 一磅奶油。③(=each) 每一。ten dollars *a* day. 每日十元。④(=some)某一；有一(指一類中之某一個)。such *a* one. 這樣一個。*a* Miss Johnson. 一位詹森小姐。⑤用在由單數形形容詞所形容的複數名詞之前。*a* hundred men. 一百人。〖注意〗用做冠詞時，a 用於以子音字母開始的字之前，如: *a* house. an 用於以不發音的 h 或母音字母開始的字之前，如: *an* honest man, *an* orange. 但開始的母音字母發〔j〕或〔w〕音時，仍須用a，如: *a* European, such *a* one.

a- 〖字首〗表下列諸義: ① =on, in, *or* at. 如: abed. ②表某種情況。如: afire. ③表某種行動。如: ahunting. ④表某種方式或態度。如: aloud. ⑤置於動詞前，形成形容詞。如: aglaze. ⑥ **ab-**之異體。

A. ① Absolute. ②Academy. ③acre. ④ America. ⑤American. ⑥angstrom unit. ⑦April. ⑧artillery. **a.** ①about. ②acre(s). ③active. ④adjective. ⑤alto. ⑥ampere. ⑦anonymous. ⑧answer. ⑨are².

@ 〖商〗 at each. 單價。

A 1 〔'e'wʌn; 'ei'wʌn〕〖俗〗第一的；極佳的。(亦作 **A one**)

A.A. ①Actors' Association. ②Angling Association. ③antiaircraft. ④Associate in (*or* of) Arts. ⑤Automobile Association. ⑥air-to-air (rockets or missiles). 空對空(火箭或飛彈)。**AAA** ①Agricultural Adjustment Administration (*or* Agency). ②antiaircraft artillery. 高射砲兵。**AAA, A.A.A.** ①Amateur Athletic Association. ②American Athletic Association. ③American Automobile Association. ④Automobile Association of America. ⑤American Arbitration Association. **A.A.A.L.** American Academy of Arts and Letters. 美國文藝協會。**A.A.A.S.** ①American Association for the Advancement of Science. ② American Academy of Arts and Sciences. **A.A.F.** 〖美〗 Army Air Forces. 陸軍航空隊。**AAM** air-to-air missile.

a & h 〖保險〗 accident and health.

A & P Great Atlantic and Pacific Tea Company. 經營美國一流超級市場的公司。

A.A. of A. Automobile Association of America.

aard·vark 〔'ɑrd,vɑrk; 'ɑːdvɑːk〕 *n.* 〖動物〗土豬(南非所產之一種食蟻獸)。

aard·wolf 〔'ɑrd,wulf; 'ɑːdwulf〕 *n.* 〖動物〗南非土狼。

Aar·on 〔'ɛrən; 'ɛərən〕 *n.* ①男子名。②亞倫(聖經中希伯來人之第一個祭司長)。

Aa·ron·ic 〔ɛr'ɑnɪk; ɛə'rɔnik〕 *adj.* ①亞倫的。②摩門教初級教士的。

Aaron's beard 〖植物〗金絲桃之類。

Aaron's rod ①〖聖經〗亞倫之杖。②〖植物〗麒麟草。③〖建築〗亞倫杖(有渦卷和葉飾之一種直長的嵌線)。

A.A.S. ① Academic Americanae Socius (拉=Fellow of the American Academy). ②Amateur Angling Society. ③American Academy of Science. ④ Army Air Service.

aas·vo·gel 〔'ɑs,fogl; 'ɑːsfougəl〕 *n.* 兀鷹。

A.A.U. Amateur Athletic Union.

A.A.U.P. American Association of University Professors. **A.A.U.W.** American Association of University Women. **Ab** 〖化〗元素 alabamine 之符號。**AB** 〖醫〗(血型)AB型。

ab- 〖字首〗表"脫離；離開"之義，如: abduct.

ab. ①abbreviation. ②about. ③absent. ④at bat. **A.B.** Artium Baccalaureus (拉=Bachelor of Arts). **A.B., a.b.** able-bodied (seaman).

a·ba 〔'ɑbə; 'ɑːbə〕 *n.* ①駱駝、山羊等毛織成之毛織物。②阿拉伯人所着之無袖寬袍；毛掛。

A.B.A. ①American Bar Association. ②American Bible Association. ③American Boxing Association. ④American Bankers Association.

a·ba·cá 〔,ɑbə'kɑ; ,ɑːbə'kɑː〕 *n.* 馬尼拉麻。

ab·a·cist 〔'æbəsɪst; 'æbəsist〕 *n.* 用算盤者。

a·back 〔ə'bæk; ə'bæk〕 *adv.* 向後地。***taken aback*** 吃驚；嚇了一跳。—*adj.* 〖航海〗(帆)正面迎風的。

ab·a·cus 〔'æbəkəs; 'æbəkəs〕 *n., pl.* **-cus·es, -ci** 〔-,saɪ; -sai〕. ①西洋珠串(教兒童計算用)。②算盤。③柱頭之頂板。

A·ba·dan 〔,ɑbɑ'dɑn; ,æbə'dɑːn〕 *n.* 阿巴丹(伊朗一城市)。

A·bad·don 〔ə'bædən; ə'bædən〕 *n.* 〖聖經〗①無底坑；地獄。②無底坑的使者。

a·baft 〔ə'bæft; ə'bɑːft〕 *adv.* 在船尾；向船尾。—*prep.* 〖航海〗在…後。

ab·al·ien·ate 〔æb'eljən,et; æb'eiljəneit〕 *v.t.,* **-at·ed, -at·ing.** 〖法律〗移轉；讓渡。

ab·a·lo·ne 〔,æbə'lonɪ; ,æbə'louni〕 *n.* 〖動物〗鮑魚；石決明。

·a·ban·don 〔ə'bændən; ə'bændən〕 *v.t.* ①放棄。②捨棄。I would never *abandon* my friends. 我永遠不捨棄我的朋友。③放縱；放肆。Do not *abandon* yourself to despair. 勿自暴自棄。④〖保險〗委付(將部分受損之保險物給予保險商，俾獲得全額之賠款)。—*n.* 狂放；放縱；放肆。

a·ban·doned 〔ə'bændənd; ə'bændənd〕 *adj.* ①被棄的。②放縱的。—**ly,** *adv.*

a·ban·don·ee 〔ə,bændə'ni; ə,bændə'iː〕 *n.* 〖法律〗受委付者(通常指保險業者)

a·ban·don·er 〔ə'bændənə; ə'bæ[illegible]nə〕 *n.* ①放棄者。②〖法律〗遺棄者。

a·ban·don·ment 〔ə'bændənm[illegible] ə'bændənmənt〕 *n.* ①放棄；拋棄。②[illegible]遺棄。③放縱；放肆。④〖保險〗委付。

à bas 〔a'bɑ; ɑː'bɑː〕 〖法〗打倒。

a·base 〔ə'bes; ə'beis〕 *v.t.,* [illegible] **abas·ing.** 貶抑；降低(職位、階級等)
—**ment,** *n.* —**a·bas·a·ble,** *adj.*

a·bash 〔ə'bæʃ; ə'bæʃ〕 *v.t.* 使[illegible]促不安；使困窘。—**ed·ly,** *adv.*[illegible]

a·ba·sia 〔ə'beʒə; ə'beiʒə〕 *n*[illegible]性)步行不能。—**a·bat·ic,** *adj.*

他忠於他的朋友。④繼續或保持某種狀況，態度，或關係等。—*v.t.* ①容忍；忍受。I can not *abide* such people. 我不能容忍這些人。②等待；守候。③毫無反對或疑問地接受。—**a·bid·er,** *n.*

a·bid·ing [əˈbaɪdɪŋ; əˈbaidiŋ] *adj.* 永久的；不變的。—**ly,** *adv.* —**ness,** *n.*

abiding place 住所；寓所；居住地。

Ab·i·djan [ˌæbɪˈdʒɑn; ˌæbiˈdʒɑːn] *n.* 阿必尙(象牙海岸共和國之首都)。

Ab·i·gail [ˈæbɪˌgel, ˈæbɪgl̩; ˈæbigeil] *n.* ①〖聖經〗亞比該(拿八之妻，見舊約撒母耳記上卷二十五章)。②(a-)侍女。

***a·bil·i·ty** [əˈbɪlətɪ; əˈbiliti] *n., pl.* **-ties.** ①能力；才幹。He is a man of *ability*. 他是一個能幹的人。②技能；技巧；本領。He had great *ability* as a general. 他是一個很有本領的將軍。③天才。*ability* in music. 音樂天才。

ab·i·o·chem·is·try [ˌæbioˈkɛmɪstrɪ; ˌæbioˈkemistri] *n.* 無機化學；無生化學。

ab·i·o·gen·e·sis [ˌæbɪəˈdʒɛnɪsɪs; ˌeibaiouˈdʒenəsis] *n.*〖生物〗偶發；自然發生；生物自生說。—**ab·i·o·ge·net·ic,** *adj.* —**ab·i·og·e·nist,** *n.*

ab·i·o·sis [ˌæbɪˈosɪs; ˌæbiˈousis] *n.* 無生命狀態。

ab·i·ot·ro·phy [ˌæbɪˈɑtrəfɪ; ˌæbiˈɔtrəfi] *n.* 〖醫〗營養性衰竭；生活力缺失。—**ab·i·o·troph·ic,** *adj.*

ab·ir·ri·tant [æbˈɪrətənt; æbˈiritənt] *adj.* 鎭痛的。—*n.* 〖醫〗鎭痛劑；鎭定劑。

ab·ject [æbˈdʒɛkt; ˈæbdʒekt] *adj.* ①不幸的；可憐的；難堪的。②卑鄙的；卑屈的。—**ly,** *adv.* —**ness,** **ab·jec·tion,** *n.*

ab·jec·tive [æbˈdʒɛktɪv; æbˈdʒektiv] *adj.* 不良的；令人沮喪的；可恥的。

ab·ju·ra·tion [ˌæbdʒuˈreʃən; ˌæbdʒuəˈreiʃən] *n.* 宣誓放棄；誓絕。

ab·jure [əbˈdʒur; əbˈdʒuə] *v.t.,* **-jured, -jur·ing.** ①誓絕；棄絕。②鄭重放棄或撤銷。

abl. ablative.

ab·lac·tate [æbˈlæktet; æbˈlækteit] *v.t.,* **-tat·ed, -tat·ing.** 使(嬰兒等)斷奶。

ab·lac·ta·tion [ˌæblækˈteʃən; ˌæblækˈteiʃən] *n.* 斷奶。

a·blare [əˈblɛr; əˈblɛə] *adj.* 喧鬧的。—*adv.* 喧鬧地。

ab·late [æbˈlet; æbˈleit] *v.,* **-lat·ed, -lat·ing.** —*v.t.* 使(一部分)除去。—*v.i.* (部分)消除。

ab·la·tion [æbˈleʃən; æbˈleiʃən] *n.* ①(一部分之)除去；切除。②〖地質〗消磨。③〖太空〗磨削；磨削作用(太空乘具於重入大氣層時，因高熱而部分燒毀)。

ab·la·tive [ˈæblətɪv; ˈæblətiv] *adj.* ①〖拉丁文法〗奪格的。②〖太空〗可磨削的。*ablative absolute* 奪格獨立句。—*n.* ①奪格。②奪格字；奪格短語。

ab·laut [ˈɑblaut; ˈæblaut] *n.* 〖語言〗母音變換(如 drink, drank, drunk)。(亦作 **gradation**)

a·blaze [əˈblez; əˈbleiz] *adv.* 着火。—*adj.* ①發光的。②憤激的。

‡a·ble [ˈebl̩; ˈeibl] *adj.,* **a·bler, a·blest.** ①能。I shall be *able* to come tomorrow. 明天我能來。②能幹的。③徹底完成的；詳盡的。an *able* speech. 一篇詳盡的演說。④〖法律〗有資格的。

-able 〖字尾〗用以構成形容詞：①能够…的。②適於…的；可…的。③值得…的。④有…之性質的。⑤趨於…的。(亦作 **-ible, -ble**)

a·ble-bod·ied [ˈebl̩ˈbɑdɪd; ˈeiblˈbɔdid] *adj.*强健的。an *able-bodied* man. 壯丁。

able-bodied seaman A.B. 級水手；熟練之水手。(今常作 **able seaman**)

ab·le·gate [ˈæblɪˌget; ˈæbligeit] *n.* 天主教教宗爲某特殊任務而派往外地之特使。

a·ble-mind·ed [ˈebl̩ˈmaɪndɪd; ˈeiblˈmaindid] *adj.* 有才幹的；聰慧的。

a·blep·si·a [əˈblɛpsɪə; əˈblepsiə] *n.*〖眼科〗瞎。(亦作 **ablepsy**)

a·bloom [əˈblum; əˈbluːm] *adv.* & *adj.* 開花地(的)。

A.B.L.S. Bachelor of Arts in Library Science.

ab·lu·ent [ˈæbluənt; ˈæbljuənt] *adj.* 洗滌的；洗淨的。—*n.* 〖醫〗洗滌劑。

a·blush [əˈblʌʃ; əˈblʌʃ] *adv.* & *adj.* 赧然；臉紅地(的)。

ab·lu·tion [æbˈluʃən; əˈbluːʃən] *n.*①洗身；沐浴。②〖宗教〗洗禮；齋戒沐浴。③淨水(尤指洗禮用者)。④(*pl.*)〖英〗**a.** (作 *pl.* 解) 軍營中的沐浴衞生設備。**b.** (作*sing.* 解) 軍營中的浴室，廁所。***perform*** (or ***make***) ***one's ablution*** 齋戒沐浴。

a·bly [ˈeblɪ; ˈeibli] *adv.* 能幹地；巧妙地。

ABM antiballistic missile.

ab·ne·gate [ˈæbnɪˌget; ˈæbnigeit] *v.t.,* **-gat·ed, -gat·ing.** 拒絕；放棄(權利等)。

ab·ne·ga·tion [ˌæbnɪˈgeʃən; ˌæbniˈgeiʃən] *n.* ①拒絕；棄權。②克己；自制。

Ab·ney level [ˈæbni～; ˈæbniː～] 測量山坡的高度或坡度用的輕便水平儀。

***ab·nor·mal** [æbˈnɔrml̩; æbˈnɔːməl] *adj.* 變態的；畸形的；不正常的。It is *abnormal* for a man to be seven feet tall. 一人身高七英尺卽爲畸形。—**ly,** *adv.*

ab·nor·mal·ism [æbˈnɔrməlɪzm; æbˈnɔːməlizm] *n.* 變態性；異常。

ab·nor·mal·i·ty [ˌæbnɔrˈmælətɪ; ˌæbnɔːˈmæliti] *n., pl.* **-ties.**①異常；變態。②變則；異常之人或物；畸形。

abnormal psychology 變態心理學。

ab·nor·mi·ty [æbˈnɔrmətɪ; æbˈnɔːmiti] *n.,pl.* **-ties.** ①異常；反常。②畸形。

a·board** [əˈbord, əˈbɔrd; əˈbɔːd] *adv.* ①**a.** 在船上；在飛機上。**b.** 〖美，加〗在火車上；在汽車上。②〖美棒球俚〗在壘上。All aboard!*** 車船等卽將開動時對乘客所作之警告語。—*prep.* 在船(車)上。They went *aboard* the ship. 他們乘船而行。

a·board·age [əˈbɔrdɪdʒ; əˈbɔːdidʒ] *n.* 〖航海〗兩船平行或近於平行時的相撞。

***a·bode** [əˈbod; əˈboud] *n.* ①住處；住所。He has no fixed *abode*. 他沒有固定的住所。②較久的居住。

ABO group 〖遺傳〗血液型原體。

a·boil [əˈbɔɪl; əˈbɔil] *adj.* & *adv.* 沸騰的(地)。

A-boil·er [ˈeˌbɔɪlə; ˈeiˌbɔilə] *n.* 用原子反應器加熱的鍋爐。

***a·bol·ish** [əˈbɑlɪʃ; əˈbɔliʃ] *v.t.*①廢止；革除。We must *abolish* slavery. 我們應當廢止奴隸制度。②完全破壞(人，或事物)。

a·bol·ish·a·ble [əˈbɑlɪʃəbl̩; əˈbɔliʃəbl] *adj.*可廢除的；可廢止的。

a·bol·ish·ment [əˈbɑlɪʃmənt; əˈbɔliʃmənt] *n.* 廢止；革除。

***ab·o·li·tion** [ˌæbəˈlɪʃən; ˌæbəˈliʃən] *n.* ①廢止；革除。②廢止黑奴制度。—**ar·y,** *adj.*

ab·o·li·tion·ism [ˌæbəˈlɪʃənˌɪzəm; ˌæbəˈliʃənizəm] *n.* (奴隸制度)廢止主義。—**ab·o·li·tion·ist,** *n., adj.*

ab·o·ma·sum [ˌæbəˈmesəm; ˌæbou-

ˈmeisəm〕 *n.*, *pl.* -sa 〔-sə;-sə〕. 皺胃。

A-bomb 〔ˈeˌbɑm; ˈeiˌbɔm〕 *n.*原子彈。

***a·bom·i·na·ble** 〔əˈbɑmnəbl; əˈbɔminəbl〕 *adj.*①可厭的;可惡的。an *abominable* affair. 醜行。②不愉快的;惡劣的。③庸俗的。—**a·bom·i·na·bly**, *adv.* —**ness**, *n.*

Abominable Snowman 雪人。

a·bom·i·nate 〔əˈbɑməˌnet; əˈbɔmineit〕 *v.t.*, **-nat·ed, -nat·ing.** 痛恨;痛惡。

a·bom·i·na·tion 〔əˌbɑməˈneʃən; əˌbɔmiˈneiʃən〕 *n.* ①憎惡;嫌惡。②可憎之事物或行爲。

a·bom·i·na·tor 〔əˈbɑməˌnetɚ; əˈbɔmineitə〕 *n.* 憎惡者;嫌惡的人。

ab·o·rig·i·nal 〔ˌæbəˈrɪdʒənl; ˌæbəˈridʒənl〕 *adj.* 原始的;土著的。—*n.*原始之居民;土人。—**ly**, *adv.*

ab·o·rig·i·nal·i·ty 〔ˌæbərɪdʒəˈnælətɪ; ˌæbəridʒiˈnæliti〕 *n.* 原始性;土著狀態。

ab·o·rig·i·ne 〔ˌæbəˈrɪdʒəni; ˌæbəˈridʒiniː〕 *n.* 原始居民;土人。

ab·o·rig·i·nes 〔ˌæbəˈrɪdʒəˌniz; ˌæbəˈridʒiniːz〕 *n.* *pl.*①原始的居民;土人。②(某一地區的)土生的動植物。

a·born·ing 〔əˈbɔrnɪŋ; əˈbɔːniŋ〕 *adv.*在生產中;尚未實施。—*adj.* 在生產中的;在具體化中的;在成爲事實中的。

a·bort 〔əˈbɔrt; əˈbɔːt〕 *v.i.* ①流產;墮胎。②失敗。③〖生物〗器官退化;發育不全。④中止(如某種試驗等在未完成前中止)。—*v.t.* ①使流產;使墮胎。②使失敗;使(某任務)中止。—*n.*①〖美〗放棄或中止。②〖美〗機械故障。③〖空戰〗無效架次,無效飛行,或無效任務。

a·bor·tar·i·um 〔ˌəbɔrˈtɛrɪəm; ˌəbɔːˈtɛəriəm〕 *n.* 〖美〗墮胎醫院。

a·bor·ti·cide 〔əˈbɔrtəˌsaɪd; əˈbɔːtisaid〕 *n.* 〖醫〗墮胎;墮胎藥。

a·bor·ti·fa·cient 〔əˌbɔrtəˈfeʃənt; əˌbɔːtiˈfeiʃənt〕 *adj.* 引起墮胎的。—*n.*墮胎藥。

a·bor·tion 〔əˈbɔrʃən; əˈbɔːʃən〕 *n.* ①流產;墮胎。②流產或墮胎產下之胎兒。③未成熟或未完成之事物;畸形。④〖生物〗器官發育不全。⑤(計畫等之)失敗;挫折。—**al**, *adj.*

a·bor·tion·ist 〔əˈbɔrʃənɪst; əˈbɔːʃənist〕 *n.* 施墮胎術者;爲人非法打胎者。

a·bor·tive 〔əˈbɔrtɪv; əˈbɔːtiv〕 *adj.* ①早產的。②無結果的;失敗的。③發育不全的。—*n.*①墮胎藥。②早產。—**ly**, *adv.* —**ness**, *n.*

a·bor·tus 〔əˈbɔrtəs; əˈbɔːtəs〕 *n.*, *pl.* **-tus·es.** 〖醫〗①流產兒。②流產。

a·bou·li·a 〔əˈbulɪə; əˈbuːliə〕 *n.*=**abulia.**

***a·bound** 〔əˈbaund; əˈbaund〕 *v.i.* 富於;充滿。He *abounds* in courage. 他極有勇氣。

a·bound·ing 〔əˈbaundɪŋ; əˈbaundiŋ〕 *adj.* 豐富的;大量的。—**ly**, *adv.*

:a·bout 〔əˈbaut; əˈbaut〕 *prep.* ①關於;對於。Tell me something *about* your trip. 告訴我一些關於你旅行的情形。②近於;接近;相近。He is *about* my height. 他的高度與我相近。③繞於;於四周。He planted trees *about* the house. 他種樹於那房子之四周。④卽將〖to〗. The plane is *about* to take off. 此機卽將起飛。⑤在…的近處;離…不遠;在…附近。He lives somewhere *about* here. 他住在附近。⑥在(某人)身邊;手頭。He has no money *about* him. 他身邊沒錢。⑦到處。—*adv.* ①將近。Supper is *about* ready. 晚飯就快預備好了。②近處。He must be somewhere *about*. 他一定在附近。③四處;遍於。④左右;大約。It is *about* nine o'clock now. 現在大約是九點。⑤向相反方向;反。—*adj.* ①在活動着。Few people were *about* on the streets. 街上的人很少。②存在着;流通着。③康復。eager to be up and *about* again. 渴望早日康復。***all about*** 所有關於。We know *all about* it. 我們盡知一切。***at about*** 大約。***be about*** 在近處。*Is* the manager *about?* 經理在嗎? ***bring something about*** 使發生。***go a long way about*** 繞遠路。***leave something about*** 無秩序地放置東西。***order somebody about*** 命某人做雜事。***set about*** 動手;着手。***take turns about*** 輪流。***turn and turn about*** 輪流交互;不斷旋轉。***what*** (or ***how***) ***about*** 關於…如何? My little dog is very clever, *what* (or *how*) *about* yours? 我的小狗甚爲聰明,你的如何?

a·bout-face 〔*n.* əˈbautˌfes; əˈbautˈfeis; *v.* əˌbautˈfes; əˌbautˈfeis〕 *n.* ①向後轉。②改變主意或態度。—*v.i.*①改變主意或態度。②轉至相反方向。〖注意〗英國作 **about-turn.**

about face 〖美〗向後轉(口令)。

a·bout-ship 〔əˌbautˈʃɪp; əˌbautˈʃip〕 *v.i.* 〖航海〗轉向;搶上風。

about ship 〖航海〗轉向;搶上風(口令)。

a·bout-sledge 〔əˈbautˌslɛdʒ; əˈbautˌsledʒ〕 *n.* (鐵匠用的)大鍾。

:a·bove 〔əˈbʌv; əˈbʌv〕 *adv.* ①在上;上方。The sky is *above.* 天在上。②在上文。The scientist mentioned *above* is no other than Dr. Einstein. 上文所提到的科學家,正是愛因斯坦博士。—*prep.* ①於…之上。Eagles fly *above* the white clouds. 鷹飛於白雲之上。②地位高於。A colonel is *above* a major. 上校高於少校。③在…以上;超過。④超過…之範圍。He is *above* reproach. 他是無可責難的。⑤勝於。A miser loves gold *above* his life. 一個守財奴愛財勝於其命。⑥不屑。He is *above* taking profits for himself. 他不屑爲自己謀利。⑦以北。The ship sank just *above* the Azores. 船沉沒在亞速爾羣島以北的地點。***above all*** 最重要。***above ground*** 在地上;活着。***above measure*** 非常;頂。***above price*** 無價之(寶)。***be above oneself*** 自命不凡;趾高氣揚。***keep one's head above water*** 保持安全;不負債。—*adj.* 上述的;上面的。You can find it in the examples *above.* 你可以在上面的例子中找到。—*n.* ①上述者;如上者。a diagram like the *above.* 如上圖。②上級。③上蒼。

a·bove·board 〔əˈbʌvˌbord; əˈbʌvbɔːd〕 *adv.* & *adj.* 光明磊落地(的);坦誠地(的)。

a·bove-cit·ed 〔əˈbʌvˌsaɪtɪd; əˈbʌvˈsaitid〕 *adj.*上文所引用的。

a·bove·deck 〔əˈbʌvˌdɛk; əˈbʌvˌdek〕 *adv.* & *adj.*①在甲板上。②直言無諱地(的);坦白地(的);公正地(的)。

a·bove·ground 〔əˈbʌvˌgraund; əˈbʌvˌgraund〕 *adj.* ①在地面上的;活着的。②公然露面的;顯而易見的。

a·bove-men·tioned 〔əˈbʌvˈmɛnʃənd; əˈbʌvˈmenʃənd〕 *adj.*上述的;前述的。

a·bove·stairs 〔əˈbʌvˌstɛrz; əˈbʌvˌstɛəz〕 *n.* *pl.*〖英〗主人房,上房(以別於僕人房)。—*adv.* & *adj.* 在樓上。

abp. archbishop. **A.B.P.C.** American Book Publishers Council. **abr.** ①abridge(d). ②abridgment.

ab·ra·ca·dab·ra 〔ˌæbrəkəˈdæbrə;

ˌæbrəkəˈdæbrə] *n.* ①符咒。②胡言。

a·bra·dant [əˈbredənt; əˈbreidənt] *adj.*研磨用的;有磨擦性的。—*n.* 研磨劑。

a·brade [əˈbred; əˈbreid] *v.t.* & *v.i.*, **a·brad·ed, a·bra·ing.'** 磨擦;擦傷;折磨。—**a·brad·er,** *n.*

A·bra·ham [ˈebrəˌhæm; ˈeibrəhæm] *n.* 〖聖經〗亞伯拉罕(希伯來族之始祖)。 ***in Abraham's bosom*** **a.** 與先祖同眠;在天國。**b.** 極樂;極平安。

a·bran·chi·al [əˈbræŋkɪəl; əˈbræŋkiəl] *adj.* 〖動物〗無鰓的;無鰓類的。

a·bras·er [əˈbrezə; əˈbreizə] *n.* 一種用來測定物質抗磨性的器械。

a·bra·sion [əˈbreʒən; əˈbreiʒən] *n.* ①磨擦;擦傷。②磨損;剝蝕。③剝蝕之物。

a·bra·sive [əˈbresɪv; əˈbreisiv] *adj.* 使生磨損或剝蝕的。—*n.* 磨磋物;研磨料。

ab·re·act [ˌæbrɪˈækt; ˌæbriˈækt] *v.t.* 〖精神分析〗使精神發洩(藉語言或動作將壓抑的不愉快經驗表達出來)。—**ab·re·ac·tion,** *n.*

a·breast [əˈbrɛst; əˈbrest] *adv.*①並肩;相並。②趕得上;不落伍。 「所;防空洞。」

a·bri [ɑˈbri; ɑːˈbriː] *n., pl.* **a·bris.** 避難

a·bridge [əˈbrɪdʒ; əˈbridʒ] *v.t.,* **-bridged, -bridg·ing.** ①縮短;刪節(指文字或語言)。②削減。③剝奪。 「過刪節的或削減的。」

a·bridged [əˈbrɪdʒd; əˈbridʒd] *adj.* 經

a·bridg(e)·ment [əˈbrɪdʒmənt; əˈbridʒmənt] *n.* ①縮短;刪節。②剝奪;削減。③(某書之)節本。 「滿溢地。—*adj.* 盈滿的。」

a·brim [əˈbrɪm; əˈbrim] *adv.*滿及杯口地;

a·broach [əˈbrotʃ; əˈbroutʃ] *adv.* & *adj.* ①開口地(的)。②在行動或活動着地(的);發表地(的);倡導地(的);傳播地(的)。 ***set abroach*** **a.** 開酒桶。**b.** 發表(新學說);宣洩(感情);吐露(詭計);倡導;傳播。

***a·broad** [əˈbrɔd; əˈbrɔːd] *adv.* ①在國外。to go *abroad.* 到國外去。②在戶外。③廣布;傳播。A rumor is *abroad.* 謠言四播。④遠;廣。⑤大錯特錯。I am much *abroad* in my guess. 我猜得大錯特錯。

ab·ro·gate [ˈæbrəˌget; ˈæbrougeit] *v.t.,* **-gat·ed, -gat·ing.** 廢止。—**ab·ro·ga·ble, ab·ro·ga·tive,** *adj.* —**ab·ro·ga·tion,** *n.*

***ab·rupt** [əˈbrʌpt; əˈbrʌpt] *adj.* ①突然的。②陡峭的;險峻的。an *abrupt* descent. 陡峭的斜坡。③唐突的;粗率的。an *abrupt* entrance. 闖進。④突兀的;不連貫的。⑤〖植物〗頂端平寬的。—**ly,** *adv.* —**ness,** *n.*

ab·rup·tion [əˈbrʌpʃən; əˈbrʌpʃən] *n.* 突然裂開;急斷;遽止。

abs. ①absent. ②absolute (temperature). ③absolutely. ④abstract. **A.B.S.** ①American Bible Society. ②American Bureau of Shipping.

Ab·sa·lom [ˈæbsələm; ˈæbsələm] *n.* 〖聖經〗押沙龍(猶太王 David 之第三子)。

ab·scess [ˈæbˌsɛs; ˈæbsis] *n.* 潰瘍;膿腫。—*v.i.* 形成膿腫。—**ab·scessed,** *adj.*

ab·scis·sa [æbˈsɪsə; æbˈsisə] *n., pl.* **-sas, -sae** [-si; -siː]. 〖數學〗橫坐標。

ab·scis·sion [æbˈsɪʒən; æbˈsiʒən] *n.* ①〖醫〗切除。②〖修辭〗頓斷法。③〖植物〗葉或果實之因成熟而自然脫落。

ab·scond [æbˈskɑnd; əbˈskɔnd] *v.i.* 潛逃;逃亡。—**er,** *n.*

ab·scond·ence [æbˈskɑndṇs; əbˈskɔndəns] *n.*逃亡;失蹤;潛伏。

ab·seil [ˈɑbzaɪl, ˈɑp-; ˈɑːbzail, ˈɑːp-] *n.* 〖爬山〗沿繩子滑下的方法。—*v.i.* 沿繩子滑下。

***ab·sence** [ˈæbsṇs; ˈæbsəns] *n.* ①缺席。I did not notice his *absence.* 我未注意他的缺席。②不在意;不注意。③缺乏。

‡ab·sent [*adj.* ˈæbsṇt; ˈæbsənt *v.* æbˈsɛnt; æbˈsent] *adj.* ①不在的;缺席的。He is *absent* from class today. 他今天未上課。②不存在的;缺乏的。Snow is *absent* in some countries. 有的國家沒有雪。③不關心的;茫然的。—*v.t.* 缺席;不在。Why did you *absent* yourself from school yesterday? 昨天你為甚麼不到校? —**ly,** *adv.*

ab·sen·ta·tion [ˌæbsɛnˈteʃən; ˌæbsenˈteiʃən] *n.* 不在;缺席。

ab·sen·tee [ˌæbsṇˈti; ˌæbsənˈtiː] *n.*缺席者;在外者。—*adj.* 缺席的;在外的。

***ab·sent-mind·ed** [ˈæbsṇtˈmaɪndɪd; ˈæbsəntˈmaindid] *adj.*心不在焉的;茫然的。He is *absent-minded.* 他心不在焉。 —**ly,** *adv.* —**ness,** *n.* 「(略作 AOL).」

absent over leave 〖軍〗逾假不歸

absent treatment 輕待;冷落。

absent without leave 〖軍〗擅自離職;不假外出。(略作**A.W.O.L.** 或 **a.w.o.l.**)

ab·sinth(e) [ˈæbsɪnθ; ˈæbsinθ] *n.* ①苦艾酒。②〖植物〗艾。 「zm] *n.* 苦艾中毒。」

ab·sinth·ism [ˈæbsɪnθɪzm; ˈæbsinθi-

ab·sin·thi·um [æbˈsɪnθɪəm; æbˈsinθiəm] *n.*①苦艾。②晒乾的艾葉或艾花。③苦艾油。 「〖俗〗逃亡;逃脫。」

ab·skize [æbˈskaɪz; æbˈskaiz] *v.i.* 〖美

***ab·so·lute** [ˈæbsəˌlut; ˈæbsəluːt] *adj.* ①完全的;全部的。②純粹的。*Absolute* alcohol has no water in it. 純酒精不摻水。③十全十美的。*absolute* purity. 完全純潔。④無限制的;專斷的;絕對的。⑤非與他物比較的。⑥眞正的。It is an *absolute* fact that the earth goes round the sun. 地球繞日運行是眞正的事實。⑦確定的;確實的。⑧〖文法〗獨立的。—*n.* 不受外物影響而能保持其存在,性質,大小等的事物。—**ness,** *n.*

absolute address 〖電腦〗絕對位址。

absolute altimeter 〖航空〗絕對高度表。

absolute altitude 〖航空〗絕對高度。

absolute ceiling 〖航空〗絕對升限。

absolute humidity 絕對濕度。

***ab·so·lute·ly** [ˈæbsəˌlutlɪ, ˌæbsəˈlutlɪ; ˈæbsəluːtli, -ljuː-] *adv.* ①完全地。His calculation is *absolutely* wrong. 他的算法完全錯了。②肯定地;絕對地。There is *absolutely* no way to calm him down. 絕對沒有方法使他安靜下來。③〖美俚〗是;正是如此。

absolute majority 絕對多數。

absolute monarchy 君主專制政體。

absolute music 絕對音樂。

absolute pressure 絕對壓力。

absolute scale 絕對(溫度)標度(從絕對零度開始的標度)。 「絕對溫度。」

absolute temperature 〖物理〗

absolute value 〖數學〗絕對值。

absolute zero 〖物理〗絕對零度。

ab·so·lu·tion [ˌæbsəˈluʃən; ˌæbsəˈluːʃən] *n.* ①免除;赦免;責任解除。②〖宗教〗赦罪。③赦罪文。

ab·so·lut·ism [ˈæbsəlutˌɪzəm; ˈæbsəluːtizm] *n.* 專制主義;絕對論。—**ab·so·lut·ist,** *n.* 「taiz] *v.t.* 使(某事)絕對化。」

ab·so·lu·tize [ˈæbsəluˌtaɪz; ˈæbsəluː-

ab·so·lu·to·ry [æbˈsɑljəˌtorɪ; əbˈsɔ-

lətəri] *adj.* 給予赦免的。
ab·solv·a·ble [æbˈsɑlvəbl; əbˈzɔlvəbl] *adj.* 可赦免或值得赦免的。
ab·solve [æbˈsɑlv; əbˈzɔlv] *v.t.*, **-solved, -solv·ing.** ①赦免。②解除(責任等)。③(宗教)解除(逐出教會令)。④取得學分。
ab·sol·vent [æbˈsɑlvənt; æbˈzɔlvənt] *adj.* 赦免的。—*n.* 赦免者。
ab·so·nant [ˈæbsənənt; ˈæbsənənt] *adj.* ①不諧和的。②不合理的。
***ab·sorb** [əbˈsɔrb; əbˈsɔːb] *v.t.* ①吸收；併呑。②使專心。He is *absorbed* in study. 他專心讀書。③(以化學作用)吸收。④收進；使用。⑤支付；負擔。⑥占有。This job *absorbs* all of my time. 這件工作占了我全部的時間。⑦理解。 —**a·bil·i·ty,** —**er,** *n.* —**a·ble,** *adj.*
ab·sorb·ate [əbˈsɔrbet; əbˈsɔːbeit] *n.* 被吸收的物質。
ab·sorbed [əbˈsɔrbd; əbˈsɔːbd] *adj.* ①被吸收的。②被併呑的。③被同化的。④全神貫注的。
ab·sorb·ed·ly [əbˈsɔrbɪdlɪ; əbˈsɔːbidli] *adv.* 全神貫注地。
ab·sor·be·fa·cient [əbˌsɔrbəˈfeʃənt; əbˌsɔːbiˈfeiʃənt] *adj.* 吸收性的。—*n.* 〖醫〗吸收劑。
ab·sorb·ent [əbˈsɔrbənt; əbˈsɔːbənt] *adj.* 能吸收的。—*n.* 〖醫〗吸收劑。
absorbent cotton 脫脂棉；藥棉。
ab·sorb·ing [əbˈsɔrbɪŋ; əbˈsɔːbiŋ] *adj.* ①吸收的。②極有趣的；撩人心的。
***ab·sorp·tion** [əbˈsɔrpʃən; əbˈsɔːpʃən] *n.* ①吸收。the *absorption* of water by cotton. 棉花之吸水。②全神貫注。*absorption* in one's work. 專心於工作。③〖生理〗吸收作用。④合併。—**ab·sorp·tive,** *adj.*
ab·squat·u·late [æbˈskwɑtʃəˌlet; əbˈskwɔtjuleit] *v.i.*, **-lat·ed, -lat·ing.** 〖俚〗①逃脫。②拐逃。
ab·stain [əbˈsten; əbˈstein] *v.i.* ①(自動地)戒絕〖from〗. ②棄權。—**er,** *n.*
ab·ste·mi·ous [æbˈstimɪəs; æbˈstiːmjəs] *adj.* ①飲食有度的；有節制的；適度的。②經濟的；節儉的。
ab·sten·tion [æbˈstɛnʃən; æbˈstenʃən] *n.* ①自制；節制；戒絕。②廻避；棄權。③棄權者。—**ab·sten·tious,** *adj.*
ab·sterge [æbˈstɝdʒ, əbˈstəːdʒ] *v.t.*, **-sterged, -sterg·ing.** ①使清潔。②洗淨。
ab·ster·gent [æbˈstɝdʒənt, əbˈstəːdʒənt] *adj.* 洗淨的；有去垢性的。—*n.* 洗淨劑；去垢物。
ab·ster·sion [æbˈstɝʃən; æbˈstəːʃən] *n.* 洗淨；洗淨法。
ab·ster·sive [æbˈstɝsɪv; æbˈstəːsiv] *adj.* 去垢性的；洗淨的。—*n.* 洗淨劑。
ab·sti·nence [ˈæbstənəns; ˈæbstinəns] *n.* ①禁戒酒類或其他嗜慾。②〖經濟〗節儉；省用。③〖宗教〗禁食。
ab·sti·nent [ˈæbstənənt; ˈæbstinənt] *adj.* 節慾的；禁慾的；有節制的。—*n.* 禁慾者。
abstr. ①abstract. ②abstracted.
***ab·stract** [*adj.* æbˈstrækt, ˈæbstrækt; ˈæbstrækt *v.* æbˈstrækt; æbˈstrækt *n.* ˈæbstrækt; ˈæbstrækt] *adj.* ①抽象的。Sweetness is *abstract;* sugar is concrete. "甜"是抽象的；"糖"是具體的。②理論的。*abstract* science. 理論科學。③難以了解的。Philosophy is an *abstract* subject. 哲學是一門難以了解的科目。—*v.t.* ①抽出；抽去；提煉。②摘要；節略。③使離開注意；不關心。④偷。—*n.* ①摘要。to make an *abstract* of a speech. 將演說作一摘要。②抽象；理論。③抽象藝術品。*in the abstract* 在理論方面。—**er,** *n.*
ab·stract·ed [æbˈstræktɪd; æbˈstræktid] *adj.* ①抽出了的；被分出的〖from〗. ②心不在焉的。—**ly,** *adv.* —**ness,** *n.*
Abstract Expressionism 〖美術〗抽象畫派風格或畫法。
ab·strac·tion [æbˈstrækʃən; æbˈstrækʃən] *n.* ①抽出。②抽象概念。③心不在焉。④〖美術〗抽象畫派之風格或特點；抽象派作品。⑤不切實際的觀念。
ab·strac·tion·ism [æbˈstrækʃənɪzm; æbˈstrækʃənizm] *n.* 〖美術〗抽象派。—**ab·strac·tion·ist,** *n.*
abstract noun 〖文法〗抽象名詞。
abstract number 〖數學〗不名數。
ab·struse [æbˈstrus; æbˈstruːs] *adj.* 深奧的；難解的。
ab·stru·si·ty [æbˈstrusətɪ; æbˈstruːsiti] *n.*, *pl.* **-ties.** ①深奧。②深奧的事物。
***ab·surd** [əbˈsɝd; əbˈsəːd] *adj.* 荒謬的；可笑的。Their request is *absurd.* 他們的要求是荒謬的。—**ly,** *adv.* —**ness,** *n.*
***ab·surd·i·ty** [əbˈsɝdətɪ; əbˈsəːditi] *n.*, *pl.* **-ties.** 愚蠢；荒謬；愚蠢荒謬的事物。
abt. about.
Abt system [ɑpt~; ɑːpt~] 〖鐵路〗「阿卜特式。」
a·build·ing [əˈbɪldɪŋ; əˈbildiŋ] *adj.* 興建中；醞釀中。
a·bu·li·a [əˈbjulɪə; əˈbjuːliə] *n.* 〖心理〗意志缺失。
***a·bun·dance** [əˈbʌndəns; əˈbʌndəns] *n.* 豐富；充足；多。The tree yields an *abundance* of fruit. 這樹結果甚多。
***a·bun·dant** [əˈbʌndənt; əˈbʌndənt] *adj.* 豐富的；充足的。The country is *abundant* in natural resources. 這個國家天然資源豐富。—**ly,** *adv.* —**ness,** *n.*
***a·buse** [*v.* əˈbjuz; əˈbjuːz *n.* əˈbjus; əˈbjuːs] *v.*, **a·bused, a·bus·ing,** *n.* —*v.t.* ①濫用。②虐待。A good rider never *abuses* his horse. 善騎者永不虐待其馬。③辱罵。Don't *abuse* your friends. 勿辱罵你的朋友。④非禮。⑤手淫。—*n.* ①濫用；妄用。the *abuse* of privileges. 濫用特權。②虐待。③辱罵。a term of *abuse.* 辱罵的話。④惡習；弊端。⑤强姦。
a·bu·sive [əˈbjusɪv; əˈbjuːsiv] *adj.* ①濫用的。②辱罵的。③虐待的。—**ly,** *adv.* —**ness,** *n.*
a·bus·tle [əˈbʌsl; əˈbʌsl] *adj.* 忙碌的。
a·but [əˈbʌt; əˈbʌt] *v.*, **a·but·ted, a·but·ting.** —*v.i.* 鄰接；緊靠。 —*v.t.* 與…鄰接；藉礅柱支撐。 —**ter,** *n.*
a·bu·ti·lon [əˈbjutɪˌlɑn; əˈbjuːtilən] *n.* 〖植物〗①(A-)苘麻屬。②苘麻。
a·but·ment [əˈbʌtmənt; əˈbʌtmənt] *n.* ①鄰接；接界，交接處。②〖建築〗礅柱；橋礅；橋台。③支撐點。
a·but·tal [əˈbʌtl; əˈbʌtl] *n.* ①鄰接；毗連；接界。②(*pl.*) 地界；邊境；境地。
a·but·ting [əˈbʌtɪŋ; əˈbʌtiŋ] *adj.* 鄰接的；毗連的。
a·buzz [əˈbʌz; əˈbʌz] *adj.* & *adv.* 嘈雜的(地)；匆忙的(地)。
abv. above.
a·bysm [əˈbɪzəm; əˈbizəm] *n.* 〖詩〗= abyss.
a·bys·mal [əˈbɪzml; əˈbizməl] *adj.* ①深淵的；地獄的。②深不可測的。—**ly,** *adv.*
***a·byss** [əˈbɪs; əˈbis] *n.* ①深淵；任何深不可測之事物。②智力或精神的深奧處。③地獄。
a·byss·al [əˈbɪsl; əˈbisəl] *adj.* ①深淵

的;無底的;深不可測的。②深海的。
abyssal zone 〖生物地理〗深海區。
Ac 〖化〗元素 actinium 之符號。
ac. acre or acres.
ac- 〖字首〗**ad-** 之異體。
AC, A.C. ① Air Corps. ② Alpine Club. ③Ambulance Corps. ④American Club. ⑤Ante Christum. ⑥Army Corps. ⑦Athletic Club. ⑧Atlantic Charter. ⑨ hydrocyanic acid. **AC, A.C., a-c.** alternating current. **AC.** Acceptance. **A/C, a/c** ① account. ② account current. **a.c.** ① before meals. ② alternating current.
-ac 〖字尾〗構成形容詞而表下列諸義: ①有…之特徵的。②有關…的。③受…感染的。
a·ca·cia 〔ə'keʃə; ə'keiʃə〕 *n.* ①〖植物〗樹屬。②〖植物〗刺槐之一種。③阿拉伯樹膠。④黃綠色。
acad. academy.
ac·a·deme 〔ˌækə'dim; ˌækə'di:m〕 *n.* 〖詩〗=**academy.** 「*n.*學究生涯;學術環境。」
ac·a·de·mi·a 〔ˌækə'dimɪə; ˌækə'demiə〕
Academia Sinica 〖中〗中央研究院。
***ac·a·dem·ic** 〔ˌækə'dɛmɪk; ˌækə'demik〕 *adj.* (亦作 **academical**) ①屬於各級學校的。*academic* year. 學年。②屬於有關人文研究及自然科學之大學各系的。③理論的。④傳統的。⑤學院派哲學的。—*n.* ①大學生;大學教師。②學會會員。③學院派哲學家。—**ally,** *adv.*
ac·a·dem·i·cals 〔ˌækə'dɛmək!z; ˌækə'demiklz〕 *n. pl.* 普通學士,碩士,或博士服。(亦作 **academic costume**)
academic freedom 學術研究自由。
a·cad·e·mi·cian 〔əˌkædə'mɪʃən; əˌkædə'miʃən〕 *n.* 學會會員;協會會員;院士。
ac·a·dem·i·cism 〔ˌækə'dɛməˌsɪzəm; ˌækə'demisizm〕 *n.* ①(藝術,文學,音樂上)墨守成規。②形式主義。(亦作 **academism**)
academic rank 〖美,加〗大學教師的等級。
a·cad·e·mize 〔ə'kædəˌmaɪz; ə'kædəmaiz〕 *v.i.,* **-mized, -miz·ing.** ①組成爲學會。②使…成爲傳統的。
***a·cad·e·my** 〔ə'kædəmɪ; ə'kædəmi〕 *n., pl.* **-mies.** ①私立高級中學。②專科學校。Naval *Academy.* 海軍軍官學校。③學會。④(A-)學院派哲學。
a·cal·cu·li·a 〔ˌekæl'kjulɪə; ˌeikæl'kju:liə〕 *n.* 計算力缺失;計算不能。「水母。」
ac·a·leph 〔'ækəlɛf; 'ækəlef〕 *n.* 〖動物〗
a·can·thus 〔ə'kænθəs; ə'kænθəs〕 *n., pl.* **-thus·es, -thi** 〔-θaɪ; -θai〕. ①〖植物〗爵牀;莨菪。②〖建築〗爵牀葉形的裝飾。
a cap·pel·la 〔ˌɑkə'pɛlə; ˌɑ:kə'pelə〕 〖義〗〖音樂〗不用樂器伴奏;以教堂音樂風格(指合唱而言)。(亦作 **a capella**)
ac·a·ro·pho·bi·a 〔ˌækərə'fobɪə; 'ækərə'foubiə〕 *n.* 〖精神科〗恙蟲恐怖;疥癬恐怖。 「〖植物〗不結果實的。」
a·car·pous 〔e'kɑrpəs; ei'kɑ:pəs〕 *adj.*
a·cat·a·lec·tic 〔eˌkæt!'ɛktɪk, ˌækæt!-; æˌkætə'lektik〕 *adj.* (詩行音節數)完整的。—*n.* 完整的詩行。
acc. ①acceptance. ②according. ③account. ④accountant. ⑤accusative. ⑥accelerate. ⑦acceleration. ⑧accept. ⑨accompanied. ⑩accompaniment. ⑪accordant.
acce. acceptance.
ac·cede 〔æk'sid; æk'si:d〕 *v.i.,* **-ced·ed, -ced·ing.** ①同意;允諾。②就職;繼承。③加入。
accel. accelerando.
ac·cel·er·an·do 〔ækˌsɛlə'rændo; ækˌselə'rændou〕 *adv., adj., n., pl.* **-dos.** —*adv.* 〖音樂〗漸速地。—*adj.* 〖音樂〗漸速的。—*n.* 〖音樂〗漸速音;漸速樂節。
ac·cel·er·ant 〔æk'sɛlərənt; æk'selərənt〕 *n.* ①加速器;促進劑。②〖化〗觸媒。
ac·cel·er·ate 〔æk'sɛləˌret; æk'seləreit〕 *v.,* **-at·ed, -at·ing.,** *n.* —*v.t.* ①加速進行或動作。②迫使;催促。③改變(一動體)之速率。—*v.i.* ①加速。②〖教育〗速成。—*n.* 受速成教育的學生。
accelerated depreciation 〖會計〗加速折舊(折舊率較高的)。
accelerated motion 〖物理〗加速運動。
ac·cel·er·a·tion 〔ækˌsɛlə'reʃən; ækˌselə'reiʃən〕 *n.* ①加速;促進。②〖物理〗加速度。③〖教育〗飛躍進級;特別進級。④〖經濟〗加速原理。
ac·cel·er·a·tive 〔æk'sɛləˌretɪv; æk'selərətiv〕 *adj.* 加速的;催促的。
ac·cel·er·a·tor 〔æk'sɛləˌretɚ; ək'seləreitə〕 *n.* ①加速者;加速物。②變速器。③〖解剖〗加速神經;加速筋。④〖照相〗顯像催進劑。⑤〖物理〗加速器。⑥〖化〗觸媒劑。
ac·cel·er·a·to·ry 〔æk'sɛlərəˌtɔrɪ; æk'selərətəri〕 *adj.* 加速的。
ac·cel·er·o·graph 〔æk'sɛlərəˌgræf; æk'selərəgrɑ:f〕 *n.* 發射(爆炸)壓力測量計。
ac·cel·er·om·e·ter 〔ækˌsɛlə'rɑmɪtɚ; ækˌselər'ɔmitə〕 *n.* 加速計;測震儀。
***ac·cent** 〔*n.* 'æksɛnt; 'æksənt *v.* æk'sɛnt, 'æksɛnt; æk'sent〕 *n.* ①揚音;重音。primary *accent.* 主重音。②重音符。③腔調;口音;土音。He speaks French with an English *accent.* 他說法國話帶英國的口音。④音調;語調;聲調。⑤加於字母上表示讀音的符號。⑥强調;注重〖on〗。⑦〖數學〗右肩上的符號。⑧符號(′)代表英尺或分;(″)代表英寸或秒。—*v.i.* ①重讀。The first syllable should be *accented.* 第一音節應重讀。②加音符。③着重;强調。
ac·cen·tu·al 〔æk'sɛntʃuəl; æk'sentjuəl〕 *adj.* ①重音的。②〖詩〗以重音爲節奏的。—**ly,** *adv.*
ac·cen·tu·ate 〔æk'sɛntʃuˌet; æk'sentjueit〕 *v.i.,* **-at·ed, -at·ing.** ①用重音讀。②加重;强調。—**ac·cen·tu·a·tion,** *n.*
ac·cen·tu·a·tor 〔æk'sɛntʃuˌetɚ; æk'sentjueitə〕 *n.* 强調者。
‡**ac·cept** 〔ək'sɛpt; ək'sept〕 *v.t.* ①領受;接受。He *accepted* a present from his friend. 他接受了朋友的禮物。②同意。I *accept* your excuse. 我同意你的辯解。③信受(其說)。I *accept* his words as true. 我把他的話信以爲眞。④接受;承認。His proposal was *accepted.* 他的提議被接受了。⑤承受。to *accept* an office. 承擔一個職務。⑥承兌;認付。to *accept* a note. 承兌票據。
***ac·cept·a·ble** 〔ək'sɛptəb!; ək'septəbl〕 *adj.* ①可接受的;值得接受的。②合意的。③勉强够格的。—**ac·cept·a·bil·i·ty,** *n.* —**ac·cept·a·bly,** *adv.*
***ac·cept·ance** 〔ək'sɛptəns; ək'septəns〕 *n.* ①領受。②承認;接受。③信受(學說)。*acceptance* of a theory. 信仰一種學說。④〖商〗(票據、匯票等之)承兌;認付。absolute (*or* clean) *acceptance.* 單純認付或承兌。⑤〖商〗承兌票據;已認付的期票。

ac·cept·an·cy [æk'sɛptənsɪ; ək'septənsi] *n.* ①接受。②願意接受。
ac·cept·ant [ək'sɛptənt; ək'septənt] *adj.* 接受的;容納的。—*n.* 接受者。
ac·cep·ta·tion [ˌæksɛp'teʃən;ˌæksep'teiʃən] *n.* ①公認的意義。②滿意的接受;良好的反應。③相信;信受。
ac·cept·ed [ək'sɛptɪd; ək'septid] *adj.* 爲一般公認的或使用的。**—ly,** *adv.*
ac·cept·ee ['æksɛp'ti; 'æksep'tiː] *n.* 被接受的人(如合格的役男等)。
accepting charge 承兌費。
ac·cept·ive [ək'sɛptɪv; ək'septiv] *adj.* ①易接納的。②可接受的。
ac·cep·tor [ək'sɛptɚ; ək'septə] *n.* ①(亦作 **accepter**) 領受人;接受者。②〖商〗票據承兌人。③〖無線電〗接收器。
***ac·cess** ['æksɛs; 'ækses] *n., pl.* **-es.** ①接近,進入或使用之權。Professors have free *access* to the library. 教授可以自由使用圖書館。②易於或難於接近之狀態。③接近之途徑或方法。④(疾病的)發作。*access* of a disease. 疾病的發作。⑤(怒氣的)爆發;突發。in an *access* of fury. 在發怒中。⑥增加;增長。
ac·ces·so·ry [æk'sɛsərɪ; æk'sesəri] *n., pl.* **-ries,** *adj.* =**accessory.**
access clerk 貴重物品保管處的管理員。
ac·ces·si·bil·i·ty [ækˌsɛsə'bɪlətɪ;ækˌsesi'biliti] *n.* ①易接近;可親。②可取得;可達到;可進入。③易受影響;易變。
***ac·ces·si·ble** [æk'sɛsəbl; æk'sesəbl] *adj.* ①易近的;可親的;可進入的。The White House is *accessible* to ordinary visitors. 普通遊客可以進白宮去參觀。②容易取得的;可達到的。③易受影響的; 易受引誘的 〖to〗. He is *accessible* to bribery. 他易於受賄。**—ac·ces·si·bly,** *adv.*
***ac·ces·sion** [æk'sɛʃən; æk'seʃən] *n.* ①到達。*accession* to manhood. 成年。②(權力等之)獲得;即位;就職。③增加; 增加物。*accession* of wealth. 財富之增加。④加入;加盟。⑤〖法律〗添附。⑥發作(脾氣等)。⑦雇用。⑧同意。—*v.t.* 登記於新增圖書目錄。
ac·ces·sion·al [æk'sɛʃənl; æk'seʃənl] *adj.* 新加的;額外的。
accession book (圖書館之)新到圖書目錄。
ac·ces·so·ri·al [ˌæksə'sorɪəl; ˌæksə'sɔːriəl] *adj.* ①=**accessory.** ②新加的; 附加的;增補的。
ac·ces·so·ri·ly [æk'sɛsərɪlɪ; æk'sesərili] *adv.* 從犯地;附屬地;附從地。
ac·ces·so·ri·us [ˌæksɪ'sorɪəs; ˌæksi'souriəs] *n.* 〖解剖〗 副神經;副肌;副腺。
ac·ces·so·ry** [æk'sɛsərɪ; æk'sesəri] *n., pl.* **-ries,** *adj.*—*n.* ①附件或附加物;附屬品。②從犯。He is an *accessory* to the murder. 他是這謀殺案的幫兇。③附屬裝飾品。accessory after the fact*** 隱匿或協助犯人;知情不報之從犯。***accessory before the fact*** 事前參與預謀之從犯。—*adj.* ①附加的;附屬的。②幫兇的。
access permit 〖美〗可使用機密文件或進入管制地區的許可。
access road 通入幹線道的支線道路。
access time 〖電腦〗進出時間。
ac·ci·dence ['æksədəns; 'æksidəns] *n.* ①(任何課程的)初步;入門。②〖文法〗語形變化之規則(如 foot, feet; have, has, had).
‡**ac·ci·dent** ['æksədənt; 'æksidənt] *n.* ①意外之事 (災害)。There was a motor-car *accident* yesterday. 昨天有一樁車禍。②偶然之事。③附帶之性質。④〖地理〗(地面之)起伏;高低。***by accident*** 偶然。I met him *by accident*. 我偶然遇到他。***meet with an accident*** 遭遇意外的事。
***ac·ci·den·tal** [ˌæksə'dɛntl; ˌæksi'dentl] *adj.* ①偶然的。Our meeting was quite *accidental*. 我們的相遇是很偶然的。②附帶的。③〖音樂〗臨時符的。 —*n.* ①〖音樂〗臨時符號。②次要的特性或情況。
ac·ci·den·tal·ism [ˌæksə'dɛntəˌlɪzəm; ˌæksi'dentəlizm] *n.* ①偶然; 偶然之結果。②〖哲學〗偶然論; 偶發說。③〖醫〗病徵重於病源之醫學。**—ac·ci·den·tal·ist,** *n.*
ac·ci·den·tal·ly [ˌæksə'dɛntlɪ; ˌæksi'dentəli] *adv.* ①偶然地。②附帶地。
accident boat 吊在船身外的小救生艇。
ac·ci·dent·ed ['æksəˌdɛntɪd; 'æksidentid] *adj.* 表面起伏不平的。
accident insurance 傷害保險;災害保險。
ac·ci·dent-prone ['æksədəntˌpron; 'æksidəntˌproun] *adj.* 易遭意外的。**—ness,** *n.*
ac·ci·dent·proof ['æksədəntˌpruf; 'æksidəntˌpruːf] *adj.* 可防止意外或減少意外機會的。
ac·ci·die ['æksədi; 'æksidiː] *n.* 懶洋洋;呆鈍;無感覺。
ac·cip·i·ter [æk'sɪpɪtɚ; æk'sipitə] *n., pl.* **-tres** [-triz; -triːz]. ①鷹;鷹類之海禽。②〖外科〗鷹爪帶(裹鼻繃帶)。
ac·cip·i·tral [æk'sɪpɪtrəl; æk'sipitrəl] *adj.* ①(似)鷹的。②鷹類之猛禽(性)的。
ac·claim [ə'klem; ə'kleim] *v.t.* 歡呼; 稱讚。—*v.i.* 歡呼;稱讚。—*n.* 歡呼;稱讚。
ac·cla·ma·tion [ˌæklə'meʃən; ˌæklə'meiʃən] *n.* ①歡呼;稱讚。②口頭表決。
ac·clam·a·to·ry [ə'klæməˌtorɪ; ə'klæmətəri] *adj.* 歡呼的;稱讚的。
ac·cli·mate [ə'klaɪmɪt; ə'klaimit] *v.t. & v.i.,* **-mat·ed, -mat·ing.** 〖主美〗(使)服水土;(使)習慣於新環境(生活方式);(使)適應。**—ac·cli·mat·a·ble,** *adj.*
ac·cli·ma·tion [ˌæklə'meʃən; ˌæklə'meiʃən] *n.* 〖美〗新環境適應;氣候適應。
ac·cli·ma·ti·za·tion [əˌklaɪmətə'zeʃən; əˌklaimətai'zeiʃən] *n.* 〖英〗新環境適應;氣候適應。
ac·cli·ma·tize [ə'klaɪməˌtaɪz; ə'klaimətaiz] *v.t. & v.i.,* **-tized, -tiz·ing.** 〖主英〗=**acclimate.**
ac·cliv·i·tous [ə'klɪvətəs; ə'klivitəs] *adj.* 向上傾斜的。
ac·cliv·i·ty [ə'klɪvətɪ; ə'kliviti] *n., pl.* **-ties.** 向上的斜坡(爲 declivity 之對)。**—ac·cli·vous,** *adj.*
ac·co·lade [ˌækə'led; 'ækəleid] *n.* ①武士授與式。②賞賜;讚頌。③〖音樂〗(連結譜表之)鉤線;連結括弧。④〖建築〗S 形狀的穹窿。
ac·com·mo·da·ble [ə'kɑmədəbl; ə'kɔmədəbl] *adj.* 可使適應的。
***ac·com·mo·date** [ə'kɑməˌdet; ə'kɔmədeit] *v.,* **-dat·ed, -dat·ing.** —*v.t.* ①給方便;幫助。②容納。This big room will *accommodate* six beds. 這大房間可以容納六張牀。③供給住宿。 ④使適應。 ⑤調解。—*v.i.* 適應;同意;調停。
ac·com·mo·dat·ing [ə'kɑməˌdetɪŋ; ə'kɔmədeitiŋ] *adj.* 肯通融的; 好施惠的。**—ly,** *adv.*
***ac·com·mo·da·tion** [əˌkɑmə'deʃən; əˌkɔmə'deiʃən] *n.* ①(常 *pl.*) 暫時的住宿或

膳宿。②施惠;便利。③適應。④調解。⑤貸款。⑥助人之熱誠。⑦視力調節。⑧(常*pl.*)車、船、飛機上的座位,房間,艙位等。

accommodation ladder 舷梯。

accommodation sale (貨物)轉批。

accommodation train 火車慢車。

ac·com·mo·da·tive [əˈkɑməˌdetɪv; əˈkɔmədeitiv] *adj.* ①調節的;調和的。②肯通融的。—**ness,** *n.*

ac·com·mo·da·tor [əˈkɑməˌdetɚ; əˈkɔmədeitə] *n.* ①調解者。②調節器。

ac·com·pa·ni·er [əˈkʌmpənɪɚ; əˈkʌmpəniə] *n.* 陪伴的人或物。

***ac·com·pa·ni·ment** [əˈkʌmpənɪmənt; əˈkʌmpənimənt] *n.* ①陪伴物;隨以俱來之物。②〖音樂〗伴奏。She sang to the *accompaniment* of the piano. 她演唱由鋼琴伴奏。

ac·com·pa·nist [əˈkʌmpənɪst; əˈkʌmpənist] *n.* ①〖音樂〗伴奏者;伴唱者。②同伴;伴隨物。(亦作 **accompanyist**)

‡**ac·com·pa·ny** [əˈkʌmpənɪ; əˈkʌmpəni] *v.,* **-nied, -ny·ing.** —*v.t.* ①伴;陪。Please *accompany* me on my walk. 請陪我散步。②隨。Thunder *accompanies* lightning. 雷隨閃電而來。③補充。④伴奏。—*v.i.* 伴奏;伴唱。

ac·com·plice [əˈkɑmplɪs; əˈkɔmplis] 「*n.* 從犯;同謀者。」

‡**ac·com·plish** [əˈkɑmplɪʃ; əˈkɔmpliʃ] *v.t.* 達到;完成;實現。to *accomplish* one's mission. 完成使命。—**er,** *n.* —**a·ble,** *adj.*

***ac·com·plished** [əˈkɑmplɪʃt; əˈkɔmpliʃt] *adj.* ①完成的;實現的。an *accomplished* fact. 已成的事實。②完善的;熟練的;有成就的。③善社交而多才藝的。

***ac·com·plish·ment** [əˈkɑmplɪʃmənt; əˈkɔmpliʃmənt] *n.* ①實行;完成;達到。②成就。③(常*pl.*)技藝;才能。Among her *accomplishments* were sewing, cooking, playing the piano and dancing. 她的才能包括縫紉、烹調、彈鋼琴和跳舞。

***ac·cord** [əˈkɔrd; əˈkɔːd] *v.i.* 一致;相合。His actions *accorded* with his belief. 他的行爲與信仰一致。—*v.t.* 給與。—*n.* ①一致;相合。②國際間協定(常指非正式的)。③(顏色、音調等之)調和。④(法庭外)和解。*of one's own accord* 出於自願;自動地。—**er,** *n.* —**a·ble,** *adj.*

***ac·cord·ance** [əˈkɔrdn̩s; əˈkɔːdəns] *n.* ①一致;和諧。②賦與。the *accordance* of a privilege. 特權之賦與。

ac·cord·an·cy [əˈkɔrdənsɪ; əˈkɔːdənsi] *n.* =**accord, accordance.**

ac·cord·ant [əˈkɔrdn̩t; əˈkɔːdənt] *adj.* ①一致的;調和的〖with, to〗。②〖地質〗高度相等或幾乎相等的。—**ly,** *adv.*

ac·cor·da·tu·ra [əˌkɔrdəˈturə; əˌkɔːdəˈtuːrə] *n., pl.* **-ras, -re** [-rɛ; -re]. 〖音樂〗調絃(絃樂器之調音)。

‡**ac·cord·ing** [əˈkɔrdɪŋ; əˈkɔːdiŋ] *adj.* ①相符的;一致的。②〖俗〗視…而定的。It's all *according* what you want to do. 那要看你想做甚麼而定。

according as ①依照。②如果。

***ac·cord·ing·ly** [əˈkɔrdɪŋlɪ; əˈkɔːdiŋli] *adv.* 如前所說;於是。He was told to speak briefly; *accordingly* he cut short his remarks. 叫他說話簡短,於是他把話刪簡了。

‡**according to** 依照;據。*According to* the papers, our export increases every year. 據報紙所載,我們的出口年有增加。

ac·cor·di·on [əˈkɔrdɪən; əˈkɔːdjən] *n.* 手風琴。—*adj.* 如手風琴之摺箱的;折摺的。

ac·cor·di·on·ist [əˈkɔrdɪənɪst; əˈkɔːdjənist] *n.* 手風琴師。

ac·cost [əˈkɔst; əˈkɔst] *v.t.* 向人搭訕;「招呼。」

ac·cost·a·ble [əˈkɔstəbl̩; əˈkɔstəbl] *adj.* 易於搭訕的。

ac·couche [əˈkuʃ; əˈkuːʃ] *v.,* **-couched, -couch·ing.** —*v.i.* 接生。—*v.t.* 〖美〗①產生;創造。②接生。

ac·couche·ment [əˈkuʃmɑ̃; əˈkuːʃ- 「mɑ̃ː] 〖法〗 *n.* 分娩;生產。」

ac·cou·cheur [ˌækuˈʃɝ; ˌækuːˈʃəː] 〖法〗 *n.* 產科醫生。

ac·cou·cheuse [ˌækuˈʃɝz; ˌækuː- 「ˈʃəːz] 〖法〗 *n.* 助產士。」

‡**ac·count** [əˈkaunt; əˈkaunt] *n.* ①報告;記事。Please give me an *account* of your trip. 請你告訴我你旅行的情形。②原因。I will do it on your *account.* 因你之故我願爲此。③計及;考慮。He takes no *account* of my warning. 他不理會我的警告。④價值。⑤戶頭;帳目。He opened an *account* in the bank. 他在銀行開戶頭。⑥利益。He did it on his own *account.* 他爲了自己的利益而爲此。⑦(常 *pl.*)據聞;道聽塗說。By all *accounts,* he is very rich. 據說他很富有。*balance account* **a.** 差額帳。**b.** 借方差額帳;負債差額帳。*call to account* 要求說明;責問;申斥。*give an account of oneself* 表現。*make much* (or *little*) *account of* (不)注意;(不)重視。*on account* 作爲分期付款;作爲部分付款。This is a payment *on account.* 這是付款的一部分。*on account of* 因爲。*on no account* 無論持何理由決不;切莫。You must *on no account* leave here. 你切莫離此。*take account of* **a.** 考慮;斟酌;體諒;注意。**b.** 作筆記。*take into account* 考慮;計及。*turn to account* 利用。—*v.i.* ①解釋;說明〖for〗。②對…負責;引起(某種後果)。—*v.t.* 認爲。I *account* myself well paid. 我認爲我所得的報酬尚佳。

ac·count·a·bil·i·ty [əˌkauntəˈbɪlətɪ; əˌkauntəˈbiliti] *n.* 負有義務或責任。

ac·count·a·ble [əˈkauntəbl̩; əˈkauntəbl] *adj.* ①應加解說的;有責任的。②可說明的。—**ness,** *n.* —**ac·count·a·bly,** *adv.*

ac·count·an·cy [əˈkauntənsɪ; əˈkauntənsi] *n.* accountant 之技術或職位;會計;主計。

ac·count·ant [əˈkauntənt; əˈkaun- 「tənt] *n.* 會計員;主計員。」

accountant general 會計主任。

account book 帳簿。

account current 往來帳戶(略作 A/C, 或 a/c)。

account day 付款日;結帳日。

account executive (廣告業或服務業之)業務經理。

ac·count·ing [əˈkauntɪŋ; əˈkauntiŋ] *n.* 商業會計法;會計(學);(記)帳;清理帳務。

account payable 〖會計〗應付帳款。

account receivable 〖會計〗應收帳款。

ac·cou·ter [əˈkutɚ; əˈkuːtə] *v.t.,* **-tered, -ter·ing.** 供給以服裝;裝備(尤指軍用品)。(英亦作 **accoutre**)

ac·cou·ter·ment [əˈkutɚmənt; əˈkuːtəmənt] *n.* ①(*pl.*)衣著;服裝。②(*pl.*)(武器、軍服以外之)裝備;配備。③穿;著。(英亦作 **accoutrement**)

accrd. int. accrued interest.
ac·cred·it [ə'krɛdɪt; ə'kredit] *v.t.* ①譽(某人)爲；謂(某人)有。②歸功(某事)於(某人)；謂(某事)屬於某人。③信以爲眞；信賴。④授以權狀或任命狀；委派。⑤承認合格；備案。—ment, *n.*
ac·cred·i·ta·tion [əˌkrɛdə'teʃən; əˌkredi'teiʃən] *n.* 〖美〗立案；甄別合格。
ac·cred·it·ed [ə'krɛdɪtɪd; ə'kreditid] *adj.* ①可接受的；可信賴的。②公認合格的；備案或立案的。
ac·cres·cence [ə'krɛsəns; ə'kresns] *n.* 成長；增大。—**ac·cres·cent,** *adj.*
ac·crete [ə'krit; æ'kri:t] *v.,* **-cret·ed, -cret·ing,** *adj.* —*v.i.* 共同生長；依附〖to〗. —*v.t.* (藉生長等)附加。—*adj.* 〖植物〗共同生長的。
ac·cre·tion [ə'kriʃən; æ'kri:ʃən] *n.* ①(自然的)增大。②增加物。③〖法律〗添附。④〖醫〗合生；癒合。—**ac·cre·tive, —ar·y,** *adj.*
ac·croach [ə'krotʃ; ə'kroutʃ] *v.t.* 非法占有；强占。
ac·cru·al [ə'kruəl; ə'kru:əl] *n.* 增加；增殖；增加物；增加額。
ac·crue [ə'kru; ə'kru:] *v.i.,* **-crued, -cru·ing.** 自然增殖。 —**ment,** *n.*
accrued dividend 〖會計〗應計股利。
accrued interest 〖會計〗應計利息。
accrued liability 〖會計〗應計負債。
acct. ①account. ②accountant.
ac·cul·tur·ate [ə'kʌltʃəˌret; ə'kʌltʃəreit] *v.t.* & *v.i.,* **-at·ed, -at·ing.** 藉文化傳入而變化。 —**ac·cul·tur·a·tive,** *adj.*
ac·cul·tur·a·tion [əˌkʌltʃə'reʃən; əˌkʌltʃə'reiʃən] *n.* 〖社會學〗受化；涵化；文化之傳入；文化之接受；混合型文化。 —**al,** *adj.*
ac·cum·bent [ə'kʌmbənt; ə'kʌmbənt] *adj.* ①橫臥的。②〖植物〗對位的。
***ac·cu·mu·late** [ə'kjumjəˌlet; ə'kju:mjuleit] *v.,* **-lat·ed, -lat·ing.** —*v.t.* 積；堆積；積聚。—*v.i.* 堆積；積聚。His debts *accumulated.* 他債台高築。 —**ac·cu·mu·la·ble,** *adj.*
***ac·cu·mu·la·tion** [əˌkjumjə'leʃən; əˌkju:mju'leiʃən] *n.* ①積聚。*accumulation* of books. 積聚圖書。②積聚的東西。
accumulation point 〖數學〗聚點。
ac·cu·mu·la·tive [ə'kjumjəˌletɪv; ə'kju:mjulətiv] *adj.* ①積聚的。②熱心積聚的；貪得的。—**ly,** *adv.* —**ness,** *n.*
ac·cu·mu·la·tor [ə'kjumjəˌletɚ; ə'kju:mjuleitə] *n.* ①積聚者；蓄財者。②〖英〗蓄電池。③〖機械〗蓄力器。④緩衝裝置；緩衝器。
***ac·cu·ra·cy** ['ækjərəsɪ; 'ækjurəsi] *n.* 正確性。I doubt the *accuracy* of your statement. 我懷疑你所說的話之正確性。
***ac·cu·rate** ['ækjərɪt; 'ækjurit] *adj.* 正確的。 —**ly,** *adv.* —**ness,** *n.*
ac·curs·ed [ə'kɝsɪd, -st; ə'kə:sid] *adj.* ①被咒的；不幸的。②可惡的；討厭的。(亦作 **accurst**) —**ly,** *adv.* —**ness,** *n.*
ac·cus·a·ble [ə'kjuzəbl; ə'kju:zəbl] *adj.* 可控訴的；可非難的。—**ac·cus·a·bly,** *adv.*
***ac·cu·sa·tion** [ˌækjə'zeʃən; ˌækju(:)'zeiʃən] *n.* ①控告。He made a false *accusation* against his neighbor. 他誣告他的鄰居。②指控之罪。
ac·cu·sa·ti·val [əˌkjuzə'taɪvəl; əˌkju:zə'taivəl] *adj.* 〖文法〗目的格的；受格的。
ac·cu·sa·tive [ə'kjuzətɪv; ə'kju:zətiv] *adj.* 〖文法〗目的格的；受格的。 —*n.* 〖文法〗目的格；目的格之字。
ac·cu·sa·to·ri·al [əˌkjuzə'torɪəl; əˌkju:zə'tɔ:riəl] *adj.* 告發人的。—**ly,** *adv.*
ac·cu·sa·to·ry [ə'kjuzəˌtorɪ; ə'kju:zətəri] *adj.* 告發的；告訴的；非難的。
***ac·cuse** [ə'kjuz; ə'kju:z] *v.t.* & *v.i.,* **-cused, -cus·ing.** ①控告。They *accused* him of taking bribes. 他們控他受賄。②歸咎。
ac·cused [ə'kjuzd; ə'kju:zd] *n. sing.* or *pl.* 被告。—*adj.* 被控告的。 ***the accused*** 〖法律〗被告。
ac·cus·er [ə'kjuzɚ; ə'kju:zə] *n.* 原告；控訴者；非難者。
ac·cus·ing [ə'kjuzɪŋ; ə'kju:ziŋ] *adj.* 非難的；譴責的；歸咎的。 —**ly,** *adv.*
ac·cu·sive [ə'kjusɪv; ə'kju:siv] *adj.* 好指控的；喜非難的。
***ac·cus·tom** [ə'kʌstəm; ə'kʌstəm] *v.t.* 使習慣；習慣於。to *accustom* oneself to cold weather. 使自己習慣於冷的天氣。
***ac·cus·tomed** [ə'kʌstəmd; ə'kʌstəmd] *adj.* 通常的；習慣的。This is his *accustomed* hour to go to bed. 這是他就寢的慣常時間。 —**ly,** *adv.* —**ness,** *n.*
ace [es; eis] *n.* ①紙牌或骰子上的么點。②一點；小點；微粒。③傑出的人才。④戰鬥成績卓著的空軍戰鬥員。⑤(網球賽等中的)一分。 ***ace in the hole*** 到緊要關頭可資運用的某種具有決定性的事物。 ***have*** (or ***keep***) ***an ace up one's sleeve*** 獲有重要消息或論據。***within an ace of*** 差一點；瀕於。 —*adj.* 優秀的。
a·ce·di·a [ə'sidɪə; ə'si:diə] *n.* 怠惰；憂鬱；對人生厭煩。
ace-high ['es'haɪ; 'eis'hai] *adj.* 〖俗〗最好的；極受尊重的；極受重視的。
A·cel·da·ma [ə'sɛldəmə; ə'keldəmə, ə'sel-] *n.* ①〖聖經〗血田(以猶大出賣耶穌所得賄銀購買之地)。②血戰之地。
a·cen·tric [e'sɛntrɪk; ei'sentrik] *adj.* 無中心的；離中心的。
a·ceph·a·lous [e'sɛfələs; ei'sefələs] *adj.* ①〖動物〗無頭的。②〖修辭〗欠完整的；無首句的；起始欠完全的(如詩行)。③無領袖的。
ac·e·ra·ceous [ˌæsə'reʃəs; ˌæsə'reiʃəs] *adj.* 屬於楓木科的。
ac·er·ate ['æsəˌret; 'æsəreit] *adj.* 〖植物〗針尖狀的。
a·cerb [ə'sɝb; ə'sə:b] *adj.* ①(果實未成熟之)酸澀的。②刻薄的；嚴苛的。—**ly,** *adv.*
ac·er·bate ['æsɚˌbet; 'æsəbeit] *v.,* **-bat·ed, -bat·ing,** *adj.* —*v.t.* ①使酸；使苦澀。②使怒；激怒。—*adj.* 激怒的；心懷怨恨的。
a·cer·bi·ty [ə'sɝbətɪ; ə'sə:biti] *n., pl.* **-ties.** ①苦；酸；澀。②苛刻；嚴苛。
a·ces·cent [ə'sɛsənt; ə'sesənt] *adj.* 變酸的；微酸的；有酸味的。
a·ces·o·dyne [ə'sɛsəˌdaɪn; ə'sesədain] *adj.* 止痛的。
a·ces·to·ma [ˌæsɪ'stomə; ˌæsi'stoumə] *n.* 肉芽塊；肉牙片。
ac·e·tab·u·li·form [ˌæsɪ'tæbjuləˌfɔrm; ˌæsi'tæbjuləfɔ:m] *adj.* 〖植物〗碟狀的。
ac·e·tab·u·lum [ˌæsɪ'tæbjələm; ˌæsi'tæbjuləm] *n., pl.* **-lums** or **-la** [-lə; -lə]. ①〖解剖〗髀臼。②〖動物〗吸盤。③盛醋等的小杯或瓶。—**ac·e·tab·u·lar,** *adj.*
ac·e·tal ['æsəˌtæl; 'æsitæl] *n.* 〖化〗二乙氧基烷；乙縮醛。
ac·et·al·de·hyde [ˌæsə'tældəˌhaɪd; ˌæsi'tældəhaid] *n.* 〖化〗乙醛。

ac·et·an·i·lide [ˌæsəˈtænḷˌaɪd, –lɪd; ˌæsəˈtænilaid] *n.* 〖化〗乙醯苯胺(C_8H_9ON).(亦作 **acetanilid**)
ac·e·ta·ri·ous [ˌæsəˈtɛrɪəs; ˌæsiˈtɛəriəs] *adj.* 當作生菜食用的;涼拌用的。
ac·e·tate [ˈæsəˌtet; ˈæsitit] *n.* 〖化〗醋酸鹽。
ac·e·tat·ed [ˈæsəˌtetɪd, ˈæsiteitid] *adj.* 以醋酸處理過的。
acetate rayon 醋酸人造絲。
a·ce·tic [əˈsitɪk; əˈsiːtik] *adj.* 醋的;醋質的;酸的。
acetic acid〖化〗乙醋;醋酸(CH_3COOH).
a·cet·i·fi·ca·tion [əˌsɛtəfɪˈkeʃən; əˌsetifiˈkeiʃən] *n.* 醋化;酸化。
a·cet·i·fy [əˈsɛtəˌfaɪ; əˈsetifai] *v.t.* & *v.i.*, **-fied, -fy·ing.** 醋化;使成醋;變醋;發酸。
ac·e·tone [ˈæsəˌton; ˈæsitoun] *n.* 丙酮;醋酮。
ac·e·to·ni·trile [ˌæsətɑˈnaɪtrəl; ˌæsitɔˈnaitril] *n.*〖化〗乙腈。
ac·e·tous [ˈæsɪtəs; ˈæsitəs] *adj.* ①含(產生)醋酸的。②(似)醋的。
a·ce·tum [əˈsitəm; əˈsiːtəm] *n.* 〖藥〗醋酸溶液;醋。
ac·e·tyl·cho·line [ˌæsətɪlˈkolin; ˌæsitilˈkɔliːn] *n.* 醋膽素($C_7H_{17}O_3N$, 減低血壓劑)。
a·cet·y·lene [əˈsɛtḷˌin; əˈsetiliːn] *n.* 〖化〗乙炔;電石氣。
ac·e·tyl·ic [ˌæsɪˈtɪlɪk; ˌæsiˈtilik] *adj.* 屬於乙醯基的。
A·chae·an [əˈkiən; əˈkiːən] *adj.* ①亞該亞(Achaia)的;亞該亞人的。②希臘的。—*n.*①亞該亞人。②希臘人。(亦作**Achaian**)
A·cha·ia [əˈkeə; əˈkaiə] *n.* 亞該亞(古國名,在希臘南部)。
A·cha·tes [əˈketiz; əˈkeitiːz] *n.* ①Virgil 所著 Aeneid 詩中 Aeneas 之忠實友人。②忠實之友。
***ache** [ek; eik] *v.*, **ached, ach·ing,** *n.* —*v.t.* ①疼痛。②渴望。I am *aching* to join in the game. 我渴望參加比賽。—*n.* 痛。He has an *ache* in the back. 他的背痛。
Ach·e·lo·us [ˌækəˈloəs; ˌækəˈlouəs] *n.* 〖希臘神話〗河神。
a·chene [eˈkin; eiˈkiːn] *n.* 〖植物〗瘦果。
Ach·er·on [ˈækəˌrɑn; ˈækərɔn] *n.* ①〖希臘、羅馬神話〗Hades 之一河名。②地獄;黃泉。
a·chiev·a·ble [əˈtʃivəbḷ; əˈtʃiːvəbl] *adj.* 可完成的。
***a·chieve** [əˈtʃiv; əˈtʃiːv] *v.*, **-chieved, -chiev·ing.** —*v.t.* ①完成;實現。②獲得。He finally *achieved* success. 他最後獲得成功。—*v.i.*實現希冀的結果。—**a·chiev·er,** *n.*
***a·chieve·ment** [əˈtʃivmənt; əˈtʃiːvmənt] *n.* ①完成;達成。It was impossible of *achievement*. 這是不可能完成的。②成就;事功;偉績。
achievement age 〖心理〗成績年齡。
achievement quotient 〖心理〗成績商數(以實際年齡除教育年齡所得之商數,簡寫爲 AQ).
achievement test 〖心理〗成績測驗;教學成就測驗。
Ach·il·le·an [ˌækɪˈliən; ˌækiˈli(ː)ən] *adj.* 似Achilles 的;無敵的;盛怒的;迅速的。
A·chil·les [əˈkɪliz; əˈkiliːz] *n.* 阿奇里斯(荷馬史詩 *Iliad* 中之希臘英雄,傳說除踵部外,其全身刀鎗不入)。***Achilles heel*** or ***heel of Achilles*** 唯一之弱點。
ach·ing [ˈekɪŋ; ˈeikiŋ] *adj.* 作痛的;疼痛的;心痛的。—*n.* 痛。—**ly,** *adv.*
ach·la·myd·e·ous [ˌækləˈmɪdɪəs; ˌækləˈmidiəs] *adj.*〖植物〗無花被的;裸花的。
a·chlo·ro·phyl·lous [eˌklorəˈfɪləs; eiˌklourəˈfiləs] *adj.* 〖植物〗無葉綠素的。
ach·ro·mate [ˈækrəˌmet; ˈækrəmeit] *n.* 全色盲者;色盲患者。
ach·ro·mat·ic [ˌækrəˈmætɪk; ˌækrouˈmætik] *adj.* ①無色的。②〖物理〗消色差的;消色的。③〖生物〗非染色性的。
achromatic lens 〖光學〗消色差透鏡。
achromatic vision 〖醫〗色盲。
a·chro·ma·tin [əˈkromətɪn; əˈkroumətin] *n.* 〖生物〗(細胞核內之)非染色質。
a·chro·ma·tize [əˈkroməˌtaɪz; əˈkroumətaiz] *v.t.*, **-tized, tiz·ing.** 使無色;使消色;去色。
a·chro·ma·top·si·a [əˌkroməˈtɑpsɪə; əˌkrouməˈtɔpsiə] *n.* 〖醫〗全色盲。
Ach·ro·my·cin [ˌækrəˈmaɪsɪn; ˌækrouˈmaisin] *n.* 〖藥〗白黴素(一種抗生素的商標名)。
ac·id** [ˈæsɪd; ˈæsid] *n.* ①酸性物質;酸味的東西。②酸。nitric *acid.* 硝酸。③〖俚〗迷幻藥(＝LSD). ④尖刻的話。put on the acid***〖澳俚〗竊取以供自用。—*adj.* ①〖化〗酸的;酸性的。*acid* solution. 酸性溶液。②有酸味的。③尖酸的;尖刻的。
acid anhydride 〖化〗酸酐;酐。
acid color 酸性染料。(亦作 **acid dye**)
ac·id-fast [ˈæsɪdˌfæst; ˈæsidfɑːst] *adj.* ①不易被酸褪色的。②抗酸的(指結核菌)。
ac·id·head [ˈæsɪdˌhɛd; ˈæsidhed] *n.* 〖俚〗使用迷幻藥(LSD)的人。
a·cid·ic [əˈsɪdɪk; əˈsidik] *adj.* ①含矽酸的;酸性的。②產生酸的。
a·cid·i·fi·ca·tion [əˌsɪdəfɪˈkeʃən; əˌsidifiˈkeiʃən] *n.* 酸化;發酸;轉化成酸。
a·cid·i·fi·er [əˈsɪdəˌfaɪr; əˈsidifaiə] *n.* 酸化劑。
a·cid·i·fy [əˈsɪdəˌfaɪ; əˈsidifai] *v.t.*, & *v.i.*, **-fied, -fy·ing.** 酸化;使成酸;變酸。—**a·cid·i·fi·a·ble,** *adj.*
ac·i·dim·e·ter [ˌæsɪˈdɪmətɚ; ˌæsiˈdimitə] *n.* 〖化〗酸定量器。
a·cid·i·ty [əˈsɪdətɪ; əˈsiditi] *n., pl.* **-ties.** ①酸味;酸性;酸度。②酸量過多。
acid mordant color 酸性媒染染料。
ac·i·do·phil·ic [ˌæsɪdoˈfɪlɪk; ˌæsidouˈfilik] *adj.* ①〖生物〗嗜酸的。②(細菌)在酸性環境中繁殖最快的。(亦作 **acidophilus**)
ac·i·do·sis [ˌæsɪˈdosɪs; ˌæsiˈdousis] *n.* 〖醫〗酸中毒。
ac·id·proof [ˈæsɪdˌpruf; ˈæsidˌpruːf] *adj.* 耐酸的;耐酸性的。
acid reaction 酸性反應。
acid soil 酸性土壤。
acid test ①酸性試驗。②嚴密的考查;決定性的分析。
ac·id-tongued [ˈæsɪdˈtʌŋd; ˈæsidˈtʌŋd] *adj.* 說話刻薄的;譏刺的。
acid trip 〖俚〗用迷幻藥(LSD)後之神志不清的感覺。
a·cid·u·late [əˈsɪdʒəˌlet; əˈsidjuleit] *v.t.*, **-lat·ed, -lat·ing.** ①使微酸;使有酸味。②使性情乖僻;使難受。—**a·cid·u·la·tion,** *n.*
a·cid·u·lat·ed [əˈsɪdʒəˌletɪd; əˈsidjuleitid] *adj.* ①微酸的。②性情乖僻的。
a·cid·u·lous [əˈsɪdʒələs; əˈsidjuləs] *adj.* ①微酸的。②性情乖僻的;彆扭的。③銳利的。—**ly,** *adv.* —**ness,** *n.*
ac·i·nus [ˈæsɪnəs; ˈæsinəs] *n., pl.* **-ni** [–ˌnaɪ; –nai]. ①〖植物〗小果;粒狀果。②葡萄核;小核。③〖解剖〗葡萄狀腺;腺泡。

A

ack. ①acknowledge. ②acknowledgment.

ack-ack ['æk'æk; 'æk'æk] *n.* 〖俚〗高射砲(火)。

***ac·knowl·edge** [ək'nɑlɪdʒ; ək'nɔlidʒ] *v.t.,* **-edged, -edg·ing.** ①認以爲眞;自認;承認。He *acknowledges* his belief in God. 他承認信仰上帝。②承認…之主權或主張。③承認;接受。④答謝;就…表示感謝。⑤表示注意到(所受的敬意等)。⑥〖法律〗公證。—**a·ble,** *adj.* —**ac·knowl·edg·er,** *n.*

ac·knowl·edged [ək'nɑlɪdʒd; ək'nɔlidʒd] *adj.* 公認的。—**ly,** *adv.*

***ac·knowl·edg·ment** [ək'nɑlɪdʒmənt; ək'nɔlidʒmənt] *n.* ①〖法律〗承認;承認書。②感謝;謝意;謝禮。③收條;收帖。④自認;自白;謝罪。an *acknowledgment* of fault. 承認過失。*in acknowledgment of* 領謝;答謝。(英亦作 **acknowledgement**)

a·clin·ic [e'klɪnɪk; ei'klinik] *adj.* 〖物理〗無傾角的。*aclinic* line. 無傾線;磁赤道。

A.C.L.S. American Council of Learned Societies.

ac·me ['ækmɪ; 'ækmi] *n.* 頂點;極點;極致。

ac·ne ['æknɪ; 'ækni] *n.* 〖醫〗痤瘡;粉刺。

ac·node ['æknod; 'æknoud] *n.* 〖數學〗孤點。

ac·o·lyte ['ækə,laɪt; 'ækəlait] *n.* ①〖宗教〗沙彌。②侍者;新手。③〖天文〗衞星。

ac·o·nite ['ækə,naɪt; 'ækənait] *n.* 〖植物〗附子;烏頭。

a·con·i·tine [ə'kɑnɪtin; ə'kɔnitiːn] *n.* 〖藥〗附子精;烏頭鹹(關節炎的外用藥)。

A-con·trol ['ekən'trol; 'eikən'troul] *n.* 原子能管制(=atomic energy control).

***a·corn** ['ekən; 'eikɔːn] *n.* 橡實;橡子。

acorn shell 〖動物〗籐壺。

acorn sugar 〖化〗櫟櫟糖;橡醇。

acorn tube 橡子型眞空管。

a·cos·mism [e'kɑzmɪzəm; ei'kɔzmizm] *n.* 〖哲學〗無宇宙論。—**a·cos·mist,** *n.*

a·cot·y·le·don [,ekɑtḷ'idṇ; æ,kɔti'liːdn] *n.* 〖植物〗無子葉植物。

a·cot·y·le·don·ous [,ekɑtḷ'idṇəs; æ,kɔti'liːdənəs] *adj.* 〖植物〗無子葉的。

a·cou·me·ter [ə'kumɪtɚ; ə'kuːmitə] *n.* 聽力計;聽覺計。

a·cous·tic [ə'kustɪk; ə'kuːstik] *adj.* 聽覺的;有關聲音的;聲學的。

a·cous·ti·cal [ə'kustɪkḷ; ə'kuːstikəl] *adj.* =**acoustic.** —**ly,** *adv.*

ac·ous·ti·cian [,ækus'tɪʃən; ,ækuːs'tiʃən] *n.* 音響學家;聲學家。

acoustic mine 音響水雷。(亦作**sonic mine**)

a·cous·ti·con [ə'kustɪkɑn; ə'kuːstikɔn] *n.* (聾者用的)助聽器。

acoustic phonetics 聲波語音學(從聲學觀點研究語音, 別於從發聲器官的部位分析語音之 articulatory phonetics).

a·cous·tics [ə'kustɪks; ə'kuːstiks] *n.* ①(作 *pl.* 解)建築物之傳音性。②(作 *sing.* 解)聲學。

acoustic torpedo 音響魚雷。

acoustic velocity 音速。

acousto- 〖字首〗表"與聲波有關"之義。

A. C. P. American College of Physicians. **acpt.** acceptance.

***ac·quaint** [ə'kwent; ə'kweint] *v.t.* ①告知。Let me *acquaint* you with the facts. 讓我把事實告訴你罷。②使認識;介紹。

***ac·quaint·ance** [ə'kwentəns; ə'kweintns] *n.* ①相識的人。He has a large circle of *acquaintances.* 他有很多相識的人。②熟悉。*make one's acquaintance* 結識。*make the acquaintance of* 結識。〖注意〗**acquaintance, associate, companion** 及 **friend** 均指有所接觸的人。acquaintance 是關係不深者。associate 是因工作或事業而共處者。companion 是同甘共苦者。friend 是關係親密感情深厚者。

ac·quaint·ance·ship [ə'kwentənsʃɪp; ə'kweintnʃip] *n.* 相識;交往關係。

ac·quaint·ed [ə'kwentɪd; ə'kweintid] *adj.* ①有知識的;知曉(某事)的。②結識的。

ac·quest [ə'kwɛst; ə'kwest] *n.* ①(財產等之)取得。②取得物。③〖法律〗取得財產。

ac·qui·esce [,ækwɪ'ɛs; ,ækwi'es] *v.i.,* **-esced, -esc·ing.** 默許;勉强同意。—**ac·qui·esc·ing·ly,** *adv.*

ac·qui·es·cence [,ækwɪ'ɛsṇs; ,ækwi'esns] *n.* 默許;默認。

ac·qui·es·cent [,ækwɪ'ɛsṇt; ,ækwi'esnt] *adj.* 默許的;默認的。—**ly,** *adv.*

***ac·quire** [ə'kwaɪr; ə'kwaiə] *v.t.,* **-quired, -quir·ing.** 得;獲得。You must work hard to *acquire* a good knowledge of English. 你要用功, 以期精通英語。—**ac·quir·a·ble,** *adj.*

ac·quired [ə'kwaɪrd; ə'kwaiəd] *adj.* ①獲得的;習得的。②〖生物〗後天的;獲得性的。*acquired taste* 從學習中得來的愛好。

ac·quire·ment [ə'kwaɪrmənt; ə'kwaiəmənt] *n.* ①取得;習得。②(常 *pl.*)才藝;學識。

***ac·qui·si·tion** [,ækwə'zɪʃən; ,ækwi'ziʃən] *n.* ①獲得。His chief aim was the *acquisition* of knowledge. 他的主要目的爲獲得知識。②獲得物。③(*pl.*)學識;技能。

ac·quis·i·tive [ə'kwɪzətɪv; ə'kwizitiv] *adj.* 想獲得的;貪得的。—**ly,** *adv.* —**ness,** *n.*

ac·quis·i·tor [ə'kwɪzətɚ; ə'kwizitə] *n.* 取得者;修得者。

ac·quit [ə'kwɪt; ə'kwit] *v.t.,* **-quit·ted, -quit·ting.** ①宣告無罪。②(反身式)**a.** 處己;行爲。He *acquitted* himself well. 他潔身自愛。**b.** 爲自己洗清。③卸脫(責任、義務)。④淸償(債務等)。—**ter,** *n.*

ac·quit·tal [ə'kwɪtḷ; ə'kwitəl] *n.* ①(義務之)履行;(負債之)還淸。②無罪之宣告;釋放。(亦作 **acquitment**)

ac·quit·tance [ə'kwɪtṇs; ə'kwitəns] *n.* ①宣告無罪。②免除責任;解除;債務消滅;償債。③債務消滅證;收據。

a·cral·de·hyde [ə'krældɪ,haɪd; ə'krældihaid] *n.* 〖化〗丙炔醛。

‡**a·cre** ['ekɚ; 'eikə] *n.* ①英畝(=43,560平方英尺)。②(*pl.*) **a.** 土地;地產。broad *acres.* 廣大的土地。**b.** 大量;甚多。*God's acre* 墳場。

a·cre·age ['ekərɪdʒ, 'ekrɪdʒ; 'eikəridʒ] *n.* ①英畝數;(土地的)面積。②按畝出售或分配之土地。

a·cre-foot ['ekɚ'fut; 'eikə'fut] *n.* 英畝英尺(灌漑之水量單位)。

ac·rid ['ækrɪd; 'ækrid] *adj.* 辛辣的;苦的;尖刻的;刺激的。—**ly,** *adv.* —**ness,** *n.*

ac·ri·dine ['ækrɪd,in; 'ækridiːn] *n.* 〖化〗吖啶(用於染料或藥品之合成)。

a·crid·i·ty [æ'krɪdətɪ; æ'kriditi] *n., pl.* **-ties.** ①辛辣;尖刻。②刻薄話。

ac·ri·mo·ni·ous [,ækrə'monɪəs; ,ækri'mounjəs] *adj.* 辛辣的;尖刻的。—**ly,** *adv.*

ac·ri·mo·ny ['ækrə,monɪ; 'ækriməni] *n., pl.* **-nies.** 苛刻;刻薄。
ac·ro·bat ['ækrə,bæt; 'ækrəbæt] *n.* ①表演特技者;賣藝者。②善變者。
ac·ro·bat·ic [,ækrə'bætɪk; ,ækrə'bætik] *adj.* ①賣藝者的。②似賣藝者的。
ac·ro·bat·ics [,ækrə'bæktɪks; ,ækrə'bætiks] *n. pl.* ①奇技;特技。②熟練的技巧。
ac·ro·bat·ism ['ækrə,bætɪzəm; 'ækrəbætizəm] *n.* =**acrobatics.**
ac·ro·gen ['ækrədʒən; 'ækrədʒən] *n.* 〖植物〗頂生植物。
a·crog·e·nous [ə'krɑdʒənəs; ə'krɔdʒinəs] *adj.* 〖植物〗頂生的;上端生長的。
ac·ro·lith ['ækrəlɪθ; 'ækrəliθ] *n.* 石頭石肢木身的雕像。
ac·ro·me·gal·ic [,ækromɪ'gælɪk; ,ækroumi'gælik] *adj.* 〖醫〗肢端肥大症的。—*n.* 肢端肥大病患者。
ac·ro·meg·a·ly [,ækrə'mɛgəlɪ; ,ækrə'megəli] *n.* 〖醫〗肢端肥大症。
ac·ro·nym ['ækrənɪm; 'ækrənim] *n.* 頭字語(如: radar 由 *r*adio *d*etecting *a*nd *r*anging 等字之開頭字母所組成)。
ac·ro·phobe ['ækrə,fob; 'ækrəfoub] *n.* 患高處恐怖症的人。
ac·ro·pho·bi·a [,ækrə'fobɪə; ,ækrə'foubiə] *n.* 〖醫〗高空恐怖;高處恐怖症。
a·crop·o·lis [ə'krɑpəlɪs; ə'krɔpəlis] *n.* 古希臘城市之衛城。the *Acropolis.* 雅典的衛城。
‡**a·cross** [ə'krɔs; ə'krɔs, ə'krɔːs] *prep.* ①橫過;越過。A bridge was laid *across* the river. 一座橋橫架河上。②在…那邊。He lives *across* the street. 他住在街對面。③遇到。We came *across* our friends. 我們遇到朋友。④交叉;成十字形。—*adv.* ①橫過;到對面。I came *across* in a steamer. 我乘船過來。②交叉地。He was standing with arms *across.* 他抱着臂站立着。③被瞭解。He couldn't get the idea *across* to the class. 他無法讓班上的學生懂這概念。④由某狀態到所希望的狀態。
a·cross-the-board [ə'krɔsðə'bɔrd; ə'krɔsðəbɔːd] *adj.* ①全盤的;全面的。②(廣播) 從星期一到星期五每天同一時間播放的。
a·cros·tic [ə'krɔstɪk; ə'krɔstik] *n.* 離合詩句。—*adj.* (亦作 **acrostical**)離合詩句的;似離合詩句的。
a·cryl·ic [ə'krɪlɪk; ə'krilik] *adj.* 〖化〗丙烯類(音譯"壓克力")特性的;有關丙烯類的。
acrylic acid 〖化〗丙烯酸。
acrylic fiber 〖化〗丙烯類纖維。
acrylic resin 〖化〗丙烯類樹脂。
A.C.S. ①American Cancer Society. ②American Chemical Society. ③Associate in Commercial Science.
A/cs pay. 應付帳款(=accounts payable). (亦作 **a/cs pay.**)
A/cs rec. 應收帳款 (=accounts receivable). (亦作 **a/cs rec.**)
‡**act** [ækt; ækt] *n.* ①行爲;舉動。a brave *act.* 勇敢的行爲。②動作過程。The thief was caught in the *act* of stealing. 此賊在行竊時被捕。③一幕;一齣。an *act* of a play. 戲劇之一幕。④節目。the trained dog's *act.* 這訓練有素的狗之表演節目。⑤法案。an *act* of Congress. 〖美〗國會的法案。⑥(牛津或劍橋大學)在學位考試中爲自己的學位論文所作的正式口頭辯護。—*v.i.* ①行動。②作用。The drug failed to *act.* 此藥不曾生效。③扮演。Did she ever *act* on the stage? 她曾在舞台上演過戲嗎?④行爲;表現。He *acted* badly in school. 他在校中行爲不好。⑤〖戲劇〗上演。His plays don't *act* well. 他的劇本上演效果不好。⑥假裝。Try to *act* interested. 盡力假裝有興趣。—*v.t.* 扮演;仿做;裝。He *acted* his part well. 他扮演他那個角色頗爲成功。***act as*** 充當。He *acted as* manager. 他充當經理。***act for*** 代理。He *acted for* Smith while he was ill. 史密斯病時他代理其職務。***act on*** (or ***upon***) a. 遵照(指示或勸告)行事。b. 使…產生變化;影響。***act one's age*** 行爲與年齡相稱。***act out*** 用手勢及言語表演(某事件)。***act up*** 〖俗〗 a. 行爲不良;出毛病。b. 作弄;開玩笑。***act up to*** 履行;符合。〖注意〗act 如用作舉動或行爲之意時, 是連繫動詞 (linking verb), 其後可接形容詞: He *acts* old. 他舉動老邁。
act· active.
act·a·ble ['æktəbḷ; 'æktəbl] *adj.* ①可上演的。②可實行的。—**act·a·bil·i·ty,** *n.*
ac·tin ['æktɪn; 'æktin] *n.* 〖生化〗肌動蛋白(存在於肌肉原形質中, 助肌肉收縮)。
***act·ing** ['æktɪŋ; 'æktiŋ] *adj.* ①代理的。He is our *acting* president. 他是我們的代理校長。②爲演員等改寫並補充的(劇本)。—*n.* 演戲的藝術;演技;演出。
acting area 舞台上用於演出的部分。
Ac·tin·i·a [æk'tɪnɪə; æk'tiniə] *n., pl.* **-i·ae** [-ɪi; -iiː], **-i·as.** 〖動物〗①海葵屬。②(a-)海葵;似海葵之動物。—**ac·tin·i·an,** *adj., n.*
ac·tin·ic [æk'tɪnɪk; æk'tinik] *adj.* 化學線的;化學線作用的;光化性的。
actinic rays 〖物理〗化學線。
ac·tin·ism ['æktɪn,ɪzəm; 'æktinizm] *n.* 化學線作用。
ac·tin·i·um [æk'tɪnɪəm; æk'tiniəm] *n.* 〖化〗錒(一種放射性元素, 符號 Ac)。
ac·ti·no·chem·is·try [,æktɪno'kɛməstrɪ; ,æktinou'kemistri] *n.* 〖化〗射線化學;光化學。
ac·ti·nom·e·ter [,æktə'nɑmɪtɚ; ,ækti'nɔmitə] *n.* 化學線計;感光計;露光計。
ac·ti·nom·e·try [,æktə'nɑmɪtrɪ; ,ækti'nɔmitri] *n.* 光量測定。
ac·ti·non ['æktɪ,nɑn; 'æktinɔn] *n.* 〖化〗氙(放射線元素, 符號爲 An)。
ac·ti·no·ther·a·py [,æktɪnə'θɛrəpɪ; ,æktinə'θerəpi] *n.* 〖醫〗射線療法。
ac·ti·no·u·ra·ni·um [,æktɪnoju'renɪəm; ,æktinouju'reiniəm] *n.* 〖化〗鈾的放射性同位素(原子量爲235)。
‡**ac·tion** ['ækʃən; 'ækʃən] *n.* ①行爲。②動作;行動。The machine is now in *action.* 這機器在開動中。③動作姿態。This horse has a very graceful *action.* 這馬動作的姿態甚優美。④戰鬥;小戰爭。The soldiers are in *action.* 兵士們在戰鬥中。⑤訴訟。He has brought an *action* against his partner. 他控告他的夥伴。⑥作用;影響。⑦(故事或戲劇中之)情節。⑧機器中有動作的部分。⑨〖俚〗賭博;打賭。⑩(*pl.*) 行爲。*Actions* speak louder than words. 行動勝於空談。***out of action*** 失效。***see action*** 參加戰鬥。***take action*** a. 活動。b. 採取行動;開始工作。c. 控告。***where the action is*** 活動最多或發展最快的地點。—**ist,** *n.* —**less,** *adj.*
ac·tion·a·ble ['ækʃənəbḷ; 'ækʃnəbl]

A

adj. 可引起訴訟的;可被控訴的。
action painting 無形象畫(將顏料潑灑在畫布上或用較粗筆劃以强調自然表現的畫)。
action shot 動態照片。
ac·ti·vate ['æktə,vet; 'æktiveit] *v.t.*, **-vat·ed, -vat·ing.** ①刺激;使產生活動。②創設;成立。③【物理】使具放射性。④【化】使活潑;使能起反應;使能加速反應。⑤灌氣於(水溝、汚物等)以使淨化。—**ac·ti·va·tion,** *n.* —**ac·ti·vat·ed,** *adj.*
ac·ti·va·tor ['æktɪ,vetɚ; 'æktiveitə] *n.* 【化】①觸媒;催化劑。②礦物中所含雜質能使該礦物發光者。
:ac·tive ['æktɪv; 'æktiv] *adj.* ①活動的。an *active* volcano. 活火山。②活躍的。Market is *active.* 市面活躍。③積極的;勤勉的。to take an *active* part. 積極參加工作。④【文法】主動的。⑤能起作用的;活性的。⑥有效的;有力的。*active* remedies. 有力的藥物。⑦激烈的。*active* sports. 激烈的運動。⑧尙未廢棄的。⑨能傳送信號的。an *active* communications satellite. 一個能傳送信號的通訊衛星。⑩繼續惡化的;活動性的。*active* tuberculosis. 活動性的肺癆。⑪放射性的。an *active* deposit. 放射性礦床。—*n.* 活躍的人或事物。—**ly,** *adv.* —**ness,** *n.*
active army 現役陸軍(爲 reserved army 之對)。
active capital 流動資本。
active carbon 【化】活性炭。
active duty 現役。
active immunity 【醫,生物】自動免役。
active list 現役軍人名册。
active service 現役;戰時服役。
active voice 【文法】主動語態。
ac·tiv·ism ['æktɪv,ɪzəm; 'æktivizəm] *n.* ①實踐主義。②【哲學】假設一切事物有其客觀的眞實性與積極的存在之一種哲學學說。
ac·tiv·ist ['æktɪvɪst; 'æktivist] *n.* 實踐主義者。—*adj.* 實踐主義者的。
:ac·tiv·i·ty [æk'tɪvətɪ; æk'tiviti] *n., pl.* **-ties.** ①活動;活躍。mental *activity.* 心靈活動。②活動。social *activities.* 社交活動。③活動力。with *activity.* 精神充沛地。④動作。⑤【化】活動性;旋光性;放射性。
ac·tiv·ize ['æktə,vaɪz; 'æktivaiz] *v.t.*, **-ized, -iz·ing.** 使活動;使活潑。
act of God 【保險,法律】天災;不可抗力。
act of grace ①恩典。②大赦令。
act of war 侵略行爲;侵犯。
ac·ton ['æktən; 'æktən] *n.* 鎧衣。
***ac·tor** ['æktɚ; 'æktə] *n.* ①演員;優伶。②行事的人。—**ish,** *adj.*
act psychology 唯意心理學。
***ac·tress** ['æktrɪs; 'æktris] *n.* 女演員。
Acts of the Apostles 使徒行傳(新約聖經之一卷)。(亦作 **Acts**)
:ac·tu·al ['æktʃuəl; 'æktjuəl, -tʃuəl] *adj.* ①眞實的;實際的。I can not give the *actual* figures. 我不能舉出實際的數字。②目前的。the *actual* states of affairs. 現狀。
ac·tu·al·ist ['æktʃuəlɪst; 'æktʃuəlist] *n.* 現實主義者;現實論者;實際者。
ac·tu·al·i·ty [,æktʃu'ælətɪ; ,æktju'æliti] *n., pl.* **-ties.** ①實在;眞實。②【英】現紀錄性的廣播節目、電影等。③(*pl.*)現狀;事實。*in actuality* =actually.
ac·tu·al·i·za·tion [,æktʃuələ'zeʃən; ,æktʃuəlai'zeiʃn] *n.* 實現;現實化。(亦作 **actualisation**)
ac·tu·al·ize ['æktʃuəl,aɪz; 'æktjuəlaiz] *v.t.*, **-ized, -iz·ing.** 實現。(亦作 **actualise**)
:ac·tu·al·ly ['æktʃuəlɪ; 'æktjuəli] *adv.* 眞實地;實際地。We *actually* thought that he was a thief. 我們眞以爲他是一個賊。
actual residence 【法律】住所;居所。
ac·tu·ar·i·al [,æktʃu'ɛrɪəl; ,æktju'ɛəriəl] *adj.* 保險公司統計員的;保險公司統計員所計算的;保險統計的。
ac·tu·ar·y ['æktʃu,ɛrɪ; 'æktjuəri] *n., pl.* **-ar·ies.** 保險統計專家;保險公司統計員。
ac·tu·ate ['æktʃu,et; 'æktjueit] *v.t.*, **-at·ed, -at·ing.** ①使活動;使動作。②激勵;刺激;鼓動。③促使。—**ac·tu·a·tion,** *n.*
act warning 舞台監督提醒演員上台時間的通知。(亦作 **act call**)
a·cu·i·ty [ə'kjuətɪ; ə'kju:iti] *n.* ①尖銳。②(病況之)急劇。③銳敏。
a·cu·le·at·ed [ə'kjulɪ,etɪd; ə'kju:lieitid] *adv.* ①尖銳的。②(昆蟲之)有刺的;有螫的。③【植物】有刺的。(亦作 **aculate**)
a·cu·men [ə'kjumɪn; ə'kju:men] *n.* 銳敏;聰明。
a·cu·mi·nate [*adj.* ə'kjumɪnɪt; ə'kju:minit *v.* ə'kjumɪ,net; ə'kju:mineit] *adj., v.*, **-nat·ed, -nat·ing.** —*adj.* 【生物】有尖的;尖銳的。—*v.t.* 使尖;使銳敏。—**a·cu·mi·na·tion,** *n.* —**a·cu·mi·nous,** *adj.*
ac·u·punc·ture [*n.* 'ækju,pʌŋktʃɚ; 'ækjupʌŋktʃə *v.* ,ækju'pʌŋktʃɚ; ,ækju'pʌŋktʃə] *n., v.*, **-tured, -tur·ing.** —*n.* 【醫】針術;針穿刺法。—*v.t.* 針刺;針療。
ac·u·punc·tur·ist [,ækju'pʌŋktʃərɪst; ,ækju'pʌŋktʃərist] *n.* 針療醫生。(亦作 **acupuncturator**)
a·cus ['ekəs; 'eikəs] *n., pl.* **a·cus.** 【醫】(外科)針;鍼。
***a·cute** [ə'kjut; ə'kju:t] *adj.* ①銳的;尖的。an *acute* angle. 銳角。②敏感的。③劇烈的。*acute* pain. 劇痛。④嚴重的。⑤深刻的。⑥上有(′)記號的。⑦【醫】急性的。—**ly,** *adv.* —**ness,** *n.*
ACV air cushion vehicle. 氣墊船、車。
ACWA Amalgamated Clothing Workers of America.
-acy 【字尾】用以形成抽象名詞,表"性質;狀況;職位"之義。
ad[1] [æd; æd] *n.* 【美俗】廣告(advertisement 之略)。
ad[2] *n.* 網球比賽時在平手 deuce 以後所得的第一分。*ad in* 平手後發球人所得的第一分。*ad out* 平手後接球人所得的第一分。
ad[3] *prep.* 【拉】到;按照(=to, toward; up to; according to).
ad. ①add. ②adverb. ③advertisement.
***A.D.** ['e'di; 'ei'di:] Anno Domini (拉=in the year of our Lord. 西元;紀元)。【注意】A.D. 應該寫在年數之前, B.C. 應該寫在年數之後。亦有把 A.D. 寫在年數之後者,那是俗寫。
a.d. after date.
ad- 【字首】見於拉丁語源的字,表"向…;加於…"之義。
A.D.A. ①American Dental Association. ②Americans for Democratic Action. (亦作 **ADA**)
ad·age ['ædɪdʒ; 'ædidʒ] *n.* 諺語;格言;箴言。
ad·a·gen·cy ['æd,edʒənsɪ; 'æd,eidʒənsi] *n.* 【美】廣告代理所;廣告代理業。
ad·a·gent ['æd,edʒənt; 'æd,eidʒənt] *n.* 【美】廣告代理人。
a·da·giet·to [ə,dadʒɪ'ɛto; ə,da:dʒi'etou] *adj., adv., n., pl.* **-tos.** 【音樂】—*adj.*

& *adv.* 稍慢的(地)。—*n.* 稍慢板速度之樂章或短曲。

a·da·gio [ə'dɑdʒo; ə'dɑ:dʒiou] *adj., adv., n., pl.* **-gios.** —*adj.* 〖音樂〗緩慢的。—*adv.* 〖音樂〗緩慢地。—*n.* 〖音樂〗緩慢的拍子;慢板;慢板的曲子。

Ad·am ['ædəm; 'ædəm] *n.* 亞當(聖經中所稱人類的始祖)。 ***not know a person from Adam*** 全然不認識某人。 ***the old Adam*** 原罪。

ad·a·mant ['ædə,mænt; 'ædəment] *n.* 堅石;堅硬的東西。 —*adj.* 堅硬的;牢不可破的;堅定不移的。

ad·a·man·tine [,ædə'mæntɪn; ,ædə'mæntain] *adj.* ①堅石製的;金剛石的。②似堅石的;堅定不移的。

A·dam·ic ['ædəmɪk; 'ædəmik] *adj.* 亞當(人類的始祖)的。(亦作 **Adamical**)

Ad·am·ite ['ædəm,aɪt; 'ædəmait] *n.* ①亞當(Adam)之後裔;人。②裸體者;裸體主義者。③〖宗教〗裸體生活宗派。

Adam's apple 喉結。

ad·ams·ite ['ædəmz,aɪt; 'ædəmzait] *n.* 噴嚏性毒氣之一種。

***a·dapt** [ə'dæpt; ə'dæpt] *v.t.* ①使適合;使適應。Can you *adapt* yourself to a new job? 你能適應新的工作嗎? ②改編; 改裝。—*v.i.* 適應各種不同情況或環境。She lacked the ability to *adapt* easily. 她缺少適應力。—**er,** —**ed·ness,** *n.*

a·dapt·a·bil·i·ty [ə,dæptə'bɪlətɪ; ə,dæptə'biliti] *n.* 適應性;順應性;適合性。

a·dapt·a·ble [ə'dæptəbl̩; ə'dæptəbl] *adj.* ①能適應的。②能適用的。

***ad·ap·ta·tion** [,ædəp'teʃən; ,ædæp'teiʃən] *n.* ①適應。②改編。③改編的東西。④〖生物〗適應需要或環境而發生的自然變化或此種變化的結果;順應;適應。(亦作**adaption**)

a·dapt·er, a·dap·tor [ə'dæptə; ə'dæptə] *n.* ①改作者;適應者。②調節或裝備零件之裝置;適用器;加減裝置。③誘導管。

a·dap·tive [ə'dæptɪv; ə'dæptiv] *adj.* 適應的;可適應的;適合的;能適合的。

ADC, A.D.C., a.d.c. aide-de-camp.

A.D.C. Amateur Dramatic Club.

Ad·cock antenna ['ædkɑk~; 'ædkɔk~] 〖電子〗測向天線。

ad·col·umn ['æd,kɑləm; 'ædkɔləm] *n.* 〖美〗廣告欄。

ad·craft ['æd,kræft; 'ædkrɑ:ft] *n.* 「〖俗〗廣告業者(集合稱)。」

‡add [æd; æd] *v.t.* ①增加。If the tea is too strong, *add* some more water. 茶如太濃,加些水。②加起〖常 up〗. *Add* them up. 將他們加起來。③附言;再言。That, he *added,* was a mistake. 那是個錯誤,他補充說。④得;獲。—*v.i.* ①增加。The music *added* to our enjoyment. 音樂增加我們的快樂。②加起;作加法。③累積。 ***add in*** 包括;算在內。 ***add insult to injury*** 辱上加辱;凌虐交加。 ***add to*** 成爲或作爲一種增加。 ***add up*** 與應有的總額相符;合乎情理。 ***add up to*** 總計達…;顯示。The costs *added up to* 10 million dollars. 費用計達一千萬元。—*n.* 〖新聞〗(一篇報導的)後加部分。

add. ①addenda. ②addendum. ③addition(al). ④address.

Ad·dams ['ædəmz; 'ædəmz] *n.* 亞當斯(Jane, 1860–1935, 美國女作家及社會事業家, 1931年曾獲諾貝爾和平獎)。

ad·dax ['ædæks; 'ædæks] *n.* 大羚羊。

add·ed ['ædɪd; 'ædid] *adj.* 附加的;增加的;更多的。

ad·dend ['ædɛnd; ə'dend] *n.* 〖數學〗「加數。」

ad·den·dum [ə'dɛndəm; ə'dendəm] *n., pl.* **-da** [-də; -də]. ①追加; 附加物。②補遺;附錄。③〖機械〗 **a.** 齒頂; 齒高。 **b.** 齒頂圓。

add·er[1] ['ædɚ; 'ædə] *n.* 加者; 加算器。

ad·der[2] *n.* 一種毒蛇。

ad·der's-mouth ['ædɚz,mauθ; 'ædəzmauθ] *n., pl.* **-mouths** [-mauðz; -mauðz]. 〖植物〗蛇嘴蘭。

ad·der's-tongue ['ædɚz,tʌŋ; 'ædəztʌŋ] *n.* ①〖植物〗瓶爾小草屬之羊齒植物。②〖美〗車前葉山慈姑。

add·i·ble ['ædəbl̩; 'ædəbl] *adj.* 可加的。「(亦作 **addable**)」

ad·dict [*n.* 'ædɪkt; 'ædikt *v.* ə'dɪkt; ə'dikt] *n.* ①耽溺於不良嗜好的人。②酷愛…者;…迷。—*v.t.* 使耽溺;使熱中;對…有癮的。—*v.i.* 使人上癮。

ad·dict·ed [ə'dɪktɪd; ə'diktid] *adj.* 耽溺;嗜好; 慣於。—**ness,** *n.*

ad·dic·tion [ə'dɪkʃən; ə'dikʃən] *n.* 耽溺;癖好;熱中。—**ad·dic·tive,** *adj.*

adding machine 計算器;加算器。

Ad·di·son[1] ['ædəsn̩; 'ædisn] *n.* 阿狄生 (Joseph, 1672–1719, 英國散文家及詩人)。

Ad·di·son[2] *n.* 阿狄生 (Thomas, 1793–1860, 英國醫生)。

Addison's disease 〖醫〗阿狄生病(一種腎上腺疾病,爲阿狄生醫生所發現,故名)。

‡ad·di·tion [ə'dɪʃən; ə'diʃn] *n.* ①加。The sign + stands for *addition.* 符號"十"卽代表"加"的意思。②附加物。③加法。*Addition* is easier than subtraction. 加法易於減法。④有用的添加物。⑤〖法律〗稱號;頭銜。 ***in addition*** 此外。 ***in addition to*** 加於…上;除…外。

ad·di·tion·al** [ə'dɪʃənl̩; ə'diʃənl] *adj.* 加添的; 補充的。 ***additional tax 附加稅。—**ly,** *adv.*

ad·di·tive ['ædətɪv; 'æditiv] *adj.* ①附加的;追加的;加法的。②累積的; 有累積之趨向的。—*n.* 添加物;添劑。—**ly,** *adv.*

additive group 〖數學〗加法羣。

ad·di·to·ry ['ædɪ,torɪ; 'æditəri] *adj.* 附加的;補充的。

ad·dle ['ædl̩; 'ædl] *v.,* **-dled, -dling,** *adj.* —*v.t.* ①使昏亂;使混亂。②使腐壞。—*v.i.* ①變昏亂。②變腐壞。—*adj.* (亦作 **addled**) ①昏亂的。②腐壞的。

ad·dle·brained ['ædl̩,brend; 'ædl,breind] *adj.* 頭腦不清的;糊塗的;愚笨的。

ad·dle·head ['ædl̩,hɛd; 'ædlhed] *n.* 糊塗蟲;呆漢;蠢物。(亦作**addlepate**)—**ed,** *adj.*

‡ad·dress [*n.* ə'drɛs, 'ædrɛs; ə'dres *v.* ə'drɛs; ə'dres] *n.* ①講演。The President gave an *address* over the radio. 總統廣播一篇講演。②住址。She has changed her *address.* 她已改變了住址。③說話的態度。A salesman should be a man of pleasant *address.* 推銷員應有悅人的談吐。④本領;技巧。⑤正式請願。⑥(*pl.*)(求愛時所作之)殷勤。to pay one's *addresses* to a lady. 向一女郎獻殷勤。—*v.t.* ①對(人)說話;發表演說。②寫住址。Please *address* the letter for me. 請爲我在信上寫住址。③稱呼。④忙着做。He *addressed* himself to the work in hand. 他忙着做他手邊的工作。⑤使加注意。to *address* a warning to a

friend. 向一個朋友作警告。⑥獻殷勤。⑦引導；指引。⑧呈送；呈遞。⑨〖高爾夫〗瞄準。
address book 住址簿。
ad·dress·ee 〔ədrɛsˈi; ˌædreˈsiː〕 *n.* 〖美〗收信人；收件人。
ad·dress·er, ad·dres·sor 〔əˈdrɛsɚ; əˈdresə〕 *n.* ①發信人；發言者；陳述者。②請願者。
addressing machine 姓名住址印刷機。
ad·dres·so·graph 〔əˈdrɛsəˌgræf; əˈdresəgrɑːf〕 *n.* ①姓名住址印刷機。②(A-)其商標名。
ad·duce 〔əˈdjus; əˈdjuːs〕 *v.t.*, **-duced, -duc·ing.** 引證；舉爲例證；舉出。
ad·duc·i·ble 〔əˈdjusəbl̩; əˈdjuːsəbl〕 *adj.* 可引證的；可舉例的。(亦作 **adduceable**)
ad·duct 〔əˈdʌkt; əˈdʌkt〕 *v.t.* 〖生理〗使內收(爲 abduct 之對)；併攏。
ad·duc·tion 〔əˈdʌkʃən; əˈdʌkʃən〕 *n.* ①引證；舉例。②〖生理〗內收。
ad·duc·tor 〔əˈdʌktɚ; əˈdʌktə〕 *n.* 〖解剖〗內收筋；內收肌。
Ad·e·laide 〔ˈædl̩ˌed; ˈædəleid〕 *n.* 阿得雷德(澳洲南部之一城市，爲南澳大利亞之首府)。
a·demp·tion 〔əˈdɛmpʃən; əˈdempʃən〕 *n.* 〖法律〗(遺贈的)取消或撤回。
ad·e·nine 〔ˈædənɪn; ˈædənin〕 *n.* 〖化〗腺鹼；腺嘌呤；6-氨基嘌呤。
ad·e·ni·tis 〔ˌædəˈnaɪtɪs; ˌædəˈnaitis〕 *n.* 〖醫〗淋巴腺炎；腺炎。
ad·e·noid 〔ˈædn̩ˌɔɪd; ˈædinɔid〕 *adj.* 腺狀腫的。
ad·e·noi·dal 〔ˌædn̩ˈɔɪdl̩; ˌædiˈnɔidl〕 *adj.* =**adenoid.**
ad·e·noids 〔ˈædn̩ˌɔɪdz; ˈædinɔidz〕 *n. pl.* 〖醫〗腺狀腫(尤指位於咽頭者)。
ad·e·nol·o·gy 〔ˌædəˈnɑlədʒɪ; ˌædiˈnɔlədʒi〕 *n.* 〖醫〗淋巴腺學；腺論。
ad·ept 〔əˈdɛpt; əˈdept〕 *adj.* 熟練的；老練的。*adept in* (*or at*) 擅長；精通。—*n.* 熟練之能手；專家。 —**ness,** *n.*
ad·e·qua·cy 〔ˈædəkwəsɪ; ˈædikwəsi〕 *n.* 適當；充分；足够。
***ad·e·quate** 〔ˈædəkwɪt; ˈædikwit〕 *adj.* ①適合需要之量的；足够的。His wages are not *adequate* to support his family. 他的薪水不够養家。②適當的。③令人滿意的；充分的。④差强人意的；僅僅足够的。—**ly,** *adv.* —**ness,** *n.*
a·der·min 〔eˈdɝmɪn; eiˈdəːmin〕 *n.* 維他命B_6之別名。(亦作 **adermine**)
ad·es·sive 〔ædˈɛsɪv; ædˈesiv〕 〖文法〗 *adj.* 表示位置的。—*n.* 位置格。
***ad·here** 〔ədˈhɪr; ədˈhiə〕 *v.*, **-hered, -her·ing.** —*v.i.* ①黏着；附着〖to〗. The mud *adhered* to our shoes. 我們的鞋子黏上了汚泥。②堅持；堅執〖to〗. ③忠於；皈依〖to〗. —*v.t.* 使黏着。The paper has been *adhered* to the surface with glue. 紙已經用膠水黏在表面上了。
ad·her·ence 〔ədˈhɪrəns; ədˈhiərəns〕 *n.* ①黏着；附着。②忠誠；皈依；嚴守。
ad·her·ent 〔ədˈhɪrənt; ədˈhiərənt〕 *adj.* 黏着的；附着的。—*n.* 黨徒；擁護者；皈依者。
ad·he·sion 〔ədˈhiʒən; ədˈhiːʒən〕 *n.* ①黏着；附着。②皈依；忠實。③同意。④〖物理〗附着力。⑤〖醫〗因發炎而不正常的結合；黏連。
ad·he·sive 〔ədˈhisɪv; ədˈhiːsiv〕 *adj.* ①黏著的；易黏著的；有黏性的；塗有黏性物用以膠著他物的。②難忘的。—**ly,** *adv.* —**ness,** *n.*
ad·hib·it 〔ædˈhɪbɪt; ædˈhibit〕 *v.t.* ①容許進入；帶進來。②黏貼；貼附。
ad·hi·bi·tion 〔ˌædhɪˈbɪʃən; ˌædhiˈbiʃən〕 *n.* 應用；施用；貼用；施；敷。
ad hoc 〔ˈædˈhɑk; ˈædˈhɔk〕 〖拉〗特別地(的)。
ad ho·mi·nem 〔ˈædˈhɑməˌnɛm; ˈædˈhɔminem〕 〖拉〗對人而不對事的；偏私的。
ad·i·a·bat·ic 〔ˌædɪəˈbætɪk; ˌædiəˈbætik〕 *adj.* 〖物理〗斷熱的；等熱的。
Ad·i·an·tum 〔ˌædɪˈæntəm; ˌædiˈæntəm〕 *n.* ①〖植物〗石長生屬。②(a-)石長生屬之植物；石長生。
ad·i·aph·o·ret·ic 〔ˌædɪˌæfəˈrɛtɪk; ˌædiˌæfəˈretik〕 *adj.* 止汗的。—*n.* 止汗劑。
ad·i·a·ther·man·cy 〔ˌædɪəˈθɝmənsɪ; ˌædiəˈθəːmənsi〕 *n.* 不透熱性。
***a·dieu** 〔əˈdju; əˈdjuː〕 *interj.*, *n., pl.* **a·dieus, a·dieux** 〔əˈdjuz; əˈdjuːz〕. 再會；辭別。to make (*or* take) one's *adieu*. 告別；辭行。
ad in·fi·ni·tum 〔ˈædˌɪnfəˈnaɪtəm; ˈædˌinfiˈnaitəm〕 〖拉〗無窮地；永遠地。
ad in·te·rim 〔ˈædˈɪntərɪm; ˈædˈintərim〕 〖拉〗過渡的；暫時的；臨時的。
a·di·os 〔ˌædɪˈos; ˌɑːdiˈous〕 〖西〗 *interj.* 再見!
ad·i·po·cere 〔ˈædəpəˌsɪr; ˈædipousiə〕 *n.* 屍蠟；屍油。
ad·i·pose 〔ˈædəˌpos; ˈædipous〕 *adj.* 脂肪的；似脂肪的；多脂肪的。—*n.* (動物性)脂肪。 —**ad·i·pos·i·ty,** *n.*
ad·i·po·sis 〔ˌædəˈposɪs; ˌædiˈpousis〕 *n.* 〖醫〗脂肪過多(尤指器官)。
Ad·i·ron·dacks 〔ˌædəˈrɑndæks; ˌædiˈrɔndæks〕 *n. pl.* ①阿第倫達克山(美國紐約州東北部一山脈)。②阿第倫達克族(美國東北部的一支印第安部族)。
ad·it 〔ˈædɪt; ˈædit〕 *n.* ①入口；通路。②(礦坑之)橫坑道。
ADIZ Air Defense Identification Zone.
adj. ①adjective. ②adjacent. ③adjoining. ④adjourned. ⑤adjudged. ⑥adjunct. ⑦adjutant. ⑧〖銀行〗adjustment.
ad·ja·cence 〔əˈdʒesn̩s; əˈdʒeisəns〕 *n.* 接近；毗連；鄰接。
ad·ja·cen·cy 〔əˈdʒesn̩sɪ; əˈdʒeisənsi〕 *n., pl.* **-cies.** ①接近；毗連；鄰接。②(常 *pl.*)鄰接物。③緊接在(某一節目)之前或後的另一廣播或電視節目。
***ad·ja·cent** 〔əˈdʒesn̩t; əˈdʒeisənt〕 *adj.* ①接近的；鄰接的；毗連的。The house *adjacent* to ours has been sold. 與我們家鄰接的房子已經售出。②前後緊接着的；對面的。—**ly,** *adv.*
adjacent angles 〖幾何〗鄰角。
ad·jec·ti·val 〔ˌædʒɪkˈtaɪvl̩; ˌædʒekˈtaivl〕 *adj.* ①〖文法〗形容詞的。②富於(喜用)形容詞的。—**ly,** *adv.*
***ad·jec·tive** 〔ˈædʒɪktɪv; ˈædʒiktiv〕 *n.* 〖文法〗形容詞。—*adj.* 形容詞的；作形容詞用的。*adjective* clause. 形容詞子句。
***ad·join** 〔əˈdʒɔɪn; əˈdʒɔin〕 *v.t.* & *v.i.* ①接界；臨近。The two houses *adjoin*. 此二幢房屋鄰接。②附；加。
ad·join·ing 〔əˈdʒɔɪnɪŋ; əˈdʒɔiniŋ〕 *adj.* 鄰接的；隔壁的。
ad·journ 〔əˈdʒɝn; əˈdʒəːn〕 *v.t.* & *v.i.* ①延期；延會；休會。The meeting was *adjourned* for a week. 會議延期一週。②〖俗〗遷至別處；移往。
ad·journ·ment 〔əˈdʒɝnmənt; əˈdʒəːnmənt〕 *n.* ①休會；延會。②休會期間。
adjt. adjutant.

部;口部的功能。
ad·o·ra·tion [ˌædəˈreʃən; ˌædɔː-ˈreiʃən] *n.* ①崇拜。②敬重;愛慕。③崇拜或愛慕之人。 「təri] *n.* 拜神的場所。
a·dor·a·to·ry [əˈdɔrəˌtorɪ; əˈdɔːrə-
***a·dore** [əˈdor; əˈdɔː] *v.*, **a·dored, a·dor·ing.** —*v.t.* ①敬重;敬愛。②崇拜。He is *adored* as a god by the natives. 土人崇拜他如神明。③〖俗〗極爲喜愛。 —*v.i.* 崇拜。 —**a·dor·er,** *n.*
a·dor·ing [əˈdorɪŋ; əˈdɔːriŋ] *adj.* 崇拜的;敬重的;愛慕的。—**ly,** *adv.*
***a·dorn** [əˈdɔrn; əˈdɔːn] *v.t.* 裝飾。She *adorns* herself with jewels. 她身飾珠寶。
a·dorn·ing [əˈdɔrnɪŋ; əˈdɔːniŋ] *adj.* 裝飾的;美化的。—*n.* 裝飾;裝飾物。—**ly,** *adv.*
a·dorn·ment [əˈdɔrnmənt; əˈdɔːnmənt] *n.* ①裝飾;盛飾;裝飾品。②裝飾的動作。 「〖詩〗=**down.**
a·down [əˈdaun; əˈdaun] *adv., prep.*
ADP automatic data processing.
ad·press [ædˈprɛs; ædˈpres] *v.i.* 緊壓於表面;平放。 「ceipt. 美國儲蓄證券。
ADR 〖美〗American Depository Re-
A·dram·me·lech [əˈdræməˌlɛk; əˈdræmələk] *n.* ①〖聖經〗亞得米勒(西法瓦音人所供奉諸神之一)。②〖聖經〗亞得米勒(亞述王西拿基立之子)。
Ad·ras·te·a [ˌædræsˈtiə; ˌædræsˈtiːə] *n.* 〖希臘神話〗復讎的女神。(亦作 **Nemesis**)
A·dras·tus [əˈdræstəs; əˈdræstəs] *n.* 〖希臘神話〗Argos 之王,爲遠征底比斯七英雄 (the Seven against Thebes)之領袖。(亦作 **Adrastos**)
ad·rate [ˈædret; ˈædreit] *n.* 附加稅。
ad-rate [ˈædret; ˈædreit] *n.*〖美〗廣告費。
a·dream [əˈdrim; əˈdriːm] *adj.* 做夢的;躭於幻想的。
ad ref·er·en·dum [ædˌrɛfəˈrɛndəm; ædˌrefəˈrendəm] 〖拉〗容再斟酌;留待查覆。
ad referendum contract 暫定合同。
ad·re·nal [ædˈrinḷ; əˈdriːnḷ] *n.* 副腎;腎上腺。—*adj.* ①副腎的;腎上腺的。②腎上的。—**ly,** *adv.* 「皮。
adrenal cortex 〖生理〗副腎皮;外腎
adrenal gland 腎上腺;腎上體;副腎。
ad·ren·al·in(e) [ædˈrɛnḷɪn; əˈdrenəlin] *n.* 腎上腺素。
a·dre·nin [əˈdrinɪn; əˈdriːnin] *n.* 副腎素。(亦作 **adrenine**) 「射的一面。
a·dret [æˈdre; æˈdrei] *n.* 山能受陽光照
A·dri·an [ˈedrɪən; ˈeidriən] *n.* 亞得連 (Edgar Douglas, 1889-, 英國生理學家, 1932 年得諾貝爾醫學獎)。
Adrianople red 鮮紅色。(亦作 **Levant red, Turkey red**)
A·dri·at·ic Sea, the [ˌedrɪˈætɪk~; ˌeidriˈætik~] 亞得里亞海(在義大利之東)。
a·drift [əˈdrɪft; əˈdrift] *adv. & adj.* ①(船隻之)漂泊;(隨風浪)漂流。②游移不定地(的)。 ***be all adrift*** 茫然不知所措。 ***get*** (or ***go***) ***adrift*** (船) 隨風漂流;脫節。 ***set adrift*** 使(船)逐流而漂。 ***turn*** (***a person***) ***adrift*** 逐出(某人)使漂泊無依。
a·drip [əˈdrɪp; əˈdrip] *adj.* 濕淋淋的。
a·droit [əˈdrɔɪt; əˈdrɔit] *adj.* 機巧的;熟練的。—**ly,** *adv.* —**ness,** *n.* 「右;在右。
à droite [ɑˈdrwɑt; aˈdrwat] 〖法〗向
A.D.S. 〖美〗American Dialect Society. 美國方言社團。 **ads.** advertisements.
a.d.s. autograph document, signed.
ad·sci·ti·tious [ˌædsɪˈtɪʃəs; ˌædsiˈtiʃəs] *adj.* 附加的;補充的;補遺的。—**ly,** *adv.*
ad·script [ˈædskrɪpt; ˈædskript] *adj.* ①後寫的。②隸屬的(農奴)。—*n.* 附屬於土地的農奴。 「ˈskripʃən] *n.* 隸屬。
ad·scrip·tion [ædˈskrɪpʃən; æd-
ad·smith [ˈædsmɪθ; ˈædsmiθ] *n.* 〖美俗〗作廣告文者。
ad-so·lic·i·tor [ˈædsəˈlɪsɪtə; ˈædsəˈlisitə] *n.* 〖美俗〗廣告掮客。
ad·sorb [ædˈsɔrb; ædˈsɔːb] *v.t.* 聚集(空氣、液體、或溶物)爲濃縮物於平面上;吸附。—**a·bil·i·ty,** *n.* —**a·ble,** *adj.*
ad·sorb·ate [ædˈsɔrbet; ædˈsɔːbeit] *n.* 被吸附物質。
ad·sorp·tion [ædˈsɔrpʃən; ædˈsɔːpʃən] *n.* 〖化〗吸附作用。—**ad·sorp·tive,** *adj., n.*
ad·sum [ˈædsʌm; ˈædsʌm] 〖拉〗*interj.* 到;有(=I am present. 點名時之應答用)。
ad·u·late [ˈædʒəˌlet; ˈædjuleit] *v.t.,* **-lat·ed, -lat·ing.** 諂媚;奉承;過分崇拜。—**ad·u·la·tion, ad·u·la·tor,** *n.* —**ad·u·la·to·ry,** *adj.*
***a·dult** [əˈdʌlt, ˈædʌlt; əˈdʌlt, ˈædʌlt] *adj.* ①成長的;成人的。an *adult* person. 成人。②成熟的;老成的。 ③適合成人的。—*n.* 成人。—**hood,** —**ness,** *n.*
a·dul·ter·ant [əˈdʌltərənt; əˈdʌltərənt] *adj.* 混合的;攙雜的。—*n.* 攙雜物。
a·dul·ter·ate [əˈdʌltəˌret; əˈdʌltəreit] *v.,* **-at·ed, -at·ing,** *adj.* —*v.t.* 攙混;攙以劣等或不純的物質。—*adj.* 不道德的;墮落的。—**a·dul·ter·a·tor,** *n.*
a·dul·ter·a·tion [əˌdʌltəˈreʃən; əˌdʌltəˈreiʃən] *n.* ①攙雜;僞造;改裝。②攙雜物;不純物;攙假的出品。
a·dul·ter·er [əˈdʌltərə; əˈdʌltərə] *n.* 通姦者;姦夫。 「*n.* 淫婦。
a·dul·ter·ess [əˈdʌltərɪs; əˈdʌltəris]
a·dul·ter·ine [əˈdʌltərɪn; əˈdʌltərin] *adj.* ①通姦所生的;姦淫的。②不正的;違法的。③不純的;僞造的。
a·dul·ter·ous [əˈdʌltərəs; əˈdʌltrəs] *adj.* 通姦的;不法的;不義的。—**ly,** *adv.*
a·dul·ter·y [əˈdʌltərɪ; əˈdʌltəri] *n., pl.* **-ies.** 通姦;私通。
a·dult·ly [əˈdʌltlɪ; əˈdʌltli] *adv.* 少年老成地;成熟地。
adult tooth 固齒;恒齒。
adult Western 成人看的西部電影,戲劇或小說。 「*adj.* 蔽蔭的;陰暗的。
ad·um·bral [ædˈʌmbrəl; ædˈʌmbrəl]
ad·um·brate [ædˈʌmbret; ˈædʌmbreit] *v.t.,* **-brat·ed, -brat·ing.** ①略示梗概。②預示。③蔭蔽;使暗。—**ad·um·bra·tion,** *n.* —**ad·um·bra·tive,** *adj.* —**ad·um·bra·tive·ly,** *adv.* 「劑之一種。
ad·u·rol [ˈædʒuˌrɔl; ˈædjurɔːl] *n.* 顯影
a·dusk [əˈdʌsk; əˈdʌsk] *adv. & adj.* 在黑暗中地(的)。
a·dust [əˈdʌst; əˈdʌst] *adj.* ①燒過的;烘乾的。②晒黑的;日炙的。③憂鬱的;鬱悶的。(亦作 **adusted**)
Adv. ①Advent. ②advocate (lawyer).
adv. ①adverb; adverbial; adverbially. ②advance. ③advertisement. ④ad valorem. **ad val.** ad valorem.
ad va·lo·rem [ˌædvəˈlorəm; ˈædvə-

ˈlɔːrem〕〖拉〗照價；按值。

:ad·vance 〔ədˈvæns; ədˈvɑːns〕 *v.*, **-vanced, -vanc·ing,** *n., adj.* —*v.t.* ①使前進；推前；撥進。to *advance* the hour hand. 向前撥動時針。②建議；貢獻；提出。to *advance* a plan. 提出計畫。③陞；擢升。He was *advanced* to the rank of colonel. 他陞級爲上校。④借貸；墊付；預付。⑤增加；漲價。to *advance* the price of milk. 提高牛奶價。⑥促進。⑦提前。to *advance* the time of the meeting. 提前開會時間。—*v.i.* ①前進；進行。The troops *advanced.* 軍隊前進。②增加(數量,價值,價錢)。The stock *advanced* recently. 股票最近漲價。③長進；進步；生長。Their children are *advancing* toward maturity. 他們的小孩正在逐漸成熟。④陞；升級。⑤(顏色等)醒目。Deep colors *advance.* 深的顏色能醒目。 —*n.* ①前進。②長進；進步；高陞。③騰貴；漲價。④言歸於好的表示；友好的表示。⑤(*pl.*) 接近。He made bold *advances* to a woman sitting next to him. 他大膽向坐在身邊的女人獻殷勤。⑥預支；貸款。⑦〖新聞〗事前寫好的報導。⑧〖美〗接待政治候選人的準備工作；助選團先遣人員的工作。***in advance*** **a.** 進步；在前。**b.** 預先。He wants to draw his salary *in advance.* 他要預支他的薪水。***in advance of*** 在…之前。 —*adj.* ①先期的。*advance* information. 事前的消息。 ②在前的。We sent out an *advance* party of soldiers. 我們派出一支先頭部隊。

advance copy 新書樣本。

·ad·vanced 〔ədˈvænst; ədˈvɑːnst〕 *adj.* ①在前的。②進步的；高深的。an *advanced* class in French. 法文高級班。③老的；暮的。an *advanced* age. 高齡。

advanced degree 碩士或博士學位。

advanced standing ①在他校所修習之學科的承認。②該被承認之學分。

advance fee 公司預付給答應代爲籌款的金融家的費用。

advance guard 〖軍〗前衞。

advance man 〖美〗①先遣宣傳員(戲劇,電影,馬戲等在某地上演前到達的宣傳員)②在政治候選人競選演說旅行途中預先布置的。先遣助選員。

·ad·vance·ment 〔ədˈvænsmənt; ədˈvɑːnsmənt〕 *n.* ①前進；推前；撥進。②擢升；升級；發跡；出頭。His *advancement* to captain came the following year. 第二年他便升爲上尉。③進步；進展；促進；發達。④增進；加多。⑤預付；墊付。

ad·vanc·er 〔ədˈvænsɚ; ədˈvɑːnsə〕 *n.* ①前進者。②雄鹿角的第二叉枝。

advance sheets 書籍未裝訂前送請專家審查或批評之樣張。

advance signal 准許火車在前列火車尚未完全離開時進入某一小段的信號。

:ad·van·tage 〔ədˈvæntɪdʒ; ədˈvɑːntidʒ〕 *n.* ①利益；便利。It is to his *advantage.* 這是對他有利的。②優勢〖over, of〗。He has the *advantage* of a good constitution. 他占身體好的便宜。③〖網球〗一局比賽中打成平手(deuce)而延長比賽後任何一方所得之第一分 (攻方所得稱 advantage in, 守方所得稱 advantage out)。***gain*** (or ***win***) ***an advantage over*** 勝過。***have an advantage over*** 勝於。***have the advantage of*** 單方面的認識(某人)。***take advantage of*** (***a person*** or ***thing***) **a.** 利用(指東西)。to *take advantage of* an opportunity. 利用機會。**b.** 欺騙；欺詐(指人)。***to advantage*** 有效。***to one's advantage*** 對…有利。***to the advantage of*** 有利於；有助於。***to the best advantage*** 最有益；最有效。***turn***(***a thing***) ***to advantage*** 利用。—*v.t.* ①促進。Such action will *advantage* our cause. 此種行動將促進我們的目的。②有助於；幫助。It would *advantage* him to work harder. 更努力會對他有幫助。

ad·van·taged 〔ədˈvæntɪdʒd; ədˈvɑːntidʒd〕 *adj.* 處於有利地位的。

advantage ground 地利；優勢；優「越之地位。」

·ad·van·ta·geous 〔ˌædvənˈtedʒəs; ˌædvənˈteidʒəs〕 *adj.* 有利的；有益的；便利的。It is *advantageous* to us. 這事於我們有利。—**ly,** *adv.* —**ness,** *n.*

adv. chgs. advance charges.

ad·vec·tion 〔ædˈvɛkʃən; ædˈvekʃən〕 *n.* ①熱之水平對流。②空氣之水平運動。 —**ad·vec·tive,** *adj.*

ad·vent 〔ˈædvɛnt; ˈædvənt〕 *n.* ①到來；來臨。②(A-) **a.** 耶穌降臨。**b.** 降臨節。

Ad·vent·ism 〔ˈædvɛntˌɪzəm; ˈædventizm〕 *n.* 耶穌再臨已近論；耶穌再生說。 —**Ad·vent·ist,** *n.*

ad·ven·ti·tious 〔ˌædvɛnˈtɪʃəs; ˌædvenˈtiʃəs〕 *adj.* ①偶發的；偶然的。②外來的。③〖生物〗偶生的；不定的。④〖醫〗偶發的。 —**ly,** *adv.* —**ness,** *n.*

ad·ven·tive 〔ædˈvɛntɪv; ædˈventiv〕 *adj.* 〖生物〗外來的；非土生的；偶發的。—*n.* 外來之動物或植物。

Advent Sunday 降臨節中之第一個「星期日。」

:ad·ven·ture 〔ədˈvɛntʃɚ; ədˈventʃə〕 *n., v.,* **-tured, -tur·ing.** —*n.* ①奇遇；奇異的經歷或事件。②冒險。Boys are usually fond of *adventure.* 男孩們常喜歡冒險。 ③商業的投機。***at all adventures*** 冒巨險；排除萬難。He will do it *at all adventures.* 他不惜冒險,要做這事。—*v.t.* ①敢爲；冒險嘗試。No man would *adventure* it. 沒有人敢冒險做這種事。②冒昧地說。—*v.i.* 冒險；圖僥倖〖on, upon〗. to *adventure* on unknown seas. 異海冒險。

ad·ven·ture·ful 〔ədˈvɛntʃɚfəl; ədˈventʃəful〕 *adj.* 富於驚險事件的；多奇遇的；具冒險性的。

adventure playground 〖英〗兒「童遊樂場。」

·ad·ven·tur·er 〔ədˈvɛntʃərɚ; ədˈventʃərə〕 *n.* ①冒險者。②投機者。political *adventurers.* 政壇投機分子。

ad·ven·ture·some 〔ədˈvɛntʃɚsəm; ədˈventʃəsəm〕 *adj.* 喜冒險的；極大膽的。

ad·ven·tur·ess 〔ədˈvɛntʃərɪs; ədˈventʃəris〕 *n.* 女冒險者；女投機者。

ad·ven·tur·ism 〔ədˈvɛntʃərɪzm; ədˈventʃərizm〕 *n.* 蔑視常軌；放蕩不羈；草率從事。 —**ad·ven·tur·ist,** *n.*

·ad·ven·tur·ous 〔ədˈvɛntʃərəs; ədˈventʃərəs〕 *adj.* ①愛冒險的；膽大的。an *adventurous* explorer. 大膽的探險者。②危險的；需要勇氣的。—**ly,** *adv.*

·ad·verb 〔ˈædvɝb; ˈædvəːd〕 *n.* 〖文法〗「副詞。」

ad·ver·bi·al 〔ədˈvɝbɪəl; ədˈvəːbjəl〕 *adj.* 副詞的；作副詞用的。—**ly,** *adv.*

ad·ver·bi·al·ize 〔ædˈvɝbɪəlˌaɪz; ædˈvəːbiəlaiz〕 *v.i.,* **-ized, -iz·ing.** 將(字或片語)變爲副詞。

ad ver·bum 〔ædˈvɝbəm; ædˈvəːbəm〕「〖拉〗逐字；一字不差。」

***ad·ver·sar·y** [ˈædvəˌsɛrɪ; ˈædvəsəri] *n.*, *pl.* **-sar·ies.** 對手; 仇敵。*the Adversary* 魔王;撒旦。

ad·ver·sa·tive [ədˈvɝsətɪv; ədˈvəːsətiv] *adj.* 反義的。 —*n.* 反義字。

***ad·verse** [ədˈvɝs, ˈædvɝs; ˈædvəːs] *adj.* ①逆的; 反對的; 不利的。*adverse* winds. 逆風。②有敵意的;敵對的。③〖植物〗內轉的(爲 averse 之對)。 —**ly,** *adv.* —**ness,** *n.*

adverse witness 〖法律〗對方證人。

***ad·ver·si·ty** [ədˈvɝsətɪ; ədˈvəːsiti] *n.*, *pl.* **-ties.** ①不幸; 災禍; 災難。His struggles with *adversity* are fruitless. 他徒與不幸掙扎而毫無效果。②(常 *pl.*) 不幸的事; 逆境;惡運。 「及;注意〖to〗.

ad·vert[1] [ədˈvɝt; ədˈvəːt] *v.i.* 談及;述

ad·vert[2] [ˈædvɝt; ˈædvəːt] *n.*〖英俗〗廣告。

ad·vert·ence [ədˈvɝtn̩s; ədˈvəːtəns] *n.* 談及;注意。(亦作 **advertency**)

ad·vert·ent [ədˈvɝtn̩t; ədˈvəːtənt] *adj.* 留心的;注意的。—**ly,** *adv.*

ad·ver·tise** [ˈædvɚˌtaɪz, ˌædvɚˈtaɪz; ˈædvətaiz] *v.*, **-tised, -tis·ing.** —*v.t.* ①登…的廣告。②吹噓貨好以資推銷。③通知。I *advertised* him of my plans. 我通知他我的計畫。④爲…作宣傳。⑤公告;公布。—*v.i.* 登廣告。to *advertise* for a job. 登廣告求職。advertise oneself*** 自吹。(亦作 **advertize**)

***ad·ver·tise·ment** [ˌædvɚˈtaɪzmənt; ədˈvəːtismənt] *n.* ①廣告。②宣傳。The news of this event will receive wide *advertisement.* 這消息將廣被宣傳。(亦作 **advertizement**)

ad·ver·tis·er, ad·ver·tiz·er [ˈædvɚˌtaɪzɚ; ˈædvətaizə] *n.* 廣告客戶。

***ad·ver·tis·ing** [ˈædvɚˌtaɪzɪŋ; ˈædvətaiziŋ] *n.* 廣告;廣告業。a career in *advertising.* 在廣告界的經歷。—*adj.* 廣告的。*advertising* agency (rate). 廣告公司(費)。

advertising man =**adman.**

‡ad·vice [ədˈvaɪs; ədˈvais] *n.* ①勸告;忠告。Let me give you a piece of *advice.* 容我勸你。②(*pl.*)消息。They receive *advices* from foreign countries regularly. 他們經常收到國外消息。③(商業上的)通知。shipping *advices.* 發貨通知。***a piece*** (***bit, word,*** or ***few words***) ***of advice*** 一句忠言。〖注意〗作①義解時, 不直接加不定冠詞。

advice boat 傳遞消息之快艇。(亦作 **dispatch boat**)

ad·vis·a·ble [ədˈvaɪzəbl̩; ədˈvaizəbl] *adj.*合理的;可取的;適當的。—**ad·vis·a·bil·i·ty, —ness,** *n.* —**ad·vis·a·bly,** *adv.*

***ad·vise** [ədˈvaɪz; ədˈvaiz] *v.*, **-vised, -vis·ing.** —*v.t.* ①勸告;忠告。②通知;報告。I will *advise* you of my future plans. 我將告訴你我的未來計畫。—*v.i.* ①商量。②勸告;忠告。I shall act as you *advise.* 我將按照你的忠告來做。

ad·vised [ədˈvaɪzd; ədˈvaizd] *adj.* ①深思熟慮過的。②獲得通知的;熟知的。—**ly,** *adv.* 「育〗接受選課指導的學生。

ad·vis·ee [ədˈvaɪzi; ədvaiˈziː] *n.* 〖教

ad·vise·ment [ədˈvaɪzmənt; ədˈvaizmənt] *n.* ①熟思;考慮。②忠告;輔導。

***ad·vis·er, ad·vis·or** [ədˈvaɪzɚ; ədˈvaizə] *n.* ①顧問。He is my legal *adviser.* 他是我的法律顧問。②導師 (尤指大學裏指導選課者)。

ad·vi·so·ry [ədˈvaɪzərɪ; ədˈvaizəri] *adj.* ①勸告的; 忠告的。②諮詢的; 顧問的。—*n.* ①報告 (尤指美國氣象局所發布者); 簡訊。②建議;報告。

ad vi·tam aut cul·pam [ædˈvaɪtæmɔtˈkʌlpæm; ædˈvaitəmɔtˈkʌlpəm] 〖拉〗終身;至犯過時爲止。

ad·vo·caat [ˌædvoˈkɑt; ˌædvouˈkɑːt] *n.* 一種荷蘭酒(混合白蘭地、糖及蛋而成)。

ad·vo·ca·cy [ˈædvəkəsɪ; ˈædvəkəsi] *n.* 辯護;主張;擁護;提倡。(亦作 **advocation**)

***ad·vo·cate** [*n.* ˈædvəkɪt, -ˌket; ˈædvəkit *v.* ˈædvəˌket; ˈædvəkeit] *n., v.,* **-cat·ed, -cat·ing.** —*n.* ①辯護者;律師。②提倡者;擁護者。③替人說情者。 —*v.t.* 提倡; 主張;建議;辯護。He *advocates* building more schools. 他主張建立更多學校。

ad·vo·ca·tor [ˈædvəˌketɚ; ˈædvəkeitə] *n.* 提倡者;辯護者;擁護者。

ad·voc·a·to·ry [ædˈvɑkəˌtɔrɪ, -ˌtor-; ædˈvɔkətəri] *adj.* 擁護者的;有關擁護者的。

ad·vow·son [ədˈvaʊzn̩; ədˈvauzən] *n.* 〖英國法律〗僧職授與權;牧師推薦權。—**ad-**

advt. advertisement. **vow·ee,** *n.*

advtg. ①advantage. ②advertising.

ad·wom·an [ˈædˌwʊmən; ˈædˌwumən] *n.*, *pl.* **-wom·en.** 〖美〗女廣告員。

ad·writ·er [ˈædˌraɪtɚ; ˈædˌraitə] *n.* 廣告詞撰擬者。「miə] *n.* 〖醫〗虛弱;無力。

ad·y·na·mi·a [ˌædɪˈnemɪə; ˌædaiˈnei-

ad·y·nam·ic [ˌædɪˈnæmɪk, ˌedaɪ-; ˌædaiˈnæmik] *adj.* 虛弱的;無力的。

ad·y·tum [ˈædɪtəm; ˈæditəm] *n.*, *pl.* **-ta** [-tə; -tə]. (古廟中之)密室; 內殿。

adz, adze [ædz; ædz] *n.* 手斧。—*v.t.* 以手斧劈。

Æ, æ [i; iː] *n.* A 與 E之連寫字, 如: Æsop (=Aesop), Cæsar (=Caesar). (亦寫作 AE 或 ae) 「的。

Æ 1 [ˈiˈwʌn; ˈiːˈwʌn] 第二等的;第二級

A E account executive.

A.E. ①Aeronautical Engineer. ②Agricultural Engineer. ③Associate in Education. ④Associate in Engineering.

a. e. 〖數學〗almost everywhere.

A.E. and P. Ambassador Extraordinary and Plenipotentiary.

AEC Atomic Energy Commission.

A. Ed. Associate in Education.

ae·dile [ˈidaɪl; ˈiːdail] *n.* 古羅馬管理公有建築物、街道、市場等之官吏。(亦作 **edile**)

Ae.E. Aeronautical Engineer.

AEF, A.E.F. American Expeditionary Forces. 「—*adj.* 愛琴海的。

Ae·ge·an [iˈdʒiən; iːˈdʒiːən] *n.*愛琴海。

Aegean Islands 愛琴羣島。

Aegean Sea 愛琴海。

ae·ger [ˈidʒɚ; ˈiːdʒə] *n.* (若干英國與加拿大大學發給因病不能參加考試學生之) 疾病證明書。

ae·gis [ˈidʒɪs; ˈiːdʒis] *n.* ①保護;庇護;主持;支持。②〖希臘神話〗Zeus 之楯。***under the aegis of*** 在…庇護下;得…之支持。(亦作 **egis**) 「疾病證明書。(亦作 **aeger**)

ae·gro·tat [ɪˈgrotæt; iːˈgroutæt] *n.*

Ae·ne·as [ɪˈniəs; iːˈniːæs] *n.* 〖希臘、羅馬神話〗Troy 戰爭中之一英雄。

Ae·ne·id [ɪˈniɪd; ˈiːniid] *n.* 羅馬詩人 Virgil 所著之史詩。 「〖美俗〗原子能。

A-en·er·gy [ˈeˈɛnɚdʒɪ; ˈeiˈenədʒi] *n.*

A. Eng. Associate in Engineering.
Ae·ni·us [ˈinɪəs; ˈiːniəs] *n.* (荷馬史詩中) 死於 Achilles 手下的特洛伊人之盟友。
Ae·o·li·an¹ [iˈolɪən; iːˈouliən] *adj.* Aeolis (小亞細亞一地方)的；其人民的；其語言的。—*n.* Aeolis 的居民；Aeolis 語言。(亦作 **Eolian**)
Ae·o·li·an² *adj.* ①風神 Aeolus 的；風的。②(常 a-) 因風之作用的；風成的。
aeolian harp 風奏琴(有等長之弦，因風之吹動而發音者)。(亦作 **aeolian lyre**)
Ae·ol·ic [iˈɑlɪk; iːˈɔlik] *adj.* Aeolis 的；Aeolis 語言的。—*n.* Aeolis 語言。(亦作 **Eolic**)
Ae·o·lus [ˈiələs; ˈiːouləs] *n.* 〖希臘神話〗風神。
ae·on [ˈiən; ˈiːən] *n.* 永世；極長而無法計算的時間。(亦作 **eon**)
ae·o·ni·an [iˈonɪən; iːˈouniən] *adj.* 永世的；恒久的。
aer·ate [ˈeəˌret; ˈeiəreit] *v.t.,* **-at·ed, -at·ing.** ①暴露於空氣中。②與空氣混合。③充以空氣或氣體。④使(血液)經呼吸與氧結合。—**aer·a·tion,** *n.*
aerated bread 無酵母麪包。
aerated water 炭酸水。
aer·a·tor [ˈeəˌretə; ˈeiəreitə] *n.* ①通風裝置。②充氣於液體之器械；炭酸氣飽和器。③(使穀物等去霉除蟲之)燻煙裝置。
*__aer·i·al__ [eˈɪrɪəl, ˈɛrɪəl; ˈɛəriəl] *adj.* ①空氣的；在空中的。②輕飄如空氣一般的。③夢幻的；幻想的。④與飛機有關的。an *aerial* attack. 空襲。⑤高懸的；巍峨的。⑥〖植物〗氣生的。—*n.*①天線。②(救火用)雲梯。③〖橄欖球〗向進攻方向的傳球。
aerial bar 表演空中飛人所用之鞦韆橫檔。
aerial beacon 航空標識。
aerial bomb (由飛機投下的)炸彈。
aerial camera 空中攝影機。
aerial chart 航空圖。
aerial current 氣流；天線電流。
aerial farming 利用飛機的機械化農業。
aer·i·al·ist [eˈɪrɪəlɪst, ˈɛrɪ-; ˈɛəriəlist] *n.* 表演空中飛人特技者。
aer·i·al·i·ty [ˌɛrɪˈælətɪ; ˌɛəriˈæliti] *n.* 似空氣之性質；空虛。
aerial ladder 雲梯(救火用者)；消防梯。
aerial lighthouse 航空燈塔。
aerial line ①架空線。②航空線。
aer·i·al·ly [ˈɛrɪəlɪ; ˈɛəriəli] *adv.* 在空中；如空氣地；空想地。
aerial mine ①空投水雷。②重型炸彈(尤指用降落傘下降者)。
aerial perspective 〖美術〗濃淡遠近法。
aerial photograph 空中照片。(亦作 **aerophoto**)
aerial photography 空中攝影；空中照相術。
aerial plant 氣生植物。
aerial railway 高架鐵路；空中纜車。
aerial root 〖植物〗氣根。
aerial ropeway 空中索道。
aerial sickness 暈機病；航空病。
aerial survey 空中測量。
aerial tanker 空中加油機。
aerial torpedo 空投魚雷。
aer·ie [ˈɛrɪ; ˈɛəri] *n.* ①(鷹等的)高巢。②(鷹等的)雛。③高山上之房舍、城市等。(亦作 **aery, eyrie, eyry**)
aer·i·fi·ca·tion [ˌɛrəfəˈkeʃən; ˌɛərifiˈkeiʃn, -ʃən] *n.* ①氣化。②充氣的狀態。
aer·i·form [eˈɪrəˌfɔrm; ˈɛərifɔːm] *adj.* ①氣體的；氣狀的。②無形的。
aer·i·fy [eˈɪrəˌfaɪ; ˈɛərifai] *v.t.,* **-fied, -fy·ing.** ①使與空氣化合。②使氣化。
aer·o [ˈeəro; ˈɛərou] *n.* 〖俗〗飛機；飛船；飛行。—*adj.* 飛機的；飛行的；航空的。
aero- 〖字首〗表"空氣；空中；氣體；航空"之義。如：aerodrome.
aer·o·bac·te·ri·ol·o·gy [ˌɛrobækˌtɪrɪˈɑlədʒɪ; ˌɛərəbækˌtiəriˈɔlədʒi] *n.* 大氣細菌學。
aer·o·bal·lis·tics [ˌɛrobəˈlɪstɪks; ˌɛərəbəˈlistiks] *n.* 空中彈道學。—**aer·o·bal·lis·tic,** *adj.*
aer·o·bat·ic [ˌeərəˈbætɪk; ˌɛərəˈbætik] *adj.* 飛行技藝的。*aerobatic* flight. 飛行表演。
aer·o·bat·ics [ˌeərəˈbætɪks; ˌɛərəˈbætiks] *n.* 高級飛行術；特技飛行。
aer·obe [ˈeərob; ˈeiəroub] *n.* 〖生物〗需空氣或游離氧氣始能生存的細菌或微生物。(亦作 **aerobium**)
aer·o·bic [ˌeəˈrobɪk; ˌeiəˈroubik] *adj.* ①生存於氧氣中的；好氧性細菌或微生物的。②氧氣的；因氧氣存在而導致的。
aer·o·bi·ol·o·gy [ˌeərobaɪˈɑlədʒɪ; ˌɛərəbaiˈɔlədʒi] *n.* 大氣生物學。—**aer·o·bi·ol·o·gist,** *n.*
aer·o·bi·o·sis [ˌeərobaɪˈosɪs; ˌɛərəbaiˈousis, ˌɛərou-] *n.* 〖生物〗氣生；需氣生活。
aer·o·boat [ˈeərəˌbot; ˈɛərəbout] *n.* 水上飛機。
aer·o·bus [ˈeərəˌbʌs; ˈɛərəbʌs] *n.* 〖俗〗民航機；班機；客機。
aer·o·cab [ˈeərəˌkæb; ˈɛərəkæb] *n.* 計程直升機。
aer·o·cade [ˌɛroˈked; ˌɛərəˈkeid] *n.* 飛行隊；機羣。
aer·o·cam·er·a [ˌeərəˈkæmərə; ˌɛərəˈkæmərə] *n.* 空中照相機。
aer·o·drome [ˈɛrəˌdrom; ˈɛərədroum] *n.* 〖英〗飛機場。
aer·o·dy·nam·i·cist [ˌɛrodaɪˈnæməsɪst; ˌɛərədaiˈnæmisist] *n.* 氣體力學家；空氣動力學家。
aer·o·dy·nam·ics [ˌɛrodaɪˈnæmɪks; ˈɛəroudaiˈnæmiks] *n.* 〖物理〗空氣動力學；氣體動力學。
aer·o·dyne [ˈɛrəˌdaɪn; ˈɛəroudain] *n.* 重於空氣的飛行器。
aer·o·em·bo·lism [ˌɛrəˈɛmblɪzəm; ˌɛərəˈembəlizm] *n.* 〖病理〗高空栓塞；氣泡栓塞。
aer·o·foil [ˈɛrəˌfɔɪl; ˈɛərəfɔil] *n.* 〖航空〗翼；風板。
aer·o·gram, aér·o·gramme [ˈeərəˌɡræm; ˈɛərəɡræm] *n.* ①無線電報。②航空信(郵簡)。
aer·o·graph [ˈeəroˌɡræf, ˈɛrə-; ˈɛərəɡrɑːf] *n.* ①無線電報機。②氣象記錄器。
aer·og·ra·phics [ˌeəroˈɡræfɪks; ˌɛərəˈɡræfiks] *n.* 大氣學。
aer·og·ra·phy [ˌeəˈrɑɡrəfɪ; ɛəˈrɔɡrəfi] *n.* 大氣誌；空氣誌。
aer·o·gun [ˈeəroˌɡʌn, ˈɛrə-; ˈɛərəɡʌn] *n.* 高射砲；對空射擊用之槍砲。
aer·o·lite [ˈeəroˌlaɪt; ˈɛərəlait] *n.* 隕石。(亦作 **aerolith**) —**aer·o·lit·ic,** *adj.*
aer·ol·o·gy [ˌeəˈrɑlədʒɪ; ɛəˈrɔlədʒi] *n.* 高空氣象學。—**aer·ol·o·gist,** *n.*
aer·o·ma·rine [ˌeərəməˈrin; ˌɛərəməˈriːn] *adj.* 海上飛行的。
aer·o·me·chan·ic [ˌɛromɪˈkænɪk; ˌɛərəmiˈkænik] *n.* 飛機修理技工。—*adj.* 氣體力學的。
aer·o·me·chan·ics [ˌɛromɪˈkænɪks;

ˌεərəmiˈkæniks] *n.* 氣體力學。
aer·o·med·i·cine [ˌεrəˈmεdɪsn̩; ˌεərəˈmedisin] *n.* 航空醫學。
aer·om·e·ter [ˌeəˈrɑmətɚ; εəˈrɔmitə] *n.* 氣體計;氣量計;氣體比重計。
aer·om·e·try [ˌeəˈrɑmɪtrɪ; εəˈrɔmitri] *n.* 氣體測定學;量氣學。
aeron. aeronautics.
aer·o·naut [ˈεrəˌnɔt; ˈεərənɔːt] *n.* ①飛艇或輕氣球之駕駛員。②飛艇之乘客。
aer·o·nau·ti·cal [ˌεrəˈnɔtɪkl̩; ˌεərəˈnɔːtikəl] *adj.* 飛行員的;航空的;航空術的。(亦作 **aeronautic**) **—ly,** *adv.*
aer·o·nau·tics [ˌεrəˈnɔtɪks; ˌεərəˈnɔːtiks] *n.* 航空學;航空術。
aer·o·na·val [ˌεrəˈnevl̩; ˌεərəˈneivəl] *adj.* 〖軍事〗海空的。
aer·o·neer [ˌeərəˈnɪr; ˌεərəˈniə] *n.* 〖美〗新式飛機模型設計者。
aer·o·neu·ro·sis [ˌεrənjuˈrosis; ˌεərənjuəˈrousis] *n.* 航空神經症。
aer·o·o·ti·tis me·di·a [ˌeəroəˈtaɪtɪsˈmidɪə; ˌεərououˈtaitisˈmiːdiə] 〖醫〗航空中耳炎。
aer·o·phi·lat·e·ly [ˌεrofəˈlætəlɪ; ˌεərəfiˈlætəli] *n.* 航空郵票之蒐集或研究。
aer·o·phile [ˈεrəfɪl; ˈεərəfil] *n.* 愛飛行者;飛行迷。
aer·o·pho·bi·a [ˌεrəˈfobɪə; ˌεərəˈfoubiə] *n.* 高空恐怖(症)。
aer·o·phone [ˈεrəˌfon; ˈεərəfoun] *n.* ①無線電話機。②助聽器。③聽音機(偵測接近之飛機者)。
aer·o·pho·to [ˈεrəˌfoto; ˈεərəfoutou, ˈεərou-] *n., pl.* **-tos.** ①空中攝影。②空中照片。
aer·o·pho·tog·ra·phy [ˌeərofəˈtɑgrəfɪ; ˌεərəfəˈtɔgrəfi] *n.* 空中照像術。
aer·o·phyte [ˈεrəˌfaɪt; ˈεərəfait] *n.* 〖植物〗氣生植物。
‡aer·o·plane [ˈεrəˌplen; ˈεərəplein] *n.* 〖英〗飛機。
aer·o·pol·i·tics [ˌεrəˈpɑlɪtɪks; ˌεərəˈpɔlitiks] *n.* 國際航空政策。
aer·o·sol [ˈεrəˌsɑl; ˈεərəsɔl] *n.* ①〖化〗液化氣體。②烟;霧。③裝液化氣體的罐子。
aerosol bomb 殺蟲劑噴霧器。(亦作 **aerosol container**)
aer·o·sol·ize [ˈεrəsɑlˌaɪz; ˈεərəsɔlaiz] *v.t.,* **-ized, -iz·ing.** 噴(藥品)爲霧氣。
aer·o·space [ˈεrəˌspes; ˈεərəspeis] *n.* 地球大氣層內外;大氣層及太空。
aer·o·stat [ˈεrəˌstæt; ˈεərəstæt] *n.* 飛船;輕氣球;輕飛行器。
aer·o·stat·ic [ˌεrəˈstætɪk; ˌεərəˈstætik] *adj.* ①氣體靜力學的。②航空(術)的。③氣船或輕氣球中所用的。(亦作**aerostatical**)
aer·o·stat·ics [ˌεrəˈstætɪks; ˌεərəˈstætiks] *n.* ①氣體靜力學。②氣體航空學。
aer·o·sta·tion [ˌεroˈsteʃən; ˌεərəˈsteiʃən] *n.* 輕氣球、飛艇等之駕駛術。
aer·o·ther·a·peu·tics [ˌεroˌθεrəˈpjutɪks; ˌεərəˌθerəˈpjuːtiks] *n.* 空氣治療術。(亦作 **aerotherapy**)
aer·o·tow [ˈεrəˌto; ˈεərətou] *v.t.* 在空中拖(飛機等)。—*n.* 空中拖曳。
aer·o·track [ˈεrəˌtræk; ˈεərətræk] *n.* 飛機場。
aer·o·train [ˈεrəˌtren; ˈεərətrein] *n.* 行駛在鋼筋水泥軌道上之氣墊式火車。
ae·ru·gi·nous [ɪˈrudʒɪnəs; iəˈruːdʒinəs] *adj.* 藍綠色的。
ae·ru·go [ɪˈrugo; iˈruːgou] *n.* 銅綠。
aer·y[1] [ˈεrɪ; ˈeiəri] *adj.* 〖詩〗空氣的;聳入空際的;空想的。
aer·y[2] [ˈεrɪ, ˈɪr-; ˈεəri] *n., pl.* **aer·ies.** =**aerie.**
Aes·chy·lus [ˈεskələs; ˈiːskiləs] *n.* 哀斯奇勒斯(525–456 B.C., 希臘悲劇詩人)。
Aes·cu·la·pi·an [ˌεskjəˈlepɪən; ˌiːskjuˈleipiən] *adj.* ①醫神 Aesculapius 的。②醫術的;醫藥的。—*n.* 醫生。
Aes·cu·la·pi·us [ˌεskjəˈlepɪəs; ˌiːskjuˈleipjəs] *n.* 〖羅馬神話〗①醫神。②(喻)醫生。
Ae·sir [ˈesɪr, ˈi-; ˈiːsəː] *n. pl.* 北歐神話中之衆神。
***Ae·sop** [ˈisəp; ˈiːsɔp] *n.* 伊索(620?–?560B.C., 希臘寓言作家)。**—i·an,** *adj.*
Aesop's Fables 伊索寓言。
aes·the·sia [εsˈθiʒə; iːsˈθiːʒə] *n.* 感覺;知覺;敏感性;感受性。(亦作 **aesthesis, esthesia**)
aes·thete [ˈεsθit; ˈiːsθiːt] *n.* ①審美家;唯美主義者。②裝做美術家者。(亦作 **esthete**)
aes·thet·ic [εsˈθεtɪk; iːsˈθetik] *adj.* (亦作 **esthetic**) ①美的;美學的。②(指人)審美的;愛美的;有美感的。③(指物)令人喜愛的;能引起趣味的;美術的。—*n.* ①審美的觀念。②=**aesthete. —al,** *adj.* **—al·ly,** *adv.*
aes·the·ti·cian [ˌεsθəˈtɪʃən; ˌiːsθiˈtiʃən] *n.* 美學家。(亦作 **esthetician**)
aes·thet·i·cism [εsˈθεtəsɪzəm; iːsˈθetisizəm] *n.* 唯美主義。
aes·thet·ics [εsˈθεtɪks; iːsˈθetiks] *n.* 美學;審美學。(亦作 **esthetics**)
aes·ti·val [ˈεstəvl̩; iːsˈtaivəl] *adj.* 夏季的;適於夏季的。(亦作 **estival**)
aet., aetat. aetatis.
ae·ta·tis su·ae [iˈtetɪsˈsui; iːˈteitisˈsuiː] 〖拉〗在某人(若干)歲時(= in a certain year of one's age).
ae·ther [ˈiθɚ; ˈiːθə] *n.* 醚。(亦作 **diethyl ether**)
ae·the·re·al [ɪˈθɪrɪəl; iˈθiriəl] *adj.* =**ethereal.**
ae·ti·ol·o·gy [ˌitɪˈɑlədʒɪ; ˌiːtiˈɔlədʒi] *n.* 病因學;病源論。(亦作 **etiology**)
A.E.U. Amalgamated Engineering Union. **AF** ① Air Force. ② Anglo-French. **Af.** ① Africa. ② African. **A.F.** ① Admiral of the Fleet. ② Air Force. ③Allied Forces. ④Armed Forces. ⑤ Army Form. ⑥ Anglo-French. ⑦ audio frequency. **a.f.** audio frequency. **A.F. (&) A.M.** Ancient Free and Accepted Masons.
a·far** [əˈfɑr; əˈfɑː] *adv.* ①在遠處;從遠處。②遙遠地。afar off*** 遠隔;遙遠。***from afar*** 自遠處。The light came *from afar.* 這光由遠處射來。
AFB Air Force Base. **A.F.B.** American Federation for the Blind. **AFC** ① Automatic flight control. ② Automatic frequency control. **AFD** accelerated freeze-drying. 加速冷凍乾燥法。
a·fear(e)d [əˈfɪrd; əˈfiəd] *adj.* 〖古,方〗恐懼的。
aff. ① affectionate. ② affirmative. ③ affirming.
af·fa·bil·i·ty [ˌæfəˈbɪlətɪ; ˌæfəˈbiliti] *n.* 和藹;殷勤;溫柔。
af·fa·ble [ˈæfəbl̩; ˈæfəbl] *adj.* 和藹可親的;殷勤的;溫柔的。**—af·fa·bly,** *adv.*
‡af·fair [əˈfεr; əˈfεə] *n.* ①事情。a private *affair.* 私事。②(*pl.*) 事務;任務;職務;業務。③東西。This machine is a complicated

affair. 這機器是件複雜的東西。④愛情；戀情。love *affair.* 戀情；戀愛。**affair of honor** 決鬥。**Ministry of Foreign Affairs** 外交部。**public affairs** 公務。

af·faire de coeur 〔əˈfɛrdəˈkɝ; əˈfɛədəˈkəː〕〖法〗戀愛事件；韻事。（亦作 **affaire d'amour**）

af·faire d'hon·neur 〔æˈfɛrdɔˈnɝ; æˈfɛədɔˈnəː〕〖法〗決鬥。

‡**af·fect**[1] 〔*v.* əˈfɛkt; əˈfekt *n.* ˈæfɛkt; ˈæfekt〕*v.t.* ①影響。to *affect* one's interests. 影響個人的利益。②感動。His speech *affected* the audience deeply. 聽衆深爲他的演說所感動。—*n.*〖心理〗感覺；感情。

‡**af·fect**[2] *v.t.* ①佯爲；假作。to *affect* ignorance. 佯爲不知。②愛好；嗜好。③（指動植物）生長於。Lions *affect* Africa. 非洲產獅子。 —**er,** *n.*

af·fec·ta·tion 〔ˌæfɪkˈteʃən; ˌæfekˈteiʃən〕*n.* ①虛飾；假裝。②裝腔作態。

af·fect·ed[1] 〔əˈfɛktɪd; əˈfektid〕*adj.* ①受影響的。②感動的。③感染的；感受的；罹病的。the *affected* part. 患部。

af·fect·ed[2] *adj.* ①矯飾的；不自然的。②傾心的。③愛好的。—**ly,** *adv.* —**ness,** *n.*

af·fect·ing 〔əˈfɛktɪŋ; əˈfektiŋ〕*adj.* 動人的；傷心的；可憐的。—**ly,** *adv.*

*__af·fec·tion__ 〔əˈfɛkʃən; əˈfekʃən〕*n.*①情愛；愛好；愛。the *affection* of parents for (*or* towards) their child. 父母對子女的愛。②(*pl.*) 感動；情感。③疾病。an *affection* of the throat. 喉病。 —**al,** *adj.*

*__af·fec·tion·ate__ 〔əˈfɛkʃənɪt; əˈfekʃnit〕*adj.* 摯愛的；親切的。an *affectionate* embrace. 親切的擁抱。—**ly,** *adv.* —**ness,** *n.*

af·fec·tive 〔əˈfɛktɪv; əˈfektiv〕*adj.* ①感情的。②激動情緒的。③〖心理〗情緒上的。

af·fec·tiv·i·ty 〔ˌæfɛkˈtɪvətɪ; əˌfekˈtiviti〕*n.*〖心理〗感觸性；易感性（對感情反應的相對强度）。

af·fer·ent 〔ˈæfərənt; ˈæfərənt〕*adj.* 〖生理、生物〗輸入的；向心的。

af·fet·tuo·so 〔əˌfɛtʃuˈoso; əˌfetjuˈouzou〕〖義〗*adj.* & *adv.*〖音樂〗哀婉動人的（地）。—*n.* 哀婉動人的曲子或樂章。

af·fi·ance 〔əˈfaɪəns; əˈfaiəns〕*n., v.,* **-anced, -anc·ing.** —*n.* ①誓約；婚約；訂婚。②信託；信心〖in〗. —*v.t.* 使訂婚；定親；下聘。

af·fi·ant 〔əˈfaɪənt; əˈfaiənt〕*n.*〖法律〗立誓詞者。

af·fi·da·vit 〔ˌæfəˈdevɪt; ˌæfiˈdeivit〕*n.*〖法律〗誓詞；口供。

af·fil·i·ate 〔*v.* əˈfɪlɪˌet, *n.* əˈfɪlɪɪt, -ˌet; əˈfilieit〕*v.,* **-at·ed, -at·ing,** *n.* —*v.t.* ①使有密切聯繫；聯合。②加入；聯絡；結交〖with〗. ③收爲養子。④判定私生子之父〖on, upon, to〗. ⑤溯源；追尋根源。 —*v.i.* 聯絡；密切聯繫；參加〖with〗. —*n.* ①支會；分會。②會員。③主權之一部或全部屬於另一公司之商業機構。

af·fil·i·at·ed 〔əˈfɪlɪˌetɪd; əˈfilieitid〕*adj.* 附屬的；有關連的。

affiliated company 相關公司。

af·fil·i·a·tion 〔əˌfɪlɪˈeʃən; əˌfiliˈeiʃən〕*n.*①立嗣。②親密之關係。③（私生子之）父子關係的鑑定。④入會；加入；合併。⑤聯盟；關係。⑥推溯由來；溯源。

af·fi·nal 〔əˈfaɪnl̩; əˈfainəl〕*adj.*①有婚姻關係的；姻親的。②同源的。—*n.*姻親；親屬。

af·fined 〔əˈfaɪnd; əˈfaind〕*adj.* ①成爲親戚的；姻親的。②相結合的；同盟的。

*__af·fin·i·ty__ 〔əˈfɪnətɪ; əˈfiniti〕*n., pl.* **-ties.** ①密切之關係。English has a close *affinity* to French. 英語與法語有很密切之關係。②姻親；親戚關係。③類似。④吸引力。⑤〖化〗親和力。⑥具有吸引力的人。—**af·fin·i·ta·tive, af·fin·i·tive,** *adj.*

*__af·firm__ 〔əˈfɝm; əˈfəːm〕*v.t.* ①矢言；斷言。to *affirm* one's loyalty to one's country. 矢言忠於本國。②證實；批准；確定。—*v.i.* 證實。

af·firm·a·ble 〔əˈfɝməbl; əˈfəːməbl〕*adj.* 可斷言的；可確認的。 —**af·firm·a·bly,** *adv.*

af·firm·ance 〔əˈfɝməns; əˈfəːməns〕*n.* 斷言；確認。

af·firm·ant 〔əˈfɝmənt; əˈfəːmənt〕*n.* 斷言者；確認者。

af·fir·ma·tion 〔ˌæfəˈmeʃən; ˌæfəːˈmeiʃən〕*n.* ①斷言；確言。②確定；肯定。③證明；證實。

af·firm·a·tive 〔əˈfɝmətɪv; əˈfəːmətiv〕*adj.* 斷言的；贊成的；肯定的。—*n.* ①贊成；認可。②肯定的字句。**the affirmative** 贊成的方面。—**ly,** *adv.*

affirmative flag 上有藍、白、紅、白、藍五根水平線條的旗，在國際信號中代表"是"。

af·firm·a·to·ry 〔əˈfɝməˌtorɪ; əˈfəːmətəri〕*adj.* 斷言的；肯定的。

affirming gun 戰艦在搜查商船前所發射的示意砲火。（亦作 **informing gun**）

af·fix 〔*v.* əˈfɪks; əˈfiks *n.* ˈæfɪks; ˈæfiks〕*v.t.* ①使固定；黏上；貼上。②加於末端；附加。③蓋（印）。④加上；加以；連有。—*n.* ①附加物；附件。②字首、字尾、或嵌入一字中的字腰。—**al,** *adj.* —**a·tion,** *n.*

af·fix·ture 〔əˈfɪkstʃɚ; əˈfikstʃə〕*n.*①附添；貼。②附添物；附加物。

af·flat·ed 〔əˈfletɪd; əˈfleitid〕*adj.* 來自靈感的。

af·fla·tus 〔əˈfletəs; əˈfleitəs〕*n.* （藝術家、詩人等之）靈感。

*__af·flict__ 〔əˈflɪkt; əˈflikt〕*v.t.* 使痛苦。He is *afflicted* with the gout. 他爲痛風症所苦。

af·flic·tion 〔əˈflɪkʃən; əˈflikʃən〕*n.* ①痛苦；苦難。②產生痛苦的事由。

af·flic·tive 〔əˈflɪktɪv; əˈfliktiv〕*adj.*致痛苦或災難的；苦惱的；悲傷的。

af·flu·ence 〔ˈæfluəns; ˈæfluəns〕*n.* ①富裕；豐富。②注入；匯聚。

af·flu·ent 〔ˈæfluənt; ˈæfluənt〕*adj.* ①富裕的。②暢流的。—*n.* 支流。—**ly,** *adv.*

af·flux 〔ˈæflʌks; ˈæflʌks〕*n.* ①湧流；流注。②匯集。③〖醫〗充血。

‡**af·ford** 〔əˈford, əˈfɔrd; əˈfɔːd〕*v.t.*①能堪；力足以（常與can, could, be able to 連用）。I can't *afford* to pay such a high price. 我出不起這樣高的價錢。②產生。Reading *affords* pleasure. 讀書予人快樂。③供給；給與。—**a·ble,** *adj.*

af·for·est 〔əˈfɔrɪst; əˈfɔrist〕*v.t.*造林於；使（土地）成林區。

af·for·es·ta·tion 〔əˌfɑrəsˈteʃən; əˌfɔrisˈteiʃən〕*n.*①造林；植林。②植林地區。

af·fran·chise 〔əˈfræntʃaɪz; əˈfræntʃaiz〕*v.t.,* **-chised, -chis·ing.** 恢復（某人）自由；釋放；解除（某人）義務、責任等。

af·fray 〔əˈfre; əˈfrei〕*n.* 騷動；滋擾；打架（尤指於公共場所中的吵架）。

af·freight 〔əˈfret; əˈfreit〕*v.t.* 租用（船隻而由船主負責行駛）；包租（船隻）。—**ment,** —**er,** *n.*

af·fri·cate 〔ˈæfrɪkɪt; ˈæfrikit〕*n.*〖語音〗爆擦音。

af·fright 〔əˈfraɪt; əˈfrait〕*v.t.* 〖古〗使恐怖；驚嚇。—*n.* 恐怖；驚嚇。

af·front 〔əˈfrʌnt; əˈfrʌnt〕*v.t.* ①侮辱；冒犯。②泰然面對。—*n.*侮辱。

af·fuse [ə'fjuz; ə'fju:z] *v.t.*, **-fused, -fus·ing.** 向(人或物)灌水或其他液體。
af·fu·sion [ə'fjuʒən; ə'fju:ʒən] *n.*①灌澆;灌注。②〖宗教〗灌水式。③〖醫〗灌注療法。
Afg. Afghanistan. (亦作 **Afgh.**)
Af·ghan ['æfgən; 'æfgæn] *n.* ①阿富汗人。②阿富汗語。③一種毛氈。④一種獵狗。—*adj.* (亦作 **Afghani**) 阿富汗的;阿富汗人的;阿富汗語的。 「肩。」
af·ghan ['æfgən; 'æfgæn] *n.* 毛氈或披
Af·ghan·i·stan [æf'gænə,stæn; æf'gænistæn] *n.* 阿富汗 (亞洲西南部一國家,首都喀布爾 Kabul)。
a·fi·cio·na·do [ə,fisjə'nado; ə,fi:sjə'na:dou] *n., pl.* **-dos.** ①鬥牛迷。②…迷。
a·field [ə'fild; ə'fi:ld] *adv.* ①至田野;向野外。②在遠方;離鄉背井地。③離題;離譜。④在戰場上。⑤〖棒球〗在外野。
a·fire [ə'fair; ə'faiə] *adv. & adj.* 着火地(的);燃燒地(的)。 「ation of Labor.」
AFL, A.F. of L. American Feder-
a·flame [ə'flem; ə'fleim] *adv. & adj.* ①着火地(的)。②紅似火焰地(的);熾盛地(的);發亮地(的);輝耀地(的)。③殷切;興奮。
AFL-CIO American Federation of Labor and Congress of Industrial Organizations.
a·float [ə'flot; ə'flout] *adj. & adv.* ①飄浮的(地)。The ship is *afloat.* 船漂在水上。②在船上;在海上。③爲水所淹的(地);氾濫。④漂蕩無定的(地)。⑤傳播甚廣的(地)。⑥免於經濟困難的(地)。
a·flush[1] [ə'flʌʃ; ə'flʌʃ] *adj.* 面紅的。
a·flush[2] *adj. & adv.* 平的(地);均勻的(地)。
a·flut·ter [ə'flʌtɚ; ə'flʌtə] *adj. & adv.* ①驚惶的(地)。②飄動的(地)。③充滿動盪東西的(地)。 「tion of Musicians.」
AFM, A.F.M. American Federa-
AFN Armed Forces Network.
a·fo·cal [ə'fokl; ə'foukl] *adj.* 〖光學〗無一定焦點的(如望遠鏡)。
a·foot [ə'fut; ə'fut] *adv. & adj.* ①徒步地(的)。②在進行中(的); 在準備中(的)。③行動地(的);走動地(的)。
a·fore [ə'for; ə'fɔ:] *adv., prep., conj.* 〖古,方〗前方;在先;在前;以前。
a·fore·men·tioned [ə'for'mɛnʃənd; ə'fɔ:'menʃənd] *adj.* 前述的; 上述的。
a·fore·named [ə'for,nemd; ə'fɔ:neimd] *adj.* 前述的;前舉的。
a·fore·said [ə'for,sɛd; ə'fɔ:sed] *adj.* 上面所說的;前述的。
a·fore·thought [ə'for,θɔt; ə'fɔ:θɔ:t] *adj.* 預謀的;故意的。—*n.* 預謀;預想。
a·fore·time [ə'for,taim; ə'fɔ:taim] *adv.* 往昔;從前。—*adj.* 往昔的;從前的。
a for·ti·o·ri ['e,forʃi'orai; 'ei,fɔ:ti'ɔ:rai] 〖拉〗何況;更加。
a·foul [ə'faul; ə'faul] *adv. & adj.* ①衝突地(的); 互撞地(的)。②糾纏地(的)。***run*** (or ***fall***) ***afoul of*** 和…相撞(衝突);爲…所糾纏;陷於…之困難中; 遭遇麻煩。
Afr. ①Africa. ②African.
A-Fr. Anglo-French.
‡**a·fraid** [ə'fred; ə'freid] *adj.* ①怕;畏懼的。She is *afraid* of dogs. 她怕狗。②我認爲(駁斥或糾正對方時較客氣的說法)。I am *afraid* you are wrong about that. 我想在那一方面你錯了。
af·reet ['æfrit; 'æfri:t] *n.* 〖阿拉伯神話〗惡魔;鬼。(亦作 **afrit**)
a·fresh [ə'frɛʃ; ə'freʃ] *adv.* 再;從新。
Af·ric ['æfrik; 'æfrik] *adj.* 〖詩〗非洲的。
‡**Af·ri·ca** ['æfrikə; 'æfrikə] *n.* 非洲。
***Af·ri·can** ['æfrikən; 'æfrikən] *adj.* ①非洲的;與非洲有關的;來自非洲的。②非洲人的;黑人的。—*n.* 非洲人;黑人。
Af·ri·can·ist ['æfrikənist; 'æfrikənist] *n.* 對非洲歷史、文化、藝術等研究有素的專家學者。—**Af·ri·can·ism,** *n.*
Af·ri·can·ize ['æfrikə,naiz; 'æfrikənaiz] *v.t.* 使非洲化。
African lily 愛情花。 「洲睡眠病。」
African sleeping sickness 非
Af·ri·kaans [,æfri'kanz; ,æfri'ka:ns] *n.* 南非洲所用之荷蘭語。(亦作 **the Taal**)
Af·ri·kan·der [,æfri'kændɚ; ,æfri'kændə] *n.* 生於南非的歐洲人 (特指荷蘭血統者)。 「一種茂密髮型。」
Af·ro ['æfro; 'æfrou] *n.* 仿效非洲土人的
Af·ro-A·mer·i·can ['æfroə'mɛrəkən; 'æfrouə'merikən] *adj.* 美國黑人的。—*n.* 美國黑人。(亦作 **Aframerican**)
Af·ro-A·sian [,æfro'eʃən; ,æfrou'eiʃən] *adj.* 非亞居民的。—*n.* 非亞居民。
AFROTC 〖美〗 Air Force Reserve Officers Training Corps. **AFRS** Armed Forces Radio Service.
A.F.S. American Field Service.
aft [æft; a:ft] *adv. & adj.* 在船尾;向船尾。***fore and aft*** 從船首到船尾。
aft. afternoon. **A.F.T.** American Federation of Teachers.
‡**af·ter** ['æftɚ; 'a:ftə] *prep.* ①在…之後。Please line up one *after* another. 請按順序排隊。②追求;跟蹤。He runs *after* an actress. 他追求女伶。③於…後。I will come *after* supper. 我將於晚飯後來。④以…之故。He ought to succeed *after* such labors. 他如此努力,定能成功。⑤次於。⑥雖…終;畢竟。⑦仿照; 依從。He was named *after* his uncle. 他以叔父之名爲名。⑧關於。⑨合乎。***after all*** 終究;畢竟。***after dark*** 日落後。***after one's own heart*** 正合己意;志趣相投。***After you.*** 請先行。***get after someone*** 責備某人;批評某人。***look after*** 照顧。***one after another*** 相繼地。—*adv.* ①在後 (隨後)。He came running *after.* 他跟在後面跑來。②之後;以後。—*adj.* 後面的;後來的。—*conj.* 後於;在…後。*After* he goes, we shall eat. 他走之後,我們就吃飯。
af·ter·birth ['æftɚ,bɝθ; 'a:ftəbə:θ] *n.* ①〖醫〗胞衣;胎胞。②〖法律〗遺腹子。
af·ter·body ['æftɚ,badi; 'a:ftə,bɔdi] *n.* (船的)後部。 「*n.* 〖解剖〗後腦;延髓。」
af·ter·brain ['æftɚ,bren; 'a:ftəbrein]
af·ter·burn·er ['æftɚ,bɝnɚ; 'a:ftə,bə:nə] *n.* (噴射引擎之)後燃器。
af·ter·care ['æftɚ,kɛr; 'a:ftəkɛə] *n.* 病後或產後之調養。
af·ter·clap ['æftɚ,klæp; 'a:ftəklæp] *n.* 〖俗〗(認爲事畢後之)意外事故或結果。
af·ter·crop ['æftɚ,krap; 'a:ftə-krɔp] *n.* (農作物之)第二次收穫。
af·ter·damp ['æftɚ,dæmp; 'a:ftədæmp] *n.* (礦坑內發生爆炸或火災後) 餘留的臭氣。 「*n.* 〖航海〗後甲板。」
af·ter·deck ['æftɚ,dɛk; 'a:ftədek]
af·ter-din·ner ['æftɚ'dinɚ; 'a:ftə'dinə] *adj.* 正餐後的;晚餐後的。

af·ter·ef·fect [ˈæftərəˌfɛkt; ˈɑːftəriˌfekt] *n.* ①餘效。②〖醫〗副作用。
af·ter·glow [ˈæftɚˌglo; ˈɑːftə-glou] *n.* ①晚霞。②(灼熱金屬等之)殘熾。③(玩樂後的)餘韻; 餘味。「*n.* 割後再生之草。」
af·ter·grass [ˈæftɚˌgræs; ˈɑːftəgrɑːs]
af·ter·growth [ˈæftɚˌgroθ; ˈɑːftəgrouθ] *n.* ①(樹木、農作物等砍割後的)再生。②二期農作物。「〖物理〗殘熱。」
af·ter·heat [ˈæftɚˌhit; ˈɑːftəhiːt] *n.*
af·ter·hours [ˈæftɚˌaurz; ˈɑːftəˈauəz] *adj.* 公餘的。
af·ter·im·age [ˈæftɚˌɪmɪdʒ; ˈɑːftəˈimidʒ] *n.* 〖心理〗殘像; 遺留感覺。(亦作 **aftersensation**) 「來世。②晚年。」
af·ter·life [ˈæftɚˌlaɪf; ˈɑːftəlaif] *n.* ①
af·ter·light [ˈæftɚˌlaɪt; ˈɑːftəlait] *n.* ①晚霞。②後見之明。
af·ter·mar·ket [ˈæftɚˌmarkɪt; ˈɑːftəˌmɑːkit] *n.* 〖美〗販賣零件(修理用)的市場。
af·ter·math [ˈæftɚˌmæθ; ˈɑːftəmæθ] *n.* ①割後再生之草。②(尤指不幸的)結果。
af·ter·most [ˈæftɚˌmost; ˈɑːftəˌmoust] *adj.* ①最後的。②〖航海〗近船尾的。
‡**af·ter·noon** [ˌæftɚˈnun; ˈɑːftəˈnuːn, ˌɑːftəˈnuːn] *n.* ①下午; 午後。I saw him on Sunday *afternoon.* 我在星期天下午看見他。②以後的部分。***good afternoon*** 午安; 您好(下午相遇時說); 再會(下午告別時說)。—*adj.* 下午的; 適於午後的。He took an *afternoon* walk. 他午後散步。
af·ter·noon·er [ˌæftɚˈnunɚ; ˌɑːftəˈnuːnə] *n.* 〖美俚〗晚報;下午報。
af·ter·noons [ˌæftɚˈnunz; ˌɑːftəˈnuːnz] *adv.* 經常發生在下午。
afternoon tea ①下午茶。②午後之社交集會。「下午四時之守望。」
afternoon watch 〖航海〗自中午至
af·ter·pains [ˈæftɚˌpenz; ˈɑːftəpeinz] *n. pl.* 〖醫〗產後痛。「(正戲後加演的)短劇。」
af·ter·piece [ˈæftɚˌpis; ˈɑːftəpiːs] *n.*
af·ters [ˈæftɚz; ˈɑːftəz] *n. pl.* 〖英俗〗主菜之後上來的一道菜;餐後甜點。
af·ter·sales [ˈæftɚˌselz; ˈɑːftəˈseilz] *adj.* 〖英〗出售以後的。「*n.* 餘震。」
af·ter·shock [ˈæftɚˌʃɑk; ˈɑːftəʃɔk]
af·ter·taste [ˈæftɚˌtest; ˈɑːftəteist] *n.* ①餘味;回味。②餘情;餘韻。
af·ter·thought [ˈæftɚˌθɔt; ˈɑːftəθɔːt] *n.* ①回想。②追悔。③加添物。
af·ter·time [ˈæftɚˌtaɪm; ˈɑːftətaim] *n.* 今後;將來。
af·ter·treat·ment [ˈæftɚˌtritmənt; ˈɑːftəˌtriːtmənt] *n.* 紡織品染色後之化學處理。「戰後的。」
af·ter·war [ˈæftɚˈwɔr; ˈɑːftəˈwɔː] *adj.*
‡**af·ter·ward** [ˈæftɚwɚd; ˈɑːftəwəd] *adv.* 以後。*Afterward* he explained it to me. 以後他曾向我解釋。(亦作 **afterwards**)
af·ter·wit [ˈæftɚˌwɪt; ˈɑːftəwit] *n.* 亡羊補牢之智。「*n.* 結論;書後。」
af·ter·word [ˈæftɚˌwɝd; ˈɑːftəwəːd]
af·ter·world [ˈæftɚˌwɝld; ˈɑːftəwəːld] *n.* 來世。「*n. pl.* 某一事件發生後若干年。」
af·ter·years [ˈæftɚˌjɪrz; ˈɑːftəjiəz]
AFTRA, A.F.T.R.A. American Federation of Television and Radio Artists. **Ag** 〖化〗元素 argentum (銀)之符號。**Ag.** August. **A.G.** ①Adjutant General. ②Attorney General. **ag.** agriculture. 「(亦作 **agha**)」
a·ga [ˈɑgɑ; ˈɑːgə] 〖土〗 *n.* 將軍;大人。
‡**a·gain** [əˈgɛn, əˈgen; əˈgen, əˈgein] *adv.* ①再;復。Come *again.* 請再來。②再者;此外。③回答。Bring us word *again.* 帶給我們回音。④在另一方面。It might rain, and *again* it might not. 天可能下雨,亦可能不下雨。***again and again*** 一再; 屢次。***as much*** (or ***many***) ***again*** 倍於。She earns *as much again* as I do. 她賺的錢比我多一倍。***be oneself again*** 恢復常態; 康復。***never again***; ***never...again*** 永不。***now and again*** 時時。***once again*** 再一次。***time and again*** 頻頻;常常。
‡**a·gainst** [əˈgɛnst, əˈgenst; əˈgenst, əˈgeinst] *prep.* ①逆;反對。I am *against* your plans. 我反對你的計畫。②準備。③對着;在…前面。This pine tree stands *against* our dormitory. 這棵松樹就在我們的宿舍前面。④對比。⑤對照;以…爲背景。⑥抵抗;抵禦。A fire is a protection *against* cold. 火可以禦寒。⑦靠;倚;接觸。He leaned *against* a wall. 他靠在牆上。⑧對着…打擊。Rain beats *against* the window. 雨打在窗上。⑨隔壁。the house *against* the church. 教堂隔壁的屋子。⑩對換;交換。⑪與…競爭。***against one's will*** 違反己意。
ag·a·ma [ˈɑgəmə; ˈɑːgəmə] *n.* 變色蜥蜴。
Ag·a·mem·non [ˌægəˈmɛmnən; ˌægəˈmemnən] *n.* 〖希臘神話〗Troy戰爭中的希臘統帥。「物〗一種無性生殖細胞。」
ag·am·ete [eˈgæmit; eiˈgæmiːt] *n.* 〖生
ag·a·mi [ˈægəmɪ; ˈægəmi] *n.* 鶴類。
a·gam·ic [əˈgæmɪk; əˈgæmik] *adj.* ①〖生物〗無性的;無性生殖的。②〖植物〗隱花的。(亦作 **agamous**)
ag·a·mo·gen·e·sis [ˌægəməˈdʒɛnɪsɪs; ˌægəməˈdʒenisis] *n.* 〖生物〗無性生殖。—**ag·a·mo·ge·ne·tic,** *adj.*
A·ga·ña [ɑˈgɑnjɑ; ɑːˈgɑːnjɑː] *n.* 阿加納(關島首府)。「瞪口呆的(地)。」
a·gape[1] [əˈgep; əˈgeip] *adj. & adv.* 目
a·ga·pe[2] [ˈægəpi; ˈægəpi(ː)] *n., pl.* **-pae** [-pi; -piː]. ①神對世人之愛。②教徒間兄弟之情。
a·gar [ˈegɑr; ˈeigɑː] *n.* ①〖植物〗瓊脂;細菌培養基。②海菜;燕菜;石花菜。
a·gar-a·gar [ˈegɑrˈegɑr; ˈeigɑːˈeigɑː] *n.* =**agar.**
ag·a·ric [ˈægərɪk, əˈgærɪk; *n.* ˈægərik *adj.* æˈgærik] *n.* 平茸; 磨菇。—*adj.* 平茸的;如菌的。
a·gar·i·ca·ceous [əˌgærəˈkeʃəs; əˌgærəˈkeiʃəs] *adj.* 屬於菌類的。
ag·ate [ˈægɪt, ˈægət; ˈægət] *n.* ①瑪瑙。②瑪瑙體活字($5^1/_2$ point)。③兒童玩的彈子。
agate line 〖美〗計算廣告大小的單位。
ag·ate·ware [ˈægɪtˌwɛr; ˈægitwɛə] *n.* ①家庭鋼鐵用具(外塗以瑪瑙紋飾者)。②有瑪瑙狀圖案的陶器。
ag·at·ize [ˈægəˌtaɪz; ˈægətaiz] *v.t.,* **-ized, -iz·ing.** 使變爲瑪瑙;使成爲瑪瑙狀。
a·ga·ve [əˈgevɪ; əˈgeivi] *n.* 〖植物〗龍舌蘭。「視地(的);凝視地(的)。」
a·gaze [əˈgez; əˈgeiz] *adv. & adj.* 驚
‡**age** [edʒ; eidʒ] *n., v.,* **aged, ag·ing** or **age·ing.** —*n.* ①年齡。They are of the same *age.* 他們同年齡。②壽命。③世紀;時代。the Golden *Age.* 黃金時代。④老年。

The Chinese people have great respect for *age*. 中國人敬老。⑤長時間。I haven't seen him for *ages*. 我很久未看到他。⑥成年。***over age*** 超過限定年齡。***under age*** 未達限定年齡。—*v.i.*變老;成熟。He is *aging* rapidly. 他老得很快。—*v.t.* 使老。Fear *aged* him overnight. 恐懼使他隔宿變老。

-age 〖字尾〗名詞語尾,表下列諸義:①集合: baggage. ②地位;身分;狀態: baronage. ③動作;行動: passage. ④費用: postage. ⑤…的家: orphanage.

Ag. E. Agricultural Engineer.

a·ged** [for ①'edʒɪd;'eidʒid for ② edʒd; eidʒd] *adj.* ①年老的。②有…歲的。a boy *aged* six. 六歲的男孩。the aged*** 老者;老年人。

a·ged·ness ['edʒɪdnɪs; 'eidʒidnis] *n.* 老年;高齡。

a·gee [ə'dʒi; ə'dʒi:] *adv.* 〖英〗在一邊;歪斜;半開地。(亦作 **ajee**)

age group 年齡相仿之一羣人。(亦作 **age-group**)

age-ism ['edʒɪzəm; 'eidʒizəm] *n.* 對老年人歧視之行爲。

age·less ['edʒlɪs; 'eidʒlis] *adj.* ①長生不老的。②永恆的;不滅的。

age limit 退休年齡。

age·long ['edʒ'lɔŋ; 'eidʒlɔŋ] *adj.* 持久的;永續的;綿延的。

A·ge·na [ə'dʒinə; ə'dʒi:nə] *n.* 愛琴娜火箭。

Agence France Presse 法國新聞社(簡稱法新社,略作 **AFP**).

a·gen·cy** ['edʒənsɪ; 'eidʒənsi] *n., pl.* **-cies.** ①動作;作用;力量。②代理處;經銷處。The Ford Company has *agencies* all over the world. 福特(汽車)公司在全世界都有經銷處。③經售;代理;代理業。④公私機構。sole agency*** 獨家代理。***through*** (or ***by***) ***the agency of...*** 經(某人)之手。

Agency for International Development 國際開發總署(簡稱 AID).

agency shop (雇工受工會控制的)工廠或商號。

a·gen·da [ə'dʒɛndə; ə'dʒendə] *n. pl., sing.* **-dum** [-dəm; -dəm]. ①應辦之事;議事單;議程。②〖神學〗實際所爲。〖注意〗 **agenda** 現常作單數用。

a·gen·e·sis [e'dʒɛnəsɪs; ei'dʒenəsis] *n.* ①陽萎。②器官發育不全。(亦作 **agenesia**)

ag·en·ize ['edʒə,naɪz; 'eidʒənaiz] *v.t.,* **-nized, -niz·ing.** 用漂白劑漂白。

***a·gent** ['edʒənt; 'eidʒənt] *n.* ①代理人;代理商店。We are their sole *agent*. 我們是他們的獨家代理商店。②作用者;媒介物。③原動力;原因。natural *agents* 天然力量。④藥劑。an oxidizing *agent*. 氧化劑。⑤官方工作人員(如警察、特工等)。He is an *agent* of the F.B.I. 他是美國聯邦調查局的特工。⑥〖俗〗旅行推銷員。⑦工具;方法。

a·gen·tial [e'dʒɛnʃəl; ei'dʒenʃəl] *adj.* ①代理人的。②〖文法〗表示動作者或動因的。

a·gent pro·vo·ca·teur [ɑ'ʒɑ̃prɔvɔkɑ'tɝ; ɑ:'ʒɑ̃:prɔvɔkə'tə:] 〖法〗 *pl.* **agents provocateurs.** (被雇以誘使嫌疑人犯罪使其受懲之)密探。〖注意〗複數形所加的 s 不發音。

Age of Aquarius 宇宙大同之世紀。

age of consent 〖法律〗承諾年齡。

age of discretion 〖法律〗解事年齡。

age-old ['edʒ,old; 'eidʒ,ould] *adj.* 古老的。

ag·er·a·tum [,ædʒə'retəm; ,ædʒə'reitəm] *n.* 〖植物〗藿香。

a·geu·si·a [ə'gjusɪə; ə'gjusiə] *n.* 味覺缺失。

ag·glom·er·ate [*v.* ə'glɑmə,ret; ə'glɔməreit *adj., n.* ə'glɑmərɪt;ə'glɔmərit] *v.,* **-at·ed, -at·ing,** *adj., n.* —*v.t. & v.i.* (使)成團;結塊。—*adj.* ①聚結成塊的;凝聚的。②〖植物〗羣生的。—*n.* ①團;塊。②〖地質〗凝塊岩。—**ag·glom·er·a·tive,** *adj.*

ag·glom·er·a·tion [ə,glɑmə'reʃən; ə,glɔmə'reiʃən] *n.*①凝集;結塊。②(攙雜成的)一堆;一團。

ag·glu·ti·nant [ə'glutənənt; ə'glu:tinənt] *adj.* 膠合的;黏着的。—*n.*膠合劑。

ag·glu·ti·nate [*v.* ə'glutn̩,et; ə'glu:tineit *adj.* ə'glutn̩ɪt; ə'glu:tinit] *v.,* **-nat·ed, -nat·ing,** *adj.* —*v.t. & v.i.* (使)黏着;(使)膠合。—*adj.* 黏着的;膠合的。

ag·glu·ti·na·tion [ə,glutn̩'eʃən; ə,glu:ti'neiʃən] *n.* ①黏着;膠合;凝集。②膠着物。③〖語言〗膠着法;膠着語形。④〖醫,細菌〗(細菌、血球等之)凝集作用;凝集現象。

ag·glu·ti·na·tive [ə'glutn̩,etɪv; ə'glu:tinətiv] *adj.* ①膠着的;膠合的;凝集的。②〖語言〗膠着法的;膠着語形的。

ag·glu·ti·nin [ə'glutɪnɪn; ə'glu:tinin] *n.* 〖醫,細菌〗凝集素。

ag·glu·tin·o·gen [,æglu'tɪnədʒɛn; ,æglu'tinədʒen] *n.* 〖醫,細菌〗凝集原。

ag·grade [ə'gred; ə'greid] *v.t.,* **-grad·ed,-grad·ing.** (河流、海洋因挾帶泥沙)使(山谷或海灣底面)升高;沉積於。

ag·gran·dize ['ægrən,daɪz; ə'grændaiz] *v.t.,* **-dized, -diz·ing.** ①加大;增大;增高。②擴充。—**ment,** *n.*

***ag·gra·vate** ['ægrə,vet; 'ægrəveit] *v.t.,* **-vat·ed, -vat·ing.** ①加重;增劇;使更壞。Grief *aggravated* her illness. 悲愁加重她的病勢。②〖俗〗激怒。

ag·gra·vat·ing ['ægrə,vetɪŋ; 'ægrəveitiŋ] *adj.*①增劇的;惡化的。②〖俗〗激怒的。

ag·gra·va·tion [,ægrə'veʃən;,ægrə'veiʃən] *n.* ①加重;惡化。②〖俗〗憤怒。

ag·gre·gate [*n., adj.* 'ægrɪgɪt, -,get; 'ægrigit,-geit *v.* 'ægrɪ,get; 'ægrigeit] *v.,* **-gat·ed, -gat·ing,** *adj., n.* —*v.t. & v.i.* ①集合;團聚。②合計。—*adj.* ①聚合的。②〖植物〗攢集的。③〖地質〗聚成岩的。—*n.*①集合;集合體。②總數;合計。***in the aggregate*** 總計。—**ly,** *adv.*

ag·gre·ga·tion [,ægrɪ'geʃən ,ægri'geiʃən] *n.* ①集合;總合。②集合體;集團。③生物之集體生活;(動物之)羣集。

ag·gre·ga·tive ['ægrɪ,getɪv; 'ægrigeitiv] *adj.* 集合的;集成的;集團的。

ag·gress [ə'grɛs;ə'gres] *v.i.* 侵略;進攻。

ag·gres·sion [ə'grɛʃən; ə'greʃən] *n.* ①進攻;侵略。②侵犯。

***ag·gres·sive** [ə'grɛsɪv; ə'gresiv] *adj.* ①侵略的;攻擊的;挑釁的。An *aggressive* country is always ready to start a war. 一個好侵略的國家永遠準備發動戰爭。②積極的;活潑的。—**ly,** *adv.* —**ness,** *n.*

ag·gres·sor [ə'grɛsɚ; ə'gresə] *n.* 攻擊者;侵略者;侵略國。

ag·grieve [ə'griv; ə'gri:v] *v.t.,* **-grieved, -griev·ing.** 使苦惱;迫害。—**ag·grieved,** *adj.*

a·ghast [ə'gæst; ə'gɑ:st] *adj.* 驚駭的;恐怖的。

ag·ile ['ædʒəl; 'ædʒail] *adj.* 活潑的;動作敏捷的。—**ly,** *adv.* —**ness,** *n.*

a·gil·i·ty [ə'dʒɪlətɪ; ə'dʒiliti] *n.* 動作的

敏捷;機智;機敏。 「熟的過程。
ag·ing ['edʒɪŋ; 'eidʒiŋ] *n.* ①衰老。②成
ag·i·o ['ædʒo; 'ædʒiou] *n., pl.* **-os.** ①〖商〗貼水;折扣;扣頭。②=**agiotage.**
ag·i·o·tage ['ædʒətɪdʒ; 'ædʒətidʒ] *n.* ①兌換業。②公債股票投機買賣。
***ag·i·tate** ['ædʒəˌtet; 'ædʒiteit] *v.,* **-tat·ed, -tat·ing.** —*v.t.* ①震動;使洶湧。The wind *agitated* the sea. 風使海浪高揚。②搖擺。③擾亂;煽動;激動。④熱烈討論;激烈辯論。—*v.i.* 發起運動;熱烈討論。to *agitate* for the repeal of a tax. 發起取消某一稅捐的運動。—**ag·i·ta·tive,** *adj.*
ag·i·tat·ed ['ædʒəˌtetɪd; 'ædʒiteitid] *adj.* ①激動的。②討論不休的。—**ly,** *adv.*
***ag·i·ta·tion** [ˌædʒə'teʃən; ˌædʒi'teiʃən] *n.* ①劇烈的震動;搖動;攪動。②激動;振奮;焦慮。She walked away in great *agitation.* 她感情激動地走開。③煽動;運動。an *agitation* for a strike. 煽動罷工。④熱烈討論;辯論。
a·gi·ta·to [ˌɑdʒɪ'tɑto; ˌædʒi'tɑːtou]〖義〗*adv.* & *adj.*〖音樂〗激動地(的);急速地(的)。
ag·i·ta·tor ['ædʒəˌtetɚ; 'ædʒiteitə] *n.* ①煽動者;政治運動者;宣傳員。②攪拌器。
ag·it·prop ['ædʒɪtˌprɑp; 'ædʒitprɔp] *adj.* (共黨之)煽動及宣傳的。—*n.* ①(共黨之)煽動及宣傳機構。②煽動家兼宣傳家。
a·gleam [ə'glim; ə'gliːm] *adv.* & *adj.* 光輝地(的)。
ag·let ['æglɪt; 'æglit] *n.* ①帶端的金屬尖頭。②〖植物〗葇荑花。(亦作 **aiglet**)
a·gley [ə'glaɪ; ə'glai] *adv.* 〖蘇〗歪地;乖誤地。 「*adj.* 閃爍地(的)。
a·glim·mer [ə'glɪmɚ; ə'glimə] *adv.* &
a·glint [ə'glɪnt ə'glint] *adv.* & *adj.* (由於反射)閃亮地(的);燦爛地(的)。
a·glis·ten [ə'glɪsn; ə'glisn] *adj.* 閃爍的;光輝耀目的。 「光輝燦爛的(地)。
a·glit·ter [ə'glɪtɚ; ə'glitə] *adj.* & *adv.*
a·glos·sia [ə'glɑsɪə; ə'glɔsiə] *n.* 無舌;不能言語。 「地(的);興奮地(的)。
a·glow [ə'glo; ə'glou] *adv.* & *adj.* 發紅
AGM air-to-ground missile.
AGMA, A.G.M.A. American Guild of Musical Artists.
ag·mi·nate ['ægmənɪt; 'ægmənit] *adj.* 聚集的;成羣的。(亦作 **agminated**)
agminated glands 簇性腺。
ag·nail ['ægˌnel; 'ægneil] *n.* ①(指頭上的)倒拉刺。②膿性指頭炎。
ag·nate ['ægnet; 'ægneit] *adj.* ①父系的。②同系的;同種的。—*n.* 父系的親屬;同族之人。—**ag·nat·ic,** *adj.* —**ag·na·tion,** *n.*
Ag·na·tha ['ægnəθə; 'ægnəθə] *n.* 脊椎動物中的無顎類(如海鰻、醜魚等)。
ag·na·thous ['ægnəθəs; 'ægnəθəs] *adj.*〖動物〗無顎的;屬於無顎類的。
Ag·nes ['ægnɪs; 'ægnis] *n.* ①女子名。②聖女埃格尼斯 (Saint, 一月二十一日爲其紀念日)。
ag·no·men [æg'nomɛn; æg'noumen] *n., pl.* **-mens, -nom·i·na** [-'nɑmənə; -'nɔmənə]. 綽號。
ag·nos·tic [æg'nɑstɪk; æg'nɔstik] *adj.* 不可知論的。—*n.*不可知論者。—**al·ly,** *adv.*
ag·nos·ti·cism [æg'nɑstəˌsɪzəm; æg'nɔstisizəm] *n.* 〖哲學〗不可知論。
Ag·nus De·i ['ægnəs'diaɪ; 'ɑːgnus'deiiː]〖拉〗神之羔羊 (耶穌基督之別名)。

‡**a·go** [ə'go; ə'gou] *adj.* 已往的;以前的。I met him a long time *ago.* 我很久以前遇到他。—*adv.* 已往;以前。His uncle left here long *ago.* 他的叔父離此已久。
a·gog [ə'gɑg; ə'gɔg] *adv.* & *adj.* 因渴望或好奇而極度興奮地(的)。
à·go-go [ə'goˌgo; ə'gouˌgou] *adv.* & *adj.* ①有關小型熱門夜總會地(的);熱門音樂地(的);阿哥哥舞地(的)。to dance *à-go-go.* 跳阿哥哥舞。an *à-go-go* dance. 阿哥哥舞。②動作迅捷地(的);奔放不拘地(的);瘋狂地(的)。③最新式地(的);最時髦地(的)。—*n.* =**discotheque.** (亦作 **à Gogo, à gogo, à go-go, go-go**)
a·go·ing [ə'goɪŋ; ə'gouiŋ] *adv.* & *adj.*〖俗〗運轉地(的);在進行中(的)。
ag·o·nal [ə'gɑnl; ə'gɔnəl] *adj.* 痛苦之徵兆的(如臨終前之痛苦)。 「的。
a·gon·ic [e'gɑnɪk; ei'gɔnik] *adj.* 不成角
ag·o·nis·tic [ˌægə'nɪstɪk; ˌægə'nistik] *adj.* ①(古希臘之)有獎競賽的。②論戰的;好鬥的。③勉強的。(亦作 **agonistical**)
ag·o·nize ['ægəˌnaɪz; 'ægənaiz] *v.,* **-nized, -niz·ing.** —*v.i.* ①煩惱;苦悶。②掙扎。—*v.t.* 使痛苦。
ag·o·niz·ing ['ægəˌnaɪzɪŋ; 'ægənaiziŋ] *adj.* 苦悶的;煩惱的;痛苦難忍的。—**ly,** *adv.*
***ag·o·ny** ['ægənɪ; 'ægəni] *n., pl.* **-nies.** ①極大的痛苦。He was in *agony.* 他在極大的痛苦中。②任何精神上的激動。in an *agony* of joy. 大喜;狂喜。③臨死時的掙扎。④鬥爭。
agony column (報紙之)人事廣告欄。
ag·o·ra ['ægərə; 'ægərə] *n., pl.* **-rae** [-ˌri; -riː]. (古希臘之)市場;集會所。
ag·o·ra·phobe ['ægərəfob; 'ægərəfoub] *n.* 廣場(曠野)恐怖症患者。
ag·o·ra·pho·bi·a [ˌægərə'fobɪə; ˌægərə'foubiə] *n.*〖醫〗廣場恐怖;曠野恐怖。
a·gou·ti [ə'gutɪ ə'guːti] *n., pl.* **-tis, -ties.**〖動物〗刺鼠。 「culture.
agr., agric. ①agricultural. ②agri-
a·gran·u·lo·cy·to·sis [eˌgrænjəlosaɪ'tosɪs; eiˌgrænjələsai'tousis] *n.*〖醫〗粒性白血球缺乏病。
a·graph·i·a [e'græfɪə; ei'græfiə] *n.* 〖醫〗失寫症;書寫不能;無寫字能力。
a·grar·i·an [ə'grɛrɪən; ə'grɛəriən] *adj.* ①土地的;土地之耕種或所有權的。②農業的。③生於田野間的;野生的。—*n.* 主張平均分配土地者。
a·grar·i·an·ism [ə'grɛrɪənˌɪzəm; ə'grɛəriənizəm] *n.* 田地均分法;平均地權論;平均地權運動。
a·grar·i·an·ize [ə'grɛrɪəˌnaɪz; ə'grɛəriənaiz] *v.t.,* **-ized, -iz·ing.** 重新分配(地產)。
‡**a·gree** [ə'gri; ə'griː] *v.,* **a·greed, a·gree·ing.** —*v.i.* ①同意。I can not *agree* with you on this point. 對於這一點我不能同意(你)。②相合;一致。Your story *agrees* with mine. 你所說的與我相合。③允諾;答應。He *agreed* to accompany us to the theater. 他答應陪我們去戲院。④相宜。⑤〖文法〗一致。The verb *agrees* with its subject in number and person. 在數與身方面,動詞必須同其主詞一致。⑥和好相處。—*v.t.* 承認;同意。***agree to something*** 同意某事。He ***agreed to this plan*** immediately. 他立刻同意這計畫。***agree with somebody*** 同意某人。I ***agree with you.*** 我

同意你。

a·gree·a·ble** [əˈgriəbl; əˈgriəbl] *adj.* ①令人愉快的。She has *agreeable* manners. 她的態度嫻雅。②合意；適合。Is that arrangement *agreeable* to you? 那樣安排合你的意思嗎?③願意的；欣然贊同的。make oneself agreeable to somebody*** 使自己與某人合得來。 **—a·gree·a·bil·i·ty, —ness,** *n.* **—a·gree·a·bly,** *adv.*

a·greed [əˈgrid; əˈgriːd] *adj.* ①經過協議的。②同意的。 「優待運費。」

agreed charge(鐵路、運輸公司等的)

***a·gree·ment** [əˈgrimənt; əˈgriːmənt] *n.* ①相合；一致；和諧；同意。His opinion is in *agreement* with mine. 他的意見與我相合。②契約；協議；協約；條約。③〖文法〗相應；一致(如動詞的身、數須與其主詞的身、數一致)。

a·gré·ment [agreˈmɑ̃; agreiˈmɑ̃]〖法〗 *n., pl.* **-ments** [–ˈmɑ̃; –ˈmɑ̃]. ①(駐在國政府對外國使節之)正式承認。②(*pl.*) 愉快之環境或性質。③有禮貌的舉止；裝飾。④〖音樂〗裝飾音。 「粗野的；鄙俗的；鄉土氣的。」

a·gres·tic [əˈgrɛstɪk; əˈgrestik] *adj.*

***ag·ri·cul·tur·al** [ˌægrɪˈkʌltʃərəl; ˌægriˈkʌltʃərəl] *adj.* 農業的。*agricultural* products. 農產物。**—ly,** *adv.*

agricultural paper 農業生意往來中所用的各種票據。

***ag·ri·cul·ture** [ˈægrɪˌkʌltʃɚ; ˈægrikʌltʃə] *n.* 農業；農藝；農耕。 **—ag·ri·cul·tur·ist,** *n.* 「*n.*〖植物〗龍芽草。」

ag·ri·mo·ny [ˈægrəˌmonɪ; ˈægriməni]

ag·ri·mo·tor [ˈægrɪˌmotɚ; ˈægriˌmoutə] *n.* 耕田用之曳引機車；農用拖車。

a·grin [əˈgrɪn; əˈgrin] *adv. & adj.* 微笑地(的)；咧嘴地(的)。

ag·ri·ol·o·gy [ˌægrɪˈɑlədʒɪ; ˌægriˈɔlədʒi] *n.* 原始人之風俗研究；蠻俗學。

ag·ro·bi·ol·o·gy [ˌægrəbaɪˈɑlədʒɪ; ˌægrəbaiˈɔlədʒi] *n.* 土壤生物學；農業生物學。

ag·ro·cli·ma·to·lo·gy [ˌægrəˌklaɪməˈtɑlədʒɪ; ˈægrəˌklaiməˈtɔlədʒi] *n.* 農業氣候學。 「*n.* 實用土壤學；農業土壤學。」

a·grol·o·gy [əˈgrɑlədʒɪ; əˈgrɔlədʒi]

a·gron·o·my [əˈgrɑnəmɪ; əˈgrɔnəmi] *n.* ①農藝學。②＝**agriculture.** **—ag·ro·nom·ic, ag·ro·nom·i·cal,** *adj.* **—a·gron·o·mist,** *n.*

ag·ro·tech·ny [ˈægrəˌtɛknɪ; ˈægrəˌtekni] *n.* 農產品加工學。

ag·ro·type [ˈægrəˌtaɪp; ˈægrətaip] *n.* 土壤型；農土類型。

a·ground [əˈgraʊnd; əˈgraund] *adv. & adj.* (船) 擱淺(的)；在地上(的)。

ag·ryp·not·ic [ˌægrɪpˈnɑtɪk; ˌægripˈnɔtik] *adj.* 使不能睡眠的；使失眠的。 **—*n.*** 提神劑；清醒劑。

A.G.S. Associate in General Studies.

agst. against. **Agt., agt.** ①against. ②agent. ③agreement. 「打寒戰；發冷。」

a·gue [ˈegju; ˈeigjuː] *n.* ①〖醫〗瘧疾。②

a·gued [ˈegjud; ˈeigjuːd] *adj.* 患瘧疾的；發冷的。 「瘧疾的。②打冷戰的；發冷的。」

a·gu·ish [ˈegjuɪʃ; ˈeigjuiʃ] *adj.* ①(似)

a·gush [əˈgʌʃ; əˈgʌʃ] *adj.* 〖美俚〗如泉湧的。 「hours.」

Ah, a.h. ampere-hour; ampere-

‡ah [ɑ; ɑː] *interj.* 感歎之聲。*Ah!* That is the trouble. 呀! 毛病在此。***Ah me!*** 唉呀!

A.H. anno Hegirae (拉＝ in the year of *or* from the Hegira).

a·ha [ɑˈhɑ; ɑ(ː)ˈhɑː] *interj.* 感歎之聲。

A·hab [ˈehæb; ˈeihæb] *n.* 〖聖經〗亞哈(紀元前九世紀以色列之國王, Jezebel之夫)。

‡a·head [əˈhɛd; əˈhed] *adv.* ①在前地。Walk *ahead* of me. 在我前面走。②進行。Go *ahead* with your work. 進行你的工作。③預先；在…之先；在…之前。He is *ahead* of his times. 他是走在時代前面的。④朝前。⑤超過；勝於。⑥占優勢。***get ahead*** 〖俗〗成功。***get ahead of*** 勝過。***look ahead*** 想到未來；未雨綢繆。

a·heap [əˈhip; əˈhiːp] *adv. & adj.* 堆積地(的)；重疊地(的)。 「咳(爲引起注意)。」

a·hem [əˈhɛm; əˈhem, mˈmm] *interj.* 啊

a·his·tor·ic [ˌehɪsˈtɑrɪk; ˌeihisˈtɔrik] *adj.* 不顧史實的；漠視傳統的。

a·hold [əˈhold; əˈhould] *n.* 抓；握〖常of〗. **—*adv.*** 〖航海〗迎風行駛。 「馬上。」

a·horse [əˈhɔrs; əˈhɔːs] *adj. & adv.* 在

a·hoy [əˈhɔɪ; əˈhɔi] *interj.* 〖航海〗與遠處之人打招呼或呼喊其他船隻的聲音。

AHQ ① Army Headquarters. ② Air Headquarters. 「〖法〗祕密地；禁止旁觀地。」

à huis clos [aˌwiˈklo; aˌwiːˈklou]

a·hull [əˈhʌl; əˈhʌl] *adv. & adj.* 〖航海〗(在暴風雨中)將帆捲起並將舵扣住朝風中駛去。

a·hum [əˈhʌm; əˈhʌm] *adv. & adj.* 低唱；哼着。 「嘆聲。」

ai¹ [aɪ; ai] *interj.* 表痛苦、憂傷、哀憐等之感

a·i² [ˈɑɪ; ˈɑːi] *n.* (南美產之) 三趾樹獺。

AID ①〖美〗Agency for International Development. 美國國際開發總署。②American Institute of Decorators. ③American Institute of Interior Designers. ④〖英〗(＝A.I.D.) artificial insemination donor.

‡aid [ed; eid] *v.t.* ①幫助；援助。I *aided* him with money. 我以金錢助他。②促成。Your encouragement *aided* him to success. 你的鼓勵促成他成功。 **—*v.i.*** 幫忙。They *aided* to solve the problem. 他們幫忙解決這問題。**—*n.*** ①幫助；援助。He deserves our *aid*. 他值得我們幫助。②幫助者；援助者；助手；幫助的東西。③〖美〗副官。***call in one's aid*** 求人援助；乞助。They *called in our aid*. 他們求我們援助。***come to one's aid*** 赴援；應援；援助。We *came to their aid*. 我們援助他們。**—er,** *n.* **—ful,** *adj.* **—less,** *adj.*

aide [ed; eid] *n.* (陸、海軍中之)副官。

aide-de-camp [ˈeddəˈkæmp; ˈeiddəˈkɑ̃ːŋ] *n., pl.* **aides-de-camp.** (將軍、元帥等之)副官；侍從武官。(亦作 **aid-de-camp**)

aide-mé·moire [ˌɛdˌmeˈmwar; ˌedˌmeiˈmwɑː]〖法〗*n.* (外交上之)備忘錄。

aid·man [ˈedˌmæn; ˈeidmæn] *n., pl.* **-men.** 〖軍〗救護兵；醫療隊隊員。

aid post 〖英〗救護站。

aid station 〖軍〗救護站；急救站。

ai·gret(te) [ˈegrɛt; ˈeigret] *n.* ①〖動物〗(白)鷺。②鷺毛。③(仿製之)鷺毛飾。

ai·guille [eˈgwil; ˈeigwiːl] *n.* ①針狀的岩石；尖峯。②鑽孔器；錐子。

ai·guil·lette [ˌegwɪˈlɛt; ˌeigwiˈlet] *n.* (軍服上所飾的) 紐線；綬帶。 「husband.」

A.I.H. artificial insemination by

A.I.I. Air-India International.

ail [el; eil] *v.t. & v.i.* ①(使)苦惱；(使)煩惱。What *ails* the child? 孩子那裏不舒服?

②生病。

ai·lan·thus [e'lænθəs; ei'lænθəs] *n.* 【植物】臭椿；樗。 「機平衡之)副翼。

ai·ler·on ['elə,rɑn; 'eilərɔn] *n.*(保持飛

ail·ing ['elɪŋ; 'eiliŋ] *adj.* 生病的。

ail·ment ['elmənt; 'eilmənt] *n.*疾病。

ai·lu·ro·phile[e'lʊrə,faɪl; ei'ljurəfail] *n.* 愛貓的人。(亦作 **aelurophile**)

ai·lu·ro·phil·i·a[e,lʊrə'fɪlɪə; ei,ljurə'filiə] *n.* 嗜貓癖；對貓的喜愛。(亦作 **ailurophilia**)

ai·lu·ro·phobe [e'lʊrə,fob; ei'ljurəfoub] *n.* 極怕或厭惡貓的人。(亦作 **ailurophobe**)

:aim [em; eim] *v.i.*①瞄準。②企圖；意欲。He *aimed* at honors. 他圖得榮譽。③意指。—*v.t.* ①瞄準。He *aimed* a pistol at the bandit. 他用手鎗瞄準强盜。②以…擲向。—*n.* ①瞄準。Take good *aim* with your gun. 用鎗好好瞄準。②目的。What is your *aim* in life? 你生活之目的爲何? ***take aim*** 瞄準。He *took* careful *aim*. 他細心瞄準。

aiming point 射擊或投彈時之實際瞄準點。 「的。—**ly,** *adv.* —**ness,** *n.*

aim·less ['emlɪs; 'eimlis] *adj.* 無目的

AInd Anglo-Indian.

aî·né [ɛ'ne; ei'nei] 【法】*adj.* 年長的；兄長的(常用於專有名詞後)。Dumas *aîné*.大仲馬。

ain't [ent; eint] 【俗】原爲 am not 的縮寫,現擴充爲 are not, is not, have not 和 has not 的縮寫。此字粗俗,受良好教育的人和在正式文書裏,不可用之。

:air [ɛr; ɛə] *n.* ①空氣；大氣；天空。We must breathe fresh *air*. 我們必須呼吸新鮮空氣。②微風。③曲調；旋律。our national *air*. 我們的國歌。④公開表示；顯示。He gave *air* to his feelings. 他將心裏想說的話說了出來。⑤態度；容貌。She has a melancholy *air*. 她面有愁容。⑥(*pl.*)不自然的態度；裝腔作勢。He gives himself *airs*. 他裝腔作勢。***clear the air*** 敍出事實或眞情以改正錯誤觀察；消除誤解或意見的不一致。***get the air*** a. 被開革。b.求愛被拒。***give the air*** 開革(尤指臨時工)。***in the air*** 流傳的；未確定的。It is quite *in the air*. 事尙未定。***off the air*** 廣播停止。***on the air*** 廣播。The President will be *on the air* at five o'clock. 總統將於五點鐘廣播。***put on airs*** 擺架子。***take the air*** a. 到戶外去；散步或騎馬。b.【美】開始廣播。***travel by air*** 航空旅行。***up in the air*** =in the air. ***walk*** (or ***tread***) ***on air*** 高興；快樂。 —*v.t.* ①晾；通風。We *air* our clothes on the roof. 我們在屋頂晾衣。②顯示；誇示。③散步。to *air* the dog. 牽着狗散步。④廣播。—*v.i.* ①散步；兜風。②晾着。Your suit is *airing* on the line. 你的衣服在繩上晾着。③廣播。—*adj.* ①通空氣的。②航空的。

Air Academy 美國空軍官校。

air action 空戰。

air-age ['ɛr,edʒ; 'ɛəreidʒ] *adj.* 航空時代的；空軍時代的。 「飛行行動。②空襲警報。

air alert ①等待戰鬥命令或敵機出現之

air arm 空軍；空中軍種；航空兵種。

air-a·tom·ic ['ɛrə'tɑmɪk; 'ɛərə'tɔmik] *adj.* 用轟炸機投擲原子彈的；飛彈裝有原子彈頭的；空中原子的。

air attaché 空軍武官。

air attack 空襲。

air·bag ['ɛr,bæg; 'ɛəbæg] *n.* 汽車撞擊時置於儀器板內可立即膨脹以保護乘者之氣袋。

air base 空軍根據地；空軍基地。

air bed 【英】空氣墊。

air bell 玻璃器皿中作點綴用的氣泡。

air bladder (魚之)氣囊；鰾。

air blast 噴入之空氣(用以助燃)；鼓風。

air blower 裝在機器裡的散熱風扇。

air·borne ['ɛr,born; 'ɛəbɔːn] *adj.* ①空降的；空運的。②空中傳播的。

air·bound ['ɛr,baʊnd; 'ɛəbaund] *adj.* 爲空氣所阻塞的(如水管)。

air brake 空氣制動機；空氣煞車。

air·bra·sive ['ɛr'bresɪv; 'ɛə'breisiv] *n.* 一種牙醫用來磨牙或除垢之工具。—*adj.* 上述機械的。 「料氧化的飛彈。

air breather 利用大氣中之氧氣使燃

air brick 花磚。

air bridge 空中橋樑。

air·brush ['ɛr,brʌʃ; 'ɛəbrʌʃ] *n.* 一種用以噴漆之噴霧器。(亦作 **air brush**)

air bump ①使飛機突然改變高度或航向之氣流突變。②飛機遇上述情形產生的震盪。

air burst 空中爆炸(如飛彈、原子彈等)。

air bus 空中巴士(載客用之噴射式飛機)。

air cargo 用飛機載運的貨物。

air carrier ①用作空運之飛機。②航空

air castle 空中樓閣。 「公司。

Air·cav ['ɛr,kæv; 'ɛəkæv] *n.* 【美】以飛機運送至戰場的軍隊。

air cell 【解剖】氣囊；氣胞。

air chamber ①(幫浦、救生艇、生物體內等之)氣室；氣囊；氣胞。②水壓機之氣室。

air coach (票價較低之)普通客機。

air cock 氣栓；氣嘴。

air command 【美】空軍司令部。

air-con·di·tion ['ɛrkən,dɪʃən; 'ɛə-kən,diʃən] *v.t.* 裝空氣調節設備。

air-con·di·tioned ['ɛrkən,dɪʃənd; 'ɛə-kən,diʃənd] *adj.* 裝有空氣調節設備的。

air conditioner 空氣調節機。

air conditioning 空氣調節設備。

air control ①制空權。②以空中優勢控制敵國或敵軍。③空中交通管制。

air-cool ['ɛr,kul; 'ɛə-kuːl] *v.t.* ①【機械】用空氣冷却。②以空氣調節器調節。—**er,** *n.*

air-cooled ['ɛr'kuld; 'ɛə-kuːld] *adj.* 空氣冷却的；冷氣調節的。 「空氣冷却法。

air-cool·ing ['ɛr,kulɪŋ; 'ɛə-kuːliŋ] *n.*

air corridor 空中走廊(在外國控制區中取得的飛行航線)。 「護航之空軍武力。

air cover ①空中支援。②空中支援或

·air·craft ['ɛr,kræft; 'ɛə-krɑːft] *n., pl.* **-craft.** 飛行器(飛機、飛船等)。

aircraft carrier 航空母艦。

air·craft(s)·man ['ɛr,kræft(s)mən; 'ɛə-krɑːft(s)mən] *n., pl.* **-men.** 【英】皇家空軍之一、二等兵。 「組。

air crew 飛機上之工作人員；機員；空勤

air-cure ['ɛr,kjʊr; 'ɛəkjuə] *v.t.,* **-cured, -cur·ing.** 晾晒(煙葉等)於空氣中；用空氣處

air current 氣流。 「理。

air curtain 把壓縮空氣向下噴而形成之無形門簾(其作用爲防止昆蟲飛入及保持室內溫度)。 「壓機之氣室。③空氣防震裝置。

air cushion ①氣墊；氣枕；氣褥。②水

air cushion vehicle 氣墊船、車。

air cylinder 空氣柱。

air defense 防空；空防。 「飛機場。

air-de·pot ['ɛr,dipo; 'ɛə'depou] *n.*

air detection 空中偵察網。

air distance 兩地之間最短的飛行距離。
air division 〖美〗空軍師。
air drag 空氣阻力。
air drain 防濕溝;通氣溝;通氣管;氣道。
air drill 風鑽。
air-driv·en [ˈɛrˌdrɪvən; ˈɛəˌdrivən] *adj.* 由壓縮空氣所推動的。
air·drome [ˈɛrˌdrom; ˈɛədroum] *n.*飛機場。(亦作 **aerodrome**)
air·drop [ˈɛrˌdrɑp; ˈɛə-drɔp] *n., v.,* **-dropped** or **-dropt, -drop·ping.** —*n.* 空投。—*v.t.* 以降落傘降落;空投。
air-dry [ˈɛrˌdraɪ; ˈɛə-drai] *v.,* **-dried, -dry·ing,** *adj.* —*v.t.* 晾乾;風乾。—*adj.* 其乾燥程度在空氣中再無水分蒸發的。
air duct 通氣管;通風孔。
Aire·dale [ˈɛrˌdel; ˈɛədeil] *n.*一種粗毛大狗。
air eddy 氣流之旋渦。
air edition (報章雜誌之)航空版。
air·er [ˈɛrɚ; ˈɛərə] *n.* (衣服等)乾燥裝置。
air express ①空中快遞。②空中快遞件。
air-ex·press [ˈɛrɪkˌsprɛs; ˈɛəriks-ˌpres] *v.t.* 空運(商品);空中快遞。
air ferry 空運人員與物資之空運飛機。
air-fer·ry [ˈɛrˌfɛrɪ; ˈɛəˌferi] *v.t.* 空運(人員與物資)。
air·field [ˈɛrˌfild; ˈɛə-fi:ld] *n.*飛機場。
air·fight [ˈɛrˌfaɪt; ˈɛə-fait] *n.* 空戰。
air fighter 戰鬪機。
air filter 空氣過濾裝置。
air fleet 機羣;航空機隊。
air·flow [ˈɛrˌflo; ˈɛəflou] *n.* 氣流。—*adj.* ①流線型的。②氣流產生的。
air·foil [ˈɛrˌfɔɪl; ˈɛə-fɔil] *n.* 翼面(機翼、機舵等均是)。
air force ①空軍。②〖美〗航空隊。
Air Force Academy 空軍官校。
air frame 機身。
air freight ①空中貨運。②空運之貨物。③貨物空運費。
air-freight [ˈɛrˌfret; ˈɛəfreit] *v.t.*用飛機運輸(貨品)。
air·freight·er [ˈɛrˌfretɚ; ˈɛəˌfreitə] *n.* ①裝貨物之運輸機。②從事空運貨物之公司或個人。
air gas 氣瓦斯。
air gauge 氣壓計。(亦作 **air gage**)
air·graph [ˈɛrˌgræf; ˈɛəgrɑ:f] *n.* 〖英〗拍照航空信(縮拍成軟片之信件, 送達時放大之)。—*v.t.*〖英〗以拍照航空傳遞。
air gun 氣鎗。
air hammer 氣壓釘鎚(由壓縮空氣推動的釘鎚或鑽孔機)。
air harbor 航空港;水上飛機港。
air·head [ˈɛrˌhɛd; ˈɛəhed] *n.* 空降陣地。
air hoist 氣壓起重機。
air hole ①通風坑;氣窗。②〖美〗(河、湖等)結冰面之氣穴。③〖航空〗=**air pocket.**
air·hop [ˈɛrˌhɑp; ˈɛəhɔp] *v.,* **-hopped, -hop·ping,** *n.* —*v.i.* 經常作短程空中旅行。—*n.* 短程空中旅行。
air hostess 〖英〗空中小姐。
air·house [ˈɛrˌhaʊs; ˈɛəhaus] *n.*充氣房屋。
air hunger 〖醫〗空氣飢;呼吸困難。
air·i·ly [ˈɛrəlɪ; ˈɛərili] *adv.*①輕描淡寫地。②高興地;輕鬆地。
air·i·ness [ˈɛrɪnɪs; ˈɛərinis] *n.* ①空氣流通;通風。②輕鬆;快活。③虛浮;飄逸。
air·ing [ˈɛrɪŋ; ˈɛəriŋ] *n.* ①曬乾;晾乾。②散步或駕車兜風。③公開; 公開討論。***take*** (or ***go for***) ***an airing*** 到戶外散步或駕車兜風。
air jacket ①機器上防止傳熱之氣套。②〖英〗充氣救生衣。
air·land [ˈɛrˌlænd; ˈɛəlænd] *v.t.* 用飛機載運(部隊、物資等)着陸(以別於空降)。
air lane 飛機航線。
air-launch [ˈɛrˌlɔntʃ; ˈɛəlɔ:ntʃ] *v.t.* 從飛行中的飛機發射。
air·less [ˈɛrlɪs; ˈɛəlis] *adj.* 不通風的;沒有空氣的。
air letter ①航空信。②航空郵簡。
air·lift [ˈɛrˌlɪft; ˈɛəlift] *n.* ①空運。②空運乘載的人或貨物。③空運所用的飛機。④利用空氣壓力推動液體的抽水機。—*v.t.* 空運。
air-line [ˈɛrˌlaɪn; ˈɛəlain] *adj.*①〖美〗直接的。②兩地間之飛行距離的。③筆直的。
air·line [ˈɛrˌlaɪn; ˈɛəlain] *n.* ①定期空運制度。②其飛機或飛機場。③其航空公司。④〖美〗直線。⑤供氣之空氣管或軟管。
airline hostess 〖美〗空中小姐。
***air·lin·er** [ˈɛrˌlaɪnɚ; ˈɛəˌlainə] *n.* 定期客運班機。
air·load [ˈɛrˌlod; ˈɛəloud] *n.* ①飛機在飛行時所載之總重量(不包括飛機本身重量)。②(飛機翼面在飛行時所受到的)氣動力負荷。
air lock ① 潛水箱不透氣的前室。②阻隔室。③氣塞。
air·log [ˈɛrˌlɔg; ˈɛəlɔg] *n.* ①飛行紀錄。②航行計程器。(亦作 **air log**)
air-logged [ˈɛrˌlɑgd; ˈɛəlɔgd] *adj.* (抽水機、水管等)被空氣阻塞不通的。
***air mail** 航空郵政;航空信。
air-mail [ˈɛrˌmel; ˈɛəmeil] *adj.* 航空郵政的。*air-mail* letters. 航空信。
air·mail [ˈɛrˌmel; ˈɛəmeil] *v.t.* 用航空郵寄。
air·man [ˈɛrmən; ˈɛəmæn] *n., pl.* **-men.** ①飛行家; 飛行員。②空軍中最低級之士兵。
air marshal 〖英〗空軍中將。
air mass 〖氣象〗氣團。
air mattress 空氣墊;氣褥。
air mechanic 航空技工;飛機修理技士。
air medal 〖美〗飛行勳章。
air·mind·ed [ˈɛrˌmaɪndɪd; ˈɛəˌmain-did] *adj.* ①熱心航空的。②贊成多用飛機的。
air·mo·bile [ˈɛrˌmobɪl; ˈɛəˌmoubil] *adj.* 〖美〗由直昇機空運作戰部隊的。
air motor 壓縮空氣發動機。
air·om·e·ter [ɛrˈɑmɪtɚ; ɛəˈrɔmitə] *n.* ①量氣計(測量空氣流動速度之計器)。②煤氣計量表。(亦作 **air meter**)
air·park [ˈɛrˌpɑrk; ˈɛəpɑ:k] *n.*小飛機場。
air patrol 空中偵察隊。
air pipe 通風管;通氣管。
air piracy 空中刼機。
:air·plane [ˈɛrˌplen; ˈɛə-plein] *n.* 飛機。—*v.i.* 搭飛機。
airplane carrier 航空母艦。
air plant ①氣生植物。②一種熱帶地區產的草本植物。
air plot ①〖航空〗空中測位。②(航空母艦上指揮飛機的)指揮室。(亦作 **airplot**)
air pocket 氣潭;氣井。
air police 空軍憲兵;空軍糾察隊。
air pollution 空氣汚染。
***air·port** [ˈɛrˌport; ˈɛə-pɔ:t] *n.* 飛機場。
air post =**air mail.**
air pressure (大)氣壓;風壓。
air·proof [ˈɛrˈpruf; ˈɛəpru:f] *adj.* 不通氣的;密不透氣的。—*v.t.* 使不透氣。
air propeller 航空用之推進器;空氣推進器。
air pump 排氣唧筒;抽氣機。
air raid 空襲。
air-raid [ˈɛrˌred; ˈɛə-reid] *adj.*空襲的。
air-raid precautions 空襲期間應

行注意事項。
air-raid shelter 防空洞;防空壕。
air-raid siren 空襲警報笛。
air-raid warden 防空隊員。
air resistance 空氣阻力。
air rifle (有膛線之)氣鎗。
air right(s) 空間所有權。
air route 飛機航線;航空線。
air sac ①氣袋。②(鳥等之)氣囊。③(昆蟲等之)呼吸管之膨脹部分。
air-sac disease ['ɛr,sæk~;ɛə-sæk~] 家禽的慢性呼吸器官病。
air sampling 空氣標本採集(測定原子塵量等之用)。
air·scape ['ɛr,skep; 'ɛəskeip] *n.* 鳥瞰圖;空瞰圖。
air·screw ['ɛr,skru;'ɛə-skru:] *n.* 〖英〗飛機之推進器;螺旋槳。
air-sea ['ɛr'si; 'ɛə'si:] *adv.* & *adj.* ①由空至海地(的)。②海空聯合地(的)。
air service ①(A- S-) 舊日之美國空軍部;空軍。②空勤。③空中運輸。
air shaft 通風管道。
air·ship ['ɛr,ʃɪp;'ɛə-ʃip] *n.* 飛艇;飛船。—*v.t.*〖美〗將…空運。〖注意〗在美國 **airship** 有時也指 **airplane.**
air·sick ['ɛr,sɪk;'ɛə-sik] *adj.* 航空暈的;暈機的。—**ness,** *n.*
air-slaked ['ɛr,slekt; 'ɛə-sleikt] *adj.* (生石炎等)曝露空氣中而消解的;風化的。
air space ①有空氣存在之空間。②(室內之可供呼吸的) 空氣量。③(編隊飛行中)一飛機之活動餘地。④領空。⑤無線電之頻道。
air speed 飛行速度。
air spring ①氣褥。②空氣緩衝器。
air station 飛機場;航空站。
air stop 〖英〗直昇機乘客上下站。(亦作 airstop)
air stream 氣流。
air·strip ['ɛr,strɪp;'ɛə-strip] *n.* ①飛機跑道。②臨時機場。
air support 〖軍〗空中支援。
air-taxi ['ɛr,tæksɪ;'ɛə,tæksi] *n.* 空中的士; 出租飛機(飛行於小城鎮間之小型客機)。—*v.i.* (指國內或本地間之)短程飛行;乘出租飛機。
air terminal 機場。
air·tight ['ɛr'taɪt;'ɛə-tait] *adj.* ①不透氣的。②無懈可擊的。
air time ①電影或電視節目開始時間。②播出時間。
air-to-air ['ɛrtə'ɛr;'ɛətə'ɛə] *adj.* & *adv.* 空對空。*air-to-air* missile. 空對空飛彈。
air-to-ground ['ɛrtə'graund; 'ɛətə'graund] *adv.* & *adj.* 空對地。
air-to-sur·face ['ɛrtə'sɝfɪs;'ɛətə'sə:fis] *adj.* & *adv.* 空對面;空對地。
air tractor 爲撒布或噴射農藥而設計的飛機。
air train 飛行列車;空中列車。
air transport ①空運業務。②運輸機。
air travel ①空中旅行。②某一時期內之空中旅行量。
air turbine 氣渦輪。
air umbrella 空中支援。
air·wash ['ɛr,wɑʃ; 'ɛəwɔʃ] *v.t.* 用冷空氣吹(屋頂等) 使之變涼。—*n.* 作上述用途之冷氣流。
air·waves ['ɛr,wevz;'ɛəweivz] *n. pl.* 無線電或電視廣播。
air·way ['ɛr,we; 'ɛəwei] *n.* ①航空線。*airway* beacon. 航(空)路燈塔。②通風孔(礦坑用)。③〖美〗無線電廣播用的周率。
air waybill 空運貨單。(略作 **AWB**)(亦作 **airwaybill, airbill, waybill**)
air·ways ['ɛr,wez; 'ɛəweiz] *n.* ①航空公司。②無線電廣播周率的波段。③電視臺的頻道。
air well=**air shaft.**
air-wise ['ɛr,waɪz; 'ɛə-waiz] *adj.* 熟習航空的;富有航空經驗的。
air·wom·an ['ɛr,wumən; 'ɛə,wumən] *n., pl.* **-wom·en.** 女飛行家。
air·wor·thy ['ɛr,wɝðɪ; 'ɛə,wə:ði] *adj.* 達於安全飛行標準的; 適宜航空的。—**air·wor·thi·ness,** *n.*
***air·y** ['ɛrɪ;'ɛəri] *adj.,* **air·i·er, air·i·est.** ①空氣的;像空氣的。②輕快的; 快活的;優美的。*airy* laughter. 快樂的笑。③空想的; 空幻的。④在空中的; 高的。⑤通氣的; 通風的。⑥輕而薄的。⑦〖俗〗裝腔作勢的。
aisle** [aɪl; ail] *n.* ①教堂、禮堂、教室、列車或劇院座椅中之縱直的通路。②任何狹長之通路。③教堂左右兩邊用一排石柱隔開的走廊;側廊;翼廊。down the aisle*** (走)向神壇去行婚禮。—**aisled,** *adj.*
aisle-sit·ter ['aɪl,sɪtɚ; 'ail,sitə] *n.* 〖美〗坐在靠通道座位上的人,尤指劇評者。
ait [et;eit] *n.* 〖英〗(河、湖中之)小島。
aitch [etʃ; eitʃ] *n., pl.* **aitch·es,** *adj.* —*n.* H(h) 字;h音。—*adj.* H 形的。
aitch·bone ['etʃ,bon; 'eitʃboun] *n.* 牛之臀骨;牛之臀骨肉。
a·jar[1] [ə'dʒɑr; ə'dʒɑ:] *adv.* & *adj.* (門)半開地(的);微開地(的)。
a·jar[2] *adv.* & *adj.* 不和諧地 (的); 相軋轢地(的)。to set the nerves *ajar.* 惑亂神經。
A·jax ['edʒæks;'eidʒæks] *n.* 〖希臘神話〗圍攻 Troy 的一勇士。(又名 **Great Ajax, Telamonian Ajax**)
a·jog [ə'dʒɑg; ə'dʒɔg] *adv.* & *adj.* 慢步而行地(的)。
a·jut [ə'dʒʌt; ə'dʒʌt] *adj.* 突出的; 伸出的。—**ment,** *n.*
a·ke·la [ə'kilə; ə'ki:lə] *n.* 幼童軍之領隊人。
a·kene [e'kin; ei'ki:n] *n.*=**achene.**
a·kim·bo [ə'kɪmbo; ə'kimbou] *adv.* & *adj.* 兩手叉腰。
a·kin [ə'kɪn;ə'kin] *adj.* ①同血族的。②同性質的;類似的。
a·ki·ne·sia [,ekə'niʒə; ,eiki'ni:ʒə] *n.* 〖病理〗運動不能;動作不能。(亦作 **akinesis**)
Al 〖化〗元素 aluminum 之符號。
-al 〖字尾〗①表"…的; 似…的; 適於…的; 有…性質的" 之義的形容詞字尾, 如: postal, sensational. ②將表示動作之動詞做成名詞之字尾, 如: removal, trial.
AL, A.L. ①American Legion. ②American League. ③Anglo-Latin.
a.l. autograph letter.
Ala. Alabama.
A.L.A. ①American Library Association. ②Automobile Legal Association. ③Associate in Liberal Arts. ④Authors League of America.
a·la ['elə; 'eilə] *n., pl.* **a·lae** ['eli;'eili:]. ①〖解剖, 動物〗 **a.** 翼;翅。**b.**翼狀部;翅狀部;耳垂。②〖植物〗蝶形花之二側瓣之一; 若干種子之薄翼。③古羅馬住宅中的小房間或凹室。
à la ['ɑlə; ɑ:lɑ:] 〖法〗①按…; 依照; …式的。②〖烹飪〗帶着; 有…的。
Al·a·bam·a [,ælə'bæmə; ,ælə'bæmə] *n.* ①阿拉巴馬(美國南部一州, 首府爲 Montgomery)。②阿拉巴馬河。
Al·a·bam·an [,ælə'bæmən; ,ælə'bæmən] *n.* 美國阿拉巴馬州人。—*adj.* 阿拉巴馬州的。(亦作 **Alabamian**)
al·a·bam·ine [,ælə'bæmin; ,ælə'bæmin] *n.* 〖化〗砹(稀有元素之一, 符號爲 Ab).
al·a·bas·ter ['ælə,bæstɚ; 'æləbɑ:stə] *n.* ①雪花石膏。②方解石之一種。—*adj.* (亦作 **alabastrine**)①雪花石膏製的。②如雪花

石膏的;雪白光滑的。

à la bonne heure [ɑləbɔ'nœr; ɑːləbɔː'nœː] 〖法〗①準時。②正好;好極了。

à la carte [ˌɑlə'kɑrt; ˌɑːlɑː'kɑːt] 〖法〗(照菜單上各菜之定價)點菜。

a·lac·ri·ty [ə'lækrətɪ; ə'lækriti] *n.*活潑;敏捷。

A·lad·din [ə'lædɪn; ə'lædin] *n.* 阿拉丁(天方夜譚中一少年)。

Aladdin's lamp ①如意神燈。②〖喻〗能滿足人一切希望的東西。

à la fran·çaise [alafrɑ̃'sɛz; alafrɑ̃ː'sez] 〖法〗法國式的。

A·lai Mountains [ɑ'laɪ~; ɑː'lai~] 阿力山脈(位於蘇聯西南亞吉爾吉亞省, Kirghizia, 爲中國新疆省天山山系之一部分, 最高峯約19,000英尺)。

à la king [ˌɑlə'kɪŋ; ˌɑːlə'kiŋ] 〖法〗用乳酪濃汁及青椒甘椒烹的(魚,肉丁)。

al·a·me·da [ˌælə'medə; ˌælə'meidə] *n.* 〖美〗林蔭路;公衆散步道路。

al·a·mo ['ælə,mo; 'æləmou] *n., pl.* **-mos.** 一種白楊。

à la mode [ˌɑlə'mod; ˌɑːlɑː'moud] ①流行地(的);時髦地(的)。②〖烹飪〗**a.** 加冰淇淋的(甜點心)。apple pie *à la mode.* 加冰淇淋的蘋果派。**b.** 加蔬菜紅燒然後澆以濃滷汁的(牛肉)。beef *à la mode.* 濃汁牛肉。(亦作 **a la mode** 或 **alamode**)

a·la·mode ['ælə,mod; 'æləmoud] *n.* 一種光亮的薄絹,多作頭巾或圍巾用。

Al·an ['ælən; 'ælən] *n.*男子名。

a·la·nine ['ælənin; 'æləniːn] *n.* 〖化,生化〗丙氨酸。

a·lar ['elɚ; 'eilə] *adj.* ①翼的;翅的;有翼的;翅狀的。②〖植物〗葉腋的; 腋生的。③〖解剖〗腋下的;翼狀的。

‡**a·larm** [ə'lɑrm; ə'lɑːm] *n.* ①驚慌;驚恐;恐懼。He was struck with *alarm.* 他飽受驚慌。②警報。a fire *alarm.* 火警。③警鈴;警鐘;警報器。④號召武裝起來的信號。—*v.t.* ①使驚慌; 使恐慌; 使焦慮不安。We were much *alarmed* by a fire in the neighborhood. 鄰近失火使我們甚感驚慌。②警告。③征召入伍。—**a·ble,** *adj.*

alarm bell 警鐘;警鈴。

alarm clock 鬧鐘。

alarm gauge (附於鍋爐上之)警報器。

alarm gun 警砲;信號砲。

a·larm·ing [ə'lɑrmɪŋ; ə'lɑːmiŋ] *adj.* 可驚的;危險的。

a·larm·ism [ə'lɑrmɪzəm; ə'lɑːmizm] *n.* 杞憂;大驚小怪。

a·larm·ist [ə'lɑrmɪst; ə'lɑːmist] *n.*杞憂者;大驚小怪者。

alarm post 〖軍〗緊急集合地點。

alarm signal 警報;警報器。

alarm whistle 警笛。

a·larm-word [ə'lɑrm,wɝd; ə'lɑːmwəːd] *n.* 暗號;軍隊回答暗號之口令。

a·la·ry ['elərɪ; 'æləri] *adj.* ①翼的;翅的。②似翼的;翅狀的。

Alas. Alaska.

***a·las** [ə'læs; ə'læs] *interj.* 感歎聲(表示悲哀或愁苦)。*Alas!* He was killed by the enemy! 啊呀! 他被敵人殺死了!

A·las·ka [ə'læskə; ə'læskə] *n.* 阿拉斯加 (美國一州, 首府朱諾 Juneau)。

Alaska cedar ①生長於北美洲西北部的一種常綠(黃柏)樹。②此種樹所產的木材。

A·las·kan [ə'læskən; ə'læskən] *adj.* (美國)阿拉斯加州的。—*n.* 阿拉斯加人。

A·las·tor [ə'læstɚ, -tɔr; ə'læstɔː] *n.* ①〖希臘神話〗復讎神。②Shelley之一詩篇名。

a·late ['elet; 'eileit] *adj.* ①有翼的。②有似翼之膜狀擴張物的;有翼狀物的。

Alb. ①Albania. ②Albanian. ③Albany. ④Albert.

alb. 〖處方〗白色的。

al·ba·core ['ælbə,kor; 'ælbəkɔː] *n., pl.* **-cores, -core.** 一種長鰓之鮪;大青花魚。

Al·ba·ni·a [æl'benɪə; æl'beinjə] *n.* ①阿爾巴尼亞(歐洲國名,首都地拉那 Tirana)。② 〖詩〗蘇格蘭高地。

Al·ba·ni·an [æl'benɪən; æl'beinjən] *adj.* 阿爾巴尼亞(人、語)的。 —*n.* 阿爾巴尼亞人(語)。

Al·ba·ny ['ɔlbənɪ; 'ɔːlbəni] *n.* 奧爾班尼(美國紐約州之首府)。

al·ba·ta [æl'betə; æl'beitə] *n.*洋銀。

al·ba·tross ['ælbə,trɔs; 'ælbətrɔs] *n.* 信天翁。

al·be·it [ɔl'biɪt; ɔːl'biːit] *conj.* 雖然。

Al·bert ['ælbɚt; 'ælbət] *n.* 男子名。

al·bes·cent [æl'bɛsənt; æl'besənt] *adj.*帶白色的;變白的。—**al·bes·cence,** *n.*

al·bi·ness [æl'baɪnɪs; æl'bainis] *n.* **albino** 之女性。

al·bi·nism ['ælbə,nɪzəm; 'ælbinizəm] *n.* 〖醫〗白化病(缺乏正常色素)。

al·bi·no [æl'baɪno; æl'biːnou] *n., pl.* **-nos.** ①楊白頭(皮膚、頭髮、及眼睛缺乏正常色素的人,其皮膚蒼白, 頭髮微白,眼睛呈粉紅色)。②任何缺乏正常色素之動物或植物;白變種。

Al·bi·on ['ælbɪən; 'ælbjən] *n.*〖詩〗英國;不列顛;英格蘭。

al·bite ['ælbaɪt; 'ælbait] *n.*〖礦〗曹長石。

ALBM 〖火箭學〗 air-launched ballistic missile. 由空中發射的彈道飛彈。

***al·bum** ['ælbəm; 'ælbəm] *n.* ①黏貼相片、郵票、字畫等之空白的簿册。②唱片本。③唱片集。④來賓簽名簿。

al·bu·men [æl'bjumən; 'ælbjumin] *n.*①蛋白。②〖植物〗胚乳。

al·bu·men·ize [æl'bjumən,aɪz; æl'bjuːminaiz] *v.t.,* **-ized, -iz·ing.** ①使蛋白質化。②塗以蛋白。

al·bu·min [æl'bjumɪn; 'ælbjumin] *n.* 〖生化〗蛋白質;蛋白素。(亦作 **albumen**)

al·bu·mi·nate [æl'bjumɪnɪt; æl'bjuːmineit] *n.* 〖生化〗白朊化物。

al·bu·mi·noid [æl'bjumɪ,nɔɪd; æl'bjuːminɔid] *adj.* 蛋白質的;似蛋白的。—*n.* 〖生化〗①任何一種不溶於中性溶劑的簡單蛋白質, 如生膠質等。②硬朊;硬蛋白質。

al·bu·mi·nous [æl'bjumɪnəs; æl'bjuːminəs] *adj.* ①蛋白性的;含蛋白質的。②〖植物〗有胚乳的。(亦作 **albuminose**)

al·bu·mi·nu·ri·a [æl,bjumɪ'njurɪə; ˌælbjuːmi'njuːriə] *n.*〖醫〗蛋白尿;蛋白尿症。

al·bu·mose ['ælbjumos; 'ælbjumous] *n.* 〖生化〗 任何一種因蛋白酶 (proteolytic enzyme) 作用由蛋白質誘導出的化合物。

al·bur·num [æl'bɝnəm; æl'bəːnəm] *n.* 〖植物〗白木質。(亦作 **alburn**)

Al·cae·us [æl'siəs; æl'siəs] *n.* 阿西奧斯(620-581, B. C., 希臘抒情詩人)。

al·ca·hest ['ælkə,hɛst; 'ælkəhest] *n.* =**alkahest.**

Al·ca·ic [æl'ke·ɪk; æl'keiik] *adj.* 古希臘詩人 Alcaeus 的; Alcaeus 句法的。—*n.* (*pl.*) ①Alcaeus 所寫之抒情詩。②似 Alcaeus 詩體之詩。

al·caide [æl'ked; æl'keid] 〖西班牙〗 *n.* ①要塞司令。②監獄看守。(亦作 **alcayde**)

al·cal·de [æl'kældɪ;æl'kældi] *n.* (西班牙等國兼具司法權之)市長;鎮長。

al·caz·ar [æl'kæzɚ; ˌælkə'zɑ:] *n.* (西班牙Moor 人之)宮殿。②Seville 地方 Moor 族國王之宮殿。

al·che·mist ['ælkəmɪst; 'ælkimist] *n.* 煉金術士;煉丹家。—**i·cal,** *adj.*

al·che·mize ['ælkɪˌmaɪz; 'ælkimaiz] *v.t.,* **-mized, -miz·ing.** 用煉金術使之變質。

al·che·my ['ælkəmɪ; 'ælkimi] *n., pl.* **-mies.** 中世紀之煉金術;煉丹術。—**al·chem·i·cal,** *adj.*

Alc·me·ne [ælk'mini;ælk'mi:ni:] *n.* 〖希臘神話〗Hercules 之母。

***al·co·hol** ['ælkəˌhɔl; 'ælkəhɔl] *n.* ①〖化〗酒精;乙醇。②酒。

***al·co·hol·ic** [ˌælkə'hɔlɪk, -'hɑl-; ˌælkə'hɔlik] *adj.* 酒精的;含酒精的。—*n.* 酗酒者;酗酒而病者。

alcoholic aldehyde 醇醛。

al·co·hol·ic·i·ty [ˌælkəhɔl'ɪsətɪ; ˌælkəhɔ'lisiti] *n.*含酒精之濃度。

Alcoholics Anonymous協助酗酒者戒酒的一個民間組織(略作**AA**或**A.A.**).

al·co·hol·ism ['ælkəhɔlˌɪzəm; 'ælkəhɔlizm] *n.* 酒精中毒;醇中毒。

al·co·hol·ize ['ælkəhɔlˌaɪz; 'ælkəhɔˌlaiz] *v.t.,* **-ized, -iz·ing.**化成酒精;醇化。

alcohol lamp 酒精燈。

al·co·hol·om·e·ter [ˌælkəhɔl'ɑmɪtɚ; ˌælkəhɔ'lɔmitə] *n.* 酒精計。

Al·cor [æl'kɔr;æl'kɔ:] *n.*〖天文〗大熊座。

Al·co·ran [ˌælko'rɑn; ˌælkɔ'rɑ:n] *n.* =**Alkoran.**

al·cove ['ælkov; 'ælkouv] *n.* ①凹室;房間中部分凹入的小室。②房間之牆壁凹入作書架或牀等用的一部分;壁凹。③園中小亭。

Ald. Alderman. (亦作 **Aldm.**)

Al·deb·a·ran [æl'dɛbərən; æl'debərən] *n.* 金牛宮座中之一等橙黃色星。

al·de·hyde ['ældəˌhaɪd; 'ældihaid] *n.* 〖化〗乙醛。(亦作 **acetaldehyde**)

al·der ['ɔldɚ; 'ɔ:ldə] *n.* 赤楊。

Al·der ['ɔldɚ; 'ɔ:ldə] *n.* 奧德爾 (Kurt, 1902–1958,德國化學家,曾得1950年諾貝爾獎)。

al·der·man ['ɔldɚmən; 'ɔ:ldəmən] *n., pl.* **-men.** ①〖美〗市議員。②〖英〗市府參事。—**ic,** *adj.*

al·der·man·ry ['ɔldɚmənrɪ; 'ɔ:ldəmənri] *n., pl.* **-ries.** ①市府參事或市議員之職位。②其選舉區。

al·der·man·ship ['ɔldɚmənˌʃɪp; 'ɔ:ldəmənʃip] *n.*市府參事或市議員之職位。

Al·dine ['ɔldaɪn; 'ɔ:ldain] *adj.* Aldus (16世紀威尼斯出版家) 版的;精裝本的。—*n.* Aldus 或其他早期版本。

al·dose ['ældos; 'ældous] *n.* 〖化〗醛醣。

***ale** [el;eil] *n.* 麥酒。

a·le·a·to·ry ['elɪəˌtorɪ, -ˌtɔrɪ; 'eiliətəri] *adj.* ①依機運而定的。②〖法律〗僥倖的;賭博的。

Al·eck ['ælɪk;'ælik] *n.* 男子名 (Alexander 之簡稱)。(亦作 **Alec**)

ale·con·ner ['elˌkɑnɚ; 'eilˌkɔ:nə] *n.* 〖英〗①酒類檢查官。②(倫敦各酒店之)酒類量度器的檢查員。

a·lee [ə'li; ə'li:] *adv.* & *adj.* 〖航海〗向下風。

al·e·gar ['æləgɚ; 'æligə] *n.* 麥酒醋。

ale·house ['elˌhaus; 'eilhaus] *n.* 麥酒店;酒館。

a·lem·bic [ə'lɛmbɪk; ə'lembik] *n.* ①(從前之)蒸餾器。②起變化作用之物。

a·lert** [ə'lɝt; ə'lə:t] *adj.* ①留心的;警覺的。He has an *alert* mind. 他很機警。②活潑的;靈活的;敏捷的。—*n.* ①注意;小心。②空襲警報;暴風警報;空襲或暴風警報期間。It's the *alert* signal. 這是空襲警報。on the alert*** 注意;留意。—*v.t.* ①發空襲或暴風警報給…。②警告…作…準備;警告。—**ly,** *adv.* —**ness,** *n.*

A·leu·tian [ə'luʃən;ə'lu:ʃjən] *adj.* ①阿留申羣島的。②阿留申羣島之土人的;其文化的。—*n.* ①阿留申羣島之土人(=Aleut). ②(*pl.*)=**the Aleutian Islands.**

Aleutian Islands 阿留申羣島。

ale·wife ['elˌwaɪf; 'eilwaif] *n., pl.* **-wives**[-ˌwaɪvz;-waivz].①麥酒店之主婦。②〖動物〗鱸類。

Alex. Alexander.

Al·ex·an·der [ˌælɪg'zændɚ; ˌælig'zɑ:ndə] *n.* 男子名。

al·ex·an·der [ˌælɪg'zændɚ; ˌælig'zɑ:ndə] *n.* (常 A-)一種雞尾酒之名稱。

Alexander the Great 亞歷山大大帝(古馬其頓國王 356–323 B. C.).

Al·ex·an·dri·a [ˌælɪg'zændrɪə; ˌælig'zɑ:ndriə] *n.* 亞歷山大港。

Al·ex·an·dri·an [ˌælɪg'zændrɪən; ˌælig'zɑ:ndriən] *adj.* ①亞歷山大港的。②(古代)亞歷山大地方之文化的。③亞歷山大大帝的。④ =**Alexandrine.**

Al·ex·an·drine [ˌælɪg'zændrɪn; ˌælig'zændrain] *adj.* ①〖詩〗亞歷山大詩行法的。②=**Alexandrian.** —*n.* 〖詩〗亞歷山大詩行法(抑揚格,六音步十二音節爲一行)。

Al·ex·an·dri·nus[ˌælɪgzæn'drinəs; ˌæligzæn'dri:nəs] *n.* 五世紀時一種新舊約聖經之抄本。

al·ex·an·drite[ˌælɪg'zændraɪt;ˌælig'zændrait] *n.* 〖礦〗紫翠玉;翠綠寶石;變石。

a·lex·i·a [ə'lɛksɪə; ə'leksiə] *n.* 〖醫〗失讀能;失讀症。—**ic,** *adj.*

a·lex·in [ə'lɛksɪn; ə'leksin] *n.*殺菌素。

al·ex·i·phar·mic [əˌlɛksɪ'fɑrmɪk; əˌleksi'fɑ:mik] *adj.* 〖醫〗解毒的;消毒的。—*n.*解毒藥;消毒藥。

Al·fa ['ælfə; 'ælfə] *n.* 通訊電碼,代表字母A.

al·fal·fa [æl'fælfə; æl'fælfə] *n.* 紫花苜蓿。

al fi·ne [ɑl'fine; ɑ:l'fi:nei] 〖義〗到終了。

al·for·ja [æl'fɔrdʒə; æl'fɔ:dʒə] *n.* ①皮袋;鞍袋。②(花栗鼠等之)頰囊。

Al·fra·ga·nus [ˌælfrə'genəs; ˌælfrə'geinəs] *n.* 月球上第四象限內一火山口之名。

Al·fred ['ælfrɪd; 'ælfrid] *n.* 阿佛列 (849–899, West Saxons 王, 在位期間爲871–899, 號稱 Alfred the Great).

al·fres·co [æl'frɛsko; æl'freskou] *adv.* & *adj.* 戶外地(的);露天地(的)。

Alg. ①Algerian. ②Algiers.

alg. ①algebra. ②algebraical.

al·ga ['ælgə; 'ælgə] *n.* sing. of **algae.**

al·gae ['ældʒi; 'ældʒi:] *n. pl.* 〖植物〗海藻;藻類。

al·gae·cide ['ældʒəˌsaɪd; 'ældʒəsaid] *n.*除海藻之藥。(亦作 **algicide**)

al·gal ['ælgəl;'ælgəl] *adj.* 海藻的。—*n.* 海藻。

al·gate ['ɔlget; 'ɔ:lgeit] *adv.*①始終如此地。②然而。(亦作 **algates**)

***al·ge·bra** ['ældʒəbrə; 'ældʒibrə] *n.*代數學。—**ist,** *n.*

al·ge·bra·ic [ˌældʒə'bre·ɪk; ˌældʒi'breiik] *adj.* 代數的;代數學的;代數學上的。

(亦作 **algebraical**) —**ly,** *adv.*
algebraic equation 代數方程(式)。
algebraic number 代數數。
Al·ge·ri·a [æl'dʒɪrɪə; æl'dʒiəriə] *n.* 阿爾及利亞(北非一國, 首都阿爾及耳 Algiers). —**Al·ge·ri·an,** *adj., n.*
Al·ge·rine [ˌældʒə'rin; ˌældʒiə'riːn] *adj.* 阿爾及利亞(人)的。—*n.* ①阿爾及利亞之土著。②北非海盜。③一種有鮮艷條紋的毛呢。
al·get·ic [æl'dʒɛtɪk; æl'dʒetik] *adj.* 痛的;引起疼痛的。「寒的;發冷的。」
al·gid ['ældʒɪd; 'ældʒid] *adj.* 寒冷的;嚴
al·gid·i·ty [æl'dʒɪdətɪ; æl'dʒiditi] *n.* 寒冷;發冷。「耳(阿爾及利亞之首都)。」
Al·giers [æl'dʒɪrz; æl'dʒiəz] *n.* 阿爾及
algo- 〖字首〗表"疼痛"之義, 如: algophobia.「似藻的。」
al·goid ['ælgɔɪd; 'ælgɔid] *adj.* 藻類的;
Al·gol, ALGOL ['ælgɑl; 'ælgɔl] *n.* 〖電腦〗算術語言(爲 *Algo*rithmic *L*anguage 之略)。
al·go·lag·ni·a [ˌælgə'lægnɪə; ˌælgə'lægniə] *n.* 〖精神病學〗痛淫;痛性淫亂;虐待狂或被虐待狂。
al·gol·o·gy [æl'gɑlədʒɪ; æl'gɔlədʒi] *n.* 藻類學。 —**al·gol·o·gist,** *n.*
Al·gon·ki·an [æl'gɑŋkɪən; æl'gɔŋkiən] *adj.* 〖地質〗元古紀的。 —*n.* =**Algonquian.**
Al·gon·qui·an [æl'gɑŋkɪən; æl'gɔŋkiən] *n.* 美國印第安族之最大一族, 居於美國中西部地區。(亦作 **Algonkian, Algonkin, Algonquin**)
al·go·pho·bia [ˌælgə'fobɪə; ˌælgə'foubiə] *n.* 對痛的極度恐懼;懼痛病。
al·gor ['ælgɔr; 'ælgɔː] *n.* 〖醫〗(發燒前之)寒冷。
al·go·rism ['ælgəˌrɪzəm; 'ælgərizəm] *n.* ①阿拉伯數字計數法;算術。②阿拉伯數字。
al·gous ['ælgəs; 'ælgəs] *adj.* 藻類的;如藻類的;海藻甚多的。
al·gua·zil [ˌælgwə'zil; ˌælgwə'ziːl] *n.* (西班牙之)警官。「檀香木。」
al·gum ['ælgʌm; 'ælgʌm] *n.* 檀香樹;
a·li·as ['elɪəs; 'eiliæs] *n.* 別名; 化名; 假名。—*adv.* 或稱;別稱。
al·i·bi ['æləˌbaɪ; 'ælibai] *n., pl.* **-bis,** *v.,* **-bied, -bi·ing.** —*n.* ①〖法律〗不在現場的答辯。②〖美俗〗託辭。 —*v.i.* 辯解;找託詞閃脫。—*v.t.* 爲(某人)作不在場的證詞。
al·i·ble ['æləbḷ; 'ælibl] *adj.* 有營養的。
Al·ice ['ælɪs; 'ælis] *n.* 女子名。(亦作 **Alyce, Alys**)
Alice blue 一種淺藍色。
Alice in Wonderland 愛麗絲漫遊奇境記(Lewis Carroll 著童話故事)。(亦作 **Alice's Adventures in Wonderland**)
al·i·dade ['ælɪˌded; 'ælideid] *n.* 〖測量〗指方規;照準儀。(亦作 **alidad**)
***al·ien** ['elɪən, 'eljən; 'eiljən] *n.* 外國人。—*adj.* ①外國人的;外國的。*alien* property. 外國人的財產。 ②相反的; 完全不同的〖to, from〗。 —*v.t.* 移交; 使離心; 讓渡。
al·ien·a·ble ['eljənəbḷ; 'eiljənəbl] *adj.* 可轉讓的。 —**al·ien·a·bil·i·ty,** *n.*
al·ien·age ['eljənɪdʒ; 'eiljənidʒ] *n.* 外國人之身分。
al·ien·ate ['eljənˌet; 'eiljəneit] *v.t.* **-at·ed, -at·ing.** ①離間;使疏遠。②讓渡;割讓。③改作。④〖法律〗(自願地)轉讓(多指房契、地契等之轉讓)。 —**al·ien·a·tor,** *n.*
al·ien·a·tion [ˌeljən'eʃən; ˌeiljə'neiʃən] *n.* ①離間;疏遠。②讓渡;割讓。③精神錯亂;發狂。
alienation of affections 〖法律〗第三者離間夫妻間之感情。
al·ien·a·tive ['eljənˌetɪv; 'eiljəneitiv] *adj.* 離間的;使疏遠的。
al·ien·ee [ˌeljən'i; ˌeiljə'niː] *n.* 〖法律〗(土地之)受讓人;接受者。「內之敵國人民。」
alien enemy 〖法律〗戰時居於本國境
al·ien·ism ['eljənˌɪzəm; 'eiljənizəm] *n.* ①=**alienage.** ②精神病學;精神病治療。
al·ien·ist ['eljənɪst; 'eiljənist] *n.* (供給法律證據之)精神病醫師;精神病研究者。
al·ien·or ['eljənɚ; 'eiljənə] *n.* 〖法律〗讓渡人。(亦作 **aliener**)「狀的。」
al·i·form ['ælɪˌfɔrm; 'ælifɔːm] *adj.* 翼
***a·light**[1] [ə'laɪt; ə'lait] *v.i.,* **a·light·ed, a·light·ing.** ①由車或馬上下來。②降落。The bird *alighted* on a twig. 鳥飛下來停在細樹枝上。③偶遇〖on, upon〗。 *alight on one's feet* 站穩;逃開而未受傷害。「(地)。」
a·light[2] *adj. & adv.* 發亮的(地);燃着的
a·lign, a·line [ə'laɪn; ə'lain] *v.t. & v.i.* ①排成直線; 排列成行。②使合作;聯合。③〖電〗調整;改良頻率帶之反應。
a·lign·ment, a·line·ment [ə'laɪnmənt; ə'lainmənt] *n.* ①排成直線;排列成行。②合作。③〖工程〗公路或鐵路之平面圖。
***a·like** [ə'laɪk; ə'laik] *adv.* 同樣地; 相似地。He treated all customers *alike.* 對所有顧客, 他都同樣看待。—*adj.* 同樣的; 相似的。The two brothers look very much *alike.* 兄弟二人長得很像。*share and share alike* 均分。 —**ness,** *n.*
al·i·ment [*n.* 'ælәmənt; 'ælimənt *v.* 'æləˌmɛnt; 'ælimənt] *n.* ①營養物;食物。②一般生活必需品;扶養;扶助。—*v.t.* ①供給食物。②扶養。 —**al,** *adj.*
al·i·men·ta·ry [ˌælə'mɛntərɪ; ˌæli'mentəri] *adj.* ①有關食物或營養的。②滋養的。③給予支持或扶助的。
alimentary canal (or **tract**) 消化管;消化道。
al·i·men·ta·tion [ˌæləmɛn'teʃən; ˌælimen'teiʃən] *n.* ①營養。②扶養;贍養。
al·i·men·to·ther·a·py [ˌælə'mɛntə'θɛrəpɪ; ˌæli'mentə'θerəpi] *n.* 營養療法;食物療法。
al·i·mo·ny ['æləˌmonɪ; 'æliməni] *n.* ①離婚贍養費。②生活費;扶養費。
al·i·ped ['æləˌpɛd; 'æliped] 〖動物〗 *adj.* 脚趾爲翼膜連接的。—*n.* 有翼膜脚趾的動物。
al·i·phat·ic [ˌælɪ'fætɪk; ˌæli'fætik] *adj.* 〖化〗脂肪性的;脂肪族的。
al·i·quant ['æləkwənt; 'ælikwənt] *adj.* 〖數學〗不能整除的。—*n.* 不能整除的數。
al·i·quot ['ælɪkwət; 'ælikwɔt] *adj.* 〖數學〗能整除的。—*n.* 能整除之數。
a·li·tur·gi·cal [ˌælə'tɝdʒəkḷ; ˌæli'təːdʒikl] *adj.* 〖宗教〗禁儀日。(亦作 **aliturgic**)
:a·live [ə'laɪv; ə'laiv] *adj.* ①活的。 They were captured *alive.* 他們被活捉。②活躍的。He is *alive* with enthusiasm. 他是熱情奮發的。③豐富的。 The lake was *alive* with fish. 這湖中多魚。④繼續活動的;繼續有效的。*be alive to* 敏感。*be alive with* 充滿。*look alive* 趕快! 注意! —**ness,** *n.*
a·liz·a·rin [ə'lɪzərɪn; ə'lizərin] *n.* 茜

(草色)素。*alizarin* crimson. 茜草紅。

al·ka·hest ['ælkə,hɛst; 'ælkəhest] *n.* (煉金術士所尋求之)萬物融化劑;萬能溶劑。

al·ka·le·mi·a [,ælkə'limɪə; ,ælkə'li:miə] *n.* 〖醫〗鹼血症。

al·ka·les·cent [,ælkə'lɛsn̩t; 'ælkə'lesnt] *adj.* 〖化〗鹼性的;鹼化的。 —**al·ka·les·cence, al·ka·les·cen·cy,** *n.*

*****al·ka·li** ['ælkə,laɪ; 'ælkəlai] *n., pl.* **-lis, -lies.** ①〖化〗鹼。 ②〖農〗某種土壤所含的可溶性無機鹽。—*adj.* 〖化〗鹼性的。*alkali* metals. 鹼金屬。*alkali* soil. 鹼性土壤。

al·ka·li·fy ['ælkələ,faɪ; 'ælkəlifai] *v.,* **-fied, -fy·ing.** —*v.t.* 使成鹼性。 —*v.i.* 變成鹼性。

al·ka·line ['ælkə,laɪn; 'ælkəlain] *adj.* 「含鹼的;鹼性的。」

alkaline earth 〖化〗鹼土。

alkaline-earth metals 〖化〗鹼土「金屬。」

al·ka·lin·i·ty [,ælkə'lɪnətɪ; ,ælkə'liniti] *n.* 鹼性。

al·ka·lize ['ælkə,laɪz; 'ælkəlaiz] *v.t.* & *v.i.,* **-lized, -liz·ing.** 使成鹼性;鹼化。 —**al·ka·li·za·tion,** *n.*

al·ka·loid ['ælkə,lɔɪd; 'ælkəlɔid] *n.* 〖化〗生物鹼;植物鹼基。—*adj.*似鹼的;含鹼的。

al·ka·loid·al [,ælkə'lɔɪdl̩; ,ælkə'lɔidl] *adj.* 鹼的;似鹼的;含鹼的。

al·kane ['ælken;'ælkein] *n.* 〖化〗烷屬「烴;鏈烷。」

al·ka·net ['ælkə,nɛt; 'ælkənet] *n.* ①朱草。 ②朱草根。 ③朱草染料。

al·kene ['ælkin; 'ælki:n] *n.* 〖化〗烯屬烴;鏈烯。

Al·ko·ran [,ælko'rɑn; ,ælkɔ'rɑ:n] 「*n.* 可蘭經。」

al·kyl ['ælkɪl; 'ælkil] *n.* 〖化〗烷基;烴基。

al·kyl·a·tion [,ælkə'leʃən; ,ælki'leiʃən] *n.* 〖化〗烷化;烴化。

al·kyne ['ælkaɪn; 'ælkain] *n.* 〖化〗炔屬烴。(亦作**alkine**)

‡all [ɔl; ɔ:l] *adj.* ①完全的;全部的;一切的。*All* men are equal. 凡人皆平等。 ②儘可能的。They counted the ballots with *all* speed. 他們儘速計算選舉票。 ③僅有;只有。He is *all* talk and no deed. 他只說不做。 ④〖俚〗完了。The cake is *all.* 蛋糕吃光了。 —*pron.* 全體;總數。*All* of us are going to see the game. 我們都去看比賽。***above all*** 尤其;最。*Above all,* the little girl wanted a doll. 這小女孩最想要的是一個洋娃娃。***after all*** 畢竟;究竟。*After all* he is a good man. 他畢竟是一個好人。***all in all*** a. 完全地。b. 最愛的;最珍惜的。c. 一般說來。***and all*** 連同。***at all*** a. 全然。b. 爲任何理由。Why bother *at all?* 何必勞駕? ***for all; for all that*** 雖然;縱然。*For all* you say, I still like him. 雖然你說了這些話,我仍喜歡他。***for good and all*** 永遠。***if at all*** 假如果有其事。***in all*** 合計。There were twenty *in all.* 合計有二十。***not at all*** 全不;毫不。He is *not* tired *at all.* 他全不疲倦。***once and for all*** 最後一次。***once for all*** 只此一次。—*adv.* ①全部;全體。The cake is *all* gone. 餅全吃完了。 ②同一;相等。The score of the game is two *all.* 賽球之記錄爲二對二。***all alone*** 獨自的。He did it *all alone.* 這件事是他一人做的。***all along*** a. 自始至終。I know that *all along.* 自始至終我盡知之。b. 沿途;全長。***all at once*** a. 突然;忽然。b. 同時;一下子。***all but*** a. 除了…全。We found them *all but* three. 除了三個外,其餘我們全找到。b. 差不多。***all gone*** 完了;沒有了。***all in*** 〖俗〗疲倦。I'm *all in.* 我累得要死。***all over*** a. 完畢。b. 遍於。***all over oneself*** 非常高興;過於自信。***all over with*** 完了;毀滅;瀕於死亡。***all ready*** 一切就緒。***all the better*** 更好。***all the more so*** 更加;越發。***all the same*** 仍然;一樣地。***all the time*** 始終。***all together*** 一起。***all up*** a. 完了;沒有希望了。b. 〖印刷〗已全部排版。***be all there*** 〖俗〗a. 神志清醒的。b. 能幹的。c. 合格的。***be not all there*** 低能的。

al·la bre·ve ['ɑllɑ'breve; 'ɑ:lɑ:'breivei] 〖義〗〖音樂〗二拍子(其樂譜符號爲 ₵ 或 2/2)。

Al·lah ['ælə, 'ɑlə; 'ælə, 'ɑ:lɑ:] *n.* 上帝;「神(爲回教之用字)。」

all-A·mer·i·can ['ɔlə'mɛrəkən; 'ɔ:lə'merikən] *adj.* ①代表全美國的。 ②全係美國原料製成的。 —*n.* 全美代表選手。

Al·lan ['ælən; 'ælən] *n.* 男子名。(亦作 **Alan, Allen, Allyne**)

al·lan·toid [ə'læntɔɪd; ə'læntɔid] *n.* = **allantois.** —*adj.* (亦作 **allantoidal**)尿膜的;尿囊的;臘腸樣的。

al·lan·to·is [ə'læntoɪs; ə'læntɔis] *n.* 〖解剖〗尿膜;尿囊。—**al·lan·to·ic,** *adj.*

al·lar·gan·do [,ɑlɑr'gɑndo; ,ɑ:lɑ:'gɑ:ndou] 〖義〗 *adj.* & *adv.* 〖音樂〗逐漸減慢轉强的(地)。

all-a·round ['ɔlə,raund; 'ɔ:ləraund] *adj.* 〖俗〗 ①多方面的;多才藝的。He is a good *all-around* sportsman. 他是一個擅長各種戶外運動的運動家。 ②普遍的;廣博的。 ③完全的。

al·lay [ə'le; ə'lei] *v.t.* ①使和緩。 ②使「鎮靜;解憂。—**er,** *n.*」

all clear 空襲或其他危險解除的信號。

al·le·ga·tion [,ælə'geʃən; ,ælə'geiʃən] *n.* ①空言;推諉。 ②斷言;辯解;主張。

al·lege [ə'lɛdʒ; ə'ledʒ] *v.t.,* **-leged, -leg·ing.** ①託言。 ②堅說;宣稱。

al·leged [ə'lɛdʒd; ə'ledʒd] *adj.* ①提出而尚未證實的;有嫌疑的。 ②聲稱的;宣稱的。 ③作爲理由或辯解的。—**ly,** *adv.*

al·le·giance [ə'lidʒəns; ə'li:dʒəns] *n.* ①對國家或君主的忠順。 ②忠誠。 —**al·le·giant,** *adj.*

al·le·gor·i·cal [,ælə'gɔrɪkl̩; ,æle'gɔrikəl] *adj.* 比喻的;寓言的;寓意的。(亦作 **allegoric**) —**ly,** *adv.* —**ness,** *n.*

al·le·go·rist ['ælə,gorɪst; 'æligərist] *n.* 諷喻家;寓言作家。

all·e·go·ris·tic [,æləgə'rɪstɪk; ,æligə'ristik] *adj.* 比喻的;寓言的。

al·le·go·rize ['æləgə,raɪz; 'æligəraiz] *v.,* **-rized, -riz·ing.** —*v.t.* ①以諷喻體敍述。 ②諷刺地詮釋。 —*v.i.* 使用諷喻。

al·le·go·ry ['ælə,gorɪ; 'æligəri] *n., pl.* **-ries.** 諷喻;寓言。

al·le·gret·to [,ælə'grɛto; ,æli'gretou] *adj., adv., n., pl.* **-tos.** —*adj.* & *adv.* 〖音樂〗稍快(比 allegro 慢)。—*n.* 稍快板。

al·le·gro [ə'legro; ə'leigrou] *adj.* & *adv.* 〖音樂〗活潑;快速。—*n.* 急速的調子。

al·lele [ə'lil; ə'li:l] *n.* 〖遺傳學〗由突變或變化而產生的遺傳因子。

al·le·lo·morph [ə'lilə,mɔrf; ə'li:ləmɔ:f] *n.* 〖生物〗相對形質;相對基因。

al·le·lu·ia [,ælə'lujə; ,æli'lu:jə] *interj.* 阿利路亞(讚美上帝語 =praise ye the Lord)。—*n.* 讚美上帝之聖詩。

al·le·mande 〔ˌæləˈmænd; ˈælmɑ̃ːnd〕 *n., pl.* **-mandes.** 〖法〗①十七、八世紀歐洲一種二拍板的慢舞曲。②用此種舞曲節拍寫的音樂。③德國土風舞之一種。
al·ler·gen 〔ˈæləˌdʒɛn; ˈælədʒen〕 *n.* 引起過敏症之物；變(態反)應原。
al·ler·gen·ic 〔ˌæləˈdʒɛnɪk; ˌæləˈdʒenik〕 *adj.* 使生過敏反應的。
al·ler·gic 〔əˈlɝdʒɪk; əˈləːdʒik〕 *adj.* ①過敏症的。②患過敏症的。③〖俚〗具有强烈反感的；對…極討厭的。
al·ler·gist 〔ˈælədʒɪst; ˈælədʒist〕 *n.* 治療及診斷過敏症的專科醫生。
al·ler·gy 〔ˈælədʒɪ; ˈælədʒi〕 *n., pl.* **-gies.** ①過敏症，如氣喘等。②厭惡。
al·le·vi·ate 〔əˈlivɪˌet; əˈliːvieit〕 *v.t.,* **-at·ed, -at·ing.** 使緩和；減輕(痛苦)；安慰。
al·le·vi·a·tion 〔əˌlivɪˈeʃən; əˌliːviˈeiʃən〕 *n.* ①減輕；安慰。②解痛物；慰藉物。
al·le·vi·a·tive 〔əˈlivɪˌetɪv; əˈliːvieitiv〕 *adj.* 減輕的；緩和的；安慰的。—*n.* 解痛物；緩和物；慰藉物。
al·le·vi·a·tor 〔əˈlivɪˌetɚ; əˈliːvieitə〕 *n.* 減輕者；緩和者；安慰者；緩和物；慰藉物。
al·le·vi·a·to·ry 〔əˈlivɪəˌtorɪ; əˈliːviətəri〕 *adj.* 減輕的；緩和的；安慰的。
all-ex·pense 〔ˈɔlɪkˈspɛns; ˈɔːliksˈpens〕 *adj.* 包括一切費用的。
al·ley**[1] 〔ˈælɪ; ˈæli〕 *n., pl.* **-leys.** ①弄；巷；胡同。②園林中之小徑。③保齡球之球場。 ***blind alley **a.** 死巷。**b.** 沒有進展希望的職位。***up one's alley*** 〖俚〗正合其所長。
al·ley[2] *n., pl.* **-leys.** 大彈石。
alley cat 街貓；野貓。
al·ley·way 〔ˈælɪˌwe; ˈæliwei〕 *n.* ①〖美〗巷；衖。②窄道；小過道。
All-fa·ther 〔ˈɔlˈfɑðɚ; ˈɔːlˈfɑːðə〕 *n.* 「上帝；神。」
all-fired 〔ˈɔlˈfaɪrd; ˈɔːlˈfaiəd〕 *adj.* 〖俚〗非常的；極端的。—*adv.* 過度地；極端地。
All Fools' Day 愚人節(四月一日)。
all fours ①四足；手腳。②一種紙牌遊戲。 ***be on all fours (with)*** 與…相合或一致。
All·hal·lows 〔ˌɔlˈhæloz; ˈɔːlˈhælouz〕 *n.* ① =**All Saints' Day.** ②萬聖節宴。
al·li·a·ceous 〔ˌælɪˈeʃəs; ˌæliˈeiʃəs〕 *adj.* ①〖植物〗葱屬的。②有葱等之味道的。
al·li·ance** 〔əˈlaɪəns; əˈlaiəns〕 *n.* ①聯盟；同盟國。to form an offensive and defensive *alliance.* 成立攻守同盟。②聯姻；親戚。③共通點。in alliance with*** 聯盟。
Alliance for Progress 美洲進步同盟。
al·li·cin 〔ˈæləsɪn; ˈæləsin〕 *n.* 蒜辣素；「蒜頭素。」
***al·lied** 〔əˈlaɪd, ˈælaɪd; əˈlaid, ˈælaid〕 *adj.* ①聯盟的；同盟的。*allied* nations. 同盟國。②聯姻的。③類似的；有關聯的。〖注意〗**allied** 或 **Allied** 用在名詞前時，重音常常在第一音節上。
Allied and Associated Pow·ers 協約國。
Allied Forces 盟軍；聯軍。
al·lies 〔ˈælaɪz, əˈl-; ˈælaiz, əˈl-〕 *n. pl.* ①聯盟國；同盟者。②(A-)(第一次大戰之)協約國；(第二次大戰之)同盟國。
***al·li·ga·tor** 〔ˈæləˌgetɚ; ˈæligeitə〕 *n.* ①一種產於美洲的鱷魚。②該種鱷魚之皮。③水陸兩用運兵船。—*v.i.* 龜裂成鱷魚皮狀。—*adj.* 鱷魚皮的。
all-im·por·tant 〔ˈɔlɪmˈpɔrtənt; ˈɔːlimˈpɔːtənt〕 *adj.* 最重要的；重大的；必要的。
all-in 〔ˈɔlˈɪn; ˈɔːlˈin〕 *adj.* 〖英〗①包括全部的。②無限制的；自由式的。
all-in·clu·sive 〔ˈɔlɪnˈklusɪv; ˈɔːlinˈkluːsiv〕 *adj.* 概括所有的；綜合全體的。
all-in-one 〔ˈɔlɪnˈwʌn; ˈɔːlinˈwʌn〕 *n.* (胸罩與束腰連在一起的)女用緊身。
al·lit·er·ate 〔əˈlɪtəˌret; əˈlitəreit〕 *v.,* **-at·ed, -at·ing.** —*v.i.* ①押頭韻〖with〗. ②用頭韻。—*v.t.* 以頭韻作成。
al·lit·er·a·tion 〔əˌlɪtəˈreʃən; əˌlitəˈreiʃən〕 *n.* 頭韻。
al·lit·er·a·tive 〔əˈlɪtəˌretɪv; əˈlitərətiv〕 *adj.* 頭韻的；頭韻體的。—**ly,** *adv.*
al·lium 〔ˈælɪəm; ˈæliəm〕 *n.* 葱蒜的總稱。
all-know·ing 〔ˈɔlˈnoɪŋ; ˈɔːlˈnouiŋ〕 *adj.* 全知的。—**ness,** *n.*
all-night 〔ˈɔlˈnaɪt; ˈɔːlˈnait〕 *adj.* ①整夜的。②整夜營業的。
al·lo·bar·ic 〔ˌæləˈbærɪk; ˌæləˈbærik〕 *adj.* 〖氣象〗有關氣壓變動的。
al·lo·ca·ble 〔ˈæləkəbl̩; ˈæləkəbl〕 *adj.* 可撥出的；可配置的。
al·lo·cate 〔ˈæləˌket; ˈæləkeit〕 *v.t.,* **-cat·ed, -cat·ing.** ①撥出；留下。②按計畫分配；配置。③定位置。—**al·lo·ca·tion,** *n.*
al·lo·ca·tee 〔ˌæləkeˈti; ˌæləkeiˈtiː〕 *n.* 受分配者；受分派者。
al·lo·cu·tion 〔ˌæləˈkjuʃən; ˌælouˈkjuːʃən〕 *n.* 訓示(尤指教宗的訓諭)。
al·lo·di·al 〔əˈlodɪəl; əˈloudjəl〕 *adj.* 完全私有地的；自主地的。(亦作 **alodial**)
al·lo·di·um 〔əˈlodɪəm; əˈloudjəm〕 *n., pl.* **-di·a** 〔-dɪə; -diə〕. 〖法律〗完全私有地；自由所有地；自主地。(亦作 **alodium**)
al·log·a·my 〔əˈlɑgəmɪ; əˈlɑːgəmi〕 *n.* 〖植物〗異花受精。—**al·log·a·mous,** *adj.*
al·lo·graft 〔ˈæləˌgræft; ˈæləgrɑːft〕 *n.* 人體組織移植。
al·lo·graph 〔ˈæləˌgræf; ˈæləgrɑːf〕 *n.* ①代人簽字或畫押。②非當事人手書之文契。
al·lom·er·ism 〔əˈlɑmərɪzəm; əˈlɔmərizm〕 *n.* 〖化〗異質同形現象。
al·lo·morph 〔ˈæləˌmɔrf; ˈæləmɔːf〕 *n.* 〖化〗同質異形體。
al·lo·morph·ism 〔ˌæləˈmɔrfɪzm̩; ˌælouˈmɔːfizm〕 *n.* 〖化〗同質異形現象。
al·longe 〔əˈlʌndʒ; əˈlʌndʒ〕 *n.* 〖法律〗證券等的附箋、補箋(供背書之用)。
al·lo·nym 〔ˈælənɪm; ˈælənim〕 *n.* ①(著作家的)假託之僞名。②假託僞名之著作。
al·lo·path 〔ˈæləˌpæθ; ˈæloupæθ〕 *n.* 用對抗療法之醫生。(亦作 **allopathist**)
al·lo·path·ic 〔ˌæləˈpæθɪk; ˌælouˈpæθik〕 *adj.* 對抗療法的。—**al·ly,** *adv.*
al·lop·a·thy 〔əˈlɑpəθɪ; əˈlɔpəθi〕 *n.* 〖醫〗對抗療法。
al·lo·pat·ric 〔ˌæləˈpætrɪk; ˌæləˈpætrik〕 *adj.* 〖生物〗生長或源出不同區域的。
al·lo·pe·lag·ic 〔ˌæləpəˈlædʒɪk; ˌæloupəˈlædʒik〕 *n.* (海中生物)生長於不同深度的。
al·lo·phane 〔ˈæləˌfen; ˈæləfein〕 *n.* 「含水矽酸鋁礦。」
all-or-noth·ing 〔ˈɔləˈnʌθɪŋ; ˈɔːləˈnʌθiŋ〕 *adj.* 非完全有效卽完全無效的；非此卽彼的。(亦作 **all or none**)
***al·lot** 〔əˈlɑt; əˈlɔt〕 *v.t.,* **-lot·ted, -lot·ting.** ①分配；攤派。to *allot* shares. 分配股份。②指定用途地分配。③指派。—**ment,** *n.*
al·lo·trope 〔ˈæləˌtrop; ˈælətroup〕 *n.* 〖化〗同素體；同素異形。
al·lo·trop·ic 〔ˌæləˈtrɑpɪk; ˌæləˈtrɔpik〕

adj. 同素體的;同素異形的。
al·lot·ro·py [ə'lɑtrəpɪ; ə'lɔtrəpi] *n.* 〖化〗同素異形;同素性。(亦作 **allotropism**)
al·lot·tee [əˌlɑ'ti; əˌlɔ'ti:] *n.*受分配者。
all-out ['ɔl'aʊt; 'ɔ:l'aut] *adj.* 盡可能的;完全的;全部的;徹底的。
all·o·ver [*n.* 'ɔlˌovə; 'ɔ:lˌouvə *adj.* 'ɔl'ovə; 'ɔ:l'ouvə] *adj.* 布滿全面的;有布滿全面之花樣的。 —*n.* 印花布料。
all-o·ver·ish [ˌɔl'ovərɪʃ; ˌɔ:l'ouvəriʃ] *adj.* 〖方〗無故不安的;說不出地渾身難過的。
‡**al·low** [ə'laʊ; ə'lau] *v.t.* ①允許。Smoking is not *allowed* here. 此處不准吸烟。②給與。③承認。We must *allow* that he is wrong. 我們必須承認他是錯了。④酌留;酌量增加或減少。⑤〖俗〗說;想。⑥(由於不小心而)讓某種情形發生。—*v.i.* 承認;容許〖of〗. to *allow* of no delay. 不容躭擱。***allow for*** a. 原諒;體諒。b. 斟酌;考慮。c. 準備;酌留。
al·low·a·ble [ə'laʊəbḷ; ə'lauəbl] *adj.* 可允許的;可承認的;可原諒的。—*n.* ①可允許之事。②〖美〗石油公司在某一時間內可從油井中取油之法定量。 —**al·low·a·bly,** *adv.*
*__al·low·ance__ [ə'laʊəns; ə'lauəns] *n., v.,* **-anced, -anc·ing.** —*n.* ①定量分配。②津貼;零用錢。③留餘地;預留。④承認;接受。⑤認可;寬容。⑥折扣;酌加額;酌減額。***make allowance*** (***for***) 留餘地;原諒。—*v.t.* ①給零用錢或津貼。②按定量分配。
al·low·ed·ly [ə'laʊɪdlɪ; ə'lauidli] *adv.* 經承認地;被允許地;當然。
al·loy [*n.* 'ælɔɪ, ə'lɔɪ; 'ælɔi, ə'lɔi *v.* ə'lɔɪ; ə'lɔi] *n.* ①合金。②和貴金屬混合的賤金屬。③(金銀)品位;成色。 —*v.t.* ①使成合金。②攙雜以劣質。
alloy steel 合金鋼。
all-par·ty ['ɔl'pɑrtɪ; 'ɔ:l'pɑ:ti] *adj.* 全黨派的;各黨派一致的;(支持等)超黨派的。
all-pow·er·ful ['ɔl'paʊəfəl; 'ɔ:l'pauəfl] *adj.* 全能的。
all-pur·pose ['ɔl'pɝpəs; 'ɔ:l'pə:pəs] *adj.* 可作各種用途的。
‡**all right** ①不錯;滿意。Is there anything wrong with the machine? No, it is *all right*. 這機器有甚麼毛病嗎?沒有,它沒有毛病。②是(=yes). Can you come here at once? *All right,* sir! 你能馬上來這裏嗎?是,先生。③確然(=certainly). ④健康;安全。Are you *all right?* 你好嗎?(或"你沒事吧?")⑤可以(含勉强意)。*All right!* You will be sorry for it. 好吧,不過你要後悔的。⑥〖俗〗可靠的;好的。
All Saints' Day 萬聖節(十一月一日)。
all·seed ['ɔlˌsid; 'ɔ:lsi:d] *n.* 多種子植物。
All Souls' Day (天主敎爲死人所定之)萬靈節(在十一月二日)。
all·spice ['ɔlˌspaɪs; 'ɔ:l-spais] *n.* 甜胡椒;其所製之香料。
all square 〖美俗〗①付清款項;完成應做工作。②分數拉平。
all-star ['ɔlˌstɑr; 'ɔ:lstɑ:] *adj.* 第一流演員或選手組成的。an *all-star* cast. 全是名角的演員名單(陣容)。
all-time ['ɔlˌtaɪm; 'ɔ:ltaim] *adj.* ① =**full-time.** ②空前的。an *all-time* best seller. 一本空前的暢銷書。
*__al·lude__ [ə'lud, ə'lɪud; ə'lu:d, ə'lju:d] *v.i.,* **-lud·ed, -lud·ing.** ①暗指〖to〗. I didn't *allude* to anything. 我並未暗指任何東西。②提及。
*__al·lure__ [ə'lur, -'lɪur; ə'ljuə, -'luə] *v.,* **-lured, -lur·ing,** *n.* —*v.t.* 引誘;誘惑。Rewards *allure* men to brave danger. 重賞之下必有勇夫。—*n.* 引誘;誘惑。
al·lure·ment [ə'lʊrmənt; ə'ljuəmənt] *n.* ①引誘;誘惑。②誘惑物。
*__al·lur·ing__ [ə'lurɪŋ; ə'ljuəriŋ] *adj.* 誘惑的;迷人的;銷魂的。—**ly,** *adv.* —**ness,** *n.*
*__al·lu·sion__ [ə'luʒən; ə'lu:ʒən] *n.* 引述;說及;提及。***in allusion to*** 間接提及;暗示;暗指。***make an allusion to*** 言及;提及。
al·lu·sive [ə'lusɪv; ə'lu:siv] *adj.* ①暗指的;引喻的。②多典故的;含典故的。
al·lu·vi·al [ə'luvɪəl; ə'lu:vjəl] *adj.*沖積的。—*n.* 沖積土。
alluvial fan 河口或山脚被水流沖積而成之扇形地。(亦作 **alluvial cone**)
al·lu·vi·on [ə'luvɪən; ə'lu:viən] *n.* ①沙洲;沖積地。②〖法律〗新生地。③洪水;氾濫。④(波之)沖擊。
al·lu·vi·um [ə'luvɪəm; ə'lu:viəm] *n., pl.* **-vi·ums, -vi·a** [-vɪə; -viə]. 〖地質〗沖積層;沖積地。
all·ways fuze ['ɔl'wez~; 'ɔ:l'weiz~] 「炸彈或火箭之觸爆雷管。」
all-weath·er ['ɔl'wɛðə; 'ɔ:l'weðə] *adj.* 全天候的;適於任何天氣狀況的。
*__al·ly__ [*v.* ə'laɪ; ə'lai *n.* 'ælaɪ, ə'laɪ; 'ælai, ə'lai] *v.,* **-lied, -ly·ing,** *n., pl.* **-lies.** —*v.t.* ①聯合;結合;結盟〖to, with〗. ②聯繫。③在血統或組織上發生關係。Dogs are *allied* to wolves. 狗和狼在血統上有關聯。 —*v.i.* 結盟。Many foreign powers will *ally* with us. 許多外國將與我們締盟。—*n.* ①同盟國。②同類之動植物等。③擁護者。
all-year ['ɔljɪr; 'ɔ:ljə:] *adj.* 全年度的。
al·lyl ['æləl; 'æləl] *n.*〖化〗烯丙基。
allyl alcohol 〖化〗丙烯醇。
al·ma(h) ['ælmə; 'ælmə] *n.* (埃及之)舞孃;歌舞女郎。(亦作 **alme, almeh**)
al·ma ma·ter, Al·ma Ma·ter ['ælmə'metə; 'ælmə'mɑ:tə] 母校。
*__al·ma·nac__ ['ɔlməˌnæk, 'ɔlmənɪk; 'ɔ:lmənæk] *n.* 年鑑;曆書。
al·man·dine ['ælmənˌdin; 'ælməndi:n] *n.* 〖礦〗貴石榴子石;鐵鋁(石)榴子石。(亦作 **almandite**)
*__al·might·y__ [ɔl'maɪtɪ; ɔ:l'maiti] *adj.*①萬能的;有無限權力的。God *Almighty.* 上帝。②〖俗〗非常的;甚大的。—*n.*(the A-)上帝。—*adv.*〖俗〗非常地。I'm *almighty* glad. 我非常高興。
al·mi·rah [æl'maɪrə; ɔ:l'mairə] 〖印〗*n.* 「櫃子;衣櫥。」
*__al·mond__ ['ɑmənd; 'ɑ:mənd] *n.* ①杏仁。②杏樹。③形似杏仁之物。
al·mond-eyed ['ɑməndˌaɪd; 'ɑ:məndˌaid] *adj.* 杏眼的;細長橢圓形眼的。
al·mon·er ['ælmənə; 'ɑ:mənə] *n.* ①救濟品分發員。②〖英〗附屬於醫院之社會工作者。③〖英〗皇宮中之軍官。
al·mon·ry ['ælmənrɪ; 'ɑ:mənri] *n., pl.* **-ries.** 救濟品發放處。
‡**al·most** [ɔl'most, 'ɔlˌmost; 'ɔ:lmoust] *adv.*差不多;幾乎。It is *almost* three o'clock now. 現在差不多三點了。
*__alms__ [ɑmz; ɑ:mz] *n. sing.* or *pl.* 施捨;賙濟;布施。(亦作 **almous**)
alms·deed ['ɑmzˌdid; 'ɑ:mzdi:d] *n.*①施捨;賙濟。②施捨之習慣;善行。
alms·giv·er ['ɑmzˌgɪvə; 'ɑ:mzˌgivə] *n.* 施捨者;慈善家;賙濟者。
alms·giv·ing ['ɑmzˌgɪvɪŋ; 'ɑ:mzˌgiviŋ] *n.* 施捨;濟助;賙濟。

alms·house ['ɑmzˌhaus; 'ɑ:mzhaus] *n.* 貧民院;救濟院。

alms·man ['ɑmzmən; 'ɑ:mzmən] *n., pl.* **-men.** 受救濟之貧民。

al·mug ['ælmʌg; 'ælmʌg] *n.*【聖經】檀香木。

al·ni·co, Al·ni·co ['ælnɪˌko; 'ælnikou] *n.* 鐵、鎳、鋁及鈷的合金。

al·oe ['ælo; 'ælou] *n., pl.* **-oes.** ①【植物】蘆薈。②(常 *pl.*)(作 *sing.* 解)蘆薈油(蘆薈葉汁所製成之瀉藥)。③【美】龍舌蘭。

***a·loft** [ə'lɔft; ə'lɔft] *adj. & adv.* ①到上面;在上面。②在桅上;在桅桿高處。to go *aloft.* 爬上桅桿。③【俗】在天上。

al·o·ha [ə'loə, ɑ'lohɑ; ə'louə, ɑ:'louhɑ:]【夏威夷語】*interj.* ①歡迎!喂! ②再見!珍重再見! —*n.* 愛(=love).

‡a·lone [ə'lon; ə'loun] *adj.* ①單獨的;孤單的。His house stands *alone* on the hillside. 他的房子孤零零地座落於山邊上。②獨特的;無雙的。***all alone*** 獨自的(參看 **all**)。***leave somebody*** (or ***something***) ***alone*** 聽其自然。*Leave me alone.* 不要管我。***let alone*** **a.** 聽其自然。*Let* him *alone.* 不要管他。**b.** 至於…更不必說;且莫提。He speaks Russian, *let alone* English. 他會說俄文,英文當然不在話下了。***let well enough alone*** 安於現狀。—*adv.* ①單獨地。He went home *alone.* 他獨自回家。②僅;獨。—**ness,** *n.*

‡a·long [ə'lɔŋ; ə'lɔŋ] *prep.* ①沿;循。We took a walk *along* the shore. 我們沿岸散步。②在…期間;在…過程中。③根據;按照。—*adv.* ①成一行地;縱長地。All the cars parked *along* by the stadium. 所有的汽車都靠着運動場停放成一行。②向前。Let us walk *along.* 我們向前行。③共同。④近。The afternoon was well *along.* 近下午了。⑤從某地(人)至另一地(人)。***all along*** 自始至終。***along of***【俗】**a.** 由於。**b.** 作伴。***be along*** 到一個地方。He will soon *be along.* 他馬上就來。***get along*** **a.** 過活。**b.**【俗】相當成功地管理。**c.** 同意。**d.** 離去。**e.** 成功;繁榮。***get along with*** **a.** 相處。I can *get along with* him. 我能與他相處。**b.** 進步。***right along*** 不停。The traffic moved *right along.* 車輛行人不斷地前進。

a·long·shore [ə'lɔŋˌʃor; ə'lɔŋʃɔ:] *adv.* ①沿岸;靠岸;近岸。②在岸上。

***a·long·side** [ə'lɔŋ'saɪd; ə'lɔŋ'said] *adv.* 傍;靠;沿。—*prep.* 橫傍。This ship lies *alongside* the pier. 船靠碼頭停泊。

***a·loof** [ə'luf; ə'lu:f] *adv.* 遠離;躲開。to hold oneself *aloof* from the crowd. 避開人羣;超然絕俗。—*adj.* 冷漠的;疏遠的;無情的。—**ness,** *n.*

al·o·pe·ci·a [ˌælə'piʃɪə; ˌælə'pi:ʃiə] *n.*【醫】禿頂症;脫毛症。

‡a·loud [ə'laud; ə'laud] *adv.* ①高聲。Please read *aloud* so that I can hear you. 請你高聲念,以便我聽得到。②大聲。He shouted *aloud* from downstairs. 他由樓下大聲叫。***think aloud*** 自言自語。

alp [ælp; ælp] *n.* ①高山;高峯(尤指瑞士境內者)。②阿爾卑斯山山地牧場。

al·pac·a [æl'pækə; æl'pækə] *n.* ①【動物】羊駝。②羊駝毛。③羊駝呢;羊駝毛織物。

al·pen·glow ['elpənˌglo; 'eilpənglou] *n.* (在高山頂所見之)晨曦或晚霞。

al·pen·horn ['ælpɪnˌhɔrn; 'ælpinhɔ:n] *n.* (瑞士牧童所用之)木製長角笛。(亦作 **alphorn**)

al·pen·stock ['ælpɪnˌstɑk; 'ælpinstɔk] *n.* 登山杖。

al·pha ['ælfə; 'ælfə] *n.* ①希臘字母的第一個字母(A, α). ②最初;開端。***alpha and omega*** 始終。***alpha rays***【物理】阿爾法射線;甲射線。

***al·pha·bet** ['ælfəˌbɛt; 'ælfəbit] *n.* ①字母。②初步;初階。

alphabet code 用於無線電及電話之字碼。

al·pha·bet·i·cal [ˌælfə'bɛtɪkl; ˌælfə'betikəl] *adj.* 字母的;依字母順序的。(亦作 **alphabetic**) —**ly,** *adv.*

al·pha·bet·ize ['ælfəbəˌtaɪz; 'ælfəbətaiz] *v.t.,* **-ized, -iz·ing.** ①依字母次序排列。②以字母表示。

al·pha·met·ic [ˌælfə'mɛtɪk; ˌælfə'metik] *n.* 字母算術(以字母代數字之數學難題)。

al·pha·nu·mer·ic [ˌælfənu'mɛrɪk; ˌælfənu:'merik] *adj.*【電子計算機】包括字母與號碼的。(亦作 **alphanumerical, alphameric**)

alpha particle【物理】α 質點。

alpha plus 最高級的;最上等的。

alpha ray【物理】α 射線。

al·pha·scope ['ælfəˌskop; 'ælfəskoup] *n.*【電腦】文字符號放映機。

al·pho·sis [æl'fosɪs; æl'fousis] *n.*【醫】皮膚色素缺乏症。

Al·pine ['ælpaɪn; 'ælpain] *adj.* ①阿爾卑斯山的;像阿爾卑斯山的。②(a-)高山的。*alpine* plants. 生於高山上的植物。

alpine fir 生長於高山的樅樹。

alpine garden 奇石園。

alpine hat 一種軟呢帽。

Al·pin·ist, al·pin·ist ['ælpɪnɪst; 'ælpinist] *n.* 登阿爾卑斯山者;登高山者。

***Alps** [ælps; ælps] *n. pl.* ①阿爾卑斯山脈。②月球北半球之一山脈名。

‡al·read·y [ɔl'rɛdɪ; ɔ:l'redi] *adv.* 早已;業經。I have been there *already,* so I don't want to go again. 我已經去過那裏,所以不欲再去。

al·right [ɔl'raɪt; ɔ:l'rait] *adv. & adj.* =**all right.**

Al·sace [æl'ses; 'ælsæs] *n.* 亞耳沙斯(前法國東北部之一省)。

Al·sace-Lor·raine ['ælˌseslo'ren; 'ælsæslou'rein] *n.* 法國東北部之一區,包括 Alsace 及 Lorraine.

Al·sa·tia [æl'seʃɪə; æl'seiʃjə] *n.* 倫敦中央之一區(昔爲負債者及罪犯之窩藏地)。

Al·sa·tian [æl'seʃən; æl'seiʃən] *adj.* ①Alsace 的。②Alsatia 的。—*n.*①Alsace 人。②Alsatia 人。③德國狼狗。

‡al·so ['ɔlso; 'ɔ:lsou] *adv.* 並且;又;亦。We ate and we *also* drank. 我們又吃又喝。—*conj.* =**and.** He was mean, *also* ugly. 他很卑鄙,而且長得醜。

al·so-ran ['ɔlsoˌræn; 'ɔ:lsouræn] *n.*【俗】①【賽馬】落選之馬。②失敗者;庸才。

alt [ælt; ælt] *n., adj.*【音樂】中高音(的)。***in alt*** **a.** 中高音的。**b.**【俗】趾高氣揚。

alt. ①alternate. ②altitude. ③alto.

Al·ta·ic [æl'teɪk; æl'teiik] *adj.* ①阿爾泰山脈的;其居民的。②阿爾泰語系的。

Al·tai Mountains [æl'taɪ~; æl'tai~] 阿爾泰山脈(在蒙古、新疆、西伯利亞中南部)。

Al·ta·ir [æl'tɑɪr; æl'tɛə] *n.*【天文】牽牛星;牛郎星。

***al·tar** ['ɔltɚ; 'ɔ:ltə] *n.* ①祭壇。②聖餐

檯。③祈禱之所。*lead (a woman) to the altar* 結婚。「於祭壇之祭品。②香火錢。」

al·tar·age ['ɔltəɪdʒ; 'ɔːltəridʒ] *n.*①供

altar boy 舉行彌撒時協助神父的男童。

altar bread 聖餐所用之麪餅(用以代「表聖體)。」

altar cloth 祭壇罩布。

al·tar·piece ['ɔltəˌpis; 'ɔːltəpiːs] *n.* 祭壇後方及上方畫成或雕刻的飾物。

altar stand 天主堂中放禱告書之架子。

altar wine 作彌撒時所用之聖酒。

alt·az·i·muth [ælt'æzəməθ; ælt-'æziməθ] *n.* 〖天文〗經緯儀。

***al·ter** ['ɔltə; 'ɔːltə] *v.t.* ①更改;變更。②〖美〗爲(雄性動物等)去勢; 爲(雌性動物)割去卵巢。 —*v.i.* 改變。The weather *alters* almost daily. 天氣差不多天天改變。—**a·bil·i·ty,** *n.* —**a·ble,** *adj.* —**a·bly,** *adv.*

alter. alteration.

al·ter·ant ['ɔltərənt; 'ɔːltərənt] *adj.* 使起改變的;變質性的。—*n.* 變色劑;變質劑。

***al·ter·a·tion** [ˌɔltə'reʃən; ˌɔːltə'reiʃən] *n.* 變更;改變。

al·ter·a·tive ['ɔltəˌretɪv; 'ɔːltərətiv] *adj.* ①引起改變的; 變更的; 體質改變的。②〖醫〗使身體逐漸恢復健康的。—*n.*〖醫〗改善體質之藥品;變質藥;改善體質之療法。

al·ter·cate ['ɔltəˌket; 'ɔːltəːkeit] *v.i.*, **-cat·ed, -cat·ing.** 爭論; 吵嘴〖with〗.

al·ter·ca·tion [ˌɔltə'keʃən; ˌɔːltəː'keiʃən] *n.* 口角;爭論。

al·ter e·go ['æltə'igo; 'æltə'iːgou] 〖拉〗①密友。②他我;個性之另一面。

***al·ter·nate** [*v.*'ɔltəˌnet, 'æl-; 'ɔːltəːneit *adj., n.* 'ɔltənɪt, 'æl-; ɔːl'təːnit] *v.*, **-nat·ed, -nat·ing,** *adj., n.* —*v.i.* ①輪流; 交替〖with〗. Day and night *alternate* with each other. 日夜彼此交替。②〖電〗交流。—*v.t.* 輪流;交替。He *alternates* joy with grief. 他時喜時憂。—*adj.* ①間隔的。②輪流的; 交替的。③〖植物〗互生的。④〖數學〗錯的; 交錯的。*alternate* angles. 錯角。—*n.* 〖美〗①代理者;替代者。He was my *alternate* during my absence. 我不在時, 他是我的代理人。②備用演員。—**ly,** *adv.*

alternating personality 〖心理〗多重人格。

alternating series〖數學〗交錯級數。

al·ter·na·tion [ˌɔltə'neʃən; ˌɔːltəː'neiʃən] *n.* ①交互;交替;輪流。②間隔;交錯。③〖數學〗錯列。④〖電〗交變;交變次數。

alternation of generations 〖生物〗世代交替。

***al·ter·na·tive** [ɔl'tɜnətɪv, æl-;ɔːl'təːnətiv] *adj.* ①二者任擇其一的; 兩不相容的。There is no *alternative* course. 沒有選擇餘地。②可從數個中擇其一的。③選擇的。*alternative* conjunctions. 〖文法〗選擇連接詞 (如 or, either...or 等)。 —*n.* ①二者擇一;二者之一。The *alternatives* are surrender or death. 降或死, 任擇其一。②選擇之事物。③可取之道;選擇餘地。—**ly,** *adv.*

al·ter·na·tor ['ɔltəˌnetə; 'ɔːltəneitə] *n.* 交流發電機。

al·th(a)e·a [æl'θiə; æl'θiːə] *n.* 〖植物〗蜀葵屬;木槿。「樂〗高音喇叭。」

alt·horn ['æltˌhɔrn; 'æltho:n] *n.*〖音

‡**al·though, al·tho** [ɔl'ðo; ɔːl'ðou] *conj.* 雖然;縱使。*Although* it was cold, he didn't light the fire. 天氣雖冷, 他並未舉火。〖注意〗**although** 在多數情形下, 可與 though 通用, 亦可簡寫爲 altho, 惟在正式文書中不宜用簡寫。Although 所領的副詞子句置於主要子句之前; though 所領的副詞子句置於主要子句之後。

al·tim·e·ter [æl'tɪmətə; 'æltimiːtə] *n.* 高度測量器;高度計。(亦作 **altometer**)

al·tim·e·try [æl'tɪmɪtrɪ; æl'timitri] *n.* 高度測量(法)。 「*n.* 高原地帶之平地。」

al·ti·pla·no[ˌɑltɪ'plɑno;ˌɑːlti'plɑːnou]

al·tis·si·mo [æl'tɪsəˌmo; æl'tisəmou] *adj.* 〖音樂〗最高的。

***al·ti·tude** ['æltəˌtjud;'æltitjuːd] *n.* ①高度。We are flying at a great *altitude.* 我們飛得甚高。②(常*pl.*)高處。It is difficult to breathe in these *altitudes.* 在此高處呼吸感到困難。③ 階級高權力大的職位。④〖幾何〗(三角形之)頂垂線。⑤〖天文〗地平緯度。

altitude sickness 因高處氧氣稀薄而導致的不適與疾病。

al·to ['ælto; 'æltou] *n., pl.* **-tos.** 〖音樂〗①男子最高音。②女子最低音。③唱 alto 者;男高音;女低音。

al·to-cu·mu·lus [ˌælto'kjumjələs; ˌæltou'kjuːmjuləs] *n., pl.* **-mu·li** [-mjəˌlaɪ; -mjulai].〖氣象〗高積雲。

***al·to·geth·er** [ˌɔltə'gɛðə;ˌɔːltə'geðə] *adv.* ① 完全地; 全部地。He is *altogether* wicked. 他完全是個壞人。②一起;總共。③總之。*Altogether,* I am glad it is over. 總之, 我很高興這事已成過去。—*n.* 僅見於下列成語之習慣用法。*in the altogether* 〖俗〗裸體。 —**ness,** *n.*

al·to-re·lie·vo ['ælto·rɪ'livo; 'æltou-ri'liːvou] *n., pl.* **-vos.** 高凸浮雕。(亦作 **alto-rilievo**)

al·to·stra·tus ['ælto'stretəs; 'æltou-'streitəs] *n.* 〖氣象〗高層雲。

al·tru·ism ['æltrʊˌɪzəm;'æltruizəm] *n.* 利他主義;愛他主義。—**al·tru·ist,** *n.* —**al·tru·is·tic,** *adj.* —**al·tru·is·ti·cal·ly,** *adv.*

al·u·la ['æljələ; 'æljulə] *n., pl.* **-lae** [-li; -liː].〖動物〗小翼;翼膜。

al·um[1] ['æləm;'æləm] *n.*〖化〗明礬;白礬。

a·lum[2] [ə'lʌm; ə'lʌm] *n.* =**alumnus, alumna.**

alum. aluminum. 「〖化〗礬土。」

al·u·mi·na [ə'lumɪnə; ə'ljuːminə] *n.*

***al·u·min·i·um** [ˌæljə'mɪnɪəm; ˌælju'minjəm] *n.*〖英〗=**aluminum.**

al·u·mi·nize [ə'ljuməˌnaɪz; ə'ljuːmənaiz] *v.t.,* **-nized, -niz·ing.** 將鋁加進…。

a·lu·mi·nog·ra·phy [əˌljumə'nɑgrəfɪ; əˌljuːmə'nɔgrəfi] *n.* 〖印刷〗鋁版術。

a·lu·mi·no·ther·my [ə'ljumənoˌθɜmɪ; ə'ljuːminouˌθəmi] *n.* 〖冶金〗鋁冶術。(亦作 **aluminothermics**)

a·lu·mi·nous[ə'lumɪnəs;ə'ljuːminəs] *adj.* 明礬的;礬土的;含有明礬的。

***a·lu·mi·num** [ə'lumɪnəm; ə'ljuːminəm] *n.* 〖化〗鋁。

aluminum bronze 鋁銅;礬銅。

aluminum foil 鋁箔。

a·lum·na [ə'lʌmnə; ə'lʌmnə] *n., pl.* **-nae** [-ni; -niː]. 女校友;女畢業生。

a·lum·ni association[ə'lʌmnaɪ~; ə'lʌmnai~]校友會。

a·lum·nus [ə'lʌmnəs; ə'lʌmnəs] *n., pl.* **-ni** [-naɪ; -nai]. 男校友;男畢業生。

al·um·root ['æləmˌrut; 'æləmruːt] *n.* 〖植物〗礬根草。

al·u·nite ['ælju,naɪt; 'æljunait] *n.* 〖礦〗明礬石。
al·ve·o·lar [æl'viələ; æl'viələ] *adj.* ① **a.** 〖解剖〗肺泡的;氣泡的。**b.** 齒槽的。②〖語音〗齒槽音的。
al·ve·o·late [æl'viəlɪt; æl'vi:əlit] *adj.* 有小孔的;有肺泡的。(亦作 **alveolated**)
al·ve·o·li·tis [,ælvɪə'laɪtɪs; ,ælviə'laitis] *n.* 〖醫〗齒槽炎。
al·ve·o·lus [æl'viələs; æl'viələs] *n.*, *pl.* **-li** [-,laɪ; -lai]. ①小洞;小孔。②〖解剖〗**a.** 肺泡;氣泡。**b.** 齒槽。③齒槽突起。
al·vine ['ælvɪn; 'ælvin] *adj.* 〖醫〗腸的;腹的。
al·way ['ɔlwe; 'ɔ:lwei] *adv.* 〖古,詩〗= **always.**
‡al·ways ['ɔlwɪz, -wez; 'ɔ:lwəz, -weiz] *adv.* ①永遠。He is *always* cheerful. 他永遠是高興的。②總是。They *always* come on Saturday. 他們總是星期六來。③不斷地。Near, *always* near, he came. 他不斷地走來,愈來愈近了。
a·lys·sum [ə'lɪsəm; 'ælisəm] *n.* 〖植物〗十字花科之一屬;該屬之植物。
‡am [*stressed* æm; æm *unstressed* əm; əm] *v.* be 的第一人稱, 單數, 現在, 直說法。
AM ①調幅 (=amplitude modulation). ② amendment. **Am.** ①America. ② American. **am.** ①ampere-meter. ② ammeter. **A. M.** (亦作 **M. A.**) Master of Arts. 文學碩士。
***a.m., A. M.** ['e'ɛm; 'ei'em] ①爲 ante meridiem (拉 =before noon) 之縮寫, 上午。6 a.m. 上午六點。②由午夜至中午。〖注意〗此字爲小寫, 惟在時間表中, 或作標題時, 則爲大寫。在連續字句中, 應與表示特定鐘點之數字連用: from 2 to 4 a.m.
AMA, A.M.A. ①American Medical Association. ② American Management Association. ③Automobile Manufacturers Association.
am·a·da·vat [,æmədə'væt; ,æmədə'væt] *n.* 梅花雀(印度產之一種鳴禽)。
a·mah ['ɑmə; 'ɑ:mə] *n.* 女傭; 乳母; 阿媽。
a·main [ə'men; ə'mein] *adv.* ①猛力地。②極端地;非常地。
a·mal·gam [ə'mælgəm; ə'mælgəm] *n.* ①汞合金;汞齊。②任何混合物。
a·mal·gam·ate [ə'mælgə,met; ə'mælgəmeit] *v.t.* & *v.i.*, **-at·ed, -at·ing.** ①與汞混合。②混合。—**a·mal·ga·ma·tor,** *n.*
a·mal·gam·a·tion [ə,mælgə'meʃən; ə,mælgə'meiʃən] *n.* ①合併;混合。②合併或混合後之產物。③將礦與汞混合以提煉貴金屬之方法。—**a·mal·ga·ma·tive,** *adj.*
am·a·ni·ta [,æmə'naɪtə; ,æmə'naitə] *n.* 〖植物〗毒蕈。
a·man·u·en·sis [ə,mænju'ɛnsɪs; ə,mænju'ensis] *n.*, *pl.* **-ses** [-siz; -si:z]. 筆記者;抄錄者;書記;文書。
am·a·ranth ['æmə,rænθ; 'æməræənθ] *n.* ①〖詩〗不凋花。②〖植物〗莧紫。③(食物染色用之)莧紫素。
am·a·ran·thine [,æmə'rænθɪn; ,æmə'rænθain] *adj.* ①不凋的。②莧的;似莧的。③呈紫紅色的。
am·a·ryl·lis [,æmə'rɪlɪs; ,æmə'rilis] *n.* ①〖植物〗宮人草。②(A-)牧羊女;鄉下姑娘。
a·mass [ə'mæs; ə'mæs] *v.t.* ①積聚。②收集。—*v.i.* 集合。—**ment,** *n.*
***am·a·teur** ['æmə,tʃur; 'æmətə:, -tjuə] *n.* ①業餘技藝家。②非專家。—*adj.* 業餘的;非專家的。He is an *amateur* tennis player. 他是一個業餘的網球員。—**ish,** *adj.* —**ism,** *n.*
amateur theatricals 業餘者所演之戲劇;票友演唱的戲。
am·a·tive ['æmətɪv; 'æmətiv] *adj.* ①戀愛的;好戀愛的。②色情的;好色的。
am·a·tol ['æmə,tɑl; 'æmətɔl] *n.* 黃色炸藥(TNT)與硝酸銨混合製成的炸藥。
am·a·to·ry ['æmə,torɪ; 'æmətəri] *adj.* 戀人的;戀愛的;色情的。
am·au·ro·sis [,æmɔ'rosɪs; ,æmɔ:'rousis] *n.* 〖醫〗黑內障;青盲。
***a·maze** [ə'mez; ə'meiz] *v.*, **a·mazed, a·maz·ing,** *n.* —*v.t.* 使吃驚;使驚愕。I was *amazed* at his conduct. 我對他的行爲感到驚愕。—*n.* 驚愕。
***a·mazed** [ə'mezd; ə'meizd] *adj.* 吃驚的;驚奇的。The magician made the dove disappear before our *amazed* eyes. 魔術師在我們驚奇的眼光前使鴿子不見了。—**ly,** *adv.*
***a·maze·ment** [ə'mezmənt; ə'meizmənt] *n.* ①驚愕; 驚異。He looked at us in *amazement.* 他驚愕地看着我們。②使人驚異的事物。
***a·maz·ing** [ə'mezɪŋ; ə'meiziŋ] *adj.* 可驚異的。—**ly,** *adv.*
***Am·a·zon** ['æmə,zɑn; 'æməzən] *n.* ①亞馬遜河 (在南美洲, 爲世界最大的河)。②〖希臘神話〗一族女戰士中之一員。③(亦作 **amazon**) 高大、强壯而有男子氣概的女人。—**i·an,** *adj.*
Amb. Ambassador.
am·ba·ges [æm'bedʒiz; æm'beidʒi:z] *n. pl.* 迂廻的方法或手段;迂遠;迂路。
***am·bas·sa·dor** [æm'bæsədə; æm'bæsədə] *n.* ①大使。He was appointed *ambassador* to the United States. 他奉派爲駐美大使。②專使; 特使。③代表。(亦作 **embassador**) —**i·al,** *adj.* —**ship,** *n.*
ambassador at large 無任所大使。
ambassador extraordinary 特命大使。
ambassador extraordinary and plenipotentiary 特命全權大使。
ambassador plenipotentiary 全權大使。
ambassador without destination 無任所大使。
am·bas·sa·dress [æm'bæsədrɪs; æm'bæsədris] *n.* ①女大使。②大使夫人。
***am·ber** ['æmbə; 'æmbə] *n.* ①琥珀。②琥珀色;黃色。—*adj.* ①琥珀製的。②琥珀色的;黃色的。—**like,** —**y,** —**ous,** *adj.*
am·ber·gris ['æmbə,gris; 'æmbəgri(:)s] *n.* 鯨糞;龍涎香(作香料用)。
ambi- 〖字首〗表"圍繞;雙方;兩側"之義。
am·bi·dex·ter [,æmbə'dɛkstə; 'æmbi'dekstə] *adj.* ①兩手都很靈巧的。②懷二心的;詭詐的。—*n.* ①兩手都很靈巧的人。②懷有二心者;詭詐者。
am·bi·dex·ter·i·ty [,æmbədɛks'tɛrətɪ; 'æmbideks'teriti] *n.* ①兩手都很靈巧。②懷二心;詭詐。③高度技巧。
am·bi·dex·trous [,æmbə'dɛkstrəs; 'æmbi'dekstrəs] *adj.* ①兩手都很靈巧的。②懷二心的; 詭詐的。③ 極技巧的; 熟練的。—**ly,** *adv.* —**ness,** *n.*
am·bi·ence ['æmbɪəns; 'æmbiəns] *n.*, *pl.* **-enc·es.** 環境;包圍。(亦作 **ambiance**)
am·bi·ent ['æmbɪənt; 'æmbiənt] *adj.*

①包圍的;周圍的。②自由移動的;流通的。

am·bi·gu·i·ty 〔ˌæmbɪˈgjuətɪ; ˌæmbiˈgju(ː)iti〕 *n., pl.* **-ties.**①二種或二種以上的意義;曖昧;不分明。②曖昧的語意或文句。

am·big·u·ous 〔æmˈbɪgjuəs; æmˈbigjuəs〕 *adj.* ①有兩種或兩種以上之意義的;含糊的。②可疑的。—**ly,** *adv.* —**ness,** *n.*

am·bi·sex·trous 〔ˌæmbəˈsɛkstrəs; ˌæmbiˈsekstrəs〕 *adj.* 兩性吸引的;兩性的。

am·bit 〔ˈæmbɪt;ˈæmbit〕 *n.* ①(建築物)周圍;範圍。②行動、政策等之範圍。③圓周;周際。

am·bi·tend·en·cy 〔ˌæmbəˈtɛndənsɪ; ˌæmbiˈtendənsi〕 *n., pl.* **-cies.** 〖心理〗對人或物喜厭兩種感覺的同時存在。

***am·bi·tion** 〔æmˈbɪʃən; æmˈbiʃən〕 *n.* ①野心;雄心;企圖。A boy who is filled with *ambition* always works hard. 一個有雄心的孩子總是努力工作。②所希望的東西。—*v.t.* 急於獲得;努力爭取。—**less,** *adj.* —**less·ly,** *adv.*

***am·bi·tious** 〔æmˈbɪʃəs;æmˈbiʃəs〕 *adj.* ①有雄心或野心的。②顯出野心的。③慾望强烈的;熱望的。to be *ambitious* of power. 熱望權力。④矯飾的。⑤需要極大努力或才幹的。—**ly,** *adv.* —**ness,** *n.*

am·biv·a·lent 〔æmˈbɪvələnt; ˈæmbiˈveilənt〕 *adj.* (對同一人、物)同時具有矛盾情感的。—*n.* 陰陽人。—**am·biv·a·lence,** *n.*

am·bi·vert 〔ˈæmbɪvɚt; ˈæmbivəːt〕 *n.* 〖心理〗兩向性之人。—**am·bi·ver·sion,** *n.*

am·ble 〔ˈæmbḷ; ˈæmbl〕 *n., v.,* **-bled, -bling.** —*n.*①馬之同側兩足同時並舉之步調。②緩行。—*v.i.* 漫步;緩馳。

am·bler〔ˈæmblɚ;ˈæmblə〕 *n.*漫步之人;緩馳之馬。

am·bly·o·pi·a 〔ˌæmblɪˈopɪə; ˌæmbliˈoupiə〕 *n.* 〖醫〗弱視。

am·bly·o·scope 〔ˈæmblɪəˌskop; ˈæmbliəˌskoup〕 *n.* 弱視矯正器。

am·bo 〔ˈæmbo;ˈæmbou〕*n., pl.* **-bos.** (古代教會之)讀經臺。(亦作 **ambon**)

am·bro·sia 〔æmˈbroʒɪə; æmˈbrouzjə〕 *n.*①〖希臘、羅馬神話〗供品。②美味;芳香之物。

am·bro·sial 〔æmˈbroʒɪəl; æmˈbrouzjəl〕 *adj.*①適於神用的。②似供品的。

am·bry 〔ˈæmbrɪ; ˈæmbri〕 *n., pl.* **-bries.** ①壁櫥;櫥櫃。②教堂之聖器置放櫥。

ambs·ace 〔ˈemzˌes; ˈeimzeis〕 *n.* ①雙么(擲骰之最小點)。②歹運;無價值;倒楣。③最小之距離;最小量。(亦作 **amesace**)

***am·bu·lance** 〔ˈæmbjələns; ˈæmbjuləns〕 *n.* ①救護車(船、飛機)。②昔時之野戰醫院。

ambulance chaser 〖美俗〗專辦交通事故損害賠償等之律師。

ambulance corps 野戰救護隊。

am·bu·lant 〔ˈæmbjələnt; ˈæmbjulənt〕 *adj.* ①巡行的;可移動的。②〖醫〗(病人)不必臥床的;可走動的。

am·bu·late 〔ˈæmbjəˌlet; ˈæmbjuleit〕 *v.i.,* **-lat·ed, -lat·ing.** 走;步行;移動。

am·bu·la·tion 〔ˌæmbjəˈleʃən; ˌæmbjuˈleiʃən〕 *n.* 步行;移動。

am·bu·la·to·ry 〔ˈæmbjələˌtorɪ; ˈæmbjulətəri〕 *adj., n., pl.* **-ries.** —*adj.* ①行走的;能走的。②宜於行走的。③動的。④〖醫〗不必臥床的。⑤〖法律〗可變更的;未確定的。—*n.* 迴廊;走廊;屋內散步之處。

am·bus·cade 〔ˌæmbəsˈked; ˌæmbəsˈkeid〕 *n., v.,* **-cad·ed, -cad·ing.** —*n.*①伏兵。②埋伏所。③埋伏;伏擊。④〖美俗〗爭吵。—*v.t. & v.i.* 伏擊。—**am·bus·cad·er,** *n.*

***am·bush** 〔ˈæmbuʃ; ˈæmbuʃ〕*n.* ①埋伏。They concealed themselves in *ambush.* 他們隱藏作埋伏。②伏兵。③埋伏之處。—*v.t.* ①自埋伏處出擊。We were *ambushed.* 我們遭遇了埋伏。②伏(兵)於隱處。—**ment,** *n.*

A.M.D.G. ad majorem Dei gloriam (拉=to the greater glory of God).

A.M.E. ①Advanced Master of Education. ②African Methodist Episcopal.

a·mel·io·ra·ble 〔əˈmiljərəbḷ; əˈmiːljərəbl〕 *adj.* 可改良的;可修正的。

a·mel·io·rate 〔əˈmiljəˌret; əˈmiːljəreit〕 *v.,* **-rat·ed, -rat·ing.** —*v.t.* 改善;修正。—*v.i.* 變好。—**a·mel·io·ra·tive,** *adj.*

a·mel·io·ra·tion 〔əˌmiljəˈreʃən; əˌmiːljəˈreiʃən〕 *n.* 改善;改良;修正。

A·men 〔ˈɑmən; ˈɑːmən〕 *n.* 古埃及的生命和生殖之神(即太陽神)。(亦作 **Amon**)

***a·men** 〔ˈeˈmɛn, ˈɑˈmɛn; ˈɑːˈmen, ˈeiˈmen〕 *interj.* 阿們(祈禱終了時之語);心願如是。—*adv.* 眞實地。—*n.*認可或批准之表示。—*v.t.* ①批准;核准。②完成。

a·me·na·bil·i·ty 〔əˌminəˈbɪlətɪ; əˌmiːnəˈbiliti〕 *n.* 服從;負責;願接受勸告。

a·me·na·ble 〔əˈminəbḷ; əˈmiːnəbl〕 *adj.* ①有責任的;有服從之義務的。②願服從的;肯接受勸告的。

a·me·na·bly 〔əˈminəblɪ; əˈmiːnəbli〕 *adv.* 順從地;願服從地。

amen corner ①教堂裏教壇兩側之座位。②集會處。

***a·mend** 〔əˈmɛnd;əˈmend〕 *v.t.* ①正式的修改。The regulations are *amended.* 這些規則修正了。②改正;改良。

a·mend·a·ble 〔əˈmɛndəbḷ; əˈmendəbl〕 *adj.* 可修正的;能改正的。

a·mend·a·to·ry 〔əˈmɛndəˌtorɪ; əˈmendətəri〕*adj.*〖美〗修正的;矯正的;改良的。

a·mende 〔aˈmɑ̃d; æˈmɑ̃ːnd〕 〖法〗 *n.* ①罰款;賠償。②道歉。

a·mende ho·no·ra·ble 〔ˌaˈmɑ̃dɑnɑˈrabḷ; æˈmɑ̃ːndɔnɔˈrɑːbl〕〖法〗公開及正式的道歉或賠償。

***a·mend·ment**〔əˈmɛndmənt;əˈmendmənt〕 *n.* ①修正。②改正;改良;改善。

a·mends 〔əˈmɛndz;əˈmendz〕 *n. sing.* or *pl.* 賠償;賠罪。

a·men·i·ty 〔əˈmɛnətɪ;əˈmiːniti〕 *n., pl.* **-ties.** ①(*sing.*)適意;溫和。②(*pl.*)令人愉快之事物。

a·men·or·rhe·a, a·men·or·rhoe·a 〔eˌmɛnəˈrɪə; eiˌmenəˈriə〕 *n.* 〖醫〗停經;月經停止。

a men·sa et tho·ro〔eˈmɛnsəɛtˈθoro; eiˈmensəetˈθourou〕〖拉〗(夫婦)分居。

a·ment[1] 〔ˈemənt; ˈeimənt〕 *n.*〖心理〗精神不健全的人;智力不足的人;呆子。—**al,** *adj.*

am·ent[2] 〔ˈæmənt; ˈæmənt〕 *n.* 〖植物〗葇荑花序。

a·men·ti·a 〔eˈmɛnʃɪə; eiˈmenʃiə〕 *n.*〖醫〗白癡;癡愚;精神錯亂。

Amer. ①America. ②American.

A·mer·a·sian 〔əˈmɛrəʃən; əˈmerəʃən〕 *n., adj.* 美亞混血兒(的)。

a·merce〔əˈmɝs;əˈməːs〕 *v.t.,* **a·merced, a·merc·ing.** ①罰鍰;罰金。②懲罰;罰科。

a·merce·a·ble 〔əˈmɝsəbḷ; əˈməːsəbl〕 *adj.* 可罰鍰的。(亦作 **amerciable**)

a·merce·ment〔əˈmɝsmənt; əˈməːsmənt〕 *n.* 罰鍰;罰金。

A·mer·eng·lish〔ˌəmɛˈrɪŋglɪʃ; ˌameˈriŋgliʃ〕 *n.* 美國英語。

‡A·mer·i·ca 〔ə'mɛrɪkə; ə'merikə〕 *n.* ①美國。②南美或北美。③(*pl.*)南北美洲。
‡A·mer·i·can 〔ə'mɛrɪkən; ə'merikən〕 *adj.*①美國的。②美洲的。—*n.*①美國人。②美洲人。③=**American English.**
A·mer·i·ca·na 〔əˌmɛrə'kenə; əˌmeri'kɑːnə〕 *n. pl.* 美國文獻。
American Beauty 四季紅薔薇。
American Dream 美國之夢想(以民主、平等及自由作理想的一種口號)。
American English 美國英語。
American Federation of Labor 美國勞工聯盟。
American Indian 美國印第安人。
A·mer·i·can·ism 〔ə'mɛrəkənˌɪzəm; ə'merikənizəm〕 *n.* ①美國的風俗習慣及特性等。②美國所創或常用的字與詞。③親美。
A·mer·i·can·ist 〔ə'mɛrəkənɪst; ə'merikənist〕 *n.* ①美國通。②研究美國印第安人文化之專家。③親美者。④美洲專家。
A·mer·i·can·i·za·tion 〔əˌmɛrəkənə'zeʃən; əˌmerikənai'zeiʃən〕*n.*美國化。
A·mer·i·can·ize 〔ə'mɛrəkənˌaɪz; ə'merikənaiz〕 *v.t.* & *v.i.*, **-ized, -iz·ing.** 美國化。
American Legion 美退伍軍人協會。
A·mer·i·ca·nol·o·gist 〔əˌmɛrəkə'nɑlədʒɪst; əˌmerikə'nɔlədʒist〕 *n.* 研究美國政府及其政策的專家。
A·mer·i·can·o·phobe 〔əˌmɛrə'kænəfob; əˌmeri'kænəfoub〕 *n.* 憎恨美國的人。
American plan 旅館之供膳制。
American Revolution 美國獨立戰爭(1775-83)。
am·er·i·ci·um 〔ˌæmə'rɪʃɪəm; ˌæmə'risiəm〕 *n.* 〖化〗鋂(一種放射性元素)。
A·mer·i·co·logue 〔əˌmɛrə'kɔlɔg; əˌmeri'kɔlɔg〕 *n.* 研究美國社會的學者。
am·er·is·tic 〔ˌæmə'rɪstɪk; ˌæmə'ristik〕 *adj.* 〖植物〗不分裂的;不是分裂組織的。
Amer Sp. American Spanish.
a·met·a·bol·ic 〔ˌemɛtə'bɔlɪk; ˌeimetə'bɔlik〕 *adj.* 〖動物〗不變形的;不變態的。(亦作 **ametabolous**)
am·e·thyst 〔'æməθɪst; 'æmiθist〕 *n.* ①〖礦〗紫晶;紫水晶;水碧;紫水晶質。②假紫水晶。③紫色。—*adj.* 紫色的。
am·e·thys·tine 〔ˌæmɪ'θɪstɪn; ˌæmi'θistain〕 *adj.* ①紫水晶製成的;含紫水晶的。②似紫水晶的。
am·e·tro·pi·a 〔ˌæmɪ'tropɪə; ˌæmi'troupiə〕 *n.* 〖醫〗非正視眼(如亂視、近視等)。
Am·har·ic 〔æm'hærɪk; æm'hærik〕 *n.* 阿比西尼亞之貴族的語言。
***a·mi·a·ble** 〔'emɪəbḷ; 'eimjəbl〕 *adj.* 和藹可親的;溫柔的;友善的。She has an *amiable* disposition. 她的性情溫柔。 —**a·mi·a·bil·i·ty, —ness,** *n.* —**a·mi·a·bly,** *adv.*
am·i·an·thus 〔ˌæmɪ'ænθəs; ˌæmi'ænθəs〕 *n.* 〖礦〗(上等之)石綿;石絨。(亦作 **amiantus**)
am·i·ca·ble 〔'æmɪkəbḷ; 'æmikəbl〕*adj.* 友善的;和平的。—**am·i·ca·bil·i·ty, —ness,** *n.* —**am·i·ca·bly,** *adv.*
amicable number 〖數學〗互完數(兩個數目,其約數相等)。
amicable settlement 和解。
am·ice 〔'æmɪs; 'æmis〕 *n.* ①天主教神父做彌撒時肩上所披之白麻布。②僧侶的頭巾。
a·mi·cus cu·ri·ae 〔ə'maɪkəs'kjʊrɪˌi; ə'maikəs'kjuərii:〕 〖拉〗〖法律〗法官之顧問。
***a·mid** 〔ə'mɪd; ə'mid〕 *prep.* 在其中。They built a hut *amid* the woods. 他們在樹林中蓋一茅屋。
am·ide 〔'æmaɪd; 'æmaid〕 *n.* 〖化〗醯胺;氨基化合物。(亦作 **acid amide**)
am·i·din 〔'æmɪdɪn; 'æmidin〕 *n.* 〖化〗澱粉溶液。
am·i·dine 〔'æmɪˌdin; 'æmidiːn〕*n.*〖化〗「脒。」
am·i·dol 〔'æmədɑl; 'æmədɔl〕 *n.* 〖化〗亞米多爾;二氫氯酸二胺基酚。
a·mid·ships 〔ə'mɪdʃɪps; ə'midʃips〕 *adj.* & *adv.* ①在船或飛機中部;向船或飛機中部;在船腹。②縱長的(地)。(亦作 **amidship**)
***a·midst** 〔ə'mɪdst; ə'midst〕 *prep.* =**amid.**
a·mi·go 〔ə'migo; ə'miːgou〕 *n., pl.* **-gos.** 朋友。
a·mim·i·a 〔ə'mɪmɪə; ei'mimiə〕 *n.* 〖醫〗「表情缺失。」
a·mine 〔ə'min; ə'miːn〕 *n.* 〖化〗碳氫基氨;胺。(亦作 **amin**)
a·mi·no acid 〔ə'mino～; ə'miːnou～〕 〖化〗氨基酸。
a·mir 〔ə'mɪr; ə'miə〕 *n.* (回教國家之)統「治者;王族;貴族。」
a·miss** 〔ə'mɪs; ə'mis〕 *adv.* 錯誤地;差錯地。Everything goes *amiss* with him. 他凡事不如意。take amiss*** 傷感情。—*adj.* 錯誤的;差錯的。Nothing is *amiss* with him. 他沒有甚麼差錯。
Am·i·ta·bha 〔ˌʌmɪ'tɑbə; ˌʌmi'tɑːbə〕「*n.*〖梵〗阿彌陀佛。」
am·i·to·sis 〔ˌæmə'tosɪs; ˌæmi'tousis〕 *n.* 〖生物〗(細胞之)無絲分裂;直接分裂。
am·i·ty 〔'æmətɪ; 'æmiti〕 *n., pl.* **-ties.** 友善;親睦;和睦;和好。
AMM antimissile missile. 反飛彈飛彈。
Am·man 〔æm'mæn; ə'mɑːn〕 *n.* 阿曼(約旦之首都)。
am·me·ter 〔'æmˌmitə; 'æmitə〕 *n.* 安「培計;電表。」
am·mo 〔'æmo; 'æmou〕 *n.* 〖俗〗彈藥。
Am·mon 〔'æmən; 'æmən〕 *n.* 古埃及之太陽神。
am·mo·nal 〔'æməˌnæl; 'æmənæl〕 *n.*「一種強烈炸藥。」
***am·mo·nia** 〔ə'monjə, -nɪə; ə'mounjə〕 *n.* ①氨(氣體, NH_3)。 ②(亦作 **ammonia water**) 氨水(氨溶於水的溶液, NH_3OH)。
am·mo·ni·ac 〔ə'monɪˌæk; ə'mouniæk〕 *n.* 氨樹膠。(亦作 **gum ammoniac, ammoniacum**) —*adj.* =**ammoniacal.**
am·mo·ni·a·cal 〔ˌæmə'naɪəkḷ; ˌæmou'naiəkəl〕 *adj.* 氨的;含氨的;似氨的。
ammonia liquor 〖化〗氨液。(亦作 **ammoniacal liquor, gas liquor**)
am·mo·ni·at·ed 〔ə'monɪˌetɪd; ə'mounieitid〕 *adj.* 與氨化合的。
am·mo·nite 〔'æməˌnaɪt; 'æmənait〕 *n.* ①〖古生物〗鸚鵡螺之化石;菊石。②硝銨二硝基萘炸藥。③一種含氮之肥料。
am·mo·ni·um 〔ə'monɪəm; ə'mounjəm〕 *n.* 〖化〗銨;氨鹽基(NH_4)。
ammonium chloride 〖化〗氯化銨(NH_4Cl)。(亦作 **sal ammoniac**)
ammonium hydroxide 氫氧化銨。
ammonium nitrate 硝酸銨。
ammonium sulfate 硫酸銨。
***am·mu·ni·tion** 〔ˌæmjə'nɪʃən; ˌæmju'niʃən〕 *n.* ①彈藥;軍火。*ammunition* belt. 彈帶。②投擲或射擊物。③攻擊或防禦之手段。
ammunition chest (or **box**) 彈藥箱。
ammunition wagon 彈藥車。
am·ne·sia 〔æm'niʒɪə; æm'niːzjə〕 *n.*

〖醫〗健忘症;記憶缺失。
am·nes·ty ('æm,nɛstɪ; 'æmnesti) *n., pl.* **-ties,** *v.,* **-tied, -ty·ing.** —*n.* 大赦;特赦。—*v.t.* 大赦;特赦。
am·ni·o·cen·te·sis (,æmnɪosɛn'tisəs; ,æmniousen'tiːsəs) *n.* 羊水穿刺;羊水診斷(直接採集羊水以判斷胎兒的性別)。
am·ni·on ('æmnɪən; 'æmniən) *n., pl.* **-ni·ons, -ni·a** (-nɪə; -niə). 〖解剖〗(胎兒之)羊膜;胞衣。
am·ni·ot·ic fluid (,æmnɪ'ɑtɪk~; ,æmni'outik~) 〖動物〗羊膜液;羊水。
a·moe·ba (ə'mibə; ə'miːbə) *n., pl.* **-bas, -bae** (-bi; -biː). 極小的單細胞原生動物;變形蟲。(亦作 **ameba**) **—like,** *adj.*
am·oe·b(a)e·an (,æmɪ'biən; ,æmi'biːən) *adj.* ①〖詩〗對話體的。②=**amoebic.**
a·moe·bic (ə'mibɪk; ə'miːbik) *adj.* ①變形蟲的。②似變形蟲的。③阿米巴性的疾病。(亦作 **amebic**)
amoebic dysentery 阿米巴痢疾;「變形蟲痢疾。」
a·moe·boid (ə'mibɔɪd; ə'miːbɔid) *adj.* 〖生物〗似變形蟲的。(亦作 **ameboid**)
‡**a·mong** (ə'mʌŋ; ə'mʌŋ) *prep.* ①在…中;在一類中。That book is the best *among* modern novels. 在近代小說中,那本書是最好的。②在…所圍繞之中。The town lies *among* the mountains. 此鎮位在羣山中。③於…之間(分配)。④共同聯合之動作。⑤互相。They fought *among* themselves. 他們互相殘殺。⑥及於全體。〖注意〗**among, between** 均指在…之間。among 通常指其受詞在兩個以上者。而 between 則指其受詞僅爲兩個者。但 between 之受詞有時亦有在兩個以上者,不過此等用法須强調每兩者間之關係: A treaty was concluded *between* the five powers. 五强之間已締結條約。
***a·mongst** (ə'mʌŋst; ə'mʌŋst) *prep.* = **among.**
A·mor ('emɔr; 'eimɔː) *n.* 愛神(=Cupid).
a·mor·al (e'mɔrəl; æ'mɔrəl) *adj.* 非道德的;超道德的;與道德無關的。
a·morce (ə'mɔrs; ə'mɔːs) *n.* 信管火藥;點火藥起爆劑。
am·o·rist ('æmərɪst; 'æmərist) *n.* ①情人;情郎。②愛情小說作者。
am·o·rous ('æmərəs; 'æmərəs) *adj.* ①多情的;傾向於愛情的。②在愛情中的。③表示愛情的。*amorous* glances. 秋波。④關於愛情的。*amorous* songs. 情歌。**—ly,** *adv.* **—ness,** *n.*
a·mor pa·tri·ae ('emɔr'petrɪ,i; 'eimɔː'peitriiː) 〖拉〗愛國心(=patriotism).
a·mor·phism (ə'mɔrfɪzəm; ə'mɔːfizəm) *n.* ①無定形;無組織。②非結晶。
a·mor·phous (ə'mɔrfəs; ə'mɔːfəs) *adj.* ①無定形的;無組織的;模糊的。②非結晶形的。(亦作 **amorphic**)
a·mor·ti·za·tion (,æmətə'zeʃən; ə,mɔːti'zeiʃən) *n.* ①(用減債基金等方法)逐漸償還。②償還金。(亦作 **amortizement**)
a·mor·tize ('æmə,taɪz; ə'mɔːtaiz) *v.t.,* **-tized, -tiz·ing.** ①(用減債基金等方法)逐漸償還。②〖法律〗讓渡(財產)成爲永遠管業;讓(不動產)與法人。
A·mos ('eməs; 'eimɔs) *n.* 〖聖經〗①阿摩司(希伯來先知)。②(舊約之)阿摩司書。
‡**a·mount** (ə'maunt; ə'maunt) *n.* ①總數;總額。The *amount* of seven and eight is fifteen. 七加八之總數爲十五。②效力;價值;範圍;程度;力量。③數量。There is a large *amount* of work for us to do. 大量的工作在等我們動手。④本利和。***gross amount*** 約計;概數。***in amount*** 在數量上。***net amount*** 細數。—*v.i.* ①總計;共達。Our debt *amounted* to two hundred dollars. 我們的債共達二百元。②等於;近於。③不啻。④成爲〖常 to〗.
a·mour (ə'mur; ə'muə) *n.* 戀情;姦情。
a·mour-pro·pre (amur'prɔpr; 'æmuə'prɔpr) 〖法〗*n.* 自尊;自愛。
A·moy (ə'mɔɪ; ə'mɔi) *n.* 厦門。
amp (æmp; æmp) *n.* ①=**ampere.** ②=**amplifier.** ③〖美俚〗電吉他。
amp. ①amperage. ②ampere(s).
AMPAS, A.M.P.A.S. Academy of Motion Picture Arts and Sciences.
Am·père (æm'pɪr; 'æmpɛə) *n.* 安培(André Marie, 1775–1836, 法國物理學家)。
am·pere ('æmpɪr; 'æmpɛə) *n.* 安培(計算電流强度之標準單位)。
am·pere·hour ('æmpɪr'aur; 'æmpiə'auə) *n.* 〖物理〗安(培小)時。
am·pere·me·ter ('æmpɪr,mitə; 'æmpiə,miːtə) *n.* 電流計;安培計。
ampere's law 〖物理〗安培定律。
ampere turn 〖電〗安培匝數。
am·per·sand ('æmpəs,ænd; 'æmpəsænd) *n.* 表示 and 的符號 &。
amphi- 〖字首〗表"兩;兩者;兩側"之義,如: amphiaster.
Am·phib·i·a (æm'fɪbɪə; æm'fibiə) *n.* 「*pl.* 〖動物〗兩棲類。」
am·phib·i·an (æm'fɪbɪən; æm'fibiən) *n.* ①水陸兩棲的生物。②水陸兩用的飛機或坦克。—*adj.* ①水陸兩棲的。②水陸均可升降的。
am·phib·i·ol·o·gy (æm,fɪbɪ'ɑlədʒɪ; æm,fibi'ɔlədʒi) *n.* 兩棲動物學。
am·phi·bi·ot·ic (,æmfɪbaɪ'ɑtɪk; ,æmfibai'ɔtik) *adj.* 幼時生長於水中而成長後生活於陸地的(動物)。
am·phib·i·ous (æm'fɪbɪəs; æm'fibiəs) *adj.* ①水陸兩棲的。②水陸兩用的。③陸海空軍協同作戰的。④有兩種特性、種類、性質、部分的。**—ly,** *adv.* **—ness,** *n.*
amphibious corps 水陸兩棲機動「部隊。」
amphibious warfare 兩棲作戰。
am·phi·bole ('æmfɪ,bol; 'æmfiboul) *n.* 〖礦〗角閃石。
am·phi·bol·ic (,æmfɪ'bɑlɪk; ,æmfi'bɔlik) *adj.* ①意義不明的。②角閃石的。
am·phi·bol·o·gy (,æmfɪ'bɑlədʒɪ; ,æmfi'bɔlədʒi) *n., pl.* **-gies.** 模棱兩可之言辭(文章);曖昧的文句。(亦作 **amphiboly**)
am·phib·o·lous (æm'fɪbələs; æm'fibələs) *adj.* 意義曖昧的;模棱兩可的。
am·phi·brach ('æmfɪ,bræk; 'æmfibræk) *n.* 〖詩〗抑揚抑格。
am·phi·cra·ni·a (,æmfɪ'krenɪə; ,æmfi'kreiniə) *n.* 〖醫〗兩側頭痛。
am·phi·go·ry ('æmfɪ,gorɪ; 'æmfigəri) *n., pl.* **-ries.** 無意義之詩或文章。(亦作 **amphigouri**) **—am·phi·gor·ic,** *adj.*
am·phi·mix·is (,æmfɪ'mɪksɪs; ,æmfi'miksis) *n.* 〖生物〗兩性生殖;兩性合體。
am·phi·ox·us (,æmfɪ'ɑksəs; ,æmfi'ɔksəs) *n.* 〖動物〗蛞蝓。
am·phip·ro·style (æm'fɪprə,staɪl; æm'fiprəstail) *n.* 〖建築〗兩排柱式之建築。
am·phis·bae·na (,æmfɪs'binə; ,æmfis'biːnə) *n.* ①〖動物〗無足蜥蜴。②(古典神

話之)雙頭蛇。
am·phi·the·a·ter, am·phi·the·a·tre ['æmfə,θiətɚ; 'æmfi,θiətə] *n.* ①鬥技場。②圓形劇場。③四面環有小山的平地。 —**am·phi·the·at·ri·cal,** *adj.*
Am·phit·ry·on [æm'fɪtrɪɑn; æm'fitriən] *n.* ①〖希臘神話〗底比斯之一國王。②東道主;主人。
am·pho·ra ['æmfərə; 'æmfərə] *n., pl.* **-ras, -rae** [-,ri; -riː]. (古羅馬、希臘人盛酒或油之)雙耳長頸瓶。—**am·pho·ral,** *adj.*
am·phor·ic [æm'fɑrɪk; æm'fɔrik] *adj.* 〖醫〗空甕性的。
***am·ple** ['æmpl; 'æmpl] *adj.,* **-pler, -plest.** ①富足的; 充足的。There is *ample* time, so you don't have to hurry. 時間很充足, 你用不着匆忙。②廣大的; 廣闊的。—**ness,** *n.* —**am·ply,** *adv.*
am·pli·fi·ca·tion [,æmpləfə'keʃən; ,æmplifi'keiʃən] *n.* ①擴大;擴張。②擴大率;倍率。③〖電〗增幅;擴大。
am·pli·fi·er ['æmplə,faɪɚ; 'æmplifaiə] *n.* ①擴大者。②〖無線電〗放大器;擴音機。
am·pli·fy ['æmplə,faɪ; 'æmplifai] *v.,* **-fied, -fy·ing.** —*v.t.* ①放大;擴大;擴展。②詳述;詳說。③加强;放大(聲音或電流)。④誇大其辭。—*v.i.* 詳述;詳說〖on〗.
am·pli·tude ['æmplə,tjud; 'æmplitjuːd] *n.* ①廣闊;寬大。②豐富;充足。③〖物理,電〗振幅。④〖軍〗射程;彈着距離。⑤〖數學〗偏角。⑥〖天文〗天體出沒方位角。
amplitude modulation 〖物理〗振幅調節;調幅(略作 **AM** 或 **A.M.**).
am·poule ['æmpul; 'æmpuːl] *n.* 〖醫〗壺腹玻管;安瓿。(亦作 **ampule**)
am·pul·la [æm'pʌlə; æm'pulə] *n., pl.* **-las, -lae** [-li; -liː]. ①〖解剖〗壺腹;內耳壜。②〖宗教〗**a.** 聖酒瓶;聖水瓶。**b.** 聖油瓶。③(古羅馬人用於裝油等之)細頸壜。
am·pul·la·ceous [,æmpə'leʃəs; ,æmpə'leiʃəs] *adj.* 似細頸壜的;瓶形的。(亦作 **ampullar, ampullary**)
am·pu·tate ['æmpjə,tet; 'æmpjuteit] *v.t.,* **-tat·ed, -tat·ing.** ①切斷;切除;鋸掉。②減除;修剪 (花草樹木等)。 —**am·pu·ta·tion, am·pu·ta·tor,** *n.*
am·pu·tee [,æmpjʊ'ti; ,æmpju'tiː] *n.* 被切斷手或足的人。
Am·ster·dam ['æmstɚ,dæm; 'æmstə'dæm] *n.* 阿姆斯特丹 (荷蘭的名義首都; The Hague 爲行政首都)。
A.M.S.W. Master of Arts in Social Work.
amt. amount.
am·trac ['æm,træk; 'æmtræk] *n.* 水陸兩用登陸車。(亦作 **amtrack**)
Am·trak ['æm'træk; 'æm'træk] *n.* 美國國家鐵路客運公司。
amu atomic mass unit.
a·muck [ə'mʌk; ə'mʌk] *adv. & adj.* 狂亂地(的)。***run amuck*** 發殺人狂;橫衝直撞地亂幹。(亦作 **amok**)
am·u·let ['æmjəlɪt; 'æmjulit] *n.*護身符。
A. Mus. Associate in Music.
A. Mus. D. Doctor of Musical Arts.
***a·muse** [ə'mjuz; ə'mjuːz] *v.t.,* **a·mused, a·mus·ing.** ①使笑;使樂。We were *amused* by his funny appearance. 他滑稽的樣子,使我們發笑。②消遣;娛樂。I *amused* myself by reading detective stories. 我讀偵探小說消遣。—**a·mused,** *adj.*
***a·muse·ment** [ə'mjuzmənt; ə'mjuːzmənt] *n.* 娛樂;消遣。
amusement park 遊樂園。
amusement tax 娛樂稅。
***a·mus·ing** [ə'mjuzɪŋ; ə'mjuːziŋ] *adj.* ①有趣的。It was *amusing* to me. 這對我是有趣的。②引人發笑的。—**ly,** *adv.*
a·mu·sive [ə'mjuzɪv; ə'mjuːziv] *adj.* 好笑的;有趣的。—**ly,** *adv.* —**ness,** *n.*
Am·vets ['æm,vɛts; 'æmvets] *n. pl.* 二次大戰美國退伍軍人協會(創於1944年)。
A·my ['emɪ; 'eimi] *n.* 女子名。
a·myg·da·la [ə'mɪgdələ; ə'migdələ] *n., pl.* **-lae** [-,li; -liː]. ①杏仁;扁桃。②〖解剖〗扁桃腺。
am·yl ['æmɪl; 'æmil] *n.* 〖化〗五碳烷基; 戊烷基。
am·y·la·ceous [,æmɪ'leʃəs; ,æmi'leiʃəs] *adj.* 澱粉的;澱粉質的。
amyl alcohol 〖化〗戊醇(用以作溶劑)。
am·yl·ase ['æmɪ,les; 'æmileis] *n.* 澱粉酶。
am·y·loid ['æmɪ,lɔɪd; 'æmilɔid] *adj.* 似澱粉的;含澱粉的。—*n.*澱粉質食物;澱粉體。
am·y·lol·y·sis [,æmɪ'lɑləsɪs; ,æmi'lɔləsis] *n.* 〖生化〗澱粉分解。
am·y·lop·sin [,æmɪ'lɑpsɪn; ,æmi'lɔpsin] *n.* 胰澱粉酶。
a·my·o·to·ni·a [,emaɪə'tonɪə; ,eimaiə'tounia] *n.* 〖醫〗肌强直。(亦作**myotonia**)
‡**an** [*unstressed* ən; ən *stressed* æn; æn] *adj.* or *indefinite article.* ①一;一個。*an* honest man. 一個誠實人。②每;各。
an. ①anno (拉=in the year). ②anonymous. ③answer. ④ante (拉=before).
-an 〖字尾〗加於名詞之尾構成形容詞表下列各義: ①"…的;屬於…的; 有…之特色的," 例: diocesan. ②"在…出生的;在…居住的,"例: American. ③"信仰…的; 服從…的," 例: Mohammedan. (在母音後亦作 -n)
AN, AN., A.N. Anglo-Norman.
A.N. ①Anglo-Norman. ②Associate in Nursing.
ANA, A.N.A. American Nurses Association.
-ana 〖字尾〗用於把專有名詞構成集體複數,表"言論;逸聞;實況"之義, 例: Americana.
a·na ['enə, 'ɑnə; 'ɑːnə] *n.* 語錄; 軼事。
ana- 〖字首〗表"上;後;再"之義。
An·a·bap·tism [,ænə'bæptɪzəm; ,ænə'bæptizəm] *n.* ①再洗禮派之教義;再洗禮論。②(a-) 再洗禮。
An·a·bap·tist [,ænə'bæptɪst; ,ænə'bæptist] *n.* ①再洗禮派教徒。②(*pl.*) 再洗禮派。—*adj.*再洗禮派的。
an·a·bas ['ænə,bæs; 'ænəbæs] *n.* 攀木魚。
a·nab·a·sis [ə'næbəsɪs; ə'næbəsis] *n., pl.* **-ses** [-,siz; -siːz]. ①由海岸向內陸之進軍。②(軍隊之)遠征。
an·a·bat·ic [,ænə'bætɪk; ,ænə'bætik] *adj.* 〖氣象〗上升的(氣流)。
a·nab·o·lism [ə'næbl,ɪzəm; ə'næbəlizəm] *n.* 〖生物〗養料之同化作用;組成代謝。—**an·a·bol·ic,** *adj.*
an·a·branch ['ænə,bræntʃ; 'ænəbrɑːntʃ] *n.* ①(河流之) 與主流分離又再流入之支流。②被沙地所吸收的支流。
a·nach·ro·nism [ə'nækrə,nɪzəm; ə'nækrənizəm] *n.* ①時代錯誤。②過時或不合時宜的人或事物。
a·nach·ro·nis·tic [ə,nækrə'nɪstɪk;

ə,nækrə'nistik] *adj.* 年代錯誤的。

a·nach·ro·nous [ə'nækrənəs; ə'nækrənəs] *adj.* 年代錯置的;時代錯誤的。

an·a·cid·i·ty [,ænə'sɪdətɪ; ,ænə'siditi] *n.*〖醫〗胃酸缺乏症;無酸症。

an·a·clas·tic [,ænə'klæstɪk; ,ænə'klæstik] *adj.*〖光學〗有折光性的;屈折的。②〖解剖〗反曲的;反彎的。

an·a·co·lu·thi·a [,ænəkə'luθɪə; ,ænəkə'lu:θiə] *n.*〖修辭〗缺乏文法上的層次或連貫性。

an·a·co·lu·thon [,ænəkə'luθɑn; ,ænəkə'lu:θɔn] *n.*, *pl.* **-tha** [-θə; -θə].〖文法〗破格文體。

an·a·con·da [,ænə'kɑndə; ,ænə'kɔndə] *n.*〖動物〗產於熱帶林的一種蟒蛇;森蚺。

A·nac·re·on [ə'nækrɪən; ə'nækriən] *n.*亞奈科雷昂(572?–488?B.C., 希臘抒情詩人)。

A·nac·re·on·tic [ə,nækrɪ'ɑntɪk; ə,nækri'ɑ:ntik] *adj.* ①亞奈科雷昂的;有亞奈科雷昂之風的。②讚揚愛情與美酒的。—*n.*亞奈科雷昂風格之詩。(亦作 **anacreontic**)

an·a·cru·sis [,ænə'krusɪs; ,ænə'kru:sis] *n.*〖韻律〗行首額外音節。

an·a·cu·sia [,ænə'kjuʒə; ,ænə'kjuʒiə] *n.*〖醫〗全聾。—**an·a·cu·sic,** *adj.*

an·a·dem ['ænə,dɛm; 'ænədem] *n.*〖詩〗頭飾之花圈;花冠;花環。

a·nad·ro·mous [ə'nædrəməs; ə'nædrəməs] *adj.* 由海入河產卵的;溯河性的。

a·nae·mi·a [ə'nimɪə; ə'ni:mjə] *n.*〖醫〗貧血症;貧血。

a·nae·mic [ə'nimɪk; ə'ni:mik] *adj.* 貧血的;貧血症的。

an·aer·obe [æn'eə,rob; æn'eiəroub] *n.*〖生物〗厭氧生物;厭氧菌。

an·aer·o·bic [æn,eə'robɪk; æn,eiə'roubik] *adj.*〖生物〗①厭氧性的。②無氧的;由無氧所引起的。

an·aes·the·sia [,ænəs'θiʒə; ,ænis'θi:zjə] *n.*〖醫〗麻木;麻醉;失去知覺。

an·aes·thet·ic [,ænəs'θɛtɪk; ,ænis'θetik] *n.* 麻醉劑。—*adj.*麻醉的。

an·a·gram ['ænə,græm; 'ænəgræm] *n.* ①顚倒字母而成的字或短語(如將 lived 改爲 devil 卽是)。②(*pl.*)此種遊戲或字謎。

an·a·gram·ma·tize [,ænə'græmə,taɪz; ,ænə'græmətaiz] *v.t.* & *v.i.*, **-tized, -tiz·ing.** 作字謎。

a·nal ['enl̩; 'einəl] *adj.* 肛門的;近肛門的。

anal. ①analogy. ②analysis. ③analytic.

an·a·lects ['ænə,lɛkts; 'ænəlekts] *n.* *pl.*文選;語錄;選集。(亦作 **analecta**)

an·a·lep·tic [,ænə'lɛptɪk; ,ænə'leptik] *adj.*〖醫〗①復元的;强壯的。②醒轉來的。—*n.*〖醫〗强壯劑;興奮劑。

an·al·ge·si·a [,ænæl'dʒizɪə; ,ænæl'dʒi:zjə] *n.*〖醫〗痛感缺失。

an·al·ge·sic [,ænæl'dʒizɪk; ,ænæl'dʒesik] *adj.*〖醫〗痛感缺失的;止痛的。—*n.* 鎭痛劑;止痛藥。(亦作 **analgetic**)

an·a·log·i·cal [,ænl̩'ɑdʒɪkl̩; ,ænə'lɔdʒikəl] *adj.* 類似的;相似的;類推的;類比的。(亦作 **analogic**) —**ly,** *adv.*

a·nal·o·gist [ə'nælədʒɪst; ə'nælədʒist] *n.* 類比推理者;類推或推論之人。

a·nal·o·gize [ə'nælə,dʒaɪz; ə'nælədʒaiz] *v.*, **-gized, -giz·ing.** —*v.i.* 推論;用類推法作推理。—*v.t.* 用類推法說明。

a·nal·o·gous [ə'næləgəs; ə'næləgəs] *adj.* 類似的;相似的。—**ly,** *adv.* —**ness,** *n.*

an·a·logue ['ænl̩,ɔg; 'ænəlɔg] *n.* ①相似物;類似物。②〖語言〗類似語;同源字。③〖生物〗相似器官。④地位或職務相似的人。

a·nal·o·gy [ə'nælədʒɪ; ə'nælədʒi] *n.*, *pl.* **-gies.** ①相似;類似;相似之處。②類推。③〖生物〗類似關係。④語言類推法(卽按語言形態創造新字的方法)。

an·al·pha·bet·ic [,ænælfə'bɛtɪk; 'ænælfə'betik] *adj.* ①目不識丁的;文盲的。②不按字母次序排列的。—*n.*目不識丁者;文盲。

a·nal·y·sis** [ə'næləsɪs; ə'næləsis] *n.*, *pl.* **-ses** [-,siz; -si:z]. ①分析。chemical *analysis.* 化學分析。②梗概;要略;綱領。③〖數學〗解析。in the last*** (or ***final***) ***analysis*** 總之;末了仍是。

analysis situs〖數學〗拓樸(學)。

an·a·lyst ['ænl̩ɪst; 'ænəlist] *n.* 分析者;解析者。

analyt. analytical.

an·a·lyt·ic [,ænl̩'ɪtɪk; ,ænə'litik] *adj.* 分析的;解析的。

an·a·lyt·i·cal [,ænl̩'ɪtɪkl̩; ,ænə'litikəl] *adj.* =**analytic.** —**ly,** *adv.*

analytical balance 一種極爲精密的天平(供化學分析用)。

analytical chemistry 分析化學。

analytical geometry 解析幾何學。

analytical method〖邏輯〗分析法。

an·a·lyt·ics [,ænl̩'ɪtɪks; ,ænə'litiks] *n.* ①〖數學〗解析學。②〖邏輯〗分析論。

an·a·lyz·a·ble ['ænl̩,aɪzəbl̩; 'ænəlaizəbl] *adj.* 可被分析的;可予分解的。(亦作 **analysable**)

***an·a·lyze** ['ænl̩,aɪz; 'ænəlaiz] *v.t.*, **-lyzed, -lyz·ing.** ①分析。to *analyze* a sentence. 分析句子。②審察;細察。(亦作 **analyse**)—**an·a·ly·za·tion, an·a·lyz·er,** *n.*

analyzed rhyme 四行詩中所用之半韻體(卽每隔一行子音不同而母音相同, 如: head, mat, met, had)。

an·am·ne·sis [,ænæm'nisɪs; ,ænæm'ni:sis] *n.* ①回憶;回想;想起;(尤指)假想的前世生活的回憶。②〖醫〗病歷;既往症。

an·a·mor·pho·sis [,ænə'mɔrfəsɪs; ,ænə'mɔ:fəsis] *n.*, *pl.* **-ses** [-,siz; -si:z]. ①歪形;歪像;歪像描法。②〖植物〗畸形;變體。③〖生物〗漸變進化;漸進變化。

a·na·nas [ə'nɑnəs; ə'nɑ:nəs] *n.*〖植物〗①鳳梨(=pineapple). ②(A-)鳳梨屬。

an·an·drous [æn'ændrəs; æn'ændrəs] *adj.*〖植物〗無雄蕊的;隱花的。

An·a·ni·as [,ænə'naɪəs; ,ænə'naiəs] *n.* ①〖聖經〗亞拿尼亞(因撒謊而暴斃之人)。②〖俗〗撒謊的人。

an·an·thous [æn'ænθəs; æn'ænθəs] *adj.*〖植物〗無花的。

an·a·pest, an·a·paest ['ænə,pɛst; 'ænəpest] *n.* ①〖韻律〗抑抑揚格。②抑抑揚格的一行詩。—**ic,** *adj.* —**i·cal·ly,** *adv.*

a·naph·o·ra [ə'næfərə; ə'næfərə] *n.*〖修辭〗首語重複法。

an·aph·ro·dis·i·a [æn,æfrə'dɪzɪə; æn,æfrə'diziə] *n.* 無性慾;陽萎。

an·a·plas·tic [,ænə'plæstɪk; ,ænə'plæstik] *adj.*〖外科〗成形手術的;整形術的。

an·a·ple·ro·sis [,ænəplə'rosɪs; ,ænəplə'rousis] *n.*, *pl.* **-ses** [-siz; -si:z]. 整形術。

an·arch ['ænɑrk; 'ænɑ:k] *n.* 無政府主義者。

an·ar·chi·cal [æn'ɑrkɪkl̩; æ'nɑ:kikəl] *adj.* 無政府主義的。(亦作 **anarchic**)

an·ar·chism ['ænəˌkɪzəm; 'ænəkizəm] *n.* ①無政府主義。②無政府主義的方法或其實行。③恐怖;無法無天。
an·arch·ist ['ænəkɪst; 'ænəkist] *n.* 無政府主義者。—*adj.* =**anarchistic.**
an·ar·chis·tic [ˌænə'kɪstɪk; ˌænə'kistik] *adj.* 無政府主義(者)的。
anarcho- 〖字首〗表"無政府主義者的"之義。
an·ar·chy ['ænəkɪ; 'ænəki] *n.* ①無政府(狀態)。②混亂;迷混。
an·ar·thri·a [æ'nɑrθrɪə; æ'nɑːθriə] *n.* 〖醫〗口齒不清。
an·ar·throus [æ'nɑrθrəs; æ'nɑːθrəs] *adj.* ①〖動物〗無關節的。②〖希臘文法〗用時無須加冠詞的。
an·a·sar·ca [ˌænə'sɑrkə; ˌænə'sɑːkə] *n.* 〖醫〗普遍性水腫;皮下水腫。
an·as·tig·mat [æ'næstɪgˌmæt; ə'næstigmæt] *n.* 〖照相〗去像散透鏡。
an·as·tig·mat·ic [ˌænəstɪg'mætɪk; ˌænəstig'mætik] *adj.* ①無像散性的;無像散現象的。②〖醫〗無散光的。
a·nas·to·mose [ə'næstəˌmoz; ə'næstəmouz] *v.i.* & *v.t.*, **-mosed, -mos·ing.** 藉交接或吻合而相連;接合;癒合;合流;吻合。
a·nas·to·mo·sis [əˌnæstə'mosɪs; əˌnæstə'mousis] *n.*, *pl.* **-ses** [-siz; -siːz]. ①(血管、葉脈、河之支流等之)交接;接合。②〖外科〗吻合;癒合。
anat. ①anatomy. ②anatomical.
a·nath·e·ma [ə'næθəmə; ə'næθimə] *n.*, *pl.* **-mas.** ①〖宗教〗呪逐;革出教門。②(一般之)呪罵;呪詛。③被呪逐之人或物。④遭人嫌惡的人或物。
a·nath·e·ma·tize [ə'næθəməˌtaɪz; ə'næθimətaiz] *v.t.* & *v.i.*, **-tized, -tiz·ing.** 呪;呪逐;呪詛。(亦作 **anathematise**)
An·a·to·li·a [ˌænə'tolɪə; ˌænə'touljə] *n.* ①安那托利亞(小亞細亞之舊稱)。②安那托利亞(現代土耳其之亞洲部分)。
an·a·tom·ic [ˌænə'tɑmɪk; ˌænə'tɔmik] *adj.* ①解剖的;解剖學上的。②構造上的。
a·nat·o·mist [ə'nætəmɪst; ə'nætəmist] *n.* 解剖者;解剖學者;分析者。
a·nat·o·mize [ə'nætəˌmaɪz; ə'nætəmaiz] *v.t.*, **-mized, -miz·ing.** ①解剖。②分析;細審。
***a·nat·o·my** [ə'nætəmɪ; ə'nætəmi] *n.*, *pl.* **-mies.** ①解剖。②解剖學。human *anatomy*. 人體解剖學。③(動物或植物的)構造;身體結構。④分析;細審。⑤骸骨;骨骼。⑥〖俗〗人體。
an·bur·y ['ænbərɪ; 'ænbəri] *n.* ①(牛馬等之)軟瘤。②〖植物〗塊莖腫大病。
anc. ①ancient. ②anciently.
-ance 〖字尾〗表"動作;狀態;性質"之義。
***an·ces·tor** ['ænsɛstɚ; 'ænsistə] *n.* ①祖先;祖宗。*ancestor* worship. 供奉祖先。②最初之物;起源。③始祖。
an·ces·tral [æn'sɛstrəl; æn'sestrəl] *adj.* 祖先的;祖宗傳下的。—**ly,** *adv.*
an·ces·tress ['ænsɛstrɪs; 'ænsistris] *n.* ancestor 之女性。
an·ces·try ['ænsɛstrɪ; 'ænsistri] *n.*, *pl.* **-tries.** ①祖先;世系。②門第。
an·chor** ['æŋkɚ; 'æŋkə] *n.* ①錨。②和錨相似的東西。③使人覺得穩定或安全的東西。Hope is his *anchor.* 希望是他的安定力。④拔河隊排在最後的一人。⑤接力賽中最後接棒者。⑥防線中之重要陣地。cast*** (or ***drop***) ***an anchor*** 拋錨。***come to an anchor*** 停船下碇;停泊。***ride*** (***lie,*** or ***be***) ***at anchor*** 停泊。***weigh an anchor*** **a.** 起錨。**b.** 準備離開某處。—*v.t.* ①拋錨;泊船。②使穩定;使穩固。③擔任接力賽中的最後接棒者。④固定;扣牢。—*v.i.* ①拋錨。The ship *anchored* along the shore. 這船沿岸拋錨。②固着。—**a·ble, —like,** *adj.* **—less,** *adj.*
an·chor·age ['æŋkərɪdʒ; 'æŋkəridʒ] *n.* ①停泊。②停泊所。③停泊稅。
anchor ball 船在停泊時掛在桅檣上的大黑球。
anchor bed 錨床(船頭放置錨的斜台)。
anchor bell 船在霧中停泊時用以通知其他船隻的鐘。
anchor buoy 標示下錨地點之浮筒。
anchor deck 用來操作錨的機械房。
an·cho·ress ['æŋkərɪs; 'æŋkəris] *n.* 女隱者;女隱士。(亦作 **ancress**)
an·cho·ret·ic [ˌæŋkə'rɛtɪk; ˌæŋkə'retik] *adj.* 隱士的;隱遁的。
an·chor-hold ['æŋkɚˌhold; 'æŋkəhould] *n.* ①錨力;掛錨的地基。②(喻)安全。③隱士所居之茅舍。
an·cho·rite ['æŋkəˌraɪt; 'æŋkərait] *n.* 隱者;隱士;隱遁者。(亦作 **anchoret**)
anchor light 夜間掛在船首的指示燈。
anchor man ①接力賽隊中最後接棒者。②機關、團體等成敗關鍵所繫者;中堅分子。
anchor ring 〖幾何〗環面。
anchor watch 船在停泊時值班之人。
an·cho·vy ['æntʃəvɪ; 'æntʃəvi] *n.*, *pl.* **-vies.** 鯷類。*anchovy* sauce. 鯷魚醬。
anchovy pear 一種產於西印度羣島的果實,與芒果類似。
an·chy·lose ['æŋkɪˌlos; 'æŋkilous] *v.t.* & *v.i.*, **-losed, -los·ing.** =**ankylose.**
an·chy·lo·sis [ˌæŋkaɪ'losɪs; ˌæŋkai'lousis] *n.* =**ankylosis.**
an·cienne no·blesse [ɑ̃'sjɛnˌno'blɛs; ɑːn'sjennou'bles] 〖法〗法國大革命前之貴族。
an·cien ré·gime [ɑ̃sjæ̃·re'ʒim; ɑːn'sjænrei'ʒiːm] 〖法〗法國大革命前之社會及政治制度。
‡**an·cient**[1] ['enʃənt; 'einʃənt] *adj.* ①古代的;遠古的。②舊的;古的。an *ancient* custom. 舊俗。③舊式的。—*n.* 老人。***the ancients*** 古代的人;古人。—**ness,** *n.* —**ly,** *adv.*
an·cient[2] *n.* ①扛旗者。②旗幟。
Ancient of Days 永恒之神;上帝。
an·cient·ry ['enʃəntrɪ; 'einʃəntri] *n.* ①古老;古風;古式;舊式。②古代;遠古。
an·cil·la·ry ['ænsəˌlɛrɪ; æn'siləri] *adj.* 輔助的;附隨的;附屬的〖to〗. —*n.* 輔助者;幫忙者;僕人。
an·con ['æŋkɑn; 'æŋkɔn] *n.*, *pl.* **an·co·nes** [æŋ'konɪz; æŋ'kouniz]. ①〖解剖〗肘。②〖建築〗肱木。
-ancy 〖字尾〗**-ance** 之變體。
an·cy·los·to·mi·a·sis [ˌænsɪˌlɑstə'maɪəsɪs; ˌænsiˌlɔstə'maiəsis] *n.* 〖醫〗十二指腸蟲病;鉤蟲病。(亦作 **ankylostomiasis**)
‡**and** [*stressed* ɛnd; ænd *untressed* ənd, ən; ənd, ən] *conj.* ①及;和;又;而;並;亦。I gave him one hundred *and* two dollars 我給他一百零二元。②而;則(含有結果之意)。The sun came out *and* the grass dried. 日出而草乾。③而;則(含有假定之意)。④而且(加重之意)。He did the work, *and*

he did it well. 他做此事，而且做得好。⑤而(相反之意)。He is so rich *and* lives like a beggar. 他如此之富，而生活得像乞丐。⑥於是；然後。He read for an hour *and* went to bed. 他讀了一小時書，然後就去睡了。⑦同時。to sleep *and* dream. 睡覺並(同時)做夢。⑧用在句子的開頭以表示連續性。*And* he said unto Moses. 接着他對摩西說。⑨特別用法。Come *and* see (=Come to see). 來看。***and/or*** 及(或)。***and so*** 所以；因此(=so). He aimed straight, *and so* hit the mark. 他瞄得準，所以射中目標。***and so on*** (***and so forth, and the like,*** or ***and what not***) 等等。***and then*** 然後；其次。***and yet*** 然而。***by twos and threes*** 三三兩兩地。***for miles and miles*** 好多好多英里。—*n.* ①附加條件。He accepted the job, no *and* about it. 他接受了這分工作，沒有附帶條件。②(常*pl.*)附帶的細節。〖注意〗**and** 是同位連接詞，其所連接之字、片語、或子句必須在文法上屬於同類者。

and. andante.

An·da·lu·sia [ˌændəˈluʒə; ˌændəˈluːzjə] *n.* 安大路西亞(西班牙南部之一區域)。—**An·da·lu·sian,** *n., adj.*

an·dan·te [ænˈdæntɪ; ænˈdænti] *adj. & adv.*〖音樂〗緩慢；溫和。—*n.*緩慢溫和之節拍或曲子；行板。

an·dan·ti·no [ˌændænˈtino; ˌændænˈtiːnou] *adj., adv., n., pl.* **-nos.** —*adj. & adv.*〖音樂〗微急的(地)(較 andante 稍速)。—*n.*微急之節拍或曲子；小行板。

An·de·an [ænˈdiən; ænˈdiːən] *adj.* 南美安地斯(Andes)山脈的；其居民的。—*n.* 安地斯山脈之居民。

An·der·sen [ˈændɚsn̩; ˈændəsn] *n.* 安徒生(Hans Christian, 1805–1875, 丹麥童話作家)。

An·der·son[1] [ˈændɚsn̩; ˈændəsn] *n.* 安德生(Sherwood, 1876–1941, 美國詩人及小說作家)。

An·der·son[2] *n.* 安德生夫人(Marian, 1902–, 美國黑人女低音歌唱家)。

Anderson shelter〖英〗家庭防空洞。

An·des [ˈændiz; ˈændiːz] *n. pl.* 安地斯山(南美西部之大山脈)。

an·des·ite [ˈændɪˌzaɪt; ˈændizait] *n.*〖礦〗中性長石。

and·i·ron [ˈændˌaɪɚn; ˈændaiən] *n.* 「(壁爐之)柴架。」

An·dor·ra [ænˈdɔrə; ænˈdɔrə] *n.* 安道爾共和國(在法西交界之庇里牛斯山中)；又該國之首都。

An·drew [ˈændru; ˈændruː] *n.* ①〖聖經〗安得烈(耶穌十二使徒之一)。②男子名。

An·dric [ˈandrɪk; ˈɑːndrik] *n.* 安德烈克(Ivo, 1892–, 南斯拉夫詩人兼小說家，曾得1961年諾貝爾文學獎)。

an·dro·cen·tric [ˌændrəˈsɛntrɪk; ˌændrəˈsentrik] *adj.* 爲男性所控制的；代表男性利益的。

an·droe·ci·um [ænˈdriʃɪəm; ænˈdriʃiəm] *n., pl.* **-ci·a** [-ʃɪə; -ʃiə].〖植物〗雄蕊。

an·dro·gen [ˈændrədʒən; ˈændrədʒən] *n.*〖生化〗男性素；雄性激素。—**ic,** *adj.*

an·drog·y·nous [ænˈdrɑdʒənəs; ænˈdrɔdʒinəs] *adj.* ①陰陽人的。②〖植物〗(一花序中)有雌雄兩花的；雌雄花同座的。

an·droid [ˈændrɔɪd; ˈændrɔid] *n.* 機器人。—*adj.* 陽性的；男性的。

An·drom·e·da [ænˈdrɑmɪdə; ænˈdrɔmidə] *n.* ①〖希臘神話〗衣索比亞公主。②〖天文〗仙女座。③一種常綠矮樹。

an·dro·pho·bi·a [ˌændrəˈfobɪə; ˌændrəˈfoubiə] *n.* 男性恐怖；憎惡男性病。

an·dros·ter·one [ænˈdrɑstɚˌon; ænˈdrɔstəroun] *n.* 〖生化〗雄素酮；男性酮；雄固酮。

An·dy [ˈændɪ; ˈændi] *n.* 男子名(Andrew 之暱稱)。

ane [en; ein] *adj., n., pron.*〖方〗=one.

-ane〖字尾〗形容詞語尾，係 -an 之變體，但此二種語尾俱有之字，含義不同，例：humane, human.

a·near [əˈnɪr; əˈniə] *adv.*〖方〗幾乎。—*prep.*〖方，詩〗緊接於。—*adj.* 接近的。

an·ec·dot·age [ˈænɪkˌdotɪdʒ; ˈænekˌdoutidʒ] *n.* ①逸事集；逸事(集合稱)。②〖諧〗老耄；老年。

an·ec·do·tal [ˌænɪkˈdotl̩; ˌænekˈdoutl] *adj.* ①逸事的；趣聞的。②多逸事趣聞的；含逸事趣聞的。

***an·ec·dote** [ˈænɪkˌdot; ˈænikdout] *n.* 「軼事；逸事。」

an·ec·dot·i·cal [ˌænɪkˈdɑtɪkl̩; ˌænekˈdɔtikl] *adj.* ①逸事的；趣聞的；多逸事趣聞的。②好述逸事趣聞的。(亦作 **anecdotic**)

an·ec·dot·ist [ˈænɪkˌdotɪst; ˈænikdoutist] *n.* 講述或蒐集逸事趣聞的人。

an·e·lec·tric [ˌænɪˈlɛktrɪk; ˌæniˈlektrik] *adj.* 不能因摩擦而起電的。—*n.* 不能摩擦生電之物。

a·ne·mi·a [əˈnimɪə; əˈniːmiə] *n.*〖醫〗貧血；貧血症。(亦作 **anaemia**)

a·ne·mic [əˈnimɪk; əˈniːmik] *adj.* ①貧血的；患貧血症的。②衰弱的。

an·e·moch·o·rous [ˌænəˈmɑkərəs; ˌænəˈmɔkərəs] *adj.* 由風而散布的；風媒的。(亦作 **anemochoric**)

a·nem·o·graph [əˈnɛməˌgræf; əˈneməgræf] *n.* 風力自計表；記風儀。—**ic,** *adj.*

an·e·mom·e·ter [ˌænəˈmɑmətɚ; ˌæniˈmɔmitə] *n.* 風力計；風速計；記風儀。

an·e·mo·met·ric [ˌænəməˈmɛtrɪk; ˌæniməˈmetrik] *adj.* 風力測定的。

an·e·mom·e·try [ˌænɪˈmɑmɪtrɪ; ˌæniˈmɔmitri] *n.* 風力測定；測風法。

***a·nem·o·ne** [əˈnɛməˌni; əˈneməni] *n.*〖植物〗白頭翁；秋牡丹。

an·e·moph·i·lous [ˌænəˈmɑfələs; ˌænəˈmɔfələs] *adj.*〖植物〗風媒的；藉風受粉的。*anemophilous* flower. 風媒花。

an·en·ce·pha·li·a [ˌænənsəˈfelɪə; ˌænənsəˈfeiliə] *n.*〖醫〗無腦畸形。

a·nent [əˈnɛnt; əˈnent] *prep.* 關於。

an·ep·i·graph·ic [ænˌɛpəˈgræfɪk; æˌnepəˈgræfik] *adj.* 沒有題字的。

an·er·oid [ˈænəˌrɔɪd; ˈænərɔid] *adj.*不用液體的。—*n.* 無液氣壓計；無液晴雨表。

aneroid barometer 無液氣壓計；無液晴雨表。

an·es·the·sia [ˌænəsˈθiʒə; ˌænisˈθiːziə] *n.* 麻醉；麻木。(亦作 **anaesthesia**)

an·es·the·si·ol·o·gy [ˌænəsˌθizɪˈɑlədʒɪ; ˌænəsθiːziˈɔlədʒi] *n.*〖醫〗麻醉學。

an·es·thet·ic [ˌænəsˈθɛtɪk; ˌænəsˈθetik] *n.* 麻醉劑；麻藥。—*adj.* 麻醉的；失去知覺的。(亦作 **anaesthetic**)

an·es·the·tist [əˈnɛsθətɪst; əˈnesθətist] *n.* 麻醉師。(亦作 **anaesthetist**)

an·es·the·ti·za·tion [ˌænəsˌθɛtɪˈzeʃən; ˌænəsθetiˈzeiʃən] *n.* ①麻醉狀態；知覺脫失；麻木。②麻醉之施行。

an·es·the·tize [əˈnɛsθəˌtaɪz; əˈnesθətaiz] *v.t.*, **-tized, -tiz·ing.** 使麻醉;使麻木。(亦作 **anaesthetize**)

a·neu·ri·a [əˈnuriə; əˈnuːriːə] *n.* 〖醫〗腦力衰竭。

an·eu·rin [ˈænjurɪn; ˈænjuərin] *n.* 維他命 B_1; 抗神經炎素。(亦作 **aneurine**)

an·eu·rism, an·eu·rysm [ˈænjəˌrɪzəm; ˈænjuərizəm] *n.* 〖醫〗動脈瘤。

an·eu·rys·mal, an·eu·ris·mal [ˌænjəˈrɪzməl; ˌænjuˈrizməl] *adj.* 動脈瘤的。

***a·new** [əˈnju, əˈnu; əˈnjuː] *adv.* 再;重新;另。

an·frac·tu·os·i·ty [ænˌfræktʃuˈɑsətɪ; ˌænfræktjuˈɔsiti] *n.*, *pl.* **-ties.** ①紆曲;千廻百折。②紆曲之水道、走道等。

an·frac·tu·ous [ænˈfræktʃuəs; ænˈfræktʃuəs] *adj.* 紆曲的;多彎曲的。(亦作 **anfractuose**)

A.N.G. American Newspaper Guild.

an·ga·ry [ˈæŋgərɪ; ˈæŋgəri] *n.* 〖國際法〗交戰國必要時可徵用或破壞中立國財產之權;非常徵用權。

***an·gel** [ˈendʒəl; ˈeindʒəl] *n.* ①天使;天神。②完善可愛之人。She is a perfect *angel.* 她是一個極完善可愛的人。③〖俚〗演戲的支助者;後臺老闆。④英國的古金幣名。*evil* (or *fallen*) *angel* 魔鬼。*good* (or *guardian*) *angel* 吉神;守護神。

an·gel·fish [ˈendʒəlˌfɪʃ; ˈeindʒəlfiʃ] *n.* ①神仙魚。②扁鮫。

angel food cake 〖美〗一種用蛋白和糖與麪粉做的白色薄餅。(亦作 **angel cake**)

an·gel·ic [ænˈdʒɛlɪk; ænˈdʒelik] *adj.* ①天使的;屬於天使的;天堂的。②似天使的。(亦作 **angelical**) **—al·ly,** *adv.*

an·gel·i·ca [ænˈdʒɛlɪkə; ænˈdʒelikə] *n.* ①〖植物〗羗活;白芷。②蜜餞的羗活莖。③(A-)一種白色葡萄酒。

An·ge·lus [ˈændʒələs; ˈændʒiləs] *n.* ①(天主教之)奉告祈禱。②奉告祈禱鐘。

:an·ger [ˈæŋgɚ; ˈæŋgə] *n.* ①怒;忿怒。He never speaks in *anger.* 他從不帶着怒氣說話。②〖方〗發炎或疼痛。*—v.t.* ①使憤怒;激怒。②〖方〗使發炎。*—v.i.* 發怒;忿怒。He *angers* easily. 他容易發怒。

An·ge·ro·na [ˌændʒəˈronə; ˌændʒəˈrounə] *n.* 古羅馬痛苦之女神。(亦作 **Angeronia**)

An·ge·vin [ˈændʒəvɪn; ˈændʒivin] *adj.* ①昔法國安如省(Anjou)的;安如省人的。②安如王朝的。*—n.* 安如省人;安如王室之一員。(亦作 **Angevine**)

an·gi·na [ænˈdʒaɪnə; ænˈdʒainə] *n.* 〖醫〗①咽峽炎。②心絞痛。**—al,** *adj.*

angina pec·to·ris [~ˈpɛktərɪs; ~ˈpektəris] 〖醫〗心絞痛。

an·gi·ol·o·gy [ˌændʒɪˈɑlədʒɪ; ˌændʒiˈɔlədʒi] *n.* 〖醫〗脈管學。

an·gi·o·ma [ˌændʒɪˈomə; ˌændʒiˈoumə] *n.*, *pl.* **-mas, -ma·ta** [-mətə; -mətə]. 〖醫〗血管腫;血管瘤。**—tous,** *adj.*

an·gi·o·sperm [ˈændʒɪoˌspɝm; ˈændʒiouspəːm] *n.* 〖植物〗被子植物。

Ang·kor Wat (or **Vat**) [ˈæŋkorˈvɑt; ˈæŋkɔəˈvɑːt] 吳哥窟(有古高棉王朝龐大之廟殿遺跡)。

an·glais [ɑŋˈglez; ɑːŋˈgleiz] *adj.* ①炙後未加調味汁卽上桌的。②灑以麪包屑的。

***an·gle¹** [ˈæŋgl̩; ˈæŋgl] *n.*, *v.*, **-gled, -gling.** *—n.* ①角;隅;稜。These two lines form a right *angle.* 這兩條線成一直角。②角度。③觀點;方面。to approach a topic from a new *angle.* 由一新觀點研究一個問題。④角落。⑤(球等物體之)彎曲運動。⑥新聞報導之角度或偏見。*—v.t. & v.i.* ①以一角度移動。②轉向或彎曲成一角度。to *angle* a camera. 把照像機取一角度對準。③偏重;側重;從某一觀點看。④〖美〗歪曲事實;作有成見之報導。**—an·gled,** *adj.*

an·gle² *v.i.* ①釣魚。②釣取。*—v.t.* 在…釣魚。

an·gle·doz·er [ˈæŋgl̩ˌdozɚ; ˈæŋglˌdouzə] *n.* 斜鏟推土機。

angle iron L字形鐵;角鐵。(亦作 **angle bar**)

angle of attack 〖航空〗衝角;迎角。

angle of deviation 〖光學〗偏向角。

angle of incidence 〖數學、物理〗入射角。

angle of reflection 〖光學〗反射角。

angle of refraction 〖光學〗折射角。

an·gler [ˈæŋglɚ; ˈæŋglə] *n.* ①釣者;以釣魚取樂者。②長袖善舞者;爲達目的不擇手段者。③琵琶魚;華臍魚。

An·gles [ˈæŋgl̩z; ˈæŋglz] *n. pl.* 盎格魯族。

an·gle·site [ˈæŋgl̩ˌsaɪt; ˈæŋglsait] *n.* 〖化,礦〗硫酸鉛礦;鉛礬。

an·gle·smith [ˈæŋgl̩ˌsmɪθ; ˈæŋglsmiθ] *n.* 專門打造各種造船用角鐵的鐵匠。

an·gle·worm [ˈæŋgl̩ˌwɝm; ˈæŋglwəːm] *n.* (作釣餌之)蚯蚓。

An·gli·a [ˈæŋglɪə; ˈæŋgliə] *n.* England 之拉丁名。

An·gli·an [ˈæŋglɪən; ˈæŋgliən] *adj.* ①盎格魯族(Angles)的。② Anglia 的;英國的。③盎格魯族之文化、方言等的。*—n.* ①盎格魯人。②盎格魯族之方言。

An·gli·can [ˈæŋglɪkən; ˈæŋglikən] *adj.* 英國國教的。*—n.* 英國國教徒。

An·gli·can·ism [ˈæŋglɪkənˌɪzəm; ˈæŋglikənizm] *n.* 英國國教;英國國教教義。

An·gli·cism [ˈæŋgləˌsɪzəm; ˈæŋglisizm] *n.* ①英國習語。②〖美〗英國語調。③英國化;英國式。

An·gli·cist [ˈæŋgləsɪst; ˈæŋglisist] *n.* 精通或研究英國語言或文學之人;英國通。

An·gli·cize [ˈæŋgləˌsaɪz; ˈæŋglisaiz] *v.*, **-cized, -ciz·ing.** *—v.t.* 使成英國派;使…英語化。*—v.i.* 英國化。(英亦作 **Anglicise**)

An·gli·fy [ˈæŋgləˌfaɪ; ˈæŋglifai] *v.t.*, **-fied, -fy·ing.** =**Anglicize.**

an·gling [ˈæŋglɪŋ; ˈæŋgliŋ] *n.* 釣魚。

An·glist [ˈæŋglɪst; ˈæŋglist] *n.* 英國通。

An·glis·tics [æŋˈglɪstɪks; æŋˈglistiks] *n.* (作 *sing.* 解)英語文研究;英學。

An·glo [ˈæŋglo; ˈæŋglou] *n.*, *pl.* **-glos.** 北歐裔英語系美國人。

An·glo-A·mer·i·can [ˈæŋgloəˈmɛrəkən; ˈæŋglouəˈmerikən] *adj.* ①英美兩國的。②居於美洲(尤指美國)之英國人的;英裔美國人的。*—n.* 居於美洲(尤指美國)之英國人;英裔美國人。

An·glo-Cath·o·lic [ˈæŋgloˈkæθəlɪk; ˈæŋglouˈkæθəlik] *n.* 英國國教高派教會之教徒。*—adj.* 英國國教高派教會之教徒的;其信仰及習俗的。**—ism,** *n.*

An·glo-Chi·nese [ˈæŋglotʃaɪˈniz; ˈæŋgloutʃaiˈniːz] *adj.* 中英兩國的;英華的。

An·glo-French [ˈæŋgloˈfrɛntʃ; ˈæŋglouˈfrentʃ] *adj.* 英法的。*—n.* 諾爾曼時代英國所用之法語。

An·glo-In·di·an [ˈæŋgloˈɪndɪən; ˈæŋglouˈindjən] *adj.* 英印的。*—n.* ①居於

印度之英國人。②英印混血兒。③印度英語。
An·glo·ma·ni·a [ˌæŋɡləˈmenɪə; ˈæŋglouˈmeinjə] *n.* 醉心英國;英國狂。
An·glo·ma·ni·ac [ˌæŋɡləˈmenɪˌæk; ˈæŋglouˈmeiniæk] *n.* 英國狂者。—**al,** *adj.*
An·glo-Nor·man [ˈæŋgloˈnɔrmən; ˈæŋglouˈnɔːmən] *adj.* ①諾爾曼人統治英國之時代的。②移居英國之諾爾曼人(及其語言)的。—*n.*①1066年後移居英國之諾爾曼人及其後裔。②諾爾曼時代英國所用之法語。
An·glo·phile [ˈæŋgləˌfaɪl; ˈæŋgloufail] *adj.* 親英的。—*n.* 親英(派)之人。
An·glo·phobe [ˈæŋgləˌfob; ˈæŋgloufoub] *n., adj.* 憎惡英國者(的)。
An·glo·pho·bi·a [ˌæŋgləˈfobɪə; ˌæŋglouˈfoubjə] *n.* 反英熱;恐英病。
An·glo·phone [ˈæŋgləˌfon; ˈæŋgloufoun] *n.* (英語爲官方語言之一的國家中)說英語的居民。(亦作 **anglophone**)
An·glo-Sax·on [ˈæŋgloˈsæksn̩; ˈæŋglouˈsæksn] *n.* ①屬於說英語的人。②盎格魯撒克遜族或其語文(由第五世紀至第十二世紀的英國人或其語文)。③出自此族的人。④英語;英文。—*adj.* ①盎格魯撒克遜族的。②盎格魯撒克遜語文的。
An·go·la[1] [æŋˈgolə; æŋˈgoulə] *n.* 安哥拉(西非一國名, 首都羅安達Luanda).
An·go·la[2] *n.* =**Angora.**
An·go·ra [for①ˈæŋgərə; ˈæŋgərə for ②③④æŋˈgorə; æŋˈgɔːrə] *n.* ①安哥拉(土耳其國都 Ankara 之舊名)。②安哥拉貓。③安哥拉羊。④安哥拉呢;純毛海。
Angora cat 安哥拉貓。(亦作**Angora**)
Angora goat安哥拉羊。(亦作**Angora**)
Angora wool 安哥拉呢。
an·gos·tu·ra [ˌæŋgəsˈtjurə; ˌæŋgɔsˈtjuərə] *n.* 南美產之一種芳香樹皮。(亦作 **angostura bark, angustura**)
an·gries [ˈæŋgrɪs; ˈæŋgris] *n. pl.* 反對社會或政治情況而憤怒的示威者。
***an·gri·ly** [ˈæŋgrəlɪ; ˈæŋgrili] *adv.* 忿怒地。
:an·gry [ˈæŋgrɪ; ˈæŋgri] *adj.,* **-gri·er, -gri·est.** ①怒的; 忿怒的。She was *angry* at what her husband said. 她對她丈夫所說的話很生氣。②風雨交作的。an *angry* sky. 風雨交作的天際。③(傷口) 腫脹的;痛楚的。An infected cut looks *angry*. 染毒創傷看起來非常痛楚。④忿怒所引起的。*angry* words. 氣話。⑤兇猛的。⑥强烈的。*angry* red. 鮮紅。—**an·gri·ness,** *n.* 〖注意〗對事物時, angry 後接用 at 或 about. 對人時, angry後通常用 with. 在正式用語中, angry at 係加强其憤怒本身者, 而 angry with 强調其後所接用之受詞。
angry young man ①1950年代, 其作品反映强烈的反傳統、反社會等不滿情緒的一羣英國作家之任一。②以這種態度寫作的作家。③任何有反抗情緒的人。(亦作 **Angry Young Man**)
ang·strom (unit) [ˈæŋstrəm; ˈæŋstrəm] *n.* 〖物理〗埃(光波波長之單位)。
an·guine [ˈæŋgwɪn; ˈæŋgwin] *adj.* 蛇的;似蛇的。
an·gui·ped [ˈæŋgwɪpɛd; ˈæŋgwiped] *adj.* 腿形似蛇的。
***an·guish** [ˈæŋgwɪʃ; ˈæŋgwiʃ] *n.* 心身上極度的痛苦。—*v.t.* 使痛苦;使悲痛。—*v.i.* 感痛苦;感悲痛。His heart *anguished* within him. 他很感痛苦。
an·guished [ˈæŋgwɪʃt; ˈæŋgwiʃt] *adj.* 痛苦的;煩惱的。
an·gu·lar [ˈæŋgjələ; ˈæŋgjulə] *adj.*①有角的;成角的。②以角度測量的。③消瘦的;瘦骨嶙峋的。④笨拙的;行動不自然的。
angular acceleration 〖物理〗角加速度。
an·gu·lar·i·ty [ˌæŋgjəˈlærətɪ; ˌæŋgjuˈlæriti] *n., pl.* **-ties.** ①有角;成角狀。②(*pl.*)尖角部分;有角的外形。③不屈。④笨拙。
an·gu·late [*adj.* ˈæŋgjəlɪt, -ˌlet *v.* ˈæŋgjəˌlet; ˈæŋgjuleit, -lit] *adj.* (亦作 **angulated**)有角的;角狀的。—*v.t.* 以角形成或組成。
an·gu·la·tion [ˌæŋgjəˈleʃən; ˌæŋgjuˈleiʃən] *n.* ①作成角。②角狀。
an·gu·lous [ˈæŋgjələs; ˈæŋgjuləs] *adj.*=**angular.** (亦作 **angulose**)
An·gus [ˈæŋgəs; ˈæŋgəs] *n.* 〖塞爾特神話〗愛神。
an·gus·ti·fo·li·ate [æŋˌgʌstɪˈfolɪɪt; æŋˌgʌstiˈfoulieit] *adj.* 〖植物〗窄葉的。
an·har·mon·ic ratio [ˌænhɑrˈmɑnɪk ~; ˈænhɑːˈmɔnik ~] 〖物理〗交比;非調和比;重比。
an·he·do·ni·a [ˌænhiˈdonɪə; ˌænhiːˈdouniə] *n.* 〖心理〗失樂症;快感缺乏。
an·hem·i·ton·ic [ænˌhɛmɪˈtɑnɪk; ænˌhemiˈtɔnik] *adj.* 〖音樂〗無半音的(音階)。
an·hi·dro·sis [ˌænhəˈdrosɪs; ˌænhaiˈdrousis] *n.* 〖醫〗汗閉。(亦作 **anhydrosis**)
An·hwei [ˈɑnˈhwe; ˈɑːnˈhwei] *n.* 安徽(中國之一省, 省會合肥, Hofei).
an·hy·drate [ænˈhaɪdret; ænˈhaidreit] *v.t.,* **-drat·ed, -drat·ing.** 使脫水;除去…之水分。—**an·hy·dra·tion,** *n.*
an·hy·dride [ænˈhaɪdraɪd; ænˈhaidraid] *n.* 〖化〗無水物;酐。(亦作**anhydrid**)
an·hy·drite [ænˈhaɪdraɪt; ænˈhaidrait] *n.* 硬石膏;無水石膏。
an·hy·drous [ænˈhaɪdrəs; ænˈhaidrəs] *adj.* 〖化, 礦〗無水的。
an·i·con·ism [ænˈaɪkənɪzəm; ænˈaikənizəm] *n.* ①無偶像論。②對象徵神(非偶像神)之崇拜。
an·il [ˈænɪl; ˈænil] *n.* ①〖植物〗木藍。②藍;靛;青黛。
a·nile [ˈænaɪl; ˈeinail] *adj.* 似老婦的;衰老的。
an·i·lide [ˈænəlɪd; ˈænilid] *n.* 〖化〗醯基苯胺。
an·i·line, an·i·lin [ˈænl̩ˌin; ˈæniliːn] *n.*〖化〗苯胺。—*adj.*苯胺的。
a·nil·i·ty [əˈnɪlətɪ; əˈniliti] *n., pl.* **-ties.** ①老弱;衰老。②老媼一般的動作、言談等。
anim. 〖音樂〗animato.
an·i·ma [ˈænɪmə; ˈænimə] *n.* 生命;靈魂。
an·i·mad·ver·sion [ˌænəmædˈvɝʒən; ˌænimædˈvəːʃən] *n.* 批判;譴責;非難〖on, upon〗.
an·i·mad·vert [ˌænəmædˈvɝt; ˌænimædˈvəːt] *v.i.* 批判;譴責;非難〖on, upon〗.
:an·i·mal [ˈænəml̩; ˈæniməl] *n.*①動物。②獸。*animal* of prey. 食肉獸。③殘暴的人;無理性的人。④獸性。unable to control the *animal* in himself. 無法抑制其獸性的發作。—*adj.* ①動物的。*animal* life. 動物的生活。②肉體上的;肉慾上的。
animal crackers 動物狀的餅干。
an·i·mal·cule [ˌænəˈmælkjul; ˌæniˈmælkjuːl] *n.* 微生動物。
animal faith 對於客觀世界之存在的單純信仰或非理性信仰。
animal husbandman 畜牧學家;從事畜牧業者。
animal husbandry 畜牧;畜牧學。
an·i·mal·ism [ˈænəml̩ˌɪzəm; ˈænimə-

lizm] *n.* ①獸行;獸慾;獸性。②獸性主義。③血氣;精力。
an·i·mal·ist [ˈænəməlɪst; ˈænimәlist] *n.* ①獸性主義者。②動物藝術家。—**ic,** *adj.*
an·i·mal·i·ty [ˌænəˈmælətɪ; ˌæniˈmæliti] *n., pl.* **-ties.** ①獸性。②動物界。
an·i·mal·i·za·tion [ˌænəməlɪˈzeʃən; ˌænimәlaiˈzeiʃәn] *n.*①獸性化。②(食物之)動物質化。③縱慾。
an·i·mal·ize [ˈænəmḷˌaɪz; ˈænimәlaiz] *v.t.,* **-ized, -iz·ing.** ①賦與獸性; 使耽於獸慾; 使動物化。②使成動物性物質。③〖美術〗賦與動物外形。
animal kingdom 動物界。
an·i·mal·ly [ˈænəmḷɪ; ˈænimәli] *adv.* 肉體上。
animal magnetism①催眠力。②對「異性之吸引力。」
animal passion 獸慾;肉慾。
animal spirits 血氣;精力。
animal starch〖生化〗獸臟粉;肝澱粉;牲粉;動物澱粉。
an·i·mate [*v.* ˈænəˌmet; ˈænimeit *adj.* ˈænəmɪt; ˈænimit] *v.,* **-mat·ed, -mat·ing,** *adj.* —*v.t.* ①賦予生命。②使活潑;使有生氣;使有活力。③激動;激勵。④推動。⑤繪製。⑥使活動。—*adj.* ①活的。②活潑的;愉快的。③動物的(爲植物的之對)。—**ly,** *adv.* —**ness,** *n.*
an·i·mat·ed [ˈænəˌmetɪd; ˈænimeitid] *adj.* ①有生氣的; 活生生的;活潑的; 熱烈的。②能活動(如有生命)的。—**ly,** *adv.*
animated cartoon 卡通影片。
an·i·ma·tion [ˌænəˈmeʃən; ˌæniˈmeiʃәn] *n.* ①生氣;興奮;活潑。②鼓舞;給予生氣。③〖電影〗卡通製作。
an·i·ma·tism[ˈænɪməˌtɪzəm; ˈænimәtizәm] *n.* 無生物之有意識說。
a·ni·ma·to [ˌɑnɪˈmɑto; ˌɑːniˈmɑːtou] 〖義〗 *adj.* & *adv.*〖音樂〗活潑的(地)。
an·i·ma·tor [ˈænɪˌmetɚ; ˈænimeitә] *n.* ①賦與生氣者;鼓舞者。②〖電影〗卡通片繪製者。
an·i·mé [ˈænɪˌme; ˈænimei] *n.* 樹脂。
an·i·mism [ˈænəˌmɪzəm; ˈænimizәm] *n.*①生命由超物質之精神力所創造的信仰。②萬物俱有靈魂的信仰。③靈魂獨立說。④有鬼論。—**an·i·mist,** *n.* —**an·i·mis·tic,** *adj.*
an·i·mos·i·ty [ˌænəˈmɑsətɪ; ˌæniˈmɔsiti] *n., pl.* **-ties.** 憎惡;仇恨;怨恨。
an·i·mus [ˈænəməs; ˈænimәs] *n.* ①意旨;心意。②敵意;惡意。③〖法律〗意向;意圖。
an·i·on [ˈænˌaɪən; ˈænaiәn] *n.*〖化〗陰離子;陽向游子。—**ic,** *adj.*
an·ise [ˈænɪs; ˈænis] *n.* 〖植物〗大茴香。
an·i·seed[ˈænɪˌsid; ˈænisiːd]*n.*大茴香子。
anise oil 大茴香子油精。
an·i·sette [ˌænɪˈzɛt; ˌæniˈzet] *n.*茴香酒。
an·i·so·me·tro·pi·a[ænˌaɪsəməˈtropɪə; ænˌaisәmiˈtroupiә] *n.* 〖醫〗(兩眼)屈光參差症。
A·ni·ta [əˈnitə; әˈniːtә] *n.* 女子名(Anna 的暱稱)。
An·i·us [ˈænɪəs; ˈæniәs] *n.*〖希臘神話〗Apollo 與 Rhoeo 之子, 後爲 Delos 之王。
An·ka·ra [ˈæŋkərə; ˈæŋkәrә] *n.* 安卡拉(土耳其首都)。(亦作**Angora**)
an·ker [ˈæŋkɚ; ˈæŋkә] *n.* 荷蘭、丹麥、瑞典、俄國等量酒之單位。
an·ker·ite [ˈæŋkəˌraɪt; ˈæŋkәrait] *n.*〖鑛〗鐵白雲石。
***an·kle, an·cle** [ˈæŋkḷ; ˈæŋkl] *n.*踝。He hurt his left *ankle* at broad jump. 他跳遠時傷了左踝。—*v.i.* 〖美〗走。Long-stemmed models *ankled* through the lobby. 身材修長的模特兒從廳中走過。
an·kle·bone [ˈæŋkḷˌbon; ˈæŋklboun] *n.* 踝骨;距骨。
an·kle-deep [ˈæŋkḷˈdip; ˈæŋklˈdiːp] *adj.* & *adv.* 深及踝部的(地)。
ankle jerk踝部腱反射;踝反射。
an·klet [ˈæŋklɪt; ˈæŋklit] *n.*①著於踝上之物。②(女人之)短襪。
ankle tie 以鞋帶縛於踝部的涼鞋。
an·ky·lose [ˈæŋkəˌlos; ˈæŋkilous] *v.t.* & *v.i.,* **-losed, -los·ing.** (骨骼等)黏合;(因黏合而)僵直。(亦作 **anchylose**)
an·ky·lo·sis [ˌæŋkəˈlosɪs; ˌæŋkiˈlousis] *n.* ①〖醫〗關節强硬。②〖動物〗(骨骼或纖維部分之)黏合。(亦作 **anchylosis**)
an·lace [ˈænlɪs; ˈænlis] *n.*短劍。
an·la·ge, An·la·ge [ˈɑnlɑgə; ˈɑːnlɑːgә] *n., pl.* **-gen** [-gən; -gәn]. ①〖發生學〗原基。②基本。③傾向;癖性。
Ann(e) [æn; æn] *n.* 女子名。
ann. ①annals. ②annual. ③annuity. ④years.
An·na [ˈænə; ˈænә] *n.* 女子名。
an·na [ˈænə; ˈænә] *n.* 安那(印度及巴基斯坦之貨幣名)。
An·na·bel [ˈænəˌbɛl; ˈænәbel] *n.* 女子名。
an·nal·ist [ˈænḷɪst; ˈænәlist] *n.* 紀年表之編著者;編年史之作者。—**ic,** *adj.*
***an·nals** [ˈænḷz; ˈænlz] *n. pl.* ①紀年表;年鑑。②(學會等之)年報。③歷史記載。
An·nap·o·lis [əˈnæpḷɪs; әˈnæpәlis] *n.* 亞那波里 (美國馬利蘭州首府,美海軍官校所在地)。
an·nates [ˈænets; ˈæneits] *n. pl.* 天主教就僧職者第一年之收入。(亦作 **annats**)
an·neal [əˈnil; әˈniːl] *v.t.*①加熱後緩冷使不脆;使韌化。②鍛鍊(意志、心意等)。
an·nec·tent [əˈnɛktənt; әˈnektәnt] *adj.* 連接一起的。
an·ne·lid [ˈænḷɪd; ˈænәlid] *n.*〖生物〗環節動物;環蟲。—*adj.* 環節動物的;環蟲類的。
An·nel·i·da [əˈnɛlɪdə; әˈnelidә] *n. pl.*〖生物〗環節動物門;環蟲類。
an·nel·i·dan [əˈnɛlɪdən; әˈnelidәn] *adj.* 環節動物的;環蟲的。
an·nex [*v.* əˈnɛks; әˈneks *n.* ˈænɛks; ˈæneks] *v.t.*①附加。②合併。③併呑;霸占。④蓋(印章)。The president *annexed* his seal to the document. 總統將印信蓋在文件上。⑤獲得。⑥侵占;不告自取。—*n.* (英亦作 **annexe**) 附屬物;附屬建築。Our hotel has an *annex.* 我們的旅社有一座附屬的建築物。
an·nex·a·ble [əˈnɛksəbḷ; әˈneksәbl] *adj.* 可附加的;可合併的。
an·nex·a·tion [ˌænɛksˈeʃən; ˌænekˈseiʃәn] *n.* 附加物;附加;合併。—**ist,** *n.*
an·nex·ment [əˈnɛksmənt; әˈneksmәnt]*n.*附加物。
An·nie [ˈænɪ; ˈæni] *n.* 女子名 (Ann, Anna, Anne 的暱稱)。
An·nie Oak·ley [ˈænɪˈoklɪ; ˈæniˈoukli] 〖俚〗免費入場券;優待券。
an·ni·hi·la·ble [əˈnaɪələbḷ; әˈnaiәlәbl] *adj.* 可滅絕的;可殲滅的。
***an·ni·hi·late** [əˈnaɪəˌlet; әˈnaiәleit] *v.t.,* **-lat·ed, -lat·ing.** 消滅。Napoleon's fleet was *annihilated* by Nelson. 拿破崙的艦隊爲納爾遜所消滅。—**an·ni·hi·la·tor,** *n.*
an·ni·hi·la·tion[əˌnaɪəˈleʃən; әˌnaiәˈleiʃәn] *n.* ①消滅;殲滅。②〖神學〗靈魂與肉體之毀滅。③〖核子物理〗電子與正子之毀滅;

電子與正子結合而產生珈瑪線。

an·ni·hi·la·tion·ism [ə,naɪə'leʃə-nɪzm; ə,naiə'leiʃnizm] *n.* 〖宗教〗靈魂寂滅論。—**an·ni·hi·la·tion·ist,** *n.*

an·ni·la·tive [ə'naɪə,letɪv; ə'naiəlei-tiv] *adj.* 有消滅之能力的。

anniv. anniversary.

an·ni·ver·sar·i·an [,ænəvɜ'sɛrɪən; ,ænivə:'sɛəriən] *n.* 〖美〗爲慶祝周年紀念而演說、作頌文等之人。

***an·ni·ver·sa·ry** [,ænə'vɜsərɪ; ,æni-'və:səri] *n., pl.* **-ries,** *adj.* —*n.* ①周年。November twelfth is the *anniversary* of Dr. Sun Yat-sen's birthday. 十一月十二日爲孫逸仙博士的誕辰。②周年紀念。a wedding *anniversary.* 結婚周年紀念。—*adj.* ①年年的;每年的。②周年紀念的。

an·no ae·ta·tis su·ae ['ænoɪ'tetɪs-'sjui; 'ænou i'teitis 'sju:i:] 〖拉〗在他(她)…歲時;行年…歲(=in the year of his *or* her age).

an·no Dom·i·ni ['æno'dɑmə,naɪ; 'ænou'dɔminai] ①〖拉〗耶穌紀元後;西元(=in the year of our Lord)(略作 **A.D.**)。②〖諧〗老齡。

an·no·tate ['æno,tet; 'ænouteit] *v.t. & v.i.,* **-tat·ed, -tat·ing.** 註解;評註。—**an·no·ta·tor,** *n.*

an·no·ta·tion [,æno'teʃən; ,ænou-'teiʃən] *n.*註解;評註。—**an·no·ta·tive,** *adj.*

:an·nounce [ə'nauns; ə'nauns] *v.,* **-nounced, -nounc·ing.** —*v.t.* ①正式宣告;對衆宣稱;發表。②報到;通知客到。to *announce* guests. 通知客到。③預示;預言;預告;爲…之先聲。The invention of the printing press *announced* the diffusion of knowledge. 印刷術之發明爲知識普及之先聲。④顯示;顯露。His earlier work *announced* a lyric talent of the first order. 他的較早作品顯露了一流的抒情天才。⑤廣播(電臺節目)。He *announces* three programs a week. 他每週廣播三個節目。—*v.i.* ①擔任廣播員。He *announces* for a national network. 他是一個全國性廣播網的廣播員。②宣布有意競選。

***an·nounce·ment** [ə'naunsmənt; ə'naunsmənt] *n.* ①通告;布告;發表。②正式的或私人的通知。The *announcement* of their marriage appeared in the newspapers. 他們結婚的啓事,已登在報紙上了。③宣布的行動或過程。④談話;言論。

***an·nounc·er** [ə'naunsə; ə'naunsə] *n.* 宣布、公告、發表者(人或物);廣播員。

***an·noy** [ə'nɔɪ; ə'nɔi] *v.t.*①使不樂;使苦惱。I was *annoyed* at his intrusion. 我被他的闖入所煩擾。②騷擾;傷害。Mosquitoes *annoy* us in the summer. 夏天蚊子騷擾我們。—*v.i.* 煩擾;騷擾;傷害。Some personalities antagonize; others simply *annoy.* 有些人會使人起反感,有些人祇是使你覺得討厭。—**er,** *n.* 〖注意〗annoyed 指物,用 at;指人,用 with;作"騷擾"解,用 by.

an·noy·ance[ə'nɔɪəns; ə'nɔiəns]*n.*①煩惱;騷擾;傷害。②使人煩惱之物;可厭之物。

an·noy·ing [ə'nɔɪɪŋ; ə'nɔiiŋ] *adj.*可厭的;煩惱的。—**ly,** *adv.*

***an·nu·al**['ænjuəl;'ænjuəl] *adj.* ①一年一次的。Your birthday is an *annual* event. 你的生日是一年一次的事。②年年的;全年的。*annual* income. 全年的收入。③一年生的。④一年內完成的。—*n.*①年刊書;年鑑;年報。②一年生或一季生植物。—**ly,** *adv.*

annual leave 每年一次的休假。

annual meeting (股東等之)年會。

annual ring (樹木之)年輪。

an·nu·i·tant [ə'nuətənt; ə'nju:itənt] *n.* 領受養老金者。

an·nu·it coep·tis ['ænjuɪt'sɛptɪs; 'ænju:it'septis] 〖拉〗天佑吾人基業(美國國璽背面之銘語)。

an·nu·i·ty [ə'nuətɪ; ə'nju:iti] *n., pl.* **-ties.** 年金;養老金。

annuity certain *pl.* **annuities certain.** 〖保險〗確定年金。

an·nul [ə'nʌl; ə'nʌl] *v.t.,* **-nulled, -nulling.** ①取消;宣告作廢。②抹殺。

an·nu·lar ['ænjələ; 'ænjulə] *adj.*環的;環狀的。—**ly,** *adv.*

annular saw 圓鋸;鋼絲鋸。

an·nu·late ['ænjə,let; 'ænjuleit] *adj.* ①有環的;有環紋的。②由環形成的。(亦作 **annulated**)

an·nu·la·tion [,ænjə'leʃən; ,ænju'lei-ʃən] *n.* ①成環;成環狀。②環紋;環狀物。

an·nu·let ['ænjəlɪt; 'ænjulit] *n.* ①小環。②〖建築〗(圓柱周圍之)環紋;環緣。

an·nul·ment [ə'nʌlmənt; ə'nʌlmənt] *n.* 取消;廢止;無效。

an·nu·lose ['ænju,los; 'ænjulous] *adj.* 有環節的。

an·nu·lus ['ænjələs; 'ænjuləs] *n., pl.* **-li** [-,laɪ; -lai], **-lus·es.** ①環;輪。②〖數學〗環形。③〖生物〗環帶。

an·num ['ænəm; 'ænəm] *n.* 年;歲。 *per annum* 每年。

an·nun·ci·ate [ə'nʌnʃɪ,et; ə'nʌnʃieit] *v.t.,* **-at·ed, -at·ing.** 通告;布告。

an·nun·ci·a·tion [ə,nʌnsɪ'eʃən; ə-,nʌnsi'eiʃən]*n.* ①通告;布告。②(A-)天使加百列奉告聖母以耶穌將降生事。③(A-)天使報喜節(三月二十五日)。

an·nun·ci·a·tor [ə'nʌnʃɪ,etə; ə'nʌn-ʃieitə] *n.* ①通告者;預告者。②〖美〗電動喚人裝置。

an·ode ['ænod; 'ænoud] *n.* 〖電〗陽極;正極。*anode* ray. 陽極射線。

an·o·dize ['æno,daɪz; 'ænədaiz] *v.t.* 電鍍。

an·o·don·tia [,ænə'dɑntʃə; ,ænə'dɔn-tʃə] *n.* 〖牙科〗無牙;無牙畸形。

an·o·dyne ['ænə,daɪn; 'ænoudain] *adj.* ①止痛的;鎮痛的。②緩和情緒的。③刪改過的。—*n.* ①止痛藥。②緩和苦惱之物。

a·noint [ə'nɔɪnt; ə'nɔint] *v.t.* ①塗油;搽油。②〖宗教〗塗油使神聖化。③照天意選定。***the (Lord's) Anointed*** **a.** 救世主;基督。**b.** 古猶太王;神權國王。—**or,** —**ment,** *n.*

a·nom·a·lism [ə'nɑml,ɪzəm; ə'nɔmə-lizm] *n.* 變態;反常;變則。

a·nom·a·lis·tic [ə,nɑml'ɪstɪk; ə,nɔ-mə'listik] *adj.* 變態的;反常的;例外的。

anomalistic month 〖天文〗近點月(月球自近地點至下一次近地點所需之時間,約27½日)。

anomalistic year 〖天文〗近點年(行星自近日點至近日點所費之時間,約365日6時13分53.1秒)。

a·nom·a·lo·scope [ə'nɑmlə,skop; ə'nɔmələskoup] *n.* 色盲測定器。

a·nom·a·lous [ə'nɑmələs; ə'nɔmə-ləs]*adj.* 不規則的;反常的;破格的。—**ly,** *adv.*

anomalous finite 〖文法〗變則有限式動詞。如 will, would, shall, should, may, might, must, am, did 等,因可用在 not 之前,亦可與主詞調換位置故謂變則。

anomalous verb 〖文法〗變則動詞。

a·nom·a·ly [əˈnɑməlɪ; əˈnɔməli] *n.* 反常之事物;異例。

a·non [əˈnɑn; əˈnɔn] *adv.* 〖古〗①不久;未幾。②他時。③立刻。***ever and anon*** 不時地。

anon. anonymous.

an·o·nych·i·a [ˌænəˈnɪkɪə; ˌænəˈnikiə] *n.* 〖醫〗無爪症;先天性無趾甲與指甲症。

an·o·nym [ˈænəˌnɪm; ˈænənim] *n.* ①假名;化名。②化名之人;作者不明的出版物。

an·o·nym·i·ty [ˌænəˈnɪmətɪ; ˌænəˈnimiti] *n.* 匿名;無名;作者不明。

a·non·y·mous [əˈnɑnəməs; əˈnɔniməs] *adj.* 無名的;匿名的。 **—ly,** *adv.*

an·o·op·si·a [ˌænoˈɑpsɪə; ˌænouˈɔpsiə] *n.* 〖醫〗上斜視。

a·noph·e·les [əˈnɑfəˌliz; əˈnɔfiliːz] *n., pl.* **-les.** 瘧蚊。

an·o·pi·a [ænˈopɪə; ænˈoupiə] *n.* 〖醫〗①無眼畸形。②視力缺如。③上轉斜眼。

an·o·pis·tho·graph [ˌænəˈpɪsθəˌgræf, -ˌgrɑf; ˌænəˈpisθəgrɑːf] *n.* 單面有字的書, 手稿等。**—ic,** *adj.*

an·o·rak [ˈɑnəˌrɑk; ˈɑːnərɑːk] *n.* 連兜帽的夾克。

an·o·rec·tal [ˌænoˈrɛktl; ˌænouˈrektl] *adj.* 肛門直腸的。

an·o·rex·i·ant [ˌænoˈrɛksɪənt, ˌænɑ-; ˌænouˈreksiənt] *n.* 使食慾減退的藥物。

a·no·scope [ˈenəˌskop; ˈeinəskoup] *n.* 〖醫〗肛門窺器;肛鏡。

an·os·mi·a [ænˈɑzmɪə; ænˈɔsmiə] *n.* 〖醫〗嗅覺喪失症;嗅覺缺失。

‡an·oth·er [əˈnʌðɚ; əˈnʌðə] *adj.* ①又一;再。Have *another* cooky. 請再吃一塊餅乾。②另一; 不同的。I'll come to see you at *another* time. 改日我再來看你。③同一類的。This young man is very clever; he may be *another* Edison. 這青年很聰明, 他可能成爲另一個愛迪生。 *—pron.* ① 又一。Have *another.* 請再吃一個。②另一;不同的東西。③同類。His father is a scholar and he is *another.* 他的父親是一學者, 他也是。***another world*** 來世;天國;西方極樂世界。***in another moment*** 忽然。***one after another*** 相繼地。***one another*** 彼此互相地。***one way or another*** 無論如何。He will accomplish it *one way or another.* 他無論如何要完成這事。

an·ox·e·mi·a [ˌænɑksˈimɪə; ˌænɔkˈsiːmiə] *n.* 〖醫〗缺氧血症。(亦作 **anoxaemia**)

an·ox·i·a [ænˈɑksɪə; ænˈɔksiə] *n.* 〖醫〗缺氧症;氧缺乏。

ANPA American Newspaper Publishers' Association.

ANS ① Army News Service. ② American Nuclear Society. ③American Names Society.

ans. ①answer. ②answered.

an·sa [ˈænsə; ˈænsə] *n., pl.* **-sae** [-si; -siː]. 柄;如柄狀的部分。

an·sate [ˈænset; ˈænseit] *adj.* 有柄的;有柄狀部分的。(亦作 **ansated**)

An·schau·ung [ˈɑnʃauˌʊŋ; ˈɑːnʃauˌuŋ] *n.* 〖哲學〗直覺;直觀。

an·schluss [ˈɑnʃlus; ˈɑːnʃlus] 〖德〗 *n.* ①聯合;兩國經濟的或政治的結合。 ②(A-)(1938年之)德奧合併。

an·ser·ine [ˈænsəˌraɪn; ˈænsərain] *n.* ①鵝科的。②似鵝的。③愚笨的;蠢的。(亦作 **anserous**)

An·shan [ˈɑnˈʃɑn; ˈɑːnˈʃɑːn] *n.* 鞍山(位於中國遼寧省)。

‡an·swer [ˈænsɚ; ˈɑːnsə] *n.* ①答覆;回覆。The boy gave a quick *answer* to the teacher's question. 這孩子對教師所提出的問題答得很快。②解答;答案。***in answer to*** 應…而…。The doctor came at once *in answer to* my telephone call. 醫生應我電話而立刻前來。*—v.t.* ①答覆;回答。I *answered* his letter promptly. 我立即回他的信。②適應;符合。③應付。④響應。⑤解答。Can you *answer* this riddle? 你能解答這個謎嗎? *—v.i.*①答覆;回答。②負責(某事)之結果;對(某事)有責任。I can't *answer* for his honesty. 我不能保證他誠實。 ③符合。 This house *answers* to his description. 這房子與他之描述相符。④發生作用或效果。⑤有反應。The illness did not *answer* to medical treatment. 此疾病對醫學治療毫無反應。***answer back*** 〖俗〗頂嘴。

an·swer·a·ble [ˈænsərəbl; ˈɑːnsərəbl] *adj.* ①有責任的; 當負責的。②可答覆的。③合比例的;相關的〖to〗. ④符合的;適當的〖to〗. *answerable* to expectation. 與希望相符。 **—an·swer·a·bly,** *adv.*

an·swer·er [ˈænsərɚ; ˈɑːnsərə] *n.* 答覆者;解答者;答辯者。

an·swer·ing [ˈænsərɪŋ; ˈɑːnsəriŋ] *adj.* ①回答的;答覆的。②符合的;相應的。

ant** [ænt; ænt] *n.* 蟻。have ants in one's pants*** 〖俚〗急於說話或做某事。

ant- 〖字首〗**anti-** 之變體(置於以母音或h開頭之字的前面, 例: antacid).

-ant 〖字尾〗①形成名詞, 表"做(某事)之人或物"之義。例: stimulant. ②形成形容詞, 與原字之現在分詞同義。例: ascendant.

an't [ænt; ɑːnt] 〖方, 英俗〗 are not, am not, is not 之縮寫。

ant. antonym.

ant·ac·id [æntˈæsɪd; ˈæntˈæsid] *adj.* 中和酸的;抵制酸性的。*—n.* 〖醫〗制酸劑。

an·tag·o·nism [ænˈtægəˌnɪzəm; ænˈtægənizəm] *n.* 敵對;反對。

***an·tag·o·nist** [ænˈtægənɪst; ænˈtægənist] *n.*①敵手;反對者。②〖生理〗對抗肌;反動肌。

an·tag·o·nis·tic [ænˌtægəˈnɪstɪk; ænˌtægəˈnistik] *adj.* 敵對的;相反的。(亦作 **antagonistical**) **—al·ly,** *adv.*

an·tag·o·nize [ænˈtægəˌnaɪz; ænˈtægənaiz] *v.t.* & *v.i.,* **-nized, -niz·ing.** 使成敵人;敵對;反對。**—an·tag·o·ni·za·tion,** *n.*

An·tag·o·ras [ænˈtægərəs; ænˈtægərəs] *n.* 〖希臘神話〗 向 Hercules 挑戰比武的牧羊人。

ant·al·gic [æntˈældʒɪk; æntˈældʒik] *adj.* 〖醫〗止痛的;鎭痛的。*—n.* 止痛藥。

ant·al·ka·li [æntˈælkəˌlaɪ; æntˈælkəlai] *n., pl.* **-lis, -lies.** 鹼性中和劑;解鹼劑。

ant·aph·ro·dis·i·ac [ˌæntæfrəˈdɪzɪæk; ˌæntæfrəˈdiziæk] *adj.* 抑制性慾的。*—n.* 抑制性慾之藥品;鎭慾劑。

***ant·arc·tic** [æntˈɑrktɪk; æntˈɑːktik] *adj.* 南極的;近南極的。*—n.* 南極地區。

Ant·arc·ti·ca [æntˈɑrktɪkə; æntˈɑːktikə] *n.* 南極洲。

Antarctic Circle 南極圈。

Antarctic Continent = **Antarctica.**

Antarctic Ocean 南冰洋;南極海。

Antarctic Peninsula 南極半島(位於南美洲之南)。(亦作 **Graham Land,** 舊名爲 **Palmer Peninsula**)

Antarctic Zone 南極帶;南寒帶。

ant·ar·thrit·ic [ˌæntɑrˈθrɪtɪk;

ˌæntɑ:θ'ritik] *adj.* 防關節炎的;治關節炎的。—*n.* 治關節炎的藥物。

ant·asth·mat·ic 〔ˌæntæz'mætɪk; ˌæntæz'mætik〕 *adj.* 防哮喘的; 治哮喘的。—*n.* 治哮喘的藥。

ant bear 〖動物〗南美所產之大食蟻獸。

ant cow 蚜蟲。(亦作 **ant cattle**)

an·te 〔'æntɪ; 'ænti〕 *v.*, **-ted** or **-teed, -te·ing,** *n.* —*v.t.* & *v.i.* 下賭注; 拿出(錢、意見等)。—*n.* 賭注;賭金。

ante- 〖字首〗表"在…之前的;比…較早的"之義。

ant·eat·er 〔'ænt,itɚ; 'ænt,i:tə〕 *n.* 食蟻獸。

an·te·bel·lum 〔'æntɪ'bɛləm; 'ænti'beləm〕 *adj.* 戰前的; 美國南北戰爭之前的。

an·te·cede 〔ˌæntə'sid; ˌænti'si:d〕 *v.t.* & *v.i.*, **-ced·ed, -ced·ing.** 居先;高於;勝過。

an·te·ced·ence 〔ˌæntə'sidn̩s; ˌænti'si:dəns〕 *n.* ①先行;居先。②〖天文〗逆行。(亦作 **antecedency**)

***an·te·ced·ent** 〔ˌæntə'sidn̩t; ˌænti'si:dənt〕 *adj.* 在先的;在前的〖常 to〗。—*n.* ①前事。*antecedents* and consequences of the war. 戰爭的前因後果。②(*pl.*)**a.** 祖先。**b.** 出身;經歷。③〖文法〗先行詞;前述詞。④〖數學〗前項。⑤前身。⑥〖邏輯〗前提。

an·te·ces·sor 〔ˌæntə'sɛsɚ; ˌænti'sesə〕 *n.* ①先行者;先驅者;先導者。②祖先。

an·te·cham·ber 〔'æntɪ,tʃembɚ; 'ænti,tʃeimbə〕 *n.* (後連正廳之)前堂;前廳;來賓接待室。

an·te·chap·el 〔'æntɪ,tʃæpl̩; 'ænti,tʃæpəl〕 *n.* 教堂之門廳。

an·te·date 〔'æntɪ,det; 'ænti'deit〕 *v.t.*, **-dat·ed, -dat·ing.** ①指定較早之日期於。②居先。③使較早發生。④預期;預料。

an·te·di·lu·vi·an 〔ˌæntɪdɪ'luvɪən; 'æntidi'lu:vjən〕 *adj.* ①Noah 時之大水以前的。②太古的;原始的。③陳舊的。—*n.* ①洪水時代以前的人(或物)。②老朽之人;舊式之人。

an·te·hall 〔'æntɪ,hɔl; 'æntihɔ:l〕 *n.* 前廳。

an·te·lope 〔'æntl̩,op; 'æntiloup〕 *n., pl.* **-lope** or **-lopes.** 〖動物〗羚羊。

an·te·me·rid·i·an 〔ˌæntɪmə'rɪdɪən; 'æntimə'ridiən〕 *adj.* 午前的。

an·te me·rid·i·em 〔'æmtɪmə'rɪdɪ,ɛm; 'æntimə'ridiem〕〖拉〗午前(略作 **A.M.** 或 **a.m.**). at 8 *a.m.* 上午八時。

an·te-mor·tem 〔'æntɪ'mɔrtəm; 'ænti'mɔ:təm〕 *adj.* 死前所作所爲的;臨死前的。

an·te·mun·dane 〔'æntɪ'mʌnden; ˌænti'mʌndein〕 *adj.* ①世界創造以前的。②誕生以前的。

an·te·na·tal 〔ˌæntɪ'netl̩; 'ænti'neitl〕 *adj.* 降生前的;出生前的。

***an·ten·na** 〔æn'tɛnə; æn'tenə〕 *n.* ①*pl.* **-ten·nae**〔-'tɛni; -'teni:〕. 觸鬚。②*pl.* **-ten·nas.** 無線電、電視等接收或發射機之天線。

an·ten·nal 〔æn'tɛnl̩; æn'tenl〕 *adj.* ①觸鬚的。②天線的。(亦作 **antennary**)

an·ten·nule 〔æn'tɛnjul; æn'tenju:l〕 *n.* (甲殼類之)小觸鬚。

an·te·nup·tial 〔ˌæntɪ'nʌpʃəl; 'ænti'nʌpʃəl〕 *adj.* 婚前的。

an·te·par·tum 〔ˌæntɪ'pɑrtəm; 'ænti'pɑ:təm〕 *adj.* 〖婦產科〗生產前的。

an·te·pen·di·um 〔ˌæntɪ'pɛndɪəm; ˌænti'pendiəm〕 *n., pl.* **-di·a** 〔-dɪə; -diə〕. 祭臺前之飾物(如帷幔等)。

an·te·pe·nult 〔ˌæntɪ'pinʌlt; 'æntipi'nʌlt〕 *n.* 倒數第三音節。—*adj.* 倒數第三音節的。(亦作 **antepenultimate**)

an·te·pran·di·al 〔ˌæntɪ'prændɪəl; 'ænti'prændjəl〕 *adj.* 餐前的。

an·te·ri·or 〔æn'tɪrɪɚ; æn'tiəriə〕 *adj.* ①前面(部)的。②以前的;較早的。—**ly,** *adv.*

anterior tooth 門牙或犬牙。

an·te·room 〔'æntɪ,rum; 'æntirum〕 *n.* ①較小的外室。②接待室。

an·te·ver·sion 〔ˌæntɪ'vɝʃən; ˌænti'və:ʃən〕 *n.* 〖醫〗子宮前傾。

an·te-Vic·tor·i·an 〔ˌæntɪvɪk'torɪən; ˌæntivik'tɔriən〕 *adj.* 維多利亞時代以前的。

an·te·war 〔ˌæntɪ'wɔr; ˌænti'wɔ:〕 *adj.* 戰前的。

ant·he·li·on 〔ænt'hiliən; æn'θi:ljən〕 *n., pl.* **-li·a** 〔-lɪə; -liə〕. 擬日輪;幻日。

an·thel·min·tic 〔ˌænθɛl'mɪntɪk; ˌænθel'mintik〕 *adj.* 〖醫〗殺腸蟲的。—*n.* 殺腸蟲藥。

an·them 〔'ænθəm; 'ænθəm〕 *n.* ①聖歌;讚美詩。②讚美歌。*national anthem* 國歌。

an·the·ma 〔æn'θimə; æn'θi:mə〕 *n., pl.* **-ma·ta** 〔-mətə; -mətə〕, **-the·mas.**〖醫〗疹。

an·ther 〔'ænθɚ; 'ænθə〕 *n.* 〖植物〗雄蕊之花粉囊;花藥。—**al,** *adj.*

an·ther·id·i·um 〔ˌænθə'rɪdɪəm; ˌænθə'ridiəm〕 *n., pl.* **-di·a** 〔-dɪə; -diə〕. (隱花植物之)藏精器。

an·the·sis 〔æn'θisɪs; æn'θi:sis〕 *n.* 〖植物〗開花期;開花。

ant hill 蟻丘;蟻塚。

an·thol·o·gist 〔æn'θɑlədʒɪst; æn'θɔlədʒist〕 *n.* 詩集或文選之編者。

an·thol·o·gize 〔æn'θɑlə,dʒaɪz; æn'θɔlədʒaiz〕 *v.*, **-gized, -giz·ing.** —*v.i.* 編纂詩集或文選。—*v.t.* 選…入詩集或文選。

an·thol·o·gy 〔æn'θɑlədʒɪ; æn'θɔlədʒi〕 *n.* 詩集;文選。

an·tho·ma·ni·a 〔ˌænθə'menɪə; ˌænθə'meiniə〕 *n.* 愛花狂。

An·tho·ny 〔'ænθənɪ, 'æntənɪ; 'æntəni, 'ænθəni〕 *n.* 男子名。

an·thoph·i·lous 〔æn'θɑfələs; æn'θɔfiləs〕 *adj.* ①〖植物〗蟲媒的。②〖動物〗好花的;以花爲食的。

an·tho·phore 〔'ænθə,for; 'ænθəfɔ:〕 *n.* 〖植物〗花柄。

an·thoph·o·rous 〔æn'θɑfərəs; æn'θɔfərəs〕 *adj.* 〖植物〗開花的;有花的。

an·tho·tax·y 〔'ænθə,tæksɪ; 'ænθətæksi〕 *n.* 〖植物〗花序。

An·tho·zo·a 〔ˌænθə'zoə; ˌænθə'zouə〕 *n. pl.* 〖動物〗珊瑚類。

an·thra·cene 〔'ænθrə,sin; 'ænθrəsi:n〕 *n.* 〖化〗蒽。

an·thra·cite 〔'ænθrə,saɪt; 'ænθrəsait〕 *n.* 無烟煤。

an·thra·cit·ic 〔ˌænθrə'sɪtɪk; ˌænθrə'sitik〕 *adj.* 無烟煤的;無烟煤質的。(亦作 **anthracitous**)

an·thrac·nose 〔æn'θræknos; æn'θræknous〕 *n.* 〖植物病理〗炭疽病。

an·thrax 〔'ænθræks; 'ænθræks〕 *n.* 〖醫〗癰;炭疽熱。

anthropo- 〖字首〗表"人;人類"之義, 例: anthropology. (在母音前作 **anthrop-**)

an·thro·po·cen·tric 〔ˌænθrəpə'sɛntrɪk; ˌænθrəpə'sentrik〕 *adj.* ①以人類爲宇宙中心的; 人類中心主義的。②以人類之經驗和價値以觀察、解釋萬物的。

an·thro·pog·e·ny 〔ˌænθrə'pɑdʒənɪ; ˌænθrə'pɔdʒini〕 *n.* 人種起源論。(亦作 **anthropogenesis**)

an·thro·po·ge·og·ra·phy 〔ˌæn-

θrəpədʒɪ'ɑgrəfɪ; ˌænθrəpədʒi'ɔgrəfi] *n.* 人文地理學。
an·thro·pog·ra·phy [ˌænθrə'pɑgrəfɪ; ˌænθrə'pɔgrəfi] *n.* 人類誌。
an·thro·poid ['ænθrəˌpɔɪd; 'ænθrəpɔid] *adj.* 似人類的。—*n.* 類人猿。
an·thro·po·log·ic [ˌænθrəpə'lɑdʒɪk; ˌænθrəpə'lɔdʒik] *adj.* 人類學的; 人類學上的。 **—al·ly,** *adv.*
an·thro·pol·o·gist [ˌænθrə'pɑlədʒɪst; ˌænθrə'pɔlədʒist] *n.* 人類學家。
an·thro·pol·o·gy [ˌænθrə'pɑlədʒɪ; ˌænθrə'pɔlədʒi] *n.* 人類學。
an·thro·pom·e·ter [ˌænθrə'pɑmɪtɚ; ˌænθrə'pɔmitə] *n.* 人體側量儀。
an·thro·pom·e·try [ˌæmθrə'pɑmətrɪ; ˌænθrə'pɔmitri] *n.* 人體測量學。 **—an·thro·po·met·ric,** *adj.*
an·thro·po·mor·phic [ˌænθrəpo'mɔrfɪk; ˌænθrəpə'mɔːfik] *adj.* 神人同形或同性論的。
an·thro·po·mor·phism [ˌænθrəpo'mɔrfɪzəm; ˌænθrəpə'mɔːfizəm] *n.* 神人同形或同性論。**—an·thro·po·mor·phist,** *n.*
an·thro·po·mor·phize [ˌænθrəpo'mɔrfaɪz; ˌænθrəpə'mɔːfaiz] *v.t.* & *v.i.*, **-phized, -phiz·ing.** 賦與(神)人形或人性。
an·thro·po·mor·phous [ˌænθrəpo'mɔrfəs; ˌænθrəpə'mɔːfəs] *adj.* ①有人形的; 似人形的。②神人同形或同性論的。
an·thro·poph·a·gi [ˌænθrə'pɑfəˌdʒaɪ; ˌænθrə'pɔfədʒai] *n. pl., sing.* **-a·gus** [-əgəs; -əgəs]. 食人族; 食人肉之人。
an·thro·poph·a·gous [ˌænθrə'pɑfəgəs; ˌænθrə'pɔfəgəs] *adj.* 食人肉的。
an·thro·poph·a·gy [ˌænθrə'pɑfədʒɪ; ˌænθrə'pɔfədʒi] *n.* 嗜食人肉。
an·thro·pot·o·my [ˌænθrə'pɑtəmɪ; ˌænθrə'pɔtəmi] *n.* 人體解剖學。**—an·thro·po·tom·i·cal,** *adj.* **—an·thro·pot·o·mist,** *n.*
an·ti ['æntaɪ, 'æntɪ; 'ænti] *n.* 〖俗〗持反對論者。—*adj.* 反對的。the *anti* group. 反對派。—*prep.* 反對。
anti- 〖字首〗表"反對; 抵抗; 排斥"之義。
an·ti·air·craft [ˌæntɪ'ɛrˌkræft; 'ænti'ɛə-krɑːft] *adj.* 防空的; 用以防禦敵機的。*antiaircraft* guns. 高射砲。
an·ti·a·li·en [ˌæntɪ'eljən; 'ænti'eiljən] *adj.* 排斥外人的; 排外的。
an·ti-A·mer·i·can [ˌæntɪə'mɛrəkən; 'æntiə'merikən] *adj.* 反美的。—*n.* 反美者。
an·ti-art [ˌæntɪ'ɑrt; ˌænti'ɑːt] *n.* 反藝術(如達達派, dadaist, 等全面否定傳統藝術的藝術派系)。
an·ti·bac·te·ri·al [ˌæntɪbæk'tɪrɪəl; 'æntibæk'tiəriəl] *adj.* 抗菌的。—*n.* 抗菌藥物。
an·ti·bal·lis·tic missile [ˌæntɪbə'lɪstɪk~; 'æntibə'listik~] 反飛彈飛彈(用以截擊敵方飛彈者)。(略作 **ABM**)
an·ti·bil·ious ['æntɪ'bɪljəs; 'ænti'biljəs] *adj.* 治黃膽病的。
an·ti·bi·o·sis [ˌæntɪbaɪ'osɪs; 'æntibai'ousis] *n.*〖生物〗抗生; 相剋。
an·ti·bi·ot·ic [ˌæntɪbaɪ'ɑtɪk; 'æntibai'ɔtik] *adj.* 〖生化〗抗生的。—*n.* 抗生素。
an·ti·bi·ot·ics [ˌæntɪbaɪ'ɑtɪks; 'æntibai'ɔtiks] *n. pl.* ①(作 *pl.* 解) 抗生素。②(作 *sing.* 解)抗生物質之研究; 抗生學。
an·ti·bod·y ['æntɪˌbɑdɪ; 'æntiˌbɔdi] *n., pl.* **-bod·ies.** 抗體。
an·ti-Bol·she·vik ['æntɪ'bɑlʃəvɪk; 'ænti'bɔlʃəvik] *adj.* 反共產黨的; 反布爾雪維克派的。—*n.* 反布爾雪維克派之人。
an·ti-bomb ['æntɪ'bɑm; 'ænti'bɔm] *adj.* 防彈的。
an·tic ['æntɪk; 'æntik] *n., adj., v.,* **-ticked, -tick·ing.** —*n.* ①(常 *pl.*)古怪; 滑稽的姿勢或動作。②〖古〗小丑。—*adj.* 古怪的; 滑稽的; 詼諧的。—*v.i.* 作滑稽的姿勢或動作。**—ly,** *adv.*
an·ti·car·i·ous [ˌæntɪ'kɛrɪəs; ˌænti'kɛəriəs] *adj.* 〖牙科〗抗齲的。
an·ti·ca·ta·lyst [ˌæntɪ'kætḷɪst; 'ænti'kætəlist] *n.* 〖化〗抗化劑。
an·ti·cath·ode [ˌæntɪ'kæθod; 'ænti'kæθoud] *n.* (X線管中放電時之)對陰極。
an·ti·christ ['æntɪˌkraɪst; 'æntikraist] *n.* ①反對基督者。②假基督。
an·ti·chris·tian [ˌæntɪ'krɪstʃən; 'ænti'kristjən] *adj.* 反對基督的; 反對基督敎的。—*n.* 反對基督者; 反對基督敎者。
an·tic·i·pant [æn'tɪsəpənt; æn'tisipənt] *adj.* 預期的。—*n.* 預期者; 預言者。
***an·tic·i·pate** [æn'tɪsəˌpet; æn'tisipeit] *v.t.,* **-pat·ed, -pat·ing.** ①預期; 預想。I *anticipate* great pleasure from my visit to Paris. 我預期巴黎之行將甚爲快樂。②預用。③先人一着; 占先。④預備。⑤預先考慮或說出。⑥提前。⑦使…提早發生。
***an·tic·i·pa·tion** [ænˌtɪsə'peʃən; ænˌtisi'peiʃən] *n.* ①預期; 預想。in *anticipation* of your success. 預祝你成功。②預用; 預備。③占先。in *anticipation*. 占先。④〖法律〗事前行爲; 信託基金之預先分派。⑤〖音樂〗先來音。
an·tic·i·pa·tive [æn'tɪsəˌpetɪv; æn'tisipeitiv] *adj.* 預期的; 預料的; 占先着的。
an·tic·i·pa·tor [æn'tɪsəˌpetɚ; æn'tisipeitə] *n.* 預期者; 預言者; 占先者。
an·tic·i·pa·to·ry [æn'tɪsəpəˌtorɪ; æn'tisipeitəri] *adj.* =**anticipative.**
an·ti·cler·i·cal [ˌæntɪ'klɛrɪkḷ; 'ænti'klerikl] *adj.* 反對僧侶(敎權)的。**—ism,** *n.*
an·ti·cli·mac·tic [ˌæntɪklaɪ'mæktɪk; 'æntiklai'mæktik] *adj.* 〖修辭〗(重要性、興趣等)漸減的; 漸降法的。
an·ti·cli·max [ˌæntɪ'klaɪmæks; 'ænti'klaimæks] *n.* ①突減(重要性、興趣等)。②〖修辭〗漸降法。③令人洩氣的轉變。
an·ti·cli·nal [ˌæntɪ'klaɪnḷ; 'ænti'klainḷ] *adj.* ①由中軸向兩側傾斜的; 向相反方向傾斜的。②〖地質〗背斜的。
an·ti·cline ['æntɪˌklaɪn; 'æntiklain] *n.* 〖地質〗背斜。
an·ti·clock·wise [ˌæntɪ'klɑkwaɪz; 'ænti'klɔkwaiz] *adj.* 反時針方向的。
an·ti·co·ag·u·lant [ˌæntɪko'ægjələnt; 'æntikou'ægjulənt] 〖醫〗 *adj.* (亦作 **anticoagulative**) 抗凝固的。—*n.* 抗凝劑。
an·ti-Com·in·tern [ˌæntɪ'kɑmɪnˌtɝn; 'ænti'kɔmintəːn] *adj.* 反共產黨第三國際的。
an·ti-com·mu·nism [ˌæntɪ'kɑmjuˌnɪzəm; 'ænti'kɔmjunizəm] *n.* 反共。
an·ti-com·mu·nist [ˌæntɪ'kɑmjunɪst; 'ænti'kɔmjunist] *adj.* 反共的。
an·ti·cor·ro·sive [ˌæntɪkə'rosɪv; 'æntikə'rousiv] *adj.* 防蝕的; 防腐的。—*n.* 防腐劑。
an·ti·cy·clone [ˌæntɪ'saɪklon; 'ænti'saikloun] *n.* 〖氣象〗高氣壓圈; 逆旋風。

an·ti·de·pres·sant [ˌæntidɪˈprɛsn̩t; ˈæntidiˈpresənt] *n.* 〖醫〗興奮劑。
an·ti·diph·the·rit·ic [ˌæntɪˌdɪfθəˈrɪtɪk; ˈæntiˌdifθəˈritik] *adj.* 預防白喉的。—*n.* 白喉注射劑。
an·ti·dot·al [ˈæntɪˌdotl̩; ˈæntidoutl] *adj.* 解毒的。
an·ti·dote [ˈæntɪˌdot; ˈæntidout] *n., v.,* **-dot·ed, -dot·ing.** —*n.* ①解毒劑;消毒藥。②有消除作用之物。—*v.t.*解毒;消毒。
an·ti·dump·ing [ˈæntɪˌdʌmpɪŋ; ˈæntiˌdʌmpiŋ] *adj.* 反傾銷的。
an·ti·en·zyme [ˌæntɪˈɛnzaɪm, -zɪm; ˌæntiˈenzaim] *n.* 〖化〗抗酵素。
an·ti·fe·brile [ˌæntɪˈfibrɪl; ˈæntiˈfi:brail] *adj.* 〖醫〗解熱的。—*n.* 解熱劑。
an·ti·fed·er·al·ist [ˌæntɪˈfɛdərəlɪst; ˈæntiˈfedərəlist] *n.* 反對聯邦主義者。
an·ti·for·eign [ˌæntɪˈfɔrɪn; ˈæntiˈfɔrin] *adj.* 排外的。
an·ti·freeze [ˌæntɪˈfriz; ˈæntiˈfri:z] *n.* 防凍劑。
an·ti·freez·ing [ˌæntɪˈfrɪzɪŋ; ˈæntiˈfriziŋ] *adj.* 防凍的。
an·ti·fric·tion [ˌæntɪˈfrɪkʃən; ˈæntiˈfrikʃən] *adj.* 減少磨擦的。—*n.* 減低或防止磨擦之物;滑潤劑。
an·ti·gas [ˌæntɪˈgæs; ˈæntiˈgæs] *adj.* 防毒(氣)的。
an·ti·gen [ˈæntədʒən; ˈæntidʒən] *n.* 〖生物〗抗原。
an·ti·grav·i·ty [ˌæntɪˈgrævətɪ; ˌæntiˈgræviti] *n.* 無重力(狀態)。
an·ti·grop·e·los [ˌæntɪˈgrɑpəˌloz; ˈæntiˈgrɔpilouz] *n.* (作 *sing* or *pl.* 解)防水綁腿。
an·ti-G suit [ˌæntɪˈdʒi ~; ˌæntiˈdʒi: ~] (飛行員所着之)抗G衣。(亦作**G-suit**)
an·ti·he·lix [ˌæntɪˈhilɪks; ˈæntiˈhi:liks] *n., pl.* **-hel·i·ces** [-ˈhiləsiz; -ˈhi:lisi:z], **-he·lix·es.** 〖解剖〗(耳翼之)對耳輪。
an·ti·he·ro [ˌæntɪˈhɪro; ˈæntiˈhiərou] *n., pl.* **-roes.** 小說或劇本中無英雄氣質的主角。—**ic,** *adj.*
an·ti·ic·er [ˌæntɪˈaɪsɚ; ˈæntiˈaisə] *n.* (飛機)防止結冰的裝置。
an·ti-im·pe·ri·al·ism [ˌæntɪɪmˈpɪrɪəlˌɪzəm; ˈæntiimˈpiəriəlizm] *n.* 反帝國主義。
an·ti-im·pe·ri·al·ist [ˌæntɪɪmˈpɪrɪəlɪst; ˈæntiimˈpiəriəlist] *n.*反帝國主義者。
an·ti-in·tel·lec·tu·al [ˌæntɪˌɪntəˈlɛktʃuəl; ˈæntiˌintəˈlektjuəl] *n.*反知識者;反知識分子者。—*adj.* 反知識的;反知識分子的。(亦作 **anti-intellectualist**)
an·ti·knock [ˌæntɪˈnɑk; ˈæntiˈnɔk] *n.* 減震劑(減低燃料爆音之物)。
an·ti·lith·ic [ˌæntɪˈlɪθɪk; ˈæntiˈliθik] *adj.* 〖醫〗預防結石的。—*n.* 防結石劑。
An·til·les, Greater and Less·er [ænˈtɪliz; ænˈtili:z] *n.* 大小安地列斯羣島(組成西印度羣島之二羣島)。
an·ti·log·a·rithm [ˌæntɪˈlɔgəˌrɪðəm; ˈæntiˈlɔgəriθəm] *n.* 〖數學〗反對數。
an·til·o·gy [ænˈtɪlədʒɪ; ænˈtilədʒi] *n., pl.* **-gies.** 自相矛盾。
an·ti·ma·cas·sar [ˌæntɪməˈkæsɚ; ˈæntiməˈkæsə] *n.* 罩布。
an·ti·mag·net·ic [ˌæntɪmægˈnɛtɪk; ˈæntimægˈnetik] *adj.* 抗磁的;有抗磁裝置的。
an·ti·ma·lar·i·al [ˌæntɪməˈlɛrɪəl; ˈæntiməˈlɛəriəl] *adj.* 抗瘧疾的。—*n.* 抗瘧疾劑。(亦作 **antimalaria**)
an·ti-Mar·ket·eer [ˌæntɪˌmɑrkɪtˈɪr; ˈæntiˌmɑ:kitˈiə] *n.* 反對英國加入歐洲共同市場者。
an·ti·mask, an·ti·masque [ˈæntɪˌmæsk; ˈæntimɑ:sk] *n.* (帶面具之)二幕間所穿插之喜劇或滑稽劇。
an·ti·mech·a·nized [ˌæntɪˈmɛkəˌnaɪzd; ˈæntiˈmekənaizd] *adj.* 〖軍〗反裝甲的。
an·ti·mi·cro·bi·al [ˌæntɪmaɪˈkrobɪəl; ˌæntimaiˈkroubiəl] 〖醫〗*n.* 抗菌劑;殺菌劑。—*adj.* 抗菌的;殺菌的。
an·ti·mil·i·ta·rism [ˌæntɪˈmɪlətəˌrɪzəm; ˌæntiˈmilitərizm] *n.* 反軍國主義。
an·ti·mis·sile [ˌæntɪˈmɪsəl; ˈæntiˈmisail] 〖軍〗*adj.* 反飛彈的。—*n.* 反飛彈飛彈。(亦作 **anti-missile**)
antimissile missile 反飛彈飛彈。
an·ti·mo·nar·chi·cal [ˌæntɪməˈnɑrkɪkəl; ˈæntiməˈnɑ:kikəl] *adj.* 反君主政體的。(亦作 **antimonarchic**)
an·ti·mon·arch·ist [ˌæntɪˈmɑnɚkɪst; ˈæntiˈmɔnəkist] *n.* 反對君主政體者。
an·ti·mo·ni·al [ˌæntɪˈmonɪəl; ˌæntiˈmounjəl] *adj.* 銻的;含銻的。—*n.* 含銻的化合物或藥劑。
an·ti·mo·nide [ˈæntɪməˌnaɪd, -nɪd; ˈæntimənaid] *n.* 〖化〗銻化物。
an·ti·mon·soon [ˌæntɪmɑnˈsun; ˈæntimɔnˈsu:n] *n.* 〖氣象〗反季風。
an·ti·mo·ny [ˈæntəˌmonɪ; ˈæntiməni] *n.* 〖化〗銻。
an·ti·neu·tri·no [ˌæntɪnjuˈtrino; ˈæntinju:ˈtri:nou] *n.* 〖物理〗反中微子。
an·ti·no·mi·an [ˌæntɪˈnomɪən; ˌæntiˈnoumiən] *adj.* (基督教中)主張廢棄道德律的;唯信仰論的。—*n.* (基督教中)主張廢棄道德律者;唯信仰論者。—**ism,** *n.*
an·ti·no·my [ænˈtɪnəmɪ; ænˈtinəmi] *n., pl.* **-mies.** 〖哲學〗二律相悖;矛盾。
an·ti·nov·el [ˈæntɪˌnɑvəl; ˈæntiˌnɔvəl] *n.* 用反傳統的手法寫成的小說(以生理或心理狀態爲主,動作爲輔的小說)。—**ist,** *n.*
an·ti·o·don·tal·gic [ˌæntioˌdɑnˈtældʒɪk, ˌæntaɪ-; ˈæntioudɔnˈtældʒik] 〖醫〗*n.* 止牙痛劑。—*adj.* 止牙痛的。(亦作 **antodontalgic**)
an·ti·ox·i·dant [ˌæntɪˈɑksədənt; ˈæntiˈɔksidənt] *n.* 〖化〗抗氧化劑。
an·ti·par·al·lel [ˌæntɪˈpærəˌlɛl; ˈæntiˈpærəlel] *adj.* 〖數學〗逆平行的;反平行的。
an·ti·pas·to [ˌɑntɪˈpɑsto; ˌɑ:ntiˈpɑ:stou] *n., pl.* **-tos.** 〖義〗開胃的食品。
an·ti·pa·thet·ic [ænˌtɪpəˈθɛtɪk; ænˌtipəˈθetik] *adj.* ①天性嫌惡的;天然不相容的;格格不入的。②引起憎惡的;令人起反感的。(亦作 **antipathetical**)
an·ti·path·ic [ˌæntɪˈpæθɪk; ˌæntiˈpæθik] *adj.* ①憎惡的。②〖醫〗有反對徵候的。
an·tip·a·thy [ænˈtɪpəθɪ; ænˈtipəθi] *n., pl.* **-thies.** 憎惡;反感;憎惡之物。***have an antipathy to*** 對…有反感。
an·ti·pa·tri·ot·ic [ˌæntɪˌpetrɪˈɑtɪk; ˈæntiˌpeitriˈɔtik] *adj.* 反愛國的。
an·ti·per·son·nel [ˌæntɪˌpɝsəˈnɛl; ˈæntiˌpə:səˈnel] *adj.* 〖軍〗用於對抗人的。
an·ti·per·spi·rant [ˌæntɪˈpɝspərənt; ˈæntiˈpə:spərənt] *n.* 止汗劑。
an·ti·phlo·gis·tic [ˌæntɪfloˈdʒɪstɪk; ˈæntiflouˈdʒistik] *n.*消炎劑。—*adj.* 消炎的。
an·ti·phlo·gis·tin [ˌæntɪfləˈdʒɪstɪn;

ˌæntifloˈdʒistin] *n.* 消炎軟膏;安福消腫膏。
an·ti·phon [ˈæntəˌfɑn; ˈæntifən] *n.* ①唱和詩歌。②交互輪唱之讚美詩。③回答;答覆。(亦作 **antiphony**)
an·tiph·o·nal [ænˈtifənl; ænˈtifənl] *adj.* 唱和詩歌的;交互輪唱的。—*n.*(亦作**antiphonary**)唱和詩歌集;交互輪唱之讚美詩集。
an·tiph·ra·sis [ænˈtɪfrəsɪs; ænˈtifrəsis] *n.* 〖修辭〗反語之使用;反用語意。
an·ti·pode [ˈæntɪˌpod; ˈæntipoud] *n.* 正相反的事物。
an·tip·o·des [ænˈtɪpəˌdiz; ænˈtipədi:z] *n. pl.* ①對蹠之地(地球上正相反之地區)。②對蹠地之居民。③(作 *sing.* or *pl.* 解)具有相反性質的人或物。
an·ti·pole [ˈæntɪˌpol; ˈæntipoul] *n.* ①反對極。②直接相反之物。
an·ti·pol·lu·tion [ˌæntɪpəˈluʃən; ˈæntipəˈlu:ʃən] *adj.* 反環境汚染的。
an·ti·pope [ˈæntɪˌpop; ˈæntipoup] *n.* 僭稱的羅馬教皇。
an·ti·pov·er·ty [ˌæntɪˈpɑvətɪ; ˈæntiˈpɔvəti] *adj.* 反貧窮的。—*n.* 美國政府所實施的反貧窮法案。
an·ti·py·ret·ic [ˈæntɪpaɪˈrɛtɪk; ˈæntipaiˈretik] 〖醫〗*adj.* 解熱的;退熱的。—*n.* 解熱劑;退熱劑。
an·ti·py·rin(e) [ˌæntɪˈpaɪərɪn; ˌæntiˈpaiərin]*n.* 安替比林(一種退熱及止痛劑)。
antiq. ①antiquarian. ②antiquities.
an·ti·quar·i·an[ˌæntɪˈkwɛrɪən;ˌæntiˈkwɛəriən] *adj.* 好古的;古物的;博古家的。—*n.* 好古的人;博古家。
an·ti·quar·i·an·ism [ˌæntɪˈkwɛrɪəˌnɪzəm; ˌæntiˈkwɛəriənizm] *n.* ①古物之研究。②蒐集古物之癖好。
an·ti·quar·i·an·ize [ˌæntɪˈkwɛrɪəˌnaɪz; ˌæntiˈkwɛəriənaiz] *v.i.*, **-ized, -iz·ing.** 〖俗〗醉心於古物之研究或蒐集。
an·ti·quar·y [ˈæntɪˌkwɛrɪ;ˈæntikwəri] *n.*, *pl.* **-quar·ies.** 古物專家;古董商人。
an·ti·quate[ˈæntəˌkwet; ˈæntikweit] *v.t.*, **-quat·ed, -quat·ing.** ①使作廢;廢棄。②使古舊;設計或創造成古式。
an·ti·quat·ed [ˈæntəˌkwetɪd; ˈæntikweitid]*adj.* 陳舊的;廢棄的;過時的;古風的。
***an·tique** [ænˈtik; ænˈti:k] *adj.* ①過時代的。She wore an *antique* gown to the costume party. 她在化裝舞會上穿了一件過時的長袍。②古代的;古老的。③舊式的。—*n.* ①古物;古董。②古代風格。③一種鉛字的字體。—*v.t.* 仿舊式製造、裝訂等。—**ness**, *n.* —**ly**, *adv.*
***an·tiq·ui·ty** [ænˈtɪkwətɪ; ænˈtikwiti] *n.*, *pl.* **-ties.** ①古;舊。②古代。Athens is a city of great *antiquity.* 雅典爲一古城。③(*pl.*)古物;古代的生活及風俗。④古人。
an·ti·rab·ic [ˌæntɪˈræbɪk; ˈæntiˈræbik] *adj.* 治療狂犬病的;防狂犬咬的。(亦作 **antirabies**)
an·ti·ra·chit·ic [ˌæntɪrəˈkɪtɪk; ˈæntirəˈkitik] *adj.* 預防或治療佝僂症的。
an·tir·rhi·num [ˌæntɪˈraɪnəm; ˌæntiˈrainəm] *n.* 〖植物〗金魚草。
an·ti·rust [ˌæntɪˈrʌst; ˈæntiˈrʌst] *adj.* 防銹的。—*n.* 防銹劑。
an·ti·sci·ence [ˌæntɪˈsaɪəns; ˈæntiˈsaiəns] *adj.* 反對犧牲人文價值而從事科學研究者的。
an·ti·scor·bu·tic [ˌæntɪskɔrˈbjutɪk; ˈæntiskɔ:ˈbju:tik] 〖醫〗*adj.* 抗壞血症的。—*n.* 抗壞血症劑。
an·ti-Sem·ite [ˌæntɪˈsɛmaɪt; ˈæntiˈsi:mait] *n.* 反對或排斥猶太人者。—**an·ti-Se·mit·ic**, *adj.* —**an·ti-Sem·i·tism**, *n.*
an·ti·sep·sis [ˌæntəˈsɛpsɪs; ˌæntiˈsepsis] *n.* 防腐;消毒;防腐法。
an·ti·sep·tic [ˌæntəˈsɛptɪk;ˌæntiˈseptik] *adj.* ①防腐的;殺菌的;有消毒力的。②消過毒的。—*n.*防腐劑;殺菌劑。—**al·ly**, *adv.*
an·ti·se·rum [ˌæntɪˈsɪrəm;ˈæntiˈsiərəm] *n.*, *pl.* **-se·rums, -se·ra** [-ˈsɪrə; -ˈsirə]. 抗毒血清。
an·ti·sex·u·al [ˌæntɪˈsɛkʃuəl; ˈæntiˈseksjuəl] *adj.* 敵視性慾的。(亦作**antisex**)
an·ti·slav·er·y [ˌæntəˈslevrɪ;ˈæntiˈsleivəri] *n.*, *adj.* 反對奴隸制度(的)。
an·ti·so·cial [ˌæntɪˈsoʃəl; ˈæntiˈsouʃəl] *adj.* ①不喜社交的;不擅社交的。②違反社會制度的。(亦作 **antisocialistic**)
an·ti·so·cial·ist [ˌæntɪˈsoʃəlɪst; ˈæntiˈsouʃəlist] *n.* 反對社會主義者。
an·ti·spas·mod·ic[ˌæntɪspæzˈmɑdɪk; ˈæntispæzˈmɔdik] *adj.* 〖醫〗使痙攣停止的;鎮痙的。—*n.* 鎮痙劑。
an·tis·tro·phe [ænˈtɪstrəfɪ; ænˈtistrəfi] *n.* ①(希臘歌詠隊之)中解(自左向右舞時所唱者)。②〖修辭〗逆反覆(同語顚倒覆用)。—**an·ti·stroph·ic**, *adj.*
an·ti·sub·ma·rine[ˌæntɪˈsʌbməˌrin; ˌæntiˈsʌbməri:n] *adj.* 反潛艇的。
an·ti·su·dor·if·ic [ˌæntɪsudəˈrɪfɪk; ˌæntisu:dəˈrifik] *adj.* 防汗的;止汗的。—*n.* 防汗劑;止汗劑。
an·ti·syph·i·lit·ic [ˌæntɪˌsɪfəˈlɪtɪk; ˌæntiˌsifiˈlitik] *adj.* 抗梅毒的。
an·ti·tank [ˌæntɪˈtæŋk; ˈæntiˈtæŋk] *adj.* 反戰車的。*antitank* gun. 反戰車砲。
an·ti·the·ism [ˌæntɪˈθiɪzəm; ˌæntiˈθi:izm] *n.* 無神論。
an·tith·e·sis [ænˈtɪθəsɪs; ænˈtiθisis] *n.*, *pl.* **-ses** [-ˌsiz; -si:z]. ①正相反。②對照;對比;對偶。③〖修辭〗對照格;對比法。④〖哲學〗(赫格爾辯證中"正","反","合"之)反。
an·ti·thet·i·cal [ˌæntɪˈθɛtɪkl; ˌæntiˈθetikəl] *adj.* ①對照格的;對比的。②正相反對的。(亦作 **antithetic**)
an·ti·tox·ic [ˌæntɪˈtɑksɪk; ˈæntiˈtɔksik] *adj.* ①抗毒的。②抗毒素的。
an·ti·tox·in(e) [ˌæntɪˈtɑksɪn; ˈæntiˈtɔksin] *n.* 抗毒素;含抗毒素之血漿。
an·ti·trade [ˈæntɪˌtred; ˈæntiˈtreid] *adj.* 逆貿易風的;反貿易風的。—*n.* (*pl.*)逆貿易風;反貿易風。
an·ti·trust [ˌæntɪˈtrʌst; ˈæntiˈtrʌst] *adj.* 反托辣斯的;反對資本兼併的。
an·ti·type [ˈæntəˌtaɪp; ˈæntitaip] *n.* ①由較早之原型或象徵所預示的人或事(如新約聖經中之人或事在舊約中預有型範者)。②相對之型範;對範;本體。—**an·ti·typ·ic, an·ti·typ·i·cal**, *adj.*
an·ti·un·ion [ˌæntɪˈjunjən;ˈæntiˈju:njən] *adj.* 〖美〗反對工會的。
an·ti·ven·in [ˌæntɪˈvɛnɪn; ˌæntiˈvenin] *n.* 抗蛇毒血清;抗蛇毒素。
an·ti·war [ˌæntɪˈwɔr; ˈæntiˈwɔ:] *adj.* 反戰的。
ant·ler [ˈæntlə; ˈæntlə] *n.* 鹿角;鹿角的叉枝。—**ant·lered**, *adj.*
ant lion 〖蟲〗蛟蜻蛉之幼蟲;蟻獅;沙挼子。
An·to·ni·a [ænˈtonɪə; ænˈtounjə] *n.*

女子名。

an·to·no·ma·si·a [ˌæntənoˈmeʒə; ˈæntənouˈmeiʒjə] *n.* 〖修辭〗換稱;代名(例如:his Honor 作爲 a judge 的稱呼)。

An·to·ny [ˈæntənɪ; ˈæntəni] *n.* 男子名。

an·to·nym [ˈæntəˌnɪm; ˈæntənim] *n.* 反意語;對語。**—ous,** *adj.*

an·trum [ˈæntrəm; ˈæntrəm] *n., pl.* **-tra** [-trə; -trə]. (骨之)腔;竇;房。

An·tung [ˈɑnˈduŋ; ˈɑːnˈduŋ] *n.* 安東(中國東北之一省,省會通化, Tunghwa).

A number 1 頂好;聒聒叫;第一流。

an·u·ri·a [əˈnjurɪə; əˈnjuəriə] *n.* 〖醫〗尿閉。(亦作 **anurisis**)

a·nus [ˈenəs; ˈeinəs] *n.* 肛門。

an·vil** [ˈænvɪl; ˈænvil] *n.* ①鐵砧。②〖解剖〗(耳內的)砧骨。③砧琴。 ***on the anvil 研討中;製作中。—*v.t.* 在鐵砧上錘鍊或製作。

***anx·i·e·ty** [æŋˈzaɪətɪ, æŋgˈz-; æŋˈzaiəti] *n., pl.* **-ties.** ①憂慮;不安。He was waiting for his father's return with *anxiety.* 他焦慮地等候他的父親回來。②渴望。The teacher praised him for his *anxiety* for knowledge. 老師稱讚他求知的慾望。

***anx·ious** [ˈæŋkʃəs, ˈæŋʃəs; ˈæŋkʃəs] *adj.* ①不安的;關懷的;掛念的。Her mother was *anxious* about her. 她母親掛念她。They became *anxious* at her delay. 他們對她的延遲漸感不安。 ②渴望的。He is *anxious* for her news. 他渴望知道她的消息。We were *anxious* to start on a journey. 我們渴望動身旅行。③使人不安的;使人憂慮的。 **—ly,** *adv.* 〖注意〗**anxious for** 表示渴望,後接所渴望之物。作不安或關懷解時, **anxious about** 指人, **anxious at** 指事或物。

anxious seat ①於某些教徒集會中位於講臺近旁的信心動搖者之坐位。②不安;憂慮。(亦作 **anxious bench**)

‡an·y [ˈɛnɪ; ˈeni] *adj.* ①任何一個;不論那個。*Any* book will do. 任何一本書均可。②有何;有多少。Have you *any* fresh fruit? 你有新鮮水果嗎? ③任何;每一個。The door doesn't seem to have *any* lock. 門好像沒有鎖。 ***any other*** 此外任何其他。Are there *any other* kinds? 此外尚有其他種類嗎? ***at any rate*** 無論如何。*At any rate,* we shall have enough. 無論如何我們會得到足够的數量。***in any case*** 無論如何;在任何情形之下。I shall be going there *in any case.* 無論如何我會去那邊的。—*pron.* ①任何一個;一個。Keep the cake; I don't want *any.* 將餅留起,我不要。②有何;任何。I don't think *any* of my friends have seen them. 我不以爲有任何朋友曾看到他們。***if any*** 卽有;雖有。There are very few trees, *if any.* 卽有樹亦不多。—*adv.* 略;稍。Did she cry *any?* 她哭了一下嗎? ***any good*** 有用;有益。It isn't *any good* to speak to him. 與他說無益。***any more*** **a.** =**anymore. b.** 另外;再。Let's not have *any more* fighting. 我們不要再打了。**c.** 現在。I don't smoke *any more.* 我現在已不吸煙了。***any more than*** 較…更(多,甚等)。***any which way*** 無一定方向地;隨便地。〖注意〗①**any more** 多用於談話或非正式場合中,在標準英文中,它被用在肯定的問句中或否定的陳述句中。 Do you want *any more* coffee? 你還要咖啡嗎?②在同類比較時,要用 **any other,** 如 This book is better than *any other* on the subject. 這一本書比討論此一問題的任何其他書籍爲佳。但異類比較時,則用 any 卽可,如 I think a movie is more entertaining than *any* book. 我認爲一部電影總比一本書更好看。

‡an·y·bod·y [ˈɛnɪˌbɑdɪ; ˈeniˌbɔdi] *pron., n., pl.* **-bodies.** ①任何人。Is *anybody* here? 有人在此嗎? ②重要人物。Is he *anybody?* 他是重要人物嗎? ***anybody else*** 別人。Does *anybody else* want to go? 有別人要去嗎? ***if anybody*** 若有人。Smith can do it *if anybody.* 若有人能做此,史密斯卽能。〖注意〗**anybody** 與 **somebody** 都可作"重要人物"解。 但 anybody 含有懷疑的意義。Somebody 則爲確定語氣且含有譏刺的成分。

***an·y·how** [ˈɛnɪˌhau; ˈenihau] *adv.* ①以任何方法。The answer is wrong *anyhow* you look at it. 你以何種眼光看這回答,它都是錯的。②無論如何。It may rain, but *anyhow* I shall go out. 可能下雨,但我無論如何要出門。③隨便。

an·y·more [ˈɛnɪmɔr, -mor; ˈenimɔː] *adv.* (不)再;再也(不)。

‡an·y·one [ˈɛnɪˌwʌn; ˈeniwʌn] *pron.* 任何人。*Anyone* can come here. 任何人可來這裏。〖注意〗當重音在 one 上時, any 與 one 應分寫成兩個字, one 可以指人,也可以指物。

an·y·place [ˈɛnɪˌples; ˈenipleis] *adv.* 〖俗〗無論何處;任何地方。

‡an·y·thing [ˈɛnɪˌθɪŋ; ˈeniθiŋ] *n.* & *pron.* 任何事物。Is there *anything* for me? 有東西給我嗎? ***anything but*** 並不;決不。She is *anything but* beautiful. 她並不美麗。***if anything*** 若有任何情形…;若要說,不過…罷了。He is, *if anything,* a little taller than I. 若要說他比我高,只不過稍高一點罷了。***like anything*** 〖俗〗非常。They work *like anything.* 他們非常努力。 ***not care anything for*** (=care nothing for) 不在乎。***not come to anything*** 無結果。***not have anything to do with*** (=have nothing to do with) 無關;不理。***not think anything of*** (=think nothing of) 不以爲意。—*adv.* 在任何方面;在任何程度內;有一點。Is it *anything* like mine? 有一點像我的嗎?

an·y·time [ˈɛnɪˌtaɪm; ˈenitaim] *adv.* ①任何時候;無論何時。②總是;沒有例外。

‡an·y·way [ˈɛnɪˌwe; ˈeniwei] *adv.* ①無論如何。I am coming *anyway,* no matter what you say. 不管你怎麼說,我無論如何要來。②用任何方法;以任何方式。 She told him to do the job *anyway* he wanted. 她要他用他所喜歡的任何方式做那工作。

an·y·ways [ˈɛnɪˌwez; ˈeniweiz] *adv.* 〖俗〗從任何觀點;不管怎樣。

an·y·where** [ˈɛnɪˌhwɛr; ˈeniwɛə, -hwɛə] *adv.* ① 任何地方;無論何處。You can go *anywhere* you like. 你可隨意去任何地方。②表數目之不定。 *anywhere* from 40 to 60 students. 大約四十至六十名學生。anywhere from*** 〖俗〗在一定範圍內之某點。It will take *anywhere from* two to three hours to drive there. 開車到那兒約需二至三小時。***anywhere near*** 〖俗〗將近;幾乎(僅用在否定句或問句中)。The job is not *anywhere near* done. 這件工作距完成之日尚早。***if anywhere*** 如有地方。You will find it in Taipei *if anywhere.* 你如有地方可以找

到它,臺北卽其地。 ***get anywhere***〖俗〗進展;成功。—*n.* 任何地方。

an·y·wise ['ɛnɪ,waɪz; 'eniwaiz] *adv.* 無論如何;無論怎樣;決。

An·zac ['ænzæk; 'ænzæk] *n.* 澳洲或紐西蘭之軍人。

a/o, a.o. account of. (亦作 **A/O**)

A.O.D. Army Ordnance Department.

A-OK, A-O.K. ['e,o'ke; 'eiou'kei] *adj., adv., interj.* 完美的。an *A.O.K.* rocket launching. 一次完美的火箭發射。

A one ['e'wʌn; 'ei'wʌn]〖俗〗第一等的;第一流的;極佳的。an *A one* man of music. 第一流的音樂家。(亦作 **A-l, A No. 1, A number 1**)

AOR〖醫〗(如有危險)概不負責。

a·o·rist ['eərɪst; 'ɛərist] *n.* 希臘文法中之不定過去式。

a·or·ta [e'ɔrtə; ei'ɔ:tə] *n., pl.* **-tas, -tae** [-ti; -ti:].〖解剖〗大動脈;主動脈。

a·or·tic [e'ɔrtɪk; ei'ɔ:tik] *adj.* 大動脈的;主動脈的。

a·or·ti·tis [,eɔr'taɪtɪs; ,eiɔ:'taitis] *n.*〖醫〗主動脈發炎。

a·ou·dad ['ɑu,dæd; 'ɑ:udæd] *n.* 北非洲所產之野生綿羊。

à ou·trance [a,u'trɑ̃s; ɑ:,u:'trɑ̃s]〖法〗(鬥)至最後;死而後已。

Ap. ①Apostle. ②April.

A.P. ①Associated Press. 美聯社。②Air Police.

ap-[1]〖字首〗**ad-** 的變體,用在 **p** 之前。如: appear.

ap-[2]〖字首〗**apo-** 的變體,用在母音或 **h** 之前。如:aphelion.

A/P, a/p ①account paid. ②accounts payable. ③authority to pay or purchase.

APA ①American Psychological Association. ②American Psychiatric Association.

a·pace [ə'pes; ə'peis] *adv.* 急速地;快地。

A·pach·e [ə'pætʃɪ; ə'pætʃi] *n., pl.* **A·pach·es, A·pach·e.** 阿柏支族(印第安人之一部落,在美國西南部);阿柏支族印第安人。

‡**a·part** [ə'pɑrt; ə'pɑ:t] *adv.* ①拆開。The machine was taken *apart* for inspection.這部機器被拆開檢查。②分開。The boys are fighting. Please keep them *apart.* 孩子們在打架,請把他們分開。③離開;除此。④各別;個別。View each idea *apart.* 請各別審察每一種辦法。***apart from*** 除…之外;此外。 ***joking apart*** 不說笑話;認眞地說。 ***know apart*** 認出其間的異點。 ***set apart*** 留置。 Please *set* the money *apart* for future use. 請將此款留作將來之用。***take apart*** **a.** 拆開。They *took* the bicycle *apart.* 他們將脚踏車拆開。**b.** 批評;(文字或口頭上的)攻擊。**c.** 嚴格分析或考查。—*adj.* ①異於其他的;與衆不同的(用在名詞的後面)。He is a man *apart.* 他與衆不同。②意見不合。The allies are still *apart.* 盟邦間意見仍有不合。

a·part·heid [ə'pɑrthet, -haɪt; ə'pɑ:theit, -eid] *n.* ①種族隔離制(行於南非)。②任何隔離種族的或政治團體之制度。

***a·part·ment** [ə'pɑrtmənt; ə'pɑ:tmənt] *n.*〖美〗①公寓。It is cheaper to live in an *apartment* than to stay at a hotel. 住公寓比住旅館便宜。②房間。③公寓式房屋。

apartment house〖美〗隔成公寓的建築物。(亦作 **apartment building**)

a·part·ness [ə'pɑrtnɪs; ə'pɑ:tnis] *n.* 冷漠;孤立;疏遠。

ap·a·thet·ic [,æpə'θɛtɪk; ,æpə'θetik] *adj.* 冷淡的;缺乏情感的;無動於衷的;缺乏興趣的。—**al·ly,** *adv.*

ap·a·thy ['æpəθɪ; 'æpəθi] *n., pl.* **-thies.** 冷淡;漠不關心。

ap·a·tite ['æpə,taɪt; 'æpətait] *n.*〖礦〗磷灰石。

ape** [ep; eip] *n., v.,* **aped, ap·ing.** —*n.* ①猿。②任何猴子。③模倣者。the *apes* of fashion. 時尚的模仿者。④醜陋笨拙的人;醜八怪。—*v.t.* 模仿。go ape over*** (***for***)〖美俚〗對…傾心。

a·peak [ə'pik; ə'pi:k] *adv. & adj.*〖航海〗成直立之位置或方向地(的);垂直地(的)。

Ap·en·nines ['æpə,naɪnz; 'æpinainz] *n. pl.* 亞平寧山脈(在義大利中部)。

a·pep·si·a [e'pɛpsɪə; ei'pepsiə] *n.*〖醫〗不消化;消化不良。(亦作 **apepsy**)

a·per·çu [ɑpɛr'sy; ,æpə:'sju:] *n., pl.* **-çus** [-'sy; -'sju:z].〖法〗①一瞥;一眼。②洞察。③摘要;概覽。

a·pe·ri·ent [ə'pɪrɪənt; ə'piəriənt] *adj.* 輕瀉的;通便的。—*n.* 輕瀉劑;通便藥。(亦作 **aperitive**)

a·pé·ri·tif [aperi'tif; ɑ:peiri:'ti:f]〖法〗*n.* 飯前酒。

***ap·er·ture** ['æpətʃɚ; 'æpətjuə] *n.* ①孔;隙。②〖光學〗鏡徑(球面鏡的口徑);孔徑。A camera has an *aperture.* (每一)攝影機(均)有一鏡徑。

ap·er·tured ['æpətʃɚd; 'æpətjuəd] *adj.* 有孔的;有球徑的。

ap·er·y ['epərɪ; 'eipəri] *n., pl.* **-er·ies.** ①模仿之行爲;模擬的動作。②不智的詭計。

a·pex ['epɛks; 'eipeks] *n., pl.* **a·pex·es, ap·i·ces** ['æpɪ,siz; 'eipisi:z]. 最高點;尖頂。

a·pha·ki·a [ə'fekɪə; ə'feikiə] *n.*〖眼科〗無晶狀體;缺少晶狀體。(亦作 **aphacia**)

a·pha·si·a [ə'feʒə; æ'feizjə] *n.*〖醫〗失語症;無語言能力。—**a·pha·sic,** *n., adj.*

a·phe·li·on [æ'filɪən; æ'fi:ljən] *n., pl.* **-li·a** [-lɪə; -liə].〖天文〗遠日點。

a·phe·li·o·trop·ic [ə,filɪə'trɑpɪk; ə,fi:liə'trɔpik] *adj.*〖植物〗背陽光性的。

a·pher·e·sis [ə'fɛrəsɪs; æ'fiərisis] *n.*〖文法〗非重讀字首之省略。(亦作 **aphaeresis**)

aph·e·sis ['æfəsɪs; 'æfisis] *n.*〖文法〗非重讀字首之消失。如 amend 略爲 mend.

a·phi·cide ['efəsaɪd, 'æfə-; 'eifəsaid] *n.* 殺蚜蟲藥。

a·phid ['efɪd, 'æfɪd; 'eifid, 'æfid] *n.*〖動物〗蚜蟲。

a·phis ['efɪs, 'æfɪs; 'eifis, 'æfis] *n., pl.* **a·phi·des** ['æfɪ,diz; 'æfidi:z]. =**aphid.**

a·pho·ni·a [e'fonɪə; æ'founjə] *n.*〖醫〗無發音能;失音;瘖。

a·phon·ic [ə'fɑnɪk; æ'fɔnik] *adj.* ①無聲的;靜的。②〖語音〗無音的;無聲的。③〖醫〗患失音症的。—*n.*〖醫〗失音症患者。

aph·o·rism ['æfə,rɪzəm; 'æfərizm] *n.* 格言;警語。

aph·o·rist ['æfərɪst; 'æfərist] *n.* 格言作者;警句家。

aph·o·ris·tic [,æfə'rɪstɪk; ,æfə'ristik] *adj.* ①格言的;似格言的。②喜撰造格言的。

aph·ro·di·sia [,æfrə'dɪʒə, -'dɪzɪə; ,æfrə'diziə] *n.* 性慾。

aph·ro·dis·i·ac [,æfrə'dɪzɪ,æk; ,æfrə'diziæk] *adj.* (亦作 **aphrodisiacal**) 引起性慾的。—*n.* 壯陽劑;春藥。

Aph·ro·di·te [,æfrə'daɪtɪ; ,æfrə'daiti] *n.*〖希臘神話〗愛與美之女神(相當於羅馬的 Venus).

aph·tha ['æfθə; 'æfθə] *n., pl.* **-thae** [-θi; -θi:].〖醫〗鵝口瘡。

aph·thong ['æfθɔŋ; 'æfθɔːŋ] *n.* 不讀音字母。—**al,** *adj.*
a·phyl·lous [e'fɪləs; ei'filəs] *adj.*〖植物〗無葉的;無葉性的。
a·pi·an ['epɪən; 'eipjən] *adj.* 蜜蜂的。
Ap·i·a·nus [ˌæpɪ'enəs; ˌæpi'einəs] *n.* 月球表面第四象限內之一坑名。
a·pi·ar·i·an [ˌepɪ'ɛrɪən; ˌeipi'ɛəriən] *adj.* 蜂的;養蜂的。—*n.* 養蜂者。
a·pi·a·rist ['epɪərɪst; 'eipjərist] *n.* 養蜂者。
a·pi·ar·y ['epɪˌɛrɪ; 'eipjəri] *n., pl.* **-ar·ies.** 養蜂場;蜂房。
ap·i·cal ['æpɪkl̩; 'æpikəl] *adj.* ①頂的;頂點的;絕頂的。②〖語言〗舌尖發出的。—*n.* 舌尖音(如 t, d, s, l)。
a·pi·cul·ture ['epɪˌkʌltʃə; 'eipi'kʌltʃə] *n.* 養蜂。
a·pi·cul·tur·ist [ˌepɪ'kʌltʃurɪst; ˌeipi'kʌltʃərist] *n.* 養蜂者;養蜂業者。
*__a·piece__ [ə'pis; ə'piːs] *adv.* 每人;每個;各。He gave the boys a dollar *apiece.* 他給孩子們一人一塊錢。
a·pi·ol·o·gy [ˌepɪ'ɑlədʒɪ; ˌeipi'ɔlədʒi] *n.* 蜜蜂學。
ap·ish ['epɪʃ; 'eipiʃ] *adj.* ①似猿的。②卑屈地仿效的;模擬的。③愚蠢的;笨拙的;不自然的;傻裏傻氣地裝模作樣的。
Apl. April.
a·pla·cen·tal [ˌeplə'sɛntl̩; ˌeiplə'sentəl] *adj.*〖動物〗無胎盤的。
a·plen·ty [ə'plɛntɪ; ə'plenti] *adv.*〖俚〗①豐富地。②極(=very much). —*adj.* 豐富的。—*n.*〖美〗豐富;大量(=a plenty).
ap·lite ['æplaɪt; 'æplait] *n.* 半花崗岩。
a·plomb [ə'plɑm; ə'plɔm] *n.*①鉛直;垂直。②自若;沉着。
ap·ne·a, ap·noe·a [æp'niə; æp'niːə] *n.*〖醫〗①呼吸暫停;無呼吸。②窒息。
APO, A.P.O. Army Post Office.(美國陸軍)軍郵局。
Apoc. ①Apocalypse. ②Apocrypha.
a·poc·a·lypse [ə'pɑkəˌlɪps; ə'pɔkəlips] *n.*①天啓;啓示。②天啓書;啓示文學。③(A-)〖聖經〗啓示錄。
a·poc·a·lyp·tic [əˌpɑkə'lɪptɪk; əˌpɔkə'liptik] *adj.*(亦作 **apocalyptical**)天啓的;(聖經)啓示錄的。—*n.* 天示預兆的解釋者。
ap·o·chro·mat ['æpəkroˌmæt; 'æpəkroumæt] *n.*〖光學〗高度消色鏡。
a·poc·o·pe [ə'pɑkəpɪ; ə'pɔkəpi] *n.*〖文法〗語尾省略,如 chapelle 略作 chapel.
a·poc·ry·pha [ə'pɑkrəfə; ə'pɔkrifə] *n. pl.*①任何作者可疑的著作品;僞書。②(A-)〖宗教〗僞經。
a·poc·ry·phal [ə'pɑkrəfəl; ə'pɔkrifəl] *adj.* 作者可疑的。
ap·od ['æpɑd; 'æpɔd] *n.* 無足動物;無腹鰭之魚。—*adj.* 無足的;無腹鰭的。
ap·o·dal ['æpədl̩; 'æpədəl] *adj.*〖動物〗①無足的。②無腹鰭的。
ap·o·dic·tic [ˌæpə'dɪktɪk; ˌæpou'diktik] *adj.*〖哲學,邏輯〗必然的;明白無疑的。(亦作 **apodeictic**)
a·pod·o·sis [ə'pɑdəsɪs; ə'pɔdəsis] *n., pl.* **-ses** [-ˌsiz; -siːz].〖文法〗結句(條件句子中表結論或結果之子句)。
ap·o·gee ['æpəˌdʒi; 'æpoudʒiː] *n.* ①〖天文〗遠地點。②最高點;極點。
—**ap·o·ge·an, ap·o·ge·al, ap·o·ge·ic,** *adj.*
ap·o·graph ['æpəˌgræf; 'æpəgrɑːf] *n.* 謄本。
a·po·lar [e'polə; ei'poulə] *adj.* 非極的;無極的。
ap·o·laus·tic [ˌæpə'lɔstɪk; ˌæpə'lɔːstik] *adj.* 放縱的;耽於逸樂的;享樂主義的。
a·po·lit·i·cal [ˌepə'lɪtəkl̩; ˌeipə'litikəl] *adj.* 非政治性的。—**ly,** *adv.*
A·pol·li·nar·is [əˌpɑlə'nɛrɪs; əˌpɔli'nɛəris] *n.*(德國產之)一種礦泉飲料。
A·pol·lo [ə'pɑlo; ə'pɔlou] *n.* ①〖希臘、羅馬神話〗阿波羅神;司日光、醫療、音樂、詩、預言、男性美等的神;太陽神。②美少年;美男子。
Apollo 11 太陽神十一號(實現人類首次登陸月球,由美國太空人所駕駛的太空船)。
Ap·ol·lo·ni·us [ˌæpə'lonɪəs; ˌæpə'lounjəs] *n.* 月球表面第一象限內之一坑名。
Apollo Program 太陽神計畫(包括人類之首次登陸月球在內的美國之一連串太空飛行)。
A·pol·lyon [ə'pɑljən; ə'pɔljən] *n.* ①〖聖經〗亞玻倫。②惡魔。
a·pol·o·get·ic [əˌpɑlə'dʒɛtɪk; əˌpɔlə'dʒetik] *adj.* 辯解的;道歉的;認錯的。—**al·ly,** *adv.*
a·pol·o·get·ics [əˌpɑlə'dʒɛtɪks; əˌpɔlə'dʒetiks] *n.*(基督教)護教學。
ap·o·lo·gi·a [ˌæpə'lodʒɪə; ˌæpə'loudʒiə] *n.*①(口頭或書面)正式的辯護。②道歉。
a·pol·o·gist [ə'pɑlədʒɪst; ə'pɔlədʒist] *n.*①辯護者;辯解者。②(基督教)護教學專家。
*__a·pol·o·gize__ [ə'pɑləˌdʒaɪz; ə'pɔlədʒaiz] *v.i.,* **-gized, -giz·ing.** ①道歉;謝罪。She *apologized* to her teacher for coming to school late. 她因遲到向老師道歉。②作正式的辯護。to *apologize* for oneself. 替自己辯護。
ap·o·logue ['æpəˌlɔg; 'æpəlɔg] *n.* 教訓;寓言。
*__a·pol·o·gy__ [ə'pɑlədʒɪ; ə'pɔlədʒi] *n., pl.* **-gies.** ①道歉;謝罪。I owe him an *apology.* 我應向他道歉。②辯白;辯護;辯明。③勉强的代用物。It is a sad *apology* for a hat. 這是一個勉强的帽子代用品。
ap·o·mict ['æpəˌmɪkt; 'æpəmikt] *n.* 單性繁殖的生物。—**ic,** *adj.* —**i·cal·ly,** *adv.*
ap·o·phthegm, ap·o·thegm ['æpəˌθɛm; 'æpouθem] *n.* 格言;箴言。
a·poph·y·sis [ə'pɑfəsɪs; ə'pɔfisis] *n., pl.* **-ses** [-ˌsiz; -siːz]. ①〖解剖〗骨突。②〖植物〗隆起。
ap·o·plec·tic [ˌæpə'plɛktɪk; ˌæpə'plektik] *adj.* ①中風的;患中風的。②易怒的。—*n.* ①患中風症者;易患中風者。②中風藥。
ap·o·plex·y ['æpəˌplɛksɪ; 'æpəpleksi] *n.*〖醫〗中風;卒中。 *cerebral apoplexy* 腦溢血;大腦卒中。
a·port [ə'port; ə'pɔːt] *adv.*〖航海〗向左舷;在左舷。
ap·o·si·o·pe·sis [ˌæpəˌsaɪə'pisɪs; ˌæpousaiou'piːsis] *n.*〖修辭〗頓絕法;急止法。
ap·o·spor·y ['æpəˌsporɪ; 'æpəspouəri] *n.*〖植物〗無胞子生殖。
a·pos·ta·sy [ə'pɑstəsɪ; ə'pɔstəsi] *n., pl.* **-sies.** 背教;脫黨;變節。
a·pos·tate [ə'pɑstet; ə'pɔstit] *n.* 背教者;脫黨者;變節者。—*adj.* 背教的;脫黨的;變節的。
a·pos·ta·tize [ə'pɑstəˌtaɪz; ə'pɔstətaiz] *v.i.,* **-tized, -tiz·ing.** 背教;脫黨;變節。
a pos·te·ri·o·ri ['epɑsˌtɪrɪ'oraɪ; 'eipɔsˌteri'ɔːrai]〖拉〗①自結果追溯其原因的。②歸納的(地)。③經驗的。
a·pos·til(le) [ə'pɑstɪl; ə'pɔstil] *n.* 旁註。
a·pos·tle [ə'pɑsl̩; ə'pɔsl] *n.* ①(A-)使徒(基督十二弟子之一)。②傳道者。③(主義,政策等之)提倡者;宣傳家。 *apostle* of free trade. 自由貿易之提倡者。—**ship,** *n.*

Apostles' Creed 使徒信經。
Apostle spoon 柄端有使徒像的湯匙。
a·pos·to·late [əˈpɑstlɪt; əˈpɔstəlit] *n.* ①使徒之身分。②羅馬教皇之職位。
ap·os·tol·ic [ˌæpəsˈtɑlɪk; ˌæpəsˈtɔlik] *adj.* ①使徒的。②使徒時代的。③羅馬教皇的。
Apostolic Fathers ①使徒時代的基督教教父。②他們的著作。
apostolic internunciature 教廷公使館。
apostolic internuncio 教廷公使。
apostolic nuncio 教廷大使。
*__a·pos·tro·phe__[1] [əˈpɑstrəfɪ; əˈpɔstrəfi] *n.* 〖文法〗①省略符號('), 如: *can't* 以代 cannot. ②所有格符號, 表示"所有"的關係, 如: *rat's* tail. 鼠的尾巴。③形成複數形, 如: two 0's. 兩個 0。④表示一字中之某一音不發, 如:'lectric =electric.
*__apos·tro·phe__[2] *n.* 〖修辭〗頓呼法 (敍述中忽變語氣而對並不在場之人所作的直接呼語); 對無生命物體之談話。
ap·os·troph·ic [ˌæpəsˈtrɑfɪk; ˌæpəsˈtrɔfik] *adj.* ①(使用)省略符號的; (使用) 所有格符號的。②〖修辭〗(使用) 頓呼法的。
a·pos·tro·phize [əˈpɑstrəˌfaɪz; əˈpɔstrəfaiz] *v.*, **-phized, -phiz·ing.** *—v.t.* ① 用上省略符號以縮短; 加以省略符號或所有格符號。②〖修辭〗用頓呼法稱呼。*—v.i.* ①使用省略符號或所有格符號。②〖修辭〗頓呼。
apothecaries' measure 藥劑用液量法。
apothecaries weight 藥劑用衡量法。
a·poth·e·car·y [əˈpɑθəˌkɛrɪ; əˈpɔθikəri] *n.*, *pl.* **-car·ies.** 藥劑師。
ap·o·theg·mat·ic [ˌæpəθɛgˈmætɪk; ˌæpəθegˈmætik] *adj.* 格言的; 箴言的; 含格言的; 用格言的。 (亦作 **apothegmatical, apophthegmatic**)
ap·o·them [ˈæpəˌθɛm; ˈæpəθem] *n.* 〖數學〗邊心距。
a·poth·e·o·sis [əˌpɑθɪˈosɪs; əˌpɔθiˈousis] *n.*, *pl.* **-ses** [-siz; -siːz]. ①尊崇爲神; 神聖化。②崇拜; 頌揚。③神聖之理想。 **—a·poth·e·o·size,** *v.*
ap·o·tro·pa·ic [ˌæpətrəˈpeɪk; ˌæpətrəˈpeiik] *adj.* 作驅邪用的。
ap·o·tro·pa·ion [ˌæpətrəˈpeən; ˌæpətrəˈpeijɔn] *n.*, *pl.* **-pa·ia** [-ˈpeə, -ˈpaɪə; -ˈpeijə]. 驅邪物。
A-power [ˈeˌpaur; ˈeipauə] *n.* 原子力。
app. ①appendix. ②appended. ③appointed. ④apprentice. ⑤apparent. ⑥apparently.
App. Apostles.
*__ap·pal(l)__ [əˈpɔl; əˈpɔːl] *v.t.*, **-palled, -pall·ing.** 驚嚇; 使驚駭。 They were *appalled* at the news. 他們被這消息嚇壞了。
Ap·pa·la·chi·an Mountains [ˌæpəˈlætʃɪən ~; ˌæpəˈleitʃjən ~] 阿帕拉契山脈(北美東部)。(亦作 **Appalachians**)
*__ap·pall·ing__ [əˈpɔlɪŋ; əˈpɔːliŋ] *adj.* 駭人的。When will this *appalling* war end? 這可怕的戰爭何時方可結束? **—ly,** *adv.*
ap·pa·nage, ap·a·nage [ˈæpənɪdʒ; ˈæpənidʒ] *n.* ①封地; 采邑; 祿食。②合法的額外收入。③屬國; 屬地。④從屬物; 屬性。
*__ap·pa·ra·tus__ [ˌæpəˈretəs, ˌæpəˈrætəs; ˌæpəˈreitəs] *n.*, *pl.* **-tus, -tus·es.** ①儀器; 器械; 裝置。 chemical *apparatus.* 化學儀器。②器官。 respiratory *apparatus.* 呼吸器官。③政治組織的下層組織。
*__ap·par·el__ [əˈpærəl; əˈpærəl] *n.*, *v.*, **-eled, -el·ing.** *—n.* 衣服; 裝飾。the king's *apparel.* 國王的服裝。*—v.t.* 加以裝飾。
*__ap·par·ent__ [əˈpærənt, əˈpɛrənt; əˈpærənt, əˈpɛərənt] *adj.* ①顯然的; 明白的。His guilt is *apparent.* 他的罪惡昭彰。②可見的。③外表上的; 似乎的。④(直系親屬之)絕對有權繼承王位、爵號或產業的。 ***heir apparent*** (亦作 **apparent heir**) 太子; 嗣子; 王儲。*—v.t.* 使結合; 使發生密切關係。
‡__ap·par·ent·ly__ [əˈpærəntlɪ, əˈpɛr-; əˈpærəntli, -ˈpɛər-] *adv.* ①顯然地。*Apparently* he has changed his mind. 顯然他已改變了他的意向。②外表地; 似乎。
ap·pa·ri·tion [ˌæpəˈrɪʃən; ˌæpəˈriʃən] *n.* ①妖怪; 幽靈。②出現(尤指不平常的或不意的)。③如此出現之事物。 **—al,** *adj.*
ap·par·i·tor [əˈpærətɚ; əˈpæritɔː] *n.* ①(古羅馬法院之)執行官。②(宗教裁判所之)命令送達官。③(英國大學之)捧持校長權標者。
‡__ap·peal__ [əˈpil; əˈpiːl] *n.* ①吸引力; 引起興趣。That sort of music hasn't much *appeal* for me. 那種音樂不能引起我多大的興趣。②懇求; 哀懇。an *appeal* for aid. 懇求援助。③上訴。 court of *appeal.* 上訴法庭。④訴諸。an *appeal* to arms. 訴之於武力。 *—v.i.* ①求助; 求援; 哀懇。to *appeal* for mercy. 求宥。 ②上訴。 He *appealed* against the judge's decision. 他不服法官的判決而上訴。③訴諸; 訴之於。to *appeal* to force. 訴之於武力。④引起興趣; 引人入勝; 投人所好。This color *appeals* to me. 這顏色投我所好。*—v.t.* 爲(某案)上訴。 **—a·bil·i·ty,** *n.* **—a·ble,** *adj.*
ap·peal·ing [əˈpilɪŋ; əˈpiːliŋ] *adj.* 上訴的; 哀懇的; 令人心動的。 **—ly,** *adv.*
‡__ap·pear__ [əˈpɪr; əˈpiə] *v.i.* ①出現; 呈現。 The sun *appeared* on the horizon. 太陽出現在地平線上。②似乎; 顯得。He *appears* quite old. 他顯得很老。③出版; 發表。This new book will *appear* next month. 這本新書下月出版。④公開出現。 to *appear* on the stage. 登臺(演唱)。⑤覺得; 覺察。It *appears* that we must go. 好像我們該走了。***appear in court*** 出庭(應詢或作證)。 ***as it appears*** 似乎。 He is quite well, *as it appears.* 他似乎很健康。
‡__ap·pear·ance__ [əˈpɪrəns; əˈpiərəns] *n.* ①出現; 呈現。His sudden *appearance* quite surprised me. 他的突然出現, 使我很驚奇。②外表; 外觀; 儀表。He is a man of noble *appearance.* 他是一個有高尚儀表的人。③登臺。 This is his first *appearance* on the stage. 這是他第一次登臺。 ④出版。⑤外表的虛飾; 體面。to save *appearances.* 維持面子。⑥出現之事物。⑦出庭。⑧(*pl.*) 表面跡象或徵兆。***at first appearance*** 乍眼一看; 初看。***at the appearance of*** 看見…而; 與…的出現同時; …公布後即。 ***for appearance's sake*** 爲了體面; 顧面子。***in appearance*** 外表上。***keep up appearances*** 鋪張排場; 裝場面; 保持體面; 維持面子; 裝闊氣。***make a good*** (or ***an ill***) ***appearance*** 以壯 (有礙) 觀瞻。***make*** (***enter*** or ***put in***) ***an appearance*** 出面; 出庭; 到案; 到達。***put on*** (or ***give***) ***the appearance of*** (***innocence***) 假裝 (清白)。***There is every appearance of....*** 無一處不像…。 ***There is no appearance of***(***him, rain***). 簡直不見(他)的影子; 一點都沒有(下雨) 的樣子。***to all appearances*** 顯然。
appearance bond 出庭保證金。

***ap·pease** [ə'piz; ə'pi:z] *v.t.*, **-peased, -peas·ing.** ①使平靜;使安靜;使緩和。to *appease* a certain person's anger. 緩和某人的憤怒。②使滿足。③姑息;安撫。—**ap·peas·a·ble,** *adj.* —**ment, ap·peas·er,** *n.*

ap·pel·lant [ə'pɛlənt; ə'pelənt] *n.* ①懇求者。②控訴人;上訴人。—*adj.* 〖法律〗控訴的;上訴的;上訴審的。

ap·pel·late [ə'pɛlɪt; ə'pelit] *adj.* 〖法律〗控訴的;上訴的;上訴審的。***appellate court*** 上訴法院;高等法院。

ap·pel·la·tion [ˌæpə'leʃən; ˌæpə'leiʃən] *n.* 名稱;稱呼。

ap·pel·la·tive [ə'pɛlətɪv; ə'pelətiv] *adj.* ①名稱的;命名的。②描寫的。③〖文法〗總稱的;普通名詞的。—*n.* ①名稱;通稱。②〖文法〗總稱名詞;普通名詞。

ap·pel·lee [ˌæpə'li; ˌæpə'li:] *n.* 〖法律〗被控訴人;被上訴人;(上訴案件中的)被告。

ap·pend [ə'pɛnd; ə'pend] *v.t.* 附加;增補。

ap·pend·age [ə'pɛndɪdʒ; ə'pendidʒ] *n.* ①附屬物。②〖動物〗軀幹以外之附屬肢體。③下屬(尤指僕從)。

ap·pend·ant [ə'pɛndənt; ə'pendənt] *adj.* ①添加的;附屬的;附加的。②附帶之權利的。—*n.* 附屬物。(亦作 **appendent**)

ap·pen·dec·to·my [ˌæpən'dɛktəmɪ; ˌæpen'dektəmi] *n., pl.* **-mies.** 〖外科〗闌尾切除術;蚓突截除術。(亦作**appendicectomy**)

ap·pen·di·ci·tis [əˌpɛndə'saɪtɪs; əˌpendi'saitis] *n.* 闌尾炎;盲腸炎。

***ap·pen·dix** [ə'pɛndɪks; ə'pendiks] *n., pl.* **-dix·es, -di·ces** [-dəˌsiz; -disi:z], *v.* —*n.* ①附錄。②闌尾;盲腸。—*v.t.* 附加於。

ap·pen·tice [ə'pɛntɪs; ə'pentis] *n.* 〖建築〗門前之遮簷;窗前之雨篷。

ap·per·cep·tion [ˌæpə'sɛpʃən; ˌæpə'sepʃən] *n.* ①〖哲學,心理〗統覺。②〖教育〗類化。

ap·per·tain [ˌæpə'ten; ˌæpə'tein] *v.i.* 屬於;與…有關〖to〗.

ap·pe·tence ['æpətəns; 'æpitəns] *n.* ①强烈的慾望;欲求;性慾。②(動物之)本能的傾向;自然的性癖;習性。③〖化〗親和力。(亦作 **appetency**) —**ap·pe·tent,** *adj.*

***ap·pe·tite** ['æpəˌtaɪt; 'æpitait] *n.* ①食慾。He has a good *appetite.* 他的胃口好。②慾念;肉慾。③嗜好。an *appetite* for reading. 閱讀嗜好。④慾望。

ap·pe·ti·tive ['æpəˌtaɪtɪv; 'æpətaitiv] *adj.* 食慾的;似食慾的;關於食慾的。

ap·pe·tiz·er ['æpəˌtaɪzə; 'æpitaizə] *n.* ①開胃的食物。②刺激慾望之事物。

ap·pe·tiz·ing ['æpəˌtaɪzɪŋ; 'æpitaiziŋ] *adj.* 開胃的;促進食慾的。

***ap·plaud** [ə'plɔd; ə'plɔ:d] *v.i.* ①鼓掌(或歡呼)贊成或讚許。When he finished his speech, the audience *applauded.* 他演講完畢時,聽衆鼓掌讚許。②稱讚。—*v.t.* ①鼓掌(或歡呼)贊成。②稱讚。We *applauded* him for his courage. 我們稱讚他的勇敢。

***ap·plause** [ə'plɔz; ə'plɔ:z] *n.* ①鼓掌(或歡呼)以示讚許。The performance met with *applause.* 這表演受鼓掌讚許。②稱讚。

ap·plau·sive [ə'plɔsɪv; ə'plɔ:siv] *adj.* 喝采的;稱讚的。

:ap·ple ['æpl̩; 'æpl] *n.* ①蘋果。The *apple* is a delicious fruit. 蘋果是好吃的水果。②蘋果樹。***Adam's apple*** 喉結。***apple of discord*** 禍根(希臘神話,引起紛爭之金蘋果)。***throw away the apple because of the core*** 因噎廢食。

apple butter 蘋果醬。

apple cart 販賣蘋果之手推車。***upset the*** (or ***one's***) ***apple cart*** 破壞(某人之)計畫。

apple green 蘋果綠。

ap·ple·jack ['æpl̩ˌdʒæk; 'æpldʒæk] *n.* 蘋果白蘭地;蘋果酒。(亦作 **apple brandy**)

ap·ple·knock·er ['æpl̩ˌnɑkə; 'æplnɔkə] *n.* 〖美俚〗①鄉下佬;莊稼漢。②採蘋果者;採水果者。③新手;生手。

apple of discord 爭鬥及嫉妒的根源(典出引發 Troy 戰爭的金蘋果故事)。

apple of Sodom (or **Dead Sea**) 失望的根源(典出摘下即變烟與灰的蘋果故事)。

apple of the (or **one's**) **eye** ①瞳子。②極珍愛之人或物;掌上明珠。

apple pandowdy 一種加糖蜜的蘋果糕餅。(亦作 **pandowdy**)

apple pie 蘋果派。

apple-pie bed (開玩笑)故意將床單舖短了的床。

apple-pie order 〖俗〗井然有序。

ap·ple·sauce ['æpl̩ˌsɔs; 'æplsɔ:s] *n.* ①蘋果醬。②〖美俚〗胡說;假意之恭維。

Ap·ple·ton ['æpl̩tən; 'æpltən] *n.* 阿波敦 (Sir Edward Victor, 1892–1965, 英國物理學家, 1947年獲諾貝爾獎)。

***ap·pli·ance** [ə'plaɪəns; ə'plaiəns] *n.* ①用具;器具。②電氣用具。③應用;適用。

ap·pli·ca·ble ['æplɪkəbl̩; 'æplikəbl] *adj.* 適宜的;合用的。—**ap·pli·ca·bly,** *adv.*

***ap·pli·cant** ['æpləkənt; 'æplikənt] *n.* 請求者;申請人。an *applicant* for a position. 求職者。

ap·pli·ca·tion** [ˌæplə'keʃən; ˌæpli'keiʃən] *n.* ①應用;用處;用途。Freedom is a word of wide *application.* "自由"一辭可用於多種場合。②適用;適合。This has no *application* to the case. 這不適用於那案子。③施用;敷用。the *application* of salve to a wound. 敷用藥膏於傷處。④請求;申請;申請書。to fill out an *application.* 塡寫申請書。⑤注意;專心;勤奮;不斷的努力。⑥敷用之物;應用之物;適用之物。on application to*** 向…函索。

ap·pli·ca·tor ['æpləˌketə; 'æplikeitə] *n.* ①敷用藥品等所用的器具;塗藥器。②敷用或噴射藥品等物質的人。

ap·plied [ə'plaɪd; ə'plaid] *adj.* 應用的。

ap·pli·qué [ˌæplɪ'ke; æ'pli:kei] *adj., n., v.,* **-quéd, -qué·ing.** —*adj.* (洋裝等)補花的。—*n.* ①縫飾;補花;附飾品。②縫飾或補花之細工。—*v.t.* ①飾以補花等。②置於…上作爲縫飾等。

:ap·ply [ə'plaɪ; ə'plai] *v.,* **-plied, -ply·ing.** —*v.t.* ①使接觸;敷;塗;用。to *apply* a match to powder. 用火柴點火藥。②應用;引用。You can *apply* those rules to this case. 你可引用那些規則於這件事情。③充用;使用。④專心。He *applied* himself to learning French. 他專心學法文。⑤置於他物之上;疊置。—*v.i.* ①應用;適用。The argument *applies* to this case. 這理由適用於此一情形。②請求;申請。He has *applied* to the American Consul for a visa. 他已向美國領事申請簽證。③專心;努力。

ap·pog·gia·tu·ra [əˌpɑdʒə'turə; əˌpɔdʒə'tuərə] *n.* 〖音樂〗附音;倚音。

:ap·point [ə'pɔɪnt; ə'pɔint] *v.t.* ①任命;派。He was *appointed* mayor of the city. 他被任命爲市長。②指定;約定;決定。to *ap-*

point a time for the meeting. 指定開會時間。③設備;裝備。④規定。—*v.i.* 運用任命的法定權力。

ap·point·ed [əˈpɔɪntɪd; əˈpointid] *adj.* ①指派的;約定的。at the *appointed* time. 在約定的時間。②裝備的; 設備的。a well-*appointed* house. 設備好的房屋。

ap·point·ee [əpɔɪnˈti; əpoinˈtiː] *n.* 被任命者;被指定者。

ap·poin·tive [əˈpɔɪntɪv; əˈpointiv] *adj.* 任命的(爲 elective 之對)。

***ap·point·ment** [əˈpɔɪntmənt; əˈpointmənt] *n.* ①任命。to fill a vacancy by *appointment.* 任命人員塡補空缺。②職位。③約會。④(常*pl.*) 設備。The *appointments* in this hotel are very good. 這旅館的設備甚好。

ap·por·tion [əˈporʃən; əˈpɔːʃən] *v.t.* 「分派;分攤;分配。」

ap·por·tion·ment [əˈporʃənmənt; əˈpɔːʃənmənt] *n.* ①分派;分攤;分配。②(美國衆議院等)議員人數的分配。

ap·pose [əˈpoz; æˈpouz] *v.t.*, **ap·posed, ap·pos·ing.** ①置於附近。②並列。

ap·po·site [ˈæpəzɪt; ˈæpəzit] *adj.* 適當的;適切的。—**ly,** *adv.* —**ness,** *n.*

ap·po·si·tion [ˌæpəˈzɪʃən; ˌæpəˈziʃən] *n.* ①並置;添附。②〖文法〗同格;同位。③並列;相鄰。—**al,** *adj.*

ap·pos·i·tive [əˈpɑzətɪv; əˈpɔzitiv] *n.* 〖文法〗同位語; 同格語。—*adj.* 同位的。

ap·prais·a·ble [əˈprezəbl̩; əˈpreizəbl] *adj.* 可評價的;可估價的。

ap·prais·al [əˈprezl̩; əˈpreizəl] *n.* ①鑑定;品定。②評價;估價。

ap·praise [əˈprez; əˈpreiz] *v.t.*, **-praised, -prais·ing.** ①鑑定; 品定。②估價;評價。—**ment, ap·prais·er,** *n.*

ap·pre·ci·a·ble [əˈpriʃɪəbl̩; əˈpriːʃəbl] *adj.* 可見到的;可覺得的;可估計的;有一點的。—**ap·pre·ci·a·bly,** *adv.*

***ap·pre·ci·ate** [əˈpriʃɪˌet; əˈpriːʃieit] *v.*, **-at·ed, -at·ing.** —*v.t.*①重視;寶貴;賞識。His great courage was not *appreciated.* 他的勇敢沒有被重視。②察知;覺得;辨別。③感激。Your kind answer will be highly *appreciated.* 如蒙賜覆,不勝感激。④提高(價值);抬高(價錢)。—*v.i.* 提高價值;抬高價錢。

***ap·pre·ci·a·tion** [əˌpriʃɪˈeʃən; əˌpriːʃiˈeiʃən] *n.* ①評價;鑑識。She has an *appreciation* of art and music. 她能欣賞藝術及音樂。②尊重; 讚賞。③感激。 in *appreciation* of your work. 感謝你的工作。④增值;漲價。

ap·pre·ci·a·tive [əˈpriʃɪˌetɪv; əˈpriːʃiətiv] *adj.* 有賞識力的; 表示賞識的; 表示感激的;表示重視的; 承認有價值的; 感謝的。(亦作 **appreciatory**) —**ly,** *adv.* —**ness,** *n.*

ap·pre·ci·a·tor [əˈpriʃɪˌetɚ; əˈpriːʃieitə] *n.* 鑑賞者;評價者;賞識者。

***ap·pre·hend** [ˌæprɪˈhɛnd; ˌæpriˈhend] *v.t.* ①覺察;疑慮;憂懼。to *apprehend* danger. 覺察危險。 ②捕捉。 to *apprehend* a thief. 捕捉竊賊。③了解;明瞭。—*v.i.* ①理解。②憂懼;害怕。

ap·pre·hen·si·ble [ˌæprɪˈhɛnsəbl̩; ˌæpriˈhensəbl] *adj.* 可理解的; 可了解的〖to〗. —**ap·pre·hen·si·bil·i·ty,** *n.*

***ap·pre·hen·sion** [ˌæprɪˈhɛnʃən; ˌæpriˈhenʃən] *n.* ①憂懼;恐怕。②逮捕。③了解力。 She is a girl of weak *apprehension.* 她是一個了解力很低的女孩子。④意見;看法;觀念。

ap·pre·hen·sive [ˌæprɪˈhɛnsɪv; ˌæpriˈhensiv] *adj.* ①憂慮的;恐懼的。②敏悟的;易了解的。 ③有關理解力的。④有知覺的。—**ly,** *adv.* —**ness,** *n.*

***ap·pren·tice** [əˈprɛntɪs; əˈprentis] *n., v.,* **-ticed, -tic·ing.** —*n.*①學徒。He was bound *apprentice* to a tailor. 他受約做裁縫的學徒。②初學者。—*v.t.* 使爲學徒。His father *apprenticed* him to a barber.他的父親使他做理髮師的學徒。—**ship,** —**ment,** *n.*

ap·prise [əˈpraɪz; əˈpraiz] *v.t.*, **ap·prised, ap·pris·ing.** 報告;通知〖常of〗.(亦作 **apprize**) —**ment,** *n.*

‡**ap·proach** [əˈprotʃ; əˈproutʃ] *v.t.* ①行近; 接近。As we *approached* the man, we saw that he was blind. 我們走近這人時, 看到他爲一盲者。②逼近(性質、時間、情形等)。③向…接洽; 向…提議。to *approach* the President with a suggestion. 向總統建議。④進行;致力於;研究。⑤使接近。—*v.i.* 行進;迫近。The storm is *approaching.* 暴風雨迫近了。—*n.* ①近前;行近。The enemy ran away at our *approach.* 敵人於我們行近時逃走。②靠近;相近的事。③方法;步驟。④進路;通路;入口。⑤〖保齡球〗投球姿勢。⑥〖航空〗接近; 進場(在指定地區內,航空器準備降落之動作)。⑦(*pl.*)親近。 He tried to make *approaches* to her. 他企圖向她親近。⑧(有時 *pl.*) 提議;建議。

ap·proach·a·ble [əˈprotʃəbl̩; əˈproutʃəbl] *adj.* ①可接近的;可進入的。②(人之)可親的。—**ap·proach·a·bil·i·ty,** *n.*

approach light 進近燈(飛機場跑道上之指示燈)。

ap·pro·bate [ˈæprəˌbet; ˈæproubeit] *v.t.*, **-bat·ed, -bat·ing.** 許可;嘉許;核准。

ap·pro·ba·tion [ˌæprəˈbeʃən; ˌæprouˈbeiʃən] *n.* 許可;嘉許;核准。

ap·pro·ba·to·ry [əˈprobəˌtorɪ; ˈæproubeitəri] *adj.* 許可的;嘉許的;核准的。(亦作 **approbative**)

ap·pro·pri·a·ble [əˈproprɪəbl̩; əˈproupriəbl] *adj.* 可專用的;可供私用的。

***ap·pro·pri·ate** [*adj.* əˈproprɪɪt; əˈproupriit *v.* əˈproprɪˌet; əˈprouprieit] *adj., v.,* **-at·ed, -at·ing.** —*adj.* ①適合的;適當的;正當的。*appropriate* words. 適當的字。②專屬的; 屬於某人的。 Each played his *appropriate* part. 每人做他所應做的事。—*v.t.* ①撥(款);撥爲某種用途的款〖for, to〗. ②據爲己有; 占用。He *appropriated* public funds for his own private use. 他挪用公款。—**ly,** *adv.*

ap·pro·pri·a·tion [əˌproprɪˈeʃən; əˌproupriˈeiʃən] *n.* ①指定用途的東西。②撥歸某種用途。 ③據爲己有; 占用。His *appropriation* of their money was not right. 他占用他們的錢是不對的。④撥款。

appropriation bill 〖美〗(向國會提出之)政府支出案;歲出預算案。

ap·pro·pri·a·tive [əˈproprɪˌetɪv; əˈprouprieitiv] *adj.* 有關政府支出的。

ap·prov·a·ble [əˈpruvəbl̩; əˈpruːvəbl] *adj.* 可贊成的;可核准的。

***ap·prov·al** [əˈpruvl̩; əˈpruːvəl] *n.* ①贊成。He nodded in *approval.* 他點首表示贊成。②核准;批准。**on approval** 送貨察看。

***ap·prove** [əˈpruv; əˈpruːv] *v.,* **-proved,**

-prov·ing. —*v.t.* ①贊成;贊許。The teacher looked at John's work and *approved* it. 老師看了約翰的成績表示贊許。②核准;批准。Congress *approved* the bill. (美國)國會批准了這方案。③證明爲;表明爲(常與反身代名詞連用)。—*v.i.* 贊成〖of〗. Her father will never *approve* of her marrying such a poor man. 她的父親決不會贊成她嫁給這樣窮的人。

ap·proved [ə'pruvd; ə'pru:vd] *adj.* 核准的;嘉許的;試驗證明的。

approved school 〖英〗管敎不良少年的學校。

ap·prov·er [ə'pruvɚ; ə'pru:və] *n.* ①承認者;贊成者。②〖英〗自首而告發共犯之人。

approx. approximately.

***ap·prox·i·mate** [*adj.* ə'prɑksəmɪt; ə'prɔksimit *v.* ə'prɑksə,met; ə'prɔksimeit] *adj., v.,* **-mat·ed, -mat·ing.** —*adj.* 近乎準確;近似;大概。an *approximate* estimate. 大概的估計。—*v.t.* ①使接近。②近於;逼近。③模擬。④估計。We *approximated* the distance at three miles. 我們估計距離約爲三英里。—*v.i.* 近;接近。—**ly,** *adv.*

ap·prox·i·ma·tion [ə,prɑksə'meʃən; ə,prɔksi'meiʃən] *n.* ①接近;近似;概算。②〖數學〗近似法;近似值。—**ap·prox·i·ma·tive,** *adj.*

ap·prox·i·ma·tor [ə'prɑksə,metɚ; ə'prɔksimeitə] *n.* 近似者;估計者;接近者。

ap·pur·te·nance [ə'pɝtṇəns; ə'pə:tinəns] *n.* ①附屬物。②〖法律〗從物;從屬權利。③(*pl.*)機械裝置;儀器設備。

ap·pur·te·nant [ə'pɝtṇənt; ə'pə:tinənt] *adj.* 附屬的;從屬的〖to〗. —*n.* 附屬物。

Apr. April.

a·prax·i·a [ə'prækʃɪə; ə'prækʃiə] *n.* 〖醫〗運用不能;失用症。

***a·pri·cot** ['eprɪ,kɑt, 'æprɪ,kɑt; 'eiprikɔt] *n.* ①杏。②杏樹。③杏黃色。

‡**A·pril** ['eprəl, -rɪl; 'eiprəl, -ril] *n.* ①四月。②女子名。

April fool ①在萬愚節受愚弄之人。②在萬愚節開的玩笑。

April Fools' Day 萬愚節(四月一日);愚人節。

a pri·o·ri ['epraɪ'oraɪ; 'ei-prai'ɔ:rai] 〖拉〗自原因推及結果;先驗(地)的;既定(地)的;演繹(地)的。

a·pri·o·rism [,epraɪ'orɪzəm; ,eiprai'ɔ:rizm] *n.* 先驗說;演繹之推論;自原因推及結果之推論。

a·pri·or·i·ty [,epraɪ'ɔrətɪ; ,ei-prai'ɔriti] *n.* 演繹性;演繹推理。

***a·pron** ['eprən, 'epɚn; 'eiprən] *n.* ①圍巾;圍裙。②似圍裙之物。③(車之)護板。④〖機械〗護牀。⑤用鐵片拼成的轉運帶(用於運送散裝貨)。⑥〖機場〗停機坪。⑦〖土木〗護岸。⑧〖建築〗壁脚板。⑨高爾夫球場果嶺(green)的邊緣。⑩拳賽臺圍繩外的部分。⑪長毛動物胸前的毛。⑫前舞臺。—*v.t.* 着圍裙於。

apron area 停機坪。

apron stage 〖戲劇〗前舞臺。

apron string 圍裙帶。*be tied to one's mother's* (or *wife's*) *apron strings* 由母親(妻子)支配;受裙帶影響。

ap·ro·pos [,æprə'po; 'æprəpou] *adj. & adv.* 適當的(地);恰好的(地);順便的(地)。*apropos of* 關於;至於;就…而論。

a·pros·ex·i·a [,eprɑ'sɛksɪə; ,eiprɔ'seksiə] *n.* 〖精神分析〗無法集中注意力。

A.P.S. ①American Peace Society. ②American Philatelic Society. ③American Philosophical Society. ④American Physical Society. ⑤American Protestant Society. **A.P.S.A.** American Political Science Association.

apse [æps; æps] *n.* 〖建築〗敎堂之半圓形或多邊形之凸出部分(通常在敎堂之東面)。

ap·si·dal ['æpsɪdl; 'æpsidl] *adj.* ①〖建築〗apse 的。②〖天文〗遠(近)日點的。

ap·sis ['æpsɪs; 'æpsis] *n., pl.* **-si·des** [-sɪ,diz; -saidi:z]. ①〖天文〗遠(近)日點。②〖建築〗=**apse.**

***apt** [æpt; æpt] *adj.* ①傾向;偏好;易於。Iron is *apt* to rust. 鐵易生銹。②聰明的;敏捷的。③適合的;適當的。—**ly,** *adv.* —**ness,** *n.*

apt. apartment.

ap·ter·ous ['æptərəs; 'æptərəs] *adj.* ①〖動物〗無翅的。②〖植物〗無膜質膨脹的。

ap·ti·tude ['æptə,tjud; 'æptitju:d] *n.* ①癖性;才能。②穎悟。③適當。

aptitude test 性向測驗。

aq. aqua.

AQ, A.Q. achievement quotient.

aq·ua ['ækwə; 'ækwə] *n., pl.* **aq·uas, aq·uae** ['ækwɪ; 'ækwi], *adj.* —*n.* 水;液體;溶液。(略作 **aq.**) —*adj.* 水色的。

aq·ua·cade ['ækwə,ked; 'ækwəkeid] *n.* 水上技藝表演。

aq·ua·farm ['ækwə,fɑrm; 'ækwəfɑ:m] *n.* 人工魚池。

aqua for·tis [~'fɔrtɪs; ~'fɔ:tis] *n.* 硝酸;硝礦水。

aq·ua·gun ['ækwə,gʌn; 'ækwəgʌn] *n.* 水中槍。

aq·ua·lung ['ækwə,lʌŋ; 'ækwəlʌŋ] *n.* 水肺。

aq·ua·ma·rine [,ækwəmə'rin; ,ækwəmə'ri:n] *n.* ①〖礦〗水藍寶石;藍晶;藍綠玉。②藍綠色。

aq·ua·naut ['ækwənɔt; 'ækwənɔ:t] *n.* 潛水人。

aq·ua·plane ['ækwə,plen, 'ækwəplein] *n., v.,* **-planed, -plan·ing.** —*n.* 滑水板。—*v.i.* 做滑水運動。

aqua pu·ra [~'pjurə; ~'pju:rə] 純水。

aqua re·gi·a [~'ridʒɪə; ~'ri:dʒjə] 〖化〗王水。

aq·ua·relle [,ækwə'rɛl; ,ækwə'rel] *n., pl.* **-relles.** ①透明水彩畫。②透明水彩畫法。—**aq·ua·rel·list,** *n.*

a·quar·ist [ə'kwɛrɪst; 'ækwərist] *n.* 水族館館長;魚類學者。

a·quar·i·um [ə'kwɛrɪəm; ə'kwɛəriəm] *n., pl.* **-i·ums, -i·a** [-ɪə; -iə]. ①蓄魚之池或槽。②水族館。

A·quar·i·us [ə'kwɛrɪəs; ə'kwɛəriəs] *n.* ①〖天文〗寶瓶座。②寶瓶宮。

aq·ua·show ['ækwə,ʃo; 'ækwəʃou] *n.* 〖美〗水上技藝表演。

a·quat·ic [ə'kwætɪk; ə'kwætik] *adj.* ①〖動、植物〗水生的;棲於水面或水中的。*aquatic* plants. 水生植物。②水的。③〖運動〗在水面或水中作的。*aquatic* sports. 水上運動。—*n.* ①水生的植物或動物。②(*pl.*)水中或水上運動。

aq·ua·tint ['ækwə,tɪnt; 'ækwətint] *n.* ①銅版蝕鏤法。②以上述方法蝕鏤之版或圖案。—*v.t. & v.i.* 蝕鏤。

aqua vi·tae [~'vaɪtɪ; ~'vaiti:] ①酒精。②白蘭地;烈酒。

aq·ue·duct ['ækwɪ,dʌkt; 'ækwidʌkt] *n.* ①水道;溝渠。②水管;水道橋。③〖生理〗管。

a·que·ous ['ekwɪəs; 'eikwiəs] *adj.* ①

水的;似水的;含水的。②(岩石等)水裏形成的。③水樣體的。

aqueous humor 眼前房水;(眼球中之)水樣體。

aqueous rock 水成岩。

aq·ui·cul·ture [ˈækwəˌkʌltʃɚ; ˈækwəˌkʌltʃə] *n.* 飼養水中動物;栽培水中植物。(亦作 **aquaculture**)

aq·ui·line [ˈækwəˌlaɪn, -lɪn; ˈækwilain] *adj.* ①鷹的;似鷹的。②鉤狀的;彎曲的。an *aquiline* nose. 鷹鉤鼻。

Ar 〖化〗化學元素 argon 之符號。**Ar.** ①Arabia. ②Arabic. ③Aramaic. ④argentum (拉 =silver). **ar.** ①aromatic. ②arrive. ③arrives. ④arrival. ⑤argent.

-ar 〖字尾〗①形容詞字尾, 表"…的;…性的;似…的"之義。②構成與名詞無直接關係之形容詞字尾。③名詞字尾, 表"…的人;…的物"。④表動作者之名詞字尾, 爲 **-or** 之異體。

A.R.A. ①Associate of the Royal Academy(of Arts). ②American Railway Association.

Ar·ab** [ˈærəb; ˈærəb] *n.* ①阿拉伯人。②阿拉伯馬。street Arab*** 流浪街頭的男孩或女孩。—*adj.* ①阿拉伯的。②阿拉伯人的。

ar·a·besque [ˌærəˈbɛsk; ˌærəˈbesk] *n., adj., v.,* **-besqued, -besqu·ing.** —*n.* ①錯綜圖飾。②一種芭蕾舞姿。③一種短曲。—*adj.* ①阿拉伯式的。②精巧的; 奇特的。—*v.t.* 用 arabesque 圖樣來裝飾。—*v.i.* 做出 arabesque 舞姿。

***A·ra·bi·a** [əˈrebɪə; əˈreibjə] *n.* 阿拉伯。

***A·ra·bi·an** [əˈrebɪən; əˈreibjən] *adj.* 阿拉伯的;阿拉伯人的。—*n.* ①阿拉伯人。②阿拉伯馬。

Arabian bird 鳳凰。

Arabian camel 單峯駝。

Arabian Nights 天方夜譚(一千○一夜故事)。

Arabian Sea 阿拉伯海。

Ar·a·bic [ˈærəbɪk; ˈærəbik] *adj.* ①阿拉伯的。②阿拉伯人(語文)的。—*n.* 阿拉伯語文。

ar·a·bil·i·ty [ˌærəˈbɪlətɪ; ˌærəˈbiliti] *n.* 適於耕種。

Ar·ab·ism [ˈærəˌbɪzəm; ˈærəbizm] *n.* ①阿拉伯主義;對阿拉伯文化的信奉。②阿拉伯國家的統稱;阿拉伯國家的勢力範圍。

Ar·ab·ist [ˈærəbɪst; ˈærəbist] *n.* 阿拉伯專家。

Ar·ab·i·za·tion [ˌærəbəˈzeʃən; ˌærəbiˈzeiʃən] *n.* 阿拉伯化。

Ar·ab·ize [ˈærəˌbaɪz; ˈærəbaiz] *v.t.,* **-ized, -iz·ing.** 阿拉伯化。

ar·a·ble [ˈærəbl̩; ˈærəbl] *adj.* 適於耕種的;可開墾的。—*n.* 可耕之地。—**ar·a·bil·i·ty,** *n.*

Arab League 阿拉伯聯盟。

a·rach·nid [əˈræknɪd; əˈræknid] *n.* 蜘蛛類之節肢動物。

a·rach·ni·dan [əˈræknədən; əˈræknidən] *adj.* (亦作 **arachnidian**)節肢類的。—*n.* 節肢動物。

a·rach·noid [əˈræknɔɪd; əˈræknɔid] *adj.* ①〖植物〗蜘蛛網狀的。②〖解剖〗蜘蛛膜的。③〖動物〗蜘蛛類節肢動物的。—*n.* ①〖解剖〗蜘蛛膜。②蜘蛛類節肢動物。

Ar·a·ma·ic [ˌærəˈmeɪk; ˌærəˈmeiik] *n.* 閃族語系中之阿拉姆語。

a·ra·ne·id [əˈrenɪɪd; əˈreiniid] *n.* 〖動物〗眞蜘蛛類;蜘蛛。

Ar·au·car·i·a [ˌærɔˈkɛrɪə; ˌærɔːˈkɛəriə] *n.* 〖植物〗①南洋杉屬。②(a-)南洋杉。

ar·bi·ter [ˈɑrbɪtɚ; ˈɑːbitə] *n.* 仲裁人;裁決人;決定者。

ar·bi·tra·ble [ˈɑrbətrəbl̩; ˈɑːbitrəbl] *adj.* 可仲裁的。

ar·bi·trage [ˈɑrbətrɪdʒ; ˈɑːbitridʒ ˌɑrbəˈtraʒ; ˌɑːbiˈtrɑːʒ *for* ②] *n.* ①裁決;仲裁。②股票等之套利;套匯。

arbitrage house 套利公司。

ar·bi·tra·geur [ˌɑrbətrɑˈʒɝ; ˌɑːbitrɑːˈʒəː] *n.* 從事套利套匯的人。(亦作 **arbitrager, arbitragist**)

ar·bi·tral [ˈɑrbətrəl; ˈɑːbitrəl] *adj.* 仲裁的。

ar·bit·ra·ment [ɑrˈbɪtrəmənt; ɑːˈbitrəmənt] *n.* 仲裁;裁決;裁判權。

ar·bi·trar·y [ˈɑrbəˌtrɛrɪ; ˈɑːbitrəri] *adj.* ①憑私意的;隨意的;武斷的;反覆無常的;不定的。②專制的;專斷的。an *arbitrary* government. 專制的政府。—**ar·bi·trar·i·ly,** *adv.* —**ar·bi·trar·i·ness,** *n.*

ar·bi·trate [ˈɑrbəˌtret; ˈɑːbitreit] *v.,* **-trat·ed, -trat·ing.** —*v.i.* 仲裁; 公斷。—*v.t.* 仲裁;公斷;委之仲裁;聽任公斷。—**ar·bi·tra·tive,** *adj.*

ar·bi·tra·tion [ˌɑrbəˈtreʃən; ˌɑːbiˈtreiʃən] *n.* ①仲裁;公斷。to settle a dispute by *arbitration.* 用仲裁解決爭端。②〖國際法〗調停。—**al,** *adj.*

ar·bi·tra·tor [ˈɑrbəˌtretɚ; ˈɑːbitreitə] *n.* 仲裁者;公斷人。

ar·bi·tress [ˈɑrbətrɪs; ˈɑːbitris] *n.* 女仲裁人;女公斷人。

ar·bor[1] [ˈɑrbɚ; ˈɑːbɔː, -bə] *n., pl.* **ar·bo·res** [ˈɑrbəˌriz; ˈɑːbəriːz]. ①〖植物〗樹;喬木。②〖解剖〗(小腦之)活樹體。

***ar·bor**[2] [ˈɑrbɚ; ˈɑːbə] *n.* ①涼亭。②藤架。(亦作 **arbour**)

ar·bor[3] [ˈɑrbɚ; ˈɑːbə] *n.* 〖機械〗軸;旋床之心軸。

ar·bo·ra·ceous [ˌɑrbəˈreʃəs; ˌɑːbəˈreiʃəs] *adj.* ①樹狀的。②林木繁茂的。

Arbor Day 〖美〗植樹節。

ar·bo·re·al [ɑrˈborɪəl; ɑːˈbɔːriəl] *adj.* ①樹的; 喬木的; 木本的。②生於樹上或樹間的;棲於樹木的。

ar·bored [ˈɑrbɚd; ˈɑːbəd] *adj.* 放在涼亭或樹蔭下面的。〖注意〗英國拼法爲**arboured.**

ar·bo·re·ous [ɑrˈborɪəs; ɑːˈbɔːriəs] *adj.* ①林木繁茂的;多樹林的。②樹的;樹狀的。③生於樹的;棲於樹的。

ar·bo·res·cent [ˌɑrbəˈrɛsn̩t; ˌɑːbəˈresnt] *adj.* 樹狀的;似喬木的;有枝的。—**ar·bo·res·cence,** *n.*

ar·bo·re·tum [ˌɑrbəˈritəm; ˌɑːbəˈriːtəm] *n., pl.* **-ta** [-tə; -tə], **-tums.** 植物園;樹林繁茂的公園。

ar·bo·ri·cul·ture [ˈɑrbərɪˌkʌltʃɚ; ˈɑːbərikʌltʃə] *n.* 育樹;樹木栽培。—**ar·bo·ri·cul·tu·ral,** *adj.*

ar·bo·ri·za·tion [ˈɑrbərɪˈzeʃən; ˈɑːbəriˈzeiʃən] *n.* 樹狀分歧; 樹枝狀。

ar·bor·vi·tae [ˈɑrbɚˈvaɪtɪ; ˈɑːbəˈvaiti] *n.* ①〖解剖〗小腦活樹。②〖植物〗側柏。(亦作 **arbor vitae**)

ar·bu·tus [ɑrˈbjutəs; ɑːˈbjuːtəs] *n.* ①〖植物〗楊梅。②五月花。

ARC, A.R.C. American Red Cross.

***arc** [ɑrk; ɑːk] *n., v.,* **arc(k)ed, arc(k)·ing.** —*n.* ①弧。the *arc* of a circle. 圓周的弧。②弧光。—*v.i.* ①形成弧光。②成曲線飛行。

ar·cade [ɑrˈked; ɑːˈkeid] *n., v.,* **-cad·ed, -cad·ing.** —*n.* ①〖建築〗拱廊;騎樓。②有拱廊或騎樓之街道。—*v.t.* 賦與拱廊或騎樓。

ar·cad·ed [ɑrˈkedɪd; ɑːˈkeidid] *adj.* 有

拱廊的。

Ar·ca·di·a [ɑr'kedɪə; ɑː'keidiə] *n.* ①古希臘一山區。②世外桃源。

Ar·ca·di·an [ɑr'kedɪən; ɑː'keidiən] *adj.* ①Arcadia 的。②田野的;簡樸的。—*n.* Arcadia 人。 **—ism,** *n.*

Ar·ca·dy ['ɑrkədɪ; 'ɑːkədi] *n.* 〖詩〗=**Arcadia.**

ar·cane [ɑr'ken; ɑː'kein] *adj.* 神祕的;祕密的;幽晦的。 **—ly,** *adv.*

ar·ca·num [ɑr'kenəm; ɑː'keinəm] *n., pl.* **-na** [-nə; -nə]. ①(常 *pl.*) 祕密;奥祕。②祕方;祕藥。

***arch¹** [ɑrtʃ; ɑːtʃ] *n.* ①拱門。a triumphal *arch.* 凱旋門。②彎曲的東西;彎曲的部分。the *arch* of the heavens. 穹蒼。—*v.t.* ①彎曲。②蓋以拱。—*v.i.* 成爲弓形。

arch² *adj.* ①主要的;最重要的。②奸詐的。③淘氣的;頑皮的。 **—ly,** *adv.* **—ness,** *n.*

arch- 〖字首〗表"第一;主要;大"之義。

arch. ①archaic. ②archaism. ③archery. ④archipelago. ⑤architect. ⑥architecture. ⑦architectural. ⑧archive; archives.

ar·chae·ol·o·gy [ˌɑrkɪ'ɑlədʒɪ; ˌɑːki'ɔlədʒi] *n.* 考古學。(亦作 **archeology**) **—ar·chae·o·log·i·cal,** *adj.* **—ar·chae·ol·o·gist,** *n.*

ar·cha·ic [ɑr'ke·ɪk; ɑː'keiik] *adj.* ①古的;古代的。②古文的;古語的。③已不通用的;已廢的。④(A-)古典的。⑤原始的。

ar·cha·ism ['ɑrkɪˌɪzəm; 'ɑːkeiizəm] *n.* ①古語。②文學中之古語風格。③古風。 **—ar·cha·ist,** *n.* **—ar·cha·is·tic,** *adj.*

ar·cha·ize ['ɑrkɪˌaɪz; 'ɑːkiaiz] *v.,* **-ized, -iz·ing.**—*v.t.* 使古化。—*v.i.* 用古語;用古體;仿古。(亦作 **archaise**)

arch·an·gel ['ark'endʒəl; 'ɑːkˌeindʒəl] *n.* ①天使長;大天使。②〖植物〗羌活。**—ic,** *adj.*

***arch·bish·op** ['ɑrtʃ'bɪʃəp; 'ɑːtʃ'biʃəp] *n.* 總主教。**—ric,** *n.*

arch dam 拱壩。

arch·dea·con ['ɑrtʃ'dikən; 'ɑːtʃ'diːkən] *n.* 副主教;副監督。

arch·dea·con·ry [ˌɑrtʃ'dikənrɪ; ɑːtʃ'diːkənri] *n., pl.* **-ries.** ①副主教之職位、職責或轄區。②副主教住宅。

arch·di·o·cese ['ɑrtʃ'daɪəˌsis; 'ɑːtʃ'daiəsis] *n.* 總主教之管轄區。

arch·du·cal [ˌɑrtʃ'djukl̩; 'ɑːtʃ'djuːkəl] *adj.* 大公(爵)的;公國的。

arch·duch·ess ['ɑrtʃ'dʌtʃɪs; 'ɑːtʃ'dʌtʃis] *n.* ①大公之妃。②昔奥國之公主。

arch·duch·y ['ɑrtʃ'dʌtʃɪ; 'ɑːtʃ'dʌtʃi] *n., pl.* **-duch·ies.** ①大公(爵)之地位。②大公(尤指奥國王子)之領土;大公國。(亦作 **archdukedom**)

arch·duke ['ɑrtʃ'djuk; 'ɑːtʃ'djuːk] *n.* 大公(尤指昔奥國太子)。

Ar·che·an [ɑr'kiən; ɑː'kiːən] *adj.* 〖地質〗太古代的。(亦作 **Archaean, Archaian**) —*n.* 始生代。

arched [ɑrtʃt; ɑːtʃt] *adj.* 弓形的;有拱的;彎曲的。

ar·che·go·ni·um [ˌɑrkɪ'gonɪəm; ˌɑːki'gouniəm] *n., pl.* **-ni·a** [-nɪə; -niə]. 〖植物〗藏卵器。

arch·en·e·my ['ɑrtʃ'ɛnəmɪ; 'ɑːtʃ'enimi] *n., pl.* **-mies.** ①大敵。②魔王;撒旦。

ar·ch(a)e·o·lith·ic [ˌɑrkɪə'lɪθɪk; ˌɑːkiə'liθik] *adj.* 舊石器時代的。

ar·ch(a)e·o·log·i·cal [ˌɑrkɪə'lɑdʒɪkl̩; ˌɑːkiə'lɔdʒikəl] *adj.* 考古學的。

ar·ch(a)e·ol·o·gist [ˌɑrkɪ'ɑlədʒɪst; ˌɑːki'ɔlədʒist] *n.* 考古學家。

Ar·ch(a)e·o·zo·ic [ˌɑrkɪə'zo·ɪk; ˌɑːkiə'zouik] *adj.* 〖地質〗始生代的。—*n.* 始生代;始生代層之岩石。

***arch·er** ['ɑrtʃɚ; 'ɑːtʃə] *n.* ①射手;弓箭手。He is a good *archer.* 他是一個善射者。②射水魚。③〖天文〗(A-)射手座。

arch·er·y ['ɑrtʃərɪ; 'ɑːtʃəri] *n.* ①箭術;射藝。②弓箭之集合稱。③弓、箭等。

ar·che·type ['ɑrkəˌtaɪp; 'ɑːkitaip] *n.* ①原型。②〖經濟〗基本貨幣。**—ar·che·typ·al,** *adj.*

arch·fiend ['ɑrtʃ'find; 'ɑːtʃ'fiːnd] *n.* ①大惡魔。②撒旦。

ar·chi·bald ['ɑrtʃəˌbɔld; 'ɑːtʃibəld] *n.* 〖英俗〗高射砲。(亦作 **archie**)

ar·chi·di·ac·o·nal [ˌɑrkɪdaɪ'ækənl̩; ˌɑːkidai'ækənl̩] *adj.* 副主教的;副監督的。

ar·chi·e·pis·co·pal [ˌɑrkɪə'pɪskəpl̩; ˌɑːkii'piskəpəl] *adj.* 總主教的;大監督的;總主教之管轄區的。

ar·chil ['ɑrkɪl; 'ɑːkil] *n.* ①桔梗色染料之一種。②產生桔梗色染料之苔。

ar·chi·mage ['ɑrkəmedʒ; 'ɑːkimeidʒ] *n.* 大魔術師。

ar·chi·man·drite [ˌɑrkɪ'mændraɪt; ˌɑːki'mændrait] *n.* (東方正教之)修道院院長;大修道院長。

Ar·chi·me·des [ˌɑrkə'midiz; ˌɑːki'miːdiːz] *n.* 阿基米德 (287?-212 B.C., 希臘數學家、物理學家及發明家)。

ar·chi·pel·a·go [ˌɑrkə'pɛləˌgo; ˌɑːki'peligou] *n., pl.* **-gos, -goes.** ①多島海。②列島。*the Archipelago* 愛琴海及其島嶼。

archit. architecture.

***ar·chi·tect** ['ɑrkəˌtɛkt; 'ɑːkitekt] *n.* ①建築師。②製造者;設計者;創造者。the *architect* of one's own fortune. 創造自己的命運者。—*v.t.* 設計。

ar·chi·tec·ton·ic [ˌɑrkɪtɛk'tɑnɪk; ˌɑːkitek'tɔnik] *adj.* ①建築術的;建築家的。②組織的;構造的;設計的。③建築式樣的。④知識系統的。

ar·chi·tec·ton·ics [ˌɑrkɪtɛk'tɑnɪks; ˌɑːkitek'tɔniks] *n.* ①建築學。②結構設計。③〖哲學〗體系論。

architect's table 繪圖桌。

ar·chi·tec·tur·al [ˌɑrkə'tɛktʃərəl; ˌɑːki'tektʃərəl] *adj.* 建築學的;建築術的;合建築法的。**—ly,** *adv.*

***ar·chi·tec·ture** ['ɑrkəˌtɛktʃɚ; 'ɑːkitektʃə] *n.* ①建築學;建築術。②建築的式樣。③建築的構造。 The *architecture* of our school is very substantial. 我們學校的建築甚爲堅固。④建築物。⑤結構。the *architecture* of a novel. 小說的結構。⑥建造;建築。

ar·chi·trave ['ɑrkəˌtrev; 'ɑːkitreiv] *n.* 〖建築〗軒緣;楣樑。

ar·chi·val [ɑr'kaɪvl̩; ɑː'kaivəl] *adj.* 檔案的;紀錄的。

ar·chive ['ɑrkaɪv; 'ɑːkaiv] *n.* 文件;檔案;紀錄。

ar·chives ['ɑrkaɪvz; 'ɑːkaivz] *n. pl.* ①檔案保存處。②紀錄;文件;檔案。*family archives* 家譜。

ar·chi·vist ['ɑrkəvɪst; 'ɑːkivist] *n.* 檔案保管人。

ar·chon ['ɑrkɑn; 'ɑːkən] *n.* ①古雅典之執政官。②統治者。

arch·priest ['ɑrtʃ'prist; 'ɑːtʃ'priːst] *n.* 主僧;大祭司。

arch support 置於足穹部的鞋襯。

arch·way ['ɑrtʃˌwe; 'ɑːtʃwei] *n.* 拱門;拱道。

arch·wise [ˈɑrtʃ͵waɪz; ˈɑːtʃwaiz] *adv.* 弓形地;成弧形地。

-archy 〖字尾〗表"統治"之義。

ar·ci·form [ˈɑrsɪfɔrm; ˈɑːsifɔːm] *adj.* 弓狀的;弧形的。

arc lamp 弧光燈。

arc light ①弧光燈。②弧光。

A.R.C.M., A.R.C.O. Associate of the Royal College of Music (*or* Organists).

ar·co·graph [ˈɑrkə͵græf; ˈɑːkəgrɑːf] *n.* 圓弧規。

A.R.C.S. Associate of the Royal College of Science.

***arc·tic** [ˈɑrktɪk; ˈɑːktik] *adj.* ①北極的;近北極的。the *Arctic* Ocean. 北冰洋。②極寒的。I cannot stand this *arctic* weather. 我不能忍受這種嚴寒的天氣。③冷峻的。—*n.* ①北極地區。②(*pl.*)保暖的防水套鞋。

arc·ti·col·o·gist [͵ɑrktəˈkɑlədʒɪst; ͵ɑːktəˈkɔlədʒist] *n.* 研究南北極圈的科學家。

arc·ti·co·lo·gy [͵ɑrktəˈkɑlədʒɪ; ͵ɑːktəˈkɔlədʒi] *n.* 研究南北極圈的科學。

Arc·tu·rus [ɑrkˈtjʊrəs; ɑːkˈtjuərəs] *n.* 〖天文〗牧夫座中之一等恒星。

ar·cu·ate [ˈɑrkjuɪt; ˈɑːkjuit] *adj.* 弓形的;弧狀的;拱狀的。(亦作 **arcuated**)

-ard 〖字尾〗表"…的人"之義。

ar·den·cy [ˈɑrdn̩sɪ; ˈɑːdənsi] *n.* ①熱心;熱情。②灼熱;高熱。

***ar·dent** [ˈɑrdn̩t; ˈɑːdənt] *adj.* ①熱心的;熱情的。They are *ardent* patriots. 他們是熱心愛國的人。②燃燒的;發熱的。③如焚的;激烈的。—**ly,** *adv.* —**ness,** *n.*

ardent spirits 烈酒。

***ar·dor, ar·dour** [ˈɑrdə; ˈɑːdə] *n.* ①熱情;熱心。an *ardor* for study. 對研究的熱心。②灼熱。

***ar·du·ous** [ˈɑrdʒuəs; ˈɑːdjuəs] *adj.* ①費力的;困難的。This is an *arduous* enterprise. 這是一個艱難的事業。②辛勤的。③陡峭的;峻險的。④嚴酷的。—**ly,** *adv.* —**ness,** *n.*

‡are[1] [ɑr; ɑː] *v.* be 的現在式,直說法,複數(第一人稱,第二人稱,第三人稱)或單數(第二人稱)。We *are* ready. 我們準備好了。

‡are[2] [ɛr, ɑr; ɑː] *n.* 一百平方公尺(面積單位)。

‡ar·e·a [ˈɛrɪə, ˈerɪə; ˈɛəriə] *n.* ①地區;地域;地方。②面積。This room is 150 square feet in *area*. 這房間的面積爲150平方英尺。③範圍。④平面。⑤〖英〗地下室的門或窗前之低窪處。⑥庭院。

area bombing 區域轟炸。

area code (電話之)區域號碼。

area defense 區域防護。

area fire 區域轟擊。

area study 地域學。

ar·e·a·way [ˈɛrɪə͵we; ˈɛəriəwei] *n.* ①地窖門前之凹院。②〖美〗通道;過道。

ar·e·ca [ˈærɪkə; ˈærikə] *n.* 〖植物〗檳榔(樹)。

a·re·na [əˈrinə; əˈriːnə] *n.* ①(古羅馬之)鬥技場。②任何競爭之場所或地點。③奮勉或努力之活動範圍;界。

ar·e·na·ceous [͵ærɪˈneʃəs; ͵æriˈneiʃəs] *adj.* ①砂質的;砂地的。②砂般的;乾燥無味的。③〖植物〗生長於砂中的。

arena theater 圓形劇場。(亦作 **arena stage**)

***aren't** [ɑrnt; ɑːnt] =**are not.**

ar·e·og·ra·phy [͵ɛrɪˈɑgrəfɪ; ͵ɛəriˈɔgrəfi] *n.* ①火星的描寫。②討論火星的論文。

a·re·o·la [əˈriələ; æˈriələ] *n., pl.* **-las, -lae** [-li; -liː]. ①〖生物〗結締體素之網眼;小區。②〖解剖〗乳頭輪;暈。(亦作 **areole**)

ar·e·ol·o·gy [͵ɛrɪˈɑlədʒɪ; ͵ɛəriˈɔlədʒi] *n.* 火星觀察與研究。

ar·e·om·e·ter [͵ærɪˈɑmɪtə; ͵æriˈɔmitə] *n.* 〖物理〗液體比重計。

Ar·e·op·a·gus [͵ærɪˈɑpəgəs; ͵æriˈɔpəgəs] *n.* ①雅典之一小山。②古希臘之最高法院。③任何重要之法院。

ar·e·o·phy·sics [͵ærɪoˈfɪzɪks; ͵eiriəˈfiziks] *n.* 火星物理學。

Ar·es [ˈeriz; ˈɛəriːz] *n.* 〖希臘神話〗戰神。

ar·e·thu·sa [͵ærəˈθuzə; ͵ærəˈθuːsə] *n.* ①蘭科植物。②(A-)〖希臘神話〗水神。

Arg. Argentina. **arg.** ①argent. ②argentum.

ar·ga·la [ˈɑrgələ; ˈɑːgələ] *n.* 〖動物〗印度產之鸛類。

ar·gent [ˈɑrdʒənt; ˈɑːdʒənt] *n.* 銀;銀色。—*adj.* ①銀的;似銀的。②銀白的;純白的。

ar·gen·tif·er·ous [͵ɑrdʒənˈtɪfərəs; ͵ɑːdʒənˈtifərəs] *adj.* 含銀的;產銀的。

Ar·gen·ti·na [͵ɑrdʒənˈtinə; ͵ɑːdʒənˈtiːnə] *n.* 阿根廷(南美洲的一個國家,首都爲布宜諾斯艾利斯 Buenos Aires).

Ar·gen·tine [ˈɑrdʒən͵tin; ˈɑːdʒəntain] *adj.* 阿根廷的。—*n.* 阿根廷人。 *the Argentine* =**Argentina.**

ar·gen·tine [ˈɑrdʒəntɪn; ˈɑːdʒəntain] *adj.* 銀的;似銀的;銀色的。—*n.* ①銀;銀色金屬。②銀色素。

Ar·gen·tin·e·an [͵ɑrdʒənˈtɪnɪən; ͵ɑːdʒənˈtiniən] *n.* 阿根廷人。

ar·gil [ˈɑrdʒɪl; ˈɑːdʒil] *n.* 陶土;白黏土;礬土。

ar·gil·la·ceous [͵ɑrdʒɪˈleʃəs; ͵ɑːdʒiˈleiʃəs] *adj.* ①陶土質的;黏土質的。②含黏土的;多黏土的。

Ar·give [ˈɑrdʒaɪv; ˈɑːgaiv] *adj.* 希臘一古城 Argos 市的;希臘的。—*n.* Argos 市的人;希臘人。

Ar·go [ˈɑrgo; ˈɑːgou] *n.* ①〖希臘神話〗Jason 率人往 Colchis 求取金羊毛所乘之船。②〖天文〗南船座。—**an,** *adj.*

ar·gol [ˈɑrgl̩; ˈɑːgɔl] *n.* 粗酒石。

ar·gon [ˈɑrgɑn; ˈɑːgɔn] *n.* 〖化〗氬(元素名,符號A).

Ar·go·naut [ˈɑrgə͵nɔt; ˈɑːgənɔːt] *n.* ①與 Jason 同往 Colchis 求取金羊毛之人。②1848–49年前往美國加州淘金者。—**ic,** *adj.*

ar·go·naut [ˈɑrgə͵nɔt; ˈɑːgənɔːt] *n.* 〖動物〗紅魚。

ar·go·sy [ˈɑrgəsɪ; ˈɑːgəsi] *n., pl.* **-sies.** ①大商船。②大商船隊。③豐富的供應。

ar·got [ˈɑrgo; ˈɑːgou] *n.* (黑社會所操之)暗語;隱語;切口;(某一職業或團體的)慣用語。

ar·gu·a·ble [ˈɑrgjuəbl̩; ˈɑːgjuəbl] *adj.* 可辯論的;可論證的;可辯駁的。

***ar·gue** [ˈɑrgju; ˈɑːgjuː] *v.,* **-gued, -gu·ing.** —*v.i.* ①辯論。to *argue* for (*or* against) a proposed law. 辯論贊成(反對)某法律草案。②爭論。They *argued* with each other about the best place for a holiday. 他們彼此爭論關於度假日最好的地方。—*v.t.* ①辯論。②主張。③說服;勸告。He wanted to go to India but we *argued* him out of it. 他要去印度,但我們已勸服他不去了。④證明。His accent *argues* him to be a foreigner. 他的口音證明了他是一個外國人。

ar·gu·er [ˈɑrgjuə; ˈɑːgjuə] *n.* 辯論者。

ar·gu·fy [ˈɑrgju͵faɪ; ˈɑːgjufai] *v.i.* & *v.t.,* **-fied, -fy·ing.** 〖俗,方〗爭論;辯論。(亦作 **argify**)

***ar·gu·ment** ['argjəmənt;'ɑ:gjumənt] *n.* ①辯論；爭論。They spent hours in *argument* about where to go. 他們費了幾小時辯論要去甚麼地方。②議論。③理由；論據。④導言；自序；大綱。⑤〖數學〗自變數；幅角；幅度。

ar·gu·men·ta·tion [ˌargjəmɛn'teʃən; ˌɑ:gjumen'teiʃən] *n.* ①立論；論法。②辯論；爭論；討論。③議論；論說。

ar·gu·men·ta·tive [ˌargjə'mɛntətɪv; ˌɑ:gju'mentətiv] *adj.* ①辯論的；爭論的。②好辯論的。(亦作 **argumental**) **—ly,** *adv.* **—ness,** *n.*

Ar·gus ['argəs; 'ɑ:gəs] *n.* ①〖希臘神話〗百眼巨人。②機警之看守人。

Ar·gus-eyed ['argəsˌaɪd; ˌɑ:gəs'aid] *adj.* 眼光銳利的；機警的。

Ar·gyle [ar'gaɪl; ɑ:'gail] *adj.* (織品中)有多色菱形花紋的。—*n.* ①織品中的多色菱形花紋。②有多色菱形花紋的襪子。

ar·gyr·i·a [ar'dʒɪrɪə; ɑ:'dʒiriə] *n.*〖醫〗銀中毒；銀質沉着。

Ar·gy·rol ['ardʒəˌrɔl; 'ɑ:dʒərɔl] *n.* 弱蛋白銀。

a·ri·a ['arɪə;'ɑ:riə] *n.*〖音樂〗曲調；抒情調。

Ar·i·an ['ɛrɪən; 'ɛəriən] *adj.* ①印歐語的。②印歐語族的。—*n.* 印歐語族之人。

ar·id ['ærɪd; 'ærid] *adj.* ①乾燥的；不毛的。②枯燥無味的；貧弱的。③死板的；缺乏想像力的。

a·rid·i·ty [ə'rɪdətɪ; æ'riditi] *n.* ①乾旱；不毛。②枯燥無味；無興趣。

Ar·i·el ['ɛrɪəl; 'ɛəriəl] *n.* 愛儷兒(莎翁劇本 *The Tempest* 中之精靈)。

ar·i·el ['ɛrɪˌɛl; 'ɛəriəl] *n.*〖動物〗瞪羚。

Ar·i·es ['ɛriz; 'ɛəri:z] *n.*〖天文〗①白羊座。②白羊宮。

ar·i·et·ta [ˌærɪ'ɛtə; ˌæri'etə] *n., pl.* **-et·tas, -et·te** [-'ɛtə; -'etə].〖音樂〗小抒情曲；短調。

a·right [ə'raɪt; ə'rait] *adv.* 正確地。—*v.t.* 使正確；更改。

ar·il ['ærɪl; 'æril] *n.*〖植物〗假種皮。

ar·il·late ['ærəˌlet; 'ærəleit] *adj.* 帶有假種皮的。

a·rio·so [ˌarɪ'oso; ˌɑ:ri:'ouzou] *n., pl.* **-sos,** *adj., adv.*〖音樂〗—*n.* 小抒情調；小獨唱曲。—*adj.* & *adv.* 像小抒情調的(地)；小獨唱曲的(地)。

***a·rise** [ə'raɪz;ə'raiz] *v.i.,* **a·rose, a·ris·en** [ə'rɪzn̩; ə'rizn], **a·ris·ing.** ①起來。②上升。③起源於〖from〗. Accidents *arise* from carelessness. 意外起源於疏忽。④出現；發生。

a·ris·ta [ə'rɪstə; ə'ristə] *n., pl.* **-tae** [-ti; -ti:]. ①〖植物〗穀類之芒。②〖動物〗昆蟲觸鬚上之刺；口刺。

a·ris·tate [ə'rɪstet;ə'risteit] *adj.*〖動、植物〗有芒的；有刺的。

***ar·is·toc·ra·cy** [ˌærə'stɑkrəsɪ;ˌæris'tɔkrəsi] *n., pl.* **-cies.** ①貴族。②上流社會；特殊階級。③貴族政治。④貴族統治的國家。

***a·ris·to·crat** [ə'rɪstəˌkræt, 'ærɪstəˌkræt;'æristəkræt, æ'ris-, ə'ris-] *n.* ①貴族。②主張貴族政治的人。③有貴族氣派的人。

***a·ris·to·crat·ic** [əˌrɪstə'krætɪk, ˌærɪstə-;ˌæristə'krætik] *adj.* ①適合於貴族的。②貴族的。③貴族政治的。(亦作**aristocratical**) **—al·ly,** *adv.* **—ism,** *n.*

Ar·is·to·te·lian, Ar·is·to·te·lean [ˌærɪstə'tilɪən; ˌæristɔ'ti:ljən] *adj.* 亞里斯多德的；亞里斯多德學派的。—*n.* ①亞里斯多德派之學者。②思想着重實際之人；實驗主義者。**—Ar·is·to·te·lian·ism,** *n.*

Ar·is·tot·le ['ærəˌstɑtl; 'æristɔtl] *n.* 亞里斯多德(384–322 B.C., 希臘大哲學家)。

arith. ①arithmetic. ②arithmetical.

***a·rith·me·tic** [*n.* ə'rɪθməˌtɪk;ə'riθmətik *adj.* ˌærɪθ'mɛtɪk; ˌæriθ'metik] *n.* ①算術。mental *arithmetic.* 心算。②算術教科書。—*adj.* 算術的。

ar·ith·met·i·cal [ˌærɪθ'mɛtɪkl;ˌæriθ'metikəl] *adj.* 算術的；算術上的。**—ly,** *adv.*

arithmetical invariant 不變數。

arithmetical mean 等差中項；相加平均數。

arithmetical progression 等差級數。

arithmetical series 算術級數；等差級數。

a·rith·me·ti·cian [əˌrɪθmə'tɪʃən; əˌriθmə'tiʃən] *n.* 算術家。

Ariz. Arizona.

Ar·i·zo·na [ˌærə'zonə; ˌæri'zounə] *n.* 亞利桑那(美國西南部一州，首府 Phoenix).

ark [ark; ɑ:k] *n.* ①方舟(世界大洪水時 Noah 所乘之大船，見聖經舊約創世記)。②方舟(小孩玩具)。③避難所。④大而笨重的船(或車輛)。⑤〖美〗大而無當的房子。⑥約櫃。

Ark. Arkansas.

Ar·kan·sas ['arkənˌsɔ; 'ɑ:kənsɔ:] *n.* 阿肯色(美國之一州，其首府爲 Little Rock).

arles [arlz;ɑ:lz] *n. pl.*〖蘇，英北方〗定金。

Ar·ling·ton ['arlɪŋtən; 'ɑ:liŋtən] *n.* 阿靈頓(在華盛頓郊區，該處有無名英雄墓)。

‡arm [arm; ɑ:m] *n.* ①臂。②用途或形狀上似臂之物。the *arms* of a chair. 椅子的扶手。an *arm* of the sea. 海灣。③獸類之前腿。④權力；權威。⑤一件武器；一枝槍；一把劍；一根棒。⑥兵種；兵科。⑦蓋臂之物，如衣袖。⑧某一機構的行政或執行部門。⑨錨的彎曲部分。***arm in arm*** 挽臂；携手。They walk *arm in arm.* 他們挽臂散步。***at arm's length*** 疏遠；不與之親近。***in the arms of Morpheus*** 睡着。***put the arm on*** 〖俚〗自…取款；誘使給付。***with folded arms*** 袖手(旁觀)。***within arm's reach*** 在左右；在近旁。***with open arms*** 熱烈(歡迎)。—*v.t.* ①給以武器；裝備。②準備…以便隨時應用。③裝甲。④裝上導火線。—*v.i.* 拿起武器；備戰。The soldiers *armed* for battle. 士兵們拿起武器準備作戰。

ar·ma·da [ar'madə; ɑ:'mɑ:də] *n.*①艦隊。②龐大的車隊或飛機羣。***the Armada*** 1588年西班牙派征英國之無敵艦隊。

ar·ma·dil·lo [ˌarmə'dɪlo; ˌɑ:mə'dilou] *n., pl.* **-los.**〖動物〗犰狳(中南美洲產)。

Ar·ma·ged·don [ˌarmə'gɛdn̩;ˌɑ:mə'gedn] *n.* ①〖聖經〗哈米吉多頓(善與惡之決戰場，啓示錄16章16節)。②(國際間之)大決戰。

***ar·ma·ment** ['arməmənt;'ɑ:məmənt] *n.*①兵力；軍勢。②(軍艦要塞等之)大砲。③(*pl.*)軍備。④裝甲。⑤配備。

ar·ma·ture ['armətʃɚ; 'ɑ:mətjuə] *n.* ①甲冑。②〖生物〗防禦器官。③〖電〗電動子；電樞。④〖磁學〗接極子。⑤〖建築〗補强料。⑥〖雕刻〗(支撑泥像之)支架。

arm badge 臂章。

arm band 臂章；臂環。

***arm·chair** ['armˌtʃɛr; 'ɑ:m'tʃɛə] *n.*有扶手的椅子。—*adj.* ①安逸的。②理論性的。

arme blanche ['arm'blɑ̃ʃ;'ɑ:mblɑ̃:ʃ] 〖法〗①白刃；騎兵刀(槍)。②騎兵。

armed [armd; ɑ:md] *adj.* ①武裝的；裝甲的。②裝上導火線的。③〖動物〗有保護作用之構造的。④有準備的；有…裝備的。⑤使產生安全感的。
armed forces (陸海空)三軍。
armed robbery 〖法律〗持械搶劫。
Ar·me·ni·a [ɑrˈminɪə; ɑːˈmiːnjə] *n.* 亞美尼亞(蘇聯之一共和國)。
Ar·me·ni·an [ɑrˈminɪən; ɑːˈmiːnjən] *adj.* 亞美尼亞(人)的。—*n.* 亞美尼亞人(語)。
ar·met [ˈɑrmɛt; ˈɑːmet] *n.* 古時的頭盔。
arm·ful [ˈɑrm͵fʊl, ˈɑːmful] *n.* (單臂或雙臂)一抱之量。
arm·guard [ˈɑrm͵gɑrd; ˈɑːmgɑːd] *n.* 護手。
arm·hole [ˈɑrm͵hol; ˈɑːmhoul] *n.* 衣服袖孔。
ar·mi·ger [ˈɑrmɪdʒɚ; ˈɑːmidʒə] *n.* ①有佩徽章資格之人。②替武士持甲冑者。
ar·mil·lar·y sphere [ˈɑrmɪ͵lɛrɪ～; ˈɑːmiləri～] 〖天文〗渾天儀。
arm·ing [ˈɑrmɪŋ; ˈɑːmiŋ] *n.* ①備戰狀態。②武器;裝甲。③裝備。④磁石的接極子。
ar·mip·o·tent [ɑrˈmɪpətənt; ɑːˈmipətənt] *adj.* 武力强大的;軍備充實的。
***ar·mi·stice** [ˈɑrməstɪs; ˈɑːmistis] *n.* 休戰。
Armistice Day 第一次世界大戰休戰紀念日(十一月十一日)。
arm·less [ˈɑrmlɪs; ˈɑːmlis] *adj.* ①無臂的。②無武器的;無武裝的。
arm·let [ˈɑrmlɪt; ˈɑːmlit] *n.* ①〖英〗臂環;臂釧。②小海灣。
arm·load [ˈɑrm͵lod; ˈɑːmloud] *n.* 一抱之量。
***ar·mor, ar·mour** [ˈɑrmɚ; ˈɑːmə] *n.* ①甲冑。②鐵甲。③裝甲部隊。④裝甲。⑤可保身之物,性質,特性,或情況。⑥保護電纜、電話線等的金屬套皮。—*v.t.* 裝甲。
ar·mor·bear·er [ˈɑrmɚ͵bɛrɚ; ˈɑːmə͵bɛərə] *n.* 持甲冑者;武士之扈從。
ar·mor-clad [ˈɑrmɚ͵klæd; ˈɑːməklæd] *adj.* 穿着甲冑的;裝甲的。
ar·mored [ˈɑrmɚd; ˈɑːməd] *adj.* 武裝的;裝甲的。
armored cable 有金屬套皮的電纜。
armored car 裝甲車。
armored concrete 鋼筋水泥。
armored cruiser 裝甲巡洋艦。
armored division 裝甲師。
armored forces 裝甲部隊。
armored train 裝甲列車。
armored troops 〖英〗裝甲部隊。
ar·mor·er [ˈɑrmərɚ; ˈɑːmərə] *n.* 製造或修理兵器者;軍械保管員。
ar·mo·ri·al [ɑrˈmorɪəl; ɑːˈmɔːriəl] *adj.* 紋章的;徽章的。—*n.* 紋章書。
armorial bearings 紋章;徽章。
ar·mor-pierc·ing [ˈɑrmɚ͵pɪrsɪŋ; ˈɑːmə͵piəsiŋ] *adj.*穿甲的。
armor plate 鋼板;裝甲板。
ar·mor-plat·ed [ˈɑrmɚ͵pletɪd; ˈɑːmə͵pleitid] *adj.*裝鋼板的;裝甲的。
ar·mor·y [ˈɑrmərɪ; ˈɑːməri] *n., pl.* **-mor·ies.** ①軍械庫。②兵工廠。③〖美,加〗國民兵訓練中心。④紋章學;紋章。⑤武器。
arm·pit [ˈɑrm͵pɪt; ˈɑːmpit] *n.* 腋窩。
arm·rest [ˈɑrm͵rɛst; ˈɑːmrest] *n.*扶手。
arms** [ɑrmz; ɑːmz] *n.* ①武器;軍械。②兵役。He received a call to *arms.* 他被召入伍。③紋章。④戰爭。appeal to arms*** 訴諸武力。***bear arms*** 當兵。***carry arms*** 帶武器;肩槍。***in arms*** 準備作戰。***lay down arms*** 投降。***side arms*** 刺刀;劍。***small arms*** 輕武器。***take up arms*** 準備戰鬥;戰爭。***to arms*** 準備打仗。***under arms*** 準備戰爭;配備有武器;武裝着;動員。***up in arms*** a. 準備作戰。b.暴動;起義。
arms race 軍備競賽。
Arm·strong [ˈɑrmstrɔŋ; ˈɑːmstrɔŋ] *n.* 阿姆斯壯(Neil, 1930–, 美太空人, 1969年7月20日登陸月球,爲人類身臨月球第一人)。
arm-twist·ing [ˈɑrm͵twɪstɪŋ; ˈɑːm͵twistiŋ] *n.* 壓力或影響。
‡**ar·my** [ˈɑrmɪ; ˈɑːmi] *n., pl.* **-mies.** ①軍隊。to enter the *army.* 入伍。②陸軍。③大羣;羣衆。an *army* of locusts. 蝗羣。
army commander 軍團司令官。
army corps 軍團。
army corps commander 軍長。
army day 陸軍節。
army group 集團軍。
army surplus 陸軍剩餘物資。
ar·ni·ca [ˈɑrnɪkə; ˈɑːnikə] *n.* ①山金車(菊科植物)。②山金車碘酒。
Ar·nold·son [ˈɑrnḷdsən; ˈɑːnldsən] *n.* 安諾森 (Klas Pontus, 1844–1916, 瑞典作家及政治家, 1908年諾貝爾和平獎得獎人)。
a·ro·ma [əˈromə; əˈroumə] *n.* 芳香;香氣;風韻。
ar·o·mat·ic [͵ærəˈmætɪk; ͵ærouˈmætik] *adj.* ①芳香的。②〖化〗芳香族的。—*n.* 芳香植物;香料。
a·ro·ma·tize [əˈromə͵taɪz; əˈroumətaiz] *v.t.,* **-tized, -tiz·ing.** 使芳香;加香味。
a·rose [əˈroz; əˈrouz] *v.* pt. of **arise.**
‡**a·round** [əˈraund; əˈraund] *prep.* ①環繞。②在四周;圍於。She had a coat *around* her shoulders. 她有一件外衣圍於肩上。③〖美俗〗近於;在…近處,近…時;差不多。④〖美俗〗到處。⑤在那邊。⑥在邊緣。⑦朝着各方向。⑧親近着某人;在某人身邊。⑨以便解決困難。⑩根據。—*adv.* ①環繞;在四周;繞着。His car circled *around.* 他的車在兜圈子。②到處。③近處。Please wait *around* for me; I will be back soon. 請在近處等我,我很快就回來。④周圍。⑤向相反方向地。Turn *around!* You are going the wrong way. 轉回來,你走錯路了。⑥時間的循環重現。⑦旋轉着。⑧朝着相反的方向、行爲、或意見。⑨恢復意識。⑩活躍着。He hasn't been *around* lately. 他最近不活躍。⑪到某地。He came *around* to see me. 他到這兒來看我。***have been around*** 見過世面;人生經驗豐富。
a·round-the-clock [əˈraundðəˈklɑk; əˈraundðə͵klɔk] *adj.* 不休的;日以繼夜的。(亦作 **round-the-clock**)
a·rous·al [əˈrauzḷ; əˈrauzəl] *n.* 覺醒;振作。
***a·rouse** [əˈrauz; əˈrauz] *v.,* **a·roused, a·rous·ing.** —*v.t.*①喚醒。②喚起;振作。to *arouse* attention. 喚起注意。—*v.i.* 醒來;振作。
ARP, A.R.P. air-raid precautions. 民防設施。
ar·peg·gi·o [ɑrˈpɛdʒɪ͵o; ɑːˈpedʒiou] *n., pl.* **-gi·os.** 〖音樂〗和音急速彈奏;琶音。
ar·que·bus [ˈɑrkwɪbəs; ˈɑːkwibəs] *n., pl.* **-es.** 火繩槍之一種。(亦作 **harquebus**)
arr. ①arranged. ②arrangement(s). ③arrival. ④arrive(d).
ar·rack [ˈærək; ˈærək] *n.* 燒酒(尤指以米或糖蜜釀造者)。(亦作 **arak**)
ar·raign [əˈren; əˈrein] *v.t.* ①〖法律〗提訊;傳問。②控告;責難。—*n.* =**arraignment.**
ar·raign·ment [əˈrenmənt; əˈreinmənt] *n.* 提訊;控告;指責。
‡**ar·range** [əˈrendʒ; əˈreindʒ] *v.,* **-ranged, -rang·ing.** —*v.t.* ①排列;配置;整

理。Please *arrange* my books on the shelf in order. 請將書架上我的書整理好。②處理;調解。③預備。④改寫(樂曲)。—*v.i.* ①協商。We must *arrange* about that. 關於那事,我們應協商。②安排;準備。Can you *arrange* to meet me this evening? 你能設法在今天晚上和我會晤嗎? —**a•ble,** *adj.*

ar·range·ment** 〔ə'rendʒmənt; ə'reindʒmənt〕 *n.* ①布置。②排列。③處理;調解。The parties have made an *arrangement* of their dispute. 雙方已設法調解其爭執。④(常 *pl.*)準備。He made *arrangements* for the meeting. 他作開會的準備。⑤特別安排之事物。⑥樂曲之改寫。come to an arrangement*** 商妥辦法。***flower arrangement*** 插花。

ar·rant 〔'ærənt; 'ærənt〕 *adj.* ①完全的;徹底的。②聲名狼藉的。—**ly,** *adv.*

ar·ras¹ 〔'ærəs; 'ærəs〕 *n.* 花氈;掛氈。

ar·ras² 〔'ɑrɑs; 'ærəs〕 *n.* 〖法律〗結婚時丈夫送給妻子的禮物。

ar·ray 〔ə're; ə'rei〕 *v.t.* ①裝飾;盛裝。She *arrayed* herself in her finest clothes. 她穿上最好的衣服。②排列;布署。—*n.* ①衣服;服裝。②整列;排陣。③軍隊。④序列。⑤一大批(物品);一大羣(人)。⑥一連串。⑦〖數學〗排列。 「排列之事物。」

ar·ray·al 〔ə'reəl; ə'reiəl〕 *n.* 排列;被

ar·rear 〔ə'rɪr; ə'riə〕 *n.* 未做之事;保留之事。***fall into arrear(s)*** 延滯。***in arrear(s)*** 拖欠;未付。***in arrear of*** 趕不上。***in arrear(s) with*** (***work***) (工作)躭誤。***work off arrears*** 把延誤的工作補過來。

ar·rear·age 〔ə'rɪrɪdʒ; ə'riəridʒ〕 *n.* ①給付遲延;拖延;躭擱;遲滯。②欠款;到期未付之款。③保留物。

ar·rears 〔ə'rɪrz; ə'riəz〕 *n. pl.* ①未完成之工作;該作未作之事;拖延,躭擱,遲滯。②到期未付之債;債。***in*** (or ***into***) ***arrear(s)*** 落後;拖欠。 「聽的。②豎起的。」

ar·rect 〔ə'rɛkt; ə'rekt〕 *adj.* ①傾耳細

ar·rest** 〔ə'rɛst; ə'rest〕 *v.t.* ①逮捕。②吸引(注意)。③停止;阻擋;妨礙。—*n.* ①逮捕。The police made several *arrests.* 警察逮捕了好幾個人。②停止;阻止。③任何停止機器運轉的裝置。④一種使火花不隨烟上升的裝置。under arrest*** 禁錮;拘留。***under house arrest*** 被軟禁。 「捕的人。」

ar·rest·ee 〔əˌrɛs'ti; əˌrest'iː〕 *n.* 被逮

ar·rest·er, ar·rest·or 〔ə'rɛstə; ə'restə〕 *n.* 逮捕者。 「引人注意的。」

ar·rest·ing 〔ə'rɛstɪŋ; ə'restiŋ〕 *adj.*

ar·res·tive 〔ə'rɛstɪv; ə'restiv〕 *adj.* 引人注意的。 「mənt〕 *n.* 逮捕;阻擋。」

ar·rest·ment 〔ə'rɛstmənt; ə'rest-

Ar·rhe·ni·us 〔ɑr'renɪʌs; ɑː'reiniʌs〕 *n.* 阿瑞尼阿斯(Svante August, 1859–1927, 瑞典理化學家, 1903 年獲諾貝爾化學獎)。

ar·ride 〔ə'raɪd; ə'raid〕 *v.t.,* **-rid·ed, -rid·ing.** 使喜悅;使滿意。

ar·ri·ère-pen·sée 〔arjɛrpɑ̃'se; æri-ɛəpɑ̃ːn'sei〕 〖法〗 *n.* 心意;心事。 「線。」

ar·ris 〔'ærɪs; 'æris〕 *n.* 〖建築〗稜角;稜

arris gutter V字形簷槽。

***ar·riv·al** 〔ə'raɪvl; ə'raivəl〕 *n.* ①到達;到。On my *arrival* at (*or* in) New York, I despatched a telegram home. 我到達紐約,即發一電報回家。②到的人或物。We have a new *arrival* in our family. 我們家裏添了一個小孩。I can not find your name in the list of new *arrivals.* 在新到旅客名單中,我找不到你的名字。③達到(某一目的或狀況)。

‡ar·rive 〔ə'raɪv; ə'raiv〕 *v.i.,* **-rived, -riv·ing.** ①到達;抵(指目的地)。We *arrived* at (*or* in) Taipei in the morning. 我們在早晨到達臺北。②獲得(結果);達到(目的)。We have *arrived* at an arrangement. 我們已得到協議。③達到某點或某階段。He has *arrived* at manhood. 他已成人。④來;來臨。⑤成功;著名。

ar·ri·viste 〔ɑri'vist; ˌæriː'viːst〕 *n., pl.* **-vistes.** 〖法〗暴發戶;新貴。

ar·ro·gance 〔'ærəgəns; 'ærəgəns〕 *n.* 傲慢;自大。(亦作 **arrogancy**)

ar·ro·gant 〔'ærəgənt; 'ærəgənt〕 *adj.* 傲慢的;自大的。 —**ly,** *adv.*

ar·ro·gate 〔'ærəˌget; 'ærougeit〕 *v.t.,* **-gat·ed, -gat·ing.** ①僭越;霸占;擅取。②不當地認爲歸屬某人。

ar·ro·ga·tion 〔ˌærə'geʃən; ˌærou-'geiʃən〕 *n.* 僭稱;霸占;越權;橫暴。

ar·ron·disse·ment 〔arɔ̃dis'mɑ̃; ærɔ̃dis'mɑ̃〕 *n., pl.* **-ments** 〔-'mɑ̃;-'mɑ̃ː〕. 〖法〗①法國之行政區(次於 department);郡。②(巴黎市等之)區。

***ar·row** 〔'æro; 'ærou〕 *n.* ①箭;矢。②箭號(→)。③任何箭形之物。—*v.t.* ①以箭頭指示。②如箭般地射出或行進。—*v.i.* 如箭般地迅速行動。

ar·row·head 〔'æroˌhɛd; 'ærouhed〕 *n.* ①箭頭。②〖植物〗慈姑。③箭頭狀物。④箭頭狀裝飾。⑤箭頭狀記號。

ar·row·head·ed 〔'ærəˌhɛdɪd; 'ærou-ˌhedid〕 *adj.* 箭頭狀的。 「形文字。」

arrowheaded characters 楔

ar·row·root 〔'æroˌrut; 'ærəruːt〕 *n.* ①〖植物〗葛。②葛粉。

ar·row·wood 〔'ærəˌwud; 'ærəwud〕 *n.* 箭木;荚蒾屬。「似箭的;快速的;筆直的。」

ar·row·y 〔'ærəwɪ; 'ærouі〕 *adj.* 箭的;

ar·roy·o 〔ə'rɔɪo; ə'rɔiou〕 *n., pl.* **-os.** ①乾涸之小谿谷。②小河;小溪。

ars 〔ɑrz; ɑːz〕 〖拉〗 *n.* 藝術。

arse 〔ɑrs; ɑːs〕 *n.* 〖俚〗臀部;屁股。

ar·se·nal 〔'ɑrsn̩əl; 'ɑːsinl〕 *n.* ①兵工廠;軍械庫。②(事物的)集成。 「砒酸鹽。」

ar·se·nate 〔'ɑrsn̩ˌet; 'ɑːsinit〕 *n.* 〖化〗

ar·sen·ic 〔*n.* 'ɑrsnɪk; 'ɑːsnik *adj.* ɑr-'sɛnɪk; ɑː'senik〕 *adj.* 砷(尤指五價者)的;含砷的;砒素的。—*n.* 砒;砷(符號爲As)。

arsenic acid 砒酸。

ar·sen·i·cal 〔ɑr'sɛnɪkl̩; ɑː'senikəl〕 *adj.* 砷的;含砒素的。—*n.* 砷劑;砒劑。

ar·sen·i·cate 〔ɑr'sɛnəˌket; ɑː'senə-keit〕 *v.t.,* **-cat·ed, -cat·ing.** 使與砒混合;用砒處理。

ar·se·ni·ous acid 〔ɑr'sinɪəs~; ɑː-'siːnjəs~〕 亞砒酸。 「亞砒酸鹽。」

ar·se·nite 〔'ɑrsn̩ˌaɪt; 'ɑːsinait〕 *n.* 〖化〗

ars est ce·la·re ar·tem 〔ɑrz ɛst sɪ'leri 'ɑrtɛm; ɑːz est si'leiri'ɑːtem〕 〖拉〗眞藝術將藝術隱藏(眞藝術不露斧鑿痕跡)。

ar·sis 〔'ɑrsɪs; 'ɑːsis〕 *n., pl.* **-ses** 〔-siz; -siːz〕. 〖音樂〗上拍;弱拍(爲 thesis 之對)。

A.R.S.L. Associate of the Royal Society of Literature.

ar·son 〔'ɑrsn̩; 'ɑːsn〕 *n.* (非法)放火;縱火。 「犯。(亦作 **arsonite**)」

ar·son·ist 〔'ɑrsn̩ɪst; 'ɑːsnist〕 *n.* 縱火

ars·phen·a·mine 〔ˌɑrsfɛnəˈmin; ˌɑːsfenəˈmiːn〕*n.* 〖醫〗六〇六(梅毒特效藥)。

ᵗ**art**[1] 〔ɑrt; ɑːt〕 *n.* ①藝術。②(*pl.*)文藝。History and literature are among the *arts*. 歷史和文學是屬於文科的。③人爲;人工。④技術;技巧。An architect studies the *art* of building. 建築家研究建築藝術。⑤(*pl.*)詭計;詐術。⑥(*pl.*) **a.** (作 *sing.* 解)人文學科。**b.** (作 *pl.* 解)文理科。⑦(新聞,雜誌)圖片,圖畫等。Is there any *art* with this story? 這篇文章附有圖片嗎? ⑧做作;裝模作樣。

art[2] *v.* 〖古,詩〗be 之第二人稱、單數、現在式,直陳法(與 thou 連用)。

art. ①article. ②artist. ③artificial. ④artillery.

art director ①美術設計人。②美術編輯。

ar·tel 〔ɑrˈtɛl; ɑːˈtel〕 *n.* (蘇聯之)農民或工人的合作社。

Ar·te·mis 〔ˈɑrtəmɪs; ˈɑːtimis〕 *n.* ①〖希臘神話〗月之女神。②女子名。

ar·te·ri·al 〔ɑrˈtɪrɪəl; ɑːˈtiəriəl〕 *adj.* ①動脈的;動脈系的。②動脈狀的;似動脈的。

ar·te·ri·al·i·za·tion 〔ɑrˌtɪrɪəlɪˈzeʃən; ɑːˌtiəriəliˈzeiʃən〕 *n.* 動脈血化。

ar·te·ri·al·ize 〔ɑrˈtɪrɪəlˌaɪz; ɑːˈtiəriəlaiz〕 *v.t.*, **-ized, -iz·ing.** 化(靜脈血)爲動脈血。

ar·te·ri·o·scle·ro·sis 〔ɑrˈtɪrɪˌosklɪˈrosɪs; ɑːˈtiəriouskliəˈrousis〕 *n.* 〖醫〗動脈硬化。

ar·te·ri·o·ste·no·sis 〔ɑrˌtɪrɪostəˈnosɪs; ɑːˌtiərioustəˈnousis〕 *n.* 〖醫〗動脈狹窄。

ar·te·ri·tis 〔ˌɑrtəˈraɪtɪs; ˌɑːtəˈraitis〕 *n.* 〖醫〗動脈炎。

***ar·ter·y** 〔ˈɑrtərɪ; ˈɑːtəri〕 *n.*, *pl.* **-ter·ies.** ①動脈。②渠道;孔道。A main road is sometimes called an *artery* of traffic. 幹路有時亦稱爲交通要道。

ar·te·sian well 〔ɑrˈtiʒən~; ɑːˈtiːzjən~〕 ①噴水井;鑽井。②〖美〗深水井。

art·ful 〔ˈɑrtfəl; ˈɑːtful〕 *adj.* ①狡詐的;欺人的。②巧妙的;技巧的;機敏的。③人爲的;不自然的。

art gallery 美術館;畫廊。

ar·thri·tic 〔ɑrˈθrɪtɪk; ɑːˈθritik〕 *adj.* 關節炎的;由關節炎所引起的。—*n.*關節炎患者。

ar·thri·tis 〔ɑrˈθraɪtɪs; ɑːˈθraitis〕 *n.* 關節炎。

ar·thro·pod 〔ˈɑrθrəˌpɑd; ˈɑːθrəpɔd〕 *n.* 節足動物。—*adj.* 節足動物的。

Ar·thur[1] 〔ˈɑrθɚ; ˈɑːθə〕 *n.* 男子名。

Ar·thur[2] *n.*亞瑟(昔不列顛傳說中之國王,爲圓桌武士之領袖)。—**i·an,** *adj.*

ar·ti·choke 〔ˈɑrtɪˌtʃok; ˈɑːtitʃouk〕 *n.* 〖植物〗朝鮮薊。

ᵗ**ar·ti·cle** 〔ˈɑrtɪkḷ; ˈɑːtikl〕 *n.*, *v.*, **-cled, -cling.** —*n.*①論文;文章。He contributed *articles* to *the Central Daily News* frequently. 他常向"中央日報"投稿。②條款;條目;節目。This document includes many *articles*. 這文件包括許多條款。③物品;物件。*articles* of trade. 商品。④〖文法〗加於名詞前面的冠詞,卽 a, an, the. ⑤人(非正式用法)。Who is that cute *article* over there? 那邊那個可愛的人兒是誰? —*v.t.* ①逐條陳述。②訂約雇用。③列擧(罪狀);控告。—*v.i.* ①約定。He *articled* with her that he should go away. 他與她約定,他必須離去。②訂契約。③控告;指責。

ar·tic·u·lar 〔ɑrˈtɪkjəlɚ; ɑːˈtikjulə〕 *adj.* 關節的。

ar·tic·u·late 〔*adj.*, *n.* ɑrˈtɪkjəlɪt; ɑːˈtikjulit *v.* ɑrˈtɪkjəˌlet; ɑːˈtikjuleit〕 *adj.*, *v.*, **-lat·ed, -lat·ing.** *n.* —*adj.* ①分明的;明白的;發音清晰的。②能言的。③清晰的;有條不紊的。④〖動植物,解剖〗關節相連的;有關節的。—*v.t.* ①明言。②發音清晰。③使(某物)清晰,清楚。④整理(某物)使其互相連貫,統一。⑤以關節連接。—*v.i.* ①發音(清晰)。②以關節連接。—*n.* 〖動物〗有節的無脊椎動物。

ar·tic·u·la·tion 〔ɑrˌtɪkjəˈleʃən; ɑːˌtikjuˈleiʃən〕 *n.* ①〖解剖〗節;關節;關節之結合。②發音。③有節之聲音。④語音;(尤指)子音。

ar·tic·u·la·tor 〔ɑrˈtɪkjəˌletɚ; ɑːˈtikjuleitə〕 *n.* ①發音之人或物;音節分明之人;發音矯正器。②發音器官。③接骨的人。

ar·tic·u·la·to·ry 〔ɑrˈtɪkjələˌtorɪ; ɑːˈtikjuleitəri〕 *adj.*①發音清晰的;與發音有關的;有音節的。②關節的;關節結合的。

ar·ti·fact 〔ˈɑrtɪˌfækt; ˈɑːtifækt〕 *n.* ①人工製品;加工品。②〖生物〗外來物質。③腦電波圖中非源自腦中的電波。(亦作 **artefact**)

ar·ti·fice 〔ˈɑrtəfɪs; ˈɑːtifis〕 *n.* ①技巧;巧妙。②巧計;策略;詭計。

ar·tif·i·cer 〔ɑrˈtɪfəsɚ; ɑːˈtifisə〕 *n.* ①技師;巧匠。②發明家;設計者。③〖軍〗技工。

***ar·ti·fi·cial** 〔ˌɑrtəˈfɪʃəl; ˌɑːtiˈfiʃəl〕*adj.* ①人造的;人爲的。an *artificial* flower. 人造花。an *artificial* tooth. 假牙。②虛僞的;不自然的。③武斷的;隨意決定的。*artificial* rules for dormitory residents. 武斷的宿舍管理規則。④〖生物〗人爲的。an *artificial* system of classification. 人爲的分類系統。⑤(寶石)仿造的。—**ly,** *adv.* —**ness,** *n.*

artificial fertilization 〖生物〗人工受精。

artificial heat 人造熱。

artificial insemination 〖生物〗人工受精。

artificial kidney 人造腎。

artificial language 人造語言。

artificial limb 義肢。

artificial lung 鐵肺(=iron lung).

artificial person 法人。

artificial rain 人造雨。

artificial respiration 人工呼吸。

artificial satellite 人造衛星。

ar·til·ler·ist 〔ɑrˈtɪlərɪst; ɑːˈtilərist〕 *n.* ①研究砲術者。②砲手;砲兵。

ar·til·ler·y 〔ɑrˈtɪlərɪ; ɑːˈtiləri〕 *n.* ①大砲。②砲兵;砲隊。heavy (*or* light) *artillery*. 重(輕)砲兵。③砲術。

ar·til·ler·y·man 〔ɑrˈtɪlərɪmən; ɑːˈtilərimən〕 *n.*, *pl.* **-men.** 砲手;砲兵。

ar·ti·san 〔ˈɑrtəzn̩; ˌɑːtiˈzæn, ˈɑːtiz-〕 *n.* 工匠;技工。—**al,** *adj.* —**ship,** *n.*

ᵗ**art·ist** 〔ˈɑrtɪst; ˈɑːtist〕 *n.* ①畫家。②美術家;藝術家。He is a great *artist*. 他是一個大藝術家。③長於技術的人。He is an *artist* in words. 他長於寫作。④善於欺騙的人。He's an *artist* with cards. 他是一個撲克牌郎中。

ar·tiste 〔ɑrˈtist; ɑːˈtiːst〕 *n.* ①技藝家;藝人。②極精於某一行業的人(常爲幽默語)。

***ar·tis·tic** 〔ɑrˈtɪstɪk; ɑːˈtistik〕 *adj.* ①美術的;藝術的;藝術家的。He had wide-ranging *artistic* interests. 他有廣泛的藝術興趣。②美妙的;精巧的。③有美感的;愛美的;雅的。—**al,** *adj.* —**al·ly,** *adv.*

art·ist·ry 〔ˈɑrtɪstrɪ; ˈɑːtistri〕 *n.*, *pl.* **-ries.** ①藝術之事業。②藝術之性質;藝術家

之才能；藝術家之手藝。

art·less ['artlɪs; 'ɑːtlis] *adj.* ①無藝術的；笨拙的。②自然的；天眞爛漫的。③單純的；簡明的。—**ly,** *adv.* —**ness,** *n.*

art·mo·bile ['art,mobil; 'ɑːtmoubiːl] *n.*〖美〗藝術品巡廻展覽車。

art of strategy 戰略。

arts and crafts 工藝。

art song 藝術歌曲。

art store 藝術用品店。

art theater 專演實驗性戲曲、紀錄片或外國電影的戲院。

art·y ['artɪ; 'ɑːti] *adj.,* **art·i·er, art·i·est.** 矯揉造作的；冒充藝術的；附庸風雅的。

A.R.U. American Railway Union.

Ar·um ['ɛrəm; 'ɛərəm] *n.*〖植物〗①白星海芋屬。②(a-) 白星海芋屬之植物。

A.R.V. American Revised Version (of the Bible). 美國改訂版(聖經)。

A.R.W.S. Associate of the Royal Water-color Society.

-ary〖字尾〗①表"…處所；…之人"等義之名詞字尾。例: adversary. ②表"…的；與…有關"等義之形容詞字尾。例: military.

Ar·y·an ['ɛrɪən; 'ɛəriən] *adj.* ①印歐語的。②印歐語族的。—*n.* ①印歐語族之人。②(納粹德國指)猶太人以外之白種人(尤指北歐的)。

As 化學元素 arsenic 之符號。

‡as [æz, əz; æz, əz] *adv.* ①相等；相同；同樣。His face is *as* black as coal. 他面黑如煤炭。②例如。Some animals, *as* dogs and cats, eat meat. 有些動物如狗，貓等是食肉的。***as above*** 如上；照上。Follow the rule *as above* stated. 照上面所述的規則做。***as against*** 比(對比之意)。***as*** (or ***so***)…***as*** 與…一樣…。***as compared with*** 比較。German, *as compared with* French, is difficult to learn. 德文較法文難學。***as far as*** 就…所。*As far as* I know, he is beyond reproach. 就我所知他是無可疵議的。***as follows*** 如次。***as for*** 至於。***as from*** 自(某日)起。***as good as*** a. 差不多；像；幾如。b. 可靠。***as late as*** 晚至；遲至…尙。***as long as*** 祇要。***as much*** 一樣。***as much as*** 儘多；一樣多。***as regards*** 至於。Now, *as regards* money, what is to be done? 至於錢的問題，怎麼辦？(***just***) ***as soon*** 寧可。***as soon as*** 卽刻；就。Come *as soon as* you can. 請就來。***as soon as not*** 一樣願意。***as soon as possible*** 儘快；儘早。Do it *as soon as possible.* 儘快做。***as to*** 至於。***as well*** 亦；也。***as well as*** a. 和；及。She wants a pen *as well as* a pencil. 她要一支鋼筆和一支鉛筆。b.同等的好。***as yet*** 至今；尙。***so as to*** 以便；俾可。***so***…***as to*** 致令；致使。He's not *so* foolish *as to* do that. 他不會蠢至做那件事。—*conj.* ①同樣；像。Run *as* I do. 像我這樣跑。②當；正值。She sang *as* she worked. 她一邊工作一邊唱歌。③因爲。*As* you are tired, you had better rest. 你已疲倦，最好休息。④雖；縱。Rich *as* he is, he is not happy. 他雖富，仍不樂。⑤結果。⑥以…而言。English *as* a spoken language. 將英文當作一種語言(以別於文字)。⑦到某種程度。You are as good *as* you think you are. 你正如你自己所想像的那樣好。***as a rule*** 照例；通常。***as if*** 儼若；好像。***as it is*** a. 事實上(用在句首)。b. 照原樣(用在句末)。***as it stands*** 照原樣；沒有改變。***as it were*** 好像是。***as one*** (***man***) 一致地。***as such*** 作爲…的身分或站在…地位；…的本身。***as though*** 好像；似乎。It looks *as though* it might rain. 看樣子天要下雨了。—*prep.* 充任；擔任。Who will act *as* teacher? 誰將擔任教師？—*pron.* ①如。He is very careful, *as* his work shows. 他的工作表現顯示他非常謹愼。②照；如。Do the same thing *as* I do. 照我這樣做。***not such as to*** 不致於。His illness was *not such as to* cause anxiety. 他的病尙不致於使人憂慮。***such as*** 像；如。***the same*** (…) ***as*** 與(…)相同。Your pen is *the same as* mine. 你的鋼筆與我的相同。I have *the same* problem *as* you have. 我的問題與你的相同。

as-〖字首〗=**ad-**.

As. ①Asia. ②Asiatic. **A.S.** ①Anglo-Saxon(亦作 **AS., A.-S., AS**). ②Associate in Science. **a.s.** at sight. **ASA** ①Acoustical Society of America. ②American Standards Association. **A.S.A.** Amateur Swimming Association.

as·bes·tine [æs'bɛstɪn; æz'bestain] *adj.* 石綿質的；不燃性的。(亦作 **asbestic**)

as·bes·tos [æs'bɛstəs; æz'bestɔs] *n.* (亦作 **asbestus**)石綿。—*adj.* 石綿的；石綿製成的。

as·bes·to·sis [,æsbɛs'tosɪs; ,æsbes'tousis] *n.*〖醫〗石綿沉着病；石綿入肺病。

A.S.C.A.P. American Society of Composers, Authors and Publishers.

as·ca·rid ['æskərɪd; 'æskərid] *n.*〖動物〗蛔蟲。

as·cend** [ə'sɛnd; ə'send] *v.t.* ①上升。②攀登；登。to *ascend* Mt. Everest. 攀登埃佛勒斯峯。ascend the throne*** 卽位。—*v.i.* ①上升。②回溯。③〖音樂〗由低音升至高音。

as·cend·ance, as·cend·ence [ə'sɛndəns; ə'sendəns] *n.* = **ascendancy.**

as·cend·an·cy, as·cend·en·cy [ə'sɛndənsɪ; ə'sendənsi] *n.* 權勢；主權；優越。

as·cend·ant, as·cend·ent [ə'sɛndənt; ə'sendənt] *adj.* ①上升的。②優越的；有權勢的。③〖植物〗向上的；向上生長的。—*n.* ①權位；優越；勢力。②祖先；祖宗。***in the ascendant*** 在優越地位上；權勢日隆。

as·cend·ing [ə'sɛndɪŋ; ə'sendiŋ] *adj.* 向上的；上升的；登高的。—**ly,** *adv.*

as·cen·sion [ə'sɛnʃən; ə'senʃən] *n.* ①上升；升高。②(A-)耶穌復活後四十天之升天(亦作 **the Ascension**). ③(A-)復活節後第四十日(亦作 **Ascension Day**). —**al,** *adj.*

as·cen·sive [ə'sɛnsɪv; ə'sensiv] *adj.* 上升的；騰達的；進步的。

as·cent** [ə'sɛnt; ə'sent] *n.* ①上升。I have never made an *ascent* in a balloon. 我從未乘過氣球升空。②攀登。③斜坡；斜坡路。a rapid *ascent.* 陡坡。④擢升。ascent to power.*** 得勢；取得權位。⑤回溯。

***as·cer·tain** [,æsɚ'ten; ,æsə'tein] *v.t.* 探知；發現；確定。It's difficult to *ascertain* what really happened. 事情眞象甚難探出。—**a·ble,** *adj.* —**a·bly,** *adv.* —**ment,** *n.*

as·cet·ic [ə'sɛtɪk; ə'setik] *n.* ①修道者；苦行者。②制慾者；禁止享受者。③(早期基督教)修道士。—*adj.* 苦行的；制慾的。—**ism,** *n.*

as·cet·i·cal [ə'sɛtɪkḷ; ə'setikəl] *adj.* 苦行的；制慾的。—**ly,** *adv.*

as·cid·i·an [ə'sɪdɪən; ə'sidiən] *n.* 海鞘類之動物。—*adj.* 海鞘類的。

as·cid·i·um [ə'sɪdɪəm; ə'sidiəm] *n., pl.* **-i·a** [-ɪə; -iə]. 〖植物〗囊狀器官。
as·ci·tes [ə'saɪtiz; ə'saitiːz] *n.* 〖醫〗水腹;腹水。
as·co·my·cete [ˌæskəmaɪ'sit; ˌæskə-mai'siːt] *n.* 〖植物〗子囊菌類。
a·scor·bic acid [ə'skɔrbɪk～; əs'kɔː-bik～] 抗壞血酸(卽維他命C)。
As·cot ['æskət; 'æskət] *n.* ①英國Ascot Heath 地方每年一度之賽馬。②(a-) 一種領巾。—*adj.*有關 Ascot Heath 之賽馬的。
***as·cribe** [ə'skraɪb; əs'kraib] *v.t.*, **-cribed, -crib·ing.** ①歸…於。He *ascribed* his failure to ill health. 他把失敗歸於健康不佳。②認爲…屬於。—**as·crib·a·ble,** *adj.*
as·crip·tion [ə'skrɪpʃən; əs'kripʃən] *n.* ①歸於;歸屬;歸因。②宣教終了時所說榮耀歸於上帝等詞。
as·dic, As·dic ['æzdɪk; 'æzdik] *n.*〖英〗潛水艇探索器(美國稱爲聲納, sonar)。
a·sep·sis [ə'sɛpsɪs; æ'sepsis] *n.* ①〖醫〗防腐法;無菌法。②〖醫〗無菌狀態。
a·sep·tic [ə'sɛptɪk; æ'septik] *adj.* 滅菌的;無膿毒的。—**al·ly,** *adv.*
a·sex·u·al [e'sɛkʃuəl; æ'seksjuəl] *adj.* 無性的;無性生殖的。—**ly,** *adv.*
a·sex·u·al·i·ty [eˌsɛkʃu'ælətɪ; eiˌsek-ʃu'æliti] *n.* 無性別之區分;無性(狀態)。
a·sex·u·al·ize [e'sɛkʃuəˌlaɪz; ei'sek-ʃuəlaiz] *v.t.*, **-ized, -iz·ing.** 使…無生殖能力;閹割。
asexual reproduction 〖生物〗無性生殖。
***ash**[1] [æʃ; æʃ] *n.* ①灰;灰燼。②(*pl.*)骨灰;屍體。His *ashes* are in his son's safe-keeping. 他的骨灰由他的兒子保存。③炭酸鈉。④火山灰。⑤灰色。⑥(*pl.*) 蒼白;痕跡。the *ashes* of the past. 歷史的遺跡。⑦(*pl.*) 表示懺悔的行爲、感情、言語等。
ash[2] *n.* 白楊。
***a·shamed** [ə'ʃemd; ə'ʃeimd] *adj.* ①羞恥的;慚愧的。②恥於;不願。He is *ashamed* to beg. 他恥於求乞。—**ly,** *adv.* —**ness,** *n.*
ash bin 〖英〗垃圾箱。
ash·can ['æʃˌkæn; 'æʃkæn] *n.*〖美〗①垃圾箱。②〖俚〗深水炸彈。③〖電影〗裝在反射器內的1000瓦弧光燈。***into the ashcan*** 丟棄。
ash cart 垃圾車。
ash-dry ['æʃ'draɪ; 'æʃ'drai] *adj.* 很乾燥的;枯乾的。
ash·en[1] ['æʃən; 'æʃn] *adj.* 灰色的。
ash·en[2] *adj.* 白楊樹的;白楊樹做的。
ash·en-faced ['æʃənˌfest; 'æʃnfeist] *adj.* 臉色灰白的。
ash heap 灰堆。***on the ash heap*** 丟棄;遺棄。
ash key 〖植物〗白楊之翅果。
ash·lar, ash·ler ['æʃlɚ; 'æʃlə] *n.* ①建築用之方石。②方石築成之建築物。
ash·lar·ing ['æʃlərɪŋ; 'æʃləriŋ] *n.* 用方石建築;疊方石爲牆面;用方石建成的建築物。
ash·man ['æʃmən; 'æʃmən] *n., pl.* **-men.** 清除垃圾之人。
***a·shore** [ə'ʃor; ə'ʃɔː] *adj.* & *adv.* ①向岸的(地);到岸的(地)。He went *ashore* at every port. 他每到一港埠必上岸。②在陸地上的(地);在岸上的(地)。
ash·ram ['ɑʃrəm; 'ɑːʃrəm] *n.*〖美〗嬉皮麕集的地方。
ash·tray ['æʃˌtre; 'æʃˌtrei] *n.* 煙灰缸。
Ash Wednesday 封齋期之第一日;復活節前之第七個星期三。
ash·y ['æʃɪ; 'æʃi] *adj.*, **ash·i·er, ash·i·est.** ①灰色的;灰白的。②灰做成的;灰的。③有灰撒布或覆蓋的。

‡**A·sia** ['eʃə, 'eʒə; 'eiʃə, 'eiʒə] *n.* 亞洲。
Asia Minor 小亞細亞(黑海與地中海間之亞洲部分)。
***A·sian** ['eʃən; 'eiʃən] *adj.*亞洲的;亞洲人的。—*n.* 亞洲人。
Asian flu 亞洲流行性感冒。(亦作 **Asiatic influenza**)
***A·si·at·ic** [ˌeʒɪ'ætɪk; ˌeiʒi'ætik] *adj.* 亞洲(人)的。—*n.* 亞洲人。
Asiatic cholera 眞性霍亂。(亦作 **Asian cholera**)
‡**a·side** [ə'saɪd; ə'said] *adv.* ①在旁地;在一邊地;側向地;離開地。He turned *aside* from the main road. 他離開大路。②撇開。③縱然;儘管如此。④貯存。to put some money *aside.* 留下一些錢。***aside from*** **a.** 除了。*Aside from* money, he works for fame. 除了金錢, 他爲名譽而工作。**b.** 離開。This is *aside from* the subject under discussion. 這點離開了所討論的問題。***lay aside*** 丟開。to *lay* one's book *aside.* 把書丟開。***put aside*** 收起;擱起。***set aside*** **a.** 放開;儲起。**b.**(法律)撤銷(判決等)。—*n.* ①旁白。②低聲說的話。③暫時離開話題。
as·i·nine ['æsn̩ˌaɪn; 'æsinain] *adj.* 像驢一樣的;愚魯的;冥頑的。—**as·i·nin·i·ty,** *n.*
‡**ask** [æsk; ɑːsk] *v.t.* ①詢問;問。Did you *ask* the price? 你問過價錢嗎? ②請求;央求。I must *ask* you a favor. 我須求你一件事。③要;討價。How much do you *ask* for this? 這個你要多少價錢? ④邀請。He *asked* me to dine with him. 他請我吃飯。⑤需要。This job *asks* hard work. 這工作需要勤勞。—*v.i.* ①詢問;問。*Ask* at the information office. 你可到詢問處詢問。②請求;要。He *asked* for a loan. 他要借錢。***ask about*** 查詢。***ask after*** 問候。***ask around*** 到處打聽。***ask for*** **a.** 請求;要。**b.** 訪問。He came here to *ask for* me. 他來此訪我。***ask for it*** 自討苦吃;自找麻煩。***ask for trouble*** 自尋煩惱;自討苦吃。***ask in*** (***out, up,*** or ***down***) 請進(出, 上樓, 下樓)。—**er,** *n.*
a·skance [ə'skæns; əs'kæns] *adv.* ①懷疑地;不贊許地。②側目;斜。(亦作 **askant**)
a·skew [ə'skju; əs'kjuː] *adv.* ①歪地;斜地;側地。②不贊同地;輕視地。—*adj.* 歪的;斜的;側的。
ask·ing ['æskɪŋ; 'ɑːskiŋ] *n.* ①探問;請求。②舉行結婚之公告。***for the asking*** 如果你要…就;備贈。
a·slant [ə'slænt; ə'slɑːnt] *adv.* 斜地;傾斜地。—*prep.* 斜過。—*adj.*斜的;傾斜的。
‡**a·sleep** [ə'slip; ə'sliːp] *adj.* ①睡的。He is *asleep.* 他睡着了。②不活潑的。③麻痺的。My foot is *asleep.* 我的脚麻木了。④死的。—*adv.* ①睡;眠。He fell fast *asleep.* 他熟睡了。②靜止狀態地。③進入死的狀態。
a·slope [ə'slop; ə'sloup] *adv.* 斜坡地;傾斜地。—*adj.* 傾斜的。
ASNE, A.S.N.E. American Society of Newspaper Editors.
asp[1] [æsp; æsp] *n.* 一種非洲產小毒蛇;任何毒蛇。
asp[2] *n.* 〖詩〗=**aspen.**
***as·par·a·gus** [ə'spærəgəs; əs'pærə-gəs] *n.* 〖植物〗蘆筍;龍鬚菜。
A.S.P.C.A. American Society for the Prevention of Cruelty to Animals.
***as·pect** ['æspɛkt; 'æspekt] *n.* ①外觀;形狀;形勢。the physical *aspect* of the country. 該國的地勢。②外貌;容貌;神態。

③觀點;方面。④方向;方位。⑤朝某方向的一邊。⑥〖占星〗運氣。⑦態度;神態。 warlike in *aspect*. 好戰的態度。⑧〖文法〗相;態。

aspect ratio ①〖航空〗縱橫比。②〖電視〗影像的寬與高。

as·pen ['æspɪn; 'æspən] *n.* 白楊。—*adj.* ①白楊樹的。②顫抖的。

As·per·ges [ə'spɝdʒiz; æs'pəːdʒiːz] *n.* 〖天主教〗①聖水灑注式。②行聖水灑注式時之聖歌。(亦作 **asperges**)

as·per·gil·lum [ˌæspə'dʒɪləm; ˌæspə'dʒiləm] *n., pl.* **-la** [-lə; -lə]. 〖天主教〗(灑水式所用之)灑水器。

as·per·i·ty [æs'pɛrətɪ; æs'periti] *n., pl.* **-ties.** ①粗糙;不平滑。②(氣候之)嚴酷。③(性情之)粗暴;刻薄。

as·perse [ə'spɝs; əs'pəːs] *v.t.,* **-persed, -pers·ing.** ①誹謗。②灑;撒。

as·per·sion [ə'spɝʒən; əs'pəːʃən] *n.* ①誹謗。②灑;撒。

***as·phalt** ['æsfɔlt; 'æsfælt] *n.* 土瀝青;柏油。—*adj.* 用柏油鋪成的。 an *asphalt* road. (土)瀝青路;柏油路。—*v.t.* 以土瀝青鋪(路)。(亦作 **asphaltum**)

as·phal·tic [æs'fɔltɪk; æs'fæltik] *adj.* 土瀝青的;柏油的。

asphalt jungle〖美〗都市中犯罪猖獗的區域。

asphalt rock 含沙岩,石灰石及大量土瀝青之岩石。

as·pho·del ['æsfəˌdɛl; 'æsfədel] *n.* 〖植物〗日光蘭;水仙花。

as·phyx·i·a [æs'fɪksɪə; æs'fiksiə] *n.* 〖醫〗窒息;悶死。(亦作 **asphyxy**)

as·phyx·i·al [æs'fɪksɪəl; æs'fiksiəl] *adj.* 窒息的。

as·phyx·i·ant [æs'fɪksɪənt; æs'fiksiənt] *adj.* 窒息性的;導致窒息的。—*n.* ①引起窒息的事物(如瓦斯等)。②窒息狀態。

as·phyx·i·ate [æs'fɪksɪˌet; æs'fiksieit] *v.t.,* **-at·ed, -at·ing.** 使窒息。

as·phyx·i·a·tion [æsˌfɪksɪ'eʃən; æsˌfiksi'eiʃən] *n.* 窒息。

as·phyx·i·a·tor [æs'fɪksɪˌetɚ; æs'fiksieitə] *n.* ①使人窒息的人或物;窒息裝置;動物窒息試驗器。②(利用二氧化碳器之)滅火器。③下水管漏水試驗器。

as·pic[1] ['æspɪk; 'æspik] *n.* (肉、魚、蕃茄等之)凍子。

as·pic[2] *n.* 〖詩〗=**asp**[1].

as·pic[3] *n.* 一種產於法國南部與西班牙的歐薄荷 (lavender), 用作香水原料。

as·pi·dis·tra [ˌæspɪ'dɪstrə; ˌæspi'distrə] *n.* 〖植物〗①(A-) 蜘蛛抱蛋屬。②蜘蛛抱蛋屬之植物;蜘蛛抱蛋;葉蘭。

as·pir·ant [ə'spaɪrənt; əs'paiərənt] *n.* (亦作 **aspirer**) 熱門者;抱負不凡者;候選人;考生。—*adj.* 抱大願望的。

as·pi·rate [*n., adj.* 'æspərɪt; 'æspərit *v.* 'æspəˌret; 'æspəreit] *n., adj., v.,* **-rat·ed, -rat·ing.** —*n.* ①送氣音; h 音。②送氣音字 (h 之字母)。—*adj.* 送氣音的;h音的。—*v.t.* ①〖語音〗送氣發音。②抽吸;吸出。③〖醫〗用吸引器將體腔中液體抽出;將液體吸入氣管或肺部。

as·pi·rat·ed ['æspəˌretɪd; 'æspəreitid] *adj.* 送氣音的;h音的。

***as·pi·ra·tion** [ˌæspə'reʃən; ˌæspə'reiʃən] *n.* ①呼吸;呼氣。②渴望;熱望〖for, after〗. This young man has no *aspiration* for fame. 這青年對聲名沒有什麼熱望(這青年不好名)。③〖語音〗送氣發音。④送氣音。⑤〖醫〗**a.** 用吸引器將體腔內液體(如膿汁)抽出。**b.** 吸入液體至氣管或肺部(如嘔吐後)。

as·pi·ra·tor ['æspəˌretɚ; 'æspəreitə] *n.* ①抽氣機;抽水機。②〖醫〗抽吸器;吸引器。

***as·pire** [ə'spaɪr; əs'paiə] *v.i.,* **-pired, -pir·ing.** ①熱望;抱大願望(與 to, after, 或不定詞連用)。 to *aspire* after immortality. 渴望名傳千古。②升高;高聳。

as·pi·rin ['æspərɪn; 'æspərin] *n.* 阿斯匹林(藥名);阿斯匹林錠。

as·pir·ing [əs'paɪrɪŋ; əs'paiəriŋ] *adj.* ①抱大願望的;有大志的。②上升的;高聳的。

a·squint [ə'skwɪnt; ə'skwint] *adv. & adj.* 側目地(的);睨視地(的)。

***ass** [æs; æs] *n.* ①驢。②笨人;愚人。 to make an *ass* of a person. 愚弄人。③〖俚〗臀部。④〖俚、鄙〗直腸。⑤〖俚、鄙〗性交;女人(當作性交的對象)。

ass. ① assistant. ② association. ③assorted.

as·sa·gai ['æsəˌgaɪ; 'æsəgai] *n., pl.* **-gais,** *v.,* **-gaied, -gai·ing.** —*n.* ①南非洲土人所用之長矛。②(製此種長矛的)一種山茱萸科喬木。—*v.t.* 用上述之長矛刺殺。

as·sa·i [ɑs'sɑ·i; ɑːs'sɑːi]〖義〗*adv.*〖音樂〗最;極。 ***allegro assai*** 最速;極快板。

***as·sail** [ə'sel; ə'seil] *v.t.* ①攻擊;責罵。②詰問。 to *assail* a person with questions. 以問題詰問某人。③困擾。—**a·ble,** *adj.*

as·sail·ant [ə'selənt; ə'seilənt] *n.* 攻擊者。

as·sart [ə'sɑrt; ə'sɑːt] *n.* 〖英國法律〗①開闢;開墾。②開闢地;草木清除以後之土地。—*v.t.* 開闢;斬除草萊。

as·sas·sin [ə'sæsɪn; ə'sæsin] *n.* ①暗殺者;刺客。②(A-) 回教之一派狂熱者, 1090至1272 活躍於波斯及敍利亞, 專門刺殺十字軍。

as·sas·si·nate [ə'sæsn̩ˌet; ə'sæsineit] *v.t.,* **-nat·ed, -nat·ing.** ①暗殺;行刺。②破壞;以卑鄙的手段毀壞。

as·sas·si·na·tion [əˌsæsn̩'eʃən; əˌsæsi'neiʃən] *n.* 暗殺;行刺。

as·sas·si·na·tor [ə'sæsn̩ˌetɚ; ə'sæsineitə] *n.* 暗殺者;行刺者;刺客。

***as·sault** [ə'sɔlt; ə'sɔːlt] *n.* ①攻擊;襲擊。The fort was taken by *assault*. 這砲台被攻陷。②〖法律〗人身傷害之威脅或企圖。③肉搏。④强姦。—*v.t.* 攻擊;襲擊。—**er,** *n.*

as·sault·a·ble [ə'sɔltəbl̩; ə'sɔːltəbl] *adj.* 可攻擊的;可襲擊的。

assault boat (or **barge** or **craft**)〖軍〗突擊艇。

assault carrier〖軍〗航空母艦。

as·say [*v.* ə'se; ə'sei *n.* ə'se, 'æse; ə'sei] *v.t.* ①分析。②試驗。③分析藥物。④衡量。⑤嘗試。⑥估計。—*v.i.* ①試金。②(礦苗經分析而知) 含貴金屬量。—*n.* ①分析;試金。②藥物的分析。③被試驗或化驗之物。④試驗或化驗所得之結果。

as·say·er [ə'seɚ; ə'seiə] *n.* 試金者;嘗試者;試驗者。

as·say·ing [ə'seɪŋ; ə'seiiŋ] *n.* 試金;嘗試;試驗。

as·sem·blage [ə'sɛmblɪdʒ; ə'semblidʒ] *n.* ①聚集的人或物;集會。②集合;配合;裝置。③以各種雜物之碎片湊成之藝術品。

***as·sem·ble** [ə'sɛmbl̩; ə'sembl] *v.,* **-bled, -bling.** —*v.t.* ①聚集;集會;集合。The students were *assembled* in the school hall. 學生們在學校禮堂內集合。②配合;裝置。—*v.i.* 集合;聚集。

as·sem·bler [ə'sɛmblɚ; ə'semblə] *n.* 裝配的人或機器。

assembler language〖電腦〗組合語言。(亦作 **assembly language**)

***as·sem·bly** [ə'sɛmblɪ; ə'sembli] *n.*, *pl.* **-blies.** ①集會;會合;會議。②【美】州議會的下院。③召集軍隊的鼓號;軍隊與裝備的集結。④機件的集合或配合;裝配。⑤立法團體;議會。the National *Assembly.* 國民大會。
assembly language 【電腦】組合語言。
assembly line 裝配線。
as·sem·bly·man [ə'sɛmblɪmən; ə'sembliman] *n.*, *pl.* **-men.** ①議會之議員。②(A-)【美】州議會(尤指下院)之議員。③(中國之)國民大會代表;省議員。
assembly plant 裝配廠。
***as·sent** [ə'sɛnt; ə'sent] *v.i.* ①同意;贊成;答應【常 to】. I *assent* to your views.我同意你的見解。②讓步。—*n.*同意;贊成;允許。
as·sen·ta·tion [ˌæsɛn'teʃən; ˌæsen'teiʃən] *n.* 迎合。
as·sen·tient [ə'sɛnʃənt; ə'senʃənt] *adj.* 同意的。—*n.* 同意者。
as·sen·tor [ə'sɛntɚ; ə'sentə] *n.* 同意者。(亦作 **assenter**)
As·ser ['æsɚ; 'æsə] *n.* 阿塞 (Tobias Michael Carel, 1838–1913, 荷蘭法學家, 1911年獲諾貝爾和平獎)。
as·sert** [ə'sɝt; ə'sə:t] *v.t.*①確說;斷言。②辯護;維護。assert oneself*** **a.**維護自己的權利。**b.**過分要求。**c.**出風頭。**—er, —or,** *n.*
as·sert·a·ble, as·sert·i·ble [ə'sɝtəbl̩; ə'sə:təbl] *adj.* 可斷言的; 可主張的。
***as·ser·tion** [ə'sɝʃən; ə'sə:ʃən] *n.* ①確說;斷言。②主張;辯護;維護。
as·ser·tive [ə'sɝtɪv;ə'sə:tiv] *adj.* 斷定的;斬釘截鐵的;武斷的。—**ly,** *adv.* —**ness,** *n.*
as·sess [ə'sɛs; ə'ses] *v.t.*①評估;估定(財產數額等以課稅)。②評定(罰款、稅額等)。③課(稅或其他費用)。
as·sess·a·ble [ə'sɛsəbl̩; ə'sesəbl] *adj.* ①可評估的;可估價的。②可課稅的;可徵收的。
as·sess·ment [ə'sɛsmənt; ə'sesmənt] *n.* ①估定;評估。②評估之款額(如稅額等)。
as·ses·sor [ə'sɛsɚ; ə'sesə] *n.* ①財產、收入等之估價員;估稅員。②輔佐人; 顧問;推事之特別助理。
as·set ['æsɛt; 'æset] *n.* ①有價值或有用的東西。②有兌換價值的東西。
as·sets ['æsɛts; 'æsets] *n. pl.* 財產; 資產;遺產;可以償債的資產。***assets and liabilities*** 資產與負債。***personal assets*** 動產。***real assets*** 不動產。
as·sev·er·ate [ə'sɛvəˌret; ə'sevəreit] *v.t.*, **-at·ed, -at·ing.** 鄭重而言;斷言;確言。—**as·sev·er·a·tion,** *n.*
as·si·du·i·ty [ˌæsə'djuətɪ;ˌæsi'djuiti] *n.*, *pl.* **-ties.** ①勤勉;專心;精勵。②(*pl.*)殷懃。
as·sid·u·ous [ə'sɪdʒuəs;ə'sidjuəs] *adj.* ①勤勉的;有恆的;不懈的。②專心的。—**ly,** *adv.* —**ness,** *n.*
as·si·fy ['æsəˌfaɪ; 'æsifai] *v.t.*, **-fied, -fy·ing.** 愚弄。
***as·sign** [ə'saɪn;ə'sain] *v.t.* ①分配;分派。②指定。③指派;選派。Two students were *assigned* to clean the classroom. 兩個學生被指派清掃教室。④【法律】讓渡;過戶。to *assign* a contract. 讓渡契約。⑤歸因;歸咎。⑥分發。—*v.i.* 【法律】將財產過戶(尤指過戶給債權人)。 —*n.* (財產、權利讓渡之)讓受人。—**er,** *n.*
as·sign·a·ble [ə'saɪnəbl̩; ə'sainəbl] *adj.* ①可指定的。②可追源的。
as·sig·nat ['æsɪgˌnæt; 'æsignæt] *n.* 法國大革命期中所發行之紙幣(以沒收之土地爲擔保)。
as·sig·na·tion [ˌæsɪg'neʃən; ˌæsig'neiʃən] *n.* ①分配。②(財產、權利等之)讓渡。③(會場、時間等之)指定; 選定。④約會;(尤指)幽會。⑤歸因。
assigned counsel 【美】公設辯護人。
as·sign·ee [əsaɪ'ni; ˌæsi'ni:] *n.* 【法律】受讓人;受託人;財產保管人。
***as·sign·ment** [ə'saɪnmənt; ə'sainmənt] *n.* ①分派或指定的東西;派定的工作。②分派;分配。③【法律】讓渡。
as·sign·or [əsaɪ'nɔr; əsai'nɔ:] *n.* 【法律】讓渡人;委託者。(亦作 **assigner**)
as·sim·i·la·bil·i·ty [əˌsɪml̩ə'bɪlətɪ; əˌsimilə'biliti] *n.* 可同化性;可吸收性。
as·sim·i·la·ble [ə'sɪml̩əbl̩;ə'similəbl] *adj.* 可同化的;可吸收的。
as·sim·i·late [ə'sɪml̩ˌet; ə'simileit] *v.*, **-lat·ed, -lat·ing.** —*v.t.* ①吸收;消化。②吸收思想;徹底了解。③同化。④使成一樣;使類似。⑤比較; 使相像。⑥【語音】同化。⑦使適應;使一致。—*v.i.* ①同化。②消化;吸收。③【語音】因同化而改變。
as·sim·i·la·tion [əˌsɪml̩'eʃən;əˌsimi'leiʃən] *n.* ①【生理】同化作用;吸收作用。②【語音】同化。③【植物】同化作用。④(不同文化之)同化。
as·sim·i·la·to·ry [ə'sɪml̩əˌtorɪ; ə'similətəri] *adj.* 同化的;有同化力的;有同化性的。(亦作 **assimilative**)
***as·sist** [ə'sɪst; ə'sist] *v.t.* 幫助;援助。Do you need anybody to *assist* you in your work? 你需要人幫你工作嗎? —*v.i.* ①幫助。②出席; 參加(會,典禮等)【常 at】. The congregation *assists* at divine service. 會衆參加聖禮。—*n.* ①【棒球】幫助迫使打擊手或跑壘者出局之動作。②幫助。
***as·sist·ance** [ə'sɪstəns; ə'sistəns] *n.* 幫助。 Can I be of any *assistance?* 我能有所幫助嗎?
***as·sist·ant** [ə'sɪstənt; ə'sistənt] *n.* ①助手;助教。②幫助之事物。—*adj.* ①幫助的。②輔助的;副的。He is our *assistant* manager. 他是我們的協理。
assistant professor 助教授。
as·sist·ant·ship [ə'sɪstəntˌʃɪp; ə'sistəntʃip] *n.* (大學)研究生獎學金(該研究生同時爲 assistant).
as·size [ə'saɪz; ə'saiz] *n.* ①立法機關在會期中所決定之法案、條例等。②陪審團、推事助理之偵查;其決定。③審判。
Assoc., assoc. ①associate. ②association.
as·so·ci·a·bil·i·ty [əˌsoʃɪə'bɪlətɪ; əˌsouʃiə'biliti] *n.* ①可聯合性。②聯想性。③社交性。④【醫】交感性。
as·so·ci·a·ble [ə'soʃɪəbl̩; ə'souʃjəbl] *adj.* ①可聯合的。②可聯想的。③社交性的。④【醫】交感的。
***as·so·ci·ate** [*v.* ə'soʃɪˌet;ə'souʃieit *n.*, *adj.* ə'soʃɪɪt; ə'souʃiit] *v.*, **-at·ed, -at·ing,** *n.*, *adj.* —*v.t.* ①聯想。②聯合;結交。③結合。—*v.i.* ①結交。 Don't *associate* with dishonest boys. 不要和不誠實的男孩結交。②結夥;參加;有來往。③聯合。—*n.* ①同伴;夥伴。②同志;伴侶。③預備會員;社員。④【數學】伴隨。—*adj.* ①同伴的;同事的。②預備會員的;無全權的。③副的。④聯合的。—**ship,** *n.*【注意】指與人聯合、結合或合夥時, 要用 associate with. 指在某方面合作或合夥時, 要用 associate in.

as·so·ci·at·ed [əˈsoʃɪˌetɪd; əˈsouʃieitid] *adj.* 聯合的;有關聯的;聯想的。
associate degree (某些美國大學)頒給修滿二年課程學生之證件。
Associated Press 〖新聞〗美聯社。(略作AP)
associate professor 副教授。
‡as·so·ci·a·tion [əˌsosɪˈeʃən, əˌsoʃɪˈeʃən; əˌsousiˈeiʃən, əˌsouʃiˈeiʃən] *n.* ①會;協會;團體。National Athletic *Association.* 全國體育協會。②聯合;結合。③結交。④聯想;思想或觀念的聯合。***in association with.*** 與…聯合、結交、或有關連。**—al,** *adj.*
association football 〖英〗足球(=soccer).
as·so·ci·a·tion·ism [əˌsosɪˈeʃənɪzəm; əˌsousiˈeiʃənizm] *n.* 〖哲學〗觀念聯合論;聯想說。(亦作 **associationalism**) **—as·so·ci·a·tion·ist,** *n.*
association of ideas 〖心理〗聯想。
as·so·ci·a·tive [əˈsoʃɪˌetɪv; əˈsouʃjətiv] *adj.* ①聯合的;組成的。②〖數學〗結合的。③聯想的。
as·so·ci·a·tor [əˈsoʃɪˌetɚ; əˈsouʃieitə] *n.* ①聯合之人或物;同夥;同伴。②團體、學會等的一分子。
as·soil [əˈsɔɪl; əˈsɔil] *v.t.* 〖古〗①釋放;赦免。②補償;贖。
as·so·nance [ˈæsənəns; ˈæsənəns] *n.* ①類音;協音。②〖韻律〗半韻;半諧音(母音相同而子音不同之韻)。
as·so·nant [ˈæsənənt; ˈæsənənt] *adj.* 協音的;半韻的。**—*n.*** 與另一個字合成半韻的字。
as·sort [əˈsɔrt; əˈsɔːt] *v.t.* ①分類;分等;配合。②供給(各類貨品)。**—*v.i.*** ①調和;相配;符合。②結交;來往。
as·sort·ed [əˈsɔrtɪd; əˈsɔːtid] *adj.* ①雜集的;各色俱備的。*assorted* biscuits. 什錦餅干。②分類的。③相配的;合適的。
as·sort·ment [əˈsɔrtmənt; əˈsɔːtmənt] *n.* ①分類;分配。②各色俱備之物。
ASSR, A.S.S.R. Autonomous Soviet Socialist Republic.
Asst., asst. assistant.
as·suage [əˈswedʒ; əˈsweidʒ] *v.t.,* **-suaged, -suag·ing.** 緩和。
as·suage·ment [əˈswedʒmənt; əˈsweidʒmənt] *n.* ①緩和;鎮靜。②緩和物。
as·sua·sive [əˈswesɪv; əˈsweisiv] *adj.* 安撫的;(使痛苦)減輕的;緩和的。**—*n.*** 緩和劑。
as·sum·a·ble [əˈsjuməbl; əˈsjuːməbl] *adj.* 可假定的;可承擔的。
as·sum·a·bly [əˈsjuməblɪ; əˈsjuːməbli] *adv.* 大概;多半。
‡as·sume [əˈsum, əˈsjum; əˈsjuːm, əˈsuːm] *v.,* **-sumed, -sum·ing.** **—*v.t.*** ①假定。Let us *assume* it to be true. 讓我們假定這是真實的。②擔任。③假裝。He *assumed* a look of innocence. 他裝出一副天真無邪的樣子。④僭取;擅用;霸占。⑤顯出;帶有。⑥採用。**—*v.i.*** 傲慢;逞强;伏恃。
as·sumed [əˈsumd; əˈsuːmd] *adj.* ①假裝的;裝做的。an *assumed* name. 化名。②假定的。③僭取的。
as·sum·ed·ly [əˈsjumɪdlɪ; əˈsjuːmidli] *adv.* 大概;也許。
as·sum·ing [əˈsjumɪŋ; əˈsjuːmiŋ] *adj.* 傲慢的;獨斷的;僭越的。**—*n.*** 傲慢;僭越;無禮。 **—ly,** *adv.*
as·sump·sit [əˈsʌmpsɪt; əˈsʌmpsit] *n.* 〖法律〗①契約;允諾。②要求履行契約的訴訟。
***as·sump·tion** [əˈsʌmpʃən; əˈsʌmpʃən] *n.* ①假定;假定的事物。②擔任;承當。③傲慢;僭越。④假裝;擺出某種樣子。She bustled about with an *assumption* of authority. 她擺着一副權威的樣子忙來忙去。⑤(the A-)聖母升天;聖母升天日(八月十五日)。
as·sump·tive [əˈsʌmptɪv; əˈsʌmptiv] *adj.* ①假定的;假設的。②傲慢的;僭越的。③假裝的。④僭取的。⑤〖文法〗假定的。
as·sur·a·ble [əˈʃurəbl; əˈʃuərəbl] *adj.* 可保證的;可保險的;可確信的。
***as·sur·ance** [əˈʃurəns; əˈʃuərəns] *n.* ①確信;信心;信念。②保證。I trusted to his *assurances.* 我信賴他的保證。③信任;信賴。④自信。⑤厚顏;大膽。⑥〖英〗保險。an *Assurance* Co. 保險公司。
‡as·sure [əˈʃur; əˈʃuə] *v.t.,* **-sured, -sur·ing.** ①確告;鄭重宣告。I *assure* you there is no danger here. 我確告你這裏沒有危險。②保證。③使穩定;使安全。④使相信;使確信。⑤保險。
as·sured [əˈʃurd; əˈʃuəd] *adj.* ①確信的;一定的。②大膽的;自信的;有權威性的。③保險的。**—*n.*** ①保險契約中指定之受益人。②生命財產已保險者。**—ly,** *adv.*
as·sur·ed·ness [əˈʃurɪdnɪs; əˈʃuədnis] *n.* ①確實。②確信;自信。③大膽;厚顏。
as·sur·er, as·sur·or [əˈʃurə; əˈʃuərə] *n.* ①保證人。②〖英〗保險業者。
as·sur·gent [əˈsɝdʒənt; əˈsəːdʒənt] *adj.* ①向上升的。②〖植物〗向斜上方生長的。
as·sur·ing [əˈʃurɪŋ; əˈʃuəriŋ] *adj.* 確信的;使人有自信的。**—ly,** *adv.*
Assyr. Assyrian.
As·syr·i·a [əˈsɪrɪə; əˈsiriə] *n.* 亞述(亞洲西南部之古國)。**—As·syr·i·an,** *adj., n.*
As·syr·i·ol·o·gy [əˌsɪrɪˈɑlədʒɪ; əˌsiriˈɔlədʒi] *n.* 對亞洲古國亞述之文化的研究;亞述學。 **—As·syr·i·ol·o·gist,** *n.*
a·stat·ic [eˈstætɪk; eiˈstætik] *adj.* ①不安定的。②〖物理〗無定向的。
as·ta·tine [ˈæstəˌtin; ˈæstətiːn] *n.* 〖化〗砈(元素之一,符號爲 At).
as·ter [ˈæstɚ; ˈæstə] *n.* ①紫菀。②〖生物〗星體。***China asters*** 翠菊。
aster- 〖字首〗**astro-** 之變形,表"星"之義,用在母音之前,如 asteroid.
-aster 〖字尾〗表"似是而非"或"模倣"之義,如 criticaster, poetaster.
as·ter·isk [ˈæstəˌrɪsk; ˈæstərisk] *n.* 星標;星狀物。**—*v.t.*** 加上星標。
as·ter·ism [ˈæstəˌrɪzəm; ˈæstərizəm] *n.* ①〖天文〗星羣;星宿;星座。②〖礦〗星狀光彩。③三星狀標記(⁂或⁂)。**—al,** *adj.*
a·stern [əˈstɝn; əsˈtəːn] *adv.* ①在船尾;向船尾。②在後;向後。***astern of*** 在後;落後。***fall astern*** 落後;被趕過。***full speed astern*** 全速後退。
as·ter·oid [ˈæstəˌrɔɪd; ˈæstərɔid] *adj.* 星狀的。**—*n.*** ①〖天文〗(其軌道在火星與木星間的)小行星。②〖動物〗海盤車。**—al,** *adj.*
as·the·ni·a [æsˈθinɪə; æsˈθiːnjə] *n.* 〖醫〗虛弱。
as·then·ic [æsˈθɛnɪk; æsˈθenik] *adj.* ①虛弱的。②身材細長的。
asth·ma [ˈæzmə; ˈæsmə] *n.* 哮喘。
asth·mat·ic [æzˈmætɪk; æsˈmætik] *adj.* (亦作 **asthmatical**)氣喘的;患哮喘症的。**—*n.*** 哮喘症患者。
as·tig·mat·ic [ˌæstɪgˈmætɪk; ˌæstigˈmætik] *adj.* (亦作 **astigmatical**) 亂視的;散光的;糾正散光的。**—*n.*** 有亂視的人。
a·stig·ma·tism [əˈstɪgməˌtɪzəm; æsˈtigmətizəm] *n.* ①〖醫〗散光;亂視眼。②

〖光學〗像散性;像散現象。

a·stir [ə'stɜ; ə'stəː] *adv. & adj.* 活動;起床;擾動。

a·stom·a·tous [ə'stɑmətəs; ei'stɔmətəs] *adj.* ①〖動物〗無嘴的。②〖植物〗無氣孔的。

As·ton ['æstən; 'æstən] *n.* 阿斯頓 (Francis William, 1877–1945, 英國物理學家, 1922年獲諾貝爾化學獎)。

as·ton·ied [ə'stɑnɪd; əs'tɔnid] *adj.* 〖古〗驚惶的;惶惑的。

***as·ton·ish** [ə'stɑnɪʃ; əs'tɔniʃ] *v.t.* 使驚異;使驚駭;使驚愕。

***as·ton·ish·ing** [ə'stɑnɪʃɪŋ; əs'tɔniʃiŋ] *adj.* 可驚異的;可驚的。an *astonishing* remark. 驚人的言論。**—ly,** *adv.*

***as·ton·ish·ment** [ə'stɑnɪʃmənt; əs'tɔniʃmənt] *n.* ①驚奇;驚異;驚愕。The people present stared in *astonishment.* 在場者都驚愕瞪視。②使人驚異的事物。

***as·tound** [ə'staund; əs'taund] *v.t.* 使驚異;使大驚駭。

as·tound·ing [ə'staundɪŋ; əs'taundiŋ] *adj.* 令人驚駭的;可驚的。**—ly,** *adv.*

astr(on). ①astronomer. ②astronomical. ③astronomy.

as·tra·chan ['æstrəkən; 'æstrəkən] *n.* ①=**astrakhan.** ②(A-) 一種酸蘋果,或其樹。

a·strad·dle [ə'strædl; ə'strædl] *adv., adj., prep.* =**astride.**

as·tra·gal ['æstrəgl; 'æstrəgəl] *n.* ①〖建築〗(柱頭等處之)圈線。②(砲口凸起之)圈帶。③〖解剖〗距骨。

as·trag·a·lus [æs'trægələs; æs'trægələs] *n., pl.* **-li** [-laɪ; -lai]. ①〖解剖〗距骨。②〖植物〗(A-) 紫雲英屬。③〖建築〗=**astragal.**

as·tra·khan ['æstrəkən; ˌæstrə'kæn] *n.* ①俄國 Astrakhan 地方所產之羔皮。②仿上述羔皮之織物;充羔皮。(亦作**astrachan**)

as·tral ['æstrəl; 'æstrəl] *adj.* ①星的;如星的;多星的。②星之世界的。an *astral* body. 靈體;星。*astral* spirits. 星靈;幽靈。

astral lamp 無影燈。

a·stray** [ə'stre; əs'trei] *adv.* 出正軌地;迷途地。go astray*** 走入歧途;墮落。***lead astray*** 使入迷途;使墮落。*—adj.* 出正軌的;迷途的。

as·trict [ə'strɪkt; ə'strikt] *v.t.* ①限制;束縛;約束。②緊縮;收縮。

as·tric·tion [ə'strɪkʃən; ə'strikʃən] *n.* ①限制;束縛;約束。②〖醫〗**a.** 收歛作用。**b.** 便秘。③責任;義務。

as·tric·tive [ə'strɪktɪv; ə'striktiv] *adj.* 收歛的;收歛用的。*—n.* 〖醫〗收歛劑。

a·stride [ə'straɪd; əs'traid] *adv. & adj.* 跨;騎。*—prep.* ①跨騎。②在兩旁。③占壓倒性地位。

as·tringe [ə'strɪndʒ; əs'trindʒ] *v.,* **as·tringed, as·tring·ing.** *—v.t.* 緊縛;收縮;使收歛。*—v.i.* 變成固體。

as·trin·gen·cy [ə'strɪndʒənsɪ; əs'trindʒənsi] *n.* ①收歛性。②嚴酷;苛厲。

as·trin·gent [ə'strɪndʒənt; əs'trindʒənt] *adj.* ①收歛性的。②止血的。③嚴酷的;嚴肅的。*—n.* 〖醫〗收歛劑。**—ly,** *adv.*

astro- 〖字首〗①表"星"之義。②表"與太空有關的"之義。(亦作 **aster-**)

as·tro·bi·ol·o·gy [ˌæstrobaɪ'ɑlədʒɪ; ˌæstroubai'ɔlədʒi] *n.* 天體生物學。

as·tro·dome ['æstrəˌdom; 'æstrədoum] *n.* 〖航空〗機身上部透明之圓頂(供領航員觀測星象之用)。(英亦作 **astro hatch**)

as·tro·gate ['æstrəˌget; 'æstrəgeit] *v.i. & v.t.,* **-gat·ed, -gat·ing.** 太空航行。**—as·tro·ga·tor,** *n.*

as·tro·ga·tion [ˌæstrə'geʃən; ˌæstrə'geiʃən] *n.* 太空船之航行。

astrol. ①astrologer. ②astrological. ③astrology.

as·tro·labe ['æstrəˌleb; 'æstrouleib] *n.* 星盤(昔天文觀測儀)。

as·trol·o·ger [ə'strɑlədʒɚ; əs'trɔlədʒə] *n.* 占星家。

as·trol·o·gy [ə'strɑlədʒɪ; əs'trɔlədʒi] *n.* 占星學;占星術。**—as·trol·o·gi·cal,** *adj.*

as·tro·man·cy ['æstrəˌmænsɪ; 'æstrəˌmænsi] *n.* 星卜術。

as·tro·me·te·or·ol·o·gy [ˌæstroˌmitɪə'rɑlədʒɪ; ˌæstrouˌmiːtiə'rɔlədʒi] *n.* 天體氣象學。

as·trom·e·try [æs'trɑmɪtrɪ; æs'trɔmitri] *n.* 天體測定學。

astron. ①astronomer. ②astronomical. ③astronomy.

as·tro·naut ['æstrəˌnɔt; 'æstrənɔːt] *n.* ①從事太空旅行之人;太空人。②太空學學者。

as·tro·nau·tics [ˌæstrə'nɔtɪks; ˌæstrə'nɔːtiks] *n.* 太空學;太空旅行學。

as·tro·nav·i·ga·tion [ˌæstroˌnævɪ'geʃən; ˌæstrouˌnævi'geiʃən] *n.* 太空航行。

***as·tron·o·mer** [ə'strɑnəmɚ; əs'trɔnəmə] *n.* 天文家。

as·tro·nom·i·cal [ˌæstrə'nɑmɪkl; ˌæstrə'nɔmikəl] *adj.* 天文學的;星學的。***astronomical day*** 平均太陽日。***astronomical observatory*** 天文臺。***astronomical telescope*** 天文望遠鏡。***astronomical time*** 天文時。***astronomical unit*** 地球至太陽間之平均距離(約爲 93,000,000 英里)。***astronomical year*** 回歸年。(亦作 **astronomic**) **—ly,** *adv.*

***as·tron·o·my** [ə'strɑnəmɪ; əs'trɔnəmi] *n.* 天文學。

as·tro·pho·tog·ra·phy [ˌæstrəfo'tɑgrəfɪ; ˌæstrəfou'tɔgrəfi] *n.* 天體照相術。

as·tro·phys·i·cal [ˌæstro'fɪzɪkl; ˌæstrou'fizikəl] *adj.* 天體物理學的。

as·tro·phys·i·cist [ˌæstro'fɪzɪsɪst; ˌæstrou'fizisist] *n.* 天體物理學家。

as·tro·phys·ics [ˌæstro'fɪzɪks; ˌæstrou'fiziks] *n.* 天體物理學。

as·tro·space ['æstroˌspes; 'æstrouspeis] *n.* 星際之間的空間。

as·tute [ə'stjut; əs'tjuːt] *adj.* 機敏的;狡猾的。**—ly,** *adv.* **—ness,** *n.*

a·sty·lar [e'staɪlɚ; ei'stailə] *adj.* 〖建築〗無柱式的;無支柱的。

A-sub ['eˌsʌb; 'eisʌb] *n.* 〖俗〗核子潛艇。

a·sun·der [ə'sʌndɚ; ə'sʌndə] *adj. & adv.* 分開(地)的;星散(地)的;化爲數部(地)的。Her heart was torn *asunder.* 她爲之柔腸寸斷。

***a·sy·lum** [ə'saɪləm; ə'sailəm] *n.* ①避難所;庇護所。②救濟院;養育院。③精神病院。④〖國際法〗庇護。political *asylum.* 政治庇護。

a·sym·met·ric [ˌesɪ'mɛtrɪk; ˌæsi'metrik] *adj.* ①不對稱的;不均勻的。②〖數學〗非對稱的。③〖邏輯〗表非對換關係的;表單向關係的。(亦作 **asymmetrical**)

a·sym·me·try [e'sɪmɪtrɪ; æ'simitri] *n.* ①不對稱;不均勻。②〖數學〗非對稱。

as·ymp·tote ['æsɪmˌtot; 'æsimptout] *n.* 〖數學〗漸近線。

a·syn·chro·nism [ə'sɪŋkrənɪzəm; ei'siŋkrənizəm] *n.* ①時間不一致;非同時性。②〖電〗異步(性)。

a·syn·chro·nous [e'sɪŋkrənəs; ei'siŋkrənəs] *adj.* ①時間不一致的；非同期的。②〖電〗異步的。

a·syn·de·ton [ə'sɪndətən; æ'sinditən] *n.* ①〖修辭〗連接詞省略；散珠格（例：Smile, shake hands, part). ②〖圖書館學〗目錄上對照參考資料之省略。—**as·yn·det·ic,** *adj.*

At 〖化〗元素 astatine 之符號。

‡at [æt, ət; æt, ət] *prep.* ①在(某地)；近(某處)。He is *at* school. 他在學校。②向；對準。Look *at* me. 向我看。③處於…情形或狀態。The two countries were *at* war. 兩國交戰。④工作；嘗試做。He sits *at* his desk all day. 他終日工作。⑤經由。Smoke came out *at* the chimney. 煙由煙囪逸出。⑥在或近於某一時間。*at* sunrise. 日出。⑦因爲。⑧依照；應。We did it *at* his request. 我們應他之請而做。⑨數額；價格。two books *at* a dollar each. 兩本書，每本一元。⑩從。***at a loss*** **a.** 虧本。**b.** 迷惑。***at a time*** 一次。***at all*** 全然(參看 **all**). ***at all cost*** 無論付出如何的代價。I will try to save him *at all cost.* 無論付出何種代價，我將設法救他。***at arm's length*** 疏遠。***at best*** 至多；充其量。*At best,* this car will go fifty miles an hour. 這部車每小時至多能走五十英里。***at first*** 最初。***at hand*** 現有的。***at large*** **a.** 逍遙法外；未被捕。The prisoner who escaped is still *at large.* 囚犯逃走後尙未就捕。**b.** 詳盡。to write *at large.* 詳盡地寫。**c.** 一般的。***at last*** 最後。*At last* we succeeded. 最後我們成功了。***at least*** 最少。***at length*** **a.** 後來；最後。*At length* he accepted my invitation. 後來他接受了我的邀請。**b.** 詳盡。to explain *at length.* 詳盡解釋。***at most*** 參看 **most.** ***at once*** 立刻；卽刻。She told him to leave the room *at once.* 她叫他立刻離開這房間。***at one*** 同心一意；友好；一致。***at one's best*** (or ***worst***) 最好(壞)的表現。***at random*** 隨意。***at sight*** 見到立刻。This check is payable *at sight.* 這張支票是見票卽付的。***at stake*** 在危險中。***at the earliest*** 最早。***at the latest*** 最遲。***at the mercy of*** 聽命於；被操縱於。***at times*** 有時。***at will*** 隨意。You can come and go *at will.* 你可隨意來去。***be near at hand*** 在手邊；逼近。〖注意〗**at** 與 **in** 將一個表示地方或時間的字連繫到一個句子上，當這一地方或時間是指一點時，卽用 at. 當這一地方或時間指一定範圍，卽用 in.

at. ①atmosphere. ②atomic. ③attorney.

A.T. ①Air Transportation. ②American Theater. ③antitank. ④Atlantic Time.

At·a·brine ['ætəbrɪn; 'ætəbrin] *n.* 「瘧滌平(瘧疾預防藥)。」

At·a·lan·ta [,ætḷ'æntə; ,ætə'læntə] *n.* 〖希臘神話〗一捷足善走之美女。(亦作**Atalante**)

a·ta·rac·tic [,ætə'ræktɪk; ,ætə'ræktik] *adj.* 鎭靜的。—*n.* 鎭靜劑。

at·a·vism ['ætə,vɪzəm; 'ætəvizəm] *n.* ①隔代遺傳；返祖(性)。②回復原始型態。

at·a·vis·tic [,ætə'vɪstɪk; ,ætə'vistik] *adj.* 隔代遺傳的；返祖(性)的。(亦作 **atavic**)

a·tax·i·a [ə'tæksɪə; ə'tæksiə] *n.* = **ataxy.**

a·tax·ic [ə'tæksɪk; ə'tæksik] *adj.* 〖醫〗運動失調的；共濟失調性的。—*n.* 患運動失調症之人。

a·tax·y [ə'tæksɪ; ə'tæksi] *n.* 〖醫〗①運動失調。②運動性共濟失調。

A·te ['etɪ; 'ɑːti] *n.* 〖希臘神話〗司騷亂戲謔之女神(後被視爲司復仇之女神)。

‡ate [et; et, eit] *v.* pt. of **eat.**

-ate[1] 〖字尾〗①構成相當於以 -ed 爲結尾之形容詞。②構成保有某職務、功用、威儀、權利、或特性之名詞。③構成表示某些動作之結果的名詞。④構成動詞。

-ate[2] 〖字尾〗表示由酸造成之鹽。

at ease 〖軍〗稍息。

at·e·brin ['ætəbrɪn; 'ætəbrin] *n.* = **Atabrine.**

at·el·ier ['ætḷ,je; 'ætəliei] *n.* 畫家或雕刻家之工作室；畫室。

a tem·po [ɑ'tɛmpo; ɑː'tempou] 〖義〗〖音樂〗恢復原來速度；還原速度。

A-test ['e'tɛst; 'ei'test] *n.* 原子爆炸試驗。

ath·a·na·si·a [,æθə'neʒɪə; ,æθə'neizjə] *n.* = **athanasy.**

Ath·a·na·sian [,æθə'neʒən; ,æθə'neiʃən] *adj.* Athanasius 的，或他的教義的。—*n.* 信 Athanasian Creed 者。

Athanasian Creed Athanasius 之「教條。」

Ath·a·na·sius [,æθə'neʃəs; ,æθə'neiʃəs] *n.* Saint, 296?–373, 亞歷山大港之主教，爲 Arianism (聖子聖父非同體論)之反對者。

a·than·a·sy [ə'θænəsɪ; ə'θænəsi] *n.* 「不死；不滅；不朽性。」

ath·ar ['æθɚ; 'æθə] *n.* = **attar.**

a·the·ism ['eθɪ,ɪzəm; 'eiθiizəm] *n.* 無神論；不信神。

a·the·ist ['eθɪɪst; 'eiθiist] *n.* 無神論者；不信神者。—**ic,** *adj.*

A·the·na [ə'θinə; ə'θiːnə] *n.* 〖希臘神話〗智慧、技藝及戰爭的女神。(亦作 **Athene**)

ath·e·nae·um [,æθə'niəm; ,æθiː'ni(ː)əm] *n.* ①(A–)雅典 Athena 女神廟。②提倡文學或科學的團體。③圖書館；閱覽室。(亦作 **atheneum**)

A·the·ni·an [ə'θinɪən; ə'θiːnjən] *adj.* 雅典的。—*n.* 雅典人。

Ath·ens ['æθɪnz; 'æθinz] *n.* 雅典(希臘首都)。

a·ther·man·cy [ə'θɝmənsɪ; ei'θəːmənsi] *n.* 不透輻射熱；不透輻射熱性。

ath·er·o·scle·ro·sis [,æθərosklə'rosɪs; ,æθərousklə'rousis] *n.* 〖醫〗動脈硬化。—**ath·er·o·scle·rot·ic,** *adj., n.*

a·thirst [ə'θɝst; ə'θəːst] *adj.* 渴望的〖for〗.

***ath·lete** ['æθlit; 'æθliːt] *n.* 運動家；運動員。

athlete's foot 〖醫〗脚濕氣；香港脚。

athlete's heart 〖醫〗運動員心病。(亦作 **athletic heart**)

***ath·let·ic** [æθ'lɛtɪk; æθ'letik] *adj.* ①身體活潑而强壯的。He is an *athletic* man. 他是一個活潑强壯的人。②運動的。*athletic* meeting (*or* meet). 運動會。③〖人類學〗有健壯體格的。—**al·ly,** *adv.* —**ism,** *n.*

***ath·let·ics** [æθ'lɛtɪks; æθ'letiks] *n.* ①(常作 *pl.*解) 運動(指各種競技)。*Athletics* include all kinds of sports, as running, rowing, boxing, etc. 運動包括各種競技，如賽跑、划船、拳擊等。②(常作 *sing.* 解) 運動(指體育原理或運動術)。*Athletics* is recommended for every student. 勸每個學生都參加運動。

at-home [ət'hom; ət'houm] *n.* (約定時日之) 會客；家庭招待會。(亦作 **at home**) —*adj.* 家用的；非正式的。

at-home day 會客日。

a·thwart [ə'θwɔrt; ə'θwɔːt] *adv.* ①橫穿過地；斜地；不對地；不順利地。②〖航海〗船側朝風。 —*prep.* ①橫過。②逆；反對。③〖航

海】横越航向。
a·thwart·ships [ə'θwɔrt·ʃɪps; ə'θwɔːtʃips] *adv.* 橫過地;橫過船。
-atic 〖字尾〗表"…的;…性的"之義。
a·tilt [ə'tɪlt;ə'tilt] *adj.* & *adv.* ①傾側的(地); 傾斜的(地)。②作舉鎗衝刺狀的(地)。*run* (or *ride*) *atilt at* (or *against*) 向…挺鎗衝刺。
a·tin·gle [ə'tɪŋgl;ə'tiŋgl] *adj.* 刺痛的;激動的。
-ation 〖字尾〗表"動作;過程;狀況;結果"之義的名詞字尾。例:agitation.
-ative 〖字尾〗表"趨向;性質;作用;關係;連結"之義的形容詞語尾。例:talkative.
Atl. Atlantic.
At·lan·ta [ət'læntə; ət'læntə] *n.* 亞特蘭大(美國喬治亞州之首府)。
At·lan·te·an [ˌætlæn'tiən; ˌætlæn'tiːən] *adj.* ①巨人 Atlas 的。②有巨人 Atlas 之力量的。③ Atlantis 島的。
at·lan·tes [ət'læntiz; ət'læntiːz] *n. pl., sing.* **at·las.** 〖建築〗雕成男性人像的柱。
:At·lan·tic [ət'læntɪk; ət'læntik] *n.* 大西洋。—*adj.* ①大西洋的。the *Atlantic* Ocean. 大西洋。②北大西洋公約組織的。③ Atlas 的。
Atlantic Charter 大西洋憲章。
At·lan·ti·cism [ət'læntəˌsɪzəm; ət'læntisizəm] *n.* 大西洋主義。
Atlantic Pact 北大西洋公約。
At·lan·tis [ət'læntɪs; ət'læntis] *n.* 阿特蘭提斯(大西洋中之一神祕島嶼,據云最後陸沉海底)。
At·las ['ætləs; 'ætləs] *n.* ①〖希臘神話〗受罰以雙肩掮天之巨人。②掮負重擔之人。③美國擎天神洲際飛彈。
***at·las** ['ætləs; 'ætləs] *n.* ①地圖; 地圖集。②〖解剖〗寰椎; 第一頸椎。③〖英〗長33至34英寸寬26英寸的大紙。④用圖表來說明某一事物的書。
atlas grid 空中照相上的方格(用以尋覓主要目標)。
atm. ①atmosphere(s). ②atmospheric.
at·man ['ɑtmən; 'ɑːtmən] *n.* 〖印度教〗①氣息。②生命之本源。③個人之靈魂;自我。④ (A-) 大我;宇宙我。⑤ (A-) 梵天。
atmo- 〖字首〗表"空氣"之義,用造複合詞,如 atmosphere.
at·mom·e·ter [æt'mɑmɪtə; æt'mɔmitə] *n.* 蒸發計。
***at·mos·phere** ['ætməsˌfɪr; 'ætməsfiə] *n.* ①大氣;空氣。②氣壓。③環境。We live in an *atmosphere* of freedom. 我們生活在自由的環境中。④氣氛;氛圍。
at·mos·pher·ic [ˌætməs'fɛrɪk; ˌætməs'ferik] *adj.* ①大氣的。②氣壓的。③氣氛的; 氛圍的。④朦朧的; 模糊的。(亦作 **atmospherical**) —**al·ly,** *adv.*
atmospheric discharge 空中放電。
atmospheric disturbances 〖無線電〗天電干擾。
atmospheric pressure 大氣壓力。
at·mos·pher·ics [ˌætməs'fɛrɪks; ˌætməs'feriks] *n. pl.*〖無線電〗①天電干擾。②天電。
at. no. atomic number.
at·oll ['ætɑl; 'ætɔl] *n.* 環狀珊瑚島;環礁。
***at·om** ['ætəm; 'ætəm] *n.* ①原子。②微粒;極少量的東西。There is not an *atom* of water. 一滴水都沒有。
atom bomb 原子彈。
at·om-bomb ['ætəm'bɑm; 'ætəm-bɔm] *v.t.* 用原子彈轟炸或毀滅。
atom bomber =**atomic bomber.**
***a·tom·ic** [ə'tɑmɪk; ə'tɔmik] *adj.* ①原子的。*atomic* furnace. 原子爐。②微粒的;極小的。③原子能的; 原子彈的。④分裂為原子的。(亦作 **atomical**) —**al·ly,** *adv.*
atomic age 原子時代。
atomic bomb, A-bomb 原子彈。
atomic bomber ①可裝載原子彈之轟炸機。②利用核能發動之飛機。
atomic clock 原子鐘。
atomic cloud 原子雲。
atomic cocktail 治癌用放射性內服藥。
atomic energy 原子能。
atomic engine 原子引擎。
atomic hypothesis =**atomic theory.**
at·o·mic·i·ty [ˌætə'mɪsətɪ; ˌætə'misəti] *n.* 〖化〗①(氣體分子中之)原子數。②原子價。
atomic mass unit 原子質量單位。
atomic nucleus 原子核。
atomic number 〖化〗原子序(數)。
atomic pile 原子爐;原子堆。
atomic power 原子動力。
atomic power reactor 原子動力反應器。
a·tom·ics [ə'tɑmɪks; ə'tɔmiks] *n.* 原子學。
atomic theory 〖理,化〗原子說。
atomic value 〖化〗原子價。
atomic volume 〖化〗原子體積。
atomic warfare 原子戰爭。
atomic warhead 原子彈頭。
atomic weapon 原子武器。
atomic weight 〖化〗原子量。
at·om·ism ['ætəmˌɪzəm; 'ætəmizəm] *n.* ①原子論;原子說。②〖哲學〗元子論。
at·om·ist ['ætəmɪst; 'ætəmist] *n.* 原子物理學家;原子論者;元子論者。
at·om·is·tic [ˌætəm'ɪstɪk; ˌætə'mistik] *adj.* 原子說的;元子論的。
at·om·ize ['ætəmˌaɪz; 'ætəmaiz] *v.t.,* **-ized, -iz·ing.** ①分為原子;使成原子。②〖俚〗用原子彈轟炸。③噴為霧狀。—**at·om·i·za·tion,** *n.*
at·om·iz·er ['ætəmˌaɪzə; 'ætəmaizə] *n.* 噴霧器。
atom probe 觀察一原子之活動的裝置。
at·o·my ['ætəmɪ; 'ætəmi] *n., pl.* **-mies.** ①原子。②矮人;侏儒。
a·ton·al [e'tonl̩; æ'tounl] *adj.* 〖音樂〗無調性的。—**i·ty,** *n.*
a·tone [ə'ton; ə'toun] *v.,* **a·toned, a·ton·ing.** —*v.i.* 補償;賠償;贖罪。—*v.t.* 賠償;賠罪。
a·tone·ment [ə'tonmənt; ə'tounmənt] *n.* 補償;贖罪。*the Atonement* 耶穌替世人贖罪之受難及死。
a·ton·ic [ə'tɑnɪk; æ'tɔnik] *adj.* ①〖語音〗非重讀的。②〖醫〗無緊張力的;弛緩的。—*n.* 非重讀之字、音節或聲音。
at·o·ny ['ætənɪ; 'ætəni] *n.* ①〖醫〗(收縮性器官之)無緊張力;弛緩。②〖語音〗非重讀。
a·top [ə'tɑp; ə'tɔp] *adv.* 在上地; 在頂上地;在上面地。—*prep.* 在上面;在頂上。
at·o·py ['ætəpɪ; 'ætəpi] *n.* 遺傳性過敏症。
at·ra·bil·ious [ˌætrə'bɪljəs; ˌætrə'biljəs] *adj.* ①憂鬱的。②憂鬱症的。③性情暴躁的。—**ness,** *n.*
a·trip [ə'trɪp; ə'trip] *adj.* 〖航海〗①剛起離水底的(錨)。②(帆或帆桁)揚起。
a·tri·um ['etrɪəm; 'ɑːtriəm] *n., pl.* **-tri·a** [-trɪə; -triə]. ①〖解剖〗心房; 心耳;內耳窩。②〖建築〗(古羅馬建築之)前室;前庭。

③〖動物〗排泄腔。

a·tro·cious [əˈtroʃəs; əˈtrouʃəs] adj. ①兇暴的;殘忍的。②〖俗〗惡劣的。—ly, adv.

a·troc·i·ty [əˈtrasətɪ; əˈtrɔsiti] n., pl. -ties. ①兇惡;暴行。②〖俗〗嚴重的錯誤。

a·troph·ic [əˈtrafɪk; æˈtrɔfik] adj. 萎縮的。

at·ro·phy [ˈætrəfɪ; ˈætrəfi] n., v., -phied, -phy·ing. —n. 虛脫; 萎縮;衰退。—v.t. & v.i. (使)萎縮;(使)衰退。

at·ro·pine [ˈætrəˌpin; ˈætrəpiːn] n. 阿托平;顛茄精(一種白色有毒之植物鹼)。

A.T.S. ①American Temperance Society. ② American Tract Society. ③ American Transport Service. ④U.S. Army Transport Service.

att., atty. attorney.

at·ta·boy [ˈætəˌbɔɪ; ˈætəbɔi] interj. 〖美俚〗好小子。

*at·tach [əˈtætʃ; əˈtætʃ] v.t. ①結;縛;連接;參加〖to〗. He attached labels to all his bags. 他在所有的袋子上都繫以標籤。②屬於;使附屬。③加;附;認爲有;歸…於。④使愛慕;使親暱;使依戀。He is greatly attached to his children. 他非常喜愛他的兒女。⑤〖軍〗(暫時的)委派;指派。⑥〖法律〗逮捕;拘留;查封。⑦簽署。—v.i. 附着;連屬〖to, upon〗. —a·ble, adj.

at·ta·ché [ˌætəˈʃe; əˈtæʃei] n., pl. at·ta·chés. 大使或公使之隨員;大(公)使館員。commercial attaché 商務幫辦。naval (or military) attaché (使館之)海(陸)軍武官。

attaché case 扁平的小型手提箱。

*at·tach·ment [əˈtætʃmənt; əˈtætʃmənt] n. ①附着。②情感;愛慕;忠誠。③附件。the attachments of a bicycle. 脚踏車的附件。④〖法律〗逮捕;拘留;扣押;查封。

⁑at·tack [əˈtæk; əˈtæk] v.t. ①攻擊。They attacked the enemy. 他們攻擊敵人。② 辱罵;(用文字或言語)攻擊。③侵襲(感染疾病)。④從事;着手。⑤對…有破壞性的效果。—v.i. 攻擊。The best way to defend is to attack. 防禦之上策爲攻擊。—n. ①攻擊。Attack is the best defense. 攻擊乃最好之防禦。②辱罵。He made a bitter attack on you in his speech. 他在演說中痛罵你。③(疾病之)侵襲。He has frequent attacks of malaria. 他常發瘧疾。④着手;從事。⑤(表演或競賽中)主動。—er, n.

at·ta·girl [ˈætəˌgɝl; ˈætəgəːl] interj. 〖美俚〗好姑娘。(亦作 attagal)

*at·tain [əˈten; əˈtein] v.t. ①達到;成就;完成。I hope you will attain your object. 我希望你將達到目的。②到達。—v.i. 到;達;達到;得到〖to〗. —a·bil·i·ty, —a·ble·ness, n. —a·ble, adj.

at·tain·der [əˈtendɚ; əˈteində] n. 〖法律〗財產或公權喪失。

at·tain·ment [əˈtenmənt; əˈteinmənt] n. ①達到;成就;造詣。②(常pl.)學識;技能。

at·taint [əˈtent; əˈteint] v.t. ①使喪失公權或財產。②羞辱;汚辱。—n. ①財產或公權喪失。②汚點;恥辱。

at·tar [ˈætɚ; ˈætə] n. 花油;玫瑰油;玫瑰油精。

at·tem·per [əˈtɛmpɚ; əˈtempə] v.t. ①沖淡;稀釋。②調和…之溫度;調節。③使緩和;平息(怒氣等);撫慰。

at·tem·per·a·tor [əˈtɛmpəˌretɚ; əˈtempəreitə] n. (蒸氣、水或其他液體之)保溫裝置。

⁑at·tempt [əˈtɛmpt; əˈtempt] v.t. ①嘗試;企圖;努力爲之。The prisoner attempted to escape but failed. 犯人企圖逃走,但未成功。②襲擊;攻擊;奪取;破壞。to attempt the enemy's positions. 攻擊敵人的陣地。—n. ①努力嘗試。②擊襲;攻擊〖常on, upon〗. An attempt was made on his life. 有人欲謀殺他。③〖法律〗未遂行爲。—a·bil·i·ty, n. —a·ble, adj.

Atten. Attention.

⁑at·tend [əˈtɛnd; əˈtend] v.t. ①出席;到;參加。The meeting was well attended. 到會的人數很多。②照顧; 照應; 侍候。He is attended by the doctor. 他由醫生照顧。③陪伴;隨至。The king was attended by the nobles. 貴族們伴隨國王。—v.i. ①料理; 從事; 照顧〖to〗. I have my business to attend to. 我要料理我的事務。②侍候;看護〖on, upon〗. ③注意;專心〖to〗. Attend to my words. 注意我的話。④伴;隨至〖常on, upon〗. Success usually attends on one's effort. 成功常隨人之努力而至。⑤出席參加〖at〗. to attend at a certain church. 參加某教堂禮拜。—er, n. —ing·ly, adv.

*at·tend·ance [əˈtɛndəns; əˈtendəns] n. ①到;出席。②隨侍; 隨從; 侍候。They were in attendance on the king. 他們是侍候國王的。③出席人數;出席者。④隨侍的人;隨從的人。in attendance 負責;當值。the physician in attendance. 當班醫師。dance attendance 慇懃侍候。take attendance 點名。

attendance officer 學校中負責調查曠課的職員。

*at·tend·ant [əˈtɛndənt; əˈtendənt] n. ①侍者;陪從。②伴隨事物。③出席人。—adj. ①隨侍的;陪從的。an attendant nurse. 陪從護士;專責護士。②伴隨的;附隨的。③出席的。attendant hearers. 出席的聽衆。—ly, adv.

at·tend·ing [əˈtɛndɪŋ; əˈtendiŋ] adj. 主治(醫師)的。

⁑at·ten·tion [əˈtɛnʃən; əˈtenʃən] n. ①注意;專心。You must pay attention to your study. 你當專心讀書。②(pl.)款待;慇懃。His attentions were assiduous. 他慇懃款待。③立正姿勢或口令。Attention! 立正!④禮貌。attention to a stranger. 對一個陌生人的禮貌。⑤關照。call away the attention 分其神。pay attention to one 傾耳靜聽某人講話。pay attentions to one 慇懃款待某人。stand at attention 直立不動。turn (or direct) one's attention to a subject 使某人注意某問題。

*at·ten·tive [əˈtɛntɪv; əˈtentiv] adj. ①注意的;留意的。②慇懃的;關懷的;有禮貌的。be attentive to 注意;傾聽;對…親切或關懷。—ly, adv. —ness, n.

at·ten·u·a·ble [əˈtɛnjuəbl̩; əˈtenjuəbl] adj. 可稀釋的。

at·ten·u·ant [əˈtɛnjuənt; əˈtenjuənt] adj. ①稀釋的;使變淡的。②〖醫〗致弱的;薄弱的。—n. 稀釋劑;致弱劑。

at·ten·u·ate [v. əˈtɛnjuˌet; əˈtenjueit adj. əˈtɛnjuɪt; əˈtenjuit] v., -at·ed, -at·ing, adj. —v.t. ①使細;使薄。②稀釋。③減弱;減少。—v.i. 變細;變弱;變稀薄。—adj. ①細的;薄的;稀薄的;減弱的。②〖植物〗漸尖的。

at·ten·u·a·tion [əˌtɛnjuˈeʃən; əˌtenjuˈeiʃən] n. ①細小;薄弱;衰弱。②稀薄;稀釋;稀釋度。③〖電〗衰減。④〖醫〗薄弱法;致弱法。

at·ten·u·a·tor [əˈtɛnjuˌetɚ; əˈtenjueitə] n. 〖電〗衰減器。

at·test [ə'tɛst; ə'test] *v.t.* ①證明;證實;爲…作證。The man's ability was *attested* by his rapid promotion. 這人的能力由他升遷之快得到證實。②使發誓。—*v.i.* 作證〖to〗. —**a·ble**, *adj.* —**ant**, —**a·tion**, *n.*

at·tes·ter, at·tes·tor [ə'tɛstə;ə'testə] *n.* 證人;作證者。

Att. Gen. Attorney General.

At·tic ['ætɪk; 'ætik] *adj.* ①Attica 的;雅典的。②古雅的; 文雅的。③〖美術〗盛行於紀元前七至四世紀 Attica 地方的陶器、花瓶等之花紋樣式的。***Attic bird*** 夜鶯之別稱。***Attic faith*** 絕對的忠實可靠。***Attic salt*** (or *wit*) 文雅的雋語。—*n.* ①Attica 人;雅典人。②Attica 語。

***at·tic** ['ætɪk; 'ætik] *n.* ①屋頂下小閣;頂樓。②〖解剖〗隱窩(耳鼓)。

At·ti·ca ['ætɪkə; 'ætikə] *n.* 雅地加(希臘東南地區,雅典爲其中心)。

at·ti·cism ['ætɪˌsɪzəm; 'ætisizəm] *n.* ①雅典之語風或風格。②簡明優美之詞章。(亦作 **Atticism**)

At·ti·cize, At·ti·cise ['ætəˌsaɪz; 'ætisaiz] *v.i.* ①模仿雅典語風或風格。②袒護雅典人。—*v.t.* 使與雅典語用法一致。

At·ti·la ['ætl̩ə;'ætilə] *n.* 阿提拉 (406?–453, 於433?–453爲匈奴王,世稱上帝之鞭)。

at·tire [ə'taɪr;ə'taiə] *v.,* **-tired, -tir·ing,** *n.* —*v.t.* 穿衣;盛裝。—*n.* ①衣服; 服飾; 美衣;盛裝。②〖紋章〗鹿角。

at·tired [ə'taɪrd;ə'taiəd] *adj.* 〖紋章〗鹿角的。

‡at·ti·tude ['ætəˌtjud; 'ætitju:d] *n.* ①態度。What is your *attitude* towards this problem? 你對這問題的態度如何? ②姿態。He stood there in a threatening *attitude.* 他以威脅的姿勢站在那裏。③飛機在飛行時的傾斜。④芭蕾舞中一姿勢。***strike an attitude*** 裝模作樣;矯飾。

at·ti·tu·di·nar·i·an [ˌætəˌtjudə'nɛrɪən; ˌætitju:di'nɛəriən] *n.* 裝模作樣之人;好擺架子之人。

at·ti·tu·di·nize [ˌætə'tjudn̩ˌaɪz; ˌæti'tju:dinaiz] *v.i.,* **-nized, -niz·ing.** 擺架子;裝模作樣;矜持。

at·torn [ə'tɝn; ə'tə:n] *v.i.* 〖法律〗承認新地主; 繼續作新地主之佃戶。—*v.t.* 易手他人;讓渡。

at·tor·ney** [ə'tɝnɪ; ə'tə:ni] *n., pl.* **-neys.** ①代理人。②律師;代辯人。letter of attorney*** 委任狀。***power of attorney*** 委託權;委託書;委任書。

attorney at law 律師。

attorney general ①首席檢察官;檢察長。②(A- G-)〖美〗司法部長。

at·tor·ney·ship [ə'tɝnɪʃɪp; ə'tə:niʃip] *n.* 代理人或辯護人之職務、身分等。

at·torn·ment [ə'tɝnmənt; ə'tə:nmənt] *n.* ①佃戶與新地主關係之承認。②讓渡。

***at·tract** [ə'trækt;ə'trækt] *v.t.* ①吸引。②招引;引誘;勾引。He shouted to *attract* attention. 他大聲呼喊以引人注意。—*v.i.* ①具有吸引力。It is a property of matter to *attract.* 物質具有吸引的性質。②引人注意。—**a·bil·i·ty,** —**or,** —**er,** *n.*—**a·ble,** *adj.*

at·trac·tile [ə'træktəl; ə'træktəl] *adj.* 運用吸引力的。

***at·trac·tion** [ə'trækʃən; ə'trækʃən] *n.* ①吸引力。The *attraction* of the moon for the earth causes the tides. 地球因月的吸引力而生潮汐。②吸引的東西; 誘惑物。③〖物理〗引力。

***at·trac·tive** [ə'træktɪv; ə'træktiv] *adj.* ①嫵媚的;動人的。She is a very *attractive* girl. 她是一個非常動人的女孩子。②有引誘力的。—**ly,** *adv.* —**ness,** *n.*

attrib. ①attribute. ②attributive.

at·trib·ut·a·ble [ə'trɪbjutəbl̩; ə'tribjutəbl] *adj.* 可歸於…的;可歸因的〖常to〗.

***at·trib·ute** [*v.* ə'trɪbjut; ə'tribju(:)t *n.* 'ætrəˌbjut; 'ætribju:t] *v.,* **-ut·ed, -ut·ing,** *n.*—*v.t.* 歸於;諉於;屬於;歸因〖常to〗.He *attributed* his failure to poor judgment. 他把他的失敗歸咎於判斷錯誤。—*n.* ①性質;品性;屬性。Politeness is an *attribute* of a gentleman. 溫文有禮爲紳士之品性。②象徵。The crown is an *attribute* of kingship. 王冠爲王權之象徵。③〖文法〗屬性形容詞。④(在 Spinoza 哲學裏)上帝之屬性。⑤〖邏輯〗有關主題(subject)之敍述。

at·tri·bu·tion [ˌætrə'bjuʃən; ˌætri'bju:ʃən] *n.* ①歸因; 歸屬。②屬性。③錢帑之分類。

at·trib·u·tive [ə'trɪbjətɪv; ə'tribjutiv] *adj.* ①屬性的。②〖文法〗形容的; 修飾的。—*n.* 〖文法〗形容語;修飾語。 —**ly,** *adv.*

at·trite [ə'traɪt; ə'trait] *adj.* 磨損的。—*v.t.* 磨損以使…變小。

at·trit·ed [ə'traɪtɪd;ə'traitid] *adj.* 磨損的。

at·tri·tion [ə'trɪʃən; ə'triʃən] *n.* ①摩擦;消磨;磨損。a war of *attrition.* 消耗戰。②減少。

at·tri·tus [ə'traɪtəs;ə'traitəs] *n.*經磨成微粒狀之物。

at·tune [ə'tjun; ə'tju:n] *v.t.,* **-tuned, -tun·ing.** ①使調和;使合調。②使一致;使適合。—**ment,** *n.*

atty. attorney. **Atty. Gen.** Attorney General. **at. vol.** atomic volume. **at. wt.** atomic weight.

a·typ·ic [e'tɪpɪk; ei'tipik] *adj.* 非典型的;不合型式的;不規則的;不正常的;變態的。(亦作 **atypical**)

Au 金 aurum 的化學符號。

au [o; ou] *pl.* **aux** [o; ou]. 〖法〗to the; at the; with the.

AU astronomical unit. **Au.** Augustus. **A.U.A.** American Unitarian Association.

au·bade [ˌo'bɑd; ou'bɑ:d] 〖法〗 *n.* 晨間音樂。

au·berge [ˌo'bɛrʒ; ou'bɛəʒ] 〖法〗 *n.* 客棧;旅舍。

au·ber·gine ['obɛrˌʒin;'oubəʒi:n] 〖法〗 *n.* ①茄子。②茄色。

au·burn ['ɔbən; 'ɔ:bən] *n., adj.* 赤褐色(的);赭色(的)。

au cou·rant [oku'rɑ̃; ou'kurɑ̃:] 〖法〗 ①最新的 (=in the current of events). ②熟知時事的。

***auc·tion** ['ɔkʃən; 'ɔ:kʃən] *n.* 拍賣。He sells his things by *auction.* 他拍賣他的東西。—*v.t.*競賣;拍賣〖off〗. He *auctioned* off his furniture. 他拍賣了像具。—**ar·y,** *adj.*

auc·tion·eer [ˌɔkʃən'ɪr; ˌɔ:kʃə'niə] *n.* 拍賣人;競賣人。—*v.t.* 拍賣。

aud. auditor.

***au·da·cious** [ɔ'deʃəs; ɔ:'deiʃəs] *adj.* 大膽的;無禮的;無恥的。—**ly,** *adv.* —**ness,** *n.*

***au·dac·i·ty** [ɔ'dæsətɪ; ɔ:'dæsiti] *n., pl.* **-ties.** ①大膽無恥。He had the *audacity* to pick pockets in broad daylight. 他竟敢白晝扒竊。②膽識。③(*pl.*)大膽的言行。

au·di·bil·i·ty [ˌɔdə'bɪlətɪ; ˌɔ:di'biliti]

n.①可聽見;能聽度。②聲音之高度(其單位爲decibel)。—**ness**, *n.*

***au·di·ble**〔'ɔdəbl; 'ɔːdəbl, -dib-〕*adj.* 聽得見的。

au·di·bly〔'ɔdəblɪ; 'ɔːdəbli〕*adv.* 可聽見地;聽得見地。

***au·di·ence**〔'ɔdɪəns; 'ɔːdjəns, 'ɔːdiəns〕*n.* ①聽衆;觀衆。There was a large *audience* at the theater. 戲院裏觀衆很多。②讀者;收聽者;收看者。③聽聞;聽取。④正式謁見;覲見。The ambassador was received in *audience* by the President. 這大使覲見總統。⑤愛護者;擁護者。

audience chamber (or **room**) 覲見室;接見室。

au·di·ence-proof〔'ɔdɪəns,pruf; 'ɔːdjəns,pruːf〕*adj.* (戲劇)一定賣座的。

audio-〖字首〗表"聽"之義,如 audiophile.

au·di·o〔'ɔdɪ,o; 'ɔːdiou〕*adj.* ①〖電〗成音頻率的;成音的。②〖電視〗聲音播放或接收的。—*n.*〖電視〗**a.** 錄聲。**b.** 接收機內產生聲音之回路。

audio frequency〖物理〗能聽見之音波頻率;成音頻率;音頻。

au·di·o·lin·gual〔'ɔdɪo,lɪŋgwəl; 'ɔːdiou,liŋgwəl〕*adj.* 聽覺及口述的(別於文字的)。

au·di·om·e·ter〔,ɔdɪ'ɑmətɚ; ,ɔːdi'ɔmitə〕*n.* 聽力計;音波計。

au·di·o·phile〔'ɔdɪə,faɪl; 'ɔːdiəfail〕*n.* 愛好身歷聲電唱機、收音機的人。(亦作 **audiophiliac**)

au·di·o·tape〔'ɔdɪə,tep; 'ɔːdiouteip〕*n.* 錄音帶(別於 videotape).

au·di·o-vid·e·o〔'ɔdɪo'vɪdɪo; 'ɔːdiou'vidiou〕*adj.* 視聽傳播的。

au·di·o-vis·u·al〔'ɔdɪo'vɪʒuəl; 'ɔːdiou'viʒuəl〕*adj.* 視聽的。—**ly**, *adv.*

audio-visual aids 視聽教育之教具(如電影、電視等)。

au·di·phone〔'ɔdə,fon; 'ɔːdifoun〕*n.* 助聽器。

au·dit〔'ɔdɪt; 'ɔːdit〕*v.t.* ①檢查(帳目)。②旁聽(課程)。—*v.i.* 稽核;查帳。—*n.* 稽核;檢查。

au·di·tion〔ɔ'dɪʃən; ɔː'diʃən〕*n.* ①聽;聽力;聽覺。②(鑑定音質所作之)試聽。③所聽到之事物。—*v.t.* & *v.i.* (作)試聽。

au·di·tive〔'ɔdətɪv; 'ɔːditiv〕*adj.* 聽覺的;聽覺器官的。

au·di·tor〔'ɔdɪtɚ; 'ɔːditə〕*n.* ①旁聽者。②查帳員。③聽者。

au·di·to·ri·al〔,ɔdə'torɪəl; ,ɔːdə'touriəl〕*adj.* 稽核員的;查帳員的。

***au·di·to·ri·um**〔,ɔdə'torɪəm; ,ɔːdi'tɔːriəm〕*n.* ①教堂、戲院、學校等容納聽衆或觀衆的大廳或房間。②禮堂。

au·di·tor·ship〔'ɔdɪtɚ,ʃɪp; 'ɔːditəʃip〕*n.* 稽核員之職務或身分。

au·di·to·ry〔'ɔdə,torɪ; 'ɔːditəri〕*adj.*, *n.*, *pl.* **-ries.** —*adj.* 耳的;聽覺的。—*n.* 聽衆;聽衆席;大禮堂。

au fait〔o'fɛ; ,ou'fe〕〖法〗熟諳;精通。

au fond〔o'fɔ̃; ,ou'fɔ̃〕〖法〗徹底地。

auf Wie·der·seh·en〔auf'viːdər,zeːən; auf'viːdə,zeiən〕〖德〗再會;再見。

Aug. August. **aug.** ①augmentative. ②augmented.

Au·ge·an〔ɔ'dʒiən; ɔː'dʒi(ː)ən〕*adj.* ①〖希臘神話〗Elis國王 Augeas 或其牛棚的。②汚穢的;極髒的。

Augean stables〖希臘神話〗Elis 國王 Augeas 的牛棚。***cleanse the Augean stables*** 掃除汚垢;清除積弊。

au·ger〔'ɔgɚ; 'ɔːgə〕*n.* 螺絲錐;錐子。—*v.t.* 以錐鑽洞。

aught〔ɔt; ɔːt〕*n.* ①任何事物;任何部分。②零。—*adv.* 無論如何;全然。(亦作 **ought**)

au·gite〔'ɔdʒaɪt; 'ɔːdʒait〕*n.*〖礦〗輝石。

aug·ment〔*v.* ɔg'mɛnt; ɔːg'ment *n.* 'ɔgmɛnt; 'ɔːgmənt〕*v.t.* & *v.i.* ①增大;增加。②〖音樂〗增音。—*n.*〖文法〗添字(希臘文或梵文加在動詞過去式字首之母音)。

aug·men·ta·tion〔,ɔgmɛn'teʃən; ,ɔːgmen'teiʃən〕*n.* ①增大。②增加物。③〖音樂〗增音。

aug·men·ta·tive〔ɔg'mɛntətɪv; ɔːg'mentətiv〕*adj.* ①增大的。②〖文法〗增大意義的。—*n.*〖文法〗增大語。

au grat·in〔o'grɑtn̩; ou'grɑːtn〕〖法〗裹以麪包屑或乾酪而製成焦殼的。

au·gur〔'ɔgɚ; 'ɔːgə〕*n.* ①(古羅馬)占兆官。②預言家;相命者。—*v.t.* & *v.i.* 占兆;預言;預示。***augur well*** (or ***ill***) 示吉(凶)兆。

au·gu·ral〔'ɔgjʊrəl; 'ɔːgjurəl〕*adj.* (古羅馬)占兆官的;預言的;占兆的;示兆的。

au·gu·ry〔'ɔgjərɪ; 'ɔːgjuri〕*n.*, *pl.* **-ries.** 占兆;徵兆;示兆。

‡**Au·gust**〔'ɔgəst; 'ɔːgəst〕*n.* 八月。

au·gust〔ɔ'gʌst; ɔː'gʌst〕*adj.* 威嚴的;高貴的;令人敬畏的。—**ly**, *adv.* —**ness**, *n.*

Au·gus·tan〔ɔ'gʌstən; ɔː'gʌstən〕*adj.* ①羅馬皇帝 Augustus 的;其統治期的。② Augustus 時代之文學的;文藝全盛期的。③有 Augustus 時代之文學特徵的;古典的。—*n.* 文藝全盛時期之作家。

Augustan Age 拉丁文學之全盛時代(相當於奧古斯都大帝時期27 B.C.–A.D.14)。

Au·gus·tine〔ɔ'gʌstɪn; ɔː'gʌstin〕*n.* 奧古斯丁(Saint, 354–430, 早期基督教領袖)。

Au·gus·tin·i·an〔,ɔgəs'tɪnɪən; ,ɔːgəs'tiniən〕*adj.* 早期基督教會領袖 Augustine 的;其教義的。—*n.* Augustine 之教義的信奉者; Augustine 教團之僧人。

Au·gus·tus〔ɔ'gʌstəs; ɔː'gʌstəs〕*n.* 奧古斯都 (63 B.C. –A.D.14, 羅馬第一任皇帝, 在位期間 27 B.C. –A.D.14)。

au jus〔o'ʒy; o'ʒy〕〖法〗原汁;原湯。

auk〔ɔk; ɔːk〕*n.* 海鳥(北極海鳥之一種)。

auk·let〔'ɔklɪt; 'ɔːklit〕*n.* 小海鳥。

au lait〔o'lɛ; ou'lei〕〖法〗加牛奶的。

auld〔ɔld; ɔːld〕*adj.*〖主,蘇〗老的;古的。

auld lang syne〔'ɔldlæŋ'saɪn; 'ɔːldlæŋ'sain〕〖蘇〗昔日;往時。

Au·lic Council〔'ɔlɪk～; 'ɔːlik～〕宮廷會議(神聖羅馬帝國時皇帝之私人顧問會議)。

AUM air-to-underwater missile.

au na·tu·rel〔onaty'rɛl; ounaty'rel〕〖法〗自然的;裸體的;未加烹調的。

‡**aunt**〔ænt; ɑːnt〕*n.* ①姑母;姨母;舅母;嬸母;伯母。②慈善的老婦人。③〖俚〗年老之同性戀者(指男人而言)。—**like**, *adj.*

aunt·ie, aunt·y〔'æntɪ; 'ɑːnti〕*n.* ① aunt 之暱稱。②〖火箭俚〗反飛彈飛彈。

Aunt Sally〖英〗①代人受過者。②一種節日遊戲, 參加者以棒擲向一假女人口中所啣的烟斗。③(a- s-)任何無聊的娛樂節目。

au pair〔o'pɛr; ou'pɛə〕〖法〗平等的;互惠的(如以授課換膳宿等)。

au·ra〔'ɔrə; 'ɔːrə〕*n.*, *pl.* **-ras, -rae**〔-ri; -riː〕. ①氣味;氣息。②氣氛。③〖電〗尖端放電所引起的氣流。④〖醫〗(病症之)先兆。

au·ral[1]〔'ɔrəl; 'ɔːrəl〕*adj.* 氣味的;氣息的;氛圍的;先兆的。

au·ral[2] *adj.* 耳的;聽力的;聽覺的。—**ly**, *adv.*

au·re·ate〔'ɔrɪɪt; 'ɔːriit〕*adj.* ①金色的;鍍金的。②華麗的;燦爛的。—**ly**, *adv.*

au·re·li·an [ɔˈriliən; ɔːˈriːliən] *adj.* 蛹的。—*n.* 研究蝶蛾等之專家;昆蟲採集家。

au·rene glass [ˈɔrɪn～; ˈɔːrin～] 美國製金色與藍色藝術玻璃。「reole.」

au·re·o·la [ɔˈriələ; ɔːˈriələ] *n.* =au-

au·re·ole [ˈɔrɪˌol; ˈɔːrioul] *n.* ①(神像頭上或身體四周之)光輪;光環。②(日月等之)暈。—*v.t.* 以光輪圍繞。

Au·re·o·my·cin[ˌɔrɪəˈmaɪsɪn; ˌɔːriəˈmaisin] *n.* 〖藥〗〖商標名〗金黴素。

au re·voir [ˌorəˈvɔr; ˌourəˈvwɑːr] 〖法〗再會;再見。「②〖化〗三價之金的。」

au·ric [ˈɔrɪk; ˈɔːrik] *adj.*①金的;含金的。

au·ri·cle [ˈɔrɪkl; ˈɔːrikl] *n.* ①〖解剖〗a. 外耳;耳郭。b. 心耳;心室。②〖生物〗耳狀物;耳狀部;動物之外耳。「的;有耳狀物的。」

au·ri·cled [ˈɔrɪkld; ˈɔːrikld] *adj.* 有耳

au·ric·u·la [ɔˈrɪkjələ; əˈrikjulə] *n.*, *pl.* -las, -lae [-ˌli; -liː]. ①〖植物〗櫻草之一種。②=**auricle.**

au·ric·u·lar [ɔˈrɪkjələ˞; ɔːˈrikjulə] *adj.* ①耳的;近耳的;聽覺的。②耳聽的; 私語的。③耳形的。④〖解剖〗耳郭的;心耳的。⑤傳聞的。—*n.* (*pl.*) 鳥類耳孔外的毛。—**ly,** *adv.*

au·rif·er·ous [ɔˈrɪfərəs; ɔːˈrifərəs] *adj.* 含金的;產金的。「耳形的。」

au·ri·form [ˈɔrɪˌfɔrm; ˈɔːrifɔːm] *adj.*

au·ri·fy [ˈɔrəˌfaɪ; ˈɔːrifai] *v.t.*, **-fied, -fy·ing.** ①使…像金子;鍍以金。②使變金子。

Au·ri·ga [ɔˈraɪgə; ɔːˈraigə] *n.*, *genitive,* -gae [-dʒi; -dʒiː]. 〖天文〗御夫座。

au·rist [ˈɔrɪst; ˈɔːrist] *n.* 耳科學者; 耳科醫生。「**-rochs.** 歐洲野牛。」

au·rochs [ˈɔrɑks; ˈɔːrɔks] *n.*, *pl.*

*****Au·ro·ra** [ɔˈrorə, ə-, -ˈrɔrə; ɔːˈrɔːrə, əˈr-] *n.* 〖羅馬神話〗曙光之女神。

au·ro·ra [ɔˈrorə; ɔːˈrɔːrə] *n.*, *pl.* **-ras, -rae** [-ri; -riː]. ①黎明。②極光。③開始;早期。「～ɔːsˈtreilis] 南極光。」

aurora aus·tra·lis [～ɔsˈtrelɪs;

aurora bo·re·al·is [～ˌborɪˈelɪs; ～ˌbouriˈeilis] 北極光。

au·ro·ral [ɔˈrorəl; ɔːˈrɔːrəl] *adj.* ①曙光的。②極光的。③燦爛的。

au·rous [ˈɔrəs; ˈɔːrəs] *adj.* 〖化〗(一價)金的;亞金的;含金的。「號 Au).」

au·rum [ˈɔrəm; ˈɔːrəm] *n.* 〖化〗金(符

AUS, A.U.S. Army of the United States. 美國陸軍。「trian.」

Aus. ①Australia. ②Austria. ③Aus-

aus·cul·tate [ˈɔskəlˌtet; ˈɔːskəlteit] *v.t.* & *v.i.*, **-tat·ed, -tat·ing.** 〖醫〗聽診。

aus·cul·ta·tion [ˌɔskəlˈteʃən; ˌɔːskəlˈteiʃən] *n.* 〖醫〗聽診。

aus·cul·ta·tor [ˈɔskəlˌtetə˞; ˈɔːskəlteitə] *n.* 〖醫〗聽診者。

aus·cul·ta·to·ry [ɔsˈkʌltəˌtorɪ; ɔːsˈkʌltətəri] *adj.* 聽診的。

aus·pice [ˈɔspɪs; ˈɔːspis] *n.*, *pl.* **aus·pic·es.** ① (常 *pl.*)前兆;吉兆。②(常 *pl.*)保護;贊助;主辦。③占卜(以鳥所做)。***under the auspices of*** 由…贊助或主辦。

aus·pi·cious [ɔˈspɪʃəs; ɔːsˈpiʃəs] *adj.* ①幸運的。②吉兆的。—**ly,** *adv.* —**ness,** *n.*

Aus·sie [ˈɔsɪ; ˈɔːsi] *n.*〖俚〗①澳洲人;(尤指)澳洲之軍人。②澳洲。「③Austrian.」

Aust. ①Austria.②Austria-Hungary.

Aus·ten [ˈɔstɪn; ˈɔːstin] *n.* 奥斯汀 (Jane, 1775-1817, 英國女小說家)。

aus·tere [ɔˈstɪr; ɔːˈstiə] *adj.* ①苛刻的;嚴峻的。②不苟且的;苦修的。③樸素的。④酸澀的。—**ly,** *adv.* —**ness,** *n.*

*****aus·ter·i·ty** [ɔˈstɛrətɪ; ɔːsˈteriti] *n.*, *pl.* **-ties.** ①嚴峻;苛刻;樸素;嚴肅。②(常 *pl.*)苦行;禁慾生活。

Aus·tin [ˈɔstɪn; ˈɔːstin] *n.* 奥斯丁 (Alfred, 1835-1913, 英國詩人, 於 1896-1913 榮膺桂冠詩人)。

aus·tral [ˈɔstrəl; ˈɔːstrəl] *adj.* ①南的;南方的。②(A-)澳大利亞的;澳大拉西亞的。

Aus·tral·a·sia [ˌɔstrəlˈeʒə; ˌɔːstrəˈleiʒiə] *n.* 澳大拉西亞 (澳洲、紐西蘭及附近南太平洋諸島之總稱)。

Aus·tral·a·sian [ˌɔstrəlˈeʒən; ˌɔːstrəˈleiʒiən] *n., adj.* Australasia 人(的)。

*****Aus·tral·ia** [ɔˈstreljə; ɔːsˈtreiljə] *n.* ①澳洲。②澳大利亞聯邦 (首都坎培拉 Canberra)。

*****Aus·tral·ian**[ɔˈstreljən; ɔːsˈtreiljən] *adj.* 澳洲(人、語、文化)的。—*n.* 澳洲人。

Australian ballot 上有全部候選人名字以便投票人圈選的選票(始於澳洲, 故名)。

*****Aus·tri·a** [ˈɔstrɪə; ˈɔːstriə] *n.* 奧地利 (歐洲中部一國家, 首都維也納 Vienna)。

Aus·tri·a-Hun·ga·ry [ˈɔstrɪəˈhʌŋgərɪ; ˈɔːstriəˈhʌŋgəri] *n.* 奧匈帝國。

*****Aus·tri·an** [ˈɔstrɪən; ˈɔːstriən] *adj.* 奧地利的; 奧國的; 其人民、方言、或文化的。—*n.* ①奧地利人;奧國人。②奧國之德語方言。

Aus·tro·ne·sia[ˌɔstroˈniʒə; ˌɔːstrouˈniːʒə] *n.* 中太平洋及南太平洋諸島之總稱。

Aus·tro·ne·sian [ˌɔstroˈniʒən; ˌɔːstrouˈniːʒiən] *adj.* Austronesia 的。—*n.* ①Austronesia 之住民。②一種通行於太平洋區之語言(包括印尼語);南島語。

au·ta·coid [ˈɔtəˌkɔɪd; ˈɔːtəkɔid] *n.* 〖生理〗內分泌物;內泌素。「制者;暴君。」

au·tarch [ˈɔtɑrk; ˈɔːtɑːk] *n.* 獨裁者;專

au·tar·chi·cal [ɔˈtɑrkɪkl; ɔˈtɑːkikəl] *adj.*①專制的。②專制國家的。(亦作**autarchic**)

au·tar·chist [ˈɔtɑrkɪst; ˈɔːtɑːkist] *n.* 主張獨裁制度者。

au·tarch·y [ˈɔtɑrkɪ; ˈɔːtɑːki] *n.*, *pl.* **-ies.** ①專制。②專制國家。③=**autarky.**

au·tar·ki·cal [ɔˈtɑrkɪkl; ɔːˈtɑːkikəl] *adj.* 自給自足的。(亦作 **autarkic**)

au·tar·ky [ˈɔtɑrkɪ; ˈɔːtɑːki] *n.*, *pl.* **-kies.** ①自給自足。②經濟獨立政策。

auth. ①author. ②authoress. ③authorized.

au·then·tic [ɔˈθɛntɪk; ɔːˈθentik] *adj.* ①可靠的。②有根據的;眞正的。③〖法律〗手續完備的。—**al·ly,** *adv.*

au·then·ti·cate [ɔˈθɛntɪˌket; ɔːˈθentikeit] *v.t.*, **-cat·ed, -cat·ing.** 鑑定;證明。

au·then·ti·ca·tion [ɔˌθɛntɪˈkeʃən; ɔːˌθentiˈkeiʃən] *n.* 鑑定;證明。

au·then·tic·i·ty [ˌɔθənˈtɪsətɪ; ˌɔːθenˈtisiti] *n.* 眞實性;確切性。

‡**au·thor** [ˈɔθə˞; ˈɔːθə] *n.* ①著作人;作家。Dickens is his favorite *author.* 狄更斯是他所喜歡的作家。②一個作家的書。③發起人;創始者。God, the *Author* of our being. 上帝——我們生命的創造者。—*v.t.* ①著作。②創作。—**less,** *adj.*

au·thor·ess [ˈɔθərɪs; ˈɔːθəris] *n.* 女作家。「作家的;創作者的。」

au·tho·ri·al [ɔˈθorɪəl; ɔːˈθouriəl] *adj.*

au·thor·i·tar·i·an [əˌθɔrəˈtɛrɪən; əˌθɔːrəˈtɛəriən] *adj.* ①主張服從權力的。②

獨裁的。—*n.* 獨裁主義者。
au·thor·i·tar·i·an·ism [əˌθɔrəˈtɛrɪənˌɪzəm; ɔˌθɔːrəˈtɛəriənizəm] *n.* 權力主義;獨裁主義;服從權力政策。
ˈ**au·thor·i·ta·tive** [əˈθɔrəˌtetɪv; ɔːˈθɔritətiv] *adj.* ①有權威的;可信的。②命令的;絕對的。He speaks in an *authoritative* tone. 他用命令式的語調說話。③必須相信的;必須服從的;有專門知識之權威的。—**ly,** *adv.* —**ness,** *n.*
ː**au·thor·i·ty** [əˈθɔrətɪ; ɔːˈθɔriti] *n., pl.* **-ties.** ①權威;權力。②(*pl.*)有權威的人;當局;官府。the local *authorities.* 地方當局。③引證;根據;可憑信之著作。④權威;專家。He is an *authority* on phonetics. 他是語音學專家。⑤職權。⑥(法院的)裁定。⑦作證。
au·thor·i·za·tion [ˌɔθərəˈzeʃən; ˌɔːθəraiˈzeiʃən] *n.* ①授權;認可;委任。②合法的權力或權利。
au·thor·ize [ˈɔθəˌraɪz; ˈɔːθəraiz] *v.t.,* **-ized, -iz·ing.** ①授權。②認可;許可;使合法。③裁定;證明不誤。④使…成爲正當;使…有理。—**au·thor·iz·a·ble,** *adj.* —**au·thor·iz·er,** *n.*
au·thor·ized [ˈɔθəˌraɪzd; ˈɔːθəraizd] *adj.* 經認可的;經審定的;經授權的;公認的。
Authorized Version 英王 James 一世欽定之聖經英譯本。
au·thor·ship [ˈɔθəˌʃɪp; ˈɔːθəʃip] *n.* ①著作業。②(書等之)來源。
au·tism [ˈɔtɪzəm; ˈɔːtizəm] *n.* 〖心理〗孤獨性;孤獨癖。—**au·tis·tic,** *adj.*
ˈ**au·to** [ˈɔto; ˈɔːtou] *n., pl.* **au·tos.** 汽車(=automobile). *auto* parts. 汽車零件。
auto¹- 〖字首〗表"自己;獨自;自身"之義,例:autocracy.
auto²- 〖字首〗表"汽車;車輛"之義,如:autocade.
auto. ①automatic. ②automobile. ③automotive.
au·to-a·larm [ˈɔtoəˈlɑrm; ˈɔːtouəˈlɑːm] *n.* (船上之)自動警報器。
Au·to·bahn [ˈautoˌbɑn; ˈautoubɑːn] *n., pl.* **-bahns, -bahn·en** [–ˌbɑnən; –ˌbɑːnən]. 〖德〗高速公路。(亦作 **autobahn**)
au·to·bike [ˈɔtəˌbaɪk; ˈɔːtəbaik] *n.* 〖美俚〗機器脚踏車。(亦作 **autobicycle**)
au·to·bi·og·ra·pher [ˌɔtəbaɪˈɑgrəfə; ˌɔːtoubaiˈɔgrəfə] *n.* 自傳作者。
au·to·bi·o·graph·i·cal [ˌɔtəˌbaɪəˈgræfɪkḷ; ˈɔːtouˌbaiouˈgræfikəl] *adj.* 自傳(體)的。(亦作 **autobiogarphic**) —**ly,** *adv.*
au·to·bi·og·ra·phy [ˌɔtəbaɪˈɑgrəfɪ; ˌɔːtoubaiˈɔgrəfi] *n., pl.* **-phies.** 自傳。
au·to·bus [ˈɔtoˌbʌs; ˈɔːtoubʌs] *n., pl.* **-bus·es, -bus·ses.** 〖俚〗公共汽車。
au·to·cade [ˈɔtoˌked; ˈɔːtoukeid] *n.* 汽車遊行;汽車隊。(亦作 **motorcade**)
au·to·car [ˈɔtəˌkɑr; ˈɔːtoukɑː] *n.* 汽車。
au·to·ceph·a·lous [ˌɔtəˈsɛfələs; ˌɔːtəˈsefələs] *adj.* (東方教會等)獨立的;(主教等)自治的。
au·to·chang·er [ˈɔtəˌtʃendʒə; ˈɔːtouˌtʃeindʒə] *n.* 自動換片的唱機。
au·toch·thon [ɔˈtɑkθən; ɔːˈtɔkθən] *n., pl.* **-thons, -tho·nes** [–θəˌniz; –θəniːz]. ①土著。②土生之動植物。
au·toch·tho·nal [ɔˈtɑkθənḷ; ɔːˈtɔkθənḷ] *adj.* 土著的;土生的。
au·toch·thon·ic [ˌɔtɑkˈθɑnɪk; ˌɔːtɔkˈθɔnik] *adj.* =**autochthonous.**
au·toch·tho·nism [ɔˈtɑkθənɪzəm; ɔːˈtɔkθənizəm] *n.* 土著;土生;原產。
au·toch·tho·nous [ɔˈtɑkθənəs; ɔːˈtɔkθənəs] *adj.* ①=**autochthonal.** ②〖醫〗本處發生的。③〖心理〗自我產生之觀念但似外來的。
au·to·cide [ˈɔtəˌsaɪd; ˈɔːtousaid] *n.* 自我毀滅。
au·to·clave [ˈɔtəˌklev; ˈɔːtəkleiv] *n., v.,* **-claved, -clav·ing.** —*n.* ①增壓鍋。②(烹調用之)壓力鍋。③〖醫〗消毒蒸鍋。 —*v.t.* 以上述容器消毒或烹調。
auto court 〖美〗汽車旅館(=motel).
au·toc·ra·cy [ɔˈtɑkrəsɪ; ɔːˈtɔkrəsi] *n.* ①專制政治。②獨裁政府;獨裁國家。
au·to·crat [ˈɔtəˌkræt; ˈɔːtəkræt] *n.* 專制君主;專橫霸道的人。—**ic,** —**i·cal,** *adj.* —**i·cal·ly,** *adv.*
au·to·cy·cle [ˈɔtəˌsaɪkḷ; ˈɔːtəˌsaikl] *n.* 機器脚踏車。
au·to-da-fé [ˌɔtodəˈfe; ˈɔːtoudɑːˈfei] *n., pl.* **au·tos-da-fé.** ①異教徒裁判所判決之宣布及執行。②公開焚燒異教徒。
au·to·drome [ˈɔtəˌdrom; ˈɔːtoudroum] *n.* 賽車場。
au·to·dyne [ˈɔtoˌdaɪn; ˈɔːtoudain] *adj.* 〖無線電〗自拍的;自差的。—*n.* ①自拍或自差系統。②自拍或自差接收機。
au·to·er·o·tism [ˌɔtoˈɛrətɪzəm; ˌɔːtouˈerɔtizəm] *n.* ①自體性慾;自發之色情。②自體性慾之行爲(如手淫等)。
au·tog·a·mous [ɔˈtɑgəməs; ɔːˈtɔgəməs] *adj.* 〖植物〗自花受粉的。
au·tog·a·my [ɔˈtɑgəmɪ; ɔːˈtɔgəmi] *n.* 〖植物〗自花受粉。
au·to·gen·e·sis [ˌɔtoˈdʒɛnəsɪs; ˌɔːtouˈdʒenisis] *n.* 〖生物〗自生;單性生殖。
au·tog·e·nous [ɔˈtɑdʒənəs; ɔːˈtɔdʒənəs] *adj.* ①〖生物〗自生的。②〖醫〗自體的。③熔接的。 —**ly,** *adv.*
au·tog·e·ny [ɔˈtɑdʒɪnɪ; ɔːˈtɔdʒini] *n.* 〖生物〗自生;單性生殖。
au·to·ges·tion [ˈɔtoˌdʒɛstʃən; ˈɔːtouˌdʒestʃən] *n.* 由工人委員會所主持的工廠或農場之管理。
au·to·gi·ro [ˌɔtoˈdʒaɪro; ˈɔːtouˈdʒaiərou] *n.* =**autogyro.**
au·to·graph [ˈɔtəˌgræf; ˈɔːtəgrɑːf] *n.* ①親筆;親筆簽的字。②作家之手稿。 —*adj.* 親筆寫的。—*v.t.* ①親筆簽名於。②親筆寫。—**ic,** —**i·cal,** *adj.* —**i·cal·ly,** *adv.*
au·tog·ra·phy [ɔˈtɑgrəfɪ; ɔːˈtɔgrəfi] *n.* ①親筆;筆跡。②原紙石版印刷術;眞跡版。
au·to·gra·vure [ˌɔtogrəˈvjur; ˌɔːtougrəˈvjuə] *n.* 照相版雕刻法。
au·to·gy·ro [ˌɔtoˈdʒaɪro; ˈɔːtouˈdʒaiərou] *n., pl.* **-ros.** ①直升飛機;旋翼機。②(A-)該種直升飛機的商標。
au·to·hyp·no·sis [ˌɔtohɪpˈnosɪs; ˌɔːtouhipˈnousis] *n.* 〖醫〗自我催眠。
au·toi·cous [ɔˈtɔɪkəs; ɔːˈtɔikəs] *adj.* 具有雌雄兩種花序的。
au·to·ig·ni·tion [ˌɔtoɪgˈnɪʃən; ˌɔːtouigˈniʃən] *n.* ①(汽車)自動發火。②自燃。
au·to-im·mune [ˌɔtoɪˈmjun; ˌɔːtouiˈmjuːn] *adj.* 自體免疫的。
au·to-in·fec·tion [ˌɔtoɪnˈfɛkʃən; ˌɔːtouinˈfekʃən] *n.* 〖醫〗自體感染;自染。
au·to-in·oc·u·la·tion [ˌɔtoɪnˌɑkjuˈleʃən; ˌɔːtouinˌɔkjuˈleiʃən] *n.* 〖醫〗自體接種。
au·to-in·tox·i·ca·tion [ˌɔtoɪnˌtɑksəˈkeʃən; ˌɔːtouinˌtɔksiˈkeiʃən] *n.* 〖醫〗自體中毒。

au·to·ist [ˈɔtəist; ˈɔːtəist] *n.* 汽車使用人;駕汽車者(=motorist).
au·to·ki·ne·sis [ˌɔtokɪˈnisɪs; ˌɔtəkiˈniːsis] *n.* 〖生理〗自發之動作;自然運動。
au·to·ki·net·ic [ˌɔtəkaɪˈnɛtɪk; ˌɔːtəkaiˈnetik] *adj.* 自動的。
auto lift 汽車修理廠之舉重機(俾便檢查車底)。
au·tol·y·sis [ɔˈtɑləsɪs; ɔːˈtɔlisis] *n.* 〖生化〗自溶;自體分解。
au·to·mak·er [ˈɔtəˌmekɚ; ˈɔːtəˌmeikə] *n.* 〖美〗汽車製造者。
au·to·mat [ˈɔtəˌmæt; ˈɔːtəmæt] *n.* 〖美〗①自動販賣機。②使用自動販賣機之餐館。
au·to·mate [ˈɔtəˌmet; ˈɔːtəmeit] *v.t.* & *v.i.*, **-mat·ed, -mat·ing.**(使)自動化。
***au·to·mat·ic** [ˌɔtəˈmætɪk; ˌɔːtəˈmætik] *adj.* ①自動的。②無意識的;機械的。Breathing is usually *automatic.* 呼吸通常是無意識的。—*n.* ①自動的機器。②自動步槍或手槍。
***au·to·mat·i·cal·ly** [ˌɔtəˈmætɪklɪ; ˌɔːtəˈmætikəli] *adv.* 自動地;機械地。
au·tom·a·tic·i·ty [ɔˌtɑməˈtɪsətɪ; ɔːˌtɔməˈtisiti] *n.* 〖生物〗自動性。
automatic pilot 〖航空〗自動駕駛儀。
automatic pistol 自動手槍。
automatic rifle 自動步槍。
automatic telephone 自動電話。
au·to·ma·tion [ˌɔtəˈmeʃən; ˌɔːtəˈmeiʃən] *n.* 自動操作;自動控制。
au·tom·a·tism [ɔˈtɑməˌtɪzəm; ɔːˈtɔmətizəm] *n.* ①自動;自動作用;自動力。②〖哲學〗(動物之)機械行爲說。③〖生理〗自動性。④〖心理〗自動現象;無意識行動。⑤〖醫〗自動症。
au·tom·a·tize [ˈɔtɑˌmətaɪz; ˈɔːtɔˌmətaiz] *v.t.* & *v.i.*, **-tized, -tiz·ing.** ①使有自動裝置。②自動化。—**au·tom·a·ti·za·tion,** *n.*
au·to·mat·o·graph [ˌɔtəˈmætəˌgræf; ˌɔːtəˈmætəgrɑːf] *n.* 自動性運動描記器;無意識運動描記器。
au·tom·a·ton [ɔˈtɑməˌtɑn; ɔːˈtɔmətən] *n., pl.* **-tons, -ta** [-tə; -tə]. ①自然運行之事物。②機械裝置。③機械地動作或工作之人或動物。—**au·tom·a·tous,** *adj.*
‡**au·to·mo·bile** [*n.* ˈɔtəməˌbil, ˌɔtəˈmobil, ˌɔtəməˈbil; ˈɔːtəməbiːl *adj.* ˌɔtəˈmobɪl; ˌɔːtəˈmoubiːl *v.* ˌɔtəməˈbil, ˈɔtəməbil; ˌɔːtəməˈbiːl, ˈɔːtəməbiːl] *n., adj., v.*, **-biled, -bil·ing.** —*n.* 汽車。—*adj.* 自動的。—*v.i.* 乘汽車旅行。—**au·to·mo·bil·ist,** *n.*
au·to·mo·bil·ism [ˌɔtəməˈbilɪzəm; ˌɔːtəməˈbiːlizəm] *n.* 汽車駕駛;汽車使用;汽車駕駛術。
au·to·mo·tive [ˌɔtəˈmotɪv; ˌɔːtəˈmoutiv] *adj.* ①自動(推進)的。②有關汽車的。
au·to·nom·ic [ˌɔtəˈnɑmɪk; ˌɔːtouˈnɔmik] *adj.* ①自治的。②〖生物〗自發的。③〖植物〗自發的;自律的。
au·ton·o·mist [ɔˈtɑnəmɪst; ɔːˈtɔnəmist] *n.* 自治論者;主張自治者。
au·ton·o·mous [ɔˈtɑnəməs; ɔːˈtɔnəməs] *adj.* ①有自治權的;自治的;自主的。②〖生物〗有獨立機能的;自發的。—**ly,** *adv.*
au·ton·o·my [ɔˈtɑnəmɪ; ɔːˈtɔnəmi] *n., pl.* **-mies.** ①自治;自主。②自治區。
au·to·nym [ˈɔtənɪm; ˈɔːtənim] *n.* ①眞名;本名。②以本名發表之作品。
au·to·plas·ty [ˈɔtəˌplæstɪ; ˈɔːtəˌplæsti] *n.* 〖醫〗自體成形術;自體移植。
au·top·sy [ˈɔtɑpsɪ; ˈɔːtəpsi] *n., pl.* **-sies,** *v.* —*n.* ①驗屍。②事後分析。—*v.t.* 驗(屍)。—**au·top·sic, au·top·si·cal,** *adj.*
au·top·ti·cal [ɔˈtɑptɪkl; ɔːˈtɔptikəl] *adj.* 實地勘察的;親身觀察的。(亦作**autoptic**)
au·to·sug·ges·tion [ˌɔtəsəˈdʒɛstʃən; ˈɔːtousəˈdʒestʃən] *n.* 〖心理〗自我暗示。
au·to·tel·e·graph [ˌɔtoˈtɛləˌgræf; ˌɔːtouˈteligrɑːf] *n.* 傳眞電報機。
au·to-tim·er [ˈɔtoˌtaɪmɚ; ˈɔːtouˌtaimə] *n.* 用於爐灶上的自動定時器。
au·tot·o·my [ɔˈtɑtəmɪ; ɔːˈtɔtəmi] *n.* 〖動物〗自割(如蜥蜴棄尾)。
au·to·tox·in [ˌɔtəˈtɑksɪn; ˌɔːtəˈtɔksin] *n.* 〖醫〗自體毒素。
au·to·tox·is [ˌɔtoˈtɑksɪs; ˌɔːtouˈtɔksis] *n.* 自體中毒。
au·to·truck [ˈɔtəˌtrʌk; ˈɔːtəˌtrʌk] *n.* 〖美〗運貨卡車(=〖英〗motor lorry).
au·to·type [ˈɔtəˌtaɪp; ˈɔːtoutaip] *n.* ①一種單色照相版;此種版製成之圖畫。②複寫;模寫。—*v.t.* 以上述過程複印。
au·tox·i·da·tion [ɔˌtɑksəˈdeʃən; ɔːˌtɔksiˈdeiʃən] *n.* 〖化〗自動氧化。(亦作**auto-oxidation**)
‡**au·tumn** [ˈɔtəm; ˈɔːtəm] *n.* ①(亦作fall)秋;秋季。②盛極而衰之時。the *autumn* of life. 中年。—*adj.* 秋天的;秋天來的。*autumn* rains. 秋雨。
au·tum·nal [ɔˈtʌmnḷ; ɔːˈtʌmnəl] *adj.* ①秋的;秋季的。②秋天開花的;秋熟的。③已過壯年的;中年的;近衰老的。
autumnal equinox (or **point**) 秋分。
aux. auxiliary.
aux·e·sis [ɔgˈzisɪs; ɔːgˈziːsis] *n.* ①〖生物〗成長。②〖修辭〗誇張。
auxil. auxiliary.
aux·il·ia·ry [ɔgˈzɪljərɪ; ɔːgˈziljəri] *adj., n., pl.* **-ries.** —*adj.* ①協助的。*auxiliary* verb. 助動詞。②附加的;輔助的。*auxiliary* coins. 輔幣。③作爲預備的。—*n.* ①幫助者。②助手。③助動詞。④(*pl.*)外國輔助隊。⑤輔助艦。⑥(裝有引擎的)帆船。
auxiliary tone 〖音樂〗輔助音。
aux·i·mone [ˈɔksəˌmon; ˈɔːksimoun] *n.* 〖植物, 化〗促進成長劑。
aux·in [ˈɔksɪn; ˈɔːksin] *n.* 植物生長素。
aux·o·car·di·a [ˌɔksəˈkɑrdɪə; ˌɔːksəˈkɑːdiə] *n.* 〖醫〗心臟擴大症。
av. ①avenue. ②average. ③avoirdupois.
A.V. or **AV** ①atrioventricular. ②auriculoventricular. ③Authorized Version.
a·vail** [əˈvel; əˈveil] *v.i.* 有用;有利;有效。—*v.t.* 幫助;利於;裨益於。All his efforts *avail* him nothing. 他徒勞無功。avail oneself of*** 利用。—*n.* 有用;效用;利益。a weapon of little *avail.* 一件用處很少的武器。***of*** (or ***to***) ***no avail*** 無用;無效。***without avail*** 無益;無效。
a·vail·a·bil·i·ty [əˌveləˈbɪlətɪ; əˌveiləˈbiliti] *n.* ①有效;可用;近便。②現有或可得之人或物。
***a·vail·a·ble** [əˈveləbḷ; əˈveiləbl] *adj.* ①可用的;可利用的;近便的。②有效的;有效力的。The season ticket is *available* for three months. 這月季票有效期爲三個月。—**ness,** *n.* —**a·vail·a·bly,** *adv.*
available light 〖照像,美術〗自然光線。
av·a·lanche [ˈævḷˌæntʃ; ˈævəlɑːnʃ] *n., v.*, **-lanched, -lanch·ing.** —*n.* ①雪崩;山崩。②任何似雪崩之事物。—*v.i.* 崩落;湧

至。—*v.t.* 以大量之事物克服。

a·vant-cou·ri·er [ˈævɑ̃ˈkurɪɚ; ˈæ-vɑ̃:ŋˈkuriə] 〖法〗*n.* ①先驅者。②(*pl.*)斥候隊;前鋒。

a·vant-garde [ɑvɑ̃ˈgɑrd; ˈævɑ̃:ŋ-ˈgɑ:d] 〖法〗*n.* 先鋒; 前衞 (=vanguard). —*adj.* 前衞派的。—**a·vant-gard·ism,** *n.*

av·a·rice [ˈævərɪs; ˈævəris] *n.* 貪財(慾)。

av·a·ri·cious [ˌævəˈrɪʃəs; ˌævəˈriʃəs] *adj.* 貪財的;貪婪的。—**ly,** *adv.* —**ness,** *n.*

a·vast [əˈvæst; əˈvɑ:st] *interj.* 〖航海〗停!

av·a·tar [ˌævəˈtɑr; ˌævəˈtɑ:] *n.* ①〖印度神話〗神之下凡;神之化身。②具體化。

AVC, A.V.C. American Veterans Committee.

avdp. avoirdupois.

a·ve [ˈevɪ; ˈɑ:vi] *interj.* ①歡迎! ②再見! —*n.* ①歡迎或告別之語。②(A-)=**Ave Maria.**

Ave., ave. avenue.

A·ve Ma·ri·a [ˈɑvɪməˈriə; ˈɑ:vimə-ˈriə] 追念聖母瑪利亞之祈禱(或時間);福哉瑪利亞。(亦作 **Ave Mary, Hail Mary**)

***a·venge** [əˈvɛndʒ; əˈvendʒ] *v.t. & v.i.,* **a·venged, a·veng·ing.** 為…報仇; 報…之仇;報復。I will *avenge* you. 我將為你報仇。*avenge oneself on* 報復。

a·veng·er [əˈvɛndʒɚ; əˈvendʒə] *n.* 報仇者;復讐者。

av·ens [ˈævənz; ˈævənz] *n.* 〖植物〗水楊梅屬之植物。

a·ven·tu·rin(e) [əˈvɛntʃərɪn; əˈven-tʃərin] *n.* ① 洒金玻璃。②〖礦〗砂金石。

‡**av·e·nue** [ˈævəˌnju; ˈævinju:] *n.* ①〖美〗大街。②(兩邊有樹的)通道。③方法;途徑。The best *avenue* to success is hard work. 成功最好的方法是努力工作。〖注意〗**street, avenue** 均指街道。street 指鄉村、市鎮、城市中的街道,兩旁均有房屋。avenue 指著名的大街,兩旁有漂亮的住宅或樹木。又大城市中縱橫相交的街道,南北者稱 avenue,東西者稱 street.

a·ver [əˈvɝ; əˈvə:] *v.t.,* **a·verred, a·ver·ring.** ①斷言。②〖法律〗主張;辯明;證明。

‡**av·er·age** [ˈævərɪdʒ; ˈævəridʒ] *n., adj., v.,* **-aged, -ag·ing.** —*n.* ①平均數。②普通;平常;平均的標準。On an *average* there are twenty boys present every day. 每天平均有二十個孩子出席。—*adj.* ①平均的。*average* age. 平均年齡。②普通的;平常的。*average* intelligence. 普通智慧。—*v.t.*①平均之;求平均數。②平均分配。We *average* 8 hours' work a day. 我們每天工作平均八小時。—**ly,** *adv.*

a·ver·ment [əˈvɝmənt; əˈvə:mənt] *n.* ①斷言。②主張。

A·ver·nus [əˈvɝnəs; əˈvə:nəs] *n.* ①義大利 Naples 附近之一湖(古人認係地獄之入口)。②地獄。

a·verse [əˈvɝs; əˈvə:s] *adj.* ①不願意的;嫌惡的;反對的〖to〗。②〖植物〗外轉的。—**ly,** *adv.* —**ness,** *n.*

a·ver·sion [əˈvɝʒən; əˈvə:ʃən] *n.* ①嫌惡。②厭惡之人或物。—**a·ver·sive,** *adj.*

***a·vert** [əˈvɝt; əˈvə:t] *v.t.* ①防止;避免。②避開;移轉。

a·vert·i·ble, a·vert·a·ble [əˈvɝ-təbl̩; əˈvə:tibl] *adj.* 可避免的;可防止的。

A·ves [ˈeviz; ˈeivi:z] *n. pl.* 〖動物〗鳥類。

A·ves·ta [əˈvɛstə; əˈvestə] *n.* 祆教之聖典;火教經。

avg. average.

av·gas [ˈævˌgæs; ˈævgæs] *n.* 〖美〗(飛機用)任何汽油。

a·vi·an [ˈevɪən; ˈeiviən] *adj.* 鳥(類)的。

a·vi·ar·ist [ˈevɪərɪst; ˈeiviərist] *n.* 飛禽飼養家。

a·vi·ar·y [ˈevɪˌɛrɪ; ˈeiviəri] *n., pl.* **-ar·ies.** 大鳥籠;鳥舍。

a·vi·ate [ˈevɪˌet; ˈeivieit] *v.i.,* **-at·ed, -at·ing.** 飛行;航行;駕駛飛機。

***a·vi·a·tion** [ˌevɪˈeʃən; ˌeiviˈeiʃən] *n.* ①航空;飛行。②航空術;航空學。③軍用機。④航空工業。*aviation academy* 航空學校。*aviation badge* 飛行徽章。

aviation cadet 飛行學生。

***a·vi·a·tor** [ˈevɪˌetɚ; ˈeivieitə] *n.* 飛行家;飛機駕駛員;飛機師。

aviator's ear 航空中耳炎。

a·vi·a·trix [ˌevɪˈetrɪks; ˌeiviˈeitriks] *n.* 女飛行家;女飛機駕駛員。(亦作**aviatress, aviatrice**)

a·vi·cul·ture [ˈevɪˌkʌltʃɚ; ˈeiviˌkʌl-tʃə] *n.* 鳥類飼養。

av·id [ˈævɪd; ˈævid] *adj.* 貪婪的;熱望的〖for, of〗。—**ly,** *adv.*

a·vid·i·ty [əˈvɪdətɪ; əˈviditi] *n.* ①貪婪;熱望。②〖化〗親和力;親和力强度。

a·vi·fau·na [ˌevɪˈfɔnə; ˌeiviˈfɔ:nə] *n.* 某一地區之鳥類。

av·i·ga·tion [ˌævəˈgeʃən; ˌæviˈgeiʃən] *n.* 航空;航空術。

a·vion [ˌaˈvjɔ̃; ˌaˈvjɔ̃] 〖法〗*n.* 飛機。

a·vi·on·ics [ˌevɪˈɑnɪks; ˌeiviˈɔniks] *n.* 航空電子學。

a·vir·u·lent [eˈvɪrjələnt; eiˈviərjə-lənt] *adj.* 無毒力的;不會致病的;無毒性的。

a·vi·so [əˈvaɪzo; əˈvaizou] *n., pl.* **-sos.** ①通信;通報。②通信艇。

a·vi·ta·min·o·sis [eˌvaɪtəmɪnˈosɪs; eiˌvaitəminˈousis] *n.* 〖醫〗維他命缺乏病。

av·o·ca·do [ˌɑvəˈkɑdo; ˌɑ:vəˈkɑ:dou] *n., pl.* **-dos.** 鱷梨;鱷梨樹。

av·o·ca·tion [ˌævəˈkeʃən; ˌævəˈkeiʃən] *n.* ①副業;嗜好。②〖俗〗本職;職業。—**al,** *adj.*

av·o·cet [ˈævəˌsɛt; ˈævəset] *n.* 〖動物〗一種長足長喙的水鳥。(亦作 **avoset**)

‡**a·void** [əˈvɔɪd; əˈvɔid] *v.t.* ①避免。to *avoid* bad company. 避免與惡人為伍。We *avoided* driving through large cities on our trip. 我們在旅途中避免開車穿過大城市。②〖法律〗宣布無效;廢止;取消。—**er,** *n.*

a·void·a·ble [əˈvɔɪdəbl̩; əˈvɔidəbl] *adj.* 可避免的;可使無效的;可廢止的。

a·void·ance [əˈvɔɪdn̩s; əˈvɔidəns] *n.* ①避免;廻避。②〖法律〗無效;取消。③(僧職之)出缺;缺額。

av·oir·du·pois [ˌævɚdəˈpɔɪz; ˌævədə-ˈpɔiz] *n.* ①常衡(16英兩為一磅, 2,000磅為一噸)。②〖俗〗重量;(尤指)體重。(略作**avoir.**)

avoirdupois weight 常衡。

A·von [ˈevən; ˈeivən] *n.* 阿文河(在英國中部, 流經莎士比亞出生地 Stratford).

a·vouch [əˈvautʃ; əˈvautʃ] *v.t.* ①承認。②保證。③斷言。—*v.i.* 保證。—**ment,** *n.*

a·vow [əˈvau; əˈvau] *v.t.* 承認;宣稱。—**a·ble,** *adj.*

a·vow·al [əˈvauəl; əˈvauəl] *n.* 承認;宣稱。

a·vowed [əˈvaud; əˈvaud] *adj.* 承認的;宣稱的。—**ly,** *adv.*

a·vow·ry [əˈvaurɪ; əˈvauri] *n.* 〖法律〗自認某種行為。

a·vulse [əˈvʌls; əˈvʌls] *v.t.* 撕裂;扯開。

a·vul·sion [əˈvʌlʃən; əˈvʌlʃən] *n.* ①撕裂;扯開。②撕裂物。③〖法律〗(因洪水或河流改道而致之)土地位置的變遷;分裂地。

a·vun·cu·lar [əˈvʌŋkjəlɚ; əˈvʌŋkjulə] *adj.* ①伯(叔)父的;似伯(叔)父的。②〖諧〗典當商的。

aw [ɔ; ɔː] *interj.* 表示抗議、懷疑、厭惡等。
*__a·wait__ [əˈwet; əˈweit] *v.t.* ①等候;期待。to *await* a person. 等人。②準備以待。—*v.i.* 期待;等待。—**er,** *n.*
‡**a·wake**[1] [əˈwek; əˈweik] *v.,* **a·woke** or **a·waked, a·wak·ing.** —*v.t.* ①使醒;喚醒。②喚起。Nothing can *awake* his interest in this subject. 沒有東西可喚起他對這問題的興趣。—*v.i.* ①醒;起床。I usually *awake* at six. 我通常於六點醒來。②覺悟;覺醒;奮起〖常 to〗. You must *awake* to the realities of life. 你必須覺悟人生之現實。
‡**a·wake**[2] *adj.* ①醒的;醒着的。Is he *awake* or asleep? 他是醒着還是睡着? ②覺醒;深知; 洞察〖to〗. He was fully *awake* to the danger. 他完全知道那危險。
*__a·wak·en__ [əˈwekən; əˈweikən] *v.t.* ①喚醒。Please *awaken* me at six. 請於六點喚醒我。②喚起。—*v.i.* ①醒。②覺悟;注意。
a·wak·en·ing [əˈwekənɪŋ; əˈweikəniŋ] *adj.* 喚醒的;喚起的;激勵的。—*n.* ①喚醒。②振作;復興。—**ly,** *adv.*
A-war [ˈeˌwɔr; ˈeiˌwɔː] *n.* 原子戰爭。
*__a·ward__ [əˈwɔrd; əˈwɔːd] *v.t.* ①授與;賞給。He was *awarded* the first prize. 他被授與第一獎。②判定;判斷。—*n.* ①獎賞;獎品。②判斷;裁定。—**a·ble,** *adj.* —**er,** *n.*
*__a·ware__ [əˈwɛr; əˈwɛə] *adj.* ①知道的;覺得的。He is *aware* of his rudeness. 他知道自己的粗魯。②通曉的;機警的。—**ness,** *n.*
A-war·fare [ˈeˌwɔrfɛr; ˈeiˌwɔːfɛə] *n.* 原子戰爭。
a·wash [əˈwɑʃ, əˈwɔʃ; əˈwɔʃ] *adv.* & *adj.* ①〖航海〗與水面齊平地(的)。②覆有水。③隨波逐流地(的)。④充滿地(的)。
‡**a·way** [əˈwe; əˈwei] *adv.* ①在遠方; 離開;不在。Go *away.* 走開。②轉方向;離去。③繼續不斷地。She *worked away* at her job. 她繼續不斷工作。④放棄;消逝;死亡。He gave his boat *away.* 他放棄了他的船。⑤立刻。***away back*** 早期;遠方。***away with*** 取去; 離去(用在命令句中)。*Away with* you! 滾開! ***clear away*** 清除。***do*** (or ***make***) ***away with*** a. 取消;廢除。b. 毀滅;殺害。***fade away*** 消滅;消退。***fall away*** 離去;遺棄;散去。***far and away***超過其他地。This is *far and away* the best. 這個比其他要好得多。***give away*** a. 奉送。b. 洩露。c. 出賣。***look away*** 他顧。***pass away*** 死;逝世。***right*** (or ***straight***) ***away*** 立即;即刻。***where away?***〖航海〗在哪裏? 在哪個方向? —*adj.* ①遠離的。six miles *away.* 六英里以外。②不在的。③立刻上路。④〖運動〗在對方之場地比賽。⑤〖棒球〗出局。⑥〖高爾夫〗a. 球在離洞最遠處。b. (高爾夫球手)打了上述之球而須先打。
a·way-go·ing crop [əˈweˌgoɪŋˈkrɑp; əˈweiˌgouiŋˈkrɔp]〖法律〗佃戶所種之農作物,其成熟時租約已期滿,但法律上仍歸佃農收割。(亦作 **waygoing crop**)
AWB air waybill.
AWC ①Army War College. ②Aircraft Warning Corps.
*__awe__ [ɔ; ɔː] *v.,* **awed, aw·ing,** *n.* —*v.t.* 使敬畏。—*n.* 敬畏;驚懼。***be struck with awe*** 懍然敬畏。***keep*** (***a person***) ***in awe*** 使(某人)敬畏。***stand*** (or ***be***) ***in awe of*** 敬畏;害怕。
A-weap·on [ˈeˌwɛpən; ˈeiˈwepən] *n.* 原子武器。
a·wea·ry [əˈwɪrɪ; əˈwiəri] *adj.*〖詩〗=**weary.**
a·weath·er [əˈwɛðɚ; əˈweðə] *adv.* & *adj.*〖航海〗迎風;向風。—**ly,** *adv.*
awed [ɔd; ɔːd] *adj.* 充滿或表示敬畏的。
a·weigh [əˈwe; əˈwei] *adj.*〖航海〗拔起的;剛起離水底的(指錨言)。
awe·less [ˈɔlɪs; ˈɔːlis] *adj.* 不足畏的;無畏的。(亦作 **awless**)
awe·some [ˈɔsəm; ˈɔːsəm] *adj.* 引起(表示或感覺)敬畏的。—**ly,** *adv.* —**ness,** *n.*
awe-strike [ˈɔˌstraɪk; ˈɔː-straik] *v.t.,* **-struck, -strik·ing.** 使敬畏。
awe-struck [ˈɔˌstrʌk; ˈɔː-strʌk] *adj.* 敬畏的;充滿敬畏的。(亦作 **awe-stricken**)
‡**aw·ful** [ˈɔfʊl, ˈɔfl; ˈɔːful, ˈɔːfl] *adj.* ①可怕的。②〖俗〗非常的;極點的。What an *awful* nuisance! 多討厭的東西! ③〖俗〗極壞的。What *awful* handwriting! 字寫得眞壞! ④尊嚴的;莊嚴的。—*adv.*〖俗〗非常地。—**ness,** *n.*
*__aw·ful·ly__ [ˈɔfʊlɪ, ˈɔflɪ; ˈɔːfuli, ˈɔːfli] *adv.* ①可怕地;敬畏地;尊嚴地。②〖俗〗非常地。I am *awfully* sorry to be late. 我因遲到非常抱歉。
*__a·while__ [əˈhwaɪl; əˈwail] *adv.* 暫時;片刻。Wait for me *awhile.* 等我片刻。
*__awk·ward__ [ˈɔkwɚd; ˈɔːkwəd] *adj.* ①笨拙的; 無技巧的; 不靈敏的; 不優美的。an *awkward* dancer. 一個笨拙的跳舞者。②不便的;使人感覺麻煩的。③令人困惑的;使人侷促不安的。④困難的;危險的。⑤可怕的;很難應付的。an *awkward* customer. 一個很難應付的人。—**ly,** *adv.* —**ness,** *n.*
awkward age 青年期之早期。
awl [ɔl; ɔːl] *n.* 鑽子;尖鑽。
A.W.L., a.w.l. 〖軍〗absent (*or* absence) with leave. 經准休假。
awn [ɔn; ɔːn] *n.* 〖植物〗芒; 穀刺。
awn·ing [ˈɔnɪŋ; ˈɔːniŋ] *n.* 帆布篷;雨篷;遮日篷。
awn·inged [ˈɔnɪŋd; ˈɔːniŋd] *adj.* 掛有帆布篷的。
a·woke [əˈwok; əˈwouk] *v.* pt. & pp. of **awake.**
A.W.O.L., AWOL, a.w.o.l. absent without leave.〖軍〗擅自離職;不假外出。
A.WOL, A.wol, a.wol [ˈewɔl; ˈeiwɔːl] *n.*〖軍俚〗不假外出者。—*adj.*〖俚〗不假外出的。
a·wry [əˈraɪ; əˈrai] *adj.* & *adv.* ①歪、拗、或曲的(地)。②錯誤;斜曲。
*__ax, axe__ [æks; æks] *n., pl.* **ax·es,** *v.* —*n.* 斧。***get the ax***〖俗〗被開除;被拒絕。***give the ax to***〖俗〗開除;拒絕。***have an ax to grind***〖俗〗有所企圖。—*v.t.* ①用斧造或削(某物)。②解雇。③大量裁減(預算等)。④削減。
ax. ①axiom. ②axis.
axe·man [ˈæksmən; ˈæksmən] *n., pl.* **-men.** =**axman.**
axe·stone [ˈæksˌston; ˈæksstoun] *n.* =**axstone.**
ax·i·al [ˈæksɪəl; ˈæksiəl] *adj.* 軸的;軸上的;軸性的。(亦作 **axile**) —**ly,** *adv.*
axial skeleton 頭與身體之骨架。
ax·il [ˈæksɪl; ˈæksil] *n.*〖植物〗葉腋;枝腋。
ax·ile [ˈæksɪl, -saɪl; ˈæksil, -sail] *adj.*〖植物〗軸的;在軸上的。
ax·il·la [ækˈsɪlə; ækˈsilə] *n., pl.* **-las, -lae** [-li; -liː]. ①〖解剖〗腋窩;腋。②〖植物〗葉腋;枝腋。③(鳥)翼腋。
ax·il·lar [ˈæksɪlɚ; ˈæksilə] *n.*(鳥)腋羽。
ax·il·lar·y [ˈæksɪˌlɛrɪ; ˈæksiləri] *adj.*

①〖解剖〗腋窩的;腋的。②〖植物〗葉腋的;枝腋的;腋生的。—*n.* (鳥)腋羽。

ax·i·nite ['æksɪˌnaɪt; 'æksinait] *n.* 〖礦〗斧石。

ax·i·ol·o·gy [ˌæksɪ'ɑlədʒɪ; ˌæksi'ɔlədʒi] *n.* 〖哲學〗價值論。

ax·i·om ['æksɪəm; 'æksiəm] *n.* ①〖數學〗公理。②定理。③格言。

ax·i·o·mat·ic [ˌæksɪə'mætɪk; ˌæksiə'mætik] *adj.* ①公理的。②多眞理的;多箴言的。(亦作 **axiomatical**) —**al·ly,** *adv.*

*__ax·is__ ['æksɪs; 'æksis] *n., pl.* **ax·es** ['æksiz; 'æksiːz]. ①軸。②聯盟。③〖結晶學〗晶軸。④光軸。***the Axis*** 軸心國。

axis of abscissas 〖數學〗橫坐標軸。

axis of ordinates 〖數學〗縱坐標軸。

*__ax·le__ ['æksl̩; 'æksl] *n.* 輪軸。—**ax·led,** *adj.* 「軸;軸槓。」

ax·le·tree ['æksl̩ˌtri; 'æksltriː] *n.* 輪軸;軸槓。

ax·man ['æksmən; 'æksmən] *n., pl.* **-men.** 使斧者;伐木者。

Ax·min·ster ['æksmɪnstɚ; 'æksminstə] *n.* 一種以黃麻爲底之羊毛地毯。(亦作 **Axminster carpet**)

ax·o·lotl ['æksəˌlɑtl̩; ˌæksə'lɔtl] *n.*〖動物〗美西螈。

ax·on ['æksɑn; 'æksɔn] *n.* 〖解剖〗(神經細胞之)軸突。(亦作 **axone**)

ax·stone ['æksˌston; 'æksstoun] *n.* 〖礦〗斧形軟玉石。

ay[1] [e; ei] *adv.* 〖古,詩,方〗永恆地;時常地。***for (ever and) ay*** 永久地。(亦作 **aye**)

ay[2] *interj.* (表痛苦或驚愕)唉!啊! ***Ay me!*** 哀哉!

a·yah ['ɑjə; 'ɑːjə] *n.*(印度本地之)女傭;乳母。

*__aye, ay__ [aɪ; ai] *adv., n.* 是(=yes).

aye-aye ['aɪˌaɪ; 'aiai] *n.* 指猴(一種夜出之狐猴)。

Ayr·shire ['ɛrʃɪr; 'ɛəʃiə] *n.* ①亞爾(蘇格蘭之一郡)。②該郡產之乳牛。

az. azure.

a·zal·ea [ə'zeljə; ə'zeiljə] *n.* 〖植物〗躑躅;杜鵑花。

a·zan [ɑ'zɑn; ɑː'zɑːn] *n.*祈禱的召喚。

A·zer·bai·jan [ˌɑzɚbaɪ'dʒɑn; ˌɑːzəbai'dʒɑːn] *n.* 亞塞拜然共和國(全名作 the Azerbaijan Soviet Socialist Republic, 首都巴庫 Baku).(亦作 **Azerbaidzhan**)

az·ide ['æzaɪd; 'æzaid] *n.*〖化〗疊炭化合物。

A·zil·ian [ə'zɪlɪən; ə'ziliən] *adj.*阿濟爾期(在後期舊石器時代與新石器時代之間)的。

az·i·muth ['æzəməθ; 'æziməθ] *n.* 方位;方位角。—**al,** *adj.*

azimuth angle 方位角。

azimuth circle 方位圈。

azimuth compass 方位羅盤;船用羅盤。

az·o ['æzo; 'æzou] *adj.* 〖化〗含氮的。

azo- 〖字首〗表"氮"之義,例:azobenzene.

az·o·ben·zol [ˌæzo'bɛnzol; ˌæzou'benzoul] *n.* 〖化〗偶氮苯。(亦作 **azobenzene**)

azo dyes 〖化〗(偶)氮染料。

a·zo·ic [ə'zoɪk; ə'zouik] *adj.* ①無生命的。②(有時 A-)〖地質〗無生物時代的。③含氮化合物的。

az·o·im·ide [ˌæzo'ɪmaɪd; ˌæzou'imaid] *n.* 〖化〗氮化氫;疊氮酸。

a·zon·ic [e'zɑnɪk; ei'zɔnik] *adj.* 不限於一地區的;非地方性的。

A·zores [ə'zorz; ə'zɔːz] *n. pl.* 亞速爾羣島(在北大西洋,屬葡萄牙)。

az·ote ['æzot; ə'zout] *n.* 氮(= nitrogen).

a·zot·ic [ə'zɑtɪk; ə'zɔtik] *adj.* 氮的。

az·o·tize ['æzəˌtaɪz; 'æzətaiz] *v.t.,* **-tized, -tiz·ing.** 使與氮化合。

A·zov, Sea of ['ɑzɑf; 'ɑːzɔv] *n.* 亞速海(位於黑海之東北部)。

Az·ra·el ['æzrɪəl; 'æzreiəl] *n.* (猶太教與回教中)人死時使其靈魂離開軀殼之天使。

Az·tec ['æztɛk; 'æztek] *n.* ①阿玆特克人(西班牙入侵前之墨西哥中部的印第安人)。②阿玆特克語。—*adj.* 阿玆特克人的;阿玆特克語(文化)的。—**an,** *adj.*

*__az·ure__ ['eʒɚ, 'æʒɚ; 'æʒə, 'eiʒə] *n.* ①青色;天青色。②碧空;青空。—*adj.* 天青色的。

az·u·rite ['æʒəˌraɪt; 'æʒərait] *n.* 〖礦〗石青;藍銅礦。

az·ur·y ['æʒərɪ; 'æʒəri] *adj.* 青色的。

az·y·gous ['æzɪgəs; 'æzigəs] *adj.*〖動、植物〗不成對的;單一的。

az·yme ['æzaɪm; 'æzaim] *n.* 未發酵的麪包。(亦作 **azym**)

B

B or **b** [bi; biː] *n., pl.* **B's** or **b's.** ①英文字母之第二個字母。②B狀之物。③(成績)乙。④(在某些學校)代表第二學期之符號。⑤B血型。⑥〖音樂〗C大調或A小調中之第七音。⑦(羅馬數字)代表300之符號。

B ①化學元素 boron 之符號。②西洋棋中之"主教"(bishop). ③black. **B.** ①Bass. ②Bay. ③Bible. ④Blessed. ⑤British. **b.** ①born. ②book. ③base. ④baseman. ⑤bass. ⑥bat. ⑦bay. ⑧brother. ⑨breadth.

Ba 化學元素 barium 之符號。 **B.A.** ①(亦作 **A.B.**) Bachelor of Arts. ②British America. ③British Academy. ④British Association (for the Advancement of Science).

baa [bæː; bɑː] *n., v.,* **baaed, baa·ing.** —*n.*羊咩;羊叫聲。—*v.i.* 作羊叫聲。

B.A.A. Bachelor of Applied Arts.

Ba·al ['beəl; 'beiəl] *n., pl.* **Ba·al·im** ['beəlɪm; 'beiəlim]. ①腓尼基人的最高神;太陽神。②(有時b-)邪神;偶像。

baa-lamb ['bɑlæm; 'bɑːlæm] *n.* 〖兒語〗小羊。

Ba·al·ism ['beəlɪzm; 'beiəlizəm] *n.* ①崇拜 Baal. ②崇拜偶像。

Bab·bitt, bab·bitt[1] ['bæbɪt; 'bæbit] *n.*庸俗之商人或實業家(源於 Sinclair Lewis 之小說 *Babbitt* 中之主人翁)。—**ry,** *n.*

bab·bitt[2] ['bæbɪt; 'bæbit] *n.* 巴必脫合金。—*v.t.* 塡或襯以巴必脫合金。

Babbitt metal ①巴必脫合金。②(泛指)任何防止磨擦之合金。

*__bab·ble__ ['bæbl̩; 'bæbl] *v.,* **-bled, -bling,** *n.* —*v.i.*①說話模糊不清。The infant *babbles.* 嬰兒牙牙學語。②嘮嘮叨叨。③多嘴;洩漏祕密。④作潺潺聲。—*v.t.* ①隨口洩漏。to *babble* a secret. 洩漏祕密。②模糊而言。③以潺潺聲發出。—*n.* ①模糊不清的言語。②胡說。③(溪流)潺潺之聲。④〖電話〗因混線而發生之雜音。

bab·bler ['bæblɚ; 'bæblə] *n.* ①說話模糊不清者。②胡說的人。③洩漏祕密的人。

bab·bling ['bæblɪŋ; 'bæbliŋ] *n.* ①胡說。②嬰兒牙牙之聲。—*adj.* 胡說的;喋喋不休的。—**ly,** *adv.*

babe** 〔beb; beib〕 *n.* ①嬰孩。②天眞而無經驗的人;不知世故者;易受騙的人。③〖俚〗女孩子; 女人(尤指漂亮者)。 ***babe in the woods (or ***wood***) 易受騙的人。***babes and sucklings*** 乳臭未乾的小伙子們。
Ba·bel 〔'bebl̩; 'beibəl〕 *n.* ①〖聖經〗巴別,古巴比倫之一城及該城所建之塔。②(常 b-)雜亂之聲。③混亂嘈雜之處。④不可能建造之高塔或建築。⑤無法實現之計畫。—**ic,** *adj.*
ba·boo 〔'bɑbu; 'bɑːbuː〕 *n., pl.* **-boos.** ①先生(印度人對男子之尊稱,等於 Sir, Mr., Esq.). ②印度紳士。③能寫英文之土著書記。④對於英國文化一知半解之土著。(亦作 **babu**)
ba·boon 〔bæ'bun; bæ'buːn〕 *n.* 〖動物〗狒狒。—**ish,** *adj.*
ba·boon·er·y 〔bæ'bunərɪ; bæ'buːnəri〕 *n.* 笨拙;可笑;粗魯的行爲或態度。
ba·bouche 〔bɑ'buʃ; bɑː'buːʃ〕 *n.* (土耳其之)拖鞋。(亦作 **baboosh**)
‡**ba·by** 〔'bebɪ; 'beibi〕 *n., pl.* **-bies,** *adj., v.,* **-bied, -by·ing.** —*n.* ①嬰孩;嬰兒;小兒。②一家或一團體中最幼小的人。She is the *baby* of the family. 她是全家中最小的。③有孩子氣的人。He acts like a *baby*. 他行動像小孩。④〖俗〗女孩。⑤初生動物。⑥男人;男孩; 傢伙。⑦〖俗〗發明或計畫。⑧事物; 東西。—*adj.* ①嬰孩的。②年幼的;稚嫩的。He has a *baby* face. 他有張娃娃臉。③小的。④幼稚的。 —*v.t.* 縱容; 如對嬰兒般對待。—**hood,** *n.* —**ish,** *adj.*
baby act ①〖法律〗少年法。②〖俗〗幼稚之舉動。
baby blue 〖美〗一種柔和的淺藍色。
baby book ①育嬰指南。②記載嬰兒成長情形的記事簿。
baby bunting 嬰兒用附有風帽之外衣。
ba·by-car 〔'bebɪ,kar; 'beibikaː〕 *n.* 嬰兒車;小型汽車。
baby carriage 嬰兒車。(亦作 **baby buggy**)
baby carrier 〖美〗小型航空母艦。
ba·by-doll 〔'bebɪ'dal; 'beibi'dɔl〕 *adj.* 有青春氣息的;年輕的。
baby farm 育嬰院;託兒所。
baby farmer 託兒所之管理人員。
baby grand (or **piano**)小型鋼琴。
Bab·y·lon 〔'bæbl̩ən;'bæbilən〕 *n.* ①巴比倫(古代 Babylonia 的首都)。②任何大的、富庶的或邪惡的城市。③流亡之地。
Bab·y·lo·ni·a 〔,bæbl̩'onɪə; ,bæbi'lounjə〕 *n.* 巴比倫尼亞(亞洲一古國)。
Bab·y·lo·ni·an 〔,bæbl̩'onɪən; ,bæbi'lounjən〕 *adj.* ①巴比倫的;巴比倫人的;巴比倫語的。②巨大的;奢華的;邪惡的。③巴比倫尼亞的。 —*n.*巴比倫(尼亞)人;巴比倫語。
ba·by-sit 〔'bebɪ,sɪt; 'beibi,sit〕 *v.i.,* **-sat, -sit·ting.** 充任臨時褓姆;看守嬰孩。
baby sitter 臨時看護嬰兒者。
ba·by-size(d) 〔'bebɪ,saɪz(d); 'beibisaiz(d)〕 *adj.* 很小的;小型的。
ba·by·wear 〔'bebɪ,wɛr; 'beibi,wɛə〕 *n.* 〖英〗嬰兒裝。
BAC, B.A.C. Business Advisory Council.
bac·ca·lau·re·ate 〔,bækə'lɔrɪɪt; ,bækə'lɔːriit〕 *n.* ①大學學士。②對畢業生之告別訓辭。—*adj.* 學士的。
bac·ca·ra(t) 〔,bækə'rɑ; 'bækərɑː〕 *n.* ①一種紙牌賭博戲。②法國 Baccarat 地方所製的高級水晶玻璃器皿。
bac·cate 〔'bæket; 'bækeit〕 *adj.* 〖植物〗似漿果的;結漿果的。
bac·cha·nal 〔'bækənl̩; 'bækənl̩〕 *adj.* ①屬於或像酒神 Bacchus 的。②鬧酒狂飲的。—*n.* ①信奉酒神 Bacchus 者。②酒徒。③醉後鬧酒者。④讚頌 Bacchus 之歌或舞。(亦作 **bacchanalian**)
Bac·cha·na·li·a 〔,bækə'nelɪə; ,bækə'neiliə〕 *n.* ①(古羅馬)酒神祭。②(b-)酒宴。
bac·chant 〔'bækənt; 'bækənt〕 *n., pl.* **-chants, -chan·tes** 〔-'kæntiz; -'kæntiːz〕, *adj.* —*n.* ①酒神 Bacchus 之祭司。②酒神 Bacchus 之崇拜者。③酒徒。—*adj.* ①崇拜酒神的。②喜飲酒的;嗜酒的。
bac·chan·te 〔bə'kæntɪ; bə'kænti〕 *n.* ①酒神 Bacchus 之女祭司。②酒神 Bacchus 之女崇拜者。③女酒徒。
Bac·chic 〔'bækɪk; 'bækik〕 *adj.* ①酒神 Bacchus 的;其祭典的。②(常 b-) 鬧飲的;醉酒的。(亦作 **Bacchical, bacchical**)
Bac·chus 〔'bækəs; 'bækəs〕 *n.* ①羅馬酒神。②酒。
bac·cif·er·ous 〔bæk'sɪfərəs; bæk'sifərəs〕 *adj.* 〖植物〗結漿果的;產漿果的。
bac·cy 〔'bækɪ;'bæki〕 *n., pl.* **-cies.** 〖俚〗煙草。(亦作 **bacco**)
Bach 〔bɑk, bɑx; bɑːx, bɑːk〕 *n.* 巴哈(Johann Sebastian, 1685–1750, 德國音樂家)。
bach 〔bætʃ; bætʃ〕 *n.* 〖俚〗獨身男子。***keep bach*** 保持獨身。—*v.i.* 〖俚〗過獨身生活。***bach it*** 過獨身生活。(亦作 **batch**)
***bach·e·lor** 〔'bætʃələ; 'bætʃələ〕 *n.* ①未婚男子。②學士學位。*Bachelor* of Arts. 文學士。③年輕武士。—**hood,** *n.*
bach·e·lor-at-arms 〔'bætʃələət'ɑrmz;'bætʃələt'ɑːmz〕*n., pl.* **bach·e·lors-at-arms.** 年輕武士。
bachelor girl 〖俗〗 獨立生活的未婚女子。
bach·e·lor·ship 〔'bætʃələ,ʃɪp; 'bætʃələʃip〕 *n.* 獨身狀態;獨身。
ba·cil·lar 〔bə'sɪlə; bə'silə〕 *adj.* ①桿狀的;桿狀體的。②桿狀菌的; 似桿狀菌的; 桿狀菌引起的。(亦作 **bacillary**)
ba·cil·li 〔bə'sɪlaɪ; bə'silai〕 *n.* pl. of **bacillus.**
ba·cil·li·form 〔bə'sɪlɪ,fɔrm; bə'silifɔːm〕 *adj.* 桿狀的。
ba·cil·lus 〔bə'sɪləs; bə'siləs〕 *n., pl.* **-cil·li.** ①桿狀細菌。②任何細菌。
bacillus Cal·mette-Gué·rin 〔~kæl'mɛtge'ræ̃; ~kæl'metgei'ræn〕 卡介苗(略作 **BCG**).(參看 **BCG vaccine**)
‡**back**¹ 〔bæk; bæk〕 *n.* ①背後;背部。 He can swim quicker on the *back*. 他仰泳更快。 ②動物的背上。 Some fishes have gills on the *back*. 有些魚背上有鰓。③脊背。He has a terrible pain in the *back*. 他脊背劇痛。④後衞球員。⑤後面;背面。There is a garden at the *back* of the house. 這房子後面有一花園。⑥椅背。 ***at one's back***; ***at the back of*** 在…幕後支持。***behind one's back*** 在背後;暗中。 They criticized him *behind his back*. 他們在背後批評他。***be on one's back*** **a.** 臥病在床。**b.** 挑錯;找麻煩。***break one's back*** 挫其脊背,使其負擔過重而不能勝任。 ***break the back of*** (***something***) **a.** 完成某事的最艱難部分。**b.**克服或擊敗某種制度、辯論等。***flat*** (or ***thrown***) ***on one's back*** 無能爲力;被擊敗。***get off one's back*** 不再找某人的麻煩。***get*** (or ***put***) ***one's back up*** **a.** 使某人生氣。**b.** 生氣。**c.** 固執。***having one's back to the wall*** =with one's back to the wall. ***put one's back into something*** 孜

孜不倦地做某事。*see the back of* (*someone*) 趕走(某人)。*slap* (*one*) *on the back* 拍拍某人的背以示親善、贊許、鼓勵等。*turn one's back on* 不理睬。*with one's back to the wall* 非苦戰不能脫逃。—*v.t.* ①支持;擁護。Don't worry, I will *back* you up. 不要憂慮,我將支持你。②使向後退。Please *back* your car a little. 你的車請後退一點。③襯托。This beach is *backed* by hills. 這海灘後面有山相襯。④簽名於…之背面。to *back* a check. (簽支票)背書。⑤下賭注於;打賭。⑥以…爲背景。—*v.i.* ①向後退。②〖航海〗(風向)逆轉。③堵(水)使升高。*back down* 退出或放棄(如辯論、要求等)。*back in* (or *into*) 無意中獲得;偶然取得。*back off* =**back down.** *back out* **a.** 食言;背信。He said he would help us and then *backed out.* 他說他要幫助我們,之後他又食言。**b.** 撤銷;後退。*back up* **a.**支持;擁護。**b.** 向後移動。*back water* **a.** 後退;改變主意。**b.** 改變船的航向。—*adj.* ①後面的。Please go out through the *back* door. 請由後門走出。②以前出版的;過時的;舊的。③未付的;前欠的。*back* pay. 欠薪。*back* rent. 〖美〗欠租。④未開發的;邊遠的。

‡back² *adv.* ①落後。Illness kept him *back* in his work. 疾病使他工作落後。②回溯;以往。③回原處。I like to go *back* to my old home. 我很想回故鄉。④還報。⑤隱匿。⑥退後。Please step *back* a little. 請退後一點。⑦忍住。*back and forth* 來回;往復。*back from* 遠離;在遠處。*back of* **a.** 在後邊。**b.** 支持;幫助。*go back on a friend* 背叛朋友;出賣朋友。*go back on one's word* 未能實踐諾言;食言。*hark back* **a.** 回轉。**b.** 舊事重提。*never look back* 〖俗〗永不後悔;永遠不計成敗而勇往直前。*pay a man back* (*in his own coin*) 以德報德;以怨報怨。*talk back* 〖美〗無禮貌地回答;回嘴。*there and back* 來回。

back³ *n.* (酒廠、染坊等處用之)大淺桶。

back·ache [ˈbækˌek; ˈbækeik] *n.*背痛。

back-al·ley [ˈbækˈælɪ; ˈbækˈæli] *n.* 〖英〗街後窄巷。—*adj.* 陋巷的;窮困的。

back-bench·er, back·bench·er [ˈbækˈbɛntʃɚ; ˈbækˈbentʃə] *n.* 英國國會下院中在政黨中不居於領導地位之議員(通常坐在後座)。(亦作 **back bencher**)

back·bite [ˈbækˌbaɪt; ˈbækbait] *v.t.* & *v.i.*, **-bit, -bit·ten** or **-bit, -bit·ing.** 背後誹謗(人)。—**back·bit·er,** *n.*

back·bit·ing [ˈbækˌbaɪtɪŋ; ˈbækˌbaitiŋ] *n.* 誹謗;背後造謠中傷。

back·board [ˈbækˌbord; ˈbækbɔːd] *n.* ①背板;靠背板。②〖醫〗(小兒之)背板;脊椎矯正板。—*v.t.* 〖醫〗使…帶脊椎矯正板。

***back·bone** [ˈbækˈbon; ˈbækboun] *n.* ①背脊骨。He has a pain in his *backbone.* 他脊骨痛。②主幹;中堅幹部;主力。③毅力。He is a man of *backbone.* 他是一個有毅力的人。④書脊;書背。⑤似背脊之物。*to the backbone* 純粹的。

back·boned [ˈbækˈbond; ˈbækbound] *adj.* ①有脊骨的。②剛毅的;果斷的。

back·break·er [ˈbækˌbrekɚ; ˈbækˌbreikə] *n.* ①艱苦的工作或任務。②工作極度辛苦的人。

back·break·ing [ˈbækˌbrekɪŋ; ˈbækˌbreikiŋ] *adj.* 勞力的;辛勞的。(亦作 **back-breaking, back-busting**)

back-call [ˈbækˌkɔl; ˈbækkɔːl] *n.* (指推銷員對顧客之)第二次訪問。

back·chat [ˈbækˌtʃæt; ˈbæktʃæt] *n.* 〖俗〗回嘴;頂嘴。

back-check¹ [ˈbækˌtʃɛk; ˈbækˌtʃek] *n.* (已完成工作之)檢查;查驗。—*v.t.* 查驗(工作、報告等)。

back-check² *v.i.* 〖曲棍球〗採取守勢。

back·cloth [ˈbækˌklɔθ; ˈbækklɔθ] *n.* ①〖戲劇〗〖英〗背景幕;天幕。②背景。(亦作 **back cloth**)

back-coun·try [ˈbækˌkʌntrɪ; ˈbækˌkʌntri] *adj.* 鄉下的。

back·court [ˈbækˌkɔrt; ˈbækkɔːt] *n.* 籃球場屬於守方之一半場地。

back·cross [ˈbækˌkrɔs; ˈbækkrɔs] *v.t.* & *v.i.* 將雜交種之第一代與原種交配。—*n.* 如此之交配。

back·door [ˈbækˌdɔr; ˈbækˈdɔː] *adj.* 祕密的;不正當的。—*n.* 後門。

back·down [ˈbækˌdaʊn; ˈbækdaun] *n.* 〖俗〗退却;投降;讓步。

back·drop [ˈbækˌdrɑp; ˈbækdrɔp] *n.* ①〖戲劇〗背景幕。②背景。

back·er [ˈbækɚ; ˈbækə] *n.* ①支援者。②(打字機的)墊紙。③(賽馬等的)賭手。

back·fall [ˈbækˌfɔl; ˈbækfɔːl] *n.* ①掉下。②掉下之物。③摔角時背著地的跌倒。

back-fence [ˈbækˈfɛns; ˈbækˈfens] *adj.* 鄰居間的;鄰居的。

back·field [ˈbækˌfild; ˈbækfiːld] *n.* 〖橄欖球〗衞。

back·fire [ˈbækˌfaɪr; ˈbækˈfaiə] *n.*, *v.*, **-fired, -fir·ing.** —*n.* ①(內燃機)逆火。②(鎗等)向後的爆發;後焰;回火。③放火(爲防野火蔓延而在其前面預先放火燒成平地)。—*v.i.* ①(內燃機)發生逆火。②(林火或野火來前)預先放火。③招致相反結果。

back·fisch [ˈbækˌfɪʃ; ˈbækfiʃ] *n.* 〖俗〗年輕少女;未成年的女學生。

back·flash [ˈbækˌflæʃ; ˈbækflæʃ] *v.i.* (內燃機火焰)逆流而着火。

back flip 倒翻觔斗。

back formation 〖語言〗①逆成法。②逆成字。

back·gam·mon [ˈbækˌgæmən; bækˈgæmən] *n.* 西洋雙陸棋戲。—*v.t.* 在此棋戲中打敗對方。

***back·ground** [ˈbækˌgraʊnd; ˈbækgraund] *n.* ①背景。②經驗;智識的背景。He is a man of high cultural *background.* 他是受過高等教育的人。③歷史背景。④(戲劇、電影、電視中的)配樂。⑤背地;暗中。—*v.t.* 〖美俗〗(在故事或戲劇中)加上背景或穿挿次要本事。—*adj.* (戲劇、電影等)背景的。

back·ground·er [ˈbækˌgraʊndɚ; ˈbækˌgraundə] *n.* 〖美〗①爲說明某政策或事件而舉行之記者招待會。②說明某政策或事件背景之公報。

back·hand [ˈbækˈhænd; ˈbækˈhænd] *n.* ①反手抽擊。②向左傾斜的書法。—*adj.* ①反手抽擊的。②諷刺的。③逆寫的(向左傾斜的)。—*v.t.* ①反手抽擊。②〖俚〗批評;反駁。

back·hand·ed [ˈbækˈhændɪd; ˈbækˈhændid] *adj.* ①反手打擊的。②諷刺的;挖苦的。③間接的。④逆寫的(向左傾斜的)。⑤(繩子等)反絞的。⑥笨手笨脚的。

back·hand·er [ˈbækˈhændɚ; ˈbækˈhændə] *n.* ①逆打;反手抽打的一擊。②酒瓶遞回後再斟之第二盃酒。③〖英〗回扣;賄賂。

back·house [ˈbækˌhaʊs; ˈbækhaus] *n.* 後面之小屋(尤指廁所)。

back·ing [ˈbækɪŋ; ˈbækiŋ] *n.* ①支持;

擁護。②(集合稱)支持者;幫助者。③置於背後的支持物。④〖建築〗隔板;底板;內牆。⑤〖戲院〗(遮住後臺之)帳幕或他物。⑥伴奏。⑦釣竿轉軸上長約50碼的第一段線。—*adj.* 後退的。

back·lash [ˈbækˌlæʃ; ˈbæklæʃ] *n.* ①反撞力;後座力。②反動;激烈的反應;退回。③〖美〗白人對黑人提倡種族混合運動的反感。④〖釣魚〗捲軸上釣線的結頭。—*v.i.* 引起反撞力;反動。

back·less [ˈbæklɪs; ˈbæklis] *adj.* 無背「的;無靠背的。」

back-light [ˈbækˌlaɪt; ˈbæklait] *n.*, *v.*, **-light·ed** or **-lit**, **-light·ing.** —*n.* 後光(由人或物之後方或90度方向照射之光線)。—*v.t.* 由後面照射。

back·log [ˈbækˌlɔg; ˈbæklɔg] *n.*, *v.*, **-logged**, **-log·ging.** —*n.* ①〖美〗壁爐中墊底之大木柴。②〖俗〗累積或存留之物。③備用物。—*v.t.* ①保留以備將來之用。②接受訂貨。

back matter 〖印刷〗書籍本文以外之附頁(以供記載參考書目、索引、補遺等)。

back·most [ˈbækmost; ˈbækmoust] *adj.* 最後面的。

back number ①過期出版物;舊雜誌。②〖俗〗過時之人或物;古董。

back order (現貨告罄,來日交貨的)「訂貨單。」

back-or·der [ˈbækˈɔrdɚ; ˈbækˈɔːdə] *v.t.* 訂(期貨)。

back·out [ˈbækˌaut; ˈbækaut] *n.* 拆「除(機器、裝置等)。」

back-pack [ˈbækˌpæk; ˈbækpæk] *v.t.* 背(貨物)。

back·ped·al [ˈbækˌpɛdl; ˈbækˌpedl] *v.i.*, **-aled**, **-al·ing.** ①(自行車煞車時)倒踏腳踏板。②(意見、動作等之)倒逆。③〖拳擊〗後退。

back·rest [ˈbækˌrɛst; ˈbækrest] *n.* 「背架;靠背。」

back·room [ˈbækˌrum; ˈbækˌruːm] *adj.* 〖俗〗不公開的;祕密的。

back·scratch·er [ˈbækˌskrætʃɚ; ˈbækˌskrætʃə] *n.* 〖俗〗①諂媚者。②〖英〗做賤役的人。③自己抓背用的長柄扒。

back·scratch·ing [ˈbækˌskrætʃɪŋ; ˈbækˌskrætʃiŋ] *n.* 〖俗〗爲共同利益互相利用。

back seat ①後座。②不重要之地位。

back-seat driver ①不斷地告訴汽車司機如何開車的乘客。②做不負責任的批評或勸告的人;多管閒事的人。

back·set [ˈbækˌsɛt; ˈbækset] *n.* ①挫折;逆轉。②逆流;渦流。

back·sheesh, back·shish [ˈbækʃiʃ; ˈbækʃiːʃ] *n.* =**baksheesh.**

back·side [ˈbækˈsaɪd; ˈbækˈsaid] *n.* ①背部;背後;後方。②(常 *pl.*)臀部。

back·sight [ˈbækˌsaɪt; ˈbæksait] *n.* ①〖測量〗後視;背視。②(槍之)表尺。

back slang 逆轉之俚語。

back·slap·per [ˈbækˌslæpɚ; ˈbækˌslæpə] *n.* 〖俗〗過分表示親密的人。

back·slap·ping [ˈbækˌslæpɪŋ; ˈbækˌslæpiŋ] *n.* 〖俗〗過分表示親密。—*adj.* 過分親密的。

back·slide [ˈbækˌslaɪd; ˈbækˈslaid] *v.*, **-slid**, **-slid·den** or **-slid**, **-slid·ing**, *n.* —*v.i.* ①墮落;退步。②減少宗教熱情。③再犯。—*n.* 再犯;退步;墮落。

back·space [ˈbækˌspes; ˈbækspeis] *v.*, **-spaced**, **-spac·ing**, *n.* —*v.i.* 將打字機滾筒後退一格。—*n.* ①打字機滾筒後退的格數。②打字機上使滾筒後退所按的鍵。

back·stage [ˈbækˈstedʒ; ˈbækˈsteidʒ] *adv.* ①在劇院之化裝室中。②在後臺;往後臺。—*adj.* ①在後臺的。②隱藏的;幕後的。—*n.* (戲院之)後臺。

back·stair(s) [ˈbækˌstɛr(z); ˈbækˈstɛə(z)] *adj.* 祕密的;間接的。

back stairs ①後樓梯。②詭密之手段「或方法。」

back·stay [ˈbækˌste; ˈbækstei] *n.* ①〖機械〗背控。②〖航海〗後支索。

back·stitch [ˈbækˌstɪtʃ; ˈbækstitʃ] *n.* 倒縫;倒針。—*v.t.* & *v.i.* 倒縫。

back·stop [ˈbækˌstɑp; ˈbækstɔp] *n.*, *v.*, **-stopped**, **-stop·ping.** —*n.* ①擋球網。②〖棒球〗本壘後方之網或柵。③〖俗〗棒球隊之捕手。④阻擋之物。—*v.i.* 〖俗〗作爲阻擋。—*v.t.* 支援;加强。

back street 後街;背街;小街。

back-street [ˈbækˌstrit; ˈbækstriːt] *adj.* 祕密的。an illegal *back-street* abortion. 非法的祕密墮胎。

back·stretch [ˈbækˌstrɛtʃ; ˈbækstretʃ] *n.* ①(徑賽跑道中)與終點直道平行並相對之部分。②〖美〗將橡皮管從救火車拉直至消防栓的動作。

back·stroke [ˈbækˌstrok; ˈbækstrouk] *n.* ①反擊;後座力。②仰泳。—*v.i.* 仰泳。

back·sword [ˈbækˌsord; ˈbækˈsɔːd] *n.* ①單刃刀。②木刀。③用木刀練習擊劍者。

back talk 〖俗〗回嘴;反唇相譏。

back·track [ˈbækˌtræk; ˈbæktræk] *v.i.* ①退却。②撤回。

back·up [ˈbækˌʌp; ˈbækʌp] *n.* ①支援者;後備者。②溢出;堆積。③輔助研究發展計畫。—*adj.* 預備的。

***back·ward** [ˈbækwɚd; ˈbækwəd] *adj.* ①向後的。He made a *backward* movement. 他向後退了一下。②背部在先的。③返回原地的;返回的。④逆反的。⑤遲鈍的。⑥落後的;不發達的。a *backward* country. 落後國家。⑦遲來的;晚的。⑧羞怯的;猶疑的。—*adv.* =**backwards.** —**ly**, *adv.* —**ness**, *n.*

back·ward·a·tion [ˌbækwɚˈdeʃən; ˌbækwəˈdeiʃən] *n.* (證券之)交割延期費。

back·wards** [ˈbækwɚdz; ˈbækwədz] *adv.* ①向後。He moves his arms *backwards.* 他向後揮臂。②背向前;倒;逆。③退步。Things are going *backwards.* 諸事退步。④追溯。⑤反省。backward(s) and forward(s)*** 上下地;往復地;徹底地。***fall (lean, or bend) over backwards*** 〖俗〗極力討好。〖注意〗**backward** 和 **backwards** 副詞可互用,但 backwards 不可用爲形容詞。

back·wash [ˈbækˌwɑʃ; ˈbækwɔʃ] *n.* ①反浪。②遺留的情況。③反動;反響。④〖英〗最差的部分;渣滓。—*v.t.* 以反浪衝擊、搖動等。

back·wa·ter [ˈbækˌwɔtɚ; ˈbækˌwɔːtə] *n.* ①逆水;逆流;水壩阻回之水。②〖比喩〗文化僵固。③窮鄉僻壤。④事件的餘波。—*adj.* 落後的。—*v.t.* (以逆划或逆轉推進器)停船。

back·wind[1] [ˈbækˌwɪnd; ˈbækwind] *v.t.*, **-wind·ed**, **-wind·ing.** 〖航海〗①使風轉向(下風之帆)。②操(帆)使風向下風處。

back·wind[2] [ˈbækˌwaɪnd; ˈbækwaind] *v.t.*, **-wound**, **-wind·ing.** 倒捲(照相機內之膠捲等)。

back·woods [ˈbækˈwudz; ˈbækwudz] *n. pl.* (常作 *sing.* 解)邊遠地區;遠離城鎮之森林地帶;半墾地。—*adj.* (亦作 **backwood**) ①荒地的;未開發的森林的。②粗野的。

back·woods·man [ˈbækˈwudzmən; ˈbækwudzmən] *n.*, *pl.* **-men.** ①居於邊遠

地區者。②隱居鄉間者。③粗笨之人。④從不或很少出席上院開會的英國貴族。

back-yard ['bæk'jɑrd; 'bæk'jɑ:d] *n.* ①後庭;後院。②常去之地;附近地區。(亦作 **back yard**)

Ba·con ['bekən; 'beikən] *n.* 培根(Francis, 1561-1626, 英國作家及哲學家)。

ba·con** ['bekən; 'beikən] *n.* 醃薰的豬肉(尤指脊肋肉)。bring home the bacon*** a. 供應物質上的需要。b. 完成某任務;獲得成功。***save one's bacon*** 使(某人)達成願望;使免受損傷。It was quick thinking that *saved our bacon.* 完全靠機警我們才得倖免。

Ba·co·ni·an [be'konɪən; bei'kouniən] *adj.* 培根的;培根哲學的;培根文體的。***Baconian method*** (培根所倡之)歸納法。***Baconian theory*** 認爲莎士比亞作品全爲培根所著的主張。—*n.* ①信仰培根哲學之人。②相信莎士比亞作品爲培根所著之人。**—ism,** *n.*

ba·con·y ['bekənɪ; 'beikəni] *adj.* 如醃肉的;脂肪質的。

bact. ①bacteriological. ②bacteriology.

***bac·te·ri·a** [bæk'tɪrɪə; bæk'tiəriə] *n.* pl. of **bacterium.**

bac·te·ri·al [bæk'tɪrɪəl; bæk'tiəriəl] *adj.* 細菌的。(亦作 **bacteric**) **—ly,** *adv.*

bac·te·ri·cide [bæk'tɪrə,saɪd; bæk'tiəri,said] *n.* 殺菌劑。**—bac·te·ri·cid·al,** *adj.*

bac·te·rin ['bæktərɪn; 'bæktiərin] *n.* 菌苗;疫苗。(亦作 **bacterial vaccine**)

bac·te·ri·o·log·i·cal warfare ['bæk,tɪrɪə'lɑdʒɪk|~; bæk,tiəriə'lɔdʒikəl ~] 細菌戰。

bac·te·ri·ol·o·gy ['bæk,tɪrɪ'ɑlədʒɪ; bæk,tiəri'ɔlədʒi] *n.* 細菌學。**—bac·te·ri·o·log·i·cal,** *adj.* **—bac·te·ri·o·log·i·cal·ly,** *adv.* **—bac·te·ri·ol·o·gist,** *n.*

bac·te·ri·ol·y·sis ['bæk,tɪrɪ'ɑləsɪs; 'bæk,tiəri'ɔlisis] *n.* 細菌引起之化學分解;細菌溶解;溶菌作用;細菌之分解或撲滅。

bac·te·ri·o·phage [bæk'tɪrɪə,fedʒ; bæk'tiəriəfeidʒ] *n.* 〖醫〗噬菌體。

bac·te·ri·os·co·py ['bæk,tɪrɪ'ɑskəpɪ; 'bæk,tiəri'ɔskəpi] *n.* 細菌之顯微鏡檢法。

bac·te·ri·o·ther·a·py [bæk,tɪrɪə'θɛrəpɪ; bæk,tiəriə'θerəpi] *n.* 細菌療法。

bac·te·ri·um [bæk'tɪrɪəm; bæk'tiəriəm] *n., pl.* **-te·ri·a.** 細菌。

bac·ter·oid ['bæktə,rɔɪd; 'bæktərɔid] *n.* (亦作 **bacterioid**)〖植物〗細菌樣;類似細菌體。—*adj.* (亦作 **bacteroidal**) 細菌性的;類似細菌的。

Bac·tri·an camel ['bæktrɪən~; 'bæktriən~]〖動物〗雙峯駝。

:bad [bæd; bæd] *adj.,* **worse, worst,** *n., adv.* —*adj.* ①不良的;不好的。a *bad* influence. 不良的影響。②邪惡的;不道德的。③令人厭惡的。a *bad* habit. 壞習慣。④有妨害的。⑤病痛的。to feel *bad.* 覺得不適。⑥無價值的。⑦不準確的。a *bad* shot. 不準的射擊。⑧無效的。⑨腐敗的(指食物等)。a *bad* egg. 壞了的蛋。⑩兇惡的;不祥的。⑪不適宜的;不適當的。He came at a *bad* time. 他在頗不適當的時候來。⑫難過的;遺憾的。⑬品質不佳的。a *bad* diamond. 劣等鑽石。⑭不够標準的;不適用的。⑮不正確的;錯誤的。a *bad* guess. 錯誤的猜測。⑯不健康的。⑰易怒的。a *bad* temper. 暴躁的脾氣。⑱心情不好的。⑲不服從的。⑳名譽不佳的。a *bad* name. 不佳的聲譽。㉑賠本的;不值的。㉒(膚色)有缺陷的。㉓浪費的。㉔僞造的。㉕〖俚〗好的。***be bad at*** 拙於。***be in a bad temper*** 在生氣。***be in a bad way*** 生病;不幸。***be in bad books*** 〖英俗〗不和睦。***go bad*** 壞了。The fruits have all *gone bad.* 水果全壞了。***go from bad to worse*** 每況愈下。***have a bad time*** 過焦慮不安的生活。***not half bad*** 相當好。***not so bad*** 還不壞。***too bad*** 可惜。That is *too bad.* 那殊爲可惜。—*n.* 不好的東西或狀態。***go to the bad*** 惡化(身體或道德上)。She wept at seeing her son *go to the bad.* 她看到她兒子的情況惡化後哭了。***in bad*** a. 在危急狀態中。b. 失寵。He is *in bad* with his mother-in-law. 他的岳母不喜歡他了。***to the bad*** a. 拖欠。He is now $100 *to the bad.* 他現在負債一百元。b. 垮臺;破產。—*adv.* 惡劣地(=badly). ***bad off*** 窮困。

bad actor〖俚〗壞的人或動物;無可救藥的罪犯。

bad apple〖俚〗壞人;壞蛋。

bad blood 仇視;憎恨;爭鬥。

bad check 空頭支票。

bad debt 呆帳。

bad·die ['bædɪ; 'bædi] *n., pl.* **bad·dies.** 壞人(尤指電影、電視中之惡人)。(亦作 **baddy**)

bad·dish ['bædɪʃ; 'bædiʃ] *adj.* 不甚好的。

bade [bæd; bæd] *v.* pt. of **bid.**

bad egg 〖俚〗①壞人。②無用的計畫。

Ba·den-Pow·ell ['bedn̩'poəl; 'beidn'pouəl] *n.* 貝登堡 (Sir Robert Stephenson Smyth, 1857-1941, 英國將軍, 於1908年始創童子軍運動)。

***badge** [bædʒ; bædʒ] *n., v.,* **badged, badg·ing.** —*n.* 徽章;標號;記號。Chains are a *badge* of slavery. 鎖鍊爲奴役之標誌。—*v.t.* 使佩帶徽章。**—less,** *adj.*

***badg·er¹** ['bædʒɚ; 'bædʒə] *n.* ①〖動物〗貛。②貛的毛皮。③(B-)〖俗〗美國威斯康辛州人。—*v.t.* 困擾。

badg·er² *n.* 販賣商人;小販。

badger game 仙人跳;美人計。

bad hat 〖英俚〗不老實或不道德的人。

bad·i·nage ['bædn̩ɪdʒ; 'bædinɑ:ʒ] *n., v.,* **-naged, -nag·ing.** 〖法〗—*n.* 嘲弄;開玩笑。—*v.t.* 打趣;嘲弄。

bad·lands ['bæd,lændz; 'bædlændz] *n.* (作 *pl.* 解)崎嶇不毛之地區。

bad·ly** ['bædlɪ; 'bædli] *adv.,* **worse, worst.** ①惡劣地。This was *badly* done. 這做得不好。②甚;劇。He needs money badly. 他極需要錢。badly off*** 窮困(爲 well off 之對)。

B.Adm.Eng. Bachelor of Administrative Engineering.

***bad·min·ton** ['bædmɪntən; 'bædmintən] *n.* ①羽球戲;羽毛球。②〖英〗一種清涼飲料。

bad-mouth ['bæd,maʊð; 'bædmauð] *v.t.* 〖美俚〗誹謗。

bad time 很困難或痛苦的時期。

BAE ①Bureau of Agricultural Economics. ②Bureau of American Ethnology. **B.A.E.** ①Bachelor of Aeronautical Engineering. ②Bachelor of Agricultural Engineering. ③Bachelor of Architectural Engineering. ④Bachelor of Art Education. ⑤Bachelor of Arts in Education. **B.A.Ed.** Bachelor of Arts in Education.

Bae·de·ker ['bedəkɚ; 'beidikə] *n.* ①貝的克(Kar Baedeker 德國人旅行指南創

始者)的旅行指南。②任何旅行指南。

baff [bæf; bæf] *v.i.* 〖高爾夫〗(擊球時以球桿之踵)擊地。—*n.*(使球高起的)刮地之一擊。

baf·fle** ['bæfḷ; 'bæfl] *v.*, **-fled, -fling,** *n.* —*v.t.* ①使困惑; 使迷惑。This puzzle *baffles* me. 這個謎把我困惑住了。②阻撓;妨礙。—*v.i.*徒勞。to *baffle* with the storm. 與暴風雨徒然搏鬥。 ***be baffled in 失敗。—*n.* ①障礙;困惑。②障板。③揚聲機之盒狀外殼。**—ment, baf·fler,** *n.*—**baf·fling,** *adj.*

baf·fle·board ['bæfḷ,bord; 'bæflbɔːd] *n.* ①證券交易所之行情板。②〖英〗滅音裝置。

baf·fle·plate ['bæfḷ,plet; 'bæflpleit] *n.* 障板。

baf·fle-wall ['bæfḷ,wɔl; 'bæflwɔːl] *n.* 隔音牆。

baffling wind 〖航海〗時常轉向的微風。

:**bag** [bæg; bæg] *n.*, *v.*, **bagged, bagging.** —*n.* ①袋。②一袋之量。③手提包;手提箱。I paid thirty dollars for this *bag.* 我以三十元買這隻手提包。④**a.**獵獲物。They made a good *bag.* 他們獵獲頗豐。**b.**裝獵獲物之袋子。⑤〖棒球〗壘。⑥(昆蟲體中之)囊。the honey *bag* of a bee. 蜜蜂之蜜囊。⑦(動物之)乳房。⑧汽船中裝瓦斯之袋。⑨〖俚〗貌醜而邋遢之女人。⑩〖美,俚〗少量海洛因。 ***bag and baggage*** 帶着全部財產;徹底地。I shall move *bag and baggage.* 我將帶着全部家當遷居。 ***give one the bag*** **a.** 解雇。**b.** 拒婚。 ***hold the bag*** 〖俗〗**a.** 剩下兩手空空。**b.** (被弄得)負起責任或受過。 ***in the bag*** 〖俗〗確實無疑;定能成功。 ***let the cat out of the bag*** 無意中洩露了祕密。—*v.t.* ①裝入袋中。*Bag* all the potatoes. 將所有馬鈴薯裝入袋中。②獵獲。③獲取;收集;捕捉;順手牽羊。Who has *bagged* my matches? 誰把我的火柴拿去了? —*v.i.* 膨脹; 如袋般鬆鬆垂下。

B. Ag. Bachelor of Agriculture.

ba·gasse [bə'gæs; bə'gæs] *n.* 蔗渣。

bag·a·telle [,bægə'tɛl; ,bægə'tel] *n.* ①瑣事。②一種彈子戲。③彈子。④短小的樂曲(尤指鋼琴曲)。

Bag·dad ['bægdæd; 'bægdæd] *n.* 巴格達(伊拉克的首都)。

B.Ag.E. Bachelor of Agricultural Engineering.

bag·ful ['bæg,ful; 'bægful] *n.*, *pl.* **-fuls.** ①一袋之量。②充裕。

***bag·gage** ['bægɪdʒ; 'bægidʒ] *n.* ①行李。I have not unpacked my *baggage* yet. 我尚未打開我的行李。②〖軍〗輜重。③〖俗〗年輕的女人。④(含輕視)醜而笨的老婦人。⑤妓女。⑥〖俗〗信仰、理論或特點等。

baggage allowance 行李重量限度。

baggage car 行李車。

baggage check 行李票;旅客行李上之標籤。

bag·gage·man ['bægɪdʒ,mæn; 'bægidʒmæn] *n.*, *pl.* **-men.** 脚夫。

bag·gage·mas·ter ['bægɪdʒ,mæstə; 'bægidʒ,mɑːstə] *n.* (尤指火車站之)行李管理人。

baggage office 行李房。

bag·gage-smash·er ['bægɪdʒ,smæʃə; 'bægidʒ,smæʃə] *n.* 〖美俚〗脚夫。

baggage train ①〖軍〗馱輜重的馬隊。②運行李之馬車、貨車隊。

bag·ger ['bægə; 'bægə] *n.* ①裝袋的人或物。②包裝機。

bag·ging ['bægɪŋ; 'bægiŋ] *n.* ①製袋之原料;袋布。②裝袋。

bag·gy ['bægɪ; 'bægi] *adj.*, **-gi·er, -gi·est.** ①膨脹的; 凸出的。②似袋子的; 鬆弛垂落的。—**bag·gi·ly,** *adv.*

bag·gys ['bægɪs; 'bægis] *n. pl.* 〖美〗寬鬆之短褲(如拳擊選手所穿者)。

bag·man ['bægmən; 'bægmən] *n.*, *pl.* **-men.** ①〖美俚〗替人收、送賄賂或保護費的歹徒。②〖主英〗旅行推銷員。

bagn·io ['bænjo; 'bɑːnjou] *n.*, *pl.* **-ios.** ①(土耳其或法國之) 監獄。②妓院。③(土耳其或義大利式之) 澡堂。

bag of bones 瘦骨嶙峋的人或動物。

bag·pipe ['bæg,paɪp; 'bægpaip] *n.*, *v.*, **-piped, -pip·ing.** —*n.* 蘇格蘭的風笛。—*v.i.* 吹風笛。—**bag·pip·er,** *n.*

bags [bægz; bægz] *n. pl.*〖英俚〗褲子。

B.Ag.Sc. Bachelor of Agricultural Science.

bag-sleeve ['bæg,sliv; 'bæg,sliːv] *n.* 〖英〗寬鬆之袖(袖口緊縮)。

ba·gui·o [bægɪo; bɑːgiː'ou] *n.*, *pl.* **-gui·os.** 熱帶性龍捲風 (尤指在非律賓的)。

Ba·gui·o ['bægɪo; 'bægiou] *n.* 碧瑤(非律賓之夏都)。

bag·wig ['bæg,wɪg; 'bæg,wig] *n.* 囊髮(囊裝之假髮)。

bag·wom·an ['bæg,wumən; 'bæg,wumən] *n.*, *pl.* **-wom·en.** 〖美俚〗替人傳遞賄賂或保護錢之女歹徒。

bag·worm ['bæg,wɜm; 'bægwəːm] *n.* 結草蟲。

bah [bɑ; bɑː] *interj.* 表示輕視或不耐煩的驚歎語。

Ba·ha·dur [bə'hɔdur; bə'hɑːdə] 〖印度〗 *n.* 閣下。

Ba·ha·ism [bə'hɑɪzṃ; bə'hɑːizm] *n.* 波斯泛神教之一派。

Ba·ha·mas [bə'hɑməz, bə'he–; bə'hɑː–məz] *n. pl.* ①巴哈馬羣島。②巴哈馬(西印度一國家,首都拿梭 Nassau).

Bah·rain [bɑ'ren; bɑː'rein] 巴林(波斯灣一國,首都 Manana).(亦作 **Bahrein**)

baht [bɑt; bɑːt] *n.*, *pl.* **bahts, baht.** 泰國貨幣單位。

bai [baɪ; bai] *n.* 黃霧。

bai·gnoire [,bɛ'nwar; 'beinwɑː] 〖法〗 *n.* 劇院之最下一層的包廂。

Bai·kal, Lake [baɪ'kɑl; bai'kɑːl] *n.* 貝加爾湖(在西伯利亞南境)。

bail[1] [bel; beil] *n.* ①保釋金。②保釋者。③保釋。④(貨物之) 委託。 ***admit to bail*** 准予保釋。 ***go*** (or ***stand***) ***bail for*** (***a person***) 做(某人)的保釋人。 ***jump bail*** 在保釋中逃亡。 ***out on bail*** 交保釋金獲得保釋。 ***surrender to one's bail*** 在保釋後出庭。—*v.t.* 保釋;准予交保。 ***bail*** (***a person***) ***out*** 保釋出(某人)。

bail[2] *v.t.* ①用桶汲(水)。②汲盡水〖out〗. —*v.i.* 汲水。 ***bail out*** **a.** 跳傘。**b.**〖俚〗幫助遇到緊急情況之人或公司(尤指財政上之困難)。**c.** 放棄(以逃避責任)。—*n.* ①杓;戽斗;桶。②外柵;外牆。③城寨外郭。④(廐的) 柵欄。⑤(曲棍球戲之)柱上橫木。

bail[3] *n.* ①壺或桶之半圓形把手。②半圓形的支撐物(如車篷、窗篷等)。

bail·a·ble ['beləbḷ; 'beiləbl] *adj.* 可交保的;可委託的。

bail bond 保釋書;保釋保證書。

bail·ee [bel'i; bei'liː] *n.* 受託人。

bail·er[1] ['belə; 'beilə] 戽斗;戽水者。

bail·er[2] *n.* 〖法律〗委託人。

bail·er[3] *n.* 〖板球〗擊中柱上橫木之球。

bai·ley ['belɪ; 'beili] *n.*, *pl.* **-leys.** ①外柵; (中古城堡之)外壁。②法庭; 監獄。 ***Old Bailey*** 倫敦中央刑事法庭。(亦作 **ballium**)

Bailey bridge 倍力橋(英國工程師 Sir Donald C. Bailey 所發明)。

bail·ie ['belɪ; 'beili] *n.* 蘇格蘭之市政官員。

bail·iff ['belɪf; 'beilif] *n.* ①州官的助手;

B

郡執行官的副手。②法庭的監守官。③管理或監督財產者。④(英國之)區鎮的地方長官。

bail·i·wick ['belə,wɪk; 'beiliwik] *n.* ① bailiff 之轄區。②個人之技能領域或興趣範圍;權力範圍;活動範圍。

bail·ment ['belmənt; 'beilmənt] *n.* 〖法律〗①委託;寄託。②保釋。

B

bail·or [,bel'ɔr; 'beilə] *n.* 〖法律〗委託人。

bail·out, bail-out ['bel,aut; 'beil,aut] *n.* ①跳傘。②以優先股發給股東作爲紅利之行爲。③緊急援助(尤指以金錢救人之急)。—*adj.* 挽救行動的。

bails·man ['belzmən; 'beilzmən] *n.*, *pl.* **-men.** 〖法律〗擔保人;保釋保證人。

Baird [berd; bɛəd] *n.* 拜爾德(John Logie, 1888–1946, 蘇格蘭發明家, 有"電視之父"之稱)。

bairn [bɛrn; bɛən] *n.* 〖蘇〗小孩。

*__bait__ [bet; beit] *n.* ①餌。Most people use worms as *bait* in fishing. 多數人釣魚時用蟲爲魚餌。②任何誘惑物。③馬料;芻秣。④小憩。Let us take a *bait.* 讓我們休息一些時候。⑤食物。—*v.t.* ①裝餌在(鈎上或阱中)。②於旅程中停下來餵(馬等)。③迫之使怒;縱犬迫獸(以取樂爲目的)。He let his dogs *bait* the bear. 他縱犬逗熊。④引誘;誘惑。⑤進擊;蹂躪。⑥(以言語)折磨。⑦逗;戲弄。—*v.i.* 〖英〗在旅程中休息。

bait advertising 〖美俗〗廉售某種不打算出賣的貨品,用意在誘人購買昂貴的物品。

bait-and-switch ['betən'swɪtʃ; 'beitən'switʃ] *adj.*〖美〗以廣告上的廉價品引誘顧客買更貴物品之作風的。

baize [bez; beiz] *n.* (做窗簾或桌布用的)厚羊毛氈。

Baj·er ['baɪɚ; 'baiə] *n.* 拜爾(Fredrik, 1837–1922, 丹麥政治家及作家, 1908年獲諾貝爾和平獎)。

B.A.Jour. Bachelor of Arts in Journalism.

‡**bake** [bek; beik] *v.*, **baked, bak·ing,** *n.* —*v.t.* ①烘;焙。The cook *bakes* bread and cake in the oven. 廚子用烤箱烘麪包和餅。②烘乾使硬。Bricks are *baked* in a kiln. 磚是在窯中燒成的。③曬之使乾;曬之使焦。—*v.i.* 焙。Biscuits *bake* quickly. 餅乾烘得很快。—*n.* ①烘;焙。②供餐的集會。

bake·house ['bek,haus; 'beikhaus] *n.* 烘製麪包之場所;麪包店。

Ba·ke·lite ['bekə,laɪt; 'beikəlait] *n.* 〖商標名〗膠木;電木。

bake-off ['bek,ɔf; 'beik,ɔ:f] *n.* 烘焙比賽(尤指業餘性的)。

*__bak·er__ ['bekɚ; 'beikə] *n.* ①製或賣麪包糕點等的人。②小型輕便的爐子。

bak·er-kneed ['bekɚ,nid; 'beikəni:d] *adj.* 兩膝內曲的。(亦作 **baker-legged**)

baker's dozen 十三個。

bak·er·y ['bekərɪ; 'beikəri] *n.*, *pl.* **-er·ies.** 麪包店。(亦作 **bakeshop**)

*__bak·ing__ ['bekɪŋ; 'beikiŋ] *n.* ①焙;烘。②烘乾;焙硬。③一次所烘焙之量。—*adj.* ①烘焙用的。②〖俗〗灼熱的。The weather was simply *baking.* 天氣熱得炙人。—*adv.* 灼熱地。*baking* hot. 極熱。

baking powder 醱粉。

baking sheet 烤餅所用之長方形平底鍋。

baking soda 碳酸氫鈉;發酵粉。

bak·sheesh ['bækʃiʃ; 'bækʃi:ʃ] *n.* (土耳其、埃及、印度等地之) 酒錢、小費。—*v.i.* & *v.t.* 給小費。(亦作 **backsheesh, bakshish, backshish**)

Ba·ku [bɑ'ku; bɑ:'ku:] *n.* 巴庫(蘇聯亞塞拜然共和國之首都)。

bal. balance.

Ba·laam ['beləm; 'beilæm] *n.* ①〖聖經〗巴蘭(Mesopotamia 之一先知)。②(b-)(報紙等之)補白資料。

bal·a·lai·ka [,bælə'laɪkə; ,bælə'laikə] *n.* 俄式三弦琴。

‡**bal·ance** ['bæləns; 'bæləns] *n.*, *v.*, **-anced, -anc·ing.** —*n.* ①天平; 秤。②平衡;均勢。He lost his *balance.* 他失去身體的平衡(他跌倒)。③精神上的平衡; 心志的健全。His mind has retained its *balance.* 他的精神保持常態。④(收支等的)差額。⑤〖俗〗餘數;餘額。I have still a *balance* in the bank. 我還有餘款存在銀行。⑥〖體育〗平衡運動;均衡運動。⑦〖天文〗(B-)天平座;天平宮。⑧決定性的力量。⑨絕大部分。The *balance* of the blame is on your side. 絕大部分的過失在你這一邊。⑩〖美術〗色彩、布局之調和。***balance in hand*** 餘款。***balance of payments*** 國際收支。***balance of power*** 均勢。***balance of trade*** 貿易的差額。***hold the balance*** 有決定之權。***in the balance*** 緊要關頭;危險的。***strike a balance*** 結算帳目。—*v.t.* ①以天平稱。②權衡(利害得失等)。We must *balance* the good and evil of things. 我們應當權衡事物的善與惡。③使之平衡。He *balanced* a book on his head. 他使一本書在他的頭上保持平衡。④相抵。The ups and downs of our life *balance* each other. 我們生命中的升沉起伏互相抵銷。⑤結帳。to *balance* an account. 結帳。—*v.i.* ①平衡;平準;相稱。②猶疑不決。

bal·ance·a·ble ['bælənsəbḷ; 'bælənsəbl] *adj.* 平衡的。

bal·anced ['bælənst; 'bælənst] *adj.* ①安定的。②和諧的;有條不紊的。

balanced diet 含有維持健康所需各種營養的食物。

balanced sentence 〖文法〗平衡句(由兩個平行子句構成的句子, 如: The winds blew and the rains came).

balance due 不足額。***balance due from*** 人欠。***balance due to*** 欠人。

balance on hand 庫存餘數。

bal·anc·er ['bælənsɚ; 'bælənsə] *n.* ①平衡之人或物。②走繩索者。③(蚊蠅等之)平衡器官。

balance sheet 資產負債表。

balance wheel (鐘錶等之) 平衡輪;輪擺。

bal·a·noid ['bælənɔɪd; 'bælənɔid] *adj.* 橡實形的。

bal·as ['bæləs; 'bæləs] *n.* 紅玉。(亦作 **balas ruby**)

bal·a·ta [bə'lɑtə; bə'lɑ:tə] *n.* ①(西印度產之)橡皮樹。②橡膠。

bal·bo·a [bɑl'boɑ; bɑ:l'bouɑ:] *n.* 巴拿馬之一種銀幣。

bal·brig·gan [bæl'brɪgən; bæl'brigən] *n.* ①棉織物。②(毛質之)仿棉織物。③(*pl.*) 上述織物製成之衣物。—*adj.* balbriggan 製成的。

Balch [bɔltʃ; bɔ:ltʃ] *n.* 包爾奇(Emily Greene, 1867–1961, 美國經濟及社會學家, 1946年獲諾貝爾和平獎)。

bal·co·nied ['bælkənɪd; 'bælkənid] *adj.* 有露臺的;有陽臺的。

*__bal·co·ny__ ['bælkənɪ; 'bælkəni] *n.*, *pl.* **-nies.** ①陽臺;騎樓。②戲院裏的包廂。

balcony scene ①莎士比亞劇 *Romeo and Juliet* 中陽臺談情之場面。②任何類似的戀愛場面。***do*** (***play,*** or ***put on***) ***a bal-***

cony scene〖俗〗將自己對異性之愛慕戲劇化。

***bald** 〔bɔld; bɔːld〕 *adj.* ①禿頭的。②無天然掩蔽的;光禿的。a *bald* hill. 無草木的山。③無掩飾的; 明白的。The *bald* truth is that he is a thief. 據實說,他是一個賊。④〖動物〗頭頂有白色的。—**ish,** *adj.* —**ly,** *adv.* —**ness,** *n.*

bal·da·chin 〔ˈbældəkɪn; ˈbɔːldəkin〕 *n.* ①一種織錦。②(用織錦等製成之)天蓋;廟蓋。③神龕;佛堂。(亦作 **baldaquin**)

bald coot 大鷭;骨頂鳥。

bald eagle 白頭鷹。

bal·der·dash 〔ˈbɔldɚ͵dæʃ; ˈbɔːldədæʃ〕 *n.* 胡言亂語;無意義的話。

bald·faced 〔ˈbɔld͵fest; ˈbɔːldfeist〕 *adj.* ①臉上有白斑的。②無掩飾的。

bald·head 〔ˈbɔld͵hɛd; ˈbɔːldhed〕 *n.* ①禿頭之人。②頭頂有白毛之鳥或獸。

bald·head·ed 〔ˈbɔldˈhɛdɪd; ˈbɔːldˈhedid〕 *adj.*禿頭的。—*adv.* 毫無約束地。

bal·di·coot 〔ˈbɔldɪ͵kut; ˈbɔːldikuːt〕 *n.* ①禿頭之人;和尚。②黑鴨;骨頂鳥。

bald·pate 〔ˈbɔld͵pet; ˈbɔːldpeit〕 *n.* ①禿頭之人。②赤頸鳧。—*adj.*禿頭的。

bal·dric 〔ˈbɔldrɪk; ˈbɔːldrik〕 *n.* (掛劍、號角等之)胸綬;佩帶。

***bale**[1] 〔bel; beil〕 *n., v.,* **baled, bal·ing.** —*n.* ①(貨物的)包; 綑。a *bale* of cotton. 一包棉花。②(*pl.*) 貨物。③一羣龜。—*v.t.* 將…打包。—**less,** *adj.*

bale[2] *n.* 〖詩〗①罪惡;災害。②憂愁;痛苦。

bale[3] *v.t.,* **baled, bal·ing.** 用桶汲水。

ba·leen 〔bəˈlin; bəˈliːn, bæ-〕 *n.* 鯨鬚。

bale·fire 〔ˈbel͵faɪr; ˈbeilfaiə〕 *n.* ①(在空曠地方之)大火。②烽火。③焚屍火。

bale·ful 〔ˈbelfəl; ˈbeilful〕 *adj.* 惡的;有害的。—**ly,** *adv.* —**ness,** *n.*

bale-hook 〔ˈbel͵hʊk; ˈbeilhuk〕 *n.* 碼頭工人搬運貨物所用之鉤。

Ba·li·nese 〔͵bɑləˈniz; ͵bɑːliˈniːz〕 *n., pl.* **-nese,** *adj.*—*n.*巴里島人(語)。—*adj.*巴里島的。

balk 〔bɔk; bɔːk, bɔːlk〕 *v.i.* ①停止;中止;拒絕繼續。②(馬)停蹄不前。③〖棒球〗做投球的假動作。—*v.t.* ①阻止;妨礙。②錯過;失掉(機會)。—*n.* ①障礙。②錯誤;失敗。③橫樑;大樑。④〖棒球〗投手假裝投球的犯規動作。⑤彈子(撞球)桌上開始打球的部分。⑥兩田畦間未犂之地。(亦作 **baulk**)

Bal·kan 〔ˈbɔlkən; ˈbɔːlkən, ˈbɔl-〕 *adj.* ①巴爾幹半島的; 巴爾幹各國的。②巴爾幹諸國人民的。③巴爾幹山脈的。 ***the Balkans*** 巴爾幹各國。

Balkan frame 巴爾幹架 (固定在病床上以懸掛上過夾板或石膏的斷肢用者)。

Bal·kan·ize, bal·kan·ize 〔ˈbɔlkən͵aɪz; ˈbɔːlkənaiz〕 *v.t. & v.i.,* **-ized, -iz·ing.** (使)分裂爲互相仇視之若干小政治單位; (使)割據。

Balkan Peninsula 巴爾幹半島(在歐洲東南部)。

Balkan States 巴爾幹各國。

balk·line 〔ˈbɔk͵laɪn; ˈbɔːklain〕 *n.* 〖體育〗田徑賽中的起跑線。(亦作 **balk line**)

balk·y 〔ˈbɔkɪ; ˈbɔːki〕 *adj.,* **balk·i·er, balk·i·est.** 〖美〗忽然停止不前進的;倔强的。

‡**ball**[1] 〔bɔl; bɔːl〕 *n.* ①球; 球狀物。The threads are wound into a *ball.* 纔線成球。②遊戲用的球。 He kicked the *ball* away. 他踢開球。③子彈。Extract the *ball* from your pistol. 退出你手槍裏的子彈。④地球。⑤球戲。⑥〖棒球〗壞球。⑦人體中類似球的部分。***carry the ball*** 負起主要責任。***have a lot*** (or ***something***) ***on the ball*** 擅長;有能力。***keep the ball rolling*** 使持續不懈。***on the ball*** **a.** 提高警覺。**b.** 幹練;效率高。***play ball*** **a.** 開始比賽;恢復比賽。 **b.** 開始某行爲。 **c.** 合作。***start the ball rolling*** 開始進行某種工作。—*v.t.* 製成球。—*v.i.* 成球狀。***ball the jack*** **a.** 快速地行動。 **b.** 孤注一擲。***ball up*** 擾亂; 惶惑。

***ball**[2] *n.* 跳舞會。How did you enjoy the *ball?* 你在這舞會上玩得很快樂嗎? —*v.i.* 〖美俚〗狂歡一番。

***bal·lad** 〔ˈbæləd; ˈbæləd〕 *n.* ①民歌;歌謠。②通俗敍事詩歌。③民歌音樂。—*v.i.* 寫或作民歌音樂。

bal·lade 〔bəˈlɑd, bæˈlɑd; bæˈlɑːd〕 *n.* ①三節聯韻詩。②〖音樂〗敍事曲。

bal·lad·eer 〔͵bæləˈdɪr; ͵bæləˈdiə〕 *n.* 民謠歌手。(亦作 **balladier**)

bal·lad·ist 〔ˈbælədɪst; ˈbælədist〕 *n.* ballad 的作者;唱 ballad 的人。

bal·lad·ize 〔ˈbæləd͵aɪz; ˈbælədaiz〕 *v.,* **-ized, -iz·ing.** —*v.t.* 將(某事)編成 ballad. —*v.i.* 作 ballad 詞或曲。

bal·lad·mon·ger 〔ˈbæləd͵mʌŋgɚ; ˈbæləd͵mʌŋgə〕 *n.* ①民謠之販售者 (尤指沿街叫賣者)。②劣等詩人;打油詩作者。

bal·lad·ry 〔ˈbælədrɪ; ˈbælədri〕 *n.* ①民歌;民謠(集合稱)。②民謠編造術。

ball and chain ①繫在囚犯脚部之鐵球與鐵鏈,以防其逃走。②沉重的約束。③〖俚〗黃臉婆;妻。

ball-and-sock·et joint 〔ˈbɔlənˈsɑkɪt~; ˈbɔːlənˈsɔkit~〕 杵臼關節。

bal·last 〔ˈbæləst; ˈbæləst〕 *n.*①壓艙物。②穩定氣球、飛船或飛機的沙袋。③任何使精神、道德、政治等穩定的東西。④鐵路或道路的道床。—*v.t.* ①供以壓艙物。②使穩定; 使鎮靜。③鋪沙石(於道床)。

bal·last·ing 〔ˈbæləstɪŋ; ˈbæləstiŋ〕 *n.* ①壓艙;加沙袋等(使穩定)。②壓艙物;作穩定用的沙袋等。

ballast line 船祇載壓艙物時之吃水線。

ballast tube 內裝氫氣使電流穩定之眞空管。

ball bearing 球軸承。

ball club ①職業球隊 (尤指棒球)。②支持棒球隊之團體或類似的組織。

ball cock (抽水馬桶等中之)浮球活栓。

bal·le·ri·na 〔͵bæləˈrinə; ͵bæləˈriːnə〕 *n., pl.* **-nas.** ①芭蕾舞女主角。②芭蕾舞女。

bal·let 〔ˈbælɪ, bæˈle; ˈbælei, -li〕 *n., pl.* **-lets.** ①芭蕾舞。②芭蕾舞團。③芭蕾舞曲。—**ic,** *adj.* —**i·cal·ly,** *adv.*

ballet dancer 跳芭蕾舞者;芭蕾舞家。

bal·let·o·mane 〔bəˈlɛtə͵men; bəˈletəmein〕*n.*芭蕾舞迷。—**bal·let·o·ma·ni·a,** *n.*

ball-flow·er 〔ˈbɔl͵flauɚ; ˈbɔːl͵flauə〕 *n.*〖建築〗球心花飾(花瓣中置球之模型);花球。

bal·lis·ta 〔bəˈlɪstə; bəˈlistə〕 *n., pl.*-**tae** 〔-ti; -tiː〕.(古代用以發射石塊之)弩砲。

bal·lis·tic 〔bæˈlɪstɪk; bəˈlistik〕 *adj.* ①彈道學的;彈道的。②發射物之運動及力量的。

ballistic missile 彈道飛彈。

bal·lis·tics 〔bæˈlɪstɪks; bəˈlistiks〕 *n.* (常作 *sing.* 解)彈道學。

bal·lon d'es·sai 〔bɑ͵lɔ̃dɛˈsɛ; ˈbælɔ̃ːŋdeˈse〕 〖法〗①試放之氣球。②用以試探輿情之聲明。

bal·lo·net 〔͵bæləˈnɛt; ͵bæləˈnet〕 *n.* (飛艇)輔助氣囊。

***bal·loon** 〔bə'lun; bə'lu:n〕 *n.* ①氣球；輕氣球；飛船。②(卡通、圖畫等) 氣球狀之圈(裏面寫有卡通人物的對白)。—*v.i.* ①乘輕氣球。②膨脹若氣球。③迅速增加。Membership has *ballooned* beyond all expectations. 會員的增加遠較預期爲速。—*v.t.* 充氣使如氣球。—*adj.*膨脹若氣球的。**—ist,** *n.*

bal·loon·er 〔bə'lunə; bə'lu:nə〕 *n.* 乘氣球者。

bal·loon·fish 〔bə'lunˌfɪʃ; bə'lu:nfiʃ〕 *n.* 河豚。

bal·lot** 〔'bælət; 'bælət〕 *n., v.,* **-lot·ed, -lot·ing.** —*n.* ①選擧票。I cast one *ballot* for him. 我投他一票。②投票總數。There was a large *ballot*. 票數很多。③祕密投票的選擧。④投票。⑤投票權。⑥抽籤的方法。take a ballot*** 由投票決之。—*v.i.* ①投票。I *balloted* for him. 我投他的票。②抽籤。—*v.t.* ①向…拉票。②投票〖on, for〗。③以抽籤決定(如服兵役等)。

bal·lot·age 〔'bælətɪdʒ; 'bælətidʒ〕 〖法〗*n.* 決選投票。

ball park 棒球場。***in the ball park*** 大約。

ball pen 原子筆。(亦作 **ball-point pen, ballpoint pen**)

ball·play·er 〔'bɔlˌpleə; 'bɔ:lˌpleiə〕 *n.* 球員；棒球員。

ball·proof 〔'bɔl'pruf; 'bɔ:lpru:f〕 *adj.* 防彈的。

ball·room 〔'bɔlˌrum; 'bɔ:lru:m〕 *n.* 大舞廳。

ballroom dancing 交際舞。

bal·ly 〔'bælɪ; 'bæli〕 *adj. & adv.* 〖英俚〗甚；很；極；太過的(地)；異常的(地)(詼諧或强意用語 bloody 的委婉說法)。

bal·ly·hoo 〔'bælɪˌhu; 'bælihu:〕 *n., pl.* **-hoos,** *v.,* **-hooed, -hoo·ing.**—*n.*〖俗〗①大吹大擂；大肆宣傳。②喧嚷；叫喊。—*v.t. & v.i.* 〖俗〗大吹大擂；大肆宣傳。

bal·ly·rag 〔'bælɪˌræg; 'bæliræg〕 *v.t.* ＝**bullyrag.**

balm 〔bam; ba:m〕 *n.*①用以止痛的香膏。②任何止痛的東西；安慰；慰藉。③香脂；香油。④香味。⑤薄荷一類有香味的植物。

Bal·mor·al 〔bæl'mɔrəl; bæl'mɔrəl〕 *n.* ①一種厚毛呢襯裙。②襯裙毛料。③(b-) 一種有帶之鞋。④蘇格蘭之一種無邊的圓形帽。

balm·y 〔'bamɪ; 'ba:mi〕 *adj.,* **balm·i·er, balm·i·est.** ①溫和的；柔軟的；安慰的。②芳香的。③〖俚〗愚蠢的；古怪的。 **—balm·i·ly,** *adv.* **—balm·i·ness,** *n.*

bal·ne·ol·o·gy 〔ˌbælnɪ'alədʒɪ; ˌbælni'ɔlədʒi〕 *n.*浴學；浴療學。

bal·ne·o·ther·a·py 〔ˌbælnɪo'θɛrəpɪ; ˌbælniou'θerəpi〕 *n.* 浴療法。

ba·lo·ney 〔bə'lonɪ; bə'louni〕 *n.* ①燻製臘腸。②〖俚〗胡言；荒謬。—*interj.* 胡說！

bal·sa 〔'bɔlsə; 'bɔ:lsə〕 *n.* ①(美洲產之)一種輕質木材。②(上述木材製之)筏。

bal·sam 〔'bɔlsəm; 'bɔ:lsəm〕 *n.* ①植物的香膠或香脂。②香油。③任何做醫療或慰藉的東西。④產香膠的樹。⑤鳳仙花屬之植物。⑥〖美〗一種樅樹。—*v.t.* ①以香脂塗之。②安慰；使鎮定。**—ic,** *adj.*

bal·sam·if·er·ous 〔ˌbɔlsə'mɪfərəs; ˌbɔ:lsə'mifərəs〕 *adj.* 出香液的；生香油的。

bal·sam·ine 〔'bɔlsəmɪn; 'bɔ:lsəmin〕 *n.* 〖植物〗鳳仙花。

Bal·tic 〔'bɔltɪk; 'bɔ:ltik〕 *adj.* 波羅的海(諸國)的。—*n.* 波羅的海地區之語言。

Bal·ti·more 〔'bɔltəˌmor; 'bɔ:ltimɔ:〕 *n.* 巴的摩爾 (美國馬里蘭州一海口)。

bal·us·ter 〔'bæləstə; 'bæləstə〕 *n.* ①欄杆的支柱。②(*pl.*)欄杆。

bal·us·trade 〔ˌbælə'stred; ˌbæləs'treid〕 *n.* 欄杆。

Bal·zac 〔'bælzæk; 'bælzæk〕 *n.* 巴爾札克 (Honoré de, 1799–1850, 法國小說家)。

bam 〔bæm; bæm〕 *v.,* **bammed, bam·ming,** *n., interj.* —*v.t.*〖俚〗欺騙。—*n.*〖俚〗欺騙。—*interj.* 砰然之聲。

bam·bi·no 〔bæm'bino; bæm'bi:nou〕 *n., pl.* **-ni** 〔-ni; -ni:〕.〖義〗①小孩；嬰兒。②基督幼時之像。

bam·boo** 〔bæm'bu; bæm'bu:〕 *n., pl.* **-boos,** *adj.* —*n.* 竹。Many useful things can be made from *bamboos*. 許多有用的東西可用竹製。—*adj.* 竹的；竹製的。bamboo shoots*** 竹筍。

Bamboo Curtain 竹幕(指共黨統治下之中國大陸)。

bam·boo·zle 〔bæm'buzl; bæm'bu:zl〕 *v.,* **-zled, -zling.** —*v.t.* 〖俗〗①欺騙；哄。②使迷惑；使爲難。 —*v.i.* 〖俗〗欺騙；愚弄。**—ment,** *n.*

ban 〔bæn; bæn〕 *v.,* **banned, ban·ning,** *n.* —*v.t.* ①禁止。②咒詛。—*n.*①禁令；法律。②逐出教會。③〖法律〗判決不受法律保護。④公告；布告。⑤(*pl.*) ＝**banns.** ⑥封建君主之爲戰爭而召喚其諸侯。⑦被封建君主所召喚之諸侯。

ba·nal 〔'benl; 'beinl〕 *adj.* 平凡的；陳腐的；瑣屑的。**—ly,** *adv.* **—i·ty,** *n.*

***ba·nan·a** 〔bə'nænə; bə'na:nə〕 *n.* ①香蕉。I like *banana* better than orange. 我喜歡香蕉勝於橘子。②香蕉樹。③〖美俚〗與白人同事或傾向於白人的東方人(外黃內白)；二毛子。

banana oil ①香蕉油。②〖美俚〗油腔滑調。

ba·nan·as 〔bə'nænəz; bə'na:nəz〕 *adj.* 僅見於下列成語中的習慣用法。***go bananas*** 〖美俚〗發狂的。

banana split 香蕉船(以香蕉墊底上覆冰淇淋等之甜點)。

Ba·na·ras 〔bə'narəs; bə'na:rəs〕 *n.* 巴那拉斯(印度北部之一城市，爲印度教之聖地)。

banc 〔bæŋk; bæŋk〕 *n.* 審判官席。***in banc*** (or ***banco***) 法官全體或達法定人數的審判。

‡band¹ 〔bænd; bænd〕 *n.* ①一羣人或動物；隊。a *band* of robbers. 一夥強盜。②樂隊。③帶；條紋。I want some rubber *bands*. 我要些橡皮筋。④波段；波帶(指無線電廣播周率中某一特定之範圍)。⑤〖解剖〗環；帶。***beat the band*** 精力充沛地；豐富地。It rained all day to *beat the band*. 下了一整天的大雨。—*v.t.* ①聯合；結合。②用帶結之。She *banded* her hat with a silk strip. 她用絲帶結帽。③以帶或條紋爲記。—*v.i.* 聯合；結合。

‡band² *n.* ①(常 *pl.*) 束縛人或其手足之任何物；械具；手銬；脚鐐。②義務；束縛。the nuptial *bands*. 婚約。

***band·age** 〔'bændɪdʒ; 'bændidʒ〕 *n., v.,* **-aged, -ag·ing.** —*n.* 繃帶。The doctor puts a *bandage* over my left eye. 醫生用繃帶縛在我的左眼上。—*v.t. & v.i.*縛以繃帶。

ban·dan·(n)a 〔bæn'dænə; bæn'dænə〕 *n.* (有色印花之)大手帕；大領巾或頭巾。

band·box 〔'bændˌbaks; 'bændbɔks〕 *n.* (裝帽子或衣領等之) 薄板箱或盒。

ban·deau 〔bæn'do; 'bændou〕 *n., pl.* **-deaux, -deaus** 〔-doz; -douz〕. ①細帶；束髮帶。②窄奶罩。

ban·de·role, ban·de·rol 〔'bændəˌrol; 'bændəroul〕 *n.* ①小旗；飄帶。②槍旗；葬旗；墓旗。(亦作 **bannerol**)

ban·di·coot 〔'bændɪˌkut; 'bændiku:t〕 *n.* ①(印度、錫蘭之) 大鼠。②(澳洲之)袋鼠。

*__ban·dit__ [ˈbændɪt; ˈbændit] *n., pl.* __-dits, ban·dit·ti__ [bænˈdɪtɪ; bænˈditi]. ①强盜；土匪。The town is infested with *bandits.* 這鎭爲土匪所擾害。②〖美空軍，俚〗敵機。—__ry,__ *n.*
__band·lead·er__ [ˈbænd͵lidɚ; ˈbænd͵liːdə] *n.* 領隊(尤指跳舞樂隊之領隊)。
__band·mas·ter__ [ˈbænd͵mæstɚ; ˈbænd͵mɑːstə] *n.* 樂隊隊長(指揮)。
__ban·dog__ [ˈbæn͵dɔg; ˈbændɔg] *n.* 猛犬；門犬。
__ban·do·leer, ban·do·lier__ [͵bændəˈlɪr; ͵bændəˈliə] *n.* 子彈帶。
__ban·do·line__ [ˈbændə͵lin; ˈbændouliːn] *n.* (固定髮型用的)膠水。
__band-pass filter__ 〖電〗帶通濾波器。
__bands__ [bændz; bændz] *n. pl.* 牧師、法官或博士服之領飾(有兩條寬帶垂落胸前)；此衣領之寬帶。(亦作 __neck bands__)
__band saw__ 帶鋸。
__bands·man__ [ˈbændzmən; ˈbændzmən] *n., pl.* __-men.__ 樂隊隊員。
__band spectrum__ 〖物理〗帶(光)譜。
__band·stand__ [ˈbænd͵stænd; ˈbændstænd] *n.* 音樂臺。
__Ban·dung__ [ˈbɑnduŋ; ˈbɑːnduŋ] *n.* 萬隆(印尼爪哇西部之一城市)。(亦作 __Bandoeng__)
__band·wag·on__ [ˈbænd͵wægən; ˈbænd͵wægən] *n.* (遊行等之)樂隊花車。***be* (*climb,* or *jump*) *on* (or *aboard*) *the bandwagon*** 〖俗〗轉向支持或贊助有勝利把握的候選人或運動。***on the bandwagon*** 〖俗〗立於獲勝或得勢之一方。
__ban·dy__ [ˈbændɪ; ˈbændi] *v.,* __-died, -dy·ing,__ *adj., n., pl.* __-dies.__ —*v.t.* 往復投擲；交換；傳布。—*adj.* 向外彎曲的(如腿)。—*n.* ①老式網球(戲)。②〖主英〗一種曲棍球或其球棒。
__ban·dy-leg·ged__ [ˈbændɪˈlɛgɪd, -ˈlɛgd; ˈbændilegd] *adj.* 膝內翻的。
__bane__ [ben; bein] *n.* ①致命的事物；導致毀滅的人或東西。②毒藥(用於複合詞，如 rat's-bane)。③毀滅；死亡。
__bane·ful__ [ˈbenfəl; ˈbeinful] *adj.* 致命的；有害的；有毒的。—__ly,__ *adv.* —__ness,__ *n.*
__bane·ber·ry__ [ˈben͵bɛrɪ; ˈbeinbəri] *n., pl.* __-ries.__ 〖植物〗①產有毒漿果之植物。②有毒漿果。
*__bang__[1] [bæŋ; bæŋ] *n.* ①重擊；重打；砰然重擊。②突然的巨響；轟聲。The servant shut the door with a *bang.* 僕人砰然關上門。③活力；衝力。The *bang* has gone out of my work. 我幹得已經沒有勁了。④〖俚〗樂趣；享受；刺激。⑤〖俚，鄙〗性交。***in a bang*** 趕緊；急忙。—*v.t.* ①重擊；重擊作聲。He *banged* his fist on the table. 他以拳重擊桌子。②砰然關上。He *banged* the lid of the box down. 他將箱蓋砰然關上。③〖俚，鄙〗與(女人)性交。—*v.i.* ①發巨響。The gun *banged.* 鎗發出巨響。②重擊。③〖俚，鄙〗性交。***bang* (*oneself*) *against*** 砰然撞上。***bang* (*sense*) *into one*** 把(道理)灌注給某人。***bang off*** 轟然開砲。—*adv.* ①砰然地；突然巨響地。②猛烈砰然地。③直接地；規矩地。—*interj.* 砰；轟隆一聲。"*Bang! Bang!*" shouted the boys. "砰！砰！" 孩子們喊道。
__bang__[2] *n.* (常 *pl.*) 垂前髮；劉海。—*v.t.* ①剪(髮)成劉海。②剪短(馬尾等)。
__ban·ga·lore torpedo__ [͵bæŋgəˈlor～; ͵bæŋgəˈlɔː～] 破壞筒(內裝炸藥用於爆破)。
__Bang·kok__ [ˈbæŋkɑk; ˈbæŋkɔk] *n.* 曼谷(泰國的首都)。
__Ban·gla·desh__ [ˈbæŋglə͵dɛʃ; ˈbæŋglədeʃ] *n.* 孟加拉共和國(原爲東巴基斯坦，於1971年獨立，首都達卡 Dacca)。
__ban·gle__ [ˈbæŋgl; ˈbæŋgl] *n.* ①手(脚)鐲。②環飾。
__bang on__ 〖英，俚〗好；要得。
__bang-up__ [ˈbæŋ͵ʌp; ˈbæŋ͵ʌp] *adj.* 〖俚〗上等的；最好的；一流的。
__ban·ian__ [ˈbænjən; ˈbæniən] *n.* ①印度人所着寬大的襯衫、短衫或外衣。②(不吃肉階級的)印度商人(亦作 __banya, bania__)。③榕樹。
__banian days__ 不吃肉的日子。
*__ban·ish__ [ˈbænɪʃ; ˈbæniʃ] *v.t.* ①驅逐出境；放逐。He was *banished* from Canada. 他被逐出加拿大國境。②擯棄；忘却。—__ment,__ *n.*
__ban·is·ter__ [ˈbænɪstɚ; ˈbænistə] *n.* 欄干。(亦作 __bannister__)
__ban·jo__ [ˈbændʒo; ˈbændʒou] *n., pl.* __-joes__ or __-jos,__ *adj., v.* —*n.* 班究琴；五絃琴。—*adj.* 形似五絃琴的。—*v.i.* 彈五絃琴。—__ist,__ *n.*
‡__bank__[1] [bæŋk; bæŋk] *n.* ①一長堆；堆。a *bank* of clouds. 一堆雲。②岸；堤。③淺灘；沙洲。④飛機轉彎時的傾斜。right *bank.* 右傾斜。⑤礦口周圍之地面。⑥路床之傾斜(度)。⑦撞球臺四周高起之邊。—*v.t.* ①圍以堤；築堤岸於。to *bank* up a river. 築堤於河岸。②堆起；堆積。③使(飛機)傾斜轉彎。④以灰覆火上使其慢慢焚燒。Please *bank* up the fire. 請把火養在灰裏。⑤將路床傾斜。—*v.i.* ①成堆狀；堆積。②傾斜。③(飛機)傾斜轉彎。***bank up*** 〖英〗堆積。
‡__bank__[2] *n.* ①銀行。I know he has a large deposit in the *bank.* 我知道他在銀行中有一大筆存款。②莊家的賭本。to break the *bank.* 將莊家的錢贏光。③倉庫；血庫。④撲滿。⑤(紙牌戲等)遊戲者可抽之牌堆。⑥兌換貨幣人之台子。—*v.i.* ①經營銀行業；與銀行來往。②存款於銀行。Where do you *bank?* 你在何處存款？③〖賭博〗做莊(＝to hold the bank)。—*v.t.* 存(款)於銀行。Smith *banked* __$1,000__ at the Central Bank. 史密斯在中央銀行存款一千元。***bank on*** (or ***upon***) 依賴。
__bank__[3] *n.* ①一排東西。②鍵盤。③ galley 船上槳手坐的長凳。④上述船凳上的槳手。⑤報紙標題之一行。—*v.t.* 排成一序列。
__bank·a·ble__ [ˈbæŋkəbl; ˈbæŋkəbl] *adj.* 可存於銀行的；銀行肯收的。
__bank__ (or __banker's__) __accept·ance__ 由銀行背書(向該行提款)的匯票或支票。
__bank account__ 銀行往來帳；銀行存款(英國稱 banking account)。
__bank annuity__ (or __annuities__) 〖英〗政府公債。
__bank balance__ ①存款人在銀行的存款。②〖財務〗銀行在票據交換所的存款。
__bank bill__ ①〖英〗銀行匯票。②〖美〗紙幣；鈔票。
__bank·book__ [ˈbæŋk͵bʊk; ˈbæŋkbuk] *n.* 銀行存摺。
__bank card__ 銀行發行的信用卡。
__bank deposit__ 銀行存款。
__bank discount__ 銀行貼現。
__bank draft__ 銀行匯票。
*__bank·er__[1] [ˈbæŋkɚ; ˈbæŋkə] *n.* ①銀行家。Smith is going to marry his daughter to a *banker.* 史密斯將把他的女兒嫁給一銀行家。②(賭博的)莊家；(賭博中抽頭的)頭家。
__bank·er__[2] *n.* ①鱈魚船。②〖英方〗掘溝者。
__bank·er__[3] *n.* (石匠、雕塑家等之)工作台。
*__bank·ing__ [ˈbæŋkɪŋ; ˈbæŋkiŋ] *n.* ①銀行業；銀行事務；銀行學。②築堤；堤防。③(紐芬蘭的)近海漁業。

banking house 銀行。
banking power 貸出之能力。
bank loan 銀行借款。
bank money 銀行匯兌。
bank note 鈔票。
bank of issue 由政府授權發行貨幣之銀行。
bank paper ①銀行匯票等。②可在銀行辦理貼現之商業票據。
bank rate 銀行所定之貼現率。
bank·roll [ˈbæŋkˌrol; ˈbæŋkroul] *n.* 〖美〗某人所有之錢。—*v.t.* 〖俚〗以金錢支持。
bank·rupt** [ˈbæŋkrʌpt, -rəpt; ˈbæŋkrəpt, -rʌpt] *n.* ①破產者。②無還債能力者。③無能力履行義務者。④某方面缺乏者。an intellectual *bankrupt.* 缺乏知識的人。—*adj.* ①無力還債的; 破產的。The company is *bankrupt.* 這公司已破產。②全部歸空的;缺乏的; 耗盡的〖常 of, in〗. *bankrupt* in good manners. 失態。be declared bankrupt*** 宣告破產。***go bankrupt*** 宣告破產。—*v.t.* 使破產。Foolish expenditures will *bankrupt* him. 胡亂的花費將使他破產。—**ly,** *adv.*
***bank·rupt·cy** [ˈbæŋkrʌptsɪ, -rəptsɪ; ˈbæŋkrəptsi] *n., pl.* **-cies.** ①破產;倒閉。a *bankruptcy* administrator. 破產管理人。②(地位、名聲等之)破產、失敗。
bank shot 〖籃球〗擦板球。
bank·si·a [ˈbæŋksɪə; ˈbæŋksiə] *n.* 〖植物〗山茂樫。
bank's letter of credit 銀行信用狀。
***ban·ner** [ˈbænɚ; ˈbænə] *n.*①旗幟。②書有標語或口號的旗。③報紙上橫貫全頁的大標題。④國王、貴族或騎士所用之旗幟。⑤任何代表某種主義之象徵。⑥寫在布上橫掛在街道或入口處的標幟。⑦滿洲八旗之一。—*adj.* 領先的;優越的。a *banner* year for crops. 豐年。—*v.t.* 〖俗〗以橫貫全頁之大標題來報導(某項新聞)。
ban·ner·et(te) [ˌbænəˈrɛt; ˌbænəˈret] *n.* 小旗。
banner head (橫貫全頁之)特長標題。
banner line =**banner head.**
ban·nock [ˈbænək; ˈbænək] *n.* 〖蘇,英方〗一種薄餅。
banns, bans [bænz; bænz] *n.pl.* 〖英〗在所屬教堂中的結婚預告。***call (ask, publish*** or ***put up) the banns*** 預告婚事問人有無異議。***forbid the banns*** 對別人婚事提出異議。***have one's banns called*** 請教堂公布結婚預告。
***ban·quet** [ˈbæŋkwɪt; ˈbæŋkwit] *n., v.,* **-quet·ed, -quet·ing.** —*n.* 宴會;酒宴。—*v.t.*宴客。—*v.i.*宴飲。The king *banqueted* on pheasant and wine.國王以雉與酒進膳。
ban·quette [bæŋˈkɛt; bæŋˈket] *n.* ①踏垜(胸牆內供士兵射擊時立足者)。②(驛馬車頂層之)乘客坐椅。③〖美〗人行道。④軟長椅。⑤增强堤防之護壁。
ban·shee, ban·shie [ˈbænʃi; bænˈʃiː] *n.* (愛爾蘭、蘇格蘭)預報凶信之女妖精。
bant [bænt; bænt] *v.i.* 行減肿法(諧語)。
ban·tam [ˈbæntəm; ˈbæntəm] *n.* ①(常B-)矮小的雞(原產爪哇)。②短小精悍的人。③羽量級拳師。—*adj.* ①好鬥到可笑地步的。②輕的。③小的。④小型眞空管的。
ban·tam·weight [ˈbæntəmˌwet; ˈbæntəmweit] *n.* 羽量級。—*adj.*羽量級的;小型的。
ban·ter [ˈbæntɚ; ˈbæntə] *v.t. & v.i.*嘲弄;戲謔。—*n.*嘲弄;戲謔。—**ing·ly,** *adv.*
ban·ting [ˈbæntɪŋ; ˈbæntiŋ] *n., pl.* **-tings.** 一種產於東南亞及馬來半島的野牛。(亦作 **banteng**)
Ban·ting·ism [ˈbæntɪŋˌɪzəm; ˈbæntiŋizm] *n.* (常 b-) 板汀氏療法 (減肥用)。
bant·ling [ˈbæntlɪŋ; ˈbæntliŋ] *n.* 〖蔑〗幼兒;小子。
Ban·tu [ˈbænˈtu; ˈbænˈtuː] *n., pl.* **-tu** or **-tus,** *adj.* —*n.* ①班圖人(非洲黑人)。②班圖語。—*adj.* 班圖族的;班圖語的。
ban·yan [ˈbænjən; ˈbæniən] *n.* ①榕樹。②婦女之工作服。③印度人的寬鬆襯衫、夾克或長袍。④印度某一禁食肉階級的小商人。
ban·zai [ˈbɑnˈzɑˈi; ˈbɑːnˈzɑːiː] 〖日〗*interj.* 萬歲! —*adj.*拚死的;自殺的。
ba·o·bab [ˈbeoˌbæb; ˈbeioubæb] *n.* 〖植物〗非洲產之木棉。
bap [bæp; bæp] *n.* 〖蘇〗小型的圓麪包。
Bap., Bapt. Baptist. **bap.** baptized.
***bap·tism** [ˈbæptɪzəm; ˈbæptizəm] *n.* ①浸禮;洗禮。②滌罪。③進入新生活的經驗。—**al,** *adj.* —**al·ly,** *adv.*
baptism of fire 士兵初臨戰場的經驗;折磨;考驗。
***Bap·tist** [ˈbæptɪst; ˈbæptist] *n.* ①浸信會教友。He is a *Baptist.* 他是浸信會的教友。②施洗者。John the *Baptist.* 〖聖經〗施洗約翰。—*adj.* (亦作 **Baptistic**) 浸信教會的;浸信會友的。
bap·tis·ter·y [ˈbæptɪstrɪ; ˈbæptistəri] *n., pl.* **-ter·ies.** 浸禮池;浸禮所。(亦作 **baptistry**)
bap·tize [bæpˈtaɪz; bæpˈtaiz] *v.,* **-tized, -tiz·ing.** —*v.t.*①施洗禮;行浸禮。②洗滌;入會。③命名;賜聖名。—*v.i.* 行浸禮。
‡**bar** [bɑr; bɑː] *n., v.,* **barred, bar·ring,** *prep.* —*n.* ①棒;條。a *bar* of soap. 一條肥皂。②門閂;橫木。He was placed behind prison *bars.* 他被置入監獄。③阻礙物;障礙;阻礙航行之沙灘。Superstition is a *bar* to progress. 迷信是進步之障礙。④樂譜的節線;小節。⑤條紋(顏色或光線)。⑥法庭的被告席;法院。⑦律師業。⑧酒館;酒吧;售酒櫃臺。She is a waitress at the *bar.* 她在酒吧充當女招待。⑨〖法律〗足以阻止或擊敗某種法律行爲或主張的請求或反對。⑩金屬或布條徽章。⑪靠牆之扶手(用於練習芭蕾舞者)。⑫巴(壓力單位,相當於 10^6 徽巴)。***at bar*** **a.** 在審訊中。a case *at bar.* 正在審訊中的一宗案子。**b.** 在全體法官之前。a trial *at bar.* 全體推事會審。***be tried at (the) bar*** 在法院受審。***the bar*** 律師業;所有有資格出庭的律師。—*v.t.*①用門關住;以橫木攔阻。②攔阻;阻礙;妨害。Poor health *barred* his chances of success. 不良的健康阻礙了他成功的機會。③禁止;摒除。All talking is *barred* during a study period. 讀書時,禁止談話。④飾以條紋。The sky was *barred* with black clouds. 天上點綴着條條的黑雲。⑤被拒;排斥。—*prep.* 除…之外;除外。He is the best student, *bar* none. 他是最好的學生,無人可比。
BAR Browning automatic rifle. **bar.** ①barometer. ②barometric. ③barrel. ④barrister. **B.Ar.** Bachelor of Architecture.
Ba·rab·bas [bəˈræbəs; bəˈræbəs] *n.* 〖聖經〗巴拉巴(耶穌被釘十字架前,猶太人要求釋放之一囚犯)。
bar·ag·no·sis [ˌbærægˈnosɪs; ˌbærægˈnousis] *n.* 〖醫〗重覺缺失。
bar-and-grill [ˈbɑrənˈgrɪl; ˈbɑːrən-

ˈgril] *n.* 一種出售酒類之餐廳。

barb [bab; ba:b] *n.* ①倒鉤。②髭。③修女用以遮喉部及胸部的麻布。④植物的芒刺。⑤鳥毛的羽枝。⑥魚口邊的觸鬚。⑦一種家鴿，喙短而寬。⑧石首魚屬。⑨一種由非洲 Barbary 輸入西班牙的阿拉伯馬。⑩帶刺的話。—*v.t.* 裝以倒鉤。

bar·ba [ˈbarbə; ˈba:bə] *n.*〖醫〗①鬚。②頭髮。

Bar·ba·do(e)s [barˈbedoz; barˈbeidouz] *n.* 巴貝多(原爲西印度群島之一，於1966年獨立，首都 Bridgetown)。

***bar·bar·i·an** [barˈbɛrɪən; ba:ˈbɛəriən] *n.*①野蠻人;蠻族。②異族人。③對文學、藝術等無欣賞力者。④非希臘人。⑤羅馬帝國版圖外之居民。⑥非基督教徒。⑦(文藝復興期中)非義大利人。—*adj.* 野蠻的。The *barbarian* tribes in Africa all hated the white people. 非洲的蠻族都恨白種人。—**ism,** *n.*

bar·bar·ic [barˈbærɪk; ba:ˈbærik] *adj.* ①野蠻的。②俗麗的。—**al·ly,** *adv.*

bar·ba·rism [ˈbarbə͵rɪzəm; ˈba:bərizəm] *n.* ①野蠻。②蠻行;蠻性。③粗野的語言。

bar·bar·i·ty [barˈbærətɪ; ba:ˈbæriti] *n., pl.* **-ties.** ①殘忍。②粗鄙。

bar·ba·ri·za·tion [͵barbərɪˈzeʃən; ͵ba:bəraiˈzeiʃən] *n.*①野蠻化。②蕪雜;破格。

bar·ba·rize [ˈbarbə͵raɪz; ˈba:bəraiz] *v.,* **-rized, -riz·ing.** —*v.t.* ①使野蠻、粗野。②使(言語或文體)蕪雜。 —*v.i.* ①變野蠻;變粗野。②變蕪雜。③用不雅的言語。

***bar·ba·rous** [ˈbarbərəs; ˈba:bərəs] *adj.* ①野蠻的。②殘暴的;無人道的。③粗野的;下流的。④噪雜的;(聲音)不和諧的。⑤非希臘人或事物的。 —**ly,** *adv.* —**ness,** *n.*

Bar·ba·ry [ˈbarbərɪ; ˈba:bəri] *n.* 巴巴利(北非洲沿海地區)。

Barbary Coast 北非洲海岸。

Barbary sheep 北非產大角羊。

Barbary States 北非諸國。

bar·bate [ˈbarbet; ˈba:beit] *adj.* ①有鬚的。②〖植物〗有芒的。

bar·be·cue [ˈbarbɪ͵kju; ˈba:bikju:] *n., v.,* **-cued, -cu·ing,** *adj.* —*n.* ①用燔炙全牲的野宴。②燔炙的全牛或其他牲物。③燔炙用之臺架。—*v.t.* ①燔炙全牲;全燒。②加作料炙烤(魚、肉片)。—*adj.* 全燒的;加作料炙烤的。(亦作 **barbeque**)

barbed [barbd; ba:bd] *adj.* ①有鉤的。②諷刺的。

barbed wire 有刺鐵絲網。(亦作 **barb-wire**)

barbed-wire [ˈbarbdˈwaɪr; ˈba:bdˈwaiə] *adj.* 有刺鐵絲網的。

bar·bel [ˈbarbḷ; ˈba:bəl] *n.* ①(魚唇之)觸鬚。②白魚。

bar bell (似啞鈴而桿較長之)運動器械。

***bar·ber** [ˈbarbɚ; ˈba:bə] *n.* 理髮匠。—*v.t.* 理髮;刮…之鬍子。

barber college 訓練理髮師的學校。

barber pole = **barber's pole.**

bar·ber·ry [ˈbar͵bɛrɪ; ˈba:bəri] *n., pl.* **-ries.** 〖植物〗①伏牛花。②伏牛花漿果或子。

bar·ber·shop [ˈbarbɚ͵ʃap; ˈba:bəʃɔp] *n.*理髮店。—*adj.*〖俗〗男聲和唱的。

barber's itch 鬚癬。(亦作 **barber's rash**)

barber's pole 理髮店招牌桿。

bar·ber-sur·geon [ˈbarbɚˈsɝdʒən; ˈba:bəˈsə:dʒən] *n.* ①從前兼外科醫生與牙醫的理髮匠。②庸醫。

bar·bette [barˈbɛt; ba:ˈbet] *n.* ①砲座;砲位。②(艦艇上之)固定砲塔。

bar·bi·can [ˈbarbɪkən; ˈba:bikən] *n.* 外堡;更樓。(亦作 **barbacan**)

bar·bi·tal [ˈbarbətɔl; ˈba:bitæl] *n.*〖藥〗巴比妥。

bar·bi·tu·rate [͵barbɪˈtjuret; ͵ba:biˈtjureit] *n.* 巴比妥酸鹽(用作鎮靜劑)。

bar·bi·tu·ric acid [͵barbɪˈtjurɪk～; ͵ba:biˈtjurik～] 巴比妥酸。

bar·bo·la [barˈbolə; ba:ˈboulə] *n.* 剪貼畫(剪貼裝飾物)。(亦作 **barbola work**)

bar·bule [ˈbarbjul; ˈba:bju:l] *n.* ①〖植物〗小芒刺。②鳥之小羽枝。

barb·wire [ˈbarb͵waɪr; ˈba:bwaiə] *n.* 鐵蒺藜;倒鉤鐵絲。

bar·ca·role [ˈbarkə͵rol; ˈba:kəroul] *n.* 威尼斯船夫之櫂歌;船歌。(亦作**barcarolle**)

B. Arch. Bachelor of Architecture.

bar chart = **bar graph.**

bard**[1] [bard; ba:d] *n.* ①古代 Celt 自編自彈自唱的遊唱詩人。②遊唱詩人。Bard of Avon*** 莎士比亞的別稱。

bard[2] *n.* (亦作 **barde**) ①護馬鎧甲。②加在烤肉、烤魚上的肥肉。 —*v.t.* 置護馬鎧甲於(馬)。

bard·ess [ˈbardɪs; ˈba:dis] *n.* bard[1]之女性。

bard·ol·a·ter [barˈdalətɚ; ba:ˈdɔlətə] *n.*(有時B-)莎翁崇拜者。—**bard·ol·a·try,** *n.*

‡bare [bɛr; bɛə] *adj.,* **bar·er, bar·est,** *v.,* **bared, bar·ing.** —*adj.* ①赤裸的。The hill is *bare* of trees. 這山沒有樹木。②顯露的;無隱藏的。He is *bare* to the elbow. 他赤露至肘。③空的。The room was *bare* of furniture. 屋裏空無傢具。④簡單的;無修飾的。He lived in a *bare* little house. 他住在一所陳設簡單的小房子裏。⑤僅有的;少的。⑥用舊的;穿舊的。***believe a person's bare word; believe a thing on a person's bare word*** 相信某人片面之詞。***lay bare*** 揭露;暴露;洩露。—*v.t.* 使赤裸;暴露。They *bared* him of his clothes. 他們脫光他的衣服。 —**ness,** *n.*

bare·back [ˈbɛr͵bæk; ˈbɛəbæk] *adv.* 不用馬鞍地。—*adj.* 無鞍的。

bare·backed [ˈbɛr͵bækt; ˈbɛəbækt] *adj.* 無鞍的;裸背的。

bare·boat [ˈbɛrˈbot; ˈbɛəˈbout] *adj.* 包船業中，船主將空船交給客戶，而由客戶負責人員、補給、保養、保險的。—*n.* 上述包船。

bare·bones [ˈbɛrˈbonz; ˈbɛəˈbounz] *n.* 極瘦的人;皮包骨的人。—*adj.* 貧乏的。—**bare·boned,** *adj.*

bare·faced [ˈbɛr͵fest; ˈbɛəfeist] *adj.* ①無鬚的。②無恥的。③公然的。—**ly,** *adv.*

***bare·foot** [ˈbɛr͵fut; ˈbɛəfut] *adj.* 赤足的。to be *barefoot.* 赤足。—*adv.* 赤足地。—**ed,** *adj.*

bare·hand·ed [ˈbɛrˈhændɪd; ˈbɛəˈhændid] *adj.* ①手無遮覆的;未戴手套的。②赤手空拳的;無憑藉的。—*adv.* ①未戴手套地。②空着手;無憑藉地。

bare·head·ed [ˈbɛrˈhɛdɪd; ˈbɛəˈhedid] *adj.* 光着頭的;不戴帽的。—*adv.* 光着頭地;不戴帽地。(亦作 **barehead**)

bare-kneed [ˈbɛrˈnid; ˈbɛəˈni:d] *adj.* 露着膝蓋的。

bare·leg·ged [ˈbɛrˈlɛgd; ˈbɛəˈlegd] *adj.* 露腿的;未穿襪子的。—*adv.* 光着腿。

***bare·ly** [ˈbɛrlɪ; ˈbɛəli] *adv.* ①僅;幾不能。He *barely* escaped death. 他僅免於死。②公開地;赤裸裸地。 a fact *barely* stated. 毫無隱瞞地陳述的事實。③貧乏地;零落地。

bare-necked [ˈbɛrˈnɛkt; ˈbɛəˈnekt] *adj.* 露着頸子的。

bare·sark (ˈbɛrˌsark; ˈbɛəsaːk) *n.* =**berserker.** —*adv.* 未穿鎧甲地。

barf (barf; baːf) *v.i.* & *v.t.* 〖美俚〗嘔吐。

bar·fly (ˈbarˌflaɪ; ˈbaːflai) *n., pl.* **-flies.** 流連於酒吧的人。

*__bar·gain__ (ˈbargɪn; ˈbaːgin) *n.* ①交易；合同；協議。I made a satisfactory *bargain* with him. 我和他作了一次滿意的交易。②廉售或廉買的東西。***close a bargain*** 成交；達成協議。***drive a bargain*** 講價。***into*** (or ***in***) ***the bargain*** 另外。He gave me thirty dollars *into the bargain.* 他另外給我三十元。***strike*** (***conclude,*** or ***settle***) ***a bargain*** 成交；達成協議。—*v.i.* ①議價。②交易；協議；訂約。③意料；希望；計及〖for〗. This bad weather is more than I *bargained for.* 這種壞天氣不是我所意料的。—**er,** *n.*

bargain basement (百貨店之)地下廉價商場。

bargain counter 廉價櫃臺。

bargain day 廉價日。

bar·gain·ee (ˌbargɪˈni; ˌbaːgiˈniː) *n.* 〖法律〗買主。

bar·gain·ing (ˈbargɪnɪŋ; ˈbaːginiŋ) *n.* ①議價；討價還價。②契約；交涉。—*adj.* 交涉的；議價的。

bargaining unit 集體交涉時代表工人之工會。

bargain money 保證金。

bar·gain·or (ˈbargɪnɚ; ˈbaːginə) *n.* 〖法律〗賣主。

bargain sale 大廉價。

*__barge__ (bardʒ; baːdʒ) *n., v.,* **barged, barg·ing.** —*n.* ①平底載貨船；駁船。②大型游艇。③戰艦司令官之座艇。④雙座四輪馬車。⑤〖俗〗笨重的船。⑥〖英〗船宅。—*v.t.* 由載貨船運送。—*v.i.* ①緩慢移動。②撞碰。③闖入。***barge into*** **a.** 干涉。**b.** 撞。

barge·board (ˈbardʒˌbord; ˈbaːdʒbɔːd) *n.* 〖建築〗破風板；山形牆桁端之蓋板。

bar·gee (ˌbarˈdʒi; baːˈdʒiː) *n.* ①駁船的船夫。②粗魯無禮的人。

barge·man (ˈbardʒmən; ˈbaːdʒmən) *n., pl.* **-men.** ①船夫。②經營駁船業的人。

barge·mas·ter (ˈbardʒˌmæstɚ; ˈbaːdʒˌmaːstə) *n.* 船主。

barge-pole (ˈbardʒˌpol; ˈbaːdʒpoul) *n.* (駁船上用的)撐篙。***not touch*** (***a thing***) ***with a barge-pole*** 非常討厭；碰都不要碰(某事物)。

bar·ghest (ˈbargest; ˈbaːgest) *n.* 犬形之妖怪。

bar·girl (ˈbarˌgɝl; ˈbaːgəːl) *n.* 〖美俗〗酒吧女。

bar graph (以直槓之長短或高低表示的)統計圖。(亦作 **bar chart**)

bar·hop (ˈbarˌhap; ˈbaːhɔp) *n., v.,* **-hopped, -hop·ping.** —*n.* 〖美俗〗酒吧女侍。—*v.i.* 流連於一家又一家酒吧間。

bar·i·at·ri·cian (ˌbæriæˈtrɪʃən; ˌbæriːæˈtriʃən) *n.* 治療體重過重的專家。

bar·i·at·rics (ˌbæriˈætrɪks; ˌbæriːˈætriks) *n.* 體重過重的醫藥治療。

bar·ic[1] (ˈbærɪk; ˈbærik) *adj.* 〖化〗鋇的；含鋇的。

bar·ic[2] *adj.* 〖物理〗大氣壓力的；氣壓的。

ba·ril·la (bəˈrɪlə; bəˈrilə) *n.* ①〖植物〗岡羊栖菜(一種海草)。②海草灰；蘇打灰；鈉灰。

bar·ite (ˈbɛraɪt; ˈbɛərait) *n.* 〖礦〗重晶石。(亦作 **barytes**)

bar·i·tone (ˈbærəˌton; ˈbæritoun) *n.* ①〖音樂〗上低音。②男中音。③(亦作**baritone horn**)形似喇叭的銅管樂器。—*adj.* 上低音的；男中音的。

bar·i·um (ˈbɛrɪəm; ˈbɛəriəm) *n.* 〖化〗鋇。

‡**bark**[1] (bark; baːk) *n.* ①吠聲；狗叫；似吠聲。His *bark* is worse than his bite. 他的脾氣壞，但不陰險。②咆哮。—*v.i.* ①吠；狗叫。The dog *barks* at him. 這狗對着他叫。*Barking* dogs won't bite. 愛叫的狗不咬人(愛喧囂者不一定會做事)。②咆哮；怒吼；喝叱。③〖俗〗咳嗽。④發出爆炸的聲音。⑤大聲叫喊以招徠顧客。—*v.t.* 吼叫。***bark at the moon*** 徒勞地吵鬧；空嚷。***bark up the wrong tree*** 認錯目標；看錯人；白費心思。

*__bark__[2] *n.* ①樹皮。②含有單寧酸的樹皮。③金鷄納樹皮。—*v.t.* ①剝去樹皮。②剝去一圈樹皮。③覆以樹皮。④鞣(皮)。⑤剝皮；擦破皮膚。

bark[3] *n.* ①〖航海〗三桅船；小帆船。②〖詩〗船；帆船。(亦作 **barque**)

bark beetle 小甲蟲(蛀蟲的一種)。

bar·keep·er (ˈbarˌkipɚ; ˈbaːˌkiːpə) *n.* ①酒吧店主。②酒保。(亦作 **barkeep**)

bar·ken·tine (ˈbarkənˈtin; ˈbaːkəntiːn) *n.* 三桅船。(亦作 **barkantine, barquentine, barquantine**)

bark·er[1] (ˈbarkɚ; ˈbaːkə) *n.* ①作哮聲之人或物；吵鬧者。②招徠客人者。

bark·er[2] *n.* 剝樹皮之人或機器；調製樹皮供製革用者。

Bark·la (ˈbarklə; ˈbaːklə) *n.* 巴克拉(Charles Glover, 1877–1944, 英國物理學家，獲1917年諾貝爾獎)。

bark·y (ˈbarkɪ; ˈbaːki) *adj.,* **bark·i·er, bark·i·est.** 有樹皮的；像樹皮的。

*__bar·ley__ (ˈbarlɪ; ˈbaːli) *n.* 大麥。

bar·ley-broo (ˈbarlɪˌbru; ˈbaːlibruː) *n.* 〖蘇〗大麥酒；烈性麥酒。(亦作 **barley broth**)

bar·ley·corn (ˈbarlɪˌkorn; ˈbaːlikɔːn) *n.* ①大麥之實。②一種長度名(等於1/3英寸)。***John Barleycorn*** 烈酒；威士忌(諧語，擬人稱)。

barley sugar 大麥糖。(亦作 **barley candy**)

bar·ley-sug·ar (ˈbarlɪˌʃugɚ; ˈbaːliˈʃugə) 〖英俚〗*n.* 將人之手臂扭轉到背後的行爲。—*v.t.* 扭轉(他人的手臂)。

barley water (病人用的)大麥湯。

barm (barm; baːm) *n.* 酵；酵母之泡。

bar·maid (ˈbarˌmed; ˈbaːmeid) *n.* 酒吧女侍。

bar·man (ˈbarmən; ˈbaːmən) *n., pl.* **-men.** 酒店主；調酒師。

Bar·me·cide (ˈbarməˌsaɪd; ˈbaːmisaid) *n.* ①(天方夜譚中)巴格達一波斯王子(假裝以筵席饗一窮漢但不給以食物)。②假慇懃或假慷慨者。—*adj.* 虛假的；空想的。

Barmecide feast ①以空盤饗客之宴會。②假慇懃或假慷慨。(亦作 **Barmecidal banquet**)

bar mitz·vah (barˈmɪtsvə; baːˈmitsvə) *n.* 猶太男子的成人禮(通常爲男孩之十三歲生日)。(亦作 **bar mizvah**)

barm·y (ˈbarmɪ; ˈbaːmi) *adj.,* **barm·i·er, barm·i·est.** ①有泡沫的。②〖英俚〗癡愚的；輕狂的。

*__barn__ (barn; baːn) *n.* ①穀倉。②車房。③類似穀倉的地方。④靶恩(=10^{-24} 平方厘米)。—*v.t.* 將(穀子、乾草等)存於倉內。

bar·na·cle (ˈbarnəkl̩; ˈbaːnəkl) *n.* ①附於岩石、船底的甲殼動物。②不易擺脫的人。

bar·na·cles (ˈbarnəklz; ˈbaːnəklz) *n. pl.* ①夾鼻具。②一種刑具(略似夾鼻具)。③〖英俗〗眼鏡。

barn dance 〖美〗①美國鄉間在穀倉舉行的舞會。②一種方塊舞。

barn-door (ˈbarnˈdor; ˈbaːnˈdɔː) *n.* ①穀倉門。②一種不透光，裝在電影或電視攝

影燈前的門扉。***as big as a barn-door*** 既大且寬。***not to be able to hit a barn-door*** 射術極糟。
barn-door fowl 普通家禽。
barn owl 一種梟鳥。
barn·storm〔ˈbɑrnˌstɔrm; ˈbɑːnstɔːm〕 *v.i.* 〖美俗〗①在鄉間作競選或演說旅行。②在鄉間作巡廻演出。③在鄉間作短程空中運輸或飛行表演。—*v.t.* 在鄉間演出或演說。
barn·storm·er〔ˈbɑrnˌstɔrmɚ; ˈbɑːn-stɔːmə〕 *n.* ①鄉間演說家；江湖藝人。②次等之藝人。③不受契約束縛之航空員。
barn swallow 好居於穀倉的燕子。
barn·yard〔ˈbɑrnˌjɑrd; ˈbɑːnjɑːd〕 *n.* 穀倉近旁的場地。—*adj.* 穀倉近旁地區的；髒的。***barnyard humor*** 粗俗的幽默。
baro- 〖字首〗表"壓力"之義。
bar·og·no·sis〔ˌbærɑgˈnosɪs; ˌbærɔgˈnousis〕 *n.* 〖醫〗辨重能力。
bar·o·gram〔ˈbærəˌgræm; ˈbærəgræm〕 *n.* 氣壓記錄表。
bar·o·graph〔ˈbærəˌgræf; ˈbærougrɑːf〕 *n.* 氣壓記錄計。
ba·rol·o·gy〔bəˈrɑlədʒɪ; bəˈrɔlədʒi〕 *n.* 重力論；重力學。
***ba·rom·e·ter**〔bəˈrɑmətɚ; bəˈrɔmitə〕 *n.* ①氣壓計；晴雨表。②測量器；顯示變化的事物。
bar·o·met·ric〔ˌbærəˈmɛtrɪk; ˌbærəˈmetrik〕 *adj.* 氣壓計的；氣壓計所示的。(亦作 **barometrical**) **—al·ly,** *adv.*
ba·rom·e·try〔bəˈrɑmɪtrɪ; bəˈrɔmitri〕 *n.* 氣壓測定法。
***bar·on**〔ˈbærən; ˈbærən〕 *n.* ①男爵。②中古英國因功封得采邑的貴族或其後代。③〖美〗大財主；大老闆。④英國上院議員。⑤兩側腰肉連在一起的整塊牛肉或羊肉。
bar·on·age〔ˈbærənɪdʒ; ˈbærənidʒ〕 *n.* ①英國貴族。②男爵之爵位。(亦作 **barony**)
bar·on·ess〔ˈbærənɪs; ˈbærənis〕 *n.* ①男爵夫人。②男爵之未亡人。③(歐洲)男爵之女。④有男爵爵位之婦人。(略作 **Bnss.**)
bar·on·et〔ˈbærənɪt; ˈbærənit〕 *n.* ①從男爵(低於男爵之爵位)。②從男爵爵位。
bar·on·et·age〔ˈbærənɪtɪdʒ; ˈbærənitidʒ〕 *n.* ①從男爵之位。②從男爵輩。
bar·on·et·cy〔ˈbærənɪtsɪ; ˈbærənitsi〕 *n.*, *pl.* **-cies.** 從男爵之地位或身分。
ba·ro·ni·al〔bəˈronɪəl; bəˈrouniəl〕 *adj.* ①男爵的。②適於男爵的；宏大的；華麗的。
bar·o·ny〔ˈbærənɪ; ˈbærəni〕 *n.*, *pl.* **-nies.** 男爵的領地、身分、爵位、稱謂等。
ba·roque〔bəˈrok; bəˈrɔk〕 *adj.* ①形狀不規則的(指珍珠)。②(常 B-) 巴羅克式之藝術或建築的。③(常 B-) 巴羅克式之藝術或建築之興盛期的(約1550-1750)。④巴羅克式之藝術或建築之後期的。⑤奇形怪狀地過分裝飾的；俗麗的。⑥〖音樂〗巴羅克時代的(約爲 1600-1750)。—*n.* 巴羅克式的作風、藝術等。
bar·o·scope〔ˈbærəˌskop; ˈbærəskoup〕 *n.* ①氣壓計。②空氣浮力計。
bar·o·switch〔ˈbærəˌswɪtʃ; ˈbærəswitʃ〕 *n.* 以氣壓作用操作的開關。(亦作 **barometric switch**)
ba·rouche〔bəˈruʃ; bəˈruːʃ〕 *n.* 一種四輪大馬車。
bar pin 棒形的胸針。
barque〔bark; bɑːk〕 *n.* ①〖詩〗船。②有三根桅檣的船。
bar·quen·tine〔ˈbɑrkənˌtin; ˈbɑːkəntiːn〕 *n.* = **barkentine.**
***bar·rack**〔ˈbærək; ˈbærək〕 *v.t.* ①供給以兵營；使駐紮於兵營內。②〖澳, 英〗吶喊而爲某人或某隊加油或喝倒采。—*v.i.* ①居於兵營中。②〖澳, 英〗吶喊。
***bar·racks**〔ˈbærəks; ˈbærəks〕 *n. pl.* ①兵營。②許多人居住的廣大簡陋房舍。〖注意〗**barracks** 一字可與單數或複數動詞連用。
barracks bag 士兵之衣物袋。
barracks lawyer 自命爲軍法、軍事規章、軍人權利等方面之權威的軍人。
bar·ra·coon〔ˌbærəˈkun; ˌbærəˈkuːn〕 *n.* 收容奴隸或囚犯的臨時場所。
bar·ra·cu·da〔ˌbærəˈkudə; ˌbærəˈkuːdə〕 *n.*, *pl.* **-da, -das.** 梭魚之類。
bar·rage〔*n.* ③ ˈbɑrɪdʒ; ˈbærɑːdʒ *n.* ①, ② & *v.* bəˈrɑʒ; ˈbærɑːʒ, bæˈrɑːʒ〕 *n.*, *v.*, **-raged, -rag·ing.** —*n.* ①〖軍〗掩護砲火；彈幕。②勢不可當的數量。③堰；堰堤。—*v.t.* & *v.i.* 布下彈幕(對抗)。
bar·ran·ca〔bəˈræŋkə; bəˈræŋkə〕 *n.*, *pl.* **-cas.** 峽谷。
bar·ra·tor, bar·ra·ter〔ˈbærətɚ; ˈbærətə〕 *n.* 〖法律〗①因疏忽或欺騙而使船主蒙受損失的船長或船員。②訴訟教唆犯。③聖職或官位之買賣者。(亦作 **barretor**)
bar·ra·trous〔ˈbærətrəs; ˈbærətrəs〕 *adj.* ①欺詐的；爲非作惡的。②訴訟教唆的。③收賄的；受賄的。
bar·ra·try〔ˈbærətrɪ; ˈbærətri〕 *n.* 〖法律〗①船長或船員使船主蒙受損失之疏忽或欺騙；非法行爲。②訴訟教唆。③聖職或官位之買賣。(亦作 **barretry**)
barre〔bɑr; bɑː〕 *n.* 練習芭蕾舞時之扶手。
barred〔bɑrd; bɑːd〕 *adj.* ①閂住的；有鐵條或木柵的；堵起的；有障礙物的。②有條紋的。③禁止的；不許的。
bar·rel**〔ˈbærəl; ˈbærəl〕 *n.*, *v.*, **-rel(l)ed, -rel·(l)ing.** —*n.* ①大桶；琵琶桶。②桶狀物。③一桶之量。They sent me a *barrel* of beer. 他們送我一大桶啤酒。④鎗身；鎗管。⑤大量。⑥四足動物之身軀。⑦鳥羽之翮。⑧鐘錶之主彈簧室。⑨筆身。barrel of the ear*** 耳鼓；中耳。***over a barrel*** 窘態；困難；不能反手的地步。—*v.t.* 裝入桶中。—*v.i.* 〖俚〗走或開得很快。
barrel bulk 五立方英尺之容積。
bar·rel-drain〔ˈbærəlˌdren; ˈbærəldrein〕 *n.* 筒形排水溝。
bar·rel(l)ed〔ˈbærəld; ˈbærəld〕 *adj.* ①裝入桶內的。②有軀幹的。③槍管的。
bar·rel·ful〔ˈbærəlˌful; ˈbærəlful〕 *n.* ①一桶之量。②大量。
bar·rel·house〔ˈbærəlˌhaus; ˈbærəlhaus〕 *n.* 〖美俚〗低級酒吧。
barrel organ 手風琴。
barrel roll (飛行表演時之)滾桶。
***bar·ren**〔ˈbærən; ˈbærən〕 *n.* (*pl.*)不毛之地。—*adj.* ①不生產的(指土地)。A sandy desert is *barren.* 多沙的荒野是不生產的。②不生產的(指植物)；不結實的。③不生育的；不孕的。④愚笨的；無趣味的。a *barren* mind. 愚蠢的頭腦。⑤無益的；無效果的。⑥無反應的。⑦缺乏的〖常 of〗. *barren* of tender feelings. 缺乏感情(狠心腸)。⑧無吸引力的；無興趣的。**—ly,** *adv.* **—ness,** *n.*
bar·rette〔bəˈrɛt; bəˈret〕 *n.* 女用髮夾。
bar·ri·cade〔ˌbærəˈked; ˌbæriˈkeid〕 *n.*, *v.*, **-cad·ed, -cad·ing.** —*n.* ①臨時建築的防禦工事。②阻擋通路的障礙物。—*v.t.* ①設柵防守。②阻礙；阻擋。
***bar·ri·er**〔ˈbærɪɚ; ˈbæriə〕 *n.* ①防阻的東西；障礙。High tariff is a *barrier* to international trade. 關稅過高是國際貿易

的障礙。②界線。The river is a natural *barrier* between these two countries. 這河是兩國的天然界線。③(*pl.*) 中世紀騎士比武場之圍柵。④(賽馬之)出發柵。
barrier beach 海浪所造成之沙灘。(亦作 **barrier bar**)
barrier reef 堡礁(一種珊瑚礁)。
bar·ring [ˈbarɪŋ; ˈbɑːriŋ] *prep.* ①除…以外。②除非。
bar·ris·ter [ˈbærɪstɚ; ˈbæristə] *n.* 〖英〗律師。
bar·room [ˈbarˌrum; ˈbɑːruːm] *n.* 酒館;酒吧。
bar·row¹ [ˈbæro; ˈbærou] *n.* ①雙輪手推車。②獨輪車。③裝在 barrow 上的東西。—*v.t.* 用 barrow 裝載。
bar·row² *n.*①塚;古墓。②獸穴。③山;丘。
bar·row³ *n.* 閹豬。
barrow boy 〖英〗推手推車售貨的少年或男人。(亦作 **barrow-boy**)
bar·row·man [ˈbæromən; ˈbæroumən] *n., pl.* **-men.** 沿街叫賣之小販。
bar·stool [ˈbarˌstul; ˈbɑːˌstuːl] *n.*酒吧之高腳凳。
Bart. Baronet.
bar·tend [ˈbartɛnd; ˈbɑːtend] *v.i.* 做調酒師。
bar·tend·er [ˈbarˌtɛndɚ; ˈbɑːˌtendə] *n.* (酒吧)調酒師。
bar·ter [ˈbartɚ; ˈbɑːtə] *v.i.* 交換物品。—*v.t.* ①交換; 物物交換〖for〗。②得不償失; 喪失〖away〗。—*n.* ①物物交換的貿易。②交換品;交易品。
barter system 物物交換制度。
Bar·thol·o·mew [barˈθaləˌmju; bɑːˈθɔləmjuː] *n.* 〖聖經〗聖・巴托羅繆(耶穌十二門徒之一)。
bar·ti·zan [ˈbartəzn̩; ˈbɑːtəzn, ˌbɑːtəˈzæn] *n.* 〖建築〗小望臺;城牆外之吊樓。
Bart·lett [ˈbartlɪt; ˈbɑːtlit] *n.*一種黃色多汁之梨。(亦作 **Bartlett pear**)
bar·ton [ˈbartn̩; ˈbɑːtn] *n.* 農舍庭院;倉房。
bar·y·cen·ter [ˈbærɪˌsɛntɚ; ˈbæriˌsentə] *n.*重心。(亦作**barycentre**)
bar·y·on [ˈbærɪˌan; ˈbæriˌɔn] *n.* 〖物理〗重子。
ba·ry·ta [bəˈraɪtə; bəˈraitə] *n.* 〖化〗①重土(卽氧化鋇BaO)。②鋇。③(泛指)氫氧化鋇。
ba·ry·tes [bəˈraɪtiz; bəˈraitiːz] *n.* 〖礦〗重晶石。
ba·ryt·ic [bəˈrɪtɪk; bəˈritik] *adj.* 重土的;氧化鋇的。
bar·y·tone [ˈbærəˌton; ˈbæritoun] *n., adj.*〖音樂〗=**baritone.**
B.A.S. ①Bachelor of Agricultural Science. ②Bachelor of Applied Science.
ba·sal [ˈbesl̩; ˈbeisl] *adj.* ①底部的。②基礎的;根本的。③〖生理〗基本的;基礎的。
ba·salt [bəˈsɔlt; ˈbæsɔːlt] *n.* ①〖地質〗玄武岩;柱石岩。②一種黑色陶器。
ba·sal·tic [bəˈsɔltɪk; bəˈsɔːltik] *adj.* 玄武岩的;似玄武岩的。
bas bleu [baˈblɝ; bɑːˈbləː] 〖法〗女學者。
bas·cule [ˈbæskjul; ˈbæskjuːl] *n.* 〖工程〗跳開結構(兩端均衡,一端落下他端卽高起者)。
bascule bridge 跳開式吊橋;上開橋(可以開闔之橋)。
‡base¹ [bes; beis] *n., v.,* **based, bas·ing,** *adj.* —*n.* ①底;地基;基礎。②基本原則。③根據;事物的重要部分。This is the *base* of my argument. 這是我議論的根據。④支架;架子。⑤柱脚;柱基。⑥牆脚;碑脚。⑦要點;要素。⑧器官之近接合點部分;器官與器官之接合點。⑨〖化〗鹽基;鹼。*Base* reacts with acid to form salt. 鹽基與酸起反應成鹽。⑩〖棒球〗壘。⑪(賽跑)出發點。⑫〖軍〗根據地;基地。The harbor forms an important naval *base.* 這港口成爲一個重要的海軍基地。⑬〖數學〗基數。⑭〖幾何〗底邊;底面。⑮(地形勘測的)基線。⑯(化妝或油漆等)最下面之一層。⑰主要成分。***get to first base*** 獲得初步成功。***load the bases*** 〖棒球〗使滿壘。***off base*** a.〖棒球〗不在壘上。b.〖俗〗大錯。c.(軍事基地)閑人免進。***on base*** 〖棒球〗在壘上。—*v.t.* 基於; 以…爲根據。These charges are *based* on facts. 這些控訴是以事實爲根據的。—*v.i.* ①有基礎的〖常 on, upon〗。②設有基地〖常 on, upon〗。—*adj.* 基礎的;地基的。
***base²** *adj.,* **bas·er, bas·est.** ①卑鄙的;自私的;怯懦的。His motives are *base.* 他的動機是卑鄙的。②下賤的;無價值的;劣等的。③假的。④出身微賤的。—**ly,** *adv.* —**ness,** *n.*
base bag 〖棒球〗作壘之沙囊。
‡base·ball [ˈbesˈbɔl; ˈbeisbɔːl] *n.* 棒球。
base·ball·er [ˈbesˌbɔlɚ; ˈbeisˌbɔːlə] *n.* 棒球選手;棒球隊經理;棒球隊隊主。
base·board [ˈbesˌbord; ˈbeisbɔːd] *n.* ①〖建築〗護壁板;脚板。②作爲基礎之板。
base·born [ˈbesˈbɔrn; ˈbeisbɔːn] *adj.* ①出身微賤的。②私生的。③卑下的;卑劣的。
base·bred [ˈbesˈbrɛd; ˈbeisˈbred] *adj.* 下賤的;無教養的。
base·burn·er [ˈbesˈbɝnɚ; ˈbeisˈbəːnə] *n.* 自動添煤之火爐。
base-court [ˈbesˌkort; ˈbeiskɔːt] *n.* ①農家的後院。②城堡的外庭。
Ba·se·dow's disease [ˈbazəˌdoz～; ˈbɑːzədouz～] *n.* 〖醫〗甲狀腺之突出病。
base exchange 〖美空軍〗基地福利社。
base hit 〖棒球〗安打。
base hospital 基地醫院。
base·less [ˈbeslɪs; ˈbeislis] *adj.* 無基礎的;無事實根據的。—**ly,** *adv.* —**ness,** *n.*
base line ①基準線;基線。②〖棒球〗壘線。③〖網球〗(與網平行的)基線。
base·man [ˈbesmən; ˈbeismən] *n., pl.* **-men.** 〖棒球〗壘手。
***base·ment** [ˈbesmənt; ˈbeismənt] *n.* ①地下室。It is rather damp in the *basement.* 地下室很潮濕。②牆的最下部分;牆脚。
base metal 賤金屬。
base·mind·ed [ˈbesˈmaɪndɪd; ˈbeisˈmaindid] *adj.* 卑陋的;心地卑劣的。
base on balls *pl.* **bases on balls.** 〖棒球〗(四壞球後)送上壘。
base path 〖棒球〗壘與壘間之路。
base pay 基本薪給;底薪;本俸。
base·plate [ˈbesˌplet; ˈbeisˌpleit] *n.* ①〖機械〗基礎板。②基板。
base price 基本價。
base rate 基本給與。(亦作**basic rate**)
base runner 〖棒球〗跑壘員。
base running 〖棒球〗跑壘。
base stealing 〖棒球〗盜壘。
base umpire 〖棒球〗棒球裁判。
bash [bæʃ; bæʃ] *v.t.* 〖俗〗重擊;重敲。—*n.* ①重重的一擊。②狂歡之派對。***have a bash (at)*** 〖英〗嘗試;企圖。***on the bash*** 〖英〗操賤業。
ba·shaw [bəˈʃɔ; bəˈʃɔː] *n.* ①土耳其人對權貴之尊稱(=pasha);土耳其的官員。②大人物;大亨;大官。
***bash·ful** [ˈbæʃfəl; ˈbæʃful] *adj.* 害羞的;羞怯的。—**ly,** *adv.* —**ness,** *n.*

bash·i·ba·zouk [ˌbæʃɪbəˈzuk; ˌbæʃi-bəˈzuːk] *n.* 土耳其非正規部隊之士兵。
Ba·shi Channel [ˈbɑʃɪ~; ˈbɑːʃi~] 巴士海峽。
***ba·sic** [ˈbesɪk; ˈbeisik] *adj.* ①基本的。②鹽基性的;鹼性的。③〖軍〗階級最低的。—*n.* ①基本事實;基本;要點;要素。*basics* of aircraft design. 飛機設計的要點。②〖軍〗接受基本訓練的士兵。③〖軍〗基本訓練;新兵訓練。
ba·si·cal·ly [ˈbesɪkəlɪ; ˈbeisikəli] *adv.* 基本地;主要地。
basic dress 單色女裝,可與他種服裝或飾物配合。
Basic English 基本英語。(亦作**Basic**)
ba·sic·i·ty [beˈsɪsətɪ; beiˈsisiti] *n.*〖化〗鹽基度。
basic proposition 基本命題。
basic rate 基本給與。
basic salary 基本薪俸。
basic wage 基本工資。
ba·sid·i·o·spore [bəˈsɪdɪəˌspor; bəˈsidiəspɔə] *n.*〖植物〗芽胞;孢子。
bas·i·lar [ˈbæsələ˞; ˈbæsilə] *adj.* ①〖解剖〗基部的; 頭蓋骨之底部的。②基礎的。(亦作 **basilary**)
ba·sil·i·ca [bəˈsɪlɪkə, bəˈzɪlɪkə; bəˈzilikə] *n.* ①皇宮。②(B-) 古羅馬之會堂。③〖建築〗長方形建築物。
ba·sil·i·con[bəˈsɪlɪkɑn;bəˈsilikən] *n.* 松脂軟膏。
ba·si·lic vein [bəˈsɪlɪk~; bəˈsilik~] (上臂內側的)大靜脈。
bas·i·lisk [ˈbæsəˌlɪsk, ˈbæzə-; ˈbæzilisk] *n.* ①傳說中非洲沙漠之似龍、蛇等之怪物。②一種蜥蜴。
***ba·sin** [ˈbesn̩; ˈbeisn] *n.*①盤;盆。Wash your hands in the *basin.* 在盆內洗你的手。②盤或盆的容量。③(深)潭。④流域。⑤盆地。the Taipei *Basin.* 臺北盆地。—*v.t.* 使(地殼)凹下成盆狀。—*v.i.* (地殼)因侵蝕而凹下成盆狀。—**ed,** *adj.* 圓形的鋼盔。
bas·i·net [ˈbæsənɪt; ˈbæsinit] *n.* 一種圓形的鋼盔。
ba·sin·ful [ˈbesn̩fʊl; ˈbeisnful] *n.* 滿盆之量。
basin stand 洗臉架。
ba·si·on [ˈbesɪən; ˈbeisiɔn] *n.*〖解剖〗後頭孔前緣正中央之一點。
ba·sip·e·tal [beˈsɪpətl; beiˈsipitəl] *adj.*〖植物〗由頂向底的;由上向下的。
ba·sis** [ˈbesɪs; ˈbeisis] *n., pl.* **-ses** [-siz; -siːz]. ①主要部分;基礎。②基本原理;根據。③主要成分;主藥。The *basis* of this medicine is an oil. 此藥主要成分是一種油。④起點;起源。⑤原則;制度。⑥基準;標準。the *basis* of assessment. 課稅標準。on the basis of*** 根據…。
bask [bæsk; bɑːsk] *v.i.* ①曝日;取暖。②處於某種適意情況中。—*v.t.* 使曝日。
:bas·ket [ˈbæskɪt; ˈbɑːskit] *n.* ①籃;筐。②一籃所裝的量。She bought a *basket* of peaches. 她買了一籃的桃子。③任何籃狀物。④(籃球場的)籃。⑤(籃球賽)得分。—*v.t.* 裝或投入籃中。—*adj.* ①用以製籃的。②使用籃子攜帶物品的。an old-fashioned *basket* picnic. 使用籃子攜帶物品的舊式野餐。
***bas·ket·ball** [ˈbæskɪtˌbɔl; ˈbɑːskitbɔːl] *n.* 籃球。
bas·ket·ball·er [ˈbæskɪtˌbɔlə˞; ˈbɑːskitˌbɔːlə] *n.* 籃球員;籃球隊經理或所有人。
basket carriage (車身用柳枝細工編製之)馬車。
basket chair 一種柳條製椅子。
basket dinner 〖美〗(大規模之)野餐。
bas·ket·ful [ˈbæskɪtˌfʊl; ˈbɑːskitful] *n.* ①滿籃之量。②大量。
basket hilt 籃狀刀柄(藉以掩蔽並保護手者)。
bas·ket-of-gold [ˈbæskɪtəvˌgold; ˈbɑːskitəvgould] *n.* 砂金;金粉。
bas·ket·ry [ˈbæskɪtrɪ; ˈbɑːskitri] *n.* 編籃技藝;籃工;籃類。

bas·ket·work [ˈbæskətˌwɜk; ˈbɑːskitwəːk] *n.* 柳條編織物;編籃技藝。
basking shark 一種不攻擊人的大鯊。
ba·son [ˈbesn̩; ˈbeisn] *n.*=**basin.**
Ba·sov [ˈbasəf;ˈbɑːsəf] 巴索夫(Nikolai Gennediyevich, 1922–, 蘇聯物理學家, 1964年獲諾貝爾物理獎)。
Basque [bæsk; bæsk] *n.* ①巴士克人(Pyrenees 地區西部之一種族)。②巴士克人所用之語言。③(b-) 一種婦人之緊身上衣。—*adj.* 巴士克人的;巴士克語的。
bas-re·lief [ˌbɑ·rɪˈlif; ˈbæsriliːf] *n.*浮雕;淺浮雕;雕刻之陽文。
Bass [bæs; bæs] *n.* 一種啤酒。
***bass**[1] [bes; beis] *adj., n., pl.* **bass·es.** —*adj.* ①低音的。②音樂中最低部分的。the *bass part.* 低音部。—*n.*①男子最低音。②低音歌者;低音樂器。③音樂之最低部分。
bass[2] [bæs; bæs] *n., pl.* **bass·es.**鱸魚類。
bass drum [bes~; beis~] 大鼓。
bas·set[1] [ˈbæsɪt; ˈbæsit] *n.* 腿短而身長的獵犬。(亦作 **basset hound**)
bas·set[2] *n., v.,* **-set·ed, -set·ing.** —*n.*〖地質〗(礦脈等之)露出。—*v.i.* 露出地表;露出。
basset horn 〖音樂〗巴賽管。
bass horn 一種有曲管之低音喇叭。
bas·si·net [ˌbæsəˈnɛt; ˌbæsiˈnet] *n.* ①小兒的搖籃。②小兒睡車。③=**basinet.**
bas·so [ˈbæso; ˈbæsou] *n., pl.* **-sos, -si** [-sɪ; -si].〖音樂〗低音;低音部;低音歌手。
bas·soon [bæˈsun; bəˈsuːn] *n.*〖音樂〗低音管;巴頌管。
bas·so pro·fun·do [ˈbæsopro̞ˈfʌndo; ˈbæsouprouˈfʌndou] *pl.* **bas·si pro·fun·di** [ˈbæsɪprəˈfʌndɪ; ˈbæsiprouˈfʌndi]. 最低音歌手。(亦作 **basso profondo**)
bas·so-re·lie·vo [ˈbæso·rɪˈlivo; ˈbæsouriˈliːvou] *n., pl.* **-vos.**〖義〗=**bas-relief.**
bass viol [bes~; beis~]〖音樂〗一種低音之古提琴。
bass·wood [ˈbæsˌwʊd; ˈbæswud] *n.* ①菩提樹。②菩提樹材。
bast [bæst; bæst] *n.* ①〖植物〗韌皮部。②菩提樹等之內皮;韌皮纖維。
bas·tard [ˈbæstə˞d; ˈbæstəd] *n.*①私生子。②劣等東西;贋品。③卑鄙的傢伙。—*adj.* ①私生的。②假的;劣的。
bas·tard·ize [ˈbæstə˞ˌdaɪz; ˈbæstədaiz] *v.,* **-ized, -iz·ing.** —*v.t.*①宣示爲私生子; 判爲庶出。②使墮落; 濫用。—*v.i.* 變壞;變劣。—**bas·tard·i·za·tion,** *n.*
bas·tard·ly [ˈbæstə˞dlɪ; ˈbæstədli] *adj.*①私生的;庶出的;出身微賤的。②僞造的;贋製的。③卑鄙的。
bas·tar·dy [ˈbæstə˞dɪ; ˈbæstədi] *n., pl.* **-dies.** ①私生;庶出。②產私生子。
baste [best; beist] *v.t.,* **bast·ed, bast·ing.** ①用長針作稀疏的縫紉;假縫。②〖俗〗毆打。③烤肉時潤以脂油。④公開指摘或責罵。
Bas·tille [bæsˈtil; bæsˈtiːl] *n.* ①巴黎的巴士底獄。②(b-) 古代的堡寨。③(b-) 監獄。(②, ③亦作 **bastile**)
Bastille Day 法國革命紀念日(七月十四日)。

bas·ti·na·do [ˌbæstəˈnedo; ˌbæstiˈneidou] *n., pl.* **-does,** *v.,* **-doed, -do·ing.** —*n.* ①棍;棒。②用棍棒打;笞蹠刑(東方打足心之一種刑罰)。—*v.t.*用棍棒打;加笞蹠刑於。

bast·ing [ˈbestɪŋ; ˈbeistiŋ] *n.* ①假縫;暫縫;綳。②(*pl.*)綳線。③烤肉時澆以汁使潤溼。④烤肉時所澆之汁。

bas·tion [ˈbæstʃən; ˈbæstiən] *n.* ①稜堡;基地。②防禦;防禦工事。—**ed,** *adj.*

bat**[1] [bæt;bæt] *n., v.,* **bat·ted, bat·ting.** —*n.*①棒。②〖俗〗打擊。③狂歡;縱飲。to go on a *bat.* 狂飲作樂。④(板球等之)擊球者。⑤〖英〗速度。at bat*** (棒球)爲打擊手。The second baseman was *at bat.* 正輪到二壘手打擊。***go to bat for*** 〖俚〗幫助;爲…辯護或調停。***off one's own bat*** 靠自己力量。***right off the bat*** 立刻;立卽。—*v.t.* ①用棒擊(球);擊。②有…之擊中率;有…之正確率。③草率撰寫。—*v.i.* 用棒擊球;輪到擊球。He *bats* well. 他是擊球能手。***bat around*** a. 無目的地到處旅行。b. 討論。c. 〖棒球〗在一局中每一個打擊手均能輪流上場打擊。***bat in*** 〖棒球〗擊出安打使已上壘者跑回本壘得分。

bat**[2] *n.* ①蝙蝠。②〖俚〗a. 賤婦。b. 醜婦。blind as a bat*** 近乎全瞎。***have bats in one's belfry*** 〖俚〗態度瘋狂。

bat[3] *v.t.,* **bat·ted, bat·ting.** 〖俗〗眨(眼)。***not to bat an eye*** 漫不經心;保持冷靜。

bat. ①battalion. ②battery.

bat boy 棒球隊中管理球棒及其他裝備的少年。

batch [bætʃ; bætʃ] *n.* ①一次所烘的麪包。②一批;一組。—*adj.* 整批的。—*v.i.* 過單身漢生活。—*v.t.* 計量(每批混凝土材料)。

batch processing 〖電腦〗分批處理。

bate[1] [bet; beit] *v.,* **bat·ed, bat·ing.** —*v.t.* ①壓制;屏(息)。②減弱;減少。—*v.i.* 減弱;減少。***with bated breath*** 屏息地。

bate[2] *n., v.,* **bat·ed, bat·ing.** —*n.* 〖英俚〗憤怒;生氣。—*v.i.*①(鷹類)撲翅急於飛行。②〖英俚〗吵架。

bate[3] *v.,* **bat·ed, bat·ing,** *n.* —*v.t. & v.i.* 浸於鹼性溶液中。—*n.* 鞣革用之鹼性溶液。

ba·teau [bæˈto; bæˈtou] *n., pl.* **-teaux** [-ˈtoz; -ˈtouz]. ①平底小舟。②浮舟。

bat·fowl [ˈbætˌfaul; ˈbætfaul] *v.i.* 夜間以燈火眩鳥之目而捕之。

Bath [bæθ, bɑθ; bɑːθ] *n.* ①〖英〗巴斯勳位(章)。②英國城市名(以溫泉著名)。

‡**bath** [bæθ; bɑːθ] *n., pl.* **baths** [bæðz; bɑːðz], *v.* —*n.*①洗澡。He takes a *bath* every morning. 他每晨洗澡。②洗澡的水;浴具。shower *bath.* 淋浴。③浴室。④(常*pl.*)有溫泉或礦泉之名勝地。They spent the summer at the *baths.* 他們在溫泉勝地過夏天。⑤浴場。⑥濕淋淋的狀態。⑦浸物之溶液。⑧希伯來之液量單位,約等於十至十一美國加侖。—*v.t.* 〖英〗替…洗澡。—*v.i.*〖英〗洗澡;沐浴。

Bath brick 巴斯磨石(用以琢磨金屬)。

Bath chair 〖英〗輪椅(病人用,有遮篷)。(亦作 **bath chair**)

***bathe** [beð; beið] *v.,* **bathed, bath·ing,** *n.* —*v.t.* ①浸於;洗。②浸濕。Tears *bathed* his cheeks. 他淚流滿面。③浴於。④蓋;籠罩;圍繞。The valley was *bathed* in sunlight. 山谷爲陽光所普照。—*v.i.* 入浴。—*n.* 海水浴或江河水浴。to take a *bathe.* 洗海水浴或洗河水浴(與 to take a bath "普通沐浴"有別)。—**bath·er,** *n.*

bathe·a·ble [ˈbeðəbl; ˈbeiðəbl] *adj.*可洗浴的;適於水浴的。(亦作 **bathable**)

ba·thet·ic [bəˈθɛtɪk; bəˈθetik] *adj.* ①虛僞或過分令人同情或傷感的;膚淺矯飾之感情的;陳腐的。②〖修辭〗突降法(bathos)的。

bath·house [ˈbæθˌhaus; ˈbɑːθhaus] *n.* ①公共浴室;澡堂。②更衣室。

bath·ing [ˈbeðɪŋ; ˈbeiðiŋ] *n.* 沐浴;游泳。

bathing beach 海水浴場。

bathing cap 游泳帽。

bathing drawers 游泳褲。

bathing house 更衣所。

bathing machine (英國海水浴場之)更衣馬車。

bathing suit 游泳衣。

bath mat 浴室內供踏足之墊。

ba·thom·e·ter [bəˈθɑmɪtɚ; bəˈθɔmitə] *n.* 深度計。

bat·horse [ˈbætˌhɔrs; ˈbæthɔːs] *n.* 軍中馱負行裝之馬。

ba·thos [ˈbeθɑs; ˈbeiθɔs] *n.* ①〖修辭〗比小法;突降法。②平凡而陳腐之風格。③假悲慨;過度誇張之哀惻。④高潮後之低潮。⑤最低點;最壞的地步。

bath·robe [ˈbæθˌrob; ˈbɑːθroub] *n.* 浴衣。

***bath·room** [ˈbæθˌrum; ˈbɑːθrum] *n.* 浴室。

bathroom tissue 草紙;衞生紙。

bath·tub [ˈbæθˌtʌb; ˈbɑːθtʌb] *n.* 浴盆;浴缸。

bath·y·scaphe [ˈbæθəˌskef; ˈbæθiskeif] *n.* 一種深海探測用的球形潛水乘具。

bath·y·sphere [ˈbæθɪˌsfɪr; ˈbæθisfiə] *n.* 潛水箱。

ba·tik [ˈbɑtik; ˈbætik] *n.* ①蠟染。②染有圖案之布。③所染印之圖案。—*v.t.* 以蠟染法染印。

bat·ing [ˈbetɪŋ; ˈbeitiŋ] *prep.* 除…外。

ba·tiste [bæˈtist; bæˈtiːst] *n.* 上等細麻布。

bat·man [ˈbætmən; ˈbætmən] *n., pl.* **-men.** 侍役;勤務兵。

ba·ton [bæˈtɑn; ˈbætən] *n.* ①警棍。②〖音樂〗指揮棒。③權杖。—*v.t.* (以棍)打。

Ba·tra·chi·a [bəˈtrekɪə; bəˈtreikjə] *n. pl.* 〖動物〗無尾兩棲類;蛙類。

ba·tra·chi·an [bəˈtrekɪən; bəˈtreikjən] *n., adj.* 無尾兩棲動物(的)。

bats [bæts; bæts] *adj.* 〖俚〗瘋狂的。

bats·man [ˈbætsmən; ˈbætsmən] *n., pl.* **-men.** (棒球等之)打擊手。

batt [bæt; bæt] *n.* (常*pl.*) 棉胎。

batt. ①battalion. ②battery.

***bat·tal·ion** [bəˈtæljən, bæˈtæl-; bəˈtæljən] *n.* ①營;大隊。②(*pl.*)軍隊;兵力。③營司令部。④羣。

bat·tels [ˈbætlz; ˈbætlz] *n. pl.* (牛津大學之)校內膳費;學雜費。

bat·ten[1] [ˈbætn̩; ˈbætn] *v.i.* 發育旺盛;長肥。—*v.t.* 使發育旺盛;使肥。

bat·ten[2] *n.* ①木板;板條。②(支撐帆用的)木棍。—*v.t.* 裝板條;用木條釘牢。

bat·ten[3] *n.* ①(紡織機上的)扣。②曲尺。

***bat·ter**[1] [ˈbætɚ; ˈbætə] *v.t. & v.i.* ①連擊;重擊。Someone was *battering* at the door. 有人在用力敲門。②敲碎;用壞。

bat·ter[2] *n.* 蛋、麪粉、牛奶等和成之糊狀物。

***bat·ter**[3] *n.* 擊球者;打擊手。

bat·ter[4] *v.i.* 〖建築〗(牆壁之)向後傲傾;傾斜。—*n.* (牆面向上漸薄所形成之)直傾斜。

bat·ter·cake [ˈbætɚˌkek; ˈbætəkeik] *n.* 煎餅。

bat·tered [ˈbætɚd; ˈbætəd] *adj.* ①打扁了的;敲碎的;用舊的。②(因生活困難等)

憔悴的;消瘦的。「破門撞牆等之大槌。
battering ram ①破城槌。②任何用以
batter's box 〖棒球〗打擊位置。
***bat·ter·y** [ˈbætərɪ; ˈbætəri] *n., pl.* **-ter·ies.** ①一組類似或相聯的東西。a *battery* of files. 一組銼刀。②電池。storage *battery* 蓄電池。③列砲;排砲。④砲兵連。⑤大砲的砲架;備有大砲的砲臺。⑥棒球的投手和捕手的集合稱。⑦〖法律〗毆打。He was guilty of assault and *battery*. 他犯毆打罪。⑧羣。⑨火砲隨時可發射的狀態。
battery charger 電池充電器。
bat·ting [ˈbætɪŋ; ˈbætiŋ] *n.*①擊球;打球動作。②〖棒球〗打擊率。③棉胎;毛胎。
batting average ①〖棒球〗打擊率。②成績;表現。
batting eye 〖棒球〗選球力。
‡**bat·tle** [ˈbætl̩; ˈbætl] *n., v.,* **-tled, -tling.** —*n.* ①戰爭;戰。He fought a losing *battle.* 他打敗仗。②勝利;成功。③奮鬥;爭鬥。the *battle* of life. 人生的奮鬥。—*v.i.* 戰;奮鬥。They *battled* for freedom. 他們爭取自由。—*v.t.* 戰;鬥。「鬥裝備。
battle array ①戰鬥序列;陣形。②戰
bat·tle-ax, bat·tle-axe [ˈbætl̩ˌæks; ˈbætlæks] *n.* ①戰斧。②〖俗〗苛刻的女人;母老虎。
battle cruiser 戰鬥巡洋艦;巡洋戰艦。
battle cry ①戰時助威喊殺聲;吶喊。②標語;口號。
bat·tle·dore [ˈbætl̩ˌdor; ˈbætldɔː] *n.* ①打毽板。②打毽戲。「打毽戲。
battledore and shuttlecock
battle fatigue 〖精神病學〗戰爭衰竭;戰爭精神病。(亦作 **combat fatigue**)
bat·tle·field [ˈbætl̩ˌfild; ˈbætlfiːld] *n.* 戰場。
battle front (戰爭的)前線;前方。
bat·tle·ground [ˈbætl̩ˌgraund; ˈbætlgraund] *n.*戰場;戰地。「指揮的單位。
battle group 〖美〗陸軍師中一計畫與
battle lantern 戰艦上急用的一種裝
battle line 戰線。 ⌊電池的手提燈。
bat·tle·ment [ˈbætl̩mənt; ˈbætlmənt] *n.* (常 *pl.*)城垛;鋸壁;雉堞。
battle piece 戰爭畫;戰爭記事。
bat·tle·plane [ˈbætl̩ˌplen; ˈbætlplein] *n.* 戰鬥機。「③激烈的爭論。
battle royal ①混戰。②激戰;扭鬥。
bat·tle-scarred [ˈbætl̩ˌskɑrd; ˈbætlskɑːd] *adj.* ①因戰爭而受傷的;有戰鬥傷痕的。②有戰爭痕跡的。「主力艦;戰艦。
***bat·tle·ship** [ˈbætl̩ˌʃɪp; ˈbætlʃip] *n.*
bat·tle·some [ˈbætl̩səm; ˈbætlsəm] *adj.* 好口角的;愛爭吵的。
battle station 〖軍〗海空軍人員在戰鬥或緊急情況時的指定位置。
bat·tle·wag·on [ˈbætl̩ˌwægən; ˈbætlˌwægən] *n.* 〖俚〗戰艦。
bat·tue [bæˈtu; bæˈtuː] *n.*①(獵物之)趕殺。②忙亂的團體活動。③亂殺;屠戮。
bat·ty [ˈbætɪ; ˈbæti] *adj.,* **-ti·er, -ti·est.** ①(似)蝙蝠的。②〖俚〗瘋狂的。③〖俚〗古怪的。
bau·ble [ˈbɔbl̩; ˈbɔːbl] *n.* ①美觀的廉價貨;玩具。②丑角手持之棒。
baud [bɔd; bɔːd] *n.* 〖電腦〗撥(傳達資料的速度單位)。
Bau·haus [ˈbauhaus; ˈbauhaus] *n.* 德國建築之一派(創始於 1919年, 以使科學技術適應藝術爲其特色)。
baulk [bɔk; bɔːk] *n., v.* =**balk.**
Bau·mé scale [ˌboˈme～; bouˈmei～] 波美比重標。「鐵鋁氧石;鐵礬土。
baux·ite [ˈbɔksaɪt; ˈbɔːksait] *n.* 〖礦〗
Ba·var·i·a [bəˈvɛrɪə; bəˈvɛəriə] *n.* 巴伐利亞(德國南部之一地區, 昔時爲一獨立王國)。
Ba·var·i·an [bəˈvɛrɪən; bəˈvɛəriən] *adj.* 巴伐利亞(人)的。—*n.* 巴伐利亞人;其語言。「小銅子。(亦作 **baubee**)
baw·bee [bɔˈbi; bɔːˈbiː] *n.*〖蘇〗半辨士;
bawd [bɔd; bɔːd] *n.* 鴇母;娼主。
bawd·i·ness [ˈbɔdɪnɪs; ˈbɔːdinis] *n.*淫穢;猥褻。
bawd·y [ˈbɔdɪ; ˈbɔːdi] *adj.,* **bawd·i·er, bawd·i·est.** 淫穢的。—**bawd·i·ly,** *adv.*
bawd·y·house [ˈbɔdɪˌhaus; ˈbɔːdihaus] *n.* 妓院。
bawl** [bɔl; bɔːl] *v.t. & v.i.* 大叫;大喊。The peddler *bawled* his wares in the street. 小販在街上叫售貨物。bawl out*** 〖美俚〗責罵。—*n.* 大叫;大喊;號哭。
‡**bay**[1] [be; bei] *n.* ①海灣。②凹陷之地。③一部分爲山所圍繞之平地;草原或平地有一部分伸入森林中者。—*v.t.* 築堤遏水。to *bay* water up. 築堤遏水。
bay[2] *n.* ①房屋之翼。②穀倉內堆乾草之地方。③船上之病室。④牆壁凹進之處。
bay**[3] *n.* ①狗吠聲。②窮途反噬之狀態。at bay*** 處於窮途之境。***bring to bay*** 圍困。***keep*** (or ***hold***) ***at bay*** 阻止(敵人等)不使前進。***stand at bay*** 作困獸之鬥。—*v.i.* 吠;連續狂吠。—*v.t.* ①吠…。The dogs ran mad and *bayed* the sky. 狗羣狂跑着向天空吠叫。②且吠且追。③圍困。④阻止(敵人)不使前進。
bay[4] *n.*①月桂樹。②(*pl.*)榮譽;月桂冠(用以獎飾詩人和戰勝者)。「紅棕色的。
bay[5] *n.* ①紅棕色。②紅棕色之馬。—*adj.*
ba·ya·dere [ˌbɑjəˈdɛr; ˌbɑːjəˈdɛə] *n.* ①顏色鮮艷的橫條花紋布。②〖法〗(南印度寺院的)舞妓。—*adj.* (布料)有色澤鮮艷之橫條的。(亦作 **bayadeer**)「的人。
Bay·ard [ˈbeəd; ˈbeiɑːd] *n.* 勇武異常
bay·ber·ry [ˈbeˌbɛrɪ; ˈbeibəri] *n., pl.* **-ries.** 〖植物〗①月桂樹。②月桂樹之實。③柳金孃屬植物。「限內大坑名。
Bay·er [ˈbeə; ˈbeiə] *n.* 月球表面第三象
bay·o·net** [ˈbeənɪt; ˈbeiənit, ˈbɛən-] *n., v.,* **-net·ed, -net·ing.** —*n.* 鎗尖;鎗上的刺刀。at the point of the bayonet*** 在鎗尖下。***bayonet charge*** (***fencing***) 刺刀衝鋒(刺刀術)。***Fix*** (***Unfix***) ***bayonets!*** 〖口令〗上(下)刺刀!—*v.t.* 用刺刀刺。—*v.i.* 操刺刀;使用刺刀。
bay·ou [ˈbaɪu; ˈbaijuː] *n., pl.* **-ous.** 美國南部之湖、河等的支流;緩流;灣流。
bay rum 一種刮鬍子後用的香水。
bay salt 日光晒製之粗粒鹽。
bay tree 月桂樹。「肚子。
bay window ①凸窗。②(胖子的)大
ba·zaar, ba·zar** [bəˈzɑr; bəˈzɑː] *n.* ①市場;商品陳列所。②百貨店;小工藝品商店。③義賣。charity bazar*** 慈善義賣會。
ba·zoo [bəˈzu; bəˈzuː] *n.* 〖美俚〗①嘴。②大話;誇口。
ba·zoo·ka [bəˈzukə; bəˈzuːkə] *n.* 火箭筒。
BB 一種常用於獵槍之子彈。
BB(B) 〖鉛筆〗double-(treble-)black.
B.B.C., BBC British Broadcasting Corporation.
BB gun 氣槍。

bbl. barrel. **bbls.** barrels.
B/C Bill for Collection. 託收票據。
***B.C.**[1] ['bi'si; 'bi:'si:] before Christ. 西元前;紀元前。
B.C.[2] ①British Columbia. ②Bachelor of Chemistry. ③Bachelor of Commerce. ④battery commander.
BCD 〖軍〗 bad conduct discharge.
BCG vaccine 卡介苗(預防肺結核之疫苗)。
B.Ch. Bachelor of Chemistry.
B.Ch.E. Bachelor of Chemical Engineering. **B.C.L.** Bachelor of Civil Law. **B. Com.** Bachelor of Commerce.
B complex 複合維他命B.
B.Com.Sc. Bachelor of Commercial Science. **B.C.P.** Bachelor of City Planning. **B.C.S.** Bachelor of Chemical Science. **B.D.** ①Bachelor of Divinity. ②bills discounted. **B/D** ①bank draft. ②bills discounted. **bd.** ①board. ②bond. ③bound. **bde** 〖軍〗 brigade.
bdel·li·um ['dɛlɪəm; 'deliəm] *n.* ①一種似沒藥的樹脂。②任何產上述樹脂之植物。③〖聖經〗紅玉;水晶;珍珠。
bd. ft. ①board foot. ②board feet.
bdl. bundle. **bds.** boards.
Be 化學元素 beryllium 之符號。
‡**be** [bi; bi:] *v.i.* 現在,直說法,單數, **am** (第一人稱), **are** (第二人稱), **is** (第三人稱), 複數, **are**;過去,直說法,單數, **was** (第一人稱), **were** (第二人稱), **was** (第三人稱),複數 **were**;過去分詞 **been**; 現在分詞 **being.** ①存在;生存;發生;存留;持續;等於;代表。②用以連結主詞和補語或用以成爲不定詞和分詞的片語。You *are* late. 你晚了。③用作助動詞。**a.** 與現在分詞並用,以成進行式或將來式。I *am* waiting. 我正在等候。**b.** 與過去分詞並用,以成被動語態。The date *was* fixed. 日期已定。④用以表示將來、責任、意向、可能性及事前的安排。He is to *be* there at nine. 他將於九時在該處。⑤與某些動詞之過去分詞連用,成爲完成式。⑥值。The book *is* five dollars. 這書值五元。⑦去過;來過。He has *been* to New York. 他到過紐約。⑧作命令句。*Be* quiet! 不要作聲! ***be for*** 贊成。I *am for* the second plan. 我贊成第二個計畫。***so be it*** **a.** 聽其自然。**b.** 即使如此。
be- 〖字首〗加於名詞、形容詞或其他動詞之前,形成動詞,如: become, befriend.
B.E. ① Bachelor of Engineering. ② Bachelor of Education. ③ Bank of England. ④bill of exchange.
BE, B/E, b.e. bill of exchange.
BEA(C), B.E.A.(C.) British European Airways (Corporation).
‡**beach** [bitʃ; bi:tʃ] *n.*海濱;江河或湖的水濱。We took a walk along the *beach.* 我們沿海濱散步。***on the beach*** **a.** 失業;處於困境。**b.** 擔任陸上職務。—*v.t.* ①移(船)靠岸。②使擱淺。—*v.i.* 擱淺。—*adj.* 在海濱着用的;在海濱使用的。
beach ball 水中或水邊遊戲用的皮球。
beach·bound ['bitʃ,baund; 'bi:tʃbaund] *adj.* 往海濱去的。
beach·boy ['bitʃ,bɔɪ; 'bi:tʃbɔi] *n.*海濱服務員。
beach·comb·er ['bitʃ,komə; 'bi:tʃ,koumə] *n.* ①向岸滾來之巨浪。②在海濱或碼頭求乞覓食的遊蕩者。
beach·er ['bitʃə; 'bi:tʃə] *n.* (湧向岸邊的)浪濤。
beach·front ['bitʃ,frʌnt; 'bi:tʃfrʌnt] *adj.* 靠海濱的。—*n.*海濱地區。
beach·head ['bitʃ,hɛd; 'bi:tʃhed] *n.* 〖軍〗灘頭陣地;橋頭堡。
beach house 海濱別墅。
beach-la-mar [,bitʃla'mar; 'bi:tʃlə'ma:] *n.*(太平洋中西部地區以英語爲基本的)一種雜揉語言。
beach·mas·ter ['bitʃ,mæstə; 'bi:tʃ,ma:stə] *n.* 陸戰隊之指揮官。
beach umbrella (海濱)太陽傘。
beach wagon 旅行車。
beach·wear ['bitʃ,wɛr; 'bi:tʃwɛə] *n.* 海灘裝。
bea·con ['bikən; 'bi:kən] *n.* ①烽火;信號。②無線電的信號,以引導飛機。③浮標;燈塔。④引導與警告之人、物或動作。—*v.t.* ①舉烽火;照耀。②引導;警告。—*v.i.* ①照耀;發出亮光。②以烽火燈塔指引;指導。
bea·con·ry ['bikənrɪ; 'bi:kənri] *n.* 無線電與雷達信號學。
bead** [bid; bi:d] *n.* ①有孔之小珠。②(*pl.*)念珠;珠串。③珠狀物;滴。④飲料之泡沫。⑤(槍之)照門。draw*** (or ***take***) ***a bead on*** 用槍瞄準。***tell*** (***say,*** or ***count***) ***one's beads*** 禱告;數念珠。—*v.t.* 串以珠;飾以珠。—*v.i.* ①成珠;成滴。②瞄準。
bead·ed ['bidɪd; 'bi:did] *adj.* 飾以小珠的。
bead·house ['bid,haus; 'bi:dhaus] *n.* 救濟院。(亦作 **bedehouse**)
bead·ing ['bidɪŋ; 'bi:diŋ] *n.* ①珠細工。②〖建築〗起珠線;串珠狀緣飾。
bea·dle ['bidl; 'bi:dl] *n.*教區小吏;差役。
bea·dle·dom ['bidldəm; 'bi:dldəm] *n.* 胥吏根性;小官僚作風。
bead·roll ['bid,rol; 'bi:droul] *n.* ①名冊;目錄。②〖天主教〗待禱之名單。
beads·man ['bidzmən; 'bi:dzmən] *n., pl.* **-men.** ①救濟院之受施人。②爲他人祈求冥福之人(尤指受雇者)。③乞丐。(亦作 **bedesman, bedeman**)
bead·work ['bid,wɜk; 'bi:dwə:k] *n.* ①珠飾細工。②〖建築〗珠緣;串珠緣飾。
bead·y ['bidɪ; 'bi:di] *adj.,* **bead·i·er, bead·i·est.** ①圓小晶亮如珠的。②飾有珠子的。③有泡的;多泡的。
bead·y-eyed ['bidɪ,aɪd; 'bi:di,aid] *adj.* 眼睛如珠的;目光銳利的;高度警覺的。
bea·gle ['bigl; 'bi:gl] *n.*一種獵兔用之小獵犬。—*v.i.* ①尾隨小獵犬後追蹤獵物。②〖美俚〗打聽某事始末。
bea·gler ['biglə; 'bi:glə] *n.* 攜小獵犬行獵者。
***beak** [bik; bi:k] *n.* ①鳥嘴。②鳥嘴狀物。③(古戰艦)突出之船首。④〖美俚〗鼻。
beaked [bikt; bi:kt] *adj.* ①有喙的。②鳥嘴狀的;鉤形的;突出的。
beak·er ['bikə; 'bi:kə] *n.*①有傾口之燒杯。②飲器;大杯子。
be-all and end-all ['bi,ɔl~'ɛnd,ɔl; 'bi:ɔ:l~'endɔ:l] 要義;本體;整體;全部。
beam** [bim; bi:m] *n.* ①桁;梁。②房屋的橫梁;船的梁。③天平的橫桿;秤桿;天平。④光線。⑤船幅(船的寬度)。⑥犁柄。⑦開顏;容光煥發。⑧無線電波束(用以指引飛機師或船員)。⑨臀部之寬度。fly*** (or ***ride***) ***the beam*** 藉無線電波束之指示而飛行。***off the beam*** **a.** 離正道;迷路。**b.** 錯誤的。***on her beam ends*** (船)幾乎傾覆。***on the beam*** **a.** (船)與龍骨成直角;(飛機)依指示航線或方向飛行。**b.**〖俗〗正好;恰好。—*v.t.* ①放(光);射(光)。②上梁。③廣播。—*v.i.* ①放光;照

耀。②微笑;開顏。
beam antenna 〖無線電〗定向天線。
beam compass 長脚圓規。
beamed 〔bimd; biːmd〕 *adj.* ①有梁的。②照耀的。③〖無線電〗定向的。
beam-ends 〔ˈbimˈɛndz; ˈbiːmˈendz〕 *n. pl.* 船梁末端。***on one's beam-ends; on the beam-ends; on the beam's ends*** 在無可奈何的困境中(尤指經濟上的)。
beam·ing 〔ˈbimɪŋ; ˈbiːmiŋ〕 *adj.* ①照耀的;發光的。②愉快的。**—ly,** *adv.*
beam sea 〖航海〗横浪。
beam wind 〖航海〗横風。
beam·y 〔ˈbimɪ; ˈbiːmi〕 *adj.,* **beam·i·er, beam·i·est.** ①放射光線的。②像梁一樣的;粗大的。③〖航海〗船身很寬的。④〖動物〗有叉角的(如公鹿等)。
bean** 〔bin; biːn〕 *n.* ①豆;豆實;豆莢。②產豆的植物。③豆狀的實。④〖俚〗頭。⑤〖英俚〗硬幣;一分錢;一毛錢。⑥〖俗〗些許;一點點。He doesn't know *beans* about it. 他一點也不知道。⑦〖俚〗打擊;痛擊;懲罰。full of beans*** 〖俚〗**a.** 精神飽滿;精力充沛。**b.** 愚蠢的;錯誤的;聽錯了消息的。***old bean*** 〖英俚〗老頭;老傢伙。***spill the beans*** 〖俗〗洩露祕密。*—v.t.* 擊打…之頭。*—interj.* 表不滿,不悅,輕微的憤怒。
bean·ball 〔ˈbin,bɔl; ˈbiːnbɔːl〕 *n.* 〖棒球〗擊中打擊手之頭的球。*—v.i. & v.t.* 〖棒球〗投出。
bean cake 豆粕;豆餅。
bean curd 豆腐。
bean·er·y 〔ˈbinərɪ; ˈbiːnəri〕 *n., pl.* **-er·ies.** 〖美俚〗經濟小飯店。
bean·feast 〔ˈbin,fist; ˈbiːnfiːst〕 *n.* ①〖英〗雇主款待雇工的宴會。②〖俚〗宴會。
bean·ie 〔ˈbinɪ; ˈbiːni〕 *n.* 彩色便帽。
bean·o 〔ˈbino; ˈbiːnou〕 *n., pl.* **-os.** ①〖英俚〗=**beanfeast.** ②=**bingo.**
bean-pod 〔ˈbin,pɑd; ˈbiːnpɔd〕 *n.* 豆莢。
bean·pole 〔ˈbin,pol; ˈbiːnpoul〕 *n.* ①支竿。②〖俗〗瘦長之人。(亦作 **bean pole**)
bean sprout 豆芽。
bean·stalk 〔ˈbin,stɔk; ˈbiːnstɔːk〕 *n.* 豆莖。
Bean Town 波士頓(Boston)之別稱。
:bear¹ 〔bɛr; bɛə〕 *v.,* **bore** or 〖古〗 **bare, borne** or **born, bear·ing.** *—v.t.* ①負荷;負重。A camel can *bear* a heavy burden. 駱駝能負重。②忍受。③生產。④負擔。⑤表示;具有。⑥處身;持己;舉止。⑦抬。They *bore* him to his quarters. 他們把他抬到他的住所。⑧强迫;壓迫。⑨懷有;記憶。⑩具有(某種身分或特性)。⑪享有(某種權利)或負有(某種責任)。The king *bears* sway over the empire. 國王掌握統治全國大權。⑫容許。⑬印有…;刻有…;寫有…。⑭引起;惹起。His book *bore* heavy praise. 他的書受到極大的讚譽。⑮擔任(角色)。*—v.i.* ①生;產生。This tree *bears* well. 此樹結果很多。②支持;承載。The floor will not *bear.* 這地板將支持不住。③移;向。The ship *bears* due west. 這船向正西行。④關於;涉及。⑤正對着;加諸於。⑥位於。The land *bore* due north of the ship. 陸地在船的正北方。⑦進;行。Nearer and nearer the foe are *bearing.* 敵人越來越靠近。***bear arms*** 從軍。***bear down*** 壓制;平定。***bear down on*** (or ***upon***) **a.** 向…逼進。**b.** 特別論及;强調。The lecture *bore down on* economic causes. 那演講特別論及經濟上的原因。**c.** 對…有重大影響。***bear fruit*** 產生效果。***bear in hand*** **a.** 處理;管理。**b.** 主張;控告;指責。**c.** 允諾;答應。***bear in mind*** 牢記在心。***bear in with*** 駛向。***bear out*** 證實。***bear up*** 鼓起勇氣;保持希望或信心。***bear with*** 容忍;忍耐。***bring to bear*** 作有效之運用。
bear²** *n.* ①熊。②鄙野之人。③能力、耐力或興趣等勝過他人者。a *bear* at mathematics. 數學能手。④(B-)熊星座。⑤股票市場上看跌者;跌勢策動者;空頭(爲 bull 之對)。⑥一種鐵片打孔機。⑦(B-)俄國。be a bear for*** 對(工作、辛勞等)特具耐力、興趣、才幹等。*—v.t.* 使…跌價。
bear·a·ble 〔ˈbɛrəbl; ˈbɛərəbl〕 *adj.* 可忍受的;支持得住的。**—bear·a·bly,** *adv.*
bear·bait·ing 〔ˈbɛr,betɪŋ; ˈbɛə,beitiŋ〕 *n.* 犬熊相鬥戲。
bear·ber·ry 〔ˈbɛr,bɛrɪ; ˈbɛəbəri〕 *n.* 〖植物〗石南科之一種小灌木。
bear·cat 〔ˈbɛr,kæt; ˈbɛəkæt〕 *n.* ①熊貓。②〖俗〗蠻幹者。
Beard 〔bɪrd; biəd〕 *n.* 比爾德 (Daniel Carter, 1850–1941, 美國藝術家,爲美國男童軍之創始者)。
beard** 〔bɪrd; biəd〕 *n.* ①鬚;髯。②〖美俚〗留鬍子的人(尤指知識分子)。③芒。in spite of one's beard*** 違反某人之意。***meet*** (or ***run***) ***in one's beard*** 公然反對某人。***speak in one's beard*** 喃喃地說。***take by the beard*** 大膽攻擊。***to one's beard*** 當面。*—v.t.* 勇敢面對;藐視;公然反對。
beard·ed 〔ˈbɪrdɪd; ˈbiədid〕 *adj.* ①有鬚的。②有芒的。
beard·less 〔ˈbɪrdlɪs; ˈbiədlis〕 *adj.* ①無鬚的。②無芒的。
***bear·er** 〔ˈbɛrɚ, ˈbærɚ; ˈbɛərə〕 *n.* ①送信人;持票人。②挑夫;扛夫;抬棺者。③結實或開花之植物。This tree is a good *bearer.* 此樹產果甚多。④支撐物。⑤擁有者。⑥擔任者。office *bearers.* 擔任職務者。⑦扈棺之人。
bear garden ①犬熊相鬥之遊戲場。②吵嚷混亂之處所。
bear·ing** 〔ˈbɛrɪŋ, ˈbær-; ˈbɛəriŋ〕 *n.* ①意義。②(*pl.*)方位;方向。③忍耐。④行爲;舉止;態度。⑤產子;結實;收穫。an old woman past *bearing.* 已不能生育的老婦。⑥軸承。⑦紋章;任何一種圖記。in bearing*** 結果(實)。***lose*** (or ***be out of***) ***one's bearings*** 迷失方向;(轉爲)惶惑;不知所措。***take one's bearings*** 審度環境找出自己的位置。*—adj.* 能產的;多產的。a good *bearing* year. 豐年。
bearing rein 制韁 (=checkrein).
bear·ish 〔ˈbɛrɪʃ; ˈbɛəriʃ〕 *adj.* ①粗暴的;似熊的。②使(股票等)下跌的;策動跌勢的。③期望(股票等)下跌的。
bear leader 富家子弟之私人教師或伴遊者。
bear·skin 〔ˈbɛr,skɪn; ˈbɛə-skin〕 *n.* ①熊皮。②熊皮製品。③(英國禁衛軍之)黑皮高帽。④一種做大衣用的粗呢。
:beast 〔bist; biːst〕 *n.* ①獸。②獸性的人;兇惡的人。He is a *beast.* 他是一個惡漢。③可惡的東西。④〖俚〗醜丫頭。⑤獸性。
beast·li·ness 〔ˈbistlɪnɪs; ˈbiːstlinis〕 *n.* ①獸性;殘忍;醜惡。②獸行;殘忍的行爲。③汚穢;淫猥。④惡心之食物;不潔之物。
beast·ly 〔ˈbistlɪ; ˈbiːstli〕 *adj.,* **-li·er, -li·est,** *adv.* *—adj.* ①獸(性)的。②淫猥的。③令人討厭的。*—adv.* 〖英俗〗非常地;過分地。
beast of burden 勞動用牲口;馱獸。
beast of prey 食肉獸。

‡beat [bit; biːt] *v.*, **beat, beat·en** or **beat, beat·ing,** *n., adj.* —*v.t.* ①打;連打;連擊。We *beat* the drums. 我們擊鼓。②擊敗。③〖音樂〗打拍子。to *beat* time. 打拍子。④開路;踏平。⑤〖俗〗難倒。This problem *beats* me. 這問題難倒了我。⑥欺騙;詐取。⑦極力使(某人)採取某種態度, 接受某種意見等。I'll *beat* some sense into him. 我將設法使他放明白些。⑧攪拌。⑨鼓(翼)。⑩通過;遍查。—*v.i.* ①敲;連打。②搏動;跳動。③打擊;衝擊。④(鼓)咚咚地響。⑤逆風循鋸齒狀路線行駛。The sailboat *beat* along the coast. 帆船沿岸邊逆風而駛。⑥〖俗〗得勝。***beat about*** (or ***around***) ***the bush*** 不直截了當地說或做;轉彎抹角地說或做。***beat a retreat*** 鳴鼓退兵;敗退。***beat down*** **a.** 擊敗。**b.** 以講價壓低(價錢)。***beat*** (***all***) ***hollow*** 打得落花流水。***beat it*** **a.** 逃走。**b.** 急奔;趕。***Beat it!*** 離開!走開! ***beat one's brains*** 苦思;苦苦思索。***beat out*** **a.** 踏出(路等)。**b.** 擊敗。***beat the air*** (or ***wind***) 做吃力不討好的事; 白費精力地做事。***beat the bushes*** (or ***woods***) 到處尋找。***beat the*** (or ***a***) ***drum*** 大事宣傳或談論。***beat the rap*** 逃避法律制裁。***beat up*** **a.** 毒打。**b.** 與逆風或逆流掙扎前進。**c.** 打(蛋);攪拌。**d.** 徵集;召集。—*n.* ①划; 頻擊。②搏動;跳動。③節拍。④常走之路; 巡邏。⑤〖俗〗更強者。I have never seen the *beat* of it. 我從未見過比這更厲害的。⑥= **beatnik.** ⑦〖新聞〗獨家報導。⑧〖新聞〗記者所負責採訪之範圍(亦作 **news beat** 或 **news run**)。***off one's beat*** **a.** 不再作慣常之工作。**b.** 非本行。***on the beat*** 〖音樂〗合乎節奏。—*adj.* 〖美俚〗①疲乏的。dead *beat.* 筋疲力盡。②驚訝的;受嚇的。③beatnik 的; beatnik 特有的。

beat-beat [ˈbitˌbit; ˈbiːtbiːt] *n.* 〖火箭〗「一種利用雷達追蹤飛彈的系統。」

***beat·en** [ˈbitn̩; ˈbiːtn] *v.* pp. of **beat.** —*adj.* ①被責打的。②鍛打的;被槌薄的。③被打敗的。The *beaten* enemy soon surrendered. 被打敗的敵人很快就投降了。④慣踏之(路)。⑤疲倦的。⑥破舊的;破爛的。

beat·er [ˈbitɚ; ˈbiːtə] *n.* 打的工具。

beat generation ①披頭世代(指二次大戰後, 對人生失望, 祇圖眼前歡樂, 服裝奇特, 行爲乖僻的男女青年)。②(B- G-)(文學上)被打垮的一代。

be·a·tif·ic [ˌbiəˈtɪfɪk; ˌbiəˈtifik] *adj.* 快「樂的;有福的;祝福的。」

be·at·i·fy [bɪˈætəˌfaɪ; bi(ː)ˈætifai] *v.t.*, **-fied, -fy·ing.** ①賜福;使享福。②〖天主教〗行宣福禮。—**be·at·i·fi·ca·tion,** *n.*

***beat·ing** [ˈbitɪŋ; ˈbiːtiŋ] *n.* ①打。②跳動;搏動。③打敗;敗北。

beat·ism [ˈbitɪzəm; ˈbiːtizəm] *n.* 披頭主義。—**beat·ist,** *n.*

be·at·i·tude [bɪˈætəˌtjud; bi(ː)ˈætitjuːd] *n.* ①全福;至福。②祝福。***the Beatitudes*** 聖經中之八福。

beat·nik [ˈbitnɪk; ˈbiːtnik] *n.* 披頭。

Be·a·trice [ˈbiətrɪs; ˈbiətris] *n.* 女子名。

beau [bo; bou] *n., pl.* **beaus** or **beaux** [boz; bouz], *v.*, **-ed, -ing.** —*n.* ①喜修飾者;紈袴子弟。②情郎。—*v.t.* 爲…任護花使者。

Beau·fort scale [ˈbofɚt~; ˈboufət~] ①波福風力等級(依風速分風力爲13等級或18等級)。②波福海浪等級(根據10級以內之風力等級而分)。

beau ideal *pl.* **beaus ideal, beaux ideal, beau ideals.** ①十全十美;至美。②優美之典範或典型。〖注意〗第一義複數爲 beaus ~或 beaux ~, 第二義複數爲 ~ ideals.

beau·ish [ˈboɪʃ; ˈbouiʃ] *adj.* 花花公子的;好修飾的。

beau monde [boˈmɑnd; bouˈmɔnd] 「時髦界;上流社會。」

Beau·mont *n.* [ˈbomɑnt; ˈboumɔnt] 月球表面第四象限內之一平原名。

Beaune [bon; boun] *n.* 法國 Beaune 地方製造的一種紅葡萄酒。

beaut [bjut; bjuːt] 〖俗〗 *n.* 美人;美好的東西(多用來諷刺)。

beau·te·ous [ˈbjutɪəs; ˈbjuːtiəs] *adj.* 美麗的。—**ly,** *adv.* —**ness,** *n.*

beau·ti·cian [bjuˈtɪʃən; bjuˈtiʃən] *n.* 「美容師。」

beau·ti·fi·ca·tion [ˌbjutəfɪˈkeʃən; ˌbjuːtifiˈkeiʃən] *n.* 修飾;美化。

beau·ti·fi·er [ˈbjutəˌfaɪɚ; ˈbjuːtifaiə] *n.* 使美的東西或人。

‡beau·ti·ful [ˈbjutəfəl; ˈbjuːtəful] *adj.* ①美麗的;美觀的;美的。a *beautiful* girl. 美麗的女子。②完美的。His arguments were *beautiful.* 他的議論美妙絕倫。—**ness,** *n.*

***beau·ti·ful·ly** [ˈbjutəfəlɪ; ˈbjuːtəfli] *adv.* 美麗地; 好。This work is *beautifully* done. 這工作做得好極了。

beautiful people 上流社會講究時髦的富人。(亦作 **Beautiful People**)

beau·ti·fy [ˈbjutəˌfaɪ; ˈbjuːtifai] *v.*, **-fied, -fy·ing.** —*v.t.* 美化。—*v.i.* 變美。

‡beau·ty [ˈbjutɪ; ˈbjuːti] *n., pl.* **-ties.** ①美貌。She combines wit with *beauty.* 她兼備機智與美貌。②美人。She is a *beauty.* 她是一個美人。③美。④美的事物。⑤優點;好處。⑥精采(實指"要命")的事物。

beauty art 美容術;化妝術。

beauty contest 選美會。

beauty doctor 美容師。

beauty parlor (or **shop**) 美容院。

beauty salon 美容院。

beauty sleep 〖俗〗午夜前之睡眠。

beau·ty-spe·cial·ist [ˈbjutɪˌspɛʃəlɪst; ˈbjuːtiˌspeʃəlist] *n.* 美容專家。

beauty spot ①皮膚上之斑點; 痣。②面貼;美人斑(婦人用以襯托其皮膚白皙之黑紙片或布片)。③特別美之處;美景;名勝。

beaux [boz; bouz] *n.* pl. of **beau.**

beaux-arts [boˈzaːr; bouˈzɑː] 〖法〗 *n. pl.* 美術;藝術。

beaux yeux [boˈzjœ; bouˈzjœ] 〖法〗①美目;明眸。②美貌。

bea·ver¹** [ˈbivɚ; ˈbiːvə] *n.* ①海狸;海獺。②海狸皮。③一種似海狸皮之厚毛呢。④海狸皮帽。⑤禮帽;絲製高帽。⑥〖美俚〗鬍鬚;蓄鬚的人。eager beaver*** 〖美俚〗工作勤奮的人。—*v.i.* 〖英〗努力工作。

bea·ver² *n.* 半面甲; 頭盔上所附之活動「臉罩。」

bea·ver·board [ˈbivɚˌbord; ˈbiːvəbɔːd] *n.* 建築用之厚紙板。

beaver cloth 仿海狸皮的毛織或棉織「品。」

bea·ver·ette [ˌbivəˈrɛt; ˌbiːvəˈret] *n.* 着色後如海狸皮的兔皮。

be·calm [bɪˈkɑm; biˈkɑːm] *v.t.* ①因無風而使(船)停航;使不動(常用p.p.)。②使安靜。

be·calmed [bɪˈkɑmd; biˈkɑːmd] *adj.* 平靜的;因風平浪靜而不能移動的(船)。

‡be·came [bɪˈkem; biˈkeim] *v.* pt. of **become.**

‡be·cause [bɪˈkɔz; biˈkɔz] *conj.* 因爲。I did not go out *because* it rained. 我因爲下雨沒有出門。***because of*** 因爲;由於。

The game was postponed *because of* rain. 這場比賽因下雨而延期。

bec·ca·fi·co 〔ˌbɛkəˈfiko; ˌbekəˈfiːkou〕 *n., pl.* **-cos.** 小鳴禽(在義大利視為美食)。

bé·cha·mel 〔ˌbeˌʃɑˈmɛl; ˌbeʃəˈmel〕 *n.* 一種調味汁;白汁。(亦作 **béchamel sauce**)

be·chance 〔bɪˈtʃæns; biˈtʃɑːns〕 *v.t. & v.i.,* **be·chanced, be·chanc·ing.** 〖古〗降臨(於);(使)發生。 「迷醉;使銷魂。

be·charm 〔bɪˈtʃarm; biˈtʃɑːm〕 *v.t.* 使

bêche-de-mer 〔ˌbɛʃdəˈmɛr; ˈbeʃdəˈmɛə〕 *n., pl.* **bêches-de-mer.** 〖法〗①海參;刺參。②＝**beach-la-mar.**

beck[1] 〔bɛk; bek〕 *n.* 點頭或招手以示意。 ***be at one's beck and call*** 聽人命令;受人指揮。—*v.t. & v.i.* ①打招呼。②〖英〗模仿鳥求偶之鳴聲俾誘近而射擊之。

beck[2] *n.* 小溪(尤指其底為岩石者)。

beck·et 〔ˈbɛkɪt; ˈbekit〕 *n.* 環索;把手索。

***beck·on** 〔ˈbɛkən; ˈbekən〕 *v.i. & v.t.* 招手或點頭示意〖to〗. He *beckoned* me to come nearer. 他招手叫我行近。—*n.* 招人行近之手勢。 「暗;蒙蔽。②使混亂。

be·cloud 〔bɪˈklaud; biˈklaud〕 *v.t.* ①遮

‡**be·come** 〔bɪˈkʌm; biˈkʌm〕 *v.,* **be·came, be·come, be·com·ing.** —*v.i.* ①變為;成為。He *became* wiser as he grew older. 他年紀大些,變得聰明些了。②發生。 ***become of*** 降臨;遭遇。What will *become of* her? 她將來的遭遇如何? —*v.t.* 適合;適宜;相稱。It does not *become* me to question your decision. 我不宜懷疑你的決定。

be·com·ing 〔bɪˈkʌmɪŋ; biˈkʌmiŋ〕 *adj.* 適當的;合式的。 **—ly,** *adv.*

Bec·que·rel 〔bɛkˈrɛl; ˌbekəˈrel〕 *n.* 白克瑞爾(Antoine Henri, 1852-1908, 法國物理學家, 1903年獲諾貝爾物理獎)。

Becquerel rays 白克瑞爾放射線。

be·crip·ple 〔bɪˈkrɪpl̩; biˈkripl〕 *v.t.* 使跛;使成殘廢。

‡**bed** 〔bɛd; bed〕 *n., v.,* **bed·ded, bed·ding.** —*n.* ①牀;臥牀。②就寢時間;睡眠。to take a walk before *bed.* 睡前散散步。③婚姻。④墳墓。to dig out his narrow *bed.* 挖他的墳。⑤基;底。the *bed* of a river. 河牀。⑥(花)壇;(苗)牀。a flower *bed.* 花壇。⑦層;地層。a *bed* of coal. 煤礦層。 ***be in bed*** **a.** 臥;睡。**b.** 性交。 ***get up on the wrong side of the bed*** 自早晨起便心情不好。 ***go to bed*** 就寢。*Go to bed* early and get up early. 早睡早起。 ***lie on a bed of thorns*** 如坐針氈。 ***lie on*** (or ***in***) ***the bed one has made*** 自作自受。 ***make one's bed*** 為自己的行為負責。You've *made your bed,* now lie in it. 你既然做了這件事, 現在就得負責。 ***make the bed*** 整理床鋪。 ***put ... to bed*** 使睡。 *Put* him *to bed.* 使他睡。 ***take to one's bed*** 臥病。—*v.t.* ①使睡。②安置;嵌入。③種植於苗牀或花壇。He was *bedding* out some young plants. 他種幼小的植物於苗牀。—*v.i.* ①臥;睡。②發生超友誼關係。③形成地層;形成硬層。

be·dab·ble 〔bɪˈdæbl̩; biˈdæbl〕 *v.t.,* **-bled, -bling.** 潑濕;濺污。

be·dad 〔bɪˈdæd; biˈdæd〕 *interj.* ＝**begad.**

bed and board ①膳宿。②婚姻的義務。

be·daub 〔bɪˈdɔb; biˈdɔːb〕 *v.t.* ①塗;污染。②過分裝飾;不當地修飾。

be·daze 〔bɪˈdez; biˈdeiz〕 *v.t.,* **be·dazed, be·daz·ing.** ①使全然暈眩。②使昏迷。

be·daz·zle 〔bɪˈdæzl̩; biˈdæzl〕 *v.t.,* **-zled, -zling.** 使眩;使迷惑。 **—ment,** *n.*

bed·bug 〔ˈbɛdˌbʌg; ˈbedbʌg〕 *n.* 臭蟲。

bed·cham·ber 〔ˈbɛdˌtʃembɚ; ˈbedˌtʃeimbə〕 *n.* 臥房;寢室。 「*n. pl.* 寢具。

bed·clothes 〔ˈbɛdˌkloz; ˈbedklouðz〕

bed cover ＝**bedspread.**

bed·ding 〔ˈbɛdɪŋ; ˈbediŋ〕 *n.* ①被褥。②寢具;牀。③基牀;底牀。 「麗。

be·deck 〔bɪˈdɛk; biˈdek〕 *v.t.* 裝飾;使美

be·dev·il 〔bɪˈdɛvl̩; biˈdevl〕 *v.t.,* **-il(l)ed, -il·(l)ing.** ①虐待;使苦惱。②蠱惑。③使混淆;敗壞。 「〔ˈdevlmənt〕 *n.* 着魔。

be·dev·il·ment 〔bɪˈdɛvl̩mənt; bi-

be·dew 〔bɪˈdju; biˈdjuː〕 *v.t.* 沾濕。

bed·fast 〔ˈbɛdˌfæst; ˈbedfɑːst〕 *adj.* 臥床不起的。 「①同床者。②同事;夥伴。

bed·fel·low 〔ˈbɛdˌfɛlo; ˈbedˌfelou〕 *n.*

Bed·ford cord 〔ˈbɛdfɚd～; ˈbedfəd～〕 堅實之粗條布。 「牀架。

bed·frame 〔ˈbɛdˌfrem; ˈbedfreim〕 *n.*

bed·gown 〔ˈbɛdˌgaun; ˈbedgaun〕 *n.* 寢衣。

be·dim 〔bɪˈdɪm; biˈdim〕 *v.t.,* **-dimmed, -dim·ming.** ①使昏暗;使朦朧。②蒙蔽。

be·di·zen 〔bɪˈdɪzn̩, -ˈdaɪzn̩; biˈdizn, -ˈdaizn〕 *v.t.* 俗氣地穿着或裝飾。

bed·lam 〔ˈbɛdləm; ˈbedləm〕 *n.* ①喧擾;騷亂。②瘋人院。 **—ic,** *adj.*

bed·lam·ite 〔ˈbɛdləmˌaɪt; ˈbedləmait〕 *n.* 狂人;瘋子。—*adj.* 瘋狂的。

bed·mak·er 〔ˈbɛdˌmekɚ; ˈbedˌmeikə〕 *n.* ①製床者。②(英國大學中之)寢室僕役。

bed of roses 舒適豪華的環境;工作輕易而一切令人滿意的職位(常用作反語)。

Bed·ou·in 〔ˈbɛduɪn; ˈbeduin〕 *n., pl.* **-ins, -in.** ①貝多因人或部落(居無定所的阿拉伯遊牧民族)。②流浪者。③遊牧民族中的人。

bed·pan 〔ˈbɛdˌpæn; ˈbedpæn〕 *n.* ①暖床器。②(病人用的)便盆。 「器之)座板。

bed·plate 〔ˈbɛdˌplet; ˈbedpleit〕 *n.* (機

bed·post 〔ˈbɛdˌpost; ˈbedpoust〕 *n.* 牀柱。 ***between you and me and the bedpost*** 暗地裏;秘密。

be·drag·gle 〔bɪˈdrægl̩; biˈdrægl〕 *v.t.,* **-gled, -gling.** (衣服)拖髒;拖濕;拖皺。 **—be·drag·gled,** *adj.*

bed·rail 〔ˈbɛdˌrel; ˈbedreil〕 *n.* 床旁欄杆。

bed·rid 〔ˈbɛdˌrɪd; ˈbedrid〕 *adj.* ①臥病的。②破舊的。

bed·rid·den 〔ˈbɛdˌrɪdn̩; ˈbedˌridn〕 *adj.* 臥病的;纏綿床褥的;久病不起的。

bed·rock 〔ˈbɛdˈrɑk; ˈbedˈrɔk〕 *n.* ①〖地質〗下層的堅石;巖床。②根底;基礎。③最低點;最低額。—*adj.* 基本的;根本的。

bed·roll 〔ˈbɛdˌrol; ˈbedroul〕 *n.* 鋪蓋捲。

***bed·room** 〔ˈbɛdˌrum; ˈbedrum〕 *n.* 臥房。—*adj.* 兩性關係的。

bedroom suburb 〖美〗白天在城裏工作, 僅晚上回家就寢的人們所居住的郊區。

bed·sheet 〔ˈbɛdˌʃit; ˈbedʃiːt〕 *n.* 牀單。

***bed·side** 〔ˈbɛdˌsaɪd; ˈbedsaid〕 *n.* 床側;枕邊。 —*adj.* ①臨床的。Young doctors need *bedside* practice. 年輕醫師需要臨床實習。②適合在床上閱讀的。 「止、態度。

bedside manner 醫生對病人的舉

bed-sit·ter 〔ˈbɛdˈsɪtɚ; ˈbedˈsitə〕 *n.* 〖英俗〗臥房與起居間兼用的房間。

bed-sit·ting-room 〔ˈbɛdˈsɪtɪŋˌrum; ˈbedˈsitiŋruːm〕 *n.* 〖英〗＝ **bed-sitter.**

bed·sore ['bɛd,sor; 'bedsɔ:] *n.* 褥瘡。

bed·spread ['bɛd,sprɛd; 'bedspred] *n.* 床單;床罩。

bed·spring ['bɛd,sprɪŋ; 'bedspriŋ] *n.* 彈簧床面。

bed·stand ['bɛd,stænd; 'bedstænd] *n.* 床前桌。(亦作 **night stand, night table**)

bed·stead ['bɛd,stɛd, -stɪd; 'bedsted] *n.* 床架。

bed·straw ['bɛd,strɔ; 'bedstrɔ:] *n.* ①牀薦。②〖植物〗蓬子菜。

bed·tick ['bɛdtɪk; 'bedtik] *n.* 褥套。

***bed·time** ['bɛd,taɪm; 'bedtaim] *n.* 就寢的時間。—*adj.* 適於睡前的。

bedtime story (適合於小孩就寢時讀給他們聽的)簡單童話。

bed wetter 尿床者。

bed-wet·ting ['bɛd,wɛtɪŋ; 'bed,wetiŋ] *n.* 尿床。

⁑**bee** [bi; bi:] *n.* ①蜂; 蜜蜂。The *bee* makes honey. 蜜蜂釀蜜。②〖美〗集會; 聚集。***have a bee in one's bonnet*** (or ***head***) **a.** 死心眼地祇想一件事。He *has* the presidential *bee in his bonnet.* 他一心一意想當總統。**b.** 有點瘋狂。***keep bees*** 養蜂。***put the bee on*** 在金錢方面打(某人)的主意。***queen bee*** 女王蜂。

B.E.E. Bachelor of Electrical Engineering.

bee·bee gun ['bibi~; 'bi:bi:~] 氣槍 (=BB gun).

bee bird 食蜂鳥。

bee·bread ['bi,brɛd; 'bi:bred] *n.* 花粉蜜。

***beech** [bitʃ; bi:tʃ] *n.* ①山毛櫸;椈。②其木材。

beech·en ['bitʃən; 'bi:tʃən] *adj.* 山毛櫸的;椈材的。

beech mast 椈實;椈子。

beech·nut ['bitʃnət, -,nʌt; 'bi:tʃnʌt] *n.* 椈實;椈子。

beech·wood ['bitʃ,wud; 'bi:tʃwud] *n.* 山毛櫸木材;椈材。

bee eater 食蜂鳥。

***beef** [bif; bi:f] *n., pl.* **beeves** [bivz; bi:vz] for ②, **beefs** for ⑤, *v., adj.* —*n.* ①牛肉。②長成待宰的牛。③〖俗〗膂力;筋力;力。④〖俗〗重; 重量。⑤〖美俚〗牢騷; 訴苦。—*v.i.* ①〖美俚〗發牢騷。②加强;增强〖up〗. —*adj.* ①牛類的。*beef* blood. 牛血。②供食用的。*beef* animal. 食用動物。

beef cattle 肉牛。

beef·eat·er ['bif,itɚ; 'bi:f,i:tə] *n.* ①食牛肉者。②英王之衞士。③倫敦塔之守衞人。

beef·er ['bifɚ; 'bi:fə] *n.* 〖美〗①發牢騷者。②告發者。

beef extract 濃縮牛肉汁。

beef·steak ['bif,stek; 'bi:f'steik] *n.* 牛排。

beef tea 濃牛肉湯。

beef-wit·ted ['bif'wɪtɪd; 'bi:f'witid] *adj.* 愚鈍的。

beef·y ['bifɪ; 'bi:fi] *adj.,* **beef·i·er, beef·i·est.** ①似牛肉的;多肉的。②强壯的;結實的。③沉重的;痴肥的。

bee·hive ['bi,haɪv; 'bi:haiv] *n.* ①蜂窩。②形似蜂窩的髮型。③人口驟集而熱鬧之處所。—*adj.* 狀如蜂窩的。

bee·keep·er ['bi,kipɚ; 'bi:,ki:pə] *n.* 養蜂家。

bee killer 一種捕食昆蟲的大蒼蠅。

bee·line ['bi'laɪn; 'bi:'lain] *n.* 直線;最短之路。***make a beeline for*** 走最短之路;匆匆趕赴。—*v.i.* 走最短之路。

Be·el·ze·bub [bɪ'ɛlzɪ,bʌb; bi'elzibʌb] *n.* ①〖聖經〗魔王;魔鬼。②惡魔。③(密爾頓之 *Paradise Lost* 中之)墮落天使。

bee·mas·ter ['bi,mæstɚ; 'bi:,mɑ:stə] *n.* 養蜂者。

⁑**been** [bɪn; bi:n] *v.* pp. of **be.**

beep [bip; bi:p] *n.* ①汽車喇叭聲。②尖銳短暫的音響。—*v.i.* 鳴汽車喇叭。—*v.t.* ①鳴(喇叭)。②鳴喇叭以發(警告)。

beep·er ['bipɚ; 'bi:pə] *n.* ①發出尖銳而短暫音響的儀器。②〖俚〗無人駕駛飛機之飛行控制員。

beer** [bɪr; biə] *n.* 啤酒。in beer*** 喝(啤酒)醉的。***small beer*** 不重要的人或物。to think *small beer* of someone. 輕視某人。to think no *small beer* of oneself. 自視頗高。

beer and skittles 〖英〗遊樂; 飲酒(或不飲酒)作樂。

beer engine 〖英〗=**beer pump.**

beer garden 屋外花園酒店。

beer hall 有歌舞助興之酒吧或酒店。

beer·house ['bɪr,haus; 'biəhaus] *n.* 〖英〗啤酒店。

beer money 〖英〗①(賞給僕役的)酒錢;小費。②零用錢。

beer pump 從啤酒筒抽出啤酒的唧筒;啤酒唧筒。

beer·y ['bɪrɪ; 'biəri] *adj.,* **beer·i·er, beer·i·est.** ①啤酒的; 酒醉的。②受啤酒之影響的;喝啤酒所引起的。③有啤酒味的。

beest·ings ['bistɪŋz; 'bi:stiŋz] *n. pl.* 母牛產後之初乳。

bees·wax ['biz,wæks; 'bi:zwæks] *n.* 蜂蠟。—*v.t. & v.i.* 以蜂蠟塗、擦或處理。

bees·wing ['biz,wɪŋ; 'bi:zwiŋ] *n.* ①陳年老酒表面上的薄膜。②有此種薄膜之陳年老酒。

***beet**[1] [bit; bi:t] *n.* ①甜菜。②甜菜根。

beet[2] *v.t.* ①修理。②生火;加燃料使火繼續。③改過;懺悔。④接濟;解除(饑餓、口渴等)。

Bee·tho·ven ['betovən; 'beithouvn] *n.* 貝多芬 (Ludwig van, 1770–1827, 德國大作曲家)。—**i·an, Bee·tho·vi·an,** *adj.*

***bee·tle**[1] ['bitl̩; 'bi:tl] *n.* ①甲蟲; 類似甲蟲之昆蟲。②笨人。③槌;大槌。—*v.i.* 急走。He *beetled* off to catch the train. 他急忙去趕火車。—*v.t.* 用大槌打破、撞開等。

bee·tle[2] *adj., v.,* **-tled, -tling.** —*adj.* 突出的;凸出的。—*v.i.* 突出;凸出。

bee·tle-browed ['bitl̩,braud; 'bi:tl-braud] *adj.* ①眉毛粗濃而突出的; 凸額的。②慍色的;蹙額的。

bee·tle·head ['bitl̩,hɛd; 'bi:tlhed] *n.* 愚蠢的人。

bee·tle·head·ed ['bitl̩'hɛdɪd; 'bi:tl-'hedid] *adj.* 愚鈍的。

bee·tling ['bitlɪŋ; 'bi:tliŋ] *adj.* 突出的;懸垂的。

beet·root ['bit,rut, -,rut; 'bi:tru:t] *n.* 甜菜根。

beet sugar 從甜菜根製成的糖;甜菜糖。

beeves [bivz; bi:vz] *n.* pl. of **beef.**

bef. before. **B.E.F.** British Expeditionary Force; British Expeditionary Forces.

***be·fall** [bɪ'fɔl; bi'fɔ:l] *v.,* **-fell, -fall·en, -fall·ing.** —*v.t.* 降臨; 遭遇; 加於。Be careful that no harm *befalls* you. 注意,不要遭到傷害。—*v.i.* 發生;(偶然而)起。

be·fit [bɪ'fɪt; bi'fit] *v.t.,* **-fit·ted, -fit·ting.** 適宜;合式。

be·fit·ting [bɪ'fɪtɪŋ; bi'fitiŋ] *adj.* 適合的。—**ly,** *adv.*

be·fog [bɪ'fɑg; bi'fɔg] *v.t.,* **be·fogged, be·fog·ging.** ①罩入霧中。②使之難了解;令困惑。

be·fool [bɪ'ful; bi'fu:l] *v.t.* ①愚弄。②欺蒙。③浪費。

⁑**be·fore** [bɪ'for, bɪ'fɔr; bi'fɔ:] *prep.* ①在…前面。Pride goes *before* a fall. 驕者

必敗。②以前。Things were cheaper *before* the war. 戰前百物較便宜。③當…面前;在面前。He was nervous *before* an audience. 在聽衆面前,他膽怯。④在前面;未來。⑤寧。They would die *before* yielding. 他們寧死不屈。⑥在…之前;位在…之上。We put freedom *before* fame. 我們置自由於名譽之上。⑦在…之審査下。The case went *before* the court. 那案子移到法庭辦理。⑧在…之威力下。⑨擺在…面前(待解決或考慮)。⑩在未算…之前。yearly income *before* taxes. 未扣除稅捐的歲入。***Before Christ*** 西曆紀元前(略作 **B. C.**). ***before everything*** 最先;第一。***before long*** 不久。I hope to see you *before long.* 我希望不久可以再看到你。***before one's time*** 在一個人死(生)之前。***before the world*** 公然地。—*adv.* ①在前。②以前。I never met him *before.* 以前我從未會過他。③早於。The show will begin at noon, not *before.* 戲將於中午開演,不會早於中午。—*conj.* ①以前;前於。Think well *before* you decide. 你決定以前,宜愼重考慮。②寧;與其…毋寧。I will die *before* I submit. 我寧死不屈。

be·fore·hand** 〔bɪˈforˌhænd; biˈfɔː-hænd〕 *adv.* ①事前;預先。He was informed *beforehand*. 他預先得到報告。②從前;曾經。—*adj.* ①預先的。②(在經濟上)進多於出的。be beforehand with*** 事先準備好;先發制人。

be·fore·men·tioned 〔bɪˈforˈmɛn-ʃənd; biˈfɔːˈmenʃənd〕 *adj.* 前述的;上述的。

be·fore-tax 〔bɪˈfɔrˌtæks; biˈfɔːtæks〕 *adj.* 納稅前所得的。

be·foul 〔bɪˈfaul; biˈfaul〕 *v.t.* ①汚染;汚穢。②誹謗;玷辱。③糾纏;阻撓。***befoul one's own nest*** 說自家人壞話;外揚家醜。

be·friend 〔bɪˈfrɛnd; biˈfrend〕 *v.t.* 照顧;協助;待之如友。

be·fud·dle 〔bɪˈfʌdl̩; biˈfʌdl〕 *v.t.*, **-dled, -dling.** ①使酒醉昏迷。②使昏亂;使糊塗;使迷惑。—**ment,** *n.*

‡beg 〔bɛg; beg〕 *v.,* **begged, beg·ging.** —*v.t.* ①求乞。He *begs* his bread from door to door. 他沿門求乞。②懇求。③(將未證實之事)視爲當然。④規避;躱避。—*v.i.* ①求乞。He was too lazy to work and too proud to *beg.* 他懶於工作,而又不屑求乞。②請求。He is *begging* for help. 他請求援助。***beg a favor of*** 請求…幫忙。***beg leave*** 請求准許。***beg off*** 對不能出席請求原諒。***beg the question*** 以未決定之問題爲論據;以假定爲論據的狡辯。***go begging*** 不爲人所接受。***I beg your pardon.*** **a.** 請恕我。**b.** 請再說一遍。

be·gad 〔bɪˈgæd; biˈgæd〕 *interj.* (發誓或强調用語)誓必!

‡be·gan 〔bɪˈgæn; biˈgæn〕 *v.* pt. of **begin.**

be·get 〔bɪˈgɛt; biˈget〕 *v.t.,* **be·got, be·got(ten), be·get·ting.** ①爲…父;生(子)。②引起;產生。

be·get·ter 〔bɪˈgɛtɚ; biˈgetə〕 *n.* 生產者;父。

***beg·gar** 〔ˈbɛgɚ; ˈbegə〕 *n.* ①乞丐。②很窮的人。③傢伙。a friendly little *beggar.* 一個友善的小傢伙。—*v.t.* ①使之貧窮。②使不足。③減低…之價值。

beg·gar·dom 〔ˈbɛgɚdəm; ˈbegədəm〕 *n.* ①乞丐之集合稱。②乞丐之境遇或身分。

beg·gar-lice 〔ˈbɛgɚˌlaɪs; ˈbegəlais〕 *n.* ①(作 *pl.* 解)易於黏附人衣之種子或果實。②(作 *sing.* or *pl.* 解)產生上述種子或果實的植物。(亦作 **beggar's-lice**)

beg·gar·ly 〔ˈbɛgɚlɪ; ˈbegəli〕 *adj.* ①似乞丐的;適於乞丐的。②赤貧的;貧乏的。③無價值的。—**beg·gar·li·ness,** *n.*

beg·gar-my-neigh·bor 〔ˈbɛgɚ-maɪˈnebɚ; ˈbegəmaiˈneibə〕 *n.* (把對方手中的牌全吃光卽爲全勝的)一種紙牌戲。

beg·gar-ticks 〔ˈbɛgɚˌtɪks; ˈbegə-tiks〕 *n. sing.* or *pl.* =**beggar-lice.** (亦作 **beggar's-ticks**)

beg·gar·y 〔ˈbɛgərɪ; ˈbegəri〕 *n.* ①赤貧。②乞丐的集合稱。③乞丐居住之處所。④乞食的習慣。⑤一無所有的狀況。⑥卑鄙。

‡be·gin 〔bɪˈgɪn; biˈgin〕 *v.,* **be·gan, be·gun, be·gin·ning.** —*v.i.* ①開始。School *begins* at 9. 九點開始上課。②始於;原於。***to begin with*** 第一;首則。*To begin with,* he is too young. 第一,他太年輕。***Well begun is half done.*** 好的開始是成功的一半。—*v.t.* ①開始。Have you *begun* your work yet? 你已經開始工作了嗎?②創始。③接近;近於。That suit doesn't even *begin* to fit me. 那套衣服一點也不合我的身。④位於…之首。The letter A *begins* the alphabet. A 位於英文字母之首。

***be·gin·ner** 〔bɪˈgɪnɚ; biˈginə〕 *n.* ①初學者;無經驗者。②開始者;創始者。

be·gin·ning** 〔bɪˈgɪnɪŋ; biˈginiŋ〕 *n.* ①開始。②初期;前部。③源於;起源。Humility is the *beginning* of wisdom. 智慧源於謙遜。④未發達之物;萌芽階段之物。⑤出發點;基本原則。from beginning to end*** 從頭到尾;自始至終。***the beginning of the end*** 最終結果的前兆。—*adj.*①剛開始的。②起頭的。③初級的。④新開業的。

be·gird 〔bɪˈgɝd; biˈgəːd〕 *v.t.,* **-girt** 〔-ˈgɝt;-ˈgəːt〕 or **-gird·ed, -gird·ing.** ①以帶捲繞。②包圍;圍繞。

beg·ohm 〔ˈbɛgˌom; ˈbegoum〕 *n.* 【電】貝格歐姆(電阻單位,等於十億歐姆)。

be·gone 〔bɪˈgɔn; biˈgɔn〕 *interj.* 去!走開!—*v.i.* 去;走開。

be·go·ni·a 〔bɪˈgonjə; biˈgouniə〕 *n.* ①(B-)【植物】球莖秋海棠屬。②秋海棠。

be·grime 〔bɪˈgraɪm; biˈgraim〕 *v.t.,* **-grimed, -grim·ing.** 積垢;弄髒。

be·grudge 〔bɪˈgrʌdʒ; biˈgrʌdʒ〕 *v.t.,* **-grudged, -grudg·ing.** ①嫉妒;羨慕。②吝嗇;不願或勉强給與。③不滿;出怨言。

***be·guile** 〔bɪˈgaɪl; biˈgail〕 *v.,* **-guiled, -guil·ing.** —*v.t.* ①欺騙;誘惑。He *beguiled* me into signing this contract. 他誘我簽這合同。②騙取。③消遣。④迷住。—*v.i.* 迷人。All her intent was to *beguile.* 她的用意完全在於迷人。—**ment, be·guil·er,** *n.*

be·guil·ing 〔bɪˈgaɪlɪŋ; biˈgailiŋ〕 *adj.* ①欺騙的。②有趣的。—**ly,** *adv.*

be·guine 〔bɪˈgin; biˈgiːn〕 *n.* ①一種 bolero 節奏的南美舞。②根據 beguine 的現代社交舞。③上兩項舞步的音樂。

be·gum¹ 〔ˈbigəm; ˈbiːgəm〕 *n.* ①(印度回教徒)公主;貴婦。②(英國)有錢的英印婦人。

be·gum² 〔bɪˈgʌm; biˈgʌm〕 *v.t.,* **-gummed, -gum·ming.** 以膠或膠質物塗、弄髒等。

‡be·gun 〔bɪˈgʌn; biˈgʌn〕 *v.* pp. of **begin.**

Be·haim 〔ˈbehaɪm; ˈbeihaim〕 *n.* 月球表面大坑名。

be·half** 〔bɪˈhæf; biˈhɑːf〕 *n.* ①利益;便利或援助。② 方面。in behalf of*** 爲了…

(某人之利益)。 ***on behalf of*** **a.** 作…之代表。The lawyer spoke convincingly *on behalf of* his client. 那律師代表他的當事人所說的話令人信服。**b.** =**in behalf of.**

*__be·have__ 〔bɪˈhev; biˈheiv〕 *v.*, **-haved, -hav·ing.** —*v.i.* ①立身;舉動。She *behaves* as if she were a child. 她行爲如小孩。②(機器等)開動;工作。The ship *behaves* well. 那條船航行得很好。③舉止適當或有禮貌。—*v.t.* 檢點;守規矩。*Behave* yourself! 放規矩一點!

*__be·hav·ior__ 〔bɪˈhevjɚ; biˈheivjə〕 *n.* ①行爲;品行。His good *behavior* deserves praise. 他的好品行值得稱讚。②儀態;態度。His *behavior* towards me is shameful. 他對我的態度是很可恥的。③(機器等之)活動狀態;(藥品等之)作用或功效。***be on one's good*** (or ***best***) ***behavior*** 行爲檢點。***put a person on his best behavior*** 勸誡某人以使其有良好之行爲。—**al,** *adj.*

be·hav·ior·al science 〔bɪˈhevjərəl～; biˈheivjərəl～〕 行爲科學。

be·hav·ior·ism 〔bɪˈhevjɚˌɪzəm; biˈheivjərizm〕 *n.* 〖心理〗行爲主義;行爲學派。—**be·hav·ior·ist,** *n.* —**be·hav·ior·is·tic,** *adj.*

be·head 〔bɪˈhɛd; biˈhed〕 *v.t.* 殺頭。

be·held 〔bɪˈhɛld; biˈheld〕 *v.* pt. & pp. of **behold.**

be·he·moth 〔bɪˈhiməθ; biˈhi:mɔθ〕 *n.* ①〖聖經〗巨獸。②〖美俗〗巨大或有力之人、獸、物等。

be·hest 〔bɪˈhɛst; biˈhest〕 *n.* 吩咐;要求;命令。

:__be·hind__ 〔bɪˈhaɪnd; biˈhaind〕 *prep.* ①在後。Put my walking stick *behind* the door. 把我的手杖放在門後。②隱藏在後。There must be something *behind* it. 其中必有隱情。③後於;晚於。④支持。⑤落後;不如。⑥留於身後。The dead man left a family *behind* him. 死者身後留下一家人。⑦在…之較遠的一邊。***behind one's back*** 暗中;祕密地。***behind the scenes*** 祕密地;內幕。***behind the times*** 落伍;趕不上時代。***behind time*** 過時;逾期。The train was *behind time.* 火車誤點。—*adv.* ①在後。The flood left ruins *behind.* 洪水過後遺下廢墟。②落後。You are *behind* in your work. 你的工作落後。③保存着。More supplies are *behind.* 還有供應品保存着。④遲。The train is *behind* today. 今天火車誤點。⑤拖欠。to be *behind* in one's rent. 拖欠租金。***come up from behind*** 迎頭趕上。***leave something behind*** 遺下。Are you sure you haven't *left anything behind?* 你確信沒有遺下甚麼東西嗎? —*adj.* 在後的。the man *behind.* 在後面的人。—*n.* 〖俗〗臀部。

be·hind·hand 〔bɪˈhaɪndˌhænd; biˈhaindhænd〕 *adv.* & *adj.* ①遲延;晚到。②落伍;落後。③拖欠;欠債。

be·hind-the-scenes 〔bɪˈhaɪndðəˈsinz; biˈhaindðəˈsi:nz〕 *adj.* 幕後的。

:__be·hold__ 〔bɪˈhold; biˈhould〕 *v.*, **be·held, be·hold·ing,** *interj.* —*v.t.* ①看。We *beheld* the ship sink. 我們看着這船下沉。②將…視爲。—*interj.* 注視(祈請);看呀。*Behold!* What a beautiful sight it is! 看呀!這是多麼美麗的風景!

be·hold·en 〔bɪˈholdən; biˈhouldən〕 *adj.* ①蒙恩的;銘感的。②依賴的〖常 to〗.

be·hoof 〔bɪˈhuf; biˈhu:f〕 *n.* 利益。***in*** (***for*** or ***to***) ***one's behoof*** 爲某人之故。

be·hoove 〔bɪˈhuv; biˈhu:v〕 *v.*, **-hooved, -hoov·ing.** —*v.t.* ①理應;必需。②有益於;必要的。—*v.i.* 有必要。(英亦作 **behove**)

be·hung 〔bɪˈhʌŋ; biˈhʌŋ〕 *adj.* 掛了…的;掛滿了…的〖with〗.

beige 〔beʒ; beiʒ〕 *n.* ①本色毛呢;嗶嘰。②灰棕色。—*adj.* 灰棕色的。

be-in 〔ˈbiˌɪn; ˈbi:in〕 *n.* ①一種在公共場所非正式的聚會。②嬉皮的聚集(無特殊目的,僅聚集在公園等地,做其所喜做的事)。

:__be·ing__ 〔ˈbiɪŋ; ˈbi:iŋ〕 *n.* ①生命;存在;生存。②禀性;體質。③神。spiritual *beings.* 神。④人。human *beings.* 人類。⑤本質。—*adj.* 現在。All is well, for the time *being.* 目前一切都很好。—*v.* pres. part. of **be.** *Being* hungry, he eats much. 他餓了,所以吃得很多。

be·ing·less 〔ˈbiɪŋlɪs; ˈbi:iŋlis〕 *adj.* 不存在;無實在性。

Bei·rut 〔ˈberut, beˈrut; ˈbeiru:t〕 *n.* 貝魯特(黎巴嫩之首都)。(亦作 **Beyrouth**)

be·jew·el 〔bɪˈdʒuəl; biˈdʒu:əl〕 *v.t.*, **-el(l)ed, -el·(l)ing.** 飾以珠寶。

bel 〔bɛl; bel〕 *n.* 〖物理〗裴耳(音量比率單位)。

Bel. ①Belgian. ②Belgic. ③Belgium.

be·la·bo(u)r 〔bɪˈlebɚ; biˈleibə〕 *v.t.* ①〖古〗重打;痛擊。②不斷地辱罵;不斷地嘲弄。③就…作過分冗長的討論或分析等。

be·lat·ed 〔bɪˈletɪd; biˈleitid〕 *adj.* ①誤期的;太遲的。②日暮時尚在途上的。③陳舊的;過時的。

be·laud 〔bɪˈlɔd; biˈlɔ:d〕 *v.t.* 激賞;大爲褒獎。

be·lay 〔bɪˈle; biˈlei〕 *v.*, **-layed, -lay·ing,** *n.* —*v.t.* & *v.i.* ①〖航海〗繫(繩)於栓上。②〖俗〗停! *Belay* (there)! 停!③使固定。④〖登山〗將(身體)繫於繩子之一端。—*n.* ①爬山用繩子。②爬山時藉以固定繩子的地上物。

belaying pin 〖航海〗止索栓。

bel can·to 〔bɛlˈkanto; ˌbelˈkɑ:ntou〕 〖音樂〗一種圓潤流暢的唱法。

belch 〔bɛltʃ; beltʃ〕 *v.t.* ①打噎。②噴出。—*v.i.* ①打噎。②噴出。③破口或衝口而出。—*n.* ①打噎;噴。②噴出之物。

bel·cher 〔ˈbɛltʃɚ; ˈbeltʃə〕 *n.* 一種藍色(上有白點)之頸巾。

bel·dam 〔ˈbɛldəm; ˈbeldəm〕 *n.* 老太婆;(尤指)醜老太婆。(亦作 **beldame**)

be·lea·guer 〔bɪˈligɚ; biˈli:gə〕 *v.t.* 包圍;圍攻。

bel·em·nite 〔ˈbɛləmˌnaɪt; ˈbeləmnait〕 *n.* 〖古生物〗①箭石;烏賊之化石。②一種絕跡之烏賊。

bel-es·prit 〔ˌbɛlˌɛsˈpri; ˌbelˌesˈpri:〕 *n., pl.* **beaux-es·prits** 〔ˌboˌzɛsˈpri; ˌbouˌzesˈpri:〕.〖法〗才子。

bel·fried 〔ˈbɛlfrɪd; ˈbelfrid〕 *adj.* 有鐘樓的;有鐘塔的。

bel·fry 〔ˈbɛlfrɪ; ˈbelfri〕 *n., pl.* **-fries.** ①鐘樓;鐘塔。②〖俚〗頭。

Belg. ①Belgian. ②Belgium.

Bel·gian 〔ˈbɛldʒən; ˈbeldʒən〕 *n.* 比利時人。—*adj.* 比利時的;比利時人的。

Bel·gic 〔ˈbɛldʒɪk; ˈbeldʒik〕 *adj.* ①古高盧 Belgae 族的。②荷蘭的。③比利時的。

*__Bel·gium__ 〔ˈbɛldʒɪəm; ˈbeldʒəm〕 *n.* 比利時(西歐一國,首都爲布魯塞爾, Brussels)。

Bel·grade 〔ˈbɛlgred; ˈbelgreid〕 *n.* 貝爾格勒(南斯拉夫首都)。

Bel·gra·vi·a 〔bɛlˈgrevɪə; belˈgreivjə〕 *n.* ①倫敦海德公園附近之一高尙住宅區。②中上流社會;其生活、嗜好等。

Be·li·al [ˈbiliəl; ˈbiːliəl] *n.* ①〖舊約〗邪惡;無價值;破壞。②〖新約〗惡魔;魔鬼。③(密爾頓之 *Paradise Lost* 中)墮落天使之一。

be·lie [bɪˈlaɪ; biˈlai] *v.t.*, **-lied, -ly·ing.** ①掩飾;誤表;與…不合;使人誤會。②證明…爲錯誤。③辜負。④行爲有辱(家風、祖先等)。

***be·lief** [bɪˈlif; biˈliːf] *n., pl.* **-liefs.** ①所信;意見。②相信;信以爲眞。*belief* in ghosts. 相信有鬼。③信仰;信念。④宗教信仰。What is your *belief?* 你的宗教信仰是甚麼?

‡be·lieve [bɪˈliv; biˈliːv] *v.*, **-lieved, -liev·ing.** —*v.t.* ①信;信受其說。②相信;信任。I can't quite *believe* him. 我不能十分相信他。③以爲;想。It is *believed* to be true. 一般相信這是眞的。—*v.i.* ①信;信以爲眞。Do you *believe* in ghosts? 你信有鬼嗎? ②信仰;深信。③以爲;想。***believe in*** a. 確信。b. 信任。***believe me*** 眞的;不騙你。***make believe*** 假裝。—**be·liev·a·ble,** *adj.* —**be·liev·a·bly,** *adv.*

***be·liev·er** [bɪˈlivɚ; biˈliːvə] *n.* 信者;信徒;基督教徒。

be·liev·ing [bɪˈlivɪŋ; biˈliːviŋ] *n.* 相信。—*adj.* 有信仰的;相信的。

be·lit·tle [bɪˈlɪtl; biˈlitl] *v.t.*, **-lit·tled, -lit·tling.** ①輕視;誹;貶。②使…顯得微小。

Bell [bɛl; bel] *n.* 貝爾(Alexander Graham, 1847–1922, 生於蘇格蘭的美國人, 電話發明者)。

‡bell¹ [bɛl; bel] *n.* ①鐘;鈴。②鐘聲。③輪船上報時的鐘。④鐘形之物。***bear*** (***ring*** or ***carry away***) ***the bell*** 獲得獎品;獲得冠軍;優勝。***saved by the bell*** a. (拳師)因鈴聲宣告一回合的結束而免於被對手擊倒。b. 因某種偶發事項而免於預期之災禍。(***as***) ***sound*** (***clear***) ***as a bell*** 很健康(清楚)。***There is the bell.*** 門鈴響了(客人來了)。***with bells on*** 急於;興高采烈地。—*v.t.* ①繫鈴於;置鐘於。②使腫脹成鐘形。③鳴鐘召(人)。④蓋在鐘形容器內。—*v.i.* ①變成鐘形;鼓起像鐘形。②響。***bell the cat*** 做極危險的事。***ring a bell*** 使人想起某事或引起興趣。***ring the bell*** 供給所需要的東西;成功的或滿意的。

bell² *n.* (鹿等交尾期中之)鳴叫聲。—*v.i.* (鹿等交尾期中)鳴叫。

bel·la·don·na [ˌbɛləˈdɑnə; ˌbeləˈdɔnə] *n.* ①(亦作 **deadly nightshade**)〖植物〗顚茄;莨菪(一種有毒植物)。②顚茄製劑。

belladonna lily =**amaryllis**①.

bell-bot·tom [ˈbɛlˌbɑtəm; ˌbelˈbɔtəm] *adj.* 褲管成鐘形的;喇叭式的。—*n.* (*pl.*) 水兵褲;喇叭褲。

bell·boy [ˈbɛlˌbɔɪ; ˈbelbɔi] *n.* 旅館侍者。

bell buoy 帶有鈴的浮標。

bell button 叫人鈴之按鈕。

bell captain 旅館侍者的領班。

belle [bɛl; bel] *n.* 美女;美婦。the *belle* of the ball. 舞會中最受讚賞的美人。

belles-let·tres [bɛlˈlɛtrə; ˈbelˈletr] *n. pl.* 純文學;純文藝;小說、詩歌、戲劇等。—**bel·let·rist,** *n.* —**bel·let·ris·tic,** *adj.*

bel·let·rism [ˌbɛlˈlɛtrɪzəm; ˌbelˈletrizm] *n.* 純文學至上主義。

bell·flow·er [ˈbɛlˌflauɚ; ˈbelflauə] *n.* 吊鐘花;風鈴草。

bell founder 鑄鐘者。

bell foundry 鑄鐘場。

bell glass 鐘形玻璃罩。

bell·hang·er [ˈbɛlˌhæŋɚ; ˈbelˌhæŋə] *n.* 以懸鐘或修鐘爲業者。

bell-hanger's bit 鑽小洞用的螺旋錐。

bell·hop [ˈbɛlˌhɑp; ˈbelhɔp] *n.* 〖美俚〗=**bellboy.**

bel·li·cism [ˈbɛlɪʃɪzəm; ˈbeliʃizəm] *n.* 嗜戰;好鬥的傾向。

bel·li·cose [ˈbɛləˌkos; ˈbelikous] *adj.* 好戰的;喜打鬥的;好爭吵的。—**bel·li·cos·i·ty,** *n.*

bel·lig·er·ence [bəˈlɪdʒərəns; biˈlidʒərəns] *n.* ①交戰(狀態);好戰。②戰爭。

bel·lig·er·en·cy [bəˈlɪdʒərənsɪ; biˈlidʒərənsi] *n.* =**belligerence.**

bel·lig·er·ent [bəˈlɪdʒərənt; biˈlidʒərənt] *adj.* ①好戰的;好爭吵的。②交戰的;戰爭的;與交戰的國家或個人有關的。—*n.* 交戰國;交戰者。—**ly,** *adv.*

bell jar 鐘形的玻璃容器或玻璃罩。

bell-like [ˈbɛlˌlaɪk; ˈbellaik] *adj.* ①形狀似鐘的。②(聲音)清脆的。

bell·man [ˈbɛlmən; ˈbelmən] *n., pl.* **-men.** ①鳴鐘者。②更夫。③乘洒水箱下水的人。

bell metal 鐘銅。

bell-mouthed [ˈbɛlˌmauðd; ˈbelmauðd] *adj.* 口部漸次向外張開如鈴的。

Bel·lo·na [bəˈlonə; bəˈlounə] *n.* 〖羅馬神話〗司戰女神。

Bel·lot [bɛˈlo; beˈlou] *n.* 月球表面第四象限內坑名。

***bel·low** [ˈbɛlo; ˈbelou] *v.i.* ①(牛、象等)吼叫;(牛)鳴。②作牛鳴聲;作吼叫聲。③怒吼;咆哮。—*v.t.* 吼叫〖out, forth〗. —*n.* ①(牛、象等的)吼聲。②(人的)吼叫;號;咆哮。

***bel·lows** [ˈbɛloz; ˈbelouz] *n. sing.* or *pl.* ①風箱。②照相機鏡頭後面的摺疊部分。③肺。

bell·pull [ˈbɛlˌpul; ˈbelpul] *n.* (鐘、鈴等之)拉索;鐘繩;鈴扣。

bell ringer 鳴鐘者;搖鈴者。

bell tower 鐘樓;鐘塔。

bell·weth·er [ˈbɛlˌwɛðɚ; ˈbelˌweðə] *n.* ①繫鈴之雄羊。②羣衆之首領。

bell·wort [ˈbɛlˌwɝt; ˈbelwəːt] *n.* ①任何桔梗科植物。②百合科植物。

bel·ly** [ˈbɛlɪ; ˈbeli] *n., pl.* **-lies,** *v.*, **-lied, -ly·ing.** —*n.* ①腹(部);胃。Our *bellies* are empty. 我們的肚子餓了。②任何東西的內部或鼓出的部分。③食慾。—*v.i.* ①鼓脹。②匍匐前進。—*v.t.* 使鼓脹。belly in*** 機腹着陸。

bel·ly·ache [ˈbɛlɪˌek; ˈbelieik] *n.* 腹痛。—*v.i.* 〖俗〗抱怨;發牢騷。

bel·ly·band [ˈbɛlɪˌbænd; ˈbelibænd] *n.* ①(馬之)腹帶。②肚兜。

bel·ly·but·ton [ˈbɛlɪˌbʌtn̩; ˈbeliˌbʌtn] *n.* 〖俗〗肚臍。

belly dance 肚皮舞。

belly dancer 肚皮舞孃。

belly flop 腹部與水面衝擊之跳水式。

bel·ly·ful [ˈbɛlɪˌful; ˈbeliful] *n.* ①滿腹之量。②〖俚〗充分;十足。③過多之量。

bel·ly·hold [ˈbɛlɪˌhold; ˈbelihould] *n.* 飛機客艙下的貨艙。

belly-land [ˈbɛlɪˌlænd; ˈbelilænd] *v.t.* (駕駛員)使(飛機)作機腹着陸。

belly laugh 大笑。

belly tank 機腹油箱。

bel·ly·worm [ˈbɛlɪˌwɝm; ˈbeliwəːm] *n.* 寄生腸蟲。

‡be·long [bəˈlɔŋ; biˈlɔŋ] *v.i.* ①屬於(指關係或所屬)。He *belongs* to the Republican Party. 他屬於共和黨。②屬於(指主權)。The books belong to me. 這些書是我的。③屬於(指配合)。④屬於(指社交地位)。This is a place where he doesn't *belong.* 這是不合他身分的地方。⑤適合;對…合適或有用。

***be·long·ings** [bəˈlɔŋɪŋz; biˈlɔŋiŋz] *n. pl.* ①所有物;財產。②親戚。③附屬物。

*__be·lov·ed__ [bɪ'lʌvɪd, -vd; bi'lʌvd, -vid] *adj.* 所愛的。my *beloved* country. 我所愛的國家。—*n.* 所愛的人。

‡**be·low** [bə'lo; bi'lou] *prep.* ①在…以下;不及。His name is *below* mine in the class. 他在班上的名次是低於我的。②不值得。*below* contempt. 極爲可鄙。③在…之下游。④在…之南。⑤在…之掩飾下。***below one's breath*** 悄悄地(說話); 低聲地。***below the mark*** **a.** 品質低劣。**b.** 健康不佳。—*adv.* & *adj.* ①在下面。Write your name in the place *below.* 把你的名字寫在下邊。②在世上。③在地獄中。④在書後;在頁末; 在下文;列後。See the note *below.* 見後面註。⑤由甲板到船艙內。⑥在零下(指溫度)。20 *below.* 零下 20度。***down below*** 在下面。

‡**belt** [bɛlt; belt] *n.*①帶;帶狀物。He carried a revolver in his *belt.* 他在皮帶上揷着一支左輪槍。②地帶。the cotton *belt.* (產)棉地帶。③連在機輪上的帶。④一擊。He gave the ball a terrific *belt.* 他給那球狠狠的一擊。⑤〖俚〗興奮。***hit below the belt*** 暗中傷人; 作不公平的攻擊。***tighten one's belt*** 儉省(束緊褲帶)。***under one's belt*** **a.** 在腹中;在肚裏。**b.** 爲某人之所有;在某人之手中。—*v.t.* ①圍繞以帶。②用帶繫上。③用帶打人。④將(爵位等)授給…。⑤繫以帶;以帶作記號。⑥大聲唱。—*v.i.* 衝。

belt conveyor 帶式運送機。

belt·ed ['bɛltɪd; 'beltid] *adj.* ①束帶的;佩綬帶的。②有紋帶的。

belt highway 環繞市區的公路。

belt·ing ['bɛltɪŋ; 'beltiŋ] *n.*①帶類。②帶布;製帶用之材料。③〖機械〗調帶裝置。

belt line 環狀運輸系統; 環狀之路線或巴士、電車等線。

belt·line ['bɛlt͵laɪn; 'beltlain] *n.* ①一貫作業之生產系統。②腰圍。

belt-tight·en·ing ['bɛlt͵taɪtn̩ɪŋ; 'belt͵taitəniŋ] *n.* 强制性的節約。—*adj.* 節約的;節省開支的。

be·lu·ga [bə'lugə; bə'lu:gə] *n., pl.* **-ga, -gas.** 〖動物〗①白鯨。②白色之大鱘魚。

bel·ve·dere [͵bɛlvə'dɪr; 'belvidiə] *n.* ①〖建築〗望樓。②短雪茄。

B.E.M. Bachelor of Engineering of Mines.

be·ma ['bimə; 'bi:mə] *n., pl.* **be·ma·ta** ['bimətə; 'bi:mətə]. 教堂中之高座;講壇。

be·mire [bɪ'maɪr; bi'maiə] *v.t.,* **be·mired, be·mir·ing.** ①汚。②陷於泥中。

be·moan [bɪ'mon; bi'moun] *v.t. & v.i.* ①悲悼;慟哭;嘆息;惋惜。②認爲遺憾。

be·mock [bɪ'mɑk; bi'mɔk] *v.t.* 嘲笑。

be·muse [bɪ'mjuz; bi'mju:z] *v.t.,* **be·mused, be·mus·ing.** 使困惑; 使獃; 使眩。—**be·mused,** *adj.* —**ment,** *n.*

Ben [bɛn; ben] *n.* 男子名(Benjamin的暱稱)。

ben [bɛn; ben] 〖蘇〗 *adv.* 由屋外到屋內。—*prep.* 在…內。—*n.*峰;山頂。

‡**bench** [bɛntʃ; bentʃ] *n.* ①長凳;長椅。②工作臺。③法官席;法官;法官的職位。④法院。The King's *Bench.* 英國高等法院。⑤一塊高起來而平坦的地。⑥席位。⑦狗在展覽時所站的臺。⑧畜犬展覽。***on the bench*** **a.** 在法院坐在法官的席位。**b.** 和預備球員坐在一起。—*v.t.* ①供給長凳。②給予座位或職位。③使(運動員)離場。The player was *benched* for many fouls. 此運動員犯規太多被罰離場。

bench dog 參加畜犬比賽前或後被展覽之狗。

bench·er ['bɛntʃɚ; 'bentʃə] *n.* ①英國四法學協會資深會員。②下議院議員。③槳手。

bench jockey ①〖棒球〗在場邊喊叫以擾亂對方球員或裁判的隊員。②從旁搗亂或嚴厲批評的人。

bench mark 〖測量〗水準基標。

bench show 畜犬展覽。

bench warmer 〖運動〗候補球員。

bench warrant 法院拘票。

‡**bend** [bɛnd; bend] *v.,* **bent, bend·ing,** *n.* —*v.t.* ①彎;屈;使曲。He *bends* a wire into a loop. 他把一鐵線彎爲圓圈。②使屈從。③致力;專心。He *bent* his mind to his business. 他專心於他的業務。④轉向。⑤固定;縛結。to *bend* one rope to another. 把一根繩子接上另一根。***be bent on*** 決心。He's *bent on* mastering Spanish. 他決心要學會西班牙文。***bend an ear*** 細心地聽。***bend one's ear*** (or ***the ear of***) 以高談闊論令人厭煩。—*v.i.* ①彎曲;轉。The road *bends* sharply here. 這路在此急轉。②屈身;屈向。③屈服;順從。④彎。⑤專心。He *bends* to his studies. 他專心於學業。***bend over backward(s)*** 盡最大的力量。—*n.* ①彎曲;彎轉。②彎身;鞠躬。③一種繩結。④紋章上之對角線。***around the bend*** 〖英俚〗瘋狂。***on the bend*** 〖英俚〗狂飮。***the bends*** 〖美俗〗潛水夫病。—**a·ble,** *adj.*

bend·er ['bɛndɚ; 'bendə] *n.* ①佝僂之人。②用以彎曲他物之物。③〖美俚〗宴飮。④〖美俚〗脚; 足。⑤〖棒球〗曲球。⑥〖英俚〗六辨士錢幣。⑦〖主英方〗不尋常之事物。

bene- 〖字首〗表"好"之義, 例: benediction.

‡**be·neath** [bɪ'niθ; bi'ni:θ] *adv.* 在下。the heaven above and the earth *beneath.* 天上及地下。—*prep.* ①在下。He took a knife from *beneath* his coat. 他從外衣下拿出一把刀。②不足取;不值得。His conduct is *beneath* contempt. 他的行爲極可鄙。③品級次於;低於。 He is *beneath* me in education. 他所受的教育不如我。④在…之壓力下或影響下。

ben·e·dic·i·te [͵bɛnə'dɪsətɪ; ͵beni'daisiti] *interj.* 祝福您(=Bless you)! —*n.* ①祝福;謝飯禱告。②(B-)〖宗教〗萬物頌。

Ben·e·dick ['bɛnə͵dɪk; 'benidik] *n.* ①莎士比亞 *Much Ado About Nothing* 劇中之一獨身男子。②(b-) 新婚者;有妻室者(=benedict).

Ben·e·dict ['bɛnə͵dɪkt; 'benidikt] *n.* 男子名。

ben·e·dict ['bɛnə͵dɪkt; 'benidikt] *n.* ①(尤指曾長期獨身之)新婚者。②有妻室者。

Ben·e·dic·tine [͵bɛnə'dɪktɪn; ͵beni'diktin] *n.* ①Saint Benedict 教團之僧侶。②(b-)該教團僧侶所釀之一種甜酒。

ben·e·dic·tion [͵bɛnə'dɪkʃən; ͵beni'dikʃən] *n.*①祝福。②祝禱(尤指禮拜結束時所作者)。③〖天主教〗(B-) 一種特別祝福儀式。④恩賜;幸事。

ben·e·dic·to·ry [͵bɛnɪ'dɪktərɪ; ͵beni'diktəri] *adj.* 祝福的;祝禱的。

Ben·e·dic·tus [͵bɛnɪ'dɪktəs; ͵beni'diktəs] *n.* (天主教)短讚美詩或其音樂。

ben·e·fac·tion [͵bɛnə'fækʃən; ͵beni'fækʃən] *n.* 恩惠;施惠;捐助。

ben·e·fac·tor ['bɛnə͵fæktɚ; 'benifæktə] *n.* 施主;恩人。

ben·e·fac·tress ['bɛnə͵fæktrɪs; 'benifæktris] *n.* 女施主;女恩人。

ben·e·fice ['bɛnəfɪs; 'benifis] *n.* ①牧

師之職;聖職。②僧侶之祿;聖俸。③(封建時代地主給予佃農之)土地。④禮物。—*v.t.*使就聖職。

be·nef·i·cence 〔bəˈnɛfəsn̩s; biˈnefisns〕 *n.* 善行;德行;仁慈;恩惠;慈善。

be·nef·i·cent 〔bəˈnɛfəsn̩t; biˈnefisnt〕 *adj.* 親切的;仁慈的;慈善的;結善果的;有益的。—**ly,** *adv.*

*__ben·e·fi·cial__ 〔ˌbɛnəˈfɪʃəl; ˌbeniˈfiʃəl〕 *adj.* 有益的。—**ly,** *adv.* —**ness,** *n.*

ben·e·fi·ci·ar·y 〔ˌbɛnəˈfɪʃərɪ; ˌbeniˈfiʃəri〕 *n., pl.* **-ar·ies.** ①受益人;受惠者(尤指承受遺產者)。②享受保險賠償之人;信託受益人。③(封建制度下的)家臣。—*adj.* ①家臣應爲的。②擁有封地的;身爲家臣的。

‡**ben·e·fit** 〔ˈbɛnəfɪt; ˈbenifit〕 *n., v.,* **-fit·ed, -fit·ing.** —*n.* ①利益;裨益。This is for your *benefit.* 這是爲你的利益。②恩惠。He received *benefits* from his father-in-law. 他接受了他岳父的恩惠。③善舉;救濟金。***benefit of the doubt*** 在未證實前先假定其爲眞或無罪。***for one's benefit*** 目的在使某人產生某種預期的反應。—*v.t.*裨益;有益於。He is *benefited* by your advice. 他受惠於你的勸告。—*v.i.* 獲益。

benefit of clergy 僧侶的特典(指僧侶犯罪不受普通法庭審訊之特典)。

benefit society (or **association**) 〖保險〗互助會。

be·nev·o·lence 〔bəˈnɛvələns; biˈnevələns〕 *n.* ①慈善;仁心。②善舉;捐助。③恩稅(昔英國國王藉名獻金,向民間逼捐之稅金)。

*__be·nev·o·lent__ 〔bəˈnɛvələnt; biˈnevələnt〕 *adj.* ①慈善的。②仁慈的。③和藹可親的。—**ly,** *adv.*

Beng. ①Bengal. ②Bengali.

Ben·gal 〔bɛnˈgɔl; beŋˈgɔːl〕 *n.* 孟加拉(昔爲印度東北部一省,現分爲東、西孟加拉,東孟加拉原屬巴基斯坦,現已獨立,稱孟加拉共和國,首都達卡, Dacca; 西孟加拉屬印)。

Ben·ga·lese 〔ˌbɛŋgəˈliz; ˌbeŋgəˈliːz〕 *adj.* 孟加拉 (Bengal) 的;其人民的;其語言的。—*n.* 孟加拉人。

Ben·ga·li 〔bɛnˈgɔlɪ; beŋˈgɔːli〕 *n.* ①孟加拉 (Bengal) 人。②孟加拉語。—*adj.* 孟加拉的;其人民的;其語言的。

ben·ga·line 〔ˈbɛŋgəˌlɪn, ˌbɛŋgəˈlin; ˈbeŋgəliːn〕 *n.*一種絲毛交織有凸起花紋之布。

be·night 〔bɪˈnaɪt; biˈnait〕 *v.t.* ①使陷入黑暗。②使盲。③使愚昧;使蒙昧。

be·night·ed 〔bɪˈnaɪtɪd; biˈnaitid〕 *adj.* ①趕路到天黑的;陷入黑暗中的。②愚昧的。

be·nign 〔bɪˈnaɪn; biˈnain〕 *adj.* ①親切的;令人喜悅的。②良好的;有益的。③(病等)良性的。④吉祥的。—**i·ty,** *n.* —**ly,** *adv.*

be·nig·nant 〔bɪˈnɪgnənt; biˈnignənt〕 *adj.* ①仁慈的;親切的。②有利的;有益的。—**ly,** *adv.* —**be·nig·nan·cy,** *n.*

Be·nin 〔bəˈnɪn; bəˈnin〕 *n.*比寧(非洲幾內亞灣沿岸之一共和國,昔稱達荷美, Dahomey, 首都 Porto Novo). 「幸福。

ben·i·son 〔ˈbɛnəzn̩; ˈbenizn〕 *n.*祝福;

Ben·ja·min 〔ˈbɛndʒəmən; ˈbendʒəmin〕 *n.* ①男子名。②〖聖經〗 Jacob 之幼子。

*__bent__[1] 〔bɛnt; bent〕 *v.* pt. *&* pp. of **bend.** —*adj.* ①彎曲的。②決心的;熱心的;傾心的。He is *bent* on becoming a sailor. 他決心做水手。—*n.* 嗜好;志向;傾向。a *bent* for drawing. 對繪畫之愛好。***to*** (or ***at***) ***the top of one's bent*** 到忍耐力的極限。

bent[2] *n.* ①草梗;枯莖。②硬草;雜草。

ben·thal 〔ˈbɛnθəl; ˈbenθəl〕 *n.* 海底;水底。—*adj.* 海底的;水底的。

Ben·tham 〔ˈbɛnθəm; ˈbentəm〕 *n.*邊沁 (Jeremy, 1748–1832, 英國法學家及哲學家)。

Ben·tham·ic 〔bɛnˈθæmɪk; benˈθæmik〕 *adj.* 邊沁學說的;功利主義的。

Ben·tham·ism 〔ˈbɛnθəmɪzm̩; ˈbentəmizm〕 *n.* 邊沁學說;功利主義。—**Ben·tham·ite,** *n.* 「動植物。

ben·thos 〔ˈbɛnθɑs; ˈbenθɔs〕 *n.*海底的

ben·tho·scope 〔ˈbɛnθəˌskop; ˈbenθəskoup〕 *n.* 一種球形海底探測機。

ben tro·va·to 〔ˌbɛntroˈvɑto; ˌbentrouˈvɑːtou〕 〖義〗合乎情理但不眞實的。

bent·wood 〔ˈbɛntˌwud; ˈbentwud〕 *adj.* 彎木作成的。 「使無感覺;使僵。

be·numb 〔bɪˈnʌm; biˈnʌm〕 *v.t.* 使麻木;

ben·zene 〔ˈbɛnzin; ˈbenziːn〕 *n.*〖化〗苯(從煤焦油等提出之無色液體)。

ben·zine 〔ˈbɛnzin; ˈbenziːn〕 *n.* 〖化〗輕油精;石油精。 「〖化〗安息(香)酸鹽。

ben·zo·ate 〔bɛnˈzo·ɪt; ˈbenzoueit〕 *n.*

ben·zo·ic 〔bɛnˈzo·ɪk; benˈzouik〕 *adj.* 〖化〗安息香(性)的。

benzoic acid 安息酸;苯甲酸。

ben·zo·in 〔ˈbɛnzo·ɪn; ˈbenzouin〕 *n.* 〖化〗安息香;苯基。 「息油 (=benzene).

ben·zol 〔ˈbɛnzol; ˈbenzɔl〕 *n.* 〖化〗苯;安

ben·zyl 〔ˈbɛnzəl; ˈbenzil〕 *n.* 〖化〗苯甲基;苄基。

Be·o·wulf 〔ˈbeəˌwulf; ˈbeiəwulf〕 *n.*①盎格魯撒克遜時代之一史詩。②該史詩中之主人翁。 「塗以脂粉;化妝;塗以油漆。

be·paint 〔bɪˈpent; biˈpeint〕 *v.t.* 著色;

be·praise 〔bɪˈprez; biˈpreiz〕 *v.t.* 盛稱;激賞。 「言)。

Be Prepared 隨時準備 (美國童軍格

*__be·queath__ 〔bɪˈkwið; biˈkwiːð〕 *v.t.* ①遺贈;遺留。②傳與。—**al,** —**er,** —**ment,** *n.*

be·quest 〔bɪˈkwɛst; biˈkwest〕 *n.* ①遺贈;遺傳;傳與。②遺傳物;遺產。

be·rate 〔bɪˈret; biˈreit〕 *v.t.,* **-rat·ed, -rat·ing.** 痛罵;嚴責。

Ber·ber 〔ˈbɝbɚ; ˈbəːbə〕 *n.* 北非一回教土族之土人。—*adj.* 該土族的;其語言的。

ber·ceuse 〔bɛrˈsøːz; bɛəˈsøːz〕 〖法〗*n.* 搖籃曲;催眠曲。

be·reave 〔bəˈriv; biˈriːv〕 *v.t.,* **be·reaved** or **be·reft, be·reav·ing.** 剝奪;奪去;使喪失。 「失親屬的。

be·reaved 〔bəˈrivd; biˈriːvd〕 *adj.* 喪

be·reave·ment 〔bəˈrivmənt; biˈriːvmənt〕 *n.*奪去;喪失;傷慟(親人之死亡)。

be·reft 〔bəˈrɛft; biˈreft〕 *v.* pp. of **bereave.** —*adj.* 被剝奪的。

be·ret 〔bəˈre, ˈbɛrɪt; ˈberei〕 *n.* 貝雷帽(扁圓柔軟羊毛小帽)。

berg 〔bɝg; bəːg〕 *n.* 冰山 (=iceberg).

ber·ga·mot 〔ˈbɝgəˌmɑt; ˈbəːgəmɔt〕 *n.* ①〖植物〗佛手柑。②佛手柑香油。③梨之一種。

be·rhyme 〔bɪˈraɪm; biˈraim〕 *v.t.,* **-rhymed, -rhym·ing.** 就…而作詩;以詩諷刺。(亦作 **berime**)

be·rib·boned 〔bɪˈrɪbənd; biˈribənd〕 *adj.* 飾之以帶的;有飾帶的。 「〖醫〗脚氣病。

ber·i·ber·i 〔ˈbɛrɪˈbɛrɪ; ˈberiˈberi〕 *n.*

Be·ring Sea, the 〔ˈbɪrɪŋ~; ˈberiŋ~〕 白令海。

Bering Strait 白令海峽。

ber·ke·li·um 〔bɝˈkilɪəm; ˈbəːkliəm〕

n. 〖化〗鉳(一種放射性元素)。

Berk·shire [ˈbɝkʃɪr; ˈbɑːkʃiə] *n.* ①波克夏(英國中南部之一郡)。②波克夏種之豬。

***Ber·lin** [ˈbɝlɪn, bɝˈlɪn; bəːˈlin] *n.* 柏林(德國的故都, 現爲東德之首都)。

ber·lin [bɚˈlɪn; bəːˈlin] *n.* ①一種有蓋雙座四輪馬車。②司機與後面座位以玻璃隔開的汽車。③一種柔軟的毛線(亦作 **Berlin**).

Ber·lin·er [bɝˈlɪnɚ; bəːˈlinə] *n.* 柏林市民。

berm(e) [bɝm; bəːm] *n.* 崖徑;城牆與外壕間之狹路。

Ber·mu·da [bɚˈmjudə; bəˈmjuːdə] *n.* ①百慕達羣島(位於大西洋中)。②(*pl.*) 短褲(=Bermuda shorts). (亦作 **Bermudas**)

Bermuda shorts 短褲。

Bern [bɝn; bəːn] *n.* 伯恩 (瑞士首都)。(亦作 **Berne**)

Ber·nard [ˈbɝnɚd; ˈbəːnəd] *n.* 男子名。

Ber·nard·ine [ˈbɝnɚdɪn; ˈbəːnədin] *adj.* 法國教士 Saint Bernard of Clairvaux 之 Cistercian教團(創立於 1115年)的。—*n.* 該教團之僧人。

ber·ried [ˈbɛrɪd; ˈberid] *adj.* ①結漿果的;似漿果的。②(龍蝦等)有卵的。

***ber·ry** [ˈbɛrɪ; ˈberi] *n., pl.* **-ries**, *v.* —*n.* 漿果(如草莓)。—*v.i.* ①結漿果。②採漿果。

ber·serk [ˈbɝsɝk; ˈbəːsəːk] *adj. & adv.* 發狂的(地)。—*n.* =**berserker.**

ber·serk·er [ˈbɝsɝkɚ; ˈbəːsəːkə] *n.*①〖北歐傳說〗狂暴戰士。②狂徒。

Ber·taud [bɚˈtaud; bəˈtaud] *n.* 月球表面第三象限內大坑名。

berth** [bɝθ; bəːθ] *n., pl.* **berths** [bɝθs; bəːðz], *v.* —*n.* ①火車鋪位;輪船艙位。②停泊的地方;可以有餘地使船廻轉的停泊處。③〖英, 俗〗差事;缺;職位。④安全的距離。to keep a clear *berth* of the shoals. 與淺灘保持安全距離。⑤船上職員與水手食宿之處。⑥名次;席次。give a wide berth to*** 避開;遠避。***on the berth*** (船)停泊準備裝貨。—*v.t.* ①帶到停泊之處。②供給鋪位或艙位。—*v.i.* ①停泊。②住宿。

Ber·tha [ˈbɝθə; ˈbəːθə] *n.*女子名。

ber·tha [ˈbɝθə; ˈbəːθə] *n.*女上衣之寬領。

Ber·tie, Ber·ty [ˈbɝtɪ; ˈbəːti] *n.*女子名。

Ber·til·lon [ˈbɝtḷˌɑn; ˈbəːtilɔn] *n.* 貝廸永(Alphonse, 1853-1914, 法國人類學家)。

Bertillon system (按犯人身體各部尺寸及特點等之)貝廸永式人體測定法。

Ber·trand [ˈbɝtrənd; ˈbəːtrənd] *n.* 男子名。

ber·yl [ˈbɛrəl; ˈberil] *n.* ①綠寶石。②淺藍色。③(B-)女子名。

be·ryl·li·um [bəˈrɪlɪəm; beˈriljəm] *n.* 〖化〗鈹。

Ber·ze·li·us [bəˈzelɪəs; bəˈzeiliəs] *n.* 月球表面第一象限內大坑名。

***be·seech** [bɪˈsitʃ; biˈsiːtʃ] *v.t.,* **-sought** or **-seeched, -seech·ing.** 懇求; 哀懇。He *besought* me to lend him some money. 他懇求我借錢給他。—**ing,** *adj.* —**ing·ly,** *adv.* —**ment,** *n.*

be·seem [bɪˈsim; biˈsiːm] *v.t.* 適合於。

be·set [bɪˈsɛt; biˈset] *v.t.,* **-set, -set·ting.** ①包圍; 圍困。②圍攻;環攻。③鑲嵌。—**ment,** *n.*

be·shrew [bɪˈʃru; biˈʃruː] *v.t.* 〖古〗咒詛。*Beshrew* me! 天亡我!我該死!

‡**be·side** [bɪˈsaɪd; biˈsaid] *prep.* ①在旁;在…邊。Come and stand *beside* me. 過來站在我身邊。②於…以外。③與…相比; 和…比較。 *Beside* his efforts ours seem small. 與他的努力相比, 我們的努力似不足道了。④離開;超出…以外。This is *beside* the question. 這離開了本題。⑤與…同等。***beside oneself*** 發狂; 忘形。***beside the mark*** (***point,*** or ***question***) 離題。—*adv.* ①傍。The ladies rode in the carriage, and I ran along *beside.* 女士們乘馬車, 我則跟在旁邊跑。②此外。

‡**be·sides** [bɪˈsaɪdz; biˈsaidz] *adv.* ①並且;又。I am too tired to go; *besides,* it is too late. 我已太倦不能去, 並且時間也太晚了。②外加;更;於…之外。He gave me a book, a pen, and some money *besides.* 他給我一本書、一支鋼筆, 此外還給我一些錢。③其他。—*prep.* ①於…之外。*Besides* English, he has to study German and French. 除英文外, 他還要讀德文和法文。②除却;除…以外。

***be·siege** [bɪˈsidʒ; biˈsiːdʒ] *v.t.,* **-sieged, -sieg·ing.** ①圍攻;圍。This city was *besieged* by the enemy for two years. 這城爲敵人圍困達二年之久。②圍困;困惱;包圍。—**ment,** —**be·sieg·er,** *n.*

be·slav·er [bɪˈslævɚ; biˈslævə] *v.t.*①以口涎汚濕。②諂媚。(亦作 **beslobber**)

be·smear [bɪˈsmɪr; biˈsmiə] *v.t.*搽;塗。

be·smirch [bɪˈsmɝtʃ; biˈsməːtʃ] *v.t.*①汚;使變色。②弄壞;糟蹋(名譽等)。

be·som [ˈbizəm; ˈbiːzəm] *n.* ①帚。②金雀花。—*v.t.* 以帚掃。

be·sot [bɪˈsɑt; biˈsɔt] *v.t.,* **-sot·ted, -sot·ting.** ①使糊塗;使醉。②使愚昧。

be·sot·ted [bɪˈsɑtɪd; biˈsɔtid] *adj.*①昏憒的。②沉溺酒色的。

be·sought [bɪˈsɔt; biˈsɔːt] *v.* pt. & pp. of **beseech.**

be·span·gle [bɪˈspæŋgḷ; biˈspæŋgl] *v.t.,* **-gled, -gling.** 飾以燦爛之物;使光燦。

be·spat·ter [bɪˈspætɚ; biˈspætə] *v.t.* ①玷汚;濺汚。②詆毀。

be·speak [bɪˈspik; biˈspiːk] *v.,* **-spoke, -spo·ken** or **-spoke, -speak·ing,** *n.* —*v.t.* ①〖英〗預約;預定。②表示;顯示。③預示;預言;指出。④與…正式談話;與…會談。⑤請求。⑥問(=ask for). —*n.* ①戲劇公演的請求。②〖英〗(圖書館的)借書預約。

be·spec·ta·cled [bɪˈspɛktəkḷd; biˈspektəkld] *adj.* 戴眼鏡的。

be·spoke [bɪˈspok; biˈspouk] *v.* pt. & pp. of **bespeak.** —*adj.* 〖英〗①預定的;定製的。②專門應定製要求的。

be·spread [bɪˈsprɛd; biˈspred] *v.t.,* **be·spread, be·spread·ing.** 鋪;蓋;廣被。

be·sprent [bɪˈsprɛnt; biˈsprent] *adj.* 〖詩〗撒布的 〖with〗.

be·sprin·kle [bɪˈsprɪŋkḷ; biˈspriŋkl] *v.t.,* **-kled, -kling.** ①灑布。②遍布。

Bess [bɛs; bes] *n.* 女子名。(亦作 **Bessie**)

Bes·se·mer steel [ˈbɛsəmɚ～; ˈbesimə～] 柏塞麥鋼 (英工程師 Sir Henry Bessemer 發明的鍊鋼法, 以Bessemer Process 所鍊的鋼)。

‡**best** [bɛst; best] *adj.,* superl. of **good.** ①最佳的;最好的。He is the *best* student in our class. 他是我們班上最好的學生。②最大的;最多的; 大半。We spent the *best* part of the day in fishing. 我們竟日大半消磨於釣魚。③最有用(利)的。the *best* thing to do. 可作的最有用(利)的事。***put one's best foot*** (or ***leg***) ***foremost*** (or ***forward***) 表現最佳的一面; 顯露拿手好戲。

—*adv.*, superl. of **well.** ①最好地。②最；極。I like this book *best.* 我最喜歡這本書。***as best one can*** 竭力;盡力。Do it *as best you can.* 盡你的力去做。***had best*** 應該;最好。We *had best* retire. 我們最好告退。—*n.* ①最好的部分; 最佳者; 佼佼者。Take the *best* of them. 從中把最好的拿去。②最大限度;極力。③要點;利益。That's the *best* of being honest. 那就是誠實的好處。④最好的衣服。⑤最佳品質。⑥大部分。Lin Hai-feng won the *best* of seven go series. 林海峯在七局圍棋賽中勝了四局。***at best*** 充其量。I can donate one hundred dollars *at best.* 我充其量只能捐助一百元。***at one's best*** **a.** 在一個人健康或精神最佳狀態之下。**b.** 一個人能力、力量等的巔峯狀態。***be (all) for the best*** **a.** 不若表面之惡劣。**b.** 終於變得有利。***get*** (or ***have***) ***the best of*** 勝利。Which side *gets the best of* it? 那一方勝利?***in one's Sunday best***〖英俗〗穿着最好的衣服。***make the best of*** 善用;儘量利用。***make the best of one's time*** (or ***opportunities***) 儘量利用時間(機會)。***make the best of one's way*** 以最快的速度走。***to the best of one's belief*** 儘…所信。***to the best of one's knowledge*** 就…所知。***to the best of one's power*** (or ***ability***) 盡…之力量(能力)。***with the best*** 不下於他人。—*v.t.* 擊敗。—*aux.* 最好(=had best).

best bet 最好的一着;上策。

best bib and tucker〖俗〗最好的衣服。

be·stead [bɪ'stɛd;bi'sted] *v.t.*, **-stead·ed, -stead·ed** or **-stead, -stead·ing.** 助;裨益。

best foot 最能吸引人的優點。

best girl 最喜歡的女朋友。

best gold (射箭比賽中)最佳的一射。

bes·tial ['bɛstɪəl; 'bestjəl] *adj.* ①(似)野獸的。②淫慾的;獸性的。③野蠻的。—**ize,** *v.* —**i·ty,** *n.* —**ly,** *adv.*

bes·ti·ar·y ['bɛstɪ,ɛrɪ; 'bestiəri] *n., pl.* **-ar·ies.** 中古時代之動物寓言集。

be·stir [bɪ'stɝ; bi'stə:] *v.t.*, **-stirred, -stir·ring.** 使發奮;鼓舞;鼓勵。

best-known ['bɛst'non; 'best'noun] *adj.* 最出名的 (well-known 的最高級)。

best man 男儐相。

best·ness ['bɛstnɪs; 'bestnis] *n.* 最佳。

*__be·stow__ [bɪ'sto; bi'stou] *v.t.* ①贈;給予。I do not deserve all the praises *bestowed* upon me.我不配得到這些讚譽。②用;利用。—**al,** *n.*

be·strad·dle [bɪ'strædl̩;bi'strædl] *v.t.*, **-dled, -dling.** 騎;跨。

be·strew [bɪ'stru; bi'stru:] *v.t.*, **-strewed, -strewed** or **-strewn, -strew·ing.** 撒布;布滿;散置。

be·stride [bɪ'straɪd; bi'straid] *v.t.*, **-strode** or **-strid, -strid·den** or **-strid, -strid·ing.** ①(兩足分跨而)坐;騎。②跨過;兩足分跨…而立。③支配;控制;淩駕。

best seller ①最暢銷之書、歌曲等。②暢銷書之作者; 暢銷唱片樂曲之作者或演奏者。

best-sell·ing ['bɛst'sɛlɪŋ; 'best'seliŋ] *adj.* 暢銷的。

*__bet__ [bɛt; bet] *v.*, **bet** or **bet·ted, bet·ting,** *n.* —*v.t.* ①打賭。②敢說;相信。I *bet* he'll be late. 我敢說他一定會遲到。—*v.i.* 打賭。I never *bet.* 我從不與人打賭。***bet a person on*** 與人打…的賭。***you bet!***〖俗〗當然!眞的! Are you going? *You bet!* 你去嗎?當然要去呀! —*n.* ①打賭。I will lay you a *bet.* 我和你打賭。②賭注; 賭金。He lost his *bet.* 他輸去賭金。③有希望贏的競爭者。④選擇;決定。

bet. between.

be·ta ['betə, 'bitə; 'bi:tə] *n.* ①希臘字母之第二字母(Β, β)。②一系列中之第二個。③(B-)一個星座中亮度居次的星。

be·take [bɪ'tek; bi'teik] *v.t.*, **-took, -tak·en, -tak·ing.** ①去(後接反身代名詞如:myself 等)。②致力於(後接反身代名詞)。***betake oneself to one's heels*** 逃走。

beta particle〖物理〗β質點。

beta ray〖化〗β射線。

be·ta·tron ['bitə,trɑn; 'bi:tətrɔn] *n.*〖物理〗電子廻旋加速器。

be·tel ['bitl̩;'bi:təl] *n.*〖植物〗①蒟醬(胡椒科)。②其葉。

betel nut 檳榔。

betel palm 檳榔樹。

bête noire ['bet'nwɑr; 'beit'nwɑ:]〖法〗=**bugbear.**

Beth [bɛθ; beθ] *n.* 女子名 (Elizabeth之暱稱)。

beth·el ['bɛθəl; 'beθəl] *n.* ①聖殿;聖地;靈場。②〖英〗非英國國教徒之禮拜堂。③〖美〗海員之陸上禮拜堂。

be·think [bɪ'θɪŋk;bi'θiŋk] *v.t.*, **-thought, -think·ing.** ①想;考慮。②憶起;追憶;提醒。③決定。

Beth·le·hem ['bɛθlɪəm; 'beθlihem] *n.* 伯利恆(耶路撒冷一市鎭,爲耶穌之降生地)。

be·thought [bɪ'θɔt; bi'θɔ:t] *v.* pt. & pp. of **bethink.**

be·tide [bɪ'taɪd; bi'taid] *v.*, **-tid·ed, -tid·ing.** —*v.t.* ①降臨。②預示。—*v.i.*發生。

be·times [bɪ'taɪmz; bi'taimz] *adv.* ①早;及時。②卽刻;不久。③〖主方〗偶爾;有時。

bê·tise [,be'tiz; bei'ti:z]〖法〗*n.* 愚蠢;愚行;愚言。

be·to·ken [bɪ'tokən;bi'toukən] *v.t.*①證明;指示;表示。②預示。

bet·o·ny ['bɛtənɪ; 'betəni] *n., pl.* **-nies.**〖植物〗藿香之一種。

*__be·tray__ [bɪ'tre; bi'trei] *v.t.* ①出賣。They *betrayed* their country. 他們出賣自己的國家。②不忠於; 辜負。She *betrayed* her promises. 她不遵守諾言。③洩露。④無意中暴露;顯示。⑤導入歧途。—**er,** *n.*

be·tray·al [bɪ'treəl; bi'treiəl] *n.* ①出賣;辜負。②暴露;跡象。

be·troth [bɪ'trɔθ; bi'trouð] *v.t.* 許配。

be·troth·al [bɪ'trɔθəl; bi'trouðəl] *n.* 訂婚;婚約;許配;訂婚禮。

be·trothed [bɪ'trɔθt;bi'trouðd] *n.* 訂過婚的人;許嫁的人。—*adj.* 已訂婚的。

Bet·sy ['bɛtsɪ;'betsi] *n.* 女子名 (Elizabeth 之暱稱)。

‡**bet·ter**¹ ['bɛtɚ; 'betə] *adj.*, comp. of **good.** ①更好的;較佳的;較優的。It is *better* to win than to lose. 勝利比失敗爲佳。②(病)較愈的;(健康)較佳的。Are you feeling any *better* yet? 你覺得稍好一點嗎? ③較多的; 較大的。the *bettter* part of a lifetime. 一生中的大部分。***be better than one's word*** 行過於言;比所說的話更慷慨、寬大。***have seen better days*** 處境曾經好過;曾經富有過。***no better than*** 一樣的; 實際的。He is *no better than* a beggar. 他與乞丐一樣。***no better than one should be*** 無道德的;卑鄙的;淫蕩的。***one's better feelings*** 本心;良心。***one's better self*** 良知。***the better hand*** 右手。—*adv.*, comp. of **well.** ①更好地。Do

better another time. 下一次你要做得更好。②更多地。I know her *better* than anyone else. 我知道她比任何人更清楚。***better off*** **a.** 景況更佳。**b.** 更快樂;更幸運。***go*** (***someone***) ***one better*** 勝過。***had better*** 毋寧;較爲適宜或聰明地。You *had better* go now. 你最好現在就走。***think better of*** **a.** 熟思;再考慮。**b.** 對…有更好的看法;對…有較高的評價。—*n.* ①較好的東西或情形。②(*pl.*) 長輩;勝於己者(如地位、財富、知識等)。Listen to the advice of your *betters.* 聽從長輩的勸告。***all the better*** 更好。***be the better for*** 對…反而更好;反而更好。***for better or for worse*** 無論好運與惡運;不管好壞。***for the better*** 轉好。His health changed *for the better.* 他的健康情形業已好轉。***for want of a better*** 因爲沒有更好的(暫以此代之)。***get*** (or ***have***) ***the better of*** 勝於;超過。***so much the better*** 那樣更好;這樣更好。***think the better of*** 對…更加尊敬;對…更認爲了不起。—*v.t.* ①使進步;改良。②勝於。The other classes can not *better* our grades. 其他各班不能勝過我們的成績。***better oneself*** 獲得更佳職位;擢陞;高陞;充實自己。—*v.i.* 進步;有改善。—*aux.* 〖俗〗最好(=had better). The boy felt he *better* go before the fight started. 那男孩覺得他最好在打架未開始前走開。

bet·ter² *n.* 打賭者;賭博者。(亦作**bettor**)

better half 〖俚〗(某人的)夫或妻;配偶。

bet·ter·ment [ˈbɛtəmənt; ˈbetəmənt] *n.* ①改良;改進。②〖法律〗(*pl.*) 房客對房產所作之修繕,依法日後可以索償者。

bet·ter·most [ˈbɛtəˌmost; ˈbetəmoust] *adj.* 〖俗〗①最好的。②較大的;大部分的。

bet·ter-to-do [ˈbɛtətəˈdu; ˈbetətəˈdu:] *adj.* 經濟情況較好的。

betting shop 有營業執照辦理打賭的商店。

bet·ty [ˈbɛtɪ; ˈbeti] *n.* ①做婦女所做之瑣事者;愛做婦女家事之男子。②一種甜食。

‡be·tween [bəˈtwin; biˈtwi:n] *prep.* ①在(兩者)之間(指時間或位置)。I have classes *between* nine and twelve o'clock. 九點至十二點之間我有課。②…與…間的(指關係)。the relation *between* teachers and students. 師生關係。③涉及;包括。war *between* two nations. 兩國間的戰爭。④以聯合行動。⑤共享;共有。They own the property *between* them. 他們共同擁有該財產。***between ourselves; between you and me; between you, me, and the post*** (***lamppost, gatepost, doorpost, etc.***) (這是)我們之間的祕密;別對他人講;祕密地。***between the cup and the lip*** 在緊要關頭;功敗垂成。***between two fires*** or ***between the devil and the deep sea*** 腹背受敵;進退維谷。***between whiles*** 時時;不時。—*adv.* 在其間(指時間或位置)。We could not see the moon, for a cloud came *between.* 我們看不到月亮,因爲有雲遮住了。***in between*** **a.** 在中間。**b.** 擋路。

be·tween·maid [bɪˈtwinˌmed; biˈtwi:nmeid] *n.* 〖英〗女傭助手。

between the lines 暗示;言外之意;絃外之音。

be·tween·times [bɪˈtwinˌtaɪmz; biˈtwi:ntaimz] *adv.* 在中間的時間。

be·tween·whiles [bɪˈtwinˌhwaɪlz; biˈtwi:nhwailz] *adv.* =**betweentimes.**

be·twixt [bəˈtwɪkst; biˈtwikst] *adv., prep.* 〖古〗=**between.** ***betwixt and between*** 在中間;既非此亦非彼;模稜兩可。

bev·el [ˈbɛvl; ˈbevəl] *n., v.,* **-el(l)ed, -el(l)ing,** *adj.* —*n.* ①斜角規 (=bevel square). ②斜面;斜角。—*v.t. & v.i.* 切成斜角;(使)成爲斜角。—*adj.* 成斜角的;傾斜的。

bevel gear 斜齒輪。

bev·er·age [ˈbɛvrɪdʒ; ˈbevəridʒ] *n.* 飲料。

bev·y [ˈbɛvɪ; ˈbevi] *n., pl.* **bev·ies.** ①一羣鳥。②一羣(少女或婦女)。③〖俗〗一堆東西;一羣人。

be·wail [bɪˈwel; biˈweil] *v.t. & v.i.* 哀悼;悲傷;嘆惜。—**ment,** *n.*

***be·ware** [bɪˈwɛr; biˈwɛə] *v.,* **-wared, -war·ing.** —*v.i.* 當心;小心。*Beware* of fire. 當心火燭。—*v.t.* 謹防;留意。

be·wigged [bɪˈwɪgd; biˈwigd] *adj.* 戴假髮的。

***be·wil·der** [bɪˈwɪldə; biˈwildə] *v.t.* 使迷惑;使昏亂。He was so *bewildered* that he did not know what to do. 他昏亂得不知所措。—*v.i.* 使人昏亂;使人迷惑;使人失去鎮靜。—**ing·ly,** *adv.*

be·wil·der·ment [bɪˈwɪldəmənt; biˈwildəmənt] *n.* ①迷惑。②混亂的事物。

***be·witch** [bɪˈwɪtʃ; biˈwitʃ] *v.t.* ①施魔術於;蠱惑;迷惑。②令人陶醉。We were all *bewitched* by the pretty dancer. 我們均爲那美貌的舞蹈者所迷。—**er·y,** —**ment,** *n.* —**ing,** *adj.* —**ing·ly,** *adv.*

bey [be; bei] *n., pl.* **beys.** ①土耳其人對顯要之尊稱。②突尼斯土著領袖之稱號。

‡be·yond [bɪˈjɑnd; biˈjɔnd] *prep.* ①越過;在…之較遠的一邊。He lived three doors *beyond* this place. 他住在過此三家之處。②超過;晚於。They stayed *beyond* the time limit. 他們留此超過時限。③爲…所不能及;出乎…之外。The dying man is *beyond* help. 這個將死的人已無法可救。④過甚;高於;超出。⑤較…更遠。⑥除…以外。I will pay nothing *beyond* the stated price. 我不願付比定價更多的錢。***be beyond a joke*** 不是開玩笑的(正經的事)。***beyond compare*** 無法比較(非常好)。***beyond control*** 無法控制。***beyond hope*** 無望的;絕望的。***beyond measure*** 大得無法衡量。***beyond reason*** 不合理。***beyond the seas*** 在海外。***go beyond oneself*** 忘形;失態。***live beyond one's income*** (or ***means***) 入不敷出;揮霍無度。—*adv.* 遠離;在遠處。*Beyond* were the hills. 山在遠處。***the life beyond*** 來生;再世。—*n.* ①未來。②遠方。***the*** (***great***) ***beyond*** **a.** 遠處。**b.** 來世。

bez·el [ˈbɛzl; ˈbezl] *n.* ①鑿之刃角。②寶石之斜面。③(戒指)嵌寶石之座盤;(錶面)嵌鑲玻璃之槽。

be·zique [bəˈzik; biˈzi:k] *n.* 一種紙牌戲。

b.f. ①brought forward. ②bold-faced.

B.F.A.Mus. Bachelor of Fine Arts in Music. **B.F.S.** Bachelor of Foreign Service. **B.F.T.** Bachelor of Foreign Trade. **bg.** bag. **B.G.E.** Bachelor of Geological Engineering. **B.Gen. Ed.** Bachelor of General Education.

B-girl [ˈbiˌgɜl; ˈbi:gə:l] *n.* 酒吧女郎;酒家女。

bh. 〖棒球〗base hits.

bhang, bang [bæŋ; bæŋ] *n.* 印度大麻;其乾葉及子囊(有麻醉性)。

BHC benzene hexachloride. 殺蟲劑。

b.h.p. brake horsepower. 制動馬力。

Bhu·tan [buˈtɑn; bu:ˈtɑ:n] *n.* 不丹(印度東北之半獨立國,首都 Punakha).

Bhu·tan·ese 〔ˌbutəˈniz; ˌbuːtəˈniːz〕 *n.* 不丹人;不丹語。—*adj.* 不丹(人)的;不丹語的。
Bi 化學元素 bismuth 之符號。
bi- 〖字首〗表"雙;二"之義。
bi·an·nu·al 〔baɪˈænjuəl; baiˈænjuəl〕 *adj.* ①一年二度的。②=**biennial.** —**ly,** *adv.*
***bi·as** 〔ˈbaɪəs; ˈbaiəs〕 *n., adj., adv., v.,* **-as(s)ed, -as·(s)ing.** —*n.* ①斜線。②〖保齡球〗使球斜進之力或偏重。③偏見。to be free from *bias.* 毫無偏見。④〖無線電〗柵極偏電壓。—*adj.* 傾斜的;對角的。—*adv.* 傾斜地;對角地。to cut material *bias.* 斜對角剪裁布料。—*v.t.* 影響;使存偏見;使傾向一方。
bi·ath·lete 〔baɪˈæθlit; baiˈæθliːt〕 *n.* 兩項運動員。(參看 **biathlon**)
bi·ath·lon 〔baɪˈæθlɑn; baiˈæθlɔn〕 *n.* 兩項運動(包括越野滑雪及步鎗射擊比賽)。
bi·ax·i·al 〔baɪˈæksɪəl; baiˈæksiəl〕 *adj.* 有二軸的。
***bib** 〔bɪb; bib〕 *n., v.,* **bibbed, bib·bing.** —*n.* ①圍裙或工作服之上部。②(小孩用)圍兜。—*v.t.* & *v.i.* 飲;啜飲。
Bib. ①Bible. ②Biblical.
bib·ber 〔ˈbɪbɚ; ˈbibə〕 *n.* 貪飲者;酒徒。
bib·cock 〔ˈbɪbˌkɑk; ˈbibkɔk〕 *n.* 嘴管下彎之水龍頭。
bi·be·lot 〔ˈbɪblo; ˈbiblou〕〖法〗*n.* (櫃架上陳設之)小珍品。
Bibl., bibl. ①Biblical. ②bibliographical.
***Bi·ble** 〔ˈbaɪbl; ˈbaibl〕 *n.* ①基督教之聖經(其中包括新約及舊約兩部分)。Swear on the *Bible.* 手撫聖經發誓。②(猶太人承認的)舊約聖經。③任何宗教的經典。④(b-)公認為權威的書籍;典籍。—*v.t.* 供以聖經。
Bible class (聖經)查經班。
Bible oath 鄭重其事的宣誓(尤指手按聖經的宣誓)。
Bible paper 聖經紙。
Bible Society 聖經公會。
Bib·li·cal 〔ˈbɪblɪkl; ˈbiblikəl〕 *adj.* ①聖經的;按照聖經的。②似聖經的。
Bib·li·cism 〔ˈbɪblɪˌsɪzəm; ˈbiblisizəm〕 *n.* 聖經學。—**Bib·li·cist,** *n.*
biblio- 〖字首〗表"書;聖經"之義。
bib·li·o·clast 〔ˈbɪblɪəˌklæst; ˈbibliəklæst〕 *n.* 破壞書籍者;焚書者。
bib·li·o·film 〔ˈbɪblɪəˌfɪlm; ˈbibliоufilm〕 *n.* (用以拍攝書頁等照片之)顯微膠片。
bibliog. ①bibliographer. ②bibliographic. ③bibliography.
bib·li·og·ra·pher 〔ˌbɪblɪˈɑgrəfɚ; ˌbibliˈɔgrəfə〕 *n.* 書目編作人;書誌學家。
bib·li·og·ra·phy 〔ˌbɪblɪˈɑgrəfɪ; ˌbibliˈɔgrəfi〕 *n., pl.* **-phies.** ①參考書目;參考文獻。②(某作者作品之)目錄。③書籍學;書誌學。—**bib·li·o·graph·ic,** *adj.*
bib·li·o·klept 〔ˈbɪblɪəˌklɛpt; ˈbiblіouklept〕 *n.* 盜書者。
bib·li·ol·a·ter 〔ˌbɪblɪˈɑlətɚ; ˌbibliˈɔlətə〕 *n.* 崇拜書籍者;崇拜聖經者。—**bib·li·ol·a·trous,** *adj.* —**bib·li·ol·a·try,** *n.*
bib·li·ol·o·gy 〔ˌbɪblɪˈɑlədʒɪ; ˌbibliˈɔlədʒi〕 *n.* ①聖經學。②書誌學;書目。
bib·li·o·man·cy 〔ˈbɪblɪəˌmænsɪ; ˈbibliouˌmænsi〕 *n.* 聖經占卜(以任何抽得之經書的一節以占未來)。
bib·li·o·ma·ni·a 〔ˌbɪblɪəˈmenɪə; ˌbibliouˈmeinjə〕 *n.* 藏書狂;藏書癖。
bib·li·o·ma·ni·ac 〔ˌbɪblɪəˈmenɪˌæk; ˌbibliouˈmeiniæk〕 *adj.* 藏書癖的。—*n.* 珍籍收藏家;有藏書癖者。—**al,** *adj.*
bib·li·op·e·gy 〔ˌbɪblɪˈɑpədʒɪ; ˌbibliˈɔpədʒi〕 *n.* 書籍裝訂術。
bib·li·o·phage 〔ˈbɪblɪoˌfedʒ; ˈbiblioufeidʒ〕 *n.* 熱愛讀書的人;書呆子。
bib·li·o·phile 〔ˈbɪblɪəˌfaɪl; ˈbibliоufail〕 *n.* ①珍愛書籍者。②藏書家。(亦作 **bibliophil**) —**bib·li·oph·i·lism, bib·li·oph·i·list,** *n.*
bib·li·o·pole 〔ˈbɪblɪəˌpol; ˈbibliоupoul〕 *n.* 書商;(特指)善本或舊書商。
bib·li·op·o·ly 〔ˌbɪblɪˈɑpəlɪ; ˌbibliˈɔpəli〕 *n.* 書籍販售。
bib·li·o·the·ca 〔ˌbɪblɪəˈθikə; ˌbibliouˈθiːkə〕 *n.* ①圖書室;書庫。②書商之目錄。
bib·li·o·ther·a·py 〔ˌbɪblɪoˈθɛrəpɪ; ˌbibliouˈθerəpi〕 *n.* 〖精神分析〗讀書療法。
Bib·list 〔ˈbɪblɪst; ˈbiblist〕 *n.* ①以聖經為信仰之唯一教條者。②聖經學者。
bib·u·lous 〔ˈbɪbjələs; ˈbibjuləs〕 *adj.* ①耽於酒的。②吸取性的;吸水的。—**ly,** *adv.*
bi·cam·er·al 〔baɪˈkæmərəl; baiˈkæmərəl〕 *adj.* 〖政治〗兩院制的。
bi·car·bon·ate 〔baɪˈkɑrbənɪt; baiˈkɑːbənit〕 *n.* 〖化〗重碳酸鹽。*bicarbonate* of soda ($NaHCO_3$). 小蘇打;碳酸氫鈉。
bice 〔baɪs; bais〕 *n.* ①灰藍色;灰藍色顏料。②(泛指)綠色;綠色顏料。
bi·cen·te·nar·y 〔baɪˈsɛntəˌnɛrɪ; ˈbaisenˈtiːnəri〕 *adj.* 〖英〗二百年的;存續二百年之久的。—*n.* 二百年;二百周年紀念。
bi·cen·ten·ni·al 〔ˌbaɪsɛnˈtɛnɪəl; ˌbaisenˈtenjəl〕 *adj.* ①存續二百年的。②每二百年發生一次的。—*n.* 二百年;二百周年紀念。
bi·ceph·a·lous 〔baɪˈsɛfələs; baiˈsefələs〕 *adj.* 〖動、植物〗有二頭的。
bi·ceps 〔ˈbaɪsɛps; ˈbaiseps〕 *n.* ①〖解剖〗二頭肌(尤指上臂之雙頭肌)。②膂力。
bi·chlo·ride 〔baɪˈkloraɪd; ˈbaiˈklɔːraid〕 *n.* 〖化〗二氯化物。(亦作**bichlorid**)
bi·chro·mate 〔baɪˈkromɪt; baiˈkroumit〕 *n.* 〖化〗重鉻酸鹽。
bi·cip·i·tal 〔baɪˈsɪpɪtəl; baiˈsipitəl〕 *adj.* ①有二頭的。②〖解剖〗二頭肌的。
bick·er 〔ˈbɪkɚ; ˈbikə〕 *v.i.* ①爭吵;爭論。②作潺潺聲。③碎步疾走;趕;急動。④閃爍;顫動。—*n.* ①爭吵;爭論。②潺潺聲。
bi·col·or, bi·col·our 〔ˈbaɪˌkʌlɚ; ˈbaiˈkʌlə〕 *adj.* 二色的。—*n.* 二色之物。
bi·con·cave 〔baɪˈkɑnkev; ˈbaiˈkɔnkeiv〕 *adj.* 兩面凹的。
bi·con·vex 〔baɪˈkɑnvɛks; ˈbaiˈkɔnveks〕 *adj.* 兩面凸的。
bi·cul·tur·al 〔baɪˈkʌltʃərəl; baiˈkʌltʃərəl〕 *adj.* 兩種不同文化混合的。
bi·cus·pid 〔baɪˈkʌspɪd; baiˈkʌspid〕 *adj.* 〖解剖〗雙尖的。—*n.* 雙尖牙;前臼齒。
bi·cus·pi·date 〔baɪˈkʌspɪdˌet; baiˈkʌspideit〕 *adj.* =**bicuspid.**
‡**bi·cy·cle** 〔ˈbaɪsɪkl; ˈbaisikl〕 *n., v.,* **-cled, -cling.** —*n.* 脚踏車;自行車。Do you ride a *bicycle?* 你騎脚踏車嗎? —*v.i.* & *v.t.* 騎脚踏車。—**bi·cy·cler,** *n.* 乘自行車者。
bi·cy·clist 〔ˈbaɪˌsɪklɪst; ˈbaisiklist〕 *n.* 乘自行車者。
‡**bid** 〔bɪd; bid〕 *v.,* **bade** or **bad** or **bid, bid·den** or **bid, bid·ding** for *v.t.* ①,②,⑤;**bid, bid·ding** for *v.t.* ③,④, *n.* —*v.t.* ①命令;囑咐。②說;致意。We *bade* him farewell. 我們向他告別。③出價。④叫牌(玩紙牌時所用術語)。⑤宣布。He *bade* defiance to them all. 他向他們全體挑釁。—*v.i.* ①出價;投標。②尋求〖for〗. to *bid* for support.

尋求援助。***bid defiance*** 拒絕讓步；抗拒。***bid fair*** 似乎可能；有機會。***bid in*** 在拍賣時替物主買進；物主在拍賣場中出高價以保留主權。***bid up*** 出更高叫價。—*n.* ①出價。He made the highest *bid* for this article. 這件東西他出價最高。②邀請。③玩紙牌時的叫牌。It is your *bid.* 輪到你叫牌。④嘗試。

bid bond 押標金。

bid·da·ble 〔ˈbɪdəbl; ˈbidəbl〕 *adj.* ①順從的。②〖牌戲〗可開牌的；可叫牌的。

bid·den 〔ˈbɪdn; ˈbidn〕 *v.* pp. of **bid.**

bid·der 〔ˈbɪdɚ; ˈbidə〕 *n.* ①出價人；投標人。②命令者。③(牌戲) 叫牌者；開牌者。

bid·ding 〔ˈbɪdɪŋ; ˈbidiŋ〕 *n.* ①命令；要求。②邀請。③（橋牌中之）叫牌。④出價。***at the bidding of*** 服從於；聽命於。***do one's bidding*** 服從某人。

bidding block ①拍賣場。②將貨物賣給出價最高者的任何市場。

bid·dy 〔ˈbɪdɪ; ˈbidi〕 *n., pl.* **-dies.** ①小鷄；母鷄。②〖美俗〗女傭。

bide 〔baɪd; baid〕 *v.,* **bode** or **bid·ed, bid·ed, bid·ing.** —*v.i.* 〖古方〗①居住。②留；繼續。③等待。 —*v.t.* ①忍受。②等待。***bide one's time*** 等待良機。

bi·den·tate 〔baɪˈdɛntet; baiˈdenteit〕 *adj.* 有二齒的。

bi·det 〔bɪˈde; ˈbiːdei〕 *n.* 臉盆狀澡盆；洗身盆。

bi·en·ni·al 〔baɪˈɛnɪəl; baiˈeniəl〕 *adj.* ①二年一次的。②經歷或生長二年的。—*n.*①二年一次的事。②二年生的植物。—**ly,** *adv.*

bier 〔bɪr; biə〕 *n.* ①棺架；屍架；②棺材。

biest·ings 〔ˈbistɪŋz; ˈbiːstiŋz〕 *n. pl.* 生犢後母牛之初乳（=beestings).

bi·fa·cial 〔baɪˈfeʃəl; baiˈfeiʃəl〕 *adj.* ①有二面的。②有相對之二相似表面的。③〖植物〗有不同之二面的(如葉等)。

biff 〔bɪf; bif〕 *n.* 〖美俚〗打；擊。—*v.t.* 〖美俚〗打；擊。

bif·fin 〔ˈbɪfɪn; ˈbifin〕 *n.* (英國 Norfolk 所產之)一種蘋果。

bi·fid 〔ˈbaɪfɪd; ˈbaifid〕 *adj.* 〖植物〗兩裂的；兩歧的。

bi·fo·cal 〔baɪˈfokl; baiˈfoukəl〕 *adj.* ①有兩焦點的。②基於兩種不同觀點的。—*n.* (*pl.*)遠近兩用之眼鏡。

bi·fo·li·ate 〔baɪˈfolɪɪt; baiˈfouliit〕 *adj.* 〖植物〗有雙葉的。

bi·forked 〔ˈbaɪˌfɔrkt; ˈbaifɔːkt〕 *adj.* 分兩枝的；成叉的。

bi·form 〔ˈbaɪˌfɔrm; ˈbaifɔːm〕 *adj.* 兩形的；兩體的。

bi·fur·cate 〔*adj.* ˈbaɪfɚˌket, baɪˈfɝkɪt; ˈbaifəːkeit *v.* ˈbaɪfɚˌket, baɪˈfɝket; ˈbaifəːkeit〕 *adj., v.,* **-cat·ed, -cat·ing.** —*adj.*分兩枝的；成叉的。—*v.t.* & *v.i.* 成叉；分爲兩枝。

bi·fur·ca·tion 〔ˌbaɪfɚˈkeʃən; ˌbaifəːˈkeiʃən〕 *n.* ①分歧；分叉；叉枝。②分歧點；分叉點；分枝處。③分歧的一支；分支。

:big 〔bɪg; big〕 *adj.,* **big·ger, big·gest,** *adv., n.*—*adj.* ①大的。a *big* girl. 長成的女孩子。②懷孕的(指卽將臨盆的)。The woman is *big* with child. 那女人有孕。③〖俗〗重要的；偉大的。④誇大的。*big* talk. 誇大之詞；吹牛。⑤充滿的。⑥寬大的。A *big* person forgives others. 寬宏大量的人常原諒別人。⑦響亮的。⑧緊要的；嚴重的。⑨突出的；著名的。He is a *big* liar. 他是個大撒謊者。***too big for one's breeches*** (***pants*** or ***boots***) 顯示分外的自豪。—*adv.* ①誇大。②順利；成功。Things are going *big.* 事情進行得順利。—*n.* 鉅子；大公司。

bi·gam·ic 〔baɪˈgæmɪk; baiˈgæmik〕 *adj.* 重婚的。

big·a·mist 〔ˈbɪgəmɪst; ˈbigəmist〕 *n.* 重婚者。

big·a·mous 〔ˈbɪgəməs; ˈbigəməs〕 *adj.* 重婚的。

big·a·my 〔ˈbɪgəmɪ; ˈbigəmi〕 *n.* 重婚。

big beat 〖美俚〗搖滾樂(舞)。

Big Ben 英國倫敦國會大廈鐘樓上的大鐘。

big business ①(常含貶意) **a.** 壟斷性或獨占性企業。**b.** 非商業性質的類似組織。②大企業。

big cheese 〖俚〗重要人物；具有影響力的人。

Big Five 世界五强(指第一次世界大戰巴黎會議中的美、英、法、義、日，或指第二次世界大戰後之中、美、英、法、蘇)。

bigg 〔bɪg;big〕 *n.* 一種大麥。

big game ①大的獵物。②大目標。

big gun 〖俚〗有影響力之重要人物。

big·head 〔ˈbɪgˌhɛd; ˈbighed〕 *n.* ①(動物的)大頭病。②自高；自大；自負。③自高、自大、自負者。—**big·head·ed,** *adj.*

big-heart·ed 〔ˈbɪgˌhɑrtɪd; ˈbigˈhɑːtid〕 *adj.* 親切的；寬大的；慷慨的。—**ly,** *adv.*

big·horn 〔ˈbɪgˌhɔrn; ˈbighɔːn〕 *n., pl.* **-horn, -horns.** (產於 Rocky 山脈中之)巨角野羊。

big house ①〖俚〗監獄；感化院。②地方富豪之大邸宅。

bight 〔baɪt; bait〕 *n.* ①海岸線之彎曲部分。②海灣。③彎曲；角；隅。④繩圈；兩端牢繫之繩索中間垂下的曲線。—*v.t.* 繫牢。

big idea 〖俚〗①鬼主意。②目的；意圖；用意。

big league ①〖運動〗美國二大職業棒球聯盟之一（=major league). ②（類似美國二大職業棒球聯盟的)全國性活動或組織。

big-leagu·er 〔ˈbɪgˈligɚ; ˈbigˈliːgə〕 *n.* 〖運動〗參加美國二大職業棒球聯盟之球賽選手；參加（類似美國二大職業棒球聯盟的）全國性競賽者。

big·mouthed 〔ˈbɪgˌmauðd; ˈbigmauðd〕 *adj.* 長舌的(人)。

big name 有名的人物；知名人士；名人。

big-name 〔ˈbɪgˈnem; ˈbigneim〕 *adj.* ①有名的；知名的；大名鼎鼎的。②包括知名人士的；與知名人士有關的。

big·ness 〔ˈbɪgnɪs; ˈbignis〕 *n.* ①大。②體積的大小。

big·no·ni·a 〔bɪgˈnonɪə; bigˈnouniə〕 *n.* 紫葳屬植物。

big·ot 〔ˈbɪgət; ˈbigət〕 *n.* ①盲從一種主義或教條的人。②心地狹窄的人。③頑固者。

big·ot·ed 〔ˈbɪgətɪd; ˈbigətid〕 *adj.* ①固執己見的。②心地狹窄的。—**ly,** *adv.*

big·ot·ry 〔ˈbɪgətrɪ; ˈbigətri〕 *n., pl.* **-ries.** 持偏見之行爲或態度等。

big shot 〖俚〗大人物；大亨。

big stick (政治上或軍事上的)壓力。

big talk 吹牛；自誇；大言。

big time 〖俚〗①雜耍表演。②第一流；最高級(指各行業中者言)。③愉快之時光。

big-time 〔ˈbɪgˈtaɪm; ˈbigˈtaim〕 *adj.* 〖美俚〗第一流的；職業的。

big-tim·er 〔ˈbɪgˌtaɪmɚ; ˈbigˌtaimə〕 *n.*(在某行業或領域中)成名者。a television *big-timer.* 電視紅星。

big top ①馬戲團之主帳篷。②馬戲。

big·wig 〔ˈbɪgˌwɪg; ˈbigwig〕 *n.* 〖俗〗權貴；大亨。

bi·jou 〔ˈbiʒu; ˈbiːʒuː〕 *n., pl.* **-joux** 〔-ʒuz; -ʒuːz〕, *adj.* —*n.*①珠寶。②小巧之珍物。—*adj.* 小巧的。

bi·jou·te·rie 〔bɪˈʒutəri; biːˈʒuːtəri〕 *n.* ①珠寶類。②小巧的裝飾物。

bi·ju·gate 〔ˈbaɪdʒuˌget; ˈbaidʒugeit〕 *adj.* 〖植物〗有二對小葉的。(亦作 **bijugous**)

bike 〔baɪk; baik〕 *n., v.,* **biked, bik·ing.** —*n.* 〖俗〗①脚踏車。②摩托車。

—*v.t.* & *v.i.* 〖俗〗①騎脚踏車(旅行)。②騎摩托車(旅行)。—**bik·er,** *n.*

bike·way ['baɪk,we; 'baikwei] 〖美〗自行車道。

Bi·ki·ni [bɪ'kinɪ; bi'ki:ni] *n.* ①比基尼(北太平洋中一珊瑚島, 屬馬紹爾羣島, 1946 年原子彈試驗地)。②(亦作 **bikini**)三點式女游泳裝。

bi·la·bi·al [baɪ'lebɪəl; bai'leibjəl] *adj.* ①〖植物〗有兩唇的。②〖語音〗雙唇音的。—*n.* 〖語音〗雙唇音(如 p, b, m).

bi·la·bi·ate [baɪ'lebɪ,et; bai'leibieit] *adj.* 〖植物〗有二唇的;兩唇形的。

bi·lat·er·al [baɪ'lætərəl; bai'lætərəl] *adj.* ①(在)兩邊的。②雙方的。③互惠的;對等的。④兩邊對稱的。—**ly,** *adv.*

bil·ber·ry ['bɪl,bɛrɪ; 'bilbəri] *n., pl.* **-ries.** 〖植物〗覆盆子。(亦作 **blaeberry**)

bil·bo ['bɪlbo; 'bilbou] *n., pl.* **-boes.** (常 *pl.*)一種防止囚犯逃走用的鐵製足械。

bile [baɪl; bail] *n.* ①膽汁。②壞脾氣;憤怒。***black bile*** 憂鬱。

bile·stone ['baɪl,ston; 'bailstoun] *n.* 〖醫〗膽石。

bilge [bɪldʒ; bildʒ] *n., v.,* **bilged, bilg·ing.** —*n.* ①桶之腹部;船腹。②船底的污水;船底兩側的排水槽。③〖俚〗無聊的文章;無聊的話;傻話。—*v.i.* ①(船底)破漏。②膨脹。③擱淺。④〖俚〗成績不及格而退學。—*v.t.* ①使(船底)破漏。②〖俚〗使(成績不及格的海軍學校之學生等)退學。

bil·har·zi·a [bɪl'hɑrzɪə; bil'hɑ:ziə] *n.* 血蛭;血吸蟲。

bil·i·ar·y ['bɪlɪ,ɛrɪ; 'biljəri] *adj.* ①〖生理〗膽汁的;輸送膽汁的。②〖醫〗膽汁性的。

bi·lin·e·ar [baɪ'lɪnɪr; bai'liniə] *adj.* 〖數學〗雙線性的。

bi·lin·gual [baɪ'lɪŋgwəl; bai'liŋgwəl] *adj.* ①兩種語言的。②能說兩種語言的。—*n.* 能說兩種語言的人。—**ly,** *adv.*

bi·lin·guist [baɪ'lɪŋgwɪst; bai'liŋgwist] *n.* 通二國語言者。

bil·ious ['bɪljəs; 'biljəs] *adj.* ①膽汁的;因膽汁過多所致的。②患膽病的。③壞脾氣的;不悅的。④使人厭惡的;令人不快的。

-bility 〖字尾〗由語尾爲 **-ble** 之形容詞變成名詞者用之, 如: ability, adaptability.

bilk [bɪlk; bilk] *v.t.* ①欺;騙。②挫折;使人失望。③躲避;開溜;賴(債等)。—*n.* ①欺騙;詭詐。②騙子。

Bill [bɪl; bil] *n.* 男子名(William之暱稱)。

‡**bill¹** [bɪl; bil] *n.* ①帳單;發票。I have many *bills* to pay. 我有許多帳單需要付款。②紙幣;鈔票。I have several one-dollar *bills.* 我有幾張一元的鈔票。③廣告;招貼。Post no *bills.* 禁止招貼。④項目單。a *bill* of expenditures. 支出項目單。⑤戲目。good *bill* at the theater. 戲院的好戲碼。⑥法案;議案。⑦匯票;支票。*bill* payable at sight. 即期支票。⑧〖法律〗訴狀。*bill* of indictment. 公訴狀。***fill the bill*** 〖俗〗合乎條件。***foot the bill*** 〖俗〗付帳。—*v.t.* ①記入帳;送帳單給。②用招貼通告;用傳單通告。③貼海報、招貼等。

bill²** *n.* ①鳥嘴。②類似鳥嘴之物。—*v.i.* ①(鳥類)接嘴;觸嘴。②調情。bill and coo*** 接吻、愛撫、懇談等。—*v.t.* (鳥等)用嘴啄取。

bill³ *n.* 麻鳽 (bittern) 之叫聲。

bill·board ['bɪl,bord; 'bilbɔ:d] *n.* 〖美〗告示板;廣告招貼板。

bill book ①〖會計〗出納簿。②置錢物之皮夾(=billfold).

bill broker 證券經紀人。

bill discounter 貼現業者。

bil·let¹ ['bɪlɪt; 'bilit] *n., v.,* **-let·ed, -let·ing.** —*n.* ①供軍事人員住宿之命令;住宿券。②士兵之住宿處;宿營。③工作;職位;地位;任命。a good *billet.* 好差事。④目的地。Every bullet has its *billet.* 〖喻〗中彈與否全是命定。⑤〖古〗簡短的公文;字條;短簡。—*v.t.* ①指定(士兵)住宿之處。②派定職位;任命。—*v.i.* 住宿;投宿。

bil·let² *n.* ①作燃料用的小木條。②粗木棒。③鐵條;鋼條。

bil·let-doux ['bɪlɪ'du; 'bilei'du:] *n., pl.* **bil·lets-doux.** 〖法〗情書。

bill·fold ['bɪl,fold; 'bilfould] *n.* 置錢物之皮夾。

bill·head ['bɪl,hɛd; 'bilhed] *n.* ①印有商號名稱的空白帳單。②帳單頂端所印之商號名稱、地址等。

bill·hook ['bɪl,hʊk; 'bilhuk] *n.* 鉤刀;鉤鐮。

bil·liard ['bɪljəd; 'biljəd] *adj.* 撞球戲的;彈子戲的。—*n.* (撞球戲中所得的)分數。

billiard ball 撞球。

billiard cloth 撞球枱上的綠色絨布。

billiard cue 撞球桿。

bil·liard·ist ['bɪljə·dɪst; 'biljədist] *n.* 打撞球者。

billiard marker (彈子戲中之)記分員。

***bil·liards** ['bɪljə·dz; 'biljədz] *n.* 彈子戲;撞球。*Billiards* is a good indoor game. 彈子戲是一種有益的戶內遊戲。

billiard saloon 彈子房。(亦作 **billiard room**).

billiard table 撞球枱。

Bil·li·ken ['bɪlɪkən; 'bilikən] *n.* 〖美〗被認爲能帶來好運之一種玩偶。

bill·ing ['bɪlɪŋ; 'biliŋ] *n.* ①戲院海報上之演員表。②演員表上之順序。③廣告;宣傳。④營業量。

bil·lings·gate ['bɪlɪŋz,get; 'biliŋz-git] *n.* 鄙俗之言語。

***bil·lion** ['bɪljən; 'biljən] *n.* ①十億=1,000,000,000(美國和法國計算法)。②萬億=1,000,000,000,000(英國和德國計算法)。

bil·lion·aire [,bɪljən'ɛr; ,biljə'nɛə] *n.* 十億富翁;巨富。

bil·lionth ['bɪljənθ; 'biliənθ] *adj.* ①第十億的。②十億分之一的。—*n.* ①第十億個。②十億分之一。

bill of entry 報關單。

bill of estimate 估價單。

bill of exchange 匯票。

bill of fare ①菜單。②節目單。

bill of health (船隻於航行期間所執的)健康證書。***clean bill of health*** 〖俗〗斷定(某人)爲清白、合格等之結論。

bill of lading 提單。

Bill of Rights ①〖英史〗人權條例。②〖美〗權利典章(憲法修正案前列十條之總稱)。

bill of sale 賣據。

bil·lon ['bɪlən; 'bilən] *n.*(鑄幣用)含銅較多的金銀。

***bil·low** ['bɪlo; 'bilou] *n.*①巨浪。②似巨浪之物。—*v.i.* ①(巨浪)奔騰;(波濤)洶湧。②如波浪一般地飄動。—*v.t.* 使波動;使飄動。

bil·low·y ['bɪloɪ; 'biloui] *adj.,* **-low·i·er, -low·i·est.** ①波濤洶湧的。②巨浪似的。

bill·post·er ['bɪl,postə; 'bil,poustə] *n.* 以在公共場所貼傳單廣告爲業者。(亦作 **billsticker**)

Bil·ly ['bɪlɪ; 'bili] *n.* 男子名 (William 之暱稱)。

bil·ly ['bɪlɪ; 'bili] *n., pl.* **-lies.** ①警棍。②棒。③(澳洲墾荒者在戶外燒茶用之)罐;壺。

bil·ly·cock ['bɪlɪ,kɑk; 'bilikɔk] *n.*〖英俗〗氈帽。

billy goat 〖俗〗雄山羊。

bi·lo·bate [baɪˈlobet; baiˈloubeit] *adj.* 〖植物〗二裂的；有二裂片的。(亦作 **bilobed**)
bil·tong [ˈbɪlˌtɑŋ; ˈbiltɔŋ] *n.* (南非洲之)乾肉。 「手的動物(如猿類)。」
bi·mane [ˈbaɪmen; ˈbaimein] *n.* 有二
bim·a·nous [ˈbɪmənəs; ˈbimənəs] *adj.* 〖動物〗有二手的。(亦作 **bimanal**)
bi·mes·tri·al [baɪˈmɛstrɪəl; baiˈmestriəl] *adj.* ①每兩月一次的。②連續兩月的。
bi·me·tal·lic [ˌbaɪməˈtælɪk; ˌbaimiˈtælik] *adj.* 二種金屬的；複本位制的。
bi·met·al·lism [baɪˈmɛtḷˌɪzəm; baiˈmetəlizm] *n.* ①複本位制(金銀二本位幣制)。②擁護此種制度之主義、行動或政策。
bi·met·al·list [baɪˈmɛtḷɪst; baiˈmetəlist] *n.* 主張(金銀)複本位制之人。
bi·month·ly [baɪˈmʌnθlɪ; ˈbaiˈmʌnθli] *adj. & adv.* ①兩個月一回的(地)。②一個月兩回的(地)(爲避免與第一義混淆，宜用semimonthly). —*n.* 隔月發行的雜誌。
***bin** [bɪn; bin] *n., v.,* **binned, bin·ning.** —*n.* (貯藏食物、燃料等之)箱或倉。grain *bin.* 穀倉。—*v.t.* 置或貯藏於箱或倉中。
bin- 〖字首〗**bi-** 之異體，用於母音之前，如binary.
bi·na·ry [ˈbaɪnərɪ; ˈbainəri] *adj.* ①兩重的。②〖化〗二元素的。—*n.* ①二個之一組；雙體；複體；一雙。②〖天文〗雙子星。
binary star 〖天文〗雙子星。
binary system 〖物理〗二元系。
binary theory 〖化〗二元說。「生的。」
bi·nate [ˈbaɪnet; ˈbaineit] *adj.* 〖植物〗雙
bin·au·ral [bɪnˈɔrəl; binˈɔːrəl] *adj.* ①有雙耳的；用雙耳的。②立體迴音的。
bind** [baɪnd; baind] *v.,* **bound, bind·ing,** *n.* —*v.t.* ①縛；綁。She *binds* her hair up. 她紮起她的頭髮。②束縛；約束。He is *bound* by a contract. 他受契約的約束。③使負義務；使應當。All are *bound* to obey the laws. 大家都應當遵守法律。④使受法規之拘束。⑤縛(用繃帶)。⑥綑(邊)；鑲(邊)。She had a hat *bound* with blue band. 她有一頂用藍帶鑲邊的帽。⑦裝訂。⑧使便祕。⑨使凝固；使凝結。⑩使爲學徒〖常 out〗。In his youth his father *bound* him out to a blacksmith. 他年輕時，他父親送他去當鐵匠的學徒。⑪(衣服等)使覺過緊。bind hand and foot*** **a.** 全身綑綁。**b.** 受約束。***bind oneself to*** 允諾；保證。—*v.i.* ①凝固；凝結。Clay *binds* when it is heated. 黏土燒後凝結。②約束；拘束。③(衣服等)太緊。—*n.* ①縛或綁的行動或狀態。②縛或綁之物。***in a bind*** 〖俚〗**a.** 在困境中。**b.** 進退兩難；左右爲難。
bind·er [ˈbaɪndɚ; ˈbaində] *n.* ①縛者。②活頁紙的封面。③裝訂書本者。④收割機使稻穗成束的部分。⑤用以綑綁或黏附之物。⑥保證書；保證金。
bind·er·y [ˈbaɪndərɪ; ˈbaindəri] *n., pl.* **-er·ies.** 書籍裝訂鋪(廠)。
***bind·ing** [ˈbaɪndɪŋ; ˈbaindiŋ] *n.* ①書籍的裝訂。②鑲邊；滾條。③束縛；束縛的東西。—*adj.* 有束縛力的；應遵守的；有效力的。
binding energy 〖物理〗結合能。
binding energy of nucleus 〖物理〗原子核結合能。 「攜之)鋪蓋捲。」
bin·dle [ˈbɪndḷ; ˈbindl] *n.* 〖俚〗(遊民所
bind·weed [ˈbaɪndˌwid; ˈbaindwiːd] *n.* 〖植物〗旋花類之野生草。
bind·wood [ˈbaɪndˌwʊd; ˈbaindwud] *n.* 〖植物〗常春藤。

bine [baɪn; bain] *n.* 蔓；藤；葛。
binge [bɪndʒ; bindʒ] *n.* 〖俚〗狂飲。
bin·gle [ˈbɪŋgḷ; ˈbiŋgl] *n.* 〖棒球〗安打。
bin·go [ˈbɪŋgo; ˈbiŋgou] *n.* 〖美〗賓果遊戲(一種賭博性遊戲)。 「羅盤針箱。」
bin·na·cle [ˈbɪnəkḷ; ˈbinəkl] *n.* 〖航海〗
bin·o·cle [ˈbɪnəkḷ; ˈbinɔkl] *n.* 雙目望遠鏡或顯微鏡(=binoculars).
bi·noc·u·lar [baɪˈnɑkjəlɚ; biˈnɔkjulə] *adj.* 雙眼並用的。—*n.* (*pl.*) 雙目望遠鏡或顯微鏡。
bi·no·mi·al [baɪˈnomɪəl; baiˈnoumiəl] *adj.* ①〖數學〗二項的；二項式的。②〖生物〗二種名稱的；重名的。—*n.* ①二項式。②動植物二名法(種名前加屬名者)。
binomial theorem 〖數學〗二項式定理；二項展開式。 「ology.」
bio- 〖字首〗表"生命；生物"之義，如：bi-
bi·o·as·tro·nau·tics [ˌbaɪoˌæstroˈnɔtɪks; ˌbaiouˌæstrəˈnɔːtiks] *n.* (作 *sing.* 解)太空醫學(研究太空旅行對生命之影響)。
bi·o·chem·i·cal [ˌbaɪoˈkɛmɪkḷ; ˈbaioˈkemikəl] *adj.* 生物化學的。(亦作 **biochemic**) **—ly,** *adv.*
biochemical warfare 生化戰。
bi·o·chem·ist [ˌbaɪoˈkɛmɪst; ˈbaiouˈkemist] *n.* 生物化學家。
bi·o·chem·i·stry [ˌbaɪoˈkɛmɪstrɪ; ˈbaiouˈkemistri] *n.* ①生物化學。②生化機能。 「命之摧毀。**—bi·o·ci·dal,** *adj.*」
bi·o·cide [ˈbaɪəˌsaɪd; ˈbaiousaid] *n.* 生
bi·o·cli·ma·tol·o·gy [ˌbaɪoˌklaɪməˈtɑlədʒɪ; ˈbaiouˌklaiməˈtɔlədʒi] *n.* 生物氣候學(研究氣候對生物之影響)。
bi·o·dy·nam·ics [ˌbaɪodaɪˈnæmɪks; ˈbaioudaiˈnæmiks] *n.* (作 *sing.* 解)生活機能學；生物機能學。
bi·o·e·col·o·gy [ˌbaɪoɪˈkɑlədʒɪ; ˈbaiouiˈkɔlədʒi] *n.* 生物生態學。
bi·o·en·gi·neer·ing [ˌbaɪoˌɛndʒəˈnɪrɪŋ; ˌbaiouˌendʒəˈniriŋ] *n.* 生物工程學。
biog. ①biographer. ②biographical. ③biography.
bi·o·gen·e·sis [ˌbaɪoˈdʒɛnəsɪs; ˈbaiouˈdʒenisis] *n.* ①生源論。②生物發生。
bi·o·ge·o·chem·i·stry [ˌbaɪoˌdʒɪoˈkɛmɪstrɪ; ˌbaiouˌdʒiouˈkemistri] *n.* 生物地球化學。
bi·o·ge·og·ra·phy [ˌbaɪoˌdʒɪˈɑgrəfɪ; ˌbaiouˌdʒiˈɔgrəfi] *n.* 生物地理學。
bi·o·graph [ˈbaɪəˌgræf, -ˌgrɑf; ˈbaiougrɑːf] *n.* ①初期之電影放映機或錄音機(其商標爲Biograph). ②小傳。—*v.t.* 爲…寫小傳。
bi·og·ra·pher [baɪˈɑgrəfɚ; baiˈɔgrəfə] *n.* 傳記作家。
bi·o·graph·i·cal [ˌbaɪəˈgræfɪkḷ; ˌbaiouˈgræfikəl] *adj.* 有關某人之一生的；傳記的；傳記體的。(亦作 **biographic**)
***bi·og·ra·phy** [baɪˈɑgrəfɪ; baiˈɔgrəfi] *n., pl.* **-phies,** *v.,* **-phied, -phy·ing.** —*n.* 傳記。—*v.t.* 爲…作傳。 「ology.」
biol. ①biological. ②biologist. ③bi-
bi·o·log·i·cal [ˌbaɪəˈlɑdʒɪkḷ; ˌbaiəˈlɔdʒikəl] *adj.* 生物的；生物學的；有關生物(學)的。(亦作 **biologic**) **—ly,** *adv.*
biological warfare 生物戰；細菌戰。
bi·ol·o·gist [baɪˈɑlədʒɪst; baiˈɔlədʒist] *n.* 生物學家。
***bi·ol·o·gy** [baɪˈɑlədʒɪ; baiˈɔlədʒi] *n.* ①生物學。②生物(集合稱)。③生命現象。

bi·ol·y·sis [baɪˈɑlɪsɪs; baiˈɔlisis] *n.*【生物】生命現象之破壞;死。
bi·o·me·te·or·ol·o·gy [ˌbaɪoˌmitɪəˈrɑlədʒɪ; ˈbaiouˌmiːtiəˈrɔlədʒi] *n.* 生物環境學;生物氣象學。
bi·o·met·rics [ˌbaɪəˈmɛtrɪks; ˌbaiəˈmetriks] *n.* (作 *sing.* 解)生物測定學;生物統計學。
bi·om·e·try [baɪˈɑmətrɪ; baiˈɔmitri] *n.*①壽命測定。②=**biometrics.**
bi·o·nom·ics [ˌbaɪəˈnɑmɪks; ˈbaiəˈnɔmiks] *n.* (作 *sing.* 解)生態學。
bi·on·o·my [baɪˈɑnəmɪ; baiˈɔnəmi] *n.* ①生命學。②=**bionomics.**
bi·o·phys·ics [ˌbaɪoˈfɪzɪks; ˈbaiouˈfiziks] *n.* (作 *sing.* 解)生物物理學。
bi·o·plasm [ˈbaɪoˌplæzm̩; ˈbaiouplæzm] *n.* 原生質。
bi·o·plast [ˈbaɪoˌplæst; ˈbaiouplæst] *n.* 原生質細胞。
bi·op·sy [baɪˈɑpsɪ; baiˈɔpsi] *n., pl.* **-sies.**【醫】活體檢視(法);活組織切片檢查(法)。
bi·o·sat·el·lite [ˌbaɪoˈsætḷˌaɪt; ˌbaiouˈsætəlait] *n.* 攜帶生物作太空環境研究之人造衛星。
bi·o·sci·ence [ˌbaɪoˈsaɪəns; ˈbaiouˈsaiəns] *n.* 太空生物學。—**bi·o·sci·en·tif·ic,** *adj.* —**bi·o·sci·en·tist,** *n.*
bi·o·scope [ˈbaɪəˌskop; ˈbaiəskoup] *n.*①電影放映機。②【英】電影院。
bi·os·co·py [baɪˈɑskəpɪ; baiˈɔskəpi] *n., pl.* **-pies.**【醫】生死判驗(法)。
bi·o·so·ci·ol·o·gy [ˌbaɪoˌsosɪˈɑlədʒi; ˌbaiouˌsousiːˈɔlədʒi] *n.* 生物社會學。(亦作 **biological sociology**)
bi·o·stat·ics [ˌbaɪoˈstætɪks; ˈbaiouˈstætiks] *n.* (作 *sing.* 解)生物靜力學。
bi·o·ther·a·py [ˌbaɪoˈθɛrəpɪ; ˌbaiouˈθerəpi] *n.*【醫】生物療法。
bi·ot·ic [baɪˈɑtɪk; baiˈɔtik] *adj.* 關於生命的;關於生物的。(亦作 **biotical**)
bi·o·tin [ˈbaɪətɪn; ˈbaiətin] *n.* 維他命H;生物素。
bi·o·tite [ˈbaɪəˌtaɪt; ˈbaiətait] *n.*【礦】黑雲母。
bi·o·vu·lar [baɪˈovjələ; baiˈouvjələ] *adj.* 由兩個卵巢而來的。
bip·a·rous [ˈbɪpərəs; ˈbipərəs] *adj.*①【植物】二枝的;二軸的。②【動物】雙生的。
bi·par·ti·san, bi·par·ti·zan [baɪˈpɑrtəzn̩; baiˈpɑːtizən] *adj.* 兩(政)黨的;(在兩黨政治的國家裏)代表兩黨的。
bi·par·tite [baɪˈpɑrtaɪt; baiˈpɑːtait] *adj.* ①有兩部分的;由二部組成的。②一式兩分的。③【植物】深裂爲二的。
bi·ped [ˈbaɪpɛd; ˈbaiped] *n.* 兩足動物。—*adj.* 兩足的。(亦作 **bipedal**)
bi·pet·al·ous [baɪˈpɛtḷəs; baiˈpetələs] *adj.*【植物】有二花瓣的。
bi·pin·nate [baɪˈpɪnet; baiˈpineit] *adj.*【植物】二回羽狀的;兩羽狀的。
bi·plane [ˈbaɪˌplen; ˈbaiplein] *n.* 雙翼飛機。
bi·po·lar [baɪˈpolə; baiˈpoulə] *adj.* ①【電】有兩極的;雙極的。②南北極的;南北極都找得到的。③(勢力等之)兩極的。—**i·ty,** *n.*
bi·quad·rat·ic [ˌbaɪkwɑdˈrætɪk; ˌbaikwɔˈdrætik] *adj.*【數學】四次的。—*n.* ①四乘冪。②四次方程式。
bi·ra·cial [baɪˈreʃəl; baiˈreiʃəl] *adj.*包括或代表兩個種族(尤指白人與黑人)的。
***birch** [bɝtʃ; bəːtʃ] *n.* ①樺類;樺樹;赤楊。②樺樹(之木材)。③笞責用之木條;樺條。—*v.t.*鞭笞;用樺條打。—*adj.*樺木的;赤楊的。
birch·en [ˈbɝtʃən; ˈbəːtʃən] *adj.* 樺樹的;樺木製的。
‡**bird** [bɝd; bəːd] *n.* ①鳥。②【俚】人。He's a queer *bird*. 他是個怪人。③飛行器。④【英俚】漂亮的少女或婦人。***a bird in the hand*** 有把握的事;已經獲得的東西。*A bird in the hand* is worth two in the bush. 一鳥在擒勝於二鳥在林(到手的東西才可靠)。***a little bird***【俗】消息靈通人士。***birds of a feather*** 同類之物;一丘之貉。*Birds of a feather* flock together. 物以類聚。***eat like a bird*** 食量極小;吃得很少。***for the birds***【俚】沒甚麼價值。***kill two birds with one stone*** 一舉兩得。***the bird***【俚】嘲笑;嘲弄的噓聲。He got *the bird* when he came out on stage. 他一出現在舞臺上人們便以噓聲嘲弄他。***The early bird catches the worm.***【諺】早起之鳥獲蟲(喻作事趁早者得利)。—*v.i.* 在野外觀察或鑑別鳥類。
bird·brain [ˈbɝdˌbren; ˈbəːdbrein] *n.*【俚】傻瓜;蠢貨。
bird·call [ˈbɝdˌkɔl; ˈbəːdkɔːl] *n.* ①鳥聲。②似鳥鳴聲。③吹出似鳥聲之哨子。(亦作 **bird call**)
bird dog 獵鳥用獵犬。
bird fancier ①歡喜養鳥者。②鳥商。
bird·house [ˈbɝdˌhaus; ˈbəːdhaus] *n.* 鳥屋;大鳥籠;鳥舍。
***bird·ie** [ˈbɝdɪ; ˈbəːdi] *n.* ①小鳥;鳥。②【高爾夫】較標準桿數少一桿而入洞。—*v.t.*【高爾夫】以較標準桿數少一桿的成績打進(洞)。
bird·like [ˈbɝdˌlaɪk; ˈbəːdlaik] *adj.* 似鳥的;敏捷的;輕快的。
bird·lime [ˈbɝdˌlaɪm; ˈbəːdlaim] *n., v.,* **-limed, -lim·ing.** —*n.* ①(塗於樹枝上以捕鳥的)黏鳥膠。②用以誘陷之事物;圈套。—*v.t.* 以黏膠捕(鳥)。
bird·man [ˈbɝdˌmæn; ˈbəːdmæn] *n., pl.* **-men.** ①【俗】飛行員。②鳥類研究者。③捕鳥者。
bird of ill omen 帶來壞消息的人。
bird of passage ①候鳥。②暫住一地的人;時常移居的人。
bird of peace 鴿子。
bird of prey 食肉鳥(如鷹、鳶、鷲等);猛禽。
bird·seed [ˈbɝdˌsid; ˈbəːdsiːd] *n.* 鳥食(如黍、麻實之類)。
bird's-eye [ˈbɝdzˌaɪ; ˈbəːdzai] *adj.*①凌高俯視的;鳥瞰的。②概觀的。③似鳥眼的;有鳥眼似之斑點的。—*n.*【植物】雪剜草類。
bird shot 射鳥用小粒彈丸。
bird's-nest [ˈbɝdzˌnɛst; ˈbəːdznest] *n.*①燕窩。②野參。③【航海】眺望臺。
bird strike 飛機與鳥羣之相撞。
bird·wom·an [ˈbɝdˌwumən; ˈbəːdˌwumən] *n., pl.* **-wom·en.**【俗】女飛行家。
bir·dy [ˈbɝdɪ; ˈbəːdi] *adj.* ①似鳥的。②多鳥的;富於鳥類的。
bi·reme [ˈbaɪrim; ˈbairiːm] *n.* 古代兩排槳之船。
bi·ret·ta [bəˈrɛtə; biˈretə] *n.* (天主教任僧職者所戴之)四角帽;法冠。
Bir·ming·ham [ˈbɝmɪŋˌhæm; ˈbəːmiŋəm] *n.* 伯明罕(**a.**美國阿拉巴馬州中北部的一城市;**b.**英格蘭中部之一城市)。
‡**birth** [bɝθ; bəːθ] *n.* ①出世;誕生。②開始;起源;創始。③生產;分娩。She gave *birth* to twin girls. 她生了一對孿生女孩。④身世;出身。He is a man of noble *birth*. 他出身高貴。⑤天生。He is a musician by *birth*. 他是天生的音樂家。⑥高尚門第。—*v.t.*

造成；產生；帶來。—*v.i.* 〖方〗分娩；生產。

birth certificate 出生證明書。

birth control 節育。

***birth·day** 〔ˈbɜθ͵de; ˈbəːθdei〕 *n.* 生日；誕辰。

birthday suit 〖俗〗裸體。

birth·mark 〔ˈbɜθ͵mɑrk; ˈbəːθmɑːk〕 *n.* ①胎記；胎痣。②特點；特徵。

***birth·place** 〔ˈbɜθ͵ples; ˈbəːθpleis〕 *n.* 誕生地；發源地；發祥地。

birth rate 出生率；生育率。(亦作 **birthrate**)

birth·right 〔ˈbɜθ͵raɪt; ˈbəːθrait〕 *n.* ①與生俱來的權利。②長子繼承權。***sell one's birthright for a pottage of lentils*** 爲扁豆湯而賣掉繼承權(出自聖經)；爲小失大。

birth·stone 〔ˈbɜθ͵ston; ˈbəːθstoun〕 *n.* 誕生石(象徵出生月分的寶石)。

bis 〔bɪs; bis〕〖拉〗*adv.* ①二度；二次。②〖音樂〗再次。

B.I.S. Bank for International Settlements.

***bis·cuit** 〔ˈbɪskɪt; ˈbiskit〕 *n., pl.* **-cuits** or **-cuit.** ①〖美〗小甜麪包。②〖英〗餅乾。③經首次烤焙而尙未上釉彩之瓷器。④灰棕色。

bise 〔biz; biːz〕 *n.* 自瑞士阿爾卑斯山吹下之寒風(通常爲北風或東北風)。

bi·sect 〔baɪˈsɛkt; baiˈsekt〕 *v.t.* ①分切爲二。②分爲二等分。③與…交叉。—*v.i.* 分開爲二；分叉。—**bi·sec·tion,** *n.*

bi·sec·tor 〔baɪˈsɛktɚ; baiˈsektə〕 *n.* 〖數學〗二等分線。

bi·sex·u·al 〔baɪˈsɛkʃuəl; ˈbaiˈseksjuəl〕 *adj.* 〖生物〗①兩性的。②雌雄同體的。—*n.* ①〖生物〗二性體。②〖精神病〗在性慾上受兩性吸引之人。—**i·ty,** *n.* —**ly,** *adv.*

***bish·op** 〔ˈbɪʃəp; ˈbiʃəp〕 *n.* 主教。

bish·op·ric 〔ˈbɪʃəprɪk; ˈbiʃəprik〕 *n.* ①主教之轄區。②主教之職權。

Bis·marck 〔ˈbɪzmɑrk; ˈbizmɑːk〕 *n.* 俾斯麥(Otto von, 1815–1898, 德國政治家，德國第一任首相)。

Bis·mil·lah 〔bɪsˈmɪlə; bisˈmilə〕〖阿拉伯〗*interj.* 眞主啊！(回教徒起誓之詞)。

bis·muth 〔ˈbɪzməθ; ˈbizməθ〕 *n.* 〖化〗鉍。

bismuth glance 〖化〗輝鉍礦。

bis·mu·thic acid 〔ˈbɪzməθɪk～; bizˈmjuːθik～〕〖化〗鉍酸。

bis·muth·yl 〔ˈbɪzməθɪl; ˈbizməθil〕 *n.* 〖化〗鉍醯基；鉍氧基。

bi·son 〔ˈbaɪsn; ˈbaisn〕 *n. sing.* or *pl.* 美洲或歐洲的野牛。

bisque¹ 〔bɪsk; bisk〕 *n.* ①(用魚、蝦、蛤等調製之)一種濃羹。②(用研碎之杏仁餅乾或其他核仁調製之)一種冰淇淋。(亦作 **bisk**)

bisque² *n.* ①素瓷；本色陶器。②紅黃色。

bis·sex·tile 〔bɪˈsɛkstɪl; biˈsekstail〕 *n.* 閏年。—*adj.* 閏年的；閏的。

bi·state 〔ˈbaɪ͵stet; ˈbaisteit〕 *adj.* (在美國)兩州的；代表兩州的。

bis·ter 〔ˈbɪstɚ; ˈbistə〕 *n.* ①(取自煤烟之)褐色顏料。②褐色。—*adj.* 褐色的。(亦作 **bistre**)

bis·tort 〔ˈbɪstɔrt; ˈbistɔːt〕 *n.* 〖植物〗拳參。

bis·tou·ry 〔ˈbɪsturɪ; ˈbisturi〕 *n., pl.* **-ries.** (外科手術用之)小刀。

bis·tro 〔ˈbɪstro; ˈbistrou〕 *n.* 〖俗〗①小酒館；小咖啡店。②酒保。

bi·sul·fate 〔baɪˈsʌlfet; baiˈsʌlfeit〕 *n.* 〖化〗重硫酸鹽。(亦作 **bisulphate**)

bi·sul·fide 〔baɪˈsʌlfaɪd; baiˈsʌlfaid〕 *n.* 〖化〗二硫化物。(亦作 **bisulphide**)

‡**bit¹** 〔bɪt; bit〕 *n.* ①一小塊；少許。We need only a *bit.* 我們祇需少許。②有點；些許。He is a *bit* of an artist. 他有些像藝術家。③〖俗〗片刻。Please wait a *bit.* 請稍等片刻。④〖美〗12¹/₂ 分。⑤〖英〗小銅錢。⑥鑽；螺旋錐。⑦〖俚〗標準作業。***a bit at a time*** 慢慢地；漸漸。***bit by bit*** 一點一點地。***do one's bit*** 盡一己的本分。Everybody has to *do* his own *bit.* 每人都應盡他的本分。***every bit*** 全部；全然。He is a scholar, *every bit* of him. 他是一位徹頭徹尾的學者。***give a person a bit of one's mind*** 坦白地指出一個人的錯誤，並指責之。***not a bit*** 毫不。It is *not a bit* cold. 一點不冷。***two bits*** 美金二角五分。

bit² *n., v.,* **bit·ted, bit·ting.** —*n.* ①馬嚼口；馬勒。②拘束物；控制物。***take the bit between*** (or ***in***) ***one's teeth*** **a.** (馬)逃走。**b.** 脫出羈絆；反叛。—*v.t.* 給(馬)帶嚼口；拘束。

bit³ *v.* pt. & pp. of **bite.**

B.I.T. Bachelor of Industrial Technology.

bitch 〔bɪtʃ; bitʃ〕 *n.* ①母狗；母狼；母狐。②〖俚〗賤女人。③〖俚〗困難或不快之事。—*v.t.* 〖俚〗弄壞；搞壞。—*v.i.* 〖俚〗抱怨；埋怨。***son of a bitch*** 罵人語(相當於"他媽的；狗狼養的"等，亦作 **s. o. b.**)。

bite** 〔baɪt; bait〕 *n., v.,* **bit** 〔bɪt; bit〕, **bit·ten** 〔ˈbɪtn̩; ˈbitən〕 or **bit, bit·ing.** —*n.* ①咬下的一塊；一口；少量食物；食物。Let me have a *bite* of the cake. 這餅讓我咬一口。②咬；咬傷。③魚之吞餌。Do you have a *bite?* 有魚來上鈎嗎？④劇痛。⑤(酸類對金屬之)腐蝕。⑥(齒輪等)卡緊。⑦鋒利；銳利。⑧(牙齒的)咬合狀態；咬合。The dentist said I had a good *bite.* 牙醫師說我的牙齒之咬合狀態良好。⑨〖俚〗從整體分出的一部分。⑩小吃。⑪銼的粗糙表面。put the bite on*** 〖俚〗向…敲竹槓。—*v.t.* ①咬。The mosquitoes *bit* me in the leg. 蚊子咬我的腿。②穿刺。③刺激；刺痛。Red pepper *bites* my tongue. 紅椒刺痛我的舌。④侵蝕。⑤抓緊；卡緊。The wheels *bite* the rails. 輪緊卡在軌上。⑥(用酸類)蝕刻。He *bit* his plates. 他蝕刻他的版子。⑦〖俚〗欺詐(用被動語態)。⑧〖俚〗使苦惱。What's *biting* you? 你在氣甚麼？—*v.i.* ①咬。Does his dog *bite?* 他的狗咬人嗎？②嚼。③(猜謎時)承認失敗。I'll *bite,* what is it? 我認輸，答案是甚麼？④絞緊；抓緊。***bite back*** 咬住嘴唇强忍不說出來(惡言)。***bite off*** 咬下一塊。He *bit off* a large piece of the apple. 他把這隻蘋果咬下一大口。***bite off more than one can chew*** 貪多而吃不下；從事能力所不及之工作。***bite one's lips*** 咬唇以表示厭煩。***bite some one's head off*** 嚴厲斥責。***bite the dust*** **a.** 倒於地上；被殺；陣亡。**b.** 失敗。***bite the hand that feeds one*** 忘恩負義。

bit·er 〔ˈbaɪtɚ; ˈbaitə〕 *n.* 咬者。

***bit·ing** 〔ˈbaɪtɪŋ; ˈbaitiŋ〕 *adj.* ①咬痛的；如刺的。②銳利的；辛辣的；譏刺的。—**ly,** *adv.*

bitt 〔bɪt; bit〕 *n.* 〖航海〗錨鎖柱；纜柱。

bit·ten 〔ˈbɪtn̩; ˈbitn〕 *v.* pp. of **bite.**

‡**bit·ter** 〔ˈbɪtɚ; ˈbitə〕 *adj.* ①有苦味的。Good medicines taste *bitter.* 良藥苦口。②難堪的。③諷刺的；嚴厲的；銳利的。④刺痛的；嚴酷的。⑤痛苦的；憂愁的。*bitter* pain. 劇痛。⑥懷恨的。*bitter* hatred. 痛恨。*bitter* enemy. 死敵。⑦不友善的。a *bitter* answer. 不友善的回答。***bitter against*** 强烈反對。We are *bitter against* the project. 我們强烈反對這計畫。—*n.* 苦。We

take the *bitter* with the sweet. 我們苦與甘兼嘗。—*adv.* ①嚴酷地;劇烈地。a *bitter* cold night. 嚴寒的一夜。②〖英方〗非常地。This drug is wanted *bitter* bad, sir. 先生,這藥非常需要。—*v.t.* 使帶苦味。*bittered* ale. 苦麥酒。
bitter cup 苦杯(quassia木所製之杯,酒盛後味變苦)。
bitter end ①最後。②死。
bit·ter·end [ˈbɪtɚˈɛnd; ˈbitəˈend] *adj.* 頑固的。
bit·ter-end·er [ˈbɪtɚˈɛndɚ; ˈbitəˈendə] *n.* 〖俗〗頑梗者;主張硬拚到底的人。
***bit·ter·ly** [ˈbɪtɚlɪ; ˈbitəli] *adv.* ①苦澀地。②難堪地。③悲痛地。to cry *bitterly*. 悲痛地喊叫。④殘酷地。
bit·tern[1] [ˈbɪtɚn; ˈbitən] *n.* 麻鳽。
bit·tern[2] *n.* 鹵水;鹵汁。
***bit·ter·ness** [ˈbɪtɚnɪs; ˈbitənis] *n.* ①苦味。②悲痛;酷烈;激越;諷刺。to speak with *bitterness*. 痛恨地說。
bit·ter·nut [ˈbɪtɚˌnʌt; ˈbitənʌt] *n.* 美國東部與南部所長一種山胡桃樹,其子甚苦。
bitter pill 恥辱;困惱;難以忍受之事。
bit·ter·root [ˈbɪtɚˌrut; ˈbitəruːt] *n.* 〖植物〗①一種馬齒莧。②大根草。③毒狗草。
bitter salt 硫酸鎂;瀉鹽。
bit·ter·sweet [ˈbɪtɚˌswit; ˈbitəswiːt] *n.* ①〖植物〗白英。②半苦半甜。—*adj.* 半苦半甜的;苦樂參半的。
bi·tu·men [bɪˈtjumən; ˈbitjumin] *n.* 瀝青。
bi·tu·mi·nous [bɪˈtjumənəs; biˈtjuːminəs] *adj.* ①瀝青的。②生煤的;煙煤的。
bituminous coal 煙煤;生煤。
bi·va·lence [baɪˈveləns; ˈbaiˌveiləns] *n.* 〖化〗二原子價。
bi·va·lent [baɪˈvelənt; ˈbaiˌveilənt] *adj.* ①〖化〗**a.** 二價的。**b.** 二原子價的。②〖生物〗二價(染色體)的。—*n.* 二價染色體。
bi·valve [ˈbaɪˌvælv; ˈbaivælv] *n.* ①雙殼貝類。②〖植物〗雙萌子。—*adj.* (亦作 **bivalved, bivalvular**) 雙殼的;雙萌的。
biv·ou·ac [ˈbɪvuˌæk; ˈbivuæk] *n., v.,* **-acked, -ack·ing.** —*n.* 野營;露營;露營之處。—*v.i.* 露營。
bi·week·ly [baɪˈwiklɪ; baiˈwiːkli] *adj., adv., n., pl.* **-lies.** —*adj.* ①兩週一次的;隔週的。②每週二次的。—*adv.* ①兩週一次地。②每週二次地。—*n.* 雙週出版物;雙週刊。
bi·year·ly [baɪˈjɪrlɪ; baiˈjəːli] *adj.* & *adv.* 兩年一次的(地);一年兩次的(地)。
biz [bɪz; biz] *n.* 〖俚〗=**business.** a *biz* confab. 商談。
bi·zarre [bɪˈzɑr; biˈzɑː] *adj.* 古怪的;奇怪的;奇異的。
bi·zar·re·rie [bizarəˈri; biˈzɑːrəri] 〖法〗*n.* 奇怪;古怪;奇異;異物。
Bi·zo·ni·a [baɪˈzonɪə; baiˈzouniə] *n.* (二次大戰後,德國境內)英美聯合占領區。
B.J. Bachelor of Journalism.
Bk 化學元素 berkelium 之符號。 **bk.** ①bank. ②block. ③book. **bkbndr.** bookbinder. **bkcy.** 〖法律〗bankruptcy. **bkg.** banking. **bkpr.** bookkeeper. **bks.** ①banks. ② barracks. ③ books. **bkt.** basket. **B.L.** ① Bachelor of Laws. ②Bachelor of Letters. **B/L** bill of lading. **bl.** ①bale. ②bales. ③ barrel. ④barrels. **B.L.A.** ①Bachelor of Landscape Architecture. ②Bachelor of Liberal Arts.
blab [blæb; blæb] *v.,* **blabbed, blab·bing,** *n.* —*v.t.* & *v.i.* ①洩漏(祕密)。②閑談;胡扯。—*n.* ①閑談;不慎之言。②洩漏祕密者;胡扯者。—**ber,** *n.*
blab·ber·mouth [ˈblæbɚˌmauθ; ˈblæbəmauθ] *n.* 長舌者。
:**black** [blæk; blæk] *adj.* ①黑色的。②黑暗無光的。It is a *black* night. 這是一個黑夜。③黑人的。the *black* races. 黑色人種。④汚穢的。⑤憂鬱的;悲慘的;暗淡的。Their future looked *black.* 他們的前途暗淡。⑥慍怒的。He gives me a *black* look. 他對我怒目而視。⑦兇惡的。*black* deeds. 兇惡的行爲。⑧身穿黑衣的。 the *black* prince. 黑衣王子。⑨不榮譽的。***be in a person's black books*** 失寵於某人。***black and blue*** 被打得青一塊紫一塊的。***black in the face*** 怒容;滿臉怒氣。***black or white*** 非此卽彼;無黑卽白(無妥協或折中餘地)。***look black at*** 怒視。***not so black as one is painted*** 不似傳聞中那樣壞。—*adv.* 〖英方〗非常。*black* afraid. 非常害怕。—*n.* ①黑色。②黑衣;喪服。Being in mourning, he was dressed in *black.* 他因居喪故着黑衣。③黑人。***black and white*** **a.** 書寫或印刷的東西。He gave me assurance in *black and white.* 他給我書面的保證。**b.** 用黑白兩色畫的圖畫或草圖。***in the black*** 有盈餘。New production methods put the company *in the black.* 新的生產方法使公司開始有盈餘。—*v.t.* 使黑。—*v.i.* ①變黑。②暫失知覺。***black out*** **a.** 〖軍〗實施燈火管制。**b.** 無法憶起;失去記憶。**c.** 昏厥。He *blacked out* at the sight of blood. 他看到血而昏厥。**d.** 使看不見或聽不見。—**er,** *n.*
black·a·moor [ˈblækəˌmur; ˈblækəmuə] *n.* ①黑種人。②皮膚黧黑的人。
black-and-blue [ˈblækənˈblu; ˈblækənˈbluː] *adj.* 青腫的;瘀血的。
Black and Tan ①英國政府於1920年派往愛爾蘭鎮壓革命的軍隊。②此軍隊之一員。
black-and-tan [ˈblækənˈtæn; ˈblækənˈtæn] *adj.* ①黑底有褐色斑紋的(狗)。②同樣迎合黑人及白人的。
black-and-white [ˈblækənˈhwaɪt; ˈblækənˈwait] *adj.* ①黑白的;無彩色的(圖片等)。②僅有兩種價值的。
black art 魔術;妖術。
black·ball [ˈblækˌbɔl; ˈblækbɔːl] *n.* 反對票。—*v.t.* ①投票反對。②擯於社交之外;排斥。
black beetle 蟑螂;油蟲。
black belt ①(常 B- B-)黑人地帶(美國南部黑人占人口的大多數的地帶)。②黑人地區。③〖柔道〗四段選手的黑色腰帶。
***black·ber·ry** [ˈblækˌbɛrɪ; ˈblækbəri] *n., pl.* **-ries.** 〖植物〗黑莓。
***black·bird** [ˈblækˌbɝd; ˈblækbəːd] *n.* 〖動物〗山烏類(其雄者遍體爲黑色,如畫眉、椋鳥等)。—*v.t.* 綁架(土人)作爲奴隸。—*v.i.* 從事販賣奴隸。
black·bird·ing [ˈblækˌbɝdɪŋ; ˈblækˌbəːdiŋ] *n.* 綁架土人賣至海外爲奴隸之勾當。
:**black·board** [ˈblækˌbord; ˈblækbɔːd] *n.* 黑板。
black body 〖物理〗黑體。
black book 黑名單。***in someone's black books*** 受某人之輕視;失去某人之好感。
black box 黑盒子(供自動控制用之電子裝置,如飛機上的自動儀器,用以收集情報等)。
black bread 黑麪包。
black bread mold 黑黴。(亦作 **black mold**)
black·cap [ˈblækˌkæp; ˈblækkæp] *n.* ①歐洲產之鶯類。②〖植物〗美國產之黑色覆盆子。

black capitalism 〖美〗黑人資本主義(黑人企業家對企業的控制)。
black coal 生煤。
black·coat [ˈblækˌkot; ˈblækkout] *n.* ①〖蔑〗牧師。②〖英〗從事勞心的職業者。—*adj.*〖英〗勞心的。
black·cock [ˈblækˌkak; ˈblækkɔk] *n.* 黑色雄松鷄。
Black Code 限制美國黑人權利的任何法律。
black comedy 黑色喜劇(以 black humor 編寫而成)。
Black Country 英國英格蘭中部以 Birmingham 爲中心的工業區。
black death 黑死病。(亦作 **Black Death**)
black dog 〖俗〗沮喪。
black draught 黑色瀉劑。
***black·en** [ˈblækən; ˈblækən] *v.*, **-ened, -en·ing.** —*v.t.* ①使變黑;使變暗。The house is *blackened* with smoke. 這所房子被烟燻黑。②毀謗。—*v.i.* 變黑。
Black English 黑人所講的英語。
black eye ①眼圈發黑。②〖俗〗恥辱;不名譽。③不名譽之事。
black-eyed [ˈblækˈaɪd; ˈblækaid] *adj.* ①黑眼珠的。②黑眼圈的。
black·face [ˈblækˌfes; ˈblækfeis] *n.* ①黑人音樂家;扮作黑人的演員。②扮演黑人之化粧。③黑體鉛字。
black-faced [ˈblækˌfest; ˈblækfeist] *adj.* 黑面的;有憂色的。
black·fel·low [ˈblækˌfɛlo; ˈblækˌfelou] *n.* 澳洲土人。
black·fish [ˈblækˌfɪʃ; ˈblækfiʃ] *n., pl.* **-fish, -fish·es.** ①黑鯨。②任何黑色之魚。
black flag 海盜用的骷髏旗。
Black·foot [ˈblækˌfut; ˈblækfut] *n., pl.* **-feet, -foot.** ①北美印第安人之一族。②該族之語言。
Black Forest 德國西南部之森林地區。
Black Friday 不祥的禮拜五。
black frost 使植物變黑的霜或嚴寒。
black game 歐洲產之松鷄。
black gold ①煤。②石油。
black·guard [ˈblægəd; ˈblægaːd] *n.* 粗俗可鄙的人;流氓;無賴。—*v.t.* 辱罵;以汚語罵。—*v.i.* 行爲如流氓。—*adj.* ①粗鄙的;低俗的。②辱罵的。—**ism,** *n.*
black·guard·ly [ˈblægədlɪ; ˈblægaːdli] *adj.* 粗鄙的。—*adv.* 粗鄙地。
Black Hand 〖美〗黑手黨(專營敲詐或犯罪的黑社會組織)。
black·head [ˈblækˌhɛd; ˈblækhed] *n.* ①美洲所產之一種鴨。②尖端帶黑點之面皰;黑頭粉刺。
black·heart·ed [ˈblækˌhartɪd; ˈblækˌhaːtid] *adj.* 壞心腸的;惡毒的。
black humor 黑色幽默(荒誕不經的幽默)。
black·ie [ˈblækɪ; ˈblæki] *n.* 黑人。(亦作 **blackey, blacky**)
black·ing [ˈblækɪŋ; ˈblækiŋ] *n.* ①黑色鞋油。②黑蠟。
black·ish [ˈblækɪʃ; ˈblækiʃ] *adj.* 稍黑的;帶黑色的。—**ly,** *adv.* —**ness,** *n.*
black·jack [ˈblækˌdʒæk; ˈblækdʒæk] *n.* ①用做武器的短棒。②(皮做的)大酒杯。③海盜用之骷髏旗。④美國東部所產之黑皮橡樹。⑤〖賭博〗二十一點。—*v.t.* ①棒打。②脅迫。
black lead 石墨;黑鉛。
black·leg [ˈblækˌlɛg; ˈblækleg] *n.* ①氣腫疽(家畜傳染病)。②〖俗〗騙子;郎中(尤指賭博者)。③〖英〗罷工期中上工之工人。—*v.t.* & *v.i.* 〖英〗反對(其他工人之)罷工而上工。
black letter 粗體鉛字。
black-letter day 不幸的一天。
black·list [ˈblækˌlɪst; ˈblæklist] *v.t.* 記於黑名單中。
black list 黑名單。(亦作 **blacklist**)
black·ly [ˈblæklɪ; ˈblækli] *adv.* ①黑暗地;呈暗色地。②憂鬱地;朦朧地。③邪惡地。④惱怒地。
black magic 妖術。
black·mail [ˈblækˌmel; ˈblækmeil] *n.* ①敲詐;勒索。②勒索所得之款。—*v.t.* 用威嚇手段詐取財物;敲詐;勒索。—**er,** *n.*
black man 惡魔;魔鬼。
Black Maria 運送囚犯的無窗卡車。
black market 黑市。
black-mar·ket [ˈblækˈmarkɪt; ˈblækˈmaːkit] *v.t.* & *v.i.* 作(某商品之)黑市買賣。—*adj.* 黑市的。
black marketeer 黑市商人。
black-mar·ket·eer [ˈblækˌmarkəˈtɪr; ˈblækˌmaːkiˈtiə] *v.i.* 從事黑市買賣。
black marketer 黑市商人。
black money 〖美俚〗黑錢(因來路不明而未報稅的錢)。
black monk 本篤會(Benedictines)修士;本篤會會士。(亦作 **Black Monk**)
black nationalism 〖美〗黑人民族主義(欲脫離白人而立國或自治之運動)。
black nationalist 主張黑白分治之美國黑人。
***black·ness** [ˈblæknɪs; ˈblæknis] *n.* ①黑;黑暗。②兇惡;陰險。
black·out [ˈblækˌaut; ˈblækaut] *n.* ①燈火管制;熄燈。②飛機師因速度、方向之突變而暫時失去視覺或知覺。③戲院中舞臺上之全部熄燈。④停止;中斷。⑤封鎖消息。
black pepper 黑胡椒。
Black Plague 1665年倫敦大流行的黑死病。(亦作 **Great Plague**)
black powder 黑色火藥。(亦作 **black gun powder**)
Black Sea 黑海。
black sheep ①黑羊。②汚損全體之名譽者;害羣之馬。
black shirt, Black Shirt 義大利(法西斯)或德國(納粹)黑衫隊員。
***black·smith** [ˈblækˌsmɪθ; ˈblæksmiθ] *n.* 鐵匠。
black·smith·er·y [ˈblækˌsmɪθərɪ; ˈblæksmiθəri] *n.* 打鐵術;鐵匠之行業。
black·snake [ˈblækˌsnek; ˈblæksneik] *n.* ①黑蛇。②皮鞭。
Black Stream 黑潮。(亦作 **Japan Current, Japan Stream, Kuroshio**)
black tea 紅茶。
black·thorn [ˈblækˌθɔrn; ˈblækθɔːn] *n.* ①薔薇科之一種有刺植物。②用上項植物之莖所製之杖。③〖美〗山楂。
black tie ①男子禮服之黑色領結。②男子之半正式禮服。
black-tie [ˈblækˈtaɪ; ˈblækˈtai] *adj.* 賓客需穿半正式禮服的。
black·wa·ter fever [ˈblækˌwɔtə~; ˈblækˌwɔːtə~] 〖醫〗黑尿熱。
black widow 黑寡婦(一種有毒而能殘食其配偶的雌蜘蛛)。
black·y [ˈblækɪ; ˈblæki] *n., pl.* **black·ies,** *adj.* —*n.* ①黑人;黑奴。②黑色之鳥獸。—*adj.* 稍黑的;帶黑色的。
black·y-white [ˈblækɪˈhwaɪt; ˈblækiˈwait] *adj.* 黑白混血的(有輕視之意味)。
blad·der [ˈblædə; ˈblædə] *n.* ①〖解剖〗膀胱。②水生植物的氣囊;脹大的果皮。③可充氣的囊袋。④任何空洞誇張之事物。
blad·der·wort [ˈblædəˌwɜt; ˈblæ-

dəwəːt〕*n.*〖植物〗狸藻。
blad·der·y〔ˈblædərɪ; ˈblædəri〕*adj.* 似氣囊的;膨脹的;多氣胞的。
***blade**〔bled; bleid〕*n.* ①刀鋒;刀口。②刀;劍。③精於劍術者。④槳的扁平部分;槳身。⑤葉片;葉身。⑥快樂的少年;紈袴子弟。a gay *blade* from the nearby city. 一個來自鄰城的花花公子。⑦任何東西之扁闊的部分。the shoulder *blade.* 肩胛骨。⑧舌之前葉。
blade·bone〔ˈbled,bon; ˈbleidboun〕*n.*〖解剖〗肩胛骨。
blague〔blɑg; blɑːg〕〖法〗*n.* 愚弄;欺騙。
blah〔blɑ; blɑː〕*n.*〖俚〗無意義;瞎說。—*adj.*〖俚〗無聊的; 無趣味的; 枯燥無味的。—*interj.* 瞎說!
blah-blah〔ˈblɑ,blɑ; ˈblɑːblɑː〕*v.i.* 瞎說。—*v.t.* 反覆地說。
blahs〔blɑs; blɑːs〕*n. pl.*〖美俚〗(the-) 情緒不佳或身體不適。
blain〔blen; blein〕*n.*〖醫〗膿泡;水泡。
Blake〔blek; bleik〕*n.* 布雷克(William, 1757–1827, 英國詩人及藝術家)。
blam(e)·a·ble〔ˈbleməbḷ; ˈbleiməbl〕*adj.* 可責備的;該譴責的;有過失的。
‡**blame**〔blem; bleim〕*v.*, **blamed, blam·ing,** *n.* —*v.t.* ①譴責;歸咎。If anything goes wrong, don't *blame* me. 假使有甚麼差錯, 不要歸咎於我。②咒。*Blame* this rainy weather. 這雨天眞該死。***be to blame*** 應該受責。You *are to blame* for the accident. 對於這個意外, 你應當受責。—*n.* ①過失。He is free from *blame.* 他沒有過失。②譴責;非難;歸咎。They lay the *blame* on him. 他們歸罪於他。***bear the blame*** 代受指責。***lay the blame on*** 責備;指責。
blamed〔blemd; bleimd〕*adj.*〖俗〗①該死的;混蛋的。②加强語氣用語。—*adv.*〖俗〗過分地; 極度地。〖注意〗此字在口語中用作 damned 之代用字, 但語氣較爲溫和。
blame·ful〔ˈblemfəl; ˈbleimfəl〕*adj.* ①應受責備的;值得罵的。②譴責的;歸咎的。
blame·less〔ˈblemlɪs; ˈbleimlis〕*adj.* 無可責難的;無過失的。—**ly,** *adv.* —**ness,** *n.*
blame·wor·thy〔ˈblem,wɝðɪ; ˈbleim,wəːði〕*adj.* 該受非難的;值得挨罵的。
Blanc, Mont〔blæŋk; blɑ̃ːŋ〕*n.* 白朗峯(在法國東南部, 爲阿爾卑斯山之最高峯)。
blanch〔blæntʃ; blɑːntʃ, blɑːnʃ〕*v.t.* ①漂白;使變(蒼)白。②〖烹飪〗燙之使去皮或變白。③〖園藝〗遮去陽光使植物的幹或葉變白色。④用酸類處理金屬使有白色光澤。⑤迫回; 迫至一邊;攔阻去路。—*v.i.* 變白;變蒼白。
blanc·mange〔bləˈmanʒ; bləˈmɔnʒ〕*n.* (以牛乳及澱粉質製成之)膠質狀甜點心。
bland〔blænd; blænd〕*adj.* ①溫柔的;慇懃的。②和暢的; 溫和的(氣候等)。③無刺激性的(藥物等)。④呆板的;沒精打采的。⑤不動感情的;漠然的。—**ly,** *adv.* —**ness,** *n.*
blan·dish〔ˈblændɪʃ; ˈblændiʃ〕*v.t. & v.i.* 甘言勸誘;諂媚;奉承。
blan·dish·ment〔ˈblændɪʃmənt; ˈblændiʃmənt〕*n.* 甘言勸誘。
blank**〔blæŋk; blæŋk〕*n.* ①空白(處)。Leave a *blank* after each word. 每字後均留空白。②空處;茫然; 心的空虛。③(有藥無彈頭的)空包彈。④空白紙。an application *blank.* 空白申請書。⑤沒有中獎的獎券。⑥準備製成銅幣、鑰匙等之金屬片。⑦靶心。⑧目標。draw (a) blank***〖俗〗未成功;失敗。***in blank*** 留空白以便塡寫;空白式的。—*adj.* ①空白的。②預留塡寫位置的。a *blank* application. 空白申請書。③空的。a *blank* cartridge. 無藥彈筒。④茫然的;空虛的;無興趣的;呆的。⑤完全的。a *blank* silence. 完全的肅靜。⑥不帶任何裝飾或附件的。⑦單調的;無聊的。⑧代表粗俗不雅的字(如"他×的"中之×)。I caught my finger in the *blank blank* door. 我的指頭被那扇(鬼)門挾住了。⑨不知所措的。—*v.t.* ①隱匿; 使模糊不清。②〖運動〗使(對方)不得分。③劃掉;擦掉。to *blank* out an entry. 刪掉一個項目。
blank·book〔ˈblæŋk,bʊk; ˈblæŋkbuk〕*n.*〖美〗空白之登記簿、帳簿等。
blank check ①未記入金額的簽名支票。②自由處理權;全權。
blank endorsement 背書。
blan·ket**〔ˈblæŋkɪt; ˈblæŋkit〕*n.* ①氈;毛毯。②任何如氈的東西。a *blanket* of green grass. 綠草如氈。born on the wrong side of the blanket*** 生爲私生子。***throw a wet blanket over a project*** 冷水澆頭;打破一項計畫。—*v.t.* ①蓋以氈;裹以氈。②蓋;掩蓋。The snow *blanketed* the ground. 雪蓋地面。③妨阻;使模糊不清;壓倒〖常 out〗. An electrical storm *blanketed* out the radio program. 雷雨妨阻了廣播節目的收聽。—*adj.* 包括幾項或全部的。A *blanket* insurance policy insures a car against all kinds of accidents. 一張綜合保險單保險汽車一切意外事件。
blan·ket·ing〔ˈblæŋkɪtɪŋ; ˈblæŋkitiŋ〕*n.* ①以毯覆蓋之動作。②製毯之粗料。③〖礦〗毛毯採金法。④(*pl.*)用毛毯採金法採得之金。⑤作爲遊戲或懲罰將人放在毯上之拋擲。⑥〖無線電〗干擾。⑦毛毯。
blank·et·y-blank〔ˈblæŋkətɪˈblæŋk; ˈblæŋkitiˈblæŋk〕*adj. & adv.*〖俚〗damned 之幽默婉曲語。—*n.* 傻瓜;可憐蟲。
blank·ly〔ˈblæŋklɪ; ˈblæŋkli〕*adv.* ①茫然地;呆呆地;毫無表情地。②完全地;充分地。
blank·ness〔ˈblæŋknɪs; ˈblæŋknis〕*n.* ①空白。②單調。③呆板。
blank verse 無韻詩。
blank wall 無法克服的障礙;毫無進展的狀態。
blare〔blɛr, blær; blɛə〕*v.*, **blared, blar·ing,** *n.* —*v.t. & v.i.* ①叫哮;高聲鳴叫;大聲宣述。②發(亮光)。—*n.* ①粗大的聲音;咆哮聲。②亮光。③虛張之聲勢;排場。
blar·ney〔ˈblarnɪ; ˈblɑːni〕*n., v.,* **-neyed, -ney·ing.** —*n.* 諂媚;奉承話。—*v.i. & v.t.* 諂媚;甘言哄騙。
Blar·ney stone〔ˈblarnɪ~; ˈblɑːni~〕愛爾蘭 Cork 附近 Blarney 城堡中之一塊石頭(據傳吻之即口齒伶俐動人)。
bla·sé〔blɑˈze; ˈblɑːzei〕〖法〗*adj.* (因過度享樂而)厭煩於享樂或人生的。
blas·pheme〔blæsˈfim; blæsˈfiːm〕*v.*, **-phemed, -phem·ing.** —*v.t.* ①褻瀆(神祇)。②咒罵;辱罵。—*v.i.* 出言褻瀆;口出惡言。
blas·phe·mous〔ˈblæsfɪməs; ˈblæsfiməs〕*adj.* 褻瀆神祇的; 不敬神的; 謾罵神的。—**ly,** *adv.* —**ness,** *n.*
blas·phe·my〔ˈblæsfɪmɪ; ˈblæsfimi〕*n., pl.* **-mies.** ①對上帝或神祇的褻瀆言行。②咒罵之話語或行爲。③輕視上帝或神祇。
***blast**〔blæst; blɑːst〕*n.* ①一陣疾風(或空氣);一陣暴風; 烈風。a *blast* of hot air from the furnace. 由火爐來的一陣熱空氣。②吹;吹聲(如笛、笳、喇叭、號角等)。③爆炸。There was a terrible *blast* in the coal

mines. 煤礦發生可怕的爆炸。④吹風;輸風;煽進(爐中)的風。⑤萎縮、枯萎或毀滅之原因。⑥〖俚〗狂歡的聚會。***in blast*** **a.** 在輸風(指煉爐)。**b.** 盛行。***in*** (or ***at***) ***full blast*** 在旺盛時(如爐火在輸風時)。***out of blast*** 停歇時(如爐火未在輸風時)。—*v.t.* ①炸毀;炸開;炸裂。②摧毀;摧殘;使枯萎。③按喇叭。④咒罵(常與 it 或受詞連用)。*Blast* it, there's the phone again! 該死,電話鈴又響了!⑤〖俚〗猛烈抨擊。⑥〖俚〗射擊。***blast off*** **a.** (火箭等)升空。**b.** 〖俚〗走開;走出。—*v.i.* ①枯萎。②〖俚〗吸毒。

blast area 因(原子彈等之)爆炸而受損害、死傷之地區。

blast·ed ['blæstɪd; 'blɑːstid] *adj.* ①被阻礙的;遭破壞的;枯萎的。②被咒詛的。

blast furnace 鼓風爐。

blasting cap 雷管。

blas·to·derm ['blæstəˌdɝm; 'blæstoudəːm] *n.* 胚盤;胚膜。

blast·off ['blæstˌɔf; 'blɑːstɔf] *n.* (火箭、飛彈等)升空;發射。

blast pipe ①送風管。②放氣管。

blast·proof ['blæstˌpruf; 'blɑːstpruːf] *adj.* 防爆炸的。

blast shelter 防爆炸之掩體(如防空洞等)。

blas·tu·la ['blæstʃʊlə; 'blæstʃulə] *n., pl.* **-las, -lae** [-ˌli; -liː]. 〖發生學〗囊胚。

blat [blæt; blæt] *v.,* **blat·ted, blat·ting.** —*v.i.* 〖俗〗發小牛或羊之叫聲。—*v.t.* 不加思索說出。

bla·tant ['bletn̩t; 'bleitənt] *adj.* ①喧嘩的。②炫耀的;俗麗的。③極顯著的。④〖詩〗(如羊)鳴叫的。—**bla·tan·cy,** *n.* —**ly,** *adv.*

blath·er ['blæðɚ; 'blæðə] *v.t. & v.i.* 胡說;亂道。—*n.* 胡扯;廢話。(亦作**blether**)

blath·er·skite ['blæðɚˌskaɪt; 'blæðəskait] *n.* 〖俗〗①胡扯;無意義的話;廢話。②胡說者;愛說話而又愚蠢者。

*__blaze__[1] [blez; bleiz] *n., v.,* **blazed, blaz·ing.** —*n.* ①火焰;烈火;火災。It took the firemen two hours to put the *blaze* out. 消防人員費了二小時才將火撲滅。②強烈的光;光輝;光明。③爆發;激發。a *blaze* of temper. 發脾氣;發怒。④(*pl.*)地獄。***go to blazes***〖俚〗滾開(=go to hell). ***in a blaze*** **a.** 着火;燃燒。**b.** 激發。***like blazes***〖俚〗憤怒地;猛烈地。***the blazes***〖俚〗地獄之火;地獄。—*v.i.* ①燃;發焰。A fire was *blazing* in the fireplace. 火爐的火在吐焰。②發光;放光;生輝。On Christmas Eve our house *blazed* with lights. 在聖誕夜,我們的房子燈光輝煌。③發怒;激怒;感情的激發。—*v.t.* ①使發光;使光輝。②使發火。③明顯地表現。***blaze away*** (or ***off***) **a.** 迅速開槍;不斷地射擊。The soldiers were *blazing away* at the enemy. 士兵們正向敵人不斷地射擊。**b.** 很熱情地講話或工作。***blaze up*** **a.** 突然發火。**b.** 突然發怒。

blaze[2] *n.* ①樹皮上的刻痕(用作記號)。②(馬、牛等)臉上的白點。—*v.t.* ①刻記號於樹皮(以標識道路)。②開拓;領導。***blaze a trail*** **a.** 刻記號於森林中的樹皮,以標識道路。**b.** 作開路先鋒;領導。

blaze[3] *v.t.* 使周知;傳播;公開宣示。

blaz·er ['blezɚ; 'bleizə] *n.* ①燃燒物;發光體。②顏色鮮明之運動衣上裝。③置於火上烹物之碟子。

blaz·ing ['blezɪŋ; 'bleiziŋ] *adj.* ①熾燃的。②燦爛的;輝煌的。③鮮明的;顯然的。④〖狩獵〗強烈的(狐臭)。—**ly,** *adv.*

blazing star ①(美洲產之)多種花色鮮明之植物。②極引人注意之人或物。

bla·zon ['blezn̩; 'bleizn] *v.t.* ①宣布。②誇示;顯示。③描繪或解說(紋章)。④裝飾。—*n.* ①紋章。②紋章之描繪或解說。③炫示。

bla·zon·ment ['blezn̩mənt; 'bleiznmənt] *n.* ①紋章解說;紋章裝飾。②宣揚;表彰;宣布。③宣揚之事物;受表彰之事物。

bla·zon·ry ['blezn̩rɪ; 'bleiznri] *n., pl.* **-ries.** ①紋章描畫術。②紋章;紋印。③美飾;美觀。

bldg. *pl.* **bldgs.** building.

Bldg.E. Building Engineer.

-ble 〖字尾〗**-able** 的異體。

*__bleach__ [blitʃ; bliːtʃ] *v.t.* ①去色。②漂白。—*v.i.* 變白;變為無色。—*n.* ①漂白。②漂白劑。③漂白後之褪色程度。

bleach·er ['blitʃɚ; 'bliːtʃə] *n.* ①漂白者;漂布業者。②漂白劑;漂白器。③(*pl.*)(球場等之)露天坐位。

bleach·er·ite ['blitʃəˌraɪt; 'bliːtʃərait] *n.* 〖美〗①露天坐席之觀衆。②觀衆。

bleach·er·y ['blitʃərɪ; 'bliːtʃəri] *n., pl.* **-er·ies.** 漂白工廠。

bleach·ing ['blitʃɪŋ; 'bliːtʃiŋ] *n.* 漂白法;漂白。—*adj.* 漂白的。

bleaching powder 漂白粉。

*__bleak__[1] [blik; bliːk] *adj.* ①無遮蔽的;荒涼的。②蒼白的。③寒冷的。a *bleak* wind. 寒風。④淒涼的;憂鬱的。—**ly,** *adv.* —**ness,** *n.*

bleak[2] *n.* 一種鯉屬之魚。

blear [blɪr; bliə] *adj.* 朦朧的;不清的。—*v.t.* 使模糊不清。—*n.* 模糊。—**ed·ness,** *n.*

blear·eye ['blɪrˌaɪ; 'bliərai] *n.* 〖醫〗瞼緣炎;爛眼。

blear-eyed ['blɪrˌaɪd; 'bliəraid] *adj.* ①淚眼模糊的;患瞼緣炎的。②眼光遲鈍的;目光淺近的。(亦作 **bleary-eyed**)

blear·y ['blɪrɪ; 'bliəri] *adj.,* **blear·i·er, blear·i·est.** ①患濕眼病的。②目光不明的。③疲倦的。

blear·y-eyed ['blɪrɪˌaɪd; 'bliəriaid] *adj.* 近視的。

*__bleat__ [blit; bliːt] *n.* ①牛羊之鳴聲。②任何類似之聲音。The victim gave a *bleat* of terror. 被害人發出恐懼之哀鳴。③訴苦;喋喋不休的廢話。—*v.i.* ①作牛羊鳴聲。②說廢話;哼鼻子。③埋怨;訴苦。—*v.t.* 以低微顫動之聲音說出。

bleb [blɛb; bleb] *n.* ①大皰;皰疹。②(水、玻璃等中之)氣泡。—**by,** *adj.*

*__bleed__ [blid; bliːd] *v.,* **bled** [blɛd; bled], **bleed·ing,** *n., adj.* —*v.i.* ①流血。His nose *bleeds* badly. 他的鼻流血很多。②受傷;流血而死。③悲痛。The nation *bleeds* for its dead heroes. 舉國為死去的英雄哀悼。④流汁;流出液汁。⑤(染料等)褪色。All the colors *bled* when the dress was washed. 那件衣服洗的時候顏色通通褪了。⑥〖印刷〗印刷到紙邊上去。⑦付出高價(被勒索等)。—*v.t.* ①放血;取血。Doctors used to *bleed* people when they were ill. 從前人們病時,醫生常為他們放血。②搾取金錢。He *bled* that poor old man without mercy. 他無情地搾取那個可憐的老人。③使(樹)流出汁液;抽出水、空氣、電等。***bleed white*** 花光或用盡(某人、某國)之金錢、力量等。War has *bled white* many countries of Europe. 戰爭使很多歐洲國家大傷元氣。—*n.* ①因切邊太多致將文字或插圖切去一部分的頁面。②切去之部分。—*adj.* 〖印刷〗因切邊太多致使部分文字或插圖被切去的。

bleed·er ['blidɚ; 'bli:də] *n.* ①抽(他人之)血者。②善出血者。③調節空氣或燃料量之活瓣(門)。④〖俚〗食客。
bleed·ing ['blidɪŋ; 'bli:diŋ] *n.* ①出血。②放血。 —*adj.* ①出血的。②感覺或表現過度悲痛或同情的。
bleeding heart ①荷包牡丹。②〖俚〗假裝同情者。
blem·ish ['blɛmɪʃ; 'blemiʃ] *n.* 汚點;缺點。—*v.t.* ①汚。②損傷。—**ment,** *n.*
blench[1] [blɛntʃ; blentʃ] *v.i.* 退縮;畏縮。—*v.t.* 避免。—**ing·ly,** *adv.*
blench[2] *v.t.* & *v.i.* 使變蒼白;變蒼白。
blench·er ['blɛntʃɚ; 'blentʃə] *n.* 退縮者;臉色蒼白者。
***blend** [blɛnd; blend] *v.,* **blend·ed** or **blent, blend·ing,** *n.* —*v.i.* ①混合;混雜。②配合; 溶合。 These two colors *blend* well. 這兩種顏色配合得很調和。—*v.t.* ①混合;攙雜。②調和。③溶合。—*n.* ①混合;攙雜。②〖美〗混合的威士忌。③〖語言〗由兩個字結合之字(常有共同之音節者)。④(聲音或顏色之)逐漸混合。
blende [blɛnd; blend] *n.* 〖礦〗閃鋅礦。
blend·ed ['blɛndɪd; 'blendid] *adj.* (威士忌酒等)數種混合的。
blended whisky 混合威士忌。
blend·er ['blɛndɚ; 'blendə] *n.* 混合的人;攪和器。
blend·ing ['blɛndɪŋ; 'blendiŋ] *n.* ①混合;折衷; 調合法。②混合物;混成語。③具有兩個母體之特性的交配種。
blend·ous ['blɛndəs; 'blendəs] *adj.* 含閃鋅礦的。
blend·word ['blɛnd,wɝd; 'blend-wə:d] *n.* 混合語。
Blen·heim spaniel ['blɛnəm~; 'blenim~] 一種小獵毛犬。
blen·nor·rh(o)e·a [,blɛnə'riə; ,blenə'ri:ə] *n.* ①膿性卡他。②淋病。
blen·ny ['blɛnɪ; 'bleni] *n., pl.* **-ny, -nies.** 〖動物〗 黏魚。
bleph·a·rism ['blɛfərɪzm̩; 'blefəri-zəm] *n.* 〖醫〗瞼痙攣。
‡**bless** [blɛs; bles] *v.t.,* **blessed** or **blest, bless·ing.** ①祝福; 祈禱。②賜福;降福。③讚美;頌揚。 We praise Thee, we *bless* Thee. 我們讚美你,我們頌揚你。④使幸福;使快樂。He is *blessed* with good health. 他享有良好健康的幸福。⑤保佑;庇護(表驚嘆)。Heaven *bless* this house. 求上天保護這家人。*Bless* me! 表示驚訝之感嘆詞。⑥感激;感謝; 對…表好感。 I *bless* him for his kindness. 我感謝他的恩惠。⑦在胸前畫十字。The Pope *blessed* the multitude. 教皇向羣衆畫十字 (以祝福他們)。***have not a penny to bless oneself with*** 貧無立錐之地;一文不名。 —**ing·ly,** *adv.*
bless·ed** ['blɛsɪd; 'blesid] *adj.* ①神聖的。②幸福的;快樂的;成功的。③〖宗教〗列爲眞福的;有福的。④〖俗〗 煩惱的; 受天罰的。⑤在天堂中的。 ⑥被咀咒的 (= damned). I am *blessed* if I know. 我知道才怪呢。⑦用以强調。every *blessed* cent. 每一分錢。(亦作 **blest**) ***the Blessed (天主教)受教皇宣福禮之亡故者。 —**ly,** *adv.* —**ness,** *n.*
blessed event 〖俗〗 ①嬰孩之誕生。②嬰孩。
Blessed Sacrament 聖餐禮。
Blessed Virgin 聖母瑪利亞。
bless·ing** ['blɛsɪŋ; 'blesiŋ] *n.* ①祝福;祈福。②幸福; 恩賜; 神恩。③斥責。He got quite a *blessing* from his superior. 他被上司狠狠地斥責了一番。④核准;支持。 ***a blessing in disguise 先不受歡迎而後又被視爲是幸運之事(塞翁失馬)。***ask the blessing*** 祈禱 (尤指進餐前)。
blew [blu; blu:] *v.* pt. of **blow.**
B.L.I. Bachelor of Literary Interpretation.
***blight** [blaɪt; blait] *n.* ①植物之病害。②招致植物病害之昆蟲、菌類。 ③任何招致毀滅或挫敗的原因。④使他人希望變黯淡的人或事物。—*v.t.* ①使枯萎。The potatoes were *blighted.* 馬鈴薯枯萎了。②毀壞;摧毀;毀滅。—*v.i.* 枯萎;受摧毀。—**ing·ly,** *adv.*
blight·er ['blaɪtɚ; 'blaitə] *n.* ①萎縮(或受摧殘)之人或物。②〖英俚〗可厭之人。
Blight·y, blight·y ['blaɪtɪ; 'blaiti] *n., pl.* **-ies.** 〖英俚〗①英國本土;老家。②(第一次世界大戰中) 可使士兵獲准自前線回轉英國本土之傷患或休假。
bli·mey ['blaɪmɪ; 'blaimi] *interj.* 〖英俚〗表示驚奇、驚訝之感嘆詞。(亦作 **blimy**)
blimp [blɪmp;blimp] *n.*〖俗〗①軟式(或半硬式) 小飛船。②任何飛船。③肥胖的人。④(拍電影時)攝影機及攝影師所在的隔音小房。
‡**blind** [blaɪnd; blaind] *adj.* ①瞎的。He is *blind* in the right eye. 他右眼瞎了。②缺乏判斷力的;不能或不願了解、判斷或覺察的。He is *blind* to his own defects. 他不能覺察自己的缺點。③不加思考的; 不留意的。He is *blind* to his own interest. 他不留意於自己的利益。④看不見的; 隱蔽的。⑤無孔的;閉塞的。⑥只有一個出口的。⑦盲人的;爲了盲人的。 a *blind* asylum. 盲人院。⑧別人代爲安排的。⑨〖俚〗酒醉的。⑩無餡的(如餅等)。⑪無知覺的。⑫盲目的;非根據理智的。⑬未用目視而作的。⑭事前不知而作的。a *blind* purchase. 事前不知其好壞而買的東西。⑮匿名的。⑯難於瞭解的。—*v.t.* ①使瞎;使看不見。 He was *blinded* of one eye. 他瞎了一隻眼。②蒙蔽;隱蔽。③使失去判斷力或覺察力;眩目。He was *blinded* by prejudice. 偏見使他無所覺察。—*n.* ①障蔽物;窗簾;百葉窗。②(常the-)(作 *pl.* 解)盲人。They founded an institution for the *blind.* 他們成立了一個盲人院。③獵人之埋伏處。④掩藏某一行動或企圖之物;藉口;掩飾。⑤經由 blind date 而會晤的男女。⑥誘餌。—*adv.* ①〖俗〗失去知覺地。He drank himself *blind.* 他喝得不省人事。②摸索地。③盲目地。—**ness,** *n.*
blind alley ①死巷;絕路。②無希望前進或改善的情形。
blind bombing 盲目轟炸。
blind copy 信或文件的副本(但其正本未註明曾以副本寄給他人)。
blind date ①未曾晤面過的男女經第三者介紹而作的約會。②參加此種約會的男女。
blind·er ['blaɪndɚ; 'blaində] *n.* ①遮眼者。②〖美〗馬眼罩。③〖英俚〗眩目的表演。
blind flying 儀器飛行。
blind·fold ['blaɪnd,fold; 'blaindfould] *v.t.* ①將…的眼睛蒙起;蒙起…的眼睛。②擋住…的視線。③欺騙;引入歧途。 —*adj.* ①蔽目的。②輕率的。—*n.* 蔽目的東西。
blind gut 〖解剖〗 盲腸。
blind·ing ['blaɪndɪŋ; 'blaindiŋ] *adj.* 使盲目的;使目眩的; 使昏瞶的。—*n.* 塡補路面的沙土。
***blind·ly** ['blaɪndlɪ; 'blaindli] *adv.* ①摸索地。②盲目地。③不繼續地。

blind·man [ˈblaɪndmən; ˈblaindmən] *n., pl.* **-men.**〖主英〗= **blind-reader.**
blindman's buff 捉迷藏。
blindman's holiday 黃昏(尚未點燈, 無法工作或讀書時)。
blind man's watch 供盲人使用之錶(以觸覺可知時刻的)。「作 **blind tiger**)
blind pig〖美俚〗非法售酒之沙龍。(亦」
blind-reader [ˈblaɪndˌridɚ; ˈblaind-riːdə] *n.*〖主英〗專司辨認地址姓名不明之郵件的郵務員。
blind spot ①盲點。②不明瞭、有偏見或不關心的事物。③(電視、無線電等)收視收聽不佳之地區。④視線不佳之處。
blind window 假窗。
blind·worm [ˈblaɪndˌwɝm; ˈblaind-wəːm] *n.* 無脚蜥蜴。
blink** [blɪŋk; bliŋk] *v.i.* ①霎眼;瞬目而視。②閃光。③不理睬〖常 at〗。④(牛乳等)變酸。⑤吃驚〖常 at〗。She *blinked* at his sudden fury. 她對他的突然暴怒大吃一驚。—*v.t.* ①霎眼。②使霎眼或閃光。③閃避;躲避;忽視。④以閃光傳遞(信號、消息等)。—*n.* 一瞥;霎眼;閃光。on the blink***〖俚〗壞的;需要修理的。「笨的人。」
blink·ard [ˈblɪŋkɚd; ˈbliŋkəd] *n.* 很」
blink·er [ˈblɪŋkɚ; ˈbliŋkə] *n.* ①馬眼罩。②十字路口之閃光警燈。③〖俚〗眼睛。④閃光裝置。⑤(*pl.*) 護目鏡。—*v.t.*〖俗〗使無法看見或了解。
blink·ing [ˈblɪŋkɪŋ; ˈbliŋkiŋ] *adj.* ①一眨眼的;幌眼的。②閃光的。③〖英俚〗全然的;完全的;道地的;他媽的;混蛋的;討厭的。
blip [blɪp; blip] *n.* ①(雷達幕上之)影像;光點。②電視音響干擾。③〖俚〗五分錢硬幣。
***bliss** [blɪs; blis] *n.* ①極大的幸福;極樂。Ignorance is *bliss.* 無知卽是福。②福佑;天賜的福。**—ful,** *adj.* **—ful·ly,** *adv.* **—ful·ness,** *n.* **—less,** *adj.*
***blis·ter** [ˈblɪstɚ; ˈblistə] *n.* ①膿疱;水泡。②(植物、金屬或油漆面上起的)浮泡。③用以引起水泡的藥物。④軍用機上透明的隆起部分(供觀測或射擊用)。—*v.t.* ①使生水泡;使起浮泡。②侮辱;辱罵。③嚴厲處罰小孩。—*v.i.* 起水泡。**—ing·ly,** *adv.*
blister gas (化學戰之)起泡瓦斯。
B. Lit. Bachelor of Literature.
blithe [blaɪð; blaið] *adj.* ①快樂的;活潑的;爽快的。②無憂無慮的。**—ly,** *adv.*
blith·er·ing [ˈblɪðərɪŋ; ˈbliðəriŋ] *adj.* 嘮叨不休的;胡扯的。—*n.* 胡扯。
blithe·some [ˈblaɪðsəm; ˈblaiðsəm] *adj.* 喜樂的;愉快的。**—ly,** *adv.*
blitz [blɪts; blits] *n.* ①〖軍〗(大規模攻擊性之)閃擊戰。②毀滅性攻擊。—*v.t.* 對…作迅速而强烈的攻擊。「*n., v.t.* = **blitz.**」
blitz·krieg [ˈblɪtsˌkrig; ˈblitskriːg]」
bliz·zard [ˈblɪzɚd; ˈblizəd] *n.* ①大風雪;暴風雪。②〖俚〗大打擊。**—y, —ly,** *adj.*
blk. ①black. ②block. ③bulk.
B.LL. Bachelor of Laws.
bloat [blot; blout] *v.t. & v.i.* ①(使)膨脹。②醃燻(鯡魚等)。③自誇。—*adj.* ①膨脹的;腫脹的。②自誇的;趾高氣揚的。—*n.* ①腫脹之物。②自誇者。③〖俚〗酒醉者。
bloat·ed [ˈblotɪd; ˈbloutid] *adj.* ①發脹的;腫脹的。②傲慢的。③醃燻的。
bloat·er [ˈblotɚ; ˈbloutə] *n.* 燻鯡。
blob [blɑb; blɔb] *n., v.,* **blobbed, blob·bing.** —*n.* ①一小塊;一滴。②笨人。③(管樂器的)錯音。—*v.t.* 塗;濺;汚;弄錯。
blob·ber-lipped [ˈblɑbɚˌlɪpt; ˈblɔ-bəlipt] *adj.* 有厚而突出之唇的。
bloc [blɑk; blɔk] *n.* 爲某種共同目的而取一致行動的政治組織;集團。
‡**block** [blɑk; blɔk] *n.* ①一塊(木或石等)。a block of wood. 一塊木料。②壅塞物;障礙物。I have been detained by a *block* in the street. 我爲街上的壅塞物所阻。③〖美〗(市街的)一區;街區;一區的邊距;兩條街間的距離。The station is six *blocks* away from here. 車站離此六條街。④一組同樣的東西。⑤滑車。⑥斷頭臺。⑦公開拍賣時之拍賣臺。⑧鐵路中一段有信號之鐵軌。⑨模;字模;帽楦。⑩〖俗〗頭;腦袋。⑪(運動中給對方之)阻擋。⑫木刻板。⑬積木。⑭〖集郵〗四張或四張以上連在一起, 排成長方形, 而非排成長條的郵票。⑮因情緒緊張而導致的突然思想或言語的中止。⑯〖地質〗火山口所噴出的巨大岩石。⑰〖加〗尚未測量的荒僻地區。⑱養鷹者室外繫鷹之矮架。⑲排字所用的底盤。***a chip of the old block*** 酷似其父的孩子。***block letters*** (or ***writing***) 正體字;正楷字;大寫。***go to the block*** **a.** 上斷頭臺。**b.** 拍賣。—*v.t.* ①阻塞;杜塞(裝滿使不能通)。②妨礙;阻止。③支撐;用木塊或石塊墊襯。④阻擋(對方)。⑤(以木楦)楦(帽)。⑥排演。—*v.i.* ①〖運動〗阻擋。②排演。***block out*** (or ***in***) (***a picture, drawing, etc.***) 草畫(圖畫等)略圖。***block up*** 阻塞;使(路)不通。
***block·ade** [blɑˈked; blɔˈkeid] *n., v.,* **-ad·ed, -ad·ing.** —*n.* ①封鎖。to enforce a *blockade.* 實行封鎖。②執行封鎖任務的陸軍或海軍。③障礙物。—*v.t.* ①封鎖。②阻礙。
block·ad·er [blɑˈkedɚ; blɔˈkeidə] *n.* 封鎖者;封港艦。「或人。」
blockade runner 穿過封鎖線之船」
blockade-running [blɑˈkedˌrʌnɪŋ; blɔˈkeidˌrʌniŋ] *n.* 突破封鎖線之行動。
block·age [ˈblɑkɪdʒ; ˈblɔkidʒ] *n.* 封鎖;閉塞。
block and tackle 滑輪組;滑車組。
block ball〖棒球〗球賽中, 擊出或投出而爲非球員所觸及或阻擋之球。
block booking 整批的出租或出售影片或雜誌, 而不予影院或書商有挑選之自由者。
block·bust·er [ˈblɑkˌbʌstɚ; ˈblɔkˌbʌstə] *n.* ①〖俚〗一種大型高度破壞炸彈。②引起突然而壓倒性力量的人或事;一鳴驚人者。③土地投機商。④耗費甚多的電影巨片。
block·head [ˈblɑkˌhɛd; ˈblɔkhed] *n.* 愚蠢的人。**—ed,** *adj.*
block·house [ˈblɑkˌhaus; ˈblɔkhaus] *n.* ①碉堡。②木堡。③木舍;圓木小屋。④核子試爆場或火箭發射臺旁之鋼骨水泥小房。
block·ish [ˈblɑkɪʃ; ˈblɔkiʃ] *adj.* 似木頭的;魯鈍的;固執的。**—ly,** *adv.* **—ness,** *n.*
block letter ①木版字。②方體字。
block plane 鉋平木板兩端所用的小鉋。
block·y [ˈblɑkɪ; ˈblɔki] *adj.,* **block·i·er, block·i·est.** ①短而堅實的。②(木版印刷之)濃淡不勻的。③易分裂成一塊塊的(岩石、礦石等)。「傢伙。②可鄙之人;鄙夫。」
bloke [blok; blouk] *n.*〖英俚〗①人;」
***blond, blonde** [blɑnd; blɔnd] *adj.* ①淺色的。②有金黃色毛髮, 碧眼和白晳皮膚的。—*n.* 有金黃色毛髮, 碧眼和白晳皮膚的人(女的稱爲 blonde, 男的稱爲 blond). **—ish,** *adj.*
‡**blood** [blʌd; blʌd] *n.* ①血;血液。②低等動物體中相當於血液之體液。③殺戮;殘殺;

流血。They avenged their father's *blood.* 他們爲父親報了血仇。④血統;血族;血統關係;家世。He is of royal *blood.* 他是皇族。⑤高貴的血統(尤指皇族血統)。⑥血氣;脾氣;心境。⑦血氣方剛的人;血性的人。⑧活力等的新來源。⑨果汁或樹漿。the *blood* of the grape. 葡萄汁。⑩肉體。the frailty of men's *blood.* 人類肉體的脆弱。***Blood is thicker than water.*** 血濃於水(親戚總比朋友親近)。***blue blood*** 貴族出身或血統。***draw first blood*** 先下手;先得分。***get*** (or ***have***) ***one's blood up*** 使震怒。***have someone's blood on one's head*** (or ***hands***) 應對某人之痛苦或死亡負責。***in cold blood*** **a.** 殘酷地。**b.** 故意地;有意地。He committed murder *in cold blood.* 他預謀殺人。***make one's blood boil*** 使發怒。***make one's blood run cold*** 使極度害怕。***taste blood*** 嘗到甜頭(尤指凶殘的新經驗)。—*v.t.* 使(獵犬)嘗到或看見血腥。

blood and thunder 刺激而誇張的通俗劇。

blood bank 血庫。

blood bath 大屠殺。

blood brother ①親生兄弟。②親友(指男的)。③不可分離之事。④拜把兄弟。

blood cancer =**leukemia.**

blood cell 〖生理〗血球。

blood count 血球計算。

blood·cur·dler 〔ˈblʌdˌkɝdlɚ; ˈblʌdˌkəːdlə〕 *n.* 令人毛骨悚然之電影、戲劇等。

blood·cur·dling 〔ˈblʌdˌkɝdlɪŋ; ˈblʌdˌkəːdliŋ〕 *adj.* 令人毛骨悚然的。—**ly,** *adv.*

blood·ed 〔ˈblʌdɪd; ˈblʌdid〕 *adj.* ①有(某種之)血的。②純種的。③有戰鬥經驗的。

blood feud 血仇。

blood group 血型。(亦作**blood type**)

blood grouping 血型分類;血型鑑定。(亦作 **blood typing**)

blood·guilt·y 〔ˈblʌdˌgɪltɪ; ˈblʌdˌgilti〕 *adj.* 殺人的;犯殺人罪的。

blood heat 人體血溫(爲37°C或98.6°F).

blood horse 純種馬;種馬。

blood·hound 〔ˈblʌdˌhaund; ˈblʌdhaund〕 *n.*①一種大偵察獵犬。②〖俚〗偵探。

blood·less 〔ˈblʌdlɪs; ˈblʌdlis〕 *adj.*①無血的;灰白的。②免出血的。③不動干戈的;不流血的。④沒精打采的。⑤無情的;冷血的。

blood·let·ting 〔ˈblʌdˌlɛtɪŋ; ˈblʌdˌletiŋ〕 *n.* ①〖醫〗放血(術)。②(戰爭等之)流血。

blood·line 〔ˈblʌdlaɪn; ˈblʌdlain〕 *n.* (動物之)血統。

blood·mo·bile 〔ˈblʌdməˌbil; ˈblʌdməbiːl〕 *n.* (設有醫療儀器的)巡迴捐血車。

blood money ①付給兇手的酬金。②付給被害人家屬之撫恤金。③爲免報復而付給的錢。④(在現代)因將兇犯交給警方所得的獎金。

blood plasma 血漿。

blood platelet 血小板。

blood poisoning 血中毒;血毒症。

blood pressure 血壓。

blood purge (在極權國家)整肅(常指有大規模屠殺的)。

blood-red 〔ˈblʌdˈrɛd; ˈblʌdˈred〕 *adj.* 血紅的;血染的。

blood relation 血親;骨肉。(亦作 **blood relative**)

blood·root 〔ˈblʌdˌrut; ˈblʌdruːt〕 *n.* 北美產之一種罌粟科植物。

blood royal 王族;皇家。

blood serum 血清。

blood·shed 〔ˈblʌdˌʃɛd; ˈblʌdʃed〕 *n.* 流血。

blood·shot 〔ˈblʌdˌʃɑt; ˈblʌdʃɔt〕 *adj.* (眼睛)充血的;有血絲的。

blood·stain 〔ˈblʌdˌsten; ˈblʌdstein〕 *n.* 血污;血跡。—*v.t.* 血染。

blood·stained 〔ˈblʌdˌstend; ˈblʌdsteind〕 *adj.*①血污的;有血跡的。②犯殺人罪的。

blood·stock 〔ˈblʌdˌstɑk; ˈblʌdstɔk〕 *n.* 純種之馬(尤指用於賽馬者)。

blood·stone 〔ˈblʌdˌston; ˈblʌdstoun〕 *n.* 〖礦〗①血石髓;血石。②赤鐵礦。

blood stream (循環中之)血液。

blood·suck·er 〔ˈblʌdˌsʌkɚ; ˈblʌdˌsʌkə〕 *n.* ①吸血動物(蟲);水蛭。②剝削者。

blood sugar 血糖。

blood test 驗血。

blood·thirst·y 〔ˈblʌdˌθɝstɪ; ˈblʌdˌθəːsti〕 *adj.* 嗜殺的;殘忍的。—**blood·thirst·i·ly,** *adv.* —**blood·thirst·i·ness,** *n.*

blood transfusion 輸血(法)。

blood vessel 血管。

***blood·y** 〔ˈblʌdɪ; ˈblʌdi〕 *adj.,* **blood·i·er, blood·i·est,** *adv., v.,* **blood·ied, blood·y·ing.** —*adj.* ①流血的;血污的。②殘忍的;嗜殺的。③(關於)血的。④〖英鄙〗該死的;非常的。He is a *bloody* fool! 他是個該死的蠢物。—*adv.* 〖英鄙〗非常地。—*v.t.* 使流血;爲血所污。—**blood·i·ly,** *adv.* —**blood·i·ness,** *n.*

Bloody Mary 〖美〗含蕃茄汁之混合酒。

blood·y-mind·ed 〔ˈblʌdɪˈmaɪndɪd; ˈblʌdiˈmaindid〕 *adj.* ①殘忍的;凶狠的。②〖英俚〗故意刁難的;不易親近的;不高興的。

***bloom**[1] 〔blum; bluːm〕 *n.* ①花。②花開的狀態。The cherry trees are in full *bloom.* 櫻花盛開。③青春;壯盛時期。④果實的粉衣;霜。⑤健康者面部紅潤之色。—*v.i.* ①開花。②繁盛。Only water can make the desert *bloom.* 祇有水才能使沙漠變爲綠洲。③處於最健康之時代或情況中。④有健美之色。—*v.t.* ①使繁榮;使開花。②使光采;使美麗。③在(光潔、清亮物體)上產生一片雲霧狀之區域。

bloom[2] *n.* ①鍛鐵塊。②塊鋼。

bloom·er 〔ˈblumɚ; ˈbluːmə〕 *n.* ①開花之樹。②發展與能力相當的技巧、興趣等的年輕人。③〖英俚〗大錯。

bloom·ers 〔ˈbluməz; ˈbluːməz〕 *n. pl.* ①婦女於運動時所穿之燈籠袴。②燈籠袖襯衫。

bloom·er·y 〔ˈblumərɪ; ˈbluːməri〕 *n., pl.* **-er·ies.** 鍛鐵爐;鍛鐵場。

bloom·ing 〔ˈblumɪŋ; ˈbluːmiŋ〕 *adj.*①開花的。②青春的;壯盛的;美麗的;精力充沛的。③興旺的;繁盛的;繁榮的。④〖俗〗全然的;討厭的。

bloom·y 〔ˈblumɪ; ˈbluːmi〕 *adj.,* **bloom·i·er, bloom·i·est.** ①盛開的;多花的。②(果實)有粉衣的。

bloop 〔blup; bluːp〕 *n.* (亦作 **blooper**) 〖美俚〗①在大衆之前所犯的錯誤。②〖棒球〗落在內野與外野之間的飛球。—*v.t.* & *v.i.* ①做出愚蠢的事。②〖棒球〗打出落在外野與內野之間的飛球。

***blos·som** 〔ˈblɑsəm; ˈblɔsəm〕 *n.* ①花(尤指結果實者)。②花開的時期或狀態。The roses are in full *blossom.* 玫瑰盛開。The apple tree is in *blossom* for the second time this year. 這蘋果樹開花今年是第二次。—*v.i.* ①有花;開花。②繁榮。That lonely, remote settlement has now *blossomed* into a charming city. 那個孤寂邊遠的地區現在繁榮成爲一個可愛的城市。

—less, *adj.* —y, *adj.*

blot¹** [blɑt; blɔt] *n., v.,* **blot·ted, blot·ting.** —*n.* ①汚漬;汚痕。②文字上的塗抹。③汚點。—*v.t.* ①弄髒。②(用吸墨紙)吸乾。③玷汚。blot out*** a. 遮蓋。The fog *blotted out* the view. 霧遮住了風景。b. 塗抹。c. 擦掉。d. 毀掉。—*v.i.* ①染汚。②被染汚。—less, *adj.* —ty, *adj.* —ting·ly, *adv.*

blot² *n.* ①(西洋雙陸戲)暴露之棋子。②暴露之點;弱點;缺陷。

blotch [blɑtʃ; blɔtʃ] *n.* ①大斑點。②皮膚上的紅疤;疙瘩。—*v.t.* 被以斑點或汚點;弄髒。—y, *adj.*

blot·ter [ˈblɑtɚ; ˈblɔtə] *n.* ①吸墨紙。②記事簿;記錄簿。

blotting paper 吸墨紙。

blot·to [ˈblɑto; ˈblɔtou] *adj.* 〖俚〗爛醉如泥的。

***blouse** [blaus; blauz] *n., v.,* **bloused, blous·ing.** —*n.* ①似襯衫的上衣。②寬鬆的婦女或兒童之短衫。③美軍軍服之短上衣。④歐洲農夫和工人所着之罩衫。 —*v.i.* & *v.t.* (使)寬鬆下垂。

‡**blow¹** [blo; blou] *n.* ①打;打擊。②精神上的打擊。③〖音樂〗吹奏。***at a*** (or ***one***) ***blow*** 一個動作或一次努力。He killed two robbers *at a blow.* 他一擊打死兩個强盜。***come to blows*** 互毆。***exchange blows*** 互毆。***strike a blow for*** (or ***against***) 贊成(反對)。***with one blow*** 一擊。***without striking a blow*** 未費吹灰之力。

‡**blow²** *v.,* **blew, blown, blow·ing.** —*v.i.* ①吹動;吹。The wind *blew* hard. 刮大風。②隨風飄動;爲風所捲。The dust was *blowing.* 塵埃飛揚。③吹氣;噓氣。④喘息。The horse *blew* short after the race. 賽跑後馬喘。⑤自誇。He *blows* too much. 他太自誇。⑥吹奏;響起。Stop work when the whistle *blows.* 汽笛響時,停止工作。⑦爆炸〖up〗。The bridge *blew* up after being hit. 橋被擊中後爆炸。—*v.t.* ①吹之使…移動或向前。②將空氣吹進…;使空氣吹經…之內。The boy was *blowing* bubbles. 那孩子正吹氣泡。③擤(鼻涕)。④ 自吹;自誇。He *blows* his own trumpet. 他自吹自擂。⑤使喘氣。⑥吹之使成定形。to *blow* glass. 吹玻璃(使成杯、瓶等)。⑦(昆蟲)產卵於…之上。⑧亂花(錢)。⑨鎔化。⑩傳播(消息)。***blow away*** 吹走。***blow hot and cold*** 從贊成意見而轉向反對;拿不定主意。***blow in*** (or ***into***) a. 偶然來訪;出其不意地出現。b. 浪費(金錢)。***blow off*** a. 吹散。b. 減輕緊張。***blow one's lines*** 忘記或讀錯臺詞。***blow one's top*** (or ***stack***) 大發雷霆。***blow out*** a. 吹熄。Don't *blow out* the light. 不要熄燈。b. 因電流過强而融化。c. 走氣。The worn tire *blew out.* 這舊車胎走氣了。d. 力量消失。***blow out a person's brain*** 以槍打死某人。***blow over*** 不吹;停止;被遺忘。***blow the whistle on*** a. 〖運動〗罰。b. 宣告不合法或不誠實。c. 告發。***blow up*** a. 打氣。b. 爆炸。c. 炸毀。d. 發脾氣。e. 形成。A storm *blew up.* 一個風暴形成了。f. 放大(照片)。g. 斥責;辱罵。

blow³ *v.,* **blew, blown, blow·ing,** *n.* —*v.t.* (使)開花。—*v.i.* 開花。—*n.* ①一叢花;花叢。②華麗炫耀之物。

blow·ball [ˈbloˌbɔl; ˈbloubɔːl] *n.* (蒲公英之)絮球。

blow-by-blow [ˈbloˌbaɪˈblo; ˈblouˌbaiˈblou] *adj.* (廣播或報紙報導拳賽時)將拳手每一動作都報導的。—*n.* 詳盡的敍述。

blow·er [ˈbloɚ; ˈblouə] *n.* ①吹者;吹奏之物。②風箱;吹火筒。③鼓風爐之工頭。④〖俚〗愛吹牛的人。⑤〖英俚〗電話。

blow·fly [ˈbloˌflaɪ; ˈblou-flai] *n., pl.* **-flies.** (產卵於腐肉或創口之)大蒼蠅。

blow·gun [ˈbloˌgʌn; ˈblougʌn] *n.* ①吹矢槍。②噴漆(油等)之器具。

blow-hard [ˈbloˌhard; ˈblouhɑːd] *n.* 〖俚〗大言者;吹法螺者。—*adj.* 〖俚〗大吹法螺的。

blow·hole [ˈbloˌhol; ˈblouhoul] *n.* ①(鯨等之)呼吸孔。②出氣孔;通風孔。③(由氣泡所造成之)鑄鐵等的瑕疵。④可供鯨或海狗等呼吸的冰上之孔。

blow·mo·bile [ˈbloməbil; ˈbloumə-biːl] *n.* 〖美〗一種放在滑雪屐上以螺旋槳推動之車輛。

blown [blon; bloun] *v.* pp. of **blow.** —*adj.* ①膨脹的。②喘不過氣來的。③腐臭的。④吹製的。⑤開花的;盛開的。⑥破壞的;歪的。

blow·off [ˈbloˌɔf; ˈblouɔːf] *n.* ①跑出之氣流、水流等。②使氣流水流溢出之裝置。③〖俚〗吹牛者。④暴怒;突然之發作。

blow·out [ˈbloˌaut; ˈblouˈaut] *n.* ①爆破。②車胎爆炸。③保險絲燒斷。④〖俚〗盛大宴會。⑤砂地上被風吹成之洞。⑥井中噴出之水、油等。

blow·pipe [ˈbloˌpaɪp; ˈblou-paip] *n.* ①吹風管; 吹火管。②(製造玻璃之)吹管。③吹矢槍。④〖醫〗吹管。

blow·torch [ˈbloˌtɔrtʃ; ˈbloutɔːtʃ] *n.* 一種汽油吹管(用於熔焊金屬等)。

blow·tube [ˈbloˌtjub; ˈbloutjuːb] *n.* ①(製造玻璃之)吹管。②吹矢槍。

blow·up [ˈbloˌʌp; ˈblouʌp] *n.* ①爆炸;爆發。②發怒;激怒;叱責。③〖照相〗放大。④破產。⑤(劇本等的)擴大。

blow·y [ˈbloɪ; ˈbloui] *adj.,* **blow·i·er, blow·i·est.** ①颳風的;有風的。②容易吹亂的。

blowz·y [ˈblauzɪ; ˈblauzi] *adj.,* **blowz·i·er, blowz·i·est.** ①紅臉的;日炙的。②不整潔的;邋遢的。(亦作 **blowzed, blowsy, blousy**)

BLS Bureau of Labor Statistics.

bls. ①bales. ②barrels. **B.L.S.** Bachelor of Library Science.

blub·ber¹ [ˈblʌbɚ; ˈblʌbə] *n.* 鯨脂。

blub·ber² *n.* 哭號;泣訴。—*v.i.* ①痛哭;且泣且訴。②因哭泣而弄得臉腫。—*v.t.* ①哭訴。②哭腫(臉或眼)。—*adj.* (臉、眼等因哭泣而)腫起的。—ing·ly, *adv.*

blub·ber·head [ˈblʌbɚˌhɛd; ˈblʌbəhed] *n.* 〖俚〗愚笨的人;笨蛋。—ed, *adj.*

blub·ber-lipped [ˈblʌbɚˌlɪpt; ˈblʌbəlipt] *adj.* 嘴唇厚厚的;嘴唇突出的。

blub·ber·y [ˈblʌbərɪ; ˈblʌbəri] *adj.* ①鯨脂的;多鯨脂的。②似鯨脂的;油膩的。③哭泣的;哭腫的。

blu·cher [ˈbluʧɚ; ˈbluːtʃə] *n.* 一種半統靴。

bludg·eon [ˈblʌdʒən; ˈblʌdʒən] *n.* 一端較重之短棒。—*v.t.* ①棒打。②脅迫;恫嚇。

‡**blue** [blu; bluː] *n., adj.,* **blu·er, blu·est,** *v.,* **blued, blu·ing** or **blue·ing.** —*n.* ①天藍色;青色。②藍色染料。③(常 *pl.*)憂鬱;沮喪。④天空;海洋。the *blue.* 蒼天;大海。⑤穿藍色衣服者; 藍隊隊員。Tomorrow the *blues* will play the browns. 明天藍隊將與棕隊比賽。⑥才女。⑦美國南北戰爭時北軍之一員。⑧藍色東西。***into the blue*** 至遠處;至未可知處;不見。***out of the blue*** 完全出於不意。***the Blue and the Gray*** 美國南北戰爭時之北軍與南軍。—*adj.* ①蔚藍的;青色的。

②沮喪的;憂鬱的。He looks a bit *blue.* 他稍現憂色。③(由寒冷、打傷、或恐懼而)發青的。④希望很小的;渺茫的。⑤嚴厲的(道德、宗教等)。⑥詛咒的;褻瀆神聖的。⑦〖俗〗猥褻的。⑧(B-)(美國南北戰爭時之)北軍的。***blue in the face*** 筋疲力竭得說不出話。***once in a blue moon*** 罕;極少。—*v.t.* 將…染成青色。

Blue·beard 〔ˈbluˏbɪrd; ˈbluːbiəd〕 *n.* ①藍鬍子(稗史中先後殺害六個妻子之人)。②任何無情、殘忍、變態的丈夫;謀害妻妾的丈夫。

blue·bell 〔ˈbluˏbɛl; ˈbluːbel〕 *n.* 鐘形花植物。

blue belt 〖柔道〗藍帶。

blue·ber·ry 〔ˈbluˏbɛrɪ; ˈbluːbəri〕 *v.,* **-ried, -ry·ing,** *n., pl.* **-ries.** —*v.t.* 採摘漿果。—*n.* ①越橘屬的漿果。②越橘屬的灌木。

***blue·bird** 〔ˈbluˏbɝd; ˈbluːbəːd〕 *n.* (北美產之)藍知更鳥。

blue-black 〔ˈbluˈblæk; ˈbluːˈblæk〕 *adj.* 深藍色的。

blue blood ①貴族的血統。②〖俗〗貴族。

blue-blood·ed 〔ˈbluˈblʌdɪd; ˈbluː-ˈblʌdid〕 *adj.* ①貴族的。②純種的。

blue·bon·net 〔ˈbluˏbɑnɪt; ˈbluːˌbɔnit〕 *n.* ①〖動物〗山雀之類。②〖植物〗矢車菊。③從前蘇格蘭人所戴藍色小帽。④蘇格蘭兵。

blue book ①藍皮書(英國國會之出版物,因書皮為藍色,故稱)。②美國政府官員錄。③社會知名人士錄。④若干大學所用供學生作試題答案之藍皮小册子。

Blue Book ①美國國務院每月發行一次的駐美外交人員名册。②英國官方出版物。

blue·bot·tle 〔ˈbluˏbɑtl̩; ˈbluːˌbɔtl〕 *n.* ①〖植物〗矢車菊。②青蠅。

blue-brick university 〖英俗〗有優良傳統及地位的大學(如劍橋、牛津大學等)。

blue cheese 上等的帶藍紋的乳酪。

blue chip ①(撲克)藍色的高價籌碼。②紅利穩而值錢的公司股票。③穩而可靠的財產。

blue·coat 〔ˈbluˏkot; ˈbluː-kout〕 *n.* ①着藍色衣服或制服之人。②警察。③美國早期之陸軍人員。④美國南北戰爭時之北軍。

blue-col·lar 〔ˈbluˈkɑlɚ; ˈbluːˈkɔlə〕 *adj.* 工人階級的。

Blue Cross 美國的一個非營利性會員組織,代會員繳付若干醫藥費用。

blue devils ①沮喪;憂鬱。②精神狂亂時的可怕之幻想。

blue·fish 〔ˈbluˏfɪʃ; ˈbluːfiʃ〕 *n., pl.* **-fish, -fish·es.** ①美洲大西洋海岸所產之青魚。②(一般的)青色之魚。

blue·grass 〔ˈbluˏgræs; ˈbluːgrɑːs〕 *n.* ①莓繫屬之植物。②美國南方傳統的鄉村民謠。

blue helmet 和平軍(聯合國所派遣維持和平的國際軍隊,因頭戴藍盔,故名)。

blue·jack·et 〔ˈbluˏdʒækɪt; ˈbluːˌdʒæ-kit〕 *n.* 水兵;水手。

blue·jay 〔ˈbluˏdʒe; ˈbluːdʒei〕 *n.* 北美產的一種藍背樫鳥,腹羽為灰色。

blue law 〖美〗嚴格的法律(尤指禁止星期日跳舞、宴會等)。

blue Monday 〖俗〗沮喪的星期一(因週末假期後開始工作,令人不悅,故名)。

Blue Monday 四旬節(Lent)前的最後一個星期一。

blue moon 不可能或極少來臨的時期。

blue movie 春宮電影。

blue·ness 〔ˈblunɪs; ˈbluː-nis〕 *n.* ①藍。②沮喪;憂鬱。

blue·nose 〔ˈbluˏnoz; ˈbluːnouz〕 *n.* 〖俗〗嚴謹的人。

blue-pen·cil 〔ˈbluˈpɛnsl; ˈbluːˈpensl〕 *v.t.,* **-cil(l)ed, -cil·(l)ing.** ①以藍筆刪改(稿件等)。②〖俗〗否決;不准。

blue peter 即將離港的船前桅所掛的旗。

blue pill 〖藥〗藍丸;汞丸。

blue plate ①有間隔的盤子,可同時放不同的食物。②菜單上的主菜。

blue·point 〔ˈbluˏpɔɪnt; ˈbluːpɔint〕 *n.* 一種可生食的小蚵(產於長島之南岸)。

blue·print 〔ˈbluˏprɪnt; ˈbluːˈprint〕 *n.* ①藍圖。②任何企業的詳細計畫。—*v.t.* ①製…之藍圖。②為…作詳細計畫。—**er,** *n.*

blue ribbon ①頭獎;最高榮譽。②藍綬徽章。③禁酒會會員章。

blue-rib·bon 〔ˈbluˏrɪbən; ˈbluːˈribən〕 *adj.* 頭等的;第一流的;特選的。

blue-ribbon jury 由傑出或受過高等教育之陪審員所組成之陪審團。

blues 〔bluz; bluːz〕 *n.pl.* ①憂鬱;沮喪;失望。②(常作*sing.*解)布魯士(爵士音樂及舞步之一種)。③藍色制服(美三軍穿的)。—**y,** *adj.*

blue-sky 〔ˈbluˈskaɪ; ˈbluːˈskai〕 *adj.* ①〖股票〗不可靠的;財務不健全的。②為純理論和科學發展而不為眼前利益的。③不切實際的。

blue-sky law 有關股票買賣的美國州法律,以防止財務不健全公司股票之推銷。

blue·stock·ing 〔ˈbluˏstɑkɪŋ; ˈbluː-ˌstɔkiŋ〕 *n.* 女學者;才女;炫學的女人。

blue·stone 〔ˈbluˏston; ˈbluːstoun〕 *n.* ①〖化〗膽礬;膽石。②(建築用之)青石。

blue streak ①行動很快的人或物。②連續的、凶猛的、或繼續不斷的事物。***like a blue streak*** 很快;很有效力。

blu·et 〔ˈbluɪt; ˈbluːit〕 *n.* 一種開藍花之叢生植物。

blue water 深海。

bluff[1] 〔blʌf; blʌf〕 *n.* 〖美〗①虛張聲勢;唬人;佯作有把握以騙人。②虛張聲勢的人。—*v.i.* 虛張聲勢;佯作有把握。—*v.t.* 恫嚇;虛張聲勢以嚇人。***call someone's bluff*** 揭穿某人的虛偽。—**er,** *n.*

***bluff**[2] *adj.* ①崎嶇的;陡峭的。②粗率的;坦直的;豪放的。—*n.* 絕崖;絕壁。—**ly,** *adv.* —**ness,** *n.*

blu·ing 〔ˈbluɪŋ; ˈbluːiŋ〕 *n.* 藍色漂白劑。(亦作 **blueing**)

blu·ish 〔ˈbluɪʃ; ˈbluː(ː)iʃ〕 *adj.* 帶青色的;淺藍色的。(亦作 **blueish**) —**ness,** *n.*

blun·der** 〔ˈblʌndɚ; ˈblʌndə〕 *n.* 愚蠢的錯誤;謬誤。He has made a terrible *blunder.* 他鑄成大錯。—*v.t.* ①做錯;致誤。②脫口而出。—*v.i.* ①措施失當。②盲目或愚蠢地行動。blunder against*** 慌張衝撞。***blunder away*** 因措置錯誤而失去。***blunder into*** (***on,*** or ***upon***) 無意中發現。to *blunder into* an explanation. 無意中發現一解釋。***blunder out*** 脫口而出。***blunder through*** 胡亂應付。—**er,** *n.*

blun·der·buss 〔ˈblʌndɚˏbʌs; ˈblʌn-dəbʌs〕 *n.* ①老式大口徑的散彈短槍。②蠢材。③輕率者。

blun·der·head 〔ˈblʌndɚˏhɛd; ˈblʌn-dəhed〕 *n.* 笨頭笨腦的人。

blun·der·ing 〔ˈblʌndərɪŋ; ˈblʌndə-riŋ〕 *adj.* 誤事的;笨拙的。—**ly,** *adv.*

blunge 〔blʌndʒ; blʌndʒ〕 *v.t.,* **blunged, blung·ing.** 混合(泥土與水等)。

***blunt** 〔blʌnt; blʌnt〕 *adj.* ①鈍的。a *blunt* knife. 一把鈍的小刀。②坦白的;明說的;直言的。③瞭解或感覺能力遲鈍的;愚蠢的;粗鹵的。—*v.t.* 使鈍;挫折。—*v.i.* 變鈍。—*n.* 鈍的東西。—**ly,** *adv.* —**ness,** *n.*

***blur** 〔blɝ; bləː〕 *v.,* **blurred, blur·ring,** *n.* —*v.t.* ①使污黑;污之。②使模糊;使不清楚。Mists *blurred* the hills. 霧遮羣山朦朧不清。

③使感覺遲鈍。—*v.i.* 變模糊。—*n.* ①模糊；模糊不清的事物。②汚點。 **—red·ly,** *adv.* **—red·ness,** *n.* **—ry,** *adj.*

blurb 〔blɜb; bləːb〕 *n.* 〖俗〗誇大的廣告或介紹詞。 —*v.t.* 〖俗〗在廣告等裏推薦。—*v.i.* 〖俗〗作推薦作者或書的廣告。**—ist,** *n.*

blurt 〔blɜt; bləːt〕 *v.t.* 不加思索地衝口說出〖常out〗. —*n.* 不加思索的話。

blush** 〔blʌʃ; blʌʃ〕 *n., v.,* **blush·ed, blush·ing.** —*n.* ①面赤；赧顏。He said it with a *blush.* 他說這話時面爲之赤。②紅色。③一見；一瞥。at***(or ***on***) ***first blush***一見；初見；驟觀之。—*v.t.* 以面赤來表達。She *blushed* a shy apology. 她面孔一紅, 表示了她的羞澀的歉意。 —*v.i.* ①面赤。②慚愧。He doesn't *blush* at his poverty. 他不以貧窮爲恥。③成爲紅色。④因過多的水分或過分的蒸發而顏色變爲朦朧或不鮮明。 **—ing,** *adj.* **—ing·ly,** *adv.*

blus·ter 〔ˈblʌstɚ; ˈblʌstə〕 *v.i.* ①狂吹。②咆哮；誇言。③恫嚇。—*v.t.* ①威嚇；欺凌。②咆哮地說。 —*n.* ①狂吹。 ②誇言；恫嚇。 **—ing, —y,** *adj.* **—ing·ly,** *adv.*

blus·ter·ous 〔ˈblʌstərəs; ˈblʌstərəs〕 *adj.* ①狂吹的；颳大風的。②狂暴的；咆哮的；恫嚇的。③虛張聲勢的；誇大的。**—ly,** *adv.*

blvd. boulevard. **B.M.** ①Bachelor of Medicine. ②Bachelor of Music. ③British Museum. **B.Mar.E.** Bachelor of Marine Engineering. **B.M.E.** ①Bachelor of Mechanical Engineering. ②Bachelor of Mining Engineering. ③Bachelor of Music Education. **B.M.Ed.** Bachelor of Music Education. **B.Met.** Bachelor of Metallurgy.

BMEWS 〔biˈmjuz; biːˈmjuːz〕〖美軍〗Ballistic Missile Early Warning System. 彈道飛彈早期警告系統。

B.Mgt.E. Bachelor of Management Engineering. **B.Min.E.** Bachelor of Mining Engineering. **B.M.R.** basal metabolic rate. **B.M.S.** Bachelor of Marine Science. **B.M.T.** Bachelor of Medical Technology. **B.Mus.** Bachelor of Music. **Bn.** ①Baron. ②Battalion. **bn.** battalion. **B.N.** ①Bachelor of Nursing. ②bank note. **bnk.** bank. **B.N.S.** Bachelor of Naval Science. **Bnss.** baroness.

bo 〔bo; bou〕 *interj., n., pl.* **boes.**—*interj.* 呸！(嚇人所發之聲)。—*n.* 〖美俚〗①伙計；老兄。②浪子；遊民。

b.o. ①branch office. ②buyer's option.

bo·a 〔ˈboə; ˈbouə〕 *n., pl.* **bo·as.** ①蟒蛇。②女用毛皮圍巾。

B.O.A.C. British Overseas Airways Corporation. 英國海外航空公司。

boa constrictor 大蟒蛇。

Bo·a·ner·ges 〔ˌboəˈnɜdʒiz; ˌbouəˈnəːdʒiːz〕 *n.* ①(作 *pl.*解)雷子(耶穌對門徒 James 及 John 獎譽之名)。②(作 *sing.* 解)大聲叱咤之傳敎者或演講家。

***boar** 〔bor; bɔː〕 *n.* ①雄豬。②野豬。③野豬肉。

:board 〔bord; bɔːd〕 *n.* ①寬而薄的木板。②爲某種特殊用途的木板。a notice *board.* 布告牌。③厚紙板。④飯桌。⑤膳食。The charge for *board* is quite reasonable. 膳費很公道。⑥理事會；董事會；(政府中的)部會。 He is the chairman of the *board* of directors of our company. 他是我們公司董事會的董事長。⑦船側；甲板。⑧邊緣。⑨建築用的各種板。⑩〖鐵路〗路牌。⑪〖俗〗電話總機。***across the board*** 賭一頭馬或狗可得第一, 第二, 或第三, 因此不管名次如何賭者都可得獎金。***All on board!***〖美〗請大家上車！***board and lodging*** 膳宿。***board on board***(船與船)並行。***go by the board*** **a.** 從船甲板上跌下。 **b.** 被棄；被忽視；被忽略。Formalities *went by the board.* 客套都省略了。***on board*** **a.** 上船；〖美〗上火車；在船(車)上。 At what time did he come *on board?* 他幾時上船的? **b.** 相並行。***on the boards*** 從事舞臺生涯。***sweep the board*** **a.** 通吃。**b.** 獲極大成功；贏得一切。***the boards*** **a.** 劇院中的舞臺。to tread *the boards.* 登臺演戲。**b.** 水球戲場四周的木板圍牆。**c.** 室內田徑賽用之木板跑道。—*v.t.* ①用板蓋。The floor was *boarded.* 地面已鋪好木板。②供膳；供膳宿。③上(船)；登(車)。④(與一船)並列航行；相對航行。⑤登船搜查或攻擊。—*v.i.* ① 包飯；寄膳。②(船在逆風中)屈折地航行。***board out*** 在別處吃飯。***board up*** 用木板(把門窗)釘起。

board chairman 董事長(＝chairman of the board).

***board·er** 〔ˈbordɚ; ˈbɔːdə〕 *n.* ①寄膳者；寄膳宿者。②寄宿生。③選出攀登敵艦的士兵。

board·ing 〔ˈbordɪŋ; ˈbɔːdiŋ〕 *n.* ①寄膳；寄膳宿。②供以膳宿。③以木板所建之物。④木板之集合稱。⑤上船(或火車)。⑥攻擊或擄獲敵船。

boarding card (or **pass**) 旅客登機證。

boarding gate 登機入口處。

boarding house 寄宿舍；公寓；供膳食之寄宿舍。

boarding school 供膳宿之學校。

board measure 量木材的特用計量制。

board of education ①學校董事會。②〖美〗在各州縣市負責管理小學及中學之委員會。

board of elections 〖美〗選舉事務所。

board of health 衞生局。

board of trade ①商會。②(B- T-)〖英〗工商部。

board room ①董事會會議室。②(證券行裏)置放一黑板報股票價格之房間。

board school 英國的公立小學。

board wages ①代工資的膳食。②僅够膳食的工資。③膳費。

board·walk 〔ˈbordˌwɔk; ˈbɔːdwɔːk〕 *n.* ①〖美〗木板鋪成的散步道。②任何木板鋪成之道路。

boar·hound 〔ˈborˌhaund; ˈbɔːhaund〕 *n.* 大獵犬。

boar·ish 〔ˈborɪʃ; ˈbɔːriʃ〕 *adj.* ①似野豬的。②殘忍的。③肉慾的。**—ly,** *adv.* **—ness,** *n.*

***boast** 〔bost; boust〕 *v.i.* 自誇；誇言。He *boasted* of his ancestors. 他誇耀他的祖先。—*v.t.* ①誇(其所有)。The town *boasts* a new school. 這鎭以新建學校爲榮。②誇言。 He *boasts* himself of his cleverness. 他自誇聰明。—*n.* ①自誇；誇言。It is a foolish *boast.* 這是無謂的自誇。②可誇耀的事物。

boast·er 〔ˈbostɚ; ˈboustə〕 *n.* 自詡的人；自誇的人。

boast·ful 〔ˈbostˌfəl; ˈboustful〕 *adj.* 自誇的；自負的。**—ly,** *adv.* **—ness,** *n.*

:boat 〔bot; bout〕 *n.* ①船。Let us go by *boat.* 我們乘船去罷。②船形的湯碗(盆)。a gravy *boat.* 一個盛肉汁或調味汁的盆。***burn one's boats*** 破釜沉舟；斷絕退路。***have an oar in every man's boat*** 多管閒事。

in the same boat 處同一的境遇(尤指不幸的境況)。We are all *in the same boat.* 我們境況相同(我們同舟共濟)。***miss the boat*** 〖俚〗a. 失敗。b. 無法了解。***rock the boat*** 〖俗〗破壞現狀;壞事。***take a boat for…*** 乘船去…。—*v.i.* 乘船。We *boated* down the Thames. 我們乘船順泰晤士河而下。—*v.t.* ①以舟載運。②把(槳)從水中取出橫置於船上。

boat·age [ˈbotɪdʒ; ˈboutidʒ] *n.* ①小船搬運。②小船運費。

boat·bill [ˈbotˌbɪl; ˈboutbil] *n.* (美洲熱帶產)一種蒼鷺科涉禽。

boat·er [ˈbotɚ; ˈboutə] *n.* ①乘船者。②一種硬草帽。

boat hook 一端有鐵鉤之撐篙。

boat·house [ˈbotˌhaus; ˈbouthaus] *n.* 船庫;艇庫。

boat·ing [ˈbotɪŋ; ˈboutiŋ] *n.* ①划船遊樂。②船之集合稱。—*adj.* 關於船的。

boat·load [ˈbotˌlod; ˈboutloud] *n.* ①船之載客或載貨量。②一船所載之貨物。

***boat·man** [ˈbotmən; ˈboutmən] *n.*, *pl.* **-men.** ①舟子;船夫。The *boatmen* bent to their oars. 舟子彎身划槳。②出租船者;船之管理人。(亦作 **boatsman**) **—ship,** *n.*

boat race 賽船;賽舟。

boat·swain [ˈbosn̩, ˈbotˌswen; ˈbousn, ˈboutswein] *n.* ①掌帆長;帆纜軍士長;水手長。②軍艦上之准尉。(亦作 **bo's'n, bosun**)

boat train 配合船期之列車。

boat·yard [ˈbotˌjard; ˈbout-jaːd] *n.* 製造或修理小船之工場。

Bob [bab; bɔb] *n.* 男子名。

***bob[1]** [bab; bɔb] *n., v.,* **bobbed, bob·bing.** —*n.* ①短髮;截髮。②秤錘;繩鏈一端之懸垂物。③釣竿線上的浮子;釣線上的蟲、碎布等。④(馬之)截短之尾巴。⑤連橇。⑥詩歌中之一短節。—*v.t.* 剪短。She *bobbed* her hair. 她剪短她的髮。—*v.i.* ①用牙齒咬住上下浮動的東西。②用繫有浮子的釣竿釣魚。

bob[2]** *v.t.* 使…上下或來回疾動。to *bob* a greeting. 點頭表示歡迎。—*v.i.* 上下疾動。bob up*** 突然出現。—*n.* 疾速的動作。

bob[3] *n.* 輕敲;輕叩。—*v.i.* 輕敲;輕叩。

bob[4] *n.* 〖英〗先令。

bobbed [babd; bɔbd] *adj.* ①截尾的。②剪短的;短髮的。

bob·ber·y [ˈbabərɪ; ˈbɔbəri] *n., pl.* **-ber·ies.** 〖俗〗吵鬧;騷動。

bob·bin [ˈbabɪn; ˈbɔbin] *n.* 線軸。

bob·bi·net [ˌbabəˈnɛt; ˌbɔbiˈnet] *n.* 機織花邊。

bob·bish [ˈbabɪʃ; ˈbɔbiʃ] *adj.* 〖英方〗欣然的;愉快的。

bob·ble [ˈbabl̩; ˈbɔbl] *n.* ①輕搖;微蕩。②〖俗〗失手掉落已投出或打出之棒球。③〖美俗〗錯誤。—*v.t.* 〖棒球〗失手掉落。

***bob·by** [ˈbabɪ; ˈbɔbi] *n., pl.* **-bies.** 〖英俚〗警察。

bobby calf 初生之犢。

bobby pin 一種緊的髮夾。

bob·by·socks [ˈbabɪˌsaks; ˈbɔbisɔks] *n. pl.* 〖俗〗短襪。(亦作 **bobby socks**)

bob·by·sox·er [ˈbabɪˌsaksɚ; ˈbɔbiˌsɔksə] *n.* 〖俗〗(醉心於時髦的)少女。(亦作 **bobby soxer**)

bob·cat [ˈbabˌkæt; ˈbɔbkæt] *n.* 美洲野貓。

bob·o·link [ˈbabl̩ˌɪŋk; ˈbɔbəliŋk] *n.* 食米鳥。(亦作 **ricebird**)

bob skate 有雙滑刃之冰鞋。

bob·sled [ˈbabˌslɛd; ˈbɔbsled] *n., v.,* **-sled·ded, -sled·ding.** —*n.* 連橇。—*v.i.* 乘連橇。(亦作 **bobsleigh**) **—der,** *n.*

bob·stay [ˈbabˌste; ˈbɔbstei] *n.* 〖航海〗船首斜檣支索。

Bob's your uncle 〖英〗加强語氣之詞句,尤其未明言之部分極為明顯時。If the boss sees you come in late, *Bob's your uncle.* 要是老闆看到你遲到(你就完蛋了)。

bob·tail [ˈbabˌtel; ˈbɔbteil] *n.* ①截短之尾。②截尾之動物。—*adj.* 截尾的;剪短的。—*v.t.* 截短…之尾;剪短。

bob·white [ˈbabˈhwaɪt; ˈbɔbˈhwait] *n.* 一種美洲鶉類之鳥。

bob wig 截短的假髮。

Boche, boche [baʃ; bɔʃ] *n.* 〖蔑〗德國人;德國兵。

bock [bak; bɔk] *n.* 一種烈性之黑啤酒。

bo·da·cious [boˈdeʃəs; bouˈdeiʃəs] *adj.* 〖美俚〗膽大包天的。

bode [bod; boud] *v.i.* & *v.t.,* **bod·ed, bod·ing.** 預示。***bode ill*** 兇兆。***bode well*** 吉兆。

bo·de·ga [boˈdigə; bouˈdiːgə] 〖西〗*n.* 酒窖;酒店;雜貨店。

bode·ment [ˈbodmənt; ˈboudmənt] *n.* 預兆;預言。

bod·ice [ˈbadɪs; ˈbɔdis] *n.* 女人穿的緊身胸衣。

bod·i·less [ˈbadɪlɪs; ˈbɔdilis] *adj.* 無體的;無形的。

***bod·i·ly** [ˈbadl̩ɪ; ˈbɔdili] *adj.* ①身體上的。*bodily* exercise. 體能活動;體操。②有形的;具體的。—*adv.* ①親自地。②全體地。

bod·ing [ˈbodɪŋ; ˈboudiŋ] *n.* 預兆;惡兆。—*adj.* 預兆的;不吉的;凶兆的。**—ly,** *adv.*

bod·kin [ˈbadkɪn; ˈbɔdkin] *n.* ①錐。②束髮針。③粗鈍之針。④〖印刷〗活字鋏。***sit bodkin*** 擠坐在車上兩人座位的中間。

‡bod·y [ˈbadɪ; ˈbɔdi] *n., pl.* **bod·ies,** *adj., v.,* **bod·ied, bod·y·ing.** —*n.* ①身體。We wear clothes to keep our *bodies* warm. 我們穿衣使我們的身體保持溫暖。②軀幹;軀體。③主要或最重要部分。the *body* of a speech. 演講的最重要部分。④屍體。⑤團體;隊。a *body* of troops. 一隊兵。⑥人。He is a good-natured *body.* 他是一位性情溫厚的人。⑦實質;實體;數量(許多)。A lake is a *body* of water. 湖為一片水。⑧車身;船身;機身。⑨(軍隊或人民之)大部分。⑩(酒味的)濃郁;(衣料等)結實。This wine has good *body.* 這種酒味道濃郁。⑪〖幾何〗立體。⑫天體。⑬瓷器之基本原料。⑭新聞報導第一段以後之文字。***in a body*** 全體。They moved forward *in a body.* 他們全體向前進。***keep body and soul together*** 養活自己;苟延殘喘。—*adj.* ①身體的。②主要部分的。—*v.t.* 賦以形體;使具體化。***body forth*** a. 賦予實體。b. 為…之象徵。

body blow 〖拳擊〗向對手身體的毆打。

body cavity 體腔。

body corporate 公司;法人團體。

body count 戰役中敵軍屍體之清點。

body English 〖美俗〗球員扭轉身體想改變或控制已打出或投出之球的方向。

body examination 體格檢查。

bod·y·guard [ˈbadɪˌgard; ˈbɔdigaːd] *n.* 扈從;保鏢。

body language 體語(表達內心思想的一種不自覺的手勢及姿態)。

body mike 〖美〗掛在頸上的小型麥克風。

body politic 占有一定的領土,在一個政府下有政治組織的人民(如國家)。

body snatcher 掘墓盜屍者。

body stocking 女用緊身連褲內衫。

bod·y·suit [ˈbadɪˌsut; ˈbɔdisuːt] *n.* 連身緊身女裝。

body type 用以排印正文的鉛字。
bod·y·work ['bɑdɪˌwɝk; 'bɔdiwə:k] *n.* ①打造車身之工作。②車身。
Boe·o·tian [bɪ'oʃən; bi'ouʃjən] *adj.* ① Boeotia (古希臘一城邦)的。②拙笨的。—*n.* ①Boeotia 人。②笨漢。
Boer [bor, bur; bouə, buə] *n.* 波爾人。—*adj.* 波爾人的。
Boer War 波爾戰爭。
B. of E. ①Bank of England. ②Board of Education.
***bog** [bɑg; bɔg] *n., v.,* **bogged, bog·ging.** —*n.* ①沼澤。②(常*pl.*)〖英俚〗廁所。—*v.t.* 使陷於泥淖。The cart was *bogged.* 車被陷於泥淖中。—*v.i.* 陷於泥淖〖常down〗.
bog brother 〖蔑〗愛爾蘭人。
bo·gey ['bogɪ; 'bougi] *n., pl.* **-geys,** *v.,* **-geyed, -gey·ing.** —*n.* ①鬼怪;怪物(=bogy). ②〖高爾夫〗**a.** 每洞標準桿數。**b.** 超過某洞標準桿數一桿之紀錄。③〖空軍俚〗不明機。—*v.t.* 〖高爾夫〗打出(bogey).
bo·gey·man, bo·gy·man ['bogɪˌmæn; 'bougimæn] *n., pl.* **-men.** 惡鬼。
bog·gle ['bɑgl; 'bɔgl] *v.,* **-gled, -gling,** *n.* —*v.i.* ①受驚; 驚跳。②畏縮不前。③託辭;閃爍其辭。④笨拙;拙劣地做。—*v.t.* ①弄糟; 做壞。②使吃驚。 —*n.* ①驚跳;猶豫;退縮。②〖俗〗拙劣之工作;失敗。
bog·gy ['bɑgɪ; 'bɔgi] *adj.,* **-gi·er, -gi·est.** 多沼澤的;似沼澤的。
bog house 廁所。
bo·gie ['bogɪ; 'bougi] *n., pl.* **-gies.** ①轉向車;臺車。②(戰車之)履帶輪。③〖英方〗低而堅實之拖車。
bog·(g)le ['bogl; 'bougl] *n.* 鬼;怪;妖魔。
bog·trot·ter ['bɑgˌtrɑtɚ; 'bɔgˌtrɔtə] *n.* ①住於沼地之人。②〖蔑〗愛爾蘭農人。
bo·gus ['bogəs; 'bougəs] *adj.* 〖美〗假的;僞造的。 —*n.* 贋品;僞物。
bog·wood ['bɑgˌwud; 'bɔgwud] *n.* 沼地所埋藏之橡樹。(亦作 **bog oak**)
bo·gy ['bogɪ; 'bougi] *n., pl.* **-gies.** ①妖怪。②如鬼的人或東西。③使人害怕的人或物。④〖軍俚〗國籍不明之飛機。(亦作 **bogey, bogie**)
Boh. ①Bohemia. ②Bohemian.
bo·hea [bo'hi; bou'hi:] *n.* 紅茶。
Bo·he·mi·a [bo'himɪə; bou'hi:mjə] *n.* ①波希米亞(昔中歐一國家,現爲捷克一部分)。②玩世不恭者居住之地區或社交場合。
Bo·he·mi·an [bo'himɪən; bou'hi:mjən] *adj.* ① Bohemia 人的; Bohemia 語的。②狂放不羈的。—*n.* ①Bohemia 人; Bohemia 語。②狂放者;玩世不恭者。③吉卜賽人。
Bo·he·mi·an·ism [bo'himɪənˌɪzəm; bou'hi:mjənizəm] *n.* 玩世不恭之作風或思想。
Bohr [bor; bouə] *n.* 包爾 (Niels, 1885–1962, 丹麥物理學家, 1922年得諾貝爾獎)。
bo·hunk ['boˌhʌŋk; 'bouhʌŋk] *n.* 〖美俚〗①無技術之工人。②粗野之人。
‡boil[1] [bɔɪl; bɔil] *v.i.* ①沸;沸騰爲汽。②似沸。The sea was *boiling.* 海水洶湧。③發怒;激動。He *boiled* with rage. 他怒氣沖天。④烹煮。The meat is *boiling.* 肉正在煮着。⑤狂烈地動。—*v.t.* ①煮。*Boil* me an egg soft. 給我煮一個蛋, 嫩些。②以煮沸使淨;消毒。③蒸去水分。***boil away*** **a.** 繼續沸騰。**b.** 煮乾。 ***boil down*** **a.** 蒸濃; 煮濃。 A solution of sugar was *boiling down* to a syrup. 糖水煎濃爲糖漿。**b.** 摘要。**c.** 顯示。***boil over*** **a.** 因沸溢出。**b.** 發怒。—*n.* ①沸;沸騰;沸點; 水在滾動的地方(如急流)。②因壓力而滲進已挖掘的洞穴內之水及雜質。***be at*** (or ***on***) ***the boil*** 在沸點。***come to the boil*** 開始沸騰。
boil[2] *n.* 疔;癤。
***boil·er** ['bɔɪlɚ; 'bɔilə] *n.* ①煮器。We use aluminum *boiler* to heat water. 我們用鋁鍋燒水。②汽鍋。③盛熱水的桶。④〖英〗煮沸或消毒衣服用的桶。
boiler plate 鍋爐板。(亦作 **boiler iron**)
boiler room (or **shop**) ①汽鍋室。②〖美俚〗用電話做未在證劵交易所上市之投機性股票交易之處所。
boil·ing ['bɔɪlɪŋ; 'bɔiliŋ] *n.* ①沸騰;烹煮。②一次所煮之物。—*adj.* ①沸騰的;烹煮的。②激動的;翻騰的。③極熱的。
boiling point 沸點。
boiling water 〖美俚〗麻煩事情; 亂子;紕漏。
boiling water reactor 沸騰水型原子爐。
***bois·ter·ous** ['bɔɪstərəs; 'bɔistərəs] *adj.* ①喧鬧的。*boisterous* laughter. 喧鬧的笑聲。②猛烈的;狂暴的。—**ly,** *adv.* —**ness,** *n.*
Bol. Bolivia.
bo·la(s) ['bolə(s); 'boulə(s)] *n., pl.* **-las, -las·es.** 一端繫重球之繩索(捕牛用)。
bold** [bold; bould] *adj.* ①勇敢的;無畏的;過度自信的。It is really very *bold* of him to venture to do this. 他敢冒險做這事, 眞是非常勇敢。②無禮的; 魯莽的; 大膽的;厚顏無恥的。Don't let him make *bold* with you. 不要任他對你無禮。③顯目的;著目的。 Print it in *bold* type. 用粗體字印刷。④陡峭的;險峻的。⑤〖航海〗海深得能使船駛近岸的。⑥富有想像力的; 不爲通常思想或行爲所限制的。make bold*** 膽敢;冒昧 I *made bold* to offer my suggestion. 我冒昧提出了我的建議。—**ly,** *adv.* —**ness,** *n.*
bold·face ['boldˌfes; 'bouldfeis] *n.* 〖印刷〗粗體鉛字;黑體字。
bold-faced ['bold'fest; 'bouldfeist] *adj.* ①厚顏的;莽撞的。②用粗體鉛字印刷的。
bole[1] [bol; boul] *n.* 樹幹;樹身。
bole[2] *n.* 黏泥;黏土。
bo·lec·tion [bo'lɛkʃən; bou'lekʃən] *n.* 〖建築〗凸嵌線。
bo·le·ro [bo'lɛro; bə'lɛərou *for* ① 'bɔlərou *for* ②] *n., pl.* **-ros.** ①一種輕快之西班牙舞曲或其音樂。②前面開口之短上衣。
bo·le·tic acid [bo'litɪk~; bou'li:tik~] 〖化〗反一丁烯二酸。(亦作 **fumaric acid**)
bo·lide ['bolaɪd, -lɪd; 'boulaid, -lid] *n.* 〖天文〗火流星。
bol·i·var ['bɑləvɚ; 'bɔlivə] *n.* 委內瑞拉之銀幣。
Bo·liv·i·a [bə'lɪvɪə; bə'liviə] *n.* 玻利維亞(南美一國, 首都拉巴斯, La Paz). —**Bo·liv·i·an,** *adj., n.*
bo·li·via·no [boˌlɪ'vjɑno; bouˌli:'vjɑ:nou] *n., pl.* **-nos.** 玻利維亞之標準貨幣單位。
boll [bol; boul] *n.* (棉、亞麻等之) 圓莢; 莢殼。
bol·lard ['bɑləd; 'bɔləd] *n.* ①〖航海〗繫船柱。②〖英〗阻止汽車進入某一區域的木樁或水泥柱。
boll weevil 棉子象鼻蟲。
boll·worm ['bolˌwɝm; 'boulwə:m] *n.* 螟蛉之幼蟲。
bo·lo ['bolo; 'boulou] *n., pl.* **-los.** 菲律賓之單刃大刀。
Bo·lo·gna [bə'lonə; bə'lounjə] *n.* 一種內含雜樣肉類之燻製臘腸。(亦作 **Bologna sausage**)
bo·lo·graph ['boləˌgræf; 'bouləgrɑ:f] *n.* ①輻射熱測定器之記錄。②輻射熱測定器。
bo·lom·e·ter [bo'lɑmətɚ; bou'lɔmitə]

n.〖物理〗輻射熱測定器。

bo·lo·ney 〔bəˈlonɪ; bəˈlouni〕 *n.*〖美〗胡言;荒謬。

Bol·she·vik, bol·she·vik 〔ˈbalʃəˌvɪk; ˈbɔlʃivik〕 *n., pl.* **-viks, Bol·she·vi·ki** 〔ˌbalʃəˈvikɪ; ˌbɔlʃəˈviːki〕, *adj.* —*n.* ①布爾什維克。**a.** (1903–1917) 俄國社會民主黨的多數派之一分子，主張立刻由無產階級奪取政權。**b.** (1918年後) 俄國共產黨之一分子。②任何國家的共產黨分子。③激進分子。—*adj.* 共產黨的;激烈派的。

Bol·she·vism, bol·she·vism 〔ˈbalʃəˌvɪzəm; ˈbɔlʃəvizəm〕 *n.* 布爾什維克主義;共產主義。(亦作 **Bolshevikism**)

Bol·she·vist 〔ˈbalʃəvɪst, ˈbol–; ˈbɔlʃəvist〕 *n.* 布爾什維克派黨員;共產黨員;政治上之極端急進主義者。

Bol·she·vis·tic 〔ˌbalʃəˈvɪstɪk, ˌbol–; ˈbɔlʃəˈvistik〕 *adj.* 布爾什維克派的; 布爾什維克主義的。(亦作 **bolshevistic**)

Bol·she·vize, bol·she·vize 〔ˈbalʃəˌvaɪz; ˈbɔlʃəvaiz〕 *v.t.*, **-vized, -viz·ing.** 使赤化;使共產化。—**Bol·she·vi·za·tion,** *n.*

bol·ster 〔ˈbolstɚ; ˈboulstə〕 *n.* ①長窄的枕（墊）。②墊物。③承板;承材。—*v.t.* 支持;支撐;援助;幫助〖有時up〗。

bolt**[1] 〔bolt; boult〕 *n.* ①螺釘。②門閂;門栓。③鎖中可由鑰匙推動之簧。④短而粗之箭頭; 矢。as straight as a *bolt.* 其直如矢。⑤霹靂;閃電。⑥突發;逃亡。The horse made a *bolt.* 馬突然逃走。⑦一捲布; 一捲紙。⑧〖美〗對自己政黨或黨提名之候選人的拒絕支持。⑨噴出之水, 或溶化之玻璃等。⑩閃電。⑪木板。⑫墊木。⑬槍機。a bolt from the blue*** 晴天霹靂。***make a bolt of it*** 〖俗〗急逃。***shoot one's bolt*** 盡力而爲。***thunder bolt*** 雷電。—*v.i.* ①突發;逃走;衝出;突然跳開。②〖美〗脫黨;拒絕擁護自己政黨的候選人。③急吃;吞。—*v.t.* ①閂住。②〖美〗脫離政黨; 不擁護自己政黨的政策。③射出。④急吃;吞。⑤捲起。⑥脫口說出。⑦(獵狗)將(狐狸)從隱藏處逼至曠野。—*adv.* ①突然地;猝然地。②直立地。***bolt upright*** 挺直地。

bolt[2] *n.* 篩子。—*v.t.* ①篩。②研討;細查。③分開。

bolt·er[1] 〔ˈboltɚ; ˈboultə〕 *n.* ①逃走之馬。②叛黨者; 不支持自己之黨的候選人者。③篩麪粉之布或細眼篩。

bolt·er[2] 穿許多釣鉤的長釣線。

bo·lus 〔ˈboləs; ˈbouləs〕 *n., pl.* **bo·lus·es.** ①小而圓之物塊。②〖獸醫〗大丸藥。③黏土。

Bo·marc 〔ˈbomark; ˈboumaːk〕 *n.*〖美〗一種地對空飛彈的名稱。

bomb** 〔bam; bɔm〕 *n.* ①炸彈。②(the B–)核子武器及其對人類之威脅。③突發事件;驚人事件。④〖俚〗大失敗; 徹底的失敗。⑤搬運放射性物質的鉛質容器。⑥火山口噴出的大堆熔岩。—*v.t.*① 轟炸;投彈。②〖美〗(棒球)長打。—*v.i.* ①投彈;轟炸。 ②完全失敗〖常out〗. The business *bombed* out with a $25,000 debt. 生意失敗了,還欠了二萬五千元的債。bomb load*** 炸彈裝載量。

bom·bard 〔bamˈbard; bɔmˈbaːd〕 *v.t.* ①砲轟;轟擊。②攻擊;質問。③〖物理〗以高能量粒子或放射能衝擊。—**ment,** *n.*

bom·bar·dier 〔ˌbambəˈdɪr; ˌbɔmbəˈdiə〕 *n.* ①〖軍〗投彈手。②砲兵下士。

bom·bar·don 〔ˈbambɚdən; bɔmˈbaːdn〕 *n.* ①簧舌塞子。②一種喇叭。

bom·bast 〔ˈbambæst; ˈbɔmbæst〕 *n.* 誇大之言辭;大話。—**ic,** *adj.* —**i·cal·ly,** *adv.*

Bom·bay 〔bamˈbe; bɔmˈbei〕 *n.* ①孟買(印度西部之一邦)。②孟買(該邦之首府)。

bom·ba·zine 〔ˌbambəˈzin; ˌbɔmbəˈziːn〕 *n.* 羽綢;羽緞。(亦作 **bombasine**)

bomb bay (飛機中的)炸彈艙。

bombed 〔bamd; bɔmd〕 *adj.* ①圓的;凸的。②〖俚〗(爲酒或毒品所)麻醉的。

bomb·er 〔ˈbamɚ; ˈbɔmə〕 *n.* ①轟炸機。②轟炸員。

bomber escort 〖美〗掩護轟炸機之戰鬥機或機羣。

bom·bi·nate 〔ˈbambəˌnet; ˈbɔmbəneit〕 *v.i.*, **-nat·ed, -nat·ing.** 哼;作嗡嗡聲。

bombing plane 轟炸機。

bomb lance 頭上裝配炸藥之魚銛。

bomb·let 〔ˈbamlɪt; ˈbɔmlit〕 *n.* 小炸彈。

bomb·proof 〔ˈbamˈpruf; ˈbɔmpruːf〕 *adj.* 不怕轟炸的;避彈的。—*n.* 防空壕;避彈室。—*v.t.* 使能避彈。

bomb rack (轟炸機上之)炸彈架。

bomb run 自看到目標至投下炸彈之間的一段飛行。(亦作**bombing run**)

bomb·shell 〔ˈbamˌʃɛl; ˈbɔmʃel〕 *n.* ①炸彈。②突然引起騷動的人或事。

bomb shelter 防空洞;避難室。

bomb sight 投彈瞄準器。

bom·by·cid 〔ˈbambɪsɪd; ˈbɔmbisid〕 *n.* 熱帶之蛾類。—*adj.* 熱帶蛾類的。

bon 〔bɔ̃; bɔ̃〕〖法〗*adj.* 良好的;佳的。

bo·na 〔ˈbonə; ˈbounə〕〖拉〗*adj.* 好的;佳良的。

bo·na fi·de 〔ˈbonəˈfaɪdɪ; ˈbounəˈfaidi〕〖拉〗眞誠地(的);無欺地(的)。

bo·na fi·des 〔ˈbonəˈfaɪdiz; ˈbounəˈfaidiːz〕〖拉〗眞誠;誠意。〖注意〗**bona fides** 作單數用。

bo·nan·za 〔boˈnænzə; bouˈnænzə〕 *n.* ①富礦帶。②〖俗〗致富之源;幸運。

bo·nan·za·gram 〔boˈnænzəˌgræm; bouˈnænzəgræm〕 *n.* 塡字遊戲。

Bo·na·part·ism 〔ˈbonəˌpartɪzəm; ˈbounəpaːtizm〕 *n.* ①對拿破崙的主義等之信仰或支持。②政治獨裁者之措施、學說等。

Bo·na·part·ist 〔ˈbonəˌpartɪst; ˈbounəpaːtist〕 *n.* (主張)政治獨裁者。

bon·bon 〔ˈbanˌban; ˈbɔnbɔn〕 *n.* 一種糖果。

bon·bon·nière 〔bɔ̃bɔˈnjɛr; bɔ̃bɔːˈnjɛə〕〖法〗*n.* ①糖果盒。②糖果店;糖果商。

‡**bond** 〔band; bɔnd〕 *n.* ①束縛; 結合; 連合;束縛物。a *bond* of affection between sisters. 姊妹之情。②債券。③契約; 合同;票據。 They entered into a *bond* after some negotiation. 經過磋商後, 他們訂了約。His word is as good as his *bond.* 他說話有信用(如同票據)。④保結。He was freed on *bonds.* 他被保釋。⑤(*pl.*) 禁錮;桎梏;足械。He was in *bonds* on account of bribery. 他因受賄被監禁。⑥保證人; 擔保人。⑦ (海關將貨物)扣留(待交稅後始可取出)。⑧砌磚(石)之方法;砌瓦;砌石。⑨結合;黏着。⑩在保稅倉庫裏已存放至少四年後再裝瓶的陳年威士忌。⑪〖電〗鍵。⑫二號紙; 銅版紙。⑬〖化學〗化學分子中兩個原子間的吸引力。—*v.t.* ①以證券作抵押;抵押。②結合;砌合(磚石等)。③作保。—*v.i.* 砌合。—**a·ble,** *adj.* —**er,** *n.* —**less,** *adj.*

***bond·age** 〔ˈbandɪdʒ; ˈbɔndidʒ〕 *n.* 奴役;爲習慣、情慾等的奴隸;囚禁。

bond·ed 〔ˈbandɪd; ˈbɔndid〕 *adj.* ①抵押的。②扣存於關棧以保稅的 (卽繳關稅後始可提取的)。*bonded* goods. 保稅貨物。

bonded warehouse 保稅倉庫。

bond·hold·er ['band,holdɚ; 'bɔnd,houldə] *n.* 債券持有人。—**bond·hold·ing,** *adj., n.*

bond·maid ['band,med; 'bɔndmeid] *n.* 女奴。

bond·man ['bandmən; 'bɔndmən] *n., pl.* **-men.** ①奴隸。②中世紀之農奴。

bond paper 二號紙;銅版紙。(亦作 **bond**)

bond servant 奴隸;奴僕。

bond service 奴役;奴隸之職役。

bond·slave ['band,slev; 'bɔndsleiv] *n.* 奴隸;奴僕。

bonds·man ['bandzmən; 'bɔndzmən] *n., pl.* **-men.** ①=**bondman.** ②受契約束縛之人。

bond·stone ['band,ston; 'bɔndstoun] *n.* 〖建築〗砌合之石。

Bond Street ①倫敦之一繁盛的街名。②任何都市之繁盛的街道。

bond·wom·an ['band,wumən; 'bɔnd,wumən] *n., pl.* **-wom·en.** 女奴隸。

‡**bone¹** [bon; boun] *n., v.,* **boned, bon·ing.** —*n.* ①骨。He is all skin and *bone.* 他瘦得僅存皮包骨。②骨骼;骸骨;屍骸。③似骨的東西(如象牙、傘骨等)。④(*pl.*)〖俗〗**a.** 骰子。**b.** 骨骼。**c.** 身體。⑤〖音樂〗骨柝。⑥供食用之獸骨(通常指帶肉的)。⑦支撐女人緊身褡(corsets)或襯裙的鯨骨。⑧〖俚〗骨牌戲之牌。⑨低音大喇叭。***feel in one's bones*** 確切知道,但不解其因;知其然,不知其所以然。***have a bone in the throat*** 難於開口。***have a bone to pick with*** (***someone***) 有可爭論或抱怨的事。***make no bones about*** 毫不猶疑;毫無顧忌。***near the bone*** **a.** 苛刻;卑鄙。**b.** 跡近猥褻的。***to the bone*** **a.** 完全地;極端地。**b.** 至極限。—*v.t.* ①除去骨頭。②以鯨骨支撐(衣服)。③以骨灰施肥於。④偷。⑤乞求。—*v.i.* 苦讀;用功研習。He *boned* through college. 他苦讀大學四年。

bone² *v.t.,* **boned, bon·ing.** 沿(物體)瞄準以決定是否水平或成直線。(亦作 **born**)

bone ash ①骨灰;骨粉。②磷酸鈣。

bone·black ['bon,blæk; 'bounblæk] *n.* (漂白用)骨灰。(亦作 **bone black**)

bone china 用瓷土與磷酸鈣燒成的半透明磁器。

boned [bond; bound] *adj.* ①骨骼的(常與他字連用)。small-*boned.* 小骨骼的。②去掉骨頭的。*boned* chicken. 去骨鷄肉。③用骨架撐起的。④用骨施肥的。

bone-dry ['bon'draɪ; 'boun'drai] *adj.* ①極乾燥的。②〖美俗〗絕對禁酒的。

bone dust 骨粉(肥料用)。

bone·head ['bon,hɛd; 'bounhed] *n.* 〖俚〗呆子;蠢漢。—*adj.* 〖俚〗愚蠢的。

bone·less ['bonlɪs; 'bounlis] *adj.* ①無骨的。②沒骨頭的;無力量的;不堅定的。

bone meal 磨碎的骨粉(作爲肥料)。

bone powder 骨粉(用作肥料)。

bon·er ['bonɚ; 'bounə] *n.* ①〖俚〗愚蠢之大錯。②除骨頭的人。③苦讀的人。

bone·set¹ ['bon,sɛt; 'bounset] *v.i.,* **-set, -set·ting.** 接骨;正骨。—**ter,** *n.*

bone·set² *n.* 〖植物〗蘭草。

bone·set·ting ['bon,sɛtɪŋ; 'boun,setiŋ] *n.* 接骨(術);正骨術。

bone yard ①收集牛馬骨骸之處所。②〖俗〗墓地。③棄置舊汽車、飛機等的場地。

bon·fire ['ban,faɪr; 'bɔn,faiə] *n.* 在戶外所舉的火,或爲慶祝而舉的火。

bong [baŋ, bɔŋ; bɔŋ, bɔːŋ] *n.* 如大鐘等發出之聲音。—*v.t.* 產生此種聲音。—*v.i.* 發出此種聲音。

bon·go¹ ['baŋgo; 'bɔŋgou] *n., pl.* **-gos.** (非洲產之)大羚羊。

bon·go² *n., pl.* **-gos, -goes.** 一種用手指敲打的小鼓。

bon·ho·mie, bon·hom·mie [,banə'mi; 'bɔnɔmiː] 〖法〗 *n.* 好性情;溫和;和藹。—**bon·ho·mous,** *adj.*

bon·i·face ['banə,fes; 'bɔnifeis] *n.* 旅店主人。

Bo·nin Islands ['bonɪn~; 'bounin~] 小笠原羣島。

bo·ni·to [bə'nito; bə'niːtou] *n., pl.* **-tos, -toes.** 鰹。

bon jour [bɔ̃'ʒur; bɔ̃'ʒuːr] 〖法〗早安;日安(=good morning; good day).

bon mot [bɔ̃'mo; bɔ̃'mou] *pl.* **bons mots** [bɔ̃'mo; bɔ̃'mou]. 〖法〗合適的話;聰明的話;雋語。

Bonn [ban; bɔn] *n.* 波昂(西德之首都,位於萊茵河畔)。

bonne [bɔ̈n; bɔn] *n., pl.* **bonnes.** 〖法〗保姆;女僕。

bonne a·mie [bɔna'mi; bɔna'miː] 〖法〗女朋友;愛人。

bonne nuit [bɔ̃'nwi; bɔn'nwiː] 〖法〗晚安(=good night).

***bon·net** ['banɪt; 'bɔnit] *n.* ①婦孺所戴的軟帽。②保護用之覆蓋物。③蘇格蘭男帽。④美洲印第安人頭上的羽飾。—*v.t.* 戴(軟帽)。

bon·ny, bon·nie ['banɪ; 'bɔni] *adj.,* **-ni·er, -ni·est,** *n.* —*adj.* ①美麗的。②好的。③健美的。What a *bonny* baby! 一個多麼健美的嬰兒!—*n.* 〖英,蘇〗健美的女孩,或少婦。—**bon·ni·ly,** *adv.* —**bon·ni·ness,** *n.*

bon·sai ['bansaɪ; 'bounsai] *n., pl.* **-sai.** 盆景。

bon soir [bɔ̃'swar; ,bɔn'swɑː] 〖法〗晚安(=good evening; good night).

bon ton [bɔ̃'tɔ̃; 'bɔ̃'tɔ̃] 〖法〗優雅的式樣;良好的家教;上流社會。

***bo·nus** ['bonəs; 'bounəs] *n.* ①花紅;獎金;紅利。②政府給與退役軍人的額外酬金、保險金等。③保險的餘利。④免費贈送的東西。

bon vi·vant [bɔ̃vi'vɑ̃; bɔnviː'vɑːn] *pl.* **bons vi·vants** [bɔ̃vi'vɑ̃; bɔnviː'vɑːn]. 〖法〗①喜錦衣玉食者。②樂天的伴侶。

bon vo·yage [bɔ̃vwa'jaːʒ; bɔ̃vwa'jaːʒ] 〖法〗再會;一路順風;一路平安。

bon·y ['bonɪ; 'bouni] *adj.,* **-i·er, -i·est.** ①多骨的;如骨的。②骨骼畢露的。③骨瘦如柴的。—**bon·i·ness,** *n.*

bonze [banz; bɔnz] *n.* 和尚;僧。

bon·zer ['bonzɚ; 'bounzə] *adj.* 〖澳〗①很大的。②特出的;美妙的;優異的。

boo [bu; buː] *interj., n., pl.* **boos,** *v.,* **booed, boo·ing.** —*interj.* 表輕視、不贊成或震驚之聲音。—*n.* 噓聲。—*v.i.* 作噓聲。—*v.t.* 以噓聲嚇走;向…作噓聲。

boob [bub; buːb] *n.* 〖美俚〗①愚人;笨伯。②愚蠢的錯誤。—*v.t.* 做出(蠢事)。

boo-boo ['bu,bu; 'buː'buː] *n., pl.* **-boos.** 〖俚〗①愚蠢的錯誤。②輕傷。

boo·by ['bubɪ; 'buːbi] *n., pl.* **-bies.** ①呆子;蠢物。②海鵝;塘鵝。③競賽或遊戲中之最劣者。***booby prize*** 末名獎品。—**ish,** *adj.*

booby hatch ①小艙口。②〖美俚〗瘋人院。③監獄。

boo·by-trap ['bubɪ,træp; 'buːbitræp] *n.* ①置物於微開的門上以驚打來人之惡作劇。②詭雷。—*v.t.* 在…安設陷阱。(亦作 **booby trap**)

boo·dle ['budl; 'buːdl] *n.* 〖美俚〗①〖蔑〗一羣;一組。②賄賂;非法得利。③盜贓。④僞

幣。⑤大量的東西。***kit and boodle*** 整批人或物。—*v.i.* 以非法手段得到金錢;受賄。

boog·ie-woog·ie 〔ˈbugɪˈwugɪ; ˈbugiˈwugi〕 *n.* 一種爵士樂。(亦作 **boogie**)

boo·hoo 〔ˈbuˌhu; ˈbuːhuː〕 *v.*, **-hooed, -hoo·ing,** *n.*, *pl.* **-hoos,** *interj.* —*v.i.* 號泣。—*n.* 哭號。—*interj.* 號哭。

ː**book** 〔buk; buk〕 *n.* ①書;書籍。The *book* is out. 這書已借出。②卷;篇。③簿册。④歌劇之歌詞。⑤(常 *pl.*) 帳簿。to audit the *books*. 查帳。The *book* balanced exactly. 帳目收支相符。⑥(爵士樂)樂隊之全部演唱目錄。⑦(歌舞劇等之)劇本。⑧賭帳(賽馬等的)。⑨裝訂如書之物(如支票簿, 成册之票子, 郵票, 火柴等)。⑩一捆東西。⑪紀錄。⑫〖運動〗記載有關運動員(尤其對方棒球選手)之各種資料的簿子。⑬〖俚〗＝**bookmaker**②. ***be in one's black*** (or ***bad***) ***books*** 不爲某人所喜; 失寵。***be in one's good books*** (or ***in one's books***) 爲某人所喜(所寵)。***bring to book*** **a.** 請求解釋。**b.** 斥責。***by the book*** 根據常規; 以通常的態度。***close the books*** **a.** (結帳時) 暫停記帳。**b.** 使…告結束。***in one's book*** 按某人的個人意見。***keep a book*** 開設小型 (非法的) 打賭場所。***keep books*** 記帳。***like a book*** 完全地;徹底地。***make book*** **a.** 下賭注或接受賭注(如賽馬等)。**b.** 打賭。***one for the book*** 值得記載的事蹟。***on the books*** 有記載;有案可查。***suit one's book*** 合於某人的計畫或希望。***the book*** **a.** 規定;辦法;法規。**b.** 電話簿。***the Book*** 聖經。to swear on *the Book*. 對聖經發誓。***throw the book at*** 〖俚〗 **a.** 把兇嫌處最重之刑。**b.** 嚴厲處罰或斥責。***without book*** **a.** 憑記憶。**b.** 無權;無根據。—*v.t.* ①登記。②預定; 約定。Seats for the game can be *booked* one week in advance. 球賽的座位可以在一星期前預定。③託運。His baggage was *booked* to Tainan. 他的行李託運至臺南。④控告。⑤接受賭注。—*v.i.* ①登記。②訂座。***book in*** 將雇員之到達登記於册簿內。***book off*** 〖英〗將自己下班登記在簿子上。—*adj.* ①書的。②來自書本的。③帳簿上的。—**like,** *adj.*

book account 帳簿上之貸借計算。

book·bind·er 〔ˈbukˌbaɪndɚ; ˈbukˌbaində〕 *n.* 裝訂書者。

book·bind·er·y 〔ˈbukˌbaɪndərɪ; ˈbukˌbaindəri〕 *n.*, *pl.* **-er·ies.** 釘書廠; 裝訂處。

book·bind·ing 〔ˈbukˌbaɪndɪŋ; ˈbukˌbaindiŋ〕 *n.* 裝訂術; 裝訂業。

***book·case** 〔ˈbukˌkes; ˈbukkeis〕 *n.* 「書架。」

book club ①讀書俱樂部。②一種販賣書籍之組織。

book debt 帳面上之負債。

book end 書夾;書靠。

book·er 〔ˈbukɚ; ˈbukə〕 *n.* 訂旅館、車票、戲票等的登記人。

book-hunt·er 〔ˈbuk ˌhʌntɚ; ˈbukˌhʌntə〕 *n.* 嗜書者;搜求古書者。

book·ie 〔ˈbukɪ; ˈbuki〕 *n.* 〖俚〗以賭賽馬爲生之人。

book·ing 〔ˈbukɪŋ; ˈbukiŋ〕 *n.* ①演講或表演之預約。②定票。***booking agent*** **a.** 代訂機票、戲票等的人。**b.** (演員等之)經紀人。***booking clerk*** **a.** 售票員。**b.** 安排與登記旅客、行李、貨物等之服務員。***booking office*** 售票房(英稱爲 booking hall)。

book·ish 〔ˈbukɪʃ; ˈbukiʃ〕 *adj.* ①好讀書的。②書呆子的;拘泥的;咬文嚼字的。③與書籍有關的;書上的。—**ness,** *n.* —**ly,** *adv.*

book jacket 書皮。

***book·keep·er** 〔ˈbukˌkipɚ; ˈbukˌkiːpə〕 *n.* 簿記員。

book·keep·ing 〔ˈbukˌkipɪŋ; ˈbukˌkiːpiŋ〕 *n.* 簿記。

book-learn·ed 〔ˈbukˌlɝnɪd; ˈbukˌləːnid〕 *adj.* 有書本上之知識的;無實際經驗的。

book learning ①書本上的學問。②〖俗〗正規教育。

***book·let** 〔ˈbuklɪt; ˈbuklit〕 *n.* 小册子。

book·lore 〔ˈbukˌlor; ˈbuklɔː〕 *n.* ＝**book learning.**

book louse 書蠹。

book·mak·er 〔ˈbukˌmekɚ; ˈbukˌmeikə〕 *n.* ①作者;編者。②以賭賽馬爲生的人。

book·mak·ing 〔ˈbukˌmekɪŋ; ˈbukˌmeikiŋ〕 *n.* ①編輯;著作。②賭跑馬賽之登記。

book·man 〔ˈbukmən; ˈbukmən〕 *n.*, *pl.* **-men.** ①飽學之士;學者。②〖俗〗出版商; 書商。③ (B-) 〖印刷〗一種活字體。

book·mark(·er) 〔ˈbukˌmɑrk(ɚ); ˈbukˌmɑːk(ə)〕 *n.* ①書籤。②＝**bookplate.**

book·mo·bile 〔ˈbukməˌbil; ˈbukmoubiːl〕 *n.* (在車上的)流動圖書館。

book of account 帳簿。

Book of Books 聖經。

Book of Changes 易經。

book·plate 〔ˈbukˌplet; ˈbukpleit〕 *n.* 書本標籤;書面上的貼頭。

book·rack 〔ˈbukˌræk; ˈbukræk〕 *n.* ①書架。②閱覽架;看書臺。

book·rest 〔ˈbukˌrɛst; ˈbukrest〕 *n.* 「閱書架。」

book review 書評。

book reviewer 書評人。

book reviewing 書評。

***book·sell·er** 〔ˈbukˌsɛlɚ; ˈbukˌselə〕 *n.* 書賈;書店老板。

book·shelf 〔ˈbukˌʃɛlf; ˈbukʃelf〕 *n.*, *pl.* **-shelves.** 書架;書櫥。

book·shop 〔ˈbukˌʃɑp; ˈbukʃɔp〕 *n.* 書店。

book·slide 〔ˈbukˌslaɪd; ˈbukslaid〕 *n.* 一種書架。

book·stack 〔ˈbukˌstæk; ˈbukstæk〕 *n.* 多層書架。

book·stall 〔ˈbukˌstɔl; ˈbukstɔːl〕 *n.* 書報攤。

book·stand 〔ˈbukˌstænd; ˈbukstænd〕 *n.* ①書報攤; 雜誌攤。②書架; 閱覽架。

book·store 〔ˈbukˌstor; ˈbukstɔː〕 *n.* 〖美〗書店。

book value ①公司或股票之淨值。②帳簿上之價值。

book·work 〔ˈbukˌwɝk; ˈbukwəːk〕 *n.* ①書本之研讀。②書本之印刷。

book·worm 〔ˈbukˌwɝm; ˈbukwəːm〕 *n.* ①蠹魚;書蟲。②書呆子。

***boom**¹ 〔bum; buːm〕 *n.* ①隆隆聲;營營聲。②繁榮。③景氣。④提高(候選人)聲望(之努力)。—*v.t.* ①以隆隆聲發出。②使繁榮。③廣爲宣傳。④力促;力迫。—*v.i.* ①作隆隆聲;發低沉之聲音。②趨於繁榮。Business is *booming*. 工商業日趨繁榮。—*adj.* 繁榮的;景氣的。

boom² *n.* ①帆之下桁。②阻擋浮木漂走的欄木。③船上的吊桿。④攝製電影用的活動架。—*v.t.* 以下桁張開 (帆脚)。 —*v.i.* (船隻) 以最大速度航行。***lower the boom*** 〖俚〗採取嚴厲措施;禁止。

boom-and-bust 〔ˈbumənˈbʌst; ˈbuːmənˈbʌst〕 *n.* 〖俗〗經濟繁榮與蕭條之交替循環。(亦作**boom and slump**)

boom bucket 〖美俚〗噴射機上之可自動彈出之座位。

boom·er 〔ˈbumɚ; ˈbuːmə〕 *n.* ①〖美俗〗 **a.** 發出隆隆聲者。 **b.** 到正繁榮的城市定居的

人。c. 流動的工人。②〖澳〗大的雄袋鼠。
boom·er·ang 〔ˈbuməˌræŋ; ˈbuːmə-ræŋ〕 *n.* ①回飛棒(一種澳洲土人打獵時用的彎曲堅木, 擲出後仍能返回原處)。②反跳回原處傷及使用者的東西。③傷及原提案人的辯論或建議。—*v.i.* 擲出後仍回原處。
boom·ing 〔ˈbumɪŋ; ˈbuːmiŋ〕 *adj.* ①隆隆作響的。②趨於繁榮的。③發展急速的; 暴漲的。 「然繁榮的城鎮。」
boom town 因投機事業, 開礦等而突
boom·y 〔ˈbumɪ; ˈbuːmi〕 *adj.* 景氣的。
boon[1] 〔bun; buːn〕 *n.* ①恩賜; 恩惠; 恩物。②請求或賜予的恩澤。③請求。 「快樂的。」
boon[2] *adj.* ①仁慈的; 慷慨的; 可愛的。②
boon·dog·gle 〔ˈbunˌdɑgḷ; ˈbuːnˌdɔgl〕 *v.*, **-dog·gled, -dog·gling,** *n.* —*v.i.* 〖美俚〗作瑣細無價值之事。 —*n.* 〖美〗①簡單之手工品。②(童子軍繫於頸際之)皮繩帶。③〖俚〗無價值之工作。 —**boon·dog·gler,** *n.*
boor 〔bur; buə〕 *n.* ①農民。②粗野的人。③(B-)波爾人(＝Boer).
boor·ish 〔ˈburɪʃ; ˈbuəriʃ〕 *adj.* 農民的; 鄉土氣的; 土俗的; 粗野的。—**ly,** *adv.* —**ness,** *n.*
boost 〔bust; buːst〕 *v.t.* ①〖美俗〗由後推; 推上。②〖俚〗爲之吹噓; 捧。③〖俚〗提高; 增加。④〖電〗升壓。 —*n.* ①〖美俗〗推動; 幫助; 後援。②〖美俚〗(價格、薪資、生產等之)提高; 增加。③〖俚〗在商店中行竊。
boost·er 〔ˈbustə; ˈbuːstə〕 *n.* ①〖美俚〗熱心之擁護者; 後援者。②〖電〗升壓機。③〖無線電〗增幅器的一種。④(亦作 **booster dose, booster shot**) 防疫劑之再注射或再次服用, 以維持或增强前劑之效用。⑤ a. 火箭或飛彈發射時之推動引擎。b. 該引擎及燃料所在之第一節火箭。⑥輔助油管。⑦擴炸藥。
booster station 無線電或電視的轉播臺。
boost-glide vehicle 〔ˈbustˌglaɪd~; ˈbuːstglaid~〕 由火箭推送至太空而裝有空氣動力面的乘具(可自由滑翔返回地面)。
‡**boot**[1] 〔but; buːt〕 *n.* ①皮靴; 長靴。high *boots.* 馬靴。②古代夾足刑具。③馬車中裝行李之部分。④馬車夫座前的護板或遮布。⑤踢。⑥〖俚〗美國海軍或陸戰隊之受訓中的新兵。⑦包覆狀之保護物。⑧〖俚〗解雇。⑨〖俚〗快樂。That joke gives me a *boot.* 那個笑話使我高興。 ***bet your boots*** 信賴; 確信。 ***die in one's boots*** (or ***die with one's boots on***) 因公殉職; 陣亡; 死於工作崗位。 ***get the boot*** 被解雇; 被開除。 ***give*** (***one***) ***the boot*** 解雇(某人)。***have*** (***one's***) ***heart in*** (***one's***) ***boots*** 失望; 灰心。 ***lick the boots of*** (or ***lick someone's boots***) 諂媚; 奴性的服從。 ***The boot is on the other leg.*** 情勢逆轉; 責任在他。 ***wipe one's boots on*** 以凌辱之態度對待。—*v.t.* ①穿上靴。②踢; 激勵。③〖俚〗解雇; 趕出。
boot[2] *n.* 利益; 獲益。 ***to boot*** 除…之外。
boot[3] *n.* 戰利品; 贓物。
boot·black 〔ˈbutˌblæk; ˈbuːtblæk〕 *n.* 擦鞋者。 「的。②〖俚〗被開除的; 解雇的。」
boot·ed 〔ˈbutɪd; ˈbuːtid〕 *adj.* ①着靴
Bo·o·tes 〔boˈotiz; bouˈoutiːz〕 *n.* 〖天文〗牧夫座。
***booth** 〔buθ, buð; buːθ, buːð〕 *n.*, *pl.* **booths.** ①市場內之攤棚; 商展等的攤位。②哨崗; 電話亭。③飯館中的小間隔。④臨時的選舉隔離投票所。 「脫靴器。」
boot·jack 〔ˈbutˌdʒæk; ˈbuːtdʒæk〕 *n.*
boot·lace 〔ˈbutˌles; ˈbuːtleis〕 *n.* 〖英〗靴帶。 ***by one's bootlaces*** 與極大的困難獨力奮鬥。
boot·leg 〔ˈbutˌlɛg; ˈbuːtleg〕 *n.*, *v.*, **-leg·ged, -leg·ging,** *adj.* —*n.* ①私酒。②長靴上部; 靴統。 —*v.i.* & *v.t.* 違法地製造、運輸或販賣(酒等)。—*adj.* ①違法製造、販賣或運輸的。②違法的; 祕密的。—**ger,** *n.*
boot·less[1] 〔ˈbutlɪs; ˈbuːtlis〕 *adj.* 無益的; 無用的。—**ly,** *adv.* —**ness,** *n.*
boot·less[2] *adj.* 不穿鞋的; 無靴的。
boot·lick 〔ˈbutˌlɪk; ˈbuːtlik〕 *v.t.* & *v.i.* 〖俚〗諂媚。—**er,** *n.* 「像靴的; 靴形的。」
boot·like 〔ˈbutˌlaɪk; ˈbuːtlaik〕 *adj.*
boot·mak·er 〔ˈbutˌmekə; ˈbuːtˌmei-kə〕 *n.* 製靴者; 靴匠。 「擦靴之僕役。」
boots 〔buts; buːts〕 *n.*, *pl.* **boots.** 〖英〗
boot·strap 〔ˈbutˌstræp; ˈbuːtstræp〕 *n.* 拔靴帶。 ***pull oneself up by one's*** (***own***) ***bootstraps*** 靠自己力量。
boot tree 鞋楦。
***boo·ty** 〔ˈbutɪ; ˈbuːti〕 *n.*, *pl.* **-ties.** ①勝利品; 俘獲物。②刼掠物。③獲得之有價值之物; 獎品。
booze 〔buz; buːz〕 *n.*, *v.*, **boozed, booz-ing.** —*n.* 〖俗〗①飲酒; 痛飲; 酒宴。②酒。 ***on the booze*** 痛飲。—*v.i.* 〖俗〗痛飲; 豪飲。
booz·y 〔ˈbuzɪ; ˈbuːzi〕 *adj.*, **booz·i·er, booz·i·est.** 〖俗〗①酒醉的。②耽於酒的; 嗜酒的。—**booz·i·ly,** *adv.* —**booz·i·ness,** *n.*
bop 〔bɑp; bɔp〕 *n.* 早期的爵士樂。
bo·peep 〔boˈpip; bouˈpiːp〕 *n.* 躲躲貓(面孔一隱一現以逗小孩之遊戲)。 ***play bo-peep*** (政客)要政治權術。
BOQ bachelor officers' quarters.
bor. ①boron. ②borough.
bo·ra 〔ˈborə; ˈbourə〕 *n.* 〖氣象〗布拉風。
bo·rac·ic 〔boˈræsɪk; bouˈræsik〕 *adj.* 硼砂的; 含硼的。 「璃苣。」
bor·age 〔ˈbɜɪdʒ; ˈbɔridʒ〕 *n.* 〖植物〗琉
bo·rate 〔ˈboret; ˈbɔːreit〕 *n.*, *v.*, **-rat·ed, -rat·ing.** —*n.* 〖化〗硼酸鹽; 含硼酸之任何鹽。—*v.t.* 以硼酸或硼砂處理。
bo·rat·ed 〔ˈboretɪd; ˈboureitid〕 *adj.* 以硼砂或硼酸處理的。 「酸鈉。」
bo·rax[1] 〔ˈborəks; ˈbɔːræks〕 *n.* 硼砂; 硼
bo·rax[2] *n.* 〖美俚〗廉價而低級的商品。
Bor·deaux 〔bɔrˈdo; bɔːˈdou〕 *n.* ①波爾多(法國西南部之一海港)。②該地所產的葡萄酒。③加硫酸銅於石灰中所製之一種殺蟲劑。
Bordeaux mixture 波爾多混合劑(一種殺蟲劑)。 「**-los.** 妓院。」
bor·del·lo 〔bɔrˈdɛlo; bɔːˈdelou〕 *n.*, *pl.*
‡**bor·der** 〔ˈbɔrdə; ˈbɔːdə〕 *n.* ①邊; 界線; 邊緣。They live on the *border* of starvation. 他們生活在飢餓邊緣。 He is on the *border* of fifty. 他年近五十。②邊境。 The bandits fled across the *border.* 強盜們逃過邊境。③窄邊; 滾邊。④狹長之花床; 其上之花草。⑤戲臺上的狹長繪圖帆布。 ***the Border*** a. 美國與墨西哥邊境。b. 英格蘭與蘇格蘭交界處。—*v.t.* ①加邊; 鑲邊。②接連; 毗連。 Scotland *borders* England. 蘇格蘭毗連英格蘭。③作…之疆界。—*v.i.* ①接壤; 接境。②近於; 接近。 Such an act *borders* on folly. 這種行爲近於愚蠢。 「境居民。」
bor·der·er 〔ˈbɔrdərə; ˈbɔːdərə〕 *n.* 邊
bor·der·ism 〔ˈbɔrdərɪzṃ; ˈbɔːdərizm〕 *n.* 邊境居民之特殊語言、習慣。
bor·der·land 〔ˈbɔrdəˌlænd; ˈbɔːdə-lænd〕 *n.* ①邊界之地。②模糊含混之情境。

bor·der·line [ˈbɔrdɚˌlaɪn; ˈbɔːdəlain] *n.* 界線;國界。—*adj.* ①邊境上的。②在兩類之間的;不確定的。a *borderline* case. 介乎二者之間的情形。③跡近不雅或猥褻的。

Border States ①〖美史〗美國內戰期間,那些有合法奴隸制度之州,而與聯邦妥協並未脫離聯邦者。②〖美〗接壤加拿大之州。③與蘇聯接壤的中、北歐諸國。

***bore**[1] [bor; bɔː] *v.*, **bored, bor·ing,** *n.* —*v.t.* ①穿;鑽;鑿。②排衆向前;鑽進〖常through, into〗。—*v.i.* ①鑽孔;穿孔。This gimlet *bores* well. 這把錐很利。②(物質)容納穿鑽。—*n.* ①孔。②管腔;鎗膛。③口徑;鎗砲的口徑。—**a·ble,** —**bor·a·ble,** *adj.*

bore[2] *v.*, **bored, bor·ing,** *n.* —*v.t.* 令人厭煩;打擾。—*n.* 令人討厭的人或事。

bore[3] *n.*①海嘯。②激潮;高潮。

bore[4] *v.* pt. of **bear**[1].

bo·re·al [ˈborɪəl; ˈbouriəl] *adj.* ①北方的;北風的。②(B-)Boreas 的。

Bo·re·as [ˈborɪəs; ˈbɔriæs] *n.* ①〖希臘神話〗北風之神。②北風。「討厭;厭倦;無趣。」

bore·dom[ˈbordəm; ˈbɔːdəm] *n.*厭煩;

bor·er [ˈborɚ; ˈbɔːrə] *n.* ①穿孔者;鑽孔器。②在水果中鑽孔之蟲。「人厭煩的。」

bore·some[ˈborsəm; ˈbɔːsəm] *adj.* 令

bo·ric [ˈborɪk; ˈbɔːrik] *adj.* 含硼的。

boric acid 硼酸。

bo·ride [ˈboraɪd; ˈbɔraid] *n.* 〖化〗硼化物。

bor·ing [ˈborɪŋ; ˈbɔːriŋ] *adj.* ①鑽孔用的。②令人厭倦的。—*n.* ①鑽孔;打孔。②鑽成之孔。③(*pl.*)鑽屑;鏜花。

‡**born** [born; bɔːn] *adj.* ①生來的。②天生的。He is a *born* poet. 他是個天生的詩人。—*v.* pp. of **bear**[1]. ***born yesterday*** 天眞的;缺乏經驗的。

borne [born; bɔːn] *v.* pp. of **bear**[1]. 〖注意〗**borne** 是 bear 的過去分詞。當做"生"解時,不加 by 的被動式用 born, 如:He was born in 1900. 他於1900年生。此外,仍用 borne, 如:She had borne five children. 她已生了五個小孩。「—**Bor·ne·an,** *adj.*」

Bor·ne·o[ˈbornɪˌo; ˈbɔːniou] *n.*婆羅洲。

bor·ne·ol [ˈbornɪˌol; ˈbɔːnioul] *n.* 〖化〗龍腦;冰片。「銅礦。」

born·ite [ˈbɔrnaɪt; ˈbɔːnait] *n.* 〖礦〗斑

bo·ron [ˈboran; ˈbɔːrɔn] *n.* 〖化〗硼。

boron nitride 〖化〗氮化硼。

bo·ro·sil·i·cate [ˌborəˈsɪləkɪt, -ˌket, ˌbɔr-; ˌbourəˈsilikeit] *n.* 〖化〗硼矽酸鹽。

***bor·ough** [ˈbɝo; ˈbʌrə] *n.* ①〖美〗享有自治權的市鎮。②紐約市之一區。③〖英〗**a.** 自治市鎮。**b.** 議會中有代表的市鎮。

bor·ough-Eng·lish [ˈbɝoˈɪŋglɪʃ; ˈbʌrəˈiŋgliʃ] *n.*〖英法律〗幼子繼承制。

bor·row** [ˈbaro; ˈbɔrou] *v.t.* ①借;借用;借入。He *borrows* money from me frequently. 他常向我借錢。②採取;採用。③借用外語。④〖算術〗做減法時向左邊一位數借一。—*v.i.* 借。Some people neither *borrow* nor lend. 有些人不借亦不貸。borrow trouble*** 杞人憂天;悲觀。—**a·ble,** *adj.* —**er,** *n.*

borsch [borʃ; bɔːʃ] *n.* 羅宋湯(俄式加甜菜肉湯)。(亦作 **borscht, borsht**)

Bor·stal system [ˈbɔrstəl~; ˈbɔːstl~] 〖英〗少年犯感化制度。(亦作 **Borstal institution**) 「**boart, bortz**」

bort [bort; bɔːt] *n.* 下等金剛鑽。(亦作

bor·zoi [ˈbɔrzɔɪ; ˈbɔːzɔi] *n.* 俄國狼犬。

bos·cage, bos·kage [ˈbaskɪdʒ; ˈbɔskidʒ] *n.* 密集之灌木;叢林。「話。」

bosh [baʃ; bɔʃ] *n.*, *interj.* 〖俗〗胡說;空

bosk [bask; bɔsk] *n.* 矮林;叢林。(亦作 **bosket, bosquet**)

bosk·y [ˈbaskɪ; ˈbɔski] *adj.*, **bosk·i·er, bosk·i·est.** ①林木叢生的。②蔭蔽的。

***bos·om** [ˈbuzəm; ˈbuzəm] *n.*①胸;懷。He kept the letter in his *bosom.* 他把這封信置於懷中。②(衣服的)胸襟。③中心;內部。④任何溫暖、舒適而熟悉的地方。⑤胸懷(感情之源);心裏;心腹。to speak one's *bosom.* 說出由衷之言。⑥(海、湖、河等之)表面。on the *bosom* of the ocean. 在海面上。⑦女人之乳房。—*adj.* 親密的;知己的。He is my *bosom* friend. 他是我的知友。—*v.t.* ①懷抱。②隱匿。「人)有大胸脯的。」

bos·om·y [ˈbuzəmɪ; ˈbuzəmi] *adj.* (女

***boss**[1] [bɔs; bɔs] *n.* 〖俗〗①工頭;老板。He is fired by his *boss.* 他被老板開除。②領袖;首腦;〖美〗控制某地區政黨機構的頭子。—*v.t.* 〖俗〗指揮;監督。He *bossed* them to do this. 他指揮他們做這事。—*v.i.*做老板;作威作福。—*adj.* ①〖俗〗主要的;首要的。②〖俚〗第一流的。「突起物。」

boss[2] *n.* 突起物。—*v.t.* (在平面上)飾以

bossed [bɔst, bast; bɔst] *adj.* 有浮凸之飾物的。「眼受傷的;斜視的。」

boss-eyed [ˈbasˌaɪd; ˈbɔsaid] *adj.* 一

boss·ism [ˈbasɪzəm; ˈbɔsizəm] *n.* 〖美俚〗頭子的控制(尤指政治方面)。

boss·y[1] [ˈbɔsɪ; ˈbɔsi] *adj.*, **boss·i·er, boss·i·est.** 〖俗〗擅權的;跋扈的。—**boss·i·ness,** *n.* 「浮凸之飾物的。」

boss·y[2] *adj.*, **boss·i·er, boss·i·est.** 有

Bos·ton [ˈbɔstn̩; ˈbɔstən] *n.* ①波士頓(美國麻薩諸塞州之首府)。②(b-)一種紙牌戲。③一種類似華爾玆的舞步。

Boston bag 一種旅行袋。

Bos·to·ni·an [bɔsˈtonɪən; bɔsˈtounjən] *adj.* 波士頓(人)的。—*n.* 波士頓人。

Boston Massacre 〖美史〗1775年3月5日在波士頓發生反對當時英駐軍之暴動,英軍向暴民開槍而造成死傷。「茶葉事件。」

Boston Tea Party 〖美史〗波士頓

Bos·well [ˈbazwɛl; ˈbɔzwəl] *n.* ①包斯威爾(James, 1740–1795, 蘇格蘭律師及作家,曾著 Samuel Johnson傳)。②爲知友作傳者。

BOT Bank of Taiwan. 臺灣銀行。

bot [bat; bɔt] *n.* 馬蠅之幼蟲。(亦作**bott**)

bot. ①botanical. ②botanist. ③botany.

B.O.T. Board of Trade.

***bo·tan·i·cal** [boˈtænɪkl; bəˈtænikəl] *adj.* 植物學的;植物的。a *botanical* garden. 植物園。—*n.* 植物性藥品。(亦作 **botanic**) —**ly,** *adv.* 「物學家。」

bot·a·nist [ˈbatn̩ɪst; ˈbɔtənist] *n.* 植

bot·a·nize [ˈbatn̩ˌaɪz; ˈbɔtənaiz] *v.*, **-nized, -niz·ing.** —*v.i.* 採集植物;研究植物。—*v.t.* 研究植物。

***bot·a·ny** [ˈbatn̩ɪ; ˈbɔtəni] *n.*, *pl.* **-nies.** ①植物學。②植物誌。③一地方之植物(集合稱)。④(植物之)生理。⑤一種細羊毛。

botch [batʃ; bɔtʃ] *v.t.* ①拙劣地補綴。②因工作笨拙而弄壞。—*n.* ①拙劣的補綴(處)。②拙笨之作品;笨活。③〖英方〗腫瘍。—**er·y,** *n.* 「工匠。②小鮭魚。」

botch·er [ˈbatʃɚ; ˈbɔtʃə] *n.* ①拙劣之

botch·y [ˈbatʃɪ; ˈbɔtʃi] *adj.*, **botch·i·er, botch·i·est.** 工作甚拙的;製作不精的。

bot·fly [ˈbatˌflaɪ; ˈbɔtflai] *n.*, *pl.*

-flies. 馬蠅。

:both [boθ;bouθ] *adj.* 二;兩方的。—*pron.* 二者;兩者。*Both* were there.兩個都在那邊。—*adv.* 並;又;兩皆。—*conj.* 而且;既…而又;兩皆。He is *both* strong and healthy. 他既強壯又健康。

·both·er [ˈbaðɚ; ˈbɔðə] *n.* ①麻煩;困擾。It is a needless *bother*. 這是不必要的麻煩。②可厭的人;討厭的事。③焦慮。④努力;煩心。—*v.t.* ①煩擾;攪擾。Don't *bother* him. 不要擾亂他。②使感不安;使焦慮。—*v.i.* 煩悶;煩惱。***bother one's head*** (or ***oneself***) ***about*** 焦慮。—*interj.* 〖主英〗討厭!

both·er·a·tion [ˌbaðəˈreʃən; ˌbɔðəˈreiʃən] *n.*, *interj.* 〖俗〗苦惱;麻煩。

both·er·some [ˈbaðəsəm; ˈbɔðəsəm] *adj.* 引起麻煩的;惹人煩惱的。

both·y, both·ie [ˈbaθɪ, ˈbaðɪ; ˈbɔθi] *n.*, *pl.* **both·ies.** 〖蘇〗小舍;茅屋。

bo tree [bo~; bou~]菩提樹。

Bots·wa·na [batsˈwana; bɔtsˈwaːnə] *n.* 波紮那(原名 Bechuanaland, 位於南非,首都 Gaberones)。

:bot·tle [ˈbatḷ; ˈbɔtl] *n.*, *v.*, **-tled, -tling.** —*n.* ①瓶。This *bottle* leaks badly. 這瓶漏得很厲害。②一瓶容量。He drank two *bottles* of wine. 他飲了兩瓶酒。***hit the bottle*** 〖俗〗 **a.** 酗酒。**b.** 喝醉。***the bottle*** **a.** 酒。Keep him from *the bottle*. 不要他飲酒。**b.** (嬰兒食的)裝於瓶中的牛奶。He was raised on *the bottle*. 他是吃牛奶養大的。—*v.t.* ①裝入瓶中。②隱藏;抑制。***bottle up*** **a.** 抑制;隱藏。He *bottled up* his anger. 他抑制他的憤怒。**b.** 擁塞。

bottle baby 用奶瓶養育的嬰孩。

bottle brush ①洗瓶刷。②〖植物〗天花榮;問荊。

bottle cap 瓶蓋。

bottled gas 筒裝液化瓦斯。

bot·tle-fed [ˈbatḷˌfɛd; ˈbɔtlfed] *adj.* 用牛乳養育的;人工營養的。

bottle glass 深綠色製瓶用之普通玻璃。

bottle gourd 細頸葫蘆。

bottle green 深綠色。

bot·tle-green [ˈbatḷˌgrin; ˈbɔtlgriːn] *adj.* 深綠色的。

bot·tle·hold·er [ˈbatḷˌholdɚ; ˈbɔtlˌhouldə] *n.* ①執瓶的人;瓶架。②(拳賽中)拳師之隨伴者。③〖俗〗助勢者;聲援者。

bot·tle·neck [ˈbatḷˌnɛk; ˈbɔtlnek] *n.* ①瓶頸。②狹道;隘路。③任何進步之阻礙;障礙。—*v.t.* 阻塞。—*v.i.* ①受阻。②變狹。—*adj.* 如瓶頸一般狹窄的;有阻礙的。

bot·tle·nose [ˈbatḷˌnoz; ˈbɔtlnouz] *n.* 槌鯨(鯨魚之一種)。

bottle nose 酒糟鼻子。

bot·tle-nosed [ˈbatḷˌnozd; ˈbɔtlnouzd] *adj.* 有酒糟鼻子的(人)。

bottle opener 開瓶器。

bottle party 參加者各攜酒一瓶之聚會。

bottle washer ①洗瓶人;洗瓶器。②雜役;散工。③職位低卑者;僚屬。

:bot·tom [ˈbatəm; ˈbɔtəm] *n.* ①底;底部。②基;基址。the *bottom* of a wall. 牆基。③水底。The boat sank to the *bottom*. 船沉於水底。④坐墊;坐的部分;臀部。⑤根本;基礎;來源。⑥心底深處。I thank him from the *bottom* of my heart. 我衷心感謝他。⑦船;船底。⑧最低點;最壞的地步。⑨〖棒球〗(每一局之)下半局。***at*** (***the***) ***bottom*** 實際地;基本地。***at the bottom of*** 眞正的原因;負責。***Bottoms up!*** 〖俗〗乾杯! ***go to the bottom*** (船)沉入水底。***knock the bottom out of*** (***an argument***) 證明(某一論證之)錯誤。—*adj.* ①最後的;最低的。They sold their goods at *bottom* price. 他們以最低的價錢出售貨物。②基本的。The *bottom* cause for his illness is wine. 酒是他生病的基本原因。***bet one's bottom dollar*** 〖俚〗傾囊下注;以所有的錢打賭;確信。—*v.t.* ①供以底或墊。②以…爲基礎〖常on, upon〗. They wanted to *bottom* their dreams on a solid basis. 他們要把他們的夢建立在堅固的基礎上。③使(酒艇)停在海底。④爲…追根究底;探究。—*v.i.* ①以某事爲根據或基礎〖on, upon〗. Find on what foundation the proposition *bottoms*. 找出這命題建立在甚麼基礎上。②觸底; 到底。to *bottom* on the bed of the sea. 臥於海底。

bottom grass 長在低地的草。

bottom land 有河流通過之低地。

bot·tom·less [ˈbatəmlɪs; ˈbɔtəmlis] *adj.* ①無底的。②深不可量的。③深不可解的;難解的。④無限的。

bot·tom·most [ˈbatəmˌmost; ˈbɔtəmmoust] *adj.* 最低的;最下的。

bot·tom·ry [ˈbatəmrɪ; ˈbɔtəmri] *n.* 船舶押款契約;冒險貸借。

bot·u·lin [ˈbatʃəlɪn; ˈbɔtjulin] *n.* 臘腸桿菌毒素;鹹肉毒素。

bot·u·lism [ˈbatʃəˌlɪzəm; ˈbɔtjulizəm] *n.* 〖醫〗肉類中毒;臘腸中毒。

bou·doir [buˈdwar; ˈbuːdwaː] *n.* 女性之會客室或化妝室;閨房。

Bou·gain·vil·lae·a [ˌbugənˈvɪlɪə; ˌbuːgənˈviliə] *n.* 〖植物〗①九重葛屬(南美產之一種生長小花的熱帶灌木)。②(b-)九重葛屬之任一種植物;九重葛。

·bough [bau; bau] *n.* 樹枝。a *bough* loaded with apples. 蘋果纍纍的一枝。

bough·pot [ˈbauˌpat; ˈbaupɔt] *n.* ①花瓶;花鉢。②〖英方〗花束。(亦作 **bowpot**)

:bought [bɔt; bɔːt] *v.* pt. & pp. of **buy.**

bought·en [ˈbɔtṇ; ˈbɔːtn] *adj.* 〖美方〗買來的;購進的(爲 homemade 之對)。

bou·gie [ˈbudʒɪ; ˈbuːʒiː] *n.* ①〖外科〗探條;探子。②蠟燭。

bouil·la·baisse [ˌbuljəˈbes; ˌbuːljəˈbeis] 〖法〗 *n.* 魚羹。

bouil·lon [ˈbuljan; ˈbuːjɔ̃ːŋ] 〖法〗*n.* 肉湯;牛肉湯。

·boul·der [ˈboldɚ; ˈbouldə] *n.* 大的鵝卵石(尤指圓而經水侵蝕的)。(亦作**bowlder**)

Boulder Dam 美國 Colorado 河上位於 Nevada 及 Arizona 州界的世界最高水壩。(亦作 **Hoover Dam**)

Bou·le [ˈbuli; ˈbuːliː] *n.* ①(希臘之)議會;下院。②(b-)(古代希臘之)立法會議。

boul·e·vard [ˈbuləˌvard; ˈbuːlvaː] *n.* 林蔭大道。

boul·ter [ˈboltɚ; ˈboultə] *n.* 附有多個釣鉤之釣絲。

·bounce [bauns; bauns] *v.*, **bounced, bounc·ing,** *n.*, *adv.* —*v.i.* ①跳;跳回;反躍。A ball *bounces* from the wall. 球由牆上跳回來。②上下地跳。③一躍而出;狂怒而跳;亂跳。He *bounced* out of the room. 他從房內憤然跳出。***bounce back*** 捲土重來。—*v.t.* ①使…跳;使…反躍。He *bounced* a ball. 他(拍球)使球反躍。②〖俚〗抛出…。③〖俚〗解雇;開革。④斥責。—*n.* ①跳;反躍。Catch the ball on the first *bounce*. 在球第一次回躍時,將其捉住。②自誇;吹噓。③〖俚〗解雇

to get the *bounce*. 被解雇;被開革。④彈力;彈性。⑤活力。There is *bounce* in his step. 他的脚步很有活力。⑥重擊。⑦雷達儀上目標影像之變化。—*adv.* 突然地。

bounc·er [ˈbaunsɚ; ˈbaunsə] *n.* ①很大的東西;一類中之龐然大物。②〖俗〗愛吹嘘的人;自誇者。③〖俚〗(旅館等中的)保鏢;鏢客。

bounc·ing [ˈbaunsɪŋ; ˈbaunsiŋ] *adj.* ①跳躍的。②强健的;精神飽滿的;健美的。③誇大的;巨大的;嘈雜的。**—ly,** *adv.*

bounc·y [ˈbaunsɪ; ˈbaunsi] *adj.*, **bounc·i·er, bounc·i·est.** 〖俗〗①跳躍的。②顛簸的。③有彈性的。④有活潑節奏的。⑤有生氣的。⑥有活力的。⑦充滿自信的。

bound¹** [baund; baund] *v.* pt. & pp. of **bind.** —*adj.* ①被縛的。He kicked at the *bound* prisoner. 他踢這被縛的囚犯。②裝訂好的;有封面的。③負有義務的;應盡責的;受拘束的。He is *bound* in duty to obey. 他在職務上必須服從。④一定的;必然的。⑤〖俗〗決心的;決意的。He is *bound* to go. 他決心去。⑥深愛的。She is *bound* to her family. 她深愛自己家人。⑦患便祕的。be bound up in***(or ***with***) **a.** 對…發生濃厚興趣;喜歡…;專心於…。**b.** 同…密切連繫。**c.** 相依爲命。**—ness,** *n.*

***bound²** *v.i.* ①跳躍;疾步跳躍而前行;躍上躍下。The deer *bounded* over the fence. 這鹿跳過籬笆。②回跳;反躍。—*n.*①跳;躍。Few men rise to eminence at one *bound*. 很少人一躍而成名。②反躍。

bound³** *n.*(*pl.*)①界限;境界;範圍。Scientists advance the *bounds* of knowledge. 科學家推進知識的範圍。②可以合法出入之地。out of bounds*** **a.** 禁止的;禁止入內的。**b.** 在界線之外。The ball bounced *out of bounds*. 球跳出界外。—*v.t.* ①限制。Our ideas are *bounded* by our experience. 我們的思想受經驗的限制。②爲…之疆界;形成…之限界。③指出水陸的界線;指出疆界。Can you *bound* France? 你能指出法國的疆界嗎? —*v.i.* 有一疆界;接界〖on〗. Canada *bounds* on the United States. 加拿大與美國接界。**—a·ble,** *adj.*

bound⁴ *adj.* 準備要去的;駛往的;行向的;開往的。The train is *bound* for Tainan. 這火車準備開往臺南。outward *bound*. 向外國開駛的。homeward *bound*. 駛回本國的。

***bound·a·ry** [ˈbaundərɪ; ˈbaundəri] *n., pl.* **-ries.** 界線;邊界;境界。

boundary beacon 〖電訊〗示界標。

boundary layer 〖數學、物理〗邊界流層。

boundary line 界線。

***bounded set** 〖數學〗有界集;囿集。

bounded variation 〖數學〗有界變分;有界變差;囿變。

bound·en [ˈbaundən; ˈbaundən] *adj.* ①受恩的;感恩的。②義務的;本分的。one's *bounden* duty. 某人之本分。

bound·er [ˈbaundɚ; ˈbaundə] *n.* ①定境界之人;置界標之人。②〖俗〗粗魯之人;服裝俗惡之人。③〖棒球〗跳球。

bound form 〖語言〗束縛型(恆與他型連用而不能獨立的部分,如英文之字首字尾)。

***bound·less** [ˈbaundlɪs; ˈbaundlis] *adj.* 無限的;無窮的。the *boundless* ocean. 無垠的海洋。—**ly,** *adv.* **—ness,** *n.*

boun·te·ous [ˈbauntɪəs; ˈbauntiəs] *adj.* ①慷慨的;好施的。②豐富的;充足的。

boun·ti·ful [ˈbauntəfəl; ˈbauntiful] *adj.* ①大方的;慷慨的。②豐富的;充足的。

***boun·ty** [ˈbauntɪ; ˈbaunti] *n., pl.* **-ties.** ①慷慨;好施。②施與;慷慨的布施。③獎金。

bounty hunter 爲獎金而搜捕罪犯或追取獵物者。

***bou·quet** [boˈke, buˈke *for* ①③buˈke *for* ②;ˈbukei, buˈkei] *n.* ①花束;花球。②芳香。③恭維。*bouquets* and brickbats. 恭維和譏評。

Bour·bon [ˈbʊrbən; ˈbuəbən] *n.* ①波旁皇族。②政治上之極端保守分子。③ (b-) (亦作 **bourbon whiskey**) 一種威士忌酒。**—ism,** *n.*

bour·don [ˈbʊrdn̩; ˈbuədn] *n.* 〖音樂〗①單調之低音。②風琴之最低音栓。

Bourdon-tube gauge 〖化〗壓力計。

bourg [burg; buəg] *n.* ①(中古時期,尤指近城堡之)村鎮。②法國之市集。

bour·geois¹ [burˈʒwɑ; ˈbuəʒwɑː] *n., pl.* **-geois,** *adj.* —*n.* 中等階級的人;中產階級的人;資產階級的人。***the bourgeois*** 中產階級之集合稱。—*adj.* ①屬於中等階級的;中產階級的;資產階級的。②平凡的;普通的。

bour·geois² [bɚˈdʒɔɪs; bəːˈdʒɔis] *n.* 〖印刷〗一種九磅因之活字。

bour·geoi·sie [ˌburʒwɑˈzi; ˌbuəʒwɑːˈziː] *n.* ①中產階級。②(馬克思學說中與無產階級相對之) 資產階級。③以中產階級爲主的社會秩序。

bour·geon [ˈbɝdʒən; ˈbəːdʒən] *v.i.* =**burgeon.**

bourn(e)¹ [born;buən] *n.* 〖蘇〗小溪。

bourn(e)² *n.* 〖古〗①目的地;目標。②境界;界限。

bour·rée [buˈre; ˈburei] *n.* ①法國、西班牙一種類似甘伐舞的舊式舞蹈。②此種舞曲。

bourse [burs; buəs] *n.* 商業交易中心;證券交易所。

bouse [baus; bauz] *v.t.* & *v.i.*, **boused, bous·ing.** 〖航海〗(以索具、船具等)拉;升起。(亦作 **bowse**)

bou·stro·phe·don [ˌbustrəˈfidn̩; ˌbaustrəˈfiːdən] *n.* 由左而右,復由右而左交互成行之書法(早期希臘文之寫法)。

bout [baut;baut] *n.* ①一個回合。②一次;一番;一巡。③發作。a *bout* of illness. 病的一次發作。④競爭;比賽。a *bout* at boxing. 比拳。⑤打仗。***this bout*** 此時;此次。

bou·ton·nière [ˌbutn̩ˈjɛr; ˌbuːtənˈjɛə] 〖法〗 *n.* 插於鈕孔上之花。

bouts ri·més [buriˈme; ˈbuːˈriːmei] 〖法〗一種作詩遊戲,指定押韻之字若干,由參加者補成詩句,綴成詩篇,盛於十八世紀。

bo·vine [ˈbovaɪn; ˈbouvain] *adj.* ①牛族的;牛的。②似牛的;遲鈍的;笨拙的。③無感情的。***bovine tuberculosis*** 牛結核(可由病牛之奶傳染給人類)。—*n.* 牛;似牛之動物。

bovine vaccine 牛痘苗。

Bov·ril [ˈbɑvrɪl; ˈbɔvril] *n.* 〖商標名〗保衞爾牛肉汁。

bov·ver [ˈbɑvɚ; ˈbɔvə] *n.* 〖英俚〗街頭鬥毆。

‡bow¹ [bau; bau] *v.t.* ①彎(腰);俯(首)。②鞠躬以迎送賓客。The host *bowed* his guests out (in). 主人鞠躬送(迎)客。③挫折;壓彎。④屈服。⑤以鞠躬表示。to *bow* one's thanks. 鞠躬表示謝意。—*v.i.*①鞠躬。②屈服;服從;膜拜。***bow and scrape*** 過於客氣;奴顏婢膝。***bow down*** **a.** 壓彎。**b.** 崇拜。***bow out*** **a.** 由…退出。**b.** 送出。***bow up*** 〖方〗忍無可忍而反抗。—*n.* 鞠躬。He gave me a *bow*. 他向我鞠躬。***make one's***

bow 初次公演;初次與觀衆見面。***take a bow*** 接受觀衆或聽衆之鼓掌;上前謝幕。

:bow² 〔bo; bou〕 *n.* ①弓。②彎曲;任何彎曲的形狀。the *bow* of one's lips. 嘴唇所成的弧形。③蝶形。The ribbon is tied in a *bow*. 絲帶結成蝶結。④樂弓。A violin is played with a *bow*. 小提琴是用弓奏的。⑤弓形物。⑥弓箭手。⑦〖美〗眼鏡兩側之支架。⑧〖美〗(剪刀、鑰匙等之)環狀柄。⑨樂弓在絃上之一擊。***have two strings to one's bow*** 有一個以上的計畫;準備有替換的辦法。—*v.t.* ①使彎曲。②用弓奏(如小提琴)。—*v.i.* ①彎曲。②用弓奏樂。—*adj.* ①弓形的。*bow* legs. 弓形腿。②蝶形的。a *bow* tie. 蝶形領結。

bow³** 〔bau; bau〕 *n.* 船首;飛機的前部。bows on*** 直衝地。The ship approached us *bows on*. 船向我們直衝過來。***bows under*** 船首沒於浪中。***on the bow*** 在正前方直線的45度角以內。

bow back 〔bo～; bou～〕 由一根木條所做的馬蹄形椅背。

Bow bells 〔bo～; bou～〕 倫敦 St. Mary-le-Bow 教堂之鐘。

bow·ditch 〔ˈbaudɪtʃ; ˈbauditʃ〕 *n.* 航海手册。

bowd·ler·ize 〔ˈbaudləˌraɪz; ˈbaudləraiz〕 *v.t.*, **-ized, -iz·ing.** 刪去(著作之)猥褻字句(由於 Thomas Bowdler 於 1818 年刊行莎士比亞全集之刪節本)。 **—bowd·ler·i·za·tion, bowd·ler·ism,** *n.*

bowed 〔bod; boud〕 *adj.* 彎曲如弓的;有弓的。

bow·el** 〔ˈbauəl; ˈbauəl〕 *n., v.*, **-eled, -el·ing.**—*n.* ①(常 *pl.*)腸。Do your *bowels* move? 你大便通嗎?②(*pl.*)內部。③(*pl.*)慈悲;憐憫;同情。He has no *bowels*. 他沒有慈悲心。bowel movement*** **a.** 大便;通便。**b.** 糞便;屎。—*v.t.* 將腸從(體內)取出。

***bow·er¹** 〔ˈbauɚ; ˈbauə〕 *n.* ①樹蔭的地方;園亭。②〖詩〗小屋村舍。③〖古〗閨房;寢室。④船首之錨。—*v.t.* 使成爲蔭蔽之所。**—y,** *adj.*

bow·er² *n.* 彎曲者;彎腰作揖者;鞠躬者。

bow·er³ *n.*船首二錨之任一。

bow·er⁴ 〔ˈboɚ; ˈbouə〕 *n.* 〖音樂〗提琴演奏者。

bow·er-maid 〔ˈbauɚˌmed; ˈbauəmeid〕 *n.* 侍婢。

bow·er·y 〔ˈbauərɪ; ˈbauəri〕 *n., pl.* **-er·ies.** ①紐約早期荷蘭移民之農場。②(B-)紐約之一街道名(其地多廉價之旅社、酒店等)。

bow hand 〔bo～; bou～〕 ①持弓之手(通常爲左手)。②拉琴弓之手(通常爲右手)。***on the bow hand*** 全錯了。

bow·head 〔ˈboˌhɛd; ˈbouhed〕 *n.*北極海中的一種頭與口特大之鯨。(亦作 **Greenland whale**)

bow·ie 〔ˈbo·ɪ; ˈboui〕 *n.* 一種鋼製單刃獵刀。

bow·ing 〔ˈboɪŋ; ˈbouiŋ〕 *n.* (拉提琴之)弓法。

bowing acquaintance 點頭之交。

bow·knot 〔ˈboˌnɑt; ˈbounɔt〕 *n.* 滑結;活結;蝴蝶結。

:bowl¹ 〔bol; boul〕 *n.* ①碗;缽。②一碗的容量。He can eat three *bowls* of rice. 他能吃三碗飯。③物的凹處;碗形的東西;煙斗的凹處。④大酒杯。⑤宴飲;飲酒。⑥(=bowl game) 美國於每年元旦所舉行的大學足球比賽,由當年足球季內的優秀校隊參加。⑦形似碗缽的球場、音樂廳等建築。—*v.t.* 使成盆形。

bowl² *n.* ①保齡球所用之木球。②(*pl.*)(作 *sing.* 解)滾木球戲(=lawn bowling).③(保齡球或 lawn bowling 中)球的一擲。—*v.t.* ①旋轉;滾(木球)。②〖保齡球〗用球撞倒(木瓶)。③玩(保齡球)。—*v.i.* 滑動(如球)。***bowl down*** 〖俗〗打倒。***bowl over*** 使狼狽;吃驚。

bow·leg 〔ˈboˌlɛg; ˈbouleg〕 *n.* 向外彎曲之腿;弓形腿;膝內翻。**—ged,** *adj.* **—ged·ness,** *n.*

bowl·er¹ 〔ˈbolɚ; ˈboulə〕 *n.* ①玩保齡球者。②〖板球〗投球手。

bowl·er² *n.* 〖英〗一種圓頂高帽。

bowl·ful 〔ˈbolful; ˈboulful〕 *n.* 一碗或一缽之量。

bow·line 〔ˈbolɪn; ˈboulin〕 *n.* 〖航海〗帆脚索。

bowline knot 〖航海〗帆繩結。

bowl·ing 〔ˈbolɪŋ; ˈbouliŋ〕 *n.* ①保齡球戲。②〖板球〗投球。

bowling alley ①保齡球場。②滾保齡球球槽。

bowling green lawn bowling 的草地球場。

bowling pin 保齡球戲中的木瓶(共十個)。

bow·man¹ 〔ˈbomən; ˈboumən〕 *n., pl.* **-men.** 射手;弓箭手。

bow·man² 〔ˈbaumən; ˈbaumən〕 *n., pl.* **-men.** 划船頭槳者;前槳手。

bow saw 〔bo～; bou～〕 弓鋸;弧鋸。

bow·shot 〔ˈboˌʃɑt; ˈbou-ʃɔt〕 *n.* 一箭之遙;射距。

bow·sprit 〔ˈbauˌsprɪt; ˈbou-sprit〕 *n.* 〖航海〗船首斜桅。

Bow Street 〔bo～; bou～〕 倫敦市街名(違警法庭所在地)。***Bow Street runner*** (or ***officer***) (英國早期之)警官。

bow·string 〔ˈboˌstrɪŋ; ˈbou-striŋ〕 *n., v.*, **-stringed** or **-strung, -string·ing.** —*n.* ①弓弦。②絞索。—*v.t.* 以索絞殺。

bow tie 〔bo～; bou～〕 蝶形領結。

bow window 〔bo～; bou～〕 ①弓形窗;凸窗。②〖俗〗大腹;大腹便便者。

bow·wow 〔ˈbauˈwau; ˈbauˈwau〕 *n.* ①犬吠聲。②=**dog.** ***go to the bowwows*** 變糟;落敗。—*v.i.* ①(犬)吠;作吠聲。②咆哮。—*adj.* 神氣活現的。

bow·yer 〔ˈbojɚ; ˈboujə〕 *n.* ①製弓匠。②射手。

:box¹ 〔bɑks; bɔks〕 *n.* ①箱;盒;匣。He made a *box* with paper board. 他用紙板做一個箱。②一箱的容量。I gave him two *boxes* of oranges. 我給他兩箱蜜柑。③戲院的包廂。④席。press *box*. 記者席。⑤〖機械〗箱;函;軸箱。⑥小亭;馬車上御者的坐位。⑦馬廄中供馬活動之部分。⑧〖美,棒球〗投手區;打擊區;教練區。pitcher's *box*. 投手區。⑨(報紙、雜誌上)花邊框出的文章。⑩裝於匣中的禮物。⑪困境。⑫〖英〗小屋;電話亭;衣箱。⑬爵士樂隊之絃樂器(如吉他);鋼琴。⑭〖俗〗留聲機。⑮小格信箱。⑯馬廄內栓馬之隔間。⑰(*pl.*)坐在包廂裏的觀(聽)衆。***in a*** (***tight***) ***box***處於窘境中。***in the wrong box*** 不得其所;錯誤;困難。—*v.t.* ①裝於箱中。②(於競賽中)擋住(對手使他不能超前)〖常 in〗. ***box the compass*** **a.** 依次舉示羅盤的方位。**b.** 屢屢改變而復歸原處。***box up*** 關閉;拘禁。

box² *n.* 一拳;一摑;一掌。to give a person a *box* on the ear. 摑某人一個耳光。—*v.t.* 掌擊;拳擊;摑。She *boxed* him on the ear. 她摑他的頰。—*v.i.* ①拳鬥。They *boxed* with each other. 他們彼此拳鬥。②爲職業拳擊家。

box³ *n.* 黃楊;黃楊木。

Box and Cox 輪流;交替 (Box 及 Cox 爲 J. M. Morton 所編趣劇中人物,二人同居一室,一日間外出,一夜間外出)。***Box and Cox arrangement*** 兩人輪流的辦法。

box and needle〖航海〗羅盤。
box calf 一種有方形印痕之小牛皮。
box camera 構造簡單的箱型照相機。
box·car (ˈbɑksˌkɑr; ˈbɔkskɑː) *n.* 貨車車廂。—*adj.* 龐大的。
box cloth 一種厚毛呢。
box coat 一種寬鬆的大衣。
box·er (ˈbɑksɚ; ˈbɔksə) *n.* ①將貨物裝箱之人或機器。②拳師;鬥拳者。
Boxer Indemnity 庚子賠款。
boxer shorts 男短內褲。
box·haul (ˈbɑksˌhɔl; ˈbɔkshɔːl) *v.t.*〖航海〗令(船)順風勢而小轉。
box·i·ness (ˈbɑksɪnɪs; ˈbɔksinis) *n.* 四四方方的樣子。
***box·ing**[1] (ˈbɑksɪŋ; ˈbɔksiŋ) *n.* 拳擊。Do you like *boxing?* 你喜歡拳擊嗎?
box·ing[2] *n.* ①做箱的材料。②箱形的罩子。③裝箱(之行動)。④窗的四邊。
Boxing Day〖英〗聖誕節翌日(十二月二十六日);如當日爲星期日,則指次日(十二月二十七日),是日頒禮物給雇員等。
boxing glove 拳擊手套。
boxing match 拳賽。
boxing ring 拳賽場地。
boxing weights 按拳擊人體重分的等級。
box iron 匣狀熨斗。
box·keep·er (ˈbɑksˌkipɚ; ˈbɔksˌkiːpə) *n.* 戲院包廂之管理者。
box kite 箱形風箏。
box office ①(戲院等之)票房。②票房收入。③〖俗〗叫座的人或物(如影星、影片等)。*good box office*〖俚〗能吸引觀衆或聽衆之物。
box-of·fice (ˈbɑksˌɑfɪs; ˈbɔksˌɔfis) *adj.* ①票房的。②受歡迎而賺錢的。
box plait (or **pleat**)(衣物等兩緣交互相對之)複褶。
box score〖運動〗個人成績表。
box seat 包廂內之位子。
box stall 馬廐或畜舍。
box tree 黃楊樹。
box·wood (ˈbɑksˌwʊd; ˈbɔkswud) *n.* ①黃楊木木材。②黃楊木。
box wrench 套筒老虎鉗。
box·y (ˈbɑksɪ; ˈbɔksi) *adj.*, **box·i·er, box·i·est.** (如箱子一般)四四方方的。
‡**boy** (bɔɪ; bɔi) *n.* ①男孩。②兒子。This is my little *boy.* 這是我的小兒子。③僕人;茶房;侍者。④〖俗〗男人;傢伙。⑤男朋友。⑥見習海員或漁夫。*the boys* **a.** 一家中之兒子。**b.**〖俗〗男伴。**c.** 政治上的跟班;跟着混飯吃的人。—*interj.* 好傢伙! *Boy!* Isn't it hot! 好傢伙! 眞熱得要命!
boy·cott (ˈbɔɪˌkɑt; ˈbɔikət) *v.t.* 杯葛;聯合抵制;排斥。—*n.* 杯葛;聯合抵制;排斥。
boy·friend (ˈbɔɪˌfrɛnd; ˈbɔifrend) *n.*〖俗〗男朋友;情郎。(亦作 **boy friend**)
***boy·hood** (ˈbɔɪhʊd; ˈbɔihud) *n.* ①童年;幼年;少年時代。②少年輩;兒童輩。the *boyhood* of China. 中國的少年。
***boy·ish** (ˈbɔɪɪʃ; ˈbɔiiʃ) *adj.* (似)小兒的;活潑的;孩子氣的。—**ly**, *adv.* —**ness**, *n.*
Boyle (bɔɪl; bɔil) *n.* 波義耳(Robert, 1627–1691, 英國物理學家及化學家)。
Boyle's law〖物理〗波義耳定律。
boy scout ①童子軍。②〖美俚〗過於理想而不切實際者。
Boy Scout Day 童軍節。
boy·sen·ber·ry (ˈbɔɪsn̩ˌbɛrɪ; ˈbɔisnbəri) *n.*, *pl.* **-ries.** 雜交草莓。
bo·zo (ˈbozo; ˈbouzou) *n.*〖俗〗傢伙(尤指四肢發達,頭腦簡單的)。
Bp. Bishop. **bp.** ①baptized. ②birthplace. ③bishop. **B.P.** ①Bachelor of Pharmacy. ②Bachelor of Philosophy. ③bills payable. ④blood pressure. **b.p.** (亦作 **B.P., B/P**) bills payable. **B.P.E.** Bachelor of Physical Education. **B.Ph.** Bachelor of Philosophy. **B.P.H.** Bachelor of Public Health. **B.Pharm.** Bachelor of Pharmacy.
B-pic·ture (biˈpɪktʃɚ; ˈbiːˈpiktʃə) *n.* 偷工減料之劣等電影。
B.P.O.E. Benevolent and Protective Order of Elks. **Br** 化學元素 bromine 之符號。**Br.** ① Britain. ②British. **br.** ①branch. ②brig. ③bronze. ④brother. ⑤brown. **b.r.** (亦作 **B.R., B/R**) bills receivable.
bra (brɑ; brɑː) *n.* 乳罩(=brassière).
brab·ble (ˈbræbl; ˈbræbl) *v.*, **-bled, -bling,** *n.* —*v.i.*〖方〗喧嚷;爭論;吵嘴。—*n.* 喧嚷;口角;吵嘴。
***brace** (bres; breis) *n.*, *v.*, **braced, brac·ing.** —*n.* ①緊縛或支撐的東西。②一雙;一對。③鑽子的曲柄。④大括弧(卽{})。⑤(*pl.*)〖英〗(褲子的)吊帶;背帶。⑥(礦坑中的)豎坑口。⑦(船上的)轉帆索。⑧(常 *pl.*)牙醫夾牙用的鋼絲套。⑨死板板的立正姿勢。⑩戰備狀態。*take a brace*〖美〗鼓勇;奮力。—*v.t.* ①支持;使固定;使穩固。to *brace* oneself against a wall. 靠牆撐立。②使興奮;使振作。③〖俚〗向…借貸。④使恢復疲勞;使爽快。*brace up* 奮起;振作。—*v.i.*振作。
brace and bit 曲柄鑽。
brace bit 鑽孔器。
brace game 欺詐的牌局。
***brace·let** (ˈbreslɪt; ˈbreislit) *n.* ①手鐲;臂鐲。②〖俗〗手銬。—**ed**, *adj.*
brac·er (ˈbresɚ; ˈbreisə) *n.* ①(射箭或鬥劍時之)護腕帶。②帶;索。③〖俚〗興奮劑;刺激性飲料。
bra·chi·al (ˈbrekɪəl; ˈbreikjəl) *adj.* ①臂的;上臍的。②似臂的。
bra·chi·ate (ˈbrekɪɪt; ˈbreikiit) *adj.* ①〖植物〗有交互對枝的。②〖動物〗有臂的。
brach·i·o·pod (ˈbrækɪəˌpɑd; ˈbrækiəpɔd) *n.* 腕足類動物。
bra·chi·um (ˈbrekɪəm; ˈbreikiəm) *n.*, *pl.* **-chi·a** (-kɪə; -kiə).〖解剖〗①上臂;肱。②(鳥獸的)翅膀或肢。③臂狀部分或隆起。
brach·y·ce·phal·ic (ˌbrækɪsəˈfælɪk; ˌbrækikeˈfælik) *adj.*〖人類學〗短頭的;短頭顱的。(亦作 **brachycephalous**)
bra·chyl·o·gy (brəˈkɪlədʒɪ; brəˈkilədʒi) *n.*, *pl.* **-gies.** ①(用語之)簡明。②省略語;省略句。
brac·ing (ˈbresɪŋ; ˈbreisiŋ) *adj.* 增加氣力的;興奮的;使心神清爽的。—*n.* ①緊繫、拉緊或支撐的裝置。②袴帶。③刺激。—**ly**, *adv.* —**ness**, *n.*
brack·en (ˈbrækən; ˈbrækən) *n.* 蕨;羊齒。
***brack·et** (ˈbrækɪt; ˈbrækit) *n.* ①牆上凸出的托架;三角形的托架。②括弧〔 〕之一邊。③納稅人按其收入的分類。in the low-income *bracket.* 在收入少的分類內。④夾叉(砲兵作矯正射擊時兩彈着點間之距離)。—*v.t.* ①用托架托住。②加括弧;置於括弧內。to *bracket* a word. 把一個字置於括弧內。③將二人或二人以上的名字放在一起;同被提名。④拼(成組)。⑤相提並論。⑥砲兵對目標

作夾叉射擊。 「鐘。
bracket clock 可擺設於托架上的小
brack·ish 〔ˈbrækɪʃ; ˈbrækiʃ〕 *adj.* ①混有鹽(味)的。②可厭的;作嘔的。—**ness,** *n.*
bract 〔brækt; brækt〕 *n.* 〖植物〗苞。—**e·al, —ed,** *adj.* 「*adj.* 有苞的。
brac·te·ate 〔ˈbræktɪɪt; ˈbræktiit〕
brad 〔bræd; bræd〕 *n.* 無頭釘;曲頭釘。—*v.t.* 用曲頭釘釘牢。 —**ded,** *adj.*
brad·awl 〔ˈbræd,ɔl; ˈbrædɔːl〕 *n.* 小錐。
brad·y·ki·net·ic 〔ˌbrædɪkɪˈnɛtɪk; ˌbrædikiˈnetik〕 *adj.* 行動緩慢的。—**brad·y·ki·ne·sia, brad·y·ki·ne·sis,** *n.*
brae 〔bre; brei〕 *n.*〖蘇〗傾斜處;山坡;斜坡。
***brag** 〔bræg; bræg〕 *n., v.,* **bragged, brag·ging,** *adj.,* **brag·ger, brag·gest.** —*n.* ①誇張;誇辭。to make *brag* of one's success. 自誇成功。②誇張的事物。③誇張者;自誇者。—*v.i.* 誇張。He is *bragging* of his achievements. 他誇張他的成就。—*v.t.* 誇張。—*adj.* ① 自誇的;吹牛的。②極好的。
brag·ga·do·ci·o 〔ˌbrægəˈdoʃɪ,o; ˌbrægəˈdouʃiou〕 *n., pl.* **-os.** ①自誇者;大言者。②大聲誇言;自誇。
brag·gart 〔ˈbrægət; ˈbrægət〕 *n.* 自誇者;大言者。—*adj.* 自誇的;矜誇的。—**ly,** *adv.* 「者;自誇者;吹牛者。
brag·ger 〔ˈbrægə; ˈbrægə〕 *n.* 誇張
Brah·ma 〔ˈbrɑmə; ˈbrɑːmə〕 *n.* ①〖印度神學〗梵;梵天;婆羅賀摩(一切衆生之父)。②印度產之牛。
brah·ma 〔ˈbrɑmə; ˈbrɑːmə〕 *n.* 亞洲產之一種雞。(亦作 **Brahma, brahmapootra**)
Brah·man 〔ˈbrɑmən; ˈbrɑːmən〕 *n., pl.* **-mans,** *adj.* —*n.* ①婆羅門(印度四大階級中之最高者)之一分子。②印度產之牛。—*adj.* 婆羅門的;婆羅門教的。
Brah·man·i·cal 〔brɑˈmænɪkl; brɑːˈmænikəl〕 *adj.* 婆羅門的;婆羅門教的。(亦作 **Brahmanic**)
Brah·man·ism 〔ˈbrɑmən,ɪzəm; ˈbrɑːmənizm〕 *n.* 婆羅門教。(亦作 **Brahminism**) —**Brah·man·ist,** *n.*
Brah·ma·pu·tra 〔ˌbrɑməˈputrə; ˌbrɑːməˈpuːtrə〕 *n.* 雅魯藏布江(發源於西藏,流入印度境內之恆河)。
Brah·min 〔ˈbrɑmɪn; ˈbrɑːmin〕 *n., pl.* **-min.** ①=**Brahman.** ②很有學識或社會地位者;貴族(尤指新英格蘭之世家)。—**ic,** *adj.*
Brahms 〔brɑmz; brɑːmz〕 *n.* 布拉姆斯(Johannes, 1833–1897, 德國作曲家及鋼琴家)。—**i·an,** *adj., n.*
braid** 〔bred; breid〕 *v.t.* ①(將三束以上的髮或細帶)編織在一起。to *braid* the hair 束髮。*braided* wire.〖電〗花線;包線。②束以或飾以辮帶或花等。braid St. Catherine's tresses*** 過處女生活;終身不嫁。—*n.* ①縧帶;辮條。elastic *braid.* 鬆緊帶。②辮子。③(髮上)飾帶。④高級將領(尤指海軍)之集合稱。—**er,** *n.* 「以索捲起(帆)。
brail 〔brel; breil〕 *n.*〖航海〗捲帆索。—*v.t.*
Braille 〔brel; breil〕 *n., v.,* **Brailled, Brail·ling.** —*n.* ①布雷爾(Louis, 1809–1852, 法國盲人教師, 發明點字)。②盲人所用的點字法。—*v.t.* 以點字法寫出。(亦作 **braille**) 「ˌraitə〕 *n.* 點字打字機。
Braille·writ·er 〔ˈbrel,raɪtə; ˈbreil-
Braill·ist 〔ˈbrelɪst; ˈbreilist〕 *n.* ①點字專家。②以寫點字爲職業者;點字打字員。
:**brain** 〔bren; brein〕 *n.* ①腦。②(常 *pl.*) 智慧;智力。Use your *brains.* 用你的智慧。③(*pl.*)智囊。***beat one's brains out*** 盡最大的努力去瞭解或做某事。***blow out one's brains*** 舉鎗擊頭自殺。***cudgel*** (or ***beat***) ***one's brains*** 苦思;絞腦汁。***have something on the brain*** 專心貫注於某事。***overtax one's brains*** 過度用腦。***pick someone's brains*** (自己不下工夫而去)請教他人。***turn the brains of*** 使…驕傲或愚蠢。—*v.t.* 打破…之腦殼;打…之頭。to *brain* a person with a book. 用書打人的頭。
brain box (or **case**) 頭蓋骨;腦殼。
brain cell 腦細胞。
brain·child 〔ˈbren,tʃaɪld; ˈbreintʃaild〕 *n.*〖俗〗腦力創造物(指計畫、概念、創作等而言)。
brain drain 人才外流。
brain fever 〖醫〗腦膜炎。
brain·less 〔ˈbrenlɪs; ˈbreinlis〕 *adj.* ①無腦筋的;愚笨的。②不用腦筋的。
brain·pan 〔ˈbren,pæn; ˈbreinpæn〕 *n.* 腦蓋(殼)。
brain·pow·er 〔ˈbren,pauə; ˈbrein-ˌpauə〕 *n.*①腦力;智力。②智囊;智囊團。
brain·sick 〔ˈbren,sɪk; ˈbreinsik〕 *adj.* 有腦病的;精神錯亂的。—**ly,** *adv.* —**ness,** *n.*
brain storm ①突然的精神錯亂。②〖俗〗心血來潮;突然之靈機。
brain·storm·ing 〔ˈbren,stɔrmɪŋ; ˈbreinˌstɔːmiŋ〕 *n.* 無限制的自由討論(其目的在刺激創造性的思想等)。
Brains Trust 〖英〗①=**brain trust.** ②(在電視或無線電廣播中對觀衆或聽衆所提出的問題作即席解答的)專家小組。
brain trust 智囊團。
brain truster 智囊團中之一員。
brain·wash 〔ˈbren,wɑʃ; ˈbreinwɔʃ〕 *v.t.* ①爲…洗腦。②以宣傳說服。—*n.*洗腦。
brain·wash·ing 〔ˈbren,wɑʃɪŋ; ˈbreinˌwɔʃiŋ〕 *n.* ①洗腦(共產黨用以改造他人思想之一種殘酷手段)。②類似洗腦之手段。
brain wave ①〖生理〗腦波。②〖俗〗靈感;突然之靈機。 「*n.* 勞心工作。—**er,** *n.*
brain·work 〔ˈbren,wɝk; ˈbreinwəːk〕
brain·y 〔ˈbrenɪ; ˈbreini〕 *adj.,* **brain·i·er, brain·i·est.** 〖俗〗聰明的;精明的。
braise 〔brez; breiz〕 *v.t.,* **braised, brais·ing.** 燉(肉);蒸(肉)。
***brake**[1] 〔brek; breik〕 *n., v.,* **braked, brak·ing.** —*n.* ①煞車;制動機。A child ran across the road and the driver put on the *brake* suddenly. 一個小孩跑過馬路,司機突然將車煞住。②用以分開苧麻使成纖維的器具或機器;麻梳。③大耙。④搓或滾轉的機器。⑤高大的四輪馬車。—*v.t.* ①用煞車止住或遲緩(車)的行動。to *brake* an automobile. 煞車;將汽車煞住。②用麻梳梳(麻)。③用耙耙碎。—*v.i.* 用煞車。The car *braked* to a stop. 車子煞車停下來。—**less,** *adj.*
brake[2] *n.* ①灌木叢;叢林。②蕨類植物。
brake band 煞車帶;軔帶;閘帶。
brake horsepower 制動馬力。
brake·man 〔ˈbrekmən; ˈbreikmən〕 *n., pl.* **-men.** ①火車上控制煞車者;軔手。②連橋隊中掌管制動機之隊員。(亦作**brake**)
brakes·man 〔ˈbreksmən; ˈbreiksmən〕 *n., pl.* **-men.** 〖英〗軔手。
brak·y 〔ˈbrekɪ; ˈbreiki〕 *adj.,* **brak·i·er, brak·i·est.** 多蕨的;多荊棘的;多矮灌木的。
bra·less 〔ˈbrɑlɪs; ˈbrɑːlis〕 *adj.* 贊成摒棄奶罩以表示婦女解放的。

bram·ble ['bræmbl; 'bræmbl] *n.* ①荆棘;懸鉤子。②有刺之灌木。

bram·bling ['bræmblɪŋ; 'bræmbliŋ] *n.* 花鶏。

bram·bly ['bræmblɪ; 'bræmbli] *adj.*, **-bli·er, -bli·est.** 懸鉤子的;多荆棘的。

bran** [bræn; bræn] *n., v.,* **branned, bran·ning.** —*n.* 糠;穀皮;麥麩。bolt it to the bran*** 徹底調查。—*v.t.* (製革時將生皮)浸在糠水裏;在糠水裏煮沸。

‡**branch** [bræntʃ; brɑːntʃ] *n.* ①樹枝。The monkey leaps from *branch* to *branch.* 那猴子在樹枝間跳來跳去。②枝狀物;支流。③支店;分行;分局;支部;支。The company has established a British *branch* in London. 這公司在倫敦成立了一個英國分行。④家族的分支。—*v.i.* ①分支。This tree *branched* off in all directions. 這棵樹四向分枝。The road *branches* here. 這路在這裏分岔。②逸出正軌。③分出來;發展出來。—*v.t.* 分。 ***branch off*** 分支。***branch out*** a. 發枝。 b. 擴充(事業、興趣、活動等)。

bran·chi·a ['bræŋkɪə; 'bræŋkiə] *n.*, *pl.* **-chi·ae** [-kɪˌi; -kiiː]. (魚之)鰓。

bran·chi·al ['bræŋkɪəl; 'bræŋkiəl] *adj.*鰓的;似鰓的。

bran·chi·ate ['bræŋkɪɪt; 'bræŋkiit] *adj.* 有鰓的。

branch·ing ['bræntʃɪŋ; 'brɑːntʃiŋ] *adj.* 分支的;有枝的。

branch·let ['bræntʃlɪt; 'brɑːntʃlit] *n.* ①小支。②大枝上長出來的小枝。

branch line 枝線;支線;支路。

branch point 分歧點;枝點;支點。

branch water ①小溪或山澗中的水。②調威士忌用的白水。

branch·y ['bræntʃɪ; 'brɑːntʃi] *adj.*, **-i·er, -i·est.** 多枝的;枝繁的。

brand** [brænd; brænd] *n.* ①種類。②商標;牌子。 We have the best *brands* of wines. 我們有各種最好牌子的酒。③烙印;打烙印的烙鐵。④汚辱的標記。⑤一塊燃燒中的或部分被燃燒的木頭。 ***snatch a brand from the burning 搶救以免危險或毀滅。—*v.t.* ①打烙印於…。On big farms, cattle are usually *branded.* 在大農場上, 牲畜通常打有烙印。②加以汚辱。They *branded* him as a liar. 他們汚辱他爲說謊者。③印(在心上)。④使…顯得突出。—**er,** *n.*—**less,** *adj.*

branding iron 烙鐵;火印。

bran·dish ['brændɪʃ; 'brændiʃ] *v.t.* 威脅地揮動;舞動;揮。—*v.i.* 搖動。—*n.* 威脅的揮動;舞動。

brand·ling ['brændlɪŋ; 'brændliŋ] *n.* ①紅紋蚯蚓。②〖方〗鮭。

brand name ①商標。②附有著名商標之產品。

brand-new ['brænd'nju; 'brænd'njuː] *adj.* ①全新的。②(泛指)最近獲得的。

***bran·dy** ['brændɪ; 'brændi] *n.*, *pl.* **-dies,** *v.,* **-died, -dy·ing.** —*n.*白蘭地酒。—*v.t.* 以白蘭地酒調味;用白蘭地酒醃藏。

bran·dy·ball ['brændɪˌbɔl; 'brændi-bɔːl] *n.* 〖英〗白蘭地糖塊。(亦作**brandy ball**)

brandy snap 以白蘭地酒調味之薑餅。

bran-new ['bræn'nju; 'bræn'njuː] *adj.* =**brand-new.**

bran·ny ['brænɪ; 'bræni] *adj.* (有)糠的;(有)麩的;似糠的。

brant [brænt; brænt] *n.* 黑雁。(亦作**brant goose**)

Bran·ting ['bræntɪŋ; 'bræntiŋ] *n.* 布蘭廷(Karl Hjalmar, 1860–1925, 瑞典政治家, 曾獲1921年諾貝爾和平獎)。

brash¹ [bræʃ; bræʃ] *n.* ①殘枝。②(巖石、冰等之)碎片。

brash² *adj.* ①易碎的;脆弱的。②倉促的;性急的。③粗魯的;無禮的。—*n.* ①〖醫〗胃灼熱。②驟雨。③病倒。④碎石堆;瓦礫堆。

bra·sier ['breʒɚ; 'breizjə] *n.* =**brazier.**

Bra·sil [brə'zɪl; brə'zil] *n.* Brazil 的葡萄牙及西班牙名。

Bra·sil·ia [brə'ziljə; brə'ziːljə] *n.*巴西利亞(巴西新都)。

***brass** [bræs; brɑːs] *n.* ①黃銅。②銅器;銅管樂器。③〖俗〗錢。④〖俗〗厚顏無恥。⑤〖美俚〗高級軍官;領導人物。They are the top *brass* of the steel industry. 他們是鋼鐵工業界的領導人物。⑥〖俚〗妓女。—*adj.* ①黃銅的; 黃銅製的。②黃銅色的。③銅管樂器的。—*v.t.* 鍍以黃銅。

brass·age ['bræsɪdʒ; 'brɑːsidʒ] *n.* 鑄幣費。

bras·sard ['bræsɑrd; 'bræsɑːd] *n.* ①臂章。②臂鎧(=brassart).

bras·sart ['bræsɚt; 'bræsət] *n.* 臂鎧。

brass band 〖音樂〗銅管樂隊。

brass·bound ['bræsˌbaund; 'brɑːs-baund] *adj.* ①有黃銅框架的。②嚴格的;毫無通融之餘地的。③厚顏的;厚臉皮的;無恥的。

brass hat 〖俚〗①(英軍之)參謀。②高級軍官。

brass·ie ['bræsɪ; 'bræsi] *n.* (鑲有銅板之)一種高爾夫球棒; 第二號木棒; 在範圍上所使用的掘飛棒。(亦作 **brassy, brassey**)

bras·sière [brə'zɪr; 'bræsiə] *n.* 奶罩。

brass knuckles 套於指節上作武器用的金屬帶。

brass plate 銅製門牌。

brass section 管絃樂隊中之銅管樂器部分。

brass tacks 〖俗〗基本事實; 眞正重要的事情。

brass·ware ['bræsˌwɛr; 'brɑːswɛə] *n.* 黃銅製品;銅器。

brass winds 銅管樂器。

brass·y ['bræsɪ; 'brɑːsi] *adj.*, **brass·i·er, brass·i·est.** ①黃銅的;銅製的。②厚顏的;無恥的。③廉價而華麗的。④尖銳刺耳的。⑤嘈雜的;喧鬧的。 —**brass·i·ness,** *n.* —**brass·i·ly,** *adv.*

brat [bræt; bræt] *n.* ①〖蔑〗乳臭小兒。②做圍裙或工作服用的粗布。

Braun [braun; braun] *n.* 布勞恩(Wernher von, 1912–1977, 歸化美國的德國火箭工程師)。

bra·va·do [brə'vɑdo; brə'vɑːdou] *n.*, *pl.* **-does, -dos.** 浮誇;作威。

‡**brave** [brev; breiv] *adj.*, **brav·er, brav·est,** *n., v.,* **braved, brav·ing.** —*adj.* ①勇敢的。②鮮艷的;炫耀的。 He puts on *brave* attire. 他穿着華麗的衣服。③很好的; 極成功的。 —*n.* ①勇敢的人。Only the *brave* deserves the fair. 只有英雄才配美人。②北美印第安戰士。—*v.t.* 抵抗; 勇敢地面對…; 冒。They *braved* the storm to rescue us. 他們冒大風雨來救我們。—**ness,** *n.*

***brave·ly** ['brevlɪ; 'breivli] *adv.* ①勇敢地; 英勇地。②鮮艷地; 華麗地。 *bravely* decked houses. 裝飾華麗的房子。③極成功地;極順利地。For three years matters went *bravely* on. 事情極順利地繼續了三年。

***brav·er·y** ['brevərɪ; 'breivəri] *n.*, *pl.* **-er·ies.** ①勇敢。He is unrivaled in *bravery.* 他勇敢無比。②華麗;華飾;華麗的衣服。

bra·vo¹ ['brɑvo; 'brɑː'vou] *interj., n., pl.* **-vos,** *v.,* **-voed, -vo·ing.** —*interj.* (喝采聲)好!—*n.* 叫好;喝采。—*v.i.* & *v.t.* 喝采;叫好。

bra·vo² ['brɑvo; 'brɑːvou] *n., pl.* **-vos, -voes.** 受雇的刺客;暴徒。

Bra·vo *n.* 通訊電碼,代表字母B.

bra·vu·ra [brəˈvjurə; brəˈvjuːrə]〖義〗*n.* ①勇敢的嘗試。②〖音樂〗華美的樂曲或演奏。「②衣飾華美的。」

braw [brɔ; brɔː] *adj.*〖蘇〗①好的;美的。

***brawl** [brɔl; brɔːl] *n.* ①爭吵;打架。②流水聲。—*v.i.* ①爭吵;打架。②淙淙而流(指流水言)。The river *brawled* over the rapids. 河水淙淙地流過急湍。—*v.t.* 喊叫。—**er,** *n.*

brawn [brɔn; brɔːn] *n.* ①筋肉(尤指強壯的肌肉);膂力。②醃煮之野豬肉。③人力;勞力。「流入另一國)。」

brawn drain 勞力外流(特指由一國

brawn·y [ˈbrɔnɪ; ˈbrɔːni] *adj.,* **brawn·i·er, brawn·i·est.** 強壯的;有力的。—**brawn·i·ly,** *adv.* —**brawn·i·ness,** *n.*

bray[1] [bre; brei] *n.* 驢叫;似驢叫的聲音。—*v.i.* ①驢叫。②嘶叫。③發出高而刺耳的聲音。—*v.t.* 以高而沙啞的聲音說出。

bray[2] *v.t.* ①搗碎;搗成粉。②薄塗(油墨)。

Braz. ①Brazil. ②Brazilian.

braze[1] [brez; breiz] *v.t.,* **brazed, braz·ing.** ①以銅製造。②覆以銅;飾以銅。③使似銅。「合金銲接。」

braze[2] *v.t.,* **brazed, braz·ing.** 以銅銲

bra·zen** [ˈbrezn̩; ˈbreizn] *adj.* ①黃銅的。②顏色如黃銅的。③聲音宏亮如喇叭的。④厚顏的;無恥的。—*v.t.* 使厚顏;使無恥。brazen a thing out*** (or ***through***) 厚顏無恥地幹下去。 —**ly,** *adv.* —**ness,** *n.*

bra·zen·faced [ˈbreznˈfest; ˈbreizn-feist] *adj.* 厚臉皮的;無恥的。—**ly,** *adv.*

bra·zier[1] [ˈbreʒɚ; ˈbreizjə] *n.* 火盆;炭盆。(亦作 **brasier**)

bra·zier[2] *n.* 銅匠。(亦作 **brasier**)

***Bra·zil** [brəˈzɪl; brəˈzil] *n.* 巴西(南美洲最大的國家,正式名稱為 The United States of Brazil, 首都巴西利亞 Brasilia, 舊都里約熱內盧 Rio de Janeiro).

***Bra·zil·ian** [brəˈzɪljən; brəˈziliən] *adj.* 巴西(人)的;巴西文化的。—*n.* 巴西人。

Brazil nut 巴西胡桃。

bra·zil·wood [brəˈzɪlˌwud; brəˈzil-wud] *n.*〖植物〗巴西木;蘇木。

Braz·za·ville [ˈbræzəvɪl; ˈbræzəvil] *n.* 布拉扎維(剛果共和國之首都)。

breach** [britʃ; briːtʃ] *n.* ①破裂;裂罅;罅隙。②違反(法紀);毀(約);破壞。a *breach* of faith. 毀約。③絕交;不和;口角。stand in*** (or ***throw oneself into***) ***the breach*** **a.** 準備並熱心於爭鬥;準備獨當難局。**b.** 緊急情況中代表他人採取對策。—*v.t.* ①攻破;擊破。②違反。The contract has been *breached.* 契約被違反了。—*v.i.* (鯨魚等)躍出水面。

breach of contract〖法律〗違約。

breach of promise〖法律〗背約;毀約(尤指婚約之不履行)。「治安;暴動。」

breach of the peace〖法律〗妨害

breach of trust ①〖法律〗受託人之違反義務。②〖俗〗背信;違背義務。

‡bread [brɛd; bred] *n.* ①麪包。②食物;食糧;生計。He earns his daily *bread* by hard work. 他勞苦工作以餬口。③〖俚〗錢。***bread buttered on both sides*** 鴻運高照。***break bread*** **a.** 共餐。**b.** 共享聖餐;舉行聖餐禮。***cast one's bread upon the waters*** 為善不圖報。***know which side one's bread is buttered on*** 知道自己的利益所在。***take the bread out of one's mouth*** 奪人之生計。—*v.t.* 灑以麪包屑。*Bread* the cutlet before you roast it. 灑麪包屑於薄肉塊上,然後烤之。

bread and butter ①麪包與牛油。②生計;必需品。③主要收入來源。

bread-and-butter [ˈbrɛdn̩ˈbʌtɚ; ˈbrednˈbʌtə] *adj.* ①實用的;生計的;為餬口的。②表示感激款待的。③〖俗〗青年的。④生活必需的。⑤限於基本考慮的。

bread and cheese 簡單的菜飯。

bread and scrape 塗有一層薄奶油的麪包。

bread·bas·ket [ˈbrɛdˌbæskɪt; ˈbred-ˌbɑːskit] *n.* ①產糧區。②〖俚〗胃;腹。③〖俚〗一種爆炸兼燃燒之炸彈。

bread·board [ˈbrɛdˌbɔrd; ˈbredbɔːd] *n.* 切麪包或揉麪團用的砧板。

bread·box [ˈbrɛdˌbɑks; ˈbredbɔks] *n.* 存放麪包、蛋糕等的盒子。

bread crumb ①麪包屑;麪包粉;碎麪包。②麪包之易碎部分。

bread·fruit [ˈbrɛdˌfrut; ˈbredfruːt] *n.* ①麪包樹。②麪包樹的果實。

bread line 等待分發救濟食物的隊伍。

bread stick 棒形麪包。

bread·stuff [ˈbrɛdˌstʌf; ˈbredstʌf] *n.* ①製麪包之原料。②麪包。

breadth** [brɛdθ; bredθ] *n.* ①寬度;闊度。②寬宏大度。③一塊(有一定寬度之物)。④(略去或縮小畫面的細節而產生的)寬廣效果。by a hair's breadth*** 間不容髮。***in breadth*** 寬。The room is ten feet in length and eight feet *in breadth.* 這房間十英尺長,八英尺寬。***to a hair's breadth*** 精確地。

breadth·ways [ˈbrɛdθˌwez; ˈbredθ-weiz] *adv.* 橫地。(亦作 **breadthwise**)

bread·win·ner [ˈbrɛdˌwɪnɚ; ˈbred-winə] *n.* 負擔家庭生計者。

‡break [brek; breik] *v.,* **broke, bro·ken, break·ing,** *n.* —*v.t.* ①打破;使破;使粉碎;分裂。He *broke* a dish. 他打破一碟。②干犯;違犯;違背;未遵守。③挫;傷。He *broke* his skin. 他傷了皮膚。④毀壞;弄壞。She *broke* her watch by winding it too tightly. 她把發條上得太緊因而把錶弄壞了。⑤減弱;挫殺(勢力);阻擋。The trees *break* the wind. 樹木可以擋風。⑥停止;使之中斷。I *broke* their conversation. 我打斷他們的談話。⑦馴養;使馴服。⑧超過;超越。⑨掘;挖;耕(地)。The ground was *broken* for a new library. 破土以建新的圖書館。⑩洩露。⑪兌換…成零錢。to *break* a five-dollar bill. 將一張五元的鈔票兌換成零錢。⑫降級;免職。⑬棄絕(一習慣)。She found it very hard to *break* the cigarette habit. 她發現戒煙很困難。⑭斷絕。⑮使屈服;克服。They *broke* him by blackmail. 他們以勒索使他屈服。⑯〖新聞〗發布(消息)。They will *break* the story tomorrow. 他們將於明天刊登那報導。⑰〖運動〗投(變化球)。He *broke* a curve for a strike. 他投了一個變化球而被判好球。⑱破案。The police needed only a week to *break* that case. 警察祇花一星期的工夫便將那宗案子破了。⑲證明為假或不合邏輯。⑳以大肆渲染而開始。㉑從整套中取出一部分。㉒破(密碼)。—*v.i.* ①破碎;破裂。The glass *broke* into pieces. 玻璃(杯)破碎。②闖入。③突然發生;突然改變。The spell of rainy weather has *broken.* 一連的雨天突然放晴了。④挫折;衰弱。

The dog's heart *broke* when his master died. 當主人死時,這狗傷心。⑤破曉。Day *breaks* at six. 六時天破曉。⑥散開。Let's *break* and run. 讓我們散開跑走。⑦破產;倒閉。The bank *broke*. 那銀行倒閉了。⑧分離。⑨發生故障;壞掉。The television set *broke* this afternoon. 今天下午電視機壞了。⑩奔馳;奔跑。⑪(在壓力下)屈服。He *broke* under questioning. 他在詢問的壓力下屈服了。⑫〖運動〗(球)轉向。The ball *broke* over the plate. 球在本壘板上轉向。⑬〖新聞〗被刊出;被發布。⑭突然出現。A deer *broke* into the clearing. 一頭鹿突然在林中空地出現。⑮突然發出聲音。She *broke* into a song. 她突然唱起歌來。⑯價值或價格之大幅陡降。⑰〖植物〗發生突變。***break away*** a. (如在賽跑等中)搶先開始;搶步。b. 突然而去;逃走。c. 突然改變。d. 脫離;放棄;革除。***break bulk*** 從船上卸貨。***break camp*** 拔營。***break down*** a. 失敗。The plan has *broken down*. 這計畫失敗了。b. 損壞;瓦解;崩潰。The machinery *broke down*. 這機器損壞了。c. 失去控制。She *broke down* and cried. 她忍不住而大哭起來。d. 分爲細目。***break even*** 毫無得失;不賺也不賠。***break forth*** 迸出;突然發出。***break in*** a. 訓練;馴養。They *break in* animals to labor. 他們訓練動物工作。b. 闖入。They *broke in* the door. 他們闖進門。c. 打斷。He *broke in* while we were talking. 他打斷了我們的談話。d. 開始使用;啓用。***break in on*** (or ***upon***)闖入。***break into*** a. 潛入;闖入。b. 進入新行業。c. 挿入;打斷。***break off*** a. 突然停止。b. 絕交。***break out*** a. 起始;發生。A rebellion *broke out*. 叛亂發生。b. 發疹。c. 逃走。Several prisoners have *broken out*. 幾個囚犯越獄逃走。d. 準備使用。e. 由貯藏處取出使用。***break the ice*** 打破僵局;打破冷場。***break through*** 突破;透過。***break up*** a. 停止。A meeting *breaks up*. 散會。b. 散開。c. 弄碎。d. 衰弱;衰退。e. 使哄堂大笑。***break with*** a. 絕交;斷絕友誼。b. 打破。It's difficult to *break with* old habits.打破舊習不易。—*n.* ①破;破裂;破隙。The prisoner made a *break* for freedom. 囚犯越獄。②破處;損壞處;裂縫。③中斷;暫停。④〖俚〗笨話;無禮貌;失禮。He made a bad *break*. 他說了一句失禮的話。⑤〖俚〗機會;運氣。⑥奔跑。⑦分手;斷絕關係。⑧突變。⑨停止電流;停電。⑩四輪大馬車。

break·a·ble [ˈbrekəbl; ˈbreikəbl] *adj.* 易破的;脆的。—*n.* 易碎之物。

break·age [ˈbrekɪdʒ; ˈbreikidʒ] *n.* ①破;破損;破裂處;裂口。②賠償損失費。③破損費。④損毀的物件(集合稱)。

break and entry =**breaking and entering.**

break·a·way [ˈbrekəˌwe; ˈbreikəˌwei] *n.* ①脫離。②(牛、羊等)狂奔。③離羣之獸(如鹿等)。④起跑(指賽跑言)。⑤〖戲劇〗容易拆除的布景或道具。—*adj.* ①脫離的。②〖戲劇〗容易拆除的(布景或道具等)。

break·down [ˈbrekˌdaun; ˈbreikdaun] *n.* ①體力不支;病倒。②崩潰;衰敗;損壞。③(阻礙工作或活動的)偶然事件。④一種喧鬧活潑的跳舞。⑤分析;分爲細目。—*adj.* 專門修理故障或損壞的。A *breakdown* train sped to the scene of the accident. 修護專車馳向車禍現場。

***break·er** [ˈbrekɚ; ˈbreikə] *n.* ①破碎者。a *breaker* of stone. 碎石者。②軋碎機(用以軋碎煤、石子等)。③打在岸上或礁上而成泡沫的浪。④馴服者。⑤船上盛水的罐子。

break-e·ven [ˌbrekˈivən; ˈbreikˈiːvən] *adj.* 收支平衡的。

break-even point 收支平衡點。

‡**break·fast** [ˈbrɛkfəst; ˈbrekfəst] *n.* 早餐。I did not have *breakfast* until nine. 我到九點才吃早餐。—*v.i.* 吃早餐。They sit down to *breakfast*. 他們坐下吃早餐。—*v.t.* 供以早餐;款以早膳。—**er,** *n.* —**less,** *adj.*

breakfast food 早餐食用的穀類食物。

break·ing [ˈbrekɪŋ; ˈbreikiŋ] *n.* ①破壞。②〖電〗斷線。③〖語言〗音之分裂(單母音之複母音化)。

breaking and entering 〖法律〗强行進入他人之辦公室或住宅。

breaking point 〖數學〗斷點。

breaking strength (or **stress**) 〖工程〗斷裂强度。

breaking test 〖工程〗斷裂試驗。

break·neck [ˈbrekˌnɛk; ˈbreiknek] *adj.* 非常危險的。

break of day 破曉;黎明;天亮。

break·out [ˈbrekˌaut; ˈbreikaut] *n.* ①逃走。②〖軍〗突圍。③大量或大規模的興起、出現等。

break-prom·ise [ˈbrekˌprɑmɪs; ˈbreikˌprɔmis] *n.* 常常失信的人;失信者;不守信用的人。

break·through [ˈbrekˌθru; ˈbreikˈθruː] *n.* ①突破;衝破防線。②完成;成功(尤指技術或科學上的成功)。③(價錢等之)猛漲。

break·up [ˈbrekˌʌp; ˈbreikˈʌp] *n.* ①解散;瓦解。②停止;終止。③分手;絕交。④(寒帶地區春天來臨後的)解凍。

break·wa·ter [ˈbrekˌwɔtɚ; ˈbreikˌwɔːtə] *n.* 防波堤。

bream[1] [brim; briːm] *n.* 鯛。

bream[2] *v.t.* 燒除(船底之汚垢或海草等);掃除(船底)。

‡**breast** [brɛst; brest] *n.* ①胸;胸部。The thief stabbed him on the *breast*. 這賊用刀刺他的胸。②衣服上身的前部。③乳房。She gives the *breast* to her baby. 她哺乳她的嬰兒。a child at the *breast*. 仍吃母乳的嬰兒。④心。What emotion lay in his *breast* when he made that speech? 他發表那篇演講時,他心裏的感觸究竟如何? ***make a clean breast*** 完全承認。He *made a clean breast* of the whole secret. 他將一切祕密全盤托出。—*v.t.* 奮勇抵抗。The ship *breasted* the rough sea waves. 該船乘風破浪而進。—*v.i.* 奮勇前進。ships *breasting* through the waves. 破浪前進的船隻。

breast-beat·ing [ˈbrɛstˌbitɪŋ; ˈbrestˌbiːtiŋ] *n.* 公開的感情表現。—*adj.* 公開表現感情的。

breast·bone [ˈbrɛstˈbon; ˈbrestboun] *n.* 胸骨。

breast-deep [ˈbrɛstˈdip; ˈbrestˈdiːp] *adj.* 深及胸部的;高與胸齊的。

breast drill 胸壓鑽。

breast-fed [ˈbrɛstˌfɛd; ˈbrestfed] *adj.* 母奶養育的。

breast-feed [ˈbrɛstˌfid; ˈbrestfiːd] *v.t.*, **-fed, -feed·ing.** 以母奶養育;餵奶;哺乳。

breast-high [ˈbrɛstˈhaɪ; ˈbrestˈhai] *adj.* 高與胸齊的。

breast milk 母奶。
breast-pang 〔ˈbrɛstˌpæŋ; ˈbrestpæŋ〕 *n.* 〖醫〗心絞痛;狹心症。
breast·pin 〔ˈbrɛstˌpɪn; ˈbrestpin〕 *n.* 「胸針。」
breast·plate 〔ˈbrɛstˌplet; ˈbrestpleit〕 *n.* ①(盔甲上之)護胸甲。②馬鞍的胸革帶。③龜的腹甲。
breast pump 抽乳器;吸乳器。
breast stroke 〖游泳〗俯泳;蛙式泳。
breast·sum·mer 〔ˈbrɛsəmɚ; ˈbresəmə〕 *n.* 〖建築〗大樑;橫楣。
breast wall 護壁。
breast·work 〔ˈbrɛstˌwɝk; ˈbrestwəːk〕 *n.* 〖軍〗胸牆。
:**breath** 〔brɛθ; breθ〕 *n.* ①氣息。②呼吸。His heavy *breath* disturbed our sleep. 他那沉重的呼吸擾亂我們的睡眠。③微風。There is a *breath* of air this afternoon. 今日下午有微風。④花的香氣。⑤(一次呼吸所需之)極短時間。***below*** (or ***under***) ***one's breath*** 低聲。***catch one's breath*** 鬆一口氣。***hold one's breath*** 因恐懼、緊張或興奮而屏息。***in the same breath***同時。***lose one's breath*** 喘不過氣來;喘息。***out of breath*** 氣喘的。He ran so fast that he was *out of breath.* 他跑得太快,因而氣喘。***save one's breath*** 不白費唇舌。***speak under one's breath*** 低語。***take a deep breath*** 作深呼吸。He *took a deep breath.* 他作深呼吸。***take one's breath away*** 使大爲驚訝。***waste one's breath*** 白費唇舌。
:**breathe** 〔brið; briːð〕 *v.*, **breathed, breath·ing.** —*v.i.* ①呼吸。②吐氣;呼氣。The boy *breathed* on a mirror. 這小孩呼氣於鏡上。③生存;活着。He is still *breathing.* 他還活着。④說話。⑤(風)吹。—*v.t.* ①呼吸。They *breathe* the breath of liberty again. 他們又呼吸到自由了。②吐出。The flower *breathes* fragrance. 花吐香氣。③注入。The artist *breathed* life into the statue. 藝術家使塑像栩栩欲生。④說出。⑤使鬆一口氣。⑥使運動;使喘氣。⑦表現。passages which *breathe* the spirit of poetry.有詩的精神的數節文章。⑧爲(靜脈)放血。***breathe a word against*** 對…表不平。***breathe freely*** 安心;鬆一口氣。***breathe love*** 喁喁談愛。***breathe on*** (or ***upon***) 玷汚。Her name has been *breathed upon.* 她的名譽被玷汚了。***breathe one's last*** 斷氣;死。***not to breathe a word*** (or ***syllable***)保守秘密;不洩露。—**breath·a·ble,** *adj.*
breathed 〔brɛθt; breθt ②*also* briðd; briːðd〕 *adj.* ①有(某種)氣息的。②〖語音〗有氣無聲的;氣音的。
breath·er 〔ˈbriðɚ; ˈbriːðə〕 *n.* ①生者;呼吸者。②〖俗〗使發喘之事。③〖俗〗片刻之休息。④說話者;發言者。⑤呼吸孔;呼吸裝置。
breath holding test 〖醫〗屏息試驗。
breath·ing 〔ˈbriðɪŋ; ˈbriːðiŋ〕 *n.* ①呼吸。②微風。③換一口氣的時間;片刻。④發言。⑤氣音(如子音 h 之發音)。⑥氣音符號(希臘發音符號)。⑦切望;心願。⑧歇息片刻;休息。—*adj.* 有氣息的;活的。
breathing place ①(詩句等中的)停頓。②歇息地;休息場所。③=**vent.**
breathing space 起碼的活動餘地或空間;喘息的時間。
***breath·less** 〔ˈbrɛθlɪs; ˈbreθlis〕 *adj.* ①喘氣的。②屏息的。He was *breathless* with fear. 他因恐懼而屏息。③無呼吸的;死的。④無風的。⑤令人氣喘的。—**ness,** *n.* —**ly,** *adv.*
breath-tak·ing 〔ˈbrɛθˌtekɪŋ; ˈbreθˌteikiŋ〕 *adj.* 驚人的;使人興奮的。
breath test 〖英〗酒醉程度之測定。
brec·ci·a 〔ˈbrɛtʃɪə; ˈbretʃiə〕 *n.* 〖地質〗角礫巖。
bred 〔brɛd; bred〕 *v.* pt. & pp. of 「**breed.**」
breech 〔britʃ; briːtʃ〕 *n.* ①臀部;尻;屁股。②(鎗砲之)後膛。③物之後部。—*v.t.* ①使着褲。②後膛裝配。③打…之屁股。
breech·block 〔ˈbritʃˌblɑk; ˈbriːtʃblɔk〕 *n.* (槍砲之)閂體;後膛鎖;膛栓。
breech·cloth 〔ˈbritʃˌklɔθ; ˈbriːtʃklɔθ〕 *n.* 圍下體之布;短褲。
breech·clout 〔ˈbritʃˌklaut; ˈbriːtʃklaut〕 *n.* =**breechcloth.**
breech·es** 〔ˈbrɪtʃɪz; ˈbritʃiz〕 *n. pl.* ①馬褲;長及膝蓋的褲子。②〖俗〗褲子(=trousers). (亦作 **britches**) ***wear the breeches (女人)在家庭裏,當家主事。
breeches buoy 短褲型之救生具。
breech·ing 〔ˈbrɪtʃɪŋ; ˈbriːtʃiŋ〕 *n.* ①馬之尻帶。②槍砲之後膛部。
breech·less 〔ˈbritʃlɪs; ˈbriːtʃlis〕 *adj.* ①(槍砲等)無後膛的。②無褲的。
breech·load·er 〔ˈbritʃˈlodɚ; ˈbriːtʃˈloudə〕 *n.* 〖軍〗後膛槍;後膛砲。
breech·load·ing 〔ˈbritʃˈlodɪŋ; ˈbriːtʃˈloudiŋ〕*adj.*〖軍〗後膛裝彈的(槍、砲等)。
breed** 〔brid; briːd〕 *v.*, **bred** 〔brɛd; bred〕, **breed·ing,** *n.*—*v.t.* ①生育。②飼養;繁殖。③致生;惹起。Familiarity *breeds* contempt. 親暱招致輕蔑。④養育;訓練;教育。He was *bred* a gentleman. 他受過紳士的教養。⑤交配。—*v.i.* ①繁殖;產子。Most birds *breed* in the spring. 大多數的鳥在春季繁殖。②生出;產生。breed in and in*** 血親結婚生育。—*n.* ①種;族。His horse is of the best *breed.* 他的馬是最好的種。②種類;型。Scholars are a quiet *breed.* 學者們是屬於好靜的類型。—**a·ble,** *adj.*
breed·er 〔ˈbridɚ; ˈbriːdə〕 *n.* ①飼育動物者。②產子嗣之動物。③來源;原因。
breeder pile (原子)滋生堆。
breeder reactor (原子)滋生反應器。
***breed·ing** 〔ˈbridɪŋ; ˈbriːdiŋ〕 *n.* ①生育。②養育;畜養。③教養;行爲。He is a man of good *breeding.* 他是個有良好教養的人。④教育;訓育。⑤〖原子物理〗滋生。
breed of cat(s) 種類。
breeze**[1] 〔briz; briːz〕 *n.*, *v.*, **breezed, breez·ing.** —*n.* ①微風。②騷動;爭吵。③輕易的工作;易事。That test was a *breeze.* 那測驗很簡單。bat*** (or ***shoot***) ***the breeze*** **a.** 漫談;聊天。**b.** 胡說;誇張。***in a breeze*** 輕易地。We did it *in a breeze.* 我們不費力就把它做好了。—*v.i.* ①吹風;颳微風。②〖俚〗輕鬆地行動。He *breezed* through the task. 他輕鬆地做完那工作。③漠不關心地行動。***breeze in*** **a.** 飄然而臨。**b.** 〖俚〗輕易得勝。—*v.t.* 使作輕鬆活動。—**less,** *adj.* —**like,** *adj.*
breeze[2] *n.* 炭灰;炭渣。
breeze[3] *n.* 虻;牛虻。
breeze·way 〔ˈbrizˌwe; ˈbriːzwei〕 *n.* 聯接兩棟房子的走廊或陽臺。
breez·y 〔ˈbrizɪ; ˈbriːzi〕 *adj.*, **-i·er, -i·est.** ①有微風的;通風的。②活潑的;自在的;輕鬆的。—**breez·i·ly,** *adv.* —**breez·i·ness,** *n.*
brek·ker 〔ˈbrɛkɚ; ˈbrekə〕 *n.* 〖英俚〗「早飯。」

Bre·men [ˈbreimən; ˈbremən] *n.* 不來梅(德國西北部之一邦;又,該邦之首府)。
Bren gun [brɛn~; bren~] 勃倫式輕機鎗。(亦作 Bren)
brent [brɛnt; brent] *n.* =**brant.**
brer, br'er [brɚ; brə] *n.* (美國南部方言) =**brother.**
***breth·ren** [ˈbrɛðrən; ˈbreðrən] *n. pl.* 同志;同道;同教的教友。
Bret·on [ˈbrɛtn̩; ˈbretən] *n.* ①Brittany (法國西北部一地區)人。② Brittany 半島之印歐語。 —*adj.* ①Brittany 半島的。②Brittany 人的。③Brittany 語的。
breve [briv; bri:v] *n.* ①〖音樂〗倍全音符;短音符。②〖法律〗令狀;特許狀。③(母音上之)短音符。
bre·vet [brəˈvɛt; ˈbrevit] *n., adj., v.,* **-vet·(t)ed, -vet·(t)ing.** —*n.* 〖軍〗名譽晉升;加銜(晉級而不加薪)。—*adj.* 名譽晉升的;加銜的。—*v.t.* 予以名譽晉升。
bre·vi·ar·y [ˈbrivɪˌɛrɪ; ˈbri:viəri] *n., pl.* **-ar·ies.** (天主教)每日祈禱書。
bre·vier [brəˈvɪr; brəˈviə] *n.* 〖印刷〗8 磅因(point)的活字。
brev·i·ty [ˈbrɛvətɪ; ˈbreviti] *n., pl.* **-ties.** ①短暫(時間)。②簡短;簡潔;簡略。
***brew** [bru; bru:] *v.t.* ①釀;釀造;泡。He *brewed* beer for home use. 他釀啤酒自用。②圖謀;醞釀。 —*v.i.* ①釀造;釀。②醞釀;孕育;形成;集合。 A storm is *brewing.* 暴風雨在醞釀中。—*n.* ①釀造物(如啤酒)。②釀造;醞釀。③酒的品質。
brew·age [ˈbruɪdʒ; ˈbru:idʒ] *n.* ①釀造;醞釀。②釀造之飲料。
brew·er [ˈbruɚ; ˈbru:ə] *n.* ①釀造者。②泡製用具。
brew·er·y [ˈbruərɪ; ˈbru:əri] *n., pl.* **-er·ies.** 釀造所。
brew·house [ˈbruˌhaʊs; ˈbru:haus] *n.* 釀造所。
brew·ing [ˈbruɪŋ; ˈbru:iŋ] *n.* ①釀造;醞釀。②泡製。③一次釀造之量。
brew·is [ˈbruɪs; ˈbru:is] *n.* 〖方〗①肉汁;牛肉汁。②浸於肉汁熱奶等之麪包。
brew·mas·ter [ˈbruˌmæstɚ; ˈbru:ˌmɑ:stə] *n.* 釀酒專家。
brew·ster [ˈbrustɚ; ˈbru:stə] *n.* 〖方〗製酒者。
bri·ar [ˈbraɪɚ; ˈbraiə] *n.* =**brier.**
Bri·ar·e·us [braɪˈɛrɪəs; braiˈɛəriəs] *n.* 〖希臘神話〗百手巨人。
brib·a·ble, bribe·a·ble [ˈbraɪbəbl̩; ˈbraibəbl] *adj.* 可收買的;可賄賂的。 —**brib·a·bil·i·ty,** *n.*
***bribe** [braɪb; braib] *n., v.,* **bribed, brib·ing.** —*n.* 賄賂。—*v.t.* & *v.i.* 賄賂。
brib·ee [ˌbraɪbˈi; ˌbraibˈi:] *n.* 受賄者。
brib·er [ˈbraɪbɚ; ˈbraibə] *n.* 行賄者。
brib·er·y [ˈbraɪbərɪ; ˈbraibəri] *n., pl.* **-er·ies.** 行賄或受賄之行爲。
bribery case 受賄事件;行賄事件。
bric-a-brac, bric-à-brac [ˈbrɪkəˌbræk; ˈbrikəbræk] 〖法〗*n.* 小古董;小古玩。〖注意〗**bric-a-brac** 係一集合名詞,無複數形,亦不能與不定冠詞 a 連用。
brick** [brɪk; brik] *n.* ①磚。②似磚的東西。③〖俚〗慷慨可靠的好人。 ***have a brick in one's hat 大醉;爛醉。***make bricks without straw*** 作某物而缺乏其所必需的材料;爲無米之炊。—*adj.* 磚造的。 a *brick* house. 磚造的房子。—*v.t.* 圍以磚;砌以磚。 —**like,** *adj.*
brick·bat [ˈbrɪkˌbæt; ˈbrikbæt] *n., v.,* **-bat·ted, -bat·ting.** —*n.* ①碎磚;磚片。②無情的批評;譏刺的話。—*v.t.* 譏刺;批評。
brick cheese 磚形乳酪塊。
brick clay (製磚之)黏土。
brick dust 磚灰;磚粉。
brick·field [ˈbrɪkˌfild; ˈbrikfi:ld] *n.* 製磚場。
brick·field·er [ˈbrɪkˌfildɚ; ˈbrikˌfi:ldə] *n.* (南澳洲的)强勁北風。
brick·kiln [ˈbrɪkˌkɪl, -ˌkɪln; ˈbrikkiln, -kil] *n.* 磚窰。
brick·lay·er [ˈbrɪkˌleɚ; ˈbrikˌleiə] *n.* 泥水匠;磚瓦匠。
brick·lay·ing [ˈbrɪkˌleɪŋ; ˈbrikˌleiiŋ] *n.* 砌磚。
brick·mak·er [ˈbrɪkˌmekɚ; ˈbrikˌmeikə] *n.* 製磚工人。
brick red 磚紅色。
brick-red [ˈbrɪkˈrɛd; ˈbrikˈred] *adj.* 磚紅色的。
brick tea 茶磚;磚茶。
brick·work [ˈbrɪkˌwɝk; ˈbrikwə:k] *n.* ①磚造之建築物。②砌磚。
brick·y [ˈbrɪkɪ; ˈbriki] *adj.* ①磚砌成的;多磚的。②似磚的(尤指顏色上)。
brick·yard [ˈbrɪkˌjɑrd; ˈbrikjɑ:d] *n.* 磚廠。
bri·cole [brɪˈkol; ˈbrikəl] *n.* ①一種擲石器。②間接之打擊。③〖網球〗球撞牆後之反彈。④〖撞球〗母球擊中目的球後彈回再擊中另一球。
brid·al [ˈbraɪdl̩; ˈbraidl] *adj.* 新娘的;新婚的。a *bridal* chamber. 新房;洞房。—*n.* 婚禮;婚禮之宴會。 —**ly,** *adv.*
***bride** [braɪd; braid] *n.* ①新娘。②婦女寬邊帽上之繫帶。—**less,** *adj.* —**like,** *adj.*
bride·cake [ˈbraɪdˌkek; ˈbraidkeik] *n.* 新娘蛋糕。
***bride·groom** [ˈbraɪdˌgrum; ˈbraidgru:m] *n.* 新郎。
bride price 聘金;聘禮。
brides·maid [ˈbraɪdzˌmed; ˈbraidzmeid] *n.* 女儐相。
brides·man [ˈbraɪdzmən; ˈbraidzmən] *n., pl.* **-men.** 男儐相。
bride·well [ˈbraɪdwɛl; ˈbraidwel] *n.* 感化院;拘留所;(泛指)牢獄;監牢。
‡bridge[1] [brɪdʒ; bridʒ] *n., v.,* **bridged, bridg·ing.** —*n.* ①橋。The *bridge* is now opened to traffic. 這橋現在開放通行。②船橋;艦橋(橫架於兩舷的高座,船長在此發號施令)。③鼻梁。④假牙的架子;假牙的牙牀。⑤任何橋形物。⑥眼鏡中間的鼻梁架。 ***burn one's bridges (behind one)*** 截斷一切退路;破釜沉舟。 —*v.t.* ①架橋於。②跨過;橫越。③度過。Politeness will *bridge* many difficulties. 有禮貌的態度會使你度過許多難關。—**less,** *adj.* —**like,** —**a·ble,** *adj.*
bridge[2] *n.* 一種紙牌戲;橋牌。
bridge·board [ˈbrɪdʒˌbord; ˈbridʒbɔ:d] *n.* 樓梯之側板。
bridge·build·er [ˈbrɪdʒˌbɪldɚ; ˈbridʒˌbildə] *n.* 溝通雙方意見的人。
bridge·head [ˈbrɪdʒˌhɛd; ˈbridʒhed] *n.* ①橋頭堡;灘頭陣地。②橋之任一端。③(繼續前進之)立足點。
bridge house 船橋之樓。
bridge·work [ˈbrɪdʒˌwɝk; ˈbridʒwə:k] *n.* ①橋樑工事;造橋;架橋。②假牙的架子。③(齒科)架橋;橋工。
bridg·ing [ˈbrɪdʒɪŋ; ˈbridʒiŋ] *n.* 〖建築〗剪刀撐。
Bridg·man [ˈbrɪdʒmən; ˈbridʒmən] *n.* 布立基曼(Percy Williams, 1882–1961, 美國物理學家,曾獲 1946年諾貝爾獎)。
***bri·dle** [ˈbraɪdl̩; ˈbraidl] *n., v.,* **-dled, -dling.** —*n.* ①馬勒;韁轡。The horse is broken to the *bridle.* 這馬已習慣於韁轡了。

②拘束;抑制。—*v.t.* ①繫以韁轡。②克制;控制。Try to *bridle* your temper. 設法控制你的脾氣。—*v.i.* 昂首(表示憤怒、傲慢或輕視)。—**bri·dler,** *n.*

bridle bridge 適於乘騎通過(不適行車)之橋。

bridle hand 拉韁的手;左手。

bridle path (or **way**) 供騎馬之小路。

bri·dle-wise [ˈbraɪdlˌwaɪz; ˈbraidl-waiz] *adj.* 用韁而不用銜的;訓練有素的(馬等)。

bri·doon [brɪˈdun; briˈdu:n] *n.* (軍用馬轡上之)輕勒;小轡。

Brie cheese [bri～; bri:～] 一種乾乳酪(原產於法國)。

:brief [brif; bri:f] *adj.* ①簡單的;簡短的。He gave a *brief* talk to the students. 他對學生作簡單的談話。②短的;短暫的。—*n.* ①摘要;節略;綱要。He drew up a *brief* for his speech. 他起草演講的綱要。②簡報。③(律師的)當事人。***hold a brief for*** 爲…而辯;支持;保衞。***in brief*** 簡言之;要之。***make brief of*** 使簡短。—*v.t.* ①節略;摘要。He *briefed* the whole story into a few sentences. 他將整個的故事節略爲幾句。②對…作簡報;指示。—**ness,** *n.*

brief case 公事包。(亦作 **brief bag, briefcase**)

brief·ing [ˈbrifɪŋ; ˈbri:fiŋ] *n.* ①任務講解(戰鬥出發前所頒布的任務要略)。②簡報。

brief·less [ˈbriflɪs; ˈbri:flis] *adj.* 無人以訴訟事件委託的(對律師等而言)。

brief·ly** [ˈbriflɪ; ˈbri:fli] *adv.* ①簡單扼要地;簡短地。②短時間地;短暫地。to put it briefly*** 簡言之。

brief of title 財產讓度文契之摘要。

briefs [brifs; bri:fs] *n.* 貼身的短內褲。

bri·er [ˈbraɪɚ; ˈbraiə] *n.* ①荊棘。②〖植物〗石南。③石南根製成之煙斗。(亦作**briar**)

bri·er·root [ˈbraɪɚˌrut; ˈbraiəru:t] *n.* ①石南之根。②石南根製成之煙斗。(亦作 **briar root**)

bri·er·wood [ˈbraɪɚˌwud; ˈbraiəwud] *n.* =**brierroot.** (亦作 **briarwood**)

bri·er·y, bri·ar·y [ˈbraɪərɪ; ˈbraiəri] *adj.* 多刺的;多荊棘的。

brig [brɪg; brig] *n.* ①雙桅方帆之帆船。②軍艦上之牢房。③〖軍俚〗禁閉室。

Brig. ①Brigade. ②Brigadier.

***bri·gade** [brɪˈged; briˈgeid] *n., v.,* **-gad·ed, -gad·ing.** —*n.* ①旅。the light *brigade.* 輕騎兵旅。②一隊的人。a fire *brigade.* 消防隊。—*v.t.* 將…組成(隊或旅)。

brig·a·dier [ˌbrɪgəˈdɪr; ˌbrigəˈdiə] *n.* ①旅長。②〖美軍〗陸空軍准將。(亦作 **brigadier general**)

brigadier general *pl.* **brigadier generals.** 〖美軍〗准將。

brig·and [ˈbrɪgənd; ˈbrigənd] *n.* 盜賊;土匪。

brig·and·age [ˈbrɪgəndɪdʒ; ˈbrigən-didʒ] *n.* ①搶刼;掠奪。②土匪之集合稱。(亦作 **brigandism**)

brig·an·dine [ˈbrɪgənˌdin; ˈbrigən-di:n] *n.* 鎖子鎧。

brig·and·ish [ˈbrɪgəndɪʃ; ˈbrigəndiʃ] *adj.* 似土匪的;令人聯想到盜賊的。

brig·an·tine [ˈbrɪgənˌtin; ˈbrigən-tain] *n.* 一種二桅船。

Brig. Gen. Brigadier General.

:bright [braɪt; brait] *adj.* ①光亮的;閃光的;發光的。②晴朗的。a *bright* day. 晴朗的一天。③聰明的;伶俐的。④明顯的;鮮艷的。⑤生氣勃勃的。⑥燦爛的;輝煌的。⑦活潑的;快樂的。She is *bright* and clever. 她活潑而聰明。⑧光明的(前途)。He has a *bright* future before him. 他有光明的前途。⑨著名的;輝煌的。⑩美麗的;漂亮的。⑪機警的。—*n.* ①(*pl.*)(汽車之)車燈。②一種菸葉。③一種畫筆。—*adv.* 亮。She asked which of the two lamps shone *brighter.* 她問那兩盞燈哪一盞照得較亮。—**ness,** *n.*

***bright·en** [ˈbraɪtn̩; ˈbraitn] *v.i.* ①露出開朗愉快之狀。His face *brightened.* 他面現愉快之色。②放晴。The sky *brightened.* 天放晴了。③變亮。④趨於活潑。—*v.t.* ①使愉快;使歡樂;使生輝。These flowers brighten the classroom. 這些花使教室生輝。②使光輝;擦亮。③使明顯;使鮮艷。

bright-eyed [ˈbraɪtˌaɪd; ˈbraitaid] *adj.* 天眞爛漫的;眼神明亮的。

bright-field [ˈbraɪtˌfild; ˈbraitfi:ld] *adj.* (顯微鏡)明視部分的。

bright-light district (都市的)娛樂區。

bright line 〖物理〗明線。

bright-line spectrum 〖理化〗明線光譜。

***bright·ly** [ˈbraɪtlɪ; ˈbraitli] *adv.* 光亮地;閃亮地。

***bright·ness** [ˈbraɪtnɪs; ˈbraitnis] *n.* ①明亮性。②亮度;光度。③智慧。

Bright's disease 勃萊特氏病(一種腎臟病,英人 Bright 所發現故名)。

brill [brɪl; bril] *n.* 一種鰈類之魚。

bril·liance [ˈbrɪljəns; ˈbriljəns] *n.* ①光亮;光輝。②卓越;傑出。(亦作 **brilliancy**)

***bril·liant** [ˈbrɪljənt; ˈbriljənt] *adj.* ①燦爛的;光輝的。②顯赫的。③有才能的。She is *brilliant* at language. 她有語言的天才。—*n.* (切成某種形狀使特別發亮的)寶石。—**ly,** *adv.*

bril·lian·tine [ˈbrɪljənˌtin; ˈbriljən-ˈti:n] *n.* ①美髮油。②一種用山羊毛與棉紗織成之有光澤的織物。

brim** [brɪm; brim] *n., v.,* **brimmed, brim·ming.** —*n.* ①(杯、碗等的)邊。The glass is full to the *brim.* 滿杯。②(帽的)邊。③(河、湖、川等之)邊緣。He drank at the fountain's *brim.* 他在泉邊喝水。—*v.i.* 盈;滿。—*v.t.* 使盈;使滿。He *brimmed* a cup with wine and offered it to me. 他斟滿一杯酒給我喝。brim over*** 溢出。The cup *brims over* with wine. 這杯盛滿了酒。

brim·ful [ˈbrɪmˈful; ˈbrimful] *adj.* 滿到邊際的;盈滿的。—**ly,** *adv.* —**ness,** *n.*

brim·less [ˈbrɪmlɪs; ˈbrimlis] *adj.* 無邊的。

brimmed [brɪmd; brimd] *adj.* ①有(某特種之)邊的。②滿到邊際的。

brim·mer [ˈbrɪmɚ; ˈbrimə] *n.* ①滿杯。②寬邊帽。

brim·ming [ˈbrɪmɪŋ; ˈbrimiŋ] *adj.* 盈滿的。—**ly,** *adv.*

brim·stone [ˈbrɪmˌston; ˈbrimstən] *n.* 硫黃。

brim·ston·y [ˈbrɪmˌstonɪ; ˈbrim-stəni] *adj.* ①硫黃的;似硫黃的;硫黃色的。②地獄的;惡魔的。

brin·dle [ˈbrɪndl; ˈbrindl] *n.* ①斑紋。②有斑紋的動物(尤指貓、狗、牛)。

brin·dled [ˈbrɪndld; ˈbrindld] *adj.* 有斑紋的(尤指灰色或棕色之牛、狗、貓等)。

brine [braɪn; brain] *n.* ①鹽水。②海洋;鹹水湖。—*v.t.* 以鹽水處理。

brine pan 鹽田;鹽場。

brine pit 鹹泉;鹽井。

:bring [brɪŋ; briŋ] *v.t.,* **brought,**

bring·ing. ①帶來；攜來；取來。*Bring* me some water, please. 請你給我取一點水來。Be sure to *bring* your friend with you next time.下次一定要帶你的朋友同來。②引來；使來。What *brings* you here? 你因何來此？③影響；誘致；使致。He could not *bring* himself to do it. 他不願做此事。I can't *bring* her to forgive you for your rudeness. 我不能使她原諒你的無禮。④訴諸法庭。He *brought* a charge against me. 他控告我。⑤能以(某價錢)出售。Meat is *bringing* a high price this week. 本週肉類的售價很高。⑥使(由一狀態變至另一狀態)。to *bring* the car to a stop. 使車子停下來。***bring about*** 使發生；致使。Gambling has *brought about* his ruin. 賭博使他傾家蕩產。***bring around*** (or ***round***) **a.** 使復蘇。**b.** 使相信；說服。***bring back*** 使回憶。***bring down*** **a.** 使降低。The good harvest *brought down* the price of rice. 豐收使米價下跌。**b.** 捕殺；傷害。***bring down the house*** 博得滿堂采；使哄堂大笑。***bring forth*** **a.** 提出。He *brought forth* a problem for our discussion. 他提出一個問題給我們討論。**b.** 致生。His carelessness *brought forth* an accident. 他欠謹愼，致生意外。***bring forward*** **a.** 提出。He *brings* the matter *forward* at the meeting. 他在會議上提出這問題。**b.** 出示；展示。***bring home the bacon*** 成功；勝利。***bring home to*** 使明瞭；使認清；證明。***bring in*** **a.** 產生；使賺到。His work *brought* him *in* $5,000 a year. 他的作品每年替他賺五千元。**b.** 介紹。***bring in a verdict*** 宣判。The jury *brought in its verdict.* 陪審團宣布了他們的決定。***bring off*** **a.** 拯救。**b.**〖俗〗成功。Did you *bring* it *off?* 這事你做成功了嗎？***bring on*** 致使；促成。***bring out*** **a.** 提出；顯示。**b.** 出版；使出現。When are you going to *bring out* your new book? 你何時出版你的新書？***bring over*** 使相信；說服。***bring through*** 幫助或指導…度過(危險或困難)。***bring to*** **a.** 使復蘇。**b.** 停止；阻礙。***bring to an end*** 結束。***bring to bear*** 朝向；利用；加壓力於。***bring to book*** 使供認罪狀。***bring*** (*a person*) ***to his senses*** 使(某人)認清是非利害。***bring to light*** 發現；發掘；公布。***bring to pass*** 使發生；促成。***bring under*** 使服從；降服；制服。***bring up*** **a.** 養育；撫養。**b.** 提出。He *brings* the matter *up* for discussion. 他提出這事討論。**c.** 教養。He was well *brought up.* 他受過好教養。**d.** 使突然停止。***bring up the rear*** 殿後；壓隊。〖注意〗**bring, fetch** 均指携帶某物給某人或至某地。bring 指從另一地方携帶至自己所在地。fetch 指往某處取，並將之携回。

bring·ing-up [ˈbrɪŋɪŋˈʌp; ˈbriŋiŋ-ˈʌp] *n.* 撫養；養育；教養。

*__brink__ [brɪŋk; briŋk] *n.* 邊緣。***on the brink of*** 瀕於。*on the brink of* war. 瀕於戰爭。

brink·man·ship [ˈbrɪŋkmən͵ʃɪp; ˈbriŋkmənʃip] *n.* ①外交冒險政策。②使至極限的行動。(亦作 **brinksmanship**)

brin·y [ˈbraɪnɪ; ˈbraini] *adj.*, **brin·i·er, brin·i·est.** ①鹽水的；海水的。②鹹的。③〖詩〗淚的。***the briny***〖俗〗海洋；海。—**brin·i·ness,** *n.*

bri·oche [ˈbrioʃ; ˈbriːouʃ] *n.* 奶油蛋捲。

bri·quet, bri·quette [brɪˈkɛt; briˈket] *n.* 煤餅；煤球；類似煤球之物。

brise-bise [ˈbrizˈbiz; ˈbriːzˈbiːz] *n.* 窗戶下半之窗帘。

*__brisk__ [brɪsk; brisk] *adj.* ①活潑的；敏捷的；輕快的；迅速的；興隆的。He is a *brisk* walker. 他走路輕快。②銳利的；強烈的。③起泡的。④熊熊的；旺盛的(指火)。a *brisk* fire. 熊熊的火。⑤(酒類)味濃的。—*v.i.* & *v.t.* (使)趨於活潑或興隆〖up〗. The market *brisked* up. 市場興隆起來。—**ness,** *n.*

bris·ket [ˈbrɪskɪt; ˈbriskit] *n.* 獸類之胸部；胸肉。

*__brisk·ly__ [ˈbrɪsklɪ; ˈbriskli] *adv.* ①輕快地；活潑地；敏捷地。②迅速地。The book is selling *briskly.* 書賣得很快。

bris·ling [ˈbrɪzlɪŋ; ˈbrizliŋ] *n.* 棘魚。(亦作 **bristling**)

*__bris·tle__ [ˈbrɪsḷ; ˈbrisl] *n., v.,* **-tled, -tling.** —*n.* ①剛毛；豬鬃。*Bristles* are used to make brushes. 豬鬃用以做刷子。②植物的刺毛。—*v.i.* ①(毛髮)豎立；聳起。The hog *bristled.* 豬豎其毛。②林立；充滿。The enterprise *bristled* with difficulties. 這事業困難重重。③發怒；挑戰。—*v.t.* ①使豎立。②加剛毛於。—**like,** *adj.* —**less,** *adj.*

bris·tle·tail [ˈbrɪsḷ͵tel; ˈbrislteil] *n.* 彈尾類之各種無翅昆蟲；蛀蟲；蠹蟲。

bris·tly [ˈbrɪslɪ; ˈbrisli] *adj.* ①有剛毛的；有刺毛的。②由剛毛所形成的。③易怒的；好吵的。

Bris·tol board [ˈbrɪstḷ~; ˈbristl~] 一種上等紙板。

brit [brɪt; brit] *n.* 小鯡；小鰮。

Brit. ①Britain. ②British.

*__Brit·ain__ [ˈbrɪtən; ˈbritən] *n.* 大不列顛(包括 England, Scotland, Wales). (亦作 **Great Britain**)

Bri·tan·ni·a [brɪˈtænɪə; briˈtænjə] *n.* ① Britain 之古拉丁文名。②大不列顛。③大英帝國。④〖詩〗象徵英國之女性。⑤ (b-) 一種製餐具之合金。

Bri·tan·nic [brɪˈtænɪk; briˈtænik] *adj.* 大英帝國的；不列顛的。

Brit·i·cism [ˈbrɪtə͵sɪzəm; ˈbritisizm] *n.* 不列顛語風；英國語調；英國用字；英國習語。

‡**Brit·ish** [ˈbrɪtɪʃ; ˈbritiʃ] *adj.* 大不列顛的；英國(人)的。—*n.* ①大不列顛人；英國人。the *British.* 英國人民。②不列顛人語。

British Commonwealth of Nations 英國聯邦；不列顛國協。

British Empire 大英帝國。

British English 英國英語(別於美國英語 American English).

Brit·ish·er [ˈbrɪtɪʃɚ; ˈbritiʃə] *n.* 英國人。

British Isles 不列顛羣島。

Brit·ish·ism [ˈbrɪtɪʃɪzəm; ˈbritiʃizm] *n.* ①=**Briticism.** ②英國作風。

British Museum 大英博物館。

British thermal unit〖物理〗英國熱單位(使一磅水增加華氏一度所需之熱量，略作 BTU, B.T.U., B.t.u., B.th.u. 等)。

*__Brit·on__ [ˈbrɪtən; ˈbritən] *n.* ①英國人。②不列顛人(兩千年前羅馬入侵時住在大不列顛南部的塞爾特人)。

brits·ka [ˈbrɪtskə; ˈbritskə] *n.* 一種四輪馬車。(亦作 **britzka, britzska**)

*__brit·tle__ [ˈbrɪtḷ; ˈbritl] *adj.* ①脆的；易碎的。②易怒的。—*n.* 酥糖。peanut *brittle.* 花生糖。—**ness,** *n.*

bro. *pl.* **bros.** brother.

broach [brotʃ; broutʃ] *n.* ①炙肉用的

叉子。②螺旋鑽；擴孔錐。③石匠用的尖鑿。④胸針。⑤教堂上之尖塔。—*v.t.* ①鑽孔使流出(如開桶、罐等)。②初次提起或建議。—*v.i.* 〖航海〗偏航；逸出航線〖to〗.

:broad [brɔd; brɔːd] *adj.* ①闊的；寬的。He has a table four feet long and two feet *broad*. 他有一張四英尺長二英尺寬的桌子。②廣大的。③廣闊的。the *broad* sea. 廣闊的海。④寬宏的；寬容的；寬大爲懷的；量大的。⑤主要的；大概的；大略的。⑥光明的；明亮的。She was robbed in *broad* daylight. 她在白晝被刧。⑦明顯的；坦率的。He gave me a *broad* hint. 他給我明顯的暗示。⑧粗野的。*broad* jokes. 粗野的笑話。⑨無拘無束的。⑩很重的(腔調)。—*adv.* 完全地；十分地。He was *broad* awake. 他十分清醒。—*n.* ①任何廣闊部分。②一種往時之英國金幣。③〖俚〗女人；行爲浪蕩之女人。

broad·ax(e) [ˈbrɔdˌæks; ˈbrɔːdæks] *n.* 鉞。

broad·brim [ˈbrɔdˌbrɪm; ˈbrɔːdbrim] *n.* ①寬邊帽。②(B-)〖俗〗教友派教徒。

:broad·cast [ˈbrɔdˌkæst; ˈbrɔːdkɑːst] *v.*, **-cast** or **-cast·ed, -cast·ing,** *n.*, *adj.*, *adv.* —*v.t.* ①廣播。to *broadcast* a speech. 廣播演辭。②撒播。③傳布。to *broadcast* rumors. 傳布謠言。④〖俗〗無意中洩漏。—*v.i.* 廣播無線電節目。He *broadcasts* every Thursday evening. 他每星期四晚上廣播。—*n.* ①廣播；廣播節目。These *broadcasts* will be heard in most parts of the world. 這些廣播節目，世界大部分地區都能聽到。②播種；撒播。*Broadcast* of seeds is done by hand. 用手撒播種子。—*adj.* ①廣播的。*broadcast* program. 廣播節目。②撒播的；播種的。*broadcast* sowing. 撒播的下種。③廣布的；普遍的。*broadcast* discontent. 普遍的不滿意。—*adv.* ①以撒播方式。The seeds were sown *broadcast*. 種子用撒播法下種。②以廣播方式。**—er,** *n.*

broad·cast·ing [ˈbrɔdˌkæstɪŋ; ˈbrɔːdˌkɑːstiŋ] *n.* 〖無線電〗廣播；播音。

broadcasting station 廣播電臺。

broadcasting studio 播音室。

broadcast receiver 廣播收音機；收音機。

broad·cloth [ˈbrɔdˌklɔθ; ˈbrɔːdklɔθ] *n.* ①(男用的)一種寬幅細毛織品。②(女用的)一種精細棉布或人造絲織品。

broad·en [ˈbrɔdn̩; ˈbrɔːdn] *v.i.* 變闊；放寬；增廣。—*v.t.* 使放寬。

broad-faced [ˈbrɔdˌfest; ˈbrɔːdfeist] *adj.* 寬臉的。

broad gauge ①寬軌。②寬軌之鐵路或車輛。(亦作 **broad gage**)

broad-gauge [ˈbrɔdˈgedʒ; ˈbrɔːdgeidʒ] *adj.* ①無偏見的；寬宏大量的。②廣泛的。③寬軌的。(亦作 **broadgauged**)

broad jump ①跳遠。②跳遠比賽。*running broad jump* 跑步跳遠。*standing broad jump* 立定跳遠。

broad jumper 跳遠選手。

broad·loom [ˈbrɔdˌlum; ˈbrɔːdluːm] *adj.* 寬幅的。

broad·ly [ˈbrɔdlɪ; ˈbrɔːdli] *adv.* ①寬廣地。②明白地。③概括地。④下流地；粗鄙地。

broad-mind·ed [ˈbrɔdˈmaɪndɪd; ˈbrɔːdˈmaindid] *adj.* 大量的；寬大爲懷的；無偏見的。**—ly,** *adv.* **—ness,** *n.*

broad·ness [ˈbrɔdnɪs; ˈbrɔːdnis] *n.* ①廣闊；廣大。②明白；露骨；粗野。

broad seal 國璽；中央政府之官印。

broad·sheet [ˈbrɔdˌʃit; ˈbrɔːdʃiːt] *n.* 大幅紙張或印刷物；祇一面有字的印刷品。

broad·side [ˈbrɔdˌsaɪd; ˈbrɔːdsaid] *n.*, *v.*, **-sid·ed, -sid·ing,** *adv.*, *adj.* —*n.* ①舷側。②舷側砲；舷側砲火。③凶猛的攻擊。④很寬的一面(如房屋)。⑤只有一面印刷字的大張紙。—*v.i.* ①以側面前進。②以舷側砲轟擊。—*adv.* ①側向地。②漫無計畫地；無特定對象地。*broadside on* 側向地。—*adj.* 全面的(攻擊)。

broad-spec·trum [ˈbrɔdˈspɛktrəm; ˈbrɔːdˈspektrəm] *adj.* 用途廣泛的。

broad·sword [ˈbrɔdˌsord; ˈbrɔːdsɔːd] *n.* 闊劍；腰刀；大砍刀。

Broad·way [ˈbrɔdˌwe; ˈbrɔːdwei] *n.* 百老滙(紐約大街名，爲戲院、夜總會等集中地)。

broad·way [ˈbrɔdˌwe; ˈbrɔːdwei] *n.* 大路；寬闊的公路。

broad·wise [ˈbrɔdˌwaɪz; ˈbrɔːdwaiz] *adv.* 以較寬的一面爲前；橫寬地。

Brob·ding·nag [ˈbrɑbdɪŋˌnæg; ˈbrɔbdiŋnæg] *n.* Swift 所著 *Gulliver's Travels* 中之大人國。**—i·an,** *adj.*, *n.*

bro·cade [broˈked; brəˈkeid] *n.*, *v.*, **-cad·ed, -cad·ing.** —*n.* 織錦。—*v.t.* 織成浮花錦緞。**—bro·cad·ed,** *adj.*

Bro·ca's area [ˈbrokəz~; ˈbroukəz~] 〖解剖〗布洛卡氏區(大腦中司語言器官之部分)。

broc·co·li [ˈbrɑkəlɪ; ˈbrɔkəli] *n.* 〖植物〗一種花椰菜。

bro·ché [broˈʃe; brouˈʃei] 〖法〗*adj.* 織出浮花的。

bro·chure [broˈʃʊr; brəˈʃuə] *n.* ①小册子。②(印成小册子出版的)論文。

brock [brɑk; brɔk] *n.* ①〖動物〗貛。②〖英方〗髒人；臭傢伙。

brock·et [ˈbrɑkɪt; ˈbrɔkit] *n.* ①(南美所產之)一種小鹿。②二歲之雄紅鹿。

bro·gan [ˈbrogən; ˈbrougən] *n.* 一種粗而堅固之靴。(亦作 **brogue**)

Bro·glie, de [dəˌbroˈgli; dəˌbrɔːˈgliː] *n.* 戴布勞格利(Louis Victor, 1892–, 法國物理學家，曾獲1929年諾貝爾獎)。

brogue [brog; broug] *n.* ①土腔(尤指愛爾蘭人說英語者)。②=**brogan.**

broi·der [ˈbrɔɪdɚ; ˈbrɔidə] *v.t.* 〖古〗=**embroider.**

·broil¹ [brɔɪl; brɔil] *v.t.* & *v.i.* ①烤；燒；炙。②曬；被曬。to sit *broiling* in the sun. 坐着曬太陽。—*n.* ①烤肉；炙肉。②高熱。

broil² *n.* 口角；爭鬧；騷擾。—*v.i.* 爭吵。**—ing·ly,** *adv.*

broil·er [ˈbrɔɪlɚ; ˈbrɔilə] *n.* ①燒烤食物的人；燒烤器。②適於燒烤之嫩雞。③〖俗〗酷熱的日子。—*adj.* 適於燒烤的(嫩雞)。

broil·ing [ˈbrɔɪlɪŋ; ˈbrɔiliŋ] *adj.* ①酷熱的。a *broiling* day. 酷熱天。②燒炙的。**—ly,** *adv.*

bro·kage [ˈbrokɪdʒ; ˈbroukidʒ] *n.* =**brokerage.** (亦作 **brocage**)

:broke¹ [brok; brouk] *v.* ①pt. of **break.** ②〖古〗pp. of **break.** —*adj.* 〖俚〗沒有錢的；破產的。*go broke* 〖俚〗成爲無錢的；破產。*go for broke* 盡力而爲；全力以赴。—*n.* ①〖造紙〗無法出售的劣質紙張。②(*pl.*)羊頸部與腹部剪下的劣質羊毛。

broke² *v.i.*, **broked, brok·ing.** 作掮客。

:bro·ken [ˈbrokən; ˈbroukən] *v.* pp. of **break.** —*adj.* ①破碎的。②折斷的；破裂的。*broken* leg. 折斷的腿。③衰弱的；頹喪的。a *broken* spirit. 一個頹喪的人。④不完全的。*broken* English. 說得不流利的英語。⑤

間斷的。*broken* sleep. 間斷的睡眠。⑥被制服的;馴服的。⑦凹凸不平的。⑧不守約的;失約的。⑨天空一半以上被雲遮住的。⑩突然改變方向的。The fox ran in a *broken* line. 狐狸曲折地跑 。⑪(感情激動時)講話斷斷續續的。⑫破產的。⑬〖印刷〗不到 500 或 1000 張的紙。—**ly**, *adv.* —**ness**, *n.*

bro·ken-down ['brokən'daun; 'broukən'daun] *adj.* ①毀壞的。②衰弱的。③不適用的。

bro·ken-heart·ed ['brokən'hαrtɪd; 'broukən'hα:tid] *adj.* 傷心的。—**ly**, *adv.* —**ness**, *n.*

bro·ken-wind·ed ['brokən'wɪndɪd; 'broukən'windid] *adj.* 呼吸促迫的;喘息的。

***bro·ker** ['brokɚ; 'broukə] *n.* 經紀人;掮客。—**ship**, *n.*

bro·ker·age ['brokərɪdʒ; 'broukəridʒ] *n.* ①經紀人或掮客之業務。②佣金;經紀費。(亦作 **brokage, brocage**)

brok·ing ['brokɪŋ; 'broukiŋ] *n.* 經紀;經紀業。—*adj.* 經紀業的。 「俗」傘。

brol·ly ['brαlɪ; 'brɔli] *n., pl.* **-lies.** 〖英〗

bro·ma ['bromə; 'broumə] *n.* ①去油之可可豆。②〖醫〗任何供咀嚼的固體食物(以別於流體食物)。 「三溴乙醛。

bro·mal ['broməl; 'broumæl] *n.* 〖化〗

bro·mate ['bromet; 'broumeit] *n., v.,* **-mat·ed, -mat·ing.** —*n.* 〖化〗溴酸鹽。—*v.t.* 使與溴素化合。 「的;含溴的。

bro·mic ['bromɪk; 'broumik] *adj.* 溴

bromic acid 溴酸。 「**bromide** ①.

bro·mid ['bromɪd; 'broumid] *n.* =

bro·mide ['bromaɪd; 'broumaid] *n.* ①〖化〗溴化物。②〖俚〗庸俗、陳腐之言。③庸俗之輩。④溴化鉀(一種鎮靜、催眠藥物)。

bromide paper 〖照相〗感光紙。

bro·mid·ic [bro'mɪdɪk; brou'midik] *adj.* 〖俗〗使用或含庸俗、陳腐之言的;平凡的;庸俗的。—**al·ly**, *adv.* 「〖化〗溴。

bro·mine ['bromin; 'broumi:n] *n.*

bro·mism ['bromɪzm̩; 'broumizm] *n.* 〖醫〗溴中毒。(亦作 **brominism**)

bro·my·rite ['bromə,raɪt; 'broumirait] *n.* 〖礦〗溴銀礦。 「〖解剖〗支氣管。

bron·chi·a ['brαŋkɪə; 'brɔŋkiə] *n.pl.*

bron·chi·al ['brαŋkɪəl; 'brɔŋkiəl] *adj.* 支氣管的。

bron·chi·tis [brαn'kaɪtɪs; brɔŋ'kaitis] *n.* 支氣管炎。—**bron·chit·ic**, *adj.*

bron·cho·pneu·mo·nia [,brαŋkonju'monjə; ,brɔŋkounju:'mounjə] *n.* 〖醫〗支氣管肺炎。

bron·cho·scope ['brαŋkə,skop; 'brɔŋkəskoup] *n.* 〖醫〗支氣管窺鏡。

bron·chot·o·my [brαŋ'kαtəmɪ; brɔŋ'kɔtəmi] *n.* 〖醫〗支氣管切開術。

bron·chus ['brαŋkəs; 'brɔŋkəs] *n., pl.* **-chi** [-kaɪ; -kai]. 〖解剖〗支氣管。

bron·to·sau·rus [,brαntə'sɔrəs; ,brɔntə'sɔ:rəs] *n.* 〖古生物〗雷獸(其化石發現於北美西部)。 「隆克斯(紐約市之一區)。

Bronx, the [brαŋks; brɔŋks] *n.* 布

***bronze** [brαnz; brɔnz] *n., adj., v.,* **bronzed, bronz·ing.** —*n.* ①青銅(銅與錫的合金)。This statue is made of *bronze.* 這雕像是用青銅製的。②青銅色;青銅色的顏料。③青銅器。④類似青銅之合金。⑤青銅藝術品(如銅像、半身像等)。⑥青銅幣(尤指羅馬帝國時代的)。—*adj.* ①青銅製的。②青銅色的;古銅色的。—*v.t.* 使成青銅色;使成褐色。His face was *bronzed* by the sun. 他的臉被太陽曬成褐色。—**like**, *adj.*

Bronze Age 銅器時代(在石器時代之後,鐵器時代之前)。 「smiθ] *n.* 青銅匠。

bronze·smith ['brαnz,smɪθ; 'brɔnz-

***brooch** [brotʃ, brutʃ; broutʃ, bru:tʃ] *n.* 女用胸針或領針。(亦作 **broach**)

brood** [brud; bru:d] *n.* ①一窠孵雛;同母的子女;孵。A hen gathered her *brood* under her wings. 母鷄掩藏一群小鷄於翼下。②種;類;批。—*v.t.* ①孵。The hen *broods* ten eggs this time. 此次這母鷄孵十個蛋。②沉思;籌劃。③(鳥等)用身或翼暖和、保護、或覆蓋雛鳥。④沉思;深思。He *brooded* the problem. 他對這個問題加以深思。⑤經過沉思而想出。—*v.i.* ①孵。②沉思;深思;憂思。He *broods* over his misfortunes. 他憂思他不幸的事。brood above*** (or ***over***)(氣氛)籠罩。***brood over*** (or ***on***) 憂思;沉思。—*adj.* 爲育種豢養的(家畜)。

brood·er ['brudɚ; 'bru:də] *n.* ①孵卵器。②沉思的人。③孵化的地方。

brood·ing ['brudɪŋ; 'bru:diŋ] *adj.* ①游移不去的;在附近翱翔的。②沉思的。—**ly**, *adv.*

brood·y ['brudɪ; 'bru:di] *adj.,* **brood·i·er, brood·i·est.** ①將孵卵的。②多產的。③抑鬱的;沉思的。—**brood·i·ness**, *n.*

‡**brook**[1] [bruk; bruk] *n.* 溪流;小河。—**less**, *adj.* —**like**, *adj.*

brook[2] *v.t.* 忍受;容忍;耐;捱。—**a·ble**, *adj.* 「溪;小川。

brook·let ['bruklɪt; 'bruklit] *n.* 小

brook·lime ['bruk,laɪm; 'bruklaim] *n.* 〖植物〗婆婆納(屬於玄參科)。

Brook·lyn ['bruklɪn; 'bruklin] *n.* 布魯克林(紐約市之一區)。

broom** [brum; bru:m] *n.* ①掃帚。He sweeps the floor with a *broom.* 他用掃帚掃地。②金雀花。③木樁經打擊後裂開的頂端。A new broom sweeps clean.*** 新官上任三把火。—*v.t.* ①掃。②用錘擊(木樁)使其頂部散裂。—*v.i.*(木樁等受到錘擊後)頂端散裂。

broom·corn ['brum,kɔrn; 'bru:mkɔ:n] *n.* 〖植物〗高粱;蘆粟。

broom·rape ['brum,rep; 'bru:mreip] *n.* 〖植物〗肉蓯蓉。 「*n.* 帚柄。

broom·stick ['brum,stɪk; 'bru:mstik]

broom·y ['brumɪ; 'bru:mi] *adj.* ①似帚的。②遍生金雀花的。

bros., Bros. brothers (通常用於公司、行號之名字中, 如 Smith *Bros. & Co.* 史密斯兄弟公司)。 「湯。—**bros·y**, *adj.*

brose [broz; brouz] *n.* 〖蘇〗一種麥粉

***broth** [brɔθ; brɔθ] *n.* ①煮肉的清湯。②煮魚肉蔬菜的湯。—**y**, *adj.* 「—**like**, *adj.*

broth·el ['brɔθəl; 'brɔθl] *n.* 妓院。

‡**broth·er** ['brʌðɚ; 'brʌðə] *n., pl.* **broth·ers** or 〖古〗**breth·ren**, *interj., v.* —*n.* ①兄弟。I have three elder *brothers.* 我有三個哥哥。②同胞;同道;同志;同仁;同業;會友;社友。All men are *brothers.* 四海皆兄弟。③同教會的教友。④修士。⑤〖俚〗傢伙;老兄。*Brother,* can you spare a dime? 老兄,能給我一角錢嗎? ⑥(美黑人用語)黑人同胞;黑人。***brothers in arms*** 戰友;袍澤。***half brother*** 同父異母或同母異父兄弟。—*interj.* 表示對他人之大膽、無恥之失望, 厭惡, 驚訝的感嘆詞。—*v.t.* 對待或稱呼(某人)爲兄弟。

***broth·er·hood** ['brʌðɚ,hud; 'brʌðəhud〕 *n.* ①兄弟關係;手足情誼。②如兄如弟的結合;同志;同仁;同僚。③同業公會。④四海之內皆兄弟的信念。

broth·er-in-law 〔ˈbrʌðərɪn͵lɔ; ˈbrʌðərinlɔ:〕 *n., pl.* **broth·ers-in-law.** ①夫或妻的兄(弟)。②姊或妹的丈夫。③連襟;丈夫或妻子之姊或妹的丈夫。

broth·er·ly 〔ˈbrʌðəlɪ; ˈbrʌðəli〕 *adj. & adv.* ①(如)兄弟的(地)。②友愛的(地);親切的(地)。—**broth·er·li·ness,** *n.*

brough·am 〔ˈbruəm, brum; ˈbru:əm〕 *n.* ①駕駛座在外面的四輪馬車。②駕駛座位在外之汽車。

:brought 〔brɔt; brɔ:t〕 *v.* pt. & pp. of **bring.**

***brow** 〔brau; brau〕 *n.* ①額。He knits his *brow.* 他深鎖眉梢。②眉;眉毛。③峭壁的邊緣或頂端。④(輪船之)跳板。—**less,** *adj.*

brow ague 前額神經痛。

brow·beat 〔ˈbrau͵bit; ˈbraubi:t〕 *v.t.,* **-beat, -beat·en, -beat·ing.** 嚴詞叱責。

:brown 〔braun; braun〕 *n.* ①棕色;褐色。②棕色或褐色的顏料。There is too much *brown* in the picture. 這幅畫褐色太多。③棕色或褐色之物。④〖英俚〗銅幣。—*adj.* ①褐色的;棕色的。②皮膚呈褐色的;曬黑的。***do it up brown*** 做得徹底、完善、完美。***in a brown study*** 沉思;出神。—*v.t.* 成為褐色;變為褐色。—*v.i.* 變為褐色。The potatoes *browned* in the pan. 洋芋在鍋裏被煎成褐色。***be browned off*** 〖俚〗不滿意;生氣;厭煩。***brown out*** (在城市裏)使燈火轉暗而部分管制以減低空襲之危險或為省電。—**ish,** *adj.* —**ness,** *n.*

brown-bag 〔ˈbraun͵bæg; ˈbraunbæg〕 *v.t. & v.i.* 〖美俚〗自帶酒菜到餐館、俱樂部等。

brown belt 〖柔道〗褐帶。

brown bread ①一種含糖漿的蒸饅頭。②黑麪包。

brown·ie 〔ˈbraunɪ; ˈbrauni〕 *n.* ①小精靈。②一種內有乾果的巧克力糖。③(B-) 8-11歲的女童軍。④(B-)方形廉價照相機。

Brown·ing automatic rifle 〔ˈbraunɪŋ~~; ˈbrauniŋ~~〕 白朗寧自動步槍。

brown·out 〔ˈbraun͵aut; ˈbraunaut〕 *n.* 〖美〗警戒燈火管制(部分燈火熄滅或減弱)。

brown race 棕色皮膚人種。

brown rice 糙米。

Brown Shirt ①納粹德國之衝鋒隊隊員。②希特勒之擁護者;納粹黨員。(亦作 **brown shirt**)

brown·stone 〔ˈbraun͵ston; ˈbraunstoun〕 *n.* 褐石。—*adj.* ①用褐石建造的。②富有階級的。

brown study 沉思。She stood there in a *brown study.* 她站在那裏沉思不語。

brown sugar 紅糖。

brown·y 〔ˈbraunɪ; ˈbrauni〕 *adj.* 棕色的;褐色的。

browse 〔brauz; brauz〕 *v.,* **browsed, brows·ing,** *n.* —*v.t.* ①食;嚙。②牧於。—*v.i.* ①食、嚙葉、嫩枝等。②從容瀏覽書籍、圖書館等。③漫然地觀看店內或攤上之貨。—*n.* ①(牛等所吃之)嫩枝;嫩葉。②瀏覽。—**brows·er,** *n.*

Bruce 〔brus; bru:s〕 *n.* 男子名。

bru·cel·lo·sis 〔͵brusəˈlosɪs; ͵bru:səˈlousis〕 *n.* 布魯氏桿菌病(一種波動性熱病)。

bruc·in 〔ˈbrusin; ˈbru:sin〕 *n.* 〖化〗馬錢子鹼;百路新。(亦作 **brucine**)

bru·in 〔ˈbruɪn; ˈbru:in〕 *n.* 熊(用於神仙故事中)。

***bruise** 〔bruz; bru:z〕 *v.,* **bruised, bruis·ing,** *n.* —*v.t.* ①打傷;瘀傷。He *bruised* his finger with a hammer. 他的手指受鎚擊傷。②搗碎。③使受傷(指情感)。He *bruised* her feelings. 他傷了她的情感。④碰損(金屬錠或成品)之外表。—*v.i.* ①打傷;受傷。His face *bruised* badly. 他的臉傷得很厲害。②受傷害(指情感)。—*n.* 打傷;瘀傷。He received a *bruise* on his leg. 他的腿受傷了。

bruis·er 〔ˈbruzɚ; ˈbru:zə〕 *n.* 〖俗〗①職業拳師;鬥拳家。②好鬥之人;強壯而粗暴的人。

bruit 〔brut; bru:t〕 *n.* 〖古〗①喧嚣。②謠言。③〖醫〗雜音。—*v.t.* 傳布;謠傳(常用被動式)。

bru·mal 〔ˈbruml̩; ˈbru:məl〕 *adj.* 多日的;如多日的。

brume 〔brum; bru:m〕 *n.* 霧;水蒸氣。

brum·ma·gem 〔ˈbrʌmədʒəm; ˈbrʌmədʒəm〕 *adj.* 僞造的;廉價而華麗炫目的。—*n.* 廉價而炫麗之物(尤指倣製珠寶等)。

bru·mous 〔ˈbruməs; ˈbru:məs〕 *adj.* 多日的;多霧的。

brunch 〔brʌntʃ; brʌntʃ〕 *n.* 〖俗〗早午餐(早餐與午餐合而為一)。—*v.i.* 吃早午餐。

brunch coat 長到膝蓋的家常服。

Bru·nei 〔bruˈnaɪ; bruˈnai〕 *n.* 婆羅乃(馬來西亞之一州,舊名為汶萊)。

bru·net 〔bruˈnɛt; bru:ˈnet〕 *adj.* ①暗色或褐色的。②髮、膚及眼睛呈褐色的。—*n.* 髮、膚及眼睛呈褐色的男子。

bru·nette 〔bruˈnɛt; bru:ˈnet〕 *adj.* = **brunet.** —*n.* 髮、膚及眼睛均為褐色之女子。

brunt 〔brʌnt; brʌnt〕 *n.* ①衝擊;衝力。②衝擊或衝力之主要部分。***bear the brunt of*** 首當其衝。

:brush¹ 〔brʌʃ; brʌʃ〕 *n.* ①刷子;畫筆;毛筆。I bought a toothbrush. 我買了一把牙刷。These two pictures are from the same painter's *brush.* 這兩幅畫是由同一畫家畫的。②拂拭;刷。Give my hat a *brush.* 把我的帽刷一刷。③輕擦;掠過。④小衝突;小戰。He had a *brush* with his neighbor. 他和鄰居發生小衝突。⑤動物的尾巴。⑥畫家的技藝。⑦爵士樂所使用,狀似刷子,用來打鼓或鐃的工具。⑧在鄉間的短程旅行。⑨〖電〗**a.** 炭刷。**b.** 刷形放電。⑩男人帽子上似刷子之裝飾品。—*v.t.* ①拂拭;用刷刷之。②拭去。He *brushed* away tears with his sleeve. 他用袖子拭眼淚。③輕觸;掠過;碰着。—*v.i.* ①掠過;輕觸。②疾走;急速移動。***brush aside*** (or ***away***) **a.** 排除。He *brushed aside* all objections from his opponents. 他排除對方的一切異議。**b.** 漠視;不理。***brush off*** 〖美俚〗**a.** 拒絕接見;驅逐。He had never been *brushed off* so rudely before. 他從沒有被那麼粗魯地斥拒過。**b.** 漠視;認為不重要。***brush up*** **a.** 清潔;拂拭。**b.** 溫習。***brush up on*** 溫習。—**a·ble,** —**like,** *adj.* —**er,** *n.*

brush² *n.* ①叢林。②柴枝。③未開拓地。

brush-burn 〔ˈbrʌʃ͵bɝn; ˈbrʌʃbə:n〕 *n.* 擦傷。

brush cut 一種男人髮型(似平頭)。

brush fire 灌木叢之火災。

brush·off 〔ˈbrʌʃ͵ɔf; ˈbrʌʃ͵ɔ:f〕 *n.* 〖美俚〗突然棄絕或拒絕。(亦作**brush-off**)

brush-pen·cil 〔ˈbrʌʃˈpɛnsl̩; ˈbrʌʃˈpensl〕 *n.* 畫筆。

brush·up 〔ˈbrʌʃ͵ʌp; ˈbrʌʃʌp〕 *n.* ①溫習。②檢修(小毛病等);拭抹。

brush wheel 以磨擦轉動之輪。

brush·wood 〔ˈbrʌʃ͵wud; ˈbrʌʃwud〕 *n.* ①砍下的樹枝;柴枝。②密集的小樹叢。

brush·work [ˈbrʌʃˌwɝk; ˈbrʌʃwəːk] *n.* ①繪畫。②畫法;畫風。
brush·y [ˈbrʌʃɪ; ˈbrʌʃi] *adj.*, **brush·i·er, brush·i·est.** ①如毛刷的; 粗糙的。 ②多灌木的。
brusque [brʌsk; brusk] *adj.* 唐突的;粗率的。(亦作 **brusk**) **—ly,** *adv.* **—ness,** *n.*
brus·que·rie [ˌbryskəˈri; ˌbryskəˈriː] 〖法〗 *n.* 粗鄙;無禮;唐突;突然。
Brus·sels [ˈbrʌslz; ˈbrʌslz] *n.* 布魯塞爾(比利時的首都)。
Brussels sprouts 〖植物〗芽甘藍。
*__bru·tal__ [ˈbrutl; ˈbruːtl] *adj.* ①野蠻的;殘忍的;不人道的。a *brutal* prison guard. 殘酷無情的獄卒。②野獸的。③不講理的。 **—ly,** *adv.*
bru·tal·ism [ˈbrutəlɪzm; ˈbruːtəlizm] *n.* 一種使用未裝飾,而巨大建材的建築樣式。
bru·tal·i·ty [bruˈtælətɪ; bruːˈtæliti] *n., pl.* **-ties.** ①殘忍;野蠻;不人道。②暴行;獸行;殘暴的行爲。
bru·tal·ize [ˈbrutlˌaɪz; ˈbruːtəlaiz] *v.,* **-ized, -iz·ing.** *—v.t.* 使殘忍; 使具獸性; 對(某人)採殘忍手段。 *—v.i.* 變殘忍; 變爲獸性。**—bru·tal·i·za·tion,** *n.*
*__brute__ [brut; bruːt] *n.* ①無理性的獸類。②殘暴的人;愚蠢或好色的人。He is a *brute* to his children. 他虐待子女。③人類之獸性。*—adj.* 殘忍的; 粗野的;愚蠢的; 好色的。*brute* courage. 蠻勇; 匹夫之勇。 *brute* strength. 蠻力;暴力。 **—like,** *adj.* **—ly,** *adv.* **—ness,** *n.*
bru·ti·fy [ˈbrutəˌfaɪ; ˈbruːtifai] *v.t. & v.i.* **-fied, -fy·ing.** =**brutalize.** **—brut·i·fi·ca·tion,** *n.*
brut·ish [ˈbrutɪʃ; ˈbruːtiʃ] *adj.* ①獸的;畜生的。②如禽獸的;野蠻的;殘忍的。③肉慾的。④粗俗的;愚蠢的。**—ly,** *adv.* **—ness,** *n.*
bru·tum ful·men [ˈbrutəmˈfʌlmɛn; ˈbruːtəmˈfʌlmen] 〖拉〗虛張聲勢。
Bru·tus [ˈbrutəs; ˈbruːtəs] *n.* 布魯特斯(Marcus Junius, 85–42 B.C., 羅馬政客及省行政官,暗殺凱撒者之一)。
brux·ism [ˈbrʌksɪzm; ˈbrʌksizm] *n.* 〖醫〗咬嚼牙;夜間銼牙。
bry·ol·o·gy [braɪˈɑlədʒɪ; braiˈɔlədʒi] *n.* 蘚苔學。**—bry·o·log·i·cal,** *adj.* **—bry·ol·o·gist,** *n.*
bry·o·ny [ˈbraɪənɪ; ˈbraiəni] *n., pl.* **-nies.** 歐薯蕷根(吐瀉劑)。(亦作 **briony**)
bry·o·phyte [ˈbraɪəˌfaɪt; ˈbraiəfait] *n.*蘚苔類植物。**—bry·o·phyt·ic,** *adj.*
bry·o·zo·an [ˌbraɪəˈzoən; ˌbraiəˈzouən] *adj.* 〖動物〗苔蘚蟲的。*—n.* 苔蘚蟲。
b.s. ①bill of sale. ②balance sheet.
B.S., B.Sc. Bachelor of Science.
B.S.A. ①British South Africa. ②Boy Scouts of America. ③Bachelor of Scientific Agriculture. **B.S.Arch.** Bachelor of Science in Architecture.
B.S.B.A Bachelor of Science in Business Administration. **B.S.Bus.** Bachelor of Science in Business.
B.S.Ch. Bachelor of Science in Chemistry. **B.S.Ec.** Bachelor of Science in Economics. **B.S.Ed.** Bachelor of Science in Education. **B.S.H.E.** Bachelor of Science in Home Economics.
B.S.J. Bachelor of Science in Journalism. **bskt.** basket. **Bs/L** bills of lading. **B.S.N.** Bachelor of Science in Nursing. **B.S.Phar.** Bachelor of Science in Pharmacy. **Bt.** Baronet.
bt. ①bolt. ②bought. **B.Th.** Bachelor of Theology. **btl.** bottle. **btry.** battery. **B.T.U.** (亦作 **BTU, B.t.u., B.th.u., Btu**) British thermal unit.
bu. ①bushel. ②bushels. ③bureau.
bub [bʌb; bʌb] *n.* 〖俗〗兄弟;少年;小傢伙(用於直接稱呼)。
*__bub·ble__ [ˈbʌbl; ˈbʌbl] *n., v.,* **-bled, -bling.** *—n.* ①泡沫;氣泡。He blows *bubbles* with soap water. 他用肥皂水吹氣泡。②在液體和固體內的氣泡。③起泡;沸騰;沸騰聲。④泡沫般的計畫或思想。⑤騙局。⑥圓型的覆蓋、或圓頂。⑦婦女圓形髮型。*—v.i.* ①起泡。Air *bubbles* up in the water. 空氣在水中起泡上浮。② 大聲地笑。③潺潺而流。The water *bubbles* down from the hill. 水由山上潺潺流下。④沸騰。⑤活潑、生動地講述或行動。⑥激動。*—v.t.*①使起泡;起泡。②欺騙。They *bubbled* him (out) of his money. 他們騙去他的錢。***bubble over*** a. 盈滿;洋溢。b. 熱心;熱情洋溢。
bubble bath ①起泡洗澡粉。②用起泡洗澡粉的沐浴。
bubble dance 全裸或半裸女演員表演之歌舞。
bubble gum 泡泡糖。
bub·bler [ˈbʌblɚ; ˈbʌblə] *n.*供飲用之噴水裝置。
bub·bly [ˈbʌblɪ; ˈbʌbli] *adj.,* **-bli·er, -bli·est,** *n.* *—adj.* 起泡的。*—n.* 〖英俚〗香檳酒。
bub·bly-jock [ˈbʌblɪˌdʒɑk; ˈbʌbli-dʒɔk] *n.* 〖蘇〗雄火鷄。
bub·by [ˈbʌbɪ; ˈbʌbi] *n., pl.* **-bies.** 〖俗〗① =**bub.** ②〖俚〗女人之乳房。
bu·bo [ˈbjubo; ˈbjuːbou] *n., pl.* **-boes.** 〖醫〗①橫痃; 便毒。②魚口疔。
bu·bon·ic [bjuˈbɑnɪk; bjuːˈbɔnik] *adj.* 〖醫〗橫痃的。
bubonic plague 黑死病; 淋巴腺鼠疫。
buc·cal [ˈbʌkl; ˈbʌkəl] *adj.* 頰的;口的。
buc·ca·neer [ˌbʌkəˈnɪr; ˌbʌkəˈniə] *n.* 海盜。 *—v.i.* 做海盜。
buc·ca·neer·ing [ˌbʌkəˈnɪrɪŋ; ˌbʌkəˈniəriŋ] *adj.* 海盜的。*—n.* 海盜行爲;掠奪。
buc·ci·na·tor [ˈbʌksɪˌnetɚ; ˈbʌksineitə] *n.* 頰筋; 頰肌。
bu·cen·taur [bjuˈsɛntɔr; bjuˈsentɔː] *n.* 〖神話〗半人半牛之怪物。
Bu·ceph·a·lus [bjuˈsɛfələs; bjuˈsefələs] *n.* 亞歷山大大帝所乘之戰馬。
Bu·cha·rest [ˌbukəˈrɛst; ˈbjuːkərest] *n.* 布加勒斯特 (羅馬尼亞的首都)。
Buch·man·ism [ˈbʌkmənˌɪzəm; ˈbʌkmənizm] *n.* 世界道德重整運動。**—Buch·man·ite,** *n.*
Buck [bʌk; bʌk] *n.* 賽珍珠(Pearl, 1892–1973, 本姓 Sydenstricker, 美國女小說家)。
*__buck__¹ [bʌk; bʌk] *n.* ①雄鹿;雄兔; 公羊。②紈袴子。③〖俗〗人。④〖蔑〗美國印第安人或黑人(指男性)。⑤臺架。*—v.i.*①跳躍(使背上之人或物摔落)。②振作〖up〗. ③抵抗;堅決反對。④〖俗〗(汽車)顚簸地行駛。*—v.t.* ①使…摔下。The horse *bucked* the rider off. 馬跳躍使騎者摔下馬背。②〖橄欖球〗帶球衝鋒。③頑强抵抗; 奮戰。④猛衝; 以頭衝刺。The plane *bucked* a strong head wind. 飛機衝着强烈的逆風飛行。⑤襲擊;攻擊。⑥打賭;冒險。***buck for***〖俚〗爲調升或利益而努力。***buck up*** 變爲快樂或有活力。***feel*** (or ***be***)

greatly bucked 精神大振。—*adj.*〖軍〗同一稱呼中之最低階的。

buck² *n.* 撲克牌戲中置於分牌者面前之物。*pass the buck*〖俗〗推諉責任。

buck³ *n.*〖美俗〗元。—*v.t.* 劈；鋸。

buck⁴ *n.* ①鋸木架；鋸臺。②(運動用)木馬。

buck basket 洗衣筐。

buck bean〖植物〗睡菜。

buck·board 〔ˈbʌkˌbord; ˈbʌkbɔːd〕 *n.* 一種四輪馬車。

buck·er 〔ˈbʌkɚ; ˈbʌkə〕 *n.* 好跳躍(以摔下所負之人或物)的騾馬。

buck·et** 〔ˈbʌkɪt; ˈbʌkit〕 *n., v.,* **-et·ed, -et·ing.** —*n.* ①水桶；弔桶。②水車的戽斗。③一桶的量。Pour in about four *buckets* of water. 倒進大約四弔桶水。④渦輪機上之瓣。⑤唧筒內之活塞。⑥馬鞭、卡賓槍、矛等之皮套。⑦〖俚〗船。a drop in the bucket*** 滄海一粟。The amount being spent on basic research is *a drop in the bucket.* 花費在基本研究上的錢微不足道。***give the bucket***〖俗〗解雇。***kick the bucket***〖俚〗死。—*v.t.* & *v.i.* 以弔桶汲取或攜帶。—**ful,** *n.*

bucket brigade ①(救火時)排成長龍以傳水桶的一隊人。②緊急組成的一羣人。

bucket shop 投機商店。

buck·eye 〔ˈbʌkˌaɪ; ˈbʌkai〕 *n.* ①七葉樹。②七葉樹果實。③一種蝴蝶。④(B-)〖俗〗美國 Ohio 州人。⑤低劣藝術品。⑥低級而誇張的廣告。—*adj.* 誇張的；刺耳或刺目的。

buck·horn 〔ˈbʌkˌhɔrn; ˈbʌkhɔːn〕 *n.* 鹿角。

buck·hound 〔ˈbʌkˌhaund; ˈbʌkhaund〕 *n.* 獵鹿用之獵犬。

Buck·ing·ham Palace 〔ˈbʌkɪŋˌhæm～; ˈbʌkiŋəm～〕白金漢宮(英國皇宮)。

buck·ish 〔ˈbʌkɪʃ; ˈbʌkiʃ〕 *adj.* ①有惡臭的；似公羊的。②愛時髦的；浮華的。

buck·jump 〔ˈbʌkˌdʒʌmp; ˈbʌkdʒʌmp〕 *v.i.* (馬)突然曲背使乘者跌落。—*n.* 如鹿、馬、驢等之突然跳躍。

buck-jump·er 〔ˈbʌkˌdʒʌmpɚ; ˈbʌkˌdʒʌmpə〕 *n.* ①突然躍起使乘者跌落之馬。②作buckjump 之人或動物。

***buck·le** 〔ˈbʌkl; ˈbʌkl〕 *n., v.,* **-led, -ling.** —*n.* ①鈕子；鞋鈕。Fasten the *buckles* in your pants. 把你褲子的鈕子扣好。②彎曲；膨脹；皺紋。—*v.t.* ①扣住。②努力從事。He *buckled* himself to a hard job. 他努力從事一件艱難的工作。③使彎曲或變形。—*v.i.*①努力從事。②彎曲；變形；起皺。③放棄；屈服〖常 under〗。④扣鈕鈕〖常 up〗。*Buckle* up for safety. 爲安全把鈕子扣好。⑤用鈕子扣起來。—**buck·led,** *adj.*

buck·ler 〔ˈbʌklɚ; ˈbʌklə〕 *n.*①小圓盾。②作掩護或防衛的人或物。③防禦。—*v.t.* 以盾保護；防禦。

buck·o 〔ˈbʌko; ˈbʌkou〕 *n., pl.* **buck-oes.** 惡霸；暴漢。

buck·pass·ing 〔ˈbʌkˌpæsɪŋ; ˈbʌkˌpɑːsiŋ〕 *n.* 委過於人。—**buck·pass·er,** *n.*

buck private 〖美俚〗二等兵。

buck·ram 〔ˈbʌkrəm; ˈbʌkrəm〕 *n., adj., v.,* **-ramed, -ram·ing.** —*n.* ①膠硬的粗布。②態度的僵硬；古板。—*adj.* ①驕傲的；僵硬的；古板的。②硬粗布製的。—*v.t.* 用 buckram 加强。

buck·saw 〔ˈbʌkˌsɔ; ˈbʌksɔː〕 *n.* 一種雙手使用的鋸。

buck·shee 〔ˈbʌkʃi; ˈbʌkʃiː〕 *n.*〖英軍俚〗額外之配給；意外獲得之物。—*adj.*〖英軍俚〗免費的；特別的。

buck·shot 〔ˈbʌkˌʃɑt; ˈbʌkʃɔt〕 *n.* 大型鉛彈。

buck·skin 〔ˈbʌkˌskɪn; ˈbʌkskin〕 *n.* ①鹿皮；鹿皮革。②(*pl.*) 鹿皮的褲或鞋。③(B-) 美國革命時着鹿皮衣之兵。④鹿皮色的馬。⑤穿鹿皮衣的鄉下人。⑥一種衣料。—*adj.* 鹿皮製的；鹿皮色的。

buck·thorn 〔ˈbʌkˌθɔrn; ˈbʌkθɔːn〕 *n.*〖植物〗鼠李。

buck·tooth 〔ˈbʌkˌtuθ; ˈbʌktuːθ〕 *n., pl.* **-teeth.** 齙牙。—**ed,** *adj.*

buck·wheat 〔ˈbʌkˌhwit; ˈbʌkwiːt〕 *n.* ①〖植物〗蕎麥。②蕎麥麪。

bu·col·ic〔bjuˈkɑlɪk; bjuːˈkɔlik〕*adj.*(亦作 **bucolical**)①牧人的。②田舍的；鄉村的。—*n.* ①牧歌。②田舍郎。③田園詩人。—**al·ly,** *adv.*

bud¹** 〔bʌd; bʌd〕 *n., v.,* **bud·ded, bud·ding.** —*n.* ①芽；花蕾。②發芽期；含苞狀態。The flowers are now in *bud.* 花現正含苞待放。③未成熟的人或事。The plot has been nipped in the *bud.* 陰謀未成熟，卽被消滅。④〖解剖〗芽；蕾。⑤〖動物〗芽體。in bud*** 在發芽或含苞狀態中。***in the bud*** 未成熟或未發展的狀態。***nip in the bud*** 一開始卽加以阻止。—*v.i.* ①發芽；萌芽；生芽。Trees begin to *bud* in the spring. 樹在春天時開始生芽。②發育。—*v.t.* ①發出；使發芽。②接(芽)；移植；移種。

bud² *n.*〖俗〗①兄弟。②對男性較隨便的稱呼。

Bu·da·pest 〔ˌbjudəˈpɛst, ˌbu-; ˈbjuːdəˈpest, ˈbuː-〕 *n.* 布達佩斯(匈牙利的首都)。

Bud·dha 〔ˈbudə; ˈbudə〕*n.* 佛；佛陀；浮屠。

***Bud·dhism** 〔ˈbudɪzəm; ˈbudizəm〕 *n.* 佛教；佛法。—**Bud·dhist,** *n., adj.* —**Bud·dhis·tic, Bud·dhis·ti·cal,** *adj.* —**Bud·dhis·ti·cal·ly,** *adv.*

bud·ding 〔ˈbʌdɪŋ; ˈbʌdiŋ〕 *adj.* 發芽的；發育期中的；少壯的。—*n.* 發芽；生芽；接芽(法)。

bud·dy 〔ˈbʌdɪ; ˈbʌdi〕 *n., pl.* **-dies.** ①〖美俗〗同伴。②軍中伙伴。③小孩(用於直接稱呼)。(亦作 **buddie**)

bud·dy-bud·dy 〔ˈbʌdɪˈbʌdɪ; ˈbʌdiˈbʌdi〕 *adj.*〖俚〗很親密的。

budge¹ 〔bʌdʒ; bʌdʒ〕 *v.,* **budged, budg·ing.** —*v.i.* ①移動(常用否定式)。②改變意見或立場。—*v.t.* ①使動。②使(某人)改變意見、決定或立場。

budge² *n.* ①翻毛羔皮。②革袋。—*adj.* ①羔皮作裏或裝飾的。②莊嚴的；尊大的。

***budg·et** 〔ˈbʌdʒɪt; ˈbʌdʒit〕 *n., v.,* **-et·ed, -et·ing.** —*n.* ①預算；預算表。Everybody must have a *budget* of his own. 每人都應當有他自己的預算。②堆積；存積。We have a *budget* of news today. 今天我們有許多新聞。③根據預算而做的計畫。④〖方〗皮包；袋；皮包或袋內之物。—*v.t.* 設計使用。—*v.i.*預算。to *budget* for the coming year. 定明年預算。

budg·et·ar·y〔ˈbʌdʒɪˌtɛrɪ; ˈbʌdʒitəri〕 *adj.* 預算的。

budget plan 分期付款。

Bue·nos Ai·res 〔ˈbwenɔsˈaɪres; ˈbwenəsˈaiəriz〕 布宜諾斯艾利斯(南美洲阿根廷的首都)。

buff 〔bʌf; bʌf〕 *n.* ①淺黃色之軟牛皮革。②牛皮製之軍衣。③淺黃色。④〖俚〗赤裸。⑤磨光用之棒或紡錘狀物。⑥〖俗〗對某事有研究或特別熟悉的人。⑦〖俗〗水牛。***in buff*** 裸體。***strip to the buff*** 將衣服剝光。—*v.t.* 以棒磨光；使光軟如皮革。—*adj.* 牛皮製的；淺黃色的。

***buf·fa·lo** 〔ˈbʌflˌo; ˈbʌfəlou〕 *n., pl.* **-loes, -los** or **-lo,** *v.,* **-loed, -lo·ing.** —*n.* ①牛；水牛。water *buffalo.* 水牛。②〖軍俚〗

重裝甲的兩棲車輛。—*v.t.* 〖美俚〗①恐嚇;威嚇。②使困惑;神祕化。

buffalo robe 用帶毛之美洲野牛皮做的大衣或地毯。

buff·coat [ˈbʌfˌkot; ˈbʌfkout] *n.* ①鹿皮製之厚上衣。②穿此種上衣的人;軍人。

buff·er¹ [ˈbʌfɚ; ˈbʌfə] *n.* ①緩衝器。②任何可供緩衝之事物。③緩衝國。④可保護某人、某機構或國家使其不破產的預備金、有價證券、或法律程序等。⑤被食肉動物所捕食之動物。—*v.t.* ①緩衝;保護。②減輕。

buff·er² *n.* ①磨光之人。②磨輪或磨棒。

buffer state 緩衝國。

buf·fet¹ [bʌˈfe; ˈbʌfit *for n.* ①, buˈfe, ˈbufe; ˈbufei] *n.* ①餐具櫥。②飲食店供備飲食的櫃臺。③有此種櫃臺設備的小餐館。④自助餐。—*adj.* 自助餐的。

buf·fet² [ˈbʌfɪt; ˈbʌfit] *n., v.,* **-fet·ed, -fet·ing.** —*n.* 手打;拳擊;打擊。—*v.t.* ①手打;拳擊。②反擊;與…掙扎。③奪路而進。—*v.i.* ①掙扎;奮鬥。②奪路而進。

buffet car 餐車。

buffet dinner (lunch, or **supper)** 自助餐。

buf·fle·head [ˈbʌflˌhɛd; ˈbʌflhed] *n.* ①北美產小鴨。②蠢人;笨蛋。

buf·fo [ˈbuffo; ˈbufou] *n., pl.* **buf·fi** [ˈbufi; ˈbufiː], **-fos,** *adj.* 〖義〗—*n.* 歌劇中演唱滑稽角色之男歌手。—*adj.* 滑稽的。

buf·foon [bʌˈfun; bʌˈfuːn] *n.* ①丑角;滑稽劇演員。②好講粗俗笑話的人。—*v.i.* 扮演 buffoon.

buf·foon·er·y [bʌˈfunərɪ; bʌˈfuːnəri] *n., pl.* **-er·ies.** ①滑稽。②粗俗的笑話。

bug** [bʌg; bʌg] *v.,* **bugged, bug·ging,** *n.* —*v.t.* 〖俗〗①使煩惱。②裝置竊聽設備。The room has been *bugged.* 這間房裝有竊聽器。③趕快地離開〖常 out〗. ④打擾;不停地勸說。bug off*** 〖美俚〗匆匆離開。—*n.* ①小蟲(尤指爬蟲, 如臭蟲)。②〖俗〗病菌。③機器的缺點。④興味;着迷。⑤…迷。⑥星號。⑦隱藏之麥克風。

bug·a·boo [ˈbʌgəˌbu; ˈbʌgəbuː] *n., pl.* **-boos.** 鬼怪;想像中的嚇人的東西。

bug·bear [ˈbʌgˌbɛr; ˈbʌgbɛə] *n.* ①足以引起不必要恐怖的事物。②專吃淘氣孩子的妖精。③主要的困難或難題。④爲小事而起的恨。

bug boy 〖美俚〗賽馬騎師的學徒。

bug-eyed [ˈbʌgˌaɪd; ˈbʌgaid] *adj.* 〖俚〗凸眼的。

bug·ger [ˈbʌgɚ; ˈbʌgə] *n.* ①鷄姦者;獸姦者。②可鄙之人。③夥計;傢伙。—*v.t.* 鷄姦。—*v.i.* 〖英俚〗離開;出發〖off〗. ***bugger about*** 無事忙。—**y,** *n.*

bug·gy¹ [ˈbʌgɪ; ˈbʌgi] *n., pl.* **-gies.** ①〖美〗四輪單座之馬車。②〖英〗雙輪單座之馬車。③〖俚〗老爺車。④運金屬塊之卡車。⑤運煤車。⑥嬰兒車。

bug·gy² *adj.,* **-gi·er, -gi·est.** ①多蟲的;多臭蟲的。②〖俚〗瘋的;怪僻的;愚蠢的。

bug·house [ˈbʌgˌhaus; ˈbʌghaus] *n.* 〖美俚〗精神病院。—*adj.* 〖美俚〗瘋狂的。

bug·hunt·er [ˈbʌgˌhʌntɚ; ˈbʌgˌhʌntə] *n.* 〖英俚〗昆蟲學者。

***bu·gle¹** [ˈbjugl; ˈbjuːgl] *n., v.,* **-gled, -gling.** —*n.* 號角;喇叭。—*v.t. & v.i.* ①吹號角。②以喇叭召集或發布命令。

bu·gle² *n.* 裝飾女服之黑色長形玻璃珠。—*adj.* (亦作 **bugled**)有長形玻璃珠鑲飾的。

bu·gle³ *n.* 〖植物〗夏枯草。

bu·gler [ˈbjuglɚ; ˈbjuːglə] *n.* 吹號角者;號兵;號手;喇叭手。

bu·gloss [ˈbjuglɑs; ˈbjuːglɔs] *n.* 牛舌草。

bugs [bʌgz; bʌgz] *adj.* 〖俚〗瘋狂的。

buhl [bul; buːl] *n.* 布爾細工(鑲嵌金、銀等於木材上)。

‡build [bɪld; bild] *v.,* **built, build·ing,** *n.* —*v.t.* ①建築;建造。His house was *built* after a European model. 他的房子是模仿歐洲的樣式建築的。②建立;基於。We must *build* a case on facts. 我們必須根據事實建立案件。③設立;創設;創建。He has *built* up a business of his own. 他已創設他自己的事業。—*v.i.* ①建築;營造。②信賴。We can *build* on that man's honesty. 我們可以信賴那個人的誠實。③建立一種計畫、思想體系等〖常 on, upon〗. ***build in*** 建(某物)使其成爲他物之一部分。He *built in* bookcases between the windows. 他在窗與窗之間裝設書櫥。***build up*** **a.** 增加;加強。**b.** 讚揚;捧場。**c.** 發展爲市區。—*n.* ①體格。His *build* is not suitable for hard work. 他的體格不適宜於做繁重的工作。②工程;建造的式樣。This hotel is of excellent *build.* 這旅館建築得極好。

***build·er** [ˈbɪldɚ; ˈbildə] *n.* ①建築者;營造商。He went into business as a *builder.* 他以營造商爲職業。②建立者;建造者。

‡build·ing [ˈbɪldɪŋ; ˈbildiŋ] *n.* ①建築物。②建築術;建築業。Business in *building* is dull this year. 今年建築業生意蕭條。

build-up [ˈbɪldˌʌp; ˈbildʌp] *n.* ①〖俚〗有計畫之宣傳;揄揚。②建立。③集結。④某種物質或能量的累積;形成。⑤預備工作。⑥累積。⑦壓力、强度等之增加。⑧鼓勵。

‡built [bɪlt; bilt] *v.* pt. & pp. of **build.** —*adj.* 〖俚〗身段優美的。—*n.* 〖俚〗好身段。

built-in [ˈbɪltˈɪn; ˈbiltˈin] *adj.* ①與建築結構連在一起的。②生就的;內在的。—*n.* 與建築結構連在一起的傢具或用具。

built-up [ˈbɪltˈʌp; ˈbiltˈʌp] *adj.* ①由數個部分結構而成的;合成的;增加層數而擴大的。②蓋滿了房屋或住滿了人的。

***bulb** [bʌlb; bʌlb] *n.* ①植物的球莖。②球莖狀物;電燈泡。the *bulb* of an electric lamp. 電燈泡。

bulb·ar [ˈbʌlbɑr; ˈbʌlbə] *adj.* 球莖的。

bulb·if·er·ous [bʌlˈbɪfərəs; bʌlˈbifərəs] *adj.* 生球莖的;生球根的。

bul·bi·form [ˈbʌlbɪˌfɔrm; ˈbʌlbifɔːm] *adj.* 球莖狀的。

bul·bous [ˈbʌlbəs; ˈbʌlbəs] *adj.* ①球莖的;球莖狀的。②有球莖的;從球莖而生的。(亦作 **bulbaceous**)

bul·bul [ˈbulbul; ˈbulbul] *n.* 夜鶯。

Bulg. ①Bulgaria. ②Bulgarian.

Bul·gar [ˈbʌlgɑr; ˈbʌlgɑː] *n.* 保加利亞人。

Bul·gar·i·a [bʌlˈgɛrɪə; bʌlˈgɛəriə] *n.* 保加利亞(歐洲東南一國, 首都索非亞 Sofia).

Bul·gar·i·an [bʌlˈgɛrɪən; bʌlˈgɛəriən] *adj.* 保加利亞(人)的;保加利亞語的。—*n.* ①保加利亞人。②保加利亞的語言。

bulge** [bʌldʒ; bʌldʒ] *v.,* **bulged, bulg·ing,** *n.* —*v.i.* 突出。—*v.t.* 使膨脹。The apples *bulged* his pocket. 蘋果使他的衣袋膨脹。—*n.* ①凸出。②任何突然的增加。Battle of the Bulge*** 第二次世界大戰中德國最後一次反攻。***get*** (or ***have***) ***the bulge on*** 〖美俚〗對…占優勢。

bulg·er [ˈbʌldʒɚ; ˈbʌldʒə] *n.* ①〖高爾夫〗凸面球棒。②〖美〗凸出物。

bulg·y [ˈbʌldʒɪ; ˈbʌldʒi] *adj.* 膨脹的;凸出的。

bu·lim·i·a [bjuˈlɪmɪə; bjuˈlimiə] *n.* 〖醫〗貪食症;善饑。(亦作 **bulimy, boulimia**)

bulk** [bʌlk; bʌlk] *n.* ①大小;巨大;巨大的體積。 He is a man of large *bulk.* 他是一個魁梧的人。②大部分;大半。 Sugar forms the huge *bulk* of our exports. 糖為我們出口的大宗。③堆;大量;容量。④散裝貨。 *bulk* cargo freighter. 散裝貨輪。⑤厚度。⑥軀體。⑦從建築物突起之構造。 ***in bulk a. 散裝(不加包裝)。 b. 大量;批發。 to sell *in bulk.* 整批出售;批發。 —*v.i.* ①漲大;長大;增大。②現巨形;變為重要。 His fame *bulks* large. 他的聲譽大噪。③成為一定的厚度。④溶和或混合。 —*v.t.* ①使膨脹,增大。②混合在一起。

bulk buying 大宗購買。

bulk·head [ˈbʌlkˌhɛd; ˈbʌlkhed] *n.* ①船艙之隔壁。②礦坑內之分壁。③任何箱狀結構物。 —**ed,** *adj.*

bulk·i·ness [ˈbʌlkɪnɪs; ˈbʌlkinis] *n.* 龐大;笨重。

bulk mail 大批郵寄之印刷品郵件,其郵資較低。

bulk·y [ˈbʌlkɪ; ˈbʌlki] *adj.,* **bulk·i·er, bulk·i·est.** 龐大的;笨重的。—**bulk·i·ly,** *adv.*

bull**[1] [bul; bul] *n.* ①公牛。②雄的大動物。③購買證券、股票等並圖抬高其行市以謀利者;多頭。④高壯的人;彪形大漢。⑤(B-)〖天文〗金牛座;金牛宮 (=Taurus). ⑥〖俚〗警察;偵探;刑警。⑦〖俚〗空話;假話。⑧相信經濟將好轉的人。⑨牛頭犬 (=bulldog). ⑩〖橋牌,俗〗不管手裏之牌而加分的人。 ***a bull in a china shop 動輒闖禍者;粗人。 ***bull session*** 〖俗〗自由討論;隨便討論。 ***like a bull at a gate*** 猛烈地;兇猛地。 ***shoot the bull*** 〖俚〗 a. 作無意義的談話;瞎扯。 b. 聊天;閒談。 ***sling*** (or ***throw***) ***the bull*** 〖俚〗吹牛;誇張。 ***take the bull by the horns*** 不畏艱難;冒險;毅然處斷難局。 —*v.t.* ①企圖抬高(股票、證券等)之價格;使(行情)上漲。②强迫;擠。③〖航海〗撞倒 (浮筒)。 —*v.i.* (股票、證券等) 漲價;行情上漲。 —*adj.* ①公的。②粗壯如牛的;高大如牛的;像牛一樣的。③大號的。④價格上漲的。

bull[2] *n.* ①教皇勅書所用之璽。②教皇勅書或訓諭。

bull[3] *n.* 矛盾不合邏輯之言。

bull. bulletin.

bul·lace [ˈbulɪs; ˈbulis] *n.* 一種西洋李子;野李子。

bull·bait·ing [ˈbulˌbetɪŋ; ˈbulˌbeitiŋ] *n.* 嗾犬逗牛之遊戲。

bull-calf [ˈbulˈkæf; ˈbulˈkɑːf] *n.* 小公牛。

bull dike 〖俚〗女子同性戀中扮演男人角色者。

***bull·dog** [ˈbulˌdɔg; ˈbuldɔg] *n., adj., v.,* **-dogged, -dog·ging.** —*n.* ①鬥牛犬;牛頭犬。②一種大口徑,短銷管的左輪槍。③〖英俗〗英國牛津劍橋大學訓導長之助理。 —*adj.* 似此種猛犬的。 *bulldog* courage. 不屈的勇氣。 —*v.t.* 用手握住雄牛之角,扭其頸而使之倒地;摔倒;猛攻。 —**ged·ness,** *n.*

bull·doze [ˈbulˌdoz; ˈbuldouz] *v.t.,* **-dozed, -doz·ing.** ①〖美俗〗恐嚇;威嚇。②用推土機推平。③用推土機清理。④强迫;壓制。⑤鞭打。

bull·doz·er [ˈbulˌdozɚ; ˈbulˌdouzə] *n.* 〖美俗〗①恐嚇者。②推土機。③〖俚〗大型左輪槍。

***bul·let** [ˈbulɪt; ˈbulit] *n.* ①子彈。 The *bullet* missed him by one inch. 子彈差一英寸未擊中他。②彈藥包。 —*v.i.* 迅速移動。

bul·let·head [ˈbulɪtˌhɛd; ˈbulithed] *n.* ①圓頭。②頭圓之人。③〖美俗〗頑固或愚蠢的人。

bul·let·head·ed [ˈbulɪtˌhɛdɪd; ˈbulitˌhedid] *n.* ①圓頭的。②頑固的。③愚蠢的。 —**ness,** *n.*

***bul·le·tin** [ˈbulətɪn; ˈbulitin] *n.* ①告示;公報;報告。②小型雜誌或報紙。③快報;速報。④年度報告。⑤學術團體之定期刊物。 —*v.t.* 公告;告示。

bulletin board 布告牌。

bul·let·proof [ˈbulɪtˌpruf; ˈbulitpruːf] *adj.* 防彈的。

bull·fight [ˈbulˌfaɪt; ˈbul-fait] *n.* 鬥牛戲。 —**er, —ing,** *n.*

bull·finch [ˈbulˌfɪntʃ; ˈbul-fintʃ] *n.* (鳥)照鶯。

bull·frog [ˈbulˌfrɑg; ˈbul-frɔg] *n.* 牛蛙。

bull·head [ˈbulˌhɛd; ˈbulhed] *n.* ①鯰屬之魚。②千鳥之類。③愚頑之人。

bull·head·ed [ˈbulˈhɛdɪd; ˈbulˈhedid] *adj.* ①有似公牛之頭的。②愚梗的;頑固的。

bul·lion [ˈbuljən; ˈbuljən] *n.* ①金塊;銀塊;金條;銀條。②金或銀線所編的纓綫或花邊。

bul·lion·ism [ˈbuljənɪzm̩; ˈbuljənizm] *n.* 金銀通貨主義。

bul·lion·ist [ˈbuljənɪst; ˈbuljənist] *n.* 金銀通貨主義者。

bull·ish [ˈbulɪʃ; ˈbuliʃ] *adj.* ①似公牛的。②頑梗的;愚笨的。③〖商〗看漲的。④樂觀的。 —**ly,** *adv.* —**ness,** *n.*

bull·necked [ˈbulˌnɛkt; ˈbulnekt] *adj.* 有粗短之頸項的。

bull·ock [ˈbulək; ˈbulək] *n.* 閹牛。

bull pen ①牛欄。②〖俗〗暴動發生時,感化院內集中囚犯之處所;任何監獄。③〖棒球〗接替投手練習投球之區域;接替投手。④臨時住所。

Bull·pup [ˈbulˌpʌp; ˈbulpʌp] *n.* 〖美軍〗犢牛飛彈(一種空對地導引飛彈)。

bull ring 鬥牛場。

bull-roar·er [ˈbulˌrorɚ; ˈbulˌrɔːrə] *n.* 牛吼器(於繩之一端繫以木片,旋轉舞動時發聲)。

bull's-eye [ˈbulzˌaɪ; ˈbulzai] *n.* ①鵠的;靶心。②打中靶心的一擊。③牛眼窗(船甲板上或船側的厚圓玻璃窗)。④半球形透鏡。⑤牛眼燈(裝有此透鏡者)。⑥小圓窗。⑦中心目標。⑧攻打目標之投射武器。⑨〖俗〗 a. 中肯之言行。 b. 決定性之事物。⑩颱風眼。⑪一種硬的糖果。

bull·shit [ˈbulˌʃɪt; ˈbulʃit] *n., v.,* **-shit, -shit·ting,** *interj.* 〖俚鄙〗—*n.* 胡說;謊話;誇張。 —*v.t.* & *v.i.* 說謊;胡說。 —*interj.* 表示懷疑、不贊成等之感歎詞。

bull terrier bulldog 與 terrier 雜交所生之犬。

bull trout 鮭魚之一種。

bull·whip [ˈbulˌhwɪp; ˈbulhwip] *n.* 短柄之鞭。 —*v.t.* 以短柄鞭抽打。(亦作 **bullwhack**)

***bul·ly**[1] [ˈbulɪ; ˈbuli] *n., pl.* **-lies,** *v.,* **-lied, -ly·ing,** *adj., interj.* —*n.* 欺凌弱小者;土霸。 —*v.t.* 恐嚇;威脅;欺負。 to *bully* a person into doing something. 威脅某人做某事。 —*adj.* ①〖俗〗豪俠的;勇敢的。②〖俗〗好的。 —*interj.* 〖俗〗好呀! *Bully* for us! 好呀! 妙!

bul·ly[2] *n.* 罐頭牛肉(=bully beef).

bul·ly·rag [ˈbulɪˌræg; ˈbuliræg] *v.t.,* **-ragged, -rag·ging.** ①威嚇;恫嚇。②惡罵;嘲笑。

bul·rush [ˈbulˌrʌʃ; ˈbulrʌʃ] *n.* ①蘆葦。②〖英〗香蒲。③〖聖經〗紙草。

bul·wark [ˈbulwək; ˈbulwək] *n.* ①壁

壘;堡壘。②防禦;保衞。Law is the *bulwark* of society. 法律是社會的防禦工具。③防波堤。④(*pl.*) 甲板上之船舷。—*v.t.* ①建堡壘以防禦。②防禦;保衞。

bum¹ (bʌm; bʌm) *n., v.,* **bummed, bumming,** *adj.,* **bum·mer, bum·mest.** —*n.* 〖美俗〗①遊蕩者;遊手閒者。②鬧飲。***on the bum*** **a.** 過遊蕩生活;做游民。**b.**〖俚〗損壞;故障。***the bum's rush*** 逐出;趕出。—*v.i.* 〖美俗〗①遊蕩。②縱飲。③乞食度日。—*v.t.* 〖美俗〗乞得;依人爲生。—*adj.*〖美俗〗廉價的;劣質的;錯誤的。

bum² *n.* ①嗡嗡之聲。②屁股;臀部。

bum·bail·iff (bʌmˈbelɪf; bʌmˈbeilif) *n.* 〖英蔑〗執達員;捕役。

bum·ble (ˈbʌmbḷ; ˈbʌmbl) *v.,* **-bled, -bling,** *n.* —*v.i.*①拙劣地做;弄糟。②顚躓;顚倒。—*v.t.* 拙劣地做;弄糟。—*n.* 錯誤。

bum·ble·bee (ˈbʌmbḷˌbi; ˈbʌmblbiː) *n.* 大黃蜂;土蜂。

bum·ble·dom (ˈbʌmbḷdəm; ˈbʌmbldəm) *n.* 傲慢;夜郎自大;小官僚的妄自尊大。

bum·bling (ˈbʌmblɪŋ; ˈbʌmbliŋ) *adj.*①易犯錯的。②無能的;無效的。—*n.*錯誤;笨拙。

bum·bo (ˈbʌmbo; ˈbʌmbou) *n.* 甘蔗酒或杜松子酒羼冷水和香料調和而成之冷飲。

bum·boat (ˈbʌmˌbot; ˈbʌmbout) *n.* 向停泊中的大船賣雜貨及食物等之小舟。

bum·mer (ˈbʌmɚ; ˈbʌmə) *n.* 〖美俚〗依賴他人而過活的人;怠惰無用之人。

bump** (bʌmp; bʌmp) *v.t.* ①撞;碰;擊。He *bumped* his head against the wall. 他的頭碰着了牆。②撞落。The cat *bumped* the vase off the shelf. 那隻貓把花瓶從架上撞落。③徵用低級人員之工作、權益、或住宿等。④解雇;拒絕;投票反對。⑤提高。He *bumped* the price of corn. 他提高了玉蜀黍的價錢。⑥取消(赴某地之)旅遊計畫。—*v.i.* ①碰撞;衝撞。They *bumped* against each other. 他們互相撞着。②顚簸地走。③跳富有誘惑性之舞。④突然沸騰。bump into*** 意外碰到。***bump off*** 〖俚〗殺死。—*n.* ①碰撞;猛擊。②腫塊。He made a *bump* on his head owing to a car accident.他因汽車發生意外, 頭上撞腫一塊。③〖俚〗升遷或降級。④〖俚〗增加(錢);加薪。He asked the boss for a 10-dollar *bump*. 他向老闆要求加薪十元。⑤〖航空〗上升氣流。⑥富誘惑性之舞。⑦地面隆起部分。

bump·er¹ (ˈbʌmpɚ; ˈbʌmpə) *n.* ①汽車前後之保險槓。②撞擊之人或物。③緩衝之物。④〖俗〗特大之事物。⑤用手塑造磚瓦之人。

bump·er² *n.* 滿杯。—*v.t.* ①倒滿杯。②乾杯以祝。—*v.i.* 飲祝。—*adj.* 豐盛的。

bumper jack 頂在汽車保險槓上將車身舉起的千斤頂。

bumper sticker 汽車保險槓上的招貼。

bumping race 一種追撞船賽。

bump·kin (ˈbʌmpkɪn; ˈbʌmpkin) *n.* 鄉巴佬。(亦作 **bumkin**)

bump·off (ˈbʌmpˌɔf; ˈbʌmpɔːf) *n.* 〖俚〗謀殺。

bump·tious (ˈbʌmpʃəs; ˈbʌmpʃəs) *adj.* 傲慢的;唐突的。—**ly,** *adv.*

bump·y (ˈbʌmpɪ; ˈbʌmpi) *adj.,* **bump·i·er, bump·i·est.** ①坑窪不平的;崎嶇的。②顚簸的;反跳多的。③氣壓變動多的。

bum's rush ①從某處強迫逐出。②粗魯或突然的解雇或逐出。

bun¹** (bʌn; bʌn) *n.* ①小甜圓麪包;小饅頭。②小圓圈形之捲髮式。take the bun*** 占第一位。(亦作 **bunn**)

bun² *n.* 〖俚〗酒醉。

bun³ *n.* ①松鼠。②兔。

bu·na (ˈbjunə; ˈbjuːnə) *n.* 一種人造橡膠。

Bun·bur·y (ˈbʌnbərɪ; ˈbʌnbəri) *v.i.,* **-bur·ied, -bur·y·ing.** 作觀光旅行。

bunch** (bʌntʃ; bʌntʃ) *n.* ①束;球;串。He gave me a *bunch* of grapes. 他給我一串葡萄。②羣。We saw a *bunch* of students. 我們看到一羣學生。③腫塊。best of the bunch*** 有限數量中之最佳者。***pick of the bunch*** 一批或一羣中之最佳者。—*v.t.* ①縛爲紮;縛爲束。The florist *bunched* the flowers. 這花匠將花縛成花束。②團在一起;皺起。—*v.i.* 羣集。

bunch·ber·ry (ˈbʌntʃˌbɛrɪ; ˈbʌntʃbəri) *n., pl.* **-ries.** 〖植物〗御膳橘。

Bunche (bʌntʃ; bʌntʃ) *n.* 彭區 (Ralph, 1904–1971,美外交家,1950年獲諾貝爾和平獎)。

bunch·flow·er (ˈbʌntʃˌflauɚ; ˈbʌntʃˌflauə) *n.* 〖植物〗百合科之一種。

bunch·y (ˈbʌntʃɪ; ˈbʌntʃi) *adj.,* **bunch·i·er, bunch·i·est.** ①成穗的;成束的;成串的。②腫的。

bun·co (ˈbʌŋko; ˈbʌŋkou) *n., pl.* **-cos,** *v.,* **-coed, -co·ing.** —*n.* 〖俗〗欺詐;騙局。—*v.t.* 〖俗〗設局詐騙;欺騙。(亦作 **bunko**)

bun·combe (ˈbʌŋkəm; ˈbʌŋkəm) *n.* 〖俗〗①討人歡心之演說;討好(選民)之談話。②引人喝采的詭計;虛言。(亦作 **bunkum**)

Bund (bunt, bund; bunt, bund) *n., pl.* **Bün·de** (ˈbyndə; ˈbyndə). 〖德〗聯盟。

bund (bʌnd; bʌnd) *n.* 堤岸;碼頭。

bun·dle** (ˈbʌndḷ; ˈbʌndl) *n., v.,* **-dled, -dling.** —*n.* ①捆;束;紮。a *bundle* of old clothes. 一捆舊衣。②包;包裹。We received a *bundle* from our friend. 我們收到朋友寄來的包裹。③羣。④〖俚〗一捆鈔票。⑤〖英俚〗不良少年鬥毆。—*v.t.* ①捆起;包紮。②推開;倉惶遣去〖常 off, out〗. The children were *bundled* off to bed.小孩們匆匆被遣去就寢。—*v.i.* ①急離;急去。②(早期新英格蘭之情人)穿着整齊而睡在一起。bundle one out*** (or ***off***) 匆匆趕走;攆出某人。***bundle up*** 穿着暖和衣服;裹暖;包紮。It's pretty cold outside. You'd better *bundle up* well. 外頭很冷, 你最好多穿點衣服。

bung (bʌŋ; bʌŋ) *n.* ①桶塞。②桶上之孔。—*v.t.* ①塞(桶)孔;塞住〖up〗. ②〖俚〗打腫〖up〗.

bun·ga·loid (ˈbʌŋgəˌlɔɪd; ˈbʌŋgəlɔid) *adj.* 〖蔑〗①平房的。②多平房的。

***bun·ga·low** (ˈbʌŋgəˌlo; ˈbʌŋgəlou) *n.* ①平房。②別墅;小屋。

bung·hole (ˈbʌŋˌhol; ˈbʌŋhoul) *n.* 桶口;桶孔。

bun·gle (ˈbʌŋgḷ; ˈbʌŋgl) *v.,* **-gled, -gling,** *n.* —*v.t. & v.i.* 拙劣地工作;搞壞。—*n.* ①拙劣的工作。②拙劣工作的成品。

bun·gling (ˈbʌŋglɪŋ; ˈbʌŋgliŋ) *adj.* 拙劣的。—*n.* 拙劣的工作;笨手笨脚的行動。

bun·ion (ˈbʌnjən; ˈbʌnjən) *n.* 〖醫〗大趾根黏液囊炎腫。(亦作 **bunyon**)

bunk¹ (bʌŋk; bʌŋk) *n.* 倚壁而設的床鋪(如舟、車上者)。—*v.i.* ①睡在此種鋪上。②〖俗〗睡眠。to *bunk* on the floor. 在地板上打地鋪。③同住一處。

bunk² *n.* 〖俚〗=**buncombe.** —*v.t.* 欺騙;胡說。

bunk³ *v.t.* 撞;碰。

bunk⁴ 〖英俚〗*v.t.* ①逃避。—*v.i.* 逃走;溜走。—*n.* 逃跑。

bunk bed 雙層床。

bunk·er [ˈbʌŋkɚ; ˈbʌŋkə] *n.* ①船上之煤倉。②〖高爾夫〗穴；坑窪。③大桶；任何大容器。④築於地下之碉堡。—*v.t.* ①〖高爾夫〗擊(球)入穴。②供燃料給船隻。③從船上卸(散裝貨)到倉庫。

bunk·er·age [ˈbʌŋkərɪdʒ; ˈbʌŋkəridʒ] *n.* ①供燃料給船隻。②卸船上之散裝貨。

bunk·house [ˈbʌŋkˌhaus; ˈbʌŋkhaus] *n.* 工寮。

bunk·ie [ˈbʌŋkɪ; ˈbʌŋki] *n.*〖俚〗同伴；同床之人。(亦作 **bunky**)

bun·ko [ˈbʌŋko; ˈbʌŋkou] *n.*, *pl.* **-kos,** *v.*, **-koed, -ko·ing.** =**bunco.**

bun·kum [ˈbʌŋkəm; ˈbʌŋkəm] *n.* =**buncombe.**

***bun·ny** [ˈbʌnɪ; ˈbʌni] *n.*, *pl.* **-nies.** ①〖俗〗兎子(兒語)。②〖美俗〗松鼠。③〖俚〗花瓶(喻以漂亮而受男人寵愛的女性)。

Bun·sen burner [ˈbʌnsn̩～; ˈbunsn～] 〖化〗本生燈。

bunt¹ [bʌnt; bʌnt] *v.t.* & *v.i.* ①用頭或角牴撞；牴觸。②〖棒球〗觸擊；短打。—*n.* ①牴撞；牴觸；推擠。②〖棒球〗短打之動作；用短打擊出之球。

bunt² *n.* (小麥的)黑穗病。

bunt³ *n.* 帆、網等之中央膨起部分。—*v.i.* 膨脹。

bun·ting¹ [ˈbʌntɪŋ; ˈbʌntiŋ] *n.* ①製旗用之薄布。②旗幟之集合稱(尤指船旗)。(亦作 **bentine**)

bun·ting² *n.* 雀類。

bun·ting³ *n.* (嬰兒之)睡袋。

bunt·line [ˈbʌntlɪn; ˈbʌntlain] *n.* 帆脚之索。

Bun·yan [ˈbʌnjən; ˈbʌnjən] *n.* 班揚 (John, 1628–1688, 英國傳教士及作家，"天路歷程", *The Pilgrim's Progress* 作者)。

***buoy** [bɔɪ, ˈbu·ɪ; bɔi] *n.* ①浮標；浮筒。②救生圈；救生衣；救生帶(=life buoy). —*v.t.* ①用浮標作記號；置備浮標。②使浮起。③鼓勵；支持。*buoy up* **a.** 使不沉下去。**b.** 支持。**c.** 鼓勵。

buoy·age [ˈbɔɪɪdʒ; ˈbɔiidʒ] *n.* 浮標之集合稱；浮標設置。

buoy·an·cy [ˈbɔɪənsɪ; ˈbɔiənsi] *n.* ①浮力。②支持物體不沉的力量。③升起的傾向。④輕鬆愉快的心情。⑤物體浸於液體中的失重。

***buoy·ant** [ˈbɔɪənt; ˈbɔiənt] *adj.* ①能浮的；有浮力的。*buoyant* force. 浮力。②趨於上升的；上漲的(物價)。③快樂的；活潑的；有希望的。They are *buoyant* with good news. 他們因爲好消息而快樂。

buoy boat 拉住及拖已捕到的鯨魚的小船。

bur [bɝ; bəː] *n.*, *v.*, **burred, bur·ring.** —*n.* ①帶有芒刺之果實；針毬。②黏附着不離的東西。③依人爲生者。④〖牙醫〗鑽；圓頭銼。—*v.t.* 除去…之芒刺。(亦作 **burr**)

Bur. Burma. **bur.** bureau.

Bur·ber·ry [ˈbɝˌbɛrɪ; ˈbəːbəri] *n.*, *pl.* **-ries.** 〖商標名〗①雨衣。②一種防水布。

bur·ble [ˈbɝbl̩; ˈbəːbl] *v.*, **-bled, -bling,** *n.* —*v.i.* ①作潺流之聲；起泡。②說話滔滔不絕。—*n.* ①潺潺聲；緩湧。②滔滔不絕的說話。

bur·bot [ˈbɝbət; ˈbəːbət] *n.*, *pl.* **-bots** or **-bot.** 鱈類之淡水魚。

***bur·den¹** [ˈbɝdn̩; ˈbəːdn] *n.* ①負荷；重載。A camel can carry a heavy *burden.* 駱駝能負重載。②負擔；責任；重累。③噸位；船的載貨量。They built a ship of one thousand tons *burden.* 他們建造一艘載重一千噸的船。④船上所載貨物的重量。⑤〖礦〗應被炸藥除去的岩石與土堆。—*v.t.* 使負擔。

bur·den² *n.* ①反覆重述之言；主旨。②〖音樂〗**a.** 疊句；重唱句；副歌。**b.** 低音部的伴奏(唱)。

bur·dened [ˈbɝdn̩d; ˈbəːdnd] *adj.* 〖航海〗須讓路給另一艘有優先航行權之船的。

bur·den·some [ˈbɝdn̩səm; ˈbəːdnsəm] *adj.* ①累人的；麻煩的；沉重的。②〖航海〗(船)爲裝貨的(容積優先速度次之的)。

bur·dock [ˈbɝˌdɑk; ˈbəːdɔk] *n.* 〖植物〗牛蒡。

***bu·reau** [ˈbjʊro; bjuəˈrou, ˈbjuərou] *n.*, *pl.* **-reaus, -reaux** [-roz; -ˈrouz]. ①〖美〗五斗櫃；〖英〗寫字臺。②辦公處；公事房。a travel *bureau.* 旅行社。③政府的機關；局。

bu·reauc·ra·cy [bjʊˈrɑkrəsɪ; bjuəˈrɔkrəsi] *n.*, *pl.* **-cies.** ①官僚政治。②官吏(集合稱)。③分部集權政治。④官僚作風；繁文縟節。

bu·reau·crat [ˈbjʊrəˌkræt; ˈbjuərokræt] *n.* ①官僚。②死守規則不知靈活變通的官員。

bu·reau·crat·ic [ˌbjʊroˈkrætɪk; ˌbjuəroˈkrætik] *adj.* ①官僚的；官僚氣的；官樣文章的。②武斷的。(亦作 **bureaucratical**) —**al·ly,** *adv.*

bu·reau·crat·ism [bjʊˈrɑkrətɪzm̩; bjuəˈrɔkrətizm] *n.* 官僚主義；官僚作風。—**bu·reau·crat·ist,** *n.*

Bureau of Standards〖美〗標準局。

Bureau of the Budget〖美〗預算局。

Bureau of the Census 〖美〗人口局。

bu·rette [bjʊˈrɛt; bjuəˈret] *n.* 滴管。(亦作 **buret**)

burg [bɝg; bəːg] *n.* ①〖俗〗城；鎮。②〖史〗設防之城鎮。③〖英〗=**borough.**

bur·gee [ˈbɝdʒi; ˈbəːdʒiː] *n.* 三角旗；燕尾旗。

bur·geon [ˈbɝdʒən; ˈbəːdʒən] *n.* 芽；新芽。—*v.i.* ①萌發；發芽。②突然成長或發展。—*v.t.* 發芽。(亦作 **bourgeon**)

burg·er [ˈbɝgɚ; ˈbəːgə] *n.* ①〖俗〗碎牛肉夾餅。②(用於複合詞)各種夾餅(如 turkeyburger, 火鷄夾餅)。

bur·gess [ˈbɝdʒɪs; ˈbəːdʒis] *n.* ①〖英〗市民；鎮民。②〖英〗代表市鎮或大學的國會議員。③〖美〗革命前 Virginia 及 Maryland 兩州之下院議員。

burgh [bɝg; ˈbʌrə] *n.* 市鎮。

burgh·er [ˈbɝgɚ; ˈbəːgə] *n.* 自治市鎮之公民；公民。—**ship,** *n.*

***bur·glar** [ˈbɝglɚ; ˈbəːglə] *n.* ①夜賊。②竊賊。

burglar alarm 自動警鈴。

bur·glar·i·ous [bəˈglɛrɪəs; bəːˈglɛəriəs] *adj.* 夜盜的；夜盜罪的。—**ly,** *adv.*

bur·glar·ize [ˈbɝgləˌraɪz; ˈbəːgləraiz] *v.*, **-ized, -iz·ing.** —*v.t.* 〖俗〗從(某處)竊。—*v.i.* 行竊。

bur·glar·proof [ˈbɝgləˈpruf; ˈbəːgləˈpruːf] *adj.* 防盜的。

bur·gla·ry [ˈbɝglərɪ; ˈbəːgləri] *n.*, *pl.* **-ries.** 〖法律〗夜盜罪；盜竊。

bur·gle [ˈbɝgl̩; ˈbəːgl] *v.t.* & *v.i.*, **-gled, -gling.** 〖俗〗犯竊盜罪；竊盜。

bur·go·mas·ter [ˈbɝgəˌmæstɚ; ˈbəːgəˌmɑːstə] *n.* ①(荷蘭、德國之)市長。②冰鷗。

bur·go·net [ˈbɝgəˌnɛt; ˈbəːgənet] *n.* 一種頭盔。

bur·goo [ˈbɝgu; ˈbəːguː] *n.*, *pl.* **-goos.** ①麥粥(水手所食者)。②〖美方〗一種蔬菜及肉類的濃湯；有此種濃湯之野餐。

Bur·gun·di·an [bəˈgʌndɪən; bəːˈgʌndiən] *adj.* 勃艮地(人)的。—*n.* 勃艮地人。

Bur·gun·dy [ˈbɝgəndɪ; ˈbəːgəndi] *n.*

①勃艮地(法國東部一地名)。②(b-)該地所產之葡萄酒。③勃艮地醬油。

***bur·i·al** [ˈbɛrɪəl; ˈberiəl] *n.* ①埋葬;葬禮。②墳墓。—*adj.* 埋葬的;葬禮的。a *burial* service. 葬禮。

burial mound 墳塚。

bur·ied [ˈbɛrɪd; ˈberid] *adj.* 埋葬的;「隱藏的。」

bur·i·er [ˈbɛrɪɚ; ˈberiə] *n.* 埋的人或物。

bu·rin [ˈbjurɪn; ˈbjuərin] *n.* ①雕刻刀。②雕刻風格。③類似雕刻刀之古代石器。

burke [bɝk; bəːk] *v.t.*, **burked, burk·ing.** ①悶死。②使消滅於無形;扣壓(議案等)。

burl [bɝl; bəːl] *n.* ①絲結;線頭。②樹節;木瘤。—*v.t.* 剔除(布上的)布結。

bur·lap [ˈbɝlæp; ˈbəːlæp] *n.* ①粗麻布(製袋用)。②倣粗麻布。

bur·lesque [bɚˈlɛsk; bəːˈlesk] *n., v.,* **-lesqued, -les·quing,** *adj.* —*n.* ①諷刺性或滑稽性之文字、圖畫或模倣。②〖美〗低級粗野之歌舞表演;脫衣舞。—*v.t.* 用文字、圖畫或模仿以諷刺。—*v.i.* 用漫畫、戲謔文字諷刺。—*adj.* ①諷刺性或滑稽性之模仿的。②詼諧或遊戲詩文的。③低級粗野之歌舞表演的。

bur·ley [ˈbɝlɪ; ˈbəːli] *n., pl.* **-leys.** (常B-)一種纖細之烟草(產於 Kentucky 及其附近諸州)。

bur·li·ness [ˈbɝlɪnɪs; ˈbəːlinis] *n.* 魁「梧;粗魯。」

bur·ly [ˈbɝlɪ; ˈbəːli] *adj.,* **-li·er, -li·est.** ①魁梧的;强壯的。②粗魯的。—**bur·li·ly,** *adv.*

Bur·ma [ˈbɝmə; ˈbəːmə] *n.* 緬甸(東南亞一國,首都仰光 Rangoon)。

Bur·man [ˈbɝmən; ˈbəːmən] *n., pl.* **-mans,** *adj.* =**Burmese.**

Burma Road 滇緬公路(自臘戍至昆明)。

Bur·mese [bɚˈmiz; bəːˈmiːz] *adj.* 緬甸的;緬甸人、語的。—*n.*①緬甸人。②緬甸語。

‡burn[1] [bɝn; bəːn] *v.* **burned** or **burnt, burn·ing,** *n.* —*v.i.* ①燃燒;燒燬。Dry wood *burns* easily. 乾柴容易燃燒。②覺熱;發熱。He *burned* with fever. 他發燒。③發光。④如焚;熱中;焦思。He *burned* with anger. 他怒火沖沖。⑤ **a.**〖化〗氧化。**b.**〖物理〗核子分裂或結合。⑥(某些遊戲)接近隱藏之東西,或猜中答案。⑦燒焦。⑧被曬黑或因熱而褪色。⑨下地獄。You may *burn* for that sin. 爲那個罪惡,你可能下地獄。⑩〖俗〗處電刑。⑪受燃燒。—*v.t.* ①燒燬;焚燒。②使覺熱;生灼熱。The strong wine *burned* his stomach. 烈酒使他的胃覺得發燒。③燒焦;灼傷。The meat is *burned* black. 肉燒焦了。④曬。⑤燃燒;燒穿。We *burned* coal. 我們燒煤炭。⑥燒成。⑦〖化〗燃燒;氧化。⑧〖物理〗利用(鈾等中之)原子能。⑨很快地花盡。⑩〖俗〗被騙。He was *burned* by that phony stock deal. 他上了那個假股票買賣的當。⑪過熱而損壞。⑫〖英〗在鐵器內溫(葡萄酒等)。⑬發動火箭 引擎或減速火箭。⑭〖美俚〗販賣假貨或劣等毒品。 ***burn down*** **a.**(房屋等)燒至地面;全部焚燬。**b.** 火力或燃料減弱。 ***burn into*** **a.**(酸類)侵 蝕。The acid has *burned into* the pan. 酸已經侵蝕到鍋子裡面去了。**b.** 留下不可磨滅的印象。The sight of such poverty *burned into* his soul. 這樣貧窮的景象,使他畢生難忘。 ***burn off*** (晨霧)爲太陽之溫度蒸發而消失。 ***burn on*** 以鉛銲鉛。 ***burn oneself out*** 因工作過度或生活無節制而筋疲力盡。They feared that he would *burn himself out.* 他們怕他會筋疲力盡。 ***burn out*** **a.** 燒壞。**b.** 住所或工作場所等被燒光。 ***burn up*** **a.** 燒完;燒盡;燒光。**b.** 使生氣;激怒。—*n.* ①燒傷;灼傷;(强酸之)烙傷。He died of the *burns* that he received in the fire. 他死於在火災中所受的灼傷。②曬黑。③烤焙。④〖澳〗森林火災。⑤(*pl.*)〖美俚〗=**sideburns.** ⑥火箭引擎或減速火箭之發動(其目的在使其產生推力)。

burn[2] *n.* 〖蘇〗小河;小溪;小川。

burned-out [ˈbɝndˌaut; ˈbəːndˈaut] *adj.* 用盡的; 因過度使用而損壞的。

***burn·er** [ˈbɝnɚ; ˈbəːnə] *n.* ①燈;燈頭。②火爐。gas *burner.* 煤氣爐。③燒火的人;火伕。④噴氣引擎之燃燒室。

bur·net [ˈbɝnɪt; ˈbəːnit] *n.* 〖植物〗地「榆。」

burn·ing [ˈbɝnɪŋ; ˈbəːniŋ] *adj.* ①燃燒的。②如火的;烈性的。③激烈的;熱烈的。a *burning* scent. 〖狩獵〗强烈的遺臭。④極嚴重的;極重要的。⑤不體面的。⑥鮮艷的;發亮的。—*n.*①燃燒。②陶器之最後火候。—**ly,** *adv.*

burning glass 火鏡(集中日光使之生熱之凸透鏡)。

burning point 引火點;燃燒點。

bur·nish [ˈbɝnɪʃ; ˈbəːniʃ] *v.t.* ①磨光。②使光滑。—*v.i.* 變光滑;變光亮。—*n.* 光澤;光亮。—**er,** —**ment,** *n.*

bur·noose, bur·nous(e) [bɚˈnus; bəˈnuːs] *n.*(阿拉伯人所着)連有頭巾之外衣。

burn·out [ˈbɝnˌaut; ˈbəːn-aut] *n.* ①毀滅性的火。②竭盡。③ **a.** (火箭引擎的)熄火。**b.** 此熄火之時間。**c.** 此熄火發生之地點。④(電器之被電流)燒燬。

Burns [bɝnz; bəːnz] *n.* 柏恩斯 (Robert, 1759–1796, 蘇格蘭詩人)。

burn·sides [ˈbɝnˌsaɪdz; ˈbəːnsaidz] *n. pl.* 連鬢鬍子;濃密的頰鬚。

***burnt** [bɝnt; bəːnt] *v.* pt. & pp. of **burn.** —*adj.* 〖美術〗①焦色的。*burnt* ocher. 焦赭色。②比原有顏色較深或帶灰色的。

burnt offering 燔祭。

burn·up [ˈbɝnˌʌp; ˈbəːn-ʌp] *n.* 核子反應爐中燃料之消耗。

bur oak ①北美產之一種橡樹。②其木材。

burp [bɝp; bəːp] *n.* 〖俚〗打嗝。—*v.i.* & *v.t.* 喂奶後輕拍嬰兒之背使其打嗝;打嗝。

burp gun 〖軍〗①全自動手鎗。②氣冷式衝鋒鎗。

burr[1] [bɝ; bəː] *n.*①=**bur.** ②(亦作**buhr**)粗糙孔緣。③牙醫技工等所用之鑽孔器。—*v.t.* 在…上造成粗糙邊緣。

burr[2] *n.* ①喉音。②任何粗的地方音。—*v.i.* ①用喉音說話。②用粗音說話。—*v.t.* 用喉音讀。

bur·ro [ˈbɝo; ˈbəːrou] *n., pl.* **-ros.** ①「馱貨的驢。②驢。」

***bur·row** [ˈbɝo; ˈbʌrou] *n.* ①動物所掘之地洞。Rabbits live in *burrows.* 兔子住在地洞裏面。②洞穴。—*v.t.* & *v.i.* ①掘洞穴;在地上鑽洞。②穴居;潛伏。③搜尋;尋找。

burr·stone [ˈbɝˌston; ˈbəːstoun] *n.* 磨石;臼石。(亦作 **burstone, buhrstone**)

bur·ry[1] [ˈbɝɪ; ˈbəːri] *adj.,* **-ri·er, -ri·est.** 多芒刺殼的;有針毬的;有瘤的。

bur·ry[2] *adj.,* **-ri·er, -ri·est.** 有喉音的。

bur·sa [ˈbɝsə; ˈbəːsə] *n., pl.* **-sas, -sae** [-siː; -si]. 〖解剖〗囊。

bur·sal [ˈbɝsəl; ˈbəːsəl] *adj.* 囊的。

bur·sar [ˈbɝsɚ; ˈbəːsə] *n.* ①大學內的會計員。②(中世紀時)大學生。③〖蘇〗獎學金學生。

bur·sar·i·al [bɚˈsɛrɪəl; bəːˈsɛəriəl] *adj.* 大學會計的; 付與大學會計或由大學會計支付的。

bur·sa·ry 〔ˈbɝsərɪ; ˈbəːsəri〕 *n., pl.* **-ries.** ①金庫(尤指大學或修道院者)。②(蘇格蘭各大學之)獎學金。

bur·si·tis 〔bəˈsaɪtɪs; bəˈsaitis〕 *n.*〖醫〗黏液囊炎。

‡**burst** 〔bɝst; bəːst〕 *v.,* **burst, burst·ing,** *n.* —*v.i.* ①爆炸。The boiler *burst.* 汽鍋爆炸。②脹裂。③闖入;突然而起;迸發。He *burst* into the room. 他闖入這房間。④突然而完全地顯現。—*v.t.* ①打破;突破。They *burst* the door open. 他們把門破開。②將(複寫紙與其他紙張)分開。***burst in*** a. 突然出現。b. 打斷。***burst out*** 迸發;大呼;驚歎。—*n.* ①爆炸;迸發。②(自動武器之)連續發射。③爆烈,爆炸的結果;缺口。④突然的出現。

bur·stone 〔ˈbɝˌston; ˈbəːstoun〕 *n.* = **burrstone.**

burst-up 〔ˈbɝstˌʌp; ˈbəːstʌp〕 *n.*〖俗〗破產。

bur·then 〔ˈbɝðən; ˈbəːðən〕 *v.t., n.*〖古〗= **burden.**

bur·ton 〔ˈbɝtn̩; ˈbəːtn〕 *n.* 引重物之索具;滑車。

Bu·run·di 〔bəˈrʌndɪ; bəˈrʌndi〕 *n.* 蒲隆地(中非一共和國,首都 Bujumbura)。

‡**bur·y** 〔ˈbɛrɪ; ˈberi〕 *v.t.,* **bur·ied, bur·y·ing.** ①埋;葬。They were *buried* alive by the enemies. 他們被敵人活埋。②掩蔽;隱匿;專心於。He *buried* himself in his work. 他專心工作。③遺忘;忘記。④使深入。⑤使處於不重要之地位而顯得不足輕重。⑥喪失。He has *buried* two sons. 他已經有二子死亡。***be buried in thought*** (or ***memories of the past***) 沉思(緬懷往事)。***bury oneself in the country*** 隱退;鄉居。***bury one's head in the sand*** 逃避現實。***bury the hatchet*** 議和。

bur·y·ing 〔ˈbɛrɪɪŋ; ˈberiiŋ〕 *n.* 埋;葬。

burying ground 墳場;墓地。(亦作 **burying place**)

‡**bus**[1] 〔bʌs; bʌs〕 *n., pl.* **bus·(s)es,** *v.,* **bus(s)ed, bus·(s)ing.** —*n.* ①公共汽車;巴士。to take the *bus.* 乘公共汽車。②類似巴士的馬車。③〖俗〗客運汽車或飛機。④一種矮的卷宗箱。⑤〖電〗匯流條。***miss the bus*** 未趕上公共汽車;〖俚〗失去機會。—*v.t.* 用巴士載。—*v.i.* 乘巴士。

bus[2] *v.i. & v.t.,* **bus(s)ed, bus·(s)ing.**〖美俗〗在餐廳打雜。

bus. ①bushel. ②bushels. ③business.

bus·boy 〔ˈbʌsˌbɔɪ; ˈbʌsbɔi〕 *n.* 餐廳之打雜工人。

bus·by 〔ˈbʌzbɪ; ˈbʌzbi〕 *n., pl.* **-bies.** (英「輕騎兵之)高頂皮軍帽。

bus girl 餐廳打雜之女工。

‡**bush**[1] 〔bʊʃ; buʃ〕 *n.* ①灌木;多枝的矮樹。②未開墾之地。③似灌木之東西。④狐尾。⑤以樹枝做的酒店或酒商之招牌。⑥任何酒店招牌。***beat about***(or ***around***) ***the bush*** 說話轉彎抹角。***beat the bush*** a. 撥叢尋覓(獵物)。b. 尋覓人或物。—*v.i.* 生密枝。—*v.t.* ①以灌木覆蓋或保護。②〖美俚〗使筋疲力竭。

bush[2] *n.* = **bushing.** —*v.t.* 裝以軸襯。

bush bean 菜豆。

bushed 〔bʊʃt; buʃt〕 *adj.* ①長滿灌木的。②〖俗〗疲倦;累。

***bush·el**[1] 〔ˈbʊʃəl; ˈbuʃl〕 *n.* ①蒲式耳(容量名,合八加侖,用以量穀)。②可裝一蒲式耳之容器。③相當於一蒲式耳之重量。

bush·el[2] *v.t. & v.i.,* **-el(l)ed, -el·(l)ing.** 修改;修補(衣服等)。—**(l)er,** *n.*

bush·el·ful 〔ˈbʊʃəlfʊl; ˈbuʃlful〕 *n., pl.* **-fuls.** 一蒲式耳之量。

bush·fight·ing 〔ˈbʊʃˌfaɪtɪŋ; ˈbuʃˌfaitiŋ〕 *n.* 叢林戰。

bush·ham·mer 〔ˈbʊʃˌhæmɚ; ˈbuʃˌhæmə〕 *n.* 石匠用之錘面有三角突起之錘。

bush·hook 〔ˈbʊʃˌhʊk; ˈbuʃhuk〕 *n.* 刈草之鉤刀。

bu·shi·do, Bu·shi·do 〔ˈbuʃɪˌdo; ˈbuːʃidou〕 *n.* (日本之)武士道。

bush·ing 〔ˈbʊʃɪŋ; ˈbuʃiŋ〕 *n.* ①〖機械〗軸襯;襯套。②〖電〗絕緣套。③不誠實的售貨方式。

bush·land 〔ˈbʊʃˌlænd; ˈbuʃlænd〕 *n.* 未開墾地區。

bush lawyer〖澳〗自誇對法律有研究者。

bush·man 〔ˈbʊʃmən; ˈbuʃmən〕 *n., pl.* **-men.** ①在森林裏居住謀生之人。②(澳洲之)墾荒者。③(B-)南非之一種黑人;其語言。

bush·mas·ter 〔ˈbʊʃˌmæstɚ; ˈbuʃˌmaːstə〕 *n.* 一種美洲產大毒蛇。

bush pilot 飛行於邊境無人地帶之駕駛員。

bush·rang·er 〔ˈbʊʃˌrendʒɚ; ˈbuʃˌreindʒə〕 *n.* ①林居之人。②澳洲之山賊。③潛伏於深林中之囚犯。

bush telegraph ①深林中土人之任何通信手段。②〖澳〗使潛伏深林之逃犯得知警方行動之任何通信方法。③謠言。

bush·whack 〔ˈbʊʃˌhwæk; ˈbuʃhwæk〕 *v.i. & v.t.* ①徘徊森林中。②奇襲。③以鐮刀刈雜草。—**ing,** *n.*

bush·whack·er 〔ˈbʊʃˌhwækɚ; ˈbuʃˌhwækə〕 *n.*〖美〗①徘徊森林中者。②游擊隊員(尤指美國內戰時之南方的)。③一種鐮刀。

***bush·y** 〔ˈbʊʃɪ; ˈbuʃi〕 *adj.,* **bush·i·er, bush·i·est.** ①灌木叢生的。②濃密如灌木的;毛密的。*bushy* eyebrows. 濃眉毛。—**bush·i·ness,** *n.*

bush·y-beard·ed 〔ˈbʊʃɪˈbɪrdɪd; ˈbuʃiˈbiədid〕 *adj.* 有濃鬚的。

***bus·i·ly** 〔ˈbɪzl̩ɪ; ˈbizili〕 *adv.* 忙碌地。

‡**busi·ness** 〔ˈbɪznɪs; ˈbiznis〕 *n.* ①職業;職務;責任。What is your *business?* 你的職業是甚麼? ②事;事件。private *business.* 私事。public *business.* 公事。③營業;商業。He is in *business.* 他在經商。④商店。He has a *business* in London. 他在倫敦有一店。⑤(戲劇中之)動作及表情。***business is business*** 公事公辦。***do someone's business*** 處置(某人);要(某人)的命。***get*** (or ***come***) ***down to business*** 着手工作。***go to business*** 辦公;上班。***have business with*** 與某人(事)有關。***have no business*** 無權。***It is none of one's business.*** 不關某人的事。***make it one's business*** 特別處理;特別照料。***mean business*** 認眞。I *mean business.* 我是認眞的。***mind one's own business*** 不管閒事。***on business*** 因商務;因公;有事。No admittance except *on business.* 非公莫入。***send*** (***a person***) ***about his business*** 打發(某人)走開。—*adj.* ①有關商業,或職務的。②適合於商業的。

business address 辦公地址。

business agent 代表工會會員與雇主交涉之人員。

business boom (or **prosperity**) 商業繁榮。

business card 名片。

business college〖美〗商業學院。

business cycle 商業周期。

business English 商業英文。

business hours 上班或營業時間。*Business hours,* 8 a.m. to 6 p.m. 營業時間上午八時至下午六時。

busi·ness·like 〔ˈbɪznɪsˌlaɪk; ˈbiznislaik〕 *adj.* 認眞的;井然有條的;實事求是的。

busi·ness·man 〔ˈbɪznɪsˌmæn; ˈbiznismæn〕 *n., pl.* **-men.** ①商人。②自開商

店或工廠者。
business news 商業新聞;行情報導。
business suit 西裝。
busi·ness·wom·an [ˈbɪznɪsˌwʊmən; ˈbiznisˌwumən] *n., pl.* **-wom·en.** 從事商業之女性。
busk [bʌsk; bʌsk] *n.* ①撐張婦女胸衣之鯨骨、鋼絲等。②婦女胸衣。—*v.t.* 〖蘇〗打扮;預備;裝備。—*v.i.* 〖英俚〗①沿街賣藝。②到鄉間演戲,賣藝。③以低級貨品欺騙鄉下人。
busk·er [ˈbʌskɚ; ˈbʌskə] *n.* 〖英俚〗巡廻藝人。
bus·kin [ˈbʌskɪn; ˈbʌskin] *n.* ①半統靴。②厚底靴(古希臘及羅馬悲劇演員所穿)。③悲劇演技。④(*pl.*) 主教做彌撒時所穿之繡金襪子。***put on the buskins*** 演悲劇;寫悲劇。
bus line ①巴士之路線。②巴士公司。
bus·load [ˈbʌsˌlod; ˈbʌsloud] *n.* 巴士之裝載量。
bus·man [ˈbʌsmən; ˈbʌsmən] *n., pl.* **-men.** 公共汽車之駕駛員或車掌。
busman's holiday 消磨於與日常工作類似之活動的假日。
buss [bʌs; bʌs] *n., v.t., v.i.* 〖古,方〗接吻(尤指粗魯或嬉戲地)。
bus·ses [ˈbʌsɪz; ˈbʌsiz] *n.* pl. of **bus.**
***bust**[1] [bʌst; bʌst] *n.* ①半身雕塑或畫像。②胸部(尤指女人者)。
bust[2] *v.t. & v.i.* 〖俚〗①爆裂。②(使)破產。③(使)降級。④馴服。⑤〖俚〗逮捕。⑥拳打。⑦因工作過度而崩潰。***bust up*** 分離;分居;破壞。—*n.* 〖俚〗①失敗;破產。②縱飲。③重打。④經濟之突然蕭條。—*adj.* 破產的。
bus·tard [ˈbʌstɚd; ˈbʌstəd] *n.* 鴇(鳥)。
bust·ed [ˈbʌstɪd; ˈbʌstid] *adj.* 〖美俚〗①失敗的;破產的。②被降級的。
bust·er [ˈbʌstɚ; ˈbʌstə] *n.* ①〖俚〗巨大之物;異物。②〖俚〗鬧飲。③〖俚〗(一種稱呼)小鬼;傢伙。④〖俚〗冒失鬼。⑤馴馬的人。⑥〖俗〗破壞某事的人。⑦〖澳〗寒冷猛烈的南風。
bus·tle**[1] [ˈbʌsl; ˈbʌsl] *v.,* **-tled, -tling,** *n.* —*v.i.* ①匆忙;迅速而喧擾地移動〖常 about〗。②充滿〖常 with〗. The office *bustled* with people and activity. 辦公室裏充滿着人和活動。—*v.t.* 催促他人趕快或工作。bustle about*** 在匆忙中迅速而喧擾地行動。***bustle up*** 趕快。—*n.* 緊張而喧擾的活動。to be in a *bustle.* 忙亂;雜沓。
bus·tle[2] *n.* ①裙撐。②裙子後方隆起之衣飾。
bus·tling [ˈbʌslɪŋ; ˈbʌsliŋ] *adj.* 忙碌的;騷動的。
bust-up [ˈbʌstˌʌp; ˈbʌst-ʌp] *n.* 〖俗〗①分離。②喧鬧的大集會。③吵架;鬥毆。
‡bus·y [ˈbɪzɪ; ˈbizi] *adj.,* **bus·i·er, bus·i·est,** *v.,* **bus·ied, bus·y·ing.** —*adj.* ①忙碌的。He is *busy* getting ready for the journey. 他忙於準備旅行。②被占用中的(指電話線言)。Wait a minute; the line is *busy*. 請等一等,電話線不空。③繁盛的;熱鬧的。④好管閒事的。The inquisitive woman is always *busy*. 那好打聽的女人總喜歡多管閒事。⑤亂糟糟的;不和諧的。The rug has a *busy* design. 那地毯的花樣很亂。—*v.t.* 使忙。The bees *busied* themselves at making honey. 蜜蜂忙於採蜜。
bus·y·bod·y [ˈbɪzɪˌbɑdɪ; ˈbiziˌbɔdi] *n., pl.* **-bod·ies.** 好管閒事者;多嘴者。
bus·y·ness [ˈbɪzɪnɪs; ˈbizinis] *n.* 忙碌;繁忙。
bus·y·work [ˈbɪzɪˌwɝk; ˈbiziwəːk] *n.* 費時但無價值的工作。
‡but[1] [bʌt; bʌt *unstressed* bət; bət] *conj.* ①但是;然而。He is poor *but* honest. 他雖窮但誠實。②除却。I can live anywhere *but* here. 除却這裏,無論那裏我都能住。③只有。We cannot choose *but* hear. 我們不得不聽。④=**that.** I don't doubt *but* he will do it. 我確信他將做這事。⑤=***that not***(在否定詞或問詞之後)。⑥用來强調感嘆句。—*rel. pron.* 無不 (=who not; which not). ***never ... but*** 必定。It ***never*** rains *but* it pours. 不雨則已,雨必傾盆;〖諺〗禍不單行。—*prep.* 除;除却…之外。No one replied *but* me. 除我外,無人回答。***but for*** 如非。*But for* your help, I should have failed. 如非你之助,我早已失敗了。***nothing but*** 除非。—*adv.* ①僅;不過;只有。He is *but* a child. 他不過是個小孩。②如非 (=if ... not). ③至少 (與 can, could 連用)(=at least; in any case). ***all but*** 幾乎;殆。He is *all but* drowned. 他幾乎淹死。***but that*** 要不是;如非。—*n.* 限制;反對。Do as I tell you, no *but* about it. 照我講的去做,不得反對。
but[2] *adj.* 〖蘇〗外面的。—*n.* 〖蘇〗外室(尤指茅舍之廚房)。***but and ben*** 全部房舍。
but[3] *n.* 庸鰈、比目魚等類之魚。
bu·ta·di·ene [ˌbjutəˈdaɪin; ˌbjuːtəˈdaiiːn] *n.* 〖化〗丁二烯(用製合成橡膠)。
bu·tane [ˈbjuten; ˈbjuːtein] *n.* 〖化〗丁烷。
***butch·er** [ˈbʊtʃɚ; ˈbutʃə] *n.* ①屠夫。He is a *butcher* by trade. 他的職業是屠夫。②屠宰商;肉店。③殘殺者;劊子手。④〖美〗小販(尤指在火車或運動場上兜售雜誌、糖果等者)。—*v.t.* ①屠;宰;殺。②殘殺。They *butchered* the prisoners. 他們殘殺囚犯。③隨便亂搞。
butch·er·bird [ˈbʊtʃɚˌbɝd; ˈbutʃəbəːd] *n.* 百舌類之鳥;伯勞。
butcher knife 屠刀。
butch·er·ly [ˈbʊtʃɚlɪ; ˈbutʃəli] *adj. & adv.* 如屠夫的(地);殘忍的(地)。
butcher paper 一種厚而不透水的紙。
butch·er·y [ˈbʊtʃərɪ; ˈbutʃəri] *n., pl.* **-er·ies.** ①屠宰業。②屠場。③屠殺。
butch haircut ①一種類似平頭的男人髮式。②一種較短的女人髮式。(亦作**butch**)
bu·tene [ˈbjutin; ˈbjuːtiːn] *n.* 〖化〗丁烯。
***but·ler** [ˈbʌtlɚ; ˈbʌtlə] *n.* 司膳的人;僕役長。
butler's pantry 備餐室。
butler's sideboard 餐具架。
butt[1] [bʌt; bʌt] *n.* ①粗大之一端。the *butt* of a fishing rod. 釣竿握手之一端。②殘餘部分。③烟蒂。④靶;目標。⑤〖俚〗臀;屁股。⑥〖俚〗香煙。⑦譏笑或攻擊的對象。⑧(*pl.*) 靶場內靶後之土堆;靶後之牆。***the butts*** 靶場。—*v.t. & v.i.* 接界;毗連;連接兩端。
butt[2] *n.* ①大酒桶。②大酒桶的容量(等於 126 gallons).
butt[3] *v.t.* 撞;以頭撞之。—*v.i.* ①撞;以頭撞。②突出。***butt in*** (or ***into***) 介入;闖入;干擾。***butt out*** 〖俚〗不介入;不管閑事。
‡but·ter[1] [ˈbʌtɚ; ˈbʌtə] *n.* ①奶油。to spread *butter* on bread. 塗奶油於麪包上。②似奶油之物。***butter would not melt in (one's) mouth*** 裝做害羞的樣子。***peanut butter*** 花生醬。—*v.t.* ①塗奶油於…上。*Butter* your bread. 塗奶油於你的麪包上。②〖俗〗諂媚。③塗上粘着物。***butter up*** 討好。
but·ter[2] *n.* ①用頭撞的獸。②抵撞的人(東西)。
but·ter-and-egg man [ˈbʌtɚənˈɛg～; ˈbʌtərənˈeg～] 〖俚〗到城裏來充闊的土

財主。「'bʌtərən'egz] *n.* 〖植物〗蛋黃草。

but·ter-and-eggs ['bʌtəən'ɛgz;

but·ter·ball ['bʌtə,bɔl; 'bʌtəbɔːl] *n.* ①〖美方〗＝**bufflehead.** ②〖俗〗圓胖的人。

butter boat 盛放溶解的奶油之小碟。

but·ter·cup ['bʌtə,kʌp; 'bʌtəkʌp] *n.* 〖植物〗金鳳花。「牛乳中之脂肪。

but·ter·fat ['bʌtə,fæt; 'bʌtəfæt] *n.*

but·ter·fin·gered ['bʌtə,fɪŋgəd; 'bʌtə,fiŋgəd] *adj.* 〖俗〗容易讓東西從手中滑掉的;不小心的。

but·ter·fin·gers ['bʌtə,fɪŋgəz; 'bʌtə,fiŋgəz] *n., pl.* **-gers.** (作 *sing.* 解)〖俗〗①容易將手中物滑落之人;常失球之選手。②笨手笨脚者。「*pl.* **-fish, -fish·es.** 酪魚。

but·ter·fish ['bʌtə,fɪʃ; 'bʌtəfiʃ] *n.,*

***but·ter·fly** ['bʌtə,flaɪ; 'bʌtəflai] *n., pl.* **-flies,** *v.,* **-flied, -fly·ing,** *adj.* —*n.* ①蝴蝶。②服裝鮮艷的人;遊手好閒的人。③(*pl.*)欲嘔的感覺。④蝶泳。—*v.t.* ①〖烹飪〗剖開而使像蝴蝶。②使移動。—*v.i.* (如蝴蝶般)頻頻移動。—*adj.* 〖烹飪〗剖開而像蝴蝶的。

but·ter·ine ['bʌtə,rin; 'bʌtəriːn] *n.* 人造奶油。

butter knife 塗奶油用之刀。

but·ter·milk ['bʌtə,mɪlk; 'bʌtəmilk] *n.* 提去奶油之酸乳。「*n.* 白胡桃。

but·ter·nut ['bʌtənət; 'bʌtənət]

but·ter·paste ['bʌtə,pest; 'bʌtəpeist] *n.* 牛油與麪粉揉成之糊狀物。

but·ter·scotch ['bʌtə'skɑtʃ; 'bʌtəskɔtʃ] *n.* ①奶油糖果。②奶油糖果之香味。—*adj.* 有奶油糖果香味的。

but·ter·wort ['bʌtə,wɜt; 'bʌtəwəːt] *n.* 捕蠅堇屬之植物。

but·ter·y [*adj.* 'bʌtərɪ; 'bʌtəri *n.* 'bʌtrɪ; 'bʌtəri] *adj., n., pl.* **-ies.** —*adj.* ①似奶油的;含奶油的。②〖俗〗諂媚的。—*n.* ①酒窖。②備餐室。③牛津、劍橋大學內放置將售與學生的食品、酒類等之房間。

buttery hatch 備餐室進口處供傳遞食物用的半門。「*n.*〖美〗非法販賣未稅香煙。

butt·leg·ging ['bʌtlɛgɪŋ; 'bʌtlegiŋ]

but·tocks ['bʌtəks; 'bʌtəks] *n. pl.* ①臀;屁股。②船尾外舷露於水面之部分。

‡**but·ton** ['bʌtn; 'bʌtn] *n.* ①鈕扣。He put on a coat with brass *buttons.* 他穿着一件有銅扣的上衣。②任何像鈕扣的東西;電鈕。③小蕈。④〖英俗〗(*pl.*)旅館中之侍役。⑤練劍時套在劍尖上的小扣。⑥〖拳擊俚〗下巴尖。⑦〖動物〗任何像鈕扣之部分。***not have all one's buttons*** 〖俚〗乖僻;瘋狂;精神不正常的。—*v.t.* & *v.i.* ①扣(鈕扣)。*Button* (up) your coat. 扣起你的外衣。②供鈕扣。③可用鈕扣扣。This coat *buttons,* but that one zips. 這件上衣用鈕扣,但那件用拉鍊。***button one's lips*** 一言不發。***button up*** **a.** 守口如瓶。**b.** 扣緊。**c.** 完成。

but·ton-boot ['bʌtn̩,but; 'bʌtnbuːt] *n.* 〖英〗有鈕絆的靴。

but·ton-down ['bʌtn̩,daun; 'bʌtndaun] *adj.* ①(襯衫領子)有鈕孔可扣在衫上的。②有此種領子的。

but·ton·hole ['bʌtn̩,hol; 'bʌtnhoul] *n., v.,* **-holed, -hol·ing.** —*n.* ①鈕孔。②戴於大衣襟鈕孔中的花。—*v.t.* ①開鈕孔於。②以縫鈕孔的針脚去縫。③强留人談話。

buttonhole stitch 鑲邊的針脚。

but·ton·hook ['bʌtn̩,huk; 'bʌtnhuk] *n.* 鈕鈎(牽引鈕扣穿過鈕孔者)。

but·ton-on ['bʌtn̩,ɑn; 'bʌtnɔn] *adj.* 用鈕扣扣上的。

but·ton·wood ['bʌtn̩,wud; 'bʌtnwud] *n.* 懸鈴木屬之植物。(亦作 **buttonball**)

but·ton·y ['bʌtn̩ɪ; 'bʌtni] *adj.* 鈕扣的;似扣的;多扣的。

but·tress ['bʌtrɪs; 'bʌtris] *n.* ①扶牆;拱壁。②支持物。③支持者。④任何類似扶牆之物。—*v.t.* ①以扶牆支持。②支持;加强。

but·ty ['bʌtɪ; 'bʌti] *n.* 〖英俗〗①監工;工頭。②採煤承包人。③〖英方〗伙伴;至友。

bu·tyl ['bjutɪl; 'bjuːtil] *adj.* 丁基的。

butyl alcohol 丁醇。

bu·tyl·ene ['bjutɪl,in; 'bjuːtiliːn] *n.* 〖化〗丁烯。(亦作 **butene**)

bu·tyr·al·de·hyde [,bjutə'ældə,haɪd; ,bjuːtə'rældəhaid] *n.* 〖化〗丁醛。

bu·tyr·ic [bju'tɪrɪk; bjuː'tirik] *adj.* 〖化〗酪酸的。

butyric acid 〖化〗丁酸。「酯。

butyric ether 〖化〗丁酸乙酯;酪酸乙

bu·tyr·in ['bjutərɪn; 'bjuːtərin] *n.* 〖化〗酪脂。

bu·ty·rom·e·ter [,bjutə'rɑmətə; ,bjuːti'rɔmitə] *n.* 牛乳含脂量測量器。

bux·om ['bʌksəm; 'bʌksəm] *adj.* 乳房豐滿的;健美活潑的。

‡**buy** [baɪ; bai] *v.,* **bought, buy·ing,** *n.* —*v.t.* ①買。He *bought* a book. 他買了一本書。②獲得。③賄賂;行賄。④全買。He *bought* up all the tennis balls they had. 他將他們所有的網球全部買光。—*v.i.* 購物;作買主。***buy in*** **a.** 買進。**b.** 拍賣時將自己之原物買回。***buy into*** **a.** 買進股票。**b.** 花錢活動使成某機關或團體之一分子。***buy off*** 賄賂。***buy on credit*** 賒。***buy out*** **a.** 買進。**b.** 付錢免役。He *bought* himself *out* of the army. 他花錢活動,得免陸軍徵召。***buy over*** 收買;行賄。***buy up*** 全買。—*n.* ①〖俗〗所買之物。That was a sensible *buy.* 那樣東西買得有道理。②〖俗〗交易;買賣。③合算的購買。The coat was a real *buy.* 這件大衣眞是買得便宜。

buy·a·ble ['baɪəbl̩; 'baiəbl] *adj.* 可買的。

***buy·er** ['baɪə; 'baiə] *n.* ①買主。A *buyer* is one who buys. 買的人謂之買主。②專管採買之人。「求)。

buyers' market 買主市場(供過於

buyers' strike 消費者之抵制某些商人或貨品以迫使其降低售價。

buying power 購買力。

buzz** [bʌz; bʌz] *n.* ①(蚊蠅和蜂等的)嗡嗡聲;營營聲。②多人低聲談話的雜聲。③耳語;謠言。④〖俗〗電話。—*v.i.* ①作嗡嗡聲;作營營聲。The bees were *buzzing* among the flowers. 蜜蜂在花間作嗡嗡聲。②發嘈雜聲。③匆忙地到處活動。④興高采烈地說話。⑤低聲說話。⑥〖英俚〗走開〖常 off, along〗. —*v.t.* ①使作嗡嗡聲;使作營營聲;使作低微的雜聲。②謠傳;暗中傳布。to *buzz* the rumor everywhere. 四處散布謠言。③〖俗〗打電話予。④(飛機)在…上空低飛。⑤飛機低飛以為信號或表示歡迎。⑥用 buzzer 叫人。He *buzzed* his secretary. 他按鈴叫他的秘書。buzz along*** (or ***about***) 〖俗〗匆忙而緊張地行動。***buzz off*** **a.** 掛斷(電話)。**b.** 走開!

buz·zard¹ ['bʌzəd; 'bʌzəd] *n.* ①鵰。②〖美〗兀鷹。③〖俚〗**a.** 卑鄙而好爭辯的人。**b.** 男人之間的較隨便的稱呼(通常前面帶有 old).「之聲的蟲。

buz·zard² *n.* 〖英方〗夜間出來發出嗡嗡

buzz bomb 〖軍〗火箭彈;飛彈。
buzz·er 〔ˈbʌzə; ˈbʌzə〕 *n.* ①發出似蜂音的電鈴。②發嗡嗡聲的東西。
buzz saw 電動小圓鋸。
B.V.M. Blessed Virgin Mary.
B.W.I. British West Indies. **bx.** *pl.* **bxs.** ①box. ②boxes. ③base exchange.
:by 〔baɪ; bai〕 *prep.* ①近於; 傍於。He built a house *by* the river. 他在河邊建屋。②沿;經;由。They walk *by* the lake. 他們沿湖散步。③賴以;藉以;經;由。The sewing was done *by* machine. 用機器縫級。④以量計。They buy eggs *by* the dozen. 他們買蛋以打計。⑤表示相乘(以計面積)。This table is two feet *by* four. 這桌子是二英尺寬四英尺長。⑥逐個;一一。He solved the problem step *by* step. 他逐步解決這問題。⑦依照;按照;以。Don't judge a person *by* his looks. 不要以貌取人。⑧至於…程度。to miss *by* an inch. 以一英寸之差未中的。⑨對於。She did well *by* her children. 她善待子女。⑩當…的時候; 在…的時候。They don't work *by* day but *by* night. 他們日間不工作,夜間工作。⑪不遲於;在…以前。He will come *by* six o'clock. 他將於六點以前來。⑫向。⑬由…所生。⑭進;至。***by all means*** 必定。Come to see us *by all means.* 你一定要來看我們。***by means of*** 藉;利用;靠。***by oneself*** 獨自。***by order of*** 奉令;奉命。***by reason of*** 因爲。***by the by*** 便中說起;順便提起。***by the side of*** 近旁;傍;側。***by the way*** **a.** 順便提及;便中說起。*By the way,* what are you doing tomorrow? 順便一提, 你明天做甚麼? **b.** 在旅途中;在途中。***by way of*** 經由。***close by*** 靠近;傍於。***end by*** 以…爲結局。***mean by*** 用意;意欲。***side by side*** 緊靠;並。***stand by*** (*a person*) 支持;幫助(某人)。***take by surprise*** 出其不意地攻擊;突襲。—*adv.* ①近;在旁。The spectators stood *by*. 觀衆站在旁邊。②過去; 已往。Those happy days are gone *by*. 那些快樂的日子已過去了。③(置)於旁;放開。④經過;越過。***by and by*** 不久;不一會兒。***by and large*** 就整個來說;一般說來。***by far*** 非常地;甚。
by, bye- 〖字首〗表"次要的;附帶的;離開正路的;近的"之義。
by-and-by 〔ˈbaɪənˈbaɪ; ˈbaiənˈbai〕 *n.* 未來;將來。
by-blow 〔ˈbaɪˌblo; ˈbaiblou〕 *n.* ①横打;側擊。②私生子;庶子。③意外之打擊。
bye 〔baɪ; bai〕 *n.* ①淘汰制比賽中,因比賽者爲奇數, 而不經比賽卽晉級之人。②不重要或次要的東西。***by the bye*** 順便;卻說;附帶。 —*adj.* 次要的; 偶發的。(亦作 **by**)
bye-bye 〔ˈbaɪˈbaɪ; ˈbaiˈbai〕 *interj.* 〖俗,兒語〗再會。—*n.* 床;睡覺。—*adv.* 睡覺;(指散步或乘車兜風之)外出(與 go連用)。(亦作**by-by**)
by-e·lec·tion 〔ˈbaɪɪˌlɛkʃən; ˈbaii-ˌlekʃən〕 *n.* 國會之補選。
by·gone 〔ˈbaɪˌgɔn; ˈbaigɔn〕 *adj.* 過去的;已往的。—*n.* 過去的事。
by·land 〔ˈbaɪˌlænd; ˈbailænd〕 *n.* 半島。(亦作 **biland**)
by-lane 〔ˈbaɪˌlen; ˈbailein〕 *n.* 弄;衖;僻巷。
by·law 〔ˈbaɪˌlɔ; ˈbailɔ:〕 *n.* ①〖英〗市鎮、公司等制定之法規;地方法。②次要的法規;附則;細則。(亦作 **byelaw**)
by-line 〔ˈbaɪˌlaɪn; ˈbailain〕 *n., v.,* **-lined, -lin·ing.** —*n.* ①(鐵道之)平行幹線。②(報刊等)每篇文字題目下作者之署名。—*v.t.* 署名於(報刊上之文章)。
by·lin·er 〔ˈbaɪˌlaɪnə; ˈbaiˌlainə〕 *n.* 可署名於報刊上之文章的作者或記者。
by·name 〔ˈbaɪˌnem; ˈbaineim〕 *n.* ①姓。②綽號;別名。
by-pass 〔ˈbaɪˌpæs; ˈbai-pɑ:s〕 *n., v.,* **-passed** or **-past, -pass·ing.** —*n.* ①旁道; 間道。②旁通管。③(電路中的)旁路。—*v.t.* ①設旁路。②繞道。③規避。④使從旁管流出。⑤越級(報告等)。
by-past 〔ˈbaɪˌpæst; ˈbai-pɑ:st〕 *adj.* 過去的。
by·path 〔ˈbaɪˌpæθ; ˈbai-pɑ:θ〕 *n., pl.* **-paths** 〔-ˌpæðz; -pɑ:ðz〕. 小路;僻徑。
by·play 〔ˈbaɪˌple; ˈbai-plei〕 *n.* (戲劇等中)穿插的動作或談話;枝節。
by-plot 〔ˈbaɪˌplɑt; ˈbai-plɔt〕 *n.* 副情節。
by-prod·uct 〔ˈbaɪˌprɑdəkt; ˈbaiˌprɔdəkt〕 *n.* 副產品。
byre 〔baɪr; ˈbaiə〕 *n.* 〖英〗牛棚;牛欄。
by·road 〔ˈbaɪˌrod; ˈbairoud〕 *n.* 間道;僻路。
By·ron 〔ˈbaɪrən; ˈbaiərən〕 *n.* 拜倫(George Gordon, Lord, 1788–1824, 英詩人)。
By·ron·ic 〔baɪˈrɑnɪk; baiˈrɔnik〕 *adj.* 英國詩人拜倫的; 有拜倫風格的; 拜倫式的。—**al·ly,** *adv.* —**By·ron·ism,** *n.*
bys·si·no·sis 〔ˌbɪsəˈnosɪs; ˌbisəˈnousis〕 *n.* 〖醫〗棉屑沉着病。
bys·sus 〔ˈbɪsəs; ˈbisəs〕 *n., pl.* **bys·sus·es, bys·si** 〔ˈbɪsaɪ; ˈbisai〕. ①〖動物〗(貝類之)足絲。②古代之一種亞麻;(古埃及用此種亞麻所織成之)亞麻布。③棉;絹。
by·stand·er 〔ˈbaɪˌstændə; ˈbaiˌstændə〕 *n.* 旁觀者。
by·street 〔ˈbaɪˌstrit; ˈbai-stri:t〕 *n.* 僻街;横街。
by-talk 〔ˈbaɪˌtɔk; ˈbai-tɔ:k〕 *n.* 雜談;閒話。
byte 〔baɪt; bait〕 *n.* 〖電腦〗粒子組;排。
by-time 〔ˈbaɪˌtaɪm; ˈbai-taim〕 *n.* 閒暇。
by·way 〔ˈbaɪˌwe; ˈbaiwei〕 *n.* ①旁路(爲 highway 之對)。②研究、努力等之次要或輔助部分。
by·word 〔ˈbaɪˌwɜd; ˈbaiwə:d〕 *n.* ①俗諺。②可鄙或可笑的人或物。③(含輕視的)別名。
by-work 〔ˈbaɪˌwɜk; ˈbaiwə:k〕 *n.* 副業;兼職。
By·zan·tine 〔bɪˈzæntɪn; biˈzæntain〕 *adj.* ①拜占庭帝國的。②拜占庭式建築的。—*n.* 拜占庭古城的居民。(亦作 **Byzantian**)
Byzantine Empire 拜占庭帝國。
By·zan·tin·esque 〔bɪˌzæntɪˈnɛsk; biˌzæntiˈnesk〕 *adj.* 拜占庭風格的。
By·zan·tin·ism 〔bɪˈzæntɪnˌɪzəm; biˈzæntinizəm〕 *n.* 拜占庭主義或風格。
By·zan·ti·um 〔bɪˈzænʃɪəm; biˈzæntiəm〕 *n.* 拜占庭(古城名, 今名伊斯坦堡)。
Bz. benzene.

C

C or c 〔si; si:〕 *n., pl.* **C's** or **Cs, c's, cs.** ①英文字母之第三個字母。②〖音樂〗C大調第一音階;C調。③用C表示之任何語音,如 cat 等。④C狀之物。⑤第三個。⑥(學校成績中之)丙。⑦(羅馬數字之) 100。⑧〖電〗電容。⑨〖美俚〗100元鈔票。⑩(男睡衣)大號。

⑪鞋之寬度(較D號窄而較B號寬)。
C ①化學元素 carbon 之符號。②central.
C. ① Centigrade. ② Cape. ③Catholic. ④Celtic. ⑤College. ⑥Conservative.
c. ①cent; cents. ②about. ③center. ④centimeter. ⑤cubic. ⑥copyright. ⑦catcher. ⑧candle. ⑨carat. ⑩carbon. ⑪carton. ⑫case. ⑬cathode. ⑭centigrade. ⑮centime. ⑯century. ⑰chairman. ⑱chapter. ⑲chief. ⑳child. ㉑church. ㉒(=C.) circa. ㉓cirrus. ㉔city. ㉕cloudy. ㉖cognate. ㉗gallon. ㉘copper. ㉙corps. ㉚〖處方〗with.
© 〖商〗copyrighted. 已取得版權的; 版權所有的。
CA chronological age. **Ca** calcium.
ca. (亦作 c.) about. 約。 **C.A.** ①Central America. ②Chartered Accountant. ③Chief Accountant. ④Church Association. ⑤Commercial Agent. ⑥Confederate Army. ⑦Consular Agent. ⑧Court of Appeal. ⑨Credit Advice. **C/A** ①capital account. ②cash account. ③credit account. ④current account. **C.A.A.** Civil Aeronautics Administration.
Caa·ba [ˈkɑbə; ˈkɑːbə] *n.* =**Kaaba.**
***cab¹** [kæb; kæb] *n., v.,* **cabbed, cab·bing.** —*n.* ①出租汽車;計程車。②一種二輪或四輪的單馬車。③火車頭之遮蓋部(司機與司爐所坐處)。④貨運汽車之駕駛台。—*v.i.* 乘坐計程車或出租馬車。
cab² 〖英俚〗*n.* 自修用書;有註解的(參考)書。—*v.t.* ①使用參考書。②偷竊。
ca·bal [kəˈbæl; kəˈbæl] *n., v.,* **-balled, -bal·ling.** —*n.* ①徒黨;祕密集會。②陰謀。③(藝術,文學或演劇之)派系。—*v.i.* 結黨;陰謀。
cab·a·la [ˈkæbələ; ˈkæbələ] *n.* ①猶太教之神祕哲學。②祕學;祕法。(亦作 **cabbala, kabala, kabbala**)
cab·a·lism [ˈkæbəlɪzəm; ˈkæbəlizəm] *n.* ①神祕學說。②神學的極端傳統主義。③因難解之文字而引起的模糊。
cab·a·list [ˈkæbəlɪst; ˈkæbəlist] *n.* ①猶太教之神祕哲學家。②祕術家。
cab·a·lis·tic [ˌkæbəˈlɪstɪk; ˌkæbəˈlistik] *adj.* ①猶太教神祕哲學的。②神祕的;玄妙的。(亦作 **cabalistical**) **—al·ly,** *adv.*
ca·ba·ña [kɑˈbɑnjɑ; kɑːˈbɑːnjɑː] 〖西〗*n.* ①小屋。②(海濱等處之)浴室。(亦作**cabana**)
cab·a·ret [ˈkæbəˌrɛt; ˈkæbərei] 〖法〗*n.* ①有歌舞助興之餐館。②助興歌舞;餘興。③茶具與茶几。—*v.i.* 常光顧有歌舞助興之餐館。***cabaret tax*** 娛樂稅。
***cab·bage¹** [ˈkæbɪdʒ; ˈkæbidʒ] *n., v.,* **-baged, -bag·ing.** —*n.* ①甘藍菜(俗稱包心菜)。②〖俚〗錢(尤指紙幣)。—*v.i.* 形成如甘藍菜之頭。
cab·bage² *n., v.,* **-baged, -bag·ing.** —*n.* 偷來之物;(尤指)裁縫所偷之布。—*v.t.* & *v.i.* 偷;偷布。
cab·bage·head [ˈkæbɪdʒˌhɛd; ˈkæbidʒhed] *n.* ①甘藍菜。②〖俚〗愚笨的人。③〖俗〗大而圓的頭。
cabbage net 煮包心菜時用的一種小網。
cabbage palm 〖植物〗任何末端葉芽可食之棕櫚。
cabbage rose 一種玫瑰。
cabbage tree 一種棕櫚(夏威夷草裙即用此樹之葉編成)。
cab·ba·la [ˈkæbələ; ˈkæbələ] *n.* =**cabala.**
cab·ba·lism [ˈkæbəlɪzəm; ˈkæbəlizəm] *n.* = **cabalism.**
cab·by [ˈkæbɪ; ˈkæbi] *n., pl.* **-bies.** 〖俗〗=**cabman.** (亦作 **cabbie**)
cab·driv·er [ˈkæbˌdraɪvɚ; ˈkæbˌdraivə] *n.* 計程車司機; 馬車夫。
ca·ber [ˈkebɚ; ˈkeibə] *n.* 〖蘇〗(投擲以測驗氣力之)棍棒。
‡cab·in [ˈkæbɪn; ˈkæbin] *n.* ①小屋;茅屋。②船艙。③飛機上駕駛員或乘客的艙位。④拖車或纜車上之臨時住處或座位。⑤軍艦上軍官之艙位。—*v.t.* 禁閉於小屋中;幽禁;拘束。—*v.i.* 住於 cabin 中。—*adv.* 在二等艙中。to travel *cabin.* 坐二等艙旅行。***cabin boy*** 船上侍者。***cabin class*** 二等艙。***cabin court*** 設有房艙的汽車旅館。***cabin cruiser*** 可住宿的遊艇。
cab·ined [ˈkæbɪnd; ˈkæbind] *adj.* ①關在小屋的; 受禁阻的。②有船艙的。
***cab·i·net** [ˈkæbənɪt; ˈkæbinit] *n.* ①放置杯碟等的櫥或櫃。a kitchen *cabinet.* 碗櫥。a filing *cabinet.* 檔案櫃。②(常 C-)內閣。③小私室。④電唱機或電視機的殼子。⑤浴室。⑥展覽藝術品之房間。—*adj.* ①內閣的。a *cabinet* meeting. 內閣會議。②私人的。③足以置於櫥櫃之內的。④cabinetmaker 的。
cabinet council 內閣會議。
cab·i·net·mak·er [ˈkæbənɪtˌmekɚ; ˈkæbinitˌmeikə] *n.* 製傢具之細工木匠。**—cab·i·net·mak·ing,** *n.*
cab·i·net-wood [ˈkæbənɪtˌwud; ˈkæbinitwud] *n.* 適於造細工傢具的木材。
cab·i·net·work [ˈkæbənɪtˌwɝk; ˈkæbinitwəːk] *n.* 精細傢具等之製造; 細工傢具;細木工。
ca·ble** [ˈkebl̩; ˈkeibl] *n., v.,* **-bled, -bling.** —*n.* ①金屬製的巨纜。②電纜。③海底電報。The message came by *cable.* 這消息由海底電報傳來。④=**cable's length.** ***cable address 電報掛號;海外電報略號。—*v.t.* ①用纜繫;用纜縛。②拍海底電報。We *cabled* congratulations to him. 我們打電報慶賀他。—*v.i.* 拍海底電報。He *cabled* in reply. 他拍電報回答。
cable car 纜車。
ca·ble·gram [ˈkebl̩ˌgræm; ˈkeiblgræm] *n.* 海底電報。
ca·ble-laid [ˈkebl̩ˌled; ˈkeiblleid] *n.* 九股鋼索扭成的大纜。
cable railroad (or **railway**) 纜車道。
cable's length 〖航海〗航行的長度單位(美國海軍定爲 720 英尺,英國海軍定爲608英尺)。(亦作 **cable length**)
ca·blet [ˈkeblɪt; ˈkeiblit] *n.* 小纜索。
cable tramway 纜車道。
cable TV 有線電視(付款用戶方能收視之電視)。(亦作 **cable television,** 略作 CATV)
ca·ble·way [ˈkebl̩ˌwe; ˈkeiblwei] *n.* 吊車道;索道。
ca·bling [ˈkeblɪŋ; ˈkeibliŋ] *n.* 〖建築〗有鋼索之裝飾;鋼索狀嵌線之集合稱。
cab·man [ˈkæbmən; ˈkæbmən] *n., pl.* **-men.** 車夫;駕車者;出租汽車司機。
cab·o·chon [kaboˈʃɔ̃; kabouˈʃɔ̃] 〖法〗*n., pl.* **-chons** [-ˌʃɔnz, -ˌʃɔ̃; -ʃɔz, -ʃɔ̃]. 凸圓形磨光的寶石。—*adj.* & *adv.* 凸圓形的(地)。
ca·boo·dle [kəˈbudl̩; kəˈbuːdl] *n.* 〖俚〗團;羣;組;夥。***kit and caboodle*** 〖俚〗全部。***the whole caboodle*** 全部;全體。
ca·boose [kəˈbus; kəˈbuːs] *n.* ①〖美〗載貨火車之守車。②〖英〗船上之廚房。

cab·o·tage ['kæbətɪdʒ; 'kæbətaːʒ] *n.* 沿海航運(權);沿海貿易。

ca·bre·ta [kə'brɛtə; kə'bretə] *n.* 一種較硬的羊皮。

cab·ri·ole ['kæbrɪ,ol; 'kæbrioul] *n.* 傢具之彎脚(末端刻有動物脚爪)。—*adj.* 此種樣式的。

cab·ri·o·let [,kæbrɪə'le; ,kæbriə'lei] *n.* ①篷式汽車。②有篷馬車。

cab·stand ['kæb,stænd; 'kæbstænd] *n.* 出租汽車或馬車之停車處。

ca' can·ny [kɑ'kænɪ; kɑː'kæni] *v.i.* 〖蘇〗小心進行。—*adj.*〖英〗留心的;緩慢的;猶豫的。—*n.*〖英俚〗①工人有意之怠工。②工會限制生產與員工人數以維持高待遇之政策。

ca·ca·o [kə'keo; kə'kɑːou] *n., pl.* **-ca·os.** ①美洲熱帶所產的樹;可可樹。②可可子;巧克力子。(亦作 **cocoa**)

cacao butter 由可可子搾取的油脂物質(化妝品原料)。

cach·a·lot ['kæʃə,lɑt; 'kæʃəlɔt] *n.*〖動物〗抹香鯨。

cache [kæʃ; kæʃ] *n., v.,* **cached, cach·ing.** —*n.* ①隱藏食物、彈藥等供應品的地窖;隱藏所。②隱藏之食物或供應品。—*v.t.* 隱藏;貯藏。—*v.i.* 躲藏。

ca·chet [kæ'ʃe; 'kæʃei]〖法〗*n.* ①(公文等之)封印。②特徵;標識。③藥包;膠囊。④(權威性的)允准;贊同的表示。⑤〖集郵〗印或蓋在信封的行號名稱或口號等。

cach·in·nate ['kækə,net; 'kækineit] *v.i.,* **-nat·ed, -nat·ing.** 放聲大笑。—**cach·in·na·tion, cach·in·na·tor,** *n.*

ca·chou [kə'ʃu; kə'ʃuː] *n.* ①〖植物〗= **catechu.** ②口香丸。

ca·cique [kə'sik; kə'siːk] *n.* ①(墨西哥及西印度羣島)酋長。②(西班牙與拉丁美洲)地方政治領袖。③(菲律賓)有聲望之地主。

cack·le ['kækl̩; 'kækl] *n., v.,* **-led, -ling.** —*n.* ①(母鷄生蛋後的)咯咯啼聲。②高聲喧談。③呵呵笑。—*v.i.* ①(母鷄生蛋後)咯咯啼。②喋喋而談。③呵呵笑。—*v.t.* ①呵呵笑出。②喋喋而談。

caco-〖字首〗表"惡;不佳;劣"之義。

cac·o·de·mon, cac·o·dae·mon [,kækə'dimən; ,kækə'diːmən] *n.* 惡魔;邪靈。

cac·o·ë·thes [,kæko'iθiz; ,kækou'iːθiːz] *n.* ①惡習;惡性。②…狂;…癖。

cacoëthes scri·ben·di [~skrɪ'bɛndɪ; ~skri'bendi] 著作狂。

cac·o·gas·tric [,kækə'gæstrɪk; ,kækə'gæstrik] *adj.* 胃病的;消化不良的。

cac·o·gen·e·sis [,kækə'dʒɛnəsɪs; ,kækə'dʒenisis] *n.* ①成長異常。②〖醫〗構造異常。

cac·o·gen·ics [,kækə'dʒɛnɪks; ,kækə'dʒeniks] *n.* (作 *sing.* 解)劣生學。

ca·cog·ra·phy [kə'kɑgrəfɪ; kæ'kɔgrəfi] *n.* ①拙劣的書法。②錯誤的拼寫。

ca·col·o·gy [kə'kɑlədʒɪ; kæ'kɔlədʒi] *n.* 不標準的發音或措辭;用字不當。

cac·o·nym ['kækənɪm; 'kækənim] *n.* 不合適的名稱;不雅之名稱。

ca·coph·o·nist [kə'kɑfənɪst; kə'kɔfənist] *n.* 不和諧音樂的作曲家;愛好此種音樂者。

ca·coph·o·ny [kæ'kɑfənɪ; kæ'kɔfəni] *n., pl.* **-nies.** ①不調和的聲音;刺耳的聲音。②〖音樂〗不和諧音。—**ca·coph·o·nous,** *adj.*

cac·o·rhyth·mic [,kækə'rɪðmɪk; ,kækə'riðmik] *adj.* 韻律拙劣的;節奏不合的。

cac·ta·ceous [kæk'teʃəs; kæk'teiʃəs] *adj.*〖植物〗仙人掌科的。

cac·tus ['kæktəs; 'kæktəs] *n., pl.* **-tus·es, -ti** [-taɪ; -tai]. 仙人掌。—**like, cac·toid,** *adj.*

ca·cu·mi·nal [kə'kjumənl̩; kæ'kjuːminl]〖語音〗*adj.* 捲舌的。—*n.* 捲舌音。

cad [kæd; kæd] *n.* ①下流人。②〖牛津大學俚〗市民。

ca·das·tral [kə'dæstrəl; kə'dæstrəl] *adj.* ①(地圖或測量)顯示界線、地產等的。②地籍簿的。

ca·das·tre, ca·das·ter [kə'dæstɚ; kə'dæstə] *n.* 地籍簿。

ca·dav·er [kə'dævɚ; kə'dævə] *n.* (人之)屍體。

ca·dav·er·ous [kə'dævərəs; kə'dævərəs] *adj.* ①屍體的;似屍的。②灰白如幽靈的;憔悴的。

cad·die ['kædɪ; 'kædi] *n., pl.* **-dies,** *v.,* **-died, -dy·ing.** —*n.* ①雜役;小廝。②〖高爾夫〗爲人攜球棒、拾球之小僮。—*v.i.* 供差遣;當球僮。(亦作 **caddy**)

caddie bag 高爾夫球棒袋。

cad·dis, cad·dice ['kædɪs; 'kædis] *n.* ①粗織之毛料。②粗絲帶。③蜻蛉;石蠶。

caddis fly 石蠶蛾。

cad·dish ['kædɪʃ; 'kædiʃ] *adj.* 下賤的;鄙野的。

cad·dy¹ ['kædɪ; 'kædi] *n., pl.* **-dies.** ①茶葉罐;茶葉筒。②小盒子;小罐子。

cad·dy² *n., pl.* **-dies,** *v.,* **-died, -dy·ing.** = **caddie.**

cade [ked; keid] *adj.* 離開其母而由人飼養的(小動物)。

***ca·dence** ['kedn̩s; 'keidəns] *n., v.,* **-denced, -denc·ing.** —*n.* ①韻律;聲調。②節奏;拍子。③聲音之降落;聲音之抑揚頓挫。④樂章之結尾。⑤進軍時的步度;步調。—*v.t.* 使成節奏。—**ca·denced, ca·den·tial,** *adj.*

***ca·den·cy** ['kedənsɪ; 'keidənsi] *n., pl.* **-cies.** ①= **cadence.** ②幼子之後裔。

ca·den·za [kə'dɛnzə; kə'denzə]〖義〗*n.*〖音樂〗裝飾樂段。

ca·det [kə'dɛt; kə'det] *n.* ①陸海空軍官校學生。②幼子或幼弟。③商船學校學生。④灰藍色。⑤〖俚〗淫媒。—**ship,** *n.*

cadet teacher 實習教師。

cadge [kædʒ; kædʒ] *v.t. & v.i.,* **cadged, cadg·ing.** ①〖方〗叫賣;販賣。②〖俗〗行乞;求食。

ca·di ['kɑdɪ; 'kɑːdi] *n., pl.* **-dis.** (回教國家之)法官。(亦作 **kadi**)

Cad·me·an [kæd'miən; kæd'miːən] *adj.* Cadmus 的;似 Cadmus 的。

Cadmean victory 付出與敗北者同等代價之勝利。

cad·mi·um ['kædmɪəm; 'kædmiəm] *n.*〖化〗鎘(元素名,符號Cd). —**cad·mic,** *adj.*

Cad·mus ['kædməs; 'kædməs] *n.*〖希臘神話〗Phoenicia 之一王子(將 Phoenicia 文字傳入希臘)。

ca·dre ['kɑdɚ; 'kɑːdə] *n.* ①〖軍〗負訓練之責的軍官及士兵;核心幹部。②骨架;核心。③政黨或宗教團體之幹部。

ca·du·ce·us [kə'djusɪəs; kə'djuːsjəs] *n., pl.* **-ce·i** [-sɪ,aɪ; -siai]. ①〖希臘神話〗Zeus 之使者 Mercury 的手杖(上有二蛇與雙翼)。②上述手杖之標幟。③美陸軍軍醫部隊之標誌。

ca·du·ci·ty [kə'djusətɪ; kə'djuːsiti] *n.* ①易落;易倒;易滅。②老邁;衰老。③〖植物〗早期凋落性。

ca·du·cous [kə'djukəs; kə'djuːkəs] *adj.* ①易逝的;短暫的。②〖植物〗早期脫落的;凋落性的。③〖動物〗脫落性的。

cae·cal, ce·cal ['sikəl; 'siːkəl] *adj.*

〖解剖〗盲腸的；似盲腸的。

cae·cec·to·my 〔si'sɛktəmɪ; si:'sektəmi〕 *n., pl.* **-mies.** 盲腸切除手術。

cae·ci·tis 〔si'saɪtɪs; si:'saitis〕 *n.* 〖醫〗盲腸炎。

cae·cum, ce·cum 〔'sikəm; 'si:kəm〕 *n., pl.* **-ca** 〔-kə; -kə〕. 〖解剖〗盲腸。

Cae·sar 〔'sizə; 'si:zə〕 *n.* ①凱撒（Gaius Julius, 102 or 100–44 B.C., 古羅馬的將軍, 政治家及歷史家）。②羅馬皇帝之尊號。③皇帝之尊稱。④暴君；獨裁者。***appeal to Caesar*** **a.** 向最高當局陳情。**b.** 〖政治〗藉總選訴諸國人。—**e·an,** —**i·an,** *adj.*

Cae·sar·i·an operation (or **section**) 〔sɪ'zɛrɪən～; si'zɛəriən～〕 剖腹取子術。

Cae·sar·ism 〔'sizə,rɪzəm; 'si:zərizəm〕 *n.* 獨裁君主制；專制政治；帝國主義。—**Cae·sar·ist,** *n.*

cae·si·um 〔'sizɪəm; 'si:ziəm〕 *n.* =cesium.

cae·su·ra 〔sɪ'ʒurə; si:'zjuərə〕 *n., pl.* **-ras, -rae** 〔-ri; -ri:〕. ①詩行中間之停頓。②〖音樂〗樂節中之中間休止。(亦作 **cesura**) —**cae·su·ral,** *adj.*

CAF ①Chinese Air Force. ②cost and freight. ③cost, assurance and freight.

***ca·fé** 〔kə'fe, kæ'fe; 'kæfei, 'kæfi〕 *n., pl.* **-fés** 〔-fez, -fe; -feiz, -fei〕. ①飲食店；飯館。②酒店。③咖啡店。④〖法〗咖啡。

CAFEA Commission on Asian and Far East Affairs.

ca·fé au lait 〔,kæfɪo'le; ,kæfiou'lei〕 〖法〗①牛奶咖啡。②淺褐色。

café car 設有吸烟室、休息室的餐車。

ca·fé chant·ant 〔ka'feʃɑ̃'tɑ̃; 'kæfei-'ʃɑ̃:tɑ̃:ŋ〕 〖法〗有音樂表演的餐廳。

ca·fé noir 〔ka'fe'nwar; ka'fei'nwar〕 〖法〗純咖啡。

caf·e·te·ri·a 〔,kæfə'tɪrɪə; ,kæfi'tiəriə〕 *n.* 〖美〗自助餐餐館。

caf·fe·ic 〔kæ'fiɪk; kæ'fi:ik〕 *adj.* 咖啡的。

caffeic acid 〖化〗咖啡酸。

caf·feine, caf·fein 〔'kæfiɪn; 'kæfi:n〕 *n.* 〖化〗咖啡鹼；茶精。(亦作 **caffeina**)

Caf·fre 〔'kæfɚ; 'kæfə〕 *n.* =**Kaf(f)ir.**

caf·tan 〔'kæftən; 'kæftən〕 *n.* 土耳其式長衫(長袖、腰部束帶)。(亦作 **kaftan**)

cage** 〔kedʒ; keidʒ〕 *n., v.,* **caged, cag·ing.** —*n.* ①籠；檻。②籠狀物。the *cage* of an elevator. 電梯的座廂。③監獄。④〖軍〗鎗架。⑤骨架。⑥〖棒球〗**a.** 用網圍繞的練球場。**b.** 捕手的面罩。⑦〖籃球〗籃。—*v.t.* ①入籠；入檻；監禁。②〖籃球〗向（籃圈）投籃。cage bird*** 通常養於籠中之鳥。

cage·ling 〔'kedʒlɪŋ; 'keidʒliŋ〕 *n.* 籠中之鳥。

cag·er 〔'kedʒɚ; 'keidʒə〕 *n.* 〖俗〗籃球選手。

cage·y, cag·y 〔'kedʒɪ; 'keidʒi〕 *adj.,* **cag·i·er, cag·i·est.** 〖俚〗小心的；狡猾的。

ca·hoot 〔kə'hut; kə'hu:t〕 *n.* (常 *pl.*) 〖俚〗合夥。***go cahoots; go in cahoot with; go in cahoots*** 變爲夥友；均分。***in cahoot(s)*** **a.** 合夥；結合。**b.** 同謀。

Cain 〔ken; kein〕 *n.* ①〖聖經〗該隱（亞當與夏娃之長子，殺害其弟亞伯 Abel）。②殺人者；殺兄弟者。***raise Cain*** **a.** 發怒；施暴。**b.** 擾亂；引起紛亂。

Cai·no·zo·ic 〔,kaɪnə'zo·ɪk; ,kainə'zouik〕 *adj.* =**Cenozoic.**

ca·ique 〔kɑ'ik; kai'i:k〕 *n.* ①(Bosporus 海峽之）一種輕舟。②（地中海之東所見之）一種帆船。

caird 〔kɛrd; kɛəd〕 *n.* 〖蘇〗①挑擔爲業之銅匠。②流浪者。

cairn 〔kɛrn; kɛən〕 *n.* ①圓錐形石堆(作爲紀念碑或地界界標者)。②一種源出蘇格蘭的獅子狗。(亦作 **cairn terrier**)

cairn·gorm 〔'kɛrn,gɔrm; 'kɛən'gɔ:m〕 *n.* 〖礦〗煙水晶。(亦作 **cairngorm stone**)

Cai·ro 〔'kaɪro; 'kaiərou〕 *n.* 開羅（埃及的首都）。

cais·son 〔'kesn̩; kə'su:n〕 *n.* ①火藥箱。②彈藥車。③彈藥箱。④潛水箱。⑤浮船箱。⑥船形渠門。***caisson disease*** 〖醫〗潛水夫病（由氣壓高之處至普通氣壓之處所引起之神經麻痺等症）。

cai·tiff 〔'ketɪf; 'keitif〕 *n.* 鄙漢；卑怯者。—*adj.* 鄙下的；畏怯的。

ca·jole 〔kə'dʒol; kə'dʒoul〕 *v.,* **-joled, -jol·ing.** —*v.t.* 以甜言蜜語誘惑或欺騙。—*v.i.* 誘騙。—**ment, ca·jol·er,** *n.*

ca·jol·er·y 〔kə'dʒolərɪ; kə'dʒouləri〕 *n., pl.* **-er·ies.** 甜言蜜語的誘惑；諂媚；勾引。

‡**cake** 〔kek; keik〕 *n., v.,* **caked, cak·ing.** —*n.* ①糕；蛋糕；餅。She is baking a *cake.* 她正在烘烤蛋糕。②薄扁的餅狀物。a meat *cake.* 肉餅。③塊狀的東西。a *cake* of soap. 一塊肥皂。***a piece of cake*** 容易的事。***cakes and ale*** 好東西；生活中之樂趣。***have one's cake and eat it*** 魚與熊掌兼得。***take the cake*** 〖俚〗**a.** 得第一名。**b.** 超過任何人。—*v.t.* 結有塊。He was *caked* with mud. 他滿身都是乾泥塊。—*v.i.* 結塊。

cake ink 墨。

cake·walk 〔'kek,wɔk; 'keikwɔ:k〕 *n.* ①美國黑人所創之一種走步遊藝。②該種遊藝之步法或樂曲。—**er,** *n.*

cak·y 〔'kekɪ; 'keiki〕 *adj.,* **cak·i·er, cak·i·est.** 如糕餅的；凝固了的。

CAL China Airlines. 中華航空公司。

Cal. ①California 之縮寫。②〖物理〗大卡(large calorie). **cal.** ①calendar. ②caliber. ③〖物理〗小卡(small calorie).

cal·a·bash 〔'kælə,bæʃ; 'kæləbæʃ〕 *n.* ①〖植物〗葫蘆；瓢。②由葫蘆所製之物品（如壺、瓶、煙斗等)。

cal·a·boose 〔'kælə,bus; 'kæləbu:s〕 *n.* 〖美俗〗監獄。

ca·la·di·um 〔kə'ledɪəm; kə'leidiəm〕 *n.* 〖植物〗貝母。

Ca·lais 〔'kælɪs; 'kælei〕 *n.* 加來（法國北部之一海港，與 Dover 僅隔21英里)。

cal·a·man·co 〔,kælə'mæŋko; ,kælə'mæŋkou〕 *n.* 一種有光澤之毛呢。

cal·a·mar·y 〔'kælə,mɛrɪ; 'kælə,mɛəri〕 *n., pl.* **-mar·ies, -mar** 〔-mɑr; -mɑ:〕. 〖動物〗槍烏賊。

cal·a·mine 〔'kælə,maɪn; 'kæləmain〕 *n.* 〖礦〗異極礦。

cal·a·mite 〔'kælə,maɪt; 'kæləmait〕 *n.* 〖古生物〗蘆木。

***ca·lam·i·ty** 〔kə'læmətɪ; kə'læmiti〕 *n., pl.* **-ties.** 不幸之事；災難。—**ca·lam·i·tous,** *adj.* —**ca·lam·i·tous·ly,** *adv.* —**ca·lam·i·tous·ness,** *n.*

calamity howler (or **shouter**) 〖美〗杞人憂天者。

cal·a·mus 〔'kæləməs; 'kæləməs〕 *n., pl.* **-mi.** ①〖植物〗白菖；白菖根；(C-)省藤屬。②蘆草、籐、竹等之莖。③鳥羽之翮。

ca·lan·do 〔kɑ'lɑndo; kɑ:'lɑ:ndou〕 〖義〗 *adj. & adv.* 〖音樂〗漸慢而弱。

ca·lash 〔kə'læʃ; kə'læʃ〕 *n.* ①低輪有篷之輕馬車。②該種馬車之篷。③篷形女用絲頭巾。

cal·car·e·ous 〔kæl'kɛrɪəs; kæl'kɛəriəs〕 *adj.* 石灰（質）的；含鈣（質)的。(亦作

calcarious)

Cal·ce·o·lar·i·a [ˌkælsɪəˈlɛrɪə; ˌkælsiəˈlɛəriə] *n.* 〖植物〗①荷包草屬。②(c-)荷包草。

cal·cic [ˈkælsɪk; ˈkælsik] *adj.* 鈣的；含鈣的。

cal·cif·er·ol [kælˈsɪfəˌrol; kælˈsifəroul] *n.* 〖生化〗維他命 D_2；鈣化固醇。

cal·cif·er·ous [kælˈsɪfərəs; kælˈsifərəs] *adj.*生碳酸鈣的；含碳酸鈣的；含方解石的。

cal·ci·fi·ca·tion [ˌkælsəfɪˈkeʃən; ˌkælsifiˈkeiʃən] *n.* ①石灰化。②〖生理〗鈣化。

cal·ci·fy [ˈkælsəˌfaɪ; ˈkælsifai] *v.t.* & *v.i.*, **-fied, -fy·ing.** ①(使)成石灰；變成石灰質。②(使)變頑固。

cal·ci·mine [ˈkælsəˌmaɪn; ˈkælsimain] *n., v.,* **-mined, -min·ing.** —*n.* 白粉溶液。—*v.t.* 粉刷。(亦作 **kalsomine**)

cal·ci·na·tion [ˌkælsɪˈneʃən; ˌkælsiˈneiʃən] *n.*①鍛燒。②經鍛燒之物。③被鍛燒之狀態。

cal·cine [ˈkælsaɪn; ˈkælsain] *v.t.* & *v.i.*, **-cined, -cin·ing.** 鍛燒。

cal·cite [ˈkælsaɪt; ˈkælsait] *n.* 〖礦〗方解石。

***cal·ci·um** [ˈkælsɪəm; ˈkælsiəm] *n.* 〖化〗鈣(Ca).

calcium acetate〖化〗乙酸鈣；醋酸鈣。

calcium aluminate 〖化〗鋁酸鈣。

calcium arsenate 〖化〗砷酸鈣。

calcium carbonate 〖化〗碳酸鈣。

calcium chlorate 〖化〗氯酸鈣。

calcium chloride 〖化〗氯化鈣。

calcium cyanamide 〖化〗氰氨基化鈣。

calcium dioxide 〖化〗二氧化鈣。

calcium fluoride 〖化〗氟化鈣。

calcium hydride 〖化〗氫化鈣。

calcium hydroxide〖化〗氫氧化鈣。

calcium hypophosphite〖化〗次磷酸鈣；次磷酸二氫鈣。

calcium iodide 〖化〗碘化鈣。

calcium lactate 〖化〗乳酸鈣。

calcium light 〖化〗鈣光；石灰光。

calcium nitrate 〖化〗硝酸鈣。

calcium nitride 〖化〗氮化鈣。

calcium oxide 〖化〗氧化鈣。

calcium permanganate〖化〗高錳酸鈣。

calcium phosphate 〖化〗磷酸鈣。

calcium phosphide 〖化〗磷化鈣。

calcium silicate〖化〗矽酸鈣。

calcium sulphate 〖化〗硫酸鈣。

cal·cog·ra·phy [kælˈkɑgrəfɪ; kælˈkɔgrəfi] *n.* 着色粉筆畫法；臘筆畫法。

cal·cu·la·ble [ˈkælkjələbl; ˈkælkjuləbl] *adj.* ①可計算的。②可依賴的；可靠的。—**cal·cu·la·bil·i·ty,** *n.*—**cal·cu·la·bly,** *adv.*

***cal·cu·late** [ˈkælkjəˌlet; ˈkælkjuleit] *v.,* **-lat·ed, -lat·ing.** —*v.t.* ①計算。to *calculate* the velocity of light. 計算光的速度。②估計。③〖美俗〗計劃；打算。The room is not *calculated* for such use. 這間房不是打算做這種用途的。④〖美俗〗認爲；覺得。⑤評價；估價。—*v.i.* ①計算；考慮。②預料；靠得住〖upon, on〗。

cal·cu·lat·ed [ˈkælkjəˌletɪd; ˈkælkjuleitid] *adj.* ①計算的；以計算求出的。②有意的；計畫的。③適合的。—**ly,** *adv.*

cal·cu·lat·ing [ˈkælkjəˌletɪŋ; ˈkælkjuleitiŋ] *adj.* ①計算的。②小心的；有算計的。③陰謀的；有策略的。 —**ly,** *adv.*

calculating machine 計算機。

***cal·cu·la·tion** [ˌkælkjəˈleʃən; ˌkælkjuˈleiʃən] *n.* ①計算。②計算所得的結果。③預料；謹愼的計畫。This is beyond our *calculation.* 這是出於我們意料之外的。④愼思；考慮。⑤估計。

cal·cu·la·tive [ˈkælkjəˌletɪv; ˈkælkjulətiv] *adj.* 計算(上)的；善於核算的；有計畫的。

cal·cu·la·tor [ˈkælkjəˌletɚ; ˈkælkjuleitə] *n.* ①計算者。②計算機。③工於速算者。④計算機操作者。

cal·cu·lous [ˈkælkjuləs; ˈkælkjuləs] *adj.* 〖醫〗結石性的。

cal·cu·lus [ˈkælkjələs; ˈkælkjuləs] *n., pl.*(for①) **-li** [-laɪ; -lai] or (for②) **-lus·es.** ①微積分學。②〖醫〗結石。

calculus of variations 〖數學〗變分學；變分法。

Cal·cut·ta [kælˈkʌtə; kælˈkʌtə] *n.* 加爾各答(印度東北部的港口)。

cal·da·ri·um [kælˈdɛrɪəm; kælˈdɛəriəm] *n., pl.* **-ri·a** [-rɪə; -riə]. (古羅馬之)熱浴室。

cal·de·ra [kælˈdirə; kælˈdiːrə] 〖西〗*n.* (死火山之)火山口。

cal·dron [ˈkɔldrən; ˈkɔːldrən] *n.* 大鍋。(亦作 **cauldron**)

Cal·e·do·ni·an [ˌkælɪˈdonɪən; ˌkæliˈdouniən] *adj.* ①古蘇格蘭的。②〖諧,詩〗蘇格蘭的。—*n.* 古蘇格蘭人。

cal·e·fac·tion [ˌkælɪˈfækʃən; ˌkæliˈfækʃən] *n.* ①加熱；溫暖；暖。②熱染汚。

***cal·en·dar** [ˈkæləndɚ; ˈkælində] *n.* ①曆法；日曆。②一覽表；表；記錄；開庭日程表。—*v.t.* 登記。

calendar clock 曆鐘(時間以外尚能表示月、日等)。

calendar day 曆日(始於午夜終於次日午夜的24小時)。

calendar month 曆月(一年中十二個月分之任一)。

calendar watch 曆錶。

calendar year 曆年(從元月一日至十二月三十一日的一段時間)。

cal·en·der[1] [ˈkæləndɚ, ˈkælɪn-; ˈkælində] *n.* ①砑光機。②使用砑光機之人。—*v.t.* 用砑光機壓光(紙、布等)。

cal·en·der[2] *n.* (伊朗、土耳其等回教國家之)托鉢僧。(亦作 **Calender**)

cal·ends [ˈkæləndz; ˈkælindz] *n. pl.* 羅馬古曆之朔日。(亦作 **kalends**)

Ca·len·du·la [kəˈlɛndʒələ; kəˈlendʒələ] *n.* 〖植物〗①金盞草屬。②(c-)金盞草屬之植物；金盞草。

cal·en·ture [ˈkælənˌtʃuɚ; ˈkæləntjuə] *n.* 〖醫〗熱帶地方之一種熱病。

ca·le·sa [kɑˈlesɑ; kɑːˈleisɑː] *n.* 菲律賓的一種二輪小馬車。

calf**[1] [kæf, kɑf; kɑːf] *n., pl.* **calves.** ①小牛；犢。②小象；小鯨；小海豹。③小牛皮；犢皮。④〖俗〗笨拙的男子。⑤由冰山上分裂下來的巨大冰塊。 ***kill the fatted calf 準備飲宴慶祝或歡迎。

calf[2] *n., pl.* **calves.** 腓；小腿。

calf-bound [ˈkæfˌbaund; ˈkɑːfbaund] *adj.* (書等)由小牛皮作封面的。

calf love〖俗〗少男和少女間短暫的愛情；幼戀。

calf·skin [ˈkæfˌskɪn; ˈkɑːfskin] *n.* ①犢皮；小牛皮。②犢皮所製之革。

Cal·i·ban [ˈkæləˌbæn; ˈkælibæn] *n.* 莎士比亞所著 *The Tempest* 中之醜陋、野蠻而殘忍的奴隸。

cal·i·ber, cal·i·bre [ˈkæləbɚ; ˈkælibə] *n.* ①(鎗砲)口徑。②(砲彈或子彈之)直徑。③才幹；能力。④品質；重要性。

cal·i·brate [ˈkæləˌbret; ˈkælibreit] *v.t.,* **-brat·ed, -brat·ing.** ①量…之口徑。②校準…之刻度。—**cal·i·bra·tor, cal·i·bra·ter, cal·i·bra·tion,** *n.*

cal·i·cle [ˈkælɪkl; ˈkælikl] *n.* ①〖生物〗(珊瑚等之)杯狀窩。②〖植物〗副萼(=calycle).

***cal·i·co** [ˈkæləˌko; ˈkælikou] *n., pl.* **-coes** or **-cos,** *adj.* —*n.* ①〖美〗印花布。②〖英〗白棉布。—*adj.* ①印花布或白棉布做的;似印花布的。②有斑點的。

cal·i·co·back [ˈkælәkoˌbæk; ˈkælikoubæk] *n.* 一種有斑點之甲蟲。

calico ball 着棉織品服裝的舞會。

calico printing 印花布之印染術。

Calif. California.

Cal·i·for·nia [ˌkæləˈfɔrnjə; ˌkæliˈfɔːnjə] *n.* 加利福尼亞州。—**Cal·i·for·nian,** *adj.,* *n.*

cal·i·pash [ˈkælɪˌpæʃ; ˈkælipæʃ] *n.* 甲魚背上之綠色膠質體, 可食用。(亦作 **callipash**)

cal·i·pee [ˈkælɪˌpi; ˈkælipiː] *n.* 甲魚下「殼外之黃色膠質物, 可食用。」

cal·i·per, cal·li·per [ˈkæləpɚ; ˈkælipə] *n.* (常 *pl.*)彎脚規;測徑器。—*v.t.* 用彎脚規或測徑器度量。

ca·liph [ˈkelɪf; ˈkælif] *n.* 回教主;回教國的國王。(亦作 **calif, khalif, kalif, khalifa**)

cal·iph·ate [ˈkælɪˌfet; ˈkælifeit] *n.* caliph之職、權或其統治地區。(亦作**califate**)

cal·(l)is·then·ics [ˌkæləsˈθɛnɪks; ˌkælisˈθeniks] *n.* ①(作 *pl.*解)柔軟體操;運動。②(作 *sing.* 解) 柔軟體操法。—**cal·is·then·ic, cal·is·then·i·cal,** *adj.*

ca·lix [ˈkelɪks, ˈkælɪks; ˈkeiliks] *n., pl.* **cal·i·ces** [ˈkælɪsiz; ˈkælisiːz]. 杯;聖餐杯。

calk[1] [kɔk; kɔːk] *v.t.* ①塡縫使不漏水。②以塡塞物阻塞;塡隙。(亦作 **caulk**) —**er,** *n.*

calk[2] *n.* ①(附於馬蹄鐵上防滑之)尖鐵。②〖美〗靴底或後跟之尖鐵。—*v.t.* ①加以尖鐵。②以尖鐵傷害。

calk[3] *v.t.* 用描繪法謄寫。

calk·in [ˈkɔkɪn; ˈkɔːkin] *n.* 馬蹄鐵上防「滑之尖鐵。」

‡call [kɔl; kɔːl] *v.t.* ①喊;叫。②喚醒。*Call* me in the morning. 早上喚醒我。③號令;命令。④呼喚;召喚。*Call* off your dog. 把你的狗喚走。⑤令服務;令服役。to *call* to arms. 令服兵役。⑥召集。to *call* a meeting. 召集會議。⑦打電話。He *called* me up by telephone. 他打電話給我。⑧稱之爲;定名。I *called* him a liar. 我叫他爲說謊者。⑨視爲;以爲。⑩大聲讀出;點名。The teacher *called* the roll of the class. 教師點名。⑪催付;催繳償付。The bank *called* my loan. 銀行催我還款。⑫(牌戲中)要求攤牌。⑬學(鳥或動物)叫聲以引誘之。⑭邀請。⑮引起(注意)。⑯使來;使發生。to *call* to mind. 想起來。⑰〖俗〗要求(某人)爲某事提供證據。They *called* him on his story. 他們要他爲他所說的故事提供證據。⑱〖俗〗非難;責備。⑲〖運動〗判定;裁定。The umpire *called* the pitch a strike. (棒球)裁判判那一球爲好球。⑳〖運動〗中止(比賽)。㉑事前宣布或描述;預料。—*v.i.* ①高聲說話;大叫。He *called* from downstairs. 他自樓下大聲叫喊。②訪問。Has anybody *called?* 有人來訪嗎? ③要求;命令。Obey when duty *calls.* 責任到時, 必須服從。④打電話。He promised to *call* at noon. 他答應中午打電話。⑤叫;鳴;吼。***call a halt*** 令停止。***call a person names*** 罵人。***call a spade a spade*** 直言。***call a strike*** 發起罷工。***call at*** 訪問。The ship *called at* Keelung. 這船停泊基隆。***call attention to*** 指出;使注意。***call away*** 請到別的地方。***call back*** a. 召回;喚回。b. 撤銷。***call down*** a.〖俗〗斥責。She *called* me *down* for coming late. 她怪我來得太晚。b. 導致。***call for*** a. 取;迎;接。I will *call for* you at your home. 我將去府上接你。b.求援;需要;要求。***call forth*** 喚起;振起。***call in*** a. 收集。b. 收回(不再流通)。c. 邀請。***call in question*** 認爲有問題;懷疑。***call into being*** (or ***existence***) 使產生;造成。***call off*** a. 取消。b. 命令…停止。c. 按次讀下去;逐條讀出。***call on*** (or ***upon***) a. 請求。to *call on* a person for a song. 請求某人唱一首歌。b. 拜訪。to *call on* friends. 拜訪朋友。***call out*** a. 大聲叫。b. 召集。The fire brigade was *called out* twice last night. 消防隊昨晚被召兩次。c. 使顯現。***call over*** (***names***) 點名。***call over the coals*** 責罵。***call to mind*** 記起。***call to order*** 令守秩序。***call up*** a. 打電話。Can you *call* him *up* this evening? 今天晚上你可以打電話給他嗎? b. 回憶;回想。c. 徵召…入伍。—*n.* ①呼聲;叫聲。I heard a *call* for help. 我聽到呼救聲。②號音(喇叭);鐘聲等。③邀請;召喚。an urgent *call.* 緊急的召喚;緊急的邀請。④拜訪。to make a *call* on a friend. 拜訪朋友。⑤需求。⑥需要;理由。⑦付款要求。He has many *calls* on his money. 許多人要他付款。⑧叫;喊。⑨鳥獸鳴叫之聲。⑩打電話。She sat near the telephone waiting for his *call.* 她坐在電話機旁等待他的電話。⑪〖運動〗裁定;評判。***a close call*** 千鈞一髮;死裏逃生。***on call*** a. 卽期支付的。b. 已經準備妥當的。c. 隨時待命的。Doctors are expected to be *on call* day and night. 醫生應日夜準備看病。***take a call*** 謝幕。***within call*** 叫聲能達的範圍之內。

cal·la [ˈkælə; ˈkælə] *n.* 〖植物〗水芋。(亦作 **calla lily**)

call·a·ble [ˈkɔləbl̩; ˈkɔːləbl] *adj.* ①可召喚的。②未到期可先行償還的(如債券等)。③請求卽付(款)的。

cal·lan(t) [ˈkɑlən(t); ˈkɑːlən(t)] *n.* 「〖蘇〗童子;孩子。」

call-back [ˈkɔlˌbæk; ˈkɔːlbæk] *n.* 〖美俗〗①召回休假工人之通告。②與顧客或當事人之再度會商。③產品收回檢修。

call-back pay 加班費。

call bell 呼人鈴。

call bird 媒鳥(用以引誘他鳥者)。

call·board [ˈkɔlˌbord; ˈkɔːlbɔːd] *n.* 通告板。

call·boy [ˈkɔlˌbɔɪ; ˈkɔːlbɔi] *n.* ①侍僕。「②喚演員按時上臺之人。」

call button 呼人鈴或警報鈴之按鈕。

call day 〖英〗每學期指定學生赴法庭見習之日。

call·er[1] [ˈkɔlɚ; ˈkɔːlə] *n.* ①喊叫者;鳴叫物。②召集者。③訪問者;來訪者;訪客。

cal·ler[2] [ˈkælɚ; ˈkælə] *adj.* 〖蘇〗①新鮮的。②清涼的。

call girl 應召女郎。

call house 應召女郎連絡處。

cal·li·gramme [ˈkæləˌgræm; ˈkæligræm] *n.* 圖畫詩(以詩行形成符合詩意的一種圖畫)。(亦作 **calligram**)

cal·lig·ra·pher [kəˈlɪgrəfɚ; kəˈligrəfə] *n.* 書法家。(亦作 **calligraphist**)

cal·li·graph·ic [ˌkælɪˈgræfɪk; ˌkæliˈgræfik] *adj.* 書法的。

cal·lig·ra·phy 〔kəˈlɪgrəfɪ; kəˈligrəfi〕 *n.* 書法;墨寶。

call-in 〔ˈkɔlɪn; ˈkɔːlin〕 *n.* 〖美〗將聽衆打進來的電話當場播出的廣播或電視節目。(亦作 **phone-in**)

call·ing 〔ˈkɔlɪŋ; ˈkɔːliŋ〕 *n.* ①職業。②邀請;召喚。③慾望。④(會議之)召集。

calling card 名片。

call-in pay ①加班費。②發給未告知停工而來上工的工人之費。

Cal·li·o·pe 〔kəˈlaɪəpɪ; kəˈlaiəpi〕 *n.* 〖希臘神話〗司辯論、史詩之女神。

cal·li·thump·i·an 〔ˌkælɪˈθʌmpɪən; ˌkæliˈθʌmpiən〕 *n.* 〖美〗①(亦作 **callithump**) 喧譁的遊行或夜曲。②參加此種遊行者。—*adj.* 喧譁的;遊行的。

call loan 通知放款(銀行可以隨時通知借款人償還)。

call money 隨時可付或借出之款。

call number 圖書編目號碼。

cal·los·i·ty 〔kəˈlɑsətɪ; kæˈlɔsiti〕 *n., pl.* **-ties.** ①皮膚硬化。②〖植物〗硬化之部分。③無情;鐵石心腸。

cal·lous 〔ˈkæləs; ˈkæləs〕 *adj.* ①堅硬的;變硬的。②無情的;無感覺的;硬心腸的。

cal·low 〔ˈkælo; ˈkælou〕 *adj.* ①未生羽毛的。②未長成的。③沒有經驗的。

call rate 通知放款的利率。

call-up 〔ˈkɔlˌʌp; ˈkɔːlʌp〕 *n.* ①召集令。②召集人數。

cal·lus 〔ˈkæləs; ˈkæləs〕 *n., pl.* **-lus·es,** *v.* —*n.* ①皮膚硬化或加厚的地方;胼胝。②癒合之骨質;接骨質;骨痂。③〖植物〗癒合體素;篩管之沉澱物。—*v.i. & v.t.* (使)結成胼胝、骨痂等。

‡**calm** 〔kɑm kɑːm〕 *adj.* ①安靜的;無風浪的。a *calm* sea. 平靜的海。②寧靜的;不激動的。a *calm* mind. 安靜的心。—*n.* 平靜;安靜。He said so with forced *calm.* 他故作鎮靜地如此說。—*v.t.* 使安靜。*Calm* yourself. 請你安靜下來。—*v.i.* 變安靜〖常down〗. The crying child soon *calmed* down. 哭鬧的孩子不久就安靜了。—**ly,** *adv.*

cal·ma·tive 〔ˈkælmətɪv; ˈkælmətiv〕 *adj.* 鎮靜的。—*n.* 鎮靜劑。

calm·ness 〔ˈkɑmnɪs; ˈkɑːmnis〕 *n.* 安靜;鎮靜;從容。

cal·o·mel 〔ˈkæləml̩; ˈkæləmel〕 *n.* 〖化〗甘汞。

ca·lor·ic 〔kəˈlɔrɪk; kəˈlɔrik〕 *n.* 熱。—*adj.* ①熱的。②(引擎等)由熱空氣推動的。③卡路里的。

***cal·o·rie, cal·o·ry** 〔ˈkælərɪ; ˈkæləri〕 *n., pl.* **-ries.** ①卡路里(熱的單位,有小卡small calorie, 大卡 large calorie 之分。每一小卡之熱量足以使一克之水升高攝氏一度;每一大卡之熱量足以使一千克之水升高攝氏一度)。②食物所供給的熱單位(相當於一大卡)。③能產生這樣多熱能的食物。

cal·o·rif·ic 〔ˌkæləˈrɪfɪk; ˌkæləˈrifik〕 *adj.* 生熱的;發熱的。

cal·o·rif·ics 〔ˌkæləˈrɪfɪks; ˌkæləˈrifiks〕 *n.* 〖物理〗熱學。

cal·o·rim·e·ter 〔ˌkæləˈrɪmətɚ; ˌkæləˈrimitə〕 *n.* 〖物理〗熱量計。

cal·o·rim·e·try 〔ˌkæləˈrɪmɪtrɪ; ˌkæləˈrimitri〕 *n.* 〖物理〗測熱法。

ca·lotte 〔kəˈlɑt; kəˈlɔt〕 *n.* ①無緣便帽;頭蓋帽。②〖建築〗小圓頂;屋頂塔尖之小圓蓋。

cal·trop 〔ˈkæltrəp; ˈkæltrəp〕 *n.* ①攔路鉤;鐵蒺藜。②〖植物〗蒺藜。(亦作 **caltrap**)

cal·u·met 〔ˈkæljuˌmɛt; ˈkæljumet〕 *n.* 北美印第安人所用之一種煙管(用以象徵和平)。***smoke the calumet together*** 和睦相處。(亦作 **peace pipe**)

ca·lum·ni·ate 〔kəˈlʌmnɪˌet; kəˈlʌmnieit〕 *v.t.,* **-at·ed, -at·ing.** 毀謗;中傷。—**ca·lum·ni·a·tor, ca·lum·ni·a·tion,** *n.*

ca·lum·ni·a·to·ry 〔kəˈlʌmnɪəˌtorɪ; kəˈlʌmniətəri〕 *adj.* 中傷的;毀謗的。

ca·lum·ni·ous 〔kəˈlʌmnɪəs; kəˈlʌmniəs〕 *adj.* 中傷的;毀謗的。

cal·um·ny 〔ˈkæləmnɪ; ˈkæləmni〕 *n., pl.* **-nies.** 誹謗;讒言。

cal·var·i·a 〔kælˈvɛrɪə; kælˈvɛəriə〕 *n.* 頭頂;顱頂。

Cal·va·ry 〔ˈkælvərɪ; ˈkælvəri〕 *n.* ①髑髏地(耶穌基督被釘十字架於此地)。②(c-)基督於十字架上之受難像。

calve 〔kæv; kɑːv〕 *v.,* **calved, calv·ing.** —*v.i.* ①產犢。②崩解。—*v.t.* ①產(犢)。②崩解;崩落。

calved 〔kævd; kɑːvd〕 *adj.* 有腓部的;有小腿肚的。

calves 〔kævz; kɑːvz〕 *n.* pl. of **calf**[1] and **calf**[2].

Cal·vin 〔ˈkælvɪn; ˈkælvin〕 *n.* 喀爾文(John, 1509–1564, 法國宗教改革者)。

Cal·vin·ism 〔ˈkælvɪnˌɪzəm; ˈkælvinizm〕 *n.* 法國宗教改革者喀爾文之教義。

Cal·vin·ist 〔ˈkælvɪnɪst; ˈkælvinist〕 *n.* 〖基督教〗Calvin 派之信徒。

Cal·vin·is·tic 〔ˌkælvəˈnɪstɪk; ˌkælviˈnistik〕 *adj.* 〖基督教〗Calvin 教義的;Calvin 派的。(亦作 **Calvinistical**)

cal·vi·ti·es 〔kælˈvɪʃɪˌiz; kælˈviʃiiːz〕 *n.* 〖醫〗禿頭。

calx 〔kælks; kælks〕 *n., pl.* **calx·es, cal·ces** 〔ˈkælsiz; ˈkælsiːz〕. 〖化〗金屬灰;燒渣。

Ca·lyp·so 〔kəˈlɪpso; kəˈlipsou〕 *n.* ①荷馬"奧德賽"中之一海中女神,截留 Odysseus 在其島上居留七年。②(c-)蘭之一種。

ca·lyp·so 〔kəˈlɪpso; kəˈlipsou〕 *adj., n., pl.* **-sos.** —*adj.* 千里達島上土人所演唱之歌曲的。—*n.* 此種歌曲或音樂;加力騷。

ca·lyx 〔ˈkelɪks; ˈkeiliks〕 *n., pl.* **ca·lyx·es, ca·ly·ces** 〔ˈkæləˌsiz; ˈkeilisiːz〕 ①〖植物〗花萼。②〖解剖,動物〗腎盞;杯狀部。

cam 〔kæm; kæm〕 *n.* 〖機械〗凸輪;鏗。

cam 〖軍〗camouflage.

Cam., Camb. Cambridge.

ca·ma·ra·de·rie 〔ˌkɑməˈrɑdərɪ; ˌkæməˈrɑːdəriː〕 〖法〗 *n.* 同志愛;友誼。

cam·a·ril·la 〔ˌkæməˈrɪlə; ˌkæməˈrilə〕 〖西〗 *n.* ①密室。②君王之祕密顧問團;(人數少之)祕密顧問團體;奸黨。

cam·as(s) 〔ˈkæməs; ˈkæməs〕 *n.* 北美產的百合科植物。

ca·mau·ro 〔kəˈmauro; kəˈmaurou〕 *n.* 〖天主教〗教宗(所戴之)紅帽。

cam·ber 〔ˈkæmbɚ; ˈkæmbə〕 *v.t. & v.i.* 彎作弧形;翹曲。—*n.* ①小彎曲;眉形。②略為彎曲之樑木。③(機翼之)彎曲;(汽車前輪之)垂直斜度;曲弧度。

cam·bist 〔ˈkæmbɪst; ˈkæmbist〕 *n.* ①兌換銀錢者;匯票商。②各國貨幣及度量衡便覽。

cam·bi·um 〔ˈkæmbɪəm; ˈkæmbiəm〕 *n.* 〖植物〗形成層。

Cam·bo·dia 〔kæmˈbodɪə; kæmˈboudiə〕 *n.* 高棉(東南亞之一國,原名柬埔寨,首都金邊, Phnom Penh)。

Cam·bri·an 〔ˈkæmbrɪən; ˈkæmbriən〕 〖地質〗 *adj.* 寒武紀的;寒武系的。—*n.* 寒武紀;寒武系。

cam·bric 〔ˈkembrɪk; ˈkeimbrik〕 *n.* 一種質料很薄的白色細葛布或棉布。

cambric tea (含牛奶、糖、茶之)熱飲。

Cam·bridge ['kembrɪdʒ;'keimbridʒ] *n.* ①劍橋(英格蘭東部一名城，爲 Cambridgeshire 郡之首府，因劍橋大學而著名)。②劍橋大學。③美國波士頓附近一城市，哈佛大學所在地。
Cambridge blue 淺藍。
Cambridge Platonist 〖哲學〗劍橋柏拉圖學派。
Cambridge School 〖哲學〗劍橋學派。
‡came¹ [kem; keim] *v.* pt. of **come.**
came² *n.* 彩色玻璃窗上作鑲嵌小玻璃用的細鉛條。
cam·e·ist ['kæmɪɪst;'kæmiist] *n.* ①寶石雕刻者。②寶石浮雕之收藏家或鑑賞家。
cam·el** ['kæml; 'kæməl] *n.* ①駱駝。②一種浮箱，用以打撈沉船或使擱淺船隻脫險之用。③一種防止停泊中的船與碼頭碰撞用的浮標。Arabian camel*** 單峯駱駝。***Bactrian camel*** 雙峯駱駝。
cam·el·back ['kæml,bæk; 'kæməlbæk] *n.* ①駱駝之背。②一種翻新橡膠。*adj.* & *adv.* 騎在駱駝背上的(地)。
cam·el·eer [,kæmə'lɪr;,kæmi'liə] *n.* ①駱駝夫。②駱駝騎兵。
ca·mel·lia [kə'miljə;kə'mi:liə] *n.* ①山茶花。②山茶屬。
ca·mel·o·pard [kə'mɛlə,pɑrd, 'kæmiləpɑ:d] *n.* ①〖動物〗長頸鹿。②(C-)〖天文〗鹿豹座。
Cam·e·lot ['kæmə,lɑt; 'kæmilɔt] *n.* ①傳說中 Arthur 王之宮殿及朝廷所在地。②刺激活動的時間或地點(尤指 1961–1963 甘迺迪當政時代和當時的華盛頓)。
cam·el·ry ['kæməlrɪ; 'kæməlri] *n., pl.* **-ries.** 駱駝騎兵(隊)。
camel's hair 駱駝毛；駱駝呢。(亦作 **camelhair**)
cam·el's-hair ['kæməlz,hɛr; 'kæməlzhɛə] *adj.* ①駱駝毛製成的。②松鼠尾之毛做成的(畫筆)。(亦作 **camelhair**)
Cam·em·bert ['kæməm,bɛr; 'kæməmbɛə] *n.* (法國 Camembert 地方所產)一種鬆軟乾酪。(亦作 **Camembert cheese**)
cam·e·o ['kæmɪ,o; 'kæmiou] *n., pl.* **-e·os.** ①刻有浮雕之寶石；寶石上之浮雕。②(文藝、戲劇等之)小品；片段。
cameo role (電影或戲劇中之) 配角。
cameo ware 有浮雕的陶製小裝飾品。
cam·er·a** ['kæmərə; 'kæmərə] *n., pl.* (*for* ① & ②) **-er·as,** (*for* ③) **-er·ae** [-ə,ri; -əri:]. ①照相機。②發射機中將形象轉變成電子衝 (electronic impulse) 以作電視發射之部分。③法官之私人辦公室。in camera*** **a.** 在法官私人辦公室內。**b.** 祕密地；私自地。
cam·er·a-eye ['kæmərə,aɪ; 'kæmərə'ai] *n.* (如照相機一般詳細客觀的)新聞報導能力。—*adj.* (如照相一般)客觀而詳細的。
camera lu·ci·da [~'lusɪdə; ~'lu:sidə] 投影描繪器；描畫鏡；畫鏡。
cam·er·a·man ['kæmərə,mæn;'kæmərəmæn] *n., pl.* **-men.** ①攝影者；照相師。②攝影記者。③電影或電視攝影師。④攝影器材商。
camera ob·scu·ra [~ ɑb'skjurə; ~ɔb'skjuərə] 〖照相〗暗箱。
camera tube 〖電視〗影像管。
cam·er·lin·go [,kæmə'lɪŋgo;,kæmə'liŋgou] *n.* 〖天主教〗教廷總管財政之紅衣主教。(亦作 **camerlengo**)
Ca·me·roun [,kæmə'run;'kæməru:n] *n.* 喀麥隆(非洲西部之一獨立國，首都 Yaoundé)。(亦作 **Cameroons, Cameroon**)
cam·i·knick·ers ['kæmə,nɪkəz; 'kæmi,nikəz] *n. pl.* 女人所穿之一種內衣。
cam·i·on ['kæmɪən; 'kæmiən] *n.* ①一種運貨低馬車；貨車。②軍用卡車。
cam·i·sole ['kæmə,sol; 'kæmisoul] *n.* ①婦女着用之一種飾有花邊的胸衣。②婦女化妝時所穿之短上衣。③一種拘束瘋子的緊身衣。
cam·let ['kæmlɪt; 'kæmlit] *n.* ①駝毛和絲所織的布。②羊毛和絲所織之布。③上述織品所製之衣服。
cam·o·mile ['kæmə,maɪl;'kæməmail] *n.* 〖植物〗甘菊。
Ca·mor·ra [kə'mɑrə; kə'mɔrə] *n.* ①1820 年創於義大利 Naples 之祕密結社。②(c-)任何類似之祕密結社。
cam·ou·flage ['kæmə,flɑʒ; 'kæmuflɑ:ʒ] *n., v.,* **-flaged, -flag·ing.** —*n.* ①掩飾。②〖軍〗僞裝。—*v.t.* 掩飾；僞裝。—*v.i.* 採取僞裝手段；隱藏。
ca·mou·flet [,kæmə'fle; ,kæmə'flei] *n.* ①潛炸。②潛炸洞。③潛炸地雷、炸彈或炸藥。
cam·ou·fleur ['kæmə,flɝ;'kæməflə:] *n.* 〖軍〗僞裝專家；僞裝技術人員。
‡camp [kæmp; kæmp] *n.* ①營。②搭帳幕處；營地。③住在營地的人；營兵。The *camp* slept through the storm. 暴風雨大作期間營地的人都在睡覺。④供臨時居住之營帳、茅屋等。⑤野營生活。⑥集團(意見相同或共同工作之人)。⑦軍中生活。⑧營帳(集合稱)。⑨因過於誇張、過時、天真或平庸的表現而被認爲有趣的事物。***break camp*** 拔營。We *broke camp* and returned home. 我們拔營回家。***in the same camp*** 意見相同；共同工作。—*v.i.* ①紮營。The army *camped* in the valley. 軍隊在山谷中紮營。②營宿；營居。They *camped* under the shade of trees. 他們在樹蔭下張幕營居。③過着似露營般不方便的生活；過簡樸的生活。④盤據不肯離去。—*v.t.* 使宿於營中；令紮營於。The soldiers were *camped* in front of a temple. 士兵們在寺廟前紮營。***camp out*** **a.** 過臨時的簡陋生活。**b.** 過野營生活；露營。
cam·pa·gna [kɑm'pɑnjə; kæm'pɑ:njə] *n., pl.* **-pa·gne** [-'pɑnje; -'pɑ:njei]. ①平原；曠野。②(C-)羅馬城四周的平原。
‡cam·paign [kæm'pen; kæm'pein] *n.* ①戰役。a military *campaign.* 軍隊出征。②活動；選舉的運動。a sales *campaign.* 競銷運動。—*v.i.* ①發起運動；從事運動。②參加戰役；打仗；作戰。He *campaigned* in France. 他在法國作過戰。
cam·paign·er [kæm'penɚ;kæm'peinə] *n.* ①推行運動者。②老兵；宿將。***old campaigner*** 老練者；老手。
campaign fund 競選用專款。
campaign medal 〖軍〗戰功獎章或獎牌。
campaign ribbon 表示曾參加某次戰役的顏色鮮明之短條，常佩帶於制服上。
cam·pa·ni·le [,kæmpə'nilɪ; ,kæmpə'ni:li] *n., pl.* **-ni·les, -ni·li** [-'nili;-'ni:li:]. 鐘樓；鐘塔。
cam·pa·nol·o·gy [,kæmpə'nɑlədʒɪ; ,kæmpə'nɔlədʒi] *n.* 鐘學。
cam·pan·u·la [kæm'pænjulə; kæm'pænjulə] *n.* ①〖植物〗風輪草。②〖動物〗鐘狀構造。
camp bed 行軍床。
camp chair 便於攜帶之摺椅。
camp·craft ['kæmp,kræft; 'kæmpkrɑ:ft] *n.* 露營術。
camp·er ['kæmpɚ; 'kæmpə] *n.* ①露營者。②露營車(內有廚、浴及起居設備)。
camp fever 營地所發生之熱病。
camp·fire ['kæmp,faɪr; 'kæmpfaiə]

n. 營火；營火會。
campfire girl 美國露營少女團團員。
camp follower ①隨軍商人或服雜役的平民。②營妓。③盲從者；為自私而隨聲附和者。
camp·ground [ˈkæmpˌgraund; ˈkæmpgraund] *n.* 露營地；營地。
cam·phene [ˈkæmfin; ˈkæmfi:n] *n.* 〖化〗烯莰；樟腦萜。
cam·phol [ˈkæmfɔl; ˈkæmfɔl] *n.* 〖化〗龍腦；冰片。
cam·phor [ˈkæmfɚ; ˈkæmfə] *n.* 樟腦。
cam·phor·ate [ˈkæmfəˌret; ˈkæmfəreit] *v.t.,* **-at·ed, -at·ing.** 加樟腦於；使與樟腦化合。
camphor ball 樟腦球；樟腦丸。
cam·phor·ic [kæmˈfɔrɪk; kæmˈfɔrik] *adj.* 樟腦的；含樟腦的。
camphor tree 樟腦樹。
camp·ing [ˈkæmpɪŋ; ˈkæmpiŋ] *n.* 露營；宿營；露營生活。
cam·pi·on [ˈkæmpɪən; ˈkæmpiən] *n.* 〖植物〗一種石竹科植物。
camp meeting 在室外或帳篷內舉行之布道大會，常持續數日之久。
camp·o·ree [ˌkæmpəˈri; ˌkæmpəˈri:] *n.* 童子軍露營。
cam·po san·to [ˈkɑmpoˈsɑnto; ˈkɑ:mpouˈsɑ:ntou] 〖義〗墓地；公墓。
camp-out [ˈkæmpˌaut; ˈkæmpaut] *n.* 野營；露營生活。(亦作 **campout**)
camp·site [ˈkæmpˌsaɪt; ˈkæmpsait] *n.* 露營地；露營預定地。
camp·stool [ˈkæmpˌstul; ˈkæmpstu:l] *n.* (便於携帶之)摺凳。
camp stove (便於携帶之)爐子；手提油爐。
***cam·pus** [ˈkæmpəs; ˈkæmpəs] *n.* 〖美〗①校園；學校範圍內。His home is on the university *campus.* 他的家在那大學的裏面。②大學。③大學教育；高等教育。
camp·y [ˈkæmpɪ; ˈkæmpi] *adj.* ①〖俚〗裝模作樣的；不自然的。②〖俚〗明顯地表現同性戀者之態度、言語、舉止的。③因誇張、過時、天眞或平庸的表現而認為有趣的。
Ca·mus [kaˈmy; kaˈmy] *n.* 卡繆(Albert, 1913–60, 法國短篇小說家、劇作家、散文家, 1957年諾貝爾文學獎得主)。
cam wheel 〖機械〗凸輪。
cam·wood [ˈkæmˌwud; ˈkæmwud] *n.* 一種供製紅色染料之木材。
‡**can**[1] [重讀 kæn; kæn 輕讀 kən, kn̩; kən, kn] *aux. v., pt.* **could.** ①能够。②〖俗〗可以。*Can* I speak to you a moment? 我可以和你說一會兒話嗎？③有權利。④有能力。He *can* read rapidly. 他能看書看得很快。⑤會。He *can* run that machine. 他會使用那部機器。⑥可能。*Can* it be true? 那可能是眞的嗎？ ***can but*** 祇能…罷了。I *can but* speak. 我祇能說話罷了。***can not but*** 不得不。***can not help*** 不能不；不禁。I *can not help* laughing. 我不禁大笑。***cannot ... too*** 決不會太…。We *cannot* praise him *too* much. 我們無論怎樣稱讚他也不算過分。〖注意〗⑴作②義解時, can 較 may 常用。⑵語氣上 Could you...? 較 Can you...? 為客氣。
can**[2] *n., v.,* **canned, can·ning.** —*n.* ①金屬罐；罐頭。a *can* of milk. 一罐牛奶。②罐頭食品。③酒杯。④桶。water *can.* 水桶。⑤〖俚〗監獄。He's been in the *can.* 他曾經入獄。⑥〖俚〗屁股。⑦〖俚〗廁所；洗澡間。⑧〖俚〗深水炸彈。⑨〖俚〗驅逐艦。in the can*** 〖電影〗已完成製片。—*v.t.* ①裝於罐頭；裝於罐內或瓶內。②〖美俚〗解雇；免除。③〖俚〗停止。*Can* that noise! 停止那噪音！④〖俚〗丟棄。
Can. ①Canada. ②Canadian.
can. ①canon. ②canto.
Ca·naan [ˈkenən; ˈkeinən] *n.* ①〖聖經〗迦南(現大部為以色列所在地)。②所想望之地；樂土。
Ca·naan·ite [ˈkenənˌaɪt; ˈkeinənait] *n.* ①迦南人。②迦南語。
***Can·a·da** [ˈkænədə; ˈkænədə] *n.* 加拿大(在北美洲，首都渥太華，Ottawa)。
Canada balsam 加拿大樹膠(樹脂)。
Canada goose 加拿大野鵝。

***Ca·na·di·an** [kəˈnedɪən; kəˈneidiən] *adj.* 加拿大(人)的。—*n.* 加拿大人。
ca·naille [kəˈnel; kəˈneil] *n.* 下等社會之人；暴民；愚民。
***ca·nal** [kəˈnæl; kəˈnæl] *n., v.,* **-nal(l)ed, -nal·(l)ing.** —*n.* ①運河。the Suez *Canal.* 蘇彝士運河。②(體內的)管。③水道；溝；渠。④火星上的狹長條紋。—*v.t.* ①開運河於。②疏導。
ca·nal·age [kəˈnælɪdʒ; kəˈnælidʒ] *n.* ①開掘運河。②運河(集合稱)。③運河通行稅。
canal boat 適合於在運河上行駛的平底載貨船。
can·a·lic·u·lus [ˌkænəˈlɪkjuləs; ˌkænəˈlikjuləs] *n., pl.* **-li** [-laɪ; -lai]. 〖解剖, 動、植物〗小管；細管。
ca·nal·i·za·tion [kəˌnæləˈzeʃən; ˌkænəlaiˈzeiʃən] *n.* ①開鑿運河；改為運河。②運河系統；運河網。
ca·nal·ize [kəˈnælaɪz; ˈkænəlaiz] *v.t.,* **-ized, -iz·ing.** ①開鑿運河於。②改為或使似運河。③導入水道。④予以出路；疏濬。(英亦作 **canalise**)
ca·nalled [kəˈnæld; kəˈnæld] *adj.* 開鑿成運河的。
canal root 〖解剖〗根管。
Canal Zone 運河區(美國向巴拿馬租用之巴拿馬運河及兩岸五英里寬的地區)。
can·a·pé [ˈkænəpɪ; ˈkænəpi] 〖法〗 *n.* ①加有菜餚、乾酪等之烤麵包或餅乾。②沙發椅。
ca·nard [kəˈnɑrd; kəˈnɑ:d] 〖法〗 *n.* ①虛報；妄報；謠言。②一種舊式飛機。—*v.i.* ①流傳。②學鴨叫的聲音；發出鴨叫似的刺耳聲。
***ca·nar·y** [kəˈnɛrɪ; kəˈnɛəri] *n., pl.* **-nar·ies.** ①金絲雀。②淡黃色。③Canary 羣島所產的甜白葡萄酒。④法國和英國的一種步調輕快的舞蹈。
canary bird 金絲雀。
ca·nar·y-creep·er [kəˈnɛrɪˈkripɚ; kəˈnɛəriˈkri:pə] *n.* 〖植物〗金蓮花。
Ca·nar·y Islands [kəˈnɛrɪ～; kəˈnɛəri～] 加那利羣島(在非洲之西北, 屬西班牙)。
canary yellow 淡黃色。
ca·nas·ta [kəˈnæstə; kəˈnæstə] *n.* 一種紙牌戲(使用兩套紙牌)。
ca·nas·ter [kəˈnæstɚ; kəˈnæstə] *n.* (南美產之)一種粗煙草。
Can·ber·ra [ˈkænbərə; ˈkænbərə] *n.* 坎培拉(澳大利亞之首都)。
can·can [ˈkænkæn; ˈkænkæn] *n.* 康康舞(一種高踢大腿而不高尚的法國式舞蹈)。
***can·cel** [ˈkænsl̩; ˈkænsl] *v.,* **-cel(l)ed, -cel·(l)ing,** *n.* —*v.t.* ①刪去；以線劃去。②取消。We *canceled* our appointment. 我們取消約會。③抵消；對消。④作廢；加蓋註銷戳使作廢。—*v.i.* ①互相抵消〖out〗. The pros and cons *cancel* out. 贊成與反對的議論正好互相抵消。②〖數學〗相消；相約。—*n.* ①抵消；取消；刪除；劃除。The order was quickly followed by a *cancel.* 命令發出立

被取消。②被 cancel 之部分。③〖數學〗約分。

can·cel·la·tion [ˌkænsəˈleʃən; ˌkænsəˈleiʃən] *n.* 作廢;取消。

can·cer** [ˈkænsɚ; ˈkænsə] *n.* ①癌;毒瘤。②有毒的事物。③社會上之弊端。④(C-)〖天文〗巨蟹座;巨蟹宮。the Tropic of Cancer*** 夏至線;北回歸線。

can·cered [ˈkænsɚd; ˈkænsəd] *n.* 患毒瘤的;患癌症的。

can·cer·ous [ˈkænsərəs; ˈkænsərəs] *adj.* ①癌的。②生癌的。③似癌的。

can·croid [ˈkæŋkrɔɪd; ˈkæŋkrɔid] *adj.* ①〖醫〗癌狀的。②〖動物〗似蟹的。—*n.* 〖醫〗類癌;癌樣腫;角化癌。

C & D Collection and Delivery.

can·de·la [kænˈdilə; kænˈdi:lə] *n.* 〖光〗燭光。

can·de·la·brum [ˌkændḷˈebrəm; ˌkændiˈlɑ:brəm] *n., pl.* **-brums, -bra** [-brə; -brə]. 枝狀大燭臺或燈臺。(亦作 **candelabra**)

can·des·cence [kænˈdɛsṇs; kænˈdesns] *n.* 白熱;明亮。

can·des·cent [kænˈdɛsṇt; kænˈdesnt] *adj.* 白熱的;明亮的。

C. & F. 〖商〗cost and freight. 運費在內。

***can·did** [ˈkændɪd; ˈkændid] *adj.* ①坦白的。a *candid* reply. 坦白的回答。②公正的。a *candid* decision. 公正的決定。③眞實的;非排演的;傳眞的。—**ly,** *adv.* —**ness,** *n.*

can·di·da·cy [ˈkændɪdəsɪ; ˈkændidəsi] *n., pl.* **-cies.** 候補者或候選人之地位或資格。(亦作 **candidateship, candidature**)

***can·di·date** [ˈkændəˌdet; ˈkændidit] *n.* ①候補者;候缺者;候選人。a *candidate* for president. 總統候選人。②參加考試以求獲得工作或入學者。③註定或理應遭遇某種命運或結果者。

candid camera 〖美〗一種小型照相機(用以偷拍照片)。

can·died [ˈkændɪd; ˈkændid] *adj.* ①糖煮的;蜜餞的。②變成糖的;凝成糖的。③甜蜜的;諂媚的。

‡**can·dle** [ˈkændḷ; ˈkændl] *n.* ①蠟燭。②任何蠟燭狀物。③燭光。***burn the candle at both ends*** 很快地消耗力量;過分消耗體力。***not hold a candle to*** 不能與之相比。***not worth the candle*** 不值得的。—*v.i.* 將(蛋)放在光前以看其是否新鮮。

candle end 蠟燭頭;殘燭。

candle holder 燭臺。

can·dle·light [ˈkændḷˌlaɪt; ˈkændllait] *n.* ①燭光。②黃昏時候。(亦作**candlelighting**)

Can·dle·mas [ˈkændḷməs; ˈkændlməs] *n.*〖天主教〗聖燭節(二月二日,紀念瑪利亞之聖潔的節日)。(亦作 **Candlemas Day**)

can·dle·pin [ˈkændḷˌpɪn; ˈkændlpin] *n.* ①瓶(保齡球戲中所用之一種細長似燭之木柱)。②(*pl.*)使用此種木瓶之遊戲。

candle power 燭光。

can·dle·stand [ˈkændḷˌstænd; ˈkændlstænd] *n.* 燭臺架。

can·dle·stick [ˈkændḷˌstɪk; ˈkændlstik] *n.* 燭臺。

can·dle·wick [ˈkændḷˌwɪk; ˈkændlwik] *n.* 燭芯。

can-do [ˈkænˌdu; ˈkændu:] *adj.*〖美〗熱衷的;急切的。

***can·do(u)r** [ˈkændɚ; ˈkændə] *n.* ①坦白;誠意。②公平;公正。

‡**can·dy** [ˈkændɪ; ˈkændi] *n., pl.* **-dies,** *v.,* **-died, -dy·ing.** —*n.* 糖製的食物;糖果;蜜餞。He was given *candy.* 人們給他糖果。—*v.t.* ①製成糖果;蜜餞。to *candy* fruit. 蜜餞水果。②使甜蜜。③使(糖等)結晶。④覆以糖。—*v.i.* ①結晶成糖。②覆有糖。

candy bar 單獨包裝的塊狀糖。

candy floss 〖英〗棉花糖。

candy stripe 濃淡二色相間的條紋圖案。

can·dy·tuft [ˈkændɪˌtʌft; ˈkænditʌft] *n.* 〖植物〗白蜀葵。

***cane** [ken; kein] *n., v.,* **caned, can·ing.** —*n.* ①手杖。②鞭打用的杖。③長而有節的莖(如竹和蔗等)。sugar *cane.* 甘蔗。④有這種莖的植物。⑤由這種莖編成之物件的材料。⑥細長的莖。—*v.t.* ①以杖擊;鞭笞。②以籐編製。to *cane* chairs. 編製籐椅。

cane·brake [ˈkenˌbrek; ˈkeinbreik] *n.* 籐叢;竹叢。

cane chair 籐椅。

cane field 甘蔗田。

ca·neph·o·rus [kəˈnɛfərəs; kəˈnefərəs] *n., pl.* **-ri** [-raɪ; -rai]. ①古希臘之攜籃者(特指祭神時頭頂盛有聖物之籃的少女)。②〖建築〗上述少女之雕像(有時用作柱頭)。(亦作 **canephoros, canephor, canephore,** 或 **canephora**)

can·er [ˈkenɚ; ˈkeinə] *n.* 籐工;製籐椅工人。

cane sugar 蔗糖。

can·ful [ˈkænfʊl; ˈkænful] *n.* 一罐;滿罐之量。

cangue [kæŋ; kæŋ] *n.* (中國古時之)枷。

Ca·nic·u·la [kəˈnɪkjʊlə; kəˈnikjulə] *n.* 〖天文〗天狼星。

ca·nine [ˈkenaɪn; ˈkeinain] *adj.* ①犬的;似犬的。②〖動物〗犬科的。—*n.* ①犬科動物(如犬、狐、狼等)。②犬;狗。③犬齒。

canine madness 狂犬病。

canine tooth 犬齒;獠牙。

can·ing [ˈkenɪŋ; ˈkeiniŋ] *n.* 鞭笞;打。

Ca·nis [ˈkenɪs; ˈkeinis] *n.* ①〖動物〗犬屬。②(c-)犬。

Canis Major 〖天文〗大犬星座;大狗座。

Canis Minor 〖天文〗小犬星座;小狗座。

can·is·ter [ˈkænɪstɚ; ˈkænistə] *n.* ①茶葉罐;茶葉筒。②金屬罐;筒。③(防毒面具的)濾氣罐;吸收器。④榴霰彈。

can·ker [ˈkæŋkɚ; ˈkæŋkə] *n.* ①(口部的)潰瘍;壞疽。②一種傷害樹皮、木材的植物病害。③傷害果樹的毛蟲;尺蠖。④積弊;弊害。—*v.t.* ①使腐爛。②被 canker 所蝕。—*v.i.* ①潰爛。②受 canker 之害。

can·kered [ˈkæŋkɚd; ˈkæŋkəd] *adj.* 〖古〗①敗德的;墮落的。②壞脾氣的;暴躁的。③爲毛蟲所蛀壞的;有潰爛部分的。④生潰瘡的。

can·ker·ous [ˈkæŋkərəs; ˈkæŋkərəs] *adj.* 潰瘍的;壞疽的;腐爛性的。

canker sore 〖醫〗口瘡。

can·ker·worm [ˈkæŋkɚˌwɝm; ˈkæŋkəwə:m] *n.* 尺蠖類之果樹害蟲。

Can·na [ˈkænə; ˈkænə] *n.* 〖植物〗①曇華屬。②(c-) 曇華屬之任一種植物;曇華。③(c-)曇華屬植物之根或花。

can·na·bin [ˈkænəbɪn; ˈkænəbin] *n.* 從印度大麻榨取的有毒樹脂;大麻脂;大麻素。

can·na·bis [ˈkænəbɪs; ˈkænəbis] *n.* 大麻。

canned [kænd; kænd] *adj.* ①裝罐的。②〖俚〗錄音的;灌成唱片的。③〖俚〗事前準備好的。④〖俚〗(稿子等)由資料供應社或通訊社統一發出的。⑤〖俚〗喝醉的。

can·nel [ˈkænḷ; ˈkænl] *n.* 燭煤;燭餘煤。(亦作 **cannel coal**)

can·ner [ˈkænɚ; ˈkænə] *n.* 〖美〗罐頭食

品製造者。
can·ner·y [ˈkænərɪ; ˈkænəri] *n., pl.* **-ner·ies.** 食品罐頭工廠。
Cannes [kæn, kænz; kæn, kænz] *n.* 坎城(法國東南部之一海港)。
can·ni·bal [ˈkænəbl; ˈkænibəl] *n.* ①食人肉的野蠻人。②食同類之肉的動物。—*adj.* cannibal 的;像 cannibal 的。
can·ni·bal·ism [ˈkænəblˌɪzəm; ˈkænibəlizm] *n.* ①嗜食同類。②殘忍;野蠻。③同類間之自相殘殺。—**can·ni·bal·is·tic,** *adj.*
can·ni·bal·ize [ˈkænəblˌaɪz; ˈkænibəlaiz] *v.t.* ①食…之生肉。②拆下(機器)之零件(以供他用)。③(以舊零件)裝修或裝配。
can·ni·kin [ˈkænəkɪn; ˈkænikin] *n.* 小罐;小杯。(亦作 **canikin**)
can·ning [ˈkænɪŋ; ˈkæniŋ] *n.* 保存食物於眞空的罐中或瓶中;裝罐頭。
***can·non** [ˈkænən; ˈkænən] *n., pl.* **-nons, -non,** *v.* —*n.* ①加農砲;大砲。*cannon* salute. 禮砲。②臂上的圓筒或半圓筒形鎧甲。③鐘上的鐵環。④圓形馬勒;馬勒之在馬口中部分。—*v.i.* 發砲;開砲。
can·non·ade [ˌkænənˈed; ˌkænəˈneid] *n., v.,* **-ad·ed, -ad·ing.** —*n.* ①連續發砲。②砲擊。③〖俗〗斥責。—*v.t.* 砲轟。—*v.i.* 發砲。
cannon ball 砲彈。
cannon bit 圓形馬勒。(亦作 **cannon**)
cannon bone 〖解剖〗馬脛骨。
cannon cracker 大型鞭炮。
can·non·eer [ˌkænənˈɪr; ˌkænəˈniə] *n.* 砲手;砲兵。
cannon fodder ①士兵;砲灰。②有用之材料;待磨的穀物。
can·non-proof [ˈkænənˈpruf; ˈkænənpru:f] *adj.* 能禦砲彈的;防彈的。
can·non·ry [ˈkænənrɪ; ˈkænənri] *n., pl.* **-ries.** ①大砲(集合稱)。②砲擊;砲火。
cannon shot ①砲彈。②砲擊。③砲的射程。
‡**can·not** [ˈkænɑt; ˈkænɔt] *v.* =can not. *cannot but* 難免;不能不。
can·ny [ˈkænɪ; ˈkæni] *adj.,* **-ni·er, -ni·est.** ①靈敏的;狡黠的。②小心的;謹愼的。③節儉的;儉省的。④安靜的;溫柔的。⑤熟練的。⑥舒服的。⑦美麗的;漂亮的。 —**can·ni·ly,** *adv.* —**can·ni·ness,** *n.*
ca·noe** [kəˈnu; kəˈnu:] *n., v.,* **ca·noed, ca·noe·ing.** —*n.* 小而輕的舟;獨木舟。paddle one's own canoe*** 自食其力。—*v.i.* 乘獨木舟;划獨木舟;駕獨木舟。 —*v.t.* 以獨木舟搬運。
ca·noe·ist [kəˈnuɪst; kəˈnu:ist] *n.* 盪舟者;操獨木舟之人。
***can·on** [ˈkænən; ˈkænən] *n.* ①宗教法規;教規。②法規;標準;軌範;原則。③聖典;正經;眞實作品。④聖徒名單。⑤官方名單。⑥天主教彌撒的中心。⑦一種大形印刷活字體。⑧天主教修道院中之教士。⑨公禱團員。
ca·ñon [ˈkænjən; ˈkænjən] *n.* =**canyon.**
can·on·ess [ˈkænənɪs; ˈkænənis] *n.* 寺院中之修道婦女。
ca·non·i·cal [kəˈnɑnɪkl; kəˈnɔnikəl] *adj.* ①依教規的;以寺院法規爲準的。②公認的;權威的。③正經的;聖典的。(亦作**canonic**) —**ly,** *adv.*
canonical hour ①〖宗教〗日課經時間(如早禱,晚禱等)。②〖英〗上午八時至下午三時之間之任一小時(爲合法教會婚禮時間)。
ca·non·i·cals [kəˈnɑnɪklz; kəˈnɔnikəlz] *n. pl.* 牧師禮服;法衣。
can·on·ic·i·ty [ˌkænənˈɪsətɪ; ˌkænəˈnisiti] *n.* ①合於法典;依據法規。②合於聖經。③符合教會規條。
can·on·ist [ˈkænənɪst; ˈkænənist] *n.* 精於宗教法規者;聖典學者。
can·on·is·tic [ˌkænənˈɪstɪk; ˌkænəˈnistik] *adj.* 精於宗教法規者的;精通聖典的;聖典學者的。(亦作 **canonistical**)
can·on·ize [ˈkænənˌaɪz; ˈkænənaiz] *v.t.,* **-ized, -iz·ing.** ①封爲聖徒。②褒揚。③承認合於教典或教規。④認可;認爲正式。 —**can·on·i·za·tion,** *n.*
canon law ①天主教教會法。②任何宗教之教典。
can·on·ry [ˈkænənrɪ; ˈkænənri] *n., pl.* **-ries.** ①牧師或僧侶之職位或聖俸。②牧師或僧侶(集合稱)。
ca·noo·dle [kəˈnudl; kəˈnu:dl] *v.i. & v.t.,* **-dled, -dling.** 〖俚〗擁抱;撫愛。
can opener 開罐具。
can·o·pied [ˈkænəpɪd; ˈkænəpid] *adj.* 有罩蓋的;掛有天篷的。
Ca·no·pus [kəˈnopəs; kəˈnoupəs] *n.* 〖天文〗在船底座 (Carina)星座中的一等星。
can·o·py [ˈkænəpɪ; ˈkænəpi] *n., pl.* **-pies,** *v.,* **-pied, -py·ing.** —*n.* ①床或寶座上之罩蓋。②在上面罩覆之物。the *canopy* of heaven. 蒼穹。③小型飛機之可滑動的機艙蓋。④降落傘之傘頂。—*v.t.* 遮蓋。
ca·no·rous [kəˈnorəs; kəˈnɔ:rəs] *adj.* 和諧的;調子優美的;音樂的。
canst [kænst; kænst] *v.* 〖古、詩〗爲 can 之第二人稱、單數、現在式。
cant[1] [kænt; kænt] *n.* ①僞善之言。②隱語;切口;黑話;術語或口語。③哀求唱吟聲。④蕪詞濫調;口頭禪。—*v.i.* ①做僞善的表示。②做哀求聲。③說隱語;講黑話。
cant[2] *n.* ①屋隅;外角。②斜面;斜邊。③傾斜;旋轉;招致傾斜或旋轉的動作。 —*v.t.* ①斜切。②使成斜角。③使傾斜或傾覆。④拋擲;投擲。—*v.i.* ①傾斜;傾覆。②船在航行中轉向。 ***cant over*** 傾覆。
‡**can't** [kænt; kɑ:nt] =**can not.**
Cant. ①Canterbury. ②Canticles.
Cantab. Cantabrigian.
can·ta·bi·le [kɑnˈtɑbɪˌle; kænˈtɑ:bili] *adj. & adv.* 〖音樂〗如歌的(地);可歌的(地)。
Can·ta·brig·i·an [ˌkæntəˈbrɪdʒɪən; ˌkæntəˈbridʒiən] *adj.* 英國 Cambridge 或 Cambridge 大學的。—*n.* ①英國 Cambridge 城之居民。② Cambridge 大學之學生或畢業生。
can·ta·lev·er [ˈkæntəˌlivɚ; ˈkæntəli:və] *n.* 〖建築〗懸臂。(亦作 **cantaliver**)
can·ta·loupe, can·ta·loup [ˈkæntlˌop; ˈkæntəlu:p] *n.* 一種甜瓜。
can·tan·ker·ous [kænˈtæŋkərəs; kænˈtæŋkərəs] *adj.* ①難處的;好吵鬧的;時時反對別人的。②壞脾氣的;難駕馭的。 —**ly,** *adv.* —**ness,** *n.*
can·ta·ta [kənˈtɑtə; kænˈtɑ:tə] 〖義〗*n.* 清唱劇。
can·ta·tri·ce [ˌkɑntɑˈtritʃe; ˌkɑ:ntɑ:ˈtri:tʃei] *n., pl.* **-tri·ci** [-ˈtritʃi; -ˈtri:tʃi:]. 〖義〗職業歌女。
can·teen [kænˈtin; kænˈti:n] *n.* ①隨身帶的水壺;水罐。②軍營中販賣部;軍中福利社。③軍中所用炊事用具箱。④軍營附近免費招待士兵的餐館。⑤臨時的流動餐館。
can·ter [ˈkæntɚ; ˈkæntə] *n.* ①(馬的)慢步小跑。②愛用術語、口頭禪、陳腔濫調等的人。***win (a race) at a canter*** (賽馬中)輕而易舉地獲勝。 —*v.i.* (馬)慢跑。 —*v.t.* 使(馬)慢跑。
Can·ter·bur·y [ˈkæntɚˌbɛrɪ; ˈkæn-

təbəri] n. 坎特布里(英格蘭著名教堂,爲中世紀英國之宗教聖地)。

Canterbury bell 〖植物〗風鈴草;「吊鐘花。」

Canterbury tale ①無稽之談。②冗長而乏味的故事。(亦作 **Canterbury story**)

Canterbury Tales, The 中世紀英國大詩人 Geoffrey Chaucer 之代表作。

can·thar·i·des [kænˈθærɪˌdiz; kænˈθæridiːz] n., pl. of **can·tha·ris** [ˈkænθərɪs; ˈkænθəris]. 〖藥〗斑蝥。

can·ti·cle [ˈkæntɪkl̩; ˈkæntikl] n. ①教堂禮拜用之頌歌。②小歌;短歌。③(C-)(pl.)所羅門之歌;雅歌(聖經之一卷)。

can·ti·le·ver [ˈkæntl̩ˌivɚ; ˈkæntiˌliːvə] n. 〖建築〗懸臂;懸桁。—v.i. 如懸臂似的向外伸展。—v.t. 利用懸臂建築。—adj. 利用懸臂原理形成的;利用懸臂建造的。

cantilever bridge 用兩個懸臂結構所造的橋。

can·tle [ˈkæntl̩; ˈkæntl] n. ①隅;角;段;「片;部分。②鞍後之弓形部。」

*__can·to__ [ˈkænto; ˈkæntou] n., pl. -tos. 長詩中的篇。

Can·ton [kænˈtɑn, ˈkæntən; kænˈtɔn, ˈkænˈt-] n. 廣州(中國廣東省省會)。

can·ton [n. ˈkæntən; ˈkæntɔn v. ˈkæntɑn; kænˈtɔn] n. ①州;縣;郡。②(法國的)市區;村;鎮。③(紋章的)紋地右上角之小方塊。④任何東西之一部分。—v.t. ①分爲 cantons. ②分;劃分。③(給軍隊)劃定駐區;駐紮。

can·ton·al [ˈkæntənl̩; ˈkæntənl] adj. 州的;縣的;郡的。

Canton crepe 縐紗。

Can·ton·ese [ˌkæntənˈiz; ˌkæntəˈniːz] n., pl. -ese, adj. —n.廣東人;廣州人;廣州話。—adj.廣東的;廣州(人)的;廣州話的。

Canton flannel 廣東絨;法蘭絨。

can·ton·ment [kænˈtɑnmənt; kənˈtuːnmənt] n. ①軍隊駐紮地;軍營。②駐紮。

can·tor [ˈkæntɚ; ˈkæntɔː] n. (教堂中唱詩班之)主領者。

can·to·ri·al [kænˈtorɪəl; kænˈtɔːriəl] adj. ①唱詩班主領人的。②教堂聖壇所之北側的。③〖動物〗能鳴的(鳥)。

*__can·vas__ [ˈkænvəs; ˈkænvəs] n., pl. **-vas·es** or **-vas·ses**, v.t., **-vased** or **-vassed**, **-vas·ing** or **-vas·sing**, adj. —n. ①帆布;帳幕布;畫布。②帆製的東西。③油畫。④帆。⑤馬戲。⑥比賽用的帆船之遮蓋的一端;該遮蓋部分的長度。***under canvas*** a. 在帳幕中。b. 張帆。—v.t. 以帆布鋪…之表面。—adj. 帆布製的。

can·vass [ˈkænvəs; ˈkænvəs] v.t. ①細究。②討論。③向(人)拉票;招徠(顧客)。—v.i. ①拉票;遊說。②檢票;計票。③討論。—n. ①討論。②拉票。③細究;審計(票數等)。**—er**, n.

can·y [ˈkenɪ; ˈkeini] adj. ①用籐做的。②狀似手杖、甘蔗或細莖植物的。

can·yon [ˈkænjən; ˈkænjən] n. 峽谷。(亦作 **cañon**)

can·zo·net [ˌkænzəˈnɛt; ˌkænzəˈnet] 「n. 短歌;小調。」

caou·tchouc [ˈkutʃuk; ˈkautʃuk] n. 彈性橡膠。

‡**cap** [kæp; kæp] n., v., **capped, cap·ping.** —n. ①無邊便帽。②戴以表示階級或職業的帽子。a nurse's *cap*. 護士帽。③帽狀物。④蓋;頂。a *cap* on a bottle. 瓶蓋。⑤最高部分;頂部。the polar *cap*. (南北)極頂。⑥火帽。⑦玩具槍之子彈。⑧大寫字母。⑨紙張之大小尺寸。⑩〖英〗加入運動隊。***a feather in one's cap*** 足以炫耀、自傲之事物。***cap in hand*** 謙恭地。***set one's cap for*** (or ***at***) 〖俗〗獵取丈夫。—v.t. ①覆之以蓋或帽。②覆以;蓋以。③做得比前面的更好。④完成;配合。⑤除…之蓋。to *cap* a bottle. 除瓶蓋。***cap the climax*** 製造高潮;出乎意料。—v.i. 脫帽以示敬。

cap. pl. **caps.** ①capital letter. ②capitalize. ③capital. ④capitulum. ⑤chapter. ⑥capacity. ⑦captain.

ca·pa·bil·i·ty [ˌkepəˈbɪlətɪ; ˌkeipəˈbiliti] n., pl. **-ties.** ①能力;才能;手腕。②可能;可能性。③(常 pl.)可發展之能力。

*__ca·pa·ble__ [ˈkepəbl̩; ˈkeipəbl] adj. ①有知識或有能力的;能幹的。②表露才幹的。***capable of*** a. 有能力的;有資格的。a man *capable of* judging art. 有評判藝術能力的人。b. 有…可能的。He's quite *capable of* neglecting his duty. 他很可能怠忽職務。c. 可容納…的。d. 能感覺…的;能了解…的。**—ness,** n.

ca·pa·bly [ˈkepəblɪ; ˈkeipəbli] adv. 「能幹地。」

ca·pa·cious [kəˈpeʃəs; kəˈpeiʃəs] adj. 能容大量的;寬綽的;大的。

ca·pac·i·tance [kəˈpæsətəns; kəˈpæsitəns] n. 〖電〗(導體之)電容。

ca·pac·i·tate [kəˈpæsəˌtet; kəˈpæsiteit] v.t., **-tat·ed, -tat·ing.** ①使能;使適於。②賦以權力;授以資格。

ca·pac·i·tor [kəˈpæsətɚ; kəˈpæsitə] 「n. 電容器。」

*__ca·pac·i·ty__ [kəˈpæsətɪ; kəˈpæsiti] n., pl. **-ties,** adj. —n. ①容量。The theater has a *capacity* of 400. 這戲院能容四百人。②能力;才能(與 of, for 或不定詞連用)。*capacity* for selfprotection. 自衞的能力。③性能。④地位;關係;資格。in the *capacity* of legal adviser. 以法律顧問的資格。⑤最高發電量。⑥電容。—adj. 充其量的;至最高量的。a *capacity* crowd. 擠得滿滿的觀衆(或聽衆)。

cap-a-pie [ˌkæpəˈpi; ˌkæpəˈpiː] adv. 「自頂至踵地;全然。」

ca·par·i·son [kəˈpærəsn̩; kəˈpærisn] n. ①馬衣;馬的裝飾物。②美服;裝束;行頭。—v.t. ①以馬衣遮(馬)。②以美服裝飾;打扮。

Cape [kep; keip] n. (the -)=**Cape of Good Hope.** —adj. 好望角的;有關好望角的;產於好望角的。

*__cape__[1] [kep; keip] n. 披肩;肩衣。

*__cape__[2] n. 岬;海角。

Ca·pe·a·dor [ˌkɑpeɑˈðɔr; ˌkɑːpeiɑːˈðɔː] n., pl. **-do·res** [-ˈðɔrɛs; -ˈðɔres]. 〖西〗鬥牛士之助手。

Cape buffalo 產於南非之黑色大水牛。

Cape Colony Cape of Good Hope 之舊名。

cap·e·lin [ˈkæpəlɪn; ˈkæpəlin] n. 香魚科之一種小海魚。

Cape of Good Hope 好望角(位「於非洲南端)。」

ca·per [ˈkepɚ; ˈkeipə] n. ①跳躍。②戲弄;頑皮。③〖俚〗犯罪或非法行爲。④輕鬆的插曲。***cut a caper*** 跳躍;雀躍;作傻事。—v.i. 雀躍。**—ing·ly,** adv.

cap·er·cail·lie [ˌkæpɚˈkeljɪ; ˌkæpəˈkeilji] n. 〖動物〗雷鳥;雷鷄。(亦作 **capercailzie**)

Cape·town [ˈkepˈtaun; ˈkeipˈtaun] n. 開普敦(南非聯邦南部之一城市)。(亦作 **Cape Town**)

Cape Verde Islands [~vɝd~; ~vəːd~] 維德角島(西非之一共和國, 首都 Praia).

cap·ful ['kæpful;'kæpful] *n., pl.* **-fuls.** 一帽之量。

ca·pi·as ['kepɪəs; 'keipiəs]*n., pl.*-**as·es.** 〖拉〗〖法律〗拘票。

cap·il·lar·i·ty [ˌkæpḷ'ærətɪ; ˌkæpi'læriti] *n.* ①毛細管作用;毛細管現象。②能產生毛細管現象之特性。

cap·il·lar·y ['kæpḷˌɛrɪ;kə'piləri] *adj., n., pl.* **-lar·ies.** —*adj.* ①毛狀的;毛細的。②毛細管(現象)的。—*n.* ①毛細管。②〖解剖〗微血管。

capillary attraction ①多孔物質吸收液體之能力。②促成毛細管作用之力。③毛的;有關毛的。

‡**cap·i·tal** ['kæpətḷ; 'kæpitl] *n.* ①國都;首都;省會。Washington is the *capital* of the U. S. 華盛頓爲美國國都。②在某方面處於領導地位的都市。③大寫字母。④資金;資本。⑤資本家(集合稱)。⑥資源;力量或利益之根源。***make capital of*** 利用。—*adj.* ①與資金有關的。*capital* stock. 資金股票。②重要的;主要的。the *capital* points of a report. 報告的要點。③好的;上等的。a *capital* dinner. 盛饌。④死刑的。*capital* offense. 死罪。⑤政府所在的;首都的。⑥嚴重的。a *capital* mistake. 一個嚴重的錯誤。

capital account ①固定資產帳戶;資本性帳戶。②(*pl.*)〖會計〗資本淨値。

capital asset 資本資產。

capital bonus 〖英〗紅利;股息。

capital budget ①資本預算。②學校、操場、公園等市政設施的開支預算。

capital expenditure〖會計〗資本支出。

capital gain 資本利得;資本利益。

captial goods 〖經濟〗資本財。

cap·i·tal-in·ten·sive ['kæpətḷɪn'tɛnsɪv;'kæpitlin'tensiv] *adj.* 資本密集的。

capital investment 資金總額。

cap·i·tal·ism ['kæpətḷˌɪzəm; 'kæpitəlizm] *n.* ①資本主義。②資本集中。

***cap·i·tal·ist** ['kæpətḷɪst;'kæpitəlist] *n.* ①資本家。②富人。③主張或擁護資本主義者。—*adj.* ①擁有資本的。the *capitalist* class. 資產階級。②實行資本主義的。③以資本主義爲特色的。

cap·i·tal·is·tic [ˌkæpɪtḷ'ɪstɪk; ˌkæpitə'listik] *adj.* 資本家的;資本主義的。—**al·ly,** *adv.*

cap·i·tal·ize ['kæpətḷˌaɪz;kə'pitəlaiz] *v.t.,* **-ized, -iz·ing.** ①用大寫字母寫。②大寫…之第一個字母。③變成資本;做資本用。④定(某公司之)資本額。⑤供給資本。⑥估價。⑦利用〖on〗.—**cap·i·tal·i·za·tion,** *n.*

capital levy 資本稅。

capital loss 資產出售虧損。

cap·i·tal·ly ['kæpətḷɪ; 'kæpitəli] *adv.* ①佳妙地;極佳。②以死刑;按死刑程序。

capital punishment 死刑。

capital ship 大型軍艦。

capital stock 股本;股票總額。

capital sum ①本金總額。②〖保險〗最高賠償額。

capital surplus 資本公積。

cap·i·tate ['kæpəˌtet; 'kæpiteit] *adj.* 〖植物〗頭狀的;頭狀花序的。

cap·i·ta·tion [ˌkæpə'teʃən; ˌkæpi'teiʃən] *n.* ①按人數計算。②人頭稅;丁稅。③按人數徵收的費。

capitation grant 按人計算的補助費。

Cap·i·tol ['kæpətḷ; 'kæpitl] *n.* ①美國國會議場。②(常 c-) 美國州議會會址。③古羅馬 Jupiter 神殿。

Cap·i·to·line ['kæpətḷˌaɪn; kə'pitəlain] *n.* (羅馬建於其上的)七丘之一。—*adj.* ①Capitoline的。②古羅馬 Jupiter 神殿的。

ca·pit·u·lar [kə'pɪtʃələ; kə'pitjulə] *n.* ①牧師會會員。②(*pl.*) 牧師會法規;牧師會決議。—*adj.* 牧師會的;公禱團的。(亦作 **capitulary**)

ca·pit·u·late [kə'pɪtʃəˌlet; kə'pitjuleit] *v.i.,* **-lat·ed, -lat·ing.** (有條件地)投降。

ca·pit·u·la·tion [kəˌpɪtʃə'leʃən;kəˌpitju'leiʃən] *n.* ①投降。②投降條約。③(常 *pl.*)協定;條約。④要點;要項。—**ca·pit·u·la·to·ry,** *adj.*

ca·pon ['kepɑn; 'keipən] *n.* 閹鷄。

ca·pon·ize ['kepənˌaɪz; 'keipənaiz] *v.t.,* **-ized, -iz·ing.** 除去睪丸;閹。

cap·o·ral [ˌkæpə'ræl; ˌkæpə'rɑːl] *n.* 一種煙草。

ca·pot [kə'pɑt; kə'pɔt] *n.* piquet 牌戲中之全勝。

ca·pote [kə'pot; kə'pout] *n.* ①車蓋;車篷。②連有兜帽之斗篷或外衣。③下顎處繫帶之女帽。

cap·per ['kæpɚ; 'kæpə] *n.* ①裝蓋之人或物。②製帽者;帽商。③〖美俚〗賭博時作弊之同黨。④〖美俚〗拍賣場所雇用以抬高價格之人。

cap·ric ['kæprɪk; 'kæprik] *adj.* 山羊的。

capric acid 〖化〗癸酸;羊蠟酸。

ca·pric·ci·o [kə'pritʃɪˌo; kə'pritʃiou] *n., pl.* **-ci·os, -ci** [-tʃi;-tʃiː]. 〖義〗①〖音樂〗幻想曲;隨想曲。②奇想;怪念頭。

ca·price [kə'pris; kə'priːs] *n.* ①反覆無常;無理性之觀念或慾望;幻想。②輕鬆而富幻想的文學或藝術作品。

ca·pri·cious [kə'prɪʃəs; kə'priʃəs] *adj.* 多變的;反覆無常的;任性的。—**ly,** *adv.* —**ness,** *n.*

Cap·ri·corn ['kæprɪˌkɔrn; 'kæprikɔːn] *n.* 〖天文〗磨羯宮。***the Tropic of Capricorn*** 多至線;南回歸線。(亦作 **Capricornus**)

cap·ri·fig ['kæprɪˌfɪg; 'kæprifig] *n.* 〖植物〗南歐及近東所產之野生無花果。

cap·rine ['kæpraɪn; 'kæprain] *adj.* ①山羊的;如山羊的。②寄生於山羊的。

cap·ri·ole ['kæprɪˌol; 'kæprioul] *n., v.,* **-oled, -ol·ing.** —*n.* (馬之)騰躍。—*v.t.* 騰躍。

Ca·pri pants ['kɑpri~;'kɑːpriː~] 一種女用緊身褲。(亦作**Capris**)

ca·pro·ic acid [kə'proɪk~;kə'prouik~] 〖化〗己酸;羊油酸。

caps. ①capital letters. ②capitals.

cap screw 帽螺釘。

Cap·si·cum ['kæpsɪkəm;'kæpsikəm] *n.* 〖植物〗①蕃椒屬。②(c-) 蕃椒;辣椒。

cap·size [kæp'saɪz;kæp'saiz] *v.,* **-sized, -siz·ing.** —*v.t.* 使(船)傾覆。—*v.i.* 傾覆。

cap·stan ['kæpstən;'kæpstən] *n.* 絞盤;起錨機。

capstan bar 絞盤桿。

cap·stone ['kæpˌston; 'kæpstoun] *n.* ①頂石。②極點;極致。

cap·su·lar ['kæpsələ; 'kæpsjulə] *adj.* ①蒴(狀)的;莢殼的。②被囊的;如膠囊的。(亦作 **capsulary**)

cap·su·late ['kæpsəˌlet;'kæpsjuleit] *adj.* ①爲膠囊所包被的。②〖植物〗包於蒴內的。(亦作 **capsulated**)

cap·sule ['kæpsḷ, 'kæpsjul;'kæpsjuːl] *n.* ①(藥物用的) 膠囊。②橡皮帽;瓶帽。③

蒸發皿。④〖生理〗被囊。⑤〖植物〗蒴;莢。⑥太空艙。⑦摘要;綱要。—*v.t.*①以瓶帽密封。②節略。—*adj.* ①非常簡短的。②小巧的。

Capt. Captain.

‡**cap·tain** 〔ˈkæptɪn; ˈkæptin〕 *n.* ①首領。②陸軍上尉;海軍上校;空軍上尉。③船長;艦長;機長。④隊長(球隊或田徑隊等)。⑤ =**bell captain.** ⑥侍者的領班。⑦有錢有勢者。—*v.t.* 作…之隊長;統率。Tom will *captain* the team. 湯姆將率領這球隊。

cap·tain·cy 〔ˈkæptɪnsɪ; ˈkæptinsi〕 *n.* ①captain 之職位。②隊長作風。

captain general 總司令。

cap·tain·ship 〔ˈkæptɪnʃɪp; ˈkæptinʃip〕 *n.* ①captain 之地位。②將領之統御才幹。③ captain 之技術或領導術。

cap·ta·tion 〔kæpˈteʃən; kæpˈteiʃən〕 *n.* 狡猾手段。

cap·tion 〔ˈkæpʃən; ˈkæpʃən〕 *n.* ①標題。②插圖的說明。③電影字幕。④〖法律〗起訴書中記載執行者、執行地點、時間之部分。⑤〖英〗合法的拘捕。⑥詭辯。—*v.t.* 加題目;加說明。

cap·tious 〔ˈkæpʃəs; ˈkæpʃəs〕 *adj.* ①好吹毛求疵的;好責備人的。②詭辯的。

cap·ti·vate 〔ˈkæptəˌvet; ˈkæptiveit〕 *v.t.,* **-vat·ed, -vat·ing.** 迷惑。—**cap·ti·va·tor,** *n.*

cap·ti·vat·ing 〔ˈkæptɪˌvetɪŋ; ˈkæptiveitiŋ〕 *adj.* 有迷惑力的;動人心魄的。

cap·ti·va·tion 〔ˌkæptəˈveʃən; ˌkæptiˈveiʃən〕 *n.* ①迷惑;被蠱惑。②魅力。

***cap·tive** 〔ˈkæptɪv; ˈkæptiv〕 *n.* ①俘虜。②被迷着;被困着。He was a *captive* to her beauty. 他被她的美麗所迷。—*adj.* ①被虜的;被俘的。*captive* soldiers. 戰俘。②被迷住的。③被奴役的(國家)。

captive audience (在餐館等公共場所,對廣告或宣傳等不聽也得聽的)受制聽衆。

captive balloon 繫留氣球。

captive test (火箭或飛彈等的)靜態試驗;繫留(地上)測試。

***cap·tiv·i·ty** 〔kæpˈtɪvətɪ; kæpˈtiviti〕 *n., pl.* **-ties.** ①囚禁。②被拘留的狀態。

cap·tor 〔ˈkæptɚ; ˈkæptə〕 *n.* 虜掠者;捕捉者。

cap·tress 〔ˈkæptrɪs; ˈkæptris〕 *n.* 「captor 之女性。」

***cap·ture** 〔ˈkæptʃɚ; ˈkæptʃə〕 *v.,* **-tured, -tur·ing,** *n.* —*v.t.* ①虜獲。The chief was *captured.* 首領已被俘。②捕捉;抓住。③占領。—*n.* ①被虜的人;被虜獲的東西;戰利品。②虜獲;捕獲。the *capture* of a thief. 竊賊的被捕。③占領。the *capture* of the town by the enemy. 市鎮的被敵人占領。

Cap·u·chin 〔ˈkæpjʊˌtʃɪn; ˈkæpjuʃin〕 *n.* ①聖芳濟教派之僧侶或任聖職者。②(c-)連帶頭巾之女用斗篷。③(c-)卷尾猴(亦作 **capucine**)。

ca·put 〔ˈkepət; ˈkeipət〕 *n., pl.* **ca·pi·ta** 〔ˈkæpətə; ˈkæpətə〕. 〖解剖〗頭;首。

CAR Civil Air Regulations.

‡**car** 〔kɑr; kɑː〕 *n.* ①有輪的車。②汽車。He goes to work by *car.* 他乘汽車去上班。③火車車廂。a dining *car.* 餐車。④氣球載人的懸籃。⑤有軌的車。⑥〖美〗電梯之機箱。⑦〖詩〗戰車;凱旋車。

car. ①carat. ②carpentry.

ca·ra·ba·o 〔ˌkɑrəˈbɑo; ˌkɑːrəˈbɑːou〕 *n., pl.* **-ba·os.** (菲律賓之)水牛。

car·a·bi·neer 〔ˌkærəbəˈnɪr; ˌkærəbiˈniə〕 *n.* 卡賓槍兵。(亦作 **carabinier**)

car·a·cal 〔ˈkærəˌkæl; ˈkærəkæl〕 *n.* ①〖動物〗波斯野貓。②波斯野貓之毛皮。

Ca·ra·cas 〔kəˈrɑkəs; kəˈrɑːkəs〕 *n.* 加拉卡斯(Venezuela 之首都)。

car·a·cole 〔ˈkærəˌkol; ˈkærəkoul〕 *n., v.,* **-coled, -col·ing.** —*n.* 〖馬術〗半旋轉。—*v.i.* 半旋轉;騎馬作旋轉。(亦作 **caracol**)

car·a·cul 〔ˈkærəkəl; ˈkærəkəl〕 *n.* ①中亞細亞所產之一種羊。②此種羊之毛皮。(亦作 **karakul**)

ca·rafe 〔kəˈræf; kəˈrɑːf〕 *n.* 玻璃水瓶。

***car·a·mel** 〔ˈkærəml; ˈkærəmel〕 *n.* ①焦糖。②糖與牛奶等所製之一種糖果。

car·a·mel·ize 〔ˈkærəmḷˌaɪz; ˈkærəməlaiz〕 *v.t.,* **-ized, -iz·ing.** —*v.t.* 加熱熔(糖)使焦。—*v.i.* (糖)熔化而變成焦黃。

car·a·pace 〔ˈkærəˌpes; ˈkærəpeis〕 *n.* ①甲殼;甲。②外殼。③無動於衷;不動心。

car·at 〔ˈkærət; ˈkærət〕 *n.* ①克拉(寶石重量的單位)。②開(純金爲 24 開);24 分之一。(亦作 **karat**)

***car·a·van** 〔ˈkærəˌvæn; ˈkærəvæn〕 *n., v.,* **-van(n)ed, -van·(n)ing.** —*n.* ①旅行隊。②有篷頂的大車;旅行乘用之大篷車。—*v.i.* 參加 caravan 旅行。

caravan park 〖英〗供度假者停放露營車的區域。

car·a·van·sa·ry 〔ˌkærəˈvænsərɪ; ˌkærəˈvænsəri〕 *n.* ①可以容納旅行車隊投宿的旅舍。②大旅舍。(亦作 **caravanserai**)

car·a·vel 〔ˈkærəˌvɛl; ˈkærəvel〕 *n.* (十六世紀之)輕快帆船。(亦作 **carvel**)

car·a·way 〔ˈkærəˌwe; ˈkærəwei〕 *n.* ①〖植物〗葛縷子。②(亦作 **caraway seeds**)此種植物之種子(用作香料)。

car·bam·ide 〔ˈkɑrbəˌmaɪd, kɑrˈbæmaɪd; kɑːˈbæmaid〕 *n.*〖化〗脲;尿素。

car·barn 〔ˈkɑrbɑrn; ˈkɑːbɑːn〕 *n.* 車庫。

car·be·cue 〔ˈkɑrbɪˌkju; ˈkɑːbikjuː〕 *n.* 以火熔化報廢汽車的設備。

car·bide 〔ˈkɑrbaɪd; ˈkɑːbaid〕 *n.* ①〖化〗碳化物。②碳化鈣。

car·bine 〔ˈkɑrbaɪn; ˈkɑːbain〕 *n.* 卡賓鎗;騎鎗。(亦作 **carabine, carabin**)

car·bi·neer 〔ˌkɑrbəˈnɪr; ˌkɑːbiˈniə〕 *n.* =**carabineer.**

car·bi·nol 〔ˈkɑrbəˌnol; ˈkɑːbinɔl〕 *n.* 〖化〗甲醇;原醇。

carbo- 〖字首〗表"炭"之義。

car·bo·hy·drate 〔ˈkɑrboˈhaɪdret; ˈkɑːbouˈhaidreit〕 *n.* 〖化〗醣;炭水化合物。

car·bo·lat·ed 〔ˈkɑrbəˌletɪd; ˈkɑːbəleitid〕 *adj.* 注入石炭酸的;浸以石炭酸的;含石炭酸的。

car·bol·ic 〔kɑrˈbɑlɪk; kɑːˈbɔlik〕 *adj.* 石炭酸的。

carbolic acid 〖化〗石炭酸;酚。

car·bo·lize 〔ˈkɑrbəˌlaɪz; ˈkɑːbəlaiz〕 *v.t.,* **-lized, -liz·ing.** 以石炭酸處理。

***car·bon** 〔ˈkɑrbən; ˈkɑːbən〕 *n.* ①〖化〗炭。②副本;複寫本。③複寫紙。④炭精棒。—*adj.* 炭的;如炭的;以炭處理的。

car·bo·na·ceous 〔ˌkɑrbəˈneʃəs; ˌkɑːbəˈneiʃəs〕 *adj.* ①炭的;含炭的。②含煤的;似煤的。

car·bo·na·do 〔ˌkɑrbəˈnedo; ˌkɑːbəˈneidou〕 *n., pl.* **-does,** *v.,* **-doed, -do·ing.** —*n.* ①烤肉;烤禽。②黑金剛石。—*v.t.* ①燒;烤。②砍;切;劈。

Car·bo·na·ri 〔ˌkɑrboˈnɑrɪ; ˌkɑːbəˈnɑːri〕 *n. pl.,* *sing.* **-ro** 〔-ro; -rou〕.〖義〗

炭夫黨。
car·bon·ate 〔*n.* 'karbənɪt, -ˌnet; 'kɑː-bənit *v.* 'karbəˌnet; 'kɑːbəneit〕 *n., v.,* **-at·ed, -at·ing.** —*n.* 炭酸鹽。—*v.t.* ①使變爲炭酸鹽；炭化。②燒成炭。③通以二氧化炭。—**car·bon·a·tion,** *n.*
carbon copy ①用複寫紙抄寫或打字的副本。②與另一物一模一樣之物。
carbon dioxide 二氧化炭。
car·bon·ic 〔kar'banɪk; kɑː'bɔnik〕 *adj.* 炭的；含炭素的。
carbonic acid 〖化〗炭酸。
carbonic acid gas 〖化〗炭酸氣。
carbonic oxide 一氧化炭。
carbonic water 〖化〗炭酸水。
car·bon·if·er·ous 〔ˌkarbə'nɪfərəs; ˌkɑːbə'nifərəs〕 *adj.* ①生炭或煤的；含炭或煤的。②(C-)〖地質〗石炭紀的；石炭系的。*the Carboniferous* **a.** 石炭紀。**b.** 石炭紀所成之岩石或煤層。
car·bon·i·za·tion 〔ˌkarbənɪ'zeʃən; ˌkɑːbənai'zeiʃən〕 *n.* 炭化；炭化法。
car·bon·ize 〔'karbənˌaɪz; 'kɑːbənaiz〕 *v.t.,* **-ized, -iz·ing.** ①炭化。②以炭處理。
carbon monoxide 〖化〗一氧化炭。
carbon paper 複寫紙。
carbon tet·ra·chlo·ride 〔~ˌtetrə'klɔraɪd; ~ˌtetrə'klɔːrid〕〖化〗四氯化炭。
car·bo·run·dum 〔ˌkarbə'rʌndəm; ˌkɑːbə'rʌndəm〕 *n.* 金剛砂；炭化矽。
car·box·yl 〔kar'baksɪl; kɑː'bɔksil〕 *adj.* 〖化〗羧基。
car·box·yl·ase 〔kar'baksəles; kɑː-'bɔksəleis〕 *n.* 〖化〗炭酸酵素；羧基酶。
car·boy 〔'karbɔɪ; 'kɑːbɔi〕 *n.* (有木框或籐籃保護的)大玻璃瓶；酸瓶。
car·bun·cle 〔'karbʌŋkl; 'kɑːbʌŋkl〕 *n.* ①〖醫〗疔。②粉刺。③紅玉；紅寶石。
car·bun·cled 〔'karbʌŋkld; 'kɑːbʌŋ-kld〕 *adj.* ①患疔的。②鑲有紅寶石的。
car·bun·cu·lar 〔kar'bʌŋkjulɚ; kɑː-'bʌŋkjulə〕 *adj.* ①疔的；患疔的。②似紅玉的；紅寶石的。
car·bu·ret 〔'karbəˌrɛt; 'kɑːbjuret〕 *v.t.,* **-ret·(t)ed, -ret·(t)ing.** 使與炭化合；增炭。(亦作 **carburize**)
car·bu·re·tion 〔ˌkarbə'rɛʃən; ˌkɑːbju-'reʃən〕 *n.* 與炭化合；炭化；摻炭。
car·bu·ret·(t)or 〔'karbəˌretɚ; 'kɑː-bjuretə〕 *n.* (引擎之)化油器。
car·ca·jou 〔'karkəˌdʒu; 'kɑːkədʒuː〕 *n.* ①狼獾類(北美產)。②美洲豹。③加拿大山貓。
***car·cass, car·case** 〔'karkəs; 'kɑː-kəs〕 *n.* ①動物的屍體。②〖蔑〗人的屍體。③(屋、船等之)骨架。④(廢車、廢屋等之)殘骸。*save one's carcass* 以保全生命。
car·cin·o·gen 〔kar'sɪnədʒən; kɑː-'sinədʒən〕 *n.* 〖醫〗致癌物。
car·ci·no·ma 〔ˌkarsə'nomə; ˌkɑːsi-'noumə〕 *n., pl.* **-ma·ta** 〔-mətə; -mətə〕. 〖醫〗癌。
car·ci·no·ma·to·sis 〔ˌkarsəˌnomə-'tosɪs; ˌkɑːsinoumə'tousis〕 *n.* 〖醫〗癌症。
car·ci·nom·a·tous 〔ˌkarsə'namə-təs, 'nomə-; ˌkɑːsi'nɔmətəs〕 *adj.*〖醫〗癌的。
carcinomatous degeneration 〖醫〗癌樣變化。
car coat 一種短外套。
:card¹ 〔kard; kɑːd〕 *n.* ①厚紙片；卡片。a calling (*or* visiting) *card.* 名片。a post *card.* 明信片。②紙牌。a pack of *cards.* 一副紙牌。③(紙牌戲中的)大牌；辦法；妙計。④(*pl.*)紙牌戲。⑤羅盤方位圖面。⑥〖俗〗(古怪或詼諧之)人。a queer *card.* 怪人。⑦節目單。⑧貼附火柴、鈕釦等的厚紙片。***have a card up one's sleeve*** 藏着一張好牌；有錦囊妙計。***have the cards in one's hand*** 有把握。***hold all the cards*** 支配全局。***in*** (or ***on***) ***the cards*** 卽將發生的；可能的。***leave cards*** (***on***) 拜訪；訪人不遇留名片而歸。***one's best card*** 絕招；妙策。***play one's cards*** 心懷某種目的去做某事。***play one's last card*** 採取最後手段。***put one's cards on the table*** 攤牌；對於某計畫之坦白表示。***speak by the card*** 精確地說。***tell one's fortune from cards*** 以紙牌卜卦。***the*** (***proper***) ***card*** 正好的東西。***throw up the cards*** 放棄計畫；罷手。—*v.t.* ①備置卡片。②記於卡片上。③用卡片標示。④〖運動〗得(分)。
card² *n.* ①鋼絲刷。②(刷布起毛或梳理紡線等之)梳毛機。—*v.t.* 刷；梳。
Card. Cardinal.
car·da·mom, car·da·mum 〔'kar-dəməm; 'kɑːdəməm〕 *n.* 〖植物〗小豆蔻。(亦作 **cardamon**)
***card·board** 〔'kardˌbord; 'kɑːdbɔːd〕 *n.* 紙板。—*adj.* 不眞實的；平面的；如紙板的。
card-car·ri·er 〔'kardˌkærɪɚ; 'kɑːd-'kæriə〕 *n.* 持有卡片者；正式黨員或會員。
card-car·ry·ing 〔'kardˌkærɪɪŋ; 'kɑːd'kæriiŋ〕 *adj.* 正式(獲准入黨或參加團體)的。
card·case 〔'kardˌkes; 'kɑːdkeis〕 *n.* 「名片盒；卡片箱；紙牌盒。」
card·cas·tle 〔'kardˌkæsl; 'kɑːdˌkɑː-sl〕 *n.* 卽將傾倒的建築；卽將失敗的計畫。(亦作 **cardhouse**)
card catalog (圖書館的)卡片目錄。
card-cut 〔'kardˌkʌt; 'kɑːd'kʌt〕 *adj.* 有浮雕的。
card·ed 〔'kardɪd; 'kɑːdid〕 *adj.* 經梳「毛機梳過的。」
card·er 〔'kardɚ; 'kɑːdə〕 *n.* ①梳毛之「人。②刷毛機。」
card file 卡片目錄。
card·hold·er 〔'kardˌholdɚ; 'kɑːdˌhoul-də〕 *n.* ①正式黨員或會員。②有借書證者。
car·di·ac 〔'kardɪˌæk; 'kɑːdiæk〕 *adj.* ①心臟的；近心臟的。②胃之上部的。—*n.* ①强心劑；興奮劑。②心臟病患者。
cardiac muscle 心肌。
cardiac waves 〖醫〗心波。
car·di·ec·to·my 〔ˌkardɪ'ɛktəmɪ; ˌkɑːdi'ektəmi〕 *n.* 〖醫〗①心部分切除術。②賁門切除。
car·di·gan 〔'kardɪgən; 'kɑːdigən〕 *n.* 「羊毛上衣；羊毛夾克；羊毛背心。」
***car·di·nal** 〔'kardn̩əl; 'kɑːdinl〕 *adj.* ①首要的；第一的。②鮮紅色的。—*n.* ①鮮紅色。②天主教的紅衣主教；樞機主教。③北美紅雀。④基數。
car·di·nal·ate 〔'kardənəlˌet; 'kɑːdi-nəleit〕 *n.* ①紅衣主教之職位。②〖天主教〗教廷之紅衣主教團。
cardinal flower ①〖植物〗紅山梗菜。②此種植物所開之花。
cardinal number 基數。(亦作 **cardinal numeral**)
cardinal points 基本方位(卽東西「南北)。」
cardinal red 鮮紅。
car·di·nal·ship 〔'kardənəlˌʃɪp; 'kɑː-dinəlʃip〕 *n.* 紅衣主教之職位或任期。
cardinal virtues 〖哲學〗基本道德。

cardinal vowel 〖語音〗基本母音(共十六個)。
card index 卡片索引。
card-index ['kard'ɪndɛks; 'kaːd'indeks] *v.t.* 作卡片索引。
card·ing ['kardɪŋ; 'kaːdiŋ] *n.* 梳理棉毛纖維;梳理法。
car·di·o·dyn·i·a [ˌkardɪo'dɪnɪə; ˌkaːdiou'diniə] *n.* 〖醫〗心臟痛;胸部痛。
car·di·o·gram ['kardɪəˌgræm; 'kaːdiəgræm] *n.* 心電圖。
car·di·o·graph ['kardɪəˌgræf; 'kaːdiəgraːf] *n.* 心動描記器。—**ic,** *adj.*
car·di·ol·o·gy [ˌkardɪ'alədʒɪ; ˌkaːdi'ɔlədʒi] *n.* 心臟學。—**car·di·ol·o·gist,** *n.*
car·di·o·meg·a·ly [ˌkardɪo'mɛgəlɪ; ˌkaːdiou'megəli] *n.* 〖醫〗心臟擴大症。
car·di·o·scope ['kardɪəˌskop; 'kaːdiəskoup] *n.* 〖醫〗心臟透視鏡。
car·di·o·ton·ic [ˌkardɪə'tanɪk; ˌkaːdiou'tɔnik] 〖醫〗*adj.* 强心的。—*n.* 强心劑。
car·di·o·vas·cu·lar [ˌkardɪo'væskjʊlə; ˌkaːdiou'væskjulə] *adj.* 〖醫〗心與血管的;循環系統的。
car·di·tis [kar'daɪtɪs; kaː'daitis] *n.* 心臟炎。
car·doon [kar'dun; kaː'duːn] *n.* 〖植物〗朝鮮薊。
card puncher 打卡員或打卡機。
card·sharp(·er) ['kardˌʃarp(ə); 'kaːdʃaːp(ə)] *n.* 以詐術賭紙牌爲生者。
card table 玩紙牌用之輕便小桌。
‡**care** [kɛr; kɛə] *n., v.,* **cared, car·ing.** —*n.* ①憂慮;操心。Few people are free from *care.* 很少人是無憂無慮的。②小心;謹慎;注意。This is made of glass, so please take *care* not to break it. 這是玻璃做的,所以請小心不要打破。③照顧;照管;看護;管理。④所關心之事;所顧慮之事。⑤關切;關懷。***care of*** 由…轉交(略作 c/o). Address my mail in *care of* the Chinese Embassy. 寄給我的郵件請由中國大使館轉交。***take*** (or ***have a***) ***care*** 小心;謹慎。***take care of*** a. 照顧;照管;看護。She will *take* good *care of* him. 她將好好地照顧他。b. 小心於;謹慎於。c. 處理。—*v.i.* ①關心;顧慮。②喜歡;愛好;願;欲。③照顧〖for〗. I will *care* for his education. 我將負責他的教育。
ca·reen [kə'rin; kə'riːn] *v.t.* ①(修船時)使(船)傾倒。②清潔或修理(傾側之船)。③使傾側。—*v.i.* ①傾側。②修理傾側之船。—*n.* 傾側;傾船;修理傾側之船。
ca·reen·age [kə'rinɪdʒ; kə'riːnidʒ] *n.* ①傾船;傾船修理。②修船所。③修船費。
***ca·reer** [kə'rɪr; kə'riə] *n.* ①生涯;經歷。②職業;事業。I take teaching as my life *career.* 我以教書爲終身事業。③急馳;飛奔。④所經之路;軌道。—*adj.* 職業的。a *career* diplomat. 職業外交家。a *career* girl. 職業婦女。—*v.i.* 急馳;飛奔〖about, along, through, over〗.
ca·reer·ism [kə'rɪrɪzm̩; kə'riərizm] *n.* 發跡第一主義。
ca·reer·ist [kə'rɪrɪst; kə'riərist] *n.* ①野心家。②從事某項終生事業者。
career man 職業外交家。
care·free ['kɛrˌfri; 'kɛəfriː] *adj.* ①快樂的;無憂慮的。②無責任感的;不負責的。
‡**care·ful** ['kɛrfəl; 'kɛəful] *adj.* ①謹慎的;小心的;關心的;注意的。to be *careful* about one's own health. 關心自己的健康。to be *careful* in speech. 小心說話。②用心從事工作的;切實的;徹底的。He is *careful* at his work. 他用心從事工作。③精確地或謹慎地做出來的。—**ly,** *adv.* —**ness,** *n.*
***care·less** ['kɛrlɪs; 'kɛəlis] *adj.* ①粗心的;欠思考的。②不正確的;疏忽的。a *careless* plan. 草率的計畫。③不負責的;不關心的。to be *careless* of one's own health. 不關心自己的健康。④無憂慮的;快樂的。*careless* life. 無憂無慮的生活。—**ly,** *adv.*—**ness,** *n.*
***ca·ress** [kə'rɛs; kə'res] *v.t.* 撫愛;撫抱;吻。—*n.* 撫摸;輕觸;擁抱;吻。
ca·ress·ing [kə'rɛsɪŋ; kə'resiŋ] *adj.* 安慰的;親切的。—**ly,** *adv.*
car·et ['kærət; 'kærət] *n., v.,* **-et·(t)ed, -et·(t)ing.** —*n.* 脫字符號;補註符號(如∧、∨等)。—*v.t.* 以補註符號加挿(於稿中)。
care·tak·er ['kɛrˌtekə; 'kɛəˌteikə] *n.* 看守者;管理者。
caretaker government 過渡時期的政府。
care·worn ['kɛrˌworn; 'kɛəwɔːn] *adj.* 憂思苦慮的;疲倦的;飽經憂患的。
car·fare ['karˌfɛr; 'kaːfɛə] *n.* 車資。
car ferry ①運送火車或汽車之輪渡。②運送汽車飛越海洋之運輸機。
car·ful ['karfʊl; 'kaːful] *n., pl.* **-fuls.** 一車之量。
***car·go** ['kargo; 'kaːgou] *n., pl.* **-goes, -gos.** (船、飛機等所載的)貨物。to load a *cargo.* 載貨。to unload a *cargo.* 卸貨。
car·hop ['karˌhap; 'kaːhɔp] *n.* 汽車飯館之侍者。
Car·ib ['kærɪb; 'kærib] *n.* 加勒比人(南美洲北部之土人)。
Car·ib·be·an [ˌkærə'biən; ˌkæri'biːən] *n.* ①加勒比海。②加勒比族人。—*adj.* ①加勒比海的。②加勒比族的。
Caribbean Sea 加勒比海。
car·i·bou ['kærəˌbu; 'kæribuː] *n., pl.* **-bous** or (集合稱) **-bou.** 北美馴鹿。
car·i·ca·ture ['kærɪkətʃə; 'kærikətjuə] *n., v.,* **-tured, -tur·ing.** —*n.* ①諷刺畫;漫畫;諷刺的描述。②作諷刺畫或諷刺描述的技術。③低劣的摹仿。—*v.t.* 作諷刺畫或描述。—**car·i·ca·tur·ist,** *n.*
car·ies ['kɛriz; 'kɛəriiːz] 〖拉〗 *n.* 齲;骨瘍。
car·il·lon ['kærəˌlan; kə'riljən] *n., v.,* **-lonned, -lon·ning.** —*n.* ①鐘樂器。②鐘樂。—*v.i.* 演奏鐘樂器。
car·il·lon·neur [ˌkærɪlə'nɝ; ˌkærilə'nəː] *n.* 鐘樂器演奏者。(亦作 **carilloner**)
car·i·nate ['kærɪˌnet; 'kærineit] *adj.* 〖動、植物〗有龍骨的;龍骨狀的。(亦作 **carinated, cariniform**)
car·i·o·ca [ˌkærɪ'okə; ˌkaːri'oukə] *n.* ①里約熱內盧之居民。②一種南美舞蹈。
car·(r)i·ole ['kærɪˌol; 'kærioul] *n.* ①一種小型無篷之兩輪馬車。②小篷車。
car·i·ous ['kɛrɪəs; 'kɛəriəs] *adj.* ①骨瘍性的;蛀齒的;腐爛的。②腐朽的。
cark [kark; kaːk] *n.* 煩惱;令人煩惱之事物。—*v.t.* & *v.i.* (使)煩惱。
cark·ing ['karkɪŋ; 'kaːkiŋ] *adj.* 煩惱的;困苦的;厭倦的。—**ly,** *adv.*
carl(e) [karl; kaːl] *n.* ①〖蘇, 古〗粗人。②〖蘇〗體格强壯的人。
car·lin(e) ['karlɪn; 'kaːlin] *n.* 〖蘇〗①巫婆。②老婦。
car·ling ['karlɪŋ; 'kaːliŋ] *n.* ①〖造船〗縱梁。②支持火車車頂之橫木。
car·load ['karˌlod; 'kaːloud] *n.* 一車的量。
Carl·ton Club ['karltən~; 'kaːltən~] 英國保守黨總部。
car·ma·gnole [ˌkarmən'jol; ˌkaːmə'njoul] *n.* ①卡曼紐夾克(1792年法國革命者

當作制服穿之短上衣)。②卡曼紐裝。③法國革命軍人。④卡曼紐歌舞(流行於法國革命期中的一種歌舞)。

car·man 〔ˈkɑrmən; ˈkɑːmən〕 *n., pl.* **-men.** 車夫;御者。

Car·mel·ite 〔ˈkɑrmḷˌaɪt; ˈkɑːmilait〕 *n.* ①Carmel 教派之托鉢僧或尼。②(c-)一種細羊毛織料。③(c-)一種梨。

car·min·a·tive 〔kɑrˈmɪnətɪv; ˈkɑːminətiv〕 *n.* 〖醫〗驅風劑;排氣劑;通氣瀉藥。—*adj.* 驅風的;排氣的。

car·mine 〔ˈkɑrmɪn; ˈkɑːmain〕 *n.* 洋紅色;深紅色;胭脂紅色。—*adj.* 洋紅色的;深紅色的。

car·nage 〔ˈkɑrnɪdʒ; ˈkɑːnidʒ〕 *n.* 大屠殺;殘殺。

car·nal 〔ˈkɑrnḷ; ˈkɑːnl〕 *adj.* ①肉體的;世俗的;現世的。②肉慾的。***have carnal knowledge of*** 與…發生性關係。—**ly,** *adv.* —**ism,** —**ness,** *n.*

car·nal·i·ty 〔kɑrˈnælətɪ; kɑːˈnæliti〕 *n., pl.* **-ties.** ①淫慾。②俗念。③性行為。

car·nal·ize 〔ˈkɑrnḷˌaɪz; ˈkɑːnəlaiz〕 *v.t.,* **-ized, -iz·ing.** 使耽於肉慾;誨淫。

car·nall·ite 〔ˈkɑrnḷˌaɪt; ˈkɑːnəlait〕 *n.* 〖礦〗光鹵石;砂金鹵石。

car·nap·per 〔ˈkɑrˌnæpɚ; ˈkɑːnæpə〕 *n.* 偷車賊。(亦作 **carnaper**)

car·na·tion 〔kɑrˈneʃən; kɑːˈneiʃən〕 *n.* ①荷蘭石竹(康乃馨)。②粉紅色。—*adj.* 粉紅色的。—*v.t.* 使帶微紅色。

Car·ne·gie 〔kɑrˈnegɪ; kɑːˈnegi〕 *n.* 卡內基(Andrew, 1835–1919, 美國鋼鐵工業家及慈善家)。

car·nel·ian 〔kɑrˈniljən; kəˈniːljən〕 *n.* 〖礦〗紅玉髓。

car·ne·ous 〔ˈkɑrnɪəs; ˈkɑːniəs〕 *adj.* 似肉的;肉色的。

car·ni·fy 〔ˈkɑrnəˌfaɪ; ˈkɑːnifai〕 *v.t. & v.i.,* **-fied, -fy·ing.** (使)長肉;變為肉質。

***car·ni·val** 〔ˈkɑrnəvḷ; ˈkɑːnivəl〕 *n.* ①巡廻表演的娛樂遊戲團(有雜耍、木馬、輪轉機等)。②嘉年華會;狂歡節(四旬齋前之飲宴狂歡)。③飲宴狂歡。④充溢;茂盛;熱鬧。⑤博覽會;展覽會。

car·ni·val·esque 〔ˌkɑrnəvḷˈɛsk; ˌkɑːnivəˈlesk〕 *adj.* 好像過節的;快樂的。

Car·niv·o·ra 〔kɑrˈnɪvərə; kɑːˈnivərə〕 *n. pl.* 〖動物〗食肉類。

car·ni·vore 〔ˈkɑnəˌvor; ˈkɑːnivɔː〕 *n.* ①食肉動物。②食蟲植物。

car·niv·o·rous 〔kɑrˈnɪvərəs; kɑːˈnivərəs〕 *adj.* ①食肉的。②食肉動物的。

car·ny 〔ˈkɑrni; ˈkɑːniː〕 *n., pl.* **-nies.** ①巡廻表演遊戲團的工作人員。②巡廻表演遊戲團。(亦作**carney, carnie**)

car·ob 〔ˈkærəb; ˈkærəb〕 *n.* 〖植物〗稻子豆。

***car·ol** 〔ˈkærəl; ˈkærəl〕 *n., v.,* **-ol(l)ed, -ol·(l)ing.** —*n.* ①歡樂之歌。②耶誕歌或讚美詩。Christmas *carols.* 耶誕頌歌。—*v.i.* 歡唱;囀鳴。—*v.t.* ①歌頌。②歡唱。—**(l)er,** *n.*

Car·o·li·na 〔ˌkærəˈlaɪnə; ˌkærəˈlainə〕 *n.* 卡羅來納(從前英國在北美之一殖民地)。***the Carolinas*** 美國南、北卡羅來納兩州。

Car·o·line 〔ˈkærəˌlaɪn; ˈkærəlain〕 *adj.* ①英王 Charles一世及二世的。②=**Carolingian.**

Car·o·lin·gi·an 〔ˌkærəˈlɪndʒɪən; ˌkærəˈlindʒiən〕 *adj.* Charlemagne 朝的。—*n.* Charlemagne 朝之君主。(亦作 **Carlovingian**)

Car·o·lin·i·an 〔ˌkærəˈlɪnɪən; ˌkærəˈliniən〕 *adj.* ①美國(南或北)卡羅來納州的。②=**Carolingian.** ③=**Caroline.** —*n.* 美國(南或北)卡羅來納州人。

car·om 〔ˈkærəm; ˈkærəm〕 *n.* ①〖撞球〗母球連撞二球之一擊。②碰擊而反跳。—*v.i.* ①〖撞球〗連撞二球。②碰擊而反跳。—*v.t.* 使反彈。(亦作 **carrom**)

car·oms 〔ˈkærəmz; ˈkærəmz〕 *n. pl.* 二人或四人玩的撞球。

car·o·tene 〔ˈkærəˌtin; ˈkærətiːn〕 *n.* 〖化〗胡蘿蔔素;葉紅素($C_{40}H_{56}$)。(亦作 **carotin**)

ca·rot·id 〔kəˈrɑtɪd; kəˈrɔtid〕 *n.* 〖解剖〗頸動脈。—*adj.* 頸動脈的。

ca·rous·al 〔kəˈrauzḷ; kəˈrauzəl〕 *n.* 喧鬧的酒會;狂歡的宴飲。

ca·rouse 〔kəˈrauz; kəˈrauz〕 *n., v.,* **-roused, -rous·ing.** —*n.* 喧鬧的宴飲;酒會。—*v.i.* 痛飲;參加喧鬧的宴會或酒會。—**ca·rous·er,** *n.*

carp[1] 〔kɑrp; kɑːp〕 *v.i. & v.t.* 吹毛求疵;找碴兒。

***carp**[2] *n., pl.* **carps** or **carp.** ①鯉魚。②鯉科的魚。

carp. carpentry.

car·pal 〔ˈkɑrpḷ; ˈkɑːpl〕 *n.* (亦作**carpale**)〖解剖〗腕骨。—*adj.* 腕的;腕骨的。

car·pe di·em 〔ˈkɑrpɪˈdaɪɛm; ˈkɑːpiˈdaiem〕 ①〖拉〗及時行樂。②〖文學〗鼓吹及時行樂之主題。

car·pel 〔ˈkɑrpḷ; ˈkɑːpel〕 *n.* 〖植物〗心皮。

***car·pen·ter** 〔ˈkɑrpəntɚ; ˈkɑːpintə〕 *n.* 木匠。a *carpenter's* rule. 折尺;木匠尺。a *carpenter's* square. 勾尺。—*v.i.* 作木工。—*v.t.* 以木料作。

car·pen·try 〔ˈkɑrpəntrɪ; ˈkɑːpintri〕 *n.* 木匠工作。

car·pet** 〔ˈkɑrpɪt; ˈkɑːpit〕 *n.* ①地毯;毛毯。②如毛毯鋪地的東西。a *carpet* of grass. 碧草如茵;綠茵。③裝在飛機上擾亂雷達的電子儀器。on the carpet*** **a.** 在考慮中;在討論中。**b.** 受責。—*v.t.* 鋪以地毯;鋪蓋。—*adj.* 趨逸避險的;好逸惡勞的;不出家門的。

car·pet·bag 〔ˈkɑrpɪtˌbæg; ˈkɑːpitbæg〕 *n., adj., v.,* **-bagged, -bag·ging.** —*n.* 氈製之旅行手提包。—*adj.* 投機取巧的。—*v.i.* 〖美俚〗投機取巧。

car·pet·bag·ger 〔ˈkɑrpɪtˌbægɚ; ˈkɑːpitˈbægə〕 *n.* ①美國內戰後自北方至南方尋求特別利益之政客或投機者。②到他處藉投機取巧以圖僥倖謀利者。

carpet bed 像多色圖案毛氈的花壇。

carpet beetle 金龜子科之小甲蟲。

carpet bombing 飽和轟炸(徹底摧毀之更番轟炸)。

carpet dance (在地氈上跳的)一種非正式的舞蹈。

car·pet·ing 〔ˈkɑrpɪtɪŋ; ˈkɑːpitiŋ〕 *n.* 氈布;地氈;毯。

carpet knight ①非由武功而得武士爵位者。②無功受祿者。③〖蔑〗未參戰之軍人。

carpet rod 固定梯氈的金屬條。

carpet snake 澳洲產有斑點的巨蟒。

carpet sweeper 掃毯器。

car·pet·weed 〔ˈkɑrpɪtˌwid; ˈkɑːpitwiːd〕 *n.* 〖植物〗氈草。

carp·ing 〔ˈkɑrpɪŋ; ˈkɑːpiŋ〕 *adj.* 吹毛求疵的;指責的。—*n.* 吹毛求疵。—**ly,** *adv.*

car·pol·o·gy 〔kɑrˈpɑlədʒɪ; kɑːˈpɔlədʒi〕 *n.* 果實學。

car pool 〖美〗車輛合用組織。

car·port 〔ˈkɑrˌport; ˈkɑːpɔːt〕 *n.* 屋側突出之無牆車庫。

car·pus 〔ˈkɑrpəs; ˈkɑːpəs〕 *n., pl.* **-pi** 〔-paɪ; -pai〕. 〖解剖〗腕骨;腕。

car·rack 〔ˈkærək; ˈkærək〕 *n.* 〖古〗從

前西、葡兩國用之大型帆船。

car·ra·g(h)een ['kærə,gin; 'kærəgi:n] *n.* 〖植物〗鹿角菜。

Car·rel [kə'rɛl; kə'rel, 'kærəl] *n.* 喀雷爾 (Alexis, 1873–1944, 法國外科醫生及生物學家, 曾獲1912年諾貝爾獎)。

car·rel, car·rell ['kærəl; 'kærəl] *n.* 圖書館書庫中供研讀者使用之卡座。

*__car·riage__ ['kærɪdʒ; 'kæridʒ] *n.* ①客車 (普通係指馬車, 英國亦指火車之客車)。②砲車; 砲架; (機器的)臺架。a typewriter *carriage.* 打字機的臺架。③身體的姿態; 舉止。④運輸。⑤運費。The *carriage* on these boxes will be high. 這些箱子的運費會很貴。

carriage and pair 一車和兩馬。

carriage clock 旅行時攜帶的鐘。

carriage dog 原產Dalmatia之一種狗(短毛, 黑白駁雜爲其特徵)。(亦作**Dalmatian**)

carriage drive 〖英〗①經風景區的公路。②私人車路。

carriage forward 運費由收件人負擔。

carriage free 運費免付。

carriage paid 運費已由收件人繳付。

carriage trade 富有的顧客(集合稱)。

car·riage·way ['kærɪdʒ,we; 'kæridʒwei] *n.* 〖英〗①馬路。②(道路上之)車道。

car·ried ['kærɪd; 'kærid] *adj.* 〖蘇、英方〗入神的; 忘我的。

*__car·ri·er__ ['kærɪɚ; 'kæriə] *n.* ①運送人; 搬運夫。the mail *carriers.* 郵差。②搬運的工具。③運輸機構。④盛器; 貨架。⑤帶菌者; 傳染疾病的媒介(人或物)。Water and milk are often *carriers* of disease germs. 水和牛奶往往是病菌的媒介。⑥〖無線電〗載波。⑦〖化工〗載媒劑。⑧航空母艦。⑨傳信鴿。

carrier bag 〖英〗購物袋。

carrier pigeon 傳信鴿。

carrier's note 取貨單。

carrier wave 〖無線電〗載波。

car·ri·on ['kærɪən; 'kæriən] *n.* ①腐臭的屍體(肉)。②腐敗; 穢行。③吃腐肉的動物(集合稱)。—*adj.* ①臭屍的; 腐爛的。②吃腐肉的。③腐敗的; 穢行的。

carrion crow 一種歐洲產吃腐肉的烏鴉; 黑兀鷹。(亦作 **carrion-eater**)

car·ron·ade [,kærə'ned; ,kærə'neid] *n.* 〖史〗艦砲(口徑大, 砲身短)。

car·ron oil ['kærən~; 'kærən~] 〖醫〗卡倫油; 石灰油乳劑。

*__car·rot__ ['kærət; 'kærət] *n.* ①胡蘿蔔; 紅蘿蔔。②(用以引誘的)報酬。

carrot red 紅蘿蔔特有之紅色。

car·rot-top ['kærət,tɑp; 'kærəttɔp] *n.* 〖俚〗紅髮者。

car·rot·y ['kærətɪ; 'kærəti] *adj.* ①胡蘿蔔色的; 紅黃色的。②紅髮的。

car·rou·sel [,kærə'zɛl; ,kæru'zel] *n.* 旋轉木馬。(亦作**carousel**)

‡**car·ry** ['kærɪ; 'kæri] *v.,* **-ried, -ry·ing,** *n., pl.* **-ries.** —*v.t.* ①搬運; 運送; 攜帶。to *carry* goods in a ship. 用船裝運貨物。②支持; 維持。③舉止; 舉動。The little girl *carries* herself gracefully. 這小女孩舉止大方。④勝; 獲得; 採納; 通過。⑤備辦(貨物)。⑥帶有。His judgment *carries* weight. 他的判斷有力量。⑦伸延; 延續。⑧影響; 感動。His acting *carried* the audience. 他的演技感動觀衆。⑨可裝; 可容納。⑩傳播。⑪身懷(胎兒)。The woman is *carrying* twins. 那女人身懷雙胞胎。⑫領銜主演。⑬輸送(流體)。This pipe *carries* water to the house. 這管子把水輸送到那屋子。⑭使維持。⑮〖簿記〗轉記; 結轉。⑯〖數學〗移上一位。—*v.i.* ①運送; 攜帶。②達; 及。His voice *carries* farther than mine. 他的聲音比我的聲音傳得遠。③能射及。④(馬)有某種姿勢。The horse *carries* well. 那匹馬的姿勢優美。⑤繼續不斷。***carry all before one*** 極爲成功。***carry a tune*** 唱得一絲不差; 唱得合乎節拍。***carry away*** a. 深深地影響; 感動。b. 沖去。***carry forward*** a. 〖會計〗將(一筆金錢)轉記於次頁、次欄或下一本帳簿。b. 〖會計〗將某年部分虧損移到次年帳中以減輕次年之稅額。c. 繼續。***carry off*** a. 强行帶走; 挾持; 刼持。b. 獲得(獎品或榮譽)。c. 成功地對付。d. 勇敢面對。e. 造成死亡。***carry on*** a. 經營。b. 繼續。c. 〖俗〗激動地或愚蠢地行動。***carry out*** 完成; 實行。***carry over*** a. 遺留。b. 繼續; 延續。c. 引伸。***carry the ball*** 〖美俗〗在某項計畫之實施或行動中擔任主要角色。***carry the day*** 贏得勝利; 打勝仗。***carry through*** a. 完成。b. 幫助度過難關; 使保持勇氣。c. 連續; 維持。***carry*** (***something***) ***too far*** 做得太過分。—*n.* ①射程; 途程。②運輸; 水陸聯運。③水陸聯運之地點。

car·ry·all ['kærɪ,ɔl; 'kæriɔ:l] *n.* ①一種四輪單馬雙座馬車。②兩排相對座位之一種汽車。③大袋子或籃子等。

car·ry-back ['kærɪ,bæk; 'kæribæk] *n.* 虧損補報措施; 抵前。

car·ry-for·ward ['kærɪ,fɔrwəd; 'kæri,fɔ:wəd] *n.* 虧損預報措施; 延後; 過次。

car·ry-home ['kærɪ,hom; 'kærihoum] *adj.* 〖美〗便於攜帶的(箱子等)。

car·ry·ing ['kærɪɪŋ; 'kæriiŋ] *adj.* 運送的; 運輸的。—*n.* 運送; 被運送的東西。

carrying capacity 某一自然環境所能容納的生物數目之最高限度。

car·ry·ing-on ['kærɪɪŋ'ɑn; 'kæriiŋ'ɔn] *n., pl.* **-ings-on.** 〖俗〗愚行; 輕率之行爲。

carrying trade 運輸業。

car·ry-on ['kærɪ,ɑn; 'kæriɔn] *adj.* 上飛機可隨身攜帶的。

car·ry-o·ver ['kærɪ'ovɚ; 'kæri'ouvə] *n.* ①留存之物; (穀物等)滯銷品。②〖簿記〗轉入次頁之錢數; 結轉。

car·sick, car-sick ['kɑr,sɪk; 'kɑ:-sik] *adj.* 暈車的。

*__cart__ [kɑrt; kɑ:t] *n.* 輕便送貨車; 二輪馬車; 手拉車。***put the cart before the horse*** (做事)本末倒置。—*v.t.* ①用車運送。②强制帶走。③辛苦地搬運。—*v.i.* 駕車。

cart·age ['kɑrtɪdʒ; 'kɑ:tidʒ] *n.* ①貨車運輸。②貨車運費。

carte[1] [kɑrt; kɑ:t] *n.* ①菜單。②〖蘇〗紙牌。③(*pl.*)紙牌戲。

carte[2] *n.* 〖劍術〗=**quarte.**

carte blanche ['kɑrt'blɑnʃ; 'kɑ:t'blɑ:nʃ] *pl.* **cartes blanches** ['kɑrts'blɑnʃ; 'kɑ:ts'blɑ:nʃ]. 〖法〗①署名白紙。②全權委任; 自由行動權。

car·tel ['kɑrtḷ, kɑr'tɛl; kɑ:'tel] *n.* ①卡特爾(企業聯合)。②交換俘虜等之條約。③決鬥挑戰書。

car·te·lize ['kɑrtə,laɪz; 'kɑ:təlaiz] *v.t.* & *v.i.,* **-lized, -liz·ing.** 組成卡特爾。

Car·ter ['kɑrtɚ; 'kɑ:tə] *n.* 卡特 (Jimmy, 1924—, 自1977—任美國第三十九任總統)。

car·ter ['kɑrtɚ; 'kɑ:tə] *n.* 運貨馬車夫。

Car·te·sian [kɑr'tiʒən; kɑ:'ti:zjən] *adj.* ①法國哲學家笛卡兒的。②笛卡兒哲學的。—*n.* 笛卡兒哲學之信奉者。

cart·ful ['kart,fʊl; 'kɑ:tful] *n.* 貨車滿載之量;一車之量。

Car·thage ['karθɪdʒ; 'kɑ:θidʒ] *n.* 迦太基(非洲北部一古國)。

Car·tha·gin·i·an [,karθə'dʒɪnɪən; ,kɑ:θə'dʒiniən] *adj.* 迦太基的;迦太基人的。—*n.* 迦太基人。

cart horse 拖貨車的馬。

Car·thu·si·an [kar'θjuʒən; kɑ:'θju:ʒən] *n.* 〖天主教〗1086年 St. Bruno 在法國所創教派的僧侶或修女。—*adj.* 上述教派的。

car·ti·lage ['kartlɪdʒ; 'kɑ:tilidʒ] *n.* 〖解剖〗軟骨。

car·ti·lag·i·nous [,kartə'lædʒənəs; ,kɑ:ti'lædʒinəs] *adj.* 軟骨的;軟骨質的。

cart·load ['kart,lod; 'kɑ:tloud] *n.* ①一車之載量。②〖俗〗大量;多量。

car·tog·ra·pher [kar'tagrəfɚ; kɑ:'tɔgrəfə] *n.* 製圖者;繪製地圖者。

car·to·graph·ic [,kartə'græfɪk; ,kɑ:tə'græfik] *adj.* 製圖的。(亦作 **cartographical**)

car·tog·ra·phy [kar'tagrəfɪ; kɑ:'tɔgrəfi] *n.* 製圖;繪圖法。

car·tol·o·gy [kar'talədʒɪ; kɑ:'tɔlədʒi] *n.* 地圖學;製圖學。

car·to·man·cy ['kartə,mænsɪ; 'kɑ:toumænsi] *n.* 以紙牌占卜。

car·ton ['kartṇ; 'kɑ:tən] *n.* 紙板盒(箱)。—*v.t.* & *v.i.* 用紙板盒包裝。—**er,** *n.*

car·toon [kar'tun; kɑ:'tu:n] *n.* ①諷刺畫;漫畫。②(亦作 **animated cartoon**) 卡通電影片。—*v.t.* 畫…之諷刺畫;將…漫畫化。—*v.i.* 畫漫畫;畫諷刺畫。—**ist,** *n.*

car·toon·ing [kar'tunɪŋ; kɑ:'tu:niŋ] *n.* 卡通製作。

car·top ['kar,tap; 'kɑ:tɔp] *adj.* 可置於車頂上搬運的。

car·touche [kar'tuʃ; kɑ:'tu:ʃ] *n.* ①〖建築〗渦形(卷軸)裝飾。②〖軍〗彈藥筒(包)。

car·tridge ['kartrɪdʒ; 'kɑ:tridʒ] *n.* ①〖兵〗子彈;彈藥筒。②照相軟片捲筒;一捲軟片。③裝有物料之筒。④(電唱機)針頭。⑤音樂匣。***ball cartridge*** 實心彈。***blank cartridge*** 空心彈。

cartridge belt 子彈帶。

cartridge box 子彈盒(箱)。

cartridge clip 子彈夾。

cartridge paper ①彈藥紙。②糊牆紙。③劣等畫紙。

car·tu·lar·y ['kartʃʊ,lɛrɪ; 'kɑ:tjuləri] *n., pl.* **-lar·ies.** =**chartulary.**

cart wheel ①車輪。②〖俚〗大型硬幣。③橫翻觔斗。

cart·wheel ['kart,hwil; 'kɑ:t-wi:l] *n.* =**cart wheel.** —*v.i.* ①橫翻觔斗。②如滾動之輪似的移動。

cart·wright ['kart,raɪt; 'kɑ:t-rait] *n.* 車匠;修車工。

car·un·cle ['kærʌŋkl, kə'rʌŋkl; 'kærəŋkl, kə'rʌŋkl] *n.* ①〖植物〗臍阜。②〖動物〗肉冠;肉阜。

Ca·ru·so [kə'ruso; kə'ru:zou] *n.* 卡羅素 (Enrico, 1873–1921, 義大利歌唱家)。

carve** [karv; kɑ:v] *v.,* **carved, carv·ing.** —*v.t.* ①切成碎片。②雕刻。to *carve* a block of stone into a statue. 刻石爲像。③造成;創造〖常 out〗。He *carved* out a career for himself. 他替自己創造出一種事業。to *carve* out one's (*or* a) way. 開闢道路。to *carve* out a way through the enemy. 由敵陣中殺出一條血路。—*v.i.* ①雕刻。②切肉。carve for oneself*** 自由行動。***carve up*** 分割(肉等);劃分(遺產等)。

car·vel-built ['karvl,bɪlt; 'kɑ:vəlbilt] *adj.* (船)以平平貼齊之木板造成的(外殼)。

carv·en ['karvən; 'kɑ:vən] *adj.* 〖古,詩〗雕刻的。

carv·er ['karvɚ; 'kɑ:və] *n.* ①雕刻者。②切肉者。③切肉刀。***a pair of carvers*** 一套切肉用具。

carv·ing ['karvɪŋ; 'kɑ:viŋ] *n.* 雕刻;雕刻物;切片。

carving fork 切肉叉。

carving knife 切肉刀。

car wash 洗(汽)車場;洗車臺。

car·y·at·id [,kærɪ'ætɪd; ,kæri'ætid] *n., pl.* **-ids, -i·des** [-əd,iz; -idi:z]. 〖建築〗雕成女像形之柱。

C.A.S. Certificate of Advanced Studies.

ca·sa·ba [kə'sabə; kə'sɑ:bə] *n.* 一種多季之甜瓜。(亦作 **cassaba**)

Cas·a·blan·ca [,kasə'blaŋkə; ,kæsə'blæŋkə] *n.* 卡薩布蘭加(非洲摩洛哥西部之一海港)。

cas·a·no·va [,kæzə'novə; ,kæzə'nouvə] *n.* 花花公子。(亦作 **Casanova**)

Cas·bah ['kazba; 'kɑ:zbɑ:] *n.* ①阿爾及耳城中的舊城區。②(尤指北非的)類似阿爾及耳舊城區之街道(亦作 **casbah**)。③任何彎彎曲曲似迷魂陣之物。

cas·cade [kæs'ked; kæs'keid] *n., v.,* **-cad·ed, -cad·ing.** —*n.* ①小瀑布。②(衣服上的)波狀花邊。③〖電〗串級。④〖化〗階式蒸發器。—*v.i.* 像瀑布般落下。—*v.t.* ①使落下。②將(一組類似機件)相聯結;使經過機器上一組類似之機件。

cas·car·a [kæs'kɛrə; kæs'kɑ:rə] *n.* 〖植物〗鼠李(其樹皮可作輕瀉劑用)。

‡**case**[1] [kes; keis] *n.* ①事;例。A similar *case* might happen again. 同樣的事可能再發生。②情形;狀況;場合。If you do so, you will make your *case* worse. 你如這樣做,將使你的處境更爲不利。③訟案。This is a civil (criminal) *case.* 這是民(刑)事案件。④病人;病症。The patient stated his *case.* 病人陳述病情。⑤〖文法〗格。⑥令人信服的理論。⑦〖俗〗奇人;怪人。a hard *case.* 難相處之人;難管教之人。⑧〖法律〗供詞。The plaintiff has no *case.* 原告無話可辯。***as is often the case with*** 那對…是常有之事。***as the case may be*** 看情形;隨機應變地。***be in good*** (or ***evil***) ***case*** 境況(不)好;身體(不)好。***come*** (or ***get***) ***down to cases*** 〖美〗開始討論正題。***drop a case*** 撤消訴訟。***have a good case*** 事實和證據有利於己。***in any case*** 無論如何。***in case*** a. 預防。b. 如果。***in case of*** 倘;倘使。*In case of* rain they can't go. 倘使下雨,他們就不能去。***in nine cases out of ten*** 十中之九。***in no case*** 絕不;在任何情況下決不。***in some cases*** 有些情形。***lay the case*** 陳述。***make out one's case*** 證明(剖白)自己立場。

case**[2] *n., v.,* **cased, cas·ing.** —*n.* ①箱;盒;套。Mother bought a *case* of beer. 母親買了一箱啤酒。②框。③〖美俚〗元;塊。④一對;兩個。⑤一箱之容量。There are a dozen bottles to a *case.* 每箱裝十二瓶。lower case*** 小寫活字盤。***upper case*** 大寫活字盤。—*v.t.* ①裝於箱、盒、套中;罩以箱、盒、套。②〖美俚〗事前勘察(擬搶刼之處所)。③將表面糊掩。

case·book ['kes,bʊk; 'keisbuk] *n.* 個案紀錄簿。

case bottle 有套瓶;方瓶。

case·bound [ˈkesˌbaund; ˈkeisbaund] *adj.* (書籍)精裝的。
case-dough [ˈkesˌdo; ˈkeisdou] *n.* 〖美俗〗(預備應急的)小筆存款;私房錢。
case·hard·en [ˈkesˌhardn̩; ˈkeis-ˌhaːdn] *v.t.* ①〖冶金〗使(鐵或鋼)之表面硬化。②使冷淡;使無感覺。 —**ing,** *n.*
case·hard·ened [ˈkesˌhardn̩d; ˈkeis-ˌhaːdnd] *adj.* 無動於衷的;無感覺的。
case history ①〖醫〗病歷。②〖社會〗血統紀錄;個案歷史。(亦作 **case record**)
ca·se·in [ˈkesɪɪn; ˈkeisiːin] *n.* 〖生化〗酪蛋白;乾酪素。
case knife ①有鞘之刀。②一種餐刀。
case law 〖法律〗判例法。
case·mate [ˈkesˌmet; ˈkeis-meit] *n.* ①有防彈工事之砲臺。②有裝甲之艦上砲塔。
***case·ment** [ˈkesmənt; ˈkeismənt] *n.* ①(亦作**casement window**)(兩扇的)門式窗。②〖詩〗窗。③鞘;套;框;架;箱;盒。
ca·se·ous [ˈkesɪəs; ˈkeisiəs] *adj.* 乾酪的;如乾酪的。
ca·sern(e) [kəˈzɝn; kəˈzəːn] *n.* (要塞附近之)兵營。
case shot 〖軍〗榴霰彈。
case study 個案研究。
case study method 個案研究法。
case·work [ˈkesˌwɝk; ˈkeis-wəːk] *n.* 生活環境之調查及改善。—**er,** *n.*
case·worm [ˈkesˌwɝm; ˈkeis-wəːm] *n.* 〖動物〗蠐螬;石蠶;蝶蛾類之幼蟲。
cash**[1] [kæʃ; kæʃ] *n.* ①現金;現款。I have no *cash* on me. May I pay by check? 我身上沒有帶現款, 我可以用支票付款嗎? ②錢;財富。I am very short of *cash.* 我很缺錢。He is rolling in *cash.* 他甚富有。hard cash*** 硬幣。***in the cash*** 富裕。***pay cash*** 付現款。—*v.t.* ①兌現;支現。to *cash* a check. 以支票兌現款;以支票(向銀行)支現金。②付款。***cash in*** **a.** 以籌碼兌換現金。**b.** 〖美俚〗將財產、股份等變賣以取得現金。**c.** 〖美俚〗死亡。***cash in on*** **a.** 營利;賺錢。**b.** 利用。***cash in one's checks*** (or ***chips***) 死。
cash[2] *n., pl.* **cash.** 小銅錢;方孔錢;制錢。
cash account 現金帳目。
cash-and-car·ry [ˈkæʃənˈkærɪ; ˈkæʃənˈkæri] *adj.* 現金購物自行運送的。—*n.* 現金購物自行運送。
cash assets 現金資產。
cash basis 現金制。
cash·book [ˈkæʃˌbuk; ˈkæʃbuk] *n.* 現金簿。(亦作 **cash journal**)
cash·box [ˈkæʃˌbaks; ˈkæʃbɔks] *n.* ①錢盒。②金庫。
cash·boy [ˈkæʃˌbɔɪ; ˈkæʃbɔi] *n.* 商店內傳遞金錢之小孩。
cash carrier 商店中傳遞貨款及找零之裝置。
cash credit 有擔保透支。
cash discount 現金折扣。
cash dividend 現金股利。
cash down 即付現款。
ca·shew [kəˈʃu, ˈkæʃu; kæˈʃuː] *n.* ①〖植物〗檟如樹(屬漆樹科)。②腰果。
***cash·ier**[1] [kæˈʃɪr; kæˈʃiə] *n.* 出納員。
cash·ier[2] *v.t.* ①解雇。②丟棄;拒用。
cashier's check 銀行開出的支票。(亦作 **bank check, banker's check**)
cash-in [ˈkæʃˌɪn; ˈkæʃin] *n.* 公債等的兌現。
cash·mere [ˈkæʃmɪr; kæʃˈmiə] *n.* ①喀什米爾及西藏的一種輕暖羊毛。②其圍巾或衣服。③其斜紋呢。
cash·o·mat [ˈkæʃəmæt; ˈkæʃəmæt] *n.* 〖美〗現鈔發放機(將證明卡片置入機內, 並將所需款額打在鍵盤上, 現鈔即可自機內滑出)。
cash on delivery 貨到付款。(略作 **C.O.D.**)
cash payment 現金支付。
cash price 現金交易的價錢。
cash register 現金出納機。
cas·ing [ˈkesɪŋ; ˈkeisiŋ] *n.* ①箱;套;鞘。②裝箱;入袋;納鞘。③(門窗的)框。④〖美〗汽車外胎。⑤油管;煤氣管。⑥製香腸用的腸衣。
ca·si·no [kəˈsino; kəˈsiːnou] *n., pl.* **-nos.** ①俱樂部;娛樂場。②(義大利的)別墅。③一種牌戲。
***cask** [kæsk; kæsk] *n.* ①桶。②桶之容量;滿桶。—*v.t.* 裝於桶中;存於桶中。
cas·ket [ˈkæskɪt; ˈkæskit] *n.* ①貯藏珠寶或信件的小箱。②〖美〗棺;柩。③骨灰盒。
Cas·pi·an Sea [ˈkæspɪən~; ˈkæspiən~] 裏海(歐亞兩洲間的內海)。
casque [kæsk; kæsk] *n.* 盔。
Cas·san·dra [kəˈsændrə; kəˈsændrə] *n.* ①〖希臘神話〗Troy 之女預言者。②作凶事預言而不爲人所信之人。
cas·sa·tion [kæˈseʃən; kæˈseiʃən] *n.* (案件判決、選舉等之)取消;廢除。***Court of Cassation*** (法國、比利時之)最高法院。
cas·sa·va [kəˈsavə; kəˈsaːvə] *n.* ①〖植物〗參茨;樹薯。②參茨根製成之澱粉;樹薯粉。
cas·se·role [ˈkæsəˌrol; ˈkæsəroul] *n.* ①有蓋的焙盤; 瓦蒸鍋。②放在此盤中所焙之菜飯。③〖化〗供蒸發用的有柄瓷皿。
cas·sette [kæˈsɛt; kæˈset] 〖法〗*n.* ①寶匣;珠寶箱。②〖照相〗乾板匣。③裝卡式錄音帶的長方形扁盒。
cassette TV 使用錄影帶之卡式電視。(亦作 **cassette television**)
cas·sia [ˈkæʃə; ˈkæsiə] *n.* 〖植物〗肉桂;桂皮。
cassia bark 桂皮。
cassia oil 桂皮油;肉桂油。
cas·si·mere [ˈkæsəˌmɪr; ˈkæsimiə] *n.* 卡斯密(一種斜紋毛織品)。(亦作 **casimere, casimire**)
cas·si·no [kəˈsino; kəˈsiːnou] *n.* 一種紙牌戲。(亦作 **casino**)
Cas·si·o·pe·ia [ˌkæsɪəˈpiə; ˌkæsiə-ˈpiːə] *n.* 〖天文〗仙后座。
Cassiopeia's Chair 〖天文〗仙后星座中最顯目, 排列形狀似椅之星羣。
cas·sit·er·ite [kəˈsɪtəˌraɪt; kəˈsitə-rait] *n.* 〖礦〗錫石。
cas·sock [ˈkæsək; ˈkæsək] *n.* ①教士所穿著之法衣;袈裟。②教士;牧師。
cas·socked [ˈkæsəkt; ˈkæsəkt] *adj.* 身穿法衣的。
cas·so·war·y [ˈkæsəˌwɛrɪ; ˈkæsə-wɛəri] *n., pl.* **-war·ies.** 〖動物〗食火鷄。
‡cast [kæst, kast; kaːst] *v.,* **cast, cast·ing,** *n., adj.* —*v.t.* ①投;擲;拋。to *cast* a ballot. 投票。to *cast* dice. 擲骰子。to *cast* anchor. 拋錨。②投向;投射。He *cast* me a look. 他向我一望。③鑄造; 鑄成。 to *cast* metal into coins. 將金屬鑄成錢幣。④分配脚色;派定扮演人員。 ⑤捨棄;脫落;蛻。⑥垂釣於。⑦安排;計劃。—*v.i.* ①投;擲。②鑄造。③計算。④思考; 計劃;圖謀。⑤推測;搜尋〖about〗。⑥扭轉(如木材)。⑦轉向(如船避風)。⑧產。***be cast down*** 失望;沮喪。 ***be cast in a different mold*** 性格不同。 ***be cast in a lawsuit*** 敗訴。***be cast in for damages*** 被判決賠償損失。 ***cast about*** **a.** 尋求。**b.** 計劃;盤算。***cast aside*** 棄却。***cast a thing in a person's teeth*** 責備某人。

cast away a. 丟棄；摒除；拒絕。b. 遭遇海難。c. 浪費。***cast back*** 提及過去事；復回原態。***cast behind one's back*** 忘掉。***cast into the shade*** 使黯然失色。***cast lots*** 抽籤。***cast off*** a. 放(船)；解纜。b.（編織衣物時的）收針。***cast on***編織成第一行針脚。***cast oneself (up) on*** 委身於；依賴；依從；仰仗。***cast (in) one's lot with*** 與…共患難。***cast out*** 趕出去。***cast up*** a. 加起。b. 被沖浮到上面。—*n.* ①投；擲；拋。②鑄成物；型成物。a plaster *cast.* 石膏或石膏模型。③演員的陣容。The film has a superior *cast.* 那影片演員陣容堅强。④形狀；表情；容色。a gloomy *cast.* 憂鬱的面容。⑤種類。⑥淡色。⑦斜視。a *cast* in the eye. 輕微的斜視眼。⑧計算。⑨外貌；輪廓。⑩傾向。⑪少量。⑫預測；猜測。⑬劣等羊毛。—*adj.* 鑄造的；鑄成的。

Cas·ta·li·an [kæsˈtelɪən; kæsˈteiliən] *adj.* ①神泉 Castaly 的。②詩歌的。***the Castalian Muses*** 詩之女神。

Cas·ta·ly [ˈkæstəlɪ; ˈkæstəli] *n.* 希臘 Parnassus 山上之神泉(據稱爲作詩靈感之源泉)。(亦作 **Castalia, Castalie**)

cas·ta·ne·ous [kæsˈtenɪəs; kæsˈteiniəs] *adj.* 栗色的。

cas·ta·nets [ˌkæstəˈnɛts; ˌkæstəˈnets] *n. pl.*〖音樂〗響板。

cast·a·way [ˈkæstəˌwe; ˈkɑːstəwei] *n.*①坐船遭難之人。②被逐出的人。③被棄之人或物。—*adj.* ①被人所擯棄的。②遭難的。

caste [kæst; kɑːst] *n.* ①印度的世襲階級。②(排他的)社會階級(地位)。③社會階級制度。④有社會組織的昆蟲(如螞蟻、蜜蜂)按功能分別的階級。***lose caste*** 失掉社會地位。

caste·less [ˈkæstlɪs; ˈkɑːstlis] *adj.* ①無社會階級的。②在印度,指不屬於任何階級的。

cas·tel·lan [ˈkæstələn; ˈkɑːstələr.] *n.* 城堡之監守；城主。

cas·tel·la·ny [ˈkæstəˌlenɪ; ˈkɑːstəleini] *n., pl.* **-nies.** ①城主之職位或其轄區。②城堡之轄區。(亦作 **castellate**)

cas·tel·lar [kæsˈtɛlə; kæsˈtelə] *adj.* 城堡的；似城堡的。

cas·tel·lat·ed [ˈkæstəˌletɪd; ˈkæstəleitid] *adj.* ①〖建築〗似城堡的。②有許多城堡的。—**cas·tel·la·tion,** *n.*

caste mark 階級或團體的特徵。

cast·er [ˈkæstɚ; ˈkɑːstə] *n.* ①投手；投擲者。②傢具之脚輪。③調味瓶；調味瓶架。④鑄造者。⑤鑄字機。(第二、三義亦作 **castor**) —*v.t.* 裝脚輪(如飛機、傢具)。

cas·ti·gate [ˈkæstəˌget; ˈkæstigeit] *v.t.,* **-gat·ed, -gat·ing.** ①懲治；苛評；譴責。②修訂。

cas·ti·ga·tion [ˌkæstəˈgeʃən; ˌkæstiˈgeiʃən] *n.* ①懲治；鞭打；譴責。②修訂。

cas·ti·ga·tor [ˈkæstəˌgetɚ; ˈkæstigeitə] *n.* ①懲罰者；譴責者。②修訂者。

cas·ti·ga·to·ry [ˈkæstəgəˌtorɪ; ˈkæstigətəri] *n.* ①懲罰的；譴責的。②修訂的。

Cas·tile¹ [kæsˈtil; kæsˈtiːl] *n.* 以前西班牙北部的一王國。

Cas·tile² *adj.*(常 c-) 用橄欖油和鹹製成的。—*n.* 橄欖香皂。

Castile soap 橄欖香皂。

Cas·til·ian [kæsˈtɪljən; kæsˈtiljən] *adj.* 古 Castile 王國的。—*n.* 其人或方言。

cast·ing [ˈkæstɪŋ; ˈkɑːstiŋ] *n.* ①鑄造；鑄件。②投擲。③用捲軸釣魚竿投擲的技巧或動作。④〖動物〗蛻落之物。

casting director 選擇戲劇或電影等演員的負責人。

casting net 撒網。

casting vote 決定投票。

casting wheel 鑄造廠中周圍裝有模子的輪子。

cast iron 鑄鐵；生鐵。

cast-i·ron [ˈkæstˈaɪən; ˈkɑːstˈaiən] *adj.* ①生鐵製的。②堅固的。③剛毅的。

‡cas·tle [ˈkæsl̩, ˈkɑsl̩; ˈkɑːsl] *n., v.,* **-tled, -tling.** —*n.* ①城堡；堡壘。②巨第。③西洋棋中城形之棋子。—*v.t.* ①使安全。②將…圍起來。

castle builder ①城堡建築師。②空想者。

cas·tled [ˈkæsl̩d, ˈkɑsl̩d; ˈkɑːsld] *adj.* ①有城堡的。②如城堡的；有城垛的。

castle in the air 幻想的事。(亦作 **castle in Spain**)

cast·off [ˈkæstˌɔf; ˈkɑːstˈɔːf] *adj.* 被丟棄的。—*n.* 遭遺棄之人或物。

cas·tor [ˈkæstɚ; ˈkɑːstə] *n.* ①(亦作**caster**) 傢具上的脚輪；調味瓶；調味瓶架。②海貍；海貍皮；海貍皮帽。③(C-)〖天文〗雙子星座的第一星。④(亦作 **castoreum**)海貍香。

castor bean 〖植物〗蓖麻子。

castor oil 蓖麻油。

castor-oil plant 蓖麻。

castor sugar 細白砂糖。

cas·trate [ˈkæstret; ˈkæstreit] *v.t.,* **-trat·ed, -trat·ing.** ①閹割。②删除。—**cas·tra·tion,** *n.*

Cas·tro [ˈkæstro; ˈkæstrou] *n.* 卡斯楚(Fidel, 1927–, 古巴共黨領袖, 自 1959– 任總理)。—**ism,** *n.* —**ite,** *n., adj.*

cast steel 鑄鋼。

***cas·u·al** [ˈkæʒuəl; ˈkæʒjuəl] *adj.* ①偶然的。②疏忽的；不關心的。③不定的。④不明確的。⑤隨便的；非正式的。⑥自然的；輕易的。⑦馬虎的。—*n.* ①臨時工人。②受臨時救濟的人。③分遣兵。—**ly,** *adv.* —**ness,** *n.*

cas·u·al·ism [ˈkæʒuəˌlɪzəm; ˈkæʒjuəlizəm] *n.* 偶然說；機緣說。

casual laborer 散工；零工。

cas·u·al·ty [ˈkæʒuəltɪ; ˈkæʒjuəlti] *n., pl.* **-ties.** ①意外。②災禍。③(*pl.*)〖軍〗死傷(人數)。④因意外而死傷的人或物。

casualty insurance 意外保險。

casual ward 臨時救濟所。

cas·u·ist [ˈkæʒuɪst; ˈkæzjuist] *n.* ①詭辯家；曲解者。②決疑者。

cas·u·is·tic [ˌkæʒuˈɪstɪk; ˌkæzjuˈistik] *adj.* ①有關行爲之是非問題的。②詭辯家的；決疑者的。③詭辯的；曲解的；世故的。(亦作 **casuistical**) —**al·ly,** *adv.*

cas·u·is·tics [ˌkæʒuˈɪstɪks; ˌkæʒjuˈistiks] *n.* ①決疑論；良心論。②詭辯；曲解。

cas·u·ist·ry [ˈkæʒuɪstrɪ; ˈkæzjuistri] *n., pl.* **-ries.** ①決疑論。②詭辯；曲解。

ca·sus [ˈkesəs; ˈkeisəs] *n., pl.* **ca·sus.** 〖拉〗一件發生的事件。

ca·sus bel·li [ˈkesəsˈbɛlaɪ; ˈkɑːsusˈbeliː] 〖拉〗宣戰的事件(理由)。

CAT ①clear-air turbulence. ②college ability test.

‡cat¹ [kæt; kæt] *n., v.,* **cat·ted, cat·ting.** —*n.* ①貓。②貓科動物。③貓皮。④可鄙的女人；惡婦。⑤九尾鞭。⑥鯰魚。⑦起錨上錨架的滑車。⑧〖俚〗爵士樂演奏者或狂嗜者。⑨船首有單桅而用大帆的小船。⑩六脚的架子，無論如何放置時，均有三脚着地。***bell the cat*** 試做某種艱巨或危險的事情。***lead a cat-and-dog life*** (夫妻間)經常吵架。***let the cat out of the bag*** 洩漏祕密。***no room to swing a cat*** 地方很狹小。***rain cats***

and dogs 下傾盆大雨。 ***see which way the cat jumps*** 伺機而動。 ***turn cat in the pan*** 見利思遷。 ***wait for the cat to jump*** 觀望形勢。—*v.t.* ①起(錨)。②用九尾鞭笞打。 ***cat around*** 尋樂。—*v.i.* ①〖英俚〗嘔吐。②嫖妓;宿娼。

cat² *n.* 〖俚〗履帶曳引機;任何有履帶之車輛。

cat. ①catalogue. ②catechism.

ca·tab·a·sis 〔kəˈtæbəsɪs; kəˈtæbəsis〕 *n., pl.* **-ses** 〔-ˌsiz; -siːz〕. ①軍事撤退。②下降。(亦作 **katabasis**)

ca·tab·o·lism 〔kəˈtæblˌɪzəm; kəˈtæbəlizəm〕 *n.* 〖生理,生物〗分解代謝;異化作用。(亦作 **katabolism**) —**cat·a·bol·ic,** *adj.*

cat·a·chre·sis 〔ˌkætəˈkrisɪs; ˌkætəˈkriːsis〕 *n., pl.* **-ses** 〔-ˌsiz; -siːz〕. ①〖修辭〗字語之誤用。②〖語言〗字形更改。

cat·a·clasm 〔ˈkætəˌklæzəm; ˈkætəklæzəm〕 *n.* 破裂;中斷。

cat·a·cli·nal 〔ˌkætəˈklaɪnl; ˌkætəˈklainəl〕 *adj.* 〖地質〗隨地層下凹處下降的。

cat·a·clysm 〔ˈkætəˌklɪzəm; ˈkætəklizəm〕 *n.* ①〖地質〗地球表面上的劇變。②(政治或社會的)劇變。③洪水。

cat·a·clys·mic 〔ˌkætəˈklɪzmɪk; ˌkætəˈklizmik〕 *adj.* ①氾濫的。②劇變的。(亦作 **cataclysmal**)

cat·a·comb 〔ˈkætəˌkom; ˈkætəkoum〕 *n.* (常*pl.*)地下墓穴。***the Catacombs*** 羅馬的墓窖。

cat·a·cous·tics 〔ˌkætəˈkustɪks; ˌkætəˈkuːstiks〕 *n.* 回音學。(亦作 **cataphonics**)

ca·tad·ro·mous 〔kəˈtædrəməs; kəˈtædrəməs〕 *adj.* (魚)因產卵而由河進海的。

cat·a·falque 〔ˈkætəˌfælk; ˈkætəfælk〕 *n.* 靈柩臺;靈車。

cat·a·gen·e·sis 〔ˌkætəˈdʒɛnəsɪs; ˌkætəˈdʒenisis〕 *n., pl.* **-ses** 〔-siz; -siːz〕. 〖生物〗(演進之)退化。

Cat·a·lan 〔ˈkætlən; ˈkætələn〕 *adj.* Catalonia (西班牙東北部之一地區)的;其人民或語言的。—*n.* ① Catalonia 人。②其語言。(亦作 **Catalonian**)

cat·a·lec·tic 〔ˌkætəˈlɛktɪk; ˌkætəˈlektik〕 *adj.* 〖韻律〗最後音步缺一個音節的。—*n.* 用此種韻作的詩;不完整詩行。

cat·a·lep·sy 〔ˈkætəˌlɛpsɪ; ˈkætəˌlepsi〕 *n.* 〖醫〗强直性昏厥。(亦作 **catalepsis**)

cat·a·lep·tic 〔ˌkætəˈlɛptɪk; ˌkætəˈleptik〕 *adj.* 〖醫〗强直性昏厥的。—*n.* 其患者。

cat·a·lo 〔ˈkætəˌlo; ˈkætəlou〕 *n., pl.* **-lo(e)s.** (美洲產之)雜種牛。(亦作**cattalo**)

***cat·a·logue, cat·a·log** 〔ˈkætlˌɔg; ˈkætəlɔg〕 *n., v.,* **-logued, -logu·ing, -loged, -log·ing.** —*n.* ①目錄;貨物價目表。②大學概況手册。③任何一系列之事物。—*v.t.* ①編目。②歸類。—*v.i.* 做成編目。—**cat·a·lo·gic,** *adj.*

cat·a·logu·er, ca·ta·log·er 〔ˈkætəˌlɔgɚ; ˈkætəlɔgə〕 *n.* 編目錄者。

ca·ta·logue rai·son·né 〔ˈkætəˌlɔg ˌrɛzəˈne; ˈkætəlɔg ˌrezəˈnei〕 〖法〗加註解的目錄。

Ca·tal·pa 〔kəˈtælpə; kəˈtælpə〕 *n.* 〖植物〗梓屬。

ca·tal·y·sis 〔kəˈtæləsɪs; kəˈtælisis〕 *n., pl.* **-ses** 〔-ˌsiz; -siːz〕. 〖化〗觸媒作用;催化作用;接觸反應。(亦作 **katalysis**)

cat·a·lyst 〔ˈkætlɪst; ˈkætəlist〕 *n.* 〖化〗觸媒;催化劑。

cat·a·lyt·ic 〔ˌkætlˈɪtɪk; ˌkætəˈlitik〕 *adj.* 起催化作用的。—*n.* 觸媒;催化劑。

catalytic converter 汽車廢氣淨化器。

cat·a·lyze 〔ˈkætlˌaɪz; ˈkætəlaiz〕 *v.t.,* **-lyzed, -lyz·ing.** 使起觸媒作用。

cat·a·lyz·er 〔ˈkætəˌlaɪzɚ; ˈkætəlaizə〕 *n.* 〖化〗觸媒;催化劑。

cat·a·ma·ran 〔ˌkætəməˈræn; ˌkætəməˈræn〕 *n.* ①筏。②雙船身之遊艇。③〖俗〗好吵架的人;(尤指)潑婦。

cat·a·me·ni·a 〔ˌkætəˈminɪə; ˌkætəˈmiːniə〕 *n. pl.* 〖生理〗月經。—**cat·a·me·ni·al,** *adj.*

cat·a·mite 〔ˈkætəˌmaɪt; ˈkætəmait〕 *n.* 嬖童;孌倖;孌童。

cat·am·ne·sis 〔ˌkætəmˈnisɪs; ˌkætəmˈniːsis〕 *n., pl.* **-ses** 〔-siz; -siːz〕. 後病歷。

cat·a·moun·tain 〔ˌkætəˈmaʊntɪn; ˌkætəˈmauntin〕 *n.* 〖動物〗①山貓。②豹。(亦作 **catamount**)

cat-and-dog 〔ˈkætənˈdɔg; ˈkætənˈdɔg〕 *adj.* ①如貓與狗一般敵對的。②〖俚〗(股票等之)投機性的。

cat and mouse 一種兒童遊戲。***play cat and mouse with*** **a.** 玩弄。**b.** 與…鬥智;伺機而動。(亦作 **cat and rat**)

cat-and-mouse 〔ˈkætənˈmaʊs; ˈkætənˈmaus〕 *adj.* 折磨的;一捕一放之虐待的。

cat·a·pha·si·a 〔ˌkætəˈfeʒɪə; ˌkætəˈfeiʒiə〕 *n.* 〖病理〗語言重複症。

cat·a·phon·ics 〔ˌkætəˈfɑnɪks; ˌkætəˈfɔniks〕 *n.* 回音學。

cat·a·pla·si·a 〔ˌkætəˈpleʒɪə; ˌkætəˈpleiʒiə〕 *n.* 〖生物〗細胞或組織的萎縮。

cat·a·plasm 〔ˈkætəˌplæzəm; ˈkætəplæzəm〕 *n.* 〖藥〗軟膏罨法;敷劑。

cat·a·plex·y 〔ˈkætəˌplɛksɪ; ˈkætəpleksi〕 *n.* 〖醫〗猝倒症;昏倒。

cat·a·pult 〔ˈkætəˌpʌlt; ˈkætəpʌlt〕 *n.* ①彈弩;彈弓。②古代之弩砲。③軍艦甲板上之放送飛機的裝置。—*v.t.* ①發射;彈出。②使突然上升。

cat·a·ract 〔ˈkætəˌrækt; ˈkætərækt〕 *n., v.,* **-ed, -ing.** —*n.* ①大瀑布;洪流。②〖醫〗白內障。—*v.i.* & *v.t.* 使如瀑布似的注流。

ca·tarrh 〔kəˈtɑr; kəˈtɑː〕 *n.* ①〖醫〗加答兒;鼻或喉的黏膜炎。②〖俗〗感冒。—**al,** *adj.*

ca·tarrh·al pneumonia 〔kəˈtɑrəl~; kəˈtɑːrəl~〕 〖醫〗膿性支氣管肺炎。(亦作 **broncho-pneumonia**)

cat·ar·rhine 〔ˈkætəˌraɪn; ˈkætərain〕 *adj.* 狹鼻猿的。—*n.* 狹鼻猿。

ca·tas·ta·sis 〔kəˈtæstəsɪs; kəˈtæstəsis〕 *n., pl.* **-ses** 〔-ˌsiz; -siːz〕. 戲劇之高潮。

***ca·tas·tro·phe** 〔kəˈtæstrəfɪ; kəˈtæstrəfi〕 *n.* ①異常的大災禍。②小說戲劇之結局。③悲慘的結局;毀滅。—**cat·a·stroph·ic, cat·a·stroph·i·cal,** *adj.* —**cat·a·stroph·i·cal·ly,** *adv.*

cat·a·to·ni·a 〔ˌkætəˈtonɪə; ˌkætəˈtouniə〕 *n.* 〖醫〗緊張症。—**cat·a·ton·ic,** *adj.*

Ca·taw·ba 〔kəˈtɔbə; kəˈtɔːbə〕 *n.* ①(美國產之)一種紅葡萄。②此種葡萄酒。

cat·bird 〔ˈkætˌbɝd; ˈkætbəːd〕 *n.* 貓鵲。

catbird seat 〖美方〗有權力的職位。

cat block 〖航海〗起錨用的有巨鉤之木柱。

cat·boat 〔ˈkætˌbot; ˈkætbout〕 *n.* 獨桅艇。

cat burglar 從上層樓窗或天窗進屋的盜賊。(亦作 **catman**)

cat·call 〔ˈkætˌkɔl; ˈkætkɔːl〕 *n.* 似貓叫之聲音(表示不滿或嘲弄)。—*v.t.* 作貓叫聲以奚落或嘲弄。—*v.i.* 作貓叫聲。

‡**catch** [kætʃ; kætʃ] *v.*, **caught** [kɔt; kɔːt], **catch·ing**, *n.*, *adj.* —*v.t.* ①捕捉;捉住。The policeman has *caught* the murderer alive. 警察已將兇手生擒。②得;傳;招;惹;感受。Paper *catches* fire easily. 紙易着火。I *caught* cold. 我受涼(傷風)了。③接(球,尤指棒球)。④見到;領悟;了解。He did not *catch* your point. 他沒有了解你的論點。⑤掛住;絆着。A nail *caught* my sleeve. 釘子鉤住我的袖子。⑥趕上。to *catch* a train. 趕上搭火車。⑦突然遇見;覺察。I *caught* him doing it. 他做這事時被我撞見。⑧令(人)注意。⑨握住。⑩欺騙。⑪擊中。The ball *caught* him on the head. 球擊中了他的頭。⑫突然阻止或約束。She *caught* her breath in surprise. 她在驚奇之下停住了呼吸。⑬受…的感染;感覺到。⑭吸引注意;使迷住。⑮承接。—*v.i.* ①絆住;掛住。②鎖住;握住。③攫取;搶取。to *catch* at the ball. 搶球。④着火。⑤傳染(如疾病)。⑥了解。⑦〖棒球〗充當捕手。***catch a crab*** 划船時槳下水太慢或出水太遲。***catch at*** a. 攫取;搶取。b. 急切地抓住。***catch a turn*** 〖航海〗將繩在絞盤上繞一匝。***catch (on) fire*** 着火。***catch hold of*** 抓住;握住;捉住。***catch it*** 受斥責;受罰。***catch on*** a. 理解。b. 流行。***catch one's breath*** a. 喘氣。b. 嚇一跳。***catch sight of*** 忽見;突然看到。***catch up*** a. 突然舉起或攫取。b. 向(某人)指出錯誤〖常 on〗. c. 受感染。***catch up (up with*** or ***up to)*** 追隨;追及;趕上。—*n.* ①捕捉;捕獲。Dick made a fine *catch* with one hand. 狄克以一隻手很穩地接住了球。②掛鉤;鎖鐶。③捕獲物。He had a good *catch* of fish. 他捕獲很多的魚。④〖俗〗宜於締婚的對象。⑤數人輪唱的短歌。⑥〖棒球〗接球。⑦陷阱;詐。⑧暫時停止(呼吸或說話)。⑨划船時將槳放入水中的動作(不包括划的動作)。⑩〖棒球〗捕手。⑪(歌的)片段。—*adj.* ①引人興趣的;有趣而易記住的。②迷人的;不定的;容易上當的。

catch·all [ˈkætʃˌɔl; ˈkætʃɔːl] *n.* 裝雜物之袋、框、箱等。

catch as catch can 隨便;無一定計畫或次序。

catch-as-catch-can [ˈkætʃəzˈkætʃˈkæn; ˈkætʃəzˈkætʃˈkæn] *n.* 角力時除不用幾種禁止的方法外,可用任何其他抓法的角力方式。—*adj.* 利用任何方法的;無計畫的。

catch basin 下水道入口處之鐵格子。

catch drain 〖土木〗承水渠。

catch-'em-a·live-o [ˈkætʃəməˈlaɪvo; ˈkætʃəməˈlaivou] *n.*〖英〗捕蠅紙。

***catch·er** [ˈkætʃɚ; ˈkætʃə] *n.* ①捕捉者;捕捉之機械。②接球員。③〖棒球〗捕手。

catch·fly [ˈkætʃˌflaɪ; ˈkætʃflai] *n.*, *pl.* **-flies.** 〖植物〗捕蟲草;捕蟲植物。

catch·ing [ˈkætʃɪŋ; ˈkætʃiŋ] *adj.* ①有傳染性的。②迷人的;動人的。

catch·line [ˈkætʃˌlaɪn; ˈkætʃlain] *n.* ①用以吸引注意力的短句。②滑稽臺詞。

catch·ment [ˈkætʃmənt; ˈkætʃmənt] *n.* ①集水(量)。②儲水池或水閘。

catchment basin (or **area**) 集水區域。

catch·pen·ny [ˈkætʃˌpɛnɪ; ˈkætʃˌpeni] *adj.*, *n.*, *pl.* **-nies.** —*adj.* 無價值的。—*n.* 無價值之物。

catch phrase 標語;引為標語的短句;吸引注意力的字句。(亦作 **catchphrase**)

catch pit 集水溝。

catch·pole, catch·poll [ˈkætʃˌpol; ˈkætʃpoul] *n.* 法警;執達員。

catch stitch ①連續用大針斜縫的簡單針法;假縫。②以大針斜縫。

catch·up [ˈkætʃəp; ˈkætʃəp] *n.* 食魚或肉時所用之醬。

catch·weight [ˈkætʃˌwet; ˈkætʃweit] *n.* (競賽選手)不受規則限制之體重。

catch·word [ˈkætʃˌwɝd; ˈkætʃwəːd] *n.* ①標語;口號。②〖印刷〗標字(字典或目錄等頁上端之該頁的首字或末字)。③演員之提示。

catch·y [ˈkætʃɪ; ˈkætʃi] *adj.*, **catch·i·er, catch·i·est.** ①令人喜愛而易記的;動人的。②詭詐的;令人迷惑的。③斷續的。

cate [ket; keit] *n.* 〖古〗精選的食物;美食。

cat·e·che·sis [ˌkætəˈkisɪs; ˌkætəˈkiːsis] *n.*, *pl.* **-ses** [-siz; -siːz]. ①用口授法教宗教法規及理論。②用問答法演講,尤指其講義。

cat·e·chet·i·cal [ˌkætəˈkɛtɪkl; ˌkætəˈketikəl] *adj.* ①宗教口授法的。②問答式教學法的。

cat·e·chism [ˈkætəˌkɪzəm; ˈkætikizəm] *n.* ①(基督教之)教義問答。②任何科目之一套問答。③問答教授法。***put a person through his catechism*** 嚴格盤問某人。***the Church Catechism*** 英國國教祈禱手册之教理問答。

cat·e·chist [ˈkætəkɪst; ˈkætikist] *n.* ①問答式教學者。②質問者。③〖宗教〗傳道師。

cat·e·chize, cat·e·chise [ˈkætəˌkaɪz; ˈkætikaiz] *v.t.* ①以問答法教學。②質問。

cat·e·chu [ˈkætəˌtʃu; ˈkætitʃuː] *n.* 〖植物〗兒茶(作醫藥、染色及鞣革等用)。(亦作 **cachou, cashoo**)

cat·e·chu·men [ˌkætəˈkjumən; ˌkætiˈkjuːmen] *n.* ①接受基督教教義者。②初學者。

cat·e·gor·i·cal [ˌkætəˈgɔrɪkl; ˌkætiˈgɔrikəl] *adj.* ①絕對的;無條件的;至上的。②直接的;明確的。③屬於某一範疇的。④〖邏輯〗定言判斷的(命題)。

categorical imperative (康德哲學中之)無上命令(乃良心至上的道德律)。

cat·e·go·rise, cat·e·go·rize [ˈkætəgəˌraɪz; ˈkætigəraiz] *v.t.* ①分類;分列入目錄中。②替…取名形容之。

cat·e·go·ry [ˈkætəˌgorɪ; ˈkætigəri] *n.*, *pl.* **-ries.** 類;種;部門。

ca·te·na [kəˈtinə; kəˈtiːnə] *n.*, *pl.* **-nae** [-ˌni; -niː]. ①鏈。②連鎖。

cat·e·nar·i·an [ˌkætɪˈnɛrɪən; ˌkætiˈnɛəriən] *adj.* ①垂曲線的。②鏈的。

cat·e·nar·y [ˈkætəˌnɛrɪ; kəˈtiːnəri] *n.* 〖數學〗垂曲線。—*adj.* ①垂曲線的。②鏈的。

cat·e·nate [ˈkætn̩ˌet; ˈkætineit] *v.t.*, **-nat·ed, -nat·ing.** 使形成連鎖;連接。

cat·e·na·tion [ˌkætɪˈneʃən; ˌkætiˈneiʃən] *n.* 連鎖。

ca·ter [ˈketɚ; ˈkeitə] *v.i.* ①備辦食物〖for〗. ②迎合;滿足〖to, for〗. ③〖俚〗斜走。—*v.t.* 供給酒食或服務。

cat·er-cor·nered [ˈkætɚˌkɔrnɚd; ˈkætəˌkɔːnəd] *adj.* & *adv.* 成對角線的(地);斜着放的(地)。

ca·ter-cous·in [ˈketɚˌkʌzn̩; ˈkeitəˌkʌzn] *n.* ①遠親。②密友。

ca·ter·er [ˈketərɚ; ˈkeitərə] *n.* 備辦食物的人。

cat·er·pil·lar** [ˈkætɚˌpɪlɚ; ˈkætəpilə] *n.* ①蝶或蛾之幼蟲;毛蟲。②戰車;履帶車。—*adj.* 有履帶裝置的。caterpillar belt*** 戰車之履帶。***caterpillar tractor*** 履帶牽引車。

cat·er·waul [ˈkætɚˌwɔl; ˈkætəwɔːl]

v.i. ①(貓)叫春。②發貓叫春聲。③貓般地吵鬧。—*n.* (亦作 **caterwauling**)①貓叫春聲。②類似之聲。

cat eye 〖電視〗貓眼系統。

cat·eyed 〔'kætˌaɪd; 'kætaid〕 *adj.* ①黑暗中能見物的。②眼睛像貓眼的。

cat·fall 〔'kætˌfɔl; 'kætfɔːl〕 *n.* 〖航海〗吊錨索。

cat·fish 〔'kætˌfɪʃ; 'kætfiʃ〕 *n., pl.* **-fish-es, -fish.** 鯰魚。

cat-foot 〔'kætˌfʊt; 'kætfut〕 *n.* 圓短如貓足的脚。

cat-foot·ed 〔'kætˌfʊtɪd; 'kætˌfutid〕 *adj.* ①貓足似的。②悄悄的(走路);偷偷摸摸的。

cat·gut 〔'kætˌgʌt; 'kætgʌt〕 *n.* ①(外科用之)腸線。②(弦樂器之)弦。③小提琴。④弦樂器之集合稱。⑤球拍用的弦線。

Cath. Catholic.

cath·a·rine wheel 〔'kæθrɪn~; 'kæθrin~〕 = **catherine wheel.**

ca·thar·sis 〔kə'θarsɪs; kə'θɑːsis〕 *n.* ①〖醫〗瀉法;通便。②亞里斯多德"詩學"所述之悲劇的淨化情感作用。③〖精神病〗心理分析治療;精神發洩。

ca·thar·tic 〔kə'θartɪk; kə'θɑːtik〕 *n.* 瀉藥。—*adj.* ①通便的。②解放感情的。

Ca·thay 〔kə'θe; kæ'θei〕 *n.* 〖古,詩〗中國。

cat·head 〔'kætˌhɛd; 'kæthed〕 *n.* 〖航海〗船首之繫錨架。

ca·the·dra 〔kə'θidrə; kə'θiːdrə〕 *n., pl.* **-drae** 〔-dri; -driː〕. ①主教座。②主教之職位。③權威人士之座位。④講座。

***ca·the·dral** 〔kə'θidrəl; kə'θiːdrəl〕 *n.* ①主教的座堂。②大教堂。—*adj.* (主教)座堂的。

cathedral glass 一種半透明有花紋的玻璃。

Cath·er·ine 〔'kæθrɪn; 'kæθərin〕 *n.* 女子名。(亦作 **Catharine, Katharine, Katherine, Kathryn**)

catherine wheel ①旋轉爲輪之焰火。②玩具風車。③輪狀圓窗。④自中心向外輻射的圓形刺繡。

cath·e·ter 〔'kæθɪtɚ; 'kæθitə〕 *n.* 〖醫〗尿液管;導管。

ca·thex·is 〔kə'θɛksɪs; kə'θeksis〕 *n., pl.* **-thex·es** 〔-'θɛksiz; -'θeksiːz〕. 〖精神分析〗精神貫注(對某一物體表現之本能或性慾)。

cath·ode 〔'kæθod; 'kæθoud〕 *n.* 〖電〗陰極。***cathode ray*** 陰極線。

***cath·o·lic** 〔'kæθəlɪk; 'kæθəlik〕 *adj.* ①(C-)天主教的。②一般的。③寬容的;大量的。—*n.* (C-)天主教徒。—**al·ly,** *adv.*

Catholic Church 天主教會。

Ca·thol·i·cism 〔kə'θaləˌsɪzəm; kə'θɔlisizəm〕 *n.* ①天主教之教義、信仰及組織等。② =**catholicity.**

cath·o·lic·i·ty 〔ˌkæθə'lɪsətɪ; ˌkæθə'lisiti〕 *n.* ①普遍性。②寬容。③(C-)天主教之教義。

ca·thol·i·cize 〔kə'θaləˌsaɪz; kə'θɔlisaiz〕 *v.t. & v.i.,* **-cized, -ciz·ing.** ①(使)成爲寬大;普遍化。②(C-)(使)皈依天主教;(使)爲天主教徒。

ca·thol·i·con 〔kə'θaləkən; kə'θɔlikən〕 *n.* 萬靈藥。

cat hook 〖航海〗吊錨鉤。

cat·house 〔'kætˌhaʊs; 'kæthaus〕 *n.* 妓院。

cat ice 薄冰。

cat·i·on 〔'kætˌaɪən; 'kætaiən〕 *n.* 〖化〗陽離子;陰向離子。(亦作 **kation**)

cat·kin 〔'kætkɪn; 'kætkin〕 *n.* 葇荑花。

cat-lap 〔'kætˌlæp; 'kætlæp〕 *n.* 〖蘇〗淡的飲料。

cat·like 〔'kætˌlaɪk; 'kætlaik〕 *adj.* 如貓的;輕步的。

cat·ling 〔'kætlɪŋ; 'kætliŋ〕 *n.* ①小貓。②腸線。③(絃樂器之)絃。④(亦作 **catlin**)外科用的尖細雙刃刀。

cat man ①馬戲班中的馴獸師。②飛賊。

cat·mint 〔'kætˌmɪnt; 'kætmint〕 *n.* 〖植物〗貓薄荷(=catnip).

cat nap 假寐;小睡。(亦作 **cat sleep**)

cat·nip 〔'kætnɪp; 'kætnip〕 *n.* 〖植物〗貓薄荷。(亦作 **catmint** 或 **catnep**)

cat-o'-nine-tails 〔ˌkætə'naɪnˌtelz; 'kætə'nain-teilz〕 *n., pl.* **-tails.** ①九尾鞭(用以鞭撻罪人者)。②〖植物〗香蒲。

ca·top·tric 〔kə'taptrɪk; kə'tɔptrik〕 *adj.* 反射的。—*n.* 反射光學(=catoptrics).

ca·top·trics 〔kə'taptrɪks; kə'tɔptriks〕 *n.* (作 *sing.* 解)反射光學。

cat rig 單帆小艇上之索具。

cat-rigged 〔'kætˌrɪgd; 'kæt-rigd〕 *adj.* 裝有單帆艇式之索具的。

cats and dogs 大量的;劇烈的。

cat's cradle 翻線戲。

cat-scratch disease 〖醫〗由於皮膚抓破受過濾性細菌傳染而得的一種感冒及淋巴腺發炎症。

cat's-ear 〔'kætsˌɪr; 'kæts-iə〕 *n.* 〖植物〗貓耳草。

cat's-eye 〔'kætsˌaɪ; 'kæts-ai〕 *n.* 〖礦〗貓睛石;貓兒眼。

cat's-foot 〔'kætsˌfʊt; 'kætsfut〕 *n.* 〖植物〗積雪草;連錢草。

Cats·kill Mountains 〔'kætsˌkɪl~; 'kætskil~〕 卡茲奇山(在美國紐約州之東南部,爲避暑勝地)。(亦作 **Catskills**)

cat's-paw 〔'kætsˌpɔ; 'kæts-pɔː〕 *n.* ①受人愚弄者。②〖航海〗貓爪風;使海面起輕波之和風。***make a cat's-paw of a person*** 使某人成爲傀儡。

cat·sup 〔'kætsəp; 'kætsəp〕 *n.* = **catchup.**

cat·tail 〔'kætˌtel; 'kætteil〕 *n.* 〖植物〗①葇荑花序之花。②香蒲。(亦作 **cat's-tail**)

cat·tish 〔'kætɪʃ; 'kætiʃ〕 *adj.* 似貓的;狡猾的。

‡**cat·tle** 〔'kætl; 'kætl〕 *n., pl.* **cat·tle.** (常作 *pl.* 解)①牛;家畜;牲口。a herd of *cattle.* 一羣牛。②毫無價值的人;畜生。

cattle guard (防止家畜走出而築的)淺溝。(亦作 **cattle grid**)

cat·tle-lift·er 〔'kætlˌlɪftɚ; 'kætlˌliftə〕 *n.* 偷家畜之賊;偷牛賊。

cat·tle·man 〔'kætlmən; 'kætlmən〕 *n., pl.* **-men.** 牧畜者。

cattle pen 牛舍;牛圈。

cattle plague 牛瘟。

cattle show 家畜展覽會。

cat·ty[1] 〔'kætɪ; 'kæti〕 *n., pl.* **-ties.** 斤(中國斤=$1\frac{1}{3}$磅)。

cat·ty[2] *adj.,* **-ti·er, -ti·est.** ①貓的;如貓的。②狡猾而陰險的。—**cat·ti·ness,** *n.*

cat·walk 〔'kætˌwɔk; 'kætwɔːk〕 *n.* ①橋樑旁側之步行小道。②飛機等內之甬道。

cat whisker 〖無線電〗礦石檢波器中用以接觸礦石之金屬細線。

Cau·ca·sia 〔kɔ'keʒə; kɔː'keizjə〕 *n.* 高加索。

Cau·ca·sian 〔kɔ'keʃən; kɔː'keizjən〕 *n.* ①高加索人種;白種人。②高加索地方。—*adj.* 高加索人的;白種人的。

Cau·ca·sus 〔'kɔkəsəs; 'kɔːkəsəs〕 *n.* ①高加索山脈。②=**Caucasia.**

cau·cus 〔'kɔkəs; 'kɔːkəs〕 *n.* ①〖美〗政黨預備會議。②〖英〗政黨中之決策機構。—*v.i.* 開政黨預備會議。

cau·dad 〔'kɔdæd; 'kɔːdæd〕 *adv.* 〖動物〗靠近尾端地。

cau·dal 〔'kɔdl; 'kɔːdl〕 *adj.* 〖動物,解剖〗

①尾的;近尾部的。②似尾的。
cau·date ['kɔdet; 'kɔːdeit] *adj.* 〖動物〗有尾的;有尾狀附屬物的。(亦作 **caudated**)
cau·dle ['kɔdl̩; 'kɔːdl] *n.* 病人之流質滋補食物。
‡caught [kɔt; kɔːt] *v.* pt. & pp. of catch.
caul [kɔl; kɔːl] *n.* 〖解剖〗大網膜;羊膜;肉胎。
caul·dron ['kɔldrən; 'kɔːldrən] *n.* =caldron.
cau·les·cent [kɔ'lɛsənt; kɔː'lesənt] *adj.* 〖植物〗有莖的;有顯著之地上莖的。
cau·li·flow·er ['kɔlə,flauə; 'kɔli,flauə] *n.* 花椰菜(俗名菜花)。
cauliflower ear 拳擊者因多次受傷而變畸形的耳朵。
cau·li·form ['kɔlə,fɔrm; 'kɔːlifɔːm] *adj.* 〖植物〗莖狀的。
cau·line ['kɔlɪn; 'kɔːlin] *adj.* 〖植物〗莖的;生於莖上的。
caulk [kɔk; kɔːk] *v.t.* 塡隙。(亦作**calk**) —**er,** *n.*
caus. causative.
caus·a·ble ['kɔzəbl̩; 'kɔːzəbl] *adj.* 可惹起的。
caus·al ['kɔzl̩; 'kɔːzəl] *adj.* ①原因的。②關於因果的。③〖邏輯,文法〗表示原因的。—*n.* 〖文法〗表示原因之連接詞。—**ly,** *adv.*
cau·sal·gi·a [kɔ'zældʒɪə; kɔː'zældʒiə] *n.* 〖醫〗灼狀神經痛;灼痛。
cau·sal·i·ty [kɔ'zælətɪ; kɔː'zæliti] *n., pl.* **-ties.** ①緣由;起因。②因果關係。
cau·sa·tion [kɔ'zeʃən; kɔː'zeiʃən] *n.* ①造因。②因果律。③原因。
cau·sa·tion·ism [kɔ'zeʃə,nɪzəm; kɔː'zeiʃənizəm] *n.* 〖哲學〗宇宙因果律。
cau·sa·tion·ist [kɔ'zeʃənɪst; kɔː'zeiʃənist] *n.* 〖哲學〗相信宇宙因果律的人。
caus·a·tive ['kɔzətɪv; 'kɔːzətiv] *adj.* ①原因的。②〖文法〗表原因的。—*n.* 〖文法〗使役字或形式。***causative verb*** 使役動詞。
‡cause [kɔz; kɔːz] *n., v.,* **caused, causing.** —*n.* ①原因;緣由。*cause* and effect. 因與果。②理由;動機;根據。He was angry without *cause.* 他無理由而發怒。There is no *cause* for anxiety. 不必憂慮。③理想;目標。Our army is fighting in the *cause* of justice. 我們的軍隊爲正義而戰。④訴訟;訟事。***make common cause with*** 與…團結一致;支持。***show cause*** 提出對…的反對理由。—*v.t.* 致使(發生);致令;起因於。The fire *caused* much damage. 火災招致重大的損害。
cause-and-ef·fect ['kɔzəndɪ'fɛkt; 'kɔːzəndi'fekt] *adj.* 有因果關係的。
cause cé·lè·bre ['koz,se'lɛbr̩; 'kouzsei'lebr] *n., pl.* **causes cé·lè·bres.** 〖法〗轟動一時的訴訟案件、審判、或辯論。
cause·less ['kɔzlɪs; 'kɔːzlis] *adj.* 無原因的;無正當理由的。—**ly,** *adv.* —**ness,** *n.*
cause of action 〖法律〗原告的起訴理由。
cau·se·rie [,kozə'ri; 'kouzəriː] 〖法〗*n.* ①閒談。②隨筆;短評。
cause·way ['kɔz,we; 'kɔːzwei] *n.* ①堤道。②石子路;公路。—*v.t.* 砌堤道於。
cau·sey ['kɔzɪ; 'kɔːzi] *n., pl.* **-seys.** 〖英方〗=**causeway.** —*v.t.* 用小石子鋪砌。
caus·tic ['kɔstɪk; 'kɔːstik] *adj.* ①腐蝕性的;苛性的。②刻薄的;譏刺的。—*n.* ①〖化〗苛性藥;腐蝕劑。②〖物理〗焦散曲線。—**al,** *adj.* —**al·ly,** —**ly,** *adv.* —**i·ty,** *n.*
caustic alcohol 乙醇鈉。
caustic soda 苛性鈉。
cau·ter·ize ['kɔtə,raɪz; 'kɔːtəraiz] *v.t.* 燒灼;腐蝕;灸。—**cau·ter·i·za·tion,** *n.*
cau·ter·y ['kɔtərɪ; 'kɔːtəri] *n., pl.* **-ter·ies.** 〖醫〗①烙術;燒灼;灸。moxa *cautery.* 針灸。②烙器;燒灼器。
***cau·tion** ['kɔʃən; 'kɔːʃən] *n.* ①謹愼;小心。to take *caution* against error. 謹防錯誤。②警告。③〖俗〗極不平常的人或物。—*v.t.* 警告;勸…使小心。I *cautioned* him against the danger. 我警告他防備危險。
cau·tion·ar·y ['kɔʃən,ɛrɪ; 'kɔːʃnəri] *adj.* 勸告的;警戒的;注意的。
caution money 保證金。
***cau·tious** ['kɔʃəs; 'kɔːʃəs] *adj.* 極小心的;愼重的;謹愼的。—**ly,** *adv.* —**ness,** *n.*
cav. ①cavalry. ②cavalier.
cav·al·cade [,kævl̩'ked; ,kævəl'keid] *n.* 騎兵隊、車隊等的行列;一隊人馬。
***cav·a·lier** [,kævə'lɪr; ,kævə'liə] *n.* ①騎士。②豪俠。③(C-)(英國查理一世與議會戰爭時之)保王黨黨員。—*adj.* ①豪俠的。②傲慢的。③(C-)英國查理一世時代保王黨的。—**ly,** *adv.*
***cav·al·ry** ['kævl̩rɪ; 'kævəlri] *n., pl.* **-ries.** ①騎兵;馬隊(集合稱)。②輕裝甲部隊。
cav·al·ry·man ['kævl̩rɪmən; 'kævəlrimən] *n., pl.* **-men.** 騎兵。
cavalry twill 一種用羊毛或棉紗織成的厚斜紋布,多用以做軍隊制服。
cav·a·ti·na [,kævə'tinə; ,kævə'tiːnə] *n., pl.* **-ne** [-nɛ; -ne]. 〖義〗〖音樂〗短曲。
cave¹** [kev; keiv] *n., v.,* **caved, cav·ing.** —*n.* 洞;穴;窟。*cave* period. 穴居時代。—*v.t.* ①掘洞。②使崩陷;使崩落。—*v.i.* 陷;落;圮塌。cave in*** a. 崩;塌陷。b.〖俗〗讓步;屈服。—**like,** *adj.*
ca·ve² ['kevɪ; 'keivi] *interj.* 〖英俚〗小心(老師來了)!—*n.* 守望;把風。
cave art 石器時代人留於山洞中的壁畫。
ca·ve·at ['kevɪ,æt; 'keiviæt] *n.* ①〖法律〗中止訴訟手續之申請。②警告。—*v.i.* ①申請停止手續。②警告。
ca·ve·at emp·tor ['kevɪ,æt'ɛmptɔr; 'keiviæt'emptɔː] 〖拉〗顧客留心(售出不換)。
cave dweller ①穴居者。②(住公寓的)都市人。
cave-in ['kev,ɪn; 'keivin] *n.* ①(礦坑等之)塌陷;崩陷。②塌陷處。
cave man ①石器時代之穴居人。②〖俗〗(尤指對女性)粗野者。
cav·en·dish ['kævəndɪʃ; 'kævəndiʃ] *n.* 煙草餅;板煙。
***cav·ern** ['kævən; 'kævən] *n.* ①巨穴。②大而暗的深凹處。—*v.t.* ①將…放入山洞。②將…挖出來。
cav·ern·ous ['kævənəs; 'kævənəs] *adj.* ①含有洞穴的。②深陷的。③沉濁音的。④多孔的。⑤(似)洞穴的。
cav·i·ar [,kævɪ'ɑr; 'kæviɑː] *n.* 魚子醬。***caviar to the general*** 太過高雅;曲高和寡。(亦作 **caviare**)
cav·i·corn ['kævə,kɔrn; 'kævikɔːn] *adj.* 〖動物〗有空心角的。
cav·il ['kævl̩; 'kævil] *v.,* **-il(l)ed, -il(l)ing.** *n.* —*v.i.*吹毛求疵;苛責〖at, about〗. —*v.t.* 以不充分的理由或藉口表示反對。—*n.* 無端的指摘;苛責。
cav·il·(l)er ['kævɪlɚ; 'kævilə] *n.* 吹毛求疵者;苛責者。
cav·i·ta·tion [,kævə'teʃən; ,kævi'teiʃən] *n.* ①半眞空之形成。②〖醫〗成洞。
cav·i·tron ['kævɪtrən; 'kævitrən] *n.* (治療牙齒之)一種無痛穿孔錐。
***cav·i·ty** ['kævətɪ; 'kæviti] *n., pl.* **-ties.**

①穴。②洞;槽。③〖生理〗腔;窩。
ca·vo-re·lie·vo,ca·vo-ri·lie·vo [ˈkɑvorɪˈlivo; ˈkɑːvouriˈliːvou] *n., pl.* **-vos, -vi** [-vi; -viː]. 凹浮雕。(亦作 **sunk relief**)
ca·vort [kəˈvɔrt; kəˈvɔːt] *v.i.* 〖美俗〗「騰躍。」
ca·vum [ˈkɑvəm; ˈkɑːvəm] *n., pl.* **-va** [-və;-və]. 〖解剖〗空腔。
ca·vy [ˈkevɪ; ˈkeivi] *n., pl.* **-vies.** 豚「鼠;天竺鼠。」
caw [kɔ; kɔː] *n.* 烏鴉叫聲。—*v.i.* (烏鴉)鳴叫;烏鴉似地叫。
Cax·ton [ˈkækstən; ˈkækstən] *n.* ①卡克斯頓(William, 1422?-1491, 英國第一位印刷家)。②其所印之任何書籍(全用黑體字)。③〖印刷〗(仿卡克斯頓版式之)活字。
cay [ke, ki; kei, kiː] *n.* 沙洲;岩礁;小島。
cay·enne [kaɪˈɛn; keiˈen] *n.* ①辣椒。②辣椒末。(亦作 **cayenne pepper**)
cay·man [ˈkemən; ˈkeimən] *n.*〖動物〗(中、南美所產之)鱷魚。(亦作 **caiman**)
Ca·yu·ga [keˈjugə; keiˈjuːgə] *n., pl.* **-ga** or **-gas.** ①卡育加人, 原居紐約州的印第安人之一族。②其語言。
cay·use [kaɪˈjus; kaiˈjuːs] *n., pl.* **-use, -uses.** ①(美西部之)小野馬。②(C-)俄勒崗州印第安人之一族。
Cb 化學元素 columbium之符號。**C.B.** Bachelor of Surgery. **C.B.D.** cash before delivery. **C.B.E.L., CBEL** Cambridge Bibliography of English Literature.
C-bomb [ˈsiˌbɑm; ˈsiːbɔm] *n.* 鈷彈。
C.B.S. Columbia Broadcasting System.
CBW chemical and biological warfare. 生化戰爭。**cc.** chapters. **cc., c.c.** cubic centimeter(s). 立方公分;立方糎。
C.C., c.c. ①carbon copy. ②cash credit. ③cashier's check. ④chamber of commerce. ⑤chief clerk. ⑥circuit court. ⑦city council. ⑧combat command. ⑨common carrier. ⑩common council. ⑪company commander. ⑫council of churches. ⑬country club. ⑭country court. ⑮current cost. **C.C.A.** ①Chief Clerk of the Admiralty. ②Circuit Court of Appeals. ③County Court of Appeals. **C.C.C.** ①Civilian Conservation Corps. ②Commodity Credit Corporation. **CCI.** Civil Communications Intelligence. **ccm** centimeters.
C.C.P. Court of Common Pleas.
CCR Commission on Civil Rights.
CCUS Chamber of Commerce of the United States. **Cd** 化學元素 cadmium 之符號。**cd.** ①cord. ②cords. **c.d.** cash discount. **C/D, CD** ①cash discount. ②certificate of deposit. **C.D., CD** Civil Defense. **Cdr., CDR** commander. **Ce** 化學元素 cerium 之符號。
C. E. ①Chemical Engineer. ②Chief Engineer. ③Church of England. ④Civil Engineer. ⑤Common Era. **C.E., c.e.** ①Christian Era. ②customs and excise.
‡**cease** [sis; siːs] *v.*, **ceased, ceas·ing.** —*v.i.* ①停止。②終止。—*v.t.* 停止。They *ceased* work (*or* working). 他們停止工作。*Cease* fire. 不要開鎗(停止開鎗;停火)。—*n.* 停止。without *cease.* 不停地。
cease-fire [ˈsisˌfaɪr; ˈsiːsˌfaiə] *n.* 停戰。
cease·less [ˈsislɪs; ˈsiːslis] *adj.* 永不停止的。—**ly,** *adv.* —**ness,** *n.*
ceas·ing [ˈsisɪŋ; ˈsiːsiŋ] *n.* 中斷;結束。
Cec·il [ˈsɛsl; ˈsesl] *n.* 塞梭(Edgar Algernon Robert, 1864-1958, 英國政治家, 1937年得諾貝爾和平獎)。
Ce·cil·ia [sɪˈsɪljə; siˈsiljə] *n.* 女子名。
CED Committee for Economic Development.
***ce·dar** [ˈsidɚ; ˈsiːdə] *n.* ①〖植物〗西洋杉;香柏。②類似香柏的樹木。—*adj.* 西洋杉的;西洋杉製的。
ce·dar·bird [ˈsidɚˌbɝd; ˈsiːdəbəːd] *n.* 黃連雀。(亦作 **cedar waxwing**)
ce·darn [ˈsidɚn; ˈsiːdən] *adj.* 〖詩〗西洋杉的;香柏的;杉木製的。
cede [sid; siːd] *v.t.*, **ced·ed, ced·ing.** ①放棄;讓與;割讓;讓步。②過戶;轉讓。
ce·dil·la [sɪˈdɪlə; siˈdilə] *n.* 法文等C字母下之"尾形"符號(表讀[s]音, 如:façade).
cee [si; siː] *n.* C字。—*adj.* C字形的。
cee spring C字形的彈簧。
ceil [sil; siːl] *v.t.* 裝以天花板。—**ed,** *adj.*
ceil·ing** [ˈsilɪŋ; ˈsiːliŋ] *n.* ①天花板。②飛機所能達到的最高度。③最高的限度。price *ceilings* on rent. 房租的限價。④自地面至最低雲層間之距離。⑤最高的能力。hit the ceiling*** 發怒。
ceil·inged [ˈsilɪŋd; ˈsiːliŋd] *adj.* 有天花板的。***ceilinged off*** 爲天花板或類似物所遮斷。
cel·a·don [ˈsɛləˌdɑn; ˈselədɔn] *n.* ①灰綠色。②(中國產之)青磁;仿青磁。
cel·an·dine [ˈsɛlənˌdaɪn; ˈseləndain] *n.* 〖植物〗白屈菜。
celandine green 淺灰綠色。
Cel·a·nese [ˈsɛləˌniz; ˌseləˈniːz] *n.* 〖商標名〗一種人造絲。
ce·leb [səˈlɛb; səˈleb] *n.* 〖俗〗名人(ce-「lebrity 的簡稱)。」
Cel·e·bes [ˈsɛləˌbiz; seˈliːbiz] *n.* 西里伯島(印尼之一島, 在婆羅洲之東)。
cel·e·brant [ˈsɛləbrənt; ˈselibrənt] *n.* ①(天主教)主領彌撒之神父。②主持典禮者。
***cel·e·brate** [ˈsɛləˌbret; ˈselibreit] *v.*, **-brat·ed, -brat·ing.** —*v.t.* ①慶祝;祝賀。We *celebrate* the Double Tenth, our National Day. 我們慶祝雙十節國慶日。②褒揚;稱頌。③公開擧行儀式。④宣布;發表。—*v.i.* ①慶祝。②〖俗〗狂歡;享樂。③擧行宗教儀式(尤指彌撒)。
***cel·e·brat·ed** [ˈsɛləˌbretɪd; ˈselibrei-「tid] *adj.* 著名的。」
cel·e·bra·tion** [ˌsɛləˈbreʃən; ˌseliˈbreiʃən] *n.* ①慶祝的典禮或儀式。②慶祝。in celebration of*** 爲慶祝…。
cel·e·bra·tor [ˈsɛləˌbretɚ; ˈselibreitə] *n.* 祝賀者;慶祝的人。
ce·leb·ri·ty [səˈlɛbrətɪ; siˈlebriti] *n., pl.* **-ties.** ①名人。②名譽。
ce·ler·i·ty [səˈlɛrətɪ; siˈleriti] *n.* 敏「捷;快速。」
***cel·er·y** [ˈsɛlərɪ; ˈseləri] *n.* 芹菜。
celery cabbage 白菜。
celery salt 芹子鹽(鹽中混有磨碎的芹菜子作香料)。
ce·les·ta [səˈlɛstə; səˈlestə] *n.* 〖音樂〗「鐘琴。」
***ce·les·tial** [səˈlɛstʃəl; siˈlestjəl] *adj.* ①天的;天上的。*celestial* bodies. 天體。②天國的。*Celestial* City. 天國。—*n.* ①天堂之居民。②中國人。
celestial crown 〖紋章〗星冠(皇冠每一尖角上加有星形裝飾的紋徽)。
celestial globe 星象儀。

ce·les·tial·ize 〔sə'lɛstʃəl,aɪz; si'lestjuəlaiz〕 *v.t.* 使神化;使仙化。

ce·li·ac 〔'silɪ,æk; 'si:liæk〕 *adj.* 〖解剖〗腹的;腹腔的。(亦作 **coeliac**)

celiac disease 〖醫〗幼童慢性腹瀉症。

cel·i·ba·cy 〔'sɛləbəsɪ; 'selibəsi〕 *n., pl.* **-cies.** 獨身生活。

cel·i·ba·tar·i·an 〔,sɛləbə'tɛrɪən; ,selibə'tɛəriən〕 *n., adj.* =**celibate.**

cel·i·bate 〔'sɛləbɪt; 'selibit〕 *n.*獨身者。—*adj.* 獨身的;未婚的。

ce·li·ot·o·my 〔,silɪ'ɑtəmɪ; ,si:li'ɔtəmi〕 *n., pl.* **-mies.** 剖腹術;腹腔切開術。

‡**cell** 〔sɛl; sel〕 *n.* ①寺院或監獄中的小室;密室。②小而凹的穴窩。③動植物的細胞。*cell* division. 細胞分裂。generative *cell.* 生殖細胞。④電池。dry *cells.* 乾電池。⑤團體中的小組織。⑥墳墓。—*v.i.*住在小室或牢房中。

cel·la 〔'sɛlə; 'selə〕 *n., pl.* **-lae** 〔-li; -li:〕. 〖建築〗古希臘或羅馬廟宇之內殿。

cel·lar** 〔'sɛlɚ; 'selə〕 *n.* ①地窖。②酒窖。③藏酒。to keep a good (small) *cellar.* 貯藏有大(少)量的好酒。the cellar*** 〖美俗〗運動比賽之末名。—*v.t.* 將…放入地窖中。

cel·lar·age 〔'sɛlərɪdʒ; 'seləridʒ〕 *n.* ①穴藏;地窖。②地窖貯藏費。

cel·lar·er 〔'sɛlərɚ; 'selərə〕 *n.* ①地窖看守人。②管理食物者。

cel·lar·et(te) 〔,sɛlə'ɛt; ,selə'ret〕 *n.* 酒櫥。

cell·block 〔'sɛl,blɑk; 'selblɔk〕 *n.* 監獄中一組囚犯室。

cel·list, 'cel·list 〔'tʃɛlɪst; 'tʃelist〕 *n.* 奏大提琴(cello)者。(亦作 **violoncellist**)

cel·lo 〔'tʃɛlo; 'tʃelou〕 *n., pl.* **-los.** 大提琴; 低音提琴。(亦作 **'cello** 爲 violoncello 之略)

cel·loi·din 〔sɛ'lɔɪdɪn; se'lɔidin〕 *n.* 〖化〗火棉膠。

cel·lo·phane 〔'sɛlə,fen; 'seləfein〕 *n.* ①玻璃紙。② (C-) 一種玻璃紙之商標。

cel·lu·lar 〔'sɛljəlɚ; 'seljulə〕 *adj.* ①有細胞的;細胞狀的。②有洞的;多孔的。③由許多小單位組成的。—**i·ty,** *n.*

cellular glass 一種海棉狀薄玻璃,多作防熱及隔音用。

cel·lu·lat·ed 〔'sɛljə,letɪd; 'seljuleitid〕 *adj.* =**cellular.**

cel·lule 〔'sɛljul; 'selju:l〕 *n.* ①〖解剖〗小細胞。②小室。

***cel·lu·loid** 〔'sɛljə,lɔɪd; 'seljulɔid〕 *n.* ①賽璐珞;假象牙。②(C-) 賽璐珞質料之一種商標。—*adj.* 〖俗〗電影的。

cel·lu·lose 〔'sɛljə,los; 'seljulous〕 *n.* ①〖植物〗纖維素。②〖化〗纖維素;醋酸纖維素和硝化棉的溶液。—*v.t.* 加纖維素製造。—*adj.* 由纖維素演變出來的。

cellulose acetate 〖化〗醋酸纖維素。

cellulose nitrate 〖化〗硝酸纖維素。

cel·lu·lous 〔'sɛljələs; 'seljuləs〕 *adj.* ①充滿細胞的。②由細胞組成的。

Cel·si·us 〔'sɛlsɪəs; 'selsjəs〕 *n.* 攝氏寒暑表; 攝氏之分度法。(亦作 **Celsius thermometer**)

Celt 〔sɛlt; kelt, selt〕 *n.* 塞爾特人。(亦作 **Kelt**)

celt 〔sɛlt; selt〕 *n.* 一種新石器時代的石斧或石鑿。

Cel·tic 〔'sɛltɪk; 'keltik, 'seltik〕 *adj.* 塞爾特人(語)的。—*n.*塞爾特語。(亦作 **Keltic**)

Celt·i·cism 〔'sɛltə,sɪzəm; 'keltisizəm〕 *n.* ①塞爾特風俗。②塞爾特語風。

***ce·ment** 〔sə'mɛnt; si'ment〕 *n.*①水泥。②結合物。③〖解剖〗堊質。—*v.t.* ①使結合;強固。②以水泥接合;砌以水泥。—*v.i.* 黏結。—*adj.* ①水泥的。②加水泥製成的。—**er,** *n.*

ce·men·ta·tion 〔,simən'teʃən; ,si:men'teiʃən〕 *n.* ①水泥結合。②接合;黏接。③〖冶金〗滲炭法。

cement block 〖建築〗水泥磚。

cement mixer 水泥攪拌機。

ce·men·tum 〔sə'mɛntəm; si'mentəm〕 *n.* 〖牙科〗白堊質;牙骨質。

***cem·e·ter·y** 〔'sɛmə,tɛrɪ; 'semitri〕 *n., pl.* **-ter·ies.** 墓地。

cen. ①central. ②century.

cen·o·bite 〔'sɛnə,baɪt; 'si:noubait〕 *n.* (寺院中之) 修道者。(亦作 **coenobite**) —**cen·o·bit·ism,** *n.*

cen·o·taph 〔'sɛnə,tæf; 'senətɑ:f〕 *n.* 紀念碑;衣冠塚;紀念塔。***the Cenotaph*** 第一次世界大戰陣亡將士紀念塔(該塔建於 London 之 Whitehall).

Ce·no·zo·ic 〔,sinə'zo·ɪk; ,si:nə'zouik〕 *adj.* 〖地質〗新生代的。***the Cenozoic era*** 新生代。—*n.* 新生代(岩層)。

cense 〔sɛns; sens〕 *v.t.,* **censed, censing.** ①焚香於(神等)之前。②以香薰。

cen·ser 〔'sɛnsɚ; 'sensə〕 *n.* 香爐。

cen·sor 〔'sɛnsɚ; 'sensə〕 *n.* ①檢查員(檢查新聞、書籍、戲劇、電影、廣播等者)。②羅馬監察吏(負責調查人口及人民行爲者)。③監察者。④好吹毛求疵者。—*v.t.* 檢查(新聞、書籍、戲劇、廣播等)。—**a·ble,** —**i·al,** *adj.*

cen·sored 〔'sɛnsɚd; 'sensəd〕 *adj.* 被檢查後通過(或不通過)的。

cen·so·ri·ous 〔sɛn'sorɪəs; sen'sɔ:riəs〕 *adj.* 吹毛求疵的;好非難的;愛批判的。—**ly,** *adv.* —**ness,** *n.*

cen·sor·ship 〔'sɛnsɚ,ʃɪp; 'sensəʃip〕 *n.* ①檢查。②檢查制度。③檢查人之職務。

cen·sur·a·ble 〔'sɛnʃərəbl̩; 'senʃərəbl〕 *adj.* 可非難的;應受譴責的。

***cen·sure** 〔'sɛnʃɚ; 'senʃə〕 *n., v.,* **-sured, -sur·ing.** —*n.* 不友善的批評;責難。—*v.t.* 不友善地批評; 非難。to *censure* a person for his selfishness. 責難某人的自私。—*v.i.* 責難; 非難。—**cen·sur·er,** *n.*

***cen·sus** 〔'sɛnsəs; 'sensəs〕 *n.* ①戶口調查。②古羅馬人口及財產之登記。

census paper 人口調查表;戶口調查表。

census taker 戶口調查員。

census tract 戶區 (戶口統計單位)。

‡**cent** 〔sɛnt; sent〕 *n.* 分(一元的百分之一)。

cent. ①centigrade. ②centime. ③centimeter. ④central. ⑤centum. ⑥century.

cen·tal 〔'sɛntl̩; 'sentl〕 *n.* 一百磅。

cen·taur 〔'sɛntɔr; 'sentɔ:〕 *n.* ①〖希臘神話〗人首馬身之怪物。② (C-) 〖天文〗人馬座。

cen·tau·ry 〔'sɛntɔrɪ; 'sentɔ:ri〕 *n., pl.* **-ries.** 龍膽科之植物。

cen·ta·vo 〔sɛn'tɑvo; sen'tɑ:vou〕 *n., pl.* **-vos.** ①拉丁美洲國家及菲律賓之小錢幣。②葡萄牙及巴西之小錢幣。

cen·te·nar·i·an 〔,sɛntə'nɛrɪən; ,senti'nɛəriən〕 *n.* 百歲或百歲以上之人。—*adj.* ①百歲或百歲以上的。②一百年的。

cen·te·nar·y 〔'sɛntə,nɛrɪ; sen'ti:nəri〕 *n., pl.* **-nar·ies,** *adj.* —*n.* ①一百年; 一世紀。②百年紀念。③百年紀念之慶典。—*adj.* ①一百年的。②每百年一次的。

cen·ten·ni·al 〔sɛn'tɛnɪəl; sen'tenjəl〕 *adj.* ①一百年的。②百歲的。③百年一次的。④百年紀念的。—*n.* ①百年紀念。②百年紀

念的慶典。—**ly,** *adv.*

‡**cen·ter** 〔'sɛntɚ; 'sentə〕 *n.* ①圓的中心; 球體的中心。 the *center* of a wheel. 輪的中心。②中央;中心(點);集中點。a *center* of trade. 貿易中心。③在中心位置的人或物。④站在中間位置的球員;籃球、曲棍球之中鋒。⑤(議會中之)中間派。 —*v.t.* ①置於中心位置。②集中。to *center* one's attention on certain things. 集中注意力於某些事。③標明中心位置。④將球從球場邊緣擲至球場中心。—*v.i.* ①集中。His interest *centered* in chemistry. 他的興趣集中在化學。②寄託於。***center about*** (***around*** or ***on***) 〖俗〗關於;以…爲焦點。The topic today *centers about* the crisis in the Far East. 今天的講題是關於遠東的危機。—*adj.* 中央的;位在正中的。

center bit 〖機械〗轉柄鑽。

cen·ter·board 〔'sɛntɚ,bord; 'sentəbɔːd〕 *n.* 〖航海〗活動船板。

center field 〖棒球、壘球〗中外野。

center fielder 〖棒球、壘球〗中外野手。

cen·ter·fold 〔'sɛntɚ,fold; 'sentəfould〕 *n.*雜誌或書籍中摺疊起來的大型圖畫。

center forward 排球、足球、水球、曲棍球隊頭排中間的球員。

center halfback 足球、曲棍球隊中排中間的球員。

center jump (籃球比賽開始時在球場「中心的」跳球。

center of gravity 〖物理〗重心。

cen·ter·piece, cen·tre·piece 〔'sɛntɚ,pis; 'sentəpiːs〕 *n.* 中央部位裝飾品(如餐桌中央之盆花等)。

cen·tes·i·mal 〔sɛn'tɛsəml; sen'tesiməl〕 *adj.* 百分之一的;百分法的;百進的。

cen·tes·i·mate 〔sɛn'tɛsə,met; sen'tesimeit〕 *v.t.,* **-mat·ed, -mat·ing.** 由每一百人中選(抽)出一人受罰;以一儆百。

cen·tes·i·mo 〔sɛn'tɛsə,mo; sen'tesimou〕 *n., pl.* **-mi** 〔-mi; -miː〕, **-mos.** 義大利、巴拿馬及烏拉圭之錢幣名。

centi- 〖字首〗米突制中表"百;百倍;百分「之一」等義。

cen·ti·are 〔'sɛntɪ,ɛr; 'sentiɛə〕 *n.* 一平方公尺。(亦作 **centare**)

cen·ti·grade 〔'sɛntə,gred; 'sentigreid〕 *adj.* ①分爲百度的;百分度的。②根據攝氏寒暑表的。

centigrade thermometer 攝氏寒暑表。

***cen·ti·gram** 〔'sɛntə,græm; 'sentigræm〕 *n.* (重量名)瓱(一公克的百分之一);公毫。(亦作 **centigramme**)

***cen·ti·li·ter, cen·ti·li·tre** 〔'sɛntl,itɚ; 'senti,liːtə〕 *n.* 公勺(容量名,一公升的百分之一)。

cen·time 〔'sɑntim; 'sɑːntiːm〕 〖法〗 *n.* 「生丁(法國或瑞士錢幣名)。」

***cen·ti·me·ter, cen·ti·me·tre** 〔'sɛntə,mitɚ; 'senti,miːtə〕 *n.* 公分。

cen·ti·me·ter-gram-sec·ond 〔'sɛntə,mitɚ'græm'sɛkənd; 'senti,miːtə'græm'sekənd〕 *adj.* 〖物理〗 C.G.S. 公制(即以糎爲長度單位、克爲質量單位、秒爲時間單位之公制)的。

cen·ti·mil·lion·aire 〔,sɛntə,mɪljən'ɛr; ,senti,miljə'nɛə〕 *n.* 億萬富翁。

cen·ti·mo 〔'sɛntə,mo; 'sentəmou〕 *n., pl.* **-mos.** 西班牙語系諸國之貨幣名。

cen·ti·pede 〔'sɛntə,pid; 'sentipiːd〕 *n.* 蜈蚣。(亦作 **centiped**)

cent·ner 〔'sɛntnɚ; 'sentnə〕 *n.* ①歐洲商用重量名(等於 50 公斤)。②一種公制重量名(等於100公斤)。③100磅(=cental).

cen·to 〔'sɛnto; 'sentou〕 *n., pl.* **-tos, -to·nes** 〔-to,niz; -toniːz〕, **-toes.** ①(詩、文等之)摘錄;(音樂之)組曲。②任何由不相稱部分湊成的東西。

‡**cen·tral** 〔'sɛntrəl; 'sentrəl〕 *adj.* ①(在或近)中央的。 My house is very *central.* 我的家很近市中心區。②主要的;重要的。③總管的;非局部的。*central* office. 總公司。—*n.* ①電話總機。②電話接線生。③總公司或機關。—**ly,** *adv.* —**ness,** *n.*

Central African Empire 中非帝國(先稱 Central African Republic, 1976年改今名;首都班基 Bangui).

Central America 中美洲。

Central Asia, Soviet 俄屬中亞細亞(包括烏玆別克、土克曼、達輯克、哈薩克及吉爾吉斯等地)。

Central Bank of China 中央「銀行。」

central heating 中央暖氣系統。

Central Intelligence Agency (美國)中央情報局(簡稱 **CIA**).

cen·tral·ism 〔'sɛntrəl,ɪzəm; 'sentrəlizəm〕 *n.* 中央集權主義或制度。—**cen·tral·ist,** *n., adj.*

cen·tral·i·ty 〔sɛn'trælətɪ; sen'træliti〕 *n.* ①中央;中心。②向心性;集中性。

cen·tral·ize 〔'sɛntrəl,aɪz; 'sentrəlaiz〕 *v.,* **-ized, -iz·ing.** —*v.t.* ①使集於中央;使聚於中心。②集中管理;統一。—*v.i.* 集於中央;聚於中心。 —**cen·tral·i·za·tion,** —**cen·tral·iz·er,** *n.*

central nervous system 中樞「神經系統。」

Central News Agency 中央通訊社。

Central Powers 第一次世界大戰時「的德、奧、匈三同盟國。」

Central Treaty Organization 中東(安全)條約組織(簡稱 **CENTO**).

Central Trust of China 中央信託局。

Central Weather Bureau 「中央氣象局。」

centre 〔'sɛntɚ; 'sentə〕 *n., v.,* **-tred, -tring.** 〖英〗=**center.**

cen·tric 〔'sɛntrɪk; 'sentrik〕 *adj.* ①中心的;中心點的;位於中心的。②〖生理〗神經中樞的。

cen·tri·cal 〔'sɛntrɪkl; 'sentrikəl〕 *adj.* 「=**centric.**」

cen·tric·i·ty 〔sɛn'trɪsətɪ; sen'trisiti〕 *n.* 中心;中央性。

cen·trif·u·gal 〔sɛn'trɪfjugl; sen'trifjugəl〕 *adj.* ①離心的。② 利用離心力的。—**ly,** *adv.*

centrifugal force 離心力。

centrifugal machine 離心分離機。

cen·trif·u·gate 〔sɛn'trɪfjə,get; sen'trifjugeit〕 *v.t.* 使離心;用離心力分離。—*n.* 由離心力分出之物。

cen·tri·fuge 〔'sɛntrə,fjudʒ; 'sentrəfjudʒ〕 *n., v.,* **-fuged, -fug·ing.** —*n.* 離心機。—*v.t.* 使離心;以離心機分離。

cen·trip·e·tal 〔sɛn'trɪpətl; sen'tripitl〕 *adj.* ①向心的。②利用向心力的。—**ly,** *adv.*

centripetal force 向心力。

cen·trist 〔'sɛntrɪst; 'sentrist〕 *n.* 在政治上走中間路線之人;中立派議員。—*adj.* (政治上)溫和派的;中間路線的。(亦作**Centrist**)

cen·troid 〔sɛn'trɔɪd; sen'trɔid〕 *n.* 〖物理〗①矩心。②質(量中)心。

cen·tro·some 〔'sɛntrə,som; 'sentrəsoum〕 *n.* 〖生物〗(細胞之)中心體;中央體。

cen·tro·sphere 〔'sɛntrə,sfɪr; 'sentrəsfiə] *n.* ①〖地質〗地球之中心。②〖生物〗中心球。

cen·trum [ˈsɛntrəm; ˈsentrəm] *n., pl.* **-trums, -tra** [-trə; -trə]. ①中心。②〖解剖〗椎體。③震源地。

cen·tu·ple [ˈsɛntupl; ˈsentjupl] *adj., v.,* **-pled, -pling.** —*adj.* 百倍的。—*v.t.* 使增加百倍;用百乘。

cen·tu·pli·cate [sɛnˈtjupləˌket; senˈtjuːplikeit] *v.,* **-cat·ed, -cat·ing,** *n., adj.* —*v.t.* ①以百乘之;使成百倍。②印一百分。—*n.* 百倍;百分。—*adj.* 百倍的;百分的。

cen·tu·ri·al [sɛnˈtjurɪəl; senˈtjuriəl] *adj.* 一世紀的。

cen·tu·ried [ˈsɛntʃərɪd; ˈsentʃərid] *adj.* ①維持了一百年或數百年的。②歷史悠久的。

cen·tu·ri·on [sɛnˈtjurɪən; senˈtjuəriən] *n.* 百人隊長;(古羅馬之)百夫長。

‡**cen·tu·ry** [ˈsɛntʃərɪ; ˈsentʃuri] *n., pl.* **-ries.** ①一百年;一世紀。in the latter part of the nineteenth *century.* 在十九世紀末葉。②一百個。—*adj.* =**centennial.**

ce·phal·ic [səˈfælɪk; keˈfælik] *adj.* ①頭(部)的。②向頭的;近頭的;在頭上的。

ceph·a·li·tis [ˌsɛfəˈlaɪtɪs; ˌsefəˈlaitis] *n.* 〖醫〗腦炎。(亦作 **encephalitis**)

ceph·a·lo·pod [ˈsɛfələˌpɑd; ˈsefəloupɔd] *n.* 頭足類動物。

ceph·a·lo·tho·rax [ˌsɛfələˈθoræks; ˌsefələˈθouræks] *n.* 〖動物〗(甲殼類之)頭胸部。

ce·ram·ic [səˈræmɪk; siˈræmik] *adj.* 陶器的;製陶的。—*n.* 陶器。

ceramic glaze 釉。

ce·ram·ics [səˈræmɪks; siˈræmiks] *n.* ①(作 *sing.* 解)陶器製造術;陶業。②(作 *pl.* 解)陶器。

ceramic tile 磁磚。

cer·a·mist [ˈsɛrəmɪst; ˈserəmist] *n.* 陶匠;陶工。

ce·rate [ˈsɪret; ˈsiərit] *n.* 〖藥〗蠟膏。—*adj.* =**cerated.**

ce·rat·ed [ˈsɪretɪd; ˈsiəreitid] *adj.* ①塗蠟的。②有蠟膜 (cere) 的。

Cer·ber·us [ˈsɝbərəs; ˈsəːbərəs] *n.* ①〖希臘、羅馬神話〗守衛冥府的三頭狗。②兇惡的看門人。③一種印度水蛇。***a sop to Cerberus*** 賄賂。

cere [sɪr; siə] *n., v.,* **cered, cer·ing.** —*n.* (鳥喙上之)蠟膜。—*v.t.* 裹以蠟布;以蠟封之。

***ce·re·al** [ˈsɪrɪəl; ˈsiəriəl] *n.* ①穀類。②穀實。③由穀類所做的食品。—*adj.* 穀類的。

cer·e·bel·lum [ˌsɛrəˈbɛləm; ˌseriˈbeləm] *n., pl.* **-lums, -la** [-lə; -lə]. 〖解剖〗小腦。

cer·e·bral [ˈsɛrəbrəl; ˈseribrəl] *adj.* ①〖解剖〗大腦的;腦的。②思慮深刻的;睿智的。③〖語音〗舌背音的。—*n.* 〖語音〗舌背子音。

cer·e·brate [ˈsɛrəˌbret; ˈseribreit] *v.i.,* **-brat·ed, -brat·ing.** 用腦;思考(尤指下意識的及機械的)。—**cer·e·bra·tion,** *n.*

cer·e·bro·spi·nal [ˌsɛrəbroˈspaɪnl; ˌserəbrouˈspainəl] *adj.* 〖解剖〗腦脊髓的。

cerebrospinal meningitis 腦脊髓膜炎。

cer·e·brot·o·my [ˌsɛrəˈbrɑtəmɪ; ˌserəˈbrɔtəmi] *n.* 〖醫〗腦切開術;剖腦術。

cer·e·brum [ˈsɛrəbrəm; ˈseribrəm] *n., pl.* **-brums, -bra** [-brə; -brə]. 〖解剖〗大腦。

cere·cloth [ˈsɪrˌklɔθ; ˈsiəklɔθ] *n.* ①蠟布;裹屍布。②教堂祭壇罩布下面的墊單。

cere·ment [ˈsɪrmənt; ˈsiəmənt] *n.* ①蠟布;裹屍布。②(常 *pl.*)壽衣。

cer·e·mo·ni·al [ˌsɛrəˈmonɪəl; ˌseriˈmounjəl] *adj.* ①儀式的;與禮儀有關的。②正式的;禮貌的。—*n.* 禮儀;儀式。—**ism,** —**ist,** —**ness,** *n.* —**ly,** *adv.*

cer·e·mo·ni·ous [ˌsɛrəˈmonɪəs; ˌseriˈmounjəs] *adj.* ①儀式的;正式的;隆重的。②講究儀式的。③恭敬的。—**ly,** *adv.* —**ness,** *n.*

cer·e·mo·ny** [ˈsɛrəˌmonɪ; ˈseriməni] *n., pl.* **-nies.** ①典禮;儀式。to fix a day for the *ceremony.* 擇日舉行儀式。②有禮貌的行爲。③虛禮;繁文縟節。④禮節。stand on ceremony*** 拘於禮節。Do not *stand on ceremony* with me. 不要與我拘禮節。

Ce·res [ˈsɪriz; ˈsiəriːz] *n.* 〖羅馬神話〗司穀類之女神。

ce·re·us [ˈsɪrɪəs; ˈsiəriəs] *n.* 〖植物〗仙人掌。

ce·ri·a [ˈsɪrɪə; ˈsiriə] *n.* 〖化〗鈰土;鈰氧(符號爲 CeO_2)。

cer·iph [ˈsɛrɪf; ˈserif] *n.* =**serif.**

ce·rise [səˈriz; səˈriːz] 〖法〗 *n., adj.* 鮮紅色(的);櫻桃色(的)。

ce·ri·um [ˈsɪrɪəm; ˈsiriəm] *n.* 〖化〗鈰(元素名,符號爲 Ce)。

cer·met [ˈsɝmɛt; ˈsəːmet] *n.* 一種由金屬與陶瓷混合而成的材料。

ce·ro·graph [ˈsɪrəˌgræf; ˈsiːrəgrɑːf] *n.* 蠟刻(畫或字)。

cer·o·plas·tic [ˌsɪroˈplæstɪk; ˌsiərouˈplæstik] *adj.* 蠟塑的。—*n.* (*pl.*) 蠟塑術。

cert [sɝt; səːt] *n.* 〖俚〗確實;確實之事。

cert. ① certainly. ② certificate. ③ certify.

‡**cer·tain** [ˈsɝtn̩; ˈsəːtn] *adj.* ①確實的;無疑的。He was *certain* he would succeed. 他確信他會成功。②確定的;一定的。at a *certain* hour. 在一定的時間。It is *certain* to happen. 這是一定要發生的。③可靠的。④某。to know a *certain* person. 認識某人。⑤不可避免的。⑥有相當程度的;不多亦不少的。of a *certain* age. 不太年輕,亦不太年老。***make certain*** 弄確實。—*n.* 僅見於下列成語中的習慣用法。***for certain*** 一定。I shall be there *for certain.* 我一定會在那兒的。—**ness,** *n.*

‡**cer·tain·ly** [ˈsɝtn̩lɪ; ˈsəːtnli] *adv.* 必然地;確然地;無疑地。*Certainly* our team will win the game. 我們的球隊將必然獲勝。—*interj.* 當然的。

***cer·tain·ty** [ˈsɝtn̩tɪ; ˈsəːtnti] *n., pl.* **-ties.** ①無疑;毫無疑問;確信。I lent him money with the *certainty* that he will return it in due time. 我借錢給他,相信他將按時還我。②免不了的事實;已成的事實。

cer·tes [ˈsɝtiz; ˈsəːtiz] *adv.* 〖古〗確然;當然。

certif. ①certificate. ②certificated.

cer·ti·fi·a·ble [ˈsɝtəˌfaɪəbl; ˈsəːtifaiəbl] *adj.* 可證明的;可確認的;可保證的。—**cer·ti·fi·a·bly,** *adv.*

***cer·tif·i·cate** [*n.* səˈtɪfəkɪt; səˈtifikit *v.* səˈtɪfəˌket; səˈtifikeit] *n., v.,* **-cat·ed, -cat·ing.** —*n.* 證書;憑照。a birth *certificate.* 出生證。—*v.t.* ①授證書予。a *certificated* teacher. 檢定合格教員。②以證書授權予。—**cer·ti·fi·ca·tion.** *n.*

certificate of deposit (銀行發出的)存款收據。

certificate of disability (軍方發的)殘廢證明書。

certificate of incorporation 公司合法組成證書。

certificate of origin (貨物等的)產地證明書。
cer·ti·fied ['sɝtəˌfaɪd; 'səːtifaid] *adj.* ①經證明的;有證明文件的。②保證的;立有證據的。③〖英〗經證明患精神病的。
certified check 保付支票。
certified milk 合格牛乳。
certified public accountant 〖美〗(有合格證件的)會計師。 「證明者。」
cer·ti·fi·er ['sɝtəˌfaɪɚ; 'səːtifaiə] *n.*
cer·ti·fy ['sɝtəˌfaɪ; 'səːtifai] *v.*, **-fied, -fy·ing.** —*v.t.* ①證明。②保證。③證明合格;授給執照。—*v.i.* 證明〖to〗;保證〖for〗。
cer·ti·o·rar·i [ˌsɝʃɪə'rɛrɪ; ˌsəːtiɔː'rɛərai] *n.* 〖法律〗法院案件移送之命令。
cer·ti·tude ['sɝtəˌtjud; 'səːtitjuːd] *n.* 確實之事;確實;確信。
ce·ru·le·an [sə'rulɪən; si'ruːliən] *adj.* 天青色的;蔚藍色的。 「〖解剖〗耳蠟;耳垢。」
ce·ru·men [sə'rumən; si'ruːmen] *n.*
ce·ruse ['sɪrus; 'siəruːs] 〖法〗 *n.* 鉛粉;白粉。 「'siərəsait] *n.* 〖礦〗白鉛礦。」
ce·ru·site, ce·rus·site ['sɪrəˌsaɪt;
Cer·van·tes Sa·a·ve·dra [sɚ'væntizˌsaɑ'veðrɑ; səː'væntizsaːaː'veiðraː] 塞凡帝斯 (Miguel de, 1547-1616, 西班牙小說家, *Don Quixote* 之作者)。
cer·vi·cal ['sɝvɪkḷ; 'səːvikəl] *adj.* 〖解剖〗頸的;子宮頸的。
cer·vi·ci·tis [ˌsɝvə'saɪtəs; ˌsəːvi'saitis] *n.* 〖醫〗子宮頸炎。
cer·vine ['sɝvaɪn; 'səːvain] *adj.* ①鹿的;如鹿的。②鹿毛色的;深黃褐色的。
cer·vix ['sɝvɪks; 'səːviks] 〖拉〗 *n.*, *pl.* **cer·vix·es, cer·vi·ces** [sə'vaɪsiz; səː'vaisiːz]. 〖解剖〗頸部;子宮頸。
ce·si·um ['sizɪəm; 'siːziəm] *n.* 〖化〗銫(元素名,符號爲 Cs)。(亦作 **caesium**)
cess [sɛs; ses] *n.* ①〖英方〗稅;稅率。②〖愛〗運氣(=luck). 「停止;中止;斷絕。」
ces·sa·tion [sɛ'seʃən; se'seiʃən] *n.*
ces·sion ['sɛʃən; 'seʃən] *n.* ①讓與;割讓;放棄。②讓與或割讓的東西(如領土)。③〖法律〗讓與(他人)債權。
ces·sion·ar·y ['sɛʃənˌɛrɪ; 'seʃənəri] *n.*, *pl.* **-ar·ies.** 〖法律〗受讓人。 「汚水坑。」
cess·pit ['sɛsˌpɪt; 'sespit] *n.* 垃圾坑;
cess·pool ['sɛsˌpul; 'sespuːl] *n.* 汚水池;汚水溝;化糞池;汚穢場所。(亦作**cesspit**)
ces·tode ['sɛstod; 'sestoud] *n.* 條蟲。—*adj.* 條蟲的。 「蟲的。—*n.* 條蟲。」
ces·toid ['sɛstɔɪd; 'sestɔid] *adj.* 似條
ces·tus ['sɛstəs; 'sestəs] *n.*, *pl.* **-tus.** 古羅馬拳擊者之手套。
ce·su·ra [sɪ'ʒurə; siː'zjurə] *n.* =**caesura.**
Ce·ta·ce·a [sɪ'teʃə; si'teiʃiə] *n.*, *pl.* 〖動物〗鯨類。
ce·ta·cean [sɪ'teʃən; si'teiʃiən] *adj.* 鯨類的;鯨的。—*n.* 鯨;鯨類動物。「鯨類的。」
ce·ta·ceous [sɪ'teʃəs; si'teiʃiəs] *adj.*
ce·te·ris pa·ri·bus ['sɛtərɪs'pærɪbəs; 'setəris'pæribəs] 〖拉〗其他情形相同;別無其他情形(=other things being equal).
Ce·tus ['sitəs; 'siːtəs] *n.* 〖天文〗鯨魚座。
ce·vi·tam·ic acid [ˌsivaɪ'tæmɪk~; ˌsiːvai'tæmik~] 維他命 C;丙種維他命。
Cé·zanne [se'zan; sei'zan] *n.* 塞尙 (Paul, 1839-1906, 法國畫家)。
Cf 化學元素 californium 之符號。 **cf.** compare. 比較(爲拉丁文 confer 之縮寫)。
cf. center field. **c/f, CF** 〖簿記〗carried forward. **c.f.i., C.F.I.** cost, freight, and insurance.
C flat 〖音樂〗降C調。*C flat* major. 降 C 大調。*C flat* minor. 降C小調。
C.G. ①Captain General. ②coast guard. ③combat group. ④commanding general. ⑤comptroller general. ⑥consul general. **C.G.H.** Cape of Good Hope. **C.G.M.** Conspicuous Gallantry Medal. **cgs, c.g.s., C.G.S.** ①centimeter-gram-second (system). ②chief of general staff. **C.H.** ①clearing house. ②Companion of Honor. ③Custom House. **ch., Ch.** ①chapter. ②chief. ③church. ④check. **c.h.** ①candle hours. ②clearing house. ③courthouse. ④custom house.
Cha·blis ['ʃæbli; 'ʃæbliː] *n. sing.* or *pl.* ①(法國產之)一種白葡萄酒。②他處所產之類似的白葡萄酒。
cha·b(o)uk ['tʃɑbuk; 'tʃɑːbuk] *n.* 馬鞭(特指鞭打犯人之長鞭)。
cha-cha(-cha) ['tʃɑ'tʃɑ('tʃɑ); 'tʃɑː'tʃɑː('tʃɑː)] *n.* 恰恰舞。
cha·conne [ʃæ'kɔn; ʃə'kɔn] *n.* ①夏康舞。②〖音樂〗夏康舞曲。
Chad [tʃæd; tʃæd] *n.* 查德 (非洲之一共和國, 首都恩賈納 N'Djaména).
chafe [tʃef; tʃeif] *v.*, **chafed, chaf·ing,** *n.* —*v.t.* ①擦熱;擦傷;擦痛。②激怒;煩擾。③磨擦;磨損。—*v.i.* ①擦。②發怒。③猛衝;顚簸。***chafe at*** 向…生氣。***chafe under*** 爲…生氣;發躁。—*n.* ①擦熱;擦傷;擦痛。②激怒;煩擾。③馬鞍環皮套。
chaf·er ['tʃefɚ; 'tʃeifə] *n.* ①發怒者。②擦傷之人或物。③小火爐;火鍋。
chaff [tʃæf; tʃɑːf] *n.* ①穀實之皮殼;糠。②切短之草(用作飼料);草料。③廢物;瑣屑之物。④惡作劇。⑤飛機投下之金屬碎箔(用以擾亂敵方雷達偵察者)。***be caught with chaff*** 容易上當。***chaff and dust*** 廢物。—*v.t.* & *v.i.* 愚弄;戲弄;開玩笑。 「笑者;嘲笑者。」
chaf·fer[1] ['tʃæfɚ; 'tʃæfə] *n.* 〖俗〗開玩
chaf·fer[2] *n.* ①講價。②吹毛求疵;錙銖計較。—*v.i.* ①討價還價;斤斤計較。②吵嚷;喋喋不休。—*v.t.* ①(口角時)互交(惡言)。②吵吵鬧鬧地打發掉。 **—er,** *n.*
chaf·finch ['tʃæˌfɪntʃ; 'tʃæfintʃ] *n.* 鶸類(鳴鳥,產於歐洲)。
chaff·y ['tʃæfɪ; 'tʃɑːfi] *adj.*, **chaff·i·er, chaff·i·est.** ①多糠的;如糠的。②無用的。③輕如糠的;無實體的;空的。「擦傷而)發炎。」
chaf·ing ['tʃefɪŋ; 'tʃeifiŋ] *n.* 皮膚(因
chafing dish ①火鍋。②保暖鍋。
cha·grin [ʃə'grɪn; 'ʃægrin] *n.* 煩悶;懊惱。***to one's chagrin*** 懊惱的是。—*v.t.* 使煩悶或懊惱。
Cha·har ['tʃɑ'hɑr; 'tʃɑː'hɑː] *n.* 察哈爾省(中國之一省,省會爲張垣市 Wanchuan 或張家口 Changchiakow).
:chain [tʃen; tʃein] *n.* ①鏈。②連續的事物。a mountain *chain.* 山系。a *chain* of misfortunes. 一連串的災禍。③(*pl.*)脚鏈;桎梏;監禁。The prisoners are in *chains.* 囚犯上了鐐銬。④測量用的測鏈。⑤同元素中如鏈鎖般結合在一起之原子。⑥屬於同一所有者而性質相同的機構。He owned a hotel *chain.* 他擁有多家旅館。—*v.t.* ①以鏈繫之;用鏈鎖之。②束縛。 He is *chained* to his

work. 他被束於工作中。③禁錮;奴役。④用皮尺測量地面距離。—*v.i.* 做成鏈條。—*adj.* ①連續發生的。②連串累積的;越來越…的。

chain·belt [ˋtʃen,bɛlt; ˈtʃeinbelt] *n.* 用金屬圈互相環扣之腰帶。

chain·bridge [ˋtʃenˋbrɪdʒ; ˈtʃeinˈbridʒ] *n.* 鏈吊橋。

chain cable 錨鏈。

chai·né [ʃɛˋne; ˈʃenei] 〖法〗*n.* (芭蕾舞)連續的旋轉成一直線通過舞臺。

chain gang 用鐵鏈鎖住之一羣囚犯。

chain·less [ˋtʃenlɪs; ˈtʃeinlis] *adj.* 無拘束的;自由自在的。

chain·let [ˋtʃenlɪt; ˈtʃeinlit] *n.* 小鏈。

chain letter 連鎖書信(受信人須轉致他人者)。

chain lightning 〖美〗鍊狀閃電(迅速而成的"之"字形閃電)。

chain locker ①錨鏈庫。②〖美俗〗碼頭附近便宜酒店。

chain mail 鐵環串連做成的盔甲。

chain·man [ˋtʃenmən; ˈtʃeinmən] *n., pl.* **-men.** 測量時拿皮尺或捲尺的人。

chain molding 〖建築〗鏈狀之花邊。

chain of command 有直接隸屬關係之軍事或行政機關。

chain plate 〖航海〗固定船體支桅索的金屬板。

chain pump 鏈唧筒。(亦作 **chain lift**)

chain-re·act·ing [ˋtʃenrɪ,æktɪŋ; ˈtʃeinriˈæktiŋ] *adj.* 〖物理〗可產生連鎖反應的。

chain reaction ①〖物理〗連鎖反應。②類似連鎖反應之現象。

chain reactor 〖物理〗反應爐。

chain saw 小型機器鋸。

chain shot (昔海戰用)鏈鎖彈。

chain-smoke [ˋtʃen,smok; ˈtʃeinsmouk] *v.i.* 連續不斷地吸煙。

chain smoker 連續不斷吸煙之人。

chain stitch 鏈狀之針脚;鏈縫。

chain-stitch [ˋtʃen,stɪtʃ; ˈtʃeinstitʃ] *v.t.* & *v.i.* 用鏈狀針脚縫。

chain store 聯號(一公司所經營管理的許多商號之一)。

chain wheel (脚踏車等的)飛輪。

‡chair [tʃɛr; tʃɛə] *n.* ①椅子。a rocking *chair.* 搖椅。Won't you take a *chair?* 你不坐嗎?(=請坐)。②職位;地位。③(會議)主席。The speaker addressed the *chair.* 發言者對主席說話。④轎子。⑤電椅。⑥ **a.** 鐵軌支持物。 **b.** 牆上凹鐵座。 **c.** 鋼骨的支持物。***get the chair*** 〖美俗〗被判坐電椅的死刑。***take the chair*** **a.** 會議開始。**b.**主持會議。—*v.t.*①置於椅上;坐於椅中;以轎子抬。②使就…職位。③任…之主席。

chair bed 可作牀鋪用的摺椅。

chair car 有可調整座椅之火車車廂。

chair lift (裝於轉運帶上之)升降椅。

***chair·man** [ˋtʃɛrmən; ˈtʃɛəmən] *n., pl.* **-men.** *v.,* **-man(n)ed, -man·(n)ing.** —*n.* ①開會時的主席。②會長;議長;社長;委員長;董事長。He was *chairman* of the board of directors. 他是董事會的董事長。—*v.t.* 任…之主席。—**ship,** *n.*

chair·per·son [ˋtʃɛr,pɜsn; ˈtʃɛəpə:sn] *n.* 〖美〗主席(男女通用)。

chair·warm·er [ˋtʃɛr,wɔrmɚ; ˈtʃɛə,wɔ:mə] *n.* 〖俗〗①長坐在旅館門廳中休息的人(非付錢的客人)。②懶得做事的人。

chair·wom·an [ˋtʃɛr,wumən; ˈtʃɛə,wumən] *n., pl.* **-wom·en.** chairman 之女性。〖注意〗**chairman** 作"會議或委員會的主席"解時,兩性均可用。男性稱呼 Mr. Chairman, 女性稱呼 Madame Chairman.

chaise [ʃez; ʃeiz] *n.* 一種輕便馬車。

chaise longue 躺椅。(亦作 **chaise lounge**)

chal·ced·o·ny [kælˋsɛdnɪ; kælˈsedəni] *n., pl.* **-nies.** 〖礦〗石髓。

chal·cid [ˋkælsɪd; ˈkælsid] *n.* 小蜂科之昆蟲。(亦作**chalcid fly**)

chal·co·cite [ˋkælkə,saɪt; ˈkælkəsait] *n.* 〖礦〗輝銅礦。

chal·cog·ra·phy [kælˋkɑgrəfɪ; kælˈkɔgrəfi] *n.* 雕銅術;銅版雕刻術。

chal·co·py·rite [,kælkəˋpaɪraɪt; ,kælkəˈpaiərait] *n.* 〖礦〗黃銅礦。

Chal·de·a [kælˋdiə; kælˈdi:ə] *n.* 迦勒底(位於波斯灣西北,爲古巴比倫南部一地區)。

Chal·de·an [kælˋdiən; kælˈdi:ən] *adj.* ① Chaldea 的;其人民、語言、或文化的。②有關占星術或魔術的。—*n.* ①Chaldea 人;居於 Chaldea 之閃族人。②占星家;預言家;卜者;巫。③Chaldea 人所用之閃族語。(亦作 **Chaldaic, Chaldee**)

chal·dron [ˋtʃɔldrən; ˈtʃɔ:ldrən] *n.* 一種乾物量度單位(約略等於 32或36 bushels).

cha·let [ʃæˋle; ˈʃælei] *n.* ①瑞士山中牧人所居之小屋;農舍。②簷低簷濶的瑞士小屋。③瑞士農舍式的小屋。

chal·ice [ˋtʃælɪs; ˈtʃælis] *n.* ①〖宗教〗聖餐杯。②杯;高脚酒杯。③〖植物〗杯狀花。

chal·iced [ˋtʃælɪst; ˈtʃælist] *adj.* 〖植物〗有杯狀花的。

‡chalk [tʃɔk; tʃɔ:k] *n.* ①白堊。②粉筆。a piece of *chalk.* 一支粉筆。③粉筆做的記號。④記分;記錄。***by a long chalk*** 極大程度的差別。—*v.t.* ①用粉筆寫。②和以白堊。③記錄。④使變白;漂白。—*v.i.* (油漆等)因時間過久而成粉狀。 ***chalk one up*** 獲得一項好處;得到一項便宜。***chalk out*** **a.** 標出。**b.** 計劃。***chalk up*** **a.** 記下。**b.** 歸咎於。**c.** 得分。—*adj.* 白堊的;粉筆的。*chalk* drawing. 粉筆畫。

chalk·board [ˋtʃɔk,bɔrd; ˈtʃɔ:kbɔ:d] *n.* 黑板;粉板。

chalk line ①白粉筆畫的線。②擦有粉筆灰的細繩。③用上述細繩做下的直線記號。***walk the chalk line*** **a.** 保持直線。**b.** 遵守嚴格紀律;循規蹈矩。

chalk·stone [ˋtʃɔk,ston; ˈtʃɔ:k-stoun] *n.* ①白堊之團塊。②〖醫〗堊石;痛風石。

chalk·y [ˋtʃɔkɪ; ˈtʃɔ:ki] *adj.,* **chalk·i·er, chalk·i·est.** ①白堊的; 含白堊的。②質地或顏色像白堊的。

***chal·lenge** [ˋtʃælɪndʒ; ˈtʃælindʒ] *v.,* **-lenged, -leng·ing,** *n.* —*v.t.* ①向…挑戰。to *challenge* a person to a duel. 向人挑戰決鬥。②邀請比賽。They *challenge* us to a swimming contest. 他們邀請我們作游泳比賽。③盤問。④懷疑;否認;詰難。⑤反對(對陪審員及投票等)。⑥需要。⑦宣稱(選票)無效;宣稱(投票人)無資格投票。—*v.i.* ①挑戰。②〖法律〗反對。③(獵犬發現獵物時)吠。—*n.* ①挑戰。 to give a *challenge.* 挑戰。to accept a *challenge.* 接受挑戰; 應戰。②邀請比賽。③盤問。④(對陪審員或投票等之)反對。⑤需要。⑥〖美〗聲稱選票無效或某人無資格投票之宣稱。⑦刺激人去努力克服的困難工作。⑧獵犬嗅得獵物時所發之吠聲。 **—a·ble,** *adj.* **—chal·leng·er,** *n.*

chal·leng·ing [ˋtʃælɪndʒɪŋ; ˈtʃælindʒiŋ] *adj.*①引起競爭性興趣的。②挑撥的;煽動的。 **—ly,** *adv.*

chal·lis, chal·lie [ˈʃælɪ; ˈʃælis, ˈʃæli] *n.* 印花之輕質毛料;印花絲毛料。

cha·lyb·e·ate [kəˈlɪbɪɪt; kəˈlibiit] *adj.* ①(泉水等)含鐵鹽的。②似鐵味的。—*n.* 含鐵鹽之水或藥水。

:cham·ber [ˈtʃembə; ˈtʃeimbə] *n.* ①房間;室。②臥房;寢室。a bridal *chamber.* 新房;洞房。③立法或司法機關之議事廳。the Senate *chamber.* 參議院的議事廳。④立法或司法的團體。the upper *chamber.* 上議院。⑤自由職業所組織的團體。a *chamber* of commerce. 商會。⑥鎗膛。⑦(動植物體中之)窩;穴。⑧(*pl.*)〖英〗套房。⑨(*pl.*)律師或法官的辦公室。⑩有特種用途的房間或隔間。—*v.t.* ①裝以鎗膛。②放在鎗膛內。③可以放入鎗膛。④放於室內或好似放在室內。—*adj.* ①祕密的。②〖音樂〗在小廳表演的,多爲由數人之小樂隊演奏的。

chamber concert 室內樂演奏會。

chamber council 祕密會議。

chamber counsel 〖英〗私人之法律顧問(不出庭的律師)。

cham·bered [ˈtʃembəd; ˈtʃeimbəd] *adj.* 有小室的;分成許多間隔的。

chamb·er·er [ˈtʃembərə; ˈtʃeimbərə] *n.* ① =**chambermaid.** ②常與女人廝混者。

Cham·ber·lain[1] [ˈtʃembəlɪn; ˈtʃeimbəlin] *n.* 張伯倫 (Neville, 1869–1940, 英國首相, 以與 Hitler 簽訂慕尼黑協定而著名)。

Cham·ber·lain[2] *n.* 張伯倫 (Sir Joseph Austen, 1863–1937, 英國政治家, 曾獲1925 年諾貝爾和平獎)。

cham·ber·lain** [ˈtʃembəlɪn; ˈtʃeimbəlin] *n.* ①國王之侍從;內臣;御前大臣。②貴族的管家。③會計員;收款員。Lord Chamberlain*** 侍從長。***Lord Great Chamberlain (of England)*** 英國之掌禮大臣。

cham·ber·maid [ˈtʃembəˌmed; ˈtʃeimbəmeid] *n.* (旅館等中)房間之女侍。

chamber music 〖音樂〗室內樂。

chamber of commerce 商會。

chamber opera 小型歌劇。

chamber orchestra 〖音樂〗室內樂隊;廳堂樂隊。

chamber pot 尿壺;夜壺。

cham·bray [ˈʃæmbre; ˈʃæmbrei] *n.* 一種柳條細布;條紋布。

cha·me·le·on [kəˈmilɪən; kəˈmiːljən] *n.* ①〖動物〗變色蜥蜴。②善變的人;反覆無常的人。—**ic,** *adj.*

cham·fer [ˈtʃæmfə; ˈtʃæmfə] *n.* ①槽;凹線。②斜面;切面。—*v.t.* ①在…上刻槽或凹線。②斜切;去角。

cham·ois [ˈʃæmɪ; ˈʃæmwɑː] *n., pl.* **-ois.** ①歐洲與亞洲西南部高山上之一種小羚羊。②用羊皮或鹿皮等製成之小軟皮。(亦作 **chammy, shammy**)

cham·o·mile [ˈkæməˌmaɪl; ˈkæməmail] *n.* =**camomile.**

champ[1] [tʃæmp; tʃæmp] *v.t.* ①大聲地嚼。②重嚙。—*v.i.* ①(興奮得)牙齒顫得響。②(怒得)咬牙切齒。***champ at the bit*** 顯得不耐煩。—*n.* 咀嚼有聲;重嚙。

champ[2] *n.* 〖俗〗=**champion.**

cham·pac [ˈtʃæmpæk; ˈtʃæmpæk] *n.* 〖植物〗金香木(產於東印度)。(亦作**champak**)

cham·pagne [ʃæmˈpen; ʃæmˈpein] *n.* ①香檳酒。②(C-) 香檳 (法國之一省)。

cham·paign [ʃæmˈpen; ˈtʃæmpein] *n.* ①曠野。②〖古〗戰場。—*adj.* 平坦而空曠的。

cham·per·ty [ˈtʃæmpətɪ; ˈtʃæmpəti] *n., pl.* **-ties.** 〖法律〗助訟罪(助人訴訟, 而言明於勝訴時, 分得其利益者)。

cham·pi·gnon [ʃæmˈpɪnjən; tʃæmˈpinjən] *n.* 〖植物〗香蕈。

***cham·pi·on** [ˈtʃæmpɪən; ˈtʃæmpjən] *n.* ①奪得錦標者; 冠軍。the swimming *champion* of the world. 世界游泳冠軍。②爲人或主義而奮鬥者;擁護者。a great *champion* of peace. 偉大的和平鬥士。③勇士;鬥士;戰士。④互爭長短之物。—*adj.* ①優勝的;冠軍的。a *champion* team. 冠軍隊。②〖俗〗第一流的。—*v.t.* 守衛;擁護。—**ship,** *n.*

Chanc. ①Chancellor. ②Chancery.

:chance [tʃæns; tʃɑːns] *n., v.,* **chanced, chanc·ing,** *adj.* —*n.* ①機會。He has a *chance* to go to college. 他有機會上大學。Let us leave it to *chance.* 讓其聽憑自然吧。②可能。The *chances* are two to one against us. 我們得勝的機會爲二對一(三分之一的機會)。③或然。④命運;幸運;僥倖。⑤冒險。We will take the *chances.* 我們要冒險爲之。⑥偶然事件的發生; 機緣。***by chance*** 偶然地。***on the chance*** 如果;指望。***on the off chance*** 極微的指望;萬一。***stand a chance*** 有希望。***take one's chance*** 成敗唯憑機會。***the chances are that*** 很可能。***the main chance*** 財富。—*v.i.* ①偶然發生。I *chanced* to be there. 我偶然在那裡。It *chanced* that I was out when he called. 他來訪時我恰好出去了。②不期而遇〖on, upon〗. We *chanced* upon a drunkard. 我們無意中遇一醉漢。—*v.t.* 冒險。—*adj.* 偶然的。a *chance* meeting. 偶然的相遇。—**ful,** *adj.*

chan·cel [ˈtʃænsl; ˈtʃɑːnsəl] *n.* 教堂內環繞聖壇的高壇;聖壇所。

chan·cel·ler·y [ˈtʃænsələrɪ; ˈtʃɑːnsələri] *n., pl.* **-ler·ies.** ①chancellor 之職位。②chancellor 之辦公處。③大使館、領事館等之辦公處。

chan·cel·lor [ˈtʃænsələ; ˈtʃɑːnsələ] *n.* ①貴族、大使館或國王的祕書;大臣。②〖美〗法院的首席法官。③(某些大學的)大學校長。—**ship,** *n.*

chance-med·ley [ˈtʃænsˌmɛdlɪ; ˈtʃɑːnsˌmedli] *n.* 〖法律〗過失傷害或殺人;因自衛而傷害或殺人。

chan·cer·y [ˈtʃænsərɪ; ˈtʃɑːnsəri] *n., pl.* **-cer·ies.** ①〖英〗大法官的法庭。②〖美〗衡平法院;記錄所。***a ward in chancery*** 受大法官監護中的未成年人。***in chancery*** **a.** 大法官支配下的。**b.** 向衡平法院控訴中的。**c.**〖拳擊, 摔角〗頭被對方挾在臂與身體之間。**d.** 無助的狀態。

chan·cre [ˈʃæŋkə; ˈʃæŋkə] *n.* 〖醫〗下疳。

chan·croid [ˈʃæŋkrɔɪd; ˈʃæŋkrɔid] *n.* 〖醫〗軟下疳。

chanc·y [ˈtʃænsɪ; ˈtʃɑːnsi] *adj.,* **chanc·i·er, chanc·i·est.** ①〖俗〗危險的。②靠不住的。

***chan·de·lier** [ˌʃændlˈɪr; ˌʃændiˈliə] *n.* 枝形吊燈。

chan·dler [ˈtʃændlə; ˈtʃɑːndlə] *n.* ①雜貨零售商。②蠟燭製造者;蠟燭商。

chan·dler·y [ˈtʃændlərɪ; ˈtʃɑːndləri] *n., pl.* **-dler·ies.** ①雜貨;雜貨店。②蠟燭及其他雜貨之倉庫或貯存室。

:change [tʃendʒ; tʃeindʒ] *v.,* **changed, chang·ing,** *n.* —*v.t.* ①變更;使改變。②替換;更換。③交換。Shall we *change* seats? 我們要不要交換座位? ④兌換。to *change* a

Chinese dollar into francs. 將中國的一元換爲法郎。⑤換罩蓋之物。to *change* a bed. 換被單。⑥變成〖into〗. The witch *changed* the boy into a dog. 巫婆將那男孩變成一隻狗。—*v.i.* ①變更;改變;變化。②更換;交換。A five-dollar bill *changes* into five one-dollar bills. 一張五元鈔票換爲五張一元鈔票。③換火車或其他交通工具。④換衣服。***change color*** 變色 (指感情衝動時臉變色)。***change hands*** 易手(一人給予他人)。***change one's mind*** 改變計畫;改變主意。***change over***(使)改變;轉換;更迭。***change trains*** 換(火)車。—*n.* ①變更。a sudden *change* in the weather.天氣驟變。*change* of policy. 政策的改變。You need a *change*. 你需要調節一下(生活)。②轉變;變化。③找回的餘錢。④小幣;零錢。I want some *change*. 我要些零錢。⑤(*pl.*)一組鐘可鳴奏的順序。⑥交換所。***ring the changes*** **a.** 以不同順序奏一組鐘。**b.** 以不同方法做事或說明。

change·a·bil·i·ty 〔ˌtʃendʒəˈbɪlətɪ; ˌtʃeindʒəˈbiliti〕 *n.* 可變性;易變性。

change·a·ble 〔ˈtʃendʒəbl̩; ˈtʃeindʒəbl〕 *adj.* ①可換的;可改變的。②變色的;變形的。③易變的。—**ness,** *n.* —**change·a·bly,** *adv.*

change·ful 〔ˈtʃendʒfəl; ˈtʃeindʒful〕 *adj.* ①變化多的;易變的。②不固定的;不穩的。—**ly,** *adv.*

change·less 〔ˈtʃendʒlɪs; ˈtʃeindʒlis〕 *adj.* 不變的;確定的。—**ly,** *adv.* —**ness,** *n.*

change·ling 〔ˈtʃendʒlɪŋ; ˈtʃeindʒliŋ〕 *n.* ①〖古〗難看、愚蠢或壞脾氣的孩子(迷信謂神仙刼走漂亮小孩後所留下的小孩)。②〖集郵〗顏色起化學變化之郵票。

change·mak·er 〔ˈtʃendʒˌmekɚ; ˈtʃeindʒˌmeikə〕 *n.* 換零錢機。

change of pace ①改變某人之習慣、興趣等;換口味。②〖棒球〗投手似將投快球,但實際上球速較慢而使打者難判斷球速。(亦作 **change-up**)

change·o·ver 〔ˈtʃendʒˌovɚ; ˈtʃeindʒˌouvə〕 *n.* ①(生產方法、裝備等之)完全改變。②(方針之)轉變。③(內閣之)更迭。④(形勢之)逆轉。

chang·er 〔ˈtʃendʒɚ; ˈtʃeindʒə〕 *n.*①改變他物之人或物。②電唱機上之自動換片機。

change·room 〔ˈtʃendʒˌrum; ˈtʃeindʒruːm〕 *n.* 更衣室。

***chan·nel** 〔ˈtʃænl̩; ˈtʃænl〕 *n., v.,* **-nel(l)ed, -nel·(l)ing.**—*n.*①河床。②海峽;海峇。He crossed the English *Channel*. 他渡過英吉利海峽。③水道之較深處。④溝;槽。⑤途徑;所經的路線;方面。⑥(無線電或電視中)較窄之波段;頻道。—*v.t.*①形成溝渠;鑿渠。②引導。—*v.i.*①在溝、槽中流動或好似在溝、槽中流動。②形成或刻出凹槽。

chan·nel·ize 〔ˈtʃænl̩ˌaɪz; ˈtʃænəlaiz〕 *v.t.* ①使形成溝渠。②引導。

chan·son 〔ˈʃænsən; ˈʃænsən〕〖法〗「*n.* 歌。」

chant 〔tʃænt; tʃɑːnt〕 *n.* ①歌;曲;旋律。②單調之歌。③聖歌;讚美詩。④似歌唱般的說話。—*v.i.* ①唱歌。②單調地說話。—*v.t.* ①唱。②歌頌。③單調地說。***chant the praises of*** 稱道不絕;頌揚。—**a·ble,** *adj.*

chan·tage 〔ˈtʃæntɪdʒ; ˈtʃæntidʒ〕〖法〗 *n.* 〖法律〗勒索;訛詐。

chant·er 〔ˈtʃæntɚ; ˈtʃɑːntə〕 *n.* ①歌唱者;吟誦者。②(教堂唱詩班之)領唱者。③(小教堂之)牧師。④蘇格蘭風笛之指管。

chan·te·relle 〔ˌtʃæntəˈrɛl; ˌtʃæntəˈrel〕 *n.* ①一種食用野香菇。②〖法〗小提琴之E絃,或任何絃樂器之高音琴絃。

chan·teuse 〔ʃɑ̃ˈtœz; ʃɑːˈtœz〕〖法〗 *n.* (夜總會之)歌女(爲 chanteur 之女性)。

chant·ey 〔ˈʃæntɪ; ˈtʃɑːnti〕 *n., pl.* **-eys.** 船夫曲;水手歌。(亦作 **chanty, shanty**)

chan·ti·cleer 〔ˈtʃæntɪˌklɪr; ˌtʃæntiˈkliə〕 *n.* 公鷄。

chant·ress 〔ˈtʃæntrɪs; ˈtʃɑːntris〕 *n.* 「女歌手;歌女。」

chan·try 〔ˈtʃæntrɪ; ˈtʃɑːntri〕 *n., pl.* **-tries.** ①爲某人作追思彌撒之奉獻(捐獻)。②(爲某人作追思彌撒所奉獻之)附屬禮拜堂。

chant·y 〔ˈʃæntɪ; ˈtʃɑːnti〕 *n., pl.* **-ties.** =**chantey.**

***cha·os** 〔ˈkeɑs; ˈkeiɔs〕 *n.* ①紛亂;混亂。The typhoon left *chaos* behind it. 颱風過後一片混亂。②混沌狀態(宇宙未成前之情形)。

cha·ot·ic 〔keˈɑtɪk; keiˈɔtik〕 *adj.* 混亂的;雜亂無章的。—**al·ly,** *adv.*

***chap**[1] 〔tʃæp; tʃæp〕 *v.,* **chapped, chap·ping,** *n.* —*v.t.* ①使(皮膚)皺裂粗糙及發痛。Cold weather *chaps* his skin. 冷天痛裂了他的皮膚。②使(土木等)裂開。—*v.i.* 變爲粗糙;裂開。—*n.* 皮膚皺裂處。

***chap**[2] *n.*①〖俗〗伙伴;傢伙;小伙子。Hullo! old *chap!* 喂! 老兄! ②〖方〗購買者;顧客。

chap[3] *n.* (常*pl.*)①顎。②頰。***lick one's chaps*** 見美味而垂涎。

chap. ①chapter. ②chaplain. ③chapel.

cha·pa·ra·jos, cha·pa·re·jos 〔ˌtʃɑpɑˈrɑhos; ˌtʃɑːpɑːˈrɑːhous〕 *n. pl.*美國牛仔所穿着的寬鬆皮套褲。(略作 **chaps**)

chap·ar·ral 〔ˌtʃæpəˈræl; ˌtʃæpəˈræl〕 *n.* 〖美〗①矮橡林。②荊棘叢;矮叢。

chap·book 〔ˈtʃæpˌbʊk; ˈtʃæpbuk〕*n.* 小本之詩歌集或故事書;廉價小册子。

chape 〔tʃep; tʃeip〕 *n.* ①釦鉤。②鞘端包被之金屬片。

cha·peau 〔ʃæˈpo; ʃæˈpou〕 *n., pl.* **-peaux, -peaus** 〔-poz; -pouz〕.〖法〗帽。

***chap·el** 〔ˈtʃæpl̩; ˈtʃæpəl〕 *n.* ①小禮拜堂。②在大建築物內的禮拜堂。③(學校、王宮等內之)禮拜堂。④小禮拜堂中之禮拜。⑤〖英〗(國教以外的)禮拜堂。⑥殯儀館。

chapel of ease 爲遠地教友之方便而設的附屬教堂。

chap·er·on, chap·er·one 〔ˈʃæpəˌron; ˈʃæpəroun〕 *n.* (陪少女上交際場所的)女伴;陪媼。—*v.t.* 陪隨;伴護。—**chap·er·on·age,** *n.*

chap·fall·en 〔ˈtʃæpˌfɔlən; ˈtʃæpˌfɔːlən〕 *adj.* ①下顎或頰骨下陷的。②憂鬱的;沮喪的。(亦作 **chopfallen**)

chap·i·ter 〔ˈtʃæpɪtɚ; ˈtʃæpitə〕 *n.* 〖建〗「築」柱頭。」

***chap·lain** 〔ˈtʃæplɪn; ˈtʃæplin〕 *n.* (私人、社團、醫院、監獄、貴族私人教堂、軍中等之)牧師。—**cy,** —**ship,** —**ry,** *n.*

chap·let 〔ˈtʃæplɪt; ˈtʃæplit〕 *n.* ①戴在頭上之花圈。②串珠。③祈禱時所用之唸珠。④一串(珠形的)。

chap·let·ed 〔ˈtʃæplɪtɪd; ˈtʃæplitid〕 「*adj.* 頭上戴着花圈的。」

Chap·lin 〔ˈtʃæplɪn; ˈtʃæplin〕 *n.* 卓別林(Charles S., 1889–1977, 英國諷刺滑稽劇及電影演員、導演、及製片家)。

Chap·lin·esque 〔ˌtʃæplɪnˈɛsk; ˌtʃæpliˈnesk〕*adj.*卓別林式的,尤指像卓別林主演的一個好心而笨拙又喜裝紳士儀態的窮浪人的。

chap·man 〔ˈtʃæpmən; ˈtʃæpmən〕 *n., pl.* **-men.** ①〖英〗小販。②〖古〗商人。

chap·pie, chap·py[1] 〔ˈtʃæpɪ; ˈtʃæpi〕

n., *pl.* **-pies.** ①伙伴。②花花公子。

chap·py² *adj.* 皮膚乾裂的。

:chap·ter [ˈtʃæptɚ; ˈtʃæptə] *n.* ①章；篇。The book consists of ten *chapters.* 此書分爲十章。②部分。③分會；支會；分社。④教士團體。⑤教士團體之會議。⑥鐘錶上表示小時的數目字。***a chapter of accidents*** 接踵而來之意外事件。—*v.t.* 分章。

chapter and verse ①詳細地引經據典。②〖俚〗規程；規章。③詳盡消息；詳細資料或情節。

chapter head 每章正文前之標題、目次、及引用的摘錄等之集合稱。

chapter house ①牧師會之場所或會堂。②〖美〗大學兄弟會或姐妹會集會所。

char¹ [tʃɑr; tʃɑ:]*v.*, **charred, char·ring,** *n.* —*v.t.* & *v.i.*①燒成炭。②燒焦。—*n.* ①燒焦之物。②木炭；骨炭。

char² *n.*, *v.*, **charred, char·ring.** —*n.* ①〖英〗charwoman 之簡稱。②打掃公共場所的工作。—*v.t.* & *v.i.* 做零工；打雜。

char³ *n.* 〖英俗〗茶。

char⁴, charr *n.* 鮭類。

char-à-banc [ˈʃærəˌbæŋk; ˈʃærəbæŋ] *n.*, *pl.* **-bancs.** 長形之遊覽車。

:char·ac·ter [ˈkærɪktɚ, -ək-; ˈkærik-tə, -rək-] *n.* ①品質；性質。②德性；品性；人格。He's a man of fine *character.* 他是個品性良好的人。③名譽；地位。④特徵（人或物）；特性。⑤劇中或書中的人物；角色。a *character* in Shakespeare's comedy. 莎士比亞喜劇中的人物。⑥堅强意志；自制。⑦位置；情形。⑧因與衆不同或滑稽而引人注意的人。He is a *character.* 他是一個引人注意的人物。⑨文字；記號。Chinese *characters.* 中國字。⑩人物。⑪品行或服務證明書。⑫人物或性格的描述。He gave the police a *character* of the thief. 他向警察將這賊描述了一番。***in character*** 如所期望（的）地；合適（的）地。***out of character*** 不如所期望（的）地；不合適（的）地。—*adj.* ①（劇中角色）表現或描寫某種個性的。②（演員）表演或擅於表演上述角色的。

character actor 性格男演員。

character actress 性格女演員。

character assassination 毀謗名譽。

char·ac·ter·ful[ˈkærɪktɚfəl;ˈkærik-təfəl] *adj.* ①表現性格的。②有特殊風格的。

***char·ac·ter·is·tic** [ˌkærɪktəˈrɪstɪk; ˌkæriktəˈristik] *adj.* 本性的；特性的；特有的。It's *characteristic* of him. 那是他的特性。—*n.*①特性；特徵。They have one *characteristic* in common. 他們有一共同的特徵。②（數學中對數之）首數（如在對數 2.95424 中，2 是首數，.95424 是尾數）。—**al·ly,** *adv.*

char·ac·ter·i·za·tion [ˌkærɪktərə-ˈzeʃən; ˌkæriktəraiˈzeiʃən] *n.* ①描述。②（在劇本或書籍中）人物之創造。③演員對其所飾演人物個性之表演。（英亦作 **character-isation**）

***char·ac·ter·ize** [ˈkærɪktəˌraɪz; ˈkæ-riktəraiz, -rək-] *v.t.*, **-ized, -iz·ing.** ①描述。②表特點；以…爲特性。His style is *characterized* by brevity. 簡潔是他的文體之特色。（英亦作 **characterise**）

char·ac·ter·less [ˈkærəktɚlɪs; ˈkæ-riktəlis] *adj.* 無特性的；無特質的；平凡的。

char·ac·ter·y[ˈkærɪktərɪ;ˈkæriktəri] *n.*, *pl.* **-ter·ies.** ①使用文字或符號以表達思想。②文字或符號之集合稱。

cha·rade [ʃəˈred; ʃəˈrɑ:d] *n.*①（*pl.*）（作 *sing.* 解）一種用動作表演而使對方猜的字謎遊戲。②上述遊戲的謎底。

***char·coal** [ˈtʃɑrˌkol; ˈtʃɑ:koul] *n.* ①木炭；炭。②木炭筆。③木炭畫。④深灰色。—*v.t.* ①以木炭塗黑或繪畫。②以木炭氣（一氧化炭）使窒息。

charcoal burner ①燒木炭之爐或窰。②燒木炭者。

chard [tʃɑrd; tʃɑ:d] *n.* 〖植物〗一種可供食用之甜菜。

chare [tʃɛr; tʃɛə] *n.*, *v.*, **chared, char-ing.** —*n.* ①打雜女傭；臨時女幫工。②按日計資之零工；雜務（尤指家庭雜務）。—*v.i.* ①做小工。②做按日計資之家庭雜務。—*v.t.* 做（雜工）；完成。

:charge [tʃɑrdʒ; tʃɑ:dʒ] *v.*, **charged, charg·ing,** *n.* —*v.t.* ①裝；載。②使（電池）充電；起電。to *charge* the battery. 將電池充電。③命令；指示。④控訴；加罪於；歸罪於。The driver is *charged* with speeding. 司機被控駕車超速。⑤索價；要價。He *charged* eight dollars for half a dozen of eggs. 半打蛋他要價八元。⑥記帳；記作欠項。⑦賒帳。The store permitted her to *charge* the dress. 店裏准她賒帳買這件衣服。⑧攻擊；突擊；進攻。⑨使負責；委以責任。⑩充滿某種氣氛。⑪加負擔於。—*v.i.*①猛衝；猛攻。②索價。He does not *charge* at all for his services. 他服務分文不取。③法官對陪審員命令。***charge off*** **a.** 因虧損而減少。**b.** 記下當作。—*n.*①負載；負荷。②責任；職責。③委託；照顧。Doctors have *charge* of sick people. 醫生照顧病人。④受照顧者。⑤命令。⑥控訴；加罪；歸咎。They made a *charge* against him. 他們控告他。⑦費用；索價。The medical service is free of *charge* in our school. 在我們學校醫藥費免收。⑧應付之款；債務。Taxes are a *charge* on citizens. 稅捐是國民應付之款。⑨攻擊；突擊。⑩進攻的號令。⑪電荷。***bring a charge against*** 控告。***give a person in charge*** 將某人交付警方。***in charge*** 負責。Who is *in charge* here? 這兒誰負責？***in charge of*** 負責管理。***in the charge of*** 受管理。***take charge of*** 負責保管；負責照顧。

charge·a·ble [ˈtʃɑrdʒəbḷ; ˈtʃɑ:dʒəbl] *adj.* ①可被控訴的。②可記在某項帳目上的。

charge account 商店戶頭（指顧客在商店記帳購物，定時付款的戶頭）。

char·gé d'af·faires [ʃɑrˈʒedæˈfɛr; ˈʃɑ:ʒeidæˈfɛə] *pl.* **char·gés d'af·faires** [ʃɑrˈʒezdæˈfɛr; ˈʃɑ:ʒeidæˈfɛə].〖法〗代辦；代理公使或大使。（亦作 **chargé**）

charge plate 商店戶頭證（多爲小金屬或塑膠牌，其上刻有顧客姓名地址及戶頭號碼）。（亦作 **charge-a-plate**）

charg·er [ˈtʃɑrdʒɚ; ˈtʃɑ:dʒə] *n.* ①軍馬；戰馬。②委託者。③控訴者。④突擊者或突擊物。⑤充電器。⑥〖古〗大盤。

char·i·ly [ˈtʃɛrəlɪ; ˈtʃɛərili] *adv.* ①謹愼地；小心地。②吝嗇地；省儉地。

char·i·ness [ˈtʃɛrənɪs; ˈtʃɛərinis] *n.* ①謹愼；小心。②吝嗇；省儉。

Char·ing Cross [ˈtʃærɪŋ~; ˈtʃæ-riŋ~] 倫敦市中心之一地區名。

***char·i·ot** [ˈtʃærɪət; ˈtʃæriət] *n.* ①古時雙輪戰車。②四輪馬車或轎車。—*v.t.* 用雙輪或四輪馬車載運。—*v.i.* 駕駛此類車輛。

char·i·ot·eer [ˌtʃærɪəˈtɪr; ˌtʃæriəˈtiə] *n.* ①雙輪或四輪馬車之御者。②(C-)〖天文〗

御夫座。—*v.t.* & *v.i.* 駕駛雙輪或四輪馬車。

cha·ris·ma 〔kəˈrɪzmə; kəˈrizmə〕 *n.*, *pl.* **-ma·ta** 〔-mətə; -mətə〕. ①一種神賜的特別才能(如預言、治病等)。②一種能引起大衆狂熱擁護而無法形容的領袖氣質。(亦作 **charism**)

***char·i·ta·ble** 〔ˈtʃærətəbl; ˈtʃæritəbl〕 *adj.* ①慈悲的;仁慈的;慈善的。a *charitable* institution. 慈善機關。②慷慨的。③寬恕的;寬厚的。—**ness**, *n.* —**char·i·ta·bly**, *adv.*

char·i·ty** 〔ˈtʃærətɪ; ˈtʃæriti〕 *n.*, *pl.* **-ties.** ①施與;賙濟;布施。He lives on *charity*. 他靠賙濟爲生。②慈善捐款;慈善機關。③博愛;慈悲;慈善。④寬恕;寬厚待人。cold as charity*** 冷漠;硬心腸。

charity school 貧民義務學校。

cha·ri·va·ri 〔ʃəˌrɪvəˈri; ˈʃɑːriˈvɑːri〕 *n.* ①戲謔之喧鬧聲。②任何喧雜之鬧聲。

char·la·dy 〔ˈtʃarˌledɪ; ˈtʃɑːˌleidi〕 *n.*, *pl.* **-dies.** =**charwoman.**

char·la·tan 〔ˈʃarlətn̩; ˈʃɑːlətən〕 *n.* ①走江湖者;騙子。②冒充內行者。③庸醫。—**ism**, —**ry**, *n.*

Char·le·magne 〔ˈʃarləˌmen; ˈʃɑːləˈmain〕 *n.* 查理曼(742–814, 世稱 Charles the Great 查理曼大帝)。

Charles 〔tʃarlz; tʃɑːlz〕 *n.* ①男子名(暱稱時常作 Charley, Charlie 或 Carl)。②查理 (Prince of Edinburgh and Wales, 1948–, Elizabeth II 之子,英國王位繼承人)。③查理(Prince, 1903–, 於 1944–50 爲比利時攝政王)。「(亦作 **Charles' Wain**)

Charles's Wain 〖天文〗北斗七星。

Charles·ton 〔ˈtʃarlztən; ˈtʃɑːlstən〕 *n.* 查爾斯敦舞(四分之四拍子的舞之一種)。

char·ley horse 〔ˈtʃarlɪ~; ˈtʃɑːli~〕 〖美俗〗(由於過度之肌肉運動或受傷所引起之)腿或胳膊之抽筋。(亦作**charlie horse**)

char·lock 〔ˈtʃarlək; ˈtʃɑːlək〕 *n.* 〖植物〗野芥。

Char·lotte 〔ˈʃarlət; ˈʃɑːlət〕 *n.* ①女子名。②(c-)一種水果糕或蛋乳凍糕。

‡**charm** 〔tʃarm; tʃɑːm〕 *n.* ①魔力;引誘力;誘惑力。a woman's *charm*. 女人的魔力。②(常 *pl.*)可愛的性質;女子的美色。He was infatuated with her *charms*. 他爲她的美色所迷惑。③小飾品(附於錶帶或錶鏈的)。④咒語;符咒。Some people believe in *charms*. 有些人信符咒。***like a charm*** 有神效的;極成功的。The machine worked *like a charm*. 這機器靈極了。—*v.t.* ①使迷醉;使高興;使惑於美色。He was *charmed* with the beauty of the scenery. 美麗的風景使他大爲喜悅。②施以符咒;以符咒保護。③如被符咒般影響或保護;似符咒般起作用。—*v.i.* ①迷人;悅人。②用符咒。

charm·er 〔ˈtʃarmɚ; ˈtʃɑːmə〕 *n.* ①可愛的人;迷人的人(通常指婦女)。②施魔術者。

char·meuse 〔ʃarˈmɜz; ʃarˈmœz〕 〖法〗 *n.* 一種軟而平滑之絲織物;軟緞。

***charm·ing** 〔ˈtʃarmɪŋ; ˈtʃɑːmiŋ〕 *adj.* 迷人的;嬌媚的。a *charming* manner. 迷人的姿態。—**ly**, *adv.* 「及服裝的學校)。

charm school 美姿學校(教少女儀態

char·nel 〔ˈtʃarnl̩; ˈtʃɑːnl〕 *n.* 藏骸所;停屍室。—*adj.* 藏骸所的;停屍室的;似停屍室的;陰森森的;慘怖的。

charnel house 藏骸所;停屍室。

Char·on 〔ˈkerən; ˈkeərən〕 *n.* ①〖希臘神話〗在 Styx 河上渡亡靈往冥府之船夫。②〖諧〗擺渡的船夫。

char·qui 〔ˈtʃarkɪ; ˈtʃɑːki〕 *n.* (智利之)肉乾(尤指牛肉乾)。(亦作 **charque**)

***chart** 〔tʃart; tʃɑːt〕 *n.* ①地圖(尤指水路圖,航海圖)。②圖;表。a weather *chart*. 氣象圖。—*v.t.* ①製圖(表);記入海圖。②計劃。

char·ter** 〔ˈtʃartɚ; ˈtʃɑːtə〕 *n.* ①(政府發的)特許狀。②分會或分社的設立許可(狀)。charter member*** 基本會員;發起人。***the Great Charter*** (英國)大憲章。—*v.t.* ①特許。②包租;包賃。

char·tered 〔ˈtʃartɚd; ˈtʃɑːtəd〕 *adj.* ①特許的;受特許的。②租賃的。a *chartered* ship. 包租之船。

chartered accountant 〖英〗(獲有合格證書之)特許會計師。(在美國稱爲 **certified accountant**)

chartered bank 特許銀行。

charter flight 包機(租用的整架飛機)。

Char·ter·house 〔ˈtʃartɚˌhaus; ˈtʃɑːtəhaus〕 *n.* ①(c-) 沙特爾修道院(=Carthusian monastery)。②(1611年在該院遺址修建之)一倫敦慈善醫院。

Charter of the United Nations 聯合國憲章。「的租約。②特權。

charter party ①賃船、飛機或車輛等

Chart·ism 〔ˈtʃartɪzəm; ˈtʃɑːtizəm〕 *n.* 〖英史〗1838–1848年英國改進黨之人民憲章運動或主義;民權運動主義。—**Chart·ist**, *n.*, *adj.*

chart·ism 〔ˈtʃartɪzəm; ˈtʃɑːtizəm〕 *n.* 〖美〗圖表之製作與研究(尤指有關股票交易的統計分析圖表)。—**chart·ist**, *n.*

char·tog·ra·phy 〔karˈtagrəfɪ; kɑːˈtɔgrəfi〕 *n.* 製圖法;製表法。—**char·tog·ra·pher**, *n.*

char·treuse 〔ʃarˈtrɜz; ʃɑːˈtrəːz〕 *n.* ①一種黃色、綠色或白色之酒。②微黃之淡綠色。—*adj.* 微黃之淡綠色的。

char·tu·lar·y 〔ˈkartʃuˌlɛrɪ; ˈkɑːtʃuləri〕 *n.*, *pl.* **-lar·ies.** ①特許狀登記簿。②檔案保存者。(亦作 **cartulary**)

char·wom·an 〔ˈtʃarˌwumən; ˈtʃɑːˌwumən〕 *n.*, *pl.* **-wom·en.** 雜役女傭;按日計資之女傭。

char·y 〔ˈtʃɛrɪ; ˈtʃɛəri〕 *adj.*, **char·i·er, char·i·est.** ①謹慎的。②害羞的。③節儉的;吝嗇的。④吹毛求疵的;不易滿足的。

Cha·ryb·dis 〔kəˈrɪbdɪs; kəˈribdis〕 *n.* ①〖希臘神話〗女妖。②義大利 Sicily 沿岸在Messina 海峽中之大旋渦(航海者圖避此旋渦時,又有觸及對面 Scylla 岩礁的危險)。***between Scylla and Charybdis*** 左右爲難;腹背受敵。

chase¹** 〔tʃes; tʃeis〕 *v.*, **chased, chasing**, *n.* —*v.t.* ①追捕;捕獲。Dogs like to *chase* hares. 狗喜歡追捕野兔。②追;逐。③驅逐;祛除。④追求。—*v.i.* ①追。to *chase* after someone. 追人。②〖俗〗急急掠過;急進。—*n.* ①追;追求。the *chase* for honors. 追求名譽。②狩獵。③被獵的動物。The *chase* escaped the hunter. 被獵的動物逃開獵人。give chase*** 追;追擊。***the chase*** 打獵。

chase² *n.* ①〖印刷〗鐵框;緊框;排版架。②坑;渠;壕溝。③〖軍〗槍砲之前身(包括槍及砲膛在內)。

chase³ *v.t.* ①雕鏤。②施以雕鏤之裝飾。

chase gun=**chaser¹** ③.

chas·er¹ 〔ˈtʃesɚ; ˈtʃeisə〕 *n.* ①追者;獵者。②驅逐機;驅逐艦。③追擊砲;反擊砲。④〖美俗〗酒後所飲之淸淡飲料。

chas·er² *n.* ①金屬雕刻師；雕鏤匠；浮雕師。②雕刻金屬用的工具；金屬雕鑿。③螺旋鈑；刻螺線的工具。

***chasm** 〔'kæzəm; 'kæzəm〕 *n.* ①深坑或裂罅；罅隙。②個人或團體間情感、利害等之衝突。③(時間等的)差距。**—al, —ic, —y,** *adj.*

chas·mo·phyte〔'kæzmə,faɪt; 'kæzməfait〕 *n.* 長在石縫中的植物。

chasse 〔ʃæs; ʃæs〕〖法〗 *n.* ①用以爽口的酒。②聖骨箱或貯聖骨的神祠。

chas·sé 〔ʃæ'se; 'ʃæsei〕〖法〗*n., v.,* **chas·séd, chas·sé·ing.** **—***n.*〖舞蹈〗快滑步。**—***v.i.* 作快滑步；用快滑步跳舞。

chas·seur 〔ʃæ'sɝ; ʃæ'səː〕〖法〗 *n.* ①獵戶；獵人。②輕步兵；輕騎兵。③侍從；僕歐。

chas·sis 〔'ʃæsɪ; 'ʃæsi〕 *n., pl.* **chas·sis** 〔'ʃæsɪz; 'ʃæsiz〕. ①汽車等之底盤。②砲架。③飛機之底部。④〖無線電〗無線電接收機或發射機之底盤。

***chaste** 〔tʃest; tʃeist〕 *adj.,* **chast·er, chast·est.** ①貞節的；有道德的。②純潔的。③簡潔的；樸素的。 **—ly,** *adv.* **—ness,** *n.*

chas·ten 〔'tʃesn̩; 'tʃeisn〕 *v.t.* ①懲戒；折磨；鍛鍊。②磨鍊；磨洗。③洗鍊。④緩和；抑制。

chas·ten·er 〔'tʃesn̩ɚ; 'tʃeisnə〕 *n.* 懲戒者。

chas·tise 〔tʃæs'taɪz; tʃæs'taiz〕 *v.t.,* **-tised, -tis·ing.** 責罰；鞭打。 **—chas·tis·a·ble,** *adj.* **—ment, chas·tis·er,** *n.*

chas·ti·ty 〔'tʃæstətɪ; 'tʃæstiti〕 *n.* ①貞節；節操。②純潔。③簡潔無華；優雅。

chastity belt 貞操帶。

chas·u·ble 〔'tʃæzjʊbl̩; 'tʃæzjubl〕 *n.* 十字褡(神父行彌撒時所着之一種無袖長袍)。

chat** 〔tʃæt; tʃæt〕 *n., v.,* **chat·ted, chat·ting.** **—n.* ①閒談。 I had a *chat* with him. 我與他閒談。②燕雀類中之任何一隻鳥。**—***v.i.* 閒談；暢談。

châ·teau 〔ʃæ'to;'ʃɑːtou〕 *n., pl.* **-teaux** 〔-'toz; -touz〕. ①城堡。②〖法〗鄉下大房屋；別墅；莊園。

chat·e·lain 〔'ʃætl̩,en; 'ʃætəlein〕 *n.* 「城主；堡守。」

chat·e·laine 〔'ʃætl̩,en; 'ʃætəlein〕 *n.* ①城主之妻。②城堡或別墅之女主人。③婦人腰間之飾鉤。④女服翻領上的鍊飾。

chat·tel 〔'tʃætl̩; 'tʃætl〕 *n.* ①〖法律〗動產。②奴婢。***chattel mortgage*** 動產抵押。***chattel personal*** 私人動產。 ***goods and chattels*** 傢具雜物。

chat·ter** 〔'tʃætɚ; 'tʃætə〕 *v.i.* ①喋喋。②啁啾。③震顫作聲。His teeth *chattered.* 他的齒震顫作聲。**—v.t.* ①絮絮不休地說。②使震顫作聲。**—***n.*①喋喋。②啁啾聲。③唧唧聲。④潺潺水流聲。**—er,** *n.*

chat·ter·box 〔'tʃætɚ,bɑks; 'tʃætəbɔks〕 *n.* 饒舌者；喋喋之人。

chat·ty 〔'tʃætɪ; 'tʃæti〕 *adj.,* **-ti·er, -ti·est.** 健談的；好閒談的。

Chau·cer 〔'tʃɔsɚ; 'tʃɔːsə〕 *n.* 喬塞 (Geoffrey, 1340?–1400, 第一位偉大的英國詩人, *the Canterbury Tales* 作者)。

Chau·ce·ri·an 〔tʃɔ'sɪrɪən; tʃɔː'siəriən〕 *adj.* 倣喬塞的；喬塞式的。

chaud·froid 〔ʃo'frwɑ; ʃou'frwɑː〕 *n.* 肉凍。

chauf·fer 〔'tʃɔfɚ; 'tʃɔːfə〕 *n.* 小爐；小「炭盆。」

chauf·feur** 〔'ʃofɚ, ʃo'fɝ; 'ʃoufə, ʃou'fəː〕 *n.* 汽車夫；司機。**—v.i.* 做司機；開車。

chauf·feuse 〔ʃo'fœz; ʃou'fœz〕〖法〗 *n.* 女司機。

chaul·moo·gra 〔tʃɔl'mugrə; tʃɔːl'muːgrə〕 *n.*〖植物〗大楓子。

Chau·tau·qua 〔ʃə'tɔkwə; ʃə'tɔːkwə〕 *n.* ①學托擴湖(在美國紐約西南部)。②學托擴(該湖畔之一村莊，爲夏季教育性集會之中心)。③(c-)夏季教育性野外集會。**—***adj.* (常 c-) 有關此類集會的。

chauve-sou·ris〔,ʃovsu'ri;,ʃouvsuː'riː〕 *n.* 蝙蝠。

chau·vin·ism 〔'ʃovɪn,ɪzəm; 'ʃouvinizəm〕 *n.* ①對武功之盲目醉心；愛國狂；盲目的愛國主義。②盲目的排外或排他主義。**—chau·vin·ist,** *n.* **—chau·vin·is·tic,** *adj.*

chaw 〔tʃɔ; tʃɔː〕 *v., n.*〖方〗=**chew.**

Ch.B. Bachelor of Surgery. **Ch.E., Che.E.** Chemical Engineer.

‡cheap 〔tʃip; tʃiːp〕 *adj.* ①便宜的；價廉的。②索價低廉的。a very *cheap* store. 索價甚廉的商店。③易得的；不甚費力的。④低級的；無甚價值的；卑劣的。⑤以低利率可獲得的。⑥吝嗇的。***feel cheap*** 感到慚愧；自愧不如。 ***hold cheap*** 小看；蔑視。 They *hold* life *cheap.* 他們不重視生命。**—***adv.* 便宜地。to buy a thing *cheap.* 東西買得便宜。***on the cheap*** 低廉地；經濟地。**—ly,** *adv.* **—ness,** *n.*

cheap·en 〔'tʃipən; 'tʃiːpən〕 *v.t.* ①減價；削價。②貶損價值。③〖古〗還價；講價。**—***v.i.* 減價；跌價。

cheap-jack〔'tʃip,dʒæk;'tʃiːpdʒæk〕*n.* (尤指先抬價後減價的)攤販。**—***adj.* 此種攤販的；賤的。(亦作 **cheap jack, cheap john**)

cheap·skate 〔'tʃip,sket; 'tʃiːp,skeit〕 *n.*〖俚〗吝嗇鬼。

cheat** 〔tʃit; tʃiːt〕 *v.t.* ①欺騙。②詐取；騙取。to *cheat* a man (out) of his money. 騙取他人的錢。③避開；躲避。**—v.i.* ①行騙；欺詐。②〖俚〗不守節〖常 on〗. **—***n.* ①騙子。He is a *cheat.* 他是一個騙子。②欺詐。

‡check 〔tʃɛk; tʃek〕 *v.t.*①突然停止；強制停止。②控制；抑制。He *checked* his anger. 他抑制住憤怒。③阻止；抵擋。④核對；查驗。Will you *check* these figures? 你核對一下這些數目字好嗎? ⑤做記號以表示核對無誤或選擇〖常 off〗. She *checked* off the names she wanted to invite. 她將要請的人的名字做個記號。⑥暫存。⑦使生裂縫。⑧〖美〗託運至目的地。 He *checked* his trunks to Taichung. 他將衣箱託運至臺中。⑨畫方格於。⑩攻王棋；將軍。⑪使減少，減低。⑫檢查。**—***v.i.* ①證明無誤；核對無誤。②查詢或調查以資證實；查核。I will *check* up on the matter. 我將查核此事。③停止；停頓。④付款以備離開住所(如旅館)。⑤攻王棋；將軍。⑥簽發支票；兌付支票。⑦產生裂縫。 Painted surfaces may *check* with age. 油漆的表面，因年代久遠可能產生龜裂。***check in*** 投宿旅館等。***check off*** 驗訖。 ***check (up) on*** 調查；檢查。***check out*** **a.** 付款而離開旅館等。**b.**〖俚〗死。 **c.** 檢查合格。 **d.** 提(款)。***check with*** **a.** 符合；核對無誤。**b.** 諮詢；商議。**—***n.* ①遏止；阻止；阻礙。②制止者；遏止者。③核對。to make a *check* on his calculation. 核對他的計算。④檢訖的記號。⑤對號牌；符證。The waiter took my hat and gave me a *check.* 侍者拿去我的帽子，給我一個對號牌。⑥飯館的帳單。⑦支票。order *check.* 記名支票。cross *check.* 劃線支票。⑧方格子的花樣。⑨攻王棋；將軍。⑩裂縫。⑪標準。***in check*** 在控制中；被阻止。**—***adj.* ①抑制的。②棋盤格的。

check·back 〔'tʃɛk,bæk; 'tʃekbæk〕 *n.* 複查;核對。

check·book 〔'tʃɛk,buk; 'tʃekbuk〕 *n.* 支票簿。

checked 〔tʃɛkt; tʃekt〕 *adj.* ①方格子花紋的。②〖語音〗位於以塞音爲結尾之音節的; 閉息音的。

check·er[1] 〔'tʃɛkə; 'tʃekə〕 *v.t.* ①使成格子花樣; 標作棋盤格。②使交錯。③使多變化。 —*n.* ①棋盤格花紋; 格子花。②棋子。(亦作 **chequer**) ③收款人。

check·er[2] *n.* ①阻止之人或事物。②衣帽間管理員。

check·er·ber·ry 〔'tʃɛkə,bɛrɪ; 'tʃekəbəri〕 *n., pl.* **-ries.** ①鹿蹄草之似漿果的紅色果實。②〖植物〗鹿蹄草。③蔓虎刺之一種。

check·er·board 〔'tʃɛkə,bord; 'tʃekəbɔːd〕 *n.* 西洋棋盤。—*v.t.* 標作棋盤格;排成棋盤格圖樣。

check·ered 〔'tʃɛkəd; 'tʃekəd〕 *adj.* ①有方格的;有不同顏色之方格的。②多變的;各種各式的;不規則的。

check·ers 〔'tʃɛkəz; 'tʃekəz〕 *n. pl.* 西洋棋。(亦作 **chequers, draughts**)

check·er·work 〔'tʃɛkə,wɝk; 'tʃekəwəːk〕 *n.* 方格花樣細工。

check-in 〔'tʃɛk,ɪn; 'tʃekin〕 *n.* 投宿於旅館。

check in formalities 向航空公司辦理一切出境手續。

checking account 活期存款戶頭。

check list ①〖美〗投票人名簿。②名單;清單。

check·man 〔'tʃɛkmən; 'tʃekmən〕 *n., pl.* **-men.** 〖英〗查票者;查驗入場券之人。

check mark 表已核對、選擇等的記號,如(√)。

check·mate 〔'tʃɛk,met; 'tʃek'meit〕 *v.,* **-mat·ed, -mat·ing,** *n., interj.* —*v.t.* ①圍攻(王棋);(象棋)將死。②完全擊敗。③採取對策。 —*n.* ①擒王棋。②完全失敗。—*interj.* (棋賽)將!

check nut 防鬆螺母;螺絲栓。

check·off 〔'tʃɛk,ɔf; 'tʃekɔːf〕 *n.* 資方自勞工工資中代扣工會會費之辦法。

check-out 〔'tʃɛk,aut; 'tʃekaut〕 *n.* ①付款退租旅館房間。②應退租的時間。③檢查;查驗。④核算(貨物)而付款。

checkout counter 〖美〗付帳櫃臺。

check·point 〔'tʃɛk,pɔɪnt; 'tʃekpɔint〕 *n.* 關卡。

check·rein 〔'tʃɛk,ren; 'tʃek-rein〕 *n.* 制韁。

check·roll 〔'tʃɛkrol; 'tʃekroul〕 *n.* 點名册。

check·room 〔'tʃɛk,rum; 'tʃek-rum〕 *n.* ①衣帽間。②車站之行李房。

check·row 〔'tʃɛk,ro; 'tʃekrou〕 *n.* 農作物之行列;樹列。—*v.t.* 栽植成行列。

check-string 〔'tʃɛk,strɪŋ; 'tʃekstriŋ〕 *n.* (指示巴士司機下車的)號鈴索。

check-tak·er 〔'tʃɛk,tekə; 'tʃek,teikə〕 *n.* 收票員。

check to bearer 不記名式支票。

check to order 記名式支票。

check·up 〔'tʃɛk,ʌp; 'tʃekʌp〕 *n.* 〖美〗①核對;審查;檢定。②健康檢查。

check valve 止回閥(防水逆流之活門)。

check·writ·er 〔'tʃɛk,raɪtə; 'tʃek,raitə〕 *n.* 支票數字打孔機。

Ched·dar 〔'tʃɛdə; 'tʃedə〕 *n.* 一種乾酪。(亦作 **Cheddar cheese**)

‡**cheek** 〔tʃik; tʃiːk〕 *n.* ①頰。②無禮;厚顏。He has the *cheek* to ask you to do his work for him. 他竟厚顏請你代他工作。③任何類似頰的事物。The *cheeks* of a vise. 虎頭鉗的雙邊。④〖俚〗臀部。***cheek by jowl*** **a.** 並肩;緊靠着。**b.** 親密的。***tongue in cheek*** 無誠意;說東指西。***turn the other cheek*** 忍受侮辱。—*v.t.* 〖俗〗厚顏地提出;大膽地講。

cheek·bone 〔'tʃik,bon; 'tʃiːkboun〕 *n.* 頰骨;顴骨。

cheek pouch 頰囊。

cheek tooth 臼齒。

cheek·y 〔'tʃikɪ; 'tʃiːki〕 *adj.,* **cheek·i·er, cheek·i·est.** ①〖俗〗厚顏的;無恥的。②面頰垂下的。—**cheek·i·ly,** *adv.* —**cheek·i·ness,** *n.*

cheep 〔tʃip; tʃiːp〕 *v.i.* 作唧唧聲;作吱喳聲。 —*v.t.* 唧唧地說出。—*n.* 吱吱的叫聲。—**er,** *n.*

‡**cheer** 〔tʃɪr; tʃiə〕 *n.* ①喜悅;愉快。②歡呼;喝采。They gave him three *cheers.* 他們向他三次歡呼。③食物。good *cheer.* 好的食物; 佳餚。④心情。⑤(*pl.*)〖主英〗乾杯等之用語。***be of good cheer*** 不要垂頭喪氣。***What cheer?*** 你好嗎? ***with good cheer*** 愉快地;情願地。—*v.t.* ①令人喜悅;令人愉快。②向…歡呼。③喝采。④鼓勵;爲…加油。Everyone *cheered* our team. 大家爲我們的隊加油。 —*v.i.* 喝采; 歡呼。The boys *cheered.* 小孩們歡呼。***cheer up*** 高興;歡樂。*Cheer up!* 鼓起興致來!(不要發愁!)

***cheer·ful** 〔'tʃɪrfəl; 'tʃiəful〕 *adj.* ①快樂的; 高興的。 He is *cheerful* in spite of his illness. 他雖病而興致尙佳。②樂意的;誠意的。③歡愉的; 令人愉快的。 —**ly,** *adv.* —**ness,** *n.*

cheer·i·ly 〔'tʃɪrəlɪ; 'tʃiərili〕 *adv.* 興高采烈地。

cheer·ing 〔'tʃɪrɪŋ; 'tʃiəriŋ〕 *n.* 喝采;歡呼。

cheer·ing·ly 〔'tʃɪrɪŋlɪ; 'tʃiəriŋli〕 *adv.* 令人快樂地;興高采烈地。

cheer·i·o 〔'tʃɪrɪ,o; 'tʃiəri'ou〕 *interj.* 〖英〗①喂;再見。②=**hurrah.** (亦作**cheero**)

cheer·lead·er 〔'tʃɪr,lidə; 'tʃiə,liːdə〕 *n.* 啦啦隊隊長。

cheer·lead·ing 〔'tʃɪr,lidɪŋ; 'tʃiə,liː-diŋ〕 *n.* 領導啦啦隊。

cheer·less 〔'tʃɪrlɪs; 'tʃiəlis〕 *adj.* 不愉快的;陰鬱的。—**ly,** *adv.* —**ness,** *n.*

cheer·ly 〔'tʃɪrlɪ; 'tʃiəli〕 *adv.* 高興地;愉快地(水手們用作振奮精神的呼語)。

***cheer·y** 〔'tʃɪrɪ; 'tʃiəri〕 *adj.,* **cheer·i·er, cheer·i·est.** 快樂的;高興的;愉快的。

‡**cheese**[1] 〔tʃiz; tʃiːz〕 *n.* ①乾酪。②〖俚〗頭等的人或事物。He's the big *cheese* in this outfit. 他在這個單位裏是一個頂呱呱的人。 ③〖俗〗嬰兒吐出來的半消化的凝乳。***make cheeses*** **a.** (婦女)深深欠腰作禮。**b.** 轉動身體使裙展開並蹲下。—*v.i.* 〖俗〗吐乳。

cheese[2] *v.t.,* **cheesed, chees·ing.** 〖俚〗停止;阻止。***cheese it*** **a.** 小心! **b.** 走開!

cheese·burg·er 〔'tʃiz,bɝgə; 'tʃiːz,bəːgə〕 *n.* 放有乾酪的肉餅。

cheese cake ①乾酪、蛋、糖等混於一起焙成的餅。②〖俚〗半裸的美女照片。(亦作 **cheesecake**)

cheese·cloth 〔'tʃiz,klɔθ; 'tʃiːzklɔθ〕 *n.* 薄而稀鬆之棉布。

cheesed 〔tʃizd; tʃiːzd〕 *adj.* 〖英俚〗厭煩的;厭膩的。

cheese mite 乾酪蟲。

cheese·mon·ger 〔'tʃiz,mʌŋgə; 'tʃiːz,mʌŋgə〕 *n.* 賣乾酪之店或人。

cheese·par·ing 〔'tʃiz,pɛrɪŋ; 'tʃiːz,pɛəriŋ〕 *n.* ①乾酪屑。②無價值之物。③吝嗇。—*adj.* 吝嗇的;小氣的。

cheese rennet 〖植物〗白花蓬子葉。

cheese straws 酪心麪條酥。

chees·y [ˈtʃizɪ; ˈtʃiːzi] *adj.*, **chees·i·er, chees·i·est.** ①乾酪製的;似乾酪的。②〖俚〗下等的;低級的。
chee·tah, chee·ta [ˈtʃitə; ˈtʃiːtə] *n.* 〖動物〗印度豹。(亦作 **chetah**)
cheez·it [ˈtʃizɪt; ˈtʃiːzit] *v.*〖俚〗小心;走開。
chef [ʃɛf; ʃef] *n.* ①主廚。②廚役。
chef de cui·sine [ˌʃɛdəkwiˈzin; ˌʃedəkwiːˈziːn] *n.*, *pl.* **chefs de cui·sine** [ˌʃɛdəkwiˈzin; ˌʃefdəkwiːˈziːn].〖法〗主廚。
chef-d'oeu·vre [ʃeˈdœvrə; ʃeiˈdəːvr] *n.*, *pl.* **chefs-d'oeu·vre** [ʃeˈdœvrə; ʃeiˈdəːvr].〖法〗傑作;名著。
Che·khov [ˈtʃɛkəf; ˈtʃekəf] *n.* 柴可夫 (Anton Pavlovich, 1860–1904, 俄國劇作家及小說家)。(亦作 **Tchekov**) **—i·an,** *adj.*
Che·kiang [ˈdʒʌdʒjˈɑŋ; ˈdʒʌdʒjˈɑːŋ] *n.* 浙江(中國之一省, 省會爲杭州市 Hangchow).
che·la [ˈkilə; ˈkiːlə] *n.*, *pl.* **-lae** [-ˌli; -liː]. (蝦蟹等之)螯。
che·lo·nian [kəˈlonɪən; kəˈlounian] *adj.* 〖動物〗海龜類的。**—***n.* 海龜;龜。
Chel·sea [ˈtʃɛlsɪ; ˈtʃelsi] *n.* 倫敦市文化區名(在倫敦市西南部, 泰晤士河北岸, 藝術家與作家多居於此)。
Chelsea Hospital 倫敦恰斯區的殘廢軍人院。
chem. ①chemical. ②chemist. ③chemistry.
chem- 〖字首〗=**chemo-**.
Chem.E. Chemical Engineer.
chem·i·cal** [ˈkɛmɪkl̩; ˈkemikəl] *adj.* 化學的。**—n.* 化學藥品。***chemical engineer*** 化學工程師。***chemical engineering*** 化學工程。**—ly,** *adv.*
chemical bomb 化學彈。
chemical corps 化學兵隊。
chem·i·cal·ize [ˈkɛməkl̩ˌaɪz; ˈkemikəlaiz] *v.t.*, **-ized, -iz·ing.** 以化學品處理。
chemical warfare 化學戰。
chem·i·cul·ture [ˈkɛmɪˌkʌltʃɚ; ˈkemiˌkʌltʃə] *n.* 水耕法(不用土壤, 置化學物質於水中使植物直接吸收之法)。
che·mig·ra·phy [kəˈmɪgrəfɪ; kəˈmigrəfi] *n.* 化學鐫版術(用化學藥品而不使用照相術的)。
chem·i·loon [ˌʃɛmɪˈlun; ˌʃemiˈluːn] *n.* 連短褲之女用內衣。
***che·mise** [ʃəˈmiz; ʃəˈmiːz] *n.* ①英國維多利亞時代末期女用似襯衫的內衣。②土堤的護岸。
chem·i·sette [ˌʃɛmɪˈzɛt; ˌʃemiˈzet] *n.* 婦女胸衣;緊胸襯衣。
chem·i·sorb [ˈkɛməˌsɔrb; ˈkemisɔːb] *v.t.* 以化學吸收作用吸收。
chem·i·sorp·tion [ˌkɛməˈsɔrpʃən; ˌkemiˈsɔːpʃən] *n.* 化學吸收作用。
***chem·ist** [ˈkɛmɪst; ˈkemist] *n.* ①化學家。②〖英〗藥店(雜貨店)主人或店員(即美國之 druggist).
***chem·is·try** [ˈkɛmɪstrɪ; ˈkemistri] *n.*, *pl.* **-tries.** ①化學。applied *chemistry.* 應用化學。②化學性質、反應、現象等。
chem·i·type [ˈkɛmɪˌtaɪp; ˈkemitaip] *n.* 化學鍍刻版;腐蝕版。
chemo- 〖字首〗表"化學;化學的"之義。
che·mol·y·sis [kɪˈmɑləsɪs; kiˈmɔləsis] *n.* 化學分解;化學分析。
chem·o·sur·ger·y [ˌkɛmoˈsɝdʒərɪ; ˌkemouˈsəːdʒəri] *n.* 〖外科〗化學外科。
chem·o·syn·the·sis [ˌkɛmoˈsɪnθəsɪs; ˌkeməˈsinθisis] *n.* 化學合成。
chem·o·ther·a·py [ˌkɛmoˈθɛrəpɪ; ˌkemouˈθerəpi] *n.* 化學療法。
chem·ur·gy [ˈkɛmɝdʒɪ; ˈkeməːdʒi] *n.* 農業化學(研究如何將農作物中有機體在工業上運用之化學)。
Cheng-Chu school 〖哲學〗程朱學派。
Cheng·teh [ˈtʃʌŋˈdʌ; ˈtʃʌŋˈdʌ] *n.* 承德(中國熱河省之省會)。(亦作 **Jehol**)
Cheng·tu [ˈtʃʌŋˈdu; ˈtʃʌŋˈduː] *n.* 成都(中國四川省之省會)。
che·nille [ʃəˈnil; ʃəˈniːl] *n.* ①鬆絨線。②此種絨線之織品。
cheque [tʃɛk; tʃek] *n.* 〖英〗支票。
cheque perforators 打支票機。
***cher·ish** [ˈtʃɛrɪʃ; ˈtʃeriʃ] *v.t.*①珍愛。He *cherishes* friendship. 他珍視友誼。②撫育;愛撫。③堅持;懷抱着(希望等)。**—a·ble,** *adj.*
Cher·o·kee [ˈtʃɛrəˌki; ˈtʃerəkiː] *n.* (北美印第安)柴拉基幾族人。
che·root [ʃəˈrut; ʃəˈruːt] *n.* 方頭雪茄菸。
‡cher·ry [ˈtʃɛrɪ; ˈtʃeri] *n.*, *pl.* **-ries,** *adj.* **—***n.* ①櫻桃。②櫻樹; 櫻木。③如櫻桃的鮮紅。④〖俚, 鄙〗處女膜; 處女。**—***adj.* ①鮮紅如櫻桃的。*cherry* lips. 櫻唇。②櫻木製的。③含櫻桃的(飲料、食物等)。④處女的。
cherry bay 〖植物〗月桂;桂樹。
cherry blossom 櫻花。
cherry brandy 浸過櫻桃的白蘭地酒。
cherry pie 櫻桃餅。
cherry stone 櫻桃核。
chert [tʃɝt; tʃəːt] *n.* 〖礦〗燧石;黑硅石。
cher·ub [ˈtʃɛrəb; ˈtʃerəb] *n.*, *pl.* **cher·u·bim** [ˈtʃɛrjubɪm; ˈtʃerəbim] *for* ① *and* ②, **cher·ubs** *for* ③*and*④。①〖聖經〗有翼的天使。②九級天使中之第二級天使。③天眞無邪的美麗孩童。④有豐滿無邪似孩童般容貌的人。
che·ru·bic [tʃəˈrubɪk; tʃəˈruːbik] *adj.* ①天使的;似天使的。②天眞無邪的。③胖胖的。
cher·vil [ˈtʃɝvɪl; ˈtʃəːvil] *n.* 〖植物〗山蘿蔔。
Cheshire [ˈtʃɛʃɪr; ˈtʃeʃə] *n.* 赤郡(英國郡名, 在英格蘭西部)。
Cheshire cat 經常露齒嘻笑之貓(源出"愛麗斯奇遇記" *Alice in Wonderland*).
***chess**[1] [tʃɛs; tʃes] *n.* 西洋棋。
chess[2] *n.*, *pl.* **chess, chess·es.** 浮橋上所鋪之木板條。
chess·board [ˈtʃɛsˌbord; ˈtʃesbɔːd] *n.* 西洋象棋盤。
ches·sel [ˈtʃɛsl̩; ˈtʃesl] *n.* 乾酪桶;製乾酪之模子。
chess·man [ˈtʃɛsˌmæn; ˈtʃesmæn] *n.*, *pl.* **-men.** 棋子。
chest** [tʃɛst; tʃest] *n.*①胸;胸部。I have a pain in the *chest.* 我胸部作痛。②有蓋的大箱。a carpenter's *chest.* 木匠的工具箱。③有屜的櫃。④(裝氣體之)密閉之箱。⑤金庫。⑥錢。⑦裝在箱裏的東西。⑧一箱之量。get*** (***something***) ***off one's chest*** 〖俗〗把悶在心裏的話講出來。
ches·ter·field [ˈtʃɛstɚˌfild; ˈtʃestəfiːld] *n.* ①長及膝部之外衣。②大型沙發。
Chester White 一種早熟的白豬。
chest·ful [ˈtʃɛstful; ˈtʃestful] *n.*, *pl.* **-fuls.** 能裝滿一箱之東西。
chest note 〖音樂〗胸音; 最低音調。(亦作 **chest voice**)
chest·nut** [ˈtʃɛsnət, -ˌnʌt; ˈtʃesnʌt, -stn-, -nət] *n.* ①栗樹。②栗子;栗木。③紅棕色;栗褐色。④栗色馬。⑤〖俗〗陳腐的笑話或故事。pull*** (***someone's***) ***chestnuts out of the fire*** 被迫解決別人的困難而自己承受其後果;爲人火中取栗。**—***adj.* ①栗褐色的。②(食物)含有栗子的;栗子做的。
chest of drawers 五斗櫃。

chest protector (禦寒的)護胸。
chest·y [ˈtʃɛstɪ; ˈtʃesti] *adj.*, **chest·i·er, chest·i·est.** 〖俗〗①胸部大的;肺活量大的。②〖俚〗驕傲的;自誇的。
che·val-de-frise [ʃəˈvældəˈfriz; ʃəˈvældəˈfriːz] *n.*, *pl.* **che·vaux-de-frise** [ʃəˈvodəˈfriz; ʃəˈvoudəˈfriːz]. 〖法〗①〖軍〗絆馬索;防柵。②牆頭上之鐵蒺藜或碎玻璃。
che·val glass [ʃəˈvæl~; ʃəˈvæl~] 穿衣鏡;架在橫軸上的立鏡。
chev·a·lier [ˌʃɛvəˈlɪr; ˌʃevəˈliə] *n.* ①(法國之)有勳位之人。②〖法國史〗最下位之貴族;貴族之見習軍官。③豪俠之士。
che·vet [ʃəˈvɛ; ʃəˈve] 〖法〗 *n.* 〖建築〗教堂之內室;休息室。
Chev·ro·let [ˌʃɛvrəˈle; ˈʃevrəlei] *n.* 雪佛蘭(美製汽車名)。
chev·ron [ˈʃɛvrən; ˈʃevrən] *n.* ①〖軍〗臂章。②〖紋章〗山形符號。③似山形之裝飾。
chev·ro·tain [ˈʃɛvrəˌten; ˈʃevrətein] *n.* 〖動物〗麝香鹿。
chev·y [ˈtʃɛvɪ; ˈtʃevi] *n.*, *pl.* **chev·ies,** *v.*, **chev·ied, chev·y·ing.** 〖英〗=**chivvy.**
chew** [tʃu; tʃuː] *v.t.* ①咬碎;咀嚼。②損壞;壓壞〖常 up〗。—*v.i.* ①咀嚼。②熟思;玩味〖常 over〗。③〖俗〗嚼烟草。bite off more than one can chew*** 去做自己做不了的事;輕諾。***chew out*** 〖俚〗大罵。***chew the fat*** (or ***rag***)〖俚〗聊天。—*n.* ①咬碎;咀嚼。②所嚼之物。
chewing gum 口香糖。
Chey·enne [ʃaɪˈɛn; ʃaiˈen] *n.*, *pl.* **-ennes, -enne.** ①夏安族人(北美印第安人之一族)。②夏安語。
chg. ①charge. ②change. **chgd.** charged.
chi [kaɪ; kai] *n.*, *pl.* **chis.** 希臘第二十二字母(寫作 X, *x*)。
Chiang Kai-shek [ˈdʒjɑŋˈkaɪˈʃɛk; ˈdʒjɑːŋˈkaiˈʃek] 蔣介石(1886–1975, 卽蔣中正, 中華民國行憲後之第一、二、三、四、五任總統)。
Chi·an·ti [kɪˈæntɪ; kiˈænti] 〖義〗 *n.* 義大利 Chianti 山所產之紅葡萄酒。
chi·a·ro·scu·ro [kɪˌɑrəˈskjʊro; kiˌɑːrəsˈkuərou] *n.*, *pl.* **-ros.** 〖義〗〖美術〗①明暗對照法。②用此法所繪之畫。
chi·as·mus [kaɪˈæzməs; kaiˈæzməs] *n.* 〖修辭〗(對偶句之)交錯配列法。
chi·as·tic [kaɪˈæstɪk; kaiˈæstik] *adj.* 交錯配列的。
chi·bouk, chi·bouque, chi·buk [tʃɪˈbuk; tʃiˈbuːk] *n.* (土耳其之)長煙管。
chic [ʃik; ʃiːk] *n.* 式樣;時式;別致之款式。—*adj.* 漂亮的;別致的;俏式的。
Chi·ca·go [ʃəˈkɑgo; ʃiˈkɑːgou] *n.* 芝加哥(美國中西部一大城市)。
chi·cane [ʃɪˈken; ʃiˈkein] *n.*, *v.*, **-caned, -can·ing.** —*n.* ①奸謀。②〖橋牌〗無王牌之一手牌。—*v.i.* 用詐術。—*v.t.* ①欺騙。②以詐術取得。③吹毛求疵。
chi·can·er·y [ʃɪˈkenərɪ; ʃiˈkeinəri] *n.*, *pl.* **-er·ies.** 奸計;狡猾手段。
Chi·ca·no [tʃɪˈkɑno; tʃiˈkɑːnou] *n.*, *pl.* **-nos.** 美籍墨西哥人。
chi·chi, chi-chi [ˈʃiˈʃi; ˈʃiːˈʃiː] *adj.* 裝作聰明的;故作時髦的;冒充雅致的。
chick** [tʃɪk; tʃik] *n.* ①小雞;小鳥;小孩。②〖俚〗少女;年輕婦女。hip chick*** 對新事物感興趣的少女。
chick·a·bid·dy [ˈtʃɪkəˌbɪdɪ; ˈtʃikəˌbidi] *n.*, *pl.* **-dies.** ①小雞。②乖寶寶。
chick·a·dee [ˈtʃɪkəˌdi; ˈtʃikədiː] *n.* 山雀類。
chick·a·ree [ˈtʃɪkəˌri; ˈtʃikəriː] *n.* 〖動物〗赤栗鼠。
Chick·a·saw [ˈtʃɪkəˌsɔ; ˈtʃikəsɔː] *n.* ①(北美印第安人)契卡索族。②契卡索族人。
:chick·en[1] [ˈtʃɪkɪn, -ən; ˈtʃikin] *n.* ①雛雞。to hatch *chickens.* 孵小雞。②雞。③雞肉。④雛鳥。⑤〖美俗〗年輕人(尤指年輕女人);乳臭小兒。***count one's chickens before they are hatched*** 依賴尚未到手的利益;打如意算盤。—*adj.* ①年輕的;小的。a *chicken* lobster. 小龍蝦。②(食物)用雞做的;有雞味的。③〖俚〗膽小的。—*v.i.* ***chicken out*** 因膽怯而退出;臨陣脫逃。
chick·en[2] *n.* 刺繡。
chicken breast 〖醫〗雞胸。(亦作 **pigeon breast**)—**chick·en-breast·ed,** *adj.*
chicken cholera 家禽霍亂病。
chicken colonel 〖美軍俚〗上校。(亦作 **bird colonel**)
chicken feed ①雞飼料;鳥食。②〖美俚〗不屑提的錢數。③故意供給雙重間諜或敵國間諜的假情報。
chicken heart ①怯懦;懦弱。②懦弱者。
chick·en-heart·ed [ˈtʃɪkɪnˈhɑrtɪd; ˈtʃikinˈhɑːtid] *adj.* 膽小的;懦弱的。—**ly,** *adv.* —**ness,** *n.*
chicken ladder 〖建築〗鷹架中供工人上下用的斜置木板。
chick·en-liv·ered [ˈtʃɪkɪnˈlɪvəd; ˈtʃikinˈlivəd] *adj.* 〖俗〗膽小的。
chicken pox 〖醫〗水痘。
chick·en·shit [ˈtʃɪkɪnˌʃɪt; ˈtʃikinʃit] 〖俚, 鄙〗 *n.* ①瑣碎的細節;不重要的工作。②謊話;誇張。—*adj.* 膽小的。
chicken switch 〖火箭俚〗太空人於緊急時之逃生開關(將此開關拉上, 太空人之救生囊卽彈出太空船外)。
chicken wire 農莊上用做籬笆的小方格鐵絲網。
chick·let [ˈtʃɪklɪt; ˈtʃiklit] *n.* 〖美俚〗妙齡女郎。(亦作 **chicklette**)
chick·ling [ˈtʃɪklɪŋ; ˈtʃikliŋ] *n.* ①小雞。②〖植物〗野豌豆。
chick-pea [ˈtʃɪkˌpi; ˈtʃikpiː] *n.* 〖植物〗山黎豆;雞豆。
chick·weed [ˈtʃɪkˌwid; ˈtʃik-wiːd] *n.* 〖植物〗蘩縷。
chic·le [ˈtʃɪkl; ˈtʃikl] *n.* 中美產之一種樹膠(用製口香糖)。
Chi·com [ˈtʃaɪkəm; ˈtʃaikəm] *n.*, *adj.* 〖美〗中國共產黨(的)(爲 Chinese Communist 之縮寫)。
chic·o·ry [ˈtʃɪkərɪ; ˈtʃikəri] *n.*, *pl.* **-ries.** 〖植物〗菊苣(根可爲咖啡之代用品)。(亦作 **chiccory**)
chide [tʃaɪd; tʃaid] *v.*, **chid·ed** or **chid** [tʃɪd; tʃid], **chid·ed, chid** or **chid·den, chid·ing.** —*v.t.* & *v.i.* 叱責;譴責。
:chief [tʃif; tʃiːf] *n.* 領袖;首領;主腦;頭目;首長。—*adj.* ①階級最高的;權力最大的。a *chief* engineer. 總工程師。②最重要的;主要的。
chief constable 〖英〗郡之警察局長。
chief·dom [ˈtʃifdəm; ˈtʃiːfdəm] *n.* 首領之地位或資格。(亦作 **chiefship**)
chief editor 總編輯。
Chief Executive 〖美〗總統。
chief executive 州長;政府最高首長。
Chief Justice 〖美〗最高法院院長。
chief justice 首席法官。
***chief·ly** [ˈtʃiflɪ; ˈtʃiːfli] *adv.* ①大概地;多半地。②首要地;主要地。These are manufactured *chiefly* for export. 這些東

西主要是爲出口而製造的。
chief mate 〖航海〗大副。
Chief of Staff 〖美〗陸軍或空軍參謀長(約相當於中國之陸軍或空軍總司令)。
chief of staff 參謀長。
Chief of the General Staff 參謀總長。
chief petty officer 海軍上士。
chief·tain [ˈtʃiftɪn; ˈtʃi:ftən] *n.* ①酋長。②首領;領袖(尤指强盜的頭目)。
chief·tain·cy [ˈtʃiftɪnsɪ; ˈtʃi:ftənsi] *n.* 酋長或首領之職位。(亦作 **chieftainship**)
Ch'ien Lung [ˈtʃjɛnˈlʊŋ; ˈtʃjenˈluŋ] 乾隆 (1711–1799, 中國清朝皇帝, 在位期間1736–1796)。(亦作 **Kien Lung**)
chif·fon [ʃɪˈfɑn; ˈʃifɔn] *n.* ①一種絲質或人造絲質的薄紗。②(*pl.*)女人衣服上作爲裝飾的花邊、絲邊等。—*adj.*(女裝)用 chiffon 作的。
chif·fo·nier, chif·fon·nier [ˌʃɪfəˈnɪr; ˌʃifəˈniə] *n.* 帶鏡的有屜豎櫃。
chi·gnon [ˈʃinjɑn; ˈʃi:njɔ:ŋ] 〖法〗 *n., pl.* **-gnons.** 髮髻。
chig·oe [ˈtʃɪgo; ˈtʃigou] *n., pl.* **-oes.** 沙蝨。(亦作 **chigger**)
chil·blain [ˈtʃɪlˌblen; ˈtʃilblein] *n.* 〖醫〗(常 *pl.*)手脚上之凍瘡。(亦作 **pernio**) —**ed,** *adj.*
:child [tʃaɪld; tʃaild] *n., pl.* **chil·dren** [ˈtʃɪldrən; ˈtʃildrən]. ①嬰孩。②小孩。The *child* stops crying at the sight of her (*or* his) mother. 這小孩見到母親就不哭了。③兒子或女兒。They have no *children* of their own. 他們沒有親生的兒女。④(常 *pl.*)後裔;後代。⑤(感情、興趣方面)似小孩的人。⑥受某種環境影響而定型的人。a *child* of poverty. 出身貧寒的人。⑦結果;產物。Abstract art is a *child* of the 20th century. 抽象藝術是二十世紀的產物。***child bride*** 很年輕的新娘。***with child*** 懷孕。
child·bear·ing [ˈtʃaɪldˌbɛrɪŋ; ˈtʃaildˌbɛəriŋ] *n.* 生產;分娩。—*adj.* 能生產的。
child·bed [ˈtʃaɪldˌbɛd; ˈtʃaildbed] *n.* 分娩;生產。
childbed fever 〖醫〗產褥熱。(亦作 **puerperal fever**)
child·birth [ˈtʃaɪldˌbɝθ; ˈtʃaildbə:θ] *n.* 分娩;生產。
child·hood** [ˈtʃaɪldˌhʊd; ˈtʃaildhud] *n.* 兒童時期;幼時。He lost his parents in his *childhood*. 他幼時卽喪父母。second childhood*** 老人天眞無邪之情景。
child·ing [ˈtʃaɪldɪŋ; ˈtʃaildiŋ] *adj.* 懷孕的。
***child·ish** [ˈtʃaɪldɪʃ; ˈtʃaildiʃ] *adj.* ①孩子氣的。*childish* games. 小孩玩的遊戲。②幼稚的;愚蠢的。a *childish* answer. 幼稚的答覆。—**ly,** *adv.* —**ness,** *n.*
child labor 童工。
child·less [ˈtʃaɪldlɪs; ˈtʃaildlis] *adj.* 無子的。
child·like [ˈtʃaɪldˌlaɪk; ˈtʃaildlaik] *adj.* ①如小孩的;有孩子氣的。②天眞爛漫的;率直的。③對小孩適宜的。—**ness,** *n.*
child·mind·er [ˈtʃaɪldˌmaɪndə; ˈtʃaildˌmaində] *n.* 〖英〗臨時看護嬰兒者。
child·proof [ˈtʃaɪldˌpruf; ˈtʃaildpru:f] *adj.* 兒童可安全操作或玩弄的。
child psychology 兒童心理學。
chil·dren [ˈtʃɪldrən; ˈtʃildrən] *n.* pl. of child.
chil·dren·ese [ˌtʃɪldrənˈiz; ˌtʃildrənˈi:z] *n.* 〖美〗與自己的子女交談所用的語言。
children of Israel 希伯來人;猶太人。
Children's Day 兒童節(每年六月之第二個星期日)。
child's play 容易事。
child wife 年輕之太太。
Chil·e [ˈtʃɪlɪ; ˈtʃili] *n.* 智利(南美洲西南部的一個國家, 首都聖地牙哥 Santiago).
Chil·e·an, Chil·i·an [ˈtʃɪlɪən; ˈtʃiliən] *adj.* 智利的;智利人的。—*n.* ①智利人。②智利人所說的西班牙語;智利語。
chil·e con car·ne [ˈtʃɪlɪ kɑnˈkɑrnɪ; ˈtʃili kɔnˈkɑ:ni] 〖西〗墨西哥一名菜(用肉、紅椒、香料及豆煮成);辣醬。
Chile saltpeter (or **saltpetre**) 智利硝石。
chil·i [ˈtʃɪlɪ; ˈtʃili] *n., pl.* **-es.** ① (=chili pepper) 紅番椒。② =**chile con carne.** (亦作 **chilli, chile**)
chil·i·ad [ˈkɪlɪˌæd; ˈkiliæd] *n.* ①千。②一千年。
chil·i·asm [ˈkɪlɪæzəm; ˈkiliæzəm] *n.* 〖基督教〗千年至福說;千禧年說。
chil·i·ast [ˈkɪlɪˌæst; ˈkiliæst] *n.* 千年至福說之信奉者。
chill** [tʃɪl; tʃil] *n.* ①寒冷;寒凍。He has caught a *chill*. 他受寒了。②寒慄;寒戰;身上感到的一陣寒冷。A *chill* came over me. 我身上寒冷發顫。③掃興; 沮喪。 The bad news cast a *chill* over the gathering. 這壞消息使集會的人甚爲沮喪。④冷淡; 缺乏熱情;冷漠。take the chill off*** 去寒氣;使熱起來。—*adj.* ①寒冷的;寒慄的;寒戰的。②冷淡的;冷漠的。③令人沮喪的。—*v.i.* 變冷;覺得冷。—*v.t.* ①使冷;使之冷凍;使冷凝。②令失望; 使沮喪。—**ing·ly,** *adv.* —**ness,** *n.*
chilled [tʃɪld; tʃild] *adj.* 冷凍的。
chil·ler [ˈtʃɪlɚ; ˈtʃilə] *n.* ①使寒冷之人或事物。②〖俗〗令人寒慄的兇殺故事。③冷凍機器。
***chill·y** [ˈtʃɪlɪ; ˈtʃili] *adj.,* **chill·i·er, chill·i·est,** *adv.* —*adj.* ①寒冷的。②不友好的;態度冷淡的。③恐怖的。—*adv.* 寒冷地;冷漠地。
chilo- 〖字首〗表"脣;脣狀的"之義。
chi·lo·pod [ˈkaɪləˌpɑd; ˈkailəpɔd] *n.* 〖動物〗蜈蚣。
chimb [tʃaɪm; tʃaim] *n.* 桶、樽等之凸邊或口邊。
chime**[1] [tʃaɪm; tʃaim] *n., v.,* **chimed, chim·ing.** —*n.* ①一套發諧音的鐘。②(*pl.*)該項鐘所發出的樂聲。③和諧。④門鈴。⑤諧音;音樂。—*v.t.* ①鳴(鐘); 鳴(鐘)作樂聲。②擊(鐘)以報時。—*v.i.* ①(鐘)鳴。②發出和諧之聲。③和諧; 調和。chime in***加入或插嘴。***chime in with*** 同意;一致。
chime[2] *n.* =**chimb.**
chi·me·ra [kəˈmɪrə; kaiˈmiərə] *n.* ①(C-)〖希臘神話〗 獅頭、羊身、蛇尾之吐火怪獸;任何類似此獸之怪物。②怪物。③幻想;妄想。(亦作 **chimaera**)
chi·mere [tʃɪˈmɪr; tʃiˈmiə] *n.* 一種寬大無袖之法衣(通常爲主教所穿着者)。
chi·mer·i·cal [kəˈmɪrɪkl; kaiˈmerikəl] *adj.* ①幻想的;妄想的。②荒誕不經的;不可能的。(亦作 **chimeric**)—**ly,** *adv.* —**ness,** *n.*
***chim·ney** [ˈtʃɪmnɪ; ˈtʃimni] *n., pl.* **-neys.** ①煙囪。②玻璃燈罩。③石頭、山、火山等的裂縫。④〖方〗火爐。—**ed,** *adj.* —**less,** *adj.*
chimney cap 煙囪蓋。
chimney corner 火爐的角隅;近火處。
chimney piece 壁爐架。
chimney place 〖美〗火爐;壁爐。
chimney pot 煙囪頂管。
chimney-pot hat 高頂絲質禮帽。
chimney shaft 煙囪。
chimney stack ①(有數個通煙道之)總合煙囪。②(泛指)僅一通煙道之煙囪。
chimney stalk (高出屋面之) 煙突;

工場之高煙囪。

chimney swallow 一種歐洲產的燕子。

chimney sweep(er) 掃煙囪的人。

chimney swift 一種北美洲產之燕子。

chim·pan·zee 〔ˌtʃɪmpænˈzi; ˌtʃimpənˈziː〕 *n.* 〖動物〗非洲之小人猿;黑猩猩。

chin** 〔tʃɪn; tʃin〕 *n., v.,* **chinned, chin·ning.** —*n.* ①頰;下頷;顎;頤。②〖俗〗談話。 ***keep one's chin up 在逆境中不屈不撓。***up to the chin*** 深及顎的。—*v.t.* ①引體向上。②將(小提琴等)提到顎下。—*v.i.*①閒談;閒聊天。②(單槓)引體向上。

Chin. ①China. ②Chinese.

‡**Chi·na** 〔ˈtʃaɪnə; ˈtʃainə〕 *n.* 中國。the Republic of *China.* 中華民國。

***chi·na**¹ 〔ˈtʃaɪnə; ˈtʃainə〕 *n.* ①陶瓷;瓷器;陶器。②瓷製小雕像。—*adj.* ①瓷製的。②一序列事物的第20號,如結婚之第20周年紀念。

chi·na² 〔ˈkaɪnə; ˈkainə〕 *n.* =**cinchona.**

China aster 翠菊。

chi·na·ber·ry 〔ˈtʃaɪnəˌbɛrɪ; ˈtʃainəbəri〕 *n., pl.* **-ries.** ①〖植物〗楝樹。②楝樹之果實。

china clay 陶土;瓷土。

China External Trade Development Council (中國)外貿協會。

china grass 〖植物〗苧蔴。

Chi·na·man 〔ˈtʃaɪnəmən; ˈtʃainəmən〕 *n., pl.* **-men.** ①〖蔑〗中國人;華人。②(c-)磁器商人。***a Chinaman's chance*** 〖美〗渺茫的機會。

china shop 瓷器店。

Chi·nat 〔ˈtʃaɪnæt; ˈtʃainæt〕 *n., adj.* 〖美〗中國國民黨(的)。

Chi·na·town 〔ˈtʃaɪnəˌtaun; ˈtʃainətaun〕 *n.* 唐人街。

China watcher 近代中國政治之觀察研究者。

chin·ca·pin 〔ˈtʃɪŋkəpɪn; ˈtʃiŋkəpin〕 *n.* 〖植物〗=**chinquapin.**

chinch 〔tʃɪntʃ; tʃintʃ〕 *n.* ①臭蟲。②=**chinch bug.**

chinch bug 麥虱。

chin·chil·la 〔tʃɪnˈtʃɪlə; tʃinˈtʃilə〕 *n.* ①〖動物〗南美產之栗鼠類。②栗鼠類之毛皮。③用此類毛皮做之衣服。

chin·chin 〔ˈtʃɪnˌtʃɪn; ˈtʃintʃin〕 *n., v.t. & v.i.* **-chinned, -chin·ning.** 〖中〗客套;寒暄;問安(即"請請"之音譯)。

chin·cough 〔ˈtʃɪnˌkɔf; ˈtʃinkɔːf〕 *n.* 百日咳。

chine¹ 〔tʃaɪn; tʃain〕 *n.* ①脊椎。②脊肉;排骨肉。③山脊;嶺。

chine² *n.* 〖英〗狹而深的峽谷。

Chi·nee 〔tʃaɪˈni; tʃaiˈniː〕 *n.* 〖俚〗中國人。

***Chi·nese** 〔tʃaɪˈniz; ˈtʃaiˈniːz〕 *n., pl.* **-nese,** *adj.* —*n.* ①中國人。The *Chinese* are a peace-loving people. 中國人是一個愛好和平的民族。②中國的文字;中國的語言。Foreigners find it difficult to learn *Chinese.* 外國人覺得中文很難學。—*adj.* 中國的;中國人的。 *Chinese* ink. 墨。〖注意〗(1) Chinese 是通用字,單數 a Chinese, 複數 the Chinese. (2)Chinaman(或 Chinamen)及 chinee 含有蔑視之意。Chinee 現已罕用。

Chinese cabbage 大白菜;黃芽白。(亦作 **celery cabbage**)

Chinese costume 中裝;唐裝。

Chinese jujube 棗樹;棗。

Chinese Kung·fu 〔~ ˈgʊŋ ˈfu; ~ ˈgʊŋˈfuː〕 中國功夫;國術。

Chinese lantern 能摺起之紙燈籠。

Chinese puzzle ①極複雜而難解答之事。②難解之謎。

Chinese red 朱紅色;橘紅色。

Chinese restaurant syndrome 某些外國人吃中國菜所發生的某些症狀。

Chinese Wall 長城。

Chinese watermelon 冬瓜。

Chinese white 鋅白。

Chinese wisteria 紫籐。

Ching·hai 〔ˈtʃɪŋˈhaɪ; ˈtʃiŋˈhai〕 *n.* 青海(中國西北之一省,省會西寧 Sining).

chin·ic acid 〔ˈkɪnɪk~; ˈkinik~〕 〖化〗奎寧酸。(亦作 **quinic acid**)

***chink**¹ 〔tʃɪŋk; tʃiŋk〕 *n.* 裂罅。—*v.t.* ①使成裂罅。②塞住(裂罅、裂縫等)。

chink² *n.* ①(玻璃等所發出之)叮噹聲。②〖俚〗錢幣;現款。—*v.t. & v.i.* (使)作叮噹聲。

Chin·men 〔ˈdʒɪnˈmɛn; ˈdʒinˈmen〕 *n.* 金門(中國福建省東部之一島)。(亦作 **Kinmen, Quemoy**)

Chino- 〖字首〗表"中國"之義。

Chi·nook 〔tʃɪˈnuk; tʃiˈnuk〕 *n., pl.* **-nook, -nooks.** ①契努克(北美印第安人之一族)。②該族人所使用之語言。

chin·qua·pin 〔ˈtʃɪŋkəpɪn; ˈtʃiŋkəpin〕 *n.* ①北美產之矮栗樹。②(北美沿太平洋海岸所產之)一種類似矮栗樹之灌木。③上述兩種植物所產之堅果。

chintz 〔tʃɪnts; tʃints〕 *n.* 印花棉布。(亦作 **chints**)

chin-up 〔ˈtʃɪnˌʌp; ˈtʃinʌp〕 *n.* (單槓運動時)將身體拉上直至下顎與槓平。—*adj.* 不洩氣的;保持士氣的;提高士氣的。

chip**¹ 〔tʃɪp; tʃip〕 *n., v.,* **chipped, chip·ping.** —*n.* ①碎片;碎渣;木屑。②瓷器或玻璃器破損後留下的缺口。③小片食物。potato *chips.* (油炸的)馬鈴薯片。④圓形籌碼。⑤(編籃子或帽子的)棕葉或草的細條。⑥做燃料用的乾糞。⑦無價值之物;瑣屑之物。Honors are but *chips* to him. 彼視功名如塵土。⑧鑽石或水晶的小片。⑨灌唱片時錄音針所排除的細片。a chip off*** (or ***of***) ***the old block*** 酷似父親的兒子。***as dry as a chip*** 非常乾燥無味。 ***chip on one's shoulder*** 好吵架的脾氣。—*v.t.*①切爲小片;破爲碎片。②切取小片下來。③切小片而使(某物)成形。④〖英俚〗嘲笑。⑤打賭;賭博(用籌碼等)。—*v.i.* 碎裂;破裂。These cups *chip* easily. 這些杯容易破裂。***chip in*** **a.** 集資;共同援助。**b.** 插嘴。**c.** 用籌碼打賭。

chip² *n.* 角力時摔對手的不光明手法。

chip·munk 〔ˈtʃɪpmʌŋk; ˈtʃipmʌŋk〕 *n.* 〖動物〗(北美產之)花栗鼠。(亦作**chipmuck**)

chipped beef 〖美〗燻製的牛肉片。

Chip·pen·dale 〔ˈtʃɪpənˌdel; ˈtʃipəndeil〕 *n.* 齊本德耳 (Thomas, 1718?-1779, 英國傢具設計家)。—*adj.* 齊本德耳式的。

chip·per 〔ˈtʃɪpɚ; ˈtʃipə〕 *adj.* 〖美俗〗輕快的;活潑的;愉快的。—*v.t.* 〖美俗〗使愉快;使振作〖up〗。

chip·ping 〔ˈtʃɪpɪŋ; ˈtʃipiŋ〕 *n.* ①割切;雕刻。②碎片;小片。

chip·py 〔ˈtʃɪpɪ; ˈtʃipi〕 *adj.,* **chip·pi·er, chip·pi·est,** *n., pl.* **-pies.** —*adj.* ①多屑片的。②枯燥無味的;極乾燥的。③〖俗〗酒後口渴的。④〖俗〗心情惡劣的。—*n.* ①花栗鼠;松鼠。②〖俚〗浪漫女子;娼妓。

chirk 〔tʃɝk; tʃəːk〕 *adj.* 〖美俗〗高興的;快活的。—*v.t. & v.i.* ①〖美俗〗(使)變高興〖up〗。②發出尖銳的吱喳聲。

chi·rog·no·my 〔kaɪˈrɑgnəmɪ; kaiˈrɔgnəmi〕 *n.* 手相術。

chi·ro·graph 〔ˈkaɪrəˌgræf; ˈkaiərougrɑːf〕 *n.* ①〖法律〗任何正式簽字之文件。②教皇之親筆特許證書。

chi·rog·ra·phy [kaɪˈrɑgrəfɪ; ˌkaiəˈrɔgrəfi] *n.* 書法；筆跡。—**chi·rog·ra·pher,** *n.*

chi·ro·man·cy [ˈkaɪrəˌmænsɪ; ˈkaiəromænsi] *n.*手相術。—**chi·ro·man·cer,** *n.*

chi·rop·o·dy [kaɪˈrɑpədɪ; kiˈrɔpədi] *n.* 手足病之治療。—**chi·rop·o·dist,** *n.*

chi·ro·prac·tic [ˌkaɪrəˈpræktɪk; ˌkaiərəˈpræktik] *n.* 按摩脊椎之指壓法。

chi·ro·prac·tor [ˈkaɪrəˌpræktɚ; ˈkaiərəpræktə] *n.* 按摩脊椎療病者；手醫。

Chi·rop·ter·a [kaɪˈrɑptərə; kaiˈrɔptərə] *n. pl.* 〖動物〗翼手類。

***chirp** [tʃɝp; tʃəːp] *v.i.* (鳥)吱喳而鳴；啁啾而鳴；(蟲) 唧唧而鳴；瑟瑟而鳴。—*v.t.* 吱喳鳴出或唧出。—*n.* 吱喳聲；唧唧聲。

chirp·y [ˈtʃɝpɪ; ˈtʃəːpi] *adj.,* **chirp·i·er, chirp·i·est.** ①〖俗〗快樂的。②愛吱喳而鳴的。

chirr [tʃɝ; tʃəː] *v.i.* (鳥或蟋蟀等) 唧唧叫。—*n.* (鳥或蟋蟀等之) 唧唧聲。(亦作 **chirre, churr**)

chir·rup [ˈtʃɪrəp; ˈtʃirəp] *v.,* **-ruped, -rup·ing,** *n.* —*v.i.* & *v.t.* ①(鳥或蟋蟀等) 吱喳鳴叫。②嘖嘖咂嘴(以刺激金絲雀、馬等)。—*n.* ①(鳥或蟲之)吱喳鳴聲。②咂嘴聲。

***chis·el** [ˈtʃɪzḷ; ˈtʃizl] *n., v.,* **-el(l)ed, -el·(l)ing.** —*n.* 鑿子。to cut with a *chisel.* 用鑿子鑿。—*v.t.* ①鑿；刻。②〖美俚〗詐取；騙取。—*v.i.* ①用鑿子工作。②〖美俚〗欺騙。—**er,** *n.*

chis·eled [ˈtʃɪzḷd; ˈtʃizld] *adj.* ①鑿刻的。②如鑿刻的；輪廓分明的。

chit[1] [tʃɪt; tʃit] *n., v.,* **chit·ted, chit·ting.** —*n.* ①芽。②小孩。③活潑之少女。—*v.i.* 〖方〗發芽。—*v.t.* 〖俗〗去…之芽。

chit[2] *n.* ①〖英〗短信；便條。②小額掛帳之單據；借條。(亦作 **chitty**)

chit·chat [ˈtʃɪtˌtʃæt; ˈtʃittʃæt] *n., v.i.,* **-chat·ted, -chat·ting.** 閒聊；聊天。

chi·tin [ˈkaɪtɪn; ˈkaitin] *n.* 蟹殼質；角質素；殼素。

chi·tin·ous [ˈkaɪtɪnəs; ˈkaitinəs] *adj.* 幾丁質的；(似)角質素的；(似)殼素的。

chi·ton [ˈkaɪtṇ; ˈkaitn] *n.* ①古希臘人所着之貼身衣服。②附着於岩石上的軟體動物。

chit·ter·lings [ˈtʃɪtɚlɪŋz; ˈtʃitəliŋz] *n. pl.* 豬等之小腸。(亦作 **chitlings**)

chiv·al·ric [ˈʃɪvḷrɪk; ˈʃivəlrik] *adj.* 有武士氣概的；有武士風範的。

chiv·al·rous [ˈʃɪvḷrəs; ˈʃivəlrəs] *adj.* 有武士風度的；俠義的。—**ly,** *adv.* —**ness,** *n.*

***chiv·al·ry** [ˈʃɪvḷrɪ; ˈʃivəlri] *n.* ①武士氣概。②武士制度。③武士團。④豪俠之士。

chive [tʃaɪv; tʃaiv] *n.* 〖植物〗蝦夷蔥。

chiv·vy [ˈtʃɪvɪ; ˈtʃivi] *n., pl.,* **-vies,** *v.,* **-vied, -vy·ing.** —*n.* 追獵；狩獵時之喊叫。—*v.t.* ①追逐；追獵。②使困窘。—*v.i.* 跑；疾走。(亦作 **chevy, chivy**)

Ch.J. Chief Justice.

chla·mys [ˈklæmɪs; ˈklæmis] *n., pl.* **-mys·es, -my·des** [-mədiz; -midiːz]. 古希臘男子所着之一種短斗篷或外套。

chlo·ral [ˈklorəl; ˈklɔːrəl] *n.* 〖化〗三氯乙醛。

chloral hydrate 〖化〗水合三氯乙醛(麻醉劑)。

chlo·ral·ism [ˈklorəlɪzəm; ˈklɔːrəlizəm] *n.* ①水合三氯乙醛之經常使用。②由此而引起之病態。

chlor·am·phen·i·col [ˌklɔræmˈfɛnəˌkol; ˌklɔːræmˈfenikɔl] *n.* 〖藥〗氯黴素。

chlo·rate [ˈklorɪt; ˈklɔːrit] *n.* 〖化〗氯酸鹽。

chlo·rel·la [kləˈrɛlə; kləˈrelə] *n.*綠藻。

chlo·ric [ˈklorɪk; ˈklɔːrik] *adj.* 〖化〗氯的；含氯的。

chlo·ride [ˈkloraɪd; ˈklɔːraid] *n.* 〖化〗氯化物。(亦作 **chlorid**)

chloride of lime 漂白粉。

chlo·rid·ize [ˈklorɪdˌaɪz; ˈklɔːridaiz] *v.t.,* **-ized, -iz·ing.** 使與氯化合；用氯化物處理。

chlo·rin [ˈklorɪn; ˈklɔːrin] *n.* =**chlorine.**

chlo·rin·ate [ˈklorɪˌnet; ˈklɔːrineit] *v.t.,* **-at·ed, -at·ing.** ①〖化〗使與氯化合；以氯處理。②以氯消毒。—**chlo·rin·a·tion,** *n.*

chlo·rine [ˈklorin; ˈklɔːriːn] *n.*〖化〗氯。

chlo·rite [ˈkloraɪt; ˈklɔːrait] *n.* ①〖化〗亞氯酸鹽。②〖礦〗綠泥石。

chlo·ro·dyne [ˈklorəˌdaɪn; ˈklɔːrədain] *n.* 〖藥〗哥羅顛(一種麻醉鎮痛劑)。

chlo·ro·form [ˈklorəˌfɔrm; ˈklɔːrəfɔːm] *n.* ①〖化〗三氯甲烷($CHCl_3$)。②〖醫〗氯仿；哥羅仿(一種有香味的無色流質，用作麻醉劑)。—*v.t.* ①用氯仿麻醉。②用氯仿殺死。

Chlo·ro·my·ce·tin [ˌklorəmaɪˈsitɪn; ˌklɔːroumaiˈsiːtin] *n.* 〖藥，商標名〗綠黴素；氯氨苯醇。

chlo·ro·phyll, chlo·ro·phyl [ˈklorəˌfɪl; ˈklɔrəfil] *n.* 葉綠素。

chlo·ro·phyl·lous [ˌkloraˈfɪləs; ˌklɔːrəˈfiləs] *adj.* 葉綠素的；含葉綠素的。

chlo·ro·pic·rin [ˌklorəˈpɪkrɪn; ˌklɔːrəˈpikrin] *n.* 〖化〗氯化苦劑(一種有毒性的無色液體，可造成嘔吐、流淚、頭痛，通常用於泥土之殺蟲劑)。

chlo·ro·plast [ˈklorəˌplæst; ˈklɔːrəplæst] *n.* 〖植物〗葉綠粒。

chlo·ro·prene [ˈklorəprin; ˈklɔːrəpriːn] *n.* 〖化〗氯丁二烯(合成橡膠的原料)。

chlo·ro·quine [ˈklorəkwin; ˈklɔːrəkwiːn] *n.* 治療瘧疾的一種特效藥。

chlo·ro·sis [kləˈrosɪs; kləˈrousis] *n.* ①〖醫〗萎黃病；綠色貧血。②〖植物〗變色病。

chlo·rous [ˈklorəs; ˈklɔːrəs] *adj.* 〖化〗①亞氯的；氯化的。②亞氯酸的。

chm. ①chairman. ②checkmate.

chmn. chairman.

chock [tʃɑk; tʃɔk] *n.* ①墊木；楔子 (置於圓桶下，以防止滾動者)。②船旁穿繩索的定盤；大船上安置救生艇的定盤。—*v.t.* ①用墊木或楔子墊阻。②置(小艇)於定盤上。***chock up*** **a.** 墊。**b.** 塞滿 (傢具於室內)。—*adv.* 塞滿地。

chock·a·block [ˈtʃɑkəˈblɑk; ˈtʃɔkəˈblɔk] *adj.* ①拉緊致使滑車相觸的。②過分擁擠的；十分緊的。—*adv.* 擠擁地。

chock-full [ˈtʃɑkˈfʊl; ˈtʃɔkˈful] *adj.* 塞滿了的。

***choc·o·late** [ˈtʃɔkəlɪt; ˈtʃɔkəlit] *n.* ①巧克力製品。②巧克力飲料。③巧克力糖。a box of *chocolates.* 一盒巧克力糖。④黑褐色。⑤巧克力糖漿或巧克力香料。—*adj.*①巧克力製的。②用巧克力調味的。③黑褐色的。

choc·o·late-box [ˈtʃɔkəlɪtbɔks; ˈtʃɔkəlitbɑks] *adj.* (像巧克力盒子)虛有其表的。

Choc·taw [ˈtʃɑktɔ; ˈtʃɔktɔː] *n.* ①巢克圖族人 (北美印第安人之一族)。②巢克圖語。—*adj.* 巢克圖族的；巢克圖語的。

‡**choice** [tʃɔɪs; tʃɔis] *n., adj.,* **choic·er, choic·est.** —*n.* ①選擇。Make your *choice.* 你選擇罷。②被選之人或物。This book is my *choice.* 這本書是我所選的。③選擇的機會與權利。You have no other *choice* but

to leave now. 你沒有其他的選擇，只有現在離開。④備選的量和種類。a wide *choice* of candidates. 可供選擇的候選人很多。⑤精選的或最佳的部分。—*adj.* ①慎選的;小心選擇的。The speech was delivered in *choice* words. 這篇演說措辭謹嚴。②上等的。—**less,** *adj.*

choice·ly 〔'tʃɔɪslɪ; 'tʃɔisli〕 *adv.* 精選地;卓越地。

choice·ness 〔'tʃɔɪsnɪs; 'tʃɔisnis〕 *n.* 精選; 優良。

***choir** 〔kwaɪr; 'kwaiə〕 *n.* ①(教堂中的)唱詩班; 歌唱隊。②教堂中唱詩班的席位。③任何歌唱隊或跳舞隊。a *choir* of dancers. 一隊舞蹈者。—*v.t.* & *v.i.*合唱。

choir·boy 〔'kwaɪr,bɔɪ; 'kwaiəbɔi〕 *n.* 唱詩班之男童。

choir·girl 〔'kwaɪr,gɝl; 'kwaiəgə:l〕 *n.* 唱詩班之女童。

choir·mas·ter 〔'kwaɪr,mæstə; 'kwaiə,mɑ:stə〕 *n.* 唱詩班指揮。

choir organ 伴奏唱詩之風琴。

choir screen (禮拜堂中)圍隔唱詩班之屏障或圍欄。

choke** 〔tʃok; tʃouk〕 *v.,* **choked, chok·ing,** *n.* —*v.t.* ①扼喉; 勒絞;使窒息;使不能呼吸。②因窒悶而使不能出聲(由於情感的激動)。③塞住;阻塞;塡塞。④使(火)熄滅。⑤壓制(情感)〖常 back, down〗. She *choked* back a sharp reply. 她忍住了(而未作)尖刻的答覆。⑥阻止成長、進展等。⑦裝滿。⑧高握(球棒等)(握着比通常高的地方)〖常up〗. —*v.i.* ①窒息。②阻塞。choke back*** 忍住;抑制。***choke down*** 忍住;抑制。***choke off*** a. 窒息死;悶死。b. 放棄;終止;結束。***choke up*** a. 阻塞。b. 〖俗〗因感情衝動而說不出話來。—*n.* ①阻塞之行爲或聲音。②汽油發動機內關閉空氣的活門。

choke·bore 〔'tʃok,bor; 'tʃoukbɔ:〕 *n.* ①口徑漸狹之獵槍管。②具此種槍管之獵槍。

choke·cher·ry 〔'tʃok,tʃɛrɪ; 'tʃouk,tʃeri〕 *n., pl.* **-ries.** (北美產之)野櫻; 野櫻桃。

choke collar 如索套之項圈(用來約束猛犬)。

choke·damp 〔'tʃok,dæmp; 'tʃoukdæmp〕 *n.* 礦坑內令人窒息之氣體(主要爲二氧化碳)。

choke-full 〔'tʃok'fʊl; 'tʃoukful〕 *adj.* =**chock-full.**

choke point 瓶頸;阻礙。

chok·er 〔'tʃokɚ; 'tʃoukə〕 *n.* ①阻礙之人或事物。②〖俗〗a. 緊項鍊。b. 高領。

chok·ing 〔'tʃokɪŋ; 'tʃoukiŋ〕 *adj.* ①(聲音)因感動而嘶啞的。②使人窒息的。

chok·y[1], chok·ey[1] 〔'tʃokɪ; 'tʃouki〕 *adj.,* **chok·i·er, chok·i·est.** 使人窒息的。

chok·y[2], chok·ey[2] *n., pl.* **-kies.** 〖英印,英俚〗拘留所;監獄。

cho·le·cal·cif·er·ol 〔,koləkæl'sɪfə,rol; ,kouləkæl'sifəroul〕 *n.* 維他命 D_3。

chol·e·cyst 〔'kɑlə,sɪst; 'kɔlisist〕 *n.* 〖解剖〗膽囊。

chol·e·cys·tec·to·my 〔,kɑləsɪs'tɛktəmɪ; ,kɔlisis'tektəmi〕 *n., pl.* **-mies.** 〖外科〗膽囊切除術。

cho·le·cys·ti·tis 〔,kɑləsɪs'taɪtɪs; ,kɔlisis'taitis〕 *n.* 〖醫〗膽囊炎。

chol·e·lith, chol·o·lith 〔'kɑləlɪθ; 'kɔləliθ〕 *n.* 〖醫〗膽結石。

chol·er 〔'kɑlɚ; 'kɔlə〕 *n.* ①憤怒。②〖古〗膽汁(古時認爲膽汁旺盛時,人易於發怒)。

***chol·er·a** 〔'kɑlərə; 'kɔlərə〕 *n.* 霍亂。

chol·er·a·ic 〔,kɑlə'e·ɪk; ,kɔlə'reiik〕 *adj.* 霍亂病的; 類似霍亂的。

cholera in·fan·tum 〔~ɪn'fæntəm; ~in'fæntəm〕 〖醫〗嬰兒吐瀉病。

cholera mor·bus 〔~'mɔrbəs; ~'mɔ:bəs〕 〖醫〗假霍亂; 似霍亂病。(亦作 **cholera nostras**)

chol·er·ic 〔'kɑlərɪk; 'kɔlərik〕 *adj.* ①易怒的;性急的;暴躁的。②與霍亂有關的。

chol·er·ine 〔'kɑlərɪn; 'kɔlərin〕 *n.* ①輕性霍亂。②霍亂病之初期。

cho·les·ter·ol 〔kə'lɛstə,rol; kə'lestəroul〕 *n.*〖生化〗膽固醇。(亦作 **cholesterin**)

cho·les·ter·ol·e·mi·a 〔kə'lɛstəro'limɪə; kə'lestərou'li:miə〕 *n.* 〖醫〗膽醇血症。(亦作 **cholesteremia**)

cho·li·amb 〔'kolɪæmb; 'kouliæmb〕 *n.* 〖韻律〗以揚揚格終結的不規則之抑揚格。(亦作 **scazon**)

cho·line 〔'kolin; 'kouli:n〕 *n.* 〖生化〗膽鹼;膽素;膽毒。

chol·la 〔'tʃoljɑ; 'tʃouljɑ:〕 *n.* 〖植物〗一種多刺的仙人掌(產於美國西南部及墨西哥)。

Cho·lon 〔,ʃɔ'lɔ̃; ,ʃɔ:'lɔ̃〕 *n.* 堤岸(越南西貢西南之一城市)。

choo-choo 〔'tʃu,tʃu; 'tʃu:tʃu:〕 *n., v.,* **-chooed, -choo·ing.** 〖兒語〗—*n.* ①火車。②火車發出之聲音。—*v.i.* ①發出火車之聲音。②坐火車。

choo·ra 〔'tʃʊrə; 'tʃurə〕 *n.* 印第安人用的一種單刃匕首。

‡**choose** 〔tʃuz; tʃu:z〕 *v.,* **chose** 〔tʃoz; tʃouz〕, **cho·sen** 〔'tʃozn̩; 'tʃouzn〕, **choos·ing.** —*v.t.* ①選擇。*Choose* the cake you like best. 選擇你所最喜歡的餅。②寧願。He would *choose* death before surrender. 他寧死不降。③欲; 望; 要。They *choose* to stay here. 他們願留此處。—*v.i.* ①選擇。There is not much to *choose* between the two. 二者之間無可選擇(無多大差別)。Go or stay where you are, as you *choose.* 去留任你選擇(請隨君便)。②作決定。You must *choose.* 你必須決定。***cannot choose but*** 不得不;只有。He *cannot choose but* hear. 他不得不聽命(他只有聽命)。***choose up*** 〖俗〗(運動、比賽等)分隊; 分組(常與 sides, teams 等連用)。—**choos·a·ble,** *adj.* —**choos·er,** *n.* —**choos·ing·ly,** *adv.*

choos·(e)y 〔'tʃuzɪ; 'tʃu:zi〕 *adj.,* **choos·i·er, choos·i·est.** 〖美俚〗性好挑選的;難以求悅的;苛求的。

chop[1]** 〔tʃɑp; tʃɔp〕 *v.,* **chopped, chop·ping,** *n.* —*v.t.* ①砍。②切碎。③切擊(網球)。④做疾速之動作。⑤伐木以開路。The explorer *chopped* his way through the bushes. 那探險者在矮叢中砍出一條路而前進。⑥持續而有節奏地切斷(光線、電流等)。—*v.i.* ①砍。②突然插入。③突然改變方向。④闖入;打擊。chop down*** 砍倒。***chop off*** 砍斷。—*n.* ①砍。②(切下的一塊)連骨的肉。lamb *chop,* pork *chop,* veal *chop.* 羊排、豬排、(小)牛排。③切擊。④隨風翻動的碎浪。⑤砍下之東西。⑥〖拳擊〗向下猛烈的一擊。⑦浪之不規則的運動。

chop[2] *n.* (常 *pl.*)①顎。②頰。③口腔。④海峽、山谷、深淵等的入口。***lick one's chops (over)*** 〖俚〗等待;期望。

chop[3] *n.* ①圖章;印。②〖俚〗品質; 等級。

chop[4] *v.,* **chopped, chop·ping.** —*v.i.* ①(風等)突然改變。②〖英方〗改變主意。***chop and change*** 改變策略或方法; 時時改變。***chop logic*** 詭辯;吹毛求疵。

chop block 切肉砧板。(亦作 **chop-**

board, chopping block)
chop-chop [ˈtʃɑpˈtʃɑp; ˈtʃɔpˈtʃɔp] *adv., interj.* 快;立刻(洋涇浜英語)。
chop·house [ˈtʃɑpˌhaus; ˈtʃɔphaus] *n.* 小食店(通常以供應肉排類食品爲主)。
Cho·pin [ˈʃopæn; ˈʃɔpɛ̃ːŋ] *n.* 蕭邦 (Frédéric François, 1810–1849, 波蘭鋼琴家及作曲家)。
chop·log·ic [ˈtʃɑpˌlɑdʒɪk; ˈtʃɔpˌlɔdʒik] *n.* 詭辯。—*adj.* (亦作 **choplogical**) 好辯的;好抬槓的。
chop·per [ˈtʃɑpɚ; ˈtʃɔpə] *n.* ①切物之人。②切割之機器或器具;刀;斧。③光線或電流之阻斷器。④〖俗〗直升機。⑤(*pl.*) 牙齒。—*v.i.* 〖俚〗乘直升機飛行。
chop·ping [ˈtʃɑpɪŋ; ˈtʃɔpiŋ] *adj.* ①(海) 波濤洶湧的;急變的。②〖英俗〗碩大健壯的。
chopping knife (細剁用之)菜刀。
chop·py [ˈtʃɑpɪ; ˈtʃɔpi] *adj.*, **-pi·er, -pi·est.** ①(海等) 波浪起伏的。②突變的(風等)。③急動的。④多縫的;有皺紋的。
chop·sticks [ˈtʃɑpˌstɪks; ˈtʃɔpstiks] *n. pl.* 筷子。
chop su·ey [ˈtʃɑpˈsuɪ; ˈtʃɔpˈsuːi]〖美〗雜碎(一種中國菜);雜炒菜。(亦作 **chop sooy**)
cho·ral [ˈkorəl; ˈkɔːrəl] *adj.* ①合唱隊的。②合唱隊所唱的。—*n.* ①讚美詩調;聖歌調。②合唱聖歌的簡單嚴肅曲調。—**ly,** *adv.*
cho·rale [koˈrɑl; kɔˈrɑːl] *n.* ①讚美詩調;聖歌調。②唱此種歌之合唱團。
cho·ral·ist [ˈkorəlɪst; ˈkɔːrəlist] *n.* ①聖歌歌手。②合唱隊員。③合唱曲作曲者。
choral speaking 合唱團之詩歌朗誦。
***chord** [kɔrd; kɔːd] *n.* ①樂弦;琴線。②身體內的絃狀物。vocal *chord.* 聲帶。spinal *chord.* 脊髓。③〖音樂〗和絃;和諧音。④〖數學〗弦。⑤情緒;感情。⑥〖土木〗弦材;臥材。
chor·date [ˈkɔrdet; ˈkɔːdeit] *adj.* 〖動物〗脊索動物的。—*n.* 脊索類動物。
chord organ 電子琴。
chore [tʃor, tʃɔr; tʃɔː, tʃɔə] *n., v.,* **chored, chor·ing.** —*n.* 〖美〗①小工作;零工。②(*pl.*) 家庭中或農場上之雜務。③困難而討厭的工作。—*v.i.* 作零碎工作。
cho·re·a [koˈriə; kɔˈriə] *n.* 〖醫〗舞蹈症(一種使肌肉發生痙攣的神經病)。—**cho·re·al,** —**cho·re·ic,** *adj.*
chore boy ①伙伕的幫手。②打雜的工人。
chore·man [ˈtʃormən; ˈtʃɔːmən] *n., pl.* **-men.** 工廠或伐木站的打雜工人。
cho·re·og·ra·pher [ˌkorɪˈɑgrəfɚ; ˌkɔriˈɔgrəfə] *n.* ①舞蹈之作者(指舞式、舞步等之創作者)。②舞蹈指揮(尤指芭蕾舞者)。(英亦作 **choregrapher**)
cho·re·og·ra·phy [ˌkorɪˈɑgrəfɪ; ˌkɔriˈɔgrəfi] *n.* 舞蹈術;舞蹈(尤指芭蕾舞)。(英亦作 **choregraphy**)
cho·ri·amb [ˈkorɪˌæmb; ˈkɔriæmb] *n.* 〖韻律〗揚抑抑揚格(-◡◡-)。(亦作 **choriambus**) —**ic,** *adj.*
cho·ric [ˈkorɪk; ˈkɔrik] *adj.* 合唱的;合唱曲的。
cho·rine [ˈkorin; ˈkɔriːn] *n.* 〖俚〗歌舞團女團員。
cho·ri·on [ˈkorɪˌɑn; ˈkɔːriɔn] *n.*〖胚胎〗絨毛膜。—**ic,** —**ri·al,** *adj.*
cho·rist [ˈkorɪst; ˈkɔːrist] *n.* 合唱者;合唱隊員。
chor·is·ter [ˈkɔrɪstɚ; ˈkɔristə] *n.* ①(教堂中)唱詩班之一員。②(教堂中)唱詩班之男性唱詩者。③(教堂中)唱詩班指揮者。
cho·rog·ra·phy [kəˈrɑgrəfɪ; kəˈrɔgrəfi] *n.* 地圖編製;地誌編纂;地勢圖。
cho·roid [ˈkorɔɪd; ˈkɔːrɔid] *adj.* 似絨毛膜的;(眼球之)脈絡膜的。—*n.* (眼球之)脈絡膜。(亦作 **chorioid**)
cho·rol·o·gy [kəˈrɑlədʒɪ; kəˈrɔlədʒi] *n.* 〖生物〗種類分佈學;生物分佈學。
chor·tle [ˈtʃɔrtl̩; ˈtʃɔːtl] *v.,* **-tled, -tling,** *n.* —*v.t.* & *v.i.* 咯咯而笑;歡笑。—*n.* 縱聲歡笑;咯咯的笑(聲)。
***cho·rus** [ˈkorəs; ˈkɔːrəs] *n., pl.* **-rus·es,** *v.,* **-rused, -rus·ing.** —*n.* ①和唱隊;合唱隊。②歌曲中的複句(合唱部分)。③合唱隊所唱之歌。④異口同聲;同時喊出的話。⑤a. 歌舞團。b. 歌舞團所表演之歌舞。⑥a.(古代希臘劇中之)合唱隊。b. 此種合唱隊所唱之歌或頌。*in chorus* 一起;共同。—*v.t.* ①同唱。②同說。—*v.i.* ①同唱。②同說。
chorus boy 歌舞劇中之男歌星或舞星。
chorus girl 歌舞劇中之女歌星或舞星。
chose[1] [tʃoz; tʃouz] *v.* pt. of **choose.**
chose[2] [ʃoz; ʃouz] *n.* 〖法律〗物;私產。
chose ju·gée [ʃoz ʒyˈʒe; ʃouz ʒyˈʒei] *pl.* **choses ju·gées** [ʃoz ʒyʒˈe; ʃouz ʒyˈʒei]. 〖法〗已結束的事;已結束的案子。
***cho·sen** [ˈtʃozn̩; ˈtʃouzn] *v.* pp. of choose. —*adj.* 精選的。*the Chosen People* 上帝之選民;以色列人。
chou [ʃu; ʃuː] *n., pl.* **choux** [ʃu; ʃuː]. 〖法〗①球結;花球(裝飾用)。②〖植物〗甘藍。③〖俗〗親愛的。
chough [tʃʌf; tʃʌf] *n.* 歐洲產的一種烏鴉(脚嘴均爲赤色)。
chouse [tʃaus; tʃaus] *v.,* **choused, chous·ing,** *n.* —*v.t.* 〖俗〗欺;瞞〖常 of, out of〗. —*n.* 〖俗〗詐欺;欺騙。
chow [tʃau; tʃau] *n.* ①中國狗之一種(有褐色或黑色之厚毛,舌爲深藍色)。②〖俚〗食物。③(C-)〖澳蔑〗中國人。
chow·chow [ˈtʃauˌtʃau; ˈtʃauˈtʃau] *n.* ①醃菜。②中國狗的一種(=chow)。③(在中國,印度)雜菜;食物;一餐。④蜜餞。—*adj.* 混合的;什錦的。
chow·der [ˈtʃaudɚ; ˈtʃaudə] *n.* 〖美〗用魚或蛤加豬肉、洋葱等所燉之羹。
chow·der·head [ˈtʃaudɚˌhɛd; ˈtʃaudəhed] *n.* 〖美俚〗傻瓜;愚蠢的人。
chow·hound [ˈtʃauˌhaund; ˈtʃauhaund] *n.* 〖俚〗貪吃的人。
chow line (在軍營等) 飯廳前排隊等開飯的人們。
chow mein [ˈtʃauˈmen; ˈtʃauˈmein]〖中〗炒麵。
Chr. ①Christ. ②Christian. ③Christopher.
chres·tom·a·thy [krɛsˈtɑməθɪ; kresˈtɔməθi] *n., pl.* **-thies.** ①(學習語言用之)文選。②(某作家之)文集。
Chris [krɪs; kris] *n.* ①男子名(Christopher 之暱稱)。②女子名(Christine 之暱稱)。
chrism [ˈkrɪzəm; ˈkrizəm] *n.* ①(天主教儀式用)聖油。②聖油式。(亦作 **chrisom**) —**al,** *adj.*
chris·ma·to·ry [ˈkrɪzməˌtorɪ; ˈkrizmətəri] *n., pl.* **-ries.** 裝聖油之容器。
chris·om [ˈkrɪzəm; ˈkrizəm] *n.* ①(嬰兒之)洗禮服。②〖古〗=**chrism.**
***Christ** [kraɪst; kraist] *n.* 基督。
Christ child 基督兒時之畫像。
christ·cross [ˈkrɪsˌkrɔs; ˈkriskrɔs] *n.* ①〖古〗十字記號(作+或×形)。②〖英方〗字母。
chris·ten [ˈkrɪsn̩; ˈkrisn] *v.t.* ①施洗

禮以加入教會;施洗。②施洗禮以命名。③命名(尤指船)。④〖俗〗首次使用。—**er,** *n.*

Chris·ten·dom ['krɪsn̩dəm; 'krisndəm] *n.* ①世界上信奉基督教的地區;基督教國家。②基督徒之集合稱。

chris·ten·ing ['krɪsn̩ɪŋ;'krisəniŋ] *n.* 洗禮儀式;命名儀式。

Christ·hood ['kraɪsthʊd; 'kraisthud] *n.* 基督之地位;爲救世主。

‡**Chris·tian** ['krɪstʃən; 'kristʃən] *adj.* ①基督(教)的。the *Christian* Era. 耶穌紀元。②信基督的。③表現基督之精神的。*Christian* charity. 基督的慈悲精神;博愛。④人的;非動物的。⑤高尚的;受尊敬的。***most Christian*** 法國國王之尊號。—*n.* ①基督教徒。②〖俗〗高尚的人。③男子名(暱稱 Christie).

Chris·ti·an·a [ˌkrɪstɪ'ænə; ˌkristi'ɑːnə] *n.* 女子名。

Christian Church 基督教會。

*__Chris·ti·an·i·ty__ [ˌkrɪstʃɪ'ænətɪ, krɪs'tʃænətɪ; ˌkristi'æniti, kris'tjæn-] *n., pl.* **-ties.** ①基督教;基督教的教義。②基督教的信仰;基督教的精神。

Chris·tian·ize ['krɪstʃənˌaɪz; 'kristjənaiz] *v.,* **-ized, -iz·ing.** —*v.t.* 使爲基督教徒;使基督教化。—*v.i.* 皈依基督;信基督教。—**Chris·tian·i·za·tion,** *n.*

Christian name ①教名;洗禮名(亦作 **baptismal name**). ②名(亦稱 first name, given name, 爲姓 last name, family name, surname 之對)。

Christian Science 基督科學(以信仰療法爲特色的一種宗教)。

Chris·tie's, Chris·ties ['krɪstɪz; 'kristiz] *n.* 倫敦一售賣藝術品之場所名。

Chris·ti·na [krɪs'tinə; kris'tiːnə] *n.* 女子名(暱稱 **Chrissie**).

Christ Jesus 耶穌基督。

Christ·less ['kraɪstlɪs; 'kraistlis] *adj.* 不信奉基督的;非基督徒的。—**ness,** *n.*

Christ·like ['kraɪstˌlaɪk; 'kraistlaik] *adj.* 如基督的;如耶穌一樣的。(亦作 **Christly**) —**ness,** *n.*

‡**Christ·mas** ['krɪsməs; 'krisməs, -stm-] *n.* 耶誕節;聖誕節。*Christmas* carol. 聖誕頌歌。*Christmas* day. 聖誕日。*Christmas* gifts. 聖誕禮物。「俗」耶誕節所送的禮金。

Christmas box ①耶誕禮物。②〖英〗

Christmas card 耶誕卡片。

Christmas club 一種無息存款, 存款人定期存款而在聖誕節領取以購買聖誕禮物。

Christmas disease 一種血友病(遺傳性, 血不凝固的病)。

Christmas Eve 聖誕前夕。

Christmas factor 血液凝結素。

Christmas seal 〖美〗慈善防癆票。

Christmas stocking 襪子或襪子形的袋子, 聖誕節時懸掛在壁爐或聖誕樹以放聖誕禮物。

Christ·mas·tide ['krɪsməsˌtaɪd; 'krisməstaid] *n.* 耶誕節期(自十二月二十日至一月六日)。(亦作 **Christmastime**)

Christmas tree 聖誕樹。

Christ·mas·(s)y ['krɪsməsɪ; 'krisməsi] *adj.* 〖俗〗有耶誕節氣氛的。

Chris·tol·o·gy [krɪs'tɑlədʒɪ;kris'tɔlədʒi] *n., pl.*-**gies.**〖神學〗基督論。—**Chris·to·log·i·cal,** *adj.* —**Chris·tol·o·gist,** *n.*

Chris·toph·a·ny [krɪs'tɑfənɪ; kris'tɔfəni] *n., pl.* **-nies.** 基督復活後之顯現。

Chris·to·pher ['krɪstəfɚ; 'kristəfə] *n.* 男子名。

Christ's-thorn ['kraɪstsˌθɔrn; 'kraiststθɔːn] *n.*〖植物〗濱棗。

chro·mate ['kromet; 'kroumeit] *n.* 〖化〗鉻酸鹽。

chro·mat·ic [kro'mætɪk;krou'mætik] *adj.*①色彩的。②〖生物〗核染質的。③〖音樂〗半音階的。—**al·ly,** *adv.*

chromatic aberration 〖光學〗色(像)差。

chro·mat·ics [kro'mætɪks; krou'mætiks] *n.* (作 *sing.* 解)色彩學。(亦作 **chromatology**) —**chro·ma·tist,** *n.*

chromatic scale 〖音樂〗半音階。

chro·ma·tin ['kromətɪn; 'kroumətin] *n.*〖生物〗染色質;核染質。—**ic,** *adj.*

chro·ma·tism ['kromətɪzəm; 'kroumətizəm] *n.* ①〖植物〗變色。②後起色覺;僞色覺。

chro·ma·to·graph ['kromətəˌgræf; 'kroumətəgrɑːf] *n.* 層析計;色彩計。—*v.t.* 以層析法將(物質)分層。

chro·ma·to·phore ['kromətəˌfor; 'kroumətəfɔː] *n.* ①〖動物〗色素細胞。②〖植物〗色素粒。

chro·ma·trope ['kroməˌtrop;'kroumətroup] *n.* (幻燈上用之)廻轉彩色板。

chro·ma·type ['kroməˌtaɪp;'kroumətaip] *n.* ①鉻鹽像片; 彩色像片。②彩色像片之印製。(亦作 **chromotype**)

chrome [krom;kroum] *n., v.,* **chromed, chrom·ing.** —*n.* ①=**chromium.** ②〖化〗鉻黃。③鉻鋼。—*v.t.* 鍍以鉻。***chrome green*** 鉻綠。***chrome red*** 鉻紅。***chrome yellow*** 鉻黃。

chrome steel 鉻鋼。(亦作 **chromium steel**)

chro·mic ['kromɪk; 'kroumik] *adj.* 〖化〗鉻的。*chromic* acid. 鉻酸。

chro·mite ['kromaɪt; 'kroumait] *n.* ①〖礦〗鉻鐵礦。②〖化〗亞鉻酸鹽。

chro·mi·um ['kromɪəm; 'kroumiəm] *n.* 〖化〗鉻(其化學符號爲 Cr).

chro·mo ['kromo; 'kroumou] *n., pl.* **-mos.** =**chromolithograph.**

chro·mo·gen ['kromədʒən; 'kroumədʒən] *n.* ①〖化〗發色體。②色素原;色元。

chro·mo·graph ['kroməˌgræf; 'krouməgrɑːf] *n.* 〖印刷〗膠版。—*v.t.* 以膠版複製。

chro·mo·lith·o·graph [ˌkromo'lɪθəˌgræf; 'kroumou'liθəgrɑːf] *n.*〖印刷〗石版或鋅版套色之印刷品。—**ic,** *adj.* —**y,** *n.*

chro·mo·pho·to·graph [ˌkromə'fotəˌgræf; ˌkroumə'foutəgrɑːf] *n.* 天然色照片。

chro·mo·pho·tog·ra·phy [ˌkroməfə'tɑgrəfɪ;ˌkroumoufə'tɔgrəfi] *n.*天然色照相術。—**chro·mo·pho·to·graph·ic,** *adj.*

chro·mo·some ['kroməˌsom;'krouməsoum] *n.* 〖生物〗染色體。

chro·mo·sphere ['kroməˌsfɪr; 'krouməsfiə] *n.* 〖天文〗(太陽周邊的)彩層;色球。

chro·mous ['kroməs;'krouməs] *adj.* 〖化〗含亞鉻(指二價者)的。

Chron. Chronicles.

chron. ①chronological. ②chronology.

chron·ic ['krɑnɪk; 'krɔnik] *adj.*①慢性的(acute 之對)。②長期的。③慣常的。(亦作 **chronical**) —**al·ly,** *adv.*

*__chron·i·cle__ ['krɑnɪk]; 'krɔnikl] *n., v.,* **-cled, -cling.**—*n.* 編年史;紀;年代記。—*v.t.*

記事;載入年代史。—**chron·i·cler,** *n.*

chronicle play 歷史劇。(亦作**chronicle history**)

chron·o·gram [ˈkrɑnəˌgræm; ˈkrɔnəgræm] *n.* ①用其中特別顯著之字母表年代之題銘(例如:MerCy MiXed with LoVe In hIm– MCMXLVII=1947)。②計時器所作之記錄。

chron·o·graph [ˈkrɑnəˌgræf; ˈkrɔnəgrɑːf] *n.* 記時器。

chro·nol·o·ger [krəˈnɑlədʒɚ; krəˈnɔlədʒə] *n.* 年代學者。

chron·o·log·i·cal [ˌkrɑnəˈlɑdʒɪkḷ; ˌkrɔnəˈlɔdʒikəl] *adj.* 按年代次序記載的。(亦作 **chronologic**) —**ly,** *adv.*

chro·nol·o·gist [krəˈnɑlədʒɪst; krəˈnɔlədʒist] *n.* 年代學者。

chro·nol·o·gize [krəˈnɑləˌdʒaɪz; krəˈnɔlədʒaiz] *v.t.,* **-gized, -giz·ing.** 按年代排列;作年表。

chro·nol·o·gy [krəˈnɑlədʒɪ; krəˈnɔlədʒi] *n., pl.* **-gies.** 年代記;年代表。

chro·nom·e·ter [krəˈnɑmətɚ; krəˈnɔmitə] *n.*①精密時計。②航海用之經線儀。—**chron·o·met·ri·c(al),** *adj.*

chro·nom·e·try [krəˈnɑmətrɪ; krəˈnɔmətri] *n.* 測時術;計時法。

chron·o·pher [ˈkrɑnəfɚ; ˈkrɔnəfə] *n.* 電動報時器。

chron·o·scope [ˈkrɑnəˌskop; ˈkrɔnəskoup] *n.* 測時器;計時器。—**chron·o·scop·ic,** *adj.* —**chron·o·scop·i·cal·ly,** *adv.* —**chro·nos·co·py,** *n.*

chrys·a·lid [ˈkrɪslɪd; ˈkrisəlid] *adj.* 蛹的。—*n.* 蛹。

chrys·a·lis [ˈkrɪsḷɪs; ˈkrisəlis] *n., pl.* **-es, chry·sal·i·des** [krɪˈsæləˌdiz; kriˈsælidiːz]. ①蛹。②繭。③準備期。

chry·san·the·mum [krɪsˈænθəməm; kriˈsænθəməm] *n.* 菊;菊花。

Chry·se·is [kraɪˈsiɪs; kraiˈsiːis] *n.*〖希臘神話〗Homer 著 Iliad 史詩中之一美女。

chrys·el·e·phan·tine [ˌkrɪsɛlɪˈfæntɪn; ˌkriseliˈfæntin] *adj.* 用金及象牙造成的。

chrys·o·ber·yl [ˈkrɪsəˌbɛrɪl; ˈkrisəˌberil] *n.*〖礦〗金綠寶石。

chrys·o·lite [ˈkrɪsḷˌaɪt; ˈkrisoulait] *n.*〖礦〗貴橄欖石。 —**chrys·o·lit·ic,** *adj.*

chrys·o·prase [ˈkrɪsəˌprez; ˈkrisoupreiz] *n.*〖礦〗綠石髓。

Chuang-tzu [ˈdʒwɑŋˈdzu; ˈdʒwɑːŋˈdzu] *n.* 莊子(中國古代哲學家)。

chub [tʃʌb; tʃʌb] *n., pl.* **chub, chubs.** (歐洲產之)一種淡水魚。

chub·by [ˈtʃʌbɪ; ˈtʃʌbi] *adj.,* **-bi·er, -bi·est.** 圓胖的;豐滿的。—**chub·bi·ly,** *adv.* —**chub·bi·ness,** *n.*

chuck[1] [tʃʌk; tʃʌk] *v.t.* ①輕叩;輕捏(尤指戲叩或戲捏下頷)。②拋擲;投擲。③〖英俚〗驅逐〖out〗。④〖英俚〗辭職;解雇。***chuck a friend*** 與朋友斷絕往來。***Chuck it!*** 停!住手!住口!—*n.* ①拋擲;投擲。②輕叩或輕捏下頷。

chuck[2] *n.* ①牛頸部與肩胛骨之間之肉。②作爲塞子用的木塊。③〖機械〗掐子;叉柱。

chuck[3] *n.* ①咯咯(母鷄喚雛之聲)。②心肝;寶貝(暱稱)。—*v.t. & v.i.* 作咯咯聲。

chuck[4] *n.*〖美西部俚〗食物。

chuck·er [ˈtʃʌkɚ; ˈtʃʌkə] *n.*〖美俚〗投擲者(尤指棒球投手)。

chuck·er-out [ˈtʃʌkɚˈaut; ˈtʃʌkərˈaut] *n., pl.* **chuck·ers-out.**〖英〗娛樂場所等所雇用之打手。

chuck farthing 投錢於小穴中的一種遊戲。

chuck-full [ˈtʃʌkˈful; ˈtʃʌkˈful] *adj.* =**chock-full.**

chuck·hole [ˈtʃʌkˌhol; ˈtʃʌkhoul] *n.* 街道上之孔或低窪處。(亦作 **chuck hole**)

***chuck·le** [ˈtʃʌkḷ; ˈtʃʌkl] *v.,* **-led, -ling,** *n.* —*v.i.* ①咯咯而笑;低聲輕笑。 —*n.* 低聲的輕笑。

chuck·le·head [ˈtʃʌkḷˌhɛd; ˈtʃʌklhed] *n.*〖俗〗傻子;笨人。—**ed,** *adj.*

chuck wagon〖美西部〗送食物給戶外工作者(如在牧場等)的馬車。

chud·dar [ˈtʃʌdɚ; ˈtʃʌdə] *n.* 印度製之一種毛質方圍巾。(亦作 **chudder, chuddah**)

chuff[1] [tʃʌf; tʃʌf] *n.* ①粗野之人。②農夫。③貪吝之人。

chuff[2] [tʃʌf, tʃuf; tʃʌf, tʃuf] *adj.*〖英方〗①圓胖的;肥胖的。②驕傲的。

chuff[3] [tʃʌf; tʃʌf] *n.* 蒸氣引擎排氣之聲音。 —*v.i.* (火車等)發出此種聲音。

chug [tʃʌg; tʃʌg] *n., v.,* **chugged, chug·ging.** —*n.* 軋軋聲。 —*v.i.* ①發軋軋聲。②軋軋而行。

Chu Hsi [ˈdʒuˈʃi; ˈdʒuːˈʃiː] 朱熹(1130–1200, 中國哲學家)。

Chu-Kiang [ˈdʒuˈdʒjɑŋ; ˈdʒuːˈdʒjɑːŋ] *n.* 珠江(中國東南之一河名)。

chuk·ker, chuk·kar [ˈtʃʌkɚ; ˈtʃʌkə] *n.* (馬球)一巡或一圈。

chum [tʃʌm; tʃʌm] *n., v.,* **chummed, chum·ming.**—*n.*〖俗〗同室之友;密友。—*v.i.* ①同室而居〖up〗. ②結爲好友〖up, with〗.

chum·mage [ˈtʃʌmɪdʒ; ˈtʃʌmidʒ] *n.* ①〖俗〗同室;共宿。②〖英俚〗(舊囚犯向新囚犯所收的)入夥錢。

chum·mer·y [ˈtʃʌmərɪ; ˈtʃʌməri] *n.*〖印〗共宿之處;宿舍。

chum·my [ˈtʃʌmɪ; ˈtʃʌmi] *adj.,* **-mi·er, -mi·est,** *n., pl.* **-mies.** —*adj.*〖俗〗親密的。—*n.*〖俗〗同室之友;密友(=chum)。

chump [tʃʌmp; tʃʌmp] *n.* ①厚木塊。②厚鈍之一端。③〖俚〗頭。④〖俗〗笨傢伙。***off one's chump***〖英俚〗瘋狂的。—*v.t. & v.i.* 大聲咀嚼。

Chung·king [ˈtʃʊŋˈkɪŋ; ˈtʃuŋˈkiŋ] *n.* 重慶(中國四川省之一城市)。

chunk [tʃʌŋk; tʃʌŋk] *n.* ①〖俗〗短厚之一塊(如肉等)。②〖美俗〗矮胖之人或動物。③相當大的數量。

chunk·y [ˈtʃʌŋkɪ; ˈtʃʌŋki] *adj.,* **chunk·i·er, chunk·i·est.**〖俗〗①矮胖的。②短厚的。

chun·nel [ˈtʃʌnl; ˈtʃʌnl] *n.* 海底鐵路隧道。

‡**church** [tʃɝtʃ; tʃəːtʃ] *n.* ①禮拜堂;教堂。They are proud of their new *church.* 他們以他們新建的教堂自豪。②禮拜。The Whites go to *church* every Sunday. 姓白的一家人每星期天上教堂做禮拜。③基督徒(集合稱)。④(C–)基督教的教派;教會。⑤教會的職務。⑥類似教堂的建築;類似教會的組織、團體。***enter the church*** 做牧師。—*v.t.* ①到教堂去(以舉行特別儀式)。②〖美中部〗以教堂規律來約束。③(女人生產後)到教堂去謝恩。

church·go·er [ˈtʃɝtʃˌgoɚ; ˈtʃəːtʃˌgouə] *n.* 經常按時到教堂做禮拜的人。

church·go·ing [ˈtʃɝtʃˌgoɪŋ; ˈtʃəːtʃˌgouiŋ] *adj.* ①經常上教堂的。②召喚到教堂去的。—*n.* 經常上教堂。

Church·ill [ˈtʃɝtʃɪl; ˈtʃəːtʃil] *n.* 邱吉爾(Winston L. S., 1874–1965, 英國首相, 1953年諾貝爾文學獎得主)。

church·ing [ˈtʃɝtʃɪŋ; ˈtʃəːtʃiŋ] *n.* 婦女分娩後之感恩禮拜。

church key (有三角尖頭的)罐裝飲料開罐器。 「的;禮拜的;教會的。

church·ly [ˈtʃɝtʃlɪ; ˈtʃəːtʃli] *adj.* 教堂

church·man [ˈtʃɝtʃmən; ˈtʃəːtʃmən] *n., pl.* **-men.** ①任聖職者;牧師;傳教士。②(常C-)信徒(尤指英國國教信徒)。—**ship,** *n.*

church rate 〖英〗(教區徵收的)教會維持費。

church text 〖印〗一種細黑字體。

church·ward·en [ˈtʃɝtʃˈwɔrdn̩; ˈtʃəːtʃˈwɔːdn] ①(英國國教及聖公會之)教會執事。②〖英俗〗陶土製之長煙斗。

church·wom·an [ˈtʃɝtʃˌwʊmən; ˈtʃəːtʃˌwumən] *n., pl.* **-wom·en.** 女信徒;女教友(尤指英國國教者)。

church·y [ˈtʃɝtʃɪ; ˈtʃəːtʃi] *adj.,* **church·i·er, church·i·est.** 〖俗〗①教會的。②過分拘泥教會形式的。③如教會(堂)的。

***church·yard** [ˈtʃɝtʃˌjɑrd; ˈtʃəːtʃˈjɑːd] *n.* 毗連教堂之院落;墓地。

churl [tʃɝl; tʃəːl] *n.* ①農夫;鄉下人。②粗野之人。③吝嗇鬼。

churl·ish [ˈtʃɝlɪʃ; ˈtʃəːliʃ] *adj.* ①粗野的。②吝嗇的。③難駕馭的。

churn [tʃɝn; tʃəːn] *n.* ①攪乳器。②劇烈的攪動。③類似攪乳器的器具。④〖英〗大型牛乳桶。—*v.t.* ①攪拌(牛奶)以製奶油。②攪拌以製奶油。③劇烈地攪拌。—*v.i.* ①使用攪乳器。②攪動。

churn-dash·er [ˈtʃɝnˈdæʃɚ; ˈtʃəːnˈdæʃə] *n.* 攪拌棒。(亦作 **churn-staff**)

churn·ing [ˈtʃɝnɪŋ; ˈtʃəːniŋ] *n.* ①攪拌。②一次提製之奶油。—*adj.* 攪拌的。

chut [tʃʌt; tʃʌt] *interj.* 咄(表示不耐煩)!

chute [ʃut; ʃuːt] *n., v.,* **chut·ed, chut·ing.** —*n.* ①瀑布;急流。②瀉槽;斜槽。③峻陡斜坡。④〖俗〗降落傘。—*v.t.* 用瀉槽將(東西)運下。 —*v.i.* ①以瀉槽而下。 ②跳傘。 *chute the chute(s)* 乘驚險滑梯。

chute-the-chute [ˈʃutðəˌʃut; ˈʃuːtðəʃuːt] *n.* ①(兒童樂園等之)驚險滑梯。②任何製造驚險情緒之事物。

chut·ist [ˈʃutɪst; ˈʃuːtist] *n.* 跳傘者。

chut·ney [ˈtʃʌtnɪ; ˈtʃʌtni] *n., pl.* **-neys.** 一種調味之果醬。(亦作 **chutnee**)

chutz·pa(h) [ˈhʊtspə; ˈhutspə] *n.* 〖美俚〗肆無忌憚;厚顏無恥。 「**lous,** *adj.*

chyle [kaɪl; kail] *n.* 〖生理〗乳糜。—**chy-**

chyme [kaɪm; kaim] *n.* 〖生理〗食糜(食物消化後所變成之漿狀物)。—**chy·mous,** *adj.*

Ci curie; curies. **CIA, C.I.A.** Central Intelligence Agency. (美國)中央情報局。 **Cia.** Company.

ci·bo·ri·um [sɪˈborɪəm; siˈbɔːriəm] *n., pl.* **-bo·ri·a** [-ˈborɪə; -ˈbɔːriə]. ①祭壇上之天蓋。②〖天主教〗聖體容器。

CIC ①Counter-Intelligence Corps. ②Commander-in-Chief. ③Combat Information Center.

ci·ca·da [sɪˈkedə; siˈkɑːdə] *n., pl.* **-das, -dae** [-di; -diː]. 蟬。(亦作 **cicala**)

cic·a·tri·cle [ˈsɪkəˌtrɪkl; ˈsikətrikl] *n.* ①〖胚胎〗卵斑。②〖植物〗葉痕(=cicatrix).

cic·a·trix [ˈsɪkətrɪks; ˈsikətriks] *n., pl.* **cic·a·tri·ces** [ˌsɪkəˈtraɪsiz; ˌsikəˈtraisiːz]. ①〖醫〗瘢痕。②〖植物〗葉痕。(亦作 **cicatrice**)

cic·a·tri·za·tion [ˌsɪkətrɪˈzeʃən; ˌsikətriˈzeiʃən] *n.* 瘢痕成形;結疤;結瘢。

cic·a·trize [ˈsɪkəˌtraɪz; ˈsikətraiz] *v.,* **-trized, -triz·ing.** —*v.t.* 使結瘢;使癒合。—*v.i.* 成瘢痕;癒合。 「繖形科植物。

cic·e·ly [ˈsɪslɪ; ˈsisli] *n., pl.* **-lies.** 一種

Cic·er·o [ˈsɪsəˌro; ˈsisərou] *n.* 西塞羅(Marcus Tullius, 106-43B.C., 羅馬政治家、演說家、及作家)。

ci·ce·ro·ne [ˌsɪsəˈronɪ; ˌtʃitʃəˈrouni] *n., pl.* **-nes, -ni** [-ni; -niː]. 〖義〗說明古蹟古物之嚮導。

Cic·e·ro·ni·an [ˌsɪsəˈronɪən; ˌsisəˈrouniən] *adj.* ①Cicero 的。②如 Cicero 的。—*n.* 仰慕或模倣 Cicero 之風格者。

ci·cis·be·o [ˌtʃitʃəzˈbeo; ˌtʃitʃizˈbeiou] *n., pl.* **-be·os, -be·i** [-bei; -beiː]. 〖義〗(有夫之婦的)情夫。—**ci·cis·be·ism,** *n.*

Cid, The [sɪd; sid] *n.* 西得(1040?-1099, 抵抗 Moors 戰爭中之西班牙英雄)。

C.I.D. ①Committee of Imperial Defense. ②Criminal Investigation Department.

-cide 〖字尾〗表"殺者;殺"之義。

***ci·der** [ˈsaɪdɚ; ˈsaidə] *n.* ①蘋果汁;蘋果酒。②其他果汁;果酒。(英亦作 **cyder**)

cider press 蘋果壓汁器。

ci-de·vant [ˌsidəˈvɑ̃; ˌsiːdəˈvɑ̃ː] 〖法〗 *adj.* 前的;以前的。—*n.* ①(法國革命時)頭銜被廢除前爲貴族的人。②往昔之人或物。

C.I.E. ①Companion of the (Order of the) Indian Empire. ②Civil Information and Education Section.

ciel [sil; siːl] *n.* 天藍色。(亦作**ciel blue**)

C.I.F., CIF, c.i.f. cost, insurance, and freight. **C.I.F. & C.** cost, insurance, freight, and commission. **C.I.F. & C.I.** cost, insurance, freight and commission, interest. **C.I.F. & E.** cost, insurance, freight, and exchange.

cig cigarette. 「(亦作 **cigale**)

ci·ga·la [sɪˈgɑlə; siˈgɑːlə] *n.* =**cicada.**

***ci·gar** [sɪˈgɑr; siˈgɑː] *n.* 雪茄烟。(亦作 **segar**)

cigar case 雪茄烟盒。

***cig·a·rette, cig·a·ret** [ˌsɪgəˈrɛt, ˈsɪgəˌrɛt; ˌsigəˈret] *n.* 香烟;紙烟。to light up a *cigarette*.點着香烟。a *cigarette* holder. 烟嘴。a pack of *cigarettes*. 一包烟。

cig·a·ril·lo [ˌsɪgəˈrɪlo; ˌsigəˈrilou] *n., pl.* **-los.** 小雪茄烟。

ci·gar-shaped [sɪˈgɑrˌʃept; siˈgɑːʃeipt] *adj.* 雪茄烟狀的。

cigar store 香烟店。

cil·i·a [ˈsɪlɪə; ˈsiliə] *n. pl., sing.* **cil·i·um.** ①〖解剖〗睫毛。②〖生物〗纖毛。③〖植物〗(葉等之)細毛。 「的。②〖生物〗纖毛的。

cil·i·a·ry [ˈsɪlɪˌɛrɪ; ˈsiliəri] *adj.* ①睫毛

cil·i·ate [ˈsɪlɪɪt; ˈsiliit] *adj.* (亦作 **ciliated**) 有睫毛的;有纖毛的。 —*n.* 纖毛蟲。—**cil·i·a·tion,** *n.*

cil·ice [ˈsɪlɪs; ˈsilis] *n.* 粗毛布;粗毛布所製之衣服(僧人及懺悔者所穿)。

Cim·me·ri·an [səˈmɪrɪən; siˈmiəriən] *n.* (Homer 所寫之) 古時居於永遠黑暗之陸地上之神祕人民。—*adj.* ①上述之人民的。②極黑暗的;幽暗的。

C-in-C Commander-in-Chief.

cinch [sɪntʃ; sintʃ] *n.* ①束馬鞍用之肚帶;馬之腹帶。②〖俗〗緊握;抓牢。③〖俚〗易做之事;有把握之事。④不負期望的事或人。—*v.t.* ①緊繫腹帶於;緊束。②〖俚〗確實把握住;弄清楚。—*v.i.* 束緊腹帶。

cin·cho·na [sɪnˈkonə; sinˈkounə] *n.* ①產於南美之金鷄納樹。②金鷄納樹皮。

cin·chon·i·dine 〔sɪn'konə,din; sin'kounidi:n〕 *n.*【藥】辛可尼丁(奎寧之代用品)。

cin·cho·nine 〔'sɪnkə,nin; 'sinkəni:n〕 *n.* 金鷄寧。

cin·cho·nism 〔'sɪnkənɪzəm; 'sinkənizəm〕 *n.* 金鷄納中毒。

cin·cho·nize 〔'sɪnkə,naɪz; 'sinkənaiz〕 *v.t.*, **-nized, -niz·ing.** 以金鷄納樹皮等處理。

Cin·cin·nat·i 〔,sɪnsə'nætɪ; ,sinsi'næti〕 *n.* 辛辛那提(美國 Ohio 州西南部之一城市)。

cinc·ture 〔'sɪŋktʃɚ; 'siŋktʃə〕 *n.*, *v.*, **-tured, -tur·ing.** —*n.* ①帶;圍繞之物。②【建築】環帶裝飾;邊輪。③圍繞;環繞。—*v.t.* 以帶等圍繞。

***cin·der** 〔'sɪndɚ; 'sində〕 *n.* ①已熄而尚未燃盡之焦木或煤渣;餘燼。②在燃燒但無火焰之煤炭。③火山岩燼。④(*pl.*)灰燼。—*v.t.* 使燒成煤渣或灰燼。—**ous,** —**like,** *adj.*

cinder block 空心磚。

cinder cone 火山灰燼積成的錐狀物。

Cin·der·el·la 〔,sɪndə'rɛlə; ,sində'relə〕 *n.* ①灰姑娘("仙履奇緣"中女孩名)。②才幹或美貌尚未被人賞識者。

cinder track 以細煤渣所鋪的跑道。(亦作 **cinder path**)

cin·der·y 〔'sɪndərɪ; 'sindəri〕 *adj.* 灰燼的;燼滓的;如燼滓的;含燼滓的。

cin·e 〔'sɪnə; 'sini〕 *n.* ①電影。②電影院。(亦作 **ciné**)

cin·e·cam·e·ra 〔,sɪnɪ'kæmərə; ,sini'kæmərə〕 *n.* 電影攝影機。

cin·e·film 〔'sɪnɪfɪlm; 'sinifilm〕 *n.* 電影膠片。

***cin·e·ma** 〔'sɪnəmə; 'sinəmə〕 *n.*①電影。Are you fond of the *cinema?* 你喜歡看電影嗎? ②電影院。

cin·e·mac·tor 〔,sɪnə'mæktə; ,sini'mæktə〕 *n.*【美俚】電影男演員。

cin·e·mac·tress 〔,sɪnɪ'mæktrɪs; ,sini'mæktris〕 *n.*【美俚】電影女演員。

cin·e·ma·go·er 〔'sɪnəmə,goɚ; 'sinəmə,gouə〕 *n.* 常看電影的人。

Cin·e·ma·Scope 〔'sɪnəmə,skop; 'sinəməskoup〕 *n.*【商標名】新藝綜合體(一種用弧形寬銀幕及立體音響發音的電影)。—**Cin·e·ma·Scop·ic,** *adj.*

cin·e·mat·ic 〔,sɪnɪ'mætɪk; ,sini'mætik〕 *adj.* 電影的。—**al·ly,** *adv.*

cin·e·mat·ics 〔,sɪnə'mætɪks; ,sini'mætiks〕 *n. sing.* or *pl.* 電影製作法。

cin·e·ma·tize 〔'sɪnɪmə,taɪz; 'siniməṭaiz〕 *v.t.* & *v.i.*, **-tized, -tiz·ing.** ①以電影攝影機攝影。②將…改編成電影。

cin·e·mat·o·graph 〔,sɪnə'mætə,græf; ,sini'mætəgrɑ:f〕 *n.* ①【英】電影放映機。②電影攝影機。—*v.t.* & *v.i.*【英】拍電影。(亦作 **kinematograph**) —**ic,** *adj.*

cin·e·ma·tog·ra·pher 〔,sɪnɪmə'tɑgrəfɚ; ,sinimə'tɔgrəfə〕 *n.* 電影攝影者。

cin·e·ma·tog·ra·phy 〔,sɪnəmə'tɑgrəfɪ; ,sinimə'tɔgrəfi〕 *n.* 電影(攝製)術。

cin·e·phile 〔'sɪnə,faɪl; 'sinifail〕 *n.*【英】電影迷。

cin·e·ra·di·og·ra·phy 〔,sɪnə,redɪ'ɑgrəfɪ; ,sini,reidi'ɔgrəfi〕 *n.* 愛克斯光電影攝製。

Cin·e·ra·ma 〔,sɪnə'ræmə; ,sini'ræmə〕 *n.*【商標名】(電影)超視綜合體。

cin·e·ra·ri·a 〔,sɪnə'rɛrɪə; ,sinə'rɛəriə〕 *n.* 一種菊科植物。

cin·e·rar·i·um 〔,sɪnə'rɛrɪəm; ,sinə'rɛəriəm〕 *n.*, *pl.* **-ri·a** 〔-rɪə; -riə〕. 古羅馬墓中壁上置骨灰罐處。

cin·er·ar·y 〔'sɪnə,rɛrɪ; 'sinərəri〕 *adj.* 灰的;骨灰的。

cin·er·a·tor 〔'sɪnə,retɚ; 'sinəreitə〕 *n.* 焚化爐;火葬爐。

ci·ne·re·ous 〔sɪ'nɪrɪəs; si'niriəs〕 *adj.* 似灰的;灰白色的。(亦作 **cineritious**)

Cin·ga·lese 〔,sɪŋgə'liz; ,siŋgə'li:z〕 *adj.* 錫蘭(Ceylon)的;錫蘭人的。—*n.* 錫蘭人;錫蘭語。

cin·gu·lum 〔'sɪŋgjələm; 'siŋgjələm〕 *n.*, *pl.* **-la** 〔-lə;-lə〕. ①【解剖,動物】扣帶。②舌面隆突。③【牙科】舌面嵴。

cin·na·bar 〔'sɪnə,bɑr; 'sinəbɑ:〕 *n.* ①【礦】辰砂;硃砂。②朱紅。—*adj.* 朱(紅)色的。

cin·na·mon 〔'sɪnəmən; 'sinəmən〕 *n.* ①肉桂。②肉桂皮。③肉桂色;黃褐色;紅褐色。—*adj.* ①肉桂色的;黃(紅)褐色的。②以肉桂調味的。—**ed,** —**ic,** *adj.*

cinnamon stone【礦】鈣鋁榴子石;肉桂石。

cinque 〔sɪŋk; siŋk〕 *n.* (骰子、紙牌的)五點。(亦作 **cinq**)

cin·que·cen·tist 〔,tʃɪŋkwɪ'tʃɛntɪst; ,tʃiŋkwi'tʃentist〕 *n.* 十六世紀義大利之詩人、作家或藝術家。

cin·que·cen·to 〔,tʃɪŋkwɪ'tʃɛnto; ,tʃiŋkwi'tʃentou〕 *n.* ①十六世紀義大利之文學與藝術。②此時期義大利藝術風格。—**cin·que·cen·tism,** *n.*

cinque·foil 〔'sɪŋk,fɔɪl; 'siŋkfɔil〕 *n.* ①洋莓屬之植物。②【建築】五葉形之裝飾。

C.I.O., CIO Congress of Industrial Organizations.

ci·on 〔'saɪən; 'saiən〕 *n.* 植物之嫩枝或芽(尤指栽植或接枝所用者)。(亦作 **scion**)

Ci·pan·go 〔sɪ'pæŋgo; si'pæŋgou〕 *n.* 馬可波羅所描述東方海中之一島;日本。(亦作 **Zipango, Zipangu, Zumpango**)

ci·pher 〔'saɪfɚ; 'saifə〕 *n.* ①零(=0)。②無價值的人或物。③阿拉伯數目字。④暗號;密碼。⑤解密碼或暗號的方法。⑥花押;特別方式的簽字。—*v.t.* & *v.i.* ①做算術。②以暗號寫或記載。③想出。(亦作 **cypher**)

ci·pher·key 〔'saɪfɚki; 'saifəki:〕 *n.* 解暗號(密碼)之書或註解。

cipher officer 大使館中之密碼翻譯員。

cip·o·lin 〔'sɪpəlɪn; 'sipəlin〕 *n.* (義大利產之)白綠紋大理石。

circ. ①circa. ②circuit. ③circulation. ④circumference.

cir·ca 〔'sɝkə; 'sə:kə〕【拉】*prep., adv.* 大約。(亦作 **circiter**, 常略作 **ca., c., cir.,** 或 **circ.**)

cir·ca·di·an 〔sɝ'kedɪən; sə:'keidiən〕 *adj.* 以24小時爲周期的(如生理或行爲現象等)。

Cir·ce 〔'sɝsɪ; 'sə:si〕 *n.*【希臘神話】(荷馬, Homer, 之"奧德賽" *Odyssey* 中)使人變成豬之女巫。—**an,** *adj.*

cir·ci·nate 〔'sɝsn̩,et; 'sə:sneit〕 *adj.* ①環狀的。②【植物】渦卷狀的。(亦作 **circinal**)

‡cir·cle 〔'sɝkl; 'sə:kl〕 *n.*, *v.*, **-cled, -cling.** —*n.* ①圓;圜;圓周。to draw a *circle* around a given center. 繞一個固定的中心畫一圓周。②圓形物;圜狀物。③週期;循環。④志同道合的集團;親人的集團。business *circles.* 商界。educational *circles.* 教育界。⑤範圍。to enlarge our *circle* of activities. 擴張我們活動的範圍。⑥天體的軌道;天體之循行。⑦戲院包廂中的座位。⑧圓形競技場。⑨【邏輯】循環論證。vicious *circle.* 循環論法;惡性循環。⑩子午線。—*v.t.* ①環繞;包圍。②環行;繞…而行。The moon *circles* the earth. 月球繞地球而轉。—*v.i.* ①廻轉;盤旋。②圍繞。

circle of confusion〖攝影〗模糊圈。
circle of convergence〖數學〗收斂圓。
circle of curvature〖數學〗曲率圓。
circle of least confusion〖光學〗明晰圈。
cir·clet [ˈsɝklɪt; ˈsəːklit] *n.* 小圓圈(尤指裝飾用者)。
***cir·cuit** [ˈsɝkɪt; ˈsəːkit] *n.* ①周圍。②被圍起的空間。③環行;繞行一周。④a. 巡廻;巡行。b. 做此巡廻的人。⑤巡廻區;巡行區。⑥巡廻裁判;巡廻裁判區。*circuit* court. 巡廻法院。⑦電路。an electrical *circuit*. 電路。⑧由一人所有或經營的諸戲院夜總會等,或由同一劇團作團體表演之諸影劇院等。⑨協會;聯盟。*make a circuit* 環行一周。—*v.t.* 巡廻;繞行。—*v.i.* 巡廻。—**al,** *adj.*
circuit breaker 斷路器。
circuit diagram 電路圖。
cir·cu·i·tous [sɚˈkjuɪtəs; səːˈkjuːitəs] *adj.* 迂曲的;繞行的;間接的。—**ly,** *adv.* —**ness,** *n.*
circuit rider 到處巡廻布道之衞理公會之牧師。
cir·cuit·ry [ˈsɝkɪtrɪ; ˈsəːkitri] *n.* ①電路之詳細平面圖。②電路之各部分。
cir·cu·i·ty [sɚˈkjuətɪ; səːˈkjuːiti] *n., pl.* **-ties.** 迂曲性;間接性。
***cir·cu·lar** [ˈsɝkjələ; ˈsəːkjulə] *adj.* ①圓的。②巡行的;環行的;巡廻的。a *circular* trip (*or* tour). 環行旅行。③通告的。a *circular* letter. 傳閱的函件。④間接的;迂廻的。⑤集團的。—*n.* 傳單;傳閱的函件。—**ness,** *n.*
circular function〖數學〗圓函數;三角函數。
cir·cu·lar·i·ty [ˌsɝkjəˈlærətɪ; ˌsəːkjəˈlæriti] *n., pl.* **-ties.** 圓圈形;環狀。
cir·cu·lar·ize [ˈsɝkjələˌraɪz; ˈsəːkjuləraiz] *v.t.,* **-ized, -iz·ing.** ①傳遞;送傳單給…。②將…製作爲傳單等。③使成圓形。—**cir·cu·lar·i·za·tion,** *n.*
circular letter of credit 可在全世界任何銀行提款之信用狀。
circular measure〖數學〗弧度法;弳量法。
***cir·cu·late** [ˈsɝkjəˌlet; ˈsəːkjuleit] *v.,* **-lat·ed, -lat·ing.** —*v.i.* ①流通;巡廻。Blood *circulated* in human body. 血在人體內循環。②傳布;分布。—*v.t.* 使傳播;使傳布。—**cir·cu·la·tive, cir·cu·la·to·ry,** *adj.* —**cir·cu·la·tor,** *n.*
circulating capital 流動資金;流動資本(爲固定資本 fixed capital 之對)。
circulating decimal 循環小數。
circulating library 巡廻圖書館。
circulating medium 通貨。
***cir·cu·la·tion** [ˌsɝkjəˈleʃən; ˌsəːkjuˈleiʃən] *n.* ①流通;傳布。②循環。blood *circulation.* 血液循環。③銷路;發行數;銷售量。This book has a large *circulation.* 這本書銷路很廣。④通貨;貨幣的流通。New notes have been put into *circulation.* 新鈔票業已發行。*in circulation* 在社會上或事業上活躍。
circum-〖字首〗表"環繞;周圍"等義。
cir·cum·am·bi·ent [ˌsɝkəmˈæmbɪənt; ˌsəːkəmˈæmbiənt] *adj.* 圍繞的;周圍的。
cir·cum·am·bu·late [ˌsɝkəmˈæmbjəˌlet; ˌsəːkəmˈæmbjuleit] *v.t. & v.i.,* **-lat·ed, -lat·ing.** 巡行;繞行。—**cir·cum·am·bu·la·tion,** *n.* —**cir·cum·am·bu·la·to·ry,** *adj.*
cir·cum·a·vi·ate [ˌsɝkəmˈevɪˌet; ˌsəːkəmˈeivieit] *v.t.,* **-at·ed, -at·ing.** 環繞(地球)飛行。—**cir·cum·a·vi·a·tion,** *n.*
cir·cum·bend·i·bus [ˌsɝkəmˈbɛndɪbəs; ˌsəːkəmˈbendibəs] *n., pl.* **-bus·es.**〖俗〗迂廻;委婉;迂廻的方法。
cir·cum·cir·cle [ˈsɝkəmˌsɝkl; ˈsəːkəmˌsəːkl] *n.*〖數學〗外接圓。
cir·cum·cise [ˈsɝkəmˌsaɪz; ˈsəːkəmsaiz] *v.t.,* **-cised, -cis·ing.** ①割包皮。②割陰唇。③〖宗教〗行割禮。④淨心;潔心;去邪念。
cir·cum·ci·sion [ˌsɝkəmˈsɪʒən; ˌsəːkəmˈsiʒən] *n.* ①割禮;割包皮。②心身之淨化。③(the–)(常C–)猶太人;心靈滌清的人。④(C–)〖聖經〗割禮節(紀念耶穌受割而設)。
cir·cum·col·um·nar [ˌsɝkəmkəˈlʌmnɚ; ˌsəːkəmkəˈlʌmnə] *adj.*〖建築〗圍繞圓柱的;繞柱的。
***cir·cum·fer·ence** [sɚˈkʌmfərəns; səˈkʌmfərəns] *n.* ①圓周。②周圍。③圓周內之事物。—**cir·cum·fer·en·tial,** *adj.*
cir·cum·flu·ence [sɚˈkʌmfluəns; səˈkʌmfluəns] *n.* 環流;周流。
cir·cum·flu·ent [sɚˈkʌmfluənt; səˈkʌmfluənt] *adj.* 周流的;環流的;圍繞的。
cir·cum·fo·ra·ne·ous [ˌsɝkəmfəˈrenɪəs; ˌsəːkəmfəˈreiniəs] *adj.* ①從此一市場遊蕩至另一市場的;流浪的。②密醫的;冒牌的。
cir·cum·fuse [ˌsɝkəmˈfjuz; ˌsəːkəmˈfjuːz] *v.t.,* **-fused, -fus·ing.** ①周圍澆灌;散佈。②圍繞;充溢。—**cir·cum·fu·sion,** *n.*
cir·cum·gy·rate [ˌsɝkəmˈdʒaɪret; ˌsəːkəmˈdʒaireit] *v.i. & v.t.,* **-rat·ed, -rat·ing.** (使)廻轉;(使)旋轉。—**cir·cum·gy·ra·tion,** *n.*
cir·cum·ja·cent [ˌsɝkəmˈdʒesn̩t; ˌsəːkəmˈdʒeisənt] *adj.* 周圍的;鄰接的;圍繞的。—**cir·cum·ja·cen·ce, cir·cum·ja·cen·cy,** *n.*
cir·cum·lo·cu·tion [ˌsɝkəmloˈkjuʃən; ˌsəːkəmləˈkjuːʃən] *n.* 迂廻累贅的陳述。—**cir·cum·loc·u·to·ry,** *adj.*
cir·cum·lu·nar [ˌsɝkəmˈlunɚ; ˌsəːkəmˈluːnə] *adj.* 繞月球的;繞行月球的。
cir·cum·nav·i·gate [ˌsɝkəmˈnævəˌget; ˌsəːkəmˈnævigeit] *v.t.,* **-gat·ed, -gat·ing.** 環航。—**cir·cum·nav·i·ga·tion, cir·cum·nav·i·ga·tor,** *n.* —**cir·cum·nav·i·ga·to·ry,** *adj.*
cir·cum·nu·tate [ˌsɝkəmˈnjutet; ˌsəːkəmˈnjuːteit] *v.i.,* **-tat·ed, -tat·ing.**〖植物〗垂屈廻旋。
cir·cum·po·lar [ˌsɝkəmˈpolɚ; ˌsəːkəmˈpoulə] *adj.* ①極地附近的;圍繞極地的。②〖天文〗圍繞天極的。
cir·cum·ra·di·us [ˌsɝkəmˈredɪəs; ˌsəːkəmˈreidiəs] *n., pl.* **-di·i** [-dɪaɪ; -diai], **-di·us·es.**〖數學〗外接圓半徑。
cir·cum·scribe [ˌsɝkəmˈskraɪb; ˈsəːkəmskraib] *v.t.,* **-scribed, -scrib·ing.** ①劃界線。②立界限;限制。③〖幾何〗a. 畫(一圖形)之外接圖形。b.(一圖形)爲(另一圖形)之外接圖形。
cir·cum·scrip·tion [ˌsɝkəmˈskrɪpʃən; ˌsəːkəmˈskripʃən] *n.* ①劃界。②限制;界限。③四周。④界限內之區域。⑤廻讀之銘文(如在硬幣上的)。
cir·cum·so·lar [ˌsɝkəmˈsolɚ; ˌsəːkəmˈsoulə] *adj.* 太陽周圍的;繞太陽運行的。
cir·cum·spect [ˈsɝkəmˌspɛkt; ˈsəː-

kəmspekt] *adj.* 愼重的;縝密周到的。—**cir·cum·spec·tion, —ness,** *n.* **—ly,** *adv.*

cir·cum·spec·tive [ˌsɝkəmˈspɛktɪv; ˌsəːkəmˈspektiv] *adj.* 留神的;愼重的;周到的。—**ly,** *adv.*

‡**cir·cum·stance** [ˈsɝkəmˌstæns; ˈsəːkəmstəns] *n., v.,* **-stanced, -stanc·ing.** —*n.* ①(行動或事件的)情形;情況。②(常*pl.*)現狀;環境。He was forced by *circumstances* to do this.他爲環境所迫而爲此。③(*pl.*)財力;境遇。They are in bad *circumstances.* 他們的境遇不佳。④事件;意外的事。⑤細節;瑣事;原委;始末。The explorer told of his adventure with great *circumstance.* 這個探險家詳盡地講述他的冒險故事。⑥華飾;儀式。***under*** (or ***in***) ***no circumstances*** 決不;無論在任何情形下…不可。*Under no circumstances* should you leave the room. 你決不可離開房間。***under*** (or ***in***) ***the circumstances*** 在此情形之下。—*v.t.* 置於某種情況之下。

cir·cum·stanced [ˈsɝkəmˌstænst; ˈsəːkəmstənst] *adj.* 在某種狀況或環境下的。to be awkwardly (well) *circumstanced.* 處境尷尬(順遂)。

cir·cum·stan·tial [ˌsɝkəmˈstænʃəl; ˌsəːkəmˈstænʃəl] *adj.* ①詳盡的。②依照情況的。*circumstantial* evidence. 情況證據;間接證據。③不重要的;偶然的。④有關物質(財富)環境的。—**ly,** *adv.* **—ness, —i·ty,** *n.*

cir·cum·stan·ti·ate [ˌsɝkəmˈstænʃɪˌet; ˌsəːkəmˈstænʃieit] *v.t.,* **-at·ed, -at·ing.** ①詳細說明;證實。②置於某種情形下。

cir·cum·val·late [ˌsɝkəmˈvælet; ˌsəːkəmˈvæleit] *adj., v.,* **-lat·ed, -lat·ing.** —*adj.* 有城牆或壕溝等圍着的;有城堡圍防的。—*v.t.* 圍以城牆、壕溝或城堡。—**cir·cum·val·la·tion,** *n.*

cir·cum·vent [ˌsɝkəmˈvɛnt; ˌsəːkəmˈvent] *v.t.* ①阻遏。②勝過;占上風。③欺詐;陷害;用計加以包圍。④繞行。⑤以欺詐避免(失敗等)。—**cir·cum·ven·tion,** *n.*

cir·cum·vo·lute [səˈkʌmvəˌljut; səːˈkʌmvəljuːt] *v.t.,* **-lut·ed, -lut·ing.** 纏繞;纏捲;迂廻。—**cir·cum·vo·lu·tion,** *n.*

cir·cum·volve [ˌsɝkəmˈvɑlv; ˌsəːkəmˈvɔlv] *v.t. & v.i.,* **-volved, -volv·ing.** 纏繞;繞…而轉。

***cir·cus** [ˈsɝkəs; ˈsəːkəs] *n., pl.* **-cus·es.** ①馬戲團;馬戲。a *circus* clown. 馬戲團的小丑。②〖俗〗 **a.** 有趣的人或物。**b.** 歡樂的時光。③古羅馬之圓形競技場或其娛樂節目。④圓廣場;圓環。⑤圓形劇場。⑥ **a.** (第一次大戰時之)飛行隊伍。**b.** 飛行特技小組。

Circus Max·i·mus [~ˈmæksəməs; ~ˈmæksəməs] 古羅馬巨大圓形競技場。

cirque [sɝk; səːk] *n.* ①圓形場;競技場。②〖詩〗圈;環。③〖地質〗圓谷。④馬戲。

cir·rho·sis [sɪˈrosɪs; siˈrousis] *n.*〖醫〗硬化;硬變。—**cir·rhot·ic,** *adj.*

cir·ri [ˈsɪraɪ; ˈsirai] *n.* pl. of **cirrus.**

cir·ri·ped [ˈsɪrɪˌpɛd; ˈsiriped] *n.* 蔓脚類動物。—*adj.* 蔓脚類的。(亦作 **cirripede**)

cir·ro-cu·mu·lus [ˌsɪrəˈkjumjuləs; ˌsirəˈkjuːmjuləs] *n., pl.* **-lus.** 〖氣象〗卷雲。

cir·rose [ˈsɪros; ˈsirous] *adj.* ①〖植物〗有卷鬚的。②〖動物〗有觸毛的。③〖氣象〗卷雲的;卷雲狀的。(亦作 **cirrous**)

cir·ro-stra·tus [ˌsɪroˈstretəs; ˌsirouˈstreitəs] *n., pl.* **-tus.** 〖氣象〗卷層雲。

cir·rus [ˈsɪrəs; ˈsirəs] *n., pl.* **cir·ri** [ˈsɪraɪ; ˈsirai] *for* ① & ②, **cir·rus** *for* ③. ①〖植物〗卷鬚。②〖動物〗觸毛。③〖氣象〗卷雲。

cir·soid [ˈsɝsɔɪd; ˈsəːsɔid] *adj.* 〖醫〗蔓狀的;曲張的。

cis- 〖字首〗①表"在這邊"之義。②〖化學〗表"順式"之義。

cis·al·pine [sɪsˈælpaɪn; sisˈælpain] *adj.* (從羅馬觀點言)在阿爾卑斯山這一面(南側)的;該山之義大利方面的。

cis·at·lan·tic [ˌsɪsətˈlæntɪk; ˌsisətˈlæntik] *adj.* 在大西洋這邊的(從說話者之觀點而言)。

cis·co [ˈsɪsko; ˈsiskou] *n., pl.* **-cos, -coes.** (北美大湖區產之)一種青魚。

cis·lu·nar [sɪsˈlunɚ; sisˈluːnə] *adj.* 〖天文〗地球與月球軌道之間的。

cis·mon·tane [sɪsˈmɑnten; sisˈmɔntein] *adj.* 山這邊的(尤指北面);(特指)阿爾卑斯山北側的。

cis·sy [ˈsɪsɪ; ˈsisi] *n.* 〖美俚〗脂粉氣之男子。(亦作 **sissy**)

cist¹ [sɪst; sist] *n.*〖考古〗箱;櫃(尤指古希臘裝聖器者)。

cist² [sɪst, kɪst; sist, kist] *n.* 史前之石櫃;箱形石墓。(亦作 **kist**)

Cis·ter·cian [sɪsˈtɝʃən; sisˈtəːʃiən] *n., adj.* Cistercian Order 之修道僧(的)。

Cistercian Order 西妥教團(一修道會名)。

cis·tern [ˈsɪstɚn; ˈsistən] *n.* ①水槽;貯水池。②(亦作 **cisterna**)〖解剖〗池。

cit [sɪt; sit] *n.* ①城裏人;商人;老闆。②〖軍俚〗老百姓。③(*pl.*)〖軍俚〗老百姓服裝。

cit·a·del [ˈsɪtədl; ˈsitədl] *n.* ①(保衛城市之)城堡。②有堅强防禦工事之地點;要塞。③安全地帶;避難處。④軍艦上之裝甲砲位。

ci·ta·tion [saɪˈteʃən; saiˈteiʃən] *n.* ①引證;引用文。②〖法律〗傳喚;傳票。③〖軍〗(在軍事公報中對軍人或部隊之)褒揚。④褒獎;獎狀。

***cite** [saɪt; sait] *v.t.,* **cit·ed, cit·ing.** ①引用;引證。to *cite* a passage from Shakespeare. 引用莎士比亞的一節文字。②提示;擧例;援引。③召喚。④傳詢。⑤褒揚(如作戰勇敢、爲公衆服務等)。⑥想起。—**cit·a·ble, —a·ble,** *adj.* —**cit·er,** *n.*

cith·a·ra [ˈsɪθərə; ˈsiθərə] *n.* 古希臘一種類似豎琴之樂器。(亦作 **kithara, cither**)

cith·ern [ˈsɪθɚn; ˈsiθən] *n.* 一種類似吉他之古樂器(流行於十六、七世紀)。(亦作 **cither, cittern, gittern, zittern**)

cit·ied [ˈsɪtɪd; ˈsitid] *adj.* 都市的;似都市的;有都市的。

cit·i·fied, cit·y·fied [ˈsɪtɪˌfaɪd; ˈsitifaid] *adj.* 〖美〗有城市生活習慣、風尚等的;都市化的(通常爲輕蔑語)。

‡**cit·i·zen** [ˈsɪtəzn̩; ˈsitizn] *n.* ①市民。the *citizens* of Taipei. 臺北市的市民。②公民;國民。③平民。④居民;棲息者。***citizen of the world*** 國際人(對全世界情況有興趣的人);四海爲家的人。—**ly,** *adj.*

cit·i·zen·ess [ˈsɪtəzənɪs; ˈsitiznis] *n.* citizen 之女性。

cit·i·zen·ize [ˈsɪtəzn̩ˌaɪz; ˈsitiznaiz] *v.t.,* **-ized, -iz·ing.** 〖美〗使成爲公民;賦與公民權。

cit·i·zen·ry [ˈsɪtəzn̩rɪ; ˈsitiznri] *n., pl.* **-ries.** 公民或市民(集合稱)。

***cit·i·zen·ship** [ˈsɪtəzn̩ˌʃɪp; ˈsitiznʃip] *n.* ①公民的身分。②公民的職責和權利。

citizenship papers 〖美〗公民證書。

citizen soldier 緊急情況時從軍之平

民。「Organization. 國際貿易憲章。」
CITO Charter of International Trade
cit·rate [ˈsɪtret; ˈsitrit] *n., v.,* **-rat·ed, -rat·ing.** —*n.*〖化〗檸檬酸鹽。—*v.t.* 加以檸檬酸鹽。「色的。」
cit·re·ous [ˈsɪtrɪəs; ˈsitriəs] *adj.* 檸檬
cit·ric [ˈsɪtrɪk; ˈsitrik] *adj.* 取自檸檬的;
citric acid〖化〗檸檬酸。 「檸檬的。」
cit·ri·cul·ture [ˈsɪtrəˌkʌltʃə; ˈsitriˌkʌltʃə] *n.* 柑橘屬植物之種植。
cit·rin [ˈsɪtrɪn; ˈsitrin] *n.*〖生化〗維他命 P; 檸檬素。
cit·rine [ˈsɪtrɪn; ˈsitrin] *adj.* 似檸檬的; 檸檬色的。—*n.* ①檸檬色。②〖礦〗黃水晶。
cit·ron [ˈsɪtrən; ˈsitrən] *n.* ①〖植物〗香櫞;香櫞樹。②香櫞皮蜜餞。—*adj.* 香櫞色的。
cit·ron·el·la [ˌsɪtrənˈɛlə; ˌsitrəˈnelə] *n.* 香茅。 「柑橘屬植物的。」
cit·rous [ˈsɪtrəs; ˈsitrəs] *adj.*〖植物〗
cit·rus [ˈsɪtrəs; ˈsitrəs] *n., pl.* **-rus·es,** *adj.* —*n.* ①(C-) 柑橘屬。②柑橘屬之植物(橘樹、柑樹、檸檬樹、柚樹)。③其果實。—*adj.* 柑橘屬植物的。
cit·tern [ˈsɪtən; ˈsitən] *n.* =**cithern.**
‡**cit·y** [ˈsɪtɪ; ˈsiti] *n., pl.* **cit·ies,** *adj.* —*n.* ①大城市; 要鎮; 都會。②城市居民的全體。③ (the C-)倫敦商業區。—*adj.* ①城市的;都會的。②在市內的。「經之消息。」
city article〖英〗報紙上有關商業、財
city assembly 市民大會。
cit·y-born [ˈsɪtɪˌbɔrn; ˈsitibɔːn] *adj.* 在城裏出生的。 「在城裏長大的。」
cit·y-bred [ˈsɪtɪˌbrɛd; ˈsitibred] *adj.*
cit·y·bust·er [ˈsɪtɪˌbʌstɚ; ˈsitiˌbʌstə] *n.*〖俗〗原子彈;氫彈。
city council 市議會。
city councilor 市議員。
city desk (報館之)採訪部。
city edition (報紙)本地版。
city editor ①〖美〗(報館之)採訪部主任。②〖英〗(報館之)經濟新聞欄編輯人。
city father ①〖美俗〗市參議員。②市府官員;本市聞人。
city hall 市政府大廈。
city man〖英〗①財政家;財政官;金融業者。②倫敦金融區之金融機構所雇用之人員。(亦作 **City man**)
city manager (由市議會所指派而非由人民公選之) 管理市政者。
City of David ①耶路撒冷。②伯利恒 (Bethlehem). 「堂;天。」
City of God 新耶路撒冷; 天國;天
City of Seven Hills 羅馬。
city of the dead 墓地。
city plan (or **planning**)都市計畫。
cit·y·scape [ˈsɪtɪˌskep; ˈsitiskeip] *n.* ①城市(尤指大都市)之風景。②描繪城市的圖畫。 「腔滑調的城裏人(鄉下人用語)。」
city slicker (常含輕蔑)打扮入時,油
cit·y-state [ˈsɪtɪˈstet; ˈsitiˈsteit] *n.* (古希臘或文藝復興時期義大利之)城邦。
cit·y·ward [ˈsɪtɪwəd; ˈsitiwəd] *adj.* & *adv.* 向城市。(亦作 **citywards**)
civ. ①civic. ②civil. ③civilian.
civ·et [ˈsɪvɪt; ˈsivit] *n.* ①(亦作 **civet cat**)〖動物〗麝貓。②麝貓香。③麝貓之毛皮。
***civ·ic** [ˈsɪvɪk; ˈsivik] *adj.* ①城市的。*civic* center. 市中心。②公民的; 市民的。*civic* rights. 公民權利。③公民或市民資格的。
civ·ic-mind·ed [ˈsɪvɪkˈmaɪndɪd; ˈsivikˈmaindid] *adj.*有公德心的;熱心公益的。
civ·ics [ˈsɪvɪks; ˈsiviks] *n.* (作 *sing.*解)〖美〗公民(課程)。
civic virtues 公民道德。
civ·ies [ˈsɪvɪz; ˈsiviz] *n. pl.*〖俚〗便服(指非軍服而言)。(亦作 **civvies**)
‡**civ·il** [ˈsɪvḷ; ˈsivl, ˈsivil] *adj.* ①市民的; 公民的; 平民的。He left the army and resumed *civil* life. 他脫離軍隊, 恢復平民生活。②國家的; 政府的。*civil* affairs. 內政。③民事的。*civil* case. 民事案件。④文職的。*civil* officers. 文官。⑤有禮貌的。⑥文明的;開化的。⑦仁慈的。—**ly,** *adv.*
civil action 民事訴訟。
civil code 民法。
civil death 褫奪公權終身。
civil defense ①民間防空; 民防。②民防指揮部。
civil disobedience 溫和抵抗;不合作主義(對法律之反抗如抵制行爲、不繳稅等)。
civil engineer 土木工程師。
civil engineering 土木工程。
***ci·vil·ian** [səˈvɪljən; siˈviljən] *n.* 平民。 —*adj.* 平民的。
***ci·vil·i·ty** [səˈvɪlətɪ; siˈviliti] *n., pl.* **-ties.** 禮貌; 慇懃。 to show one *civility.* 待人以禮。
***civ·i·li·za·tion** [ˌsɪvḷəˈzeʃən, ˌsɪvlaɪˈzeʃən; ˌsivilaiˈzeiʃən, -vḷ-, -liˈz-] *n.* ①文明; 文化; 教化; 教導。western *civilization.* 西方文明 (或文化)。②文明國家的集合稱。③一種族或一國家的文化和生活方式。④教養;文雅。⑤城市;有人居住的地方。⑥現代文明所提供的各種舒適。—**al,** *adj.*
***civ·i·lize** [ˈsɪvḷˌaɪz; ˈsivilaiz] *v.t.,* **-lized, -liz·ing.** ①使開化。 to *civilize* a barbarous people. 教化一個野蠻民族。②教導;使文雅。—**civ·i·liz·a·ble,** *adj.*
***civ·i·lized** [ˈsɪvḷˌaɪzd; ˈsivilaizd] *adj.* ①文明的;開化的。 a *civilized* people. 一個文明的民族。②文明國家的; 文明人民的。③有禮貌的;有教養的。
civil law 民法。
civ·il-law [ˈsɪvḷˈlɔ; ˈsivlˈlɔː] *adj.*民法的。
civil liberty 公民的言論和行動自由。
civil list ①〖英〗皇室費。②政府人事費。
civil marriage 公證結婚。
civil rights 公民權。
civil servant〖主英〗文職公務員。
civil service ①文職。②文官制度。
civil war 內戰。
civil year 日曆年(365天)。
civ·ism [ˈsɪvɪzəm; ˈsivizəm] *n.* 公德心; 公民精神。 「平民;老百姓。」
civ·vy [ˈsɪvɪ; ˈsivi] *n., pl.* **-vies.**〖俚〗
C.J. Chief Justice.
ck. ①cask. ②check. **Cl** 化學元素 chlorine 之符號。 **cl.** ①carload. ②centiliter. ③claim. ④class. ⑤classification. ⑥clause. ⑦clearance. ⑧clergyman.
C/L ①carload. ②carload lot. ③cash letter. **c.l.** ①carload. ②carload lot. ③center line. ④civil law.
clab·ber [ˈklæbɚ; ˈklæbə] *v.t.* & *v.i.* (使)(牛奶等)凝固; 凝結。 —*n.* 凝結而發酸之牛奶。
clack [klæk; klæk] *n.* ①畢剝聲;短而尖之響聲。②嘮叨。③鷄鳴聲。—*v.i.* ①發畢剝聲。②嘮叨。③鷄鳴。 —*v.t.* ①饒舌。②使(某物)發出短而尖的聲音或畢剝聲。

clad[1] [klæd; klæd] *v.* pt. & pp. of **clothe.** 「覆於或鍍於另一金屬。」
clad[2] *v.t.*, **clad, clad·ding.** 將一種金屬
clad·o·phyll [ˈklædəˌfɪl; ˈklædəfil] *n.* 〖植物〗兼具葉之功能的葉狀莖(如蘆筍之莖)。
‡claim [klem; kleim] *v.t.* ①要求;請求。to *claim* payment of debt. 要求還債。②聲言(或主張) 應予承認 (事實或權利)。He *claimed* that he was right. 他聲言他是對的。Does anybody *claim* this umbrella? 有人來認領這把傘嗎?③需要。—*v.i.*①提出要求。②聲言; 聲稱。—*n.* ①要求。to make a *claim* for damages. 要求賠償損害。②要求的權利。They have no *claim* on us. 他們無向我們要求的權利。③所要求的東西。④使用者占有之公有土地。⑤保險等所請求之賠償。⑥聲言。***lay claim to*** **a.** 爭…之所有權。**b.** 宣稱屬己。***set up a claim to*** 提出…的要求。—**a·ble,** *adj.*
claim·ant [ˈklemənt; ˈkleimənt] *n.* 請求者;申請者。(亦作 **claimer**)
claiming race (比賽前可以預約購買出場比賽之馬的)一種賽馬。
clair·au·di·ence [klɛrˈɔdɪəns; klɛər-ˈɔːdjəns] *n.* (尤指催眠中)特別敏銳之聽力。
clair·au·di·ent [klɛrˈɔdɪənt; klɛər-ˈɔːdjənt] *adj., n.* 有特別敏銳之聽力的(人)。
clair·voy·ance [klɛrˈvɔɪəns; klɛə-ˈvɔiəns] *n.* ①(傳說中的) 能看到異時異地事物的能力。②機敏;敏感;迅速之直覺洞察力。
clair·voy·ant [klɛrˈvɔɪənt; klɛə-ˈvɔiənt] *adj.* 具有超人之目力或洞察力的;機敏的。—*n.* 具有上述能力之人。
clam**[1] [klæm; klæm] *n., v.,* **clammed, clam·ming.** —*n.* ①〖動物〗蛤; 蚌; 蚶。②〖美俗〗沈默之人;嘴緊之人。③〖美俗〗銀幣;一元。④冷濕。as close as a clam*** 吝嗇的。—*v.i.* 拾蛤;掘蛤。***clam up***〖俚〗不講話;不提供消息。
clam[2] *n.* 〖英〗鉗;夾子。
cla·mant [ˈklemənt; ˈkleimənt] *adj.* ①吵鬧的;喊叫的。②緊急的;亟需改正的。
clam·bake [ˈklæmˌbek; ˈklæmbeik] *n.* 〖美〗 ①以烤蚌蛤爲主菜之海濱野宴。②〖諧〗社交集會(尤指歡佚者)。③〖俚〗(尤指無線電或電視節目之)拙劣之播放或演出。
***clam·ber** [ˈklæmbə; ˈklæmbə] *v.i.* 攀爬; 攀登。 to *clamber* up a wall. 爬牆。—*n.* 爬上;攀登。
clam face 〖美〗膽小鬼。「蚌蛤者。」
clam·mer [ˈklæmə; ˈklæmə] *n.* 捕拾
clam·my [ˈklæmɪ; ˈklæmi] *adj.*, **-mi·er, -mi·est.** ①濕冷而黏的; 冷而濕的。②病態的。 —**clam·mi·ness,** *n.*
clam·o(u)r** [ˈklæmə; ˈklæmə] *n.* ①喧鬧。②大聲的要求或責難; 輿論嘩然。 the *clamor* of the press. 報紙上輿論嘩然。—*v.i.* & *v.t.* 喧鬧;大聲的要求或責難。clamor*** (***a person***) ***down*** 叱止 (某人) 說話。—**er,** —**ist,** *n.*
clam·or·ous [ˈklæmərəs; ˈklæmərəs] *adj.* ①吵鬧的; 叫喊的。②大聲要求或抗議的。—**ly,** *adv.* —**ness,** *n.*
clamp[1] [klæmp; klæmp] *n.* 鉗;夾子。—*v.t.* 用夾子夾住。***clamp down*** (***on***)〖俗〗箝制;嚴辦;取締。
clamp[2] *n.* (曬乾或準備燒的)一堆磚瓦。
clamp-down, clamp·down [ˈklæmpˌdaun; ˈklæmpdaun] *n.* 嚴禁。
clam·shell [ˈklæmˌʃɛl; ˈklæmʃel] *n.* ①蛤殼。②蛤殼式挖泥器。
***clan** [klæn; klæn] *n.* ①宗族; 部落。②黨派;團體。③家族。—**like,** *adj.*
clan·des·tine [klænˈdɛstɪn; klæn-ˈdestin] *adj.* 祕密的;暗中的。—**ly,** *adv.*
***clang** [klæŋ; klæŋ] *n.* ①玎瑺聲。②刺耳的喇叭聲。③鶴或鵝之叫聲。—*v.t.* 使發玎瑺聲。—*v.i.* 發玎瑺聲。
clan·go(u)r [ˈklæŋgə; ˈklæŋgə] *n.* ①玎瑺聲。②喧鬧聲。—*v.i.*作玎瑺聲。—**clan·gor·ous,** *adj.* —**clan·gor·ous·ly,** *adv.*
clank [klæŋk; klæŋk] *n.* 玎瑺聲; 磕隆磕隆(較 clang 聲爲小)。—*v.i.* ①作玎瑺聲;磕隆磕隆地響。②走動時發出玎瑺聲。—*v.t.* 使作玎瑺聲;使磕隆磕隆地響。
clan·nish [ˈklænɪʃ; ˈklæniʃ] *adj.* ①氏族的;宗親的。②(宗親間)團結的。③排他的;有偏見的。—**ly,** *adv.* —**ness,** *n.*
clan·ship [ˈklænʃɪp; ˈklænʃip] *n.* 族黨之團結、制度或精神。
clans·man [ˈklænzmən; ˈklænzmən] *n., pl.* **-men.** 同宗;族人。
clap**[1] [klæp; klæp] *n., v.,* **clapped, clap·ping.** —*n.* ①突然的轟聲 (如雷鳴)。a *clap* of thunder. 雷聲轟隆。②拍手聲; 擊掌聲; 碰撞聲。The audience gave him a loud *clap*. 聽衆大聲爲他鼓掌。③一擊;一拍。—*v.t.* ①鼓(掌); 拍(手)。②輕拍。to *clap* him on the shoulder. 拍他的肩。③急置;急爲。④(面對面地)碰在一起。She *clapped* the book shut. 她拍的一聲把書合上了。⑤(鳥)振翅飛翔。⑥〖俗〗急速地安排〖常 up, together〗。 —*v.i.* ①擊; 拍。②鼓掌。clap eyes on*** 注視;看。
clap[2] *n.* 〖俚〗(常 the-)淋病。
clap·board [ˈklæbəd; ˈklæpbɔːd] *n.*①護牆板。②〖電影〗(亦作 **clap-stick**)場記板;拍板。—*v.t.*裝以護牆板。—*adj.* 裝有護牆板的。
clap·net [ˈklæpˌnɛt; ˈklæpnet] *n.* 捕鳥之網。
clap·per [ˈklæpə; ˈklæpə] *n.* ①拍擊之人或物;鼓掌者。②鐘或鈴之舌。③〖俚〗舌。④(常 *pl.*)響板。
clap·per·claw [ˈklæpəˌklɔ; ˈklæpə-klɔː] *v.t.* 〖方〗①抓打。②痛罵。
clap·trap [ˈklæpˌtræp; ˈklæp-træp] *n.* ① 爲引人注意或喝采而天花亂墜的空話或謊言。②噱頭。 —*adj.* 空有噱頭的。
claque [klæk; klæk]〖法〗*n.* ①受雇於戲院中喝采之一班人。②一羣景慕者或奉承者。
Clar·a [ˈklɛrə; ˈklɛərə] *n.* 女子名。
clar·a·bel·la [ˌklærəˈbɛlə; ˌklærəˈbelə] *n.* 〖音樂〗一種發出柔美音調之風琴音栓。
Clare [klɛr; klɛə] *n.* ①男子名(Clarence 之暱稱)。②女子名 (Clara 之暱稱)。
Clar·ence [ˈklærəns; ˈklærəns] *n.* 男子名。「一種雙座四輪馬車。」
clar·ence [ˈklærəns; ˈklærəns] *n.*
clar·en·don [ˈklærəndən; ˈklærən-dən] *n.* 〖印刷〗一種粗體活字。
clar·et [ˈklærət; ˈklærət] *n.* ①紅葡萄酒。②深紫紅色。③〖俚〗血。—*adj.* 紫紅色的。
clar·et-col·ored [ˈklærətˌkʌləd; ˈklærətˌkʌləd] *adj.* 深紫紅色的。
claret cup (紅葡萄酒、蘇打水、檸檬汁、白蘭地酒、水果、糖等之)混合飲料。
claret red 深紫紅色。
cla·rif·i·cant [klæˈrɪfəkənt; klæˈri-fikənt] *n.* 〖化〗澄清劑。
clar·i·fy [ˈklærəˌfaɪ; ˈklærifai] *v.,* **-fied, -fy·ing.** —*v.t.* ①使清淨; 使澄清。②使明

瞭；解釋。 —*v.i.* ①澄清。②明瞭。—**clar·i·fi·ca·tion, clar·i·fi·er,** *n.*

clar·i·net [ˌklærəˈnɛt; ˌklæriˈnet] *n.* 豎笛；單簧管。(亦作 **clarionet**)—**clar·i·net-(t)ist,** *n.*

clar·i·on [ˈklærɪən; ˈklærian] *n.* ①尖音小號。②〖詩〗尖音小號所發出之聲音。③〖詩〗此種響亮清澈之聲音。—*adj.* 響亮清澈的。

clar·i·ty [ˈklærətɪ; ˈklæriti] *n.* ①(思想、文體等之)明晰。②(音色之)清澄。③(寶石等之)純粹；透明。

cla·ro [ˈklɑro; ˈklɑːrou] *adj., n., pl.* **-ros.** —*adj.* 色味俱淡的(雪茄煙)。—*n.* 此種雪茄煙。

clar·y [ˈklɛrɪ; ˈklɛəri] *n., pl.* **-ies.** 鼠尾草屬之植物。

***clash** [klæʃ; klæʃ] *n.* ①撞擊聲(如刀劍等金屬的鏗然聲)。②衝突。The *clash* of arguments between them is unavoidable. 他們議論的衝突是無可避免的。③戰鬥。—*v.i.* ①作撞擊聲。②衝突。Their interests *clashed* with ours. 他們的利益與我們的衝突。③相撞；相遇。—*v.t.* ①撞擊。②發撞擊聲。

***clasp** [klæsp; klɑːsp] *n.* ①釦；鉤。②緊握；緊抱。 He gave my hand a warm *clasp.* 他熱切地緊握我的手。③〖外科〗把持鉤。—*v.t.* ①用臂緊抱。②用手緊握。③用釦或鉤搭住。 —**er,** *n.*

clasp hook 抱合鉤；彎腳鉤。

clasp knife 可摺疊之小刀。

‡class [klæs, klɑs; klɑːs] *n.* ①種類；門類。to arrange goods in *classes.* 將貨物分類。②班；級。She is at the head of her *class.* 她名冠全班。③上課；上課時間；講授和講習之科目。We have an English *class* every morning. 我們每天上午都有英文課。④階級。They belong to the middle *class.* 他們屬於中等階級。⑤等級。Shall we get a ticket for the first *class?* 我們要買頭等票嗎？⑥綱(動植物的分類)。⑦同年次的國民兵或徵兵。⑧〖俚〗優秀；卓越；風度。⑨教室。***in a class by itself*** (or ***oneself***) 獨一無二的。***the classes*** 上流的人士。He is liked by *the classes* and the masses. 上流的人士和普通的民衆都喜歡他。—*v.t.* ①分等級；分類。②將…分班或編級。—*v.i.* 列爲；隸屬於某一階級。those who *class* as believers. 列爲信徒的人們。

class. ①classic. ②classical. ③classification. ④classified.

class·a·ble [ˈklæsəbl̩; ˈklɑːsəbl] *adj.* 可分類的；可分組的。

class·book [ˈklæsˌbuk; ˈklɑːsbuk] *n.* ①(學校之)點名記分簿。②畢業班紀念册。

class-con·scious [ˈklæsˈkɑnʃəs; ˈklɑːsˈkɔnʃəs] *adj.* 有階級意識的。

class consciousness 階級意識。

class day 〖美〗畢業紀念日。

class·fel·low [ˈklæsˌfɛlo; ˈklɑːsˌfelou] *n.* =**classmate.**

clas·sic** [ˈklæsɪk; ˈklæsik] *adj.* ①第一等的；最高等的；最優的；典雅的；高尚的(尤指文學藝術作品)。②模範的。③屬於古希臘羅馬的文學、藝術或生活方面的。④古典的；古典文學的。⑤在文學與歷史方面著名的。⑥基本的。⑦保持持久興趣、品質或風尚的。⑧傳統的；典型的。⑨有權威的。—*n.* ①第一流的文學作家或著作。ancient and modern *classics.* 古今名著。②第一等的藝術作家或作品。③〖俚〗傳統式樣的女裝。④最重要而每年舉行的體育競賽。⑤值得注意或記憶之事物。⑥有權威性之著作。the Chinese classics*** 四書五經；中國經書。 ***the classics*** 古希臘、羅馬的文學或語言；古典文學。

***clas·si·cal** [ˈklæsɪkl̩; ˈklæsikəl] *adj.* ①第一等的；最高等的(=classic)。②精通古代典籍的。a *classical* scholar. 精通古典的學者。③正統的(與新奇的有別)；標準的。④古典的；典雅的。 *classical* school. 古典派。⑤(C-)合於西元前5世紀至4世紀時之希臘藝術繪畫、雕刻等標準的。⑥〖建築〗古希臘羅馬公共建築樣式的。⑦仿此種樣式的。 —**ly,** *adv.*

classical architecture 古典建築。

classical economics 古典經濟學(主張自由競爭及政府應竭力避免干涉)。

clas·si·cal·ism [ˈklæsɪkl̩ˌɪzəm; ˈklæsikəlizəm] *n.* =**classicism.**

clas·si·cal·i·ty [ˌklæsəˈkælətɪ; ˌklæsiˈkæliti] *n., pl.* **-ties.** ①第一；卓越。②文雅；典雅。③古典文學之學識。

classical music 古典音樂。

clas·si·cism [ˈklæsəˌsɪzəm; ˈklæsisizəm] *n.* ①古典主義。②模倣古典；擬古主義。③古典之語風或形式。④古典學。

clas·si·cist [ˈklæsəsɪst; ˈklæsisist] *n.* 古典學者；古典主義者。(亦作 **classicalist**)

clas·si·cize [ˈklæsəˌsaɪz; ˈklæsisaiz] *v.t.* & *v.i.,* **-cized, -ciz·ing.** (使)具有古典風格；古典化。

***clas·si·fi·ca·tion** [ˌklæsəfəˈkeʃən; ˌklæsifiˈkeiʃən] *n.* ①分類；類別。②被分類之事物。③〖美軍〗保密區分。④〖圖書館學〗編目。 —**al, clas·si·fi·ca·to·ry,** *adj.*

clas·si·fied [ˈklæsəˌfaɪd; ˈklæsifaid] *adj.* ①分類的。②〖俗〗保密的。

classified ad 分類廣告。

classified advertising ①分類廣告。②分類廣告業務。③分類廣告部。④分類廣告欄。

***clas·si·fy** [ˈklæsəˌfaɪ; ˈklæsifai] *v.t.,* **-fied, -fy·ing.** ①分類；列等；類別。to *classify* books by subjects. 書按科目分類。②〖美政府、軍〗 **a.** 將(文件等)列入保密區分。 **b.** 將(情報文件等)之閱覽限於授權人員。 —**clas·si·fi·er,** *n.* —**clas·si·fi·a·ble,** *adj.*

clas·sis [ˈklæsɪs; ˈklæsis] *n., pl.* **-ses** [-siz; -siːz]. 〖基督教〗長老監督會。

class·less [ˈklæslɪs; ˈklɑːslis] *adj.* ①無階級差別的。②不屬於任何階級的。

class·list [ˈklæsˌlɪst; ˈklɑːslist] *n.* 班級名册。

class·man [ˈklæsmən; ˈklɑːsmən] *n., pl.* **-men.** 班上之學生。

***class·mate** [ˈklæsˌmet, ˈklɑsˌmet; ˈklɑːsmeit] *n.* 同班班友；同級級友。

***class·room** [ˈklæsˌrum; ˈklɑːsrum] *n.* 教室。

class struggle 階級鬥爭。

class·work [ˈklæsˌwɝk, ˈklɑs-; ˈklɑːswəːk] *n.* ①在教室做的功課。②老師與學生一起在教室做的功課。

class·y [ˈklæsɪ; ˈklɑːsi] *adj.,* **class·i·er, class·i·est.** 〖俚〗上等的；時髦的；典雅的；精美的。

clas·tic [ˈklæstɪk; ˈklæstik] *adj.* ①〖生物〗分裂的；裂成碎片的。*clastic* action. 分解作用。②人體解剖模型的；(人體模型)由可以拆散的部分組成的。③〖地質〗碎片性的。

clath·rate [ˈklæθˌret; ˈklæθreit] *adj.* 〖植物〗如窗格子的；窗格形的。

***clat·ter** [ˈklætɚ; ˈklætə] *n.* ①噼啪聲；嘩喇聲。 the *clatter* of machinery. 機器之隆隆聲。②嘈雜的笑鬧聲。③閒談。 —*v.i.* ①發出噼啪聲。②喧鬧而急促地談話。—*v.t.*

使噼啪或嗶喇作響。—**er,** *n.* —**ing·ly,** *adv.*
Clau·di·us I 〔'klɔdɪəs; 'klɔːdiəs〕克勞第阿斯一世（10 B.C.–A.D. 54，羅馬皇帝，在位期間 A.D. 41–54）。
***clause** 〔klɔz; klɔːz〕 *n.* ①〖文法〗子句。noun *clause.* 名詞子句。②(法律、條約等的)條款。saving *clause.* 保留條款；附條。—**claus·al,** *adj.*
claus·tral 〔'klɔstrəl; 'klɔːstrəl〕 *adj.* ①修道院的；似修道院的。②幽閉於修道院中的；遁世的。
claus·tro·pho·bi·a 〔ˌklɔstrə'fobɪə; ˌklɔːstrə'foubjə〕 *n.* 〖醫〗幽閉恐怖。—**claus·tro·pho·bic,** *adj.*
cla·vate 〔'klevet; 'kleiveit〕 *adj.* 棍棒狀的；一端膨大的。(亦作 **clavated**)
clave 〔klev; kleiv〕 *v.* pt. of **cleave.**
clav·e·cin 〔'klævəsɪn; 'klævisin〕 *n.* 大鍵琴。—**ist,** *n.*
cla·ver 〔'klevɚ; 'kleivə〕 *n.* 〖蘇〗饒舌；喋喋不休。—*v.i.* 〖蘇〗饒舌；閒談。
clav·i·chord 〔'klævəˌkɔrd; 'klævikɔːd〕 *n.* 〖音樂〗翼琴(爲鋼琴之前身)。
clav·i·cle 〔'klævək]; 'klævikl〕 *n.* 〖解剖〗鎖骨。—**cla·vic·u·lar,** *adj.*
cla·vi·er 〔*for* ① 'klævɪɚ, *for* ② & ③ klə'vɪr; *for* ① 'klæviə, *for* ② & ③ klə'viə〕 *n.* ① 鍵盤。②有鍵盤之樂器。③僅有鍵盤然不能發聲之樂器(供練習指法用)。(亦作 **klavier**)
***claw** 〔klɔ; klɔː〕 *n.* ①爪。②(龍蝦、蟹等的)鉗。③有爪之腳。④似爪之物。—*v.t.* 用爪搔；用爪撕；用爪鉗；用爪挖。*claw hold of* 以爪抓緊。—**er,** *n.* —**less,** *adj.* —**like,** *adj.*
claw foot 有爪之腳。
claw hammer ①拔釘鎚。②〖美俗〗燕尾服上裝。
claw hatchet 背部有鉤可拔釘用的斧。
***clay** 〔kle; klei〕 *n.* ①黏土。②土；泥。③〖聖經〗肉體；人身。④體質與天賦。—*v.t.* ①與黏土混合。②濾過黏土。—**ish,** —**like,** *adj.*
clay·bank 〔'kleˌbæŋk; 'kleibæŋk〕 *n.* ①土堤。②棕黃色。③此種顏色之馬。
clay-cold 〔'kle'kold; 'klei'kould〕 *adj.* 冷如泥土的；冷冰冰的；死的。
clay court 泥土網球場。
clay·ey 〔'kleɪ; 'kleii〕 *adj.,* **clay·i·er, clay·i·est.** (敷有)黏土的；多黏土的；黏土質的。
clay pigeon ①一種飛靶。②〖俚〗處於易爲他人所乘之情況中的人。
clay stone 泥鐵石；黏土石。
-cle 〖字尾〗=**-cule.**
‡clean 〔klin; kliːn〕 *adj.* ①潔淨的；清潔的。②清白的；無瑕的。He has a *clean* record. 他有清白的記錄。③有潔淨習慣的。④適於做食物的。⑤勻稱的；整齊的。A sharp knife makes a *clean* cut. 利刃切得整整齊齊。⑥新的；沒有用過的；洗淨的。Give me a *clean* sheet of paper. 給我一張沒有用過的乾淨紙。⑦完全的。⑧俐落的；巧妙的。a *clean* leap. 靈巧的一跳。⑨不挾雜物的。⑩不產生放射塵的。⑪(稿子等)無刪改而易讀的。a *clean* copy. 一分謄清稿。⑫不作弊的。⑬(文體等)優雅的；不俗的。⑭徹底的。⑮〖俚〗有技巧的。⑯〖俚〗不吸毒的。⑰未遭遇意外困難的。⑱不含色情或瀆神字眼的。⑲〖俚〗未暗藏武器的。⑳〖俚〗無錢的。㉑(船)未載貨的。*clean sweep* 完全的勝利。*come clean* 〖俚〗全部招供。*keep the hands clean* 廉潔清正。*make a clean breast of* 徹底懺悔；吐露一切詳情。*make a clean sweep of* 一掃而光。—*adv.* ①乾淨地。to sweep *clean.* 掃得乾淨。②完全地；整個地。I *clean* forgot about it. 我完全忘記了它。③技巧地；熟練地。—*v.t.* 使清潔；使乾淨。to *clean* one's hands. 洗淨自己的手。—*v.i.*打掃；除汙〖up〗. to *clean* up for dinner. 收拾乾淨，以備開飯。*be cleaned out* 〖俗〗一文不名。*clean down* (從牆上)把汚物掃下。*clean house* 肅清貪汚。*clean out* **a.** 清除。**b.** 用完；用盡。**c.**〖俗〗將(不良分子)趕出。**d.**〖俚〗使一文不名。**e.** 將…清場。*clean up* **a.**使潔淨。**b.** 做完；整理。**c.** 賺錢；獲利。**d.** 肅清不法分子。—**a·ble,** *adj.* —**a·bil·i·ty,** —**ness,** *n.*
clean bill of health ①無傳染病的健康證明書。②〖俗〗某團體或個人經調查後，被確認無不道德行爲而適於擔任公職。
clean·bred 〔'klinˌbrɛd; 'kliːnbred〕 *adj.* 純種的。
clean-cut 〔'klin'kʌt; 'kliːn'kʌt〕 *adj.* ①輪廓鮮明的。②形狀美好的。③清晰的。④爽朗的；爽利的。⑤毫無疑義的。
***clean·er** 〔'klinɚ; 'kliːnə〕 *n.* ①清除汚物者。②乾洗店。③除汚物；清潔劑。④掃除器；吸塵器。⑤乾洗店經營人。*take to the cleaners* 〖俚〗使失去金錢或財物。
clean-fin·gered 〔'klin'fɪŋgɚd; 'kliːn'fiŋgəd〕 *adj.* ①廉潔的；不苟的；誠實的。②熟練的(指扒手)。
clean·hand·ed 〔'klin'hændɪd; 'kliːn'hændid〕 *adj.* 清廉的。—**ness,** *n.*
clean hands 老實；無罪。
***clean·ing** 〔'klinɪŋ; 'kliːniŋ〕 *n.* ①清潔；洗濯；掃除。dry *cleaning.* 乾洗。②(*pl.*)垃圾。③(牛、羊等的)胞衣。④〖俚〗**a.** 慘敗。**b.** 財務上慘重的損失(常與 good 連用)。
cleaning rod (槍口的)通條。
cleaning woman 打掃房間的女僕。
clean·li·ly 〔'klɛnlɪlɪ; 'klenlili〕 *adv.* 清潔地。
clean-limbed 〔'klin'lɪmd; 'kliːn'limd〕 *adj.* 四肢勻稱的；姿勢優美的。
clean-liv·ing 〔'klin'lɪvɪŋ; 'kliːn'liviŋ〕 *adj.* 過着老實生活的。
***clean·ly** 〔*adj.* 'klɛnlɪ; 'klenli *adv.* 'klinlɪ; 'kliːnli〕 *adj.,* **-li·er, -li·est,** *adv.* —*adj.* ①潔淨的；清潔的。a *cleanly* hotel. 清潔的旅館。②習慣於清潔的；有清潔習慣的。—*adv.* 清潔地；純潔地；俐落地。—**clean·li·ness,** *n.*
clean room 經過消毒的房間。
***cleanse** 〔klɛnz; klenz〕 *v.t.,* **cleansed, cleans·ing.** ①使清潔。②使純潔。—**cleans·a·ble,** *adj.*
cleans·er 〔'klɛnzɚ; 'klenzə〕 *n.* ①清潔劑。②使清潔的人或物。
clean-shav·en 〔'klin'ʃevn; 'kliːn'ʃeivn〕 *adj.* 刮光鬍鬚的。
cleans·ing 〔'klɛnzɪŋ; 'klenziŋ〕 *n.* ①清淨；齋戒。②(常 *pl.*)(家畜之)胞衣；胎膜。—*adj.* ①有清潔效能的；洗滌用的。②淨化的。
clean-up 〔'klinˌʌp; 'kliːnʌp〕 *n.* ①清掃；清潔。②〖俚〗贏利；賺錢(尤指暴利)。
‡clear 〔klɪr; kliə〕 *adj.* ①晴朗無雲的；清亮的。a *clear* day. 晴天。②易看穿的；透明的。③白皙的。④易聽清楚的；嘹亮的。⑤清晰的；明確的。a *clear* idea. 清晰明確的思想。⑥確然的；無疑的。It is *clear* that it is going to rain. 顯然就要下雨了。⑦無障礙的；一覽無餘的。⑧暢通無阻的。The roads were *clear* of traffic. 條條大路暢通無阻。⑨安全通過的；未受阻礙的。⑩清白的；無罪的；無疚的。⑪不負債的。⑫無可指責的。⑬純利的；

淨得的。clear profit. 純利。⑭無限制的;全然的。a clear month. 一整月。⑮醇的(酒)。⑯無節瘤的(木材,樹)。⑰無瑕疵的。⑱心平氣和的。⑲易懂的。⑳貨物已卸完的。㉑遠離的。***keep clear of*** 避開;躲開。***The coast is clear.*** 已無危險;已無困難;可以行事。—*adv.* ①完全地。The prisoner got *clear* away. 囚犯逃得無影無蹤。②不含糊地;乾淨俐落地。—*v.t.* ①使乾淨。to *clear* one's throat. 清嗓子。②移去;移除。③越過;跳過。④宣告…無罪;證明…無罪。⑤除卻疑慮。⑥逐退;掃蕩。⑦淨得;獲得純利。⑧使(船)辦理出港手續。⑨交換清算(票據)。⑩使易懂得。⑪吃完。⑫洗清。to *clear* one's name. 洗清某人的名譽。⑬處理(郵件、電話等)。⑭使了卻債務。⑮獲得授權或批准。⑯授權或准許。⑰(法庭)處理積案。⑱賣完;買光。—*v.i.* ①變晴;雲散。②出港;啓碇。③交換;清算。④逃走。⑤明白。⑥清除餐桌。⑦通過。⑧售完;賣光。***clear away*** a. 消釋。b. 清除。c. 消散。***clear expenses*** 掙足够之錢以供支出。***clear off*** a. 清除;掃除。b. 償清。c. 放晴;雲霧消散。d. 售清。e. 離開;逃走。***clear out*** a. 售清。b. 離開。c. 掃除;清除。d. 使囊空如洗。e. 趕走。***clear the air*** a. 使空氣清潔。b. 清除誤解。***clear the decks*** 準備作戰;準備行動。***clear the ground*** 砍伐樹林;開墾土地。***clear up*** a. 轉晴;放晴。The weather *clears up*. 天氣轉晴。b. 使明瞭;解釋。c. 打掃;掃除。—*n.* ①空隙;空間。②內部之長寬深。***in the clear*** a. 內部之長寬深。b. 自由的。c. 明碼的。d. 無罪。—**a-ble,** *adj.* —**ness,** *n.*

clear air turbulence 晴空亂流。(略作 CAT)

clear·ance [ˈklɪrəns; ˈkliərəns] *n.* ①距離;間隔。②清除。*clearance* sale. 減價清售存貨。③=**clearance papers.** ④純益;淨利。⑤支票或期票的交換。⑥森林中無樹木之地方。⑦〖政府,軍〗授權允許閱覽機密文件。⑧〖醫〗肅清作用;肅清力;肅清試驗。

clearance papers 出港單。

clear-cut [ˈklɪrˈkʌt; ˈkliəˈkʌt] *adj.* ①輪廓分明的。②清晰的;明白的;確定的。

clear-eye [ˈklɪrˈaɪ; ˈkliərˈai] *n., pl.* **-eyes.** =**clary.**

clear-eyed [ˈklɪrˈaɪd;ˈkliərˈaid] *adj.* ①明眼的。②聰明的。

clear·head·ed [ˌklɪrˈhɛdɪd; ˈkliəˈhedid] *adj.* 頭腦清楚的;聰明的。

***clear·ing** [ˈklɪrɪŋ; ˈkliəriŋ] *n.* ①開墾的土地。②銀行之票據交換。③(*pl.*)票據交換所所交換之總額。④清除;掃除。

clearing hospital 野戰醫院。

clearing house 票據交換所。

‡**clear·ly** [ˈklɪrlɪ; ˈkliəli] *adv.* ①明亮地;清澄地。②明白地;明確地。It is too dark to see *clearly*. 天太黑看不清楚。③無疑地;明顯地。It was *clearly* a mistake. 它顯然錯誤。④無誤地;是那樣地。

clear-sight·ed [ˈklɪrˈsaɪtɪd; ˈkliəˈsaitid] *adj.* 視力銳敏的;聰明的。—**ly,** *adv.* —**ness,** *n.*

clear·sto·ry [ˈklɪrˌstorɪ;ˈkliəstəri] *n., pl.* **-ries.**〖建築〗高窗。

clear text (電報之)明碼。

cleat [klit; kliːt] *n.* ①楔;栓。②〖航海〗索栓。③〖電〗磁夾板。—*v.t.* ①栓住。②加栓於。

cleav·a·ble [ˈklivəbl; ˈkliːvəbl] *adj.* 可割的;可裂的;可打通的;可劈開的。

cleav·age [ˈklivɪdʒ; ˈkliːvidʒ] *n.* ①劈開;分裂。②劈開處。③不協和。④〖化〗分解。⑤〖生物〗(受精卵)細胞分裂。

***cleave** [kliv; kliːv] *v.,* **cleft** [klɛft; kleft] or **cleaved** or **clove** [klov; klouv], **cleft** or **cleaved** or **clo·ven** [ˈklovn; ˈklouvn], **cleav·ing.** —*v.t.* ①割開;劈開;分開。②穿過;通經。③劈通;打通。They *cleaved* a path through the wilderness. 他們在荒野中打通一條路。④砍下。—*v.i.* ①分裂;裂開。②忠於;固守。to *cleave* to an idea. 忠於一思想。

cleav·er [ˈklivɚ; ˈkliːvə] *n.* ①屠刀。②切割者。

cleav·ers [ˈklivɚz; ˈkliːvəz] *n. sing.* or *pl.*〖植物〗豬殃殃。(亦作 **clivers**)

cleek [klik; kliːk] *n., v.,* **claught** or **cleeked, cleek·ing.** —*n.* ①〖蘇,北英〗鐵鉤。②一種有鐵頭之高爾夫球棒。③〖蘇〗抽筋。—*v.t.*抓住;緊握。

clef [klɛf; klef] *n.* 〖音樂〗音部記號。

***cleft**[1] [klɛft; kleft] *v.* pt. & pp. of **cleave.**

cleft[2] *n.* 裂縫;裂口。—*adj.* 裂開的;劈開的。***be in a cleft stick*** 進退維谷。

cleft lip 兔脣。

cleg [klɛg; kleg] *n.* 〖英方〗馬蠅;牛蠅;虻。

cleis·tog·a·mous [klaɪsˈtɑgəməs; klaisˈtɔgəməs] *adj.* 〖植物〗閉花受精的。

cleis·tog·a·my [klaɪsˈtɑgəmɪ;klaisˈtɔgəmi] *n.* 〖植物〗閉花受精。

clem·a·tis [ˈklɛmətɪs; ˈklemətis] *n.* 〖植物〗女萎;鐵線蓮。

clem·en·cy [ˈklɛmənsɪ; ˈklemənsi] *n., pl.* **-cies.** ①仁慈。②溫和。③和藹。

Clem·ens [ˈklɛmənz; ˈklemənz] *n.* 克里門斯 (Samuel Langhorne, 1835–1910, 筆名 Mark Twain, 馬克吐溫, 美幽默小說家)。

clem·ent [ˈklɛmənt; ˈklemənt] *adj.* ①仁慈的。②(氣候或天氣) 溫和的。—**ly,** *adv.*

***clench** [klɛntʃ; klentʃ] *v.t.* ①緊握;咬緊。to *clench* one's teeth. 咬緊牙關。②牢牢地抓住。③確定。to *clench* a bargain. 定契約。—*v.i.* 握緊。—*n.* ①牢牢抓住。②釘緊。

clench·er [ˈklɛntʃɚ; ˈklentʃə] *n.* = **clincher.**

Cle·o·pat·ra [ˌkliəˈpetrə;kliəˈpɑːtrə] *n.* 克麗佩脫拉 (69–30 B.C., 古埃及女王, 51–49B.C. 及 48–30B.C. 統治埃及)。

Cleopatra's Needle 古埃及方尖形碑,一在紐約市中央公園,一在倫敦泰晤士河畔。

clep·sy·dra [ˈklɛpsɪdrə; ˈklepsidrə] *n., pl.* **-dras, -drae** [-ˌdri;-driː]. 漏壺;水時計。

clere·sto·ry [ˈklɪrˌstorɪ;ˈkliəstəri] *n., pl.* **-ries.**〖建築〗高窗。

***cler·gy** [ˈklɝdʒɪ; ˈkləːdʒi] *n., pl.* **-gies.** 僧侶;牧師(集合稱)。

***cler·gy·man** [ˈklɝdʒɪmən; ˈkləːdʒimən] *n., pl.* **-men.** 牧師;教士。

cler·gy·wom·an [ˈklɝdʒɪˌwʊmən; ˈkləːdʒiˌwumən] *n., pl.* **-wom·en.** ①女教士。②牧師之女眷。

cler·ic [ˈklɛrɪk; ˈklerik] *n.* 牧師;傳教士。—*adj.* 牧師的。

cler·i·cal [ˈklɛrɪkl; ˈklerikəl] *adj.* ①書記的;抄寫員的。②牧師的。③支持政治中教權或教會影響的。—*n.* ①牧師。②支持政治中教權或教會影響者。③(*pl.*)教士之服裝。④小錯誤。

cler·i·cal·ism [ˈklɛrɪkəlɪzəm; ˈklerikəlizəm] *n.*①教權主義。②任聖職者之不正當的政治影響力。③對此種力量之支持。—**cler·i·cal·ist,** *n.*

cler·i·cal·ize [ˈklɛrɪkəlaɪz; ˈklerikəlaiz] *v.t.,* **-ized, -iz·ing.** ①使教權化。②在

…中提高教權之影響力。

cler·i·hew [ˈklɛrɪˌhju; ˈklerihju:] *n.* 一種幽默押韻的四行詩。

cler·i·sy [ˈklɛrɪsɪ; ˈklerisi] *n.* 知識分子(集合稱);知識階級。

‡clerk [klɝk; klɑ:k] *n.* ①售貨員;店員。He is a *clerk* of that department store. 他是那間百貨公司的店員。②書記;錄事。③辦事員;記帳員。a bank *clerk.* 銀行的辦事員。④在法院或立法機關管理記錄的官員。⑤教會的執事(非牧師)。⑥教士;牧師。⑦〖古〗**a.** 識字的人。**b.** 學者。 —*v.i.* 做 clerk 的工作。

clerk in holy orders 牧師;教士。

clerk·ly [ˈklɝklɪ; ˈklɑ:kli] *adj.*, **-li·er, -li·est,** *adv.* —*adj.* 店員的;書記的。—*adv.* 像店員地;像書記地。

clerk of the weather 〖英〗想像中的被幽默地認爲可控制天氣的官員。

clerk·ship [ˈklɝkʃɪp; ˈklɑ:kʃip] *n.* ① clerk 之職位或身分。②醫科學生之實習。③〖古〗**a.** 學問。**b.** 牧師;教士。

Cleve·land [ˈklivlənd; ˈkli:vlənd] *n.* 克利夫蘭(美國 Ohio 州東北部之一都市)。

***clev·er** [ˈklɛvɚ; ˈklevə] *adj.* ①聰明的。②巧妙的。③擅長的。He is *clever* at painting. 他擅長繪畫。④〖方〗性情和順的;態度溫和的。⑤身手靈活的。**—ly,** *adv.* **—ness,** *n.*

clev·er·ish [ˈklɛvərɪʃ; ˈklevəriʃ] *adj.* 聰明的;巧妙的。 **—ly,** *adv.*

clev·is [ˈklɛvɪs; ˈklevis] *n.* 一種U形連接裝置。

clew [klu; klu:] *n.* ①(解決問題的)線索。②線團;繩團。③帆的下角。④帆下角上的金屬圈。***from clew to earing*** 〖航海〗**a.** 從方形帆之底部到頂部。 **b.** 徹底地。***spread a large clew*** 〖航海〗張滿帆。***spread a small clew*** 〖航海〗張少量帆。 —*v.t.* ①以 clew 張或收帆。②將…纏成線團。(亦作 **clue**)

cli·ché [kliˈʃe; ˈkli:ʃei] *n.*, *pl.* **-chés** [-ˈʃez; -ʃeiz], *adj.* 〖法〗—*n.* ①陳腔濫調。②〖印刷〗鉛版;電氣版。—*adj.* 陳腐的。

***click** [klɪk; klik] *n.* ①克啦聲;滴答聲。②掣子。③(*pl.*)〖英,無線電〗大氣中之短暫的干擾。—*v.i.* ①作滴答聲;作拍答聲。The door *clicked* shut. 這門拍答關起。②〖俚〗情形良好;成功。③〖俗〗**a.** 合得來。**b.** 變爲清晰的。 —*v.t.* 使作滴答聲;使作拍答聲。**—less,** *adj.*

click·e·ty-clack [ˈklɪkətɪˈklæk; ˈklikitiˈklæk] *n.* 克力克啦之聲音。—*v.i.* 發出此種聲音。(亦作 **clickety-click**)

***cli·ent** [ˈklaɪənt; ˈklaiənt] *n.* ①委託律師訴訟之當事人;訴訟委託人。②顧客。③受人保護之人;食客。④隨從。

cli·en·tele [ˌklaɪənˈtɛl; ˌkli:ɑ̃ˈteil] *n.* ①(醫師、律師等之)顧客;(商店、旅社、娛樂場所之)常客(集合稱)。②隨從(集合稱)。(亦作 **clientage**)

***cliff** [klɪf; klif] *n.* 懸崖;絕壁。

cliff dweller ①居於絕壁洞穴中的人。②〖美俗〗大城市中公寓居民;都市居民。

cliff-hang·er [ˈklɪfˌhæŋɚ; ˈklifˌhæŋə] *n.* ①緊張懸宕的情節。②結果到最後才分曉的一件事或競賽。—*adj.* 緊張懸宕的。(亦作 **cliffhanger**)

cliff-hang·ing [ˈklɪfˌhæŋɪŋ; ˈklifˌhæŋiŋ] *adj.* 緊張懸宕的;勝敗相差極微的。(亦作 **cliffhanging**)

cliff·side [ˈklɪfˌsaɪd; ˈklifsaid] *n.* 懸崖之邊或面。

cliffs·man [ˈklɪfsmən; ˈklifsmən] *n.*, *pl.* **-men.** 善攀登懸崖者。

cliff swallow 崖燕(築巢於懸崖上)。

cliff·y [ˈklɪfɪ; ˈklifi] *adj.*, **cliff·i·er, cliff·i·est.** 有岩峻的;崎嶇的。

cli·mac·ter·ic [klaɪˈmæktərɪk; klaiˈmæktərik] *n.* ①更年期;經絕期。②任何緊要時期。③水果成熟期。***the grand climacteric*** 一生之六十三歲(臆斷斯時有重大變化發生)。 —*adj.* ①更年期的;經絕期的。②似更年期的;重要時期的;緊要的;高潮的。

cli·mac·tic [klaɪˈmæktɪk; klaiˈmæktik] *adj.* 頂點的;極點的;高潮的。(亦作 **climactical**)

***cli·mate** [ˈklaɪmɪt; ˈklaimit] *n.* ①氣候。tropical *climate.* 熱帶性氣候。 ②特殊氣候的地區。③某一團體,時期或地區的特殊情況或環境。investment *climate.* 投資環境。

cli·mat·ic [klaɪˈmætɪk; klaiˈmætik] *adj.* 氣候(上)的。(亦作 **climatical, climatal**) **—al·ly,** *adv.*

cli·ma·ti·za·tion [ˌklaɪmətəˈzeʃən; ˌklaimətiˈzeiʃən] *n.* ①順應氣候。②機器設計而使其能在任何氣候下的某溫度範圍內作業。

cli·ma·tize [ˈklaɪməˌtaɪz; ˈklaimətaiz] *v.t.* & *v.i.*, **-tized, -tiz·ing.** (使)順應氣候。

cli·ma·tol·o·gy [ˌklaɪməˈtɑlədʒɪ; ˌklaiməˈtɔlədʒi] *n.* 氣候學;風土學。

***cli·max** [ˈklaɪmæks; ˈklaimæks] *n.* ①頂點;極點。②〖修辭〗漸進法;層進法。③高潮。④興奮之頂點。—*v.t.* 使達頂點。—*v.i.* 達頂點。

‡climb [klaɪm; klaim] *v.*, **climbed** or (古) **clomb; climbed** or (古) **clomb, climb·ing,** *n.* —*v.t.* ①攀高;攀登。to *climb* a mountain. 登山。②攀緣。 —*v.i.* ①攀登;上升。②攀緣。The grapevine *climbed* up along wall. 葡萄藤沿牆攀緣而上。***climb down*** **a.** 攀緣而下。 **b.** 放棄自己的地位;自認錯誤;屈服。—*n.* ①攀登。He made a difficult *climb.* 他作一次艱難的攀登。 ②攀登的地方。The path is an easy *climb.* 這小徑是容易攀登的地方。

climb·a·ble [ˈklaɪməbl̩; ˈklaiməbl] *adj.* 可攀登的。

climb·down [ˈklaɪmˌdaun; ˈklaimdaun] *n.* 〖俗〗①攀緣而下。②讓步;作罷;撤回。(亦作 **climb-down**)

climb·er [ˈklaɪmɚ; ˈklaimə] *n.* ①登山者。②攀緣植物。③力求上進的人;有野心者。④＝**climbing irons.**

climb indicator (飛機之)升降率指示儀。

climb·ing [ˈklaɪmɪŋ; ˈklaimiŋ] *adj.* 攀緣而上的;上升的。—*n.* 攀登。

climbing fish 攀木魚。(亦作 **climbing perch**)

climbing irons 繫於鞋、腿或膝上供攀高之鐵鉤。

***clime** [klaɪm; klaim] *n.* 〖詩〗①氣候。②地方;地域。

clinch [klɪntʃ; klintʃ] *v.t.* ①敲彎(釘頭等)使釘牢。②如此釘牢(東西)。③確定。 —*v.i.* ①打下釘頭使釘牢。②揪扭;扭住。③〖俚〗熱烈的擁吻。 —*n.* ①釘牢。②揪扭;扭住。③釘牢的釘。④〖航海〗一種繩結。⑤拳擊手之扭住對方使不能出手。⑥〖俚〗擁吻。⑦證實;決定性的解決。(亦作 **clench**)

clinch·er [ˈklɪntʃɚ; ˈklintʃə] *n.* ①敲平或敲彎釘頭之人或其工具。②釘牢物品之釘等。③〖俗〗任何有決定力之物;決定性之言辭。

cling** [klɪŋ; kliŋ] *v.*, **clung, cling·ing,** *n.* —*v.i.* ①黏着;固執;堅守;堅持。to *cling* to a hope. 不放棄希望;抱着希望。②貼近;靠近;依附〖to〗。③緊握;擁抱。cling on to*** 緊緊抓住。—*n.* ①黏附;堅守。②＝**clingstone.** **—er,** *n.* **—ing·ly,** *adv.*

clinging vine 〖俗〗完全依附男人之婦女。

cling·stone ['klɪŋ,ston; 'kliŋstoun] *adj.* 果肉緊貼於核的。—*n.* ①果肉緊貼於核之桃或梅子。②此種桃或梅核。

cling·y ['klɪŋɪ; 'kliŋi] *adj.*, **cling·i·er, cling·i·est.** 黏着(性)的;緊貼的;易黏的。

*__clin·ic__ ['klɪnɪk; 'klinik] *n.* ①醫院或醫學院的貧民義診所。②專門醫治某些人或某些病的診療所。a dental *clinic.* 齒科醫院。③臨床教授。④臨床教授的班。⑤臨床的講義。⑥臨床教授班之學生。⑦診所。⑧講習班。—*adj.* 診所的;臨床的。

clin·i·cal ['klɪnɪkḷ; 'klinikəl] *adj.* ①臨床的。*clinical* medicine. 臨床醫學。②在病房所用的或所作的。③與觀察並研究病人病狀有關的。④極度客觀的。⑤【宗教】**a.**(指聖禮)施於臨終時的。**b.**(信仰的改變)在病床或臨終時所做的。—**ly,** *adv.*

clinical thermometer 體溫計。

cli·ni·cian [klɪ'nɪʃən; kli'niʃən] *n.* 臨床醫生。

clink [klɪŋk; kliŋk] *n.* ①玎璫聲。②【俗】監獄。③用來挖路面之尖棒。—*v.t.* 使作玎璫聲。—*v.i.* 玎璫作響。***clink off*** 急急走開。

clink-clank ['klɪŋk,klæŋk; 'kliŋk-klæŋk] *n.* 連續的玎璫聲。—*v.i.* 發出連續的玎璫聲。

clink·er ['klɪŋkɚ; 'kliŋkə] *n.* ①一種表面光澤如玻璃之煉磚。②熔滓; 鐵渣。③火山熔岩。④發出玎璫聲之物或人。⑤【俚】**a.** 錯誤。**b.** 失敗;低劣之東西。**c.**【英俚】很好或很受歡迎的東西。—*v.i.* 燒成熔滓。

clink·er-built ['klɪŋkɚ,bɪlt; 'kliŋkə-,bilt] *adj.* 以重疊之木板造成的;鱗狀搭造的(指木船言)。

clink·ing ['klɪŋkɪŋ; 'kliŋkiŋ] *adj.* ①玎璫作響的。②【俚】極好的; 至上的。—*adv.*【俚】很;極。

cli·nom·e·ter [klaɪ'nɑmətɚ; klai-'nɔmitə] *n.* 傾斜儀;測斜器。

Cli·o ['klaɪo; 'klaiou] *n.*【希臘神話】司史詩及歷史之女神。

*__clip__[1] [klɪp; klip] *v.,* **clipped, clipped** or **clipt** [klɪpt; klipt], **clip·ping,** *n.* —*v.t.* ①剪;剪短;修剪;修剪…之毛。to *clip* sheep. 剪羊毛。②【俗】用力一擊。③(在發音中)省略(聲音)。④削下(硬幣的邊)。⑤縮短。—*v.i.* ①剪髮。②【俗】迅速行動。③剪報。—*n.* ①剪;剪短。②一次剪下之羊毛。③【俗】迅速行動。④【俗】用力一擊;一次。⑤(*pl.*)剪刀。⑥【俗】步伐;速率。—**pa·ble,** *adj.*

clip[2] *v.,* **clipped, clip·ping,** *n.* —*v.t.* & *v.i.* ①緊握;夾住。②包圍。—*n.* ①夾子。②血管夾。③【軍】子彈卡;彈夾。④可別在衣服上的裝飾品。⑤【古】擁抱。

clip joint【俚】欺騙顧客或敲竹槓的公共娛樂場所。

clip·per ['klɪpɚ; 'klipə] *n.* ①剪取者。②(*pl.*)剪子;剪毛器。③快船;快馬;大而快的飛機。④【俗】第一流的人或物。⑤【電】削波器。

clip·per-built ['klɪpɚ,bɪlt; 'klipə-bilt] *adj.* 快艇型構造的(船等);流線型的。

clipper ship 快船。

clip·pie ['klɪpɪ; 'klipi] *n.*【英俚】巴士或電車的女車掌。

clip·ping ['klɪpɪŋ; 'klipiŋ] *n.* ①剪下的報紙、雜誌等。②剪下的東西。③剪(之動作)。—*adj.* ①剪的。②【俗】快的。③【俗】一等的。

clique [klik; kli:k] *n., v.,* **cliqued, cliqu·ing.** —*n.* 朋黨;派系。—*v.i.*【俗】結成派系。

cli·quish ['klikɪʃ; 'kli:kiʃ] *adj.* ①派系的。②分成派系的。③屬於派系的。

cli·quy ['klikɪ; 'kli:ki] *adj.* ①結黨的;喜結黨的。②排外的;排他的。(亦作 **cliquey, cliquish**)

cli·to·ris ['klaɪtərɪs; 'klaitəris] *n.*【解剖】陰核;陰蒂。

cliv·ers ['klɪvɚz; 'klivəz] *n.* = **cleavers.**

clo·a·ca [klo'ekə; klou'eikə] *n., pl.* **-cae** [-si; -si:]. ①【動物】排泄腔。②下水道。③廁所。

*__cloak__ [klok; klouk] *n.* ①外衣;斗篷。②掩飾;藉口;僞託。—*v.t.* ①用外衣遮蔽。②掩飾;隱匿。—**ed·ly,** *adv.* —**less,** *adj.*

cloak-and-dag·ger ['klokən'dægɚ; 'kloukən'dægə] *adj.* (尤指戲劇性的)有關陰謀或間諜的。

*__cloak·room__ ['klok,rum; 'klouk-rum] *n.* ①衣帽間。②車站中之行李暫存處。③【英】盥洗室;便所。

clob·ber[1] ['klɑbɚ; 'klɔbə] *v.t.* ①毆打。②慘敗。

clob·ber[2]【英,澳】【俚】*n. pl.* 衣服。—*v.i.* 穿衣服。

cloche [kloʃ; klouʃ] *n.* ①(園藝用之)鐘形玻璃罩。②鐘形之婦人帽。

‡__clock__[1] [klɑk; klɔk] *n.* ①鐘;時計。to set a *clock.* 校準時鐘。②(C-)【天文】時鐘星座(Horologium). ***around the clock*** 二十四小時連續地;不斷地;不眠不休地。***run out the clock*** 故意拖延時間以阻止對方得分。—*v.t.* 爲…計時。—*v.i.* 僅見於下列成語中的習慣用法。***clock in*** 上班打卡。***clock out*** 下班打卡。

clock[2] *n.* 襪上腳踝處的織花。—*v.t.* 繡上 clock.

clock-hour ['klɑk,aur; 'klɔk,auə] *n.*【教育】60分鐘之上課。

clock·ing ['klɑkɪŋ; 'klɔkiŋ] *adj.* 孵蛋的;伏窩的(母鷄)。

clock·mak·er ['klɑk,mekɚ; 'klɔk-,meikə] *n.* 製造或修理鐘錶者。

clock radio 帶時鐘的收音機(可定時開關)。

clock tower 鐘樓。

clock watch 報時錶;自鳴錶。

clock watcher 作事不起勁老盼望着下班的雇員。

clock·wise ['klɑk,waɪz; 'klɔkwaiz] *adv.* & *adj.* 順時針移動方向地(的);右旋地(的)。

clock·work ['klɑk,wɝk; 'klɔkwə:k] *n.* 鐘錶的機械;發條裝置。***like clockwork*** 規律的;順利地。—*adj.* 自動的;規律的。

clod [klɑd; klɔd] *n.* ①土塊; 泥塊。②肉體。③傻瓜;老粗。

clod·dish ['klɑdɪʃ; 'klɔdiʃ] *adj.* ①如土塊的。②粗魯無禮的;愚昧的。

clod·dy ['klɑdɪ; 'klɔdi] *adj.* 多土塊的;如土塊的。

clod·hop·per ['klɑd,hɑpɚ; 'klɔd-,hɔpə] *n.* ①農夫; 莊稼漢。②笨拙之人; 粗人。③(*pl.*)堅實笨重的鞋。

clod·hop·ping ['klɑd,hɑpɪŋ; 'klɔd-,hɔpiŋ] *adj.* 粗魯的;不合禮節的。

clod·pate ['klɑd,pet; 'klɔdpeit] *n.* 笨人;呆子。(亦作 **clodpoll, clodpole**)

clog[1] [klɑg; klɔg] *n.* ①木屐;木底鞋。②木屐舞。—*v.i.* 跳木屐舞。

clog[2] *v.,* **clogged, clog·ging,** *n.* —*v.t.* ①妨礙;阻礙。②塞住。—*v.i.* ①發生阻礙;容易受阻。②黏住。—*n.* ①障礙。②縛於人或動物腿部的重物。

clog·gy ['klɑgɪ; 'klɔgi] *adj.,* **-gi·er, -gi·est.** ①阻礙的;易生阻塞的。②有黏性的。

cloi·son·né [,klɔɪzə'ne; ,klɔizə'nei] *adj.* 景泰藍製的。—*n.* 景泰藍;景泰藍磁器。

*__clois·ter__ ['klɔɪstɚ; 'klɔistə] *n.* ①廻廊。②修道院;寺院。③遠離塵世之地。—*v.t.* ①幽閉於修道院中;隱遁。②築廻廊。③使成爲修道院。—**less,** *adj.* —**like,** *adj.*

clois·tered ['klɔɪstɚd; 'klɔistəd] *adj.*

①隱居的;遁世的。②有廻廊的。

clois·tral [ˈklɔɪstrəl; ˈklɔistrəl] *adj.* ①修道院的; 似修道院的。②幽閉於修道院中的。③遁世的;隱居的。

clomb [klom; kloum] *v.* 〖古〗 pt. & pp. of **climb.**

clon(e) [klon; kloun] *n.,v.,* **cloned, clon·ing.** 〖生物〗 —*n.* 由無性生殖繁殖的生物。 —*v.t.* & *v.i.* 由無性生殖繁殖。

clon·ic [ˈklanɪk; ˈklɔnik] *adj.* 抽筋的;有陣攣現象的。

clo·nus [ˈklonəs; ˈklounəs] *n., pl.* **-nuses.** 〖醫〗陣攣;抽筋。(亦作 **clonos**)

cloop [klup; klu:p] *n.* 拔瓶塞所發之砰然聲。—*v.i.* 發出砰然之聲。

:close¹ [kloz; klouz] *v.,* **closed, clos·ing,** *n.* —*v.t.* ①關;閉。②靠緊;靠攏。③結束。④使閉塞。⑤辦妥。to *close* a sale on a car. 辦妥一部車子的出售。⑥關店。⑦〖航海〗靠近。—*v.i.* ①關閉。The store *closes* at 9 p.m. 店鋪於晚上九時關門。②完畢。The meeting *closed* at six o'clock. 會議於六時結束。③圍集; 圍困〖about, round〗。④格鬥; 扭住互毆〖with〗。⑤同意; 和解〖on, upon, with〗。⑥接近;靠近。⑦〖股票〗收盤。 ***close about*** 包圍; 圍攏。***close down*** (or ***up***) **a.** 關門。**b.** 停止做生意。**c.** 設法控制或消滅。***close in on*** (or ***upon***)圍住;迫近。***close on*** (or ***upon***) 遮蔽。 ***close out*** **a.** 賣完(底貨);出清。**b.** 減價以求脫手。 **c.** 結束買賣。 ***close with*** **a.** 同意於。**b.** 搏鬥。—*n.* 完畢; 終了。The summer vacation is drawing to a *close.* 暑假快完了。

:close² [klos; klous] *adj.,* **clos·er, clos·est,** *adv.* —*adj.* ①近的; 接近的; 密接的。to keep in *close* contact with a person. 與某人密切接觸。②密閉的; 狹窄的。③緊密的。④親近的;親密的。*close* friends. 密友。*close* relatives. 近親。⑤準確的;正確的。⑥徹底的;謹嚴的;密切的。*close* attention. 密切注意。⑦欠缺新鮮空氣的。⑧難以呼吸的;窒息的。⑨不喜多言的; 不談自己的。⑩祕密的;隱藏的。⑪吝嗇的。⑫勢均力敵的;幾乎相當的。⑬嚴密的;精細的。*close* investigation. 精密的調查。⑭不公開的。a *close* meeting. 不公開的會。⑮少的。⑯受限制的; 嚴格限制的。⑰〖語音〗閉口的。⑱乾乾淨淨的。⑲貼身的。⑳很緊的。Money is *close.* 銀根很緊。㉑關緊的。㉒嚴密監禁的。㉓嚴格的。*close* questioning. 嚴格的盤查。 ***a close thing*** 幾乎失敗或造成災禍的事。 ***keep oneself close*** 不與人相往來。—*adv.* 接近地;緊密地;嚴密地。They sit *close* together. 他們緊靠着坐。***lie close*** 密藏着。***press a man close*** 嚴對某人。***run a man close*** 趕上某人。—**ness,** *n.*

close-at-hand [ˈklosətˈhænd; ˈklousətˈhænd] *adj.* 在附近的; 即將來臨的。

close-by [ˈklosˈbaɪ; ˈklousˈbai] *adj.* 附近的。

close call 〖美俗〗千鈞一髮。

close corporation 家族公司(股票由公司自己把持,不對外公開)。

close-cropped [ˈklosˈkrapt; ˈklousˈkrɔpt] *adj.* 剪的短短的(頭髮、草等); 頭髮等剪的短短的。(亦作 **close-cut**)

closed [klozd; klouzd] *adj.* ①關閉的;密閉的。with *closed* doors. 禁止旁聽。②關門的; 休業的。③〖語音〗(音節之)以子音爲結尾的。④已結束的。

closed circuit 〖電視〗閉路(以電線連絡,限於少數特定收視者之設備)。

closed circuit television 閉路電視。

closed-door [ˈklozdˈdor; ˈklouzdˈdɔː] *adj.* 門戶關閉的; 禁止旁聽的;祕密的。a *closed-door* session. 祕密會議。

closed-end [ˈklozdˈɛnd; ˈklouzdˈend] *adj.* 閉鎖式的(信託投資);資本額固定的。

close·down [ˈklozˈdaun; ˈklouzˈdaun] *n.* 關店;歇業。

close fighting 白刃戰。

close-fist·ed [ˈklosˈfɪstɪd; ˈklousˈfistid] *adj.* 吝嗇的。—**ly,** *adv.* —**ness,** *n.*

close-fit·ting [ˈklosˈfɪtɪŋ; ˈklousˈfitiŋ] *adj.* 緊身的;貼合身體的。

close-grained [ˈklosˈgrend; ˈklousˈgreind] *adj.* 木理細緻的;密實的。

close-hauled [ˈklosˈhɔld; ˈklousˈhɔːld] *adj.* 〖航海〗張滿帆的;迎風航行的。

close-lipped [ˈklosˈlɪpt; ˈklousˈlipt] *adj.* 閉口不言的;沉默的。

:close·ly [ˈkloslɪ; ˈklousli] *adj.* ①接近地。②緊密地。③親密地;親近地。They are *closely* related. 他們係屬近親。④嚴密地;密切地。⑤節省地;吝嗇地。

close-mouthed [ˈklosˈmauðd; ˈklousˈmauðd] *adj.* 閉口不言的;緘默的。

close·out [ˈklozˌaut; ˈklouzaut] *n.* ①出清存貨。②出清某種貨品。

close-packed [ˈklosˈpækt; ˈklousˈpækt] *adj.* 擠得水洩不通的。

close quarters ①狹窄或擁擠之處。②肉搏戰;白刃戰。

close season 禁止捕獵某些魚類或鳥獸的時期。

close shave 幸免;間不容髮的險事。

close·stool [ˈklosˌstul; ˈklousstuːl] *n.* 有蓋馬桶;室內用便器。

clos·et** [ˈklazɪt; ˈklɔzit] *n.* ①小櫥;小房間。②祕密研究或會客之小室。*closet* consultation. 祕密會議。③廁所;便所(=water closet). —*v.t.*關在私室中作密談。be closeted with*** 與…密談。—*adj.* ①私室的; 祕密的。②適於在私室內用或享受的。③沉思的;不實際的。

closet homosexual 祕密的同性戀者。

close-up [ˈklosˌʌp; ˈklousʌp] *n.* ①〖電影〗特寫。②精密的觀察。

clos·ing [ˈklozɪŋ; ˈklouziŋ] *adj.* 閉鎖的;終止的;結尾的; 締結的; 決算的。—*n.* 閉鎖;終止;結尾;締結;決算。

closing price 〖股票〗收盤價格。

clo·sure [ˈkloʒɚ; ˈklouʒə] *n., v.,* **-sured, -sur·ing.** —*n.* ①封閉;封鎖。②封閉物。③終止。④終止討論以付表決之方法。—*v.t.* & *v.i.* 終止辯論;對(議案)終止辯論而付諸表決。

clot [klat; klɔt] *n., v.,* **clot·ted, clot·ting.** —*n.* ①凝塊。②一小羣。—*v.i.* 凝結。—*v.t.* 使凝結。

:cloth [klɔθ; klɔθ, klɔːθ] *n., pl.* **cloths** [klɔðz, klɔθs; klɔːðz, klɔːθs], *adj.* —*n.* ①布。a piece of cotton *cloth.* 一塊棉布。②特種用途的布(如 tablecloth 桌布等)。③某一行業中人所常穿的服裝。***lay the cloth*** 鋪桌布準備開飯。***the cloth*** 教士(職)。—*adj.* 布的;布做的。

cloth binding 布面精裝本。

cloth·bound [ˈklɔθˈbaund; ˈklɔθˈbaund] *adj.* 布面精裝的。

:clothe [kloð; klouð] *v.t.,* **clothed** or **clad, cloth·ing.** ①着(衣)。He was *clad* in rags. 他衣服襤褸。②供以衣着。③覆蓋。The fields are *clothed* with trees. 樹木蔽野。④以適當言語表達。⑤供以;授以。

‡**clothes** 〔kloz, kloðz; klouðz, klouz〕 *n. pl.* ①衣服。to put *clothes* on. 穿衣。to take *clothes* off. 脫衣。②被褥。

clothes·bag 〔'kloz,bæg; 'klouðzbæg〕 *n.* 裝換洗衣物的袋子。「之籃子。」

clothes basket 置放或搬運髒衣服之籃子。

clothes·brush 〔'kloz,brʌʃ; 'klouðzbrʌʃ〕 *n.* 衣刷。「乾機。」

clothes dryer (or **drier**) 濕衣烘乾機。

clothes·hook 〔'kloz,huk; 'klouðzhuk〕 *n.* 掛衣鉤。

clothes·horse 〔'kloz,hɔrs; 'klouðzhɔːs〕 *n.* ①晒衣架。②好穿着入時的人。

clothes·line 〔'kloz,laɪn; 'klouðzlain〕 *n.* 晒衣繩。

clothes moth 蠹蟲;蠹魚子。

clothes-peg 〔'kloz,pɛg; 'klouðzpeg〕 *n.* 〖英〗=**clothespin.**

clothes·pin 〔'klozpɪn; 'klouðzpin〕 *n.* 晒衣繩上夾衣服之夾子。

clothes pole 晒衣繩之支柱。

clothes·press 〔'kloz,prɛs; 'klouðzpres〕 *n.* 衣櫃;衣樹。

clothes·prop 〔'kloz,prɑp; 'klouðzprɔp〕 *n.* 〖英〗晒衣繩之支架。

clothes tree 衣帽架。

clothes wringer 衣服絞乾器。

cloth·ier 〔'kloðjɚ; 'klouðiə〕 *n.* ①製或賣衣服之人。②織布商;布商。

‡**cloth·ing** 〔'kloðɪŋ; 'klouðiŋ〕 *n.* 衣服之集合稱。Our warm *clothing* protects us against the cold. 我們的溫暖的衣服保護我們不受寒。

cloth measure 布尺(量布之尺寸)。

Clo·tho 〔'kloθo; 'klouθou〕 *n.* 〖希臘神話〗司命運三女神之一。

cloth yard (衣料之)一碼。

clot·ty 〔'klɑtɪ; 'klɔti〕 *adj.* ①多凝塊的;含凝塊的。②易凝結的。

clo·ture 〔'klotʃɚ; 'kloutʃə〕 *n., v.,* **-tured, -tur·ing.** —*n.* 終結辯論以付表決之方法。—*v.t.* 對(某議案等)終結辯論而付諸表決。

‡**cloud** 〔klaud; klaud〕 *n.* ①雲。The plane climbed into the *cloud.* 飛機昇入雲中。②煙雲。a *cloud* of dust. 一片揚塵。③大羣。a *cloud* of birds in flight. 成羣的飛鳥。④令起暗晦之事物。a *cloud* of suspicion. 疑雲重重。⑤(*pl.*)天空。to sail up into the *clouds.* 升入空中。⑥朦朧不清的地方。⑦汚點。***in the clouds*** **a.** 心不在焉;陷入幻想。 **b.** 幻想的;不現實的。***on a cloud*** 〖俚〗興高采烈。***under a cloud*** **a.** 受到懷疑。 **b.** 失體面。—*v.t.* ①被雲遮蔽。The sky is darkly *clouded.* 黑雲遮天。②蒙蔽。③使暗澹;使陰沈。His face was *clouded* with anger. 他怒容滿面。④玷汚。⑤加斑紋;攙雜斑點。—*v.i.* ①起雲;雲蔽。②變爲陰沉;陰鬱。The sky *clouded* over. 天爲雲所蔽。—**like,** *adj.*

cloud·ber·ry 〔'klaud,bɛrɪ; 'klaud,beri〕 *n., pl.* **-ries.** 野生之黃色草莓。

cloud-built 〔'klaud,bɪlt; 'klaudbilt〕 *adj.* 如雲的;空虛的;幻想的。

cloud·burst 〔'klaud,bɝst; 'klaudbəːst〕 *n.* 驟雨;豪雨。

cloud-capped 〔'klaud,kæpt; 'klaudkæpt〕 *adj.* 聳入雲霄的。

cloud castle 空中樓閣。

cloud chamber 〖物理〗雲室。

cloud drift 浮雲;流雲。

cloud·ed 〔'klaudɪd; 'klaudid〕 *adj.* ①模糊的。②混亂的。③被雲遮住的。④有斑點或條紋的。「雲地;如雲地;朦朧地;憂鬱地。」

cloud·i·ly 〔'klaudɪlɪ; 'klaudili〕 *adv.* 多雲地;如雲地;朦朧地;憂鬱地。

cloud·i·ness 〔'klaudɪnɪs; 'klaudinis〕 *n.* 陰暗;朦朧。

cloud·ing 〔'klaudɪŋ; 'klaudiŋ〕 *n.* (染色面之)雲狀花紋;光澤面之暗晦;悶光。

cloud-kiss·ing 〔'klaud'kɪsɪŋ; 'klaud'kisiŋ〕 *adj.* 高聳雲霄的。

cloud·land 〔'klaud,lænd; 'klaudlænd〕 *n.* 仙境;神祕之國;夢幻之世界。

cloud·less 〔'klaudlɪs; 'klaudlis〕 *adj.* ①無雲的;晴朗的。②無憂鬱的;無煩惱的。

cloud·let 〔'klaudlɪt; 'klaudlit〕 *n.* 薄雲;片雲。「(亦作**Cloud Nine**)」

cloud nine 〖俚〗無上幸福之狀態〖常on〗(亦作**Cloud Nine**)。

cloud rack 一團浮雲。

cloud·scape 〔'klaud,skep; 'klaudskeip〕 *n.* 雲景。

cloud stone 隕石。

cloud·ward(s) 〔'klaudwɚd(z); 'klaudwəd(z)〕 *adv.* 朝着雲地。

cloud·world 〔'klaud,wɝld; 'klaudwəːld〕 *n.* =**cloudland.**

‡**cloud·y** 〔'klaudɪ; 'klaudi〕 *adj.,* **cloud·i·er, cloud·i·est.** ①有雲的;多雲的。It was a *cloudy* day. 那是一個陰天。②如雲的;雲的。③不清爽的;不明朗的;朦朧的。④有斑紋的。⑤混亂的;不清的。⑥憂鬱的;煩惱的。⑦被猜疑的;名譽不好的。—**cloud·i·ly,** *adv.* —**cloud·i·ness,** *n.* 「谷;峽谷;谿谷。」

clough 〔klʌf, klau; klʌf〕 *n.* 〖英方〗山谷;峽谷;谿谷。

clout 〔klaut; klaut〕 *n.* ①〖俗〗敲;打。②白布製成之箭靶。③中的之射。④〖古〗布;破布。⑤〖棒球俚〗長打。—*v.t.* 敲;打。

clove[1] 〔klov; klouv〕 *v.* pt. of **cleave.**

clove[2] *n.* 〖植物〗①丁香。②丁香花苞。③乾丁香花苞。④鱗莖;珠芽。⑤樹木。

clove[3] *n.* 英國棉布、乾酪等之重量單位(等於 8 磅)。

clove hitch 〖航海〗卷結(一種結繩法)。

clo·ven 〔'klovən; 'klouvən〕 *v.* pp. of **cleave.** —*adj.* ①分裂的。②偶蹄的。

cloven foot =**cloven hoof.**

clo·ven-foot·ed 〔'klovən'futɪd; 'klouvn'futid〕 *adj.* ①分趾蹄的;偶蹄的。②窮凶極惡的;似惡魔的。「的誘惑的象徵。」

cloven hoof ①偶蹄。②撒旦或邪惡的誘惑的象徵。

clo·ven-hoofed 〔'klovən'huft; 'klouvn'huːft〕 *adj.* =**cloven-footed.**

clo·ver** 〔'klovɚ; 'klouvə〕 *n., pl.* **-vers, -ver.** ①〖植物〗苜蓿。②苜蓿科之植物。be*** (or ***live***) ***in clover*** 生活逸樂奢華。***pigs in clover*** 暴發戶。

clo·ver·leaf 〔'klovɚ,lif; 'klouvəliːf〕 *n., pl.* **-leaves,** *adj.* —*n.* 狀似四葉苜蓿的公路立體交叉點。—*adj.* 類似苜蓿葉的。

***clown** 〔klaun; klaun〕 *n.* ①丑角;小丑。②粗魯笨拙而無知識的人。③好開玩笑的人。④鄉下人。—*v.i.* 做小丑;行如小丑(常與 it 連用)。—**ish,** *adj.* 「過多享樂而生厭。」

cloy 〔klɔɪ; klɔi〕 *v.t.* ①使過飽。②使因過多享樂而生厭。

‡**club** 〔klʌb; klʌb〕 *n., v.,* **clubbed, club·bing,** *adj.* —*n.* ①棒;棍。②擊球棒;體操用的棍。He hit the ball with his *club.* 他用棒打球。③會社;俱樂部。to organize an athletic *club.* 組織體育俱樂部。④會所。⑤印有黑色三葉形(亦稱梅花)的紙牌。⑥(*pl.*)(作 *sing.* or *pl.* 解)此種紙牌之一組。⑦夜總

會；舞廳。—*v.t.* ①用棒擊。to *club* a person. 用棒打人。②形成棒狀物。③組織；聯合。④共同出錢。⑤分攤。⑥拿着槍身，將槍托當棍子使用。—*v.i.* ①為共同目的而結合。②共同出資。—*adj.* ①俱樂部的。②客飯性質的；以固定價格供應所配合之食物的。

club·(b)a·ble 〔ˈklʌbəbl;ˈklʌbəbl〕 *adj.* 〖俗〗①好交際的。②適於為俱樂部會員的。

clubbed 〔klʌbd; klʌbd〕 *adj.* ①棍棒狀的。②末端較粗的。

club·by 〔ˈklʌbɪ; ˈklʌbi〕 *adj.*, **-bi·er, -bi·est.** ①俱樂部的。②很友善的。③小圈子的；排他性的。④好加入俱樂部的。

club car 有沙發、牌桌、小餐館的火車廂。

club·foot 〔ˈklʌbˈfʊt; ˈklʌbˈfut〕 *n.*, *pl.* **-feet.** 畸形足。—**ed,** *adj.*

club·haul 〔ˈklʌbˌhɔl; ˈklʌbhɔːl〕 *v.t.* 〖航海〗緊急時拋下風之錨使(船)向上風換向。

club·house 〔ˈklʌbˌhaʊs; ˈklʌbˈhaus〕 *n.*, *pl.* **-hous·es** 〔-ˌhaʊzɪz;-ˈhauziz〕. 俱樂部的房屋；會所。

club·land 〔ˈklʌbˌlænd;ˈklʌblænd〕 *n.* 俱樂部區；俱樂部街。

club law 暴力政治；私刑法律。

club moss 〖植物〗石松。

club·root 〔ˈklʌbˌrʊt; ˈklʌb-ruːt〕 *n.* (甘藍類等之)根瘤病。

club sandwich 總會三明治。

club soda 汽水；蘇打水。

club steak 小牛排。

club·wom·an 〔ˈklʌbˌwʊmən; ˈklʌbˌwumən〕 *n.*, *pl.* **-wom·en.** 俱樂部女會員。

***cluck**[1] 〔klʌk; klʌk〕 *n.* ①咯咯聲。②類此之聲音。—*v.t.* 以咯咯聲呼叫。—*v.i.* 作咯咯叫聲。

cluck[2] *n.* 〖俚〗愚笨的人。

clue 〔klu; kluː〕 *n.*, *v.*, **clued, clu·ing.** —*n.* ①線索；端倪。②線團。—*v.t.* ①藉線索指出。②將…捲成線團。(亦作 **clew**)

clum·ber 〔ˈklʌmbɚ; ˈklʌmbə〕 *n.* 一種短腿厚毛之獵犬。(亦作 **clumber spaniel**)

***clump** 〔klʌmp; klʌmp〕 *n.* ①草叢；樹叢。a *clump* of trees. 一叢樹。②塊；團。③笨重的腳步聲。④多加的一層厚鞋底。—*v.i.* ①叢生。②重踏着走。—*v.t.* ①密植成叢。②使成塊。③於鞋底加貼一層皮。

clump foot=**clubfoot.**

clump·y 〔ˈklʌmpɪ; ˈklʌmpi〕 *adj.*, **clump·i·er, clump·i·est.** (土等)多塊的；多草樹叢的。

***clum·sy** 〔ˈklʌmzɪ; ˈklʌmzi〕 *adj.*, **-si·er, -si·est.** ①笨拙的。②樣子不好看的。—**clum·si·ly,** *adv.* —**clum·si·ness,** *n.*

clung 〔klʌŋ;klʌŋ〕 *v.* pt. & pp. of **cling.**

***clus·ter** 〔ˈklʌstɚ; ˈklʌstə〕 *n.* ①串；束；叢；羣；團。in a *cluster*. 成串(束，叢，羣，團)的。a *cluster* of grapes. 一串葡萄。②子母照明彈。③星團。—*v.i.* 叢生；羣聚。—*v.t.* 使密集；使羣聚。

cluster point 〖數學〗聚點。

***clutch** 〔klʌtʃ; klʌtʃ〕 *v.i.* ①抓牢；抓緊〖常 at〗. A drowning man will *clutch* at a straw. 急不暇擇(將溺死之人連一根草也要去抓)。②踩汽車之離合器。③〖俚〗突然緊張起來〖常 up〗. —*v.t.* ①抓住；緊抱住。②〖俚〗使迷住；使感動。③孵小雞。—*n.* ①突然抓取。to make a *clutch* at something. 突然抓取某物。②緊握；緊抓。③掌握。to fall (*or* get) into the *clutches* of. 遭…毒手。within *clutch*. 在伸手可及處；在近處。④〖機械〗鰡合子；離合器。⑤一次所孵之小雞或一窩之卵，通常為十三個。⑥抓東西之任何裝置。⑦〖體育〗競賽中之緊要關頭。⑧〖俗〗任何緊要關頭。*in the clutches* 危難時；危難狀態下。—*adj.* ①(手提包等)無手提帶的；可用手抓住的。②(衣服等)無鈕釦的；用手拉住的。—**ing·ly,** *adv.* —**y,** *adj.*

clut·ter 〔ˈklʌtɚ; ˈklʌtə〕 *v.t.* 使散亂；使雜亂。—*v.i.* ①忙亂。②喧鬧。③說話過快因而模糊不清。④亂跑。 —*n.* ①混亂。②喧鬧。③雜亂。

Clydes·dale 〔ˈklaɪdzˌdel;ˈklaidzdeil〕 *n.* 一種健壯之馱馬。

cly·sis 〔ˈklaɪsɪs; ˈklaisis〕 *n.*, *pl.* **-ses** 〔-siz; -siːz〕. 〖醫〗①灌腸法。②肌肉注射以彌補營養，體液，控制血壓等。

clys·ter 〔ˈklɪstɚ;ˈklistə〕 *n.* 〖醫〗灌腸劑；灌腸法。

Cm 化學元素 curium 之符號。 **cm.** centimeter(s). **C.M.G.** Companion of the Order of St. Michael and St. George. **C/N** ①circular note. ②credit note. **CND** Campaign for Nuclear Disarmament. **CNO, C.N.O.** Chief of Naval Operations. **Co** 化學元素cobalt之符號。**Co., co.** ①company. ②county. **C/O** ①cash order. ②certificate of origin. **C.O.** ①Commanding Officer. ②cash order. ③conscientious objector. ④〖英〗Colonial Office. **c.o., c/o** ①care of. 由…轉。②carried over. 轉下頁；轉入。

co- 〖字首〗表"聯合；伴同"之義。

***coach** 〔kotʃ; koutʃ〕 *n.* ①轎式大馬車；轎式汽車。②鐵路的客車廂。③教導；教練。He is our chief *coach* in football.他是我們的足球總教練。④為準備某種考試之私人教師。⑤演員或歌星之教師。⑥驛車。⑦公共汽車。⑧〖航海〗船長室。⑨(飛機上之)二等艙。—*v.t.* ①以 coach 載運。②教授；訓練。—*v.i.* ①做教練。②在私人教師指導下讀書。③乘坐 coach. —*adv.* 乘坐 coach；乘坐二等艙。—**a·ble,** *adj.* —**a·bil·i·ty,** *n.*

coach-and-four 〔ˈkotʃənˈfor; ˈkoutʃənˈfɔː〕 *n.* 四匹馬牽引的馬車。

coach box 馬車夫的座位。

coach dog 守護馬車之犬。

coach·er 〔ˈkotʃɚ; ˈkoutʃə〕 *n.* ①教練；練習指導員。②拉車之馬。

coach·fel·low 〔ˈkotʃˌfɛlo; ˈkoutʃˌfelou〕 *n.* ①馬車所用一對馬中之一匹。②伴侶；夥伴。

coach house 車房。(亦作 **carriage house**)

***coach·man** 〔ˈkotʃmən; ˈkoutʃmən〕 *n.*, *pl.* **-men.** ①馬車夫；車夫。②人造蠅(垂釣用之魚餌)。

co·act 〔koˈækt; kouˈækt〕 *v.t.* & *v.i.* 採取共同行動。

co·ad·ju·tant 〔koˈædʒətənt; kouˈædʒətənt〕 *adj.* 互助的；合作的。 —*n.* 助手；夥伴。

co·ad·ju·tor 〔koˈædʒətɚ;kouˈædʒutə〕 *n.* ①助手；夥伴。②主教之助理。③協助另一主教之主教。

co·ad·u·nate 〔koˈædʒunɪt;kouˈædʒunit〕 *adj.* 〖動、植物〗連生的；連結的。

co·a·gent 〔koˈedʒənt; kouˈeidʒənt〕 *n.* 合作者；共事者；夥伴。

co·ag·u·lant 〔koˈægjələnt;kouˈægjulənt〕 *n.* 促凝劑；凝血劑。(亦作 **coagulator**)

co·ag·u·lase 〔koˈægjəˌles; kouˈægjuleis〕 *n.* 〖生化〗凝固酶；凝固酵素。

co·ag·u·late 〔koˈægjəˌlet; kouˈægjuleit〕 *v.*, **-lat·ed, -lat·ing.** —*v.t.* 使凝結。—*v.i.* 凝結；凝固。

co·ag·u·la·tion 〔koˌægjəˈleʃən;kou-

ˌægjuˈleiʃən] *n.* ①凝固;凝結。②凝固物;凝塊。

:coal [kol; koul] *n.* ①煤;煤炭。②燃燒中或燒過的煤塊等。③焦炭。***call*** (***haul, drag, rake,*** or ***take***) ***over the coals*** 責罵。***carry coals to Newcastle*** 多此一舉(Newcastle 是產煤地)。***heap coals of fire on one's head*** 以德報怨而使人悔悟。—*v.t.* 供給煤炭。—*v.i.* 裝煤;加煤。—**less,** *adj.*

coal bed (熔爐中之)置煤處;煤層。

coal-black [ˈkolˌblæk; ˈkoulblæk] *adj.* 深黑的;烏黑的。

coal·box [ˈkolˌbɑks; ˈkoulbɔks] *n.* ①煤箱。②〖軍俚〗發黑煙的炸彈。

coal breaker 碎煤機;碎煤夫。(亦作 **coal cracker**)

coal bunker 煤庫;煤倉。

coal car 煤車。

coal cellar 地下煤庫。

coal dust 煤灰。

coal·er [ˈkolɚ; ˈkoulə] *n.* ①運煤之船(車、鐵道等)。②煤商。③〖英〗煤工。

co·a·lesce [ˌkoəˈlɛs; ˌkouəˈles] *v.*, **-lesced, -lesc·ing.** —*v.i.* ①合生。②聯合;合併。—*v.t.* 使合併。—**co·a·les·cence,** *n.*

co·a·les·cent [ˌkoəˈlɛsn̩t; ˌkouəˈlesnt] *adj.* ①合生的。②聯合的;合併的。—*n.* 與另一母音聯合而成爲一個單音的有子音傾向之母音(如 ***house*** 中之 u).

coal-face [ˈkolˌfes; ˈkoulfeis] *n.* ①因採礦而露出的煤面。②採煤之礦區。

coal factor 賣煤者;煤炭商人。

coal field 煤礦區;煤田。

coal·fish [ˈkolˌfɪʃ; ˈkoulfiʃ] *n.* 黑鱈魚。

coal flap 〖英〗地下煤庫入口之板蓋。

coal gas 煤氣。

coal heaver 搬運煤炭之人;煤夫。

coal hole ①由人行道通到煤庫的洞穴。②〖英〗(地下的)煤庫。

coaling station 船舶或火車之加煤站。

co·a·li·tion [ˌkoəˈlɪʃən; ˌkouəˈliʃən] *n.* ①聯合;結合。②聯盟。

coalition cabinet 聯合內閣。

coal-mas·ter [ˈkolˌmæstɚ; ˈkoulˌmɑːstə] *n.* 煤礦主。

coal measures 〖地質〗炭層。

coal mine 煤礦;煤礦坑。

coal miner 煤礦工人。

coal mining 採煤。

coal oil 煤油;石油。

coal pit ①煤礦;煤礦坑。②〖美〗燒焦炭處。

coal·sack [ˈkolˌsæk; ˈkoulsæk] *n.* ①煤炭袋。②(C-)〖天文〗煤袋(銀河中之黑點區域)。

coal scuttle 煤簍。(亦作 **coal vase**)

coal tar 煤焦油。

coal-whip·per [ˈkolhwɪpɚ; ˈkoulˌwipə] *n.* 〖英〗起煤工人或機器。

coal·y [ˈkolɪ; ˈkouli] *adj.*, **coal·i·er, coal·i·est.** 多煤的;煤的;含煤的;似煤的;黑色的。

coam·ing [ˈkomɪŋ; ˈkoumiŋ] *n.* (艙口、水井、天窗等防水流入之)欄圍裝置;邊材。

***coarse** [kors, kɔrs; kɔːs, kɔəs] *adj.*, **coars·er, coars·est.** ①粗的;粗糙的。②質粗的。*coarse* cloth. 粗布。③普通的;劣等的。④粗魯的;粗俗的。Don't use *coarse* words before a lady. 在婦女前不要講粗魯的話。⑤(金屬等)未精鍊的。⑥不愉快的。—**ly,** *adv.* —**ness,** *n.*

coarse-grained [ˈkorsˈgrend; ˈkɔːsgreind] *adj.* ①質地粗糙的。②粗野的;鄙俗的。

coars·en [ˈkorsn̩; ˈkɔːsn] *v.t.* & *v.i.* (使)變粗糙。

:coast [kost; koust] *n.* ①海岸。The land is barren on the east *coast.* 東海岸的土地貧瘠。②溜下山;滑下坡。③坡。***the Coast*** 〖美〗太平洋海岸;西海岸。***the coast is clear*** 無人阻礙;危險已過。—*v.i.* ①沿海岸而行。②向下溜行。You can *coast* downhill on a bicycle. 你可騎脚踏車滑下坡。③滑行。④不需努力而上昇或前進。—*v.t.* ①使…靠動量滑行。②沿海岸而行。

coast·al [ˈkostl̩; ˈkoustl] *adj.* 海岸的;沿岸的。

coast artillery ①海岸砲。②海岸砲兵。

coast defence 海岸防禦。

coast·er [ˈkostɚ; ˈkoustə] *n.* ①沿岸航行者。②沿岸貿易的船。③滑行橇。④供遊戲用之小鐵路。⑤茶杯墊。⑥放酒瓶的盤子。

coaster brake (脚踏車的)倒煞車。

coast guard ①(C-G-) 美國海岸巡邏隊。②以救生及緝私爲任務的任何組織。③(亦作 **coastguardsman**) 此項組織的分子。

coast·guards·man [ˈkostˌgɑrdzmən; ˈkoustˌgɑːdzmən] *n.* 美海岸巡邏隊員。

coast·ing [ˈkostɪŋ; ˈkoustiŋ] *adj.* 沿岸航行的;近海航路的。—*n.* ①沿岸航行;沿海貿易。②海岸線(圖)。③滑雪運動。④滑降。

coasting pilot 沿岸領港者。

coasting trade 沿海貿易。

coast·land [ˈkostˌlænd; ˈkoustlænd] *n.* 沿海岸地區。

coast·line [ˈkostˌlaɪn; ˈkoust-lain] *n.* 海岸線。

coast pilot ①(=pilot) 美政府所出版有關潮水,港口設施等之手册;沿岸航線指南。②=**coasting pilot.**

Coast Ranges 海岸山脈(在北美洲太平洋沿岸)。

coast·ward [ˈkostwɚd; ˈkoustwəd] *adj.* & *adv.* 向岸的(地)。(亦作**coastwards**)

coast·ways [ˈkostˌwez; ˈkoust-weiz] *adv.* 沿岸地(=coastwise).

coast·wise [ˈkostˌwaɪz; ˈkoust-waiz] *adj.* & *adv.* 沿岸的(地)。

:coat [kot; kout] *n.* ①外衣。②獸皮;獸毛;羽毛。③樹皮。④表層。He gave the wall a *coat* of white paint. 他將牆塗上一層白漆。⑤果皮;洋葱瓣。—*v.t.* ①披以外衣;外塗一層。②覆;蓋;塗。—**less,** *adj.*

coat card 紙牌中繪有人像之牌。

coat·ed [ˈkotɪd; ˈkoutid] *adj.* ①着外衣的;有皮的。②(紙)光滑的。③加一層化學塗料使不透水的。

coat·ee [koˈti; ˈkoutiː] *n.* 緊身上衣;短衣。

coat hanger 掛衣鉤;衣架。

co·a·ti [koˈɑtɪ; kouˈɑːti] *n.*, *pl.* **co·a·tis** or **co·a·ti.** 長鼻浣熊。(亦作 **coatimondi, coati-mundi**)

coat·ing [ˈkotɪŋ; ˈkoutiŋ] *n.* ①被覆物;外層。②衣料。

coat of arms ①〖紋章〗盾形紋徽。②中古武士甲胄外面之罩袍,上有刺繡之紋章。

coat·rack [ˈkotˌræk; ˈkout-ræk] *n.* 衣帽架。

coat·room [ˈkotˌrum; ˈkoutrum] *n.* 衣帽間。

coat·tail [ˈkotˌtel; ˈkoutteil] *n.* ①(男人上衣之)背尾。②(男人燕尾禮服之)尾。***on the coattails of*** (or ***on one's coattails***) **a.** 隨着…之後。**b.** 得到…之幫助。***ride on someone's coattails*** 利用或依靠別人的聲望達到自己之上進。—*adj.*〖美政治〗讓實力薄弱之競選者藉實力雄厚者之力量一同當選的。

co·au·thor [koˈɔθɚ; kouˈɔːθə] *n.* 合著者。—*v.t.* 合著。

***coax** 〔koks; kouks〕 *v.t.* ①用巧言誘哄;甘言勸誘。to *coax* a person to do (*or* into doing). 誘哄某人去做…。to *coax* a thing out of a person. 哄騙某人東西。②以巧言誘哄得到。③巧妙地做。—*v.i.* 誘哄;勸誘。—*n.* 同軸電纜。

co·ax·i·al 〔ko'æksɪəl; kou'æksiəl〕 *adj.* 同軸的;共軸的。(亦作 **coaxal**)

coaxial cable 同軸電纜。

cob¹ 〔kɑb; kɔb〕 *n.* ①硬固之圓塊。②雄天鵝。③〖英俗〗要人;領袖。④矮而肥之小馬。⑤〖美〗玉蜀黍的穗軸。⑥〖英俗〗蜘蛛。⑦〖英〗泥土與稻草之混合物。

cob² *v.t.*, **cobbed, cob·bing.** 打(尤指用扁的東西打臀部)。

co·balt 〔'kobɔlt; kou'bɔːlt〕 *n.* ①〖化〗鈷(符號為Co). ②由鈷製的深藍顏色。

cobalt 60 鈷之放射性同位素;鈷60。

cobalt blue 鈷藍。

co·bal·tic 〔kə'bɔltɪk; kou'bɔːltik〕 *adj.* 〖化〗(含三價之)鈷的。

co·bal·tite 〔kə'bɔltaɪt; kə'bɔːltait〕 *n.* 〖礦〗輝砷鈷礦。(亦作 **cobaltine**)

cob·ber 〔'kɑbɚ; 'kɔbə〕 *n.* 〖澳〗好友(指男子);合夥人。

cob·ble¹ 〔'kɑbl̩; 'kɔbl〕 *n., v.,* **-bled, -bling.** —*n.* 圓石子。—*v.t.* 鋪以圓石子。

cob·ble² *v.t.,* **-bled, -bling.** ①補綴。②粗劣的修補。

***cob·bler** 〔'kɑblɚ; 'kɔblə〕 *n.* ①補鞋匠。②粗笨的工人。③〖美〗在一種深碟中焙的水果餅。④酒、水、果汁等混成之一種冷飲。⑤因染色或加工不佳而被剔除的布匹。

cob·ble·stone 〔'kɑbl̩ˌston; 'kɔblstoun〕 *n.* 圓石。

co·bel·lig·er·ent 〔ˌkobə'lɪdʒərənt; ˌkoubə'lidʒərənt〕 *n.* 協助他國或他人作戰的國家或個人。

co·ble 〔'kobl̩; 'koubl〕 *n.* ①〖英〗一種小魚船。②〖蘇〗一種平底船。(亦作 **cobble**)

cob·nut 〔'kɑbˌnʌt; 'kɔbnʌt〕 *n.* 〖植物〗大榛子。

Co·bol, COBOL 〔'kobl̩; 'koubl〕 *n.* 〖電腦〗通用商業語言(為 *C*ommon *B*usiness *O*riented *L*anguage 之略)。

co·bra 〔'kobrə; 'koubrə〕 *n.* 眼鏡蛇;毒帽蛇。

cob·web** 〔'kɑbˌwɛb; 'kɔbweb〕 *n., v.,* **-webbed, -web·bing.** —*n.* ①蜘蛛網;蛛絲。②薄細如蛛網的東西。③陳腐;陳舊。④陰謀;陷阱。⑤(*pl.*)混亂。blow (away) the cobwebs from one's brain*** 去戶外呼吸新鮮空氣以使頭腦清醒。—*v.t.* ①用蜘蛛網蓋住。②使混亂。

cob·web·by 〔'kɑbˌwɛbɪ; 'kɔbˌwebi〕 *adj.* ①(如)蛛網的。②覆滿蛛網的。③陳舊的。

co·ca 〔'kokə; 'koukə〕 *n.* ①古柯(南美及西印度羣島所產之藥用植物)。②古柯之乾葉。

Co·ca Co·la 〔'kokə'kolə; 'koukə'koulə〕 〖商標名〗可口可樂(一種清涼飲料)。

co·cain(e) 〔ko'ken; kə'kein, kou-〕 *n.* 古柯鹼。

co·cain·ism 〔ko'kenɪzəm; kou'keinizəm〕 *n.* 〖醫〗古柯鹼中毒。

co·cain·i·za·tion 〔koˌkenɪ'zeʃən; kouˌkeini'zeiʃən〕 *n.* 〖醫〗古柯鹼麻醉。

co·cain·ize 〔ko'kenaɪz; kou'keinaiz〕 *v.t.,* **-ized, -iz·ing.** 以古柯鹼麻醉。

coc·co·ba·cil·lus 〔ˌkɑkobə'sɪləs; ˌkɔkoubə'siləs〕 *n.* 〖醫〗球桿菌。

coc·cus 〔'kɑkəs; 'kɔkəs〕 *n., pl.* **-ci** 〔-saɪ; -sai〕. ①〖植物〗小乾果。②〖細菌〗球菌。

coc·cyg·e·al 〔kɑk'sɪdʒɪəl; kɔk'sidʒiəl〕 *adj.* 〖解剖〗尾骨的。

coc·cyx 〔'kɑksɪks; 'kɔksiks〕 *n., pl.* **coc·cy·ges** 〔kɑk'saɪdʒiz; kɔk'saidʒiːz〕. 〖解剖〗尾骨;尾骶骨。

coch·i·neal 〔ˌkɑtʃə'nil; 'kɔtʃiniːl〕 *n.* ①胭脂蟲。②洋紅。

coch·le·a 〔'kɑklɪə; 'kɔkliə〕 *n., pl.* **-le·ae** 〔-lɪˌi; -liiː〕. 〖解剖〗耳蝸。—**coch·le·ar,** *adj.*

‡**cock¹** 〔kɑk; kɔk〕 *n.* ①公鷄。②雄鳥。a turkey *cock.* 雄火鷄。③首領。the *cock* of the school. 學生中的首領。④龍頭;活栓。⑤鎗的扳機。⑥翹起(鼻子);斜翻(眼睛);翻起(帽邊)。⑦風信鷄。—*v.t.* ①豎起;歪斜。to *cock* the ears. 豎起耳朵。to *cock* one's eye at somebody. 斜視某人。to *cock* one's hat. 歪戴帽子。②扣扳機準備發射。—*v.i.* ①扣扳機。②顯著地站立或豎起。③〖方〗昂首闊步而行。***cock a snoot*** 看不起;不屑一顧〖常 at〗。

cock² *n.* (乾草等之)錐形小堆。—*v.t.* 堆(乾草等)成小堆。

cock·ade 〔kɑk'ed; kɔ'keid〕 *n.* 帽章。

cock-a-doo·dle-doo 〔'kɑkəˌdudl̩'du; 'kɔkəduːdl'duː〕 *interj., n., pl.* **-doos,** *v.,* **-dooed, -doo·ing.** —*interj., n.* ①公鷄啼聲。②(兒語)公鷄。—*v.i.* (公鷄)啼叫。

cock-a-hoop 〔ˌkɑkə'hup; 'kɔkə'huːp〕 *adj. & adv.* ①自負的(地)。②彎斜的(地)。

Cock·aigne, Cock·ayne 〔kɑ'ken; kɔ'kein〕 *n.* 理想之逸樂鄉;蓬萊島。

cock·a·leek·ie 〔ˌkɑkə'likɪ; ˌkɔkə'liːki〕 *n.* 〖蘇〗一種和韭菜(或蔥)煮的鷄湯。(亦作 **cockie-leekie, cocky-leeky**)

cock·a·lo·rum 〔ˌkɑkə'lorəm; ˌkɔkə'lɔːrəm〕 *n.* ①小公鷄。②自負的人。

cock·a·ma·my, cock·a·ma·mie 〔ˌkɑkə'memɪ; ˌkɔkə'meimi〕 *adj.* 荒謬的;可笑的;荒唐的。

cock-and-bull 〔'kɑkən'bʊl; 'kɔkən'bul〕 *adj.* 荒誕無稽的。***cock-and-bull story*** 無稽之談。

cock·a·too 〔ˌkɑkə'tu; ˌkɔkə'tuː〕 *n., pl.* **-toos.** ①(澳洲及東印度產之)一種鸚鵡。②〖澳〗**a.** 小農(牧)場主人。**b.**〖俚〗把風者。

cock·a·trice 〔'kɑkətrɪs; 'kɔkətrais〕 *n.* ①傳說中之一種毒蛇(具瞪視致人於死之能力)。②(聖經)不知名之毒蛇。

cock·boat 〔'kɑkˌbot; 'kɔkbout〕 *n.* 小船。(亦作 **cockleboat**)

cock·chaf·er 〔'kɑkˌtʃefɚ; 'kɔkˌtʃeifə〕 *n.* 小金蟲;金龜子。

cock·crow 〔'kɑkˌkro; 'kɔkkrou〕 *n.* 鷄鳴之時刻;黎明;清晨。(亦作 **cockcrowing**)

Cock·er 〔'kɑkɚ; 'kɔkə〕 *n.* 柯克爾(Edward, 1631–1675, 英國著名之數學教師)。***according to Cocker*** 正確地說。

cock·er¹ 〔'kɑkɚ; 'kɔkə〕 *v.t.* 嬌養;溺愛。

cock·er² *n.* ①喜好或舉辦鬥鷄的人。②=**cocker spaniel.**

cock·er·el 〔'kɑkərəl; 'kɔkərəl〕 *n.* 小公鷄。

cocker spaniel 一種短腿、長毛、大耳下垂的小獵犬。

cock·eyed 〔'kɑkˌaɪd; 'kɔkaid〕 *adj.* ①斜眼的;鬥鷄眼的。②〖俚〗歪斜的;扭曲的。③〖俚〗愚昧的;荒謬的;瘋狂的。

cock·fight 〔'kɑkˌfaɪt; 'kɔkfait〕 *n.* 鬥鷄。

cock·horse 〔'kɑk'hɔrs; 'kɔk'hɔːs〕 *n.* 玩具木馬;搖馬。

cock·i·ly 〔'kɑkɪlɪ; 'kɔkili〕 *adv.* 〖俗〗驕傲地;自大地。

cock·ish 〔'kɑkɪʃ; 'kɔkiʃ〕 *adj.* 〖俗〗像公鷄的;傲慢的;自負的。

cock·le¹ 〔'kɑkl̩; 'kɔkl〕 *n.* ①〖動物〗海

扇(殼)。②小舟。③〖植物〗瞿麥。④〖植物〗莠草。⑤〖美〗一種糖果。⑥一種火爐。***warm the cockles of one's heart*** 使某人振奮。

cock·le² *v.t. & v.i.,* **-led, -ling.** ①(使)皺;起皺。②(使)起小浪。

cock·le·shell [ˈkakl̩ˌʃɛl; ˈkɔklʃel] *n.* ①海扇;海扇殼。②=**cockboat.** ③小舟。

cockle stairs 螺旋梯。「樓;閣樓。

cock·loft [ˈkakˌlɔft; ˈkɔklɔft] *n.* 頂

cock·ney [ˈkaknɪ; ˈkɔkni] *n., pl.* **-neys,** *adj.* —*n.* ①倫敦人。②倫敦話;倫敦語腔。—*adj.* 倫敦人的;倫敦話的。(亦作**Cockney**)

cock·ney·dom [ˈkaknɪdəm; ˈkɔknidəm] *n.* ①倫敦人之社會;倫敦人居住之區域。②倫敦人之集合稱。

cock·ney·ism [ˈkaknɪˌɪzəm; ˈkɔkniizəm] *n.* 倫敦人之作風、口音等。

cock of the walk 〖俗〗一羣人中之領導人(尤指自負,作威作福者)。

cock·pit [ˈkakˌpɪt; ˈkɔkpit] *n.* ①飛機駕駛員的座艙。②鬥鷄場。③舊式軍艦中之傷兵室。④屢經戰役的戰場。⑤小船上後部船員或部分旅客可休息之地方。「*n.* 蟑螂。

cock·roach [ˈkakˌrotʃ; ˈkɔkroutʃ]

cocks·comb [ˈkaksˌkom; ˈkɔkskoum] *n.* ①鷄冠。②〖植物〗鷄冠花。③丑角所戴之鷄冠帽。④花花公子。⑤起碼有四個火口的瓦斯爐。

cock·shy [ˈkakˌʃaɪ; ˈkɔkʃai] *n., pl.* **-shies.** ①投棒戲(擲棒打靶)。②其靶。③其投擲。④嘲笑或譏評的對象。(亦作 **cockshot**)

cock·spur [ˈkakˌspɝ; ˈkɔkspəː] *n.* ①公鷄之距。②〖植物〗山楂類。

cock·sure [ˈkakˈʃʊr; ˈkɔkˈʃuə] *adj.* ①絕對可靠的;必定的。②過於自信的。

*__cock·tail¹__ [ˈkakˌtel; ˈkɔkteil] *n.* ①鷄尾酒。a *cocktail* party. 鷄尾酒會。②開胃的食品。③混合水果;以濃烈之醬調製之貝類食物。—*v.t.* 開鷄尾酒會。—*v.i.* 喝鷄尾酒。—*adj.* 半正式款式的。a *cocktail* dress. 鷄尾酒會穿的衣裳。

cock·tail² *n.* ①尾剪短的馬。②雜種馬。③無教養而冒充紳士的人。

cocktail hour 晚飯前喝鷄尾酒及其他酒類的時間,約五至八時。「酒吧間。

cocktail lounge 飯館、機場大厦之

cock·up [ˈkakˌʌp; ˈkɔkʌp] *n.* ①翹起之末端。②前端翹起之帽。

cock·y [ˈkakɪ; ˈkɔki] *adj.,* **cock·i·er, cock·i·est.** 〖俗〗傲慢的;自負的。(亦作 **cocksy**)

cock·y·ol·(l)y bird [ˌkakɪˈalɪ~; ˌkɔkiˈɔli~] 小鳥之暱稱。「椰子樹。

co·co [ˈkoko; ˈkoukou] *n., pl.* **co·cos.**

*__co·coa__ [ˈkoko; ˈkoukou] *n.* ①可可粉。②可可樹。*cocoa* bean. 可可豆。③棕色;棕黃色。—*adj.* ①可可的。②棕黃色的;棕色的。

‡**co·co·nut, co·coa·nut** [ˈkokənət; ˈkoukənʌt] *n.* 椰子。(英亦作 **cokernut**)

coconut milk 椰子汁。

coconut oil 椰子油。

coconut palm 椰子樹。

co·coon [kəˈkun; kəˈkuːn] *n.* 繭;蠶繭;(蜘蛛類的)子囊;(蚯蚓等的)土房。—*v.i.* 產繭。—*v.t.* ①封緊(如繭)。②將塑膠等噴射(槍或機器等)以保護之。「*n.* 養蠶所。

co·coon·er·y [kəˈkunərɪ; kəˈkuːnəri]

co·cotte [koˈkat; kouˈkɔt] *n., pl.* **-cottes.** 〖法〗①妓女。②一種土鍋。

*__cod¹__ [kad; kɔd] *n.* 鱈;鰵。*cod*-liver oil. 鰵魚肝油。

cod² *n.* ①陰囊。②〖方〗莢;殼;蒴。

cod³ *v.t. & v.i.* 〖俗〗欺騙;愚弄。

C.O.D., c.o.d. ①〖美〗collect on delivery. 貨到收款。②〖英〗cash on delivery. 送到付現。

co·da [ˈkodə; ˈkoudə] 〖義〗 *n.* ①〖音樂〗尾聲。②芭蕾舞結局部分。③文學、戲劇之結局。

cod·dle [ˈkadl̩; ˈkɔdl] *v.,* **-dled, -dling,** *n.* —*v.t.* ①嬌養;溺愛;珍護。②半煮;軟煮。—*n.* 嬌生慣養者;身體虛弱者。

*__code__ [kod; koud] *n., v.,* **cod·ed, cod·ing.** —*n.* ①法典;法規。civil *code.* 民法。criminal *code.* 刑法。②章程;規則。③禮儀;禮法;道德。moral *code.* 道德律。④海陸軍信號制度。⑤暗號;電碼。a secret *code.* 密碼。a telegraphic *code.* 電碼。—*v.t.* 譯爲電碼。

code·book [ˈkodˌbʊk; ˈkoudbuk] *n.* 電報密碼本。

code·break·er [ˈkodˌbrekɚ; ˈkoudˌbreikə] *n.* 譯電碼員(解密碼者)。

co·de·fend·ant [ˌkodɪˈfɛndənt; ˌkoudiˈfendənt] *n.* 共同被告。

co·de·ine, co·de·in [ˈkodɪˌin; ˈkoudiːn] *n.* 〖化〗可待因(鎮靜劑或麻醉劑)。

co·de·ter·mi·na·tion [ˌkodɪˌtɝmɪˈneʃən; ˌkoudiˌtəːmiˈneiʃən] *n.* 勞工應參加大企業經營主義。

co·dex [ˈkodɛks; ˈkoudeks] *n., pl.* **-di·ces** [-dɪˌsiz; -disiːz]. (聖書、古代典籍之)抄本。「**es, -fish.** 鱈。

cod·fish [ˈkadˌfɪʃ; ˈkɔdfiʃ] *n., pl.* **-fish-**

codg·er [ˈkadʒɚ; ˈkɔdʒə] *n.* ①〖俗〗有怪癖之(老)人。②〖英方〗卑吝之人。

cod·i·cil [ˈkadəsl̩; ˈkɔdisil] *n.* ①〖法律〗遺囑附錄。②附加條款。—**la·ry,** *adj.*

cod·i·fy [ˈkadəˌfaɪ; ˈkɔdifai] *v.t.,* **-fied, -fy·ing.** 編成法典;編纂;整理。—**cod·i·fi·ca·tion,** *n.*

cod·lin [ˈkadlɪn; ˈkɔdlin] *n.* ①〖英〗(供烹調之)長形蘋果。②未成熟之蘋果。

cod·ling¹ [ˈkadlɪŋ; ˈkɔdliŋ] *n.* 幼鱈。

cod·ling² *n.* =**codlin.**

cod oil 鱈魚肝油。

co·ed, co-ed [ˈkoˈɛd; ˈkouˈed] *n.* 〖美俗〗男女同校的學校之女生。「合編者。

co·ed·i·tor [ˈkoˈɛdɪtɚ; ˈkouˈeditə] *n.*

co·ed·u·ca·tion [ˌkoɛdʒəˈkeʃən; ˈkouˌedju(ː)ˈkeiʃən] *n.* 男女合校教育。—**al,** *adj.*

co·ef·fi·cient [ˌkoəˈfɪʃənt; ˌkouiˈfiʃənt] *n.* ①〖數學〗係數。②〖物理〗率;係數。—*adj.* 合作的。—**ly,** *adv.*

coe·len·ter·ate [sɪˈlɛntəˌret; siˈlentəreit] *n.* 腔腸動物。—*adj.* 腔腸動物的。

coe·li·ac [ˈsilɪˌæk; ˈsiːliæk] *adj.* 在腹腔裏面的;腹腔的。(亦作 **celiac**) 「修道士。

coe·no·bite [ˈsɛnəˌbaɪt; ˈsiːnəbait] *n.*

coe·no·bit·ism [ˈsinəˌbaɪtɪzəm; ˈsiːnəbaitizəm] *n.* 修道院之制度;修道士生活。

co·en·zyme [koˈɛnzaɪm; kouˈenzaim] *n.* 〖生化〗輔酵素;輔酶。

co·e·qual [koˈikwəl; kouˈiːkwəl] *adj., n.* (地位或能力)相等的(人或物)(=equal).

co·e·qual·i·ty [ˌkoɪˈkwalətɪ; ˌkoui(ː)ˈkwɔliti] *n.* 同等;同地位;同身分。

co·erce [koˈɝs; kouˈəːs] *v.t.,* **co·erced, co·erc·ing.** ①强迫。②抑制,壓制。

co·er·ci·ble [koˈɝsəbl̩; kouˈəːsibl] *adj.* 可强迫的;可壓制的。

co·er·cion [koˈɝʃən; kouˈəːʃən] *n.* ①强制。②高壓政治。—**ar·y,** *adj.* —**ist,** *n.*

co·er·cive [koˈɝsɪv; kouˈəːsiv] *adj.*

強制的;高壓的。

coercive force 〖物理〗抗磁力。

co·es·sen·tial [ˌkoəˈsɛnʃəl; ˌkouiˈsenʃəl] *adj.* 同素的;同體的;同質的。

co·e·ta·ne·ous [ˌkoɪˈtenɪəs; ˌkoiˈteiniəs] *adj.* 同時代的;同年的;同期的。—**ly,** *adv.* —**ness,** *n.*

co·e·ter·nal [ˌko·iˈtɝnl; ˌkoui(ː)ˈtəːnl] *adj.* 永遠共存的。

co·e·val [koˈivl; kouˈiːvəl] *adj.* 同時代的;同年代的。—*n.* 同時代者;同年代者。

co·ex·ec·u·tor [ˌko·ɪgˈzɛkjətɚ; ˈkouigˈzekjutə] *n.* 〖法律〗共同執行者。

co·ex·ec·u·trix [ˌko·ɪgˈzɛkjətrɪks; ˈkouigˈzekjutriks] *n., pl.* **-ex·ec·u·tri·ces** [-ɪgˌzɛkjəˈtraɪsiz; -igˌzekjuˈtraisiːz]. coexecutor 之女性。

co·ex·ist [ˌko·ɪgˈzɪst; ˈkouigˈzist] *v.i.* 同時存在;共存。—**ent,** *adj.*

co·ex·ist·ence [ˌko·ɪgˈzɪstəns; ˈkouigˈzistəns] *n.* 共存。

co·ex·tend [ˌko·ɪkˈstɛnd; ˈkouiksˈtend] *v.t. & v.i.* 時間或空間的共同擴展或伸張。—**co·ex·ten·sion,** *n.*

co·ex·ten·sive [ˌko·ɪkˈstɛnsɪv; ˈkouiksˈtensiv] *adj.* 有同等範圍的。—**ly,** *adv.*

:**cof·fee** [ˈkɔfɪ; ˈkɔfi] *n.* ①咖啡飲料;咖啡。②咖啡子或粉末。③咖啡樹。④咖啡色。

cof·fee-and [ˈkɔfɪˈænd; ˈkɔfiˈænd] *n.* 〖俚〗咖啡和糕餅等的點心。

coffee bean 咖啡豆。

coffee break 工作時之喝咖啡休息時間。

coffee cup 咖啡杯。

coffee grinder 咖啡磨研機。

coffee grounds 咖啡渣。

coffee hour 正式會議、學術講演等以後之自由交談聚會(參加者有咖啡招待)。

coffee house 咖啡館;咖啡屋。

coffee maker (煮)咖啡壺。(亦作 **coffeemaker**)

coffee mill 磨咖啡機。

coffee pot 咖啡壺。(亦作 **coffeepot**)

coffee room =**coffee shop.**

coffee shop =**coffee house.**

coffee stall 賣咖啡及點心之活動攤位。

coffee table 茶几。

coffee-table book 一種置於茶几上之特大號而插圖豐富的昂貴書籍。

cof·fee-tav·ern [ˈkɔfɪˌtævɚn; ˈkɔfiˌtævən] *n.* 〖英〗①(不賣酒的)簡易食堂。②飲茶店。

coffee tree 咖啡樹。

cof·fer [ˈkɔfɚ; ˈkɔfə] *n.* ①存放金錢或其他貴重物品之箱櫃。②天花板等之飾板。③〖建築〗藻井。④(*pl.*)資金;財寶;國庫。⑤沉箱。—*v.t.* ①放入櫃中收藏。②飾以藻井。

cof·fer·dam [ˈkɔfɚˌdæm; ˈkɔfədæm] *n.* ①圍堰。②沉箱;潛水箱。

*__cof·fin__ [ˈkɔfɪn; ˈkɔfin] *n.* 棺;柩。***drive a nail into one's coffin*** 促人早死。—*v.t.* ①納入棺中;收殮。②將…緊閉。

coffin bone (馬等之)蹄骨。

coffin joint (馬等的)蹄關節。

coffin nail 〖俚〗香煙。

coffin plate 棺蓋上之金屬名牌。

cof·fle [ˈkɑfl; ˈkɔfl] *n.* (被鍊在一起的)奴隸或獸類。

co·found·er [koˈfaundɚ; kouˈfaundə] *n.* 共同開辦人;共同創立人。

cog [kɑg; kɔg] *n., v.,* **cogged, cog·ging.** —*n.* ①〖機械〗鈍齒。②〖機械〗鈍齒輪。③枘;榫;筍。④小船。***slip a cog*** 做錯事。—*v.t.* 裝齒輪;打榫。—*v.i.* 欺騙(特指擲骰子時之詐欺)。

cog. cognate.

co·gent [ˈkodʒənt; ˈkoudʒənt] *adj.* ①強有力的;使人信服的。②中肯的;恰到好處的;對題的。—**co·gen·cy,** *n.* —**ly,** *adv.*

cogged [kɑgd; kɔgd] *adj.* ①有齒輪的。②作弊的;騙人的。

cog·i·ta·ble [ˈkɑdʒətəbl; ˈkɔdʒitəbl] *adj.* 可思考的;可想像的。

cog·i·tate [ˈkɑdʒəˌtet; ˈkɔdʒiteit] *v.,* **-tat·ed, -tat·ing.** —*v.i.* 慎思;思考;沉思。—*v.t.* 計畫;設計。—**cog·i·ta·tion,** *n.*

cog·i·ta·tive [ˈkɑdʒəˌtetɪv; ˈkɔdʒitətiv] *adj.* ①能思想的。②好思想的;善用心思的。

cog·i·ta·tor [ˈkɑdʒəˌtetɚ; ˈkɔdʒiteitə] *n.* 好沉思之人;深思熟慮的人。

co·gnac [ˈkonjæk; ˈkounjæk] *n.* 法國 Cognac 地方所產之白蘭地酒。

cog·nate [ˈkɑgnet; ˈkɔgneit] *adj.* ①同源的。②同性質的。③同族的;同父母的。—*n.* 同源之人、物或字。—**cog·nat·ic,** *adj.*

cog·na·tion [kɑgˈneʃən; kɔgˈneiʃən] *n.* 同族;同源;同系;親族。

cog·ni·tion [kɑgˈnɪʃən; kɔgˈniʃən] *n.* ①認識;認識力。②所認識之事物;知識。

cog·ni·tive [ˈkɑgnətɪv; ˈkɔgnitiv] *adj.* 認識(力)的。(亦作 **cognitional**) —**ly,** *adv.*

cog·ni·za·ble [ˈkɑgnəzəbl; ˈkɔgnizəbl] *adj.* ①可認知的;可知覺的。②〖法律〗在審判權限內的;可審問的。

cog·ni·zance [ˈkɑgnəzəns; ˈkɔgnizəns] *n.* ①認識;知覺;察知。②認知之範圍。③〖法律〗審理;審理權。④紋章。⑤管轄權;指揮權。***have cognizance of*** 知道;察覺。***take cognizance of*** 注意到;覺察到。

cog·ni·zant [ˈkɑgnəzənt; ˈkɔgnizənt] *adj.* ①認識的;認知的。②〖法律〗審理(權)的。

cog·nize [ˈkɑgˌnaɪz; kɔgˈnaiz] *v.t.,* **-nized, -niz·ing.** 認識;認知。

cog·no·men [kɑgˈnomən; kɔgˈnoumən] *n.* ①(古羅馬人之)姓。②名字;綽號。

co·gno·scen·te [ˌkonjoˈʃɛnte; ˌkɔnjouˈʃenti] *n., pl.* **-ti** [-ti; -tiː]. 〖義〗鑑賞家。

cog·nos·ci·ble [kɑgˈnɑsəbl; kɔgˈnɔsibl] *adj.* 可知的;可認知的。

cog·no·vit [kɑgˈnovɪt; kɔgˈnouvit] *n.* 〖法律〗被告承認書(被告承認原告請求為正當所具之結)。

cog·wheel [ˈkɑgˌhwil; ˈkɔgwiːl] *n.* 〖機械〗齒輪。

co·hab·it [koˈhæbɪt; kouˈhæbit] *v.i.* (男女)同居。

co·hab·it·ant [koˈhæbətənt; kouˈhæbitənt] *n.* 同居者。

co·hab·i·ta·tion [koˌhæbəˈteʃən; ˌkouhæbiˈteiʃən] *n.* 同居。

co·heir [koˈɛr; ˈkouˈɛə] *n.* 共同繼承人。

co·heir·ess [koˈɛrɪs; ˈkouˈɛəris] *n.* 女性共同繼承人。

co·here [koˈhɪr; kouˈhiə] *v.i.,* **-hered, -her·ing.** ①黏着;附着;凝結。②連貫;結合。

co·her·ence [koˈhɪrəns; kouˈhiərəns] *n.* ①連貫性。②黏着。③語言或文字之連貫。

co·her·ent [koˈhɪrənt; kouˈhiərənt] *adj.* ①一致的;連貫的;合於邏輯的。②黏着的;附着的。—**ly,** *adv.*

co·her·er [koˈhɪrɚ; kouˈhiərə] *n.* 〖無線電〗檢波器。

co·he·sion [koˈhiʒən; kouˈhiːʒən] *n.* ①附着;團結;凝結;凝結力;結合力。②〖物理〗內聚力。—**co·he·sive,** *adj.*

Cohn [kon; koun] *n.* 柯恩 (Ferdinand Julius, 1828–1898, 德國植物學家,為細菌學創始者)。

co·hort [ˈkohɔrt; ˈkouhɔːt] *n.* ①古羅馬

馬軍團(legion)中之一區分(約有 300 至 600 人)。②一隊兵。③一隊。④〖俗〗同事;同黨。

coif 〔kɔɪf; kɔif〕 *n.* ①(修女)戴於頭巾下緊箍着頭的布帽。②(歐洲農婦)緊箍着頭的帽子。③高級律師所戴之白帽。④高級律師的職位。⑤鐵盔或皮帽。—*v.t.* ①覆以頭巾;戴緊帽。②整理(頭髮)。「理髮師。」

coif·feur 〔kwɑˈfɝ; kwɑːˈfəː〕 〖法〗 *n.*

coif·fure 〔kwɑˈfjʊr; kwɑːˈfjuə〕 *n., v.,* **-fured, -fur·ing.** —*n.* 〖法〗①頭髮式樣。②婦女之頭飾。—*v.t.* ①做成某種髮型。②戴以頭飾。

coign, coigne 〔kɔɪn; kɔin〕 *n.* ①外角;隅;隅石。②楔。***coign of vantage*** 有利之地位。

*__coil__[1] 〔kɔɪl; kɔil〕 *v.t.* 盤繞;將…捲起。to *coil* a rope. 將繩索捲起。—*v.i.* 盤繞;捲。—*n.* ①捲。a *coil* of cable. 一捲巨纜。②螺旋。③〖電〗線圈。④髮捲。⑤成捲筒形發行的郵票。「囂煩忙。」

coil[2] *n.* 〖古〗騷動。***mortal coil*** 塵世之喧

‡**coin** 〔kɔɪn; kɔin〕 *n.* 貨幣;鑄幣;硬幣;錢。silver *coins.* 銀幣。***pay (a person) back in his own coin*** 以其人之道還治其人之身。—*v.t.* ①鑄(幣)。②造(字)。***coin money*** 〖俗〗發大財。—*v.i.* ①鑄幣。②〖英〗造假鈔。

coin·age 〔ˈkɔɪnɪdʒ; ˈkɔinidʒ〕 *n.* ①貨幣之鑄造。②貨幣鑄造權。③硬幣。④幣制。decimal *coinage.* 十進幣制。⑤創造。⑥新創字及成語等。

coin assorter 大小硬幣分類器。

co·in·cide 〔ˌkoɪnˈsaɪd; ˌkouinˈsaid〕 *v.i.,* **-cid·ed, -cid·ing.** ①空間上相合。②時間上相合。③一致;符合。My views do not *coincide* with theirs.我的意見與他們不一致。

*__co·in·ci·dence__ 〔koˈɪnsədəns; kouˈinsidəns〕 *n.* ①一致;符合。②同時發生或同時存在之事。a mere *coincidence.* 祇是巧合而已。

co·in·ci·dent 〔koˈɪnsədənt; kouˈinsidənt〕*adj.* ①同時發生的。②一致的;巧合的。③占同一地方或位置的。—**al,** *adj.* —**al·ly,** *adv.*

coin·er 〔ˈkɔɪnɚ; ˈkɔinə〕 *n.* ①造幣者。②偽幣製造者。③製造者;發明者。

co·in·her·it·ance 〔ˌkoɪnˈhɛrətəns; ˌkouinˈheritəns〕 *n.* 共同繼承。「機器。」

coin machine 投下硬幣卽發生作用的

coin-op·er·at·ed 〔ˈkɔɪnˌɑpəˌretɪd; ˈkɔinˌɔpəreitid〕 *adj.* (機器)投入硬幣卽發生作用的。

co·in·stan·ta·ne·ous 〔ˌkoɪnstənˈtenɪəs; ˌkouinstənˈteiniəs〕 *adj.* 同時的;同時發生的。「inˈʃuərəns〕 *n.* 共同保險。」

co·in·sur·ance 〔ˌkoɪnˈʃurəns; ˌkou-

co·in·sure 〔ˌkoɪnˈʃur; ˌkouinˈʃuə〕 *v.t. & v.i.,* **-sured, -sur·ing.** 共同保險。

coir 〔kɔɪr; kɔiə〕 *n.* ①椰子殼之纖維。②椰子殼纖維所製之蓆或繩。

co·i·tion 〔koˈɪʃən; kouˈiʃən〕 *n.* 性交。

co·i·tus 〔ˈkoɪtəs; ˈkouitəs〕〖拉〗*n.* 性交。

coitus in·ter·rup·tus 〔~ˌɪntəˈrʌptəs; ~ˌintəˈrʌptəs〕 *pl.* **coitus in·ter·rup·ti** 〔~-taɪ; ~-tai〕. 未射精前卽中止性交之行爲;間斷式交媾。

coke 〔kok; kouk〕 *n., v.,* **coked, cok·ing.** —*n.* ①焦炭。②〖俚〗古柯鹼。③(C-)〖俚〗可口可樂 (Coca Cola). —*v.t.* 將…變爲焦炭。—*v.i.* 變爲焦炭。「壓谷。」

col 〔kɑl; kɔl〕 *n.* ①峽路;峽。②〖氣象〗氣

Col. ①Colombia. ②Colonel. ③Colorado.

col. ①collected. ②collector. ③college. ④colonial. ⑤colony. ⑥color. ⑦colored. ⑧column. 「collateral.」

col- 〖字首〗 **com-** 之異體,用於 l 前,如:

co·la 〔ˈkolə; ˈkoulə〕 *n.* ①〖植物〗可樂樹(其子含咖啡鹼)。②可樂(飲料)。

co·la·bor·er 〔koˈlebərɚ; kouˈleibərə〕 *n.*勞工同事。「器;濾鍋。(亦作 **cullender**)」

col·an·der 〔ˈkʌləndɚ; ˈkʌləndə〕*n.* 濾

co·lat·i·tude 〔koˈlætəˌtjud; kouˈlætitjuːd〕 *n.* 〖天文〗餘緯度(某地之緯度與 90° 之差)。「*n.* 秋水仙素。」

col·chi·cine 〔ˈkɑltʃəsin; ˈkɔltʃəsiːn〕

col·chi·cum 〔ˈkɑltʃɪkəm; ˈkɔltʃikəm〕 *n.* ①〖植物〗秋水仙。②秋水仙之種子或球莖(用於治療風濕與痛風)。

‡**cold** 〔kold; kould〕 *adj.* ①寒冷的;涼的。If you feel *cold,* come and sit by the fire. 如果你覺得冷,來坐在火爐邊。②冷淡的;冷漠的;不友誼的。a *cold* reply. 冷淡的答覆。③冷靜的。④輕微的。⑤寒色的。⑥失去知覺的。⑦令人沮喪的。⑧無偏見的。⑨〖俚〗死亡。⑩(女人)性冷感的。***give (a person) the cold shoulder*** 冷淡相對。***have cold feet*** 怯懦起來 (=to become timid). ***in cold blood*** 冷靜地;鎮靜地。***make one's blood run cold*** 令人寒心;令人害怕。***throw (pour or dash) cold water on*** 潑冷水;使沮喪 (=to discourage). —*n.* ①寒冷。He is afraid of *cold.* 他怕冷。②寒冷的天氣。③寒冷的感覺。He was shivering with *cold.* 他凍得發抖。④受寒;感冒;傷風。I had a *cold* last night. 我昨夜受寒;我昨夜傷風。⑤〖物理〗結冰點;冰點之下。***catch*** (or ***take***) ***cold*** 着涼;患傷風或感冒。***come in from the cold*** 時來運轉(脫離孤立或被閒置的境地)。***out in the cold*** 遭受冷落。—**ness,** *n.*

cold bath 冷水浴。

cold-blood·ed 〔ˈkoldˈblʌdɪd; ˈkouldˈblʌdid〕 *adj.* ①冷血的。②殘忍的。—**ly,** *adv.* —**ness,** *n.*

cold chisel 鏨。

cold comfort 令人洩氣之事;不值得高興之事。

cold cream 雪花膏;冷霜(化妝品)。

cold cuts 冷吃的肉片或乾酪片。

cold-drawn 〔ˈkoldˈdrɔn; ˈkouldˈdrɔːn〕 *adj.* ①(金屬等)不加熱力以延展的。②(油等)不加熱抽取的;冷抽的。

Cold Duck 〖美〗葡萄酒與香檳混合的一種較便宜的酒。

cold feet 〖俗〗信心或勇氣之喪失;害怕。***have*** (or ***get***) ***cold feet*** 失去信心或勇氣。

cold frame 保護幼嫩植物之罩子。

cold front 〖氣象〗冷鋒;冷面。

cold-heart·ed 〔ˈkoldˈhɑrtɪd; ˈkouldˈhɑːtid〕 *adj.* 冷淡無情的。「的;略冷的。」

cold·ish 〔ˈkoldɪʃ; ˈkouldiʃ〕 *adj.* 微冷

*__cold·ly__ 〔ˈkoldlɪ; ˈkouldli〕 *adv.* 冷淡地;冷靜地;無情地。「巾、冰袋等。」

cold pack ①一種食物裝罐法。②冷毛

cold-pack 〔ˈkoldˌpæk; ˈkouldpæk〕 *v.t.* ①以冷毛巾、冰袋等敷用。②以低溫裝罐法處理食物。

cold rubber 一種很硬的人造橡皮。

cold-short 〔ˈkoldˈʃɔrt; ˈkouldˈʃɔːt〕 *adj.* 一冷卽脆的(金屬等)。

cold shoulder 〖俗〗冷淡;輕視。

cold-shoul·der 〔ˈkoldˈʃoldɚ; ˈkouldˈʃouldə〕 *v.t.* 〖俗〗冷淡;冷遇;輕視。

cold snap 一時突然寒冷的天氣。

cold sore (傷風時嘴邊生的)小水疱。
cold steel 鋼製的武器。
cold storage 冷藏。
cold sweat 冷汗。
cold turkey 〖俚〗①突然斷絕毒品供應,以戒絕毒癮之方法。②曉以利害。
cold war 冷戰。
cold-wa·ter [ˈkoldˌwɔtɚ; ˈkould-ˌwɔːtə] *adj.* (公寓等)祇供應冷水的;無熱水供應設備的。
cold wave ①寒流; 寒流滯留之時期。②冷燙。
cole [kol; koul] *n.* 芥菜類之蔬菜;(尤指)油菜。(亦作 **colewort**)
Co·le·op·ter·a [ˌkolɪˈɑptərə; ˌkɔli-ˈɔptərə] *n. pl.* 〖動物〗甲蟲類; 鞘翅類。—**co·le·op·ter·ous,** *adj.*
Cole·ridge [ˈkolrɪdʒ; ˈkoulridʒ] *n.* 柯爾雷基 (Samuel Taylor, 1772–1834, 英國詩人及哲學家)。
cole·seed [ˈkolˌsid; ˈkoulsiːd] *n.* 〖植物〗①油菜籽。②油菜。
cole·slaw [ˈkolˌslɔ; ˈkoulslɔː] *n.* 涼拌生菜絲。
co·le·us [ˈkolɪəs; ˈkouliəs] *n.* 〖植物〗薄荷科植物。
col·ic [ˈkɑlɪk; ˈkɔlik] *n.* 〖醫〗肚腹絞痛;疝痛。—*adj.* 腹痛的;疝痛的。
col·ick·y [ˈkɑlɪkɪ; ˈkɔliki] *adj.* 肚腹絞痛的;疝痛的。
col·i·form [ˈkɑləˌfɔrm; ˈkɔləfɔːm] *adj.* 大腸桿菌的;似大腸桿菌的。
coliform bacillus 大腸桿菌。
C.O.L. index Cost of Living index.
col·i·se·um [ˌkɑləˈsiəm; ˌkɔliˈsiəm] *n.*①競技場;大表演場。②(C-)=**Colosseum.**
co·li·tis [koˈlaɪtɪs; kɔˈlaitis] *n.* 〖醫〗結腸炎。
coll. ①colleague. ②collect. ③collection. ④collective. ⑤collector. ⑥college. ⑦colloquial. ⑧〖處方〗=an eyewash.
col·lab·o·rate [kəˈlæbəˌret; kəˈlæbəreit] *v.i.,* **-rat·ed, -rat·ing.** ①合作。②與敵人合作;資敵;通敵。—**col·lab·o·ra·tor, col·lab·o·ra·tion,** *n.*
col·lab·o·ra·tion·ist [kəˌlæbəˈreʃənɪst; kəˌlæbəˈreiʃənist] *n.* 通敵賣國者。
col·lage [kəˈlɑʒ; kəˈlɑːʒ] *n.*(用報紙、布、壓平之花等碎片合成之)美術拼貼。
*__col·lapse__ [kəˈlæps; kəˈlæps] *v.,* **-lapsed, -laps·ing,** *n.* —*v.i.* ①倒塌;崩潰;陷縮。②突然失敗;病倒。 His business *collapsed* within a year. 他的生意在一年內完全失敗。③摺疊。—*v.t.* 使倒塌;摺疊起。—*n.* ①倒塌;崩潰;陷縮。 A heavy flood caused the *collapse* of the bridge. 洪水使這橋倒塌。②失敗;體力不支。
col·laps·i·ble [kəˈlæpsəbl̩; kəˈlæpsəbl] *adj.* (傢具等)可摺疊的;摺疊式的。(亦作 **collapsable**)
*__col·lar__ [ˈkɑlɚ; ˈkɔlə] *n.* ①衣領。*collar* badge. 領章。②項飾。③狗、馬等之項圈。④畜牲頸部皮毛之一圈顏色。⑤軸鉗;環管。⑥銜接兩管之短管。***against the collar*** 冒着困難。***hot under the collar*** 怒;激動。***keep a person up to the collar*** 把人當作牛馬。***slip the collar*** 逃避困難;逃脫。—*v.t.* ①扭住…的衣領;捉住。②〖俗〗拿去。③裝領於;加項圈於。④强留(他人)談話。
collar beam 〖建築〗繫樑;維樑。
col·lar·bone [ˈkɑlɚˈbon; ˈkɔləboun] *n.* 〖解剖〗鎖骨。
col·lar·et, col·lar·ette [ˌkɑləˈrɛt; ˌkɔləˈret] *n.* 婦女之圍巾、項飾、毛披肩等。
collar work 困難而吃力的工作。
collat. ①collateral. ②collaterally.
col·late [kɑˈlet, ˈkɑlet; kɔˈleit] *v.i.,* **-lat·ed, -lat·ing.** ①對照; 校勘。②整理;檢點。—**col·la·tor,** *n.*
col·lat·er·al [kəˈlætərəl; kɔˈlætərəl] *adj.* ①並行的;附隨的;副的。②旁系的;間接的。—*n.* ①旁系親屬。②擔保物;抵押品。③〖解剖〗側枝。—**ly,** *adv.*
col·lat·er·al·ize [kəˈlætərəˌlaɪz; kəˈlætərəlaiz] *v.t.,* **-ized, -iz·ing.** ①將…作抵押。②借款時提供抵押。
col·la·tion [kɑˈleʃən; kɔˈleiʃən] *n.* ①校勘;整理。②圖書館對書籍、卷頁、挿圖等之描述。③齋期中可獲准之小食。④便餐。⑤牧師職之委任。
*__col·league__ [ˈkɑlig; ˈkɔliːg] *n.* 同事;同僚。
‡__col·lect__ [*v., adj., adv.* kəˈlɛkt; kəˈlekt *n.* ˈkɑlɛkt; ˈkɔlekt] *v.t.* ①集合;收集。②集(款);收回(款);催繳(租稅等)。③蒐集。I like to *collect* stamps. 我喜歡蒐集郵票。④使(心神)鎮靜或安靜;使(思想)集中。⑤接走;取走。They *collected* their mail. 他們取走了他們的郵件。—*v.i.* ①聚集;積聚。②收款〖常on〗。 He *collected* on the damage to his house. 他收到房屋損害賠償費。—*adj.* & *adv.* 向收件人收款的(地)。—*n.* 某些宗教儀式中很短的祈禱文。
col·lect·a·ble, col·lect·i·ble [kəˈlɛktəbl̩; kəˈlektəbl] *adj.* 可收集的; 可徵集的。
col·lec·ta·ne·a [ˌkɑlɛkˈtenɪə; ˌkɔlek-ˈtɑːnjə] *n. pl.* 選集;雜錄。
col·lect·ed [kəˈlɛktɪd; kəˈlektid] *adj.* ①聚集的;積聚的。②鎮靜的;泰然的。—**ly,** *adv.* —**ness,** *n.*
collected edition (作家之)全集。
*__col·lec·tion__ [kəˈlɛkʃən; kəˈlekʃən] *n.* ①收集;收取。②蒐集的東西。He has a fine *collection* of stamps. 他蒐集了一些精美的郵票。③聚集;積聚。④募集之款。***make*** (or ***take up***) ***a collection*** 募集捐款。
collection agency 爲其他公司代收欠款的公司。
collection item 支票存款。
*__col·lec·tive__ [kəˈlɛktɪv; kəˈlektiv] *adj.* 集合的; 聚集的; 共同的; 集體的。*collective* efforts. 共同努力;集體努力。—*n.* ①集合名詞。②集體經營之農場、工廠等組職。—**ly,** *adv.*
collective agreement ①工會代表全體工人與資方訂的協議。②此等協議事項。
collective bargaining 勞方與資方對工作之時間、工資等所作之協商。
collective farm (蘇聯之)集體農場。
collective fruit 〖植物〗聚果。
collective noun 集合名詞。
collective security 集體安全。
col·lec·tiv·ism [kəˈlɛktɪvˌɪzəm; kəˈlektivizəm] *n.* 集產主義;集體主義。—**col·lec·tiv·ist,** *n.* —**col·lec·tiv·is·tic,** *adj.*
col·lec·tiv·i·ty [ˌkɑlɛkˈtɪvətɪ; ˌkɔlekˈtiviti] *n.* ①聚集。②總體。③全體人民。④集產主義。
col·lec·ti·vize [kəˈlɛktɪˌvaɪz; kəˈlektivaiz] *v.t.,* **-ized, -iz·ing.** 按集產主義原則而組織(人民、工業、經濟等)。
collect on delivery 貨到收款。(略作 **C.O.D., c.o.d.**)
*__col·lec·tor__ [kəˈlɛktɚ; kəˈlektə] *n.* ①

收集者；蒐集者。a stamp *collector.* 郵票收藏家。②被雇收款的人。③集電器；集電極。

col·lec·tor·ship [kə'lɛktɚ,ʃɪp; kə'lektəʃip] *n.*徵收人之職務或負責地區。(亦作 **collectorate**)

collector's (or **collectors'**) **item** 珍品。

col·leen ['kɑlin; 'kɔliːn] *n.* 〖愛〗女孩。

‡col·lege ['kɑlɪdʒ; 'kɔlidʒ] *n.* ①大學內的學院。②獨立的高等學府；獨立的學院。Teachers *College.* 師範學院。③學會；社團。the *College* of Surgeons. 〖英〗外科醫師學會。④法國之中等學校。⑤有某種權力或權利，且從事某種工作之集團。⑥〖英俚〗監獄。⑦任何集團。***give (something) the college try*** 〖俗〗盡力去做(某事)。

College of Cardinals 〖天主教〗樞機團。

col·leg·er ['kɑlɪdʒɚ; 'kɔlidʒə] *n.* ①大學生；大學或學院中之一分子。②英國 Eton 學校中由該校資助之學生。

college widow 〖美俚〗曾經和本地大學歷屆男生交遊而尚未結婚之婦女。

col·le·gian [kə'lidʒən; kə'liːdʒjən] *n.* ①大學生。②大學畢業生。③大學或學院中之一分子。④〖英俚〗監獄中同監房的人。

col·le·gi·ate [kə'lidʒɪɪt; kə'liːdʒiit] *adj.* ①大學的；學院的。②大學生的；供大學生用的。③大學之組織的；高等程度的；社團的。(亦作 **collegial**)

***col·let** ['kɑlɪt; 'kɔlit] *n., v.,* **-let·ed, -let·ing.** —*n.* ①鑲嵌寶石之底座。②〖機械〗筒夾；夾頭。—*v.t.* ①鑲進底座。②裝以筒夾或夾頭。

***col·lide** [kə'laɪd; kə'laid] *v.i.,* **-lid·ed, -lid·ing.** ①碰撞；互撞。②衝突；抵觸。

col·lie ['kɑlɪ; 'kɔli] *n.* 〖動物〗一種牧羊犬。(亦作 **colly**)

col·lier ['kɑljɚ; 'kɔliə] *n.* 〖英〗①運煤船。②煤礦工人。

col·lier·y ['kɑljərɪ; 'kɔljəri] *n., pl.* **-lier·ies.** 煤礦場及其建築與設備。

col·li·gate ['kɑlɪ,get; 'kɔligeit] *v.t.,* **-gat·ed, -gat·ing.** ①紮；綁；縛；束。②〖邏輯〗總括；綜合(各種事實)。—**col·li·ga·tion,** *n.*

col·li·mate ['kɑlə,met; 'kɔlimeit] *v.t.,* **-mat·ed, -mat·ing.** ①對準；調節。②使平行。—**col·li·ma·tion,** *n.*

col·li·ma·tor ['kɑlɪ,metɚ; 'kɔlimeitə] *n.* 準直儀；準直管；平行光管。

col·lin·e·ar [kə'lɪnɪɚ; kɔ'linjə] *adj.* 〖幾何〗在同一直線上的；共線的。

Col·lins ['kɑlɪnz; 'kɔlinz] *n.* ①〖英俗〗(客人寄來的)謝函。②(c-)(一種混合糖、碳酸水、檸檬汁、酒精等調成的)碳酸酒。

col·li·sion [kə'lɪʒən; kə'liʒən] *n.* ①撞；碰；猛烈相撞。②衝突；抵觸。***come into collision with*** 與…衝突；抵觸。

collision mat 〖航海〗(船撞破時用的)防水墊。

col·lo·cate ['kɑlo,ket; 'kɔləkeit] *v.t.,* **-cat·ed, -cat·ing.** ①配置。②排列。

col·lo·ca·tion [,kɑlo'keʃən; ,kɔlə'keiʃən] *n.* ①排列；安排；布置。②連語。

col·lo·di·on [kə'lodɪən; kə'loudjən] *n.* 火棉膠。(亦作 **collodium**)

col·logue [kə'log; kə'loug] *v.i.,* **-logued, -logu·ing.** 〖方〗密謀；密議。

col·loid ['kɑlɔɪd; 'kɔlɔid] *n.* 〖化〗膠體；類膠質。—*adj.*膠體的；膠質的；膠狀的。—**al,** *adj.*

col·lop ['kɑləp; 'kɔləp] *n.* ①小片；小塊。②小肉片；小肉塊。

colloq. ①colloquial. ②colloquialism. ③colloquially.

col·lo·qui·al [kə'lokwɪəl; kə'loukwiəl] *adj.* 俗語的；會話的。—**ly,** *adv.*

col·lo·qui·al·ism [kə'lokwɪəl,ɪzəm; kə'loukwiəlizəm] *n.* 俗語；白話；口語。—**col·lo·qui·al·ist,** *n.*

col·lo·qui·um [kə'lokwɪəm; kə'loukwiəm] *n., pl.* **-qui·ums, -qui·a** [-kwɪə; -kwiə]. 非正式之會議；座談會；研討會。

col·lo·quy ['kɑləkwɪ; 'kɔləkwi] *n., pl.* **-quies.** ①談話。②會議。③以對話體寫的文章。

col·lo·type ['kɑlə,taɪp; 'kɔloutaip] *n.* 〖印刷〗珂羅版。—*v.t.* 將…做成珂羅版。

col·lude [kə'lud; kə'luːd] *v.i.,* **-lud·ed, -lud·ing.** 共謀；串騙。

col·lu·sion [kə'luʒən; kə'luːʒən] *n.* 共謀；串騙；勾結。—**col·lu·sive,** *adj.*

collut. 〖處方〗漱口水。

collyr. 〖處方〗洗眼水；眼藥水。

col·lyr·i·um [kə'lɪrɪəm; kə'liriəm] *n., pl.* **-i·a** [-ɪə; -iə]. 點眼水；洗眼劑。

col·ly·wob·bles ['kɑlɪ,wɑbl̩z; 'kɔli,wɔblz] *n. pl.* 〖俗〗肚痛。

Colo. Colorado.

col·o·cynth ['kɑləsɪnθ; 'kɔləsinθ] *n.* ①〖植物〗苦西瓜(屬葫蘆科)。②苦西瓜瓤。③苦西瓜瓤所製之瀉劑。(亦作 **coloquintida**)

Co·logne [kə'lon; kə'loun] *n.* 科倫(德國西部一城市，濱萊茵河，以其天主教堂著名)。②(c-)一種香水。

Co·lom·bi·a [kə'lʌmbɪə; kə'lɔmbiə] *n.* 哥倫比亞(南美洲之一國，首都波哥大Bogotá)。

Co·lom·bo [kə'lʌmbo; kə'lʌmbou] *n.* 可倫坡(斯里蘭卡之首都)。

co·lon¹ ['kolən; 'koulən] *n.* 冒號(:)。

co·lon² ['kolən; 'koulən] *n., pl.* **-lons, -la** [-lə; -lə]. 〖解剖〗結腸。

***colo·nel** ['kɝnl̩; 'kəːnl̩] *n.* (陸空軍及海軍陸戰隊)上校。—**cy,** —**ship,** *n.*

***co·lo·ni·al** [kə'lonɪəl; kə'lounjəl] *adj.* ①殖民地的。②英屬十三州殖民地的；美國初期的。③〖生物〗羣體的。—*n.* 殖民地居民。

co·lo·ni·al·ism [kə'lonɪəl,ɪzəm; kə'lounjəlizəm] *n.* 殖民政策；殖民地主義。

***col·o·nist** ['kɑlənɪst; 'kɔlənist] *n.* ①開發殖民地者。②殖民地居民；移住之人民。

col·o·ni·tis [,kɑlə'naɪtɪs; ,kɔlə'naitis] *n.* 〖醫〗結腸炎。

col·o·ni·za·tion [,kɑlənaɪ'zeʃən; ,kɔlənai'zeiʃən] *n.* 殖民；拓殖。

col·o·nize ['kɑlə,naɪz; 'kɔlənaiz] *v.t. & v.i.* **-nized, -niz·ing.** ①殖民；拓殖。②建立殖民地。—**col·o·niz·er,** *n.*

col·on·nade [,kɑlə'ned; ,kɔlə'neid] *n.* ①〖建築〗柱廊；一列柱子。②雙行的樹。—**col·on·nad·ed,** *adj.*

‡col·o·ny ['kɑlənɪ; 'kɔləni] *n., pl.* **-nies.** ①殖民。②殖民地。③居留民；僑居於外國的同國人；同職業的一羣人。the Chinese *colony* in San Francisco. 在舊金山的中國僑民。④一羣動物或植物。⑤〖細菌〗菌叢；菌集落。***the Colonies*** 北美之英國十三個殖民地。

col·o·phon ['kɑlə,fɑn; 'kɔləfən] *n.* ①書籍末尾之題記。②印於書籍前頁或後頁之出版者的標誌。***from title page to colophon*** (全書)從頭至尾。

col·o·pho·ny ['kɑlə,fonɪ; 'kɔləfouni] *n.* 樹脂；松脂(=rosin).

‡col·or, col·our ['kʌlɚ; 'kʌlə] *n.* ①顏色；色；色彩；色素。②(*pl.*) 顏料。water *colors.*水彩顏料。③面色；(害羞的)臉紅；紅潤。④外表；樣子。The story has some *color* of truth. 這故事似有幾分眞實。⑤特色;生動之品質。⑥(*pl.*) 徽章;有顏色的制服、帽;賽馬之主人所有的色彩標幟。⑦(*pl.*) 艦旗;軍旗。to salute the *colors*. 向軍旗致敬。⑧藉口。⑨(某一時期或地區之) 色彩。a novel with much local *color*. 一部富於地方色彩的小說。⑩美海軍之升降旗典禮。⑪〖印刷〗所用油墨之量。⑫音色。***call to the colors*** 號召從軍。***change color*** 變色 (面色變紅或蒼白)。***come off with flying colors*** 奏凱歌;凱旋;大爲成功。***desert one's colors*** 變節;逃走。***get one's colors*** 榮獲徽章、帽等,以示屬於學校中某種球隊或運動隊。***give a false color to*** 曲解;歪曲原意。***join the colors*** 從軍。***lend*** (or ***give***) ***color to*** 使之似可能;使之像眞;加以渲染。***lose color*** 面色變爲蒼白。***lower one's colors*** 退讓。***nail the colors to the mast*** 決不投降。***paint in bright*** (***dark***) ***colors*** 加以褒詞(貶詞)。***sail under false colors*** 打着假招牌騙人。***serve with the colors*** 從軍。***show one's true colors*** **a.** 現出本來面目。**b.** 宣布自己的意見或計畫。***stick to one's colors*** 嚴守黨律;堅持己見。***strike one's colors*** 投降。***under the color of*** 託詞;藉口;以…爲口實。—*v.t.* ①爲…染色;爲…着色。②加以渲染;曲解。News is often *colored*. 新聞常被渲染。③使帶顯著特性。—*v.i.* 變色;臉紅。The leaves have begun to *color*. 樹葉開始變色。

col·or·a·ble [ˈkʌlərəbl̩; ˈkʌlərəbl] *adj.* ①可着色的。②似眞的;似是而非的。③僞造的。—**col·or·a·bly,** *adv.*

Col·o·ra·do [ˌkɑləˈræd̩o; ˌkɔləˈrɑːdou] *n.* ①科羅拉多(美國西部之一州)。②美國西南部之一河流。③源於美國 Texas 州之西部,流入墨西哥灣之一河流。—**Col·o·rad·an,** *adj.,n.*

col·o(u)r·a·tion [ˌkʌləˈreʃən; ˌkʌləˈreiʃən] *n.* 染色;着色;色澤。

col·o·ra·tu·ra [ˌkʌlərəˈtjurə; ˌkɔlərəˈtuərə] *n.* (亦作 **coloratura**)〖音樂〗①華彩;花腔。②具有華彩之樂曲。③花腔女高音。—*adj.* & *adv.* 華彩音的(地)。

col·or-bear·er [ˈkʌləˌbɛrə; ˈkʌləˌbɛərə] *n.* 旗手。

col·o(u)r-blind [ˈkʌləˌblaɪnd; ˈkʌləblaind] *adj.* ①色盲的。②不加區別的。③沒有種族偏見的。

colo(u)r blindness 色盲。

color box 顏料盒。

col·or·cast [ˈkʌləˌkæst; ˈkʌləkɑːst] *n., v.,* **-cast** or **-cast·ed, -cast·ing.** —*n.* 〖電視〗彩色廣播。—*v.i.* 廣播彩色節目。

col·o(u)red [ˈkʌləd; ˈkʌləd] *adj.* ①有色的;着色的。②黑皮膚的;黑人的。③帶有偏見的;虛飾的。④(樹葉)非綠色的。—*n.* (亦作 **Colored**) 南非共和國的有色人種之人。

colored stone 鑽石以外之其他寶石。

col·or·fast [ˈkʌləˌfæst; ˈkʌləfɑːst] *adj.* 不褪色的。

color film 彩色影片;彩色軟片。

color filter 〖照相〗濾光鏡頭。

***col·o(u)r·ful** [ˈkʌləfəl; ˈkʌləful] *adj.* ①富有色彩的。②活現的;生動的;如畫的。

color guard 〖美〗護旗隊。

col·or·if·ic [ˌkʌləˈrɪfɪk; ˌkʌləˈrifik] *adj.* ①產生顏色的;賦與顏色的。②色彩的。

col·or·im·e·ter [ˌkʌləˈrɪmətə; ˌkʌləˈrimətə] *n.* 色度計;色量計。

col·o(u)r·ing [ˈkʌlərɪŋ; ˈkʌləriŋ] *n.* ①着色;施色;配色。②顏料。③虛飾。

coloring matter 顏料;染料。

col·or·ist [ˈkʌlərɪst; ˈkʌlərist] *n.* ①着色者。②專門研究彩色之藝術家。

col·o(u)r·less [ˈkʌləlɪs; ˈkʌləlis] *adj.* ①無色的。②無趣味的。③蒼白的。④無偏見的;公正的。

color line 〖美〗(亦作 **color bar**) 白人與黑人在社會、政治及經濟上之界限。***draw the color line*** 分黑白種族界限。

col·or·man [ˈkʌləmən; ˈkʌləmən] *n., pl.* **-men.** ①〖英〗顏料商。②調染料工人。

color photography 彩色照相。

color printing 彩色版;彩色印刷。

color sergeant 〖軍〗護旗士官。

color television 彩色電視。

color transparency 彩色幻燈片。

col·or·y [ˈkʌlərɪ; ˈkʌləri] *adj.* ①〖俗〗色澤甚濃的。②〖商〗有優良品質之色澤的。

***co·los·sal** [kəˈlɑsl̩; kəˈlɔsl] *adj.* 巨大的。*colossal* folly. 大大的荒唐。—**ly,** *adv.*

Col·os·se·um [ˌkɑləˈsiəm; ˌkɔləˈsiəm] *n.* 古羅馬之圓形大劇場。

co·los·sus [kəˈlɑsəs; kəˈlɔsəs] *n., pl.* **-los·si** [-ˈlɑsaɪ; -ˈlɔsai], **-los·sus·es.** ①巨大石像。②(C-) Rhodes 島 (土耳其西南) 上 Apollo 神之巨像。③任何巨大之物或人。

co·los·to·my [kəˈlɑstəmɪ; kəˈlɔstəmi] *n., pl.* **-mies.** 〖醫〗結腸造口術;結腸造瘻術。

co·los·trum [kəˈlɑstrəm; kəˈlɔstrəm] *n.* 初乳。

co·lot·o·my [kəˈlɑtəmɪ; kəˈlɔtəmi] *n., pl.* **-mies.** 〖醫〗結腸切開術。

col·pi·tis [kolˈpaɪtɪs; koulˈpaitis] *n.* 〖醫〗陰道炎。

col·por·teur [ˈkɑlˌportə; ˈkɔlˌpɔːtə] *n.* 販賣書籍者;分送宗教書籍者。

Colt [kolt; koult] *n.* 柯爾特公司之左輪槍及其他火器。

***colt** [kolt; koult] *n.* ①雄馬駒 (四歲或五歲以下者);小驢駒;小斑馬。②無經驗的年輕人。③〖航海〗末端有結的繩子。

col·ter [ˈkoltə; ˈkoultə] *n.* 犂刃;犂頭鐵。(亦作 **coulter**)

colt·ish [ˈkoltɪʃ; ˈkoultiʃ] *adj.* 似小馬的;輕佻的;放蕩的。

colts·foot [ˈkoltsˌfʊt; ˈkoultsfut] *n.* 〖植物〗款冬。

col·u·brine [ˈkɑljəˌbraɪn; ˈkɔljubrain] *adj.* 蛇的;似蛇的。

col·um·bar·i·um [ˌkɑləmˈbɛrɪəm; ˌkɔləmˈbɛəriəm] *n.* ①古羅馬地下墓窟中之藏骨灰所。②鴿房。

Co·lum·bi·a [kəˈlʌmbɪə; kəˈlʌmbiə] *n.* ①哥倫比亞 (**a.** 美國西北部一河流。**b.** 美國南卡羅來納州之首府。**c.** 美國米蘇里州中部一城市)。②〖詩〗美洲;美國。③一種雜種羊。***District of Columbia*** (略作 **D. C.**) (美國)哥倫比亞特區。

Co·lum·bi·an [kəˈlʌmbɪən; kəˈlʌmbiən] *adj.* ①美洲的;美國的。②哥倫布 (Columbus)的。—*n.* 〖印刷〗一種活字。

col·um·bine [ˈkɑləmˌbaɪn; ˈkɔləmbain] *n.* 〖植物〗耬斗菜。—*adj.* 鴿的;似鴿的。

co·lum·bi·um [kəˈlʌmbɪəm; kəˈlʌmbiəm] *n.* 〖化〗鈳(元素名,現改稱niobium).

Co·lum·bus [kəˈlʌmbəs; kəˈlʌmbəs] *n.* ①哥倫布 (Christopher, 1446?–1506, 義大利人, 於1492年發現美洲)。②美國俄亥俄州 (Ohio) 首府。

Columbus Day 哥倫布發現美洲紀念日(十月十二日)。

col·u·mel·la [ˌkɑljuˈmɛlə; ˌkɔljuˈme-

lə] *n., pl.* **-lae** [-li; -liː]. ①小柱。②〖植物〗果軸；子柱。③〖動物〗殼軸；軸柱。
—col·u·mel·lar, *adj.*

***col·umn** [ˈkɑləm; ˈkɔləm] *n.* ①圓柱；柱。②細長而直如柱的東西。a *column* of mercury in a thermometer. 寒暑表的水銀柱。③欄；段。There are two *columns* on each page of this book. 這本書每頁有二欄。④軍隊的縱隊；艦隊的縱列。⑤報紙上的一欄。⑥專欄文章。

co·lum·nar [kəˈlʌmnɚ; kəˈlʌmnə] *adj.* ①如柱的。②(圓) 柱構成的。③分欄印刷或書寫的。

col·umned [ˈkɑləmd; ˈkɔləmd] *adj.* ①有柱的；立有圓柱的。②＝**columnar.**

co·lum·ni·a·tion [kə,lʌmnɪˈeʃən; kə,lʌmniˈeiʃən] *n.* 〖建築〗①柱之使用。②柱之集合稱。

col·umn·ist [ˈkɑləmɪst; ˈkɔləmnist] *n.* 專欄作家。

co·lure [koˈljur; kəˈljuə] *n.* 〖天文〗分至圈。the equinoctial *colure.* 二分圈。

col·za [ˈkɑlzə; ˈkɔlzə] *n.* ①芥菜之類；菜籽。②菜籽油。***colza oil*** 菜籽油；菜油。

Com. ①Commander. ②Commission. ③Commissioner. ④Committee. ⑤Commodore. ⑥Communist. **com.**[1] ①comedy. ②comma. **com.**[2] ①command; commander. ②commentary. ③commerce. ④commercial. ⑤common. ⑥commonly. ⑦commune. ⑧communication. ⑨community. ⑩communist. ⑪commission.

com- 〖字首〗表"共同；聯合；組合"之義。

co·ma[1] [ˈkomə; ˈkoumə] *n., pl.* **co·mas.** 〖醫〗昏迷；昏睡。

co·ma[2] *n., pl.* **-mae** [-mi; -miː]. ①〖光學〗彗形像差。②〖植物〗種髮；種芒。

co·mate [koˈmet; kouˈmeit] *n.* 同伴。

com·a·tose [ˈkɑmə,tos; ˈkoumətous] *adj.* ①昏睡的；昏迷的。②似昏迷的。

comb** [kom; koum] *n.* ①頭梳。②用以清理毛、棉、麻等的梳。③梳狀的東西；用途如梳的東西 (如馬梳)。④蜂房；蜂巢。⑤鷄冠。⑥浪頭。 ***cut the comb of a person 挫人銳氣；使屈服。 *—v.t.* ①梳 (髮)；刷 (馬毛等)。to *comb* one's hair. 梳(某人的)頭髮。②到處搜尋。③除去。to *comb* out head lice. 除去頭蝨。④當梳子用。⑤橫掃；掃射。 *—v.i.* 起浪花；起浪。***comb one's hair the wrong way*** 使人發怒。***comb one's head*** 打人。

comb. ①combination. ②combining.

***com·bat** [ˈkɑmbæt, ˈkʌm-, *for v. also* kəmˈbæt; ˈkɔmbət, ˈkʌm-, -æt] *v.,* **-bat(t)ed, -bat·(t)ing,** *n.* *—v.i.* 格鬥；爭鬥〖with, against〗. to *combat* with one's opponents. 與敵手格鬥。*—v.t.* 格鬥；爭鬥；對抗；極力反對。*—n.* 戰鬥；爭鬥。a mortal *combat.* 生死之戰。

com·bat·ant [ˈkɑmbətənt; ˈkɔmbətənt] *adj.* ①戰鬥的。②好鬥的。*—n.* 戰鬥員。

combat boot 短統軍靴。

combat car 裝甲車。

combat command 戰鬥指揮部。

combat duty 戰鬥任務。

combat fatigue 前線士兵的神經疲倦。(亦作 **battle fatigue**)

combat intelligence 戰鬥情報。

com·bat·ive [kəmˈbætɪv; ˈkɔmbətiv] *adj.* ①好鬥的。②鬥志旺盛的。 **—ly,** *adv.* **—ness,** *n.*

com·ba·tiv·i·ty [,kɑmbəˈtɪvətɪ; ,kɔmbəˈtiviti] *n.* ①好鬥性。②鬥志。

combat orders 戰鬥命令。

combat plane 戰鬥機。

combat ration 野戰口糧。

com·bat-read·y [ˈkɑmbæt,rɛdɪ; ˈkɔmbət,redi] *adj.* 有戰備的。

combat team 戰鬥聯隊；團戰鬥羣。

combat unit 戰鬥部隊；戰鬥單位。

combat zone 戰區。

combe [kum; kuːm] *n.* 〖英〗峽谷；深谷。

comb·er [ˈkomɚ; ˈkoumə] *n.* ①梳刷之人或器具。②捲浪。

com·bi·na·tion** [,kɑmbəˈneʃən; ,kɔmbiˈneiʃən] *n.* ①聯合；結合；組合。②組合物。③化合。chemical *combination.* 化合。④團體。⑤汗衫與褲子連於一起之內衣。⑥〖數學〗配合。⑦(開鎖時之)暗碼。the *combination* of a safe. 保險箱的暗碼。⑧保險箱的鎖。in combination with*** 與…共同。*—adj.* ①組合的；混合的；結合的；合併的。②兼兩用的。

combination car (具有兩種以上不同用途之)混合車廂。

combination lock 暗碼鎖。

com·bi·na·tive [ˈkɑmbə,netɪv; ˈkɔmbinətiv] *adj.* ①結合的；聯合的；組合的。②有結合力的；有化合力的。③由於結合、聯合或化合而造成的。

‡com·bine [*v.* kəmˈbaɪn; kəmˈbain *n.* ˈkɑmbaɪn, kəmˈbaɪn; ˈkɔmbain, kəmˈbain] *v.,* **-bined, -bin·ing,** *n.* *—v.t.* ①聯合；結合。to *combine* theory with practice. 將理論與實踐合而爲一。②同時具有；同時顯示。*—v.i.* ①化合。②聯合；結合；混合。Oil and water do not readily *combine.* 油和水不易混合。*—n.* ①〖美俗〗團體；組合。②〖美〗聯合收割打穀機。

combined action 聯合行動；協同戰鬥。

combined fleet 聯合艦隊。

combined operations 聯合作戰。

comb·ing [ˈkomɪŋ; ˈkoumiŋ] *n.* ①梳刷；梳洗。②(*pl.*) 梳下之毛或髮。

combing machine 刷毛機。

combining form 〖文法〗連結型(只見於複合字而從不單獨使用之語型)；字素。

com·bo [ˈkɑmbo; ˈkɔmbou] *n., pl.* **-bos.** ①小型爵士樂隊。②〖俗〗聯合之物；聯合組織。

comb-out [ˈkom,aut; ˈkoum-aut] *n.* ①梳理頭髮；做頭髮。②尋查；清除。

com·bust [kəmˈbʌst; kəmˈbʌst] *v.t.* 消耗(燃料)。*—v.i.* ①燃燒。②消耗燃料。

com·bus·ti·ble [kəmˈbʌstəbl̩; kəmˈbʌstəbl] *adj.* ①易燃的。②易激動的；易怒的。*—n.* 易燃物。**—com·bus·ti·bil·i·ty,** *n.*

com·bus·tion** [kəmˈbʌstʃən; kəmˈbʌstʃən] *n.* ①燃燒。②伴以高溫度和發光的氧化。③無高溫度和光的慢氧化。④喧囂；爭擾。 ***spontaneous combustion 自燃。
—com·bus·tive, *adj.*

com·bus·tor [kəmˈbʌstɚ; kəmˈbʌstə] *n.* 噴射引擎之燃燒室。

comdg. commanding.

Comdr., comdr. commander.

Comdt., comdt. commandant.

‡come [kʌm; kʌm] *v.,* **came, come, com·ing.** *—v.i.* ①來。*Come* here! 來這裏！②到。He hasn't *come* yet. 他尚未到。③出現。④伸至；及。⑤發生。What will *come,* let *come.* 要發生的事，讓它發生好了。⑥結

果。⑦出身。The boy *comes* of a poor family. 這小孩出身貧家。⑧成爲;變爲。His dream *came* true. 他的夢想實現了。⑨進入。to *come* into use. 被用。⑩思及;發見。⑪等於;總共。The total *comes* to $100. 總數共一百元。⑫有;裝;存。This dress *comes* in four sizes. 這衣服有四種尺寸。⑬(要做到或得到)是(容易、困難等)。Good clothes *come* high. 好衣服需付高價。⑭注意(常作命令式)。*Come,* we must hurry. 聽我講,我們得趕快。⑮心變軟;開始同情。He'll relent; he's *coming.* 他會寬恕的;他開始軟化了。⑯〖俚〗(性交時)達到興奮之頂點。—*v.t.* ①〖俗〗做;爲。He tried to *come* a trick over his old pal. 他想對自己的老友來個惡作劇。②達到(某一年齡)。a pretty child *coming* eight years old. 快八歲的漂亮孩子。③扮演。④〖英〗完成;達成。***come about*** **a.** 發生。**b.** 改變方向。***come across*** **a.** 偶然遇到;找到。**b.**〖俗〗交付;償付。***come again***〖俚〗你說甚麼?請再說一遍。***come*** (***up***) ***against*** **a.** 遇到。**b.** 攻擊。***come along*** **a.** 伴隨;陪伴。**b.** 進行;進步。**c.** 趕快。***come around*** (or ***round***) **a.** 恢復知覺或健康。**b.** 讓步;同意;屈服。**c.** 轉方向。***come at*** **a.** 攻擊;撲向。**b.** 得到;找到。***come away*** **a.** 散開。**b.** 離開。**c.** 發芽。***come back*** **a.** 回來。**b.**〖俗〗恢復原狀或原位;捲土重來;憶起。**c.**〖俚〗回口。***come between*** **a.** 分開;離間。**b.** 居…間。***come by*** **a.** 獲得。**b.** 走近;經過。**c.** 藉…爲交通工具而來;由…來。***come down*** **a.** 下來;降下。**b.** 下得大(如雨)。**c.** 失掉(階級、金錢、地位)。**d.** 傳遞;傳給。**e.** 生病。**f.** 減價;跌價。***come down on*** (or ***upon***) **a.** 斥責;重責。**b.** 突然攻擊。**c.** 表示反對。***come down with*** 付款。***come for*** **a.** 爲某種目的而來。**b.** 取;攜;接。***come forward*** 提出;自願效勞。***come from*** **a.** 來自。**b.** 出生於。***come in*** **a.** 開始;開始使用…。**b.** 進入。**c.**(競賽中)獲選。**d.** 開始生產。***come in for*** 得到;接受。***come in handy*** 可能有用。***come into*** **a.** 承繼。**b.** 進入。***come into effect*** (or ***force***) 生效。***come into one's own*** 獲得有權得到的東西。***come into sight*** 出現;進入視線所及範圍之內。***come of*** 出身。***come of age*** 成年。***come off*** **a.** 舉行。**b.** 結果。**c.** 成功。**d.** 離開。***come off it***〖俚〗停止假裝高尚。***come on*** (or ***upon***) **a.** 進行;進展;發展。**b.** 遇到;發現。**c.** 上臺。**d.** 開始;出現。**e.**〖俗〗趕快(常用命令式)。*Come on,* before it rains! 趕快,趁着天還未下雨。**f.**〖俗〗請(常用懇求語氣)。**g.**〖俚〗產生某種效果;予人某種印象。***come on to*** 開始。It *came on to* rain. 開始下雨。***come out*** **a.** 出現。**b.** 刊出。**c.** 參加。**d.** 初入社會;初次出現於交際界。**e.** 結果。***come out with*** **a.** 被伴隨着。**b.** 洩露。**c.** 說出。**d.** 向大衆提供。***come over*** **a.** 訪問。**b.** 發生。**c.** 占住;侵占。**d.** 占上風。***come round*** **a.** 訪問;來訪。**b.** 恢復知覺。***come short of*** **a.** 缺少。**b.** 失敗;失望。He *came short of* my expectation. 他使我失望。***come through*** **a.** 成功。**b.** 交出;付。**c.** 經歷宗教信仰的改變。***come to*** **a.** 恢復知覺。**b.** 發生。**c.** 憶及。**d.** 停止;下錨。**e.** 總數達…。***come to a decision*** 作一決定。***come to an agreement*** 達成協議。***come to an end*** 終止。***come to a standstill*** 陷入僵局;停止。***come to blows*** 開始交戰;打起架來。***come to grief*** (or ***harm***) 遭遇不幸;遇到意外事件。***come to light*** 顯露眞相;明朗化。***come to one's notice*** 注意及;注意到。***come to one's senses; come to oneself*** **a.** 蘇醒。**b.** 變聰明;變機智。***come to pass*** 發生。***come to terms*** (***with***)(與…)獲致協議。The employers and their workmen at last *came to terms.* 雇主與工人最後獲得了協議。***come under*** **a.** 應列入…;應屬於…。**b.** 應歸…管或處理。***come up*** **a.** 前來。**b.** 生長;發展。**c.** 被提及;出現。**d.** 被提出討論。***come up to*** 達到某一水準。***come up with*** **a.** 追及。**b.** 取出。**c.** 建議。***come what may*** 無論有何變化。

come-and-go [ˈkʌmənˈgo; ˈkʌmənˈgou] *adj.* 不定的。

come-at-a·ble [kʌmˈætəbl; kʌmˈætəbl] *adj.*〖俗〗易接近的;易獲得的;可近的。

come·back [ˈkʌmˌbæk; ˈkʌmbæk] *n.* ①〖俗〗回復;重返;東山再起。②〖俚〗機智的回答;反唇相譏;辯駁。③〖美俚〗抱怨或不滿之理由或根據。

co·me·di·an [kəˈmidiən; kəˈmiːdjən] *n.* ①喜劇演員。②喜劇作家。③滑稽人物;有趣的人(往往有諷刺之意)。

co·me·dic [kəˈmidɪk; kəˈmiːdik] *adj.* 喜劇(性)的;有關喜劇的。(亦作 **comedical**)

co·me·di·enne [kəˌmidɪˈɛn; kəˌmediˈen] *n.* 喜劇女演員。

co·me·di·et·ta [kəˌmidɪˈɛtə; kəˌmediˈetə] *n.* 小喜劇;短滑稽戲。

com·e·dist [ˈkɑmədɪst; ˈkɔmidist] *n.* 喜劇作家。

com·e·do [ˈkɑmɪˌdo; ˈkɔmidou] *n., pl.* **-dos, com·e·do·nes** [ˌkɑmɪˈdoniz; ˌkɔmiˈdouniːz]. 黑頭粉刺;面皰。

come·down [ˈkʌmˌdaun; ˈkʌmdaun] *n.* 零落;衰落;退步;(階級、地位等之)降落。

***com·e·dy** [ˈkɑmədɪ; ˈkɔmidi] *n., pl.* **-dies.** ①喜劇。I prefer *comedy* to tragedy. 我喜歡喜劇甚於悲劇。②喜劇性。③有趣的事情;好玩的事;任何令人發噱的事。

comedy of manners (起源於十七世紀英國之)諷刺某社會階級習俗的喜劇。

come-hith·er [ˌkʌmˈhɪðə; ˌkʌmˈhiðə] *adj.* 引誘的。—*n.* 引誘;誘惑。

come·ly [ˈkʌmlɪ; ˈkʌmli] *adj.,* **-li·er, -li·est.** ①漂亮的;美麗的;悅目的。②合宜的;適宜的。③令人愉快的。—**come·li·ness,** *n.*

come-on [ˈkʌmˌɑn; ˈkʌmɔn] *n.*〖美俚〗①勸誘;誘惑。②〖俚〗騙子。③誘人之外貌或姿態。④用作誘惑之物;誘餌。

come-out·er [ˌkʌmˈautə; ˌkʌmˈautə] *n.*〖美俗〗脫離者(尤指脫離宗教團體者);激進改革者。

com·er [ˈkʌmə; ˈkʌmə] *n.* ①來者;新來者。First *comers* will be served first. 先來的人先吃。②〖俚〗有成功希望的人或事。

co·mes·ti·ble [kəˈmɛstəbl; kəˈmestibl] *adj.* 可食的;食用的。—*n.* (常 *pl.*)食品;食物。—**ar·y, —ic,** *adj.*

***com·et** [ˈkɑmɪt; ˈkɔmit] *n.* 彗星。

come·up·pance [kʌmˈʌpəns; kʌmˈʌpəns] *n.*〖美俚〗應得之責罰;因果報應。

com·fit [ˈkʌmfɪt; ˈkʌmfit] *n.* 糖果;蜜餞。

‡**com·fort** [ˈkʌmfət; ˈkʌmfət] *v.t.* ①安慰;鼓舞。②使安逸;使舒適。③〖法律〗幫助;支持。—*n.* ①安慰;慰藉。②安樂;舒適。He lives in *comfort.* 他生活很舒適。③使生活安樂之人或物;舒適的設備。The hotel possesses every modern *comfort.* 這旅館有各種新式的舒適設備。④棉被;被褥。⑤〖法律〗

幫助;支持。

:com·fort·a·ble ['kʌmfətəbl; 'kʌmfətəbl] *adj.* ①安逸的;安樂的;舒適的;愉快的。He lives a *comfortable* life. 他過着舒適的生活。②(覺得)舒服的。③容易相處的。She's a *comfortable* person to be with. 她是個容易相處的人。④充裕的;豐富的。a *comfortable* income. 相當豐富的收入。—**ness,** *n.*

***com·fort·a·bly** ['kʌmfətəblɪ; 'kʌmfətəbli] *adv.* 舒舒服服地;安樂地;安逸地。They live plainly but *comfortably*. 他們的生活簡單但舒適。

com·fort·er ['kʌmfətə; 'kʌmfətə] *n.* ①安慰者;安慰之物。②〖美〗棉被;尼龍被。③一種很長的羊毛圍巾。④(the C-) 聖靈。

com·fort·less ['kʌmfətlɪs; 'kʌmfətlis] *adj.* 不愉快的;不安適的;不舒服的。—**ly,** *adv.* —**ness,** *n.*

comfort station 公共盥洗室或休息室。

comfort stop 〖美〗(公路長途客車方便旅客的)休息停車。

com·frey ['kʌmfrɪ; 'kʌmfri] *n., pl.* **-freys.** 紫草科植物。

com·fy ['kʌmfɪ; 'kʌmfi] *adj.,* **-fi·er, -fi·est.** 〖俗〗 =**comfortable.**

com·ic** ['kamɪk; 'kɔmik] *adj.* ①使人發笑的;有趣的;滑稽的。a *comic* song. 滑稽的歌曲。②喜劇的。③連環圖畫的。—*n.(pl.)* (亦作 **comic strips**) 連環圖畫。the comic*** 文學、人生等滑稽有趣的一面。

***com·i·cal** ['kamɪkl; 'kɔmikəl] *adj.* 滑稽的;詼諧的;可笑的。—**ly,** *adv.*

com·i·cal·i·ty [ˌkamɪ'kælətɪ; ˌkɔmi'kæliti] *n.* ①滑稽性;詼諧。②滑稽可笑之事物。

comic book 連環圖畫册。

comic opera 喜歌劇。

comic paper 報紙之連環圖畫版。

comic relief ①喜劇性穿插(悲劇中給觀衆暫時性鬆懈之有趣穿插)。②喜劇性鬆懈(由此種穿插所產生)。

comic strip 連續漫畫;連環圖畫。

COMINCH 〖美海軍〗Commander in Chief. **Com. in Chf.** Commander in Chief.

Com·in·form ['kamɪnˌfɔrm; 'kɔminfɔ:m] *n.* 共產黨情報局(爲 Communist Information Bureau 之略)。

:com·ing ['kʌmɪŋ; 'kʌmiŋ] *n.* 來。—*adj.* ①其次的;將來的。the *coming* year. 來年。②〖俗〗將成爲重要的;將成名的。a *coming* young actor. 一個即將露頭角的年輕演員。

com·ing-out ['kʌmɪŋˌaut; 'kʌmiŋaut] *n.* (少女的)初次在社交場合露面。a *coming-out* ball. 爲 coming-out 而舉行的舞會。

comings and goings 活動。

Com·in·tern ['kamɪnˌtɜn; 'kɔmintə:n] *n.* 共產主義國際;共產黨第三國際(1919年成立於莫斯科, 1943 年解散)。(亦作 **Komintern**)

co·mi·ti·a [kə'mɪʃɪə; kə'miʃiə] *n. pl.* 「(古羅馬之)國民會議;公民會議。」

com·i·trag·e·dy [ˌkamə'trædʒədɪ; ˌkɔmi'trædʒidi] *n.* 喜悲劇。

com·i·ty ['kamətɪ; 'kɔmiti] *n., pl.* **-ties.** ①禮讓;禮儀。②團結;聯合。

comity of nations ①國際間之禮儀及互相尊重。②履行此種禮儀之國家。

coml. commercial. **comm.** 參看 **com.**

***com·ma** ['kamə; 'kɔmə] *n.* 逗點(,)。

comma bacillus 霍亂弧菌;撇菌。

:com·mand [kə'mænd; kə'ma:nd] *v.t.* ①命令。He *commanded* silence. 他命令大家肅靜。②統率;指揮。③臨視;俯視。④把握;支配。He cannot *command* so large a sum of money. 他不能支配這樣大筆的款子。⑤應得;博得。to *command* respect. 使人敬仰。⑥控制;克制。—*v.i.* ①指揮。Who *commands* here? 誰負責這兒的指揮任務? ②俯視。—*n.* ①命令。to obey *command.* 服從命令。②統率權;指揮權。The general is in *command* of the army. 此將軍負責指揮陸軍。③管轄下的軍隊、艦隊或地區。④控制。⑤支配;使用;運用。She had a good *command* of French. 她精通法文。⑥俯視。the *command* of the valley from the hill. 從山上對山谷的鳥瞰。⑦口令。⑧司令部。the Taiwan Garrison *Command.* 臺灣警備司令部。***at one's command*** 供某人支配;擁有。—*adj.* ①指揮的;用於指揮的。②指揮官的。③君主所命令的;奉敕令的;似奉敕令的;迫於情勢的。—**a·ble,** *adj.*

com·man·dant [ˌkamən'dænt; ˌkɔmən'dænt] *n.* ①司令官;指揮官。②軍事學校校長。③〖美〗海軍陸戰隊司令。(亦作 **comandante**)

command car 指揮車。

com·man·deer [ˌkamən'dɪr; ˌkɔmən'diə] *v.t.* ①徵募(兵丁等)。②徵用。③〖俗〗奪占;霸占。

***com·mand·er** [kə'mændə; kə'ma:ndə] *n.* ①司令官;指揮官。②海軍中校;副艦長。③某些社團中的資深會員。—**ship,** *n.*

commander in chief *pl.* **commanders in chief.** ①統帥;總司令;大元帥。②陸軍、海軍或空軍某部分的司令官。

command guidance 導向飛彈等飛行時的電子遙控系統。

com·mand·ing [kə'mændɪŋ; kə'ma:ndiŋ] *adj.* ①指揮的;有權威的。②有威儀的;堂堂的。③眺望無阻的;居高臨下的。

commanding officer 〖美軍〗任何自少尉至上校階級之指揮官。

com·mand·ment** [kə'mændmənt; kə'ma:ndmənt] *n.* ①戒律。②〖聖經〗聖誡。③命令;指令;法律。the Ten Commandments*** 〖聖經〗十誡。

command mod·ule [~'madjul; ~'mɔdju:l] (登月太空船之)指揮艙;駕駛艙。

com·man·do [kə'mændo; kə'ma:ndou] *n., pl.* **-dos** or **-does.** ①〖英〗突擊兵;突擊隊。②突擊;突襲。③(南非之)民兵。

command paper 〖英〗內閣大臣奉王命向國會提出之報告或文件。

command performance 御前演出。

command post 〖美軍〗戰地指揮所。

comme il faut [kɔmil'fo; kɔmi:l'fou] 〖法〗當然的(地);適當的(地)。

com·mem·o·ra·ble [kə'mɛmərəbl; kə'memərəbl] *adj.* 値得記憶的;値得紀念或慶祝的。

com·mem·o·rate [kə'mɛməˌret; kə'meməreit] *v.t.,* **-rat·ed, -rat·ing.** ①紀念;慶祝。②表揚。—**com·mem·o·ra·tor,** *n.*

com·mem·o·ra·tion [kəˌmɛmə'reʃən; kəˌmemə'reiʃən] *n.* 紀念;慶祝。***in commemoration of*** 紀念。

com·mem·o·ra·tive [kə'mɛməretɪv; kə'memərətiv] *adj.* (亦作 **commemoratory**) 紀念的;慶祝的。—*n.* 紀念之物。

***com·mence** [kə'mɛns; kə'mens] *v.,* **-menced, -menc·ing.** —*v.t.* 開始;着手。to *commence* learning English. 開始學英文。—*v.i.* 開始。The second term *commences* in March. 第二學期自三月開始。

***com·mence·ment** [kə'mɛnsmənt; kə'mensmənt] *n.* ①開始。at the *commencement* of the twentieth century. 二十世紀開始時。②畢業式;畢業典禮。When will be your *commencement?* 你們幾時行畢業典禮? ③畢業日;文憑或學位授予日。

***com·mend** [kə'mɛnd; kə'mend] *v.t.* ①稱讚。His work was highly *commended.* 他的工作大受稱讚。②推薦。to *commend* a person to one's friend. 推薦某人於朋友。③委託;付託。④吸引;引起興趣;給以良好印象。—**a·ble,** *adj.* —**a·bly,** *adv.*

com·men·da·tion [ˌkamən'deʃən; ˌkɔmen'deiʃən] *n.* ①稱讚;讚揚。②獎狀。***commendation of the soul*** 臨終時之祈禱。

com·mend·a·to·ry [kə'mɛndəˌtorɪ; kə'mendətəri] *adj.* 推薦的;稱讚的。a *commendatory* letter. 推薦信。

com·men·sal [kə'mɛnsəl; kə'mensəl] *adj.* ①共餐的;同食的。②〖生物〗共生的。—*n.* ①同桌進餐的人。②共生的動物或植物。—**ism,** —**i·ty,** *n.*

com·men·su·ra·ble [kə'mɛnʃərəbḷ; kə'menʃərəbl] *adj.* ①有同量的;有公度的;能較量的。②相稱的;適當的〖to〗。③可通約的。—**com·men·su·ra·bil·i·ty,** *n.*

commensurable number 〖數學〗盡數。

commensurable quantity 〖數學〗盡量。

com·men·su·rate [kə'mɛnʃərɪt; kə'menʃərit] *adj.* ①同量的;同大小的。②相稱的;適當的;相當的。③可以用同一標準比較的。—**com·men·su·ra·tion,** *n.* —**ly,** *adv.*

***com·ment** ['kamɛnt; 'kɔment] *n.* ①註解;註釋;批評。He made no *comment* on the subject. 他對這問題未作批評。②閒談;談話;談論。—*v.i.* ①註釋;批評〖on, upon〗. to *comment* on current events. 評論時事。②談論。—*v.t.* 談論;評論。—**er,** *n.*

com·men·tar·y ['kamənˌtɛrɪ; 'kɔməntəri] *n., pl.* **-tar·ies.** ①註解;註釋。②評註;評語。③(常 *pl.*)紀事。—**com·men·tar·i·al,** *adj.*

com·men·ta·tor ['kamənˌtetɚ; 'kɔmenteitə] *n.* ①註釋者;評註者。②時事評論家。

‡**com·merce** ['kamɝs; 'kɔməːs] *n.* ①商業;商務;貿易。international *commerce.* 國際貿易。②交往;社交。

***com·mer·cial** [kə'mɝʃəl; kə'məːʃəl] *adj.* ①商業的;與商業有關的;商務的。New York is a *commercial* city. 紐約是一個商業的城市。②出售的;商用的;工業用的。a *commercial* product. 商業產品。③由廣告資助的。a *commercial* radio program. 無線電營業廣告節目。—*n.* 無線電或電視的商業廣告。—**ly,** *adv.*

commercial agency 商業徵信機構。

commercial art 商業美術。

commercial attaché (大使館或公使館的)商務幫辦。

commercial club 商會 (=chamber of commerce).

commercial code 商業電碼。

commercial college 商學院;商業專科學校。

commercial credit 商業貸款。

com·mer·cial·ism [kə'mɝʃəlˌɪzəm; kə'məːʃəlizm] *n.* ①商業主義;重商主義。②商業精神。③商業慣例或用語。—**com·mer·cial·ist,** *n.*

com·mer·cial·ize [kə'mɝʃəlˌaɪz; kə'məːʃəlaiz] *v.t.,* **-ized, -iz·ing.** ①使商業化。②以商業主義使變低俗。③使商品化。—**com·mer·cial·i·za·tion,** *n.*

commercial law 商法。

commercial letter of credit 信用狀。

commercial museum 商品博覽館。

commercial paper 商業本票;商業票據。

commercial traveler 〖英〗旅行推銷員。

com·mie ['kamɪ; 'kɔmi] *n., pl.* **-mies.** 共產黨員;共產黨徒。(亦作 **Commie, commy**)

com·mi·nate ['kaməˌnet; 'kɔmineit] *v.t. & v.i.,* **-nat·ed, -nat·ing.** 威嚇;詛咒。—**com·mi·na·tion,** *n.* —**com·min·a·to·ry,** *adj.*

com·min·gle [kə'mɪŋgḷ; kə'miŋgl] *v.i. & v.t.,* **-gled, -gling.** 混合;摻合;混雜。

com·mi·nute ['kaməˌnjut; 'kɔminjuːt] *v.t.,* **-nut·ed, -nut·ing.** 弄成粉末;粉碎;分割;細分。

com·mi·nu·tion [ˌkamə'njuʃən; ˌkɔmi'njuːʃən] *n.* ①粉碎。②磨損。

com·mis·er·ate [kə'mɪzəˌret; kə'mizəreit] *v.,* **-at·ed, -at·ing.** —*v.t.* 憐憫;同情。—*v.i.* 弔慰;慰問〖with〗. to *commiserate* with a person on his loss. 慰問一個人的損失。—**com·mis·er·a·tive,** *adj.*

com·mis·er·a·tion [kəˌmɪzə'reʃən; kəˌmizə'reiʃən] *n.* 憐憫;同情。

com·mis·sar [ˌkamə'sar; ˌkɔmi'saː] *n.* ①部長(蘇聯各共和國中各部首長,現稱爲 minister). ②共產政權機關中主管政治事務的官員。

com·mis·sar·i·al [ˌkamə'sɛrɪəl; ˌkɔmi'sɛəriəl] *adj.* commissary 的;蘇聯之委員或代表的;軍需官的;供應糧食或日用品之商店的。

com·mis·sar·i·at [ˌkamə'sɛrɪət; ˌkɔmi'sɛəriət] *n.* ①〖軍〗聯合勤務;軍需處。②蘇聯政府之部會。③食物供應;給養。

com·mis·sar·y ['kaməˌsɛrɪ; 'kɔmisəri] *n., pl.* **-sar·ies.** ①蘇聯之各部部長;委員;代表。②軍需官。③(軍隊、礦場、林場中的)供應食物及日用品的商店。④〖宗教〗主教之特別代理。

‡**com·mis·sion** [kə'mɪʃən; kə'miʃən] *n.* ①委託;委任;委任狀。a *commission* to serve as notary public. 充當公證人的委任狀。②陸海軍的任命書。③陸海軍的職位和權力。④授權;授予之權力。⑤委託代辦的事。⑥考察團;調查團;委員會。⑦行爲。the *commission* of a crime. 犯罪。⑧佣金;酬勞金。Some salesmen in big shops receive a *commission* of 10% on everything they sell, as well as a salary. 大商店中有些店員得到所售貨物百分之十的佣金,還有薪金。⑨商業上的代理權。***in commission*** **a.** 服役的。**b.** 可用的。***on commission*** 委託。to sell goods *on commission.* 出賣寄售的貨物。***out of commission*** **a.** 退役的。**b.** 不能用的。The motor is *out of commission.* 發動機壞了。***put in*** (or ***into***) ***commission*** 使船艦服現役。—*v.t.* ①委任;授權;委託。②任命。*commissioned* officers. 少尉以上的軍官。③使(船艦)服役。

com·mis·sion·aire [kəˌmɪʃən'ɛr; kəˌmiʃə'nɛə] *n.* 〖英〗(電影院、戲院、旅館、百

貨店等的)門警;聽差;信差。

***com·mis·sion·er** [kəˈmɪʃənə; kəˈmiʃənə] *n.* ①委員;(考察團等之)團員。②政府中某一部門的長官;廳長;處長;局長。*Commissioner* of Customs. 海關稅務司長。

commission house 證券經紀公司。

commission merchant 掮客;代銷商。

Commission on Human Rights (聯合國)人權委員會。

Commission on the Status of Women (聯合國)婦女地位委員會。

commission plan 由選出之委員會執掌市政之制度。

com·mis·su·ral [kəˈmɪʃərəl; ˌkɔmiˈsjuərəl] *adj.* 接合的;縫合的。

com·mis·sure [ˈkɑmɪˌʃʊr; ˈkɔmisjuə] *n.* ①接合處;縫口。②〖解剖〗接合纖維組織。

***com·mit** [kəˈmɪt; kəˈmit] *v.t.*, **-mit·ted, -mit·ting.** ①委託;委任。He *committed* himself to the doctor's care. 他將自己(健康)委請醫生照料。②藏於;付於。to *commit* it to writing. 將它寫下來。③監禁;下獄。 to *commit* him to jail. 將他監禁。④授與;付託。⑤作;犯。 to *commit* an error. 做錯事。⑥發交(議案等)於委員會。⑦束縛;受拘束。 ⑧將(軍隊)投入(戰場)。—**ta·ble,** —**ti·ble,** *adj.*

com·mit·ment [kəˈmɪtmənt; kəˈmitmənt] *n.* ①行爲;犯罪。②委託;委任。③監禁;禁閉。④約定;承諾。⑤獻身。

com·mit·tal [kəˈmɪtl; kəˈmitl] *n.* ①監禁;禁閉。②獻身。③埋葬。

:com·mit·tee [kəˈmɪtɪ; kəˈmiti] *n.* 委員會。He is a member of the *Committee* on Education. 他是教育委員會的委員。***standing committee*** 常務委員會。

com·mit·tee·man [kəˈmɪtɪmən; kəˈmitimən] *n., pl.* **-men.** 委員。

committee of the whole (立法機構等之)全體委員會。

Committee of (or **on**) **Ways and Means** (立法機構之)財政委員會。

Committee on Children's Emergency Funds (聯合國)兒童基金委員會。

Committee on the Admission of New Members (聯合國)新會員國准許入會委員會。

com·mit·tee·wom·an [kəˈmɪtɪˌwʊmən; kəˈmitiˌwumən] *n., pl.* **-wom·en.** 女委員。

com·mix·ture [kəˈmɪkstʃə; kəˈmikstʃə] *n.* 混合;混合物。

com·mode [kəˈmod; kəˈmoud] *n.* ①有抽屜之櫥或櫃。②洗臉臺。③室內用之便溺器。④廁所;盥洗室(委婉語)。

com·mo·di·ous [kəˈmodɪəs; kəˈmoudiəs] *adj.* ①寬敞的。②方便的。③合宜的。—**ly,** *adv.* —**ness,** *n.*

***com·mod·i·ty** [kəˈmɑdətɪ; kəˈmɔditi] *n., pl.* **-ties.** 商品;物品。The prices of the *commodities* are quite stable this year. 今年各種物價尙稱穩定。

commodity dollar 商品美元(商品貨幣單位)。

commodity exchange ①商品交易所。②期貨交易。

commodity money 商品貨幣。

com·mo·dore [ˈkɑməˌdor; ˈkɔmədɔː] *n.* ①〖美〗海軍代將。②〖英〗暫時指揮分艦隊之司令官。③巡弋船隊或商船隊中年資最深之船長。④船隊司令官。⑤遊艇俱樂部的主席之敬稱。

:com·mon [ˈkɑmən; ˈkɔmən] *adj.* ①公有的;共有的。Parks in a town are *common* property. 城中的公園爲公有的財產。②聯合的;團結的。to make *common* cause against the enemy. 協力抵抗敵人。③共同的。*common* knowledge. 常識。④常見的;熟識的。⑤普通的;無職位的。⑥劣等的;低等的;下賤的。*common* clothes. 劣等的衣服。⑦粗俗的。*common* manners. 俗態。⑧〖數學〗公有的。⑨聲名狼藉的。a *common* thief. 一個聲名狼藉的小偷。⑩陳腔濫調的。—*n.* ① 公地。② 普通股(集合稱)。Additional shares of *common* will be sold privately. 追加的普通股將私自出售。***in common*** **a.** 相同;相似。**b.** 共有的;公用的。***on short commons*** 缺乏足够的食物。***out of the common*** 不平常的。—**ness,** *n.*

com·mon·age [ˈkɑmənɪdʒ; ˈkɔmənidʒ] *n.* ①共同使用;(牧地)公用權。②公用(牧)地;公地。③平民;大衆。

com·mon·al·ty [ˈkɑmənəltɪ; ˈkɔmənl̩ti] *n., pl.* **-ties.** ①平民;庶民。②人民之集合稱。③共同團體;社會。④社團法人;團體。⑤平凡瑣碎之事物。

common alum 〖化〗硫酸鋁鉀;明礬。

common carrier 運輸業者或公司。

common cold 傷風。

common council 市議會;市民大會。

common denominator ①〖數學〗公分母。②共同特性;共有的特質。

common difference 〖數學〗公差。

common divisor 〖數學〗公約;公約數。

com·mon·er [ˈkɑmənə; ˈkɔmənə] *n.* ①平民。②(牛津大學)普通學生(指無奬學金者)。③有權使用共有地者。***the Great Commoner*** 指英國政治家 William Pitt.

common factor 〖數學〗公因子;公因數。

common gender 〖文法〗(名詞之)通性。

com·mon·land [ˈkɑmənˌlænd; ˈkɔmənlænd] *n.* 公共用地。

common law 不成文法;習慣法。

com·mon-law [ˈkɑmənˈlɔ; ˈkɔmənˈlɔː] *adj.* 習慣法的;有關(依據)習慣法的。

common logarithm 〖數學〗常用對數。

***com·mon·ly** [ˈkɑmənlɪ; ˈkɔmənli] *adv.* 通常地;普通地;普遍地。

Common Market 歐洲共同市場。

Common Marketeer 贊成加入歐洲共同市場的(尤指英國)人。

common measure ①〖數學〗公度;公測度。②〖音樂〗普通拍子;4/4 拍子。(亦作 **common time**)

common multiple 〖數學〗公倍;公倍數。

common noun 〖文法〗普通名詞。(亦作 **common name**)

***com·mon·place** [ˈkɑmənˌples; ˈkɔmənpleis] *adj.* ①普通的;平凡的。a *commonplace* person. 平庸的人。②陳腐的。—*n.* ①老生常談;陳腐之言。What he has said is a mere *commonplace.* 他所說的不過老生常談而已。②普通的事物。

commonplace book 劄記簿。

common pleas 〖法律〗民事訴訟。

common property ①公共財產;公共所有物;屬於大衆的人物。②人人共知之事。

common room 〖主英〗公共休息室。

com·mons [ˈkɑmənz; ˈkɔmənz] *n.*

pl. ①平民。②公共食堂(尤指大學內者)。③公共食堂中的食物。 ***the Commons*** (英國、北愛爾蘭或加拿大的)下議院 (= House of Commons).

common salt 食鹽。

common saying 俗諺。

common school 〖美〗公立小學。

common sense 常識(尤指判斷力)。

com·mon·sense 〔ˈkɑmənˈsɛns; ˈkɔmənˈsens〕 *adj.* 常識的。the *commonsense* interpretation. 基於常識的解釋。(亦作 **common-sense**)

common tangent 〖數學〗公切線。

common touch 平易近人的特徵。

com·mon·weal 〔ˈkɑmən,wil; ˈkɔmənwiːl〕 *n.* 大衆福利。

***com·mon·wealth** 〔ˈkɑmən,wɛlθ; ˈkɔmənwelθ〕 *n.* ①國民的整體; 國家的全體公民。②共和政治。③聯邦。④美國的一州。⑤由某種共同利益而結合的一羣人或國家。⑥(the C-)〖英史〗(自 1649–1660 間 Oliver Cromwell 父子統治下的)共和政體。

Commonwealth of Australia 澳洲聯邦。

Commonwealth of Nations 不列顛國協。(亦作 **the British Commonwealth of Nations**)

common year 平年(閏年之相對語)。

***com·mo·tion** 〔kəˈmoʃən; kəˈmouʃən〕 *n.* ①騷動;暴動;騷擾。to be in *commotion.* 在動盪之中。②政治或社會的擾亂;叛變。civil *commotion.* 民變。

com·move 〔kəˈmuv; kəˈmuːv〕 *v.t.*, **-moved, -mov·ing.** 激動;擾亂。

commr. ①commander. ②commissioner.

com·mu·nal 〔ˈkɑmjʊnl; ˈkɔmjunl〕 *adj.* ①公有的。②公社內的; 社區內的。③社區或公社間的。**—ly,** *adv.*

com·mu·nal·ism 〔ˈkɑmjʊnl,ɪzəm; ˈkɔmjunəlizm〕 *n.* 地方自治主義。**—com·mu·nal·ist,** *n.*

com·mu·nal·is·tic 〔,kɑmjʊnlˈɪstɪk; ,kɔmjunəˈlistik〕 *adj.* 地方自治的。

com·mu·nal·ize 〔ˈkɑmjʊnl,aɪz; ˈkɔmjunəlaiz〕 *v.t.*, **-ized, -iz·ing.** 使公有; 使(某物)歸屬公衆;使公社化。

communal marriage 集團結婚。

com·mu·nard 〔ˈkɑmjunəd; ˈkɔmjuːnəd〕 *n.* 公社的居民。

com·mune[1] 〔*v.* kəˈmjun; kəˈmjuːn *n.* ˈkɑmjun; ˈkɔmjuːn〕 *v.*, **-muned, -mun·ing,** *n.* —*v.i.* ①密談。I would *commune* with you of such matters. 我要和你密談這些事。②感覺同(某人或物)有密切關係。③接受聖餐。—*n.* ①交換思想、意見。②懇談。

com·mune[2] 〔ˈkɑmjun; ˈkɔmjuːn〕 *n.* ①(法國、比利時、義大利、西班牙等國的)最小地方行政區; 自治村。②此種行政區之政府或公民。③原始部落中之代表羣體。④公社。⑤與他人分擔費用或工作而暫時寄居的處所。***the Paris Commune*** 巴黎公社(於 1792及 1871 曾推翻政府)。

com·mu·ni·ca·ble 〔kəˈmjunɪkəbl; kəˈmjuːnikəbl〕 *adj.* ①可傳達的; 可相傳授的。②可傳染的。

com·mu·ni·cant 〔kəˈmjunɪkənt; kəˈmjuːnikənt〕 *n.* ①(基督教)領受聖餐者;教友。②報音信者。—*adj.* 交通的; 相通的〖with〗.

***com·mu·ni·cate** 〔kəˈmjunə,ket; kəˈmjuːnikeit〕 *v.*, **-cat·ed, -cat·ing.** —*v.t.* ①傳染;傳授; 傳遞。to *communicate* a disease. 傳染疾病。②傳達; 通知; 告知。to *communicate* news. 傳達消息。③授聖體給…。—*v.i.* ①聯絡; 通信; 報告。to *communicate* with a person. 與人通信; 與人聯絡。②相通;相連。③接受聖餐;領聖體。④喚起興趣或共鳴。

com·mu·ni·ca·tion** 〔kə,mjunəˈkeʃən; kə,mjuːniˈkeiʃən〕 *n.* ①傳達或交換思想、意見、消息等 (口頭的或書面的)。I am in *communication* with him on this subject. 對於這問題我正與他交換意見。②書信公文或電訊等。③交通; 聯絡; 交通工具;聯絡方法。All *communication* with the east has been stopped by the earthquake. 與東部的一切交通均因地震而斷絕。④傳染疾病。⑤〖宗教〗聖餐之拜受。mass communication*** 大衆傳播(學)。

communication cord (火車內的)緊急通報索。

communication engineering 通信工程。

communications gap 思想上的鴻溝。

communications zone 〖軍〗後勤區。

com·mu·ni·ca·tive 〔kəˈmjunɪ,ketɪv; kəˈmjuːnikətiv〕 *adj.* ①愛說話的。②傳達的;通信的;來往的。

com·mu·ni·ca·tor 〔kəˈmjunə,ketɚ; kəˈmjuːnikeitə〕 *n.* ①傳達之人或物; 通信員;報知器。②發報機。

com·mu·ni·ca·to·ry 〔kəˈmjunə,ketorɪ; kəˈmjuːnikətəri〕 *adj.* 有關通信的。

com·mun·ion 〔kəˈmjunjən; kəˈmjuːnjən〕 *n.* ①共有;共享。②交際;友誼;交換思想和情感。③教友;教會。④領聖餐禮;聖餐(式)。***hold communion with oneself*** 深思(尤指道德和精神方面)。***Holy Communion*** 聖餐。***in communion with nature*** 與自然同化。

communion cup 〖基督教〗聖餐杯。

communion hymn 〖基督教〗領聖餐之前所唱的聖歌。

com·mun·ion·ist 〔kəˈmjunjənɪst; kəˈmjuːnjənist〕 *n.* ①領聖餐者。②對參加聖餐禮者所應具有之條件持有特殊觀點者。

Communion Service 聖餐禮。

Communion Sunday 領聖餐的星期天。

communion table 聖餐檯;祭壇。

com·mu·ni·qué 〔kə,mjunəˈke; kəˈmjuːnikei〕 *n.* 官報;公報。

***com·mu·nism** 〔ˈkɑmjʊ,nɪzəm; ˈkɔmju(ː)nizm〕 *n.* ①共產主義。②(C-) 國際共產黨之共產主義。

***com·mu·nist** 〔ˈkɑmjʊnɪst; ˈkɔmju(ː)nist〕 *n.* ①共產主義者。②(C-) 共產黨員。—*adj.* (C-)共產黨的。**—ic,** *adj.* **—i·cal·ly,** *adv.*

Communist International =**Comintern.**

com·mu·ni·tar·i·an 〔kə,mjunɪˈtɛrɪən; kə,mjuːniˈtɛəriən〕 *n.* ①共產社會之一分子。②提倡共產社會者。

‡**com·mu·ni·ty** 〔kəˈmjunətɪ; kəˈmjuːniti〕 *n., pl.* **-ties.** ①同住一地,具相同文化和歷史背景的民衆;社區。the foreign *community* in Taipei. 在臺北市的外僑。②團體。the business *community.* 實業界。③共有;共享; 共同的責任。④同居一起之動物; 同生一處之植物。⑤共同的性質; 相同; 一致。***the community*** 公衆。

community center 社區活動中心。
community chest 社區福利基金。
community college 社區大學。
community property (美國若干州中的法律規定的)夫妻共有共享的財產。
community singing (未經演練的)團體合唱。
com·mu·nize [ˈkɑmjuˌnaɪz; ˈkɔmju:naiz] *v.t.*, **-nized, -niz·ing.** 使爲社會公有;使共產化。—**com·mu·ni·za·tion,** *n.*
com·mut·a·ble [kəˈmjutəbl̩; kəˈmju:təbl] *adj.* 可交換的;可代替的;可折償的。—**com·mut·a·bil·i·ty,** *n.*
com·mu·tate [ˈkɑmjuˌtet; ˈkɔmjuteit] *v.t.*, **-tat·ed, -tat·ing.** ①轉換(電流)之方向。②轉變(交流電)爲直流電。
com·mu·ta·tion [ˌkɑmjuˈteʃən; ˌkɔmjuˈteiʃən] *n.* ①變換。*commutation* of iron into silver. 點鐵爲銀。②交換。③折算;代換償付。④〖美〗以月季車票旅行。⑤〖法律〗減刑。⑥〖電〗整流;換向。
commutation ticket 〖美〗月季車票(英亦作 **season-ticket**).
com·mu·ta·tive [kəˈmjutətɪv; kəˈmju:tətiv] *adj.* 交換的;代替的。
com·mu·ta·tor [ˈkɑmjuˌtetɚ; ˈkɔmjuteitə] *n.* 〖電〗整流器;換向器。
com·mute [kəˈmjut; kəˈmju:t] *v.*, **-mut·ed, -mut·ing.** —*v.t.* ①變換。②減刑。③代換償付;折償。—*v.i.* ①代換;折償。②〖美〗使用月季票乘車。③〖美〗每天往返上班(通常使用月季車票往返);定期往返於兩地間。
com·mut·er [kəˈmjutɚ; kəˈmju:tə] *n.* 〖美〗①有長期車票經常乘車往返者。②持月季票者。
com·mu·ter·ville [kəˈmjutɚˌvɪl; kəˈmju:təvil] *n.* commuter 居住的郊區。
com·my [ˈkɑmɪ; ˈkɔmi] *n.*, *pl.* **-mies.** 〖俗〗=**communist.**
co·mose [ˈkomos; ˈkoumous] *adj.* 〖植物〗多毛的。
comp[1] [kɑmp; kɔmp] *n.* 〖俗〗①=**compositor.** ②=**composition.** —*v.t.* 排(版)。
comp[2] *n.* 〖俚〗贈送券;免費票。
comp. ①companion. ②comparative. ③compare. ④compiled. ⑤compiler. ⑥composer. ⑦composition. ⑧compositor. ⑨compound. ⑩compounded.
***com·pact**[1] [*adj.*, *v.* kəmˈpækt; kəmˈpækt *n.* ˈkɑmpækt; ˈkɔmpækt] *adj.* ①固結的;緊密的。a *compact* package. 一個紮得緊密的包裹。②簡潔的。a *compact* speech. 一篇簡潔的演說。③〖詩〗組成的;做成的。④小巧的。a *compact* car. 小型車。⑤結實的。—*v.t.* ①壓緊;束緊;結緊;塞緊。②簡化;使簡潔。③由…組成。—*v.i.* 結緊;固結。—*n.* ①有鏡小粉盒。②小型汽車。—**ly,** *adv.*
com·pact[2] [ˈkɑmpækt; ˈkɔmpækt] *n.* 合同;契約;協定。
com·pac·tion [kəmˈpækʃən; kəmˈpækʃən] *n.* 壓緊;結緊。
com·pact·ness [kəmˈpæktnɪs; kəmˈpæktnis] *n.* 緊湊;結實;緊密;(面積等之)小。
com·pact·or [kəmˈpæktɚ; kəmˈpæktə] *n.* 壓土機;夯土機。(亦作 **compacter**)
‡**com·pan·ion**[1] [kəmˈpænjən; kəmˈpænjən] *n.* ①同伴;伴侶;朋友。A dictionary is his constant *companion.* 字典是他經常的同伴。②情趣相投者。③種類、大小、顏色等能相匹配的東西。④受雇的伴從(常指女性的)。⑤手册;指南。He bought a Traveler's *Companion.* 他買了一本"旅行指南"。⑥武士中最低級的一員。—*v.i.* 伴從;結交。to *companion* with fools. 與愚人爲伍。—*v.t.* 伴隨。
com·pan·ion[2] *n.* 甲板通船艙之梯路;比梯路頂部之蓋。
com·pan·ion·a·ble [kəmˈpænjənəbl̩; kəmˈpænjənəbl] *adj.* 友善而好交往的;適於做朋友的。
com·pan·ion·ate [kəmˈpænjənɪt; kəmˈpænjənit] *adj.* ①同伴的;似同伴的。②友愛的;共享的。③和諧的。
companionate marriage 同意不生育,並可自由離婚的一種婚姻制度。
***com·pan·ion·ship** [kəmˈpænjənˌʃɪp; kəmˈpænjənʃip] *n.* 友誼;交往。
com·pan·ion·way [kəmˈpænjənˌwe; kəmˈpænjənwei] *n.* 〖造船〗甲板通往船艙之梯路。
‡**com·pa·ny** [ˈkʌmpənɪ; ˈkʌmpəni] *n.*, *pl.* **-nies.** ①一羣人。Among the *company* was an old man. 這羣人中有一老者。②爲社交目的而聚集的人;爲某種目的結合一起的一羣人。③同伴;陪伴。He kept me *company.* 他陪伴我。④〖俗〗賓客;來客;訪客。We have *company* today. 今日我們有客來。⑤連(陸軍單位)。⑥全體船員。⑦公司;行號。We organized a publishing *company.* 我們組織一出版公司。⑧(公司行號之名稱中)其他關係人。J. J. Smith and *Company.* J. J. Smith 公司。⑨同一羣中之其他人們。***be good*** (***poor*** or ***bad***) ***company*** 良伴(無趣的同伴)。***company manners*** 虛禮;過分之禮。***for company*** 陪伴;伴隨。***in company*** 在人中;當衆。***in company*** (***with***) (與…)一同;一起。We went there *in company.* 我們一起去那裏。***keep*** (or ***bear***) ***a person company*** 與人爲伴。***keep company*** **a.** 與人結交;與人爲伍。**b.** (戀愛期中之)形影不離。***keep good*** (or ***bad***) ***company*** 與好人(或壞人)爲伍。***part company with*** **a.** 與人離別。**b.** 分道揚鑣;斷絕交往。**c.** 持反對意見。—*v.t.* 伴隨。May fair winds *company* your safe return. 願和風伴你平安歸來。
company commander 〖軍〗連長。
company man 着重公司利益甚於同事利益者。
company officer 〖美國陸軍〗尉官。
company store 員工福利社。
company union ①商店、工廠等員工組成的獨立工會。②被雇主所控制的工會。
compar. ①comparative. ②comparison.
com·pa·ra·bil·i·ty [ˌkɑmpərəˈbɪlətɪ; ˌkɔmpərəˈbiliti] *n.* 可相比;相似。
***com·pa·ra·ble** [ˈkɑmpərəbl̩; ˈkɔmpərəbl] *adj.* ①可比的;能比的。No horse has a speed *comparable* to that of his. 沒有一匹馬的速度能與他的馬相比。②可供比較的。—**com·pa·ra·bly,** *adv.*
***com·par·a·tive** [kəmˈpærətɪv; kəmˈpærətiv] *adj.* ①比較的。He lived in *comparative* comfort recently. 近來他的生活過得比較舒適。②比較研究的。—*n.* 比較級。"Better" is the *comparative* of "good". "Better" 爲 "good" 之比較級。
comparative degree 〖文法〗比較級。
comparative linguistics 比較語言學。
comparative literature 比較文學。
***com·par·a·tive·ly** [kəmˈpærətɪvlɪ;

kəm'pærətivli) *adv.* ①比較地。*Comparatively* speaking, he is a good man. 比較地說，他是一個好人。②有幾分地；相當地；稍微地。He is *comparatively* rich. 他相當富有。

comparative method 〖語言〗比較研究法。

comparative religion 比較宗教學。

com·pa·ra·tor ('kɑmpə,retə; 'kɔmpəreitə) *n.* (機械之)精密度測量器。

‡**com·pare** (kəm'pɛr; kəm'pɛə) *v.*, **-pared, -par·ing,** *n.* —*v.t.* ①比較〖常 with〗. to *compare* one thing with another.將一物與另一物比較。②喻；比擬〖常to〗. Man's life is often *compared* to a candle. 人生常被喻爲蠟燭。—*v.i.* ①匹敵；相比。②競爭。***compare notes*** 交換意見。***not to be compared with*** a. 相差極遠。b. 不如；不及。—*n.* 比較；匹敵。The grandeur of Niagara Falls is beyond *compare*. 尼加拉大瀑布的奇觀，世無其匹。

com·par·i·son** (kəm'pærəsn̩; kəm'pærisn) *n.* ①比較。He is rather dull in *comparison* with the others. 他和別人比較起來有一點遲鈍。②比擬；相似。③〖文法〗比較。by comparison*** 同其他比較時。***in comparison with*** 較之；比較。

comparison shopper 派往同業店中去購物，以探聽行情的雇員。

com·part (kəm'pɑrt; kəm'pɑːt) *v.t.* 分隔。

***com·part·ment** (kəm'pɑrtmənt; kəm'pɑːtmənt) *n.* ①間隔；區劃；格。②火車中的小房間。③分立而不相屬的機能、作用等。the *compartments* of the human mind. 人類智性的各種機能。—*v.t.* ①分成間隔；分隔。a *compartmented* box. 有分格的盒子。②分類。—**al,** *adj.*

com·part·men·tal·ize (,kəmpɑrt'mɛntl̩aɪz; ,kəmpɑːt'mentəlaiz) *v.t.*, **-ized, -iz·ing.** 區分；區劃；劃分。—**com·part·men·tal·i·za·tion,** *n.*

com·part·men·ta·tion (kəm,pɑrtmən'teʃən; kəm,pɑːtmən'teiʃən) *n.* ①分爲小房；區劃。②分門別類。

***com·pass** ('kʌmpəs; 'kʌmpəs) *n.* ①指南針。②境界；周圍。A prison is within the *compass* of its walls. 監獄是在其圍牆的周圍以內。③範圍。④(聲音或樂器所能達及的)音域。⑤(*pl.*)兩脚規；圓規。⑥迂迴；繞行。—*v.t.* ①環行。Magellan's ship *compassed* the earth. 麥哲倫的船環行了地球。②圍繞；包圍。③完成；得到；達到。to *compass* one's object. 達其目的。④圖謀。⑤理會；完全瞭解。

com·pass·a·ble ('kʌmpəsəbl̩; 'kʌmpəsəbl) *adj.* ①可圍繞的。②可達成的；可得到的。

compass card (航海羅盤之)盤面。

***com·pas·sion** (kəm'pæʃən; kəm'pæʃən) *n.* 憐憫；同情。I had *compassion* on him. 我憐憫他。

com·pas·sion·ate (*v.* kəm'pæʃənet; kəm'pæʃəneit *adj.* kəm'pæʃənɪt; kəm'pæʃənit) *v.*, **-at·ed, -at·ing,** *adj.* —*v.t.* 憐憫；體恤；同情。—*adj.* 慈悲的；有同情心的。—**ly,** *adv.*

compass saw 開孔鋸；截圓鋸。

compass window 〖建築〗弓形窗；半圓形凸窗。

com·pat·i·ble (kəm'pætəbl̩; kəm'pætəbl) *adj.* ①能共處的；能共存的；相容的。②(彩色電視廣播)黑白與彩色電視機均可收看到的。—**com·pat·i·bil·i·ty,** *n.*

compatible color 黑白電視機亦能收看的彩色電視節目。

com·pa·tri·ot (kəm'petrɪət; kəm'pætriət) *n.* 同胞。—*adj.* 同國的。

com·peer (kəm'pɪr; kɔm'piə) *n.* ①地位相等的人或物。②同志；夥伴。

‡**com·pel** (kəm'pɛl; kəm'pel) *v.*, **-pelled, -pel·ling.** —*v.t.* ①强迫；迫使。I was *compelled* to do so. 我被迫如此做。②以强力獲得或引起。He *compelled* obedience. 他迫使別人服從。—*v.i.* 驅策；驅使。—**la·ble,** *adj.* —**la·bly,** *adv.* —**ler,** *n.*

com·pel·la·tion (,kɑmpə'leʃən; ,kɔmpə'leiʃən) *n.* ①稱呼；呼名。②名稱；敬稱。

com·pel·ling (kəm'pɛlɪŋ; kəm'peliŋ) *adj.* ①驅使人的；使人不能不行動的；促人行動的。②引人注目的；令人佩服的。—**ly,** *adv.*

com·pend ('kɑmpɛnd; 'kɔmpend) *n.* =**compendium.**

com·pen·di·ous (kəm'pɛndɪəs; kəm'pendiəs) *adj.* 簡潔的；簡要的；摘要的。(亦作 **compendiary**) —**ly,** *adv.* —**ness,** *n.*

com·pen·di·um (kəm'pɛndɪəm; kəm'pendiəm) *n.*, *pl.* **-di·ums, -di·a** (-dɪə; -diə). 梗概；摘要；概略；撮要。

com·pen·sa·ble (kəm'pɛnsəbl̩; kəm'pensəbl) *adj.* ①可補償的。②依法可補償的。—**com·pen·sa·bil·i·ty,** *n.*

***com·pen·sate** ('kɑmpən,set; 'kɔmpenseit) *v.*, **-sat·ed, -sat·ing.** —*v.t.* ①償還；賠償。②報酬。The company *compensates* her for extra work. 公司因她的額外工作而報酬她。③(改變黃金成色或儲備黃金以)穩定(貨幣)購買力。④〖物理〗補整…之變差；補償；補助。—*v.i.* 補償；抵補〖for〗. Nothing can *compensate* for the loss of one's health. 沒有甚麼可以補償一個人的健康的損失。

***com·pen·sa·tion** (,kɑmpən'seʃən; ,kɔmpen'seiʃən) *n.* ①補償；賠償。②賠償金；賠償物。③報酬；酬金。Equal *compensation* should be given to men and women for equal work. 男女同工應同酬。④補整；補充；抵償。*compensation* pendulum. 補整振子；抵償擺。—**al, com·pen·sa·tive, com·pen·sa·to·ry,** *adj.* —**com·pen·sa·tor,** *n.*

com·père ('kɑmpɛr; 'kɔmpɛə) *n.*, *v.*, **com·pèred, com·pèr·ing.** 〖廣播、電視〗—*n.* 節目主持人。—*v.t.* 主持(節目)。—*v.i.* 做節目主持人。

***com·pete** (kəm'pit; kəm'piːt) *v.i.*, **-pet·ed, -pet·ing.** ①競爭。to *compete* with others for a prize. 與人競爭得獎。②比賽。to *compete* in a race. 賽跑。

com·pe·tence ('kɑmpətəns; 'kɔmpitəns) *n.* ①能力。②相當的財產；足以過舒適生活的財產。③資格；合法的權力；權限；權能。

com·pe·ten·cy ('kɑmpətənsɪ; 'kɔmpitənsi) *n.* =**competence.**

***com·pe·tent** ('kɑmpətənt; 'kɔmpitənt) *adj.* ①能幹的；勝任的。a *competent* cook. 能幹的厨子。a *competent* teacher. 勝任的教師。②有資格的。Two *competent* witnesses testified. 兩個有資格的證人作證。—**ly,** *adv.*

***com·pe·ti·tion** (,kɑmpə'tɪʃən; ,kɔmpi'tiʃən) *n.* ①競爭；角逐。②比賽。He takes part in a swimming *competition.* 他參加游

泳比賽。③競爭者;敵手。***free competition*** 自由競爭。***open competition*** 公開競爭。

***com·pet·i·tive** [kəm'pɛtətɪv; kəm'petitiv] *adj.* ①競爭的。Some kinds of business are *competitive.* 有些工商業是要競爭的。②經得起競爭的。 **—ly,** *adv.* **—ness,** *n.*

***com·pet·i·tor** [kəm'pɛtətɚ; kəm'petitə] *n.* 競爭者;敵手。

com·pet·i·to·ry [kəm'pɛtə,torɪ; kəm'petitəri] *adj.* 競爭的(=competitive).

com·pi·la·tion [,kɑmpɪ'leʃən; ,kɔmpi'leiʃən] *n.* ①編輯;編纂。②編纂物。

com·pi·la·to·ry [kəm'paɪlə,torɪ; kəm'pailətəri] *adj.* 編纂的;編輯的。

***com·pile** [kəm'paɪl; kəm'pail] *v.t.,* **-piled, -pil·ing.** ①編輯;編纂。②編列。

com·pil·er [kəm'paɪlɚ; kəm'pailə] *n.* ①編纂者;編輯人。②〖電腦〗編譯程式。*compiler* language. 編譯程式語言。

compl. complement.

com·pla·cence [kəm'plesn̩s; kəm'pleisns] *n.* =**complacency.**

com·pla·cen·cy [kəm'plesn̩sɪ; kəm'pleisnsi] *n.* ①自滿;自足;自得。②心滿意足。

com·pla·cent [kəm'plesn̩t; kəm'pleisnt] *adj.* 自滿的;自得的;得意的。**—ly,** *adv.*

com·plain** [kəm'plen; kəm'plein] *v.i.* ①抱怨;不滿。They *complained* of high prices. 他們抱怨物價太高。②訴苦。③控訴;控告。**—v.t.* 抱怨說。**—er,** *n.*

com·plain·ant [kəm'plenənt; kəm'pleinənt] *n.* ①訴苦者。②原告。

***com·plaint** [kəm'plent; kəm'pleint] *n.* ①訴苦。②控訴;控告。He brought a *complaint* against his neighbor. 他控告他的鄰居。③疾病;不適。

com·plai·sance [kəm'plezn̩s; kəm'pleizəns] *n.* 慇懃;順從;彬彬有禮。

com·plai·sant [kəm'plezn̩t; kəm'pleizənt] *adj.* ①慇懃的;彬彬有禮的。②順從的。**—ly,** *adv.* **—ness,** *n.*

com·plect·ed [kəm'plɛktɪd; kəm'plektid] *adj.* 〖美方〗有(某種之)膚色的。

com·ple·ment** [*n.* 'kɑmpləmənt; 'kɔmplimənt *v.* 'kɑmplə,mɛnt; 'kɔmpliment] *n.* ①補足物;補充物;附添物。Love is the *complement* of the law. 法律中需有愛的精神,始爲完備。②足量;全數;足額。③〖數學〗餘角;餘弧;餘子式;補數。④〖文法〗補助語。**—v.t.* 補足;補充。The museum is *complemented* by a spacious garden. 廣大的花園爲博物館增色不少。

com·ple·men·tal [,kɑmplə'mɛntl̩; ,kɔmpli'mentl] *adj.* =**complementary.** **—ly,** *adv.*

com·ple·men·ta·ry [,kɑmplə'mɛntərɪ; ,kɔmpli'mentəri] *adj.* ①補足的;補充的。②互相依賴的。③有一定關係的。④〖文法〗有補語作用的。

complementary angle 〖幾何〗餘角。

complementary color 補色。

‡**com·plete** [kəm'plit; kəm'pli:t] *adj., v.,* **-plet·ed, -plet·ing.** **—***adj.* ①完整的;全部的。Is this a *complete* story? 這是一個完整的故事嗎? the *complete* works of Shakespeare. 莎士比亞全集。②徹底的;絕對的。a *complete* success. 徹底的成功。③完畢;終了。④技藝高明的;有技巧的。He's a *complete* horseman. 他是個技藝高明的騎師。⑤完美的;十全十美的。a *complete* scholar. 無懈可擊的學者。⑥〖文法〗完全(包括修飾語)的。**—***v.t.* ①完成。to *complete* one's work. 完成工作。②使完全;使完整。The good news *completed* my happiness. 這好消息使我太高興了。③〖橄欖球〗傳(球)成功。**—com·plet·a·ble,** *adj.* **—com·plet·ed·ness, —ness,** *n.*

‡**com·plete·ly** [kəm'plitlɪ; kəm'pli:tli] *adv.* ①完全地。The cask is *completely* filled with wine. 這桶盛滿了酒。②徹底地;十分地。

***com·ple·tion** [kəm'pliʃən; kəm'pli:ʃən] *n.* ①完成(的狀態);圓滿。The work is near *completion.* 工作將近完成。②完成(指行爲)。

com·plex** [*adj., v.* kəm'plɛks, 'kɑmplɛks; 'kɔmpleks *n.* 'kɑmplɛks; 'kɔmpleks] *adj.* ①合成的;複合的。a *complex* term. 複合名詞。②複雜的;錯綜的。Life is getting more *complex* and difficult. 生活變得越加複雜而困難。**—n.* ①複雜的事物。②深的成見;嫉惡。I have a *complex* about dish washing. 我很討厭洗碟盤。③情結。④〖數學〗複合形;叢。⑤綜合物;複合物。vitamin B *complex.* 複合維他命B. ***inferiority complex*** 自卑感。***superiority complex*** 優越感。**—***v.t.* 使化爲複雜;使複雜化。**—ly,** *adv.* **—ness,** *n.*

complex fraction 〖數學〗繁分數。

com·plex·ion** [kəm'plɛkʃən; kəm'plekʃən] *n.* (亦作 **complection**) ①面色;膚色;氣色。a good *complexion.* 很好的面色。②外觀;形勢。the *complexion* of the war. 戰況。③思想;態度;趨向。**—v.t.* 微染以某顏色或特色。Propaganda *complexioned* his views. 他的看法多少受了宣傳的影響。**—al,** *adj.*

com·plex·ioned [kəm'plɛkʃənd; kəm'plekʃənd] *adj.* 有…膚色的。a light-*complexioned* person. 膚色淺淡的人。

com·plex·i·ty [kəm'plɛksətɪ; kəm'pleksiti] *n.* ①錯綜;複雜。②錯綜複雜之事。

complex sentence 〖文法〗複句。

com·pli·ance [kəm'plaɪəns; kəm'plaiəns] *n.* ①順從;聽從。②應允;答應。***in compliance with*** 聽從;依照。(亦作 **compliancy**)

com·pli·ant [kəm'plaɪənt; kəm'plaiənt] *adj.* 順從的;依從的;應允的。(亦作 **compliable**) **—ly,** *adv.*

com·pli·ca·cy ['kɑmpləkəsɪ; 'kɔmplikəsi] *n., pl.* **-cies.** ①錯綜;複雜。②複雜的事(物)。

com·pli·cate** ['kɑmplə,ket; 'kɔmplikeit] *v.,* **-cat·ed, -cat·ing,** *adj.* **—v.t.* ①使複雜;使起糾紛。That will *complicate* the matter. 那將使事情趨於複雜。②使更壞;使惡化;併發。**—***v.i.* 變複雜。**—***adj.* ①組成的。②複雜的。a *complicate* problem. 複雜的問題。

***com·pli·cat·ed** ['kɑmplə,ketɪd; 'kɔmplikeitid] *adj.* 複雜的。The mechanism of a watch is very *complicated.* 錶的機件甚爲複雜。**—ly,** *adv.* **—ness,** *n.*

***com·pli·ca·tion** [,kɑmplə'keʃən; ,kɔmpli'keiʃən] *n.* ①糾紛;難以解決的紛擾或糾葛。②併發病;併發症。Pneumonia is the *complication* we most fear. 肺炎是我們最畏懼的併發症。③趨於複雜的過程。④新增之問題或困難。*Complications* arose on all sides. 新問題從各方面發生。⑤使故事或劇情

變爲複雜之因素。⑥【心理】不同知覺之聯合(如進食時嗅覺與味覺之聯合)。

com·plic·i·ty [kəm'plɪsətɪ; kəm'plisiti] *n., pl.* **-ties.** 共謀;串通作弊。

com·pli·ment** ['kampləmənt; 'kɔmplimənt] *n.* ①恭維;敬意;稱讚。They paid him a high *compliment.* 他們非常恭維他。②(*pl.*) 致意; 問候; 道賀。Give my best *compliments* to your father. 請代我向你的父親問候。the compliments of the season*** 敬賀佳節 (聖誕節及年節間的致意語)。***With the compliments of*** 敬贈(作者或出版者贈送新書給他人時用語)。—*v.t.* ①稱讚; 恭維。to *compliment* a woman on her new hat. 稱讚一婦女的新帽。②送禮;餽贈。He *complimented* us with tickets for the football game. 他送給我們足球比賽入場券。③祝賀;致問;問候。—*v.i.* 稱讚;恭維。—**er,** *n.*

com·pli·men·tal [ˌkamplə'mɛntl; ˌkɔmpli'mentəl] *adj.* 讚美的; 恭維的 (= complimentary). —**ly,** *adv.*

com·pli·men·ta·ry [ˌkamplə'mɛntərɪ; ˌkɔmpli'mentəri] *adj.* ①讚美的;恭維的; 表示敬慕的。②【美】贈送的; 免費的。—**com·pli·men·ta·ri·ly,** *adv.* —**com·pli·men·ta·ri·ness,** *n.*

complimentary address 祝賀「辭;頌辭。」

complimentary close 書信結尾之問候語,如:"Yours truly" 或 "Sincerely yours." (亦作 **complimentary closing**)

complimentary copy 贈送本。

complimentary ticket (免費)招待券;優待券。

com·plin, com·pline ['kamplɪn; 'kɔmplin] *n.* 【宗教】晚禱;晚禱的時間。

com·plot [*n.* 'kamplat; 'kɔmplɔt *v.* kəm'plat; kəm'plɔt] 【古】*n., v.,* **-plot·ted, -plot·ting.** —*n.* 共謀; 陰謀。—*v.i.* & *v.t.* 共謀;陰謀。

***com·ply** [kəm'plaɪ; kəm'plai] *v.i.,* **-plied, -ply·ing.** 應允;同意;順從【with】. to *comply* with the rules. 遵守規則。

com·po ['kampo; 'kɔmpou] *n., pl.* **-pos.** ①混合塗料; 混合物 (爲composition之略)。②製造撞球用的象牙代用品。

com·po·nent [kəm'ponənt; kəm'pounənt] *adj.* 組成的; 成分的。—*n.* ①成分。②【物理】分力。—**ial,** *adj.*

com·port [*v.* kəm'port; kəm'pɔːt *n.* 'kampɔrt; 'kɔmpɔːt] *v.t.* 舉動;持(躬);持(己)。—*v.i.* 適合;相稱。—*n.* 果碟。

com·port·ment [kəm'pɔrtmənt; kəm'pɔːtmənt] *n.*①舉止;舉動。②習慣;行爲。

***com·pose** [kəm'poz; kəm'pouz] *v.,* **-posed, -pos·ing.** —*v.t.* ①組成; 構成。Water is *composed* of hydrogen and oxygen. 水由氫和氧所組成。②著; 撰;作曲。③使安靜;鎮定(心神)。to *compose* oneself to read a book. 鎮定心神讀書。④調停; 和解;調解。to *compose* a dispute. 調解爭執。⑤【印刷】排(字)。—*v.i.* 寫作;作曲。

***com·posed** [kəm'pozd; kəm'pouzd] *adj.* 安靜的;鎮靜的;泰然自若的。—**ly,** *adv.*

com·pos·ed·ness [kəm'pozɪdnɪs; kəm'pouzidnis] *n.* 鎮靜;泰然自若。

***com·pos·er** [kəm'pozə; kəm'pouzə] *n.*①作曲家。a *composer* of popular songs. 流行歌曲之作曲家。②作家; 著作者。③調停者;調解者。

com·pos·ing [kəm'pozɪŋ; kəm'pouziŋ] *n.* ①組成;配合。②【印刷】排字。***composing machine***【印刷】自動排字機。***composing room***【印刷】排字房。***composing stick***【印刷】排字盤。

com·pos·ite [kəm'pazɪt; 'kɔmpəzit] *adj.* ①混合成的; 湊集成的。②【植物】菊科的。—*n.* ①合成物;混合物。②菊科植物。③合成數。—**ly,** *adv.* —**ness,** *n.*

composite number【數學】合成數。

composite photograph (由兩張以上照片合併而成的)合成照片。

composite portrait 拼湊肖像 (據見證人描述疑犯的各部特徵而繪成的肖像)。

composite shot 電影 (或電視) 中將兩個鏡頭並列同時放射在銀幕(螢光幕)上的手法。(亦作 **split screen**)

***com·po·si·tion** [ˌkampə'zɪʃən; ˌkɔmpə'ziʃən] *n.* ①組織;組成;成分。Scientists study the *composition* of the soil. 科學家研究土壤的成分。②著作;作品。③(學生在學校所練習的)作文。④寫作。⑤(藝術作品等之)結構;布局。⑥混合物。⑦性質;素質。He has a touch of madness in his *composition.* 他在素質上有一點神經病。⑧調停;和解。⑨【印刷】排字。⑩組合(的狀態或性質)。⑪樂曲。⑫折中(尤指債權人對債務人還債的打折扣)。⑬經打折扣後償還債權人的錢。—**al,** *adj.* —**al·ly,** *adv.*

com·pos·i·tive [kəm'pazətɪv; kəm'pɔzitiv] *adj.* 組成的;集成的;合成的。

com·pos·i·tor [kəm'pazɪtə; kəm'pɔzitə] *n.* ①排字工人。②排字機。

com·pos men·tis ['kampəs'mɛntɪs; 'kɔmpəs'mentis]【拉】【法律】精神健全的。

com·post ['kampost; 'kɔmpɔst] *n.* 混合肥料; 堆肥。—*v.t.* ①將…做堆肥。②用堆肥施肥於。

***com·po·sure** [kəm'poʒə; kəm'pouʒə] *n.* 泰然自若; 鎮靜; 沉着。to keep one's *composure.* 保持鎮靜。

com·po·ta·tion [ˌkampə'teʃən; ˌkɔmpə'teiʃən] *n.* 聚飲;共飲。

com·po·ta·tor ['kampəˌtetə; 'kɔmpəteitə] *n.* 同飲者。

com·pote ['kampot; 'kɔmpout] *n.* ①煮熟的糖漬水果。②裝糖果的高脚盤子。

com·pound** [*adj.* 'kampaund, kam'paund; 'kɔmpaund, kɔm'paund *n.* 'kampaund; 'kɔmpaund *v.* kam'paund; kɔm'paund] *adj.* 合成的; 複合的; 混合的。Soap is a *compound* substance. 肥皂是種合成物質。—*n.* ①複合字。②混合物。A medicine is usually a *compound.* 藥常爲混合物。③化合物。④圍地; 圍場。—*v.t.* ①混合;攙合;調合。②調停;調解(尤指雙方讓步以解決)。③增加。④算複利;以複利計算。⑤組成;構成。compound a felony***【法律】接受金錢以私了訴訟。—*v.i.* ①結合。②調停;和解。—**a·ble,** *adj.* —**ed·ness,** —**er,** *n.*

com·pound-com·plex sentence ['kampaund'kamplɛks~; 'kɔmpaund'kɔmpleks~]【文法】複合複句。

compound eye (昆蟲等之)複眼。

compound fraction【數學】繁分數。

compound fracture【醫】哆開骨「折;穿破骨折。」

compound interest 複利。

compound number 複名數(如4英尺5英寸)。

compound sentence【文法】複「合句。」

compound word 複合字(如steamship 由 steam 及 ship 複合而成)。

com·pra·dor(e)〔ˌkɑmprəˈdɔr; ˌkɔmprəˈdɔː〕*n.* (中國及東方其他國家之) 洋商的經紀人;買辦。

Com·preg〔ˈkɑmprɛg; ˈkɔmpreg〕*n.* 〖商標名〗高壓夾板。

***com·pre·hend**〔ˌkɑmprɪˈhɛnd; ˌkɔmpriˈhend〕*v.t.* ①了解; 領悟。He *comprehends* geometry and algebra. 他了解幾何和代數。②包括;包含。**—er,** *n.* **—ing·ly,** *adv.*

com·pre·hen·si·ble〔ˌkɑmprɪˈhɛnsəbḷ; ˌkɔmpriˈhensəbl〕*adj.* 能理解的;易了解的。(亦作 **comprehendible**) **—com·pre·hen·si·bly,** *adv.* **—com·pre·hen·si·bil·i·ty,** *n.*

com·pre·hen·sion〔ˌkɑmprɪˈhɛnʃən; ˌkɔmpriˈhenʃən〕*n.* ①理解;理解力。②包含; 包括; 含蓄。③〖邏輯〗內涵(與"外延" extent 或 extension 相對)。④廣被性。

com·pre·hen·sive**〔ˌkɑmprɪˈhɛnsɪv; ˌkɔmpriˈhensiv〕*adj.* ①包羅豐富的; 廣博的。The term's work ended with a *comprehensive* review. 這學期的功課全部溫習後結束。②有理解力的。**—n.* (常 *pl.*)(亦作 **comprehensive examination**) 總括考試;總考;綜合測驗。**—ly,** *adv.* **—ness,** *n.*

comprehensive school (課程內包括普通中學與職校學科的)綜合制中學。

com·press**〔*v.* kəmˈprɛs; kəmˈpres *n.* ˈkɑmprɛs; ˈkɔmpres〕*v.t.* ①緊壓;壓縮;壓榨。②鎮壓。to *compress* an angry mob. 鎮壓憤怒的暴民。**—v.i.* (受壓力而)縮小。**—***n.* ①壓在傷患處之繃帶; 壓布。②壓棉成包的機器。**—i·ble,** *adj.* **—i·bly, —ing·ly,** *adv.*

com·pressed〔kəmˈprɛst; kəmˈprest〕*adj.* ①壓縮的。*compressed* gases. 壓縮氣體。②緊合的。③壓扁的。**—ly,** *adv.*

compressed petroleum gas 液化瓦斯。(亦作**liquefied petroleum gas**)

com·pres·si·bil·i·ty〔kəmˌprɛsəˈbɪlətɪ; kəmˌpresiˈbiliti〕*n.* 壓縮性。

com·pres·sion〔kəmˈprɛʃən; kəmˈpreʃən〕*n.* ①壓榨; 壓縮。②抑制; 壓抑。**—al,** *adj.*

com·pres·sive〔kəmˈprɛsɪv; kəmˈpresiv〕*adj.* 有壓縮力的;壓榨的。

com·pres·sor〔kəmˈprɛsɚ; kəmˈpresə〕*n.* ①壓縮物; 壓縮器; 壓榨器。②〖解剖〗收縮肌。

com·prise, com·prize**〔kəmˈpraɪz; kəmˈpraiz〕*v.,* **-prised, -pris·ing; -prized, -priz·ing.** **—v.t.* ①包括;包含。The United States *comprises* 50 states. 美國包括五十州。②構成。**—***v.i.* 由…所構成〖of〗. The funds of the association shall *comprise* of members' subscriptions. 協會基金將由會員的捐款所構成。

com·pro·mise**〔ˈkɑmprəˌmaɪz; ˈkɔmprəmaiz〕*v.,* **-mised, -mis·ing,** *n.* **—v.t.* ①和解;妥協。②危及;連累。**—***v.i.* ①和解。to *compromise* with a person. 與人和解。②姑息;妥協;退讓。I would rather die than *compromise.* 我寧死不妥協。**—***n.* ①和解; 互讓了事。to make a *compromise.* 和解。②連累; 危及。He did it without *compromise* of his dignity. 他做這事而不損及他的尊嚴。③折衷物; 中間物。④調停的結果; 協議。**—com·pro·mis·er,** *n.* **—com·prom·is·sa·ry,** *adj.*

com·pro·vin·cial〔ˌkɑmprəˈvɪnʃəl; ˌkɔmprəˈvinʃəl〕*adj.* 〖天主教〗屬同一教省(由同一總主教管轄)的。**—***n.* 屬於同一教省的任一主教。

Comp·tom·e·ter〔kɑmpˈtɑmətɚ; kɔmpˈtɔmitə〕*n.* 〖商標名〗一種自動計算機。

Comp·ton〔ˈkɑmptən; ˈkɔmptən〕*n.* 康普頓 (Arthur Holly, 1892-1962, 美國物理學家,曾獲1927年諾貝爾獎)。

comp·trol·ler〔kənˈtrolɚ; kənˈtroulə〕*n.* 主計官。

compu- 〖字首〗表"電腦"之義。

com·pul·sion〔kəmˈpʌlʃən; kəmˈpʌlʃən〕*n.* ①强迫;强制。②動人的力量。③〖心理〗不可抗拒的衝動。**—ist,** *n.*

com·pul·sive〔kəmˈpʌlsɪv; kəmˈpʌlsiv〕*adj.* ①强迫的; 强制的。②禁不住的。**—***n.* 驅迫力。**—ly,** *adv.*

***com·pul·so·ry**〔kəmˈpʌlsərɪ; kəmˈpʌlsəri〕*adj.* ①强迫的;强制的。*compulsory* education. 義務教育。②必修的。Which subjects are *compulsory* in your school? 在你們學校裏, 那些課程是必修的? **—com·pul·so·ri·ly,** *adv.*

com·punc·tion〔kəmˈpʌŋkʃən; kəmˈpʌŋkʃən〕*n.* 追悔;懊悔;良心不安。**—less,** *adj.*

com·punc·tious〔kəmˈpʌŋkʃəs; kəmˈpʌŋkʃəs〕*adj.* ①出於懊悔的;有關懊悔的。②感到懊悔的;良心不安的。**—ly,** *adv.*

com·pur·ga·tion〔ˌkɑmpɝˈgeʃən; ˌkɔmpəːˈgeiʃən〕*n.* 〖法律〗根據數人之證詞對嫌疑犯作無罪之判決。

com·put·a·ble〔kəmˈpjutəbḷ; kəmˈpjuːtəbl〕*adj.* 可計算的;可推測的。

com·pu·ta·tion〔ˌkɑmpjəˈteʃən; ˌkɔmpjuˈteiʃən〕*n.* ①計算。②算法。**—al, com·put·a·tive,** *adj.*

com·pute**〔kəmˈpjut; kəmˈpjuːt〕*v.,* **-put·ed, -put·ing,** *n.* **—v.t.* & *v.i.* 計算; 估計。I *compute* my losses at $500. 我估計我的損失有五百元。**—***n.* 計算;估計。It is beyond *compute.* 那是無法估計的。**—com·put·ist,** *n.*

com·put·er〔kəmˈpjutɚ; kəmˈpjuːtə〕*n.* ①計算者。②電子計算機; 電腦 (=electronic computer).

computer dating 〖電腦〗電腦約會。

com·put·er·i·za·ble〔kəmˈpjutəˌraɪzəbḷ; kəmˈpjuːtəraizəbl〕*adj.* 〖電腦〗可以電腦程式製作以供電腦分析或控制的。

com·pu·ter·ize〔kəmˈpjutəˌraɪz; kəmˈpjuːtəraiz〕*v.t.,* **-ized, -iz·ing.** 使電腦化。**—com·pu·ter·i·za·tion,** *n.*

computer language 〖電腦〗電腦語言。(亦作 **programming language**)

com·put·er·man〔kəmˈpjutəmən; kəmˈpjuːtəmən〕*n.* =**computer scientist.**

computer science 〖電腦〗電腦科學。

computer scientist 〖電腦〗電腦科學家。

computing machine 電子計算機;計算機(=computer).

***com·rade**〔ˈkɑmræd, ˈkɑmrɪd; ˈkɔmrid〕*n.* ①同伴;夥友;同事;至友;同志;社友。②共產黨員。

comrade in arms 武裝同志;戰友。

com·rade·ly〔ˈkɑmrædlɪ; ˈkɔmridli〕*adj.* 表現同志愛的;親熱的。

com·rade·ship〔ˈkɑmrædˌʃɪp; ˈkɔmridʃip〕*n.* 友誼;同志之誼;朋友關係。

com·sat〔ˈkɑmˌsæt; ˈkɔmsæt〕*n.* 通訊

衞星(由 *com*munications *sat*ellite 合成)。

com·stock·er·y [ˈkʌmˌstɑkərɪ; ˈkʌmˌstɔkəri] *n.* 對危害社會風紀之文藝、戲劇等的强烈反對。—**com·stock·er,** *n.*

Comte [kɔnt, kōt; kɔːnt, kɔ̃ːt] *n.* 孔德 (Auguste, 1798–1857, 法國數學家及哲學家)。

comte [kɔnt; kɔːnt] 〖法〗*n.* 伯爵。

com·tesse [kɔnˈtɛs; kɔnˈtes] 〖法〗 *n.* 女伯爵;伯爵夫人。

Com·ti·an [ˈkɔntɪən; ˈkɔːntiən] *adj.* 孔德 (Comte) 的;孔德哲學的;實證哲學的。

Comt·ism [ˈkɔntɪzəm; ˈkɔːntizəm] *n.* 孔德之學說;實證哲學。

Comt·ist [ˈkɔntɪst; ˈkɔːntist] *n.* 信奉孔德學說者; 實證哲學家。—*adj.* 孔德學說的;實證哲學的。

Co·mus [ˈkoməs; ˈkouməs] *n.* 〖羅馬、希臘神話〗司酒宴之神。

con[1] [kɑn; kɔn] *adv.* 反對。***pro and con*** 正反兩面地。—*adj.* 反對的。—*prep.* 反對。—*n.* 反對; 反對者; 反對的理由。 ***pros and cons*** 正反兩面。

con[2] *v.t.,* **conned, con·ning.** ①細心閱讀; 精讀;研讀。②諳記。③沉思;考慮;細查。

con[3] *v.,* **conned con·ning,** *n.* —*v.t. & v.i.* 〖航海〗指揮操舵;指揮(船)之航路。—*n.* 指揮操舵;指揮操舵者之位置。

con[4] *adj., v.,* **conned, con·ning.** —*adj.* 〖美俚〗詐欺的。—*v.t.* 〖美俚〗詐欺;騙取(某人)之財物。

con[5] *n.* 〖俚〗=**convict.**

con[6] *n.* 敲;(用指節之)敲頭。

con. ①concerto. ②conclusion. ③connection. ④consol. ⑤consolidated. ⑥consul. ⑦contra(拉=against).

CONAD Continental Air Defense(美國三軍聯合組成之防空組織, 防衞美國大陸使不受空襲;可譯作"本土防空司令部")。

co·na·tion [koˈneʃən; kouˈneiʃən] *n.* 〖心理〗意動(努力之本能)。

con·cat·e·nate [kɑnˈkætn̩ˌet; kɔnˈkætineit] *v.,* **-nat·ed, -nat·ing,** *adj.* —*v.t.* 連結;連鎖。—*adj.* 連結在一起的;連鎖的。

con·cat·e·na·tion [ˌkɑnkætn̩ˈeʃən; kɔnˌkætiˈneiʃən] *n.* ①連結;連鎖。②相關連之事物。③一連串之事物。

con·cave [kɑnˈkev, ˈkɑnkev; ˈkɔnˈkeiv, ˈkɔnkeiv] *adj.* 凹的。—*n.* 凹面;凹。

concave mirror 凹鏡。

concave polygon 凹多邊形。

con·cav·i·ty [kɑnˈkævətɪ; kɔnˈkæviti] *n., pl.* **-ties.** 凹;凹狀;凹面。

con·ca·vo-con·cave [kɑnˈkevo-kɑnˈkev; kɔnˈkeivou ˈkɔnkeiv] *adj.* 兩面凹進的;雙凹的。

con·ca·vo-con·vex [kɑnˈkevokɑnˈvɛks; kɔnˈkeivouˈkɔnveks] *adj.* 凹凸的;一面凹一面凸的。

***con·ceal** [kənˈsil; kənˈsiːl] *v.t.* ①隱藏;隱匿。He *concealed* himself behind the trees. 他藏身樹後。②對…保守祕密。—**a·ble,** *adj.* —**er,** *n.*

con·ceal·ment [kənˈsilmənt; kənˈsiːlmənt] *n.* ①隱藏;隱匿。 to remain in *concealment.* 隱藏着。②隱匿之方法或處所。

***con·cede** [kənˈsid; kənˈsiːd] *v.,* **-ced·ed, -ced·ing.** —*v.t.* ①承認;認以爲眞。Everyone *concedes* that 2 and 2 make four. 每個人都承認二加二等於四。②讓與;容許。③勉强承認。④放棄贏得(選舉等)之希望。—*v.i.* 讓步。—**con·ced·er,** *n.*

con·ced·ed·ly [kənˈsidɪdlɪ; kənˈsiːdidli] *adv.* 毫無疑問地;不容置疑地。

con·ceit** [kənˈsit; kənˈsiːt] *n.* ①自誇;自負。No one admires a man who is full of *conceit.* 沒有人喜歡一個十分自負的人。②觀念;意念。③意見。④想像; 幻想。 He is wise in his own *conceit.* 他自認爲聰明。be out of conceit with something*** 對某物(事)不再滿意;對某物(事)厭倦。***put one out of conceit with something*** 使某人厭倦某事。—*v.t.* ①自誇。②〖方〗想像。

con·ceit·ed [kənˈsitɪd; kənˈsiːtid] *adj.* ①自誇的; 自負的。②〖俗〗幻想的;奇想的。—**ly,** *adv.* —**ness,** *n.*

***con·ceiv·a·ble** [kənˈsivəbl̩; kənˈsiːvəbl] *adj.* 可想像的; 可料到的; 可了解的;可相信的。We took every *conceivable* precaution against fire. 我們以所有可想像的預防方法防火。—**con·ceiv·a·bly,** *adv.* —**con·ceiv·a·bil·i·ty,** *n.*

***con·ceive** [kənˈsiv; kənˈsiːv] *v.,* **-ceived, -ceiv·ing.** —*v.t.* ①想像; 構思; 設想。Such a badly *conceived* scheme is sure to fail. 設想得這樣壞的計畫一定要失敗。②以爲;相信;了解;想。③表明;表示;表達。④懷孕。to *conceive* a child. 懷孕。⑤養成或體驗(一種情感)。⑥引起;產生。—*v.i.* ①想像;設想〖of〗. ②懷孕。—**con·ceiv·er,** *n.*

con·cen·ter, con·cen·tre [kɑnˈsɛntɚ; kɔnˈsentə] *v.t. & v.i.* 集中;集於一點;聚集。

***con·cen·trate** [ˈkɑnsn̩ˌtret; ˈkɔnsentreit] *v.,* **-trat·ed, -trat·ing,** *n.* —*v.t.* ①集中。②注意; 專心。to *concentrate* one's mind on some work. 專心致意於某種工作。③濃縮。—*v.i.* ①集中;集於中心。He is unable to *concentrate* upon academic work. 他不能全神貫注於學術工作。②密集;濃縮。—*n.* 濃縮物。

con·cen·trat·ed [ˈkɑnsn̩ˌtretɪd; ˈkɔnsentreitid] *adj.* ①濃縮的。②强烈的。③專心的。④擁擠在一起的。

concentrated feed 濃縮飼料。

concentrated milk 煉乳。

***con·cen·tra·tion** [ˌkɑnsn̩ˈtreʃən; ˌkɔnsenˈtreiʃən] *n.* ①集中。②注意;專心。He reads with deep *concentration.* 他專心讀書。③濃縮。④集中之物。⑤在短時間內砲兵集中射擊之火力;火力集中;集中射擊目標。

concentration camp 集中營。

con·cen·tra·tive [ˈkɑnsn̩ˌtretɪv; ˈkɔnsentreitiv] *adj.* 集於中心的;集中的;聚集性的。

con·cen·tra·tor [ˈkɑnsɛnˌtretɚ; ˈkɔnsentreitə] *n.* ①專心致志之人。②集中或濃縮溶液、礦砂等之各種機械。

con·cen·tric [kənˈsɛntrɪk; kənˈsentrik] *adj.* 同中心的。(亦作 **concentrical**) —**al·ly,** *adv.* —**i·ty,** *n.*

con·cept [ˈkɑnsɛpt; ˈkɔnsept] *n.* 概念;觀念。

***con·cep·tion** [kənˈsɛpʃən; kənˈsepʃən] *n.* ①想像; 想像力。His cruelty is beyond our *conception.* 他的殘忍非你我所能想像。②觀念; 概念。He has a wrong *conception* of life. 他的人生觀是錯誤的。③懷孕。to prevent *conception.* 避孕。④計畫。⑤開始; 發源。⑥想像圖。⑦想像或設計的產物。—**al,** *adj.*

con·cep·tive [kənˈsɛptɪv; kənˈseptiv] *adj.* ①有想像力的。②想像的;構思的。

con·cep·tu·al [kənˈsɛptʃuəl; kən-

ˈseptjuəl] *adj.* 概念的。 **—ly,** *adv.*

con·cep·tu·al·ism [kənˈsɛptʃuəlˌɪzəm; kənˈseptjuəlizm] *n.* 〖哲學〗概念論。 **—con·cep·tu·al·ist,** *n.*

‡**con·cern** [kənˈsɝn; kənˈsəːn] *v.t.* ①關係;與之有關;關涉。That doesn't *concern* me. 那與我無關。②使擔心;使關心。***as concerns*** 關於。***as far as...is concerned*** 關於;至於。*As far as* they themselves *are concerned* they are safe and sound. 至於他們自身,則安然無恙。***concern oneself*** **a.** 注意。**b.** 顧慮;介懷。*—n.* ①事務;事。②利害;關係。It interferes with his personal *concerns.* 這與他的利害衝突。③顧慮;憂慮;關懷;掛念。④關心之所在;關心之事。⑤公司;商店。This is a money-making *concern.* 這是賺錢的商店。⑥股份。He has a *concern* in the business. 他在這商店內有股份。⑦東西;玩意。***of concern*** 重要的;有利害關係的(=of importance; of interest). 〖注意〗concern 與 in 或 with連用,以表示"參與"或"與…有關"。concern與 for 或 about 連用時,表示"關懷"或"擔憂"。

***con·cerned** [kənˈsɝnd; kənˈsəːnd] *adj.* ①掛念的;憂慮的。a *concerned* look (air). 擔憂的神色(態度)。②有關的。the authorities *concerned.* 有關當局。the persons(*or* parties) *concerned.* 當事人;關係人。③被牽累的。**—ly,** *adv.* **—ness,** *n.*

con·cern·ful [kənˈsɝnfəl; kənˈsəːnful] *adj.* 重要的。

***con·cern·ing** [kənˈsɝnɪŋ; kənˈsəːniŋ] *prep.* 關於。

con·cern·ment [kənˈsɝnmənt; kənˈsəːnmənt] *n.* ①關係;參與。②擔憂;懸念〖about, for〗。③重大;重要性。④所關心之事。

con·cert** [*n., adj.* ˈkɑnsɝt; ˈkɔnsət *v.* kənˈsɝt; kənˈsəːt] *n.* ①音樂會。②一致;和諧。in concert*** 一致;共同。to work *in concert* with others. 與他人協力工作。*—adj.*音樂會用的;為音樂會的。*concert* hall. 音樂廳。*—v.t.* 協議設計或進行。*—v.i.* 協同工作〖常 with〗。

con·cer·tan·te [ˌkɑntʃəˈtɑnti; ˌkɔntʃəˈtɑːntiː] *adj.* (樂曲)適於發揮高度技巧的。

con·cert·ed [kənˈsɝtɪd; kənˈsəːtid] *adj.* ①協同的;一致的。②〖音樂〗協調的。**—ly,** *adv.*

concert grand 平臺鋼琴。(亦作**concert grand piano**)

con·cer·ti·na [ˌkɑnsəˈtinə; ˌkɔnsəˈtiːnə] *n.* 一種六角形手風琴。

concertina table 可伸縮的桌子。

con·cert·mas·ter [ˈkɑnsətˌmæstə; ˈkɔnsətˌmɑːstə] *n.* 交響樂隊之第一提琴手(其地位僅次於樂隊指揮);樂隊首席。

con·cer·to [kənˈtʃɛrto; kənˈtʃəːtou, -tʃɛə-] *n., pl.* **-tos.** 〖音樂〗協奏曲。

concert pitch ①〖音樂〗合奏調(比平常音調稍高)。②(機器、身體等之)極佳狀況。

concert tour 演奏旅行。

***con·ces·sion** [kənˈsɛʃən; kənˈseʃən] *n.* ①讓步。②特許權;讓給之物。③租界;租地。

con·ces·sion·aire [kənˌsɛʃənˈɛr; kənˌseʃəˈnɛə] *n.* 受讓人;特許權所有者。

con·ces·sive [kənˈsɛsɪv; kənˈsesiv] *adj.* 讓步的;讓與的;許可的。**—ly,** *adv.*

concessive clause〖文法〗讓步子句。

conch [kɑŋk, kɑntʃ; kɔŋk, kɔntʃ] *n., pl.* **conchs** [kɑŋks; kɔŋks], **conch·es**[ˈkɑntʃɪz; ˈkɔntʃiz]. ①〖動物〗海螺;貝類。②介殼;貝殼。③〖羅馬神話〗海神 Tritons 用作號角之貝殼。

con·cha [ˈkɑŋkə; ˈkɔŋkə] *n., pl.* **-chae** [-ki; -kiː]. 〖解剖〗貝殼狀結構;(尤指)外耳;耳殼。

con·chie [ˈkɑntʃɪ; ˈkɔntʃi] *n.* =**conchy.**

con·chif·er·ous [kɑŋˈkɪfərəs; kɔŋˈkifərəs] *adj.* 有介殼的。

con·chol·o·gist [kɑŋˈkɑlədʒɪst; kɔŋˈkɔlədʒist] *n.* 介類學者;貝類學者。

con·chol·o·gy [kɑŋˈkɑlədʒɪ; kɔŋˈkɔlədʒi] *n.* 介類學;貝類學。

con·chy [ˈkɑntʃɪ; ˈkɔntʃi] *n., pl.* **-chies.** 〖俚〗=**conscientious objector.**

con·ci·erge [ˌkɑnsɪˈɛrʒ; ˌkɔ̃ːsiˈɛəʒ] 〖法〗*n.* ①看門人。②(公寓)管理人員。

con·cil·i·ate [kənˈsɪlɪˌet; kənˈsilieit] *v.,* **-at·ed, -at·ing.** *—v.t.* ①安慰;取悅於。②調解;調停。*—v.i.* 取得好感;修好;和好。

con·cil·i·a·tion [kənˌsɪlɪˈeʃən; kənˌsiliˈeiʃən] *n.* ①撫慰;安慰。②修好;和好。③和解;懷柔。

con·cil·i·a·tive [kənˈsɪlɪˌetɪv; kənˈsiliətiv] *adj.* =**conciliatory.**

con·cil·i·a·tor [kənˈsɪlɪˌetə; kənˈsilieitə] *n.* 撫慰者;和解者。

con·cil·i·a·to·ry [kənˈsɪlɪəˌtorɪ; kənˈsiliətəri] *adj.* ①撫慰的;安慰的。②願修好的;有和解趨勢的。

con·cin·ni·ty [kənˈsɪnətɪ; kənˈsiniti] *n., pl.* **-ties.** ①(各部分間之巧妙的)調和安排;和諧。②(文體之)優雅;優美。

***con·cise** [kənˈsaɪs; kənˈsais] *adj.* 簡明的;概括的。**—ly,** *adv.* **—ness,** *n.*

con·ci·sion [kənˈsɪʒən; kənˈsiʒən] *n.* 簡明;簡潔;簡略。

con·clave [ˈkɑnklev; ˈkɔnkleiv] *n.* ①樞機主教互選教皇之密室及會議。②祕密會議。***sit in conclave*** 舉行祕密會議。

‡**con·clude** [kənˈklud; kənˈkluːd] *v.,* **-clud·ed, -clud·ing.** *—v.t.* ①結束;使完畢。to *conclude* a speech. 結束演講。②結論;推論;推斷。③訂立;締結。to *conclude* a treaty. 締結條約。④決定;斷定。She *concluded* that she would wait. 她決定等候。*—v.i.*①終結;結束。The meeting *concluded* at six. 會議在六時結束。②推斷。It is hard to *conclude.* 這是難以推斷的。③決定。

con·clu·sion** [kənˈkluʒən; kənˈkluːʒən] *n.* ①完結;終了。at the *conclusion* of the war. 戰爭終了時。②結論。to arrive at a *conclusion.*得到結論。③結果。to bring to a *conclusion.* 使終結;談定(買賣等)。④訂立;締結。⑤最後的決定。⑥推論;推斷。in conclusion*** 最後;總之。***try conclusions with*** 與…爭勝負。**—al,** *adj.* **—al·ly,** *adv.*

con·clu·sive [kənˈklusɪv; kənˈkluːsiv] *adj.* 確定的;決定性的;最後的。**—ly,** *adv.* **—ness,** *n.*

con·coct [kɑnˈkɑkt; kənˈkɔkt] *v.t.* ①調製;混合。②編造;虛構。③計畫。**—con·coc·tive,** *adj.* **—er,** *n.*

con·coc·tion [kɑnˈkɑkʃən; kənˈkɔkʃən] *n.* ① concoct 之動作或過程。② concoct 而成之產物。

con·col·or·ous [kɑnˈkʌlərəs; kənˈkʌlərəs] *adj.* 單色的;同色的(尤指昆蟲各部之顏色)。

con·com·i·tance [kɑnˈkɑmətəns; kənˈkɔmitəns] *n.* ①相伴;併立;共存;附隨。②附隨之物。(亦作 **concomitancy**)

con·com·i·tant [kɑnˈkɑmətənt;

kən'kɔmitənt] *adj.* 相伴的；伴隨的；附隨的。 —*n.* 相伴物；附隨物。 —**ly,** *adv.*

*__con·cord__ ['kankɔrd, 'kaŋ-; 'kɔŋkɔːd, 'kɔn-] *n.* ①和諧；協調；同意。②(國與國間的)友善；親睦；親善。③〖音樂〗諧和；和聲。④〖文法〗(人稱、性、數、格等之)一致。⑤條約；公約。***in concord*** 和諧。

con·cord·ance [kan'kɔrdn̩s; kən'kɔːdəns] *n.* ①和諧；一致。②重要語詞索引(以字母次序排列，註明該語詞之出處者)。

con·cord·ant [kan'kɔrdn̩t; kən'kɔːdənt] *adj.* 和諧的；一致的〖with〗. —**ly,** *adv.*

con·cor·dat [kan'kɔrdæt; kɔn'kɔːdæt] *n.* ①協定；協約；契約。②羅馬教皇與各國政府間所訂的有關宗教事務的協定。③宗派間之協定。

con·course ['kankors; 'kɔŋkɔːs] *n.* ①流集；合流；會流。②集合；羣集。③車站或公園內的空地。④競技場。⑤寬闊的大道。

con·cres·cence [kan'krɛsəns; kɔn'kresns] *n.* 〖生物〗癒合；合生。

*__con·crete__ ['kankrit, kan'krit; 'kɔnkriːt *v.* ② & ③ kan'krit; kən'kriːt] *adj., n., v.,* **-cret·ed, -cret·ing.** —*adj.* ①實在的；具體的。*concrete* facts. 具體的事實。②混凝土的；水泥的。③凝結的；固結的。—*n.*①混凝土；水泥。reinforced *concrete.* 鋼筋水泥。②凝結物。③具體物。***in the concrete*** 具體上；實際上。—*v.t.*①鋪以混凝土；塗以水泥。②凝固；凝結。③使結合。—**ly,** *adv.* —**ness,** *n.*

concrete mixer 混凝土拌合機。

concrete noun 〖文法〗具體名詞。

concrete number 〖數學〗名數。

con·cre·tion [kan'kriʃən; kən'kriːʃən] *n.* ①凝固；固結。②凝固物；固結物。③固結之程度；凝結度。④〖醫〗結石。⑤〖地質〗凝塊。⑥〖哲學〗具體；具體化。 —**ar·y,** *adj.*

con·cre·tive [kan'kritɪv; kɔn'kriːtiv] *adj.* 有凝固力的；凝結的；凝結性的。—**ly,** *adv.*

con·cu·bi·nage [kan'kjubənɪdʒ; kɔn'kjuːbinidʒ] *n.* ①蓄妾；姘居。②與男人姘居；爲妾。

con·cu·bine ['kaŋkjuˌbaɪn; 'kɔŋkjubain] *n.* ①妾。②姘婦。

con·cu·pis·cent [kan'kjupəsn̩t; kən'kjuːpisnt] *adj.* 慾望强烈的；色慾强的；好色的。 —**con·cu·pis·cence,** *n.*

con·cur [kən'kɝ; kən'kəː] *v.i.,* **-curred, -cur·ring.** ①同意；意見一致。②同時發生。③協力；聯合。④贊成。—**rer,** *n.*

con·cur·rence [kən'kɝəns; kən'kʌrəns] *n.* ①同意；贊同；一致。②同時發生。③〖幾何〗數直線的共交點。④〖法律〗權力或利益之均分。⑤聯合動作或效果。⑥競爭。

con·cur·rent [kən'kɝənt; kən'kʌrənt] *adj.* ①同時發生的；共存的。②協力的；合作的。③和諧的；一致的。④〖數學〗共交於一點的。⑤〖法律〗有相等的裁判權的。—*n.* ①同時發生或並存的原因。②同心協力者；競爭者。 —**ly,** *adv.* —**ness,** *n.*

concurrent resolution 由國會兩院所通過而不需總統或首相簽署的決議案(此種決議案僅係兩院意見的表達，並非法律)。

con·cuss [kən'kʌs; kən'kʌs] *v.t.* ①震動；震盪。②使(腦)震傷。

con·cus·sion [kən'kʌʃən; kən'kʌʃən] *n.* ①震動；衝擊。②(打擊、跌交或其他震動而致之)腦震盪。 —**con·cus·sive,** *adj.*

*__con·demn__ [kən'dɛm; kən'dem] *v.t.* ①反對；責難。We *condemned* him for his bad conduct. 我們因爲他行爲不良而責備他。②招禍；致令有罪。③宣告不合用或不宜服役。④宣告有罪；判罪。He was *condemned* to life imprisonment. 他被判無期徒刑。⑤宣告無可救藥。⑥沒收；充公。⑦使處於(某種地位或境界)。 —**ing·ly,** *adv.* —**er,** *n.*

con·dem·na·ble [kən'dɛmnəbl̩; kən'demnəbl] *adj.* 可定罪的；該受責備的。

con·dem·na·tion [ˌkandɛm'neʃən; ˌkɔndem'neiʃən] *n.* ①責難；非難。②定罪；判罪。③定罪或非難之理由。④〖美〗充公；沒收。—**con·dem·na·to·ry,** *adj.*

con·demned [kən'dɛmd; kən'demd] *adj.* ①被責難的；被判罪的。②用於被判罪者的。③無可救藥的。

con·den·sa·bil·i·ty [kənˌdɛnsə'bɪlətɪ; kənˌdensə'biliti] *n.* 凝縮性。

con·den·sa·ble [kən'dɛnsəbl̩; kən'densəbl] *adj.* 可凝結的；可壓縮的；可濃縮的。(亦作 **condensible**)

con·den·sa·tion [ˌkandɛn'seʃən; ˌkɔnden'seiʃən] *n.* ①凝結；凝縮；縮短。②凝塊；濃縮物。③(文體等之)緊湊。④摘要；節錄；縮寫。⑤節略。 —**al,** *adj.*

*__con·dense__ [kən'dɛns; kən'dens] *v.,* **-densed, -dens·ing.** —*v.t.* ①使壓縮；使凝縮；使縮緊。②縮寫；使簡潔。③使冷凝；使凝結。④使强；使聚集(如光線等)。—*v.i.* 凝縮；冷凝；凝結。

con·densed [kən'dɛnst; kən'denst] *adj.* ①縮小的；縮短的。②凝縮的(尤指氣體液化)。③濃縮的。

condensed milk 煉乳。

con·dens·er [kən'dɛnsɚ; kən'densə] *n.* ①冷凝器；凝結器。②聚光器；聚光鏡。③電容器。

con·den·ser·y [kən'dɛnsərɪ; kən'densəri] *n.* 煉乳工廠。

con·de·scend [ˌkandɪ'sɛnd; ˌkɔndi'send] *v.i.* 屈尊；俯就；降格相從。

con·de·scend·ing [ˌkandɪ'sɛndɪŋ; ˌkɔndi'sendiŋ] *adj.* 屈尊的；降格相從的。—**ly,** *adv.* —**ness,** *n.*

con·de·scen·sion [ˌkandɪ'sɛnʃən; ˌkɔndi'senʃən] *n.* 謙卑；謙讓；慇懃；屈尊。

con·dign [kən'daɪn; kən'dain] *adj.* 相當的；應受的；適宜的。—**ly,** *adv.*

con·di·ment ['kandəmənt; 'kɔndimənt] *n.* 調味品；佐料。

‡**con·di·tion** [kən'dɪʃən; kən'diʃən] *n.* ①情形；情況；狀態。Weather *conditions* were good. 天氣情況良好。②健康情形。He is at the top of his *condition.* 他的健康情形達於最佳地步。③地位；身分。He is a man of humble *condition.* 他是一個地位低微的人。④條件。Ability and effort are *conditions* of success. 才能與努力是成功的條件。⑤不正常的狀態；不利情況。⑥需補考之分數。⑦〖文法〗條件子句。⑧〖邏輯〗前提。⑨〖美〗補考或補修。***change one's condition*** 結婚。***in condition*** 健康情形良好。***on*** (or ***upon***) ***condition that*** 假使。***on no condition*** 無論如何均不；絕不。***out of condition*** 健康不佳。I'm *out of condition.* 我身體不太好。—*v.t.* ①置於適當情形；調節；訓練。②附以條件；以…爲條件。He *conditioned* his going upon the weather. 他能去與否，視天氣好壞而定。③需補考。He was *conditioned* in English. 他的英文需補考。④作成條件。⑤〖心理〗制約；因制約作用而。

con·di·tion·al [kən'dɪʃənl̩; kən'diʃənl] *adj.* ①有條件的。②〖數學〗條件的。③〖文法〗**conditional clause.** 條件子句。**conditional sentence.** 條件句。—*n.*〖文法〗條件句;條件語。

con·di·tion·al·i·ty [kən,dɪʃə'næləti; kən,diʃə'næliti] *n.* 受限制性;制約。

con·di·tion·al·ly [kən'dɪʃənlɪ; kən'diʃṇəli] *adv.* 有條件地。

con·di·tioned [kən'dɪʃənd; kən'diʃənd] *adj.* ①受條件限制的;制約的。②〖美〗暫行入學或升級的;試讀的。③情形…的;境遇…的。④(暖房、冷氣室)被調節的。⑤置於良好情況之下的。⑥適於…的。

conditioned reflex 〖心理〗條件反射(如飼狗時常搖鈴,則其聞鈴聲卽分泌唾液)。(亦作 **conditioned response**)

con·di·tion·er [kən'dɪʃənɚ; kən'diʃənə] *n.* ①調節者。②調節劑。③調節器。air *conditioner.* 空氣調節器。

con·do·la·to·ry [kən'dolə,torɪ; kən'doulətəri] *adj.* 弔唁的;弔慰的。

con·dole [kən'dol; kən'doul] *v.,* **-doled, -dol·ing.** —*v.i.* 同情;哀悼;弔慰;慰問。I *condole* with you upon the loss of your mother. 我向你弔慰令堂之死。—*v.t.*〖古〗哀悼。—**ment, con·dol·er,** *n.*

con·do·lence [kən'doləns; kən'douləns] *n.* 弔;弔慰;哀悼;弔詞。Her friends sent her many *condolences.* 她的朋友對她弔慰頻頻。

con·do·lent [kən'dolənt; kən'doulənt] *adj.* 弔慰的;哀悼的。

con·dom ['kɑndəm; 'kɔndəm] *n.* (男性爲避孕,防性病用的)橡皮套子;陰莖套;如意套;保險套;小夜衣。

con·do·min·i·um [,kɑndə'mɪnɪəm; ,kɔndə'miniəm] *n.* ①共有權。②〖國際法〗共同管轄權。③共同管轄區。④〖美〗土地爲公司所有而每層住宅爲私有的公寓建築。

con·do·na·tion [,kɑndo'neʃən; ,kɔndou'neiʃən] *n.* ①寬恕;赦免;原諒。②〖法律〗(夫對妻,或妻對夫的)通姦宥恕。

con·done [kən'don; kən'doun] *v.t.,* **-doned, -don·ing.** 寬恕;赦免;原諒。—**ment, con·don·er,** *n.*

con·dor ['kɑndɚ; 'kɔndɔː] *n.* (美洲產之)兀鷹。

con·duce [kən'djus; kən'djuːs] *v.i.,* **-duced, -duc·ing.** 助成;貢獻;引起〖to, toward〗.

con·du·cive [kən'djusɪv; kən'djuːsiv] *adj.* 促成的;有助益的〖to〗. —**ly,** *adv.* —**ness,** *n.*

‡**con·duct** [*n.* 'kɑndʌkt; 'kɔndəkt, -dʌkt *v.* kən'dʌkt; kən'dʌkt] *n.* ①行爲;擧動。good *conduct.* 良好的行爲。②處理;經營。the *conduct* of a business. 商業的經營。③指引;引導;嚮導。④基於理性的行爲。—*v.t.* ①行爲;持(身)。She always *conducts* herself like a lady. 她擧止經常似淑女。②處理;經營。to *conduct* a business. 經營商業。③指揮。to *conduct* an orchestra. 指揮樂隊。④引導;嚮導。⑤傳導。Glass *conducts* heat. 玻璃傳熱。—*v.i.* ①領導;指揮。②傳導。

con·duct·ance [kən'dʌktəns; kən'dʌktəns] *n.* ①〖電〗電導。②傳導。

con·duct·i·bil·i·ty [kən,dʌktə'bɪlətɪ; kən,dʌkti'biliti] *n.* (電、熱等之)傳導性。

con·duct·i·ble [kən'dʌktəbl; kən'dʌktəbl] *adj.* ①可傳導(電、熱等)的。②可被傳導的。

con·duc·tion [kən'dʌkʃən; kən'dʌkʃən] *n.* ①傳導。②輸送。

con·duc·tive [kən'dʌktɪv; kən'dʌktiv] *adj.* 傳導性的;有傳導力的;傳導的。

con·duc·tiv·i·ty [,kɑndʌk'tɪvətɪ; ,kɔndʌk'tiviti] *n.* ①傳導性;傳導係數。②〖電〗電導係數。

***con·duc·tor** [kən'dʌktɚ; kən'dʌktə] *n.* ①領導者;指揮者;管理者。②樂隊指揮者;音樂隊或合唱隊的隊長。③車掌;火車、電車、公共汽車的管理員(兼收票或收費)。④傳導體;導體。Metals are good *conductors* of heat and electricity. 金屬爲熱和電的良導體。⑤避雷針。—**ship,** *n.* —**less,** *adj.*

conductor rail (電動火車的)電導軌道。

con·duc·tress [kən'dʌktrɪs; kən'dʌktris] *n.* conductor 之女性。

con·duit ['kɑndɪt; 'kɔndit] *n.* ①導管;水管;油管。②線管(藏納電線者)。

con·du·pli·cate [kɑn'djupləkɪt; kɔn'djuːplikit] *adj.* 〖植物〗摺合的。

con·dyle ['kɑndəl, -daɪl; 'kɔndil, -dail] *n.* 〖解剖〗髁狀突;骨節;骨阜。

***cone** [kon; koun] *n.* ①〖數學〗圓錐;錐面。②圓錐體。③毬果(如松毬等)。④任何似圓錐形的東西(如尖峯等)。an ice-cream *cone.* 甜筒;冰淇淋捲。—*v.t.* ①使成錐形;使帶斜角。②捲於圓錐。—**less,** *adj.* —**like,** *adj.*

cone·nose ['kon,noz; 'kounnouz] *n.* 〖動物〗錐鼻蟲(產於北美南部及西南部之一種大形吸血蟲)。

Con·es·to·ga wagon [,kɑnə'stogə~; ,kɔnəs'tougə~] 一種寬輪的篷車。

Co·ney Island ['konɪ~; 'kouni~] 科尼島(屬紐約市之一小島,爲一遊樂場地)。

con·fab ['kɑnfæb; 'kɔnfæb] *n., v.,* **con·fabbed, con·fab·bing.** —*n.* 〖俗〗= **confabulation.** —*v.i.* 〖俗〗= **confabulate.**

con·fab·u·late [kən'fæbjə,let; kən'fæbjuleit] *v.i.,* **-lat·ed, -lat·ing.** 談論;閒談;會談;談心〖with〗.

con·fab·u·la·tion [kən,fæbjə'leʃən; kən,fæbju'leiʃən] *n.* (隨便的)聚談;會談;閒談。(亦作 **confab**)

con·fab·u·la·tor [kən'fæbjə,letɚ; kən'fæbjuleitə] *n.* 聚談者;會談者;閒談者。

con·fect [*n.* 'kɑnfɛkt; 'kɔnfekt *v.* kən'fɛkt; kən'fekt] *n.* 〖廢〗蜜餞;糖果。—*v.t.* ①混合調製。②把…做成糖果、蜜餞等。③湊成。

con·fec·tion [kən'fɛkʃən; kən'fekʃən] *n.* ①糖果;點心;蜜餞。②混和;調製。③女裝或帽(通常爲精製者)。④多種藥物調製的口服軟膏。

con·fec·tion·ar·y [kən'fɛkʃən,ɛrɪ; kən'fekʃənəri] *adj.* 蜜餞、糖果的。—*n.* 蜜餞製造、出售或存放場所;蜜餞;糖果。

con·fec·tion·er [kən'fɛkʃənɚ; kən'fekʃənə] *n.* 糖果餅點類之製造人或販賣人。

confectioners' sugar 特級細砂糖。

con·fec·tion·er·y [kən'fɛkʃən,ɛrɪ; kən'fekʃənəri] *n., pl.* **-er·ies.** ①糖果餅點等之集合稱。②糖果餅點製造業。③糖果店。

Confed. Confederate.

con·fed·er·a·cy** [kən'fɛdərəsɪ, -'fɛdrəsɪ; kən'fedərəsi] *n., pl.* **-cies.** ①聯盟;同盟。②共謀;私黨。the Confederacy*** 美國南部邦聯(1860-61年間,美國南部退出合衆國因而導致內戰之十一州)。

***con·fed·er·ate** [*adj. & n.* kən'fɛdərɪt; kən'fedərit *v.* kən'fɛdə,ret; kən'fedəreit] *adj., n., v.,* **-at·ed, -at·ing.** —*adj.* ①同盟的;聯合的。②(C-)美國南北戰爭時

南部同盟的。 ***the Confederate States of America*** = **the Confederacy.** —*n.* ①同盟者;聯合者;同盟國。②共犯;同謀者。③(C-)美國南北戰爭時擁護南部邦聯者。—*v.t.* & *v.i.* 同盟;聯合。

con·fed·er·a·tion** [kən͵fɛdə'reʃən; kən͵fedə'reiʃən] *n.* ①同盟; 聯合。②同盟國;聯合者。 ***the Confederation 1781-89年間之北美合衆國。

***con·fer**[1] [kən'fɝ; kən'fəː] *v.*, **-ferred, -fer·ring.** —*v.t.* ①賜予; 頒給。to *confer* an honorary degree upon a person. 頒榮譽學位給一個人。②賦與。—*v.i.* 商量;商議。I *confer* with him about a certain matter. 我與他商量某事。「作 **cf., conf.**)」

con·fer[2] 〖拉〗*v.t.* 比較;參照;參較。(略

con·fer·(r)ee [͵kɑnfə'ri; ͵kɔnfə'riː] *n.* ①〖美〗參加會議者;評議員。②受賜者;(榮譽、學位等之)接受人。

***con·fer·ence** ['kɑnfərəns; 'kɔnfərəns] *n.* ①會議; 談判; 討論會。a peace *conference.* 和平會議。The director is in *conference* now. 主任在開會。②〖運動〗聯盟;協會;聯合會。—**con·fer·en·tial,** *adj.*

con·fer·ment [kən'fɝmənt; kən'fəːmənt] *n.* (學位、榮譽、贈品、特權等之)授與;頒給。

***con·fess** [kən'fɛs; kən'fes] *v.t.* ①承認;供認;自白;自認。to *confess* a crime. 承認罪行。②表示;聲明。③認過;認罪;懺悔;告解(尤指對神父告解)。to *confess* a sin. 認罪;懺悔罪。④聽告解。The priest *confessed* her. 神父聽她的告解。—*v.i.* ①承認;自認。②懺悔。—**a·ble,** *adj.*

con·fessed [kən'fɛst; kən'fest] *adj.* ①公認的;有定評的;明白的。a *confessed* fact. 明白的事實。②自己承認的;自白的;告解的。a *confessed* thief. 認罪的竊盜。He stood *confessed.* 他已認罪。—**ly,** *adv.*

***con·fes·sion** [kən'fɛʃən; kən'feʃən] *n.* ①承認;自認;自白。The prisoner made a full *confession.* 犯人全部招供。②認過;認罪;懺悔。③承認之事物,如悔過書或口供等。*confession* of faith. 信仰聲明(正式獲准進入教會前所作)。④告解(對神父懺悔,以求赦免)。

con·fes·sion·al [kən'fɛʃənəl; kən'feʃənəl] *n.* ①(宗教之) 懺悔; 告解。②懺悔室。 —*adj.* 懺悔的;自白的。

con·fes·sor [kən'fɛsɚ; kən'fesə] *n.* ①自白者。②聽告解的神父。③ (C-) = **Edward the Confessor.** (亦作 **confesser**)

con·fet·ti [kən'fɛtɪ; kən'feti] *n. pl., sing.* **-fet·to** [-'fɛto; -'fetɔː]. (婚禮或狂歡時所投擲之)五彩碎紙。

con·fi·dant [͵kɑnfə'dænt, 'kɑnfə͵dænt; ͵kɔnfi'dænt, 'kɔnfidænt] *n.* 密友;知己;心腹之人。

con·fi·dante [͵kɑnfə'dænt, 'kɑnfə͵dænt; ͵kɔnfi'dænt, 'kɔnfidænt] *n.* confidant 之女性。

***con·fide** [kən'faɪd; kən'faid] *v.*, **-fid·ed, -fid·ing.** —*v.i.* ①信任;信賴〖in〗。He *confided* in your honesty. 他信任你的誠實。②告以祕密或私事以示信賴。—*v.t.* ①信賴(告知祕密)。to *confide* a secret to a friend. 將祕密告知朋友。②交託;託付。

‡**con·fi·dence** ['kɑnfədəns; 'kɔnfidəns] *n.* ①信任;信賴。The servant enjoyed his master's *confidence.* 這傭人深得主人的信任。②自信;大膽。She has great *confidence* in her success. 她極自信能成功。③祕密。to exchange *confidences.* 交換祕密。***in confidence*** 當作祕密。***take a person into one's confidence*** 對某人吐露私事或祕密;以某人為心腹。

confidence game (獲得對方信任之後的)欺詐。(英亦作 **confidence trick**)

confidence man 騙子。

***con·fi·dent** ['kɑnfədənt; 'kɔnfidənt] *adj.* ①確信的; 完全相信的。We are *confident* of victory. 我們確信能勝利。I feel *confident* that we will win. 我確信我們將勝利。②自信的;大膽的。—*n.* 密友;知己。—**ly,** *adv.*

***con·fi·den·tial** [͵kɑnfə'dɛnʃəl; ͵kɔnfi'denʃəl] *adj.* ①機密的; 祕密的。a *confidential* correspondence. 祕密通信。②獲信任的;參與機密的。a *confidential* secretary. 機要祕書。③信任他人的; 以他人為心腹的。—**ness,** *n.*

confidential communication 不能對第三者洩露之祕密(如當事人對律師或懺悔者對神父所說的話)。「員。」

confidential employee 機要人

confidential inquiry 祕密調查。

con·fi·den·ti·al·i·ty [͵kɑnfɪ͵dɛnʃɪ'ælɪtɪ; ͵kɔnfi͵denʃi'æliti] *n.* 機密性;祕密性。

con·fi·den·tial·ly [͵kɑnfə'dɛnʃəlɪ; ͵kɔnfi'denʃəli] *adv.* 要告知祕密似地; 好像有祕密相告一般地。

con·fid·ing [kən'faɪdɪŋ; kən'faidiŋ] *adj.* 深信的;易信的。—**ly,** *adv.* —**ness,** *n.*

con·fig·u·ra·tion [kən͵fɪgjə'reʃən; kən͵figju'reiʃən] *n.* 輪廓;外貌;形狀;方位。—**al·ly,** *adv.* —**al, con·fig·u·ra·tive,** *adj.*

***con·fine** [*v.* kən'faɪn; kən'fain *n.* 'kɑnfaɪn; 'kɔnfain] *v.*, **-fined, -fin·ing,** *n.* —*v.t.* ①限制。②監禁。③臥病;分娩。He is *confined* to his room. 他病了不能出房。She expects to be *confined* soon. 她很快就要分娩。④控制。—*n.*(常 *pl.*) ①疆界;境界。the *confines* of our country. 我國的疆界。②邊疆區;邊緣。—**con·fin·er,** *n.* —**con·fin·a·ble,** *adj.* —**less,** *adj.*

con·fined [kən'faɪnd; kən'faind] *adj.* 分娩中的; 生產中的。—**ly,** *adv.* —**ness,** *n.*

con·fine·ment [kən'faɪnmənt; kən'fainmənt] *n.* ①限制。②拘留; 監禁。③臥病。④分娩。

***con·firm** [kən'fɝm; kən'fəːm] *v.t.* ①證實。This *confirms* my suspicions. 這證實了我的疑心。②認可;批准。to *confirm* an appointment. 批准任命。③加强; 使堅定。④〖宗教〗付堅振;施堅信禮。⑤證明確實收到。The order has been *confirmed* by the manufacturer. 定貨單已由廠方證明確實收到。⑥確定;訂妥。to *confirm* a plane reservation. 證實訂妥機位。

con·firm·a·ble [kən'fɝməbl; kən'fəːməbl] *adj.* 可確定的; 能證實的。

***con·fir·ma·tion** [͵kɑnfɚ'meʃən; ͵kɔnfə'meiʃən] *n.* ①認可;證實;確定。We are waiting for *confirmation* of the report. 我們在等待這報告的證實。②證明;證據。③〖宗教〗堅振;堅信禮。

con·firm·a·tive [kən'fɝmətɪv; kən'fəːmətiv] *adj.* 確證的; 確定的; 確認的;批准的。—**ly,** *adv.*

con·firm·a·to·ry [kən'fɝmə͵torɪ; kən'fəːmətəri] *adj.* ①確證的;確定的;確認

的(=confirmative). ②〖宗教〗堅信禮的。
con·firmed 〔kən'fɜmd; kən'fə:md〕 *adj.* ①證實的; 確認的。②習慣的。③長久的;慢性的(疾病)。—**ness,** *n.*
confirmed habit 積習。
confirming charge 保兌費。
con·fis·ca·ble 〔kən'fɪskəbl̩; kən'fiskəbl〕 *adj.* 可沒收的; 應充公的。
*__con·fis·cate__ 〔'kɑnfɪsˌket; 'kɔnfiskeit〕 *v.t.*, **-cat·ed, -cat·ing.** 充公;沒收。—**con·fis·cat·a·ble,** *adj.*
con·fis·ca·tion 〔ˌkɑnfɪs'keʃən; ˌkɔnfis'keiʃən〕 *n.* 沒收;充公。
con·fis·ca·to·ry 〔kən'fɪskəˌtorɪ; kən'fiskətəri〕 *adj.* 沒收的;充公的。
con·fi·ture 〔'kɑnfɪˌtʃur; 'kɔnfitʃuə〕 *n.* 糖果;蜜餞。
con·fla·grant 〔kən'flegrənt; kən'fleigrənt〕 *adj.* 燃燒的; 熾燃的。
con·fla·gra·tion 〔ˌkɑnflə'greʃən; ˌkɔnflə'greiʃən〕 *n.* 大火;火災。
con·fla·tion 〔kən'fleʃən; kən'fleiʃən〕 *n.* 根據兩種版本把兩個異文合併而成爲一個新的文句;此種形成的文句。
*__con·flict__ 〔*v.* kən'flɪkt; kən'flikt *n.* 'kɑnflɪkt; 'kɔnflikt〕 *v.i.* ①爭鬥; 戰鬥。France *conflicted* with England. 法國與英國爭鬥。②爭執;意見衝突;抵觸。His point of view *conflicts* with mine. 他的觀點與我的抵觸。—*n.* ①爭鬥;戰爭(尤指長期的)。②爭執;意見衝突;抵觸。a *conflict* of opinions. 意見衝突。—**con·flic·tion,** *n.* —**con·flic·to·ry,** *adj.*
con·flict·ing 〔kən'flɪktɪŋ; kən'fliktiŋ〕 *adj.* 衝突的;矛盾的;抵觸的。—**ly,** *adv.*
conflict of interest ①利害衝突。②從事公務者可能因執行公務而獲私利之情況。
conflict of laws ①法律間之相抵觸。②處理相抵觸法律之法律。
con·flu·ence 〔'kɑnfluəns; 'kɔnfluəns〕 *n.* ①(河流之)合流;匯流處。②羣集;羣衆。—**con·flu·ent,** *adj.*
con·flux 〔'kɑnflʌks; 'kɔnflʌks〕 *n.* ①(河流之)合流;匯流處。②羣集;羣衆。
*__con·form__ 〔kən'fɔrm; kən'fɔ:m〕 *v.t.* 使相似;使一致;使順應。—*v.i.* ①遵從;依照。You must *conform* to the rules. 你應遵從規則。②相合; 一致。③相配。His way of life *conforms* to his income. 他的生活方式與他的收入相配(量入爲出)。—**er,** *n.* —**ing·ly,** *adv.*
con·form·a·ble 〔kən'fɔrməbl̩; kən'fɔ:məbl〕 *adj.* 相似的;適應的;一致的;溫順的;服從的。—**con·form·a·bil·i·ty, —ness,** *n.* —**con·form·a·bly,** *adv.*
con·form·ance 〔kən'fɔrməns; kən'fɔ:məns〕 *n.* =**conformity.**
con·for·ma·tion 〔ˌkɑnfɔr'meʃən; ˌkɔnfɔ:'meiʃən〕 *n.* ①構造;形態;組成。②一致;適應。
con·form·ist 〔kən'fɔrmɪst; kən'fɔ:mist〕 *n.* ①遵奉傳統者;信奉因襲者。②(C-)英國國教徒。—*adj.* 因襲的。
con·form·i·ty 〔kən'fɔrmətɪ; kən'fɔ:miti〕 *n., pl.* **-ties.** ①相似; 一致。②服從;遵照。③〖英史〗信奉國教。
*__con·found__ 〔kɑn'faund; kən'faund〕 *v.t.* ①使驚訝;使惶惑;使狼狽。②混淆;使混亂;分不清。③使不純;使變質。④打敗;打破;破壞(敵人、計畫、希望等)。⑤討厭;該死(表煩惱或忿怒)。⑥推翻(理論等); 駁斥。***Confound it!*** 討厭!該死的! ***Confound you!*** 天罰你! 你混蛋! —**er,** *n.*
con·found·ed 〔kən'faundɪd; kən'faundid〕 *adj.* ①驚惶失措的; 困惑的。②討厭的;該死的(罵人之委婉語)。—**ness,** *n.*
con·found·ed·ly 〔kən'faundɪdlɪ; kən'faundidli〕 *adv.* 非常地;…得要命。
con·fra·ter·ni·ty 〔ˌkɑnfrə'tɜnətɪ; ˌkɔnfrə'tə:niti〕 *n., pl.* **-ties.** ①友愛之結合;志同道合之關係。②會社;團體。
con·frere 〔'kɑnfrɛr; 'kɔnfrɛə〕 *n.* 會員;社員;同仁;同志。
*__con·front__ 〔kən'frʌnt; kən'frʌnt〕 *v.t.* ①面對;使碰面。I am *confronted* by many difficulties. 我面對許多困難。②勇敢而冷靜地面對;對抗。③相對。④對照;比較。⑤使怒;使不愉快。—**a·tion,** *n.*
Con·fu·cian 〔kən'fjuʃən; kən'fju:ʃən〕 *adj.* 孔子的;孔子思想的;儒家的;儒家思想的。—*n.* 儒家學者。
Con·fu·cian·ism 〔kən'fjuʃənˌɪzəm; kən'fju:ʃənizm〕 *n.* 孔子思想; 儒家思想。
Con·fu·cius 〔kən'fjuʃəs; kən'fju:ʃəs〕 *n.* 孔子。
*__con·fuse__ 〔kən'fjuz; kən'fju:z〕 *v.t.*, **-fused, -fus·ing.** ①使混亂。So many people talking to me at once *confused* me. 這樣多人同時與我說話使我迷惑。②二者之中不能辨別;誤認;混同。to *confuse* dates. 弄錯日期。③使羞赧不安。—**con·fus·able,** *adj.* —**con·fus·a·bly, con·fus·ing·ly,** *adv.*
con·fused 〔kən'fjuzd; kən'fju:zd〕 *adj.* 混淆不清的;混亂的;紊亂的。—**ly,** *adv.*
*__con·fu·sion__ 〔kən'fjuʒən; kən'fju:ʒən〕 *n.* ①混亂;騷亂。②迷惑;惶惑。He is in a state of *confusion.* 他在惶惑狀態中。③混淆不清。④令人迷惑或混亂之事。⑤不安;羞慚。Her *confusion* led to blushes. 她的羞慚使她面紅耳赤。—**al,** *adj.*
con·fu·ta·tion 〔ˌkɑnfju'teʃən; ˌkɔnfju:'teiʃən〕 *n.* ①辯駁; 駁倒。②用以駁倒之事物。
con·fute 〔kən'fjut; kən'fju:t〕 *v.t.*, **-fut·ed, -fut·ing.** ① 證明(某人)錯誤;辯倒(某人)。② 證明(論據、證言等)爲錯誤;駁倒;駁住。—**con·fut·a·ble, con·fu·ta·tive,** *adj.* —**con·fu·ta·tor,** *n.*
Cong. ①Congregation(al). ②Congregationalist. ③Congress.
con·ga 〔'kɑŋgə; 'kɔŋgə〕 *n., v.,* **-gaed, -ga·ing.** —*n.* ①康加舞(舞者排成一行或成對, 向前走三步然後一踢脚)。②跳康加舞時的音樂。—*v.i.* 跳康加舞。
con·gé 〔'kɑnʒe; 'kɔ̃:ʒei〕〖法〗*n.* ①撤職;免職;辭職。②正式之告別;辭行。③〖建築〗一種凹形嵌線。
con·geal 〔kən'dʒil; kən'dʒi:l〕 *v.t.* ①使凝結;使凍僵。②使癱瘓。—*v.i.* ①凝結;凍僵。②變冷。—**ment,** *n.*
con·gee[1] 〔'kɑndʒi; 'kɔndʒi:〕 *v.i.,* **-geed, -gee·ing.** 告別;鞠躬告別。
con·gee[2] *n.* 稀飯。(亦作 **conjee**)
con·ge·la·tion 〔ˌkɑndʒə'leʃən; ˌkɔndʒi'leiʃən〕 *n.* ①凝固; 凝結。②凝結物; 凝塊。③凝凍;凍傷。
con·ge·la·tive 〔ˌkɑndʒə'letɪv; ˌkɔndʒi'leitiv〕 *adj.* 會凝固的;有凝結作用的。
con·ge·ner 〔'kɑndʒɪnə; 'kɔndʒinə〕 *n.* 同種之人或物。

con·ge·ner·ic 〔ˌkɑndʒɪˈnɛrɪk; ˌkɔndʒiˈnerik〕 *adj.* 同種的; 同屬的; 同族的;同源的。(亦作**congenerical**)

***con·gen·ial** 〔kənˈdʒinjəl; kənˈdʒiːniəl〕 *adj.* ①性格相同的(人);氣質相似的;意氣相投的; 同情的。He found few persons *congenial* to him. 他發現沒幾個人和他意氣相投。②適合的(事物);適意的。③令人快樂的;宜人的。④友善的; 好客的。—**ly**,*adv.*—**ness**,*n.*

con·ge·ni·al·i·ty 〔kənˌdʒinɪˈælətɪ; kənˌdʒiːniˈæliti〕 *n.* 同性質;意氣相投;氣質相似;適合;適意。

con·gen·i·tal 〔kənˈdʒɛnətl̩; kənˈdʒenitl〕 *adj.* 天生的; 先天的; 天賦的; 與生俱來的(指疾病、缺陷等)。—**ly**, *adv.*

con·ger 〔ˈkɑŋgɚ; ˈkɔŋgə〕 *n.* 海鰻。(亦作 **conger eel**)

con·ge·ries 〔kɑnˈdʒɪriz; kɔnˈdʒiəriːz〕 *n. sing.* or *pl.* 聚集;堆積;團塊。

con·gest 〔kənˈdʒɛst; kənˈdʒest〕 *v.t.* ①充滿; 擁塞。②(使)充血。 —*v.i.* 擁塞;阻塞。—**i·ble**, *adj.*

con·ges·tion 〔kənˈdʒɛstʃən; kənˈdʒestʃən〕 *n.* ①充滿; 擁塞。②充血。

con·ges·tive 〔kənˈdʒɛstɪv; kənˈdʒestiv〕 *adj.* 〖醫〗充血的;充血性的。

con·glo·bate 〔kɑnˈglobet; ˈkɔnglouˌbeit〕 *v.*, **-bat·ed**, **-bat·ing**, *adj.* —*v.t.* & *v.i.* (亦作 **conglobe**)(使)成球形;堆成圓堆。—*adj.* 成球形的;堆成圓堆的。—**ly**, *adv.*

con·glo·ba·tion 〔ˌkɑngloˈbeʃən; ˌkɔnglouˈbeiʃən〕 *n.* 球體;團塊;圓形物。

con·glom·er·a·cy 〔kənˈglɑmərəsɪ; kənˈglɔmərəsi〕 *n.*多元混合商業組織之形成。

con·glom·er·ate 〔*adj., n.* kənˈglɑmərɪt; kənˈglɔmərit *v.* kənˈglɑməˌret; kənˈglɔməreit〕 *v.*, **-at·ed**, **-at·ing**, *adj., n.* —*v.t.* & *v.i.* (使)成一團;使成圓塊;集聚。—*adj.* ①聚成一團的。②集聚而成的。 —*n.* ①集成物; 聚集物。②多元混合組成之龐大商業公司。③〖地質〗礫岩。

con·glom·er·a·tion 〔kənˌglɑməˈreʃən; kənˌglɔməˈreiʃən〕 *n.* ①聚集; 凝聚。②聚集物;凝體;團塊。

con·glom·er·a·tor〔kənˈglɑmərɪtɚ; kənˈglɔməritə〕 *n.*多元混合組成的龐大商業公司之首腦人物。

con·glu·ti·nate〔kənˈglutəˌnet; kənˈgluːtineit〕*v.*, **-nat·ed**, **-nat·ing**, *adj.*—*v.t.* & *v.i.* (使)癒合;(使)結合;(使)黏着。—*adj.* 結合的; 黏着的。—**con·glu·ti·na·tion**, *n.*

Con·go 〔ˈkɑŋgo; ˈkɔŋgou〕 *n.* ①剛果(中非一共和國, 首都布拉薩, Brazzaville). ②剛果河(非洲中部一大河)。

Con·go·lese 〔ˌkɑŋgoˈliz, -ˈlis; ˌkɔŋgəˈliːz〕 *adj.* 剛果的;剛果人的; 剛果語的。—*n.* 剛果人。

Congo paper 一種化學試紙,遇酸變藍色,遇鹼則變紅色。

con·gou 〔ˈkɑŋgu; ˈkɔŋguː〕〖中〗*n.*工夫茶 (中國產之一種紅茶)。(亦作 **congo**)

con·grat·u·lant 〔kənˈgrætʃələnt; kənˈgrætjulənt〕 *adj.* 祝賀的; 慶賀的。—*n.* 祝賀者。

***con·grat·u·late** 〔kənˈgrætʃəˌlet; kənˈgrætjuleit〕 *v.t.*, **-lat·ed**, **-lat·ing**. ①慶賀; 祝賀。 I *congratulate* you on your engagement. 我賀你訂婚。②自慶; 私自慶幸。I *congratulate* my escape. 我深自慶幸得以脫逃。

***con·grat·u·la·tion** 〔kənˌgrætʃəˈleʃən; kənˌgrætjuˈleiʃən〕 *n.* ①祝賀; 慶賀。②(*pl.*)賀詞;祝詞。Please accept my *congratulations*. 請接受我的祝賀。*Congratulations!* 恭喜! —**al**, *adj.*

con·grat·u·la·tor〔kənˈgrætʃəˌletɚ; kənˈgrætjuleitə〕 *n.* 祝賀者;慶賀者。

con·grat·u·la·to·ry〔kənˈgrætʃələˌtorɪ; kənˈgrætjuleitəri〕 *adj.* 慶賀的;祝賀的。a *congratulatory* telegram. 賀電。

con·gre·gate 〔ˈkɑŋgrɪˌget; ˈkɔŋgrigeit〕 *v.*, **-gat·ed**, **-gat·ing**, *adj.* —*v.t.* 集合; 聚集。—*v.i.* 會集; 聚集。—*adj.* ①集合的;聚集的。②集體的。

***con·gre·ga·tion** 〔ˌkɑŋgrɪˈgeʃən; ˌkɔŋgriˈgeiʃən〕 *n.* ①集合;會集。②集合的人或東西;集會。③宗教的集會或會衆。

con·gre·ga·tion·al〔ˌkɑŋgrɪˈgeʃənl̩; ˌkɔŋgriˈgeiʃənl〕 *adj.* ①會衆的; 集合的。②(C-) 〖基督教〗公理(教會)的。 —**ly**, *adv.* —**ist**, *n.*, *adj.*

Congregational Church (基督教之)公理教會。

con·gre·ga·tion·al·ism 〔ˌkɑŋgrɪˈgeʃənl̩ˌɪzəm; ˌkɔŋgriˈgeiʃənl̩izm〕 *n.* ①組合教會。②(C-) 公理教會之主義或制度;會衆自治主義。

‡**con·gress** 〔ˈkɑŋgrəs; ˈkɔŋgres〕 *n.* ①國家立法的機關(尤指共和國的)。②(C-)美國的國會;美國國會會期。③集會。International *Congress* of Medicine. 國際醫學會議。④協會。⑤羣。—*v.i.* 聚集;集合。

***con·gres·sion·al** 〔kənˈgrɛʃənl̩; kɔŋˈgreʃənl〕 *adj.* ①會議的;集會的。②(C-)美國國會的。—**ist**, *n.* —**ly**, *adv.*

***con·gress·man** 〔ˈkɑŋgrəsmən; ˈkɔŋgresmən〕 *n.*, *pl.* **-men**. (常C-)美國國會議員(尤指衆院議員)。

con·gress·wom·an 〔ˈkɑŋgrəsˌwumən; ˈkɔŋgresˌwumən〕 *n.*, *pl.* **-wom·en**. 國會女議員(尤指衆院女議員)。

con·gru·ence 〔ˈkɑŋgruəns; ˈkɔŋgruəns〕 *n.* ①適合;一致;相合性。②〖數學〗符合;全等。(亦作 **congruency**)

con·gru·ent 〔ˈkɑŋgruənt; ˈkɔŋgruənt〕 *adj.* ①一致的;相合的。②〖幾何〗全等的。*congruent* triangles. 全等三角形。

con·gru·ous 〔ˈkɑŋgruəs; ˈkɔŋgruəs〕 *adj.* ①符合的; 一致的 〖to, with〗. ②適當的。③和諧的;前後一貫的。④〖數學〗符合的;全等的。—**ly**, *adv.* —**ness**, *n.*

con·ic 〔ˈkɑnɪk; ˈkɔnik〕 *adj.* 圓錐的;圓錐形的。—*n.* 〖數學〗 =**conic section.**

con·i·cal 〔ˈkɑnɪkl̩; ˈkɔnikəl〕 *adj.* 圓錐的;圓錐形的。—**ly**, *adv.*

conical surface 〖數學〗 錐式曲面。

con·i·coid 〔ˈkɑnəˌkɔɪd; ˈkɔnikɔid〕 *n.* 〖幾何〗二次曲面。

con·ics 〔ˈkɑnɪks; ˈkɔniks〕 *n.* 〖數學〗 錐線法;錐線論。

conic section 〖數學〗錐線;二次曲線。

co·ni·fer 〔ˈkonəfɚ; ˈkounifə〕 *n.* 針葉樹;松柏科植物。

co·nif·er·ous 〔koˈnɪfərəs; kouˈnifərəs〕 *adj.* 〖植物〗針葉科的;松柏科的。

co·ni·form 〔ˈkonɪˌfɔrm; ˈkounifɔːm〕 *adj.* 圓錐形的。

conj. ①conjunction. ②conjugation. ③conjunctive.

con·jec·tur·a·ble 〔kənˈdʒɛktʃərəbl̩; kənˈdʒektʃərəbl〕 *adj.* 可推測的。

con·jec·tur·al 〔kənˈdʒɛktʃərəl; kənˈdʒektʃərəl〕 *adj.* ①揣度的;推測的。②喜揣度的;喜推測的。—**ly**, *adv.*

***con·jec·ture** 〔kən'dʒɛktʃɚ; kən'dʒektʃə〕 *n., v.,* **-tured, -tur·ing.** —*n.* 推測;臆測;猜想。—*v.t.*推測;猜想。—*v.i.*臆測;猜想。

con·join 〔kən'dʒɔɪn; kən'dʒɔin〕 *v.t. & v.i.* 結合;連接;聯合。

con·joint 〔kən'dʒɔɪnt; kən'dʒɔint〕 *adj.* 連合的;相聯的;共同的。—**ly,** *adv.*

con·ju·gal 〔'kɑndʒʊgl̩; 'kɔndʒugəl〕 *adj.* 婚姻的;夫婦的。

con·ju·gate 〔*v.* 'kɑndʒə,get; 'kɔndʒugeit *adj., n.* 'kɑndʒʊgɪt, -,get; 'kɔndʒugit, -geit〕 *v.,* **-gat·ed, -gat·ing,** *adj., n.* —*v.t.* ①〖文法〗把一個動詞的各形式作有系統的排列。②配合;結合。—*adj.* ①結合的;配合的。②從同一字根變來的。③〖數學〗共軛的。—*n.* 從同一字根變化而來的另一字。

conjugate axis 〖數學〗共軛軸。

conjugate complex number 〖數學〗共軛複數。

conjugate hyperbola 〖數學〗共軛雙曲線。

conjugate lines 〖數學〗共軛直線。

conjugate point 〖數學〗共軛點。

***con·ju·ga·tion** 〔,kɑndʒə'geʃən; ,kɔndʒu'geiʃən〕 *n.* ①連合;配合。*conjugation* of the sexes. 兩性之配合。②〖文法〗動詞之變化。—**al,** *adj.* —**al·ly,** *adv.*

con·junct 〔kən'dʒʌŋkt; kən'dʒʌŋkt〕 *adj.* 連合的;結合的。

con·junc·tion** 〔kən'dʒʌŋkʃən; kən'dʒʌŋkʃən〕 *n.* ①連合;連結;連接。②〖文法〗連接詞。③〖天文〗合;天體之間顯著的接近。a *conjunction* of Mars and Jupiter. 火星與木星的接近。④一連串事件或情況之結合。in conjunction with*** 連同;共同。—**al,** *adj.*

con·junc·ti·va 〔,kɑndʒʌŋk'taɪvə; ,kɔndʒʌŋk'taivə〕 *n., pl.* **-vas, -vae** 〔-vi; -viː〕.〖解剖〗(眼球之)結合膜。

con·junc·tive 〔kən'dʒʌŋktɪv; kən'dʒʌŋktiv〕 *adj.* ①連結的;連接的。②互相配合的;聯合的。③〖文法〗有連接作用的。—*n.* 〖文法〗連接詞。—**ly,** *adv.*

conjunctive adverbs 〖文法〗連接副詞,卽本爲副詞而用作複合句之連接詞,但其副詞之意義仍甚爲顯著。

conjunctive phrase 〖文法〗連接片語,乃作連接詞用之片語。

conjunctive pronoun 〖文法〗連接代名詞,卽關係代名詞。

con·junc·ti·vi·tis〔kən,dʒʌŋktə'vaɪtɪs; kən,dʒʌŋkti'vaitis〕 *n.* 〖醫〗結合膜炎。

con·junc·ture 〔kən'dʒʌŋktʃɚ; kən'dʒʌŋktʃə〕 *n.* ①連接。②局面;時機;危機。

con·ju·ra·tion 〔,kɑndʒʊ'reʃən; ,kɔndʒuə'reiʃən〕 *n.* ①以聖名召喚。②符咒;魔法。

con·jur·a·tor〔'kɑndʒə,retɚ; 'kɔndʒəreitə〕 *n.*①魔法師。②〖法律〗陰謀者;同謀者。

***con·jure** 〔'kʌndʒɚ, 'kɑndʒɚ; 'kʌndʒə. *for v.t.* ④ kən'dʒʊr; kən'dʒuə〕 *v.,* **-jured, -jur·ing.** —*v.t.* ①行魔術。②以咒召遣〖常 up〗。③回憶;追憶〖常 up〗。④懇求;懇切祈求。—*v.i.* ①行魔術;用咒召遣靈魂或魔鬼。②以敏捷手法變戲法。

con·jur·er 〔*for* ① kən'dʒʊrɚ; kən'dʒuərə. 'kʌndʒərɚ; 'kʌndʒərə〕 *n.* ①懇求者。②魔術師。③奇術家,行咒法者。④〖俗〗聰明俐落之人。(亦作 **conjuror**)

conk 〔kɑŋk; kɔŋk〕 *n.* 〖俚〗①〖英〗鼻。②頭。③頭上之一擊。④一種由黴菌引起的植物病。—*v.t.* 〖俚〗打擊…之頭部。***conk out*** **a.** 〖俚〗突然失靈;突然發生故障。**b.** 死亡。**c.** 失去知覺。**d.** 停止或慢下來。

con man 〖俚〗騙子。

Conn. Connecticut.

con·nate 〔'kɑnet; 'kɔneit〕 *adj.* ①先天的;與生俱來的。②同時發生的;同時開始存在的。③性質一致的;同源的。④〖生物〗合生的;合體的;並蒂的。⑤性質相合或有關係的。⑥〖地質〗在沉澱物形成時被封在裏面的。

con·nat·u·ral 〔kə'nætʃərəl; kə'nætʃrəl〕 *adj.*①與生俱來的;固有的;自然的〖to〗.②同性質的;同種的。

‡con·nect 〔kə'nɛkt; kə'nekt〕 *v.t.* ①連接;聯合;結合〖常 with〗. ②聯繫;聯想。③聯貫;貫通。④接通。⑤使有關。⑥使發生(商業上的或人與人間的)關係。to *connect* oneself with a group of like-minded persons. 使自己與一羣志同道合者建立關係。—*v.i.* ①連結;連接。The two parts do not *connect* properly. 這兩部分連接不好。②聯絡;接駁(如火車、汽車的聯運)。

con·nect·ed 〔kə'nɛktɪd; kə'nektid〕 *adj.* ①連在一起的。②按次序連接的。③有人事關係的。—**ly,** *adv.*

con·nect·er, con·nec·tor 〔kə'nɛktɚ; kə'nektə〕 *n.* 連接之人或物;連接器。

con·nect·i·ble 〔kə'nɛktəbl̩; kə'nektibl〕 *adj.* 可以聯結的。(亦作 **connectable**)

Con·nect·i·cut 〔kə'nɛtɪkət; kə'netikət〕 *n.* 康乃狄克(美國東北部一州,首府爲 Hartford).

connecting rod 〖機械〗連桿。

con·nec·tion** 〔kə'nɛkʃən; kə'nekʃən〕 *n.* ①連接;連合;聯繫。②通信工具;交通工具。③(方便旅客)車船等的聯運。④關係。a business *connection.* 商業上的關係;業務上的關係。I have no *connection* with that firm. 我和那個公司沒有關係。⑤親戚。He is my intimate *connection.* 他是我的近親。⑥派系;宗派;政治或宗教的關係。⑦連接的東西。⑧顧客。⑨聯想。⑩上下文關係。⑪性交。⑫(常 *pl.*)人事關係。He has *connections* in the Senate. 他在參議院中有人事關係。⑬通訊線路。a bad telephone *connection.* 電話線路不佳。⑭〖美俚〗毒販;毒品的來源。in connection with*** 關於。(英亦作 **connexion**) —**al,** *adj.*

con·nec·tion-peg 〔kə'nɛkʃən,pɛg; kə'nekʃənpeg〕 *n.* 臨時接通電流之插頭。

con·nec·tive 〔kə'nɛktɪv; kə'nektiv〕 *adj.* ①連接的。②聯合的;結合的。③連接詞的。—*n.* ①用以連接之物。②〖文法〗連結詞(用以連接字、片語、子句及句等)。

connective tissue 〖生物〗結締體素。

conn·ing tower〔'kɑnɪŋ~; 'kɔniŋ~〕 ①(軍艦)司令塔;駕駛臺。②(潛艇)瞭望塔。

con·nip·tion 〔kə'nɪpʃən; kə'nipʃən〕 *n.* ①(常 *pl.*)(亦作 **conniption fit**)〖美俗〗陣怒;一陣發狂。②(*pl.*) =**hysterics.**

con·niv·ance, con·niv·ence 〔kə'naɪvəns; kə'naivəns〕*n.* ①默許;縱容。②〖法律〗**a.** 知情不報;對犯罪之鼓勵或同意。**b.** 對配偶通姦行爲之縱容。(亦作 **connivancy**)

con·nive 〔kə'naɪv; kə'naiv〕 *v.i.,* **-nived, -niv·ing.** ①假裝不見;默許;縱容。②共謀。③〖生物〗逐漸集中於一處或點。

con·nois·seur 〔,kɑnə'sɝ; ,kɔni'səː〕 *n.* (藝術品之)鑑定家;行家。

con·no·ta·tion 〔,kɑnə'teʃən; ,kɔnə'teiʃən〕 *n.* 涵意;暗示。

con·not·a·tive 〔'kɑnə,tetɪv; 'kɔnou-

teitiv] *adj.* ①含蓄的;暗示的〖of〗. ②〖邏輯〗內包的;內涵的。
con·note [kə'not; kɔ'nout] *v.t.*, **-not·ed, -not·ing.** ①暗示;含意;包涵。②〖邏輯〗內涵;包攝。
con·nu·bi·al [kə'nubɪəl; kə'njuːbiəl] *adj.* 婚姻的;夫婦的。—**ly,** *adv.*
con·nu·bi·al·i·ty [kəˌnjubɪ'ælətɪ; kəˌnjuːbi'æliti] *n., pl.* **-ties.** ①婚姻。②有關婚姻之事。
co·noid ['konɔɪd; 'kounɔid] *adj.* 圓錐形的。—*n.*①錐形體;圓錐物。②〖幾何〗劈錐曲面。
con·plane [kɑn'plen; kɔn'plein] *adj.* 〖數學〗位於同一個平面的。
***con·quer** ['kɑŋkə, 'kɔŋkə; 'kɔŋkə] *v.t.* ①攻取;略取。②征服;克服。to *conquer* an enemy. 征服敵人。to *conquer* bad habits. 克服不良的習慣。—*v.i.* 得勝。
con·quer·a·ble ['kɑŋkərəbḷ; 'kɔŋkərəbl] *adj.* 可勝的;可克服的。
con·quer·ess ['kɑŋkərɛs; 'kɔŋkəres] *n.* 女征服者。
con·quer·ing·ly ['kɑŋkərɪŋlɪ; 'kɔŋkəriŋli] *adv.* 勝利地;征服姿態地。
con·quer·or** ['kɑŋkərə; 'kɔŋkərə] *n.* 征服者;勝利者。the Conqueror*** 英王威廉一世之稱號。
con·quest** ['kɑŋkwɛst; 'kɔŋkwest] *n.* ①征服; 戰勝。They succeeded in the *conquest* of that city. 他們征服了那城。the *conquest* of difficulties. 克服困難。②略取的土地; 戰利品。③愛情的勝利; 恩寵之贏得。④愛情的俘虜。the Conquest*** 英國之征服(指 1066 年開始,英國爲 Normandy 征服之事實)。
con·quis·ta·dor [kɑn'kwɪstəˌdɔr; kɔn'kwistədɔə] *n., pl.* **-dors, -dores.** 〖西〗①十六世紀征服墨西哥和秘魯之西班牙人。②征服者。
Con·rad ['kɑnræd; 'kɔnræd] *n.* 康拉德(Joseph,1857–1924,生於波蘭之英國小說家)。
Cons. ① Conservative. ② Consul.
cons. ①consecrated. ②consolidated. ③consonant. ④constitution. ⑤constitutional. ⑥construction. ⑦constable. ⑧consul. ⑨consulting.
con·san·guin·e·ous [ˌkɑnsæŋ'gwɪnɪəs; ˌkɔnsæŋ'gwiniəs] *adj.* ①同血統的; 同族的; 同祖先的。②血緣的; 血親的。(亦作 **consanguine, consanguined**)
con·san·guin·i·ty [ˌkɑnsæŋ'gwɪnətɪ; ˌkɔnsæŋ'gwiniti] *n.* 血親;同族;親族。
con·science** ['kɑnʃəns; 'kɔnʃəns] *n.* 良心。a good (*or* clear) *conscience.* 問心無愧。a bad (*or* guilty) *conscience.* 有愧於心。for conscience' sake*** 爲良心起見。***go against one's conscience*** 違背良心。***have something on one's conscience*** 問心有愧;內疚。***in all conscience*** 〖俗〗**a.** 當然。**b.** 正當地;合理地。***make something a matter of conscience*** 依照良心行某事。—**less,** *adj.*
conscience clause 說明因良心關係而不能守某規定時可不受處分之法律條文。
conscience money 爲使良心獲得安寧而付出的錢。
con·science-strick·en ['kɑnʃənsˌstrɪkən; 'kɔnʃənsˌstrikən] *adj.* 良心不安的;受良心譴責的。(亦作**conscience-struck, conscience-smitten**)
***con·sci·en·tious** [ˌkɑnʃɪ'ɛnʃəs; ˌkɔnʃi'enʃəs, kɔn'ʃjen-] *adj.* ①從良心的; 正直的。②謹愼的;盡責的。—**ly,** *adv.* —**ness,** *n.*
conscientious objector 因反對戰爭或基於宗教信仰而不肯服兵役的人。
con·scion·a·ble ['kɑnʃənəbḷ; 'kɔnʃṇəbl] *adj.* 〖罕〗合乎良心的;公正的。
***con·scious** ['kɑnʃəs; 'kɔnʃəs] *adj.* ①覺得的;知道的。to be *conscious* of a sharp pain. 覺得刺痛。②自覺的。He spoke with *conscious* superiority. 他帶着自覺的優越感說話。③有知覺的;有意識的。He was badly hurt, but he still remained *conscious.* 他傷得很厲害, 但仍未失去知覺。④有意的。⑤羞怯的;窘困的。⑥故意的。—**ly,** *adv.*
***con·scious·ness** ['kɑnʃəsnɪs; 'kɔnʃəsnis] *n.* ①知覺;意識。to regain *consciousness* after a swoon. 昏厥後恢復知覺。②個人或集體的思想和意識;自覺。
con·scribe [kən'skraɪb; kən'skraib] *v.t.*, **-scribed, -scrib·ing.** 徵服兵役。
con·script [*adj.*, *n.* 'kɑnskrɪpt; 'kɔnskript *v.* kən'skrɪpt; kən'skript] *adj.* 被徵入伍的; 徵召的。—*n.* 徵集入伍的兵士;應徵的兵。—*v.t.* ①徵召; 徵集。②强徵爲政府之用;徵用。
conscript fathers 參議員;立法委員。
con·scrip·tion [kən'skrɪpʃən; kən'skripʃən] *n.* 徵集;徵兵;徵用;徵發。*conscription* age.兵役年齡。*conscription* system. 徵兵制度。*conscription* of wealth. (未應召者所納之)兵役稅。
conscription law 兵役法。
***con·se·crate** ['kɑnsɪˌkret; 'kɔnsikreit] *v.t.*, **-crat·ed, -crat·ing.** ①奉爲神聖;尊崇;供獻。②行宗教儀式以任(某人)爲主教等;任聖職。③獻(身);委(身)。He *consecrated* his life to the service of the country. 他獻身爲國家服務。④使成爲神聖。
con·se·cra·tion [ˌkɑnsɪ'kreʃən; ˌkɔnsi'kreiʃən] *n.* ①奉爲神聖。②聖職授任。
con·se·cra·to·ry ['kɑnsɪkrəˌtorɪ; 'kɔnsikrətəri] *adj.* ①奉爲神聖的;奉獻的。②聖職授任的。
con·se·cu·tion [ˌkɑnsɪ'kjuʃən; ˌkɔnsi'kjuːʃən] *n.* ①連續; 順序; 邏輯上的聯貫;論理之一貫; 推理上的連系。②〖文法〗(措辭、時態等之)一貫;一致。
con·sec·u·tive [kən'sɛkjətɪv; kən'sekjutiv] *adj.* ①連續的; 始終一貫的。②〖文法〗表示結果的(如子句)。—**ly,** *adv.* —**ness,** *n.*
consecutive clause 〖文法〗表示「結果的副詞子句。」
consecutive points 〖數學〗相鄰點。
con·sen·su·al [kən'sɛnʃuəl; kən'senʃuəl] *adj.* ①〖法律〗由雙方同意而成立的。②〖生理〗交感性的;交感作用的。—**ly,** *adv.*
con·sen·sus [kən'sɛnsəs; kən'sensəs] *n.* ①一致;意見的一致。②一般的意見;輿論。
‡**con·sent** [kən'sɛnt; kən'sent] *v.i.* 同意;答應; 允許(與 to 或 infinitive 連用)。They *consented* to buy this house. 他們同意買這所房子。—*n.* 同意;答應;許可。Her parents would not give their *consent* to her marriage. 她的父母不同意她的婚姻。***age of consent*** 〖法律〗結婚年齡。***Silence gives consent.*** 沉默卽認可。***with one consent*** 一致。
con·sen·ta·ne·ous [ˌkɑnsɛn'tenɪəs; ˌkɔnsen'teiniəs] *adj.* 相合的;一致同意的。

con·sent·er 〔kən'sɛntɚ; kən'sentə〕 *n.* ①同意者。②參與者。

con·sen·tient 〔kən'sɛnʃənt; kən'senʃənt〕 *adj.* 同意的; 一致的; 協同的。—**con·sen·tience,** *n.*

con·sent·ing 〔kən'sɛntɪŋ; kən'sentiŋ〕 *adj.* 同意的;准許的。

con·se·quence** 〔'kɑnsə,kwɛns; 'kɔnsikwəns〕 *n.* ①結果;影響。The *consequence* of his fall is a broken leg. 他跌下的結果是斷了一條腿。②重要。a matter of little (*or* no) *consequence.* 無關重要(或不重要)的事。③重要的地位;顯要。a person of *consequence.* 重要的人物。as a consequence*** 其結果是; 因此。***in consequence*** (***of***) 由於…。*In consequence of* his bad conduct he was dismissed. 他由於行爲不良被開除了。***take the consequences*** 接受後果;自作自受。

***con·se·quent** 〔'kɑnsə,kwɛnt; 'kɔnsikwənt〕 *adj.* ①是由於; 是來自。His financial embarrassment is *consequent* upon his careless spending.他經濟上的困難是由於胡亂花錢。②邏輯上一貫的。—*n.* ①結果;影響。② **a.** 〖數學〗後項。**b.** 〖邏輯〗(假言命題之)後件。

con·se·quen·tial 〔,kɑnsə'kwɛnʃəl; ,kɔnsi'kwenʃəl〕 *adj.* ①結果的;相因而生的;邏輯上一致的。②自大的;自傲的。③重要的。—**i·ty,** *n.* —**ly,** *adv.*

***con·se·quent·ly** 〔'kɑnsə,kwɛntlɪ; 'kɔnsikwəntli〕 *adv.* 因此;所以。

con·serv·an·cy 〔kən'sɝvənsɪ; kən'səːvənsi〕 *n., pl.* **-cies.** ①保存;保藏;保護。②〖英〗(河川、港灣之)管理委員會。

con·ser·va·tion 〔,kɑnsɚ'veʃən; ,kɔnsə(ː)'veiʃən〕 *n.* ①保存;保藏。②政府對於森林、水利的保護。③受如上保護的森林或區域。—**al,** *adj.*

con·ser·va·tion·ist 〔,kɑnsɚ'veʃənɪst; ,kɔnsə(ː)'veiʃənist〕 *n.* (資源之)保護管理論者;自然風景之保護論者。

conservation of energy 能量不滅。

conservation of mass 質量不滅。

con·serv·a·tism 〔kən'sɝvətɪzəm; kən'səːvətizəm〕 *n.* 守舊性;保守主義。

***con·serv·a·tive** 〔kən'sɝvətɪv; kən'səːvətiv〕 *adj.* ①(政黨)保守的;守舊的。②謹慎的;保守的。a *conservative* estimate. 保守的估計。③缺乏時新款式的。④有保存力的;防腐的。—*n.* ①保守者;守舊者。②(C-)英國保守黨員。③防腐劑。—**ly,** *adv.* —**ness,** *n.*

Conservative Party ①英國之保守黨。②加拿大之保守黨。

con·ser·va·toire 〔kən,sɝvə'twɑr; kən'səːvətwɑː〕〖法〗*n.* 音樂學校;藝術學校。

con·ser·va·tor 〔'kɑnsɚ,vetɚ, kən'sɝvətɚ; 'kɔnsə(ː)veitə, *for* ③kən'səːvətə〕 *n.*①保護者。②(博物館等之)管理員;〖英〗(河川等之)管理委員。③〖法律〗監護人。

con·serv·a·to·ry 〔kən'sɝvə,torɪ; kən'səːvətri〕 *n., pl.* **-ries,** *adj.* —*n.* ①溫室;暖房。②音樂學校。—*adj.* 保存的;有保護作用的。

***con·serve** 〔*v.* kən'sɝv; kən'səːv *n.* 'kɑnsɝv, kən'sɝv; kən'səːv, 'kɔnsəːv〕 *v.,* **-served, -serv·ing,** *n.* —*v.t.* ①保存; 保全。②使成蜜餞。—*n.* (常 *pl.*) 蜜餞;果醬。—**con·serv·a·ble,** *adj.* —**con·serv·er,** *n.*

:con·sid·er 〔kən'sɪdɚ; kən'sidə〕 *v.t.* ①思考;考慮。②以爲;認爲;視爲。I *considered* him a rascal. 我認爲他是一個流氓。③注意; 顧及; 爲…着想。He never *considers* others. 他從不顧及他人。④尊重;重視。⑤考慮接受。I'll *consider* your offer. 我將考慮你的提議。⑥留意; 研究。 —*v.i.* 考慮;熟思。—**er,** *n.*

:con·sid·er·a·ble 〔kən'sɪdərəbl; kən'sidərəbl〕 *adj.* ①值得考慮的; 重要的; 值得注意的。 The mayor is a *considerable* citizen. 市長是一位重要的公民。②不少的;多的。a *considerable* sum of money. 一筆相當可觀的錢。—*n.*〖美俗〗多。He has done *considerable* for me. 他爲我做了不少事。

***con·sid·er·a·bly** 〔kən'sɪdərəblɪ; kən'sidərəbli〕 *adv.* 非常地;頗。It's *considerably* colder this morning. 今天早晨冷得多了。

***con·sid·er·ate** 〔kən'sɪdərɪt; kən'sidərit〕 *adj.* 體諒的;體貼的;顧慮週到的。We should be *considerate* of the comfort of old people. 我們應顧慮到老年人的舒適。—**ly,** *adv.* —**ness,** *n.*

con·sid·er·a·tion** 〔kən,sɪdə'reʃən; kən,sidə'reiʃən〕 *n.* ①考慮;熟思。②原因;理由;考慮之事物。③體恤; 顧及他人; 斟酌。to show great *consideration* for one's friends. 對朋友表示甚深的體念。④重要。It's of no *consideration* at all. 它是毫不重要的。 ⑤報酬;酬資。 ⑥尊敬。in consideration of*** **a.** 顧及;體恤;體諒;因爲。**b.** 報酬。***leave*** (or ***put***) ***out of consideration*** 置之度外;不顧。***on no consideration*** 決不。*On no consideration* will he sell this house. 他決不出售這所房子。***out of consideration*** 顧及; 顧念。***take into consideration*** 顧及;考慮。We must *take* his children *into consideration.* 我們應該顧及他的兒女。***under consideration*** 在考慮中。

con·sid·ered 〔kən'sɪdɚd; kən'sidəd〕 *adj.* ①經考慮的;經熟思的。②受尊敬的。

***con·sid·er·ing** 〔kən'sɪdərɪŋ; kən'sidəriŋ〕 *prep.* 顧及;就…而論;照…情形而言。The price of this hat is not high, *considering* its quality. 就品質而言, 這頂帽子的價錢並不貴。—*adv.* 總而言之。—**ly,** *adv.*

con·sign 〔kən'saɪn; kən'sain〕 *v.t.* ①交付;移交。②移交他人看管; 付託;委託。③指定或留作。④存款。⑤送;寄;傳遞。⑥寄售;託賣。 —*v.i.* 同意。***consign the body to the grave*** 埋葬。***consign to oblivion*** 置於腦後;忘記了。—**a·ble,** *adj.*

con·sig·na·tion 〔,kɑnsɪg'neʃən; ,kɔnsig'neiʃən〕 *n.* 委託;託送。

con·sign·ee 〔,kɑnsaɪ'ni; ,kɔnsai'niː〕 *n.* 收件人;收貨者;承銷人; 代售人;受託者。

con·sign·er, con·sign·or 〔kən'saɪnɚ; kən'sainə〕 *n.* 委託人;寄件人。

con·sign·ment 〔kən'saɪnmənt; kən'sainmənt〕 *n.* ①交託;寄售;運送;委託。②交託之物;託賣之貨品。***on consignment*** 寄售。

con·sil·i·ence 〔kən'sɪlɪəns; kən'siliəns〕 *n.* 符合;一致;協調。

:con·sist 〔kən'sɪst; kən'sist〕 *v.i.* ①組成;爲…所製 〖of〗. Man *consists* of soul and body. 人由靈魂和肉體組成。②存在; 在於 〖in〗. True charity doesn't *consist* in almsgiving. 眞的慈善不在於施捨。③相容;並存; 符合 〖with〗. His actions do not *consist* with words. 他的言行不相符。—*n.* 一列火車之車廂。

con·sist·en·cy [kən'sɪstənsɪ; kən'sistənsi] *n., pl.* **-cies.** ①堅固;堅實。②堅度;濃度。③一致;一貫。④和諧;調和。(亦作 **consistence**)

***con·sist·ent** [kən'sɪstənt; kən'sistənt] *adj.* ①前後一貫的;不矛盾的;一致的。He is not *consistent* in his statements.他的聲明前後不一致。You are not *consistent* with yourself. 你自相矛盾。②相合的。—**ly,** *adv.*

con·sis·to·ry[kən'sɪstərɪ;kən'sistəri] *n., pl.* **-ries.** ①開會處;開庭處。②宗教會議;宗教法庭。③由教皇主持之樞機主教全體會議。

con·so·ci·ate [*v.* kən'soʃɪˌet; kən'souʃieit *adj., n.* kən'soʃɪɪt, -ˌet; kən'souʃiit, -ʃieit] *v.,* **-at·ed, -at·ing,** *n., adj.* —*v.t.* & *v.i.* (使)聯合; 組合。 —*n.* 同伴;合夥人;有來往者。—*adj.* 聯合的; 組合的。—**con·so·ci·a·tion,** *n.*

consol. consolidated.

con·sol·a·ble [kən'soləbḷ; kən'souləbl] *adj.* 可安慰的;可慰藉的。

***con·so·la·tion** [ˌkɑnsə'leʃən; ˌkɔnsə'leiʃən] *n.* ①安慰;慰藉。②可以安慰的人、事、物。The little girl is a great *consolation* to her parents. 這小女孩是大可以安慰她父母的人。③〖運動〗落選賽。

consolation game 〖運動〗落選賽。(亦作 **consolation match**)

consolation prize 精神獎;安慰獎。

con·sol·a·to·ry [kən'sɑləˌtorɪ; kən'sɔlətəri] *adj.* 安慰的; 撫慰的。 a *consolatory* letter. 慰問信;慰勞信。

***con·sole**[1] [kən'sol; kən'soul] *v.t.,* **-soled, -sol·ing.** 安慰。—**con·sol·er,** *n.* —**con·sol·ing,** *adj.* —**con·sol·ing·ly,** *adv.*

con·sole[2] ['kɑnsol; 'kɔnsoul] *n.* ①裝飾用的支柱。②風琴之書桌式的架子。③收音機或留聲機的座架。

console table ①用橫支柱固着於牆上之小枱子。②螺形脚之靠牆小桌。

con·so·lette [ˌkɑnsə'lɛt; ˌkɔnsə'let] *n.* 小型的收音機或留聲機的座架。

con·sol·i·date [kən'sɑləˌdet; kən'sɔlideit] *v.,* **-dat·ed, -dat·ing.** —*v.t.* ①(使)堅强;(使)鞏固;强化。②結合;統一;合併;聯合。—*v.i.* 合併。—**con·sol·i·dat·or,** *n.*

consolidated annuities 〖英〗統一公債。

consolidated school 由若干小學校合併而成的鄉間公立學校。(亦作 **centralized school**)

con·sol·i·da·tion [kənˌsɑlə'deʃən; kənˌsɔli'deiʃən] *n.* 鞏固;團結;統一;合併;聯合。

con·sol·ing [kən'solɪŋ; kən'souliŋ] *adj.* 安慰的;慰藉的。—**ly,** *adv.*

con·sols ['kɑnsɑlz; kən'sɔlz] *n. pl.* 英國統一公債。

con·som·mé [ˌkɑnsə'me;kən'sɔmei] 〖法〗 *n.* 肉煮成的清湯。

con·so·nance ['kɑnsənəns; 'kɔnsənəns] *n.* ①協調; 一致。②聲音之和諧。③〖物理〗共振; 共鳴。(亦作 **consonancy**)

***con·so·nant**['kɑnsənənt;'kɔnsənənt] *n.* 子音;子音字母。—*adj.* ①一致的;和諧的〖to, with〗。②〖物理〗共振的;共鳴的。—**ly**,*adv.*

con·so·nan·tal [ˌkɑnsə'næntḷ; ˌkɔnsə'næntl] *adj.* 子音的;似子音的。

con·sort [*n.* 'kɑnsɔrt; 'kɔnsɔːt *v.* kən'sɔrt; kən'sɔːt] *n.* ①配偶;夫或妻。②國王或女王之配偶。prince *consort.* 女王之夫;皇夫。③同事;夥伴。④伴隨之船;僚艇;僚艦。⑤演奏古曲的一組樂器與歌唱者。⑥音樂會中同類的一組樂器。—*v.t.* & *v.i.* ①陪伴;相交;結交。②調和;協調。

con·sor·ti·um [kən'sɔrʃɪəm; kən'sɔːtjəm] *n., pl.* **-ti·a** [-ʃɪə; -tjə]. ①銀行團;財團。②合股;合夥。③會社;俱樂部。④結合。

con·spec·tus [kən'spɛktəs; kən'spektəs] *n.* ①大綱;概略。②概觀。

***con·spic·u·ous** [kən'spɪkjuəs; kən'spikjuəs] *adj.* ①顯著的; 顯而易見的; 顯明的。②引人注目的; 值得注意的。 She is a *conspicuous* figure. 她是引人注目的人物。—**ly,** *adv.* —**ness,** *n.*

conspicuous consumption 公開享受昂貴之物以炫示財富。

conspicuous waste 炫耀奢侈生活以示富有;排場。

***con·spir·a·cy** [kən'spɪrəsɪ; kən'spirəsi] *n., pl.* **-cies.** 陰謀;共謀;謀叛。

con·spir·a·tor [kən'spɪrətɚ; kən'spirətə] *n.* 共謀者;陰謀者;謀叛者。(亦作 **conspirer**)

con·spir·a·to·ri·al [kənˌspɪrə'torɪəl; kənˌspirə'tɔːriəl] *adj.* 陰謀者的;陰謀的。(亦作 **conspiratory**)

con·spir·a·tress [kən'spɪrətrɪs; kən'spirətris] *n.* conspirator 之女性。

***con·spire** [kən'spaɪr; kən'spaiə] *v.,* **-spired, -spir·ing.** —*v.i.* ①共謀; 圖謀;陰謀。to *conspire* against the government. 共同圖謀推翻政府。②協同;一致行動。—*v.t.* 〖罕〗圖謀;共謀。

Const. ①constable. ②Constantinople. ③constitution. **const.** ①constable. ②constant. ③constitution.

con·sta·ble** ['kɑnstəbḷ; 'kʌnstəbl] *n.* ①〖英〗警察;警官。②(中古之)高級軍官。③管城堡者;皇家堡壘之管理人。 ***special constable 特別巡警;臨時警察。 —**con·stab·u·lar,** *adj.* —**ship,** *n.*

con·stab·u·lar·y [kən'stæbjəˌlɛrɪ; kən'stæbjuləri] *n., pl.* **-lar·ies,** *adj.* —*n.* ①警察所管轄之地區。② 地區警察。③ 具有軍隊組織性質之警察部隊; 警察隊; 保安隊。—*adj.* 警察的;警官的;警察隊的。

***con·stan·cy** ['kɑnstənsɪ; 'kɔnstənsi] *n.* ①不變; 恆久性; 堅定。②忠誠;堅忍不拔;不屈不撓。③永久之物,尤指固定工作。

‡**con·stant** ['kɑnstənt; 'kɔnstənt] *adj.* ①不變的; 一定的。 I keep the speed of my car *constant.* 我使我的汽車保持速度不變。②時常的;不斷的。③繼續的;持久的;有恆的。to be *constant* in love. 愛情持久。④忠實的;忠貞的。to be *constant* to one's occupation. 忠於自己的職業。—*n.*①不變的事物。②〖數學、物理〗常數;恆量;恆定。

con·stant·an ['kɑnstənˌtæn; 'kɔnstəntæn] *n.* 用以作抗電器的一種銅鎳合金。

Con·stan·tine I ['kɑnstənˌtaɪn; 'kɔnstəntain] 君士坦丁大帝 (280?–337, 羅馬皇帝,在位期間爲 306–337)。

Con·stan·ti·no·ple [ˌkɑnstæntə'nopḷ; ˌkɔnstænti'noupl] *n.* 君士坦丁堡(昔爲土耳其之首都,今名Istanbul伊斯坦堡)。

***con·stant·ly**['kɑnstəntlɪ;'kɔnstəntli] *adv.* ①不變地。②不斷地。③時常地。

constant of gravitation (萬有)引力恆量。

con·stel·late ['kɑnstəˌlet; 'kɔnstəleit] *v.t.* & *v.i.*, **-lat·ed, -lat·ing.** ①集爲星座。②以羣星裝飾。

***con·stel·la·tion** [ˌkanstəˈleʃən; ˌkɔnstəˈleiʃən] *n.* ①【天文】星座;星羣。②明麗如星之一羣。③(C-)美國星座式客運飛機。—**con·stel·la·to·ry,** *adj.*

con·ster·nate [ˈkanstəˌnet; ˈkɔnstə(ː)neit] *v.t.*, **-nat·ed, -nat·ing.** 使驚恐;使驚愕。

con·ster·na·tion [ˌkanstəˈneʃən; ˌkɔnstə(ː)ˈneiʃən] *n.* 驚愕;恐怖;狼狽。

con·sti·pate [ˈkanstəˌpet; ˈkɔnstipeit] *v.t.*, **-pat·ed, -pat·ing.** ①閉塞;壅塞。②【醫】使便祕;祕結。

con·sti·pat·ed [ˈkanstəˌpetɪd; ˈkɔnstipeitid] *adj.* 患便祕的。

con·sti·pa·tion [ˌkanstəˈpeʃən; ˌkɔnstiˈpeiʃən] *n.* 【醫】便祕;大便祕結。

con·stit·u·en·cy [kənˈstɪtʃuənsɪ; kənˈstitjuənsi] *n.*, *pl.* **-cies.** ①選舉區之全體選民。②選舉區。③顧客;贊助者;支持者。

***con·stit·u·ent** [kənˈstɪtʃuənt; kənˈstitjuənt] *adj.* ①有選舉權的;有任命權的。②有創制權的;有更改政治制度之權的。a *constituent* assembly. 創制憲法或修改憲法之議會;國民代表大會。③組成的;成分的。a *constituent* part. 組成之部分。—*n.*①要素;構成分子;成分。②選民;選舉者。—**ly,** *adv.*

***con·sti·tute** [ˈkanstəˌtjut; ˈkɔnstitjuːt] *v.t.*, **-tut·ed, -tut·ing.** ①組成;構成。Seven days *constitute* a week. 七天構成一星期。②任命;選定。They *constituted* him president of the club. 他們選他爲俱樂部的會長。③設立。④制定。

***con·sti·tu·tion** [ˌkanstəˈtjuʃən; ˌkɔnstiˈtjuːʃən] *n.* ①構成;構造。②體質;體格。③性情;性質。④設立;設定。⑤憲法。⑥法律;命令。⑦任命;推選。

***con·sti·tu·tion·al** [ˌkanstəˈtjuʃənḷ; ˌkɔnstiˈtjuːʃənḷ] *adj.* ①憲法的;法治的。*constitutional* government. 立憲政體。②體質的;生來的。a *constitutional* weakness. 體質的虛弱。—*n.*【俗】爲維持健康而舉行的散步或其他運動。—**ly,** *adv.*

con·sti·tu·tion·al·ism [ˌkanstəˈtjuʃənḷɪzəm; ˌkɔnstiˈtjuːʃṇəlizəm] *n.* ①立憲制度;立憲政體;立憲主義;憲法論。②憲政之維護。

con·sti·tu·tion·al·ist [ˌkanstəˈtjuʃənḷist; ˌkɔnstiˈtjuːʃṇəlist] *n.* ①憲法擁護者;立憲主義者。②研究憲法者;憲法學者。

con·sti·tu·tion·al·i·ty [ˌkanstəˌtjuʃənˈælətɪ; ˌkɔnstiˌtjuːʃəˈnæliti] *n.* 立憲;法治;符合憲法。

constitutional monarchy 「君主立憲政體。」

con·sti·tu·tive [ˈkanstəˌtjutɪv; ˈkɔnstitjuːtiv] *adj.* ①構成的;組織的;基本的;要素的。②有制定、任命等權的。③必要的。

con·sti·tu·tor [ˈkanstəˌtjutə; ˈkɔnstitjuːtə] *n.* 構成…之人或物。

constr. ①construction. ②construed.

con·strain [kənˈstren; kənˈstrein] *v.t.* ①强迫。②受拘束;受束縛;拘禁。③抑制;壓制。—**a·ble,** *adj.* —**er,** *n.*

con·strained [kənˈstrend; kənˈstreind] *adj.*①被强迫的;受壓制的。②僵硬的;不自然的。—**ly,** *adv.*

con·straint [kənˈstrent; kənˈstreint] *n.* ①强迫;被迫。He did this under *constraint.* 他被迫而爲此。②束縛。③態度不自然;忸怩不安。④拘禁。⑤拘束或限制之事物。

con·strict [kənˈstrɪkt; kənˈstrikt] *v.t.* ①壓縮;使收緊。②使緩慢或停止。—**ed,** *adj.*

con·stric·tion [kənˈstrɪkʃən; kənˈstrikʃən] *n.* ①壓縮;收緊;收縮。②緊壓之感覺。③被縮緊之部分。④能壓縮或縮緊之物。

con·stric·tive [kənˈstrɪktɪv; kənˈstriktiv] *adj.* 緊縮的;收斂性的。—**ly,** *adv.*

con·stric·tor [kənˈstrɪktə; kənˈstriktə] *n.* ①壓迫之人或物;壓縮物。②【解剖】括約肌。③緊繞獵物使其窒息而死之蛇。

con·stringe [kənˈstrɪndʒ; kənˈstrindʒ] *v.t.*, **-stringed,-string·ing.** 收縮;緊縮;壓縮。

con·strin·gen·cy [kənˈstrɪndʒənsɪ; kənˈstrindʒənsi] *n.* 收縮;收斂性。

con·strin·gent [kənˈstrɪndʒənt; kənˈstrindʒənt] *adj.* ①緊縮的;收斂性的。②使緊縮的;使收斂的。

con·stru·a·ble [kənˈstruəbḷ; kənˈstruːəbl] *adj.* 可分析的;能解釋的。

***con·struct** [*v.* kənˈstrʌkt; kənˈstrʌkt *n.* ˈkanstrʌkt; ˈkɔnstrʌkt] *v.t.* ①組成;構造;建築;敷設;設計。to *construct* a bridge. 造橋。②作(圖)。—*n.* ①構造而成之物。②抽象名詞;觀念;概念。—**er,** *n.*

***con·struc·tion** [kənˈstrʌkʃən; kənˈstrʌkʃən] *n.*①建築;構造。A dam is under *construction.* 水壩在建築中。②建築法;結構;建築式。③建築物。④解釋。⑤【文法】造句法。

con·struc·tion·al [kənˈstrʌkʃənḷ; kənˈstrʌkʃənḷ] *adj.* ①建設的;構造上的。②解釋的。

***con·struc·tive** [kənˈstrʌktɪv; kənˈstrʌktiv] *adj.* ①建設性的。②構造上的;組織的;構成的。③肯定的;積極的。④解釋的;推斷的。—**ly,** *adv.* —**ness,** *n.*

constructive fraud 【法律】推斷「的欺詐。」

con·struc·tiv·ism [kənˈstrʌktɪvɪzəm; kənˈstrʌktivizəm] *n.* 【藝術】構成派。

con·struc·tor [kənˈstrʌktə; kənˈstrʌktə] *n.* 建設者;建造者;營造商;造船技師。

con·strue [kənˈstru; kənˈstruː] *v.*, **-strued, -stru·ing,** *n.* —*v.t.* ①分析。②解釋;推斷。③翻譯。—*v.i.* ①分析句子的結構。②可被解釋;可被分析。—*n.* ①解釋;推斷。②文句之分析。③翻譯。

con·sub·stan·tial [ˌkansəbˈstænʃəl; ˌkɔnsəbˈstænʃəl] *adj.* 同質的;同體的。—**ism,** —**ist,** *n.*

con·sub·stan·ti·al·i·ty [ˌkansəbˌstænʃɪˈælətɪ; ˌkɔnsəbˌstænʃiˈæliti] *n.* 同質;同體(尤指神學中之三位一體而言)。

con·sub·stan·ti·ate [ˌkansəbˈstænʃɪˌet; ˌkɔnsəbˈstænʃieit] *v.*, **-at·ed, -at·ing.** —*v.t.* ①使同體;使同質。②視之爲同體或同質。—*v.i.* ①信奉聖體合質說或聖體共在說。②成同體;成同質。

con·sub·stan·ti·a·tion [ˌkansəbˌstænʃɪˈeʃən; ˈkɔnsəbˌstænʃiˈeiʃən] *n.*【神學】聖體合質;聖體共在。

con·sue·tude [ˈkanswɪˌtjud; ˈkɔnswitjuːd] *n.* 習慣;慣例。

con·sue·tu·di·nar·y [ˌkanswɪˈtjudṇˌɛrɪ; ˌkɔnswiˈtjuːdnəri] *adj.* 習慣的;慣例的。

***con·sul** [ˈkansḷ; ˈkɔnsəl] *n.* ①領事。②古羅馬的執政官。③法蘭西共和國自1799年至1804年間三執政官之一。

con·su·lar ['kɑnsl̩ɚ, 'kɑnsjəlɚ; 'kɔnsjulə] *adj.* ①領事的；領事館的；領事職務的。②〖史〗執政官的；執政的。

consular agent 領事代辦。 「權。

consular jurisdiction 領事裁判

con·su·late ['kɑnsl̩ɪt; 'kɔnsjulit] *n.* ①領事館。②領事之職權或任期。③(常C-)執政官政府。

consul general *pl.* **consuls general.** 總領事。 「*n.* 領事之職權或任期。

con·sul·ship ['kɑnsl̩ˌʃɪp; 'kɔnsəlʃip]

***con·sult** [kən'sʌlt; kən'sʌlt] *v.t.* ①請教；就教於。②諮詢。③參考；查閱。to *consult* a dictionary. 參考字典。④顧及；顧念。—*v.i.* 考慮；磋商；商量〖with〗. I *consulted* with him about the matter. 我與他商量這事。—**a·ble,** *adj.*

con·sult·ant [kən'sʌltənt; kən'sʌltənt] *n.* ①諮詢者。②貢獻意見之專家；顧問。③專員。

***con·sul·ta·tion** [ˌkɑnsl̩'teʃən; ˌkɔnsəl'teiʃən, -sʌl-] *n.* ①請教；諮詢。②商議；會議。③參考；調查。④〖英法律〗將案件由普通法庭移送教會法庭的裁定書。

con·sult·a·tive [kən'sʌltətɪv; kən'sʌltətiv] *adj.* 諮詢的；協議的。(亦作 **consultatory, consultive**) —**ly,** *adv.*

con·sult·ing [kən'sʌltɪŋ; kən'sʌltiŋ] *adj.* ①諮詢的；就教的。②作顧問的。a *consulting* engineer. 顧問工程師。③專門診視的。a *consulting* room. 診室。

con·sum·a·ble [kən'suməbl̩; kən'sju:məbl] *adj.* 可消耗的；能用盡的；消費的。—*n.* (常 *pl.*)消耗品。

con·sume** [kən'sum; kən'sju:m] *v.,* **-sumed, -sum·ing.** —*v.t.* ①消耗；消費；耗盡；用壞。 He is *consumed* with age. 他因年老而衰弱。His old car *consumed* much gasoline. 他的舊汽車耗油很多。②食盡或飲完；吞。③毀滅；燒毀。④浪費。consumed with*** 被…所充滿。—*v.i.* 憔悴而死〖away〗. to *consume* away with grief. 抑鬱以終。

con·sum·ed·ly [kən'sumɪdlɪ; kən'sju:midli] *adv.* 非常地；極度地；無拘束地。

***con·sum·er** [kən'sumɚ; kən'sju:mə] *n.* ①消費者；消耗者。②以植物或其他動物爲食的動物。

consumer credit 消費者信用。

con·sum·er·ism [kən'sumərɪzəm; kən'sju:mərizəm] *n.* 保護消費者主義。

con·sum·er·ist [kən'sumərɪst; kən'sju:mərist] *n.* 贊成保護消費者主義的人。

consumer price index 消費者物價指數。 「**society** 消費合作社。

consumers' cooperative

consumers' goods 〖經濟〗消費財。(亦作 **consumer goods**)

consumer strike 消費者罷購。

con·sum·mate [*adj.* kən'sʌmɪt; kən'sʌmit *v.* 'kɑnsəˌmet; 'kɔnsʌmeit, -səm-] *v.,* **-mat·ed, -mat·ing,** *adj.* —*v.t.* ①成就；完成。②新婚夫婦發生性行爲使(婚姻)成爲事實。—*v.i.* 完成。—*adj.* ①至上的；完全的；圓滿的。*consummate* happiness. 無上的幸福。*consummate* ass. 無比的傻瓜。②有成就的；技藝高超的。—**ly,** *adv.*

con·sum·ma·tion [ˌkɑnsə'meʃən; ˌkɔnsə'meiʃən] *n.* 完全；成就；完成。

***con·sump·tion** [kən'sʌmpʃən; kən'sʌmpʃən] *n.* ①消耗；用盡；消滅。This is produced for domestic *consumption.* 這是爲國內的消費而生產的。②消耗量。③肺病。④憔悴。

con·sump·tive [kən'sʌmptɪv; kən'sʌmptiv] *adj.* ①害肺病的；患癆病的。②消費的；消耗的。 —*n.* 肺病患者；癆病患者。—**ly,** *adv.* —**ness,** *n.*

Cont. Continental. **cont.** ①containing. ②contents. ③continent. ④continental. ⑤continue(d). ⑥contract.

***con·tact** ['kɑntækt; 'kɔntækt] *n.* ①接觸。to come into frequent *contact* with people. 與人常接觸。②聯繫。to bring them into closer *contact.* 使他們更密切聯繫。③〖電〗電路中之接觸。④〖電〗連接器。⑤鄰近。⑥可幫助得到消息或恩寵的親戚、朋友。⑦〖醫〗接觸者；與傳染病接觸者。—*v.t.*〖俗〗與人接觸；與人交接。—*v.i.* 發生接觸。—*adj.*〖航空〗可看到地面景物的。*contact* flying. 可看到地面景物的飛行。—**u·al,** *adj.* —**u·al·ly,** *adv.*

contact breaker 電流遮斷器。

contact dermatitis 因接觸引起過敏症物質而起的皮膚炎。

contact flight 〖航空〗接觸飛行(駕駛員藉觀察地面、河流、建築物等以定航線者)。

contact lenses 隱形眼鏡。

contact maker 電流開關裝置。

contact man 連絡人。

contact mine 觸發(水)雷。

con·tac·tor ['kɑntæktɚ; 'kɔntæktə] *n.* 〖電〗接觸器。

con·ta·gion [kən'tedʒən; kən'teidʒən] *n.* ①接觸傳染病。②傳染；傳染之方法或媒介。③任何影響的蔓延。④不良影響；道德敗壞。

***con·ta·gious** [kən'tedʒəs; kən'teidʒəs] *adj.* ①接觸傳染的。Scarlet fever is a *contagious* disease. 猩紅熱是一種接觸傳染病。②易感染的；蔓延的。③造成傳染病的；傳播疾病的。—**ly,** *adv.* —**ness,** *n.*

‡**con·tain** [kən'ten; kən'tein] *v.t.* ①包含。 This purse *contains* much money. 這個錢包裏有很多錢。②容納。That pitcher will *contain* a quart of milk. 那個水瓶能盛一夸特的牛奶。③等於。A pound *contains* sixteen ounces. 一磅等於十六英兩。④控制；含忍；容忍。He *contained* his anger. 他忍怒。He couldn't *contain* himself for joy. 他不禁喜形於色。⑤可被除盡。—*v.i.* 自制。—**a·ble,** *adj.*

con·tained [kən'tend; kən'teind] *adj.* 泰然自若的；從容不迫的。—**ly,** *adv.*

con·tain·er [kən'tenɚ; kən'teinə] *n.* 箱；罐；貨櫃；容器。

container car 貨櫃車。

con·tain·er·i·za·tion [kənˌtenərə'zeʃən; kənˌteinərai'zeiʃən] *n.* 貨櫃運輸；貨櫃裝貨。

con·tain·er·ize [kən'tenɚˌaɪz; kən'teinəraiz] *v.t.,* **-ized, -iz·ing.** ①將貨物裝入貨櫃。②以貨櫃運送貨物。

container ship 貨櫃船。

con·tam·i·nant [kən'tæmənənt; kən'tæmənənt] *n.* 染汚(他物)之物。

con·tam·i·nate [kən'tæməˌnet; kən'tæmineit] *v.t.,* **-nat·ed, -nat·ing.** ①汚損；弄髒；染汚。②以放射性物質加入使有害或無法使用。

con·tam·i·na·tion [kənˌtæmə'neʃən; kənˌtæmi'neiʃən] *n.* ①汚穢；染汚；混

淆。②汚穢物;汚染物。

con·tam·i·na·tive [kən'tæmɪˌnetɪv; kən'tæminətiv] *adj.* 汚損的;弄髒的。

con·tan·go [kən'tæŋgo;kən'tæŋgou] *n., pl.* **-gos, -goes.** 交易延期費;延期付款先付之利息。(亦作 **continuation**)

contango day 交割限期日。

contd. continued.

conte [kɔ̃t; kɔ̃ːt] *n., pl.* **contes** [kɔ̃t; kɔ̃ːt]. 〖法〗短篇故事;短篇小說。

con·temn [kən'tɛm; kən'tem] *v.t.* 輕視。

contemp. contemporary.

***con·tem·plate** ['kɑntəmˌplet; 'kɔntempleit] *v.,* **-plat·ed, -plat·ing.** —*v.t.* ①注視。②沉思;默想;考慮。③期待;預期。④意欲;打算。She *contemplated* going to America after graduation. 她意欲畢業後去美國。—*v.i.* 沉思;默想。

con·tem·pla·tion** [ˌkɑntəm'pleʃən; ˌkɔntem'pleiʃən] *n.* ①凝視;沉思;冥想。②期待;希望。③研討;考慮。have*** (*a thing*) ***in contemplation*** 籌劃(某事物);企圖做…。

con·tem·pla·tive ['kɑntəmˌpletɪv; 'kɔntempleitiv] *adj.*沉思的;默想的;冥想的。***the contemplative life*** 宗教上冥想的生涯。—*n.* 好冥想或致力於冥想的人。

contemplative faculties 思想力;思考力。

con·tem·pla·tor ['kɑntəmˌpletɚ; 'kɔntempleitə] *n.* 熟思者;凝視者;沉思者。

con·tem·po·ra·ne·i·ty [kənˌtɛmpərə'niətɪ;kənˌtempərə'niːiti] *n.* 同時代;當代。

con·tem·po·ra·ne·ous [kənˌtɛmpə'renɪəs;kənˌtempə'reinjəs] *adj.* 同時代的;屬同一時期的。(亦作 **cotemporaneous**) —**ly,** *adv.* —**ness,** *n.*

***con·tem·po·rar·y** [kən'tɛmpəˌrɛrɪ; kən'tempərəri] *adj., n., pl.* **-rar·ies.**—*adj.* ①同時代的。*contemporary* records of events. 同時代的大事記。②同年齡的;同日期的。③現代的;現時期的。—*n.* ①同時代的人。②同年齡的人。③同時代或同日期的雜誌或報紙。(亦作 **cotemporary**)

con·tem·po·rize [kən'tɛmpəˌraɪz; kən'tempəraiz] *v.,* **-rized, -riz·ing.** —*v.t.* 置於或認爲同時代的。—*v.i.* 成爲同時代的。

con·tempt** [kən'tɛmpt; kən'tempt] *n.* ①輕視。②恥辱。③藐視。He was fined for *contempt* of court. 他因藐視法庭被罰。fall*** (or ***bring***) ***into contempt*** (使)蒙恥辱。***in contempt of*** 輕視;蔑視。

con·tempt·i·bil·i·ty [kənˌtɛmptə'bɪlətɪ; kənˌtemptə'biliti] *n.* 可輕視;可鄙。

con·tempt·i·ble[kən'tɛmptəbḷ;kən'temptəbl] *adj.* 可輕視的;可鄙的。

con·tempt·i·bly [kən'tɛmptəblɪ; kən'temptəbli] *adv.* 可輕視地;可鄙地。

contempt of Congress 〖美〗〖法律〗藐視國會。

***con·temp·tu·ous** [kən'tɛmptʃuəs; kən'temptjuəs] *adj.* 表示輕蔑的;侮慢的;藐視的。a *contemptuous* look. 表示輕蔑的眼色。—**ly,** *adv.*

***con·tend** [kən'tɛnd; kən'tend] *v.i.* ①爭鬥;競爭。to *contend* with an enemy. 與敵人爭鬥。to *contend* for a prize. 爲獎品而競爭。②爭論;辯論。to *contend* with a person about something. 爲某事與人爭論。—*v.t.* 主張;力辯;堅信…爲事實。

‡**con·tent¹** [kən'tɛnt; kən'tent] *v.t.* 使滿足;使安心;使滿意。Nothing *contents* her; she is always complaining. 沒有甚麼能使她滿足,她總是訴苦。—*adj.* ①滿意的;滿足的;安心的。He is *content* with very little. 他易於滿足。②願意的。③〖英〗同意的。—*n.* ①滿意;滿足;安心。②(英國上議院)投贊成票者;贊成票。***to one's heart's content*** 如意地;盡情地。

***con·tent²** ['kɑntɛnt, kən'tɛnt; 'kɔntent] *n.* ①(常 *pl.*)所容之物;內容。②(*pl.*)書籍、報紙、雜誌、公文等的內容;目次;目錄。table of *contents.* 目次。③面積;容積。linear *content(s).* 長;長度。④含量。⑤意義;深度。⑥內含的事物;事物之可認知部分。

***con·tent·ed** [kən'tɛntɪd;kən'tentid] *adj.* 知足的;滿意的;安心的。a *contented* look. 滿足的表情。—**ly,** *adv.* —**ness,** *n.*

***con·ten·tion** [kən'tɛnʃən; kən'tenʃən] *n.* ①爭論;辯論。This is not a time for *contention.* 現在不是爭論的時候。②爭端;爭點。③爭;競爭。④爭論或辯論之行爲。

con·ten·tious [kən'tɛnʃəs; kən'tenʃəs] *adj.* ①好爭吵的;愛議論的;好辯的。②足以引起爭論的。③〖法律〗關於兩造間之爭執原因的。

***con·tent·ment** [kən'tɛntmənt;kən'tentmənt] *n.* 滿意;知足。They lived in perfect *contentment.* 他們生活十分滿意。

con·ter·mi·nous [kən'tɝmənəs; kən'təːminəs] *adj.* ①有共同邊界的;毗連的;鄰接的。②(空間、時間、或範圍上)同樣擴展的。(亦作 **conterminal, coterminous**)

***con·test** [*n.*'kɑntɛst; 'kɔntest *v.* kən'tɛst; kən'test] *n.* ①競爭;比賽。a tug of war *contest.* 拔河競賽。to enter the *contest.* 參加比賽。②爭鬥;爭勝。③爭論;爭辯。—*v.t.* ①爭取;爭奪。②爭論;爭辯。The lawyer *contested* every point. 律師逐點爭辯。③駁斥;對…提出疑問。④競取;爭取…的勝利。—*v.i.* 競爭;爭論〖with, against〗. to *contest* with a person. 與人爭論;與人競爭。—**a·ble,** *adj.*

con·test·ant [kən'tɛstənt; kən'testənt] *n.* ①競爭者;爭論者;選手。②在遺囑認證法庭上對遺囑之有效性提出異議的人。

con·tes·ta·tion [ˌkɑntɛs'teʃən;ˌkɔntes'teiʃən] *n.* 爭論;論戰;爭訟。

con·test·ee [ˌkɑntɛs'ti; ˌkɔntes'tiː] *n.* 〖美〗被認爲非法當選的人。

con·text ['kɑntɛkst; 'kɔntekst] *n.* ①上下文;文之前後關聯。②某事之前後關係、情況。***in this context*** 關於此點;就此而論。***quote out of context*** 斷章取義。—**u·al,** *adj.* —**u·al·ly,** *adv.*

con·tex·ture [kən'tɛkstʃɚ;kən'tekstʃə] *n.* ①組織;構成;構造。②編織;織物。—**con·tex·tur·al,** *adj.*

con·ti·gu·i·ty [ˌkɑntə'gjuətɪ; ˌkɔnti'gjuːiti] *n.* ①接近。②接觸。③連綿不斷之物。

con·tig·u·ous [kən'tɪgjuəs; kən'tigjuəs] *adj.* ①接觸的。②接近的;鄰近的。*contiguous* angle. 鄰角。—**ly,** *adv.* —**ness,** *n.*

con·ti·nence ['kɑntənəns; 'kɔntinəns] *n.* ①自制;節制。②節慾。(亦作 **continency**)

con·ti·nent¹** ['kɑntənənt;'kɔntinənt] *n.* ①洲。②大陸。the Continent*** 歐洲大陸。

con·ti·nent² *adj.* 自制的;節慾的。

con·ti·nen·tal** 〔ˌkantəˈnɛntl; ˌkɔntiˈnentl〕 *adj.* ①洲的；大陸的。②(常 C-)歐洲大陸的。*Continental* customs differ from those of England. 歐洲大陸習俗與英國習俗不同。③(C-) 美國獨立戰爭前後之原十三州殖民地的。④北美洲大陸的。—*n.* ①(C-)美國獨立戰爭時的軍人。②美國獨立戰爭時發行的紙幣。③(常 C-) 歐洲大陸人。④大陸人。not worth a continental***〖俗〗毫無價值。 「麪包與熱飲的早餐。」
continental breakfast 包括
con·ti·nen·tal·ism 〔ˌkantəˈnɛntlˌɪzəm; ˌkɔntiˈnentəlizəm〕 *n.* ①大陸(尤指歐洲)的態度、表現、特性等。②偏袒大陸的態度或政策。—**con·ti·nen·tal·ist,** *n.*
continental shelf 大陸礁層。
con·ti·nent·ly 〔ˈkantənəntlɪ; ˈkɔntinəntli〕 *adv.* 適度地；溫和地。
con·tin·gence 〔kənˈtɪndʒəns; kənˈtindʒəns〕 *n.* ①接觸。② =**contingency.**
con·tin·gen·cy 〔kənˈtɪndʒənsɪ; kənˈtindʒənsi〕 *n., pl.* **-cies.** ①臨時事故發生之可能性；偶然性。②意外事故；偶然之事故。③可能附帶發生之事件。
con·tin·gent 〔kənˈtɪndʒənt; kənˈtindʒənt〕 *adj.* ①偶然的；意外的。Such risks are *contingent* to the trade. 此種危險對於該行業是偶然會有的。②有條件的；須依仗的。③可能而不定的。④備用的。—*n.* ①(部隊、艦隊、工人等之)分遣隊。②分得或分攤之部分。③代表團(指整個會議人員之一部分)。④意外之事。—**ly,** *adv.*
contingent beneficiary〖保險〗第二受益人。 「ˈtinjuəbl〕 *adj.* 可繼續的。」
con·tin·u·a·ble 〔kənˈtɪnjuəbl; kən-
***con·tin·u·al** 〔kənˈtɪnjuəl; kənˈtinjuəl〕 *adj.* ①不停的；連續的。②時常的；頻頻的。*Continual* smoking is bad to health. 頻頻的抽烟有害於健康。—**ly,** *adv.*
***con·tin·u·ance** 〔kənˈtɪnjuəns; kənˈtinjuəns〕 *n.* ①連續；繼續；繼續期間；繼續的逗留。②續篇。the *continuance* of a story. 故事的續篇。③〖法律〗延期。
con·tin·u·ant 〔kənˈtɪnjuənt; kənˈtinjuənt〕 *n.* 〖語音〗連續音。
***con·tin·u·a·tion** 〔kənˌtɪnjuˈeʃən; kənˌtinjuˈeiʃən〕 *n.* ①連續；延長。②續前；續篇。③添附物；建築物之增建部分。④間斷後之繼續；恢復。⑤=**contango.**
continuation school 補習學校。
con·tin·u·a·tive 〔kənˈtɪnjuˌetɪv; kənˈtinjuətiv〕 *adj.* 使連續的；繼續的；延長的。—*n.* ①連續的事物。②接續句。—**ly,** *adv.*
continuative relative clause〖文法〗接續關係子句。
con·tin·u·a·tor 〔kənˈtɪnjuˌetɚ; kənˈtinjueitə〕 *n.* 繼續的事物或人。
‡con·tin·ue 〔kənˈtɪnju; kənˈtinju(ː)〕 *v.,* **-tin·ued, -tin·u·ing.** —*v.t.* ①繼續；連續。to *continue* one's subscription to a magazine. 繼續訂閱一雜誌。②(中斷後) 繼續；恢復。③續作；續登。to be *continued.* 未完待續。④留住；使持續。He was *continued* in office. 他得保留職位。⑤延期。⑥擴展(空間)。—*v.i.* ①繼續；連續。②依然不變；持久。③留。④延續。⑤(中斷後)繼續。 「數。」
continued fraction〖數學〗連分
continued multiplication〖數學〗連乘法。 「連比例。」
continued proportion〖數學〗
con·ti·nu·i·ty 〔ˌkantəˈnuətɪ; ˌkɔntiˈnjuːiti〕 *n., pl.* **-ties.** ①連續；密切的關連。②電影分景劇本；影片組合。③廣播節目中間做的挿白。④〖數學〗連續性；綿續性。
continuity equation〖數學〗連續(性)方程。「(亦作 **continuity clerk**)」
continuity girl〖電影〗場記小姐。
***con·tin·u·ous** 〔kənˈtɪnjuəs; kənˈtinjuəs〕 *adj.* ①不斷的；連續的。*continuous* progress. 不斷的進步。②〖數學〗連續；綿續。—**ly,** *adv.*
con·tin·u·um 〔kənˈtɪnjuəm; kənˈtinjuəm〕 *n., pl.* **-u·a** 〔-juə; -juə〕. ①連續。②〖數學〗連續統；閉聯集。
con·to 〔ˈkanto; ˈkɔntou〕 *n., pl.* **-tos.** 巴西及葡萄牙之錢款數目(在巴西等於一千 cruzeiros, 在葡萄牙等於一千 escudos).
con·tort 〔kənˈtɔrt; kənˈtɔːt〕 *v.t.* 扭歪；使彎。—**ed,** *adj.* 「ʃən〕 *n.* 扭歪；彎曲。」
con·tor·tion 〔kənˈtɔrʃən; kənˈtɔː-
con·tor·tion·ist 〔kənˈtɔrʃənɪst; kənˈtɔːʃənist〕 *n.* ①作軟體表演者。②做彎曲或歪曲者。
con·tour 〔ˈkantur; ˈkɔntuə〕 *n.* 輪廓；外形界線；海岸線。—*v.t.* ①畫輪廓；畫地形線。②依地形建築(公路等)。—*adj.* ①沿等高線的(指梯田等)。②以等高線表示的。
contour coach 太空船中與太空人體型完全適合的座位。
contour line(s) 等高線。
contr. ①contract. ②contracted. ③contraction. ④contralto. ⑤contrary. ⑥contrasted. ⑦control. ⑧controller.
con·tra 〔ˈkantrə; ˈkɔntrə〕 *prep.* 相反；反對。—*adv.* 相反地。—*n.* 帳簿之右欄。
contra-〖字首〗表"反對；相反"之義。
con·tra·band 〔ˈkantrəˌbænd; ˈkɔntrəbænd〕 *n.* ①違法交易；走私。②走私貨；違禁品。③(美國內戰時) 逃入或被帶入北方的黑奴。***absolute contraband*** 絕對禁運品。***occasional contraband*** 戰時特別禁運品。***unconditional contraband*** =**absolute contraband.** —*adj.* ①禁止進口或入口的；禁運的。②違法的(交易)。
con·tra·band·age 〔ˈkantrəˌbændɪdʒ; ˈkɔntrəˌbændidʒ〕 *n.* ①違禁品之買賣。②走私。 「之物品；走私貨。」
contraband goods 禁止進出口
con·tra·band·ist 〔ˈkantrəˌbændɪst; ˈkɔntrəˌbændist〕 *n.* 買賣違禁品者；走私者。
contraband of war 戰時禁運品。
con·tra·bass 〔ˈkantrəˌbes; ˈkɔntrəbeis〕 *n.* (亦作 **contrabasso**)①低音大提琴。②任何低於低音的樂器。—*adj.* 此類樂器的。
con·tra·cept 〔ˈkantrəsɛpt; ˈkɔntrəsept〕 *v.t.* 避孕。
con·tra·cep·tion 〔ˌkantrəˈsɛpʃən; ˌkɔntrəˈsepʃən〕 *n.* 避孕；避孕法。
con·tra·cep·tive 〔ˌkantrəˈsɛptɪv; ˌkɔntrəˈseptiv〕 *adj.* 避孕的。—*n.* 避孕用具；避孕藥。
con·tra·clock·wise 〔ˌkantrəˈklakˌwaɪz; ˌkɔntrəˈklɔkˌwaiz〕 *adj.* & *adv.* 反時針方向的(地)。
‡con·tract 〔*v.* kənˈtrækt; kənˈtrækt *v.t.* ⑤ˈkantrækt; ˈkɔntrækt *n.* ˈkantrækt; ˈkɔntrækt〕 *v.t.* ①收縮。②皺。③縮短；省略。④感受；感染；沾染；招致；得。to *contract* a disease. 得病。⑤締結；訂立。to *contract* an alliance. 訂盟。—*v.i.* ①收縮。Metals

contract on cooling. 金屬冷則收縮。②訂約。—*n.* ①合約;合同。to sign a *contract.* 簽約。②正式契約。③婚約。④=**contract bridge.** —**a·ble,** *adj.*

contract bridge 合約橋牌。

con·tract·ed [kən'træktɪd; kən'træktid] *adj.* ①收縮的;皺縮的。②省略的;縮短的。a *contracted* noun. 〖文法〗省略之名詞(如 ma'am 等)。③褊狹的;小氣的。④貧窮的;困苦的。⑤訂過約的;協定的。—**ly,** *adv.*

con·tract·i·bil·i·ty [kənˌtræktə'bɪlətɪ; kənˌtræktə'biliti] *n.* 收縮性;收縮。

con·tract·i·ble [kən'træktəbl̩; kən'træktəbl] *adj.* 可縮的;收縮的。

con·trac·tile [kən'træktl̩; kən'træktail] *adj.* ①有收縮性的。②致使收縮的。

con·trac·til·i·ty [ˌkɑntræk'tɪlətɪ; ˌkɔntræk'tiliti] *n.* 收縮性;收縮力。

***con·trac·tion** [kən'trækʃən; kən'trækʃən] *n.* ①收縮;縮短。②〖文法〗(一字中字母之)省略;省略字。③緊縮(貸款、資金等)。④約束;限制。⑤〖醫〗攣縮;收縮。

con·trac·tive [kən'træktɪv; kən'træktiv] *adj.* 有收縮性的;收縮的。

contract miner 按工計酬的礦工。

con·trac·tor ['kɑntræktɚ; 'kɔntræktə *for* ② kən'træktɚ; kən'træktə] *n.* ①承造者;承辦者;立約者;包商。②〖解剖〗收縮肌。③〖橋牌〗**a.** 莊家。**b.** 夢家。

con·trac·tu·al [kən'træktʃuəl; kən'træktʃuəl] *adj.* 契約上(性)的。—**ly,** *adv.*

con·trac·ture [kən'træktʃɚ; kən'træktʃə] *n.* 〖醫〗攣縮。

***con·tra·dict** [ˌkɑntrə'dɪkt; ˌkɔntrə'dikt] *v.t.* ①否認。②反駁。③相反;牴觸;矛盾。He *contradicted* himself. 他自相矛盾。—*v.i.* 矛盾;衝突。

***con·tra·dic·tion** [ˌkɑntrə'dɪkʃən; ˌkɔntrə'dikʃən] *n.* ①反駁;否定;否認;反對。②矛盾;牴觸;相反。*contradiction* in terms. 〖邏輯〗名辭之矛盾。③由矛盾要素組成的人或物。④〖邏輯〗矛盾對立;正相反。

con·tra·dic·tious [ˌkɑntrə'dɪkʃəs; ˌkɔntrə'dikʃəs] *adj.* 好反駁的;喜爭辯的。—**ly,** *adv.* —**ness,** *n.*

con·tra·dic·tive [ˌkɑntrə'dɪktɪv; ˌkɔntrə'diktiv] *adj.* 傾向於矛盾的;矛盾的。—**ly,** *adv.* —**ness,** *n.*

con·tra·dic·to·ry [ˌkɑntrə'dɪktərɪ; ˌkɔntrə'diktəri] *adj., n., pl.* **-ries.** —*adj.* ①矛盾的;對立的。②正反對的;相反的。③好反駁的。—*n.* 〖邏輯〗矛盾對立的命題;正相反的命題(名辭)。—**con·tra·dic·to·ri·ly,** *adv.* —**con·tra·dic·to·ri·ness,** *n.*

con·tra·dis·tinc·tion [ˌkɑntrədɪ'stɪŋkʃən; ˌkɔntrədis'tiŋkʃən] *n.* 對比;對照之區別。

con·tra·dis·tin·guish [ˌkɑntrədɪ'stɪŋgwɪʃ; ˌkɔntrədis'tiŋgwiʃ] *v.t.* 以比較分別;以對比區分。

con·trail ['kɑntrel; 'kɔntreil] *n.* 〖航空〗凝結尾(飛機在飛行時尾部形成之似雲物)。(亦作 **condensation trail, vapor trail**)

con·tra·in·di·cate [ˌkɑntrə'ɪndəˌket; ˌkɔntrə'indikeit] *v.t.,* **-cat·ed, -cat·ing.** 〖醫〗(病徵等)顯示(治療)不當。—**con·tra·in·di·ca·tion,** *n.*

con·tral·to [kən'trælto; kən'træltou] *n., pl.* **-tos.** ①最低之女低音。②用此低音唱的部分。③唱此低音之女子。

con·tra·or·bi·tal [ˌkɑntrə'ɔrbɪtl̩; ˌkɔntrə'ɔːbitəl] *adj.* (火箭、飛彈等之)與正常軌道相反的。

con·tra·pose ['kɑntrəˌpoz; 'kɔntrəpouz] *v.t.,* **-posed, -pos·ing.** 置於相對之位置。

con·tra·po·si·tion [ˌkɑntrəpə'zɪʃən; ˌkɔntrəpə'ziʃən] *n.* ①對偶;相對之位置。②對換;換位。

con·tra·pos·i·tive [ˌkɑntrə'pɑzətɪv; ˌkɔntrə'pɔzitiv] *adj.* 〖邏輯〗對換的。—*n.* 對換句。

con·trap·tion [kən'træpʃən; kən'træpʃən] *n.* 〖俗〗機巧品;(新奇的)機械。

con·tra·pun·tal [ˌkɑntrə'pʌntl̩; ˌkɔntrə'pʌntl] *adj.* 〖音樂〗對位法的。

con·tra·pun·tist [ˌkɑntrə'pʌntɪst; ˌkɔntrə'pʌntist] *n.* 〖音樂〗對位法家。

con·tra·ri·e·ty [ˌkɑntrə'raɪətɪ; ˌkɔntrə'raiəti] *n., pl.* **-ties.** ①相反;不相容;矛盾。②相反或矛盾的事物或言論。

con·tra·ri·wise ['kɑntrɛrɪˌwaɪz; 'kɔntrəriwaiz] *adv.* ①相反地;反對地;背逆地。②剛愎地;執拗地。

con·tra·ro·tate [ˌkɑntrə'rotet; ˌkɔntrə'routeit] *v.i.,* **-tat·ed, -tat·ing.** ①朝相反之方向旋轉。②逆旋轉。—**con·tra·ro·ta·tion,** *n.*

con·tra·ry** ['kɑntrɛrɪ, *for adj.* ③ *also* kən'trɛrɪ; 'kɔntrəri, *for adj.* ③kən'trɛəri] *adj., adv., n., pl.* **-ries.** —*adj.* ①反對的;相反的;矛盾的。*contrary* to facts. 與事實相反;與事實矛盾。②逆的;不順的。*contrary* winds. 逆風。③固執的;剛愎的。④〖植物〗成直角的。—*adv.* 反對地;相反地;矛盾地。to act *contrary* to the rules. 行動違反規則。—*n.* 相反的事物;矛盾。There is not enough evidence to the *contrary.* 相反的證據不够。by contraries*** 與願望相反。***on the contrary*** **a.** 反之;反是。**b.** 從另一觀點看來。***to the contrary*** 有相反的情形。—**con·tra·ri·ly,** *adv.* —**con·tra·ri·ness,** *n.*

***con·trast** [*n.* 'kɑntræst; 'kɔntrɑːst *v.* kən'træst; kən'trɑːst] *n.* ①差別;明顯的差異。the *contrast* between black and white. 黑白之間的差別。②對比;對照;反襯。③對照物。Black hair is a sharp *contrast* to white skin. 黑頭髮和白皮膚是一明顯的對照。—*v.t.* 對比;對照。*Contrast* birds with fishes. 將鳥和魚對比。—*v.i.* 對比時顯示差別;成對照。

con·tra·stim·u·lant [ˌkɑntrə'stɪmjələnt; ˌkɔntrə'stimjələnt] *n.* 抗興奮劑;鎮靜劑。—*adj.* 有鎮靜作用的。

con·tras·tive [kən'træstɪv; kən'trɑːstiv] *adj.* 對比的。

con·trast·y [kən'træstɪ; kən'træsti] *adj.* 〖照相〗明暗差別强烈的。

con·tra·vene [ˌkɑntrə'vin; ˌkɔntrə'viːn] *v.t.,* **-vened, -ven·ing.** ①違反;抵觸。②破壞;侵犯。③否定;反駁。

con·tra·ven·tion [ˌkɑntrə'vɛnʃən; ˌkɔntrə'venʃən] *n.* ①違反;矛盾。②違警罪。***in contravention of*** 與…相抵觸。

con·tre·danse [kõtrə 'dɑ̃s; kõtrə'dɑ̃ːs] *n., pl.* **-dans·es.** 〖法〗對舞(諸舞伴對面成列而跳之一種土風舞);對舞曲。(亦作 **contradance**)

con·tre·temps [kõtrə'tɑ̃, 'kõtrəˌtɑ̃; 'kɔ̃ːtrətɑ̃ː] *n., pl.* **-temps.** 不幸的意外之

事;令人尷尬的事。

*con·trib·ute [kən'trɪbjut; kən'tribju(:)t] v., -ut·ed, -ut·ing. —v.t. ①捐助;貢獻。to *contribute* clothing for the relief of the poor. 捐衣以濟貧。②投(稿)。—v.i. ①捐助。②助成;促成。Good health *contributed* to his success. 良好的健康助成他的成功。③投稿。

*con·tri·bu·tion [ˌkɑntrə'bjuʃən; ˌkɔntri'bju:ʃən] n. ①捐助;貢獻。*contribution* box. 捐獻箱。②捐助的東西。③投稿。④稅。***lay under contribution*** 强迫繳稅。

con·trib·u·tive [kən'trɪbjutɪv; kən'tribjutiv] adj. ①貢獻的; 捐助的。②促成的; 增進的。

con·trib·u·tor [kən'trɪbjətɚ; kən'tribjutə] n. ①捐助者;貢獻者。②投稿人。

con·trib·u·to·ry [kən'trɪbjəˌtorɪ; kən'tribjutəri] adj. ①有貢獻的; 有捐助之性質的;有助於…的;促成…的。②雇主與被雇者共同出錢的。③可課稅的。—n. 貢獻者;捐助者。

con·trite ['kɑntraɪt;'kɔntrait] adj. 悔罪的;痛悔的;表示懺悔的。—**con·tri·tion,** n.

con·triv·a·ble [kən'traɪvəbl̩; kən'traivəbl] adj. 可設計的;可發明的。

*con·triv·ance [kən'traɪvəns; kən'traivəns] n. ①發明物;機械裝置。②設計;籌畫。③設計或發明的才能。④計畫; 圖謀。

*con·trive [kən'traɪv; kən'traiv] v., -trived, -triv·ing. —v.t. ①發明;設計。②圖謀。③以計謀達成。He *contrived* to gain their votes. 他設法獲得了他們的選票。—v.i. ①設法; 計劃。②圖謀。③料理家務; 治家。—**con·triv·er,** n.

‡con·trol [kən'trol; kən'troul] n., v., -trolled, -trol·ling. —n. ①管理;管轄;監督;支配。②抑制;克制。He lost *control* of his temper. 他不能抑制他的脾氣。③(*pl.*) 駕馭機件的裝置;操縱裝置。④(確定科學實驗之結果的) 對照標準; 核對。⑤招魂術中,驅使靈媒的精靈。⑥控制。remote *control.* 遙控。⑦管理員。⑧〖棒球〗制球能力。***be beyond control*** 不能控制。***be out of control*** 失去控制; 不能操縱。***be under control*** 受控制;受鎭壓。***birth control*** 節育。***control room*** 控制室。***control stick*** (飛機之)操縱桿。***control tower*** (機場之)指揮塔臺。***Control Yuan*** (中國之) 監察院。***get*** (or ***gain***) ***control over*** (or ***of***)控制;鎭壓;制服。***get under control*** 鎭壓;控制;使平服。***keep under control*** 抑制;克制。***lose control over*** (or ***of***) 不能控制。—v.t. ①指揮;監督;管理;支配。②抑制;約束。to *control* oneself. 抑制自己。③調節;操縱。④核對(帳目);撙節(支出)。

control board 儀器板。(亦作 **control panel**)

control center 控制中心。

control experiment 核對其他實驗結果所作之實驗。

con·trol·la·ble [kən'troləbl̩; kən'trouləbl] adj. 可管理的; 可控制的; 能操縱的;可支配的;可抑制的。

con·trolled [kən'trold; kən'trould] adj. 受約束的;克制的。

con·trol·ler [kən'trolɚ; kən'troulə] n. ①主計員; 查帳員。②管理者; 指揮者。③管制機器的機件;操縱器。④〖航海〗(錨鍊)之制鍊器。⑤〖航空〗飛航管制員。***controller general*** 主計長。—**ship,** n.

con·tro·ver·sial [ˌkɑntrə'vɝʃəl; ˌkɔntrə'və:ʃəl] adj. ①爭論的;引起爭論的。②好爭論的。—**ist,** n.

*con·tro·ver·sy ['kɑntrəˌvɝsɪ; 'kɔntrəvə:si] n., pl. -sies, v. —n. 爭論;辯論。This problem is beyond *controversy.* 這問題是無庸置辯的。—v.t. & v.i. 爭論;辯論。

con·tro·vert ['kɑntrəˌvɝt; 'kɔntrəvə:t] v.t. ①駁擊;否定;反證。②辯論;討論。—v.i. 辯論;爭辯。

con·tro·vert·i·ble [ˌkɑntrə'vɝtəbl̩; ˌkɔntrə'və:tibl] adj. 可爭論的; 可辯論的。

con·tu·ma·cious [ˌkɑntju'meʃəs; ˌkɔntju:'meiʃəs] adj. ①不服從命令的; 頑固的。②〖法律〗抗傳的;反抗法院命令的。

con·tu·ma·cy ['kɑntjuməsɪ;'kɔntjuməsi] n., pl. -cies. 堅不服從;抗命;頑抗。

con·tu·me·li·ous [ˌkɑntju'milɪəs; ˌkɔntju:'mi:ljəs] adj. 侮慢的;無禮的。

con·tu·me·ly ['kɑntjuməlɪ; 'kɔntjumli] n., pl. -lies. ①(言語或行爲上之)傲慢;無禮。②侮辱。

con·tuse [kən'tjuz; kən'tju:z] v.t., -tused, -tus·ing. 打傷;撞傷;挫傷。—**con·tu·sion,** n. —**con·tu·sive,** adj.

co·nun·drum [kə'nʌndrəm; kə'nʌndrəm] n. (含詼諧、雙關之意的)謎語。

con·ur·ba·tion [ˌkɑnɚ'beʃən; ˌkɔnə:'beiʃən] n. (幾個)集合都市。

con·va·lesce [ˌkɑnvə'lɛs; ˌkɔnvə'les] v.i., -lesced, -lesc·ing. 恢復健康;漸癒。

con·va·les·cence [ˌkɑnvə'lɛsns; ˌkɔnvə'lesns] n. ①漸癒。②病後復原期。

con·va·les·cent [ˌkɑnvə'lɛsn̩t; ˌkɔnvə'lesnt] adj. (有益於) 漸癒的。—n. 恢復健康中的病人。

con·vect [kən'vɛkt; kən'vekt] v.t. 以對流傳(熱或液體)。—v.i. (指液體) 以對流傳熱。

con·vec·tion [kən'vɛkʃən; kən'vekʃən] n. ①傳達。②〖氣象〗對流。③〖物理〗(熱或電之)對流。—**con·vec·tive,** adj.

con·vec·tor [kən'vɛktɚ; kən'vektə] n. 以對流傳熱之液體或儀器。

con·ven·a·ble [kən'vinəbl̩; kən'vi:nəbl] adj. 可召集的;可召喚的。

con·ve·nance ['kɑnvəˌnans; 'kɔ̃:ŋvinɑ̃:ns] 〖法〗 n. ①適當。②(*pl.*) 慣例;習俗。

con·vene [kən'vin; kən'vi:n] v., -vened, -ven·ing. —v.i. 集會;集合。—v.t. 召集;票傳。

*con·ven·ience¹ [kən'vinjəns; kən'vi:njəns] n. ①方便;適合。to await one's *convenience.* 等待他人方便的時候。②便利的事物。It is a great *convenience* to have a doctor living next door. 有醫生住在隔鄰,是一大便利的事。③〖英〗厠所。***as a matter of convenience*** 爲了方便。***at one's convenience*** 在方便的時候。You may pay me *at your convenience.* 你可以在方便時付款給我。***for convenience' sake*** 爲方便起見。***for the convenience of*** 爲…的方便起見。***make a convenience of*** (***a person***)〖俗〗任意利用(某人)。***marriage of convenience*** 以實利爲本位的結婚;政略結婚。***suit one's convenience*** 合某人便利。if it *suits your convenience.* 若對你方便。***suit*** (or ***consult***) ***one's own convenience*** 只圖一己方便。

con·ven·ience² v.t., -ven·ienced, -ven·ienc·ing. 使方便。

***con·ven·ient** [kən'vinjənt; kən'vi:njənt] *adj.* ①方便的；合宜的；舒適的。It is not *convenient* for me to return the book now. 現在還書對我不方便。②近便的；易得的。—**ly,** *adv.*

con·vent** ['kɑnvɛnt; 'kɔnvənt] *n.* ①修女(或修士)之團體。②(多指女)修道院。go into a convent*** 作修女；作尼姑。

con·ven·ti·cle [kən'vɛntɪkl̩; kən'ventikl] *n.* ①非國教徒之聚會。②聚會所。—*v.i.* 在聚會所聚集。

‡**con·ven·tion** [kən'vɛnʃən; kən'venʃən] *n.* ①集會；(正式派代表出席的)會議。to join the *convention* on wireless telegraphy. 參加無線電報會議。②(會議的)代表；使節。③條約；協約；契約。to conclude a military *convention.* 締結軍事協定。④習俗；習慣。⑤〖美政治〗政黨提名大會。

***con·ven·tion·al** [kən'vɛnʃənl̩; kən'venʃənl] *adj.* ①傳統的；習慣的。②協定上的；依條約的；會議的。*conventional* neutrality. 約定中立。③形式上的。④陳舊的；因襲的。⑤任意選擇的。—**ly,** *adv.*

con·ven·tion·al·ism [kən'vɛnʃənl̩ˌɪzəm; kən'venʃn̩əlizəm] *n.* ①因襲之思想、習慣、或文句。②墨守成規；因襲之風。

con·ven·tion·al·ist [kən'vɛnʃənəlɪst; kən'venʃənəlist] *n.* 拘泥習俗者；遵守慣例者；墨守成規者。

con·ven·tion·al·i·ty [kənˌvɛnʃən'ælətɪ; kənˌvenʃə'næliti] *n., pl.* **-ties.** 隨俗；因襲；慣例；老套。

con·ven·tion·al·ize [kən'vɛnʃənl̩ˌaɪz; kən'venʃn̩əlaiz] *v.t.,* **-ized, -iz·ing.** ①使從習俗或慣例。②〖美術〗依傳統筆法作畫。

con·ven·tion·er [kən'vɛnʃənɚ; kən'venʃənə] *n.* 參加集會的人。(亦作 **conventioneer**)

con·ven·tu·al [kən'vɛntʃuəl; kən'ventʃuəl] *adj.* 女修道院的。—*n.* ①修女；修士。②(C-)聖芳濟會修士。

con·verge [kən'vɝdʒ; kən'və:dʒ] *v.,* **-verged, -verg·ing.** —*v.i.* ①集中於一點。②收斂。③趨於相同的目標。—*v.t.* 使輻合。

con·ver·gence [kən'vɝdʒəns; kən'və:dʒəns] *n.* ①集中；輻合；收斂。②〖生物〗趨同作用。(亦作 **convergency**)

con·ver·gent [kən'vɝdʒənt; kən'və:dʒənt] *adj.* ①輻合的；會聚的。②包圍集中的。③〖數學, 物理〗收斂的；會聚的。

con·vers·a·ble [kən'vɝsəbl̩; kən'və:səbl] *adj.* ①可與交談的；易與交談的。②善於辭令的；喜交談的。③(適於)談話的。

con·ver·sant ['kɑnvɚsn̩t; kən'və:sənt] *adj.* ①精通…的；嫻熟的；熟識…的〖with〗。②親近的；與…有交情的。—**con·ver·sance, con·ver·san·cy,** *n.*

‡**con·ver·sa·tion** [ˌkɑnvɚ'seʃən; ˌkɔnvə'seiʃən] *n.* ①會話；談話；會談。I had a pleasant *conversation* with him. 我和他有很愉快的談話。②親密；親近。③談話的技巧。—**al,** *adj.* —**al·ly,** *adv.*

con·ver·sa·tion·ist [ˌkɑnvɚ'seʃənɪst; ˌkɔnvə'seiʃənist] *n.* 有口才的人；健談者。(亦作 **conversationalist**)

conversation piece ①人物畫。②「話題。」

con·ver·sa·zi·o·ne [ˌkɑnvɚˌsɑtsɪ'onɪ; 'kɔnvəˌsætsi'ouni] *n., pl.* **-nes, -ni** [-nɪ; -ni].〖義〗(文藝、學術性等之)座談會。

***con·verse**[1] [*v.* kən'vɝs; kən'və:s *n.* 'kɑnvɝs; 'kɔnvə:s] *v.,* **-versed, -vers·ing,** *n.* —*v.i.* 談話。I *conversed* with him on a certain problem. 我與他談論某一問題。—*n.* 談話。

con·verse[2] [*adj.* kən'vɝs; 'kɔnvə:s *n.* 'kɑnvɝs; 'kɔnvə:s] *adj.* 倒轉的；方向或行動相反的。—*n.* ①相反的事物。②反轉來的事物。—**ly,** *adv.*

con·ver·sion** [kən'vɝʃən; kən'və:ʃən] *n.* ①轉變；變換；改變。②信仰的改變。③〖法律〗變更；强占。④換算。conversion table*** 換算表。

***con·vert** [*v.* kən'vɝt; kən'və:t *n.* 'kɑnvɝt; 'kɔnvə:t] *v.t.* ①轉變；改變。to *convert* sugar into alcohol. 將糖變爲酒精。②使改變信仰、黨派或意見等。③兌換；交換。④反轉；倒置；置換。⑤〖法律〗侵占；占用。⑥變更(用途等)。—*n.* 改變信仰或意見的人。—**ed,** *adj.*

con·vert·er [kən'vɝtɚ; kən'və:tə] *n.* ①轉換者。②(生鐵鍊鋼用之)轉化爐。③〖電〗變流器。④織物加工之販售業者。(亦作 **convertor**)

con·vert·i·bil·i·ty [kənˌvɝtə'bɪlətɪ; kənˌvə:tə'biliti] *n.* 可改變(性)；可轉換(性)；可兌換(性)。

con·vert·i·ble [kən'vɝtəbl̩; kən'və:təbl] *adj.* ①可改變的。②可改造的。③改變信仰的。④可兌換的；可交換的。⑤(汽車)有摺篷的。⑥同意義的。—*n.* ①可改變或變換之事物。②敞篷車。***convertible note*** (or ***paper***) 兌現券。

con·vert·i·bly [kən'vɝtəblɪ; kən'və:təbli] *adv.* ①可改變地；可改造地。②可兌換地；可交換地。

con·vex [*adj.* kɑn'vɛks; kɔn'veks *n.* 'kɑnvɛks; 'kɔn'veks] *adj.* 凸出的。—*n.* 凸面。—**i·ty,** *n.* —**ly,** *adv.*

con·vex·o-con·cave [kən'vɛkso-kɑn'kev; kən'veksoukɔn'keiv] *adj.* (透鏡)一面凸出，另一面凹的。

con·vex·o-con·vex [kən'vɛkso-kɑn'vɛks; kən'veksoukɔn'veks] *adj.* 雙凸面的。

con·vex·o-plane [kən'vɛkso'plen; kən'veksou'plein] *adj.* (透鏡)一面凸出，另一面平的。

***con·vey** [kən've; kən'vei] *v.t.* ①運送；運輸。②傳遞；傳達。Please *convey* to her my best regards. 請轉達我對她的問候。③通知；通報。④(經合法的手續)讓與。⑤傳導。

con·vey·a·ble [kən'veəbl̩; kən'veiəbl] *adj.* 可搬運的；可傳達的；可轉讓的。

con·vey·ance [kən'veəns; kən'veiəns] *n.* ①運送；運輸。②傳達；傳遞。③〖法律〗讓與；讓與證書。④舟車；交通工具。

con·vey·anc·er [kən'veənsɚ; kən'veiənsə] *n.* ①運送業者；傳遞者。②〖法律〗辦理不動產等讓與事務之律師。

con·vey·anc·ing [kən'veənsɪŋ; kən'veiənsiŋ] *n.*〖法律〗讓與證書製作(業)；財產或其他權益讓與之法律事務。

con·vey·er [kən'veɚ; kən'veiə] *n.* 運送者(機)；搬運器；轉運帶。(亦作 **conveyor**)

conveyor belt 轉運帶。

***con·vict** [*v.* kən'vɪkt; kən'vikt *n.* 'kɑnvɪkt; 'kɔnvikt] *v.t.* ①證明有罪。②判爲有罪；宣告有罪。The jury *convicted* the prisoner of murder. 陪審員宣告這犯人犯謀殺罪。③使知罪。—*n.* 罪犯。

convict goods 囚犯生產之貨物。
con·vic·tion** 〔kənˈvɪkʃən; kənˈvikʃən〕 *n.* ①定罪；判罪。②說服；信服。③堅信；信念。carry conviction*** 頗有道理。***in the (full) conviction that*** 堅信…。***open to conviction*** 服理。—**al,** *adj.*
***con·vince** 〔kənˈvɪns; kənˈvins〕 *v.t.,* **-vinced, -vinc·ing.** 使相信；說服。He is *convinced* of its truth. 他深信這事實的眞情。—**con·vinced,** *adj.* —**con·ivnc·ed·ly,** *adv.* 〖注意〗**convince** 與 **of** 連用，再接名詞或與連接詞 that 之名詞子句連用。
con·vin·ci·ble 〔kənˈvɪnsəbl̩; kənˈvinsəbl, -sib-〕 *adj.* 可使相信的；可說服的。
***con·vinc·ing** 〔kənˈvɪnsɪŋ; kənˈvinsiŋ〕 *adj.* 令人心服的；能說服人的。—**ly,** *adv.* —**ness,** *n.*
con·vive 〔ˈkɑnvaɪv; ˈkɔnvaiv〕 *n., pl.* **-vives.** 同桌吃飯的人。
con·viv·i·al 〔kənˈvɪvɪəl; kənˈviviəl〕 *adj.* ①歡宴的；歡樂的。②友善的；愉快的。—**i·ty,** *n.* —**ly,** *adv.*
con·vo·ca·tion 〔ˌkɑnvəˈkeʃən; ˌkɔnvouˈkeiʃən〕 *n.* ①(會議之)召集。②會議（尤指宗教或學術上的）。③(C-) 英國教士會議。④出席會議的地區。
con·vo·ca·tor 〔ˈkɑnvəˌketɚ; ˈkɔnvəkeitə〕 *n.* ①召集會議的人。②與會者。
con·voke 〔kənˈvok; kənˈvouk〕 *v.t.,* **-voked, -vok·ing.** 召集(會議)。
con·vo·lute 〔ˈkɑnvəˌlut; ˈkɔnvəluːt〕 *adj., v.,* **-lut·ed, -lut·ing.** —*adj.* 旋繞的；回旋狀的。—*v.t. & v.i.* 旋繞。
con·vo·lut·ed 〔ˈkɑnvəˌlutɪd; ˈkɔnvəluːtid〕 *adj.* 旋繞的；回旋狀的。
con·vo·lu·tion 〔ˌkɑnvəˈluʃən; ˌkɔnvəˈluːʃən〕 *n.* ①旋繞；盤旋。②一捲；一旋。③〖解剖〗腦回。
con·volve 〔kənˈvɑlv; kənˈvɔlv〕 *v.t. & v.i.,* **-volved, -volv·ing.** 捲；盤；旋繞。
con·vol·vu·lus 〔kənˈvɑlvjələs; kənˈvɔlvjuləs〕 *n., pl.* **-lus·es, -li** 〔-laɪ; -lai〕. 〖植物〗旋花植物。
con·voy 〔*v.* kənˈvɔɪ; ˈkɔnvɔi, kənˈvɔi *n.* ˈkɑnvɔɪ; ˈkɔnvɔi〕 *v.t.* 護送；護衛；護航。—*n.* ①護送；護衛。②護送隊。③被護送之船隊或車隊等。
convoy fleet 護航艦隊。
con·vul·sant 〔kənˈvʌlsənt; kənˈvʌlsənt〕 *adj.* 引起痙攣的。—*n.* 引搐藥。
con·vulse 〔kənˈvʌls; kənˈvʌls〕 *v.t.,* **-vulsed, -vuls·ing.** ①震動；使騷動。②痙攣；抽搐。③使…哄堂大笑。
con·vul·sion 〔kənˈvʌlʃən; kənˈvʌlʃən〕 *n.* ①震動；騷動。②〖醫〗痙攣；驚風症。③(*pl.*) 大笑。***throw into convulsions*** 使起痙攣；使捧腹大笑。
con·vul·sion·ar·y 〔kənˈvʌlʃənˌɛrɪ; kənˈvʌlʃn̩əri〕 *adj., n., pl.* **-ar·ies.** —*adj.* 震動的；痙攣的。—*n.* 痙攣性之人。
con·vul·sive 〔kənˈvʌlsɪv; kənˈvʌlsiv〕 *adj.* 痙攣的；騷動的。—**ly,** *adv.* —**ness,** *n.*
co·ny 〔ˈkonɪ; ˈkouni〕 *n., pl.* **-nies.** ①家兔。②兔的毛皮。（亦作 **coney**）
coo**[1] 〔ku; kuː〕 *n., v.,* **cooed, coo·ing.** —*n.* 咕咕聲（如鴿子）。—*v.i.* ①作咕咕聲。②喁喁情話。—*v.t.* 低聲而言或表示。bill and coo*** 調情。—**ing·ly,** *adv.*
coo[2] *interj.* 〖英俚〗表示驚訝的感歎詞。
coo·ee 〔ˈkuɪ; ˈkuːi〕 *n., v.,* **coo·eed, coo·ee·ing.** —*n.* 澳洲土人呼喊之聲。—*v.i.* 作此呼喊聲。（亦作 **cooey**）
Cook 〔kuk; kuk〕 *n.* 科克(Capt. James, 1728–1779, 英國航海家及探險家)。
‡**cook** 〔kuk; kuk〕 *n.* 廚子。—*v.t.* ①烹調；煮。②〖俗〗**a.** 竄改；捏造。**b.** 毀壞。—*v.i.* ①烹調；煮。Meat doesn't *cook* as quickly as an egg. 肉不能像蛋煮熟得那麼快。②作廚子。③〖俗〗發生。***cook off*** （子彈）未經扣扳機即發射或爆炸。***cook one's goose*** 破壞…計畫；使…徹底失敗。***cook up*** 〖俗〗**a.** 計劃。**b.** 捏造。to *cook up* a story. 捏造故事。
cook·book 〔ˈkukˌbuk; ˈkukbuk〕 *n.* 食譜。（英亦作 **cookery-book**）
cook·er 〔ˈkukɚ; ˈkukə〕 *n.* ①鍋；炊具。②爲烹食而非生食所種植之水果。
***cook·er·y** 〔ˈkukərɪ; ˈkukəri〕 *n., pl.* **-er·ies.** 烹飪；烹調術；烹調業。
cook·house 〔ˈkukˌhaus; ˈkukhaus〕 *n.* 炊事房；(特指)船上之廚房。
***cook·ie** 〔ˈkukɪ; ˈkuki〕 *n.* =**cooky.**
cook·ing 〔ˈkukɪŋ; ˈkukiŋ〕 *adj.* 烹調用的。—*n.* 烹調；烹調法。
cook·out 〔ˈkukˌaut; ˈkukaut〕 *n.* ①在野外烹調飲食的聚會。②此種聚會之食物。—*adj.* 此種聚會的。
cook·room 〔ˈkukˌrum; ˈkukrum〕 *n.* 廚房。
cook·shop 〔ˈkukˌʃɑp; ˈkukʃɔp〕 *n.* 小飯館；小菜館。
Cook's tour 安排好的走馬看花式的遊覽。
cook·stove 〔ˈkukˌstov; ˈkukstouv〕 *n.* 烹調用之爐。
***cook·y** 〔ˈkukɪ; ˈkuki〕 *n., pl.* **cook·ies.** ①餅乾。②〖蘇〗一種小麪包。③〖俗〗情人(暱稱)。④〖俚〗人（尤指男人）；傢伙。⑤(*pl.*)〖俚〗一個人胃內之食物。（亦作 **cookie**）
cooky pusher 〖美俚〗置工作不顧而留連茶會、宴會者。
‡**cool** 〔kul; kuːl〕 *adj.* ①微冷的；涼的。②涼爽的。③冷靜的。a *cool* head. 冷靜的頭腦。④冷淡的。⑤大膽的；厚顏的；無禮的。He is a *cool* hand. 他是一個厚顏的人。What *cool* cheek! 多麼無禮！⑥〖俗〗不折不扣的。We walked a *cool* twenty miles. 我們整整走了二十英里。⑦寒色的。⑧從容的。⑨〖俚〗好的；棒的。⑩未被放射線汚染的。—*n.* ①涼爽；涼爽的部分、地方、或時間。the *cool* of the evening. 晚間的涼爽。②〖俚〗自制。***blow one's cool*** 激動。***keep one's cool*** 保持冷靜。***lose one's cool*** =**blow one's cool.** —*v.t.* ①使冷。②使冷靜。to *cool* one's anger. 息怒。③使失去興趣。—*v.i.* ①冷却。The hot syrup *cooled* off gradually. 熱糖漿漸漸冷却。②冷靜；止息；緩和（情感）。His affection *cooled* down. 他的愛情冷淡下來。③興趣減低。***cool it*** 〖俚〗冷靜下來。***cool off*** 〖俗〗變冷靜。***cool one's heels*** 等候良久。—*adv.* 〖俗〗=**coolly.**
cool·ant 〔ˈkulənt; ˈkuːlənt〕 *n.* ①冷却劑。②冷却用之潤滑油。
cool·er 〔ˈkulɚ; ˈkuːlə〕 *n.* ①冷却器。②清涼劑。③〖俚〗監獄。④冷氣機。
cool-head·ed 〔ˈkulˈhɛdɪd; ˈkuːlˈhedid〕 *adj.* 頭腦冷靜的。—**ly,** *adv.* —**ness,** *n.*
Coo·lidge 〔ˈkulɪdʒ; ˈkuːlidʒ〕 *n.* 柯立芝（John Calvin, 1872–1933, 美國第30任總統，其任期爲 1923–29)。
coo·lie, coo·ly 〔ˈkulɪ; ˈkuːli〕 *n., pl.* **-lies.** 苦力；小工。
cool·ing 〔ˈkulɪŋ; ˈkuːliŋ〕 *adj.* 冷的；冷却的。*cooling* drinks. 清涼飲料。

cool·ing-off [ˈkulɪŋˈɔf, -ˈɑf; ˈku:liŋ-ˈɔ:f] *adj.* 可使頭腦冷靜的。 *cooling-off* period. 勞資爭執雙方爲協商而緩和的期間。

***cool·ly** [ˈkullɪ, ˈkulɪ; ˈku:lli, ˈku:li] *adv.* ①冷然;鎮靜地。②鹵莽地;厚顏地。

cool·ness [ˈkulnɪs; ˈku:lnis] *n.* ①冷;涼爽。②冷靜;沉着。③冷淡。(亦作 **coolth**)

coomb [kum; ku:m] *n.* 〖方〗山谷;峽谷。(亦作 **combe, comb**)

coon [kun; ku:n] *n.* 〖俗〗①〖動物〗浣熊;樹狸。②黑人(帶有輕蔑之意)。③粗漢。 ***a coon's age*** 〖俗〗悠久的歲月。 ***a gone coon*** 〖俚〗陷於絕望的人或物。 ***go the whole coon*** 〖俚〗徹底地做。 ***hunt the same old coon*** 〖俗〗繼續作同樣的事。

coon·can [ˈkunˌkæn; ˈku:nkæn] *n.* 一種紙牌戲。

coon dog 獵浣熊之獵犬。(亦作 **coon-er, coonhound**)

coon·skin [ˈkunˌskɪn; ˈku:nskin] *n.* ①浣熊皮。②浣熊皮的衣物。—*adj.* 浣熊皮的。

coon songs 美國黑人歌曲。

coop [kup; ku:p] *n.* ①(鷄、兔等之)籠、欄等。②〖俚〗監獄。 ***fly the coop*** 越獄。 —*v.t.* ①關入籠或欄內〖常 up, in〗。②拘禁〖常 up, in〗。

co·op [koˈɑp; kouˈɔp] *n.* 〖俗〗消費合作社。(亦作 **co-op**)

co-op. ①co-operation. ②co-operative (society).

coop·er [ˈkupɚ, ˈkʊ-; ˈku:pə] *n.* 箍桶匠。—*v.t. & v.i.* 修理(桶類);製桶。 ***cooper up*** 修飾;磨光。

coop·er·age [ˈkupərɪdʒ; ˈku:pəridʒ] *n.* ①桶匠工作;桶業。②桶店。③桶匠製品。

***co·op·er·ate** [koˈɑpəˌret; kouˈɔpəreit] *v.i.*, **-at·ed, -at·ing.** ①合作;協力;協同。to *cooperate* with somebody in some work. 與某人合作做某事。②相助。③實行經濟合作。—**co·op·er·a·tor,** *n.*

***co·op·er·a·tion** [koˌɑpəˈreʃən; kouˌɔpəˈreiʃən] *n.* ①合作;協力;協同。Let us work in close *cooperation* with our friends. 我們和朋友們密切合作罷。②合作社。consumers' *cooperation.* 消費合作社。

***co·op·er·a·tive** [koˈɑpəˌretɪv; kouˈɔpərətiv] *adj.* 合作的;協力的;協同的。a producers' *cooperative* society. 生產合作社。—*n.* 合作社。—**ly,** *adv.*

cooperative bank 合作金庫。

cooperative store ①福利社。②農民合作社商店。

co-opt [koˈɑpt; kouˈɔpt] *v.t.* (由原委員)選舉(新委員)。(亦作**co-optate**)—**a·tion,** *n.*

co·op·ta·tive [koˈɑptətɪv; kouˈɔptətiv] *adj.* 由原任委員投票的;互選的。

co·or·di·nal [koˈɔrdn̩əl; kouˈɔ:dinəl] *adj.* ①(生物分類上)同科的;同目的。②〖數學〗坐標的。

***co·or·di·nate** [*adj., n.* koˈɔrdn̩ɪt; kouˈɔ:dn̩it *v.* koˈɔrdn̩ˌet; kouˈɔ:dineit] *adj., n., v.*, **-nat·ed, -nat·ing.** —*adj.* ①同等的;同格的。②〖文法〗對等的;同位的。*coordinate* conjunction. 對等連接詞。③〖數學〗坐標的。—*n.* ①同等的人或物。②〖數學〗坐標。—*v.t.* ①使同等。②調和。

coordinate paper 坐標紙。

coordinate system 坐標法。

co·or·di·na·tion [koˌɔrdn̩ˈeʃən; kouˌɔ:diˈneiʃən] *n.* ①同等;同格;同位。②調和;協調。

co·or·di·na·tive [koˈɔrdn̩ˌetɪv; kouˈɔ:dinətiv] *adj.* 同等的;同格的。

co·or·di·na·tor [koˈɔrdəˌnetɚ; kouˈɔ:dineitə] *n.* ①同等之人或物。②協調者。

coot [kut; ku:t] *n.* ①大鷭(水鳥)。②〖俗〗愚人。

coot·ie [ˈkutɪ; ˈku:ti] *n.* ①〖俚〗虱。②〖蘇〗木碗。(亦作 **cooty**)

cop[1] [kɑp; kɔp] *n., v.,* **copped, cop·ping.** —*n.* 〖俚〗警察。—*v.t.* 〖俚〗①抓;捉;獲得。②偷;竊。

cop[2] *n.* ①山丘之頂;物之頂端;禽類之冠毛。②(繞於紡錘之)圓錐形線團。

co·pai·ba [koˈpaɪbə; kɔˈpaibə] *n.* 古巴香(樹脂,作藥用)。(亦作 **copaiva**)

co·pal [ˈkopl̩, ˈkopæl; ˈkoupəl, kouˈpæl] *n.* 岩樹脂;柯巴脂(樹脂,供製漆)。

co·par·ce·nar·y [koˈpɑrsn̩ˌɛrɪ; kouˈpɑ:sinəri] *n.* 〖法律〗①共同繼承。②所有權共有。—*adj.* 共同繼承的。

co·par·ce·ner [koˈpɑrsn̩ɚ; ˈkouˈpɑ:sinə] *n.* 〖法律〗土地共同繼承人。

co·part·ner [koˈpɑrtnɚ; ˈkouˈpɑ:tnə] *n.* 合作者;合夥人。

co·part·ner·ship [koˈpɑrtnɚˌʃɪp; ˈkouˈpɑ:tnəʃip] *n.* 協同;合作;合夥。

***cope**[1] [kop; koup] *v.,* **coped, cop·ing.** —*v.i.* ①對抗;抗衡〖with〗。②對付;應付〖with〗。—*v.t.* 〖英俗〗應付。

cope[2] *n., v.,* **coped, cop·ing.** —*n.* ①(教士主禮時穿着之)長袍。②蒼穹。③覆蓋;遮隱。—*v.t.* 覆罩。

co·peck [ˈkopɛk; ˈkoupek] *n.* 蘇聯硬幣名(等於 1/100 盧布)。(亦作 **kopeck**)

Co·pen·ha·gen [ˌkopənˈhegən; ˌkoupnˈheigən] *n.* 哥本哈根(丹麥的首都)。

co·pe·pod [ˈkopəˌpɑd; ˈkoupəpɔd] *n.* 橈脚類之動物。—*adj.* 橈脚類動物的。

cop·er [ˈkopɚ; ˈkoupə] *n.* 〖英〗馬販(尤指不誠實者)。

Co·per·ni·can [koˈpɝnɪkən; kouˈpə:nikən] *adj.* 哥白尼(學說)的。

Co·per·ni·cus [koˈpɝnɪkəs; kouˈpə:nikəs] *n.* 哥白尼(Nicolaus, 1473–1543, 波蘭人,現代天文學之創始者)。

cope·stone [ˈkopˌston; ˈkoupstoun] *n.* ①牆帽;冠石。②〖喩〗頂點;極點;最後完成工作。(亦作 **coping stone**)

cop·i·er [ˈkɑpɪɚ; ˈkɔpiə] *n.* ①謄寫者。②剽竊者;仿效者。

co·pi·lot [koˈpaɪlət; kouˈpailət] *n.* (飛機之)副駕駛員。(亦作 **first officer**)

cop·ing [ˈkopɪŋ; ˈkoupiŋ] *n.* 〖建築〗牆之頂部。

coping saw 弓鋸。

co·pi·ous [ˈkopɪəs; ˈkoupjəs] *adj.* ①豐富的;饒多的。②長篇累牘的。—**ly,** *adv.* —**ness,** *n.*

co·pla·nar [koˈplenɚ; kouˈpleinə] *adj.* 〖數學〗共面的。

co·pol·y·mer [koˈpɑləmɚ; kouˈpɔliməl] *n.* 〖化〗異量分子聚合物。—**ize,** *v.*

cop out ①犯罪而被逮捕。②認罪。③〖美俚〗解脫干係;不履行承諾〖常 on, of〗。

***cop·per**[1] [ˈkɑpɚ; ˈkɔpə] *n.* ①銅。②銅器。③銅幣。④銅色。⑤〖英〗大銅鍋。⑥有銅色翅之小蝴蝶。—*v.t.* ①用銅板被覆;用銅皮包。②〖俗〗做兩面投機以免損失。—*adj.* ①銅的;銅製的。②銅色的。

cop·per[2] *n.* 〖俚〗警察。

cop·per·as [ˈkɑpərəs; ˈkɔpərəs] *n.* 〖化〗綠礬;硫酸亞鐵。

cop·per-bath [ˈkɑpɚˌbæθ; ˈkɔpəbɑ:θ] *n.* 〖化〗電鍍用硫酸銅溶液。

cop·per-bot·tomed [ˈkɑpɚ-

ˈbɑtəmd; ˈkɔpəˈbɔtəmd] *adj.* ①(船)底包銅皮的。②耐航的;結實的。

cop·per·head [ˈkɑpɚˌhɛd; ˈkɔpəhed] *n.* ①(北美之毒蛇)銅斑蛇。②(C-) 美國內戰時同情南方之北方人。

cop·per·plate [ˈkɑpɚˌplet; ˈkɔpəpleit] *n.* 〖印刷〗銅版;銅版印刷;銅版雕刻。—*v.t.* 製成銅版。

copper pyrites 黃銅礦。

cop·per·smith [ˈkɑpɚˌsmɪθ; ˈkɔpəsmiθ] *n.* 銅匠。

copper sulphate 硫酸銅。

cop·per·y [ˈkɑpərɪ; ˈkɔpəri] *adj.* 銅的;似銅的;含銅的;銅色的。

cop·pice [ˈkɑpɪs; ˈkɔpis] *n.* =**copse.**

cop·ra [ˈkɑprə; ˈkɔprə] *n.* 乾椰子肉。

co·pro·duce [ˌkoprəˈdus; ˌkouprəˈdjuːs] *v.t.*, **-duced, -duc·ing.** 〖電影〗共同製(片)。「*n.* 糞石(古動物糞之化石)。

cop·ro·lite [ˈkɑprəˌlaɪt; ˈkɔprəlait]

cop·rol·o·gy [kɑpˈrɑlədʒɪ; kɔpˈrɔlədʒi] *n.* 〖醫〗糞便學。

cop·roph·a·gous [kɑpˈrɑfəgəs; kɔpˈrɔfəgəs] *adj.* (昆蟲) 以糞爲食的。

cop·ros·ta·sis [kɑpˈrɑstəsɪs; kɔpˈrɔstəsis] *n.* 便祕;糞積。「盜遊戲。

cops and robbers 兒童之警察捕

copse [kɑps; kɔps] *n.* 矮樹叢。(亦作 **coppice**)

Copt [kɑpt; kɔpt] *n.* ①埃及土人。②(Coptic 教派之)埃及基督徒。「機。

cop·ter [ˈkɑptɚ; ˈkɔptə] *n.* 〖俗〗直升

Cop·tic [ˈkɑptɪk; ˈkɔptik] *n.* 埃及古語。—*adj.* 埃及土人的;埃及基督徒的。「派。

Coptic Church 埃及之土著基督教

cop·u·la [ˈkɑpjələ; ˈkɔpjulə] *n.*, *pl.* **-las, -lae** [-li; -liː]. ①連接之物。②〖文法、邏輯〗連繫辭。③〖解剖〗介體;接合部。

cop·u·lar [ˈkɑpjəlɚ; ˈkɔpjulə] *adj.* 連接的;連繫辭的。

cop·u·late [ˈkɑpjəˌlet; ˈkɔpjuleit] *v.*, **-lat·ed, -lat·ing.** 交媾;性交。

cop·u·la·tion [ˌkɑpjəˈleʃən; ˌkɔpjuˈleiʃən] *n.* ①連接;結合。②交媾;性交。

cop·u·la·tive [ˈkɑpjəˌletɪv; ˈkɔpjulətiv] *adj.* (亦作 **copulatory**) ①〖文法〗連繫的; 連繫辭的。②交媾的; 性交的。—*n.* 連繫辭;繫語之接續詞。

‡**cop·y** [ˈkɑpɪ; ˈkɔpi] *n.*, *pl.* **cop·ies,** *v.*, **cop·ied, cop·y·ing.** —*n.* ①複本; 抄本; 謄本;模倣複製品。 a fair *copy.* 謄清的稿本。a rough *copy.* 草稿。②摹本;範本。③(一次刊行的)部;册;分。Over one thousand *copies* of the book were sold. 這書銷數超過一千册。④〖電影〗拷貝。The picture now showing is a new *copy.* 現在上映的電影是個新拷貝。 ⑤要付印的東西;原稿。 ⑥寫作的題材。That will make good *copy.* 那是寫作的好題材。⑦〖新聞〗(人或事之)新聞價值。—*v.t.* & *v.i.* ①抄寫。*Copy* these sentences in your notebook. 把這幾句抄在你的筆記簿上。②摹倣。You should *copy* his good points. 你應效法他的優點。

cop·y·book [ˈkɑpɪˌbʊk; ˈkɔpibuk] *n.* 字帖;習字簿。—*adj.* 平凡的;老套的。

cop·y·boy [ˈkɑpɪˌbɔɪ; ˈkɔpibɔi] *n.* 報館內送稿件的工友。

cop·y·cat [ˈkɑpɪˌkæt; ˈkɔpikæt] *n.*, *v.*, **-cat·ted, -cat·ting.** —*n.* 〖俗〗模倣他人動作或工作的人。—*v.t.* 盲目地模倣。

cop·y·cut·ter [ˈkɑpɪˌkʌtɚ; ˈkɔpiˌkʌtə] *n.* 〖新聞〗將新聞稿剪成條狀以便排版的工人。

copy desk 〖新聞〗馬蹄形之編輯桌子。

cop·y-ed·it [ˈkɑpɪˌɛdɪt; ˈkɔpiˌedit] *v.t.* 改寫;編輯。—**or,** *n.* 「*n.* 油印機。

cop·y·graph [ˈkɑpɪˌgræf; ˈkɔpigrɑːf]

cop·y·hold [ˈkɑpɪˌhold; ˈkɔpihould] *n.* 〖英〗①〖法律〗依據官册享有之不動產產權。②此種不動產。

cop·y·hold·er [ˈkɑpɪˌholdɚ; ˈkɔpiˌhouldə] *n.* 依據官册享有不動產者。

copying paper 謄寫紙;複寫紙。

cop·y·ist [ˈkɑpɪɪst; ˈkɔpiist] *n.* ①抄寫者;謄寫者。②摹倣者;剽竊者。

copy paper 稿紙。

cop·y·read·er [ˈkɑpɪˌridɚ; ˈkɔpiˌriːdə] *n.* 〖新聞〗編輯;校訂人。

***cop·y·right** [ˈkɑpɪˌraɪt; ˈkɔpirait] *n.* 版權;著作權。*copyright* reserved. 版權所有。 —*adj.* 受著作權保護的; 有著作權的。—*v.t.* 取得版權。

cop·y·writ·er [ˈkɑpɪˌraɪtɚ; ˈkɔpiˌraitə] *n.* (報社之) 寫稿人 (尤指廣告文字)。(亦作 **copymaker**)

co·quet [koˈkɛt; kouˈket] *v.*, **-quet·ted, -quet·ting,** *adj.* —*v.i.* (亦作 **coquette**) (女子)賣俏;賣弄風情;獻媚;玩弄。—*adj.* 賣弄風情的。

co·quet·ry [ˈkokɪtrɪ; ˈkoukitri] *n.*, *pl.* **-ries.** (女子) 玩弄男子;賣弄風情。

co·quette [koˈkɛt; kouˈket] *n.* 賣弄風情之女子。 「*adj.* 賣俏的;賣弄風情的。

co·quet·tish [koˈkɛtɪʃ; kouˈketiʃ]

co·qui·na [koˈkinə; kouˈkiːnə] *n.* (建築用之)介殼石。 「**-tos.** 〖植物〗智利棕櫚。

co·qui·to [koˈkito; kouˈkiːtou] *n.*, *pl.*

Cor. ①Corinthians. ②Coroner. **cor.** ①corner. ②cornet. ③coroner. ④corpus. ⑤correct. ⑥corrected. ⑦correction. ⑧correlative. ⑨correspondence. ⑩correspondent. ⑪corresponding.

cor- 〖字首〗**com-** 之異體 (用在 r 之前)。

cor·a·cle [ˈkɔrəkḷ; ˈkɔːrəkl] *n.* 用枝條作骨架外覆防水布的短闊小船。

cor·a·coid [ˈkɑrəˌkɔɪd; ˈkɔrəkɔid] *n.* 〖解剖,動物〗烏喙骨;喙突。—*adj.* 烏喙狀的。

***cor·al** [ˈkɑrəl; ˈkɔrəl] *n.* ①珊瑚;珊瑚樹;珊瑚蟲。②珊瑚製品。③桃紅色。—*adj.* ①珊瑚製的。*coral* ring. 珊瑚戒指。②桃紅色的。

cor·al·line [ˈkɑrəlɪn; ˈkɔrəlain] *n.* ①珊瑚;珊瑚狀之動物。②〖植物〗珊瑚藻。—*adj.* ①珊瑚(組成)的。②似珊瑚的;珊瑚色的。

cor·al·lite [ˈkɑrəˌlaɪt; ˈkɔrəlait] *n.* 珊瑚蟲之骨架;珊瑚石;珊瑚化石。

cor·al·loid [ˈkɑrəˌlɔɪd; ˈkɔrəlɔid] *adj.* 珊瑚狀的。 —*n.* 珊瑚類之生物。

coral reef 珊瑚礁。

Coral Sea 珊瑚海(在澳洲東北)。

coral snake (美洲產之)一種小毒蛇。

co·ram [ˈkorəm; ˈkɔːrəm] 〖拉〗*prep.* 在…面前。

coram ju·di·ce [~ˈdʒudɪsɪ; ~ˈdʒuːdisi] 〖拉〗在有權審判(該案)之法庭上。

coram non judice [~nɑn~; ~nɔn~] 〖拉〗在無權審判(該案)之法庭上。

coram po·pu·lo [~ˈpɑpjʊlo; ~ˈpɔpjulou] 〖拉〗在公衆面前。

cor·beil [ˈkɔrbɛl; ˈkɔːbel] *n.* 〖建築〗花籃或果籃之雕飾。(亦作 **corbeille**)

cor·bel ['kɔrbl; 'kɔːbəl] *n., v.,* **-bel(l)ed, -bel·(l)ing.** —*n.* 〖建築〗承材。—*v.t.* 以承材支撐。「以承材支撐的。」

cor·bel(l)ed ['kɔrbḷd; 'kɔːbəld] *adj.*

cor·bel·(l)ing ['kɔrblɪŋ; 'kɔːbəliŋ] *n.* 〖建築〗①承材工程。②承材結構。

cor·bie ['kɔrbɪ; 'kɔːbi] *n., pl.* **-bies.** 〖蘇〗烏鴉。

cor·bie·step ['kɔrbɪˌstɛp; 'kɔːbistep] *n.* 〖建築〗山形牆側邊之梯形突出物。

***cord** [kɔrd; kɔːd] *n.* ①細繩；索；絃。②絕緣的小電線。③腱；索狀組織。the vocal *cords.* 聲帶。the spinal *cord.* 脊髓。④楞條(布)。⑤柴薪或木材等的容量單位(8×4×4立方英尺)。—*v.t.* ①用繩索縛起。②堆積(柴薪)。—**er,** *n.* 「集合稱；索具。」

cord·age ['kɔrdɪdʒ; 'kɔːdidʒ] *n.* 繩索

cor·date ['kɔrdet; 'kɔːdeit] *adj.* 〖植物〗(葉等)心形的。

cord·ed ['kɔrdɪd; 'kɔːdid] *adj.* ①用繩綑的。②繩製的。③有棱條的。④(木材依 cord 爲單位)成堆的。⑤(肌肉)拉緊的。

Cor·del·ia [kɔr'diljə; kɔː'diːljə] *n.* ①女子名。②莎士比亞所著李爾王中之人物，爲李爾王三女中最小而惟一忠心於彼者。

Cor·de·lier [ˌkɔrdə'lɪr; ˌkɔːdi'liə] *n.* ①St. Francis 教派之修道士。②(*pl.*)法國革命時期中一激進派之政治俱樂部。

***cor·dial** ['kɔrdʒəl; 'kɔːdjəl, -diəl] *n.* ①興奮劑；補品；强心劑。②利久酒(liqueur). —*adj.* ①熱心的；熱誠的；眞誠的；友善的。a *cordial* welcome. 熱誠的歡迎。②興奮的；提神滋補的。—**ly,** *adv.*

cor·dial·i·ty [kɔr'dʒælətɪ; ˌkɔːdi'æliti] *n., pl.* **-ties.** ①熱誠；懇摯。②熱誠之言行。

cor·dil·le·ra [kɔr'dɪlərə; ˌkɔːdi'ljɛərə] *n.* 山脈；山系。「藥；紐形火藥。」

cord·ite ['kɔrdaɪt; 'kɔːdait] *n.* 線狀火

Cor·do·ba ['kɔrdəvə; 'kɔːdəvə] *n.* 哥多華(西班牙南部之一城市)。(亦作 **Cordova**)

cor·don ['kɔrdṇ; 'kɔːdn] *n.* ①飾帶；綬帶。②〖軍事〗警戒線；哨兵線。③〖建築〗飛簷層。

cor·don bleu [kɔr'dɔ̃ 'blœ; kɔː'dɔ̃ 'blœ] *pl.* **cor·dons bleus.** 〖法〗①(法國波旁王朝時授與騎士之)最高勳章。②帶此種勳章的人。③某行業之傑出者(尤指廚師)。

Cor·do·van ['kɔrdəvən; 'kɔːdəvən] *adj.* ①西班牙之哥多華城的。②(c-)哥多華皮革製的。—*n.* ①西班牙之哥多華人。②哥多華皮革。③(*pl.*)此種皮革所製之鞋。

cor·du·roy [ˌkɔrdə'rɔɪ; 'kɔːdərɔi] *n.* ①燈心絨。②(*pl.*)燈心絨所縫成之褲子。—*adj.* ①燈心絨的。②橫排木段築成的(道路、橋)。—*v.i.* 橫排木段以築成(道路)。

cord·wain ['kɔrdwen; 'kɔːdwein] *n.* 〖古〗哥多華皮革。

cord·wain·er ['kɔrdwenə; 'kɔːdweinə] *n.* ①〖古〗哥多華皮革鞣製者。②鞋匠。

cord·wood ['kɔrdˌwud; 'kɔːdwud] *n.* ①按128立方英尺(cord)一堆出售或堆積之木材。②鋸成4英尺長之木材。

***core** [kor; kɔː, kɔə] *n., v.,* **cored, cor·ing.** —*n.* ①果心(如梨、蘋果等含子的果心)。②中心或最重要的部分。He is true to the *core.* 他是絕對忠實的。He is rotten to the *core.* 他壞透了。③〖電〗心；心線。—*v.t.* 去(果)心。

Co·re·a [ko'riə; kə'riə] *n.* =**Korea.**

Co·re·an [ko'riən; kə'riən] *adj., n.* =**Korean.**

co·re·la·tion [ˌkorɪ'leʃən; ˌkouri'leiʃən] *n.* =**correlation.**

co·re·li·gion·ist [ˌkorɪ'lɪdʒənɪst; 'kouri'lidʒənist] *n.* 信奉同一宗教之人。

cor·e·op·sis [ˌkorɪ'ɑpsɪs; ˌkɔri'ɔpsis] *n.* 〖植物〗波斯菊。

cor·er ['korə; 'kɔːrə] *n.* 去果核之器具。

co·re·spond·ent [ˌkorɪ'spɑndənt; 'kourisˌpɔndənt] *n.* 〖法律〗離婚案件中被控通姦之共同被告。

corf [kɔrf; kɔːf] *n., pl.* **corves** [kɔrvz; kɔːvz]. 〖英〗搬運煤炭等之簍筐；(現指)煤車。

Co·ri ['korɪ; 'kɔːri] *n.* 葛里(Carl Ferdinand, 1896–, 生於捷克之美國生物化學家，與 Houssay 合得 1947 年諾貝爾醫學獎)。

cor·i·a·ceous [ˌkorɪ'eʃəs; ˌkɔri'eiʃəs] *adj.* 皮革的；似革的；强韌的。

cor·i·an·der [ˌkorɪ'ændə; ˌkɔri'ændə] *n.* 〖植物〗胡荽。「(希臘南部之一城市)。」

Cor·inth ['kɑrɪnθ; 'kɔrinθ] *n.* 科林斯

Co·rin·thi·an [kə'rɪnθɪən; kə'rinθiən] *adj.* ①古希臘城市科林斯的；科林斯人的；科林斯文化的。②優雅的。③科林斯式之建築的。—*n.* ①科林斯人(以放蕩著稱)。②(*pl.*)聖經新約中哥林多前書及後書。

co·ri·um ['korɪəm; 'kɔːriəm] *n., pl.* **-ri·a** [-rɪə; -riə]. 〖解剖〗眞皮。

***cork** [kɔrk; kɔːk] *n.* ①軟木。*Cork* can float on water. 軟木能浮於水。②軟木製的東西。③軟木塞。④瓶塞(泛指玻璃、橡皮等所製成者)。⑤栓皮。⑥釣魚用之小浮標。—*v.t.* ①用瓶塞塞緊。②限制；阻止；抑制。③用軟木炭塗黑。—*adj.* 以軟木製成的。

cork·age ['kɔrkɪdʒ; 'kɔːkidʒ] *n.* (客人自備酒類時)旅館或食堂收取之開瓶費。

corked [kɔrkt; kɔːkt] *adj.* ①塞以軟木的。②用燒焦之軟木塗黑的。③有軟木塞氣味的(酒等)。

cork·er ['kɔrkə; 'kɔːkə] *n.* ①塞瓶之人或器具。②〖俚〗特出之人或物。③〖俚〗決斷性之言論；定論；定局。④〖俚〗大謊。⑤〖俚〗傑出之事物或人。

cork·ing ['kɔrkɪŋ; 'kɔːkiŋ] *adj., adv., interj.* 〖俚〗極好的；特佳的；非常。

cork·screw ['kɔrkˌskru; 'kɔːk-skruː] *n.* 拔塞鑽；螺絲錐。—*adj.* 螺旋形的。—*v.i.* 彎曲而進。—*v.t.* 作彎曲的前進。

cork tree 〖植物〗軟木槲。

cork·y ['kɔrkɪ; 'kɔːki] *adj.,* **cork·i·er, cork·i·est.** ①(似)軟木的；似瓶塞的。②〖俗〗快活的；活潑的。③(酒等)有軟木塞氣味的。

corm [kɔrm; kɔːm] *n.* 〖植物〗球莖。

cor·mo·rant ['kɔrmərənt; 'kɔːmərənt] *n.* ①〖動物〗鸕鶿。②貪心的人；饕餮者。—*adj.* 貪婪的；貪吃的。

‡corn[1] [kɔrn; kɔːn] *n.* ①〖美〗玉蜀黍。②玉蜀黍粒。③〖英〗一般的穀類，尤指小麥。④〖蘇,愛〗燕麥。⑤〖俗〗老套而陳舊的笑話、故事、音樂等。—*v.t.* ①用濃鹽水醃。②使成爲粒狀。③種玉蜀黍。④餵玉蜀黍。

corn[2] *n.* 脚上生的鷄眼。***step*** (or ***tread***) ***on one's corns*** 觸及某人的傷心處。

Corn. ①Cornish. ②Cornwall.

corn binder 玉蜀黍收割機。

corn·brash ['kɔrnˌbræʃ; 'kɔːnbræʃ] *n.* 〖地質〗粗石灰質沙層。

corn bread 〖美〗玉蜀黍粉製成之麪包。

corn cake 〖美〗玉蜀黍製成之餅。

corn chandler 〖英〗糧食零售商。

corn·cob ['kɔrnˌkɑb; 'kɔːnkɔb] *n.* 〖美〗

①玉蜀黍之穗軸。②此種穗軸所製之煙斗。

corn cockle〖植物〗瞿麥。

corn-crack·er [ˈkɔrnˌkrækɚ; ˈkɔːnˌkrækə] *n.*〖蔑〗美國南方之窮苦白人。

corn crake 秧鷄。

corn·crib [ˈkɔrnˌkrɪb; ˈkɔːnkrib] *n.* 「玉蜀黍穀倉。」

corn·dodg·er [ˈkɔrnˌdɑdʒɚ; ˈkɔːnˌdɔdʒə] *n.*〖美〗玉蜀黍製之一種硬餅。(亦作 **corn-dodger, corn dodger**)

cor·ne·a [ˈkɔrnɪə; ˈkɔːniə] *n.*〖解剖〗(眼球之)角膜。—**cor·ne·al,** *adj.*

corned [kɔrnd; kɔːnd] *adj.* ①鹽醃的;醃藏的。②〖英俚〗酒醉的。

cor·nel [ˈkɔrnəl; ˈkɔːnəl] *n.*〖植物〗山「茱萸。」

cor·nel·ian [kɔrˈniljən; kɔːˈniːljən] *n.*〖礦〗紅玉髓。

cor·ne·ous [ˈkɔrnɪəs; ˈkɔːniəs] *adj.* 「角質的;似角的。」

‡**cor·ner** [ˈkɔrnɚ; ˈkɔːnə] *n.* ①角;隅。Meet me at the *corner* of the street. 請於大街轉角處會我。②隱僻之處。to hide money in odd *corners.* 將錢隱藏在偏僻之處。③遠處;地區。in every *corner* of the earth. 在地球上每個角落。④窮境;窘境。to drive somebody into a *corner.* 迫人入窘境。⑤壟斷;囤積。⑥兩條街連接處。⑦邊緣。***a tight corner*** 危險或困難之處境。***cut corners*** **a.** 穿小路;走近路。**b.** 節省時間、金錢、力氣等。***hole and corner*** 不誠實的;欺詐的(方法、交易等)。***rough corners*** 粗獷的性格;粗裏粗氣的態度或作風等。***turn the corner*** 脫險;度過危機。—*adj.* ①在拐角處的。②適於角隅的。—*v.t.* ①迫至一隅。②使之困窘。③壟斷;獨佔。④〖俚〗(汽車)急轉彎。—*v.i.* ①位於角上。②形成一個角。③壟斷;「囤積居奇。」

corner boy 游蕩者。

corner chisel 角鑿。

cor·nered [ˈkɔrnɚd; ˈkɔːnəd] *adj.* ①有角的(常用作字尾)。a six-*cornered* room. 有六個角落的房間。②被迫至困境的。

cor·ner·er [ˈkɔrnərɚ; ˈkɔːnərə] *n.* 囤積居奇者。

corner man 無業游民;游蕩者。

cor·ner·stone [ˈkɔrnɚˌston; ˈkɔːnəstoun] *n.* ①基石;隅石。②基礎;要素。

cor·ner·wise [ˈkɔrnɚˌwaɪz; ˈkɔːnəwaiz] *adv.* 斜地;對角地。(亦作**cornerways**)

cor·net [ˈkɔrnɪt; ˈkɔːnit] *n.* ①〖音樂〗一種有音栓之小銅喇叭。②圓錐形之紙袋。③〖航海〗信號旗。④〖英〗古時騎兵掌旗官。⑤圓錐形之(冰淇淋)蛋捲。

cor·net-à-pis·tons [ˈkɔrnɪtəˈpɪstn̩z; ˈkɔːnitəˈpistənz] *n., pl.* **cor·nets-à-pis·tons.** 一種有音栓之小銅喇叭。

cor·net·(t)ist [kɔrˈnɛtɪst; kɔːˈnetist] *n.* 小銅喇叭之吹奏者。

corn-ex·change [ˈkɔrnɪksˈtʃendʒ; ˈkɔːniksˈtʃeindʒ] *n.* 糧食交易所。

corn factor〖英〗糧食批發商。

corn·fed [ˈkɔrnˌfɛd; ˈkɔːnfed] *adj.* ①餵以玉蜀黍的。②看來營養良好、健康而不狡猾的。

corn·field [ˈkɔrnˌfild; ˈkɔːnfiːld] *n.* 「稻田;麥田;玉蜀黍田。」

corn flag〖植物〗水仙菖蒲。

corn·flakes [ˈkɔrnˌfleks; ˈkɔːnfleiks] *n.* 玉蜀黍片(拌糖、牛奶等當早餐吃的)。

corn flour ①玉蜀黍粉。②〖英〗米或其他穀物的粉。

corn·flow·er [ˈkɔrnˌflauɚ; ˈkɔːnflauə] *n.*〖植物〗矢車菊。

corn·husk [ˈkɔrnˌhʌsk; ˈkɔːnhʌsk] *n.* 玉蜀黍之外殼。

corn·husk·ing [ˈkɔrnˌhʌskɪŋ; ˈkɔːnˌhʌskiŋ] *n.*〖美〗去玉蜀黍之外殼。

cor·nice [ˈkɔrnɪs; ˈkɔːnis] *n., v.,* **-niced, -nic·ing.** —*n.* ①〖建築〗飛簷;檐板。②(凍結在岩石邊的)雪簷。—*v.t.* 蓋以飛簷;以飛簷爲頂。

corn·loft [ˈkɔrnˌlɔft; ˈkɔːnlɔːft] *n.* 「穀倉。」

corn meal ①玉蜀黍粗粉。②〖美〗玉米片。③〖蘇〗麥片(=oatmeal).

corn picker 去玉蜀黍之穗及外殼之「機器。」

corn plaster 鷄眼膏藥。

corn pone 玉蜀黍粉製成之麪包。

corn popper 做爆米花之鍋。

corn rent〖英〗以穀代金之地租。

corn shock 一堆直放的玉蜀黍莖。

corn silk 玉蜀黍穗上之絲狀花柱。

corn·stalk [ˈkɔrnˌstɔk; ˈkɔːnstɔːk] *n.* ①玉蜀黍之莖。②(C-)〖澳俗〗白人。

corn·starch [ˈkɔrnˌstɑrtʃ; ˈkɔːnstɑːtʃ] *n.* 玉蜀黍澱粉。

corn sugar 右旋糖。

corn syrup 玉蜀黍糖漿。

cor·nu·co·pi·a [ˌkɔrnəˈkopɪə; ˌkɔːnəˈkoupiə] *n.* ①〖希臘神話〗哺乳 Zeus 神之羊的角。②(繪畫或雕刻中)滿裝花果表示豐饒的羊角狀物。③豐富;豐饒。—**cor·nu·co·pi·an,** *adj.*

cor·nut·ed [kɔrˈnjutɪd; kɔːˈnjuːtid] 「*adj.* 有角的;角狀的。」

corn·y[1] [ˈkɔrnɪ; ˈkɔːni] *adj.,* **corn·i·er, corn·i·est.** ①生穀的;多穀的;穀製的。②〖俚〗鄉野的;單純的;天眞的。③〖俚〗陳腔濫調的;老生常談的;平凡的;不佳的。④〖俚〗過於傷感的;過分多愁善感的。

corn·y[2] *adj.* 脚上之鷄眼的;脚上生鷄眼的。

co·rol·la [kəˈrɑlə; kəˈrɔlə] *n.*〖植物〗花冠。

cor·ol·la·ceous [ˌkɑrəˈleʃəs; ˌkɔrəˈleiʃəs] *adj.* 花冠的;似花冠的。

cor·ol·lar·y [ˈkɔrəˌlɛrɪ; kəˈrɔləri] *n., pl.* **-lar·ies.** ①〖數學〗系。②推論。③自然之結果。

co·rol·late [ˈkɔrəˌlet; kəˈrɔleit] *adj.*〖植物〗有花冠的。(亦作 **corollated**)

co·ro·na [kəˈronə; kəˈrounə] *n., pl.* **-nas, -nae** [-ni; -niː]. ①日月之暈;日冕。②〖古羅馬〗授與有功之人的冠或花冠。③〖建築〗飛簷。④圓形燭架。⑤〖解剖〗(齒等之)冠。⑥長雪茄煙。⑦修士剃光頭髮之圓頂。⑧一種有同心圓架之吊燈。

cor·o·nach [ˈkɔrənəx; ˈkɔrənək] *n.* 「〖蘇,愛〗葬歌;輓歌。」

cor·o·nal [*n.* ˈkɔrənl̩; ˈkɔrənl̩ *adj.* kəˈronl̩; ˈkɔrənl̩, *for* ②kəˈrounl̩] *n.* ①冠;花冠。②冠狀物;花圈。③〖解剖〗冠狀縫。—*adj.* ①冠的;花冠的。②〖天文〗日冕的;日月之暈的。③〖解剖〗頭顱的;冠狀縫的。

coronal suture〖解剖〗冠狀縫。

cor·o·nar·y [ˈkɔrəˌnɛrɪ; ˈkɔrənəri] *adj.* ①冠的;花冠的。②〖解剖〗冠狀的。—*n.* =**coronary thrombosis.**

coronary arteries (veins) (心臟之)冠狀動脈(靜脈)。

coronary thrombosis (心臟之)「冠狀動脈血栓症。」

***cor·o·na·tion** [ˌkɑrəˈneʃən; ˌkɔrəˈneiʃən] *n.* 加冕;加冕禮。

cor·o·ner [ˈkɔrənɚ; ˈkɔrənə] *n.* 驗屍「官。」

coroner's inquest 驗屍。

cor·o·net [ˈkɔrənɪt; ˈkɔrənit] *n.* ①小冠冕(如公爵、伯爵等所戴者)。②冠狀頭飾。

cor·o·net(t)·ed [ˈkɔrənɪtɪd; ˈkɔrənitid] *adj.* ①戴小冠的。②貴族的。

Corp., corp. ①Corporal. ②Corpo「ration.」

***cor·po·ral**[1] ['kɔrpərəl, 'kɔrprəl; 'kɔː-pərəl] *adj.* ①肉體的；身體的。*corporal* punishment. 體罰。②個人的。—*n.* 聖餐布。

***cor·po·ral**[2] *n.* ①〖軍〗下士。②一羣信徒或擁護者。

cor·po·ral·i·ty [ˌkɔrpə'rælətɪ; ˌkɔː-pə'ræliti] *n., pl.* **-ties.** ①具體性；有形體之存在。②形體；肉身；肉體。③(*pl.*)與肉體有關之事物；肉體之慾望。

cor·po·ral·ly ['kɔrpərəlɪ; 'kɔːpərəli] *adv.* 肉體上；身體上。

cor·po·rate ['kɔrpərɪt; 'kɔːpərit] *adj.* ①團體的；法人組織的。②共同的；全體的。—**ly,** *adv.*

***cor·po·ra·tion** [ˌkɔrpə'reʃən; ˌkɔːpə-'reiʃən] *n.* ①團體；公司；社團。②法人（許多人行使職權時如一人）。③〖俗〗凸出之腹部。

corporation cork 煤氣管或水管之總開關。

cor·po·ra·tive ['kɔrpəˌretɪv; 'kɔː-pəreitiv] *adj.* =**corporate.**

cor·po·ra·tor ['kɔrpəˌretə; 'kɔːpə-reitə] *n.* 社團或公司中之一分子。

cor·po·re·al [kɔr'porɪəl; kɔː'pɔːriəl] *adj.* ①肉體的。②物質的。③有形的；具體的。—**ly,** *adv.*

cor·po·re·al·i·ty [kɔrˌporɪ'ælətɪ; kɔːˌpɔːri'æliti] *n.* ①有形體之存在；具體性。②〖諧〗身體。

cor·po·re·i·ty [ˌkɔrpə'riətɪ; ˌkɔːpə-'riːiti] *n.* 物質或形體之性質；實質。

cor·po·sant ['kɔrpəˌzænt; 'kɔːpə-zænt] *n.* ①(暴風雨時船上之)桅頂燈光。②尖頂電光(=St. Elmo's fire)。③環形放電。

***corps** [kor; kɔː] *n., pl.* **corps** [korz; kɔːz]. ①軍中的特種部隊。Marine *Corps.* 海軍陸戰隊。②軍團；兵團。③共同工作者的團體。

corps de bal·let [ˈkɔrdəbæ'le; 'kɔː-dəbæ'lei] (非單獨表演之)芭蕾舞團體舞星(集合稱)。

corps di·plo·ma·tique [~ˌdɪplə-ˌmæ'tik; ~ˌdipləˌmæ'tiːk]〖法〗外交使節團(=diplomatic corps).

***corpse** [kɔrps; kɔːps] *n.* 屍體(通常指人的)。

corpse candle ①埋葬前燃於死者四周之蠟燭。②〖英〗燐火(鬼火)。

corps·man ['kormən; 'kɔːmən] *n., pl.* **-men.** ①〖美海軍〗醫藥兵。②〖美陸軍〗醫務兵。③任何 corps 之一員。

cor·pu·lence ['kɔrpjələns; 'kɔːpju-ləns] *n.* 肥胖。(亦作 **corpulency**)

cor·pu·lent ['kɔrpjələnt; 'kɔːpjulənt] *adj.* 肥胖的；肥大的。—**ly,** *adv.*

cor·pus ['kɔrpəs; 'kɔːpəs] *n., pl.* **-po·ra** [-pərə; -pərə]. ①體；身體(尤指屍體)。②(文獻、法典等之)全集。③任何事物之主體。④財產或投資之總值(以別於利息或收益)。⑤〖解剖〗物體；體。

Cor·pus Chris·ti ['kɔrpəs'krɪstɪ; 'kɔːpəs'kristi]〖天主教〗聖體節。

cor·pus·cle ['kɔrpəsl; 'kɔːpʌsl] *n.* ①血球。②微粒子。(亦作 **corpuscule**)

cor·pus·cu·lar [kɔr'pʌskjələ; kɔː-'pʌskjulə] *adj.* 微粒的；由微粒組成的。

corpus ju·ris [~'dʒurɪs; ~'dʒuəris] 法典大全。

corr. ①corrected. ②correspond. ③correspondence. ④correspondent. ⑤corresponding. ⑥corrupt. ⑦corrupted. ⑧corruption.

cor·rade [kə'red; kə'reid] *v.,* **-rad·ed, -rad·ing.** —*v.t.* & *v.i.* (水、風、冰川等)侵蝕。

cor·ral [kə'ræl; kɔː'rɑːl] *n., v.,* **-ralled, -ral·ling.** —*n.* ①畜欄。②(捕捉象等之)圍欄。③防禦攻擊之圓形車陣。—*v.t.* ①驅入畜欄。②〖俚〗捕捉。③排成圓形車陣。

‡cor·rect [kə'rɛkt; kə'rekt] *adj.* ①正確的；無誤的。He gave *correct* answers to the questions. 他提供了問題的正確答案。②適當的。*correct* manners. 適當的禮貌；合式的儀態。—*v.t.* ①改正；修正。*Correct* any wrong spellings that you find. 你發現拼字錯誤的地方請改正。②校正。③指出錯誤並譴責或懲罰之。④醫治；克服；消解(毒物)。—**ness,** *n.* —**ly,** *adv.*

cor·rec·tion** [kə'rɛkʃən; kə'rekʃən] *n.* ①改正；修正；校正。②改正的東西；正誤。③懲戒。house of correction*** 懲戒所；感化院。***under correction*** 可能有誤；尚待訂正。I speak *under correction.* (= I may be wrong.) 我所說的可能不正確。

cor·rec·tion·al [kə'rɛkʃənl; kə'rek-ʃənl] *adj.* 修正的；矯正的。—*n.* 教養院。

cor·rect·i·tude [kə'rɛktəˌtjud; kə-'rektitjuːd] *n.* (品行)端正；適宜；得體。

cor·rec·tive [kə'rɛktɪv; kə'rektiv] *adj.* ①改正的；矯正的。②中和的(藥)。—*n.* ①矯正物；改善法。②中和劑；中和物。

cor·rec·tor [kə'rɛktə; kə'rektə] *n.* ①改正者；修正者。②矯正者；懲治者。③〖醫〗中和劑。

correl. correlative.

cor·re·late ['kɔrəˌlet; 'kɔrileit] *v.,* **-lat·ed, -lat·ing,** *adj., n.* —*v.i.* 關連。—*v.t.* 使相關連。—*adj.* 關連的；相關的。—*n.* 有相互關係之人或物。

cor·re·la·tion [ˌkɔrə'leʃən; ˌkɔri-'leiʃən] *n.* ①相互關連；關連。②〖數學〗異射；異素射(影)變(換)。

correlation ratio 〖統計〗相關比。

cor·rel·a·tive [kə'rɛlətɪv; kə'relə-tiv] *adj.* ①關連的；相關的。②〖數學〗異素射變的。—*n.* 有相互關係之人或物。—**ly,** *adv.*

correlative conjunctions 〖文法〗相關連接詞(如：either...or...).

cor·rel·a·tiv·i·ty [kəˌrɛlə'tɪvətɪ; kəˌrelə'tiviti] *n.* 相互關係；相關的程度。

***cor·re·spond** [ˌkɔrə'spɑnd; ˌkɔris-'pɔnd] *v.i.* ①調合；符合〖with, to〗. This house exactly *corresponds* with my needs. 這房子正符合我的需要。②相當；相稱；相配；相似〖to〗. The American Congress *corresponds* to the British Parliament. 美國的國會相當於英國的議院。③通信。

***cor·re·spond·ence** [ˌkɔrə'spɑn-dəns; ˌkɔris'pɔndəns] *n.* ①符合；一致；相當；相稱；相似。②通信。I have been in *correspondence* with him about the matter. 關於這事，我與他通過信。③信件；信札。I have a good deal of *correspondence.* 我有許多信件。

correspondence course 函授課程。

correspondence school 函授學校。

***cor·re·spond·ent** [ˌkɔrə'spɑndənt; ˌkɔris'pɔndənt] *n.* ①通信者。He is a good (bad) *correspondent.* 他是一個勤(懶)於通信的人。②訪員；通信記者。a war *correspondent.* 戰地通訊記者。③商務關係者。④與他物相當或相似的東西。—*adj.* 一致的；相當的。

***cor·re·spond·ing** [ˌkɔrə'spɑndɪŋ;

ˌkɔrisˈpɔndiŋ〕 *adj.* ①相當的；一致的〖to, with〗. the *corresponding* period of last year. 去年同一期間。②〖數學〗同位的；對應的。*corresponding* angles. 同位角。③通信的；掌管通信的。a *corresponding* member (of a society). (學會的)通訊會員。

cor·re·spond·ing·ly 〔ˌkɔrəˈspɑndɪŋlɪ; ˌkɔrisˈpɔndiŋli〕 *adv.* 相當地。

cor·re·spon·sive 〔ˌkɔrəˈspɑnsɪv; ˌkɔrisˈpɔnsiv〕 *adj.* 相應的；相當的。

*__cor·ri·dor__ 〔ˈkɔrədɚ, -ˌdɔr, ˈkɑr-; ˈkɔridɔː〕 *n.* ①〖建築〗走廊；迴廊。②〖英〗火車一側之走廊(以便進入各房間者)。③〖地理〗走廊；地帶。④通道；通路。***the Polish Corridor*** 波蘭走廊（第一次大戰後，波蘭為求得一出海口，乃在德國與東普魯士間劃一寬三公里之非軍事區，通往波羅的海沿岸之旦澤，此一地區稱為波蘭走廊)。

cor·rie 〔ˈkɔrɪ; ˈkɔri〕 *n.* 〖蘇〗山腹之凹處。

cor·ri·gen·dum 〔ˌkɔrɪˈdʒɛndəm; ˌkɔriˈdʒendəm〕 *n., pl.* **-da** 〔-də; -də〕. ①需改正之錯（尤指文稿或書中者)。②(*pl.*) 勘誤表。

cor·ri·gi·ble 〔ˈkɔrədʒəbl̩; ˈkɔridʒəbl〕 *adj.* 可改正的；易矯正的。

cor·ri·val 〔kəˈraɪvl̩; kəˈraivəl〕 *n.* 競爭之對手。—*adj.* 競爭的。—*v.t.* 與…競爭。

cor·rob·o·rant 〔kəˈrɑbərənt; kəˈrɔbərənt〕 *adj.* ①確證的；使確實的。②强壯性的；使强固的(藥劑或補藥)。—*n.* ①確證之事實；確事。②補藥；强壯劑。

cor·rob·o·rate 〔kəˈrɑbəˌret; kəˈrɔbəreit〕 *v.,* **-rat·ed, -rat·ing.** —*v.t.* ①確定；確證。②堅定；鞏固。

cor·rob·o·ra·tion 〔kəˌrɑbəˈreʃən; kəˌrɔbəˈreiʃən〕 *n.* ①確定；確證。②堅定；鞏固。③〖法律〗加强證據。

cor·rob·o·ra·tive 〔kəˈrɑbəˌretɪv; kəˈrɔbərətiv〕 *adj.* (亦作 **corroboratory**) 確定的；確證的；强壯性的。—*n.* 補劑。

cor·rob·o·ra·tor 〔kəˈrɑbəˌretɚ; kəˈrɔbəreitə〕 *n.* 確證之人或物。

cor·rob·o·ree 〔kəˈrɑbərɪ; kəˈrɔbəri〕 *n.* ①澳洲土人之跳舞夜宴。②澳洲之任何熱鬧宴會。③吵鬧；騷動。(亦作 **corrobori**)

cor·rode 〔kəˈrod; kəˈroud〕 *v.,* **-rod·ed, -rod·ing.** —*v.t.* ①腐蝕；侵蝕。②損害；損傷。—*v.i.* ①腐蝕。②發生腐蝕作用。

cor·rod·i·bil·i·ty 〔kəˌrodəˈbɪlətɪ; kəˌroudəˈbiliti〕 *n.* 可腐蝕性。

cor·rod·i·ble 〔kəˈrodəbl̩; kəˈroudəbl〕 *adj.* 會腐蝕的；可腐蝕的。(亦作 **corrosible**)

cor·ro·sion 〔kəˈroʒən; kəˈrouʒən〕 *n.* ①腐蝕；侵蝕。②衰敗；漸失。③腐蝕物。

cor·ro·sive 〔kəˈrosɪv; kəˈrousiv〕 *adj.* ①腐蝕的；侵蝕的。②逐漸為害的。③刻薄的；譏刺的。—*n.* ①腐蝕物；腐蝕劑。②有害因素；禍害。(亦作 **corrodent**) —**ly,** *adv.*

corrosive sublimate 〖化〗昇汞。

cor·ru·gate 〔*v.* ˈkɔrəˌget; ˈkɔrugeit *adj.* ˈkɔrəgɪt, -ˌget; ˈkɔrugeit, -git〕 *v.,* **-gat·ed, -gat·ing,** *adj.* —*v.t.* & *v.i.* 使起皺紋；起皺紋。—*adj.* 〖古〗皺的。

cor·ru·gat·ed 〔ˈkɔrəˌgetɪd; ˈkɔrugeitid〕 *adj.* 皺的；有皺紋的；波狀的。

corrugated iron 波狀鐵皮。

corrugated paper 波狀紙或紙板。

cor·ru·ga·tion 〔ˌkɔrəˈgeʃən; ˌkɔruˈgeiʃən〕 *n.* ①起皺紋。②(波狀表面之)起伏。

*__cor·rupt__ 〔kəˈrʌpt; kəˈrʌpt〕 *adj.* ①腐敗的；貪汚的；敗德的。*corrupt* practices. 敗德的行為(如受賄等)。②不潔的。③訛誤及塗改太多的。④語言轉訛的。⑤腐爛的；潰爛的。—*v.t.* ①使腐爛；使腐敗。②使變壞(道德)；使敗壞；使墮落。③用賄賂收買。④使(言語)轉訛。⑤使不潔。⑥使訛誤。—*v.i.* 腐敗；腐爛。—**ly,** —**ed·ly,** —**ing·ly,** *adv.* —**ness,** *n.*

cor·rupt·i·bil·i·ty 〔kəˌrʌptəˈbɪlətɪ; kəˌrʌptəˈbiliti〕 *n.* 腐敗性；易賄賂性；易壞。

cor·rupt·i·ble 〔kəˈrʌptəbl̩; kəˈrʌptəbl〕 *adj.* 會腐敗的；可賄賂的；易毀壞的。—**cor·rupt·i·bly,** *adv.*

*__cor·rup·tion__ 〔kəˈrʌpʃən; kəˈrʌpʃən〕 *n.* ①腐化；墮落；貪汚。We cannot tolerate *corruption* in the government. 我們不能容忍政府的腐化。②賄賂。③腐爛。④轉訛或誤用(指語言)。⑤促成腐化敗壞之不良影響；頹敗的風氣。

cor·rup·tion·ist 〔kəˈrʌpʃənɪst; kəˈrʌpʃənist〕 *n.* 政治腐化之支持者或實行者。

cor·rup·tive 〔kəˈrʌptɪv; kəˈrʌptiv〕 *adj.* 使腐敗的；使墮落的；腐敗性的。

cor·sage 〔kɔrˈsɑʒ; kɔːˈsɑːʒ〕 *n.* ①女用緊身上衣。②女性裝飾在腰部或肩部的花束。③女服的腰部。

cor·sair 〔ˈkɔrsɛr; ˈkɔːsɛə〕 *n.* ①海盜。②海盜船。③私掠船。

corse 〔kɔrs; kɔːs〕 *n.* 〖古，詩〗=**corpse.**

Cor. Sec. Corresponding Secretary.

corse·let 〔ˈkɔrslɪt; ˈkɔːslit〕 *n.* ①甲冑；胸甲。②昆蟲之胸部。(亦作 **corslet**)

*__cor·set__ 〔ˈkɔrsɪt; ˈkɔːsit〕 *n.* (常 *pl.*)(女性用)緊身褡；束腹。—*v.t.* ①穿緊身褡。②束縛；嚴格控制。

Cor·si·ca 〔ˈkɔrsɪkə; ˈkɔːsikə〕 *n.* 科西嘉（地中海中之一島，為拿破崙誕生地)。

Cor·si·can 〔ˈkɔrsɪkən; ˈkɔːsikən〕 *adj.* ①Corsica 的。②科西嘉島人的。③科西嘉島方言的。—*n.* ①科西嘉島人或居民。②科西嘉島之義大利方言。***the Corsican*** 拿破崙 (Napoleon Bonaparte) 之別稱。

cor·tège 〔kɔrˈteʒ; kɔːˈteiʒ〕〖法〗*n.* ①行列；儀仗。②扈從；隨從。

Cor·tes 〔ˈkɔrtɪz; ˈkɔːtiz〕 *n. pl.* (西班牙或葡萄牙之)國會；議會。

cor·tex 〔ˈkɔrtɛks; ˈkɔːteks〕 *n., pl.* **-ti·ces** 〔-tɪˌsiz; -tisiːz〕. ①(植物之) 皮層；樹皮。②(腦或腎等之) 皮層；皮質。

cor·ti·cal 〔ˈkɔrtɪkl̩; ˈkɔːtikəl〕 *adj.* ①皮層的；皮質的。②有關腦皮層的。

cor·ti·cate 〔ˈkɔrtɪkɪt, -ˌket; ˈkɔːtikit, -keit〕 *adj.* 有外皮的；有皮層的；有樹皮的。(亦作 **corticated**)

cor·ti·le 〔kɔrˈtile; kɔːˈtiːlei〕〖義〗*n.* 中庭；內院。

cor·tin 〔ˈkɔrtɪn; ˈkɔːtin〕 *n.* 〖生化〗腎上腺皮質激素；皮層素；皮質素。

cor·ti·sone 〔ˈkɔrtɪˌson; ˈkɔːtisoun〕 *n.* 可體松（一種荷爾蒙，自腎上腺提取，或用若干熱帶植物人工製造之，用以治療關節病)。

co·run·dum 〔kəˈrʌndəm; kəˈrʌndəm〕 *n.* 〖礦〗金剛砂；剛玉。

cor·us·cate 〔ˈkɔrəsˌket; ˈkɔrəskeit〕 *v.i.,* **-cat·ed, -cat·ing.** ①閃光；閃鑠。②(才氣的)煥發。

cor·us·ca·tion 〔ˌkɔrəˈskeʃən; ˌkɔrəsˈkeiʃən〕 *n.* ①閃光；亮光。②才氣煥發；機智閃現；諧趣橫生。

cor·vée 〔kɔrˈve; kɔːˈvei〕〖法〗*n.* 强迫勞役。

cor·vet(te) 〔kɔrˈvɛt; kɔːˈvet〕 *n.* ①舊時中型巡洋艦。②千噸級之小軍艦（用於驅逐潛水艇或護航)。

cor·vine 〔ˈkɔrvaɪn; ˈkɔːvain〕 *adj.* 烏鴉的；似烏鴉的。

Cor·vus ['kɔrvəs; 'kɔːvəs] *n.* 【天文】烏鴉座。

Cor·y·bant ['kɔrə,bænt; 'kɔribænt] *n., pl.* **-bants, -bant·es** [-'bæntiz; -'bæntiːz]. ①【希臘神話】**a.** 女神 Cybele 之從者。**b.** 祭祀 Cybele 之祭司。②(c-)縱樂之人;飲鬧之人。—**ic,** *adj.*

Cor·y·don ['kɔrədn̩; 'kɔridən] *n.* ①(牧歌或田園詩中之)牧人。②鄉下青年。

cor·ymb ['kɔrɪmb; 'kɔrimb] *n.* 【植物】繖房花序。

co·rym·bose [kə'rɪmbos; kə'rimbous] *adj.* 【植物】繖房花序的;繖房狀的。

cor·y·phae·us [,kɔrə'fiəs; ,kɔri'fiːəs] *n., pl.* **-phae·i** [-'fiaɪ; -'fiːai]. ①(古希臘劇)合唱之主唱者。②(合唱隊之)主唱者。

cor·y·phee [,kɔrə'fe; ,kɔri'fei] 【法】 *n.* (芭蕾舞)首席舞星。

co·ry·za [kə'raɪzə; kə'raizə] *n.* 【醫】鼻炎;鼻傷風。

cos [kɑs, kɔs; kɔs] *n.* 一種萵苣。

cos 【數學】 cosine.

C.O.S., c.o.s. cash on shipment.

cose [kos; kous] *v.,* **cosed, cos·ing,** *n.* —*v.i.* 閒談;聊天。—*n.* 閒談;聊天。(亦作 coze)

cosec cosecant.

co·se·cant [ko'sikənt; 'kou'siːkənt] *n.* 【數學】餘割。

co·sey ['kozɪ; 'kouzi] *adj.,* **co·si·er, co·si·est,** *n., pl.* **co·seys.** =**cozy.**

cosh [kɑʃ; kɔʃ] *n.* 【主英俚】(用做武器的)短棒。—*v.t.* 用短棒打(某人的)頭。

cosh·er ['kɑʃɚ; 'kɔʃə] *v.t.* 給以美味;飽以美食;縱容;姑息。—*v.i.* 靠他人生活。

co·sig·na·to·ry [ko'sɪgnə,torɪ; 'kou'signətəri] *adj., n., pl.* **-ries.** —*adj.* 連名簽署的。—*n.* 連署人;連署國。

co·si·ly ['kozɪlɪ; 'kouzili] *adv.* 溫暖而舒服地。

co·sine ['kosaɪn; 'kousain] *n.* 【數學】餘弦。

co·si·ness ['kozɪnɪs; 'kouzinis] *n.* 溫暖而舒適;安逸。

cos·met·ic [kɑz'mɛtɪk; kɔz'metik] *n.* (常*pl.*)化粧品。—*adj.* 化粧用的。—**al,** *adj.* —**al·ly,** *adv.*

cos·me·ti·cian [,kɑzmə'tɪʃən; ,kɔzmi'tiʃən] *n.* ①製造或出售化粧品者。②化粧師。

cosmetic surgery 美容手術。

cos·me·tol·o·gist [,kɑzmɪ'tɑlədʒɪst; ,kɔzmi'tɔlədʒist] *n.* 美容專家;美容師。(亦作 **beautician**) —**cos·me·tol·o·gy,** *n.*

cos·mic ['kɑzmɪk; 'kɔzmik] *adj.* ①宇宙的。②廣大無邊的。③秩序井然的;和諧的。

cos·mi·cal ['kɑzmɪk!; 'kɔzmikəl] *adj.* ①=**cosmic.** ②日出之際發生的。—**ly,** *adv.*

cosmic dust 【天文】宇宙塵。

cosmic radiation 宇宙射線;宇宙線。(亦作 **cosmic ray**)

cosmic speed 物體擺脫地心引力所需之速度(人造衞星爲每秒五英里,太空船爲每秒七英里)。

cosmic year 【天文】宇宙年(約等於兩億年)。

cos·mism ['kɑzmɪzm̩; 'kɔzmizəm] *n.* 【哲學】宇宙論;宇宙演進論。—**cos·mist,** *n.*

cos·mo·drome ['kɑzmə,drom; 'kɔzmədroum] *n.* (蘇聯)太空船發射基地。

cos·mog·o·ny [kɑz'mɑgənɪ; kɔz'mɔgəni] *n., pl.* **-nies.** 宇宙之發生;宇宙開創論。—**cos·mog·o·nist,** *n.*

cos·mog·ra·phy [kɑz'mɑgrəfɪ; kɔz'mɔgrəfi] *n.* 宇宙誌。—**cos·mog·ra·pher,** *n.* —**cos·mo·graph·ic, cos·mo·graph·i·cal,** *adj.*

cos·mo·log·i·cal [,kɑzmə'lɑdʒɪk!; ,kɔzmə'lɔdʒikəl] *adj.* 宇宙論的;宇宙哲學的。

cos·mol·o·gist [kɑz'mɑlədʒɪst; kɔz'mɔlədʒist] *n.* 宇宙論者。

cos·mol·o·gy [kɑz'mɑlədʒɪ; kɔz'mɔlədʒi] *n.* 宇宙論;宇宙哲學。

cos·mo·naut ['kɑzmə,nɔt; 'kɔzmənɔːt] *n.* (蘇聯)太空人(別於 astronaut 美國太空人)。

cos·mop·o·lis [kɑz'mɑpəlɪs; kɔz'mɔpəlis] *n.* 國際都市。

cos·mo·pol·i·tan [,kɑzmə'pɑlətn̩; ,kɔzmə'pɔlitən] *adj.* ①四海爲家的;無地方或國家之偏見的。②見聞很廣大的。③分布於世界各地的。—*n.* 四海爲家的人。

cos·mo·pol·i·tan·ism [,kɑzmə'pɑlətn̩,ɪzəm; ,kɔzmə'pɔlitənizm] *n.* 世界大同主義;四海一家主義。

cos·mo·pol·i·tan·ize [,kɑzmə'pɑlətn̩,aɪz; ,kɔzmə'pɔlitənaiz] *v.t.* 使國際化。

cos·mop·o·lite [kɑz'mɑpə,laɪt; kɔz'mɔpəlait] *n.* ①=**cosmopolitan.** ②遍布於世界之動植物。—*adj.* =**cosmopolitan.**

cos·mop·o·lit·ism [kɑz'mɑpəlɪ,tɪzm̩; kɔz'mɔpəlitizm] *n.* =**cosmopolitanism.**

cos·mo·ra·ma [,kɑzmə'ramə; ,kɔzmə'rɑːmə] *n.* 展示世界各地景物之西洋鏡;世界景物照片展覽。

cos·mos ['kɑzməs; 'kɔzmɔs] *n.* ①(井然有序之)宇宙(爲混沌之對)。②秩序。③【植物】大波斯菊。

co·sov·er·eign·ty [ko'sɑvərɪntɪ; 'kou'sɔvrənti] *n.* 共同主權。

co·spon·sor [ko'spɑnsɚ; 'kou'spɔnsə] *n.* 共同主辦人。—*v.t.* 共同主辦;共同提供。

Cos·sack ['kɑsæk; 'kɔsæk] *n.* 哥薩克人(在蘇聯南部的民族)。

cos·set ['kɑsɪt; 'kɔsit] *n.* ①親手飼養之羔羊;寵愛之小羊。②任何寵愛之小動物。—*v.t.* 寵愛;珍愛;溺愛;縱容。

‡**cost** [kɔst; kɔst] *n., v.,* **cost, cost·ing.** —*n.* ①價;價值;費用。The *cost* of living is much higher now than it was two years ago. 現在的生活費用比兩年前的高得多。②損失;犧牲。The battle was won at great *cost* of life. 犧牲了許多生命,才打了這場勝仗。③(*pl.*)訴訟費。***at all costs*** 無論作何犧牲(=at any cost). ***at the cost of*** 損失;犧牲。***count the cost*** 考慮一切細節;盤算費用;愼密考慮。***prime*** (or ***first***) ***cost*** 主要成本。***to one's cost*** 對某人有損失、損傷或不利;算作某人的損失;歸某人負擔。—*v.t.* ①值(若干);需(價若干)。A motorcar *costs* a great deal of money. 一部汽車值很多錢。②費;需。The journey *cost* more than ten hours. 這次旅行費時十餘小時。③令遭損失;令受犧牲。His dissipation *cost* him his fortune. 他的揮霍浪費使他損失全部財產。—*v.i.* 估計成本。

cos·ta ['kɑstə; 'kɔstə] *n., pl.* **-tae** [-ti; -tiː]. ①【解剖】肋骨;似肋骨之構造。②【植物】(葉之)主脈;葉肋。

cost accountant 【商】成本會計員。

cost accounting 【商】成本會計。

cos·tal ['kɑst!; 'kɔstl] *adj.* 【解剖】肋骨的;肋骨附近的。

cost and freight 貨價包括運費。(略作 C. & F.)

co-star ['ko'stɑr; 'kou'stɑː] *n.* 共演者;配角。—*v.i.* 共演;當配角。—*v.t.* 使(名

氣相當的幾個演員)共演。

cos·tard ['kastəd; 'kʌstəd] *n.* 英國產之一種大蘋果。

Cos·ta Ri·ca ['kastə'rikə; 'kɔstə'riːkə] 哥斯大黎加(在中美洲的一個國家,首都爲聖約瑟 San José).

Cos·ta Ri·can ['kastə'rikn̩; 'kɔstə'riːkən] *adj.* ①哥斯大黎加的。②哥斯大黎加人的。—*n.* 哥斯大黎加人。

cos·tate ['kastet; 'kɔsteit] *adj.* ①〖解剖〗肋骨的; 肋骨狀的。②〖植物〗(葉之)主脈的;葉肋的。

cost-benefit analysis 成本效率分析。

cost book 成本帳簿。

cost control 成本控制。

cost efficiency 成本效率。(亦作**cost effectiveness**)

cos·ter ['kastə; 'kɔstə] *n.* 沿街叫賣水果、蔬菜、魚等之小販(或推車或擺攤)。

cos·ter·mon·ger ['kastə'mʌŋgə; 'kɔstə'mʌŋgə] *n.* =**coster.**

cost-free ['kast'fri; 'kɔstfriː] *adj.* & *adv.* 免費的(地)。

cost inflation 成本膨脹(產品需求未增加,而勞力及生產成本提高之現象)。

cos·tive ['kastɪv; 'kɔstiv] *adj.* ①便祕的;祕結的。②吝嗇的。**—ly,** *adv.* **—ness,** *n.*

cost keeper =**cost accountant.**

***cost·ly** ['kɔstlɪ; 'kɔstli] *adj.,* **-li·er, -li·est.** ①寶貴的; 貴重的。*costly* jewels. 貴重的珠寶。*costly* garments. 貴重的衣服。②昂貴的。③奢侈的;浪費的。*costly* habits. 奢侈的習慣。**—cost·li·ness,** *n.*

cost of living 生活費。

cost-of-liv·ing ['kastəv'lɪvɪŋ; 'kɔstəv'liviŋ] *adj.* 生活費的。

cost-of-living index 生活費指數。

cost-plus ['kast'plʌs; 'kɔst'plʌs] *adj.* (對實際成本)利益增加的計算方式的。

cost price 成本價格。

cost-push ['kɔst,pʊʃ; 'kɔstpuʃ] *n.* = **cost inflation.**

cos·trel ['kastrəl; 'kɔstrəl] *n.* (皮製、陶製或木製)酒壺(有耳可懸在腰部等處)。

cost sheet 成本單。(亦作 **cost card**)

***cos·tume** [*n.* 'kastjum; 'kɔstjuːm, kɔs'tjuːm *v.* kas'tjum; 'kɔstjuːm] *n., v.,* **-tumed, -tum·ing,** *adj.* —*n.* ①服裝;服裝的式樣。He was in academic *costume.* 他着學士服。②舞臺裝; 劇裝。③戶外的服裝。—*v.t.* 供給服裝; 供給適當的服裝; 着服裝。—*adj.*①以服裝爲特色的。a *costume* ball. 化裝舞會。a *costume* movie. 古裝影片。②配合服裝的。

costume jewelry 人造珠寶。

costume piece 古裝劇。

cos·tum·er [kas'tjumə; kɔs'tjuːmə] *n.* 衣商(特指裁製、售賣或出租劇裝、舞衣等者)。

cos·tum·i·er [kas'tjumɪə; kɔs'tjuːmiə] *n.* =**costumer.**

cost unit 成本單位。

co·sy ['kozɪ; 'kouzi] *adj.,* **co·si·er, co·si·est,** *n., pl.* **co·sies.** —*adj.* 溫暖而舒適的; 安逸的。—*n.* 茶壺上保暖的棉墊; 暖罩。

***cot**¹ [kat; kɔt] *n.* ①窄的牀(尤指帆布牀)。②〖英〗兒童臥床(四圍常有欄杆者)。

cot² *n.* ①小屋;茅屋。②(保護或裹傷用之)手指套。

cot cotangent.

co·tan·gent [ko'tændʒənt; 'kou'tændʒənt] *n.* 〖數學〗餘切。

cot bed 輕便小牀。

cote [kot; kout] *n.* ①(家禽和獸的)棚;窩;欄。②〖方〗茅屋。

co·tem·po·ra·ne·ous [ko,tɛmpə'renɪəs; 'kou,tempə'reinjəs] *adj.* =**contemporaneous.**

co·tem·po·rar·y [ko'tɛmpə,rɛrɪ; 'kou'tempərəri] *adj., n., pl.* **-rar·ies.** = **contemporary.**

co·ten·ant [ko'tɛnənt; kou'tenənt] *n.* 共同租地人;共同佃戶;合租人。

co·te·rie ['kotərɪ; 'koutəri] *n.* 由共同興趣而組織的小團體。

co·ter·mi·nous [ko'tɝmənəs; kou'təːminəs] *adj.* =**conterminous.**

co·thur·nus [ko'θɝnəs; kou'θəːnəs] *n., pl.* **-ni** [-naɪ; -nai]. ①(古羅馬及希臘悲劇演員所穿之)半統靴。②悲劇; 悲劇風格。(亦作 **cothurn**)

co·til·lion [ko'tɪljən; kə'tiljən] *n.* ①(十九世紀時之)一種活潑輕快之舞。②此種舞曲。(亦作 **cotillon**)

Cots·wold ['katswold; 'kɔtswould] *n.* (原產於英國之)一種長毛綿羊。

***cot·tage** ['katɪdʒ; 'kɔtidʒ] *n.* ①小屋。②別墅。③醫院中供患者住的個別小屋。

cottage cheese (由脫脂凝乳作成的)鬆軟白乾酪。(亦作 **Dutch cheese**)

cottage fried potatoes 油炸馬鈴薯片。(亦作 **home fried potatoes**)

cottage industry 家庭工業。

cottage pudding 覆有熱甜醬的布丁。

cot·tag·er ['katɪdʒə; 'kɔtidʒə] *n.* ①住茅屋者。②〖英〗農場雇工;佃農。③〖美〗在度假勝地有別墅之人。

cot·ter¹ ['katə; 'kɔtə] *n.* ①住茅屋者。②〖蘇〗佃農。③〖愛〗=**cottier.**(亦作**cottar**)

cot·ter² *n.* ①楔; 鍵。② =**cotter pin.**(亦作 **cotterel**)

cotter pin 〖機械〗開尾栓。

cot·ti·er ['katɪə; 'kɔtiə] *n.* (英國及愛爾蘭)居於茅屋之農夫。

‡**cot·ton** ['katn̩; 'kɔtn] *n.*①棉花。Japan imports raw *cotton* and exports *cotton* goods. 日本輸入原棉而輸出棉織品。②棉樹。③棉紗;棉線。④棉布。—*adj.* 棉的;棉製的。—*v.i.*〖俗〗①交友。②喜歡;贊成〖to, with〗。③一致; 協調。④繁榮。***cotton on to***〖主英俚〗了解;明白。

cotton batting 棉胎。

cotton belt 美國南部產棉地帶。

cotton candy 棉花糖。

cotton gin 軋棉機。

cotton grass 〖植物〗棉菅(薹、菖蒲、白菖等植物)。

cotton grower 棉花栽培者;棉農。

cotton mill 紗廠;紡織廠。

cot·ton·mouth ['katn̩,maʊθ; 'kɔtnmauθ] *n.* 南美產之一種有毒大水蛇。

cot·ton·oc·ra·cy [,katn̩'akrəsɪ; ,kɔtn'ɔkrəsi] *n.*大棉紗業者(集合稱)。

Cot·ton·op·o·lis [,katn̩'apəlɪs; ,kɔtn'ɔpəlis] *n.* 〖謔〗紡織首都(英國之 Manchester).

cot·ton·seed ['katn̩,sid; 'kɔtənsiːd] *n., pl.* **-seed, -seeds.** 棉子。

cottonseed oil 棉子油。

cotton spinner ①紡織工人。②紡織廠廠主;紡織業者。

cot·ton·tail ['katn̩,tel; 'kɔtnteil] *n.* 美國產之白尾野兔。

cotton tree 木棉樹。

cot·ton·wood ['katn̩,wʊd; 'kɔtnwud] *n.* 〖植物〗白楊。

cotton wool ①棉花;原棉。②〖英〗脫脂棉花。③安逸的生活。
cot·ton·y [ˈkɑtn̩ɪ; ˈkɔtni] *adj.* ①棉的;棉製的。②似棉的;柔軟的。
cot·y·le·don [ˌkɑtl̩ˈidn̩; ˌkɔtiˈliːdən] *n.* ①〖植物〗子葉。②〖解剖〗絨毛葉。—**ous,** *adj.*
*__couch__ [kautʃ; kautʃ] *n.* ①臥榻; 長椅; 長沙發; 睡椅。②隱藏之所; 睡眠或休息的所在;獸穴。—*v.t.* ①措辭;表達。His refusal was *couched* in very polite words. 他用非常委婉的語言表達拒絕之意。②放平; 放低(矛等)預備攻擊。③使橫臥;使偃臥。—*v.i.* ①橫臥;偃臥。②俯伏;屈身。③埋伏;潛伏。④堆置(如樹葉)以備分解或發酵。
couch·ant [ˈkautʃənt; ˈkautʃənt] *adj.* ①俯伏的;蹲着的(特指動物言)。②〖紋章〗抬頭伏臥狀的。
cou·chette [kuˈʃɛt; kuːˈʃet] *n.* 有臥鋪的火車廂。
couch grass 〖植物〗茅草。
cou·gar [ˈkugə; ˈkuːgə] *n.* 〖動物〗美洲豹。
*__cough__ [kɔf; kɔf] *v.i.* ①咳嗽。He *coughs* badly. 他咳嗽得很厲害。② (引擎等) 爆發不連續的噗噗聲。—*v.t.* 咳出〖up, out〗. ***cough down*** 故意咳嗽以掩沒演講者的聲音而使其中止。***cough up*** **a.** 咳出。**b.** 付出。**c.** 吐露。—*n.* ①咳; 咳嗽。②咳嗽病。He had a bad *cough.* 他咳得很厲害。③咳聲。④(引擎等之)不連續爆發聲。***give a*** (***slight***) ***cough*** 以咳嗽引起注意或警告。
cough drop 止咳藥片。
cough syrup 止咳糖漿。
‡**could** [kud; kud] *v.* pt. of **can.** ①表示簡單過去(常用於附屬子句)。He said he would go if he *could.* 他說如果可能他就會去。②表示客氣。*Could* you do this for me? 你能爲我做這事嗎? ③表示假定。If you *could* come we would be pleased. 如果你能來,我們會很高興。④表示沒有把握。Perhaps I *could* write a poem, but I doubt it.也許我可以寫一首詩,但我沒有把握。
*__could·n't__ [ˈkudn̩t; ˈkudnt]＝**could not.**
cou·lee [ˈkulɪ; ˈkuːli] *n.* ①〖地質〗熔岩流。②〖美西部〗深谷;斜壁谷。
cou·lisse [kuˈlis; kuːˈliːs] *n.* ①有槽之木材。②〖戲劇〗**a.** 側面布景; **b.** 二側面布景間的地方; **c.** 後臺。
cou·loir [kuˈlwar; ˈkuːlwɑː] 〖法〗 *n.* 深谷;壑。
cou·lomb [kuˈlɑm; ˈkuːlɔm] *n.* 庫;庫侖(電量之實用單位)。
cou·lom·e·ter [kuˈlɑmɪtə; kuːˈlɔmitə] *n.*電量計;庫侖計。(亦作 **coulombmeter**)
coul·ter [ˈkoltə; ˈkoultə] *n.* 犁刀。
‡**coun·cil** [ˈkaunsl̩; ˈkaunsl] *n.* ①會議。*council* of war. 軍事會議。②市或鎮的議會。city *council.* 市議會。③顧問委員會。
council board 會議桌;會議。
council chamber 會議室。
coun·cil·man [ˈkaunsl̩mən; ˈkaunslmən] *n., pl.* **-men.** ①市議會議員; 鎮民代表。②參議;議員。
coun·ci·lor, coun·cil·lor [ˈkaunsl̩ə; ˈkaunsilə] *n.* (州、市、鎮等議會之)議員;評議員;顧問。
coun·ci(l)·lor·ship [ˈkaunsələˌʃɪp; ˈkaunsiləʃip] *n.* councilor 之職或地位。
council school 〖英〗公立學校。
coun·cil·wom·an [ˈkaunsl̩ˌwumən; ˈkaunslˌwumən] *n., pl.* **-wom·en** [-wɪmən; -wimin]. (市議會等之)女議員。
*__coun·sel__ [ˈkaunsl̩; ˈkaunsəl] *n., v.,* **-sel(l)ed, -sel·(l)ing.** —*n.* ①商議;商量。②勸告; 忠告。He gave me good *counsel* on this matter. 對於這事,他給我很好的忠告。③(作 *sing.* or *pl.* 解)法律顧問; 律師。④計畫;企圖。***keep one's own counsel*** 守祕密。***take*** (or ***hold***) ***counsel with*** 與…商量。—*v.t.* ①勸告;忠告。②建議;主張。—*v.i.* ①商議; 商量; 商討。②提出或接受建議、忠告等。
coun·sel·ing [ˈkaunsl̩ɪŋ; ˈkaunsliŋ] *n.* 輔導服務。
*__coun·se·lor, coun·sel·lor__ [ˈkaunsl̩ə; ˈkaunsələ] *n.* ①顧問;(使館)參事。②法律顧問;律師。
‡**count**[1] [kaunt; kaunt] *v.t.* ①點數;數。②計算;清點。③計及;包括。There are ten people here, not *counting* the children. 小孩不計,這裏共有十人。④以爲;想;視爲。I *count* it foolish to let him go. 我認爲讓他走是不智的。—*v.i.* ①數;計算。②信賴;憑藉;期望〖on, upon〗. You had better not *count* on an increase in your salary at present. 你最好不要期望現在加薪。③有價值;有用。Every minute *counts.* 每分鐘都不可錯過。④總計達某數目。⑤得分。***count as*** (or ***for***) ***dead*** (or ***lost***) 視爲已死。I'm afraid we must *count* him *as lost.* 我想我們應該當他已死。***count for much*** (***little,*** or ***nothing***) 算是重要的(或無關重要的)。***count in*** 包括。***count off*** 挑出;選出;點出。***count out*** **a.** 宣告失敗(拳賽時,被對手打倒,數至十秒仍不能起立)。**b.** 出席者不足法定人數而宣告延會。**c.** 計算投票時,非法地使一部分選票失效,從而控制選舉。**d.** 忽略;不算在內。***count the cost*** 預算費用。***count up*** 數。—*n.* ①數;計算。②總計;總數。③控訴的條款。④顧慮;重視;考慮;注意。⑤事項。⑥〖拳擊〗(爲給與被打倒者再起的機會) 數十秒。⑦〖棒球〗好壞球之報數。***keep*** (***lose***) ***count of*** 數(不)清。***the*** (***full***) ***count*** 〖拳擊〗＝**count out a.**
*__count__[2] *n.* 伯爵(歐洲大陸的稱號, 相當於英國的 earl)。
count·a·ble [ˈkauntəbl̩; ˈkauntəbl] *adj.* 可數的。—*n.* 〖文法〗可數名詞。
count·down [ˈkauntˌdaun; ˈkauntdaun] *n.*(按預定時間實行計畫之)倒數計時。
*__coun·te·nance__ [ˈkauntənəns; ˈkauntinəns] *n., v.,* **-nanced, -nanc·ing.** —*n.* ①面容;面部表情。②面貌;容貌。The king had a noble *countenance.* 這國王容貌高貴。③應許;鼓勵。He gave *countenance* to our plan, but no active help. 他對我們的計畫予以鼓勵,但無實際的幫助。④鎮靜;沉着。***keep one's countenance*** 保持鎮靜;不露喜怒之色。***lose countenance*** 緊張起來;現於形色。***put*** (***a person***) ***out of countenance***使之跼促不安。—*v.t.*應許;鼓勵;贊助。
*__count·er__[1] [ˈkauntə; ˈkauntə] *n.* ①籌碼。②〖美〗櫃臺。③計算機。④計算者。⑤劣幣;僞幣。***under the counter*** 非法地;祕密地;偷偷地。
coun·ter[2] *adv.* 相反地; 反對地。—*adj.* ①相反的;反對的。②還擊的;反擊的。③背後的;背面的。④與前令相反的。⑤副本的;複印的。—*n.* ①反對;反對物。②〖拳擊〗還擊。③(鞋底之)後跟。④相反的方向。⑤相反之事。—*v.t.* ①反對。②(拳擊或打架時)還擊一拳。③鞋底後跟。④阻遏。⑤抵抗。⑥答辯;抗辯。—*v.i.* 還擊。
counter- 〖字首〗表"相反; 相對"之義, 如

counterattack, counterpart.

coun·ter·ac·cu·sa·tion [ˌkauntə-ˌækjuˈzeʃən; ˈkauntərˌækjuˈzeiʃən] *n.* 反控。

***coun·ter·act** [ˌkauntəˈækt; ˌkauntəˈrækt] *v.t.* 抵消;消除;消解;抵制。

coun·ter·ac·tion [ˌkauntəˈækʃən; ˌkauntəˈrækʃən] *n.* ①(藥之)中和作用;消解。②反作用;反動。

coun·ter·ac·tive [ˌkauntəˈæktɪv; ˌkauntəˈræktiv] *adj.* 中和性的;反作用的。—*n.* 反作用劑;中和藥劑;中和力。

coun·ter·a·gent [ˈkauntəˌedʒənt; ˈkauntərˌeidʒənt] *n.* 反抗力;抵制者;消解者;反作用劑;中和劑;反對動因。

coun·ter·ap·peal [ˈkauntərəˌpil; ˈkauntərəˌpiːl] *n.* 〖法律〗抗告。

coun·ter·at·tack [*n.* ˈkauntərəˌtæk; ˈkauntərəˌtæk *v.* ˌkauntərəˈtæk; ˌkauntərəˈtæk] *n.* 反攻;反擊。—*v.t.* & *v.i.* 反攻;反擊。

coun·ter·at·trac·tion [ˌkauntərəˈtrækʃən; ˈkauntərəˌtrækʃən] *n.* 反引力。

coun·ter·bal·ance [*n.* ˈkauntəˌbæləns; ˈkauntəˌbæləns *v.* ˌkauntəˈbæləns; ˌkauntəˈbæləns] *n.*, *v.*, **-anced, -anc·ing.** —*n.* ①平衡;平衡力。②平衡裝置。—*v.t.* ①使平衡;使抵消。②配以平衡裝置。

coun·ter·blast [ˈkauntəˌblæst; ˈkauntə-blɑːst] *n.* ①反對氣流。②猛烈之反對。

count·er·boy [ˈkauntəˌbɔɪ; ˈkauntəbɔi] *n.* 在櫃檯值班的服務員。

coun·ter·change [ˌkauntəˈtʃendʒ; ˌkauntəˈtʃeindʒ] *v.t.*, **-changed, -chang·ing.** ①交易;交換。②使交錯;使有方格紋。

coun·ter·charge [*n.* ˈkauntəˌtʃɑrdʒ; ˈkauntə-tʃɑːdʒ *v.* ˌkauntəˈtʃɑrdʒ; ˌkauntəˈtʃɑːdʒ] *n.*, *v.*, **-charged, -charg·ing.** —*n.* ①反擊;逆襲。②〖法律〗反訴。—*v.t.* 反擊;反訴。

coun·ter·check [*n.* ˈkauntəˌtʃɛk; ˈkauntə-tʃek *v.* ˌkauntəˈtʃɛk; ˌkauntəˈtʃek] *n.* ①抑制物;制止物。②再驗證;覆核。—*v.t.* ①(以反作用)制止。②再驗證;覆核。

coun·ter·claim [*n.* ˈkauntəˌklem; ˈkauntə-kleim *v.* ˌkauntəˈklem; ˌkauntəˈkleim] *n.* 反要求;反訴。—*v.i.* & *v.t.* 反訴。

coun·ter·clock·wise [ˌkauntəˈklɑkˌwaɪz; ˈkauntəˈklɔkwaiz] *adj.* & *adv.* 反時針方向的(地)。

coun·ter·cur·rent [ˈkauntəˌkɝənt; ˈkauntəˌkʌrənt] *n.* ①逆流。②逆電流。—*adj.* & *adv.* 逆流的(地);相反的(地)。

coun·ter·es·pi·o·nage [ˌkauntəˈɛspɪənɪdʒ; ˈkauntərˌespiəˈnɑːʒ] *n.* 反間諜(活動);策反。

coun·ter·ev·i·dence [ˈkauntəˌɛvədəns; ˈkauntərˌevidəns] *n.* 反證。

coun·ter·feit [ˈkauntəfɪt; ˈkauntəfit] *adj.* 贋造的;假冒的;冒牌的。—*v.t.* & *v.i.* 贋造;僞造;模仿;僞裝。—*n.* 贋品;僞造品。—**er,** *n.*

coun·ter·flow [ˈkauntəˌflo; ˈkauntəflou] *n.* 逆流。

coun·ter·foil [ˈkauntəˌfɔɪl; ˈkauntəfɔil] *n.* 〖英〗支票存根;(收據、匯票等之)存根。(美亦作 **stub**)

coun·ter·fort [ˈkauntəˌfort; ˈkauntəfɔːt] *n.* ①〖建築〗扶壁;撐垛;支撐。②山之突出處;山嘴。

count·er·girl [ˈkauntəˌgɝl; ˈkauntəgəːl] *n.* 在櫃檯值班的服務小姐。

coun·ter·guard [ˈkauntəˌgɑrd; ˈkauntəgɑːd] *n.* (碉堡之)壁障。

coun·ter·in·tel·li·gence [ˌkauntərɪnˈtɛlədʒəns; ˈkauntərinˌtelidʒəns] *n.* 〖軍〗①反情報;反間諜活動。②反情報機構。

coun·ter·ir·ri·tant [ˌkauntəˈɪrətənt; ˌkauntərˈiritənt] *n.* 〖藥〗反刺激劑。

coun·ter·ir·ri·tate [ˌkauntəˈɪrəˌtet; ˌkauntərˈiriteit] *v.t.*, **-tat·ed, -tat·ing.** 用反刺激劑刺激。—**coun·ter·ir·ri·ta·tion,** *n.*

coun·ter·jump·er [ˈkauntəˌdʒʌmpə; ˈkauntəˌdʒʌmpə] *n.* 〖蔑〗店員。

coun·ter·man [ˈkauntəˌmæn; ˈkauntəmæn] *n.* 在櫃檯值勤的服務員。

coun·ter·mand [*v.* ˌkauntəˈmænd, *n.* ˈkauntəˌmænd; ˌkauntəˈmɑːnd, ˈkauntəˈm-] *v.t.* ①撤回或取消(已發出之命令)。②下令撤回;下令取消;下令停止。③〖廢〗違反…之命令。—*n.* 收回成命。

coun·ter·march [*v.* ˌkauntəˈmɑrtʃ; ˌkauntəˈmɑːtʃ *n.* ˈkauntəˌmɑrtʃ; ˈkauntəmɑːtʃ] *v.i.* & *v.t.* 後退。—*n.* 後退。

coun·ter·mark [ˈkauntəˌmɑrk; ˈkauntəmɑːk] *n.* 戳記。—*v.t.* 加蓋戳記。

coun·ter·meas·ure [ˈkauntəˌmɛʒə; ˈkauntəˌmeʒə] *n.* 抵制手段;對策。

coun·ter·mine [*n.* ˈkauntəˌmaɪn; ˈkauntəmain *v.* ˌkauntəˈmaɪn; ˌkauntəˈmain] *n.* ①裝有炸藥的坑道(用以炸毀敵人之坑道)。②沉入水中用以炸毀敵人水雷的炸藥。③破壞對方陰謀的陰謀。—*v.i.* & *v.t.* ①挖坑道禦敵。②以計破壞敵人陰謀。③在某地區布雷(以破壞敵人之布雷)。

coun·ter·mis·sile [ˈkauntəˌmɪsl; ˈkauntəˌmisail] *n.* 反飛彈之飛彈。

coun·ter·move [*n.* ˈkauntəˌmuv; ˈkauntəmuːv *v.* ˌkauntəˈmuv; ˌkauntəˈmuːv] *n.* 反動議;對抗之手段。—*v.t.* & *v.i.* 提反議;反動議。—**ment,** *n.*

coun·ter·of·fen·sive [ˌkauntərəˈfɛnsɪv; ˈkauntərəˈfensiv] *n.* 〖軍〗(守軍之)反攻;反擊;逆襲。

coun·ter·pane [ˈkauntəˌpen; ˈkauntəpein] *n.* 床罩;床單。

coun·ter·part [ˈkauntəˌpɑrt; ˈkauntəpɑːt] *n.* ①副本。②極相似的人或物;互相配對的東西。③互相補充的東西。—*adj.*(接受資金援助時之)相對基金的。

coun·ter·plot [ˈkauntəˌplɑt; ˈkauntəplɔt] *v.i.* & *v.t.* 將(計)就計;用反計。—*n.* 反計;對抗策略。

coun·ter·point [ˈkauntəˌpɔɪnt; ˈkauntəpɔint] *n.* ①〖音樂〗對位法;旋律配合法。②對應(物)。—*v.t.* 用對照法强調。

coun·ter·poise [ˈkauntəˌpɔɪz; ˈkauntəpɔiz] *n.*, *v.*, **-poised, -pois·ing.** —*n.* ①平均;平衡;平衡力。②足以抗拒之力。③砝碼;秤錘。—*v.t.* 使平衡;使均衡;使平均。

coun·ter·pro·duc·tive [ˌkauntəprəˈdʌktɪv; ˌkauntəprəˈdʌktiv] *adj.* ①反生產的。②使達不到預期目標的。

coun·ter·prop·a·gan·da [ˈkauntəˌprɑpəˈgændə; ˈkauntəˌprɔpəˈgændə] *n.* 反宣傳。

coun·ter·pro·pos·al [ˈkauntəprəˌpozl; ˈkauntəprəˈpouzəl] *n.* 對案;反建議。

coun·ter·punch [ˈkauntəˌpʌntʃ; ˈkauntəpʌntʃ] *n.* 反擊。

coun·ter·ref·or·ma·tion [ˌkaun-

tə͵rɛfəˈmeʃən; ˈkauntə͵refəˈmeiʃən) *n.* 反改革。
coun·ter·rev·o·lu·tion 〔͵kauntə͵rɛvəˈluʃən; ˈkauntərevə͵luːʃən〕 *n.* 反革命。
coun·ter·scarp 〔ˈkauntə͵skɑrp; ˈkauntə-skɑːp〕 *n.* (堡壘壕溝之)外岸。
coun·ter·shaft〔ˈkauntə͵ʃæft;ˈkauntəʃɑːft〕 *n.* (機器中之)副軸;間軸。
coun·ter·sign 〔ˈkauntə͵saɪn;ˈkauntəsain〕 *n.* ①〖軍〗口令; 答號(對答哨兵之暗號)。②連署;副署。—*v.t.* 連署;副署。
coun·ter·sig·na·ture 〔͵kauntəˈsɪgnətʃə; ͵kauntəˈsignitʃə〕 *n.* 副署;連署。
coun·ter·sink 〔ˈkauntə͵sɪŋk;ˈkauntəsiŋk〕 *v.*, **-sunk, -sink·ing,** *n.* —*v.t.* ①鑽大(孔)以便旋入螺絲釘。②將(螺絲釘頭)裝入孔眼。—*n.* 鑽孔工具;裝螺絲釘頭之孔眼。
coun·ter·spy 〔ˈkauntə͵spaɪ; ˈkauntəspai〕 *n.* 反間諜。
coun·ter·ten·or 〔ˈkauntəˈtɛnə; ˈkauntəˈtenə〕 *n.* 〖音樂〗男聲中音。
coun·ter·ter·ror·ism 〔͵kauntəˈtɛrə͵rɪzəm; ͵kauntəˈterərizəm〕 *n.* 報復性恐怖主義。
coun·ter·vail 〔͵kauntəˈvel; ˈkauntəveil〕 *v.t.* ①抵銷。②補償。③對抗。—*v.i.* 對抗; 均等。
coun·ter·vi·o·lence 〔͵kauntəˈvaɪələns; ͵kauntəˈvaiələns〕 *n.* 以暴制暴。
coun·ter·weigh〔͵kauntəˈwe; ͵kauntəˈwei〕 *v.t.* & *v.i.* 抵消;彌補。
coun·ter·weight 〔ˈkauntə͵wet; ˈkauntəweit〕 *n.* ①秤錘; 砝碼。②平衡; 平衡力。 —*v.t.* =**counterbalance.**
coun·ter·work 〔*v.* ͵kauntəˈwɜk; ͵kauntəˈwəːk *n.* ˈkauntə͵wɜk; ˈkauntəwəːk〕 *v.i.* & *v.t.* 對抗;妨害。—*n.* ①對抗; 反對行動。②〖軍〗對抗工事;對峙之碉堡。
coun·ter·work·er〔ˈkauntə͵wɜkə; ˈkauntə͵wəːkə〕 *n.* 對手;敵手。
*__count·ess__ 〔ˈkauntɪs; ˈkauntis〕 *n.* 伯爵夫人;女伯爵。
count·ing 〔ˈkauntɪŋ; ˈkauntiŋ〕 *n.* 計算;開票。
count·ing·house 〔ˈkauntɪŋ͵haus; ˈkauntiŋhaus〕 *n.* 帳房; 會計室。 (亦作 **counting room**)
counting machine 計算機。
counting room 帳房;會計室。
*__count·less__ 〔ˈkauntlɪs; ˈkauntlis〕 *adj.* 無數的。
coun·tri·fied, coun·try·fied 〔ˈkʌntrɪ͵faɪd; ˈkʌntrifaid〕 *adj.* ①鄉野的。②粗俗的;鄉下人的。
‡**coun·try**〔ˈkʌntrɪ;ˈkʌntri〕*n., pl.* **-tries,** *adj.* —*n.* ①國;國家。We are willing to die for our *country.* 我們願意為國家而死。②地方;地域。③國民;全國。④家鄉;故土。to return to one's *country.* 回到自己的家鄉。⑤鄉村; 鄉間。 I like to live in the *country.* 我喜歡住在鄉間。⑥〖法律〗(代表公衆的)陪審團。—*adj.* ①鄉間的;田舍的。②在農莊土製的。
coun·try-and-west·ern 〔ˈkʌntrɪənˈwɛstən; ˈkʌntrienˈwestən〕 *n.* = **country music.**
coun·try-bred 〔ˈkʌntrɪˈbrɛd;ˈkʌntriˈbred〕 *adj.* 在鄉下長大的。
country club 鄉間俱樂部。
country cousin 鄉巴佬。
coun·try-dance 〔ˈkʌntrɪˈdæns; ˈkʌntridɑːns〕 *n.* 土風舞。
coun·try·folk 〔ˈkʌntrɪ͵fok;ˈkʌntrifouk〕 *n. pl.* ①鄉下人。②同胞;國人。
country gentleman 鄉紳。
country house 別墅。
*__coun·try·man__〔ˈkʌntrɪmən; ˈkʌntrimən〕 *n., pl.* **-men.** ①鄉間人。②同國人。
country mile 很遠的距離。
country music 鄉村音樂 (以電吉他伴奏的美國西部民謠音樂)。
Country Party 英王查理二世時之一政黨,為 Whig Party 之前身。
country rock 美國西部民謠與搖滾樂混合的曲調。
coun·try·seat 〔ˈkʌntrɪ͵sit; ˈkʌntriˈsiːt〕 *n.* ①別墅。②〖英〗鄉紳的住宅。
*__coun·try·side__ 〔ˈkʌntrɪ͵saɪd; ˈkʌntriˈsaid〕 *n.* ①鄉間。②村民。③地方。
coun·try-wide〔ˈkʌntrɪˈwaɪd;ˈkʌntriˈwaid〕 *adj.* 遍及全國的。
coun·try·wom·an 〔ˈkʌntrɪ͵wumən; ˈkʌntri͵wumən〕 *n., pl.* **-wom·en.** ①村婦。②女同胞。
count·ship 〔ˈkaunt·ʃɪp; ˈkaunt-ʃip〕 *n.* 伯爵之地位。
‡**coun·ty** 〔ˈkauntɪ;ˈkaunti〕 *n., pl.* **-ties.** ①〖美〗郡(僅次於州的行政區)。②〖英、愛〗州或郡。③〖英〗(the-) 全郡居民。 ***home counties*** 〖英〗倫敦周圍的六郡。
county borough 〖英〗人口在五萬以上的自治市。
county council 郡議會。
county court 州(郡)法院;地方法院。
coun·ty-court〔ˈkauntɪˈkort;͵kauntiˈkɔːt〕 *v.t.* 〖英俗〗向地方民事法院控告。
county fair 郡一年一度之農產品展覽會。
county family 郡世居望族。
county seat 郡政府所在地。
county town 郡的首邑。
coup[1] 〔ku; kuː〕 *n., pl.* **coups.** ①突然而有效的一擊;出乎意料的行動;策略。②政變。
coup[2] 〔kop, kup; koup, kuːp〕 *v.t.* 使顛倒;使傾斜。—*v.i.* 推倒;溢出;傾斜。
coup de grâce 〔kudəˈgrɑs; kuːdəˈgrɑːs〕〖法〗①致死之一擊。②任何最後的或決定性之一擊。
coup de main 〔kudəˈmæ; kuːdəˈmæ〕〖法〗突擊;奇襲。
coup d'é·tat 〔ˈkudeˈtɑ; ˈkuːdeiˈtɑː〕〖法〗武力政變。
cou·pé 〔kuˈpe;ˈkuːpei〕〖法〗*n.* 有車廂的四輪馬車;小汽車。
coupe 〔kup; kuːp〕 *n.* 〖美俗〗=**coupé.**
‡**cou·ple** 〔ˈkʌpl̩; ˈkʌpl〕 *n., v.,* **-pled, -pling,** *adj.* —*n.* ①一對;一雙。②配偶;夫婦;情侶;(男女)舞伴。a married *couple.* 夫婦。③〖俗〗數個;幾個。 I have a *couple* of things to do. 我有幾件事情要做。④交媾。⑤〖物理〗力偶。⑥栓兩隻獵狗的拉犬繩。⑦〖獵狐〗兩隻獵犬。—*v.t.*①連合;連接。②聯繫;聯想。—*v.i.*①成對。②交媾。—*adj.* (與 a 連用)二;兩。a *couple* nights ago. 兩夜前。〖注意〗在日常談話中, couple 相等於數目字 two: a *couple* of weeks. 兩週。 但俗用亦作"數個"或"幾個"解(=a few, several): a *couple* of days. 數天;幾天。
cou·pler 〔ˈkʌplə; ˈkʌplə〕 *n.* ①連結者;配合者;聯結器。②(連結二節火車車廂的)車鉤器。③〖無線電〗耦合器。
cou·plet 〔ˈkʌplɪt; ˈkʌplit〕 *n.* ①〖詩〗對句;雙韻。②雙; 對。 ***heroic couplet*** 英雄雙行體(每句有五音步十音節)。

cou·pling [ˈkʌplɪŋ; ˈkʌpliŋ] *n.* ①聯結。②聯結器;聯軸節。③(連結車廂的)輓鉤;車鉤。④馬或狗自股至肩部間之身體。

cou·pon [ˈkupɑn; ˈkuːpɔn] *n.* ①可以撕下的利息單、聯票等。②商家的優待券。③配給券。④(試驗材料所用之)試料。

:cour·age [ˈkɝɪdʒ; ˈkʌridʒ] *n.* 勇敢;勇氣;無畏。to lose *courage.* 失去勇氣;氣餒。***Dutch courage*** 酒後之勇氣;爲時極短的勇氣。***have the courage of one's convictions*** 有敢作敢爲自以爲是的勇氣。***pluck up*** (or ***take***) ***courage*** 鼓起勇氣。***take courage in both hands*** 鼓足勇氣作事;敢作敢爲。〖注意〗**courage, bravery** 均表勇敢。courage 指精神的力量。bravery 指處於危難中以大膽無畏的行動表現出來的勇敢。

***cou·ra·geous** [kəˈredʒəs; kəˈreidʒəs] *adj.* 勇敢的。—**ly,** *adv.* —**ness,** *n.*

cou·rant [kuˈrænt; kuˈrænt] *n.* 新聞;報紙(僅用於報紙名稱)。

cour·i·er [ˈkʊrɪɚ; ˈkuriə] *n.* ①送遞快信的信差。②旅行時被雇用之從僕。③替間諜傳遞消息之人。④信差之交通工具。

:course [kors, kɔrs; kɔːs] *n., v.,* **coursed, cours·ing.** —*n.* ①過程。The new road is in the *course* of construction. 這條新的路在修築中。②方向; 方針。③行爲; 做法。He took to evil *courses.* 他行爲放蕩。④所經之路。⑤連續的事物。⑥課程。⑦一道菜。 The main *course* is a steak. 主菜爲牛排。⑧跑馬場或球場。⑨磚、瓦、石等的層列。⑩船帆。⑪依正常次序排列的一些相類似之物。⑫正常的程序。⑬生涯;一生。⑭(獵狗之)追逐獵物〖常 at, of〗。⑮(*pl.*) **a.** 指南針上的位置。 **b.** 月經。⑯編織物之經線。***as a matter of course*** 自然地。***follow*** (or ***adopt***) ***a middle course*** 採取中庸之道。 ***follow*** (or ***pursue***) ***her course*** (船)照一定航線航行。 ***hold*** (or ***keep on***) ***one's course*** 不變方向; 抱定宗旨。 ***in course*** **a.** =**in due course. b.** 修得的(學位)。 a degree taken *in course,* not an honorary one. 修得的學位, 而不是名譽學位。 ***in due course*** 在適當的時候; 不久以後。 ***in mid course*** 在中途; 在半路。 ***in the course of*** 當…期間; 在…過程中。 ***in the ordinary course of events*** 按照平常情形的趨勢。 ***of course*** 自然; 當然。 ***run*** (or ***take***) ***its course*** (聽其)自然發展。***shape one's course*** 確定自己方針。 ***stay the course*** 貫徹始終。 ***walk over the course*** (賽馬因無勁敵而)輕易獲勝。—*v.i.* ①運行;馳行; 流行。②狩獵。 —*v.t.* ①奔過;奔經。②追逐;用犬狩獵。③砌(磚等)。

cours·er [ˈkorsɚ; ˈkɔːsə] *n.* ①獵犬;狩獵者。②〖詩〗駿馬;戰馬。

cours·ing [ˈkorsɪŋ; ˈkɔːsiŋ] *n.* ①運行;奔馳;追逐。②使用獵犬之狩獵。

:court [kort, kɔrt; kɔːt] *n.* ①庭院; 天井。②短街;死巷。③場。④宮院;朝廷。⑤廷臣;朝臣。⑥法院;法庭。to hold a *court.* 開庭。⑦法官。The *court* found the prisoner not guilty. 法官判決犯人無罪。⑧求寵; 殷勤;求愛。to pay *court* to a pretty woman. 對美婦獻殷勤。***court dress*** 朝服。 ***court fool*** 宮中弄臣。***Court of Admiralty***〖英〗海軍法庭。 ***court of appeal*** 上訴法庭。***Court of Claims***〖美〗(華盛頓)行政法院。***Court of Common Pleas***〖英〗高等民事裁判所。***court of justice*** (or ***judicature***) 法院。***Crown Court***〖英〗刑事法庭。***High Court of Parliament*** (等於最高法院的)英國國會。***in open court*** 公開地。***laugh out of court*** 一笑了之。***order the court to be cleared*** 命令旁聽人退席。 ***out of court*** **a.** 不經審判。**b.** 不值得討論。 ***pay court to*** **a.** 向…討好。**b.** 向…求愛。 ***put oneself out of court*** 做出(說出)遭人白眼的事(話)。 ***put out of court*** 不顧;蔑視。***summary court*** 簡易審判庭。—*v.t.* ①求愛; 獻殷勤。②乞惠;求得。③惹;招致。④引誘。—*v.i.* ①求愛。②乞惠。 —*adj.* ①宮廷的。②法庭的。a *court* decision. 法庭的判決。③球場的。a *court* star. 明星球員。

court card〖英〗紙牌中之king, queen, 和 jack.

court circular (英國皇家給新聞界「之」宮廷公報。)

court dress 宮廷服;朝服。

***cour·te·ous** [ˈkɝtɪəs; ˈkəːtjəs] *adj.* 有禮貌的;謙恭的;殷勤的。—**ly,** *adv.* —**ness,** *n.*

cour·te·san [ˈkortəzn̩; ˌkɔːtiˈzæn] *n.* 高等娼妓。(亦作 **courtezan**)

cour·te·sy** [ˈkɝtəsɪ, *for n.* ④ ˈkɝtsɪ; ˈkəːtisi] *n., pl.* **-sies,** *adj.* —*n.* ①禮貌;殷勤。②恩惠;允許。③禮儀;謙恭。④=**curtsy.** ***be granted the courtesy (or ***courtesies***) ***of the port***〖美〗免受海關檢查。 ***by*** (or ***of***) ***courtesy*** 禮貌上;好意上;情面上。—*adj.* 禮貌上的。***courtesy call*** 禮貌上的拜訪。***courtesy title*** 禮貌上的稱呼、爵號。

courtesy card 優待券。

court·house [ˈkortˌhaus; ˈkɔːtˈhaus] *n.* ①法院。②〖美〗郡政府所在地。

***cour·ti·er** [ˈkortɪɚ, ˈkɔr-, -tjɚ; ˈkɔːtjə] *n.* ①廷臣; 朝臣。②奉承者; 諂媚者。—**ly,** *adj.* —**ship,** *n.*

court·ly [ˈkortlɪ; ˈkɔːtli] *adj.,* **-li·er, -li·est,** *adv.* —*adj.* ①適於做朝臣的。②有禮貌而威嚴的;謙恭的;優雅的。③奉承的。—*adv.* 有禮貌地。—**court·li·ness,** *n.*

court-mar·tial [ˈkortˈmɑrʃəl; ˈkɔːtˈmɑːʃəl] *n., pl.* **courts-mar·tial,** *v.,* **-tialed, -tial·ing.** —*n.* ①軍事法庭。②軍事審判。—*v.t.* 軍事審判。

court of inquiry 軍事調查庭。

Court of St. James 英國王宮。

court plaster 橡皮膏。

court·room [ˈkortˌrum; ˈkɔːt-ruːm] *n.* 法庭;審判室。

court·ship [ˈkort·ʃɪp; ˈkɔːt-ʃip] *n.* ①求愛; 求愛時期。②求支持;求友誼。

court tennis 室內網球。

***court·yard** [ˈkortˌjɑrd; ˈkɔːtˈjɑːd] *n.* 庭院;天井。

:cous·in [ˈkʌzn̩; ˈkʌzn] *n.* ①堂(表)兄、弟、姊、妹。②遠親。③一國之主對他國君主或其貴族的敬稱。④同輩;同類。⑤同族者;同種者;同胞。⑥性情相似之人或物。***call cousins*** (***with***) 稱兄道弟。***cousin once removed*** =**second cousin.** ***first*** (or ***full***) ***cousin*** =**cousin-german.** ***second cousin*** (第二代)遠堂(表)兄、弟、姊、妹。***third cousin*** (第三代)堂(表)兄、弟、姊、妹。

cous·in-ger·man [ˈkʌzn̩ˈdʒɝmən; ˈkʌznˈdʒəːmən] *n., pl.* **cous·ins-ger·man.** (第一代)親堂(表)兄、弟、姊、妹。

cous·in·hood [ˈkʌzn̩hud; ˈkʌznhud] *n.* =**cousinship.**

cous·in-in-law [ˈkʌzn̩ɪnˌlɔ; ˈkʌzn-inˌlɔː] *n.* 表(堂)姊(妹)夫;表(堂)嫂;表(堂)

弟媳。

cous·in·ly [ˈkʌzn̩lɪ; ˈkʌznli] *adj.* 堂(表)兄弟(姊妹)的;似表親的。—*adv.* 似堂兄弟(姊妹)地;作爲表親地。

cous·in·ship [ˈkʌzn̩ˌʃɪp; ˈkʌznʃip] *n.* 堂(表)兄弟(姊妹)之關係;表親關係。

coûte que coûte [ˌkutkəˈkut; ˈkuːtkəˈkuːt] 〖法〗無論代價如何;不惜任何犧牲。

cou·tu·rier [kutyˈrje; kuːtyˈrjei] 〖法〗 *n.* 女服設計師。

cou·tu·rière [kutyˈrjɛːr; kuːtyˈrjɛr] 〖法〗 *n.* 女性之女服設計師。

cove [kov; kouv] *n.* ①小海灣;小灣。②〖英俚〗傢伙;人。

co·vel·line [koˈvɛlɪn; kouˈvelin] *n.* 〖礦〗銅藍;靛銅礦。

cov·e·nant [ˈkʌvənənt; ˈkʌvinənt] *n.* 契約;盟約;契約書。—*v.i.* 締結盟約。—*v.t.* ①誓約;保證。②要求以…爲條件。—**er,** *n.*

cov·ent [ˈkʌvənt, ˈkɑv-; ˈkɔvənt] *n.* 女修道院。

Covent Garden ①英國倫敦之一廣場。②該廣場中之一劇院。

Cov·en·try [ˈkɑvəntrɪ; ˈkɔvəntri] *n.* 科芬特里(英格蘭中部一城市)。***send (a person) to Coventry*** 拒絕同(某人)講話或來往。

‡**cov·er** [ˈkʌvə; ˈkʌvə] *v.t.* ①蓋。*Cover* this box with a wide board. 用一塊寬的板將這箱蓋起來。②遮蔽。③占(時間或空間)。④穿衣;包裹起。⑤掩飾;掩藏。He tried to *cover* his mistakes. 他設法掩飾他的錯誤。⑥掩護;庇護。⑦通過;行過。⑧包括;論及。⑨供給;抵償;足敷。⑩對…瞄準;使在火力距離以內;掩護(部隊等)。to *cover* a person with a pistol. 用手槍對某人瞄準。⑪戴帽於。*Cover* your head when you are in the sun. 你在太陽下須戴帽。⑫採訪(新聞)。⑬下與對方相等的賭注;接受賭注。⑭購買(貨物、股票等)以備將來交貨或以防將來損失。⑮孵(蛋)。⑯淹沒。Floodwaters *covered* the town. 洪水淹沒了那市鎮。⑰與(雌性)交配。⑱吃掉(對方的牌)。—*v.i.* ①展延。②代替別人。③〖拳擊〗掩護臉部。***cover against*** 抵償。***cover (the) ground*** a. (以足够速度)執行一區域之防衞。b. 討論問題。***cover in*** 用泥土填(洞等)。***cover (up) one's tracks*** 掩蔽蹤跡或證據。***cover over*** 蓋起;被覆。***cover up*** a. 隱藏。b. 包庇別人。***remain covered*** 仍戴着帽。—*n.* ①蓋子;封面。②隱蔽;掩蔽;隱伏的地方。③(餐桌上的)一分餐具。④(馬蹄鐵之)全寬。***break cover*** (動物等)由樹叢或樹林中出來。***from cover to cover*** 自始至終(指書籍等)。***take cover*** 託庇;隱藏。***under cover*** a. 在安全地方。b. 祕密地;藉口。c. 裝在信封中。***under cover of*** a. 在…掩蔽下。b. 假託;假藉;藉口。***under separate cover*** 在另一信封或信袋中;另函。***under the same cover*** 隨函。

cov·er·age [ˈkʌvərɪdʒ, ˈkʌvrɪdʒ; ˈkʌvəridʒ] *n.* ①某事物所包含或掩蓋之量、範圍、程度等。②〖保險〗保險項目。③賠償債務之準備金總額。④〖財政〗通貨發行之準備金。⑤〖新聞〗報導之分量。⑥〖新聞〗報導。⑦〖新聞〗採訪。⑧有效範圍;影響範圍。⑨綜述。

cov·er·all [ˈkʌvəˌɔl; ˈkʌvərɔːl] *n.* (常 *pl.*)有袖之上下身連在一起的工作服。

cov·er-all [ˈkʌvəˌɔl; ˈkʌvərɔːl] *adj.* 包羅甚廣的;無所不包的。

cover charge 服務費或娛樂費。

cover crop (作物之)間作。

cov·ered [ˈkʌvəd; ˈkʌvəd] *adj.* ①有覆蓋的。②遮蔽的;隱藏的。③戴帽的。④覆蓋…的;蓋滿…的(複合用語)。a snow-*covered* mountain. 覆雪之山。⑤被包括在內的。

covered wagon 有篷大馬車;篷車。

cov·er·er [ˈkʌvərə; ˈkʌvərə] *n.* 包裝工人。

cover girl 〖俗〗(雜誌的)封面女郎。

***cov·er·ing** [ˈkʌvərɪŋ; ˈkʌvəriŋ] *n.* 遮蔽之物;覆蓋物。

covering fire 〖軍〗掩護砲火。

covering letter 說明書或附信。

cov·er·let [ˈkʌvəlɪt; ˈkʌvəlit] *n.* 床單;被單。(亦作 **coverlid**)

cov·er-point [ˈkʌvəˌpɔɪnt; ˈkʌvəˈpɔint] *n.* 〖板球〗後衞;後衞之位置。

cover story (雜誌的)封面故事。

cov·ert [ˈkʌvət; ˈkʌvət] *adj.* ①暗地的;隱密的;掩蔽的;半掩的。②〖法律〗在丈夫保護下的。—*n.* ①掩蔽處;庇護所。②鳥獸隱藏之叢林。③(*pl.*)蔽覆羽翮基部之覆羽。

cov·ert·ly [ˈkʌvətlɪ; ˈkʌvətli] *adv.* 偷偷地;悄悄地。

cov·er·ture [ˈkʌvətʃə; ˈkʌvətjuə] *n.* ①覆蓋;庇護;庇護所。②隱蔽;隱匿;掩飾。③〖法律〗有夫之身分。

cov·er-up [ˈkʌvəˌʌp; ˈkʌvərʌp] *n.* 隱蔽;隱藏;掩飾。

***cov·et** [ˈkʌvɪt; ˈkʌvit] *v.t.* & *v.i.* 貪;垂涎;妄圖。All *covet* all lose. 貪多則無得。—**a·ble,** *adj.* —**ing·ly,** *adv.* —**er,** *n.*

cov·et·ous [ˈkʌvətəs; ˈkʌvitəs] *adj.* 貪婪的;貪心的。—**ly,** *adv.* —**ness,** *n.*

cov·ey [ˈkʌvɪ; ˈkʌvi] *n., pl.* **-eys.** ①一羣鳥(尤指鷓鴣、鶉等)。②一羣人;一隊;一批。

‡**cow**[1] [kau; kau] *n.* ①母牛。②牛(不分公母老幼)。③大的雌性動物。④〖澳俚〗搗蛋的傢伙;不討人喜歡的人、物或工作。⑤〖鄙〗子女多的女人。⑥〖俚〗肥而不潔的女人。***till the cows come home*** 永久;長時間。

cow[2] *v.t.* 恐嚇;嚇。

***cow·ard** [ˈkauəd; ˈkauəd] *n.* 膽小的人;膽怯者。—*adj.* 膽怯的;害怕的。

***cow·ard·ice** [ˈkauədɪs; ˈkauədis] *n.* 怯懦;膽小。(亦作 **cowardliness**)

***cow·ard·ly** [ˈkauədlɪ; ˈkauədli] *adj.* & *adv.* 卑怯的(地);膽小的(地)。—**cow·ard·li·ness,** *n.*

cow·bane [ˈkauˌben; ˈkaubein] *n.* 〖植物〗毒芹;長命竹。

cow·bell [ˈkauˌbɛl; ˈkaubel] *n.* 母牛之頸鈴。

cow·ber·ry [ˈkauˌbɛrɪ; ˈkaubəri] *n., pl.* **-ries.** 〖植物〗越橘。

cow·bird [ˈkauˌbɝd; ˈkaubəːd] *n.* 〖動物〗(北美產之)椋鳥。(亦作 **cow blackbird, cow bunting**)

***cow·boy** [ˈkauˌbɔɪ; ˈkaubɔi] *n.* 〖美〗①牛仔;牧童。②駕車亂闖者。—*v.i.* 駕車亂闖。

cowboys and Indians 牧場騎士打紅蕃(兒童槍戰遊戲之一種)。

cowboy suit 牛仔裝(兒童服裝之一種)。

cow·catch·er [ˈkauˌkætʃə; ˈkauˌkætʃə] *n.* (火車機車前之)排障器。

cow college 〖俚〗①農學院。②偏僻無名而規模小的大學。

cow·er [ˈkauə; ˈkauə] *v.i.* 畏縮;退縮;抖縮。

cow·fish [ˈkauˌfɪʃ; ˈkaufiʃ] *n., pl.* **-fish, -fish·es.** 〖動物〗①海牛;江豚。②角魚。

cow·girl [ˈkauˌgɝl; ˈkaugəːl] *n.* 在牧場上照料牛馬的婦女。

cow grass 〖植物〗瓜槌草。

cow·hand [ˈkauˌhænd; ˈkauhænd] *n.* 牛仔。

cow·heel [ˈkauˌhil; ˈkauhiːl] *n.* 炖牛

蹄筋(菜名)。 「牧牛者。
cow·herd ['kau,hɝd; 'kauhə:d] *n.*
cow·hide ['kau,haɪd; 'kauhaid] *n., v.,* **-hid·ed, -hid·ing.** —*n.* ①牛皮。②牛皮鞭。—*v.t.* 用牛皮鞭子鞭撻。
cowl [kaul; kaul] *n.* ①連有頭巾的修道士服;頭布。②煙筒頂上的旋轉罩;通風帽。③汽車中包括擋風玻璃和儀器板(dashboard)的部分。④飛機引擎上的金屬罩。***take the cowl*** 出家修道。 「曲的頭髮。
cow·lick ['kau,lɪk; 'kaulik] *n.* 一簇扭
cowl·ing ['kaulɪŋ; 'kauliŋ] *n.* 飛機引擎之罩。
cow·man ['kaumən; 'kaumən] *n., pl.* **-men.** ①牧場主人;牧牛業者。②〖英〗牧牛者。
co-work·er [ko'wɝkɚ; 'kou'wə:kə] *n.* 合作者;共同工作者。 「黎豆;牛豆。
cow·pea ['kau,pi; 'kaupi:] *n.* 〖植物〗
cow pony 牧童騎的馬。 「牛痘。
cow·pox ['kau,pɑks; 'kaupɔks] *n.*
cow·punch·er ['kau,pʌntʃɚ; 'kau,pʌntʃə] *n.* 〖美俗〗 =**cowboy.**
cow·rie, cow·ry ['kaurɪ; 'kauri] *n.* 〖動物〗子安貝(印度及非洲用做貨幣)。
cow·skin ['kau,skɪn; 'kauskin] *n.* ①牛皮。②牛皮鞭。 「物〗野櫻草。
cow·slip ['kau,slɪp; 'kauslip] *n.* 〖植
cow tree 〖植物〗乳樹(產於南美洲)。
cox [kɑks; kɔks] *n., pl.* **coxes,** *v.* —*n.* 〖俗〗舵手 (coxswain 之縮寫)。—*v.t. & v.i.* 做舵手;掌舵。
cox·a ['kɑksə; 'kɔksə] *n., pl.* **cox·ae** ['kɑksi; 'kɔksi:]. ①〖解剖〗髖;無名骨;臀部。②(節肢動物腿的)基節;腰節。—**cox·al,** *adj.*
cox·comb ['kɑks,kom; 'kɔkskoum] *n.* ①〖植物〗鷄冠花。②花花公子;紈袴子。
cox·comb·i·cal [kɑks'kɑmɪkl; kɔks'koumikəl] *adj.* 花花公子的;虛飾的;浮誇的。(亦作 **coxcombic**)
cox·comb·ry ['kɑks,komrɪ; 'kɔkskoumri] *n., pl.* **-ries.** (男子之)虛飾;浮誇。
cox·swain ['kɑksn̩; 'kɔkswein] *n.* 舵手;艇長。(亦作 **cockswain**)
cox·y ['kɑksɪ; 'kɔksi] *adj.,* **cox·i·er, cox·i·est.** =**cocky.**
coy [kɔɪ; kɔi] *adj.* ①害羞的。②賣弄風情的;獻媚的。 —**ness,** *n.* —**ly,** *adv.*
coy·o·te [kaɪ'ot; 'kɔiout] *n.* ①(北美大草原之)土狼。②〖美〗奸詐之歹徒;惡棍。
coy·pu ['kɔɪpu; 'kɔipu:] *n., pl.* **-pu, -pus.** 〖動物〗(產於南美洲之)河鼠。
coz [kʌz; kʌz] *n.* 〖俗〗 =**cousin.**
coze [koz; kouz] *v.,* **cozed, coz·ing,** *n.* —*v.i.* 聊天;閒談。 —*n.* 聊天;閒談。
coz·en ['kʌzn̩; 'kʌzn] *v.t. & v.i.* 欺騙;欺哄。 「欺騙;欺哄。
coz·en·age ['kʌzn̩ɪdʒ; 'kʌznidʒ] *n.*
***co·zy** ['kozɪ; 'kouzi] *adj.,* **-zi·er, -zi·est,** *n., pl.* **-zies,** *v.,* **-zied, -zy·ing.** —*adj.* =**cosy.** —*n.* =**cosy.** —*v.i.* 得…之歡心〖up to〗. —**co·zi·ly,** *adv.* —**co·zi·ness,** *n.*
cp. ①compare. ②coupon. **C.P.** ①Chief Patriarch. ②Command Post. ③Common Pleas. ④Common Prayer. ⑤Communist Party. **c.p.** ①candle power. ②chemically pure. ③circular pitch. **CPA** Cathay Pacific Airways. 國泰航空公司。**C.P.A., c.p.a.** Certified Public Accountant. **cpd.** compound. **C.P.H.** Certificate in Public Health.

C.P.I. Consumer Price Index. **Cpl., cpl.** Corporal. **c.p.m., cpm** cycles per minute. **CPO, c.p.o.** chief petty officer. **cpr.** copper. **cps** cycles per second. **C.P.S.** Consumer Price Survey. **CPSU, C.P.S.U.** Communist Party of the Soviet Union. **cpt.** ①captain. ②counterpoint. **cptr.** carpenter. **CQ** call to quarters. 〖美〗業餘無線電廣播聯絡之信號。 **Cr** 化學元素 chromium 之符號。**cr.** ①credit. ②creditor. ③creek. ④crown. ⑤crowns.
crab** [kræb; kræb] *n., v.,* **crabbed, crab·bing.** —*n.* ①蟹。②脾氣乖戾的人。③起重機;絞車。④〖天文〗巨蟹座。⑤吹毛求疵;批評;抱怨。⑥=**crab apple.** ***catch a crab 〖划船〗下槳時用力不當。—*v.i.* ①捉蟹。②斜行。③〖俗〗抱怨;吹毛求疵;批評。She often *crabs* without cause. 她經常無緣無故的抱怨。—*v.t.* ①〖俗〗弄壞;糟蹋。②抱怨;批評。③使乖戾。④使斜行。 「蘋果。②其樹。
crab apple 〖植物〗①山查子;(野生)酸
crab·bed ['kræbɪd; 'kræbid] *adj.* ①乖戾的;暴躁的。②潦草難讀的。③複雜而難解的。 —**ly,** *adv.* —**ness,** *n.*
crab·ber ['kræbɚ; 'kræbə] *n.* ①捕蟹者。②捕蟹船。③〖俗〗吹毛求疵者。
crab·by ['kræbɪ; 'kræbi] *adj.,* **-bi·er, -bi·est.** 執拗的;暴躁的;乖戾的。
crab louse 〖動物〗毛蝨。 「果樹。
crab tree 〖植物〗山查子樹;(野生)酸蘋
crab·wise ['kræb,waɪz; 'kræbwaiz] *adv.* ①橫斜地。②小心地。
crack** [kræk; kræk] *n.* ①裂縫;龜裂。②爆炸聲;噼啪聲。③突然的重擊。④〖俗〗瞬息;頃刻。in a *crack.* 馬上。⑤〖美俚〗嘗試;努力。⑥〖美俚〗笑話;玩笑。⑦小縫。⑧瘋子;怪人。⑨〖英俚〗極優的人或物;好手;上品。the crack of doom*** 世界末日之雷聲。—*v.i.* ①破裂。②作破裂聲;作噼啪聲。③變聲(倒嗓)。④斷。⑤(體力、耐力等)崩潰。⑥〖化〗分餾。—*v.t.* ①破裂。②重擊。③使發噼啪聲;使發爆裂聲。④打開;撬開。⑤解明;解破。⑥破壞;毀壞。⑦微開。⑧研讀(書本)。***crack a bottle*** 打開酒瓶喝酒。***crack a joke*** 說笑話。***crack a person*** (or ***thing***) ***up*** 盛讚一個人(物)。He *cracked up* Whitehead to the stars. 他把 Whitehead 捧上了天。***crack a smile*** 笑;微笑。***crack down***〖美俚〗採取嚴厲手段。***crack the whip*** 突然採取嚴厲措施或態度。***crack up*** **a.** 墜毀。**b.** 身心疲憊;解體。**c.** 使汽車粉碎。 **d.** 〖美俚〗 捧腹大笑。***crack wise*** 發妙語。—*adj.* 〖俗〗最好的;第一流的。
crack·a·jack ['krækə,dʒæk; 'krækədʒæk] *n., adj.* 〖俚〗 =**crackerjack.**
crack·brain ['kræk,bren; 'krækbrein] *n.* 頭腦不正常者。
crack·brained ['kræk'brend; 'krækbreind] *adj.* 顚狂的;精神錯亂的。
crack·down ['kræk,daun; 'krækdaun] *n.* 嚴厲手段;懲罰行動。
cracked [krækt; krækt] *adj.* ①破碎的;破裂的。②破損的;損壞的。③聲音嘶啞的;嗓音起變化的。④〖俗〗瘋狂的; 精神失常的。
***crack·er** ['krækɚ; 'krækə] *n.* ①薄而脆的餅乾。②鞭砲。③一種裝有糖果、小字籤等物的紙筒(拉扯兩端即起爆炸)。④居住美國 Georgia, Florida 等州山地或森林地帶之窮苦白人。⑤敲破者;撬開者;破碎器。⑥吹牛者。
crack·er·jack ['krækɚ,dʒæk; 'krækə-

dʒæk] *adj.*, *n.*〖俚〗能力極强的(人); 極佳的(物)。(亦作 **crackajack**)

crack·ers [ˈkrækəz; ˈkrækəz] *adj.* 〖英俚〗瘋狂的;狂熱的。

crack·ing [ˈkrækɪŋ; ˈkrækiŋ] *adj.* 〖美俚〗猛烈的; 極大的。 ***get cracking*** 〖俚〗開始動或做。—*n.*〖化〗裂煉;熱裂;裂化。—*adv.* 極(常與 good 連用)。a *cracking* good race 極快之賽跑。 「*adj.*〖俗〗讀音困難的。」

crack·jaw [ˈkræk,dʒɔ; ˈkrækdʒɔː]

***crack·le** [ˈkrækl; ˈkrækl] *v.*, **-led, -ling,** *n.* —*v.i.* ①發噼啪聲; 發爆裂聲。②充滿。③產生裂紋。—*v.t.* 使發爆裂聲。—*n.* ①爆裂聲。②裂紋。

crack·le·ware [ˈkrækl,wɛr; ˈkræklwɛə] *n.* 有裂紋花飾之瓷器或陶器;碎瓷。

crack·ling [ˈkræklɪŋ; ˈkrækliŋ] *n.* ①連續的爆裂或噼啪聲。②烤豬肉的脆皮。③(*pl.*)〖方〗豬油渣。

crack·ly [ˈkræklɪ; ˈkrækli] *adj.* 發爆裂聲的;易發噼啪聲的。

crack·nel [ˈkræknl; ˈkræknəl] *n.* ①一種薄而脆之餅乾。②(*pl.*) 脆炸豬肉片。

crack of dawn 天初亮;破曉。

crack·pot [ˈkræk,pɑt; ˈkrækpɔt] *n.* 〖俗〗狂想之人; 顛狂的人。—*adj.*〖俗〗狂想的;想入非非的;顛狂的。

cracks·man [ˈkræksmən; ˈkræksmən] *n.*, *pl.* **-men.**〖俚〗盜賊;竊賊。

crack-up [ˈkræk,ʌp; ˈkrækʌp] *n.* ①(飛機等之) 撞碎;粉碎。②〖俗〗精神或體力崩潰。③失敗;崩潰。

crack·y [ˈkrækɪ; ˈkræki] *adj.*, **crack·i·er, crack·i·est,** *interj.* —*adj.* ①有龜裂的;易裂的。②〖俗〗精神錯亂的;發狂的。③多言的; 嘮叨的。—*interj.* 表示驚喜之語(常用於 by cracky 中,以强調語氣)。

cra·dle** [ˈkredl; ˈkreidl] *n.*, *v.*, **-dled, -dling.** —*n.* ① 嬰孩的搖籃。② 發源地。③淘金器。④支船架。⑤附於大鐮刀上的配禾架;此種大鐮刀。⑥(電話的)掛聽筒架。from*** (or ***in***) ***the cradle*** 由(在)襁褓時。***from the cradle to the grave*** 從生到死;一生中。***rob the cradle*** 與年齡遠較自己爲輕者作伴或結婚。***stifle in the cradle*** 防患於未然。***the cradle of the deep***〖詩〗海洋。—*v.t.* ①搖小兒使睡; 置小兒於搖籃內。②撫育; 生長。③刈割。④在淘金器內淘洗。⑤置於支架上。⑥捧;抱。

cradle scythe 帶有配禾架之鐮刀。

cra·dle·song [ˈkredl,sɔŋ; ˈkreidlsɔŋ] *n.* 搖籃曲;催眠曲。

cra·dling [ˈkredlɪŋ; ˈkreidliŋ] *n.* ①(砂金之)淘洗;選鑛。②撫養;育成。③〖建築〗鞍座;船床。

craft** [kræft; krɑːft] *n.* ①技巧;技術;手藝。②行業;職業。③(同業的)行會;公會(集合稱)。④詭計;奸狡。⑤ **a.** 船。 **b.** 船的集合稱。The harbor is full of all kinds of *craft*. 這港口泊滿各種船舶。⑥ **a.** 飛機。 **b.** 飛機的集合稱。arts and crafts*** 美術與工藝。***the gentle craft*** 釣魚術;釣魚同好。—*v.t.* 靠技術製作;精製。 「carrier).」

craft carrier 航空母艦(=aircraft

craft·i·ly [ˈkræftılı; ˈkrɑːftili] *adv.* 狡猾地;詭詐地。 「*n.* 狡猾;詭詐。」

craft·i·ness [ˈkræftınıs; ˈkrɑːftinis]

crafts·man [ˈkræftsmən; ˈkrɑːftsmən] *n.*, *pl.* **-men.** ①工匠;手工匠;手藝精巧的人。②藝術家 (=artist).

crafts·man·like [ˈkræftsmən,laɪk; ˈkrɑːftsmənlaik] *adj.* 表露手藝的;精巧的。

crafts·man·ship [ˈkræftsmən,ʃɪp; ˈkrɑːftsmənʃip] *n.* 技巧; 技術。

craft union 同業工會。

craft·work [ˈkræftwɜk; ˈkrɑːftwəːk] *n.* ①工藝(尤指手工藝)。②(手)工藝品。

***craft·y** [ˈkræftɪ; ˈkrɑːfti] *adj.*, **craft·i·er, craft·i·est.** 狡猾的;善騙人的。He is as *crafty* as a fox. 他狡猾如狐狸。

***crag** [kræg; kræg] *n.* 峭壁;危岩。

crag·ged [ˈkrægɪd; ˈkrægid] *adj.* 多峭壁的;崎嶇的。—**ly,** *adv.* —**ness,** *n.*

crag·gy [ˈkrægɪ; ˈkrægi] *adj.*, **-gi·er, -gi·est.** ①多峭壁的;崎嶇的。②粗的。③暴躁的。—**crag·gi·ly,** *adv.* —**crag·gi·ness,** *n.*

crags·man [ˈkrægzmən; ˈkrægzmən] *n.*, *pl.* **-men.** 善於攀登危岩、峭壁者。

crake [krek; kreik] *n.*, *pl.* **crake, crakes,** *v.*, **craked, crak·ing.** —*n.* ①秧鷄。②秧鷄之叫聲。—*v.i.* 像秧鷄似的叫。

cram [kræm; kræm] *v.*, **crammed, cram·ming,** *n.* —*v.t.* ①塡塞; 塞入。②充滿;塞滿;擁擠。③吃得太快或太多。④〖俗〗倉卒用功,預備考試;匆匆記誦。⑤灌滿;注滿(知識)。—*v.i.* ①貪食。②倉卒準備應試〖常up〗. ***cram*** (***a thing***) ***down one's throat*** 反覆對人說(某事)。***cram oneself*** 塞滿肚皮。***cram up*** (***a subject***) 强記。—*n.* ①擁擠。②倉卒用功。—**ming·ly,** *adv.*

cram·bo [ˈkræmbo; ˈkræmbou] *n.* ①索韻遊戲。②同韻字;韻語。 「*adj.* 充滿。」

cram-full [ˈkræmˈfʊl; ˈkræmˈful]

cram·mer [ˈkræmɚ; ˈkræmə] *n.* ①倉卒用功應付考試的學生。②倉卒將知識灌輸學生以應付考試的教師。 「塡鴨式之教育。」

cram·ming [ˈkræmɪŋ; ˈkræmiŋ] *n.*

cramp¹ [kræmp; kræmp] *n.* ①抽筋; 痙攣。②(*pl.*) 腹部絞痛;發痧。③(*pl.*) 月經痛。—*v.t.* 使抽筋。

cramp²** *n.* ①鐵搭;鐵箍;夾子。②約束(之事物)。—*v.t.* ①以鐵箍扣緊。②妨礙; 阻止; 限制;抑制。③監禁;約束。④使(車前輪)向右或向左。cramp one's style*** 因受阻礙而無法施展。—*adj.* ①狹窄的;受限制的。②(字體的)潦草難認的;難解的。

cramped [kræmpt; kræmpt] *adj.* ①狹窄的。②偏狹的。③(字體)難辨認的。

cramp·fish [ˈkræmp,fɪʃ; ˈkræmpfiʃ] *n.*, *pl.* **-fish, -fish·es.** 電魚。(亦作 **electric ray, torpedo fish**)

cramp iron 鐵搭;大鉗。

cram·pon [ˈkræmpən; ˈkræmpən] *n.* ①(用以起重之)鐵鉤。②(常 *pl.*) 靴鐵(防滑用)。③〖植物〗用以攀緣之氣根。(亦作 **crampoon**)

cran·age [ˈkrenɪdʒ; ˈkreinidʒ] *n.* ①起重機之使用。②使用起重機之費用。

cran·ber·ry [ˈkræn,bɛrɪ; ˈkrænbəri] *n.*, *pl.* **-ries,** *v.* —*n.*蔓越橘。—*v.i.*採蔓越橘。

crane** [kren; krein] *n.*, *v.*, **craned, cran·ing.** —*n.* ①〖動物〗鶴。②起重機;活動吊鉤。floating crane*** 水上起重機。***gantry crane*** 高架移動起重機。***hammer*** (or ***hammer-head***) ***crane*** 鎚形起重機。***water crane*** 水力起重機。—*v.t.* ①以起重機搬動。②伸(頸)。—*v.i.* ①(鶴般)伸頸。②〖俚〗躊躇。

crane fly 似大蚊之蠅。

crane's-bill [ˈkrenz,bɪl; ˈkreinzbil] *n.* 〖植物〗牻牛兒苗。(亦作 **cranesbill**)

crane ship 起重機船。

cra·ni·al ['krenɪəl; 'kreinjəl] *adj.* 頭蓋骨的。

cra·ni·ate ['krenɪɪt; 'kreiniit] *adj.* 有頭蓋骨的; 有脊椎骨的。—*n.* 有頭蓋骨之動物;脊椎動物。

cra·ni·ol·o·gist [ˌkrenɪ'ɑlədʒɪst; ˌkreini'ɔlədʒist] *n.* 頭蓋學家;頭蓋骨研究者。

cra·ni·ol·o·gy [ˌkrenɪ'ɑlədʒɪ; ˌkreini'ɔlədʒi] *n.* 頭蓋學;人類頭蓋骨研究。

cra·ni·om·e·ter [ˌkrenɪ'ɑmətɚ; ˌkreini'ɔmitə] *n.* 頭蓋測量器。

cra·ni·om·e·try [ˌkrenɪ'ɑmətrɪ; ˌkreini'ɔmitri] *n.* 頭蓋測量學。—**cra·ni·o·met·ri·cal,** *adj.*

cra·ni·um ['krenɪəm; 'kreinjəm] *n., pl.* **-ni·a** [-nɪə; -niə]. 頭蓋;頭蓋骨。

crank** [kræŋk; kræŋk] *n.* ①〖機械〗曲柄。②(言語、思想等之)反覆無常;怪異之行動或思想。③〖美俗〗瘋狂或古怪的人。④〖美俗〗暴躁的人。—*adj.* ①〖航海〗不穩的;易翻的。②活潑的; 有精神的。③困難的。④〖主蘇〗彎曲的。⑤狀況不佳的; 鬆弛的。—*v.t.* ①製成曲柄形。②裝以曲柄。③以曲柄轉搖。④加速。—*v.i.* ①搖曲柄。②彎曲而行。crank out*** 機械地完成或推出。

crank·case ['kræŋkˌkes; 'kræŋkkeis] *n.* 〖機械〗曲軸箱。

crank·i·ly ['kræŋkɪlɪ; 'kræŋkili] *adv.* ①任性地;暴躁地。②搖盪不穩地。③鬆弛地。④古怪地。

crank·i·ness ['kræŋkɪnɪs; 'kræŋkinis] *n.* ①任性; 暴躁; 易怒。②搖盪; 易覆。③不穩;鬆弛。④古怪;奇癖。

cran·kle ['kræŋkl; 'kræŋkl] *v.,* **-kled, -kling,** *n.* —*v.i.* & *v.t.* 彎曲。—*n.* 彎曲。

crank·pin ['kræŋkˌpɪn; 'kræŋkpin] *n.* 〖機械〗曲柄針;曲柄梢。

crank·shaft ['kræŋkˌʃæft; 'kræŋkʃɑːft] *n.* 〖機械〗機軸。

crank·y ['kræŋkɪ; 'kræŋki] *adj.,* **crank·i·er, crank·i·est.** ①任性的;暴躁的;壞脾氣的。②〖航海〗搖蕩不穩的;易翻覆的。③(建築物、機器等) 不穩的; 鬆弛的。④奇癖的; 奇怪的;有怪而愚的念頭的。⑤彎彎曲曲的。

cran·nied ['krænɪd; 'krænid] *adj.* 有裂縫的。

cran·ny ['krænɪ; 'kræni] *n., pl.* **-nies,** *v.,* **-nied, -ny·ing.** —*n.* 裂縫;裂隙。—*v.i.* ①起裂縫。②經裂縫等而入。

crap [kræp; kræp] *v.i.,* **crapped, crapping.** ①〖鄙〗排泄。②〖俚〗做愚事。

crape [krep; kreip] *n., v.t.,* **craped, crap·ing.** =**crepe.**

crape·hang·er ['krepˌhæŋɚ; 'kreipˌhæŋə] *n.* 〖俚〗悲觀者;澆冷水者;掃興者。(亦作 **crepehanger**)

crape myrtle 〖植物〗紫薇。

craps [kræps; kræps] *n.* 〖美〗雙骰子的賭博。(亦作 **crap game, crapshooting**)

crap·shoot·er ['kræpˌʃutɚ; 'kræpˌʃuːtə] *n.* 賭雙骰 (craps) 之人。

crap·u·lence ['kræpjʊləns; 'kræpjuləns] *n.* ①過量飲食所致之病。②飲食無度;酗酒。

crap·u·lent ['kræpjʊlənt; 'kræpjulənt] *adj.* =**crapulous.**

crap·u·lous ['kræpjʊləs; 'kræpjuləs] *adj.* 過量飲食的;酗酒的。

crap·y ['krepɪ; 'kreipi] *adj.* 似縐紗的;縐褶的。

***crash¹** [kræʃ; kræʃ] *n.* ①突然的轟聲;破碎聲;砰磅聲。The dishes fell with a *crash.* 盤碟墮地作砰磅聲。②飛機的墜落或不慎降落; 碰撞; 猛撞。③失敗; 破產。stock market *crash.* 股票行情大跌價。—*v.t.* ①猛使破裂;猛使破碎。②猛力前進〖in, through, out〗. to *crash* one's way through a thicket. 向叢林猛進。③〖俗〗不買票進(場)。to *crash* the gate (*or* a party). 不買票進門;未經邀請而擅自參加集會;不請而至。④〖航空〗使(飛機)緊急降落或墜毀。—*v.i.* ①打碎;撞碎。②(飛機) 迫降;墜毀。The airplane *crashed* on a hillside. 飛機在山邊墜毀。③衝撞作聲。④轟然作響。⑤闖。⑥失敗 (指金錢與商業)。—*adj.* 全力以赴的;緊急的。

crash² *n.* (用作毛巾或窗帘等之)粗布。

crash boat 空難救助船。

crash dive (潛艇之)緊急潛水。

crash-dive ['kræʃ'daɪv; 'kræʃ'daiv] *v.i.* (潛艇)緊急潛水。—*v.t.* (飛機)向…俯衝。

crash·er ['kræʃɚ; 'kræʃə] *n.* ①猛力碰擊之人或物; 發猛烈聲響的東西。②〖俚〗= **gate crasher.**

crash helmet (警察、摩托車騎士等所戴用之)安全帽。

crash·ing ['kræʃɪŋ; 'kræʃiŋ] *adj.* ①非凡的;異常的。②徹底的;絕對的。

crash-land ['kræʃˌlænd; 'kræʃlænd] *v.t.* & *v.i.* 〖航空〗(使飛機) 緊急降落。—**ing,** *n.*

crash truck (or **wagon**) 空難救助車。

crash·wor·thy ['kræʃˌwɝðɪ; 'kræʃˌwəːði] *adj.* 打不碎的。

cra·sis ['kresɪs; 'kreisis] *n., pl.* **-ses** [-siz; -siːz]. ①〖文法〗母音縮合;二母音之綴合。②體質;氣質。

crass [kræs; kræs] *adj.* 愚蠢的;笨的。—**ly,** *adv.* —**ness,** *n.*

cras·si·tude ['kræsəˌtjud; 'kræsitjuːd] *n.* 粗大;愚鈍。

-crat 〖字尾〗表"參與或支持某種政府或政治者"之義, 如: democrat.

crate [kret; kreit] *n., v.,* **crat·ed, crat·ing.** —*n.* ①板條箱。②〖美俚〗舊汽車;破飛機。—*v.t.* 裝入大板條箱。

cra·ter ['kretɚ; 'kreitə] *n.* ①火山口。②(爆炸炸成的)彈坑。③(C-)〖天文〗巨爵座。—*v.i.* 成坑狀;成坑。—*v.t.* 使成坑。

cra·ter·i·form [krə'tɛrɪfɔrm; 'kreitərifɔːm] *adj.* 似火山口的;漏斗狀的。

crater lake 火山口形成的深湖。

crat·er·wall ('kretɚ'wɔl; 'kreitə'wɔːl] *n.* 火口壁。

C-ra·tion ['siˌræʃən; 'siːˌræʃən] *n.* 〖美軍〗丙種口糧(罐裝和包裝的野戰乾糧)。

cra·vat [krə'væt; krə'væt] *n., v.,* **-vat·ted, -vat·ting.** —*n.* ①領結。②領巾。—*v.t.* 使穿有領結之服裝;使結領結。

***crave** [krev; kreiv] *v.,* **craved, crav·ing.** —*v.t.* ①渴望;熱望。②請求;懇求。③要求。④〖主蘇〗向…討債。—*v.i.* 渴望〖for, after〗. to *crave* for good food. 渴望好食物。

cra·ven ['krevən; 'kreivən] *adj.* 懦弱的;怯懦的;膽小的。—*n.* 懦夫。***cry craven*** 投降。—**ly,** *adv.*

crav·en·ette [ˌkrævə'nɛt; ˌkrævə'net] *n.* 一種防水布。—*v.t.* 施防水處理於…。

cra·ven·heart·ed ['krevən'hɑrtɪd; 'kreivn'hɑːtid] *adj.* 怯懦的;膽小的。

crav·ing ['krevɪŋ; 'kreiviŋ] *n.* 熱望;懇求。—*adj.* 熱望的。—**ly,** *adv.* —**ness,** *n.*

craw [krɔ; krɔː] *n.* ①(鳥或昆蟲之)嗉囊。②任何動物之胃。***stick in one's craw*** 不能容忍;受不了。

craw·fish ['krɔˌfɪʃ; 'krɔːfiʃ] *n., pl.*

-fish·es, -fish, *v.* —*n.* ①小龍蝦。②〖美俗〗退縮者。—*v.i.* 〖俗〗撤退;退縮〖常 out〗.

*__crawl¹__ [krɔl;krɔ:l] *v.i.* ①爬;爬行。Worms and snakes *crawl.* 蟲類和蛇爬行。②匍匐。③徐行;緩行。④充滿爬行的東西。The ground was *crawling* with ants. 滿地都是螞蟻在爬行。⑤感覺若有蟲爬。⑥(以不光明的行動)鑽營。⑦用自由式游。—*v.t.* ①行於…之上。②〖俚〗責怪。—*n.* ①爬行;匍匐。②徐行;緩行。to go at a *crawl.* 匍匐而行。③自由式(游泳)。***go for a crawl*** 去散步。***the crawl*** 自由式游法。

crawl² *n.* 淺水中的圍籬(用以範圍龍蝦等)。

crawl·er ['krɔlɚ;'krɔ:lə] *n.* ①爬行者;匍匐者。②爬行動物;爬蟲。③懶人;賤卑者。④〖美俗〗跛脚乞丐。⑤〖英俗〗沿街緩行兜攬生意的出租汽車。⑥(常 *pl.*)(幼兒之)罩服。⑦自由式之游泳者。

crawl·y ['krɔlɪ;'krɔ:li] *adj.*, **crawl·i·er, crawl·i·est.** 〖俗〗有蟲爬肌膚之感的;悚然的。

cray·fish ['kre,fɪʃ; 'kreifiʃ] *n., pl.* **-fish·es, -fish.** 小龍蝦。(亦作 **crawfish**)

*__cray·on__ ['kreən;'kreiən] *n., v.,* **-oned, -on·ing.** —*n.* ①有色的粉筆;蠟筆;炭筆。②此種筆作的畫。—*v.t.* ①以此種筆畫。②策劃。

*__craze__ [krez; kreiz] *n., v.,* **crazed, craz·ing.** —*n.* ①爲時不久的强烈興趣。②一時的風尙。Gliding is the latest *craze.* 駕滑翔機爲最近流行的玩意兒。③顚狂;瘋狂。④陶器之裂痕。—*v.t.* ①使發狂。②使(陶、瓷器)生裂痕。—*v.i.* ①發狂。②破裂。

*__cra·zy__ ['krezɪ; 'kreizi] *adj.,* **-zi·er, -zi·est,** *adv., n., pl.* **-zi·es.** —*adj.* ①顚狂的;發狂的。to be *crazy* with pain. 因痛苦而發狂。②〖俗〗狂熱的。He is *crazy* about swimming. 他極好游泳。③不穩固的;搖搖欲墜的。④彎彎曲曲的。⑤混亂的。⑥不實際的。⑦橫衝直闖的。⑧〖俚〗了不起的;好極的。That's *crazy,* man, *crazy.* 那眞是妙極了,伙計,妙極了。⑨奇特的。⑩衰弱的;有病的。***crazy as a bedbug*** 〖美〗非常靠不住。***like crazy*** 〖俚〗極度;非常起勁或賣力。—*adv.*①〖俚〗非常地;極度地。②〖俚〗瘋狂地。—*n.* 〖俚〗性情怪異之人。—**cra·zi·ly,** *adv.* —**cra·zi·ness,** *n.*

crazy bone 上膊骨(尺骨神經通過處,觸之則臂及手常會發麻)。(亦作 **funny bone**)

crazy cat 〖美〗笨蛋;傻瓜。

crazy house 〖俚〗瘋人院;精神病醫院。

crazy pavement (花園中)碎紋石道。

crazy quilt ①碎布縫成的坐褥。②雜亂不完整之物。

*__creak__ [krik; kri:k] *v.i.* ①作輾軋聲。②勉强進行或發展。—*v.t.* 使發輾軋聲。—*n.* 輾軋聲。

creak·y ['krikɪ; 'kri:ki] *adj.* ①吱吱作響的。②搖搖欲墜的。

‡**cream** [krim;kri:m] *n.* ①乳酪;乳脂;乳皮。②乳酪所製的食品。ice *cream.* 冰淇淋。③滑潤皮膚的油質製品。face *cream.* 面霜。④精華;最好的部分。⑤乳酪色;淡黃色。***cream of the crop*** 最佳部分。***get the cream of*** 提取…之精華;拔萃。—*v.i.* ①成乳皮。②起泡沫。—*v.t.* ①撇(乳酪);掬取(乳皮)。②加乳酪於(茶、咖啡等)。③擷取精華。④和以奶油、糖等使成乳脂狀的東西。⑤使起泡沫。⑥塗以面霜。⑦〖俚〗痛擊;使受重大損害。—*adj.* ①含乳酪或牛奶的;像乳酪的。②乳酪色的;淡黃色的。

cream·col·o(u)red ['krim,kʌlɚd; 'kri:m,kʌləd] *adj.* 乳酪色的;淡黃色的。

cream·cups ['krim,kʌps;'kri:mkʌps] *n., pl.* **-cups.** 一種罌粟科植物。

cream·er ['krimɚ; 'kri:mə] *n.* ①裝乳酪之小瓶。②乳酪分離器。③冷凍乳酪之冰箱。④撇取乳酪之人或器具。

cream·er·y ['krimərɪ; 'kri:məri] *n., pl.* **-er·ies.** ①乳酪製造廠。②乳酪販賣處。

cream puff 〖俚〗①懦夫。②不足取之物。③保養得極好的舊車。④乳油卷。

cream separator 乳酪分離器。

*__cream·y__ ['krimɪ; 'kri:mi] *adj.,* **cream·i·er, cream·i·est.** 似乳酪的;含乳酪的。—**cream·i·ness,** *n.*

crease¹ [kris; kri:s] *n., v.,* **creased, creas·ing.** —*n.* ①摺痕;皺摺。②〖板球〗投球者與擊球者間的界線。—*v.t.* ①使皺;使有摺痕。②使擦傷。—*v.i.* 變皺。—**creas·y,** *adj.* —**less,** *adj.*

crease² *n.* =creese.

‡**cre·ate** [krɪ'et; kri(:)'eit] *v.,* **-at·ed, -at·ing.** —*v.t.* ①創造;建立。She *created* this garden in the desert. 她在沙漠裏創造了這花園。②製造;產生;致使。Do not *create* a disturbance. 不要製造麻煩。③封爵。—*v.i.* ①創造;創作。②〖英俚〗發牢騷。

cre·a·tin(e) ['kriə,tin; 'kri:ətin] *n.* 〖生化〗肌(氨)酸。

*__cre·a·tion__ [krɪ'eʃən; kri(:)'eiʃən] *n.* ①(指上帝的)創造。②世界;宇宙;萬物。Man is sometimes called the lord of *creation.* 人有時稱爲萬物之靈。③開創;創立;創作;產生;致使。④封爵。⑤作品。***the Creation*** 上帝創造天地。—**al,** —**ar·y,** *adj.*

cre·a·tion·ism [krɪ'eʃən,ɪzəm;kri(:)'eiʃənizəm] *n.* ①上帝創造人類靈魂說。②〖生物〗特創說。

*__cre·a·tive__ [krɪ'etɪv; kri(:)'eitiv] *adj.* 有創造力的;創造的;創作的。*creative* work. 創作。—*n.* 〖美〗有創造力的人。—**ly,** *adv.* —**ness,** *n.*

cre·a·tiv·i·ty [,krie'tɪvətɪ; ,kri:ei'tiviti] *n.* 創造力。

*__cre·a·tor__ [krɪ'etɚ; kri(:)'eitə] *n.* 創造者;創作者。***the Creator*** 上帝。

‡**crea·ture** ['kritʃɚ; 'kri:tʃə] *n.* ①人;動物。a lovely *creature.* 可愛的人(指女人)。②傀儡;聽人驅使者;依人爲生者。③受造之物。④(常 the-)〖主方〗酒;威士忌。***a drop of the creature.*** 一滴威士忌酒。***creature comforts*** 物質的享受(尤指食物)。—**crea·tur·al,** —**ly,** *adj.*

crèche [kreʃ;kreiʃ] 〖法〗*n.* ①託兒所。②棄兒教養院。

cre·dence ['kridn̩s; 'kri:dəns] *n.* ①相信。②可信任。③憑證;證件。④〖宗教〗置放聖餐、聖餅的小桌。***letter of credence*** 介紹信;(大、公使等所呈遞的)國書。

cre·den·tial [krɪ'dɛnʃəl; kri'denʃəl] *n.* (常 *pl.*)證件;外國使臣所遞的國書;介紹信。

cred·i·bil·i·ty [,krɛdə'bɪlətɪ; ,kredi'biliti] *n.* 確實性;可靠性。

cred·i·ble ['krɛdəbl̩; 'kredəbl] *adj.* 可信的;可靠的。

cred·i·bly ['krɛdəblɪ; 'kredəbli] *adv.* 可信地;確實地。

‡**cred·it** ['krɛdɪt; 'kredit] *n.* ①信託;信任。②信用。His *credit* is good. 他的信用好。③存款;貸方。He placed one thousand dollars to my *credit.* 他存一千元於我的帳上。④延緩付款的期限。90 days' *credit.* 90 天的延緩付款期限。⑤貸款。⑥名譽;名望;光榮。⑦帶給榮譽之事物。⑧學分。He needs three more *credits* to graduate. 他需要再修三個學分始能畢業。⑨(戲劇、電影等)對原作者及

其他有貢獻者的謝啓或姓名表。*add to one's credit* 增加一人之聲譽。*be to one's credit* 是某人的光榮。*do one credit* (or *do credit to one*) 致譽;成名。His new book *does him credit.* 他的新書爲人稱譽。*get* (or *have*) *the credit of* 得到…的光榮或名譽。*give* (*a person*) *credit for* 以爲(某人)是。*give credit to* 相信;信賴。*letter of credit* 信用狀。*on credit* 掛帳;賒帳。*put* (or *place*) *credit in* 相信。*reflect credit on* 使…光榮;爲…增光。*take* (or *get*) *credit for* 因…而獲得光榮或盛譽。*take credit to oneself* 把功勞歸於自己。—*v.t.* ①相信;信賴。to *credit* a story. 相信一個故事。②記於帳簿之貸方;存入貸方。to *credit* a man with $5 (to *credit* $5 to a man). 於貸方記明某人存款五元。③給予學分。④歸功於;讚頌。He is *credited* with the invention. 那發明該歸功於他。*credit to a person* 相信某人有…;將…歸功於某人。*credit* (*a person*) *with* 相信(某人)有…。—**less,** *adj.*

cred·it·a·ble ['krɛdɪtəbl̩; 'kreditəbl] *adj.* ①可稱譽的;值得稱贊的;帶來聲譽光榮的。②可歸功(於某人或某事)的。—**ness,** *n.*

cred·it·a·bly ['krɛdɪtəblɪ; 'kreditəbli] *adv.* 可稱譽地;有好名聲地。

credit agency 徵信所。

credit card 信用卡;記帳卡。

credit hour 〖教育〗學分。

credit insurance 債權保險。

credit line 作者姓名或來源附註。

credit man 信用部工作員。

***cred·i·tor** ['krɛdɪtɚ; 'kreditə] *n.* 債主;債權人;貸方。

credit rating 信用估計。

credit sale 賒賣。

credit standing 信譽。

credit union 信用合作社。

cre·do ['krido; 'kri:dou] *n., pl.* **-dos.** ①〖宗教〗信條。②任何信條。

cre·du·li·ty [krə'dulətɪ; kri'dju:liti] *n.* 輕信;易信。

cred·u·lous ['krɛdʒələs; 'kredjuləs] *adj.* ①輕信的。②有輕信特徵的。—**ly,** *adv.* —**ness,** *n.*

Cree [kri; kri:] *n., pl.* **Cree, Crees.** ①(北美印第安之)克里族人。②該族之語言。

***creed** [krid; kri:d] *n.* ①〖宗教〗教條。②任何信仰的信條。③宗教;宗派。*the Creed* (or *the Apostles' Creed*) 使徒信條。

Creek [krik; kri:k] *n.* 克里克聯盟之印第安人(現居於美國 Oklahoma).

***creek** [krik; kri:k] *n.* ①小溪;小河。②〖主英〗小港;小灣。③〖主英〗祕密的角落。*up the creek* 〖美俚〗在困境。—**y,** *adj.*

creel [kril; kri:l] *n.* ①柳條魚籃。②〖紡織〗線軸架。—*v.t.* 捕到;捉到。

***creep** [krip; kri:p] *v.,* **crept, creep·ing,** *n.* —*v.i.* ①爬行;匍匐。A tiger *creeps* toward its prey. 一隻老虎向着它的獵物爬行。②蔓延;盤旋。The grapevine *creeps* along the wall. 葡萄藤沿牆蔓延。③皮膚有蟲爬的感覺。④緩行。⑤(時間、歲月等)不知不覺地來臨或消逝。Time *creeps* on. 時間在不知不覺中過去。⑥潛行。⑦逐漸變形。—*n.* ①爬行;緩慢地移動。traffic moving at a *creep.* 緩慢流動的交通。②(*pl.*)若有蟲爬的感覺。③變形;蠕動。④〖俚〗討厭的傢伙。*give one the creeps* 使某人驚恐、戰慄、或厭惡。

creep·er ['kripɚ; 'kri:pə] *n.* ①匍匐之人或物;爬蟲。②蔓草。③〖動物〗旋木雀。④鐵鉤;鐵耙。⑤繫於鞋底用以防滑之有釘鐵板。

creeper title 電影電視等由下方顯現而向上緩慢移動的字幕。(亦作**creeping title**)

creep·hole ['krip,hol; 'kri:phoul] *n.* ①(動物之)竄匿處;逃穴。②託辭;藉口。

creep·ing ['kripɪŋ; 'kri:piŋ] *adj.* ①爬行的;匍匐的;遍地蔓延的。*creeping* things. 爬蟲類。②緩慢的;悄悄的。③諂媚的;奉承的。④悚然的。

creeping paralysis 漸次性癱瘓;「漸漸的癱木。」

creep·y ['kripɪ; 'kri:pi] *adj.,* **creep·i·er, creep·i·est.** ①爬行的;匍匐的。②皮膚上有蟲在爬行之感的;悚然的。③緩行的;蠕動的。④鬼鬼祟祟的。—**creep·i·ly,** *adv.*

creep·y-crawl·y ['kripɪ'krɔlɪ; 'kri:pi'krɔ:li] *n.* 〖英俗〗爬蟲。

creese [kris; kri:s] *n.* (馬來亞人用之)「短劍。」

cre·mains [krɪ'menz; kri'meinz] *n. pl.* 人體火化後的骨灰。

cre·mate ['krimet; kri'meit] *v.t.,* **-mat·ed, -mat·ing.** 火葬;燒成灰。

cre·ma·tion [krɪ'meʃən; kri'meiʃən] *n.* ①火葬。②焚毀。

cre·ma·tion·ist [krɪ'meʃənɪst; kri'meiʃənist] *n.* 主張火葬者。

cre·ma·tor ['krimetɚ; kri'meitə] *n.* ①燒屍工人。②火葬爐;垃圾焚化爐。

cre·ma·to·ri·um [,krimə'torɪəm; ,kremə'tɔ:riəm] *n., pl.* **-ri·a** [-rɪə; -riə]. 〖英〗火葬場。(亦作 **crematory**)

cre·ma·to·ry ['krimə,torɪ; 'kremətəri] *n., pl.* **-ries,** *adj.* —*n.* 火葬場;焚屍爐。—*adj.* 火葬的。

crème [krɛm; krem] 〖法〗*n.* ①=**cream.** 「②芬芳之烈酒。」

Cre·mo·na [krɪ'monə; kri'mounə] *n.* ①格里摩那(義大利北部之一城市)。②Cremona 城所製之小提琴。

cre·nate ['krinet; 'kri:neit] *adj.* 〖植物〗(葉等)鈍鋸齒狀的。(亦作 **crenated**)

cre·na·tion [krɪ'neʃən; kri'neiʃən] *n.* 鈍鋸齒狀。

cren·a·ture ['krɛnətʃɚ; 'krenətʃə] *n.* ①葉緣之鈍鋸齒狀突出。②葉緣之兩鈍鋸齒間的凹缺。

cren·el ['krɛnl̩; 'krenl] *n.* 城或牆頂之「垛口;槍眼;砲門。」

cren·el·(l)ate ['krɛnl̩,et; 'krenileit] *v.t.,* **-(l)at·ed, -(l)at·ing.** ①開以垛口;設槍眼或砲門。②〖建築〗使成鈍鋸齒形。

cren·el·(l)a·tion [,krɛnl̩'eʃən; ,kreni'leiʃən] *n.* 開垛口;裝設槍眼或砲門。

cren·el·et ['krɛnlɪt; 'krenilit] *n.* 小垛口。

Cre·ole ['kriol; 'kri:oul] *n.* ①生長於西印度羣島和西屬美洲的歐洲人後裔。②美國路易西安那州之法國人後裔。③(c-)沿墨西哥灣各州歐洲人與黑人之混血兒。④上述各州中所用的法國方言。—*adj.* Creole 的。

cre·o·sol ['kriə,sol; 'kri:əsɔl] *n.* 〖化〗木餾油醇;木焦油醇(用作防腐劑)。

cre·o·sote ['kriə,sot; 'kri(:)əsout] *n.* 木餾油;木焦油(防腐劑)。—*v.t.* 以木餾油處理。

crepe, crêpe [krep; kreip] *n., v.,* **creped, crep·ing.** —*n.* ①縐紗;縐綢。②縐紋紙。③黑喪章;孝布。—*v.t.* ①使縐。②覆以縐紗。③使佩帶孝布。

crepe de Chine 廣東縐紗。

crepe·hang·er ['krep,hæŋɚ; 'kreip,hæŋə] *n.* 悲觀者。

crepe paper 縐紋紙。

crepe rubber 一種做鞋底的生膠。

crep·i·tant ['krɛpətənt; 'krepitənt] *adj.* 作爆裂聲的。

crep·i·tate ['krɛpə,tet; 'krepiteit] *v.i.*, **-tat·ed, -tat·ing.** 作一連串之小爆裂聲。—**crep·i·ta·tion,** *n.*

cré·pon ['krepɑn; 'krepɔ̃:ŋ] 〖法〗 *n.* 一種似縐紗但質地較厚之織物。

crept [krɛpt; krept] *v.* pt. & pp. of **creep.**

cre·pus·cu·lar [krɪ'pʌskjələ˞; kri'pʌskjulə] *adj.* ①晨曦的; 黃昏的; 朦朧的。②〖動物〗在晨曦或薄暮活動的。③曙光時代的;未充分開化的。

cre·pus·cule [krɪ'pʌskjul; 'krepəskju:l] *n.* 黃昏;朦朧。

cres., cresc. crescendo.

cre·scen·do [krə'ʃɛndo; kri'ʃendou] *adj., adv., n., pl.* **-dos.** —*adj.* & *adv.* 漸強的(地);漸響的(地)。—*n.* ①〖音樂〗(音之)漸響;漸次加强。②漸趨高潮。③高潮。

cres·cent** ['krɛsn̩t; 'kresnt] *n.* ①新月;彎月;半鈎月。②新月形的東西。③回教勢力;土耳其帝國勢力。the Cross and the Crescent*** 基督教與回教。—*adj.* ①新月形的。②逐漸生長的;逐漸增加的。

cres·cent·ade [,krɛsn̩t'ed; ,kresn'teid] *n.* 土耳其帝國時代之回教軍;新月軍。

cres·cent-shaped ['krɛsn̩t,ʃept; 'kresnt-ʃeipt] *adj.* 新月形的。

cre·sol ['krisol; 'kri:soul] *n.* 〖化〗甲酚。

cress [krɛs; kres] *n.* 〖植物〗水芹;水堇。

cres·set ['krɛsɪt; 'kresit] *n.* 篝燈; 標燈;號燈。

***crest** [krɛst; krest] *n.* ①鳥的冠。②盔上的裝飾(如羽毛);盔。③頂。④盾形徽號、紋章等上端的飾章。⑤馬、狗等的頸脊。⑥動物頸脊上長的毛(如馬鬃)。⑦任何物體之頂部。⑧洪水之最高點(如河中水位)。⑨同類事物中之最高或最佳者。—*v.t.* ①加以頂飾。②在…之頂; 爲…之頂。③到達…之頂。—*v.i.* ①形成頂;上升;(浪)起浪頭。②〖方〗傲然直立。

crest·ed ['krɛstɪd; 'krestid] *adj.* 有冠毛的;有頂飾的。

crest·fall·en ['krɛst,fɔlən; 'krest,fɔ:lən] *adj.* 垂頭喪氣的;沮喪的;氣餒的。

crest·less ['krɛstlɪs; 'krestlis] *adj.* ①無冠毛的;無頂飾的; 無飾章的。②卑賤的; 出身低下的。

cre·ta·ceous [krɪ'teʃəs; kri'teiʃəs] *adj.* ①白堊質的。②(C-)〖地質〗白堊紀的;白堊系的。—*n.* (C-)〖地質〗白堊紀;白堊系。

Cre·tan ['kritən; 'kri:tən] *adj.* 克里特島 (Crete) 的; 克里特島人的。—*n.* 克里特島人。

Crete [krit; kri:t] *n.* 克里特(地中海東部之一島,屬希臘)。

cre·tic ['kritɪk; 'kri:tik] *n.* 〖韻律〗揚抑揚的音步。—*adj.* 揚抑揚音步的。

cre·tin ['kritɪn; 'kretin] *n.* 矮呆病者;白癡。

cre·tin·ism ['kritɪn,ɪzəm; 'kretinizəm] *n.* 〖醫〗矮呆病;癡呆症。

cre·tin·ous ['kritɪnəs; 'kri:tinəs] *adj.* 矮呆病的;癡呆症的。

cre·tonne [krɪ'tɑn; kre'tɔn] *n.* (做窗帘等之)印花棉布。

cre·vasse [krə'væs; kri'væs] *n., v.,* **-vassed, -vass·ing.** —*n.* (冰河、堤壩等之)裂縫;罅隙。—*v.t.* 在…中造成裂縫。

crev·ice ['krɛvɪs; 'krevis] *n.* 裂縫;罅隙;破口。—**crev·iced,** *adj.*

crew**¹ [kru; kru:] *n.* ①水手;船員的全體(包括官長); 飛機上的全體機員。The *crew* abandoned the ship after a hard struggle. 經過一場艱苦奮鬥,全體船員放棄這船。②一羣共同工作的人。③一羣; 一組; 一羣暴民;一羣流氓。④划船隊的隊員。⑤團體划船比賽。crew cut*** 海軍髮式;平頭。—*v.t.* 用船員操作。—**less,** *adj.*

crew² *v.* pt. of **crow.**

crew·el ['kruəl; 'kru:il] *n.* 刺繡用之鬆細毛線。

crew·man ['krumən; 'kru:mən] *n., pl.* **-men.** 船員;機員。

crew·mate ['krumet; 'kru:meit] *n.* 同船(機)工作之船(機)員。

crib [krɪb; krib] *n., v.,* **cribbed, crib·bing.** —*n.* ①(嬰兒之)有欄小床。②小屋。③秣槽;芻槽;牛欄。④(貯藏穀物、鹽等之)木桶;倉。⑤〖俗〗(學生用之)逐字對照譯本。⑥〖俗〗剽竊; 抄襲(他人之文字或思想)。⑦〖俚〗保險箱。⑧狹窄之空間。⑨貯水庫。⑩(考試時之)夾帶。⑪建築用之木架。⑫礦坑內之護壁棚架。—*v.t.* ①關進(狹小地方); 拘禁。②裝設以秣槽。③偷; 剽竊。—*v.i.* ①剽竊; 抄襲。②〖俗〗翻譯時參考對照譯本。

crib·bage ['krɪbɪdʒ; 'kribidʒ] *n.* 一種紙牌戲。

crib·ber ['krɪbə˞; 'kribə] *n.* ①剽竊者;抄襲者;夾帶者。②咬槽之馬。

crib-bite ['krɪb,baɪt; 'kribbait] *v.i.,* **-bit, -bit·ten** or **-bit, -bit·ing.** (指馬)咬槽。

crib biting 馬咬食槽並吸氣出聲之惡癖。

crib note 考試時夾帶的紙條。(亦作 **crib sheet**)

crib·ri·form ['krɪbrɪ,fɔrm; 'kribrifɔ:m] *adj.* 篩狀的;有小孔的。

crib·work ['krɪb,wɜk; 'kribwə:k] *n.* 筏狀木排;(接頭處成直角的)筐籠工。

crick [krɪk; krik] *n.* 肌肉痙攣。—*v.t.* 引起痙攣;扭傷。

***crick·et**¹ ['krɪkɪt; 'krikit] *n.* 蟋蟀。

***crick·et**² *n.* ①板球(盛行於英國之戶外遊戲,雙方各十一人參加)。②〖俗〗公正; 運動精神。—*v.i.* 玩板球戲。—*adj.* 〖俗〗公正的;符合運動精神的。

***crick·et**³ *n.* 小脚凳。

crick·et·er ['krɪkɪtə˞; 'krikitə] *n.* 玩板球者。

cri·coid ['kraɪkɔɪd; 'kraikɔid] *adj.* 〖解剖〗環狀的。—*n.* 環狀軟骨。

cri·er ['kraɪə˞; 'kraiə] *n.* ①傳令員;叫賣者。②哭喊者。

crim. criminal.

‡**crime** [kraɪm; kraim] *n.* ①罪;犯罪行爲;罪行。to commit a *crime.* 犯罪。He was sent to prison for his *crimes.* 他因犯罪下獄。②罪惡;犯罪。③罪惡的行爲;錯誤的行爲(非犯罪行爲)。It would be a *crime* to send the boy out on such a cold, wet night. 在這麼寒冷的雨夜裏把孩子遣走是一種罪惡的行爲。—**ful,** *adj.* —**less,** *adj.*

Cri·me·a [kraɪ'miə, krɪ-; krai'miə, kri-] *n.* 克里米亞(蘇聯西南部黑海中一半島)。—**Cri·me·an,** *adj.*

crime-rid·den ['kraɪm,rɪdn̩; 'kraim-ridən] *adj.* 充滿犯罪行爲的。

***crim·i·nal** ['krɪmənl̩; 'kriminl] *n.* 罪犯;犯罪者。The *criminal* was sentenced to life imprisonment. 這罪犯被判終身監禁。—*adj.* ①犯罪的;犯法的。②與犯罪有關的。*criminal* cases. 刑事案件。③錯誤的;如罪惡的。—**ly,** *adv.*

criminal conversation 〖法律〗通姦。

crim·i·nal·ist ['krɪmənl̩ɪst; 'kriminəlist] *n.* 刑事專家;罪犯學者。

crim·i·nal·is·tics [,krɪmənl̩'ɪstɪks; ,kriminə'listiks] *n.* (作 *sing.*解)刑事學。

crim·i·nal·i·ty 〔ˌkrɪmə'nælətɪ; ˌkrimi'næliti〕 *n., pl.* **-ties.** ①犯罪;犯罪行爲。②有罪;犯罪性。
crim·i·nal·i·za·tion〔ˌkrɪmənəlaɪ'zeʃən;ˌkriminəlai'zeiʃən〕*n.* 使成爲犯罪行爲。
crim·i·nal·ize 〔'krɪmənḷˌaɪz; 'kriminəlaiz〕 *v.t.,* **-ized, -iz·ing.** ①使人犯罪。②宣布(某人)爲罪犯或宣布(某種行動)爲犯罪。
criminal law 刑法。
crim·i·nate 〔'krɪməˌnet; 'krimineit〕 *v.t.,* **-nat·ed, -nat·ing.** ①告發;使負罪;歸罪;定罪。②陷人於罪; 表示有罪; 牽累。③責備(行爲等)。—**crim·i·na·tion,** *n.*
crim·i·na·to·ry 〔'krɪmənəˌtorɪ; 'kriminətəri〕 *adj.* 使負罪的; 控告的; 責備的。(亦作 **criminative**)
crim·i·no·log·i·cal〔ˌkrɪmənə'lɑdʒɪkḷ; ˌkriminə'lɔdʒikl〕 *adj.* 犯罪學(上)的。
crim·i·nol·o·gist 〔ˌkrɪmə'nɑlədʒɪst; ˌkrimi'nɔlədʒist〕 *n.* 刑事學家。
crim·i·nol·o·gy 〔ˌkrɪmə'nɑlədʒɪ; ˌkrimi'nɔlədʒi〕 *n.* 犯罪學;刑事學。
crimp¹ 〔krɪmp; krimp〕 *v.t.* ①使摺縐。②使減少。③使(頭髮等)捲縮。—*n.* ①摺疊;摺縐。②摺縐物;波紋。③(*pl.*)鬈髮。***put a crimp in*** 〖美俗〗干涉;干擾;阻礙。—**er,** *n.*
crimp² *n.* 誘迫他人當兵之人; 兵販子。—*v.t.* 誘迫(人)充當水手或士兵。
crimping iron 鬈髮器;鬈髮夾子。
crim·ple 〔'krɪmpḷ; 'krimpl〕 *n., v.,* **-pled, -pling.** —*n.* 縐;摺痕。—*v.t. & v.i.* 縮緊;鬈縮。
crimp·y 〔'krɪmpɪ;'krimpi〕*adj.,* **crimp·i·er, crimp·i·est.** 有小褶的; 捲縮了的。
***crim·son** 〔'krɪmzn̩; 'krimzn〕 *n.* 深紅色。—*adj.* 深紅色的。—*v.t.* 使染爲深紅色。—*v.i.* 變爲深紅色;面赧。
cringe 〔krɪndʒ; krindʒ〕 *v.,* **cringed, cring·ing,** *n.* —*v.i.* ①畏縮;抖縮。②奉承;諂媚;卑躬。—*n.* 畏縮;奉承。
crin·gle 〔'krɪŋgḷ; 'kriŋgl〕 *n.* 〖航海〗帆緣之環孔;索眼。
cri·nite 〔'kraɪnaɪt; 'krainait〕 *adj.* ①有毛的。②有毛尾的。—*n.* 化石海百合。
crin·kle 〔'krɪŋkḷ; 'kriŋkl〕 *v.,* **-kled, -kling,** *n.* —*v.t. & v.i.* ①(使)縐;(使)縮。②(使)作沙沙聲;(使)作瑟瑟聲。—*n.* ①縐;波紋。②沙沙聲;瑟瑟聲。
crin·kly 〔'krɪŋklɪ;'kriŋkli〕*adj.,* **-kli·er, -kli·est.** 多皺褶的;起皺的;捲縮的;起伏的。
crin·kum-cran·kum 〔'krɪŋkəm'kræŋkəm; 'kriŋkəm'kræŋkəm〕 *n.* 〖俗〗多曲折之物;盤曲有趣之飾物。
cri·noid 〔'kraɪnɔɪd; 'krainɔid〕 *adj.* ①百合狀的。②〖動物〗海百合的。 —*n.* 〖動物〗海百合。
crin·o·lette 〔ˌkrɪnə'lɛt; ˌkrinə'let〕 *n.* 裙襯。
crin·o·line 〔'krɪnḷɪn; 'krinəli:n〕 *n.* ①襯布或襯架;裙襯。②帶襯的裙。
***crip·ple** 〔'krɪpḷ; 'kripl〕 *n., v.,* **-pled, -pling.** —*n.* 跛者;跛的人或動物。—*v.t.* ①使跛;使成殘廢。He was *crippled* in the war. 他在戰爭中變爲跛者。②使失戰鬥力;受損失;受損傷;削弱。The team was *crippled* by his absence. 他的缺席使這球隊實力削弱。
cris 〔krɪs; kris〕 *n.* =**creese.**
cri·sis** 〔'kraɪsɪs; 'kraisis〕 *n., pl.* **-ses** 〔-siz; -si:z〕. ①(疾病的)轉變期。②危機;難關;危急存亡之際。a political *crisis.* 政治上的危機。③(歷史上的)轉捩點; 決定性事件。bring to a crisis*** 使事情發展至非作決定不可的地步;使緊迫;使危急。
***crisp** 〔krɪsp; krisp〕 *adj.* (亦作 **crispy**) ①脆的;乾硬而易碎的。②新鮮的。③活潑的;明確的;爽快的。④起皺的;捲曲的;起波紋的。⑤新鮮而令人爽快的;使精神爽快的。*crisp* air. 新鮮宜人的空氣。—*v.i. & v.t.* 使脆;變得活潑爽朗;捲起。—**ly,** *adv.* —**ness,** *n.*
cris·pate 〔'krɪspet; 'krispeit〕 *adj.* 捲縮的;縐的。
cris·pa·tion 〔krɪs'peʃən; kris'peiʃən〕 *n.* ①捲縮。②(皮膚或肌肉上之)皺。
crisp·er 〔'krɪspɚ; 'krispə〕 *n.* ①使脆或捲曲之人或物。②捲髮夾。③冰箱內存放蔬菜水果的抽屜。
criss·cross 〔'krɪsˌkrɔs; 'kriskrɔs〕 *adj.* 作十字記號的;成十字狀的。—*adv.* 互相交叉。 —*v.t.* ①用十字線作記號; 交叉成爲十字狀。 ②來回旅行。 ③在…交織。—*v.i.* 來回交織。—*n.* 十字記號;交叉。
cris·tat·ed 〔'krɪstetɪd; 'kristeitid〕 *adj.* 有冠的;有冠狀突起的。(亦作 **cristate**)
cri·te·ri·on 〔kraɪ'tɪrɪən;krai'tiəriən〕 *n., pl.* **-ri·a** 〔-rɪə; -riə〕, **-ri·ons.** (評斷之)標準;定規;準繩。
***crit·ic** 〔'krɪtɪk; 'kritik〕 *n.* ①批評家;評論家。②非難者;吹毛求疵者。
***crit·i·cal** 〔'krɪtɪkḷ; 'kritikl〕 *adj.* ①吹毛求疵的。②長於批評或鑑定的; 有判斷力的。③危急的;生死關頭的。*critical* moment. 危機; 重要關頭。④決定性的; 重要的。⑤批評的;批判的。⑥危險的; 困難的。⑦〖物理〗**a.** 臨界的。**b.** 中肯的。—**ly,** *adv.* —**ness,** *n.*
critical angle 〖光學〗臨界角。
critical size 〖物理〗中肯大小。
critical temperature 〖物理〗臨界溫度。
critical velocity 〖物理〗①臨界速度。②中肯速度。
crit·ic·as·ter 〔'krɪtɪkˌæstɚ; 'kritikˌæstə〕 *n.* 卑劣之批評者。
***crit·i·cism** 〔'krɪtəˌsɪzəm; 'kritisizəm〕 *n.* ①吹毛求疵;非難。His *criticisms* robbed her of self-confidence. 他的吹毛求疵, 使她失去自信。②批評;評論;書評;批評的文章。③文藝批評的理論;評論或鑑定的法則。
***crit·i·cize** 〔'krɪtəˌsaɪz; 'kritisaiz〕 *v.t. & v.i.,* **-cized, -ciz·ing.** 批評;非難;吹毛求疵。His policies were severely *criticized.* 他的政策受到嚴酷的批評。(英亦作 **criticise**) —**crit·i·ciz·a·ble,** *adj.* —**crit·i·ciz·er,** *n.*
cri·tique 〔krɪ'tik; kri'ti:k〕 *n.* ①批評;評論。②批評法;評論技術。
***croak** 〔krok; krouk〕 *n.* ①(蛙、鴉等的)哇哇叫;嗄聲。②怨言;凶事之預報。—*v.t. & v.i.* ①哇哇叫;嗄聲。②預報凶事;抱怨。③悽慘地說;哭喪着說。④〖俚〗死;殺死。 —**er,** *n.* —**y,** *adj.*
Cro·at 〔'kroæt; 'krouət〕 *n.* Croatia 人或其語言。
Cro·a·tia 〔kro'eʃə; krou'eiʃjə〕 *n.* 克羅埃西亞(歐洲東南部一地區)。
Cro·a·tian 〔kro'eʃən; krou'eiʃjən〕 *adj.* Croatia 的。—*n.* Croatia 人或其語言。
cro·chet 〔*v.* kro'ʃe, *n.* 'krɑtʃɪt; 'krouʃei〕 *v.,* **-cheted** 〔-'ʃed; -ʃeid〕, **-chet·ing** 〔-'ʃeɪŋ; -ʃeiiŋ〕, *n.* —*v.t. & v.i.* 用鉤針織。—*n.* 鉤針織物。
crochet work 鉤針織品。
cro·cid·o·lite 〔kro'sɪdəˌlaɪt; krou'sidəlait〕 *n.* 〖礦〗青石棉;虎睛石。
crock¹ 〔krɑk;krɔk〕 *n.* ①瓦罐。②碎瓦片。

crock² *n.* ①廢馬;無用之人。②〖英俚〗殘廢人。—*v.t.* & *v.i.* 〖英〗(使)無用;(使)衰弱。

crock³ *n.* ①〖方〗煤煙; 油煙; 汚物。②從有色布上擦下來的顏料。—*v.t.* 〖方〗以油煙等汚損。—*v.i.* 〖方〗放出油煙或汚物。—**y,** *adj.*

crock·er·y 〔ˈkrakərɪ; ˈkrɔkəri〕 *n.* 陶器;瓦器。

crock·et 〔ˈkrakɪt; ˈkrɔkit〕 *n.* ①〖建築〗捲葉花樣或捲花形之浮雕。②雄鹿角端之節。

croc·o·dile** 〔ˈkrakəˌdaɪl; ˈkrɔkədail〕 *n.* ①鱷魚。②鱷魚皮。③假慈悲者。④〖英俗〗一縱列人（尤指女學童）。crocodile tears*** 假哭;假慈悲。***crocodile bird*** 鱷鳥。

croc·o·dil·i·an 〔ˌkrakəˈdɪlɪən; ˌkrɔkəˈdiliən〕 *adj.* ①鱷魚的;似鱷魚的。②假善的;假慈悲的。—*n.* 鱷魚類之動物;鱷。

cro·cus 〔ˈkrokəs; ˈkroukəs〕 *n., pl.* **cro·cus·es, cro·ci** 〔-saɪ; -sai〕. ①〖植物〗番紅花。②橘黃色。③磨光粉; 氧化鐵粉末。

crocus cloth 珠寶匠用以磨光珠寶之厚布(上有一層過氧化鐵粉末,故名)。

Croe·sus 〔ˈkrisəs; ˈkriːsəs〕 *n.* ①克里薩斯(古 Lydia 王,極富有)。②大富豪。

croft 〔krɔft; krɔft〕 *n.* 〖英〗(住宅附近之)小農地;租來的小農場。

croft·er 〔ˈkrɔftɚ; ˈkrɔftə〕 *n.* 〖英〗(蘇格蘭之)小農場佃農。

croix de guer·re 〔krwadˈgɛːr; krwɔdˈgeə〕 〖法〗法國之軍功十字章。

Cro-Mag·non 〔kroˈmægnɑn; krouˈmægnɔn〕 *n., adj.* 古石器時代居於歐洲大陸之原始人(的)。

crom·lech 〔ˈkramlɛk; ˈkrɔmlek〕 *n.* ①史前大石坊。②史前環狀列石。

Crom·well 〔ˈkramwəl; ˈkrɔmwəl〕 *n.* 克倫威爾 (Oliver, 1599–1658, 英國將領、政治家,1653–58任英國監國)。

Crom·well·i·an 〔kramˈwɛlɪən; krɔmˈweljən〕 *adj.* ①克倫威爾的。②(傢具) 十七世紀英國式的。—*n.* ①克倫威爾擁護者。②在克倫威爾領導下作戰之士兵。

crone 〔kron; kroun〕 *n.* 乾癟老太婆。

Cro·nos, Cro·nus 〔ˈkronəs; ˈkrounəs〕 *n.* 〖希臘神話〗 Titan 神之一 (簒其父 Uranus 而爲統治宇宙之神,後復被其子 Zeus 取而代之)。

cro·ny 〔ˈkronɪ; ˈkrouni〕 *n., pl.* **-nies.** 「密友;親密的伙伴。」

cro·ny·ism 〔ˈkronɪɪzəm; ˈkrouniizəm〕 *n.* 任用親信(不論被任用者之才幹)。

crook** 〔krʊk; kruk〕 *n.* ①彎; 鉤; 曲。②任何物之彎曲部分。③惡棍; 賊; 騙子;不誠實之人。④牧人用之手杖。 ***by hook or by crook 以任何一種方法;不擇手段。 ***on the crook*** 狡詐地;詭譎地;以不正當方法。—*v.t.* ①彎曲。②用鉤鉤住。③〖俚〗欺騙; 詐取。—*v.i.* 彎曲。

crook·back 〔ˈkrʊkˌbæk; ˈkrukbæk〕 「*n.* 駝背。—**ed,** *adj.*」

***crook·ed** 〔ˈkrʊkɪd; ˈkrukid〕 *adj.* ①屈曲的;彎的;扭曲的。②〖美,俗〗不誠實的;行爲不正的。③歪斜的; 偏向一邊的。④(錢幣) 多邊或多角形的。—**ly,** *adv.* —**ness,** *n.*

crook·neck 〔ˈkrʊkˌnɛk; ˈkruknek〕 *n.* 〖美〗一種頸長而彎曲之南瓜。

croon 〔krun; kruːn〕 *v.t.* & *v.i.* 輕哼;「低唱。」

croon·er 〔ˈkrunɚ; ˈkruːnə〕 *n.* ①淺哼低唱者。②用低聲唱流行抒情歌曲之男歌手。

‡**crop** 〔krap; krɔp〕 *n., v.,* **cropped, crop·ping.** —*n.* ①收成; 收穫。 a good *crop.* 豐收。②農作物。 Farm *crops* were badly damaged by the flood. 洪水使農作物受到很大的損害。③鳥的嗉囊。④帶圈而不帶皮條之馬鞭;鞭柄。⑤剪短的髮。⑥一組;一羣。 The prime minister's statement produced a *crop* of questions. 首相的言論引起了許多問題。⑦家畜耳上所剪之記號。⑧一個動物身上的整塊皮。⑨露出地面之礦脈。⑩動物之消化器官。⑪修剪。***neck and crop*** 〖俗〗完全地;一齊地。—*v.t.* ①種植。②刈;割;剪短。to *crop* one's hair. 剪短頭髮。③(動物)吃(草)。④將(相片或底片上不要部分)剪掉或遮蔽。⑤剪(動物)之耳或毛。—*v.i.* ①無意中出現。②收成。③(礦脈)露出地面〖常out, up〗. ***crop out*** **a.** 露出地面。 **b.** 使可見; 出現。 ***crop up*** 突然出現;不期而出現。—**less,** *adj.*

crop-dust 〔ˈkrapˌdʌst; ˈkrɔpˌdʌst〕 *v.t.* 撒農藥(尤指由飛機撒播)。—*v.i.* 從事撒農藥之工作。—**ing,** *n.*

crop duster 撒農藥用之小飛機或其「駕駛員。」

crop-ear 〔ˈkrapˌɪr; ˈkrɔpˌiə〕 *n.* ①有剪記的耳朵。②耳朵剪有記號之馬或犬。

crop-eared 〔ˈkrapˈɪrd; ˈkrɔpˈiəd〕 *adj.* ①耳朵剪有記號的; 有耳印的。②毛髮剪短耳露於外的。

crop·per 〔ˈkrapɚ; ˈkrɔpə〕 *n.* ①種植者。②農作物;莊稼。③〖俗〗重摔;慘敗;崩潰。

crop·py 〔ˈkrapɪ; ˈkrɔpi〕 *n., pl.* **-pies.** 剪短髮之人。

crop rotation 〖農事〗輪作;輪流栽種。

cro·quet 〔kroˈke; ˈkroukei〕 *n.* 槌球遊戲;循環球戲。

cro·quette 〔kroˈkɛt; krouˈket〕 *n.* 「炸肉丸;炸魚丸。」

cro·qui·gnole 〔ˈkrokəˌnol; ˈkroukənoul〕 *n.* 將髮由髮梢向內捲至頭皮之捲髮法。

crore 〔kror; krɔː〕 〖印度〗 *n.* 一千萬。

cro·sier 〔ˈkroʒɚ; ˈkrouʒə〕 *n.* 牧杖(主教或修道院長所持用者)。(亦作 **crozier**)

‡**cross** 〔krɔs; krɔs, krɔːs〕 *n.* ①十字架。②各種似十字形的東西。 the Distinguished Service *Cross.* 十字勳章。③十字形;十字記號。④磨難;苦難。⑤交叉路;十字街。⑥異種雜交的混合種。 A mule is a *cross* between a horse and a donkey. 騾爲馬與驢雜交的混合種。⑦不幸之事;麻煩。⑧〖俚〗〖運動〗事先決定勝負的比賽。⑨電線走火。⑩用右手在空氣中劃的十字記號。⑪反對;阻礙;失敗。***bear*** (or ***take up***) ***one's cross*** 忍受苦難。***take the cross*** 宣誓參加十字軍。***the Cross*** **a.** 釘死耶穌的十字架。**b.** 耶穌的受難和死;耶穌救贖世人。**c.** 基督教。to follow *the Cross.* 信耶穌教。 —*v.t.* ① 作十字於。 ②劃橫線。 He *crossed* out the wrong words. 他劃去錯字。③交叉。 to *cross* one's legs. (疊起)交叉兩腿。④橫過;越過;渡過。to *cross* a street. 越過馬路。⑤錯過。 We *crossed* each other on the way. 我們在途中錯過了。⑥阻礙。 If anyone *crosses* him, he gets very angry. 如任何人和他作梗,他即大怒。⑦使雜交。⑧公開反對;打擊;使挫折。⑨〖俚〗出賣 (朋友、國家等)。⑩運送。⑪劃十字。***cross a check*** 劃線於支票上。 ***cross a person's hand with a piece of money*** 給某人(尤指卜者)錢。 ***cross a person's path*** 遇到; 與某人有瓜葛。 ***cross oneself*** 在胸前劃十字。***cross one's fingers*** 交叉手指(表示但願不出亂子,或說話中有隱瞞之處)。 ***cross one's heart*** (***and hope to die***) 〖俗〗(兒童習語, 說時常於胸前劃十字) 憑良心說;說老實話。***cross one's mind*** 想起。 ***cross one's palm*** 賄賂。 ***cross one's t's and dot one's i's*** 劃 t 字上的橫線,加 i 字上

的點,喻言行謹愼周詳。***cross swords*** (***with***) 與人爭鬥;與人辯論。***cross up*** a.〖俚〗欺騙。b. 迷惘。—*v.i.* ①交叉;相叉。②橫過;渡過。③錯過。④雜交。—*adj.* ①橫的。*cross* street. 橫街。②乖戾的;不高興的。Why are you so *cross* with me? 你爲甚麼對我這樣不高興? ③逆的;相反的;反對的。④雜交的。⑤〖俚〗不誠實的。⑥不幸的;不利的。***as cross as two sticks*** 脾氣極壞。—**a·ble,** *adj.*

cross action 〖法律〗反訴。

cross·bar [ˈkrɔsˌbɑr; ˈkrɔsbɑː] *n., v.,* **-barred, -bar·ring.** —*n.* ①閂;橫木。②足球場的球門橫木。③跳高架之橫竿。④單槓。⑤男用腳踏車兩輪間之橫檔。⑥橫線或橫條;若干字母中之橫線(如 H). —*v.t.* 劃以橫線或橫條。

cross·beam [ˈkrɔsˌbim; ˈkrɔsbiːm] *n.* 橫梁;大梁。

cross-bear·er [ˈkrɔsˌbɛrɚ; ˈkrɔsˌbɛərə] *n.* 宗教遊行時擎十字架者。

cross·belt [ˈkrɔsˌbɛlt; ˈkrɔsbelt] *n.* 由肩頭斜越胸前之帶;斜皮帶。

cross-bench [ˈkrɔsˌbɛntʃ; ˈkrɔsbentʃ] *n.* (英國上下兩院之)中立議員席。—*adj.* 中立的;獨立的。***have the cross-bench mind*** 公平無私;不偏不倚。

cross-bench·er [ˈkrɔsˌbɛntʃɚ; ˈkrɔsˌbentʃə] *n.* 中立議員;中立人士。

cross·bill [ˈkrɔsˌbɪl; ˈkrɔsbil] *n.* 交喙鳥。

cross bond (砌磚時)十字式堆疊。

cross·bones [ˈkrɔsˌbonz; ˈkrɔsbounz] *n. pl.* (通常畫於骷髏下)二股骨交叉之圖形。

cross·bow [ˈkrɔsˌbo; ˈkrɔsbou] *n.* 石弓;弩。

cross·bow·man [ˈkrɔsˌbomən; ˈkrɔsˌboumən] *n., pl.* **-men.** 弩手。

cross·bred [ˈkrɔsˌbrɛd; ˈkrɔsbred] *adj.* 雜種的;雜交的。—*n.* 雜種。

cross·breed [ˈkrɔsˌbrid; ˈkrɔsbriːd] *v.,* **-bred, -breed·ing,** *n.* —*v.t. & v.i.* (亦作 **cross-mate**) 異種交配;雜交。—*n.* 雜種。

cross bun 上有十字架花飾的圓麪包。

cross·but·tock [ˈkrɔsˌbʌtək; ˈkrɔsˌbʌtək] *n.* (角力之)一種攔腰抛擲。

cross-check [ˈkrɔsˌtʃɛk; ˈkrɔstʃek] *v.t.* ①從各方面查證某事之可靠性。②再次核對。—*n.* ①多方求證。②多方求證之方法或手段。③再次核對。

cross-coun·try [ˈkrɔsˌkʌntrɪ; ˈkrɔsˌkʌntri] *adj.* ①橫過田野的;越野的。②橫越國境的。—*n.* 越野賽。

cross cousins 姑表及舅表兄弟姐妹。

cross-cul·tur·al [ˈkrɔsˈkʌltʃərəl; ˈkrɔsˈkʌltʃərəl] *adj.* 超越某一種文化界限的;多種文化的。

cross·cut [ˈkrɔsˌkʌt; ˈkrɔskʌt] *n., adj., v.,* **-cut, -cut·ting.** —*n.* ①直路;捷徑。②橫鋸。③〖電影、電視〗剪接。④〖數學〗交;正交。—*adj.* 橫鋸的;橫切的。—*v.t.* 橫切;橫越。—*v.i.* 剪接影片。

crosscut saw 橫切鋸。

crosse [krɔs; krɔs] *n.* 曲棍球(lacrosse)之球棒。

crossed [krɔst; krɔst] *adj.* ①十字的;交叉的。②劃橫線的。a *crossed* check. 劃線支票。③作十字押的。④被阻礙的。

cross-ex·am·ine [ˈkrɔsɪgˈzæmɪn; ˈkrɔsigˈzæmin] *v.t.,* **-ined, -in·ing.** ①盤詰;嚴密詢問。②〖法律〗詰問對方證人。—**cross-ex·am·i·na·tion,** *n.*

cross-eye [ˈkrɔsˌaɪ; ˈkrɔs-ai] *n.* 對視眼。

cross-eyed [ˈkrɔsˌaɪd; ˈkrɔs-aid] *adj.* 對視眼的;斜視的。

cross-fade [ˈkrɔsˌfed; ˈkrɔsfeid] *v.,* **-fad·ed, -fad·ing,** *n.* —*v.t.* 〖電影、電視〗使(影像或聲音)逐漸消失之同時,使另一明確之影像或聲音出現。—*n.* 此等動作。

cross-fer·ti·lize [ˈkrɔsˈfɝtlˌaɪz; ˈkrɔsˈfəːtilaiz] *v.t. & v.i.,* **-lized, -liz·ing.** (使)異花受精;(使)異體受精。—**cross-fer·ti·li·za·tion,** *n.*

cross-file [ˈkrɔsˌfaɪl; ˈkrɔsfail] *v.i.,* **-filed, -fil·ing.** 〖美〗在初選中登記爲敵對黨之候選人。

cross fire ①〖軍〗交叉射擊。②內心衝突引起的困境。③交相指責。

cross-grained [ˈkrɔsˈgrend; ˈkrɔsgreind] *adj.* ①木材紋理不規則的;扭絲的。②執拗的;倔强的;脾氣大的。

cross·hatch [ˈkrɔsˌhætʃ; ˈkrɔshætʃ] *v.t. & v.i.* 用兩組以上之平行線相交作(雕刻或繪畫)之陰影。—*n.* 此等平行線之任一。

cross·head [ˈkrɔsˌhɛd; ˈkrɔshed] *n.* ①〖機械〗聯桿器;丁字頭。②小標題;子題。

cross index 前後參照之索引。

cross·ing [ˈkrɔsɪŋ; ˈkrɔsiŋ, ˈkrɔːsiŋ] *n.* ①橫過;橫渡。②街道河流等之過渡處或穿越道。③交叉點。railroad *crossing.* 鐵路交叉點。④阻礙;反對。⑤雜交。⑥鐵路路軌交叉點之銜接;道岔。

cross·ing-sweep·er [ˈkrɔsɪŋˌswipɚ; ˈkrɔsiŋˌswiːpə] *n.* 十字路口之清道夫。

cross·jack [ˈkrɔsˌdʒæk; ˈkrɔsdʒæk] *n.* 〖航海〗繫於後桅下桁之大橫帆。

cross keys 交叉鑰匙(敎皇徽章)。

cross-leg·ged [ˈkrɔsˈlɛgɪd, -ˈlɛgd; ˈkrɔslegd] *adj. & adv.* 盤着腿的(地);翹着腿的(地)。

cross·let [ˈkrɔslɪt; ˈkrɔslit] *n.* 〖紋章〗小十字形。(亦作 **croslet**)

cross-li·cense [ˈkrɔsˌlaɪsəns; ˈkrɔsˌlaisəns] *n., v.,* **-censed, -cens·ing.** —*n.* 握有專利權者之間的交換使用對方產品之權利。—*v.i.* 作上述權利之交換。

cross·light [ˈkrɔsˌlaɪt; ˈkrɔslait] *n.* ①交叉之光線。②(*pl.*)關於一問題的種種意見。

cross·line [ˈkrɔsˌlaɪn; ˈkrɔslain] *n.* ①交叉線;連接兩點之線。②英文報之一欄單行標題。③〖數學〗正交線。

cross-link [ˈkrɔsˌlɪŋk; ˈkrɔsliŋk] *n., v.* 交叉結合。

cross·ly [ˈkrɔslɪ; ˈkrɔsli] *adv.* ①橫地;斜地。②逆對地;不利地。③乖戾地;執拗地。

cross·ness [ˈkrɔsnɪs; ˈkrɔsnis] *n.* ①橫過;橫斷。②倔强;執拗;彆扭;壞脾氣。

cross·o·ver [ˈkrɔsˌovɚ; ˈkrɔsˌouvə] *n.* ①(鐵路之)轉線軌。②〖生物〗同型染色體之局部交換。③連接之物(如橫越公路之陸橋)。④U形管。⑤男女雙方交換位置的一種舞步。

cross·patch [ˈkrɔsˌpætʃ; ˈkrɔspætʃ] *n.* 〖俗〗脾氣乖戾的人。

cross·piece [ˈkrɔsˌpis; ˈkrɔspiːs] *n.* 橫木;橫檔;閂。

cross-pol·li·nate [ˈkrɔsˈpɑləˌnet; ˈkrɔsˈpɔlineit] *v.t. & v.i.,* **-nat·ed, -nat·ing.** (使)異花受粉。

cross-pol·li·na·tion [ˈkrɔsˌpɑləˈneʃən; ˈkrɔsˌpɔliˈneiʃən] *n.* 〖植物〗異花受粉。

cross product 〖數學〗交叉乘積。

cross-pur·pose [ˈkrɔsˈpɝpəs; ˈkrɔsˈpəːpəs] *n.* ①反對之目的。②(*pl.*)滑稽問答遊戲。***at cross-purposes*** 互相誤解;齟齬。

cross-ques·tion [ˈkrɔsˈkwɛstʃən; ˈkrɔsˈkwestʃən] *v.t.* =**cross-examine.** —*n.* =**cross-examination.**

cross·rail [ˈkrɔsˌrel; ˈkrɔsreil] *n.* 橫木。
cross ratio 〖數學〗交比;重比。
cross-re·fer [ˌkrɔsrɪˈfɝ; ˌkrɔsriˈfəː] *v.t. & v.i.*, **-re·ferred, -re·fer·ring.** 參照;對照;互參。
cross reference 對照;前後參照。
cross-re·sist·ance [ˈkrɔsrɪˈzɪstəns; ˈkrɔsriˈzistəns] *n.* 〖細菌〗抗力移轉。
cross·road [ˈkrɔsˌrod; ˈkrɔsroud] *n.* ①交叉路;岔路。②(常*pl.*)(作 *sing.* or *pl.* 解)十字路口。③(常*pl.*)(作 *sing.* or *pl.* 解)面臨抉擇的關頭。④鄉村的市集。⑤(常 *pl.*)(作 *sing.* or *pl.* 解)活動中心。***at the crossroads*** 面臨抉擇。
cross·ruff [ˈkrɔsˌrʌf; ˈkrɔsrʌf] *n.* 〖橋牌〗交互用王牌贏墩。—*v.t. & v.i.* 用上述方法打橋牌。
cross sea 逆浪;橫浪。
cross section ①橫斷面;橫截面。②典型人物;樣品。③〖物理〗(原子)核(被撞)截面。
cross-sec·tion·al [ˈkrɔsˈsɛkʃənəl; ˈkrɔsˈsekʃənəl] *adj.* 代表性人物的。
cross-sell·ing [ˈkrɔsˈsɛlɪŋ; ˈkrɔsˈseliŋ] *n.* 汽車商人越區出售同型汽車之不道德行爲。
cross-shaped [ˈkrɔsˌʃept; ˈkrɔsˌʃeipt] *adj.* 十字架形的。
cross-staff [ˈkrɔsˌstæf; ˈkrɔsstaːf] *n., pl.* **-staves, -staffs.** 一種測量天體角度之儀器。
cross-stitch [ˈkrɔsˌstɪtʃ; ˈkrɔsstitʃ] *n.* 一種十字形針法。—*v.t. & v.i.* 以此種針法縫。
cross talk ①(無線電之)他處傳來之干擾;漏話(電話之別條線漏過來的話)。②閑談;聊天。③〖英〗戲劇或表演中的詼諧對白。
cross·tie [ˈkrɔsˌtaɪ; ˈkrɔstai] *n.* ①〖美〗橫放之支柱。②〖鐵路〗枕木。
cross-town [ˈkrɔsˌtaʊn; ˈkrɔstaun] *adj.* 橫越市鎮的。
cross traffic 道路交叉點彼此穿越的交通。
cross·trees [ˈkrɔsˌtriz; ˈkrɔstriːz] *n. pl.* 〖航海〗桅頂橫桁。
cross·walk [ˈkrɔsˌwɔk; ˈkrɔswɔːk] *n.* 行人穿越道;斑馬線。
cross·way [ˈkrɔsˌwe; ˈkrɔswei] *n.* =**crossroad.**
cross wind 逆風。
cross·wise [ˈkrɔsˌwaɪz; ˈkrɔswaiz] *adv.* ①橫亙地;交叉地。②作十字形。③相反地。(亦作 **crossways**)
cross·word puzzle [ˈkrɔsˌwɝd～; ˈkrɔswəːd～] 塡字遊戲;縱橫字謎(各方格塡入字母,使之縱橫皆成字)。(亦作 **crossword**)
cross·yard [ˈkrɔsˌjɑrd; ˈkrɔsjɑːd] *n.* 橫桁。
crotch [krɑtʃ; krɔtʃ] *n.* ①叉狀物;叉桿;叉柱。②(樹枝之)交叉處;枒叉。③人體兩腿分叉處;袴部。—**ed,** *adj.*
crotch·et [ˈkrɑtʃɪt; ˈkrɔtʃit] *n.* ①鉤狀物;小鉤。②怪想;奇思。③〖音樂〗四分音符。④(外科用)鉤鑷;產科鉤。
crotch·et·eer [ˌkrɑtʃəˈtɪr; ˌkrɔtʃiˈtiə] *n.* 耽於幻想之人;固守偏執之人。
crotch·et·y [ˈkrɑtʃətɪ; ˈkrɔtʃiti] *adj.* 耽於幻想的;懷怪癖的。
cro·ton [ˈkrotn̩; ˈkroutən] *n.* 〖植物〗巴豆。
croton bug 一種小蟑螂。
cro·ton·ic acid [kroˈtɑnɪk～; krouˈtɔnik～] 〖化〗巴豆酸;丁烯醛。
croton oil 巴豆油(用作瀉劑)。
***crouch** [kraʊtʃ; krautʃ] *v.i.* ①蹲伏;彎身。②畏縮;卑屈。—*v.t.* 使低彎。—*n.* 蹲伏;屈膝姿勢。
croup[1] [krup; kruːp] *n.* 〖醫〗格魯布性喉頭炎;義膜性喉炎。
croup[2] *n.* (馬等之)臀部。(亦作 **croupe**)
crou·pi·er [ˈkrupɪɚ; ˈkruːpiə] *n.* ①賭桌上收付賭注之人。②公宴時的副主席。
croup·ous [ˈkrupəs; ˈkruːpəs] *adj.* 〖醫〗①患格魯布性之病的。②格魯布性的。(亦作 **croupy**)
crou·ton [kruˈtɑn; kruːˈtɔn] 〖法〗 *n.* 油煎之麪包碎塊(通常放入湯中)。
Crow [kro; krou] *n.* ①北美印第安人之一族(屬於 Siouan 語族)。②該族語言。
***crow**[1] [kro; krou] *n., v.,* **crowed** or **crew, crowed, crow·ing.** —*n.* ①鷄叫;作喔喔聲。②嬰孩歡呼聲。—*v.i.* ①鷄叫。②自鳴得意。They *crowed* over a victory. 他們因勝利而自鳴得意。③(嬰孩)歡呼。〖注意〗鷄啼的過去式是 **crew,** 不是 **crowed.**
crow**[2] *n.* ①烏鴉。②類似烏鴉之鳥(如喜鵲、樫鳥等)。③鐵撬。as the crow flies*** 成直線地;取捷徑地。***eat crow*** 〖俗〗被迫作所厭惡或羞辱之事;被迫認錯。***have a crow to pick with*** 〖俗〗對…不滿。***white crow*** 珍奇之物。
crow·bar [ˈkroˌbɑr; ˈkroubɑː] *n.* 鐵撬;撬棍。
crow·ber·ry [ˈkroˌbɛrɪ; ˈkroubəri] *n., pl.* **-ries.** 〖植物〗一種黑色草莓。
crow·bill [ˈkroˌbɪl; ˈkroubil] *n.* 一種外科手術用之鉗子。(亦作 **crow's-bill**)
‡**crowd** [kraʊd; kraud] *n.* ①羣衆。②平民;民衆(集合稱)。Many newspapers appeal to the *crowd.* 許多報紙迎合大衆趣味。③〖俗〗一夥;一班。④許多;一羣;一堆。a *crowd* of papers and books. 一堆文件和書。⑤觀衆;聽衆。⑥古塞爾特人(Celts)的一種長方形絃樂器。—*v.i.* ①聚集。②擠進。They *crowded* into a small room. 他們擠進一小房間裏。—*v.t.* ①擠滿。The room was *crowded* with guests. 這房間擠滿了客人。②擁擠。③排擠;推擠。④〖俗〗追;催。***crowd (on) sail*** 揚起更多的帆,以增加船的速度。—**ed,** *adj.*
crowd puller 吸引群衆的人、事或物。
crow·foot [ˈkroˌfʊt; ˈkrou-fut] *n., pl.* **-feet, -foots.** ①〖植物〗毛茛。②〖軍〗鐵蒺藜。
Crow Jim 〖美俚〗黑人對白人之偏見。
crow·keep·er [ˈkroˌkipɚ; ˈkrouˌkiːpə] *n.* ①趕烏鴉之雇工。②田間之稻草人。
‡**crown** [kraʊn; kraun] *n.* ①王冠;皇冕。②王權;君權。③國王;王后。④冠狀物(如錨頂)。⑤花冠。⑥榮譽;獎賞;褒獎。⑦頭。a bald *crown.* 禿頭。⑧頂。the *crown* of a hill. 小山的頂。⑨英國的銀幣(值五先令)。⑩帽之頂端。⑪顚峯狀態。⑫齒冠。⑬樹葉與樹枝。⑭鳥冠。⑮寬15英寸長19英寸之印刷紙。***the Crown*** 王權;君權。—*v.t.* ①使爲王或后;加冕。They *crowned* him as king. 他們立他爲國王。②加榮譽於;褒獎;表彰。③加冠於。④完成;結束。Success *crowned* his efforts. 他的努力終於得到成功。⑤鑲牙。⑥處於…之頂;籠罩…之頂。⑦〖俗〗擊…之頭部。—*adj.* 皇冕的;王室的。—**ed,** *adj.*
crown cap 邊緣成鋸齒狀之金屬瓶蓋。(亦作 **crowncork**)
crown colony 英國直轄殖民地。
crown·er [ˈkraʊnɚ; ˈkraunə] *n.* ①〖英方〗驗屍官。②加冕者;加冠者。③加蓋之物。④重大事件。
crown·ing [ˈkraʊnɪŋ; ˈkrauniŋ] *adj.* ①無上的;至高的。crowning glory. 無上光榮。②凸起的。③在頂端的。

crown land 君主的土地。
crown octavo 一種書籍的尺寸(長約 7½ 英寸,寬約 5 英寸)。
crown·piece ['kraun,pis; 'kraunpi:s] *n.* ①構成頭冠或頂部之部分。②馬兩頰之韁繩。
crown prince 皇太子;皇儲。
crown princess ①皇太子之妃。②將繼承王位的公主。
crown saw (外科用)冠狀鋸;環鋸。
crown wheel 鐘錶等內部之齒輪。
crow-quill ['kro,kwɪl; 'krou-kwil] *n.* ①鴉之翮。②翮筆。
crow's-foot ['kroz,fut; 'krouzfut] *n., pl.* **crow's-feet.** ①(*pl.*) 成人眼外角之皺紋;魚尾紋。②衣服接縫末端之三角花樣。③〖軍〗鐵蒺藜。
crow's-nest ['kroz,nɛst; 'krouznest] *n.* ①〖航海〗桅樓;眺望臺;守望處。②交通崗亭及類似之陸上小亭。
crow·toe ['kro,to; 'kroutou] *n.* 〖植物〗百脈根。
crs. ①credits. ②creditors.
cru·cial ['kruʃəl; 'kru:ʃjəl] *adj.* ①嚴重的;艱苦的。②有決定性的;極重要的。—**ly,** *adv.*
cru·ci·ate ['kruʃɪɪt; 'kru:ʃiit] *adj.* ①〖植物〗有十字形葉或花瓣的;十字形的;十字狀的。②〖動物〗交叉的(翼)。—**ly,** *adv.*
cru·ci·ble ['krusəbl̩; 'kru:sibl] *n.* ①坩堝。②嚴酷的考驗。
crucible steel 坩堝鋼。
cru·ci·fer ['krusəfɚ; 'kru:sifə] *n.* ①〖宗教〗執十字架之人。②〖植物〗十字花科之植物。—**ous,** *adj.*
Cru·cif·er·ae [kru'sɪfə,ri; kru:'sifəri:] *n. pl.* 〖植物〗十字花科。
cru·ci·fix ['krusə,fɪks; 'kru:sifiks] *n.* ①苦像(耶穌釘於十字架的像)。②十字架。
cru·ci·fix·ion [,krusə'fɪkʃən; ,kru:si'fikʃən] *n.*①釘死於十字架。②(C-) 耶穌之釘死於十字架;耶穌被釘十字架之圖畫或塑像。
cru·ci·form ['krusə,fɔrm; 'kru:sifɔ:m] *adj.* 十字形的。—**i·ty,** *n.* —**ly,** *adv.*
cru·ci·fy ['krusə,faɪ; 'kru:sifai] *v.t.,* **-fied, -fy·ing.** ①釘死十字架上。②壓抑;克制。③虐待。
*__crude__ [krud; kru:d] *adj.,* **crud·er, crud·est.** ①未提煉的;未熟的;生的。*crude* oil. 原油。②粗的。*crude* manners. 粗魯的態度。—**ly,** *adv.* —**ness,** *n.*
cru·di·ty ['krudətɪ; 'kru:diti] *n., pl.* **-ties.** ①粗糙;粗野;生硬;未熟。②粗糙或未成熟之東西。③粗野之行爲或言詞。
‡**cru·el** ['kruəl;kruəl, 'kru:əl] *adj.* ①殘忍的。He is very *cruel* to the prisoners. 他對待犯人非常殘忍。②使痛苦的;使受苦的。③殘酷的。a *cruel* war. 殘酷的戰爭。—**ly,** *adv.* —**ness,** *n.*
cru·el·heart·ed ['kruəl'hɑrtɪd; 'kru:əl'hɑ:tid] *adj.* 狠心的;鐵石心腸的。
*__cru·el·ty__ ['kruəltɪ; 'kruəlti, 'kru:əl-] *n., pl.* **-ties.** ①虐待;殘忍。②殘忍的行爲。③嚴酷;殘酷。the *cruelty* of fate. 命運的殘酷安排。
cru·et ['kruɪt; 'kru:it] *n.* ①餐桌上用的調味瓶。②調味瓶架。
cruet stand 調味瓶架。
*__cruise__ [kruz; kru:z] *v.,* **cruised, cruis·ing,** *n.* —*v.i.* ①往返航行;海上遊弋。②一地又一地旅行。③乘坐飛機以最省油之速度飛行。④慢速行車以招攬生意或巡査。⑤〖俗〗在街道上或公共場所尋找性的尋歡對象。—*v.t.* ①航行;飛行。②巡視(林區)以勘察森林資源。—*n.* 巡航;遊弋;海上巡邏。
cruise car 警察巡邏車。
cruise missile 巡弋飛彈。
*__cruis·er__ ['kruzɚ; 'kru:zə] *n.* ①巡洋艦。②往返航行或巡弋的飛機、出租汽車、機動船艇等。③警察巡邏車。④巡廻之人或車船等。⑤估計某一森林地帶內木材價值之人。⑥〖俚〗沿街拉客之妓女。
cruis·er·weight ['kruzɚ,wet; 'kru:zəweit] *n.* ①〖英〗輕重量級拳擊手。②〖美〗重量級拳擊手(體重在177至186磅之間者)。
cruise ship 載運遊客作長程航行的郵輪。
cruis·ing ['kruzɪŋ; 'kru:ziŋ] *adj.* 〖航空〗省油量最大之飛行的。*cruising* speed. 省油量最大之飛行速度。
crul·ler ['krʌlɚ; 'krʌlə] *n.* 一種油煎小圓餅。(亦作 **kruller**)
*__crumb__ [krʌm; krʌm] *n.* ①麪包屑;餅屑。②麪包心。③小量;少許。a *crumb* of comfort. 少許安慰。④一無是處之人。—*v.t.* ①捏碎;弄碎。②覆以麪包屑。③〖俗〗將麪包屑等從桌布上拂拭掉。—*v.i.* 變成碎屑。
crumb·cloth ['krʌm,klɔθ; 'krʌmklɔθ] *n.* 鋪於桌下以承麪包屑之布。
*__crum·ble__ ['krʌmbl̩; 'krʌmbl] *v.,* **-bled, -bling,** *n.* —*v.t.* 弄碎;碎爲細屑。—*v.i.* 粉碎;崩潰。—*n.* ①正在碎裂或已碎裂之物。②〖方〗小片;碎片;碎粒。
crum·bly ['krʌmblɪ; 'krʌmbli] *adj.,* **-bli·er, -bli·est.** 易碎的;脆的。
crumb·y ['krʌmɪ; 'krʌmi] *adj.,* **crumb·i·er, crumb·i·est.** ①多麪包屑的。②柔軟的。③〖俚〗劣等的。
crum·my ['krʌmɪ;'krʌmi] *adj.,* **-mi·er, -mi·est,** *adv.* —*adj.* 〖俚〗①質劣的;難看的;卑鄙的;骯髒的。②不滿意的;無價値的。—*adv.* 〖俚〗不佳地;差勁地。
crump [krʌmp;krʌmp] *v.t.* ①用齒咯赤咯赤地咬嚼。②重擊。—*v.i.* 發出咯赤咯赤的壓、磨、或踩踏之聲。—*n.* ①咯赤之聲。②重擊。
crum·pet ['krʌmpɪt; 'krʌmpit] *n.* 一種鬆脆之圓餅。
*__crum·ple__ ['krʌmpl̩;'krʌmpl] *v.,* **-pled, -pling,** *n.* —*v.t.* ①壓皺;弄皺。He *crumpled* the letter into a ball. 他把信捏得皺成一團。②使崩潰。—*v.i.* ①變皺;成摺。②突然倒下。*crumple up* **a.** 揉皺;使皺。**b.** 征服;擊敗。**c.** 崩潰;損害。—*n.* 皺紋。
crunch [krʌntʃ; krʌntʃ] *v.t.* ①嘎扎有聲地吃。②(脚、輪等)嘎扎地碾踏過;壓、磨或踩踏有聲。—*v.i.* ①吃時發出嘎扎聲。②壓、踩、碾時發嘎扎聲。—*n.* ①咬嚼;咬碎;咬嚼聲。②壓磨;踩踏;嘎扎聲。③危機;轉捩點。④關鍵。—**ing·ly,** *adv.* —**ing·ness,** *n.*
crunch·y ['krʌntʃɪ; 'krʌntʃi] *adj.,* **crunch·i·er, crunch·i·est.** 〖俗〗鬆脆的;易裂的。—**crunch·i·ness,** *n.*
cru·or ['kruɔr; 'kru:ɔ:] *n.* 凝血。
crup·per ['krʌpɚ;'krʌpə] *n.* ①兜在馬尾下之皮帶。②馬之臀部。③保護馬臀部之鎧甲。④臀部。
cru·ral ['krurəl; 'krurəl] *adj.* 〖解剖〗脚部的;小腿的;後腿的。
crus [krʌs;krʌs] *n., pl.* **cru·ra** ['krurə; 'krurə]. 〖解剖〗小腿;後腿。
*__cru·sade__ [kru'sed; kru:'seid] *n., v.,* **-sad·ed, -sad·ing.** —*n.* ①(常 C-)十字軍。②社會除惡運動。③宗教戰爭。—*v.i.* 加入十字軍。—**cru·sad·er,** *n.*
cru·sa·do [kru'sedo; kru:'seidou] *n., pl.* **-dos, -does.** 葡萄牙之鑄有十字架的古幣。

cruse 〔kruz; kruːz〕 *n.* 瓶；罐；罈子。*widow's cruse* 無盡之藏(聖經列王紀)。

***crush** 〔krʌʃ; krʌʃ〕 *v.t.* ①壓破。to *crush* nuts with a nutcracker. 用堅果鉗壓破堅果。②壓皺；揉皺。③壓碎；磨細。④征服；壓服。⑤壓平。⑥欺壓。⑦緊抱。He *crushed* her in his arms. 他將她緊抱在懷裡。⑧喝(酒等)。*crush down* 壓碎；壓倒；壓制。*crush out* 搾出。*crush up* 壓碎；捏成一團。—*v.i.* ①起皺紋。②擠入。They *crushed* into a small room. 他們擠入一小房間。—*n.* ①壓破；壓碎。②擁擠。③〖俗〗迷戀；迷戀之對象。He has had a *crush* on her ever since they met at that party last summer. 自從去夏宴會邂逅後，他一直迷戀着她。④壓搾。—**a·ble,** *adj.*

crush hat 可摺疊而不致損壞的帽子。

crush·ing〔ˈkrʌʃɪŋ; ˈkrʌʃiŋ〕*adj.* ①壓破的；壓碎的。②決定性的。③壓倒性的；凌辱的。

crush room(劇場等處之)休息室。

Cru·soe 〔ˈkruso; ˈkruːsou〕 *n.* 克魯素(Daniel Defoe 著"魯濱遜飄流記"之主角)。

***crust** 〔krʌst; krʌst〕 *n.* ①麪包皮。②任何麪餅的外殼。③堅硬的外殼、外皮或外層。④〖俚〗厚顏；厚臉皮。*earn one's crust* 謀生；掙錢餬口。*have a crust*〖俗〗過分大膽；太過冒失；太鹵莽。—*v.t.* ①蓋以硬皮；使結硬皮。②在冰雪地上獵(鹿等)。—*v.i.* 結硬皮。—**less,** *adj.*

Crus·ta·ce·a〔krʌsˈteʃɪə; krʌsˈteiʃjə〕*n. pl.* 〖動物〗甲殼類。

crus·ta·cean 〔krʌsˈteʃən; krʌsˈteiʃjən〕*n.* 〖動物〗甲殼類動物。—*adj.* 甲殼類的。

crus·ta·ceous 〔krʌsˈteʃəs; krʌsˈteiʃiəs〕 *adj.* ①外皮的；有外殼的。②〖動物〗甲殼類的。

crust·ed 〔ˈkrʌstɪd; ˈkrʌstid〕 *adj.* ①有外皮或外殼的。②(酒等)有浮渣的；有酒垢的。③古色古香的；陳腐的。

crust·y 〔ˈkrʌstɪ; ˈkrʌsti〕 *adj.*, **crust·i·er, crust·i·est.** ①有硬皮的；似外殼的。②乖戾的；粗暴的。

***crutch** 〔krʌtʃ; krʌtʃ〕 *n.* ①拐杖。②支持物。③〖航海〗船尾肘木；叉柱；槳架。④叉狀物。⑤任何彌補缺陷或不足之物。—*v.t.* 支撐；支持。

crutched 〔krʌtʃt; krʌtʃt〕 *adj.* ①撐拐杖的。②帶十字架的。

crux 〔krʌks; krʌks〕 *n., pl.* **crux·es, cru·ces** 〔ˈkrusiz; ˈkruːsiːz〕. ①緊要關頭。②要點。③難題。④(C-)〖天文〗十字座。⑤〖紋章〗十字形。

cru·zei·ro 〔kruˈzero; kruːˈzeirou〕 *n., pl.* **-ros.** 巴西貨幣單位(等於 1 milreis)。

‡**cry** 〔kraɪ; krai〕 *v.,* **cried, cry·ing,** *n., pl.* **cries.** —*v.i.* ①呼；喊；大聲呼號(因痛、怒、恐懼或憂慮而致)。②號哭；哭泣。Stop *crying*. 不要哭。③(動物)叫；啼；鳴；嗥。—*v.t.* ①乞；求；懇求。②大叫；大聲呼喊。③叫賣；叫買；叫修理；公開宣告。Peddlers *cried* their wares in the streets. 小販沿街叫賣貨物。④使哭至某種程度。She *cried* herself to sleep. 她哭倦而睡。*cry down* a. 喝止。b. 輕視。*cry for* a. 哭着要；要求。b. 急需。*cry for the moon* 妄想不可能的東西。*cry havoc* 警告禍難或危險之來臨。*cry off* 停止；撤回；取消；食言；毁約。*cry one's eyes* (or *heart*) *out* 痛哭。*cry out* 大叫；埋怨。*cry over* 慟哭。*cry over spilled* (or *spilt*) *milk* 作無益之後悔或譴責。*cry quits* 同意停止爭辯。*cry to* 呼籲；禱告。*cry up* 稱讚；大聲稱讚。—*n.* ①呼；喊；叫(表示痛、怒、驚恐或憂慮等)。He uttered a *cry* of triumph when he found the treasure. 他找到寶藏時，發出勝利的歡呼。②哭泣；號泣；啼哭。to have a good *cry*. 痛哭一場；盡情大哭。③動物的啼叫聲。④大叫；大聲呼號。a *cry* for help. 大聲呼救。⑤標語；口號。⑥大聲說話或叫喊。a peddler's *cry*. 小販的叫賣聲。⑦公意。⑧懇求。*a far cry* a. 遠的距離。b. 大的差別。*all the cry* 流行；時尚。*hue and cry* a. 追捕犯人。b. 公憤；責難。*in full cry* 緊追。*within cry* (*of*) 在呼聲可以達到的地方。

cry·ba·by 〔ˈkraɪˌbebɪ; ˈkraiˌbeibi〕 *n., pl.* **-bies.** ①愛哭之人(尤指小孩)。②軟弱之人；愛訴苦者。

cry·ing 〔ˈkraɪɪŋ; ˈkraiiŋ〕 *adj.* ①號泣的。②顯著的；緊急的。—**ly,** *adv.*

cry·o·gen 〔ˈkraɪədʒən; ˈkraiədʒən〕 *n.* 〖化〗冷劑；凍劑(產生低溫之物)。

cry·o·gen·ics〔ˌkraɪəˈdʒɛnɪks; ˌkraiəˈdʒeniks〕 *n.* 低溫學。—**cry·o·gen·ic,** *adj.*

cry·o·lite 〔ˈkraɪəˌlaɪt; ˈkraiəlait〕 *n.* 〖礦〗冰晶石。

cry·on·ics 〔kraɪˈɑnɪks; kraiˈɔniks〕 *n.* 屍體冷凍保存法。

cry·o·sur·ger·y 〔ˌkraɪoˈsɝdʒərɪ; ˌkraiouˈsəːdʒəri〕 *n.* 以低溫消除或破壞人體組織之外科手術。

crypt 〔krɪpt; kript〕 *n.* ①地窖；地穴；地下墓。②〖解剖〗腺窩；小囊。③〖俗〗密碼。

crypt·a·nal·y·sis 〔ˌkrɪptəˈnæləsɪs; ˌkriptəˈnælisis〕 *n.* ①密碼翻譯法之研究。②密碼翻譯程序或方法。

cryp·tic 〔ˈkrɪptɪk; ˈkriptik〕 *adj.* ①祕密的；隱藏的；神祕的。②〖動物〗潛隱的(如體形或顏色等)。

cryp·ti·cal 〔ˈkrɪptɪkl; ˈkriptikəl〕 *adj.* =**cryptic.**

crypto- 〖字首〗表"祕密；隱匿"之義。(在母音前作 **crypt-**)

cryp·to-Com·mu·nist 〔ˈkrɪptəˈkɑmjʊnɪst; ˈkriptouˈkɔmjunist〕 *n.* 共產黨祕密黨員。

cryp·to·gam 〔ˈkrɪptəˌgæm; ˈkriptəgæm〕 *n.* 隱花植物。

cryp·to·gam·ic 〔ˌkrɪptəˈgæmɪk; ˌkriptəˈgæmik〕 *adj.* 隱花植物的。(亦作 **cryptogamous**)

cryp·to·gram 〔ˈkrɪptəˌgræm; ˈkriptougræm〕 *n.* ①密碼；暗號。②此類記載或符號。

cryp·to·graph〔ˈkrɪptəˌgræf; ˈkriptougrɑːf〕 *n.* ①密碼文件。②密碼。

cryp·tog·ra·pher 〔krɪpˈtɑgrəfɚ; kripˈtɔgrəfə〕 *n.* 精於密碼之人；使用密碼者。

cryp·tog·ra·phy 〔krɪpˈtɑgrəfɪ; kripˈtɔgrəfi〕 *n.* 密碼法；密碼；暗號。

cryp·to·me·ri·a 〔ˌkrɪptəˈmɪrɪə; ˌkriptəˈmiriə〕 *n.* 〖植物〗①(C-)日本杉屬。②日本杉屬之植物；日本杉；杉。

cryp·to·nym 〔ˈkrɪptəˌnɪm; ˈkriptənim〕 *n.* 化名；假名。—**ous,** *adj.*

***crys·tal** 〔ˈkrɪstl; ˈkristl〕 *n., adj., v.,* **-tal(l)ed, -tal·(l)ing.** —*n.* ①水晶；水晶製之裝飾品。②錶面玻璃。③精製的玻璃。④結晶；結晶體。⑤〖無線電〗晶體(檢波用礦石)。—*adj.* ①水晶製的。②透明如水晶的。③〖無線電〗晶體檢波器的。④第十五的(如結婚十五周年)。—*v.t.* ①使結晶。②罩以結晶體或水晶〖常 over〗。—**like,** *adj.*

crystal ball (占卜者用之)水晶球。

crys·tal-ball 〔ˈkrɪstlˈbɔl; ˈkristlˈbɔːl〕 *v.t.* 〖俚〗預言。—*v.i.* 作預言。

crystal-ball gazer 〖俗〗預言家。

crystal detector 晶體檢波器。
crys·tal-gaz·er [ˈkrɪstl̩ˌgezɚ; ˈkristəlˌgeizə] *n.* 注視水晶球占卜者。
crystal gazing ①水晶球占卜術。②揣測；預測。
crys·tal·line [ˈkrɪstl̩ɪn; ˈkristəlain] *adj.* ①水晶的；晶質的；結晶狀的。②透明的；澄澈的。—**crys·tal·lin·i·ty,** *n.*
crystalline lens (眼球中的)晶狀體。
crys·tal·lize [ˈkrɪstl̩ˌaɪz; ˈkristəlaiz] *v.,* **-lized, -liz·ing.** —*v.t.* ①使結晶。*crystallized* sugar. 冰糖。②覆以糖霜；包以糖。*crystallized* fruits. 蜜餞果類。③使(計畫等)具體化。—*v.i.* ①結晶。②具體化；形象化。—**crys·tal·li·za·tion,** *n.*
crys·tal·log·ra·phy [ˌkrɪstl̩ˈɑgrəfɪ; ˌkristəˈlɔgrəfi] *n.* 結晶學；結晶論。
crys·tal·loid [ˈkrɪstl̩ˌɔɪd; ˈkristəlɔid] *adj.* 結晶狀的；晶體的。—*n.* ①〖化〗晶性體；晶質。②〖植物〗假結晶。—**al,** *adj.*
crystal set 礦石收音機。
crystal violet 龍膽紫。
crystal vision ①由水晶球占卜術所引起之視覺，可看見遠處或未來發生之事。②如此所見之事。
Cs 化學元素 cesium 之符號。 **C.S.** ①Chemical Society. ②Christian Science. ③Civil Service. ④Court of Session.
C/s cases. **C.S.A.** ①Confederate States Army. ②Confederate States of America. **C.S.T., CST** Central Standard Time. **Ct.** ①Connecticut. ②Count. ③Court. **ct.** ①cent. ②centum (=a hundred). ③certificate. ④county. ⑤court. **C.T.C.** Cyclists' Touring Club.
cte·noid [ˈtinɔɪd; ˈtiːnɔid] *adj.* 櫛狀的；有櫛齒狀之邊緣的。
ctn cotangent. **Cu** 化學元素 copper 之符號。**cu.** cubic. **C.U.** ①Cambridge University. ②Communications Unit.
*__cub__ [kʌb; kʌb] *n.* ①(獅、熊、狐、虎等之)幼兒；仔。②〖諧〗小伙子；小傢伙；生手；初出茅廬者。an unlicked *cub.* 無經驗之小伙子。③幼童軍。④新進記者。⑤學徒。
Cu·ba [ˈkjubə; ˈkjuːbə] *n.* 古巴(西印度羣島中最大的島國，首都哈瓦那 Havana).
cub·age [ˈkjubɪdʒ; ˈkjuːbidʒ] *n.* ①體積計算；立體求積法。②容積；體積。
Cu·ban [ˈkjubən; ˈkjuːbən] *adj.* 古巴的；古巴人的。—*n.* 古巴人。
cu·ba·ture [ˈkjubətʃɚ; ˈkjuːbətʃə] *n.* =**cubage.**
cub·bish [ˈkʌbɪʃ; ˈkʌbiʃ] *adj.* 似小熊等的；無經驗的；笨拙的。—**ly,** *adv.* —**ness,** *n.*
cub·by [ˈkʌbɪ; ˈkʌbi] *n., pl.* **-bies.** 小而幽閉之處；小房間。(亦作 **cubbyhole**)
*__cube__ [kjub; kjuːb] *n., v.,* **cubed, cub·ing.** —*n.* ①正六面體；立方體。②立方。—*v.t.* ①使成立方體。②用一數自乘三次。*cube root* 立方根。
cu·beb [ˈkjubɛb; ˈkjuːbeb] *n.* 〖植物〗畢澄茄。
cub·hood [ˈkʌbhud; ˈkʌbhud] *n.* (獸類之)幼兒期。
cub·hunt·ing [ˈkʌbˌhʌntɪŋ; ˈkʌbˌhʌntiŋ] *n.* 獵幼狐。
*__cu·bic__ [ˈkjubɪk; ˈkjuːbik] *adj.* ①立方體的。a *cubic* foot. 立方英尺。②有長、寬、高三面的。*cubic content* 體積；容積。*cubic equation*〖數學〗三次方程式。(亦作 **cubical**)
cu·bi·cle [ˈkjubɪkl̩; ˈkjuːbikl] *n.* 小寢室。
cubic measure 容量。
cubic sugar 方糖。
cubic system 〖礦〗等軸晶系。
cu·bi·form [ˈkjubɪˌfɔrm; ˈkjuːbifɔːm] *adj.* 立方形的。
cub·ism [ˈkjubɪzəm; ˈkjuːbizəm] *n.* 〖美術〗立體派圖畫作風。
cub·ist [ˈkjubɪst; ˈkjuːbist] *n.* 立體派藝術家。—*adj.* 立體藝術(家)的。—**ic,** *adj.*
cu·bit [ˈkjubɪt; ˈkjuːbit] *n.* 腕尺(自肘至中指端之長，約十八英寸至二十二英寸)。
cu·boid [ˈkjubɔɪd; ˈkjuːbɔid] *adj.* 立方形的；骰子形的。—*n.* ①〖解剖〗骰骨。②〖數學〗矩體；長方體。
cu·boi·dal [kjuˈbɔɪdl̩; kjuːˈbɔidəl] *adj.* ①立方形的；骰子形的。②骰骨的。
cub reporter 初出茅蘆的新聞記者。
cub scout 幼童軍(8–11 歲的童子軍)。
cuck·old [ˈkʌkl̩d; ˈkʌkəld] *n.* 妻子與人通姦的男人；烏龜。—*v.t.* 與(某人)之妻通姦。
cuck·old·ry [ˈkʌkl̩drɪ; ˈkʌkəldri] *n.* ①與有夫之婦通姦；私通。②戴綠頭巾；當烏龜。
*__cuck·oo__ [ˈkuku, kuˈku; ˈkukuː] *n., pl.* **-oos,** *adj., v.,* **-ooed, -oo·ing.** —*n.* ①布穀鳥；杜鵑。②布穀鳥之鳴聲。—*adj.* 〖美俚〗瘋狂的；愚蠢的。—*v.i.* 學布穀鳥鳴聲。
cuckoo clock 布穀鳥自鳴鐘。
cuck·oo·flow·er [ˈkukuˌflauɚ; ˈkukuːˌflauə] *n.* 〖植物〗酢漿草。
cuck·oo·pint [ˈkukuˌpɪnt; ˈkukuːpint] *n.* 〖植物〗白星海芋。
cuckoo spit(tle) ①吐泡蟲之活動蛹分泌於葉上之泡沫。②吐泡蟲。
cu. cm., cu cm cubic centimeter(s).
cu·cul·late [ˈkjukəˌlet; ˈkjuːkəleit] *adj.* =**cucullated.**
cu·cul·lat·ed [ˈkjukəˌletɪd; ˈkjuːkəleitid] *adj.* ①戴頭巾的；有僧帽的。②頭巾狀的；似僧帽的。
*__cu·cum·ber__ [ˈkjukʌmbɚ; ˈkjuːkəmbə] *n.* ①〖植物〗胡瓜(俗稱黃瓜)。②胡瓜的果實。*cool as a cucumber* 冷靜。
cu·cur·bit [kjuˈkɝbɪt; kjuˈkəːbit] *n.* ①〖植物〗葫蘆；南瓜。②〖化〗蒸餾瓶。
cu·cur·bi·ta·ceous [kjuˌkɝbɪˈteʃəs; kjuˌkəːbiˈteiʃəs] *adj.* 葫蘆科的。
cud [kʌd; kʌd] *n.* ①反芻動物從胃中吐出重嚼之食物。②(反芻動物之)瘤胃。*chew the* (or *one's*) *cud* 反芻；細想；熟思。
cud·bear [ˈkʌdˌbɛr; ˈkʌdbɛə] *n.* ①〖植物〗一種地衣。②地衣紫；苔蘚紫質。
cud·dle [ˈkʌdl̩; ˈkʌdl] *v.,* **-dled, -dling,** *n.* —*v.t.* 撫愛地擁抱。—*v.i.* ①擁抱；撫抱。②貼着身睡；蜷曲着睡。—*n.* 擁抱；摟抱。
cud·dle·some [ˈkʌdl̩səm; ˈkʌdlsəm] *adj.* 適於擁抱的；令人想擁抱的。
cud·dly [ˈkʌdlɪ; ˈkʌdli] *adj.,* **-dli·er, -dli·est.** ①愛擁抱的。②=**cuddlesome.**
cud·dy¹ [ˈkʌdɪ; ˈkʌdi] *n., pl.* **-dies.** ①船上之小房間或廚房。②小房間；食櫥；壁櫥。
cud·dy² *n., pl.* **-dies.** 〖蘇〗①驢。②愚人。
cud·dy³ *n., pl.* **-dies.** 〖蘇〗黑鱈。
cudg·el [ˈkʌdʒəl; ˈkʌdʒəl] *n., v.,* **-el(l)ed, -el·(l)ing.** —*n.* 粗短的棍。*take up the cudgels for* 保衛；極力辯護。—*v.t.* 以粗短的棍擊之。*cudgel one's brains* 絞腦汁；苦思。
cud·weed [ˈkʌdˌwid; ˈkʌdwiːd] *n.* 〖植物〗鼠麴草。
cue¹ [kju; kjuː] *n., v.,* **cued, cu·ing.** —*n.* ①暗示。②演員說白的尾語。③任何動作的暗示，使演員出場或開始說白或歌唱。④劇中的脚色。⑤行動的方向；方針。⑥性情；心情。⑦刺激。*miss a cue* **a.** 未能接受暗示。**b.**〖俗〗

未抓到要點。—*v.t.* ①給…暗示。②插進（歌劇、戲劇）〖常 in, into〗. ***cue* (*someone*) *in*** 通知；告訴；指示。

cue² *n.* ①髮辮。②（劇場等售票處等候購票者所排之）長龍。—*v.t.* 編成辮子。

cue³ *n.* 〖撞球〗球桿。

cue ball 〖撞球〗母球（以球桿擊打之白色球）。

cue·ist 〔ˈkjuist; ˈkjuːist〕 *n.* 精於撞球者。

*__cuff¹__ 〔kʌf; kʌf〕 *n.* ①袖口；袖頭；硬袖。②西裝褲脚的反摺部分。③手銬。***off the cuff*** 〖俚〗 **a.** 不加準備；即席（致詞）。**b.** 非正式地透露消息或表示意見。***on the cuff*** 〖俚〗 **a.** 欠帳；賒帳。**b.** 白送；不指望償付。—*v.t.* ①將褲管加反摺。②銬上手銬。

cuff² *n.*, *v.t.* 掌擊；掌摑；撞擊。

cuff button （襯衫的）袖扣。

cuff link 男子襯衫袖的鏈扣。

cu. ft. cubic foot (*or* feet).

cui bo·no 〔ˈkwiˈbono; ˈkwiːˈbɔnou〕 〖拉〗 ①何人得益？(= for whose benefit?) ②有何益處？(= for what use? of what good?)

cu. in. cubic inch(es).

cui·rass 〔kwɪˈræs; kwiˈræs〕 *n.* ①保護身軀之胸冑與背冑（亦作 **corselet**）。②保護船身之鋼甲。③動物之甲殼。—*v.t.* 披以甲冑；被以鋼甲。

cui·rassed 〔kwɪˈræst; kwiˈræst〕 *adj.* 着甲冑的；裝甲的。

cui·ras·sier 〔ˌkwɪrəˈsɪr; ˌkwirəˈsiə〕 *n.* 着甲冑之騎兵。

cuish 〔kwɪʃ; kwiʃ〕 *n.* =**cuisse.**

cui·sine 〔kwɪˈzin; kwiˈziːn〕 *n.* ①烹調；烹飪法。②食品。③廚房。

cuisse 〔kwɪs; kwis〕 *n.*, *pl.* **cuiss·es.** （常 *pl.*）保護大腿之腿甲。（亦作 **cuish**）

cul-de-sac 〔ˈkʌldəˈsæk; ˈkuldəˈsæk〕 *n.* ①死巷。②無通路之處境；死路。③〖軍〗軍隊之三面受敵，僅有後路可退之情況。

-cule 〖字尾〗表"微小"之義。

cu·lex 〔ˈkjulɛks; ˈkjuːleks〕 *n.* 〖動物〗（歐洲與北美常見的）蚊子。

cu·li·nar·y 〔ˈkjuləˌnɛrɪ; ˈkʌlinəri〕 *adj.* 廚房的；烹調的；烹調用的。

cull¹ 〔kʌl; kʌl〕 *v.t.* 選擇；揀出；採摘（花）。—*n.* 剔除之物；揀剩之物；揀開之物。

cull² *n.* 〖方〗傻瓜；笨蛋。

cul·len·der 〔ˈkʌləndə; ˈkʌlində〕 *n.* =**colander.**

cul·ly 〔ˈkʌlɪ; ˈkʌli〕 *n.*, *pl.* **-lies.** ①〖罕〗易受騙之人。②〖英俚〗人；傢伙（=fellow）；同伴；夥伴。

culm¹ 〔kʌlm; kʌlm〕 *n.* ①煤屑；碎煤。②（尤指下等之）無煙煤。③(C-)〖地質〗頁岩系。

culm² *n.* 草稈。—*v.i.* 長成草稈。

cul·mi·nate 〔ˈkʌlməˌnet; ˈkʌlmineit〕 *v.*, **-nat·ed, -nat·ing.** —*v.i.* ①達於頂點；達最高潮〖in〗. ②升至最高點；形成最高點〖常 in〗. ③〖天文〗（天體）達到子午線；升至最高度。—*v.t.* 結束；完成；到達高潮。

cul·mi·nat·ing 〔ˈkʌlməˌnetɪŋ; ˈkʌlmineitiŋ〕 *adj.* 達於最高點的；終極的。

cul·mi·na·tion 〔ˌkʌlməˈneʃən; ˌkʌlmiˈneiʃən〕 *n.* ①頂點；極點；終極。②最高潮；全盛。③〖天文〗中天。

cu·lottes 〔kjuˈlɑts; kjuˈlɔts〕 *n. pl.* （女用）褲裙。

cul·pa·ble 〔ˈkʌlpəbl; ˈkʌlpəbl〕 *adj.* 該受譴責的。 —**cul·pa·bly,** *adv.* —**cul·pa·bil·i·ty,** *n.*

cul·prit 〔ˈkʌlprɪt; ˈkʌlprit〕 *n.* ①刑事被告。②犯罪者。③導致不良後果之人或事物。

cult 〔kʌlt; kʌlt〕 *n.* ①〖宗教〗禮拜儀式。②（對人或主義）崇拜。③時尚；風靡一時的嗜好。④信徒；教派。⑤崇拜者（集合稱）。—**ic,—ish,** *adj.* —**ism,** —**ist,** *n.*

cultch 〔kʌltʃ; kʌltʃ〕 *n.* ①垃圾；廢物。②牡蠣殼屑。③牡蠣之卵。（亦作 **culch**）

cul·ti·va·ble 〔ˈkʌltəvəbl; ˈkʌltivəbl〕 *adj.* 可耕種的；可培養的。—**cul·ti·va·bil·i·ty,** *n.* —**cul·ti·va·bly,** *adv.*

*__cul·ti·vate__ 〔ˈkʌltəˌvet; ˈkʌltiveit〕 *v.t.*, **-vat·ed, -vat·ing.** ①耕種。②教化；培養。to *cultivate* a taste for music. 培養音樂的興趣。to *cultivate* friendship with a person. 與人締交。③致力（音樂、藝術、科學等）。

cul·ti·vat·ed 〔ˈkʌltəˌvetɪd; ˈkʌltiveitid〕 *adj.* ①在耕種中的；耕耘的。*cultivated* land. 耕地。②栽植的；由栽培而生長的。③有教養的；優雅的。a *cultivated* person. 有教養之人。

*__cul·ti·va·tion__ 〔ˌkʌltəˈveʃən; ˌkʌltiˈveiʃən〕 *n.* ①耕種。The land is under *cultivation.* 此地在耕種中。②教化；培養。*cultivation* of the mind. 修養心性。

cul·ti·va·tor 〔ˈkʌltəˌvetɚ; ˈkʌltiveitə〕 *n.* ①耕種者；培養者。②鬆土除草機。

cult of personality 個人崇拜。

*__cul·tur·al__ 〔ˈkʌltʃərəl; ˈkʌltʃərəl〕 *adj.* ①栽培的。②教養的。③文化的；人文的。Literature, art, and music are *cultural* studies. 文學、藝術與音樂是人文方面的研究。

cul·tur·al·ize 〔ˈkʌltʃərəˌlaɪz; ˈkʌltʃərəlaiz〕 *v.t.*, **-ized, -iz·ing.** 使受文明或文化之薰陶。

cul·tu·ra·ti 〔ˌkʌltʃəˈrɑti; ˌkʌltʃəˈrɑːtiː〕 *n. pl.* 文化人士；有教養的人士。

*__cul·ture__ 〔ˈkʌltʃɚ; ˈkʌltʃə〕 *n.*, *v.*, **-tured, -tur·ing.** —*n.* ①修養；文雅。a man of *culture.* 有文學藝術修養的人。②文明；文化。Chinese *culure.* 中國的文化。③培養；教化；教育；訓練。pearl *culture.* 養殖眞珠。④耕種。water *culture.* 水耕。⑤細菌的培養。a *culture* of cholera germs. 霍亂菌的培殖。⑥以培養基培殖之物。—*v.t.* ①耕種。②〖生物〗以培養基培殖。③以…作培養基。

culture area 文化區。

culture center 文化中心。

culture complex 文化結叢（多種文化特質相互關聯而以其中某一特質爲主導者）。

cul·tured 〔ˈkʌltʃɚd; ˈkʌltʃəd〕 *adj.* 有修養的。

cultured pearl 養殖珠。

culture medium 培養基（微生物之養料）。

culture shock 文化震盪（對外國或某種新文化不能適應的情況）。

culture trait 文化特質。

cul·tur·ist 〔ˈkʌltʃərɪst; ˈkʌltʃərist〕 *n.* ①培養者；耕種者。②文化之擁護者。

cul·tus 〔ˈkʌltəs; ˈkʌltəs〕 *n.*, *pl.* **-tus·es, -ti** 〔-taɪ; -tai〕. =**cult.**

cul·ver 〔ˈkʌlvɚ; ˈkʌlvə〕 *n.* 〖英方〗鴿；斑鳩。

cul·vert 〔ˈkʌlvɚt; ˈkʌlvət〕 *n.* ①暗渠；陰溝；涵洞。②地下電纜。

cum 〔kʌm, kum; kʌm〕 〖拉〗 *prep.* 連同；附帶；兼（=with, including）.

cum·ber 〔ˈkʌmbɚ; ˈkʌmbə〕 *v.t.* ①阻礙。②拖累。—*n.* 阻礙；拖累。

Cum·ber·land 〔ˈkʌmbɚlənd; ˈkʌmbələnd〕 *n.* ①坎伯蘭（英格蘭西北部一郡）。②坎伯蘭（美國 Maryland 州西北部一城市）。

cum·ber·some 〔ˈkʌmbɚsəm; ˈkʌmbəsəm〕 *adj.* 笨重的；累贅的。 —**ly,** *adv.*

Cum·bri·an 〔ˈkʌmbrɪən; ˈkʌmbriən〕 *n.* Cumberland 人。—*adj.* Cumberland 的。

cum·brous [ˈkʌmbrəs; ˈkʌmbrəs] *adj.* 笨重的;累贅的。—**ly**, *adv.*

cum·in [ˈkʌmɪn; ˈkʌmin] *n.* 〖植物〗小茴香。

cum·mer [ˈkʌmɚ; ˈkʌmə] *n.* 〖蘇〗①教母。②女伴;女友。③婦女;女郎。

cum·mer·bund [ˈkʌmɚˌbʌnd; ˈkʌməbʌnd] *n.* 〖英印〗圍腰之帶;腹帶。(亦作 **kummerbund**)

cum·min [ˈkʌmɪn; ˈkʌmin] *n.* =**cumin.**

cum·quat [ˈkʌmkwɑt; ˈkʌmkwɔt] *n.* 〖植物〗金橘。

cum·shaw [ˈkʌmʃɔ; ˈkʌmʃɔː] *n.* 賞錢;小帳(由閩南語"感謝"訛轉而來)。

cu·mu·late [*v.* ˈkjumjəˌlet; ˈkjuːmjuleit *adj.* ˈkjumjəlɪt; ˈkjuːmjulit] *v.*, **-lat·ed, -lat·ing,** *adj.* —*v.t.* & *v.i.* 累積;堆積。—*adj.* 堆積的。—**cu·mu·la·tion,** *n.*

cu·mu·la·tive [ˈkjumjəˌletɪv; ˈkjuːmjulətiv] *adj.* 累積的。—**ly**, *adv.* —**ness,** *n.*

cumulative evidence 〖法律〗①重覆以前之證詞。②證明或加强前一證據之證據。③各部分彼此加强可靠性之證據。

cumulative stock 累積股(因股利累積而價值亦隨之增高的股票)。

cumulative voting 選民所領選票數與候選人數相同之選舉制(選民可將所有選票投給一人,亦可分投數人)。

cu·mu·lo-cir·rus [ˌkjumjəloˈsɪrəs; ˌkjuːmjulouˈsirəs] *n.* 〖氣象〗積卷雲。

cu·mu·lo-nim·bus [ˌkjumjəloˈnɪmbəs; ˌkjuːmjulouˈnimbəs] *n.* 〖氣象〗積雨雲。

cu·mu·lo-stra·tus [ˌkjumjəloˈstretəs; ˌkjuːmjulouˈstreitəs] *n.* 〖氣象〗積層雲。

cu·mu·lous [ˈkjumjələs; ˈkjuːmjuləs] *adj.* 〖氣象〗積雲狀的。

cu·mu·lus [ˈkjumjələs; ˈkjuːmjuləs] *n.*, *pl.* **-li** [-laɪ; -lai]. ①〖氣象〗積雲。②堆積;累積。

C.U.N. Charter of the United Nations.

cu·ne·ate [ˈkjunɪɪt; ˈkjuːniit] *adj.* 〖植物〗楔形的(葉)。(亦作 **cuneated**)

cu·ne·i·form [ˈkjunɪəˌfɔrm; ˈkjuːniifɔːm] *adj.* ①楔形的。②楔形文字的。—*n.* (古波斯、亞述等國之)楔形文字。—**ist,** *n.*

cun·ner [ˈkʌnɚ; ˈkʌnə] *n.* 青鱸(產於英格蘭及北美洲大西洋沿岸)。

***cun·ning** [ˈkʌnɪŋ; ˈkʌniŋ] *adj.* ①狡猾的;奸詐的。a *cunning* trick. 詭計;狡計。②熟練的;巧妙的。③〖美俗〗美麗的;可愛的;迷人的;甜蜜的。—*n.* ①狡猾;奸詐。②〖古〗熟練;聰明。—**ly,** *adv.* —**ness,** *n.*

‡**cup** [kʌp; kʌp] *n.*, *v.*, **cupped, cup·ping.** —*n.* ①杯;酒杯。He bought a set of *cups*. 他買了一套杯子。②一杯;一杯的量。a *cup* of coffee. 一杯咖啡。③杯形物。④杯中物;酒。He is too fond of the *cup*. 他太嗜酒。⑤銀杯;獎杯。to win the *cup*. 優勝;得錦標。⑥〖宗教〗聖爵。⑦〖宗教〗聖餐酒。⑧命運;必須經歷之事。a bitter *cup*. 苦命;苦事。His *cup* of happiness was full. 他的命中充滿幸福。⑨(*pl.*) 飲易醉之酒。⑩高爾夫球洞;洞內之鐵杯。***between cup and lip*** 事在將成未成之間。***in one's cups*** 醉酒。—*v.t.* ①使成杯形。②以杯盛;放置杯中。③用吸血器替…放血。—*v.i.* 成爲杯形。—**like,** *adj.*

cup·bear·er [ˈkʌpˌbɛrɚ; ˈkʌpˌbɛərə] *n.* 司酒者;嘗酒者。

cup·board** [ˈkʌbɚd; ˈkʌbəd] *n.* 碗櫥;食櫥;小櫥。cupboard love*** 有所企圖的愛。

cup·cake [ˈkʌpˌkek; ˈkʌpkeik] *n.* 小糕餅(有時在紙杯中烤之)。

cu·pel [ˈkjupɛl; ˈkjuːpəl] *n.*, *v.*, **-pel(l)ed, -pel·(l)ing.** —*n.* 灰皿;骨灰所製之坩堝。—*v.t.* 用灰皿加熱或煉製。

cu·pel·la·tion [ˌkjupəˈleʃən; ˌkjuːpəˈleiʃən] *n.* (分析或精鍊貴金屬之)灰皿法;灰吹法。

***cup·ful** [ˈkʌpˌful; ˈkʌpful] *n.*, *pl.* **-fuls.** 一滿杯;一滿杯之量。

Cu·pid [ˈkjupɪd; ˈkjuːpid] *n.* ①羅馬神話中的愛神。②(c-) 用爲愛情表徵的持弓箭的美童。

cu·pid·i·ty [kjuˈpɪdətɪ; kju(ː)ˈpiditi] *n.* 貪婪;貪得。

cup of tea 〖英俗〗①愛好之物或活動。②命運。③應當心的人物或值得懷疑之事。

cu·po·la [ˈkjupələ; ˈkjuːpələ] *n.* ①圓屋頂。②圓頂閣。③小型之鎔鐵爐。④(軍艦與砲臺上的)迴旋砲塔。—**t·ed,** *adj.*

cup·ping [ˈkʌpɪŋ; ˈkʌpiŋ] *n.* 〖醫〗杯吸法;吸器放血法。

cupping glass 〖醫〗玻璃吸杯;放血杯。

cu·pre·ous [ˈkjuprɪəs; ˈkjuːpriəs] *adj.* ①銅的;似銅的;含銅的。②銅色的。

cu·pric [ˈkjuprɪk; ˈkjuːprik] *adj.* 〖化〗(尤指二價之)銅的;含銅的。

cupric sulfate 硫酸銅。

cu·prif·er·ous [kjuˈprɪfərəs; kju(ː)ˈprifərəs] *adj.* 含銅的。

cu·prite [ˈkjupraɪt; ˈkjuːprait] *n.* 〖礦〗赤銅礦。

cu·pro·nick·el [ˌkjuproˈnɪkḷ; ˌkjuːprouˈnikəl] *n.* 含鎳量最高達百分之四十的任何銅合金。—*adj.* 含銅與鎳的。

cu·prous [ˈkjuprəs; ˈkjuːprəs] *adj.* 〖化〗一價銅的;亞銅的。

cu·prum [ˈkjuprəm; ˈkjuːprəm] 〖拉〗*n.* 銅,化學符號爲 Cu.

cu·pule [ˈkjupjul; ˈkjuːpjuːl] *n.* ①〖動物〗吸盤。②〖植物〗(苔蘚植物等之杯形)子器。

cur [kɝ; kəː] *n.* ①雜種狗。②〖蔑〗下流坯子。

cur. ①currency. ②current.

cur·a·ble [ˈkjʊrəbḷ; ˈkjuərəbl] *adj.* 可醫治的(病);可矯正的(缺點)。—**cur·a·bly,** *adv.* —**cur·a·bil·i·ty,** —**ness,** *n.*

cu·ra·çao [ˌkjʊrəˈso; ˌkjuərəˈsou] *n.* (加苦橙皮所釀成之)柑香酒。(亦作 **curaçoa**)

cu·ra·cy [ˈkjʊrəsɪ; ˈkjuərəsi] *n.*, *pl.* **-cies.** 副牧師之職位或職務。

cu·ra·re [kjʊˈrɑrɪ; kjuəˈrɑːri] *n.* ①美洲箭毒(南美土人用以製毒箭之毒質)。②產此等毒質之樹。(亦作 **curara, curari**)

cu·ras·sow [ˈkjʊrəˌso; ˈkjuərəsou] *n.* (中、南美所產之)一種似火鷄之大鳥。

cu·rate [ˈkjʊrɪt; ˈkjuərit] *n.* 〖宗教〗副牧師;助理牧師。

cur·a·tive [ˈkjʊrətɪv; ˈkjuərətiv] *adj.* 治病的;有治病效力的。—*n.* 藥物;補救;補救方法。—**ly,** *adv.* —**ness,** *n.*

cu·ra·tor [kjʊˈretɚ; kjuəˈreitə] *n.* ①(博物館、圖書館、美術館等之)館長。②〖法律〗(未成年人或無行爲能力者之)監護人。

cu·ra·to·ri·al [ˌkjʊrəˈtorɪəl; ˌkjuərəˈtɔːriəl] *adj.* 主持者的;監護人的。

cu·ra·tor·ship [kjʊˈretɚʃɪp; kjuəˈreitəʃip] *n.* curator 之職。

***curb** [kɝb; kəːb] *n.* ①馬勒;馬銜。②抑制;控制;阻擋或抑制的東西。Put (*or* Keep) a *curb* to your anger. 抑制住你的憤怒。③路的邊欄;邊石。④〖美〗(證券股票的)場外市場。—*v.t.* ①勒(馬)。②抑制。to *curb* one's tongue. 不要饒舌;少說話。③加邊石。—**a·ble,** *adj.* —**less,** *adj.* —**er,** *n.*

curb exchange =curb market.
curb·ing ['kɝbɪŋ; 'kə:biŋ] *n.* 路之邊欄的石材;邊石材料。(亦作 **kerbing**)
curb market 股票場外交易市場。
curb roof 〖建築〗複折屋頂。
curb service 路旁小吃店對坐在車裏的顧客提供之服務。
curb·stone ['kɝb,ston; 'kə:bstoun] *n.* 邊石。
cur·cu·li·o [kɝ'kjulɪ,o; kə:'kju:liou] *n., pl.* **-li·os.** 象鼻蟲。
cur·cu·ma ['kɝkjumə; 'kə:kjumə] *n.* 〖植物〗薑黃。
curcuma paper 薑黃紙; 試驗紙。
cur·cu·min ['kɝkjumɪn; 'kə:kjumin] *n.* 〖化〗薑黃素。
curd [kɝd; kə:d] *n.* ①(常 *pl.*) 凝乳。②任何類似凝乳之物。
cur·dle ['kɝdl; 'kə:dl] *v.,* **-dled, -dling.** —*v.i.* ①凝結。②變稠;變濃厚。—*v.t.* 使凝結。 ***curdle the*** (or ***one's***) ***blood*** 嚇得戰慄。
curd·y ['kɝdɪ; 'kə:di] *adj.,* **curd·i·er, curd·i·est.** ①多凝乳的。 ②凝結了的; 似凝乳的。—**curd·i·ness,** *n.*
***cure** [kjur, kɪur; kjuə, kjɔə, kjɔ:] *v.,* **cured, cur·ing,** *n.* —*v.t.* ①醫癒。 to *cure* a child of a cold. 醫癒小孩的傷風。②治療;祛除(惡習)。to *cure* a cold. 治療傷風。to *cure* society of a social evil. 爲社會除公害。③醃;晒乾或燻製。④使(新敷的水泥)保持潮濕以助其硬化。—*v.i.* ①治療。②痊癒。—*n.*①醫治;治療;痊癒。②醫法;治療方法;補救方法。a rest *cure.* 靜養。③藥劑。Aspirin is a wonderful *cure* for colds.阿斯匹靈是治傷風的妙藥。④精神上的監督;宗教上之職務。the *cure* of souls. (監督靈魂)牧師的職務。
cu·ré [kju're; kju'rei] 〖法〗 *n.* 牧師。
cure-all ['kjur,ɔl; 'kjuərɔ:l] *n.* 萬靈藥;百寶丹。
cure·less ['kjurlɪs;'kjuəlis] *adj.* 不治的;不可救藥的。
cu·rette [kju'rɛt; kju'ret] *n., v.,* **-ret·ted, -ret·ting.** —*n.* (外科用之) 刮匙。—*v.t.* 用刮匙刮。
cur·few ['kɝfju; 'kə:fju:] *n.* ①古代晚間令人熄燈安睡的鐘鳴。②作此種鳴聲的鐘。③鳴鐘熄燈安睡的時間。④宵禁。—**ed,** *adj.*
cu·ri·a ['kjurɪə; 'kjuəriə] *n., pl.* **-ri·ae** [-rɪ,i; -rii:]. ①(古羅馬之) 政治區分之一;古羅馬元老院。②中世紀時之法庭。③主教之行政助理。④(C-)羅馬教廷; 教皇高級助理之集合稱。—**cu·ri·al,** *adj.* —**l·ism,**—**l·ist,** *n.*
Cu·rie[1] ['kjuri, kju'ri; 'kjuəri, kjuə'ri:] *n.* 居里 (Pierre, 1859–1906, 女科學家 Marie 之夫,法國物理學家及化學家)。
Cu·rie[2] *n.* 居里夫人 (Marie, 1867–1934, 本姓 Marja Sklodowska, 生於波蘭之法國女物理學家及化學家,爲鐳的發現者)。
cu·rie ['kjuri; 'kjuəri] *n.* 〖物理〗 居里 (質射單位)。
cu·ri·o ['kjurɪ,o; 'kjuəriou] *n., pl.* **-ri·os.** 古玩;古董;珍品。
***cu·ri·os·i·ty** [,kjurɪ'ɑsətɪ; ,kjuəri'ɔsiti] *n., pl.* **-ties.** ①求知慾。②好奇;好奇心。I bought it out of *curiosity.* 我因好奇心而買了它。③新奇的事物;珍品。
‡**cu·ri·ous** ['kjurɪəs, 'kɪurɪ-; 'kjuəriəs, 'kjɔər-] *adj.* ①求知的; 好問的;好奇的。He is a *curious* student. 他是個好學的學生。②好管閒事的;好窺探的。The old woman is too *curious* about other people's business. 這位老太婆太愛管人家的閑事。③奇特的; 古怪的; 反常的。What a *curious* mistake! 多奇怪的錯誤呀!④十分仔細的;精細的。a jewel of *curious* workmanship. 精工鑲造的珠寶。⑤(書籍等)淫穢的; 黃色的。—**ly,** *adv.* —**ness,** *n.*
cu·ri·um ['kjurɪəm; 'kjuəriəm] *n.* 〖化〗鋦(元素名,符號爲Cm)。
curl** [kɝl; kə:l] *v.t.* ①捲成小圈(如頭髮)。to *curl* one's lips. 抿嘴;撇嘴。②捲曲;盤旋;盤繞。—*v.i.* ①捲曲。Her hair *curled* into a lock. 她的頭髮捲成鬈髮。②環繞;盤旋。③彎曲;起波紋。 ***curl up **a.** 捲起。**b.** 彎曲雙腿; 蜷伏。The child *curled up* on the sofa. 小孩蜷伏於沙發上。**c.** 損壞;放棄。—*n.* ①捲成的小圈(如頭髮)。to keep the hair in *curls.* 保持鬈髮。②盤旋;彎曲如環狀的東西。a *curl* of smoke. 煙圈。③圈繞。 ***in curl*** 捲曲的。—**a·ble,** *adj.*
curl·er ['kɝlɚ; 'kə:lə] *n.* ①捲曲之人或物。②捲髮夾。③參加 curling 遊戲的人。
cur·lew ['kɝlu; 'kə:lu:] *n., pl.* **-lews, -lew.** 〖動物〗麻鷸。
cur·li·cue ['kɝlɪ,kju; 'kə:likju:] *n.* (書法等之)旋曲;花體。(亦作 **curlycue**)
curl·i·ness ['kɝlɪnɪs; 'kə:linis] *n.* 捲曲;捲縮;旋渦。
curl·ing ['kɝlɪŋ; 'kə:liŋ] *n.* 〖蘇〗一種在冰上滑滾石塊的遊戲。
curling iron(s) 捲髮或燙髮之鉗。
curling tongs =curling iron.
curl·pa·per ['kɝl,pepɚ; 'kə:l,peipə] *n.* 捲髮用之軟紙。
***curl·y** ['kɝlɪ; 'kə:li] *adj.,* **curl·i·er, curl·i·est.** ①捲曲的; 有波紋的。②有捲曲物的;有捲髮的。—**curl·i·ly,** *adv.*
cur·mudg·eon [kɚ'mʌdʒən; kə:-'mʌdʒən] *n.* 守財奴;脾氣壞而愛爭吵的人。—**ly,** *adv.*
cur·rach, cur·ragh ['kɝrəx; 'kʌrə] *n.* 〖蘇, 愛〗 =**coracle.**
***cur·rant** ['kɝənt; 'kʌrənt] *n.* ①一種小而無核的葡萄乾。②〖植物〗紅醋栗。
***cur·ren·cy** ['kɝənsɪ; 'kʌrənsi] *n., pl.* **-cies.** ①通貨; 貨幣(硬幣或紙幣)。hard *currency.* 硬幣。②流通;流布。③通用;通行。④某一事物流行之時期。
‡**cur·rent** ['kɝənt; 'kʌrənt] *n.* ①水流或氣流。He swam with (against) the *current.* 他順(逆)流游泳。②電流。 direct *current.* 直流。③趨向;趨勢。—*adj.* ①流通的;通行的。②目下的;現在的。 the *current* month. 本月。*current* expenses (=*current* expenditure). 經常費。the *current* price. 時價。③公認的。④流傳中的; 傳布中的。 ***current account*** 往來帳。 —**ness,** *n.*
current assets 流動資產(可隨時,通常在一年內,變賣爲現金而不會虧蝕之資產)。
current cost 現時成本(以目前原料價格、工資等爲依據的成本)。
current deposit 活期存款(爲定期存款 fixed deposit 之對)。
current English 現代英語。
current liabilities 〖商業〗流動負債(一年內必須償付的債務)。
cur·rent·ly ['kɝəntlɪ; 'kʌrəntli] *adv.* ①眼前地;目前地。②容易地;順利地。
cur·ri·cle ['kɝɪkl; 'kʌrikl] *n.* 一種雙馬二輪之馬車。
cur·ric·u·lar [kə'rɪkjəlɚ; kə'rikjulə] *adj.* 課程的;功課的。
cur·ric·u·lum [kə'rɪkjələm; kə'rikjuləm] *n., pl.* **-lums, -la**[-lə; -lə]. 課程。
curriculum vi·tae [~'vaɪti; ~'vaiti:] *pl.* **cur·ric·u·la vi·tae.** 履歷;簡歷。
cur·ried ['kɝɪd; 'kʌrid] *adj.* (食物)用咖哩粉烹調的。

cur·ri·er 〔ˈkɝɪə; ˈkʌriə〕 *n.* ①鞣皮匠；硝皮者；製革者。②梳刷馬毛之人。

cur·rish 〔ˈkɝɪʃ; ˈkəːriʃ〕 *adj.* ①惡狗似的。②脾氣壞的；下賤的。—**ly,** *adv.*

cur·ry¹ 〔ˈkɝɪ; ˈkʌri〕 *n., pl.* **-ries,** *v.,* **-ried, -ry·ing.** —*n.* ①咖哩醬；咖哩粉。②咖哩醬所調製的食品。—*v.t.* 用咖哩醬調製。

cur·ry² *v.t.,* **-ried, -ry·ing.** ①梳刷(馬等之毛)。②硝(皮)；製(革)。③擊打；鞭打。***curry favor (with)*** 曲意逢迎；拍馬屁。

cur·ry·comb 〔ˈkɝɪˌkom; ˈkʌrikoum〕 *n.* 梳刷馬毛之梳；馬梳；馬櫛。—*v.t.* 用馬梳梳刷。

curry powder 咖哩粉。

curse** 〔kɝs; kəːs〕 *v.,* **cursed** or **curst, curs·ing,** *n.* —*v.t.* ①祈禱上帝降禍於。②詛咒。③使受罪；使感痛苦。He was *cursed* with boils. 他爲疔瘡所苦。④將…逐出教會。—*v.i.* 詛咒；咒罵。—*n.* ①祈求上帝降禍於人；詛咒；咒罵。②殃禍。③禍因；災源。Gambling is a *curse.* 賭博是一禍因。④怒時所作的惡言；褻瀆的語言。⑤被詛咒之物。⑥逐出教會。⑦(常 the~)〔俚〕月經；經期。Curses come home to roost.*** 害人反害己。***not to care*** (or ***give***) ***a curse for*** 毫不顧及；不以…爲意。—**curs·er,** *n.*

curs·ed 〔ˈkɝsɪd, kɝst; ˈkəːsid, kəːst〕 *adj.* ①被咒的；受詛的。②可憎的；可厭的。③痛苦的；悲慘的。—**ness,** *n.*

cur·sive 〔ˈkɝsɪv; ˈkəːsiv〕 *adj.* 草書的；草書體的。—*n.* 行書；草書原稿。—**ly,** *adv.*

cur·so·ri·al 〔kɝˈsorɪəl; kəˈsɔːriəl〕 *adj.* 〔動物〕①適於奔跑的(如犬、馬等之足與骨骼)。②生有適於行走之肢的。

cur·so·ry 〔ˈkɝsərɪ; ˈkəːsəri〕 *adj.* 匆促的；粗略的。—**cur·so·ri·ly,** *adv.* —**cur·so·ri·ness,** *n.*

curst 〔kɝst; kəːst〕 *v.* pt. & pp. of **curse.** —*adj.*=**cursed.** —**ly,** *adv.*

curt 〔kɝt; kəːt〕 *adj.* ①簡短的；草率的。②簡慢的。—**ly,** *adv.* —**ness,** *n.*

cur·tail 〔kɝˈtel; kəːˈteil〕 *v.t.* 縮短；減縮。***curtailed words*** 簡筆字(如 bike, flu, math 等)。—**ed·ly,** *adv.* —**er,** —**ment,** *n.*

‡cur·tain 〔ˈkɝtn̩, -tɪn; ˈkəːtn, -tən, -tin〕 *n.* ①帳；幕；窗帘。The *curtain* falls (*or* drops). 閉幕。②掩蔽；隔絕；掩蔽之物。a *curtain* of smoke. 煙幕。③(兩稜堡間的)中堤。④(*pl.*)〔俚〕死亡。⑤戲劇開幕之時間或動作。⑥戲劇結束時之臺詞劇情或效果等。***bring down the curtain on*** 結束。***draw a curtain over*** (***something***) 隱瞞(某事)；不再提(某事)。***iron curtain*** 鐵幕。***raise*** (or ***lift***) ***the curtain on*** a. 揭露。b. 開始。***safety curtain*** 防火窗帘(或布幕)。—*v.t.* ①掛幕於。*curtained windows.* 掛有窗帘的窗。②掩蔽；隱藏。***curtain off*** 用幕布隔開。—**less,** *adj.*

curtain call 觀衆要求演員出場謝幕時的呼聲。

curtain fire 彈幕。

curtain lecture 妻子在枕邊對丈夫之責備。

curtain raiser 正戲前之配戲；開場戲。

curtain speech (劇作者、演員或演出人)劇終在幕前所發表之演說。

Cur·ta·na 〔kɝˈtɑnə; kəːˈtɑːnə〕 *n.* 無尖之刀；慈悲之劍(英王加冕時捧持於王前，以作仁慈之表徵者)。

cur·te·sy 〔ˈkɝtəsɪ; ˈkəːtisi〕 *n., pl.* **-sies.** 〔法律〕鰥夫產(妻死後丈夫運用妻子繼承得來之不動產的權利)。

cur·ti·lage 〔ˈkɝtl̩ɪdʒ; ˈkəːtilidʒ〕 *n.* 〔法律〕庭園；宅地。

curt·sy, curt·sey 〔ˈkɝtsɪ; ˈkəːtsi〕 *n., pl.* **-sies, -seys,** *v.,* **-sied, -sy·ing; -sey·ed, -sey·ing.** —*n.* 女人行的鞠躬禮(包括彎身和屈膝)。***drop a curtsey*** (女人)行鞠躬禮。***make one's curtsey to*** (女人)向…行鞠躬禮。—*v.i.* 行女人鞠躬禮。

cu·rule 〔ˈkjurul; ˈkjuəruːl〕 *adj.* ①(古羅馬之)高官的。②最高階級的。

cur·va·ceous 〔kɝˈveʃəs; kəːˈveiʃəs〕 *adj.* 〔俗〕婀娜多姿的；曲線玲瓏的。

cur·va·ture 〔ˈkɝvətʃɚ; ˈkəːvətʃə〕 *n.* ①彎曲；屈曲。②〔數學〕曲度；曲率。

***curve** 〔kɝv; kəːv〕 *n., v.,* **curved, curv·ing,** *adj.* —*n.* ①曲線。②彎曲。③繪圖者所用的曲線用具。④〔棒球〕曲球(路線彎曲的投球)。—*v.t.* 使彎曲。—*v.i.* 彎。The road *curves* to the west. 路向西彎。—*adj.* 彎曲的。—**curved,** *adj.* —**less,** *adj.*

cur·vet 〔*n.* ˈkɝvɪt; kəːˈvet *v.* ˈkɝvɪt, kɚˈvɛt; kəːˈvet〕 *n., v.,* **-vet·ted, -vet·ting.** —*n.* 馬之騰躍。—*v.i.* 騰躍。—*v.t.* 使(馬)騰躍。

cur·vi·lin·e·ar 〔ˌkɝvəˈlɪnɪɚ; ˌkəːviˈliniə〕 *adj.* 曲線的。

cu·sec 〔ˈkjusɛk; ˈkjuːsek〕 *n.* 每秒一立方英尺。

cush·at 〔ˈkʌʃət; ˈkʌʃət〕 *n.* (歐洲產之)斑鳩。

***cush·ion** 〔ˈkuʃən, -ɪn; ˈkuʃən, -in〕 *n.* ①墊子；坐褥。②形狀或用途如褥墊的東西。an air *cushion.* 氣墊。③撞球桌面四周之彈性襯裏。④任何足以減輕撞擊震動之物。⑤任何足以減輕痛苦、負擔或有助於舒適之事物。⑥電臺或電視廣播稿中可節略或完全免去之部分。—*v.t.* ①裝置褥墊於。②隱忍；壓制。③以褥隱藏或遮蓋。④減輕…之效力。⑤放低聲音。

cush·y 〔ˈkuʃɪ; ˈkuʃi〕 *adj.,* **cush·i·er, cush·i·est.** 〔俚〕容易的；舒適的。

cusk 〔kʌsk; kʌsk〕 *n., pl.* **cusk, cusks.** 鱈類之魚。

cusp 〔kʌsp; kʌsp〕 *n.* ①尖端；尖頭。②〔解剖〕**a.** 牙尖。**b.** (心臟之)瓣尖。③〔天文〕(新月之)尖角。—**al,** *adj.*

cus·pid 〔ˈkʌspɪd; ˈkʌspid〕 *n.* 〔解剖〕尖牙；犬牙。—*adj.* = **cuspidate.**

cus·pi·dal 〔ˈkʌspɪdl; ˈkʌspidl〕 *adj.* ①尖的；有尖端的。②〔幾何〕歧點的。

cus·pi·date 〔ˈkʌspɪˌdet; ˈkʌspideit〕 *adj.* ①有尖端的；有尖頭的。②末端尖銳的。

cus·pi·dat·ed 〔ˈkʌspɪˌdetɪd; ˈkʌspideitid〕 *adj.* =**cuspidate.**

cus·pi·dor 〔ˈkʌspəˌdɔr; ˈkʌspidɔː〕 *n.* 〔美〕痰盂。

cuss 〔kʌs; kʌs〕 *n.* 〔美俗〕①詛咒。②奇怪或討厭的人或動物。③任何人或動物。—*v.t.* 〔美俗〕①詛咒；咒罵。②嚴厲地批評或責備〔常 out〕。—*v.i.* 咒罵。

cuss·ed 〔ˈkʌsɪd; ˈkʌsid〕 *adj.* 〔俗〕①= **cursed.** ②執拗的；彆扭的；頑固的。—**ly,** *adv.* —**ness,** *n.*

cus·tard 〔ˈkʌstɚd; ˈkʌstəd〕 *n.* 鷄蛋牛乳和糖製成的軟凍。

custard apple 〔植物〕番荔枝。

cus·to·di·al 〔kʌsˈtodɪəl; kʌsˈtoudjəl〕 *adj.* 保管的；監視的；監督人的；保管人的。—*n.* 裝遺骸之容器。

cus·to·di·an 〔kʌsˈtodɪən; kʌsˈtoudjən〕 *n.* 監督人；保管人；管理人。

cus·to·di·an·ship 〔kʌsˈtodɪənˌʃɪp; kʌsˈtoudjənʃip〕*n.* custodian之職務或地位。

cus·to·dy 〔ˈkʌstədɪ; ˈkʌstədi〕 *n., pl.* **-dies.** ①監督；監視；保護。②監禁；拘留。***be in custody*** 爲警方所扣留；在獄中。***take***

into custody 逮捕;監禁。

‡cus·tom [ˈkʌstəm; ˈkʌstəm] *n.* ①習慣。It was his *custom* to rise early. 早起是他的習慣。②習俗;風俗;慣例。Is this the *custom* here? 這是這裏的風俗嗎?③主顧的經常照顧。I shall withdraw (*or* take away) my *custom* from this shop. 我將停止(不再)光顧此店。④顧客的集合稱。⑤進口稅。⑥封建時代佃農對封主按時繳的捐稅或提供的服務。—*adj.* ①定製的。*custom* shoes (clothes, etc.). 定製的鞋(衣等)。②專做定製的。a *custom* tailor. 專做定製衣服的裁縫。

***cus·tom·ar·y** [ˈkʌstəm͵ɛrɪ; ˈkʌstəməri] *adj.* 習常的;慣常的。*customary* law. 習慣法。—**cus·tom·ar·i·ly,** *adv.*—**cus·tom·ar·i·ness,** *n.*

***cus·tom·er** [ˈkʌstəmɚ; ˈkʌstəmə] *n.* ①顧客;主顧。to secure *customers* by advertising. 用廣告招徠顧客。②〖俗〗傢伙;人。He is a queer *customer*. 他是一個怪傢伙。

custom house 海關。

custom house broker 代理報關「人;報關行。」

cus·tom-made [ˈkʌstəmˈmed; ˈkʌstəmˈmeid] *adj.* 定做的;訂製的。

‡cus·toms [ˈkʌstəmz; ˈkʌstəmz] *n. pl.* ①進口稅。②〖罕〗出口稅。③(the C-)(作*sing.*解)海關。How long will it take us to pass (get through) the *Customs?* 我們要花多久時間才通過海關檢查? The *Customs* formalities are simple. 海關檢查手續簡單。

customs broker 報關行(爲進、出口商報關而賺取佣金者)。(亦作 **customhouse broker**)

customs duties 進口稅。

customs tariffs 關稅表。

customs union 關稅聯盟。

‡cut [kʌt; kʌt] *v.*, **cut, cut·ting,** *adj.*, *n.* —*v.t.* ①割;切。He *cut* his finger. 他割傷了他的手指。②劈開。③縮減;減少。to *cut* expenses. 減少費用。④分開;穿過。⑤刺。The cold wind *cut* me to the bone. 寒風刺骨。⑥(球戲)斜打;削擊;切擊。⑦傷感情。⑧〖俗〗不與交往;不睬。⑨缺席;缺課。⑩溶解。⑪(牌戲)將洗好的牌分爲兩部分(而上下顚倒之);切(牌)。⑫〖俗〗做;表演。⑬縮短。⑭快走。⑮停止;制止。⑯砍伐。⑰修剪。to *cut* one's hair. 理髮。⑱相交。⑲〖無線電與電視〗刪剪(節目)。⑳稀釋。㉑挖空;掘。㉒長牙。㉓停止(引擎的轉動或液體的流動)。㉔〖俗〗不再繼續〖常 out〗. Let's *cut* out the pretense. 我們不要再假裝了。㉕剪輯(影片)。㉖(電影檢查員)剪去影片禁映的部分。㉗將…錄音。—*v.i.* ①割;切;裁。The scissors *cut* well. 這剪刀很快。②被割;被切。Meat *cuts* easily. 肉容易切。③取捷徑;走近路〖across, through〗. to *cut* across an empty lot. 取捷徑越過空地。④猛打;猛擊;刺。⑤長牙。⑥將洗好的牌分爲兩部分; 切牌。⑦〖運動〗**a.** 擊球或擲球使其廻旋。 **b.** 跑時忽然轉方向。⑧〖電影, 電視〗突然轉變鏡頭。⑨傷害(情感)。⑩〖俗〗匆匆離開。***be cut out for*** 適於;勝任。He *is* not *cut out for* that sort of work. 他不適於那種工作。***cut a caper*** (or ***figure***) 手舞足蹈。***cut across*** **a.** 參看 *v.i.* 第三義。**b.** 超越(黨派、階級等)。***cut a figure*** 給人一種印象。***cut after*** (***something*** or ***somebody***) 急追;追趕。***cut a loss*** (or ***one's losses***) 重新做起;相機撤手;知難而退。***cut and come again*** 〖俗〗請儘量吃;請多吃一點東西(尤指肉類)。***cut and run*** **a.** 急忙逃竄。**b.** 匆匆解纜啓航。***cut a poor*** (***grand*** or ***ridicule***) ***figure*** 顯出低劣(威風、滑稽)的樣子。***cut at*** (以刀、棍等)對準猛打;傷害;毀滅。***cut away*** **a.** 砍掉;切除;切去;移去。**b.** 逃走;逃逸。***cut adrift*** 使獨立;使斷。***cut a swathe*** 吸引注意;使產生印象。***cut back*** **a.** 剪去其一端使短(如樹枝)。**b.**忽然重提前事(如小說、電影等)。**c.**減少或停止。***cut both ways*** 有好處也有壞處。***cut down*** **a.** 砍倒。**b.** 使減少。I shall *cut* his allowance *down* to ten dollars a week. 我要把他的津貼減爲每星期十元。**c.** 毀滅;破壞。**d.** 修改(衣服)使小。***cut down to size*** **a.** 縮減至所希望的大小或數目。**b.** 打擊(某人的)自大。***cut...free*** 割斷以獲自由。***cut in*** **a.** 突入;衝入。**b.** 攙言;插嘴。**c.** 在跳舞中的一對男女舞伴, 其中一人(常爲女的)突然爲人邀去共舞;截舞。**d.** 搶先;搶頭;超車。**e.** 連接(尤指機器)。***cut in half*** (or ***into halves***) 切爲相等之兩半。***cut in*** (or ***into***) ***pieces*** 切成許多塊。***cut into*** 打斷(談話);插嘴。***cut it fine*** 〖俗〗 只有僅僅足够的任何東西(尤指時間)。***cut it out*** 〖俚〗停止。***cut...loose*** 割離。***cut no*** (***not much***) ***ice*** 〖俗〗一無(少有)所成;毫無(少有)效果;不中用。***cut off*** **a.** 切去;截斷;使不連接。**b.** 使終止。**c.** 隔斷;隔絕。**d.** 隔離。**e.** 剝奪繼承權。***cut off a corner*** 抄近路;走捷徑。***cut on*** 趕路;趕忙。***cut one's coat to fit*** (or ***according to***) ***one's cloth*** 依自己財力作事;量入爲出。***cut one's eye*** 斜視。***cut one's eyeteeth*** 變成老於世故。***cut one's profits*** 知足;獲少量(或絲毫沒有)利益而感滿足。***cut*** (***one's***) ***stick*** 逃走。***cut one's teeth on*** 從小學習;一開頭便學習。***cut one's wisdom teeth*** 到達成年之齡; 成年; 及冠。***cut*** (***something***) ***open*** 切破;切傷。***cut out*** **a.** 切去;刪去。**b.** 造成…形狀。**c.**〖俚〗停止。The doctor said I must *cut* tobacco right *out*. 醫生說我必須立刻戒煙。**d.** 取代;占…之優勢;擊敗。**e.** 計劃;安排。**f.** 非常適合。**g.** (家畜等)離羣。**h.** (許多車輛行進時)不予他人警告而離開行列。***cut*** (***something***) ***short*** 切(刪)短(某事物); 打斷; 插嘴。***cut teeth*** 長牙。***cut the ground from under one*** (or ***from under a person's feet***) 使某人處於不鞏固之地位;推翻某人計畫、理論等的根據。***cut the*** (***Gordian***) ***knot*** 以最快方法解決一問題; 快刀斬亂麻。***cut the record*** 打破紀錄。***cut to pieces*** 切碎以毀壞;切毀。***cut to the bone*** 減至最低(少)限度。***cut up*** **a.** 切碎。**b.** 予以嚴酷的批評;尋人之短。**c.** 〖俗〗傷害。**d.**〖俚〗賣弄; 炫耀; 耍花樣。**e.** 頑皮; 惡作劇。***cut up rough*** 〖俗〗吵鬧;發脾氣;有危險。***cut up well*** 〖俗〗死後留下一大筆遺產。—*adj.* ①切過的。a *cut* pie. 一個切好的派。②琢磨過的。③降低的; 減縮的。*cut* prices. 減價。④去勢的;閹割的。⑤〖俚〗酒醉的。***cut and dried*** **a.** 預先準備的;卽可應用的。**b.** 呆板的;缺乏趣味的。***cut out for*** 〖俗〗適合。—*n.* ①割傷;切傷;傷口; 傷痕。a *cut* in one's finger. 手指傷痕。②溝渠;渠道(由開掘而成的)。③切開的片、塊等; 割下的東西; 剪下的東西。a nice *cut* of meat. 一塊上等的肉。④(裁剪的)樣式。I don't like the *cut* of this coat. 我不喜歡這外衣的樣式。⑤降低;減少。I shall be pleased to see a *cut* in prices. 我甚望物價能降低。⑥重擊; 猛擊(用刀劍或鞭等)。⑦斜擊; 切擊(如網球、板球等)。⑧傷人感情的言行;中傷。That was a *cut* at me. 那是中傷我的話。

⑨〖俗〗佯爲不識。⑩圖版;刻版;刻板印出之圖。⑪〖俗〗缺課。⑫切牌。⑬〖美,俗〗分贓。⑭分兒。His agent's *cut* is 20 per cent. 他的代理人的佣金是百分之二十。⑮種類;態度;風格。⑯捷徑。⑰刪節的部分。⑱抽籤用的籤。⑲電影、電視中鏡頭的轉變。⑳(擊劍時)双邊的一擊。***a cut above***〖俗〗勝過一籌。***a short cut*** 近路;捷徑。***cut of one's jib***〖俚〗面容。***give*** (***a person***) ***the cut directly*** 當面不認(某人);不睬。

cu·ta·ne·ous [kju'tenıəs; kju(:)'teinjəs] *adj.* 皮膚的。

cut·a·way ['kʌtə,we; 'kʌtəwei] *adj.* (衣服之)下擺裁成圓角的。a *cutaway* coat. 常禮服。—*n.* ①常禮服。②揭去外殼之機器(使參觀者能看到內部的結構)。③上述機械之圖示。④電影中鏡頭之轉移。

cut·back ['kʌt,bæk; 'kʌtbæk] *n.* ①剪去末端;剪尾。②(電影、故事等)重複以前之事故;重現。③減低;減少。④(契約等之)取消。

cut·down ['kʌt,daun; 'kʌtdaun] *adj.* ①縮小的;縮短的。②刪節的。

***cute** [kjut; kju:t] *adj.*, **cut·er, cut·est.** ①〖美〗美麗嬌小而可愛的。②聰明的;狡猾的。③裝模做樣的。—**ly,** *adv.* —**ness,** *n.*

cut glass 刻花玻璃。

cu·ti·cle ['kjutıkḷ; 'kju:tikl] *n.* ①〖解剖〗表皮;外皮。②〖植物〗上皮。—**cu·tic·u·lar,** *adj.*

cu·tin ['kjutın; 'kju:tin] *n.*〖植物〗上皮之蠟狀質;表皮素。

cut-in ['kʌt,ın; 'kʌtin] *n.* ①〖電影〗有關物件之特寫。②廣播或電視聯播節目中本地電臺所挿進的消息或廣告。③兩人在跳舞時,另一人(通常爲男人)之挿入。

cu·tis ['kjutıs; 'kju:tis] *n.*〖解剖〗眞皮。

cut·lass, cut·las ['kʌtləs; 'kʌtləs] *n.* (古時水手所用之)短厚而微彎的刀。

cut·ler ['kʌtlɚ; 'kʌtlə] *n.* 刀剪等之製造、修理或販賣者。

cut·ler·y ['kʌtlərı; 'kʌtləri] *n.* ①刀、剪等利器之集合稱。②刀、劍製造業。③餐具(如刀、叉、匙等)。

cut·let ['kʌtlıt; 'kʌtlit] *n.* 供燒烤或煎炸的薄肉片。

cut·line ['kʌt,laın; 'kʌtlain] *n.* 圖片說明。

cut man〖美〗拳賽時在回合與回合之間替拳擊手治傷的人。

cut·off ['kʌt,ɔf; 'kʌtɔ:f] *n.* ①捷徑;近路。②新河道。③〖機械〗停汽;切斷。

cut·out ['kʌt,aut; 'kʌtaut] *n.* ①〖電〗斷流器;保險開關。②(內燃機之)排氣閥。③布或紙上剪下或可剪下的圖案花樣等。

cut·o·ver ['kʌt,ovɚ; 'kʌt,ouvə] *adj.* 樹木被砍光的。—*n.* 樹木被砍光的土地。

cut-price ['kʌt,praıs; 'kʌtprais] *adj.* ①價格已經降低的。②減價出售的。

cut·purse ['kʌt,pɝs; 'kʌtpə:s] *n.* =pickpocket.

cut rate〖美〗低價。

cut·ter** ['kʌtɚ; 'kʌtə] *n.* ①切割者;截切器。a meat *cutter.* 切肉機。②裁剪衣服者。③〖電影〗影片剪輯者。④快艇。⑤輕便的雪橇。⑥軍艦上的駁船。⑦〖美〗老牛;老牛身上的肉(多作製罐頭用)。coast-guard cutter*** 海防巡邏艇。***revenue cutter*** 緝私船。

cut·ter-lid ['kʌtɚ,lıd; 'kʌtəlid] *n.* (罐頭上)附有罐頭起子的蓋子。

cut·throat ['kʌt,θrot; 'kʌtθrout] *n.* 兇手;刺客。—*adj.* ①殺人的;兇狠的。②激烈的;拚命的。③三人參加的(紙牌)。

cut·ting ['kʌtıŋ; 'kʌtiŋ] *n.* ①切;割。②切下或割下之部分。③〖電影〗剪接。④從山丘中開鑿出來的道路。⑤〖英〗剪報。⑥〖園藝〗切下供挿或移植的小枝;挿木法。—*adj.* ①銳利的。②刺骨的。a *cutting* wind. 刺骨之寒風。③尖刻的。a *cutting* criticism. 苛刻的批評。—**ly,** *adv.*

cut·tle ['kʌtḷ; 'kʌtl] *n.* =**cuttlefish.**

cut·tle·bone ['kʌtḷ,bon; 'kʌtlboun] *n.* 墨魚骨;海螵蛸。

cut·tle·fish ['kʌtḷ,fıʃ; 'kʌtlfiʃ] *n., pl.* **-fish·es, -fish.**〖動物〗烏賊;墨魚。(亦作 **cuttle**)

cut·ty ['kʌtı; 'kʌti] *adj., n., pl.* **-ties.** —*adj.*〖蘇,方〗①短的;急的。②性急的;易怒的。—*n.* ①短匙。②短煙斗。③不正經女子。

cutty stool〖蘇〗①矮凳。②古時蘇格蘭教堂爲不守婦道之女人而設的坐席。

cut·up ['kʌt,ʌp; 'kʌtʌp] *n.*〖美俚〗扮小丑或開玩笑以引人注意的人(或動作)。

cut·wa·ter ['kʌt,wɔtɚ; 'kʌt,wɔ:tə] *n.* ①船首之破浪處。②橋脚的分水角。

cut·worm ['kʌt,wɝm; 'kʌtwə:m] *n.*〖動物〗糖蛾之幼蟲。

C.V. Common Version (of the Bible).

c.w.o. cash with order. **cwt.** hundredweight. **Cy.** Country.

-cy〖字尾〗表"狀態;品質;職位;階級"之義。

cy·an·am·ide [,saıə'næmaıd; ,saiə'næmaid] *n.*〖化〗氰胺。

cy·a·nate ['saıə,net; 'saiəneit] *n.*〖化〗氰酸鹽。

cy·an·ic [saı'ænık; sai'ænik] *adj.* ①〖化〗氰的;含氰的。②〖植物〗藍色的。

cy·a·nide ['saıə,naıd; 'saiənaid] *n.*〖化〗氰化物。(亦作 **cyanid**)

cy·a·nine ['saıə,nin; 'saiəni:n] *n.* 氰藍;藍色素。

cy·a·nite ['saıə,naıt; 'saiənait] *n.*〖礦〗藍晶石。

cy·an·o·gen [saı'ænədʒən; sai'ænədʒin] *n.*〖化〗①氰(C_2N_2)。②氰根(CN)。

cy·a·no·sis [,saıə'nosıs; ,saiə'nousis] *n.*〖醫〗發紺病;蒼藍症;青紫。—**cy·a·not·ic,** *adj.*

cy·an·o·type [saı'ænə,taıp; sai'ænətaip] *n.* 氰版照相。

Cyb·e·le ['sıbḷ,i; 'sibəli:] *n.* (古時小亞細亞人民所崇奉之)女性大神;諸神之母。

cy·ber·na·tion [,saıbɚ'neʃən; ,saibə'neiʃən] *n.* (以電子計算機)控制。full automation and *cybernation.* 全自動控制。

cy·ber·net·ics [,saıbɚ'nεtıks; ,saibə:'netiks] *n.*(作 *sing.* 解)神經機械學(電腦與人類神經系統之比較研究)。

cy·cad ['saıkæd; 'saikæd] *n.* 蘇鐵科之植物;蘇鐵。—**a·ceous,** *adj.*

cyc·la·men ['sıkləmən; 'sikləmən] *n.*〖植物〗櫻草屬之植物。

cy·cle** ['saıkḷ; 'saikl] *n., v.,* **-cled, -cling.** —*n.* ①周期;循環周。one Chinese *cycle.* 一甲子(六十年)。②循環;周而復始。business *cycle.* 商業盛衰的循環。③成套的有關英雄或重要事蹟之故事、詩歌或稗史等作品。④〖電〗周波。⑤〖植物〗輪周。⑥〖天文〗天體之循環期;旋道。⑦一段很長之時期;時代。solar cycle*** **a.** 太陽曆循環(每二十八年一次之月日與星期完全相同)。**b.** 太陽循環期(太陽內部之變動,約每十一年一次)。—*v.i.* ①循環。②騎脚踏車。

cy·cle·car ['saıkḷ,kɑr; 'saiklkɑ:] *n.* 一種三輪或四輪之輕便汽車。

cy·cler ['saıklɚ; 'saiklə] *n.*〖美〗=**cyclist.**

cy·clic ['saıklık; 'saiklik] *adj.* ①循環的;周期的。②〖植物〗輪狀的;輪周的。③〖化〗環式的。④有關成套之史詩或傳說的。(亦作

cyclical) —al·ly, *adv.* 「車者。」
cy·clist ['saɪklɪst; 'saiklist] *n.* 騎脚踏
cy·clo·graph ['saɪklə,græf; 'saiklougrɑːf] *n.* ①輪轉全景照相機。②一種測定金屬硬度之電子儀器。
cy·cloid ['saɪklɔɪd; 'saiklɔid] *n.* 〖幾何〗擺線;旋輪線。—*adj.* 圓形的。
cy·cloi·dal [saɪ'klɔɪdḷ; sai'klɔidl] *adj.* 〖幾何〗擺線的;旋輪線的。
cy·clom·e·ter [saɪ'klɑmətɚ; sai'klɔmitə] *n.* ①圓弧測定器。②計程表。
cy·clone ['saɪklon; 'saikloun] *n.* ①旋風。②颶風;暴風。—**cy·clon·ic,** *adj.*
cyclone cellar 地下避風室。
cy·clo·nite ['saɪklənaɪt; 'saiklənait] *n.* 一種高性能的炸藥。
Cy·clo·pe·an [,saɪklə'piən; sai'kloupjən] *adj.* ①Cyclops 的。②(c-) 巨大的。
cy·clo·p(a)e·di·a [,saɪklə'pidɪə; ,saiklə'piːdjə] *n.* 百科全書;百科辭典 (encyclopedia 之簡體)。
cy·clo·p(a)e·dic [,saɪklə'pidɪk; ,saiklə'piːdik] *adj.* ①百科全書的;百科辭典的。②廣泛的; 淵博的。
Cy·clops ['saɪklɑps; 'saiklɔps] *n., pl.* **Cy·clo·pes** [saɪ'klopiz; sai'kloupiːz]. ①〖希臘神話〗獨眼巨人。②(c-) 水蚤; 獨眼水蚤。③(c-)獨眼畸胎。
cy·clo·ram·a [,saɪklə'ræmə; ,saiklə'ræmə] *n.* ①陳列於圓形室內之風景或戰爭畫。②舞臺上之弧形畫幕。—**cy·clo·ram·ic,** *adj.*
cy·clo·style ['saɪklə,staɪl; 'saiklə-stail] *n., v.,* **-styled, -styl·ing.** —*n.* 模版 (stencil) 複印機。—*v.t.* 以模版複印。
cy·clo·tron ['saɪklə,trɑn; 'saiklətrɔn] *n.* 〖物理〗廻旋磁力加速器 (一種使原子核分裂之裝置)。
cyg·net ['sɪgnɪt; 'signit] *n.* 小天鵝。
Cyg·nus ['sɪgnəs; 'signəs] *n.* 〖天文〗天鵝座。
cyl. ①cylinder. ②cylindrical.
*__cyl·in·der__ ['sɪlɪndɚ; 'silində] *n.* ①圓筒。②〖幾何〗圓柱體。③〖機械〗汽缸。a six-*cylinder* motorcar. 一輛六汽缸的汽車。④〖印刷〗滾筒。—**cy·lin·dric, cy·lin·dri·cal,** *adj.* —**cy·lin·dri·cal·ly,** *adv.*
cylinder press 滾筒印刷機。
cyl·in·droid ['sɪlɪn,drɔɪd; 'silindrɔid] *n.* 〖幾何〗圓柱性面。—*adj.* 圓柱性的。
cy·ma ['saɪmə; 'saimə] *n., pl.* **-mas, -mae** [-mi; -miː]. ①〖建築〗反曲線脚。②〖植物〗聚繖花序。
cy·ma·ti·um [sɪ'meʃɪəm; si'meiʃiəm] *n., pl.* **-ti·a** [-ʃɪə; -ʃiə]. 〖建築〗①拱頂花邊。②反曲線脚(=cyma)。
cym·bal ['sɪmbḷ; 'simbəl] *n.* 鐃;鈸(常成對使用)。—**eer,** —**er,** —**ist,** *n.*
cyme [saɪm; saim] *n.* 〖植物〗聚繖花序。
cy·mose ['saɪmos; 'saimous] *adj.* 〖植物〗聚繖狀的;聚繖花序的。
cy·mous ['saɪməs; 'saiməs] *adj.* 「=**cymose.**」
Cym·ric ['sɪmrɪk; 'kimrik] *adj.* 威爾斯之塞爾特人(Celt)的; 其語言的。—*n.* 威爾斯之塞爾特語。
Cym·ry ['sɪmrɪ; 'kimri] *n. pl.* 威爾斯「之塞爾特人;威爾斯人。」
cyn·ic ['sɪnɪk; 'sinik] *n.* ①憤世嫉俗的人。②(C-) 犬儒學派的人。—*adj.* ①好譏諷的。②(C-) 犬儒學派的。
cyn·i·cal ['sɪnɪkəl; 'sinikəl] *adj.* ①懷疑人生之價值的; 懷疑人之誠意或善意的。②譏刺的;冷嘲的。—**ly,** *adv.* —**ness,** *n.*
cyn·i·cism ['sɪnəsɪzəm; 'sinisizəm] *n.* ①(C-) 犬儒主義; 犬儒哲學。②譏誚的言詞或見解。
cy·no·ceph·a·lus [,sɪno'sɛfələs; ,sainou'sefələs] *n.* ①(神話中之) 犬首人。②〖動物〗犬面狒狒。
cy·no·sure ['saɪnə,ʃʊr; 'sinəzjuə] *n.* ①指針;引導物。②衆目之的。③(C-)〖天文〗小熊星座。④ (C-)〖天文〗北極星。
Cyn·thi·a ['sɪnθɪə; 'sinθiə] *n.* ①月之女神 Diana 之別名。②〖詩〗月。
cy·pher ['saɪfɚ; 'saifə] *n., v.i. & v.t.* 「=**cipher.**」
cy·press ['saɪprəs; 'saipris] *n.* ①柏樹。②柏樹木。③(用作誌哀之) 柏樹枝。
Cyp·ri·an ['sɪprɪən; 'siprian] *adj.* ①塞浦路斯 (Cyprus) 的;塞浦路斯人的; 塞浦路斯語的。②淫蕩的; 放縱的。—*n.* ①塞浦路斯人。②希臘之塞浦路斯方言。③ **a.** 放蕩之人。**b.** 妓女;神女。
cyp·ri·noid ['sɪprə,nɔɪd; 'siprinɔid] *adj.* 鯉科之魚的;似鯉魚的。—*n.* 鯉科之魚。
Cyp·ri·ot ['sɪprɪət; 'sipriɔt] *n., adj.* =**Cypriote.**
Cyp·ri·ote ['sɪprɪ,ot; 'sipriout] *n.* ①塞浦路斯島人。②塞浦路斯島之希臘方言。—*adj.* 塞浦路斯島的;其居民或其語言的。
Cy·prus ['saɪprəs; 'saiprəs] *n.* 塞浦路斯 (地中海東部之一島, 原屬英, 於1960 年宣布獨立成爲共和國, 其首都爲尼科西亞, Nicosia)。
Cyr·e·na·ic [,saɪrə'ne·ɪk; ,saiərə'neiik] *adj.* ①北非之古地區 Cyrenaica 或其首府 Cyrene 的。②(Cyrene 之 Aristippus 所倡之)快樂主義之哲學的。—*n.* ①北非一古地區 Cyrenaica 或首府 Cyrene 之人。②快樂主義派之哲學家。
Cy·ril·lic [sɪ'rɪlɪk; si'rilik] *adj.* 古代斯拉夫語之字母的。
cyst [sɪst; sist] *n.* 〖生物〗胞囊;包囊;囊「腫。 —**ic,** *adj.*」
cys·ti·cer·coid [,sɪstɪ'sɝkɔɪd; ,sisti'səːkɔid] *adj.* 類似囊尾蚴的;擬囊蟲的。—*n.* 類似囊尾蚴之蟲;擬囊蟲。
cys·ti·cer·cus [,sɪstɪ'sɝkəs; ,sisti'səːkəs] *n., pl.* **-cer·ci** [-'sɝsaɪ; -'səːsai]. 〖動物〗囊尾蚴;囊蟲(某些絛蟲之幼蟲)。
cys·ti·form ['sɪstɪ,fɔrm; 'sistifɔːm] *adj.* 胞狀的;囊狀的。
cys·ti·tis [sɪs'taɪtɪs; sis'taitis] *n.* 〖醫〗膀胱炎。
cys·to·cele ['sɪstə,sil; 'sistəsiːl] *n.* 「〖醫〗膀胱膨出。」
cyst·oid ['sɪstɔɪd; 'sistɔid] *adj.* 囊樣的; 似胞囊的。
cys·to·scope ['sɪstə,skop; 'sistəskoup] *n.* 〖醫〗膀胱鏡;檢膀胱鏡。
cys·to·scop·ic [,sɪstə'skɑpɪk; ,sistə'skɔpik] *adj.* 膀胱鏡的。
cys·tot·o·my [sɪs'tɑtəmɪ; sis'tɔtəmi] *n.* 膀胱切開術。
Cyth·er·e·a [,sɪθə'riə; ,siθə'riə] *n.* 「=**Aphrodite.**」
cy·tol·o·gy [saɪ'tɑlədʒɪ; sai'tɔlədʒi] *n.* 細胞學。—**cy·to·log·ic, cy·to·log·i·cal,** *adj.* —**cy·tol·o·gist,** *n.*
cy·to·plasm ['saɪtə,plæzəm; 'saitə,plæzəm] *n.* 〖生物〗細胞質;細胞漿。—**ic,** *adj.*
C.Z. Canal Zone.
czar [zɑr; zɑː] *n.* ①沙皇。②舊時俄國皇帝的稱號。(亦作 **tsar, tzar**) —**dom,** *n.*
czar·e·vitch ['zɑrɪvɪtʃ; 'zɑːrivitʃ] *n.* 俄皇太子;俄皇長子之稱。(亦作 **tsarevitch, tzarevitch**)
cza·rev·na [zɑ'rɛvnə; zɑː'revnə] *n.* 「俄公主;俄太子妃。」

cza·ri·na [zɑ'rinə; zɑː'riːnə] *n.* ①沙皇之妻。②舊時俄國女王之稱號。

czar·ism ['zɑrɪzəm; 'zɑːrizəm] *n.* 專制政治;獨裁政治。

cza·rit·za [zɑ'rɪtsə; zɑː'ritsə] *n.* [=czarina.]

Czech [tʃɛk; tʃek] *n.* ①捷克人。②捷克語。—*adj.* 捷克斯拉夫(人或語言)的。

Czech·ish ['tʃɛkɪʃ; 'tʃekiʃ] *adj.* =Czech.

Czech·o·slo·vak, Czech·o-Slo·vak [ˌtʃɛkə'slovæk; 'tʃekou'slouvæk] *adj.* 捷克斯拉夫的;其人民或語言的。—*n.* ①捷克斯拉夫人。②捷克斯拉夫語。

Czech·o·slo·va·ki·a, Czech·o-Slo·va·ki·a [ˌtʃɛkəslo'vækɪə; 'tʃekouslou'vækiə] *n.* 捷克斯拉夫共和國(歐洲中部的國家,首都爲布拉格, Prague). —**Czech·o·slo·va·ki·an, Czech·o-Slo·va·ki·an,** *adj.*, *n.*

D

D or **d** [di; diː] *n.*, *pl.* **D's** or **d's.** ①英文字母之第四個字母。②〔音樂〕C 大調音階中之第二個音或音符。

D 化學元素 didymium 之符號。

D. ①December. ②Dutch. ③Democrat. ④day. ⑤density. **d.** ①day;days. ②dead. ③died. ④dollar. ⑤diameter. ⑥daughter. ⑦degree. ⑧dime. ⑨〔英〕penny or pence 便士。⑩dose. ⑪dyne. ⑫dialect; dialectal. ⑬dividend. **'d** had, should 或 would 之縮寫。

da [dɑ; dɑː] *n.* 〔英俚〕=**dad.**

D.A. ①District Attorney. ②Delayed Action. ③direct action. ④documents against acceptance. ⑤documents for acceptance. **D/A, d. a.** deposit account.

dab[1] [dæb; dæb] *v.*, **dabbed, dab·bing.** *n.* —*v.t.* & *v.i.* 輕拍;輕撫;塗敷。—*n.* ①輕拍;塗敷。②小量的東西(指軟者言)。

dab[2] *n.* 孫鰈。

dab[3] *n.* 〔俗〕能手;專家;老手。

dab·ber ['dæbɚ; 'dæbə] *n.* ①輕拍之人或物;塗敷者。②(印刷或鐫板)上墨滾子。

dab·ble ['dæbḷ; 'dæbl] *v.*, **dab·bled, dab·bling.** —*v.t.* 使濺濕;玩水。—*v.i.* ①戲水。②涉獵; 涉足; 淺嘗。③竄改。 —**dab·bler,** *n.*

dab·chick ['dæbˌtʃɪk; 'dæbtʃik] *n.* [鸊鷉類之小鳥。]

dab·ster ['dæbstɚ; 'dæbstə] *n.* ①〔英方〕能手;妙手。②〔俗〕淺嘗者;生手。

da ca·po [dɑ'kɑːpo; dɑː'kɑːpou] 〔義〕〔音樂〕①反始。②反始記號。

Dac·ca ['dækə; 'dækə] *n.* 達卡(孟加拉共和國首都)。

dace [des; deis] *n.*, *pl.* **dac·es,** (集合稱) [**dace.** 鰷魚。]

dachs·hund ['dɑksˌhund; 'dækshund] 〔德〕*n.* 一種身長腿短的獵犬; 獵獾狗。

da·coit [də'kɔɪt; də'kɔit] *n.* 印度或緬甸之土匪。(亦作 **dakoit**)

da·coit·y [də'kɔɪtɪ; də'kɔiti] *n.*, *pl.* **da·coit·ies.** 印、緬盜匪之掠奪; 强盜行爲。(亦作 **dakoity**)

Da·cron ['dekrɑn; 'deikrɔn] *n.* 〔商標名〕達克龍。

dac·tyl ['dæktɪl; 'dæktil] *n.*〔詩〕揚抑抑格(英文詩中一個長音節後接二短音節或一個重音節後接二輕音節之韻律, 如: "Gēntlў ănd | hūmănlў").

dac·tyl·ic [dæk'tɪlɪk; dæk'tilik] *adj.* 〔韻律〕揚抑抑格的。—*n.* 揚抑抑格之詩。

dac·ty·log·ra·phy [ˌdæktɪ'lɑgrəfɪ; ˌdækti'lɔgrəfi] *n.* 指紋學;指紋法。—**dac·ty·log·ra·pher,** *n.* —**dac·tyl·o·graph·ic,** *adj.*

dac·ty·lol·o·gy [ˌdæktɪ'lɑlədʒɪ; ˌdækti'lɔlədʒi] *n.*, *pl.* **-gies.** 指語術(以手指傳話之法)。

dac·ty·los·co·py [ˌdæktə'lɑskəpɪ; ˌdæktə'lɔskəpi] *n.* 以指紋認明罪犯等。

***dad** [dæd; dæd] *n.* 〔俗〕①爸爸; 爹爹。②傢伙;人;朋友(常用以稱呼陌生人)。

Da·da·ism, da·da·ism ['dɑdəɪzm; 'dɑːdəizm] *n.* 達達派; 達達主義(第一次大戰後一文藝運動,藉狂怪、象徵之手法以表達潛意識之事物, 且運用虛無主義之諷刺)。(亦作 **Dada, dada**) —**Da·da·ist,** *n.* —**Da·da·is·tic,** *adj.* —**Da·da·is·ti·cal·ly,** *adv.*

dad-blamed ['dæd'blemd; 'dæd'bleimd] *adj.* & *adv.* 表示驚異、厭惡或生氣之咒駡語。

***dad·dy** ['dædɪ; 'dædi] *n.*, *pl.* **-dies.** ①〔俗〕爸爸; 爹爹。②〔俚〕以金錢換取少女歡心之中年人。

dad·dy-long·legs ['dædɪ'lɔŋlɛgz; 'dædi'lɔŋlegz] *n. sing.* or *pl.* ①〔美〕盲蜘蛛。②〔英方〕一種長脚似蚊之蠅。

da·do ['dedo; 'deidou] *n.*, *pl.* **-does, -dos.** ①〔建築〕臺座之腰部。②護壁。③〔木匠〕挿木板之槽。—*v.t.* 僅見於下列成語的習慣用法。 ***dado in*** 將(木板)挿入槽內。

DAE, D.A.E. Dictionary of American English.

dae·dal ['didəl; 'diːdəl] *adj.* ①〔詩〕巧妙的;有技巧的。②狡獪的。③複雜的。

Daed·a·lus ['dɛdḷəs; 'diːdələs] *n.* 〔希臘神話〕德狄勒斯(在 Crete 建造迷宮之雅典名匠)。—**Dae·da·li·an, Dae·da·le·an,** *adj.*

dae·mon ['dimən; 'diːmən] *n.* =**demon.** —**is·tic,** *adj.*

dae·mon·ic [dɪ'mɑnɪk; di'mɔnik] *adj.* =**demonic.** —**al·ly,** *adv.*

***daf·fo·dil** ['dæfədɪl; 'dæfədil] *n.* 水仙花。—*adj.* 水仙花色的。

***daf·fo·dil·ly** ['dæfəˌdɪlɪ; 'dæfədili] *n.*, *pl.* **-lies.** 〔詩〕=**daffodil.**

daff·y ['dæfɪ; 'dæfi] *adj.*, **daff·i·er, daff·i·est.** 〔俗〕瘋狂的;愚笨的;癡傻的。

daft [dæft; dɑːft] *adj.* ①愚笨的。②懦弱的。③瘋狂的。 to go *daft.* 發狂。—**ly,** *adv.* —**ness,** *n.*

dag. decagram(me).

dag·ger** ['dægɚ; 'dægə] *n.* ①短劍;匕首。②書籍中作附註記號的劍號(†)。 ***at daggers drawn 準備戰鬥;敵意的。 ***look daggers at*** 怒目相視。 —*v.t.* ①以匕首刺。②〔印刷〕加劍形符號(†)。

dag·gle ['dægḷ; 'dægl] *v.t.* & *v.i.*, **-gled, -gling.** 在泥水中拖汚;拖髒。

da·go, Da·go ['dego; 'deigou] *n.*, *pl.* **-gos, -goes.** 〔美,蔑〕南歐人(指義大利、西班牙或葡萄牙人)。

da·go·ba ['dɑgəbə; 'dɑːgəbə] 〔印〕*n.* [佛骨堂;舍利塔。]

da·guerre·o·type [də'gɛrəˌtaɪp; də'geroutaip] *n.*, *v.*, **-typed, -typ·ing.** —*n.* ①銀版照相。②銀版照相法。 —*v.t.* 以

銀版照相法拍攝。

da·ha·be·ah, da·ha·bee·yah, da·ha·bi·ah [ˌdɑhəˈbiə; ˌdɑːhəˈbiːə] *n.* (尼羅河上之)一種大客船。

***dahl·ia** [ˈdæljə, ˈdɑl-, ˈdel-; ˈdeiljə,-liə] *n.* 天竺牡丹;大利花。

dai [daɪ; dai] *n.* 〖英印〗乳母。

Dail Eir·eann [ˈdɔɪlˈerən; dailˈɛərən] 愛爾蘭國會之下院。

‡dai·ly [ˈdelɪ; ˈdeili] *adj., n., pl.* **-lies,** *adv.* —*adj.* 每日的;週日的(除星期日)。*daily* newspapers. 日報。—*n.* ①日報。②〖英〗不寄宿的僕人;白天做家務的女傭。—*adv.* 每日地。Most newspapers appear *daily.* 大多數報紙每日出版。

***dain·ty** [ˈdentɪ; ˈdeinti] *adj.,* **-ti·er, -ti·est,** *n., pl.* **-ties.** —*adj.* ①美麗而易斷的;漂亮而不牢的;嬌美的。②優美的;雅緻的。③講究的。She is *dainty* about her eating. 她甚講究飲食。④美味的;適口的。—*n.* 適口的食物。—**dain·ti·ly,** *adv.*—**dain·ti·ness,** *n.*

dai·qui·ri [ˈdaɪkərɪ; ˈdaikəri] *n., pl.* **-ris.** 一種雞尾酒(由蘭酒、檸檬或萊姆汁及糖調配而成)。

Dai·ren [ˈdaɪˈrɛn; ˈdaiˈren] *n.* 大連(中國遼東半島之一海港)。

***dair·y** [ˈdɛrɪ; ˈdɛəri] *n., pl.* **-ies.** ①牛奶棚;製奶油和乾酪的工場。②產牛奶、乳酪和製奶油乾酪的農場。③牛奶公司;售牛奶、乳酪、奶油、乾酪的商店。*dairy* cattle. 乳牛。*dairy* farm. 牛奶場;製酪場。④牛奶場之乳牛。

dairy farmer 牛奶場之業主或工人。

dairy farming 乳酪生產事業。

dair·y·ing [ˈdɛrɪɪŋ; ˈdɛəriiŋ] *n.* 製售牛奶、奶油或乾酪之業。

dair·y·maid [ˈdɛrɪˌmed; ˈdɛərimeid] *n.* 牛奶場女工;製酪女工。

dair·y·man [ˈdɛrɪmən; ˈdɛərimən] *n., pl.* **-men.** ①奶棚的雇員。②奶棚的棚主。③賣牛奶、乳酪、牛油、乾酪的人。

da·is [ˈde·ɪs, des; ˈdeiis, deis] *n.* 講臺;壇;高座(尤指設於廳或房之一端者)。

Dai·sy [ˈdezɪ; ˈdeizi] *n.* 女子名。

dai·sy** [ˈdezɪ; ˈdeizi] *n., pl.* **-sies,** *adj.* —*n.*①雛菊;延命菊。②〖俚〗第一流之物。push up daisies*** 〖俗〗死。—*adj.* 〖俚〗第一流的。

daisy chain 雛菊花環。

daisy cutter 〖俚〗①舉足距地甚近之馬。②掠地而過之球。③〖軍〗殺傷彈。

dak [dɔk, dɑk; dɑːk, dɔːk] *n.* =**dawk**[1].

Dak. Dakota.

da·koit [dəˈkɔɪt; dəˈkɔit] *n.* =**dacoit.**

Da·ko·ta [dəˈkotə; dəˈkoutə] *n.* 美國南達科塔州或北達科塔州。***the Dakotas*** 美國南、北達科塔二州。—**Da·ko·tan,** *adj., n.*

dal. decaliter.

Da·lai La·ma [dəˈlaɪˈlɑmə; ˈdælaiˈlɑːmə] 達賴喇嘛(西藏喇嘛教首領之一)。

Dale [del; deil] *n.* 德爾 (Sir Henry Hallett, 1875–1968, 英國生理學家, 曾獲1936年諾貝爾醫學獎)。

dale [del; deil] *n.* 山谷;谷。

dales·man [ˈdelzmən; ˈdeilzmən] *n., pl.* **-men.** (尤指英格蘭北部諸郡之)山谷中之居民。

dalles [dælz; dælz] *n. pl.* (美國西部之)急流;峽谷間之絕壁。(亦作 **dells**)

dal·li·ance [ˈdælɪəns; ˈdæliəns] *n.* ①戲弄;狎遊。②荒唐度日;荒嬉時日。

dal·ly [ˈdælɪ; ˈdæli] *v.,* **-lied, -ly·ing.** —*v.i.* ①嬉戲。②戲弄;調笑。③玩忽;遷延。④閑蕩。—*v.t.* 荒廢(時光)〖away〗。

Dal·ma·tia [dælˈmeʃɪə; dælˈmeiʃjə] *n.* 達爾馬希亞(南斯拉夫西南部一地區)。

Dal·ma·tian [dælˈmeʃɪən; dælˈmeiʃjən] *adj.* ①Dalmatia 的。②Dalmatia人的。—*n.* ①Dalmatia 人。②原產於 Dalmatia 之一種狗。

dal·mat·ic [dælˈmætɪk; dælˈmætik] *n.* ①〖天主教〗(助祭者或主教所着之)一種法衣。②英國國王加冕時所穿之袍。

dal se·gno [dɑlˈsenjo; dɑːlˈseinjou] 〖義〗〖音樂〗連續記號。

Dal·ton [ˈdɔltn̩; ˈdɔːltən] *n.* 道爾頓 (John, 1766–1844, 英國化學家及物理學家)。—**i·an,** *adj.*

Dal·ton·ism [ˈdɔltn̩ɪzm; ˈdɔltnizm] *n.* 色盲(尤指不辨紅、綠二色)。(亦作 **daltonism**) —**Dal·ton·ist,** *n.*

Dalton plan (or **system**) 〖教育〗道爾頓制(一種教育方式, 每一學生按其自訂計畫完成學業, 創始於美國麻省之Dalton中學)。

Dalton's Law 道爾頓定律。

Dam [dæm; dæm] *n.* 達姆(Henrik, 1895–, 丹麥生物化學家, 曾獲 1943 年諾貝爾醫學獎)。

***dam**[1] [dæm; dæm] *n., v.,* **dammed, dam·ming.** —*n.* ①水壩; 堤; 堰。②爲壩所蓄阻的水。③似水壩之物。—*v.t.* ①築堤;築壩;用堤壩防水。to *dam* a river. 築堤防河水。②控制;抑制〖up〗. to *dam* up one's feelings. 控制自己的情感。

dam[2] *n.* ①母獸。②〖蔑〗母親。

***dam·age** [ˈdæmɪdʒ; ˈdæmidʒ] *n., v.,* **-aged, -ag·ing.** —*n.* ①損害;傷害;損失。The accident didn't do much *damage* to either of the motorcars. 這兩部汽車無一部受到此次意外事件的重大損害。②(*pl.*)賠償損失費。They sued for *damages.* 他們提起訴訟要求賠償損失。③〖俚〗(常 *pl.*)價錢;價格;開支。—*v.t.* 損害; 毀傷。He has a *damaged* reputation. 他的名譽很受損害。—*v.i.*損壞。—**dam·ag·ing,** *adj.* —**dam·ag·ing·ly,** *adv.*

dam·age·a·ble [ˈdæmɪdʒəbl̩; ˈdæmidʒəbl] *adj.* 可損壞的; 易破壞的; 易受損的。

damage suit 要求賠償的訴訟。

dam·a·scene [ˈdæməˌsin; ˈdæməsiːn] *adj., n., v.,* **-scened, -scen·ing.** —*adj.* 金屬鑲嵌的;波紋裝飾的。—*n.* ①金屬鑲嵌法;波紋裝飾;金屬鑲嵌製品。②西洋李子(=damson). —*v.i.* ①用波紋裝飾(金屬)。②以貴重金屬鑲嵌(鋼鐵用品)。

Da·mas·cus [dəˈmæskəs; dəˈmɑːskəs] *n.* 大馬士革(敍利亞之首都)。

Damascus steel 一種鑄劍等用之鋼。

dam·ask [ˈdæməsk; ˈdæməsk] *n.* ①花緞; 錦緞。②花布。③大馬士革鋼。④深薔薇色;粉紅色。—*v.t.* ①以花紋裝飾(鋼鐵);以金屬鑲飾。②飾以彩色。③蓋印銷毀。—*adj.* ①大馬士革鋼鑄造的; 如大馬士革鋼的。②深薔薇色的。

dam·a·skeen [ˌdæməˈskin; ˌdæməˈskiːn] *v.t.* =**damascene.**

damask steel =**Damascus steel.**

dame [dem; deim] *n.* ①已婚的婦女; 夫人(常作稱號)。②婦女(尤指貴族或有地位的婦女)。③老婦。④〖俚〗女人。

***damn** [dæm; dæm] *v.t.* ①貶責;指摘。②咒罵。*Damn* it all! 該死。*Damn* you! 該死! I'll be *damned* if I'll go. 我絕不去。③遭天譴;被罰下地獄。May you be *damned!*

希望你下地獄!④使失敗;破壞。—*v.i.* 咒罵。***damn with faint praise*** 用冷淡的稱讚反對(貶責)。—*n.*咒罵;詛咒。It is not worth a *damn*.一文不值。I don't care a *damn*. 我絕不在乎。***not to give a damn*** 認爲毫無關係。—*adj.*討厭的。—*adv.* 非常地;極。

dam·na·ble [ˈdæmnəbl; ˈdæmnəbl] *adj.* ①該死的。②討厭的。③〖俗〗很壞的。—**ness,** *n.* —**dam·na·bly,** *adv.*

dam·na·tion [dæmˈneʃən; dæmˈneiʃən] *n.* ①指責;詛咒。②毀壞;破滅。③永遠的處罰。—*interj.* =**damn.**

dam·na·to·ry [ˈdæmnəˌtorɪ; ˈdæmnətəri] *adj.* ①定罪的; 處罰的。②應墮地獄的;應受永罰的。③喝罵的。

damned [dæmd; dæmd] *adj.,* **damned·er, damn(e)d·est.** ①應罰的; 應受永罰的; 被罰的; 被墮地獄的。②討厭的。③〖俗〗被咒的;該咒罵的;該死的。 a *damned* shame. 該受咒罵的可恥之人或物。 ***the damned*** 地獄中之靈魂。 —*adv.* 〖俗〗非常地; 極。It was so *damned* hot. 天太熱了。

damned·est [ˈdæmdɪst; ˈdæmdist] *n.* 〖俗〗最大的努力。They did their *damnedest* to finish on time. 他們盡了最大的努力使(工作)如期完成。(亦作 **damndest**)

dam·ni·fi·ca·tion [ˌdæmnəfɪˈkeʃən; ˌdæmnifiˈkeiʃən] *n.* 〖法律〗損傷;侵害。

dam·ni·fy [ˈdæmnəˌfaɪ; ˈdæmnifai] *v.t.,* **-fied, -fy·ing.** 〖法律〗損傷;侵害。

damn·ing [ˈdæmɪŋ; ˈdæmiŋ] *adj.* 定罪的;使負罪的。—**ly,** *adv.* —**ness,** *n.*

dam·no·sa he·red·i·tas [dæmˈnosə hɪˈrɛdɪtæs; dæmˈnousə hiˈreditæs] 〖拉〗債務的繼承。

Dam·o·cle·an [ˌdæməˈkliən; ˌdæməˈkliːən] *adj.* 關於 Damocles 的;(因居高位而)危險不安的。

Dam·o·cles [ˈdæməˌkliz; ˈdæməkliːz] *n.* 達摩克利玆(古代 Syracuse 暴君 Dionysius 一世之諂臣, 常言王者多福, 其君因以一髮懸劍, 命其燕飲其下, 藉喩王者之福猶斯也)。***sword of Damocles*** 幸福中所隱藏的危險。

Da·mon and Pyth·i·as [ˈdemən ən ˈpɪθɪəs; ˈdeimən ən ˈpiθiəs] ①〖羅馬神話〗此兩人係刎頸之交。②生死之交。

damp** [dæmp; dæmp] *adj.* ①潮濕的。②沮喪的;不起勁的。—*n.* ①濕空氣;水分;濕度。There is too much *damp* here. 這裏太濕。②礦中毒氣。③沮喪; 失望。④令人消沉、沮喪之物。cast a damp over*** 使沮喪。***fire damp*** 煤礦內爆發的氣體(主要爲沼氣)。—*v.t.* ①使潮濕。②阻滯;妨礙;挫折。③使窒息;熄滅。***damp off*** (植物因過於冷濕而)腐爛。—**ly,** *adv.* —**ness,** *n.*

damp-dry [*v.* ˈdæmpˈdraɪ; ˈdæmpˈdrai *adj.* ˈdæmpdraɪ; ˈdæmpdrai] *v.t.* 使(洗濯物)半乾。—*adj.* 半乾的。

damp·en [ˈdæmpən; ˈdæmpən] *v.t.* ①使潮濕。②使沮喪。—*v.i.* 變潮濕。—**er,** *n.*

damp·er [ˈdæmpɚ; ˈdæmpə] *n.* ①使人沮喪的人或物。②(火爐或鍋爐上用的)節氣閘。③(鋼琴上的)斷音裝置; 制振器。***put a damper on*** 壓抑;壓制。

damp·proof [ˈdæmpˌpruf; ˈdæmpˌpruːf] *adj.* 防濕的。

dam·sel [ˈdæmzl̩; ˈdæmzəl] *n.* 少女;「處女。」

dam·son [ˈdæmzn̩; ˈdæmzən] *n.* 西洋李子; 西洋李子樹。(亦作 **dampson plum**)

Dan [dæn; dæn] *n.* 巴勒斯坦北端之古都。***from Dan to Beersheba*** 從一端至他端(Beersheba 係巴勒斯坦南端之一城市)。

dan 指示漁網位置之小浮標(浮標上有桿,白天懸旗,夜間掛燈)。

Dan. ①Daniel. ②Danish. ③Danzig.

:**dance** [dæns; dɑːns] *v.,* **danced, dancing,** *n., adj.* —*v.i.* ①跳舞。②跳躍。She *danced* for joy. 她因快樂而跳躍。***dance on air*** 〖俚〗被絞死。***dance to another tune*** 改變主意或態度。—*v.t.* 使跳舞;使(小兒等)跳動。***dance attendance on*** 小心侍候;奉承。—*n.* ①跳舞;舞蹈。②一回跳舞;一輪跳舞。May I have the next *dance* with you? 下一回我可以和你共舞嗎?③舞曲;舞樂。④舞會。to give a *dance*. 開舞會。⑤舞步。⑥跳躍;雀躍;搖動。—*adj.* 跳舞用的。*dance* music. 跳舞音樂。—**danc·er,** *n.*

dance hall 跳舞場;舞廳(尤指公共的)。

dance of death 象徵死亡權威的舞蹈。

***danc·ing** [ˈdænsɪŋ; ˈdɑːnsiŋ] *n.* 跳舞。

dancing girl 舞女。

dancing party 舞會。

D & D deaf and dumb. 〖美俚〗裝聾作啞(因恐懼報復而不提供線索給警方)。

***dan·de·li·on** [ˈdændɪˌlaɪən; ˈdændilaiən] *n.* 〖植物〗蒲公英。

dan·der [ˈdændɚ; ˈdændə] *n.* 〖俗〗①怒氣。②脾氣。***get one's dander up*** 〖俗〗發怒;發脾氣。

Dan·die Din·mont (terrier) [ˈdændɪˈdɪnmɑnt; ˈdændiˈdinmɔnt] 一種短足長身之小獵犬。(亦作 **dandie**)

dan·di·fy [ˈdændɪˌfaɪ; ˈdændifai] *v.t.,* **-fied, -fy·ing.** 使打扮得像紈袴子;盛裝。

dan·dle [ˈdændl; ˈdændl] *v.t.,* **-dled, -dling.**(在膝上或懷抱中)播弄(嬰兒)。②撫愛。

dan·druff [ˈdændrəf; ˈdændrəf] *n.* 頭皮屑。(亦作 **dandriff**)

dan·dy [ˈdændɪ; ˈdændi] *n., pl.* **-dies,** *adj.,* **-di·er, -di·est.** —*n.* ①好修飾的人;花花公子。②〖俚〗優良的或上等的東西。—*adj.* ①漂亮的; 上等的。②花花公子的; 紈袴子的; 好修飾的。

dandy brush 刷馬之硬毛刷。

dandy cart 送牛奶的二輪貨車。

dan·dy·ism [ˈdændɪɪzm̩; ˈdændiizəm] *n.* 紈袴子之作風及態度。

dandy roll 造幣機中做水印的滾筒。(亦作 **dandy roller**)

Dane [den; dein] *n.* 丹麥人。 ***Great*** 「***Dane*** 大丹犬。」

:**dan·ger** [ˈdendʒɚ; ˈdeindʒə] *n.* ①危險。Is there any *danger* of fire? 有遭火災的危險嗎? ②危險的事物; 危險的原因。 Hidden rocks are a *danger* to ships. 暗礁對船隻是一種危險。 ***in danger (of)*** 在危險中。He is *in danger*. 他在危險中。to be *in danger of* being killed. 有被殺的危險。 ***out of danger*** 出險;脫險。

:**dan·ger·ous** [ˈdendʒ(ə)rəs; ˈdeindʒrəs] *adj.*危險的。It is *dangerous* to walk on thin ice in a lake. 在湖中薄冰上走是很危險的。to look *dangerous*. 現出兇相;看起來有危險。—**ly,** *adv.* —**ness,** *n.* 〖注意〗 **dangerous** 通常指對人有危險的事物。指某人有危險,應說 He is in danger; 若說 He is *dangerous*, 則意爲"他是一個危險人物"。

danger signal 危險信號。

danger zone 危險區。

***dan·gle** [ˈdæŋgl; ˈdæŋgl] *v.,* **-gled, -gling,** *n.* —*v.i.* ①懸擺; 搖擺; 懸垂。②追

隨;依附。—*v.t.* 使懸擺。—*n.* ①搖擺。②搖擺之物。—**dan·gling·ly**, *adv.*
dan·gler ['dæŋglɚ; 'dæŋglə] *n.* ①懸擺物;振子。②追隨者;追逐女人的男子。
dangling participle 〖文法〗不連結分詞(如: Plunging 1,000 feet into the gorge, we saw the Yosemite Falls. 句中之 plunging 爲 dangling participle, 因其應修飾 Yosemite Falls, 而在結構上却修飾 we)。
Dan·iel ['dænjəl; 'dænjəl] *n.* ①〖聖經〗但以理(舊約所載之希伯來先知, 因其極忠於神, 故曾困於獅窟而未受害, 見但以理書六章十六節及十七節)。②舊約但以理書。③男子名。
Dan·ish ['denɪʃ; 'deiniʃ] *adj.* 丹麥國的;丹麥人的;丹麥語的。—*n.* ①丹麥語。②〖俗〗一種丹麥點心。
dank [dæŋk; dæŋk] *adj.* 陰濕的。—**ly**, *adv.* —**ness**, *n.*
danse ma·ca·bre ['dɑ̃sˌmə'kɑbrə; 'dɑ̃sˌmə'kɑ:brə] 〖法〗=**dance of death.**
dan·seur [dɑ̃'sœr; dɑ̃'sø] 〖法〗*n.* 男性芭蕾舞蹈家。
dan·seuse [dɑn'sɜz; dɑ:n'sə:z] 〖法〗*n.* 女性芭蕾舞蹈家。
Dan·te ['dæntɪ; 'dænti] *n.* 但丁 (Alighieri, 1265–1321, 義大利詩人)。
Dan·te·an ['dæntɪən; 'dæntiən] *adj.* 但丁 (Dante) 的;但丁之風格的;但丁之作品的。—*n.* 但丁之研究者;但丁之崇拜者。
Dan·tesque [dæn'tɛsk; dæn'tesk] *adj.* 但丁的;但丁之著作的;但丁之風格的;莊嚴細密而情感高尚的。
Dan·ube ['dænjub; 'dænju:b] *n.* 多瑙河(由德經奧、匈、南、保、羅等國流入黑海)。
dap [dæp; dæp] *v.*, **dapped, dap·ping.** —*v.i.* ①輕放魚餌於水上而垂釣。②在水面上漂跳。③迸跳。④突然衝入水中(如鳥之捕魚)。—*v.t.* ①使入水又提起。②使在水面飛掠。
Daph·ne ['dæfnɪ; 'dæfni] *n.* ①〖希臘神話〗女神名(河神 Peneus 之女, 爲 Apollo 神所襲, 乃化身爲月桂樹而遁去)。②(d-) 月桂樹。
dap·per ['dæpɚ; 'dæpə] *adj.* ①漂亮整潔的。②矯健活潑的。—**ly**, *adv.* —**ness**, *n.*
dap·per·ling ['dæpəlɪŋ; 'dæpəliŋ] *n.* 矯健活潑的小夥子。
dap·ple ['dæpl̩; 'dæpl] *adj.*, *v.*, **-pled, -pling,** *n.* —*adj.* 有斑點的。—*v.t.* 加斑點於。—*n.* ①斑紋。②有斑點之馬 (並非指斑馬)。
dap·pled ['dæpl̩d; 'dæpld] *adj.* 有斑點的;斑駁的。
dap·ple-gray ['dæpl̩'gre; 'dæpl'grei] *adj.* 灰色而有黑斑的。
dar·by ['dɑrbɪ; 'dɑ:bi] *n.*, *pl.* **-bies.** ①〖古俚〗現金;錢。②(*pl.*)〖英俚〗手銬。
Dar·by and Joan ['dɑrbɪ ənd 'dʒon; 'dɑ:bi ənd 'dʒoun] 夫唱婦隨的老夫婦(原出於一首古歌名, 1753年)。
:dare [dɛr; dɛə] *v.*, **dared** or **durst, dared, dar·ing,** *n.* —*v.i.* 敢;膽敢。He *dare* not jump (*or* He does not *dare* to jump) from the top of that wall. 他不敢從那牆頭跳下。He does not *dare* (to) speak. 他不敢說。—*v.t.* ①敢冒;不懼。He will *dare* any danger. 他敢冒任何危險。②挑戰;挑激。He *dared* me to jump over the stream. 他挑激我跳過河。***I dare say*** 我以爲;我想。You are tired, *I dare say*. 我想你已疲倦。—*n.* 挑激。I took his *dare* to jump. 我接受他的挑激而跳了。—**dar·er**, *n.* 〖注意〗**dare** 及 **need** 用法:(1)否定及疑問句中, 常作助動詞, 與不帶 to 的不定詞連用, 無過去式, 第三人稱單數, 現在式不加 s. 此二字作助動詞用, 英語較美語爲常見。(2)否定及疑問句中, 作動詞用時, 其後接之不定詞的 to, 有時可省。
dare·dev·il ['dɛrˌdɛvl̩; 'dɛəˌdevl] *n.* 蠻勇之徒。—*adj.* 膽大的。—**ry**, —**try**, *n.*
***dar·ing** ['dɛrɪŋ; 'dɛəriŋ] *n.* 勇敢。—*adj.* ①勇敢的。②膽大的。—**ly**, *adv.* —**ness**, *n.*
Da·ri·us I [də'raɪəs; də'raiəs] 大流士 (Hystaspis, 558? –?486 B.C., 古波斯王)。
:dark [dɑrk; dɑ:k] *adj.* ①黑暗的。②暗色的;帶黑色的;淺黑的。*dark* brown. 深棕色。She is *dark* in complexion. 她的膚色微黑。③祕密的。He tried to keep the matter *dark* from us. 他設法隱瞞這事, 不使我們知道。④不易了解的;曖昧的。⑤兇惡的;邪惡的。*dark* deeds. 惡行。He made *dark* confessions. 他承認罪惡。⑥悲觀的;憂鬱的。He was a peddler in his *dark* days. 在不得意時, 他做過小販。⑦愚昧的;無知的。*Dark* Ages (or *dark* ages). 黑暗時代(歐史, 約紀元476 年至1000 年, 或紀元476年至文藝復興)。⑧ (電臺等)無廣播的。⑨沉默的。⑩有黑髮的。—*n.* ①黑暗。Women and children are often afraid of the *dark*. 婦孺常怕黑暗。②夜;日暮。I don't go out after *dark*. 夜間我不出門。③祕密;無知;愚昧。④暗色。There is too much *dark* in this painting. 這畫顏色太暗。***at dark*** 日暮時;天黑時。***in the dark*** **a.** 在黑暗中。**b.** 不爲人所知的。***keep dark*** 保守祕密。***keep (a person) in the dark*** 將事隱瞞不使某人知道。He kept me *in the dark* about it. 他將此事隱瞞不使我知道。
Dark Continent, The 非洲。
dark·en** ['dɑrkən; 'dɑ:kən] *v.i.* 變黑暗;變更黑;變陰沉。—*v.t.* ①使黑暗;使更黑暗。②使帶黑色;使微黑;使加深。③使難懂;使曖昧;使不易了解。④使瞎;使失去視覺。⑤使陰沉;使憂鬱。to *darken* mirth. 掃興。darken one's door*** 拜訪某人。Don't *darken my door* again. 別再進我家的門(別再來我家)。—**er**, *n.*
dark·ey, dark·ie ['dɑrkɪ; 'dɑ:ki] *n.* =**darky.**
dark horse 〖俗〗①黑馬(賽馬或比賽中, 不知名而出人意外得勝之馬或人)。②(政治)意外獲得提名之人。
dark·ish ['dɑrkɪʃ; 'dɑ:kiʃ] *adj.* 微暗的;淺黑的。—**ness**, *n.*
dark lantern 可用罩子等遮蓋使光線不外射的燈籠。
dar·kle ['dɑrkl̩; 'dɑ:kl] *v.i.*, **dar·kled, dar·kling.** ①漸暗;漸呈陰晦。②顯得陰暗;模糊不清。
dark·ling ['dɑrklɪŋ; 'dɑ:kliŋ] *adv.* 在黑暗中。—*adj.* 黑暗中的;模糊的。
dark·ly ['dɑrklɪ; 'dɑ:kli] *adv.* ①黑暗地。②神祕地。③態度略帶威脅地。④微弱地。
:dark·ness ['dɑrknɪs; 'dɑ:knis] *n.* ①黑暗。The room was in *darkness*. 房間一片漆黑。②罪惡。Satan, the prince of *darkness*. 撒旦, 罪惡之尤。③不明;含蓄。④無知。⑤盲。
dark·room ['dɑrkˌrum; 'dɑ:k'rum] *n.* (沖洗底片的)暗室;暗房。
dark·some ['dɑrksəm; 'dɑ:ksəm] *adj.* 〖詩〗①憂愁的;鬱鬱不樂的。②模糊不清的。③稍暗的;陰暗的。—**ness**, *n.*
dark·y ['dɑrkɪ; 'dɑ:ki] *n.*, *pl.* **dark·ies.** ①黑暗的東西。②〖俚〗夜。③〖蔑〗黑人。
***dar·ling** ['dɑrlɪŋ; 'dɑ:liŋ] *n.* 親愛的人。Come here, my *darling!* 親愛的, 過來罷! —*adj.* 鍾愛的;可愛的。—**ly**, *adv.* —**ness**, *n.*
***darn**[1] [dɑrn; dɑ:n] *v.t.* 縫補;補綴。—*n.*

補釘;補綴之布片。

darn² *v.t., n.* 〖美俗〗=**damn.** —*adj.* & *adv.* =**darned.**

darned [dɑrnd; dɑ:nd] *adj.* 〖美俗〗被詛咒的;可厭的。—*adv.* 〖美俗〗非常地。

dar·nel [ˈdɑrnḷ; ˈdɑ:nḷ] *n.* 〖植物〗毒麥。

darn·er [ˈdɑrnɚ; ˈdɑ:nə] *n.* ①補綴者;補綴用針。②蜻蜓。

darn·ing [ˈdɑrnɪŋ; ˈdɑ:niŋ] *n.* ①縫補;補綴。②縫補之衣物。

darning needle ①補綴用針。②〖美〗〖方〗蜻蜓。

***dart** [dɑrt; dɑ:t] *n.* ①標槍;箭;鏢。②突然而快的動作;突進;急發;急射。③(昆蟲的)螯;刺。④怒目;尖刻之語。⑤(*pl.*)(作 *sing.* 解)擲鏢遊戲。—*v.t.* ①投擲;急射。②投射;放出;發出。—*v.i.* 急飛;突發;急馳。—**ing,** *adj.* —**ing·ly,** *adv.* —**ing·ness,** *n.*

dart·er [ˈdɑrtɚ; ˈdɑ:tə] *n.* ①急飛、突發、投射之人或物。②鵜類之鳥。③射水魚。

dar·tle [ˈdɑrtḷ; ˈdɑ:tl] *v.t.* & *v.i.*, **-tled, -tling.** 反覆投射;不斷突進。

Dar·win [ˈdɑrwɪn; ˈdɑ:win] *n.* 達爾文 (Charles Robert, 1809–1882, 英國博物學家,進化論之創立者)。

Dar·win·i·an [dɑrˈwɪnɪən; dɑ:ˈwiniən] *adj.* 達爾文的;達爾文學說的。***Darwinian theory*** 達爾文之進化論。—*n.* 崇奉達爾文之學說者;進化論者。

Dar·win·ism [ˈdɑrwɪnˌɪzəm; ˈdɑ:winizəm] *n.* 達爾文學說;進化論。

Dar·win·ist [ˈdɑrwɪnɪst; ˈdɑ:winist] *n., adj.* =**Darwinian.** —**ic,** *adj.*

:dash [dæʃ; dæʃ] *v.t.* ①擲;猛撞;撞破。The ship was *dashed* to pieces. 這船被撞成碎片。②濺潑;澆;淋。③使失望;使沮喪。④破壞;挫折。⑤使與其他物質少許混合;摻雜。to *dash* wine with water. 在酒裏摻水。⑥迅速完成。to *dash* off a letter. 匆匆地寫一封信。⑦使狼狽。—*v.i.* 衝撞;衝進;突進。He *dashed* out of the room at the sight of a snake. 他看到蛇急衝出房外。***dash against*** 向…撞。***dash down***=**dash off** (**a.**). ***dash off*** **a.** 急寫;急草。**b.** 匆匆離開。I must *dash off* now. 我必須立刻離開。—*n.* ①少許;少量。Give him a glass of water with a *dash* of whisky in it. 給他一杯水,加少許威士忌酒。②突進;突擊。③衝撞。④短跑。the 100-meter *dash.* 百米短跑。⑤銳氣;氣力。⑥長畫符號(—)。⑦潑;濺。⑧使人沮喪之物。⑨一擊。⑩(電報中之)長音。⑪虛飾之外表或行爲。⑫有力之動作。⑬汽車之儀器板。***at a dash*** 急進;速發。***cut a dash*** 〖俗〗賣弄自己;炫耀。***make a dash for*** (or ***at***) 向…急進;衝向。

dash·board [ˈdæʃˌbord; ˈdæʃbɔ:d] *n.* ①(馬車等前部之)遮泥板。②〖航海〗防波板;遮水板。③(汽車等之)儀器板。

dash·er [ˈdæʃɚ; ˈdæʃə] *n.* ①猛撞之人或物。②攪拌器。③擋泥板。④〖俗〗打扮入時者。

dash·ing [ˈdæʃɪŋ; ˈdæʃiŋ] *adj.* ①勇敢的;活躍的。②時髦的;炫耀的。—**ly,** *adv.*

dash·y [ˈdæʃɪ; ˈdæʃi] *adj.*, **dash·i·er, dash·i·est.** 華麗的;炫耀的;浮華的。

das·tard [ˈdæstɚd; ˈdæstəd] *n.* 懦夫;膽小的人。—*adj.* 怯懦的;畏縮的。

das·tard·ly [ˈdæstɚdlɪ; ˈdæstədli] *adj.* 怯懦的;卑鄙的;鬼祟的。

das·y·ure [ˈdæsɪjur; ˈdæsijuə] *n.* 〖動物〗袋貓(澳洲產)。

dat. dative.

***da·ta** [ˈdetə; ˈdeitə] *n.* pl. of **datum.** 資料;材料;作爲論據之事實。The *data* are insufficient. 資料不足。〖注意〗在非正式英語中, data 常與單數動詞連用。但在正式英語中,仍視 data 爲一複數名詞。

data bank 〖電腦〗資料銀行。

data-bank [ˈdetəˌbæŋk; ˈdeitəbæŋk] *v.t.* 輸入或儲存於資料銀行。

da·ta·phone [ˈdetəˌfon; ˈdeitəfoun] *n.* 〖電腦〗資料聽器。

:date¹ [det; deit] *n., v.,* **dat·ed, dat·ing.** —*n.* ①日期;年月日。*date* of birth. 出生日期。②年代;時代。③〖俗〗約會(尤指與異性的約會)。I have a *date* with him next week. 我和他在下星期有一個約會。④〖俗〗相與約會之人(異性)。She is my *date.* 她跟我有約會。⑤(*pl.*)生死年代。***of even date*** 同一日期的。***out of date*** 過時的;陳舊的。***to date*** 到目前爲止。***up*** (or ***down***) ***to date*** 及時的;最新式的;直至最近的。You must have *up to date* ideas. 你的思想應當趕上時代。—*v.i.* ①有日期;記日期;載日期。②屬於某時期。③始自某時期。④與異性作社交約會。—*v.t.* ①記日期;載日期。Don't forget to *date* your letters. 不要忘了在你的信上寫明日期。②定時期;斷定時代。③與…約會。④顯出…的年齡;使…顯得保守。〖注意〗美國日期的通常寫法: December 7, 1977。非正式寫法用數字: 12/7/77。順序爲月、日、年(美軍語、科學用語和英國寫法: 7/12/77。順序爲日、月、年)。正式文體中,如不書年份,則日子常拼爲: December seven或December seventh. 一般除正式社交通告、請帖等外,常不書年份。

date² *n.* ①棗椰樹之果。②棗椰樹。

date·book [ˈdetˌbuk; ˈdeitbuk] *n.* 記事册(記載重要日期、約會等)。

dat·ed [ˈdetɪd; ˈdeitid] *adj.* ①載明日期的。②過時的。—**ly,** *adv.* —**ness,** *n.*

date·less [ˈdetlɪs; ˈdeitlis] *adj.* ①無日期的;未記月日的。②無限期的。③太古的;無法計算日期的。④歷久而趣味不減的。

date line ①國際換日線(即距 Greenwich 180度之子午線)。②=**dateline.**

date·line [ˈdetˌlaɪn; ˈdeitlain] *n., v.,* **-lined, -lin·ing.** —*n.* 書信或新聞通信稿上所註明之書寫(發稿)日期與地點。—*v.t.* 註明發稿(信)日期與地點。

date of maturity 〖商〗(支票、匯票等之)兌現日期。

dat·er [ˈdetɚ; ˈdeitə] *n.* ①約會者。②打日期之戳子。

date slip 向圖書館借得之書籍後面註明借書與還書日期之附條。

date stamp ①郵戳。②郵戳所註明之日期與地點。

dating bar 〖美〗供男女約會的酒館。

da·ti·val [deˈtaɪvəl; dəˈtaivəl] *adj.* 〖文法〗與格的。

da·tive [ˈdetɪv; ˈdeitiv] *adj.* 〖文法〗與格的。—*n.* ①〖文法〗與格。②〖法律〗可隨意贈予或處置的。

da·tum [ˈdetəm; ˈdeitəm] *n., pl.* **da·ta.** ①資料;材料;論據。②(*pl.*)觀察所得之事實。

da·tu·ra [dəˈtjurə; dəˈtjuərə] *n.* 蔓陀羅屬之植物。

dau. daughter.

daub [dɔb; dɔ:b] *v.t.* & *v.i.* ①塗;搽。②弄污。③(拙劣地)繪畫;裝飾。—*n.* ①粉塗之物。②拙劣之畫。③塗、搽(之動作)。—**er,** *n.* —**ing·ly,** *adv.*

daub·ster [ˈdɔbstɚ; ˈdɔ:bstə] *n.* 笨拙(庸)畫匠。

daub·y [ˈdɔbɪ; ˈdɔ:bi] *adj.*, **daub·i·er, daub·i·est.** ①膠黏的。②亂畫的;潦草的。

:daugh·ter [ˈdɔtɚ; ˈdɔ:tə] *n.* ①女兒。②女性的後裔。③關係如女兒者。*daughters* of the church. 教會的女會友。④產物。—*adj.* ①如女兒的。②〖生物〗第一代的。

daugh·ter-in-law ['dɔtərɪn,lɔ; 'dɔːtərinlɔː] *n., pl.* **daugh·ters-in-law.** 兒媳婦。

daugh·ter·ly ['dɔtəlɪ; 'dɔːtəli] *adj.* 女兒的;似女兒的;盡女職的;孝順的。

daunt [dɔnt; dɔːnt] *v.t.* ①恐嚇。②使失去勇氣或信心。

daunt·less ['dɔntlɪs; 'dɔːntlis] *adj.* 大膽的;勇敢的。—**ly,** *adv.*

dau·phin ['dɔfɪn; 'dɔːfin] *n.* 法國皇太子的稱號(用於1349年至1830年間)。

dau·phin·ess ['dɔfɪnɪs; 'dɔːfinis] *n.* 法國之太子妃。

dav·en·port ['dævən,port; 'dævənpɔːt] *n.* ①〖美〗長沙發。②〖英〗小型寫字檯。

Da·vid ['devɪd; 'deivid] *n.* ①男子名。②〖聖經〗大衛(以色列第二代國王)。

Da·vis cup ['devɪs～; 'deivis～] 戴維斯杯(美國人 D.F. Davis 所捐贈之大銀杯,網球賽優勝者所獲之獎)。

Da·vis·son ['devɪsn; 'deivisn] *n.* 大衞生(Clinton Joseph, 1881–1958, 美國物理學家, 1937年獲諾貝爾物理獎)。

dav·it ['dævɪt; 'dævit] *n.* (船旁的)吊柱;吊艇架。

Da·vy ['devɪ; 'deivi] *n.* 男子名。

da·vy ['devɪ; 'deivi] *n.* 〖俚〗=**affidavit.**

Davy Jones 海神;海魔。

Davy Jones's locker ①海底;淹死於海中之人的墓地。②海洋。

Davy lamp 礦坑中用的一種安全燈。

daw [dɔ; dɔː] *n.* ①〖動物〗鴉之一種。②〖古〗愚人;呆子。

daw·dle ['dɔdl; 'dɔːdl] *v., -dled, -dling, n.* —*v.i. & v.t.* 浪費光陰;閒蕩;怠惰〖常away〗. —*n.* ①閒蕩。②浪費光陰者。—**daw·dler,** *n.*

Dawes [dɔz; dɔːz] *n.* 道斯 (Charles Gates, 1865–1951, 美國律師及財政家, 於1925–29 任美國副總統, 曾獲1925年諾貝爾和平獎)。

dawk[1] [dɔk; dɔːk] *n.* 〖英印〗①驛遞。②郵政;郵件。

dawk[2] *n.* 〖美〗不喜歡戰爭亦不願對戰爭表示反對的人。

:dawn [dɔn; dɔːn] *n.* ①天初亮;黎明;曙;破曉。He got up at *dawn.* 他黎明卽起。②開始;發端。the *dawn* of civilization. 文化的發端。—*v.i.* ①天曙;破曉。The day was *dawning.* 天剛亮。②覺醒;了解〖on〗。③開始發展;出現;初現。

dawn·ing ['dɔnɪŋ; 'dɔːniŋ] *n.* ①黎明;破曉。②出現;開始。

dawn patrol ①〖軍〗清晨偵察飛行。②無線電或電視臺之早晨節目工作者。

:day [de; dei] *n.* ①日出至日沒;日間。The sun gives us light during the *day.* 日間太陽給我們陽光。②一日;晝夜二十四小時。What *day* of the week is it? 今天禮拜幾?③工作日。④紀念日。New Year's *Day.* 元旦。⑤競爭之日;競爭;爭鬥;勝利。⑥(常 *pl.*) 時期;時代。in these *days.* 現在;如今。⑦(常 *pl.*)生命或活動的時期;壽命。His *days* are numbered. 他的壽命已可指日而計(壽命不長了)。⑧某事發生之日。⑨幸運或順利的時期。He had his *day.* 他也曾飛黃騰達過 (即全盛時代已過)。***all* (*the*) *day long*** 終日。***before day*** 天未明。***by day*** 日間。***by the day*** 按日計算地。He is paid *by the day.* 他按日支薪。***call it a day*** 結束一日之工作;暫時停止。***day after day*** 一天又一天;一連許多天。***day after tomorrow*** 後天。***day and night*** (or ***night and day***) 晝夜;日夜。***day before yesterday*** 前天。***day in and day out*** 每天;繼續不斷地。***end one's days*** 死。***every day*** 每日。***from day to day*** a. 從第一到第二天。b. 每日;日日;一日之間。***have one's day*** 有過輝煌的時代。***one day*** 某日;有一日。***one of these days*** 將來有一天;最近的將來。***pass the time of day*** 與人閒聊。***some day*** 他日;將來有一天。***the other day*** 前幾日。***this day fortnight*** 兩星期後。***this day week*** 下星期的這一天;從今天算起一星期;一星期後。***to a day*** 恰好;剛好。***win the day*** 獲得勝利。

day bed 〖美〗坐臥兩用長椅。(亦作 **daybed**)

day·bill ['de,bɪl; 'deibil] *n.* 戲劇或其他娛樂節目之廣告招貼;海報。

day blindness 〖醫〗晝盲。

day-board·er ['de,bordə; 'dei,bɔːdə] *n.* 通學生;走讀生。

day·book ['de,bʊk; 'deibuk] *n.* ①日記。②〖簿記〗流水帳;日記簿。

day boy 〖主英〗寄宿學校之走讀生。

***day·break** ['de,brek; 'dei-breik] *n.* 破曉;黎明。He gets up at *daybreak.* 他黎明卽起。

day-by-day ['debaɪ'de; 'deibai'dei] *adj.* 逐日的;每天的。

day camp 白晝兒童夏令營 (參加者在家過夜)。

day-care ['de,kɛr; 'dei,kɛə] *adj.* 〖美〗日間照料學前兒童的。

day-care center 託兒所。

day coach 〖美〗普通客車。

day·dream ['de,drim; 'dei-driːm] *n.* 白日夢;幻想;想像;妄想。—*v.i.* 作白日夢;耽於幻想;妄想。—**er,** *n.* —**y,** *adj.*

day·fly ['de,flaɪ; 'deiflai] *n., pl.* **-flies.** 蜉蝣。

day labo(u)r ①按日計酬的勞工。②其工作。

day labo(u)rer 按日計酬的勞工(尤指非技術性工人)。

day letter 〖美〗晝間書信電報(較普通電報低廉但稍遲緩)。(亦作 **day telegram**)

day·light** ['de,laɪt; 'deilait] *n.* ①日光。It is better to read by *daylight* than by lamplight. 用日光讀書較用燈光好。②破曉;黎明。He was up at *daylight.* 他黎明卽起。③白晝;日間。④公開;公然。⑤空間;空隙;缺口。beat* (*knock, frighten* or *scare*) *the daylights out of* (*someone*)** 將(某人) 打(毆、嚇) 得半死。***see daylight*** 〖俗〗a. 明瞭;了解。b. 行將結束一項困難枯燥的工作;接近完成。

daylight-saving time 日光節約時間。

day lily 萱草。

day·long ['de,lɔŋ; 'deilɔŋ] *adj. & adv.* 終日的(地)。

day nursery 日間託兒所。

day-off ['de'ɔf; 'dei'ɔːf] *n.* 休息日。

day room 兵營中之士兵閱讀或消遣室。(亦作 **dayroom**)

day school ①日校。②無宿舍學校。

day·spring ['de,sprɪŋ; 'dei-spriŋ] *n.* 〖詩〗黎明;破曉。

day·star ['de,stɑr; 'dei-stɑː] *n.* ①晨星;金星。②〖詩〗太陽。

***day·time** ['de,taɪm; 'deitaim] *n.* 日間;白晝。Baby sleeps even in the *daytime.* 嬰兒在白晝也要睡覺。

day-to-day ['detə'de; 'deitə'dei] *adj.* ①每日的;逐日的。②祇顧目前需要的(不作長遠打算的)。

day·work ['de,wɝk; 'deiwəːk] *n.* ①白晝工作。②按日或按小時計酬的工作。

day·work·er ['de,wɝkə; 'dei,wəːkə] *n.* 按日或小時計酬之工人。

***daze** [dez; deiz] *v.,* **dazed, daz·ing,** *n.*

—*v.t.* 使惶惑；使眩暈。—*n.* 眩迷；目眩；恍惚。—**daz•ed•ly, daz•ing•ly,** *adv.*
***daz•zle** ['dæzl; 'dæzl] *v.,* **-zled, -zling,** *n.* —*v.t.* ①以强光使目眩。②使迷惑。—*v.i.* ①受强光而目眩。②閃耀。—*n.* 閃耀；眩目的强光。—**ment, daz•zler,** *n.*
daz•zling ['dæzlɪŋ; 'dæzliŋ] *adj.* 眩目的；燦爛的。—**ly,** *adv.*
d.b. daybook. **D. C.** ①District of Columbia. ②direct current. ③Deputy Consul. ④District Court. **D.C.L.** Doctor of Civil Law. **D.C.M.** Distinguished Conduct Medal. **dd., d/d** deliverd. **D.D.** Doctor of Divinity. **d.d.** ①days after date. ②days after delivery. ③dono dedit (拉 =present as a gift). **d-d** danned.
D-Day ['di,de; 'di:-dei] *n.* ①二次世界大戰中盟軍進攻西歐之開始日(1944年6月6日)。②攻擊發起日。(亦作 **D-day**)
D.D.S. Doctor of Dental Surgery.
DDT, D.D.T. 一種殺蟲藥 (dichlorodiphenyl-trichloroethane之簡寫)。
de, De [dɪ, də, di; di:] 〖法〗 *prep.* 的；從；屬於(多用於法國人之姓氏前以表示世居地)。
de- 〖字首〗①剝奪；分離。②否定；相反。③下；貶。④衍出。⑤爭；倍。
dea•con ['dikən, 'di:kən] *n.* 教會中之執事。—*v.t.* ①〖俗〗(唱詩前)朗讀(聖詩)。②〖俚〗將最好的裝在上面做樣子以包裝(水果等)。③〖俚〗以次貨冒充上等貨；欺騙。
dea•con•ess ['dikənɪs; 'di:kənis] *n.* 教會之女執事。
dea•con•ry ['dikənrɪ; 'di:kənri] *n., pl.* **-ries.** ①教會執事之職。②教會執事之集合稱。
dea•con•ship ['dikən,ʃɪp; 'di:kən-ʃip] *n.* 教會執事之職。
de•ac•ti•vate [di'æktə,vet; di'æktiveit] *v.t.,* **-vat•ed, -vat•ing.** ①使無效。②解散；撤銷。③使(炸彈等)不能爆炸。
:dead [dɛd; ded] *adj.* ①死的。He is *dead.* 他死了。②無生命的。*dead* matter. 無生命的東西。*dead* leaves. 枯葉。③如死的。*dead* sleep. 酣睡；沉睡如死。④不新鮮的；不活潑的；無生氣的。*dead* water. 不流動的水；死水。*dead* market. 冷落的市場；蕭條的市場。⑤麻木的；無感覺的。He is *dead* to all sense of shame. 他毫無羞恥的感覺。⑥(語言)不通行的。Latin and Greek are *dead* languages. 拉丁文和希臘文是死的文字。⑦無彈性的。⑧缺乏趣味、熱心或色彩的；無風趣的。⑨荒蕪的；不生產的；無利益的。⑩準確的；無誤的。⑪完全的；絕對的。a *dead* failure. 完全失敗。⑫無法投遞的。⑬一端不通的。⑭熄滅的。⑮直的；直接的。⑯〖電〗無電流通過的；未充電的。⑰不在使用中的；失效的。⑱〖俗〗累極的。⑲無味的。⑳無動於衷的。㉑不再感覺的。㉒突然的。The train came to a *dead* stop. 火車突然停住。㉓無放射性的。㉔〖印刷〗已經用過或不再需要的。㉕不停止的。—*adv.* ①全然地；絕對地；完全地。I was *dead* tired. 我極為疲倦。②突然停止地。③直接地；正對地。—*n.* ①(the-) 死人 (集合稱)。to mourn for the *dead.* 哀悼死亡者。②最暗或最冷的時期。the *dead* of winter. 隆冬。
dead air ①〖無線電、電視〗廣播停止期間。②不流通的空氣。
dead-a•live ['dɛdə'laɪv; 'dedə'laiv] *adj.* 無生氣的；不景氣的。(亦作 **dead-and-alive**)
dead angle 〖軍〗死角。
dead-beat ['dɛd'bit; 'ded'bi:t] *adj.* 〖俗〗筋疲力盡的。
dead beat 〖俗〗①賴債者；延不償付者。②遊手好閒者。
dead•beat ['dɛd,bit; 'ded'bi:t] *adj.* 〖機械〗①不擺的。②(計量器指針之)速指作用的。
dead•born ['dɛd,bɔrn; 'dedbɔ:n] *adj.* =**stillborn.**
dead duck 〖俚〗失去使用價值之人或物。
dead•ee [dɛd'i; ded'i:] *n.* 根據照片所繪的遺像。
dead•en ['dɛdn; 'dedn] *v.t.* ①使鈍；使弱；減緩。②隔阻；防住。—*v.i.* ①變得如死一般。②失去活力。—**er,** *n.*
dead end ①一端不通之管或道路；死巷。②僵局；絕境。
dead•eye ['dɛd,aɪ; 'dedai] *n.* 〖航海〗三眼轆轤；三孔滑車。—*adj.* 精確的。
dead•fall ['dɛd,fɔl; 'dedfɔ:l] *n.* ①陷阱。②〖美〗因年久或腐爛而倒落的林木。③(美國西部之)下級酒館。
dead fire 桅頭電光(暴風雨夜見於桅頭，為死之預兆)。
dead•head ['dɛd,hɛd; 'dedhed] *n.* ①木浮標。②(使用優待證)看戲或乘車不付錢者。③無能力者；庸人。④行駛中的空火車。—*v.t.* ①優待…免費入場或乘車。②〖鐵路〗放空車。—*v.i.* 免費入場或乘車。—**er,** *n.*
dead heat 並列名位(二個以上之競爭者同時到達終點之賽跑)。
dead•house ['dɛd,haʊs; 'dedhaus] *n.* 陳屍所；太平間。
dead letter ①無法投遞的信件。②失效的法令。③失去原有力量或意義的文件。
dead lift ①不藉助機械之力舉起。②須盡最大努力之情勢；須全力以赴的艱巨工作。
dead•light ['dɛd,laɪt; 'dedlait] *n.* 〖航海〗船窗之防水屏。
dead•line ['dɛd,laɪn; 'dedlain] *n.* ①截限時間；(付款等之) 最後時間。②(不可越過的)界線。
dead•li•ness ['dɛdlɪnɪs; 'dedlinis] *n.* ①致命；性命攸關。②不共戴天；深讎。
dead load 靜載重；靜負荷。
dead•lock ['dɛd,lɑk; 'dedlɔk] *n.* 完全停頓。*be at* (or *come to*) *a deadlock* 停頓；相持不下。—*v.t.* 使相持不下；使停頓。—*v.i.* 相持不下；停頓。
***dead•ly** ['dɛdlɪ; 'dedli] *adj.,* **-li•er, -li•est,** *adv.* —*adj.* ①致命的。a *deadly* poison. 烈性毒藥。②深仇的；勢不兩立的。*deadly* enemy. 深仇；死敵。③如死的。④極度的。*deadly* haste. 至急。⑤使靈魂死亡的。*deadly* sins. 死罪；大罪(卽驕傲、貪婪、邪淫、憤怒、貪饕、嫉妬、懶惰)。⑥絕對精確的。⑦非常令人生厭的。—*adv.* ①如死地。*deadly* pale. 蒼白如死人。②〖俗〗非常地；極度地。
dead mail 無法投遞之郵件。
dead-mail office ['dɛd'mel~; 'ded'meil~] 郵局處理無法投遞郵件的部門。(亦作 **dead-letter office**)
dead•ness ['dɛdnɪs; 'dednis] *n.* ①無生氣；死。②無精神；衰敗。③(酒等)走脫氣味。
dead nettle 葉似蕁蔴而無刺之薄荷科植物。
dead pan 〖俚〗①無表情的面孔。②面孔無表情的人(如演員等)。
dead-pan, dead•pan ['dɛd,pæn; 'dedpæn] *adj.* & *adv.* 〖俚〗面部無表情的(地)；缺乏幽默的(地)。—*v.i.* & *v.t.* 面部無表情地做或表演。
Dead Sea 死海(巴勒斯坦東邊的一鹽湖，為世界上最低之湖)。
dead set ①獵犬於指示獵物方位時所採取的固定姿勢。②認眞的嘗試；堅定的努力。
dead stick 〖航空〗停止旋轉的螺旋槳。

dead-stick landing ['dɛd,stɪk~; 'ded,stik~]〖航空〗滑翔着陸(引擎已關閉或失效時之飛機降落)。
dead storage (貨物之)長期存庫。
dead weight ①不活動之人或物的重量。②重負;重載。③車重;皮重。④按重量計算運費之貨物。
dead weight ton 長噸;載重噸(等於2,240磅)。
dead wind 〖航海〗逆風。
dead·wood ['dɛd,wud; 'dedwud] *n.* ①樹上之枯枝。②無用之人或物。③(尤指船尾)龍骨以上之木材。④〖保齡球〗被球擊倒但仍留在槽內的柱。
***deaf** [dɛf; def] *adj.* ①聾的。②不願聽的;不理會的。He turned a *deaf* ear to all requests for help. 他不理會一切求援的呼籲。*deaf and dumb* 聾且啞的。—**ness,** *n.*
***deaf·en** ['dɛfən;'defn] *v.t.* ①使聾;使不能聽。②被噪聲震聾。③(大聲)淹沒(小聲)。④使…能隔音。
deaf·en·ing ['dɛfənɪŋ;'defniŋ] *n.* 隔音裝置;止響物。—*adj.* 令人耳聾的。—**ly,** *adv.*
deaf-mute ['dɛf'mjut; 'def'mju:t] *n.* 聾啞之人。—*adj.* 聾啞的。
‡deal[1] [dil; di:l] *v.,* **dealt, deal·ing,** *n.* —*v.i.* ①與…有關;涉及;論及;討論〖with〗. This book *deals* with the Far East. 這本書討論遠東問題。②處分;懲處;對付;對待;待人〖with〗. He *deals* fairly with others. 他待人公道。③交易;經營;買賣〖with, in〗. ④處理;考慮〖with〗. ⑤分配(尤指分紙牌)。—*v.t.* ①分配。②給以;加於。③發紙牌。***deal a blow*** 加以打擊。 ***deal in*** 買與賣;經售。This garage *deals in* oil, tyres and petrol. 這個汽車修理廠經售油、車胎和汽油。 ***deal out*** 分配。***deal someone in*** 〖俚〗 算一分兒;算在內。***deal with*** **a.** 對付;來往;打交道。**b.** 處理;考慮。**c.** 對待。**d.** 討論;論及。—*n.* ①〖俗〗交易。Do you have a *deal* with Smith? 你和史密斯有交易嗎? ②〖俗〗(商業的或政治的)協議(尤指密約)。③〖俗〗分配;待遇。He gave me a square *deal.* 他給我公平的待遇。④量;數量。⑤發紙牌。⑥(D-)政治、經濟或社會政策。the New *Deal.* (羅斯福的)新政。***a great deal*** (or ***a good deal***) 許多。It took him *a great deal* of trouble. 這事給他很多麻煩。
deal[2] *n.* 松木木材(英國:寬7英寸,長6英尺,厚3英寸以下;美、加兩國:寬11英寸,長12英尺,厚2½英寸)。
***deal·er** ['dilɚ; 'di:lə] *n.* ①行爲者;處已者。②商人;交易者。a *dealer* in furs. 毛皮商。a wholesale (retail) *dealer.* 批發(零售)商。③發牌者;莊家。
***deal·ing** ['dilɪŋ; 'di:liŋ] *n.* ①對人的態度;應接。②(*pl.*)交往;交際;友誼的關係。business *dealings.* 商業上的往來。③交易;買賣。④分配。⑤發牌。
dealt [dɛlt; delt] *v.* pt. & pp. of **deal.**
dean [din; di:n] *n.* ①教務主任;教務長;學院院長。②訓導長;學監。③教會中高級職員。④團體中資格最老者(習慣上充任該團領袖)。
dean·er·y ['dinərɪ; 'di:nəri] *n., pl.* **-er·ies.** dean 之職務、邸宅或管區。
dean·ship ['dinʃɪp; 'di:nʃip] *n.* dean 之職位或任期。
‡dear [dɪr; diə] *adj.* ①親愛的;可愛的。②寫信時的稱呼。*Dear* sir. 執事先生台鑒;敬啓者。*Dear* Mr. Chang. 張先生大鑒。③昂貴的;索價高的(店鋪)。④寶貴的;珍視的。They hold their lives *dear.* 他們珍視生命。⑤內心的;誠懇的。my *dearest* wish. 我最誠懇的願望。—*n.* 親愛的人。Come here, my *dear.* 親愛的,這裏來。—*adv.* ①親愛地。②昂貴地;高價地。The accident cost him *dear.* 這意外使他損失很重。—*interj.* 啊呀。Oh, *dear!* (*Dear* me! *Dear, dear!*) 啊呀!(天呀!不得了!) —**ly,** *adv.* —**ness,** *n.*
dear·ie ['dɪrɪ; 'diəri] *n.* =**deary.**
Dear John 〖俚〗(指女子)絕情信(通知男友或未婚夫以後不再來往)。
dearth [dɝθ; də:θ] *n.* ①缺乏;少。②饑饉。
dear·y ['dɪrɪ; 'diəri] *n., pl.* **dear·ies.** 〖俗〗親愛的人;親親;小寶貝(母親稱小孩)。
‡death [dɛθ; deθ] *n.* ①死;死亡。*Death* comes to all men. 人皆有死。②消滅;毀滅。the *death* of one's hopes. 希望的毀滅。③死亡的狀態。④死亡的方式。a hero's *death.* 英雄式的死。⑤死亡的原因。⑥瘟疫。a black *death.* 黑死病。⑦謀殺;流血。⑧(D-)死神。***as sure as death*** 確定。***be at death's door*** 與死爲鄰;瀕於死亡。***catch one's death of cold*** 受涼甚重,可能致死。***do to death*** **a.** 謀殺;殺死。**b.** 重複地說(做、表演)以至令人感到極度厭煩。***put to death*** 處死。***to death*** 到極點;極度的;非常的。***to the death*** 至死方休。
death ash (dust or **sand)** 放射塵。
death·bed ['dɛθ,bɛd;'deθbed] *n.* ①臨死時所臥之床。②臨死之時。—*adj.* 臨終時所做的。
death bell ①喪鐘。②耳鳴(其聲若鐘,迷信認係死亡先兆)。
death benefit 受益人領的死亡保險金。
death·blow ['dɛθ,blo; 'deθblou] *n.* 致命之打擊。
death cell 死囚牢房。
death certificate 死亡證書。
death chair (處決死囚的)電椅。
death chamber ①監獄中的行刑室。②瀕死者之臥房。
death cup 〖植物〗一種極毒的蘑菇。
death·day ['dɛθ,de; 'deθdei] *n.* 忌辰。
death duty 〖英〗(常 *pl.*) 遺產稅。
death·ful ['dɛθfəl; 'deθful] *adj.* ①多死亡的;殘殺的;流血的。②如死的。—**ly,** *adv.* —**ness,** *n.*
death·less ['dɛθlɪs; 'deθlis] *adj.* 不死的;不朽的。
death·like ['dɛθ,laɪk; 'deθlaik] *adj.* 如死的;可致死的;不幸的。
death·ly ['dɛθlɪ; 'deθli] *adj.* ①如死的。②致死的。—*adv.* ①如死地。②非常地。—**death·li·ness,** *n.*
death mask 死後所製成之面型。
death penalty 死刑。
death rate 死亡率。
death rattle 臨死時從喉間發出的不清楚的聲音。
death ray 死光。
death roll 死亡名簿。
death's-head ['dɛθs,hɛd; 'deθshed] *n.* 骷髏;象徵死亡之骷髏畫。
death·trap ['dɛθ,træp; 'deθtræp] *n.* ①危險場所;危險之建築物。②危險之情況。
death warrant 死刑判決書。
death·watch ['dɛθ,watʃ; 'deθwɔtʃ] *n.* ①守屍。②死囚行刑前夜之看守者。③死亡之蟲(發滴答叫聲,迷信者認係死亡之兆)。
death-wound ['dɛθ,wund; 'deθ-wu:nd] *n.* 致命傷。
deb [dɛb; deb] *n.* 〖美俗〗=**debutante.**
deb. debenture.
de·ba·cle [de'bakḷ, -'ba:kḷ; dei'ba:kl]

n.①突然的大災難;大混亂。②崩潰。③(河水的)氾濫。④(冰河的)潰裂。⑤〖地質〗山崩。
de·bar [dɪ'bar; di'bɑː] *v.t.*, **-barred, -bar·ring.** 阻止;禁止;排除。
de·bark [dɪ'bark; di'bɑːk] *v.i.* & *v.t.* 「登陸;上岸。」
de·bar·ka·tion [ˌdibar'keʃən; ˌdiː-bɑː'keiʃən] *n.* 登陸;上岸。
de·base [dɪ'bes; di'beis] *v.t.*, **-based, -bas·ing.** ①貶低;貶降。②貶值。—**ment,** *n.*
de·bat·a·ble [dɪ'betəbl; di'beitəbl] *adj.* 可爭辯的;成問題的。—**de·bat·a·bly,** *adv.*
***de·bate** [dɪ'bet; di'beit] *v.*, **-bat·ed, -bat·ing,** *n.* —*v.i.* ①討論;辯論。to *debate* on a question. 討論或辯論一個問題。②考慮。—*v.t.* ①討論;辯論;爭論。②沉思;考慮。—*n.* ①討論。②辯論。③思考;考慮。—**de·bat·er,** *n.*
de·bauch [dɪ'bɔtʃ; di'bɔːtʃ] *v.t.* ①使誤入歧途;誘使放蕩。②姦淫;敗壞。—*v.i.* 放蕩;荒淫。—*n.* ①放蕩;荒唐。②暴飲;暴食。
deb·au·chee [ˌdɛbɔ'tʃi; ˌdebɔː'tʃiː] *n.* 放蕩者;邪淫者。
de·bauch·er·y [dɪ'bɔtʃərɪ; di'bɔːtʃəri] *n., pl.* **-er·ies.** ①放蕩;淫亂。②敗德;腐敗。③(*pl.*)墮落荒唐的期間或行爲。
de·ben·ture [dɪ'bɛntʃɚ; di'bentʃə] *n.* ①債券。②(海關發給的)退稅憑單。
de·bil·i·tate [dɪ'bɪləˌtet; di'biliteit] *v.t.*, **-tat·ed, -tat·ing.** 使衰弱;使虛弱。
de·bil·i·ty [dɪ'bɪlətɪ; di'biliti] *n., pl.* **-ties.** 衰弱;虛弱。
deb·it ['dɛbɪt; 'debit] *n.* 借方;負債。—*v.t.* ①使負債。②〖簿記〗登入借方。
deb·o·nair(e) [ˌdɛbə'nɛr; ˌdebə'nɛə] *adj.* ①快樂的;心境愉快的。②溫文有禮的。
Deb·o·rah ['dɛbərə; 'debərə] *n.* ①女子名。②〖聖經〗底波拉(希伯來女先知及法官)。
de·bouch [dɪ'buʃ; di'bautʃ] *v.i.* ①〖軍〗由隘路或閉塞地區進至開闊地區;出發。②流注(至開闊地區)。③從…出來;從…出現。—*v.t.* 使出發;使出現;使流注。
de·bouch·ment [dɪ'buʃmənt; di-'bautʃmənt] *n.* ①〖軍〗進行;出發。②(河之)出口;出路。
de·brief [di'brif; diː'briːf] *v.t.* 向(飛行員、情報官等於任務完畢歸來時)提出詢問。—*v.i.* (飛行員、情報官等於任務完畢歸來時)接受詢問。
de·bris [də'bri, 'debri; 'debriː] *n.* ①殘「骸;瓦礫堆。②〖地質〗岩屑。」
:debt [dɛt; det] *n.* ①債;債務。I owe him a *debt* of gratitude for all he has done to help me. 爲了他的一切幫助,我欠了他一筆人情債。②罪。*get* (or *run*) *into debt* 負債。It is easier to *get into debt* than to get out of debt. 負債容易還債難。*in debt* 欠債;負債。He is deeply *in debt.* 他負債很多。—**less,** *adj.*
debt collector 收帳人。
debt of honor 信用欠款;賭債。
debt·or ['dɛtɚ; 'detə] *n.* 債務人;借方(爲 creditor 之對)。—**ship,** *n.*
de·bunk [di'bʌŋk; 'diː'bʌŋk] *v.t.* 〖美俗〗①除去有關…之不確的情緒或意見;暴露;揭穿。②揭…之短;反駁。—**er,** *n.*
de·bus [di'bʌs; diː'bʌs] *v.t.* & *v.i.*, **-bus(s)ed, -bus·(s)ing.** 〖英〗(從巴士或卡車等)卸下。
de·but, dé·but [dɪ'bju; 'deibuː] 〖法〗 *n.* ①初次在社交場露面。②初次登臺。③任何事物之初次出現。—*v.i.* 初次露面;首次出現。—*v.t.* 將…作首次公演。

deb·u·tante, dé·bu·tante [ˌdɛbju'tant; 'debju(ː)tɑːnt] 〖法〗 *n.* ①初入社會之少女。②初次登臺之女子。
De·bye [də'baɪ; də'bai] *n.* 狄白 (Peter Joseph Wilhelm, 1884-1966, 荷蘭物理學家, 1936年獲諾貝爾化學獎)。
Dec. December. **dec.** ①deceased. ②decimeter. ③decorative. ④declination. ⑤decrease. ⑥decrescendo.
deca- 〖字首〗表"十;十倍"之義。
***dec·ade** ['dɛked, dɛk'ed; 'dekeid, di-'keid] *n.* ①十年。②由十所構成的一組。
de·ca·dence [dɪ'kedns; 'dekədəns] *n.* 衰落;墮落;衰微;頹廢。
de·ca·dent [dɪ'kednt; 'dekədənt] *adj.* ①衰落的;墮落的。②十九世紀末葉之文藝頹廢期的;頹廢派的。—*n.* ①衰落者;式微者。②頹廢派之作家或藝術家。—**ly,** *adv.*
dec·a·gon ['dɛkəˌgɑn; 'dekəgən] *n.* 十角形;十邊形。—**al,** *adj.*
dec·a·gram(me) ['dɛkəˌgræm; 'de-kəgræm] *n.* 十克;兙。
dec·a·he·dron [ˌdɛkə'hidrən; ˌdekə-'hiːdrən] *n., pl.* **-drons, -dra** [-drə; -drə]. 十面體。—**dec·a·he·dral,** *adj.*
de·cal ['dikæl, dɪ'kæl; 'diːkæl, di'kæl] *n.* =**decalcomania.**
de·cal·ci·fy [di'kælsəˌfaɪ; diː'kælsifai] *v.t.*, **-fied, -fy·ing.** 自…除去石灰質。
de·cal·co·ma·ni·a [dɪˌkælkə'menɪə; diˌkælkə'meiniə] *n.* ①將圖畫由特製之紙上移印於玻璃器、陶器等之上。②上項用之圖畫。
dec·a·li·ter, dek·a·li·ter, dek·a·li·tre ['dɛkəˌlitɚ; 'dekəˌliːtə] *n.* 十竔;公斗。
Dec·a·log, Dec·a·logue ['dɛkəˌlɔg; 'dekəlɔg] *n.* 十誡 (=the Ten Commandments). (亦作 **decalog, decalogue**)
De·cam·er·on [dɪ'kæmərən; di'kæ-mərən] *n.* ①十日談 (義大利 Boccaccio 所著, 包括一百個故事)。②(d-) 十日談式之著作;色情文學。—**ic,** *adj.*
dec·a·me·ter, dek·a·me·ter, dec·a·me·tre ['dɛkəˌmitɚ; 'dekəˌmiː-tə] *n.* 十公尺;公丈。
de·camp [dɪ'kæmp; di'kæmp] *v.i.* ①逃亡。②離營;撤營。—**ment,** *n.*
dec·a·nal ['dɛkənl; di'keinl] *adj.* ①dean的;deanery 的。②教堂內壇(chancel)之南側的。—**ly,** *adv.*
de·cant [dɪ'kænt; di'kænt] *v.t.* ①將(液體)慢慢倒出(俾將沉澱留於原容器中)。②將(液體等)由一容器倒入另一容器。③卸貨;下客。
de·cant·er [dɪ'kæntɚ; di'kæntə] *n.* 玻璃酒瓶;傾注器;傾析器。
de·cap·i·tate [dɪ'kæpəˌtet; di'kæpi-teit] *v.t.*, **-tat·ed, -tat·ing.** 斬首;砍頭。—**de·cap·i·ta·tion,** *n.*
dec·a·pod ['dɛkəˌpɑd; 'dekəpɔd] *n.* ①十腳類之動物(如龍蝦、螃蟹等)。②十腕類之動物(如墨魚、槍鯽等)。—*adj.* ①〖動物〗十腳類的。②有十腳的。
de·car·bon·ate [di'karbənˌet; diː-'kɑːbəneit] *v.t.*, **-at·ed, -at·ing.** 〖化〗從…中除去二氧化碳或碳酸。
de·car·bon·ize [di'karbənˌaɪz; diː-'kɑːbənaiz] *v.t.* 〖化〗除去炭素。
dec·are ['dɛkɛr; 'dekɛə] *n.* 法國制土地丈量單位 (等於10 ares 或 0.2471 英畝)。
dec·a·stere ['dɛkəˌstɪr; 'dekəstiə] *n.*

十立方公尺(＝10 steres).

dec·a·syl·lab·ic [ˌdɛkəsɪˈlæbɪk; ˈdekəsiˈlæbik] *adj.* ①有十音節的。②十音節之詩行的。—*n.* ＝**decasyllable.**

dec·a·syl·la·ble [ˈdɛkəˌsɪləbl̩; ˈdekəsiləbl] *n.* 有十音節之詩行。

de·cath·lete [dɪˈkæθˌlit; diˈkæθˌliːt] *n.* 十項運動員。

de·cath·lon [dɪˈkæθlɑn; diˈkæθlɔn] *n.* 十項運動。

de·cay** [dɪˈke; diˈkei] *v.i.* ①衰落;衰微;衰弱;衰敗;退化。②腐敗;腐爛。—*v.t.* 使衰退或腐爛。—*n.* ①漸漸衰落;漸漸衰敗;漸漸退化。②衰弱;衰頹。③腐敗;腐爛。④〖物理〗衰變。⑤數量、强度等之減少。be in decay*** 漸漸衰敗;漸漸損壞。***fall into decay*** 漸漸衰落;退化。—**a·ble,** *adj.* —**less,** *adj.*

de·cayed [dɪˈked; diˈkeid] *adj.* 腐朽的;衰敗的;頹廢的。*decayed* teeth. 蛀牙;齲齒。

***de·cease** [dɪˈsis; diˈsiːs] *n., v.,* **-ceased, -ceas·ing.** —*n.* 死亡。—*v.i.* 死亡。

de·ceased** [dɪˈsist; diˈsiːst] *adj.* 死的;死亡的;已故的。the deceased*** 死者。

de·ce·dent [dɪˈsidn̩t; diˈsiːdnt] *n.* 〖法律〗死者。

***de·ceit** [dɪˈsit; diˈsiːt] *n.* ①欺騙。②詭計;狡詐;虛僞。He is full of *deceit.* 他詭計多端。③欺詐的手段;欺詐的行爲;謊話。

de·ceit·ful [dɪˈsitfəl; diˈsiːtful] *adj.* 欺詐的;多僞的。—**ly,** *adv.*

de·ceiv·a·ble [dɪˈsivəbl̩; diˈsiːvəbl] *adj.* 可欺騙的;易受騙的。—**de·ceiv·a·bly,** *adv.* —**de·ceiv·a·bil·i·ty,** *n.*

***de·ceive** [dɪˈsiv; diˈsiːv] *v.,* **-ceived, -ceiv·ing.** —*v.t.* 欺騙。—*v.i.* 欺詐;行騙。Don't *deceive* under any circumstances. 任何情形之下都不要欺騙。—**de·ceiv·er,** *n.* —**de·ceiv·ing·ly,** *adv.*

de·cel·er·ate [diˈsɛləˌret; diːˈseləreit] *v.t. & v.i.,* **-at·ed, -at·ing.** 減速;減緩。—**de·cel·er·a·tion, de·cel·er·a·tor,** *n.*

‡De·cem·ber [dɪˈsɛmbɚ; diˈsembə] *n.* 十二月。

de·cem·vir [dɪˈsɛmvɚ; diˈsemvə] *n., pl.* **-virs, -vir·i** [-vəˌraɪ; -vərai]. ①古羅馬十大行政官之一。②十人當政團體中之一人。

de·cem·vi·rate [dɪˈsɛmvərɪt; diˈsemvirit] *n.* ①古羅馬之十大行政官之職位或任期。②十人當政團體;十頭政治。

de·cen·cy [ˈdisn̩sɪ; ˈdiːsnsi] *n., pl.* **-cies.** ①行爲之正當;端莊;莊重;恭而有禮。②(*pl.*)正當的行爲。

de·cen·na·ry [dɪˈsɛnərɪ; diˈsenəri] *n., pl.* **-ries,** *adj.* —*n.* 十年間;十年。—*adj.* 十年間的;十週年紀念的。

de·cen·ni·al [dɪˈsɛnɪəl; diˈsenjəl] *adj.* 十年間的;十年一度的。—*n.* 十週年紀念。—**ly,** *adv.*

***de·cent** [ˈdisn̩t; ˈdiːsnt] *adj.* ①合式的;適合的。②正當的;適當的。It is not *decent* to laugh at a funeral. 在葬禮時發笑是失禮的。③可尊重的;可敬的。④尙可的;尙佳的。⑤正經的;不猥褻的。⑥不太嚴厲的;寬大的。⑦相當漂亮的。⑧〖俗〗(穿足够的衣服)可以見人的。—**ly,** *adv.* —**ness,** *n.*

de·cen·tral·ize [diˈsɛntrəlˌaɪz; diːˈsentrəlaiz] *v.t.,* **-ized, -iz·ing.** ①劃分;分散(權力等)。②疏散。—**de·cen·tral·i·za·tion,** *n.*

de·cep·tion [dɪˈsɛpʃən; diˈsepʃən] *n.* ①欺騙。②虛幻騙人的東西。③詭計。

de·cep·tive [dɪˈsɛptɪv; diˈseptiv] *adj.* 虛僞的;欺騙的。—**ly,** *adv.* —**ness,** *n.*

deci- 〖字首〗表"十分之一"之義。

dec·i·bel [ˈdɛsəˌbɛl; ˈdesibel] *n.* 〖物理〗分貝(音量之單位)。

de·cid·a·ble [dɪˈsaɪdəbl̩; diˈsaidəbl] *adj.* 可決定的。

‡de·cide [dɪˈsaɪd; diˈsaid] *v.,* **-cid·ed, -cid·ing.** —*v.t.* ①決定;決心;決意。Nothing is *decided* yet. 一切均未決定。②解決;判決。③使決定。His honesty *decided* me to employ him. 他的誠實使我決定用他。—*v.i.* ①決定。He has *decided* on a different plan. 他決定改變計畫。②判決。

***de·cid·ed** [dɪˈsaɪdɪd; diˈsaidid] *adj.* ①無疑的;確定的。a *decided* victory. 決定性的勝利。②堅定的;堅決的。—**ly,** *adv.* —**ness,** *n.*

de·cid·u·ous [dɪˈsɪdʒuəs; diˈsidjuəs] *adj.* ①每年落葉的。②(按季節或生長期)脫落的(如毛髮、牙、角等)。③非永久性的;短暫的。—**ly,** *adv.* —**ness,** *n.*

deciduous tooth 乳齒。

dec·i·gram(me) [ˈdɛsəˌgræm; ˈdesigræm] *n.* 公釐(十分之一克)。

dec·i·li·ter, dec·i·li·tre [ˈdɛsəˌlitɚ; ˈdesiˌliːtə] *n.* 公合(十分之一竔)。

de·cil·lion [dɪˈsɪljən; diˈsiljən] *n.* ①〖美,法〗一千之11次乘方(1後加33個0)。②〖英,德〗100 萬之 10次乘方(1後加 60個0)。—*adj.* 數達 1 decillion 的。—**de·cil·lionth,** *adj.*

dec·i·mal [ˈdɛsəml̩; ˈdesiməl] *adj.* 十進的。—*n.* 小數;十進小數。

dec·i·mal·ism [ˈdɛsəməlɪzm̩; ˈdesiməlizm] *n.* 十進法;十進制。—**dec·i·mal·ist,** *n.*

dec·i·mal·i·za·tion [ˌdɛsəmələˈzeʃən; ˌdesimlaiˈzeiʃən] *n.* 化爲十進位制;十進位制之採用。

dec·i·mal·ize [ˈdɛsəml̩ˌaɪz; ˈdesiməlaiz] *v.t.,* **-ized, -iz·ing.** 使成十進位制;十進化。

dec·i·mal·ly [ˈdɛsəmlɪ; ˈdesiməli] *adv.* 十進地;用小數;每十。

dec·i·mate [ˈdɛsəˌmet; ˈdesimeit] *v.t.,* **-mat·ed, -mat·ing.** ①毁掉大部分。②減去十分之一。③(以抽籤決定)殺(叛變者)十分之一。—**dec·i·ma·tion, dec·i·ma·tor,** *n.*

dec·i·me·ter, dec·i·me·tre [ˈdɛsəˌmitɚ; ˈdesiˌmiːtə] *n.* 公寸($^1/_{10}$公尺)。

de·ci·pher [dɪˈsaɪfɚ; diˈsaifə] *v.t.* ①釋明(不懂之語言、文字及令人迷惑之事)。②譯(密碼等)成普通文字。—**er,** *n.*

de·ci·pher·a·ble [dɪˈsaɪfərəbl̩; diˈsaifərəbl] *adj.* 可闡釋的;可迻譯的。

de·ci·pher·ment [dɪˈsaɪfɚmənt; diˈsaifəmənt] *n.* ①(對難解文字、語言之)釋明。②(密碼之)翻譯。

de·ci·sion** [dɪˈsɪʒən; diˈsiʒən] *n.* ①決定。What is your *decision?* 你的決定爲何?②決心;果斷。He is a man of *decision.* 他是有決心的人。③判決。④決議。with decision*** 堅決地;迅速而有力地。—**al,** *adj.*

***de·ci·sive** [dɪˈsaɪsɪv; diˈsaisiv] *adj.* ①決定性的。to win a *decisive* battle. 贏得有決定性的戰役。②堅決的。—**ly,** *adv.* —**ness,** *n.*

dec·i·stere [ˈdɛsəˌstɪr; ˈdesiˌstiə] *n.* $^1/_{10}$ 立方公尺(體積單位,等於$^1/_{10}$ stere).

‡deck¹ [dɛk; dek] *n.* ①甲板;艙面。②(紙牌之)一組或一副(通常爲 52 張)。③〖俚〗一小包毒品(尤指海洛英)。***clear the decks*** 準備戰鬥;準備行動。***hit the deck*** 〖俚〗 **a.** 起床;起身。**b.** 被擊倒;摔倒。***on deck*** 〖俗〗 **a.** 準備妥當。**b.** 準備出場(如棒球賽中投手之接

替等)。**stack the deck**〖俗〗**a.** 事先準備或安排。**b.** 以欺騙方式做牌。**sweep the deck** 浪把甲板上的一切均捲去;獲全勝。

deck² *v.t.* ①裝飾;打扮。②〖俗〗擊倒。

deck apprentice〖航海〗駕駛實習生。

deck chair 輕便折疊躺椅。

deck·er [ˈdɛkɚ; ˈdekə] *n.* ①裝飾者;裝飾物。②有…層甲板之船艦。

deck hand ①船上屬於駕駛部之海員。②在舞臺上搬移道具、調整燈光等之工作人員。

deck·house [ˈdɛk͵haus; ˈdekhaus] *n.* 甲板室。

deck·le, deck·el [ˈdɛkl̩; ˈdekl] *n.* ①(製紙用之)定紙框。② =**deckle edge.**

deckle edge 手工製紙之毛邊。

deck·le-edged [ˈdɛkl̩ˈɛdʒd; ˈdeklˈedʒd] *adj.* 有毛邊的。

deck passenger 統艙旅客。

de·claim [dɪˈklem; diˈkleim] *v.t.* 高聲朗誦。—*v.i.* ①(用美麗的辭藻)演說;巧辯。②叱責;抗辯〖against〗。③唱高調。—**er,** *n.*

dec·la·ma·tion [͵dɛkləˈmeʃən; ͵dekləˈmeiʃən] *n.* 演說;雄辯;唱高調。

de·clam·a·to·ry [dɪˈklæmə͵torɪ; diˈklæmətəri] *adj.* ①演說的;朗誦的;雄辯的。②着重修辭的;誇飾的。

de·clar·ant [dɪˈklɛrənt; diˈklɛərənt] *n.* ①聲明者。②在法庭中正式宣告願加入美國國籍者。

***dec·la·ra·tion** [͵dɛkləˈreʃən; ͵dekləˈreiʃən] *n.* ①宣言;聲明。②宣言書。*declaration* of war. 宣戰(書)。*Declaration* of Independence.(美國)獨立宣言。③〖橋牌〗叫牌。④報稅;報關。

de·clar·a·tive [dɪˈklærətɪv; diˈklærətiv] *adj.* ①宣言的;申告的。②〖文法〗陳述的。*declarative* sentence. 陳述句。—**ly,** *adv.*

de·clar·a·to·ry [dɪˈklærə͵torɪ; diˈklærətəri] *adj.* =**declarative.**

‡de·clare [dɪˈklɛr; diˈklɛə] *v.,* **-clared, -clar·ing.** —*v.t.* ①公告;布告;宣告。②確言;斷言;聲稱。The boys *declared* themselves against cheating. 孩子們聲稱他們決不欺騙。③詳報;申報(應納稅的東西等)。Have you anything to *declare?* 你有甚麼應申報納稅的東西嗎?—*v.i.* 宣言;表示;自白。**declare for** (or **against**) 贊成(反對)。**declare war** (or **peace**) 宣戰(或宣布和平)。—**de·clar·a·ble,** *adj.* —**de·clar·er,** *n.*

de·clared [dɪˈklɛrd; diˈklɛəd] *adj.* 宣言的;公布過的;公然的。*declared* value. 申報價格。—**ly,** *adv.* —**ness,** *n.*

dé·clas·sé [deklaˈse; deiklaˈsei]〖法〗*adj.* 失去社會地位的;落魄的。—*n.* 落魄者。

dé·clas·sée [deklaˈse; deiklaˈsei]〖法〗*n., adj.* déclassé 之女性(的)。

de·clas·si·fy [diˈklæsə͵faɪ; diːˈklæsifai] *v.t.,* **-fied, -fy·ing.** 撤銷(文件等之)機密。

de·clen·sion [dɪˈklɛnʃən; diˈklenʃən] *n.* ①〖文法〗**a.** 名詞、代名詞、形容詞之語尾變化(如 who, whose, whom)。**b.** 一個此等字之所有語尾變化。**c.** 一羣語尾變化相同的字。②傾斜;傾斜面。③衰微;墮落。④謝絕。⑤宗教、政治等信仰的背棄。—**al,** *adj.*

de·clin·a·ble [dɪˈklaɪnəbl̩; diˈklainəbl] *adj.*〖文法〗可以變化語尾的;有語尾之格變化的。

dec·li·na·tion [͵dɛkləˈneʃən; ͵dekliˈneiʃən] *n.* ①傾斜;斜面。②衰微;衰落。③偏差;逸出。④謝絕;婉辭。⑤〖天文〗赤緯。⑥〖物理〗磁偏角;偏角;偏差。—**al,** *adj.*

‡de·cline [dɪˈklaɪn; diˈklain] *v.,* **-clined, -clin·ing,** *n.* —*v.t.* ①拒絕;謝絕;婉謝。He *declined* the invitation with thanks. 他辭謝邀請。②使傾斜;低垂(頭)。—*v.i.* ①婉拒;婉謝。②傾斜。The sun *declined* toward the west. 日已西斜。③衰落;衰微;減退。④減低;降落;跌落。⑤屈尊;降格。⑥接近終了;近尾聲。—*n.* ①衰落;衰微;衰退。②任何東西的最末一部分。the *decline* of life. 老年。③下跌;下落。a *decline* in prices. 物價的下跌。④消耗性的疾病;肺病。**fall into a decline** 體力衰退(尤指因患肺病而衰弱)。—**de·clin·a·ble,** *adj.* —**de·clin·er,** *n.*

de·clin·ing [dɪˈklaɪnɪŋ; diˈklainiŋ] *adj.* 傾斜的;衰微的;衰退的;下坡的。*declining* fortune. 衰運。*declining* years. 晚年。

dec·li·nom·e·ter [͵dɛkləˈnɑmɪtɚ; ͵dekliˈnɔmitə] *n.* 磁偏計;方位計。

de·cliv·i·ty [dɪˈklɪvətɪ; diˈkliviti] *n., pl.* **-ties.** 下傾的斜面。

de·cli·vous [dɪˈklaɪvəs; diˈklaivəs] *adj.* 下傾的;有斜坡的。

de·clutch [diˈklʌtʃ; ˈdiːˈklʌtʃ] *v.i.* 使離合器離開(使汽車發動機同輪子間的連繫斷掉);(駕駛汽車時)放空檔。

de·coc·tion [dɪˈkɑkʃən; diˈkɔkʃən] *n.* ①煎;熬。②煮成物;煎劑;熬汁。

de·code [diˈkod; ˈdiːˈkoud] *v.t.,* **-cod·ed, -cod·ing.** 將(密碼等)譯成普通文字。—**de·cod·er,** *n.*

de·col·late [dɪˈkɑlet; diˈkɔleit] *v.t.,* **-lat·ed, -lat·ing.** 將…斬首。—**de·col·la·tion, de·col·la·tor,** *n.*

dé·colle·tage [͵dekɑlˈtɑʒ; ͵deikɔlˈtɑːʒ]〖法〗*n.* ①袒胸露背之低領。②袒胸露背之低領女服。

dé·colle·té [͵dekɑlˈte; deiˈkɔltei]〖法〗*adj.* 露出頸部和肩部的(衣服);穿袒胸露肩的衣服的(女人)。

de·col·o(u)r [diˈkʌlɚ; diːˈkʌlə] *v.t.* 使脫色;漂白。

de·col·o(u)r·ize [diˈkʌlə͵raɪz; diːˈkʌləraiz] *v.t.,* **-ized, -iz·ing.** 去色;漂白。

de·com·pen·sa·tion [͵dikɑmpɛnˈseʃən; ͵diːkɔmpenˈseiʃən] *n.*〖醫〗代償機能減退;代償失調。

de·com·pose [͵dikəmˈpoz; ͵diːkəmˈpouz, ˈdiː-] *v.,* **-posed, -pos·ing.** —*v.i.* ①分解。②腐爛。—*v.t.* ①使分解。②使腐爛。

de·com·pos·ite [͵dikəmˈpɑzɪt; ͵diːkəmˈpɔzit] *adj.* ①再混合的;再合成的。②〖植物〗數回分裂的;重複狀的。—*n.* 再混合物;二重複合物。

de·com·po·si·tion [͵dikɑmpəˈzɪʃən; ͵diːkɔmpəˈziʃən] *n.* ①分解。②腐爛。

de·com·pound [͵dikəmˈpaund; ͵diːkəmˈpaund, ˈdiː-] *v.t.* ①二重混合;使與混合物相混。② =**decompose.** —*adj., n.* =**decomposite.**

de·con·cen·trate [diˈkɑnsn̩͵tret; diːˈkɔnsentreit] *v.t.,* **-trat·ed, -trat·ing.** 使從中央分散。

de·con·cen·tra·tion [di͵kɑnsn̩ˈtreʃən; diː͵kɔnsenˈtreiʃən] *n.* 分散;經濟力量的排除集中。

de·con·tam·i·nate [͵dikənˈtæmə͵net; ˈdiːkənˈtæmineit] *v.t.,* **-nat·ed, -nat·ing.** ①(化學戰爭中之)消除毒氣毒液。②(原子爆炸後之)清除輻射塵。③將…消毒。

④刪去(機密文件之)機密部分以便發表。

de·con·trol 〔ˌdikən'trol; 'diː-kən'troul〕 *v.*, **-trolled, -trol·ling,** *n.* —*v.t.* 解除(政府)管制。—*n.* 撤除管制。—**ler,** *n.*

dé·cor 〔de'kɔr; dei'kɔː〕〖法〗 *n.* ①舞臺裝飾。②裝飾之格調。③裝飾品。

***dec·o·rate** 〔'dɛkəˌret; 'dekəreit〕 *v.t.*, **-rat·ed, -rat·ing.** ①裝飾。The streets were all *decorated* with flags on October the Tenth. 雙十節滿街懸掛國旗。②爲…作室內裝修。③授以勳章。—**dec·o·ra·tor,** *n.*

***dec·o·ra·tion** 〔ˌdɛkə'reʃən; ˌdekə'reiʃən〕 *n.* ①裝飾。②裝飾品。Christmas *decorations.* 耶誕節裝飾品。③勳章。

Decoration Day 美國紀念內戰陣亡士兵之紀念日(五月三十日)。

***dec·o·ra·tive** 〔'dɛkəˌretɪv; 'dekərətiv〕 *adj.* 裝飾的;產生美或藝術效果的;裝潢的。

decorative surgery 整容外科。(亦作**cosmetic surgery**)

dec·o·rous 〔'dɛkərəs; 'dekərəs〕 *adj.* 合宜的; 相稱的; 有禮的; 有威儀的; 端莊的。—**ly,** *adv.* —**ness,** *n.*

de·co·rum 〔dɪ'korəm; di'kɔːrəm〕 *n.* ①禮節;禮儀。②(*pl.*)上流社會中遵守的一切慣例和禮儀。③合宜;相稱。

de·cou·page 〔ˌdeku'pɑʒ; ˌdeikuː'pɑːʒ〕 *n.* ①剪紙裝飾術。②以剪紙裝飾之物。

de·cou·ple 〔dɪ'kʌpḷ; di'kʌpl〕 *v.t.*, **-pled, -pling.** 吸收(核子爆炸之)震力。

de·coy 〔*n.* dɪ'kɔɪ, 'dikɔɪ; di'kɔi *v.* dɪ'kɔɪ; di'kɔi〕 *n.* ①獵鳥時用以引誘別的鳥(特別是野鴨)集於一地的眞鳥或假鳥。②誘捕水鳥的池塘。③引誘他人(陷於危險中)的人或物。④用以干擾雷達偵察之物(如假飛機、飛彈等)。—*v.t.* ①以眞鳥或假鳥做餌引誘(鳥獸)而捕捉之。②以詭計引誘使陷於危險中。—*v.i.* 被誘。

decoy duck ①作餌用之眞或假鴨。②「誘人入彀者。」

***de·crease** 〔*v.* dɪ'kris, ˌdi'kris; diː'kriːs, 'diːk- *n.* 'dikris, ˌdi'kris; 'diː-kriːs, diː-'kriːs〕 *v.*, **-creased, -creas·ing,** *n.* —*v.i.* 減少。—*v.t.* 使減少。—*n.* 減少;減少之量。*on the decrease* 在減少中。

de·creas·ing 〔dɪ'krisɪŋ; diː'kriːsiŋ〕 *adj.* 減少的;漸減的。—**ly,** *adv.*

***de·cree** 〔dɪ'kri; di'kriː〕 *n.*, *v.*, **-creed, -cree·ing.** —*n.* ①命令;法令;布告。②〖法律〗判決;裁判。③天命。—*v.t.* & *v.i.* 頒令;判定;天命註定。—**a·ble,** *adj.* —**de·cre·er,** *n.*

dec·re·ment 〔'dɛkrəmənt; 'dekrimənt〕 *n.* ①漸減;減少;消耗。②減少之量;消耗量。③〖數學〗減少率。

de·crep·it 〔dɪ'krɛpɪt; di'krepit〕 *adj.* ①衰老的。②破舊的;用舊的。—**ly,** *adv.*

de·crep·i·tate 〔dɪ'krɛpəˌtet; di'krepiteit〕 *v.*, **-tat·ed, -tat·ing.** —*v.t.* 鍛燒(鹽、礦等)至發出爆裂聲或至爆裂聲終止。—*v.i.* 燒裂;發出炸裂聲。

de·crep·i·tude 〔dɪ'krɛpɪˌtjud; di'krepitjuːd〕 *n.* 衰老;老弱;破舊。

de·cre·scen·do 〔ˌdikrə'ʃɛndo; 'diː-kri'ʃendou〕 *adv.*, *adj.*, *n.*, *pl.* **-dos.**〖音樂〗—*adj.* & *adv.* 漸弱的(地)。—*n.* ①音量之漸弱。②漸弱之樂節。

de·cres·cent 〔dɪ'krɛsṇt; di'kresnt〕 *adj.* ①變小的;變少的。②虧缺的;下弦的(月)。

de·cre·tal 〔dɪ'kritḷ; di'kriːtl〕 *adj.* 法令的; 法規的。—*n.* ①教皇之敎令。②(*pl.*)敎令集。

de·cre·tive 〔dɪ'kritɪv; di'kriːtiv〕 *adj.* 命令的;法令的;有法令之權力的。—**ly,** *adv.*

de·cry 〔dɪ'kraɪ; di'krai〕 *v.t.*, **-cried, -cry·ing.** ①責難;公開譴責。②輕視;貶低。③使(金錢等)貶值。—**de·cri·er,** *n.*

de·cum·bence 〔dɪ'kʌmbəns; di'kʌmbəns〕 *n.* 橫臥。—**de·cum·bent,** *adj.*

dec·u·ple 〔'dɛkjupḷ, dɛk'jupḷ; 'dekjupl〕 *n.*, *adj.*, *v.*, **-pled, -pling.** —*n.* 十倍;十倍之量。—*adj.* 十倍的。—*v.t.* 乘以十。

de·cus·sate 〔dɪ'kʌset; di'kʌseit〕 *v.*, **-sat·ed, -sat·ing,** *adj.* —*v.t.* & *v.i.* (使)成交叉形;交叉。—*adj.* ①十字形的;直角交叉的。②〖植物〗對生的;互生的。—**ly,** *adv.*

de·dans 〔də'dɑ̃; də'dɑ̃〕 *n.*, *pl.* **-dans.** 〖法〗網球的觀衆席。***the dedans*** (網球的)觀衆。

***ded·i·cate** 〔'dɛdəˌket; 'dedikeit〕 *v.t.*, **-cat·ed, -cat·ing.** ①供奉; 奉獻。②獻身;委身;致力。to *dedicate* one's life to the service of one's country. 獻身爲國家服務。③題獻。to *dedicate* a book to a certain person. 將(所著的)書題獻於某人。—**ded·i·cant,** *n.*

ded·i·ca·tion 〔ˌdɛdə'keʃən; ˌdedi'keiʃən〕 *n.* ①供奉;奉獻;祝聖。②獻身;委身;致力。③題獻辭;獻詞。—**al,** *adj.*

ded·i·ca·tive 〔'dɛdəˌketɪv; 'dedikeitiv〕 *adj.* 奉獻的;獻納的;供奉的。

ded·i·ca·tor 〔'dɛdəˌketɚ; 'dedikeitə〕 *n.* 奉獻者; 獻身者;題獻者。

ded·i·ca·to·ry 〔'dɛdəkəˌtorɪ; 'dedikətəri〕 *adj.* =**dedicative.**

de·duce 〔dɪ'djus; di'djuːs〕 *v.t.*, **-duced, -duc·ing.** ①演繹;推論。②對…追本溯源;探索…之過程。

de·duc·i·ble 〔dɪ'djusəbḷ; di'djuːsəbl〕 *adj.* 可推知的;可推斷的;可推論的。

de·duct 〔dɪ'dʌkt; di'dʌkt〕 *v.t.* ①扣除;減除。②使減低〖常 from〗. —**i·ble,** *adj.*

de·duc·tion 〔dɪ'dʌkʃən; di'dʌkʃən〕 *n.* ①減除;扣除。②扣除額。③推論; 推斷。④演繹;演繹法。

de·duc·tive 〔dɪ'dʌktɪv; di'dʌktiv〕 *adj.* 推定的;推斷的;演繹的。—**ly,** *adv.*

deductive method 〖邏輯〗演繹法。

deductive reasoning 演繹推理。

dee 〔di; diː〕 *n.*①D 或 d 字; D 形物。②D 形電極。

‡deed 〔did; diːd〕 *n.* ①行爲。②事業;功績。*deeds* of arms. 武功。③實行;事實。He is a good leader in *deed* as well as in name. 他是名實相符的好領袖。④證書;契據。⑤以契據讓渡。***in deed*** 事實地;眞正地;誠然地。—*v.t.* 立契約讓與(田產等)。—**less,** *adj.*

deem 〔dim; diːm〕 *v.i.* 認爲;視爲; 以爲;想;判。We *deem* very highly of him. 我們非常重視他。—*v.t.* 認爲;視爲;想。I *deem* it my duty to help my needy friends. 我認爲幫助窮苦朋友是我的責任。—**er,** *n.*

deem·ster 〔'dimstɚ; 'diːmstə〕 *n.* 在英國 Isle of Man島上之法官。—**ship,** *n.*

‡deep 〔dip; diːp〕 *adj.* ①深的(爲 shallow 之對)。He drew a *deep* breath. 他深吸一口氣。②深長;縱深。This plot of land is 100 feet *deep.* 這塊地縱深100英尺。③深奧的;難懂的。He is a *deep* one. 他是一個莫測高深的人。④銘心的;深感的。*deep* gratitude. 深深感激。⑤專心的。He is *deep* in reading. 他正專心讀書。⑥極度的;濃厚的;强烈

D

的。The sea was *deep* blue. 海是深藍色的。⑦深刻的(指知識)。⑧低調的;聲音沈濁的。⑨狡猾的。⑩聰明的;深謀遠慮的。⑪深陷的。He is *deep* in debt. 他債臺高築。⑫嚴重的。⑬神祕的。***go off the deep end*** a. 躍入深水。b.【俗】魯莽地參加某種工作。c.【俗】發怒。d. 做得或說得太多。***in deep water*** 遭遇困難或麻煩;在困境中。—*adv.* ①深深地。Still waters run *deep*. (諺)靜水流深;大智若愚。②深遠地(時間)。He went on studying *deep* into the night. 他繼續讀書至深夜。③深邃地;強烈地。to drink *deep*. 豪飲。—*n.* ①(指河海)深處。②任何深處。the *deep* of night. 深夜。③最嚴酷的部分。the *deep* of winter. 隆冬;嚴冬。***in deep*** 牽涉極深;無法擺脫干係。***the deep***【詩】海洋。—**ness,** *n.*

***deep·en** [ˈdipən; ˈdiːpən] *v.t.* ①使深;使加深。to *deepen* a canal. 使運河加深。②使濃。③使強烈。④使低沈。—*v.i.* ①變深。②變濃;變深(顏色)。③變強烈;變醇。Wine *deepens* on aging. 酒久藏而益醇。④變低沈。—**er,** *n.* —**ing·ly,** *adv.*

deep freeze 靜止狀態;冬眠狀態。

deep kiss 深吻(張口將舌伸至對方口內之吻)。

deep-laid [ˈdipˈled; ˈdiːpˈleid] *adj.* 深遠的;精巧的;祕密作成的。

***deep·ly** [ˈdiplɪ; ˈdiːpli] *adv.* ①在深處;到深處。②強烈地;深刻地。*deeply* in love. 深陷在戀愛中。③發沉重聲音地。④巧妙地;繁複地。

deep mourning 全身黑色之喪服。

deep·mouthed [ˈdipˈmauðd; ˈdiːpˈmauðd] *adj.* 聲音洪亮的。

deep-root·ed [ˈdipˈrutɪd; ˈdiːpˈruːtid] *adj.* ①植根甚深的。②根深蒂固的。—**ness,** *n.*

deep-sea [ˈdipˈsi; ˈdiːpˈsiː] *adj.* 深海的。

deep-seat·ed [ˈdipˈsitɪd; ˈdiːpˈsiːtid] *adj.* ①深層的。②根深蒂固的;由來已久的。

deep-set [ˈdipˌsɛt; ˈdiːpset] *adj.* ①根深蒂固的。②深陷的。

Deep South 美國南部(尤指與墨西哥接壤之各州)。

deep space 太陽系以外之太空。

deep·wa·ter [ˈdipˌwɔtɚ; ˈdiːpˌwɔːtə] *adj.* ①深水的。②深海的。③靠近海洋的。

***deer** [dɪr; diə, djəː] *n., pl.* **deer** or (罕) **deers.** 鹿。a drove of *deer*. 鹿羣。

deer·hound [ˈdɪrˌhaund; ˈdiəhaund] *n.* (獵鹿的)大獵犬。

deer·skin [ˈdɪrˌskɪn; ˈdiəskin] *n.* 鹿皮。

deer·stalk·er [ˈdɪrˌstɔkɚ; ˈdiəˌstɔːkə] *n.* ①用偷襲法獵鹿之人。②一種獵帽。

de-es·ca·late [diˈɛskəˌlet; diˈeskəleit] *v.t. & v.i.,* **-lat·ed, -lat·ing.** 緩和;降低;縮小。—**de-es·ca·la·tion,** *n.* —**de-es·ca·la·to·ry,** *adj.*

def. ①defect. ②definition. ③defendant. ④deferred. ⑤defined. ⑥definite.

de·face [dɪˈfes; diˈfeis] *v.t.,* **-faced, -fac·ing.** ①傷毀(外表或美觀)。②銷毀;毀滅。—**a·ble,** *adj.* —**ment,** *n.*

de fac·to [diˈfækto; diːˈfæktou] 事實上;實際上(爲 de jure 之對)。

de·fal·cate [dɪˈfælket; ˈdiːfælkeit] *v.i.,* **-cat·ed, -cat·ing.**【法律】盗用公款。

de·fal·ca·tion [ˌdifælˈkeʃən; ˌdiːfælˈkeiʃən] *n.*【法律】①盗用公款;監守自盜。②盗用之公款數額。

de·fal·ca·tor [dɪˈfælˌketɚ; ˈdiːfælkeitə] *n.* 盗用公款者;監守自盜者。

def·a·ma·tion [ˌdɛfəˈmeʃən; ˌdefəˈmeiʃən] *n.* 誹謗;中傷;破壞名譽。

de·fam·a·to·ry [dɪˈfæməˌtorɪ; diˈfæmətəri] *adj.* 誹謗的;中傷的;損傷名譽的。

de·fame [dɪˈfem; diˈfeim] *v.t.,* **-famed, -fam·ing.** 誹謗;中傷;損毀名譽。—**de·fam·er,** *n.* —**de·fam·ing·ly,** *adv.*

de·fat [diˈfæt; diːˈfæt] *v.t.,* **-fat·ted, -fat·ting.** ①除去脂肪。②使得不到脂肪。

de·fault [dɪˈfɔlt; diˈfɔːlt] *n.* ①不履行責任;不履行契約。②拖債;不還債。③缺席;(球賽中)不出場。④不出庭;不到案。⑤缺乏;短少。⑥玩忽;不採取行動;怠職。***judgment by default*** 缺席裁判。—*v.t. & v.i.* ①疏怠職責;不履行(條約)。②拖欠(債務)。③缺席;不出場。④不出庭;缺席裁判。⑤宣布…缺席或欠債。—**er,** *n.*

de·fea·sance [dɪˈfizəns; diˈfiːzəns] *n.*【法律】①廢除;宣布(契約)無效。②毀約之條件;毀約之證書。

de·fea·si·ble [dɪˈfizəbl; diˈfiːzəbl] *adj.* 可作廢的;可取消的。

‡de·feat [dɪˈfit; diˈfiːt] *v.t.* ①擊敗。②破壞;打破。Our hopes were *defeated*. 我們的希望未實現。③使失敗。④【法律】使無效。—*n.* ①失敗;敗北。Our baseball team has never yet suffered a *defeat*. 我們的棒球隊尚未遭遇一次失敗。②征服;傾覆。③【法律】無效。—**er,** *n.*

de·feat·ism [dɪˈfitɪzəm; diˈfiːtizəm] *n.* 失敗主義。—**de·feat·ist,** *n., adj.*

de·fea·ture [dɪˈfitʃɚ; diˈfiːtʃə] *n.* ①【古】損壞外貌;毀容。②【廢】敗北;挫折。

def·e·cate [ˈdɛfəˌket; ˈdefəkeit] *v.,* **-cat·ed, -cat·ing.** —*v.t.* 澄清;除去(汚物)。—*v.i.* ①澄清;除汚。②通便。—**def·e·ca·tion, def·e·ca·tor,** *n.*

***de·fect¹** [dɪˈfɛkt, ˈdifɛkt; diˈfekt, ˈdiːfekt] *n.* 過失;缺點。He has some *defect* in eyesight. 他目力不佳。—**or,** *n.*

***de·fect²** *v.i.* 變節;叛變;投奔敵方〖常to〗.

de·fec·tion [dɪˈfɛkʃən; diˈfekʃən] *n.* ①缺點;失敗。②背叛;叛離;脫黨;變節。

de·fec·tive [dɪˈfɛktɪv; diˈfektiv] *adj.* ①有缺點的;不完美的。②智慧或行爲不健全的。—*n.* 身體或精神不健全的人。—**ly,** *adv.* —**ness,** *n.*

defective verb【文法】變化不完全的動詞。如: "can", "may", "must", "ought" 等。

‡de·fence [dɪˈfɛns; diˈfens] *n.*【英】=**defense.**

‡de·fend [dɪˈfɛnd; diˈfend] *v.t.* ①保護;保衛〖常 from, against〗. They *defended* the city against the enemy. 他們保衛這城以禦敵。The duty of a soldier is to *defend* his country. 保衛國家爲軍人的責任。②辯護。③【法律】作…之辯護律師。—*v.i.*【法律】作辯護。—**a·ble,** *adj.*

de·fend·ant [dɪˈfɛndənt; diˈfendənt] *n.* 被告。—*adj.* 辯護的;爲自己辯護的。

***de·fend·er** [dɪˈfɛndɚ; diˈfendə] *n.* ①保護者;防守者。②【運動】衞冕者。

‡de·fense [dɪˈfɛns; diˈfens] *n.* ①防護;防禦。There can be no real *defense* against attacks from the air. 對來自空中的攻擊不可能有眞正有效的防禦。②防禦物。The best *defense* is to attack. 攻擊爲最佳之防禦。③(拳賽與鬥劍中)自衞。④(球賽中的)防守員;守方。⑤辯護。⑥【法律】答辯;抗辯。⑦被告及其律師。***in defense of*** 保

衞。Is there any man unwilling to fight *in defense of* his country? 難道有任何人不願爲保衞國家而戰? ***make a defense*** 防禦。

de·fense·less [dɪˈfɛnslɪs; diˈfenslis] *adj.* 無防備的; 不設防的; 不能保衞自己的。**—ly,** *adv.* **—ness,** *n.*

de·fen·si·ble [dɪˈfɛnsəbl̩; diˈfensəbl] *adj.* ①可防禦的;可保衞的。②可辯護的。**—de·fen·si·bly,** *adv.* **—de·fen·si·bil·i·ty, —ness,** *n.*

de·fen·sive** [dɪˈfɛnsɪv; diˈfensiv] *adj.* ①防禦用的; 防護用的。②守勢的; 自衞的。*defensive* war. 保衞戰;自衞戰。*—n.* ①防禦物。②守勢。act on the defensive*** 取自衞行爲。***be on the defensive*** 準備自衞的狀態。**—ly,** *adv.* **—ness,** *n.*

***de·fer**[1] [dɪˈfɝ; diˈfəː] *v.,* **-ferred, -fer·ring.** *—v.t.* 延緩;展期。to *defer* payment. 延期付款。*deferred* telegrams. 慢遞電報。*—v.i.* 遲緩;延遲。

de·fer[2] *v.i.,* **-ferred, -fer·ring.** ①服從;順從〖to〗。②由…作決定。

de·fer·(r)a·ble [dɪˈfɝəbl̩; diˈfəːrəbl] *adj.* 可延遲的;可緩征的。*—n.* 緩征者。

def·er·ence [ˈdɛfərəns; ˈdefərəns] *n.* ①服從;順從。②敬意;尊重。

def·er·ent[1] [ˈdɛfərənt; ˈdefərənt] *adj.* =**deferential.**

def·er·ent[2] *adj.* 輸送的。*—n.* 輸送或「傳導之物。」

def·er·en·tial [ˌdɛfəˈrɛnʃəl; ˌdefəˈrenʃəl] *adj.* 恭順的。**—ly,** *adv.*

de·fer·ment [dɪˈfɝmənt; diˈfəːmənt] *n.* 延期;遷延。

de·ferred [dɪˈfɝd; diˈfəːd] *adj.* ①延期的。②緩召的。③暫時取消或不發表的。

deferred charge 〖會計〗遞延借項(爲未來業務而作的開支)。

de·fi·ance** [dɪˈfaɪəns; diˈfaiəns] *n.* 挑戰; 輕視; 違抗。He shouted *defiance* at the enemy. 他大聲呼喊着向敵人挑戰。bid defiance to*** 不服從;蔑視。***in defiance of*** 不服從; 違抗; 輕視; 蔑視。***set at defiance*** 不服從;蔑視。

de·fi·ant [dɪˈfaɪənt; diˈfaiənt] *adj.* 大「膽反抗的;挑釁的。」

***de·fi·cien·cy** [dɪˈfɪʃənsɪ; diˈfiʃənsi] *n., pl.* **-cies.** ①缺乏;不完全;不足。②不足的量;不足的數額。

deficiency disease 缺乏某種維他命所發生的病症(如脚氣病等)。

***de·fi·cient** [dɪˈfɪʃənt; diˈfiʃənt] *adj.* ①有缺點的; 不完全的。②不足的; 不充分的; 缺乏的。He is *deficient* in courage. 他缺乏勇氣。**—ly,** *adv.*

def·i·cit [ˈdɛfəsɪt; ˈdefisit, diˈfisit] *n.* (收支之)不足;不足額;赤字。

def·i·lade [ˌdɛfəˈled; ˌdefiˈleid] *v.,* **-lad·ed, -lad·ing,** *n.* *—v.t.* 以人工或天然物掩護使不受敵軍火力傷害。*—n.* 遮蔽;掩護。

***de·file**[1] [dɪˈfaɪl; diˈfail] *v.t.,* **-filed, -fil·ing.** ①弄髒。②褻瀆。③使受損。**—de·fil·er,** *n.*

de·file[2] *v.i.* 以縱隊前進。*—n.* 小路;狹谷。

de·file·ment [dɪˈfaɪlmənt; diˈfailmənt] *n.* ①汚辱;受辱;褻瀆。②髒物。

de·fin·a·ble [dɪˈfaɪnəbl̩; diˈfainəbl] *adj.* 可限定的;可闡釋其意義的;可下定義的。

***de·fine** [dɪˈfaɪn; diˈfain] *v.t.,* **-fined, -fin·ing.** ①下定義; 闡釋。A dictionary *defines* words. 字典闡釋字的意義。②詳細說明。③立界限;定範圍。④使清楚;使顯明。⑤爲…之特質或因素。Perseverance usually *defines* success. 毅力常爲成功之因素。**—de·fin·er, —ment,** *n.*

***def·i·nite** [ˈdɛfənɪt; ˈdefinit, -fn̩it] *adj.* ①明白的; 正確的; 明確的。I want a *definite* answer, "yes" or "no". 我要明確的答覆,"是" 或 "否"。②一定的。③有明確界限的。**—ly,** *adv.* **—ness, de·fin·i·tude,** *n.*

definite article 〖文法〗定冠詞,卽**the.**

***def·i·ni·tion** [ˌdɛfəˈnɪʃən; ˌdefiˈniʃən, -fn̩ˈiʃ-] *n.* ①確定。②定義;釋義。③(透鏡的)鮮明度。④(收音機收音的)精確度;(電視機影像的)清晰度。⑤輪廓、影像等的清晰。Good photographs have *definition.* 好的照片都很清晰。**—al,** *adj.*

de·fin·i·tive [dɪˈfɪnətɪv; diˈfinitiv] *adj.* ①確定的;最後的。②限定的。*—n.* 〖文法〗限定詞。**—ly,** *adv.* **—ness,** *n.*

def·la·grate [ˈdɛfləˌgret; ˈdefləgreit] *v.t. & v.i.,* **-grat·ed, -grat·ing.** (使)爆燃;燃燒;突然地燃燒。

de·flate [dɪˈflet; diˈfleit] *v.t.,* **-flat·ed, -flat·ing.** ①放出(氣球、車胎)中之空氣;使坍陷。②減消(通貨膨脹等)。③挫(某人之)銳氣或自大感。**—de·flat·a·ble,** *adj.*

de·fla·tion [dɪˈfleʃən; diˈfleiʃən] *n.* ①放出空氣。②通貨緊縮。③物價之低廉(尤指成本不降低時之反常情形)。**—ar·y,** *adj.*

de·fla·tion·ist [dɪˈfleʃənɪst; diˈfleiʃənist] *n.* 主張通貨緊縮者。

de·flect [dɪˈflɛkt; diˈflekt] *v.t. & v.i.* (使)偏斜;(使)偏離;(使)轉向。**—a·ble,** *adj.*

de·flec·tion [dɪˈflɛkʃən; diˈflekʃən] *n.* ①偏向; 偏離; 轉斜。②偏向或偏離之量。③〖兵學〗(鎗、砲彈等之)偏差。④(光的)曲折;(磁石之)偏角。⑤〖機械〗撓曲;偏轉。

de·flec·tive [dɪˈflɛktɪv; diˈflektiv] *adj.* 致使偏向的;引起偏差的。

de·flec·tor [dɪˈflɛktɚ; diˈflektə] *n.* 使轉向之物;轉折板;偏向器;偏針儀。

de·flex·ion [dɪˈflɛkʃən; diˈflekʃən] *n.* 〖英〗=**deflection.**

def·lo·ra·tion [ˌdɛfləˈreʃən; ˌdiːflɔːˈreiʃən] *n.* ①採花;折花。②姦汚;蹂躪童貞。③吸取精華;奪美。④褻瀆;毀汚。

de·flow·er [dɪˈflauɚ; diːˈflauə] *v.t.* ①摧毀…之花。②奪去(婦女)之貞節;蹂躪。③吸取精華;奪美。④褻瀆;毀汚。**—er,** *n.*

De·foe [dɪˈfo; dəˈfou] *n.* 狄福(Daniel, 1659?-1731, 英國小說家)。

de·fog [ˈdiˈfɔg; ˈdiːˈfɔːg] *v.t.,* **-fogged, -fog·ging.** 除(玻璃上的)霧。

de·fo·li·ant [dɪˈfolɪənt; diˈfouliənt] *n.* 去葉劑;落葉劑。

de·fo·li·ate [dɪˈfolɪˌet; diˈfoulieit] *v.,* **-at·ed, -at·ing.** *—v.t.* 去…之葉; 除葉。*—v.i.* 落葉。**—de·fo·li·a·tion,** *n.*

de·fo·li·a·tor [dɪˈfolɪˌetɚ; diˈfoulieitə] *n.* ①除葉劑。②食葉之昆蟲。

de·for·est [dɪˈfɔrɪst; diːˈfɔrist] *v.t.* 採伐森林;清除樹林。**—a·tion, —er,** *n.*

de·form [dɪˈfɔrm; diːˈfɔːm] *v.t.* ①使不成形; 使失原形; 使殘廢。②使醜;使變形。**—a·ble, —a·tive,** *adj.* **—er,** *n.*

de·for·ma·tion [ˌdifɔrˈmeʃən; ˌdiːfɔːˈmeiʃən] *n.* ①毀壞。②殘廢;畸形。③〖物理〗變形。

de·formed [dɪˈfɔrmd; diˈfɔːmd] *adj.* ①畸形的;殘廢的;醜陋的。②醜惡的;討厭的;可恨的。**—ly,** *adv.*

de·form·i·ty 〔dɪˈfɔrmətɪ; diˈfɔːmiti〕 *n., pl.* **-ties.** ①畸形;殘廢。②畸形或殘缺的部分。③畸形的人或物。④醜陋;瑕疵。

de·fraud 〔dɪˈfrɔd; diˈfrɔːd〕 *v.t.* 詐取;欺詐;欺騙。—**er,** —**a·tion,** —**ment,** *n.*

de·fray 〔dɪˈfre; diˈfrei〕 *v.t.* 付給;支付。—**a·ble,** *adj.* —**er,** *n.*

de·fray·al 〔dɪˈfreəl; diˈfreiəl〕 *n.* 支付;支出。

de·fray·ment 〔dɪˈfremənt; diˈfreimənt〕 *n.* =**defrayal.**

de·frost 〔diˈfrɔst; diːˈfrɔst〕 *v.t.* ①去冰或霜。②使(凍的食物)融化。—**er,** *n.*

deft 〔dɛft; deft〕 *adj.* 熟練的;敏捷的;靈巧的。—**ly,** *adv.* —**ness,** *n.*

de·funct 〔dɪˈfʌŋkt; diˈfʌŋkt〕 *adj.* ①死的;亡故的。②已倒閉的;非現存的。***the defunct*** 死人(法律名詞)。—**ness,** *n.*

***de·fy** 〔dɪˈfaɪ; diˈfai〕 *v.,* **-fied, -fy·ing,** *n.* —*v.t.* ①不服從;公然反抗;公然蔑視;不顧。②足以抵禦。The problem *defied* solution. 這問題無法解答。③挑;激;惹。to *defy* someone to do something. 激某人做某事。—*n.* 〖俗〗挑戰;公然反抗。—**de·fi·a·ble,** *adj.* —**ing·ly,** *adv.*

deg. ①degree. ②degrees.

dé·ga·gé 〔degaˈʒe; deigaˈʒei〕 〖法〗 *adj.* 瀟洒的;無拘束的。

de·gas 〔diˈgæs; diːˈgæs〕 *v.t.,* **-gassed, -gas·sing.** ①除去氣體。②除去毒氣。

de·gas·i·fi·er 〔diˈgæsəˌfaɪɚ; diːˈgæsifaiə〕 *n.* 消除毒氣劑。

de Gaulle 〔dəˈgol; dəˈgoul〕 戴高樂(Charles André Joseph Marie, 1890–1970, 法國將軍, 於 1945–46 任法國臨時總統, 1959–69, 任法國第五共和首任總統)。—**de Gaull·ism,** *n.*

de Gaull·ist 〔dəˈgolɪst; dəˈgoulist〕 法國戴高樂派黨員。

de·gauss 〔diˈgaus; ˈdiːˈgaus〕 *v.t.* 中和(船)四周之磁場以防禦磁雷。—**er,** *n.*

de·gen·er·a·cy 〔dɪˈdʒɛnərəsɪ; diˈdʒenərəsi〕 *n.* 退化;墮落;退步。

***de·gen·er·ate** 〔*v.* dɪˈdʒɛnəˌret; diˈdʒenəreit *adj., n.* dɪˈdʒɛnərɪt; diˈdʒenərit〕 *v.,* **-at·ed, -at·ing,** *adj., n.* —*v.i.* ①退步;墮落;衰敗。Liberty often *degenerates* into lawlessness. 自由常淪爲無法無天。②〖生物〗退化。—*adj.* ①退步的;墮落的;卑賤的。②退化的。—*n.*墮落者;退步的東西;退化的東西。

de·gen·er·a·tion 〔dɪˌdʒɛnəˈreʃən; diˌdʒenəˈreiʃən〕 *n.* ①退化;退步;墮落。②〖生物〗退化。③〖生理〗變質;變性。

de·gen·er·a·tive 〔dɪˈdʒɛnəˌretɪv; diˈdʒenərətiv〕 *adj.* ①變壞的;退化的;衰敗的。②使變壞的;使退化的;使衰敗的。

de·glu·ti·tion 〔ˌdigluˈtɪʃən; ˌdiːgluːˈtiʃən〕 *n.* 吞;嚥;嚥下。

de·grad·a·ble 〔dɪˈgredəbl; diˈgreidəbl〕 *adj.* 〖化〗可降解的;可減解的。—**de·grad·a·bil·i·ty,** *n.*

***deg·ra·da·tion** 〔ˌdɛgrəˈdeʃən; ˌdegrəˈdeiʃən〕 *n.* ①惡化;退步。②免職;罷黜。③(岩石、土壤的)剝蝕;漸崩。—**al,** *adj.*

***de·grade** 〔dɪˈgred; diˈgreid〕 *v.,* **-grad·ed, -grad·ing.** —*v.t.* ①降級;降格;免職。②使墮落;使惡化。③〖地質〗剝蝕;使漸崩。④減低價格、力量、純度等。⑤〖化〗降解;減解。—*v.i.* 墮落;退化;降等。—**de·grad·er,** *n.*

de·grad·ed 〔dɪˈgredɪd; diˈgreidid〕 *adj.* ①被貶謫的;被免職的。②下賤的;墮落的。③〖生物〗退化的。④〖地質〗漸崩的;剝蝕的。—**ly,** *adv.* —**ness,** *n.*

de·grad·ing 〔dɪˈgredɪŋ; diˈgreidiŋ〕 *adj.* 退化的;墮落的;可恥的。—**ly,** *adv.*

:de·gree 〔dɪˈgri; diˈgriː〕 *n.* ①等級;階段;程度。②親等。a relation in the third *degree.* 三親等。③地位。She is a lady of high *degree.* 她是一個地位甚高的婦女。④度數。There are 90 *degrees* in a right angle. 直角有九十度。⑤學位。He got the *degree* of Master of Arts from that university. 他由那個大學得到文學碩士學位。⑥〖數學〗次。⑦〖音樂〗階;音度;音差。⑧〖文法〗級。superlative *degree.* 最高級。***by degrees*** 漸漸地;漸次。***in the slightest degree*** 毫(不)。***to a degree*** **a.** 非常地。**b.** 有限地;有些兒。***to a high degree*** 非常。***to the last degree*** 非常。He is corrupt *to the last degree.* 他非常腐敗。***to what degree*** 至何種程度;多少。

de·gree-day 〔dɪˈgriˈde; diˈgriːˈdei〕 *n.* 戶外每日平均溫度之單位。

de·gres·sion 〔dɪˈgrɛʃən; diˈgreʃən〕 *n.* ①漸減;下降。②(課稅之)遞減;累減。

de·hire 〔dɪˈhaɪr; diˈhaiə〕 *v.t.,* **-hired, -hir·ing.** 〖美〗解雇。

de·hisce 〔dɪˈhɪs; diˈhis〕 *v.i.,* **-hisced, -hisc·ing.** 張口;(植物莢角之)裂開。—**de·his·cence,** *n.* —**de·his·cent,** *adj.*

de·horn 〔diˈhɔrn; diːˈhɔːn〕 *v.t.* 去(動物)之角。—**er,** *n.*

de·hu·man·ize 〔diˈhjuməˌnaɪz; diːˈhjuːmənaiz〕 *v.t.,* **-ized, -iz·ing.** 使失掉人性;獸化。—**de·hu·man·i·za·tion,** *n.*

de·hu·mid·i·fy 〔ˌdihjuˈmɪdəˌfaɪ; ˌdiːhjuːˈmidifai〕 *v.t.,* **-fied, -fy·ing.** 除溼氣。—**de·hu·mid·i·fi·er, de·hu·mid·i·fi·ca·tion,** *n.*

de·hy·drate 〔diˈhaɪdret; diːˈhaidreit〕 *v.,* **-drat·ed, -drat·ing.** —*v.t.* 去掉…之水分;脫水;使乾。—*v.i.* 失水;變乾。—**de·hy·dra·tion, de·hy·dra·tor,** *n.*

de·hyp·no·tize 〔diˈhɪpnəˌtaɪz; ˈdiːˈhipnətaiz〕 *v.t.,* **-tized, -tiz·ing.** 解除催眠狀態;令覺醒。

de·ice 〔diˈaɪs; ˈdiːˈais〕 *v.t.,* **de·iced, de·ic·ing.** 防冰;除冰。

de·ic·er 〔diˈaɪsɚ; diːˈaisə〕 *n.* 防冰器;除冰器。

de·i·cide 〔ˈdiəˌsaɪd; ˈdiːisaid〕 *n.* ①殺神。②殺神者;害死耶穌的人。

deic·tic 〔ˈdaɪktɪk; ˈdaiktik〕 *adj.* ①〖邏輯〗直接的;直證的。②〖文法〗直示的;直指的;指示的。

de·i·fi·ca·tion 〔ˌdiəfəˈkeʃən; ˌdiːifiˈkeiʃən〕 *n.* 神化。

de·i·fy 〔ˈdiəˌfaɪ; ˈdiːifai〕 *v.t.,* **-fied, -fy·ing.** ①奉爲神;祀爲神。②崇拜如神。—**de·i·fi·er,** *n.*

deign 〔den; dein〕 *v.i.* 認爲適合其身分或尊嚴(作某事);以爲值得。—*v.t.* 俯賜;恩賜。

de·ism 〔ˈdiɪzəm; ˈdiːizəm〕 *n.* ①自然神論;自然神教。②〖哲學〗理神論(信仰理性足以證明神之存在)。

de·ist 〔ˈdiɪst; ˈdiːist〕 *n.* 奉自然神教者;理神論者。

de·is·tic 〔diˈɪstɪk; diːˈistik〕 *adj.* 自然神教的;理神論的。(亦作 **deistical**)

de·i·ty** 〔ˈdiətɪ; ˈdiːiti, ˈdiːəti, ˈdiəti〕 *n., pl.* **-ties.** ①神性。②神。the Deity*** 上帝。

de·ject 〔dɪˈdʒɛkt; diˈdʒekt〕 *v.t.* 使沮喪;使落膽。—*adj.* 〖古〗頹喪的。

de·jec·ta 〔dɪˈdʒɛktə; diˈdʒektə〕 *n. pl.* 排泄物;糞便。

de·ject·ed [dɪˈdʒɛktɪd; diˈdʒektid] *adj.* 失望的;沮喪的;萎靡的。—**ly,** *adv.* —**ness,** *n.*
de·jec·tion [dɪˈdʒɛkʃən; diˈdʒekʃən] *n.* 頹喪;沮喪;憂鬱。
dé·jeu·ner [ˈdeʒəˌne; ˈdeiʒənei]〖法〗*n.* ①早餐。②(歐洲大陸之)午餐。
de ju·re [diˈdʒurɪ; diːˈdʒuəri] 法理上;權利上(爲 de facto 之對)。
deka-〖字首〗=**deca-.**
dek·a·li·ter [ˈdɛkəˌlitɚ; ˈdekəˌliːtə] *n.* =**decaliter.**
dek·a·li·tre [ˈdɛkəˌlitɚ; ˈdekəˌliːtə] *n.* =**decaliter.**
dek·a·me·ter [ˈdɛkəˌmitɚ; ˈdekəˌmiːtə] *n.* =**decameter.**
Del. Delaware. **del.** ①delete. ②delegate.
de·laine [dəˈlen; dəˈlein] *n.* (一種羊毛與棉紗織成之)細布。
de·late [dɪˈlet; diˈleit] *v.t.*, **-lat·ed, -lat·ing.** ①〖蘇〗彈劾;控訴。②敍述;宣布;公開。 —**de·la·tion,** *n.*
Del·a·ware [ˈdɛləˌwɛr; ˈdeləwɛə] *n.* ①德拉瓦(美國東部濱大西洋之一州,首府爲 Dover)。②德拉瓦河(從美國 New York 州東南,經 Pennsylvania 州及 New Jersey 州間交界處,流入德拉瓦灣)。
‡**de·lay** [dɪˈle; diˈlei] *v.t.* ①延期;延緩。We will *delay* the party for a week. 我們要把會期延後一週。②阻滯;耽擱。—*v.i.* 遷延。It is getting late; don't *delay*. 時間已晚,不要遷延。—*n.* 耽擱;遲滯。***without delay*** 勿延;趕緊;立卽。We must start *without delay*. 我們必須立刻開始。—**a·ble,** *adj.* —**er,** *n.* —**ing·ly,** *adv.*
de·layed-ac·tion [dɪˈledˈækʃən; diˈleidˈækʃən] *adj.* (炸彈等)延期爆炸的。(亦作 **delay-action**)
delaying action〖軍〗拖延戰(一面撤退,一面予優勢敵軍以最大可能的打擊)。
de·le [ˈdilɪ; ˈdiːli(ː)] *v.*, **de·led, de·le·ing,** *n.* —*v.t.* (校對用語)刪除。—*n.* 刪除符號。(ꝺ, 𝔡)
de·lec·ta·ble [dɪˈlɛktəbl; diˈlektəbl] *adj.* 令人愉快的;使人高興的。
de·lec·ta·tion [ˌdilɛkˈteʃən; ˌdiːlekˈteiʃən] *n.* 愉快;款待。
de·lec·tus [dɪˈlɛktəs; diˈlektəs] *n.* 文選讀本(尤指習拉丁或希臘文所用者)。
del·e·ga·cy [ˈdɛləgəsɪ; ˈdeligəsi] *n.*, *pl.* **-cies.** ①代表。②代表權。③代表團。
***del·e·gate** [*n.* ˈdɛləˌget, ˈdɛləgɪt; ˈdeligit, -geit *v.* ˈdɛləˌget; ˈdeligeit] *n.*, *v.*, **-gat·ed, -gat·ing.** —*n.* ①代表。a *delegate* to a conference. 赴會的代表。②美國衆議院中一地區(未設州)的代表。③美國 Maryland, Virginia 及 West Virginia 州議會下院之代表。—*v.t.* ①指令…作代表;委派…爲代表。to *delegate* a person to a convention. 委派一人代表參加會議。②授權;委託。to *delegate* power to an envoy. 授權與使者。—**del·e·ga·ble,** *adj.* —**ship,** **del·e·ga·tor,** *n.*
del·e·ga·tion [ˌdɛləˈgeʃən; ˌdeliˈgeiʃən] *n.* ①授權;委託;派遣代表。②代表團。Each country sent a *delegation* to the convention. 每國派一代表團赴會。
de·lete [dɪˈlit; diˈliːt] *v.t.*, **-let·ed, -let·ing.** 消除;刪去。
del·e·te·ri·ous [ˌdɛləˈtɪrɪəs; ˌdeliˈtiəriəs] *adj.* 有害的;有毒的。—**ly,** *adv.* —**ness,** *n.*

de·le·tion [dɪˈliʃən; diˈliːʃən] *n.* ①刪除;刪掉。②被刪除之字句章節。
delf(t) [dɛlf(t); delf(t)] *n.* 彩色陶器(荷蘭 Delft 地方所產)。
delft·ware [ˈdɛlftˌwɛr; ˈdelftˌwɛə] *n.* =**delf(t).**
Del·hi [ˈdɛlɪ; ˈdeli] *n.* 德里(印度之舊都)。
del·i [ˈdɛli; ˈdeliː] *n.*〖美〗=**delicatessen.**
***de·lib·er·ate** [*adj.* dɪˈlɪbərɪt; diˈlibərit *v.* dɪˈlɪbəˌret; diˈlibəreit] *adj.*, *v.*, **-at·ed, -at·ing.** —*adj.* ①深思熟慮的;有意的。②愼重而遲緩的;不慌不忙的;從容不迫的。A statesman should be *deliberate* in his speeches. 政治家的演說應從容不迫。③審愼的。—*v.t.* 考慮;熟思;硏討。—*v.i.* ①愼重考慮。②商議;商討。—**ly,** *adv.* —**ness,** **de·lib·er·a·tor,** *n.*
de·lib·er·a·tion [dɪˌlɪbəˈreʃən; diˌlibəˈreiʃən] *n.* ①愼思熟慮;熟思;熟籌。②商議;商討;審議。③從容;遲緩。***with deliberation*** 愼重地。
de·lib·er·a·tive [dɪˈlɪbəˌretɪv; diˈlibərətiv] *adj.*①愼重的;熟慮的。②討論的;評議的。—**ly,** *adv.* —**ness,** *n.*
***del·i·ca·cy** [ˈdɛləkəsɪ; ˈdelikəsi] *n.*, *pl.* **-cies.** ①細緻;纖美;精緻;柔軟;優美;纖細;細嫩。②靈敏;敏感。③微妙;精巧;精細;細心;周密。This is a matter of great *delicacy*. 這是一件需要謹愼處理的事情。④關心;體諒。⑤柔弱;虛弱;易病或易傷。⑥佳餚;美味。table *delicacies*. 佳餚。⑦易破;易損壞。⑧非禮勿視,非禮勿聞;一本正經。
del·i·cate** [ˈdɛləkət, -kɪt; ˈdelikit] *adj.* ①纖細的;纖美的;精美的;精緻的。A pretty girl usually has very *delicate* skin. 一個漂亮的女子常有細嫩的皮膚。②美味的;佳餚的。③纖弱的;易傷的;薄弱的;脆弱的。He is a *delicate* child. 他是一個柔弱的小孩。④微妙的;需要愼重處理的。The international situation is very *delicate* at present. 現在國際情勢甚爲微妙。⑤輕淡的。⑥靈敏的;敏感的。She has *delicate* sense of smell. 她有靈敏的嗅覺。⑦賢淑的;幽嫻的。⑧關心的;有同情心的;體諒的。⑨得體的。—*n.* ①〖古〗美味的食物。②〖廢〗奢侈。give a delicate hint*** 微露暗示。—**ly,** *adv.* —**ness,** *n.*
del·i·ca·tes·sen [ˌdɛləkəˈtɛsn̩; ˌdelikəˈtesn] *n. pl.* ①(作 *sing.* 解)賣熟菜的店鋪。②(常作*pl.*解)熟菜;現成菜餚。
***de·li·cious** [dɪˈlɪʃəs; diˈliʃəs] *adj.* ①美味的;精美的。Doesn't it smell *delicious!* 好香的味道!②極爲悅人的;使人愉快的;宜人的;悅目的。—*n.* ①(D-) 一種有香味的紅色或黃色蘋果。②此種蘋果樹。—**ly,** *adv.* —**ness,** *n.*
de·lict [dɪˈlɪkt; diˈlikt] *n.*〖法律〗輕罪;違警罪;不法行爲。
‡**de·light** [dɪˈlaɪt; diˈlait] *n.* ①欣喜;樂趣;愉快;娛樂。Moving pictures give *delight* to millions of people. 電影給數以百萬計的人們以娛樂。②使喜悅的東西;使喜悅的原由;嗜好的東西。Boxing is his chief *delight*. 拳擊是他主要的嗜好。***take delight in*** 樂於;好;嗜。He *takes* great *delight in* painting. 他好繪畫。***to the delight of*** 使喜悅。—*v.t.* 使喜悅;使樂。Her singing *delighted* everybody. 她的歌唱爲人人所喜歡。—*v.i.* 喜;嗜;好〖in〗. He is a naughty boy and *delights* in teasing his little sister. 他是一個頑皮的小孩,好以戲弄他的小妹妹爲樂。—**er,** *n.* —**ing·ly,** *adv.* —**less,**

adj. 「欣喜的;快樂的。
de·light·ed [dɪˈlaɪtɪd; diˈlaitid] *adj.*
de·light·ed·ly [dɪˈlaɪtɪdlɪ; diˈlaitidli] *adv.* 大喜地;快樂地。
***de·light·ful** [dɪˈlaɪtfəl; diˈlaitful] *adj.* ①歡樂的;愉快的。②令人愉快的;悅人的;可愛的。—**ly,** *adv.* —**ness,** *n.*
de·light·some [dɪˈlaɪtsəm; diˈlaitsəm] *adj.* =**delightful.** —**ly,** *adv.*
De·li·lah [dɪˈlaɪlə; diˈlailə] *n.* ①〖聖經〗大利拉(迷惑大力士 Samson 之妖婦)。②妖婦。 「劃界。
de·lim·it [dɪˈlɪmɪt; diːˈlimit] *v.t.* 定界;
de·lim·i·tate [dɪˈlɪmɪˌtet; diˈlimiteit] *v.t.,* **-tat·ed, -tat·ing.** =**delimit.** —**de·lim·i·ta·tion,** *n.*
de·lin·e·ate [dɪˈlɪnɪˌet; diˈlinieit] *v.t.,* **-at·ed, -at·ing.** 描畫;畫出輪廓;記述。
de·lin·e·a·tion [dɪˌlɪnɪˈeʃən; diˌliniˈeiʃən] *n.* ①描畫;記述。②描寫。
de·lin·e·a·tor [dɪˈlɪnɪˌetɚ; diˈlinieitə] *n.* ①描寫之人或器具;製圖者;記述者。②(裁縫師所用之)裁製各種大小衣物的模型。
de·lin·quen·cy [dɪˈlɪŋkwənsɪ; diˈliŋkwənsi] *n., pl.* **-cies.** ①怠忽職務。②過失;錯誤。③違法;犯罪。④ **a.** 無法如期付出應付款項。**b.** 過期未付之款項、稅款等。
de·lin·quent [dɪˈlɪŋkwənt; diˈliŋkwənt] *adj.* ①怠忽職務的。②犯法的。③有過失的。④(稅款、應付款等)過期未付的。—*n.* 犯過的人;犯法的人。a juvenile *delinquent.* 少年罪犯。
del·i·quesce [ˌdɛləˈkwɛs; ˌdeliˈkwes] *v.i.,* **-quesced, -quesc·ing.** ①溶化;融解。②〖化〗潮解;液化。③〖植物〗分枝;生小枝。
del·i·ques·cence [ˌdɛləˈkwɛsn̩s; ˌdeliˈkwesns] *n.* 溶化;融解;潮解;溶化或潮解生成之液體。—**del·i·ques·cent,** *adj.*
de·lir·i·ous [dɪˈlɪrɪəs; diˈliriəs] *adj.* ①昏迷的;不省人事的。②精神錯亂的;發狂的。③狂言囈語的。④特別興奮的。—**ly,** *adv.*
de·lir·i·um [dɪˈlɪrɪəm; diˈliriəm] *n., pl.* **-lir·i·ums, -lir·i·a** [-ˈlɪrɪə; -ˈliriə]. ①(暫時的)精神狂亂。②狂語;囈語。③極度的興奮。
del·i·tes·cence [ˌdɛlɪˈtɛsəns; ˌdeliˈtesəns] *n.* ①匿伏;隱藏。②〖醫〗(炎症等之)隱匿;消匿。(亦作 **delitescency**)
del·i·tes·cent [ˌdɛlɪˈtɛsənt; ˌdeliˈtesənt] *adj.* 匿伏的;隱藏的。
‡**de·liv·er** [dɪˈlɪvɚ; diˈlivə] *v.t.* ①遞送;交付。A postman is a man who *delivers* letters and parcels. 郵差是遞送信件和郵包的人。②發言;陳述;發表。③加(重擊);投;射。④拯救;釋放。May God *deliver* us from all evil spirits. 願上帝救我們出魔掌。⑤爲…接生。She was *delivered* of a child. 她產下一孩。⑥交給;交出;放棄。⑦出產。⑧〖俗〗爲某候選人拉(選票)。—*v.i.* ①分娩。②送貨。③〖美〗達成願望;使成事實。***deliver oneself of*** 說出;發表(意見)。***deliver (oneself) up*** 自首。The thief *delivered himself up* to the police. 這賊向警察局自首。***deliver up*** 讓與。to *deliver up* the city to the enemy. 將城讓與敵人。—**a·ble,** *adj.* —**a·bil·i·ty,** —**er,** *n.*
de·liv·er·ance [dɪˈlɪvərəns; diˈlivərəns] *n.* ①釋放;救出。②意見;判決。
delivered price 交貨價格(廠商對貨物所報之價格,包括自工廠至交貨地之運費)。
de·liv·er·y** [dɪˈlɪvərɪ; diˈlivəri] *n., pl.* **-er·ies.** ①分送;遞送。②分娩。③演說的態度;演說時的聲調和姿態。④打擊或投球;打擊或投球的姿態。⑤拯救;釋放。⑥交納。⑦交付;交付之物;交付之貨。⑧〖法律〗財產等之正式移交。cash on delivery***(略作 **C.O.D.**)貨到付款。***special delivery***(郵件)快遞;專送。
delivery book 交貨簿;送貨簿。
delivery boy 少年送貨員。
de·liv·er·y·man [dɪˈlɪvərɪˌmən, -mæn; diˈlivərimən, -mæn] *n., pl.* **-men.** 送貨員(如牛奶、冰塊等以卡車送貨者)。
delivery on term 定期交貨。
delivery order 出棧憑單。
delivery receipt 送達回條。
dell [dɛl; del] *n.* 兩邊有樹的小谷;幽谷。
de·louse [diˈlaus; ˈdiːˈlaus] *v.t.,* **-loused, -lous·ing.** 自…除虱;去虱。
Del·phi [ˈdɛlfaɪ; ˈdelfai] *n.* 特耳菲(古希臘一都城,因 Apollo 的神殿著稱)。
Del·phi·an [ˈdɛlfɪən; ˈdelfiən] *adj.* =**Delphic.** —*n.* 特耳菲之居民。
Del·phic [ˈdɛlfɪk; ˈdelfik] *adj.* ①Delphi 的;阿波羅神(Apollo)的;阿波羅神殿的。②(意義)含混不清的;深奧的。(亦作**Delphian**)
del·phin·i·um [dɛlˈfɪnɪəm; delˈfiniəm] *n., pl.* **-i·ums, -i·a** [-ɪə; -iə]. 飛燕草;飛燕草子;翠雀花。
***del·ta** [ˈdɛltə; ˈdeltə] *n.* ①三角洲。the Nile *Delta.* 尼羅河三角洲。②希臘字母中的第四個字母(△或 δ)。③三角形(如希臘字母)之物。④通訊中代表D之代號。⑤(D-)〖天文〗四等星。—**del·tal,** *adj.*
del·ta-winged [ˈdɛltəˌwɪŋd; ˈdeltəˌwiŋd] *adj.* (飛機)翼作三角形設計的;有三角形翼的。
del·toid [ˈdɛltɔɪd; ˈdeltɔid] *adj.* (亦作 **deltoidal**)①三角形的。②〖解剖〗三角肌的。—*n.* 〖解剖〗三角肌(=deltoid muscle).
de·lude [dɪˈlud; diˈluːd] *v.t.,* **-lud·ed, -lud·ing.** 欺騙;迷惑。—**de·lud·a·ble,** *adj.* —**de·lud·er,** *n.*
del·uge [ˈdɛljudʒ; ˈdeljuːdʒ] *n., v.,* **-uged, -ug·ing.** —*n.* ①大水災;洪水。②豪雨。③狂湧而至的東西。a *deluge* of questions. 一連串的問題。***the Deluge*** 聖經創世紀中諾亞時代的大洪水。—*v.t.* ①泛濫。②湧至。③充盈;壓倒。to be *deluged* with questions. 被許多問題所困惑。
***de·lu·sion** [dɪˈluʒən, -ˈlɪuʒən; diˈluːʒən, -ˈljuː-] *n.* ①欺瞞;迷惑。②謬見;妄念;幻想。—**al,** *adj.*
de·lu·sive [dɪˈlusɪv; diˈluːsiv] *adj.* 欺騙的;虛妄的;令人錯解的。—**ly,** *adv.* —**ness,** *n.* 「=delusive.
de·lu·so·ry [dɪˈlusərɪ; diˈluːsəri] *adj.*
de·luxe [dɪˈlʊks; dəˈluks] *adj.* 華美的;華麗的。—*adv.* 豪華地。(亦作 **de luxe**)
delve [dɛlv; delv] *v.,* **delved, delv·ing.** —*v.t.* 〖古〗掘。—*v.i.* ①〖古〗掘;耕。②蒐求;發掘。
Dem. ①Democrat. ②Democratic.
de·mag·net·i·za·tion [ˌdimægnətəˈzeʃən; ˈdiːˌmægnitaiˈzeiʃən] *n.* 去磁。
de·mag·net·ize [diˈmægnəˌtaɪz; ˈdiːˈmægnitaiz] *v.t.,* **-ized, -iz·ing.** 去磁。—**de·mag·net·iz·a·ble,** *adj.*
dem·a·gog(ue) [ˈdɛməˌgɔg; ˈdeməgɔg] *n.* ①利用情緒或偏見以煽動民衆以期獲得領導地位及達到私人目的的人;煽動政治家。②〖古史〗民衆領袖。

dem·a·gog·ic 〔ˌdɛməˈgɑdʒɪk; ˌdeməˈgɔgik〕 *adj.* 煽動羣衆的; 煽惑的。(亦作 **demagogical**) —**al·ly,** *adv.*

dem·a·gog·ism 〔ˈdɛməˌgɔgɪzəm; ˈdeməgɔgizəm〕 *n.* 煽動民衆; 煽動行爲; 煽動主義。(亦作 **demagoguism**)

dem·a·gog·uer·y 〔ˈdɛməˌgɔgərɪ; ˈdeməgɔgəri〕 *n.* =**demagogy.**

dem·a·go·gy〔ˈdɛməˌgodʒɪ;ˈdeməgɔgi〕 *n.* ①煽動家的方法與行爲。②一羣煽動家。

‡**de·mand** 〔dɪˈmænd; diˈmɑːnd〕 *v.t.* ①要求。He *demanded* immediate payment. 他要求立刻付款。②詰問;查詢。③需要。This sort of work *demands* great patience. 這種工作需要很大的耐心。④〖法律〗 **a.** 召喚。**b.** 提出正式要求。—*v.i.* 查問。—*n.* ①要求;請求。It is impossible to satisfy all *demands.* 滿足所有的要求是不可能的事。②需要;需求。supply and *demand.* 供與求。③〖法律〗徵收; 正式要求。④〖古〗詢問。 ***in great demand*** 需要甚股;需要甚大。***on demand*** 來取卽付。

de·mand·a·ble 〔dɪˈmændəbl; diˈmɑːndəbl〕 *adj.*可要求的;可請求的。

de·mand·ant 〔dɪˈmændənt;diˈmɑːndənt〕 *n.*①要求者;請求者。②〖法律〗原告。

demand bill (draft, or **note)** 見票卽付的支票或匯票等。

demand deposit 活期存款;隨時可提取的存款。

de·mand·er 〔dɪˈmændɚ; diˈmɑːndə〕 *n.* 要求者;請求者。

demand loan 不定期借款;雙方隨時可索取或歸還的借款。(亦作 **call loan**)

de·mand-pull 〔dɪˈmændˌpʊl; diˈmɑːndpul〕 *n.* 景氣性通貨膨脹(由於對貨物及服務需求過多而引起)。(亦作**demand-pull inflation**)

de·mar·cate 〔dɪˈmɑrket;ˈdiːmɑːkeit〕 *v.t.*, **-cat·ed, -cat·ing.** ①劃界;定界線;劃分;劃歸。②區別;區分。—**de·mar·ca·tor,** *n.*

de·mar·ca·tion 〔ˌdimɑrˈkeʃən; ˌdiːmɑːˈkeiʃən〕 *n.* ①定界限; 定界線。②界限;界線。③分開。(亦作 **demarkation**)

de·marche 〔deˈmɑrʃ; ˈdeimɑːʃ〕 *n.*①行動方針。②〖外交〗行動新方針;政策之改變。

de·ma·te·ri·al·ize 〔ˌdiməˈtɪrɪəlˌaɪz; ˈdiːməˈtiəriəlaiz〕 *v.t. & v.i.*, **-ized,-iz·ing.** (使)喪失物質形態;非物質化。

de·mean 〔dɪˈmin; diˈmiːn〕 *v.t.* ①舉止;行爲。②貶抑;降低。

***de·mean·o(u)r** 〔dɪˈminɚ; diˈmiːnə〕 *n.* ①行爲; 態度;風度。The girl had a quiet, modest *demeanour.* 這個女孩子有一種嫻靜而謙遜的態度。②臉上的表情。

de·ment·ed 〔dɪˈmɛntɪd; diˈmentid〕 *adj.* 失本性的; 瘋狂的; 精神錯亂的。—**ly,** *adv.* —**ness,** *n.*

dé·men·ti 〔demɑ̃ˈti; deimɑ̃ˈtiː〕 *n., pl.* **-tis.**〖法〗〖外交〗(謠言等之)正式否認。

de·men·tia 〔dɪˈmɛnʃɪə; diˈmenʃiə〕 *n.* 〖醫〗癡呆。

dementia pr(a)ecox 〖醫〗精神分裂症。

de·mer·it 〔diˈmɛrɪt;diːˈmerit〕 *n.* ①過失;缺點;失德。②因品行或學業不佳的處罰分數;記過。

de·mesne 〔dɪˈmen; diˈmein〕 *n.* ①土地的領有。②不動產(尤指留爲自用之地產)。③封建時代郡主房舍及其鄰接之土地(歸其直接使用者)。④區域;領地。***land held in demesne*** 領有地。***Royal demesne*** 〖英〗王餒。***State demesne*** 國有地。

De·me·ter 〔dɪˈmitɚ; diˈmiːtə〕 *n.* 〖希臘神話〗司農業、豐饒及保護婚姻之女神。

de·mi 〔ˈdimaɪ;ˈdiːmai〕 *n.* pl. of **demos.**

dem·i·god 〔ˈdɛməˌgɑd; ˈdemigɔd〕 *n.* 半神半人;神人。(女性爲 demigoddess)

dem·i·john 〔ˈdɛməˌdʒɑn; ˈdemidʒɔn〕 *n.* 一種細頸大罎(常用柳條編護且編有把手)。

de·mil·i·ta·ri·za·tion 〔diˌmɪlətərɪˈzeʃən;ˈdiːˌmilitəraiˈzeiʃən〕 *n.* 廢除軍備;解除軍事控制。

de·mil·i·ta·rize 〔diˈmɪlətəˌraɪz;ˈdiːˈmilitəraiz〕 *v.t.*, **-rized, -riz·ing.** ①廢除軍備;撤除軍隊及軍事設施。②解除軍事控制。

dem·i·lune 〔ˈdɛmɪˌlun; ˈdemiluːn〕 *n.* ①新月; 半月。②半月形堡壘。③新月形之事物。—*adj.* 新月狀的;半月形的。

dem·i·mon·daine 〔ˌdɛmɪmɑnˈden; ˌdemimɔːnˈdein〕 *n., pl.* **-daines.** *adj.* —*n.* 行爲放蕩的女人。—*adj.* 花街柳巷的。

dem·i·monde 〔ˈdɛmɪˌmɑnd; ˈdemiˈmɔ̃d〕 *n.* 下流婦女之社會;花柳界。

dem·i·rep 〔ˈdɛmɪˌrɛp; ˈdemirep〕 *n.* 貞潔可疑之婦女;名譽不佳之婦女。

de·mise〔dɪˈmaɪz; diˈmaiz〕*n., v.,* **-mised, -mis·ing.** —*n.* ①死亡。②君權之轉移或授與;讓位;傳位;禪讓。③(產業之)讓與;讓授;遺贈;遺傳。④終止。—*v.t.* ①遺贈、遺傳、租讓或讓與(產業)。②轉移或授與(君權); 讓(王位);傳(位);禪讓。—*v.i.* 遺贈; 遺傳; 讓授。

dem·i·sem·i·qua·ver 〔ˌdɛmɪˈsɛməˌkwevɚ; ˈdemisemiˌkweivə〕 *n.* 〖音樂〗三十二分音符。***demisemiquaver rest*** 三十二分休止符。

de·mis·sion 〔dɪˈmɪʃən; diˈmiʃən〕 *n.* 〖古〗放棄;辭職。

de·mit 〔dɪˈmɪt; diˈmit〕 *v.*, **-mit·ted, -mit·ting.** —*v.t.* ①放棄;辭(職)。②〖古〗開除。—*v.i.* 辭職。

dem·i·tasse 〔ˈdɛməˌtæs; ˈdemitæs〕 *n.* ①盛黑咖啡之小杯。②一小杯之黑咖啡。

dem·i·tint 〔ˈdɛmɪˌtɪnt; ˈdemitint〕 *n.* (色調)半濃半淡;中色。

dem·i·urge 〔ˈdɛmɪˌɝdʒ; ˈdiːmiəːdʒ〕 *n.* ①(D-)〖哲學〗 **a.** 造物主。**b.** 物質世界之創造者。②(古希臘之)行政官。(亦作 **demiurgos, demiurgus**)—**dem·i·ur·gic, dem·i·ur·gi·cal,** *adj.*

de·mi·world 〔ˈdɛmɪˌwɝld; ˈdemiwəːld〕 *n.* 低層社會。

dem·o 〔ˈdɛmo; ˈdemou〕 *n., pl.* **dem·os.** 〖俗〗①示威。②示威者。

de·mob 〔diˈmɑb; ˈdiːˈmɔb〕 *n., v.,* **-mobbed, -mob·bing.** —*n.* 〖英俗〗①(軍隊等之)遣散;復員(=demobilization). ②遣散者;復員者。—*v.t.* 〖英俗〗 =**demobilize.**

de·mo·bi·li·za·tion 〔ˌdimobləˈzeʃən; ˈdiːˌmoubilaiˈzeiʃən〕 *n.* (軍隊等的)遣散;復員。

de·mo·bi·lize 〔diˈmoblˌaɪz; diːˈmoubilaiz〕 *v.t.*, **-lized, -liz·ing.** 遣散;改編(軍隊等);使復員。

***de·moc·ra·cy** 〔dəˈmɑkrəsɪ; diˈmɔkrəsi〕 *n., pl.* **-cies.** ①民主政治;民主政體。②民主國家。③民主精神;以平等對待。④(D-)美國的民主黨;該黨的精神與政策;該黨黨員。⑤民衆。

***dem·o·crat** 〔ˈdɛməˌkræt;ˈdeməkræt〕 *n.* ①民主主義者。②以平等待人者。③(D-)美國民主黨黨員。④一種高而輕的雙座馬車。

‡**dem·o·crat·ic**〔ˌdɛməˈkrætɪk; ˌdeməˈkrætik〕 *adj.* ①民主主義的; 民主政體的;像

民主政治的。②信仰民主主義的。Schools in the United States are *democratic.* 美國的學校是民主的。③以平等待人的。④(D-)美國民主黨的。(亦作 **democratical**) *the Democratic Party* 美國民主黨。

dem·o·crat·i·cal·ly [ˌdɛməˈkrætɪklɪ; ˌdeməˈkrætikəli] *adv.* 民主地。

de·moc·ra·tism [dɪˈmɑkrətɪzəm; diˈmɔkrətizəm] *n.* 民主主義;民主制度。

de·moc·ra·tize [dəˈmɑkrəˌtaɪz; diˈmɔkrətaiz] *v.t.* & *v.i.*, **-tized, -tiz·ing.** (使) 民主化; 平民化。 **—de·moc·ra·ti·za·tion,** *n.*

dé·mo·dé [demɔˈde; deimɔːˈdei] 〖法〗 *adj.* 陳舊的;老式的。

De·mo·gor·gon [ˌdiməˈgɔrgən; ˈdiːmouˈgɔːgən] *n.* (古神話之)魔王;魔神。

de·mo·graph·ic [ˌdiməˈgræfɪk; ˌdiːməˈgræfik] *adj.* 人口統計的; 人口學的。(亦作 **demographical**)

de·mog·ra·phy [dɪˈmɑgrəfɪ; diːˈmɔgrəfi] *n.* 人口統計;人口學。

dem·oi·selle [ˌdɛmwɑˈzɛl; ˌdemwɑːˈzel] 〖法〗 *n.* ①處女;閨秀。②蓑羽鶴。③豆娘(蜻蜓之一種)。

de·mol·ish [dɪˈmɑlɪʃ; diˈmɔliʃ] *v.t.* ①毀壞;破壞;削平;推翻。②〖俗〗吃光。

de·mol·ish·ment [dɪˈmɑlɪʃmənt; diˈmɔliʃmənt] *n.* =**demolition.**

dem·o·li·tion [ˌdɛməˈlɪʃən; ˌdeməˈliʃən] *n.* ①破壞; 毀壞。②(*pl.*) 被破壞或毀壞之物;廢墟。—*adj.* 破壞的;毀壞的。

***de·mon** [ˈdimən; ˈdiːmən] *n.* ①惡鬼;惡魔。②兇惡的人; 極殘忍的人。③惡劣的影響。④護靈;守護神。⑤精力充沛的人;有能力的人。He is a *demon* for work. 他工作不倦。⑥希臘的次要之神。—*adj.* ①惡鬼的;惡魔的。②受惡鬼控制的。

de·mon·e·ti·za·tion [diˌmɑnətɪˈzeʃən; diːˌmʌnitaiˈzeiʃən] *n.* 廢止通用之通貨;廢用;廢止流通。

de·mon·e·tize [diˈmɑnəˌtaɪz; diːˈmʌnitaiz] *v.t.*, **-tized, -tiz·ing.** ①使(通貨)失去標準價值;廢止(通用之通貨)。②停止(金、銀等)充作貨幣。③廢止(郵票)。

de·mo·ni·ac [dɪˈmonɪˌæk; diˈmouniæk] *adj.* (亦作 **demoniacal**) ①魔鬼的; 似魔鬼的。②着魔的; 凶惡的。—*n.* 着魔之人;狂暴者;瘋狂者。**—al·ly,** *adv.*

de·mon·ic [diˈmɑnɪk; diːˈmɔnik] *adj.* ①魔鬼的; 似魔鬼的。②有魔力的。③受靈感的。(亦作 **daemonic, demonical**)

de·mon·ism [ˈdimənˌɪzəm; ˈdiːmənizəm] *n.* ①對鬼怪之信仰。②對鬼怪之崇拜。③鬼怪論;鬼神學 (=demonology).

de·mon·ize [ˈdimənˌaɪz; ˈdiːmənaiz] *v.t.*, **-ized, -iz·ing.** ①使爲魔鬼; 使似魔鬼。②使爲魔鬼所附。

de·mon·ol·a·try [ˌdimənˈɑlətrɪ; ˌdiːməˈnɔlətri] *n.* 鬼神崇拜。**—de·mon·ol·a·trous,** *adj.*

de·mon·ol·o·gy [ˌdimənˈɑlədʒɪ; ˌdiːməˈnɔlədʒi] *n.* 魔鬼之研究;鬼怪論;鬼神學。(亦作 **daemonology**)

de·mon·stra·ble [ˈdɛmənstrəbl̩; ˈdemənstrəbl] *adj.* 可證明的;可表明的;可示範的。**—de·mon·stra·bil·i·ty,** *n.* **—de·mon·stra·bly,** *adv.*

***dem·on·strate** [ˈdɛmənˌstret; ˈdemənstreit] *v.*, **-strat·ed, -strat·ing.** —*v.t.* ①證明。②(用標本或實驗)施教;演示;示範。③當衆表演;誇示…之好處(以求出售貨物)。④表露(情緒)。—*v.i.* ①作示威運動。The workers marched through the streets *demonstrating* against the rising cost of living. 工人們遊街, 作反對生活費用高漲示威。②炫耀軍力(以欺騙或阻嚇敵人)。**—dem·on·stra·tor,** *n.*

***dem·on·stra·tion** [ˌdɛmənˈstreʃən; ˌdemənsˈtreiʃən] *n.* ①證明。②表演;示範。③感情之表現或流露。 *demonstration* of affection. 情愛的表示。④示威運動。⑤炫耀武力。**—al,** *adj.*

dem·on·stra·tion·ist [ˌdɛmənˈstreʃənɪst; ˌdemənsˈtreiʃənist] *n.* 參加示威運動者。

de·mon·stra·tive [dɪˈmɑnstrətɪv; diˈmɔnstrətiv] *adj.* ①明白表示的;說明的;指示的。②予以證明的; 證實的; 令人信服的〖常 of〗。③與論證有關的;論證的;實驗的。④公開而坦率地表露出感情的;坦率的。⑤〖文法〗指示的。*demonstrative* adjective. 指示形容詞。—*n.* 〖文法〗 指示代名詞; 指示形容詞。(略作 **demon.**) **—ly,** *adv.* **—ness,** *n.*

de·mor·al·i·za·tion [dɪˌmɔrələˈzeʃən; diˌmɔrəlaiˈzeiʃən] *n.* ①風俗敗壞;道德墮落。②士氣低落。

de·mor·al·ize [dɪˈmɑrəlˌaɪz; diˈmɔrəlaiz] *v.t.*, **-ized, -iz·ing.** ①敗壞(道德)。②使沮喪;使消沉;使無鬥志。③使陷於混亂。④使迷惑。**—de·mor·al·iz·er,** *n.*

de·mos [ˈdimɑs; ˈdiːmɔs] *n.*, *pl.* **-mi** [-maɪ;-mai]. 人民;民衆;庶民。

De·mos·the·nes [dɪˈmɑsθəˌniz; diˈmɔsθəniːz] *n.* 狄摩西尼斯(385?–322 B.C., 古希臘之演說家及政治家)。

De·mos·then·ic [ˌdɛməsˈθɛnɪk; ˌdeməsˈθenik] *adj.* 希臘演說家 Demosthenes 之雄辯的;有愛國之熱忱的。

de·mote [dɪˈmot; diˈmout] *v.t.*, **-mot·ed, -mot·ing.** 降級 (爲 promote 之對)。

de·mot·ic [diˈmɑtɪk; di(ː)ˈmɔtik] *adj.* ①民衆的; 通俗的。②經過簡化的古埃及象形文字的。—*n.* ①經過簡化的古埃及象形文字。②(D-) 現代希臘方言 (=Romaic).

de·mo·tion [dɪˈmoʃən; diˈmouʃən] *n.* 降級;降官階。

de·mount [diˈmaʊnt; diːˈmaunt] *v.t.* ①卸下。②拆開;拆卸。

de·mount·a·ble [diˈmaʊntəbl̩; diːˈmauntəbl] *adj.* 可卸下的;可拆開的。

de·mul·cent [dɪˈmʌlsn̩t; diˈmʌlsnt] *adj.* (藥物等) 緩和的;鎮靜的。 —*n.* 刺激緩衝劑;潤藥;潤劑。

de·mur [dɪˈmɝ; diˈməː] *v.*, **-murred, -mur·ring,** *n.* —*v.i.* ①躊躇;猶豫〖at, to〗. ②提出異議;抗議;反對〖at, to〗. —*n.* ①躊躇;遲疑不決。②異議;抗議。

de·mure [dɪˈmjʊr; diˈmjuə] *adj.*, **-mur·er, -mur·est.** ①嚴肅的;端莊的;不苟言笑的。②假裝正直的;假裝謹愼的;佯作端莊的。**—ly,** *adv.* **—ness,** *n.*

de·mur·rage [dɪˈmɝɪdʒ; diˈmʌridʒ] *n.* 〖商〗①(車、船等因裝卸貨物逾越預定時間而)停留過久。②因上項逾時而付之賠償;延期停泊費;貨車停留費。

de·mur·rer [dɪˈmɝə; diˈməːrə] *n.* ①抗辯者;反對者。②異議;抗議。③〖法律〗對起訴之異議;抗辯。

de·my [dɪˈmaɪ; diˈmai] *n.*, *pl.* **-mies.** ①(英國牛津大學 Magdalen 學院之)受資助之學生。②一種特定大小的紙 (美國爲16×21

英寸,英國爲 $17^1/_2 \times 22$ 英寸)。

***den** [dɛn; den] *n., v.,* **denned, den·ning.** —*n.* ①獸窟;獸穴。a tiger's *den.* 虎穴。②舒適之私室。③汚穢的所在;藏垢納汚之所。*dens* of misery. 貧民窟。④藏匿的處所。a *den* for thieves. 賊窩。⑤幼童軍之一單位。—*v.i.* 住於汚穢的地方。*den up*〖美〗**a.**(野獸)到洞中去過多(去多眠)。**b.** 回至私室。—**like,** *adj.*

Den. Denmark.

de·nar·i·us [dɪ'nɛrɪəs; di'nɛəriəs] *n., pl.* **-nar·i·i** [-'nɛrɪ,aɪ;-'nɛəriai]. ①古羅馬之銀幣名。②(英國錢幣計算中之)辨士(penny 之符號 d 由此義而來)。③古羅馬之金幣。

de·na·ry ['dɛnərɪ; 'di:nəri] *adj.* ①十的;十倍的。②十進的。

de·na·tion·al·i·za·tion [di,næʃənələ'zeʃən; 'di:,næʃn̩əlai'zeiʃən] *n.* ①剝奪國籍;褫奪公民資格。②解除國有化。③失去獨立國資格;國際化。

de·na·tion·al·ize [di'næʃənḷ,aɪz; di:'næʃn̩əlaiz] *v.t.,* **-ized, -iz·ing.** ①剝奪國籍;褫奪公民資格。②解除國有;使成民有。③使失去獨立國資格;使國際化。—**de·na·tion·al·iz·er,** *n.*

de·nat·u·ral·ize [di'nætʃrəl,aɪz; di:'nætʃrəlaiz] *v.t.,* **-ized, -iz·ing.** ①使違本性;使不自然。②剝奪公民權;剝奪國籍。—**de·nat·u·ral·i·za·tion,** *n.*

de·na·tur·ant [di'netʃərənt;di:'neitʃərənt] *n.* 變性劑。

de·na·ture [di'netʃɚ; di:'neitʃə] *v.t.,* **-tured, -tur·ing.** ①使變性;除去…之特性。②使(酒精等)不適飲用而仍不損其他用途。③使(蛋白質等)改變其特性。④加不核裂物質於核裂物質使其不適於爲原子武器而可利用其原子動力。—**de·na·tur·a·tion,** *n.*

de·na·zi·fy [di'nɑtsə,faɪ;di:'nɑ:tsifai] *v.t.,* **-fied, -fy·ing.** 解除納粹制度;使脫離納粹影響。—**de·na·zi·fi·ca·tion,** *n.*

den·drite ['dɛndraɪt; 'dendrait] *n.* ①〖礦〗樹枝石。②〖解剖〗樹狀突。

den·drit·ic [dɛn'drɪtɪk; den'dritik] *adj.* ①〖解剖〗樹狀突的;似樹狀突的。②樹枝狀的。(亦作 **dendritical**)

den·droid ['dɛndrɔɪd; 'dendrɔid] *adj.* 樹木狀的;樹枝狀的。(亦作 **dendroidal**)

den·dro·lite ['dɛndrə,laɪt; 'dendrəlait] *n.* 植物之化石。

den·drol·o·gy [dɛn'drɑlədʒɪ; den'drɔlədʒi] *n.* 樹木學。

den·drom·e·ter [dɛn'drɑmɪtɚ;den'drɔmitə] *n.* 測樹器(測樹之大小高低)。

dene [din; di:n] *n.*〖英〗(海濱之)沙地。

de·neu·tral·ize [di'njutrəl,aɪz; di:'nju:trəlaiz] *v.t.,* **-ized, -iz·ing.** 解除…之中立;使脫離中立地位。

den·gue ['dɛŋgɪ; 'deŋgi] *n.*〖醫〗登革熱(熱帶傳染病,關節及肌肉奇痛)。

de·ni·a·ble [dɪ'naɪəbḷ; di'naiəbl] *adj.* 可否認的;可拒絕的;可反對的。

***de·ni·al** [dɪ'naɪəl; di'naiəl] *n.* ①否認;否定;打消。to give a *denial* to the rumor. 否認謠傳。②謝絕;拒絕。Your *denial* of her request hurt her. 你拒絕她的請求傷了她的感情。③抑制。

de·nic·o·tin·ize [di'nɪkətɪn,aɪz; di:'nikətinaiz] *v.t.,* **-ized, -iz·ing.** (從烟草)除去尼古丁。

de·ni·er[1] [dɪ'naɪɚ;di'naiə] *n.* 否認者;反對者;拒絕者。

de·nier[2] [də'nɪr; di'niə] *n.* ①一種測定絲、尼龍等細度之重量單位。②極微之量。

den·i·grate ['dɛnə,gret; 'denigreit] *v.t.,* **-grat·ed, -grat·ing.** ①塗汚;塗黑。②毀壞(他人)之名譽;玷辱。

den·im ['dɛnəm; 'denim] *n.* ①厚而粗之斜紋棉布。②(*pl.*) 以此種棉布做的衣服。

de·ni·trate [di'naɪtret; di:'naitreit] *v.t.,* **-trat·ed, -trat·ing.** 除去硝酸。

de·ni·tri·fy [di'naɪtrə,faɪ; di:'naitrifai] *v.t.,* **-fied, -fy·ing.** 除氮;除去氮化物。

den·i·zen ['dɛnəzn̩; 'denizn] *n.* ①公民;居民。②歸化者;入籍者。③外來語;外來之動植物。—*v.t.* ①給予永住權。②移植(植物)。③使歸化;使入籍。

***Den·mark** ['dɛnmɑrk;'denmɑ:k] *n.* 丹麥(北歐一國,首都哥本哈根 Copenhagen).

de·nom·i·nate [*v.* dɪ'nɑmə,net; di'nɔmineit *adj.* dɪ'nɑmənɪt; di'nɔminit] *v.,* **-nat·ed, -nat·ing,** *adj.* —*v.t.* 命名;取名。—*adj.* 有名稱的;具體的。

***de·nom·i·na·tion** [dɪ,nɑmə'neʃən; di,nɔmi'neiʃən] *n.* ①名稱;命名。②派別;宗派;分派。③(重量、長度、貨幣等之)單位;面額。money of small *denominations.* 零錢。④(人或物之)種類。—**al,** *adj.*

de·nom·i·na·tion·al·ism [dɪ,nɑmə'neʃənḷ,ɪzəm; di,nɔmi'neiʃn̩əlizəm] *n.* ①宗派主義。②宗派制度。③對宗派主義或制度之接受或支持。④宗派之區分。

de·nom·i·na·tive [dɪ'nɑmə,netɪv; di'nɔminətiv] *adj.* ①命名的;有名稱的;可命名的。②〖文法〗出自名詞或形容詞的。—*n.*〖文法〗出自名詞或形容詞之字(尤指動詞)。

de·nom·i·na·tor [dɪ'nɑmə,netɚ;di'nɔmineitə] *n.* ①〖數學〗分母。②命名者;據以命名之物。③共同點;標準。

de·no·ta·tion [,dino'teʃən;,di:nou'teiʃən] *n.* ①表示;指示;指定。②名稱;符號。③(辭句之)意義。④〖邏輯〗外延;概述。⑤命名。

de·no·ta·tive [dɪ'notətɪv; di'noutətiv] *adj.* ①指示的;表示的。②〖邏輯〗外延的;概述的。—**ly,** *adv.* —**ness,** *n.*

de·note [dɪ'not; di'nout] *v.t.,* **-not·ed, -not·ing.** ①指示;表示。②意義。—**de·not·a·ble,** *adj.* —**ment,** *n.*

de·noue·ment [de'numɑ̃; dei'nu:mɑ:ŋ] *n.* ①(小說、戲劇等之)結局;收場。②結局或收場之部分。③結果;終場。

***de·nounce** [dɪ'nauns; di'nauns] *v.t.,* **-nounced, -nounc·ing.** ①公開指摘;當衆指責。He was *denounced* as a rascal. 他被當衆指責爲無賴。②告發;揭發。to *denounce* a person to the police. 向警局告發某人。③通知廢止(如條約等)。—**ment, de·nounc·er,** *n.*

***dense** [dɛns; dens] *adj.,* **dens·er, dens·est.** ①緊密的;濃密的;嚴密的。a *dense* population. 稠密的人口。a *dense* fog. 濃霧。②密緻的;密實的。③愚鈍的。④强烈的。⑤半透明的。⑥〖數學〗稠密。—**ly,** *adv.* —**ness,** *n.*

den·sim·e·ter [dɛn'sɪmətɚ; den'simitə] *n.* 比重計;密度計。

***den·si·ty** ['dɛnsətɪ; 'densiti] *n., pl.,* **-ties.** ①稠密;濃密;密實。②密度。Mercury has a much greater *density* than water. 水銀的密度比水大得多。③(影的)濃度。④愚鈍。⑤電流的密度。

dent [dɛnt; dent] *n.* ①凹;缺口。②齒狀突出物。③弱點;損害。***make a dent*** **a.** 引起注意。**b.** (工作、思考等) 略有進展;越過起

始階段。—*v.t.* ①使成缺口。②使凹下。③使受輕傷。—*v.i.* ①凹下;成鋸齒狀。②穿入。

dent. ①dental. ②dentist. ③dentistry.

den·tal [ˈdɛntl̩; ˈdentl] *adj.* ①牙齒的;齒科醫術的。a *dental* surgeon. 牙醫;齒科醫師。②〖語音〗齒音的。—*n.* 〖語音〗齒音。—**i·ty,** *n.*

「齒的;鋸齒狀的。」

den·tate [ˈdɛntet; ˈdenteit] *adj.* 有牙

den·ta·tion [dɛnˈteʃən; denˈteiʃən] *n.* 〖動、植物〗齒狀突;齒狀構造。

den·ti·care [ˈdɛntɪˌkɛr; ˈdentikɛə] *n.* 〖加〗政府對兒童所提供的免費牙齒防治及醫療計畫。

「齒;齒狀裝飾。」

den·ti·cle [ˈdɛntɪkl̩; ˈdentikl] *n.* 小

den·tic·u·late [dɛnˈtɪkjəlɪt; denˈtikjuleit] *adj.* 〖植物〗小齒的;鋸齒狀的。(亦作 **denticulated**) —**ly,** *adv.*

den·tic·u·la·tion [dɛnˌtɪkjəˈleʃən; denˌtikjuˈleiʃən] *n.* 小齒;齒狀裝飾;小齒狀突起。

「*adj.* 齒形的。」

den·ti·form [ˈdɛntɪˌfɔrm; ˈdentifɔːm]

den·ti·frice [ˈdɛntəˌfrɪs; ˈdentifris] *n.* 牙膏、牙粉、洗牙的藥水等。

「狀裝飾。」

den·til [ˈdɛntɪl; ˈdentil] *n.* 〖建築〗齒

den·tin(e) [ˈdɛntin; ˈdentiːn] *n.* 牙本質;齒骨質;象牙質。

den·ti·na·sal [ˌdɛntəˈnezl̩; ˌdentəˈneizəl] *adj.* 齒鼻音的。—*n.* 齒鼻音。

***den·tist** [ˈdɛntɪst; ˈdentist] *n.* 牙科醫生。—**ic,** —**i·cal,** *adj.*

den·tist·ry [ˈdɛntɪstrɪ; ˈdentistri] *n.* 齒科學;牙科學;牙醫術。

den·ti·tion [dɛnˈtɪʃən; denˈtiʃən] *n.* ①齒之發育;生齒。②齒列;齒系。③個人或動物之齒的集合稱。

den·ture [ˈdɛntʃɚ; ˈdentʃə] *n.* 一副牙齒;(尤指)一副假牙。***partial* (*full*) *denture*** 部分(全部)假牙。

de·nude [dɪˈnjud; diˈnjuːd] *v.t.*, **-nud·ed, -nud·ing.** ①使裸露;剝下;脫去。②剝奪。③〖地質〗磨剝;侵蝕。—**den·u·da·tion,** *n.*

de·nun·ci·ate [dɪˈnʌnsɪˌet; diˈnʌnsieit] *v.t.*, **-at·ed, -at·ing.** =**denounce.**

de·nun·ci·a·tion [dɪˌnʌnsɪˈeʃən; diˌnʌnsiˈeiʃən] *n.* ①公開的指責。②告發。③廢止條約等的正式通知。④警告;威脅。

de·nun·ci·a·tor [dɪˈnʌnʃɪˌetɚ; diˈnʌnsieitə] *n.* 非難者;恫嚇者;斥責者。

de·nun·ci·a·to·ry [dɪˈnʌnsɪəˌtorɪ; diˈnʌnsiətəri] *adj.* 非難的;攻擊的;斥責的。(亦作 **denunciative**)

:de·ny [dɪˈnaɪ; diˈnai] *v.t.*, **-nied, -ny·ing.** ①否認;否定。to *deny* that it is so. 否認事實是如此的。②拒絕相信;不信;不承認。to *deny* one's signature. 不承認自己的簽名。③拒絕給予。She can *deny* her son nothing. 她對其子百依百順。④拒絕接受。⑤使(某人)不接見訪客。***deny oneself*** 自制;克己;放棄;捨棄;摒棄。He had to *deny himself* many of the comforts of life. 他必須放棄自己生活上的許多享受。***deny oneself to*** 拒絕會見;不會(客)。Illness forced Mrs. Smith to *deny herself to* all callers. 疾病使史密斯太太不能會客。

de·o·dar [ˈdiəˌdɑr; ˈdioudɑː] *n.* 〖植物〗喜馬拉雅山所產之杉。

de·o·dor·ant [diˈodərənt; diːˈoudərənt] *adj.* 除臭氣的。—*n.* 除臭劑;防臭劑。

de·o·dor·ize [diˈodəˌraɪz; diːˈoudəraiz] *v.t.*, **-ized, -iz·ing.** 除…之臭;防臭。—**de·o·dor·i·za·tion,** *n.*

de·o·dor·iz·er [diˈodəˌraɪzɚ; diːˈoudəraizə] *n.* 防臭物;除臭劑。

De·o gra·ti·as [ˈdioˈgreʃɪˌæs; ˈdiːouˈgreiʃiæs] 〖拉〗蒙神之佑;託天之福(=thanks to God).

de·on·tol·o·gy [ˌdiɑnˈtɑlədʒɪ; ˌdiːɔnˈtɔlədʒi] *n.* 義務論;道義學(倫理學之一)。

De·o vo·len·te [ˈdiovoˈlɛntɪ; ˈdiːouvouˈlenti] 〖拉〗如蒙上帝恩允;悉聽神意(=God willing; if God wills it).

de·ox·i·dize [diˈɑksəˌdaɪz; diːˈɔksidaiz] *v.t.*, **-dized, -diz·ing.** 除氧;使還原;脫氧。

「ˈɔksidaizə] *n.* 還原劑;去氧劑。」

de·ox·i·diz·er [diˈɑksəˌdaɪzɚ; diː-

de·ox·y·gen·ate [diˈɑksədʒənˌet; diːˈɔksidʒəneit] *v.t.*, **-at·ed, -at·ing.** =**deoxidize.**

de·ox·y·ri·bo·nu·cle·ic acid [diˈɑksɪˌraɪbonʊˌkliɪk～; diːˈɑːksiˌraibounjuˌkliːik～] =**DNA.** (亦作 **deoxyribose nucleic acid**)

de·ox·y·ri·bose [dɪˌɑksəˈraɪbos; diˌɔksəˈraibous] *n.* 去氧核糖(分子式 $C_5H_{10}O_4$)。

dep. ①departed. ②department. ③departs. ④departure. ⑤deponent. ⑥depot. ⑦deputy.

:de·part [dɪˈpɑrt; diˈpɑːt] *v.i.* ①離去;離開;出發。to *depart* for America. 動身去美國。The train *departs* at 6 a.m. 火車早晨六時開。②違反;放棄〖from〗. Old people don't like to *depart* from old customs. 老人們不願意放棄舊習慣。③死。to *depart* from this life. 死亡;辭世。—*v.t.* 離開(很少用,僅用於下列辭句)。to *depart* this life. 死去。—*n.* 〖古〗出發;死亡。

de·part·ed [dɪˈpɑrtɪd; diˈpɑːtid] *n. sing.* or *pl.* 死人。—*adj.* 死的;過去的。

:de·part·ment [dɪˈpɑrtmənt; diˈpɑːtmənt] *n.* ①部分;部門。②系;科;所。We have twelve *departments* in our college. 我們學院有十二系。③部;局;處;司;科。④行政區(如法國等的)。⑤(D-)〖美軍〗衛戍區。⑥專長;專責。

de·part·men·tal [dɪˌpɑrtˈmɛntl̩; ˌdiːpɑːtˈmentl] *adj.* ①部分的;局、處、司、科、系、所等的。②分類的。—**ly,** *adv.*

「院。」

Department of State 〖美〗國務

Department of Trusteeship Council (聯合國)託管理事會。

department store 百貨商店;百貨公司。(英亦作 **departmental store**)

de·par·ture** [dɪˈpɑrtʃɚ; diˈpɑːtʃə] *n.* ①離去;離開;出發;分別。②改變;變更;違反〖from〗. ③新行動或方針的開始。new *departure.* 新政策;新方針。take one's departure*** 離去。

de·pas·ture [dɪˈpæstʃɚ; diːˈpɑːstʃə] *v.*, **-tured, -tur·ing.** —*v.t.* ①食掉(某地)之草。②牧(畜);放(牛、羊)。—*v.i.* 食草。

:de·pend [dɪˈpɛnd; diˈpend] *v.i.* ①信賴;信任〖on, upon〗. Can I *depend* on you? 我可以信賴你嗎? ②依賴;依靠〖on, upon〗. Children *depend* on their parents for food and clothing. 小孩的衣食均依賴父母。③視…而定〖on, upon〗. Whether he can go to America or not *depends* on the amount of money he can have. 他能去美國與否端視他能有多少錢而定。④懸;垂

〖from〗. ⑤〖文法〗附屬於其他字句。⑥無法決定;懸宕。I may go to Europe or I may not, it all *depends*. 我去不去歐洲,要看情形(決定)。*depend upon it* 無疑地。—**er,** *n.*

de·pend·a·bil·i·ty [dɪ͵pɛndəˈbɪlətɪ; di͵pendəˈbiliti] *n.* 可信任;可靠性。

de·pend·a·ble [dɪˈpɛndəbl̩; diˈpendəbl] *adj.* 可信賴或可靠的。—**ness,** *n.* —**de·pend·a·bly,** *adv.*

***de·pend·ant** [dɪˈpɛndənt; diˈpendənt] *adj., n.* =**dependent.** —**ly,** *adv.*

***de·pend·ence** [dɪˈpɛndəns; diˈpendəns] *n.* ①信賴;信任。We have firm *dependence* upon the will of God. 我們堅定信賴上帝的意旨。②依賴;依靠。③視…而定 ④隸屬;順從;服從。⑤所依賴的人或東西。(亦作 **dependance**)

de·pend·en·cy [dɪˈpɛndənsɪ; diˈpendənsi] *n., pl.* **-cies.** ①依賴;信任;信賴。②附屬物。③屬國;屬地;附庸。④房屋之一翼。(亦作 **dependancy**)

***de·pend·ent** [dɪˈpɛndənt; diˈpendənt] *adj.* ①依賴的;倚靠的。A child is *dependent* on its parents. 小孩依賴其父母。②關連的;受影響的;受控制的。③懸垂的;下垂的。—*n.* ①依賴他人者;侍從;隨員。②家眷。(亦作 **dependant**) —**ly,** *adv.*

dependent clause 〖文法〗從屬子句(從屬子句具備主詞和述詞,但不能獨立)。(亦作 **subordinate clause**)

de·pict [dɪˈpɪkt;diˈpikt] *v.t.* ①描畫。②敍述。—**er,** —**or,** **de·pic·tion,** *n.* —**de·pic·tive,** *adj.*

de·pic·ture[1] [dɪˈpɪktʃɚ; diˈpiktʃə] *v.t.,* **-tured, -tur·ing.** 想像。

de·pic·ture[2] *n.* ①描畫。②敍述。

dep·i·late [ˈdɛpə͵let; ˈdepileit] *v.t.,* **-lat·ed, -lat·ing.** 去…之髮;爲…去毛。—**dep·i·la·tion, dep·i·la·tor,** *n.*

de·pil·a·to·ry [dɪˈpɪlə͵torɪ;diˈpilətəri] *adj., n., pl.* **-ries.** —*adj.* 去毛髮的;除毛性的。—*n.* 除毛劑;脫毛劑。

de·plane [diˈplen; diːˈplein] *v.i.,* **de·planed, de·plan·ing.** 下飛機;從飛機卸下。

de·plete [dɪˈplit; diˈpliːt] *v.t.,* **-plet·ed, -plet·ing.** ①使空虛;用盡。②〖醫〗放血。

de·ple·tion [dɪˈpliʃən; diˈpliːʃən] *n.* ①空虛;涸竭。②〖醫〗放血;減液法。

de·ple·tive [dɪˈplitɪv; diˈpliːtiv] *adj.* (亦作 **depletory**) 使空虛的;放血的;減液的。—*n.* 減血藥;放血之物。

de·plor·a·ble [dɪˈplorəbl̩;diˈplɔːrəbl] *adj.* ①悲哀的;可嘆的。②不幸的;可憐的。—**de·plor·a·bly,** *adv.*

de·plore [dɪˈplor;diˈplɔː] *v.t.,* **-plored, -plor·ing.** 悲痛;深悔。

de·ploy [dɪˈplɔɪ; diˈplɔi] *v.t. & v.i.* ①〖軍〗散開成戰鬥隊形。②布署。③展開。—**ment,** *n.*

de·plume [dɪˈplum; diːˈpluːm] *v.t.,* **-plumed, -plum·ing.** ①剝去…之羽毛;拔毛。②剝奪…之榮譽、財富等。

de·po·lar·i·za·tion [di͵polərəˈzeʃən; ˈdiː͵pouləraiˈzeiʃən] *n.* ①〖磁學,電〗去極;去偏極。②〖光學〗去偏光。

de·po·lar·ize [diˈpolə͵raɪz; diːˈpouləraiz] *v.t.,* **-ized, -iz·ing.** ①〖磁學,電〗去極;去偏極。②〖光學〗去偏光。③攪亂;消解(偏見等)。

de·pol·lute [͵dipəˈlut;͵diːpəˈluːt] *v.t.,* **-lut·ed, -lut·ing.** 免除汚染。

de·pone [dɪˈpon; diˈpoun] *v.t. & v.i.,* **-poned, -pon·ing.** 〖法律〗作證;發誓證明。

de·po·nent [dɪˈponənt; diˈpounənt] *adj.* (希臘文和拉丁文之動詞)有被動之形而含自動之意的;相異的。—*n.* ①(希臘文和拉丁文法中)有被動之形而含自動之意的動詞;相異動詞。②證人;作證者。

de·pop·u·late [diˈpɑpjə͵let; diːˈpɔpjuleit] *v.t.,* **-lat·ed, -lat·ing.** 減少…之人口;使人口減少。

de·pop·u·la·tion [͵dipɑpjəˈleʃən; diː͵pɔpjuˈleiʃən] *n.* 人口減少。

de·port [dɪˈport; diˈpɔːt] *v.t.* ①驅逐出境。②放逐;充軍。③擧止;處己;持身(與反身代名詞連用)。—**a·ble,** *adj.*

de·por·ta·tion [͵diporˈteʃən;͵diːpɔːˈteiʃən] *n.* 移送;充軍;放逐。

de·por·tee [͵diporˈti; ͵diːpɔːˈtiː] *n.* 被放逐者。

de·port·ment [dɪˈportmənt;diˈpɔːtmənt] *n.* ①風度;行爲;態度。②學生在校之品行。

de·pos·a·ble [dɪˈpozəbl̩; diˈpouzəbl] *adj.* 可廢黜的;可革職的。

de·pos·al [dɪˈpozl̩; diˈpouzl] *n.* 免職;廢位。

***de·pose** [dɪˈpoz; diˈpouz] *v.t.,* **-posed, -pos·ing.** ①免職;革職;廢(王位)。The king was *deposed* by the revolution. 那國王由於革命而被廢除王位。②宣誓作證。—*v.i.* 作證(尤指以書面的)。

***de·pos·it** [dɪˈpɑzɪt; diˈpɔzit] *v.t.* ①放下;置下。②貯存;存儲。He always *deposits* half of his salary in the bank. 他總是將一半薪水存儲於銀行。③沈澱;沈積。④抵押;交保證金。⑤放硬幣於以硬幣操作之機器內。⑥留下。Please *deposit* your returned books with the librarian. 請將你要還的書留在圖書館管理員處。—*v.i.* ①堆積;沈澱;附着。②抵押;留下;放下。—*n.* ①堆積物;沈澱物。②〖礦〗礦床。③存放物;存款。current *deposit*. 活期存款。fixed *deposit*. 定期存款。trust *deposit*. 信託存款。④押金;保證金。⑤保管處。*on deposit* 置存;存於銀行。to place money *on deposit*. 存貯款項。

de·pos·i·tar·y[1] [dɪˈpɑzə͵tɛrɪ; diˈpɔzitəri] *n., pl.* **-tar·ies.** ①保管人;受託人;信託公司。②存放處;貯藏所;倉庫。

de·pos·i·tar·y[2] *adj.* ①接受存款的(銀行)。②礦脈的。

dep·o·si·tion [͵dɛpəˈzɪʃən; ͵depəˈziʃən] *n.* ①廢位;革職。②堆積;沈澱。③證據;證明;口供;證言。④堆積物;沈澱物。⑤耶穌降架(由十字架上解下);其畫、用狀等。

deposit money 即可兌現之支票、信用狀等。

de·pos·i·tor [dɪˈpɑzɪtɚ; diˈpɔzitə] *n.* ①寄託者;存款者。②沈澱器;鍍金槽。

de·pos·i·to·ry [dɪˈpɑzə͵torɪ; diˈpɔzitəri] *n., pl.* **-ries.** ①受託者;保管者。②儲藏室;倉庫;寶庫。a *depository* of learning. 知識的寶庫。

deposit slip 存款單。(亦作 **credit slip**)

***de·pot** [ˈdipo, ˈdɛpo; ˈdepou] *n.* ①庫房;倉庫。②火車站;公共汽車站;航空站。③軍械庫;補給站。④新兵訓練站。

depot ship 〖海軍〗補給艦;母艦。

dep·ra·va·tion [͵dɛprəˈveʃən; ͵deprəˈveiʃən] *n.* 惡化;頹廢;墮落。

de·prave [dɪˈprev; diˈpreiv] *v.t.,* **-praved, -prav·ing.** 使敗壞;使腐敗。

de·praved [dɪˈprevd; diˈpreivd] *adj.*

敗壞的;墮落的;邪惡的。
de·prav·i·ty [dɪ'prævətɪ; di'præviti] *n., pl.* -ties. 墮落;腐敗;邪惡。
dep·re·cate ['dɛprə,ket; 'deprikeit] *v.t.,* **-cat·ed, -cat·ing.** 抗議;駁斥;不贊成。
dep·re·cat·ing·ly ['dɛprɪ,ketɪŋlɪ; 'deprikeitiŋli] *adv.* 大不贊成地;反對地;深悔地。 「pri'keiʃən] *n.* 不贊成;反對。
dep·re·ca·tion [,dɛprə'keʃən; ,de-
dep·re·ca·to·ry ['dɛprəkə,torɪ; 'deprikeitəri] *adj.* ①不贊成的; 反對的。②表示歉意的;求恕的。
de·pre·ci·ate [dɪ'priʃɪ,et; di'pri:ʃieit] *v.t. & v.i.,* **-at·ed, -at·ing.** ①減價;跌價。②輕視;毀謗。③貶值。④〖美〗〖會計〗折舊;以折舊準備減縮(固定資產)的成本。
de·pre·ci·a·tion [dɪ,priʃɪ'eʃən; di,pri:ʃi'eiʃən] *n.* ①跌價;貶值。*depreciation* of the currency. 通貨貶值。②輕視;毀謗。③折舊。
de·pre·ci·a·to·ry [dɪ'priʃɪə,torɪ; di'pri:ʃieitəri] *adj.* ①跌價的; 貶值的;折舊的。②輕視的;毀謗的。
dep·re·date ['dɛprɪ,det; 'deprideit] *v.t. & v.i.,* **-dat·ed, -dat·ing.** 刼掠;掠取;蹂躪。
dep·re·da·tion [,dɛprɪ'deʃən; ,depri'deiʃən] *n.* 搶奪;刼掠;蹂躪;毀滅。
***de·press** [dɪ'prɛs; di'pres] *v.t.* ①壓下;降低。to *depress* the price of rice. 抑低米價。②使沮喪。③使不活潑; 使蕭條。④減價;貶值。⑤〖音樂〗降調。
de·pres·sant [dɪ'prɛsn̩t; di'presnt] *adj.* ①有鎮靜作用的。②蕭條的; 不景氣的。③令人沮喪的。—*n.* 抑制劑;鎮靜劑。
de·pressed [dɪ'prɛst; di'prest] *adj.* ①憂傷的; 抑鬱的; 精神不振的。②壓下的;降低的。③〖動、植物〗扁平的。④經濟蕭條的。
de·press·i·ble [dɪ'prɛsəbl̩; di'presibl] *adj.* 可壓抑的;可抑低的。
de·press·ing [dɪ'prɛsɪŋ; di'presiŋ] *adj.* 壓抑的;鬱悶的。—**ly,** *adv.*
de·pres·sion** [dɪ'prɛʃən; di'preʃən] *n.* ①降低。②窪穴;凹陷。③愁苦;沮喪。He is in a state of deep *depression* on account of his failure to pass the examination. 他因考試失敗而深為沮喪。④〖商業〗蕭條; 不景氣。Business *depressions* usually cause misery among the working classes. 商業的不景氣,常使勞工階級受苦。⑤〖醫〗抑鬱症。⑥盆地。⑦〖氣象〗低氣壓;低氣壓區。the Depression*** or ***Great Depression*** 一九二九年開始的世界經濟蕭條(恐慌)。
de·pres·sive [dɪ'prɛsɪv; di'presiv] *adj.* ①沮喪的;(令人)抑鬱的。②壓抑的; 降低的。③不景氣的。
de·pres·sor [dɪ'prɛsɚ; di'presə] *n.* ①壓抑者。②〖解剖〗壓低肌;下掣肌。③減壓神經。④〖醫〗(檢驗或手術用)壓板;壓器。a tongue *depressor.* 壓舌器;壓舌板。⑤血壓下降劑;抑壓劑。
de·pres·sur·ize [dɪ'prɛʃə,raɪz; di'preʃəraiz] *v.t.,* **-ized, -iz·ing.** (飛機內部等)減壓。(亦作 **depressurise**)
de·priv·a·ble [bɪ'praɪvəbl̩; di'praivəbl] *adj.* 可剝奪的。「=deprivation.
de·priv·al [dɪ'praɪvl̩; di'praivl] *n.*
dep·ri·va·tion [,dɛprɪ'veʃən; ,depri'veiʃən] *n.* ①奪去;剝奪。②損失;喪失。③撤職。④清苦之生活。
***de·prive** [dɪ'praɪv; di'praiv] *v.t.,* **-prived, -priv·ing.** ①奪去; 剝奪; 使喪失〖of〗. An accident *deprived* him of his sight. 意外的事使他失明。②使不能有;使不能享受。③撤職。 「deponent.
dept. ①department. ②deputy. ③
depth** [dɛpθ; depθ] *n.* ①深;深度。The snow is five feet in *depth.* 雪深五英尺。②縱深。③最內部; 深處。in the *depth* of winter. 在嚴冬。④深奧;奧妙。⑤深厚;濃厚。⑥低沉。⑦(常 *pl.*) 知識或道德上之低落。⑧嚴重性。⑨球隊之潛力(指預備隊員之人數及技術)。beyond*** (or ***out of***) ***one's depth*** **a.** 入水至沒頂的深度。**b.** 不能理解;力所不及。***in depth*** 廣泛地;徹底地。 「炸彈。
depth bomb (or **charge**) 深水
dep·u·rate ['dɛpjə,ret; 'depjureit] *v.,* **-rat·ed, -rat·ing.** —*v.t.* 使清潔; 使純潔。—*v.i.* 變清潔;變純潔。
dep·u·ta·tion [,dɛpjə'teʃən; ,depju:'teiʃən] *n.* ①代理者;代表團。②代表或代理人之指派。
de·pute [dɪ'pjut; di'pju:t] *v.t.,* **-put·ed, -put·ing.** ①指定或委託(某人)為代理或代表。②以(權、職等)授(或委)予代理人。
dep·u·tize ['dɛpjə,taɪz; 'depjutaiz] *v.,* **-tized, -tiz·ing.** —*v.t.* 委託…為代表; 授權為…代理。—*v.i.* 充任代理或代表〖for〗.
***dep·u·ty** ['dɛpjətɪ; 'depjuti] *n., pl.* **-ties.** ①代理人; 代表。②副主官;副主管。③議員。Chamber of *Deputies.* (法國等的)衆議院。④副警長。—*adj.* 代理的; 副的。a *deputy* mayor. 副市長。
der. ① derivation. ② derivative. ③ derive. ④derived.
de·rail [di'rel; di'reil] *v.t.* 使(火車)出軌。—*v.i.* 出軌。—*n.* 緊急時可使機車出軌的軌道裝置。 「mənt] *n.* 出軌。
de·rail·ment [di'relmənt; di'reil-
de·range [dɪ'rendʒ; di'reindʒ] *v.t.,* **-ranged, -rang·ing.** ①使錯亂;擾亂。②使精神錯亂;使發狂。
de·ranged [dɪ'rendʒd; di'reindʒd] *adj.* ①混亂的;錯亂的。②瘋狂的。
de·range·ment [dɪ'rendʒmənt; di'reindʒmənt] *n.* ①混亂; 精神錯亂; 發狂。②擾亂。 「**-rat·ing.** 減免(稅)。
de·rate [di'ret; di:'reit] *v.t.,* **-rat·ed,**
de·ra·tion [di'reʃən; 'di:'ræʃən] *v.t.* 停止(物品之)配給。
Der·by ['dɑrbɪ; 'dɑ:bi] *n., pl.* **-bies.** ①德貝(英格蘭中部的城市)。②英國之大賽馬會(德貝伯爵所創立,與賽之馬年齡均為三歲,是日稱為 Derby Day)。③賽馬會。④(d-)有獎的公開賽。 「質之禮帽。
der·by ['dɝbɪ; 'dɑ:bi] *n.* 圓頂窄邊絲
der·e·lict ['dɛrə,lɪkt; 'derilikt] *adj.* ①被棄的。②疏忽職務的; 不忠的。 —*n.* ①被棄漂流於海上之船。②被遺棄的人或物。③疏忽職務的人。④海水退落而露出之新土地。
der·e·lic·tion [,dɛrə'lɪkʃən; ,deri'likʃən] *n.* ①放棄; 遺棄。②玩忽職務; 曠職。③〖法律〗**a.** (因海水漸退而致之)陸地之擴展。**b.** 海浦新生地。
de·req·ui·si·tion [di,rɛkwə'zɪʃən; di:,rekwi'ziʃən] *n.* 〖英〗退還曾被徵收之財產(尤指自軍方退還民間)。 —*v.t. & v.i.* 退還曾被徵收之財產、事業等給民間。
de·ride [dɪ'raɪd; di'raid] *v.t.,* **-rid·ed, -rid·ing.** 嘲笑;愚弄。

de·rid·ing·ly [dɪˈraɪdɪŋlɪ; diˈraidiŋli] *adv.* 嘲笑地;愚弄地。
de·ri·sion [dɪˈrɪʒən; diˈriʒən] *n.* ①嘲笑;愚弄。②被嘲弄之人或物;笑柄。
de·ri·sive [dɪˈraɪsɪv; diˈraisiv] *adj.* ①嘲笑的;愚弄的。②可笑的;值得嘲弄的。**—ly,** *adv.* **—ness,** *n.*
de·ri·so·ry [dɪˈraɪsərɪ; diˈraisəri] *adj.* =**derisive.**
deriv. ① derivation. ② derivative. ③ derive. ④ derived.
de·riv·a·ble [dɪˈraɪvəbl̩; diˈraivəbl] *adj.* 可引出的;可誘導的;可推考的。
der·i·va·tion [ˌdɛrəˈveʃən; ˌderiˈveiʃən] *n.* ①引出;誘導;轉來;得來。②起源;由來。③引出的事物。④〖數學〗求導;微分法。⑤〖文法〗引申;引申語。
de·riv·a·tive [dəˈrɪvətɪv; diˈrivətiv] *adj.* 引出的;轉來的。—*n.* ①引出之物;誘導而來之物;轉來之物。②衍生字;引申字;轉生字。③〖化〗衍生物。④〖數學〗導數;微商;紀數。**—ly,** *adv.* **—ness,** *n.*
***de·rive** [dəˈraɪv; diˈraiv] *v.t.,* **-rived, -riv·ing.** ①獲得;得來〖from〗. to *derive* pleasure from reading. 由讀書獲得快樂。②起源;由來;出自。Many English words are *derived* from Latin. 許多英文字是源於拉丁文。③推論;推究。④追溯根源;溯源。⑤〖化〗衍生。—*v.i.* 起源;發生〖常from〗.
derm- 〖字首〗表"皮;膜"之義。(亦作 **dermat-, dermato-, dermo-**)
-derm 〖字尾〗表"皮;膜"之義。
der·ma [ˈdɜmə; ˈdəːmə] *n.* 〖解剖,動物〗①眞皮。②(一般之)皮膚。**—der·mal,** *adj.*
der·ma·ti·tis [ˌdɜməˈtaɪtɪs; ˌdəːməˈtaitis] *n.* 皮炎。
der·ma·toid [ˈdɜməˌtɔɪd; ˈdəːmətɔid] *adj.* 皮狀的。
der·ma·tol·o·gy [ˌdɜməˈtɑlədʒɪ; ˌdəːməˈtɔlədʒi] *n.* 皮膚病學;皮膚學。**—der·ma·tol·o·gist,** *n.*
der·mis [ˈdɜmɪs; ˈdəːmis] *n.*=**derma.**
der·nier res·sort [dɛrˌnjerəˈsɔr; dɛrˌnjei rəˈsɔːr] 〖法〗最後的辦法;最後的手段(=last resort).
der·o·gate [ˈdɛrəˌget; ˈderəgeit] *v.,* **-gat·ed, -gat·ing.** —*v.i.* ①取去;減除;減損〖常from〗. to *derogate* from rights. 喪失權利。②變壞;減退;退步〖常 from〗. —*v.t.* 減去;損毀。**—der·o·ga·tion,** *n.*
de·rog·a·tive [dɪˈrɑgətɪv; diˈrɔgətiv] *adj.* =**derogatory.**
de·rog·a·to·ry [dɪˈrɑgəˌtorɪ; diˈrɔgətəri] *adj.* ①損毀(人之名譽)的;誹謗的。②降低價值的;有損…的。*derogatory* from authority. 有損權威的。
der·rick [ˈdɛrɪk; ˈderik] *n.* ①起重機。②鑽探油井或煤氣井用之井口上的鐵架塔。
der·ring-do [ˈdɛrɪŋˈdu; ˈderiŋˈduː] *n.* 大膽行爲;蠻勇。(亦作 **derring do**)
der·rin·ger [ˈdɛrɪndʒɚ; ˈderindʒə] *n.* 〖美〗大口徑短筒之手槍。(亦作 **deringer**)
der·ris [ˈdɛrɪs; ˈderis] *n.* 〖植物〗魚藤(根莖可作殺虫劑)。
der·vish [ˈdɜvɪʃ; ˈdəːviʃ] *n.* (回教之)苦修僧人。
des·cant[1] [dɛsˈkænt; disˈkænt] *v.i.* ①詳論;絮說〖on, upon〗. ②合唱;合奏。③唱。(亦作 **discant**)
des·cant[2] [ˈdɛskænt; ˈdeskænt] *n.* ①批註;通考;論說。②〖音樂〗**a.** 高音部;轉變之歌曲或旋律。**b.** 歌;旋律。—*adj.* 〖主英〗①女高音的。②最高音的。

Des·cartes [deˈkart; deiˈkɑːt, ˈdeikɑːt] *n.* 笛卡爾 (René, 1596–1650, 法國哲學家及數學家)。
***de·scend** [dɪˈsɛnd; diˈsend] *v.i.* ①降。②傳;傳下來;由來;出自〖from〗. He (is) *descended* from a good family. 他出自名門。③屈身。He *descended* to inferior position. 他屈就低微的職位。④突擊;襲擊。⑤逐漸減少;遞減。⑥(討論等)由一般性的至具體的題目。⑦向下傾斜。⑧下凡。—*v.t.* 降落。**descend upon** (or **on**) 突襲。Our soldiers *descended upon* the enemy. 我們的士兵突擊敵人。
***de·scend·ant** [dɪˈsɛndənt; diˈsendənt] *n.* ①後裔。②傳衣鉢之人或物。③追隨者。—*adj.* 相傳的;下降的。
de·scend·ent [dɪˈsɛndənt; diˈsendənt] *adj.* ①降落的;下降的。②自祖先傳下的。
de·scend·er [dɪˈsɛndɚ; diˈsendə] *n.* ①下降或傳下之人或事物。②〖印刷〗部分筆畫伸向基線下面之字母(如 p, q, j, y 等)。
de·scend·i·ble [dɪˈsɛndəbl̩; diˈsendəbl] *adj.*(可)遺傳的。(亦作 **descendable**)
***de·scent** [dɪˈsɛnt; diˈsent] *n.* ①降下;降落。The balloon made a slow *descent.* 氣球慢慢降落。②傾斜。③下坡的路;下降的方法或工具。④遺傳;遺留;代代相傳。⑤世系;出身;血統。He is of good *descent.* 他出自名門。⑥襲擊。The pirates made frequent *descents* upon the coasts. 海盜時常襲擊該海岸。⑦零落;式微;墮落;屈身。⑧〖法律〗產業之繼承。
de·scrib·a·ble [dɪˈskraɪbəbl̩; disˈkraibəbl] *adj.* 可敍述的;可描畫的;可表明的。
‡**de·scribe** [dɪˈskraɪb; disˈkraib] *v.t.,* **-scribed, -scrib·ing.** ①敍述;記述;描寫;形容。He was *described* as being very clever. 他被形容爲非常聰明。②畫;描;摹;作圖。③畫輪廓;畫成…之形狀。His arm *described* an arc in the air. 他的手臂在空中畫了一個弧形。
de·scrip·tion** [dɪˈskrɪpʃən; disˈkripʃən] *n.* ①敍述;描寫;說明。②種類。The harbor was crowded with vessels of every *description.* 這海港擠滿各種各式的船。③〖幾何〗摹狀。answer to a description*** 與說明或描述的相合。***beyond description*** 難以描寫;難以形容。
de·scrip·tive [dɪˈskrɪptɪv; disˈkriptiv] *adj.* 描寫的;敍述的;說明的。**—ly,** *adv.* **—ness,** *n.*
descriptive geometry 〖數學〗圖形幾何學。
de·scrip·tor [dɪˈskrɪptɚ; disˈkriptə] *n.* 〖電腦〗述語(指認物體之符號)。
de·scry [dɪˈskraɪ; disˈkrai] *v.t.,* **-scried, -scry·ing.** 察看;發現;遠遠看到。
des·e·crate [ˈdɛsɪˌkret; ˈdesikreit] *v.t.,* **-crat·ed, -crat·ing.** 褻瀆;汚辱;把(神物)供俗用。**—des·e·crat·er, des·e·crat·or,** *n.*
des·e·cra·tion [ˌdɛsɪˈkreʃən; ˌdesiˈkreiʃən] *n.* 汚辱神物;褻瀆神聖。
de·seg·re·gate [diˈsɛgrəˌget; diːˈsegrigeit] *v.t.* & *v.i.,* **-gat·ed, -gat·ing.** 取消種族隔離。
de·seg·re·ga·tion [diˌsɛgrəˈgeʃən; ˌdiːsegriˈgeiʃən] *n.* 取消種族隔離。
de·sen·si·tize [diˈsɛnsəˌtaɪz; diːˈsensitaiz] *v.t.,* **-tized, -tiz·ing.** ①除去…之感覺;使較不敏感。②〖生理〗使(人、動物、體素等)對外來刺激不起反應或不敏感。③〖照相〗

使減低感光性。

‡**de·sert¹** ['dɛzət; 'dezət] *n.* ①沙漠。the Sahara *Desert.* 撒哈拉沙漠。an oasis in a *desert.* 沙漠中的綠洲。②不毛之地。③海洋中魚類無法生存之處。④缺乏某事之地方。—*adj.*①沙漠的;荒蕪不毛的。a *desert* island. 荒島。②荒地的;荒漠的。③生長於沙漠的。

***de·sert²** [dɪ'zɝt; di'zə:t] *v.t.* ①放棄;遺棄。He *deserted* his wife. 他遺棄他的妻。②〖軍〗開小差;逃亡;潛逃。③失去;離去。All his courage *deserted* him. 他勇氣盡失。—*v.i.* ①〖軍〗開小差;逃亡;棄職潛逃。A soldier who *deserts* is punished. 士兵逃亡要受懲罰。②離開;他往。Many *deserted* during the food shortage. 飢荒中許多人逃往他鄉。—**er,** *n.*

de·sert³ [dɪ'zɝt; di'zə:t] *n.* ①(常 *pl.*)應得的賞罰。Some people failed to get their *deserts.* 有的人沒有得到應得的賞罰。②功或過。③功;德。He is a man of *desert.* 他是一個有功的人。

de·sert·ed [dɪ'zɝtɪd; di'zə:tid] *adj.* ①荒蕪的;荒廢的;爲人所棄的。a *deserted* village 荒村。②人跡罕至的;荒僻的。

de·ser·tion [dɪ'zɝʃən; di'zə:ʃən] *n.* ①放棄;背棄;遺棄。②擅離職守;開小差。

***de·serve** [dɪ'zɝv; di'zə:v] *v.,* **-served, -serv·ing.** —*v.t.* 應得;應受(賞罰等)。If you do wrong, you *deserve* punishment. 你如做錯事,你應受罰。—*v.i.* 應得報酬。His good conduct is *deserving* of the highest praise. 他的良好品行應得最高的稱讚。

de·served [dɪ'zɝvd; di'zə:vd] *adj.* 應得的;當然的。—**ly,** *adv.*

de·serv·ing [dɪ'zɝvɪŋ; di'zə:viŋ] *n.* 應得之賞罰;功績。—*adj.* ①相當的;值得的〖of〗。②有功的;功績的。③應得幫助、酬勞等的。—**ly,** *adv.*

des·ha·bille [ˌdɛzə'bil; 'dezæbi:l] *n.* =**dishabille.**

des·ic·cant ['dɛsəkənt; 'desikənt] *adj.* 使乾燥的。—*n.* 乾燥劑。

des·ic·cate ['dɛsəˌket; 'desikeit] *v.,* **-cat·ed, -cat·ing.** —*v.t.* ①使完全乾涸;使乾。②乾貯(食物)。—*v.i.* 變乾。—**des·ic·ca·tion,** *n.*

des·ic·cat·ed ['dɛsəˌketɪd; 'desikeitid] *adj.* 脫水的;粉狀的。

des·ic·ca·tive ['dɛsəˌketɪv; de'sikətiv] *adj., n.* =**desiccant.**

des·ic·ca·tor ['dɛsəˌketɚ; 'desikeitə] *n.* ①使乾燥之人或物。②乾燥器;防潮之容器。

de·sid·er·a·ta [dɪˌsɪdə'retə; diˌzidə'reitə] *n.* pl. of **desideratum.**

de·sid·er·ate [dɪ'sɪdəˌret; di'zidəreit] *v.t.,* **-at·ed, -at·ing.** 渴望;亟需。

de·sid·er·a·tive [dɪ'sɪdəˌetɪv; di'zidəreitiv] *adj.* ①慾望的;有慾求的;表示願望的。②〖文法〗願望的。—*n.* 〖文法〗願望動詞。

de·sid·er·a·tum [dɪˌsɪdə'retəm; diˌzidə'reitəm] *n., pl.* **-ta.** 所願望之事物;缺乏之物;迫切需要之事物。

‡**de·sign** [dɪ'zaɪn; di'zain] *n.* ①圖案;圖樣;美術工藝品等的設計。②美術工藝品、建築等之形式、顏色和細節的配置。③製作模型、圖案、圖樣等技術。④藝術的產品。⑤計畫;腹案。⑥(*pl.*)企圖;圖謀〖on, upon〗。The thief had *designs* upon the safe. 這賊對保險箱打主意。⑦計畫;故意;目的。***have designs on*** (or ***against***) (有野心或惡意的)圖謀。He *had designs on* your life. 他有意謀害你的命。—*v.t.* ①作圖案;打圖樣;設計(圖案、圖樣等)。②(在心中)計劃;設計;盤算。③企圖;圖謀。④意欲;指定;預定。His parents *designed* him for the navy. 他的父母意欲使他習海軍。—*v.i.* ①作圖案;打圖樣;設計(圖案、圖樣等)。She *designs* for a coat manufacturer. 她爲外衣製造廠家設計圖樣。②企圖;志願。My brother *designs* to be an engineer. 我的弟弟志願做工程師。

***des·ig·nate** [*v.* 'dɛzɪgˌnet; 'dezigneit *adj.* 'dɛzɪgnɪt, -ˌnet; 'dezignit, -neit] *v.,* **-nat·ed, -nat·ing,** *adj.* —*v.t.* ①指出;指定;指示;標明。②指派;派定;任命。to *designate* a person for some office. 任命某人任某職。③指名;命名。—*adj.* 指派好的;選派好的。a bishop *designate.* 尚未就任的主教。

des·ig·na·tion [ˌdɛzɪg'neʃən; ˌdezig'neiʃən] *n.* ①指示;指定。②任命;選任。③名稱;稱呼。

des·ig·na·tor ['dɛzɪgˌnetɚ; 'dezigneitə] *n.* ①指示者;指定者。②古羅馬之儀注官。

de·signed [dɪ'zaɪnd; di'zaind] *adj.* 計畫的;原意的。

de·sign·ed·ly [dɪ'zaɪnɪdlɪ; di'zainidli] *adv.* 有計畫地;故意地。

***de·sign·er** [dɪ'zaɪnɚ; di'zainə] *n.* ①設計家;計劃者;打圖樣的人。②陰謀者。

de·sign·ing [dɪ'zaɪnɪŋ; di'zainiŋ] *adj.* ①狡猾的;詭譎的;陰謀的。②表現有計畫的或蓄意的。—*n.* 設計;陰謀。

***de·sir·a·bil·i·ty** [dɪˌzaɪrə'bɪlətɪ; diˌzaiərə'biliti] *n.* 可取之處;有想望之價值;優點;妙處。Nobody doubts the *desirability* of good health. 沒有人對健康的好處表示懷疑。

***de·sir·a·ble** [dɪ'zaɪrəbl; di'zaiərəbl] *adj.* 值得要的;合意的;悅人心意的;良好的;優良的。a quiet, *desirable* neighborhood. 一個幽靜、合意的區域。—*n.* 合意的人或事物。—**ness,** *n.*

de·sir·a·bly [dɪ'zaɪrəblɪ; di'zaiərəbli] *adv.* 合意地;願望地。

‡**de·sire** [dɪ'zaɪr; di'zaiə] *v.,* **-sired, -sir·ing,** *n.* —*v.t.* ①想要;意欲;願望。He *desires* a college education. 他欲受大學教育。②請求;要求。He *desires* that you should see him at once. 他請求你立即見他。***leave much to be desired*** 缺點不少。***leave nothing to be desired*** 一點缺點也沒有。—*v.i.* 有慾望。—*n.* ①願望;渴望。His *desire* is to travel. 他熱望旅行。②請求;祈求。③想要的東西。I hope you will get your *desire.* 我希望你將得到你所想要的東西。④肉慾;情慾。

de·sired [dɪ'zaɪrd; di'zaiəd] *adj.* ①渴望的;想得到的。②合適的;適宜的。

de·sir·ous [dɪ'zaɪrəs; di'zaiərəs] *adj.* 渴望的;希望的。We are all *desirous* of success. 我們都渴望成功。

de·sist [dɪ'zɪst; di'zist] *v.i.* 止;停止〖from〗;休想;斷念。

‡**desk** [dɛsk; desk] *n.* ①書桌;辦公桌。②教堂內講道時擺書之桌子。③說教壇。④政府機關或報館內負責某方工作的部門。city *desk.* 採訪部。foreign *desk.* 外電部。⑤樂譜架。⑥(交響樂團中的)位子。—*adj.* ①書桌的。a *desk* drawer. 書桌的抽屜。②在辦公桌的;坐辦公桌的。—*v.t.* 派(某人)做辦公室工作。

desk·bound ['dɛskˌbaund; 'deskbaund] *adj.* ①(工作等)坐辦公桌的。②(坐辦公桌)與實際情況脫節的。③無戰鬥任務的。

desk·man ['dɛskˌmæn; 'deskmæn]

n., pl. **-men** [ˈ-ˌmɛn;-men]. ①(新聞)助理編輯。②坐辦公桌的人。

desk·mate [ˈdɛskˌmet; ˈdeskmeit] *n.* 同坐一張課桌之學生。

desk work ①書桌上之工作。②書寫「之工作。」

***des·o·late** [*adj.* ˈdɛslɪt; ˈdesəlit *v.* ˈdɛslˌet; ˈdesəleit] *adj., v.,* **-lat·ed, -lat·ing.** —*adj.* ①荒涼的;無人烟的。The island was *desolate.* 此島荒無人烟。②荒蕪的;荒廢的。③被棄的; 孤獨的。④不幸的; 可憐的;絕望的。⑤淒涼的;枯寂的。—*v.t.* ①使荒蕪;使無人烟。②使悲慘。③遺棄。—**ly,** *adv.* —**ness, des·o·lat·er, des·o·la·tor,** *n.*

***des·o·la·tion** [ˌdɛslˈeʃən; ˌdesəˈleiʃən] *n.* ①無人烟;荒蕪;荒廢。②悲慘;毀滅。③孤寂。He lost his wife and was in *desolation.* 他因妻死而孤寂一身。④荒地;廢墟。⑤憂傷;悲哀。

de·sorb [dɪˈsɔrb; diˈsɔːb] *v.t.* 〖化〗釋出被吸收之物。—**de·sorp·tion,** *n.*

***de·spair** [dɪˈspɛr; disˈpɛə] *n.* ①失望;絕望。He gave up the attempt in *despair.* 他失望地放棄嘗試。②令人失望的人或物。—*v.i.* 失望;絕望;斷念〖of〗. They *despaired* of winning the game. 他們不抱比賽得勝的希望。

***de·spair·ing** [dɪˈspɛrɪŋ; disˈpɛəriŋ] *adj.* 感覺絕望的; 表現絕望的; 失望的。a *despairing* look. 失望的神情。—**ly,** *adv.*

***des·patch** [dɪˈspætʃ; disˈpætʃ] *v., n.* =**dispatch.**

des·per·a·do [ˌdɛspəˈredo; ˌdespəˈrɑːdou] *n., pl.* **-does, -dos.** 惡漢;亡命徒。

***des·per·ate** [ˈdɛspərɪt; ˈdespərit] *adj.* ①失望的; 絕望的;嚴重的; 危險的。②預備冒險的; 因無望而不惜冒險的。a *desperate* criminal. 亡命之徒。③極度的;非常的;極壞的。a *desperate* fool. 極愚的人。④無望的;絕望的; 不抱希望的。⑤孤注一擲的。The doctor made a last, *desperate* attempt to save the child's life. 醫生做最後孤注一擲的努力,希望能挽救這孩子的生命。—**ly,** *adv.* —**ness,** *n.*

des·per·a·tion [ˌdɛspəˈreʃən; ˌdespəˈreiʃən] *n.* ①不顧一切以赴;冒險。②失望;絕望。③絕望之事。***in desperation*** 拚命。

des·pi·ca·ble [ˈdɛspɪkəbl; ˈdespikəbl] *adj.* 可鄙的;卑劣的。—**des·pi·ca·bly,** *adv.*

***de·spise** [dɪˈspaɪz; disˈpaiz] *v.t.,* **-spised, -spis·ing.** 輕視;蔑視。

de·spite** [dɪˈspaɪt; disˈpait] *n.* 侮辱;危害。in despite of*** (=in spite of) 不管;不顧。—*prep.* 不顧;雖有;縱使。

de·spite·ful [dɪˈspaɪtfəl; disˈpaitful] *adj.* 〖古〗可鄙的; 可恨的; 惡毒的; 輕侮的。—**ly,** *adv.*

de·spoil [dɪˈspɔɪl; disˈpɔil] *v.t.* 奪取;掠「奪;搶刼。—**ment,** —**er,** *n.*」

de·spo·li·a·tion [dɪˌspolɪˈeʃən; diˌspouliˈeiʃən] *n.* 奪取;掠奪。

de·spond [dɪˈspand; disˈpɔnd] *v.i.* 失掉勇氣;失去希望;沮喪。—*n.* 僅見於下列用語。slough of *despond.* 失望;灰心。

de·spond·ence [dɪˈspandəns; disˈpɔndəns] *n.* =**despondency.**

de·spond·en·cy [dɪˈspandənsɪ; disˈpɔndənsi] *n., pl.* **-cies.** 失望;失去勇氣;意氣消沉。

de·spond·ent [dɪˈspandənt; disˈpɔndənt] *adj.* 失望的;沮喪的; 失去勇氣的;消沉的。—*n.* 心灰意懶者。—**ly,** *adv.*

de·spond·ing [dɪˈspandɪŋ; disˈpɔndiŋ] *adj.* =**despondent.** —**ly,** *adv.*

des·pot [ˈdɛspət; ˈdespɔt] *n.* ①暴君;專制君主。②〖歷史〗拜占庭皇帝及其家屬之名譽稱號。

des·pot·ic [dɪˈspatɪk; desˈpɔtik] *adj.* 專制的;暴虐的;專橫的。(亦作 **despotical**) —**al·ly,** *adv.*

des·pot·ism [ˈdɛspətˌɪzəm; ˈdespətizəm] *n.* ①專制;專制政治;專制政府;暴政。②專制政治統治下之國家。

des·qua·mate [ˈdɛskwəˌmet; ˈdeskwəmeit] *v.i.,* **-mat·ed, -mat·ing.** 脫屑;脫皮。—**des·qua·ma·tion,** *n.*

***des·sert** [dɪˈzɝt; diˈzəːt] *n.* 餐後的甜「點心。」

des·sert·spoon [dɪˈzɝtˌspun; diˈzəːtspuːn] *n.* 中匙(餐後食甜點心之用)。

des·sert·spoon·ful [dɪˈzɝtˌspunful; diˈzəːtˌspuːnful] *n.* 中匙之量 (2½drams).

dessert wine 甜酒 (吃dessert時或餐時飲用者)。

de·ster·i·li·za·tion [diˌstɛrələˈzeʃən; diːˌsterəlaiˈzeiʃən] *n.* 解除貨幣管制;解除禁止使用;(黃金等之)解禁。

de·ster·i·lize [diˈstɛrəˌlaɪz; diːˈsterilaiz] *v.t.,* **-lized, -liz·ing.** 解除凍結;解禁(封存之黃金等)以供發行貨幣之用。

***des·ti·na·tion** [ˌdɛstəˈneʃən; ˌdestiˈneiʃən] *n.* ①目的地。②預定的目的; 意圖。③注定;預定。

des·tine** [ˈdɛstɪn; ˈdestin] *v.t.,* **-tined, -tin·ing.** ①指定;預定。②命運注定。They were *destined* never to meet again. 命運注定他們永不再相逢。be destined for*** **a.** 指定;預定。**b.** 開往。Those ships *were destined for* Cuba. 那些船係開往古巴的。

des·ti·ny** [ˈdɛstənɪ; ˈdestini] *n., pl.* **-nies.** ①命運。②定數;天命。It was his *destiny* to die in a foreign country. 他命定客死異國。③(D-) 命運之女神(司"定數"或事之發展過程之神)。the Destinies*** 命運之三女神。

des·ti·tute [ˈdɛstəˌtjut; ˈdestitjuːt] *adj., v.,* **-tut·ed, -tut·ing.** —*adj.* ①缺乏(食物、衣服、房屋等)的;窮困的。②無;沒有〖常of〗. A bald head is *destitute* of hair. 禿頭就是沒有頭髮。***the destitute*** 貧民。—*v.t.* ①使窮困。②剝奪(職位等)。

des·ti·tu·tion [ˌdɛstəˈtjuʃən; ˌdestiˈtjuːʃən] *n.* 缺乏;貧困。

‡de·stroy [dɪˈstrɔɪ; disˈtrɔi] *v.t.* ①毀壞;破壞。All his hopes were *destroyed.* 所有他的希望都破滅了。②毀滅;消滅。Their army was beaten and *destroyed.* 他們的軍隊被打敗並消滅。③殺戮。 Many lives were *destroyed* by the robbers. 強盜殺死許多人。④抵銷…的效果; 使無效。—*v.i.* 從事於破壞。

de·stroy·er [dɪˈstrɔɪɚ; disˈtrɔiə] *n.* ①破壞者;毀滅者。②驅逐艦。

de·struct [dɪˈstrʌkt; disˈtrʌkt] *adj.* 破壞的。—*n.* 故意或有計畫的破壞。—*v.t.* 破壞。

de·struct·i·ble [dɪˈstrʌktəbl; disˈtrʌktəbl] *adj.* 可破壞的; 易毀壞的。—**de·struct·i·bil·i·ty,** *n.*

***de·struc·tion** [dɪˈstrʌkʃən; disˈtrʌkʃən] *n.* ①毀壞;毀滅。②被毀的原因或方法。Gambling was his *destruction.* 賭博爲他毀滅的原因。

de·struc·tion·ist [dɪˈstrʌkʃənɪst;

disˈtrʌkʃənist] *n.* 破壞主義者。

***de·struc·tive** [dɪˈstrʌktɪv; disˈtrʌktiv] *adj.* ①破壞的;毀壞的(爲 constructive 之對)。②消極的;否定的;有害的。Drinking is *destructive* to health. 飲酒有害於健康。—**ly,** *adv.*

destructive distillation 〖化〗分解蒸餾;乾餾。

de·struc·tor [dɪˈstrʌktɚ; disˈtrʌktə] *n.* ①〖英〗垃圾焚化爐。②破壞者。

des·ue·tude [ˈdɛswɪˌtjud; diˈsjuːitjuːd] *n.* 廢止;廢(爲 consuetude 之對)。

de·sul·fu·rize [diˈsʌlfəˌraɪz; diːˈsʌlfəraiz] *v.t.,* **-ized, -iz·ing.** 自…除去硫磺。(亦作 **desulphurize**)

des·ul·to·ry [ˈdɛslˌtorɪ; ˈdesəltəri] *adj.* ①無次序的;不連貫的;散漫的;無目的的;無方法的。②突然出現的。—**des·ul·to·ri·ly,** *adv.* —**des·ul·to·ri·ness,** *n.*

***de·tach** [dɪˈtætʃ; diˈtætʃ] *v.t.* ①分開;解開;分離(爲 attach 之對)。to *detach* a watch from a chain. 將錶與錶鏈分開。②指派擔任特種任務;分遣。—**er,** *n.*

de·tach·a·ble [dɪˈtætʃəbl; diˈtætʃəbl] *adj.* 可分開的; 可分離的; 可分遣的。a notebook with *detachable* leaves. 活葉筆記簿。—**de·tach·a·bil·i·ty,** *n.*

de·tached [dɪˈtætʃt; diˈtætʃt] *adj.* ①分開的;分離的。He lives in a *detached* house. 他住在一所孤立的房屋中。②不受他人影響的;超然的;公平的。—**ly,** *adv.* —**ness,** *n.*

***de·tach·ment** [dɪˈtætʃmənt; diˈtætʃmənt] *n.* ①分開;解開;分離。②〖軍〗支隊;分遣的艦隊。a *detachment* of army. 分遣部隊。③分遣;擔任特殊任務。④脫俗;不過問他人的事。⑤公平;超然;客觀。

:de·tail [*n.* ˈditel, dɪˈtel; ˈdiːteil, diˈteil *v.* dɪˈtel; ˈdiːteil, diˈt-] *n.* ①細節;細事;瑣碎。②細目;條款;整體中的一小部分。Please let me know all the *details.* 請讓我知道所有的條款。③詳委;詳情。④分圖;細圖。⑤〖軍〗特派的小隊。⑥複雜而精細的裝飾。⑦細部。***go*** (or ***enter***) ***into details*** 詳述。***in detail*** 詳細地。There isn't time to explain *in detail.* 沒有時間詳細解釋。—*v.t.* ①詳述;縷陳。②(陸海軍)選派;特派。③列舉。④加以複雜而工細的裝飾。

detail drawing (房屋、機器)細部圖。

de·tailed [dɪˈteld; ˈdiːteild, diˈteild] *adj.* ①詳細的; 明細的。a *detailed* account (report). 詳細的記述(報告)。②錯綜複雜的;千頭萬緒的。—**ly,** *adv.* —**ness,** *n.*

***de·tain** [dɪˈten; diˈtein] *v.t.* ①使延遲;留住;阻止。②拘留;扣押。The police *detained* the suspected thief for further questioning. 警方將竊嫌拘留作進一步之訊問。

de·tain·ee [dɪˌteˈni; ˌdiːteiˈniː] *n.* 被拘留者。

de·tain·er [dɪˈtenɚ; diˈteinə] *n.* ①阻止者;拘留者。②〖法律〗非法之留置; 非法占有;續行監禁犯人之令狀。

de·tain·ment [dɪˈtenmənt; diˈteinmənt] *n.* =**detention.**

***de·tect** [dɪˈtɛkt; diˈtekt] *v.t.* ①發見;查明;查出;探獲。We *detected* him in the act of breaking into our neighbor's house. 我們當場發現他闖入鄰居的房子。②〖電〗以檢波器檢(波)。

de·tect·a·ble [dɪˈtɛktəbl; diˈtektəbl] *adj.* 可探出的;可查覺的;可查明的。

de·tec·ta·phone [dɪˈtɛktəˌfon; diˈtektəfoun] *n.* 竊聽機;偵聽器。

de·tec·tion [dɪˈtɛkʃən; diˈtekʃən] *n.* ①發覺; 探出; 查知。②〖化〗檢出。③〖電〗檢波;整流;調整。

***de·tec·tive** [dɪˈtɛktɪv; diˈtektiv] *n.* 偵探。to hire a private *detective.* 雇一名私人偵探。—*adj.* ①偵探的。a *detective* story. 偵探小說。②偵查的;探究的。

de·tec·tor [dɪˈtɛktɚ; diˈtektə] *n.* ①探出(事件)之人;發現者。②〖無線電〗檢波器。③〖電〗電流計;檢電器。④(鍋爐中之)水深計。⑤〖化〗檢察器。

de·tent [dɪˈtɛnt; diˈtent] *n.* 〖機械〗爪;掣子。

dé·tente [deˈtɑ̃t; deiˈtɑ̃t] 〖法〗 *n.* 國際上緊張關係之緩和。

de·ten·tion [dɪˈtɛnʃən; diˈtenʃən] *n.* ①阻止;延遲。②監禁; 拘留;(罰學生)關學。③扣押(他人之物)。—*adj.* 阻止的; 拘留的。

detention barracks 軍中拘留所。

detention home 少年感化院。

detention hospital (傳染病之)隔離醫院。

detention house (移民)臨時扣留所。

de·ter [dɪˈtɝ; diˈtəː] *v.t.,* **-terred, -ter·ring.** ①妨礙; 阻礙; 脅阻。②防止;延緩。

de·terge [dɪˈtɝdʒ; diˈtəːdʒ] *v.t.,* **de·terged, de·terg·ing.** 清淨;洗淨(傷口等)。

de·ter·gent [dɪˈtɝdʒənt; diˈtəːdʒənt] *adj.* 潔淨的; 洗淨的;有洗淨力的。—*n.* 清潔劑;去垢劑。

de·te·ri·o·rate [dɪˈtɪrɪəˌret; diˈtiəriəreit] *v.,* **-rat·ed, -rat·ing.** —*v.t.* 使變壞(品質或品性)。—*v.i.* 變壞;退化;墮落。

de·te·ri·o·ra·tion [dɪˌtɪrɪəˈreʃən; diˌtiəriəˈreiʃən] *n.* 變壞;退化;墮落;衰頹。

de·ter·ment [dɪˈtɝmənt; diˈtəːmənt] *n.* ①妨礙;阻礙;脅阻。②阻礙物;障礙。

de·ter·mi·na·ble [dɪˈtɝmɪnəbl; diˈtəːminəbl] *adj.* ①可決定的; 可確定的。②可終止的;有限期的(=terminable).

de·ter·mi·nant [dɪˈtɝmənənt; diˈtəːminənt] *adj.* 決定的; 有決定力的; 限定的。—*n.* ①決定因素。②〖數學〗行列式。

de·ter·mi·nate [*adj.* dɪˈtɝmənɪt; diˈtəːminit *v.* dɪˈtɝməˌnet; diˈtəːməneit] *adj., v.,* **-nat·ed, -nat·ing.** —*adj.* ①一定的;有限的;確定的。②〖植物〗有限花序的。③最後的。④堅決的。—*v.t.* ①確定; 確保。②認明。—**ly,** *adv.* —**ness,** *n.*

***de·ter·mi·na·tion** [dɪˌtɝməˈneʃən; diˌtəːmiˈneiʃən] *n.* ①決心;決意;決斷。You must carry out your plan with *determination.* 你必須有決心實行你的計畫。②決定;確定;判決。③測定。④對某對象或目的的傾向。⑤〖法律〗終結;裁定。

de·ter·mi·na·tive [dɪˈtɝməˌnetɪv; diˈtəːminətiv] *adj.* 決定的;限定的;指定的。—*n.* ①決定者;限定者。②〖文法〗指示代名詞;限定詞。

:de·ter·mine [dɪˈtɝmɪn; diˈtəːmin] *v.,* **-mined, -min·ing.** —*v.t.* ①決心;決意;下決心; 作決定。They *determined* to learn English. 他們決心學習英文。②決定;決斷。His fate has not yet been *determined.* 他的命運尚未決定。③確定;限定;規定。④使下決心。The news *determined* him against further delay. 這消息使他下決心不再延擱。⑤測定。⑥了結;使終結。⑦限制。That hill *determines* our view. 那座山擋住我們的視線。—*v.i.* ①決心;決定。②終結;終止。

***de·ter·mined** [dɪˈtɝmɪnd; diˈtəː-mind] *adj.* ①有決心的；已下決心的。②堅決的。His *determined* look showed that he had made up his mind. 他堅決的表情顯示他已下了決心。③〖文法〗(指語音性質)可由上下文預測的。—**ness,** *n.* —**ly,** *adv.*

de·ter·min·ism [dɪˈtɝmɪn,ɪzəm; diˈtəːminizəm] *n.* 〖哲學〗決定論。—**de·ter·min·is·tic,** *adj.*

de·ter·min·ist [dɪˈtɝmɪnɪst;diˈtəːminist] *n.* 〖哲學〗決定論者。—*adj.* 決定論的。

de·ter·rent [dɪˈtɝrənt;diˈterənt] *adj.* 妨礙的；阻止的；制止的。—*n.* ①阻礙之物；制止物。②嚇阻武力。—**ly,** *adv.*

de·ter·sive [dɪˈtɝsɪv; diˈtəːsiv] *adj.* 洗淨的；使清潔的。—*n.* 清潔劑。—**ly,** *adv.* —**ness,** *n.*

***de·test** [dɪˈtɛst; diˈtest] *v.t.* 深深憎恨；深惡；憎惡。—**er,** *n.*

de·test·a·ble [dɪˈtɛstəbl; diˈtestəbl] *adj.* 極可恨的；極可厭的；極可惡的。—**de·test·a·bly,** *adv.* —**de·test·a·bil·i·ty,** *n.*

de·tes·ta·tion [,ditesˈteʃən; ,diːtesˈteiʃən] *n.* ①深惡；厭惡。②深惡或憎恨的人或物。

de·throne [dɪˈθron; diˈθroun] *v.t.*, **-throned, -thron·ing.** 廢(君)；廢立(某王)；推翻權威地位。—**de·thron·er,** *n.*

de·throne·ment [dɪˈθronmənt; diˈθrounmənt] *n.* 廢立；權威地位之推翻。

det·i·nue [ˈdɛtɪ,nju; ˈdetinjuː] *n.* 〖法律〗①(他人動產之)非法占有。②取回非法被人强占之財產的訴訟。

det·o·nate [ˈdɛtə,net; ˈdetouneit] *v.t.* & *v.i.*, **-nat·ed, -nat·ing.** (使)突然大聲爆炸；使爆裂。—**det·o·na·bil·i·ty, det·o·nat·a·bil·i·ty,** *n.* —**det·o·na·ble,** *adj.*

det·o·na·tion [,dɛtəˈneʃən; ,detouˈneiʃən] *n.* ①爆裂；爆炸。②爆炸聲。—**det·o·na·tive,** *adj.*

det·o·na·tor [ˈdɛtə,netə; ˈdetouneitə] *n.* ①起爆管；雷管。②任何一種爆炸物；炸藥。

de·tour [ˈditur, dɪˈtur; ˈdeituə, deiˈtuə] *n.* 便道；繞行之路(幹路在修理時，臨時代用之路)；迂路。*make a detour* 繞行。—*v.t.* & *v.i.* 繞道而行；由便道而過；迂迴。

de·tract [dɪˈtrækt; diˈtrækt] *v.t.* ①去掉；減損。②轉移。—*v.i.* 減損；貶抑〖常from〗。—**ing·ly,** *adv.*

de·trac·tion [dɪˈtrækʃən; diˈtrækʃən] *n.* ①減除。②誹謗。

de·trac·tive [dɪˈtræktɪv; diˈtræktiv] *adj.* 誹謗的；惡言的。—**ly,** *adv.* —**ness,** *n.*

de·train [diˈtren; diːˈtrein] *v.t.* 自火車卸下(如隊伍等)。—*v.i.* 下火車。—**ment,** *n.*

det·ri·ment [ˈdɛtrəmənt; ˈdetrimənt] *n.* 損害；傷害；損害的原因。

det·ri·men·tal [,dɛtrəˈmɛntl; ,detriˈmentl] *adj.* 有害的；傷害的。—**i·ty,** —**ness,** *n.* —**ly,** *adv.*

de·tri·tion [dɪˈtrɪʃən; diˈtriʃən] *n.* 消耗；損耗。

de·tri·tus [dɪˈtraɪtəs; diˈtraitəs] *n.* ①〖地質〗岩屑。②瓦礫；碎片。

De·troit [dɪˈtrɔɪt; diˈtrɔit] *n.* ①底特律(美國 Michigan 州東南部之一城市，位於底特律河流上)。②底特律河（從 St. Clair 湖流入 Erie 湖，爲美國及加拿大一部分的國界，是世界上最頻繁的內河航運)。—**er,** *n.*

deuce [djus; djuːs] *n.* ①二點(骰子或紙牌)。②(網球)雙方各勝三球(即 40-40) 或各贏五局時的記點數；平。③〖俗〗惡運；魔鬼（用於較溫和的詛咒)。④〖美俚〗 **a.** 兩元紙幣。 **b.** 兩元。***Go to the deuce!*** 滾你的! ***The weather played the deuce with our plans.*** 天氣對我們的計畫開起玩笑來了。***What the deuce is that?*** 那究竟是甚麼東西? —*adj.* 兩個的(尤指各種遊戲、競賽中的)。

deuc·ed [ˈdjusɪd; djuːst] *adj.* & *adv.* 過度的(地)；非常的（地)；極；魔鬼様的（地)。*in a deuced hurry* 極速地。

deuc·ed·ly [ˈdjusɪdlɪ; ˈdjuːsidli] *adv.* 過度地；非常地；極。

Deut. Deuteronomy.

deu·te·ri·um [djuˈtɪrɪəm; djuːˈtiəriəm] *n.* 〖化〗氘；重氫（D 或 H², 爲氫之同位素)。

deu·ter·og·a·my [,djutəˈrɑgəmɪ; ,djuːtəˈrɔgəmi] *n.* 再婚；再嫁；再娶。—**deu·ter·og·a·mist,** *n.*

deu·ter·on [ˈdjutə,rɑn; ˈdjuːtərɔn] *n.* 〖物理〗重氫子；氘(原子之)核子。

Deu·ter·on·o·my [,djutəˈrɑnəmɪ; ,djuːtəˈrɔnəmi] *n.* 〖聖經〗申命記（舊約中之一卷)。—**Deu·ter·o·nom·ic,** *adj.*

Deut·sche mark [ˈdɔɪtʃə~; ˈdɔitʃə~] 德國馬克（西德幣值單位，略作 **DM**)。(亦作 **Deutchemark**)

Deutsch·land [ˈdɔɪtʃ,lɑnt; ˈdɔitʃlɑːnt] 〖德〗 *n.* =**Germany.**

deut·zi·a [ˈdjutsɪə; ˈdjuːtsiə] *n.* 溲疏屬的植物。

de·val·u·ate [diˈvælju,et; diːˈvæljueit] *v.t.*, **-at·ed, -at·ing.** ①減少…之價值；使減價。②使(錢幣)減值；使貶值。—**de·val·u·a·tion,** *n.*

***dev·as·tate** [ˈdɛvəs,tet; ˈdevəsteit] *v.t.*, **-tat·ed, -tat·ing.** ①使荒廢；毀滅；蹂躪；破壞。②壓倒；征服；擊敗。—**dev·as·ta·tive,** *adj.*

dev·as·ta·tion [,dɛvəsˈteʃən; ,devəsˈteiʃən] *n.* 毀壞；蹂躪。

dev·el [ˈdɛvəl; ˈdevəl] *n.* 〖蘇〗重擊。—*v.t.* 以重擊擊倒。

‡de·vel·op [dɪˈvɛləp; diˈveləp] *v.t.* ①發展。Fresh air and exercise *develop* healthy bodies. 新鮮空氣和運動可以發展健康的身體。②使顯影；沖洗。③顯示。④揭露；披露。⑤逐漸擴大或擴充。⑥〖生物〗進化；發育。⑦〖數學〗展開。⑧(西洋棋開始時)落子。⑨詳述。⑩在新礦區作開採準備工作。—*v.i.* ①進步；發展；進展。He is *developing* into a good citizen. 他正發展成一個好公民。②發育；生長。Plants *develop* from seeds. 植物發育於種子。③變化；進化。④顯影。This type of film *develops* in twenty minutes. 此種軟片顯影需二十分鐘。 —**a·bil·i·ty,** *n.* —**a·ble,** *adj.*

de·vel·ope [dɪˈvɛləp; diˈveləp] *v.t.* & *v.i.* **-oped, -op·ing.** =**develop.**

developed country 已開發國家。

de·vel·op·er [dɪˈvɛləpɚ; diˈveləpə] *n.* ①發展者；顯示者。②〖照相〗顯像劑；顯色劑。③都市或郊區之發展者；開發公司。

developing country 開發中國家。

‡de·vel·op·ment [dɪˈvɛləpmənt; diˈveləpmənt] *n.* ①發展；開拓；擴張。He is engaged in the *development* of his business. 他正努力發展營業。②發育；發達；成長；進化。③發展階段。④發展的事；發展的結果。What are the latest *developments?* 最近所發展的事有那些? ⑤顯影。⑥新社區。⑦(西洋棋開始時之)落子；佈局。(亦作 **developement**) —**a·ry,** *adj.*

de·vel·op·men·tal 〔dɪˌvɛləpˈmɛntəl; diˌveləpˈmentəl〕 *adj.* 發展的；發育的；進化的；啓發的。—**ly,** *adv.*

de·vi·ate 〔ˈdivɪˌet; ˈdiːvieit〕 *v.,* **-at·ed, -at·ing,** *adj., n.* —*v.i.* 逸出正軌；不符事實；離題〖from〗。—*v.t.* 使逸出正軌。—*adj.*(行爲等)逸出正軌的。—*n.* ①逸出正軌的人或事。②性變態者。—**de·vi·a·bil·i·ty, de·vi·a·tor,** *n.* —**de·vi·a·ble,** *adj.*

de·vi·a·tion 〔ˌdivɪˈeʃən; ˌdiːviˈeiʃən〕 *n.* ①逸出正軌；離題。②逸出正軌之程度；偏差量。③(思想之)偏差。—**de·vi·a·to·ry, de·vi·a·tive,** *adj.*

de·vi·a·tion·ism 〔ˌdivɪˈeʃənˌɪzm; ˌdiːviˈeiʃənizəm〕 *n.* (共產主義思想)偏差。—**de·vi·a·tion·ist,** *n.*

*__de·vice__ 〔dɪˈvaɪs; diˈvais〕 *n.* ①發明或創造的東西；精巧的東西或裝置。safety *devices.* 安全裝置。a *device* for catching flies or rats. 捕蠅或捕鼠的裝置。②策略；詭計。by *device* of diplomacy. 用外交的策略。③圖案；紋章。④題銘。***leave a person to his own devices*** 聽其自由行動。

‡**dev·il** 〔ˈdɛvl̩; ˈdevl〕 *n., v.,* **-il(l)ed, -il·(l)ing,** *interj.* —*n.* ①魔鬼；惡魔。the *Devil.* 魔王；撒旦(＝Satan)。②惡人；殘暴的人。③聰明、活潑、精力充沛而好妄動或惡作劇的人。④醜惡的事；惡勢力或惡影響等。⑤替他人寫文章而名利不歸於自己的人。⑥印刷所的使童或學徒。⑦可憐的人。He has lost his job, poor *devil!* 他失業了，可憐的人！⑧有利齒的機器(如用以撕裂破布等)。⑨〖俗〗表示驚歎。How (*or* What, Where, Why) the *devil* is it? 究竟如何?(到底怎樣?) We had the *devil* of a time! 我們眞苦透了！⑩鐵工廠等所使用之可携帶之火爐。***between the devil and the deep sea*** 進退兩難；進退維谷。***devil of a*** 可惡的；可恨的。***give the devil his due*** 對於我們不喜歡的人或惡人，仍宜待以公平，承認其優點。***go to the devil*** a. (道德上的)墮落；染惡習。b. 滾開。c. 徹底失敗；成功希望全部落空。***play the devil with*** 〖俗〗傷害。Smoking *plays the devil with* one's health. 吸煙有害於健康。***printer's devil*** 印刷所的使童。***raise the devil*** 〖俗〗a. 引起大騷擾。b. 狂歡。c. 强烈抗議；採取極端的措施。***the devil take the hindmost*** a. 魔鬼抓那落後的人(喻：後下手遭殃)。b. 聽天由命。***the devil to pay*** 前途艱巨；大難。If inflation becomes much worse there will be *the devil to pay.* 如果通貨膨脹更趨惡化，其後果將不堪設想。***work like the devil*** 拚命工作。—*v.t.* ①〖俗〗戲弄；困擾；虐待。②(用機器)撕碎。③和以辛辣的調味煎煮食物。—*interj.* 表示厭惡、憤怒、驚訝等之感歎詞。—**hood,** *n.*

devil dog 〖美〗陸戰隊隊員。

dev·il(l)ed 〔ˈdɛvl̩d; ˈdevld〕 *adj.* 加有辛辣之調味品的。

dev·il·fish 〔ˈdɛvl̩ˌfɪʃ; ˈdevlfiʃ〕 *n., pl.* **-fish, -fish·es.** ①章魚。②灰鯨。③大鷂魚。

devil horse 螳螂。

dev·il·ish 〔ˈdɛvlɪʃ; ˈdevl̩iʃ〕 *adj.* ①如惡魔的；窮兇極惡的；殘酷的。②〖俗〗過度的；非常的；巨大的。③〖俗〗惡作劇的；淘氣的；精力充沛的；鹵莽的；無所顧慮的。—*adv.*〖俗〗過度地；極端地。—**ly,** *adv.* —**ness,** *n.*

dev·il-may-care 〔ˈdɛvlmɪˈkɛr; ˈdevlmeiˈkɛə〕 *adj.* ①不在意的；無所顧慮的；輕蔑的。②隨遇而安的；歡愉的。

dev·il·ment 〔ˈdɛvlmənt; ˈdevlmənt〕 *n.* ①惡行。②詭計；惡作劇。「＝**deviltry.**」

dev·il·ry 〔ˈdɛvlrɪ; ˈdevlri〕 *n., pl.* **-ries.**

devil's bones 骰子。

dev·il·try 〔ˈdɛvltrɪ; ˈdevltri〕 *n., pl.* **-tries.** ①惡行；兇暴之行爲；惡作劇；胡爲。②極惡。③邪術；魔法。④鬼神學(＝demonology)。(亦作 **devilry**)

de·vi·ous 〔ˈdivɪəs; ˈdiːvjəs〕 *adj.* ①繞道的；遙遠的；偏僻的。②不正直的；彎曲的；有偏差的。③無一定路線的。—**ly,** *adv.* —**ness,** *n.*

de·vir·il·ize 〔diˈvɪrəlˌaɪz; diːˈvirəlaiz〕 *v.t.,* **-ized, -iz·ing.** ①使失去精力或活力。②使失去男性氣概或特質。

*__de·vise__ 〔dɪˈvaɪz; diˈvaiz〕 *v.,* **-vised, -vis·ing,** *n.* —*v.t.* ①想出；設法；計劃；發明。②遺囑贈予或遺傳(財產)。—*v.i.* 計劃。—*n.* ①財產的遺贈。②遺囑中之遺贈條款。③遺贈的財產。「〖律〗接受遺贈者。」

dev·i·see 〔dɪˌvaɪzˈi; ˌdeviˈziː〕 *n.* 〖法

de·vis·er 〔dɪˈvaɪzɚ; diˈvaizə〕 *n.* ①設計者；發明者；圖謀者。② ＝**devisor.**

de·vi·sor 〔dɪˈvaɪzɚ; ˌdeviˈzɔː〕 *n.* 〖法律〗遺贈人；遺產贈與者。

de·vi·tal·ize 〔diˈvaɪtl̩ˌaɪz; diːˈvaitəlaiz〕 *v.t.,* **-ized, -iz·ing.** 殺死；使無生命；減少…之活力；使弱。—**de·vi·tal·i·za·tion,** *n.*

de·vit·ri·fy 〔diˈvɪtrəˌfaɪ; diːˈvitrifai〕 *v.t.,* **-fied, -fy·ing.** ①使不透明；使無光澤。②使(玻璃等)成不透明而結晶。—**de·vit·ri·fi·ca·tion,** *n.* 「空的；無的〖of〗。」

de·void 〔dɪˈvɔɪd; diˈvɔid〕 *adj.* 缺乏的；

de·voir 〔dəˈvwɑr, ˈdɛvwɑr; diˈvwɑː, ˈdevwɑː〕 *n.* ①禮貌；尊重。②(*pl.*)敬意；問候；祝賀。③職守；本分。

dev·o·lu·tion 〔ˌdɛvəˈluʃən; ˌdiːvəˈluːʃən〕 *n.* ①滾下；落下。②依次傳下；相傳。③(官職、權利、財產等之)移轉；移交；轉讓。④(議會對於委員會等之)委付。⑤〖生物〗退化；衰落。⑥中央政府對地方政府之授權。—**ar·y,** *adj.*

de·volve 〔dɪˈvɑlv; diˈvɔlv〕 *v.,* **-volved, -volv·ing.** —*v.t.* 傳下；授與；委任；移交；使負擔。—*v.i.* ①傳下；授與；移歸。②〖古〗滾下。—**ment,** *n.*

De·vo·ni·an 〔dəˈvonɪən; deˈvouniən〕 *adj.* ①英國之 Devon 郡的。②〖地質〗泥盆紀(古生代之一時期)的。—*n.* 該郡之人。

‡**de·vote** 〔dɪˈvot; diˈvout〕 *v.t.,* **-vot·ed, -vot·ing.** ①專心從事；獻身。The students *devote* themselves to their lessons. 這些學生專心於他們的功課。②供奉；供獻。③將…作某種專用。

*__de·vot·ed__ 〔dɪˈvotɪd; diˈvoutid〕 *adj.* ①忠實的；摯愛的；專心的。A mother is *devoted* to her children. 母親摯愛她的兒女。②獻身於某種目的的；祝聖的。③專供…之用的。—**ly,** *adv.* —**ness,** *n.* 「心從事者；獻身者。」

dev·o·tee 〔ˌdɛvəˈti; ˌdevouˈtiː〕 *n.* 專

*__de·vo·tion__ 〔dɪˈvoʃən; diˈvouʃən〕 *n.* ①摯愛；熱愛。the *devotion* of parents to (*or* for) their children. 父母對於兒女的摯愛。②忠實；專心；熱誠。a scholar's *devotion* to study. 學者專心於學問。③(*pl.*)祈禱。The priest was at his *devotions.* 牧師在祈禱。④信仰；虔敬。⑤奉獻。

de·vo·tion·al 〔dɪˈvoʃənl̩; diˈvouʃənl̩〕 *adj.* 專心的；獻身的；忠誠的。—**i·ty,** —**ism,** *n.* —**ly,** *adv.*

*__de·vour__ 〔dɪˈvaur; diˈvauə〕 *v.t.* ①吃；吞食(尤指動物)；貪食；狼吞虎嚥。②破壞；破

滅。The fire *devoured* the forest. 火焚毀了森林。③貪婪地注視或諦聽；凝視；耽讀；傾聽。—**er,** —**ing·ness,** —**ment,** *n.*

de·vour·ing·ly [dɪˈvaurɪŋlɪ; diˈvauəriŋli] *adv.* 貪婪地；貪食地；吞噬地。

de·vout [dɪˈvaut; diˈvaut] *adj.* ①虔敬的；虔誠的。②表示虔敬的。③忠誠的；熱心的。—**ly,** *adv.* —**ness,** *n.*

***dew** [dju; djuː] *n.* ①露。②新鮮如露的東西；小粒的水珠(如淚珠、汗珠等)。③〖俗〗**a.** 蘇格蘭威士忌。**b.** 玉蜀黍威士忌(尤指非法釀造者)。—*v.t.* 用露水等沾濕；沾潤。—**less,** *adj.*

DEW [dju, du; djuː, duː] distant early warning. (參看 **DEW line**)

de·wan [dɪˈwɑn; diˈwɑːn] *n.* 〖英印〗長官；官員。(亦作 **diwan**)

dew·ber·ry [ˈdjuˌbɛrɪ; ˈdjuːberi] *n., pl.* **-ries.** 懸鉤子屬之植物；其果實。

dew·claw [ˈdjuˌklɔ; ˈdjuː-klɔː] *n.* (鹿等之)假蹄；(狗等之)上爪。

dew·drop [ˈdjuˌdrɑp; ˈdjuː-drɔp] *n.* 露滴；露珠。

Dew·ey [ˈdjuɪ; ˈdju(ː)i] *n.* 杜威(John, 1859-1952, 美國教育家及哲學家)。

dew·fall [ˈdjuˌfɔl; ˈdjuːˌfɔːl] *n.* ①降露；結露。②降露之時；薄暮。

dew·i·ness [ˈdjuɪnɪs; ˈdjuːinis] *n.* 露狀；多露；潮濕；涼爽。

dew·lap [ˈdjuˌlæp; ˈdjuːlæp] *n.* ①(牛等)喉部之垂肉。②胖人喉部鼓出之肥肉。

DEW line 美加兩國國防用雷達防衞線。

dew point 露點(一定濕度內，凝結爲露珠之溫度)。(亦作 **dew point temperature**)

dew pond 露池(英格蘭南部高地，人工開鑿之淺池)。

***dew·y** [ˈdjuɪ; ˈdjuːi] *adj.,* **-i·er, -i·est.** ①帶露水的；露濕的。②有露之性質的；似露的。③〖詩〗清爽的；輕降的。④露的；降露的。—**dew·i·ly,** *adv.*

dex·ter [ˈdɛkstɚ; ˈdekstə] *adj.* ①右手的；右側的。②〖紋章〗右邊的。③好徵兆的。

dex·ter·i·ty [dɛksˈtɛrətɪ; deksˈteriti] *n.* ①機巧；靈敏；妙手。②腦筋靈活；聰慧；善於運用心智。③用右手之習慣。

dex·ter·ous [ˈdɛkstərəs; ˈdekstərəs] *adj.* ①機巧的；靈敏的。②腦筋靈活的；聰慧的；善於運用心智的。③慣用右手的。(亦作 **dextrous**) —**ly,** *adv.* —**ness,** *n.*

dex·tral [ˈdɛkstrəl; ˈdekstrəl] *adj.* ①右側的；右邊的。②右手的；用右手的。③右旋的(軟體動物之貝殼)。—**ly,** *adv.*

dex·tral·i·ty [dɛkˈstrælətɪ; deksˈtræliti] *n.* ①右側之優於左側；慣用右手。②〖動物〗右旋。

dex·tran [ˈdɛkstrən; ˈdekstrən] *n.* 〖化、藥〗葡萄聚糖；葡聚糖。

dex·trin(e) [ˈdɛkstrɪn; ˈdekstrin] *n.* 〖化〗糊精。—**ous,** *adj.*

dex·trose [ˈdɛkstros; ˈdekstrous] *n.* 〖化〗葡萄糖。

dex·trous [ˈdɛkstrəs; ˈdekstrəs] *adj.* =**dexterous.** —**ly,** *adv.* —**ness,** *n.*

dey [de; dei] *n.* ①1830 年法人征服 Algiers 以前該地之統治者。②昔 Tunis 及 Tripoli 之統治者。—**ship,** *n.*

D/F, D.F., DF 〖無線電〗direction finding. **D.F.** ①Defender of the Faith. ②Distrio Federal. ③ Doctor of Forestry. **D.F.A.** Doctor of Fine Arts. **D.F.C., DFC** Distinguished Flying Cross. **D.F.M.** Distinguished Flying Medal. **dft.** ①defendant. ②draft. **D. G.** ①Dei gratia (拉=by the grace of God). ②Deo gratias (拉 =thanks to God). ③Director-General. **dg, dg.** ①decigram(me). ②decigrams. **D.H.** ①Doctor of Humanics. ②Doctor of Humanities.

dhar·ma [ˈdɑrmɑ; ˈdɑːmə] *n.* ①〖印度教、佛教〗**a.** 律法；教規。**b.** 遵守教規；德性。②(D-)達摩(古代印度之聖者)。

dho·bi [ˈdobɪ; ˈdoubi] *n., pl.* **-bis.** 〖英印〗洗衣服之男人。(亦作 **dhobie**)

dhole [dol; doul] *n.* 印度野犬之一種。

dho(o)·ti [ˈdotɪ; ˈdouti] *n., pl.* **-tis.** 印度男子所纏之腰布。(亦作 **dhootie, dhuti**)

dhow [dau; dau] *n.* (阿拉伯沿海之)單桅帆船。(亦作 **dau, dow**)

DI ①Department of the Interior. ②drill instructor.

di- 〖字首〗①表"二次；二倍；二"之義。②**dis-** 或 **dia-** 之變體。

dia- 〖字首〗表"通過；完全；離開；中間；橫切"之義(母音前作 **di-**)。

di·a·base [ˈdaɪəˌbes; ˈdaiəbeis] *n.* 〖礦〗輝綠岩。—**di·a·ba·sic,** *adj.*

di·a·be·tes [ˌdaɪəˈbitɪs; ˌdaiəˈbiːtiːz] *n.* 〖醫〗糖尿病；多尿症。

di·a·bet·ic [ˌdaɪəˈbɛtɪk; ˌdaiəˈbetik] *adj.* (患)糖尿病的。—*n.* 糖尿病患者。

di·a·ble·rie [dɪˈɑblərɪ; diˈɑːbləri] *n.* ①魔法；妖術。②鬼怪談集；鬼怪學。③惡作劇；邪惡的行爲。④鬼怪之領域。(亦作 **diablery**)

di·a·bol·ic [ˌdaɪəˈbɑlɪk; ˌdaiəˈbɔlik] *adj.* 殘酷的；窮兇惡極的。

di·a·bol·i·cal [ˌdaɪəˈbɑlɪkl; ˌdaiəˈbɔlikəl] *adj.* =**diabolic.** —**ly,** *adv.* —**ness,** *n.*

di·ab·o·lism [daɪˈæbəˌlɪzəm; daiˈæbəlizəm] *n.* ①魔術。②信仰魔鬼。③兇暴之行爲；魔行；魔力。④魔鬼之性格或狀況。

di·ab·o·lo [dɪˈæbəˌlo; diˈɑːbəlou] *n., pl.* **-los.** 響簧(玩具)。

di·ach·y·lon [daɪˈækəˌlɑn; daiˈækəlɔn] *n.* 〖醫〗鉛膏。

di·ach·y·lum [daɪˈækələm; daiˈækələm] *n.* =**diachylon.**

di·ac·o·nal [daɪˈækənəl; daiˈækənl] *adj.* (教會中之)執事的；助祭的。

di·ac·o·nate [daɪˈækənɪt; daiˈækənit] *n.* ①(教會)執事之職。②執事們；執事會。

di·a·crit·ic [ˌdaɪəˈkrɪtɪk; ˌdaiəˈkritik] *n.* =**diacritical mark.** —*adj.* ①=**diacritical.** ②〖醫〗診斷的；徵候的。

di·a·crit·i·cal [ˌdaɪəˈkrɪtɪkl; ˌdaiəˈkritikəl] *adj.* ①示區別的；能分辨的。②〖語音〗附加於字母之發音記號的。—**ly,** *adv.*

diacritical mark 附加於字母之發音記號(如 ä, â, é 所加之"¨, ^, ˊ"等)。

di·ac·tin·ic [ˌdaɪækˈtɪnɪk; ˌdaiækˈtinik] *adj.* 〖物理〗光化性的。

di·a·dem [ˈdaɪəˌdɛm; ˈdaiədem] *n.* ①王冠；冕。②王權；王位。—*v.t.* 加冠。

di·aer·e·sis [daɪˈɛrəsɪs; daiˈiərisis] *n., pl.* **-ses** [-siz; -siːz]. =**dieresis.**

di·ag·nose [ˌdaɪəgˈnos; ˈdaiəgnouz] *v.,* **-nosed, -nos·ing.** —*v.t.,* ①〖醫〗診斷。②找出毛病。③根據科學資料分類或決定。④判斷；分析。—*v.i.* 診斷；分類；判斷。—**di·ag·nos·a·ble,** *adj.*

di·ag·no·sis [ˌdaɪəgˈnosɪs; ˌdaiəgˈnousis] *n., pl.* **-ses** [-siz; -siːz]. ①診斷。②審察；細心研究；慎辨；查究眞象。③診斷或審察後所作之決定或判斷。④調查；分析。

di·ag·nos·tic [ˌdaɪəgˈnɑstɪk; ˌdaiəgˈnɔstik] *adj.* 診斷的；在診斷上有價值的；特

徵的。—*n.* ①診斷；診斷學。②病之徵候。—**al·ly,** *adv.*

di·ag·nos·ti·cian [ˌdaɪəgnɑsˈtɪʃən; ˌdaiəgnɔsˈtiʃən] *n.* 診斷家。

di·ag·o·nal [daɪˈægənḷ; daiˈægənl] *adj.* ①斜的；斜紋的。②對角線的。—*n.* ①對角線。②斜紋布。—**ly,** *adv.*

*__di·a·gram__ [ˈdaɪəˌgræm; ˈdaiəgræm] *n., v.,* **-gram(m)ed, -gram·(m)ing.** —*n.* 圖樣；圖表。—*v.t.* 用圖表示；作成圖表。

di·a·gram·mat·ic [ˌdaɪəgrəˈmætɪk; ˌdaiəgrəˈmætik] *adj.* ①圖樣的；圖表的。②概略的；大體的。

di·a·gram·mat·i·cal [ˌdaɪəgrəˈmætɪkḷ; ˌdaiəgrəˈmætikəl] *adj.* =**diagrammatic.** —**ly,** *adv.*

di·a·gram·ma·tize [ˌdaɪəˈgræməˌtaɪz; ˌdaiəˈgræmətaiz] *v.t.,* **-tized, -tiz·ing.** 圖解；作成圖形。

di·a·graph [ˈdaɪəˌgræf; ˈdaiəgrɑːf] *n.* ①作圖器；分度尺。②放大繪圖器。

*__di·al__ [ˈdaɪəl; ˈdaiəl] *n., v.,* **-al(l)ed, -al(l)ing.** —*n.* ①日規；日晷儀（=sundial）。②（鐘錶、羅盤、磅秤、電表等的）針盤、標度盤。③自動電話的號碼盤。a telephone *dial.* 電話號碼盤。④收音機上的刻度盤。⑤（礦工用的）地下測量用的羅盤（=miner's dial）。—*v.t.* ①撥自動電話號碼；與…通電話。We *dialed* the police station. 我們打電話給警察局。②收聽（某一廣播或電視節目）。③顯示在針面，針盤等。④〖礦業〗用羅盤測量。—*v.i.* ①撥自動電話號碼。②收聽廣播或電視節目。—**er,** *n.*

dial. ①dialect. ②dialectal. ③dialogue.

*__di·a·lect__ [ˈdaɪəˌlɛkt; ˈdaiəlekt] *n.* ①方言。He speaks several *dialects.* 他會說好幾種方言。②同語系的語言。③某特殊行業、階級的人所用之字眼或發音。—*adj.* =**dialectal.**

di·a·lec·tal [ˌdaɪəˈlɛktḷ; ˌdaiəˈlektl] *adj.* 方言的；有方言之特徵的。—**ly,** *adv.*

dialect atlas 表示方言分布的地圖。

di·a·lec·tic [ˌdaɪəˈlɛktɪk; ˌdaiəˈlektik] *adj.* ①辯證的；辯證法的。② =**dialectal.** —*n.* ①（常 *pl.*）論理學；邏輯。②論理之辯論法。③〖哲〗辯證法。

di·a·lec·ti·cal [ˌdaɪəˈlɛktɪkḷ; ˌdaiəˈlektikəl] *adj.* ①辯證的；辯證法的（=dialectic）。②方言的（=dialectal）。—**ly,** *adv.*

di·a·lec·ti·cian [ˌdaɪəlɛkˈtɪʃən; ˌdaiəlekˈtiʃən] *n.* 辯證學者；論理學家。

di·a·lec·tol·o·gy [ˌdaɪəlɛkˈtɑlədʒɪ; ˌdaiəlekˈtɔlədʒi] *n.* 方言學；方言研究。

di·a·log·i·cal [ˌdaɪəˈlɑdʒɪkəl; ˌdaiəˈlɔdʒikəl] *adj.* 問答的；對話體的。（亦作 **dialogic**）

di·al·o·gist [daɪˈælədʒɪst; daiˈælədʒist] *n.* 問答者；對話者；問答體書籍之作者。

*__di·a·logue__ [ˈdaɪəˌlɔg; ˈdaiəlɔg] *n., v.,* **-logued, -logu·ing.** —*n.* ①對話。②對話式文學作品；對話體。③戲劇上的對白；小說中的對話。Plays are written in *dialogue.* 劇本是用對白寫的。④關於某些題目的意見交換。—*v.i.* 對話。—*v.t.* 以對話體寫成。（亦作 **dialog**）—**di·a·logu·er,** *n.*

dial telephone (or **phone**) 自動電話。

dial tone （自動電話）受話器拿起後話機中之嗡嗡聲。

di·a·lyse [ˈdaɪəˌlaɪz; ˈdaiəlaiz] *v.t.,* **-lysed, -lys·ing.** =**dialyze.**

di·al·y·sis [daɪˈæləsɪs; daiˈælisis] *n., pl.* **-ses** [-siz; -siːz]. ①分離；分解。②〖化〗濾膜分析；滲析。「〖化〗濾膜分析的；滲析的。

di·a·lyt·ic [ˌdaɪəˈlɪtɪk; ˌdaiəˈlitik] *adj.*

di·a·lyze [ˈdaɪəˌlaɪz; ˈdaiəlaiz] *v.t. & v.i.,* **-lyzed, -lyz·ing.** 〖化〗濾膜分析；滲析。

di·a·lyz·er [ˈdaɪəˌlaɪzɚ; ˈdaiəlaizə] *n.* 滲析器。（亦作 **dialyzator**）

diam. diameter.

di·a·mag·net·ic [ˌdaɪəmægˈnɛtɪk; ˌdaiəmægˈnetik] *adj.* 〖物理〗反磁的；反磁性的。—*n.* 反磁性體。

di·a·mag·net·ism [ˌdaɪəˈmægnəˌtɪzəm; ˌdaiəˈmægnitizəm] *n.* 〖物理〗反磁性；反磁現象；反磁現象之研究。「*n.* 直徑。

*__di·am·e·ter__ [daɪˈæmətɚ; daiˈæmitə]

di·am·e·tral [daɪˈæmətrəl; daiˈæmitrəl] *adj.* 直徑的。—**ly,** *adv.*

di·a·met·ric [ˌdaɪəˈmɛtrɪk; ˌdaiəˈmetrik] *adj.* =**diametrical.**

di·a·met·ri·cal [ˌdaɪəˈmɛtrɪkḷ; ˌdaiəˈmetrikəl] *adj.* ①直徑的；沿直徑的。②直接的；絕對的。③正相反的。

di·a·met·ri·cal·ly [ˌdaɪəˈmɛtrɪklɪ; ˌdaiəˈmetrikəli] *adv.* ①作爲直徑地。②直接地；完全地；正。

‡__di·a·mond__ [ˈdaɪmənd, ˈdaɪə-; ˈdaiəmənd] *n.* ①金剛鑽；鑽石。②亮晶如鑽石的小東西。③（紙牌）紅色的方塊。He called *diamond* four.（橋牌）他叫方塊四。④〖棒球〗棒球場內野；棒球場（含內外野）。⑤菱形；菱飾。⑥〖印刷〗鑽石體活字（4½磅因）。⑦（切玻璃用的）鑽刀。⑧（*pl.*）（紙牌中的）方塊牌。***black diamond*** 煤炭。***diamond cut diamond*** 强中更有强中手；勢均力敵。***diamond in the rough***（亦作 **rough diamond**）有好資質而態度壞的人。—*adj.* ①鑲鑽石的。She wears a *diamond* ring. 她戴一只鑽石戒指。②菱形的。—*v.t.* 鑲以鑽石。—**like,** *adj.*

di·a·mond·back [ˈdaɪməndˌbæk; ˈdaiəməndbæk] *adj.* 有菱紋之背的。—*n.* 菱紋背蛾。

diamond drill 鑽石穿岩機。

diamond dust 鑽石沙（用作磨料）。

diamond field 金剛鑽產地。

diamond jubilee 第六十或第七十五周年紀念。「鑽石，於金屬板上劃線時用）。

diamond pencil 鑽石鉛筆（筆尖鑲有

dia·mond-point [ˈdaɪməndˌpɔɪnt; ˈdaiəməndpɔint] *adj.* ①有鑽石尖的。②以鑽石尖工具所做的。

dia·mond-shaped [ˈdaɪməndˌʃept; ˈdaiəmendʃeipt] *adj.* 鑽石形的；菱形的。

diamond wedding 鑽石婚（結婚第六十、七十或七十五周年紀念）。

di·a·mor·phine [ˌdaɪəˈmɔrfin; ˌdaiəˈmɔːfiːn] *n.* 〖藥〗海洛因。

Di·an [ˈdaɪən; ˈdaiən] *n.* 〖詩〗=**Diana.**

Di·an·a [daɪˈænə; daiˈænə] *n.* ①戴安娜（羅馬神話中之處女性守護神，狩獵女神及月亮女神）。②〖詩〗月。③（亦作 **Diane, Dyana, Dyane**）女子名。

di·a·pa·son [ˌdaɪəˈpezṇ; ˌdaiəˈpeisn] *n.* 〖音樂〗①悅耳之曲調；諧音。②音域。③標準調。④有管風琴之主要音栓。

di·a·per [ˈdaɪəpɚ; ˈdaiəpə] *n.* ①（嬰兒之）尿布。②勻列菱形花紋之麻布或棉布。③勻列之菱形花紋。—*v.t.* ①爲（嬰兒）包尿布。②飾以勻列之菱形花紋。—*adj.* ①diaper 的。②包着尿布的；飾有勻列之菱形花紋的。③尿布上用的。「由尿布內之糞便引起）。

diaper rash 尿布疹（嬰兒臀部之紅疹，

di·aph·a·nous 〔daɪ'æfənəs; dai'æfənəs〕 *adj.* 透明的；清澄的。 —**ly,** *adv.* —**ness,** *n.*

di·a·pho·re·sis 〔ˌdaɪəfə'risɪs; ˌdaiəfə'ri:sis〕 *n.* 〖醫〗發汗。

di·a·pho·ret·ic 〔ˌdaɪəfə'rɛtɪk; ˌdaiəfə'retik〕 *adj.* 發汗性的。—*n.* 發汗劑。

di·a·phragm 〔'daɪəˌfræm; 'daiəfræm〕 *n.* ①〖解剖〗橫隔膜。②〖機械〗隔板。③電話機的振動板。④子宮托（一種避孕裝置）。⑤（照相機之）快板；快門。—*v.t.* ①裝以隔板等。②因橫隔膜而影響。③縮小（照相機之）快門〖down〗. —**at·ic,** *adj.*

di·ar·chi·al 〔daɪ'ɑrkɪəl; dai'ɑ:kiəl〕 *adj.* 兩頭政治的；由兩個統治者管理的。（亦作 **diachal, diarchic**）

di·ar·chy 〔'daɪɑrkɪ; 'daiɑ:ki〕 *n., pl.* **-arch·ies.** 兩頭政治。（亦作 **dyarchy**）

di·a·rist 〔'daɪərɪst; 'daiərist〕 *n.* 寫日記者；記日記的人。—**ic,** *adj.*

di·ar·rhe·a, di·ar·rhoe·a 〔ˌdaɪə'riə; ˌdaiə'riə〕 *n.* 腹瀉。 —**di·ar·rhe·al, di·ar·rhoe·al,** *adj.*

***di·a·ry** 〔'daɪərɪ; 'daiəri〕 *n., pl.* **-ries.** 日記；日記簿。It takes great patience to keep a *diary* without interruption. 寫日記不間斷需要很大的耐心。

Di·as·po·ra 〔daɪ'æspərə; dai'æspərə〕 *n.* ①猶太人受巴比倫人放逐後之散居世界各地。②散居世界各地之猶太人。③使徒時代未居住於巴勒斯坦之猶太籍基督徒。④（d-）與另一宗教信徒雜處而居於少數地位之教徒。

di·a·stase 〔'daɪəˌstes; 'daiəsteis〕 *n.* 〖生化〗澱粉酵素；澱粉酶；糖化素。

di·as·to·le 〔daɪ'æstəˌli; dai'æstəli〕 *n.* （心臟之）舒張。—**di·as·tol·ic,** *adj.*

di·as·tro·phism 〔daɪ'æstrəˌfɪzəm; dai'æstrəfizəm〕 *n.* 〖地質〗地殼變動；因地殼變動而成之地形。—**di·a·stroph·ic,** *adj.*

di·a·ther·man·cy 〔ˌdaɪə'θɝmənsɪ; ˌdaiə'θə:mənsi〕 *n.* 〖物理〗透輻射熱性；傳熱性。（亦作 **diathermance**）

di·a·ther·ma·nous 〔ˌdaɪə'θɝmənəs; ˌdaiə'θə:mənəs〕 *adj.* 〖物理〗熱線透過性的；透熱性的。

di·a·ther·mic 〔ˌdaɪə'θɝmɪk; ˌdaiə'θə:mik〕 *adj.* ①〖醫〗透熱法的。②〖物理〗=**diathermanous.**

di·a·ther·my 〔'daɪəˌθɝmɪ; 'daiəˌθə:mi〕 *n.* 〖醫〗透熱法；電氣透熱療法。（亦作 **diathermia**）

di·ath·e·sis 〔daɪ'æθɪsɪs; dai'æθisis〕 *n., pl.* **-ses** 〔-siz; -si:z〕. 〖醫〗素因；素質。

di·a·tom 〔'daɪətəm; 'daiətəm〕 *n.* 〖植物〗硅藻。

di·a·to·ma·ceous 〔ˌdaɪətə'meʃəs; ˌdaiətə'meiʃəs〕 *adj.* ①硅藻類的。②硅藻土的；矽藻土的。

di·a·tom·ic 〔ˌdaɪə'tɑmɪk; ˌdaiə'tɔmik〕 *adj.* 〖化〗①二原子的。②二價的。—**i·ty,** *n.*

di·a·ton·ic 〔ˌdaɪə'tɑnɪk; ˌdaiə'tɔnik〕 *adj.* 〖音樂〗全音階的。

di·a·tribe 〔'daɪəˌtraɪb; 'daiətraib〕 *n.* 惡罵；激烈之爭論；苛評；誹謗；冗長之議論。—**di·a·trib·ist,** *n.*

di·a·zine 〔'daɪəˌzin; 'daiəzi:n〕 *n.* 〖化〗二氮三烯陸圜。（亦作 **diazin**）

dib 〔dɪb; dib〕 *v.i.,* **dibbed, dib·bing.** 輕輕垂釣。

di·ba·sic 〔daɪ'besɪk; dai'beisik〕 *adj.* 〖化〗二鹽基的。 —**i·ty,** *n.*

dib·ber 〔'dɪbɚ; 'dibə〕 *n.* =**dibble**[1].

dib·ble[1] 〔'dɪbl; 'dibl〕 *n., v.,* **-bled, -bling.** —*n.* 小鍬；挖洞鑽。—*v.t.* ①用小鍬等在（地）中挖洞。②用小鍬等種植。

dib·ble[2] *v.i.* ①在水中划或游動。②輕輕垂釣。

dibs 〔dɪbz; dibz〕 *n. pl.* 〖俚〗①小錢；零錢。②一種用葡萄汁或棗做的濃糖漿。 ***dibs on (something)*** 對（某物）之所有或使用權。

dice** 〔daɪs; dais〕 *n.* pl. of **die**[2], *v.,* **diced, dic·ing.** —*n.* ①骰子；骰子戲；賭博。②骰子形；小方塊。no dice*** 〖俚〗拒絕；不成功。—*v.i.* 擲骰子；賭博。—*v.t.* ①切成骰子形（小方塊）。②賭骰子輸掉。③以方塊爲飾；做方塊記號。

dice·box 〔'daɪsˌbɑks; 'daisbɔks〕 *n.* 骰子筒（擲骰子用）。

dic·er 〔'daɪsɚ; 'daisə〕 *n.* ①賭骰子者。②切方塊之工具。③〖俚〗硬帽。

di·chlo·ride 〔daɪ'kloraɪd; dai'klɔ:raid〕 *n.* 〖化〗二氯化物。（亦作 **dichlorid**）

di·chog·a·my 〔daɪ'kɑgəmɪ; dai'kɔgəmi〕 *n.* 〖植物〗雌雄蕊異時成熟。

di·chot·o·mous 〔daɪ'kɑtəməs; dai'kɔtəməs〕 *adj.* ①二分的。②〖植物,解剖〗叉狀的；對生的。 —**ly,** *adv.*

di·chot·o·my 〔daɪ'kɑtəmɪ; di'kɔtəmi〕 *n., pl.* **-mies.** ①兩斷；兩半；二分。②〖邏輯〗二分法。③〖植物〗對生。④〖天文〗星等之半輪；弦月。

di·chro·mate 〔daɪ'kromet; dai'kroumeit〕 *n.* 〖化〗重鉻酸鹽。

di·chro·mat·ic 〔ˌdaɪkro'mætɪk; ˌdaikrou'mætik〕 *adj.* 二色的；現二色的。

dichromatic vision 〖醫〗色盲；二色眼。

di·chro·mic 〔daɪ'kromɪk; dai'kroumik〕 *adj.* 二色的。

Dick 〔dɪk; dik〕 *n.* Richard 之暱稱。

dick 〔dɪk; dik〕 *n.* ①〖美俚〗偵探。②〖俗〗人；傢伙。③〖俚,鄙〗男人性器；鷄巴。

Dick·ens 〔'dɪkɪnz; 'dikinz〕 *n.* 狄更斯（Charles, 1812-1870, 英國小說家）。

dick·ens 〔'dɪkɪnz; 'dikinz〕 *n., interj.* （常the-）〖俗〗惡魔（=devil）；溫婉之詛咒語。What the *dickens* is it? 它究竟是甚麼？The *dickens!* 惡魔！畜生！

dick·er[1] 〔'dɪkɚ; 'dikə〕 *n.* ①交易；小生意。②礎商。③交易之商品。④政治上之討價還價。—*v.t.* & *v.i.* ①交易；做小生意。②討價還價；斤斤較量。

dick·er[2] *n.* 十個；十枚；（特指）十張（皮革）。

dick·ey 〔'dɪkɪ; 'diki〕 *n., pl.* **-eys.** ①婦人襯衣胸前之胸衿。②男子之襯衣虛衿。③小孩之涎圍；涎巾。④小鳥。⑤驢；公驢。⑥馬車中供僕人等乘坐之後座。（亦作 **dicky, dickie**）

dick·ey·bird 〔'dɪkɪˌbɝd; 'dikibə:d〕 *n.* 小鳥。

dick·y 〔'dɪkɪ; 'diki〕 *adj.* 〖俗〗弱的；不好的；不穩的。

di·cot·y·le·don 〔ˌdaɪkɑtl̩'idn̩; 'daiˌkɔti'li:dən〕 *n.* 雙子葉植物。

di·cot·y·le·don·ous 〔ˌdaɪkɑtl̩'idn̩əs; ˌdaikɔti'li:dənəs〕 *adj.* 有雙子葉的；雙子葉植物的。

di·cou·ma·rin 〔daɪ'kumərɪn; dai'ku:mərin〕 *n.* 〖化〗雙香豆素；丁香素（用於防止血液凝結）。

dict. ① dictation. ② dictator. ③ dictionary.

dic·ta 〔'dɪktə; 'diktə〕 *n.* pl. of **dictum.**

dic·ta·graph 〔'dɪktəˌgræf; 'diktəgrɑ:f〕 *n.* 竊聽器。

Dic·ta·phone 〔'dɪktəˌfon; 'diktəfoun〕 *n.* 〖商標名〗錄音機；口授留聲機。

***dic·tate** 〔*v.* 'dɪktet; dik'teit *n.* 'dɪktet; 'dikteit〕 *v.,* **-tat·ed, -tat·ing,** *n.* —*v.t.* &

v.i. ①口授令人筆錄。Businessmen often *dictate* their letters. 商人常口授信稿令人筆錄。②指定;命令。These workmen refused to be *dictated* to. 這些工人拒受命令。—*n.* ①命令;指揮。②要求;原則。—**dic·tat·ing·ly,** *adv.*

***dic·ta·tion** [dɪkˈteʃən; dikˈteiʃən] *n.* 命令;口授令人筆錄;聽寫。—**al,** *adj.*

***dic·ta·tor** [dɪkˈtetɚ; dikˈteitə] *n.* ①獨裁者; 獨夫。②口授令人筆錄者。③(古羅馬)緊急時被授權掌管國政的人(音譯作"狄克推多")。④左右風尚習俗的人。

dic·ta·to·ri·al [ˌdɪktəˈtorɪəl; ˌdiktəˈtɔːriəl] *adj.* 獨裁的;專橫的;傲慢的;蠻橫的。—**ly,** *adv.* —**ness,** *n.*

dic·ta·tor·ship [dɪkˈtetɚˌʃɪp; dikˈteitəʃip] *n.* ①獨裁者之職位、任期或尊嚴。②獨裁政府;獨裁政治。③獨裁權;絕對權。

dic·ta·to·ry [ˈdɪktəˌtorɪ; ˈdiktətəri] *adj.* =**dictatorial.**

dic·ta·tress [dɪkˈtetrɪs; dikˈteitris] *n.* dictator 之女性。

dic·tion [ˈdɪkʃən; ˈdikʃən] *n.* ①語法;句法;用字;措辭。poetic *diction.* 詩的詞藻。②發音。

‡dic·tion·ar·y [ˈdɪkʃənˌɛrɪ; ˈdikʃənri] *n., pl.* **-ar·ies.** 字典;辭典。to consult a *dictionary.* 查字典。

dictionary catalog 圖書館之圖書目錄(列有作者、書名、內容等)。

Dic·to·graph [ˈdɪktəˌgræf; ˈdiktəgrɑːf] *n.* 〖商標名〗(電話)偵聽器。

dic·tum [ˈdɪktəm; ˈdiktəm] *n., pl.* **-tums, -ta** [-tə; -tə]. ①金言;格言。②權威的斷言; 意見; 定見; 正式聲明。 ③〖法律〗(對本案無直接關係之)審判官的意見。

‡did [dɪd; did] *v.* pt. of **do.**

di·dac·tic [daɪˈdæktɪk; diˈdæktik] *adj.* ①教誨的;教訓的。②好教誨的。

di·dac·ti·cal [daɪˈdæktɪkl; diˈdæktikəl] *adj.* =**didactic.**

di·dac·ti·cal·ly [daɪˈdæktɪklɪ; diˈdæktikəli] *adv.* 教訓地;訓誨地。

di·dac·ti·cism [daɪˈdæktəsɪzəm; diˈdæktisizəm, dai-] *n.* 教訓主義;啓蒙主義。

di·dac·tics [daɪˈdæktɪks; diˈdæktiks] *n.* (作 *sing.* 解)教授法。

di·dap·per [ˈdaɪˌdæpɚ; ˈdaidæpə] *n.* 鸊鷉;鸊鷉類之小鳥。

did·dle [ˈdɪdl; ˈdidl] *v.t.* & *v.i.,* **-dled, -dling.** ①〖俗〗欺;騙;哄。to *diddle* a person out of his money. 騙某人之錢。②毀滅(某人)。③虛度(時光);虛擲光陰;浪蕩。*diddle away* 浪費。

‡did·n't [ˈdɪdn̩t; ˈdidnt] =**did not.**

di·do [ˈdaɪdo; ˈdaidou] *n., pl.* **-dos, -does.** (常*pl.*)〖俗〗惡作劇。

didst [dɪdst; didst] *v.* 〖古, 詩〗do 之第二人稱, 單數, 過去式。

‡die¹ [daɪ; dai] *v.i.,* **died, dy·ing.** ①死亡;死。to *die* at one's post. 殉職。to *die* by one's own hand. 自殺而死。to *die* for one's country. 爲國殉難。to *die* a natural death. 善終。to *die* a glorious death. 光榮而死。to *die* a dog's death. 潦倒而死。②枯萎;凋謝。③消失;漸息〖常 away, out, down〗. The storm slowly *died* down. 暴風雨逐漸地停息了。④〖俗〗渴望;切望。He is *dying* to go to sea. 他切望航海。He is *dying* for a drink. 他渴望一飲。⑤强烈地感覺到。They are *dying* with curiosity. 他們好奇得要死。⑥消逝。The laughter *died* on their lips. 笑聲從他們的唇邊消失了。⑦失去興味。to *die* to worldly matters. 看破紅塵。⑧〖神學〗失去信仰。⑨停止作用。*die away* 漸漸消失。*die down* **a.** 漸息;漸漸衰亡。**b.** 枯萎。*die from* 因…致死。to *die from* a wound. 因傷致死。*die happy* (*rich, young,* or *poor*) 死時快樂(富有、年輕、貧窮)。He *died young.* 他早死。*die hard* (觀念信仰等之) 不易根絕。*die in harness* 死時猶在做事;殉職。*die in one's bed* 壽終正寢;善終。*die in the last ditch* 奮鬥至終而死。*die of* 因…而死。He *died of* cancer. 他死於癌症。to *die of* hunger. 餓死。*die off* 相繼死亡。*die out* **a.** 漸漸消滅。**b.** 完全停止或終結。*die standing up* 演劇中不獲得喝采。*die to self* 捨己;無我。*die to shame* 恬不知恥。*die to the world* 遁世;不問人間事。*die with one's boots on* 參看 **boot.** *never say die* 不灰心;不失去希望。

die² *n., pl.* **dice** for ①, **dies** for ②③, *v.,* **died, die·ing.** —*n.* ①骰子。②小立方塊。③印模;螺絲模;壓穿臺。*the die is cast* 已做決定,不能再改。—*v.t.* 用印模或機械造型、鑄造或削切。—**di·er,** *n.*

die-a·way [ˈdaɪəˌwe; ˈdai-əwei] *adj.* 沒精神的;頹喪的;憂鬱的。

di·e·cious [daɪˈiʃəs; daiˈiːʃəs] *adj.* =「**dioecious.**」

die-hard [ˈdaɪˌhɑrd; ˈdaihɑːd] *adj.* 頑強的; 死不屈從的; 抵抗到底的。—*n.* 頑強的人;死不屈從者。—**ism,** *n.*

di·e·lec·tric [ˌdaɪəˈlɛktrɪk; ˌdaiəˈlektrik] *adj.* 〖電〗介體的; 介質的;不導電的;絕緣的。—*n.* 〖電〗介體;介質;非導體;絕緣體。

die·mak·er [ˈdaɪˌmekɚ; ˈdaiˌmeikə] *n.* 雕刻印模者(=diesinker).

di·en·ceph·a·lon [ˌdaɪɛnˈsɛfəˌlɑn; ˌdaienˈsefələn] *n.* 〖解剖〗間腦;中腦。

di·er·e·sis [daɪˈɛrəsɪs; daiˈiərisis] *n., pl.* **-ses** [-siz; -siːz]. ①二連續母音之分開。②分音符(在二連續母音之第二個上加"¨",表須分開發音, 如 coöperate).

di·es [ˈdaɪiz; ˈdaiiːz] 〖拉〗*n. sing.* or *pl.* 「日(=day).」

Die·sel [ˈdizl; ˈdiːzəl] *n.* ①笛塞爾(Rudolf, 1858–1913, 德國工程師, 發明笛塞爾內燃機)。②(亦作 d-)笛塞爾內燃機;柴油機。—*adj.* 由柴油引擎推動的。

die·sel-e·lec·tric [ˈdizlɪˈlɛktrɪk; ˈdiːzliˈlektrik] *adj.* (亦作 D-) 裝有電動柴油引擎的。*diesel-electric* locomotive. (火車之)電動柴油機車。

Die·sel engine (or **motor**) [ˈdizl~; ˈdiːzəl~] 笛塞爾內燃機;柴油機。

die·sel·ize [ˈdizlˌaɪz; ˈdiːzlaiz] *v.t.,* **-ized, -iz·ing.** (亦作D-) 裝以柴油引擎(或電動柴油引擎)。—**die·sel·i·za·tion,** *n.*

diesel oil (or **fuel**) 柴油。(亦作 **Diesel~**)

die·sink·er [ˈdaɪˌsɪŋkɚ; ˈdai-siŋkə] *n.* 雕刻印模者。—**die·sink·ing,** *n.*

Di·es I·rae [ˈdaɪizˈaɪri; ˈdiːeizˈiərai] 〖拉〗①最後審判日。②中世紀之拉丁文讚美詩。

di·e·sis [ˈdaɪəsɪs; ˈdaiisis] *n., pl.* **-ses** [-siz; -siːz]. 〖印刷〗雙劍符號(卽‡)。(亦作 **double dagger**)

di·es non [ˈdaɪizˈnɑn; ˈdaiiːzˈnɔn] 〖拉〗〖法律〗不開庭之日;法定假日。

***di·et¹** [ˈdaɪət; ˈdaiət] *n., v.,* **-et·ed, -et·ing.** —*n.* ①飲食。a low-calory *diet.* 低熱

量飲食。②選定的飲食（指養病或設法增減體重時所規定的飲食）。He is on a *diet.* 他的飲食受着限制。③供給之事物。—*v.i.* 照規定而飲食。She got so fat that she had to *diet.* 她太胖,故須節食。—*v.t.* 規定飲食。

***di·et²** *n.* ①會議。②國會。the Japanese *Diet.* 日本議會。

di·e·tar·y 〔ˈdaɪəˌtɛrɪ; ˈdaiətəri〕 *adj., n., pl.* **-tar·ies.** —*adj.* 有關飲食的; 照規定飲食的。—*n.* (醫院、監獄等中規定之)日常飲食;伙食;膳食。

di·e·tet·ic 〔ˌdaɪəˈtɛtɪk; ˌdaiiˈtetik〕 *adj.* ①有關飲食衞生的;營養的。②飲食學的;營養學的。③適合節食者的。

di·e·tet·ics 〔ˌdaɪəˈtɛtɪks; ˌdaiiˈtetiks〕 *n.* (作 *sing.* 解) 營養學。

di·e·ti·tian 〔ˌdaɪəˈtɪʃən; ˌdaiiˈtiʃən〕 *n.* 飲食學家; 營養學家。(亦作 **dietician**)

di·e·to·ther·a·py 〔ˌdaɪətəˈθɛrəpɪ; ˌdaiətouˈθerəpi〕 *n.* 〖醫〗食物療法。

diet pill 〖美〗節食丸。

diff. ①difference. ②different.

dif·fer** 〔ˈdɪfɚ; ˈdifə〕 *v.i.* ①相異;不同。to *differ* in opinion. 意見相左。②意見相左;意見不合。I *differ* with (*or* from) you entirely. 我的意見與你完全不合。I beg to *differ.* 我未敢苟同。agree to differ*** 不再互相說服。

‡dif·fer·ence 〔ˈdɪfərəns; ˈdifərəns〕 *n.* ①不同; 相異。②差數; 差額;差量;差異。There are many *differences* between English and Chinese. 英文與中文有很多的差異。③爭論;意見衝突。④重要改變;重要後果或影響; 重要性。What's the *difference* whether I go or not? 我之走與否有甚麼關係? ***make some*** (***no*** or ***a great***) ***difference*** 有些(沒有,甚大)差別(重要)。It *makes no difference.* 這沒有什麼差別 (無關重要)。***settle differences*** 調停。***split the difference*** a. 折中。b. 互讓;妥協。—*v.t.* ①使不同。②區別;辨別。

‡dif·fer·ent 〔ˈdɪfərənt; ˈdifərənt〕 *adj.* ①不同的〖from〗. His second book is *different* from his first. 他的第二本書和第一本不同。②差異的;各別的。There are three *different* answers. 有三種不同的答案。③與衆不同的。—*adv.* 以不同方法;以不同作法。They do things *different* here. 他們在此有另一套做法。〖注意〗**different** 在標準美國用語中,後邊的 preposition 爲 from (見第一義例句)。在非正式的用法中則不一致,有時用 from, 有時用 to (英國習用 to). 而更常用的是 than: She was *different than* any other girl he had ever known. 她跟他所認識的女孩子都不同。如果受詞爲名詞子句時, than 已變得愈來愈通用了: The house was a good deal *different than* he remembered it. 這房子和他所記憶的已有很大不同了。

dif·fer·en·ti·a 〔ˌdɪfəˈrɛnʃɪə; ˌdifəˈrenʃiə〕 *n., pl.* **-ti·ae** 〔-ʃɪˌi; -ʃiiː〕. ①不同之點;特點。②〖邏輯〗種差;特異性。

dif·fer·en·tial 〔ˌdɪfəˈrɛnʃəl; ˌdifəˈrenʃəl〕 *adj.* ①與差別有關的; 基於差別的。②有區別之作用的。③〖機械〗差動的;應差的。④〖數學〗微分的。⑤比率不同的;數量不同的;速度不同的。—*n.* ①(可相比的事物間之)差別。②〖機械〗差動齒輪。

differential calculus 微分學。

differential diagnosis 〖醫〗鑑別診斷。

differential gear 差動齒輪;差速齒輪。

dif·fer·en·ti·ate 〔ˌdɪfəˈrɛnʃɪˌet; ˌdifəˈrenʃieit〕 *v.,* **-at·ed, -at·ing.** —*v.t.* ①使有區別;使變異。②辨別;區分。to *differentiate* one from another. 區別兩者。③求微分;微分。—*v.i.* ①變爲有分別;變成不同;分化。②辨別〖between〗.

dif·fer·en·ti·a·tion 〔ˌdɪfəˌrɛnʃɪˈeʃən; ˌdifərenʃiˈeiʃən〕 *n.* ①差別;區別。②變異;分化。③〖數學〗微分法。

***dif·fer·ent·ly** 〔ˈdɪfərəntlɪ; ˈdifərəntli〕 *adv.* 不同地;有差別地;…的不同。They do *differently* from (*or* to) us. 他們的做法與我們不同。They think *differently* than we do. 他們的想法跟我們不同。

dif·fi·cile 〔ˌdɪfəˈsil; ˈdifisiːl〕 *adj.* 困難的;難以相處的;難以處理的;難以滿足的。

‡dif·fi·cult 〔ˈdɪfəˌkʌlt; ˈdifikəlt〕 *adj.* ①困難的;費力的;難懂的。He finds it *difficult* to stop smoking. 他覺得戒烟是件難事。The place is *difficult* of access. 那地方不易到達。②難以取悅的;難以共處的。③煩擾的;令人憂煩或焦慮的 (情勢或環境)。—**ly,** *adv.*

‡dif·fi·cul·ty 〔ˈdɪfəˌkʌltɪ; ˈdifikəlti〕 *n., pl.* **-ties.** ①困難。You will find the house without much *difficulty.* 你會無甚困難找到這房子。②難事; 難題; 障礙。The book is full of *difficulties.* 這書難解處甚多。③(常 *pl.*)逆境;經濟上的困難。He is always in *difficulties.* 他總是在窘迫中。④爭論;爭吵。⑤麻煩。***make*** (or ***raise***) ***a difficulty*** 不願;反對。

dif·fi·dence 〔ˈdɪfədəns; ˈdifidəns〕 *n.* ①羞怯;缺乏自信。②謙虛。

dif·fi·dent 〔ˈdɪfədənt; ˈdifidənt〕 *adj.* ①羞怯的;缺乏自信的。②謙虛的。—**ly,** *adv.*

dif·fract 〔dɪˈfrækt; diˈfrækt〕 *v.t.* ①分解;分散。②使(光等)繞射。

dif·frac·tion 〔dɪˈfrækʃən; diˈfrækʃən〕 *n.* 〖物理〗(光、聲等之)繞射。

diffraction grating 〖物理〗繞射柵。

dif·frac·tive 〔dɪˈfræktɪv; diˈfræktiv〕 *adj.* 使繞射的;繞射的。—**ly,** *adv.* —**ness,** *n.*

***dif·fuse** 〔*v.* dɪˈfjuz; diˈfjuːz *adj.* dɪˈfjus; diˈfjuːs〕 *v.,* **-fused, -fus·ing,** *adj.* —*v.t.* ①流布;傳播;廣布。to *diffuse* knowledge. 傳播知識。②擴散;散布。—*v.i.* ①傳播。②擴散。③(氣體、油等)因擴散而混合。—*adj.* ①散布的;擴散的。②冗長的。③展開的。—**ly,** *adv.* —**ness,** *n.*

dif·fused 〔dɪˈfjuzd; diˈfjuːzd〕 *adj.* 流布的;廣布的;普及的。

dif·fus·i·bil·i·ty 〔dɪˌfjuzəˈbɪlətɪ; diˌfjuːzəˈbiliti〕 *n.* ①可流布; 可傳播。②〖生物〗瀰漫性。③〖物理〗擴散率。

dif·fus·i·ble 〔dɪˈfjuzəbl̩; diˈfjuːzəbl〕 *adj.* ①可流布的; 可傳播的; 可擴散的。②〖生物〗瀰漫性的。—**dif·fus·i·bly,** *adv.*

dif·fu·sion 〔dɪˈfjuʒən; diˈfjuːʒən〕 *n.* ①流布; 普及。②(文體等之) 散漫。③〖物理〗擴散(作用)。—**al,** *adj.*

dif·fu·sive 〔dɪˈfjusɪv; diˈfjuːsiv〕 *adj.* ①流布的;普及的。②擴散的;擴散性的。③散漫的;冗贅的。—**ly,** *adv.* —**ness,** *n.*

‡dig 〔dɪg; dig〕 *v.,* **dug, dig·ging,** *n.* —*v.t.* ①掘;鑿。to *dig* a well. 鑿井。②用鋤翻(土)。The old gardener *dug* the soil thoroughly. 老園丁將土徹底翻過。③掘出。④發現;發掘(事實)〖up, out〗. to *dig* up facts from books. 由書中發掘事實。⑤穿刺;衝刺;插入。

⑥〖俚〗看;注意。⑦〖俚〗懂;了解。⑧〖俚〗喜歡;佩服。People seem to *dig* it. 人們似乎喜歡這個。—*v.i.* ①掘;翻(土)。The miners were *digging* for gold. 礦工們在掘礦尋金。②鑿通〖through, into, under〗. ③〖俗〗苦讀。to *dig* in one's books. 苦讀;用功讀書。④〖俚〗住。This is the inn where I *dig*. 這是我住的旅館。⑤〖俚〗奔跑。***dig down*** 掏腰包。The customers will not *dig down* for such entertainment. 顧客不會爲這種娛樂節目掏腰包。***dig for*** **a.** 掘尋。**b.** 探求。to *dig for* information. 探求消息(或知識)。***dig in*** 〖俗〗 **a.** 苦讀。**b.** 掘壕自衞。**c.** 埋。***dig into*** 〖俗〗 **a.** 努力於。**b.** 動用。**c.** 苦心研究。***dig out*** **a.** 挖出;掘出。**b.** 奔跑。**c.** 匆匆出發;匆匆地走。***dig up*** **a.** 掘出。**b.** 掘;翻(土)。**c.** 尋出。**d.** 捐款;出錢。—*n.* ①〖俗〗衝;刺。to give one a *dig* in the ribs. 戳戳他人的肋骨(以引起其注意)。②諷刺;譏刺。This was a *dig* at him. 這是諷刺他的。③〖美俗〗苦讀的學生。④〖主英〗(*pl.*)寄宿舍。Are you living at home or in *digs?* 你住在家裏還是住在寄宿舍?⑤(考古學之)探掘。

dig·a·my [ˈdɪgəmɪ; ˈdigəmi] *n.* 再婚。

di·gen·e·sis [daɪˈdʒɛnɪsɪs; daiˈdʒenisis] *n.* 〖生物〗無性有性交迭生殖;複殖。

***di·gest** [*v.* dəˈdʒɛst; diˈdʒest *n.* ˈdaɪdʒɛst; ˈdaidʒest] *v.t.* ①消化。②了解;融會。③忍受。These insults are more than we can *digest*. 這些侮辱是我們所難忍受的。④浸漬。⑤摘要;分類。—*v.i.* ①消化。Some foods *digest* more easily than others. 有些食物較其他食物容易消化。②消化食物。—*n.* 分類;摘要。a *digest* of the week's news. 一週新聞摘要。

di·gest·er [dəˈdʒɛstɚ; diˈdʒestə] *n.* ①摘要作者。②消化劑;促進消化力之食物。③〖化學〗浸漬器;蒸鍋。

di·gest·i·bil·i·ty [də,dʒɛstəˈbɪlətɪ; di,dʒestəˈbiliti] *n.* 能消化;可消化性;可分類性。

di·gest·i·ble [dəˈdʒɛstəbl; diˈdʒestəbl] *adj.* 可消化的;可分類的;可了解的。—**ness,** *n.* —**di·gest·i·bly,** *adv.*

***di·ges·tion** [dəˈdʒɛstʃən; diˈdʒestʃən] *n.* ①消化。This food is easy of *digestion*. 這食物容易消化。②消化力。He has a good *digestion*. 他消化力好。

***di·ges·tive** [dəˈdʒɛstɪv; diˈdʒestiv] *adj.* ①消化的。He suffers from *digestive* trouble. 他消化不好。②助消化的。—*n.* 助消化的東西。

***dig·ger** [ˈdɪgɚ; ˈdigə] *n.* ①挖掘者;掘地獸。a gold *digger*. 淘金者;以姿色或手段向男人索取財物之女人。②掘鑿的器具。③穴蜂(=digger wasp). ④(D-)(亦作 **Digger Indian**) 掘食土人(住於美國西北部之一種印第安人,因其專掘植物之根爲食,故名)。⑤〖俗〗澳大利亞或紐西蘭的兵。⑥〖俚〗替戲票黃牛購票者。

dig·ging [ˈdɪgɪŋ; ˈdigiŋ] *n.* ①挖掘。②挖出之物。③挖掘之處。

dig·gings [ˈdɪgɪŋz; ˈdigiŋz] *n. pl.* ①(常作 *sing.* 解)採礦場所或地方。②(作 *sing.* or *pl.*解)礦區;礦地(尤指金礦)。③(作*pl.*解)從礦中採出之物。④(亦作 **digs**)(作 *pl.* 解)〖主英,俗〗寓所;住處;寄宿舍。

dight [daɪt; dait] *v.t.,* **dight** or **dight·ed, dight·ing.** ①〖詩〗使就緒;預備。②〖古〗調理;裝飾。③〖方〗清理;擦拭。〖注意〗此字目前主用於過去分詞形式。

dig·it [ˈdɪdʒɪt; ˈdidʒit] *n.* ①手指或足趾。②阿拉伯數目字(即 0,1,2,3,4,5,6,7,8,9;有時 0 除外)。③一指寬(約¾英寸)。④〖天文〗蝕分(太陽或月的直徑的 1/12)。

dig·i·tal [ˈdɪdʒətl; ˈdidʒitəl] *adj.* ①手指的。②(阿拉伯)數字的。—**ly,** *adv.*

dig·i·tal·is [,dɪdʒəˈtelɪs; ,didʒiˈteilis] *n.* ①〖植物〗洋地黃;毛地黃。②毛地黃之乾葉(用作强心劑)。

dig·i·tate [ˈdɪdʒə,tet; ˈdidʒiteit] *adj.* ①〖動物〗有指(趾)的。②〖植物〗掌狀的。③指狀的;掌狀的。(亦作**digitated**) —**ly,** *adv.*

dig·i·ti·grade [ˈdɪdʒɪtə,gred; ˈdidʒitigreid] *adj.* 趾行(類)的。—*n.* 趾行動物。

dig·ni·fied [ˈdɪgnə,faɪd; ˈdignifaid] *adj.* 威嚴的;莊嚴的;高貴的。—**ly,** *adv.* —**ness,** *n.*

dig·ni·fy [ˈdɪgnə,faɪ; ˈdignifai] *v.t.,* **-fied, -fy·ing.** 使尊榮;使顯貴;加以尊號。

dig·ni·tar·y [ˈdɪgnə,tɛrɪ; ˈdignitəri] *n., pl.* **-tar·ies.** 高貴的人物;顯要的人物。—*adj.* 尊榮的。—**dig·ni·tar·i·al,** *adj.*

dig·ni·ty** [ˈdɪgnətɪ; ˈdigniti] *n., pl.* **-ties.** ①高尙的品德;可敬的品格;高貴。②威嚴;尊嚴。③高位;顯爵。④光榮;神聖。Honest work has *dignity*; idleness has none. 忠實工作有光榮;怠惰則無。⑤〖古〗達官貴人;名流;要人。*dignities* of church. 教會中的要人。beneath one's dignity*** 有傷尊嚴;有失身分。***stand upon*** (or ***on***) ***one's dignity*** 保持尊嚴。

di·graph [ˈdaɪgræf; ˈdaigrɑːf] *n.* 兩個字母發一音(如 ship 中的 sh, beat 中的 ea等)。—*adj.* 兩個字母發一音的。—**ic,** *adj.* —**ic·al·ly,** *adv.*

di·gress [dəˈgrɛs; daiˈgres] *v.i.* 離開本題〖from〗.

di·gres·sion [dəˈgrɛʃən; daiˈgreʃən] *n.* 離開本題;枝節。—**al,** —**ar·y,** *adj.*

di·gres·sive [dəˈgrɛsɪv; daiˈgresiv] *adj.* 離題的;枝節的。—**ly,** *adv.*

digs [dɪgz; digz] *n. pl.*〖英俚〗寓所;住處;寄宿舍。

di·he·dral [daɪˈhidrəl; daiˈhiːdrəl] *adj.* ①由二平面構成的;二面的。②二面角的;有二面角的。—*n.*①〖數學〗二面角。②〖航空〗飛機雙翼與其橫軸水平面所成之角。

di·hy·dro·strep·to·my·cin [daɪ,haɪdro,strɛptəˈmaɪsɪn; dai,haidrou,streptəˈmaisin] *n.* 二氫連絲菌素(二氫鏈黴素)。

dike¹ [daɪk; daik] *n., v.,* **diked, dik·ing.** —*n.* ①堤。②溝。③低的土牆或石牆;堤道。④障礙物;屛障。⑤〖地質〗壁狀巖塊。—*v.t.*圍以堤;設堤(防水)。(亦作 **dyke**)

dike² *v.t.,* **diked, dik·ing.** 使穿漂亮衣服。〖常 out, up〗.

di·lap·i·date [dəˈlæpə,det; diˈlæpideit] *v.,* **-dat·ed, -dat·ing.** —*v.t.* 使荒廢;浪費;使部分毁壞。—*v.i.* 變爲荒廢;變破爛。—**di·lap·i·da·tor,** *n.*

di·lap·i·dat·ed [dəˈlæpə,detɪd; diˈlæpideitid] *adj.* 毁壞的;倒塌的;破舊的。

di·lap·i·da·tion [də,læpəˈdeʃən; di,læpiˈdeiʃən] *n.* 倒塌;毁壞。

di·lat·a·ble [daɪˈletəbl; daiˈleitəbl] *adj.* 可膨脹的;可擴大的。—**di·lat·a·bil·i·ty,** *n.*

dil·a·ta·tion [,dɪləˈteʃən; ,daileiˈteiʃən] *n.* ①擴張;膨脹;蔓衍。②〖醫〗舒張;擴張。—**al,** *adj.*

di·late [daɪˈlet; daiˈleit] *v.,* **-lat·ed, -lat·ing.** —*v.t.* ①使擴大;使膨脹。②〖古〗詳述。—*v.i.* ①擴大;膨脹。②詳述;誇張〖常 on, upon〗. to *dilate* on one's view. 詳述意見。

di·la·tion [daɪˈleʃən; daiˈleiʃən] *n.* ①

擴張;膨脹。②擴大部分;膨脹部分。

dil·a·tom·e·ter [ˌdaɪlə'tɑmɪtɚ; ˌdilə'tɔmitə] *n.* 膨脹計。

di·la·tor [daɪ'letɚ; dai'leitə] *n.* ①〖外科〗擴張器。②〖解剖〗擴張肌。③使擴大或膨脹的人。

dil·a·to·ry ['dɪləˌtorɪ; 'dilətəri] *adj.* ①慢的;不慌不忙的。②遲緩的;拖延的。 **—dil·a·to·ri·ly,** *adv.* **—dil·a·to·ri·ness,** *n.*

***di·lem·ma** [də'lɛmə, daɪ-; di'lemə, dai-] *n.* ①左右爲難的狀況;困難的選擇。to put one in a *dilemma.* 使人左右爲難。②兩端論法;雙關論法;二重體(提出均不利於對方之兩端,迫使選取其一之辯論法)。

dil·et·tan·te [ˌdɪlə'tæntɪ; ˌdili'tænti] *n., pl.* **-tes, -ti** [-tɪ; -ti], *adj., v.,* **-ted, -te·ing.** *—n.* ①藝術愛好者。②業餘藝術愛好者。*—adj.* 業餘藝術愛好的。*—v.i.* 作業餘藝術愛好者;對藝術產生業餘性愛好。(亦作 **dilettant**) **—dil·et·tant·ish,** *adj.*

dil·et·tant(e)·ism [ˌdɪlə'tæntɪzəm; ˌdili'tæntizəm] *n.* 業餘的藝術愛好。

***dil·i·gence**[1] ['dɪlədʒəns; 'dilidʒəns] *n.* 勤勉。We should study with *diligence.* 我們應該勤讀。

dil·i·gence[2] *n.* (尤指法國之)公共馬車。

***dil·i·gent** ['dɪlədʒənt; 'dilidʒənt] *adj.* 勤勉的;細心而繼續不斷的。**—ly,** *adv.*

dill [dɪl; dil] *n.* 〖植物〗蒔蘿。

dil·ly ['dɪlɪ; 'dili] *n.* 〖俗〗極好的東西或人。

dil·ly·dal·ly ['dɪlɪˌdælɪ; 'dilidæli] *v.i.,* **-lied, -ly·ing.** 三心二意地浪費時間。

dil·u·ent ['dɪljuənt; 'diljuənt] *adj.* 稀薄的;沖淡的。*—n.* 〖醫〗稀釋劑。

di·lute [dɪ'lut; dai'lju:t] *v.,* **-lut·ed, -lut·ing,** *adj.* *—v.t.* ①稀釋;沖淡。②使(顏色)變淡。③使變弱;使變低劣。*—v.i.* 變稀薄;變淡。*—adj.* ①稀薄的;淡的。②無力的。

di·lu·tee [dəˌlu'ti; daiˌlju:'ti:] *n.* 〖英〗從事技術工作之半技術或無技術工人;生手或半生手。

di·lu·tion [dɪ'luʃən; dai'lu:ʃən] *n.* ①稀釋;沖淡。②(一般之)變弱;薄弱化。③稀釋之物;用水沖淡之物。④〖英〗勞動稀釋(用生手或半生手代替熟手之方式)。

di·lu·vi·al [dɪ'luvɪəl; dai'lu:vjəl] *adj.* ①洪水的;(特指) Noah 時之洪水的。②洪水作用的。③〖地質〗洪水所積成的;洪積的。(亦作 **diluvian**)

di·lu·vi·um [dɪ'luvɪəm; dai'lu:vjəm] *n., pl.* **-vi·a** [-vɪə; -viə]. 〖地質〗洪積物;洪積土;洪積層。

dim** [dɪm; dim] *adj.,* **dim·mer, dim·mest,** *v.,* **dimmed, dim·ming,** *n.—adj.* ①微暗的;不亮的。②不明顯的;模糊的;不清楚的。③朦朧的;意識不清的。④微弱的(聲音)。⑤看不清的(視力)。Her eyes were *dim* with tears. 她眼中含淚,視線模糊。⑥暗淡無光澤的(顏色)。⑦了解不清楚的。⑧不容樂觀的。take a dim view of*** 對…無動於中或持悲觀或懷疑的看法。*—v.t.* 使暗淡;使模糊。Her eyes were *dimmed* with tears. 眼淚使她的眼力模糊。*—v.i.* 變暗淡;變模糊。*—n.* 汽車停時所用之弱光。

dim., dimin. ①diminuendo. ②diminutive.

dime** [daɪm; daim] *n.* 〖美〗一角的銀幣;一角。They made hardly a *dime.* 他們幾乎連一毛錢也沒有賺到。a dime a dozen*** 多得不稀罕。Heroes were *a dime a dozen* that day. 那時期英雄多如過江之鯽。***on a dime*** **a.** 極小地方。This car can turn *on a dime.* 這部車能在極小地方轉彎。**b.** 立卽。He stopped *on a dime.* 他立卽停止。

dime museum 〖美〗簡易博物館。

dime novel 故事動人但毫無文學價值的小說。

di·men·sion** [də'mɛnʃən; di'menʃən] *n.* ①尺寸(長、寬、厚);(空間的)度(數);維(數)。What are the *dimensions* of the room? 這房間的長闊高尺寸有多少? ②(*pl.*)大小;範圍。A rich man's house is usually of considerable *dimensions.* 一個富人的房屋常是很寬大的。③〖代數〗次。x^3, x^2y, and xyz are all of three *dimensions.* x^3, x^2y 和 xyz 都是三次式。④幅員;廣延(性)。⑤重要性。⑥(*pl.*)〖俗〗女人之三圍。The beauty queen's dimensions were 38-24-36. 那美女的三圍是38, 24, 36英寸。live in the fourth dimension*** 生活在第四度空間中(生活於幻想之中)。*—v.t.* 作成某種尺寸。**—less,** *adj.*

di·men·sion·al [dɪ'mɛnʃənl; di'menʃənl] *adj.* (長、寬、高之)尺寸的;…次元的。

dimensional sound 立體音響。

dime store 專售廉價貨物的商店。

dim·e·ter ['dɪmətɚ; 'dimitə] *n.* 〖韻律〗含有二音步之詩行;二步格。

di·mid·i·ate [dɪ'mɪdɪˌet; di'midieit] *adj., v.,* **-at·ed, -at·ing.** *—adj.* 兩半的;兩分的。*—v.t.* 兩分;分爲兩半。

di·mid·i·a·tion [dɪˌmɪdɪ'eʃən; diˌmidi'eiʃən] *n.* 分爲兩半;切半。

***di·min·ish** [də'mɪnɪʃ; di'miniʃ] *v.t.* ①減少;縮小;使變小。②詬病;貶抑。*—v.i.* 減少;縮小。**—a·ble,** *adj.* **—ment,** *n.*

di·min·u·en·do [dəˌmɪnju'ɛndo; diˌminju'endou] *adj., n., pl.* **-dos,** *v.,* **-doed, -do·ing.** *—adj.* 〖音樂〗漸弱的。*—n.* 〖音樂〗漸弱。*—v.i.* (聲音)漸弱。

dim·i·nu·tion [ˌdɪmə'njuʃən; ˌdimi'nju:ʃən] *n.* 縮小;減少;變小。

***di·min·u·tive** [də'mɪnjətɪv; di'minjutiv] *adj.* ①小的。②縮小的;變小的。③表示"小"的(如 -let, -kin 等語尾稱爲 *diminutive* suffixes). *—n.* ①極小的人或物。②表示"小"的字或字中的一部分(如 streamlet 指小溪)。**—di·min·u·ti·val,** *adj.* **—ly,** *adv.*

di·mis·sion [dɪ'mɪʃən; di'miʃən] *n.* 離職;退職。

dim·is·so·ry ['dɪməˌsorɪ, də'mɪsərɪ; 'dimisəri] *adj.* 准許離去的;退職的;(特指)(主教准許教士之)轉任許可的。

dim·i·ty ['dɪmətɪ; 'dimiti] *n., pl.* **-ties.** 一種薄棉布。

***dim·ly** ['dɪmlɪ; 'dimli] *adv.* 不清楚地;隱約地;朦朧地;模糊地;含糊地。

dim·mer ['dɪmɚ; 'dimə] *n.* ①使暗淡之人或物。②〖電〗減光器;制光裝置。

dim·ness ['dɪmnɪs; 'dimnis] *n.* 微暗;朦朧。

di·mor·phic [daɪ'mɔrfɪk; dai'mɔ:fik] *adj.* 同種二形的。

di·mor·phism [daɪ'mɔrfɪzəm; dai'mɔ:fizəm] *n.* ①〖動、植物〗同一種類有兩種形狀的現象;同種二形。②〖結晶學〗同質二像。

di·mor·phous [daɪ'mɔrfəs; dai'mɔ:fəs] *adj.* =**dimorphic.**

dim-out ['dɪmˌaut; 'dimaut] *n.* ①部分的燈火管制。②管制;限制。(亦作**dimout**)

***dim·ple** ['dɪmpl; 'dimpl] *n., v.,* **-pled, -pling.** *—n.* ①靨;臉上之酒渦。This pretty girl has *dimples* on her cheeks. 這個美麗的女子兩頰都有酒渦。②地或水面上的微凹處。③波紋。—*v.t.* ①使現頰渦;使生靨。A smile *dimpled* her cheeks. 微笑使她臉上現出酒渦。②使起波紋。—*v.i.* ①微笑而現酒渦;生靨。She *dimpled* up at them shyly. 她向他們羞澀地微笑而現出酒渦。②起微波;生波紋。

dim·ply ['dɪmplɪ; 'dimpli] *adj.*, **-pli·er, -pli·est.** ①有頰渦的; 有酒渦的。②起波紋的;多波紋的。

dim-sight·ed ['dɪm'saɪtɪd; 'dim'saitid] *adj.* ①視力朦朧的。②缺少洞察力的。

dim·wit ['dɪm,wɪt; 'dimwit] *n.* 傻瓜。

dim-wit·ted ['dɪm,wɪtɪd; 'dimwitid] *adj.* 愚蠢的; 愚笨的。—**ly,** *adv.* —**ness,** *n.*

***din** [dɪn; din] *n., v.,* **dinned, din·ning.** —*n.* 喧聲;嘈聲。—*v.i.* 喧嘩;作嘈聲。 The noise *dinned* in my ears. 喧聲聒耳。—*v.t.* 聒;絮聒不休地說。The shouts of the boys *dinned* his ears. 小孩們的叫聲聒他的耳。

Di·nah ['daɪnə; 'dainə] *n.* 女子名。

di·nar [dɪ'nɑr; 'di:nɑ:] *n.* ①東方的古錢(特指流通於回教國家的古金幣)。②伊拉克貨幣名。③南斯拉夫硬幣名。

‡**dine** [daɪn; dain] *v.,* **dined, din·ing.** —*v.i.* 用餐;進膳。 When do you *dine?* 你們甚麼時候吃飯? —*v.t.* 宴請。 Our school *dined* the famous scholar. 我們學校宴請這位有名的學者。 *dine out* 在外邊(不在家)吃飯。

din·er ['daɪnə; 'dainə] *n.* ①用膳者。②〖美〗火車的餐車。

din·er-out ['daɪnə'aut; 'dainər'aut] *n., pl.* **din·ers-out.** 在夜總會、飯館等用膳者。

di·nette [daɪ'nɛt; dai'net] *n.* 小飯廳。

ding [dɪŋ; diŋ] *v.t. & v.i.* ①鳴(鐘);叮叮噹噹地響。②〖俗〗一再地說;反覆强調使生印象。—*n.* 鐘聲;叮噹聲。

ding·bat ['dɪŋ,bæt; 'diŋbæt] *n.* 〖俗〗①可投擲之物(如石、木棍等)。②器具;傢伙。

ding·dong ['dɪŋ,dɔŋ; 'diŋ'dɔŋ] *n.* ①(鐘聲的) 叮噹。②任何與鐘聲相似的聲音。—*adj.* ①連續反覆的。②〖俗〗猛烈的 (鬥爭、競爭等)。 —*adv.* 熱心地。 —*v.i.* ①叮噹地響。②反覆行走。③嘮叨。

din·ghy, din·gey ['dɪŋgɪ; 'diŋgi] *n., pl.* **-ghies.** 軍艦或大船上帶的小艇; 小舟;輕舟。(亦作 **dingy, dinky**)

din·gle ['dɪŋgl; 'diŋgl] *n.* 小峽谷。

din·go ['dɪŋgo; 'diŋgou] *n., pl.* **-goes.** 澳洲產之一種野犬。

din·gus ['dɪŋgəs; 'diŋgəs] *n.* 〖俚〗器具;精巧之物;玩意。

***din·gy**[1] ['dɪndʒɪ; 'dindʒi] *adj.,* **-gi·er, -gi·est.** ①骯髒的。②昏暗的。

din·gy[2] ['dɪŋgɪ; 'diŋgi] *n.* =**dinghy.**

din·ing alcove ['daɪnɪŋ~; 'dainiŋ~] 小飯廳。

dining car (火車之)餐車。

dining hall 大餐廳。

dining room 飯廳。

dining table 餐桌。

dink·ey ['dɪŋkɪ; 'diŋki] *n., pl.* **-eys.** 〖俗〗①細小之物。②小型之機車或電動車。(亦作 **dinky**)

din·kum ['dɪŋkəm; 'diŋkəm] *adj.* 〖澳俚〗誠實的; 可靠的;公平的。 ***dinkum oil*** 可靠的眞相。—*adv.* 〖澳俚〗誠實地;眞實地。

dink·y ['dɪŋkɪ; 'diŋki] *adj.,* **dink·i·er, dink·i·est,** *n., pl.* **dink·ies.** —*adj.* ①〖俚〗小型的;小的;不重要的;無意義的。②〖英俗〗整齊的;整潔的;精緻的;漂亮的。 —*n.* ① =**dinkey.** ② =**dinghy.**

‡**din·ner** ['dɪnə; 'dinə] *n.* ①一日的主餐(午餐或晚餐)。It is time for *dinner.* 是吃晚飯的時候了。②宴會。We gave a *dinner* in honor of our new president. 我們設筵款待新會長。〖注意〗在英國和美國的工人階級和中下層階級的 dinner 指午餐;有閒階級和中上層階級 (尤其在大城市中) 的 dinner 指晚餐。 注意上邊例句中冠詞之應用及省略;有冠詞時表示係一頓一頓的飯食, 不用冠詞時通常表示吃飯這件事。

dinner bell 通知開膳之鐘(或鈴); 吃飯鐘。

dinner bucket (or **pail**) 便當盒。

dinner cloth 正餐桌巾。

dinner clothes 餐服。

dinner dress 一種半正式之婦女餐服(通常有袖或短外衣)。

dinner fork 有四個叉齒的大桌叉。

dinner hour 正餐之時刻。

dinner jacket (or **coat**) 男子無尾晚禮服。

dinner knife 桌刀; 餐刀。

dinner party 宴會。

dinner plate 西餐用大盤。

dinner service (or **set**) 一套特別的餐具。

dinner table 食桌;餐桌。

dinner time =**dinner hour.**

dinner wag(g)on 裝有脚輪之食器臺。

din·ner·ware ['dɪnə,wɛr; 'dinəwɛə] *n.* 食器類。

di·noc·er·as [daɪ'nɑsərəs; dai'nɔsərəs] *n.* 〖古生物〗①恐角獸。② (D-) 恐角獸屬。

di·no·saur ['daɪnə,sɔr; 'dainəsɔ:] *n.* 恐龍。

di·no·sau·ri·an [,daɪnə'sɔrɪən; ,dainə'sɔ:riən] *adj.* (似)恐龍的。 —*n.* 恐龍。

di·no·sau·ric [,daɪnə'sɔrɪk; ,dainə'sɔ:rik] *adj.* 恐龍一般巨大的;龐大的。

di·no·there ['daɪnə,θɪr; 'dainəθiə] *n.* 〖古生物〗一種似象之恐龍(第三紀哺乳動物)。

dint [dɪnt; dint] *n.* ①(由一擊或壓而成的)凹痕;凹處。②力;力量。 ***by dint of*** 由於;憑藉。 You succeeded *by dint of* hard work. 你由於努力工作而成功。—*v.t.* 在…上擊出凹痕。

di·oc·e·san [daɪ'ɑsəsn; dai'ɔsisən] *adj.* 主教轄區的。—*n.* 主教(轄有教區者)。

di·o·cese ['daɪə,sis; 'daiəsi:s] *n.* 主教轄區。

di·ode ['daɪod; 'daioud] *n.* 〖電〗兩極眞空管。

di·oe·cious [daɪ'iʃəs; dai'i:ʃəs] *adj.* 〖生物〗雌雄異體的;雌雄異株的。

Di·og·e·nes [daɪ'ɑdʒə,niz; dai'ɔdʒini:z] *n.* 戴奧眞尼斯(412?–323B.C., 希臘犬儒學派, Cynic, 哲學家)。—**Di·og·e·ne·an,** *adj.*

Di·o·me·des [,daɪə'midiz; ,daiə'mi:di:z] *n.* 〖希臘神話〗戴奧米底斯 (荷馬史詩Illiad中之希臘英雄, 其武藝僅次於Achilles).

Di·o·ny·si·a [,daɪə'nɪʃɪə; ,daiə'niziə] *n. pl.* (古希臘之) 狂歡節;酒神節。

Di·o·nys·i·ac [,daɪə'nɪsɪ,æk; ,daiə'niziæk] *adj.* (古希臘之) 狂歡節的; 酒神節的;酒神的。

Di·o·ny·sian [,daɪə'nɪʃən; ,daiə'niziən] *adj.* ①酒神 Dionysus 或 Bacchus 的。② (d-) 狂飲的;騷鬧的。

Di·o·ny·si·us [,daɪə'nɪʃɪəs; ,daiə'nisiəs] *n.* 戴奧尼夏 (the Elder, 430?–367 B.C., 古希臘 Syracuse 之暴君)。

Di·o·ny·sus, Di·o·ny·sos [,daɪə'naɪsəs; ,daiə'naisəs] *n.* 戴奧尼索斯(古希

臘酒神與戲劇之神)。

di·op·ter, di·op·tre [daɪ'ɑptɚ; dai'ɔptə] *n.* 〖光學〗屈光度。

di·op·tric [daɪ'ɑptrɪk; dai'ɔptrik] *adj.* 光線折射的;光線屈折學的;屈光學的。

di·op·trics [daɪ'ɑptrɪks; dai'ɔptriks] *n.* (作 *sing.* 解) 光線屈折學;屈光學。

di·o·ram·a [ˌdaɪə'ræmə; ˌdaiə'rɑːmə] *n.* ①西洋鏡 (從小孔窺看裝設之圖畫)。②透視圖畫。③實景模型。 **—di·o·ram·ic,** *adj.*

di·o·rite ['daɪəˌraɪt; 'daiərait] *n.* 〖礦〗閃長岩。**—di·o·rit·ic,** *adj.*

di·ox·ide [daɪ'ɑksaɪd; dai'ɔksaid] *n.* 二氧化物。

dip** [dɪp; dip] *v.,* **dipped** or **dipt, dip·ping,** *n.* —*v.t.* ①沾;浸。Mary *dipped* her head into the clear pool. 瑪麗將頭浸入清水池中。②降後復升起。③行浸禮。④掬;汲。He *dipped* up the clear water. 他汲出清澈之水。⑤伸(入)。⑥浸(某物)於液體以染之。to *dip* a garment. 染衣服。⑦使陷入經濟困難。She was *dipped* as badly as her father. 她的經濟狀況跟他父親一樣困難。—*v.i.*①沾水;擊水;浸水。②傾斜。The land *dips* gently to the south. 這地微向南方傾斜。③下降。The sun *dipped* below the horizon. 日落於地平線下。④伸入掬取。⑤涉獵;瀏覽。to *dip* into a book. 瀏覽一本書。⑥請安;行禮。dip into the future***預想將來。***dip one's hand into one's purse*** 浪費。—*n.* ①浸。②浸液。③傾斜;斜坡。a *dip* in a road. 路的斜坡。④地面之凹處。⑤急降。The plane made a *dip* and then descended. 飛機急降,然後便降落了。⑥浸心蠟燭。⑦短時的嘗試或經驗;涉獵。his early *dip* into politics. 他早期對政治的涉獵。⑧掬取。***have*** (or ***take***)***a dip*** 游泳;海浴。

diph·the·ri·a [dɪf'θɪrɪə; dif'θiəriə] *n.* 白喉。**—diph·the·ri·al,** *adj.*

diph·ther·ic [dɪf'θɛrɪk; dif'θerik] *adj.* =**diphtheritic.**

diph·the·rit·ic [ˌdɪfθə'rɪtɪk; ˌdifθi'ritik] *adj.* ①白喉的;像白喉的。②患白喉的。

diph·the·roid ['dɪfθəˌrɔɪd; 'difθərɔid] *adj.* 似白喉的。

diph·thong ['dɪfθɔŋ; 'difθɔŋ] *n.* 雙元音(如 ɔi, au 等)。**—al,** *adj.*

diph·thong·ize ['dɪfθɔŋˌaɪz; 'difθɔŋgaiz] *v.,* **-ized, -iz·ing.** —*v.t.* 化(單元音)爲雙元音;讀作雙元音。 —*v.i.* 變爲雙元音。

dip·lo·coc·cus [ˌdɪplə'kɑkəs; ˌdiplə'kɔkəs] *n., pl.* **-ci** [-saɪ; -sai]. 雙球菌。**—dip·lo·coc·cal, dip·lo·coc·cic,** *adj.*

di·plo·ma [dɪ'plomə; di'ploumə] *n., pl.* **-mas, -ma·ta** [-mətə; -mətə]. ①文憑;畢業證書。②證明權力、特權、榮譽等的證書;獎狀。

***di·plo·ma·cy** [dɪ'ploməsɪ; di'plouməsi] *n., pl.* **-cies.** ①外交。courses in *diplomacy.* 外交課程。②外交的手腕;權謀。③外交使節團。members of UN *diplomacy.* 聯合國之各國代表人員。

di·plo·ma'd, di·plo·maed[dɪ'plomәd; di'ploumәd] *adj.* 有文憑或證書的。

di·plo·ma·ism [dɪ'ploməɪzəm; di'plouməizəm] *n.* 文憑主義。

diploma mill ①學店(有錢即可獲得學位者)。②龐大而鬆懈的大學或學院。

diploma piece 爲文憑而寫的論文。

dip·lo·mat ['dɪpləˌmæt; 'dipləmæt] *n.* ①外交家。②有權謀的人。

***dip·lo·mat·ic** [ˌdɪplə'mætɪk; ˌdiplə'mætik] *adj.* ①外交的;與外交有關的。*diplomatic* service. 外交官的集合稱;外交界。②有外交手腕的;靈敏的;機智的;圓滑的。a *diplomatic* answer. 圓滑的答覆。**—al·ly,** *adv.*

diplomatic corps 外交使節團。(亦作 **diplomatic body**)

diplomatic immunity 外交人員免受種種外國法律約束的自由;外交豁免權。

diplomatic pouch 外交文件遞送袋。

dip·lo·mat·ics [ˌdɪplə'mætɪks; ˌdiplə'mætiks] *n.*① =**diplomacy.** ②考證古代文獻的一門學問。

di·plo·ma·tist [dɪ'plomətɪst; di'ploumətist] *n.* =**diplomat.**

di·plo·ma·tize [dɪ'plomәˌtaɪz; di'ploumәtaiz] *v.,* **-tized, -tiz·ing.** —*v.i.* 運用外交手腕。—*v.t.* 以外交手腕行之。

dip·lon ['dɪplɑn; 'diplɔn] *n.* 〖化〗二重核(重氫之原子核)。

di·plo·pi·a [dɪ'plopɪə; di'ploupiə] *n.* 〖醫〗複視。—**di·plop·ic,** *adj.*

dip·no·an ['dɪpnoən; 'dipnouən] *adj.* 肺魚類的。—*n.* 肺魚;肺魚類之魚。**—dip·no·ous,** *adj.*

di·pole ['daɪˌpol; 'daipoul] *n.* 〖理化〗偶極子。**—di·po·lar,** *adj.*

dip·per ['dɪpɚ; 'dipə] *n.* ①浸者;汲取者。②長柄杯或勺。③〖動物〗川烏類之鳥。④〖攝影〗顯影槽。⑤ (D-)〖天文〗**a.** (大熊星座之)北斗七星(=the Big Dipper). **b.** (小熊星座之)北斗七星(=the Little Dipper). ⑥(讀書不求甚解之)略讀者。

dip·ping needle['dɪpɪŋ～;'dipiŋ～] 磁傾針。

dip·so·ma·ni·a [ˌdɪpsə'menɪə; ˌdipsou'meinjə] *n.* 耽酒狂;酗酒病。

dip·so·ma·ni·ac [ˌdɪpsə'menɪˌæk; ˌdipsou'meiniæk] *n.* 耽酒狂之人;酗酒病患者。**—al,** *adj.*

dip·sy-do, dip·sy-doo [ˌdɪpsɪ'du; ˌdipsi'duː] *n.* 〖美俚〗①〖棒球〗極慢或極快之曲球。②狡猾之手法。

dip·sy doo·dle [ˌdɪpsɪ'dudḷ; ˌdipsi'duːdl] ①〖俚〗大幅波動。②〖俚〗欺騙手段。(亦作 **dipsy-doodle**)

Dip·ter·a ['dɪptərə; 'diptərə] *n.* 雙翅類。

dip·ter·al ['dɪptərəl; 'diptərəl] *adj.* ①〖生物〗有雙翅的;雙翅類的(=dipterous). ②〖建築〗雙排柱式的。

dip·ter·ous ['dɪptərəs;'diptərəs] *adj.* ①雙翅類的。②〖植物〗(種子、莖等) 有二翅狀物的。

dip·tych['dɪptɪk;'diptik]*n.* ①古羅馬之記事板。②有雙葉之摺疊物;(特指)雙連圖畫。

Di·rac [dɪ'ræk; di'ræk] *n.* 狄雷克(Paul Adrien Maurice, 1902-, 英國物理學家, 曾獲 1933 年諾貝爾獎)。

***dire** [daɪr; 'daiə] *adj.,* **dir·er, dir·est.** ①可怕的;可悲的。②非常的;極度的。He is in *dire* need of help. 他非常需要援助。

:di·rect [də'rɛkt, daɪ-; di'rekt, dai'r-] *v.t.* ①管理;指導;指揮;命令。②指示方向;指引。Can you *direct* me to the post office? 你能指示我去郵局的方向嗎? ③指向;針對。Please *direct* your attention to what I'm saying. 請注意我正講的話。④書寫住址。—*v.i.* ①指揮。Who *directed* at yesterday's concert? 誰指揮昨天的音樂會?②指導;引導。—*adj.* ①直的。Our house is in a *direct* line with the school. 我們的房子和學校是在一直線上。②最近的;最短的;捷徑的。This is a *direct* route to the station. 這是去車站的捷徑。③直接的。a *direct* hit. 直接命中。④直系的。a *direct* descendant. 直系子孫。⑤坦白的;確實的。I want a *direct* answer, "yes" or "no." 我要一個確實的答覆"是"或"否"。⑥剛好;恰好。This is the *direct* opposite of that. 這個剛好與那個相反。⑦〖文法〗a. 直接敍述法 (*direct* quotation or discourse). b. 直接受詞 (*direct* object). —*adv.* 直接地。Send it *direct* to me. 把它直接送給我。The train goes there *direct*. 火車直接開往那裡。—**a·ble,** *adj.*

direct action 有組織之工人對抗雇主之直接行動(如罷工、怠工、破壞等)。

direct cost 直接成本 (別於 indirect cost).

direct current 直流電。

di·rect·ed [dəˈrɛktɪd; diˈrektid] *adj.* 經指導的;經管理的。

directed economy 管制經濟。

di·rec·tee [dəˌrɛkˈti; diˌrekˈtiː] *n.* 受指導者;受指揮者。

direct evidence (證人所提的)直接證據。

direct examination 〖法律〗當事人或辯護人對己方證人所作之初度詰問。

:di·rec·tion [dəˈrɛkʃən, daɪ-; diˈrekʃən, dai-] *n.* ①管理;監督;指揮。We are under his *direction*. 我們受他管轄。②指導;指引;命令;說明。He gave me full *directions* how to reach the station. 他向我詳細指示如何到達車站。③方向。In which *direction* did he go? 他向那方向走?④住址。⑤趨勢;傾向。Of late, international politics have taken a new *direction*. 近來國際政治活動已有一新趨勢。⑥方面。The town shows improvement in many *directions*. 這小城在許多方面均表現了進步。⑦董事會。—*v.t.* 給以方向。—**less,** *adj.* —**less·ly,** *adv.*

di·rec·tion·al [dəˈrɛkʃənḷ; diˈrekʃənḷ] *adj.* ①方向的。②〖無線電〗定向的。③指示方向的。④賦予方向的。⑤導演的。—**i·ty,** *n.*

directional antenna 〖無線電〗指向天線;定向天線。

direction finder 〖無線電〗定向儀。

di·rec·tive [dəˈrɛktɪv; diˈrektiv] *adj.* ①指揮的;指導的。②指向的。—*n.* 指令;訓令;指導。

:di·rect·ly [dəˈrɛktlɪ, daɪ-; diˈrektli, dai-] *adv.* ①直接地。He was looking *directly* at me. 他直望着我。②卽刻地。Come in *directly*. 請卽刻進來。③〖英俗〗立卽(=as soos as). Let me know *directly* he comes. 他來到時立卽通知我。④全然地。*directly* opposite. 全然相反;恰好相反。

direct mail (分別向廣大羣衆投寄的)直接郵件。

direct method (語言等之)直接教學法。

di·rect·ness [dəˈrɛktnɪs; diˈrektnis] *n.* 率直;坦白;直接。

direct object 〖文法〗直接受詞。

Di·rec·toire [dirɛkˈtwar; diːrekˈtwar] 〖法〗*n.* 法國第一共和時代之五人執政團。—*adj.* 五人執政團之時期的(指服式、傢具等而言)。

·di·rec·tor [dəˈrɛktə, daɪ-; diˈrektə, dai-] *n.* ①指揮者;指導者;管理者(如局長、校長、主管等)。②理事;董事。Board of *Directors*. 董事會。③影、劇的導演。④〖軍〗(控制火砲的)指揮儀。(亦作 **directer**)

di·rec·to·rate [dəˈrɛktərɪt; diˈrektərit] *n.* ①董事會。②董事的地位或身分。

director general 處長或局長(尤指某些政府機構之主管)。

di·rec·to·ri·al [dəˌrɛkˈtorɪəl; diˌrekˈtɔːriəl] *adj.* ①指揮者的;管理者的;理事的;董事的。②(D-)(從 1795-1799 年間統治法國之)五人執政團的。—**ly,** *adv.*

di·rec·tor·ship [dəˈrɛktəˌʃɪp; diˈrektəʃip] *n.* director 之職位或任期。

di·rec·to·ry [dəˈrɛktərɪ; diˈrektəri] *n., pl.* **-ries,** *adj.* —*n.* ①人名住址簿。a telephone *directory*. 電話簿。②(記載規則或指令的)指南;寶鑑。③一羣董事;董事會。④(D-)從 1795 到1799年間統治法國的五人執政團。—*adj.* 指導的;勸告的。

direct proportion 正比例;正比。

direct question 〖文法〗直接問句。

direct reaction 〖化〗直接反應;正反應。

di·rec·tress [dəˈrɛktrɪs; diˈrektris] *n.* director 之女性。

di·rec·trix [dəˈrɛktrɪks; diˈrektriks] *n., pl.* **-trix·es, -tric·es** [-ˈtraɪsiz; -ˈtraisiːz]. ①〖幾何〗準線。②director 之女性。

direct tax 直接稅。

dire·ful [ˈdaɪrfəl; ˈdaiəfəl] *adj.* 可怕的;悲慘的;不幸的。—**ly,** *adv.* —**ness,** *n.*

dirge [dɝdʒ; dəːdʒ] *n.* 喪曲;輓歌。

dir·i·gi·bil·i·ty [ˌdɪrədʒəˈbɪlətɪ; ˌdiridʒəˈbiliti] *n.* 可操縱性。

dir·i·gi·ble [ˈdɪrədʒəbḷ; ˈdiridʒəbl] *n.* 可駕駛的輕氣球;飛船。—*adj.* 能被指導的。

dirigible balloon 飛船(=airship).

dir·i·ment [ˈdɪrɪmənt; ˈdirimənt] *adj.* 〖法律〗使絕對無效的。

dirk [dɝk; dəːk] *n.* 短劍;匕首。—*v.t.* 以短劍刺。

dirn·dl [ˈdɝndḷ; ˈdəːndl] *n.* 一種女裝。

·dirt [dɝt; dəːt] *n.* ①垃圾;污穢物(如灰塵、糞便、泥土等)。Wash the *dirt* off. 洗去污物。②泥土;鬆的土。③無價值的東西。as cheap as *dirt*. 賤如糞土。④污行;卑鄙。⑤地面。⑥〖俚〗流言蜚語;穢聞。***eat dirt*** 忍辱含詬。***throw*** (or ***fling***) ***dirt at somebody*** 誹謗人。—**less,** *adj.*

dirt-cheap [ˈdɝtˈtʃip; ˈdəːtˈtʃiːp] *adj.* 毫無價值的;賤如糞土的。

dirt eating 食土病;(非洲黑人)以土爲食之習俗。

dirt farmer 〖俗〗實地耕作之農夫(爲 gentleman farmer 之對)。

dirt-poor [ˈdɝtˈpʊr; ˈdəːtˈpuə] *adj.* 很窮的。

dirt road 未加鋪路面的道路。

·dirt·y [ˈdɝtɪ; ˈdəːti] *adj.,* **dirt·i·er, dirt·i·est.,** *v.,* **dirt·ied, dirt·y·ing.** —*adj.* ①不潔的;污穢的;髒的。Children playing in mud get *dirty*. 在爛泥中玩的孩子弄得很骯髒。②卑劣的;淫猥的;齷齪的。Don't mix with boys who have *dirty* minds. 不要與思想卑劣的男孩混在一起。③暴風雨的;暴風的。I don't want to go out on such a *dirty* night. 如此暴風雨的夜晚,我不願出去。④(顏色)不鮮明的;有雲翳的。⑤凶狠的。—*v.t.*弄髒。***dirty one's hands*** 幹不正當之事。—*v.i.* 變髒。Soft cloths *dirty* easily. 軟布易髒。—**dirt·i·ly,** *adv.* —**dirt·i·ness,** *n.*

dirty pool 〖美俚〗卑鄙或不正當的手段或策略。

dirty work 〖美俚〗欺詐行爲;不法行爲。

dis. ① discipline. ② discount. ③ distance.

dis- 〖字首〗①表"分開;分離;離去;全然"或"否定;相反"之義。②表"兩次;雙"之義

(爲 **di-** 之異體用於 **s** 之前, 如: dissyllable).

dis·a·bil·i·ty [ˌdɪsəˈbɪlətɪ; ˌdisəˈbiliti] *n., pl.* **-ties.** ①無力;無能;缺乏活力。②〖法律〗無能力;無資格。③使喪失資格之事。

disability clause 壽險被保人殘廢時可停付保險費的規定。

disability insurance 殘廢保險。

***dis·a·ble** [dɪsˈebl̩; disˈeibl] *v.t.,* **-bled, -bling.** ①使無能力; 使殘廢; 使失去能力。Old age *disabled* him for hard labor. 年邁使他不能勝任繁重工作。②使在法律上無資格。**—ment,** *n.*

dis·a·bled [dɪsˈebl̩d; disˈeibld] *adj.* 殘廢的。*disabled* soldiers. 傷殘軍人。

dis·a·buse [ˌdɪsəˈbjuz; ˌdisəˈbju:z] *v.t.,* **-bused, -bus·ing.** 解惑;釋疑;矯正。

dis·ac·cord [ˌdɪsəˈkɔrd; ˌdisəˈkɔ:d] *v.i.* 不一致;不同意;不和。**—***n.* 不一致;不同意;不和。

dis·ad·van·tage** [ˌdɪsədˈvæntɪdʒ; ˌdisədˈvɑ:ntidʒ] *n.* ①不便;不利;不利情況。Jenny's shyness puts her at a *disadvantage* in company. 珍妮的害羞使得她在人羣中處於不利的地位。②傷害; 損失(如名譽、信用、金錢等)。They created a rumor to his *disadvantage.* 他們造謠言中傷他。③缺點;缺陷。**—v.t.* 使處於不利地位。

dis·ad·van·taged [ˌdɪsədˈvæntɪdʒd; ˌdisədˈvɑ:ntidʒd] *adj.* 貧窮的。

dis·ad·van·ta·geous [dɪsˌædvənˈtedʒəs; ˌdisædvɑ:nˈteidʒəs] *adj.* 不利的;招致傷害的。**—ly,** *adv.* **—ness,** *n.*

dis·af·fect [ˌdɪsəˈfɛkt; ˌdisəˈfekt] *v.t.* ①使不滿意;使生惡感;使生二心。②〖罕〗不喜歡;不贊成。**—dis·af·fec·tion,** *n.*

dis·af·fect·ed [ˌdɪsəˈfɛktɪd; ˌdisəˈfektid] *adj.* 不友善的;不忠實的;不滿意的;憤憤不平的。 **—ly,** *adv.* **—ness,** *n.*

dis·af·fil·i·ate [ˌdɪsəˈfɪlɪˌet; ˌdisəˈfilieit] *v.t. & v.i.,* **-at·ed, -at·ing.** (使)脫離;(使)退出。

dis·af·firm [ˌdɪsəˈfɝm; ˌdisəˈfə:m] *v.t.* ①抗議; 反駁。②〖法律〗否認; 註銷; 廢棄。**—ance, —a·tion,** *n.*

dis·af·for·est [ˌdɪsəˈfɑrɪst; ˌdisəˈfɔrist] *v.t.* ①〖英法律〗使成不受森林法拘束之普通地;取消林地特權。②砍伐…之森林;開闢(林地)。

dis·ag·gre·gate [dɪsˈægrəˌget; disˈægrigeit] *v.t.* 使崩潰。**—dis·ag·gre·ga·tion,** *n.*

***dis·a·gree** [ˌdɪsəˈgri; ˌdisəˈgri:] *v.i.,* **-greed, -gree·ing.** ①不合;不一致〖with〗. The conclusions *disagree* with the facts. 結論與事實不一致。②意見不合;爭論。③不適宜。Cheese *disagrees* with some people. 乾酪對有些人不適宜。

***dis·a·gree·a·ble** [ˌdɪsəˈgriəbl̩; ˌdisəˈgri:əbl] *adj.* ①不合意的; 討厭的。What *disagreeable* weather! 好討厭的天氣! ②令人不愉快的; 不爲人所喜愛的; 脾氣不好的。**—dis·a·gree·a·bil·i·ty, —ness,** *n.*

dis·a·gree·a·bles [ˌdɪsəˈgriəbl̩z; ˌdisəˈgri:əblz] *n. pl.* 不愉快的事物。

dis·a·gree·a·bly [ˌdɪsəˈgriəblɪ; ˌdisəˈgri:əbli] *adv.* 不愉快地。

dis·a·gree·ment [ˌdɪsəˈgrimənt; ˌdisəˈgri:mənt] *n.* ①意見不同;不合。②爭論。③不適宜。④不一致。

dis·al·low [ˌdɪsəˈlaʊ; ˈdisəˈlau] *v.t.* ①不允;不許可。②拒絕接受;拒絕。**—ance,** *n.*

dis·an·nul [ˌdɪsəˈnʌl; ˌdisəˈnʌl] *v.t.,* **-nulled, -nul·ling.** 取消;使作廢;廢棄。

‡dis·ap·pear [ˌdɪsəˈpɪr; ˌdisəˈpiə] *v.i.* ①不見; 消失; 隱沒。A ship *disappeared* below the horizon. 一隻船隱沒於水平線下。②不存在;絕跡;失去。My rheumatism has *disappeared.* 我的風濕病已癒。**—er, —ance,** *n.*

disappearing bed 立體萬能床。

***dis·ap·point** [ˌdɪsəˈpɔɪnt; ˌdisəˈpɔint] *v.t.* ①使失望。His conduct *disappoints* us. 他的行爲使我們失望。②使受挫折;阻礙。③對…失信。You promised to come; do not *disappoint* me. 你答應來的;不要失信於我。

dis·ap·point·ed [ˌdɪsəˈpɔɪntɪd; ˌdisəˈpɔintid] *adj.* 失望的;沮喪的。I was *disappointed* in him. 我對他甚感失望。**—ly,** *adv.*

dis·ap·point·ing [ˌdɪsəˈpɔɪntɪŋ; ˌdisəˈpɔintiŋ] *adj.* 令人失望的; 掃興的。**—ly,** *adv.*

***dis·ap·point·ment** [ˌdɪsəˈpɔɪntmənt; ˌdisəˈpɔintmənt] *n.* ①失望;挫折。To my great *disappointment,* it rained on Sunday. 星期日下雨,使我大爲失望。②造成使人失望原因的人或事物。③令人失望的事實或行爲。

dis·ap·pro·ba·tion [ˌdɪsæprəˈbeʃən; ˌdisæprouˈbeiʃən] *n.* 不贊同;不認可。

***dis·ap·prov·al** [ˌdɪsəˈpruvl̩; ˌdisəˈpru:vəl] *n.* 不承認;不贊成。He shook his head in *disapproval.* 他不贊成地搖搖頭。

***dis·ap·prove** [ˌdɪsəˈpruv; ˈdisəˈpru:v] *v.t. & v.i.,* **-proved, -prov·ing.** 不贊成; 不准許; 非難。I'm sorry I must *disapprove* (of) your action. 很抱歉,我必須指責你的行動。

dis·ap·prov·ing·ly [ˌdɪsəˈpruvɪŋlɪ; ˈdisəˈpru:viŋli] *adv.* 以非難的態度; 以不贊成的眼光、口吻等。She eyed him *disapprovingly.* 她不以爲然地看着他。

dis·arm** [dɪsˈɑrm; disˈɑ:m] *v.t.* ①繳械。The police *disarmed* them. 警察將他們繳械。②解除武裝;消除軍備;裁減軍備。③驅除敵意或懷疑等。④使無害。**—v.i.* 裁減軍備;解除武裝。Which country will be the first to *disarm?* 那一國將先裁減軍備?

***dis·ar·ma·ment** [dɪsˈɑrməmənt; disˈɑ:məmənt] *n.* 解除武裝;裁減軍備。

dis·arm·ing [dɪsˈɑrmɪŋ; disˈɑ:miŋ] *adj.* 排除警戒心或懷疑心的; 使人不緊張的。**—ly,** *adv.*

dis·ar·range [ˌdɪsəˈrendʒ; ˈdisəˈreindʒ] *v.t.,* **-ranged, -rang·ing.** 擾亂;弄亂。**—ment,** *n.*

dis·ar·ray [ˌdɪsəˈre; ˈdisəˈrei] *n.* ①雜亂; 毫無秩序。②不整齊之服裝; 無服飾。**—***v.t.* ①使亂;使無秩序。②剝脫衣服;脫衣。

dis·ar·tic·u·late [ˌdɪsɑrˈtɪkjəˌlet; ˈdisɑ:ˈtikjuleit] *v.t. & v.i.* (使)關節脫落;截斷關節。**—dis·ar·tic·u·la·tor,** *n.*

dis·as·sem·ble [ˌdɪsəˈsɛmbl̩; ˌdisəˈsembl] *v.,* **-bled, -bling.** **—***v.t.* 解離; 分解。 **—***v.i.* 可拆開;可分解。

dis·as·so·ci·ate [ˌdɪsəˈsoʃɪˌet; ˌdisəˈsouʃieit] *v.,* **-at·ed, -at·ing.** **—***v.t.* 使分離;使分解;使分裂(=dissociate). **—***v.i.* 分離;分裂;脫離關係。**—dis·as·so·ci·a·tion,** *n.*

***dis·as·ter** [dɪzˈæstɚ; diˈzɑ:stə] *n.* ①災禍;不幸。They kept a record of earthquake *disasters.* 他們記錄地震所發生的災禍。②失敗。

disaster area 災區。

***dis·as·trous** [dɪzˈæstrəs, –ˈɑs–; diˈzɑːstrəs] *adj.* 造成災禍的; 招致不幸的; 造成重大傷害的; 致令痛苦的。 Carelessness in driving often results in *disastrous* accidents. 駕駛不愼常招致不幸的意外。 **—ness,** *n.* **—ly,** *adv.*

dis·a·vow [ˌdɪsəˈvau; ˈdisəˈvau] *v.t.* 不承認;否認;推翻(前言)。**—al, —er,** *n.*

dis·band [dɪsˈbænd; disˈbænd] *v.t.* 解散(軍隊)。*—v.i.* ①解散。②潰散。**—ment,** *n.*

dis·bar [dɪsˈbɑr; disˈbɑː] *v.t.,* **-barred, -bar·ring.** ①使失資格。②〖法律〗取消律師資格;取消(律師)出庭權利。**—ment,** *n.*

dis·be·lief [ˌdɪsbəˈlif; ˈdisbiˈliːf] *n.* 不信;懷疑;疑惑。

dis·be·lieve [ˌdɪsbəˈliv; ˈdisbiˈliːv] *v.t. & v.i.,* **-lieved, -liev·ing.** 不信;懷疑;疑惑。**—dis·be·liev·er,** *n.*

dis·be·liev·ing [ˌdɪsbɪˈlivɪŋ; ˈdisbiˈliːviŋ] *adj.* 懷疑的;疑惑的;不信的。

dis·bench [dɪsˈbɛntʃ; disˈbentʃ] *v.t.* ①使離座。②〖英法律〗使喪失法學協會會員資格。

dis·bos·om [dɪsˈbuzəm; disˈbuzəm] *v.t.* 招供;吐露;公開。

dis·branch [dɪsˈbræntʃ; disˈbrɑːntʃ] *v.t.* 折(枝);剪去(樹等)之枝。

dis·bud [dɪsˈbʌd; disˈbʌd] *v.t.,* **-bud·ded, -bud·ding.** 摘去嫩芽;去蕾。

dis·bur·den [dɪsˈbɝdn̩; disˈbəːdn] *v.i. & v.t.* 解除(責任、重擔); 擺脫; 卸除。 ***disburden one's mind to*** 向…吐露心懷。 **—ment,** *n.*

dis·burse [dɪsˈbɝs; disˈbəːs] *v.t. & v.i.,* **-bursed, -burs·ing.** ①支出;付出。②分配。 **—dis·burs·a·ble,** *adj.*

dis·burse·ment [dɪsˈbɝsmənt; disˈbəːsmənt] *n.* 支出;付出之款。

dis·burs·er [dɪsˈbɝsɚ; disˈbəːsə] *n.* 支出者;付出者。

disc [dɪsk; disk] *n.* =**disk.**

disc. ① discount. ② discovered. ③ discoverer.

dis·cal [ˈdɪskəl; ˈdiskəl] *adj.* 圓盤的; 圓盤狀的;在圓盤上的。

dis·card** [*v.* dɪsˈkɑrd; disˈkɑːd *n.* ˈdɪskɑrd; ˈdiskɑːd, disˈkɑːd] *v.t.* ①拋棄; 棄絕;摒除。to *discard* prejudices. 摒除偏見。 ②(紙牌戲)擲出無用的牌。*—v.i.* 擲出無用的牌。 *—n.* ①棄去; 拋棄。 *discard* of old beliefs, prejudices. 拋棄舊信念、偏見。 ②被棄的人或物。the *discards* of society. 爲社會所棄者。③擲出的無用之紙牌。into the discard*** 成爲無用之物。 **—er,** *n.*

***dis·cern** [dɪˈzɝn, –ˈsɝn; diˈsəːn, –ˈzəːn] *v.t.* ①目睹;認識;洞悉。②辨別;辨識。*—v.i.* 辨別。 to *discern* between truth and falsehood. 辨別眞僞。 **—er,** *n.*

dis·cern·i·ble, dis·cern·a·ble [dɪˈzɝnəbl̩; diˈsəːnəbl] *adj.* 可辨別的;可認識的。**—dis·cern·i·bly, dis·cern·a·bly,** *adv.* **—ness,** *n.*

dis·cern·ing [dɪˈzɝnɪŋ; diˈsəːniŋ] *adj.* 有辨識能力的;聰敏的。**—ly,** *adv.*

dis·cern·ment [dɪˈzɝnmənt; diˈsəːnmənt] *n.* ①認識;識別。②洞察力。

***dis·charge** [dɪsˈtʃɑrdʒ; disˈtʃɑːdʒ] *v.,* **-charged, -charg·ing,** *n.* *—v.t.* ①將(貨)從船上卸下。②發射。③放出; 流出。 ④完成任務; 執行職務。 We have to *discharge* ourselves of our duties. 我們要盡我們的職責。⑤解除職務; 開除; 開釋。 The servant was *discharged* for being dishonest. 這僕人因不誠實而被解雇。⑥還債。 He was unable to *discharge* his debts. 他無力還債。 ⑦送走; 放行 〖from〗. The patient was *discharged* from hospital after his complete recovery. 這病人痊癒後,醫院請他出院。⑧放電。⑨流出(膿)。 The wound *discharges* pus. 傷口流膿。⑩洗除(布之顏色)。⑪免除(破產者)償還舊債。 ⑫解約。 *—v.i.* ①卸載; 卸貨。The vessel is *discharging.* 船在卸貨。②放出;流出。③出膿。④發射。The soldiers loaded and *discharged* with great rapidity. 兵士們迅速裝子彈發射。⑤(染料)可洗除。*—n.* ①卸貨。How long will the *discharge* of the cargo take? 卸貨需要多少時間? ②發射;爆炸。 ③釋放; 放行。The prisoners were glad to get their *discharges.* 犯人們獲釋都很高興。④開除。⑤放電。⑥放出;流出;流出量;流出之物。⑦盡職。⑧償還。⑨(布色之)洗除。**—a·ble,** *adj.*

dis·charg·er [dɪsˈtʃɑrdʒɚ; disˈtʃɑːdʒə] *n.* ①卸貨人;卸貨之器具。②發射者;射手。③排出裝置。④履行者。⑤〖電〗放電器。

***dis·ci·ple** [dɪˈsaɪpl̩; diˈsaipl] *n.* ①信徒; 門徒; 弟子。②耶穌十二使徒之任一。③(D-)基督門徒會 (Disciples of Christ) 教友。

dis·ci·ple·ship [dɪˈsaɪpl̩ˌʃɪp; diˈsaiplʃip] *n.* ①disciple 之身分、地位。②作 disciple 之期間。

dis·ci·plin·a·ble [ˈdɪsəˌplɪnəbl̩; ˈdisiplinəbl] *adj.* ①可訓練的;可薰陶的。②可懲罰的; 應懲罰的。 **—dis·ci·plin·a·bil·i·ty, —ness,** *n.*

dis·ci·pli·nar·i·an [ˌdɪsəplɪnˈɛrɪən; ˌdisipliˈnɛəriən] *n.* ①訓練者;維持紀律者。②信仰嚴格訓練者。*—adj.* 訓練的;紀律的。

dis·ci·pli·nar·y [ˈdɪsəplɪnˌɛrɪ; ˈdisiplinəri] *adj.* ①懲戒的。②紀律的;有關紀律的。③嚴格的。④有紀律的。⑤學術的;科學的。

***dis·ci·pline** [ˈdɪsəplɪn; ˈdisiplin] *n., v.,* **-plined, -plin·ing.** *—n.* ①教訓;訓練(尤指人格與思想者)。②服從規律; 紀律; 風紀。③懲戒;懲罰。The naughty boy needs a little *discipline.* 這頑皮的小孩需略加懲戒。 ④修行; 宗教戒律。 ⑤方法。 ⑥學科; 學問。 ⑦規律性。 *—v.t.* ①懲罰。 ②訓練; 控制。 **—dis·ci·pli·nal,** *adj.* **—dis·ci·plin·er,** *n.*

dis·claim [dɪsˈklem; disˈkleim] *v.t.* ①拒絕承認;否認;否認與…有關。The motorist *disclaimed* responsibility for the accident. 該駕駛人否認對車禍有責任。 ②放棄權利。 *—v.i.* 否認;拒絕承認。

dis·claim·er [dɪsˈklemɚ; disˈkleimə] *n.* ①否認。②否認者。③否認之聲明或文件。

dis·cla·ma·tion [ˌdɪskləˈmeʃən; ˌdiskləˈmeiʃən] *n.* 放棄;拒絕;不承認;不承受。

***dis·close** [dɪsˈkloz; disˈklouz] *v.t.,* **-closed, -clos·ing.** 揭發; 洩露; 宣露。 This letter *discloses* a secret. 這封信揭露了一個祕密。**—dis·clos·er,** *n.*

dis·clo·sure [dɪsˈkloʒɚ; disˈklouʒə] *n.* ①揭發; 洩露; 顯露。②揭發之物;顯露之物。

dis·co [ˈdɪsko; ˈdiskou] *n., pl.* **dis·cos.** =**discotheque.**

dis·cob·o·lus [dɪsˈkɑbələs; disˈkɔbələs] *n., pl.* **-li** [–ˌlaɪ; –lai]. (古希臘及羅馬之)擲鐵餅者。

dis·cog·ra·phy 〔dɪsˈkɑgrəfɪ; disˈkɔgrəfi〕 *n.* ①某一作曲家或演出者之全部唱片錄音目錄。②音樂唱片之歷史、分析或分類。③音樂唱片之分析或分類法。—**dis·cog·ra·pher,** *n.* —**dis·co·graph·i·cal,** *adj.*
dis·coid 〔ˈdɪskɔɪd; ˈdiskɔid〕 *n.* 圓盤狀之物。—*adj.* 圓盤狀的。
dis·col·or 〔dɪsˈkʌlɚ; disˈkʌlə〕 *v.t.* 使變色；使褪色；弄髒。—*v.i.* 變色；褪色。—**ment,** *n.*
dis·col·or·a·tion 〔ˌdɪskʌləˈreʃən; disˌkʌləˈreiʃən〕 *n.* ①變色；染汚。②汚點。
dis·col·ored 〔dɪsˈkʌlɚd; disˈkʌləd〕 *adj.* 變色的；汚染的。—**ness,** *n.*
dis·com·fit 〔dɪsˈkʌmfɪt; disˈkʌmfit〕 *v.t.* ①挫敗；擾亂；擊潰；推翻(計畫等)。②使混亂；使困窘。
dis·com·fi·ture 〔dɪsˈkʌmfɪtʃɚ; disˈkʌmfitʃə〕 *n.* ①挫敗。②失望；困苦。③困窘；狼狽。④混亂。
***dis·com·fort** 〔dɪsˈkʌmfɚt; disˈkʌmfət〕 *n.* ①不舒服；不適；不快；難過。He gave every sign of intense *discomfort.* 他處處顯得非常不舒服。②招致不安之物；困苦。—*v.t.* 使覺不舒服；使難過。
dis·com·mode 〔ˌdɪskəˈmod; ˌdiskəˈmoud〕 *v.t.,* **-mod·ed, -mod·ing.** 使煩惱；使不方便；擾亂。
dis·com·mon 〔dɪsˈkɑmən; disˈkɔmən〕 *v.t.* ①(英國牛津及劍橋大學)禁止(商人)與學生交易。②〖法律〗**a.** 褫奪對公地之使用權(如放牧牛羊)。**b.** 使成爲私有。
dis·com·pose 〔ˌdɪskəmˈpoz; ˌdiskəmˈpouz〕 *v.t.,* **-posed, -pos·ing.** ①使不安；使失常；使心亂。②弄亂；使不整齊。—**dis·com·po·sure,** *n.*
dis·com·pos·ed·ly 〔ˌdɪskəmˈpozɪdlɪ; ˌdiskəmˈpouzidli〕 *adv.* 不安地；心緒不寧地。
dis·con·cert 〔ˌdɪskənˈsɝt; ˌdiskənˈsəːt〕 *v.t.* ①使驚惶；使張皇失措；使不安。②妨礙；破壞；擾亂。—*n.* 慌亂。—**dis·con·cer·tion,** —**ment,** *n.* —**ed,** *adj.*
dis·con·cert·ing 〔ˌdɪskənˈsɝtɪŋ; ˌdiskənˈsəːtiŋ〕 *adj.* 令人驚慌失措的；令人緊張的。—**ly,** *adv.* —**ness,** *n.*
dis·con·firm 〔ˌdɪskənˈfɝm; ˌdiskənˈfəːm〕 *v.t.* 證明爲不確。
dis·con·nect 〔ˌdɪskəˈnɛkt; ˈdiskəˈnekt〕 *v.t.* 使分離；使脫離；斷絕。
dis·con·nect·ed 〔ˌdɪskəˈnɛktɪd; ˈdiskəˈnektid〕 *adj.* ①分離的；脫離的。②無系統的；不連貫的。—**ly,** *adv.*
dis·con·nec·tion 〔ˌdɪskəˈnɛkʃən; ˌdiskəˈnekʃən〕 *n.* 分離；分開；斷絕；切斷。(英亦作 **disconnexion**)
dis·con·so·late 〔dɪsˈkɑnsḷɪt; disˈkɔnsəlit〕 *adj.* ①孤獨的；絕望的；哀傷的；不快的。②令人哀傷的；淒涼的。—**ly,** *adv.*
***dis·con·tent** 〔ˌdɪskənˈtɛnt; ˈdiskənˈtent〕 *adj.* 不滿意的。He is *discontent* with his position. 他對於他的位置不滿意。—*n.* 不滿意的情緒。—*v.t.* 使不滿足。
dis·con·tent·ed 〔ˌdɪskənˈtɛntɪd; ˈdiskənˈtentid〕 *adj.* 不滿意的；不滿足的；不平的。—**ly,** *adv.* —**ness,** *n.*
dis·con·tent·ment 〔ˌdɪskənˈtɛntmənt; ˈdiskənˈtentmənt〕 *n.* 不滿；不平。
dis·con·tin·u·ance 〔ˌdɪskənˈtɪnjuəns; ˌdiskənˈtinjuəns〕 *n.* ①停止；中止；截止；廢止；放棄。②〖法律〗訴訟之中止。
dis·con·tin·u·a·tion 〔ˌdɪskənˌtɪnjuˈeʃən; ˈdiskənˌtinjuˈeiʃən〕 *n.* ＝**discontinuance.**
dis·con·tin·ue 〔ˌdɪskənˈtɪnju; ˈdiskənˈtinjuː〕 *v.t. & v.i.,* **-tin·ued, -tin·u·ing.** 停止；廢止；放棄。
dis·con·ti·nu·i·ty 〔ˌdɪskɑntəˈnuətɪ; ˈdisˌkɔntiˈnjuːiti〕 *n.* ①不接續；間斷。②〖數學〗不連續。
dis·con·tin·u·ous 〔ˌdɪskənˈtɪnjuəs; ˈdiskənˈtinjuəs〕 *adj.* 中斷的；不連續的。—**ly,** *adv.* —**ness,** *n.*
dis·co·phile 〔ˈdɪskəˌfaɪl; ˈdiskəfail〕 *n.* 唱片愛好家或收藏家。(亦作 **diskophile**)
***dis·cord** 〔*n.* ˈdɪskɔrd; ˈdiskɔːd *v.* dɪsˈkɔrd; disˈkɔːd〕 *n.* ①不一致。These two answers are in *discord.* 這兩個答案不一致。②意見不合；爭論。③〖音樂〗音調不和諧。④雜亂的聲音。—*v.i.* 不一致；不合。
dis·cord·ance 〔dɪsˈkɔrdṇs; disˈkɔːdəns〕 *n.* 不調和；不一致；不和諧。
dis·cord·an·cy 〔dɪsˈkɔrdṇsɪ; disˈkɔːdənsi〕 *n.* ＝**discordance.**
dis·cord·ant 〔dɪsˈkɔrdṇt; disˈkɔːdənt〕 *adj.* ①不調和的；不一致的。②〖音樂〗不悅耳的；不和諧的。③嘈雜的。—**ly,** *adv.*
dis·co·theque 〔ˌdɪskəˈtɛk; ˌdiskəˈteik〕 *n.* 用唱片伴奏的小型夜總會。
dis·count** 〔*v.* ˈdɪskaunt, dɪsˈkaunt; ˈdiskaunt, disˈkaunt *n.* ˈdɪskaunt; ˈdiskaunt〕 *v.t.* ①折扣。to *discount* 5% for cash payment. 現金付款，打九五折。②貼現。③不全置信。④減少(因預知而減少興趣、價值或效用)。—*n.* ①折扣。We give 10% *discount* for cash payment. 現金付款，我們予以九折優待。②貼現。③不全置信。 ***at a discount **a.** 打折扣。to sell *at a discount.* 打折扣出售。 **b.** 不受重視。 **c.** 不全置信。—**er,** *n.* 〖注意〗 **discount** 折扣，中英文表達方式不同，中文以折價後所剩餘之十分之幾的分數，言明其折扣，英文則以所減之百分比言明其折扣：10% *discount.* 九折。
dis·count·a·ble 〔ˈdɪskauntəbl; ˈdiskauntəbl〕 *adj.* 可以折扣的；不可全信的。
dis·coun·te·nance 〔dɪsˈkauntənəns; disˈkauntinəns〕 *n., v.,* **-nanced, -nanc·ing.** —*n.* ①不贊成；不支持。②羞愧。—*v.t.* ①不贊成；不支持。②使羞愧；使丟臉。
discount house 廉價商店。(亦作 **discount store**)
discount rate 貼現率。
***dis·cour·age** 〔dɪsˈkɝɪdʒ; disˈkʌridʒ〕 *v.,* **-aged, -ag·ing.** —*v.t.* ①使失去勇氣；使沮喪；使氣餒。Try again! Don't let one failure *discourage* you. 再試試！不要因一次失敗卽使你氣餒。②勸阻；使不敢做〖from〗. We tried to *discourage* him from climbing the mountain without a guide. 我們設法勸他不要無嚮導而去爬山。③阻礙；妨礙。Low prices *discourage* industry. 低物價不利於工業。—*v.i.* 灰心；失去勇氣。—**a·ble,** *adj.* —**dis·cour·ag·er,** *n.*
dis·cour·age·ment 〔dɪsˈkɝɪdʒmənt; disˈkʌridʒmənt〕 *n.* ①氣餒；沮喪。There are moments of *discouragement* in us all. 我們大家都會有氣餒的時刻。②使人氣餒之事物；障礙。③阻止。
dis·cour·ag·ing 〔dɪsˈkɝɪdʒɪŋ; disˈkʌridʒiŋ〕 *adj.* ①令人失意的；使人氣餒的；使人沮喪的。②阻止的。—**ly,** *adv.*
***dis·course** 〔*n.* ˈdɪskors, dɪˈskors; dis-

ˈkɔːs, ˈdiskɔːs *v.* dɪˈskors; disˈkɔːs〕 *n., v.,* **-coursed, -cours·ing.** —*n.* ①演講;論述;論文;講道。②談話;會話。Let your *discourse* with men of business be short and comprehensive. 你對企業界人士的談話務必簡單明瞭。—*v.i.* ①談話;談論。Let us *discourse* beneath this tree. 我們在這樹下談話吧。②演講;論述。—*v.t.* 發出(樂音)。

dis·cour·te·ous 〔dɪsˈkɝtɪəs; disˈkəːtjəs〕 *adj.* 無禮貌的;不恭敬的;粗魯的。—**ly,** *adv.* —**ness,** *n.*

dis·cour·te·sy 〔dɪsˈkɝtəsɪ; disˈkəːtisi〕 *n., pl.* **-sies.** 無禮貌;不恭;粗野。

‡dis·cov·er 〔dɪˈskʌvɚ; disˈkʌvə〕 *v.t.* ①發見;看到。Columbus *discovered* America. 哥倫布發見美洲。②〖古〗顯露;洩露。—*v.i.* 看到實情。The rumor is false, as far as I can *discover.* 就我所看到的實情來說,那傳聞是虛假的。 —**a·ble,** *adj.* —**a·bly,** *adv.* —**er,** *n.*

dis·cov·ert 〔dɪˈskʌvɚt; disˈkʌvət〕 *adj.* 〖法律〗無丈夫的(指未婚或離婚之女人或寡婦言)。—**dis·cov·er·ture,** *n.*

‡dis·cov·er·y 〔dɪˈskʌvərɪ; disˈkʌvəri〕 *n., pl.* **-er·ies.** ①發見;發明。the *discovery* of making synthetic rubber by chemists. 化學家之發明製造人造橡皮。②發見或發明的東西。He made several important *discoveries* in science. 他完成幾件重要的科學發見。

Discovery Day 新大陸發見紀念日(10月12日)。(亦作 **Columbus Day**)

dis·cred·it 〔dɪsˈkrɛdɪt; disˈkredit〕 *v.t.* ①不信任;懷疑。②玷辱;給予恥辱。③使失去權威性;使發生動搖。—*n.* ①懷疑;不信任。②玷辱;恥辱;丟面子;失名譽。③破壞名譽的人或物。You are a *discredit* to your school. 你是破壞學校名譽的人。

dis·cred·it·a·ble 〔dɪsˈkrɛdɪtəbl̩; disˈkreditəbl〕 *adj.* ①不名譽的;無信用的。②恥辱的;傷害名譽的。—**dis·cred·it·a·bly,** *adv.*

dis·cred·it·ed 〔dɪsˈkrɛdɪtɪd; disˈkreditid〕 *adj.* ①失去名譽的。②失去權威性的。③被視爲卑鄙的。

***dis·creet** 〔dɪˈskrit; disˈkriːt〕 *adj.* 言行謹愼的;小心的;賢明的。He followed her at a *discreet* distance. 他小心地保持距離跟蹤她。—**ness,** *n.*

dis·creet·ly 〔dɪˈskritlɪ; disˈkriːtli〕 *adv.* 愼重地;謹愼地;小心地。

dis·crep·an·cy 〔dɪˈskrɛpənsɪ; disˈkrepənsi〕 *n., pl.* **-cies.** ①不同;不符合;矛盾。②矛盾之點;不符合之點。

dis·crep·ant 〔dɪˈskrɛpənt; disˈkrepənt〕 *adj.* 不同的;矛盾的;極懸殊的。—**ly,** *adv.*

dis·crete 〔dɪˈskrit; disˈkriːt〕 *adj.* ①各別的;分立的。②無連續的;不關連的。③〖植物〗非合生的。④〖哲學〗抽象的。⑤由不相關的各部分組成的。

dis·crete·ly 〔dɪˈskritlɪ; disˈkriːtli〕 *adv.* 各別地;分別地。

discrete smallpox 稀疏痘;稀疏性天花。

dis·cre·tion** 〔dɪˈskrɛʃən; disˈkreʃən〕 *n.* ①隨意處理;自由選擇或決定。Use your own *discretion.* 由你自作決定。②謹愼;明辨。*Discretion* is the better part of valour. 勇敢貴審愼。at discretion*** 隨意地。***at the discretion of*** 由…隨意決定。***surrender at discretion*** 無條件投降。***use one's discretion*** 隨意處理;自由決定。***years*** (or ***age***) ***of discretion*** 成年。

dis·cre·tion·al 〔dɪˈskrɛʃənl̩; disˈkreʃənl〕 *adj.* =**discretionary.** —**ly,** *adv.*

dis·cre·tion·ar·y 〔dɪˈskrɛʃənˌɛrɪ; disˈkreʃənəri〕 *adj.* 隨意的;無條件的;自由裁量的;無限制或束縛的。

dis·crim·i·na·ble 〔dɪˈskrɪmənəbl̩; disˈkriminəbl〕 *adj.* 可辨別的;可分別的。

dis·crim·i·nate 〔*v.* dɪˈskrɪməˌnet; disˈkrimineit *adj.* dɪˈskrɪmənɪt; disˈkriminit〕 *v.,* **-nat·ed, -nat·ing,** *adj.* —*v.i.* ①歧視;區別待遇。②分別;辨別。to *discriminate* between right and wrong. 辨別是非。—*v.t.*分別;區別。—*adj.*有辨識力的。—**ly,** *adv.*

dis·crim·i·nat·ing 〔dɪˈskrɪməˌnetɪŋ; disˈkrimineitiŋ〕 *adj.* ①有辨識力的。②辨別的。③不同的;有差別的;有差等的。*discriminating* duties. 差別稅。

dis·crim·i·na·tion 〔dɪˌskrɪməˈneʃən; disˌkrimiˈneiʃən〕 *n.* ①辨別;分別;區別。②歧視;差別的待遇。③辨別力;鑑別的能力。—**al,** *adj.*

dis·crim·i·na·tive 〔dɪˈskrɪməˌnetɪv; disˈkriminətiv〕 *adj.* ①有差異的;有差別的。②有辨識力的。③區別的;特殊的。—**ly,** *adv.*

dis·crim·i·na·tor 〔dɪˈskrɪməˌnetɚ; disˈkrimineitə〕 *n.* ①區別之人或物;分畛域者;立異者。②〖無線電〗鑑別器。

dis·crim·i·na·to·ry 〔dɪˈskrɪmənəˌtorɪ; disˈkriminətəri〕 *adj.* 歧視的;差別的;不公平的。

dis·crown 〔dɪsˈkraun; disˈkraun〕 *v.t.* 罷黜…之王位;使退位。

dis·cul·pate 〔dɪsˈkʌlpet; disˈkʌlpeit〕 *v.t.,* **-pat·ed, -pat·ing.** 爲…脫罪;爲…辯護。—**dis·cul·pa·tion,** *n.*

dis·cur·sive 〔dɪˈskɝsɪv; disˈkəːsiv〕 *adj.* ①散漫的;無層次的。②〖哲學〗推論的;辯論的。—**ly,** *adv.* —**ness,** *n.*

dis·cus 〔ˈdɪskəs; ˈdiskəs〕 *n., pl.* **-cus·es, -ci** 〔-saɪ; -sai〕. 鐵餅;擲鐵餅。

***dis·cuss** 〔dɪˈskʌs; disˈkʌs〕 *v.t.* ①討論;商討;議論。to *discuss* a question with friends. 和朋友們討論一問題。②享受(飲食)之滋味。—*v.i.* 談話;討論;談論。—**er,** *n.*

dis·cuss·i·ble 〔dɪˈskʌsəbl̩; disˈkʌsibl〕 *adj.* 可討論的;可議論的。

***dis·cus·sion** 〔dɪˈskʌʃən; disˈkʌʃən〕 *n.* 討論;商討;辯論;議論。Don't deviate from the subject under *discussion.* 不要離開所討論之問題。—**al,** *adj.*

***dis·dain** 〔dɪsˈden; disˈdein〕 *v.t.* ①鄙視;輕視。A great man should *disdain* flatterers. 一個偉人應輕視諂媚者。②不屑爲。We *disdained* to notice the insult. 我們不屑計較這侮辱。—*v.i.* 遭輕視;遭鄙視。—*n.* 輕視;蔑視;輕蔑。No one likes to be treated with *disdain.* 沒有人喜歡被輕視。

dis·dain·ful 〔dɪsˈdenfəl; disˈdeinfəl〕 *adj.* 輕視的;蔑視的;傲慢的。—**ly,** *adv.*

‡dis·ease 〔dɪˈziz; diˈziːz〕 *n.* ①病;疾病;不適。The business of doctors is to prevent and cure *diseases.* 醫生的職責爲預防和治療疾病。②植物的病。*Diseases* sometimes attack plants. 植物有時亦受病之侵害。③變質(變壞)。④(心靈、道德、公共事務等之)敗壞;壞的傾向。—*v.t.* 使生病;傳染。—**less,** *adj.*

dis·eased 〔dɪˈzizd; diˈziːzd〕 *adj.* ①患病的;有病的。the *diseased* part. 患部。②有毛病的;有弊病的;不健全的。—**ly,** *adv.* —**ness,** *n.*

disease germ 病菌。

dis·em·bark 〔ˌdɪsɪm'bɑrk; 'disim'bɑːk, ˌdis-〕 *v.t. & v.i.* 登岸;上岸;離船;(自船上)卸貨。

dis·em·bar·ka·tion 〔ˌdɪsɛmbɑr'keʃən; ˌdisembɑː'keiʃən〕 *n.* 登岸;上岸;離船。(亦作 **disembarkment**)

dis·em·bar·rass 〔ˌdɪsɪm'bærəs; 'disim'bærəs, ˌdis-〕 *v.t.* 使免於困窘;使脫離困境;使解脫。—**ment,** *n.*

dis·em·bod·y 〔ˌdɪsɪm'bɑdɪ; 'disim'bɔdi, ˌdis-〕 *v.t.,* **-bod·ied, -bod·y·ing.** ①使(靈魂、精神等)脫離肉體。②臨時解散。—**dis·em·bod·i·ment,** *n.*

dis·em·bogue 〔ˌdɪsɛm'bog; ˌdisim'boug〕 *v.,* **-bogued, -bogu·ing.** —*v.t.* 注入;流注。—*v.i.* 流入海洋;流注。—**ment,** *n.*

dis·em·bos·om 〔ˌdɪsəm'bʊzəm; ˌdisim'buzəm〕 *v.t. & v.i.* 洩露(祕密等);吐露(心事);說出。

dis·em·bow·el 〔ˌdɪsɪm'baʊəl; ˌdisim'bauəl〕 *v.t.,* **-el(l)ed, -el·(l)ing.** ①切腹取腸。②將內部機件取出。—**ment,** *n.*

dis·em·broil 〔ˌdɪsɛm'brɔɪl; ˌdisim'brɔil〕 *v.t.* 使免於紛亂;解難。

dis·en·chant 〔ˌdɪsɪn'tʃænt; 'disin'tʃɑːnt〕 *v.t.* 解除魔法;使醒悟。—**ment,** *n.*

dis·en·cum·ber 〔ˌdɪsɪn'kʌmbɚ; ˌdisin'kʌmbə〕 *v.t.* 排除障礙;解除負擔;清除憂煩。

dis·en·dow 〔ˌdɪsɛn'daʊ; 'disin'dau〕 *v.t.*沒收(教會等)之基金;剝奪基金。—**er,** —**ment,** *n.*

dis·en·fran·chise 〔ˌdɪsɪn'fræntʃaɪz; 'disin'fræntʃaiz, ˌdis-〕 *v.t.,* **-chised, -chis·ing.** ①剝奪…之公民權。②剝奪…之權利或特權。—**ment,** *n.*

dis·en·gage 〔ˌdɪsɪn'gedʒ; 'disin'geidʒ〕 *v.,* **-gaged, -gag·ing.** —*v.t.* ①使解約。②釋放;解脫。③〖化〗使游離。④使脫離戰鬥。—*v.i.* 脫離;斷絕關係。

dis·en·gaged 〔ˌdɪsɪn'gedʒd; 'disin'geidʒd〕 *adj.* ①自由的;空閒的。②脫離的;無關係的;淡然的。

dis·en·gage·ment 〔ˌdɪsɪn'gedʒmənt; ˌdisin'geidʒmənt〕 *n.* ①解脫;解雇;解約;解除婚約。②〖化〗游離。③閒暇。④優雅。

dis·en·tail 〔ˌdɪsɛn'tel; 'disin'teil, ˌdis-〕 *v.t.*〖法律〗使(地產)免於限定繼承;解除繼嗣之限定。

dis·en·tan·gle 〔ˌdɪsɪn'tæŋgḷ; 'disin'tæŋgl, ˌdis-〕 *v.,* **-tan·gled, -tan·gling.** —*v.t.* 清理(混亂);解開;解決(糾紛)。—*v.i.* 解開;鬆開。—**ment,** *n.*

dis·en·thral(l) 〔ˌdɪsɛn'θrɔl; ˌdisin'θrɔːl〕 *v.t.,* **-thralled, -thral·ling.** 解放;釋放。—**ment,** *n.*

dis·en·throne 〔ˌdɪsɛn'θron; ˌdisin'θroun〕 *v.t.,* **-throned, -thron·ing.** = **dethrone.**

dis·en·tomb 〔ˌdɪsɛn'tum; ˌdisin'tuːm〕 *v.t.*自墓中掘出;挖墓;掘墓。

dis·en·twine 〔ˌdɪsɛn'twaɪn; ˌdisin'twain〕 *v.t. & v.i.,* **-twined, -twin·ing.** 解開;解紛。

dis·e·qui·lib·ri·um 〔dɪsˌikwə'lɪbrɪəm; disˌiːkwə'libriəm〕 *n.* 失去平衡或安定。

dis·es·tab·lish 〔ˌdɪsə'stæblɪʃ; 'disis'tæbliʃ〕 *v.t.* ①廢除;廢止;取消。②廢除政府對國教教會之支持。—**ment,** *n.*

dis·es·teem 〔ˌdɪsə'stim; ˌdisis'tiːm〕 *v.t.* 輕視;蔑視;厭惡。—*n.* 輕視;不敬。

dis·fa·vo(u)r 〔dɪs'fevɚ; 'dis'feivə〕 *n.* ①不喜歡;不贊成。②失寵;失衆望;輕視。He cheated at the examination and is in great *disfavor.* 他考試作弊,因之受到蔑視。—*v.t.* ①不贊成;不喜歡。②輕視;蔑視。

dis·fig·ure 〔dɪs'fɪgjɚ; dis'figə〕 *v.t.,* **-ured, -ur·ing.** 破壞(姿容、形狀、價值等)。

dis·fig·ure·ment 〔dɪs'fɪgjɚmənt; dis'figəmənt〕 *n.* 損形;毁容;破相;被毁損之醜處。

dis·for·est 〔dɪs'fɑrɪst; dis'fɔrist〕 *v.t.* 使成童山;砍伐…之森林。

dis·fran·chise 〔dɪs'fræntʃaɪz; 'dis'fræntʃaiz〕 *v.t.,* **-chised, -chis·ing.** ①褫奪…之公權(特別是選舉權)。②剝奪…之特權。—**ment,** *n.*

dis·frock 〔dɪs'frɑk; dis'frɔk〕 *v.t.* 剝奪…之俗職。

dis·gorge 〔dɪs'gɔrdʒ; dis'gɔːdʒ〕 *v.t. & v.i.,* **-gorged, -gorg·ing.** ①吐出。②噴出;流出。③不自願地放棄;交出;交還。

***dis·grace** 〔dɪs'gres; dis'greis〕 *n., v.,* **-graced, -grac·ing.** —*n.* ①不名譽;恥辱。to bring *disgrace* upon one's family. 玷辱家族。②失寵;罷黜;貶斥。He told a lie and is in *disgrace.* 他說謊而受斥。③招致恥辱的原因或事物。The dirty walls are a *disgrace* to the school. 這些髒的牆乃學校之恥辱。—*v.t.* ①玷辱。②解職。

dis·grace·ful 〔dɪs'gresfəl; dis'greisful〕 *adj.* 不名譽的;可恥的。—**ly,** *adv.*

dis·grun·tle 〔dɪs'grʌntḷ; dis'grʌntl〕 *v.t.,* **-tled, -tling.** (常使用過去分詞形式)使不悅;使不滿。

dis·grun·tled 〔dɪs'grʌntḷd; dis'grʌntld〕 *adj.* 不高興的;不悅的;心境不佳的。

***dis·guise** 〔dɪs'gaɪz; dis'gaiz〕 *v.,* **-guised, -guis·ing,** *n.* —*v.t.* ①改裝;假扮。to *disguise* oneself as a monk. 假扮爲僧人。②僞裝。③隱匿;掩飾。—*n.* ①假裝;假扮;化裝。We went among the enemy in *disguise.* 我們化裝混入敵人中。②掩飾物;僞裝之行動。③假託;託辭;佯裝。She made no *disguise* of her feelings. 她不掩飾她的情感。④僞裝之狀態。a blessing in *disguise.* 因禍得福;塞翁失馬。

***dis·gust** 〔dɪs'gʌst; dis'gʌst〕 *n.* 厭惡;嫌惡;令人作嘔。We feel *disgust* for bad odors. 我們厭聞惡臭。—*v.t.* 使厭惡;使嫌惡。I'm *disgusted* at her affectation. 我討厭她的裝腔作勢。—*v.i.* 令人厭惡。

***dis·gust·ed** 〔dɪs'gʌstɪd; dis'gʌstid〕 *adj.* 充滿厭惡心的。—**ly,** *adv.*

dis·gust·ful 〔dɪs'gʌstfəl; dis'gʌstfəl〕 *adj.* 令人作嘔的;討厭的。

dis·gust·ing 〔dɪs'gʌstɪŋ; dis'gʌstiŋ〕 *adj.* 令人厭惡的;令人作嘔的。—**ly,** *adv.*

‡dish 〔dɪʃ; diʃ〕 *n.* ①碟;盤;皿。②碟中的菜;肴;饌。The main *dish* is a steak. 主菜爲牛排。③一碟的量。He finished two *dishes* of ice cream. 他吃了兩碟冰淇淋。④碟狀的東西。⑤凹陷;凹入。⑥〖俚〗美女。What a *dish!* 好漂亮的妞兒!—*v.t.* ①盛於碟中。②使呈碟形。③〖俗〗擊潰;使沮喪;欺騙。—*v.i.* 凹陷;凹入。***dish it out*** 〖俚〗責罵;體罰。***dish out*** **a.** 上(菜)。**b.** 供應;供給。**c.**〖俚〗說得極爲動聽。

dis·ha·bille 〔ˌdɪsə'bil; ˌdisæ'biːl〕 *n.* ①便裝。②一種寬大的晨衣。(亦作 **deshabille**)

dis·har·mon·ic 〔ˌdɪshɑr'mɑnɪk; ˌdishɑː'mɔnik〕 *adj.*①不和諧的。②奇形怪狀的。

dis·har·mo·nize 〔dɪs'hɑrməˌnaɪz; 'dis'hɑːmənaiz〕 *v.t. & v.i.,* **-nized, -niz-**

ing. (使) 不調和;(使)不融合;不諧調。

dis·har·mo·ny 〔dɪs'harmənɪ; 'dis'hɑːməni〕 *n., pl.* **-nies.** ①不調和;不融合。②不調和之物。—**dis·har·mo·ni·ous,** *adj.*

dish·cloth 〔'dɪʃ,klɔθ; 'diʃklɔθ〕 *n.* (擦洗盤碟用之)抹布。

dishcloth gourd 絲瓜。

dish·clout 〔'dɪʃ,klaut; 'diʃklaut〕 *n.* =**dishcloth.**

dis·heart·en 〔dɪs'hartn̩; dis'hɑːtn〕 *v.t.* 使沮喪;使氣餒。—**ment,** *n.*

dis·heart·en·ing·ly 〔dɪs'hartn̩ɪŋlɪ; dis'hɑːtniŋli〕 *adv.* 使人氣餒地;令人沮喪地。

dished 〔dɪʃt; diʃt〕 *adj.* ①凹下的。②(兩個平行的車輪)上部距離大於下部距離的。③〖俚〗打敗的;遭挫折的。

di·shev·el 〔dɪ'ʃɛvl̩; di'ʃevəl〕 *v.t.,* **-el(l)ed, -el·(l)ing.** 使(髮等)蓬亂;使(某人)之衣或髮凌亂。

di·shev·eled 〔dɪ'ʃɛvl̩d; di'ʃevəld〕 *adj.* ①凌亂的;不整潔的;蓬亂的。*disheveled* hair. 蓬亂的頭髮。②組織不佳的;脫節的。

dish·ful 〔'dɪʃ,ful; 'diʃful〕 *n.* 一碟;一碟之量。

dish·mop 〔'dɪʃ,map; 'diʃmɔp〕 *n.* 洗碟刷。

***dis·hon·est** 〔dɪs'anɪst; dis'ɔnist〕 *adj.* 不誠實的;欺詐的。—**ly,** *adv.*

dis·hon·es·ty 〔dɪs'anɪstɪ; dis'ɔnisti〕 *n., pl.* **-ties.**①不誠實。②欺詐;偷竊。

***dis·hon·or** 〔dɪs'anɚ; dis'ɔnə〕 *n.* ①不名譽;不名譽的行爲;恥辱。He would rather die than live in *dishonor.* 他寧死不願忍辱偷生。②不名譽的原因。③侮辱。—*v.t.* ①侮辱;玷辱。②拒絕支付或接受(支票、匯票等);不兌現。③失信;不遵守。④强姦或誘拐。

dis·hon·or·a·ble 〔dɪs'anərəbl̩; dis'ɔnərəbl〕 *adj.* 不名譽的; 可鄙的; 可恥的。—**dis·hon·or·a·bly,** *adv.*

dishonorable discharge 〖軍〗不榮譽免職。

dishonored check 不兌現支票。

dis·horn 〔dɪs'hɔrn; dis'hɔːn〕 *v.t.* 去(動物)之角。

dis·house 〔dɪs'hauz; dis'hauz〕 *v.t.,* **-housed, -hous·ing.** 使無家可居。

dish·pan 〔'dɪʃ,pæn; 'diʃpæn〕 *n.* 洗碗、碟等物之淺桶。

dishpan hands 家庭主婦因家務操勞而造成之粗糙的手。

dish·rag 〔'dɪʃ,ræg; 'diʃræg〕 *n.* 抹布。

dish·tow·el 〔'dɪʃ,tauəl; 'diʃ,tauəl〕 *n.* (揩乾碗碟等)乾毛巾布;乾抹布。

dish·wash·er 〔'dɪʃ,waʃɚ; 'diʃ,wɔʃə〕 *n.* 洗碗碟之人或機器。

dish·wa·ter 〔'dɪʃ,watɚ; 'diʃ,wɔːtə〕 *n.* ①洗碗碟等之水。②無趣味之事。

dish·y 〔'dɪʃɪ; 'diʃi〕 *adj.,* **dish·i·er, dish·i·est.** 〖俚〗很棒的;精采的。

dis·il·lu·sion 〔,dɪsɪ'luʒən; ,disi'ljuːʒən〕 *v.t.* 使從迷夢、幻思、錯誤信任等中醒悟。—*n.* 覺醒;消除迷夢。

dis·il·lu·sion·ar·y 〔,dɪsɪ'luʒə,nɛrɪ; ,disi'luːʒənəri〕 *adj.* 令人感到失望的。

dis·il·lu·sion·ize 〔,dɪsɪ'luʒən,aɪz; ,disi'luːʒənaiz〕 *v.t.,* **-ized, -iz·ing.** =**disillusion.**

dis·il·lu·sion·ment 〔,dɪsɪ'luʒənmənt; ,disi'luːʒənmənt〕 *n.* 消除幻想;覺醒。

dis·im·pas·sioned 〔,dɪsɪm'pæʃənd; ,disim'pæʃənd〕 *adj.* 不激動的;冷靜的。

dis·im·pri·son 〔,dɪsɪm'prɪzn̩; ,disim'prizən〕 *v.t.* 使自獄中釋放。—**ment,** *n.*

dis·in·cen·tive 〔,dɪsɪn'sɛntɪv; ,disin'sentiv〕 *n.* 障礙。

dis·in·cli·na·tion 〔,dɪsɪnklə'neʃən; ,disinkli'neiʃən〕 *n.* 不高興;厭惡;不中意。

dis·in·cline 〔,dɪsɪn'klaɪn; 'disin'klain〕 *v.t. & v.i.,* **-clined, -clin·ing.** (使)厭惡;(使)不願。

dis·in·clined 〔,dɪsɪn'klaɪnd; ,disin'klaind〕 *adj.* 不願的;厭惡的。

dis·in·cor·po·rate 〔,dɪsɪn'kɔrpə,ret; ,disin'kɔːpəreit〕 *v.t.,* **-rat·ed, -rat·ing.** 解除團體關係;剝奪法人資格;使與團體分離;除名。

dis·in·fect 〔,dɪsɪn'fɛkt; ,disin'fekt〕 *v.t.* ①將…消毒。②淨化。

dis·in·fect·ant 〔,dɪsɪn'fɛktənt; ,disin'fektənt〕 *n.* 消毒劑。—*adj.* 消毒的。

dis·in·fec·tion 〔,dɪsɪn'fɛkʃən; ,disin'fekʃən〕 *n.* 消毒;殺菌(作用)。

dis·in·fec·tor 〔,dɪsɪn'fɛktɚ; ,disin'fektə〕 *n.* 消毒者;消毒劑;消毒器具。

dis·in·fest 〔,dɪsɪn'fɛst; ,disin'fest〕 *v.t.* 驅除害蟲(如蚤等)。

dis·in·fla·tion 〔,dɪsɪn'fleʃən; ,disin'fleiʃən〕 *n.* =**deflation.**

dis·in·for·ma·tion 〔,dɪsɪnfɚ'meʃən; ,disinfə'meiʃən〕 *n.* (故意供給敵方諜報人員的)錯誤情報。

dis·in·gen·u·ous 〔,dɪsɪn'dʒɛnjuəs; ,disin'dʒenjuəs〕 *adj.* 不正直的;不坦白的;不誠懇的。—**ly,** *adv.*

dis·in·her·it 〔,dɪsɪn'hɛrɪt; 'disin'herit〕 *v.t.* ①剝奪…之繼承權。②剝奪…之人權。③剝奪…之特權。—**ance,** *n.*

dis·in·te·grate 〔dɪs'ɪntə,gret; dis'intigreit〕 *v.,* **-grat·ed, -grat·ing.** —*v.t.* ①使分裂成小塊或小粒。②使瓦解。—*v.i.* ①分裂;崩潰;風化。②〖物理〗蛻變。③瓦解。

dis·in·te·gra·tion 〔dɪs,ɪntə'greʃən; dis,inti'greiʃən〕 *n.* ①分解;分裂;崩潰。②〖地質〗風化作用。③〖物理〗蛻變。

dis·in·te·gra·tor 〔dɪs'ɪntə,gretɚ; dis'intigreitə〕 *n.* 使碎裂之人或物;粉碎機。

dis·in·ter 〔,dɪsɪn'tɝ; 'disin'təː〕 *v.t.,* **-terred, -ter·ring.** ①從墳墓中挖出。②使顯現;發現。—**ment,** *n.*

dis·in·ter·est 〔dɪs'ɪntərəst; dis'intrist〕 *n.*①不利。②公正無私。③漠不關心。

dis·in·ter·est·ed 〔dɪs'ɪntərəstɪd; dis'intristid〕 *adj.* ①公正的; 不偏的; 無私的。② 漠不關心的。—**ly,** *adv.* —**ness,** *n.*

dis·in·vest·ment 〔,dɪsɪn'vɛstmənt; ,disin'vestmənt〕 *n.* 蝕本;收回投資。

dis·join 〔dɪs'dʒɔɪn; dis'dʒɔin〕 *v.t. & v.i.* 分離;拆散;散開。

dis·joint 〔dɪs'dʒɔɪnt; dis'dʒɔint〕 *v.t.* ①使關節脫離。②使分裂; 使解體。③使失去連繫。—*v.i.* ①脫離; 脫節。②失去連繫。

dis·joint·ed 〔dɪs'dʒɔɪntɪd; dis'dʒɔintid〕 *adj.* ①脫節的;脫臼的。②無連繫的;無系統的;雜亂的。

dis·junc·tion 〔dɪs'dʒʌŋkʃən; dis'dʒʌŋkʃən〕 *n.* ①分離;分裂。②〖邏輯〗a. 選言命題。b. 選言命題中諸名辭之關係。

dis·junc·tive 〔dɪs'dʒʌŋktɪv; dis'dʒʌŋktiv〕 *adj.* ①分離的。②〖文法〗反意的。③〖邏輯〗選言的。—*n.*①〖文法〗反意連接詞。②〖邏輯〗選言命題。—**dis·junc·tiv·i·ty,** *n.*

***disk** 〔dɪsk; disk〕 *n.* ①薄平的圓板; 圓盤;平圓面。the sun's *disk.* 日輪。the moon's *disk.* 月輪。a metal *disk.* 金屬圓盤。②植物或動物的圓平部分; 花盤。③似圓盤之物。

④唱片。⑤鐵餅(=discus).(亦作 **disc**)

disk jockey 電臺之唱片音樂節目主持人。(亦作 **disc jockey**)

***dis·like** [dɪsˈlaɪk; disˈlaik] *n., v.,* **-liked, -lik·ing.** —*n.* 嫌惡;憎嫌。I have taken a strong *dislike* to (of, *or* for) him. 我極不喜歡他。—*v.t.* 嫌惡;憎嫌。

dis·lo·cate [ˈdɪslo,ket, dɪsˈloket; ˈdisləkeit] *v.t.,* **-cat·ed, -cat·ing.** ①使脫關節。②使混亂。③使變位;使歪斜;使歪曲。

dis·lo·ca·tion [,dɪsloˈkeʃən; ,disləˈkeiʃən] *n.* ①脫節;脫臼。②紛亂;擾亂。③〖地質〗斷層。

dis·lodge [dɪsˈlɑdʒ; disˈlɔdʒ] *v.,* **-lodged, -lodg·ing.** —*v.t.* ①驅逐;逐出;逐退。②移出。—*v.i.* ①逃出;退却。②鬆開;鬆落。③離開住處。

dis·lodge·ment [dɪsˈlɑdʒmənt; disˈlɔdʒmənt] *n.* 〖英〗=**dislodgment.**

dis·lodg·ment [dɪsˈlɑdʒmənt; disˈlɔdʒmənt] *n.* 逐出;被逐出之狀態。

dis·loy·al [dɪsˈlɔɪəl; disˈlɔiəl] *adj.* 不忠的;無信的;背叛的。—**ly,** *adv.*

dis·loy·al·ty [dɪsˈlɔɪəltɪ; disˈlɔiəlti] *n., pl.* **-ties.** ①不忠不義;背叛。②背叛行爲。

***dis·mal** [ˈdɪzml; ˈdizməl] *adj.* ①憂鬱的;黯淡的。②陰暗的;陰沉的。What *dismal* weather! 天氣眞陰沈! —*n.* (the-)(常 *pl.*) 沮喪;頹喪。He is suffering from an attack of the *dismals.* 他正心灰意懶。

dis·mal·ly [ˈdɪzmḷɪ; ˈdizməli] *adv.* 憂鬱地;憂愁地。

dismal science 經濟學。

dis·man·tle [dɪsˈmæntl; disˈmæntl] *v.t.,* **-tled, -tling.** ①拆除(房屋等)之傢具、裝飾、設備等;拆卸(船)上的設備。②拆散。③剝脫(衣服、遮蓋等)。④廢除;撤銷。

dis·mast [dɪsˈmæst; disˈmɑːst] *v.t.* 除去…之桅檣;折毀桅桿。

***dis·may** [dɪsˈme; disˈmei] *n.* ①喪膽;驚慌。He was filled with *dismay* at the news. 聽到這消息他十分驚慌。②希望之突然幻滅。—*v.t.* 使喪膽;使驚慌。He was *dismayed* at the sad news. 這悲慘的消息使他驚慌。

dis·mem·ber [dɪsˈmɛmbɚ; disˈmembə] *v.t.* ①割斷四肢;肢解。②分裂;分割;使四分五裂;瓜分。

dis·mem·ber·ment [dɪsˈmɛmbɚmənt; disˈmembəmənt] *n.* ①解體;肢解。②分割;瓜分。

***dis·miss** [dɪsˈmɪs; disˈmis] *v.t.* ①解散。The teacher *dismissed* the class as soon as the bell rang. 鈴聲一響老師卽下課。②使告退。③開除;革退;罷免。to *dismiss* a servant for being dishonest. 因佣人不誠實而予以解雇。④摒除;放棄。to *dismiss* fear from one's mind. 摒除心中的恐懼。⑤〖法律〗不受理。⑥拒絕。to *dismiss* a suitor. 拒絕一個求婚者。⑦擱置。⑧不予考慮。He *dismissed* the story as a rumor. 他將這個消息當作謠言而不予考慮。—*v.i.* 解散。

dis·miss·al [dɪsˈmɪsḷ; disˈmisəl] *n.* ①開除;免職;解雇。②免職令。

dismissal wage 離職津貼。

dis·miss·i·ble [dɪsˈmɪsəbḷ; disˈmisəbl] *adj.* 可解職的。

dis·mis·sion [dɪsˈmɪʃən; disˈmiʃən] *n.* =**dismissal.**

***dis·mount** [dɪsˈmaunt; ˈdisˈmaunt, disˈmaunt] *v.i.* 下馬;下車。—*v.t.* ①使從馬上落下。②使失去馬。③拆卸。—*n.* 下馬;下車。

Dis·ney [ˈdɪznɪ; ˈdizni] *n.* 狄斯耐(Walt, 1901-1966, 美國電影監製人,卡通電影家)。

Dis·ney·esque [ˈdɪznɪˈɛsk; ˈdizniˈesk] *adj.* 有華德狄斯耐影片之風格或特色的。

Dis·ney·land [ˈdɪznɪ,lænd; ˈdizni-lænd] *n.* 狄斯耐樂園。

dis·o·be·di·ence [,dɪsəˈbidɪəns; ,disəˈbiːdjəns] *n.* 不服從;違命。

dis·o·be·di·ent [,dɪsəˈbidɪənt; ,disəˈbiːdjənt] *adj.* 不服從的;違命的。—**ly,** *adv.*

***dis·o·bey** [,dɪsəˈbe; ˈdisəˈbei, ,dis-] *v.t.* 不服從;違命。to *disobey* one's conscience. 違背良心。—*v.i.* 不服從;違命。

dis·o·blige [,dɪsəˈblaɪdʒ; ˈdisəˈblaidʒ] *v.t.,* **-bliged, -blig·ing.** ①不施惠於人;不通融。②得罪。③爲難;使感不便。—**dis·o·blig·ing,** *adj.*

***dis·or·der** [dɪsˈɔrdɚ; disˈɔːdə] *n.* ①無秩序;缺乏秩序;雜亂。The accounts were in *disorder.* 帳目紊亂。②騷亂;騷動。③疾病;不適。④行爲不檢;持身不正。—*v.t.* ①使紊亂;擾亂。②致病。Anxiety may *disorder* the stomach. 焦慮會引起胃病。

dis·or·dered [dɪsˈɔrdɚd; disˈɔːdəd] *adj.* ①紛亂的。②不正常的。—**ly,** *adv.*

dis·or·der·li·ness [dɪsˈɔrdɚlɪnɪs; disˈɔːdəlinis] *n.* 紊亂;雜亂。

dis·or·der·ly [dɪsˈɔrdɚlɪ; disˈɔːdəli] *adj.* ①不整齊的;無秩序的;混亂的。②不守法的;不守秩序的;騷動的。—*adv.* 不整齊地;紊亂地。—*n.* 不守法律秩序者。

disorderly house ①妓院。②賭場。

dis·or·gan·i·za·tion [dɪs,ɔrgənəˈzeʃən; dis,ɔːgənaiˈzeiʃən] *n.* ①分裂;瓦解;破壞組織。②被瓦解之狀態;紊亂。

dis·or·gan·ize [dɪsˈɔrgə,naɪz; disˈɔːgənaiz] *v.t.,* **-ized, -iz·ing.** 擾亂;破壞規律或組織;使紊亂。

dis·o·ri·ent [dɪsˈɔrɪ,ɛnt; disˈɔːrient] *v.t.* ①使失去方位。②使失去判斷力;使迷惑。③使偏歪。(亦作 **disorientate**)

dis·own [dɪsˈon; disˈoun] *v.t.* 否認;不承認爲己所有。

dis·par·age [dɪˈspærɪdʒ; disˈpæridʒ] *v.t.,* **-aged, -ag·ing.** ①輕視;蔑視。②毀謗;貶抑;責難。

dis·par·age·ment [dɪˈspærɪdʒmənt; disˈpæridʒmənt] *n.* ①非難;輕視;毀謗。②使尊嚴或名譽受損之事。③與身分較低之人所締之婚姻。

dis·par·ag·ing·ly [dɪˈspærɪdʒɪŋlɪ; disˈpæridʒiŋli] *adv.* 以貶抑的口吻;以輕視的態度。

dis·pa·rate [ˈdɪspərɪt; ˈdisparit] *adj.* 不同的;不相像的;異種(類)的。

dis·par·i·ty [dɪsˈpærətɪ; disˈpæriti] *n., pl.* **-ties.** 不同;不等;不一致;懸殊。

dis·park [dɪsˈpɑrk; disˈpɑːk] *v.t.* ①開放(私人園囿)。②解放;釋放。

dis·part [dɪsˈpɑrt; disˈpɑːt] *v.t.* & *v.i.* (使)破裂;分離。

dis·pas·sion [dɪsˈpæʃən; disˈpæʃən] *n.* 冷靜;公平;冷淡;不介意;不動感情。

dis·pas·sion·ate [dɪsˈpæʃənɪt; disˈpæʃənit] *adj.* 不動感情的;沒有偏見的;公平的;冷靜的。

dis·pas·sion·ate·ly [dɪsˈpæʃənɪtlɪ; disˈpæʃənitli] *adv.* 不動感情地;冷靜地。

***dis·patch** [dɪˈspætʃ; disˈpætʃ] *v.t.* ①

派遣；發；送。to *dispatch* a telegram. 拍發電報。②速辦；速了；解決。③殺；處死。④〖俗〗吃掉。—*n.* ①派遣；發送。②快信；快郵；急件(公文)；新聞專電；電報。He sent his letter by *dispatch.* 他以快郵寄出他的信。③速了；速辦；迅速；急速。to do something with *dispatch.* 趕辦某事。④殺戮；處死。⑤發送代理者。(亦作 **despatch**)

dis·patch·box 〔dɪsˈpætʃbɑks; disˈpætʃbɔks〕 *n.* 公文遞送箱。(亦作 **dispatch box, dispatchcase**)

dis·patch·er 〔dɪsˈpætʃɚ; disˈpætʃə〕 *n.* ①派遣者。②(車輛、電梯等之) 調度負責人。

dispatch rider 〖軍〗騎馬或機器脚踏車之傳信者。

dis·pel 〔dɪˈspɛl; disˈpel〕 *v.t.*, **-pelled, -pel·ling.** 祛除；驅散。

dis·pen·sa·ble 〔dɪˈspɛnsəbl; disˈpensəbl〕 *adj.* ①能分配的。②可寬恕的。③可省却的。④不必要的；不重要的。

dis·pen·sa·ry 〔dɪˈspɛnsərɪ; disˈpensəri〕 *n., pl.* **-ries.** ①藥房。②施診所；施藥所；醫務所。

dis·pen·sa·tion 〔ˌdɪspənˈseʃən; ˌdispenˈseiʃən〕 *n.* ①分與；賜與。②分配的東西；天道。③處理；處置；安排；統治。④免除；特赦(尤指天主教)。⑤〖宗教〗教規；教條。

dis·pen·sa·to·ry 〔dɪˈspɛnsəˌtorɪ; disˈpensətəri〕 *n., pl.* **-ries.** ①藥方書；藥譜。②藥房；施診所。

*__dis·pense__ 〔dɪˈspɛns; disˈpens〕 *v.*, **-pensed, -pens·ing.** —*v.t.* ①分配；分與；施與；給與。②實施；執行。③配(藥)。to *dispense* medicine. 配藥。④赦免；免除。to *dispense* a person from some obligation. 豁免某人之義務。—*v.i.* 特免；宥恕。***dispense with*** **a.** 免除；省却；拋棄(=do without). to *dispense with* formalities. 免除禮節。**b.** 無需；不用(=do away with).

dis·pens·er 〔dɪsˈpɛnsɚ; disˈpensə〕 *n.* ①分配者；施與者。②實施者；執行者。③販賣機。④發藥者；藥劑師。

dis·peo·ple 〔dɪsˈpipl; ˈdisˈpiːpl〕 *v.t.*, **-pled, -pling.** 使人口稀少；使無人烟或棲居者。

dis·per·sal 〔dɪˈspɝsl; disˈpəːsəl〕 *n.* 解散；散布；傳布；疏散；分布。

*__dis·perse__ 〔dɪˈspɝs; disˈpəːs〕 *v.*, **-persed, -pers·ing,** *adj.* —*v.t.* ①使散；解散；驅散。②使分散。Veins are *dispersed* through the body. 血管散布全身。③傳播；散布；傳布。④使消散；使散失。The fog is *dispersed.* 霧氣消散。⑤將(白色光)析爲色線。—*v.i.* ①四散；分散。The crowd *dispersed* at the sight of the police. 羣衆看到警察而四散。②消散；消失。—*adj.* 分散的；稀疏的。

dis·pers·ed·ly 〔dɪˈspɝsɪdlɪ; disˈpəːsidli〕 *adv.* 散亂地；四散地。

dis·pers·i·ble 〔dɪsˈpɝsəbl; disˈpəːsibl〕 *adj.* 可分散的。

dis·per·sion 〔dɪˈspɝʃən; disˈpəːʃən〕 *n.* ①散布；散亂；離散。②〖物理〗色散；分散。③〖醫〗(炎症等之) 消散。④〖統計〗離勢。⑤〖軍〗(砲彈之)散布；疏開。***the Dispersion*** 散居異邦之猶太人(=Diaspora).

dis·per·sive 〔dɪˈspɝsɪv; disˈpəːsiv〕 *adj.* 分散的；散亂的；散布性的。

dis·pir·it 〔dɪˈspɪrɪt; disˈpirit〕 *v.t.* 使乏勇氣；使喪志。

dis·pir·it·ed 〔dɪˈspɪrɪtɪd; disˈpiritid〕 *adj.* 沮喪的；喪膽的；無精打采的。

dis·pir·it·ed·ly 〔dɪˈspɪrɪtɪdlɪ; disˈpiritidli〕 *adv.* 沮喪地；喪志地。

dis·pit·e·ous 〔dɪsˈpɪtɪəs; disˈpitiəs〕 *adj.* 殘酷的；無憐憫心的。

*__dis·place__ 〔dɪsˈples; disˈpleis〕 *v.t.*, **-placed, -plac·ing.** ①代替。②移置；移換；排(水)。③免職。④使離鄉背井。⑤〖化〗置換。

displaced person (戰爭、暴政等下之)難民。(略作 **DP**)

dis·place·ment 〔dɪsˈplesmənt; disˈpleismənt〕 *n.* ①移置；換替；代替。②免職；罷免。③(船的)排水量。a ship of 5,000 tons *displacement.* 一艘排水量五千噸的船。④變形；變位。⑤脫臼。⑥〖化〗置換。⑦〖物理〗位移。

displacement tonnage 排水噸數。

‡**dis·play** 〔dɪˈsple; disˈplei〕 *v.t.* ①展示；展覽；陳列。to *display* goods for sale. 陳列出售的貨物。②展開；張開。to *display* a sail. 張帆。③顯露；洩露；表現出。His son *displays* great intelligence. 他的兒子顯得很聰明。④誇示。⑤使顯明(印刷時用特別的排列)。—*n.* ①陳列；展覽；表現。a *display* of radios. 無線電收音機的展覽。a fashion *display.* 時裝展覽。②誇示；炫耀。Some people like to make a *display* of their knowledge. 有些人愛賣弄他們的知識。③特別引人注意的印刷排列。—*adj.* ①作樣品陳列的。*display* goods. 作樣品陳列的貨品。②陳列的。—**er,** *n.*

display ad 以醒目的方式刊載之廣告。(亦作 **display advertisement**)

*__dis·please__ 〔dɪsˈpliz; disˈpliːz〕 *v.*, **-pleased, -pleas·ing.** —*v.t.* 使不快；使厭煩；使生氣。Your teacher will be *displeased* with you. 你的老師會對你不高興。—*v.i.* 使人不快；使人生氣。

dis·pleas·ing 〔dɪsˈplizɪŋ; disˈpliːziŋ〕 *adj.* 不愉快的；令人不悅的。—**ly,** *adv.*

*__dis·pleas·ure__ 〔dɪsˈplɛʒɚ; disˈpleʒə〕 *n.* ①微怒；不快；不滿。We feel *displeasure* at something we dislike. 我們對於不喜歡的東西會感到不快。②不愉快的事；煩惱事。

dis·plume 〔dɪsˈplum; disˈpluːm〕 *v.t.*, **-plumed, -plum·ing.** ①除去羽毛。②剝奪勳位、名譽等。

dis·port 〔dɪˈsport; disˈpɔːt〕 *v.t.* ①以…自娛；嬉戲(與反身代名詞連用)。②展示。—*v.i.* 遊戲；嬉戲；玩。—*n.* 娛樂；玩樂；嬉戲。

dis·pos·a·ble 〔dɪˈspozəbl; disˈpouzəbl〕 *adj.* ①可自由處置的；可隨意使用的。②用後卽可丟棄的。

disposable income 扣完所得稅後之收入。

*__dis·pos·al__[1] 〔dɪˈspozl; disˈpouzəl〕 *n.* ①排列；陳列；布置。②清理；處置；處理；使用；支配。the *disposal* of property. 財產的處理。③出售；售賣。***at one's disposal*** 聽其使用；聽其支配。I am *at your disposal* the whole morning. 整個上午我聽你使喚。

dis·pos·al[2] *n.* 厨房水槽中之碎骨機。(亦作 **disposer**)

*__dis·pose__ 〔dɪˈspoz; disˈpouz〕 *v.*, **-posed, -pos·ing.** —*v.t.* ①陳列；排列；配置；布署。②處分；處置；使用。③使傾向；使心向。④使易患(某病)；使易陷於。Getting your feet wet *disposes* you to catching cold. 將脚弄濕使你易傷風。⑤使適於。—*v.i.* 處置；布置；決定。Man proposes, (but) God *disposes.* 謀事在人，成事在天。***dispose of*** **a.** 處分；處理；支配。The business has been *disposed of* successfully. 事務處理甚爲成功。**b.** 移去；除去；收拾。to *dispose of* rub-

bish. 除去垃圾。c. 放棄;賣去。d. 吃;喝。
dis·posed 〔dɪ'spozd; dis'pouzd〕 *adj.* ①有某種健康狀態的。I found him not well *disposed.* 我發現他身體不太舒適。②有…傾向的;有意的。to be *disposed* to go. 有意去。Do you feel *disposed* for a walk? 你願意散步嗎? ***be well (ill) disposed towards*** 對…(不)友善。
***dis·po·si·tion** 〔ˌdɪspə'zɪʃən; ˌdispə'ziʃən〕 *n.* ①性情;脾氣。He has a cheerful *disposition.* 他性情愉快。②布置;排列;配置。③傾向。④意向。⑤處置。⑥處理權。Who has the *disposition* of these buildings? 誰有這些房屋之處理權? ⑦(對少年罪犯之)判決。⑧(*pl.*)軍隊之部署。
dis·pos·sess 〔ˌdɪspə'zɛs; ˌdispə'zes〕 *v.t.* ①强奪(他人財產)。②剝奪;使失去。Fears *dispossessed* him of his senses. 恐懼使他失去理性。③逐出。
dis·pos·sessed 〔ˌdɪspə'zɛst; ˌdispə'zest〕 *adj.* ①無依無靠的。②失去產業的。③被逐出的。
dis·pos·ses·sion 〔ˌdɪspə'zɛʃən; ˌdispə'zeʃən〕 *n.* 强奪;剝奪。
dis·praise 〔dɪs'prez; dis'preiz〕 *v.*, **-praised, -prais·ing,** *n.* —*v.t.* 誹謗;非議;責備。—*n.* 誹謗;非議;責備。
dis·pread 〔dɪs'prɛd; di'spred〕 *v.t.*, **-pread, -pread·ing.** 向四方張開;向各方展開。
dis·proof 〔dɪs'pruf; dis'pru:f〕 *n.* 反證;反駁。
dis·pro·por·tion 〔ˌdɪsprə'porʃən; ˌdisprə'pɔ:ʃən〕 *n.* 不平衡;不相稱;不成比例。—*v.t.* 使失均衡;使不相稱。
dis·pro·por·tion·al 〔ˌdɪsprə'porʃənl̩; ˌdisprə'pɔ:ʃənl̩〕 *adj.* 不均衡的;不相稱的。—**ly,** *adv.*
dis·pro·por·tion·ate 〔ˌdɪsprə'porʃənɪt; ˌdisprə'pɔ:ʃənit〕 *adj.* 不成比例的;不相稱的;不平衡的。—**ly,** *adv.*
dis·prov·al 〔dɪs'pruvəl; dis'pru:vəl〕 *n.* ①反證。②證明爲誤(之行爲)。
dis·prove 〔dɪs'pruv; dis'pru:v〕 *v.t.*, **-proved, -prov·ing.** 證明爲誤;證明爲僞;反證。
dis·put·a·ble 〔dɪ'spjutəbl̩, 'dɪspjutəbl̩; dis'pju:təbl〕 *adj.* 易引起辯論的;不能確定的;成問題的。—**dis·put·a·bly,** *adv.*
dis·pu·tant 〔'dɪspjutənt, dɪ'spjutn̩t; dis'pju:tənt〕 *n.* 參加辯論者;爭論者。—*adj.* 爭論的;參加爭論的。
dis·pu·ta·tion 〔ˌdɪspju'teʃən; ˌdispju:'teiʃən〕 *n.* ①爭論;爭辯。②討論;辯論。
dis·pu·ta·tious 〔ˌdɪspju'teʃəs; ˌdispju:'teiʃəs〕 *adj.* 好議論的;好爭論的。
dis·pu·ta·tive 〔dɪ'spjutətɪv; dis'pju:tətiv〕 *adj.* =**disputatious.**
dis·pute** 〔dɪ'spjut; dis'pju:t〕 *v.*, **-put·ed, -put·ing,** *n.* —*v.i.* ①辯論;爭論。to *dispute* with a person. 與人辯論(或爭論)。②競爭。to *dispute* for a prize. 競爭獎品。③爭吵;吵鬧。—*v.t.* ①討論;辯論。②反駁;駁斥;懷疑。③抵抗;反抗。to *dispute* an advance by the enemy. 抵抗敵軍之推進。④競爭。Our team *disputed* the victory right to the end. 我們的球隊爭取勝利到底。⑤爭奪。—*n.* ①辯論;爭論。②爭吵;吵鬧。beyond dispute*** 無可爭論;無爭論餘地;無疑。This is *beyond dispute* the best book on the subject. 這本書無疑是關於此問題的最好的書。***in dispute*** 在爭論中。The matter *in dispute* is the possession of the house. 在爭論中的事爲房屋之所有權。
dis·qual·i·fi·ca·tion 〔ˌdɪskwɑləfə'keʃən; disˌkwɔlifi'keiʃən〕 *n.* ①無資格;無能力;不合格。②使不合格之事物或原因。
dis·qual·i·fy 〔dɪs'kwɑləˌfaɪ; dis'kwɔlifai〕 *v.t.*, **-fied, -fy·ing.** ①使不適合;使不能做事。②剝奪資格;取消資格。
dis·qui·et 〔dɪs'kwaɪət; dis'kwaiət〕 *v.t.* 使不安;使憂煩。—*n.* 憂慮;不安;動搖。
dis·qui·et·ing 〔dɪs'kwaɪətɪŋ; dis'kwaiətiŋ〕 *adj.* 令人不安的。—**ly,** *adv.*
dis·qui·e·tude 〔dɪs'kwaɪəˌtjud; dis'kwaiitju:d〕 *n.* 憂慮;不安;動搖。
dis·qui·si·tion 〔ˌdɪskwə'zɪʃən; ˌdiskwi'ziʃən〕 *n.* ①論文;專論。②正式之演講;專題演講。
dis·rate 〔dɪs'ret; dis'reit〕 *v.t.*, **-rat·ed, -rat·ing.** 〖航海〗使降級;使降低。
***dis·re·gard** 〔ˌdɪsrɪ'gɑrd; 'disri'gɑ:d〕 *v.t.* 不注意;不理;不顧;忽視。He *disregarded* my warnings and met with an accident. 他忽視我的警告,結果發生意外。—*n.* 不理;不顧;忽視;輕視。
dis·re·gard·ful 〔ˌdɪsrɪ'gɑrdfəl; ˌdisri'gɑ:dful〕 *adj.* 不顧的;忽視的。
dis·rel·ish 〔dɪs'rɛlɪʃ; dis'reliʃ〕 *v.t.* 厭惡;嫌。—*n.* 厭惡;嫌〖for〗.
dis·re·mem·ber 〔ˌdɪsrɪ'mɛmbɚ; ˌdisri'membə〕 *v.t.* & *v.i.* 〖方,俗〗遺忘;忘却;無法記憶。
dis·re·pair 〔ˌdɪsrɪ'pɛr; ˌdisri'pɛə〕 *n.* 失修;頹廢;破爛。
dis·rep·u·ta·ble 〔dɪs'rɛpjətəbl̩; dis'repjutəbl〕 *adj.* ①名譽不好的;可恥的。②不體面的;鄙陋的。—*n.* 名譽不好的人。—**dis·rep·u·ta·bil·i·ty, —ness,** *n.* —**dis·rep·u·ta·bly,** *adv.*
dis·re·pute 〔ˌdɪsrɪ'pjut; 'disri'pju:t〕 *n.* 名譽壞;汚名;無信用;不受歡迎。
dis·re·spect 〔ˌdɪsrɪ'spɛkt; 'disris'pekt〕 *n.* 不敬;無禮;粗暴;輕蔑。—*v.t.* 無禮對待;輕蔑。
dis·re·spect·a·ble 〔ˌdɪsrɪ'spɛktəbl̩; ˌdisris'pektəbl〕 *adj.* 不體面的;不值得尊重的。—**dis·re·spect·a·bil·i·ty,** *n.*
dis·re·spect·ful 〔ˌdɪsrɪ'spɛktfəl; ˌdisris'pektful〕 *adj.* 不敬的;無禮的;粗暴的。—**ly,** *adv.* —**ness,** *n.*
dis·robe 〔dɪs'rob; 'dis'roub〕 *v.t.* & *v.i.*, **-robed, -rob·ing.** 脫衣(尤指官服);使裸露。—**ment,** *n.*
dis·root 〔dɪs'rut; dis'ru:t〕 *v.t.* 連根拔起;拔除;根除。
dis·rupt 〔dɪs'rʌpt; dis'rʌpt〕 *v.t.* ①使分裂;使破裂;使裂開。②使中斷。③使陷入混亂。—*adj.* 中斷的。—**er,** *n.*
dis·rup·tion 〔dɪs'rʌpʃən; dis'rʌpʃən〕 *n.* ①分裂;破裂;瓦解。②(the D-) 1843 年之蘇格蘭教會的分裂。③中斷。
dis·rup·tive 〔dɪs'rʌptɪv; dis'rʌptiv〕 *adj.* ①引起分裂的;破裂的。②由分裂而產生的。—**ly,** *adv.* —**ness,** *n.*
dis·sat·is·fac·tion 〔ˌdɪssætɪs'fækʃən; 'disˌsætis'fækʃən〕 *n.* 不滿意;不滿足。
dis·sat·is·fac·to·ry 〔ˌdɪssætɪs'fæktərɪ; 'disˌsætis'fæktəri〕 *adj.* 令人不滿的。
dis·sat·is·fied 〔dɪs'sætɪsˌfaɪd; 'dis'sætisfaid〕 *adj.* 不滿意的;不高興的。
dis·sat·is·fy 〔dɪs'sætɪsˌfaɪ; 'dis'sætisfai〕 *v.t.*, **-fied, -fy·ing.** 使不滿意;使不滿足。
dis·sav·ing 〔dɪs'sevɪŋ; dis'seiviŋ〕 *n.*

花用儲蓄;支出多於收入。 「奪席位。

dis·seat (dɪs'sit; dis'si:t) *v.t.* 使離席;

***dis·sect** (dɪ'sɛkt; di'sekt) *v.t.* ①切開;解剖。②詳細研究;分析。③分辨出來〖常out〗. **—or,** *n.*

dis·sect·ed (dɪ'sɛktɪd; di'sektid) *adj.* ①切開的;分開的。②〖植物〗全裂的(葉)。③〖地質〗被山谷斷開的;開析的。

dis·sec·tion (dɪ'sɛkʃən; di'sekʃən) *n.* ①切開;解剖。②解剖體;解剖標本。③詳細查究;分析。 「ʃənəl) *adj.* 解剖的;剖析的。

dis·sec·tion·al (dɪ'sɛkʃənl; di'sek-

dis·seize (dɪs'siz; dis'si:z) *v.t.*, **-seized, -seiz·ing.** 〖法律〗强奪(某人)之產業;霸占。

dis·sei·zee (ˌdɪssi'zi; ˌdissi:'zi:) *n.* 財產被强占者;被逐出者。

dis·sei·zin, dis·sei·sin (dɪs'sizɪn; 'dis'si:zin) *n.* 〖法律〗①(地產之)强占;强奪;霸占。②(地產等)被强占之狀態。

dis·sem·ble (dɪ'sɛmbl̩; di'sembl) *v.*, **-bled, -bling.** —*v.t.* ①隱藏;掩飾(眞情、行爲等)。②假裝;矇混。—*v.i.* 掩飾眞情、行爲等。

dis·sem·bler (dɪ'sɛmbl̩ɚ; di'semblə) *n.* 假裝者;掩飾者。

dis·sem·i·nate (dɪ'sɛməˌnet; di'semineit) *v.*, **-nat·ed, -nat·ing.** —*v.t.* 散布;傳播。—*v.i.* 散布。

dis·sem·i·na·tion (dɪˌsɛmə'neʃən; diˌsemi'neiʃən) *n.* 散布;傳播。

dis·sem·i·na·tive (dɪ'sɛməˌnetɪv; di'semәneitiv) *adj.* 散布的;傳播的。

dis·sem·i·na·tor (dɪ'sɛməˌnetɚ; di'semineitə) *n.* 傳播者;播種者;播種器。

***dis·sen·sion** (dɪ'sɛnʃən; di'senʃən) *n.* 衝突;紛爭。Political questions often cause *dissension.* 政治問題常引起紛爭。

dis·sent (dɪ'sɛnt; di'sent) *v.i.* ①不同意;持異議。②不服從國教;反對國教。—*n.* ①不同意;異議。②不從國教;反叛國教。

dis·sent·er (dɪ'sɛntɚ; di'sentə) *n.* 持異議者。

dis·sen·tient (dɪ'sɛnʃənt; di'senʃiənt) *adj.* 不贊成的;持異議的(尤指不贊成大多數之意見者)。—*n.* 不贊成者;反對者;持異議者。—**ly,** *adv.* —**dis·sen·tience, dis·sen·tien·cy,** *n.* 「=dissentient. —**ly,** *adv.*

dis·sent·ing (dɪ'sɛntɪŋ; di'sentiŋ) *adj.*

dis·sen·tious (dɪ'sɛnʃəs; di'senʃəs) *adj.* 好爭論的。

dis·sep·i·ment (dɪ'sɛpəmənt; di'sepimənt) *n.* 〖動、植物〗隔膜。 **—al,** *adj.*

dis·sert (dɪ'sɝt; di'sə:t) *v.i.* 〖罕〗= **dissertate.**

dis·ser·tate ('dɪsɚˌtet; 'disəteit) *v.i.*, **-tat·ed, -tat·ing.** 〖罕〗正式談論;討論。

dis·ser·ta·tion (ˌdɪsɚ'teʃən; ˌdisə:'teiʃən) *n.* ①論文;學位論文。②議論;論說;正式之演講。**—al,** *adj.* **—ist,** *n.*

dis·serve (dɪs'sɝv; dis'sə:v) *v.t.*, **-served, -serv·ing.** ①不盡力侍奉。②冷待;虐待;傷害。

dis·serv·ice (dɪs'sɝvɪs; dis'sə:vis) *n.* 損害;傷害;虐待。**—a·ble,** *adj.*

dis·sev·er (dɪ'sɛvɚ; dis'sevə) *v.t.* & *v.i.* 分離;分裂;割開。 「vərəns) *n.* 分離;隔離。

dis·sev·er·ance (dɪ'sɛvərəns; di'se-

dis·si·dence ('dɪsədəns; 'disidəns) *n.* ①不一致;異議。②背離國教。

dis·si·dent ('dɪsədənt; 'disidənt) *adj.* 不相合的;倡異議的;背離國教的。—*n.* ①倡反調者。②背離國教者。 「爆裂的。

dis·sil·ient (dɪ'sɪlɪənt; di'siliənt) *adj.*

dis·sim·i·lar (dɪ'sɪmələ; 'di'similə) *adj.* 不同的;異樣的;不相似的。**—ly,** *adv.*

dis·sim·i·lar·i·ty (dɪˌsɪmə'lærətɪ; ˌdisimi'læriti) *n.*, *pl.* **-ties.** 不同;異點;不相似。

dis·sim·i·late (dɪ'sɪməˌlet; di'simileit) *v.i.* & *v.t.*, **-lat·ed, -lat·ing.** (使)不同;(使)變得不同。**—dis·sim·i·la·tive,** *adj.*

dis·sim·i·la·tion (dɪˌsɪmə'leʃən; 'disimi'leiʃən) *n.* 異化;異化作用。

dis·si·mil·i·tude (ˌdɪssɪ'mɪləˌtjud; ˌdissi'militju:d) *n.* ①相違;不同。②相違或不同之點。

dis·sim·u·late (dɪ'sɪmjəˌlet; di'simjuleit) *v.t.* & *v.i.*, **-lat·ed, -lat·ing.** 假裝;掩飾(眞情等);欺瞞。**—dis·sim·u·la·tor,** *n.* **—dis·sim·u·la·tive,** *adj.*

dis·sim·u·la·tion (dɪˌsɪmjə'leʃən; diˌsimju'leiʃən) *n.* 假裝;掩飾;欺瞞。

dis·si·pate ('dɪsəˌpet; 'disipeit) *v.*, **-pat·ed, -pat·ing.** —*v.t.* ①使消散;驅散。②浪費。—*v.i.* ①消散。②放蕩;耽於遊樂。

dis·si·pat·ed ('dɪsəˌpetɪd; 'disiˌpeitid) *adj.* ①放蕩的。②浪費的。**—ly,** *adv.*

dis·si·pa·tion (ˌdɪsə'peʃən; ˌdisi'peiʃən) *n.* ①分散;消散。②浪費。③放蕩;娛樂(尤指不正當者)。

dis·si·pa·tor ('dɪsəˌpetɚ; 'disipeitə) *n.* 放蕩者;浪子;使散開之物。(亦作**dissipater**)

dis·so·ci·a·ble (dɪ'soʃɪəbl̩; di'souʃjəbl) *adj.* ①可分立的;可分離的。②不善交際的;孤僻的。③不調和的;不能相合的。**—dis·so·ci·a·bil·i·ty,** *n.*

dis·so·cial (dɪ'soʃəl; di'souʃəl) *adj.* 不善交際的;不喜社交的;孤僻的。

dis·so·ci·ate (dɪ'soʃɪˌet; di'souʃieit) *v.*, **-at·ed, -at·ing,** *adj.* —*v.t.* ①斷絕關係;分離;分開來想。②〖化〗加熱分解;分離。***dissociate oneself from*** 斷絕和…之關係;否認和…有關係。—*adj.* 無關的;分開的。

dis·so·ci·a·tion (dɪˌsosɪ'eʃən; diˌsousi'eiʃən) *n.* ①分解;分離。②〖心理〗分裂。③〖化〗分離。

dis·so·ci·a·tive (dɪ'soʃɪˌetɪv; di'souʃiətiv) *adj.* ①〖化〗分離的。②〖心理〗分裂的。③反社會的。

dis·sol·u·bil·i·ty (dɪˌsɑljə'bɪlətɪ; diˌsɔlju'biliti) *n.* 可溶性。

dis·sol·u·ble (dɪ'sɑljəbl̩; di'sɔljubl) *adj.* ①可分解的;可分離的。②可解除的。③可溶解的;溶解性的。**—ness,** *n.*

dis·so·lute ('dɪsəˌlut; 'disəlu:t) *adj.* 放蕩的;淫樂的。**—ly,** *adv.* **—ness,** *n.*

***dis·so·lu·tion** (ˌdɪsə'luʃən; ˌdisə'lu:ʃən) *n.* ①分離;分解;分裂。②解除;(議會、團體等之)解散。the power of *dissolution* of a legislature. 解散議會之權。③毀滅;瓦解。④死亡。⑤溶化;鎔化;融解。the *dissolution* of ice. 冰的融解。**—dis·so·lu·tive,** *adj.*

dis·solv·a·ble (dɪ'zɑlvəbl̩; di'zɔlvəbl) *adj.* ①可溶解的。②可解散的。③可解除的。

***dis·solve** (dɪ'zɑlv; di'zɔlv) *v.*, **-solved, -solv·ing,** *n.* —*v.t.* ①溶解。②解散;解除;解開。to *dissolve* a partnership. 拆散合夥(散夥)。③分解(成許多部分)。The company was *dissolved* into smaller units. 此公司分解成許多較小單位。④〖法律〗宣告無效;取

消。⑤使衰弱；使無力。⑥消滅。⑦使熔化。⑧感動。⑨消除。—*v.i.*①溶解。②消散;消失。The view *dissolved* in mist. 景色消失在霧中。③解散。The assembly *dissolved.* 議會解散了。④熔化。⑤流淚。***dissolve*** (or ***be dissolved***) ***in tears*** 眼淚汪汪;成爲淚人兒。—*n.*〖電影〗漸隱;溶暗。—**dis·solv·er,** *n.*

dis·sol·vent [dɪˈzɑlvənt; diˈzɔlvənt] *adj.* 有溶解力的。—*n.* ①溶解劑。②有消除力之事物。

dissolving view 〖電影〗漸隱畫面。

dis·so·nance [ˈdɪsənəns; ˈdisənəns] *n.* ①不調和;不協調。②〖音樂〗不諧和音。

dis·so·nant [ˈdɪsənənt; ˈdisənənt] *adj.* ①不和諧的；不悅耳的。②不融洽的；不一致的。—**ly,** *adv.*

dis·suade [dɪˈswed; diˈsweid] *v.t.*, **-suad·ed, -suad·ing.** 勸阻；勸戒；阻止〖常from〗。—**dis·suad·er,** *n.*

dis·sua·sion [dɪˈsweʒən; diˈsweiʒən] *n.* 勸止;諫言;忠告。

dis·sua·sive [dɪˈswesɪv; diˈsweisiv] *adj.* 勸戒的;阻止的。—*n.* 勸戒的言談；勸阻的言論。—**ly,** *adv.* —**ness,** *n.*

dis·syl·lab·ic [ˌdɪsɪˈlæbɪk; ˈdisiˈlæbik] *adj.* 二音節的。(亦作 **disyllabic**)

dis·syl·la·ble [dɪˈsɪləbl̩; diˈsiləbl] *n.* 二音節之字。(亦作**disyllable**)

dis·sym·met·ri·cal [ˌdɪsɪˈmɛtrɪkl̩; ˈdisiˈmetrikəl] *adj.* ①不均衡的;不對稱的。②相反對稱的。

dis·sym·me·try [dɪsˈsɪmɪtrɪ; ˈdiˈsimitri] *n., pl.* **-tries.** ①不均衡;不對稱。②相反對稱(如人之左右手)。

dist. ①distance. ②distinguish. ③distinguished. ④district.

dis·taff [ˈdɪstæf; ˈdistɑːf] *n.* ①(手紡用之)繞桿；捲線桿。②婦女之事務。③婦女；女性。④母方親戚。—*adj.* 女性的；婦女的。***distaff side*** 女系;母系。

dis·tain [dɪˈsten; disˈtein] *v.t.* 〖古〗①使變色;染(色)。②玷辱;貽羞。

dis·tal [ˈdɪstl̩ ˈdistl] *adj.* 〖解剖〗末梢部的;遠側的。—**ly,** *adv.*

‡**dis·tance** [ˈdɪstəns; ˈdistəns] *n., v.,* **-tanced, -tanc·ing.** —*n.* ①距離。The *distance* from the farm to the city is ten miles. 由農場至市鎮之距離爲十英里。My house is within walking *distance* of the school. 我的房子和學校在步行可及的距離內。②遠;遙遠;遠處。The farm is at a *distance* from any railroad. 農場距任何鐵路線均甚遠。*Distance* lends enchantment. (遠)距離增添魅力(遠道的和尚會念經)。③時間的距離。at this *distance* of time. 在這樣長久的時間。④〖音樂〗兩音符間之音程。⑤冷淡；疏遠；敬鬼神而遠之的態度。⑥差異。***a long distance call*** 長途電話。***from*** (***at***) ***a distance*** 由(在)遠處。***go*** (or ***last***) ***the distance*** 賽到底。***in the distance*** 在遠處。We saw a light *in the distance.* 我們看到遠處有光。***keep a person at a distance*** 冷待某人(不與親近)。***keep one's distance*** 不與親近。—*v.t.* ①越過;超過;遠勝。The black horse soon *distanced* the others. 這匹黑馬很快就遙遙領先其他各馬。②使遠離;使不接近。

distance post 賽馬時用之距離標示。

‡**dis·tant** [ˈdɪstənt; ˈdistənt] *adj.* ①遠離的;遠隔的〖from〗. The moon is *distant* from the earth. 月球與地球距離甚遠。The city is 10 miles *distant* from Chicago. 這城市距芝加哥十英里。The town is three miles *distant.* 這鎮遠在三英里外。②遙遠的。He lives in a *distant* city. 他住在一個很遠的城市中。*distant* thoughts. 遠慮。③遠族的。a *distant* relative. 遠親。④冷漠的；冷淡的。⑤不同種的;不同的。⑥分明的;不連接的。⑦從遠方來的或往遠方去的。—**ly,** *adv.* —**ness,** *n.*

dis·taste [dɪsˈtest; disˈteist] *n.* ①嫌惡;憎厭。②不喜飲、食。

dis·taste·ful [dɪsˈtestfəl; disˈteistful] *adj.* ①不愉快的;令人可厭的。②味道不佳的。③表現厭惡的。—**ly,** *adv.* —**ness,** *n.*

dis·tem·per¹ [dɪsˈtɛmpɚ; disˈtempə] *n.* ①犬熱病;犬瘟熱。②病;(身心之)不健康。③不安;騷動。—*v.t.* 使病;使不安。

dis·tem·per² *n.* ①以水、蛋或膠等所調和之顏料(繪畫於內壁等使用者)。②用上項材料所作之畫；用上項材料作畫之畫法。—*v.t.* (用上項材料)畫或在…上着色。

dis·tend [dɪˈstɛnd; disˈtend] *v.i. & v.t.* (使)擴張;膨脹。—**er,** *n.*

dis·ten·si·ble [dɪˈstɛnsəbl̩; disˈtensəbl] *adj.* 膨脹性的;可擴大的。

dis·ten·sion, dis·ten·tion [dɪˈstɛnʃən; disˈtenʃən] *n.* 膨脹;延伸。

dis·tich [ˈdɪstɪk; ˈdistik] *n.* 〖韻律〗兩行爲一節的詩或格言。

dis·till, dis·til [dɪˈstɪl; disˈtil] *v.,* **-tilled, -till·ing; -tiled, -til·ing.** —*v.t.* ①蒸餾。②由蒸餾而得;精煉。③摘出;精選出。④流出;分泌出。⑤使滴下。⑥由蒸餾而除去。⑦加以濃縮。—*v.i.* ①蒸餾。②滴下。③一點一滴地產生。

dis·til·late [ˈdɪstl̩ɪt; ˈdistilit] *n.* ①由蒸餾氣化後再凝縮而得之液體;蒸餾物。②精華。

dis·til·la·tion [ˌdɪstl̩ˈeʃən; ˌdistiˈleiʃən] *n.* ①蒸餾。②蒸餾物。③精華。

dis·til·la·to·ry [dɪsˈtɪləˌtorɪ; disˈtilətəri] *adj.* 蒸餾的;蒸餾用的。

distilled liquor 蒸餾而得之酒(如威士忌)。

distilled water 蒸餾水。

dis·till·er [dɪˈstɪlɚ; disˈtilə] *n.* ①蒸餾器。②蒸餾(酒)者。

dis·till·er·y [dɪˈstɪlərɪ; disˈtiləri] *n., pl.* **-er·ies.** 蒸餾所;釀酒廠。

***dis·tinct** [dɪˈstɪŋkt; disˈtiŋkt] *adj.* ①分開的；分別的；不同的。Fortitude is *distinct* from valor. 剛毅(堅忍不拔)與剛勇(勇猛)有別。②清楚的;明晰的。③確切的。④非凡的；稀有的。—**ness,** *n.*

dis·tinc·tion** [dɪˈstɪŋkʃən; disˈtiŋkʃən] *n.* ①區別;分別。There is a *distinction* between the two. 兩者之間有區別。②差別之點；不同的特點；特徵。③優待;優遇。④高貴;卓越;有名聲。He was a writer of *distinction.* 他是一個卓越的作家。⑤榮譽;殊勳。to graduate from college with *distinction.* 以優異成績從大學畢業。distinction without a difference*** 假的區別；人爲的區別。—**less,** *adj.*

***dis·tinc·tive** [dɪˈstɪŋktɪv; disˈtiŋktiv] *adj.* 示區別的；特殊的；有特色的。actions *distinctive* of a brutal man. 殘忍者特有的行動。—**ness,** *n.*

dis·tinc·tive·ly [dɪˈstɪŋktɪvlɪ; disˈtiŋktivli] *adv.* 特有地;特殊地。

***dis·tinct·ly** [dɪˈstɪŋktlɪ; disˈtiŋktli] *adv.* ①清楚地。Please speak *distinctly.* 請

清楚地說。②無疑地；不錯地。③特有地。

dis·tin·gué 〔ˌdɪstæŋˈge; disˈtæŋgei〕 〖法〗 *adj.* 高尚的；上流的(指舉止儀態)。

***dis·tin·guish** 〔dɪˈstɪŋgwɪʃ; disˈtiŋgwiʃ〕 *v.t.* ①區別；辨別 〖from〗. to *distinguish* right from wrong. 辨別是非。②認明；辨識；看清楚。③使有別於…；做爲…之特徵；表特性。Speech *distinguishes* man from the animals. 語言使人有別於動物。④使揚名；使顯著。He *distinguished* himself by his bravery. 他因勇敢而揚名。⑤分類。—*v.i.* 區別；辨別 〖between〗. to *distinguish* between right and wrong. 辨別是非。

dis·tin·guish·a·ble 〔dɪˈstɪŋgwɪʃəbl; disˈtiŋgwiʃəbl〕 *adj.* 可區別的；可辨識的；有分別的；有特徵的。 **—ness,** *n.* **—dis·tin·guish·a·bly,** *adv.*

***dis·tin·guished** 〔dɪˈstɪŋgwɪʃt; disˈtiŋgwiʃt〕 *adj.* ①著名的；卓越的；傑出的。a *distinguished* writer. 著名的作家。②有要人的模樣的。 **—ly,** *adv.*

dis·tin·guish·ing 〔dɪˈstɪŋgwɪʃɪŋ; disˈtiŋgwiʃiŋ〕 *adj.* 特殊的；特異的；區別的。 **—ly,** *adv.*

***dis·tort** 〔dɪsˈtɔrt; disˈtɔːt〕 *v.t.* ①扭歪；扭曲；使變形。 Her face was *distorted* by rage. 她因發怒而面容大變。②曲解；誤傳。a *distorted* interpretation. 曲解的詮釋。

dis·tor·tion 〔dɪsˈtɔrʃən; disˈtɔːʃən〕 *n.* ①扭曲；變形；曲解。②變形之物；曲解之事。 **—al,** *adj.*

dis·tor·tion·ist 〔dɪsˈtɔrʃənɪst; disˈtɔːʃənist〕 *n.* 漫畫家。

***dis·tract** 〔dɪˈstrækt; disˈtrækt〕 *v.t.* ①分心；轉移(意向)。The music of the radio *distracted* me from my reading. 無線電收音機的音樂使我不能專心讀書。 ②擾亂；困惱；迷惑。He was *distracted* with business. 他爲事務所煩擾。③使精神錯亂。④使輕鬆；使娛樂。

dis·tract·ed 〔dɪˈstræktɪd; disˈtræktid〕 *adj.* ①意亂情迷的；精神錯亂的；發狂的。to drive a person *distracted*. 迫使某人發狂；使人困擾。②精神或注意力分散的。 **—ness,** *n.*

dis·tract·ed·ly 〔dɪˈstræktɪdlɪ; disˈtræktidli〕 *adv.* 心情紛亂地。

dis·tract·ing·ly 〔dɪˈstræktɪŋlɪ; disˈtræktiŋli〕 *adv.* 令人分心地；令人心情不安地；惱人地。

dis·trac·tion 〔dɪˈstrækʃən; disˈtrækʃən〕 *n.* ①分散注意力。②分心之事物。③心情不安。④狂亂；心智不清。⑤困惑。⑥娛樂；輕鬆；舒適。 ***to distraction*** …到發狂。

dis·trac·tive 〔dɪˈstræktɪv; disˈtræktiv〕 *adj.* 分散注意力的；擾亂的。

dis·train 〔dɪˈstren; disˈtrein〕 *v.t.* 〖法律〗扣押(動產等)。—*v.i.* 〖法律〗扣押財產。 **—a·ble,** *adj.*

dis·train·ee 〔ˌdɪstreˈni; ˌdistreiˈniː〕 *n.* 〖法律〗財產被扣押者。

dis·train·er, dis·train·or 〔dɪˈstrenə; disˈtreinə〕 *n.* 〖法律〗扣押人。

dis·train·ment 〔dɪˈstrenmənt; disˈtreinmənt〕 *n.* 〖法律〗扣押財產。

dis·traint 〔dɪˈstrent; disˈtreint〕 *n.* 〖法律〗扣押；强制執行。

dis·trait 〔dɪˈstre; disˈtrei〕 *adj.* ①心不在焉的；心神恍惚的。②心神分散的。

dis·traught 〔dɪˈstrɔt; disˈtrɔːt〕 *adj.* ①心神分散的；煩憂的。②發狂的。 **—ly,** *adv.*

***dis·tress** 〔dɪˈstrɛs; disˈtres〕 *n.* ①痛苦；悲痛；憂愁。②使痛苦或焦慮之事物與原因。③窮困；因窮而發生的痛苦。④危險；困難。—*v.t.* ①使痛苦；使悲愁。Don't *distress* yourself. 你自己不要難過了。②逼使；迫使。

distress call 求救呼號；遇難呼號。(亦作 **distress signal**)

dis·tressed 〔dɪˈstrɛst; disˈtrest〕 *adj.* ①痛苦的。②賤賣的。 **—ly,** *adv.*

distressed area 災區。

distress flag 遇難信號旗。

distress frequency 〖無線電〗求救頻率。

dis·tress·ful 〔dɪˈstrɛsfəl; disˈtresful〕 *adj.* ①痛苦的；苦惱的。②不幸的；悲慘的。 **—ly,** *adv.* **—ness,** *n.*

distress gun 遇難信號砲。

dis·tress·ing 〔dɪˈstrɛsɪŋ; disˈtresiŋ〕 *adj.* 悲慘的；悲痛的；困苦的。

distress merchandise 廉價出售(以求現款)的商品。

distress rocket 遇難信號火箭。

distress selling 廉價出售(以求現款)。

distress warrant 〖法律〗扣押令狀。

dis·trib·u·tar·y 〔dɪˈstrɪbjuˌtɛrɪ; disˈtribjutəri〕 *n.*, *pl.* **-tar·ies.** (河之) 支流。

***dis·trib·ute** 〔dɪˈstrɪbjʊt; disˈtribjuːt〕 *v.t.*, **-ut·ed, -ut·ing.** ①分配；分送；分發。②分布；散開；散布。*Distribute* the paint evenly over the wall. 將漆均匀地刷於牆上。③分類；類別。④分開。The soldiers were *distributed* into three ranks. 這些士兵分爲三列。

***dis·tri·bu·tion** 〔ˌdɪstrəˈbjuʃən; ˌdistriˈbjuːʃən〕 *n.* ①分配；頒發。②分布；散布。③(消費品的)供銷。④分配的東西。⑤分類。⑥銷售量。 **—al,** *adj.* **—ly,** *adv.*

dis·trib·u·tive 〔dɪˈstrɪbjətɪv; disˈtribjutiv〕 *adj.* ①分配的；普及的；廣衍的。②〖文法〗個別的；分配的。—*n.* 〖文法〗個別詞。〖注意〗個別詞包括(1) *distributive* adjective, 個別形容詞, 如修飾名詞用的 each, every, either, neither 等；(2) *distributive* pronoun, 個別代名詞, 如作代名詞用的each, every, either, neither 等。 **—ly,** *adv.*

dis·trib·u·tor 〔dɪˈstrɪbjətə; disˈtribjutə〕 *n.* ①分配者；分送之人。②〖商〗貨物之配售人或商號。 exclusive *distributor.* 總代理。③〖印刷〗拆版之人或機器。④〖機械〗配電器；分電盤。(亦作**distributer**) **—ship,** *n.*

‡dis·trict 〔ˈdɪstrɪkt; ˈdistrikt〕 *n.* ①行政區；郡(英)；縣；地方；管區。*district* court. 地方法院。②區域；地域。This is a purely agricultural *district*. 這是一個純粹的農業區域。—*v.t.* 分爲區域。

district attorney 地方法院檢察官。

district man 負責某一地區新聞採訪之記者。

District of Co·lum·bi·a 〔~~kəˈlʌmbɪə; ~~kəˈlʌmbiə〕 哥倫比亞特區(美國聯邦地區, 與美首都華盛頓同其範圍, 屬聯邦政府, 由國會管轄, 略作 **D.C.**)。

***dis·trust** 〔dɪsˈtrʌst; disˈtrʌst〕 *n.* 不信；疑惑。—*v.t.* 不信；猜疑。

dis·trust·ful 〔dɪsˈtrʌstfəl; disˈtrʌstful〕 *adj.* 不信任的；懷疑的。 ***be distrustful of*** 對…缺乏信心；不信…。 **—ly,** *adv.*

***dis·turb** 〔dɪˈstɝb; disˈtəːb〕 *v.t.* ①使紊亂；攪動；擾亂。②妨礙；妨害。I am sorry to *disturb* you. 我很抱歉妨礙你的工作。③使困擾；使煩惱；使心亂。 **—er,** *n.*

***dis·turb·ance** 〔dɪˈstɝbəns; disˈtəːbəns〕 *n.* ①擾亂；滋擾。②騷動；動亂。③憂慮；

激動;不安;恐慌。He showed no *disturbance* over the sad news. 他聽了這悲慘消息之後,並未表示焦慮不安的樣子。④失常;不正常。

disturbances of apprehension〖醫〗領會障礙。

disturbances of attention 「〖醫〗注意障礙。」

disturbances of intelligence〖醫〗智力障礙。

di·sul·fide 〔daɪˈsʌlfaɪd; daiˈsʌlfaid〕 *n.*〖化〗二硫化物。(亦作 **disulphide**)

dis·un·ion 〔dɪsˈjunjən; ˈdisˈjuːnjən〕 *n.* ①分裂;分離。②不統一;不和合。

dis·un·ion·ist 〔dɪsˈjunjənɪst; disˈjuːniənist〕 *n.* 反對統一者(尤指美國南北戰爭前南方之主張脫離聯邦者)。

dis·u·nite 〔ˌdɪsjuˈnaɪt; ˈdisjuːˈnait〕 *v.*, **-nit·ed, -nit·ing.** —*v.t.* 使分離;使分裂;使不合作。—*v.i.* 分離;分散。

dis·u·ni·ty 〔dɪsˈjunɪtɪ; disˈjuːniti〕 *n.* 不統一;不團結。

dis·use 〔*n.* dɪsˈjus; ˈdisˈjuːs *v.* dɪsˈjuz; ˈdisˈjuːz〕 *n.*, *v.*, **-used, -us·ing.** —*n.* 不用;廢止。—*v.t.* 停用(常用於被動式)。

di·syl·lab·ic 〔ˌdɪsəˈlæbɪk; ˈdisiˈlæbik〕 *adj.* 二音節的。

di·syl·la·ble 〔dɪˈsɪləbl̩; diˈsiləbl〕 *n.* 「二音節的字。」

dis·yoke 〔dɪsˈjok; disˈjouk〕 *v.t.*, **-yoked, -yok·ing.** 使脫離桎梏。

*__ditch__ 〔dɪtʃ; ditʃ〕 *n.* 壕溝。***die in a ditch*** 死於溝壑;窮困潦倒而死。***die in the last ditch*** 戰至最後而死。—*v.t.* ①以壕溝圍繞。②使墜溝中。He *ditched* his car while learning to drive. 他在學習駕駛時,將車墜入溝中。③使(飛機)迫降於水面上。④放棄;丟開。⑤〖俚〗擺脫;逃避;逃開。Let's *ditch* school today. 今天我們來逃學吧。⑥〖俚〗藏起來。—*v.i.* ①掘溝。②(指非水上飛機)水面迫降。—**less,** *adj.*

ditch·er 〔ˈdɪtʃɚ; ˈditʃə〕 *n.* ①挖溝人;掘壕人。②掘壕機(=ditching machine).

ditch·wa·ter 〔ˈdɪtʃˌwɔtɚ; ˈditʃˌwɔːtə〕 *n.* 溝中之死水。

di·the·ism 〔ˈdaɪθiɪzm̩; ˈdaiθiizəm〕 *n.* ①二神論;二神教。②善惡二元論。—**di·the·is·tic,** *adj.* —**di·the·ist,** *n.*

dith·er 〔ˈdɪðɚ; ˈdiðə〕 *n.*, *v.i.* 戰慄;震動。

dith·er·y 〔ˈdɪðərɪ; ˈdiðəri〕 *adj.* ①戰慄的。②遲疑不決的。

dith·y·ramb 〔ˈdɪθəˌræm; ˈdiθiræm〕 *n.* ①古希臘祭酒神之狂熱的合唱歌。②感情強烈之詩歌、演說或文字。—**ic,** *adj.*

dit·ta·ny 〔ˈdɪtənɪ; ˈditəni〕 *n.*, *pl.* **-nies.** 薄荷類植物;白鮮。

dit·to 〔ˈdɪto; ˈditou〕 *n.*, *pl.* **-tos,** *v.*, **-toed, -to·ing,** *adv.* —*n.* ①同上;同前(略作 do., d°). ②代表同上之符號(")。③同樣物;複製品。***say ditto to*** 〖俗〗對…表示同意。—*v.t.* 重複;複製。—*adv.* 同前地;同樣地。

dit·tog·ra·phy 〔dɪˈtɑgrəfɪ; diˈtɔgrəfi〕 *n.*, *pl.* **-phies.** 重複的誤寫;誤寫之重複文字。—**dit·to·graph·ic,** *adj.*

ditto machine 複印機。

ditto mark 同上、同前之符號(")。

dit·ty 〔ˈdɪtɪ; ˈditi〕 *n.*, *pl.* **-ties.** 小曲;歌謠。—**dit·tied,** *adj.*

ditty bag 水手等用之針線袋。

ditty box 水手等用之針線盒。

di·u·ret·ic 〔ˌdaɪjuˈrɛtɪk; ˌdaijuəˈretik〕 *adj.*〖醫〗利尿的。—*n.* 利尿劑。

di·ur·nal 〔daɪˈɝnl̩; daiˈəːnl〕 *adj.* ①每日的。②白晝的。③〖植物〗晝開夜合的(花、葉等)。④〖動物〗晝間活動的。—*n.*〖宗教〗日課書。—**i·ty,** *n.* —**ly,** *adv.*

diurnal motion (因地球自轉而產生的星球由東向西之)視移動。

div. ①divide. ②divided. ③division. ④divergence. ⑤diversion. ⑥dividend. ⑦divine. ⑧divinity. ⑨divorce.

di·va 〔ˈdivə; ˈdiːvə〕 *n.*, *pl.* **-vas, -ve** 〔-vɛ; -ve〕.〖義〗歌劇中之首席女角。

di·va·gate 〔ˈdaɪvəˌget; ˈdaivəgeit〕 *v.i.*, **-gat·ed, -gat·ing.** ①漫遊;漂泊;入歧途。②(談話)離題;涉入枝節。③逸出。—**di·va·ga·tion,** *n.*

di·va·lent 〔daɪˈvelənt; ˈdaiˌveilənt〕 *adj.*〖化〗二價的。—**di·va·lence,** *n.*

di·van 〔ˈdaɪvæn, dɪˈvæn; diˈvæn〕 *n.* ①無靠背之長沙發椅。②(東方國家之)國務會議;會議室;法庭。③吸煙室(吸煙、喝咖啡等用)。④(波斯或其他東方詩人之)詩集。

di·var·i·cate 〔dəˈværəˌket; daiˈværikeit〕 *v.*, **-cat·ed, -cat·ing,** *adj.* —*v.i.* ①分歧;分開。②〖動、植物〗分枝;分爲兩叉。—*v.t.* 使分成兩枝;使分叉;分開。—*adj.* ①分歧的;分開的。②〖動、植物〗分叉的;成叉角的。—**ly,** *adv.* —**di·var·i·ca·tor,** *n.*

di·var·i·ca·tion 〔daɪˌværəˈkeʃən, də-; daiˌværiˈkeiʃən〕 *n.* ①分支。②分歧。

*__dive__ 〔daɪv; daiv〕 *v.*, **dived** or **dove, dived, div·ing,** *n.* —*v.i.* ①(頭部向下)跳水。②俯衝。③潛水(利用特種潛水設備潛入水中)。The submarine *dived.* 潛水艇潛水了。④突然挿入。⑤突然跑進;突然消失。He *dived into* an alley. 他突然跑進一小巷而消失。⑥潛心於;專心於;探究。⑦驟降。—*v.t.* ①插入。He *dived* his hand into the earth. 他將手插入泥土中。②使俯衝。He *dived* his plane. 他駕機俯衝。—*n.* ①潛水。②(飛機之)俯衝。③〖美俗〗下等的飲酒賭博處所。④〖英〗餐館、旅館中賣特殊食物之地下室。⑤埋頭研究。⑥急奔。He made a *dive* for the ditch. 他向壕溝急奔。⑦驟降。⑧〖俚〗(於拳賽中)假裝被擊倒。He took a *dive* in the third round. 他在第三回合假裝被擊倒。

dive-bomb 〔ˈdaɪvˌbɑm; ˈdaivbɔm〕 *v.t.* & *v.i.* 俯衝轟炸。

dive bomber 俯衝轟炸機。

dive·keep·er 〔ˈdaɪvˌkipɚ; ˈdaivˌkiːpə〕 *n.* 下等酒家、賭窟之老板。

div·er 〔ˈdaɪvɚ; ˈdaivə〕 *n.* ①潛水者。②潛水鳥。③〖俗〗潛水艇。④俯衝轟炸機。

di·verge 〔dəˈvɝdʒ; daiˈvəːdʒ〕 *v.*, **-verged, -verg·ing.** —*v.i.* ①分歧;分出。②差異。③逸出正軌。—*v.t.* 使偏向。

di·ver·gence 〔dəˈvɝdʒəns; daiˈvəːdʒəns〕 *n.* 分歧;分離;背馳;差異。

di·ver·gen·cy 〔dəˈvɝdʒənsɪ; daiˈvəːdʒənsi〕 *n.*, *pl.* **-cies.** =**divergence.**

di·ver·gent 〔dəˈvɝdʒənt; daiˈvəːdʒənt〕 *adj.* ①分歧的;差異的。②發散的。③分向不同方向的。—**ly,** *adv.*

*__di·vers__ 〔ˈdaɪvɚz; ˈdaivəːz〕 *adj.* 不同的;種種的。—*pron.* (作 *pl.* 解) 若干。

*__di·verse__ 〔dəˈvɝs, daɪ-; daiˈvəːs, ˈdaivəːs〕 *adj.* ①不同的;互異的。②種種的;有變化的。—**ly,** *adv.*

di·ver·si·fi·ca·tion 〔dəˌvɝsəfəˈkeʃən; daiˌvəːsifiˈkeiʃən〕 *n.* ①變化;不同;多樣。②投資於不同類之事業;分散投資;各種產品之製造。

di·ver·si·fied 〔daɪˈvɝsəˌfaɪd; daiˈvəːsifaid〕 *adj.* ①多變化的;種種色色的。②投資於不同類之事業的。

di·ver·si·form 〔daɪˈvɝsəˌfɔrm; daiˈvəːsifɔːm〕 *adj.* 多樣的;具備種種形狀的。

di·ver·si·fy 〔dəˈvɝsəˌfaɪ; daiˈvəːsifai〕 *v.*, **-fied, -fy·ing.** —*v.t.* 使變化;使有變異。 —*v.i.* 作多樣性投資或種植。 —**di·ver·si·fi·er,** *n.*

***di·ver·sion** 〔dəˈvɝʒən; daiˈvəːʃən〕 *n.* ①轉向; 轉變; 變更。②注意力分散;分心。③娛樂;消遣。Chess and billiards are his favorite *diversions.* 棋和撞球是他所喜愛的消遣。④離正題;逸出本題。⑤〖軍〗聲東擊西。

di·ver·sion·ar·y 〔dəˈvɝʃənˌɛrɪ; daiˈvəːʃənəri〕 *adj.*轉向的;分心的;聲東擊西的。

di·ver·sion·ist 〔daɪˈvɝʃənɪst; daiˈvəːʃənist〕 *n.* 背離黨規者; 敵後工作者; 從事叛亂活動者。

di·ver·si·ty 〔dəˈvɝsətɪ, daɪ-; daiˈvəːsiti〕 *n., pl.* **-ties.** ①完全不同;異樣。②變化多端;多樣。a great *diversity* of methods. 各種不同之方法。

di·vert** 〔dəˈvɝt, daɪ-; daiˈvəːt, di-〕 *v.t.* ①使轉向;轉入。②使轉變注意力或思想、目的等。Some people are easily *diverted.* 有的人很容易轉變。③消遣;娛樂。I have neither friends nor books to *divert* me. 我沒有朋友或書籍可資消遣。④竊盜; 私吞(公款)。—*v.i.* 轉向; 轉入。Traffic was forced to *divert* to side streets. 往來之行人車輛被迫轉入小街。divert oneself*** **a.** 轉向。He *diverts himself* into a new field of study. 他轉入新的研究領域。**b.**自娛;消遣。—**i·ble,** *adj.*

di·vert·ing 〔dəˈvɝtɪŋ; daiˈvəːtiŋ〕 *adj.* 有趣的; 娛樂的。 —**ly,** *adv.* —**ness,** *n.*

di·ver·tisse·ment 〔divɛrtisˈmɑ̃; diːvɛrtisˈmɑ̃ː〕〖法〗 *n.* ①消遣;娛樂。②戲劇兩幕間之短暫表演(如芭蕾舞等)。

di·ver·tive 〔daɪˈvɝtɪv; daiˈvəːtiv〕 *adj.* 有趣的; 消遣的。

Di·ves 〔ˈdaɪviz; ˈdaiviːz〕 *n.* ①〖聖經〗寓言中之一富豪(見新約路加福音16章 19-31節)。②(一般之)富豪;財主。

di·vest 〔dəˈvɛst; daiˈvest〕 *v.t.* ①剝除; 脫去。②除去;放棄。③搶奪;剝奪。—**i·ble,** *adj.* —**ment,** *n.*

di·ves·ti·ture 〔dəˈvɛstətʃɚ; daiˈvestitʃə〕 *n.* ①剝奪。 ②脫衣。(亦作 **divestment, divesture**)

‡**di·vide** 〔dəˈvaɪd; diˈvaid〕 *v.*, **-vid·ed, -vid·ing,** *n.* —*v.t.* ①分割;分切;剖分;分。②分開; 分界; 隔開。 A brook *divides* my land from his. 一溪隔開我的地與他的地。③分配; 分給。You may *divide* the blame among you. 你們可分任其過。④等分;除。If you *divide* 30 by 5, the answer is 6. 你如以5 除30,答案爲6。⑤分類;分別;類分。⑥分…成不同之羣。⑦使不合; 使意見不同。—*v.i.*①分開;分界。②分歧。Their opinions *divided.* 他們的意見分歧。③〖英〗分正反表決。The House again *divided.* 議會再度分正反表決。④分享利益。⑤分裂。—*n.* ①〖美〗分水嶺。②分歧點;分界線。***the Great Divide*** **a.** 大分水嶺(指北美的 Rocky 山脈)。**b.**(命運的)關鍵。**c.** 死。—**di·vid·a·ble,** *adj.*

di·vid·ed 〔dəˈvaɪdɪd; diˈvaidid〕 *adj.* ①分開的;分離的;分裂的。②〖植物〗裂開的(葉)。③意見不一致的;不團結的。 —**ness,** *n.*

divided highway 分道公路(中間有安全島分開的雙向公路)。

divided ownership (土地之) 分割所有。

divided payments 分期付款。

divided skirt 褲裙。

div·i·dend 〔ˈdɪvəˌdɛnd; ˈdividend〕 *n.* ①股息。The company paid a 10% *dividend* last year. 該公司去年付出一成股息。②附贈品。③報酬;效益。④〖數學〗被除數。

di·vid·er 〔dəˈvaɪdɚ; diˈvaidə〕 *n.* ①分開者;分配者。②隔離者;隔離物。

di·vid·ing 〔dəˈvaɪdɪŋ; diˈvaidiŋ〕 *adj.* 區分的;分劃的;分開的。

div·i·na·tion 〔ˌdɪvəˈneʃən; ˌdiviˈneiʃən〕 *n.* ①預言;占卜;先兆。②先知;先見。

di·vine** 〔dəˈvaɪn; diˈvain〕 *adj., n., v.,* **-vined, -vin·ing.** —*adj.* ①神的; 如神的。②神聖的。③超人的;非凡的。④〖俗〗極好的。a *divine* hat. 一頂極好的帽子。the Divine*** **a.** 上帝。**b.**(有時d-) 人之精神方面的特質。***the divine Being*** 神;上帝。***the divine will*** 神意; 天命。—*n.* ①神學者。②牧師。—*v.t.* 預言; 推測。to *divine* a person's intentions. 推測某人的意向。—*v.i.* 預言。—**di·vin·er,** —**ness,** *n.*

di·vine·ly 〔dəˈvaɪnlɪ; diˈvainli〕 *adv.* ①如神一般地。②非常地。③…得極美妙。④藉上帝;由於上帝的恩惠。

di·vin·er 〔dəˈvaɪnɚ; diˈvainə〕 *n.* ①預言者;占卜者。②用探礦杖探測水脈或礦脈者。

divine service 禮拜式;祈禱禮式。

div·ing 〔ˈdaɪvɪŋ; ˈdaiviŋ〕 *n.* 潛水;跳水。

diving bell 潛水箱; 潛水鐘(內儲空氣,人們可於其中在水下工作)。

diving dress 潛水衣。

diving helmet 潛水帽。

diving plane (潛艇)浮沉控制舵。(亦作 **diving rudder**)

diving suit 潛水衣。

di·vin·ing 〔dəˈvaɪnɪŋ; diˈvainiŋ〕 *n.* 占卜。 —*adj.*占卜的;預言的;推測的。

divining rod 探礦杖。

***di·vin·i·ty** 〔dəˈvɪnətɪ; diˈviniti〕 *n., pl.* **-ties.** ①神性;神力。the *divinity* of Christ. 基督之神性。②神;上帝。 a *divinity.* 神(非基督徒尊奉者)。the *Divinity.* 基督教徒尊奉之上帝。③神學。Doctor of *Divinity.* 神學博士。—**ship,** *n.*

divinity school 神學院。

div·i·nize 〔ˈdɪvəˌnaɪz; ˈdivinaiz〕 *v.t.,* **-nized, -niz·ing.**賦以神性;崇拜;讚美。

di·vis·i·ble 〔dəˈvɪzəbl̩; diˈvizəbl〕 *adj.* ①可分的。 ②〖數學〗可除盡的〖by〗. —**di·vis·i·bil·i·ty,** —**ness,** *n.*

‡**di·vi·sion** 〔dəˈvɪʒən; diˈviʒən〕 *n.* ①分開;劃分; 切分。②分配; 分派; 分給。Is that a fair *division* of the money? 那樣分款公平嗎? ③除法。 Thirty divided by five is a simple *division.* 三十除以五是簡單除法。④分界;界限;分界線;分別。⑤區分; 部分; 片段;章節。⑥〖軍〗師。⑦分裂;分離; 離異; 分歧; 不和。There is a *division* of opinions among them. 他們之間有歧見。⑧〖英〗分組表決(議院分贊成反對兩組表決)。The bill was passed without a *division.* 這議案未經分組表決卽通過了。⑨〖運動〗級。⑩(公司、機關等之) 部門。 the sales *division* of a company. 公司之售貨部。 ***division of labor*** 分工。—**ar·y,** *adj.*

di·vi·sion·al 〔dəˈvɪʒənl̩; diˈviʒənl〕 *adj.* ①分劃的;區分的。②〖數學〗除法的。③

部分的; 片段的。④〖軍〗師的。⑤零碎的。 —ly, *adv.* —i·za·tion, *n.*

di·vi·sion·ist [dɪ'vɪʒənɪst; di'viʒənist] *n.* 反對統一者。

division mark =**division sign.**

division sign 除號(÷)。

di·vi·sive [də'vaɪsɪv; di'vaisiv] *adj.* ①區劃的; 分區的。②離間的; 造成不和的。 —ly, *adv.* —ness, *n.* 「學〗除數;約數。

di·vi·sor [də'vaɪzə; di'vaizə] *n.* 〖數

di·vi·so·ry [də'vaizərɪ; di'vaɪzəri] *adj.* ①劃分的。②分配的。③造成意見不合的。

***di·vorce** [də'vors; di'vɔːs] *n., v.,* **-vorced, -vorc·ing.** —*n.* ①離婚。②分離; 分裂。They demanded the *divorce* of the subsidiary from the parent firm. 他們要求子公司與母公司分離。—*v.t.*①使離婚;和…離婚。Did he *divorce* his wife or did she *divorce* him? 是他要和他太太離婚的,還是他太太要和他離婚的?②分離;分開。In sports, exercise and play are not *divorced.* 在運動中,練習和比賽是分不開的。 —**a·ble,** *adj.* —**di·vorc·er,** *n.* 「離了婚的男子。

di·vor·cé [də,vor'se;di'vɔːsei] 〖法〗*n.*

di·vor·cée [də,vor'se; di'vɔːsei] 〖法〗 *n.* 離了婚的女子。 「了婚的人。

di·vor·cee [də,vor'si;divɔː'siː] *n.* 離

di·vorce·ment [də'vorsmənt; di'vɔːsmənt] *n.* ①離婚。②分離。

div·ot ['dɪvət; 'divət] *n.* ①〖高爾夫〗(擊球時削起之)草皮斷片。②〖蘇〗一塊草皮。

di·vul·gate [də'vʌlget; di'vʌlgeit] *v.t.,* **-gat·ed, -gat·ing.** 洩漏;揭穿;公開。

div·ul·ga·tion [,dɪvəl'geʃən; ,divʌl'geiʃən] *n.* 〖罕〗洩漏;暴露;揭露。

di·vulge [də'vʌldʒ; dai'vʌldʒ] *v.t.,* **-vulged, -vulg·ing.** ①〖古〗宣布。②洩露; 揭穿; 走漏。—**ment, di·vulg·er,** *n.*

di·vul·sion [də'vʌlʃən; dai'vʌlʃən] *n.* 撕裂; 扯裂; 扯開。 —**di·vul·sive,** *adj.*

div·vy ['dɪvɪ; 'divi] *v.,* **-vied, -vy·ing,** *n., pl.* **-vies.** —*v.t.* & *v.i.* 〖俚〗分享;分攤〖常 up〗。 —*n.* 〖俚〗分配。

Dix·ie ['dɪksɪ; 'diksi] *n.* ①美國南部各州之別稱 (亦作 **Dixie Land**)。②美國南北戰爭時南部聯邦流行的軍歌。 —*adj.* 美國南方的。 「外作炊之鍋。

dix·ie ['dɪksɪ; 'diksi] *n.* 〖英俚〗士兵野

Dixie (or **dixie**) **cup** ①裝飲料、冰淇淋等之紙杯。②(D- C-)其商標名。

Dix·ie·land ['dɪksɪ,lænd; 'diksilænd] *n.* 一種爵士音樂。(亦作 **Dixieland jazz**) —**er,** *n.* 「扮。—**ment,** *n.*

di·zen ['dɪzn̩; 'daizn] *v.t.* 〖古〗修飾;裝

diz·zi·ly ['dɪzəlɪ; 'dizili] *adv.* ①令人暈眩地。②暈眩地。③搖搖擺擺地。

***diz·zy** ['dɪzɪ; 'dizi] *adj.,* **-zi·er, -zi·est,** *v.,* **-zied, -zy·ing.** —*adj.* ①暈眩的; 昏亂的;迷惑的。Riding on a merry-go-round makes you feel *dizzy.* 乘旋轉木馬使你覺得暈眩。②使人暈眩的。③令人迷惑的; 令人昏亂的。④〖俗〗愚蠢的;笨的。 —*v.t.* ①使暈眩。We were *dizzied* by the beating wind. 我們被猛烈的風勢吹得頭昏眼花。②使昏亂。 —**diz·zi·ness,** *n.*

DJ ①disc jockey. ②district judge.

Dja·kar·ta [dʒə'kɑrtə; dʒə'kɑːtə] *n.* 雅加達(印尼之首都)。(亦作 **Jakarta**)

Dji·bou·ti or **Ji·bu·ti** [dʒə'butɪ; dʒə'buːti] *n.* 吉布地(東非之一共和國,首都吉布地 Djibouti)。

D.Journ. Doctor of Journalism.

D.J.S. Doctor of Juridical Science.

D.J.T. Doctor of Jewish Theology.

dk. ①deck. ②dock. **dl.** deciliter; deciliters. **D.L.** Deputy Lieutenant.

D. Lit.,D. Litt. Doctor of Literature. **D.L.O.** Dead-Letter Office.

dlr. dealer. **D.L.S.** Doctor of Library Science. **DM** (亦作 **Dm., D-Mark**) Deutsche mark. **dm.** ①decimeter(s). ② delta metal. **D.M.** ① Doctor of Mathematics. ② Doctor of Medicine. ③Drafted Man. ④Daily Mail. **D.M.D.** Doctor of Dental Medicine. **DME** distance measuring equipment. **D.M.L.** Doctor of Modern Languages. **D.M.S.** ①Director of Medical Services. ②Doctor of Medical Science. **D. Mus.** Doctor of Music. **DN** debit note. **DNA** deoxyribonucleic acid. 去氧核糖核酸。**D.N.B.** Dictionary of National Biography.

‡do[1] [du; duː] *v.,* **did, done** [dʌn; dʌn], **do·ing,** *n., pl.* **dos, do's.** —*v.t.* ①做; 搞;工作;實行;執行。What are you *doing* now? 現在你在做甚麼? ②勉力而爲; 盡力而爲。 *Do* your best. 盡力做。③完畢; 完成(用被動式及完成式)。Dinner has been *done* for an hour. 晚餐已預備好了一個鐘頭。④演出;扮演;製片。We *did Hamlet.* 我們演"哈姆雷特"。⑤致有;致使。Your work *does* you credit. 你的工作使你博得好名譽。It *does* him no harm. 這無害於他。⑥翻譯。He *did* Shakespeare into Chinese. 他將莎士比亞的作品譯成中文。⑦給與 (=to give, render). We must *do* him justice. 我們不可寃枉他。⑧處理; 料理; 照應 (=to attend to). She *does* her hair every morning. 她每天早晨梳頭。⑨適合;便於 (=to suit; to be convenient to). This hat will *do* me very well. 這帽子對我非常適合。⑩解決 (=to solve). He *did* the problem. 他解決了這問題。⑪烹調; 煮 (=to cook). The roast will be *done* in an hour. 烤肉一小時內可以烤好。⑫通過; 行經 (=to traverse). We *did* eighty miles in an hour. 我們一小時走了八十英里(指乘汽車)。⑬欺騙。You have been *done!* 你受騙了! ⑭參觀; 觀光。Have you *done* Paris yet? 你去巴黎觀光過嗎? ⑮招待;款待。 They *do* you well at that hotel. 那個旅館招待得很好。⑯毁掉。That has *done* me. 那把我(的機會等)毁了。⑰使疲憊不堪。⑱服(刑)。He's *doing* five years in Sing Sing. 他正在辛辛監獄裏服五年徒刑。⑲任(職)。⑳創造;畫。 She *does* lovely oil portraits. 她的油畫像畫得很好。 —*v.i.* ①行;爲;實行。He *does* well when treated well. 待他好時他做得好。②進行 (=to proceed); 行動 (=to behave). *Do* wisely. 行動要聰明。③起居;經過 (指健康); 度日。How do you *do?* 你好嗎? ④適合; 可用; 可; 足 (表示滿意)。The black dress will *do.* 黑的衣服也可穿。⑤發生。⑥完成。When you have *done,* let me know. 你做完時, 跟我說一聲。⑦〖文法〗作助動詞。**a.** 加重動詞的語氣。Please *do* stay. 務請留此。**b.** 用於疑問句。*Do* you feel cold? 你覺得冷嗎? **c.** 用於表示否定句。*Don't* go now. 現在不要去。 **d.** 用以替代前述之動詞, 以避免重複。 My dog goes where I *do.* 我去那裏，我的狗跟到那裏。**e.** 用於倒裝句，在 rarely, hardly, little 等字之後。Rarely *did* she laugh. 她難得笑。***do any*** (or ***no***) ***good*** (不)產生效果或影響。That won't *do any good.* 那不會產生甚麼好結果。***do away with*** **a.** 廢除。**b.** 殺。The man *did away with* himself. 這個人自殺了。***do by*** 待(人)。He *did* very well *by* me. 他待我甚好。***do down*** 打敗；擊敗。If it's a game of skill, you'll *do* me *down.* 如果這是技能的比賽，你會擊敗我。***do for*** (***a person***) 照料；照顧。He's old enough to *do for himself.* 他大得足以照顧自己。***do for*** (***someone***) 〖俚〗殺死或傷害(某人)。***do for*** (***something***) 處理；設法。How shall we *do for* food? 我們如何得到食物呢? ***do good*** 爲善。She prefers to *do good* by stealth. 她喜祕密行善。***do in*** **a.** 欺騙。We were *done in* that time. 那次我們受騙了。**b.** 疲乏至死；累得要命。**c.** 〖俗〗殺。They *did* him *in* when they caught him. 他們捉到他時，殺了他。***do one's best*** 盡最大努力；盡力而爲(參看及物動詞第二義)。***do one's damnedest*** 以全力爲之。***do one's worst*** 任(他)爲害；任(他)反對。***do or die*** 盡最大努力。***do out of*** 〖俚〗欺騙。***do over*** 重新做過。I should *do* it *over* with green paint if I were you. 如果我是你，我就再用綠色塗過。***do proud*** (or ***credit***)更足以自豪；更值得讚美。Your neat appearance *does* you *proud.* 整潔的儀容使你更足以自豪。***do up***〖俗〗**a.** 扣起；束起；結好。*Do up* your coat. 扣起你的外衣。**b.** 重新裝修(如油漆等)。**c.** 收拾齊整。*Do up* your hair. It is all loose. 你的頭髮散了，把它梳理齊整。**d.** 疲乏；力竭。I am *done up.* The work was too much for me. 我已力竭；這工作非我所能勝任。**e.** 包好。Please *do up* these books. 請把這些書包好。***do with*** **a.** 利用。Can you *do with* a ten-dollar note? 十元的票你够用嗎? **b.** 忍受。**c.** 需要；樂於做。***do without*** 免除；不用。The workmen find it hard to *do without* tobacco. 這些工人覺得戒煙困難。***do wonders*** 產生奇特的結果。Patience and hard work will *do wonders.* 耐性與努力工作會產生很好的成績。***have something*** (or ***nothing***) ***to do with*** 和…有(無)關係。I advise you to *have nothing to do with* him. 我勸你不要和他有來往。***isn't done*** 爲習俗，禮貌等所不容許。Picking one's teeth *isn't done* in public. 在公衆場所剔牙是不高雅的舉動。***make do with*** 對…將就。She can't afford a new coat and so will have to *make do with* the old one. 她買不起新大衣，因此祇好將就去穿那件舊大衣。—*n.* ①〖主方〗騷動。②〖主英〗熱鬧的聚會。③作戰；演習。He was there for the big *do.* 他在那裏參加那次大會戰。④應行之事。***dos and don'ts*** 風俗，規章，法令等。

do² [do; dou] *n.* 〖音樂〗①固定唱法時之C音。②首調唱法時指任何大音階之第一音，或任何小音階之第三音。

do. ditto. **D/o; d.o.** delivery order.

DOA dead on arrival.

do·a·ble [ˈduəbl̩; ˈduːəbl] *adj.* 可爲的；可行的。

do-all [ˈduˌɔl; ˈduːɔːl] *n.* 雜役；總務員。

doat [dot; dout] *v.i.* =**dote.**

dob·ber [ˈdɑbɚ; ˈdɔbə] *n.* 〖美〗釣魚線上之浮子。

dob·bin [ˈdɑbɪn; ˈdɔbin] *n.* 農場用之馴良的馬。

Do·ber·man pin·scher [ˈdobɚmənˈpɪnʃɚ; ˈdoubəmənˈpinʃə] 㹴之一種(毛短而潤，呈暗色，帶棕色斑點)。

dob·son fly [ˈdɑbsn̩~; ˈdɔbsn~] 一種翅色灰白之昆蟲(其幼蟲常用爲釣餌)。

do·cent [ˈdosn̩t, doˈtsɛnt; douˈsent] *n.* ①(美國某些大學之)講師(常係研究生充任，而不算正式教職員)。②博物館、畫廊等處的嚮導兼講解人。—**ship,** *n.*

doc·ile [ˈdɑsl̩; ˈdousail] *adj.* ①聽話的；溫順的；馴良的。②可教的。—**ly,** *adv.*

do·cil·i·ty [doˈsɪlətɪ; douˈsiliti] *n.* 溫順；馴良。

dock¹** [dɑk; dɔk] *n.* ①〖美〗碼頭。②船塢。dry dock*** 乾船塢(塢中水可排去，供修船造船之用)。***floating dock*** 浮船塢。***naval dock*** 海軍船塢。***shipping dock*** 裝卸碼頭。***wet dock*** 有水的船塢。—*v.t.* 拖船入船塢；將(船)靠碼頭。—*v.i.* ①進入船塢；靠碼頭。The ship *docked* here. 船停靠在這裏。②(兩艘太空船)連接或啣接。

dock² *n.* 法庭中的被告席。

dock³ *n.* 動物尾巴的多肉而結實之部分。—*v.t.* ①剪短(尾巴)。②減少；減低。③從…奪去。

dock⁴ *n.* 〖植物〗酸模；羊蹄。

dock·age¹ [ˈdɑkɪdʒ; ˈdɔkidʒ] *n.* ①使用船塢之費用。②船塢之設備。③(船)進塢。

dock·age² (薪俸等之)減少；扣除。

dock·en [ˈdɑkən; ˈdɔkən] *n.* 〖主蘇〗無價值之物。

dock·er [ˈdɑkɚ; ˈdɔkə] *n.* 船塢工人；碼頭工人。

dock·et [ˈdɑkɪt; ˈdɔkit] *n., v.,* **-et·ed, -et·ing.** —*n.* ①〖法律〗(待判決之)訴訟事件表。②判決之摘錄。③行事程序表。④(一般之)摘要；概略。⑤標籤；牌子。***clear the docket*** 〖美〗清理積案。***on the docket*** 〖美俗〗考慮中；執行中；實行中。—*v.t.* ①記載要領；摘記。②加標籤。

dock-glass [ˈdɑkˌglæs; ˈdɔkglɑːs] *n.* 〖英〗大號飲酒杯。

dock·hand [ˈdɑkˌhænd; ˈdɔkhænd] *n.* 碼頭工人(尤指起卸貨物者)。

dock·ing [ˈdɑkɪŋ; ˈdɔkiŋ] *n.* ①入塢。②(兩艘太空船之)接合或連接。—*adj.* 入塢的。

dock·side [ˈdɑkˌsaɪd; ˈdɔksaid] *n.* 碼頭邊；碼頭側鄰區。

dock-tailed [ˈdɑkˌteld; ˈdɔkteild] *adj.* 尾巴剪短的。

dock-wal·lop·er [ˈdɑkˌwɑləpɚ; ˈdɔkˌwɔləpə] *n.* 〖俚〗在船塢等處作散工者。

dock warrant 船塢倉庫存貨憑單。

dock·yard [ˈdɑkˌjɑrd; ˈdɔkjɑːd] *n.* 造船所；修船所。

‡**doc·tor** [ˈdɑktɚ; ˈdɔktə] *n.* ①醫生。If you are ill, go to see a *doctor* at once. 你如生病，即刻去看醫生。②任何醫療疾病者。③博士。④博士學位。⑤博學之士。⑥神學家。⑦修護者；補修者。—*v.t.* ①醫治。②〖俗〗修理。③〖俗〗假造；竄改；攙混；攙雜。④以博士稱呼。His false humility made him *doctor* all his associates. 他的假謙虛使他以博士稱呼所有同事。—*v.i.* ①〖俗〗行醫。My grandfather *doctored* there for over 50 years. 我的祖父在那裡行醫五十年以上。②就醫。

doc·tor·al [ˈdɑktərəl; ˈdɔktərəl] *adj.* ①博士的。②有博士學位的。③醫生的。

doc·tor·ate [ˈdɑktərɪt; ˈdɔktərit] *n.* 博士學位。

Doctor of Laws 法學博士。(略作LL.D.)

Doctor of Philosophy ①(美國

的)博士學位。②獲有(美國的)博士學位者。(略作 Ph.D.)
Doctor of Science 理學博士。(略作 Sc.D.)
doctor's degree ①博士學位。②醫學士學位。
doc·tress ['daktrɪs; 'dɔktris] *n.* 〖罕〗doctor 之女性。
doc·tri·naire [ˌdaktrɪ'nɛr; ˌdɔktri'nɛə] *n.* 純理論家;空論家。—*adj.* 空論的;純理論的。
doc·tri·nair·ism [ˌdaktrɪ'nɛrɪzm; ˌdɔktri'nɛərizəm] *n.* 空論主義;教條主義;空論家之作爲。
doc·tri·nal ['daktrɪnl; dɔk'trainl] *adj.* 教義上的;學理的;教條的。
doc·tri·nar·i·ly [ˌdaktrə'nɛrəlɪ; 'dɔktrinərili] *adv.* 在基本原則上;在主義上。
doc·trine** ['daktrɪn; 'dɔktrin] *n.* ①教義;教旨;教條。②學說;學理。③主義。the Monroe Doctrine*** 門羅主義(不讓歐洲各國干涉美洲大陸的主張)。
***doc·u·ment** [*n.* 'dakjəmənt; 'dɔkjumənt *v.* 'dakjəˌmɛnt; 'dɔkjument] *n.* 公文;文書;證件。a public *document.* 公文。—*v.t.* ①使(小說、影片等)包含史實。The book is highly *documented.* 這本書有許多史實記載。②用文書證明。③爲…引證。—**a·ble,** *adj.*
doc·u·men·tal [ˌdakjə'mɛntl; ˌdɔkju'mentl] *adj.* =**documentary.**
doc·u·men·tar·i·ly [ˌdakjə'mɛntərɪlɪ; ˌdɔkju'mentərili] *adv.* 在記錄上;在文書上。
doc·u·men·ta·ry [ˌdakjə'mɛntərɪ; ˌdɔkju'mentəri] *adj.* ①文件的;文書上的。②用藝術手法記錄或表現的。③多引證的;喜引證的。***documentary film*** 記錄影片。—*n.* 照實錄製之書籍、影片、廣播、電視節目等。
doc·u·men·ta·tion [ˌdakjəmɛn'teʃən; ˌdɔkjumen'teiʃən] *n.* ①文書、證件等之提供。②文件、證明之應用。
dod·der[1] ['dadɚ; 'dɔdə] *v.i.* ①(因老弱等而)搖擺;蹣跚;震顫。②竄劣。
dod·der[2] *n.* 〖植物〗菟絲子。
dod·dered ['dadəd; 'dɔdəd] *adj.* ①(樹)禿枝的。②脆弱的;軟弱的;損壞的。
do·dec·a·gon [do'dɛkəˌgan; dou'dekəgən] *n.* 十二角形;十二邊形。
do·dec·a·he·dron [ˌdodɛkə'hidrən; ˌdoudikə'hedrən] *n., pl.* **-drons, -dra** [-drə; -drə]. 〖幾何〗十二面體。
do·dec·a·phon·ic [ˌdodɛkə'fanɪk; ˌdoudekə'founik] *adj.* =**twelve-tone.**
***dodge** [dadʒ; dɔdʒ] *v.,* **dodged, dodg·ing,** *n.* —*v.i.* ①躲閃;閃避。②逃避責任。He never *dodges.* 他從不逃避責任。—*v.t.* ①躲避。②規避;推託;作遁辭。—*n.* ①躲避;閃避。He made a sudden *dodge* aside as the door swung to. 門關上時他迅速向旁閃避。②〖俗〗巧計;詭計。
dodge ball 躲避球。
dodg·em ['dadʒəm; 'dɔdʒəm] *n.* 樂園中供遊客乘坐之小型車輛。(亦作 **dodgem car**)
dodg·er ['dadʒɚ; 'dɔdʒə] *n.* 躲避者;閃避者;規避者。
dodg·er·y ['dadʒərɪ; 'dɔdʒəri] *n.* 巧計;詭計。
dodg·y ['dadʒɪ; 'dɔdʒi] *adj.,* **dodg·i·er, dodg·i·est.** ①閃避的;支吾的;詭譎的。②〖俚〗巧妙的;精緻的。—**dodg·i·ness,** *n.*
do·do ['dodo; 'doudou] *n., pl.* **-does, -dos.** ①古代之一種巨鳥(今已絕跡)。②〖俗〗老頑固;守舊者。
doe [do; dou] *n.* 雌鹿;雌兔。
do·er ['duɚ; 'du:ə] *n.* 行爲者;作事者;實行家。
‡**does** [dʌz; dʌz] *v.* do 的第三人稱,單數,現在式,直說法。
doe·skin ['doˌskɪn; 'dou-skin] *n.* 雌鹿皮;一種質似雌鹿皮之細軟毛織品。
‡**does·n't** ['dʌznt; 'dʌznt] =**does not.**
do·est ['duɪst; 'du:ist] *v.* 古語中 do 之第二人稱,單數,現在式,直說法(與 thou 連用,作aux. 時縮寫爲 dost)。
do·eth ['duɪθ; 'du:iθ] *v.* 古語中 do 之第三人稱,單數,現在,直說法。
doff [daf; dɔf] *v.t.* ①脫;除去(衣、帽等)。②(從紡織機)取下。
‡**dog** [dɔg; dɔg] *n., v.,* **dogged, dog·ging,** *adv.* —*n.* ①犬;狗。②任何犬科動物(包括狼、狐、胡狼等)。③雄狗;雄狐;雄狼等。④類似犬之動物。⑤卑鄙的人;小人。a lazy *dog.* 懶漢。⑥人。He is a gay *dog.* 他是個快樂的人。⑦鋪張。There was a lot of *dog* about the affair. 那件事鋪張得很。⑧鐵鉤;薪架。⑨(D-)〖天文〗大小犬星座。⑩(*pl.*)〖俚〗脚。⑪(*pl.*)毀滅。It's enough to drive anyone to the *dogs.* 這足以使任何人毀滅。***be top dog*** 位居要津。***be under dog*** 居於低位(永遠聽命他人)。***die a dog's death*** 潦倒而死。***dog eat dog*** 同類相殘。***dog in the manger*** 狗占馬槽。***dog it*** 〖俗〗躲懶;推卸責任。***Every dog has his day.*** 每人在一生中皆有得意之日。***give to the dogs*** 因無價值而擲去。***go to the dogs*** 變壞;變糟。***help a lame dog over a stile*** 助人於危難之時。***lead a dog's life*** 度窮苦的生活。***lead someone a dog's life*** 使無安靜;令人苦惱。***Let sleeping dogs lie.*** 別惹麻煩。***not even a dog's chance*** 毫無機會。***put on the dog*** 〖俚〗充門面;裝闊;擺威風。***teach an old dog new tricks*** 使老頑固接受新知識或新方法。***throw to the dogs*** 不屑而棄之;棄如敝屣。***work like a dog*** 拚命工作。—*v.t.* ①追蹤;追隨。to *dog* a person's steps. 尾隨一人。②使困惱。③=**damn.** *Dog* it all! (咀咒語)該死的! ④以鐵鉤弄緊。—*adv.* 非常地。
do·gate ['dogɪt; 'dougit] *n.* 〖史〗共和國總督或首長的職位或職權。
dog·bane ['dɔgˌben; 'dɔgbein] *n.* 〖植物〗毒狗草。
dog·ber·ry ['dɔgˌbɛrɪ; 'dɔgberi] *n., pl.* **-ries.** 〖植物〗山茱萸之實;山茱萸樹。
dog biscuit ①飼狗之硬餅乾(含骨粉、肉等)。②〖俚〗軍中配給之硬餅乾。
dog·cart ['dɔgˌkart; 'dɔgkɑ:t] *n.* ①狗拖之輕便小車。②一種雙輪小馬車。
dog·catch·er ['dɔgˌkætʃɚ; 'dɔgˌkætʃə] *n.* 捕狗人。
dog-cheap ['dɔgˌtʃip; 'dɔgtʃi:p] *adj.* 奇廉的;大減價的。
dog collar 犬之頸圈。
dog days 一年中最酷熱難過的日子(七、八月間)。
doge [dodʒ; doudʒ] *n.* (古 Genoa 及 Venice 共和國之)總督;首長。—**ship,** *n.*
dog-ear ['dɔgˌɪr; 'dɔgiə] *n.* 書頁之摺角。—*v.t.* 將書頁摺起角。(亦作 **dog's-ear**)
dog·eared ['dɔgˌɪrd; 'dɔgiəd] *adj.* ①書頁有很多摺角的書。②破舊的;襤褸的。
dog-eat-dog ['dɔgitˌdɔg; 'dɔgi:t-'dɔg] *n.* 自相殘殺;殘忍;兇惡;暴烈。—*adj.* 自相殘殺的;殘忍的;兇惡的。
dog·face ['dɔgˌfes; 'dɔgfeis] *n.* 〖俚〗小兵(尤指步兵)。

dog·fight [ˈdɔgˌfaɪt; ˈdɔgfait] *n.*, *v.*, **-fought, -fight·ing.** —*n.* ①(如兩惡犬等之間的)猛烈糾鬥。②【軍】(戰鬥機之)近距離激戰。—*v.t.* & *v.i.* 作近距離戰鬥;打架。

dog·fish [ˈdɔgˌfɪʃ; ˈdɔgfiʃ] *n.*, *pl.* **-fish, -fish·es.** 小鮫。

dog·ged [ˈdɔgɪd; ˈdɔgid] *adj.* 頑强的;固執的。***It's dogged that does it.*** 天下無難事,只怕有心人。—**ly,** *adv.* —**ness,** *n.*

dog·ger [ˈdɔgɚ; ˈdɔgə] *n.* 一種雙桅漁船。

dog·ger·el [ˈdɔgərəl; ˈdɔgərəl] *n.* 拙句;打油詩。—*adj.* 拙劣不合詩律的。—**ist,** *n.*

dog·ger·y [ˈdɔgərɪ; ˈdɔgəri] *n.*, *pl.* **-ger·ies.** ①卑劣行爲;詭詐。②犬之集合稱;犬類。③下等社會;賤民。④【美俚】下等酒吧。

dog·gie [ˈdɔgɪ; ˈdɔgi] *n.* =**doggy.** (亦作 **dogey**)

dog·gish [ˈdɔgɪʃ; ˈdɔgiʃ] *adj.* ①犬的;似犬的。②乖戾的;鄙野的。③【俗】時髦的;炫耀的。—**ly,** *adv.* —**ness,** *n.*

dog·go [ˈdɔgo; ˈdɔgou] *adv.* 【俚】隱匿地;隱祕地。

dog·gone [ˌdɔgˈgɔn; ˌdɔgˈgɔn] *adj.*, **-gon·er, -gon·est,** *adv.*, *interj.*, *v.*, **-goned, -gon·ing.** 【美俚】 —*adj.* 可惡的。—*adv.* 很;極端地。—*interj.* 表忿怒、激動、驚異、快樂等。—*v.t.* 降罰;定罪。

dog·gy [ˈdɔgɪ; ˈdɔgi] *adj.*, **-gi·er, -gi·est,** *n.*, **-gies.** —*adj.* ①似犬的。②愛犬的。③【俗】虛飾的;浮華的。—*n.* (亦作**doggie**)【兒語】小犬;小狗。

doggy bag【美】餐館給顧客裝剩餘食物帶回家餵狗的袋子。

dog·hole [ˈdɔgˌhol; ˈdɔghoul] *n.* ①僅適於犬住之處。②煤礦之通風穴。

dog·house [ˈdɔgˌhaus; ˈdɔghaus] *n.* 犬舍。***in the doghouse*** 【俚】失寵。

do·gie [ˈdogɪ; ˈdougi] *n.* (美國西部之)失去母牛的小牛;迷失的小牛。(亦作 **dogy**)

dog killer 瘋犬及野犬撲殺者。

dog-leg·ged [ˈdɔgˌlɛgɪd; ˈdɔglegd] *adj.* 彎曲如犬後足的;く形的。

dog·like [ˈdɔgˌlaɪk; ˈdɔglaik] *adj.* ①似犬的。②頑强的。③忠實的。

dog·ma [ˈdɔgmə; ˈdɔgmə] *n.*, *pl.* **-mas, -ma·ta** [-mətə; -mətə]. ①教條;信條;教理。②獨斷之見。

dog·man [ˈdɔgmən, ˈdɑg-; ˈdɔgmən] *n.*, *pl.* **-men.** ①狗專家。②狗屋管理人。

dog·mat·ic [dɔgˈmætɪk; dɔgˈmætik] *adj.* ①教條的;教理的。②武斷的。

dog·mat·i·cal [dɔgˈmætɪkl; dɔgˈmætikəl] *adj.* =**dogmatic.** —**ly,** *adv.*

dog·mat·ics [dɔgˈmætɪks; dɔgˈmætiks] *n.* (作 *sing.* 解) 教理神學;教義論。

dog·ma·tism [ˈdɔgməˌtɪzəm; ˈdɔgmətizəm] *n.* ①教條主義。②獨斷主義。

dog·ma·tist [ˈdɔgmətɪst; ˈdɔgmətist] *n.* ①武斷的人;獨斷主義者。②教條主義者。

dog·ma·tize [ˈdɔgməˌtaɪz; ˈdɔgmətaiz] *v.t.* & *v.i.*, **-tized, -tiz·ing.** 武斷;獨斷地主張。

dog·meat [ˈdɔgˌmit; ˈdɔgmiːt] *n.* ①餵狗的碎肉。②狗肉;香肉。(亦作 **dog's meat**)

do-good [ˈduˌgud; ˈduːgud] *adj.* (不切實際的)社會改革的。

do-good·er [ˈduˌgudɚ; ˈduːˌgudə] *n.* (不切實際的)社會改革家。

do-good·ism [ˈduˌgudɪzm; ˈduːˌgudizm] *n.* (不切實際的) 社會改革主義。(亦作 **do-goodery**)

dog paddle 手划腳蹬並將頭保持於水面上的一種基本游泳式(俗稱狗扒式)。

dog-poor [ˈdɔgˈpur, ˈdɑg-; ˈdɔgˈpuə] *adj.* 極其貧窮的;赤貧的。

dog pound 關迷失之狗的地方。

dog rose 歐洲產之一種野生薔薇。

dog's chance 【俗】極少的機會。

dog's-ear [ˈdɔgzˌɪr; ˈdɔgz-iə] *n.*, *v.t.* =**dog-ear.** —**ed,** *adj.*

dog·shore [ˈdɔgˌʃor; ˈdɔgʃɔː] *n.* 【造船】(滑船進水用的)支船木。

dog·skin [ˈdɔgˌskɪn; ˈdɔgskin] *n.* 狗皮。—*adj.* 狗皮的。

dog·sleep [ˈdɔgˌslip; ˈdɔgsliːp] *n.* 假寐;淺睡。

dog's life 潦倒的生活。

dog's meat =**dogmeat.**

dog's-nose [ˈdɔgzˌnoz; ˈdɔgznouz] *n.* 一種混合酒(由啤酒或麥酒與杜松子酒或糖酒混合而成)。

Dog Star 【天文】天狼星。

dog tag ①狗之識別牌。②【俚】軍人佩帶之識別牌。

dog-tired [ˈdɔgˈtaɪrd; ˈdɔgˈtaiəd] *adj.* 【俗】極疲的;甚倦的。

dog·tooth [ˈdɔgˌtuθ; ˈdɔgtuːθ] *n.*, *pl.* **-teeth.** ①犬牙;狗牙。②【建築】齒飾。

dog·track [ˈdɔgˌtræk; ˈdɔgtræk] *n.* 賽狗場。

dog·trot [ˈdɔgˌtrɑt; ˈdɔgtrɔt] *n.* 小跑;慢跑步。

dog·watch [ˈdɔgˌwɑtʃ; ˈdɔgwɔtʃ] *n.* 【航海】二小時輪換之當值(午後4–6, 6–8 時,爲通常輪值時間之折半)。

dog·wood [ˈdɔgˌwud; ˈdɔgwud] *n.* 【植物】山茱萸。

do·gy [ˈdogɪ; ˈdougi] *n.* =**dogie.**

doi·ly [ˈdɔɪlɪ; ˈdɔili] *n.*, *pl.* **-lies.** (墊於餐盤、飾物等下面之)小布巾;墊子。

***do·ings** [ˈduɪŋz; ˈduːiŋz] *n. pl.* 行爲;活動;所做之事。Tell me about all your *doings* in Europe. 告訴我所有你在歐洲的活動。

Doi·sy [ˈdɔɪzɪ; ˈdɔizi] *n.* 杜伊基 (Edward Adelbert, 1893–, 美國生物化學家,曾獲1943年諾貝爾醫學獎)。

doit [dɔɪt; dɔit] *n.* ①昔日荷蘭之一種小銅幣。②價值甚微之物;瑣事。

doit·ed [ˈdɔɪtɪd; ˈdɔitid] *adj.* 【蘇】衰邁的;昏愚的;昏朽的。

do-it-your·self [ˌduɪtjɚˈsɛlf; ˌduːitjɔːˈself] *adj.* 爲業餘者使用或裝配而設計的。—*n.* 自己做(裝配、修理等)。

do-it-your·self·er [ˌduɪtjɚˈsɛlfɚ; ˌduːitjɔːˈselfə] *n.* 實行 do-it-yourself 者。

do-it-your·self·er·y [ˌduɪtjɚˈsɛlfərɪ; ˌduːitjɔːˈselfəri] *n.* do-it-yourselfer 的活動。

dol. ①dolce. ②dollar.

dol·ce [ˈdoltʃe; ˈdɔltʃi] 【義】【音樂】*adj.* 悅耳而柔和的。—*n.* ①悅耳而柔和之記號。②(風琴之)柔聲音栓。

dol·ce far nien·te [doltʃefɑrˈnjɛnte; ˈdɔltʃifɑːˈnienti] 【義】無爲;逸居;休閒。

dol·drums [ˈdɑldrəmz; ˈdɔldrəmz] *n. pl.* ①憂悶;消沉。②不景氣;低潮。③近赤道之海洋無風帶。

dole[1] [dol; doul] *n.*, *v.*, **doled, dol·ing.** —*n.* ①賑濟品;布施之物。②分額;小部分。③失業救濟金。④賑濟;布施。⑤【古】命運;天命。***go*** (or ***be***) ***on the dole*** 接受政府的失業救濟金。—*v.t.* 布施;微量分配【常 out】.

dole[2] *n.* 【古】悲哀;悲嘆。

dole·ful [ˈdolfəl; ˈdoulfəl] *adj.* 悲哀的;憂愁的;陰鬱的。—**ly,** *adv.* —**ness,** *n.*

dol·er·ite [ˈdɑləˌraɪt; ˈdɔlərait] *n.* 【礦】粗粒玄武岩。—**dol·er·it·ic,** *adj.*

dole·some [ˈdolsəm; ˈdoulsəm] *adj.* =**doleful.**

dol·i·cho·ce·phal·ic [ˌdɑlɪˌkosəˈfælɪk; ˈdɔlikoukeˈfælik] *adj.* 〖解剖〗長頭的。(亦作 **dolichocephalous**)

‡**doll** [dɑl; dɔl] *n.* ①洋娃娃。②美麗而無知識的女人。③美麗的孩子。④溫柔體貼的女人。⑤〖俚〗美男子。He is tall, handsome, and muscular. In short, he is a *doll.* 他高大,英俊而強壯。總之他是個美男子。—*v.t.* & *v.i.* 穿戴漂亮入時之服裝〖up, out〗. She insisted that he must *doll* up for this party. 她堅持他必須穿戴整齊地去參加這個晚會。—**like,** *adj.*

‡**dol·lar** [ˈdɑlɚ; ˈdɔlə] *n.* ①元;圓(美國和加拿大,墨西哥等所用的貨幣單位)。One hundred cents make a *dollar.* 一百分等於一元。②價值一元的銀幣或紙幣。③美金。④美國之經濟利益。

dol·lar(s)-and-cent(s) [ˈdɑlɚ(z)ənd ˈsɛnt(s); ˈdɔlə(z)əndˈsent(s)] *adj.* 以金錢衡量的;以金錢表示的。

dollar bloc 美元集團(以美金爲匯率基礎的國家)。

dollar diplomacy ①財力外交;金元外交。②維護商務利益的外交。

dol·lar·fish [ˈdɑlɚˌfɪʃ; ˈdɔləfiʃ] *n., pl.* **-fish, -fish·es.** 一種短而扁的海魚。

dollar gap (一國在國際貿易上之)美金虧空。(亦作 **dollar shortage**)

dollar mark (or **sign**) 美元記號(即 $ 或 $)。

dol·lar·wise [ˈdɑlɚˌwaɪz; ˈdɔləwaiz] *adv.* (就某事物之)金錢價值而言。

doll baby ①洋娃娃。②情人;愛人。③漂亮可愛的少婦。

doll·face [ˈdɑlfes; ˈdɔlfeis] *n.* 娃娃臉(的大人)。

dol·lop [ˈdɑləp; ˈdɔləp] *n.* ①塊;團。②〖方〗衣著不整的懶女人。

Dol·ly [ˈdɑlɪ; ˈdɔli] *n.* 女子名。

doll·y [ˈdɑlɪ, ˈdɔlɪ; ˈdɔli] *n., pl.* **doll·ies,** *v.,* **-lied, -ly·ing.** —*n.* ①〖兒語〗洋娃娃。②轆車;小機車。③〖機械〗釘頭型。④(洗衣用之)攪拌棒。⑤(打樁用之)墊盤。⑥〖電影、電視〗安裝攝影機之矮盤車。—*v.t.* 以轆車搬動。—*v.i.* ①以矮盤車搬動攝影機。②(攝影機等)被用矮盤車搬動。

Doll·y Var·den [ˌdɑlɪˈvɑrdn; ˈdɔliˈvɑːdn] ①一種女服。②一種闊邊女帽。③一種鱒魚。

dol·man [ˈdɑlmən; ˈdɔlmən] *n., pl.* **-mans.** ①土耳其長袍。②一種披肩式女外套。

dol·men [ˈdɑlmɛn; ˈdɔlmen] *n.* 史前時期用石架成的紀念物(一般認定爲墳墓)。

dol·o·mite [ˈdɑləˌmaɪt; ˈdɔləmait] *n.* 〖礦〗白雲石。

do·lo(u)r [ˈdolɚ; ˈdoulə] *n.* ①〖詩〗悲哀;憂愁。②〖醫〗痛。

dol·or·ous [ˈdɑlərəs; ˈdɔlərəs] *adj.* 悲哀的;憂愁的;悲痛的。—**ly,** *adv.*

dol·phin [ˈdɑlfɪn; ˈdɔlfin] *n.* ①海豚。②鯕鰍。③(碼頭上之)繫船樁;繫船浮筒。④(D-)〖天文〗海豚座。

dolt [dolt; doult] *n.* 笨拙之人;傻瓜。

dolt·ish [ˈdoltɪʃ; ˈdoultiʃ] *adj.* 笨重的;愚鈍的。—**ly,** *adv.* —**ness,** *n.*

Dom [dɑm; dɔm] *n.* ①天主教僧侶之一種榮銜。②巴西及葡萄牙昔日由敕令賦與的一種榮銜(與名字連用)。

dom. ①domain. ②domestic. ③dominion.

-dom 〖字尾〗表下列諸義:①階級;地位;管轄權;管轄區。②存在。③羣體;狀態。

Do·magk [ˈdomɑk; ˈdoumɑːk] *n.* 杜馬克(Gerhard, 1895–1964, 德國化學家, 曾奉納粹政府之命拒領 1939 年諾貝爾醫學獎)。

***do·main** [doˈmen; dəˈmein] *n.* ①領土;領地;版圖。②思想或活動的範圍。③所有地;田地。④〖數學〗區域。—**do·ma·ni·al,** *adj.*

***dome** [dom; doum] *n., v.,* **domed, dom·ing.** —*n.* ①圓頂。②如圓頂的東西。—*v.t.* ①覆以圓頂。②使成圓頂形。—*v.i.* 呈圓頂形。

dome car 裝有玻璃圓頂之火車車廂(供旅客觀看沿途風景者)。

dome·lin·er [ˈdomˌlaɪnɚ; ˈdoumˌlainə] *n.* 有一輛或多輛玻璃圓頂車廂的列車。

Domes·day Book [ˈdumzˌde~; ˈduːmzdei~] (英國 William the Conqueror 下令,約於 1086 年編成,確定土地之所有權、範圍及價值等之)英格蘭土地勘查記錄書。(亦作 **Doomsday Book**)

dome-shaped [ˈdomˌʃept; ˈdoumʃeipt] *adj.* 圓頂狀的。

***do·mes·tic** [dəˈmɛstɪk; dəˈmestik] *adj.* ①屬於家的;屬於家務的。He had many *domestic* troubles. 他有許多家庭糾紛。②專心家庭的;善理家務的;喜歡家庭生活的。She is a very *domestic* sort of woman. 她是專心家務的一種婦女。③與人同處的;馴良的。④寄生人類住處的。⑤屬於本國的。*domestic* news. 本國消息。⑥國內製造的。The government urged the people to buy *domestic* goods. 政府勸導人民購買國貨。—*n.* ①僕人。②(*pl.*) a. 國貨(本國所製或出產的)。b. 〖美〗家內布質物品(如毛巾、床單等)。

do·mes·ti·cal·ly [dəˈmɛstɪklɪ; dəˈmestikəli] *adv.* ①在家庭方面;在國內方面。②在國內問題方面。

domestic animal 家畜。

do·mes·ti·cate [dəˈmɛstəˌket; dəˈmestikeit] *v.,* **-cat·ed, -cat·ing.** —*v.t.* ①使習於家事;使喜歡家庭生活。②養馴;馴服;培育(野生植物)。③使感覺舒服自由(如在家中)。—*v.i.* ①定居。②(外國公司等)獲得法人資格。—**do·mes·ti·cat·or,** *n.*

do·mes·ti·ca·tion [dəˌmɛstəˈkeʃən; dəˌmestiˈkeiʃən] *n.* 馴養;教化。

domestic economy 家政;家庭經濟。

domestic fowl 家禽。

do·mes·tic·i·ty [ˌdomɛsˈtɪsətɪ; ˌdoumesˈtisiti] *n., pl.* **-ties.** ①家庭生活;家居之愛好。②(*pl.*)家務;家事。

domestic science 家政學。

domestic trade 國內貿易。

dom·i·cal [ˈdoməkl; ˈdoumikəl] *adj.* ①似圓屋頂的。②有圓頂的;圓頂式的。

dom·i·cile [ˈdɑməsl; ˈdɔmisail] *n., v.,* **-ciled, -cil·ing.** —*n.* ①家;住所。②〖法律〗正式居住地。***domicile of origin*** 原籍(地);本籍(地)。—*v.t.* 定居。—*v.i.* 居住〖at, in〗.

dom·i·ciled [ˈdɑməsld; ˈdɔmisaild] *adj.* 指定支付地點的。

dom·i·cil·i·ar·y [ˌdɑməˈsɪlɪˌɛrɪ; ˌdɔmiˈsiljəri] *adj.* 家宅的;住所的。

dom·i·cil·i·ate [ˌdɑməˈsɪlɪˌet; ˌdɔmiˈsilieit] *v.t.* & *v.i.,* **-at·ed, -at·ing.** =**domicile.** —**dom·i·cil·i·a·tion,** *n.*

dom·i·nance [ˈdɑmənəns; ˈdɔminəns] *n.* ①統治;支配;優越。②俯視。

dom·i·nan·cy [ˈdɑmənənsɪ; ˈdɔminənsi] *n.* =**dominance.**

***dom·i·nant** [ˈdɑmənənt; ˈdɔminənt] *adj.* ①有統治權的;有支配力量的;最有勢力

的。the *dominant* partner in a business. 公司中最有勢力的股東。②占重要位置的。③卓越的;顯著的。*dominant* race. 優秀民族。④高於其他的(樹、山峯等)。⑤〖音樂〗全音階之第五調的。—*n.* 處於最主要地位的人、物、因素等。—**ly,** *adv.* 「勢遺傳性質;主宰形質。」

dominant character 〖遺傳〗優

***dom·i·nate** [ˈdɑməˌnet; ˈdɔmineit] *v.*, **-nat·ed, -nat·ing.** —*v.t.* ①統治;支配;管轄。②凌駕;俯臨。—*v.i.* ①管轄;支配。The strong usually *dominate* over the weak. 强者常支配着弱者。②占重要的位置。

dom·i·nat·ing [ˈdɑməˌnetɪŋ; ˈdɔmineitiŋ] *adj.* ①有領導作風的。②專制的。

dom·i·na·tion [dɑməˈneʃən; ˌdɔmiˈneiʃən] *n.* ①統治;統制;支配;管轄。②(*pl.*)〖神學〗天使之第四階級。

dom·i·na·tive [ˈdɑməˌnetɪv; ˈdɔmineitiv] *adj.* 統治的;管轄的;喜支配他人的。

dom·i·na·tor [ˈdɑməˌnetɚ; ˈdɔmineitə] *n.* 統治者;支配者;統治權。

dom·i·neer [ˌdɑməˈnɪr; ˌdɔmiˈniə] *v.i.* 壓倒;凌駕;弄權;作威作福。—*v.t.* 控制;專制統治。—*n.* 專制或極權的態度。—**er,** *n.*

dom·i·neer·ing [ˌdɑməˈnɪrɪŋ; ˌdɔmiˈniəriŋ] *adj.* 專制的;跋扈的。—**ly,** *adv.*

Dom·i·nic [ˈdɑmənɪk; ˈdɔminik] *n.* 聖・多明我(1170–1221, 西班牙神父, Dominican 修會之創始人)。

Dom·i·ni·ca [dəˈmɪnɪkə; ˌdɔmiˈniːkə] *n.* 多明尼加(英屬西印度羣島, 迎風羣島內之一島, 首府爲 Roseau).

do·min·i·cal [dəˈmɪnɪk]; dəˈminikəl] *adj.* 主的;主日的。—*n.* =**dominical letter.**

dominical letter 主日字母(教曆上表示星期日用之 A至 G 七字母中的一字母)。

Do·min·i·can [dəˈmɪnɪkən; dəˈminikən] *adj.* ①西班牙神父聖・多明我的; Dominican 修會的。②多明尼加共和國的。—*n.* ①Dominican 修會之神父。②多明尼加共和國國民。

Dominican Republic 多明尼加共和國(在西印度羣島, 首都爲聖多明各 Santo Domingo). (亦作 **Santo Domingo**)

dom·i·nie [ˈdɑmənɪ; ˈdɔmini] *n.* ①〖蘇〗教師。②〖美〗牧師。

***do·min·ion** [dəˈmɪnjən; dəˈminjən] *n.* ①主權;統治權。②支配;控制。③領土。④自治領。⑤(D-)英國自治領。

Dominion Day 七月一日, 係 1867 年宣布加拿大自治領成立之紀念日。

dom·i·no¹ [ˈdɑməˌno; ˈdɔminou] *n., pl.* **-noes, -nos.** ①帶面罩及頭巾之外衣。②假面具。③戴面具或頭巾之人。—**ed,** *adj.*

dom·i·no² *n., pl.* **-noes.** ①(*pl.*)(作*sing.*解)一種骨牌戲。②此種牌戲之牌。③完結。

domino effect 骨牌效果。

domino theory 骨牌理論(在强大侵略者威脅下, 某一地區諸國中如有一國被征服, 其他諸國亦將相繼覆亡之理論)。

***don**¹ [dɑn; dɔn] *n.* ①(D-)先生(西班牙人所用之尊稱)。②西班牙紳士。③西班牙人。④著名的人。⑤〖俗〗(牛津或劍橋大學的)導師;院長;得獎學金的研究生。

don² *v.t.,* **donned, don·ning.** 穿(衣)。

Do·ña [ˈdonja; ˈdounjaː] 〖西〗 *n.* ①小姐;太太(西班牙之敬稱語, 與名字連同使用)。②(d-)西班牙之婦女。 「人;情婦。」

do·na(h) [ˈdonə; ˈdounə] *n.* 〖英俚〗婦

Don·ald [ˈdɑnəld; ˈdɔnəld] *n.* 男子名。

do·nate [ˈdonet; douˈneit] *v.t.*, **-nat·ed, -nat·ing.** 捐贈;贈與。

do·na·tion [doˈneʃən; douˈneiʃən] *n.* ①捐贈。②捐贈的東西;捐款。

don·a·tive [ˈdɑnətɪv; ˈdounətiv] *n.* 捐贈物;捐款。—*adj.* 捐贈的。 「贈者。」

do·na·tor [ˈdonətɚ; douˈneitə] *n.* 捐

‡done [dʌn; dʌn] *v.* pp. of **do.** Easier said than *done.* 說來容易做來難。No sooner said than *done.* 即說即做。Well begun is half *done.* 好的開始即完成了一半。—*adj.* ①妥當。②已完成工作;已達到目的;已到耐力或能力之極點。Just one more question and I'm *done.* 再來一個問題我就完了。③疲倦;疲乏。④已成過去;已完結。The day of the circus big top is *done.* 馬戲團大公演的時代已成過去。⑤註定失敗。—*adv.* 〖方〗已經。He *done* had his dinner. 他已經吃過晚飯。***done for*** 完蛋;完了。***done in*** 〖俗〗精疲力竭。***done with*** 完全結束。In my craft a thing done is a thing *done with.* 在我的行業內, 一件事情要完全做完才算做完。***have done with*** 結束。

do·nee [ˌdoˈni; douˈniː] *n.* 受贈者。

don·ga [ˈdɑŋgə; ˈdɔŋgə] *n.* 〖南非〗壑;谷;峽。 「世紀城堡之主樓。」

don·jon [ˈdʌndʒən; ˈdɔndʒən] *n.* 中

Don Ju·an [dɑnˈdʒuən; dɔnˈdʒuːən] ①唐璜(西班牙傳奇故事中之風流漢)。②略誘婦女者;淫蕩者。—**esque,** *adj.* 〖注意〗 Don Juan 通常讀作 [dɑnˈwɑn; dɔnˈwɑːn] 或 [dɑnˈhwɑn; dɔnˈhwɑːn], 但在拜倫詩中則應讀作 [dɑnˈdʒuən; dɔnˈdʒuːən].

***don·key** [ˈdɑŋkɪ; ˈdɔŋki] *n., pl.* **-keys.** ①驢。②蠢人;頑强的人;頑固的人。③補助汽鍋(=donkey boiler). ④輕便引擎(=donkey engine). ⑤補助唧筒(=donkey pump).

don·key·back [ˈdɑŋkɪˌbæk; ˈdɔŋkibæk] *n.* 驢背。—*adv.* 在驢上;騎在驢背上。

don·key·work [ˈdɑŋkɪwɝk; ˈdɔŋkiwəːk] *n.* 苦役。 「義大利婦女之尊稱。」

don·na [ˈdɑnə; ˈdɔnə] *n.* ①貴婦。②(D-)

don·nish [ˈdɑnɪʃ; ˈdɔniʃ] *adj.* ①(大學之)導師的; 院長的; 得獎學金之研究生的。②賣弄學識的; 自矜的。—**ly,** *adv.* —**ness,** *n.*

Don·ny·brook Fair [ˈdɑnɪˌbrʊk～; ˈdɔnibruk～] ①迄 1855 年止每年一度舉行於愛爾蘭 Donnybrook 地方之賽會(以騷亂放蕩著稱)。②任何騷亂放蕩之場合。

do·nor [ˈdonɚ; ˈdounə] *n.* ①給予者;捐贈者。②〖化學〗原料物質。

do-noth·ing [ˈduˌnʌθɪŋ; ˈduːˌnʌθiŋ] *n.* 游手好閒之人;無爲者;懶惰者。—*adj.* 游手好閒的;無爲的;懶惰的。—**ness,** *n.*

Don Quix·ote [dɑnˈkwɪksət,ˌdɑnkɪˈhotɪ; dɔnˈkwiksət, ˌdɔnkiˈhouti] ①唐・吉訶德(西班牙文學家 Cervantes 所著小說的主角)。②(d- q-)俠義而不切實際或有理想而不能實現的人。

don't [dont; dount] =**do not.**

doo·dad [ˈdudæd; ˈduːdæd] *n.* 〖俗〗①小飾物;小玩意兒。②美觀而無用的東西。

doo·dle [ˈdudl; ˈduːdl] *v.,* **-dled, -dling,** *n.* —*v.t.* ①〖方〗愚弄;逗弄。②混過(時間)。—*v.i.* ①閒蕩;偷懶。②胡寫亂畫;不用心地畫。—*n.* ①愚人;笨漢。②亂畫之物;亂寫的符號。—**doo·dler,** *n.* 「*n.* 蟻獅之幼蟲。」

doo·dle·bug [ˈdudlˌbʌg; ˈduːdlbʌg]

doo·hick·ey [ˈduˌhɪkɪ; ˈduːˌhiki] *n.* 〖美俚〗①小東西;小玩意。②小機關;小發明。

doo·lie, doo·ly [ˈdulɪ; ˈduːli] *n., pl.* **-lies.** 印度之一種肩輿;轎式擔架。

***doom** [dum; duːm] *n.* ①命運(尤指惡運);劫數。His *doom* is sealed. 他的劫數已定。②毀滅;死亡。③判罪。④世界末日的審判。—*v.t.* ①註定命運(尤指惡運)。He was *doomed* to ill fortune. 他命中註定走惡運。②註定失敗、衰敗、死亡等。③判罪;判定有罪。

dooms·day [ˈdumzˌde; ˈduːmzdei] *n.* ①世界末日。②〖古〗定罪日;判決日。

Doomsday Book =**Domesday Book.**

‡**door** [dor, dɔr; dɔː, dɔə] *n.* ①門;戶。back *door.* 後門。front *door.* 前門。②任何門狀的可移動部分。③進口;入口。④有門的房屋、建築物。His house is three *doors* down the street. 他的房子在沿街第三家。⑤通路;途徑;門路。⑥(*pl.*) 室。The air is foul in (*or* within) *doors.* 室內空氣汚濁。⑦(一個人的)門楣。He is striving to keep scandal from his *door.* 他努力杜絕醜聞於門外。***be at death's door*** 垂死;將死。***be next door to*** **a.** 甚近於。My house *is next door to* the school. 我家距學校甚近。**b.** 幾乎;簡直。*next door to* impossible. 簡直不可能。***foot in the door*** 保持成功的機會。***lay*** (***something***) ***at a person's door*** 歸咎某人。They *laid the fault at his door.* 他們歸咎於他。***lie at someone's door*** 歸咎於某人;某人應負責。One's mistakes generally *lie at one's own door.* 一個人的錯誤通常祇能怪自己。***show a person the door*** 下逐客令;要某人離去。

door·bell [ˈdorˌbɛl; ˈdɔːbel] *n.* 門鈴。

door·case [ˈdorˌkes; ˈdɔːkeis] *n.* 門框。(亦作 **doorframe**)

door chain 防盜鍊。

do-or-die [ˈduəˈdaɪ; ˈduːəˈdai] *adj.* 不幹毋寧死的。

door·frame [ˈdɔrˌfrem; ˈdɔːfreim] *n.* 門框。

door·jamb [ˈdorˌdʒæm; ˈdɔːdʒæm] *n.* 門框兩側之直木。

door·keep·er [ˈdorˌkipɚ; ˈdɔːˌkiːpə] *n.* 守門人;門房。

door·knob [ˈdorˌnɑb; ˈdɔːnɔb] *n.* 門之把手。

door·man [ˈdorˌmæn; ˈdɔːmæn] *n., pl.* **-men.** 看門人;門房;傳達。

door·mat [ˈdorˌmæt; ˈdɔːmæt] *n.* ①門前擦去鞋底泥汚之墊子。②乖乖忍受虐待者。③〖俚〗經常居於末位的球隊。

door money 入場費。

door·nail [ˈdorˌnel; ˈdɔːneil] *n.* 門釘。***dead as a doornail*** 死得僵硬了。***deaf as a doornail*** 全聾。

door opener ①(救火員等所使用之)開門器。②推銷員爲進門推銷而贈送的廉價禮物。

door·plate [ˈdorˌplet; ˈdɔː-pleit] *n.* 門牌(有門牌號碼、居住人姓名等)。

door·post [ˈdorˌpost; ˈdɔː-poust] *n.* 門柱。***deaf as a doorpost*** 全聾。

door prize 娛樂場所入場劵所中之獎。

door·sill [ˈdorˌsɪl; ˈdɔːsil] *n.* 門限;閾。

door·step** [ˈdorˌstɛp; ˈdɔː-step] *n.* 門階。at one's doorstep*** 在某人之家門。

door·stone [ˈdorˌston; ˈdɔː-stoun] *n.* 門前之階石;門限石。

door·stop [ˈdorˌstɑp; ˈdɔː-stɔp] *n.* 制止門扉過開之物;制門物。

door-to-door [ˈdortəˈdor; ˈdɔːtəˈdɔː] *adj.* 挨戶訪問的。

***door·way** [ˈdorˌwe; ˈdɔːwei] *n.* 門口;門廊。Don't stand in the *doorway.* 不要站在門口。

door·yard [ˈdorˌjɑrd; ˈdɔːjɑːd] *n.* 〖美〗庭園;天井。

dope [dop; doup] *n., v.,* **doped, dop·ing.** —*n.* ①濃液;(塗機翼等之)明膠。②油脂(如潤滑油等)。③〖俚〗麻醉藥物(鴉片、嗎啡等)。④〖美俚〗情報;密告。⑤〖美俚〗笨人;傻子。—*v.t.* ①用藥物等使顯得更好。②〖俚〗擬定;想出;預測〖out〗。③使麻醉。—*v.i.* 慣用鴉片等麻醉劑。***dope off*** **a.** 如麻醉一般地打瞌睡。**b.** 變愚蠢。**c.** 不注意。

dope addict 吸毒成癮者。

dope fiend 〖俚〗麻醉劑慣用者。

dope·head [ˈdophɛd; ˈdouphed] *n.* 慣用鴉片者。

dope pusher 販毒者。

dor [dɔr; dɔː] *n.* 金蜣類昆蟲。

Dor·a [ˈdorə, ˈdɔrə; ˈdɔːrə] *n.* 女子名。

D.O.R.A. the Defence of the Realm Act.

do·ra·do [dəˈrɑdo; dəˈrɑːdou] *n.* ①鯕鰍;劍魚。②(D-)〖天文〗劍魚座。

Dor·cas [ˈdɔrkəs; ˈdɔːkəs] *n.* ①〖聖經〗多加(廣施賙濟之女子)。②女子名。

Do·ri·an [ˈdorɪən; ˈdɔːriən] *adj.* ①Doris 地區的。②Doris 族人的。③Doris 方言的。—*n.* ①Doris居民。②Doris族人。③男子或女子名。

Dor·ic [ˈdɔrɪk, ˈdɑr-; ˈdɔrik] *adj.* ①Doris 或其居民的。②希臘建築之最古樸形式的。③鄉下的;粗野的。—*n.* ①Doris 之希臘方言。②蘇格蘭方言(別於標準英語)。

Do·ris [ˈdɔrɪs; ˈdɔris] *n.* ①古希臘之一地區。②女子名。

Dor·king [ˈdɔrkɪŋ; ˈdɔːkiŋ] *n.* 多輕鷄(家禽名)。

dorm [dɔrm; dɔːm] *n.* 〖俗〗宿舍(=dormitory).

dor·man·cy [ˈdɔrmənsɪ; ˈdɔːmənsi] *n.* 蟄伏;休止;隱匿。

dor·mant [ˈdɔrmənt; ˈdɔːmənt] *adj.* ①蟄伏的;睡眠狀態的。②休止的。③隱伏的;匿名的。④不動的;靜止的。

dor·mer [ˈdɔrmɚ; ˈdɔːmə] *n.* (屋頂斜坡上凸出之)天窗;老虎窗。(亦作 **dormer window**)

dormer window =**dormer.**

***dor·mi·to·ry** [ˈdɔrməˌtorɪ; ˈdɔːmitri] *n., pl.* **-ries.** 寄宿舍;宿舍。

dormitory car 供火車上服務人員使用有床等設備之車廂。

dor·mouse [ˈdɔrˌmaus; ˈdɔːmaus] *n., pl.* **-mice.** 多眠鼠;睡鼠。

dor·my [ˈdɔrmɪ; ˈdɔːmi] *adj.* 〖高爾夫〗占先對方穴數與尙待將球擊入穴數相等的。

Dor·o·the·a [ˌdɔrəˈθiə; ˌdɔrəˈθiːə] *n.* 女子名。(亦作 **Dorothy, Dorothee**)

Dor·o·thy [ˈdɑrəθɪ; ˈdɔrəθi] *n.* 女子名。

dorp [dɔrp; dɔːp] *n.* 村落;小村。

dor·sal[1] [ˈdɔrsl̩; ˈdɔːsəl] *adj.* ①〖動物〗背脊的。②〖植物〗(葉等)背面的;背生的。—**ly,** *adv.*

dor·sal[2] *n.* =**dossal.**

do·ry [ˈdorɪ; ˈdɔːri] *n., pl.,* **-ries.** ①平底小漁船。②魴。

do·ry·man [ˈdorɪmən, ˈdɔr-; ˈdɔːrimən] *n., pl.* **-men.** 平底小漁船之漁夫。

dos-à-dos [ˌdozaˈdo; ˌdouzəˈdou] *adv., n., pl.* **-dos** [-ˈdoz; -ˈdouz].〖法〗—*adv.* 背對背地。—*n.* ①鄉村舞蹈中的一種舞步(一對舞者相對前進,然後後退至原來地位)。②背對背坐的坐椅、沙發、馬車等。

dos·age [ˈdosɪdʒ; ˈdousidʒ] *n.* ①配藥。②劑量;一服之量。③加於酒中之糖漿或香料。

***dose** 〔dos; dous〕 *n., v.,* **dosed, dos·ing.** —*n.* ①一服（藥）；一劑（藥）。The bottle contains six *doses* of liquid medicine. 瓶內含有六次服量的藥水。②部分；一次給予或接受之一分。—*v.t.* ①配藥。②令服藥。The doctor *dosed* the boy with quinine. 醫生令孩子服奎寧。③混雜；攙入。④懲戒；教訓。—*v.i.* 服藥。—**dos·er,** *n.*

do·sim·e·ter 〔doˈsɪmətɚ; douˈsimətə〕 *n.* 用量計（尤指測量人或物在某一時間內所受之放射量所用者）。（亦作 **dosemeter**）

do·sim·e·try 〔doˈsɪmətrɪ; douˈsimətri〕 *n.* 劑量測定法；（放射線等之）用量測定。—**do·si·me·tri·cian, do·sim·e·trist,** *n.*

doss 〔dɑs; dɔs〕 *n.* 〖英俚〗①臥處；（尤指小客棧的）床鋪。②睡眠。—*v.i.* 〖英俚〗睡臥；就寢。

dos·sal 〔ˈdɑsəl; ˈdɔsəl〕 *n.* 祭壇背後裝飾用之掛布。

dos·si·er 〔ˈdɑsɪˌe; ˈdɔsiei〕〖法〗 *n.* 有關文件；案卷。

dost 〔dʌst; dʌst〕 *v.* 古語中 do 之第二人稱，單數，現在式，直陳法。

Do·sto·ev·ski 〔ˌdɑstəˈjɛfskɪ; ˌdɔstɔːˈjefski〕 *n.* 杜斯妥也夫斯基（Feodor Mikhailovich, 1821–1881，俄國小說家）。

dot¹** 〔dɑt; dɔt〕 *n., v.,* **dot·ted, dot·ting.** —*n.* ①點；小點。②如小點的東西。③極小之物。in the year dot*** 〖英〗很久以前。***off one's dot*** 精神失常。***on the dot*** 〖俗〗準時。—*v.t.* ①加小點於。Please sign your name on the *dotted* line. 請在虛線上簽名。②星散於（地上）；點綴。The field was *dotted* with sheep. 遍地綿羊。③（匆匆）記下。*Dot* down these notes. 請記下這些註解。—*v.i.* 打小點；作小點記號。***dot the i*** 明確指出。***dot the i's and cross the t's*** 把事情作得有條不紊；一絲不苟。—**ter,** *n.*

dot² *n.* 〖法律〗妝奩。—**al,** *adj.*

dot·age 〔ˈdotɪdʒ; ˈdoutidʒ〕 *n.* ①老弱；老朽。②溺愛；癡愛。③深愛之人或物。

dot-and-dash 〔ˈdɑtənˈdæʃ; ˈdɔtənˈdæʃ〕 *adj.* 點與短橫（・—・—・—）的；點與短橫所構成的。—*v.t.* 作點與短橫交互的記號於。

do·tard 〔ˈdotɚd; ˈdoutəd〕 *n.* 老耄者；年老昏憒之人。

dote 〔dot; dout〕 *v.i.,* **dot·ed, dot·ing.** ①顯得愚蠢或低能（尤指因年老之故）。②溺愛〖on, upon〗。③（樹木等）開始腐朽。

doth 〔dʌθ; dʌθ〕 *v.* 〖古〗=**does.**

dot·ing 〔ˈdotɪŋ; ˈdoutiŋ〕 *adj.* ①過於喜愛的；溺愛的。②因老而愚弱的；遲鈍的。③〖植物〗因年久而衰枯的。—**ly,** *adv.*

dot·tle, dot·tel 〔ˈdɑtl̩; ˈdɔtl〕 *n.* （煙斗中吸剩的）煙渣。

dot·t(e)r·el 〔ˈdɑtərəl; ˈdɔtrəl〕 *n.* ①睢鳩。②〖方〗愚人；易受欺騙的人。

dot·ty 〔ˈdɑtɪ; ˈdɔti〕 *adj.,* **-ti·er, -ti·est.** ①上有小點的；以點記的；用點所造成的。②〖俗〗柔軟的；不穩的。③〖俗〗心志不堅的；怪誕的；瘋狂的。

dou·ane 〔duˈɑn; duːˈɑːn〕〖法〗 *n.* （國境之）海關。

Dou·ay Bible 〔ˈdue～; ˈduːei～〕 拉丁聖經的英譯本（爲羅馬天主教學者所譯）。（亦作 **Douay Version**）

‡dou·ble 〔ˈdʌbl̩; ˈdʌbl〕 *adj., adv., n., v.,* **-bled, -bling.** —*adj.* ①雙重的；雙層的。②加倍的。He is *double* her age. 他的歲數比她大一倍。③兩面的；表裏的。④雙重的；兩用的。⑤兩人用的。⑥由二重不同性質聯合起來的。a man with a *double* character. 有雙重性格的人。⑦懷貳心的；不誠實的。to wear a *double* face. 不誠實的人。⑧摺疊爲二的。⑨〖植物〗重瓣的。***double talk*** 含糊的騙人話；花言巧語。—*adv.* ①加倍地。②雙重地。to sleep *double.* 兩人共寢。③（彎）向下前方。He was bent *double* with pain. 他因痛苦而彎身。—*n.* ①二倍；加倍。Ten is the *double* of five. 十爲五之兩倍。②相像的人或物。③（*pl.*）（作*sing.*解）（網球、桌球等之）雙打。④急轉彎；突然的向後轉。⑤摺疊。⑥〖棒球〗二壘安打。⑦〖橋牌〗叫加倍。***advance at the double*** 跑步前進。***double or quits*** （亦作 **double or nothing**）（賭注之）加倍輸贏或輸贏相銷。***on the double*** **a.** 趕快。**b.** 跑步。—*v.t.* ①使加倍；兩倍於。Money in the bank earning good interest will *double* itself in a few years. 在銀行中的優利存款，幾年之內將加一倍。②（在一劇中）扮演二種角色。He is *doubling* the part of a preacher and a teacher. 他扮演牧師和教師兩角色。③擔任（某角色之）替身。④摺；彎。⑤使彎身。⑥反覆。⑦繞行。⑧〖橋牌〗增加（對方叫牌）所贏或所負之分數。⑨〖棒球〗以二壘安打獲得（分數）。⑩〖棒球〗以二壘安打護送（隊友）。The batter walked and was *doubled* to third base. 打擊手以四壞球進壘並被隊友以二壘安打護送至三壘。⑪〖棒球〗以雙殺使出局。He was *doubled* up at first base. 他在一次雙殺中在一壘被刺殺。—*v.i.* ①增加一倍。Our income *doubled* in one year. 一年內我們的收入增了一倍。②摺疊。The carpet won't *double* up. 這地氈不能摺起來。③跑步。Squad—quick march! Squad—*double!* 全班，快步！全班，跑步！④兼有其他用途。⑤在一劇中扮演兩種角色。⑥擔任某角色之替身。***double back*** **a.** 循原路倒退；向後急跑（以避危險）。**b.** 拉回；摺疊。***double in brass*** 〖俚〗**a.** 演奏非自己通常所演奏的樂器。**b.** 兼有某種作用或任務。***double up*** **a.** 彎；屈。**b.** 摺疊。He *doubled up* a sheet of paper. 他將紙摺疊。**c.** 與別人共宿一床、一室等。

dou·ble-act·ing 〔ˈdʌbl̩ˈæktɪŋ; ˈdʌblˈæktiŋ〕 *adj.* 兩面動作的；複式作用的。

double agent ①反間諜。②雙重間諜。

double ax 雙口斧。

double bar 〖音樂〗樂譜上之雙縱線（樂章或整個樂曲結束之記號）。

double-bar·rel 〔ˈdʌbl̩ˈbærəl; ˈdʌblˈbærəl〕 *n.* 雙管的槍。

dou·ble-bar·reled 〔ˈdʌbl̩ˈbærəld; ˈdʌblˈbærəld〕 *adj.* ①雙管的（槍）；雙筒的（望遠鏡）。②兩用的；雙重目的的；兩方面的；雙重的。③模稜兩可的；模糊不清的。

double bass 〖音樂〗低音提琴。

double bassoon 〖音樂〗倍低音管（較普通低音管低八度音管）。

double bed 雙人床。

dou·ble-bed·ded 〔ˈdʌbl̩ˈbɛdɪd; ˈdʌblˈbedid〕 *adj.* 有二床的；有雙人床的。

double bill 同場演出的兩部影片或兩齣戲；同場演出而不同的兩個節目。

dou·ble-bit·ted 〔ˈdʌbl̩ˈbɪtɪd; ˈdʌblˈbitid〕 *adj.* 雙口的；雙刃的。

double boiler 雙層鍋。

dou·ble-breast·ed 〔ˈdʌbl̩ˈbrɛstɪd; ˈdʌblˈbrestid〕 *adj.* 雙排鈕扣的；對襟的。

double chair 雙人椅。

double check 仔細的檢查。

dou·ble-check 〔ˈdʌbl̩ˈtʃɛk; ˈdʌbl-

ˈtʃek〕*v.t.* & *v.i.* 仔細檢查。
double chin 雙下巴。
double clutch 〖機器〗雙離合器。
dou·ble-crop 〔ˈdʌbl̩ˈkrɑp; ˈdʌblˈkrɔp〕*v.t.* & *v.i.*, **-cropped, -crop·ping.** 於同一季內種兩種農作物(於同一土地)。
double cross 欺騙;出賣。
dou·ble-cross 〔ˈdʌbl̩ˈkrɔs; ˈdʌblˈkrɔs, -ˈkrɔːs〕*v.t.* 〖俚〗欺騙;出賣。
double crosser 欺騙者;出賣者。
double dagger 雙短劍的記號(‡)。
double date 〖俗〗兩對男女同來同往的社交。
dou·ble-deal·er 〔ˈdʌbl̩ˈdilɚ; ˈdʌblˈdiːlə〕*n.* 口是心非者;言行不一者。
dou·ble-deal·ing 〔ˈdʌbl̩ˈdilɪŋ; ˈdʌblˈdiːliŋ〕*adj.* 言行不符的;奸詐的。—*n.* 表裏不一的言行;奸詐。
dou·ble-deck 〔ˈdʌbl̩ˈdɛk; ˈdʌblˈdek〕*adj.* 兩層的;雙層的。
dou·ble-deck·er 〔ˈdʌbl̩ˈdɛkɚ; ˈdʌblˈdekə〕*n.* ①兩層甲板之船隻; 兩層座位之車輛或飛機;雙層公共汽車。②〖俗〗兩層夾心之三明治。③共有兩卷的長篇小說。
dou·ble-du·ty 〔ˈdʌbl̩ˈdjutɪ, -ˈdu-; ˈdʌblˈdjuːti〕*adj.* 可作兩種用途的。
dou·ble-dyed 〔ˈdʌbl̩ˈdaɪd; ˈdʌblˈdaid〕*adj.* ①染二次的。②完全的;徹底的。
dou·ble-edged 〔ˈdʌbl̩ˈɛdʒd, -ˈɛdʒɪd; ˈdʌblˈedʒd〕*adj.* ①雙口的; 兩刃的。②有表裏二義的;有正反兩面的。③雙重的。
dou·ble-en·ten·dre 〔ˈdublɑnˈtɑndrə; ˈduːblɑ̃ːnˈtɑ̃ːndr〕〖法〗*n.* ①雙關語(尤指其中一義有壞意者)。②雙關語之使用。
double entry 複式簿記。
dou·ble-faced 〔ˈdʌbl̩ˈfest; ˈdʌblfeist〕*adj.* ①僞裝的; 奸詐的;口是心非的;不誠意的。②兩副面孔的; 有兩表面的。③兩面都可用的(布料)。④有二義的;含糊的。
double first ①英國大學中兩科之最高榮譽。②獲得此等榮譽之學生。
double gun 雙管獵槍。
dou·ble-head·er 〔ˈdʌbl̩ˈhɛdɚ; ˈdʌblˈhedə〕*n.* ①(兩棒球隊同日連續舉行的)兩場比賽。②兩火車頭拖的列車。③拖同一列車的兩火車頭。
dou·ble-heart·ed 〔ˈdʌbl̩ˈhɑrtɪd; ˈdʌblˈhɑːtid〕*adj.* 欺詐的; 陰險的。
double indemnity 保險費之雙倍付給(如被保人之意外死亡者)。
dou·ble-job·ber 〔ˈdʌbl̩ˈdʒɑbɚ; ˈdʌblˈdʒɔbə〕*n.* 〖英〗兼差以增加收入者(美國稱爲 moonlighter).
dou·ble-joint·ed 〔ˈdʌbl̩ˈdʒɔɪntɪd; ˈdʌblˈdʒɔintid〕*adj.* 有特大屈曲性之關節的。
dou·ble-lead·ed 〔ˈdʌbl̩ˈlɛdɪd; ˈdʌblˈledid〕*adj.* 〖印刷〗(爲醒目)加挿兩鉛條的。
dou·ble-lock 〔ˈdʌbl̩ˈlɑk; ˈdʌblˈlɔk〕*v.t.* 將鑰匙轉動兩次以便鎖上。
dou·ble-mind·ed 〔ˈdʌbl̩ˈmaɪndɪd; ˈdʌblˈmaindid〕*adj.* 心緒不定的; 反覆無常的。—**ness,** *n.*
dou·ble·ness 〔ˈdʌbl̩nɪs; ˈdʌblnis〕*n.* 二倍;二重;貳心;詭詐。
dou·ble-park 〔ˈdʌbl̩ˈpɑrk; ˈdʌblˈpɑːk〕*v.i.* & *v.t.* (與停在路邊的車)並排停車。
double personality 〖心理〗雙重人格。
double play 〖棒球〗雙殺。
dou·ble-quick 〔ˈdʌbl̩ˈkwɪk; ˈdʌblˈkwik〕*adj.* 快速的;極快的。—*adv.* 快速地。—*n.* 跑步;快步(=double time). —*v.t.* & *v.i.* (使)跑步; (使)快步。
dou·bler 〔ˈdʌblɚ; ˈdʌblə〕*n.* 加倍裝置。
dou·ble-re·fine 〔ˈdʌblrɪˈfaɪn; ˈdʌbliˈfain〕*v.t.*, **-re·fined, -re·fin·ing.** 再精製。
dou·ble-ring 〔ˈdʌbl̩ˈrɪŋ; ˈdʌblˈriŋ〕*adj.* 新郎新娘交換結婚戒指的。
dou·ble-rip·per 〔ˈdʌbl̩ˈrɪpɚ; ˈdʌblˈripə〕*n.* 一種雙橇(二橇一前一後以木板連接者)。(亦作 **double-runner**)
double room 由相連的二房所構成的大房。
double salt 〖化〗重鹽。
double sentry 複哨(由二哨兵組成)。
double shift 兩班制;二部制。
dou·ble-shift 〔ˈdʌbl̩ˈʃɪft; ˈdʌblˈʃift〕*adj.* 兩班制的;二部制的。
dou·ble-sid·ed 〔ˈdʌbl̩ˈsaɪdɪd; ˈdʌblˈsaidid〕*adj.* 兩方面的。
dou·ble·speak 〔ˈdʌbl̩ˌspik; ˈdʌblspiːk〕*n.* 欺人之談。
double standard 雙重標準。
double star 〖天文〗雙星(緊密相連之二星,藉望遠鏡始可分辨者)。
double steal 〖棒球〗雙盜壘。
double summer time 〖英〗比格林威治時間提早兩小時或較日光節約時間提早一小時的時間。
dou·blet 〔ˈdʌblɪt; ˈdʌblit〕*n.* ①(十五、六世紀歐洲男子穿的)緊身上衣。②一對。③一對中之一;相似物之一。④(同源而異形或異義之)對似語(如 hospital 和 hostel, fragile 和 frail 等)。⑤〖印刷〗字語之重複。⑥(*pl.*)朝上的一面點數相同的兩顆骰子。
double take ①經短時的心不在焉後突然注意到而驚訝的行動; 反應遲鈍的驚訝。②回頭再看的行動。—**dou·ble-take,** *n.*
dou·ble-talk 〔ˈdʌbl̩ˌtɔk; ˈdʌbltɔːk〕*n.* 含糊其詞的言談;不知所云的話。—*v.i.* 避重就輕或虛與委蛇地說話; 含糊其詞地說話。
double taxation 雙重課稅。
dou·ble-team 〔ˈdʌbl̩ˈtim; ˈdʌblˈtiːm〕*v.t.*(球賽中)以兩球員防守(對方之一球員)。
Double Ten 雙十節。(亦作 **Double Tenth**)
dou·ble·think 〔ˈdʌbl̩ˌθɪŋk; ˈdʌblθiŋk〕*n.* 思想矛盾。
double time ①〖軍〗跑步(每分鐘180步,每步 36 英寸)。②快步。③〖俗〗跑;疾行。
dou·ble-time 〔ˈdʌbl̩ˌtaɪm; ˈdʌbltaim〕*v.i.* 快步行走。—*v.t.* 使快步行走;使奔跑。
dou·ble-tongued 〔ˈdʌbl̩ˈtʌŋd; ˈdʌblˈtʌŋd〕*adj.* 欺詐的;欺騙的。
dou·ble-track 〔ˈdʌbl̩ˈtræk; ˈdʌblˈtræk〕*v.t.* 〖鐵路〗使成雙軌。
dou·ble·tree 〔ˈdʌbl̩ˌtri; ˈdʌbltriː〕*n.* 車上之橫木(其兩端繫駕馬之橫木)。
dou·bling 〔ˈdʌblɪŋ; ˈdʌbliŋ〕*n.* ①倍加;倍增。②摺。③兩重物。④廻航。⑤轉回。⑥再蒸餾。⑦襯裏。
dou·bloon 〔dʌˈblun; dʌˈbluːn〕*n.* 昔西班牙之金幣名。
dou·bly 〔ˈdʌblɪ; ˈdʌbli〕*adv.* 加倍地。
‡**doubt** 〔daut; daut〕*v.t.* 懷疑;猶疑;不信。I *doubt* if he will come. 我恐怕他不會來了。—*v.i.* 懷疑〖of〗. I do not *doubt* of your success. 我不懷疑你的成功。—*n.* 疑慮;疑懼;懷疑。I have no *doubt* that he will succeed. 我相信他將成功。***beyond*** (***a*** or ***the shadow of a***) ***doubt*** 無疑地。***give a person the benefit of the doubt*** 未有確證前,假定其無罪。***in doubt*** 懷疑的;未確定的。***no doubt*** 無疑地。***without doubt*** 無疑地;毫無問題。—**a·ble,** *adj.* —**a·bly,** *adv.* —**er,** *n.* 〖注意〗**doubt** 的習語有:⑴否定的

(沒有眞正的懷疑存在)。**doubt that**: I do not *doubt that* he means well. 我相信(毫不懷疑)他爲意甚善。⑵肯定的(有眞正懷疑存在)。**doubt that, doubt whether** (正式用法): I *doubt whether* he meant that way. 我懷疑他是否那種意思。I *doubt that* he meant that way. 我不相信他竟會是那種意思。**doubt if** (一般用法): I *doubt if* he meant that way. 我懷疑他是否有那種意思。

***doubt·ful** ['dautfəl; 'dautfəl] *adj.* ①可疑的;未確定的。It is *doubtful* whether I shall go or stay. 我之去留尙未確定。②懷疑的;疑懼的。He was *doubtful* of the patient's recovery. 他懷疑病人能否痊癒。③狐疑的;猶豫不決的。④(結果如何)難以預測的;不明朗的。⑤不可靠的;有問題的。⑥不明瞭的;曖昧的。—*n.* 懷疑者。—**ly,** *adv.*—**ness,** *n.*

doubt·ing ['dautıŋ; 'dautiŋ] *adj.* 有疑心的; 不信的。***doubting Thomas*** 不信無證據之事物的人;懷疑者。—**ly,** *adv.*

***doubt·less** ['dautlıs; 'dautlis] *adv.* 無疑地;確定地。—*adj.* 確定的。—**ly,** *adv.*

douce [dus; du:s] *adj.* 〖蘇〗文雅的; 愼重的; 殷勤的。

dou·ceur [du'sɝ; du:'sə:] 〖法〗 *n.* ①賞錢;小費。②賄金;懷柔之禮物;苞苴。③(態度的)溫柔;可親。

douche [duʃ; du:ʃ] *n., v.,* **douched, douch·ing.** —*n.* 〖醫〗①灌洗之(噴)水。②灌洗療法。③灌洗器。 —*v.t. & v.i.* 行灌洗療法。

***dough** [do; dou] *n.* ①生麪糰;麪漿糰。②任何如生麪糰之物。③〖美俚〗錢;金錢。

dough·boy ['do,bɔı; 'doubɔi] *n.* 〖美俚〗步兵。

dough·face ['do,fes; 'doufeis] *n.* ①〖俗〗柔順的人;易受人左右的人。②〖美史〗願意容忍南方蓄奴制度的北方政客。③生麪糰狀的面孔。

dough·head ['do,hɛd; 'douhed] *n.* 〖美俚〗笨人;智力低者。

***dough·nut** ['donət, -,nʌt; 'dounʌt] *n.* 油煎圈餅。

dough·ty ['dautı; 'dauti] *adj.,* **-ti·er, -ti·est.** 〖古,謔〗勇敢的;堅强的。

dough·y ['doı; 'doui] *adj.,* **dough·i·er, dough·i·est.** ①如麪糰的;糊狀的; 軟弱而蒼白的。②含有生麪的;未焙透的。

Doug·las ['dʌgləs; 'dʌgləs] *n.* 男子名。

Douglas fir (pine or **spruce)** 〖植物〗洋松(常超過二百英尺高)。

dour [dur, dʊr; duə] *adj.* ①冷峻的; 陰鬱的。②〖蘇〗嚴厲的;倔强的;頑固的。

douse [daus; daus] *v.,* **doused, dous·ing,** *n.* —*v.t.* ①浸…入水;潑水。②〖俚〗熄滅(燈)。③〖俗〗脫去(衣服等)。④〖航海〗急速降下(帆等)。—*v.i.* 投入水中;被浸入水中;泡在水裏。—*n.* 傾倒的一盆水。(亦作 **dowse**)

***dove¹** [dʌv; dʌv] *n.* ①鴿;鳩。②〖俗〗主張和平者;非戰者(爲 hawk 之對)。③純潔可愛的女人或小孩。④(D-)聖靈。

dove² [dov; douv] *v.* 〖俗〗pt. of **dive.**

dove color [dʌv~; dʌv~] 淺灰而略帶紫紅之色。

dove·cote ['dʌv,kɑt; 'dʌvkɔt] *n.* 鴿舍;鴿房。***flutter the dovecotes*** 引起驚擾。(亦作 **dovecot**)

dove-eyed ['dʌv,aıd; 'dʌvaid] *adj.* 目光柔和的。

Do·ver ['dovə; 'douvə] *n.* 多佛(**a.** 英國東南部之一海港。**b.** 美國德拉瓦州之首府)。

dove·tail ['dʌv,tel; 'dʌvteil] *n.* 〖木工〗鳩尾榫; 楔形榫頭。—*v.i.* ①用鳩尾榫接合。②密合;切合。—*v.t.* ①與…密合;與…吻合。②作成鳩尾榫;作成楔形榫頭。

dov·ish ['dʌvıʃ; 'dʌviʃ] *adj.* 非戰主義的。(亦作 **doveish**)

dow·a·ger ['dauədʒɚ; 'dauədʒə] *n.* ①富孀;受有遺產或爵位之寡婦。②〖俗〗貴婦;年長之婦女。***Empress Dowager*** 皇太后。

dow·dy ['daudı; 'daudi] *adj.,* **-di·er, -di·est,** *n., pl.* **-dies.** —*adj.* 衣衫襤褸的;粗鄙的;不整潔的。—*n.* 衣服襤褸或不整潔之婦女;衣着不合時尙之女性。—**dow·di·ly,** *adv.* —**dow·di·ness,** *n.*

dow·el ['dauəl; 'dauəl] *n., v.,* **-el(l)ed, -el·(l)ing.**—*n.* ①合板釘;夾縫釘。②嵌入牆內以受釘之木片。—*v.t.* 裝合板釘; 以夾縫釘釘合。

dow·er ['dauɚ; 'dauə] *n.* ①寡婦得自亡夫維持生活之財產。②嫁妝;粧奩。③稟賦;天分。—*v.t.* ①給寡婦應得之財產;給嫁妝與。②資助。③賦予(才能)〖with〗. —**less,** *adj.*

Dow-Jones average 道瓊指數(紐約市 Dow-Jones 公司所發表,表示美國證券市場漲跌情形)。(亦作 **Dow-Jones index**)

‡down¹ [daun; daun] *adv.* ①由上而下地。The sun goes *down* in the west. 太陽在西邊落下。②在下邊地。*Down* in the valley the fog still lingers. 下面山谷裏,霧還瀰漫未散。③在(或去)屬於南方的地方。He lives in Taipei, but goes *down* to Tainan every winter. 他住在臺北,但每年冬天均去臺南。④致於困難或危險之境地。⑤自古至今;由前傳後(指時間)。⑥由大至小;由多至少;由上至下(指數量、地位、程度等)。The temperature has gone *down*. 溫度已降低。⑦確實地;認眞地。Stop talking, and get *down* to work. 停止空談,認眞工作。⑧寫下;記下。Take *down* what I say. 寫下我所說的話。⑨付現。⑩病倒。⑪抑制;壓制。They held him *down*. 他們抑制他。⑫付印;發排。***be*** (or ***feel***) ***down*** (***in spirits***) 悲傷;不愉快。***come down in the world*** 失掉社會地位。***come down on a person*** 責備、懲罰某人。***come*** (or ***get***) ***down to business*** 認眞談正事。***down in the mouth*** 〖俗〗面容憂戚的。***down on one's luck*** 不幸; 倒楣。***down to the ground*** 完全地。That suits me *down to the ground*. 那完全適合我。***down under*** **a.** 在世界另一邊的。**b.** 澳洲或紐西蘭。**c.** 在(到)澳洲或紐西蘭(去)。***down with*** 打倒。*Down with* the dictator! 打倒獨裁者! ***hit a man when he's down*** 打落水狗;落井下石。***let a person down*** **a.** 見人陷於不幸而不救;任其失敗。**b.** 使人坍臺;使人丟面子。***put a person down*** 叱責某人。***put something down*** 撲滅;剷除;停止(惡習等)。***send a person down*** (大學中)革除某人。***shout a person down*** 拒聽某人講話;高聲喊叫使某人的話不能被聽到。—*prep.* ①順沿而下;下向;下經,下循,下入(朝向下方或認爲下方之處)。to sail *down* a stream. 順流下航。②由較遠的至較近的(指時間)。*down* the ages. 經過若干時代(由古至今)。③到…中;到…裏。He went *down* town. 他上街了。—*adj.* ①向下的。a *down* train. 下行車。②在下的。③病倒的。She is *down* with a cold. 她患傷風。④意志消沈的;沮喪的。He felt *down* about his failure. 他因失敗而覺得沮喪。⑤不再用的(橄欖球)。⑥低於對方若干分的。⑦衰微;減少。New construction is sharply *down.* 新工程急速地減少。⑧減弱。The wind is *down.* 風勢已減弱。⑨停業;休業。⑩已落;已沉。⑪跌價。⑫頭次的(付款)。a *down* payment of $10. 10 元的頭次付款。⑬送到印刷室。The paper was *down* in the afternoon. 報紙於下午送到印刷室。***down and out*** **a.** 貧病潦倒(健康、金錢、朋友、希望、一無所有)。**b.** 拳賽時被打倒。***down on***〖俗〗**a.** 對…發怒。**b.** 懷敵意;仇視;對…存偏見。***on the down grade*** 走下坡;日趨潦倒。—*v.t.* ①擊敗;打倒。to *down* one's enemy. 擊敗敵人。②吞下。③抑制;克制;消除。He could not *down* his regrets. 他不能抑制悔恨之情。④擊落。⑤放下。***down tools*** 停止工作。—*v.i.* ①開胃。②被克制;被消除。His regret may never *down.* 他的悔恨可能永遠不會消除。—*n.* ①下;向下的行動。②失敗;厄運。***have a down on someone*** 不喜歡某人;怨恨某人。

down² *n.* 軟毛;柔毛;軟髮。***in the down*** (雛鳥)身體包在軟毛中。—*v.t.* 覆以軟毛。

down³ *n.* ①沙丘。②(*pl.*)草原。

down-and-out [ˈdaunənˈaut, ˈdaunəndˈaut; ˈdaunəndˈaut] *adj.* ①窮困潦倒的。②〖拳賽〗被擊倒的。③無力氣的;殘廢的。

down-and-out·er [ˈdaunənˈautɚ; ˈdaunənˈautə] *n.* 窮困潦倒者。

down·beat [ˈdaun,bit; ˈdaunbiːt] *adj.* 哀愁的;悲觀的;悲劇的。

down·cast [ˈdaun,kæst; ˈdaunkaːst] *adj.* ①向下的;垂視的。②沮喪的;憂鬱的。—*n.* ①垂視;向下看。②覆沒;瓦解。③〖礦冶〗通風坑。—**ness,** *n.*

down-curve [ˈdaun,kɝv; ˈdaunkəːv] 「*n.*〖棒球〗下垂球。」

down·draft [ˈdaun,dræft; ˈdaundrɑːft] *n.* ①朝下之氣流或風。②下降之趨勢(尤指商業活動)。

down·drift [ˈdaun,drɪft; ˈdaundrift] *n.* 朝下漂流;逐漸下降。

down·er [ˈdaunɚ; ˈdaunə] *n.*〖美俚〗「鎮靜劑。」

***down·fall** [ˈdaun,fɔl; ˈdaunfɔːl] *n.* ①毀滅;敗亡;衰落。His *downfall* was caused by gambling. 他因賭博而身敗名裂。②落下;降下。③造成毀滅或敗亡之原因。

down·fall·en [ˈdaunˈfɔlən; ˈdaunˈfɔːlən] *adj.* 毀滅的;敗亡的。

down·flow [ˈdaun,flo; ˈdaunflou] *n.* ①向下流。②向下流之物。

down·grade [ˈdaun,gred; ˈdaungreid] *n., adj., adv., v.,* **-grad·ed, -grad·ing.** —*n.* 向下之斜坡。***on the downgrade*** 走下坡地;日趨潦倒。—*adj. & adv.* 向下坡的(地)。—*v.t.* ①將(某人)降級減薪。②減少;降低…之重要性。—**down·grad·ing,** *n.*

down·heart·ed [ˈdaunˈhɑrtɪd; ˈdaunˈhɑːtid] *adj.* 鬱悶的;沮喪的;無精打采的。—**ly,** *adv.* —**ness,** *n.*

down·hill [ˈdaun,hɪl; ˈdaunhil] *adv. & adj.* 向下地(的);下坡地(的)。***go downhill*** **a.** 下坡。**b.** 衰頹;每況愈下。

Down·ing Street [ˈdaunɪŋ~; ˈdauniŋ~] ①(英國)唐寧街(首相官邸所在)。②英國政府。

down payment 分期付款的首次款。

down·play [ˈdaun,ple; ˈdaunplei] *v.t.* 不重視。

down·pour [ˈdaun,por; ˈdaunpɔː] 「*n.* 大雨。」

down·range [ˈdaunˈrendʒ; ˈdaunˈreindʒ] *adj. & adv.* 沿已定路線由(火箭或飛彈)發射台向目標發射的(地)。

down·right [ˈdaun,raɪt; ˈdaunrait] *adj.* ①徹底的;完全的。②坦白的;正直的。—*adv.* 徹底地;全然地。—**ly,** *adv.* —**ness,** *n.*

down·riv·er [ˈdaun,rɪvɚ; ˈdaunˈrivə] *adj.* 下游的。—*adv.* 向下游。

down·side [ˈdaunˈsaɪd; ˈdaunˈsaid] *adj.* 下側的。—*n.* 下邊;底面。***on the downside*** 衰落中;在走下坡。

down·slope [ˈdaun,slop; ˈdaun-sloup] *adj.* 下坡的。—*adv.* 向着坡下。

down·stage [ˈdaunˈstedʒ; ˈdaunˈsteidʒ] *adv.* 向舞臺前;在舞臺前。—*adj.* 前臺的。

down·stair [ˈdaunˈstɛr; ˈdaunˈstɛə] *adj.* 樓下的。(亦作 **downstairs**)

***down·stairs** [*adj., adv.* ˈdaunˈstɛrz *n.* ,daunˈstɛrz; ˈdaunˈstɛəz] *adv.* 樓下地。to go *downstairs.* 下樓。—*adj.* 樓下的。*downstairs* rooms. 樓下的房間。—*n.* 樓下。He rushed to *downstairs* on hearing his boy's scream. 他聽到他小孩的尖叫, 衝下樓去。

down·state [ˈdaunˈstet; ˈdaunˈsteit] *adj. & adv.*〖美〗在州裏的鄉下或偏僻地區的(地)。—*n.*〖美〗一州裏的較鄉下部分或偏僻地區。—**down·stat·er,** *n.*

down·stream [ˈdaunˈstrim; ˈdaunˈstriːm] *adj. & adv.* 下流的(地);順流的(地)。

down·street [ˈdaunˈstrit; ˈdaunˈstriːt] *adv.* 到鬧區。—*n.* 街之下段。

down·stroke [ˈdaun,strok; ˈdaunstrouk] *n.* ①向下打的一擊。②向下寫的一筆。

down·sun [ˈdaunˈsʌn; ˈdaunˈsʌn] *adv.* 「*& adj.* 背着太陽地(的)。」

down·swing [ˈdaun,swɪŋ; ˈdaunswiŋ] *n.* ①〖高爾夫〗球棍向下之一揮。②衰落。

down·throw [ˈdaun,θro; ˈdaunθrou] *n.* ①投下;陷沒;敗北;顛倒。②〖地質〗坍陷;斷層。

down·time [ˈdaunˈtaɪm; ˈdauntaim] *n.* 工廠上班時間內機器停止生產的時間(如因修理、缺乏原料等)。

down-to-earth [ˈdauntəˈɝθ; ˈdauntəˈəːθ] *adj.* ①樸實的;不傲慢的。②實際的;現實的。

down town 商業區;鬧區。

***down·town** [ˈdaunˈtaun; ˈdaunˈtaun] *adj.* 在商業區的;屬於商業區的。*downtown* stores. 商業區商店。—*adv.* 到(在)商業區。to go *downtown.* 到商業區去。—**er,** *n.*

down·trend [ˈdaun,trɛnd; ˈdauntrend] *n.* 衰微的趨向。

down·trod(den) [ˈdaunˈtrɑd(n̩); ˈdaun,trɔd(n)] *adj.* 受壓制的;被蹂躪的。—**ness,** *n.*

down·turn [ˈdaun,tɝn; ˈdauntəːn] *n.* 「①向下彎曲。②降低;衰落。」

***down·ward** [ˈdaunwɚd; ˈdaunwəd] *adj.* 向下的;下降的。—*adv.* ①向下地。②衰微地。Then he fell from grace and went *downward* in life. 然後他失去寵信,生活也就每況愈下了。③自…以降。—**ly,** *adv.* —**ness,** *n.*

***down·wards** [ˈdaunwɚdz; ˈdaunwədz] *adv.* ①向下地。The river flows *downwards* toward the sea. 這條河向海流去。②自…以來;自…以下。

down·wind [ˈdaunˈwɪnd; ˈdaunˈwind] *adj. & adv.* 順風的(地)。—*n.* 順風。

down·y¹ [ˈdaunɪ; ˈdauni] *adj.,* **down·i·er, down·i·est.** ①似軟毛之性質的;柔軟的。②軟毛做成的。③覆有軟毛的;有茸毛的。④柔和的;撫慰的;平靜的。—**down·i·ness,** *n.*

down·y² *adj.,* **down·i·er, down·i·est.** 多丘崗的;丘原的。

dow·ry [ˈdaurɪ; ˈdauəri] *n., pl.* **-ries.** ①妝奩;陪嫁物。②稟賦;天才。(亦作 **dower, dowery**)

dowse¹ [daus; daus] *v.t.* =**douse.**

dowse² *v.i.* 用探條探測水源、礦藏等。

dows·er [ˈdauzɚ; ˈdauzə] *n.* ①用探條或探礦杖探測水源、礦藏等之人。②探測水源、礦藏等之探條或探礦杖。

dox·ol·o·gy [dɑksˈɑlədʒɪ; dɔkˈsɔlədʒi] *n., pl.* **-gies.** ①(讚頌上帝的)讚美詩。②讚美。—**dox·o·log·i·cal,** *adj.*

dox·y¹ [ˈdɑksɪ; ˈdɔksi] *n., pl.* **dox·ies.** ①意見;學說。②教義;教旨。(亦作 **doxie**)

dox·y² *n., pl.* **dox·ies.** 〖俚〗情婦;娼婦。

doy·en [ˈdɔɪən, dwɑˈjæ̃; ˈdɔiən] *n.* 首席;領袖。

Doyle [dɔɪl; dɔil] *n.* 柯南道爾(Sir Arthur Conan, 1859–1930, 英國醫生、及偵探小說家)。

doz. ①dozen. ②dozens.

doze** [doz; douz] *v.,* **dozed, doz·ing,** *n.* —*v.i.* 小睡;微睡。doze off*** 打瞌睡。—*v.t.* 瞌睡中度過〖out, away〗. to *doze* away one's time. 在瞌睡中虛度時間。—*n.* 微睡;假寐。He fell into a *doze.* 他打瞌睡。—**doz·er,** *n.*

‡doz·en [ˈdʌzn̩; ˈdʌzn] *n.* ①一打;十二個。He bought two *dozen* bottles of wine. 他買二十四瓶酒。②十來個;十幾個。***a baker's dozen*** 十三個。***dozens of*** 一大堆的;很多的。I have *dozens of* things to do. 我有一大堆事情要做。〖注意〗 **dozen** 的複數爲 dozens. 但在數目字後則仍爲 dozen.

doz·enth [ˈdʌzn̩θ; ˈdʌznθ] *adj.* 第十二的 (=twelfth).

doz·y [ˈdozɪ; ˈdouzi] *adj.,* **doz·i·er, doz·i·est.** ①欲眠的;困倦的。②腐爛的(水果);枯朽的(林木)。

D.P., DP displaced person.

D.Ph(il). Doctor of Philosophy.

D.P.I. Director of Public Institution.

DPT 白喉、百日咳及破傷風混合血清。

dpt. ①department. ②deponent.

D.P.W. Department of Public Works.

***Dr** doctor. ***Dr.** ①debit. ②debtor. ③doctor. **dr.** ①debtor. ②dram. ③drams. ④drawer.

drab¹ [dræb; dræb] *n., adj.,* **drab·ber, drab·best.** —*n.* ①暗黃灰色;土褐色。②單調。—*adj.* ①單調的;枯澀的;簡陋的。②暗黃灰色的;土褐色的。—**ly,** *adv.* —**ness,** *n.*

drab² *n., v.,* **drabbed, drab·bing.** —*n.* ①不整潔之婦女;邋遢女子。②娼妓。—*v.i.* 嫖妓。

drab³ *n.* 極少金額;極少數量。***dribs and drabs*** 極少金額。

drab·ble [ˈdræbl̩; ˈdræbl] *v.t. & v.i.,* **-bled, -bling.** 將(衣裳等)拖髒;(使)變髒濕。

drachm [dræm; dræm] *n.* ①=**drachma.** ②〖英〗=**dram.**

drach·ma [ˈdrækmə; ˈdrækmə] *n., pl.* **-mas, -mae** [-mi; -miː]. ①希臘貨幣名。②古希臘硬幣名。③古希臘衡名(約等於一個dram).

Dra·co [ˈdreko; ˈdreikou] *n.* ①〖天文〗天龍座。②(d-)〖動物〗飛龍。③德拉寇(公元前七世紀之雅典政治家及立法者)。

Dra·co·ni·an [dreˈkonɪən; dreiˈkounjən] *adj.* ①雅典立法者德拉寇(Draco)的。②德拉寇(Draco)所草擬之嚴峻法典的。③(亦作d-)苛刻的;嚴峻的。④(d-)龍的;似龍的(=draconic). —**ism,** *n.*

dra·con·ic [dreˈkɑnɪk; dreiˈkɔnik] *adj.* ①龍的;似龍的。②(D-)=**Draconian.**

draff [dræf; dræf] *n.* 糟粕;渣滓。—**y,** *adj.*

draft** [dræft; drɑːft] *n.* ①氣流;通風。②調節空氣的設備。③圖樣;設計。a *draft* for a machine. 一部機器的圖樣。④草稿。a *draft* for a speech. 一篇演說的草稿。⑤徵募兵士。⑥所徵的兵。⑦(物品、體力、金錢、時間等的)消耗。⑧拉;曳;所拉曳的東西。⑨(=draught) **a.** 拉網。**b.** 一網所獲的魚量。⑩匯票;支票。a *draft* for $500. 五百元的一張匯票。⑪船底沒入水中的深度;(船的)吃水(=draught). a ship of 10 feet *draft.* 吃水十英尺的船。⑫飲;一飲的量(=draught). He emptied the glass at one *draft.* 他一飲而乾杯。⑬吸進;吸進之空氣(=draught). ⑭吸入之煙(=draught). ⑮從桶中汲飲啤酒等(=draught). ***on draft 直接從桶中。beer to be served *on draft.* 從桶中直接供應的啤酒。—*v.t.* ①作草案;作草圖;起草;起稿。to *draft* a petition. 草擬請願書。②拉開;曳去。③徵募。He was *drafted* as a soldier. 他被徵召當兵。—*v.i.* 擬草稿。—*adj.* ①適於拖曳重載的。②草稿的。③從桶中汲飲的。

draft·a·ble [ˈdræftəbl̩; ˈdrɑːftəbl] *adj.* 可徵召入伍的。

draft board 兵役委員會(負責徵選合格壯丁入伍的官方或民間組織)。

draft·ee [dræfˈti; drɑːfˈtiː] *n.* 被徵召之士兵。

draft·er [ˈdræftɚ; ˈdrɑːftə] *n.* ①起草者。②駄馬。

draft horse 駄馬。

draft·i·ness [ˈdræftɪnɪs; ˈdrɑːftinis] *n.* 多罅縫風;通風。

drafting machine 製圖器。

drafting paper 製圖紙。

drafting room 製圖室。

drafting table 製圖桌。

drafts·man [ˈdræftsmən; ˈdrɑːftsmən] *n., pl.* **-men.** ①(國會法案等的)起草者。②製圖員。(亦作 **draughtsman**)

drafts·man·ship [ˈdræftsmənˌʃɪp; ˈdrɑːftsmənʃip] *n.* ①作圖術。②起草術。

draft·y [ˈdræftɪ; ˈdrɑːfti] *adj.* 通風良好的;有罅縫風吹入的。(亦作 **draughty**) —**draft·i·ly,** *adv.*

‡drag [dræg; dræg] *v.,* **dragged, drag·ging,** *n.* —*v.t.* ①拖曳;用力徐拖。The horse was *dragging* a heavy load. 馬拖曳着重載。②勉强捱過;困難地繼續。③(用網或爪錨)在…中撈物。④耙耕。—*v.i.* ①被拖曳而進。The anchor *drags.* 船拖錨而進。②困難地或用力地徐進;單調無趣地進行。③拖延;落後。④拖網撈取。⑤〖俗〗吸一口烟。***drag an anchor*** (船)拖着錨。***drag down*** 〖俚〗賺(錢)。***drag in*** 插入討論中。***drag on*** (or ***out***) 冗長乏味地延長;拖延太久。***drag one's feet*** 拖步而行(累而不能舉足)。***drag one's heels*** 故意延遲行動。***drag up a child*** 〖俗〗對一孩子未盡教養之責。—*n.* ①拖曳;牽引。②拖曳的東西(如網、撬等);耕土用的笨重的耙;四輪馬車。③被拖曳的東西。④阻礙物;拖累的東西。⑤吃力的前進。It was a long *drag* up the hill. 上山是一段長而吃力的路程。⑥阻力。⑦一吸。⑧一飲。⑨〖俚〗勢力;背景。He must have lots of *drag.* 他一定有很大的勢力。⑩〖俚〗街;路。⑪〖俚〗男扮女裝用之服飾。⑫〖俚〗女朋友。⑬〖俚〗令人討厭的人。⑭四匹馬以上拉的大馬車。⑮〖打獵〗 **a.** 獵物所留的氣味。**b.** 讓獵犬聞而跟蹤的人造氣味。—**ger,** *n.*

dra·gée [drɑ'ʒe; drɑː'ʒei]〖法〗*n.* ①(外包有糖衣之)糖果。②〖藥〗糖衣丸。

drag·gle ['dræg!; 'drægl] *v.t. & v.i.*, **-gled, -gling.** ①拖汚;拖溼;拖曳。②落後。

drag·gle·tail ['dræg!,tel; 'drægl teil] *n.* 拖着不整潔之長裙的女子;邋遢女人。

drag·line ['dræg,laɪn; 'dræglain] *n.* ①一種挖泥機械。②=**dragrope.**

drag·net ['dræg,nɛt; 'drægnet] *n.* ①拖網。②搜捕之羅網;警網。

drag·o·man ['drægəmən; 'drægoumən] *n., pl.* **-mans, -men.** (東方諸國之)譯員;通譯;導遊。

drag·on** ['drægən;'drægən] *n.* ①龍。②兇惡的人。③嚴厲而有警覺性的女人;嚴厲的女監管人。④(D-)〖天文〗天龍座。⑤撒旦;魔王。sow dragon's teeth*** 撒下不和或毀滅的種子,對己對他人均不利。**—ish,** *adj.*

Dragon Boat Festival (中國)端午節。

drag·on·ess ['drægənɪs; 'drægənis] *n.* dragon 之女性。

drag·on·et ['drægənɪt; 'drægənit] *n.* ①小龍;幼龍。②鰕虎魚之類(有明亮顏色之小海魚)。

***drag·on·fly** ['drægən,flaɪ;'drægən-flai] *n., pl.* **-flies.** 蜻蜓。

drag·on·nade [,drægə'ned; ,drægə'neid] *n.* ①(法王路易十四使用龍騎兵)對新教徒之迫害。②武力迫害。

dragon's blood 麒麟竭(一種產於馬來亞之紅色樹脂)。

dra·goon [drə'gun; drə'guːn] *n.* ①騎兵。②凶暴的男人。*—v.t.* 以武力逼迫;彈壓。

drag·rope ['dræg,rop; 'drægroup] *n.* ①(飛機或砲的)拉繩;拖索。②(氣球之)導索。

drail [drel; dreil] *n.*〖美〗加重量使餌沉入水中之釣魚鈎。

drain** [dren; drein] *v.t.* ①使徐徐流出;漸次排出(水)。A farmer must *drain* his land well for certain crops. 對於某些作物,農人須將田地做適當的排水。②使乾竭;使流盡。③剝奪;使耗盡。Four years of war *drained* the country of men and resources. 四年的戰事使國家耗盡壯丁和資源。④飲。*—v.i.* ①徐徐流出;流去。The water will soon *drain* away. 水將很快流去。②漸次流盡。*—n.* ①水管;陰溝;任何排水的東西。②〖醫,外科〗排膿的管。③精力、時間、金錢的消耗。Military expenditure has been a great *drain* on the country's wealth. 軍費消耗國家的財富甚大。④流出。⑤〖俗〗一口之量。Don't drink it all; leave me a *drain!* 不要都喝掉;給我留一口!⑥排出之水。⑦(*pl.*) =**dregs.** ***go down the drain 化爲烏有。**—a·ble,** *adj.*

***drain·age** ['drenɪdʒ; 'dreinidʒ] *n.* ①排水;排泄。②排水的裝置。③排水的區域。④排出的東西(如水或膿等)。⑤消耗。⑥漸流。

drainage basin 排水盆地;流域。

drainage system 排水系統。

drained [drend; dreind] *adj.* ①已排水的。②失去活力的。

drain·er ['drenə; 'dreinə] *n.* 排水裝置。

drain·pipe ['dren,paɪp; 'dreinpaip] *n.* 排水管。

drake¹** [drek; dreik] *n.* 公鴨。play ducks and drakes*** 打水漂。

drake² *n.* =**drake fly.**

drake fly 蜉蝣。

dram [dræm;dræm] *n., v.,* **drammed, dram·ming.** *—n.* ①特拉姆(衡量的單位;在藥衡中等於八分之一唡;常衡中等於十六分之一唡)。②液體容量單位(等於 1/123 品脫)。③少量之酒。④少許;微量。*—v.t.* 勸酒。*—v.i.* 飲烈酒。

***dra·ma** ['dræmə, 'drɑmə; 'drɑːmə] *n.* ①在舞臺上演的戲。②戲劇;戲劇文學。He is a student of *drama.* 他是研究戲劇的人。③一連串緊張而有趣的事。④趣味;刺激。

Dram·a·mine ['dræmə,min;'dræməmiːn] *n.*〖商標名〗防暈車藥。

***dra·mat·ic** [drə'mætɪk; drə'mætik] *adj.* ①戲劇的;有關戲劇的。*dramatic* performance. 戲劇的表演。②似戲劇的;戲劇性的。*dramatic* changes in the international situation. 國際情勢之戲劇性變化。**—al·ly,** *adv.*

dra·mat·ics [drə'mætɪks; drə'mætiks] *n.* ①(作 *sing.* or *pl.* 解)演劇技術。②(作 *pl.* 解)業餘者演出之戲劇。③(作 *pl.* 解)〖美俗〗裝腔作勢之行爲;做作。

dram·a·tis per·so·nae ['dræmətɪs pə'soni; 'drɑːmətis-pəː'sounai]〖拉〗登場人物;劇中人物。

dram·a·tist ['dræmətɪst; 'dræmətist] *n.* 戲劇家;戲劇作者。

dram·a·ti·za·tion [,dræmətə'zeʃən; ,dræmətai'zeiʃən] *n.* ①編爲戲劇;戲劇化。②戲劇化之事物;(小說等之)戲劇本。

dram·a·tize ['dræmə,taɪz; 'dræmətaiz] *v.,* **-tized, -tiz·ing.** *—v.t.* ①編爲戲劇。②使戲劇化。③戲劇性地表示。*—v.i.* 被編爲戲劇。

dram·a·turge ['dræmə,tɝdʒ; 'dræmətəːdʒ] *n.* 劇作家。(亦作 **dramaturgist**)

dram·a·tur·gic [,dræmə'tɝdʒɪk; ,dræmə'təːdʒik] *adj.* 編劇法的。

dram·a·tur·gy ['dræmə,tɝdʒɪ;'dræmətəːdʒi] *n.* 編劇法;演出法。

dram·shop ['dræm,ʃɑp; 'dræmʃɔp] *n.* 酒店;酒吧。

‡**drank** [dræŋk; dræŋk] *v.* pt. of **drink.**

drape [drep; dreip] *v.,* **draped, draping,** *n.* *—v.t.* ①覆以摺綴的布。②摺綴(衣服);整理(衣服)。③懸掛。*—v.i.* 垂下。*—n.* ①帘子。②垂下狀。

drap·er ['drepɚ; 'dreipə] *n.* ①懸掛者;整理者。②〖英〗布商。

***dra·per·y** ['drepərɪ;'dreipəri] *n., pl.* **-per·ies.** ①織物;帳;幃。②〖英〗布業;呢絨業。③摺綴的帘子或衣着。④帘子。⑤裝飾或掩飾的外貌。

dras·tic ['dræstɪk; 'dræstik] *adj.* 激烈的;(藥性等)猛烈的;徹底的。*drastic* remedies to cure an illness. 烈性的藥物。**—al·ly,** *adv.*

drat [dræt; dræt] *v.,* **drat·ted, drat·ting,** *interj.* *—v.t.*〖俗〗咒罵。*Drat* you! 討厭!你這畜生! *—interj.* (表示惱怒之委婉咒語)討厭!

***draught** [dræft; drɑːft] *n., v., adj.* =**draft.** **—er,** *n.*〖注意〗**draught** 在美國多用在 a *draught* of fish (一網所得之魚), a ship's *draught* (船的吃水), a *draught* of ale (一口酒)等意義;用作其他意義時,則多用 draft. 但 *draftsman* 或 *draughtsman* 當用作"起草者"時,則兩種拼法通用。

draught·board ['dræft,bord; 'drɑːftbɔːd] *n.*〖英〗西洋碁盤。

draught horse 曳馬;馱馬。

draughts [dræfts; drɑːfts] *n. pl.*〖英〗

=checkers.

draughts·man ['dræftsmən; 'drɑːftsmən] *n.*, *pl.* **-men.** ①西洋棋之棋子。②=**draftsman.**

draught·y ['dræftɪ; 'drɑːfti] *adj.* =**drafty.**

drave [drev; dreiv] *v.* 〖古〗pt. of **drive.**

:draw [drɔ; drɔː] *v.*, **drew, drawn, draw·ing,** *n.* —*v.t.* ①拉；曳；拖。The horse *drew* the wagon. 馬拖貨車。②拉起(如張帆)；拉下(如窗帘)；拉開(如窗帘)；拉進(如收網)；拉後(如挽弓)；拉出(如拔劍)。*Draw* the curtains across the window. 把窗帘拉下遮住窗。③(船)吃(水)。④吸引；使趨於；使走向。⑤吸入(空氣)。The diver *drew* a deep breath. 這潛水者深深吸口氣。⑥引起。⑦拔出。A dentist *draws* teeth. 牙醫拔牙。⑧汲(水)；取。They *drew* water from the pond. 他們由池中取水。⑨使流出。⑩取出(臟腑)。⑪支領；提取。He *draws* a good salary. 他支領優厚的薪金。⑫寫(支票、匯票等)。to *draw* a check. 開支票。⑬產生；使有收入。⑭推論；引出；獲得。He *draws* his inspiration from nature. 他從自然中獲得靈感。⑮發出(聲)。He *drew* a deep sigh. 他長嘆一聲。⑯拉長；引長；拉緊。⑰拉之使變形；使縮；使變小。His face is *drawn* with anxiety. 他滿面愁容。⑱畫。⑲起草；草擬。⑳使(茶)多泡一會兒而味更濃。㉑區別。㉒〖運動〗成和局；分數拉平。㉓抽籤。㉔使乾涸。㉕(在樹林中)尋找獵物。㉖以文火鍊(鋼)；回火鍊(鋼)。㉗〖軍〗領取(給養、裝備)等。—*v.i.* ①拉；曳；拖。A sail *draws* by being filled with wind. 帆鼓風而曳行(船隻)。②移動〖on, off, out, near〗. We *drew* near to town. 我們走近市鎮。③通風。The chimney *draws* well. 這煙囪很通風。④拔出(刀、鎗等)〖on〗. ⑤作畫。⑥收縮。⑦不分勝負。The two teams *drew.* 這兩隊打成平手。⑧在開水中泡之而味變濃。⑨拈鬮決定。Shall we *draw* for partners? 我們拈鬮決定誰爲一組好嗎? ⑩汲水。⑪吸引人(尤指觀衆)。⑫(船)吃水。Greater ships *draw* deep. 大船吃水深。***draw a bead on*** 以…爲攻擊的目標；攻擊。***draw a blank*** 一無所得。***draw a distinction between...*** 指出…之間的不同。***draw a parallel between...*** 指出…之間的相同。***draw*** (***a thing*** or ***person***) ***aside*** 拉至旁邊。***draw away*** **a.** 拉走；退走。**b.** (於比賽中)超出對手。***draw back*** **a.** 拉起；退後。**b.** 遲疑；猶豫；不守諾言。***draw blood*** 傷人；使憤怒。***draw down*** **a.** 拉下。**b.** 招致。***draw down the curtain*** **a.** 閉幕。**b.** 無話可說了。It's time to *draw down the curtain.* 說得已很多了，現在已無話可說了。***draw first blood*** 先動手攻擊。***draw forth*** 招致；使出現。***draw from*** **a.** 引出消息。**b.** 拔取；取下。The tooth was *drawn from* the upper jaw. 這牙是由上顎取下。**c.** 推論。***draw in*** **a.** 變短。**b.** 儉省。I shall have to *draw in.* 我必須儉省。***draw*** (***something***) ***in*** **a.** 吸引；拉進；縮進；收縮。The fisherman *drew* his net *in.* 漁夫收網。**b.** 特別留意；更加小心。**c.** 收回；令歸還。***draw it mild*** 〖俚〗不誇張。***draw lots*** 抽籤決定。Someone must go. Let us *draw lots.* 必須有人去，讓我們抽籤決定誰(去)。***draw off*** **a.** 撤退；退去。**b.** 排除(水)。***draw on*** **a.** 使出現；惹起；招致。**b.** 穿起。**c.** 依賴。I shall *draw on* you for assistance. 我依賴你的援助。**d.** 接近。Winter is *drawing on.* 冬季卽將來臨。***draw oneself up*** 站直；坐直。***draw one's first*** (or ***last***) ***breath*** 誕生(死)。***draw one's time*** (被迫)辭職。Get to work or *draw your time* right now. 快去工作否則請馬上辭職。***draw out*** **a.** 拉長。**b.** 使說出(實情)。***draw round*** 湊近。***draw the fangs*** 使無害；使無力。***draw the*** (or ***a***) ***line*** 劃出界限；限制。***draw the long bow*** 誇張。***draw the sword*** 宣戰。***draw the teeth*** 使無害。***draw to an end*** 完了；終止。***draw together*** **a.** 靠近；駛近；走近。**b.** 協力。***draw up*** **a.** 草擬。I will *draw up* a scheme of it for you. 我將替你草擬這事的計畫。**b.** 靠近。**c.** 停止。The car *drew up* at the door. 這車停在門外。**d.** 排列。**e.** 提取；汲取。—*n.* ①拉；拖；曳；抽；拔。He is quick on the *draw.* 他拔鎗很快。②吸引注意的東西。③不分勝負。The game ended in a *draw.* 這球賽結果勝負未分。④吊橋可以移動的部分。⑤抽籤；抓鬮。⑥優勢。⑦(弓之)張力。***beat someone to the draw*** 捷足先登。***be fast*** (or ***quick***) ***on the draw*** **a.** 拔鎗快。**b.** 機警；思想敏捷。The debater *was fast on the draw.* 辯論者思想敏捷。—**a·ble,** *adj.*

draw·back ['drɔ͵bæk; 'drɔːbæk] *n.* ①缺點；障礙。②退還的關稅；退款。

draw·bar ['drɔ͵bɑr; 'drɔːbɑː] *n.* 列車間之掛鈎。

draw·bridge ['drɔ͵brɪdʒ; 'drɔːbridʒ] *n.* (可開合之)吊橋。

draw·card ['drɔ͵kɑrd; 'drɔːkɑːd] *n.* ①叫座的節目；精采節目。②受歡迎的演員。(亦作 **drawing card**)

draw·ee [drɔ'i; drɔː'iː] *n.* (支票、匯票等之)付款人。

***draw·er** [*for* ① & ② drɔr; drɔː *for* ③ 'drɔɚ; 'drɔːə] *n.* ①抽屜。chest of *drawers.* (有抽屜的)衣櫃。②(*pl.*)內褲。③畫家。

***draw·ing** ['drɔ·ɪŋ; 'drɔːiŋ] *n.* ①製圖。out of *drawing.* 畫錯。②圖畫。③素描術。④泡茶用的少量茶葉。

drawing account ①(股東或員工的)提款帳單。②商店預付薪金、佣金等之帳戶。

drawing block 圖畫紙册。

drawing board 製圖板。***on the drawing board*** 在設計階段；在初步籌備階段。

drawing compasses 製圖用之兩脚規。

drawing paper 圖畫紙；製圖用紙。

drawing pen (製圖用之)鴨嘴筆；繪圖筆。

drawing pin 〖英〗圖釘。

drawing room *pl.* **drawing rooms.** ①客廳。②聚於客廳中的客人。③〖美〗臥車中的私用車室。④正式的接待。⑤(*pl.*)上流社交界。

draw·ing-room ['drɔ·ɪŋ͵rum; 'drɔːiŋruːm] *adj.* ①客廳的。②上流社會的。

drawing table ①製圖桌。②大小可憑拉動調整之餐桌。

draw·knife ['drɔ͵naɪf; 'drɔːnaif] *n.*, *pl.* **-knives.** (兩端有柄之)刨刀。(亦作 **drawingknife**)

drawl [drɔl; drɔːl] *v.t.* & *v.i.* 慢吞吞地說；拉長語調說。—*n.* 說時緩慢而拉長的語調。

drawl·ing ['drɔlɪŋ; 'drɔːliŋ] *adj.* 慢吞吞的；有氣無力的；沒精打采的。—**ly,** *adv.*

:drawn [drɔn; drɔːn] *v.* pp. of **draw.**

drawn work 抽絲織花手工。

draw·shave ['drɔ͵ʃev; 'drɔːʃeiv] *n.* =**drawknife.**

draw·string ['drɔ͵strɪŋ; 'drɔːstriŋ]

n. 穿在袋口、褲腰等的拉繩。

draw well 深井;汲水井。

dray [dre; drei] *n.* ①一種載重的馬車。②橇。—*v.t.* 以馬車運;以橇運。

dray·age [ˈdreɪdʒ; ˈdreiidʒ] *n.* 載貨馬車之搬運;載貨馬車之搬運費。

dray·man [ˈdremən; ˈdreimən] *n., pl.* **-men.** 貨運馬車之車夫。

dread** [drɛd; dred] *v.t. & v.i.* 害怕;恐懼。—*n.* ①畏懼;恐怖。Doubt and anxiety changed into *dread.* 懷疑和焦慮變成恐懼。②可怕的人或事物。be*** (or ***live***) ***in dread*** (***of***) 常在恐怖中。—*adj.* ①可怕的。②令人敬畏的。—**er,** *n.* —**ing·ly,** —**ly,** *adv.*

***dread·ful** [ˈdrɛdfəl; ˈdredful] *adj.* ①可怕的。a *dreadful* story. 可怕的故事。②〖俗〗不愉快的;不合意的。③非常的;極度的。—*adv.* 非常地。a *dreadful* good man. 非常好的人。—*n.* 低級恐怖小說。a shilling *dreadful.* 廉價的低級恐怖小說。

dread·ful·ly [ˈdrɛdfəlɪ; ˈdredfuli] *adv.* ①充滿恐怖地。②非常地。I am *dreadfully* tired. 我累得要命。

dread·nought, dread·naught [ˈdrɛdˌnɔt; ˈdrednɔːt] *n.* ①無畏艦(英國於 1906 年建造第一艘此種重級戰艦,命名曰 Dreadnaught,因而得名)。②大膽的人;天不怕地不怕的人。③一種厚呢;厚呢外衣。

:dream [drim; driːm] *n., v.,* **dreamed** or **dreamt, dream·ing.** —*n.* ①夢。to have bad *dreams.* 做惡夢。②幻想;夢想;空想。He had *dreams* of being a hero. 他夢想作英雄。③想望的人或事;夢境中之人或事物;極美之人物。—*v.i.* ①夢;做夢。②夢想;幻想〖of〗. The soldiers *dreamed* of home. 兵士們想家。③顯得似在夢境;顯得極爲寧靜。—*v.t.* ①夢見。He *dreamed* that he was a rich man. 他夢見他爲一富人。②夢想;幻想。***dream away one's time*** (or ***life***) 虛度光陰(一生)。***dream up*** 〖俗〗構思;創造;設計(發明物等)。

dream·er [ˈdrimə; ˈdriːmə] *n.* ①作夢者。②夢想家。

dream·i·ly [ˈdrimɪlɪ; ˈdriːmili] *adv.* 如夢地;朦朧地。

dream·land [ˈdrimˌlænd; ˈdriːmlænd] *n.* ①夢境;夢鄉。②想像中可愛的地方;幻想世界。

dream·less [ˈdrimlɪs; ˈdriːmlis] *adj.* 無夢的。

dream·like [ˈdrimˌlaɪk; ˈdriːmlaik] *adj.* 似夢中的。

dream-read·er [ˈdrimˌridə; ˈdriːmˈriːdə] *n.* 解夢者;斷夢者;詳夢者。

dreamt [drɛmt; dremt] *v.* pt. & pp. of **dream.**

dream·world [ˈdrimˈwɜld; ˈdriːmwəːld] *n.* 夢境;幻想世界。

dream·y [ˈdrimɪ; ˈdriːmi] *adj.,* **dream·i·er, dream·i·est.** ①夢的;多夢的。②如夢的;幻想的。③模糊的;朦朧的。④喜歡幻想的;不務實際的。⑤安慰的;慰藉的。⑥理想的;合乎理想的。—**dream·i·ness,** *n.*

drear [drɪr; driə] *adj.* 〖詩〗=**dreary.**

***drear·y** [ˈdrɪrɪ, ˈdrirɪ; ˈdriəri] *adj.,* **drear·i·er, drear·i·est.** ①憂鬱的;淒涼的;陰沉的。a *dreary* scenery. 淒涼的景色。②寡歡的。—**drear·i·ly,** *adv.* —**drear·i·ness,** *n.*

dredge[1] [drɛdʒ; dredʒ] *n., v.,* **dredged, dredg·ing.** —*n.* ①挖泥機;撈泥機。②撈網。—*v.t.* ①撈取;挖(泥)。②疏浚。—*v.i.* 挖;撈。

dredge[2] *v.t.* 〖烹飪〗篩或撒(麪粉等)於…之上。

dredg·er[1] [ˈdrɛdʒə; ˈdredʒə] *n.* ①挖泥船;疏浚機。②疏浚夫。

dredg·er[2] *n.* 一種有孔容器,用以撒布粉狀物者;撒粉匣。

dredging machine 挖泥機;疏浚機。

dree [dri; driː] *v.t.* 〖蘇,古〗忍耐;忍受。to *dree* one's weird. 甘心認命。—*adj.* 〖蘇,古〗淒涼的;冗長的。

dreg·gy [ˈdrɛgɪ; ˈdregi] *adj.,* **-gi·er, -gi·est.** 多渣滓的;渾濁的。

dregs [drɛgz; dregz] *n. pl.* ①渣滓;糟粕。②最無用的部分。③少量;微量。***drink*** (or ***drain***) ***to the dregs*** 喝乾;受盡苦痛;歷盡辛酸。

***drench** [drɛntʃ; drentʃ] *v.t.* ①浸;浸透。A heavy rain *drenched* the campers. 一陣大雨把露營者都淋濕了。②令(牛、馬等)飲(藥水)。—*v.i.* (雨雪)大作。—*n.* ①浸;浸液;浸透的東西。②一服藥水(尤指牛、馬等所服用者)。③大雨。a *drench* of rain. 豪雨。

drench·er [ˈdrɛntʃə; ˈdrentʃə] *n.* ①令水浸濕者。②灌藥器(灌牛、馬用)。③〖俗〗驟雨;豪雨。

Dres·den [ˈdrɛzdən; ˈdrezdən] *n.* ①德勒斯登(德國 Saxony 邦之首府)。②德勒斯登附近產之陶瓷。

:dress [drɛs; dres] *n., adj., v.,* **dressed** or **drest, dress·ing.** —*n.* (尤指婦女或小孩的)外衣;衣服;禮服。What a lot of nice *dresses* she has! 她有好多精美的衣服啊! ***evening dress*** 晚禮服。***full dress*** 大禮服;盛裝。—*adj.* ①衣服的。*dress* material. 衣料。②盛裝的。The graduation will be a *dress* affair. 畢業典禮將是穿着正式服裝之盛典。—*v.t.* ①使穿衣;爲…着衣。She *dresses* herself quickly. 她迅速地穿好衣服。②供給衣服。③裝飾。④處理;準備。⑤整理。⑥烹調;調製。⑦整列(隊伍)。⑧爲…施肥。—*v.i.* ①穿衣。②穿燕尾服;着晚禮服。You have just time to *dress* before banquet. 你剛好還有時間着晚禮服赴宴。③〖軍〗整隊。Right, *dress!* 向右看齊。***dress down*** 〖俗〗 **a.** 斥責;指斥。**b.** 打;鞭打。***dress ship*** 將船從頭至尾懸旗。***dress up*** **a.** 盛裝。to *dress up* for a party. 盛裝赴會。**b.** 粉飾;僞裝;隱瞞。

dress circle 戲院內之前排包廂(專備穿禮服者坐的特座)。

dress coat 燕尾服。

dress·er[1] [ˈdrɛsə; ˈdresə] *n.* ①(爲自己或他人)穿衣者;佈置商店之窗飾者;裹傷者。a careful *dresser.* 服裝講究者。②整理東西用之工具或機器。

dress·er[2] *n.* ①〖美〗鏡臺;化妝臺。②盛碗碟之櫃櫥。③厨房中放做好菜肴的桌子。

dresser set 成套的梳妝用具。

dress·i·ness [ˈdrɛsɪnɪs; ˈdresinis] *n.* 〖俗〗考究服飾;時髦。

dress·ing [ˈdrɛsɪŋ; ˈdresiŋ] *n.* ①着衣;衣服。②調味品。fish *dressing.* 魚的調味品。③塞入鷄腹內調味的東西。④繃帶;藥膏;敷藥。⑤肥料。⑥用以漿絲布等的材料。⑦裝飾表面之物。

dressing case 化妝箱;梳妝盒。

dress·ing-down [ˈdrɛsɪŋˈdaʊn; ˈdresiŋˈdaun] *n.* 〖俗〗①譴責;懲戒。②打;打擊。***give one a good dressing-down*** 責罵某人;痛打某人。

dressing gown (or **sack**) 晨衣。

dressing room 整容室;化妝室。

dressing station 〖軍〗(接近火線的)

包紮站;急救站。

dressing table 化妝臺。

***dress·mak·er** [ˈdrɛsˌmekɚ; ˈdresˌmeikə] *n.* 製女服與童裝的裁縫。

dress·mak·ing [ˈdrɛsˌmekɪŋ; ˈdresmeikiŋ] *n.* 女衣裁製;女衣裁縫業。

dress parade 閱兵式。

dress rehearsal (戲劇之) 正式預演;彩排。

dress shirt 男子襯衫(着於禮服內者)。

dress suit 一種男子晚間所穿的禮服。

dress·y [ˈdrɛsɪ; ˈdresi] *adj.*, **dress·i·er, dress·i·est.** 〖俗〗①服飾考究的。②時髦的。③盛裝的。

drest [drɛst; drest] *v.* pt. & pp. of **dress.**

‡**drew** [dru; druː] *v.* pt. of **draw.**

drib [drɪb; drib] *n.* 小滴;微量。***dribs and drabs*** 一點一滴;零星微量。

drib·ble [ˈdrɪbl; ˈdribl] *v.*, **-bled, -bling,** *n.* —*v.i.* ①滴下。②流口水;垂涎。③〖籃球〗運球。④(足球等)盤球。—*v.t.* ①使滴下。②〖籃球〗運(球)。③(足球等)盤(球)。—*n.* ①一滴。②少量;涓滴。③運球;盤球。④〖俗〗細雨;毛毛雨。

drib·(b)let [ˈdrɪblɪt; ˈdriblit] *n.* ①零星;微量。②小滴。***by*** (or ***in***) ***driblets*** 一點一點地;漸漸地。

dried [draɪd; draid] *v.* pt. & pp. of **dry.**

dried beef 牛肉乾。

dried milk 奶粉。(亦作 **milk powder, powdered milk**)

dri·er [ˈdraɪɚ; ˈdraiə] *n.* ①使乾燥的人或東西;乾燥劑。②乾燥機。(亦作 **dryer**) —*adj.* compar. of **dry.**

drift** [drɪft; drift] *n.* ①沖流;風捲。②意向;意義;主旨。③(被風吹積的)雪堆;沙堆。④猶豫;觀望。The government's policy is one of *drift.* 政府的政策是觀望。⑤趨向;傾向。⑥漂流;飄動;移動。⑦漂流物;隨風而飄之物。⑧漸變。⑨(因水流或氣流使)船或飛機離開航路之偏差;航差。⑩〖礦〗導坑;橫坑。⑪〖地質〗堆積物。on the drift*** 無固定目標或職業;隨波逐流。—*v.t.* ①沖漂。②吹積。③覆以吹積物。—*v.i.* ①漂流。We *drifted* down the stream. 我們順流而下。②盲目前進。③被吹積。④偏歪。⑤(物價等)不安定。

drift·age [ˈdrɪftɪdʒ; ˈdriftidʒ] *n.* ①漂流。②流程(船、飛機等偏離航路之距離)。③漂流物;沖積物。

drift·er [ˈdrɪftɚ; ˈdriftə] *n.* ①漂流物。②流浪者;漂泊者。③漂網漁船。④一種掃雷船。

drift ice 流冰;浮冰。

drift·ing [ˈdrɪftɪŋ; ˈdriftiŋ] *adj.* ①漂流的;飄動的。②漂泊無定的;無目標的。

drift·less [ˈdrɪftlɪs; ˈdriftlis] *adj.* ①無目標的;無定向的。②無飄積之冰雪的。

drift net 漂網;流網。

drift·wood [ˈdrɪftˌwud; ˈdriftwud] *n.* ①被潮水沖到河岸的木頭;水上浮木。②(社會變動所產生之)無用的人。

***drill**[1] [drɪl; dril] *n.* ①鑽;錐。②訓練;操練。The soldiers were at *drill.* 兵士們在操練。③練習。④尖銳的連續打擊或摩擦聲。—*v.t.* ①鑽;穿。②鑽孔於。③訓練;教練。to *drill* students in English grammar. 使學生練習英文文法。—*v.i.* ①鑽;穿〖through〗。②訓練;操練。

drill[2] *n.* ①播種機。②播種時地上挖出的淺畦。③一排播下的種子。—*v.t.*以播種機播(種)。

drill[3] *n.* 一種堅實的斜紋棉布或麻布。

drill[4] *n.* 黑面狒狒(產於非洲西部)。

drill bit 〖機械〗鑿孔器。

drill book 〖軍〗操典。

drill·er [ˈdrɪlɚ; ˈdrilə] *n.* ①鑽孔者;鑽孔機。②訓練人者;教官;教練。③列植之人;列植機;條播機。

drill·ing[1] [ˈdrɪlɪŋ; ˈdriliŋ] *n.* ①鑽孔;錐鑽。②(常*pl.*)鑽屑。③操練;訓練。④按列播種。⑤尖銳的連續音響。—*adj.* ①尖銳的。②尖刻的。③鑽孔的。

drill·ing[2] *n.* 一種斜紋布。

drilling machine 鑽床;穿孔機。

drill instructor =**drillmaster.**

drill·mas·ter [ˈdrɪlˌmæstɚ; ˈdrilˌmɑːstə] *n.* ①訓練者;教練。②〖軍〗教官。

drill press 〖機械〗鑽床。

drill yard 鐵路貨車調車場。

dri·ly [ˈdraɪlɪ; ˈdraili] *adv.* =**dryly.**

‡**drink** [drɪŋk; driŋk] *v.*, **drank, drunk, drink·ing,** *n.* —*v.i.* ①飲酒。He *drinks* but does not smoke. 他喝酒但不抽煙。②飲水或其他液體。③舉杯祝賀〖to〗。to *drink* to one's health. 舉杯祝賀某人健康。—*v.t.*①飲。to *drink* water. 飲水。②吸收。③耗費在飲酒上。④以飲酒虛度(時間)。⑤吸入心中。⑥飲酒祝賀。to *drink* a toast. 舉杯祝人健康。***drink deep*** 大量的飲酒。***drink hard*** 痛飲。***drink*** (***something***) ***in*** **a.** 吸入;吸取。**b.** 欣賞。—*n.* ①飲料;水;酒。Give him a *drink* of water. 給他一點水喝。②(常the-)大海;海洋。He slipped off the rock and into the *drink.* 他在岩石上滑了一跤掉入海中。***in drink*** 醉酒。He talks too much when he is *in drink.* 他酒醉時說話太多。

drink·a·ble [ˈdrɪŋkəbl; ˈdriŋkəbl] *adj.* 可飲用的。—*n.* (常*pl.*) 飲料。eatables and *drinkables.* 飲食品。

drink·er [ˈdrɪŋkɚ; ˈdriŋkə] *n.* ①飲者;飲酒者。②酒徒。

drink·er·y [ˈdrɪŋkərɪ; ˈdriŋkəri] *n.*, *pl.* **-er·ies.** 〖俗〗酒店。

drink·ing [ˈdrɪŋkɪŋ; ˈdriŋkiŋ] *n.* ①飲;飲用。suitable for *drinking.* 適於飲用。②飲酒;豪飲;酒會;酒宴。—*adj.* ①飲用的。②嗜酒的;好飲酒的。

drinking bout 縱飲。

drinking fountain 自動飲水器。

drinking song 飲酒歌。

drinking water 飲用水。

drink money 酒錢;賞錢。

drink offering 祭獻之酒。

***drip** [drɪp; drip] *v.*, **dripped** or **dript, drip·ping,** *n.* —*v.i.* 滴落;滴下。—*v.t.* ①使滴落。He was *dripping* sweat. 他揮汗如雨。②將(濕淋淋的衣服)掛起來使乾。—*n.* ①水滴;點滴。②水滴聲。③屋簷。④〖美俗〗乏味的人。⑤〖美俗〗無聊之談。

drip-dry [ˈdrɪpˌdraɪ; ˈdripdrai] *v.*, **-dried, -dry·ing,** *adj.* —*v.i.* 隨洗隨乾。—*adj.* 隨洗隨乾的。

drip·ping [ˈdrɪpɪŋ; ˈdripiŋ] *n.* ①滴落;滴落之物。②(*pl.*)炙肉時滴落之油脂;機器滴下的油。—*adj.* ①濕透的。*dripping* wet. 濕透的。②落雨的。

drip·stone [ˈdrɪpˌston; ˈdripstoun] *n.* ①〖建築〗簷溜石;滴水石。②〖礦〗濾石。

dript [drɪpt; dript] *v.* pt. & pp. of **drip.**

‡**drive** [draɪv; draiv] *v.*, **drove, dri·ven, driv·ing,** *n.* —*v.t.* ①驅使;迫使。Hunger *drove* him to steal. 饑餓迫使他偷竊。②駕

駛。to *drive* a car. 駕車。③發動;推動。This machinery is *driven* by steam. 這機器是用蒸汽推動。④趕走;驅逐。The enemy were *driven* out of the city. 敵人被逐出城。⑤努力經營。He is *driving* a roaring trade. 他生意興隆。⑥打(球);擊(球)。⑦(大規模)開掘(隧道等)。⑧釘入;打進;鑽入(釘子、螺絲、木樁等)。With one blow he *drove* the nail home. 祇一下他就把釘子釘進去了。⑨盡力完成。to *drive* a good bargain. 作一筆有利的交易。⑩使(木頭)沿河漂下。—*v.i.* ①駕駛;乘車。②打球;擊球。③向前疾駛;被風吹送。***drive a person into a corner*** 追逼某人使無法逃遁;駁倒某人;難倒某人。***drive at*** 用意所在。***drive away at*** 努力做。***drive on*** 繼續進行。***drive out*** 逐出。***let drive*** 射擊;打擊;瞄準。—*n.* ①駕駛;駕遊。We had a very pleasant *drive.* 我們的乘車旅行非常愉快。②車路(尤指 driveway "從花園中通到房屋的車路或林中開闢之通路")。③力量;精力;能力。④爲某一目標而發起的運動。⑤驅策力。⑥驅策。⑦重擊。⑧〖軍〗大規模攻勢。⑨(被驅的)一羣;一堆。a *drive* of cattle. 一羣牛。⑩驅趕獸羣的跋涉。⑪(球之)一擊。⑫驅動方式。front-wheel *drive.* (汽車)前輪驅動。

drive-in [ˈdraɪvˌɪn; ˈdraivin] *n.* 免下車餐館;免下車電影院。

driv·el [ˈdrɪvl; ˈdrivl] *v.,* **-el(l)ed, -el(l)ing,** *n.* —*v.i.* ①流涎;流涕。②胡說八道;說無聊話。—*v.t.* ①笨拙地說。②荒廢;浪費。—*n.* ①流涎。②無聊的話。

driv·el·(l)er [ˈdrɪvlə; ˈdrivlə] *n.* 流涎者;胡說的人;呆子。

‡**driv·en** [ˈdrɪvən; ˈdrivən] *v.* pp. of drive. —*adj.* ①難以阻遏的;勢不可當的。②吹積的;飄積的。

***driv·er** [ˈdraɪvɚ; ˈdraivə] *n.* ①馬車夫。②司機。③牧人。④監工;工頭。⑤〖機械〗主動輪;傳動輪。⑥一種高爾夫球棒。⑦驅使者。

driv·er·ship [ˈdraɪvɚʃɪp; ˈdraivəʃip] *n.* (汽車)駕駛技術或修養。

driver's license (汽車)駕駛執照。

driver's seat ①駕駛員坐位。②領導地位;控制性地位。

drive·way [ˈdraɪvˌwe; ˈdraivwei] *n.* ①私用車道。②馬路;汽車道。

driv·ing [ˈdraɪvɪŋ; ˈdraiviŋ] *adj.* ①推進的;有推進力的。②充滿活力的;精力充沛的。③驅策別人的。④感人的;動人的。—*n.* 開車;駕駛。—**ly,** *adv.*

driving iron 一種鐵頭高爾夫球棒。

driving wheel 傳動輪;主動輪。(亦作 **drive wheel**)

driz·zle [ˈdrɪzl; ˈdrizl] *v.,* **-zled, -zling,** *n.* —*v.i.* 下細雨;下毛毛雨。—*v.t.* ①使成細滴降下。②以細滴潤濕。—*n.* 細雨;毛毛雨。

driz·zly [ˈdrɪzlɪ; ˈdrizli] *adj.* 雨濛濛的。

dro·gher [ˈdrogɚ; ˈdrougə] *n.* ①(西印度羣島等地之笨重而緩慢)沿岸航行之小帆船。②挑夫。

drogue [drog; droug] *n.* = **sea anchor.**

droit [drɔɪt; drɔit] *n.* ①(法律上之)權利;所有權。②所有物;對之可主張權利之物。③法律;正義;衡平。④(*pl.*)稅;關稅。

droll [drol; droul] *adj.* 有趣的;滑稽的。—*n.* ①小丑。②小鬧劇。—*v.i.* 逗笑;開玩笑。

droll·er·y [ˈdrolərɪ; ˈdrouləri] *n., pl.* **-er·ies.** ①滑稽之事;詼諧之事。②笑話。③幽默;詼諧。 「幽默;詼諧。」

droll·ness [ˈdrolnɪs; ˈdroulnis] *n.*

drol·ly [ˈdrolɪ; ˈdrouli] *adv.* 幽默地;詼諧地。 「場。—*v.i.* 飛行;起飛。」

drome [drom; droum] *n.* 〖俚〗飛機

drom·e·dar·y [ˈdrɑməˌdɛrɪ; ˈdrʌmədəri] *n., pl.* **-dar·ies.** 單峯駝。

drone [dron; droun] *n., v.,* **droned, dron·ing.** —*n.* ①雄蜂。②依賴他人勞力而生活的人;怠惰的人。③作嗡嗡聲。the *drone* of a bee. 蜜蜂的嗡嗡聲。④單調的低音。⑤無線電控制的無人飛機;靶機。—*v.i.* ①閑散度日。②作嗡嗡聲。③(時間)單調平板地過去。—*v.t.* ①以單調的低聲說出。②於閑散中虛度。 「手好閑的;懶惰的。」

dron·ish [ˈdronɪʃ; ˈdrouniʃ] *adj.* 遊

drool [drul; druːl] *v.i.* ①流涎;流口水。②(口水)自口中流下。③〖俚〗胡言;說無聊話。④顯露過度快樂或預期之快樂。—*v.t.* ①讓…自口中流下。②〖俚〗愚蠢地說;無聊地說;胡言。—*n.* ①口水;流涎。②〖俚〗無聊話;傻話。

***droop** [drup; druːp] *v.i.* ①下垂;低垂。②憔悴;消沈;枯萎。His spirits *drooped.* 他精神不振。③變弱;精力喪生。④〖詩〗下沉。—*v.t.* 〖罕〗使下垂;使沉下。—*n.* 下垂;低垂。—**ing·ly,** *adv.*

droop·y [ˈdrupɪ; ˈdruːpi] *adj.,* **droop·i·er, droop·i·est.** ①下垂的。②無精打采的。

‡**drop** [drɑp; drɔp] *n., v.,* **dropped** or **dropt, drop·ping.** —*n.* ①滴;點。There were a few *drops* of rain. 下了幾滴雨。②下降;落下。There was a sudden *drop* of temperature. 溫度驟降。③下降的距離;高低兩物間的距離。④少量的液體。⑤如滴點的東西。fruit *drops.* 果汁糖。⑥(*pl.*)以滴計量的藥水。⑦陡坡。⑧投寄中心。a mail *drop.* 投郵處。⑨〖軍〗**a.** 一次戰役中空降的部隊。**b.** 空投補給;空投補給之量。**c.** 空降。⑩(信箱等的)投遞口。⑪剛生下之動物。***a drop in the bucket*** (or ***ocean***) 滄海一粟。***at the drop of a hat*** **a.** 發出信號時。**b.** 立刻;動輒…;動不動就…。***get*** (or ***have***) ***the drop on*** 〖俚〗**a.** 先發制人。**b.** 占上風;占優勢。***in drops*** 一滴滴地。—*v.i.* ①滴下;滴落。②落下。③跌傷;跌倒;跌死。④終止;作罷。Let the matter *drop.* 這事聽其作罷。⑤退出;離開;不見〖常 out〗。⑥蹲踞;彎身(如獵犬見到獵物時)。⑦下降;下跌;減低;減少。The prices *drop* sharply. 物價驟跌。⑧不用力而轉入某種狀態。⑨緩緩流下。⑩退後;落後;墜下;貶降。⑪不期而至;過訪〖常 in, by, over〗. *Drop* over to our house for a visit sometime. 有工夫請到我們家來玩。⑫生產。—*v.t.* ①使滴下;使滴入。②使跌下;失落;使落下;擲下;放開。③生下;生產。④有意無意地或偶然地說出;暗示。to *drop* a hint on the subject. 對於這問題予以暗示。⑤投寄;簡略寫寄。Please *drop* me a line whenever you have time. 暇時祈惠我短信。⑥射擊;射落。⑦使(人或物)離開船車;卸(貨)。Where shall I *drop* you? 我應在甚麼地方讓你下車?⑧脫落;漏掉;去掉;刪去(字母)。⑨放低聲音。⑩棄去;終止;作罷。⑪〖美〗開除(學生);解雇;斥退。He was *dropped* from the college. 他被這學院開除。⑫退修。⑬投進;踢進;射進。⑭輸。⑮空投(人員、物資等)。⑯〖航海〗超前。⑰使落後。⑱放下(飛機的起落架)。⑲將(衣服的滾邊)放長。⑳將(蛋)加水打勻。㉑〖足球〗球着地未及彈起卽將(球)踢出去;如此踢球而得分。***drop across*** (***a person***) 〖俗〗偶遇(某人)。***drop a line*** 垂釣。***drop anchor*** 拋錨。***drop away*** 離開;減少。***drop behind***

落伍;落後。*drop in* 偶然過訪;不先期預告的拜訪。He *dropped in* on us occasionally. 他不時來訪我們。*drop off* a. 減退;減低;減少。Sales have *dropped off*. 銷路減退。b. 睡着。to *drop off* into a doze. 打瞌睡。c. 失蹤;離開。*drop out* 不參與;離去;放棄。*drop through* 崩潰;失敗。

drop curtain 舞臺前之垂幕。

drop-forge ['drɑp'fɔrdʒ; 'drɔp'fɔːdʒ] *v.t.*, **-forged, -forg·ing.** 以落鎚鍛鍊(燒熱的金屬)。

drop hammer 一種用重力壓金屬的機器;落鎚。

drop·head ['drɑp,hɛd; 'drɔphed] *n.* 【英】有活動摺篷之汽車。

drop-in ['drɑp,ɪn; 'drɔpin] *n.* ①(亦作 **dropper-in**) 偶然過訪者。②偶然過訪處。

drop kick 【足球】落地踢中。

drop-kick ['drɑp,kɪk; 'drɔpkik] *v.t.* & *v.i.* 【足球】球着地時未及彈起卽踢出去。

drop leaf 桌面可以放下的延展部分。

drop·let ['drɑplɪt; 'drɔplit] *n.* 小滴。

drop letter 【美】由同一郵局收發的信件。

drop·light ['drɑp,laɪt; 'drɔplait] *n.* 可上下移動之吊燈。

drop-off ['drɑp,ɑf; 'drɔpɔf] *n.* ①降低;減少。②陡然的下降。

drop-out, drop·out ['drɑp,aʊt; 'drɔpaut] *n.* ①中途退學。②中途退學學生。③脫離傳統社會加入急進分子或嬉皮集團者。

drop·per ['drɑpɚ; 'drɔpə] *n.* ①使液體或溶液滴落之人或物。②【醫】滴管。

drop·ping ['drɑpɪŋ; 'drɔpiŋ] *n.* ①(使)滴落;(使)滴下;降下。②落下之物; 滴下物。③ (*pl.*) 獸糞;鳥糞。

drop·scene ['drɑp,sin; 'drɔpsiːn] *n.* ①(垂於戲臺之)景幕。②戲劇每一幕之結局。

drop shot 【網球】過網卽落地而甚少反躍之球。

drop shut·ter [~'ʃʌtɚ; ~'ʃʌtə] 【照相】瞬間開閉器;快門。

drop·si·cal ['drɑpsɪkl; 'drɔpsikəl] *adj.* 水腫性的;患水腫的。—**ly,** *adv.*

drop·sy ['drɑpsɪ; 'drɔpsi] *n.* 【醫】水腫; 浮腫。

dropt [drɑpt; drɔpt] *v.* pt. & pp. of **drop.**

drosh·ky ['drɑʃkɪ; 'drɔʃki] *n., pl.* **-kies.** 俄國四輪敞篷馬車。(亦作 **drosky**)

dro·soph·i·la [dro'sɑfələ; drɔ'sɔfilə] *n., pl.* **-lae** [-li; -liː]. 果蠅。

dross [drɔs; drɔs] *n.* ①渣滓。②無用之物。③【英】無價值之煤。

dross·y ['drɔsɪ; 'drɔsi] *adj.,* **dross·i·er, dross·i·est.** 無價值的;含渣滓的;不純淨的。

***drought** [draʊt; draut] *n.* ①久旱。②乾;乾燥。【注意】在正式英語中, 通用 **drought.** 在非正式英語中, 常用 **drouth.**

drought·y ['draʊtɪ; 'drauti] *adj.,* **drought·i·er, drought·i·est.** ①乾的; 乾燥的。②缺乏雨水的;旱的。③【方】口渴的。

drouth [draʊθ; drauθ] *n.* =**drought.**

‡**drove**[1] [drov; drouv] *v.* pt. of **drive.**

drove[2] *n., v.,* **droved, drov·ing.** —*n.* ①一羣動物(如牛、羊等)。②一羣的人。③(亦作 **drove chisel**) 石匠用的一種鑿子。④(亦作 **drove work**) 經石匠用鑿子處理過的石頭表面。—*v.t.* & *v.i.* 做牲畜買賣;趕牲畜。

dro·ver ['drovɚ; 'drouvə] *n.* 牲畜販子; 驅牛、羊等入市的人。

***drown** [draʊn; draun] *v.i.* 淹溺;溺死。He jumped into the river to save the *drowning* man. 他跳入河中, 去救將溺斃的人。—*v.t.* ①淹死;溺死。②消滅;消除。He *drowned* his cares in wine. 他以酒消愁。③使氾濫。Her eyes were *drowned* in tears. 她熱淚盈眶。④加太多的水。⑤淹沒;壓制。⑥(在生石灰上)加水(使變熟石灰)。—**er,** *n.* —**ing·ly,** *adv.*

drown·ing ['draʊnɪŋ; 'drauniŋ] *n.* 溺死。

drowse [draʊz; drauz] *v.,* **drowsed, drows·ing,** *n.* —*v.i.* ①假寐;打瞌睡。②發呆。—*v.t.* ①使昏睡。②糊里糊塗地度過【away】. —*n.* 瞌睡。

***drow·sy** ['draʊzɪ; 'drauzi] *adj.,* **-si·er, -si·est.** ①半睡的;昏昏欲睡的。②沉寂的;呆滯的。③令人昏昏欲睡的。—**drow·si·ness,** *n.*

drub [drʌb; drʌb] *v.,* **drubbed, drub·bing,** *n.* —*v.t.* ①棒打; 毆打。②强迫灌注。③徹底打敗。④踏;頓(足)。—*v.i.* ①連敲;打。②咚咚踏聲。—*n.* 短棒的敲打。

drub·bing ['drʌbɪŋ; 'drʌbiŋ] *n.* ①痛毆。②徹底擊敗。

drudge [drʌdʒ; drʌdʒ] *n., v.,* **drudged, drudg·ing.** —*n.* 服賤役的人;作苦工的人。—*v.i.* 服賤役;作苦工。

drudg·er·y ['drʌdʒərɪ; 'drʌdʒəri] *n., pl.* **-er·ies.** 沉悶、辛苦、或無興趣之工作。

***drug** [drʌg; drʌg] *n., v.,* **drugged, drug·ging.** —*n.* ①藥物; 藥材; 藥劑。②麻醉藥(如鴉片、嗎啡等)。*a drug on* (or *in*) *the market* (因供應太多而難銷的)滯銷貨。—*v.t.* ①混麻醉藥或毒藥於食物或飲料中。②用藥使麻醉;用藥使昏迷。—*v.i.* 【俗】吸毒。

drug addict 吸毒者; 癮君子。

drug·get ['drʌgɪt; 'drʌgit] *n.* (印度產之)粗地毯;厚毯。

drug·gist ['drʌgɪst; 'drʌgist] *n.* 藥商;藥劑師。

drug·gy ['drʌgɪ; 'drʌgi] *n.* 【美】吃麻醉藥者;吸毒者。

drug·push·er ['drʌg,puʃɚ; 'drʌg,puʃə] *n.* 販賣毒品者。

drug·store ['drʌg,stor; 'drʌgstɔː] *n.* 【美】藥房;雜貨店。

drugstore cowboy 【美俗】①愛吹牛的年輕人; 討女人歡喜的男人; 女人氣的男人。②閒蕩者; 無業遊民。③穿牛仔服而實際非牛仔的人。

dru·id ['druɪd; 'dru(ː)id] *n.* ①督伊德教(古時 Gaul 人與 Briton 人的宗教)之教徒。② (D-) 1781 年倫敦成立的共濟會會員。

dru·id·ic [dru'ɪdɪk; dru(ː)'idik] *adj.* 督伊德教(徒)的。(亦作 **druidical**)

dru·id·ism ['druɪdɪzm; 'dru(ː)idizəm] *n.* 督伊德教; 該教之教義或儀式。

***drum** [drʌm; drʌm] *n., v.,* **drummed, drum·ming.** —*n.* ①鼓。②鼓聲; 類似鼓聲的聲音。③鼓形的東西。④【機械】鼓輪。⑤盛裝油、食物等之鼓狀容器。⑥【解剖】鼓膜。⑦【解剖】鼓室。*beat the drum* 宣傳。*beat the drums for* 竭力擁護;鼓吹;主張。—*v.i.* ①擊鼓。②作鼓聲。to *drum* with one's finger on the table. 以指彈桌上作鳴鼓聲。—*v.t.* ①擊鼓奏(曲);擊…使發出咚咚聲。②鳴鼓召集。③反覆進言;絮絮不休。to *drum* lessons into a boy's head. 將功課反覆溫習, 使小孩記住。*drum out* 開除。*drum up* a. 召集。b. 招徠(生意)。c. 喚起;爭取。

drum·beat ['drʌm,bit; 'drʌmbiːt] *n.* 鼓音;打鼓。

drum-beat·er ['drʌm,bitɚ; 'drʌm,biːtə] *n.* 【俗】①宣傳員。②對某種政策、主張等大事宣傳者。

drum·beat·ing ['drʌm'bitɪŋ; 'drʌm'biːtiŋ] *n.* 廣告;宣傳。

drum corps 鼓樂隊。

drum·fire 〔'drʌm,faɪr; 'drʌm,faiə〕 *n.* ①(似鼓聲般之)連續不斷的砲火。②不斷的猛烈攻擊。

drum·head 〔'drʌm,hɛd; 'drʌmhed〕 *n.* ①鼓皮。②耳鼓。③絞盤之頂部。—*adj.* 簡短而直接的;迅速而不注重形式的。

drum·lin 〔'drʌmlɪn; 'drʌmlin〕 *n.*〖地質〗冰河堆積成之橢圓形冰丘。

drum major 樂隊指揮;鼓樂隊隊長。

drum ma·jor·ette 〔~,medʒə'rɛt; ~,meidʒə'ret〕 drum major 之女性。(亦作 **majorette**)

drum·mer 〔'drʌmɚ; 'drʌmə〕 *n.* ①鼓手。②〖美〗旅行推銷員。

drum·stick 〔'drʌm,stɪk; 'drʌmstik〕 *n.* ①鼓槌。②鼓槌形之物(如鷄腿等)。

‡**drunk** 〔drʌŋk; drʌŋk〕 *v.* pp. of **drink.** —*adj.* ①醉的。He is *drunk.* 他醉了。②陶醉。***drunk as a lord*** 酣醉。***get drunk*** 醉。—*n.* ①醉酒者。②酒宴。〖注意〗**drunk, drunken** 作形容詞用而置於所形容之名詞前面時, drunken 較爲合適。

***drunk·ard** 〔'drʌŋkəd; 'drʌŋkəd〕 *n.* 醉漢;酒徒。

***drunk·en** 〔'drʌŋkən; 'drʌŋkən〕 *adj.* ①醉的。②由於醉酒的。a *drunken* quarrel. 醉後爭吵。③常常酗酒的;常醉的。—**ness,** *n.*

drunk·om·e·ter 〔drʌŋ'kɑmɪtɚ; drʌŋ'kɔmətə〕 *n.* 測酒計(測量駕車者是否喝酒及其所喝酒量多寡之儀器)。

dru·pa·ceous 〔dru'peʃəs; druː'peiʃəs〕 *adj.* 核果狀的;結核果的。

drupe 〔drup; druːp〕 *n.* 核果。

drupe·let 〔'druplɪt; 'druːplit〕 *n.*〖植物〗小核果。

‡**dry** 〔draɪ; drai〕 *adj.,* **dri·er, dri·est,** *v.,* **dried, dry·ing,** *n.* —*adj.* ①乾的。*Dry* wood will burn. 乾柴可燃。②缺少雨水的;乾旱的;乾燥的。a *dry* climate. 乾燥的氣候。③乾涸的。④缺奶的;無奶的。The cow is *dry.* 母牛缺奶。⑤無淚的;不哭的。⑥口渴的。⑦不在水中的。on *dry* land. 在陸地。⑧枯燥無味的;缺乏趣味的。a *dry* book. 枯燥無味的書。⑨毫無表情的。⑩不加甜味的。⑪禁酒的。⑫明白的;不加修飾的。⑬漠然的;冷淡的。⑭引起口渴的。⑮(麪包、餅干等)陳的;不新鮮的。⑯(英國餅干)不甜的。⑰(鷄尾酒)未加苦艾酒的。⑱(建築)不用水泥或混凝土的。⑲(瓷器)未上釉或上釉不足的。⑳(作家、藝術家等)沒有作品發表的。㉑(藝術作品)生硬的。㉒〖軍〗非實彈演練的。㉓付現款的。***dry as a bone*** 非常乾的。***not dry behind the ears*** 未成熟的;不懂世故的。—*v.t.* 使乾。*Dry* your eyes. 拭乾你的眼睛。—*v.i.* 乾。***dry out*** 變乾。***dry up*** **a.** 乾涸;枯竭。**b.** 停止說話。*Dry up!* 住口!**c.** 忘記臺詞或動作。**d.** (作家或藝術家等)失去創造力。—*n.* ①〖美俗〗主張禁酒者。②乾燥區。—**ness,** *n.*

Dry·ad, dry·ad 〔'draɪəd; 'draiəd〕 *n., pl.* **-ads, -a·des** 〔-ə,diz; -ədiːz〕.〖希臘神話〗森林女神。

dry·as·dust 〔'draɪəz,dʌst; 'draiəzdʌst〕 *n.* 研究枯燥無味問題的學者;無趣味的腐儒。—*adj.* 枯燥無味的;賣弄學問的。

dry battery 乾電池。

dry-bones 〔'draɪ,bonz; 'draibounz〕 *n.* 骨瘦如柴之人。

dry bread 無牛油的麪包。

dry cell 乾電池。

dry-clean 〔'draɪ'klin; 'drai'kliːn〕 *v.t.* 乾洗。

dry cleaner ①乾洗用的揮發油。②乾洗商店或工人。

dry cleaning 乾洗。

dry-cure 〔'draɪ,kjur; 'drai,kjuə〕 *v.t.,* **-cured, -cur·ing.** 晒乾醃藏(魚、肉等)。

Dry·den 〔'draɪdn̩; 'draidn〕 *n.* 德萊敦(John, 1631–1700, 英國詩人及劇作家, 1670–88 爲桂冠詩人)。

dry distillation 乾餾。

dry-dock 〔'draɪ'dɑk; 'drai'dɔk〕 *v.t.* ①使入乾船塢。②使停職。—*v.i.* ①入乾船塢。②被停職。

dry dock 乾船塢。

dry·er 〔'draɪɚ; 'draiə〕 *n.* =**drier.**

dry-farm 〔'draɪ,fɑrm; 'draifɑːm〕 *v.t.* & *v.i.* 在(土地)上從事乾燥農耕。

dry farmer 作乾燥農耕的農夫。

dry farming 乾燥農耕(在乾燥區的耕作,不藉助於灌溉,多靠土壤本身保留自然濕氣而耕種耐乾作物)。

dry fly 釣魚時用的浮在水面上的假蠅餌。

dry goods ①〖美〗布疋或毛織物等。②〖英〗穀類。

dry hole 出油量不足的新油井。

dry ice 乾冰。

dry law 禁酒令。

***dry·ly** 〔'draɪlɪ; 'draili〕 *adv.* ①乾燥地。②枯燥無味地。③冷淡地。(亦作 **drily**)

dry measure 乾量(量乾物的量)。

dry nurse ①(不餵奶的)褓姆。②〖俗〗教導無經驗之上級長官的人。

dry plate 舊式照相用的玻璃底片。

dry point ①用針雕刻(非用酸腐蝕)的銅版。②雕刻銅版用的針。

dry rot 乾枯;乾蝕;內部之逐漸腐敗(如道德墮落)。

dry run ①不用實彈之輕武器演習。②任何演練;排演。

dry-salt 〔'draɪ,sɔlt; 'draisɔːlt〕 *v.t.* = **dry-cure.**

dry·salt·er 〔'draɪ,sɔltɚ; 'drai,sɔːltə〕 *n.*〖英〗乾貨商;鹹貨商;藥品染料商。

dry shaver 〖英〗電動刮鬍刀。

dry-shod 〔'draɪ'ʃɑd; 'drai'ʃɔd〕 *adj.* & *adv.* 所穿之鞋未濕的(地);脚未致濕的(地)。

dry wall 未使用灰泥(mortar)建造的牆(現通常指工廠中預造的牆)。

dry wash 洗過而尚未燙過的乾衣服。

dry well =**dry hole.**

Ds (亦作 **Dy**) 化學元素 dysprosium 之符號。 **D.S.** ①Doctor of Science. ②Dental Surgeon. ③Distinguished Service. ④〖音樂〗dal segno(義 =from the sign). **d.s.** ①daylight saving. ②day's sight. ③days after sight. **D.Sc.** Doctor of Science. **D.S.C.** Distinguished Service Cross. **D.S.M.** Distinguished Service Medal. **D.S.O.** Distinguished Service Order. **D.S.S.** Doctor of Social Science. **D.S.T.** Daylight Saving Time. **D. Surg.** Dental Surgeon. **D.T.** ①Daily Telegraph. ②Doctor of Theology. **d.t., d.t.'s** delirium tremens. 震戰性譫妄;酒狂。 **D.Th., D. Theol.** Doctor of Theology. **Du.** ① Dutch. ②duke.

du·ad 〔'djuæd; 'djuːæd〕 *n.* ①包括二個之一組;一對。②〖化〗二價元素。

du·al 〔'djuəl; 'dju(ː)əl〕 *adj.* ①二的;二重的;二體的;兩層的。②〖文法〗雙數的。

du·al·in 〔'djuəlɪn; 'dju(ː)əlin〕 *n.* (一種由硝化甘油、硝石、及鋸屑配製成之)雙硝炸藥。(亦作 **dualine**)

du·al·ism 〔'djuəl,ɪzəm; 'dju(ː)əlizəm〕

n. 〖哲學、神學〗二元論。**—du·al·ist,** *n.*
du·al·is·tic 〔ˌdjuəlˈɪstɪk; ˌdju(:)əˈlistik〕 *adj.* 二元的; 二元論的。 「二重性;二元性。」
du·al·i·ty 〔djuˈælətɪ; dju(:)ˈæliti〕 *n.*
dual nationality 雙重國籍。
dub[1] 〔dʌb; dʌb〕 *v.t.*, **dubbed, dub·bing.** ①授以勳爵(在授勳典禮中以劍輕擊其肩)。②授以稱號;呼名;起綽號。③削光;磨光;打光。
dub[2] *n.* 笨拙之人。 ④置餌於釣鉤。
dub[3] *v.t.* ①〖電影〗改換影片之錄音;爲(影片)配音。②將(錄音)製成唱片。③加(聲音)於。—*n.* 所加配之聲音。
dub[4] *v.*, **dubbed, dub·bing,** *n.* —*v.t.* & *v.i.* 刺;推;蔽打。—*n.* ①刺;推;蔽打。②鼓聲。
dub[5] *n.* 〖蘇〗水潭;污水坑。
dub·bin 〔ˈdʌbɪn; ˈdʌbin〕 *n.* = **dubbing.**
dub·bing 〔ˈdʌbɪŋ; ˈdʌbiŋ〕 *n.* 皮革用防水油。 「*n., pl.* **-ties.** ①懷疑。②疑點。」
du·bi·e·ty 〔djuˈbaɪətɪ; dju(:)ˈbaiəti〕
du·bi·ous 〔ˈdjubɪəs; ˈdju:biəs〕 *adj.* ①懷疑的。②可疑的。③曖昧的。④結果未定的。**—ly,** *adv.*
du·bi·ta·ble 〔ˈdjubɪtəbl; ˈdju:bitəbl〕 *adj.* 可疑的;不確定的;不切實的。
du·bi·ta·tion 〔ˌdjubəˈteʃən; ˌdju:biˈteiʃən〕 *n.* 懷疑;疑慮。
Dub·lin 〔ˈdʌblɪn; ˈdʌblin〕 *n.* 都柏林(愛爾蘭共和國的首都)。 「公爵之領地的。」
du·cal 〔ˈdjukl; ˈdju(:)kəl〕 *adj.* 公爵的;
duc·at 〔ˈdʌkət; ˈdʌkət〕 *n.* ①古歐洲之金或銀幣名;貨幣。②〖俗〗票(=ticket)。③(*pl.*)〖俚〗錢。 「女公爵;公爵之未亡人。」
*__duch·ess__ 〔ˈdʌtʃɪs; ˈdʌtʃis〕 *n.* 公爵夫人;
duch·y 〔ˈdʌtʃɪ; ˈdʌtʃi〕 *n., pl.* **duch·ies.** 公爵所管轄的領地;公國。
*__duck__[1] 〔dʌk; dʌk〕 *n.* ①鴨;母鴨。②做食物之鴨肉。③親愛的人或小動物。④〖俚〗人;傢伙。 ***a duck's egg*** 零分。 ***a fine day for young ducks*** 下雨的天氣。 ***a lame duck*** **a.** 行動失靈的人或船。 **b.** 任期未滿而不能再競選連任或競選失敗者。 ***a sitting duck*** 無助或無法還擊之人或物。 ***like water off a duck's back*** 無效果;無結果。 (***take to something***) ***like a duck to water*** 自然地;毫不猶疑。
duck[2] *v.i.* ①沒入水中;入水卽出。②急速俯身。③閃避(打擊等)。 ***duck out*** 逃避。—*v.t.* ①投入水中;浸(頭)入水卽出。②急速低(頭)或彎(身)。③閃避(打擊)。④〖俗〗逃避。—*n.* 俯身閃避或略浸入水中卽出的動作。
duck[3] *n.* ①細帆布;堅韌的棉布或麻布。②(*pl.*)(作 *pl.* 解)細帆布製成的褲子。
duck[4] *n.* 水鴨子(水陸兩用之軍用卡車,用以運送軍需品或軍隊者)。
duck·bill 〔ˈdʌkˌbɪl; ˈdʌkbil〕 *n.* 鴨嘴獸。
duck·board 〔ˈdʌkˌbɔrd; ˈdʌkbɔ:d〕 *n.* 戰壕上的遮泥板;鋪於泥濘道路或地面之木板。
duck·er[1] 〔ˈdʌkɚ; ˈdʌkə〕 *n.* ①潛水者。②潛水之鳥;鷿鷈。
duck·er[2] *n.* ①飼鴨者。②獵野鴨者。
duck hawk 〖美〗鷹隼。
duck·ing 〔ˈdʌkɪŋ; ˈdʌkiŋ〕 *n.* ①濕透;浸沒水中。②獵野鴨。③急速低頭。
ducking stool 浸水椅(古刑具)。
duck·ling 〔ˈdʌklɪŋ; ˈdʌkliŋ〕 *n.* 小鴨。
duck·pin 〔ˈdʌkˌpɪn; ˈdʌkpin〕 *n.* 〖保齡球〗①(*pl.*)(作 *sing.* 解)十瓶之保齡球(戲)。②此球戲所用之木瓶。
duck soup 〖美俚〗輕而易擧之事。
duck·weed 〔ˈdʌkˌwid; ˈdʌkwi:d〕 *n.* 〖植物〗水萍。
duck·y[1] 〔ˈdʌkɪ; ˈdʌki〕 *adj.*, **duck·i·er, duck·i·est.** 〖俚〗最好的;令人愉快的;可愛的。
duck·y[2] *n., pl.* **duck·ies.** 〖英俚〗親愛的。
duct 〔dʌkt; dʌkt〕 *n.* ①(導水、空氣等的)管;輸送管。②排泄管。③包電纜之管。**—less,** *adj.*
duc·tile 〔ˈdʌktl; ˈdʌktail〕 *adj.* ①(金屬等)可延展的。②柔軟的;易於塑鑄的。③馴順的。 「延展性;柔和性;順從。」
duc·til·i·ty 〔dʌkˈtɪlətɪ; dʌkˈtiliti〕 *n.*
ductless gland 無管腺;內分泌腺。
duct·work 〔ˈdʌktˌwɝk; ˈdʌktwə:k〕 *n.* 通風系統之通風管。
dud 〔dʌd; dʌd〕 *n.* ①〖俗〗衣服的一件。②(*pl.*)服裝的集合稱(尤指破舊者)。③(*pl.*)一般的財物。④〖俗〗失敗之人或事。⑤發射出而未爆炸的砲彈或炸彈。⑥失望;失敗。
dude 〔djud; dju:d〕 *n.* ①花花公子。②〖美西俚〗都市人;在牧場度假之都市人(尤指東部人)。 「製之短柄煙斗。」
du·deen 〔duˈdin; du:ˈdi:n〕 *n.* 〖愛〗陶
dude ranch 作爲遊覽區而經營的牧場。
dudg·eon 〔ˈdʌdʒən; ˈdʌdʒən〕 *n.* 憤怒。 ***in high dudgeon*** 極爲憤怒。
du·dheen 〔duˈdin; du:ˈdi:n〕 *n.* = **dudeen.**
dud·ish 〔ˈdjudɪʃ; ˈdju:diʃ〕 *adj.* 花花公子的;有紈袴氣的;好修飾的。
‡**due** 〔dju; dju:〕 *adj.* ①到期的;應付給的。When is the rent *due?* 房租應於何時付給? ②適當的;合宜的。in *due* time. 在適當的時期。in *due* course. 順序;及時。Respect is *due* to older people. 年長者應受尊敬。③應到的;預期的。Our train is *due* at Taichung at 7 a.m. 我們的火車應於早晨七時到臺中。④充分的。⑤由於;起因於〖to〗。The accident was *due* to careless driving. 這意外事件起因於駕駛疏忽。 ***become*** (or ***fall***) ***due*** 應給付。 ***due to*** 由於;因…而產生。—*n.* ①應得的東西。②(*pl.*)到期應付的款;稅;按期應繳的費。I have paid my club *dues.* 我已繳會費。 ***give*** (***a person***) ***his due*** **a.** 公平待人;善待他人。 **b.** 不抹煞自己不喜歡的人的功勞或優點。 ***give the devil his due*** 不掩沒惡人的長處。—*adv.* 正向地;直接地。The wind is *due* east. 這風是向正東吹。
due bill 借據。
*__du·el__ 〔ˈdjuəl; ˈdju(:)əl〕 *n., v.*, **-el(l)ed, -el·(l)ing.** —*n.* 決鬥;相鬥。I challenge you to a *duel.* 我向你挑戰;作一決鬥。—*v.i.* 決鬥。
du·el·(l)ing 〔ˈdjuəlɪŋ; ˈdju(:)əliŋ〕 *n.* 決鬥;決鬥術。 「決鬥者;精於決鬥者。」
du·el·(l)ist 〔ˈdjuəlɪst; ˈdju(:)əlist〕 *n.*
du·en·na 〔djuˈɛnə; dju(:)ˈenə〕 *n.* ①(西班牙及葡萄牙之)少女的媬姆。②女傅;陪媼。
du·et 〔djuˈɛt; dju(:)ˈet〕 *n.* ①二部合唱;二重奏。②二部合唱或二重奏之歌曲。
du·et·tist 〔djuˈɛtɪst; dju(:)ˈetist〕 *n.* 二部合唱(奏)者。 「= **duet.**」
du·et·to 〔djuˈɛto; dju(:)ˈetou〕 *n.*
duff[1] 〔dʌf; dʌf〕 *n.* ①一種布丁。②林地上之半腐的植物質。③煤屑。
duff[2] *v.t.* 〖俚〗①虛飾(貨品)以欺人;改裝;欺騙。②〖澳〗偷盜(牛、羊等)並改變其烙印。③〖高爾夫〗未擊中(球)。
duff[3] *n.* 〖俗〗笨拙者;倔強不講理之人。
duf·fel, duf·fle 〔ˈdʌfl; ˈdʌfl〕 *n.* ①有厚毛之粗毛衣。②運動員或露營者之裝具。
duffel bag 行李袋。

duff·er [ˈdʌfɚ; ˈdʌfə] *n.* ①〖英俚〗行動笨拙者;不能勝任者; 愚人。②〖俚〗贋品;品質粗劣之物品。③以劣質或贋品冒充上等商品之小販。
duffle coat 連風帽之粗呢大衣。(亦作 **duffel coat**)
dug¹ [dʌg; dʌg] *v.* pt. *&* pp. of **dig.**
dug² *n.* 雌性哺乳動物之乳頭。
Du Gard [dyˈgar;dyˈgɑː] 杜嘉(Roger Martin, 1881–1958, 法國小說家, 1937 年獲諾貝爾文學獎)。
du·gong [ˈdugɑŋ; ˈduːgɔŋ] *n.* 儒艮(水棲食草之哺乳動物)。(亦作 **sea cow**)
dug·out [ˈdʌgˌaut; ˈdʌgaut] *n.* ①防空洞; 避彈的壍壕。②獨木刳成的小舟。③棒球場邊供球員休憩之所。
:duke [djuk; djuːk] *n.* ①公爵。②公國之君主。③(*pl.*)〖俚〗手;拳頭。Put up your *dukes*. 將你的手舉起來。
duke·dom [ˈdjukdəm; ˈdju(ː)kdəm] *n.* ①公爵所管轄之地區;公國。②公爵之爵位;公國之君主的地位。
dul·cet [ˈdʌlsɪt; ˈdʌlsit] *adj.* ①愉快的;美妙的; 悅耳的。②〖古〗美味的; 有香味的。—*n.* 一種形似 dulciana 而高八度之音栓。
dul·ci·an·a [ˌdʌlsɪˈænə; ˌdʌlsiˈænə] *n.* 〖音樂〗一種音調優美之風琴音栓。
dul·ci·fi·ca·tion [ˌdʌlsɪfɪˈkeʃən; ˌdʌlsifiˈkeiʃən] *n.* 使甜美。
dul·ci·fy [ˈdʌlsəˌfaɪ; ˈdʌlsifai] *v.t.*, **-fied, -fy·ing.** ①使和好;使喜悅; 使柔和。②使甜美。
dul·ci·mer [ˈdʌlsəmɚ; ˈdʌlsimə] *n.* (用小錘擊打的絃琴)德西馬琴;楊琴;蝴蝶琴。
dul·cin·e·a [dʌlˈsɪnɪə;ˌdʌlsiˈniə] *n.* ①情人;愛人。②(D-) Don Quixote 稱呼其所愛農婦之名。
***dull** [dʌl; dʌl] *adj.* ①不銳的;鈍的。a *dull* razor. 鈍的剃刀。②無光彩的;不清楚的;暗晦的;陰沈的。a *dull* weather. 陰沉的天氣。③不聰明的;笨的。④無趣味的;單調的;枯燥無味的。a *dull* book. 枯燥無味的書。⑤不活潑的;不景氣的。Business is *dull*. 生意蕭條。⑥不太感覺得到的。a *dull* pain. 不太感覺得到的痛苦。⑦感覺遲鈍的;不敏感的。Your ears are *dull*. 你的聽覺不靈。⑧(貨物)滯銷的。—*v.t.* ①使鈍。②使暗晦;使不活潑;使麻木。—*v.i.* 變鈍。This cheap knife *dulls* easily. 這把便宜的刀容易變鈍。—**ness, dul·ness,** *n.* —**y,** *adv.*
dull·ard [ˈdʌlɚd;ˈdʌləd] *n.* 愚人;蠢物。
dull·ish [ˈdʌlɪʃ; ˈdʌliʃ] *adj.* 略遲鈍的;稍暗晦的;無趣味的。
dulse [dʌls; dʌls] *n.* 〖植物〗紅藻類之一種(可供食用)。
***du·ly** [ˈdjulɪ; ˈdjuːli] *adv.* ①正當地;適當地; 恰當地。②及時地;按時地。Your letter has been *duly* received. 來信已如期收到。③足够地;足量地;足够所需地。
Du·ma [ˈdumə; ˈduːmə] *n.* ①俄國自1905至1917 年之國會。②(d-) 國會;議會。(亦作 **Douma, douma**)
Du·mas [djuˈmɑ; ˈdjuːmɑː] *n.* ①大仲馬(Alexandre, 世稱 *Dumas père,* 1802–70, 法國小說家及劇作家)。②小仲馬(Alexandre, 世稱 *Dumas fils,* 1824–1895, 法小說家、劇作家,爲大仲馬之子)。
du Mau·ri·er [djuˈmɔrɪˌe, du-; djuːˈmɔːriei, ˈmɔr-] 杜莫里哀 (George Louis Palmella Busson, 1834–1896, 英國藝術家及小說家)。
***dumb** [dʌm; dʌm] *adj.* ①啞的。②沉默的(由於恐懼、驚奇或害羞等)。He was struck *dumb* with horror. 他因恐怖而嚇得不能出聲。③〖美俗〗愚笨的。④(車船等)無動力的。⑤缺乏某種特性的。—**ly,** *adv.* —**ness,** *n.*
Dum·bar·ton Oaks [dʌmˈbartn̩~; dʌmˈbɑːtn~] 頓巴敦橡園 (在美京華盛頓郊外, 1944年曾舉行國際會議於此)。
dumb·bell [ˈdʌmˌbɛl; ˈdʌmbel] *n.* ①啞鈴。②〖美俗〗笨漢。
dumb·found [dʌmˈfaund; dʌmˈfaund] *v.t.* =**dumfound.**
dumb millions 人民。
dumb piano 練習指法用之無聲鋼琴。
dumb show ①默劇;啞劇。②做手勢。
dumb-struck [ˈdʌmˌstrʌk; ˈdʌmstrʌk] *adj.* 張口結舌的;迷惘的。
dumb-wait·er [ˈdʌmˈwetɚ; ˈdʌmˈweitə] *n.* ①輕便之食品臺 (可置於食桌近處)。②遞送食物之升降機。
dum·dum [ˈdʌmdʌm; ˈdʌmdʌm] *n.* 達姆彈 (一種擊中目標卽行擴散而致嚴重傷害之子彈)。(亦作 **dumdum bullet**)
dum·found [dʌmˈfaund; dʌmˈfaund] *v.t.* 使人啞然失聲;使人驚惶失色。
dum·my [ˈdʌmɪ; ˈdʌmi] *n., pl.* **-mies,** *adj., v.,* **-mied, -my·ing.** —*n.* ①啞子。②(服裝店用的)人像模型;(劈刺用的)人形靶。③〖美俗〗愚笨的人。④(橋牌中的)夢家;將牌攤出的人;夢家的牌。⑤(機關中的)傀儡人物。⑥名義上的人物;用作幌子的人物。⑦冒充貨。⑧作陳列用的貨品模型或空盒等。⑨〖印刷〗大樣。⑩一種舊式火車頭。⑪〖軍〗演習用的假炸彈。 —*adj.* 仿造的;假的; 名義上的; 無聲的。—*v.t.* ①將…做大樣〖常 up〗. to *dummy* up a book. 將一本書印成大樣。②將…在大樣中印出來〖常 in〗. —*v.i.* 〖澳〗替別人占領土地。
***dump** [dʌmp; dʌmp] *v.t.* ①倒下;傾倒。②賤賣;傾銷。③丢棄;放棄。④開除。⑤〖拳擊〗**a.** 擊倒。**b.** 放水給(對方);故意輸給(對方)。—*v.i.* ①突然下降。②傾倒垃圾、廢物等。③以低價傾銷。—*n.* ①垃圾堆;垃圾場。②臨時軍需品供應站。③傾銷; 傾倒。④〖俚〗破舊不潔之處所或色情場合。
dump·cart [ˈdʌmpˌkart; ˈdʌmpkɑːt] *n.* 一種車身可以斜豎而傾出裝載物的車輛。
dump·ing [ˈdʌmpɪŋ; ˈdʌmpiŋ] *n.* ①傾棄。②海外傾銷。
dump·ish [ˈdʌmpɪʃ;ˈdʌmpiʃ] *adj.* ①遲鈍的。②憂鬱的。
dump·ling [ˈdʌmplɪŋ;ˈdʌmpliŋ] *n.* ①蒸或煮的麪糰。②蘋果或其他水果裹以麪糊,煮或烤而成的點心。③〖俗〗矮而壯的人或動物。
dumps [dʌmps; dʌmps] *n.* 〖俗〗憂鬱。(前面常加 in the).
dump truck 傾卸卡車(其裝貨之車身可向後傾斜)。
dump·y [ˈdʌmpɪ; ˈdʌmpi] *adj.,* **dump·i·er, dump·i·est,** *n.* —*adj.* ①矮而肥的。②悶悶不樂的;鬱鬱不歡的。—*n.* (蘇格蘭產的)一種矮脚鷄。
dun¹ [dʌn; dʌn] *adj., n., v.,* **dunned, dun·ning.** —*adj.*①黃褐色的; 暗褐色的。②陰暗的。—*n.* ①黃褐色。②假蚊餌(釣魚用之人造餌)。③蜉蝣。—*v.t.* 使成黃褐色。
dun² *v.,* **dunned, dun·ning,** *n.* —*v.t.* (一再的)催討(債款)。—*v.i.* 糾纏不放。—*n.* 討債;催討;催討者;收債人。
dun³ *n.* 山丘。
dunce [dʌns; dʌns] *n.* 愚蠢的人; 劣等的學生。
dunce cap 頑劣的學生受罰時所戴的圓椎形紙帽。(亦作**dunce's cap, fool's cap**)

dun·der·head ['dʌndə,hɛd; 'dʌndə-hed] *n.* 愚人；蠢物。
dun·der·pate ['dʌndə,pet; 'dʌndə-peit] *n.* =**dunderhead.**
dune [djun; dju:n] *n.* 沙丘(尤指海邊爲風吹積而成者)。
dun fly 釣魚用的假蚊餌；蜉蝣。
dung [dʌŋ; dʌŋ] *n.* ①(牛馬等之)糞便；糞肥。②汚穢；醜惡。—*v.t.*(給土地)施肥；上糞。
dun·ga·ree [,dʌŋgə'ri; ,dʌŋgə'ri:] *n.* ①粗布。②(*pl.*)粗布製的工作服。
dung beetle 蜣螂。
***dun·geon** ['dʌndʒən; 'dʌndʒən] *n.* ①地牢；囚禁犯人的地下暗牢。②城堡上防禦堅牢之塔。—*v.t.* 囚於地牢中。
dung·hill ['dʌŋ,hɪl; 'dʌŋhil] *n.* ①糞堆；堆肥。②下賤的地方、人、環境。—*adj.* 下賤的；卑賤的。
dung·y ['dʌŋɪ; 'dʌŋi] *adj.,* **dung·i·er, dung·i·est.** 滿是糞的；汚穢的。
dun·ie·was·sal ['dunɪ'wɑsəl; 'du:ni-'wɔsəl] *n.* 〖蘇〗蘇格蘭高地之二流鄉紳。
dunk [dʌŋk; dʌŋk] *v.t. & v.i.* ①浸泡(麪包、餅等)於咖啡、牛奶等中。②下水；浸。
Dun·kirk ['dʌnkɝk; dʌn'kə:k] *n.* 敦克爾克(法國北部的海口，英國駐法遠征軍於1940年由此撤退)。
dun·lin ['dʌnlɪn; 'dʌnlin] *n.* 鷸類。
dun·nage ['dʌnɪdʒ; 'dʌnidʒ] *n., v.,* **-naged, -nag·ing.** —*n.* ①行李；隨身物件。②〖航海〗包墊船貨以防受損之墊木；襯料。③〖俚〗水手或流浪漢之衣服。—*v.t.* 覆(或墊)以襯料。
dunn·ite ['dʌnaɪt; 'dʌnait] *n.* 一種有高度爆炸性之炸藥。
dun·nock ['dʌnək; 'dʌnək] *n.* 籬雀。
dun·ny ['dʌnɪ, 'dunɪ; 'dʌni, 'duni] *adj.* 〖英方〗聾的；魯鈍的。
du·o ['du:o; 'dju(:)ou] *n., pl.* **du·os, du·i** ['du:i; 'dju(:)i:].〖義〗〖音樂〗二重奏(唱)(=duet).
duo- 〖字首〗表"二"之義。
du·o·dec·i·mal [,djuə'dɛsəml, ,duə-; ,dju(:)ou'desiməl] *adj.* 十二的；十二分之一的；十二進法的。—*n.* ①十二分之一。②(*pl.*)〖數學〗十二進法。
du·o·dec·i·mo [,djuə'dɛsə,mo; ,dju(:)-ou'desimou] *n., pl.* **-mos,** *adj.* —*n.* ①十二開。②十二開之書。—*adj.* 十二開的。
du·o·de·nal [,djuə'dinl; ,dju(:)ou-'di:nəl] *adj.* 十二指腸的。
du·o·den·a·ry [,djuə'dɛnərɪ; ,dju(:)-ou'di:nəri] *adj.* =**duodecimal.**
du·o·de·ni·tis [,djuədi'naɪtɪs; ,dju(:)-oudi:'naitis] *n.* 〖醫〗十二指腸炎。
du·o·de·num [,djuə'dinəm; ,dju(:)ou-'di:nəm] *n., pl.* **-na** [-nə; -nə]. 十二指腸。
du·o·logue ['djuə,lɔg; 'djuəlɔg] *n.* ①對話(=dialogue). ②(限於二人之)對話劇。
duo·mo ['dwɔmɔ; 'dwɔ:mɔ:] *n., pl.* **-mi** [-mi; -mi:].〖義〗教區中之首要教堂；大教堂。
dup. duplicate.
dup·a·ble ['djupəbl; 'dju:pəbl] *adj.* 可欺的；易騙的。(亦作 **dupeable**)
dupe [djup, dup; dju:p] *v.,* **duped, dup·ing,** *n.* —*v.t.* 欺騙；詐欺。—*n.* (易)受欺騙的人。
dup·er ['djupɚ; 'dju:pə] *n.* 詐欺者；騙子。
dup·er·y ['djupərɪ; 'dju:pəri] *n., pl.* **-er·ies.** ①欺詐。②被騙。
du·ple ['djupl; 'dju:pl] *adj.* ①二倍的；二重的。②〖音樂〗二拍子的。
duple time (or **measure**) 二拍子。
du·plex ['djuplɛks; 'dju:pleks] *adj.* ①雙倍的；二重的。*duplex* apartment. 兩層樓的公寓。②〖機械〗二聯式的。—*n.* ①兩面顏色、表面等不同的紙。②一次可印刷紙的兩面之印刷機。
duplex house 〖美〗二家合住的房屋。
***du·pli·cate** [*adj., n.* 'djupləkɪt, -,ket; 'dju:plikit *v.* 'djuplə,ket; 'dju:plikeit] *adj., n., v.,* **-cat·ed, -cat·ing.** —*adj.* ①完全相同的；副的。We have *duplicate* keys for the front door. 我們有幾把開前門用的相同的鑰匙。②雙重的；成雙的。—*n.* 相同的東西；副本；複本。We mailed the letter but kept a *duplicate.* 我們寄出了信，但留了副本。—*v.t.* ①製複本；複製。②倍之；加倍。③使再發生；重複；重犯。She *duplicated* her former success. 她又獲得和以前一樣的成功。
duplicating machine ①複寫機。②複製機。
du·pli·ca·tion [,djuplə'keʃən; ,dju:-pli'keiʃən] *n.* ①加倍；重複。②複寫；複製；複寫物；複製物；副本；複本。
du·pli·ca·tor ['djuplə,ketɚ; 'dju:pli-keitə] *n.* ①複寫器。②複本製作人。
du·plic·i·ty [dju'plɪsətɪ; dju(:)'plisiti] *n., pl.* **-ties.** ①欺騙；口是心非；言行不一。②〖法律〗重覆而無用之陳述或答辯。
du·ra·bil·i·ty [,djurə'bɪlətɪ; ,djuərə-'biliti] *n.* 耐久性；堅固。
***du·ra·ble** ['djurəbl; 'djuərəbl] *adj.* 耐久的；不易傷損的；持久的。a *durable* pair of shoes. 一雙耐穿的鞋。—*n.* (*pl.*) 耐久之貨物。Household furnishings and appliances are *durables.* 家庭陳設及用具是耐久貨物。—**ness,** *n.* —**du·ra·bly,** *adv.*
durable goods 耐用之貨物。
du·ral·u·min [dju'ræljumɪn; djuə-'ræljumin] *n.* 一種輕而堅固之鋁合金。
du·ra ma·ter ['djurə'metɚ; 'djuərə-'meitə] 〖解剖〗硬腦膜。(亦作 **dura**)
du·ra·men [dju'remɛn; djuə'reimen] *n.*〖植物〗木心；中心木質；心材。
du·rance ['djurəns; 'djuərəns] *n.* 禁錮；監禁。
du·ra·tion** [dju'reʃən; djuə'reiʃən] *n.* 持續的時間。We hope the war will be of short *duration.* 我們希望戰爭係短期的。for the duration*** 直到結束時(尤指戰爭)。
dur·a·tive ['djurətɪv; 'djuərətiv] *adj.* 〖文法〗(動詞之)持續性的。
dur·bar ['dɝbɑr; 'də:bɑ:] *n.* 〖英印〗①覲見。②覲見之處。③本地統治者之王宮。
du·ress ['djurɪs; djuə'res] *n.* ①威脅；强迫。②監禁；束縛。(亦作 **duresse**)
du·ri·an, du·ri·on ['durɪən; 'djuə-riən] *n.* ①(東南亞所產之)榴槤果樹。②榴槤果(上述果樹所產之可食的果實)。
‡**dur·ing** ['djurɪŋ; 'djuəriŋ] *prep.* ①在…期間。The boys played *during* the afternoon. 整個下午小孩們在玩。②在…期間中的某一時間。He called *during* my absence. 我不在的時候，他來訪過。
Du·roc-Jer·sey ['djurɑk'dʒɝzɪ; 'djuərɔk'dʒə:zi] *n.* 美國產之一種紅色大猪。(亦作 **Duroc**)
dur·ra ['durə; 'durə] *n.*〖植物〗黍；玉米。(亦作 **doura, dourah**)
durst [dɝst; də:st] *v.* pt. of **dare.**
du·rum ['djurəm; 'djuərəm] *n.* 一種麩質堅硬之小麥(用於做通心粉等)。(亦作 **durum wheat**)

***dusk** [dʌsk; dʌsk] *n.* ①傍晚;黃昏;薄暮。②昏暗。She was invisible in the *dusk* of the room. 她在昏暗的房間裏別人看不到她。—*adj.* 昏暗的;黃昏的。—*v.t.* 使昏暗。—*v.i.* 變昏暗。

***dusk·y** [ˈdʌskɪ; ˈdʌski] *adj.*, **dusk·i·er, dusk·i·est.** 薄暗的;幽黑的(膚色);悽慘的。—**dusk·i·ly,** *adv.* —**dusk·i·ness,** *n.*

‡dust [dʌst; dʌst] *n.* ①灰塵;塵埃。His clothes were covered with *dust.* 他的衣服上布滿了灰塵。②紛擾;混亂。Wait until the *dust* is cleared. 等待局勢澄清。③花粉。④遺骸。⑤大地。⑥低賤的地位。⑦無價值的廢物。He treated me like *dust.* 他不把我放在眼裏。⑧〖俚〗錢。⑨土地;陸地。⑩金粉。***be in the dust*** 被羞辱;受屈辱。***bite the dust*** 被打倒;打敗;倒斃。***lick the dust*** a. 倒斃;受傷而倒。b. 奴顏婢膝地自辱。***make*** (or ***raise***) ***a dust*** 揚起灰塵;引起騷動。***make the dust fly*** 用力或加速做。***shake the dust off one's feet*** 傲然而去;憤然而去。***throw dust in a person's eyes*** 欺騙他人。—*v.t.* ①拂去灰塵;拭去灰塵。②灑以粉;撒粉於…上。③撒灰塵於…上;使多灰塵;以灰塵弄污之。—*v.i.* ①拂拭灰塵。②浴於塵土中(如鳥類)。***dust a person's jacket for him*** 用棍子好好揍一頓。***dust off*** 〖俚〗a.〖棒球〗(投手)有意將球投得與打擊手非常的近。b. 痛毆。c. 久藏後取出重用。

dust bag 眞空吸塵器內存垃圾之袋。

dust·bin [ˈdʌstˌbɪn; ˈdʌstbin] *n.* 〖英〗垃圾箱。〖注意〗在美國稱爲 ash can, garbage can 或 garbage box.

dust bowl 美國大草原 (Great Plains) 中之長久乾旱的乾燥地帶。(亦作**Dust Bowl**)

dust·brand [ˈdʌstˌbrænd; ˈdʌst-brænd] *n.* 〖植物〗黑穗病。

dust cart 〖英〗垃圾車。〖注意〗在美國稱爲 garbage wagon.

dust cloak 防灰塵之輕便外衣;罩衫。

dust-coat [ˈdʌstˌkot; ˈdʌstkout] *n.* 〖英〗風衣;防灰塵之輕便外衣。

dust color 暗褐色。

dust cover ①〖英〗(傢具等的) 防塵布套。②書皮;包書紙。

dust·er [ˈdʌstɚ; ˈdʌstə] *n.* ①打掃灰塵的人;除塵器;撣子。②防塵之長外衣。③撒粉(除蟲粉等)器。④空中撒藥粉的人。⑤婦女之輕外套。⑥〖俗〗不產油或產油量不足的油井。⑦〖棒球〗有意投得太靠近打擊手的球。⑧=**dust storm.**

dust·heap [ˈdʌstˌhip; ˈdʌsthi:p] *n.* ①垃圾堆。②默默無聞;閑置。

dust·ing [ˈdʌstɪŋ; ˈdʌstiŋ] *n.* ①拂拭;清掃。②撒粉。③〖喩〗暴風雨;船在暴風雨中之擺動。④〖俗〗毆打;擊敗。

dusting powder 撒布劑;撒粉(敷在傷口以吸水分之撲粉);爽身粉。

dust jacket 包書紙;書皮。

dust·man [ˈdʌstmən; ˈdʌstmən] *n.*, *pl.* **-men.** 〖英〗①清道夫。② =**sandman.**

dust mop (擦地板用的)長柄拖把。

dust·pan [ˈdʌstˌpæn; ˈdʌstpæn] *n.* 畚箕;糞斗。

dust·proof [ˈdʌstˈpruf; ˈdʌstpru:f] *adj.* 防塵的。

dust storm 〖氣象〗塵暴(空中充滿塵灰的風暴)。

dust·up [ˈdʌstˌʌp; ˈdʌstʌp] *n.* 〖俗〗騷動;吵鬧。

dust·y** [ˈdʌstɪ; ˈdʌsti] *adj.*, **dust·i·er, dust·i·est.** ①多灰塵的;灰塵厚積的。②如灰塵的;如粉的。③灰色的。not so dusty*** 〖英俚〗還好;還過得去。—**dust·i·ness,** *n.*

Dutch** [dʌtʃ; dʌtʃ] *adj.* ①荷蘭的;荷蘭人的;荷蘭語的或文化的。②〖俚〗德國的;條頓民族的。go Dutch*** 〖俗〗各人付各人的帳。***talk to someone like a Dutch uncle*** 嚴厲地教訓某人。—*n.*①荷蘭人(集合稱)。②〖俚〗德國人。③荷蘭語。④〖俚〗德國語。***beat the Dutch*** 〖俗〗a. 做奇異或驚人之事。b. 超過以前所聞所見的任何東西。***double Dutch*** 糊塗話;莫名其妙的話。***High Dutch*** 德國中部或南部的;高地德語。***in Dutch*** 〖俚〗a. 受辱;失體面。b.在困難中。***Low Dutch*** 德國北部、荷蘭及法蘭德斯(Flanders)的;低地德語。

Dutch auction 拍賣者自動落價,直到發現有人願出資購買的拍賣。

Dutch courage 〖俗〗酒後的勇氣。

Dutch door 上下兩扇可分別開關之門。

Dutch gold 一種銅與鋅的薄片狀金色合金。(亦作 **Dutch foil, ~leaf, ~metal**)

Dutch·man [ˈdʌtʃmən; ˈdʌtʃmən] *n.*, *pl.* **-men.** ①荷蘭人;荷蘭船。②〖俚〗德國人。③〖航海俚〗德國船。④(d-)〖木工〗用以塞孔補缺之零片。

Dutch·man's-breech·es [ˈdʌtʃmənzˈbrɪtʃɪz; ˈdʌtʃmənzˈbritʃiz] *n. sing.* or *pl.* 罌粟科之一種野生植物。

Dutch oven ①一種鐵製之焙鍋。②一種烤炙肉等之金屬容器。③一種磚灶。

Dutch treat 〖俗〗各自付費之聚餐。

du·te·ous [ˈdjutɪəs; ˈdju:tjəs] *adj.* 盡職的;服從的。—**ly,** *adv.* —**ness,** *n.*

du·ti·a·ble [ˈdjutɪəbl̩; ˈdju:tjəbl] *adj.* 應納稅的(進口貨);有稅的。

du·ti·ful [ˈdjutɪfəl; ˈdju:tiful] *adj.* ①盡責的;孝順的;服從的。②責任所規定的;發自責任感的。—**ly,** *adv.* —**ness,** *n.*

‡du·ty [ˈdjutɪ; ˈdju:ti] *n.*, *pl.* **-ties.** ①義務;責任;本分。②職務;任務。③孝順;忠順;忠貞;尊敬;敬意。Don't forget your *duty* to your parents. 不要忘記對父母盡孝。④(舊式或正式的)表示尊敬之客套用語。⑤稅(尤指關稅)。payment of *duty.* 報關。import and export *duties.* 進口稅和出口稅。customs *duties.* 關稅。⑥〖軍〗指派之任務;值勤。He was on radar *duty* for two years. 他操作雷達爲時兩年。⑦兵役。⑧〖俗〗大便(尤指兒童)。⑨=**duty of water.** ***do duty for*** 充作;當…用。***off duty*** 下班;不值班。***on duty*** 值班;上班。

du·ty-free [ˈdjutɪˈfri; ˈdju:tiˈfri:] *adj.* & *adv.* 免稅的(地);免關稅的(地)。*duty-free* shop. 免稅店。

duty of water 某一定區域內某種作物所需灌漑之水量。

du·um·vir [djuˈʌmvɚ; dju(:)ˈʌmvə] *n.*, *pl.* **-virs, -vir·i** [-vəˌraɪ; -virai]. 古羅馬同任一職之二官員中之一人。

du·um·vi·rate [djuˈʌmvərɪt; dju(:)ˈʌmvirit] *n.* 二人共職;二頭政治。

du·ve·tyn, du·ve·tyne, du·ve·tine [ˈduvəˌtin; ˈdu:vəti:n] *n.* 一種表面有柔毛之棉、毛、絲或尼龍織物。

D.V. ①〖拉〗Deo volente (=God willing). 如上帝願意。②discharged veteran. 退役軍人。③Douay Version 的耶教聖經。

***dwarf** [dwɔrf; dwɔ:f] *n.* 矮子;侏儒;較同類遠爲矮小的動物或植物。—*adj.* 矮小的。—*v.t.* ①阻礙發育;使矮小。②相形之下使現矮小;相形之下爲之減色。

dwarf·ish [ˈdwɔrfɪʃ; ˈdwɔ:fiʃ] *adj.* 似侏儒的;矮小的。

***dwell** 〔dwɛl; dwel〕 *v.i.*, **dwelt** or **dwelled, dwell·ing.** ①居;住;住宿。②注意;凝思;評述;詳論〖on, upon〗. Don't allow your mind to *dwell* upon past failures. 不要老想過去的失敗。③久留於某一狀態中。

***dwell·er** 〔ˈdwɛlɚ; ˈdwelə〕 *n.* 居住者;居民。

***dwell·ing** 〔ˈdwɛlɪŋ; ˈdweliŋ〕 *n.* 住宅;寓所。He had his *dwelling* there. 他的住宅在那邊。

dwelling house 住宅。

dwelling place 住所;住址。

dwelt 〔dwɛlt; dwelt〕 *v.* pt. & pp. of **dwell.**

***dwin·dle** 〔ˈdwɪndl; ˈdwindl〕 *v.*, **-dled, -dling.** —*v.i.* 縮減;減少。—*v.t.* 使減少;使縮小。Failing health *dwindles* ambition. 健康衰退使人喪志。

dwt. pennyweight(s).

DX, D.X. distance.

Dy 化學元素 dysprosium 之符號。(亦作 **Ds**)

dy·ad 〔ˈdaɪæd; ˈdaiæd〕 *n.* ①對;雙;成對之物。②〖化〗二價元素。③〖生物〗二分體;一對染色體。—*adj.* ①對的;雙的;成對之物的。②〖化〗二價元素的。

dy·ar·chy 〔ˈdaɪɑrkɪ; ˈdaiɑːki〕 *n.* = **diarchy.**

dye** 〔daɪ; dai〕 *n., v.*, **dyed, dye·ing.** —*n.* ①顏料;染料。②色;色彩;(染成之)顏色。of the deepest*** (or ***blackest***) ***dye*** 最卑鄙的;最兇惡的。—*v.t.* ①染;染色於。to *dye* a white dress blue.將白色的衣服染爲藍的。②着色於。③染污。—*v.i.*①染色。②被染;受染。

dyed-in-the-wool 〔ˈdaɪdn̩ðəˈwʊl; ˈdaidinðəˈwul〕 *adj.* ①未紡織以前即染色的。②徹底的。

dye·house 〔ˈdaɪˌhaʊs; ˈdaihaus〕 *n.* 「染坊。」

dye·ing 〔ˈdaɪɪŋ; ˈdaiiŋ〕 *n.* 染色;染色法;染色業。

dy·er 〔ˈdaɪɚ; ˈdaiə〕 *n.* 染業者;染工。

dye·stuff 〔ˈdaɪˌstʌf; ˈdai-stʌf〕 *n.* 染料。

dye·wood 〔ˈdaɪwʊd; ˈdaiwud〕 *n.* 任何產顏料之樹。

***dy·ing** 〔ˈdaɪɪŋ; ˈdaiiŋ〕 *adj.* ①將死的;瀕死的;臨終的。②將終的;近於結束的。the *dying* year. 歲暮。—*n.* 死;死亡。

dyke[1] 〔daɪk; daik〕 *n., v.t.* =**dike.**

dyke[2] *n.*〖俚〗女子同性戀者。

dyn(am). dynamics.

dy·nam·e·ter 〔daɪˈnæmətɚ; daiˈnæmitə〕 *n.*〖光學〗(望遠鏡之)擴度計。

dy·nam·ic 〔daɪˈnæmɪk; daiˈnæmik〕 *adj.* ①活動的;精力充沛的;精悍的。②動力的;動力學的。*dynamic* electricity. 動電。*dynamic* engineering. 機械學。③〖哲學〗力本說的;物力論的。④〖醫〗官能的。—*n.* 動力;原動力。

dy·nam·i·cal 〔daɪˈnæmɪkl; daiˈnæmikəl〕 *adj.* =**dynamic.** —**ly,** *adv.*

dy·nam·ics 〔daɪˈnæmɪks; daiˈnæmiks〕 *n.*①(作 *sing.*解)〖物理〗動力學。②(作 *pl.*解)任何事物之成長、變遷及發展史。

dy·na·mism 〔ˈdaɪnəˌmɪzəm; ˈdainəmizəm〕 *n.* ①〖哲學〗力能論(以力與能解釋一切現象之根本)。②有活力之特質;活力。

***dy·na·mite** 〔ˈdaɪnəˌmaɪt; ˈdainəmait〕 *n., v.*, **-mit·ed, -mit·ing.** —*n.* ①炸藥。②〖俚〗能產生不凡效果之人或物。—*v.t.* 用炸藥爆炸。

dy·na·mit·er 〔ˈdaɪnəˌmaɪtɚ; ˈdainəˌmaitə〕 *n.* 使用炸藥之人(尤指革命者)。(亦作 **dynamitist**)

***dy·na·mo** 〔ˈdaɪnəˌmo; ˈdainəmou〕 *n.*, *pl.* **-mos.** ①發電機。an alternating (direct) current *dynamo.* 交(直)流發電機。②〖俗〗有活力有個性的人(尤指能鼓舞他人者)。

dy·na·mo·e·lec·tric 〔ˌdaɪnəmo·ɪˈlɛktrɪk; ˌdainəmouiˈlektrik〕 *adj.* 電能與機械能互相轉換的;動電的。

dy·na·mom·e·ter 〔ˌdaɪnəˈmɑmətɚ; ˌdainəˈmɔmitə〕 *n.*〖物理〗①測力計。②功率計。

dy·na·mom·e·try 〔ˌdaɪnəˈmɑmətrɪ; ˌdainəˈmɔmitri〕 *n.* 力之測量;肌力測定法。

dy·na·mo·tor 〔ˈdaɪnəˌmotɚ; ˈdainəˌmoutə〕 *n.*〖物理〗電動發電機。

dy·nast 〔ˈdaɪnæst; ˈdinəst, ˈdain-〕 *n.* 統治者(尤指世襲者)。

dy·nas·tic 〔daɪˈnæstɪk; diˈnæstik, dai-〕 *adj.* 朝代的;王朝的。(亦作 **dynastical**)

***dy·nas·ty** 〔ˈdaɪnəstɪ; ˈdinəsti, ˈdai-〕 *n.*, *pl.* **-ties.**朝代;王朝。to establish a *dynasty.* 創建王朝。

dy·na·tron 〔ˈdaɪnəˌtrɑn; ˈdainətrɔn〕 *n.* ①〖電〗帶那特龍管(三極眞空管之一種)。②〖物理〗間子(一種不穩定之質點,其質量介於電子與質子之間)。

dyne 〔daɪn; dain〕 *n.*〖物理〗達因(力之「單位)。」

dys-〖字首〗表"困難;狀況不佳"之義(特別用於醫藥上)。

dys·che·zi·a, dys·chi·zi·a 〔dɪsˈkizɪə; disˈkiːziə, -ʒə〕 *n.*〖醫〗大便疼痛;大便困難。

dys·en·ter·y 〔ˈdɪsn̩ˌtɛrɪ; ˈdisntri〕 *n.* 痢疾;赤痢。—**dys·en·ter·ic,** *adj.*

dys·func·tion 〔dɪsˈfʌŋkʃən; disˈfʌŋkʃən〕 *n.*〖醫〗官能不良;官能紊亂。

dys·gen·ic 〔dɪsˈdʒɛnɪk; disˈdʒenik〕 *adj.* 妨礙優生的;劣生的(爲 eugenic 之對)。

dys·lex·i·a 〔dɪsˈlɛksiə; disˈleksiːə〕 *n.*〖醫〗閱讀能力部分喪失;讀字困難。

dys·lo·gis·tic 〔ˌdɪsloˈdʒɪstɪk; ˌdislouˈdʒistik〕 *adj.* 非難的;非議的。(爲 eulogistic 之對)。

dys·lo·gy 〔ˈdɪslodʒɪ; ˈdisloudʒi〕 *n.* 非難;非議;貶抑(爲 eulogy 之對)。

dys·men·or·rhe·a 〔ˌdɪsmɛnəˈriə; ˌdismenəˈriːə〕 *n.* 經痛;月經困難。(亦作 **dysmenorrhoea**)

dys·pep·si·a 〔dɪˈspɛpʃə; disˈpepsiə〕 *n.* 消化不良症。(亦作 **dyspepsy**)

dys·pep·tic 〔dɪˈspɛptɪk; disˈpeptik〕 *adj.* ①消化不良的。②憂鬱的。—*n.* 患消化不良症的人。

dys·pho·ni·a 〔dɪsˈfonɪə; disˈfouniə〕 *n.*〖醫〗發音困難。

dys·pho·ri·a 〔dɪsˈforɪə; disˈfɔːriə〕 *n.* 一種精神病(感覺不適、焦急、不滿、侷促不安)。

dysp·ne·a 〔dɪspˈniə; disˈpni(ː)ə〕 *n.*〖醫〗呼吸困難。(亦作 **dyspnoea**) —**dyspne·ic,** *adj.*

dys·pro·si·um 〔dɪsˈprosɪəm; disˈprousiəm〕 *n.*〖化〗鏑(元素名,符號爲 Dy)。

dys·tro·phi·a 〔dɪsˈtrofɪə; disˈtroufiə〕 *n.* =**dystrophy.**

dys·tro·phy 〔ˈdɪstrəfɪ; ˈdistrəfi〕 *n.* 營養不良;營養性退化。

dys·u·ri·a 〔dɪsˈjʊrɪə; disˈjuəriə〕 *n.*〖醫〗小便困難。

dz. ①dozen. ②dozens.

E

E or **e** [i; iː] *n., pl.* **E's** or **e's** [iz; iːz]. ①英文字母之第五個字母。②〖音樂〗C長調的第三音。③東方(=East). ④美國學校予學生之成績。

E. ①Earl. ②East. ③Eastern. ④Easter. ⑤English. ⑥excellence. ⑦excellent. ⑧earth. **e.** ①eldest. ②errors. ③export. ④east. ⑤eastern. ⑥electron. ⑦engineer. ⑧engineering. ⑨entrance. ⑩〖棒球〗error.

e- 【字首】為 **ex-** 之變體 (用於拉丁字源之子音前,但 c, f, p, q, s, t 除外, 如 emit).

‡**each** [itʃ; iːtʃ] *adj.* 每; 每一; 各個。*Each* man may try twice. 每人可以試兩次。—*pron.* 各個;各人;每人。He gave two to *each*. 他給每人兩個。—*adv.* 每人;每件(物)。They cost one shilling *each*. 它們每件價值一先令。 ***each other*** 互相; 相互。They saw *each other* every day. 他們每天相見。〖注意〗**each other** 與 **one another** 有時也有混用的,但嚴格說來 each other 限於二者之間, one another 則用於三者以上之間。

***ea·ger** [ˈigɚ; ˈiːgə] *adj.* ①渴想的; 切望的。I am *eager* to do it. 我極想作這件事。②焦急的;急切的。—**ly,** *adv.* —**ness,** *n.*

eager beaver 〖美俗〗努力工作者(尤指目的在討好,希望超過別人者)。

***ea·gle** [ˈigl; ˈiːgl] *n.* ①鷹。②鷹狀之圖案。③鷹旗。④美國十元金幣(今已不通用)。⑤〖高爾夫〗比標準少兩次之桿數。⑥(*pl.*) 美國陸軍上校之領章或肩章。

ea·gle-eyed [ˈiglˌaɪd; ˈiːglˈaid] *adj.* 目光銳利的。

eagle owl 歐洲產之大鵰鴞。

ea·glet [ˈiglɪt; ˈiːglit] *n.* 小鷹。

ea·gle·wood [ˈiglˌwud; ˈiːglwud] *n.* 〖植物〗沉香。

ea·gre [ˈigɚ, ˈegɚ; ˈeigə, ˈiːgə] *n.* (河口之)急潮;高潮。

E. & O. E. errors and omission excepted.

‡**ear¹** [ɪr; iə] *n.* ①耳。②聽覺; 聽力。We have good *ears*. 我們的聽覺很好。③辨音力。④注意;傾聽。He was all *ears*. 他專心地傾聽。⑤耳狀物。⑥報紙首頁左右上角印氣象報告、口號等的小格。***A word in your ear.*** 讓我偷偷地告訴你一件事。***be all ears*** 傾聽。She *was all ears* when the scandal was revealed. 當醜聞被說出時, 她全神傾聽。***believe one's ears*** 相信所聽得的話。***bend an ear*** 留心聽。to *bend an ear* to a request for aid. 留心聽要求協助的申請。***bend one's ear*** 〖俚〗絮絮不休令人生厭。***fall on deaf ears*** 未受注意。***gain the ear of*** 使(人)相信。***give ear to*** 聽;傾聽 (= listen to). ***go in one ear and out the other*** 左耳進右耳出; 未留任何印象。***have*** (or ***keep***) ***an ear to the ground*** 〖俗〗注意別人所說或所想之事俾能據以行動。***have*** (or ***win***) ***a person's ear*** 受人寵顧。***lend an ear*** 注意聽。***over head and ears*** 深陷於…之中;全神貫注於…。***pin someone's ears back*** 〖俚〗痛毆;徹底擊敗。***play by ear*** **a.** 彈奏樂器而不用樂譜 (憑記憶)。**b.** 無適當之準備或遵循即做事。***set people by the ears*** 使人不和; 挑撥離間。His choice of a wife *set his family by the ears*. 他的擇妻造成家庭不和。***turn a deaf ear*** 不聽;不注意。He *turns a deaf ear* to requests of loans. 他對借錢的要求一概不理。***up to the ears*** 深陷於…之中;沈溺於…之中。***wet behind the ears*** 幼稚;不成熟。

ear² *n.* 穗。*ear* of corn. 玉蜀黍穗。to be in (the) *ear*. 正在長穗。—*v.i.* 出穗; 成穗。

ear·ache [ˈɪrˌek; ˈiəreik] *n.* 耳痛。

ear·clip [ˈɪrˌklɪp; ˈiəklip] *n.* 用夾子夾在耳上的耳環或飾物。

ear·drop [ˈɪrˌdrɑp; ˈiədrɔp] *n.* 有垂飾的耳環;耳墜。

ear drops 滴耳用的藥水。

ear·drum [ˈɪrˌdrʌm; ˈiədrʌm] *n.* ①中耳。②耳鼓;鼓膜。

eared [ɪrd; iəd] *adj.* 有耳的; 有耳狀物的; 有穗的(常用於結合字中)。long-*eared*. 長耳的。***eared owls*** 有穗狀羽毛之梟鳥。***eared seals*** 有外耳的海豹。

ear·flap [ˈɪrˌflæp; ˈiəflæp] *n.* 耳罩(附於帽側)。

ear·ful [ˈɪrful; ˈiəful] *n., pl.* **-fuls.** 〖俗〗①聽膩了的消息傳聞等。②重要消息; 聳人聽聞之吹嘘。③責罵;斥責。

ear·ing [ˈɪrɪŋ; ˈiəriŋ] *n.* 〖航海〗耳索。

***earl** [ɝl; əːl] *n.* 〖英〗伯爵。

ear·lap [ˈɪrˌlæp; ˈiəlæp] *n.* ①兩片耳罩之一 (=earflap). ②耳垂 (=ear lobe). ③外耳;耳殼。

earl·dom [ˈɝldəm; ˈəːldəm] *n.* ①伯爵的爵位或尊號。②伯爵的采邑。

ear·less [ˈɪrlɪs; ˈiəlis] *adj.* ①無耳的;無耳狀物的。②聾的。

ear lobe 耳垂。

‡**ear·ly** [ˈɝlɪ; ˈəːli] *adv.* & *adj.*, **-li·er, -li·est.**—*adv.* ①開始;開端;初;早。The sun is not hot *early* in the day. 清晨陽光不熱。②較慣常或指定時間為早。Call me *early*. 早一點叫我。③很久以前; 古代。④不久; 最近;即將。***early on*** 〖主英〗不久以前;剛纔。—*adj.* ①早;初。in one's *early* life. 在某人之早年。②較通常或指定時間為早的。an *early* dinner. 早吃的正餐。③不久的; 最近之將來的。④很久以前的。—**ear·li·ness,** *n.*

early bird ①〖俗〗早起者。②早到者。

ear·mark [ˈɪrˌmɑrk; ˈiəmɑːk] *n.* ①(加於牛、羊等耳朵上的)耳號(表示屬於何人所有)。②特殊的記號;特徵;特色。—*v.t.* ①加以耳號;加以記號。②特別指定(做某種特殊用途);指撥(款項)。

ear·muff [ˈɪrˌmʌf; ˈiəmʌf] *n.* 〖美〗耳套(覆於耳上以禦寒之兩塊布片或毛皮之一)。

‡**earn** [ɝn; əːn] *v.t.* ①(用勞力)賺(錢);謀(生)。He *earns* a lot of money. 他賺很多錢。②應得; 獲得。He is paid more than he really *earns*. 他所賺的錢多於他所應得之數。—*v.i.* 獲得收入。***earn a*** (***good***) ***living*** 謀生。It is not easy to *earn a living*. 謀生不易。***earn one's living*** 自行謀生;自立。He began to *earn his living* early. 他很早便開始自行謀生。

earned income 薪水、工資或其他用勞力與服務所換取的收入(非由營利所得或存款等的利息收入)。

earned run 〖棒球〗非因對方犯錯而獲得的分數。

ear·nest¹** [ˈɝnɪst; ˈəːnist] *adj.* ①熱心的;誠摯的。an *earnest* worker. 熱心的工作者。②重要的。Life is real! Life is *earnest!* 人生是真實的! 人生是重要的! —*n.* 嚴肅性。in earnest*** 熱心地; 認真地。I am *in ear-*

nest. 我是很鄭重的(非開玩笑)。 —**ly,** *adv.* —**ness,** *n.* 「金。②保證;預兆。
ear·nest² *n.* ①(=earnest money)定
***earn·ing** [ˈɝnɪŋ; ˈəːniŋ] *n.* ①賺;掙錢。②(*pl.*)工資;薪水;所賺的錢。He soon spent all his *earnings.* 他不久便把所賺得的錢都花掉了。
ear·phone [ˈɪrˌfon; ˈiəfoun] *n.* (電話機、電報機、收音機等之)耳機。 「耳垢器)。
ear·pick [ˈɪrˌpɪk; ˈiəpik] *n.* 耳挖(除
ear·piece [ˈɪrˌpis; ˈiəpiːs] *n.* 眼鏡架掛於耳上之彎曲部分。 「用之棉花、橡皮等。
ear·plug [ˈɪrˌplʌg; ˈiəplʌg] *n.* 塞耳孔
ear·ring [ˈɪrˌrɪŋ; ˈiəriŋ] *n.* 耳環。
ear·shot [ˈɪrˌʃɑt; ˈiəʃɔt] *n.* 聽力所及之距離;聽力所及處。 「*adj.* 震耳欲聾的。
ear·split·ting [ˈɪrˌsplɪtɪŋ; ˈiəˌsplitiŋ]
‡earth [ɝθ; əːθ] *n.* ①(亦作 **Earth**)地球。How far is the *earth* from the sun? 地球距離太陽有多遠? ②世界上的人類。③人世間;塵世(與 heaven 及 hell相對)。④陸地。⑤地。Bury it in the *earth.* 把它埋在地下。⑥泥土。⑦(狐狸或其他獸類之)洞穴;地洞。to stop an *earth.* 塡塞狐穴。⑧世俗;世事。⑨〖化〗土類。⑩〖電〗接地。***come back*** (or ***down***) ***to earth*** 重返現實中。***down to earth*** 實際的;不加渲染的。***how*** (***why, where, who, etc.***) ***on earth*** 究竟如何(爲甚麼,甚麼地方,誰等)? *How on earth* can one accomplish such a feat? 一個人怎能完成如此偉大的工作呢? ***move heaven and earth*** 想盡辦法;盡力。***on earth*** 全世界;世界上。***run*** (***a thing***) ***to earth*** **a.** 追尋(獵物)直至捕獲。**b.** 窮究到底。—*v.t.* ①覆以土。to *earth* up a plant or its root. 將植物或其根以土蓋住。②將電線或導體埋入地中。③〖方〗藏或埋在土中。④將狐狸趕入洞中。—*v.i.* 躲進洞裏。The fox *earthed.* 狐狸躲進洞裏。
earth·born [ˈɝθˌbɔrn; ˈəːθbɔːn] *adj.* ①地面所生的;土中長出的。②人類的;必死的。③世俗的;塵世的。
earth·bound, earth-bound [ˈɝθˌbaund; ˈəːθbaund] *adj.* ①爲世俗所束縛的;爲俗慾所縛的。②固着於地的。③前往地球的。
earth closet 以乾土防污之廁所。
***earth·en** [ˈɝθən; ˈəːθən] *adj.* ①土的;土製的。②陶製的。③人世間的;地球上的。
earth·en·ware [ˈɝθənˌwɛr; ˈəːθənwɛə] *n.* ①陶器;瓦器。②製陶器的原料;陶土。—*adj.* 陶製的。
earth·fall [ˈɝθˌfɔl; ˈəːθfɔːl] *n.* 坍方。
earth·light [ˈɝθˌlaɪt; ˈəːθlait] *n.* 〖天文〗地球反照(新月暗部所現之微光)。
earth·ling [ˈɝθlɪŋ; ˈəːθliŋ] *n.* ①世人;凡人。②俗人;俗物。
***earth·ly** [ˈɝθlɪ; ˈəːθli] *adj.,* **-li·er, -li·est.** ①大地的;地球的。②塵世的;俗世的;肉身的。He thinks only of *earthly* affairs. 他只顧塵世的事。③可知的;可能的。That rubbish is of no *earthly* use. 那些垃圾根本沒有用。—**earth·li·ness,** *n.*
earth·mov·er [ˈɝθˌmuvɚ; ˈəːθˌmuːvə] *n.* 推土機。(亦作 **earth mover**)
earth·nut [ˈɝθˌnʌt; ˈəːθnʌt] *n.* 〖植物〗落花生。 「花生。
earth·pea [ˈɝθˌpi; ˈəːθpiː] *n.* 〖植物〗
***earth·quake** [ˈɝθˌkwek; ˈəːθkweik] *n.* 地震。Taiwan suffers from *earthquakes.* 臺灣時遭地震災害。
earth·quake-proof [ˈɝθkwek-ˈpruf; ˈəːθkweikpruːf] *adj.* 耐震的。
earth·rise [ˈɝθˌraɪz; ˈəːθraiz] *n.* 從月球上或太空船中所看到的地球景象。
earth satellite 人造衛星。
earth·shak·ing [ˈɝθˌʃekɪŋ; ˈəːθˌʃeikiŋ] *adj.* 重大的;驚天動地的。
earth·shine [ˈɝθˌʃaɪn; ˈəːθʃain] *n.* =**earthlight.**
earth·ward [ˈɝθwɚd; ˈəːθwəd] *adv.* (亦作 **earthwards**) 向地面地;向地下地;向地球地。—*adj.* 向地的;向地球的。
earth·work [ˈɝθˌwɝk; ˈəːθ-wəːk] *n.* ①土木工程中挖土或築堤等工程。②〖軍〗泥土工事。 「*n.* ①蚯蚓。②卑鄙的人。
***earth·worm** [ˈɝθˌwɝm; ˈəːθ-wəːm]
earth·y [ˈɝθɪ; ˈəːθi] *adj.,* **earth·i·er, earth·i·est.** ①泥土的;土質的。②有泥土之特徵的。③居住於土中的。④現世的;世俗的;塵世的。⑤粗俗的;純樸的。
ear trumpet 喇叭狀助聽器。 「耳蠟。
ear·wax [ˈɪrˌwæks; ˈiəwæks] *n.*耳垢;
ear·wig [ˈɪrˌwɪg; ˈiəwig] *v.,* **-wigged, -wig·ging,** *n.* —*v.t.* 偸偸唆使;暗中諷示。—*n.* 小蜈蚣;蠼螋。
‡ease [iz; iːz] *n., v.,* **eased, eas·ing.** —*n.* ①舒適;安逸。He led a life of *ease.* 他過着舒適的生活。②容易;不費力。③不緊張;態度從容自然;無拘束。***at*** (***one's***) ***ease*** 安逸;自由自在。***ill at ease*** 侷促不安;心神不寧。***stand at ease*** 〖軍〗稍息。***take one's ease*** 無拘束;休息。***with ease*** 容易地。—*v.t.* ①使舒適;減輕(痛苦等)。to *ease* the pain of a wound. 減輕傷口的疼痛。②放鬆;減低(速度、努力等)。③慢慢而小心地移動。④使容易。—*v.i.* ①減輕;減緩〖常 off, up〗。②小心移動。***ease off*** (or ***up***) **a.** 減少;減輕。 **b.** 放鬆。***ease out*** 以比較體面(不傷和氣)的方法免人職務。 「逸樂的。②怠惰的;懶散的。
ease·ful [ˈizfəl; ˈiːzful] *adj.* ①安適的;
ea·sel [ˈizl; ˈiːzl] *n.* 畫架;黑板架。
ease·ment [ˈizmənt; ˈiːzmənt] *n.* ①緩和;減輕。②舒適;安逸;便利品;慰勞品;慰藉。③〖法律〗地役權。
‡eas·i·ly [ˈizɪlɪ; ˈiːzili] *adv.* ①容易地。They won *easily.* 他們很容易地就得勝了。②安適地;安樂地。③平靜地;自由地。④無疑地。She is *easily* the best singer in the choir. 她無疑是這歌詠隊中最佳的歌手。⑤很可能地。A war may *easily* begin. 很可能有一次戰爭發生。 「②安適;從容;流暢。
eas·i·ness [ˈizɪnɪs; ˈiːzinis] *n.* ①容易。
‡east [ist; iːst] *n.* ①東;東方。The sun rises in the *east.* 太陽出在東方。② (the E-)亞洲諸國。③(the E-)美國東部。***to the east of...*** 在…之東。Japan lies (*to the*) *east of* China. 日本在中國之東。—*adj.* ①靠東的;在東方的。②從東方來的。③向東方的。Take the *east* road. 走那條向東去的路。—*adv.*向東方地。 to face *east.* 朝東方。
east·a·bout [ˈistəˌbaut; ˈiːstəbaut] *adv.* 向東方地。
East China Sea 東海。
East End 倫敦之東端(爲一貧民區)。
***East·er** [ˈistɚ; ˈiːstə] *n.* (基督教的)復活節(在三月二十一日或是日以後的月圓之後第一個星期日)。 —*adj.* 復活節的。*Easter* week. 復活節日起算的一星期。
Easter egg 彩色蛋(用作復活節之裝飾品或禮品)。

east·er·ly [ˈistəlɪ; ˈi:stəli] *adj.* ①東方的;東向的。②由東方來的。—*adv.* ①向東方。②自東方。 —*n.* 東風。

:east·ern [ˈistən; ˈi:stən] *adj.* ①東方的;東邊的; 自東方來的。the *eastern* side of a building. 建築物的東側。② (E-) 東羅馬正教的。③(常 E-) 東方的; 東方國家的;亞洲國家的。 —*n.* ①東方人; 東部人。②(E-) 東羅馬正教之教友。

Eastern Church 東羅馬教;希臘正教。

East·ern·er [ˈistənə; ˈi:stənə] *n.* ①美國東部之居民。②(e-)東部或東方之居民。

east·ern·most [ˈistənˌmost; ˈi:stənmoust] *adj.* 最東的;極東的。

East·er·tide [ˈistəˌtaɪd; ˈi:stətaid] *n.* 復活節季(復活節後40–57日之期間)。

East Germany 東德(1945 年蘇聯在德國之占領區所成立的共產國家, 正式名稱 German Democratic Republic, 首都爲東柏林 East Berlin)。

East Indies 東印度羣島。

East·man color [ˈistmən~; ˈi:stmən~] 伊士曼彩色。

East·side [ˈistˌsaɪd; ˈi:stsaid] *adj.* 紐約市曼哈坦東區的。

***east·ward** [ˈistwəd; ˈi:stwəd] *adv.*(亦作 **eastwards**) 向東; 向東地。We were traveling *eastward(s)*. 我們向東旅行。—*adj.* 向東的。

east·ward·ly [ˈistwədlɪ; ˈi:stwədli] *adj.* ①向東的;朝東的。②從東方來的。—*adv.* 向東方地。②來自東方地。

***east·wards** [ˈistwədz; ˈi:stwədz] *adv.* =**eastward.**

:eas·y [ˈizɪ; ˈi:zi] *adj.*, **eas·i·er, eas·i·est,** *adv.* —*adj.* ①容易的;輕易的。That's an *easy* question. 那是一個易答的問題。②輕鬆的;舒適的;安樂的。③不嚴的;不認眞的。an *easy* master. 不嚴的教師。④從容自如的。*easy* manners. 從容自如的擧止。⑤緩慢的;從容不迫的。an *easy* pace. 緩緩的步子。⑥鬆弛的;不緊的。an *easy* fit. 寬鬆地恰好合身。⑦容易得到的。⑧愛逸樂的。an *easy* disposition. 愛逸樂的個性。⑨清晰流利的。an *easy* style of writing. 清晰流利的文體。***on easy street*** 在舒適的環境中。—*adv.* 輕易地;安適地。***go easy on*** **a.** 以溫和對待(不要使…太難堪)。**b.** 循中庸之道。***take it*** (or ***things***) ***easy*** 輕鬆一點; 不要緊張。

easy chair 安樂椅。

eas·y·go·ing [ˈizɪˈgoɪŋ; ˈi:ziˌgouiŋ] *adj.* ①做事懶散的; 隨遇而安的。②步伐從容不迫的(馬)。

easy mark 〖俗〗易受欺騙的人;易受利用的人。

easy money ①不費大力賺得的錢。②用欺詐得來的錢。

:eat [it; i:t] *v.*, **ate** [et; eit], **eat·en** [ˈitn̩; ˈi:tn], **eat·ing.** —*v.t.* ①吃; 食。Is there anything to *eat?* 有甚麼可吃的東西嗎? ②嚙;呑。③蛀蝕成。④侵蝕;腐蝕。This acid *eats* metal. 這種酸能腐蝕金屬。—*v.i.* ①吃; 食;吃飯。②侵蝕;腐蝕。The sea has *eaten* into the north shore. 海侵蝕了北岸。***be eating someone*** 使某人不安或不悅。***eat away*** (or ***into***) 侵蝕。***eat one out of house and home*** 將某人吃窮。***eat one's heart out*** 極度悔恨或悲痛。He is *eating his heart out* over the defeat. 他對那次失敗極感悔恨。***eat one's terms*** 〖英俗〗攻讀法律。***eat one's words*** 食言;背信。***eat out of another's hand*** 完全聽命於某人。***eat up*** **a.** 把…吃光;食盡。*Eat up* your food. 把你的食物吃光罷。**b.** 用盡;浪費掉。**c.** 〖俚〗迫切或貪婪地接受。

eat·a·ble [ˈitəbl; ˈi:təbl] *adj.* 可食的;可吃的。—*n.*(常 *pl.*) 食物;食品。

:eat·en [ˈitn̩; ˈi:tn] *v.* pp. of **eat.**

eat·er [ˈitə; ˈi:tə] *n.*食者。a big (good, *or* great) *eater.* 飯量很大的人。

eat·er·y [ˈitərɪ; ˈi:təri] *n., pl.* **-er·ies.** 〖俚〗小餐館;食堂。

eat·ing [ˈitɪŋ; ˈi:tiŋ] *n.* ①吃;食。②食物;吃食。—*adj.* ①食用的。*eating* apples. 生食的蘋果(與煮菜用的蘋果cooking apples 相對稱)。②腐蝕的;咬嚙般的。

eating house 飲食店。

eats [its; i:ts] *n. pl.* 〖俗〗食物;餐食。

eau [o; ou] *n., pl.* **eaux** [o; ou]. 〖法〗水。

eau de Co·logne [ˌodəkəˈlon; ˈoudəkəˈloun] 一種用酒精和香油做成之香水 (=cologne).

eau de vie [ˌodəˈvi, ˌodˈvi; ˈoudəˈvi:] 〖法〗白蘭地酒。

***eaves** [ivz; i:vz] *n. pl.* 屋簷。

eaves·drop [ˈivzˌdrɑp; ˈi:vzdrɔp] *v.*, **-dropped, -drop·ping,** *n.* —*v.i.* 偸聽。—*n.* ①屋簷流下之水滴。②此等水滴掉落之地面。(亦作 **eavesdrip**)

eaves·drop·per [ˈivzˌdrɑpə; ˈi:vzˌdrɔpə] *n.* 竊聽者。

eaves·drop·ping [ˈivzˌdrɑpɪŋ; ˈi:vzˌdrɔpiŋ] *n.* 竊聽。

E.B. Encyclop(a)edia Britannica.

ebb** [ɛb; eb] *n.* ①退潮; 落潮。②衰落; 衰退。His fortunes were at an *ebb.* 他家道中衰。ebb tide*** 退潮;落潮。—*v.i.* ①(潮)落;(潮)退。②衰落;衰退。

ebb and flow ①漲潮與退潮; 潮汐。②人事滄桑。

E-boat [ˈiˌbot; ˈi:bout] *n.* 〖英〗魚雷快艇。

eb·on [ˈɛbən; ˈebən] *adj., n.* 〖詩〗= **ebony.**

eb·on·ite [ˈɛbənˌaɪt; ˈebənait] *n.* 硬橡膠。

eb·on·ize [ˈɛbənˌaɪz; ˈebənaiz] *v.t.*, **-ized, -iz·ing.** 使(木材等)成黑色;使似烏木。

eb·on·y [ˈɛbənɪ; ˈebəni] *n., pl.* **-on·ies.** 〖植物〗烏木; 黑檀。 —*adj.* ①烏木製的;烏木色的。②純黑而亮的。***ebony wood*** 烏木。

e·bri·e·ty [iˈbraɪətɪ; i(:)ˈbraiəti] *n.* 酒醉;酩酊。

e·bul·li·ence [ɪˈbʌljəns; iˈbʌljəns] *n.* 沸騰;熱情洋溢;興高采烈。

e·bul·li·en·cy [ɪˈbʌljənsɪ; iˈbʌljənsi] *n.* =**ebullience.**

e·bul·li·ent [ɪˈbʌljənt; iˈbʌljənt] *adj.* 沸騰的;興高采烈的;熱情充溢的。

eb·ul·li·tion [ˌɛbəˈlɪʃən; ˌebəˈliʃən, -bʊˈl-] *n.* ①沸騰。②激發;洋溢。③(溶岩、水等)湧溢;噴出。

E.C. ①East Central (London之一郵區)。②Established Church. ③Engineering Corps.

ec- 〖字首〗**ex-** 之變體。

ECA ①European Cooperative Administration. ②Economic Cooperation Administration. (亦作 **E.C.A.**)

ECAFE Economic Commission for Asia and the Far East. 聯合國亞洲暨遠東經濟委員會;聯合國遠東經濟委員會。

é·car·té [ˌekɑrˈte; eiˈkɑ:tei] 〖法〗 *n.* 一種(二人)紙牌戲。

ec·bol·ic [ɛkˈbɑlɪk; ekˈbɔlik] *adj.* 〖醫〗催生的。—*n.*催生藥。

ec·ce ho·mo [ˈɛksɪˈhomo; ˈeksiˈhoumou] 〖拉〗①你們看這個人 (=Behold the man!)(Pilate 將戴荆冕之耶穌指示猶太人時之語)。②戴荆冕之耶穌像。

***ec·cen·tric** 〔ɪk'sɛntrɪk; ik'sentrik〕 *adj.* ①古怪的;怪癖的。②不同中心的(圓)。③離中心的;偏心的。 —*n.* ①古怪的人。 He is an *eccentric.* 他是一個古怪的人。②偏心圓。③離心圈。—**al·ly,** *adv.*

ec·cen·tric·i·ty 〔ˌɛksən'trɪsɪtɪ; ˌeksen'trisiti〕 *n.* ①怪癖性;古怪性。②離心率;偏心距離。

ec·chy·mo·sis 〔ˌɛkə'mosɪs; ˌeki'mousis〕 *n., pl.* **-ses** 〔-siz; -si:z〕.〖醫〗瘀斑。

Eccl., Eccles. Ecclesiastes.

eccl., eccles. ecclesiastical.

ec·cle·si·a 〔ɪ'kliʒɪə; i'kli:zjə〕 *n., pl.* **-ae** 〔-ˌi; -i:〕. ①古希臘城邦之人民大會。②教會會友;會衆。③教堂。

Ec·cle·si·as·tes 〔ɪˌklizɪ'æstiz; iˌkli:zi'æsti:z〕 *n.* 傳道書(舊約聖經中之一卷)。

ec·cle·si·as·tic 〔ɪˌklizɪ'æstɪk; iˌkli:zi'æstik〕 *n.* 牧師;傳教士。 —*adj.* 牧師的;教會的。

ec·cle·si·as·ti·cal 〔ɪˌklizɪ'æstɪkl; iˌkli:zi'æstikəl, -i'ɑ:s-〕 *adj.* ①教會的(組織、權力等)。②牧師的;教士的。—**ly,** *adv.*

ec·cle·si·as·ti·cism 〔ɪˌklizɪ'æstəˌsɪzəm; iˌkli:zi'æstisizəm〕 *n.* ①教會之主義、習俗、或禮儀。②恪守教規;教會精神。

Ec·cle·si·as·ti·cus 〔ɪˌklizɪ'æstɪkəs; iˌkli:zi'æstikəs〕 *n.* 〖聖經〗次經(或稱僞經)中之一卷。(亦作 **Wisdom of Jesus**)

ec·cle·si·ol·o·gy 〔ɪˌklizɪ'ɑlədʒɪ; iˌkli:zi'ɔlədʒi〕 *n.* ①教會學;教會建築學;教堂裝飾學。②有關教堂之專論。

Ecclus. Ecclesiasticus.

ec·dy·sis 〔'ɛkdɪsɪs; 'ekdisis〕 *n., pl.* **-ses** 〔-ˌsiz; -si:z〕.〖動物〗表皮脫落;蛻皮。

ECG, E.C.G. electrocardiogram 心電圖。

ech·e·lon 〔'ɛʃəˌlɑn; 'eʃəlɔn〕 *n.* 〖軍〗①指揮階層。②梯隊。③梯次隊形。④特勤部隊。 *in echelon* 排成梯次隊形。—*v.t. & v.i.* 列成梯隊。—*adj.* ①成梯隊形的。②梯隊的。

e·chid·na 〔ɪ'kɪdnə; e'kidnə〕 *n.* 〖動物〗針鼴;食蟻蝟。

ech·i·nate 〔'ɛkənet; e'kineit〕 *adj.* 多刺的;蝟棘狀。

e·chi·no·derm 〔ɛ'kaɪnəˌdɝm; e'kainədə:m〕 *n.* 〖動物〗棘皮動物。

E·chi·no·der·ma·ta 〔ɪˌkaɪnə'dɝmətə; iˌkainə'də:mətə〕 *n.* 〖動物〗棘皮類。

e·chi·nus 〔ɛ'kaɪnəs; e'kainəs〕 *n., pl.* **-ni** 〔-naɪ; -nai〕. ①〖動物〗海膽。②〖建築〗凸圓線脚。

***ech·o** 〔'ɛko; 'ekou〕 *n., pl.* **ech·oes,** *v.,* **-oed, -o·ing.** —*n.* ①回聲;回音。②附和者;應聲蟲。He is an *echo* of his master. 他是他主人的隨聲附和者。③附和;摹仿。④〖無線電〗回波。 *cheer to the echo* 大聲歡呼。—*v.i.* 發回聲;共鳴。—*v.t.* 隨聲附和。

echo sounder 回音測深器。

é·clair 〔e'klɛr; 'eikleə〕〖法〗 *n.* (乳酪餡,糖霜衣之)一種指形小餅。

é·clair·cisse·ment 〔eklɛrsis'mɑ̃; eiklersi:s'mɑ̃〕〖法〗 *n.* 解釋;說明。

é·clat 〔ɪ'klɑ; 'eiklɑ:〕〖法〗 *n.* ①顯赫之成功;輝煌之成就。②喝采;讚揚。③榮譽;聲名。④醜聞;狼藉之聲名。 *with great éclat* 在大聲喝采中;盛大地。

ec·lec·tic 〔ɪk'lɛktɪk; ek'lektik〕 *adj.* ①選擇的;自不同材料加以挑選的。②由選自不同來源之資料做成的;選編的。③〖哲學,藝術〗折衷的;不拘於一家之言的。—*n.* 折衷派之人。—**al·ly,** *adv.*

ec·lec·ti·cism 〔ɪk'lɛktɪˌsɪzəm; ek'lektisizəm〕 *n.* ①贊成或運用選擇方法。②(醫學、哲學的)折衷主義。

e·clipse** 〔ɪ'klɪps; i'klips〕 *n., v.,* **-clipsed, -clips·ing.** —*n.* (日、月)蝕;晦暗。lunar *eclipse.* 月蝕。solar *eclipse.* 日蝕。 ***be under an eclipse 命運乖張;命舛。—*v.t.* ①蝕;遮掩。②使失色;凌駕。—**e·clips·er,** *n.*

e·clip·tic 〔ɪ'klɪptɪk; i'kliptik〕 *n.* 〖天文〗黃道。—*adj.* ①黃道的。②蝕的。

e·clip·ti·cal 〔ɪ'klɪptɪkl; i'kliptikl〕 *adj.* =**ecliptic.**

ec·logue 〔'ɛklɔg; 'eklɔg〕 *n.* (尤指兩牧人對話體之)牧歌;田園詩。

ECM, E.C.M. European Common Market.

e·col·o·gy 〔ɪ'kɑlədʒɪ; i'kɔlədʒi〕 *n.* ①〖生物〗生態學。②社會生態學。—**ec·o·log·i·cal,** *adj.* —**e·col·o·gist,** *n.*

econ. ①economic. ②economics. ③economy.

e·con·o·met·rics 〔ɪˌkɑnə'mɛtrɪks; iˌkɔnə'metriks〕 *n.*(作 *sing.* 解)計量經濟學。

‡e·co·nom·ic 〔ˌikə'nɑmɪk, ˌɛk-; ˌi:kə'nɔmik, ˌek-〕 *adj.* ①經濟學的。②經濟的;經濟上的。the government's *economic* policy. 政府的經濟政策。③影響物資的。④實用的;實際的。*economic* geography. 實用地理學。⑤儉省的(=economical).

***e·co·nom·i·cal** 〔ˌikə'nɑmɪkl, ˌɛk-; ˌi:kə'nɔmikəl, ˌek-〕 *adj.* ①經濟的;節儉的;節省的。An efficient engine is *economical* of fuel. 效率高的機器節省燃料。②經濟學的。—**ly,** *adv.*

economic bankruptcy 經濟破產。

economic blockade 經濟封鎖。

economic impact 經濟衝擊力。

economic recession 經濟萎縮。

***e·co·nom·ics** 〔ˌikə'nɑmɪks, ˌɛk-; ˌi:kə'nɔmiks, ˌek-〕 *n.* ①(作 *sing.* 解)經濟學。②(作 *pl.* 解)財務上的考慮;經濟上的要素。What are the *economics* of such a project? 這一計畫的經濟要素何在(經濟上有何利弊)?

***e·con·o·mist** 〔ɪ'kɑnəmɪst, i-; i(:)'kɔnəmist〕 *n.* ①經濟學家。②節約者;儉省的人。

e·con·o·mi·za·tion 〔ɪˌkɑnəmɪ'zeʃən; iˌkɔnəmi'zeiʃən〕 *n.* 節約;經濟化。

e·con·o·mize 〔ɪ'kɑnəˌmaɪz; i(:)'kɔnəmaiz〕 *v.,* **-mized, -miz·ing.** —*v.t.* 節儉;節約;儉省。—*v.i.* 節儉;儉省;節省經費。—**e·con·o·miz·er,** *n.*

e·con·o·my** 〔ɪ'kɑnəmɪ, i-; i(:)'kɔnəmi〕 *n., pl.* **-mies.** ①經濟;節約。By various little *economies,* she managed to save a few pounds. 賴各種瑣碎的節約方法,她設法節省了好幾鎊錢。②經濟制度。 ***domestic economy 家庭經濟;家政。 ***feudal economy*** 封建經濟。 ***national economy*** 國家經濟。

economy class 二等座次(尤指客機艙位)。

ECOSOC Economic and Social Council.

ec·ru 〔'ɛkru; 'eikru:〕 *adj.* 淡褐色的;亞麻色的。—*n.* 淡褐色。(亦作 **écru**)

ec·sta·size 〔'ɛkstəˌsaɪz; 'ekstəsaiz〕 *v.,* **-sized, -siz·ing.** —*v.t.* 使大感奮;使狂喜。—*v.i.* 出神;狂喜。

***ec·sta·sy** 〔'ɛkstəsɪ; 'ekstəsi〕 *n., pl.* **-sies.** ①狂喜。②忘形;恍惚;出神;入迷。to be in (*or* go into) *ecstasies* over something. 對某事心醉神迷。

ec·stat·ic 〔ɪk'stætɪk; eks'tætik〕 *adj.*

狂喜的；出神的；入迷的。—*n.* ①易發狂喜或神情恍惚之人。②(*pl.*)狂喜或神情恍惚之突發狀態。—**al·ly,** *adv.*

ec·to·blast [ˈɛktəˌblæst; ˈektəblæst] *n.*〖生物〗外胚葉；外胚層；外板。

ec·to·derm [ˈɛktəˌdɝm; ˈektədəːm] *n.*〖生物〗外胚層；(腔腸動物等之)外細胞層。

ec·to·morph [ˈɛktəˌmɔrf; ˈektəmɔːf] *n.* 修長而瘦弱的人。—**ic,** *adj.*

ec·to·plasm [ˈɛktəˌplæzəm; ˈektouplæzəm] *n.* ①〖生物〗外質；外胞漿；細胞外層質。②心靈學上假想靈媒體放射之物質。

E.C.U. English Church Union.

Ec·ua·dor [ˈɛkwəˌdɔr; ˌekwəˈdɔː] *n.* 厄瓜多爾（國名，位於南美洲西北部，首都爲基多，Quito).

Ec·ua·do·ri·an [ˌɛkwəˈdorɪən; ˌekwəˈdɔːriən] *adj.* 厄瓜多爾的；其人民的；其文化的。—*n.* 厄瓜多爾人或居民。（亦作 **Ecuadoran, Ecuadorean**)

ec·u·men·i·cal [ˌɛkjuˈmɛnɪkəl; ˌiːkjuˈmenikəl] *adj.* ①一般的；普遍的。②〖宗教〗全基督教會的。③促進基督教團結的。（亦作 **ecumenic**)

ec·ze·ma [ˈɛksəmə; ˈeksimə] *n.*〖醫〗濕疹；熱疹。

Ed [ɛd; ed] *n.* 男子名(Edmund, Edward, Edwin 等之暱稱)。

ed. ①edited. ②(*pl.* eds.) editor. ③edition. ④educated.

-ed〖字尾〗①表動詞的過去式。②表動詞的過去分詞。③加於名詞之後作成形容詞。

e·da·cious [ɪˈdeʃəs; iˈdeiʃəs] *adj.* 貪食的；饕餮的；狼吞虎嚥的。—**e·dac·i·ty,** *n.*

E·dam [ˈidəm; ˈiːdæm] *n.* 一種用紅蠟包封的黃色乳酪。（亦作 **Edam cheese**)

Ed.B. Bachelor of Education. **EDC, E.D.C.** European Defense Community. **Ed.D.** Doctor of Education.

Ed·da [ˈɛdə; ˈedə] *n., pl.* **-das.** 古代冰島二文學集之一。***the Elder*** (or ***Poetic***) ***Edda*** 古冰島之詩集。***the Younger*** (or ***Prose***) ***Edda*** 古冰島之散文集。

***ed·dy** [ˈɛdɪ; ˈedi] *n., pl.* **-dies,** *v.,* **-died, -dy·ing.** —*n.* ①逆流；旋渦。②旋風；渦流。*Eddies* of mist rose from the valleys. 捲捲霧氣從谷間升起。—*v.i.* & *v.t.* ①成逆流。②洄旋。

e·del·weiss [ˈedlˌvaɪs; ˈeidlvais] *n.*〖植物〗薄雪草之一種。

e·de·ma [ɪˈdimə; iˈdiːmə] *n., pl.* **-ma·ta** [-mətə; -mətə].〖醫〗水腫；浮腫。

***E·den** [ˈidn; ˈiːdn] *n.*〖聖經〗伊甸園；樂園。

e·den·tate [iˈdɛntet; iːˈdenteit] *n.* 貧齒類哺乳動物。—*adj.*〖生物〗①無齒的。②貧齒類動物的。

‡**edge** [ɛdʒ; edʒ] *n.* ①邊緣；端。Don't walk too near the *edge.* 不要太走近邊緣。②刀刃；鋒。③尖銳；銳利。The knife has lost its *edge.* 刀已經變鈍了。④〖俗〗占上風。He gained the *edge* on his opponent. 他與他的對手相較已占了上風。⑤言語等的尖刻。Her voice had an *edge* to it. 她的語調尖刻。***have an edge on*** 微醉。***on edge*** **a.** 被困擾的；緊張的。**b.** 渴望的；不耐的。***on the edge of*** 在…的邊緣上。***set on edge*** **a.** 使興奮或不舒服；擾亂。**b.** 使不耐煩；使急於…。***set*** (or ***put***) ***one's teeth on edge*** **a.** 引起不愉快的感覺。**b.** 刺激。***take the edge off*** 挫其銳氣；使斂鋒芒。—*v.i.* 徐進；側進。She *edged* through the crowd.她側身擠過了人羣。—*v.t.* ①加邊於。②加刃於。③側身擠進；漸移。***edge in*** 設法進入；擠身於。***edge out*** 小勝。

edge·bone [ˈɛdʒˌbon; ˈedʒboun] *n.* =**aitchbone.**

edge(d) tool 有刃之工具；利器；危險之事物。

edge·ways [ˈɛdʒˌwez; ˈedʒweiz] *adv.* 以刃(或邊緣)向前地；向邊緣地。(亦作**edgewise**)

edge·wise [ˈɛdʒˌwaɪz; ˈedʒwaiz] *adv.* 邊朝前；朝邊緣。***get a word in edgewise*** 插嘴。

edg·ing [ˈɛdʒɪŋ; ˈedʒiŋ] *n.* ①裝飾邊緣。②飾邊。

edg·y [ˈɛdʒɪ; ˈedʒi] *adj.,* **edg·i·er, edg·i·est.** ①有刃的；鋒利的。②(藝術品如雕刻、繪畫等)線條過於明顯的。③易怒的；躁急的。—**edg·i·ness,** *n.*

ed·i·bil·i·ty [ˌɛdəˈbɪlətɪ; ˌediˈbiliti] *n.* 可食性。

ed·i·ble [ˈɛdəbl; ˈedibl] *adj.* 可食的。*edible* seaweeds. 海帶。—*n.*（常 *pl.*）可吃的東西；食品。

e·dict [ˈidɪkt; ˈiːdikt] *n.* 敕令；布告；詔書。

ed·i·fi·ca·tion [ˌɛdəfəˈkeʃən; ˌedifiˈkeiʃən] *n.* 陶冶；薰陶；啓廸。

ed·i·fice [ˈɛdəfɪs; ˈedifis] *n.* ①大廈。②(比喻)心中構思的東西。

ed·i·fi·er [ˈɛdəˌfaɪɚ; ˈedifaiə] *n.* 陶冶者；教化者。

ed·i·fy [ˈɛdəˌfaɪ; ˈedifai] *v.t.,* **-fied, -fy·ing.** 陶冶；薰陶；教化；訓誨。

ed·i·fy·ing [ˈɛdəˌfaɪɪŋ; ˈedifaiiŋ] *adj.* 有益教化的；訓誨的；陶冶的。

e·dile [ˈidaɪl; ˈiːdail] *n.* =**aedile.**

Ed·in·burgh [ˈɛdn̩ˌbɝo; ˈedinbərə] *n.* 愛丁堡(蘇格蘭之首府)。

Ed·i·son [ˈɛdəsn̩; ˈedisn] *n.* 愛廸生 (Thomas Alva, 1847–1931, 美國發明家)。

***ed·it** [ˈɛdɪt; ˈedit] *v.t.* ①編輯；編纂。②主編(報紙、雜誌等)。③剪接(影片、錄音帶等)。④修改；修正(草稿等)。⑤剔除〖常 out〗.

edit. ①edited. ②edition. ③editor.

***e·di·tion** [ɪˈdɪʃən; iˈdiʃən] *n.* 版本；版。de luxe *edition.* 精裝版。pocket *edition.* 袖珍版。popular *edition.* 普及版。revised *edition.* 修訂版。

‡**ed·i·tor** [ˈɛdɪtɚ; ˈeditə] *n.* ①編者；主筆。chief *editor* or *editor* in chief. (*pl. editiors* in chief). 主編；總編輯。②一種檢查和接影片用的工具。

***ed·i·to·ri·al** [ˌɛdəˈtorɪəl, -ˈtɔr-; ˌediˈtɔːriəl] *adj.* 編輯的；主筆的。*editorial* staff. 編輯人員。—*n.* 社論；時評。—**ly,** *adv.*

ed·i·to·ri·al·ize [ˌɛdəˈtorɪəlˌaɪz; ˌediˈtɔːriəlaiz] *v.t.* & *v.i.,* **-ized, -iz·ing.** ①寫社論；作時評。②作社論式之新聞報導。

editorial writer 社論作者；主筆。

ed·i·tress [ˈɛdətrɪs; ˈeditris] *n.* 女編輯；女主筆。

Ed·mund [ˈɛdmənd; ˈedmənd] *n.* 男子名。

eds. editors. **E.D.S.** English Dialect Society. **EDT, E.D.T., edt.** Eastern Daylight Time. **educ.** ①education. ②educational. ③educated.

ed·u·ca·bil·i·ty [ˌɛdʒəkəˈbɪlətɪ; ˌedju(ː)kəˈbiliti] *n.* ①可教育性；可塑性。②受教育之機會。

ed·u·ca·ble [ˈɛdʒəkəbl; ˈedjukəbl] *adj.* 可教育的；可塑的。(亦作 **educatable**)

***ed·u·cate** [ˈɛdʒəˌket, -dʒu-; ˈedju(ː)keit, -dʒu(ː)-] *v.,* **-cat·ed, -cat·ing.** —*v.t.* ①教育；訓練；培育；培養(愛好等)。He was *educated* in England. 他是在英國受的教育。to *educate* the ear. 訓練耳朵。to *educate* oneself. 自修。②送…上學；付(某人)之學費。

—*v.i.* 教育。

ed·u·cat·ed [ˈɛdʒəˌketɪd; ˈedju(:)-keitid] *adj.* ①受過教育的;有學識的;有教養的。self-*educated.* 自修出身的。②根據資料或經驗的。an *educated* guess. 有所根據的推測。

ed·u·ca·tee [ˌɛdʒəkeˈti; ˌedju(:)kei-ˈti:] *n.* 受教育者。

:ed·u·ca·tion [ˌɛdʒəˈkeʃən, -dʒʊ-; ˌedju(:)ˈkeiʃən, -dʒu(:)-] *n.* ①教育;訓練。*Education* is an important thing. 教育是一件重要的事情。②教養;修養。He had a good *education.* 他有良好的教養。③教育學。④教育程度。

***ed·u·ca·tion·al** [ˌɛdʒəˈkeʃənl, -dʒʊ-; ˌedju(:)ˈkeiʃənl, -dʒu(:)-] *adj.* 教育的; 教育上的; 有教育價值的。an *educational* motion picture. 有教育意義的電影。—**ly,** *adv.*

ed·u·ca·tion·al·ist [ˌɛdʒəˈkeʃənlɪst; ˌedju(:)ˈkeiʃnəlist] *n.* 教育家;教育學者。

educational park 〖美〗教育公園(在一大片土地上設立許多中學及小學, 並共同使用各種設施)。(亦作 **education park**)

educational system 教育制度。

ed·u·ca·tion·ist [ˌɛdʒəˈkeʃənɪst; ˌedju(:)ˈkeiʃənist] *n.* =**educationalist.**

ed·u·ca·tive [ˈɛdʒəˌketɪv; ˈedju(:)kətiv] *adj.* ①教育的。②教育上的;含有教育意義的。

ed·u·ca·tor [ˈɛdʒəˌketɚ; ˈedju(:)keitə] *n.* ①從事教育者;教師。②教育專家。

e·duce [ɪˈdjus; i(:)ˈdju:s] *v.t.,* **e·duced, e·duc·ing.** ①引出; 令顯出。②推斷; 演繹。③〖化〗析出。—**e·duc·i·ble,** *adj.* —**e·duction,** *n.*

ed·u·crat [ˈɛdʒəˌkræt; ˈedʒukræt] *n.* 〖美〗教育機構的官員或代表。

e·duct [ˈidʌkt; ˈi:dʌkt] *n.* ①引出之物。②推斷;推論的結果。③〖化〗游離物。

e·dul·co·rate [ɪˈdʌlkəˌret; iˈdʌlkəreit] *v.t.,* **-rat·ed, -rat·ing.** ①去酸味;使甜。②〖化〗洗去酸類、鹽類或其他溶解性物質;洗淨。

Ed·ward [ˈɛdwəd; ˈedwəd] *n.* 男子名。

Ed·ward·i·an [ɛdˈwɔrdɪən; edˈwɔ:djən] *adj.* 〖英史〗愛德華時代的; (尤指) **a.** 愛德華一至三世之建築形式的。**b.** 愛德華七世時代的(就文學、藝術等而言)。—*n.* 愛德華七世時代之人。

E.E. ①Early English. ②Electrical Engineer(ing). ③errors excepted.

e.e. errors excepted.

-ee 〖字尾〗表"動作接受者"之義。

EEC, E.E.C. European Economic Community.

***eel** [il; i:l] *n.* 鰻;鱔魚。

eel·fare [ˈilˌfɛr; ˈi:lfɛə] *n.* ①幼鰻羣之逆流而上。②一羣幼鰻。

eel·grass [ˈilˌgræs; ˈi:lgrɑ:s] *n.* 〖美〗〖植物〗①大葉藻。②苦草。

eel·pout [ˈilˌpaut; ˈi:lpaut] *n.* ①黏魚之類。②鱈類之淡水魚。

eel·spear [ˈilˌspɪr; ˈi:l-spiə] *n.* 捕鰻叉。

eel·y [ˈilɪ; ˈi:li] *adj.* 似鰻的;蠕動的;滑行的。

e'en [in; i:n] *adv.* 〖詩, 方〗=**even.**

-eer 〖字尾〗①用以造成名詞, 以表"與…有關之人或物; 寫作者; 製作者"之義。②用以造成動詞, 以表"與…有關係"之義。

e'er [ɛr; ɛə] *adv.* 〖詩〗=**ever.**

ee·rie, ee·ry [ˈɪrɪ; ˈiəri] *adj.,* **-ri·er, -ri·est.** ①奇異的;怪誕的;可怖的。②膽小的;畏怯的。—**ee·ri·ness,** *n.*

ef- 〖字首〗**ex-** 之異體(用於以f起首字之前)。

ef·fa·ble [ˈɛfəbl; ˈefəbl] *adj.* 可解釋的;可說明的。

ef·face [ɪˈfes; iˈfeis] *v.t.,* **-faced, -facing.** ①塗抹;消除;抹殺;沖淡。②使自己不受人注意。—**ment,** *n.*

:ef·fect [əˈfɛkt, ɪ-, ɛ-; iˈfekt] *n.* ①結果; 效果; 效力。The *effect* of morphine is to produce sleep. 嗎啡的效力在使人入睡。②感觸;印象。③(*pl.*)家財; 動產。personal *effects.* 私人所有物。④影響;效驗。The medicine had an immediate *effect.* 那藥立即起效驗。⑤意旨;意思;大意(前面加 to). He wrote to that *effect.* 他寫的大意如此。**for effect** 做樣子; 使人發生預期之印象。**give effect to** 使生效。**in effect** **a.** 實際上(=in fact). **b.** 生效; 有效。The law is still *in effect.* 那法律仍然有效。**c.** 結果。**into effect** 實行。**of no effect** 無效。**take effect** **a.** 生效; 奏效。The prescribed medicine failed to *take effect.* 醫生開的藥沒有生效。**b.** 開始發生作用;開始工作。**to the effect** 大意是。—*v.t.* 實現;產生(效果)。The change was *effected* peacefully. 該項改革和平地實現了。—**i·ble,** *adj.*

***ef·fec·tive** [əˈfɛktɪv, ɪ-; iˈfektiv] *adj.* ①有效的。*effective* measures. 有效的方策。②生效的。③有力的;印象深刻的。an *effective* speech. 有力的演說。④能戰鬥的。—*n.* 〖軍〗①能作戰之步兵或海軍人員。②實員; 兵員。—**ly,** *adv.* —**ness, ef·fec·tiv·i·ty,** *n.*

ef·fec·tor [əˈfɛktɚ; iˈfektə] *n.* 〖解剖〗受動器(神經末端之器官, 其功能爲傳播興奮, 促進肌肉收縮及腺分泌)。(亦作 **effecter**)

ef·fec·tu·al [əˈfɛktʃuəl; iˈfektjuəl] *adj.* ①有效的; 收效的。②有法律效力的。—**ly,** *adv.*

ef·fec·tu·ate [əˈfɛktʃuˌet; iˈfektjueit] *v.t.,* **-at·ed, -at·ing.** 使實現;使有效;實踐;貫徹。—**ef·fec·tu·a·tion,** *n.*

ef·fem·i·na·cy [əˈfɛmənəsɪ; iˈfeminəsi] *n.* 優柔;溫柔;女人氣質。

ef·fem·i·nate [*adj.* əˈfɛmənɪt; iˈfeminit *v.* əˈfɛmənet; iˈfemineit] *adj., v.,* **-nat·ed, -nat·ing.** —*adj.* ①無丈夫氣的;優柔的; 柔弱的。②頹廢的(藝術)。 —*v.t.* (亦作 **effeminize**)使柔弱; 使無丈夫氣。—*v.i.* 流於柔弱。—**ly,** *adv.*

ef·fer·ent [ˈɛfərənt; ˈefərənt] *adj.* 〖生理〗輸出的;傳出的。—*n.* 傳出神經。

ef·fer·vesce [ˌɛfəˈvɛs; ˌefəˈves] *v.i.,* **-vesced, -vesc·ing.** ①沸騰; 冒泡;生泡沫。②激動;活潑;興奮。—**ef·fer·ves·cence,** *n.* —**ef·fer·ves·cent,** *adj.*

ef·fete [ɛˈfit; eˈfi:t] *adj.* ①疲憊的;筋疲力盡的。②不能再生產的; 枯竭的; 衰微的。—**ness,** *n.*

ef·fi·ca·cious [ˌɛfəˈkeʃəs; ˌefiˈkeiʃəs] *adj.* 有效的。—**ly,** *adv.* —**ness,** *n.*

ef·fi·ca·cy [ˈɛfəkəsɪ; ˈefikəsi] *n., pl.* **-cies.** 功效;效能;功能;效力。(亦作**efficacity**)

***ef·fi·cien·cy** [əˈfɪʃənsɪ, ɪ-; iˈfiʃənsi] *n.* ①效能;效率。②=**efficiency apartment.**

efficiency apartment 包括一個或兩個房間之公寓(通常包括生活必需之設施以供單人或夫婦居住者)。

efficiency expert 效率專家。(亦作 **efficiency engineer**)

***ef·fi·cient** [əˈfɪʃənt, ɪ-; iˈfiʃənt] *adj.* ①有效率的; 最經濟的。*efficient* methods. 經濟而有效的方法。②能勝任的; 有能力的。③產生結果的;肇因的。—**ly,** *adv.*

ef·fi·gy [ˈɛfədʒɪ; ˈefidʒi] *n., pl.* **-gies.**

肖像；雕像；畫像。 ***burn*** (or ***hang***) ***in effigy*** 焚燒(或縊)某人之像以洩公憤。

ef·flo·resce [ˌɛfloˈrɛs; ˌeflɔːˈres] *v.i.*, **-resced, -resc·ing.** ①開花。②〖化〗風化；(因蒸發或其他變化而)表面生鹽類結晶；晶化。

ef·flo·res·cence [ˌɛfloˈrɛsn̩s; ˌeflɔːˈresns] *n.* ①開花；開花期；花族。②〖化〗風化；晶化；風化物。③〖醫〗發疹；風化性。(亦作 **efflorescency**) **—ef·flo·res·cent,** *adj.*

ef·flu·ence [ˈɛfluəns; ˈefluəns] *n.* ①流出；放出。②流出物。

ef·flu·ent [ˈɛfluənt; ˈefluənt] *adj.* 流出的；放出的。—*n.* ①流出物。②自河、湖等流出之水道；支流。③工廠等之廢水；污水。

ef·flu·vi·al [ɛˈfluvɪəl; eˈfluːviəl] *adj.* 臭氣的；穢氣的。

ef·flu·vi·um [ɛˈfluvɪəm; eˈfluːvjəm] *n., pl.* **-vi·ums, -vi·a** [-vɪə; -viə]. 惡臭；臭氣。

ef·flux [ˈɛflʌks; ˈeflʌks] *n.* ①流出；流出物。②時光之流逝；時間之經過。③期滿；終了。(亦作 **effluxion**)

‡ef·fort [ˈɛfɚt; ˈefət] *n.* ①努力；奮力。Their *efforts* were rewarded with success. 他們的努力獲得成功。②(努力所得的)成果；作品(尤指文學，藝術)。③〖主英〗募款運動；有組織的社團行動或成就。 **—ful,** *adj.*

ef·fort·less [ˈɛfɚtlɪs; ˈefətlis] *adj.* ①不須費力的；容易的。②不努力的；不盡力的；消極的。

ef·frac·tion [ɛˈfrækʃən; eˈfrækʃən] *n.* 用力打開。

ef·frac·tor [ɪˈfræktɚ; iˈfræktə] *n.* 〖法律〗竊賊。

ef·fron·ter·y [əˈfrʌntərɪ; eˈfrʌntəri] *n., pl.* **-ter·ies.** 厚顏無恥。

ef·fulge [ɛˈfʌldʒ, ɪ-; eˈfʌldʒ, i-] *v.t. & v.i.,* **-fulged, -fulg·ing.** 閃閃發光；發出燦爛之光。

ef·ful·gent [ɛˈfʌldʒənt; eˈfʌldʒənt] *adj.* 光輝的；燦爛的。 **—ef·ful·gence,** *n.* **—ly,** *adv.*

ef·fuse [*v.* ɛˈfjuz; eˈfjuːz *adj.* ɛˈfjus; eˈfjuːs] *v.,* **-fused, -fus·ing,** *adj.* —*v.t.* ①流出；瀉出。②散布。—*v.i.* 瀉流；流出。—*adj.* 〖植物〗疏展的；散開的。

ef·fu·sion [əˈfjuʒən; iˈfjuːʒən] *n.* ①流出；瀉出。the *effusion* of blood. 血之流出。②流出物。③(思想、感情之)迸發。④〖醫〗(從腺體、血管中)滲出；滲出之液。⑤〖物理〗瀉流；溢出。

ef·fu·sive [ɛˈfjusɪv; iˈfjuːsiv] *adj.* ①流出的；噴出的。②感情橫溢的；流溢着感情的。**—ly,** *adv.* **—ness,** *n.*

eft [ɛft; eft] *n.* 〖動物〗①〖美〗(在陸地生活時期之)水蜥。②〖廢〗蜥蜴。

EFTA, E.F.T.A. European Free Trade Association.

eft·soon(s) [ɛftˈsun(z); eftˈsuːn(z)] *adv.* 〖古〗①不久；卽刻。②又；再。③間或地；常。

Eg. ①Egypt. ②Egyptian.

e.g. exampli gratia (拉= for example). 例如(句中插語)。〖注意〗**e.g.** 讀作 for example.

e·gad [ɪˈgæd; iˈgæd] *interj.* 一種溫和之誓語。

e·gal·i·tar·i·an [ɪˌgælɪˈtɛrɪən; iˌgæliˈtɛəriən] *adj.* 相信人人平等的。 —*n.* 平等主義。 **—ism,** *n.*

‡egg [ɛg; eg] *n.* ①蛋；卵。②卵形物。③〖俚〗炸彈；水雷。 ***a bad egg*** 〖俚〗壞蛋；壞人。 ***in the egg*** 在早期；尚未發展的。 ***lay an egg*** 〖俚〗徹底失敗(尤指在觀衆之前)。 ***put all one's eggs in one basket*** 孤注一擲。 ***teach one's grandmother to suck eggs*** 班門弄斧。 ***tread*** (or ***walk***) ***upon eggs*** 小心翼翼；當心。—*v.t.* ①慫恿；鼓勵〖on〗。The other boys *egged* him on to fight. 其他的孩子慫恿他去打架。②以打碎的雞蛋混合食物烹調。③投擲雞蛋。

egg albumin 卵蛋白質。

egg beater ①攪蛋器。②〖美俚〗直昇機。

egg·crate [ˈɛgˌkret; ˈegkreit] *n.* ①運蛋用的分格箱。②天花板嵌燈下的方格架。

egg·cup [ˈɛgˌkʌp; ˈegkʌp] *n.* 蛋杯(用以盛半煮熟的帶殼蛋)。

egg·er [ˈɛgɚ; ˈegə] *n.* 幼蟲食葉子的蛾類昆蟲。(亦作 **eggar**)

egg flip 蛋酒。(亦作 **eggnog**)

egg foo yung [ˈɛgˈfuˈjʌŋ; ˈegˈfuːˈjʌŋ] 芙蓉蛋(中國菜名)。

egg·head [ˈɛgˌhɛd; ˈeghed] *n.* 〖美俚〗書獃子；書生；理想主義者。

egg·head·ed [ˈɛgˌhɛdɪd; ˈegˌhedid] *adj.* 〖俗〗書生之見的；書獃子氣的。

egg·plant [ˈɛgˌplænt; ˈegplɑːnt] *n.* 〖植物〗茄。

egg roll 蛋皮春捲。

egg·shell [ˈɛgˌʃɛl; ˈegʃel] *n.* 蛋殼。—*adj.* 似蛋殼的；脆的。

egg spoon 食蛋小匙。

egg whisk 〖英〗攪蛋器。(亦作 **egg whip**)

egg white 蛋白。

eg·lan·tine [ˈɛglənˌtaɪn; ˈegləntain] *n.* ①〖植物〗野薔薇。②〖化〗苯乙酸異丁酯。

e·go [ˈigo; ˈegou] *n., pl.* **e·gos.** ①我；自我。②〖俗〗自大；自私。③自尊心。

e·go·cen·tric [ˌigoˈsɛntrɪk; ˌegouˈsentrik] *adj.* 自我中心的；利己主義的。—*n.* 自我中心之人。

e·go·ism [ˈigoˌɪzəm; ˈegouizəm] *n.* ①自我主義；利己主義。②自私。③自負；自大狂。

e·go·ist [ˈigoɪst; ˈegouist] *n.* ①自我主義者；利己主義者。②自負者；自傲者；愛自我吹噓者。

e·go·is·tic [ˌigəˈɪstɪk; ˌegouˈistik] *adj.* ①利己主義的；自我中心的。②自私自利的。(亦作 **egoistical**) **—al·ly,** *adv.*

e·go·tism [ˈigəˌtɪzəm; ˈegoutizəm] *n.* ①自負；自大。②自我吹噓。③自私。

e·go·tist [ˈigətɪst; ˈegoutist] *n.* ①自負者；自誇者；自大者。②自私自利者。

e·go·tis·tic [ˌigəˈtɪstɪk; ˌegouˈtistik] *adj.* ①自負的；自大的。②自我吹噓的。③自私自利的。(亦作 **egotistical**) **—al·ly,** *adv.*

e·gre·gious [ɪˈgridʒəs; iˈgriːdʒəs] *adj.* ①非常的；太過的；過分的。②〖古〗超羣的；卓越的。 **—ly,** *adv.* **—ness,** *n.*

e·gress [*n.* ˈigrɛs; ˈiːgres *v.* ɪˈgrɛs; iˈgres] *n.* ①出；出去；出現。②外出權。③出口。④〖天文〗出離。 ***egress and ingress*** 出入。 —*v.i.* 出現；出去。

e·gres·sion [ɪˈgrɛʃən; i(ː)ˈgreʃən] *n.* 外出；出去。

e·gret [ˈigrɪt; ˈiːgret] *n.* ①白鷺。②白鷺羽毛(做裝飾物)。③〖植物〗冠毛。

***E·gypt** [ˈidʒəpt, ˈidʒɪpt; ˈiːdʒipt] *n.* 埃及(非洲東北部之一國，首都開羅 Cairo).

Egypt. Egyptian.

***E·gyp·tian** [ɪˈdʒɪpʃən, i-; iˈdʒipʃən] *adj.* 埃及的；埃及人的；埃及語的。*Egyptian* architecture. 埃及式的建築。 —*n.* ①埃及人。②古埃及語。

Egyptian darkness 完全的黑暗。

E·gyp·tol·o·gy [ˌidʒɪpˈtɑlədʒɪ; ˌiːdʒipˈtɔlədʒi] *n.* 埃及古物學。—**E·gyp·tol-**

o·gist, *n.*
eh [e, ɛ; ei] *interj.* (表疑問和驚訝)呃? 啊!
Ehr·lich [ˈerlɪx; ˈeirlix] *n.* 艾爾利希(Paul, 1854–1915, 德國細菌學家, 曾獲1908年諾貝爾醫學獎)。
E.I. ①East India. ②East Indian. ③East Indies.
EIB (W) Export-Import Bank of Washington.
ei·der [ˈaɪdɚ; ˈaidə] *n.* ①棉鳧(北冰洋的雁類)。②棉鳧之絨毛。
eider down ①棉鳧之絨毛。②鳧絨被。③〖美〗一種厚絨布。
ei·det·ic [aɪˈdɛtɪk; aiˈdetik] *adj.* 清晰地保留於記憶中之視覺的。
ei·do·lon [aɪˈdolən; aiˈdoulɔn] *n., pl.* **-la** [-lə; -lə]. 幻像; 幽靈; 妖怪。
Eif·fel Tower [ˈaɪfl~; ˈaifəl~] 巴黎愛費爾鐵塔(建於1889年, 高 984 英尺)。
‡eight [et; eit] *n., adj.* 八; 八個; 8。
eight·ball [ˈet,bɔl; ˈeitbɔːl] *n.* ①撞球中有"8"記號之黑球。②〖俗〗一種無定向之圓形擴音器。***behind the eightball*** 〖俚〗處於不利地位。(亦作**eight ball**)
‡eight·een [eˈtin, ˈeˈtin; ˈeiˈtiːn, eiˈtiːn] *n., adj.* 十八; 十八個; 18。
eight·een·mo [eˈtin,mo; eiˈtiːnmou] *n.* 〖印刷〗十八開。
***eight·eenth** [ˈeˈtinθ; ˈeiˈtiːnθ] *adj.* 第十八(分之一)的。 —*n.* 第十八(分之一)。on the *eighteenth* of this month. 本月十八日。
eight·fold [ˈetˈfold; ˈeitfould] *adj.* & *adv.* 八倍的(地); 八重的(地)。
‡eighth [etθ; eitθ] *adj.* 第八的; 八號的; 八分之一的。—*n.* ①第八; 八分之一。②〖音樂〗第八音; 第八度音程。—**ly**, *adv.*
eighth note 〖音樂〗八分音符。
eighth rest 〖音樂〗八分休止符。
***eight·i·eth** [ˈetɪɪθ; ˈeitiiθ] *n., adj.* 第八十(的); 八十分之一(的)。
eight·score [ˈetˈskor; ˈeitˈskɔː] *n., adj.* 二十之八倍(的); 百六十(的)。
‡eight·y [ˈetɪ; ˈeiti] *n., pl.* **eight·ies**, *adj.* —*n., adj.* 八十; 八十個; 80。〖注意〗**eighties** 表80至89, 尤指壽命或某世紀的第80至第89年。the *eighties*. 80年代。
ei·kon [ˈaɪkɑn; ˈaikɔn] *n., pl.* **-kones**, **-ko·nes** [-kəniz; -kəniːz]. =**icon.**
E. Ind. East Indian.
Ein·stein [ˈaɪnstaɪn; ˈainstain] *n.* 愛因斯坦(Albert, 1879–1955, 美國物理學家, 爲相對論發明者)。—**i·an**, *adj.*
Einstein equation 〖物理〗愛因斯坦方程式。
ein·stein·i·um [aɪnˈstaɪnɪəm; ainˈstainiəm] *n.* 〖化〗鑀(放射性元素, 符號Es)。
Einstein theory 〖物理〗相對論。
Eir·e [ˈerə; ˈɛərə] *n.* 愛爾蘭共和國之舊稱(首都爲都柏林 Dublin)。
ei·ren·i·con [aɪˈrinɪkɑn; aiˈriːnikɔn] *n.* 和平建議(尤指宗教鬥爭中之和平建議)。
Ei·sen·how·er [ˈaɪzn,hauɚ; ˈaizən,hauə] *n.* 艾森豪(Dwight D., 1890–1969, 美國第34任總統, 任期 1953–1961 年)。
‡ei·ther [ˈiðɚ, ˈaɪðɚ; ˈaiðə, ˈiːðə] *adj.* (二者之)任一; 每一; 二者。You may go by *either* road.(兩條路)你可走任何一條。—*pron.* 二者之一。I don't want *either.* 二者我都不想要。—*adv.* 也; 亦(僅用於否定句, 且須置於句末)。I haven't seen it, *either.* 我也沒有看見它。—*conj.* (與 or 連用) 抑; 或。He is *either* in London or in Paris. 他或在倫敦或在巴黎。
ei·ther-or [ˈiðɚˈɔr; ˈaiðərˈɔː] *adj.* 〖英〗只能選擇二者之一的; 別無他途的。
e·jac·u·late [ɪˈdʒækjə,let; iˈdʒækjuleit] *v.,* **-lat·ed, -lat·ing,** *n.* —*v.i.* ①突然排出(液體); 射出。②突然說出; 喊叫。—*n.* 〖生理〗射精。
e·jac·u·la·tion [ɪ,dʒækjəˈleʃən; i,dʒækjuˈleiʃən] *n.* ①分泌液射出; 射精。②突然的說; 絕叫; 失聲。
e·jac·u·la·tor [ɪˈdʒækjə,letɚ; iˈdʒækjuleitə] *n.* ①突然射出者; 突然叫喊者。②〖生理〗射出肌。③〖畜牧〗人工取精器。
e·jac·u·la·to·ry [ɪˈdʒækjələ,torɪ; iˈdʒækjulətəri] *adj.* ①射出的; 射精的。②突發的; 突然說出的; 感嘆的。
e·ject [*v.* ɪˈdʒɛkt; i(ː)ˈdʒekt *n.* ˈidʒɛkt; ˈiːdʒekt] *v.t.* ①噴出; 投出。②逐出; 罷黜。—*n.* 〖心理〗投覩(他人之心理狀態, 自其身體動作等直接推知者)。—**e·jec·tive**, *adj.*
e·jec·ta [iˈdʒɛktə; iˈdʒektə] *n. pl.* 噴出物; 排泄物; 渣滓。(亦作 **ejectamenta**)
e·jec·tion [ɪˈdʒɛkʃən; i(ː)ˈdʒekʃən] *n.* ①噴出; 投出。②逐出; 罷黜。③噴出物; 排泄物。
ejection capsule 飛機上救生用之緊急彈出艙。
ejection seat 緊急情況時連駕駛員一同彈出飛機之座位。(亦作 **ejector seat**)
e·ject·ment [ɪˈdʒɛktmənt; iˈdʒektmənt] *n.* ①噴出; 投出; 罷黜。②〖法律〗收回地產之訴訟。
e·jec·tor [iˈdʒɛktɚ; iˈdʒektə] *n.* ①投出者; 逐出者。②〖機械〗噴射器。③排彈器。
eke¹ [ik; iːk] *v.t.,* **eked, ek·ing.** 增加; 補充〖out〗。
eke² *adv., conj.* 〖古〗亦; 又。
el [ɛl; el] *n.* ①側房。②〖俗〗高架鐵道。
***e·lab·o·rate** [*adj.* ɪˈlæbərɪt; iˈlæbərit *v.* ɪˈlæbə,ret; iˈlæbəreit] *adj., v.,* **-rat·ed, -rat·ing.** —*adj.* 用心作成的; 精巧的; 複雜的。 an *elaborate* machine. 精巧的機器。—*v.t.* 用心地作; 苦心經營。—*v.i.* 詳盡地說明〖常 on, upon〗。—**ly**, *adv.* —**ness**, *n.* —**e·lab·o·ra·tor**, *n.*
e·lab·o·ra·tion [ɪ,læbəˈreʃən; i,læbəˈreiʃən] *n.* ①苦心經營。②其成果。③精密; 精緻。
e·lab·o·ra·tive [ɪˈlæbə,retɪv; iˈlæbərətiv] *adj.* 苦心經營的; 精緻的。
é·lan [eˈlɑ̃; eiˈlɑ̃ːŋ] 〖法〗 *n.* 銳氣; 熱情。
e·land [ˈilənd; ˈiːlənd] *n., pl.* **-lands, -land.** 〖動物〗(非洲產之)大羚羊。
el·a·pid [ˈɛləpɪd; ˈeləpid] *n.* 〖動物〗毒蛇 (cobra, 眼鏡蛇, coral snake, 美洲產的一種小毒蛇等屬之)。
e·lapse [ɪˈlæps; iˈlæps] *v.,* **e·lapsed, e·laps·ing,** *n.* —*v.i.* (時間)溜走; (光陰)逝去。—*n.* (光陰之)逝去。
e·las·mo·branch [ɪˈlæsmə,bræŋk; iˈlæsməbræŋk] *n.* 〖動物〗 板鰓類之魚。—*adj.* 板鰓類的。
***e·las·tic** [ɪˈlæstɪk; iˈlæstik] *adj.* ①有彈性的。②可以伸縮的。an *elastic* rule. 有伸縮性的規則。③跳彈的。④易於復原的。—*n.* 鬆緊帶; 橡皮筋。a piece of *elastic.* 一條鬆緊帶(橡皮筋)。—**al·ly**, *adv.*
e·las·tic·i·ty [ɪ,læsˈtɪsətɪ; ,elæsˈtisiti] *n.* 彈性; 伸縮性。
e·las·tin [ɪˈlæstɪn; iˈlæstin] *n.* 〖生化〗彈性蛋白質。
e·late [ɪˈlet; iˈleit] *v.,* **e·lat·ed, e·lat·ing,** *adj.* —*v.t.* 使興奮; 使得意; 使驚喜。—*adj.* 興奮的; 得意的; 感到驚喜的。—**e·lat·er**, *n.*

e·lat·ed 〔ɪˈletɪd; iˈleitid〕 *adj.* 興高采烈的。—**ly,** *adv.* —**ness,** *n.*

e·la·tion 〔ɪˈleʃən; iˈleiʃən〕 *n.* 得意揚揚；昂然自得。

El·be 〔ɛlb, ˈɛlbə; elb, ˈelbə〕 *n.* 易北河(自捷克西部經德國入北海)。

el·bow** 〔ˈɛlˌbo; ˈelbou〕 *n.* ①肘。②肘狀物(如烟囱之轉接處等)。 ***be at one's elbow 在近旁；緊靠於其旁。 ***bend*** (***lift,*** or ***crook***) ***an eblow*** 〖俚〗縱飲。 ***be out at the elbows*** (or ***out at elbows***) **a.** 衣衫襤褸的。 **b.** 貧窮。 ***be up to the elbows*** **a.** 極爲忙碌。He *is up to the elbows* in work. 他正在埋頭工作。 **b.** 極有關連。 ***rub elbows with*** 與…來往；與…雜處。—*v.t.* 以肘推；擠。 to *elbow* one's way through a crowd. 從人羣中擠過去。—*v.i.* 推擠。

elbow grease 〖俗〗費體力的工作。

el·bow·room 〔ˈɛlboˌrum; ˈelbourum〕 *n.* 可自由伸肘的地方；足够活動或工作之空間；充裕的場所或範圍。

eld 〔ɛld; eld〕 *n.* 〖古〗①年紀；年齡。②老年；年邁。③往古；古代；古人。

***eld·er**[1] 〔ˈɛldɚ; ˈeldə〕 *adj.* ①年紀較長的；前輩的。my *elder* brother. 我的哥哥。②較優先的。③古的；從前的。—*n.* ①前輩。Children should respect their *elders.* 孩子們應該尊敬長輩。②年長者。③祖先。④一個團體中有影響力之人；領袖；族長。⑤某些教會中的高級職員；長老。〖注意〗 **elder** 特指兄弟姊妹間的較長者，但表長幼關係時，不能以之代替 older.

el·der[2] *n.* 〖植物〗接骨木。

el·der·ber·ry 〔ˈɛldɚˌbɛrɪ; ˈeldəˌberi〕 *n., pl.* **-ries.** 〖植物〗接骨木之果實；接骨木。

***eld·er·ly** 〔ˈɛldəlɪ; ˈeldəli〕 *adj.* 稍老的；甫逾中年的；老年人的。—**eld·er·li·ness,** *n.*

eld·er·ship 〔ˈɛldɚˌʃɪp; ˈeldəʃip〕 *n.* ①教會長老之身分或地位。②長老之集合稱。

***eld·est** 〔ˈɛldɪst; ˈeldist〕 *adj.* 年最長的。the *eldest* daughter (son). 長女(子)。

eldest hand 牌戲中坐發牌者左方的人。

El·do·ra·do, El Do·ra·do 〔ˌɛldəˈrɑdo; ˌeldoˈrɑːdou〕 〖西〗 *n., pl.* **-dos.** ①理想中的黃金國(相傳在南美內陸，盛產黃金寶石)。②傳說中的寶山。

el·dritch 〔ˈɛldrɪtʃ; ˈeldritʃ〕 *adj.* 〖蘇〗可畏的；不祥的；妖魔的。(亦作**eldrich, elritch**)

elec., elect. ①electric. ②electrical. ③electrician. ④electricity.

el·e·cam·pane 〔ˌɛləkəmˈpen; ˌelikæmˈpein〕 *n.* ①〖植物〗土木香。②以土木香之根調味製成之糖果。

‡e·lect 〔ɪˈlɛkt; iˈlekt〕 *v.t.* ①推選；選舉。He was *elected* chairman. 他被選舉爲主席。(注意 chairman 在此不加冠詞)。②選擇；決定。He *elected* to stay. 他決定留下了。—*adj.* 選出的；被選出而尙未就職的。 the President *elect.* 總統當選人。—*n.* (the ~) ①上帝的選民。②被選或值得被選的人。

***e·lec·tion** 〔ɪˈlɛkʃən; iˈlekʃən〕 *n.* 選擇；選舉。*election* campaign. 競選活動。

Election Day ①美國總統及國會議員選舉日。②(e- d-) 任何舉行選舉之日。

e·lec·tion·eer 〔ɪˌlɛkʃənˈɪr; iˌlekʃəˈniə〕 *v.i.* 競選；作競選活動。—**er,** *n.*

e·lec·tive 〔ɪˈlɛktɪv; iˈlektiv〕 *adj.* ①被選出的；選任的。②可任意選擇的。③有選舉權的。—*n.* 選修科目。—**ly,** *adv.* —**ness,** *n.*

***e·lec·tor** 〔ɪˈlɛktɚ; iˈlektə〕 *n.* ①有選舉權者；合格選舉人。②美國總統與副總統的選舉人。③神聖羅馬帝國之有權選舉皇帝的諸侯。

e·lec·tor·al 〔ɪˈlɛktərəl; iˈlektərəl〕 *adj.* 選舉的；選舉人的。

electoral college 〖美〗選舉總統與副總統的選舉團(其代表由各州選舉)。

electoral vote 〖美〗選舉團所投的票(按 electoral votes 每州均有規定數目，總統與副總統候選人各獲得某一州之多數選民票，卽獲得該州之全部 electoral votes).

e·lec·tor·ate 〔ɪˈlɛktərɪt; iˈlektərit〕 *n.* ①選民；選舉團。②選舉區。③神聖羅馬帝國選帝侯之地位或領地。

electr. ①electrical. ②electricity.

E·lec·tra complex 〔ɪˈlɛktrə~; iˈlektrə~〕 〖心理分析〗戀父情結。

e·lec·tress 〔ɪˈlɛktrɪs; iˈlektris〕 *n.* ①女選民。②神聖羅馬帝國選帝侯 (elector)之妻或遺孀。

‡e·lec·tric 〔ɪˈlɛktrɪk, ə–; iˈlektrik〕 *adj.* ①電的；用電的；生電的。②令人興奮的；刺激的；緊張的；感動的。an *electric* eloquence. 令人感動的口才。—*n.* ①〖火車〗 **a.** 電動火車頭。 **b.** 〖俚〗用電操縱的鐵路。②電動車輛。

***e·lec·tri·cal** 〔ɪˈlɛktrɪkl; iˈlektrikəl〕 *adj.* ①=**electric.** ②與電有關的。an *electrical* consultant. 電氣顧問。—**ly,** *adv.*

electrical engineer 電機工程師。

electrical engineering 電機工程。

electrical machine 發電機。

electrical transcription ①用錄音片之無線電廣播。②是項錄音片。

electrical transmission (照相之)傳眞。

electric automobile 電動汽車。

electric battery 電池。

electric bell 電鈴。

electric blanket 電毯。

electric brain 電腦。

electric cable 電纜。

electric chair 電椅(刑具)。

electric current 電流。

electric eye 〖物理〗電眼；光電池；光電管(一種置於電路上之裝置，用以操縱機械活動)。

electric fan 電扇。

electric furnace 電爐。

e·lec·tri·cian 〔ɪˌlɛkˈtrɪʃən; ilekˈtriʃən〕 *n.* 〖美〗電工技師；電機師。

electric iron 電熨斗。

***e·lec·tric·i·ty** 〔ɪˌlɛkˈtrɪsətɪ, ə–, ˌilɛk–; ilekˈtrisiti, ˌelek–, ˌiːle–〕 *n.* ①電；電力；電流；電子流。This machine goes by *electricity.* 這機器是用電發動的。②電學。

e·lec·tri·cize 〔ɪˈlɛktrəˌsaɪz; iˈlektrisaiz〕 *v.t.,* **-cized, -ciz·ing.** 充電；使帶電；使電化。

electric lamp 電燈。

electric light 電光；電燈。

electric meter 電錶。

electric shaver 電動刮鬍刀。

electric wave 電波。

electric wire 電線。

e·lec·tri·fi·ca·tion 〔ɪˌlɛktrəfəˈkeʃən; iˌlektrifiˈkeiʃən〕 *n.* ①充電；帶電。②電化；電力使用。③驚駭；震撼。

e·lec·tri·fy 〔ɪˈlɛktrəˌfaɪ; iˈlektrifai〕 *v.t.,* **-fied, -fy·ing.** ①充電；使帶電。②使電化。③使驚駭；使感動；震撼。

e·lec·trize 〔ɪˈlɛktraɪz; iˈlektraiz〕 *v.t.,* **-trized, -triz·ing.** =**electrify.**

e·lec·tro 〔ɪˈlɛktro; iˈlektrou〕 *n., pl.* **-tros.** ①=**electrotype.** ②=**electroplate.**

electro- 〖字首〗表"電"之義。

e·lec·tro·a·nal·y·sis 〔ɪˌlɛktroə'næləsɪs; iˌlektrouə'næləsis〕 *n.* 〖化〗電析。
e·lec·tro·bath 〔ɪ'lɛktrəˌbæθ; i'lektrəbɑːθ〕 *n.* (電版或電鍍用之)電液;電解液。
e·lec·tro·car·di·o·gram 〔ɪˌlɛktro'kɑrdɪəˌgræm; iˌlektrou'kɑːdiəgræm〕 *n.* 心電圖;心動電流圖。(亦作 **cardiogram**)
e·lec·tro·car·di·o·graph 〔ɪˌlɛktro'kɑrdɪəˌgræf; iˌlektrou'kɑːdiəgrɑːf〕 *n.* 〖醫〗心動電流描記器。(亦作 **cardiograph**)
e·lec·tro·chem·is·try 〔ɪˌlɛktro'kɛmɪstrɪ; iˌlektrou'kemistri〕 *n.* 電化學。—**e·lec·tro·chem·i·cal,** *adj.*
e·lec·tro·chron·o·graph 〔ɪˌlɛktrə'krɑnəˌgræf; iˌlektrə'krɔnəgrɑːf〕 *n.* 電氣計時器。
e·lec·tro·cute 〔ɪ'lɛktrəˌkjut; i'lektrəkjuːt〕 *v.t.,* **-cut·ed, -cut·ing.** ①施以電刑。②誤觸電致死。
e·lec·tro·cu·tion 〔ɪˌlɛktrə'kjuʃən; iˌlektrə'kjuːʃən〕 *n.* 施電刑。
e·lec·trode 〔ɪ'lɛktrod; i'lektroud〕 *n.* 電極。
e·lec·tro·de·pos·it 〔ɪˌlɛktrodɪ'pɑzɪt; iˌlektroudi'pɔzit〕 *v.t.* 以電解積貯(金屬等)。—*n.* 電積物(如銅、鎳等)。
e·lec·tro·dy·nam·ic 〔ɪˌlɛktrodaɪ'næmɪk; i'lektroudai'næmik〕 *adj.* 電動力學的。
e·lec·tro·dy·nam·ics 〔ɪˌlɛktrodaɪ'næmɪks; i'lektroudai'næmiks〕 *n.* (作 *sing.* 解)電動力學。(亦作 **electrodynamism**)
e·lec·tro·dy·na·mom·e·ter 〔ɪˌlɛktroˌdaɪnə'mɑmətɚ; iˌlektrouˌdainə'mɔmətə〕 *n.* ①電功率計。②力測電流計。③變流作用計。
e·lec·tro·en·ceph·a·lo·gram 〔ɪˌlɛktroɛn'sɛfələgræm; iˌlektrouen'sefələgræm〕 *n.* 〖醫〗腦電波;腦電像;腦電圖。
e·lec·tro·en·ceph·a·lo·graph 〔ɪˌlɛktroɛn'sɛfələˌgræf; iˌlektrouen'sefələgrɑːf〕 *n.* 腦電描記器。—**ic, —i·cal,** *adj.*
e·lec·tro·graph 〔ɪ'lɛktroˌgræf; i'lektrougrɑːf〕 *n.* ①電位記錄;電氣記錄。②電氣雕刻器。③電傳照相機;傳眞機。④電傳照片。⑤ X 光照片。—**ic,** *adj.* —**y,** *n.*
e·lec·tro·ki·net·ics 〔ɪˌlɛktrokɪ'nɛtɪks; iˌlektroukai'netiks〕 *n.* (作 *sing.* 解)動電學。—**e·lec·tro·ki·net·ic,** *adj.*
e·lec·tro·lier 〔ɪˌlɛktro'lɪr; iˌlektrou'liə〕 *n.* (有多個燈泡之)電燈架;吊燈架。
e·lec·trol·o·gy 〔ɪˌlɛk'trɑlədʒɪ; iˌlek'trɔlədʒi〕 *n.* 電學。
e·lec·trol·y·sis 〔ɪˌlɛk'trɑləsɪs; ilek'trɔlisis〕 *n.* ①電解。②〖外科〗以電針毀掉瘤腫、痣、毛根等。—**e·lec·trol·o·gist,** *n.*
e·lec·tro·lyte 〔ɪ'lɛktrəˌlaɪt; i'lektroulait〕 *n.* 電解質;電解液。
e·lec·tro·lyt·ic 〔ɪˌlɛktrə'lɪtɪk; iˌlektrou'litik〕 *adj.* 電解的;電解質的。
e·lec·tro·lyt·i·cal 〔ɪˌlɛktrə'lɪtɪk]; iˌlektrou'litikl〕 *adj.* =**electrolytic.** —**ly,** *adv.*
e·lec·tro·lyze 〔ɪ'lɛktrəˌlaɪz; i'lektroulaiz〕 *v.t.,* **-lyzed, -lyz·ing.** 電解。—**e·lec·tro·ly·za·tion,** *n.*
e·lec·tro·mag·net 〔ɪˌlɛktro'mægnɪt; i'lektrou'mægnit〕 *n.* 電磁石;電磁鐵。
e·lec·tro·mag·net·ic 〔ɪˌlɛktromæg'nɛtɪk; i'lektroumæg'netik〕 *adj.* ①電磁的;電磁鐵的。②電磁學的。—**al·ly,** *adv.*
e·lec·tro·mag·net·ics 〔ɪˌlɛktromæg'nɛtɪks; i'lektroumæg'netiks〕 *n.* (作 *sing.* 解)電磁學。
e·lec·tro·mag·net·ism 〔ɪˌlɛktro'mægnəˌtɪzəm; i'lektrou'mægnətizəm〕 *n.* 電磁;電磁學。—**e·lec·tro·mag·net·ist,** *n.*
e·lec·tro·met·al·lur·gy 〔ɪˌlɛktro'mɛtḷˌɝdʒɪ; iˌlektroume'tælədʒi〕 *n.* 電氣冶金(術);電氣冶金學。
e·lec·trom·e·ter 〔ɪˌlɛk'trɑmətɚ; ilek'trɔmitə〕 *n.* 靜電計。
e·lec·tro·mo·tive 〔ɪˌlɛktrə'motɪv; i'lektroumoutiv〕 *adj.* 電動的;起電的。—*n.* 電動機車。—**e·lec·tro·mo·tiv·i·ty,** *n.*
e·lec·tro·mo·tor 〔ɪˌlɛktrə'motɚ; i'lektrou'moutə〕 *n.* 電動機;發電機。
*__e·lec·tron__ 〔ɪ'lɛktrɑn; i'lektrɔn〕 *n.* 〖物理〗電子。Atoms are made up of *electrons* and protons. 原子由電子和質子構成。
e·lec·tro·nar·co·sis 〔ɪˌlɛktronɑr'kosɪs; iˌlektrounɑː'kousis〕 *n.* 〖醫〗電流麻醉;電性麻醉。
e·lec·tro·neg·a·tive 〔ɪˌlɛktro'nɛgətɪv; i'lektrou'negətiv〕 *adj.* ①〖電、化〗有陰電荷的;陰電的。②〖物理〗非金屬的。③〖化〗酸性的。—*n.* 帶陰電荷之物質;非金屬物質;酸性物質。—**ly,** *adv.*
electron gun 電子槍。
e·lec·tron·ic 〔ɪˌlɛk'trɑnɪk; ilek'trɔnik〕 *adj.* ①電子的。②由電子作用的。
electronic brain (構造複雜之)電子計算機;電腦。
electronic computer =**electronic brain.**
electronic music 電子音樂。
e·lec·tron·ics 〔ɪˌlɛk'trɑnɪks, ə–; iˌlek'trɔniks, ˌel–, ˌiːl–〕 *n.* (作 *sing.* 解)電子學。
electron lens 電子透鏡。
electron microscope 電子顯微鏡。
electron tube 眞空管;電子管。
electron volt 電子伏(特)。
e·lec·tro·op·tics 〔ɪˌlɛktro'ɑptɪks; iˌlektrou'ɔptiks〕 *n.* (作 *sing.* 解)電場光學。
e·lec·trop·a·thy 〔ɪˌlɛk'trɑpəθɪ; iˌlek'trɔpəθi〕 *n.* =**electrotherapeutics.** —**e·lec·tro·path·ic,** *adj.*
e·lec·tro·pho·re·sis 〔ɪˌlɛktrofə'risɪs; iˌlektroufə'riːsis〕 *n.* 〖物理〗電泳(質點在液體中,因通電而起之運動)。
e·lec·troph·o·rus 〔ɪˌlɛk'trɑfərəs; ilek'trɔfərəs〕 *n., pl.* **-ri** 〔-ˌraɪ; -rai〕. 〖物理〗起電盤。
e·lec·tro·plate 〔ɪ'lɛktrəˌplet; i'lektroupleit〕 *v.,* **-plat·ed, -plat·ing,** *n.* —*v.t.* 電鍍。—*n.* 被電鍍的物品;(特指)鍍銀餐具。—**e·lec·tro·plat·er,** *n.*
e·lec·tro·plat·ing 〔ɪ'lɛktrəˌpletɪŋ; i'lektroupleitiŋ〕 *n.* 電鍍。
e·lec·tro·pos·i·tive 〔ɪˌlɛktrə'pɑzətɪv; i'lektrou'pɔzətiv〕 *adj.* ①有陽電荷的;陽電的。②〖化〗鹽基性的。③〖物理〗金屬的。—*n.* 帶陽電荷之物質;鹽基性物質;金屬物質。
e·lec·tro·scope 〔ɪ'lɛktrəˌskop; i'lektrəskoup〕 *n.* 驗電器。
e·lec·tro·shock 〔ɪ'lɛktroˌʃɑk; i'lektrouʃɔk〕 *n.* 〖醫〗(治療精神病的)電擊療法。
e·lec·tro·stat·ic 〔ɪˌlɛktrə'stætɪk; i'lektrou'stætik〕 *adj.* 靜電的。
e·lec·tro·stat·ics 〔ɪˌlɛktrə'stætɪks; i'lektrou'stætiks〕 *n.* (作 *sing.* 解) 靜電學。

e·lec·tro·ther·a·peu·tics 〔ɪˌlɛktroˌθɛrəˈpjutɪks; iˈlektrouθerəˈpjuːtiks〕 *n.* (作 *sing.* 解)〖醫〗電療學;電療法。

e·lec·tro·ther·a·py 〔ɪˌlɛktroˈθɛrəpɪ; iˈlektrouˈθerəpi〕 *n.* 〖醫〗電療;電療學。

e·lec·tro·type 〔ɪˈlɛktrəˌtaɪp; iˈlektroutaip〕 *n., v.,* **-typed, -typ·ing.** —*n.* ①電版。②電版術。③電版印刷物。—*v.t.* 製…之電版。—*v.i.* 製電版。

e·lec·trum 〔ɪˈlɛktrəm; iˈlektrəm〕 *n.* ①琥珀金(琥珀色之金銀合金)。②含銀之金礦。③洋銀(銅、鎳與鋅之合金)。

e·lec·tu·ar·y 〔ɪˈlɛktʃuˌɛrɪ; iˈlektjuəri〕 *n., pl.* **-ar·ies.** 〖醫〗舐劑;煉製之藥劑。

el·ee·mos·y·nar·y 〔ˌɛləˈmɑsnˌɛrɪ; ˌeliiːˈmɔsinəri〕 *adj.* ①慈善的;賙濟的。②捐助的;不收費的。③依賴救濟而生活的。

***el·e·gance** 〔ˈɛləgəns; ˈeligəns〕 *n.* ①文雅;高雅。②優美;雅潔。③優美之物;雅事。

***el·e·gan·cy** 〔ˈɛləgənsɪ; ˈeligənsi〕 *n., pl.* **-cies.** = **elegance.**

***el·e·gant** 〔ˈɛləgənt; ˈeligənt〕 *adj.* ①(指人)文雅的;高雅的。*elegant* manners. 文雅的舉止。②(指物)優美的;雅潔的。③〖俗〗佳的;好的;上等的。—**ly,** *adv.*

el·e·gi·ac 〔ɪˈlidʒɪˌæk; ˌeliˈdʒaiək〕 *adj.* ①輓詩的;輓歌的。②屬於輓詩(歌)的;合於輓詩(歌)的。③哀悼的。—*n.* (*pl.*)輓歌;輓詩。

el·e·gist 〔ˈɛlɪdʒɪst; ˈelidʒist〕 *n.* 輓歌作者。

el·e·gize 〔ˈɛləˌdʒaɪz; ˈelidʒaiz〕 *v.,* **-gized, -giz·ing.** —*v.i.* 作輓歌。—*v.t.* 以輓歌紀念或哀悼。

el·e·gy 〔ˈɛlədʒɪ; ˈelidʒi〕 *n., pl.* **-gies.** 輓歌;輓詩;悲歌。

elem. ①element. ②elementary. ③elements.

‡el·e·ment 〔ˈɛləmənt; ˈelimənt〕 *n.* ①元素。Gold, iron, tin, oxygen and hydrogen are *elements.* 金、鐵、錫、氧與氫是元素。②要素;成分。Honesty, industry, and kindness are *elements* of a good life. 誠實、勤勉與仁慈是美好生活的要素。③(常 *pl.*)自然的力量(指風、雨等)。④(常 *pl.*)基礎;基本原理;初步;大綱。⑤小量。There is an *element* of truth in his account of what happened. 他對所發生之事的敍述,有一些是確實的。⑥〖軍〗部隊中較小之單位。⑦生活環境。***be in one's element*** 得其所哉;如魚得水。***be out of one's element*** 不得其所;如魚出水。***the elements*** 聖餐中之麪包與酒。***the four elements*** 四元素;四行(卽土、水、風、火)。

el·e·men·tal 〔ˌɛləˈmɛntl; ˌeliˈmentl〕 *adj.* ①元素的;原質的。②要素的;成分的。③自然力的。④基礎的;原理的。⑤可與自然力比擬的。—**ist,** —**ism,** *n.* —**ly,** *adv.*

***el·e·men·ta·ry** 〔ˌɛləˈmɛntərɪ; ˌeliˈmentəri〕 *adj.* ①基礎的;基本的。②初步的;未發展的;未成熟的。He has only an *elementary* knowledge of grammar. 他對文法祇有一點初步的知識。③元素的。

elementary arithmetic 初等算術。

elementary education 初等教育。

elementary school 小學。

el·e·mi 〔ˈɛlɪmɪ; ˈelimi〕 *n., pl.* **-mis.** 欖香(熱帶產之芳香樹脂)。

e·len·chus 〔ɪˈlɛŋkəs; iˈleŋkəs〕 *n., pl.* **-chi** 〔-kaɪ; -kai〕. ①〖邏輯〗反對論證(藉證明某命題之結論爲僞從而否定該命題爲眞實之論辯)。②詭辯。

e·lenc·tic 〔ɪˈlɛŋktɪk; iˈleŋktik〕 *adj.* ①〖邏輯〗反對論證的。②詭辯的。③對質的。

‡el·e·phant 〔ˈɛləfənt; ˈelifənt〕 *n., pl.* **el·e·phants,** (集合稱) **el·e·phant.** 象。***a white elephant*** 大而無用之物或禮品。

el·e·phan·ti·a·sis 〔ˌɛləfənˈtaɪəsɪs; ˌelifənˈtaiəsis〕 *n.* 〖醫〗象皮病;結節癩。

el·e·phan·tine 〔ˌɛləˈfæntin; ˌeliˈfæntain〕 *adj.* ①象的;如象的。②巨大的;沉重的;笨拙的。

el·e·phant's-ear 〔ˈɛlɪfəntsˌɪr; ˈelifəntsˌiə〕 *n.* 葉大呈象耳狀之植物(如芋等)。

***el·e·vate** 〔ˈɛləˌvet; ˈeliveit〕 *v.t.,* **-vat·ed, -vat·ing.** ①舉起;提高。②擢陞;提拔。The soldier was *elevated* to a higher rank for bravery. 此士兵因勇敢而被擢陞。③提高品質。④使興高采烈;使精神興奮。

el·e·vat·ed 〔ˈɛləˌvetɪd; ˈeliveitid〕 *adj.* ①高起的。②高尙的;崇高的。③高興的;愉快的。—*n.*〖俗〗高架鐵路。

elevated railroad (or **railway**) 高架鐵路。

***el·e·va·tion** 〔ˌɛləˈveʃən; ˌeliˈveiʃən〕 *n.* ①高地。②高度;海拔。The *elevation* of Denver is 5,300 feet. Denver 的海拔是 5,300 英尺。③提高;擢陞。④高超。⑤〖建築〗(建築物的正面、側面及背面等之)圖。

***el·e·va·tor** 〔ˈɛləˌvetɚ; ˈeliveitə〕 *n.* ①升降運送機。②電梯。③〖美〗穀倉。④(飛機的)升降舵。〖注意〗作"電梯"解時, **elevator** 爲美語, **lift** 爲英語。

el·e·va·to·ry 〔ˈɛlɪˌvetərɪ; ˈeliveitəri〕 *adj.* 高舉的;舉起的。

‡e·lev·en 〔ɪˈlɛvən; iˈlevn〕 *adj.* 十一。—*n.* ①十一個。②由十一個人組成的球隊。

e·lev·en·fold 〔ɪˈlɛvənˌfold; iˈlevnfould〕 *adj. & adv.* ①十一倍的(地)。②十一重的(地)。

e·lev·enth** 〔ɪˈlɛvənθ; iˈlevnθ〕 *adj.* 第十一;十一號;十一分之一的。eleventh hour*** 最後一刻;接近截止時間。—*n.* 第十一;十一分之一。—**ly,** *adv.*

el·e·von 〔ˈɛləvɑn; ˈeləvɔn〕 *n.* 〖航空〗兩用襟翼。

***elf** 〔ɛlf; elf〕 *n., pl.* **elves.** ①小精靈。②喜歡惡作劇的孩子。③侏儒;矮子。

elf bolt 石鏃(傳爲小鬼所用者)。(亦作 **elf arrow, elf dart**)

elf child 小妖精(將原小孩竊去後)所換留之小孩。

elf·in 〔ˈɛlfɪn; ˈelfin〕 *adj.* 小精靈的;像小精靈的。—*n.* = **elf.**

elf·ish 〔ˈɛlfɪʃ; ˈelfiʃ〕 *adj.* 似小精靈的;惡作劇的。

elf·land 〔ˈɛlfˌlænd; ˈelflænd〕 *n.* 小妖國;魔境。

elf·lock 〔ˈɛlfˌlɑk; ˈelflɔk〕 *n.* 鬈髮;糾結之髮。

e·lic·it 〔ɪˈlɪsɪt; iˈlisit〕 *v.t.* 誘出;引出;抽出。

e·lic·i·ta·tion 〔ɪˌlɪsəˈteʃən; iˌlisiˈteiʃən〕 *n.* 誘出;引出;抽出。

e·lide 〔ɪˈlaɪd; iˈlaid〕 *v.t.,* **-lid·ed, -lid·ing.** ①省略(一母音或一音節)。②略去。

el·i·gi·bil·i·ty 〔ˌɛlədʒəˈbɪlətɪ; ˌelidʒəˈbiliti〕 *n., pl.* **-ties.** 合格;適任。

el·i·gi·ble 〔ˈɛlɪdʒəbl; ˈelidʒəbl〕 *adj.* 合格的。—*n.*合格者。—**el·i·gi·bly,** *adv.*—**ness,** *n.*

E·li·jah 〔ɪˈlaɪdʒə; iˈlaidʒə〕 *n.* 〖聖經〗以利亞(希伯來先知)。

e·lim·i·na·ble 〔ɪˈlɪmənəbl; iˈliminəbl〕 *adj.* 可除去的;可忽略的;可淘汰的。

***e·lim·i·nate** 〔ɪˈlɪməˌnet; iˈlimineit〕 *v.t.,* **-nat·ed, -nat·ing.** ①除去;削減(不適人員);剔除;淘汰。The new bridge over the railroad tracks *eliminated* danger in crossing. 這座新築跨越鐵軌的橋，免除了越過鐵軌時的危險。②忽略；不予考慮。③【數學】(代數中)消去(未知數)。④【生理】排洩。

e·lim·i·na·tion 〔ɪˌlɪmə'neʃən; iˌlimi'neiʃən〕 *n.* ①除去；削減。②排除；排泄。③【數學】消去(法)。④【運動】淘汰。

e·lim·i·na·tor 〔ɪ'lɪməˌnetɚ; i'limineitə〕 *n.* ①除去者；排除器。②【無線電】交流接收裝置。

El·i·ot 〔'ɛlɪət, 'ɛljət; 'eljət, 'eliət〕 *n.* ①艾略特 (George, 1819–1880, 眞名 Mary Ann Evans, 英國小說家)。②艾略特 (Thomas Stearns, 1888–1965, 生於美國之英國詩人及批評家)。

E·li·sha 〔ɪ'laɪʃə; i'laiʃə〕 *n.*【聖經】以利沙 (受教於 Elijah 之先知)。

e·li·sion 〔ɪ'lɪʒən; i'liʒən〕 *n.* ①省略。②(一母音或一音節的)省略。

e·lite 〔ɪ'lit, e'lit; ei'li:t〕 *n.* ①精華。②(常作 *pl.* 解) 社會中或行業中最傑出的人物。—*adj.* 最上等的；最優秀的。

e·lix·ir 〔ɪ'lɪksɚ; i'liksə〕 *n.* ①鍊金藥液。②長生不老藥 (或作 *elixir* vitae, *elixir* of life)。③萬靈藥。④精髓；精華。⑤【藥】數種藥物浸製之醇劑。

Eliz. ①Elizabeth. ②Elizabethan.

E·liz·a·beth 〔ɪ'lɪzəbəθ; i'lizəbəθ〕 *n.* ①Elizabeth I, 伊利莎白一世 (1533–1603, 自 1558 至 1603 之英女王)。②Elizabeth II, 伊利莎白二世 (1926–, 1952 卽位之英女王)。③女子名。(亦作 **Elisabeth**)

E·liz·a·be·than 〔ɪˌlɪzə'biθən; iˌlizə'bi:θən〕 *adj.* 伊利莎白 (一世) 女王的；伊利莎白 (一世) 時代的。—*n.* 其時代的人。

elk 〔ɛlk; elk〕 *n., pl.* **elks, elk.** ①【動物】麋鹿；角鹿。②輕而韌的皮革。

ell[1] 〔ɛl; el〕 *n.* 厄爾 (長度名)。***Give him an inch and he'll take an ell.*** 得寸進尺。

ell[2] *n.* ①字母 L. ②L 形之物；(特指) **a.** 邊廂；側房。**b.**【機械】矩管。

el·lipse 〔ɪ'lɪps; i'lips〕 *n.* 橢圓；橢圓形。

el·lip·sis 〔ɪ'lɪpsɪs; i'lipsis〕 *n., pl.* **-ses** 〔-siz; -si:z〕. ①【文法】省略法。②省略符號 (…或＊＊＊)。

el·lip·soid 〔ɪ'lɪpsɔɪd; i'lipsɔid〕 *n.*【幾何】橢面；橢球。—*adj.* 橢面的；橢球的；橢面形的；橢球形的。

el·lip·tic 〔ɪ'lɪptɪk; i'liptik〕 *adj.* ＝**elliptical.**

el·lip·ti·cal 〔ɪ'lɪptɪkḷ; i'liptikl〕 *adj.* ①橢圓的；橢圓形的。②【文法】省略的。

el·lip·ti·cal·ly 〔ɪ'lɪptəklɪ; i'liptikli〕 *adv.* ①橢圓形地。②省略地；精簡地。③(語氣、思想等)不銜接地。

El·lis Island 〔'ɛlɪs～; 'elis～〕 艾利斯島(紐約港之一小島，昔至美國之移民登陸處)。

***elm** 〔ɛlm; elm〕 *n.* 榆樹；榆木。—**y,** *adj.*

el·o·cu·tion 〔ˌɛlə'kjuʃən; ˌelə'kju:ʃən〕 *n.* ①辯論術；演說術。②演說法或狀態；朗誦法。③說話時之矯揉做作。—**ar·y,** *adj.*

el·o·cu·tion·ist 〔ˌɛlə'kjuʃənɪst; ˌelə'kju:ʃnist〕 *n.* ①縱橫家；善辯者；演說家。②教授講演術者。

é·loge 〔e'loʒ; ei'louʒ〕【法】*n.* 追悼演說。

E·lo·him 〔ɛ'lohɪm; e'louhim〕 *n.* 上帝；神(希伯來聖經用語)。

E. lon(g). East longitude.

e·lon·gate 〔'ɪlɔŋget; 'i:lɔŋgeit〕 *v.,* **-gat·ed, -gat·ing,** *adj.* —*v.t.* & *v.i.* 延長；伸延。—*adj.* ①延長的。②修長的。

e·lon·ga·tion 〔ɪˌlɔŋ'geʃən; ˌi:lɔŋ'geiʃən〕 *n.* ①延長；伸長。②延長之物；延長的部分。③【天文】離日度(與太陽的距離)。

e·lope 〔ɪ'lop; i'loup〕 *v.i.,* **-loped, -lop·ing.** ①私奔；淫奔。②逃亡；私逃。—**ment,** *n.*

***el·o·quence** 〔'ɛləkwəns; 'eləkwəns, 'elou-〕 *n.* 雄辯；口才。

***el·o·quent** 〔'ɛləkwənt; 'eləkwənt, 'elou-〕 *adj.* 雄辯的；動人的。—**ly,** *adv.*

El Sal·va·dor 〔ɛl'sælvəˌdɔr; el'sælvədɔ:〕 薩爾瓦多 (中美洲一國，首都聖薩爾瓦多 San Salvador)。

‡**else** 〔ɛls; els〕 *adj.* 別的；其他。anybody *else.* 別的人。nobody *else.* 沒有別的人。somebody *else.* 別的人。Who *else* is coming? 還有甚麼別人要來？—*adv.* 此外；別的。Where *else* did you go? 你還去了別的甚麼地方？—*conj.* 否則；不然的話 (亦作 **or else**)。Hurry, *else* you will be late. 快點，不然你就要遲到了。【注意】**else** 用於其所形容之名詞(常爲代名詞)後面時，可帶有所有格之記號：He finally decided the book was somebody *else's.* 最後他斷定這書是別人的。

***else·where** 〔'ɛlsˌhwɛr; 'els'wɛə〕 *adv.* 在別處；在別的地方；往別的地方。Can you find anything like this *elsewhere?* 你能在別處找到像這樣的東西嗎？(亦作 **elsewhither**)

e·lu·ci·date 〔ɪ'lusəˌdet; i'lu:sideit〕 *v.t.,* **-dat·ed, -dat·ing.** 闡明；說明。—**e·lu·ci·da·tion,** *n.*

e·lu·ci·da·tive 〔ɪ'lusəˌdetɪv; i'lu:sideitiv〕 *adj.* 闡釋的；說明的。(亦作 **elucidatory**)

e·lu·ci·da·tor 〔ɪ'lusəˌdetɚ; i'lu:sideitə〕 *n.* 闡釋者；說明者。

e·lude 〔ɪ'lud; i'lu:d〕 *v.i.,* **-lud·ed, -lud·ing.** ①躲避；規避；逃脫。②困惑；使迷離。The idea *eludes* me. 那意思使我困惑。

e·lu·sion 〔ɪ'luʒən; i'lu:ʒən〕 *n.* 躲避；規避。

e·lu·sive 〔ɪ'lusɪv; i'lu:siv〕 *adj.* ①規避的；躲避的。②難懂的；難記憶的；令人困惑的；難捉摸的。—**ly,** *adv.* —**ness,** *n.*

e·lu·so·ry 〔ɪ'lusərɪ; i'lu:səri〕 *adj.* ＝**elusive** (尤用於心理印象方面)。

e·lu·tri·ate 〔ɪ'lutrɪˌet; i'lu:trieit〕 *v.t.,* **-at·ed, -at·ing.** ①洗淨；淘淨。②冲洗以使…之細粒與粗粒分開。

el·ver 〔'ɛlvɚ; 'elvə〕 *n.*【動物】幼鰻。

elves 〔ɛlvz; elvz〕 *n.* pl. of **elf.**

elv·ish 〔'ɛlvɪʃ; 'elviʃ〕 *adj.* 小妖精的；惡作劇的。

E·ly·sée 〔eli'ze; eili:'zei〕【法】*n.* 巴黎之一宮殿(法國總統官邸)。

E·ly·sian 〔ɪ'lɪʒən; i'liziən〕 *adj.* 天堂的；幸福的；快樂的。***the Elysian Fields***【希臘神話】天堂樂土；極樂世界。

E·ly·si·um 〔ɪ'lɪʒɪəm; i'liziəm〕 *n.* ①【希臘神話】善人死後所居之樂土。②天堂；樂土。

El·ze·vir 〔'ɛlzəvɚ; 'elziviə〕 *n.* ①厄爾澤維 (Louis, 1540?–1617, 荷蘭之一著名印刷廠的創辦人)。②該廠出版之書籍。③該廠所使用之活字。—*adj.* 厄爾澤維家族的；該家族創始之活字的。

EM ①enlisted men. ②East Mark. 東德之馬克。

Em. emanation.

em 〔ɛm; em〕 *n.* ①M 字母。②【印刷】全方 (一鉛字所占之面積)。—*adj.* ①M 形的。②【印刷】有全方之面積的。

E.M. Engineer of Mines.

'em 〔əm; əm〕 *pron.*【俗】＝**them.**

em-【字首】**en-** 之異體。

e·ma·ci·ate 〔ɪ'meʃɪˌet; i'meiʃieit〕 *v.t.,*

-at·ed, -at·ing. 使瘦弱; 使憔悴。
e·ma·ci·at·ed 〔ɪ'meʃɪˌetɪd; i'meiʃieitid, e'm-〕 *adj.* 瘦弱的;憔悴的。
e·ma·ci·a·tion 〔ɪˌmeʃɪ'eʃən; iˌmeisi'eiʃən〕 *n.* 瘦弱;憔悴。
em·a·nate 〔'ɛməˌnet; 'eməneit〕 *v.i.*, **-nat·ed, -nat·ing.** 流出;發出;發散。
em·a·na·tion 〔ˌɛmə'neʃən; ˌemə'neiʃən〕 *n.* ①流出;發出;散發;發射。②發出物;流出物。③〖化〗放射性物質解體時放出之氣體。
em·a·na·tive 〔'ɛməˌnetɪv; 'eməneitiv〕 *adj.* 流出性的;發散的;放射的。
e·man·ci·pate 〔ɪ'mænsəˌpet; i'mænsipeit〕 *v.*, **-pat·ed, -pat·ing,** *adj.* —*v.t.* ①解放(奴隸);解除(束縛)。②〖羅馬法〗解除父母對兒童之管教。—*adj.* 解放的。
e·man·ci·pa·tion 〔ɪˌmænsə'peʃən; iˌmænsi'peiʃən〕 *n.* 解放;解脫;解除。
Emancipation Proclamation (1863年1月1日美國林肯總統所頒布之)黑奴解放令。
e·man·ci·pa·tion·ist 〔ɪˌmænsə'peʃənɪst; iˌmænsi'peiʃənist〕 *n.* 解放主義者。
e·man·ci·pa·tive 〔ɪ'mænsəˌpetɪv; i'mænsipeitiv〕 *adj.* 有助於解放的; 旨在解放的。
e·man·ci·pa·tor 〔ɪ'mænsəˌpetɚ; i'mænsipeitə〕*n.* 解放者;釋放者。***the Great Emancipator*** 大解放者(Abraham Lincoln 之尊稱)。
e·man·ci·pa·to·ry 〔ɪ'mænsəpəˌtorɪ; i'mænsipeitəri〕 *adj.* 解放的; 解除的。
e·mas·cu·late 〔*v.* ɪ'mæskjəˌlet; i'mæskjuleit *adj.* ɪ'mæskjəˌlɪt; i'mæskjulit〕 *v.*, **-lat·ed, -lat·ing,** *adj.* —*v.t.* ①閹割;去勢。②使柔弱。③使(文章)失去雄偉氣勢。—*adj.* ①去勢的;柔弱的。②失去雄偉氣勢的(文章)。 —**e·mas·cu·la·to·ry, e·mas·cu·la·tive,** *adj.* —**e·mas·cu·la·tion,** *n.*
em·balm 〔ɪm'bɑm; im'bɑːm〕 *v.t.* ①塗敷香料藥物等於(屍體)以防腐; 薰香。②使香; 使瀰漫香味。 ③銘記; 銘刻於心。(亦作 **imbalm**) —**ment,** *n.*
em·bank 〔ɪm'bæŋk; im'bæŋk〕 *v.t.* 築堤;築(鐵路的)路基。—**ment,** *n.*
em·bar 〔ɛm'bɑr; em'bɑː〕 *v.t.*, **-barred, -bar·ring.** ①囚禁;關入。②阻遏;使停止。
em·bar·go 〔ɪm'bɑrgo; em'bɑːgou〕 *n.*, *pl.* **-goes,** *v.*, **-goed, -go·ing.** —*n.* ①禁止船舶出入港口;封港令; 禁運。②禁止通商; 禁止貿易。a gold *embargo.* 禁止或限制黃金交易。③禁止;限制;阻礙。***lift*** (***raise,*** or ***take off***) ***the embargo on*** 對…解禁。—*v.t.* ①禁止(船舶)出入港口;禁止(通商)。②扣押(船舶、貨物等)。
***em·bark** 〔ɪm'bɑrk; im'bɑːk, em-〕 *v.i.* ①乘船; 搭載。 ②着手; 從事。 to *embark* upon an action. 着手一項行動。 —*v.t.* ①裝於船上。The ship *embarked* passengers and cargo. 該船裝載客貨。②邀(某人)入夥;投(資)於某企業。—**ment,** *n.*
em·bar·ka·tion 〔ˌɛmbɑr'keʃən; ˌembɑː'keiʃən〕 *n.* ①乘船;搭載。②着手;從事。(亦作 **embarcation**)
embarkation deck 緊急情況時乘客與船員搭乘救生艇之甲板。
***em·bar·rass** 〔ɪm'bærəs; im'bærəs, em-〕 *v.t.* ①使困窘; 使侷促不安。 He has been *embarrassed* by debts for years. 他爲債務困窘多年了。②阻礙;妨礙。③使複雜;使錯綜;使困難。
em·bar·rass·ing 〔ɪm'bærəsɪŋ; im'bærəsiŋ〕 *adj.* 令人困窘的。—**ly,** *adv.*
***em·bar·rass·ment** 〔ɪm'bærəsmənt; im'bærəsmənt, em-〕 *n.* ①困窘;困難;困惑。Blushes showed her *embarrassment.* 她的困窘由她面頰發紅表現出來。②妨害。③令人困窘之事。④太多的數量。
em·bas·sa·dor 〔ɪm'bæsədɚ; im'bæsədə〕 *n.* =**ambassador.**
***em·bas·sy** 〔'ɛmbəsɪ; 'embəsi〕 *n.*, *pl.* **-sies.** ①大使館的全體人員。②大使館。Chinese *Embassy* in Washington. 駐華盛頓的中國大使館。③大使之地位及職務。④特使;特別使節團。⑤特別使命;重要任務。
em·bat·tle¹ 〔ɛm'bætl̩; im'bætl〕 *v.t.*, **-tled, -tling.** ①布陣。②備戰; 設防(城市等)。
em·bat·tle² *v.t.*, **-tled, -tling.** 築以城垛;設雉堞於。
em·bay 〔ɛm'be; im'bei〕 *v.t.* ①使(船)等庇護於港灣內。②環繞;圍繞。③使形成港灣狀。—**ment,** *n.*
em·bed 〔ɪm'bɛd; im'bed, em-〕 *v.t.*, **-bed·ded, -bed·ding.** ①埋入;埋於土中。②嵌於;插入。③使銘記於心。(亦作 **imbed**)
em·bel·lish 〔ɪm'bɛlɪʃ; im'beliʃ〕 *v.t.* ①裝飾;布置。②修飾;潤色。
em·bel·lish·ment 〔ɪm'bɛlɪʃmənt; im'beliʃmənt〕 *n.* ①裝飾;布置。②裝飾品。③故事敍述中之想像的細節。
***em·ber** 〔'ɛmbɚ; 'embə〕 *n.* ①燃屑。②(*pl.*)餘燼。—*adj.* 四季大齋日的。*Ember* days. 四季大齋日。
em·bez·zle 〔ɪm'bɛzl̩; im'bezl〕 *v.t.*, **-zled, -zling.** 盗用(公款、公物);監守自盜;侵吞。—**ment, em·bez·zler,** *n.*
em·bit·ter 〔ɪm'bɪtɚ; im'bitə〕 *v.t.*①使苦;使痛苦;使難受。②使更苦;激怒。—**ment,** *n.*
em·bla·zon 〔ɛm'blezn̩; im'bleizən〕 *v.t.* ①飾以紋章。②盛飾;使炫耀。③頌揚;稱讚。—**ment,** *n.*
em·bla·zon·ry 〔ɛm'blezn̩rɪ; im'bleizənri〕 *n.*, *pl.* **-ries.** ①紋章描畫; 紋章之裝飾。②炫耀之裝飾;美飾。
em·blem 〔'ɛmbləm; 'embləm〕 *n.* ①象徵。②紋章;徽章。—*v.t.* 以象徵或徽章代表。
em·blem·at·ic 〔ˌɛmblə'mætɪk; ˌembli'mætik〕 *adj.* 象徵的;表記的〖of〗. (亦作 **emblematical**) —**al·ly,** *adv.*
em·blem·a·tist 〔ɛm'blɛmətɪst; em'blemətist〕 *n.* 設計、製造或使用標號、徽章等者。
em·blem·a·tize 〔ɛm'blɛməˌtaɪz; em'bleməta iz〕 *v.t.*, **-tized, -tiz·ing.** 象徵;表以記號;作爲…之表記。
em·ble·ments 〔'ɛmblɪmənts; 'emblimənts〕 *n. pl.* 〖法律〗耕作地之收穫或孳息。
em·bod·i·ment 〔ɪm'bɑdɪmənt; im'bɔdimənt〕 *n.* ①賦與形體;具體化。②化身。③組成之系統;體系。
***em·bod·y** 〔ɪm'bɑdɪ; im'bɔdi, em-〕 *v.t.*, **-bod·ied, -bod·y·ing.** ①使具體化; 具體表現。Words *embody* thought. 言語具體表現思想。②編入;搜集在內。
em·bold·en 〔ɪm'boldn̩; im'bouldən〕 *v.t.* 增加勇氣;鼓勵;助長(某人)的氣勢;壯膽。
em·bo·lism 〔'ɛmbəˌlɪzəm; 'embəlizəm〕 *n.* ①閏;置閏。②〖醫〗栓塞。
em·bo·lis·mi·cal year 〔ˌɛmbə'lɪzmək l̩~; ˌembə'lizməkəl~〕 陰曆閏年。
em·bo·lize 〔'ɛmbəlaɪz; 'embəlaiz〕 *v.t.* 以栓塞阻止流通。

em·bo·lus [ˈɛmbələs; ˈembələs] *n., pl.* **-li** [-ˌlaɪ; -lai]. ①〖醫〗栓子;栓(血液中之氣泡或其他不溶性物質)。②楔;活塞;挿入物。

em·bon·point [ɑ̃bɔ̃ˈpwæ̃; ˌɔ̃:mbɔ̃:mˈpwɛ̃:ŋ]〖法〗*n.* (女子的)豐滿之體態(肥胖之婉轉語)。

em·bosk [ɛmˈbɑsk; emˈbɔsk] *v.t.* 藏「在樹葉叢中。

em·bos·om [ɛmˈbuzəm; imˈbuzəm] *v.t.* ①包圍;環繞。a house *embosomed* in (*or* with) trees. 被樹木環繞着的屋子。②納諸懷中;珍護。

em·boss [ɪmˈbɔs; imˈbɔs] *v.t.* ①加浮雕花紋於其上。②使隆起;印浮凸文字或圖樣。*embossed* printing. 浮凸印刷術。**—ment,** *n.*

em·bou·chure [ˌɑmbuˈʃʊr; ˌɔmbuˈʃuə]〖法〗*n.* ①河口;谷口。②任何口狀之物。③〖音樂〗**a.** 吹口。**b.** 運唇法。

em·bow·el [ɛmˈbauəl; imˈbauəl] *v.t.,* **-el(l)ed, -el·(l)ing.** 切腹取腸。

em·bow·er [ɛmˈbauɚ; imˈbauə] *v.t.* 以樹葉遮蓋;隱於樹葉中。—*v.i.* 棲息於涼亭中;憩於樹蔭。

*__em·brace__ [ɪmˈbres; imˈbreis, em-] *v.,* **-braced, -brac·ing,** *n.* —*v.t.* ①擁抱。He *embraced* her in his arms. 他擁抱她。②接受。③包含;包括。④圍繞。⑤利用。to *embrace* an opportunity. 利用一個機會。⑥信奉。to *embrace* Buddhism. 信仰佛教。—*v.i.*互相擁抱。—*n.* 擁抱。He held her to him in a warm *embrace.* 他熱烈的擁抱她。

em·brace·or [ɪmˈbresɚ; imˈbreisə] *n.*〖法律〗企圖以非法手段影響法庭或陪審團的人。

em·brac·er [ɪmˈbresɚ; imˈbreisə] 「*n.* ①擁抱者。② =**embraceor.**

em·brac·er·y [ɪmˈbresərɪ; imˈbreisəri] *n.*〖法律〗以非法手段影響法庭或陪審團之企圖。

em·bran·gle [ɛmˈbræŋgl; emˈbræŋgl] *v.t.,* **-gled, -gling.** 使紛亂;使生糾紛。(亦作 **imbrangle**)

em·bra·sure [ɛmˈbreʒɚ; imˈbreiʒə] *n.* ①〖築城〗(碉堡等之)砲眼。②〖建築〗(門、窗之)內寬外窄之開口。

em·brit·tle [ɛmˈbrɪtl; emˈbritl] *v.t.,* **-tled, -tling.** 使(金屬)變脆。

em·bro·cate [ˈɛmbroˌket; ˈembroukeit] *v.t.,* **-cat·ed, -cat·ing.** 塗敷;塗擦。

em·bro·ca·tion [ˌɛmbroˈkeʃən; ˌembrouˈkeiʃən] *n.* ①擦劑。②擦劑的塗擦。

*__em·broi·der__ [ɪmˈbrɔɪdɚ; imˈbrɔidə, em-] *v.t.* ①刺繡;繡花於…。②潤飾(語言);鋪張。—*v.i.* 刺繡。**—er,** *n.*

em·broi·der·ess [ɪmˈbrɔɪdərɪs; imˈbrɔidəris] *n.* 刺繡的婦女。

*__em·broi·der·y__ [ɪmˈbrɔɪdərɪ; imˈbrɔidəri, em-] *n., pl.* **-der·ies.** ①刺繡。②刺繡藝品。③鋪張之詞;誇大。***embroidery frame*** 刺繡架。

em·broil [ɛmˈbrɔɪl; imˈbrɔil] *v.t.* ①拖累;捲入糾紛中;牽連。②使混亂;使複雜。

em·broil·ment [ɛmˈbrɔɪlmənt; imˈbrɔilmənt] *n.* 混亂;糾紛;捲入漩渦。

em·brown [ɛmˈbraun; imˈbraun] *v.t.* 着褐色於;使暗。—*v.i.* 成褐色;變暗。

em·brute [ɛmˈbrut; emˈbru:t] *v.,* **-brut·ed, -brut·ing.** —*v.t.* 使如禽獸;使殘忍。—*v.i.* 變爲禽獸;變殘忍。(亦作**imbrute**)

em·bry·o [ˈɛmbrɪˌo; ˈembriou] *n., pl.* **-bry·os,** *adj.* —*n.* ①〖植物〗胚芽。②〖動物〗幼蟲;胚胎。③初期;萌芽期。***in embryo*** 初期的;萌芽的;在考慮中。—*adj.* ①胚胎的;幼蟲的。②初期的;未發達的。

em·bry·oc·to·ny [ˌɛmbrɪˈɑktənɪ; ˌembriˈɔktəni] *n.* 殺胎;墮胎。

em·bry·oid [ˈɛmbrɪˌɔɪd; ˈembriɔid] *adj.* 胚胎的;胚胎狀的。

em·bry·ol·o·gy [ˌɛmbrɪˈɑlədʒɪ; ˌembriˈɔlədʒi] *n.* 胚胎學;發生學。**—em·bry·ol·o·gist,** *n.* **—em·bry·o·log·ic, em·bry·o·log·i·cal,** *adj.*

em·bry·on·ic [ˌɛmbrɪˈɑnɪk; ˌembriˈɔnik] *adj.* ①胚芽的;胚胎的;幼蟲的。②萌芽期的;未發達的。

embryo sac〖植物〗胚囊。

em·bus [ɛmˈbʌs; emˈbʌs] *v.t. & v.i.*〖軍〗裝入或登乘大卡車。

em·cee [ˈɛmˈsi; ˈemˈsi:] *v.,* **-ceed, -cee·ing,** *n.* —*v.t.*〖俚〗作(廣播節目等)之節目主持人。—*n.*〖俚〗司儀;節目主持人。

e·mend [ɪˈmɛnd; i(:)ˈmend] *v.t.* 修訂;修正;(特指文稿之)詮正;校訂。**—a·ble,** *adj.*

e·men·date [ˈimənˌdet; ˈi:məndeit] *v.t.,* **-dat·ed, -dat·ing.** =**emend.**

e·men·da·tion [ˌimɛnˈdeʃən; ˌi:menˈdeiʃən] *n.* ①修正;修改。②校訂。

e·men·da·tor [ˈimənˌdetɚ; ˈi:mendeitə] *n.* 修正者;校訂者。

e·men·da·to·ry [ɪˈmɛndəˌtorɪ; i(:)ˈmendətəri] *adj.* 修正的;校訂的。

*__em·er·ald__ [ˈɛmərəld; ˈemərəld, ˈemrəld] *n.* ①翡翠;綠寶石。an *emerald* ring. 翡翠戒指。②翠綠色。③一種印刷鉛字(6½ 磅因)。—*adj.* 翠綠色的。the *Emerald* Isle. 綠島(愛爾蘭的別稱)。

*__e·merge__ [ɪˈmɝdʒ; iˈmə:dʒ] *v.i.,* **e·merged, e·merg·ing.** ①出現;露出。The sun *emerged* from behind the clouds. 太陽自雲後出現。②(自卑微、貧窮等)出人頭地;脫穎而出。Many distinguished men have *emerged* from slums. 很多名人都出身於貧民窟。

e·mer·gence [ɪˈmɝdʒəns; iˈmə:dʒəns] *n.* ①現出;露出。②〖植物〗外部突出物。

*__e·mer·gen·cy__ [ɪˈmɝdʒənsɪ; iˈmə:dʒənsi] *n., pl.* **-cies.** 緊急事件;緊急需要。*emergency* door. 太平門。*emergency* measures. 緊急應變措施。***in case of emergency*** 在緊急時。

e·mer·gent [ɪˈmɝdʒənt; iˈmə:dʒənt] *adj.* ①現出的;露出的。②意外的;緊急的。③爲必然之後果而發生的。④剛獲得獨立的。the *emergent* nations of Africa. 非洲新獨立的國家。

e·mer·i·tus [ɪˈmɛrətəs; i(:)ˈmeritəs] *adj., n., pl.* **-ti** [-taɪ; -tai]. —*adj.* 名譽退休的;保留銜稱而退休的。—*n.* 名譽退休者。〖注意〗**emeritus** 作形容詞用時,常置於名詞後,但亦可置於名詞前: (a) professor *emeritus* 或 (an) *emeritus* professor. 退休名譽教授。複數作 professors *emeriti.*

e·mer·sion [ɪˈmɝʃən; i(:)ˈmə:ʃən] *n.* ①出現;浮出。②〖天文〗(日蝕、月蝕後或其他天體受遮掩後之)復明。

Em·er·son [ˈɛmɚsn̩; ˈeməsn] *n.* 愛默生 (Ralph Waldo, 1803–1882, 美國哲學家、散文家及詩人)。

Em·er·so·ni·an [ˌɛmɚˈsonɪən; ˌemə:ˈsouniən] *adj.* 愛默生的;與愛默生有關的。—*n.* ①愛默生之擁護者或模仿者。②研究愛默生著作之專家。

em·er·y [ˈɛmərɪ;ˈeməri] *n.*〖礦〗金剛砂。
emery cloth 金剛砂布;鑪布。
emery paper 金剛砂紙;鑪紙。
emery wheel 金剛砂旋轉磨石;鑪輪。
em·e·sis [ˈɛməsɪs;ˈeməsis] *n.*〖醫〗嘔吐。
e·met·ic [ɪˈmɛtɪk; iˈmetik] *adj.*〖醫〗使人嘔吐的。—*n.* 催吐劑。
é·meute [eˈmœt; eiˈməːt]〖法〗*n.* 暴動;騷動。
E.M.F., e.m.f. electromotive force.
e·mic·tion [ɪˈmɪkʃən; iˈmikʃən] *n.* ①小解。②尿。
***em·i·grant** [ˈɛməgrənt;ˈemigrənt] *n.* 移居他國者;移民;僑民。—*adj.* 移居他國的;移民的。*emigrant* laborers. 移居他國的勞工。
em·i·grate [ˈɛməˌgret;ˈemigreit] *v.i.*, **-grat·ed, -grat·ing.** 遷居他國;移居。〖注意〗**emigrate** 指自本國移出。**immigrate** 指自他國移入。
em·i·gra·tion [ˌɛməˈgreʃən; ˌemiˈgreiʃən] *n.* ①向國外移居。②僑民們。
em·i·gra·to·ry [ˈɛməgrəˌtorɪ; ˈemigrətəri] *adj.* 移民的;遷居出境的;移棲的。
é·mi·gré [ˈɛməˌgre, emiˈgre; ˈemigrei] *n., pl.* **-grés.**〖法〗①(因政治迫害而)移居者。②(因法國大革命而)逃亡者;亡命者。
Em·i·ly [ˈɛmɪlɪ; ˈemili] *n.* 女子名。
***em·i·nence** [ˈɛmənəns; ˈeminəns] *n.* ①高地;山丘。②高位;顯職;令名;卓越。Edison won *eminence* as an inventor. 愛迪生以發明家之身分而聞名。③(E-)天主教對紅衣主教之尊稱。
***em·i·nent** [ˈɛmənənt; ˈeminənt] *adj.* ①聞名的;顯赫的。an *eminent* person. 知名之士。②高的;巍峨的。③顯著的;可察的。④明顯的;突出的。**—ly,** *adv.*
eminent domain〖法律〗國家徵用私產權(業主應獲得補償)。
e·mir [əˈmɪr; eˈmiə] *n.* ①阿拉伯之酋長、王侯或統帥。②穆罕默德(Mohammed)後裔的尊號。③土耳其高官的尊號。(亦作 **emeer**)
e·mir·ate [əˈmɪrɪt; əˈmiərit] *n.* ①阿拉伯酋長或王子之職位或階級。②阿拉伯酋長或王子之轄地;酋長國。(亦作 **emeerate**)
em·is·sar·y [ˈɛməˌsɛrɪ; ˈemisəri] *n., pl.* **-sar·ies,** *adj.* —*n.* ①密使;使者。②特務;間諜。—*adj.* 密使的;特務的。
e·mis·sion [ɪˈmɪʃən; iˈmiʃən] *n.* ①發出;發射;發光。②發布;發行(紙幣)。③放射物;發射物;流出物。④〖醫〗身體內排出液體;(尤指)遺精。nocturnal *emission.* 夢遺。
e·mis·sive [ɪˈmɪsɪv; iˈmisiv, iːˈm-] *adj.* 發射的;放射(性)的。
e·mit [ɪˈmɪt; iˈmit, iːˈm-] *v.t.*, **-mit·ted, -mit·ting.** ①放射(光、熱等);噴射。②發出(聲音)。③吐露(意見、思想等)。④發布(命令);發行(紙幣)。
Emm [ɛm; em] **Em·mie** [ˈɛmɪ; ˈemi] *n.* 女子名(Emma 之暱稱)。
Em·ma [ˈɛmə; ˈemə] *n.* 女子名。
Em·man·u·el [ɪˈmænjuəl; iˈmænjuəl] *n.* ①男子名。②基督(=Immanuel).
em·mar·ble [ɪˈmɑrbl̩; iˈmɑːbl] *v.t.*, **-bled, -bling.** 以大理石裝飾;用大理石雕刻;刻成大理石像。
em·men·a·gogue [əˈmɛnəgɔg; əˈmenəgɔg] *n.*〖醫〗通經劑;調經藥。
em·men·i·a [əˈmɛnɪə;əˈmeniə] *n.* 月經。
em·men·i·op·a·thy [əˌmɛnɪˈɑpəθɪ; əˌmeniˈɔpəθi] *n.*〖生理〗月經不調。
em·me·tro·pi·a [ˌɛməˈtropɪə; ˌeməˈtroupiə] *n.* 正視眼。
Em·my [ˈɛmɪ; ˈemi] *n., pl.* **-mies, -mys.** 艾美獎(美國電視之最高榮譽獎)。
e·mol·lient [ɪˈmɑljənt;iˈmɔliənt] *adj.* 使柔軟的;使柔和的。—*n.*(皮膚的)緩和藥;鎮痛劑。
e·mol·u·ment [ɪˈmɑljəmənt; iˈmɔljumənt] *n.* 薪俸;報酬;費。
e·mote [ɪˈmot; iˈmout] *v.i.*, **e·mot·ed, e·mot·ing.**〖俗〗激情地作爲;表演重感情之角色(常爲幽默用語)。
***e·mo·tion** [ɪˈmoʃən; iˈmouʃən] *n.* 情感;情緒;激情;感情。Love, hate, joy, fear and grief are *emotions.* 愛、恨、喜、懼與悲都是情感。
***e·mo·tion·al** [ɪˈmoʃənl̩; iˈmouʃənl] *adj.* ①情感的;情緒的。*emotional* expression. 表情。②訴諸情感的;感動人的。③易受感動的。an *emotional* woman. 多愁善感的女人。**—ly,** *n.*
e·mo·tion·al·ism [ɪˈmoʃənl̩ˌɪzəm; iˈmouʃn̩əlizəm] *n.* ①感人性。②訴諸感情。③動情之傾向(尤指病態者)。④感情表現。⑤〖倫理〗情緒本位說。
e·mo·tion·al·ist [ɪˈmoʃənəlɪst;iˈmouʃənəlist] *n.* ①訴諸感情之人。②易受感動之人;易動感情之人。③〖倫理〗情緒本位說者。
e·mo·tion·al·i·ty [ɪˌmoʃənˈælətɪ; iˌmouʃənˈæliti] *n.* 情感性;感動性。
e·mo·tion·al·ize [ɪˈmoʃənl̩ˌaɪz, -ʃnəl-;iˈmouʃənəlaiz] *v.t.*, **-ized, -iz·ing.** ①激動;使動情。②視爲純感情之事;感情化。
e·mo·tive [ɪˈmotɪv; iˈmoutiv] *adj.* 情感的;表現感情的;令人感動的。**—ly,** *adv.*
Emp. ① Emperor. ② Empire. ③ Empress.
e.m.p.〖處方〗照方處理(=as directed).
em·pai·stic [ɛmˈpestɪk; emˈpeistik] *adj.*(裝飾品)有隆地花紋的;鑲嵌的;銘刻的。
em·pan·el [ɪmˈpænl̩; imˈpænl, em-] *v.t.*, **-el(l)ed, -el·(l)ing.** ①登錄…之姓名於陪審員名簿。②從陪審員名簿挑選(陪審員)。
em·pa·thy [ˈɛmpəθɪ; ˈempəθi] *n.*〖心理〗神入。
em·pen·nage [ɑ̃pɛˈnɑʒ; ɑ̃peˈnɔʒ]〖法〗*n.*〖航空〗機尾;尾部。
***em·per·or** [ˈɛmpərɚ; ˈempərə] *n.* 皇帝;君主。
em·per·y [ˈɛmpərɪ; ˈempəri] *n., pl.* **-per·ies.**〖詩〗①至高無上之權力。②帝國(之領土)。
***em·pha·sis** [ˈɛmfəsɪs; ˈemfəsis] *n., pl.* **-ses** [-ˌsiz; -siːz]. ①强調;重要。Some schools lay special *emphasis* on language study. 有些學校特別注重語文學科。②加重語氣;重讀。③强調之事物。Morality was the *emphasis* of his speech. 道德是他演講的重點。
***em·pha·size** [ˈɛmfəˌsaɪz; ˈemfəsaiz] *v.t.*, **-sized, -siz·ing.** ①特別着重地說;强調;重讀。Pronouns are not usually *emphasized.* 代名詞通常不重讀。②喚起注意。
em·phat·ic [ɪmˈfætɪk; imˈfætik] *adj.* ①有力的;强調的。②引人注意的;驚人的。**—al·ly,** *adv.*
em·phy·se·ma [ˌɛmfɪˈsimə; ˌemfiˈsiːmə] *n.*〖醫〗氣腫;肺氣腫。
‡**em·pire** [ˈɛmpaɪr; ˈempaiə] *n.* ①帝國。the Roman *Empire.* 羅馬帝國。②絕對權力;最高威權。③大企業。
Em·pire *adj.*(服裝、傢具等)第一法蘭西帝國時期之款式的。

Empire Day 英帝國節(5月24日)。
Empire State 美國紐約州之別名。
em·pir·ic [ɛmˈpɪrɪk; emˈpirik, im-] *n.* ①沒有科學知識而只憑經驗行事的人；經驗主義者。②沒有受過正式訓練的人；庸醫；江湖醫生。—*adj.* =**empirical.**
em·pir·i·cal [ɛmˈpɪrɪkl̩; emˈpirikl, im-] *adj.* ①只憑經驗的。②經驗主義的；憑實驗的。*empirical* philosophy. 經驗哲學。—**ly,** *adv.*
empirical formula 〖化學〗實驗式。
em·pir·i·cism [ɛmˈpɪrəˌsɪzəm; emˈpirisizəm, im-] *n.* ①經驗主義。②〖哲學〗經驗論。③專靠經驗；以經驗爲主。④經驗醫術；庸醫之醫術。
em·pir·i·cist [ɛmˈpɪrəsɪst; emˈpirisist] *n.* 經驗論者；經驗主義者；經驗醫術者。
Em·pi·rin [ˈɛmpərɪn; ˈemparin] *n.* 〖商標名〗阿斯匹靈之商標。
em·place [ɛmˈples; emˈpleis] *v.t.,* **-placed, -plac·ing.** 放；置。
em·place·ment [ɪmˈplesmənt; imˈpleismənt, em-] *n.* ①定位置。②〖軍〗砲位；砲兵之掩體。
em·plane [ɛmˈplen; emˈplein] *v.t.* & *v.i.,* **em·planed, em·plan·ing.** 裝(乘)飛機。
em·plas·tic [ɛmˈplæstɪk; emˈplæstik] *adj.* 黏性的。—*n.* 黏性物質。
:**em·ploy** [ɪmˈplɔɪ; imˈplɔi, em-] *v.t.* ①雇用；使用。I *employ* my spare time in reading. 我利用空閒時間讀書。②使專心；使忙於；使從事。She *employed* herself in reading. 她勤於閱讀。—*n.* 雇用。I have more than 200 persons in my *employ.* 我雇用了兩百多人。*out of employ* 失業。—**a·bil·i·ty,** *n.* —**a·ble,** *adj.*
·**em·ploy·e(e)** [ɪmˈplɔɪ·i, ˌɛmplɔɪˈi; ˌemplɔiˈiː, emˈplɔiiː, imˈplɔiiː] *n.* 被雇者；雇工；職員。The firm has 200 *employees.* 這公司擁有二百員工。
·**em·ploy·er** [ɪmˈplɔɪɚ; imˈplɔiə, em-] *n.* 雇主；老板。
·**em·ploy·ment** [ɪmˈplɔɪmənt; imˈplɔimənt] *n.* ①職業；工作。He is looking for *employment.* 他正在找工作。②雇用。in the *employment* of. 受雇於。③使用；利用。the *employment* of capital. 資金的運用。④消遣。***get*** (or ***obtain***) ***employment*** 尋得職業。***lose employment*** 失業。***out of employment*** 失業。***take*** (***a person***) ***into employment*** 雇用(某人)。***throw*** (***a person***) ***out of employment*** 解雇(某人)；使(某人)失業。
employment agency 職業介紹所。
em·poi·son [ɛmˈpɔɪzn̩; emˈpɔizn] *v.t.* ①置毒；令染毒；令污染。②使懷恨。
em·po·ri·um [ɛmˈporɪəm; emˈpɔːriəm] *n., pl.* **-ri·ums, -ri·a** [-rɪə; -riə]. ①商業中心區；商場。②大百貨商店。
em·pow·er [ɪmˈpauɚ; imˈpauə] *v.t.* ①授權與。②使能；允許。(亦作 **impower**)
·**em·press** [ˈɛmprɪs; ˈempris] *n.* ①皇后。②女皇。③有至高無上權力的女人。
em·presse·ment [ɑ̃prɛsˈmɑ̃; ɑ̃presˈmɑ̃] 〖法〗*n.* 熱誠；熱心。
em·prise [ɛmˈpraɪz; emˈpraiz] *n.* 〖古〗冒險事業；武俠；勇武。(亦作 **emprize**)
:**emp·ty** [ˈɛmptɪ; ˈempti] *adj.,* **-ti·er, -ti·est,** *v.,* **-tied, -ty·ing,** *n., pl.* **-ties.**—*adj.* ①空的。It's gradually getting *empty.* 它漸漸空了。②空虛的。An *empty* promise is insincere. 空虛的諾言是無誠意的。③〖俗〗餓的。④缺少某種特質的〖常 of〗. Theirs is a life *empty* of happiness. 他們的生活缺少快樂。⑤無所事事的。*empty* summer days. 閒散的夏日。⑥輕浮的；無知的；愚蠢的。*empty* head. 愚蠢的頭腦。⑦無感情的；感情耗盡的。***be empty of*** 毫無。—*v.t.* 騰空；飲乾。He *emptied* his glass. 他乾杯。—*v.i.* ①變空；成空。②流入；注入。③乾涸。***empty out*** 騰空；騰出來。—*n.* 空的東西(如空瓶、空車等)。—**emp·ti·ly,** *adv.* —**emp·ti·ness,** *n.*
emp·ty-hand·ed [ˈɛmptɪˈhændɪd; ˈemptiˈhændid] *adj.* 徒手的；空手的。
emp·ty-head·ed [ˈɛmptɪˈhɛdɪd; ˈemptiˈhedid] *adj.* 無頭腦的；愚笨的。
emp·ty·ing [ˈɛmptɪɪŋ; ˈemptiiŋ] *n.* ①倒空；空出。②倒出之物(如瓶中之酒，船上之貨)。③(*pl.*)〖美俗〗用啤酒糟做的酵素。
emp·ty·sis [ˈɛmptɪsɪs; ˈemptisis] *n.* 〖醫〗咯血；吐血。
empty word (尤指中文文法之)虛字。
em·pur·ple [ɛmˈpɝpl̩; emˈpəːpl] *v.t.,* **-pled, -pling.** 着紫色；染紫色。
em·pye·ma [ˌɛmpɪˈimə; ˌempaiˈiːmə] *n.* 〖醫〗積膿。
em·pyr·e·al [ɛmˈpɪrɪəl; ˌempaiˈri(ː)əl] *adj.* ①尊貴的；崇高的。②最高天的；天空的。③由純淨之火或光所形成的。
em·py·re·an [ˌɛmpəˈriən; ˌempaiˈri(ː)ən] *n.* ①最高天(古人認由純火形成)。②天神居處。③天空；宇宙。
E.M.U., e.m.u., emu electromagnetic unit(s).
e·mu [ˈimju; ˈiːmjuː] *n.* 〖動物〗食火雞。(亦作 **emeu**)
em·u·la·ble [ˈɛmjələbl̩; ˈemjuləbl] *adj.* 可效法的；可趕上或超過的。
em·u·lant [ˈɛmjələnt; ˈemjulənt] *n.* 效法他人者；競爭者。
em·u·late [ˈɛmjəˌlet; ˈemjuleit] *v.t.,* **-lat·ed, -lat·ing.** 趕上或超過；與…競爭。
em·u·la·tion [ˌɛmjəˈleʃən; ˌemjuˈleiʃən] *n.* 競爭；爭勝。
em·u·la·tive [ˈɛmjəˌletɪv; ˈemjulətiv] *adj.* 有競爭心的；好勝的。—**ly,** *adv.*
em·u·la·tor [ˈɛmjəˌletɚ; ˈemjuleitə] *n.* 競爭者。
em·u·la·to·ry [ˈɛmjələˌtorɪ; ˈemjulətəri] *adj.* 競爭的；好勝的。
em·u·lous [ˈɛmjələs; ˈemjuləs] *adj.* ①競爭的；好勝的。②出於好勝心的。—**ly,** *adv.* —**ness,** *n.*
e·mul·si·fi·ca·tion [ɪˌmʌlsəfəˈkeʃən; iˌmʌlsifiˈkeiʃən] *n.* 乳化；化爲乳劑。
e·mul·si·fy [ɪˈmʌlsəˌfaɪ; iˈmʌlsifai] *v.t.,* **-fied, -fy·ing.** 使成乳狀；使成乳劑。
e·mul·sion [ɪˈmʌlʃən; iˈmʌlʃən] *n.* ①乳狀液。②乳劑。③〖攝影〗感光乳劑。—**e·mul·sive,** *adj.*
e·munc·to·ry [ɪˈmʌŋktərɪ; iˈmʌŋktəri] *n., pl.* **-ries,** *adj.* —*n.* 〖解剖〗排泄器官；排泄管。—*adj.* 排泄的。
en [ɛn; en] *n.* ①N 字母。②〖印刷〗半方。—*adj.* ①N 形的。②〖印刷〗有半方之面積的。
en- 〖字首〗在 p, b, m 前作 **em-**. 置名詞前，形成表"置於…之內(或之上)"的動詞，如 enthrone；置名詞或形容詞前，形成表"使成…"的動詞，如 endanger；置動詞前，使該動詞具有"在…之中；進入…之中"之義，如 enclose. 不及物動詞可由此形成及物動詞。〖注意〗英語中許多以 en- 爲開始之字，亦拼作 in-，如：enquire=inquire.

-en 【字尾】①構成動詞,表"變為;使為"(加於形容詞之後),如: weaken. "變為有;使有"(加於名詞之後),如: strengthen. ②把具體名詞構成形容詞,表"由…做成的",如: wooden. ③構成若干動詞之過去分詞,如: written. ④構成複數,如: children. ⑤構成名詞之陰性,如: vixen. ⑥構成表示"小"之字,如: chicken.

***en·a·ble** [ɪn'ebl̩; i'neibl, e'n-] *v.t.*, **-bled, -bling.** 使能够。This will *enable* him to do it. 這將使他能够做(某事)。

en·act [ɪn'ækt; i'nækt, e'n-] *v.t.* ①制定為法律;頒布(法律);通過(法律);(法律所)規定。②扮演。③發生(通常用於被動式中)。

en·ac·tive [ɪn'æktɪv; i'næktiv] *adj.* 有制定權的;制定法律的。

en·act·ment [ɪn'æktmənt; i'næktmənt] *n.* ①(法律之)創制;制定;頒布;通過。②制定之法律或法令。

***en·am·el** [ɪ'næml̩; i'næməl] *n., v.*, **-el(l)ed, -el·(l)ing.** —*n.* ①瓷釉;珐瑯;搪瓷。②搪瓷製品。③牙齒上之珐瑯質。④任何硬而有光澤的表面。⑤染指甲油。⑥亮漆;光漆。—*v.t.* ①塗以瓷釉;漆以亮漆。②使發光澤。③加上瓷釉般的表面。

en·am·el·ware [ɪ'næml̩ˌwɛr; i'næməlˌwɛə] *n.* 搪瓷器。

en·am·o(u)r [ɪn'æmɚ; i'næmə] *v.t.* 引起愛憐;迷住。He became (*or* was) *enamored* of Jenny. 他愛上珍妮了。

en·an·ti·o·sis [ɛnˌæntɪ'osɪs; enˌænti'ousis] *n.* 【修辭】反語;諷刺語。

en·ar·thro·sis [ˌɛnɑr'θrosɪs; ˌenɑː'θrousis] *n., pl.* **-ses** [-siz; -siːz]. 【解剖】杵臼關節。

e·nate [i'net; iː'neit] *adj.* 母系親戚的。「—*n.* 母系親戚。」

en bloc [ɛn'blɑk; en'blɔk] 【法】全體;總。***resign en bloc*** 全體辭職;總辭。

enc. ①enclosed. ②enclosure. ③encyclopedia.

en·cae·ni·a [ɛn'sinɪə; en'siːnjə] *n.* ①(作*pl.*解)城市之建立慶典;教堂之落成慶典。②(E-)(常作 *sing.* 解)為牛津大學之建校者或捐贈者舉行的紀念性慶典。

en·cage [ɛn'kedʒ; in'keidʒ] *v.t.*, **-caged, -cag·ing.** 關入籠中;監禁。

en·camp [ɪn'kæmp; in'kæmp, en-] *v.i.* 紮營;宿營;露營。—*v.t.* ①置於營幕中。②搭成營房。

en·camp·ment [ɪn'kæmpmənt; in'kæmpmənt] *n.* ①營房;營帳。②紮營;露營。

en·cap·sule [ɛn'kæpsl̩; en'kæpsjuːl] *v.t.*, **-suled, -sul·ing.** 裝入膠囊;做成囊狀;納入囊中。

en·case [ɪn'kes; in'keis] *v.t.*, **-cased, -cas·ing.** ①裝於箱;納入鞘。②包裹;包圍;包起。

en·case·ment [ɪn'kesmənt; in'keismənt] *n.* ①包圍;包起。②被包起之狀態。③【生物】預成論。④外殼;外膜;被罩。(亦作 **incasement**)

en·cash [ɛn'kæʃ; en'kæʃ] *v.t.* 兌現;「付現。」

en·cast·age [ɛn'kæstɪdʒ; en'kæstidʒ] *n.* (在窯中)將陶胚或瓷胚排列。

en·caus·tic [ɛn'kɔstɪk; en'kɔːstik] *adj.* 蠟畫的;燒入色彩的;以熱力固着色彩的。*encaustic* brick. 玻璃磚。—*n.* 蠟畫;以熱力固着彩色之畫。

en·cave [ɛn'kev; en'keiv] *v.t.*, **-caved, -cav·ing.** 藏於洞內。

-ence 【字尾】與 **-ance** 相同(為名詞字尾,與形容詞字尾 -ent 相當)。

en·ceinte¹ [ɛn'sent; en'seint] 【法】*n.* 【築城】圍廓;圍廓內之地區。

en·ceinte² 【法】*adj.* 妊娠的。

en·ce·phal·ic [ˌɛnsə'fælɪk; ˌenke'fælik, ˌense'f-] *adj.* 頭的;腦的。

en·ceph·a·li·tis [ˌɛnsɛfə'laɪtɪs; ˌenkefə'laitis, ˌensef-] *n., pl.* **-ti·des** [-təˌdiz; -tədiːz]. 【醫】腦炎。(亦作 **encephalitis lethargica**)

en·ceph·a·lo·gram [ɛn'sɛfələˌgræm; en'sefələgræm] *n.* 【醫】腦照相。

en·ceph·a·lo·graph [ɛn'sɛfələˌgræf; en'sefələgrɑːf] *n.* ①=**encephalogram.** ②=**electroencephalograph.**

en·ceph·a·lon [ɛn'sɛfəˌlɑn; en'kefəlɔn] *n., pl.* **-la** [-lə; -lə]. 【解剖】腦。

en·chain [ɛn'tʃen; in'tʃein] *v.t.* ①加鎖鍊於;束縛。②抓牢;吸引(注意等)。

en·chant** [ɪn'tʃænt; in'tʃɑːnt, en-] *v.t.* ①蠱惑;施魔法於。the *enchanted* palace. (神話中的)魔宮。②使迷醉;使銷魂。She was *enchanted* by the flowers you sent her. 你所送給她的花,她極為喜歡。be enchanted with*** 被…迷住。—**er,** *n.*

en·chant·ing [ɪn'tʃæntɪŋ; in'tʃɑːntiŋ] *adj.* ①嫵媚的;迷人的。②迷惑人的;令人銷魂的。—**ly,** *adv.*

***en·chant·ment** [ɪn'tʃæntmənt; in'tʃɑːntmənt] *n.* ①施魔法;行妖術。②魔法;妖術。③銷魂。④使人銷魂的東西。⑤大的喜悅或樂趣。

en·chant·ress [ɪn'tʃæntrɪs; in'tʃɑːntris] *n.* ①妖婦;女巫。②迷人的女人;令人銷魂之女子。

en·chase [ɛn'tʃes; en'tʃeis] *v.t.*, **-chased, -chas·ing.** ①鑲嵌。②雕刻;鏤刻。

en·chi·rid·i·on [ˌɛnkaɪ'rɪdɪən; ˌenkaiə'ridiən] *n., pl.* **-rid·i·ons, -rid·i·a** [-'rɪdɪə; -'ridiə]. 手册;便覽。

en·ci·pher [ɛn'saɪfɚ; en'saifə] *v.t.* 譯「成密碼。」

en·cir·cle [ɪn'sɝkl̩; in'səːkl] *v.t.*, **-cled, -cling.** ①環繞;包圍。②繞行。—**ment,** *n.*

encl. ①enclosed ②enclosure.

en clair [ɑ̃'klɛər; ɑ̃'klɛə] 【法】(外交電報等)用實字(為用密碼之對)。

en·clasp [ɛn'klæsp; in'klɑːsp] *v.t.* 緊握;環抱。(亦作 **inclasp**)

en·clave ['ɛnklev; 'enkleiv] *n., v.*, **-claved, -clav·ing.** —*n.* (被包圍在他國領土內之)被包領土。—*v.t.* 包圍。

en·clit·ic [ɛn'klɪtɪk; in'klitik] *adj.* 【文法】(因結合於前字而失去重音之)附屬的。—*n.* (因結合於前字而失去重音之)附屬字(如 layman 中之 man)。

***en·close** [ɪn'kloz; in'klouz] *v.t.*, **-closed, -clos·ing.** ①圍繞。②圍以籬(牆等)。③(隨函)封入;附寄。He *enclosed* a check. 他附寄支票一紙。

***en·clo·sure** [ɪn'kloʒɚ; in'klouʒə] *n.* ①圍繞。②圍場。Those cages are *enclosures* for the monkeys. 這些籠子是養猴子用的圍籠。③圍牆;籬;圈。④附件。

en·clothe [ɛn'kloð; en'klouð] *v.t.*, **en·clothed, en·cloth·ing.** =**clothe.**

en·cloud [ɛn'klaud; en'klaud] *v.t.* 以雲蔽之;使暈。

en·code [ɛn'kod; en'koud] *v.t.*, **-cod·ed, -cod·ing.** 譯成密碼。

en·cof·fin [ɛn'kɔfɪn; en'kɔfin] *v.t.* 放「入棺材中。」

en·coi·gnure [ˌɑnkwɑ'njʊr; ˌɑːnkwɑː-

ˈnjuə〕〖法〗*n.* 置於牆角之裝飾傢具(如三角几、牆角小櫃等)。

en·co·mi·ast 〔ɛnˈkomɪˌæst; enˈkoumiæst〕 *n.* 宣讀或寫作頌辭之人;讚頌者。

en·co·mi·as·tic 〔ɛnˌkomɪˈæstɪk; enˌkoumiˈæstik〕 *adj.* 讚頌的;稱頌的。

en·co·mi·um 〔ɛnˈkomɪəm; enˈkoumiəm〕 *n., pl.* **-mi·ums, -mi·a** 〔-mɪə; -miə〕. 讚頌;頌辭。

en·com·pass 〔ɪnˈkʌmpəs; inˈkʌmpəs〕 *v.t.* ①包圍;圍繞;團團圍住。②封入;包含。—**ment,** *n.*

en·coop 〔ɛnˈkup; enˈkuːp〕 *v.t.* 將…圍住;圍以欄。

en·co·pre·sis 〔ɛnˌkoˈprisɪs; enˌkouˈpriːsis〕*n.* 大便失禁;漏便(不能自制的排便)。

en·core 〔ˈɑŋkor; ɔŋˈkɔː〕 *interj., n., v.,* **-cored, -cor·ing.** —*interj.* 再 (=again). *Encore!* 再演(唱)一次! —*n.* ①要求再演。②經要求而再演之歌曲等。③經要求而加演之歌曲等。—*v.t.* 要求再演或唱;要求(演員、歌唱者等)再演(唱)一次。

***en·coun·ter** 〔ɪnˈkauntɚ; inˈkauntə〕 *v.t.* ①遭遇(困難);邂逅(友人)。②迎(戰);迎(敵)。—*v.i.* ①邂逅;偶晤。We *encountered* at Rome. 我們在羅馬相遇。②遭遇;會戰。—*n.* ①邂逅;遭遇。②會戰。

***en·cour·age** 〔ɪnˈkɝɪdʒ; inˈkʌridʒ〕 *v.t.,* **-aged, -ag·ing.** ①鼓勵;激勵。to *encourage* a man to work harder. 鼓勵一個人使更加努力工作。②援助;支持;促進;助長。

***en·cour·age·ment** 〔ɪnˈkɝɪdʒmənt; inˈkʌridʒmənt, en-〕 *n.* ①鼓勵;激勵。②獎勵;慫恿。③幫助;支持。

en·cour·ag·ing 〔ɪnˈkɝɪdʒɪŋ; inˈkʌridʒiŋ〕 *adj.* 鼓勵的;獎勵的;給予希望的。—**ly,** *adv.*

en·crim·son 〔ɛnˈkrɪmzn̩; enˈkrimzn〕 *v.t.* 使成深紅色。

en·cri·nite 〔ˈɛnkrəˌnaɪt; ˈenkrinait〕 *n.* ①石蓮(海百合之化石)。②海百合。

en·croach 〔ɪnˈkrotʃ; inˈkroutʃ〕 *v.i.* 侵占。—**ment,** *n.*

en·crust 〔ɪnˈkrʌst; inˈkrʌst〕 *v.t.* & *v.i.* =**incrust.**

en·cul·tu·ra·tion 〔ɛnˌkʌltʃəˈreʃən; enˌkʌltʃəˈreiʃən〕 *n.* 對某種文化之適應。

en·cum·ber 〔ɪnˈkʌmbɚ; inˈkʌmbə〕 *v.t.* ①阻礙行動;妨害;阻礙。②煩擾。③負累;繫累。He is *encumbered* with a large family. 他被龐大家庭所繫累。④堆滿。⑤負債。He is *encumbered* with debts. 他負債纍纍。⑥(財產的)帶有(抵押權)。

en·cum·brance, in·cum·brance 〔ɪnˈkʌmbrəns; inˈkʌmbrəns〕 *n.* ①阻礙物;累贅。②(家室之)負累。③〖法律〗(財產上設定之)負擔;財產留置權;財產的抵押權。

en·cur·tain 〔ɛnˈkɝtn̩; enˈkəːtən〕 *v.t.* 懸門簾;掛幕簾。

ency., encyc., encycl. encyclopedia.

-ency 〖字尾〗=**-ence.**

en·cyc·li·cal 〔ɛnˈsɪklɪkl̩; enˈsiklikəl〕 *n.* 羅馬教皇之通諭。—*adj.* 爲廣傳布的;傳閱的;通諭的。(亦作 **encyclic**)

***en·cy·clo·p(a)e·di·a** 〔ɪnˌsaɪkləˈpidɪə; enˌsaiklouˈpiːdiə〕 *n.* 百科全書。

en·cy·clo·p(a)e·dic 〔ɪnˌsaɪkləˈpidɪk; enˌsaiklouˈpiːdik〕 *adj.* ①百科全書的。②百科全書式的;知識廣泛的;博學的。(亦作 **encyclop(a)edical**)

en·cy·clo·p(a)e·dist 〔ɪnˌsaɪkləˈpidɪst; enˌsaiklouˈpiːdist〕*n.* 百科全書編纂者。

en·cyst 〔ɛnˈsɪst; enˈsist〕 *v.t.* & *v.i.* 〖生物〗囊入;包在囊內。—**ment,** —**a·tion,** *n.*

ː**end** 〔ɛnd; end〕 *n.* ①端點;末梢;末尾。the *end* of the year. 歲末。②目的。The *end* justifies the means. 爲達到目的可不擇手段。③結局;結果。④限度;極限。to be at one's wits' (*or* wit's) *end.* 困惑;智窮;不知所措。⑤死亡;毀滅;廢除。⑥殘片;殘屑;殘餘。⑦死亡、毀滅等之肇因。⑧工作之一部分。⑨目標。⑩〖俚〗容忍之極點。⑪〖俚〗最佳之事物。That music is the *end.* 那音樂之妙無出其右。***all ends up*** 完全地;徹底地。***at a loose end*** 〖俗〗無固定職業;無特別工作。***at loose ends*** **a.** 在不確定之狀態中;困惑的;雜亂的。**b.** 無職業;不安定。***at the end*** 最後;終於。***be at an end*** 結束;完成;告一段落。***begin at the wrong end*** 着手錯誤。***be no end to*** 沒有止境。***come to an end*** 結束;完了。***end for end*** 顛倒地;相反地。***end on*** 一端朝着。***end-to-end*** 頭尾相接;銜接。***from end to end*** 自始至終;都。***get hold of the wrong end of the stick*** 想錯;誤解。***give one a rope's end*** 處罰某人。***go off the deep end*** 〖俗〗**a.** 趨於極端。**b.** 失去情緒上的控制;異常激動。***have an end in view*** 有所企圖。***in the end*** 最後;終於。***jump*** (or ***go***) ***off the deep end*** 〖俚〗不加思索而突然地鹵莽從事。***keep*** (or ***hold***) ***one's end up*** **a.** 做好分內工作;盡責任。**b.** 能保衞自己。***make an end of*** 停止;廢除;消滅。***make both ends meet*** 使收支相抵;量入爲出。***meet one's end*** 死;遇難。***no end*** 無限;非常。***no end of*** (=a lot of; much; many) 很多;許多;無盡的。***odds and ends*** 竹頭木屑;雜俎;零星雜物。***on end*** **a.** 豎起;直立着。**b.** 繼續地;一連地。***put an end to*** 結束;停止;中止。***right on end*** (or ***straight on end***) 接連;繼續;立即。***the ends of the earth*** 地球最遙遠之處;到處。They searched for him to *the ends of the earth.* 他們到處尋找他。***to no end*** 無結果。***to the bitter end*** 到最後;到死。***to the end of time*** 永久地。***to what end*** 爲甚麼。***without end*** 無盡的;無限的。trouble *without end.* 無盡的困難。***world without end*** 永久;無窮之世。—*v.i.* ①結束;終止;終結。How will the matter *end?* 這事將如何終結? ②死。—*v.t.* ①結束;終止;終結。②毀滅;殺死。③作爲…之終結。***end in*** 終於;終歸;終成。***end in smoke*** 被燒光;(轉義指)終歸失敗;終成泡影。***end off*** 完成;結束;完畢。***end up*** 結果;結束。If you continue to steal, you'll *end up* in prison. 假如你繼續偷竊,結果必定坐牢。***end up with*** 結束;以…爲結束。

end-all 〔ˈɛndˌɔl; ˈendɔːl〕 *n.* ①一切事物之終了;結束;結局。②使一切終了之事物;導致結束之因素。

en·dam·age 〔ɛnˈdæmɪdʒ; enˈdæmidʒ〕 *v.t.,* **-aged, -ag·ing.** 損害 (=damage).

en·da·moe·ba 〔ˌɛndəˈmibə; ˌendəˈmiːbə〕 *n., pl.* **-bae** 〔-bi; -biː〕. 內阿米巴屬。

end·an·ge·i·tis 〔ˈɛndændʒiˈaɪtɪs; ˈendændʒiːˈaitis〕 *n.* 〖醫〗血管內膜炎。

en·dan·ger 〔ɪnˈdendʒɚ; inˈdeindʒə〕 *v.t.* 使受危險;危及;危害。

end-con·sum·er 〔ˌɛndkənˈsumɚ; ˌendkənˈsjuːmə〕 *n.* 最終消費者。

en·dear 〔ɪnˈdɪr; inˈdiə〕 *v.t.* 使親蜜;使受鍾愛。

en·dear·ing 〔ɪnˈdɪrɪŋ; inˈdiəriŋ〕 *adj.* 使人愛的;可愛的。—**ly,** *adv.*

en·dear·ment [ɪnˈdɪrmənt; inˈdiəmənt] *n.* ①鍾愛;寵愛。②令人鍾愛的行爲。③表示鍾愛的行爲、話語、文字等。

***en·deav·o(u)r** [ɪnˈdɛvɚ; inˈdevə] *v.i.* 努力;竭力。He *endeavors* to keep things nice about his place. 他努力把他的環境整理得很優美。—*n.* 努力;竭力。Make every *endeavor* to be here early. 盡一切力量早來此地。—**er,** *n.*

en·dem·ic [ɛnˈdɛmɪk; enˈdemik] *adj.* (亦作 **endemical**) 某一國家、地區或一羣人中所特有的; 地方性的。—*n.* 風土病; 地方性的病。—**al·ly,** *adv.* —**en·de·mism,** *n.*

en·de·mic·i·ty [ˌɛndɪˈmɪsətɪ; ˌendiˈmisiti] *n.* 地方特殊性;風土性。

en·der·mic [ɛnˈdɝmɪk; enˈdə:mik] *adj.* 〖醫〗皮下的; 藉皮下吸收而作用的。

end game 西洋棋之尾聲。

***end·ing** [ˈɛndɪŋ; ˈendiŋ] *n.* ①終結; 結局。The story has a happy *ending.* 這故事有一個快樂的結局。②字尾;語尾(如-ed, -ing等)。③死亡;毁滅。

en·dive [ˈɛndaɪv; ˈendiv] *n.* 〖植物〗菊萵苣。

***end·less** [ˈɛndlɪs; ˈendlis] *adj.* ①不停的;無窮盡的;無止境的。The story of his troubles seemed to be *endless.* 他的困苦的故事似乎是無止境的。②兩端連接成圈狀而循環不息的;環狀的。—**ly,** *adv.* —**ness,** *n.*

end·long [ˈɛndˌlɔŋ; ˈendlɔŋ] *adv.* 從此端到彼端;全長地。

end man ①行列中排在最後之人。②化裝黑人之樂隊排在首排兩端說滑稽笑話者。

end·most [ˈɛndˌmost; ˈendmoust] *adj.* 最末端的;極遠的;最後的。

end·note [ˈɛndˌnot; ˈendnout] *n.* 附註。

endo- 〖字首〗表"內部"之義。

en·do·car·di·tis [ˌɛndokɑrˈdaɪtɪs; ˌendoukɑ:ˈdaitis] *n.* 〖醫〗心內膜炎。

en·do·car·di·um [ˌɛndoˈkɑrdɪəm; ˌendouˈkɑ:diəm] *n.* 〖解剖〗心內膜。

en·do·carp [ˈɛndoˌkɑrp; ˈendoukɑ:p] *n.* 〖植物〗內果皮。

en·do·crine [ˈɛndoˌkraɪn; ˈendoukrain] *n.* ①內分泌腺。②內分泌物;內分泌。—*adj.* 內分泌的。

endocrine gland 內分泌腺。

en·do·cri·nol·o·gy [ˌɛndokraɪˈnɑlədʒɪ; ˌendoukraiˈnɔlədʒi] *n.*內分泌學。

en·do·derm [ˈɛndoˌdɝm; ˈendoudə:m] *n.* ①〖發生學〗內胚葉。②〖植物〗內皮層。(亦作 **entoderm**)

end-of-day glass [ˌɛndəvˈde~; ˌendəvˈdei~] 彩色玻璃。

en·dog·a·my [ɛnˈdɑgəmɪ; enˈdɔgəmi] *n.* 同族結婚; 同族婚姻。—**en·dog·a·mous, en·do·gam·ic,** *adj.*

en·do·gen [ˈɛndəˌdʒɛn; ˈendədʒen] *n.* 〖植物〗單子葉植物;內長莖植物。

en·dog·e·nous [ɛnˈdɑdʒənəs; enˈdɔdʒənəs] *adj.* ①由內部發展的。②〖生物〗內生的。③〖生理,生化〗細胞之新代作用的;內源的。—**en·do·ge·nic·i·ty,** *n.* —**ly,** *adv.*

en·do·lymph [ˈɛndoˌlɪmf; ˈendoulimf] *n.* 〖解剖〗內淋巴液。

en·do·me·tri·tis [ˌɛndomɪˈtraɪtɪs; ˌendoumiˈtraitis] *n.* 〖醫〗子宮內膜炎。

en·do·morph [ˈɛndəˌmɔrf; ˈendəmɔ:f] *n.* 〖礦〗內容礦物。—**ic,** *adj.* —**y,** *n.*

end-on [ˈɛndˈɔn; ˈendˈɔn] *adj.* 在端點的;端點的。

en·do·plasm [ˈɛndoˌplæzəm; ˈendouˌplæzəm] *n.* (細胞質之) 內質; 內胞漿。—**ic,** *adj.*

en·dorse [ɪnˈdɔrs; inˈdɔ:s] *v.t.,* **-dorsed, -dors·ing.** ①簽名於(票據等)的背面;背書。②認可;贊同;支持。 —**en·dors·a·ble,** *adj.* —**en·dors·er,** *n.*

en·dor·see [ɪnˌdɔrˈsi; ˌendɔ:ˈsi:] *n.* (票據之) 被背書人 (承受背書票據者)。(亦作 **indorsee**)

en·dorse·ment [ɪnˈdɔrsmənt, inˈdɔ:smənt] *n.* ①票據等後面之簽名;背書。②認可;支持。

en·do·scope [ˈɛndəˌskop; ˈendəskoup] *n.* 〖醫〗內窺鏡;內診鏡。

en·do·skel·e·ton [ˌɛndəˈskɛlətən; ˌendəˈskelətən] *n.* 〖解剖〗內骨骼。

en·do·sperm [ˈɛndəˌspɝm; ˈendəspə:m] *n.* (植物種子之)內胚乳。

en·do·the·li·um [ˌɛndoˈθilɪəm; ˌendouˈθi:liəm] *n., pl.* **-li·a** [-lɪə; -liə]. 〖解剖〗內皮;內皮細胞。

***en·dow** [ɪnˈdaʊ; inˈdau, en-] *v.t.* ①捐助; 捐贈基金。②賦與; 天賦。Nature has *endowed* him with great ability. 天賦與他很大的才能。

en·dow·ment [ɪnˈdaʊmənt; inˈdaumənt] *n.* ①捐贈; 捐助。②捐贈之基金或財產。③(常 *pl.*) 天資;禀賦;才能。

endowment insurance 養老保險。

end paper 書籍卷首及卷尾之對摺空頁。(亦作 **end leaf, end sheet**)

end product (一連串變化、程序、或化學反應之)最後結果;最後生成物。

end-stopped [ˈɛndˌstɑpt; ˈendstɔpt] *adj.* 末尾標有段落符號的(指詩行而言)。

end table (置於大型傢具旁之) 小桌。

en·due [ɪnˈdju; inˈdju:] *v.t.,* **-dued, -du·ing.** ①賦予 (才能等)。②穿着;使穿着;被以。(亦作 **indue**)

en·dur·a·ble [ɪnˈdjʊrəbl; inˈdjuərəbl] *adj.* ①可忍受的;可耐的。②耐久的;持久的。—**ness,** *n.* —**en·dur·a·bly,** *adv.*

en·dur·ance** [ɪnˈdjʊrəns; inˈdjuərəns] *n.* ①耐久力。Cheap cloth has little *endurance.* 廉價的布不能耐久。②忍耐力。③忍耐;容忍之舉動。④耐久的時期;持續的時間。beyond*** (or ***past***) ***endurance*** 不可忍耐的;忍無可忍的。His cruelty is *beyond* (or *past*) *endurance.* 他的殘暴令人忍無可忍。

en·dur·ant [ɪnˈdjʊrənt; inˈdjuərənt] *adj.* 忍耐的;能忍的。

***en·dure** [ɪnˈdjʊr; inˈdjuə] *v.,* **-dured, -dur·ing.** —*v.i.* ①持久; 耐久。②忍耐; 忍受。—*v.t.* 忍耐; 忍受。I can't *endure* him (*i.e.* I hate him). 我不能忍受他(我討厭他)。—**en·dur·er,** *n.*

***en·dur·ing** [ɪnˈdjʊrɪŋ; inˈdjuəriŋ] *adj.* 忍耐的;耐久的;長久不變的。—**ly,** *adv.*

end use (產品之) 主要用途或基本用途。

end-us·er [ɛndˈjuzɚ; endˈju:zə] *n.* =**end-consumer.**

end·ways [ˈɛndˌwez; ˈendweiz] *adj.* & *adv.* =**endwise.**

end·wise [ˈɛndˌwaɪz; ˈendwaiz] *adj.* & *adv.* ①直立的(地)。②末端向前或向上的(地)。③縱的(地)。④兩端相接的(地)。

En·dym·i·on [ɛnˈdɪmɪən; enˈdimiən] *n.* 〖希臘神話〗月神所愛的美少年。

E.N.E., ENE, e.n.e. east-northeast.

en·e·ma [ˈɛnəmə; ˈenimə] *n., pl.* **-mas, -ma·ta** [-mətə; -mətə]. 〖醫〗灌腸劑;灌腸

器;灌腸法。

:en·e·my 〔'ɛnəmɪ; 'enimi, -nəm-〕 *n., pl.* **-mies,** *adj.* —*n.* ①敵人;敵軍;敵國。The *enemy* were (*or* was) forced to retreat. 敵軍被迫撤退。②有害物。Frost is the *enemy* of plants. 霜對植物是有害的。***be an enemy to*** 討厭;仇視。He *is an enemy to* work. 他討厭工作。***be no enemy to*** 喜歡。***lifelong*** (***mortal*** or ***sworn***) ***enemy*** 不共戴天之仇人。***public*** (***King's*** or ***Queen's***) ***enemy*** 公敵。***the Enemy*** **a.** 撒旦。**b.** (the e-)〖俚〗時間。How goes *the enemy?* 現在是甚麼時刻?—*adj.* 敵人的;敵國的。〖注意〗the enemy 作"敵軍"解時,動詞用複數或單數均可。

***en·er·get·ic** 〔ˌɛnɚ'dʒɛtɪk; ˌenə'dʒetik〕 *adj.* ①精力充沛的;有活力的。He is constitutionally *energetic.* 他的體質是富有活力的。②積極的;有力的。**—al·ly,** *adv.*

en·er·get·ics 〔ˌɛnɚ'dʒɛtɪks; ˌenə'dʒetiks〕 *n.* 〖物理〗唯能說。

en·er·gic 〔ɛ'nɝdʒɪk; e'nəːdʒik〕 *adj.* 顯得精力充沛的。

en·er·gize 〔'ɛnɚˌdʒaɪz; 'enədʒaiz〕 *v.,* **-gized, -giz·ing.** —*v.t.* 給與精力;使活動。—*v.i.* 用力;活動;盡力而爲。**—en·er·giz·er,** *n.*

en·er·gu·men 〔ˌɛnɚ'gjumɛn; ˌenəː'gjuːmen〕 *n.* ①着魔之人。②狂熱者。

***en·er·gy** 〔'ɛnɚdʒɪ; 'enədʒi〕 *n., pl.* **-gies.** ①活力;精力;氣力;力量。②〖物理〗能。conservation of *energy.* 能量不滅。

en·er·vate 〔*v.* 'ɛnɚˌvet; 'enəːveit *adj.* ɪ'nɝvɪt; 'enəːvit〕 *v.,* **-vat·ed, -vat·ing,** *adj.* —*v.t.* 使衰弱;使虛弱;使無力;使失去活力。—*adj.* 衰弱的;虛弱的。

en·er·va·tion 〔ˌɛnɚ'veʃən; ˌenəː'veiʃən〕 *n.* 衰弱;虛弱;無力。

en·fant ter·ri·ble 〔ɑ̃'fɑ̃tɛ'ribl; ɑ̃ː'fɑːte'riːbl〕〖法〗①難管的、愛惡作劇的小孩;發奇問而無忌諱之兒童。②肆無忌憚之人;無責任心之人。

en·fee·ble 〔ɪn'fibl; in'fiːbl〕 *v.t.,* **-bled, -bling.** 使弱;使衰。**—ment,** *n.*

en·feoff 〔ɛn'fɛf, -'fif; in'fef, en-, -'fiːf〕 *v.t.* 〖法律〗①賜以封地;授以采邑。②讓渡。**—ment,** *n.*

en·fet·ter 〔ɛn'fɛtɚ; en'fetə〕 *v.t.* 加桎梏;束縛;加鎖鍊於。

en·fi·lade 〔ˌɛnfə'led; ˌenfi'leid〕 *n., v.,* **-lad·ed, -lad·ing.** —*n.* 〖軍〗①側射砲火。②易受側射之排列。—*v.t.* 〖軍〗側射;占側射位置。

en·fold 〔ɪn'fold; in'fould〕 *v.t.* =in**fold.** **—er, —ment,** *n.*

***en·force** 〔ɪn'fors; in'fɔːs〕 *v.t.,* **-forced, -forc·ing.** ①強行;執行;實施(法律等)。Policemen and judges *enforce* the laws. 警察與法官執行法律。②強迫;迫使。③極力主張;力勸;加強;強調。**—en·forc·er,** *n.* **—a·ble,** *adj.*

en·force·ment 〔ɪn'forsmənt; in'fɔːsmənt〕 *n.* 強迫;強制;實施;加強;執行。

en·frame 〔ɛn'frem; en'freim〕 *v.t.,* **en·framed, en·fram·ing.** 配以框;裝於框內。

en·fran·chise 〔ɛn'fræntʃaɪz; in'fræntʃaiz〕 *v.t.,* **-chised, -chis·ing.** ①釋放;解放。②給予投票權;授以公民權。**—en·fran·chis·er,** *n.*

en·fran·chise·ment 〔ɛn'fræntʃɪzmənt; in'fræntʃizmənt〕 *n.* ①釋放;解放。②公民權(選舉權)之授與。

Eng. ①England. ②English. **eng.** ①engine. ②engineer. ③engineering. ④engraved. ⑤engraver. ⑥engraving.

:en·gage 〔ɪn'gedʒ; in'geidʒ, en-〕 *v.,* **-gaged, -gag·ing.** —*v.i.* ①允諾;保證。Don't *engage* to do it unless you have time. 不要答應做它,除非你有時間。②從事;活動。She *engaged* in dramatics. 他從事戲劇活動。③〖機械〗啣接;嚙合。④交戰。—*v.t.* ①與…訂婚(用被動式)。Miss A is *engaged* to Mr. B. A小姐與B先生訂婚了。②約束;使忙;正忙於。He *engaged* her in conversation. 他正和她交談。③預定;訂(座);雇。This seat is *engaged.* 此座位已爲人所定。④吸引;引起(興趣)。⑤攻擊;與交戰。Our army presently *engaged* the enemy. 我軍立卽與敵軍交戰。⑥占去。Work *engages* much of his time. 工作占去他許多時間。⑦〖機械〗啣接;嚙合。⑧保證;答應。He *engaged* himself to pay his debt within a month. 他答應在一個月內償還他的債務。***engage for*** 保證;負責。That's more than I can *engage for.* 那事我不能保證。**—en·gag·er,** *n.*

en·gaged 〔ɪn'gedʒd; in'geidʒd〕 *adj.* ①已訂婚的。②有保證的;有約束的。③忙碌的;忙於工作的。④被占用的;使用中的。⑤在交戰中的。⑥〖機械〗相嚙合的。⑦已訂約的。

en·gage·ment** 〔ɪn'gedʒmənt; in'geidʒmənt〕 *n.* ①保證;諾言。An honest person fulfills all his *engagements.* 誠實的人履行他一切的諾言。②訂婚。③約會。I have numerous *engagements* for next week. 下週我有很多約會。④交戰。⑤訂定、預訂、使用、雇用之期間。⑥〖機械〗銜接。⑦(*pl.*) 財務上的義務。be under an engagement*** (***to***) 與…有約。***break off an engagement*** 解約;作廢。***break one's engagements*** 違約;爽約。***enter into*** (or ***make***) ***an engagement*** (***with***)(與…)訂約。

engagement ring 訂婚戒指。

en·gag·ing 〔ɪn'gedʒɪŋ; in'geidʒiŋ〕 *adj.* 美麗動人的;逗人喜愛的;迷人的。**—ly,** *adv.* **—ness,** *n.*

en·gar·land 〔ɛn'gɑrlənd; en'gɑːlənd〕 *v.t.* 圍以花環。

Eng·el 〔'ɛŋəl; 'eŋəl〕 *n.* 安格爾 (Ernst, 1821–1896, 德國經濟學家)。

Eng·els 〔'ɛŋəls; 'eŋəls〕 *n.* 恩格爾斯 (Friedrich, 1820–1895, 德國社會主義者)。

Engel's law 安格爾定律(卽家庭收入增加,其用於食物開支之比例相對減少)。

en·gen·der 〔ɪn'dʒɛndɚ; in'dʒendə〕 *v.t.* 產生;釀成。—*v.i.* 生成;發生。**—er, —ment,** *n.*

:en·gine 〔'ɛndʒən; 'endʒin〕 *n.* ①引擎;發動機。a steam *engine.* 蒸汽機。②機車。③機器;器械;器具。④救火車。—*v.t.* 裝以引擎。

engine driver 〖英〗火車司機。

***en·gi·neer** 〔ˌɛndʒə'nɪr; ˌendʒi'niə〕 *n.* ①機械師;技師。②工程師。a mechanical *engineer.* 機械工程師。③〖軍〗工兵;輪機官;機械員。corps of *engineer.* 工兵軍團。④有技巧的策劃者。a political *engineer.* 一個有智謀的政客。—*v.t.* ①設計;監督;建造;指揮。②機巧地處理;操縱;圖謀。

***en·gi·neer·ing** 〔ˌɛndʒə'nɪrɪŋ; ˌendʒi'niəriŋ〕 *n.* ①工程學;工程師業。civil *engineering.* 土木工程學。②幕後策劃;技巧的操縱。

engine house 消防車車房。

engine room 機器房;機艙。

en·gine·ry 〔'ɛndʒənrɪ; 'endʒənəri〕 *n.* ①機械(集合稱)。②軍用器械(集合稱)。③計略;計謀。

en·gird [ɛnˈgɝd; inˈgəːd] *v.t.*, **-girt** or **-gird·ed, -gird·ing.** 環繞;圍繞。

en·gir·dle [ɛnˈgɝdl̩; enˈgəːdl] *v.t.*, **-dled, -dling.** =**engird.**

:Eng·land [ˈɪŋglənd; ˈiŋglənd] *n.* 英格蘭;(通常卽指)英國(首都倫敦 London).

Eng·land·er [ˈɪŋgləndɚ; ˈiŋgləndə] *n.* 英格蘭人。

:Eng·lish [ˈɪŋglɪʃ; ˈiŋgliʃ] *adj.* 英國的;英國人的; 英語的。an *English* dictionary. 英文字典。—*n.* ① (the–)英國人(集合稱)。The *English* belong to the white race. 英國人屬於白種人。②英語;英文。Do you speak *English?* 你會說英語嗎? ③十四磅因的大活字。④撞球邊緣被擊後所發生之旋轉。***the King's English*** 純正英語。—*v.t.* ①譯爲英文;以淺近英文書寫。②採(外國語)入英文。③〖美〗使(撞球)旋轉。—**ness,** *n.*

English Canadian 〖主加〗①祖籍英國之加拿大人(的)。②說英語的加拿大人。

English Channel 英吉利海峽。

Eng·lish·ism [ˈɪŋglɪʃɪzm; ˈiŋgliʃizm] *n.* ①英國風格;英國主義。②拘守英國式。③英國英語語法。

Eng·lish·ize [ˈɪŋglɪʃaɪz; ˈiŋgliʃaiz] *v.t.*, **-ized, -iz·ing.** 使英國化。

***Eng·lish·man** [ˈɪŋglɪʃmən; ˈiŋgliʃmən] *n.*, *pl.* **-men.** ①英國人。②祖籍爲英國的人。

Eng·lish·wom·an [ˈɪŋglɪʃˌwʊmən; ˈiŋgliʃˌwumən] *n.*, *pl.* **-wom·en.** ①英國女人。②祖籍英國的女人。

en·gorge [ɛnˈgɔrdʒ; enˈgɔːdʒ] *v.*, **en·gorged, en·gorg·ing.** —*v.t.* ①貪婪地吞食。②〖醫〗使充血。—*v.i.* 吞食;貪婪地食。—**ment,** *n.*

engr. ①engineer. ②engraved. ③engraver. ④engraving.

en·graft [ɛnˈgræft; inˈgrɑːft] *v.t.* ①接(枝);插…之枝條。②樹立;灌輸。—**a·tion,** —**ment,** *n.*

en·grail [ɛnˈgrel; inˈgreil] *v.t.* 鑲以花邊(特指鋸齒形者)。—**ment,** *n.*

en·grain [ɪnˈgren; inˈgrein] *v.t.* =**ingrain.**

en·grained [ɪnˈgrend; inˈgreind] *adj.* =**ingrained.** —**ly,** *adv.*

en·gram [ˈɛngræm; ˈengræm] *n.*〖心理〗印象。

***en·grave** [ɪnˈgrev; inˈgreiv] *v.t.*, **-graved, -grav·ing.** ①雕刻;刻。②銘記(於心)。The scene is *engraved* on my memory. 那情景印刻在我的記憶中。

en·grav·er [ɪnˈgrevɚ; inˈgreivə] *n.* 雕刻師;雕板工;雕工。

en·grav·ing [ɪnˈgrevɪŋ; inˈgreiviŋ] *n.* ①雕刻術;鐫版術。②木刻版;銅版。③木刻畫;版畫。***engraving shop*** 刻字店。

en·gross [ɪnˈgros; inˈgrous] *v.t.* ①使全神貫注。②以大字寫;正式謄寫。③壟斷。—**ment,** *n.*

en·gross·ing [ɛnˈgrosɪŋ; enˈgrousiŋ] *adj.* ①令人神往的;吸引人的。②獨占的;在全部控制下的。—**ly,** *adv.*

en·gulf [ɪnˈgʌlf; inˈgʌlf] *v.t.* ①陷入(深淵)。②吞噬。(亦作 **ingulf**) —**ment,** *n.*

en·hance [ɪnˈhæns; inˈhɑːns] *v.t.*, **-hanced, -hanc·ing.** 增加;提高。

en·hance·ment [ɪnˈhænsmənt; inˈhɑːnsmənt] *n.* 增加;提高。

en·har·mon·ic [ˌɛnhɑrˈmɑnɪk; ˌenhɑːˈmɔnik] *adj.* 〖音樂〗①四分音的。②等音的。—**al·ly,** *adv.*

EN·I·AC [ˈɛnɪæk; ˈeniæk] *n.*〖商標名〗第一部電子指數電腦計算機(*E*lectronic *N*umerical *I*ntegrator *A*nd *C*omputer之略)。

e·nig·ma [ɪˈnɪgmə; iˈnigmə] *n.*, *pl.* **-mas, -ma·ta** [–mətə; –mətə]. ①謎;謎般的話。②難解的事或人。

en·ig·mat·ic [ˌɛnɪgˈmætɪk; ˌenigˈmætik] *adj.* =**enigmatical.**

en·ig·mat·i·cal [ˌɛnɪgˈmætɪkl̩; ˌenigˈmætikəl] *adj.* 謎的;像謎般的;難解的;不可思議的。—**ly,** *adv.*

e·nig·ma·tize [ɪˈnɪgməˌtaɪz; iˈnigmətaiz] *v.t.* & *v.i.*, **-tized, -tiz·ing.** 作謎;說隱語;使成謎;使難解。

en·isle [ɛnˈaɪl; enˈail] *v.t.*, **-isled, -isl·ing.** ①使成島;使如島。②置於島上;使孤立。

en·join [ɪnˈdʒɔɪn; inˈdʒɔin] *v.t.* ①命令;吩咐;迫使。②禁止。—**er,** —**ment,** *n.*

:en·joy [ɪnˈdʒɔɪ; inˈdʒɔi] *v.t.* ①享受;欣賞;歡喜。to *enjoy* oneself. 享樂。to *enjoy* swimming (fishing). 喜歡游泳(釣魚)。I *enjoyed* it very much. 我高興極了。②享有;享用。③獲得某種利益。④與(婦人)性交。—**er,** *n.* —**ing·ly,** *adv.*

en·joy·a·ble [ɪnˈdʒɔɪəbl̩; inˈdʒɔiəbl] *adj.* 可享受的;令人感愉快的。—**ness,** *n.* —**en·joy·a·bly,** *adv.*

***en·joy·ment** [ɪnˈdʒɔɪmənt; inˈdʒɔimənt] *n.* ①快樂;樂趣;喜歡。He takes great *enjoyment* in hunting. 他極喜狩獵。②令人喜歡之事物。③享受;享有;享用;使用。

en·kin·dle [ɛnˈkɪndl̩; inˈkindl] *v.t.* & *v.i.*, **-dled, -dling.** ①燃點(燈、火等);着火;發火。②燃熾;煽動;激起。—**en·kin·dler,** *n.*

en·lace [ɪnˈles; inˈleis] *v.t.*, **en·laced, en·lac·ing.** ①纏繞;包圍。②糾纏;交錯。③鑲以邊。—**ment,** *n.*

***en·large** [ɪnˈlɑrdʒ; inˈlɑːdʒ, en–] *v.*, **-larged, -larg·ing.** —*v.t.* 擴大;增大;擴充。an *enlarged* edition. 增訂版。—*v.i.* ①擴大;擴充。②詳述〖on, upon〗. —**a·ble,** *adj.*

en·large·ment [ɪnˈlɑrdʒmənt; inˈlɑːdʒmənt] *n.* ①擴大;擴充。②(照相)放大的照片。③增添之物。

en·larg·er [ɛnˈlɑrdʒɚ; inˈlɑːdʒə] *n.* ①擴大者;增補者;詳述者。②〖照相〗放大機。

***en·light·en** [ɪnˈlaɪtn̩; inˈlaitn] *v.t.* 啓迪;開導;敎化;啓蒙。Can you *enlighten* me on this subject? 關於這一題目,你能指點我一番麼? —**er,** *n.* —**ing·ly,** *adv.*

en·light·ened [ɪnˈlaɪtn̩d; inˈlaitnd] *adj.* ①開明的;開通的;文明的。②有知識的;明悉的。—**ly,** *adv.* —**ness,** *n.*

en·light·en·ment [ɪnˈlaɪtnmənt; inˈlaitnmənt] *n.* ①啓迪;啓蒙;敎化;開導。②開明的狀態。③(the E–) 歐洲十八世紀思想上之啓蒙運動。

***en·list** [ɪnˈlɪst; inˈlist, en–] *v.t.* ①使入伍;徵募;使參加。We'll *enlist* him in our movement. 我們要他參加我們的運動。②得…的助力。—*v.i.* ①從軍;應徵募。Many students *enlisted* in the army. 許多學生從軍了。②參加。③贊助;支持。

enlisted man 士兵。

enlisted woman 女兵(在軍中服務而無官階的婦女)。

en·list·ee [ɪnˌlɪsˈti; enlisˈtiː] *n.* 入伍者。

en·list·er [ɪnˈlɪstɚ; inˈlistə] *n.* ①應募者;入伍者。②募兵者;徵兵者。

en·list·ment [ɪnˈlɪstmənt; inˈlistmənt] *n.* ①登入兵籍。②兵士之應徵(募)。③應徵服役之期限。

en·liv·en [ɪnˈlaɪvən; inˈlaivn] *v.t.* 使活潑;使愉快;使有生氣;使有趣味;使有光輝。**—er, —ment,** *n.* **—ing·ly,** *adv.*

en·mesh [ɛnˈmɛʃ; inˈmeʃ] *v.t.* 使陷入網;使絆住。**—ment,** *n.*

en·mi·ty [ˈɛnmətɪ; ˈenmiti] *n., pl.* **-ties.** 敵意;敵對;不和;仇恨。to be at *enmity* with one's neighbors. 同鄉人不和睦。

en·ne·ad [ˈɛnɪˌæd; ˈeniæd] *n.* ①九個一組之人或物。②(E-) 埃及宗教之九神。**—ic,** *adj.*

en·no·ble [ɪˈnobḷ; iˈnoubl] *v.t.,* **-bled, -bling.** ①使尊貴;使受尊敬。②使(某人)成為貴族;授以爵位。③抬高。**—ment,** *n.*

en·nui [ˈɑnwi; ɑ̃ːˈnwiː] *n., v.,* **-nuied** or **-nuyed, -nuy·ing.** *—n.* 怠倦;無聊。*—v.t.* 使無聊。

e·nor·mi·ty [ɪˈnɔrmətɪ; iˈnɔːmiti] *n., pl.* **-ties.** ①極惡;殘暴。②暴行。③廣大;深重。

***e·nor·mous** [ɪˈnɔrməs; iˈnɔːməs] *adj.* ①極大的;巨大的。The war cost an *enormous* sum of money. 戰爭用去巨額的金錢。②極惡的;橫暴的。**—ly,** *adv.*

e·no·sis [ɛˈnosɪs; eˈnousis] *n.* 合併(尤指塞浦路斯與希臘之合併)。

‡e·nough [əˈnʌf, ɪˈnʌf; iˈnʌf, əˈnʌf] *adj.* 足够的;充分的。We haven't *enough* time. 我們沒有充足的時間。*—n.* 够;充足。I've had *enough,* thank you. 我已經(吃)够了,謝謝你。*—adv.* 够;充分。Is this good *enough?* 這個够好嗎? ***sure enough*** 的確地;確實地。*—interj.* 停止! 住手! 不要再繼續!〖注意〗在複數主詞的句子中,enough 如用作述語的形容詞(predicate adjective)時,其前面動詞可作複數或單數:Five boxes of apples are (*or* is) *enough* for the camp. 五箱蘋果足够該營食用。目前之一般趨勢,將形容詞 enough 置於其所形容之名詞後面,將副詞 enough 置於其所形容之形容詞或副詞之後面:You have room *enough.* 你有足够的地方。Her sewing is good *enough* for me. 她的縫工對我是够好的。You don't get up early *enough.* 你起身不够早。

e·nounce [iˈnauns; i(ː)ˈnauns] *v.t.,* **e·nounced, e·nounc·ing.** ①宣布;聲明。②發聲;讀出。**—ment,** *n.*

e·now [ɪˈnau; iˈnau] *adj. & adv.*〖古〗=**enough.**

en·plane [ɛnˈplen; enˈplein] *v.i.,* **en·planed, en·plan·ing.** 登(飛)機。

en·quire [ɪnˈkwaɪr; inˈkwaiə] *v.,* **-quired, -quir·ing.** *—v.i.* ①詢問;探問;問明。②調查;查究。*—v.t.* 詢問;問明。***enquire after*** 問候。***enquire for*** **a.** 尋訪;索取。**b.** 問候。***enquire into*** 查究;調查。**—en·quir·er,** *n.* **—en·quir·ing·ly,** *adv.*

en·quir·y [ɪnˈkwaɪrɪ; inˈkwaiəri] *n., pl.* **-quir·ies.** ①詢問;探問;問題。②調查;查究。***make enquiries about*** 詢問;探問。

en·rage [ɪnˈredʒ; inˈreidʒ] *v.t.,* **-raged, -rag·ing.** 激怒;使暴怒。to be *enraged* at an insult (with a person). 因侮辱(向某人)發怒。**—ment,** *n.*

en·rapt [ɛnˈræpt; inˈræpt] *adj.* 狂喜的;不自勝的;恍惚迷離的;神魂顛倒的。

en·rap·ture [ɪnˈræptʃɚ; inˈræptʃə] *v.t.,* **-tured, -tur·ing.** 使狂喜;使高興;使迷惑。**—en·rap·tur·er,** *n.*

***en·rich** [ɪnˈrɪtʃ; inˈritʃ, en-] *v.t.* ①使富足;使豐裕;使華麗;使肥沃。Commerce *enriches* a nation. 商業使一國富足。②充實。③加入維他命以增強食物價值。

en·rich·ment [ɪnˈrɪtʃmənt; inˈritʃmənt] *n.* ①使富足;使肥沃。②富足;肥沃。③致富足(肥沃)之物。

en·robe [ɛnˈrob; inˈroub] *v.t.,* **-robed, -rob·ing.** 穿以衣袍;着以華服。**—ment,** *n.*

***en·rol(l)** [ɪnˈrol; inˈroul, en-] *v.,* **-rolled, -roll·ing.** *—v.t.* ①登記。②加入;參加(與 oneself 連用)。He *enrolled* himself in the army. 他從軍了。③徵募。④列入;記錄。⑤捲起;包起。*—v.i.* 參加;加入。**—ee,** *n.*

en·rol(l)·ment [ɪnˈrolmənt; inˈroulmənt] *n.* 參加;註册人數。

en route [ɑnˈrut; ɑːnˈruːt]〖法〗在途中。

Ens. Ensign.

en·san·guine [ɛnˈsæŋgwɪn; inˈsæŋgwin] *v.t.,* **-guined, -guin·ing.** 血汚;血染。

en·sconce [ɛnˈskɑns; inˈskɔns] *v.t.,* **en·sconced, en·sconc·ing.** ①藏匿;庇護。②安置;使安坐。

en·sem·ble [ɑnˈsɑmbḷ; ɑːnˈsɑːmbl] *n.* ①整體;總效果。②全套服裝。③〖音樂〗**a.** 重奏;重唱。**b.** 合奏;合唱。**c.** 合奏的諸樂器;合唱的諸部聲音。④整個劇團;整個劇團在舞臺上之表現。

en·shrine [ɪnˈʃraɪn; inˈʃrain] *v.t.,* **-shrined, -shrin·ing.** ①置於神龕內;奉祀於廟堂中。②奉爲神聖;珍藏;銘記。

en·shrine·ment [ɪnˈʃraɪnmənt; inˈʃrainmənt] *n.* ①置於神龕中。②珍藏;銘記。③供作神龕之物;放珍藏品的東西。

en·shroud [ɛnˈʃraud; inˈʃraud] *v.t.* (以壽衣)掩蓋;掩蔽;遮蔽;覆蓋。

en·sign [ˈɛnsaɪn, ˈɛnsṇ; ˈensain, ˈensn] *n.* ①國旗;軍旗;艦旗;商船旗。②〖美〗海軍少尉。③昔英國陸軍中之掌旗官。④徽章。⑤階級、地位或權力等之標誌。***the blue ensign*** 英國海軍預備艦隊隊旗。***the red ensign*** 英國商船旗。***the white ensign*** 英國皇家海軍旗。**—cy, —ship,** *n.*

en·si·lage [ˈɛnsḷɪdʒ; ˈensilidʒ] *n., v.,* **-laged, -lag·ing.** *—n.* ①秣草之保藏。②保藏於地窖之秣草。*—v.t.* 窖藏(秣草)。

en·sile [ɛnˈsaɪl; enˈsail] *v.t.,* **-siled, -sil·ing.** =**ensilage.**

en·slave [ɪnˈslev; inˈsleiv] *v.t.,* **-slaved, -slav·ing.** ①奴役;使爲奴隸;剝奪…自由。②束縛;沉溺。

en·slave·ment [ɪnˈslevmənt; inˈsleivmənt] *n.* 奴役;束縛。

en·slav·er [ɪnˈslevɚ; inˈsleivə] *n.* 奴役人者;使人失去自由之事物。

en·snare [ɛnˈsnɛr; inˈsnɛə] *v.t.,* **-snared, -snar·ing.** 使陷於羅網;誘入陷阱。(亦作 **insnare**) **—ment, en·snar·er,** *n.*

en·sphere [ɛnˈsfɪr; enˈsfiə] *v.t.,* **-sphered, -spher·ing.** ①置於球中;包圍。②使成球形。(亦作 **insphere**)

en·sue [ɛnˈsu, ɛnˈsju; inˈsjuː, en-, -ˈsuː] *v.i.,* **-sued, -su·ing.** 隨起;結果;因而發生。the *ensuing* year. 翌年。

en·sure [ɪnˈʃur; inˈʃuə] *v.t.,* **-sured, -sur·ing.** ①保證。②擔保獲得。③保護;使得安全。**—en·sur·er,** *n.*

-ent〖字尾〗=**-ant.**

en·tab·la·ture [ɛnˈtæblətʃɚ; enˈtæblətʃə] *n.*〖建築〗柱頂線盤;臺口。

en·ta·ble·ment [ɛnˈtebḷmənt; enˈteiblmənt] *n.* ①=**entablature.** ②雕像座;

承雕像之平臺。

en·tail [ɪn'tel, ɛn–; in'teil, en–] *v.t.* ①惹起；使負擔；使需要。②〖法律〗限制繼承。—*n.* ①惹起；負擔；需要。②〖法律〗限定繼承之財產。③〖法律〗預定繼承人之順序。—**er,** —**ment,** *n.*

***en·tan·gle** [ɪn'tæŋgḷ, ɛn–; in'tæŋgl, en–] *v.t.*, **-gled, -gling.** ①使糾纏；與…糾纏在一起。②牽累；連累；困惑。The villain tried to *entangle* the hero in evil scheme. 這個惡棍企圖把這位英雄牽連在邪惡的陰謀中。③使複雜。—**a·ble,** *adj.* —**en·tan·gler,** *n.*

en·tan·gle·ment [ɪn'tæŋgḷmənt; in'tæŋglmənt] *n.* ①糾纏；牽累。②糾纏物。③(*pl.*)〖軍〗鐵絲網。

en·ta·sis ['ɛntəsɪs; 'entəsis] *n.* 〖建築〗圓柱收分曲線(柱之隆起或陽紋)。

en·tel·lus [ɛn'tɛləs; en'teləs] *n.* 〖動物〗聖猿(東印度羣島產，土人視爲神聖)。

en·tente [ɑn'tɑnt; ɑːn'tɑːnt] *n., pl.* **-tentes.**〖法〗①協定；協約。②參加協約之國。

en·tente cor·diale [ɑn'tɑntkɔr'djɑl; ɑːn'tɑːntkɔː'djɑːl] (政府間之)友善的了解。

‡**en·ter** ['ɛntɚ; 'entə] *v.t.* ①進入。He *entered* the house. 他進入屋內。②加入；參加。Shall you *enter* the Army or the Navy? 你將投效陸軍還是海軍? ③使(某人)參加或進入；報(名)參加。Parents *enter* their children in school. 父母使子女報名入學。④註明；登記。⑤開始；着手。After years of training, the doctor *entered* the practice of medicine. 經過多年的訓練，這醫生開始行醫。⑥編入。A dictionary *enters* words in alphabetical order. 字典依字母次序刊印字彙。⑦〖法律〗a. 正式提出。b. 正式占有(土地等)。c. 提出(對公地之)申請。⑧報關；申報海關。⑨貫穿。⑩插入。⑪參悟。—*v.i.* ①進入。Let them *enter*. 讓他們進來(進去)。②(演戲)上場。③入學；參加競賽。④開始〖on, upon〗. ***enter into*** a. 着手處理；研究。b. 開始；着手。to *enter into* conversation with someone. 與某人開始交談。c. 參加。d. 參與；同情；了解；領略。e. 討論；考慮。***enter upon*** (or ***on***) a. 開始；着手。The boy had left school and was about to *enter upon* a business life. 那孩子已離校，即將從商。to *enter upon* a new career. 開始一種新事業。b. 承受；得到。—**a·ble,** *adj.* —**er,** *n.*

en·ter·ic [ɛn'tɛrɪk; en'terik] *adj.* 腸的。—*n.* 腸熱病(=enteric fever).

enteric fever 傷寒；腸熱病。

en·ter·i·tis [ˌɛntə'raɪtɪs; ˌentə'raitis] *n.* 〖醫〗腸炎。

en·ter·op·to·sis [ˌɛntərɑp'tosɪs; ˌentərɔp'tousis] *n.* 〖醫〗腸下垂。

***en·ter·prise** ['ɛntɚˌpraɪz; 'entəpraiz] *n.* ①企業；計畫。②事業心；進取心。We need a spirit of *enterprise*. 我們需要進取精神。③從事企業；參加企業。private *enterprise*. 民營企業。④重要、艱難、或危險的工作。⑤公司。

en·ter·pris·ing ['ɛntɚˌpraɪzɪŋ; 'entəˌpraiziŋ] *adj.* ①富於創業精神的；有進取心的。②富於想像力和主動的。—**ly,** *adv.*

***en·ter·tain** [ˌɛntɚ'ten; ˌentə'tein] *v.t.* ①使娛樂；助興。We were all *entertained* by his tricks. 我們大家對他的把戲都感興趣。②款待；招待。to *entertain* friends at (*or* to) dinner. 招待(請)朋友們吃飯。③懷抱；心存；考慮。—*v.i.* 招待客人。

en·ter·tain·er [ˌɛntɚ'tenɚ; ˌentə'teinə] *n.* ①招待人。②表演娛樂節目的人。

en·ter·tain·ing [ˌɛntɚ'tenɪŋ; ˌentə'teiniŋ] *adj.* 娛樂的；有趣的。—**ly,** *adv.*

en·ter·tain·ment** [ˌɛntɚ'tenmənt; ˌentə'teinmənt] *n.* ①遊藝；技術表演；娛樂。He fell into the water, much to the *entertainment* of the onlookers. 他跌進水中，旁觀者大樂。②款待；招待。This hotel is famous for its *entertainment*. 此旅館以慇懃待客著稱。entertainment tax*** 娛樂稅。

en·thral(l) [ɪn'θrɔl; in'θrɔːl] *v.t.*, **-thralled, -thral·ling.** ①迷惑；迷住。②使服從；奴役。(亦作 **inthral, inthrall**) —**ment,** —**er,** *n.*

en·throne [ɪn'θron; in'θroun] *v.t.*, **-throned, -thron·ing.** ①擁立爲國王；使登極。②〖宗教〗任命爲主教。③尊崇；推崇。(亦作 **inthrone**)

en·throne·ment [ɪn'θronmənt; in'θrounmənt] *n.* ①使卽王位；登極。②授予主教職；就主教職。

en·thron·i·za·tion [ɛnˌθronɪ'zeʃən; inˌθrounai'zeiʃən] *n.* =**enthronement.**

en·thuse [ɪn'θjuz; in'θjuːz] *v.*, **en·thused, en·thus·ing.** —*v.i.* 〖美俗〗熱心；熱中。—*v.t.* 〖美俗〗使熱心。

***en·thu·si·asm** [ɪn'θjuzɪˌæzəm; in'θjuːziæzəm] *n.* ①熱心；狂熱。We are received with great *enthusiasm*. 我們受到熱烈的歡迎。②酷嗜之事物。Music is my great *enthusiasm*. 音樂是我最熱愛的東西。③〖古〗(宗教的)狂信。

en·thu·si·ast [ɪn'θjuzɪˌæst; in'θjuːziæst] *n.* ①熱心家；狂熱者。②〖古〗狂信者。

***en·thu·si·as·tic** [ɪnˌθjuzɪ'æstɪk; inˌθjuːzi'æstik, en–, -θuː–, -i'ɑːs–] *adj.* 熱心的；滿腔熱誠的。an *enthusiastic* admirer of Dr. Sun Yat-sen. 孫中山先生之熱烈的仰慕者。(亦作 **enthusiastical**) —**al·ly,** *adv.*

en·thy·meme ['ɛnθəˌmim; 'enθəˌmiːm] *n.* 〖邏輯〗省略推理法；省略之三段論法。—**en·thy·me·mat·ic,** *adj.*

en·tice [ɪn'taɪs, ɛn–; in'tais, en–] *v.t.*, **-ticed, -tic·ing.** 誘惑；誘入；誘出。to *entice* a person to do (*or* into doing) something wrong. 誘使一個人做壞事。—**a·ble,** *adj.* —**en·tic·er,** *n.*

en·tice·ment [ɪn'taɪsmənt; in'taismənt] *n.* ①誘惑；誘出。②引誘物；誘惑物。

‡**en·tire** [ɪn'taɪr; in'taiə] *adj.* ①整個的；全部的；完全的。I was in *entire* ignorance of what had happened. 我完全不知道發生些甚麼事。②〖植物〗無齒缺的(葉)。③未斷的；一整片的。④完整的。⑤未閹割的。an *entire* horse. 未閹割的馬。⑥〖廢〗純的；未含雜物的。—*n.* ①整體；全部。②未閹割的馬。③〖英〗一種麥芽酒。—**ly,** *adv.* —**ness,** *n.*

en·tire·ty [ɪn'taɪrtɪ; in'taiəti] *n., pl.* **-ties.** ①全部。②完全。***in its entirety*** 整個地；完全地。

***en·ti·tle** [ɪn'taɪtḷ; in'taitl] *v.t.*, **-tled, -tling.** ①定(著作的或人的)名稱。The new book is *entitled How To Write Letters*. 這新書名叫"怎樣寫信"。②使有資格；使有權。This ticket *entitles* you to a free lunch. 憑此券你可免費午餐一次。③稱呼。④以榮譽銜稱呼(某人)。(亦作 **intitle**) —**ment,** *n.*

en·ti·ty ['ɛntətɪ; 'entiti] *n., pl.* **-ties.**

①存在;實存。②實體;實存物。③本質;精義。
en·tomb [ɪn'tum; in'tu:m] *v.t.* ①埋葬;安放墓中。②作爲…之墓。—**ment,** *n.*
en·to·mo·log·ic [ˌɛntəmə'lɑdʒɪk; ˌentəmə'lɔdʒik] *adj.* =**entomological.**
en·to·mo·log·i·cal [ˌɛntəmə'lɑdʒɪkl; ˌentəmə'lɔdʒikəl] *adj.* 昆蟲學的。
en·to·mol·o·gist [ˌɛntə'mɑlədʒɪst; ˌentə'mɔlədʒist] *n.* 昆蟲學家。
en·to·mol·o·gize [ˌɛntə'mɑlədʒaɪz; ˌentə'mɔlədʒaiz] *v.i.,* **-gized, -giz·ing.** 研究昆蟲學;採集昆蟲。
en·to·mol·o·gy [ˌɛntə'mɑlədʒɪ; ˌentə'mɔlədʒi] *n.* 昆蟲學。
en·to·moph·i·lous [ˌɛntə'mɑfələs; ˌentə'mɔfələs] *adj.* 〖植物〗蟲媒的。—**en·to·moph·i·ly,** *n.*
en·tou·rage [ˌɑntu'rɑʒ; ˌɔntu'rɑ:ʒ] 〖法〗*n.* ①周遭;環境。②周圍之人(指隨員等)。
en-tout-cas [ɑ̃tu'kɑ; ɑ̃:tu:'kɑ:] 〖法〗*n.* 晴雨兩用傘。 —*adj.* ①晴雨兩用的。②(網球場)鋪有易排水物質的。
en·tr'acte [ɑn'trækt; 'ɔntrækt] 〖法〗*n.* ①幕間休息。②插演節目。
en·trails ['ɛntrəlz, 'ɛntrelz; 'entreilz] *n. pl.* ①內臟。②腸。③內部結構。
en·train[1] [ɪn'tren; in'trein] *v.i.* 乘火車;上火車。—*v.t.* 以火車輸送(部隊等)。—**er,** *n.*
en·train[2] *v.t.* 吸走;隨流帶走。
‡**en·trance**[1] ['ɛntrəns; 'entrəns] *n.* ①入口;大門。Where is the *entrance* to this building? 這大厦入口在何處? ②進;入。③入場權;准許進入。*Entrance* to the college is by examination only. 入此學院僅能經由考試。④船首在水線下之部分。***entrance fee*** 入場費。***No entrance!*** 不准入內(標語)。
en·trance[2] [ɪn'træns; in'trɑ:ns] *v.t.,* **-tranced, -tranc·ing.** ①使恍惚;使失神。②使狂喜;使驚奇。—**ment,** *n.* —**en·tranc·ing·ly,** *adv.*
en·trance·way ['ɛntrənsˌwe; 'entrənswei] *n.* 入口。
en·trant ['ɛntrənt; 'entrənt] *n.* ①進入者。②參加競爭或比賽者。③加入一種組織或職業者。④新分子;大學的新同學。
en·trap [ɪn'træp; in'træp] *v.t.,* **-trapped,-trap·ping.** ①以網或陷阱捕捉;誘陷。②使陷入困難或危險。—**per,—ment,** *n.*
*__en·treat__ [ɪn'trit; in'tri:t] *v.t. & v.i.* 懇求;乞求。He *entreated* a favor of me. 他求我開恩幫忙。(亦作 **intreat**) —**ment,** *n.*
*__en·treat·y__ [ɪn'tritɪ; in'tri:ti] *n., pl.* **-treat·ies.** 懇求;乞求。The robbers paid no attention to his *entreaties* for mercy. 强盗不理睬他的懇求施恩。
en·tre·chat [ɑ̃trə'ʃa; ˌɑ̃trə'ʃa] *n., pl.* **-chats** [-'ʃa; -'ʃa]. 〖法〗芭蕾舞之一種跳躍舞姿(舞者躍起兩足騰空交叉數次)。
en·tre·côte [ɑ̃trəkōt; 'ɔntrəkout] *n., pl.* **-cotes** [-kōt; -kouts]. 〖法〗肋肉;附肋之肉。
en·tree, en·trée ['ɑntre; 'ɔntrei] *n.* ①入場權。②〖美〗宴客之主菜。③兩道菜(魚與肉)之間所上之菜。④芭蕾舞中之開場舞。
en·tre·mets ['ɑntrəˌme; 'ɔntrəmei] *n., pl.* **-mets** [-ˌmez; -meiz]. 〖法〗①小菜或與燒烤食物同進之菜。②餐後之甜食。
en·trench [ɪn'trɛntʃ; in'trentʃ] *v.t.* ①以壕溝防護;挖壕溝。②確立。—*v.i.* ①侵害;侵犯〖常on, upon〗. ②〖古〗近乎;在嚴格定義之內〖on, upon〗.(亦作 **intrench**) —**er,** *n.*
en·trench·ment [ɪn'trɛntʃmənt; in'trentʃmənt] *n.* ①修壕溝防護。②壍壕;防禦工事。(亦作 **intrenchment**)
en·tre nous [ɑ̃trə'nu; ɑ̃trə'nu:] 〖法〗祕密地(=between ourselves).
en·tre·pôt ['ɑntrəˌpo; 'ɔntrəpou] *n., pl.* **-pôts** [-ˌpoz; -pouz]. 〖法〗①倉庫。②貨物集散地。(亦作 **entrepot**)
en·tre·pre·neur [ˌɑntrəprə'nɝ; ˌɔntrəprə'nə:] *n., pl.* **-neurs** [-'nɝz; -'nə:z]. 〖法〗①包辦人。②企業家。—**ship,** *n.*
en·tre·sol ['ɛntrəˌsɑl; 'ɔntrəsɔl] *n., pl.* **-sols** [-ˌsɑlz; -sɔlz]. 〖法〗〖建築〗假樓;中層(通常在一樓二樓之間)。
en·tro·py ['ɛntrəpɪ; 'entrəpi] *n.* ①〖物理〗熵(熱力學函數)。②相同之程度。③一致性;統一性。
en·trust, in·trust [ɪn'trʌst; in'trʌst, en-] *v.t.* 信賴;信託;交託。Can I *entrust* you with the task? 我可將此事交給你辦嗎? —**ment,** *n.*
*__en·try__ ['ɛntrɪ; 'entri] *n., pl.* **-tries.** ①進;入。The army made a triumphant *entry* into the enemy's capital. 該軍得勝進入敵人京城。②進口;入口;門。③(書、表中的)條目;記載;字、辭典中的字。This dictionary has over 90,000 *entries.* 這辭典含有九萬多字。④參加競賽之人或物。⑤〖法律〗土地占領;侵入家宅。⑥貨物報關。⑦進入之權。***double (single) entry***(簿記)複(單)式。***make an entry in*** 登入;記入。
en·try·way ['ɛntrɪˌwe; 'entriwei] *n.* 入口;入口處。
en·twine [ɪn'twaɪn; in'twain] *v.t. & v.i.,* **-twined, -twin·ing.** 使纏繞;編織。—**ment,** *n.*
en·twist [ɛn'twɪst; in'twist] *v.t.* 纒;絞;撚合。(亦作 **intwist**)
e·nu·cle·ate [*v.* ɪ'njuklɪˌet; i'nju:klieit *adj.* ɪ'njuklɪɪt; i'nju:klieit, -it] *v.,* **-at·ed, -at·ing,** *adj.* —*v.t.* ①〖生物〗除去…之細胞核 (nucleus). ②剜出 (腫瘤等)。③〖古〗解明;闡釋。—*adj.* 無細胞核的。—**e·nu·cle·a·tion, e·nu·cle·a·tor,** *n.*
*__e·nu·mer·ate__ [ɪ'njuməˌret; i'nju:məreit] *v.t.,* **-at·ed, -at·ing.** ①枚舉;列舉。②計算;數。—**e·nu·mer·a·tor,** *n.* —**e·nu·mer·a·tive,** *adj.*
e·nu·mer·a·tion [ɪˌnjumə'reʃən; iˌnju:mə'reiʃən] *n.* ①枚舉;列舉。②計算;數。③目錄;細目;一覽表。
e·nun·ci·ate [ɪ'nʌnsɪˌet; i'nʌnsieit] *v.,* **-at·ed, -at·ing.** —*v.i.* 發音。—*v.t.* ①發音。②宣布;發表。—**e·nun·ci·a·ble,** *adj.* —**e·nun·ci·a·bil·i·ty,** *n.*
e·nun·ci·a·tion [ɪˌnʌnsɪ'eʃən; iˌnʌnsi'eiʃən] *n.* ①發音。②宣布;發表。
e·nun·ci·a·tive [ɪ'nʌnʃɪˌetɪv; i'nʌnʃieitiv] *adj.* ①發音的。②宣布的;陳明的。
e·nun·ci·a·tor [ɪ'nʌnʃɪˌetɚ; i'nʌnsieitə] *n.* 發音者;宣布者。
en·ure [ɪn'jur; i'njuə] *v.t. & v.i.,* **en·ured, en·ur·ing.** =**inure.**
en·u·re·sis [ˌɛnju'risɪs; ˌenju'ri:sis] *n.* 〖醫〗遺尿。—**en·u·ret·ic,** *adj.*
*__en·vel·op__ [ɪn'vɛləp; in'veləp] *v.,* **-oped, -op·ing,** *n.* —*v.t.* ①包;包裝。②圍繞;包圍;掩藏。Our soldiers *enveloped* the enemy. 我們的兵已包圍了敵人。③作爲圍繞的東西(如黏膜、鞘等)。—*n.* =**envelope.**—**er,** *n.*
*__en·ve·lope__ ['ɛnvəˌlop; 'enviloup] *n.*

①信封。②封套;封袋。③飛艇或氣球之氣囊;囊套。④【植物】(樹葉等之)圍繞部分。⑤【數學】包絡(線面);包跡。⑥【電子】眞空管之封套。(亦作 **envelop**)

envelope table 四邊附有摺葉可以放大的桌子。

en·vel·op·ment [ɪnˈvɛləpmənt; inˈveləpmənt] *n.* ①包;封。②包封物;封皮;包裝紙。

en·ven·om [ɛnˈvɛnəm; inˈvenəm] *v.t.* ①使有毒。②使含惡意;使懷恨。

en·vi·a·ble [ˈɛnvɪəbl̩; ˈenviəbl] *adj.* 可羨慕的。—**ness,** *n.* —**en·vi·a·bly,** *adv.*

***en·vi·ous** [ˈɛnvɪəs; ˈenviəs, -vjəs] *adj.* ①嫉妒的;羨慕的。to be *envious* of another person's success. 羨慕他人的成功。②【廢】好勝的;好成爲對等的。—**ly,** *adv.* —**ness,** *n.*

en·vi·ron [ɪnˈvaɪrən; inˈvaiərən] *v.t.* 包圍;環繞。to be *environed* by (*or* with) perils. 危機四伏。

***en·vi·ron·ment** [ɪnˈvaɪrənmənt; inˈvaiərənmənt] *n.* ①圍繞;環繞。The *environment* of our enemy is almost complete. 對敵人之包圍將近完成。②環境;周遭的狀況。I know little about his home *environment.* 我不大曉得他的家庭環境。③包圍之物。

en·vi·ron·men·tal [ɪnˌvaɪrənˈmɛntl̩; inˌvaiərənˈmentl] *adj.* 環境的;環繞的。—**ly,** *adv.*

en·vi·ron·men·tal·ism [ɪnˌvaɪrənˈmɛntəlɪzəm; inˌvaiərəˈmentəlizəm, en-] *n.* 環境決定一切論。

en·vi·ron·men·tal·ist [ɪnˌvaɪrənˈmɛntəlɪst; inˌvaiərənˈmentəlist] *n.* ①環境決定一切論者。②主張保持環境清潔主義者。

environmental resistance 對人口增加的環境上的限制。

en·vi·rons [ɪnˈvaɪrənz; ˈenvirənz] *n. pl.* 郊外;近郊;郊野。New York and its *environs.* 紐約及其近郊。

en·vis·age [ɛnˈvɪzɪdʒ; inˈvizidʒ] *v.t.,* **-aged, -ag·ing.** ①正視;熟視;面對。②擬想。③【哲】直覺;直觀。—**ment,** *n.*

en·vi·sion [ɛnˈvɪʒən; enˈviʒən] *v.t.* 擬想(尚未實現之事)。

en·voy[1] [ˈɛnvɔɪ; ˈenvɔi] *n.* ①使者。②特使;公使。***envoy extraordinary and minister plenipotentiary*** 特命全權公使。***peace envoy*** 和平使者。—**ship,** *n.*

en·voy[2] *n.* ①(結束一首詩之)煞尾的短節。②文學作品之後記。(亦作 **envoi**)

en·vy** [ˈɛnvɪ; ˈenvi] *n., pl.* **-vies,** *v.,* **-vied, -vy·ing.** —*n.* ①嫉妬;羨慕。He did that out of *envy.* 他由於嫉妬而那樣做。②可羨慕的東西;被羨慕者。—*v.t.* ①嫉妬;羨慕。You're lucky; I *envy* you. 你眞幸運,我羨慕你。②因…而嫉妬。not to envy a person something*** 對某人之…並不羨慕(對…甚感慶幸)。—**en·vi·er,** *n.* —**ing·ly,** *adv.*

en·womb [ɛnˈwum; enˈwuːm] *v.t.* 【詩】深藏;包藏。

en·wrap [ɛnˈræp; inˈræp] *v.t.,* **-wrapped, -wrap·ping.** ①包;裝封;圍繞。②吸引;使心神貫注;沉溺於。

en·wreathe [ɛnˈrið; inˈriːð] *v.t.,* **-wreathed, -wreath·ing.** 繞以花圈;圈之。

en·zo·ot·ic [ˌɛnzəˈɑtɪk; ˌenzəˈɔtik] *n.* 地方性之獸類疾病。—*adj.* 獸類的地方病的。

en·zyme [ˈɛnzaɪm; ˈenzaim] *n.* 【化】酵素;酶。(亦作 **enzym**)

E·o·cene [ˈiəˌsin; ˈiːosiːn] *adj.* 【地質】第三紀之始新世的。—*n.* 【地質】始新世;始新世之岩石;始新統。

E·o·li·an [ɪˈolɪən; iˈouliən] *adj., n.* =**Aeolian.**

e·o·lith·ic [ˌiəˈlɪθɪk; ˌiːouˈliθik] *adj.* 【考古】原始石器時代的。the *Eolithic* era. 原始石器時代。

e·on [ˈiən, ˈiɑn; ˈiːən, ˈiːɔn] *n.* ①世;紀;代。②無限長之時期;永刼。

e·o·ni·an [ɪˈonɪən; iˈouniən] *adj.* 永世的;無窮的。(亦作 **aeonian**)

E·os [ˈiɑs; ˈiːɔs] *n.* 【希臘神話】黎明之女神。

e·o·sin [ˈiəsɪn; ˈiːəsin] *n.* 【化】曙紅;伊紅(一種染料)。(亦作 **eosine**)

E·o·zo·ic [ˌiəˈzoɪk; ˌiːəˈzouik] *n., adj.* 【地質】元古代(的);始生代(的)。

ep- 【字首】 **epi-** 之異體(用於母音之前)。

EP extended play. EP 盤唱片(每分鐘 45 轉)。 **Ep.** Epistle.

e·pact [ˈipækt; ˈiːpækt] *n.* ①閏餘;每年陽曆超過陰曆之日數。②歲首月齡(陽曆元旦回溯至陰曆當月初一之日數)。

ep·arch [ˈɛpɑrk; ˈepɑːk] *n.* ①(今希臘之)郡長。②(古希臘之)省長。③(東正教之)大主教。

ep·ar·chy [ˈɛpɑrkɪ; ˈepɑːki] *n., pl.* **-chies.** ①今希臘之郡。②古希臘之省。③(東正教之)大主教管區。—**ep·ar·chi·al,** *adj.*

ep·au·let, ep·au·lette [ˈɛpəˌlɛt; ˈepoulet] *n.* ①【軍】肩章。②女人衣服上類似肩章之飾物。***win one's epaulets*** 升爲軍官。

é·pée [eˈpe; eiˈpei] 【法】 *n.* ①尖頭劍。②使用此種劍的劍術比賽。

ep·en·the·sis [ɛpˈɛnθɪsɪs; eˈpenθisis] *n., pl.* **-ses** [-ˌsiz; -siːz]. 【語言】①字或音節之插入。②插入字;插入之音節。—**ep·en·thet·ic,** *adj.*

e·pergne [ɪˈpɜn; iˈpəːn] *n.* 食桌中央之飾架(盛花、糖果等)。

ep·ex·e·ge·sis [ɛpˌɛksɪˈdʒisɪs; eˌpeksiˈdʒiːsis] *n., pl.* **-ses** [-ˌsiz; -siːz]. 【修辭】①說明語之加添。②附加之說明語。

Eph. Ephesians.

e·phed·rine [ɛˈfɛdrɪn; eˈfedrin] *n.* 【藥】鹽酸麻黃素(治枯草熱、氣喘等)。(亦作 **ephedrin**)

e·phem·er·a [əˈfɛmərə; iˈfemərə] *n., pl.* **-er·as, -er·ae** [-əˌri; -əriː]. ①生命短促之物;朝生暮死者。②蜉蝣。

e·phem·er·al [əˈfɛmərəl; iˈfemərəl] *adj.* ①朝生暮死的;瞬息的。②繼續一天的。—*n.* 朝生暮死的東西。—**ly,** *adv.* —**ness,** *n.*

e·phem·er·al·i·ty [əˌfɛməˈrælətɪ; iˌfeməˈræliti] *n., pl.* **-ties.** ①朝生暮死;短命。②不持久之事物。

e·phem·er·id [əˈfɛmərɪd; iˈfemərid] *n.* 蜉蝣科之蟲。

e·phem·er·is [ɪˈfɛmərɪs; iˈfeməris] *n., pl.* **eph·e·mer·i·des** [ˌɛfəˈmɛrɪdiz; ˌefiˈmeridiːz]. ①【天文】星曆表。②載有星曆表之曆書。

e·phem·er·on [ɪˈfɛməˌrɑn; iˈfemərɔn] *n., pl.* **-er·ons, -er·a.** =**ephemera.**

E·phe·sians [ɪˈfiʒənz; iˈfiːʒjənz] *n. pl.* (作 *sing.* 解)【聖經】以弗所書。

eph·od [ˈɛfɑd; ˈiːfɔd] *n.* 猶太敎大祭司所穿之法衣。

eph·or [ˈɛfɔr; ˈefɔː] *n., pl.* **-ors, -or·i** [-əˌraɪ; -ərai]. ①古希臘之民選長官。②(今希臘之)政府官員。

epi- 【字首】表"在上;向;反"之義。

ep·i·blast [ˈɛpəˌblæst; ˈepiblæst] *n.* 【發生學】外胚層;外胚葉。—**ic,** *adj.*

***ep·ic** [ˈɛpɪk; ˈepik] *n.* ①敍事詩；描寫英雄事蹟的長詩；史詩。Homer's *Iliad* and Milton's *Paradise Lost* are *epics.* 荷馬的"伊利亞德"和密爾頓的"失樂園"都是史詩。②值得以敍事詩頌揚的事蹟。—*adj.* ①敍事詩的。②宏偉壯麗的。③不平常的。—**like,** *adj.*

ep·i·cal [ˈɛpɪkl̩; ˈepikəl] *adj.* =**epic.** —**ly,** *adv.*

ep·i·ca·lyx [ˌɛpɪˈkelɪks; ˌepiˈkeiliks] *n., pl.* **-lyx·es, -lyces** [-lɪˌsiz;-lisiːz].〖植物〗苞之小總苞或環生體。

ep·i·carp [ˈɛpɪˌkɑrp; ˈepikɑːp] *n.*〖植物〗外果皮。

ep·i·ce·di·um [ˌɛpəˈsidɪəm; ˌepiˈsiːdiəm] *n., pl.* **-se·di·a** [-ˈsidɪə; -ˈsiːdiə]. 哀歌；輓歌。—**ep·i·ce·di·al, ep·i·ce·di·an,** *adj.*

ep·i·cene [ˈɛpəˌsin; ˈepisiːn] *adj.* ①屬於兩性的；有兩性特徵的。②(希臘與拉丁語之)通性的。③軟弱的。④女性化的。—*n.* ①陰陽人。②兩性名詞。—**ep·i·cen·ism,** *n.*

ep·i·cen·ter, ep·i·cen·tre [ˈɛpɪˌsɛntɚ; ˈepisentə] *n.* ①震源；震央。②中心；焦點。—**ep·i·cen·tral,** *adj.*

ep·i·cen·trum [ˌɛpɪˈsɛntrəm; ˌepiˈsentrəm] *n., pl.* **-trums, -tra** [-trə; -trə].〖英〗= **epicenter.**

ep·i·cure [ˈɛpɪˌkjʊr; ˈepikjuə] *n.* ①嗜美食醇酒的人；貪口腹之慾者。②對食物、藝術、音樂有良好趣味的人。

ep·i·cu·re·an [ˌɛpɪkjʊˈriən; ˌepikjuəˈriːən] *adj.* ①好美食的；享樂主義的。②(食物)精美的。—*n.* 享樂主義者；美食主義者。

Ep·i·cu·re·an·ism [ˌɛpɪkjʊˈriənˌɪzəm; ˌepikjuəˈriːənizəm] *n.* ①Epicurus之哲學。②快樂主義；美食主義。③(e-)享樂主義者之癖好或習慣。

Ep·i·cur·ism [ˈɛpɪkjʊˌrɪzəm; ˈepikjuərizəm] *n.* ①=**Epicureanism.** ②(e-)享樂主義者之癖好或習慣。

Ep·i·cu·rus [ˌɛpɪˈkjʊrəs; ˌepiˈkjuərəs] *n.* 伊璧鳩魯(紀元前 342?–270 希臘哲學家)。

ep·i·cy·cle [ˈɛpəˌsaɪkl̩; ˈepisaikl] *n.* 周轉圓。—**ep·i·cy·clic, ep·i·cy·cli·cal,** *adj.*

ep·i·cy·cloid [ˌɛpɪˈsaɪklɔɪd; ˈepiˈsaiklɔid, ˌepiˈs-] *n.*〖數學〗外擺線；圓外旋輪線。

***ep·i·dem·ic** [ˌɛpəˈdɛmɪk; ˌepiˈdemik] *n.* ①疾疫流行；時疫；流行性傳染病。②思想、式樣等的流行。—*adj.* 流行性的；傳染性的。—**i·ty,** *n.*

ep·i·dem·i·cal [ˌɛpəˈdɛmɪkl̩; ˌepiˈdemikəl] *adj.* =**epidemic.** —**ly,** *adv.*

ep·i·de·mi·ol·o·gy [ˌɛpɪˌdimɪˈɑlədʒɪ; ˌepiˌdiːmiˈɔlədʒi] *n.* 流行病學；傳染病學。

ep·i·der·mal [ˌɛpəˈdɝml̩; ˌepiˈdəːməl] *adj.* 表皮的；皮上的。

ep·i·der·mic [ˌɛpəˈdɝmɪk; ˌepiˈdəːmik] *adj.* =**epidermal.**

ep·i·der·mis [ˌɛpəˈdɝmɪs; ˌepiˈdəːmis] *n.*〖解剖，生物〗表皮；上皮；外皮。

ep·i·di·a·scope [ˌɛpɪˈdaɪəˌskop; ˌepiˈdaiəskoup] *n.* 實物幻燈機。

ep·i·gas·tric [ˌɛpəˈgæstrɪk; ˌepiˈgæstrik] *adj.*〖解剖〗腹上部的。

ep·i·gas·tri·um [ˌɛpɪˈgæstrɪəm; ˌepiˈgæstriəm] *n., pl.* **-tri·a** [-trɪə; -triə].〖解剖〗腹上部。

ep·i·gen·e·sis [ˌɛpəˈdʒɛnəsɪs; ˌepiˈdʒenəsis] *n.* ①〖生物〗新生論；(胚胎之)漸成說。②〖地質〗外力變質。

ep·i·glot·tis [ˌɛpəˈglɑtɪs; ˌepiˈglɔtis] *n., pl.* **-glot·tis·es, -glot·ti·des** [-ˈglɑtɪˌdiz; -ˈglɔtidiːz].〖解剖〗會厭(軟骨)。

ep·i·gone [ˈɛpɪˌgon; ˈepigoun] *n.* 重要作家或畫家的平凡模倣者。(亦作 **epigon**)

ep·i·gram [ˈɛpəˌgræm; ˈepigræm] *n.* ①雋語；警句。②諷刺短詩。

ep·i·gram·mat·ic [ˌɛpəgrəˈmætɪk; ˌepigrəˈmætik] *adj.* ①雋語的；(多)警句的。②諷刺的。—**al·ly,** *adv.*

ep·i·gram·ma·tist [ˌɛpəˈgræmətɪst; ˌepiˈgræmətist] *n.* 說雋語的人；警句家；諷刺詩人。

ep·i·gram·ma·tize [ˌɛpɪˈgræməˌtaɪz; ˌepiˈgræmətaiz] *v.t. & v.i.*, **-tized, -tiz·ing.** 寫警句；作諷刺短詩；以警句表白；將…作成警句或諷刺短詩。

ep·i·graph [ˈɛpəˌgræf; ˈepigrɑːf] *n.* 碑文；題銘；題詞。—**ic, —i·cal,** *adj.*

e·pig·ra·phy [ɪˈpɪgrəfɪ; iˈpigrəfi] *n.* ①題銘之研究；金石學。②題銘之集合稱。

ep·i·lep·sy [ˈɛpəˌlɛpsɪ; ˈepilepsi] *n.*〖醫〗癲癎症。(亦作 **epilepsia**)

ep·i·lep·tic [ˌɛpəˈlɛptɪk; ˌepiˈleptik] *adj.* 癲癎的；患癲癎症的。—*n.* 癲癎症患者。

ep·i·logue [ˈɛpəˌlɔg; ˈepilɔg] *n.* ①結語；尾聲。②(戲劇的)收場白。③(戲劇中)念收場白的演員。(亦作 **epilog**)

E·piph·a·ny [ɪˈpɪfənɪ; iˈpifəni] *n., pl.* **-nies.** ①(基督教每年一月六日之)主顯節。②(e-)(神等之)顯現。

ep·i·phe·nom·e·non [ˌɛpɪfɪˈnɑmɪˌnɑn; ˌepifiˈnɔminɔn] *n., pl.* **-na** [-nə; -nə]. ①副現象。②〖醫〗併發症。

ep·i·phyte [ˈɛpɪˌfaɪt; ˈepifait] *n.* ①〖植物〗附生植物。②〖醫〗皮上寄生菌。—**ep·i·phy·tal, ep·i·phyt·ic, ep·i·phyt·i·cal,** *adj.*

Epis. ①Episcopal. ②Episcopalian. ③Epistle.

Episc. ①Episcopal. ②Episcopalian.

e·pis·co·pa·cy [ɪˈpɪskəpəsɪ; iˈpiskəpəsi] *n., pl.* **-cies.**〖宗教〗①主教統轄制度。②主教之職位、任期等。③主教之集合稱。

e·pis·co·pal [ɪˈpɪskəpl̩; iˈpiskəpəl] *adj.* ①主教的。②主教統轄的。③(E-)英國國教的；監督派的。the *Episcopal* Church. 英國國教。***Methodist Episcopal Church*** 美以美監督派教會。***Protestant Episcopal Church*** 新教徒監督教會。

E·pis·co·pa·li·an [ɪˌpɪskəˈpelɪən; iˌpiskəˈpeiliən] *n.* ①(e-)主教派教友。②聖公會教徒。—*adj.* ①(e-)主教統轄的。②=**Episcopal. *Episcopalian Church*** 聖公會；監督派教會。—**ism,** *n.*

e·pis·co·pate [ɪˈpɪskəpɪt; iˈpiskəpit] *n.* 主教之職；主教任期；主教轄區；主教團。

***ep·i·sode** [ˈɛpəˌsod, -ˌzod; ˈepisoud] *n.* ①(人生、小說或詩歌中的)插曲。②〖音樂〗插入曲。③希臘悲劇中二段合唱間的部分。④〖電影、廣播、電視〗某一影集中之一齣。⑤(小說、故事等中的)主要情節。—**ep·i·sod·ic, ep·i·sod·i·cal,** *adj.*

ep·i·spas·tic [ˌɛpɪˈspæstɪk; ˌepiˈspæstik] *adj.* 起泡的；發泡的。—*n.* 發泡藥。

e·pis·te·mol·o·gy [ɪˌpɪstəˈmɑlədʒɪ; iˌpistəˈmɔlədʒi] *n.*〖哲〗認識論。

***e·pis·tle** [ɪˈpɪsl̩; iˈpisl] *n.* ①書信。②(E-)(新約聖經中的)使徒書。

e·pis·to·lar·y [ɪˈpɪstəˌlɛrɪ; iˈpistələri] *adj.* ①書信的。②書信體的。

e·pis·tro·phe [ɪˈpɪstrəfɪ; iˈpistrəfi] *n.*〖修辭〗結句重疊；(結尾的)疊句。

ep·i·style [ˈɛpɪˌstaɪl; ˈepistail] *n.* = architrave. **—ep·i·sty·lar,** *adj.*

***ep·i·taph** [ˈɛpəˌtæf; ˈepitaːf, –tæf] *n.* ①墓誌銘。②墓誌銘體小詩或短文。**—ic,** *adj.* **—ist,** *n.* **—less,** *adj.*

ep·i·tha·la·mi·um [ˌɛpɪθəˈlemɪəm; ˌepiθəˈleimiəm] *n., pl.* **-mi·ums, -mi·a** [–mɪə; –miə]. 祝婚詩歌。

ep·i·the·li·al [ˌɛpɪˈθilɪəl; ˌepiˈθiːliəl] *adj.* 上皮的;上皮細胞的。

ep·i·the·li·um [ˌɛpəˈθilɪəm; ˌepiˈθiː-liəm] *n., pl.* **-li·ums, -li·a** [–lɪə; –liə]. 〖解剖〗上皮;上皮細胞。

ep·i·thet [ˈɛpəˌθɛt; ˈepiθet] *n.* ①描述特性之名詞、形容詞或片語。②附加於人名後之描述詞。③帶有侮辱性之稱呼或字句。**—ic, —i·cal,** *adj.*

e·pit·o·me [ɪˈpɪtəmɪ; iˈpitəmi] *n.*①梗概; 大要。②縮影; 典型。 **—ep·i·tom·i·cal, ep·i·tom·ic,** *adj.*

e·pit·o·mize [ɪˈpɪtəˌmaɪz; iˈpitəmaiz] *v.t.,* **-mized, -miz·ing.** 摘要;爲…之縮影。

ep·i·zo·on [ˌɛpɪˈzoɑn; ˌepiˈzouɔn] *n., pl.* **-zo·a** [–ˈzoə; –ˈzouə]. 〖動物〗體外寄生蟲;皮上寄生物。(亦作 **epizoön**)

ep·i·zo·ot·ic [ˌɛpɪzəˈɑtɪk; ˌepizəˈɔtik] *adj.* 動物流行病的。**—n.** 動物流行病。(亦作 **epizoötic**)

e plu·ri·bus u·num [iˈplurɪbəsˈju-nəm; iːˈpluribəsˈjuːnəm] 〖拉〗合衆爲一(=one out of many, 昔爲美國之國訓)。

***ep·och** [ˈɛpək; ˈiːpɔk] *n.* ①紀元。The invention of the atomic bomb begins (*or* marks) a new *epoch* in history. 原子彈的發明給歷史開了一個新紀元。②時代; 時期。③〖地質〗期;紀。④值得紀念的時期。⑤重大事故發生之時期。⑥〖物理〗**a.** 初相。**b.** 時紀。

ep·och·al [ˈɛpəkl̩; ˈepɔkəl] *adj.* ①紀元的;時代的。②開新紀元的;劃時代的。**—ly,** *adv.*

ep·och-mak·ing [ˈɛpəkˌmekɪŋ; ˈiːpɔkˌmeikiŋ] *adj.* 開新紀元的;劃時代的。

ep·ode [ˈɛpod; ˈepoud] *n.* 〖古韻律〗①長短句交替之抒情詩體。②希臘抒情歌謠之第三段。**—ep·od·ic,** *adj.*

ep·o·nym [ˈɛpəˌnɪm; ˈepounim] *n.* 名祖(地方、民族、機構等因以得名之人)。

ep·on·y·mous [ɛˈpɑnəməs; iˈpɔni-məs] *adj.* 以己名賜與其地方、民族、機構等的;名祖的。

ep·o·pee [ˈɛpəˌpi; ˈepoupiː] *n.* 敍事詩。

ep·os [ˈɛpɑs; ˈepɔs] *n.* ①敍事詩。②口傳之原始史詩。③以敍事詩相傳的一連串事件。

ep·ox·y [ɛpˈɑksɪ; epˈɔksi] *adj., n., pl.* **-ox·ies.** **—adj.** 〖化〗環氧基的。**—n.** 環氧基樹脂。

ep·si·lon [ˈɛpsələn; epˈsailən] *n.* 希臘語之第五字母(E, ε)。

Ep·som [ˈɛpsəm; ˈepsəm] *n.* 艾普孫(英格蘭東南部之一市鎮)。

Epsom salt(s) 瀉鹽。

eq. ①equal. ②equalizer. ③equitable. ④equation. ⑤equivalent.

eq·ua·bil·i·ty [ˌɛkwəˈbɪlətɪ; ˌekwə-ˈbiliti] *n.* 無變動;一致;穩定;平靜。

eq·ua·ble [ˈɛkwəbl̩; ˈekwəbl] *adj.* ①寧靜的;穩定的;一致的;均勻的。②(法律等) 公平的。**—ness,** *n.* **—eq·ua·bly,** *adv.*

‡**e·qual** [ˈikwəl; ˈiːkwəl] *adj., n., v.,* **-qual(l)ed, -qual·(l)ing.** **—adj.** ①相等的;同樣的;同等的〖常 to, with〗. All men are not *equal* in ability. 人的能力並非全一樣的。②平靜的。③公平的。④始終如一的;一致的。⑤均勻的; 勢均力敵的。⑥足够的。The supply is *equal* to the demand. 供應足够滿足需要。⑦平坦的(如平原等)。***equal to***能勝任…的; 有…之能力的。He is *equal to* doing that (to his work). 他能勝任該事(他的工作)。***equal to the occasion*** 能處理局勢;能應急。**—n.** 對手;匹敵;相等物。Is he your *equal* in strength?他的力量是你的對手嗎? **—v.t.** ①等於。If *x equals* 6, then 6*x equals* 36. 如 *x* 等於 6, 則 6*x* 等於 36. ②使相等。

e·qual·i·tar·i·an [ɪˌkwɑləˈtɛrɪən; iˌkwɔliˈtɛəriən] *adj.* 平等主義的。**—n.** 平等主義者。**—ism,** *n.*

e·qual·i·ty** [ɪˈkwɑlətɪ; i(ː)ˈkwɔliti] *n.* ①相等;平等。②(平面、運動等) 均勻。on a footing of equality with*** (or ***on an equality with***) 與…基於平等地位; 與…平等。

Equality State 美懷俄明 (Wyoming) 州之別稱。

e·qual·i·za·tion [ˌikwələˈzeʃən; ˌiːkwəlaiˈzeiʃən] *n.* ①平均;平等化。②一律。***equalization fund*** 〖經濟〗(外匯)平準基金。***equalization of landownership*** 平均地權。

e·qual·ize [ˈikwəlˌaɪz; ˈiːkwəlaiz] *v.t.,* **-ized, -iz·ing.** ①使平等; 使平均; 使平衡。②使整齊均一;劃一。

e·qual·iz·er [ˈikwəlˌaɪzɚ; ˈiːkwəlaizə] *n.* ①使平等者。②均值器。③〖電〗均壓器。④〖俚〗武器(手槍、彈簧刀、短棒等)。

***e·qual·ly** [ˈikwəlɪ; ˈiːkwəli] *adv.* 相等地;同樣地。Divide it *equally.* 等分之。

e·qual-sign [ˈikwəlˌsaɪn; ˈiːkwəlˌsain] *n.* 〖數學〗等號(=)。

e·qua·nim·i·ty [ˌikwəˈnɪmətɪ; ˌiːkwə-ˈnimiti] *n.* 平靜;鎮定。

e·quate [ɪˈkwet; iˈkweit] *v.t.,* **-quat·ed, -quat·ing.** ①使相等。②視爲同等;相提並論。③立方程式;以方程式表示。**—e·quat·a·bil·i·ty,** *n.* **—e·quat·a·ble,** *adj.*

e·qua·tion [ɪˈkweʒən; iˈkweiʃən] *n.* ①〖數學〗等式; 方程式。②化學方程式。③相等;平衡。

e·qua·tion·al [ɪˈkweʒənəl; iˈkweiʃə-nəl] *adj.* ①平均的;平衡的。 ②方程式的。③〖生物〗(細胞之) 均等分裂的。**—ly,** *adv.*

***e·qua·tor** [ɪˈkwetɚ; iˈkweitə] *n.* ①赤道。②日夜平分線。

E·qua·to·ri·a Guinea [ˌikwə-ˈtorɪə～; ˌekwəˈtɔːriə～] 赤道幾內亞(中非一國, 首都 Sant Isabel)。

e·qua·to·ri·al [ˌikwəˈtorɪəl; ˌekwə-ˈtɔːriəl] *adj.* ①赤道的;近赤道的。②似赤道或赤道附近的。**—n.** 赤道儀。**—ly,** *adv.*

eq·uer·ry [ˈɛkwərɪ; iˈkweri] *n., pl.* **-ries.** ①英國皇室之侍從武官。②掌馬官。

e·ques·tri·an [ɪˈkwɛstrɪən; iˈkwes-triən] *adj.* ①騎馬的;騎在馬上的。②騎術的。③騎兵的;騎士的。④(古羅馬之) 騎士團的。**—n.** 騎馬者;騎術家;騎手。**—ism,** *n.*

e·ques·tri·enne [ɪˌkwɛstrɪˈɛn; iˌkwestriˈen] *n.* 女馬師;女騎術家。

equi- 〖字首〗表"平等"之義。

e·qui·an·gu·lar [ˌikwɪˈæŋgjəlɚ; ˌiːkwiˈæŋgjulə] *adj.* 等角的。

e·qui·dis·tance [ˌikwəˈdɪstəns; ˈiːkwiˈdistəns] *n.* 等距。

e·qui·dis·tant [ˌikwəˈdɪstənt; ˈiːkwi-

ˈdistənt] *adj.* 等距的;距離相等的。—**ly,** *adv.*

e·qui·lat·er·al [ˌikwəˈlætərəl; ˈiːkwiˈlætərəl] *adj.* 等邊的。—*n.* ①等邊形。②相等的邊。—**ly,** *adv.*

e·quil·i·brant [iˈkwɪləbrənt; iːˈkwilibrənt] *n.* 〖物理〗平衡力;平衡。

e·qui·li·brate [ˌikwəˈlaɪbret; ˌiːkwiˈlaibreit] *v.t.* & *v.i.,* **-brat·ed, -brat·ing.** (使)均衡;(使)相稱。

e·qui·li·bra·tion [ˌikwɪlɪˈbreʃən; ˌiːkwilaiˈbreiʃən] *n.* 均衡;相稱。

e·qui·li·bra·tor [ˌikwɪˈlaɪbretɚ; ˌiːkwiˈlaibreitə] *n.* 保持平衡之物;安定裝置。

e·qui·li·bra·to·ry [ˌikwəˈlaɪbrəˌtorɪ; ˌiːkwiˈlaibrətəri] *adj.* (有助)產生平衡的。

e·quil·i·brist [ɪˈkwɪləbrɪst; iːˈkwilibrist] *n.*①擅長保持身體平衡者。②走繩索者。

e·qui·lib·ri·um [ˌikwəˈlɪbrɪəm; ˌiːkwiˈlibriəm] *n., pl.* **-ums, -ri·a** [-rɪə; -riə]. ①平衡;均衡。②(對抗因素、力量的)均勢。③心理的平衡。④〖化〗平衡。—**e·qui·lib·ri·ous,** *adj.*

e·qui·mul·ti·ple [ˌikwɪˈmʌltəpḷ; ˈiːkwiˈmʌltipl] *n.* 等倍數;等倍量。—*adj.* 乘以同數的;等倍數的。

e·quine [ˈikwaɪn; ˈiːkwain] *adj.* 馬的;似馬的。—*n.* 馬。—**ly,** *adv.* —**e·quin·i·ty,** *n.*

e·qui·noc·tial [ˌikwəˈnɑkʃəl; ˌiːkwiˈnɔkʃəl] *adj.* ①晝夜平分的。②晝夜平分時的;春分的;秋分的。③晝夜平分線的;赤道的。④〖植物〗(花)經常在某時間開放的。***equinoctial circle*** (or ***line***) 晝夜平分線;赤道。***equinoctial point*** (春分或秋分之)二分點。—*n.* ①晝夜平分線;赤道。②春(秋)分時之暴風雨。

e·qui·nox [ˈikwəˌnɑks; ˈiːkwinɔks] *n.*①春(秋)分。②晝夜平分點(＝equinoctial point). ***autumnal equinox*** 秋分。***spring*** (or ***vernal***) ***equinox*** 春分。

***e·quip** [ɪˈkwɪp; iˈkwip] *v.t.,* **-quipped, -quip·ping.** ①設備;裝備。*Equip* your bicycle with a head light. 在你的脚踏車上裝前燈。②提供知識上或情感上之需要。③穿着。—**per,** *n.*

eq·ui·page [ˈɛkwəpɪdʒ; ˈekwipidʒ] *n.* ①馬車。②馬車及其馬匹、車夫、及車僕等之集合稱。③裝備;設備。④成套之家庭用具(如磁器等)。⑤成套之個人用品(如裝飾品等)。

***e·quip·ment** [ɪˈkwɪpmənt; iˈkwipmənt] *n.* ①設備;裝備。②設備品;供應品;全套器具。③知識或技藝;才能;素養。He has the necessary *equipment* for law. 他具備從事律師的知識和才能。④鐵路機車。

e·qui·poise [ˈɛkwəˌpɔɪz; ˈekwipɔiz] *n., v.,* **-poised, -pois·ing.** —*n.* ①平衡。②平衡物;平衡力;秤錘;砝碼。—*v.t.* 使成平衡。

e·qui·pol·lence [ˌikwəˈpɑləns; ˌiːkwiˈpɔləns] *n.* (力量、價值、意義等之)相等;等力;等值;等義。(亦作 **equipollency**)

e·qui·pol·lent [ˌikwəˈpɑlənt; ˌiːkwiˈpɔlənt] *adj.* ①(力量、重量、效力等之)相等的。②等義的;結果相同的。—*n.* 相等之物。

e·qui·pon·der·ance [ˌikwɪˈpɑndərəns; ˌiːkwiˈpɔndərəns] *n.* 均重;平衡。—**e·qui·pon·der·ant,** *adj.*

e·qui·pon·der·ate [ˌikwɪˈpɑndərˌet; ˌiːkwiˈpɔndəreit] *v.t.,* **-at·ed, -at·ing.** 使(重量、力量、重要性等)相等或抵銷。

e·qui·po·tent [ɪˈkwɪpətənt; iˈkwipətənt] *adj.* (力量、能力、效果等)相等的。

e·qui·po·ten·tial [ˌikwɪpoˈtɛnʃəl; ˌiːkwipəˈtenʃəl] *adj.* 〖物理〗等位的;等勢的。—**i·ty,** *n.*

Eq·ui·se·tum [ˌɛkwəˈsitəm; ˌekwiˈsiːtəm] *n., pl.* **-tums, -ta** [-tə; -tə]. 〖植物〗①木賊屬。②(e-)木賊屬植物;木賊;問荆。

eq·ui·ta·ble [ˈɛkwɪtəbḷ; ˈekwitəbl] *adj.* ①公平的;公正的。②〖法律〗衡平法的。—**ness,** *n.* —**eq·ui·ta·bly,** *adv.*

eq·ui·ta·tion [ˌɛkwɪˈteʃən; ˌekwiˈteiʃən] *n.* 騎馬;騎術。

eq·ui·ty [ˈɛkwətɪ; ˈekwiti] *n., pl.* **-ties.** ①公平;公正。②公平或公正之事。③〖法律〗衡平法。④衡平法上之權利。⑤〖美〗財產超過其負債之剩餘價額。⑥公司普通股所有人之利益。⑦(E-)演員協會。***equity court*** 衡平法庭。

equity capital ①股東資本(非借來的資金)。②股東持有之證劵或股票。

e·quiv·a·lence [ɪˈkwɪvələns; iˈkwivələns] *n.* ①等價;等值;等量;同義。②〖化〗等價;當量。③〖數學〗等勢;等積。—*adj.* 〖數學,邏輯〗對稱的。

e·quiv·a·len·cy [ɪˈkwɪvələnsɪ; iˈkwivələnsi] *n.* ＝**equivalence.**

***e·quiv·a·lent** [ɪˈkwɪvələnt; iˈkwivələnt] *adj.* ①相等的。Nodding your head is *equivalent* to saying yes. 點頭就等於説贊同。②有相等面積的。③相當的。—*n.* ①相等物。②〖化〗當量。—**ly,** *adv.*

e·quiv·o·cal [ɪˈkwɪvəkḷ; iˈkwivəkəl] *adj.* ①意義不明顯的;模稜兩可的。②未決的;不確定的。③靠不住的;可疑的。—**e·quiv·o·ca·cy, —i·ty, —ness,** *n.* —**ly,** *adv.*

e·quiv·o·cate [ɪˈkwɪvəˌket; iˈkwivəkeit] *v.i.,* **-cat·ed, -cat·ing.** 用雙關語;説模稜兩可之話;矇混;推托。—**e·quiv·o·ca·tor,** *n.* —**e·quiv·o·cat·ing·ly,** *adv.*

e·quiv·o·ca·tion [ɪˌkwɪvəˈkeʃən; iˌkwivəˈkeiʃən] *n.* ①用雙關語。②〖邏輯〗基於語義雙關之誤謬推理;一語多義之謬誤。③雙關語。—**e·quiv·o·ca·to·ry,** *adj.*

eq·ui·voque, eq·ui·voke [ˈɛkwəˌvok; ˈekwivouk] *n.* ①雙關語;含糊之措辭。②文字遊戲;作雙關諧語。③雙關含義。

ER ①earned run. ②en route.

Er 化學元素 erbium 之符號。

er [ə, əː, ʌ, ʌː; ʌː, əː] *interj.* 表示停頓、猶豫、無把握等義。

-er 〖字尾〗①加於名詞後表與某物有關或居於某地之人, 如:hatter, cottager, New Yorker. ②加於名詞、名詞複合語或名詞片語之後表相屬之物或動作, 如:diner, doubleheader. ③加於動詞之後表做該動作之人或物, 如:sprayer, roller. ④加於若干形容詞及副詞之後形成比較級, 如:later, greater.

E.R. ①East Riding (Yorkshire). ②East River (New York City). ③King Edward (Edwardus Rex). ④Queen Elizabeth (Elizabeth Regina).

***e·ra** [ˈɪrə; ˈiərə] *n.* ①歷史上的時代。an *era* of progress. 進步的時代。②紀元。Christian *era.* 耶穌紀元。③〖地質〗代。

e·ra·di·ate [ɪˈredɪˌet; iˈreidieit] *v.t.* & *v.i.,* **-at·ed, -at·ing.** 放射(光線等);發射。

e·ra·di·a·tion [ɪˌredɪˈeʃən; iˌreidiˈeiʃən] *n.* (光、熱等之)發射;放射。

e·rad·i·ca·ble [ɪˈrædɪkəbḷ; iˈrædikəbl] *adj.* 可根絕的;可拔去的。

e·rad·i·cate [ɪˈrædɪˌket; iˈrædikeit] *v.t.,* **-cat·ed, -cat·ing.** ①根除;撲滅。②連根拔除。—**e·rad·i·ca·tive,** *adj.* —**e·rad-**

i·cant, *adj.*, *n.*

e·rad·i·ca·tion [ɪˌrædɪˈkeʃən; iˌrædiˈkeiʃən] *n.* 根除;撲滅;連根拔起。

e·rad·i·ca·tor [ɪˈrædɪˌketə; iˈrædikeitə] *n.* 除草器;根絕者。

e·ras·a·ble [ɪˈresəbl̩; iˈreizəbl] *adj.* 可擦掉的;可抹去的。 —**e·ras·a·bil·i·ty,** *n.*

e·rase [ɪˈres; iˈreiz] *v.*, **-rased, -ras·ing.** —*v.t.* ①擦掉;抹去。②(錄音帶等)將所錄之音擦掉。③〖俚〗謀殺;殺害。—*v.i.* ①容易被擦掉。②擦掉;抹去。—**ment,** *n.*

***e·ras·er** [ɪˈresə; iˈreizə] *n.* ①橡皮擦;黑板擦。②擦去之人或物。

E·ras·mus [ɪˈræzməs; iˈræzməs] *n.* 伊拉斯莫斯 (Desiderius, 眞名爲 Gerhard Gerhards, 1466?–1536, 荷蘭學者, 文藝復興運動領導者之一)。

E·ras·tian [ɪˈræstʃən; iˈræstiən] *adj.* Thomas Erastus 或其學說(倡宗教受國家支配說)的。—*n.* 信奉 Erastus 之學說者。

e·ra·sure [ɪˈreʒə; iˈreiʒə] *n.* ①抹去;擦掉。②被擦掉的字或字母。③字或字母被擦掉的地方。

Er·a·to [ˈɛrəˌto; ˈerətou] *n.* 〖希臘神話〗司抒情詩及戀愛詩之女神。

er·bi·um [ˈɜbɪəm; ˈəːbiəm] *n.* 〖化〗鉺(稀土金屬元素之一, 化學符號爲 Er)。

ere [ɛr; ɛə] *prep.* 前於…。***ere long*** 不久;一會兒。 —*conj.* ①在…以前。②與其…(寧願…)。

Er·e·bus [ˈɛrəbəs; ˈeribəs] *n.* 〖希臘神話〗塵世通往冥府之暗界。

***e·rect** [ɪˈrɛkt; iˈrekt] *adj.* 直立的;豎起的。to sit *erect.* 端坐。—*v.t.* ①豎立;使直立。②建築;建立。③拼起;裝起。When the missing parts arrived we *erected* the machine.當缺少的零件運到時,我們把機器裝起。④正式成立〖常 into〗. ⑤實現;建造。—*v.i.*直立。—**a·ble,** *adj.* —**er,** —**ness,** *n.* —**ly,** *adv.*

e·rec·tile [ɪˈrɛktɪl; iˈrektail] *adj.* ①可建立的;可豎起的。②〖生理〗易勃起的;勃起性的。—**e·rec·til·i·ty,** *n.*

e·rec·tion [ɪˈrɛkʃən; iˈrekʃən] *n.* ①直立。②建築。③建築物。④〖生理〗勃起。

e·rec·tor [ɪˈrɛktə; iˈrektə] *n.* ①建立者;設立者。②〖解剖〗勃起肌。(亦作**erecter**)

ere·long [ɛrˈlɔŋ; ɛəˈlɔŋ] *adv.* 〖古,詩〗不久;須臾。

er·e·mite [ˈɛrəˌmaɪt; ˈerimait] *n.* 隱修士;隱者。—**er·e·mit·ic, er·e·mit·i·cal, er·e·mit·ish,** *adj.* —**er·e·mit·ism,** *n.*

er·e·thism [ˈɛrəˌθɪzm̩; ˈeriθizm] *n.* 〖醫〗興奮增盛;容易興奮性。

ere·while [ɛrˈhwaɪl; ɛəˈwail] *adv.* 〖古〗片刻之前;頃間。(亦作 **erewhiles**)

erg [ɜg; əːg] *n.* 〖物理〗爾格(功之單位)。

er·go [ˈɜgo; ˈəːgou] 〖拉〗 *adv., conj.* 因此;由是;所以。

er·got [ˈɜgət; ˈəːgət] *n.* ①(穀類)麥角病。②麥角菌。③〖藥〗麥角(乾燥之麥角菌,用於止血及子宮收縮)。—**ic,** —**ed,** *adj.*

er·got·ism [ˈɜgətɪzm̩; ˈəːgətizm] *n.* 〖醫〗麥角中毒。

er·i·ca·ceous [ɛrəˈkeʃəs; ˌeriˈkeiʃəs] *adj.* 石南屬植物的。

E·rie [ˈɪrɪ; ˈiəri] *n.* ①伊利湖(在美國與加拿大間)。②伊利城(在美國 Pennsylvania 州西北境)。③印第安伊利族人(從前居住於伊利湖之南岸)。

Er·in [ˈɛrɪn; ˈiərin] *n.* 〖詩,古〗愛爾蘭。

er·is·tic [ɛˈrɪstɪk; eˈristik] *adj.* (亦作 **eristical**)不和的;好爭論的。—*n.* ①爭論者;辯論家。②辯論術。—**al·ly,** *adv.*

erl·king [ˈɜlˌkɪŋ; ˈəːlkiŋ] *n.* 〖北歐、日耳曼神話〗(加害兒童之)魔王。

er·mine [ˈɜmɪn; ˈəːmin] *n., pl.* **-mines, -mine.** ①〖動物〗貂;銀鼠。②貂皮。③國王、貴族或法官之位置、階級或職責。④(*pl.*)貂皮製衣服。—*adj.* 用貂皮做的;用貂皮裝飾的。

ern, erne [ɜn; əːn] *n.* 海鷲。

e·rode [ɪˈrod; iˈroud] *v.t.*, **e·rod·ed, e·rod·ing.** ①侵蝕;腐蝕。②藉腐蝕形成。—*v.i.* 被腐蝕。

E·ros [ˈɪrɑs; ˈerɔs] *n.* ①〖希臘神話〗愛神(與羅馬之 Cupid 相當)。②(e-)性慾。③求生之本能。

e·rose [ɪˈros; iˈrous] *adj.* ①不平坦的(如被咬去似的)。②〖植物〗樹葉等之邊緣不平的。—**ly,** *adv.*

e·ro·sion [ɪˈroʒən; iˈrouʒən] *n.* ①侵蝕;腐蝕;沖蝕。②〖醫〗糜爛;磨耗。—**al, e·ro·sive,** *adj.*

e·rot·ic [ɪˈrɑtɪk; iˈrɔtik] *adj.* 性愛的;色情的;好色的。(亦作 **erotical**) —*n.* ①好色之徒。②情詩。—**al·ly,** *adv.*

e·rot·i·cism [ɪˈrɑtəˌsɪzəm; eˈrɔtisizəm] *n.* ①情慾;情慾之情緒或傾向。②性慾亢進。③(藝術、文學、戲劇中)引起情慾之文字、情況等之使用。

er·o·tism [ˈɛrətɪzm̩; ˈerətizm] *n.* ①〖精神分析〗性慾之亢進與滿足。②性慾;漁色。

e·ro·to·ma·ni·a [ɪˌrotəˈmenɪə; iˌroutəˈmeiniə] *n.* 〖醫〗色情狂;花癡。

ERP, E.R.P. European Recovery Program.

***err** [ɜ; əː] *v.i.* ①做錯;犯錯。It's better to *err* on the side of mercy. 過於仁慈總比過於嚴厲好。②走入歧途;犯罪。③偏差;未中的。—**a·bil·i·ty,** *n.* —**a·ble,** *adj.*

er·ran·cy [ˈɛrənsɪ; ˈerənsi] *n., pl.* **-cies.** 錯誤;易誤。

er·rand** [ˈɛrənd; ˈerənd] *n.* ①出差;差使。He was sent on an *errand.* 他被派出差。②使命;任務。a fool's errand*** 無眞正目的之任務;一定失敗之任務。

er·rand-boy [ˈɛrəndˌbɔɪ; ˈerəndbɔi] *n.* 供差遣之僮僕。

er·rant [ˈɛrənt; ˈerənt] *adj.* ①漂泊的;遊俠的。②錯誤的;離正途的。③巡遊的。④漫無目的地移動的。—**ly,** *adv.*

er·rant·ry [ˈɛrəntrɪ; ˈerəntri] *n., pl.* **-ries.** 遊俠行爲;武士精神。

er·ra·ta [ɪˈretə; eˈrɑːtə] *n.* pl. of **erratum.**

er·rat·ic [əˈrætɪk; iˈrætik] *adj.* ①不穩定的;不確定的;不規律的。②奇僻的;奇怪的。③〖地質〗移離原位的。④〖醫〗移動的;變動的。—*n.* ①古怪的人。②漂泊無定的人。③〖地質〗漂石。—**al·ly,** *adv.* —**ism,** *n.*

er·ra·tum [ɪˈretəm; eˈrɑːtəm] *n., pl.* **-ta.** 書寫或印刷中之錯誤。

err·ing [ˈɜɪŋ; ˈəːriŋ] *adj.* 錯誤的;犯錯的。

er·ro·ne·ous [əˈronɪəs; iˈrounjəs] *adj.* ①錯誤的。②〖古〗走入歧途的。—**ly,** *adv.* —**ness,** *n.*

***er·ror** [ˈɛrə; ˈerə] *n.* ①錯誤;謬誤。to commit (*or* make) an *error.* 犯錯。②過失。③歧途。to lead a person into *error.* 引人入歧途。④謬見;誤信。⑤〖數學〗誤差。⑥〖棒球〗失誤。⑦〖法律〗審判上之錯誤。⑧變體郵票。

er·satz [ɛrˈzɑts; ˈɛəzæts] *adj.* 代用的(常指劣質之代用品言)。—*n.* 代用品。

Erse [ɜs; əːs] *n.* 蘇格蘭高地之 Celt 語;愛爾蘭語。

erst 〔ɝst; əːst〕 *adj.* 【古】 =erstwhile.
erst·while 〔ˈɝstˌhwaɪl; ˈəːst-wail〕 *adj.* 以前的;過去的。—*adv.* 以前;往昔。
e·ruct 〔ɪˈrʌkt; iˈrʌkt〕 *v.t.* & *v.i.* 打噎;噴出。
e·ruc·tate 〔ɪˈrʌktet; iˈrʌkteit〕 *v.t.* & *v.i.*, **-tat·ed, -tat·ing.** =eruct.
e·ruc·ta·tion 〔ɪˌrʌkˈteʃən; ˌiːrʌkˈteiʃən〕 *n.* ①打噎;噴出。②噴出物。
er·u·dite 〔ˈɛrʊˌdaɪt; ˈeru(ː)dait〕 *adj.* 博學的;飽學的。—**ly,** *adv.* —**ness,** *n.*
er·u·di·tion 〔ˌɛrʊˈdɪʃən; ˌeru(ː)ˈdiʃən〕 *n.* 學識;博學;飽學。—**al,** *adj.*
e·rupt 〔ɪˈrʌpt; iˈrʌpt〕 *v.i.* ①爆發;迸出。②發出疹子。③長牙;生齒。—*v.t.* 迸出;噴出。—**i·ble,** *adj.*
***e·rup·tion** 〔ɪˈrʌpʃən; iˈrʌpʃən〕 *n.* ①(火山之)爆發;噴火。②(泉水之)噴出。③出疹。Scarlet fever causes an *eruption* on the body. 猩紅熱使身上發疹。④生牙。⑤勃發;突發。⑥噴出之物。—**al,** *adj.*
e·rup·tive 〔ɪˈrʌptɪv; iˈrʌptiv〕 *adj.* ①爆發的;噴火的。②噴出的;迸出的。③【地質】火成的。④【醫】發疹的。—*n.* 【地質】火山爆發所噴出之岩石;火成岩。—**ly,** *adv.*
-ery 【字尾】表"職業;商業;情況;場所;產品;物之集合稱;性質;動作"之義。
er·y·sip·e·las 〔ˌɛrəˈsɪpl̩əs; ˌeriˈsipiləs〕 *n.* 【醫】丹毒。
er·y·the·ma 〔ˌɛrəˈθimə; ˌeriˈθiːmə〕 *n.* 【醫】紅斑;發紅。
Es. einsteinium.
E·sau 〔ˈisɔ; ˈiːsɔː〕 *n.* 【聖經】以掃(Isaac之長子)。
ESC Economic and Social Council (of the United Nations).
es·ca·drille 〔ˌɛskəˈdrɪl; ˌeskəˈdril〕 *n.* ①飛行小隊(通常由六機編成)。②海軍分隊(通常由八艘艦艇編成)。
es·ca·lade 〔ˌɛskəˈled; ˌeskəˈleid〕 *n.*, *v.*, **-lad·ed, -lad·ing.** —*n.* ①用梯攀登。②【軍】雲梯攻戰。—*v.t.* 用梯攀登(城牆);以雲梯攻入(設防地)。—**es·ca·lad·er,** *n.*
es·ca·late 〔ˈɛskəˌlet; ˈeskəleit〕 *v.t.* & *v.i.*, **-lat·ed, -lat·ing.** ①增强;升高;擴大。②抬高,降低,升起,或下落。—**es·ca·la·tion,** *n.*
***es·ca·la·tor** 〔ˈɛskəˌletɚ; ˈeskəleitə〕 *n.* ①自動梯。②升降之方法、工具。
escalator clause 勞資協定中有關工資等的伸縮條款。(亦作 **escalation clause**)
es·cal·lop 〔ɛˈskɑləp; isˈkɔləp〕 *n.*, *v.t.*, =**scallop.** (亦作 **escalop**)
es·ca·pade 〔ˈɛskəˌped; ˌeskəˈpeid〕 *n.* ①胡作非爲的惡作劇;大膽妄爲。②逃脫。
‡**es·cape** 〔əˈskep, ɪ-, ɛ-; isˈkeip〕 *v.*, **-caped, -cap·ing,** *n.*, *adj.* —*v.i.* ①逃脫;逃走;逃出。We *escaped* from the enemy. 我們從敵人手中逃出。②逸出;漏出。③免除;避免(懲罰、艱苦工作等)。④溜走;消滅。The words *escaped* from memory. 記不起字眼了。⑤(移植的植物)變成野生。—*v.t.* ①逃避;避免。He *escaped* punishment. 他避免懲罰。②免受。We all *escaped* the measles. 我們統統未出疹子。③逸出。A cry *escaped* her lips. 她不自禁地喊起來。④未注意;忘記。—*n.* ①脫逃;逃。No *escape* was possible. 不可能逃出(避免)。②逃走之路;逃脫之方法。③解悶;消遣。④漏水;漏氣。There is an *escape* of air. 有點漏氣。⑤原爲栽培之植物變爲野生。***a fire escape*** 太平門;太平梯。***make one's escape*** 逃走;逃出。He *made his escape* successfully. 他順利地逃出了。—*adj.* 供以逃脫機會的。—**es·cap·a·ble,** *adj.* —**less,** *adj.* —**es·cap·ee, es·cap·er,** *n.*
escape artist ①表演脫逃的藝人。②屢次越獄的慣犯。
escape clause 契約中言明在某種情況下簽字者可不負責任之條款。
escape hatch ①飛機上之緊急逃生出口。②逃避之道路或方法。
es·cape·ment 〔əˈskepmənt; isˈkeipmənt〕 *n.* ①鐘錶內控制擺或擺輪速度之裝置。②打字機管制捲軸活動之裝置。③【古】**a.** 逃走;逃避。**b.** 逃路。
escape velocity 物體脫離地心吸力所需之最低速度(約爲每小時25,000英里)。
es·cape·way 〔əˈskepˌwe; isˈkeipwei〕 *n.* ①逃路。②太平門;太平梯。
es·cap·ism 〔əˈskepɪzəm; isˈkeipizəm〕 *n.* 逃避現實。
es·cap·ist 〔əˈskepɪst; isˈkeipist〕 *adj.* 逃避主義的。—*n.* 逃避現實者。
es·car·got 〔ɛskarˈgo; eskarˈgou〕 *n.*, *pl.* **-gots** 〔-go; gou〕.【法】食用蝸牛。
es·ca·role 〔ˈɛskərol; ˈeskəroul〕 *n.* =**endive.**
es·carp 〔ɛˈskɑrp; isˈkɑːp〕 *n.* ①【築城】(堡壘外壕之)內壁。②似內壁之斜面;急斜面。—*v.t.* 使成急斜面;築以內壁。—**ment,** *n.*
-esce 【字尾】動詞字尾,表"開始成爲或做某事物;尚未完成"之義。
-escence 【字尾】名詞字尾,表"動作;歷程;變化;情狀"之義。
-escent 【字尾】與 **-esce** 同義之形容詞字尾。
esch·a·lot 〔ˈɛʃəˌlɑt; ˈeʃəlɔt〕 *n.* =**shallot.**
es·cha·tol·o·gy 〔ˌɛskəˈtɑlədʒɪ; ˌeskəˈtɔlədʒi〕 *n.* 【神學】末世學;終世論(研究死亡、世界末日、來生等之學問)。
es·cheat 〔ɛsˈtʃit; isˈtʃiːt〕 *v.t.* 使(無人繼承之土地、財產等)歸屬國家;充公。—*v.i.* 歸屬國家;被充公。—*n.* ①歸屬土地、財產等於國家;充公。②充公之產業。—**a·ble,** *adj.* —**ment,** *n.* —**al,** *adj.*, *n.* —**er,** *n.*
es·chew 〔ɛsˈtʃu; isˈtʃuː〕 *v.t.* 避開;遠離。
***es·cort** 〔*n.* ˈɛskɔrt; ˈeskɔːt *v.* ɪˈskɔrt; isˈkɔːt〕 *n.* ①護送者;護衛隊。②護送;護衛。③在公共場所陪伴女子的男人;護花使者。He is to be my *escort* for the dance tonight. 他將陪我去今晚的舞會。—*v.t.* 護送;護航。Will you *escort* this young lady home? 你願意護送這位小姐回家嗎?
escort carrier 【海軍】護航航空母艦。
es·cri·toire 〔ˌɛskrɪˈtwɑr; ˌeskriːˈtwɑː〕 *n.* 寫字檯;書桌。
es·crow 〔ˈɛskro; ˈeskrou〕 *n.*【法律】(寄存於第三人處,以待某種條件完成後始交付受讓人的)未完蓋印證書。***in escrow*** 寄存於第三人處以待某種條件完成而交付受讓人。
es·cu·do 〔ɛsˈkudo; esˈkuːdou〕 *n.*, *pl.* **-dos.** (西、葡、智利等國之)一種貨幣單位。
es·cu·lent 〔ˈɛskjələnt; ˈeskjulənt〕 *adj.* 適於食用的;可食的。—*n.* 適於食用的東西(尤指蔬菜)。
es·cutch·eon 〔ɪˈskʌtʃən; isˈkʌtʃən〕 *n.* ①飾有紋章的盾。②鑰匙孔周圍的金屬板。③船尾的船名牌。***a blot on one's escutcheon*** 令名之玷。His crime was *a blot on the family escutcheon.* 他的犯罪有辱家門。
E.S.E., ESE, e.s.e. east-southeast.
-ese 【字尾】名詞或形容詞語尾,表"地方;國家;語言;文體;人民或居住者"之義。

Es·ki·mo** [ˈɛskəˌmo; ˈeskimou] *n., pl.* **-mos, -mo,** *adj.* —*n.* 愛斯基摩人(北美洲、亞洲東北部頂端及北冰洋沿岸民族)。—*adj.* 愛斯基摩人的。Eskimo dog*** 愛斯基摩人用以拉雪橇的狗。(亦作 **Esquimau**) —**Es·ki·moid,** *adj.*

e·soph·a·gus [iˈsɑfəgəs; iːˈsɔfəgəs] *n., pl.* **-gi** [-ˌdʒaɪ; -dʒai]. 食道;食管。(亦作 **oesophagus**)

es·o·ter·ic [ˌɛsəˈtɛrɪk; ˌesouˈterik] *adj.* ①祕傳的;奧祕的。②私的;祕密的。③祕教的。—*n.* ①神祕教,神祕論。②傳授祕教之人。—**al·ly,** *adv.*

esp. especially.

es·pal·ier [ɛˈspæljɚ; isˈpæljə] *n.* ①樹牆;樹棚(用以整飭果樹等生長之棚架)。②(用樹牆整飭過的)樹木或植物;牆式果樹;棚式果樹。—*v.t.* ①用樹牆整飭。②供以樹牆。

es·par·to [ɛsˈpɑrto; esˈpɑːtou] *n., pl.* **-tos.**〖植物〗一種長而粗大之草(盛產於北非,可供製繩索及紙等)。(亦作 **esparto grass**)

espec. especially.

***es·pe·cial** [əˈspɛʃəl; isˈpeʃəl, es-] *adj.* 特別的;特殊的。a matter of *especial* importance. 特別重要的事情。—**ness,** *n.*

:es·pe·cial·ly [əˈspɛʃəlɪ; isˈpeʃəli, es-] *adv.* 特別地;主要地;多半;尤其。I like the country, *especially* in spring. 我喜愛鄉間,尤其在春天。

Es·pe·ran·tist [ˌɛspəˈrɑntɪst; ˌespəˈræntist] *n.* (1887年 Dr. Zamenhof 所創之)世界語的學者;使用世界語者。

Es·pe·ran·to [ˌɛspəˈrɑnto; ˌespəˈræntou] *n.* 一種世界語 (1887 年 Dr. Zamenhof所創)。—**Es·pe·ran·tic,** *adj.* —**Es·pe·ran·tism,** *n.*

es·pi·al [ɪˈspaɪəl; isˈpaiəl] *n.* ①偵察;監視。②看出;發見。

es·piè·gle [ɛsˈpjɛglə; esˈpjeglə]〖法〗*adj.* 好戲謔的。

es·pi·o·nage [ˈɛspɪənɪdʒ; ˌespiəˈnɑːʒ] *n.* 間諜活動。

es·pla·nade [ˌɛspləˈned; ˌespləˈneid] *n.* ①(海邊)遊憩場。②(要塞與城市房屋間之)空地。

es·pous·al [ɪˈspauzl; isˈpauzəl] *n.* ①(主義、學說的)採取。②訂婚或結婚典禮。③(*pl.*)訂婚;訂婚典禮;結婚;結婚典禮。—*adj.* 婚禮的;訂婚典禮的。

es·pouse [ɪˈspauz; isˈpauz] *v.t.,* **-poused, -pous·ing.** ①嫁;娶。②採取;贊助。③信奉。—**es·pous·er,** *n.*

es·pres·so [ɛsˈprɛso; esˈpresou] *n.* 一種濃咖啡。

es·prit [ɛˈspri; ˈespriː] *n.* 機智;聰明。

es·prit de corps [ɛˈsprɪdəˈkor; ˈespriːdəˈkɔː]〖法〗團體精神。

es·prit fort [ɛsˈpriˈfɔr; esˈpriːˈfɔː]〖法〗個性極强的人。

es·py [əˈspaɪ; isˈpai] *v.t.,* **-pied, -py·ing.** 看出;探出(因遙遠、微小、或隱匿而不易看出之東西)。

Esq., Esqr. Esquire.〖注意〗在寫信時,將 Esq. 或 Esquire 放在收信者的名字後邊是正式用法,而含古風或英國作風之意味;但在美國主要用於指專門職業者,尤指律師。既用 Esq.之後,就不得再加 Mr., Dr., Hon. 等之稱呼;如 Harry A. Kinne, Esq.

-esque〖字尾〗形容詞語尾,表"式樣;風格;特性"之義。

Es·qui·mau [ˈɛskəˌmo; ˈeskimou] *n., pl.* **-maux** [-ˌmo, -ˌmoz; -mou, -mouz]. =**Eskimo.**

Es·quire [əˈskwaɪr; isˈkwaiə] *n.* ①放在一個男人姓名後面的尊稱,例如:John Jones, *Esquire*=Mr. John Jones (在美常用於律師,在英用於士紳)。②(e-)(中世紀時)騎士之隨從(而想成爲騎士者)。③英士紳階級(次於騎士)之一員。④〖古〗鄉紳(=squire).—*v.t.* ①提拔(某人)爲騎士隨從,鄉紳等。②稱呼(某人)爲 Esquire. ③護從;護衞。

ess [ɛs; es] *n.* ①字母 S. ②S形之物。

-ess〖字尾〗名詞字尾,表"陰性;女性"之義。

***es·say** [*n. for* ①, ③ ˈɛsɪ, ˈɛse, *for* ② ɛˈse, ˈɛse; ˈesei, ˈesi *v.* əˈse, ɛˈse; eˈsei, ˈesei] *n.* ①文章;論說文。②試驗;企圖;嘗試。His *essays* at friendship were met with suspicion. 他想交朋友之嘗試受到懷疑。③〖郵票〗經考慮而未正式採用之郵票設計。—*v.t.* ①嘗試;企圖。to *essay* to do something. 企圖做某事。②試驗。—**er,** *n.*

es·say·ist [ˈɛse·ɪst; ˈeseiist] *n.* ①論說文作家;隨筆作家;散文家。②〖罕〗試驗者。

es·se [ˈɛsɪ; ˈesi]〖拉〗*n.* 存在;實在。

es·sence** [ˈɛsn̩s; ˈesns] *n.* ①本質;精髓;原素。The *essence* of morality is right intention. 道德的精髓在於心正。②香氣;香水。③精;素。in essence*** 在本質上。***of the essence*** **a.** 絕對需要的;不可缺少的。**b.** 必要之物。Time is *of the essence* of this agreement. 時間因素爲本協議中之要點。

Es·sene [ˈɛsin, ɛˈsin; ˈesiːn, eˈsiːn] *n.* 古猶太之一苦修教派教徒。—**Es·se·ni·an, Es·sen·ic,** *adj.*

***es·sen·tial** [əˈsɛnʃəl; iˈsenʃəl] *adj.* ①基本的;重要的;必要的。Is wealth *essential* to happiness? 財富對於幸福是必要的嗎? ②本質的;實質的。—*n.* 要素;要點;本質;精髓。the *essentials* of English grammar. 英文文法要義。—**ly,** *adv.* —**ness,** *n.*

es·sen·ti·al·i·ty [əˌsɛnʃɪˈælətɪ; iˌsenʃiˈæliti] *n., pl.* **-ties.** ①本質;本體;重要性。②要點;要件。

E.S.T., EST, e.s.t. Eastern Standard Time.

est. ①established. ②estate. ③estimated. ④estuary.

-est〖字尾〗表最高級之形容詞或副詞字尾。

:es·tab·lish [əˈstæblɪʃ; isˈtæbliʃ, es-] *v.t.* ①建立;設立。②確立;認可;固定。His honesty is well *established.* 他的忠實已確立(爲人所信任)。③證實。④使成爲國教。⑤執業;開業。A new doctor has *established* himself on this street. 一個新的醫生已在這條街上開業。⑥住定;定居。We are now comfortably *established* in our new house. 我們遷居新屋業已安頓下來。⑦安置;使任…職。—**a·ble,** *adj.* —**er,** *n.*

es·tab·lished [əˈstæblɪʃt; isˈtæbliʃt] *adj.* ①已確立的;基礎鞏固的。②常設的。③已制定的;已設立的。④已定爲國教的。***established church*** 國教;(the E- C-)英國國教(會)。

establishing shot〖電影、電視〗確定鏡頭。

es·tab·lish·ment** [əˈstæblɪʃmənt; isˈtæbliʃmənt] *n.* ①建立;確立;固定。②建立物(如工廠、商店、教會、軍隊等)。He keeps a large *establishment.* 他經營一個雇用很多人的大機構(工廠、商號等)。③承認爲國教;國教。④〖軍隊〗編制;組織。war *establishment.* 戰時編制。⑤員額;定員。⑥家庭(包括傢具、土地等)。⑦固定收入。⑧成家立業;安身立命。the Establishment*** 社會上現存的權力機構;某一行業之當權派。

es·tab·lish·men·tar·i·an [əsˌtæblıʃmɛn'tɛrıən; es,tæbliʃmən'tɛəriən] *adj.* 國教的（尤指英國國教會的）。—*n.* 支持國教者。—**ism,** *n.*

es·ta·mi·net [ɛstami'nɛ; estɑ:mi'ne] 〖法〗 *n.* 酒店;咖啡館（=café).

es·tate** [ə'stet; is'teit] *n.* ①地產;財產。②身分;地位。A boy attains man's *estate* at 21. 一個男孩於二十一歲卽屆成年。③社會階級。④〖英〗新社區。⑤〖古〗榮貴。⑥〖廢〗高貴的社會地位。personal estate*** 動產。He died leaving very little *personal estate.* 他死時留下很少的動產。***real estate*** 房地產;不動產。***the three estates***（英國）貴族、僧侶與平民三階級。—*v.t.* 〖廢〗使有地產、地位。

estate agent 〖英〗①代管房地產者。②房地產經紀人。

estate tax 房地產稅（尤指向繼承人徵收者）。

***es·teem** [ə'stim; is'ti:m] *v.t.* ①尊敬;尊重。Your *esteemed* letter has reached me. 尊示業已收到。②認爲;想;諒。I *esteem* it an honor to address this audience. 我認爲向諸位演講是一種光榮。—*n.* ①尊重;尊敬。Please accept this picture as a mark of our high *esteem.* 請將此照片收下,作爲我們最高敬意的表示。②〖古〗判斷;珍重。

es·ter ['ɛstɚ; 'estə] *n.* 〖化〗酯。

Esth. ①Esther. ②Esthonia.

Es·ther ['ɛstɚ; 'estə] *n.* ①女子名。②〖聖經〗以斯帖（波斯王 Xerxes 之猶太籍妻子）。③以斯帖書（舊約聖經之一卷）。

es·thete ['ɛsθit; 'i:sθi:t] *n.* 審美者; 唯美主義者（=aesthete).

es·thet·ic [ɛs'θɛtɪk; i:s'θetik] *adj.* ①美的。②美學的。③富美感的。

es·thet·i·cal [ɛs'θɛtɪkl; i:s'θetikəl] *adj.* =**esthetic.** —**ly,** *adv.*

es·thet·ics [ɛs'θɛtɪks; i:s'θetiks] *n.*（作 *sing.* 解）美學;審美學。（亦作 **aesthetics**)

Es·tho·ni·a [ɛs'tonɪə; es'touniə] *n.* =**Estonia.** —**Es·tho·ni·an,** *adj., n.*

es·ti·ma·ble ['ɛstəməbl; 'estiməbl] *adj.* ①值得尊敬的。②可估計的。

es·ti·mate** [*n.* 'ɛstəmɪt; 'estimit, -meit *v.* 'ɛstə,met; 'estimeit] *n., v.,* **-mat·ed, -mat·ing.** —*n.* 意見;估計;評價;判斷。I hope the builders won't exceed their *estimate.* 我希望建築者不要超出了他們的估計。by estimate*** 照估計。***the Estimates***（政府之）歲費預算。—*v.t. & v.i.* 評價;評定;估計。He *estimated* the cost of my new suit at $1,200. 他估計我的新衣服需一千二百元。

***es·ti·ma·tion** [,ɛstə'meʃən; ,esti'meiʃən] *n.* ①判斷; 意見; 估計。In my *estimation,* your plan will not work. 依我判斷,你的計畫行不通。②尊敬; 敬重。He stands high in my *estimation.* 我很欽敬他。③預算; 概算。

es·ti·val ['ɛstəvl, ɛs'taɪvl; i:s'taivəl] *adj.* 夏天的; 夏季特有的。

es·ti·vate ['ɛstə,vet; 'estiveit] *v.i.,* **-vat·ed, -vat·ing.** ①度夏。②〖動物〗夏眠。

es·ti·va·tion [,ɛstə'veʃən; ,esti'veiʃən] *n.* ①〖動物〗夏眠。②〖植物〗花芽層(花之各部分在苞內之排列)。（亦作 **aestivation**)

Es·to·ni·a [ɛs'tonɪə; es'touniə] *n.* 愛沙尼亞(波羅的海沿岸小國,首都爲 Tallinn, 於 1940 年爲蘇聯兼併)。

Es·to·ni·an [ɛs'tonɪən; es'touniən] *adj.* 愛沙尼亞的;其人民、語言或文化的。—*n.* 愛沙尼亞人; 愛沙尼亞語。

es·top [ɛ'stap; is'tɔp] *v.t.,* **-topped, -top·ping.** ①〖法律〗禁止翻供(卽不許爲與以前相反之主張或否認)。②禁止;防止。

es·top·pel [ɛ'stapl; is'tɔpl, es-] *n.* 〖法律〗禁止反言。

es·to·vers [ɛ'stovɚz; es'touvəz] *n. pl.* 〖法律〗必要物; 必需供給品(如給妻之贍養費等)。

es·trade [ɛs'trad; es'trɑ:d] *n.* 講臺;壇。

es·trange [ə'strendʒ; is'treindʒ] *v.t.,* **-tranged, -trang·ing.** ①疏遠。②隔離;遠離。③轉用他途;轉手。

es·trange·ment [ə'strendʒmənt; is'treindʒmənt, es-] *n.* 疏遠。

es·tray [ɪ'stre; is'trei] *n.* ①離開本來位置之人或物; 迷失物。②〖法律〗迷失之家畜。—*v.i.* 〖古〗迷途;漂泊。

es·treat [ɪ'strit; is'tri:t] *n.* 〖法律〗裁判紀錄副本、謄本或節本。—*v.t.* ①摘抄(罰金等)裁判紀錄以便執行。②課(罰金);徵收。

es·tri·ol ['ɛstraɪ,ol; 'estraioul] *n.* 〖生化〗雌素三醇;三氫氧動情激素。

es·tro·gen ['ɛstrədʒən; 'estrədʒən] *n.* 〖生化〗雌激素;動情激素。

es·trone ['ɛstron; 'estroun] *n.* 〖生化〗雌素酮（一種促進女性性慾之荷爾蒙）。

es·trus ['ɛstrəs; 'estrəs] *n.* 〖動物〗①(雌性動物之)動情期; 求偶期。②動情周期。(亦作 **estrum, oestrus**)

es·tu·ar·y ['ɛstʃu,ɛrɪ; 'estjuəri] *n., pl.* **-ar·ies.** ①海灣。②(河流的) 入海口。

e·su·ri·ent [ɪ'sjurɪənt; i'sjuəriənt] *adj.* 饑餓的; 貪吃的; 貪婪的。—*n.* 饑餓的人;貪吃者;貪婪者。

et¹ [ɛt; et] 〖拉〗 *conj.* =**and.**

et² [e; ei] 〖法〗 *conj.* =**and.**

-et 〖字尾〗表"小"之義。如 isle, islet(小島)。

E.T. ①English Translation. ②Eastern Time.

e.t. ①eastern time. ②electrical transcription.

e·ta ['etə, 'itə; 'i:tə] *n.* 希臘語之第七字母 (H, η).

E.T.A., ETA estimated time of arrival.

et al. ①et alibi(拉=and elsewhere). ② et alii (=and others).

***etc.** 〖拉〗及其他; 等等 (=et cetera). The case is suitable for prints, maps, blueprints, *etc.* 此匣子宜於放置板畫、地圖、藍圖等。〖注意〗 **etc.** 通常讀作 and so forth (*or* on);前面加 comma, 但不可再加 and.

et cet·er·a [ɛt'sɛtərə, -'sɛtrə; it'setrə, et-, ət-] 〖拉〗及其他;等等。

et·cet·er·as, et·caet·er·as [ɛt'sɛtrəz; it'setrəz] *n. pl.* 其餘之人或物。

etch [ɛtʃ; etʃ] *v.t.* ①(用酸類在金屬或玻璃上) 蝕刻(圖案、圖畫等)。②蝕刻; 蝕鏤(玻璃或金屬)。③刻畫(如某人之容貌、性格等)。④牢記心中。⑤由腐蝕在地面上造成新地形。—*v.i.* 以蝕刻術作圖案、圖畫等。

etch·er ['ɛtʃɚ; 'etʃə] *n.* 蝕刻師;銅版工。

etch·ing ['ɛtʃɪŋ; 'etʃiŋ] *n.* ①以蝕刻版印出之圖畫或圖案。②蝕刻版; 蝕刻圖畫或圖案。③蝕刻術; (以酸類於金屬或玻璃上)蝕刻(圖畫或圖案)之方法。

***e·ter·nal** [ɪ'tɝnl; i(:)'tə:nl] *adj.* ①永恆的;不變的。②不滅的;永生的。③不停的。Stop this *eternal* chatter. 不要囉囉唆唆說個不停。—*n.* ①(the E-)上帝。②永恆不變之事物。—**i·ty,** —**ness,** *n.* —**ly,** *adv.*

Eternal City, The 羅馬之別稱。

e·ter·nal·ize [ɪ'tɝnḷ͵aɪz; iː'təːnəlaiz] *v.t.*, **-ized, -iz·ing.** =**eternize.**

***e·ter·ni·ty** [ɪ'tɝnətɪ; iː'təːniti, i'təː-] *n., pl.* **-ties.** ①永恆;無窮。It seemed an *eternity* before news that he had been saved reached her. 在她得到他獲救的消息前，那段時間好像是無限長的。②來世；永世。③很長久的時間。We had to wait an *eternity* for the ship to sail. 我們須等很久船才開。④(*pl.*) 不變的眞理或事實。 the *eternities.* 永恆不滅的眞理。

e·ter·nize [ɪ'tɝnaɪz; iː'təːnaiz] *v.t.*, **-nized, -niz·ing.** ①使永恆;使不變。②使不朽。—**e·ter·ni·za·tion,** *n.*

e·te·sian [ɪ'tiʒən; i'tiːʒjən] *adj.* 例年的;每年一定季節吹的。

Eth. Ethiopia.

-eth 【字尾】①古時表第三人稱、單數、直述法動詞的現在簡單式。② **-th** 之異體。

eth·ane ['εθen; 'eθein] *n.* 【化】乙烷。

e·ther ['iθɚ; 'iːθə] *n.* ①【化】醚。②上空；大氣以外之上層空間。③【物理】以太。④【俗】無線電廣播。—*v.t.* 【俗】無線電廣播。

e·the·re·al [ɪ'θɪrɪəl; iː'θiəriəl] *adj.* ①輕的；如空氣的。②纖弱的;靈妙的;清輕的。③非人世的；天上的。④上空的；蒼天的。⑤【化】醚的。(亦作 **aethereal**) —**ness,** *n.* —**ly,** *adv.*—**e·the·re·ous,** *adj.*

e·the·re·al·i·ty [ɪ͵θɪrɪ'ælətɪ; i͵θiəri'æliti] *n.* 如空氣;無形體;輕妙;靈妙。

e·the·re·al·i·za·tion [ɪ͵θɪrɪəlɪ'zeʃən; i͵θiəriəli'zeiʃən] *n.* 氣化;醚化。

e·the·re·al·ize [ɪ'θɪrɪəl͵aɪz; iː'θiəriəlaiz] *v.t.*, **-ized, -iz·ing.** ①使氣化。②使輕妙;使靈妙。③使醚化。

e·ther·i·fy [ɪ'θεrə͵faɪ; i'θerifai] *v.t.*, **-fied, -fy·ing.** 【化】使化爲醚;使化爲醇精。—**e·ther·i·fi·ca·tion,** *n.*

e·ther·ize ['iθə͵raɪz; 'iːθəraiz] *v.t.*, **-ized, -iz·ing.** ①使化爲醚。②【醫】以醚麻醉。—**e·ther·iz·er, e·ther·i·za·tion,** *n.*

eth·ic ['εθɪk; 'eθik] *adj.* =**ethical.** —*n.* ① =**ethics.** ②某一文化或團體的道德規範;倫理。③個人的道德準繩。

eth·i·cal ['εθɪkḷ; 'eθikəl] *adj.* ①倫理的;道德的。②倫理學的。③【藥】憑處方出售的。—**ly,** *adv.* —**ness,** —**i·ty,** *n.*

ethical drug 有醫生處方才能出售的「藥物。

***eth·ics** ['εθɪks; 'eθiks] *n.* ①(常作 *sing.* 解) 倫理學。*Ethics* deals with moral conduct. 倫理學研討道德行爲。②(*pl.*)倫常;道德。 Medical *ethics* do not permit doctor and surgeons to advertise.醫德不許醫師和外科醫生登廣告宣傳。—**e·thi·cian, eth·i·cist,** *n.*

E·thi·o·pi·a [͵iθɪ'opɪə; ͵iːθi'oupjə] *n.* 衣索比亞 (卽阿比西尼亞,爲非洲東部之一國,其首都爲亞底斯亞貝巴 Addis Ababa).

E·thi·o·pi·an [͵iθɪ'opɪən; ͵iːθi'oupjən] *adj.* 衣索比亞的。—*n.* ①衣索比亞人。②古人認爲來自埃及之南的皮膚黑的人。③黑人。

E·thi·op·ic [͵iθɪ'ɑpɪk; ͵iːθi'ɔpik] *adj.* 衣索比亞(語)的。 —*n.* 衣索比亞語。

eth·moid ['εθmɔɪd; 'eθmɔid] *adj.* 【解剖】篩骨的。—*n.* 篩骨。

eth·nic ['εθnɪk; 'eθnik] *adj.* ①種族的;人種的。②人種學的。③非猶太人亦非基督徒的;異敎徒的。④民族的(尤指原始的)。(亦作 **ethnical**) —**i·ty,** *n.* —**al·ly,** *adv.*

ethno- 【字首】表"種族;民族"之義。

eth·no·cen·trism [͵εθnə'sεntrɪzəm; ͵eθnə'sentrizəm] *n.* 【社會】民族優越感。

eth·nog·e·ny [εθ'nɑdʒɪnɪ; eθ'nɔdʒini] *n.* ①人種起源學。②種族之起源。

eth·nog·ra·pher [εθ'nɑgrəfɚ; eθ'nɔgrəfə] *n.* 人種誌學者;研究人種誌的人。

eth·nog·ra·phy [εθ'nɑgrəfɪ; eθ'nɔgrəfi] *n.* 人種誌。

ethnol. ①ethnologic. ②ethnology.

eth·no·lin·guis·tics [͵εθnolɪŋ'gwɪstɪks; ͵eθnouliŋ'gwistiks] *n.* (作 *sing.* 解) 文化語言學 (研究語言與文化關係的)。

eth·no·log·ic [͵εθnə'lɑdʒɪk; ͵eθnou'lɔdʒik] *adj.* =**ethnological.**

eth·no·log·i·cal [͵εθnə'lɑdʒɪkḷ; ͵eθnə'lɔdʒikəl] *adj.* 人種學的。

eth·nol·o·gist [εθ'nɑlədʒɪst; eθ'nɔlədʒist] *n.* 人種學家。

eth·nol·o·gy [εθ'nɑlədʒɪ; eθ'nɔlədʒi] *n.* 人種學。

eth·no·mu·si·col·o·gy [͵εθno͵mjuzɪ'kɑlədʒɪ; ͵eθnou͵mjuːzi'kɔlədʒi] *n.*人種音樂學(研究民謠、原始音樂與種族文化關係的)。

eth·no·psy·chol·o·gy [͵εθnəsaɪ'kɑlədʒɪ; ͵eθnəsai'kɔlədʒi] *n.* 人種心理學。

e·thos ['iθɑs; 'iːθɔs] *n.* ①性格；氣質。②【社會】民族精神；社會思潮；風氣。

eth·yl ['εθəl; 'eθil] *n.* 【化】乙基。

ethyl alcohol 普通酒精;【俗】威士忌。

eth·yl·ene ['εθə͵lin; 'eθiliːn] *n.* 【化】乙烯。(亦作 **ethene**)

e·ti·o·late ['itɪə͵let; 'iːtiouleit] *v.*, **-lat·ed, -lat·ing.** —*v.t.* 使(植物)不見陽光而蒼白。—*v.i.* (植物) 缺乏陽光變蒼白。—**e·ti·o·la·tion,** *n.*

e·ti·ol·o·gy [͵itɪ'ɑlədʒɪ; ͵iːti'ɔlədʒi] *n., pl.* **-gies.** =**aetiology.** —**e·ti·o·log·i·cal,** *adj.*

***et·i·quette** ['εtɪ͵kεt; ͵eti'ket, 'etiket] *n.* ①禮節。 *Etiquette* requires a man to rise when a woman enters the room. 按照禮節,一個女人進到屋裡,男人應該起立。②規則；成規。

et·na ['εtnə; 'etnə] *n.* 酒精燈煮水器。

E·ton ['itn̩; 'iːtn] *n.* 伊頓(英國倫敦以西一城市，爲 Eton College 所在地)。***Eton collar*** (掛於 Eton jacket 衣領外面的)寬硬衣領。***Eton jacket*** 一種童裝短上衣。

E·to·ni·an [i'tonɪən; iː'tounjən] *adj.* Eton 學院的。—*n.* Eton 學院學生; Eton 學院出身者。

E·tru·ri·a [ɪ'trurɪə; i'truəriə] *n.* 義大利西部之一古國。

E·trus·can [ɪ'trʌskən; i'trʌskən] *adj.* Etruria 的；其人民或語言的。 —*n.* ①古代 Etruria 人。② Etruria 語。(亦作 **Etrurian**)

et seq. *pl.* **et seqq., et sqq.** et sequēns (拉 =and the following).

Et·ta ['εtə; 'etə] *n.* 女子名 (Henrietta 之暱稱)。

-ette 【字尾】①表有 **-et** 字尾的名詞之陰性。②表"小"之義。

é·tude [e'tjud; ei'tjuːd] *n., pl.* **é·tudes.** 【法】【音樂】練習曲。

e·tui [ə'twi; e'twiː] *n., pl.* **e·tuis.** 小匣；小盒;針線盒;化妝品盒。(亦作 **etwee**)

etym., etymol. ①etymological. ② etymology.

et·y·mo·log·ic [͵εtəmə'lɑdʒɪk; ͵etimə'lɔdʒik] *adj.* =**etymological.**

et·y·mo·log·i·cal [͵εtəmə'lɑdʒɪkḷ; ͵etimə'lɔdʒikəl] *adj.* 語源學的。—**ly,** *adv.*

et·y·mol·o·gist [͵εtə'mɑlədʒɪst; ͵eti-

ˈmɔlədʒist] *n.* 語源學者；語源專家。
et·y·mol·o·gize [ˌɛtəˈmɑlə,dʒaɪz; ˌetiˈmɔlədʒaiz] *v.*, **-gized, -giz·ing.** —*v.t.* 追溯(字)之語源。 —*v.i.* 舉出（字）之語源；研究語源。 —**et·y·mol·o·giz·a·ble,** *adj.*
***et·y·mol·o·gy** [ˌɛtəˈmɑlədʒɪ; ˌetiˈmɔlədʒi] *n.*, *pl.* **-gies.** ①語源。②語源學。
et·y·mon [ˈɛtə,mɑn; ˈetimɔn] *n.*, *pl.* **-mons, -ma** [-mə; -mə]. 語源；字根；字之原形。
Eu 化學元素 europium 之符號。
eu- 〖字首〗表"良好"之義。
eu·caine [juˈken; juːˈkein] *n.* 〖藥〗優卡因(一種局部痲醉劑)。
eu·ca·lyp·tus [ˌjukəˈlɪptəs; ˌjuːkəˈliptəs] *n.*, *pl.* **-tus·es, -ti** [-taɪ; -tai]. 〖植物〗有加利樹。
Eu·cha·rist [ˈjukərɪst; ˈjuːkərist] *n.* ①聖餐。②聖餐之麪包與酒。—**ic,** —**i·cal,** *adj.*
eu·chre [ˈjukɚ; ˈjuːkə] *n.*, *v.*, **-chred, -chring.** —*n.* 一種牌戲。 —*v.t.* ①趁（對方)疏忽時取勝。②〖美俗〗以計取勝〖常out〗。
Euck·en [ˈɔɪkən; ˈɔikən] *n.* 奧伊鏗 (Rudolf Christoph, 1846–1926, 德國哲學家，曾獲1908年諾貝爾文學獎)。
Eu·clid [ˈjuklɪd; ˈjuːklid] *n.* ①歐幾里得(希臘數學家，約生於紀元前三世紀，被稱爲幾何學之父)。②歐氏幾何學。
Eu·clid·e·an [juˈklɪdɪən; juˈklidiən] *adj.* 歐幾里得 (Euclid) 的；歐幾里得幾何學的。(亦作 **Euclidian**)
eu·d(a)e·mo·ni·a [ˌjudɪˈmonɪə; ˌjuːdiˈmouniə] *n.* ①幸福。②(亞里斯多德哲學)因理性而積極生活所帶來的幸福。
eu·d(a)e·mon·ics [ˌjudɪˈmɑnɪks; ˌjuːdiˈmɔniks] *n.* (常作*sing.* 解) ①幸福學。②獲得幸福之方法；幸福獲致術。
eu·d(a)e·mon·ism [juˈdimənɪzəm; juˈdiːmənizəm] *n.* 〖倫理〗幸福論；快樂說。
eu·di·om·e·ter [ˌjudɪˈɑmətɚ; ˌjudiˈɔmitə] *n.*〖化〗測氣管(度量或分析氣體用者)。
Eu·gene, Eu·gène [juˈdʒin; ˈjuːdʒiːn] *n.* 男子名。
Eu·ge·ni·a [juˈdʒinɪə; juːˈdʒiːniə] *n.* 女子名。(亦作 **Eugenie**)
eu·gen·ic [juˈdʒɛnɪk; juːˈdʒenik] *adj.* ①優生的。②有優良之遺傳質的。(亦作 **eugenical**) —**al·ly,** *adv.*
eu·gen·ics [juˈdʒɛnɪks; juːˈdʒeniks] *n. sing.* or *pl.* 優生學；人種改良學。
eu·ge·nist [ˈjudʒənɪst; ˈjuːdʒənist] *n.* 優生學者；優生學專家。
Eu·ler-Chel·pin [ˈɔɪləˈkɛlpɪn; ˈɔiləˈkelpin] *n.* 奧伊勒凱賓 (Hans August Simon von, 1873–1964, 生於德國之瑞典化學家，曾獲1929年諾貝爾化學獎)。
eu·lo·gist [ˈjulədʒɪst; ˈjuːlədʒist] *n.* 述說或寫作頌詞之人；頌揚者。
eu·lo·gis·tic [ˌjuləˈdʒɪstɪk; ˌjuːləˈdʒistik] *adj.* 頌詞的；頌揚的。
eu·lo·gis·ti·cal [ˌjuləˈdʒɪstɪkl; ˌjuːləˈdʒistikəl] *adj.* ＝**eulogistic.** —**ly,** *adv.*
eu·lo·gi·um [juˈlodʒɪəm; juːˈloudʒiəm] *n.*, *pl.* **-ums, -gi·a** [-dʒɪə; -dʒiə]. ＝**eulogy.**
eu·lo·gize [ˈjulə,dʒaɪz; ˈjuːlədʒaiz] *v.t.*, **-gized, -giz·ing.** 稱讚；頌揚。—**eu·lo·giz·er, eu·lo·gi·za·tion,** *n.*
eu·lo·gy [ˈjulədʒɪ; ˈjuːlədʒi] *n.*, *pl.* **-gies.** 頌詞；頌德文；頌揚。
eu·nuch [ˈjunək; ˈjuːnək] *n.* ①閹人。②太監；宦官。

eu·pep·si·a [juˈpɛpʃə; juːˈpepsiə] *n.* 消化良好。(亦作 **eupepsy**)
eu·pep·tic [juˈpɛptɪk; juːˈpeptik] *adj.* ①消化良好的。②有助消化的。
eu·phe·mism [ˈjufə,mɪzəm; ˈjuːfimizəm] *n.* ①委婉話；婉言。②委婉的說法。
eu·phe·mist [ˈjufə,mɪst; ˈjuːfimist] *n.* 用婉曲語之人；說話委婉的人。
eu·phe·mis·tic [ˌjufəˈmɪstɪk; ˌjuːfiˈmistik] *adj.* 婉曲的；委婉說法的。(亦作 **euphemistical**) —**al·ly,** *adv.*
eu·phe·mize [ˈjufə,maɪz; ˈjuːfimaiz] *v.t.* & *v.i.*, **-mized, -miz·ing.** 委婉而言。
eu·phon·ic [juˈfɑnɪk; juːˈfɔnik, juˈf-] *adj.* ①和諧的；悅耳的。②使發音變爲容易的。(亦作 **euphonical**) —**al·ly,** *adv.*
eu·pho·ni·ous [juˈfonɪəs; juːˈfouniəs] *adj.* 和諧的；悅耳的。
eu·pho·ni·um [juˈfonɪəm; juːˈfounjəm] *n.* 〖音樂〗粗管上低音號(一種喇叭)。
eu·pho·nize [ˈjufə,naɪz; ˈjuːfənaiz] *v.t.*, **-nized, -niz·ing.** 使悅耳；使和諧。
eu·pho·ny [ˈjufənɪ; ˈjuːfəni] *n.*, *pl.* **-nies.** ①諧音；悅耳之音。②使聲音變爲容易發出之趨勢。
eu·pho·ri·a [juˈforɪə; juˈfouriə] *n.* 〖心理〗(尤指虛幻的) 幸福感；陶醉。
eu·phra·sy [ˈjufrəsɪ; ˈjuːfrəsi] *n.*, *pl.* **-sies.** 〖植物〗小米草(可治眼疾)。
Eu·phra·tes [juˈfretiz; juːˈfreitiːz] *n.* 幼發拉底河(在亞洲西南部)。
eu·phu·ism [ˈjufjuɪzm; ˈjuːfjuːizəm] *n.* 誇飾之文體；華麗之詞藻。
eu·phu·ist [ˈjufjuɪst; ˈjuːfjuːist] *n.* 寫誇飾文體之人；用華麗詞藻之人。
eu·phu·is·tic [ˌjufjuˈɪstɪk; ˌjuːfjuːˈistik] *adj.* 誇飾體的；華麗的。
eu·phu·is·ti·cal [ˌjufjuˈɪstɪkl; ˌjuːfjuːˈistikəl] *adj.* ＝**euphuistic.** —**ly,** *adv.*
Eur. ①Europe. ②European.
Eur·af·ri·can [juˈræfrɪkən; juːˈræfrikən] *adj.* ①歐非大陸的。②歐非混血的；黑白混血的。—*n.* 歐非混血兒；黑白混血兒。
Eur·a·mer·i·can [ˌjurəˈmɛrɪkən; ˌjuərəˈmerikən] *adj.* 歐美共通的。(亦作 **Euro-American**)
Eur·a·sia [juˈreʒə; juəˈreiʒiə] *n.* 歐亞大陸。
Eur·a·sian [juˈreʒən; juəˈreiʒiən] *adj.* ①歐亞大陸的；歐亞人的。②歐亞混血的。—*n.* 歐亞混血人。
Eur·at·om [juˈrætəm; juərˈætəm] *n.* 1957 由法、荷、比利時、盧森堡、及西德組成的原子能發展組織 (＝*Eur*opean *At*omic Energy Community).
eu·re·ka [juˈrikə; juəˈriːkə] *interj.* 我找到了 (＝I have found it! 遇有新發現時勝利的歡呼)。
eu·rhyth·mic [juˈrɪðmɪk; juəˈriðmik] *adj.* ①韻律和諧的。②韻律舞蹈體操的。(亦作 **eurythmic**)
eu·rhyth·mics [juˈrɪðmɪks; juːˈriðmiks] *n.* (作*pl.* or *sing.* 解) 韻律舞蹈體操(通常藉助於音樂)。(亦作 **eurythmics**)
Eu·rip·i·des [juˈrɪpə,diz; juəˈripidiːz] *n.* 尤里披蒂 (480?–406 B.C., 希臘悲劇作家)。
eu·ri·pus [juˈraɪpəs; juəˈraipəs] *n.*, *pl.* **-pi** [-paɪ; -pai]. 海峽（尤指水流湍急者)。
Eu·ro·cheque [ˈjuro,tʃɛk; ˈjuərou-tʃek] *n.* 〖英〗在歐洲國家使用的信用卡。
Eu·ro·cra·cy [ˈjurə,kræsɪ; ˈjuərə-

kræsi〕 *n.* 歐洲共同市場的全體官員。
Eu·ro·crat 〔ˈjurəkræt; ˈjuərəkræt〕 *n.* 歐洲共同市場之官員或代表。
Eu·ro·cur·ren·cy 〔ˈjurəˌkɝənsɪ; ˈjuərəˌkʌrənsi〕 *n.* 存入歐洲各銀行並通行歐洲金融市場的各國通貨。(亦作 **Euromoney**)
Eu·ro·pa 〔juˈropə; juəˈroupə〕 *n.* 〖希臘神話〗尤蘿芭(腓尼基公主, Zeus 愛之且將伊刼至 Crete 島)。(亦作 **Europe**)
‡**Eu·rope** 〔ˈjurəp; ˈjuərəp〕 *n.* 歐洲。
***Eu·ro·pe·an** 〔ˌjurəˈpiən; ˌjuərəˈpi:ən〕 *adj.* 歐洲的; 歐洲人的。—*n.* 歐洲人。
European Coal and Steel Community 於 1952 成立的歐洲經濟組織(將比利時、法、義、盧森堡、荷、西德之煤、鐵、鋼鐵統籌使用)。
European (Economic) Community 歐洲共同市場之正式名稱。(亦作 **European Common Market**)
Eu·ro·pe·an·ism 〔ˌjurəˈpiənɪzm̩; ˌjuərəˈpi:ənizm〕 *n.* ①歐洲主義;歐洲風氣;歐洲精神。②歐洲之特色或習慣;歐式。
Eu·ro·pe·an·ize 〔ˌjurəˈpiənˌaɪz; ˌjuərəˈpi:ənaiz〕 *v.t.*, **-ized, -iz·ing.** 使爲歐洲式;歐化。
European plan 〖美〗歐洲式(指旅館固定向客人收住宿費及服務費, 客人可自由選擇是否在該旅館開膳, 且可自由在該旅館之餐廳選擇所喜之食物而付費)。
eu·ro·pi·um 〔juˈropɪəm; juˈroupi:əm〕 *n.* 〖化〗銪(稀土金屬元素, 化學符號爲Eu)。
eu·ryg·na·thous 〔juˈrɪgnəθəs; juˈrignəθəs〕 *adj.* 有寬廣之上顎的。
eu·sol 〔ˈjusol; ˈju:soul〕 *n.* 〖藥〗攸瑣(一種防腐劑)。
Eu·sta·chi·an tube 〔juˈstekɪən～; ju:sˈteikiən～〕〖解剖〗耳咽管;歐氏管。
eu·tec·tic 〔juˈtɛktɪk; ju:ˈtektik〕 *adj.* ①鎔點最低的(指成分相同之諸合金中, 以某種比例合成者其鎔點最低而言)。②最低鎔合金的;共鎔混合物的。—*n.* 最低鎔合金;易鎔物。
eu·tec·toid 〔juˈtɛktɔɪd; ju:ˈtektɔid〕 *n., adj.* 類似最低鎔合金(的)。
Eu·ter·pe 〔juˈtɝpɪ; ju:ˈtə:pi〕 *n.* 〖希臘神話〗司音樂及抒情詩之女神。
eu·tex·i·a 〔juˈtɛksɪə; juˈteksiə〕 *n.* 易鎔性。
eu·tha·na·si·a 〔ˌjuθəˈneʒə; ˌju:θəˈneiziə〕 *n.* ①無痛苦之死亡。②安死術。
eu·then·ics 〔juˈθɛnɪks; ju:ˈθeniks〕 *n.* (作*sing.*解) 環境優生學。
eu·to·ci·a 〔juˈtoʃɪə; ju:ˈtouʃiə〕 *n.* 〖醫〗安產; 順產。
Eu·to·pi·a 〔juˈtopɪə; ju:ˈtoupiə〕 *n.* 烏托邦。
eu·troph·ic 〔juˈtrɑfɪk; ju:ˈtrɔfik〕 *adj.* ①發育營養正常的。②(湖等) 有充足營養可供植物動物之生長的。—*n.* 促進發育營養正常之藥。
EV, ev electron-volt.
E. V. (聖經) English Version.
E·va 〔ˈivə; ˈi:və〕 *n.* 女子名。
EVA extravehicular activity. 太空人在太空船外之活動。
e·vac·u·ant 〔ɪˈvækjuənt; iˈvækjuənt〕 *adj.* 〖醫〗促進排泄的。—*n.* 瀉藥; 排泄藥。
e·vac·u·ate 〔ɪˈvækjuˌet; iˈvækjueit〕 *v.*, **-at·ed, -at·ing.** —*v.t.* ①撤退; 撤離。②撤空。③疏散。④使空; 清除。⑤剝奪。—*v.i.* ①撤退。②使空。
e·vac·u·a·tion 〔ɪˌvækjuˈeʃən; iˌvækjuˈeiʃən〕 *n.* ①撤退; 撤離;撤空。②清除; 排泄。③排泄物; 瀉出物。④失效。⑤廢除。
e·vac·u·ee 〔ɪˈvækjuˌi; iˌvækju(:)ˈi:〕 *n.* 撤離的人;疏散者。
***e·vade** 〔ɪˈved; iˈveid〕 *v.*, **e·vad·ed, e·vad·ing.** —*v.t.* 規避;逃避;閃避。Criminals try to *evade* the law. 罪犯想逃避法律制裁。—*v.i.* 作逃避行爲。—**e·vad·er,** *n.*
e·vag·i·nate 〔ɪˈvædʒɪˌnet; iˈvædʒineit〕 *v.t.*, **-nat·ed, -nat·ing.** 使外突; 使裏翻出外面。
e·val·u·ate 〔ɪˈvæljuˌet; iˈvæljueit〕 *v.t.*, **-at·ed, -at·ing.** ①評價;估價;估計。②〖數學〗求值;定數值;以數字表示。
e·val·u·a·tion 〔ɪˌvæljuˈeʃən; iˌvæljuˈeiʃən〕 *n.* ①評價;估計。②〖數學〗定數值。
ev·a·nesce 〔ˌɛvəˈnɛs; ˌi:vəˈnes〕 *v.i.*, **-nesced, -nesc·ing.** 逐漸消失;消散。
ev·a·nes·cence 〔ˌɛvəˈnɛsn̩s; ˌi:vəˈnesns〕 *n.* ①消失; 消散。②消失性;消散性。
ev·a·nes·cent 〔ˌɛvəˈnɛsnt; ˌi:vəˈnesnt〕 *adj.* ①易消散的。②僅能持續短時的;暫時的。③〖植物〗易凋零的 (花等)。④〖數學〗無限小的。
e·van·gel 〔ɪˈvændʒəl; iˈvændʒel〕 *n.* ①福音; 佳音。②(E-) 四福音書之一。③主義;指導原則。④=**evangelist.**
e·van·gel·i·cal 〔ˌivænˈdʒɛlɪkl̩; ˌi:vænˈdʒelikəl〕 *adj.* (亦作 **evangelic**) ①福音的。②新教會的(强調信基督而得救, 儀式爲次要者)。③熱衷的。—*n.* 信福音主義者。—**ly,** *adv.*
e·van·gel·i·cal·ism 〔ˌivænˈdʒɛlɪkəlɪzm̩; ˌi:vænˈdʒelikəlizəm〕 *n.* 福音主義; 福音派之教義。
E·van·ge·line 〔ɪˈvændʒəˌlin; iˈvændʒili:n〕 *n.* 女子名。(亦作 **Evangelina**)
e·van·ge·lism 〔ɪˈvændʒəˌlɪzəm; iˈvændʒəlizəm〕 *n.* ①傳播福音。②福音主義。③傳教之熱誠或活動。
e·van·ge·list 〔ɪˈvændʒəlɪst; iˈvændʒilist〕 *n.* ①傳福音者。②旅行傳道者。③(E-) 四福音作者之中任一人。④(原始教會)第一個將福音傳到某一城市或地區者。⑤喚醒宗教信仰者。⑥對某些主張具有如傳教者之熱誠者。
e·van·ge·lis·tic 〔ɪˌvændʒəˈlɪstɪk; iˌvændʒiˈlistik〕 *adj.* ①傳福音者的。②=**evangelical.** ③試圖使罪犯改宗的; 傳道的。④(常 E-) 四福音作者的。
e·van·ge·li·za·tion 〔ɪˌvændʒəlɪˈzeʃən; iˌvændʒilaiˈzeiʃən〕 *n.* 傳福音;使皈依基督教。
e·van·ge·lize 〔ɪˈvændʒəˌlaɪz; iˈvændʒilaiz〕 *v.*, **-lized, -liz·ing.** —*v.t.* ①以福音教化之;布道。②使皈依基督教。—*v.i.* 傳福音。
e·van·ish 〔ɪˈvænɪʃ; iˈvæniʃ〕 *v.i.* 〖詩〗消失;消滅。—**ment,** *n.*
e·vap·o·ra·ble 〔ɪˈvæpərəbl̩; iˈvæpərəbl〕 *adj.* 可蒸發的;有蒸發性的。
e·vap·o·rate** 〔ɪˈvæpəˌret; iˈvæpəreit〕 *v.*, **-rat·ed, -rat·ing.** —*v.t.* ①蒸發。Heat *evaporates* water. 熱蒸發水。②去…的水分;煉。③使消失。evaporated milk*** 煉乳。—*v.i.* ①失去水分;蒸乾。The water soon *evaporated.* 水不久便蒸乾了。②散發濕氣。③消失。
***e·vap·o·ra·tion** 〔ɪˌvæpəˈreʃən; iˌvæpəˈreiʃən〕 *n.* ①蒸發;蒸乾;脫水。to thicken by *evaporation.* 因蒸發而變濃。②消散;消失。
e·vap·o·ra·tive 〔ɪˈvæpəˌretɪv; iˈvæpəreitiv〕 *adj.* 蒸發的;使蒸發的。
e·vap·o·ra·tor 〔ɪˈvæpəˌretɚ; iˈvæpəreitə〕 *n.* 蒸發者; 蒸發器;乾燥器。

e·va·sion 〔ɪˈveʒən; iˈveiʒən〕 *n.* ①逃避;規避。②遁詞;推托;藉口。③逃避之方法。④逃稅。tax *evasion.* 逃稅。

e·va·sive 〔ɪˈvesɪv; iˈveisiv〕 *adj.* ①逃避的; 迴避的; 推托的。 "Perhaps" is an *evasive* answer. "也許"爲一遁詞。②易消失的;不可捉摸的。**—ness,** *n.* **—ly,** *adv.*

Eve 〔iv; iːv〕 *n.* ①夏娃(亞當 Adam 之妻,聖經中所謂世界最初的女人)。②女子名。

eve** 〔iv; iːv〕 *n.* ① 前夕; 前日。 New Year's *Eve.* 除夕。②〖詩〗=**evening.** ***on the eve of 正當…前夕。

e·vec·tion 〔ɪˈvɛkʃən; iˈvekʃən〕 *n.* 〖天文〗出差(由於太陽吸力所致之月亮周期性不均衡運行)。

‡**e·ven**[1] 〔ˈivən; ˈiːvən〕 *adj.* ①平的; 平坦的。②相齊的;同高的。The snow is *even* with the window. 積雪與窗平齊。③正規的;均勻的;沉靜的。This boy has an *even* temper. 此男孩性情是沉靜的。④相等的。They had *even* shares of the money. 他們所分得之錢彼此相等。⑤(數目)偶數的。2, 4, 6, 8 are *even* numbers. 二,四,六,八是偶數。⑥整數的。 an *even* mile. 恰好一英里。⑦公正的。Justice is *even* treatment. 公平即是公正的待人處事。⑧不欠情的;兩相抵的。***be even*** **a.** 不欠。**b.** 報復。***of even date*** 同一日。 *—v.t.* ①使平;使相等。②使平坦。 to *even* a board with a plane. 刨平一塊木板。③使得失相等〖常up〗. to *even* up accounts. 平衡帳目。*—v.i.* 成爲平衡。*—adv.* ①正(當);恰好。*Even* as he spoke, it began to rain. 正當他說話時,下雨了。②即使; 甚至; 就是。*Even* a child can understand it. 即使小孩也能懂得。③愈加; 更加〖more, better〗. You can do it *even* better if you try hard. 你若努力,你會做得更加好。④完全地;很。He was faithful *even* unto death. 直到死他都很忠實。⑤平坦地。 The road ran *even* over the fields. 那路平坦地越過田野。⑥〖古〗正確地。 ***break even*** 得失相等;不輸也不贏。***even if*** (or ***though***) 縱使;即令。I shan't mind *even if* he doesn't come. 縱使他不來,我也不介意。***get even*** **a.** 不欠債。**b.** 報復。 ***get even with*** 報復。I'll *get even with* him for his insulting remarks. 他的侮辱的話,我一定要報復。

e·ven[2] 〔ˈivən; ˈiːvən〕 *n.* 〖古〗晚; 暮。

e·ven·fall 〔ˈivən͵fɔl; ˈiːvən͵fɔːl〕 *n.* 〖詩〗薄暮; 黃昏。

e·ven·hand·ed〔ˈivənˈhændɪd;ˈiːvənˈhændid〕 *adj.* 不偏不倚的;公正的。

‡**eve·ning** 〔ˈivnɪŋ; ˈiːvniŋ〕 *n.* ①晚間;夕;暮。the *evening* of life. 晚年。②晚間的應酬或交際。Her *evenings* at home were extremely fashionable. 她的家庭晚會是很時髦的。***make an evening of it*** 歡度夜晚。*—adj.* 晚間的;晚間用的。

evening dress 晚禮服。

evening gown (女人之)晚禮服。

evening paper 晚報。

evening primrose 〖植物〗月見草。

eve·nings 〔ˈivnɪŋz; ˈiːvniŋz〕 *adv.* 晚間經常地。

evening school (學校的)夜間部。

evening wear 晚禮服。

***e·ven·ly** 〔ˈivənlɪ; ˈiːvənli〕 *adv.* ①平坦地;平衡地; 公平地; 平等地; 均勻地。 The cloth is woven *evenly.* 這塊布織得均勻。②速度大約相等地。

e·ven-mind·ed 〔ˈivənˈmaɪndɪd; ˈiːvənˈmaindid〕 *adj.* 頭腦平靜的; 心平氣和的;性情平和的;寧靜的;安詳的。

even money ①賭博者所押的同額賭注。②賭博時機會相等;成功與失敗機會均等。

e·ven·ness 〔ˈivənnɪs; ˈiːvənnis〕 *n.* 平坦;平均;平等;公平;坦蕩。

even page 書本之偶數頁。

e·ven·song 〔ˈivən͵sɔŋ; ˈiːvənsɔŋ〕 *n.* ①(常 E-)英國國教之晚禱。②天主教之晚禱。③〖古〗夕;暮。

e·ven-ste·ven 〔ˈivənˈstivən; ˈiːvənˈstiːvən〕 *adj.* 〖俗〗機會相等的; 和的; 分數拉平的。

‡**e·vent** 〔ɪˈvɛnt; iˈvent〕 *n.* ①發生的事;事件。 The discovery of America was a great *event.* 發現美洲是一件重要的事。②結果。 We made careful plans and awaited the *event.* 我們做了審慎計畫並靜待結果。③運動會日程中的一項競賽。 Have you entered your name for any of the *events?* 你報名參加任何競賽項目沒有? ***at all events*** 無論如何。 ***in any event*** =**at all events.** ***in the event of*** 設若。***In the event of*** rain, the game will be postponed. 如果天雨,球賽將延期。

e·ven-tem·pered 〔ˈivənˈtɛmpɚd; ˈiːvnˈtempəd〕 *adj.* 鎭靜的;不易生氣的。

e·vent·ful 〔ɪˈvɛntfəl; iˈventful, -fəl〕 *adj.* ①多事故的。②重大的;重要的。

e·ven·tide 〔ˈivən͵taɪd; ˈiːvəntaid〕 *n.* 〖詩〗日暮; 黃昏。

e·vent·less 〔ɪˈvɛntlɪs;iˈventlis〕 *adj.* 「平靜無事的。」

e·ven·tu·al 〔ɪˈvɛntʃuəl; iˈventjuəl, -tʃuəl〕 *adj.* ①結果的;最後的。②可能的;視…而定的。**—ly,** *adv.*

e·ven·tu·al·i·ty 〔ɪ͵vɛntʃuˈælətɪ; i͵ventjuˈæliti〕 *n., pl.* **-ties.** 可能性;可能發生的事件。

e·ven·tu·al·ize 〔ɪˈvɛntʃuəl͵aɪz;iˈventjuəlaiz〕 *v.i.,* **-ized, -iz·ing.** 結果終於發生。

e·ven·tu·ate 〔ɪˈvɛntʃu͵et; iˈventjueit〕 *v.i.,* **-at·ed, -at·ing.** 結果; 終歸〖常in〗.

‡**ev·er** 〔ˈɛvɚ; ˈevə〕 *adv.* ①曾; 曾經 (用於現在, 現在完成及過去疑問句中); 無論何時(用於條件句及否定句中)。 Have you *ever* been there? 你曾經到過那裏嗎? ②究竟;到底(與疑問詞連用);的確。Why *ever* didn't you go? 你到底爲甚麼沒有去? He is *ever* such a clever man. 他的確是一個聰明人。③永遠。You will find me *ever* at your service. 你會發現我永遠聽命於你。④如果;要是(用以强調驚奇、不耐等)。If the band *ever* plays again, we will dance. 如果樂隊再演奏的話, 我們將相偕起舞。 ***ever and again*** 偶爾 (亦作 **ever and anon**). ***ever since*** 自從 (較單用 since 語氣爲强)。***ever so*** 非常 (=very). Thank you *ever so* much. 非常感謝你。 ***ever such*** 〖俚〗= **ever so.** He is *ever such* a rich man. 他是個很富有的人。***for ever*** (***and ever***) 永遠; 永久 (亦作 **for ever and a day**). ***hardly ever*** 很少; 殆無; 幾乎不 (較單用 hardly 語氣爲强)。I *hardly ever* see him nowadays. 近來我很少見他。

Ev·er·est, Mount 〔ˈɛvrɪst; ˈevərist〕 *n.* 埃弗勒斯峯 (喜馬拉雅山主峯之一,世界最高峯,又稱聖母峯, 高 29,028 英尺)。

ev·er·glade 〔ˈɛvɚ͵gled; ˈevəgleid〕

n. 澤地; 溼地。 ***the Everglades*** (美國 Florida 州南部之) 大沼澤地。

***ev·er·green** ['ɛvə,grin; 'evəgri:n] *adj.* 常綠的(樹)。—*n.* ①常綠植物;常綠樹; 冬青。②(*pl.*)紮綵用的常綠樹枝。

Evergreen State 美國華盛頓州的別稱。

ev·er·last·ing** [,ɛvə'læstɪŋ; ,evə'lɑ:stiŋ] *adj.* ①持久的; 永恒的。②持續太久的; 重複太多的; 令人厭倦的。I'm tired of his *everlasting* jokes. 我厭倦他那說個不完的笑話。 —*n.* 永恆。 ***the Everlasting 上帝 (=God). —**ly,** *adv.*

ev·er·more** [,ɛvə'mor; 'evə'mɔ:] *adv.* ①經常。②永久; 永遠。③從此以後; 將來。 ***for evermore 永遠。

ev·er-pres·ent ['ɛvə'prɛznt; 'evə'preznt] *adj.* (威脅等)常在的。

e·ver·si·ble [ɪ'vɜsəbl; i'və:sibəl] *adj.* 可外翻的。

e·ver·sion [ɪ'vɜʃən; i'və:ʃən] *n.* 外翻。*eversion* of the eyelids. 眼皮之外翻。

e·vert [i'vɜt; i'və:t] *v.t.* 外翻; 翻轉。

‡eve·ry ['ɛvrɪ, 'ɛvərɪ; 'evri] *adj.* ①每; 每一; 所有的。 He has read *every* book in the school. 學校裏所有的書, 他都讀過。②所有可能的;最大可能的。*every* prospect of success. 成功之最大可能的展望。 ***every bit*** **a.** 全部。He ate up *every bit* of it. 他把它全吃掉了。**b.** 完全。 This is *every bit* as good as that. 這一個同那一個一樣好。 ***every last*** 〖俗〗絕對全部;每一個。 ***every now and then*** (or ***and again***) 時時; 不時。 ***every other*** **a.** 每隔一。**b.** 所有其他的。Tom was early; *every other* boy was late. 湯姆一人早到; 所有別的孩子都遲到。 ***every time*** 〖俗〗無例外地。He has heard the story often but he laughs *every time.* 他常常聽到這個故事, 但他每次都笑。 ***every way*** 從各方面看。 This is *every way* better than that. 這一個從各方面看都比那一個好。 ***every which way*** 朝着各方向地; 零亂地。〖注意〗**every** 與 **all** 在意義上是相同的, 不過 every 之後須用單數名詞, all 之後則用複數名詞。

‡eve·ry·bod·y ['ɛvrɪ,bɑdɪ; 'evribɔdi, -bədi] *pron.* 每個人; 人人。*Everybody* admired him. 人人都欽佩他。 ***everybody else*** 別的每一個人。 *Everybody else* returned. 別的人都回來了。〖注意〗**everybody** 作主詞時, 動詞必須用單數, 但在其附近之代名詞則可能用複數形式: *Everybody* dresses in their best clothes. 每個人都穿上他們的最好的衣服。

***eve·ry·day** ['ɛvrɪ'de; 'evri'dei, 'evridei] *adj.* ①每天的;日常的;平凡的。*everyday* phrases and sentences. 日常的成語和語句。②平日的(非禮拜天或假日的)。〖注意〗**everyday** 合寫一字是 *adj.*, 分寫成兩字時, every 則形容名詞 day:如 *Every day* seemed a year. 度日如年。

eve·ry·how ['ɛvrɪ,hau; 'evrihau] *adv.* 各種各樣地; 各方面地。

Eve·ry·man ['ɛvrɪ,mæn; 'evrimæn] *n.* ①昔英國劇名及其主角名。②(e-)普通人。

‡eve·ry·one ['ɛvrɪ,wʌn; 'evriwʌn] *pron.* 每個人; 人人。 *Everyone* took his purchases home. 每個人都把他所買的東西帶回家了。 ***everyone else*** 每個別的人。〖注意〗**everyone** 可以合寫成一字, 也可分寫爲兩字; 其代名詞可用單數形 his, 也可用複數形 their.

eve·ry·place ['ɛvrɪ,ples; 'evripleis] *adv.* 到處; 各處。

‡eve·ry·thing ['ɛvrɪ,θɪŋ; 'evriθiŋ] *pron.* 每樣事物;一切事物。 He knows *everything.* 他無所不知。—*n.* 最主要者;重於一切者。 Money is not *everything.* 金錢並非重於一切。〖注意〗**everything** 作 pronoun 及 noun 用時是一個字, 如果 thing 的讀音加强或强調 thing 時, 則爲兩個字。

eve·ry·way ['ɛvrɪwe; 'evriwei] *adv.* 無論怎樣看法;不管從那一方面來看。

eve·ry·when ['ɛvrɪ,hwɛn; 'evriwen] *adv.* 經常地;時時地。

‡eve·ry·where ['ɛvrɪ,hwɛr; 'evriwɛə, -hwɛə] *adv.* 各處;到處; 處處。 They go *everywhere.* 他們到處都去。 ***the everywhere*** 無限; 無限之空間。 —*conj.* 所到之處。 *Everywhere* I go, I find the same thing. 凡我所到之處, 均發現同樣的事情。

eve·ry·whith·er ['ɛvrɪ,hwɪðə; 'evri,hwiðə] *adv.* 到處;各處;每一個方向地。

e·vict [ɪ'vɪkt; i:'vikt] *v.t.* ①(依法律程序自土地或建築物中) 逐出;驅逐(租戶)。②追還(財產)。

e·vict·ee [ɪ,vɪk'ti; i,vik'ti:] *n.* 被逐出的人。

e·vic·tion [ɪ'vɪkʃən; i:'vikʃən] *n.* 逐出;追還。

e·vic·tor [ɪ'vɪktə; i:'viktə] *n.* 驅逐者;收回(產業等)之人。

‡ev·i·dence ['ɛvədəns; 'evidəns] *n., v.,* **-denced, -denc·ing.** —*n.* ①證據。②(法庭所認可的)證據;證詞;作證。Mr. X was the first witness who was called to give *evidence.* 某先生爲第一個被傳作證的證人。③跡象; 痕跡。 A smile gives *evidence* of pleasure. 微笑乃愉快之證明。 ***in evidence*** 顯然可見。 Smith was nowhere *in evidence.* 史密斯顯然不見了。 ***turn state's*** (***queen's*** or ***king's***) ***evidence*** 共犯反成爲檢方之證人。 —*v.t.* ①顯示。 Her smiles *evidenced* her pleasure. 她的微笑顯示她的快樂。②證明;以證據支持。

***ev·i·dent** ['ɛvədənt; 'evidənt] *adj.* 明白的;明顯的;顯然的。It must be *evident* to everybody that somebody has been here. 有人到這裏來過, 這乃是人人可見的極明顯的事。 —**ly,** *adv.*

ev·i·den·tial [,ɛvə'dɛnʃəl; ,evi'denʃəl] *adj.* ①證據的;作證據用的;根據證據的。②供給證據的。(亦作 **evidentiary**)

‡e·vil ['ivl; 'i:vl, -il] *adj.* ①邪惡的; 罪惡的; 不善的。 to lead an *evil* life. 過着罪惡的生活。②有害的;不吉的。an *evil* plan. 一個惡毒的計畫。③不幸的。④聲名狼藉的。⑤凶暴的。He is known for his *evil* disposition. 他的暴躁脾氣是有名的。 ***the Evil One*** 惡魔 (指撒旦 Satan). —*n.* ①邪惡;不善。 to return good for *evil.* 以德報怨。②災禍; 不幸。③疾病。 ***speak evil of*** 講(人)壞話;中傷。 Don't *speak evil of* people behind their backs. 不要背後說人壞話。—*adv.* 邪惡地。—**ness,** *n.*

e·vil-dis·posed ['ivḷdɪs,pozd; 'i:vl-dis,pouzd] *adj.* 性惡的;懷惡意的;心壞的。

e·vil·do·er [,ivḷ'duə; 'i:vl'du:ə] *n.* 惡人; 做壞事者。

e·vil·do·ing [,ivḷ'duɪŋ; 'i:vl'du:iŋ] *n.* 惡行;惡事。

evil eye 根據迷信的說法, 有些人具有目視他人而使之遭殃的能力。

e·vil-eyed ['ivḷ'aɪd; 'i:vl'aid] *adj.* 目光凶惡的;有凶眼的。

e·vil·ly [ˈivl̩;ˈiːvli] *adv.* 邪惡地;凶惡地。
e·vil-mind·ed [ˈivl̩ˈmaɪndɪd; ˈiːvlˈmaindid] *adj.* ①惡毒的;黑心的。②過度色情的。—**ly,** *adv.* —**ness,** *n.*
e·vince [ɪˈvɪns; iˈvins] *v.t.,* **e·vinced, e·vinc·ing.** ①表明。②表明具有(某特點或感覺等);表示;表現。
e·vin·ci·ble [ɪˈvɪnsəbl̩; iˈvinsəbl] *adj.* 可表明的;可表現的。
e·vin·cive [ɪˈvɪnsɪv; iˈvinsiv] *adj.* 表明的;顯示的。
e·vis·cer·ate [ɪˈvɪsəˌret; iˈvisəreit] *v.,* **-at·ed, -at·ing,** *adj.* —*v.t.* ①取出…之腸;剜除內臟。②取出…之重要部分;使失去力量或意義。—*adj.* 內臟被剜除的。—**e·vis·cer·a·tion,** *n.*
ev·i·ta·ble [ˈɛvətəbl̩; ˈevitəbl] *adj.* 可避免的。
ev·o·ca·ble [ˈɛvəkəbl̩; ˈevəkəbl] *adj.* 可喚起的;可引出的。
ev·o·ca·tion [ˌɛvoˈkeʃən; ˌevouˈkeiʃən] *n.* ①喚起;召喚。②〖法律〗訴訟案件之移送。
e·voc·a·tive [ɪˈvɑkətɪv; iˈvɔkətiv] *adj.* 喚起的;召喚的。
ev·o·ca·tor [ˈɛvəˌketɚ; ˈevəˌkeitə] *n.* 喚起人;招鬼魂的人。
e·voke [ɪˈvok; iˈvouk] *v.t.,* **e·voked, e·vok·ing.** ①喚起;引起。②使追憶到。
ev·o·lute [ˈɛvəˌlut; ˈiːvəluːt] *n.* 〖數學〗漸屈線。*evolute of a surface* 漸屈面。
***ev·o·lu·tion** [ˌɛvəˈluʃən, -ˈlju-; ˌiːvəˈluːʃən, ˌev-, -ˈljuː-] *n.* ①進化;演化;發展。In politics, England prefers *evolution* to revolution. 在政治方面,英國採取漸進而不喜歡革命。②演變之結果或產物。③進化論。④〖軍〗機動演習;操演;布署。⑤動作;旋轉。⑥放出;射出。⑦〖數學〗開方。—**al,** *adj.*
ev·o·lu·tion·a·ry [ˌɛvəˈluʃənˌɛrɪ; ˌiːvəˈluːʃnəri] *adj.* ①進化的;開展的。②進化論的。③機動演習的。
ev·o·lu·tion·ism [ˌɛvəˈluʃənɪzm̩; ˌiːvəˈluːʃənizəm] *n.* 進化論;進化說。
ev·o·lu·tion·ist [ˌɛvəˈluʃənɪst; ˌiːvəˈluːʃənist] *n.* ①進化論者。②信政治與社會漸進改革論者。—*adj.* (亦作 **evolutionistic**) ①進化論的。②進化論者的。
ev·o·lu·tive [ˈɛvəˌljutɪv; ˈiːvəˌluːtiv] *adj.* 進化的;發展的。
***e·volve** [ɪˈvɑlv; iˈvɔlv] *v.,* **e·volved, e·volv·ing.** —*v.t.* ①發展;計劃。The boys *evolved* a plan for earning money during their summer vacation. 孩子們做了一個暑假時掙錢的計畫。②放出;放射出;釋出。③引出;推理。④〖生物〗進化。—*v.i.* 演進;演變;進化。—**e·volv·ment,** *n.* —**e·volv·a·ble,** *adj.*
e·vul·sion [ɪˈvʌlʃən; iˈvʌlʃən] *n.* 拔出;拔去;强拔。
ewe [ju; juː] *n.* 母羊。*ewe lamb* **a.** 幼母羊。**b.** 獨生子(女)。
ewe-necked [ˈjuˌnɛkt; ˈjuːnekt] *adj.* 頸如母羊的;(馬等)頸部瘦長而曲的。
ew·er [ˈjuɚ; ˈjuːə, ˈjuə] *n.* 大口水罐。
ex[1] [ɛks; eks] *n.* ①字母X. ②X形物。
ex[2] *prep.* ①〖財政〗無;不包括;無權得到。②〖商〗在…前免費;交貨。③(美國專科及大學中)肄業於;曾就讀…班級(但未正式畢業)。
ex[3] *n.* 〖俗〗前夫;前妻。
ex- 〖字首〗①表"由…出來;從;出"之義。如 export 等字之字首。②表"完全;徹底"之義。如exasperate 等字之字首。③表"從前的地位"之義。如 exsoldier 字之字首。④**exo-**之異形。
Ex., Exod. Exodus.
ex. ①examination. ②examined. ③example. ④except. ⑤exception. ⑥exchange. ⑦excursion. ⑧executed. ⑨executive. ⑩exercise.
ex·ac·er·bate [ɪgˈzæsɚˌbet; eksˈæsəːbeit] *v.t.,* **-bat·ed, -bat·ing.** ①使(病、痛等)加劇;加重。②激怒。—**ex·ac·er·ba·tion,** *n.*
***ex·act** [ɪgˈzækt; igˈzækt, eg-] *adj.* ①正確的;準確的;精確的。What is the *exact* size of the room? 這間房子到底有多大? ②嚴格的;嚴厲的。③〖數學〗恰當微分方程的。—*v.t.* ①需要。A hard piece of work *exacts* patience. 一件困難工作需要耐心才能完成。②要求;堅持地要求。—**a·ble,** *adj.*
ex·act·ing [ɪgˈzæktɪŋ; igˈzæktiŋ] *adj.* ①苛求的;難取悅的。②需要留神和注意力的;費力的。③强取的;勒索的。
ex·ac·tion [ɪgˈzækʃən; igˈzækʃən] *n.* ①勒索;强取;榨取。②索取之物;勒索之物;榨取之錢;稅;費。
ex·act·i·tude [ɪgˈzæktəˌtjud; igˈzæktitjuːd] *n.* 正確;精密;嚴正。
‡**ex·act·ly** [ɪgˈzæktlɪ; igˈzæktli, igˈzækli] *adv.* 精確地;正確地;完全地。His answer was *exactly* right. 他的答案完全對。
ex·act·ness [ɪgˈzæktnɪs; igˈzæktnis] *n.* =**exactitude.**
ex·ac·tor [ɪgˈzæktɚ; igˈzæktə] *n.* 强求者;强索者;强取者;收稅人;稅吏。(亦作 **exacter**)
exact science 精密科學(如數學、物理、化學等)。
***ex·ag·ger·ate** [ɪgˈzædʒəˌret; igˈzædʒəreit] *v.,* **-at·ed, -at·ing.** —*v.t.* ①誇大;誇張。②使過大或過量。Those shoes *exaggerate* the size of her feet. 那雙鞋使她的腳顯得特別大。—*v.i.* 誇大;誇張。
ex·ag·ger·at·ed [ɪgˈzædʒəˌretɪd; igˈzædʒəreitid] *adj.* ①誇張的;誇大的。②過度擴大的。—**ly,** *adv.*
***ex·ag·ger·a·tion** [ɪgˌzædʒəˈreʃən; igˌzædʒəˈreiʃən, eg-] *n.* ①誇張;過大。②誇大詞。③〖美術〗誇大之表現。
ex·ag·ger·a·tive [ɪgˈzædʒəˌretɪv; igˈzædʒərətiv] *adj.* 誇張的;誇大的;好誇大的。(亦作 **exaggeratory**) —**ly,** *adv.*
ex·ag·ger·a·tor [ɪgˈzædʒəˌretɚ; igˈzædʒəreitə] *n.* 誇張者;言過其實之人。
***ex·alt** [ɪgˈzɔlt; igˈzɔːlt] *v.t.* ①擢升;提高。②使得意。He was *exalted* with pride. 他充滿了驕傲。③讚揚。④刺激(想像力等)。The lyrics of Shakespeare *exalted* the audience. 莎士比亞的詩詞刺激了觀衆的想像力。⑤加强(如顏色等)。
ex·al·ta·tion [ˌɪgzɔlˈteʃən; ˌegzɔːlˈteiʃən] *n.* ①(階級、榮譽、權力等之)提高;擢升;讚揚。②意氣揚揚;狂喜。with great *exaltation.* 狂喜地。③〖醫〗(器官、機能等之)異常亢奮。④〖冶金〗純化;精鍊。
ex·alt·ed [ɪgˈzɔltɪd; igˈzɔːltid] *adj.* ①地位(身分)高尚的;高貴的。②崇高的;高尚的。③意氣揚揚的;狂喜的。—**ly,** *adv.*
ex·am [ɪgˈzæm; igˈzæm] *n.* 〖俗〗考試;試驗;測驗(=examination).
exam. ①examination. ②examine. ③examined. ④examinee. ⑤examiner.
ex·am·i·nant [ɪgˈzæmənənt; igˈzæminənt] *n.* 審問者;檢查者;審查者;檢察官。
ex·am·i·nate [ɪgˈzæmənet; igˈzæmineit] *n.* 受檢查者;應訊者。
***ex·am·i·na·tion** [ɪgˌzæməˈneʃən;

ig,zæmiˈneiʃən] *n.* ①檢查。He made an *examination* of the room. 他對這房間作了一番檢查。②審問；訊問。③考試；測驗。The *examination* lasted two hours. 考試繼續了兩個鐘頭。④試題。⑤答案。***entrance examination*** 入學考試。***make-up examination*** 補考。***oral examination*** 口試。***physical examination*** 體格檢查。***written examination*** 筆試。

ex·am·i·na·to·ri·al 〔ɛg,zæmənəˈtorɪəl; eg,zæminəˈtouriəl〕 *adj.* ①考試的；審查的。②考試官的；檢查者的；審訊者的。

‡**ex·am·ine** 〔ɪgˈzæmɪn; igˈzæmin, eg–〕 *v.t.*, **-ined, -in·ing.** ①檢查。He *examined* the room. 他檢查過這房間。②考試；測驗。He *examined* the boys in English. 他考學生的英文。③詰問；審問。He was *examined* by the police. 他受警察的審問。④驗屍。⑤研究；調查。

ex·am·i·nee 〔ɪg,zæməˈni; ig,zæmiˈniː〕 *n.* 受試驗者；應試者；受檢者。

ex·am·in·er 〔ɪgˈzæmɪnɚ; igˈzæminə〕 *n.* 主考者；審問者；檢查者；審查者；驗屍官。

‡**ex·am·ple** 〔ɪgˈzæmpḷ; igˈzɑːmpl, eg–〕 *n.* ①例證；實例。Give me an *example* of what you mean. 給我舉個實例說明你的意思。②樣本；樣子；標本。Show me an *example* of your work. 把你的作品給我一個樣本看看。③模範；楷模。You should follow Tom's *example* and work harder. 你應該以湯姆爲模範，更加努力工作。④警告。Let this be an *example* to you. 這是給你的一個警告。⑤先例。an action without *example.* 無先例的行爲。***for example*** 譬如；例如（爲句中挿語）。***make an example of somebody*** 懲一以儆百。***set an example to somebody*** 給某人樹立一個楷模。***without example*** 無前例的。

ex·an·i·mate 〔ɪgˈzænəmɪt; igˈzænimit〕 *adj.* ①無生氣的；意氣消沉的。②已死的。

ex a·ni·mo 〔ɛksˈænɪmo; eksˈænimou〕〖拉〗出自內心地；懇摯地（＝from the heart; sincerely）。

ex·an·the·ma 〔,ɛksænˈθimə; ,eksænˈθiːmə〕 *n. pl.*, **-mas, -ma·ta** 〔–mətə; –mətə〕.〖醫〗疹。

ex·arch 〔ˈɛksark; ˈeksɑːk〕 *n.* ①（東羅馬帝國之）太守；總督。②（東正教之）大主教；主教（大主教之代理）。

ex·arch·ate 〔ˈɛksar,ket; ˈeksɑːkeit〕 *n.* exarch 之職權或轄區。

ex·ar·tic·u·la·tion 〔,ɛksar,tɪkjuˈleʃən; ,eksɑː,tikjuˈleiʃən〕 *n.*〖外科〗①脫臼。②關節截斷。

ex·as·per·ate 〔ɛgˈzæspə,ret, ɪg–; igˈzɑːspəreit, eg–, –ˈzæs–〕 *v.*, **-at·ed, -at·ing,** *adj.* —*v.t.* 激怒；使（痛苦、憤怒等）增劇。It is very *exasperating* to lose a train by half a minute. 以半分鐘之差誤了火車是很使人惱火的。—*adj.*〖植物〗（樹葉等之）粗糙的。—**ex·as·per·at·ing,** *adj.* —**ex·as·per·at·ing·ly,** *adv.*

ex·as·per·at·er, ex·as·per·a·tor 〔ɛgˈzæspə,retɚ; igˈzɑːspəreitə〕 *n.* 激怒他人者；惹人生氣者。

ex·as·per·a·tion 〔ɪg,zæspəˈreʃən; ig,zɑːspəˈreiʃən〕 *n.* 憤怒；憤激。

Exc. Excellency. **exc.** ①excellent. ②except. ③exception. ④excudit（拉＝he or she engraved this）. ⑤excursion.

ex ca·the·dra 〔,ɛkskəˈθidrə; ,ekskəˈθiːdrə〕〖拉〗有權威；用權威；由職權。

ex·cau·date 〔ɛksˈkɔdet; eksˈkɔːdeit〕 *adj.*〖動物〗無尾巴的。

ex·ca·vate 〔ˈɛkskə,vet; ˈekskəveit〕 *v.t.*, **-vat·ed, -vat·ing.** ①挖空。②挖掘；掘出；挖出。They *excavated* an ancient buried city. 他們發掘一古代被埋於地下之城市。

***ex·ca·va·tion** 〔,ɛkskəˈveʃən; ,ekskəˈveiʃən〕 *n.* ①挖掘；發掘。②挖掘之洞穴；發掘物。The *excavation* was six feet deep. 挖掘之洞有六英尺深。

ex·ca·va·tor 〔ˈɛkskə,vetɚ; ˈekskəveitə〕 *n.* ①挖掘者。②挖土機。③〖牙醫〗挖出器。

***ex·ceed** 〔ɪkˈsid; ikˈsiːd, ek–〕 *v.t. & v.i.* 越過；超過；駕乎…之上。Their success *exceeded* all expectations. 他們的成功超出一切預料之外。

***ex·ceed·ing** 〔ɪkˈsidɪŋ; ikˈsiːdiŋ, ek–〕 *adj.* 非常的；過度的。Helen is a girl of *exceeding* beauty. 海倫是一個極度美麗的女孩。—**ly,** *adv.*

***ex·cel** 〔ɪkˈsɛl; ikˈsel〕 *v.*, **-celled, -cel·ling.** —*v.t.* 優於；勝過。to *excel* others in courage. 勇氣過人。—*v.i.* 特出；擅長。to *excel* at sports. 長於運動。

***ex·cel·lence** 〔ˈɛksḷəns; ˈeksələns〕 *n.* 特優；傑出。He received a prize for *excellence* in English. 他因英文特優而得獎。

ex·cel·len·cy** 〔ˈɛksḷənsɪ; ˈeksələnsi〕 *n.*, *pl.* **-cies.**（常 E–）對顯貴者之尊稱。A governor is formally spoken of as His *Excellency.* 正式提起州長要用"大人"稱呼。Your Excellency*** 大人；閣下（對總統、省長、大使、主教等之尊稱語，注意不用姓名）。

‡**ex·cel·lent** 〔ˈɛksḷənt; ˈeksələnt〕 *adj.* 最優的；特優的。His English is *excellent.* 他的英文好極了。—**ly,** *adv.*

ex·cel·si·or[1] 〔ɪkˈsɛlsɪɔr; ekˈselsiɔː〕 *adj.* 更上的；永遠向上的；精益求精的（用作箴言，如紐約州璽上者）。

ex·cel·si·or[2] 〔ɪkˈsɛlsɪɚ; ekˈselsiə〕 *n.* ①細鉋花（用以塡充墊子等者）。②〖印刷〗一種（3 point 之）鉛字。***as dry as excelsior*** 乾透的。

‡**ex·cept** 〔ɪkˈsɛpt; ikˈsept, ek–〕 *prep.* 除…之外。We all went *except* Tom. 除湯姆之外，我們都去了。***except for*** 除去…一點之外；祇是（有表惋惜之意）。The letter is good *except for* the spelling. 該信很通順，祇是拼法有誤。***except that*** 除去…一點之外；祇可惜（後接名詞子句）。It's a very satisfactory hat, *except that* it doesn't fit me. 那是一頂很令人滿意的帽子，只可惜不適合於我。—*v.t.* 把…除外；不包括…在內。Of course I *except* you. 我當然把你除外。***present company excepted*** 在席者不算。—*v.i.* 反對〖常 to, against〗. to *except* against a statement. 反對一聲明。—*conj.*〖古〗除非（＝unless）.〖注意〗**except** 與 **but** 均意爲除外。except 着重於"除去；除掉"。but 則着重於"不予計入"，而非"除掉；除去"之意。

ex·cep·tant 〔ɛkˈsɛptənt; ekˈseptənt〕 *adj.* 例外的；除外的。—*n.* 例外者。

ex·cept·ing 〔ɪkˈsɛptɪŋ; ikˈseptiŋ〕 *prep.* 除…外（＝except，可用於 not, without 及 always 之後）。—*conj.*〖古〗除非。

***ex·cep·tion** 〔ɪkˈsɛpʃən; ikˈsepʃən,

ek-] *n.* ①例外。There is one *exception* to this rule. 這條規則有個例外。②反對。③【法律】(審判過程中)異議。a statement liable to *exception.* 易引起批評(反對)的一個聲明。***above*** (or ***beyond***) ***exception*** 無可非議的。***make an exception of*** 把…除外。***take exception to*** **a.** 反對。I *take exception to* your statement that I am bad-tempered. 我反對你說我脾氣不好。**b.** 生氣。***without exception*** 沒有例外。***with the exception of*** 除…之外。

ex·cep·tion·a·ble [ɪkˈsɛpʃənəbl̩; ikˈsepʃnabl] *adj.* ①可反對的; 可非難的; 可抗議的。②例外的。—**ex·cep·tion·a·bly,** *adv.*

***ex·cep·tion·al** [ɪkˈsɛpʃənl̩; ikˈsepʃənl, ek-] *adj.* ①例外的; 特別的; 異常的。This warm weather is *exceptional* for January. 這樣熱的天氣在正月是很異常的。②優秀的。③【教育】(兒童)特殊的(天才的或有缺陷的)。—**ly,** *adv.*

ex·cep·tious [ɛkˈsɛpʃəs; ekˈsepʃəs] *adj.* 好責備人的; 好吹毛求疵的; 易於得罪的。

ex·cep·tive [ɛkˈsɛptɪv; ikˈseptiv] *adj.* ①例外的; 除外的。②好反對的; 吹毛求疵的。

ex·cerpt [*n.* ˈɛksɝpt; ˈeksəːpt *v.* ɪkˈsɝpt; ekˈsəːpt] *n.* 選錄; 引述; 摘錄。—*v.t.* 摘錄。—**ex·cerp·tion,** *n.* 「摘要; 大綱; 摘錄。」

ex·cerp·ta [ɪkˈsɝptə; ikˈsəːptə] *n. pl.*

ex·cess** [*n.* ɪkˈsɛs; ikˈses, ek- *adj.* ˈɪksɛs, ɪkˈsɛs; ˈikses, ikˈses] *n.* ①過多之量; 過度; 過分。Pour off the *excess.* 把多餘的倒掉。②超額; 超過數。*excess* of import. 入超。*excess* of export. 出超。③過度之行爲; 暴行。④飲食烟酒等的無節制; 無節制; 無節度。His *excesses* shortened his life. 他以飲食無度而致夭壽。in excess of*** 較…爲多。***to excess*** 過度。He drinks *to excess.* 他飲酒過度。—*adj.* 超額的。*excess* fare. 補票費。*excess* luggage (baggage). 過重的行李。*excess* postage. (郵票)欠資。

***ex·ces·sive** [ɪkˈsɛsɪv; ikˈsesiv] *adj.* 過度的; 極度的。Wise people will not buy when prices are *excessive.* 物價過高時, 聰明的人不會去買東西。—**ness,** *n.* —**ly,** *adv.*

ex·cess-prof·its tax [ˈɛksɛsˈprɑfɪts~; ˈeksesˈprɔfits~] 超額所得稅; 過分利得稅。

exch. ①exchange. ②exchequer.

‡ex·change [ɪksˈtʃendʒ; iksˈtʃeindʒ, eks-] *v.,* **-changed, -chang·ing,** *n.* —*v.t.* ①交換; 互換; 交互。John *exchanges* gifts with Mary at Christmas. 約翰在耶誕節同瑪麗交換禮物。②換取。She *exchanged* honor for wealth. 她犧牲榮譽以換取財富。③掉換。We can *exchange* no yard goods. 我們不能換零頭布。—*v.i.* ①交換。②調換。to *exchange* from one regiment into another. 從甲團調換到乙團。③兌換。The currency of this country *exchanges* at par. 這個國家的貨幣可按票面價值兌換。—*n.* ①交換; 交易。*exchange* of prisoners during a war. 戰爭中俘虜的交換。②所交換之物。The car was a fair *exchange.* 交換來的車還算公平(沒有吃虧)。③交易所。a stock *exchange.* 股票交易所。④電話總局的交換臺; 電話總機。⑤(外幣的)兌換。A bank that sells foreign money is called an *exchange* bank. 賣外幣的銀行叫做匯兌銀行。⑥(外幣的)匯率。⑦票據交換所。⑧票據交換所中的票據。***in exchange*** (***for***) 交換。I am giving him English lessons *in exchange for* French lessons. 我教他英文, 他教我法文。

ex·change·a·bil·i·ty [ɪksˌtʃendʒəˈbɪlətɪ; iksˌtʃeindʒəˈbiliti] *n.* 可交易; 可兌換; 可交換。

ex·change·a·ble [ɪksˈtʃendʒəbl̩; iksˈtʃeindʒəbl] *adj.* 可交換的; 可更換的; 可兌換的。「ˈdʒiː] *n.* 被交換者(如學生、俘虜等)。」

ex·chang·ee [ˌɛkstʃenˈdʒi; ˌekstʃein-

exchange rate 匯率。

exchange student 交換學生。

ex·cheq·uer [ɪksˈtʃɛkɚ; iksˈtʃekə] *n.* ①國庫。②資財。③【俗】財源。④(E-)英國的財政部。⑤(E-)英國政府之債券。⑥【英史】有關稅收之民事法庭。

ex·cide [ɪkˈsaɪd; ikˈsaid] *v.t.,* **-cid·ed, -cid·ing.** 切除; 割除。「【數學】外圓。」

ex·cir·cle [ˈɛksˌsɝkl̩; ˈeksˌsəːkəl] *n.*

ex·cis·a·ble [ɛkˈsaɪzəbl̩; ekˈsaizəbl] *adj.* ①應課稅的。②可切除的。

ex·cise[1] [ɪkˈsaɪz; ekˈsaiz] *n., v.,* **-cised, -cis·ing.** —*n.* ①國產稅; (煙、酒等之)消費稅。the *Excise.* (英國之)國產稅局。②執照稅。—*v.t.* 課以國產稅。

ex·cise[2] *v.t.,* **-cised, -cis·ing.** ①切去; 除去。to *excise* the tonsils. 割除扁桃腺。②剔除; 删除。

ex·cise·man [ˈɛksaɪzmən; ekˈsaizmæn] *n., pl.* **-men.** 【英】稅務官。

ex·ci·sion [ɪkˈsɪʒən; ekˈsiʒən] *n.* ①删除; 除去。② =**excommunication.** ③【外科】截除; 切除; 割除術。

ex·cit·a·bil·i·ty [ɪkˌsaɪtəˈbɪlətɪ; ikˌsaitəˈbiliti] *n.* ①易激動; 易興奮。②敏感; (對刺激之)反應。

ex·cit·a·ble [ɪkˈsaɪtəbl̩; ikˈsaitəbl] *adj.* 易激動的; 能興奮的。—**ex·cit·a·bly,** *adv.*

ex·cit·ant [ɛkˈsaɪtənt; ˈeksitənt] *adj.* 刺激性的。—*n.* 刺激物; 興奮劑。

ex·ci·ta·tion [ˌɛksaɪˈteʃən; ˌeksiˈteiʃən] *n.* ①刺激; 鼓舞。②【電】激發。

ex·cit·a·to·ry [ɛkˈsaɪtəˌtorɪ; ekˈsaitətəri] *adj.* 刺激的; 使興奮的。(亦作 **excitative**)

‡ex·cite [ɪkˈsaɪt; ikˈsait, ek-] *v.t.,* **-cit·ed, -cit·ing.** ①激動; 鼓舞; 使興奮。The news *excited* everybody. 這消息使人人爲之鼓舞。②引起; 招致; 招惹。Don't *excite* the dog; let him keep still. 不要招惹那隻狗; 讓它耽着吧。③【物理】激(電、磁)。*excited* atom. 受激原子。④【生理】刺激。

ex·cit·ed [ɪkˈsaɪtɪd; ikˈsaitid] *adj.* ①興奮的; 激動的。②活躍的。

ex·cit·ed·ly [ɛkˈsaɪtɪdlɪ; ikˈsaitidli, ek-] *adv.* 激憤地; 激昂地; 興奮地。

***ex·cite·ment** [ɪkˈsaɪtmənt; ikˈsaitmənt, ek-] *n.* ①興奮; 刺激; 煽動; 騷動。The fire caused great *excitement.* 火警引起大騷動。②引起刺激或騷動之事物。

ex·cit·er [ɛkˈsaɪtɚ; ikˈsaitə] *n.* ①刺激者; 激勵者。②刺激物; 興奮劑。③【電】激發機。

***ex·cit·ing** [ɪkˈsaɪtɪŋ, ɛk-; ikˈsaitiŋ, ek-] *adj.* 鼓舞的; 興奮的。an *exciting* news. 使人興奮之消息。「易激動的。」

ex·ci·tive [ɛkˈsaɪtɪv; ikˈsaitiv] *adj.*

excl. ①exclamation. ②excluding. ③exclusive. ④exclusively.

‡ex·claim [ɪkˈsklem; iksˈkleim, eks-] *v.i. & v.t.* 呼喊; 驚叫; 大呼。"What!" he *exclaimed,* "Are you leaving without me?" "甚麼!" 他喊道,"你要丟下我離開嗎?"

exclam. ①exclamation. ②exclamatory.

*__ex·cla·ma·tion__ 〔ˌɛkskləˈmeʃən; ˌeksklәˈmeiʃən〕 *n.* ①呼喊;感嘆。②驚嘆詞;感嘆詞(如 Ah, Oh 等)。③驚嘆句;感嘆句。例如:Oh, how terrible! 哦,多麼可怕啊! ***exclamation mark*** (or ***point***) 驚嘆號;感嘆號"!"。

ex·clam·a·to·ry 〔ɪkˈsklæməˌtorɪ; eksˈklæmətəri〕 *adj.* 驚嘆的;感嘆的。

ex·clave 〔ˈɛksklev; ˈekskleiv〕 *n.* 孤立於外地的領土。

ex·clo·sure 〔ɛksˈkloʒɚ; iksˈklouʒə〕 *n.* (防範獸類或害蟲侵入的)圍地。

*__ex·clude__ 〔ɪkˈsklud; iksˈklu:d〕 *v.t.*, **-clud·ed, -clud·ing.** ①拒絕;除去;除外。to *exclude* immigrants from a country. 拒絕移民進入國境。②逐出;排除。

ex·clu·sion 〔ɪkˈskluʒən; iksˈklu:ʒən〕 *n.* ①拒絕;除去。②排斥;排外。***to the exclusion of*** 排除;排斥;把…除外。

exclusion clause 〖保險〗契約中聲明不屬保險範圍事項之條款。

ex·clu·sion·ism 〔ɪkˈskluʒənˌɪzəm; iksˈklu:ʒənizəm〕 *n.* 排他主義;排外主義。

*__ex·clu·sive__ 〔ɪkˈsklusɪv; iksˈklu:siv, eks-〕 *adj.* ①不許外人加入的。an *exclusive* school. 限於某些人(可以進入)的學校。②獨有的;獨享的。an *exclusive* right. 獨占權。③限制嚴格的。He moves in very *exclusive* social circles. 他活動於限制很嚴格的社交圈子內。④除外的。⑤孤芳自賞的。That man is rather *exclusive* in his manner. 那人的態度十分孤高。⑥唯一的;排他的。—*n.* ①〖新聞〗獨家消息。The *Times* has been granted an interview as an *exclusive*. 時報已獲准獨家接見。②公司行號等之特有商品、計畫等。—**ness, ex·clu·siv·i·ty,** *n.*

*__ex·clu·sive·ly__ 〔ɪkˈsklusɪvlɪ, ɛk-; iksˈklu:sivli, eks-〕 *adv.* 排外地;獨占地;專有地。That selfish girl looks out for herself *exclusively*. 那自私的女孩祇管她自己的利益。

ex·clu·siv·ism 〔ɪkˈsklusɪvɪzəm; iksˈklu:sivizm〕 *n.* 排他主義;獨占主義。

ex·cog·i·tate 〔ɛksˈkɑdʒəˌtet; eksˈkɔdʒiteit〕 *v.t.*, **-tat·ed, -tat·ing.** ①設計;想出;發明。②仔細或努力研究以求徹底明瞭。

ex·cog·i·ta·tion 〔ɛksˌkɑdʒəˈteʃən; eksˌkɔdʒiˈteiʃən, iks-〕 *n.* 設計;發明;設計物;發明物。

ex·com·mu·ni·ca·ble 〔ˌɛkskəˈmjunɪkəbl̩; ekskəˈmju:nikəbl〕 *adj.* ①可逐出教會的。②應逐出教會的。

ex·com·mu·ni·cant 〔ˌɛkskəˈmjunɪkənt; ˌekskəˈmju:nikənt〕 *n.* 被逐出教會者。

ex·com·mu·ni·cate 〔ˌɛkskəˈmjunəˌket; ˌekskəˈmju:nikeit〕 *v.*, **-cat·ed, -cat·ing,** *n., adj.* —*v.t.* ①逐出教會。②逐出任何團體。—*n.* 被逐出教會者。—*adj.* 被逐出教會的。

ex·com·mu·ni·ca·tion 〔ˌɛkskəˌmjunəˈkeʃən; ˈekskəˌmju:niˈkeiʃən〕 *n.* ①逐出教會。②開除(會籍、黨籍等)。

ex·com·mu·ni·ca·tive 〔ˌɛkskəˈmjunəˌketɪv, -kətɪv; ˌekskəˈmju:nikeitiv〕 *adj.* 開除的;逐出教會的。(亦作 **excommunicatory**)

ex·com·mu·ni·ca·tor 〔ˌɛkskəˈmjunəˌketɚ; ˌekskəˈmju:nikeitə〕 *n.* (將他人)開除者;除名者;將他人逐出教會者。

ex·co·ri·ate 〔ɪkˈskorɪˌet; eksˈkɔ:rieit〕 *v.t.*, **-at·ed, -at·ing.** ①磨損或擦去…之皮;脫皮。②痛詆;責罵。—**ex·co·ri·a·tion,** *n.*

ex·cor·ti·cate 〔ɛkˈskɔrtɪˌket; eksˈkɔ:tikeit〕 *v.t.*, **-cat·ed, -cat·ing.** ①剝樹皮、外殼。②〖外科〗剝皮。

ex·cre·ment 〔ˈɛkskrɪmənt; ˈekskrimənt〕 *n.* 排泄物;糞。

ex·cre·men·ti·tious 〔ˌɛkskrɪmɛnˈtɪʃəs; ˌekskrimenˈtiʃəs〕 *adj.* 糞便的;排泄物的;像糞便般的。(亦作 **excremental**)

ex·cres·cence 〔ɪkˈskrɛsn̩s; iksˈkresns〕 *n.* ①瘤;贅肉。②長出物(如指甲等)。③贅疣;多餘物。—**ex·cres·cent,** *adj.*

ex·cres·cen·cy 〔ɪkˈskrɛsn̩sɪ; iksˈkresənsi〕 *n.* ①排泄。②排泄物。

ex·cre·ta 〔ɛkˈskritə; eksˈkri:tə〕 *n. pl.* 〖生理〗排泄物;糞便;汗;尿;腺分泌物。

ex·crete 〔ɛkˈskrit; eksˈkri:t〕 *v.t.*, **-cret·ed, -cret·ing.** 排泄;分泌。

ex·cre·tion 〔ɪkˈskriʃən; eksˈkri:ʃən〕 *n.* ①排泄;分泌。②排泄物;分泌物。—**excre·tive,** *adj.*

ex·cre·to·ry 〔ˈɛkskrɪˌtorɪ; eksˈkri:təri〕 *adj.* 排泄的;分泌的。—*n.* 排泄器官。

ex·cru·ci·ate 〔ɪkˈskruʃɪˌet; iksˈkru:ʃieit〕 *v.t.*, **-at·ed, -at·ing.** ①施酷刑;拷打。②使煩惱;使痛苦。

ex·cru·ci·at·ing 〔ɪkˈskruʃɪˌetɪŋ; iksˈkru:ʃieitiŋ〕 *adj.* ①極痛苦的;使極痛苦的。②繁文褥節的。—**ly,** *adv.*

ex·cru·ci·a·tion 〔ɪkˌskruʃɪˈeʃən; iksˌkru:ʃiˈeiʃən〕 *n.* ①酷刑;拷問。②苦惱;痛苦;慘痛。

ex·cul·pate 〔ˈɛkskʌlˌpet; ˈekskʌlpeit〕 *v.t.*, **-pat·ed, -pat·ing.** 剖白;辯解。to *exculpate* a person from a charge. 辯白某人無罪。

ex·cul·pa·tion 〔ˌɛkskʌlˈpeʃən; ˌekskʌlˈpeiʃən〕 *n.* 剖白;辯解;雪冤。

ex·cul·pa·to·ry 〔ɪkˈskʌlpəˌtorɪ; eksˈkʌlpətəri〕 *adj.* 剖白的;辯解的;雪冤的。

ex·cur·rent 〔ɛksˈkɝənt; eksˈkʌrənt〕 *adj.* ①流出的;向外流的。②〖動物〗作爲外流之通道的。③〖植物〗**a.** 莖軸延長成爲主幹的。**b.** 突出葉尖的(指葉之中肋言)。

*__ex·cur·sion__ 〔ɪkˈskɝʒən, -ʃən; iksˈkə:ʃən, eks-〕 *n.* ①遠足;旅行;遊覽。to go on (*or* make) an *excursion*. 舉行遠足。②一羣遠足旅行的人。③有折扣之火車或輪船之旅行。④〖軍〗侵入;侵奪。⑤離開本題。*excursions* from the major theme. 離開主題。—*v.i.* 旅行;遠足。—*adj.* 旅行的;優待的。an *excursion* fare. 優待票價。〖注意〗**excursion, tour** 皆指旅遊而言。excursion 指短程一日可來回之團體旅行,通常有各種優待(如票價之折扣等)。tour 指有計畫之長程旅行,目的在觀光風景名勝。

ex·cur·sion·ist 〔ɛksˈkɝʒənɪst; iksˈkə:ʃnist〕 *n.* 旅行者;遊覽者。

excursion ticket 優待票(尤指至名勝地之優待票價)。

excursion train 供持優待票乘客搭的列車。

ex·cur·sive 〔ɪkˈskɝsɪv; eksˈkə:siv〕 *adj.* ①遊覽之性質的;漫遊的。②散漫的;無連貫的。③離正途的;逸出正軌的。—**ness,** *n.* —**ly,** *adv.*

ex·cur·sus 〔ɛkˈskɝsəs; eksˈkə:səs〕 *n., pl.* **-sus·es, -sus.** ①卷末附註;附記。②脫離本題。

ex·cus·a·ble [ɪk'skjuzəbḷ; iks'kju:zəbl] *adj.* 可恕的;可原諒的。

ex·cus·al [ɛk'skjusəl; ek'skju:səl] *n.* ①原諒;諒解。②辯解;辯白。

ex·cus·a·to·ry [ɪk'skjuzəˌtorɪ; iks'kju:zətəri] *adj.* 辯解的;申辯的。

:ex·cuse [*v.* ɪk'skjuz; iks'kju:z, eks- *n.* ɪk'skjus; iks'kju:s, eks-] *v.*, **-cused, -cus·ing,** *n.* —*v.t.* ①原諒;寬恕;諒宥(過失等)。We *excused* him for being late. 我們原諒他遲到。②辯解;辯白;託故。I cannot *excuse* his laziness. 我無法替他的懶惰辯白。③作爲…之理由。Sickness *excused* his absence from school. 患病是他不來學校的理由。④免除。I cannot *excuse* you from attending my classes. 我不能准許你不來上我的課。⑤不需要;可以不要。We will *excuse* your presence. 我們可以讓你不出席。***Excuse me*** 對不起;借光。*Excuse me,* sir, will you tell me the way to the station? 對不起,先生,請問到車站去怎麼走? ***excuse oneself*** **a.** 請求原諒。**b.** 請求准予離開。**c.** 請求准予不參加。—*n.* ①藉口;託辭。That is not a good *excuse.* 那不是一個好的藉口。②辯解;解釋。③某事物之簡陋的替身;劣質的樣品。That coward is barely an *excuse* for a man. 那個懦夫不配稱爲一個男人。〖注意〗(1) **excuse, pardon** 均表原諒、寬恕。excuse 指原諒較輕微之過失或錯誤。pardon 語氣較正式,指對罪刑之赦免。(2) **excuse, apology**均指對過錯之辯解。excuse 指爲避免責咎而辯解。apology 則指承認錯誤而表示遺憾。(3) **excuse** 與 **pardon** 稍有區別。"Pardon me" 較 "Excuse me" 高雅。"I beg (your) pardon." 是當沒聽清楚對方所說的話時常用的一句話。"Excuse me" 另含請求"允許離去"之意。

ex·cus·ing [ɪk'skjuzɪŋ; iks'kju:ziŋ] *adj.* 作託辭的;辯解的。

ex div. ①ex dividend. ②without dividend.

ex dividend 〖股票〗除息;股利除外。(亦作 **ex-dividend,** 略作 **ex dev.**)

ex·e·at ['ɛksɪæt; 'eksiæt] *n.* ①〖英〗(學期中之)外宿許可;缺席許可。②主教之允許傳教士離開其教區。

ex·ec [ɛg'zɛk; eg'zek] *n.* 〖美俗〗=executive.

exec. ①executive. ②executor.

ex·e·cra·ble ['ɛksɪkrəbḷ; 'eksikrəbl] *adj.* 討厭的;可惡的;可咒的。—**ex·e·cra·bly,** *adv.*

ex·e·crate ['ɛksɪˌkret; 'eksikreit] *v.*, **-crat·ed, -crat·ing.** —*v.t.* ①咒罵。②憎惡。—*v.i.* 咒罵。

ex·e·cra·tion [ˌɛksɪ'kreʃən; ˌeksi'kreiʃən] *n.* ①詛咒。②憎惡。③被詛咒之人或物;討厭的人或物。

ex·e·cra·tive ['ɛksəˌkretɪv; 'eksikreitiv] *adj.* ①詛咒的;厭惡的。②好詛咒的。

ex·ec·u·tant [ɪg'zɛkjutənt; ig'zekjutənt] *n.* ①執行者;實行者。②〖音樂〗演奏者。—*adj.* ①表演(者)的。②演奏者的。

·ex·e·cute ['ɛksɪˌkjut; 'eksikju:t] *v.t.*, **-cut·ed, -cut·ing.** ①實現;完成;執行;實施。He *executed* the captain's orders. 他執行了船長的命令。②執行(法律)。Congress makes the laws; the President *executes* them. 國會創制法律;總統執行法律。③處決;處死。④(根據計畫或設計)製作(藝術品等)。An artist *executes* a painting or statue. 藝術家繪製圖畫或製作雕像。⑤演奏(樂曲);演(戲)。The part of Hamlet was badly *executed.* Hamlet 這角色演得不好。⑥(以簽章而)使(契約、遺囑等文件)生效。

·ex·e·cu·tion [ˌɛksɪ'kjuʃən; ˌeksi'kju:ʃən] *n.* ①實現;完成。The *execution* of the plan was a failure. 該計畫之實施不令人滿意。②執行。③技巧;熟練。The pianist has marvelous *execution.* 此鋼琴家技巧極爲熟練。④執行死刑。⑤(根據計畫或設計的)製作。⑥經簽章而在法律上生效。⑦法院的執行命令。⑧效力(尤指武器之效力,前面常用 do). ***carry* (*something*) *into execution*** =**put (something) in execution.** 完成(一件事);依照計畫實施(某事)。***do execution*** **a.** 有摧毀的效果。Our machine guns *did* great *execution* among the enemy. 我們的機槍在敵人中發生了極大的摧毀力。**b.** 發生效果。

ex·e·cu·tion·er [ˌɛksɪ'kjuʃənɚ; ˌeksi'kju:ʃənə] *n.* 行刑者;劊子手。

·ex·ec·u·tive [ɪg'zɛkjutɪv; ig'zekjutiv, eg-] *adj.* ①實行的;執行的。an *executive* committee. 執行委員會。②行政的。③管理能力很强的;行政能力很强的。④供主管人員使用的。an *executive* dining room. 高級職員膳廳。—*n.* ①行政官。②執行者;管理者;經理主管級人員。The president of a company is an *executive.* 一個公司的經理是一個管理公司業務者。③(the~)(政府中的)行政部門;行政院。***the Executive***〖美〗總統。

Executive Mansion〖美國〗①白宮。②(某些州的)州長官邸。

executive officer 〖軍〗執行官。

executive order 美國總統對陸海空軍或政府各部門之命令。

Executive Yu·an [~y'æn; ~y'æn] (中華民國之)行政院。

ex·ec·u·tor [*for* ②'ɛksɪˌkjutɚ; 'eksikjutə *for* ①ɪg'zɛkjətɚ; ig'zekjutə] *n.* ①〖法律〗被指定執行遺囑者。②執行者。

ex·ec·u·to·ri·al [ɛgˌzɛkjə'torɪəl; igˌzekju'tɔ:riəl] *adj.* ①執行者的。②執行命令的;執行法律程序的。

ex·ec·u·to·ry [ɪg'zɛkjəˌtorɪ; ig'zekjutəri] *adj.*①行政上的。②在施行中的;有效的(如法律、命令等)。③〖法律〗將來可生效的。

ex·ec·u·trix [ɪg'zɛkjətrɪks; ig'zekjutriks] *n., pl.* **-trix·es, ex·ec·u·tri·ces** [ɪgˌzɛkjə'traɪsiz; igˌzekju'traisi:z]. ①〖法律〗被指定執行遺囑之婦女。②女執行者。

ex·e·ge·sis [ˌɛksə'dʒisɪs; ˌeksi'dʒi:sis] *n., pl.* **-ses** [-siz; -si:z]. 註釋(特指經典上者);訓詁。

ex·e·get·ic [ˌɛksə'dʒɛtɪk; ˌeksi'dʒetik] *adj.* 註釋的;訓詁的。(亦作 **exegetical**) —**al·ly,** *adv.*

ex·em·plar [ɪg'zɛmplɚ; ig'zemplə] *n.* 模範;範本;榜樣;例。

ex·em·pla·ri·ly [ɛg'zɛmplərɪlɪ; ig'zemplərili] *adv.* ①作爲模範地。②可作鑑戒地。

ex·em·pla·ri·ness [ɛg'zɛmplərɪnɪs, ɪg-; ig'zemplərinis] *n.* 可爲模範;可作鑑戒。

ex·em·pla·ry [ɪg'zɛmplərɪ; ig'zempləri] *adj.* ①可爲模範的。②可作鑑戒的。③代表性的;典型的。

ex·em·pli·fi·ca·tion [ɪgˌzɛmpləfə'keʃən; igˌzemplifi'keiʃən] *n.* ①例示;例證;例。②〖法律〗正式謄本。—**al,** *adj.*

ex·em·pli·fy [ɪg'zɛmpləˌfaɪ; ig'zemplifai] *v.t.*, **-fied, -fy·ing.** ①例示;例

證。②製作…之正本。—**ex·em·pli·fi·er**, *n.* —**ex·em·pli·fi·a·ble**, *adj.*

ex·em·pli gra·ti·a [ɪgˈzɛmplaɪˈgreʃɪə; igˈzemplaiˈgreiʃiə]〖拉〗例如 (=for example, 略作 **e.g.**).

ex·empt [ɪgˈzɛmpt, ɛg-; igˈzempt, eg-] *v.t.* 使免除(責任、義務等)。—*adj.* 被免除(責任、義務等)的。—*n.* 被免除義務者;免稅者。—**i·ble**, *adj.*

ex·emp·tion [ɪgˈzɛmpʃən; igˈzempʃən] *n.* 免除;解除。 —**ex·emp·tive**, *adj.*

ex·e·qua·tur [ˌɛksɪˈkwetɚ; ˌeksiˈkweitə] *n.* ①(駐在國對外國領事等的)認可書。②統治者對教皇敕書等之認可書。

ex·e·quies [ˈɛksɪkwɪz; ˈeksikwiz] *n.* pl. of **exequy**.

ex·e·quy [ˈɛksɪkwɪ; ˈeksikwi] *n.*, *pl.* **-quies.** ①葬儀。②出殯行列。

ex·er·cis·a·ble [ˈɛksɚˌsaɪzəbl̩; ˈeksəsaizəbl] *adj.* 可運用的;可操作的。

‡**ex·er·cise** [ˈɛksɚˌsaɪz; ˈeksəsaiz] *n.*, *v.*, **-cised, -cis·ing.** —*n.* ①運動;體操。②運用。The *exercise* of patience is essential in diplomatic negotiations. 在外交談判中,運用忍耐力是必要的。③練習問題;習題。He is engaged in doing his French *exercises.* 他正忙於做法文練習。④練習。*exercise* for the violin. 小提琴練習。⑤(*pl.*)〖美〗儀式;典禮。⑥演習。The third cruiser squadron has left port for a series of *exercises.* 第三巡洋艦隊已離港作一連串之演習。⑦心智活動或訓練。*Exercise* of the mental faculties is just as important as *exercise* of the body. 智能的訓練與身體的運動是同等重要的。—*v.t.* ①訓練;操練。②鍛鍊;運用;使用。③履行;實踐。④產生(作用);影響。What others think *exercises* a great influence on most of us. 他人作如何想對我們多半產生很大的影響。⑤吸引…之注意。This is a problem which is much *exercising* the minds of fathers. 這是一個很吸引父親們注意的問題。⑥憂愁;惶恐。I'm very much *exercised* about the future. 我對於將來深爲惶恐。—*v.i.* 訓練;鍛鍊;運動。You don't *exercise* enough. 你運動不够。

ex·er·cis·er [ˈɛksɚˌsaɪzɚ; ˈeksəsaizə] *n.* ①做運動的人。②鍛鍊肌肉的器械。

exercise book〖主英〗筆記簿。

ex·ergue [ɛgˈzɝg; ekˈsəːg] *n.* 貨幣、獎牌等圖案之底部與邊緣之間用以記年月日及鑄造局所之處。 —**ex·er·gual**, *adj.*

***ex·ert** [ɪgˈzɝt; igˈzəːt, eg-] *v.t.* 運用;施行。A ruler *exerts* authority. 統治者運用權威。—**ive**, *adj.*

***ex·er·tion** [ɪgˈzɝʃən; igˈzəːʃən] *n.* ①努力;用力;盡力;費力。It was so hot that it seemed too much *exertion* even to breathe. 天氣如此的熱,連呼吸都似乎太吃力。②行使;運用。

ex·es [ˈɛksɪz; ˈeksiz] *n. pl.*〖俚〗費用(=expenses).

ex·e·unt [ˈɛksɪənt; ˈeksiʌnt]〖拉〗*v.i.*〖戲劇〗退場;下 (=they go out or off. 常用在劇中人前)。

ex·fo·li·ate [ɛksˈfolɪˌet; eksˈfoulieit] *v.t.* & *v.i.*, **-at·ed, -at·ing.** 剝落。

ex·fo·li·a·tion [ɛksˌfolɪˈeʃən; eksˌfouliˈeiʃən] *n.* ①剝落;鱗落;落屑。②剝落之物(如鱗、樹皮等)。

ex. gr. 例如 (=exempli gratia).

ex·hal·ant [ɛksˈhelənt; eksˈheilənt] *adj.* 呼出的;吐出的;排出的。—*n.* 排出器官(如某些軟體動物的導管)。

ex·ha·la·tion [ˌɛksəˈleʃən; ˌekshəˈleiʃən] *n.* ①呼出;呼氣;發出;蒸發。②發散物;蒸發物(如空氣、蒸汽、氣味等)。

ex·hale [ɛksˈhel; eksˈheil] *v.*, **-haled, -hal·ing.** —*v.t.* ①呼出;呼(氣)。②發出(氣、煙、味等)。—*v.i.* ①呼氣。②蒸發。③發出;散發。—**ment**, *n.*

***ex·haust** [ɪgˈzɔst, ɛg-; igˈzɔːst, eg-] *v.t.* ①用盡;耗盡。②使力竭;使疲憊。The long war *exhausted* the country. 長期的戰爭使這國家民窮財盡。③抽盡;汲盡。④評論;闡述詳盡。—*v.i.* ①逸出;放出。Steam *exhausts.* 蒸氣逸出來。②排出氣體;放出氣體。The engine *exhausts* through a muffler. 引擎從消音器排氣。—*n.* ①廢氣。②廢氣之逸出或放出。③廢氣口;排氣口;排氣管。

ex·haust·ed [ɪgˈzɔstɪd; igˈzɔːstid] *adj.* ①用盡的。My patience is *exhausted.* 我的耐心已竭。②疲憊的。—**ness**, *n.* —**ly**, *adv.*

ex·haust·er [ɪgˈzɔstɚ; igˈzɔːstə] *n.*〖機械〗洩氣器。

exhaust fan 抽風機。

ex·haust·i·bil·i·ty [ɪgˌzɔstəˈbɪlətɪ; igˌzɔːstəˈbiliti] *n.* 可耗盡;被耗費性。

ex·haust·i·ble [ɪgˈzɔstəbl̩; igˈzɔːstəbl] *adj.* 可用盡的; 可耗盡的; 可枯竭的。—**ness**, *n.*

ex·haust·ing [ɪgˈzɔstɪŋ; igˈzɔːstiŋ] *adj.* ①使竭盡的。②令人疲乏不堪的。—**ly**, *adv.*

***ex·haus·tion** [ɪgˈzɔstʃən, ɛg-; igˈzɔːstʃən, eg-] *n.* ①竭盡。②疲憊。The soldiers were in a state of *exhaustion* after five days' continuous fighting. 在五天不斷的戰鬥後,兵士均感疲憊。

ex·haus·tive [ɪgˈzɔstɪv; igˈzɔːstiv] *adj.* ①無遺漏的;徹底的;廣泛的。②消耗的;使枯竭的。—**ness**, *n.* —**ly**, *adv.*〖注意〗**exhaustive** 與 **exhausting** 不同。前者意爲徹底的、包羅無遺的,後者意爲使人疲乏的。

ex·haust·less [ɪgˈzɔstlɪs; igˈzɔːstlis] *adj.* 取之不盡的; 用之不竭的; 無盡藏的。—**ly**, *adv.* —**ness**, *n.*

exhaust pipe 排氣管。

***ex·hib·it** [ɪgˈzɪbɪt; igˈzibit, eg-] *v.t.* ①表現; 顯示。 Our men *exhibited* great bravery in the battle. 我們的士兵在戰鬥中表現了極大的勇敢。②展覽; 陳列。③呈上…以供考慮者檢閱。④提示(證據)。⑤解釋。⑥配(藥)。—*v.i.* 展覽; 顯露。This artist *exhibits* in all the art galleries. 這位藝術家在所有美術館中展出作品。—*n.* ①展覽品或陳列品。②陳列; 展覽。③〖法律〗證物;物證。The prosecution introduced the weapons into evidence as *exhibits* A and B. 檢察當局將那些武器拿出作物證甲及物證乙。④表現; 顯露。—**a·ble**, *adj.* —**ant**, *n.*

***ex·hi·bi·tion** [ˌɛksəˈbɪʃən; ˌeksiˈbiʃən] *n.* ①表現;顯露。You're making an *exhibition* of yourself. 你是在出醜。②展覽會;博覽會。 The art school holds an art *exhibition* every year. 藝術學校每年舉行一次美術展覽會。③陳列品。④英國大學中之獎學金。 —**al, ex·hib·i·to·ry**, *adj.*

ex·hi·bi·tion·er [ˌɛksəˈbɪʃənɚ; ˌeksiˈbiʃənə] *n.* (英國大學之)獲得獎學金學生。

ex·hi·bi·tion·ism [ɛksəˈbɪʃənˌɪzəm; ˌeksiˈbiʃənizəm] *n.* ①風頭主義。②〖精神

病〗a. 陰部顯露慾。b. 顯露陰部。—**ex·hi·bi·tion·is·tic,** *adj.*

ex·hi·bi·tion·ist 〔ˌɛksəˈbɪʃənɪst; ˌeksiˈbiʃənist〕 *n.* ①風頭主義者。②〖精神病〗陰部顯露症患者。 —*adj.* 風頭主義者的; 陰部顯露症患者的。

ex·hib·i·tive 〔ɪgˈzɪbɪtɪv; igˈzibitiv〕 *adj.* ①供展覽的;作爲陳列的。②有陳列或展示之傾向的。—**ly,** *adv.*

ex·hib·i·tor, ex·hib·it·er 〔ɪgˈzɪbɪtɚ; igˈzibitə〕 *n.* ①展覽者; 顯示者。②提供者; 提出者。③電影院之老闆或經理人。

ex·hil·a·rant 〔ɪgˈzɪlərənt; igˈzilərənt, eg-〕 *adj.* 令人興奮的; 令人歡喜的。—*n.* 令人興奮或歡喜之物;興奮劑。

ex·hil·a·rate 〔ɪgˈzɪləˌret; igˈziləreit〕 *v.t.,* **-rat·ed, -rat·ing.** 使高興;使快活;使興奮。 —**ex·hil·a·ra·tor,** *n.*

ex·hil·a·rat·ing 〔ɪgˈzɪləˌretɪŋ; igˈziləreitiŋ〕 *adj.* 令人歡喜的; 令人快樂的。—**ly,** *adv.*

ex·hil·a·ra·tion 〔ɪgˌzɪləˈreʃən; igˌziləˈreiʃən〕 *n.* ①高興;快活。②令人高興。

ex·hil·a·ra·tive 〔ɪgˈzɪləˌretɪv; igˈzilərətiv〕 *adj.* 使高興的; 令人興奮的。(亦作 **exhilaratory**)

ex·hort 〔ɪgˈzɔrt; igˈzɔːt〕 *v.t. & v.i.* 勸告;勸誡。—**er,** *n.* —**ing·ly,** *adv.*

ex·hor·ta·tion 〔ˌɛgzɔrˈteʃən; ˌegzɔːˈteiʃən〕 *n.* 勸誡; 勸誡人之演說、布道等。

ex·hor·ta·tive 〔ɪgˈzɔrtətɪv; igˈzɔːtətiv〕 *adj.* 勸誡的;用以勸誡的。—**ly,** *adv.*

ex·hor·ta·to·ry 〔ɪgˈzɔrtəˌtorɪ; igˈzɔːtətəri〕 *adj.* =**exhortative.**

ex·hu·ma·tion 〔ˌɛkshjuˈmeʃən; ˌekshjuːˈmeiʃən〕 *n.* 發掘;掘墓。

ex·hume 〔ɪgˈzjum; eksˈhjuːm〕 *v.t.,* **-humed, -hum·ing.** ①從墓中掘出。②從默默無聞中發掘;從被遺忘的狀態中掘出。—**ex·hum·er,** *n.*

ex·i·gence 〔ˈɛksədʒəns; ˈeksidʒəns〕 *n.* =**exigency.**

ex·i·gen·cy 〔ˈɛksədʒənsɪ; ˈeksidʒənsi〕 *n., pl.* **-cies.** ①(*pl.*)急切之需要。②迫切;急切; 緊急。③緊急事件。

ex·i·gent 〔ˈɛksədʒənt; ˈeksidʒənt〕 *adj.* ①急切的; 緊急的; 急需的; 危急的。②所需極多的。(亦作 **exigeant**) —**ly,** *adv.*

ex·i·gi·ble 〔ˈɛksədʒəbl̩; ˈeksidʒibl〕 *adj.* 可要求的;可勒逼的。

ex·i·gu·i·ty 〔ˌɛksəˈgjuətɪ; ˌeksiˈgjuːiti〕 *n.* 稀少;微細;些須。

ex·ig·u·ous 〔ɪgˈzɪgjuəs; egˈzigjuəs〕 *adj.* 稀少的; 微細的;些須的。—**ly,** *adv.*

ex·ile** 〔ˈɛgzaɪl, ˈɛksaɪl, *for v. also* ɪgˈzaɪl; ˈeksail, ˈegz-〕 *v.,* **-iled, -il·ing,** *n.* —*v.t.* 放逐; 流放。He was *exiled* for life. 他被放逐終身。—*n.* ①放逐; 流放。Napoleon's *exile* to Elba was brief. 拿破崙之放逐厄爾巴島是很短暫的。②被放逐者。He has been an *exile* for ten years. 他已過了十年放逐者的生活。③流亡國外者; 流亡。the Exile*** 紀元前597–538年間猶太人之被巴比倫奴役。

ex·il·i·an 〔ɛgˈzɪlɪən; egˈziliən〕 *adj.* =**exilic.**

ex·il·ic 〔ɛgˈzɪlɪk; egˈzilik〕 *adj.* 亡命的; 放逐的(尤指猶太人之亡命於巴比倫)。

‡ex·ist 〔ɪgˈzɪst; igˈzist〕 *v.i.* ①存在;實有。Do you believe that God *exists?* 你相信上帝存在嗎? ②生存; 活着。We cannot *exist* without air, food and water. 我們不能離開空氣、食物和水而生存。③發生;有。Does life *exist* on the planets? 各星球上有生物嗎? Crime and poverty still *exist* in our big cities. 罪行與貧窮仍發生在我們的大城市中。—**er,** *n.*

ex·ist·ence** 〔ɪgˈzɪstəns; igˈzistəns, eg-〕 *n.* ①存在;實在。This is the largest ship in *existence.* 這是全世界現有最大的船。②生存; 生活。Air and warmth are necessary for *existence.* 空氣與溫暖對於生存是必要的。③發生。④存在之物。call*** (or ***bring***) ***into existence*** 使產生; 使成立。***come into existence*** 產生; 發生。Nobody knows how this world *came into existence.* 沒有人知道這個世界是怎樣產生的。***put out of existence*** 滅絕;使絕跡。

ex·ist·ent 〔ɪgˈzɪstənt; igˈzistənt〕 *adj.* ①存在的; 生存的。②實存的; 現存的。—*n.* 存在者;生存物。

ex·is·ten·tial 〔ˌɛgzɪsˈtɛnʃəl; ˌegzisˈtenʃəl〕 *adj.* ①存在的。②〖邏輯〗存在上的; 實體論的。—**ly,** *adv.*

ex·is·ten·tial·ism 〔ˌɛgzɪsˈtɛnʃəlɪzm; ˌegzisˈtenʃəlizəm〕 *n.* 〖哲〗實存主義;存在主義。

ex·is·ten·tial·ist 〔ˌɛgzɪsˈtɛnʃəlɪst; ˌegzisˈtenʃəlist〕 *n.* 實存主義者;存在主義者。—*adj.* 實存主義的;存在主義的。

ex·ist·ing 〔ɪgˈzɪstɪŋ; igˈzistiŋ〕 *adj.* 現在的;現存的;目前的。

***ex·it** 〔ˈɛgzɪt, ˈɛksɪt; ˈeksit, ˈegzit〕 *n.* ①出口。②出;離去。He made his *exit.* 他離去了。③(演員的)退場。The actor made a graceful *exit.* 該演員退場動作十分優美。—*v.i.*(劇中人自舞臺)下;退場。*Exit* Hamlet. 哈姆雷特下(劇本中用語)。

ex lib. ex libris.

ex li·bris 〔ɛksˈlaɪbrɪs; eksˈlaibris〕 *pl.* **-bris.**〖拉〗①屬於(某人)藏書(=belonging to the library of)。②藏書標籤(略作 **ex lib.**)

exo-〖字首〗表"外"之義。

ex·o·bi·ol·o·gy 〔ˌɛksəbaɪˈɑlədʒɪ; ˌeksəbaiˈɔlədʒi〕 *n.* 太空生物學。—**ex·o·bi·ol·o·gist,** *n.*

ex·o·crine 〔ˈɛksəkraɪn; ˈeksəkrain〕 *adj.*〖生理〗外分泌的。

exocrine gland〖生理〗外分泌腺。

Exod. Exodus.

ex·o·don·tia 〔ˌɛksəˈdɑnʃə; ˌeksəˈdɔnʃə〕 *n.* 拔牙術;拔牙學。

ex·o·dus 〔ˈɛksədəs; ˈeksədəs〕 *n.* ①成羣外出;大批離去。②(E-)以色列人隨摩西之離開埃及。③(E-) 出埃及記(舊約聖經第二卷)。

ex of·fi·ci·o 〔ˌɛksəˈfɪʃɪˌo; ˌeksəˈfiʃiou〕〖拉〗依官職的;當然的。

ex·og·a·mous 〔ɛksˈɑgəməs; ekˈsɔgəməs〕 *adj.* 異族結婚的。(亦作 **exogamic**)

ex·og·a·my 〔ɛksˈɑgəmɪ; ekˈsɔgəmi〕 *n.* ①異族結婚;外族通婚。②〖生物〗異種生殖細胞之結合。

ex·o·gen 〔ˈɛksədʒən; ˈeksədʒən〕 *n.*〖植物〗外長植物。

ex·og·e·nous 〔ɛksˈɑdʒɪnəs; ekˈsɔdʒinəs〕 *adj.* ①外長的; 外長植物的。②起於外部的;外來的。—**ex·og·e·nism,** *n.* —**ly,** *adv.*

ex·on·er·ate 〔ɪgˈzɑnəˌret; igˈzɔnəreit〕 *v.t.,* **-at·ed, -at·ing.** ①免罪;證明無罪。②免除(責任、義務等)。—**ex·on·er·a·tor,** *n.*

ex·on·er·a·tion 〔ɪgˌzɑnəˈreʃən; igˌzɔnəˈreiʃən〕 *n.* ①釋罪; 免罪。②免除; 責任之解除。

ex·on·er·a·tive [ɪɡ'zɑnəˌretɪv; iɡ'zɔnərətiv] *adj.* 釋罪的;免除的。
ex·o·ra·ble ['ɛksərəbl̩; 'eksərəbl] *adj.* 易說服的;可由請求而感動的;心軟的。
ex·or·bi·tance [ɪɡ'zɔrbətəns; iɡ'zɔːbitəns] *n.* (要求、價格等)過高;過度。
ex·or·bi·tan·cy [ɪɡ'zɔrbətənsɪ; iɡ'zɔːbitənsi] *n., pl.* **-cies.** =**exorbitance.**
ex·or·bi·tant [ɪɡ'zɔrbətənt; iɡ'zɔːbitənt] *adj.* 過度的;荒唐的。—**ly,** *adv.*
ex·or·cise, ex·or·cize ['ɛksɔrˌsaɪz; 'eksɔːsaiz] *v.t.,* **-cised** or **-cized, -cis·ing** or **-ciz·ing.** ①驅(邪);除(怪)。②祓除(人、地等)之邪怪。—**ment,** *n.* —**ex·or·cis·er,** *n.*
ex·or·cism ['ɛksɔrˌsɪzəm; 'eksɔːsizəm] *n.* ①驅邪;伏魔。②驅邪所用之咒語。
ex·or·cist ['ɛksɔrsɪst; 'eksɔːsist] *n.* 驅邪之人;伏魔者。
ex·or·di·um [ɪɡ'zɔrdɪəm; ek'sɔːdjəm] *n., pl.* **-di·ums, -di·a** [-dɪə; -diə]. ①開端。②序言。
ex·o·skel·e·ton [ˌɛkso'skɛlətn̩; ˌeksou'skelitn] *n.* 〖解剖〗皮骨骼;外骨骼(如甲殼、魚鱗等)。
ex·o·sphere ['ɛksəsˌfɪə; 'eksəsfiə] *n.* 大氣之最外層。
ex·o·ter·ic [ˌɛksə'tɛrɪk; ˌeksou'terik] *adj.* ①外界的;外部的。②適於外圍人士的;非局限於少數子弟的。③一般人易於了解的;通俗的;公開的。(亦作 **exoterical**)
ex·ot·ic [ɪɡ'zɑtɪk; eɡ'zɔtik] *adj.* ①外來的;外國產的。②〖俗〗奇特、華麗而動人的。—*n.* 舶來品;外國種。—**al·ly,** *adv.*
exotic dancer 脫衣舞孃。
ex·ot·i·cism [ɪɡ'zɑtəˌsɪzm̩; eɡ'zɔtisizəm] *n.* ①外國化傾向。②異國趣味;異國情調。③外來語;外來語法。—**ex·ot·i·cist,** *n.*
exp. ①expenses. ②export. ③exported. ④express. ⑤experience. ⑥experiment; experimental. ⑦expiration. ⑧explosive. ⑨exponential. ⑩exposure.
***ex·pand** [ɪk'spænd; iks'pænd, eks-] *v.t.* ①擴張;擴大;擴展。He is trying to *expand* his business. 他正努力發展他的營業。②展開。The bird *expanded* its wings. 那隻鳥展開了它的兩翼。③增訂;增述。The writer *expanded* one sentence into a paragraph. 那作者將原來的一句話增述爲一整段。④闡述。⑤將(簡寫字等)完全拼出來。—*v.i.* ①膨脹。Metals *expand* when they are heated. 金屬加熱則膨脹。②開放。The petals of this flower *expand* in the sunshine. 此花之花瓣在陽光中開放。③擴大;擴張;擴展。The river *expands* and forms a lake. 該河漸形寬廣而形成一湖。④加以闡述〖on, upon〗。⑤感到心花怒放。The flattery made him *expand* and glow. 那些阿諛使他心花怒放而容光煥發。—**er,** *n.*
***ex·panse** [ɪk'spæns; iks'pæns] *n.* 茫茫一片;寬闊之空間;廣袤。the blue *expanse* of the sky. 一望無際的藍天。
ex·pan·si·bil·i·ty [ɪkˌspænsə'bɪlətɪ; iksˌpænsə'biliti] *n.* 膨脹性;擴展性。
ex·pan·si·ble [ɪk'spænsəbl̩; iks'pænsəbl] *adj.* 可膨脹的;可擴展的。
ex·pan·sile [ɪk'spænsl̩; iks'pænsail] *adj.* ①擴張的;膨脹的。②能膨脹的。
***ex·pan·sion** [ɪk'spænʃən; iks'pænʃən] *n.* ①擴張;開展;脹大。The *expansion* of the factory made room for more machines. 工廠之擴充俾有更大的地方安裝機器。②擴大之量或程度。③擴大之部分或形式。This book is an *expansion* of a series of articles. 這本書是擴大一系列的獨立文章而成的。④〖數學〗展開;展開式。—**al,** *adj.*
ex·pan·sion·ism [ɪks'pænʃənɪzm̩; iks'pænʃənizəm] *n.* ①(通貨之)膨脹主義。②領土擴張主義。—**ex·pan·sion·is·tic,** *adj.*
ex·pan·sion·ist [ɪks'pænʃənɪst; iks'pænʃənist] *n.* ①通貨膨脹主義者。②領土擴張主義者。—*adj.* 主張領土擴張的;侵略性的。
ex·pan·sive [ɪk'spænsɪv; iks'pænsiv] *adj.* ①可擴張的;可擴展的;可膨脹的。②能促起膨脹的。③廣濶的。④(胸襟)開濶的。⑤主張擴張領土的(=expansionist). —**ly,** *adv.* —**ness,** *n.*
ex par·te [ɛks'pɑrtɪ; 'eks'pɑːti] 〖拉〗片面的;偏袒一方的。
ex·pa·ti·ate [ɪk'speʃɪˌet; eks'peiʃieit] *v.i.,* **-at·ed, -at·ing.** ①詳述;鋪陳〖on, upon〗。②〖罕〗漫遊。—**ex·pa·ti·a·tor,** *n.*
ex·pa·ti·a·tion [ɪkˌspeʃɪ'eʃən; iksˌpeiʃi'eiʃən] *n.* ①詳述;鋪陳。②〖罕〗漫遊。
ex·pa·ti·a·to·ry [ɪk'speʃɪəˌtorɪ; iks'peiʃjətəri] *adj.* ①詳述的。②擴張的。
ex·pa·tri·ate [ɛks'petrɪˌet; eks'pætrieit] *v.,* **-at·ed, -at·ing,** *n., adj.* —*v.t.* ①驅逐(某人)離開本國;放逐。②使(自己)背棄本國;脫離國籍。—*v.i.* 背離母國。—*n.* ①被放逐的人;亡命國外者。②背棄本國者;脫離國籍者。—*adj.* 被放逐的;亡命國外的。
ex·pa·tri·a·tion [ɛksˌpetrɪ'eʃən; eksˌpætri'eiʃən] *n.* ①旅居國外;亡命國外。②放棄國籍。
‡ex·pect [ɪk'spɛkt; iks'pekt, e-] *v.t.* ①預期;期待;希望。I never *expected* such unkindness. 我從未預料有如此之不仁。②堅持;要求。I don't *expect* him to do impossibilities. 我並非要他做不可能的事情。③〖俗〗認爲。Who has eaten all the cake? Oh, I *expect* it was Tom. 誰把餅全吃了?哦,我想是Tom. —*v.i.* ①期望;期待;希望。We love to *expect.* 我們喜歡期待。②懷孕。His wife is *expecting.* 他太太有喜。—**ing·ly,** *adv.*
ex·pect·a·ble [ɪk'spɛktəbl̩; iks'pektəbl] *adj.* 可預想的;意料中的。—**ex·pect·a·bil·i·ty,** *n.* —**ex·pect·a·bly,** *adv.*
ex·pect·an·cy [ɪk'spɛktənsɪ; iks'pektənsi] *n., pl.* **-cies.** ①期望;預期;期待。*Expectancy* darkened into anxiety. 期待轉成了焦慮。②期望之目的物;希冀物。Each of us came with his own purposes and *expectancies.* 我們每個人都有自己的目的與希望。(亦作 **expectance**)
ex·pect·ant [ɪk'spɛktənt; iks'pektənt] *adj.* ①期待的。②卽將生孩子的。—*n.* 期待之人。—**ly,** *adv.*
ex·pec·ta·tion** [ˌɛkspɛk'teʃən; ˌekspek'teiʃən] *n.* ①期望;預料。②(常 *pl.*)預期之物;希望。We have great *expectations* of you. 我們對你期望甚殷。③可能性。④被期望之狀態。⑤假想;假定。The *expectation* that you are always from home prevents my writing to you. 我以爲你經常不在家所以沒有寫信給你。⑥〖古〗等待。against*** (or ***contrary to***) ***expectation(s)*** (事)與願違。***answer*** (***meet,*** or ***come up to***) ***one's expectation*** 合乎理想;達到理想。***beyond expectation(s)*** 出乎意料。***fall short of one's expectation*** 不如理想。***in expectation*** 預期;想望。

expectation of life 平均壽命;平均餘年(某一年齡的人尚可期望活的平均年數,常由統計資料顯示)。

ex·pect·a·tive [ɛk'spɛktətɪv; eks'pektətiv] *adj.* 期望的;預期的。

ex·pec·to·rant [ɪk'spɛktərənt; eks'pektərənt] *adj.* 〖醫〗祛痰的。—*n.* 祛痰劑。

ex·pec·to·rate [ɪk'spɛktə,ret; eks'pektəreit] *v.t.* & *v.i.*, **-rat·ed, -rat·ing.** 咳而吐(痰等);吐痰;吐唾液。

ex·pec·to·ra·tion [ɪk,spɛktə'reʃən; eks,pektə'reiʃən] *n.* ①咳吐;吐痰;吐唾液。②吐出之物;痰。—**ex·pec·to·ra·tive,** *adj.*

ex·pe·di·ence [ɪk'spidɪəns; iks'pi:djəns] *n., pl.* **-enc·es.** =**expediency.**

ex·pe·di·en·cy [ɪk'spidɪənsɪ; iks'pi:djənsi] *n., pl.* **-cies.** ①權宜;方便。②(事之)利害。

ex·pe·di·ent [ɪk'spidɪənt; iks'pi:djənt] *adj.* ①權宜的;方便的。②有利的;合算的。—*n.* 權宜之計。

ex·pe·di·en·tial [ɛks,pidɪ'ɛnʃəl; iks,pi:di'enʃəl] *adj.* 權宜主義的;爲利益或便利起見的。—**ly,** *adv.*

ex·pe·dite ['ɛkspɪ,daɪt; 'ekspidait] *v.,* **-dit·ed, -dit·ing,** *adj.* —*v.t.* ①使加速。②速辦。③正式發布(公文等)。④發送。—*adj.* ①無阻礙的。②迅速的;機敏的。③便利的。

ex·pe·dit·er ['ɛkspɪ,daɪtɚ; 'ekspidaitə] *n.* ①(政府、工廠等雇用之)加速完成緊急或繁雜計畫之人。②官方發布文件之人。

***ex·pe·di·tion** [,ɛkspɪ'dɪʃən; ,ekspi'diʃən] *n.* ①遠征;探險。to go on an *expedition.* 去遠征(探險)。②遠征隊;探險隊。a hunting *expedition.* 狩獵隊。③有效而迅速的行動。She put her things on with remarkable *expedition.* 她動作極爲迅速地穿戴整齊。

ex·pe·di·tion·ar·y [,ɛkspɪ'dɪʃən,ɛrɪ; ,ekspi'diʃənəri] *adj.* 遠征的;探險的。—*n.* 遠征隊員;探險隊員。

ex·pe·di·tion·er [,ɛkspɪ'dɪʃənɚ; ,ekspi'diʃənə] *n.* =**expeditionary.**

ex·pe·di·tion·ist [,ɛkspɪ'dɪʃənɪst; ,ekspi'diʃənist] *n.* =**expeditionary.**

ex·pe·di·tious [,ɛkspɪ'dɪʃəs; ,ekspi'diʃəs] *adj.* 迅速的;敏捷的。—**ly,** *adv.* —**ness,** *n.*

***ex·pel** [ɪk'spɛl; iks'pel, eks-] *v.t.*, **-pelled, -pel·ling.** ①驅逐;逐出。②開除。to *expel* a bad boy from school. 開除一壞學生。—**la·ble,** *adj.*

ex·pel·lee [,ɛkspɛ'li; ,ekspe'li:] *n.* 被「驅逐出境者;被開除者。」

ex·pel·lent [ɪk'spɛlənt; iks'pelənt] *adj.* 驅除的;有驅逐力的;有排毒性的。—*n.* 驅除劑;排毒劑。(亦作 **expellant**)

ex·pel·ler [ɛk'spɛlɚ; eks'pelə] *n.* ①逐出者;開除者。②榨油機。

ex·pend [ɪk'spɛnd; iks'pend] *v.t.* 用;花費;消耗(時間、金錢等)。—*v.i.* 花錢。

ex·pend·a·ble [ɪk'spɛndəbḷ; iks'pendəbl] *adj.* ①可消費的。②〖軍〗爲達成某項目標而放棄或犧牲的。—*n. pl.* ①消耗品。②可放棄或犧牲的人員或裝備。—**ex·pend·a·bil·i·ty,** *n.*

***ex·pend·i·ture** [ɪk'spɛndɪtʃɚ; iks'penditʃə, eks-] *n.* ①消費;費用。*Expenditure* on armaments is increasing. 軍費正增加中。②經費;開支。Limit your *expenditures* to what is necessary. 節縮你的開支在必要範圍之內。

:ex·pense [ɪk'spɛns; iks'pens, eks-] *n.* ①費用;代價。Most children are educated at public *expense.* 大多數的兒童都靠公費受教育。②消費。A boy at college puts his father to considerable *expense.* 孩子上大學使其父親負一重擔。③消費之原因;經濟上的負擔。Running an automobile is an *expense.* 有汽車是經濟上的一個負擔。④犧牲;損失。⑤(*pl.*)做某事所需的費用;津貼。The salesman gets *expenses* besides his salary. 推銷員除薪水外還得到津貼。***at one's expense*** 嘲弄某人。We had a good laugh *at his expense.* 我們着實嘲笑了他一番。***at the expense of*** 犧牲。He became a brilliant scholar only *at the expense of* his health. 他成了有學問的學者,却犧牲了他的健康。***go to the expense of*** 花費於。

expense account 〖會計〗費用帳戶;用費表。

***ex·pen·sive** [ɪk'spɛnsɪv; iks'pensiv, eks-] *adj.* 昂貴的;奢華的;費用浩大的。—**ly,** *adv.* —**ness,** *n.*

:ex·pe·ri·ence [ɪk'spɪrɪəns; iks'piəriəns, eks-] *n., v.,* **-enced, -enc·ing.** —*n.* ①經歷;閱歷。Please tell us about your *experiences* in Africa. 請告訴我們你在非洲的經歷。②經驗;體驗。We all learn by *experience.* 我們都是從經驗中學習。—*v.t.* ①經驗;經歷;感受。The reason death was feared was because no man could twice *experience* it. 死亡之所以爲人懼怕乃是因爲無人能經歷兩次。②由經驗中發覺;體驗。—**a·ble,** *adj.* —**less,** *adj.* —**ex·pe·ri·enc·er,** *n.*

***ex·pe·ri·enced** [ɪk'spɪrɪənst; iks'piəriənst] *adj.* ①已有經驗的。②由經驗中學得的。③熟練的;老練的。to be *experienced* in teaching. 對教學有經驗。

ex·pe·ri·en·tial [ɪk,spɪrɪ'ɛnʃəl; iks,piəri'enʃəl] *adj.* 經驗(上)的;得諸經驗的;實驗得來的。—**ly,** *adv.*

:ex·per·i·ment [ɪk'spɛrəmənt; iks'perimənt, eks-] *v.i.* 實驗;試驗。He *experimented* in painting at home. 他在家中試驗繪畫。—*n.* 實驗;試驗。Scientists test out theories by *experiment.* 科學家藉實驗證明理論。—**er,** *n.*

ex·per·i·men·tal [ɪk,spɛrə'mɛntḷ; eks,peri'mentl] *adj.* ①實驗的;做實驗的;根據經驗的。an *experimental* farm. 實驗農場。②試驗性的。—*n.* 實驗性之事物。

ex·per·i·men·tal·ism [ɪk,spɛrə'mɛntḷ,ɪzəm; eks,peri'mentəlizəm] *n.* 〖哲〗實驗主義。

ex·per·i·men·tal·ist [ɪk,spɛrə'mɛntḷɪst; eks,peri'mentəlist] *n.* 實驗主義者;做實驗者。

ex·per·i·men·tal·ize [ɪk,spɛrə'mɛntḷ,aɪz; eks,peri'mentəlaiz] *v.i.*, **-ized, -iz·ing.** 作實驗。

ex·per·i·men·tal·ly [ɪk,spɛrə'mɛntḷɪ; eks,peri'mentəli] *adv.* 以實驗;從實驗中。

experimental psychology 實驗心理學。

ex·per·i·men·ta·tion [ɪk,spɛrəmɛn'teʃən; eks,perimen'teiʃən] *n.* 實驗;試驗。

experiment station 試驗所;實「驗站。」

***ex·pert** [*n.* 'ɛkspɝt; 'ekspə:t *adj.* ɪk'spɝt, 'ɛkspɝt; 'ekspə:t, eks'p-, i- *v.* ɪk'spɝt; eks'pə:t] *n.* 專家。a chemical *ex-*

pert. 化學專家。—*adj.* ①老練的；熟練的。The acting was fresh and *expert.* 演出新穎而老練。②需要專門知識的。—*v.t.* 以專家身分處理或應付。—*v.i.* 擔任專家。—**ly,** *adv.* —**ness,** *n.*

ex·per·tise 〔ˌɛkspɚˈtiz; ˌekspəˈtiːz〕 *n.* ①專家之見解。②專門技術或知識。

ex·pert·ize 〔ˈɛkspɝˌtaɪz; ˈekspətaiz〕 *v.i.* ①任專家；提供專門性意見；作專門性判斷。—*v.t.* 爲…提供專門性意見；爲…作專門性判斷。

ex·pi·a·ble 〔ˈɛkspɪəbl̩; ˈekspiəbl〕 *adj.* 可贖的；可補償的。

ex·pi·ate 〔ˈɛkspɪˌet; ˈekspieit〕 *v.t.,* **-at·ed, -at·ing.** ①贖；補償。②避開；躲避。

ex·pi·a·tion 〔ˌɛkspɪˈeʃən; ˌekspiˈeiʃən〕 *n.* ①補償；贖罪。②贖罪之方式。—**al,** *adj.*

ex·pi·a·to·ry 〔ˈɛkspɪəˌtorɪ; ˈekspiətəri〕 *adj.* 補償的；贖罪的。

ex·pi·ra·tion 〔ˌɛkspəˈreʃən; ˌekspaiəˈreiʃən〕 *n.* ①滿滿；終止。②呼出；放出。

ex·pir·a·to·ry 〔ɪkˈspaɪrəˌtorɪ; iksˈpaiərətəri〕 *adj.* 呼氣的；吐氣的。

***ex·pire** 〔ɪkˈspaɪr; iksˈpaiə〕 *v.,* **-pired, -pir·ing.** —*v.i.* ①滿期；終止。His furlough *expires* on Tuesday. 他的假期於星期二屆滿。②熄滅；斷氣；死亡。He *expired* at midnight. 他午夜死去。③呼氣。—*v.t.* 排出；呼氣。

ex·pi·ry 〔ɪkˈspaɪrɪ; iksˈpaiəri〕 *n., pl.* **-ries.** 期滿；告終。

‡**ex·plain** 〔ɪkˈsplen; iksˈplein〕 *v.t.* ①解釋；說明；講解。Please *explain* this rule to me. 請將此規則解釋給我聽。②辯解；辯護；辯明。Can you *explain* your behavior? 你能給你的行爲作什麼辯解嗎？—*v.i.* 說明；解釋。***explain away*** 以解釋將…却除。***explain oneself*** a. 使自己說的話清楚明瞭。b. 爲自己的行爲作辯護或解釋。—**a·ble,** *adj.* —**er,** *n.* —**ing·ly,** *adv.*

***ex·pla·na·tion** 〔ˌɛkspləˈneʃən; ˌekspləˈneiʃən〕 *n.* ①解釋；說明；辯解；剖白。Can you understand this passage without *explanation?* 你能不待解釋而懂這一段嗎？②爲消除彼此之誤解而作的會談。

ex·plan·a·to·ry 〔ɪkˈsplænəˌtorɪ; iksˈplænətəri〕 *adj.* ①解釋的；說明的。②樂於解釋的。—**ex·plan·a·to·ri·ly,** *adv.*

ex·ple·tive 〔ˈɛksplɪtɪv; eksˈpliːtiv〕 *n.* ①虛字；助詞(常指 it, there 等)。②咒罵語；感歎詞(如 "Damn," "my goodness"等是)。—*adj.* 僅有文法功用而無實際意義的。〖文法〗如下列各句中之 it, there等字，僅有文法功用而無實際的意義，文法上就稱做 expletive. 如：*There* is some paper on the desk. 桌上有一些紙。*It* is said that he has resigned. 據說他已辭職了。

ex·pli·ca·ble 〔ˈɛksplɪkəbl̩; ˈeksplikəbl〕 *adj.* 可說明的；可解釋的。

ex·pli·cate 〔ˈɛksplɪˌket; ˈeksplikeit〕 *v.t.,* **-cat·ed, -cat·ing.** ①解說；說明。②分析。

ex·pli·ca·tion 〔ˌɛksplɪˈkeʃən; ˌekspliˈkeiʃən〕 *n.* 描述；說明。

ex·pli·ca·tive 〔ˈɛksplɪˌketɪv, ɪkˈsplɪkətɪv; eksˈplikətiv, ˈeksplikeitiv〕 *adj.* 解釋的；說明的。(亦作 **explicatory**)

ex·plic·it 〔ɪkˈsplɪsɪt; iksˈplisit〕 *adj.* ①明白表示的；明確的。②直爽的；說話無保留的。③有外形可見的；可明顯地觀察到的。***explicit faith*** 徹底了解教義後之信仰，爲 implicit faith(妄信)之對。—**ly,** *adv.* —**ness,** *n.*

ex·plode** 〔ɪkˈsplod; iksˈploud, e-〕 *v.,* **-plod·ed, -plod·ing.** —*v.i.* ①爆發；爆炸。I heard that a bomb *exploded.* 我聽說有一炸彈爆炸。②發作。At last his anger *exploded.* 他的怒氣終於發作了。③特別引人注目。④迅速擴張。Suburbs are *exploding* outward. 市郊迅速地向外擴張。⑤〖高爾夫〗將球從沙坑中擊出。—*v.t.* ①使爆發；使爆炸。②駁倒；推翻；打破。to *explode* an idea. 駁倒一種觀念。③〖高爾夫〗將(球)從沙坑中擊出。explode a bombshell*** 作意外的透露、建議等。

ex·plod·er 〔ɪkˈsplodɚ; iksˈploudə〕 *n.* ①爆炸人；爆發物。②爆炸裝置；雷管。

ex·ploit 〔*n.* ˈɛksplɔɪt, ɪkˈsplɔɪt; ˈeksplɔit *v.* ɪkˈsplɔɪt; iksˈplɔit〕 *n.* 功績；功勞；勳業。—*v.t.* ①開發。②剝削。③利用。—**er,** *n.* —**a·ble,** *adj.*

ex·ploi·ta·tion 〔ˌɛksplɔɪˈteʃən; ˌeksplɔiˈteiʃən〕 *n.* ①剝削；搾取。②開發；採掘；拓墾。③利用。④廣告；宣傳。

***ex·plo·ra·tion** 〔ˌɛkspləˈreʃən; ˌeksplɔːˈreiʃən〕 *n.* ①探險。②仔細檢查；研究。③〖醫〗體內器官之檢查。

ex·plor·a·to·ry 〔ɪkˈsploraˌtorɪ; iksˈplɔːrətəri〕 *adj.* ①探險的；探究的。②好探險的；好探究的。③試探性的；初步的。(亦作 **explorative**)

***ex·plore** 〔ɪkˈsplor, -ˈsplɔr; iksˈplɔː, eks-, -ˈplɔə〕 *v.,* **-plored, -plor·ing.** —*v.t.* ①探險；探測。to *explore* the Arctic regions. 探險北極地帶。②探究；研究；仔細察看。to *explore* a problem. 深刻研究一項問題。—*v.i.* 實行探勘；實行探險。to *explore* for oil. 探勘石油。

***ex·plor·er** 〔ɪkˈsplorɚ; iksˈplɔːrə〕 *n.* ①探險者；探究者。an arctic *explorer.* 北極探險家。②探索器具；探查器；(醫學用之)探針。

ex·plo·si·ble 〔ɪkˈsplozəbl̩; iksˈplouzəbl〕 *adj.* ①可爆炸的。②易於爆炸的。

***ex·plo·sion** 〔ɪkˈsploʒən; iksˈplouʒən〕 *n.* ①爆發；爆炸。the *explosion* of a bomb. 炸彈的爆炸。②爆發聲；爆炸聲。③發出；爆出。an *explosion* of laughter. 發笑。④(學說等之)推翻。⑤劇增；急速擴張。

explosion shot 〖高爾夫〗將陷入沙坑中的球擊出來的一擊。

***ex·plo·sive** 〔ɪkˈsplosɪv; iksˈplousiv〕 *adj.* ①爆炸的；易爆炸的；富爆炸性的。an *explosive* substance. 易炸物。②易發脾氣的。③爆發音的。④劇增的；急速擴張的。the *explosive* increase of population. 人口的劇增。—*n.* ①爆炸物；爆炸藥。②爆發音(如 b,p,t,d等)。—**ly,** *adv.* —**ness,** *n.*

ex·po 〔ˈɛksˌpo; ˈekspou〕 *n., pl.* **ex·pos.** 博覽會；展覽會(＝exposition).

ex·po·nent 〔ɪkˈsponənt; eksˈpounənt〕 *n.* ①解釋者；說明者。②代表者；代表物；典型。③〖代數〗指數；冪。

ex·po·nen·tial 〔ˌɛkspoˈnɛnʃəl; ˌekspouˈnenʃəl〕 *adj.* 〖代數〗指數的；冪的。

***ex·port** 〔*v.* ɪksˈport, ˈɛksport; eksˈpɔːt, i-, ˈekspɔːt *n., adj.* ˈɛksport; ˈekspɔːt〕 *v.t.* ①輸出；外銷。We now *export* all kinds of industrial products. 我們現在輸出各種工業產品。②排出。—*v.i.* 輸出；出口。—*n.* ①輸出品；出口貨。Sugar is one of the chief *exports* of China. 糖是中國的主要輸出品之一。②輸出；出口。He is engaged in *export.* 他從事出口貿易。—*adj.* 輸出的；外銷的。

ex·port·a·ble 〔ɛksˈportəbl̩; eksˈpɔːtəbl〕 *adj.* 可輸出的。

ex·por·ta·tion [ˌɛkspor'teʃən; ˌekspɔː'teiʃən] *n.* ①輸出。②輸出品。

ex·port·er [ɪk'sportɚ; iks'pɔːtə] *n.* 輸出(業)者;出口者。

export exchange 出口外匯。

export tax (or **duty**) 出口關稅。

***ex·pose** [ɪk'spoz; iks'pouz] *v.t.*, **-posed, -pos·ing.** ①暴露。The soldiers in the open field were *exposed* to the enemy's gunfire. 在曠野中的士兵們暴露在敵人砲火之下。②展覽; 陳列。to *expose* goods in a shop window. 陳列貨物於店窗中。③揭穿(祕密等)。He *exposed* their plot. 他揭穿了他們的陰謀。④曝光;使(底片等)感光。⑤遺棄。⑥使受影響; 使冒感染之危險。to *expose* children to good books. 使兒童受好書的薰陶。—**ex·pos·er,** *n.*

ex·po·sé [ˌɛkspo'ze; eks'pouzei] 〖法〗*n.* ①(罪惡、騙局等的) 揭發。②闡述;闡明。

ex·posed [ɪk'spozd; iks'pouzd] *adj.* 暴露的;無掩蔽的。

***ex·po·si·tion** [ˌɛkspə'zɪʃən; ˌekspə'ziʃən] *n.* ①展覽;陳列。②博覽會;展覽會。an industrial *exposition.* 工業展覽會。③說明;解釋。④說明文。a splendid piece of *exposition.* 一篇絕妙的說明文。

ex·pos·i·tive [ɛks'pɑzətɪv; eks'pɔzitiv] *adj.* =**expository.**

ex·pos·i·tor [ɪk'spɑzɪtɚ; eks'pɔzitə] *n.* 解釋者;註解者;一段註解。

ex·pos·i·to·ry [ɪk'spɑzɪˌtorɪ; eks'pɔzitəri] *adj.* 註解的; 說明的。

ex post fac·to ['ɛksˌpost'fækto; 'eks poust 'fæktou] 〖拉〗事後的(地); 追溯的(地)。

ex·pos·tu·late [ɪk'spɑstʃəˌlet; iks'pɔstjuleit] *v.i.*, **-lat·ed, -lat·ing.** 勸戒;忠告;抗議〖about, for, on, upon〗. —**ex·pos·tu·la·tor,** *n.*

ex·pos·tu·la·tion [ɪkˌspɑstʃə'leʃən; iksˌpɔstju'leiʃən] *n.* ①告戒;抗議。②諫言;忠告。

ex·pos·tu·la·to·ry [ɪk'spɑstʃələˌtorɪ; iks'pɔstjulətəri] *adj.* 告戒的;諫言的。

***ex·po·sure** [ɪk'spoʒɚ; iks'pouʒə, e-] *n.* ①曝露。His face was brown from *exposure* to the weather. 他的臉因飽經風霜而成褐色。②揭露;揭發。The *exposure* of the real criminal cleared the innocent man. 眞正罪犯的揭露洗清了那個無辜的人。③(照相的)曝光;晒像;曝光的時間。an *exposure* of $^1/_{10}$ second. 十分之一秒的曝光。④(房屋的)方向。⑤(嬰兒等的) 遺棄。⑥發表。⑦置人於某事物之影響下。⑧暴露之表面; 暴露之物。(亦作 **exposal**)

exposure meter (照相機)曝光表。

exposure suit 絕緣材料做的禦寒衣。

ex·pound [ɪk'spaund; iks'paund] *v.t.* ①解釋;說明。to *expound* a theory (*or* one's views, etc.). 解釋一理論(某人觀點等)。②詳細說明; 逐項敍述。—*v.i.* 發表見解;作說明。They *expounded* on the subject. 他們就那問題發表見解。

ex-pres·i·dent ['ɛks'prɛzədənt; 'eks'prezidənt] *n.* 前任總統。

:**ex·press** [ɪk'sprɛs; iks'pres, eks-] *v.t.* ①表示;表達。I can't *express* it properly. 我無法把它適當地表達出來。②代表。The sign "=" *expresses* equality. "=" 號代表相等。③〖美〗以快郵寄遞。You'd better *express* the letter; it's urgent. 你還是以快郵寄那封信好; 那是很緊急的。④擠出。to *express* the juice from grapes to make wine. 從葡萄中擠出汁來做酒。—*adj.* ①表明的;確定的。It is his *express* wish that we should go without him. 他明確的願望是要我們不帶他一起走。an *express* provision. (法律) 明文。②特別的;特殊的。She came for the *express* purpose of seeing you. 她特地爲看你而來。③正確的。He is the *express* image of his father. 他極像他父親。④運送的。an *express* company. 運送公司。⑤快速的; 特別快的。an *express* train. 特別快車。⑥供快速旅行用的。an *express* highway. 快車公路。⑦〖英〗限時的(郵件等)。*express* letter. 限時信。—*n.* ①〖英〗專差。②快遞法。③快車。by *express.* 快遞; 乘快車。④運送公司或系統。⑤以快遞運送之物(如信件、包裹等)。—*adv.* ①直接地。②快遞地。to send a parcel *express.* 以快遞寄包裹。

ex·press·age [ɛks'prɛsɪdʒ; iks'presidʒ] *n.* ①捷運;快遞。②捷運業。③捷運之費用;快遞費。

express delivery 〖主英〗(郵件之)「限時專送;快遞。」

ex·press·i·ble [ɪk'sprɛsəbl̩; iks'presəbl] *adj.* ①可表白的;可表達的。②可擠出的。(亦作 **expressable**)

:**ex·pres·sion** [ɪk'sprɛʃən; iks'preʃən] *n.* ①說明。②表現法; 措辭; 辭句。a very curious (interesting) *expression.* 很奇特的(有趣的)措辭。③表情;面色。He looked at me with a very strange *expression.* 他以一種非常奇怪的表情望着我。④表現。the proper *expression* of one's thoughts. 思想之適當表現。⑤感情。Poetry should be read with *expression.* 讀詩應該有感情。⑥〖數學〗式。⑦擠出。the *expression* of oil from plants. 從植物中榨油。***beyond*** (or ***past***) ***expression*** 非言語或筆墨所能形容的。It was beautiful *beyond expression.* 它美得無法形容。***find expression in*** 以…表現;以…發洩。***give expression to*** 表示;說明。Her sobs prevented her from *giving expression to* her gratitude. 她的飲泣使她不能表明感激之情。

ex·pres·sion·al [ɛk'sprɛʃənl̩; iks'preʃənl̩] *adj.* ①表現的。②表情的。

ex·pres·sion·ism [ɪk'sprɛʃənˌɪzəm; iks'preʃənizəm] *n.* (文學藝術等之) 表現主義;表現派。

ex·pres·sion·ist [ɪk'sprɛʃənɪst, ɛk-; iks'preʃənist] *adj.* 表現派的; 表現主義的。—*n.* 表現派藝術家。

ex·pres·sion·less [ɪk'sprɛʃənlɪs; iks'preʃənlis] *adj.* 無表情的; 缺乏表情的。

ex·pres·sive [ɪk'sprɛsɪv; iks'presiv] *adj.* ①表現的;表示的。the *expressive* function of language. 言語之表達功能。②富有表情的;有含意的。an *expressive* silence. 含情脈脈的沉默。—**ly,** *adv.* —**ness,** *n.*

ex·press·ly [ɪk'sprɛslɪ, ɛk-; iks'presli] *adv.* ①明白地;顯然地;確切地。②特意地;專誠地。She came *expressly* to see you. 她專誠來看你。

ex·press·man [ɪk'sprɛsmən, ɛk-; iks'presmæn] *n.*, *pl.* **-men.** ①營捷運業者。②捷運業公司收送貨物之工人。

ex·press·way [ɪk'sprɛsˌwe, ɛk-; iks'preswei] *n.* 高速公路。

ex·pro·pri·ate 〔ɛks'proprɪˌet; eks'proupriet〕 *v.t.*, **-at·ed, -at·ing.** ①沒收；徵用(土地、財產)。②剝奪…之所有權。③讓渡；移轉(財產)。④侵占；據爲己有。He *expropriated* my ideas for his own article. 他竊取我的意見來寫他自己的文章。—**ex·pro·pri·a·tion,** *n.*

ex·pulse 〔ɪk'spʌls; iks'pʌls〕 *v.t.* 逐出；驅逐。

ex·pul·sion 〔ɪk'spʌlʃən; iks'pʌlʃən〕 *n.* ①驅逐；逐出。②開除。

ex·pul·sive 〔ɪk'spʌlsɪv; iks'pʌlsiv〕 *adj.* 驅逐的；開除的；有驅逐或開除權的。

ex·punge 〔ɪk'spʌndʒ; eks'pʌndʒ〕 *v.t.*, **-punged, -pung·ing.** ①除去；删掉；擦去。②消毀；消滅。

ex·pur·gate ['ɛkspɚˌget; 'ekspəːgeit〕 *v.t.*, **-gat·ed, -gat·ing.** ①修訂；删除(書籍等)不妥處。an *expurgated* edition. 修訂版。②廓清；使潔淨。

ex·pur·ga·tion 〔ˌɛkspɚ'geʃən; ˌekspəː'geiʃən〕 *n.* 删訂；廓清；消滅。

ex·pur·ga·tor ['ɛkspɚˌgetɚ; 'ekspəːgeitə〕 *n.* 删訂者；廓清者。

ex·pur·ga·to·ri·al 〔ɛkˌspɝgə'torɪəl; eksˌpəːgə'tɔːriəl〕 *adj.* 删訂或廓清(者)的。

ex·pur·ga·to·ry 〔ɛks'pɝgəˌtorɪ; eks'pəːgətəri〕 *adj.* 删訂的；廓清的。

***ex·qui·site** ['ɛkskwɪzɪt, ɪk's-; 'ekskwizit, eks'k-, iks'k-〕 *adj.* ①精美的；纖美的。an *exquisite* design. 精緻的圖案。②劇烈的；極度的。③高尙的。She has *exquisite* tastes and manners. 她有高尙的情趣與舉止。④極度靈敏的。an *exquisite* ear for music. 對音樂辨別極爲靈敏的耳朶。—*n.* 衣飾過度講究者。—**ly,** *adv.* —**ness,** *n.*

ex·san·gui·nate 〔ɛks'sæŋgwəˌnet; eks'sæŋgwəneit〕 *v.*, **-nat·ed, -nat·ing.** —*v.t.* 使血流盡。—*v.i.* 流血過多而死。

ex·san·guine 〔ɛks'sæŋgwɪn; eks'sæŋgwin〕 *adj.* 貧血的；無血的。

ex·scind 〔ɛk'sɪnd; ek'sind〕 *v.t.* 割去；切除；滅盡；拔除。

ex·sert 〔ɛk'sɝt; ek'səːt〕 *v.t.* 突出；伸出。—*adj.* 〖生物〗突出的(如雄蕊等)。

ex·sert·ed 〔ɛk'sɝtɪd; ek'səːtid〕 *adj.* 伸出的；突出的。

ex-ser·vice ['ɛks'sɝvɪs; 'eks'səːvis〕 *adj.* 退伍的；退役的。

ex-ser·vice·man ['ɛks'sɝvɪsmən; 'eks'səːvismən〕 *n., pl.* **-men.** 退役軍人。

ex·sic·cate ['ɛksɪˌket; 'eksikeit〕 *v.*, **-cat·ed, -cat·ing.** —*v.t.* 使乾；弄乾。—*v.i.* 失去水分；變乾。

ext. ①extension. ②external. ③extinct. ④extra. ⑤extract.

ex·tant 〔ɪk'stænt; eks'tænt〕 *adj.* 現存的；未失的。

ex·tem·po·ral 〔ɪk'stɛmpərəl; eks'tempərəl〕 *adj.* 〖古〗=**extemporaneous.**

ex·tem·po·ra·ne·ous 〔ɪkˌstɛmpə'renɪəs; iksˌtempə'reinjəs〕 *adj.* ①無準備的；隨口說的；卽席的。an *extemporaneous* speech. 卽席演說。②一時的；臨時作成的。—**ly,** *adv.*

ex·tem·po·rar·i·ly 〔ɛk'stɛmpəˌrɛrɪlɪ; iks'tempərərili〕 *adv.* 臨時地；卽興地；隨口而出地。

ex·tem·po·rar·y 〔ɪk'stɛmpəˌrɛrɪ; iks'tempərəri〕 *adj.* =**extemporaneous.**

ex·tem·po·re 〔ɪk'stɛmpərɪ; ɛks'tempəri〕 *adv.* 臨時地；卽席地；無準備地。—*adj.* 卽席而講的；臨時作成的。

ex·tem·po·ri·za·tion 〔ɪkˌstɛmpərə'zeʃən; eksˌtempərai'zeiʃən〕 *n.* ①卽席作成。②卽席作成之事物。

ex·tem·po·rize 〔ɪk'stɛmpəˌraɪz; iks'tempəraiz〕 *v.*, **-rized, -riz·ing.** —*v.i.* 卽席演說；隨意演奏或演唱。to *extemporize* in verse. 卽席賦詩。—*v.t.* 臨時製作；卽席作成。

‡**ex·tend** 〔ɪk'stɛnd; iks'tend, e-〕 *v.t.* ①伸出。to *extend* your hand. 伸出你的手。②伸展；延長；擴大。to *extend* one's business. 擴大其營業。③致；施；給。to *extend* help to poor people. 幫助窮人。④(與反身代名詞連用)勉强。⑤加入他物以增加(某物之)分量。⑥展期；寬限。—*v.i.* ①伸延；延長。The road *extends* for miles and miles. 此路延展若干英里之遙。②伸出；突出。Fruit trees *extended* out over the farm fences. 果樹從農場圍牆伸出。

ex·tend·ed 〔ɪk'stɛndɪd; iks'tendid〕 *adj.* ①(在空間上或時間上)很長的。an *extended* tale. 很長的故事。②伸出的。③廣大的。④廣博的；廣泛的。an *extended* vocabulary. 廣博的字彙。

ex·ten·si·ble 〔ɪk'stɛnsəbl; iks'tensəbl〕 *adj.* 可伸展的；可擴張的。an *extensible* measuring rule. 曲尺。—**ex·ten·si·bil·i·ty,** *n.*

ex·ten·sile 〔ɛk'stɛnsɪl; eks'tensail〕 *adj.* ①〖動物, 解剖〗伸出的；可伸展的。②=**extensible.**

***ex·ten·sion** 〔ɪk'stɛnʃən; iks'tenʃən, eks-〕 *n.* ①延長；伸展；擴充。②增加之物。the *extension* of a railroad. 鐵路的支線。③大學補習部。*extension* courses. 大學補習部所開的課程。④範圍。the *extension* of the human mind. 人類智力的範圍。⑤〖物理〗塡充性；廣袤性。⑥〖生理, 外科〗牽引法；肢之伸張。⑦〖醫〗(病之)蔓延。⑧(電話)分機。⑨〖邏輯〗外延。"Plant" is a word with wider *extension*. "plant" 是個外延較廣大的字。

extension ladder 伸縮梯子。

extension table 兩端可拉開以增長桌面之桌；伸縮桌子。

extension telephone 電話分機。

ex·ten·si·ty 〔ɛk'stɛnsətɪ; iks'tensiti〕 *n.* ①廣闊性；擴張性。②範圍；大小。③〖心理〗形成空間感之感覺屬性；空間性。

***ex·ten·sive** 〔ɪk'stɛnsɪv; iks'tensiv, eks-〕 *adj.* ①廣闊的；廣博的；廣泛的。an *extensive* view. 廣闊的視野。②影響廣遠的。③大量的；大規模的。*Extensive* funds will be needed. 我們將需要大筆經費。④〖農〗疏種的。—**ly,** *adv.* —**ness,** *n.*

ex·ten·sor 〔ɪk'stɛnsɚ; iks'tensə〕 *n.* 〖解剖〗伸肌。

***ex·tent** 〔ɪk'stɛnt; iks'tent〕 *n.* ①程度；範圍。I agree with you to a certain *extent.* 我在某種程度內同意你。②廣闊；淵博。③〖邏輯〗外延(=extension ⑨)。

ex·ten·u·ate 〔ɪk'stɛnjʊˌet; eks'tenjueit〕 *v.t.*, **-at·ed, -at·ing.** ①使(罪過等)顯得輕微；使人原諒。Nothing can *extenuate* his guilt. 他的罪無法減輕。②減少；減弱。③爲…提供理由；爲…找藉口；爲…辯解。④〖古〗使細瘦；使弱。

ex·ten·u·a·tion 〔ɪkˌstɛnjʊ'eʃən; eksˌtenju'eiʃən〕 *n.* ①(過失、罪狀等的)減輕。②能減輕過失之事物；藉口。

ex·ten·u·a·to·ry 〔ɪk'stɛnjʊəˌtorɪ, -ˌtɔrɪ; eks'tenjuətəri, iks-〕 *adj.* 輕微的；可原諒的。

***ex·te·ri·or** 〔ɪk'stɪrɪɚ; eks'tiəriə〕 *n.*

①外部；外面；外表。a good man with a rough *exterior.* 外粗內秀的人。②(電影等之)外景；在野外拍製的電影。—*adj.* 外部的；外在的；外來的。

exterior angle 〖數學〗外角。

ex·te·ri·or·i·ty 〔ɛksˌtɪrɪ'ɑrətɪ; eksˌtiəri'ɔriti〕 *n., pl.* **-ties.** =**externality.**

ex·te·ri·or·ize 〔ɪk'stɪrɪəˌraɪz; eks'tiəriəraiz〕 *v.t.,* **-ized, -iz·ing.** =**externalize.**

ex·te·ri·or·ly 〔ɪk'stɪrɪəlɪ; iks'tiəriəli〕 *adv.* ①在外。②就外表而言；就外部而言。

ex·ter·mi·nate 〔ɪk'stɝməˌnet; iks'tə:mineit〕 *v.t.,* **-nat·ed, -nat·ing.** ①消滅。②消除。

ex·ter·mi·na·tion 〔ɪkˌstɝmə'neʃən; iksˌtə:mi'neiʃən〕 *n.* 消滅；根絕。

ex·ter·mi·na·tor 〔ɪk'stɝməˌnetɚ; eks'tə:mineitə〕 *n.* 消滅者；根除者；(尤指)以撲滅老鼠、蟑螂等害蟲爲業的人；殺蟲粉；驅蟲藥；老鼠藥。

ex·ter·mi·na·to·ry 〔ɪk'stɝmənəˌtorɪ; eks'tə:minətəri〕 *adj.* 消滅的；根除的；消滅性的。

ex·tern 〔'ɛkstɝn; eks'tə:n〕 *n.* 通勤者；通學生；非住院醫師。—*adj.* 〖詩〗外面的；外部的。

***ex·ter·nal** 〔ɪk'stɝnḷ; eks'tə:nḷ〕 *adj.* ①外部的。The *external* features of the building are very attractive. 該建築物的外觀很吸引人。②外用的。a lotion for *external* use only. 限於外用的藥水。③外來的。*external* stimuli. 外來的刺激。④外界的；客觀的。the *external* world.〖哲學〗外界(對精神世界言)。⑤外表的；形式上的。⑥國外的；有關國際關係的。⑦〖解剖〗外的；外側的。the *external* ear. 外耳。⑧〖數學〗外的。an *external* angle. 外角。⑨〖法律〗外證的。*external* evidence. 外證。—*n.*①外部；外面。②(*pl.*)外表；表面。—**ly,** *adv.*

ex·ter·nal·ism 〔ɛk'stɝnḷɪzm; eks'tə:nəlizəm〕 *n.*①形式主義。②〖哲學〗現象論。

ex·ter·nal·i·ty 〔ˌɛkstɚ'nælətɪ; ˌekstə:'næliti〕 *n., pl.* **-ties.** ①在外；在外性；客觀性。②外在之物；外形；外貌。③崇尚外表；拘泥虛禮。

ex·ter·nal·ize 〔ɪk'stɝnḷˌaɪz; eks'tə:nəlaiz〕 *v.t.,* **-ized, -iz·ing.** ①賦予形體；具體化。Language *externalizes* thought. 語言使思想具體化。②祇注重…之外表。③使趨於外向。to *externalize* the individual. 使個人趨於外向。—**ex·ter·nal·i·za·tion,** *n.*

ex·ter·ri·to·ri·al 〔ˌɛkstɛrə'torɪəl; 'eksˌteri'tɔ:riəl〕 *adj.* 治外法權的；享有治外法權者的。

ex·ter·ri·to·ri·al·i·ty 〔ɛksˌtɛrəˌtorɪ'ælətɪ; ˌeksˌteriˌtɔ:ri'æliti〕 *n.* 治外法權。

***ex·tinct** 〔ɪk'stɪŋkt; iks'tiŋkt〕 *adj.* ①滅種的；滅絕的。Many animals and birds are now *extinct.* 許多鳥獸現已絕種。②熄滅了的。③不再活動的。an *extinct* volcano. 死火山。④已亡故的。⑤已不風行的。a fashion long *extinct.* 久已不風行的時樣。⑥已失去原來面目的。

ex·tinc·tion 〔ɪk'stɪŋkʃən; iks'tiŋkʃən〕 *n.* ①熄滅。②撲滅。③消滅；毀滅。④絕滅；死滅。

ex·tinc·tive 〔ɪk'stɪŋktɪv; iks'tiŋktiv〕 *adj.* 消滅性的；消滅的。***extinctive prescription*** 〖法律〗消滅時效。

***ex·tin·guish** 〔ɪk'stɪŋgwɪʃ; iks'tiŋgwiʃ, eks-〕 *v.t.* ①熄滅；撲滅。to *extinguish* a light. 熄燈。②消滅；滅絕。③使暗淡無色；使減色。He was *extinguished* by his brother. 他的兄弟使他相形見絀(他的兄弟一切都比他好)。④使沉默。⑤使(所有權等)無效。—**a·ble,** *adj.* —**ment,** *n.*

ex·tin·guish·er 〔ɪk'stɪŋgwɪʃɚ; iks'tiŋgwiʃə〕 *n.* ①滅火器。②消滅者；消滅物。

ex·tir·pate 〔'ɛkstɚˌpet; 'ekstə:peit〕 *v.t.,* **-pat·ed, -pat·ing.** 拔除；連根拔起；根除；除盡；滅絕。to *extirpate* weeds (a social evil, a wrong belief). 除盡雜草(社會弊病、錯誤信仰)。

ex·tir·pa·tion 〔ˌɛkstɚ'peʃən; ˌekstə:'peiʃən〕 *n.* 拔除；剷除。

ex·tol, ex·toll 〔ɪk'stɑl; iks'tɔl〕 *v.t.,* **-tolled, -tol·ling.** 頌揚；極口稱讚。***extol one to the skies*** 把某人捧上天。

ex·tort 〔ɪk'stɔrt; iks'tɔ:t〕 *v.t.* ①勒索；敲詐。to *extort* money from a person. 向某人勒索錢財。②强索；逼(供)。He *extorted* a promise from me. 他硬要我答應。③(對某字或某事)牽强附會。

ex·tor·tion 〔ɪk'stɔrʃən; iks'tɔ:ʃən〕 *n.* ①强取；勒索。②强取或勒索之財物、保證等。③〖法律〗假借職務勒索罪。

ex·tor·tion·ate 〔ɪk'stɔrʃənɪt; iks'tɔ:ʃənit〕 *adj.* ①勒索的；敲詐性的。②過高的；太大的。an *extortionate* price. 過高的價格。(亦作 **extortionary**)

ex·tor·tion·er 〔ɪk'stɔrʃənɚ, ɛk-; iks'tɔ:ʃənə, eks-〕 *n.* 强取者；勒索者。(亦作 **extortionist**)

***ex·tra** 〔'ɛkstrə, -trɪ; 'ekstrə〕 *adj.* ①額外的；特別的。②不包括在價目內的。Room service is *extra.* 房價不含小費。③特佳的。*extra* quality. 特佳的品質。—*n.* ①額外的事物或人員。Your boarding is an *extra.* 膳費在外。②〖美〗(報紙的)號外。③特級品。This hi-fi set is a real *extra.* 這部高度傳眞收音機是眞正的特級品。—*adv.* 格外地。

extra- 〖字首〗表"在外；外面；此外"之義。

***ex·tract** 〔*v.* ɪk'strækt; iks'trækt, eks- *n.* 'ɛkstrækt; 'ekstrækt〕 *v.t.* ①拔取；摘取；抽出。He *extracted* a letter from his pocket. 他從口袋中掏出一封信。②得到。③榨取；吸取。We can *extract* oil from olive. 我們可自橄欖中榨油。④選取；摘錄。to *extract* examples from a grammar book. 從文法書上摘錄例子。⑤〖數學〗開方。⑥推論。to *extract* a principle from a collection of facts. 從一堆事實中推理出一原則。—*n.* ①摘取物；選粹。②濃縮物；濃汁；精；素。beef *extract.* 濃縮牛肉汁。〖注意〗**extract**和**extort**均作拔取、榨取解。extract着重於"用力拔出使之鬆動"。extort 則指"强向某人索取彼所不願給予之物"。

ex·tract·a·ble 〔ɪk'stræktəbḷ, ɛk-; iks'træktəbl〕 *adj.* 可拔取的；可榨取的；可抽出的；可選取的。(亦作 **extractible**)

ex·trac·tion 〔ɪk'strækʃən, ɛk-; iks'trækʃən, eks-〕 *n.* ①拔出；摘出。the *extraction* of a tooth. 牙齒之拔出。②煎出；提鍊。③拔出物；摘出品；精萃。④血統；家世；祖系。people of humble *extraction.* 貧寒家世的人們。⑤(穀類磨粉時之)成粉率。

ex·trac·tive 〔ɪk'stræktɪv, ɛk-; iks'træktiv〕 *adj.* ①可拔取的；可選取的。②蒸餾的；煎汁的；拔萃的。*extractive* processes. 提鍊過程。—*n.* 拔取物；提出物；煎汁；精華。

ex·trac·tor 〔ɛk'stræktɚ; iks'træktə〕

n. ①拔取者；抽出者。②抽出裝置；抽出器。an oil *extractor.* 抽油器。③選取者；摘錄者。④(槍砲等之)退彈器。⑤〖外科〗萃取器；取出器；鉗子。

ex·tra·cur·ric·u·lar 〔ˏɛkstrəkəˈrɪkjələ; ˌekstrəkəˈrikjulə〕 *adj.* ①課外的；課程以外的。 *extracurricular* activities. 課外活動。②業餘的。③本分以外的。(亦作 **extracurriculum**)

ex·tra·dit·a·ble 〔ˈɛkstrəˏdaɪtəbl; ˈekstrədaitəbl〕 *adj.* 可引渡的；可送還的；可引渡逃犯的。an *extraditable* criminal. 可引渡的罪犯。

ex·tra·dite 〔ˈɛkstrəˏdaɪt; ˈekstrədait〕 *v.t.*, **-dit·ed, -dit·ing.** ①引渡(逃犯)。②獲得(逃犯)之引渡。

ex·tra·di·tion 〔ˏɛkstrəˈdɪʃən; ˌekstrəˈdiʃən〕 *n.* 引渡逃犯。an *extradition* treaty. 引渡條約。

ex·tra·dos 〔ɛkˈstredɑs; eksˈtreidɔs〕 *n.*, *pl.* **-dos, -dos·es.** 〖建築〗拱背；外弧線。

ex·tra·es·sen·tial 〔ˈɛkstrɪəˈsɛnʃəl; ˈekstrəiˈsenʃəl〕 *adj.* 非主要的；本質以外的。

ex·tra·ju·di·cial 〔ˏɛkstrədʒuˈdɪʃəl; ˈekstrədʒu(ː)ˈdiʃəl〕 *adj.* ①法院以外的；法院管轄以外的。②裁判外的；裁判權以外的。③未照法定程序的。(亦作 **extrajural**)

ex·tra·le·gal 〔ˏɛkstrəˈligl; ˌekstrəˈliːgəl〕 *adj.* 超出法律管轄範圍的。

ex·tral·i·ty 〔ɛksˈtrælətɪ; eksˈtræliti〕 *n.* 治外法權(=extraterritoriality)。

ex·tra·mar·i·tal 〔ˏɛkstrəˈmærətl; ˌekstrəˈmæritəl〕 *adj.* 婚姻外的(性經驗等)。

ex·tra·mun·dane 〔ˏɛkstrəˈmʌnden; ˌekstrəˈmʌndein〕 *adj.* 超越現世的；物質界以外的。

ex·tra·mu·ral 〔ˏɛkstrəˈmjurəl; ˈekstrəˈmjuərəl〕 *adj.* ①城鎮以外的；城牆外的。②大學校牆外的；校外的。*extramural* classes. 大學(對校外人士提供)之公開課程。③校際的(比賽等)。*extramural* athletics. 校際運動競賽。④醫院外的。⑤閨房外的；不貞的。a husband's *extramural* affair. 丈夫的拈花惹草。

ex·tra·ne·ous 〔ɪkˈstrenɪəs; eksˈtreinjəs〕 *adj.* ①外來的。*extraneous* aid. 外來援助。②體外的。③無關係的。*extraneous* to the subject. 無關本題的。

ex·tra·of·fi·cial 〔ˏɛkstrɪəˈfɪʃəl; ˌekstrəəˈfiʃəl〕 *adj.* 職務外的；職權外的。

***ex·traor·di·nar·y** 〔ɪkˈstrɔrdn̩ˏɛrɪ, ˏɛkstrəˈɔr–; iksˈtrɔːdnri, ˌekstrəˈɔː–〕 *adj.* ①非常的；特別的；驚人的。He is a man of *extraordinary* strength. 他是一個具有驚人力氣的人。②特任的；特命的。an envoy *extraordinary.* 特使。③臨時的；額外的。—**ex·traor·di·nar·i·ly,** *adv.* —**ex·traor·di·nar·i·ness,** *n.*

ex·trap·o·late 〔ɪksˈtræpəˏlet; eksˈtræpəleit〕 *v.t.* ①延伸。②推延。③推測。

ex·tra·po·la·tion 〔ɛkˏstræpoˈleʃən; ˌekstrəpouˈleiʃən〕 *n.* ①延伸；推延；推測。②〖統計〗外推法。

ex·tra·sen·so·ry 〔ˏɛkstrəˈsɛnsərɪ; ˌekstrəˈsensəri〕 *adj.* 超感覺的。***extrasensory perception*** 〖心理〗超感覺力。

ex·tra·ter·res·tri·al 〔ˏɛkstrətəˈrɛstrɪəl; ˌekstrətiˈrestriəl〕 *adj.* 地球以外的。

ex·tra·ter·ri·to·ri·al·i·ty 〔ˏɛkstrəˏtɛrəˏtorɪˈælətɪ; ˈekstrəˌteriˌtɔːriˈæliti〕 *n.* 治外法權。—**ex·tra·ter·ri·to·ri·al,** *adj.*

***ex·trav·a·gance** 〔ɪkˈstrævəgəns; iksˈtrævigəns〕 *n.* ①揮霍無度；奢侈；浪費。His *extravagance* kept him always in debt. 他的揮霍無度使他常常負債。②過度。③放縱。to live in idle *extravagance.* 生活在懶散放縱之中。④昂貴的事物；奢侈品。(亦作 **extravagancy**)

***ex·trav·a·gant** 〔ɪkˈstrævəgənt; iksˈtrævigənt〕 *adj.* ①奢侈的；浪費的；放縱的。to be *extravagant* in living. 生活奢侈。②過度的。③茂盛的。a tropical island with *extravagant* vegetation. 植物茂盛的熱帶島嶼。—**ly,** *adv.*

ex·trav·a·gan·za 〔ɪkˏstrævəˈgænzə, ɛk–; eksˌtrævəˈgænzə〕 *n.* ①狂妄之藝術作品(如樂曲、喜劇等)；狂詩；狂文；幻想曲；鬧劇。②狂言；癡想。③盛典；盛事。④豪華飾物。

ex·trav·a·sate 〔ɛkˈstrævəˏset; eksˈtrævəseit〕 *v.*, **-sat·ed, -sat·ing.** —*v.t.* ①〖醫〗放(血)。②〖地質〗噴出(岩漿等)。—*v.i.* ①〖醫〗自血管溢出；外滲。②〖地質〗噴出岩漿。

ex·trav·a·sa·tion 〔ɛkˏstrævəˈseʃən; ekˌstrævəˈseiʃən〕 *n.* 溢出；流出；噴出。

ex·tra·ve·hic·u·lar 〔ˏɛkstrəviˈhɪkjələ; ˌekstrəviˈhikjulə〕 *adj.* 宇宙飛船(或座艙)外的。

ex·treme** 〔ɪkˈstrim; iksˈtriːm, eks–〕 *adj.*, **-trem·er, -trem·est,** *n.* —*adj.* ①盡頭的；最遠的。the *extreme* border. 極遠的邊界。②極早的或極晚的。③最高的；最大的。*extreme* patience (kindness, love). 極度的耐心(慈悲、愛)。④極端的；偏激的。the *extreme* left. 極左分子。⑤極度嚴厲的。⑥最後的。—*n.* ①極端之事；完全相反之事物。Love and hate are two *extremes* of feeling. 愛與恨乃感情中兩完全相反的狀態。②極端。It's annoying in the *extreme.* 討厭之極。③〖數學〗(比例的)外項；第一及第四項。go to extremes*** 走極端。〖注意〗**extreme** 之比較級及最高級有兩種，一爲 extremer 與 extremest. 一爲 more extreme 與 most extreme. 兩者中，後者較爲常用。—**ness,** *n.*

***ex·treme·ly** 〔ɪkˈstrimlɪ; iksˈtriːmli, eks–〕 *adv.* 極端地；非常地。It is *extremely* good (*or* kind) of you to invite me. 承你邀請我，實在太客氣了。

ex·trem·ism 〔ɪkˈstrimɪzəm; iksˈtriːmizəm〕 *n.* ①極端性。②極端主義；過激主義。

ex·trem·ist 〔ɪkˈstrimɪst, ɛk–; iksˈtriːmist, eks–〕 *n.* 走極端者；極端主義者；急進黨人。—*adj.* 極端主義者的；急進黨人的。

***ex·trem·i·ty** 〔ɪkˈstrɛmətɪ; iksˈtremiti, eks–〕 *n.*, *pl.* **-ties.** ①末端；極點。②極度；極限。in the *extremity* of hunger. 在極度饑餓中。③窮境。I hope you will help them in their *extremity.* 我希望你能幫助陷於極端窮困的他們。④極端的手段；激烈的行爲。to resort to *extremities.* 採極端的手段。⑤極端性。⑥(*pl.*)手足；四肢。circulation of blood in the *extremities.* 四肢的血液循環。

ex·tri·ca·ble 〔ˈɛkstrɪkəbl; ˈekstrikəbl〕 *adj.* 可救出的；可解脫的。

ex·tri·cate 〔ˈɛkstrɪˏket; ˈekstrikeit〕 *v.t.*, **-cat·ed, -cat·ing.** ①解脫；救出。to *extricate* oneself from difficulties. 使自己從困難中解脫出來。②〖化〗使(氣體等)游

離;放出。③分辨出來。—**ex·tri·ca·tion,** *n.*

ex·trin·sic 〔ɛk'strɪnsɪk; eks'trinsik〕 *adj.* ①非固有的; 不緊要的。That's something *extrinsic* to the subject. 那事對這問題並不緊要。②外來的; 外界的; 附帶的。*extrinsic value* 〖經濟〗外在價值。

ex·trin·si·cal 〔ɛk'strɪnsɪkḷ; eks'trinsikəl〕 *adj.* =**extrinsic.** —**ly,** *adv.* —**ness,** —**i·ty,** *n.*

ex·trorse 〔ɛk'strɔrs; eks'trɔ:s〕 *adj.* 〖植物〗外向的; 向軸外的。

ex·tro·ver·sion 〔ˌɛkstro'vɝʃən; ˌekstrou'və:ʃən〕 *n.* ①〖心理〗外傾; 外傾性。②〖醫〗外翻。③外向。(亦作 **extraversion**)

ex·tro·vert 〔'ɛkstroˌvɝt; 'ekstrouvə:t〕 *n.* (亦作 **extravert**) 喜活動而不喜思想之人; 外傾之人。—*adj.* 個性外傾的。—*v.t.* 使(思想等)外傾; 使外向。

ex·trude 〔ɪk'strud; eks'tru:d〕 *v.,* **ex·trud·ed, ex·trud·ing.** —*v.t.* ①逼出; 擠出。②逐出。—*v.i.* ①突出。②被擠出。③被壓製。

ex·tru·sion 〔ɪk'struʒən; eks'tru:ʒən〕 *n.* ①擠出; 壓出。②被擠出或壓出之物。③噴出地面之岩漿或其他火山之物質。

ex·tru·sive 〔ɪk'strusɪv; eks'tru:siv〕 *adj.* 〖地質〗由地中流出的。

ex·u·ber·ance 〔ɪg'zjubərəns; ig'zju:bərəns〕 *n.* 茂盛; 豐富; 充溢。(亦作 **exuberancy**)

ex·u·ber·ant 〔ɪg'zjubərənt, -'zu-; ig'zju:bərənt〕 *adj.* ①繁茂的; 茂盛的。②豐富的; 充溢的; 充滿活力的。children in *exuberant* spirits. 精神充溢的孩子。—**ly,** *adv.* —**ness,** *n.*

ex·u·ber·ate 〔ɛg'zjubəˌret, -'zu-, ɪg-; ig'zju:bəreit, eg-〕 *v.i.,* **-at·ed, -at·ing.** ①充溢; 繁茂。②顯得精神飽滿; 顯得熱情洋溢。an actor who knows how to *exuberate.* 知道如何表現得熱情洋溢的演員。

ex·u·da·tion 〔ˌɛksju'deʃən; ˌeksju:'deiʃən〕 *n.* ①滲出; 發出。②滲出物; 流出物; 汗水。

ex·ude 〔ɪg'zjud, -'zud, ɪk'sjud, -'sud; ig'zju:d, ek's-, eg'z-〕 *v.t. & v.i.,* **-ud·ed, -ud·ing.** ①滲出; 流出。to *exude* sweat. 流汗。②滲出。Some successful men *exude* self-confidence. 有些成功的人流露出自信。

ex·ult 〔ɪg'zʌlt; ig'zʌlt〕 *v.i.* 歡騰; 狂歡; 大喜。to *exult* in a victory. 因勝利而歡騰。—*v.t.* 使高興。

ex·ult·an·cy 〔ɪg'zʌltṇsɪ, ɛg-; ig'zʌltənsi, eg-〕 *n.* =**exultation.**

ex·ult·ant 〔ɪg'zʌltṇt, ɛg-; ig'zʌltənt, eg-〕 *adj.* 歡騰的; 狂歡的; 大喜的。He gave an *exultant* shout. 他發出狂歡的呼喊。—**ly,** *adv.*

ex·ul·ta·tion 〔ˌɛgzʌl'teʃən, ˌɛksʌl-; ˌegzʌl'teiʃən, ˌeksʌl-〕 *n.* 狂歡; 大喜; 歡騰。

ex·urb 〔'ɛksɝb; 'eksə:b〕 *n.* 市郊之外。the city, the suburbs, and the *exurbs.* 市區、市郊以及市郊之外。—**an,** *adj.*

ex·ur·ban·ite 〔ɛk'sɝbənˌaɪt; ek'sə:bənait〕 *n.* 住於市郊之外者; 半鄉半城的居民。

ex·u·vi·ae 〔ɪg'zjuvɪˌi; ig'zju:vii:〕 *n. pl.* 動物脫落之皮、甲殼等; (蛇之)蛻皮; (蟬、蟹等之)脫殼。—**ex·u·vi·al,** *adj.*

ex·u·vi·ate 〔ɛg'zjuvɪˌet; ig'zju:vieit, eg-〕 *v.t. & v.i.,* **-at·ed, -at·ing.** 蛻(皮); 脫(殼); 脫落(羽毛)。—**ex·u·vi·a·tion,** *n.*

-ey 〖字尾〗 **-y** 之異體。

ey·as 〔'aɪəs; 'aiəs〕 *n.* ①小鷹; 鷹仔。②巢中之鶵。

‡**eye** 〔aɪ; ai〕 *n., v.,* **eyed, ey·ing** or **eye·ing,** *interj.* —*n.* ①眼睛。We see with our *eyes.* 我們用眼看。②眼珠。a girl with blue *eyes.* 藍眼的女孩子。③眼眶。The blow gave him a black *eye.* 那一擊把他的眼眶打青了。④對光有反應的器官。⑤視力。to have sharp *eyes.* 視力極佳。⑥精細的辨別力或判斷力。to have an *eye* in one's head. 有判斷力。⑦眼光; 看。The boy was peering through the window with an eager *eye.* 那男孩以渴望的眼光自窗戶窺視。⑧嚴密的監視。under the *eyes* of. 在…監視下。⑨意見; 判斷; 觀點。Stealing is a crime in the *eye* of the law. 就法律觀點而言, 偷竊即犯罪。⑩眼狀物(如針孔等)。⑪颱風中心; 颱風眼; 風的中心。the *eye* of the storm. 暴風中心。⑫〖俚〗偵探。a private *eye.* 私家偵探。***an eye for an eye*** 以牙還牙; 以眼還眼。***be all eyes*** 極欲看到; 極注意。***close one's eyes to*** 拒絕看; 拒絕考慮。***give an eye to*** 照顧。***give the eye to*** 向…眉目傳情。***have an eye for*** 能夠瞭解。***have an eye to*** 着眼於。***have in one's eye*** 在心中想。I *have* one particular friend *in my eye* at this moment. 我現在正想着一個朋友。***in a pig's eye*** 〖俚〗決不; 絕對不。***in the public eye*** **a.** 常公開出現的。**b.** 衆所周知的。***keep an eye on*** 注意; 留意看。***keep an eye out for*** 密切注意。***keep one's eyes open*** 提高警覺。***make a person open his eyes*** 使之驚異。***make eyes at*** 眉目傳情。***mind one's eye*** 注意。*Mind your eye.* 你要注意。***open one's eyes to*** 使之注意。***pipe one's eye*** 哭泣。***run one's eyes over*** 迅速地閱覽或檢查。***see eye to eye*** 完全同意。We *see eye to eye* in everything we do. 我們無論做甚麼事意見完全相同。***see something with half an eye*** 極容易地瞭解某事; 一目了然。***set eyes on*** 瞧; 看。***shut one's eyes to*** 不管; 不理。***throw eyes*** (or ***the eye***) ***at*** 向…眉目傳情。***to the eye*** 表面上看起來。These problems are *to the eye* rather complex. 這些問題在表面上看起來相當複雜。***under one's eye*** 在某人面前。***up to the eyes in*** 深陷於…之中。***with an eye to*** 爲了(某目的)。I entered *with an eye to* saving him. 我爲了救他而進入。***with one's eyes open*** 瞭解…之危險或不利。—*v.t.* 看; 注視。to *eye* a person with suspicion. 懷疑地看着一個人。—*interj.* 表"反對""驚訝"之聲。Oh, my *eye!* 啊呀! 啊喲!

eye appeal 對視覺之吸引力。

eye·ball 〔'aɪˌbɔl; 'aibɔ:l〕 *n.* 眼球。—*v.t.* 〖俚〗注視。***eyeball to eyeball*** 〖俚〗直接衝突。

eye bank 眼庫。

eye bath 〖英〗=**eyecup.**

eye·bright 〔'aɪˌbraɪt; 'aibrait〕 *n.* 〖植物〗小米草(昔日用以療目疾)。

***eye·brow** 〔'aɪˌbrau; 'aibrau〕 *n.* 眉毛。

eyebrow pencil 眉筆。

eye catcher 〖俗〗引人注意之物。(亦作 **eye-catcher**)

eye chart 視力檢查表。

eye·cup 〔'aɪˌkʌp; 'aikʌp〕 *n.* 洗眼杯; 洗眼器。

eyed 〔aɪd; aid〕 *adj.* 有眼的。

eye·drop 〔'aɪˌdrɑp; 'ai-drɔp〕 *n.* 眼淚。

eye·drop·per 〔'aɪˌdrɑpɚ; 'aiˌdrɔpə〕

n. 眼藥水滴管。

eye·ful [ˈaɪˌful; ˈaiful] *n.* ①一眼之容量;滿眼。②一瞥見及之量。③〖俚〗顯眼或奇特的人或物(尤指美麗女郎)。***get an eyeful***〖俗〗**a.** 仔細看。**b.** 看有趣之物。

eye·glass [ˈaɪˌglæs; ˈaiglɑːs] *n.* ①(一片)眼鏡;單眼鏡。②洗眼杯。③(望遠鏡等之)接目鏡。④(*pl.*)一副眼鏡。

eye·hole [ˈaɪˌhol; ˈaihoul] *n.* ①眼窩。②視孔;窺視之孔。③=**eyelet.**

eye·lash [ˈaɪˌlæʃ; ˈailæʃ] *n.* 睫毛。

eye·less [ˈaɪlɪs; ˈailis] *adj.* ①無眼的。②瞎的;失明的。③無眼光的。an *eyeless* leader. 無眼光的領袖。④無針孔的。

eye·let [ˈaɪlɪt; ˈailit] *n.* ①眼孔;小孔(尤指穿帶子者)。②(嵌於孔眼之)小金屬圈;氣眼。③(牆上或面罩上的)視孔。—*v.t.* 開眼孔;裝氣眼。

eye·let·eer [ˌaɪlɪˈtɪr; ˌailiˈtiə] *n.* 穿小孔用的鑽。

***eye·lid** [ˈaɪˌlɪd; ˈailid] *n.* 眼瞼;眼皮。

eye·lin·er [ˈaɪˌlaɪnɚ; ˈaiˌlainə] *n.* 眼線筆;眼線膏。

eye·mind·ed [ˈaɪˈmaɪndɪd; ˈaiˈmain-did] *adj.* 視覺特別敏銳的;視覺記憶特强的。

eye opener ①〖美〗令人眼開之新奇或美麗事物。She was a real *eye opener.* 她的確是個令人眼開的美人。②令人恍然大悟之事;有啓發作用的事物。③〖俚〗一次所飲之酒(尤指清晨所飲者)。

eye-o·pen·ing [ˈaɪˌopənɪŋ; ˈaiˌoupə-niŋ] *adj.* 啓廸的;振聾發聵的;揭露的。

eye·piece [ˈaɪˌpis; ˈai-piːs] *n.* (望遠鏡、顯微鏡等之)接目鏡。

eye·reach [ˈaɪˌritʃ; ˈairiːtʃ] *n.* 視界;視域;視野。

eye·serv·ant [ˈaɪˌsɝvənt; ˈaiˌsəːvənt] *n.* 陽奉陰違的僕人;當有人看到時才做事的人。(亦作 **eyeserver**)

eye·serv·ice [ˈaɪˌsɝvɪs; ˈaiˌsəːvis] *n.* ①陽奉陰違的工作。②讚美之眼色或神情。

eye·shade [ˈaɪˌʃed; ˈai-ʃeid] *n.* ①護眼用的(半)透明鴨舌帽簷。② =**eye shadow.**

eye shadow (婦女化妝用之)眼影。

eye·shot [ˈaɪˌʃɑt; ˈai-ʃɔt] *n.* 視界;視野。

eye·sight [ˈaɪˌsaɪt; ˈai-sait] *n.* ①視力;目力。②視界。③見;見到。

eyes left〖軍、口令〗(一種行進間之敬禮)向左看!

eye socket 眼眶。

eye·sore [ˈaɪˌsor; ˈai-sɔː] *n.* 難看的東西;礙眼的東西。

eye splice (繩之)環眼結。

eye·spot [ˈaɪˌspɑt; ˈai-spɔt] *n.* ①(無脊椎動物之)視覺器官。②眼狀之斑點(如孔雀之尾羽上者)。

eyes right〖軍、口令〗(一種行進間之敬禮)向右看!

eye·stalk [ˈaɪˌstɔk; ˈai-stɔːk] *n.*〖動物〗(蝦等之)眼柄。

eye·strain [ˈaɪˌstren; ˈai-strein] *n.* (由久視等而生之)眼疲倦感覺;眼睛疲勞。

eye·strings [ˈaɪˌstrɪŋz; ˈai-striŋz] *n. pl.* 眼肌、眼筋或眼神經。

eye·tooth [ˈaɪˌtuθ; ˈai-tuːθ] *n., pl.* **-teeth.** 犬齒;上尖牙;上犬牙。***cut one's eye-tooth*** **a.** 年事漸長;世故漸深。**b.** (= cut one's eyeteeth on) 獲得第一次經驗;初次登臺獻藝。***draw one's eyetooth*** 挫某人之驕氣。***give one's eyeteeth for*** 極願。

eye·wash [ˈaɪˌwɑʃ; ˈaiwɔʃ] *n.* ①洗眼水 (=eyewater). ②無稽之談。③言不由衷之談;阿諛。

eye·wink [ˈaɪˌwɪŋk; ˈaiwiŋk] *n.* ①瞬眼;霎眼。②一瞥。

eye·wink·er [ˈaɪˌwɪŋkɚ; ˈaiˌwiŋkə] *n.* ①睫毛 (=eyelash). ②引起霎眼之物。

eye·wit·ness [ˈaɪˈwɪtnɪs; ˈaiˈwitnis] *n.* 目擊者;見證人。—*v.t.* 親眼看到。

ey·ot [ˈaɪət, et; eit, ˈeiət] *n.*〖英方〗小島。

eyre [ɛr; ɛə] *n.*〖英史〗巡廻;巡廻法院。

ey·rie, ey·ry [ˈɛrɪ; ˈaiəri] *n.* =**aerie.**

Ez., Ezr. Ezra. **Ezek.** Ezekiel.

E·ze·ki·el [ɪˈzikɪəl; iˈziːkjəl] *n.*〖聖經〗①以西結(紀元前六世紀時之希伯來先知)。②以西結書(舊約之一卷)。③男子名。

Ez·ra [ˈɛzrə; ˈezrə] *n.*〖聖經〗①以斯拉(紀元前五世紀時之希伯來預言家)。②以斯拉書(舊約之一卷)。

F

F or **f** [ɛf; ef] *n., pl.* **F's** or **f's** [ɛfs; efs]. ①英文字母之第六個字母。②〖音樂〗C 長調的第四音。

F〖化〗(亦作 **Fl**)氟 (=fluorine). **F.** ①Fahrenheit. ②February. ③French. ④Friday. **f.** ①female. ②feminine. ③forte. ④franc. ⑤farthing. ⑥following.

fa [fɑ; fɑː] *n.*〖音樂〗全音階之長音階的第四音。

FA, F.A. ①Field Artillery. ②Football Association. ③Fine Arts. ④freight agent. **f.a.a.** free of all average.

Fa·bi·an [ˈfebɪən; ˈfeibjən] *adj.* ①使用延宕方式以達目標的;謹慎的;遲緩的。②Fabian Society 的。***Fabian Society*** 費邊學社(主張以和平緩進手段實現社會主義, 1884 年創立於英國)。—*n.* 費邊學社會員。

Fa·bi·an·ism [ˈfebɪənˌɪzəm; ˈfeibjə-nizəm] *n.* 費邊主義。

Fa·bi·an·ist [ˈfebɪənɪst; ˈfeibiənist] *n.* =**Fabian.**

***fa·ble** [ˈfebḷ; ˈfeibl] *n., v.,* **-bled, -bling.** —*n.* ①寓言。②無稽之談。③傳說;神話。We may take the story of Job for a history or a *fable.* 我們可以把約伯的故事當做歷史或傳說。④人人所談及的人或事。He became the chief *fable* of the village. 他變成了村裏之主要話題。⑤無實在性之事物。—*v.i.* 寫或說寓言;說謊。—*v.t.* 傳說。It is *fabled* that Norsemen built the tower. 相傳古代斯堪的那維亞人建了那座塔。

fa·bled [ˈfebḷd; ˈfeibld] *adj.* ①寓言中的;傳說的;神話的。②虛構的;子虛的。

fab·li·au [ˈfæblɪo; ˈfæbliou] *n., pl.* **-aux** [-oz; -ouz]. 故事詩(十二、三世紀起於法國)。

Fa·bre [ˈfɑbɚ; ˈfɑːbə] *n.* 法布爾 (Jean Henri, 1823–1915, 法國昆蟲學家及著作家)。

***fab·ric** [ˈfæbrɪk; ˈfæbrik] *n.* ①布;織物。woolen (silk) *fabric.* 毛(絲)織物。②(編織物之)質地或紋理。③結構。Unwise loans weakened the financial *fabric* of the bank. 不穩妥的貸款削弱了這銀行的金融基礎。④建築材料。The usual *fabric* was timber. 通常的建築材料是木材。⑤建築物。⑥建築方法。⑦建築(之動作)。

fab·ri·cant [ˈfæbrəkənt; ˈfæbrikənt] *n.* 製造者。

fab·ri·cate [ˈfæbrɪˌket; ˈfæbrikeit] *v.t.,* **-cat·ed, -cat·ing.** ①建造;製造;裝配。②捏造;僞造。③創造。—**fab·ri·ca·tor,** *n.*

fab·ri·ca·tion [ˌfæbrɪˈkeʃən; ˌfæbriˈkeiʃən] *n.* ①建造;製造;構造。②捏造。③虛構之物;謊言;捏造的托詞。

fab·ri·koid [ˈfæbrɪˌkɔɪd; ˈfæbrikɔid] *n.* ①一種防雨布。②(F-)該種防雨布之商標名。

fab·u·list [ˈfæbjəlɪst; ˈfæbjulist] *n.* ①寓言家;編寓言者。②說謊者。

fab·u·los·i·ty [ˌfæbjəˈlɑsətɪ; ˌfæbjuˈlɔsiti] *n.* ①〖罕〗述說寓言之嗜好。②寓言;杜撰的故事。

fab·u·lous [ˈfæbjələs; ˈfæbjuləs] *adj.* ①神話中的;想像的;寓言的。The phoenix is a *fabulous* bird. 長生鳥是一種想像的鳥。②難以置信的;驚人的。③神話似的。**—ness,** *n.*

fabulous age 一個國家開國初期之神話時代。

fab·u·lous·ly [ˈfæbjələslɪ; ˈfæbjuləsli] *adv.* 非常地;令人驚訝地。

fac. ①facsimile. ②factor. ③factory. ④faculty.

fa·çade, fa·cade [fəˈsɑd, fæˈsɑd; fəˈsɑːd] 〖法〗 *n.* ①〖建築〗建築物的正面。②虛僞、浮面或做作的外表。*—v.t.* 裝飾…之正面;裝飾…之外表。

:face [feis; fes] *n., v.,* **faced, fac·ing.** *—n.* ①面部;臉。The eyes, nose, and mouth are parts of the *face.* 眼、鼻和口都是臉上的部分。②面容;表情。Her *face* was sad. 她的面容是悲傷的。③表面。④正面;前面。⑤大膽;厚顏。⑥尊嚴;面子。*Face* is very important to Oriental peoples. 東方人很講面子。⑦票面價值。⑧外表。The whole village presented a *face* of placid contentment. 全莊呈現一片寧靜而滿足的外表。⑨面具。The children bought some funny *faces* for the party. 孩子們爲晚會買了一些滑稽的面具。⑩面部化妝。She will be here as soon as she gets her *face* on. 她化妝好就會來。***be unable to look someone in the face*** 不敢正視某人(感到慚愧)。***face to face*** 面對面。We sent for the man to accuse him *face to face.* 我們喚那人來當面指控他。***fly in the face of*** 公開反抗;詆毁。***in*** (***the***) ***face of*** 面臨。He remained calm even *in the face of* dangers. 就是面臨危險,他也鎮定自若。***in one's face*** **a.** 正對着。The sun was shining *in our faces.* 太陽光正對着我們照射。**b.** 公開地。She'll only laugh *in your face* if you say that. 如果你說那件事的話,祇落得她當面笑你而已。***keep a straight face*** 不露笑容。***look someone in the face*** 直視某人。***lose face*** 失面子;丢臉。***make a face*** 做厭惡的表情。***make faces at*** 扮鬼臉。Instead of eating, the two children sat at the table *making faces at* each other. 孩子們坐在桌旁,不吃東西,儘扮鬼臉。***on the face of*** 就表面看。*On the face of* it the document seemed genuine. 就表面看來,這文件像是眞的。***pull*** (***make,*** or ***wear***) ***a long face*** 拉長臉;不高興。***put a bold*** (or ***good***) ***face on something*** 使面目一新;面對某事物顯出勇氣;大膽去幹。***put a new face on*** 使改觀。That *puts* an entirely *new face on* the matter. 那使這問題整個改觀了。***put on a bold face*** 假裝不在乎。***save one's face*** 挽回面子。***set one's face against*** 反對。***show one's face*** 露面。If you ever *show your face* around here again, I'll throw you out bodily. 如果你敢再在這一帶露面,我要把你整個地擲出去。***to one's face*** 當着一個人的面。I dare you to say those same things *to his face.* 我看你敢不敢當着他的面說這同樣的話。*—v.t.* ①朝;向;臨。The house *faces* the street. 該屋面朝街。②面對;對付。A crisis *faced* us. 一項危機面臨着我們。③覆蓋。a wooden house *faced* with brick. 表面覆蓋着磚之木房。④使(隊伍)轉向。The captain *faced* his company to the left. 上尉令他的連向左轉。⑤使面對。We are *faced* with the same problem. 我們遭遇到同樣的問題。⑥將(水果、青菜等)排放容器內使露出同一面。Berries are much more salable when neatly *faced.* 漿果如整齊陳列則比較有人買。⑦將(撲克牌)翻過來使牌面朝上。⑧將(石的)表面鑿光滑。*—v.i.* ①將臉轉向。She quickly *faced* to her right. 她迅速地將臉轉向右邊。②朝某一方向。The house *faced* south. 房子朝南。***About face!*** 〖軍〗向後轉! ***face down*** = **browbeat.** ***face out*** 堅持到底。He is determined to *face out* the situation. 他決心堅持到底。***face the music*** 勇敢地面對艱難困苦。He had made a mistake and now had to *face the music.* 他曾犯了錯誤而今他必須勇敢地面對艱苦。***face up to*** **a.** 勇敢面對。He was forced to *face up to* the situation. 他只好勇敢地面對那情況。**b.** 承認。***Left*** (***Right***) ***face!*** 〖軍〗向左(右)轉!

face-ache [ˈfesˌek; ˈfeis-eik] *n.* 面部神經痛。

face card 繪有人面之紙牌(如 King, Queen 及 Jack 等)。

face·cloth [ˈfesˌklɔθ; ˈfeis-klɔːθ] *n.* 面巾;洗臉毛巾。

face·down [ˈfesˌdaun; ˈfeisdaun] *n.* 〖美〗敵對雙方之對峙。

face guard (工廠工人或鬥劍者所戴之)護面罩。

face-hard·en [ˈfesˌhɑrdn̩; ˈfeisˌhɑːdn] *v.t.* (冷卻或鑄造)使金屬表面堅硬。

face·less [ˈfeslɪs; ˈfeislis] *adj.* ①無面的;無臉的。②無個人特性的;無法辨認的。③隱名的;不知名的。

face-lift [ˈfesˌlɪft; ˈfeis-lift] *v.t.* ①爲(建築物、汽車等)作外觀上的改善。②作面部整形手術。*—n.* =**face lifting.**

face lifting ①整形美容術。②外觀上之改善。(亦作 **face-lifting**)

face-off [ˈfesˌɔf; ˈfeisɔːf] *n.* 〖美〗①對立;對峙;敵對。②面對面會議。③(冰球賽等中)開球。

face powder 撲面粉。

fac·er [ˈfesɚ; ˈfeisə] *n.* 〖俗〗①(拳擊等中之)面部之突然一擊。②意外之障礙;難題。

face-sav·er [ˈfesˌsevɚ; ˈfeisˌseivə] *n.* 〖俗〗保全面子之事。

face-sav·ing [ˈfesˌsevɪŋ; ˈfeisˌseiviŋ] *n.* 面子之保全。*—adj.* 保全面子的。

fac·et [ˈfæsɪt; ˈfæsit] *n., v.,* **-et·(t)ed, -et·(t)ing.** *—n.* ①(寶石等之)小平面;刻面。②(昆蟲複眼中的一個)小眼。③(事物之)一面。*—v.t.* 在…上雕琢小平面。

fac·et·ed [ˈfæsɪtɪd; ˈfæsitid] *adj.* 有小刻面的。

fa·ce·ti·ae [fəˈsiʃɪˌi; fəˈsiːʃiiː] *n. pl.* ①詼諧語;雋語。②粗鄙詼諧之書籍;猥褻作品。

fa·ce·tious [fəˈsiʃəs; fəˈsiːʃəs] *adj.* ①好開玩笑的。②玩笑性質的。③不認眞的;輕浮的。**—ly,** *adv.* **—ness,** *n.*

face-to-face [ˈfestəˈfes; ˈfeistəˈfeis] *adj.* 面對面的;直接接觸的。*—adv.* 面對面地。

face towel 洗臉用毛巾。

face value ①票面額。②表面之價値、意義等。

fa·ci·a [ˈfæʃɪə; ˈfæʃə] *n., pl.* **fa·ci·ae** [ˈfæʃɪˌi; ˈfæʃiiː]. ①商店前店主之名牌；招牌。②＝**fascia.**

fa·cial [ˈfeʃəl; ˈfeiʃəl] *adj.* ①臉面的；容顏的；面部用的。②表面的。—*n.* 〖俗〗面部按摩或治療。—**ly,** *adv.*

facial index 面長指數(面部長度與寬度之比,將面部長度乘以100,然後以面部寬度除之)。

facial tissue 面紙;化妝紙。

fac·ile [ˈfæsl̩; ˈfæsail] *adj.* ①輕而易舉的;易得的。②靈巧的; 敏捷的; 能幹的。③隨和的。—**ness,** *n.*

fac·ile·ly [ˈfæsl̩ɪ; ˈfæsaili] *adv.* ①輕而易舉地。②未加思考地。③〖廢〗隨和地。

***fa·cil·i·tate** [fəˈsɪləˌtet; fəˈsiliteit] *v.t.,* **-tat·ed, -tat·ing.** ①使容易;使便利。Modern inventions *facilitate* housework. 現代的許多發明使家事操作便利了。 ②幫助(他人)。 —**fa·cil·i·ta·tor,** *n.* —**fa·cil·i·ta·tive, fa·cil·i·ta·to·ry,** *adj.*

fa·cil·i·ta·tion [fəˌsɪləˈteʃən; fəˌsiliˈteiʃən] *n.* ①容易化;簡化。②使更容易之事物。③〖生理〗促進;促進作用。

***fa·cil·i·ty** [fəˈsɪlətɪ; fəˈsiliti] *n., pl.* **-ties.** ①熟練;敏捷;靈巧。②(常*pl.*) 設備。In the country one has no *facilities* for study. 在鄉下沒有讀書的設備(如沒有圖書設備等)。③容易; 方便。The *facility* of communication is far greater now than it was a hundred years ago. 今日之交通比一百年前方便多了。④隨和的性格。⑤自然。

fac·ing [ˈfesɪŋ; ˈfeisiŋ] *n.* ①面飾; 覆面物(如覆牆等)。②覆面、飾邊等之材料。③(衣服的)飾邊; 貼邊。④(*pl.*)(軍服之)領飾;袖飾。⑤〖軍〗(軍隊操演時, 向左或向右看齊的)看齊。

facing slip 郵包上註明目的地、日期等的標籤。

fac·sim·i·le [fækˈsɪməlɪ; fækˈsimili] *n., v.,* **-led, -le·ing,** *adj.* —*n.* ①精摹; 複製。②無線電傳眞。*in facsimile* 逼眞的;一模一樣。—*v.t.* 精摹; 複製。—*adj.* ①如複製的。②製造複製本的。—**fac·sim·i·list,** *n.*

facsimile telegraph 傳眞發報機。

‡**fact** [fækt; fækt] *n.* ①事實;眞情;眞實;眞相。*Facts* speak louder than words. 事實勝於雄辯。②所主張之事。His *facts* are open to question. 他所主張之事有問題。*after the fact* 〖法律〗犯罪之後。*as a matter of fact* 事實上。*As a matter of fact,* I was the one who broke it. 事實上,我就是打破它的人。*before the fact* 〖法律〗犯罪之前。*fact of life* 基本事實;無法更改之事。*facts of life* 性知識; 生殖方面之常識。*in fact* 說得確切點; 實際上。I saw him not long ago; *in fact* I saw him yesterday. 我不久前見過他,說得確切點,就是昨天我見過他。*in point of fact* 眞實地;實際地。*the fact that*…之事實。〖注意〗the fact that 有時略爲 that: He was quite conscious (of *the fact*) *that* his visitor has some other reason for coming. 他頗知來客另有原由。

fact-find·er [ˈfæktˌfaɪndɚ; ˈfæktˌfaində] *n.* 實情調查者。

***fac·tion** [ˈfækʃən; ˈfækʃən] *n.* ①(政黨或任何組織中的)小派別; 小圈子; 小黨派。②(政黨或任何組織中的) 傾軋; 磨擦; 不和。*Faction* almost broke up the club. 內部磨擦幾乎使俱樂部解體。

fac·tion·al [ˈfækʃənl̩; ˈfækʃənl] *adj.* ①小派別的;小派別間的。②導致派別磨擦的。—**ist,** *n.*

fac·tion·al·ism [ˈfækʃənəˌlɪzəm; ˈfækʃənəlizəm] *n.* 傾軋;內爭。

fac·tious [ˈfækʃəs; ˈfækʃəs] *adj.* ①好植黨派的; 好亂的。②黨派性的。—**ly,** *adv.* —**ness,** *n.*

fac·ti·tious [fækˈtɪʃəs; fækˈtiʃəs] *adj.* ①人爲的; 人工的。②不自然的;勉强的;虛假的。—**ness,** *n.*

fac·ti·tious·ly [fækˈtɪʃəslɪ; fækˈtiʃəsli] *adv.* 人爲地;勉强地。

fac·ti·tive [ˈfæktətɪv; ˈfæktitiv] *adj.* 〖文法〗作爲的; 致使的。*factitive verb* 作爲動詞(含有"作爲;稱爲;以爲"等意,並須有受詞補充詞者 : to paint the house red 中之paint 是)。—*n.* 作爲動詞。—**ly,** *adv.*

***fac·tor** [ˈfæktɚ; ˈfæktə] *n.* ①因素;原動力。Wealth and opportunity were the chief *factors* in (*or* of) his success. 富有和機會是他成功的兩大因素。②〖數學〗因數;因子。5, 3, and 4 are *factors* of 60. 五、三和四是六十的因子。③代理人。④〖生物〗遺傳因子。⑤ ＝**factor of production.** —*v.t.* ①〖數學〗分解因子或因式。 ②爲…擔任代理人;經管。He *factored* his cousin's estate for five years. 他經管他表兄弟的財產有五年之久。—**a·ble,** *adj.* —**ship,** *n.*

fac·tor·age [ˈfæktərɪdʒ; ˈfæktəridʒ] *n.* ①代理商之業;代理買賣。②代理商之佣金。

fac·to·ri·al [fækˈtorɪəl; fækˈtɔːriəl] *adj.* ①代理店的;代理商的。②〖數學〗a. 因子的;因數的。b. 階乘的。—*n.* 〖數學〗階乘。

fac·tor·ize [ˈfæktəˌraɪz; ˈfæktəraiz] *v.t.,* **-ized, -iz·ing.** ①〖數學〗分解因子。② ＝**garnishee.**

factor of production 生產要素。

factor of safety (建造物等之)安全率;安全因數。

‡**fac·to·ry** [ˈfæktrɪ, -tərɪ; ˈfæktəri] *n., pl.* **-ries.** ①工廠; 製造廠。The city's air is polluted by its many *factories.* 這城市的空氣爲市內許多工廠汚染。②製造處; 產生處。The leaf is a *factory* for carbohydrate production. 葉子是炭水化合物之製造所。③代理店;駐外代理商。

factory ship 有處理鯨魚設備之捕鯨船。

fac·to·tum [fækˈtotəm; fækˈtoutəm] *n.* 雜役;聽差。

fac·tu·al [ˈfæktʃuəl; ˈfæktjuəl] *adj.* 事實的;實際的;實在的;確實的。—**ly,** *adv.*

fac·tu·al·ism [ˈfæktʃuəˌlɪzəm; ˈfæktjuəlizm] *n.* 着重事實的作風。 —**fac·tu·al·is·tic,** *adj.* —**fac·tu·al·ist,** *n.*

fac·u·la [ˈfækjulə; ˈfækjulə] *n., pl.* **-lae** [-ˌli; -liː]. 〖天文〗(太陽之)光斑。—**fac·u·lar,** *adj.*

fac·ul·ta·tive [ˈfækl̩ˌtetɪv; ˈfækəltətiv] *adj.* ①給予權能的; 容許的。②任意的;自由選擇的。③偶發的;在某種情況下發生的。④〖生物〗在另一種環境中亦可生存的。⑤選修的(課程)。—**ly,** *adv.*

***fac·ul·ty** [ˈfækl̩tɪ; ˈfækəlti] *n., pl.* **-ties.** ①才能;天賦; 能力; 技能。She has a *faculty* for making friends. 她善於交友。②(大學中的)分科;院;系。③一學校中的全體教員; 大學或學院的全體教授。④任一種專業之全體從業人員。The medical *faculty* is made up of doctors, surgeons, etc. 醫藥從業員包括內、外科醫生等。

faculty adviser 〖美〗指導教授。

fac·ul·ty·man 〔ˈfækḷtɪmən; ˈfækəltimən〕 *n., pl.* **-men.** 教員；教授。

fad 〔fæd; fæd〕 *n.* ①(一時流行之)狂熱；時尚。②嗜好。③奇想；怪念頭；突然的念頭。

fad·dish 〔ˈfædɪʃ; ˈfædiʃ〕 *adj.* ①趨於時尚的。②風行的；流行的。—**ly,** *adv.*

fad·dist 〔ˈfædɪst; ˈfædist〕 *n.* 趨於時尚者；好新奇之人。—*adj.* 好趨附時尚的。

fad·dy 〔ˈfædɪ; ˈfædi〕 *adj.,* **-di·er, -di·est.** ＝**faddish.**

ˈ**fade** 〔fed; feid〕 *v.,* **fad·ed, fad·ing.** —*v.i.* ①褪色；退光；消退。The colors *fade* into one another. 各色消退得分不清了。②凋謝；枯萎；衰弱。The flowers have *faded.* 花已凋謝。③消失。④後退。You can *fade* away and the sergeant and I will take over. 你可以走了，軍士和我會來接管。—*v.t.* 使褪色。The sun *faded* the carpet. 太陽使地毯褪了色。***fade in***(電影、無線電及電視中之)漸强。***fade out*** 漸弱。—**fad·a·ble,** *adj.* —**d·ly,** *adv.* —**d·ness,** *n.*

fade·a·way 〔ˈfedəˌwe; ˈfeidəwei〕 *n.* 〖棒球〗看起來投得很快的內彎下墜球。

fade-in 〔ˈfedˌɪn; ˈfeidin〕 *n.* 〖電影、電視、廣播〗淡顯；漸顯；漸强。

fade·less 〔ˈfedlɪs; ˈfeidlis〕 *adj.* 不褪色的；不衰凋的；不朽的。—**ly,** *adv.*

fade-out 〔ˈfedˌaut; ˈfeidˈaut〕 *n.* ①〖電影、電視、廣播〗淡沒；漸隱；漸弱。②漸衰。

fae·cal 〔ˈfikḷ; ˈfiːkəl〕 *adj.* ＝**fecal.**

fae·ces 〔ˈfisiz; ˈfiːsiːz〕 *n. pl.* ＝**feces.**

fa·er·ie 〔ˈfeərɪ; ˈfeiəri〕 *n., pl.* **-ies,** *adj.* —*n.* 仙人；仙女；仙境；仙國。—*adj.* 仙人的；似仙人的；纖巧可愛的。(亦作 **faërie, faery, fäery**)

fag[1] 〔fæg; fæg〕 *v.,* **fagged, fag·ging.** —*v.t.* 勞役；使疲勞。—*v.i.* ①努力工作至疲倦。②(爲高年級生)服務；服勞役。—**ger,** *n.*

fag[2] *n.* 〖英俗〗①(僅 *sing.*) 苦工；費力之工作。②服勞役者。③(英 public school 爲高年級生服務之)低年級生。

fag[3] *n.* 〖英俚〗紙煙；香煙。

fag[4] 〖美俚〗男性同性戀者。

fag end ①沒用之剩餘物；末端。②布疋頭尾之散口邊。③繩索等之散端。④上當；吃虧。⑤〖英俗〗香煙；煙蒂。

fag·(g)ot 〔ˈfægət; ˈfægət〕 *n.* ①柴把；束薪。②一綑熟鐵。—*v.t.* & *v.i.* ①捆；使成束。②以抽紗裝飾。「抽紗法；抽紗製品。」

fag·(g)ot·ing 〔ˈfægətɪŋ; ˈfægətiŋ〕 *n.*

fag·got·ry 〔ˈfægətrɪ; ˈfægətri〕 *n.* 〖俚〗男性同性戀。—**fag·go·ty, fag·gy,** *adj.*

Fahr. Fahrenheit.

ˈ**Fahr·en·heit** 〔ˈfærənˌhaɪt, ˈfɑrən-; ˈfærənhait, ˈfɑːr-〕 *adj.* 華氏(寒暑表)的。(略作 **F.**) 32° *F.* is the freezing point of water and 212° *F.* the boiling point. 華氏 32 度是水的冰點，212 度是沸點。—*n.* ①(Gabriel Daniel, 1686–1736) 德國物理學家，華氏寒暑表的設計者。②華氏寒暑表。***Fahrenheit thermometer*** 華氏寒暑表。

fa·ience 〔faɪˈɑns; faiˈɑːns〕 *n.* 一種彩陶。(亦作 **faïence**)

ː**fail** 〔fel; feil〕 *v.i.* ①失敗；未能成功。He *failed* to follow our advice. 他未聽從我們的忠告。②不足；缺乏；毀壞。Our water supply has *failed.* 我們的飲水供應不足。③轉弱；衰退。His sight is beginning to *fail.* 他的眼力開始衰退。④破產；倒閉。That company will *fail.* 那家公司將要倒閉。⑤沒有；缺乏。He's a clever man but *fails* in perseverance. 他是個聰明人，但是缺乏毅力。⑥忘記；忽略。He never *fails* to write to his mother every week. 他永不忘記每禮拜給他母親寫信。⑦不及格。He *failed* in arithmetic. 他算術不及格。—*v.t.* ①無助於；使失望。The wind *failed* us. 風使我們失望(風勢不足吹動船)。②給…不及格；使失敗。After some consideration, the teacher *failed* him. 經過一番考慮之後，老師給他不及格。③於…不及格。He *failed* chemistry. 他化學不及格。④缺少。Our youth never *failed* an invincible courage. 我們的青年從不缺少大無畏的精神。***fail of*** 不能獲得；缺乏。The debater's argument *failed of* logical connection. 辯論者的論點缺乏邏輯的連貫性。—*n.* 遲誤(僅用於 without fail 一語中)。I'll pay you tomorrow without *fail.* 我明天一定付你不誤。—**er,** *n.*

fail·ing 〔ˈfelɪŋ; ˈfeiliŋ〕 *n.* ①失敗。②過失；缺點。—*prep.* ①如果沒有。②如果在…中失敗。—*adj.* 衰退的；失敗的；不及格的。

faille 〔faɪl, fel; feil〕 *n.* 一種素織之軟綢。

fail safe (機器)在發生故障或停電時，有保護工作人員免受傷或機器本身免受損之裝置的。(亦作 **failsafe**)

ˈ**fail·ure** 〔ˈfeljɚ; ˈfeiljə〕 *n.* ①失敗。What was the cause of his *failure?* 他失敗的原因爲何？②失敗者。The man is a complete *failure.* 此人一事無成。③減退；不足。④衰退。⑤破產；倒閉。⑥未做；忽略。⑦不存在；不在。Through the *failure* of heirs, most of the noble families disintegrated. 由於沒有繼承人，大部分貴族家族都解體了。***end in*** (or ***meet with***) ***failure*** 結果失敗。All his efforts *ended in* (or *met with*) *failure.* 他的全部努力失敗了。

failure of issue 〖法律〗死亡時沒有在世的子女。

ˈ**fain** 〔fen; fein〕 *adv.* 〖古，詩〗欣然地；樂意地(與 would 連用，後接無 to 的不定詞)。He would *fain* go. 他樂意去。—*adj.* ①高興的；願意的(與不定詞連用)。He was *fain* to acknowledge my right. 他樂於承認我的權利。②因不得已而願意的；迫於環境的。Men were *fain* to eat horseflesh. 人們因不得已而吃馬肉。③熱心的；渴望的。—**ness,** *n.*

fai·né·ant 〔ˈfenɪənt; feineiˈɑ̃ːŋ〕 *adj.* 不活動的；無所爲的；不管事的；懶惰的。—*n.* 懶惰者；無所事事者。

ː**faint** 〔fent; feint〕 *adj.* ①模糊的；不清楚的。We heard *faint* sounds in the distance. 我們聽見遠處有模糊的聲音。②微弱的；昏暈的。His breathing became *faint.* 他的呼吸變得微弱了。③無力的；似不會有結果的。④即將昏暈的。⑤令人昏暈的。⑥無勇氣的；無精神的(通常僅用於 faint heart)。—*v.i.* ①昏暈；昏厥。Several boys *fainted* because of the heat. 幾個孩子因受熱而昏倒。②〖古〗逐漸微弱；失却勇氣。—*v.t.* 〖古〗使昏暈。—*n.* 昏厥。She went off in a *faint.* 她昏過去了。

faint·heart 〔ˈfentˈhɑrt; ˈfeintˈhɑːt〕 *n.* 怯懦者；膽小者。

faint·heart·ed 〔ˈfentˈhɑrtɪd; ˈfeintˈhɑːtid〕 *adj.* 無勇氣的；怯懦的；膽小的。—**ly,** *adv.* —**ness,** *n.*

faint·ing 〔ˈfentɪŋ; ˈfeintiŋ〕 *n., adj.* 昏厥(的)；失神(的)。

faint·ish 〔ˈfentɪʃ; ˈfeintiʃ〕 *adj.* ①微

覺發暈的;衰弱的。②略爲模糊的;微弱的。

***faint·ly** ['fentlı;'feintli] *adv.* ①微弱地;無力地。For a few seconds he *faintly* struggled with the man. 他無力地與那人搏鬥了幾秒鐘。②微微地。

faint·ness ['fentnıs; 'feintnis] *n.* ①無勇氣;懦弱。②不鮮明;淺淡。

‡**fair**[1] [fɛr; fɛə] *adj.* ①公平的; 正直的。He was not quite *fair* to me. 他對我不十分公平。②應當的;應得的。He has a *fair* complaint. 他的牢騷不過分。③美好的;晴朗的。④相當的;尚可的。There is a *fair* crop of wheat this year. 今年麥子收成還不錯。⑤淡色的; 白的。⑥金髮碧眼白皮膚的。She is *fair*, with great wavy masses of golden hair. 她是皮膚白皙金髮捲曲如雲的美人。⑦整潔的;整齊的。⑧清晰的;清白的。⑨可能的;有利的。He is in a *fair* way to succeed. 他頗有成功希望。⑩彬彬有禮的。⑪開闊的; 無遮掩的。⑫似眞而實非的。His *fair* promises proved false. 他虛與委蛇的允諾畢竟是假的。***fair and square***〖俗〗正直的; 公平的。 ***fair to middling*** 尚可; 中等; 馬馬虎虎。—*adv.* ①誠實無欺地。②照直地。③〖古〗有禮貌地。④清晰地。⑤美麗地;愉快地。The sun shone *fair*. 陽光美麗地照耀。⑥完全; 徹底地。It *fair* takes one's breath away. 這使人完全屏住氣息。 ***bid fair*** 甚有…的希望。***play fair*** 以誠實無欺的態度對人。—*n.* ①〖古〗女人; 愛人。②〖古〗公正。 ***for fair*** 〖俗〗的確; 完全。What you say is true, *for fair!* 你說得完全不錯! ***no fair*** 不應該之事。That's *no fair.* 那是不應該的事。

***fair**[2] *n.* ①博覽會; 展覽會。②市集。The village has a *fair* once a month. 那村莊每月有一次市集。③義賣會。Our church held a *fair* to raise money. 我們的教會舉行一義賣會以籌款。

fair ball 〖棒球〗界內球;有效球。

fair employment 公平的雇用政策(不因受雇者之膚色、信仰等而有所歧視)。

fair·ground['fɛr,graund;'fɛəgraund] *n.* 舉行賽會之場所;露天市場。

fair-haired ['fɛr'hɛrd; 'fɛə'hɛəd] *adj.* ①金髮的。②受寵愛的; 討人喜歡的。***fair-haired boy*** **a.** 受上司寵愛者; 親信。**b.** 努力工作者;取悅於上司者。

fair·i·ly ['fɛrılı; 'fɛərili] *adv.* 如小神仙地;優雅地 (=gracefully).

fair·ing ['fɛrıŋ; 'fɛəriŋ] *n.* ①〖機械〗(裝置於飛機等上之)減阻裝置。②〖英〗(市場購得之)禮物; 酬謝物品。

fair·ish ['fɛrıʃ; 'fɛəriʃ] *adj.* 還好的; 尚佳的;頗大的。—**ly,** *adv.*

‡**fair·ly** ['fɛrlı; 'fɛəli] *adv.* ①公平地;光明正大地。He did not act *fairly* towards me. 他沒有公平地對待我。②相當地;尚可地。He is a *fairly* good actor. 他是一個相當好的演員。③正直地;誠實地。④實在地;宛若;眞可謂。⑤清楚地;清晰地。I *fairly* caught sight of him. 我清楚地看到他。⑥徹底地;完全地。We were *fairly* in the trap. 我們完全陷於陷阱中。⑦美麗地;漂亮地。She likes to be overlooking the table with its *fairly* set dishes and silver. 她喜歡觀看美麗地擺放着盤碟和銀器的桌子。⑧應當地。His services have *fairly* earned him promotion. 其服務恰如其分地使他獲得晉陞。⑨精確地。One of the salvos smashed *fairly* into a large warship. 齊發的砲彈之一精確地擊中了一艘大戰艦。

fair-mind·ed ['fɛr'maındıd; 'fɛə'maindid] *adj.* 公正的; 公平的; 坦白的。—**ly,** *adv.* —**ness,** *n.*

fair·ness ['fɛrnıs; 'fɛənis] *n.* ①公平;正直。②美好;晴朗;明亮。③清晰;潔白;鮮麗。④適當;有禮。

fair sex 婦女。

fair-spo·ken ['fɛr'spokən;'fɛə'spoukən] *adj.* 甜言蜜語的;利口的; 婉言的; 奉承的;客氣的;有禮的。

fair trade 根據fair-trade agreement而作的貨物銷售。

fair-trade ['fɛr'tred; 'fɛə'treid] *v.t.,* **-trad·ed, -trad·ing.** ①訂定(商品之)最低零售價格。②按 fair-trade agreement 之規定銷售貨物。

fair-trade agreement (廠商與零售商所訂)不擅減商品零售價格之協定。

fair·way ['fɛr,we; 'fɛəwei] *n.* ①通路; 無阻礙之路。②〖高爾夫〗球座與終點間修整過的草地。③(川、港內之)航路。

fair-weath·er ['fɛr,wɛðə;'fɛə,weðə] *adj.* ①晴天的; 適於晴天的。②可共安樂而難以共患難的。

***fair·y** ['fɛrı; 'fɛəri] *n., pl.* **fair·ies,** *adj.* —*n.* 小仙子; 小神仙。—*adj.* ①小神仙的。②如小神仙的;纖巧的。

***fair·y·land** ['fɛrı,lænd; 'fɛərilænd] *n.* ①仙國;仙境。②樂園。

fair·y·like ['fɛrı,laık; 'fɛərilaik] *adj.* 如小仙的;優美的;靈妙的。

fairy tale ①神仙故事。②虛傳。

fair·y-tale ['fɛrı,tel; 'fɛəriteil] *adj.* 美麗如在神仙故事中的。

fait ac·com·pli [fɛtakõ'pli; fɛtakõ'pli:] *pl.* **faits ac·com·plis** [fɛtakõ'pli; fɛtakõ'pli:]. 〖法〗(無庸反對之)既成事實。

‡**faith** [feθ; feiθ] *n.* ①信仰; 信心。Have you any *faith* in what he tells you? 你相信他告訴你的事嗎? ②宗教信仰。③信靠之事物。④宗教。⑤忠誠。⑥保證; 諾言。He gave his *faith* that he would come on the appointed day. 他保證他會在約定的日子來。***bad faith*** 欺詐。It was an act of *bad faith* to betray one's friend. 出賣朋友乃是欺詐行爲。 ***breach of faith*** 背約。It was a *breach of faith* to reveal the story I told you. 把我對你講的事洩露出去乃是背信行爲。***break*** (***one's***) ***faith with somebody*** 對某人不守信實。***in faith*** 實在(=indeed). *In faith,* he is a fine lad. 他實在是個好孩子。***in good faith*** 老實地; 誠懇地。I told you *in* all *good faith* that my father was dead. 我已經老實地告訴你,我的父親已死。***keep*** (***one's***) ***faith with somebody*** 對某人講信實。***lose faith in*** 對…失去信心。I've *lost faith in* that fellow. 我對那傢伙已失信心。***put*** (***one's***) ***faith in*** 相信。I advise you not to *put your faith in* such a remedy. 我奉勸你切勿相信這樣的藥。 ***shake*** (or ***hatter***) ***one's faith*** 使失去信心。 What you tell me *shakes my faith* in human nature. 你對我所說的話使得我對人性失去信心。***on faith*** 不加懷疑地。You will have to accept my statements *on faith.* 你得完全相信我的話。

faith cure (or **healing**)信仰治療法。

***faith·ful** ['feθfəl; 'feiθful] *adj.* ①忠實的; 守信的。②詳實的。 a *faithful* account of what happened. 對所發生事件之確實報

導。③有信心的;虔誠的。④誠心誠意的(行爲等)。a *faithful* promise. 誠心誠意的諾言。—*n.* ①信徒。②忠誠分子。Only the party *faithfuls* favored his plan. 只有黨的忠誠分子贊成他的計畫。—**ness,** *n.*

faith·ful·ly** [ˈfeθfəlɪ; ˈfeiθfuli, -fəli] *adv.* 忠實地。He kept his promise *faithfully*. 他很忠實地守信約。Yours faithfully*** (or ***Faithfully yours***) 書信中之結尾語,相當於中文之"頓首; 拜上"等。

faith·less [ˈfeθlɪs; ˈfeiθlis] *adj.* ①無信的; 不忠的; 不守約的。②不眞的;不傳眞的。③無信仰的。—**ly,** *adv.* —**ness,** *n.*

fake[1] [fek; feik] *n., adj., v.,* **faked, fak·ing.** —*n.* ①作僞;欺詐。②贋品;僞造物。③佯裝之人。④魔術師之道具。—*adj.* 僞造的。—*v.t.* ①僞造。②假裝。—*v.i.* 佯裝。

fake[2] *n., v.,* **faked, fak·ing.** —*n.* 〖航海〗盤索之一捲。—*v.t.* 盤捲〖常 down〗。

fake·ment [ˈfekmənt; ˈfeikmənt] *n.* 〖俗〗①作僞;欺詐。②假冒(僞造、騙人)的東西。

fak·er [ˈfekɚ; ˈfeikə] *n.* 〖俗〗①作僞者;僞造者。②欺詐者;騙徒。③小販;攤販。

fa·kir[1] [fəˈkɪr; ˈfɑːkiə] *n.* 托鉢僧;行者。

fak·ir[2] [ˈfekɚ; ˈfeikə] *n.* =**faker.**

fal·cate [ˈfælket; ˈfælkeit] *adj.* 鐮形的;鉤狀的。(亦作 **falcated**) —**fal·ca·tion,** *n.*

fal·chion [ˈfɔltʃən; ˈfɔːltʃən] *n.* ①偃月刀; 鐮形刀。②〖詩〗刀;劍。

F

fal·ci·form [ˈfælsɪˌfɔrm; ˈfælsifɔːm] *adj.* 鐮形的; 鉤狀的。

fal·con [ˈfɔlkən; ˈfɔːlkən] *n.* 鷹;獵鷹。

fal·con·er [ˈfɔlkənɚ, ˈfɔkənɚ; ˈfɔːlkənə] 鷹者;放鷹者。

fal·co·net [ˈfɔlkənˌɛt; ˈfɔːlkənet] *n.* ①小獵鷹。②一種舊式小砲。

fal·con·ry [ˈfɔlkənrɪ; ˈfɔːlkənri] *n.* ①放鷹捕獵。②訓練鷙鷹捕獵術。

fal·de·ral [ˈfældəˌræl; ˈfældəˈræl] *n.* ①瑣細小巧之物;裝飾品。②無意義;廢話。③古歌謠中無意義的反覆。(亦作 **falderol**)

fald·stool [ˈfɔldˌstul; ˈfɔːldstuːl] *n.* ①(主教之)無背椅。②讀經檯。③小案;跪拜臺。

Fa·ler·ni·an [fəˈlɝnɪən; fəˈləːnjən] *n.* (義大利產之)一種白葡萄酒。

‡**fall** [fɔl; fɔːl] *v.,* **fell, fall·en, fall·ing,** *n.* —*v.i.* ①落下; 跌下; 下降。The snow *falls* fast. 雪下得很緊。②倒下。Many trees *fell* in the storm. 那次風雨中許多樹倒了。③掛下;垂下。Her curls *fell* upon her shoulders. 她的卷髮垂於兩肩。④低垂。She blushed and her eyes *fell*. 她臉紅了, 雙眼低垂。⑤變壞; 墮落; 走入歧途。He was tempted and *fell*. 他被引誘而走入歧途。⑥失勢; 失尊嚴。The governor *fell* from the people's favor. 總督失掉了人民的擁戴。⑦被占領; 推翻; 毀壞。The fort *fell* to the enemy. 該碉堡爲敵人所占領。⑧因傷亡而倒下; 死亡。Many men *fell* in battle. 許多人在那次戰役中陣亡。⑨變爲;成爲。The baby *fell* asleep. 那嬰兒入睡了。⑩臨; 來到。When the night *falls*, the stars appear. 夜晚來到時, 星星出現。⑪偶然遇到; 碰上。Our choice *fell* on him. 我們碰巧選中了他。⑫發生。Christmas *falls* on Sunday this year. 今年的耶誕是禮拜天。⑬留傳。The money *fell* to the only son. 那筆錢留傳給了那個獨子。⑭置;放;在。⑮降低; 減少; 減弱。Prices *fell* sharply. 物價銳跌。⑯分裂; 分開。The story *falls* into five parts. 那故事分成五段。⑰顯得憂愁或失望。His face *fell* at the bad news. 聽到那壞消息時, 他的臉色變得陰沉了。⑱下斜;流下;注入。The land *falls* gradually to the beach. 該地逐漸下斜直至海灘。⑲向;照向。The light *falls* on my book. 燈光照在我的書上。⑳說出; 透露。Not a word *fell* from his lips. 他甚麼也沒有說出。㉑停止。The conversation *fell* for a few minutes. 談話停止了幾分鐘。㉒〖俚〗被捕。He *fell* twice, for theft and burglary. 他因偷竊和夜盜罪而入獄兩次。***fall aboard*** 〖航海〗**a.** 攻擊。**b.** 與…相撞。***fall among*** 淪於…手中。to *fall among* thieves. 淪於盜賊之手;被刼。***fall apart*** 分裂;崩潰。***fall asleep*** 睡着了; 入了夢鄉。***fall away*** **a.** 減少; 消減; 消退。Trade always *falls away* during the summer. 在夏季生意總是要減少的。**b.** 變爲不認眞。**c.** 疏遠; 遺棄。All his friends *fell away* from him. 他的朋友們全對他疏遠了。**d.** 被毀。***fall back*** 後退。***fall back on*** (or ***upon***) **a.** 依靠。In an emergency we can always *fall back on* our savings. 在緊急時我們總可以依靠我們的積蓄。**b.** (亦作 **fall back to**) 退守。The soldiers were ordered to *fall back on* the second line of defence. 兵士們奉令退守第二道防線。***fall behind*** **a.** 落後。He always *falls behind* when we are going uphill. 我們上山時, 他總是落後。**b.** 拖欠。I've *fallen behind* my rent. 我的房租逾期未繳。***fall by the wayside*** 受挫;失敗。Many party stalwarts *fell by the wayside* on election day. 許多黨的忠誠分子於選舉中受挫。***fall down on*** 失敗; 做得不滿意。He was doing well on the exam until he *fell down on* the last question. 他考得很順利, 可是最後一道題可將他考垮了。***fall due*** 到期。When does the money *fall due?* 該款甚麼時候到期? ***fall flat*** **a.** 臥倒; 平臥。As the firing began I *fell flat* to avoid the bullets. 一開槍之後, 我便臥倒, 以躲避子彈。**b.** 未能產生預期效果。This play will *fall flat*. 這部戲怕不會令人感趣味。***fall for*** 〖俚〗**a.** 傾倒;受誘惑。He always *falls for* a pretty face. 他見到美貌便爲之傾倒。**b.** 受騙。His story was so convincing that everybody *fell for* it. 他說得非常動聽, 人人都受騙了。***fall foul*** (or ***afoul***) ***of*** **a.** (船)撞碰。**b.** 與…發生衝突。This new clerk will soon *fall foul of* the manager. 這新來的職員不久就會和經理衝突。***fall from grace*** **a.** 失寵。**b.** 〖宗教〗再度陷入罪惡生活。***fall heir to*** 繼承。***fall home*** 向內彎曲。***fall in*** **a.** 排隊。At two o'clock the men *fell in*. 兩點鐘兵士們就排隊了。**b.** 塌陷。After the fire the roof *fell in*. 大火過後, 屋頂塌陷了。**c.** 遇見。**d.** 同意。**e.** 跌入。There was a big hole and she *fell in*. 有一個大坑, 她跌進去了。***fall in battle*** 陣亡。***fall in love*** (***with***) (與)…相愛; 喜愛。He *fell in love with* an actress. 他與一女伶相戀。***fall into*** **a.** 陷入;落入。**b.** 養成。**c.** 分成。**d.** 開始。**e.** 排成隊。The soldiers *fell into* line. 兵士們排好隊。***fall in with*** 遇見。On my way home I usually *fall in with* that man. 我在回家途中總是遇見那個人。***fall off*** **a.** 減色; 消減; 退步。The quality of his painting has *fallen off* greatly. 他的圖畫

的品質已大大退步。b. 掉下。His hat *fell off*. 他的帽子掉下了。c.（健康）衰退。d. 離開。They *fell off* one by one. 他們一一離開。e. 分手；背棄。My readers will never *fall off* from me. 我的讀者將不會背棄我。***fall off the roof***（婦女）行經；來月經。***fall on*** a. 發生。Christmas *fell on* Sunday last year. 去年的耶誕節是星期日。b. 攻擊。They *fell on* the enemy vigorously. 他們猛烈攻擊敵人。c. 遭遇。***fall on one's face*** 完全失敗。Efforts to increase production have up to now *fallen on their face*. 增產的努力至今都完全失敗。***fall on one's feet*** 有好運道；化險爲夷。Some people always seem to *fall on their feet*. 有些人好像永遠運氣很好。***fall on one's knees*** 屈膝；下跪。***fall out*** a. 吵架。Husband and wife often *fall out* over small matters. 夫妻常因細故吵架。b. 解散。After a long drill the captain told his squad to *fall out*. 長時間操練之後，隊長令他的隊伍解散。c. 發生。It *fell out* that I could not be present. 結果是我不能出席。***fall over oneself*** a. 因行動笨拙而跌倒。b. 急於做某事。They almost *fell over themselves* in the anxiety to get there quickly. 他們急欲快點到那裏。***fall*** (or ***come***) ***short*** 不够；不足。The performance *fell* far *short* of our expectations. 這場表演遠不及我們預期之佳。***fall sick*** 生病。***fall through*** 失敗；不能實現。Owing to lack of funds the scheme *fell through*. 因款項支絀，計畫未能實現。***fall to*** a. 開始工作。As soon as the work was distributed each man *fell to*. 工作一經分配，每人即開始工作。b. 開始吃。He *fell to* ravenously. 他開始狼吞虎嚥地吃。c. 開始攻擊。d. 落在。It *fell to* me to tell him. 去通知他的責任落在我身上了。***fall to pieces*** 破碎；崩潰。After the death of Napoleon his empire *fell to pieces*. 拿破崙死後，其帝國即行崩潰。***fall under*** a. 屬於（某一項目）之下。b. 爲…之責任。***fall upon*** (or ***on***) 進攻。The police *fell upon* the rioters. 警察向暴徒進攻。—*n.* ①落；跌落；跌倒。He had been hurt by a *fall*. 他因跌跤而受傷了。②跌落之距離。③下垂。④適當的部位。⑤下降；降低。⑥下坡。⑦〖美〗秋季。⑧摔角中之被摔倒；角力中之競爭。⑨(*pl.*)瀑布。the Niagara *Falls*. 尼加拉大瀑布（在美國與加拿大之間）。⑩(*pl.*)大船上用以收放小船之裝置。⑪墮落；變壞。*fall* from virtue. 道德之墮落。⑫衰落；滅亡。⑬敗亡之因。His stubbornness was his *fall*. 他的頑固是他敗亡之因。⑭〖俚〗被捕入獄。She served time on narcotics and prostitution *falls*. 她因吸毒與賣淫而被捕入獄。***ride for a fall*** 註定失敗。He is proud, but he is *riding for a fall*. 他很驕傲，但他這樣準會失敗。***the Fall*** 亞當與夏娃受引誘而吃禁果之墮落。〖注意〗**falls** 作瀑布解時，在形式上雖是複數，在意義上則是單數，或者視爲一集合名詞。在名詞中，通常用 *a* falls, 但在句中常接用複數動詞：The falls *are* almost dry in August. 八月中瀑布幾乎乾了。作專有名詞時，falls 後常用單數動詞：The Niagara Falls *is* receding. 尼加拉瀑布正減弱中。

fal·la·cious 〔fəˈleʃəs; fəˈleiʃəs〕 *adj.* ①欺騙的；使人誤解的。②邏輯上不健全的；謬誤的。③令人失望的；不可靠的。—**ly**, *adv.* —**ness**, *n.*

fal·la·cy 〔ˈfæləsɪ; ˈfæləsi〕 *n., pl.* **-cies.** ①謬見；謬誤。②謬誤之推理；謬論。③不鞏固。

fal·lal 〔ˌfælˈlæl; ˈfæˈlæl〕 *n.* 無用之飾物。（亦作 **fal-lal, fallol**）

‡fall·en 〔ˈfɔlən; ˈfɔːlən〕 *v.* pp. of **fall.** —*adj.* ①落下的；倒下的。②被推翻的；被毀滅的。③死的。④墮落的。⑤憔悴的。

fal·li·bil·i·ty 〔ˌfæləˈbɪlətɪ; ˌfæliˈbiliti〕 *n.* 可誤性；不可靠性。

fal·li·ble 〔ˈfæləbl; ˈfæləbl〕 *adj.* 可能犯錯的。—**fal·li·bly**, *adv.*

fall·ing 〔ˈfɔlɪŋ; ˈfɔːliŋ〕 *n.* ①落下；跌下；倒下；陷落；顚覆；墮落。②墜下之物。—*adj.* 落下的；垂下的；減退的；降低的。

falling leaf 〖航空〗落葉式之降落。

fall·ing-off 〔ˈfɔlɪŋˈɔf; ˈfɔːliŋˈɔːf〕 *n.* 下降；減退；衰退。

falling sickness 癲癇症。

falling star 隕星；流星。

Fal·lo·pi·an tube 〔fəˈlopɪən～; fəˈloupiən～〕〖解剖、動物〗輸卵管。

fall·out 〔ˈfɔlˈaut; ˈfɔːlˈaut〕 *n.* ①輻射性微塵。②剩餘之物。（亦作 **fall-out**）

fal·low[1] 〔ˈfælo; ˈfælou〕 *adj.* ①犁過而不耕種的；休耕的。②無教養的。③久未生育的。—*n.* ①休耕地。②休耕法。—*v.t.* 使（田地）休耕。

fal·low[2] *adj.* 淡黃（褐）色的。

fallow deer （歐洲產的淡黃帶白斑之）小鹿。

‡false 〔fɔls; fɔːls〕 *adj.*, **fals·er, fals·est,** *adv.* —*adj.* ①不對的；錯的。②謊騙的；不實的；欺騙的。③不忠實的；虛僞的。a *false* friend. 不忠實的朋友。④假的；人造的。a *false* coin. 假錢。⑤誤稱的；誤命名的。⑥臨時的；代用的。***sail under false colors*** a.（船）懸別國國旗而航行。b. 冒充；假裝。—*adv.* 錯誤地；欺騙地。***play false*** 欺騙。If you *play* them *false* in this matter, they will not trust you again. 假若你在這件事上欺騙他們，他們便不會再信任你了。—**ness**, *n.* 〖注意〗**false** 與 **counterfeit** 均作"假的"解。false 說明某物"看似眞的"，不一定有用以冒充謊騙之意。counterfeit 着重於冒充眞的，而常有用以謊騙之意。

false alarm ①虛報的火警。②一場虛驚。

false arrest 不合法逮捕。

false bottom （箱子、抽屜等祕密藏物用的）夾層底。

false colors ①別國之國旗。②冒充。

false face 面具。

false·heart·ed 〔ˈfɔlsˈhɑrtɪd; ˈfɔːlsˈhɑːtid〕 *adj.* 不誠實的；背信的；欺騙的。

***false·hood** 〔ˈfɔls·hud; ˈfɔːlshud〕 *n.* ①虛假；不實。Truth, if exaggerated, may become *falsehood*. 眞理若加誇大，可能變成虛假。②謊言。How can you utter such *falsehoods*? 你怎能說出這樣的謊話？③虛假之事物。④作僞；欺詐。He was convicted of *falsehood*. 他因欺詐而被判有罪。

false imprisonment 違法拘禁或限制自由。

false keel 〖造船〗副龍骨。

false·ly 〔ˈfɔlslɪ; ˈfɔːlsli〕 *adv.* ①錯誤地。②不眞實地。③冤枉地。④虛僞地。

false pretenses 〖法律〗意存欺詐而作之不實言論。

false step ①失足；蹿倒；絆跌。②錯誤；失着。

false teeth 假牙。

fal·set·to 〔fɔlˈsɛto; fɔːlˈsetou〕 *n., pl.* **-tos,** *adj., adv.* —*n.* 〖音樂〗①假聲。②假

聲歌手。—*adj.* 假聲的；以假聲歌唱的。—*adv.* 假聲地。

fals·ies [ˈfɔlsɪz; ˈfɔːlsiz] *n. pl.* 〖俗〗假奶；義乳。

fal·si·fi·ca·tion [ˌfɔlsəfəˈkeʃən; ˌfɔːlsifiˈkeiʃən] *n.* 僞造；竄改；曲解；說謊；反證；揭破。

fal·si·fy [ˈfɔlsəˌfaɪ; ˈfɔːlsifai] *v.*, **-fied, -fy·ing.** —*v.t.* ①僞造；竄改；曲解。②證明爲虛妄；反證。—*v.i.* 作僞；說謊。—**fal·si·fi·a·ble,** *adj.* —**fal·si·fi·ca·tor, fal·si·fi·er,** *n.*

fal·si·ty [ˈfɔlsətɪ; ˈfɔːlsiti] *n., pl.* **-ties.** ①錯誤；不正確。②不誠實；欺騙；奸詐。③詐僞的行爲；錯誤的事物。

Fal·staff [ˈfɔlstæf; ˈfɔːlstɑːf] *n.* (莎士比亞戲劇 *Henry IV* 及 *Merry Wives of Windsor* 中)愛吹嘘、大膽、歡樂而肥胖之武士。

falt·boat [ˈfɑltˌbot; ˈfɑːltbout] *n.* 一種可摺疊之小艇。(亦作 **foldboat**)

***fal·ter** [ˈfɔltɚ; ˈfɔːltə] *v.i.* ①膽怯；動搖。②吶吶而語；支吾而語。His voice *faltered* as he tried to speak. 他要說話的時候聲音發抖。③蹣跚而行。—*v.t.* 支吾地說出；口吃地說出。He *faltered* out a few words. 他支吾地說出了幾個字。—*n.* ①遲疑的行動。I did what was required of me without *falter.* 我毫不遲疑地做了我所應做之事。②支吾。—**er,** *n.*

fal·ter·ing [ˈfɔltərɪŋ; ˈfɔːltəriŋ] *adj.* 口吃的；躊躇的；戰慄的；顫聲的。

fal·ter·ing·ly [ˈfɔltərɪŋlɪ; ˈfɔːltəriŋli] *adv.* 遲疑地；支吾地。

FAM foreign air mail.

‡**fame** [fem; feim] *n.* ①名聲；名氣；聲譽。His *fame* spread all over the country. 他名震全國。②〖古〗風聞；傳說。The *fame* of this brave act soon spread. 關於這英勇行爲的傳說，立刻傳遍各地。***come to fame*** 成名。—*v.t.* 傳揚…之名聲；使有名氣。—**less,** *adj.*

famed [femd; feimd] *adj.* 著名的；聞名的；負有盛名的。

‡**fa·mil·iar** [fəˈmɪljɚ; fəˈmiljə] *adj.* ①日常的；見慣的。a *familiar* figure at the opera. 歌劇中常見的人物。②熟悉的；通曉的。I'm not very *familiar* with botanical names. 我不太熟悉植物學上的名稱。③親密的。He has very few *familiar* friends. 他很少親密的朋友。④非正式的。*familiar* essays. 隨筆。⑤過分親密的；冒失的。He made himself much too *familiar* with my wife. 他對我的妻子太冒失了。⑥適於家族的。—*n.* ①熟人；親密的朋友。With *familiars* he is very candid. 他對知友很坦白。②專爲某人服務之精靈。A black cat was thought to be a witch's *familiar.* 黑貓曾被認爲是爲巫婆服務的精靈。③常到某地者。—**ness,** *n.*

***fa·mil·i·ar·i·ty** [fəˌmɪlɪˈærətɪ; fəˌmiliˈæriti] *n., pl.* **-ties.** ①親密。*Familiarity* breeds contempt. 親密易趨侮慢。②熟悉；精通。His *familiarity* with modern languages was remarkable. 他對近代語言之精通是驚人的。③親密之舉動；不拘形式的行爲。④過分親密；冒失。⑤男女間之親密行動。She is unwise enough to permit affectionate *familiarities* when she is with boys. 她很不聰明，與男孩子在一塊時容許超友誼的親密行動。

fa·mil·iar·i·za·tion [fəˌmɪljərəˈzeʃən; fəˌmiljəraiˈzeiʃən] *n.* 使熟識；通俗化。

fa·mil·iar·ize [fəˈmɪljəˌraɪz; fəˈmiljəraiz] *v.t.* ①使熟識。②使成爲家喻戶曉。

fa·mil·iar·ly [fəˈmɪljɚlɪ; fəˈmiljəli] *adv.* ①親密地。②一般地；通常地。③不拘禮地。④冒失地。⑤不畏懼地。

‡**fam·i·ly** [ˈfæməlɪ; ˈfæmili] *n., pl.* **-lies.** ①家；家庭；家屬。Almost every *family* in the village had sent a man to the army. 村裏差不多每家都送了一個人去當兵。②子女。Tom is the eldest of the *family.* 湯姆是這家最大的孩子。③家族；家世。④〖生物〗族；科。⑤語系。⑥〖化〗族。⑦〖數學〗族。⑧幕僚。I was invited to join his military *family* as aide-de-camp. 我被邀以副官身分加入他的軍事幕僚。⑨學派。He belongs to the Kantian *family.* 他屬於康德學派。—*adj.* 家庭的；適於家庭的。*family* dances. 家庭舞。***among the family of nations*** 在國際間。

family Bible 家用聖經。

family circle 某一家之男女老幼全體。

family doctor 家庭特約醫師。(亦作 **family physician**)

family name 姓。

family planning 家庭計畫。

family skeleton 不願外揚的家醜。

family style 按照自助餐方式(的)。

family tree 系圖；家譜。

family way 有孕；有喜(常與定冠詞或不定冠詞連用)。

***fam·ine** [ˈfæmɪn; ˈfæmin] *n.* ①饑荒；饑餓。Thousands died of *famine.* 千萬人死於饑荒。②缺乏；荒。—*adj.* 因缺乏而致的。

fam·ish [ˈfæmɪʃ; ˈfæmiʃ] *v.i.* 饑餓；挨餓。—*v.t.* 使餓(常用於被動語態)。—**ment,** *n.*

‡**fa·mous** [ˈfeməs; ˈfeiməs] *adj.* ①著名的。a *famous* man (place, town, etc.). 著名的人(地方、城鎮等)。②〖俗〗好的；優越的。The singer gave a *famous* performance. 那歌星唱得極爲精彩。—**ness,** *n.* 〖注意〗**famous, notorious** 與 **noted.** famous 指在好的方面出名。notorious 指在壞的方面出名。noted 指由於某一特殊事物而出名，不一定好，也不一定壞。

fa·mous·ly [ˈfeməslɪ; ˈfeiməsli] *adv.* ①著名地。②很好地。③非常地。

fam·u·lus [ˈfæmjuləs; ˈfæmjuləs] *n., pl.* **-li** [-ˌlaɪ; -lai].〖拉〗(中世紀魔術師或學者之)助手；侍從。

***fan** [fæn; fæn] *n., v.,* **fanned, fan·ning.** —*n.* ①扇；風扇；扇狀形。②〖美，俗〗迷；狂熱者。③簸穀機。—*v.t.* ①扇；以扇驅。She *fanned* the flies from the sleeping child. 她以扇趕走睡着的孩子身上的蒼蠅。②鼓動；煽動；引起。Bad treatment *fanned* their dislike into hate. 虐待將他們的不悅激成了恨。③簸(穀)。④把…展成扇形。⑤〖俚〗搜查。The guard *fanned* him for weapons. 守衞在他身上搜查武器。⑥〖棒球〗將(打擊手)三振出局。—*v.i.* ①作扇形散開〖常 out〗。②〖俚〗〖棒球〗(打擊手)被三振出局。③擺動；飄動。

fa·nat·ic [fəˈnætɪk; fəˈnætik] *n.* 盲信者；宗教狂熱者。—*adj.* 盲信的；熱狂的。—**al,** *adj.* —**al·ly,** *adv.* —**al·ness,** *n.*

fa·nat·i·cism [fəˈnætəˌsɪzəm; fəˈnætisizəm] *n.* 狂熱；盲目；盲從；宗教狂熱。

fa·nat·i·cize [fəˈnætəˌsaɪz; fəˈnætisaiz] *v.*, **-cized, -ciz·ing.** —*v.t.* 使狂熱。—*v.i.* 如狂熱者行動。

fan·cied [ˈfænsɪd; ˈfænsid] *adj.* ①空

想的;非事實的。②所喜愛的。

fan·ci·er 〔ˈfænsɪɚ; ˈfænsiə〕①有特別癖好者;玩賞家。②飼養並販賣鳥、狗等之人。③空想者; 好想像的人。

fan·ci·ful 〔ˈfænsɪfəl; ˈfænsiful〕 *adj.* ①希奇的;奇怪的; 設計奇特的。②想像的;夢想的;富於幻想的。—**ly,** *adv.* —**ness,** *n.*

‡**fan·cy** 〔ˈfænsɪ; ˈfænsi〕 *n., pl.* **-cies,** *v.,* **-cied, -cy·ing,** *adj.,* **-ci·er, -ci·est.** —*n.* ①想像; 幻想;想像力。That's only your *fancy.* 那不過是你的想像。②幻想的東西; 觀念。Did I really hear someone come in or was it only a *fancy?* 我眞聽到有人進來呢,抑或衹是一種幻想? ③愛好; 喜歡。I have a *fancy* for some wine with my dinner. 我喜歡在吃飯的時候喝一點酒。④想像之結果。What a pretty *fancy* her drawing is! 她的繪畫是多麼美麗的想像作品啊! ⑤鑑賞力。***take*** (or ***catch***) ***the fancy of*** 討好某人;使某人注意。The new musical comedy *took the fancy of* the public. 那部新的歌舞喜劇很受大衆的注意。—*v.t.* ①想像;以爲;想。I *fancy* (that) he won't come. 我想他不會來。②想想看(表示驚訝等)。*Fancy* his believing it! 他竟相信了, 多麼希奇啊! ③喜歡。I don't *fancy* this place at all. 我一點兒也不喜歡這個地方。***fancy oneself*** 自以爲(了不起)。—*v.i.* 幻想;空想。Let me *fancy* while I may. 讓我在可幻想的時候儘情幻想吧。—*adj.* ①特製的; 外表特別好看的。②特別裝飾的。③需要特殊技巧的;花式的。*fancy* skating. 花式溜冰。④特選而昂貴的。a *fancy* price. 高昂的價格。⑤特別培育的。

fancy dress 化裝舞會所着之服裝。

fancy (dress) ball 化裝舞會。

fan·cy-free 〔ˈfænsɪˈfri; ˈfænsiˈfriː〕 *adj.* ①未受(愛情)影響的; 可自由談愛的; 未結婚的;未訂婚的。②無憂的。

fancy goods ①僅有裝飾價值而無實際用途之貨物。②奢侈品;精巧玩意兒。

fancy man ①女人養的漢子;吃軟飯者。②情郞。

fancy woman 情婦或妓女。(亦作 **fancy lady**)

fan·cy-work 〔ˈfænsɪˌwɝk; ˈfænsiwəːk〕 *n.* (用作裝飾之)鈎針織品;刺繡。

fan dance (裸體或半裸舞女之)扇舞。

fan·dan·go 〔fænˈdæŋgo; fænˈdæŋgou〕 *n., pl.* **-gos,** *v.* —*n.* ①(西班牙之)輕快的三步舞。②其舞曲。③〖俗〗舞會。④愚行;兒戲。—*v.i.* 跳 fandango 或作類似的運動。

fane 〔fen; fein〕 *n.* 〖古、詩〗寺院;神殿。

fan·fare 〔ˈfænˌfɛr; ˈfænfɛə〕 *n.* ①喇叭聲; 號角的短疾之聲。②虛張之聲勢;誇耀;鋪張。—*v.t.* 熱熱鬧鬧地宣布或介紹。

fan·fa·ron·ade 〔ˌfænfərəˈned; ˌfænfærəˈnɑːd〕 *n.* 大言;壯語;虛誇。

fan·fold 〔ˈfænˌfold; ˈfænfould〕 *n.* 複寫簿;複寫本。

fang 〔fæŋ; fæŋ〕 *n.* ①尖牙。②某物之長、細、尖的部分。③齒根。—*v.t.* ①以尖牙咬。②配以尖牙或尖牙般的東西。—**less,** *adj.*

fanged 〔fæŋd; fæŋd〕 *adj.* 有毒牙的;有尖牙的; 有爪的。

fan·light 〔ˈfænˌlaɪt; ˈfænlait〕 *n.* 扇形窗;氣窗。

fan mail 影星等收到的崇拜者之郵件(=fan letters).

fan·ner 〔ˈfænɚ; ˈfænə〕 *n.* ①扇者; 簸者。②送風機;通風機;簸穀機;簸箕。

Fan·ny, Fan·nie 〔ˈfænɪ; ˈfæni〕 *n.* 女子名。

fan·tail 〔ˈfænˌtel; ˈfænteil〕 *n.* ①扇狀尾。②扇尾鴿、鳥或魚等。③〖建築〗扇狀結構物; (特指)拱架; 放射形架。④〖英〗(運煤工人之) 扇形帽。

fan-tan 〔ˈfænˌtæn; ˈfænˈtæn〕〖中〗 *n.* 番攤(盛行於中國廣東省之一種賭博)。

fan·ta·si·a 〔fænˈteʒɪə; fænˈteizjə〕 *n.* ①〖音樂〗幻想曲。②奇幻事物。

fan·tast 〔ˈfæntæst; ˈfæntæst〕 *n.* 幻想者; 夢想者。

***fan·tas·tic** 〔fænˈtæstɪk; fænˈtæstik〕 *adj.* ①奇異的; 怪誕的;不合理的。The idea that machines could be made to fly seemed *fantastic* a hundred years ago. 機器能飛起來的想法, 在一百年前似乎是怪誕的。②奇形怪狀的。③空想的; 幻想的。Superstition causes *fantastic* fears. 迷信造成無中生有的恐懼。④難以置信的。The bomb did *fantastic* damage. 那炸彈造成了難以置信的損害。⑤愚蠢的。He has a *fantastic* idea of his own importance. 他對自己的重要性存有愚蠢的想法。—**al·ness,** —**ism,** *n.*

***fan·tas·ti·cal** 〔fænˈtæstɪkl; fænˈtæstikəl〕 *adj.* =**fantastic.**

fan·tas·ti·cal·i·ty 〔fænˌtæstɪˈkælətɪ; fænˌtæstiˈkæliti〕 *n.* ①空想; 變化無常。②奇妙。

fan·tas·ti·cal·ly 〔fænˈtæstɪklɪ; fænˈtæstikəli〕 *adv.* ①奇特地。②非常地。

fan·ta·sy 〔ˈfæntəsɪ; ˈfæntəsi〕 *n., pl.* **-sies.** ①想像; 幻想; 狂想。②想像的東西。③幻想曲。(亦作 **phantasy**)

fan·toc·ci·ni 〔ˌfæntəˈtʃinɪ; ˌfæntəˈtʃiːni〕〖義〗 *n. pl.* 傀儡;傀儡戲。

fan·wise 〔ˈfænˌwaɪz; ˈfænwaiz〕 *adv.* & *adj.* (張開)如扇形地(的)。

FAO Food and Agriculture Organization.

fa·quir 〔fəˈkɪr; ˈfɑːkiə〕 *n.* =**fakir**¹.

‡**far** 〔fɑr; fɑː〕 *adj.,* **far·ther, far·thest,** *adv.* —*adj.* ①遠的;遠方的。②較遠的。③久遠的。the *far* past. 太古。④廣遠的; 遠大的。a man of *far* vision. 眼光遠大的人。—*adv.* ①甚遠地;久遠地。The house is not *far* away. 該屋離此不遠。②很; 大大地。③很晚地。He often works *far* into the night. 他常工作到深夜。***as*** (or ***so***) ***far as*** **a.** 像…那樣遠。We did not go *so far as* the bridge. 我們沒有走到橋那麼遠。**b.** 就…而論。*So far as* I know, he has not much money. 就我所知, 他沒有很多錢。***by far*** **a.** 遠超過其他地; 顯然地。This is *by far* the best. 這一個顯然是最好的。**b.** 很;極高。***far and away*** (=by far) 遠超過其餘之上地。This one is *far and away* better. 這一個比較好得多。***far and near*** 遠遠近近; 到處。They searched *far and near* for the missing airman. 他們到處搜尋那失蹤的航空員。***far and wide*** 廣布;普遍。He has traveled *far and wide.* 他足跡遍天下。***far be it from me*** 我不敢;我不要。***far from*** 遠非; 絕非。It is *far from* perfect. 那絕算不得是完善。***far from it*** 一點也不。I don't blame him—*far from it.* 我不責備他——一點也不。***far out***〖俚〗**a.** 不尋常的;不合常規的。**b.** 極端的; 激進派的。**c.** 奧祕的;祕傳的。***far to seek*** 不易找到; 難找。A really conscientious man is *far to seek.* 眞正正直而盡責的人不易找到。***from far*** 來自遠處。***go far*** **a.** 成功; 成名。

F

That man will *go far.* 那個人將來大有希望。**b.** 保持長時間的。**c.** 大有幫助。***go far towards*** 對…有大大的貢獻。***how far*** 至於甚麼距離、程度等。She didn't know *how far* to trust him. 她不知道應該相信他到甚麼程度。***in so far as*** 至於…程度。***so far*** 到目前爲止。*So far,* you have been successful. 到目前爲止，你是成功了。***so far so good*** 到目前爲止一切尙稱良好。***thus far*** 到目前爲止。He has had good luck *thus far.* 到目前爲止他事事如意。

far. ① farad. ② farthing.

far·ad [ˈfærəd, ˈfæræd; ˈfærəd] *n.* 法拉(電容量的單位)。

Far·a·day [ˈfærədɪ; ˈfærədi] *n.* 法拉第(Michael, 1791–1867, 英國物理學家、化學家)。

far·a·day [ˈfærədɪ; ˈfærədi] *n.* 〖物理〗法拉第(電量單位)。

fa·rad·ic [fəˈrædɪk, fæ–; fəˈrædik] *adj.* 〖電〗感應電流的。

far·a·dize [ˈfærəˌdaɪz; ˈfærədaiz] *v.t.*, **-dized, -diz·ing.** 〖醫〗以感應電流治療。

far·a·way [ˈfɑrəˈwe; ˈfɑːrəwei] *adj.* ①久遠的；遙遠的。②恍惚的；如夢的。

far-be·tween [ˈfɑrbɪˌtwin; ˈfɑːbiˈtwiːn] *adj.* 隔離的；遠隔的；久隔的；稀有的。

farce [fɑrs; fɑːs] *n.* ①笑劇；滑稽劇；鬧劇。The place of *farce* in the modern theater is disputable. 鬧劇在現代戲劇中的地位尙未確定。②無謂之事；滑稽可笑之事；諷刺；胡鬧。The trial was a mere *farce.* 那次審判簡直是胡鬧。③詼諧；滑稽。

far·ceur [fɑrˈsœ; fɑːˈsœ] 〖法〗 *n.* 詼諧家；滑稽劇作者；滑稽劇演員。

far·ci·cal [ˈfɑrsɪkl; ˈfɑːsikəl] *adj.* 滑稽劇的；詼諧的；引人發笑的。—**ly,** *adv.*

far·ci·cal·i·ty [ˌfɑrsɪˈkælətɪ; ˌfɑːsiˈkæliti] *n., pl.* **-ties.** ①滑稽；諧謔。②滑稽之行爲或言詞。

far cry 長距離。

far·cy [ˈfɑrsɪ; ˈfɑːsi] *n.* 〖獸醫〗馬皮疽。

far·del [ˈfɑrdl; ˈfɑːdl] *n.* 〖古〗①束；包。②重擔；不幸。

‡fare [fɛr; fɛə] *n., v.,* **fared, far·ing.** —*n.* ①車費；船費；旅客票價。The *fare* from London to Paris is £6. 從倫敦到巴黎的票價爲六鎊。②旅客；乘客。The taxi-driver had only six *fares* all day. 那計程車司機一天祇載了六個乘客。③飲食；食品。The *fare* in this restaurant is terrible. 這家餐館的食物壞極了。—*v.i.* ①享受飲食。He usually *fares* sumptuously. 他平常飲食很豐富。②處境；遭遇；經營；經歷。He *fared* well in his business. 他生意做得不壞。③〖古〗行；旅行。

Far East 遠東。

fare-thee-well [ˈfɛrðiˌwɛl; ˈfɛəðiːˈwel] *n.* ①完美的狀態。②最大效果；極限。(亦作 **fare-you-well, fare-ye-well**)

***fare·well** [ˈfɛrˈwɛl, ˌfɛrˈwɛl; ˈfɛəˈwel, ˌfɛəˈwel] *interj.* 再會；祝你平安。—*n.* ①告別辭；臨別贈言。The visitors made their *farewells* and left. 訪客們互相告別然後離開了。②離別；辭別。③歡送會。They held a great *farewell* for the retiring senator. 他們爲將退休的參議員舉行盛大的歡送會。—*adj.* 告別的；臨別的。a *farewell* speech. 告別演說。—*v.t.* 向…道別。to *farewell* the parting guests. 向將離開的客人道別。—*v.i.* 道別。

fare-you-well [ˈfɛrjʊˌwɛl; ˈfɛəjuˈwel] *n.* =**fare-thee-well.**

far-famed [ˈfɑrˌfemd; ˈfɑːˈfeimd] *adj.* 名聞遠方的；著名的。

far-fetched [ˈfɑrˈfɛtʃt; ˈfɑːˈfetʃt] *adj.* ①牽强的；不自然的。②自遠方帶來的；來自遠方的。

far-flung [ˈfɑrˈflʌŋ; ˈfɑːˈflʌŋ] *adj.* 廣布的；範圍極廣的。

far-gone [ˈfɑrˈgɔn; ˈfɑːˈgɔn] *adj.* ①遙遠的。②疲乏不堪。③磨損不堪。④程度已深的。

fa·ri·na [fəˈrinə; fəˈrainə] *n.* ①穀類磨成之粉。②澱粉。③〖植物〗花粉。

far·i·na·ceous [ˌfærəˈneʃəs; ˌfæriˈneiʃəs] *adj.* ①穀粉做成的；穀粉的。②含澱粉的。③穀粉性的。

far·i·nose [ˈfærəˌnos; ˈfærinous] *adj.* ①澱粉性的；生澱粉的。② 〖動、植物〗覆有白粉的。

far·kle·ber·ry [ˈfɑrklˌbɛrɪ; ˈfɑːklˌberi] *n.* 〖植物〗(美國南部產之)一種白莓。

farl(e) [fɑrl; fɑːl] *n.* 一種燕麥粉薄餅。

‡farm [fɑrm; fɑːm] *n.* ①農田；農場；飼養場。He worked on a *farm.* 他在農場作工。②〖美〗隸屬於大棒球比賽聯盟之小聯盟。—*v.i.* 種田；飼畜。He is *farming* in South America. 他在南美務農。—*v.t.* ①耕(田)；種植；豢養(家畜)。He *farms* 100 acres of land. 他耕種一百英畝田。②租佃。The estate was broken up and *farmed.* 該田產被分租出去了。③招人承包(收租稅等)；承包(收租稅等)。④寄養(幼兒等)。***farm out*** 〖棒球〗派至小聯盟(接受訓練)。—**a·ble,** *adj.*

farm belt (美國等之)農業區。

farm bloc 美國國會中主張保護農民利益之集團。

‡farm·er [ˈfɑrmɚ; ˈfɑːmə] *n.* ①農夫；農人；佃農。a leading dairy *farmer.* 主要酪農。②賦稅承包人。〖注意〗**peasant** 爲"小農"或"農工"，僅適用於歐洲大陸。在英、美通稱 **farmer.**

farm·er·ette [ˌfɑrməˈrɛt; ˌfɑːməˈret] *n.* 〖俗〗農婦；種田的婦女。

far·mer·ly [ˈfɑrməlɪ; ˈfɑːməli] *adj.* 像農人的。

farm hand 農場勞動者；農家之雇工。(亦作 **farmhand**)

***farm·house** [ˈfɑrmˌhaus; ˈfɑːmhaus] *n.* 農舍。

farm·ing [ˈfɑrmɪŋ; ˈfɑːmiŋ] *n.* ①農業；農作；耕作。②賦稅之承包。③出租。—*adj.* 農業的；耕種的。

farm·land [ˈfɑrmˌlænd; ˈfɑːmlænd] *n.* 農地。

farm·stead [ˈfɑrmˌstɛd; ˈfɑːmsted] *n.* 農場及其建築物。(亦作 **farmsteading**)

farm stock 農業資產。

farm·work·er [ˈfɑrmˌwɝkɚ; ˈfɑːmˌwəːkə] *n.* 〖英〗=**farm hand.**

***farm·yard** [ˈfɑrmˌjɑrd; ˈfɑːmjɑːd] *n.* 農家之庭院。

far·o [ˈfɛro; ˈfɛərou] *n.* 一種紙牌戲(入局者對莊家之一組牌，猜測其出現之順序而加注之賭博)。

***far-off** [ˈfɑrˈɔf; ˈfɑːˈɔːf] *adj.* 久隔的；遙遠的。

fa·rouche [faˈruʃ; fəˈruːʃ] 〖法〗 *adj.* ①兇野的；不馴的。②不善社交的；羞澀的。③悒鬱寡歡的。

far-out [ˈfɑrˈaut; ˈfɑːˈaut] *adj.* 〖美俚〗①非常特別的；走在時代前面的。②極度理論性的；奧祕的。③深受感動的；出神的。

far·ra·go [fəˈrego; fəˈrɑːgou] *n., pl.* **-goes.** 混成物；雜合物；混雜。

far-reach·ing [ˈfɑrˈritʃɪŋ; ˈfɑːˈriːtʃiŋ] *adj.* 影響廣大的；遠達的。—**ly,** *adv.*

far·ri·er ['færɪɚ; 'færiə] *n.* 〖英〗①蹄鐵匠。②獸醫。

far·ri·er·y ['færɪərɪ; 'færiəri] *n., pl.* **-er·ies.** ①蹄鐵術;獸醫術。②蹄鐵場;馬掌鋪。

far·row ['færo; 'færou] *n.* 一窩小豬。—*v.t.* 產(小豬)。—*v.i.* 產小豬〖常 down〗.

far-see·ing ['fɑr'siɪŋ; 'fɑː'siːiŋ] *adj.* ①有遠見的;有先見之明的。②能看得遠的。

far-sight·ed ['fɑr'saɪtɪd; 'fɑː'saitid] *adj.* ①遠視的(眼)。②眼光遠大的。—**ly,** *adv.* —**ness,** *n.*

fart [fɑrt; fɑːt] *n.* 〖俗〗屁。—*v.t.* & *v.i.* 〖俗〗放屁。

‡**far·ther** ['fɑrðɚ; 'fɑːðə] comp. of **far.** —*adj.* ①(用指距遠)更遠的; 較遠的。②(=further) 進一步的; 另外的。Do you need *farther* help? 你還需要進一步的幫助嗎? —*adv.* ①更遠地; 較遠地。They were so tired that they could go no *farther.* 他們太疲倦了,所以不能再向前行。②更加地;進一步地。③此外(=further). ***farther on*** 再向前;更向前。The village is about two miles *farther on.* 那村子還在前面約兩英里遠的地方。〖注意〗在正式文字裏 **farther** 僅限於指具體的距離,而 **further** 則偏於抽象的程度。但在俚俗之用法中,兩者常混用,且有以 further 代替 farther 之趨勢。

far·ther·most ['fɑrðɚ,most; 'fɑːðə-moust] *adj.* 最遠的。

far·thest** ['fɑrðɪst;'fɑːðist] superl. of **far.** *adj.* & *adv.* 最遠的(地);最久的(地)。See who could jump the *farthest.* 看誰能跳得最遠。at*** (***the***) ***farthest*** 最多;至遲。

far·thing ['fɑrðɪŋ; 'fɑːðiŋ] *n.* ①英國小錢幣名。②價值微小之物。***not to care*** (or ***matter***) ***a farthing*** 毫不在乎。***not worth a farthing*** (or ***brass***) 一文不值。

far·thin·gale ['fɑrðɪŋ,gel;'fɑːðiŋgeil] *n.* ①十六、七世紀時用以撐大女裙之鯨骨環。②用鯨骨環撐大之女裙。

f.a.s., F.A.S. free alongside ship. 船邊交貨。

fas·ces ['fæsiz; 'fæsiːz] *n. pl.* ①(棒、桿等之)一束。②古羅馬代表權威之束棒。

fas·ci·a ['fæʃɪə; 'feiʃə] *n., pl.* **fas·ci·ae** ['fæʃɪ,i; 'feiʃiː]. ①帶;飾帶。②〖外科〗繃帶。③〖建築〗線脚間之扁平石材或木材;封簷底板。④〖解剖〗筋膜;肌膜。⑤〖動物〗濶條之色帶。—**fas·ci·al,** *adj.*

fas·ci·ate ['fæʃɪ,et; 'fæʃieit] *adj.* ①以帶束的。②〖植物〗叢生的;由異狀生長而扁平的。③〖動物〗有闊條之色帶的。—**ly,** *adv.* —**fas·ci·a·tion,** *n.*

fas·ci·at·ed ['fæʃɪ,etɪd; 'fæʃieitid] *adj.* =**fasciate.**

fas·ci·cle ['fæsɪkl; 'fæsikl] *n.* ①小束。②(書籍等之)分册。③〖植物〗(花、葉等之)束;簇;團。④〖解剖〗纖維束。

fas·cic·u·lar [fə'sɪkjulɚ; fə'sikjulə] *adj.* ①〖植物〗叢生的。②〖解剖〗纖維束的。—**ly,** *adv.*

fas·cic·u·late [fə'sɪkju,let; fə'sikju-lit] *adj.* 叢生的;成束而生的。(亦作 **fasciculated**) —**ly,** *adv.* —**fas·cic·u·la·tion,** *n.*

fas·ci·cule ['fæsɪ,kjul; 'fæsikjuːl] *n.* =**fasciculus.**

fas·cic·u·lus [fə'sɪkjuləs; fə'sikjuləs] *n., pl.* **-li** [-,laɪ; -lai]. ①〖解剖〗纖維束。②(書籍等之)分册。

***fas·ci·nate** ['fæsn,et; 'fæsineit] *v.,* **-nat·ed, -nat·ing.** —*v.t.* ①使迷惑;對…有極大魔力。The actress's beauty and cleverness *fascinated* everyone. 那女伶的美與聰明迷住了每一個人。②蠱惑;施魔術於。—*v.i.* 迷人; 令人入神。The very style of the book *fascinates.* 該書的風格本身就令人入神。

fas·ci·nat·ing ['fæsn,etɪŋ; 'fæsineitiŋ] *adj.* 迷人的;吸引人的。—**ly,** *adv.*

***fas·ci·na·tion** [,fæsn'eʃən; ,fæsi'neiʃən] *n.* ①迷惑; 蠱惑; 銷魂。②魅力;魔力;嬌媚。They found a certain *fascination* in combat. 他們發現戰鬥有某種魅力。

fas·ci·na·tor ['fæsə,netɚ;'fæsineitə] *n.* ①有迷惑力者;蠱惑者。②婦女之一種頭巾。

fas·cine [fæ'sin; fæ'siːn] *n.* ①束薪;柴把。②〖築城〗柴把;木排;柴綑。

fascine dwelling 湖上的筏上住戶。

Fas·cism ['fæʃ,ɪzəm; 'fæʃizəm] *n.* 法西斯主義(1919年創於義大利,1922年在墨索里尼 Mussolini 的領導下奪取義大利政權)。

Fa·scis·mo [fɑ'ʃizmo; fæ'ʃiːzmou] 〖義〗*n.* 法西斯主義 (=Fascism).

Fas·cist, fas·cist ['fæʃɪst; 'fæʃist] *n.* ①法西斯主義者。②法西斯黨員。—*adj.* 法西斯主義的;法西斯黨的。

Fa·scis·ti [fə'ʃɪsti; fæ'ʃistiː] *n.pl.* 法西斯政黨;黑衫黨 (1919 年義大利 Mussolini 所創之反民主獨裁政黨)。

fas·cis·tic [fə'ʃɪstɪk; fæ'ʃistik] *adj.* =**fascist.**

fash [fæʃ; fæʃ] *v.t.* & *v.i.* 〖蘇〗困惱;窘困; 使氣惱。***fash oneself; fash one's thumb*** 〖蘇〗自尋煩惱。—*n.* 〖蘇〗煩惱;苦惱。

‡**fash·ion** ['fæʃən;'fæʃən] *n.* ①姿態;方式。He walks in a peculiar *fashion.* 他走路的姿態很奇特。②時樣; 風尚; 時髦(尤指裝束或擧止)。Short skirts were the *fashion* in 1919. 短裙乃是 1919 年的流行時樣。③時髦人物;上流社會。④形狀。⑤種類。You can fix it with a drill or something of that *fashion.* 你可以用鑽或類似工具來修理。***after*** (or ***in***) ***a fashion*** 略略地;不太令人滿意地。He speaks English very much *after a fashion.* 他說英文不太高明。***after the fashion of*** 模仿; 仿效。***be all the fashion*** 非常流行。***be the fashion*** 很流行;很時髦。It *is* not *the fashion* to do this. 這樣做是不合潮流的。***follow the fashion*** 趕時髦。***in*** (***out of***) ***fashion*** (不)流行。When did this style of dress go *out of fashion?* 這種衣服的式樣甚麼時候變爲不流行了? ***man of fashion*** 時髦人物。***set the fashion*** 出新花樣以創先例; 開風氣之先。—*v.t.* ①做成…的形狀。②使配合。

***fash·ion·a·ble** ['fæʃənəbl;'fæʃənəbl] *adj.* ①時髦的;流行的(服裝等)。a *fashionable* dress. 時髦的服裝。②時髦人物用的; 像時髦人物的。—*n.* 時髦人物。to keep up with the *fashionables* of the city. 跟上城裏的時髦人物。

fash·ion·a·bly ['fæʃənəblɪ; 'fæʃə-nəbli] *adv.* 時髦地;流行地。

fashion book 時裝錄。

fashion designer 時裝設計師。

fash·ioned ['fæʃənd; 'fæʃənd] *adj.* ①…式的;…風的。②(織物之)作…形式的。

fash·ion·mon·ger ['fæʃən,mʌŋgɚ; 'fæʃən,mʌŋgə] *n.* 追隨時尚者;研究時尚者;提倡時尚者。

fashion plate ①時裝圖樣。②穿着時髦的人。

fashion show 時裝表演會。

‡**fast¹** [fæst, fɑst; fɑːst] *adj.* ①快的;迅速的。My watch is *fast.* 我的錶快了。②牢固的;緊的。Make the door *fast.* 把門拴牢

或關牢。③忠實的。④放蕩的。He led a *fast* life, drinking and gambling. 他過放蕩的生活，又飲酒又賭博。⑤不易褪色的;維持長久的。Good cloth is dyed with *fast* color. 好的布料是以不褪色的顏料染的。⑥激烈的。⑦深沉的;熟睡的。***pull a fast one*** 欺詐;詭計。He *pulled a fast one* on his best friend and lost his friendship. 他對他最好的朋友耍詭計而失去了他的友誼。—*adv.* ①快地;迅速地。Don't speak so *fast.* 不要說這樣快。②堅定地;穩固地。③完全地;徹底地。He was *fast* asleep. 他正熟睡着。④激烈地。He was living too *fast* for his health. 對他的健康來說，他生活得太過緊張。***play fast and loose*** (***with***) 玩弄;行爲不負責任。to *play fast and loose with* someone else's money. 胡亂花別人的錢。***stand fast*** 立穩。***stick fast*** 無法前進。—*n.* 繫結物(如鎖、門、鉤等)。

fast[2] *v.i.* 斷食;齋戒;禁食。—*v.t.* 使絕食;禁食。—*n.* ①斷食;齋戒;禁食。②齋戒日;齋戒期。

fast[3] *n.* 拴船之鐵鍊或繩。

fast·back [ˈfæstbæk; ˈfɑːstbæk] *n.* ①車篷向後傾斜的汽車。②此等汽車之車篷。

fast day 齋戒日。

fas·ten** [ˈfæsn̩, ˈfɑsn̩; ˈfɑːsn] *v.t.* ①裝牢;關鎖;縛;繫。*Fasten* the door. 把門關牢或鎖上。②連結;加諸於。He tried to *fasten* the blame on me. 他想把罪過加在我身上。③盯住;使朝向。He *fastened* his attention upon a fire in the distance. 他集中注意盯住遠方的火。④使(顏色)不褪。We *fastened* the dyes into the cloth. 我們使染色不從布上脫落。—*v.i.* ①牢;緊;附着。The door will not *fasten.* 此門關不牢。②緊抓;堅持〖on, upon〗。He *fastened* on the idea. 他堅持那種想法。③集中注意〖on, upon〗。His blue eyes *fastened* upon the general. 他的藍眼盯住將軍。fasten a crime on*** (or ***upon***) ***a person*** 歸罪於某人。***fasten*** (***something***) ***off*** 用結繫牢。***fasten one's eyes on*** 注視。***fasten*** (***something***) ***up*** 關緊並鎖牢。

fas·ten·er [ˈfæsn̩ɚ; ˈfɑːsnə] *n.* ①牢繫者;使固着者。②使牢繫之物;使固着之物。

fas·ten·ing [ˈfæsn̩ɪŋ, ˈfɑsn̩ɪŋ; ˈfɑːsniŋ] *n.* 繫結物。

fast-food [ˈfæstˌfud; ˈfɑːstfuːd] *adj.* 〖美〗速食的;快餐的。

fas·tid·i·ous [fæsˈtɪdɪəs; fæsˈtidiəs] *adj.* 難以取悅的;吹毛求疵的;苛求的。

fas·tid·i·ous·ly [fæsˈtɪdɪəslɪ; fæsˈtidiəsli] *adv.* 嚴正地;一絲不苟地。

fas·tid·i·ous·ness [fæsˈtɪdɪəsnɪs; fæsˈtidiəsnis] *n.* 嚴正;一絲不苟。

fas·tig·i·ate [fæsˈtɪdʒɪɪt; fæsˈtiːdʒiit] *adj.* 成錐狀上升的;向上逐漸變窄的。(亦作 **fastigiated**)

fast·ness [ˈfæstnɪs; ˈfɑːstnis] *n.* ①鞏固;堅牢。②要塞;堡壘;城砦。③迅速;急速。④浪漫;放蕩。

:fat [fæt; fæt] *adj.,* **fat·ter, fat·test,** *n., v.,* **fat·ted, fat·ting.** —*adj.* ①肥的;胖的。This meat is too *fat.* 這肉太肥了。②豐富的;充實的。The *fat* job pays well. 這肥缺待遇優厚。③愚蠢的。④給予好機會的。⑤厚的;寬的。⑥〖俚〗幾乎等於零的。⑦肥沃的。Everything grows in this *fat* soil. 在這種肥沃的土壤中任何東西都會生長。⑧富;有錢。He grew *fat* on dishonest profits. 他發不義之財。***a fat chance*** 〖俚〗希望甚少;機會極小。*A fat chance* he has of winning the title! 他奪得冠軍的機會極少! ***a fat lot*** 〖俚〗幾乎不;簡直不;壓根兒不。*A fat lot* they care about anyone else's troubles! 他們對別人的麻煩一點兒也不關心! —*n.* ①肥肉;脂肪。I do not like *fat* (of meat). 我不喜歡吃肥肉。②油類。Fried potatoes are cooked in deep *fat.* 炸洋芋是放在油裏炸的。③多餘之物;多餘部分。***chew the fat*** 〖俚〗閒談;聊天。***live on the fat of the land*** 過豪華的生活。***The fat is in the fire.*** **a.** 生米已成熟飯;木已成舟。**b.** 危機迫在眉睫。**c.** 無可挽救之行動或事件業已開始。—*v.t.* 使肥胖。*Fat* her up and kill her. 餵肥她再殺她。—*v.i.* 變肥胖。***kill the fatted calf*** 竭誠地歡迎。

fa·tal** [ˈfetl; ˈfeitl] *adj.* ①致命的;不幸的。②毀滅性的;毀壞性的。The loss of all our money was *fatal* to our plan. 丟了錢把我們的計畫也毀了。③重大的;決定的;決定命運的。④命運的。⑤不可避免的;宿命的。fatal sisters*** 〖希臘神話〗司命運的三女神。

fa·tal·ism [ˈfetl̩ˌɪzəm; ˈfeitəlizəm] *n.* ①宿命論。②對宿命論之信仰;由此信仰產生的順從命運的行爲。

fa·tal·ist [ˈfetl̩ɪst; ˈfeitəlist] *n.* 宿命論者。

fa·tal·is·tic [ˌfetl̩ˈɪstɪk; ˌfeitəˈlistik] *adj.* ①宿命論的;宿命論者的。②相信宿命論的。—**al·ly,** *adv.*

fa·tal·i·ty [feˈtælətɪ; fəˈtæliti] *n., pl.* **-ties.** ①災禍;死亡。②關係生命;致命。③命運。④宿命;命數。⑤災禍中之死者。

fa·tal·ly [ˈfetl̩ɪ; ˈfeitəli] *adv.* ①宿命地;命運注定地。②致命地。③無可補救地。

Fa·ta Mor·ga·na [ˈfɑtəmɔrˈgɑnə; ˈfɑːtə mɔːˈgɑːnə] 〖義〗①中世紀稗史或傳奇中之精怪。②(f- m-)(義大利與西西里之間的海峽上常出現之)海市蜃樓。

fat cat 〖俚〗①捐獻大宗政治款項之富戶。②有勢有名之人。③因財富而獲得某種特權者。

:fate [fet; feit] *n.* ①命運;運數;天命。He doesn't believe in *fate.* 他不相信命運之說。②吉凶;禍福;安危。They met their various *fates.* 他們遭遇到各種不同的禍福。③死;毀滅。④結局。The Congress decided the bill's *fate* by a single vote. 國會以一次的投票決定了那議案的結局。***go to one's fate*** 死。***meet one's fate*** 死。***the irony of Fate*** 命運的播弄。—*v.t.* 注定。The deep antipathy *fates* them to antagonism. 深沉的反感注定他們處於敵對地位。

fat·ed [ˈfetɪd; ˈfeitid] *adj.* 命運決定了的;命數的;宿命的。***be fated*** (***that***) 命定。

fate·ful [ˈfetfəl; ˈfeitful] *adj.* ①命運注定的。②重大的;決定性的。③不幸的;招致毀滅的;致死的。④預示的;預言的。—**ly,** *adv.*

Fates [fets; feits] *n. pl.* 〖希臘、羅馬神話〗司命運之三女神。

fat-faced [ˈfætˌfest; ˈfætfeist] *adj.* 面孔圓胖的。

fat·head [ˈfætˌhɛd; ˈfæthed] *n.* 愚鈍者;傻瓜。

fat·head·ed [ˈfætˌhɛdɪd; ˈfætˈhedid] *adj.* 愚鈍的;笨的。

:fa·ther [ˈfɑðɚ; ˈfɑːðə] *n.* ①父親。Like *father,* like son. 有其父，必有其子。②祖先。③創始者;發明者。④神父。⑤對教士之尊稱。⑥對長者之尊稱。⑦古羅馬之參議員。⑧〖俗〗岳父;繼父;義父。⑨扶養者;養育者。a *father* to the poor. 窮人之父。⑩元老;德高望重者。⑪起源。⑫原始形態;鼻祖。The horseless carriage was the *father* of all modern automobiles. 無馬之馬車爲一切現代汽車之鼻祖。***sleep with one's fathers*** 死。***The child is father to the man.*** 一個人的兒童時代決定其未來。***the Father*** 上帝 (=God). ***the fathers*** 基督教的最初六世紀之主要作家。***the Pilgrim Fathers*** 美國的開國先驅。***The wish is father to the thought.*** 願望決定思想。—*v.t.* ①爲…之父。He *fathered* eleven sons. 他生了十一個兒子。②扶養;養育。③創造;負責;擔任。Edison *fathered* many inventions. 愛迪生有許多發明。④認某人爲…之父。Investigation *fathered* the child upon her lover. 調查的結果得知她的情人就是那小孩之父。⑤將…歸咎或歸功於某人。

Father Christmas 〖英〗聖誕老人。

father confessor ①〖天主教〗聽告解的神父;解罪神父。②聽人傾訴私衷之人。

fa·ther·hood 〔ˈfɑðə͵hud; ˈfɑːðəhud〕 *n.* 父親之身分、資格;父權;父道。

fa·ther-in-law 〔ˈfɑðərɪn͵lɔ; ˈfɑːðərinlɔː〕 *n., pl.* **fa·thers-in-law.** ①公公;翁(夫之父)。②岳父。

fa·ther·land 〔ˈfɑðə͵lænd; ˈfɑːðəlænd〕 *n.* 祖國。〖注意〗 **fatherland** 係從德語 Vaterland 而來, 在英語用法中, mother country 較通用。

fa·ther·less 〔ˈfɑðəlɪs; ˈfɑːðəlis〕 *adj.* 無父的。

fa·ther·like 〔ˈfɑðə͵laɪk; ˈfɑːðəlaik〕 *adj. & adv.* 如父的(地)。

fa·ther·li·ness 〔ˈfɑðəlɪnɪs; ˈfɑːðəlinis〕 *n.* 如父;父道;父心。

fa·ther·ly 〔ˈfɑðəlɪ; ˈfɑːðəli〕 *adj.* ①父親的。②如父親的;慈愛的。

˙fath·om 〔ˈfæðəm; ˈfæðəm〕 *n., pl.* **fath·oms** or **fath·om,** *v.* —*n.* 噚(長度名, =6英尺, 多用以量水深)。—*v.t.* ①量(水)的深淺。②徹底明白。I cannot *fathom* his meaning. 我不能徹底明白他的意思。

fath·om·a·ble 〔ˈfæðəməbl̩; ˈfæðəməbl〕 *adj.* 可測的;可洞悉的。

fa·thom·e·ter 〔fæˈðɑmətə; fæˈðɔmitə〕 *n.* 回音測深儀;水深計。

fath·om·less 〔ˈfæðəmlɪs; ˈfæðəmlis〕 *adj.* ①深不可測的。②不可瞭解的。—**ly,** *adv.* —**ness,** *n.*

˙fa·tigue 〔fəˈtig; fəˈtiːg〕 *n., v.,* **-tigued, -ti·guing,** *adj.* —*n.* ①疲倦; 疲乏; 疲勞。bodily (mental) *fatigue.* 身體的(精神的)疲勞。②令人勞累的工作或努力。a *fatigue* such as floor scrubbing or potato peeling. 如拖地板或削馬鈴薯等令人勞累的工作。③經長期操勞或緊張而發生之(心智)衰弱。④軍中雜務(=fatigue duty)。⑤(*pl.*)〖軍〗工作服。—*v.t.* 使疲勞; 使(心智)衰弱。—*adj.* 疲勞的;疲累的。

fa·tigued 〔fəˈtigd; fəˈtiːgd〕 *adj.* 疲乏的。

fatigue dress 〖軍〗工作服。(亦作 **fatigues, fatigue clothes**)

fatigue party 〖軍〗雜役班。

fat·ling 〔ˈfætlɪŋ; ˈfætliŋ〕 *n.* 肥畜。

fat·ness 〔ˈfætnɪs; ˈfætnis〕 *n.* ①肥胖。②豐富。③肥沃。

fat·so 〔ˈfætso; ˈfætsou〕 *n., pl.* **-sos.** 〖美俚〗胖子。

fat·ten 〔ˈfætn̩; ˈfætn〕 *v.t.* ①催肥;養肥〖常 up〗。②使增大(多)。—*v.i.* ①變肥。②增大(多);成長。

fat·tish 〔ˈfætɪʃ; ˈfætiʃ〕 *adj.* 稍肥的;略胖的。

fat·ty 〔ˈfætɪ; ˈfæti〕 *adj.,* **-ti·er, -ti·est,** *n.* —*adj.* ①脂肪的;含脂肪的;多脂肪的。②如脂肪的;油質的;油膩的。③在成分上與脂肪有關的。—*n.* 〖俗〗胖子。—**fat·ti·ness,** *n.*

fa·tu·i·ty 〔fəˈtjuətɪ, -ˈtu-; fəˈtjuːiti〕 *n., pl.* **-ties.** ①愚頑;昏庸;愚而自滿。②愚昧之事物。③〖罕〗白癡;低能。

fat·u·ous 〔ˈfætʃuəs; ˈfætjuəs〕 *adj.* ①愚庸而自滿的。②不實在的;空虛的。—**ly,** *adv.* —**ness,** *n.*

fat-wit·ted 〔ˈfætˈwɪtɪd; ˈfætˈwitid〕 *adj.* 遲鈍的;愚魯的。

fau·bourg 〔foˈbur; fouˈbuːə〕 〖法〗 *n.* (城市之)郊區;郊外;近郊。

fau·cal 〔ˈfɔkəl; ˈfɔːkəl〕 *adj.* ①咽喉的。②〖語音〗喉音的。—*n.* 喉音。

fau·ces 〔ˈfɔsiz; ˈfɔːsiːz〕 *n.pl.* 咽門;咽喉。

fau·cet 〔ˈfɔsɪt; ˈfɔːsit〕 *n.* (自來水管等之)龍頭。

fau·cial 〔ˈfɔʃəl; ˈfɔːʃəl〕 *adj.* 咽喉的。a *faucial* tonsil. 扁桃腺。

faugh 〔fɔ; fɔː〕 *interj.* 呸; 嘘(表示輕蔑、嫌惡之聲音)。(亦作 **foh**)

Faulk·ner 〔ˈfɔknə; ˈfɔːknə〕 *n.* 佛克納 (William, 1897–1962, 美國名小說家, 1949年獲諾貝爾文學獎)。(亦作 **Falkner**) —**i·an,** *adj.*

‡fault 〔fɔlt; fɔːlt〕 *n.* ①過錯;過失。It was my *fault.* 那是我的過錯。②缺點; 毛病; 錯誤。She loves him in spite of his *faults.* 他雖有缺點, 她仍愛他。③〖地質〗斷層。④(網球等之)發球失誤。***at fault*** **a.** 失錯;咎有應得。**b.** 茫然不知所措。I am *at fault* as to where to go. 我不知究竟該往那裏去。***find fault*** 批評;吹毛求疵。He is always *finding fault.* 他老是吹毛求疵。***in fault*** 錯了。***to a fault*** 甚;過分。He is generous *to a fault.* 他過分慷慨。—*v.i.* ①犯錯。His tongue stammered and *faulted* with rage. 他講話因生氣而口吃並出錯。②〖地質〗發生斷層。—*v.t.* ①批評; 認爲不妥。I *fault* this speech in three ways. 我認爲這演講有三方面不妥。②將…做錯。③〖地質〗使發生斷層。

fault·find·er 〔ˈfɔlt͵faɪndə; ˈfɔːlt͵faində〕 *n.* ①揭人短處者;吹毛求疵者。②〖電〗檢示電流障礙之裝置。

fault·find·ing 〔ˈfɔlt͵faɪndɪŋ; ˈfɔːlt͵faindiŋ〕 *adj.* 揭人短處的; 吹毛求疵的。—*n.* 找錯;揭短。

fault·i·ly 〔ˈfɔltɪlɪ; ˈfɔːltili〕 *adv.* 有缺點地;有過失地;可指責地。

fault·i·ness 〔ˈfɔltɪnɪs; ˈfɔːltinis〕 *n.* 有錯誤;不完全。

fault·less 〔ˈfɔltlɪs; ˈfɔːltlis〕 *adj.* 毫無瑕疵的;完美的。—**ly,** *adv.* —**ness,** *n.*

fault·y 〔ˈfɔltɪ; ˈfɔːlti〕 *adj.,* **fault·i·er, fault·i·est.** 有缺點的;有錯誤的。

faun 〔fɔn; fɔːn〕 *n.* 〖羅馬神話〗(半人半羊狀之)農牧神。

fau·na 〔ˈfɔnə; ˈfɔːnə〕 *n., pl.* **-nas, -nae** 〔-ni; -niː〕. ①(the–)(某區域、某時代的)動物(集合稱);動物區系。②討論某區域、某時代動物的論文;某區系之動物誌。

fau·nal 〔ˈfɔnl̩; ˈfɔːnəl〕 *adj.* 動物區系的;動物誌的。—**ly,** *adv.*

fau·nis·tic 〔fɔˈnɪstɪk; fɔːˈnistik〕 *adj.* =**faunal.**

Faust 〔faust; faust〕 *n.* 浮士德(**a.** 日爾曼故事中之一人物, 曾將其靈魂售與魔鬼以換取權力及知識; **b.** Goethe 著之一悲劇; **c.** Gounod 所作之歌劇名)。—**i·an,** *adj.*

fau·teuil 〔ˈfotəl; ˈfoutəl〕 〖法〗 *n.* 安樂椅;太師椅。

faux pas 〔ˈfoˈpɑ; ˈfouˈpɑː〕 *pl.* **faux pas** 〔~ˈpɑz; ~ˈpɑːz〕. 〖法〗失言;失禮;失態。

fa·ve·la 〔fəˈvɛlə; fəˈvelə〕 *n.* (巴西的)

貧民區。 「毒；豆類中毒。」

fa·vism ['fevɪzəm; 'feivizəm] *n.* 豆中

:fa·vo(u)r ['fevɚ; 'feivə] *n.* ①恩寵；愛護；善意。to win a person's *favor.* 得某人好感或恩寵。May I ask a *favor* of you? 我可以請你幫幫忙嗎？②喜歡；同意；贊成。They will look with *favor* on your plan. 他們對你的計畫會表贊成的。③偏好；私好。④來函；大札。⑤贈品；紀念物。⑥特權。⑦利益。a man who acts only in his own *favor.* 一個只爲自己利益打算的人。⑧有利的差別。⑨(常 *pl.*)(婦女)以身相許。***be* (or *stand*) *high in one's favor*** 頗受某人之尊重。***by* (or *with*) *your favor*** 蒙你的允許。***find favor in a person's eyes*** 邀寵於某人。***in favor of*** **a.** 贊成；支持。I am *in favor of* a change. 我贊成改變。**b.** 有利於。He resigned *in favor of* a better man. 他辭職讓賢。**c.** 支付給。to write a check *in favor of* the bank. 簽一張付給銀行的支票。***out of favor*** 不受歡迎。A fashion in favor this year may be *out of favor* next year. 今年受人歡迎的式樣明年可能便不受人歡迎了。—*v.t.* ①眷顧；愛護；贊成。Fortune *favors* the brave. 命運眷顧勇者。②偏愛；徇私。A teacher must not *favor* any of his pupils. 教師不可偏愛任何學生。③於…有利；幫助。The weather *favored* our voyage. 天氣使我們的航行順利。④肖；似（指面貌）。The girl *favors* her mother. 這女孩面貌像她的母親。⑤善爲照顧。

F

***fa·vo(u)r·a·ble** ['fevərəbl; 'feivərəbl] *adj.* ①贊成的；贊許的；嘉許的。The teacher made a *favorable* report on the boy's work at school. 教師報告該生在校成績優良。②有幫助的；順利的。a *favorable* wind. 順風。③良好的。④前途有望的。*favorable* conditions for opening a new business. 對開創新事業的有利條件。—**fa·vor·a·bly,** *adv.*

fa·vo(u)r·a·ble·ness ['fevərəblnɪs; 'feivərəblnis] *n.* 有利；順利；如願以償。

fa·vo(u)red ['fevɚd; 'feivəd] *adj.* 有利的；占優勢的；有特權的。a most *favored* nation clause. 最惠國條款。

fa·vo(u)r·er ['fevərɚ; 'feivərə] *n.* 愛顧者；保護者；援助者；贊成者。

fa·vo(u)r·ing ['fevərɪŋ; 'feivəriŋ] *adj.* 順利的；有幫助的。*favoring* winds. 順風。—**ly,** *adv.*

:fa·vo(u)r·ite ['fevərɪt; 'feivərit] *adj.* 最喜愛的。Who is your *favorite* novelist? 你最喜愛的小說家是誰？—*n.* ①最被喜愛之人或物。He is a general *favorite.* 他是一個孚衆望的人。This book is a great *favorite* of mine. 這本書是我所最喜歡讀的。②享受特殊待遇的人。③可望贏得競賽的人、馬等。

favorite son （美國政黨提名競選總統時）獲得當地代表所擁護之候選人；本州的政治寵兒。

fa·vo(u)r·it·ism ['fevərɪt,ɪzəm; 'feivəritizəm] *n.* 偏愛；徇私；偏袒；不公平。

fa·vus ['fevəs; 'feivəs] *n.* 〖醫〗黃癬；瘌痢。 「憐。②巴結；奉承。—**er,** *n.*」

fawn¹ [fɔn; fɔːn] *v.i.* ①（犬之）搖尾乞

fawn² *n.* ①未滿一歲之幼鹿；麑。②淡黃褐色。—*adj.* 淡黃褐色的。

fawn-col·o(u)red ['fɔn,kʌlɚd; 'fɔːn,kʌləd] *adj.* 麑色的；淡黃褐色的。

fawn·ing ['fɔnɪŋ; 'fɔːniŋ] *adj.* 巴結的；奉承的；搖尾乞憐的。—**ly,** *adv.* —**ness,** *n.*

fax [fæks; fæks] *n.* 無線電傳眞機。

fax-mail ['fæks,mel; 'fæksmeil] *n.* 無線電傳眞郵件。

fay¹ [fe; fei] *n.* =**fairy.**

fay² *v.t.* & *v.i.* 〖造船〗密接。

faze [fez; feiz] *v.t.*, **fazed, faz·ing.** 〖美俗〗使困擾；煩擾。

F.B.A. Fellow of the British Academy. **FBI, F.B.I.** Federal Bureau of Investigation. 美國聯邦調查局。**F.C.** ① Football Club. ② Free Church.

fcap., fcp. foolscap. **FCC, F.C.C.** Federal Communications Commission.

F clef 〖音樂〗F譜號；低音部記號。**F.D.** Fidei Defensor (拉=Defender of the Faith). **FDR, F.D.R.** Franklin Delano Roosevelt. **Fe** 化學元素 ferrum (拉=iron)之符號。

fe·al·ty ['fiəltɪ; 'fiːəlti] *n., pl.* **-ties.** ①(封建時代臣僕對主上之)效忠；忠節。②忠誠；信實；忠貞。

:fear [fɪr; fiə] *n.* ①懼怕；恐懼。There is no reason for your *fears.* 你的恐懼沒有理由。②敬畏。the *fear* of God. 對上帝的敬畏。③擔心；憂慮。I have a *fear* that the boy will not make out well in his examination. 我擔心那男孩不會考得很好。④可能；機遇。There's not much *fear* of that. 那件事發生的可能不大。⑤令人懼怕之事物。***for fear* (*that*)** 因恐；免得。He's working hard *for fear* (*that*) he should fail. 他因恐失敗而努力工作。***for fear of*** 因恐；恐有…之虞。He ran away *for fear of* being hurt. 他因恐受傷而跑開。***in fear of*** 懼怕。He was *in fear of* his enemies. 他懼怕他的敵人。***without fear or favor*** 不偏不倚；公平地。—*v.t.* ①懼怕。Our cat *fears* big dogs. 我們的貓怕大狗。He did not *fear* to die. 他不怕死。②擔心；恐怕。He *fears* that the children will be sick. 他怕孩子們會生病。③敬畏。*Fear* God. 敬畏上帝。④〖方〗使駭怕。Be careful not to *fear* the horse by shouting. 別大聲喊叫以免馬匹受驚。—*v.i.* ①懼怕。*Fear* not, my dear, for I am here. 不要害怕，親愛的，因我在這裏。②擔心。I *fear* for his life (safety). 我爲他的生命(安全)而擔心。

***fear·ful** ['fɪrfəl; 'fiəful] *adj.* ①可怖的；可怕的。a *fearful* accident. 可怖的慘禍。②懼怕的；膽怯的。I am *fearful* of his doing it. 我怕他做這事。a *fearful* child. 一個膽怯的孩子。③〖俗〗很壞的；醜陋的；極端的。What a *fearful* mess! 多亂七八糟！④〖俗〗非常的。⑤擔心的；憂慮的。⑥〖俚〗敬畏的。—**ness,** *n.*

***fear·ful·ly** ['fɪrfəlɪ; 'fiəfəli] *adv.* 〖俗〗頗；極；非常地。a *fearfully* hot day. 非常熱的日子。

***fear·less** ['fɪrlɪs; 'fiəlis] *adj.* 無畏的；勇敢的。to be *fearless* of.... 無畏於…。—**ness,** *n.* 「勇敢地；無畏地。」

fear·less·ly ['fɪrlɪslɪ; 'fiəlisli] *adv.*

fear·mon·ger ['fɪr,mʌŋgɚ; 'fiə,mʌŋgə] *n.* 散布恐懼心理者。

fear·nought, fear·naught ['fɪr,nɔt; 'fiənɔːt] *n.* ①一種粗呢。②此種粗呢製成之外衣。

fear·some ['fɪrsəm; 'fiəsəm] *adj.* ①

可怕的；可怖的。②膽怯的；害怕的。③極大的；極深的；極高的。
fea·sance ['fizṇs; 'fi:zəns] *n.* 〖法律〗(條件、責任、義務等之)履行。
fea·si·bil·i·ty [ˌfizə'bɪlətɪ; ˌfi:zə'biliti] *n., pl.* **-ties.** 易實現性；可行性；可能性。
fea·si·ble ['fizəbḷ; 'fi:zəbl] *adj.* ①可實行的；易實現的；切實可行的。②可能的；或然的；合理的。③合宜的；方便的。
***feast** [fist; fi:st] *n.* ①饗宴；祝宴；宴樂。②〖宗教〗節期；節日。③賞心樂事。a *feast* of reason. 雋語；清談；高論。a *feast* for the eyes. 賞心悅目的事。—*v.t.* 款宴；使享受。to *feast* one's friends. 款宴朋友。to *feast* one's eyes on beautiful scenes. (使眼)飽賞美景。—*v.i.* 宴樂；享受。He sat there *feasting*.他坐在那兒大吃大喝。—**er,** *n.* 〖注意〗**feast** 與 **banquet** 均爲宴會，但前者着重於飲食之豐美，後者着重於儀式之堂皇。
feast day 節日；宗教節日。
feast·ful ['fistfəl; 'fi:stfəl] *adj.* 祝宴的；過節的。
feast-or-fam·ine ['fistɔr'fæmɪn; 'fi:stɔə'fæmin]*adj.*時飽時餓的；好壞不定的。
***feat** [fit; fi:t] *n.* ①功績；偉業。He achieved a *feat*. 他作成了一項偉績。②技藝的表演。*feats* of agility. 敏捷的表演。
feath·er** ['fɛðɚ; 'feðə] *n.* ①羽毛。a *feather* fan. 羽毛扇。②鳥類。③輕如羽毛的東西。④〖划船〗槳葉的水平運動。⑤種類。His clients were of the same *feather*. 他的顧客都屬同一類型的人物。⑥情緒；心情。She woke up in good *feather*. 她覺醒時心情愉快。⑦服裝。⑧箭翎；裝翎之箭末梢。a feather in one's cap*** 值得驕傲的事物；榮譽。Winning the scholarship was *a feather in his cap.* 得到獎學金是他的榮譽。***as light as a feather*** 輕如鴻毛。***be in high*** (***fine,*** or ***good***) ***feather*** 得意的；高興的。He *is in high feather* at the chance of going abroad. 他有機會出國很是得意。***birds of a feather*** 一類的人；一丘之貉。*Birds of a feather* flock together. 〖諺〗物以類聚。***crop one's feathers*** 挫某人銳氣。***cut a feather*** 船頭破浪前進。***Fine feathers make fine birds.*** 馬靠鞍裝，人靠衣裳。***in full feather*** 長滿了毛的(雛等)；盛裝；精神抖擻。***make the feathers fly*** 引起大騷亂；使雞飛狗跳。***not care a feather*** 毫不介意。***show the white feather*** 表示膽怯；示弱。***smooth one's ruffled*** (or ***rumpled***) ***feathers*** 鎮定下來。—*v.t.* ①飾以羽毛；插羽毛於。to *feather* an arrow. 上箭翎。②〖划船〗放平(槳面)。③〖航空〗順槳。—*v.i.* ①長羽毛；成羽毛狀生長〖常 out〗. birds *feathering* out. 正在長羽毛的鳥。②像羽毛似地動搖。③像羽毛似地覆蓋。***feather one's nest*** 營私中飽。***feather out*** 減弱；逐漸消失。***feather up to*** 〖美俚〗追求。—**like,** *adj.*
feather bed 鴨(鵝)絨牀墊。
feath·er·bed ['fɛðɚˌbɛd; 'feðəbed] *v.i.* & *v.t.,* **-bed·ded, -bed·ding.** 强迫雇用(較實際需要爲多之工人)。
feath·er·bed·ding ['fɛðɚˌbɛdɪŋ; 'feðəˌbediŋ] *n.* 强迫雇用(工會迫使雇主雇用較實際需要爲多之工人，並限制工人之工作或產量，以避免失業)。
feath·er·brain ['fɛðɚˌbren; 'feðəbrein] *n.* 愚人；低能者。
feath·er·brained ['fɛðɚˌbrend; 'feðəbreind] *adj.* 愚笨的。
feath·er·cut ['fɛðɚˌkʌt; 'feðəkʌt] *n.* (婦女)羽毛式髮型。
feath·ered ['fɛðɚd; 'feðəd] *adj.* ①有羽的；飾以羽毛的；有羽狀附加物的。②有翼的；迅速的。③(箭)裝翎的。
feath·er·edge ['fɛðɚˌrɛdʒ; 'feðəredʒ] *n., v.,* **-edged, -edg·ing.** —*n.* (易折或易曲之)薄邊。—*v.t.* 使有薄邊。—**feath·er-edged,** *adj.*
feath·er-foot·ed ['fɛðɚˌfutɪd; 'feðəˌfutid] *adj.*脚步輕快的。
feath·er·head ['fɛðɚˌhɛd; 'feðəhed] *n.* 輕率之人；愚蠢之人。
feath·er·head·ed ['fɛðɚˌhɛdɪd; 'feðəˌhedid] *adj.* 愚笨的；呆頭呆腦的。
feath·er·i·ness ['fɛðərɪnɪs; 'feðərinis] *n.* 如羽毛(之性質)；輕薄；被覆羽毛。
feath·er·ing ['fɛðərɪŋ; 'feðəriŋ] *n.* ①飾以羽毛；插羽。②羽毛(集合稱)。③(獵犬等)脚及尾之毛叢。④箭翎。⑤〖音樂〗提琴之輕而弱的弓法。
feather merchant 〖美俗〗懶惰的人；逃避責任的人。
feath·er·stitch ['fɛðɚˌstɪtʃ; 'feðəstitʃ] *n.* 刺繡之羽狀針法。—*v.t.* & *v.i.* 繡成羽毛狀。
feath·er·weight ['fɛðɚˌwet; 'feðəweit] *n.* ①極輕之人或物。②不重要之人或物。③輕乙級(體重在 126 磅與 118 磅之間)的拳擊家；羽量級拳師。—*adj.* ①極輕的。②輕乙級的。③不重要的。
feath·er·y ['fɛðərɪ; 'feðəri] *adj.* ①生羽毛的；覆蓋羽毛的。②柔軟的。③輕脆的。④輕如羽毛的。⑤(外形)羽毛狀的。
‡**fea·ture** ['fitʃɚ; 'fi:tʃə] *n., v.,* **-tured, -tur·ing.** —*n.* ①容貌之一部。Her eyes are her best *feature.* 她容貌生得最好的一部分是她的眼睛。②(*pl.*)容貌；相貌。a man of handsome *features.* 美貌男子。③特徵；外貌。④要點；特別節目。⑤故事電影片；情節片；長片。There are two *feature* films and three cartoons in the program. 節目單上訂有兩部故事片及三部卡通片。⑥(報章上的)特寫文字、專欄或連環圖畫等。***make a feature of*** 以…爲號召。—*v.t.*①以…爲特色；爲…之特色。②〖俗〗以…爲號召。The scenery is *featured* in railroad advertising. 鐵路廣告以風景爲號召。③與…相貌相似。④想像。⑤給以顯著地位。The newspaper *featured* the story of the murder. 報紙以顯著地位報導那謀殺案。—*v.i.* 扮演角色。
fea·tured ['fitʃɚd; 'fi:tʃəd] *adj.* ①被形成的。②作爲特色的；作爲號召的。③有…之面貌的。well-*featured.* 面目姣好的。
fea·ture·less ['fitʃɚlɪs; 'fi:tʃəlis] *adj.* 無特色的；平淡無奇的；平凡的。
fea·ture·ly ['fitʃəlɪ; 'fi:tʃəli] *adj.* 英俊的；美貌的。
feaze [fiz; fi:z] *v.i.* & *v.t.,* **feazed, feaz·ing.** 將繩端拆散。
Feb. February.
feb·ri·fuge ['fɛbrɪˌfjudʒ; 'febrifju:dʒ] *n.* ①退燒劑。②冷飲。—*adj.* 止熱的；退燒的。
fe·brile ['fibrəl; 'fi:brail] *adj.* 發燒的；熱病的。
‡**Feb·ru·ar·y** ['fɛbruˌɛrɪ; 'februəri] *n., pl.* **-ar·ies.** 二月。
fec. fecit
fe·cal ['fikḷ; 'fi:kəl] *adj.* ①渣滓的。②糞便的。(亦作 **faecal**)
fe·ces ['fisiz; 'fi:si:z] *n. pl.* ①渣滓。②排泄物；糞便。(亦作 **faeces**)

F

fe·cit [ˈfisɪt; ˈfiːsit] 〖拉〗 *v.* (某人)作(=he, *or* she, made, *or* did, it).(略作 **fec**)

feck·less [ˈfɛklɪs; ˈfeklis] *adj.* ①無能的;無精力的。②無思想的;無憂慮的。③無目標的;無意義的。

fec·u·lence [ˈfɛkjʊləns; ˈfekjuləns] *n.* ①不潔;污濁。②污物;渣滓;糞便。

fec·u·lent [ˈfɛkjʊlənt; ˈfekjulənt] *adj.* 不潔的;污濁的;髒而臭的。

fe·cund [ˈfikənd; ˈfiːkənd] *adj.* 多產的;肥沃的;豐富的。

fe·cun·date [ˈfikənˌdet; ˈfiːkəndeit] *v.t.,* **-dat·ed, -dat·ing.** ①使多產;使豐饒。②〖生物〗使受孕;授精。

fe·cun·da·tion [ˌfikənˈdeʃən; ˌfiːkənˈdeiʃən] *n.* 受胎作用;受胎;受精;授精。

fe·cun·di·ty [fɪˈkʌndətɪ; fiˈkʌnditi] *n.* ①生產力;生殖力。②多產;肥沃。③豐富。

fed [fɛd; fed] *v.* pt. & pp. of **feed.**

*__fed·er·al__ [ˈfɛdərəl; ˈfedərəl] *adj.* ①聯邦制的; 聯合的。The American Federation of Labor is a *federal* organization of labor unions. 美國勞工聯盟是工會的聯合組織。②聯邦政府的; 國家的。Congress is the *federal* lawmaking body of the United States. (美國)國會是美國聯邦政府的立法機構。③(F-)〖美〗聯邦政府的擁護憲法的;南北戰爭中擁護聯邦政府的。***make a Federal case out of*** 〖美俗〗小題大做。I was only a little late but she *made a Federal case out of* it. 我祇不過遲到一會兒,她就小題大做起來。—*n.* (F-) ①〖美〗南北戰爭中擁護聯邦政府的人士或士兵。*Federals* and Confederates lie buried together. 聯邦政府的人和南方政府的人都同葬在一起。②〖美〗聯邦政府人員。

Federal agent 〖美〗聯邦調查局員;聯邦探員(=G-man).(亦作 **Federal cop, Federal dick, Federal officer**)

Federal Bureau of Investigation 〖美〗聯邦調查局。(略作 **FBI**)

Federal City 華盛頓市的別名。

Federal Constitution 美國憲法。

fed·er·al·ese [ˌfɛdərəˈliz; ˌfedərəˈliːz] *n.* (常F-)〖俚〗美國聯邦政府特有的官樣文章。

fed·er·al·ism [ˈfɛdərəlˌɪzəm; ˈfedərəlizəm] *n.* ①聯邦政治;聯邦制度。②(F-)(美國聯邦黨所倡之)聯邦主義。

fed·er·al·ist [ˈfɛdərəlɪst; ˈfedərəlist] *n.* ①(F-)聯邦黨黨員;擁護聯邦黨者。②擁護聯邦主義者。—*adj.* 聯邦主義的;聯邦黨員的。

fed·er·al·i·za·tion [ˌfɛdərəlɪˈzeʃən; ˌfedərəlaiˈzeiʃən] *n.* ①同盟;聯合。②聯邦組織。

fed·er·al·ize [ˈfɛdərəlˌaɪz; ˈfedərəlaiz] *v.t.,* **-ized, -iz·ing.** ①使聯合;使成同盟;使成聯邦。②置之於聯邦政府之權力下。

Federal Party 聯邦黨(美國擁護採用憲法及建立強大之中央集權政府之政黨,其存在時期約 1791–1816)。(亦作 **Federalist Party**)

Federal Republic of Cameroon 喀麥隆聯邦共和國。

Federal Republic of Germany 德意志聯邦共和國(為西德之正式國名)。

Federal Reserve Bank (美國)聯邦準備銀行。

Federal Reserve Board (美國)聯邦準備金監察小組。

Federal Reserve System (美國)聯邦準備銀行制度。

fed·er·ate [*v.* ˈfɛdəˌret; ˈfedəreit *adj.* ˈfɛdərɪt; ˈfedərit, -reit] *v.,* **-at·ed, -at·ing,** *adj.* —*v.t. & v.i.* 組成聯邦; 聯盟。—*adj.* 聯盟的; 聯合的; 聯邦的。

*__fed·er·a·tion__ [ˌfɛdəˈreʃən; ˌfedəˈreiʃən] *n.* 聯盟;聯邦;聯合總會;聯邦政府。

fed·er·a·tion·ist [ˌfɛdəˈreʃənɪst; ˌfedəˈreiʃənist] *n.*聯盟主義者;聯邦主義者。

fed·er·a·tive [ˈfɛdəˌretɪv; ˈfedərətiv] *adj.* 同盟的;聯盟的;聯邦的。—**ly,** *adv.*

fe·do·ra [fɪˈdorə; fiˈdɔːrə] *n.* 一種男式軟呢帽。

*__fee__ [fi; fiː] *n., v.,* **feed, fee·ing.** —*n.* ①薪金;稅;費(如律師、醫生等所收之費)。The doctor's *fee* is $5.00 a visit. 這醫生的出診費每次五元。②賞金; 小費; 小帳。③采邑;封地。④世襲地。⑤所有權。***fee absolute*** 〖法律〗無條件繼承地。***fee of permit*** 執照稅; 牌照稅。***fee simple*** 〖法律〗無條件繼承的不動產(權)。***fee tail*** 〖法律〗指定繼承人繼承的不動產(權)。***hold in fee*** 永遠繼承;擁有。***qualified fee*** 〖法律〗有條件繼承地。—*v.t.* ①交費給。to *fee* a lawyer. 交費給律師。②給小費。

*__fee·ble__ [ˈfibl̩; ˈfiːbl] *adj.,* **-bler, -blest.** 微弱的; 衰弱的; 無效的; 無益的。a *feeble* mind. 薄弱的意志。

fee·ble-mind·ed [ˈfibl̩ˈmaɪndɪd; ˈfiːblˈmaindid] *adj.* 意志薄弱的; 低能的。

fee·ble·ness [ˈfiblnɪs; ˈfiːblnis] *n.* 微弱;衰弱;無力。

*__fee·bly__ [ˈfiblɪ; ˈfiːbli] *adv.* ①無力地;不够積極地;無效地。Nations have tried *feebly* to humanize war.許多國家想促使戰爭人道化,可是沒有效。②微微地。③微弱地。

‡**feed** [fid; fiːd] *v.,* **fed, feed·ing,** *n.* —*v.t.* ①飼育; 餵養; 供養。We *fed* the birds yesterday. 我們昨天餵了鳥。②供…以原料。This moving belt *feeds* the machine with raw material. 這條輸送帶供給機器所需之原料。③使滿足。Praise *fed* his vanity.稱讚滿足了他的虛榮心。④培養;增長。He *fed* his anger with thoughts of revenge.復仇的意念增長了他的忿怒。⑤供以糧食。The pasture *fed* the cows poorly. 那牧場不能充分餵飽牛羣。⑥將…給動物吃。⑦向(演員)作提示。⑧〖運動〗向隊友傳球。⑨以虛偽之希望安慰(某人)。—*v.i.* ①吃;食(指畜牲言,指人言則為俗語或諧語)〖on, upon, off〗. The sheep *feed* on grass. 羊以草為食。②供養;飼養。③注入;流入;灌入。The river *feeds* into the Atlantic Ocean. 那河流注入大西洋。***be fed to the gills*** (or ***teeth***) 受够了。I *am fed to the teeth* with this little pension.我受够了(無法再忍受)這一點點養老金。***be fed up*** (***with***)〖俚〗忍耐够了;厭煩。I'm *fed up with* your grumbling! 我聽够了你的咕嚕怨言。***be well*** (or ***poorly***) ***fed*** 吃得好(不好)。***Feed a cold and starve a fever.*** 傷風要吃,發燒要餓。***feed a person*** (or ***thing***) ***on*** 以…餵人(物)。What do you *feed your dog on?* 你用甚麼餵你的狗? ***feed a person up*** 給吃飽。There are hundreds of children in the slums who need *feeding up.* 貧民窟裏有好幾百個孩子需要養活。***feed at the public trough*** 吃公家飯;尸位素餐。***feed fat on*** (***wonders***) 飽看(珍奇)。***feed high*** (or ***well***) 吃得好。***feed on*** (***hope***) 寄託於(希

望)。**feed oneself** 自己吃(不須別人餵)。The baby can't *feed itself* yet. 這個嬰孩尙不能自己吃。**feed with the money** 賄賂。**Well fed, well bred.** 衣食足然後禮義興。—*n.* ①飼料。*feed* for the horses. 餵馬的飼料。②吃飼料。We stopped to let the horses have a *feed.* 我們停下來,令馬吃一頓飼料。③一次所吃的飼料。④〖俗〗人的一餐。We had a good *feed.* 我們飽餐了一頓。⑤〖機械〗(原料的)供給; 輸送原料的管子; 加原料的輸送槽。**at one feed** 一頓。**be off one's feed** a. 胃口不好。The child *was off his feed* and cried a good deal. 那小孩胃口不好而常常哭。 b. 憂愁的; 頹喪的。c. 身體不適;有病。He's *been off his feed* ever since the party. 自從那次開派對後他一直身體不適。**be out at feed** (牛等) 在牧場上吃着草。**feed bag** (掛在馬首之) 食料袋。**feed crop** 牧草。**feed pipe** 〖機械〗供水管。**feed pump** 供水唧筒。**feed water** 給水。—**a·ble,** *adj.*

feed·back [ˈfidˌbæk; ˈfiːdbæk] *n.* 〖無線電〗(眞空增幅器的)反饋。

feed·er [ˈfidɚ; ˈfiːdə] *n.* ①餵養者。②輸送材料的裝置; 材料輸送機; 給油器。③支流;支脈;支線。④〖電〗饋電線。⑤(嬰兒的)奶瓶。⑥餵養器; 給食器。⑦飲食者; 好吃者。The man is a prodigious *feeder.* 那人是個老饕。⑧煽動者; 促成者。⑨供應者; 供應之源。It was thought that Broadway had become a *feeder* for Hollywood. 人們以爲百老匯已成爲好萊塢的供應之源。**large feeder** a. 食量大的人。b. 需大量肥料的植物。

feeder line (鐵路等之)支線。

feed-in [ˈfidˌɪn; ˈfiːdin] *adj.* 用以輸入材料或資料於機器中的。—*n.* 領救濟食品的人群。

feed·ing [ˈfidɪŋ; ˈfiːdiŋ] *n.* ①飼育; 供養。②供水;供電。③滋長; 增大。a *feeding* storm. 一陣緊過一陣之暴風雨。④牧場。

feeding bottle 哺乳瓶;餵奶瓶。

feed·lot [ˈfidˌlɑt; ˈfiːdlɔt] *n.* (家畜的)飼養場。

feed·stuff [ˈfidˌstʌf; ˈfiːdstʌf] *n.* 飼料。Carbohydrate, fat and protein are the *feedstuffs.* 碳水化合物、脂肪和蛋白質乃是基本飼料。

fee-faw-fum [ˈfiˈfɔˈfʌm; ˈfiːˈfɔːˈfʌm] *interj.* (童話中之巨人) 表示要吃人的喊聲。—*n.* 用以恐嚇無知或怯懦者之事物。(亦作 **fee-fo-fum**)

‡feel [fil; fiːl] *v.,* **felt** [fɛlt; felt], **feel·ing,** *n.* —*v.i.* ①摸着是;感覺着是。Ice and snow *feel* cold. 冰雪摸着是冷的。②感覺;覺得。I *feel* so cold (warm, etc.). 我感覺冷(熱等) 得很。③有知覺; 有感情作用。The dead cannot *feel.* 死人沒有知覺。④用手摸索。He *felt* in his pockets for a dime. 他用手在衣袋裏摸找一角錢。⑤同情; 憐憫。She *feels* for all who suffer. 她同情一切受苦的人。⑥訴諸感情。He is a man who *feels* but seldom thinks. 他是個凡事多訴諸感情而少用理智的人。—*v.t.* ①感覺到。②易感;敏感。She *feels* the heat very much. 她甚易感覺熱。③觸;摸;摸摸看。*Feel* whether the water is warm enough yet. 摸摸看水是不是够熱了。④摸索;探尋。He *felt* his way across the room when the lights went out. 當燈熄了他摸索着走過房間。⑤觸試;摸試。Just *feel* the edge of this knife. 觸一觸這刀的鋒刃。⑥受影響於。The whole region *felt* the storm. 整區受到暴風雨的影響。⑦以爲;相信;想。I *feel* that we shall win. 我認爲我們將得到勝利。⑧有…之感覺(常與反身代名詞連用)。**feel after** 摸索; 探尋。**feel an interest in** 對…感興趣。**feel at** 用手摸摸看。**feel at home** 感到很暢快;舒鬆。**feel for** 同情於。I *feel for* him in his sorrow. 我同情他的悲痛。**feel like** a. 摸着像是。It *feels like* wood (glass, etc.). 那摸着像是木頭 (玻璃等)。b. 欲;想。He doesn't *feel like* taking a walk (a meal, etc.). 他不欲散步(進餐等)。**feel like oneself** 心情、健康等和平常一樣。**feel like thirty cents** 〖俗〗害燥;臉紅。**feel no pain** 酒醉。**feel of** 摸摸…看。**feel (quite) oneself** 覺得康健;安康。He isn't *feeling quite himself* this morning. 今天早上他感到有點不舒服。**feel one's legs** (or **feet**) 以爲自己站得穩;自信無事。**feel one's oats** 感到精神飽滿。**feel one's way** 摸索着走。**feel out** 摸清楚;探明。**feel strongly about** 對…抱强硬態度。**feel the need of** (or **for**) 對…感到需要。**feel up** 〖鄙,俚〗撫摸 (異性之)大腿、生殖器等。**feel up to** 以爲承當得了…; 以爲吃得消…。I don't *feel up to* a long hike today. 我今天不能走遠路。**feel with** 對…有同感;同情。**make...felt** 使…讓人認識清楚; 發揚。—*n.* ①觸摸。I like the *feel* of silk. 我喜歡觸摸絲織品。②感觸; 感覺。③知覺;觸覺。④直覺。**by the feel** 由於觸摸; 靠觸覺。I can tell that this is silk *by the feel.* 由於觸摸我曉得這是綢子。

feel·er [ˈfilɚ; ˈfiːlə] *n.* ①〖動物〗觸角;觸毛;觸鬚。②探人意見之言語、行動或暗示問題等。

‡feel·ing [ˈfilɪŋ; ˈfiːliŋ] *n.* ①感覺; 感觸。a *feeling* that something is going to happen. 感覺得某事將要發生。②同情;憐憫。He's a man of *feeling.* 他是一個富有同情心的人。③(*pl.*) 感情。I said it in that way so as not to hurt his *feelings.* 我那樣說爲的是不要傷他的感情。④感想; 意見。⑤知覺。He had lost all *feeling* in the left leg. 他的左腿完全失去了知覺。⑥心情; 情緒。a *feeling* of happiness. 愉快的情緒。⑦興奮; 憤激。The speech roused strong *feeling* on all sides. 這番話引起各方面的忿慨。⑧感受性;敏感。He has a deep *feeling* for beauty. 他對美有很深的感受力。⑨事物給人的感覺。**enter into one's feelings** 表同情;體諒。**good feeling** 好感。**have a feeling of** 覺得。**have no feeling for** 對…沒有同情。**ill feeling** 惡感;反感。—*adj.* ①易感動的; 有同情心的。②動人的。③有感情的。He is not a mere lump of clay but a *feeling* creature. 他不僅具有血肉之軀而且是個有感情的人。④表達感情的。—**ful,** *adj.* —**less,** *adj.*

feel·ing·ly [ˈfilɪŋlɪ; ˈfiːliŋli] *adv.* 充滿「感情地;激動地。」

fee simple *pl.* **fees simple.** 〖法律〗繼承者有全權(可任意處置)的地產。

***feet** [fit; fiːt] *n.* pl. of **foot.**

fee tail *pl.* **fees tail.** 〖法律〗繼承權有限制的地產。

feeze [fiz; fiːz] *v.t.,* **feezed, feez·ing.** 「=**faze.**」

***feign** [fen; fein] *v.t.* ①假裝;裝作。Some animals *feign* death when in danger. 有些動物遇危險時便裝死。②虛構; 杜撰; 假造。③想像。—*v.i.* 做假; 佯裝。

feigned [fend; feind] *adj.* 假的;做作的; 虛僞的;杜撰的;想像的。

feint [fent; feint] *n.* ①僞裝;假裝。②聲東擊西的行動。—*v.i.* 聲東擊西;作假擊;佯攻。—*v.t.* 騙。

feist [faɪst; faist] *n.* 〖美方〗小犬。

feld·spar ['fɛld,spɑr, 'fɛl–; 'feldspɑ:] *n.* 〖礦〗長石。(亦作 **feldspath**)

feld·spath·ic [fɛld'spæθɪk, fɛl–; feld'spæθik] *adj.* 長石的;含長石的;似長石的。

fe·lic·i·tate [fә'lɪsә,tet; fi'lisiteit] *v.t.*, **-tat·ed, -tat·ing.** 祝賀;道賀;恭賀;慶賀。

fe·lic·i·ta·tion [fә,lɪsә'teʃәn; fi,lisi'teiʃәn] *n.* 祝賀;慶賀。***offer one's felicitations*** 道賀;致祝辭。

fe·lic·i·tous [fә'lɪsәtәs; fi'lisitәs] *adj.* ①適當的;得體的;恰切的。②幸福的。③令人快樂的。

fe·lic·i·tous·ly [fә'lɪsәtәslɪ; fi'lisitәsli] *adv.* 恰切地;適切地。

fe·lic·i·ty [fә'lɪsәtɪ; fi'lisiti] *n., pl.* **-ties.** ①幸福;幸運;快樂。②(措辭)適當;巧妙。③巧妙的思想;措辭巧妙的辭句。

fe·lid ['filɪd; 'fi:lid] *n.* 貓科之動物。

fe·line ['filaɪn; 'fi:lain] *adj.* ①貓科的;貓的。②似貓的;輕行的。③狡詐的;陰險的。***feline amenities*** 笑裏藏刀的好話;委婉隱祕之罵詈。—*n.* 貓。—**ly,** *adv.* —**ness,** *n.*

:fell¹ [fɛl; fel] *v.* pt. of **fall.**

fell² *v.t.* ①打倒;推倒。②砍伐(樹木)。③縫起(縫邊)。—*n.* ①一個季節中砍下來之木材。②縫邊。

fell³ *adj.* ①殘忍的;兇猛的。②致死的;毀滅的。

fell⁴ *n.* 獸皮;毛皮。***fell of hair*** 蓬髮。

fell⁵ *n.* 〖蘇〗①荒野;澤池。②小山;丘陵。

fel·lah ['fɛlә; 'felә] *n., pl.* **fel·la·hin, fel·la·heen** [,fɛlә'hin; ,felә'hi:n], **fel·lahs.** 阿拉伯、埃及等地之土著農夫或勞工。

fell·er¹ ['fɛlә; 'felә] *n.* ①採伐者;伐木機。②縫邊者(機)。

fell·er² *n.* 〖俚,方〗人;漢子;傢伙;男人;男孩(=fellow).

fell·mon·ger ['fɛl,mʌŋgә; 'fel,mʌŋgә] *n.* 皮革商;毛皮商;(特指)羊皮商。

fel·loe ['fɛlo; 'felou] *n.* 輪圈;輞。

:fel·low ['fɛlo; 'felou] *n.* ①〖俗〗人;漢子。He's a very pleasant *fellow.* 他是個很和氣的人。②同伴;夥友;同事;同儕。We were *fellows* at school. 我們從前是同學。③一對中之一;一雙中之一;相配物之一。Where is the *fellow* of this glove? 這手套還有一隻在那裏? ④〖俗〗情人;情郎(常用爲親暱之稱)。⑤傢伙(用稱兒童及動物等)。I fired twice but the big *fellow* got away and we lost his trail. 我開了兩鎗,還是給那大傢伙逃脫了,然後我們失去了牠的踪跡。⑥卑賤漢;無用之人。⑦類似之(人)物;相等者。The world has not his *fellow.* 世界上沒有跟他一樣的人。⑧(得獎學金的)研究生。⑨學術團體之榮譽會員。***be hail fellow well met*** (*with*) (與…)友善。***old fellow*** 老友。***young fellow-me*** (or ***-my***) ***lad*** 相好的朋友。—*adj.* 同伴的;同事的;同類的;同階級的。a *fellow* man. 人類;同胞。*fellow* students. 同學。***fellow feeling*** 同情;同感。***fellow heir*** 〖法律〗共同繼承人。***our fellow creatures*** 人類(=human beings).

·fel·low·ship ['fɛlo,ʃɪp; 'felouʃip] *n.* ①交情;友誼;同伴關係。good *fellowship.* 厚誼。②參加;共處;協助。*fellowship* in prosperity or adversity. 甘苦與共的精神。③同好;同志。④大學內給研究生的一種獎學金。⑤會;團體。***bear*** (***one***) ***fellowship*** 與(某人)有交情。***offer a person the hand of fellowship*** 對某人伸出友誼之手。

fellow traveler 同情某一政治運動或政黨之人;同路人。

fel·ly ['fɛlɪ; 'feli] *n., pl.* **-lies.** =**felloe**

fe·lo-de-se ['filodi'si; 'fi:loudi:'si:] *n., pl.* **fel·o·nes-de-se** [fi'lo,nizdi'si; fi:,louni:zdi:'si:], **fe·los-de-se** ['filozdi'si; 'fi:louzdi:'si:]. 〖拉〗①自殺者。②自殺。

fel·on ['fɛlәn; 'felәn] *n.* ①〖法律〗重罪犯;罪犯。②〖醫〗蛇頭疔;瘭疽;甲溝炎。—*adj.* 邪惡的;殘忍的;卑劣的;犯法的。

fe·lo·ni·ous [fә'lonɪәs; fi'lounjәs] *adj.* ①〖法律〗犯重罪的;犯罪的。②極惡的;横暴的。—**ly,** *adv.* —**ness,** *n.*

fel·on·ry ['fɛlәnrɪ; 'felәnri] *n.* 重罪犯(集合稱)。

fel·o·ny ['fɛlәnɪ; 'felәni] *n., pl.* **-nies.** 〖法律〗重罪。

fel·site ['fɛlsaɪt; 'felsait] *n.* 〖礦〗珪長石。(亦作 **felstone**)

fel·spar ['fɛl,spɑr; 'felspɑ:] *n.* =**feldspar.**

:felt¹ [fɛlt; felt] *v.* pt. & pp. of **feel.**

***felt²** *n.* ①毛氈。②毛氈所製之物。—*v.t.* ①作成氈。②覆以氈。—*adj.* 用毛氈做的。a *felt* hat. 氈帽。

felt·ing ['fɛltɪŋ; 'feltiŋ] *n.* 製氈材料;製氈法;氈。

fe·luc·ca [fә'lʌkә; fe'lʌkә] *n.* 地中海沿岸之小帆船。

fem. ①female. ②feminine.

***fe·male** ['fimel; 'fi:meil] *n.* ①婦人;女性。More than half of the employees were *females.* 大半員工是女性。②雌獸。③雌性植物;雌花。—*adj.* ①婦女的;女性的。*female* operatives. (工廠裏的)女工。②女性的;雌性的。③〖植物〗雌的;雌本的;有雌蕊的。④〖機械〗凹的;陰的;雌的。*female* screw. 陰螺旋;母螺。〖注意〗**female, woman, lady** 皆表婦女。female 着重於性別的區分,除用於科學及統計之外,大半含有輕蔑的意思。woman 是成年女性的通稱。lady 意爲淑女。

feme [fɛm; fi:m] *n.* 〖法律〗①妻。②婦女。

feme covert 〖法律〗有夫之婦;已婚女性。

feme sole 〖法律〗①未婚女性;已離婚之女性;未亡人。②經濟上獨立的已婚女性。

fem·i·nal·i·ty [,fɛmә'nælәtɪ; ,femi'næliti] *n., pl.* **-ties.** 女性;女人之氣質;柔弱。

fem·i·ne·i·ty [,fɛmә'niәtɪ; ,femi'ni:iti] *n., pl.* **-ties.** =**feminality.**

***fem·i·nine** ['fɛmәnɪn; 'feminin] *adj.* ①婦女的;適於婦女的;爲婦女所特有的。*feminine* curiosity. 女人之好奇心。②婦女似的;柔弱的。③〖文法〗陰性的;女性的。"Actress" is a *feminine* noun. Actress 是一個陰性名詞。④〖詩〗弱韻的(句尾)。—*n.* ①女性。②溫柔的女性。③女性名詞;女性代名詞;女性形。—**ness,** *n.* 〖注意〗**female** 指性別,如男性女性;**feminine** 指性質,此性質爲女性所特具,如溫柔、嬌小等。

fem·i·nine·ly ['fɛmәnɪnlɪ; 'femininli] *adv.* 適合女性地。

feminine rhyme 弱韻(押韻之兩音節字之第二節爲非重音,或三音節字之第二、三音節爲非重音,如 motion, notion; happily, snappily).

fem·i·nin·i·ty [,fɛmә'nɪnәtɪ; ,femi'niniti] *n.* ①婦女氣質;柔弱。②婦女(集合稱)。③娘娘腔。

fem·i·nism ['fɛmә,nɪzәm; 'feminizәm] *n.* ①女權主義;男女平等主義;提高女權運動。②女子特性。

fem·i·nist ['fɛmənɪst; 'feminist] *n.* 男女平權主義者;提高女權論者。—*adj.* 主張男女平等的。

fe·min·i·ty [fɪ'mɪnətɪ; fi'miniti] *n.* =**femininity.**

fem·i·nize ['fɛmə,naɪz; 'feminaiz] *v.t. & v.i.*, **-nized, -niz·ing.** ①(使)成女性; 女性化。②使女性在…占多數。—**fem·i·ni·za·tion,** *n.*

femme de cham·bre [famdə'ʃɑ̃:br; famdə'ʃɑ̃:br]〖法〗侍女;女婢。

femme fa·tale [,famfa'tal; famfa'tal] *pl.* **femmes fa·tales** [,famfa'tal; famfa'tal].〖法〗妖姬。

fem·o·ral ['fɛmərəl; 'femərəl] *adj.* 股骨的;大腿骨的。

fe·mur ['fimɚ; 'fi:mə] *n., pl.* **fe·murs, fem·o·ra** ['fɛmərə; 'femərə].〖解剖〗股骨。

fen[1] [fɛn; fen] *n.*〖英〗沼澤; 沼地。***fen fire*** 鬼火。***the fens*** 英格蘭 Cambridgeshire 及 Lincolnshire 兩郡內之沼澤地區。

fen[2]〖中〗分(一毛錢的十分之一)。

F.E.N., FEN Far East Network.

‡**fence** [fɛns; fens] *n., v.,* **fenced, fenc·ing.** —*n.* ①圍牆; 籬笆; 柵欄。The horse jumped over the *fence.* 此馬跳過了籬笆。②劍術; 擊劍。books on *fence.* 劍術書。③巧辯;詭辯術;敏答。④買賣贓物者。⑤贓品買賣處;黑貨市場。*fence* shops. 贓品店。***come down on the right side of the fence*** 附於勝者方面。***fence month*** 禁獵期。***mend*** (or ***look after***) ***one's fences*** a.(美國國會議員)整頓自己地盤。b. 加强與他人之關係或提高自己之聲望。***on one's fence*** 幫助某人。***on the fence***〖俗〗未決定幫助那一方;躊躇;猶豫;騎牆。***on the other side of the fence*** 加入反對黨。***sit on the fence*** 騎牆;觀望。—*v.t.* ①圍以柵籬;築圍牆防衛;用柵籬防護。Farmers *fence* their fields. 農夫用柵籬來防護他們的田園。②保衞;警衞;保護。③在贓品買賣處出售。The gang stole cars and *fenced* them themselves. 盜賊偷了車, 然後在贓品買賣處出售。④閃避。The chairman *fences* awkward questions. 主席閃避了棘手的問題。—*v.i.* ①鬥劍;舞劍。I am learning how to *fence.* 我正在學怎樣鬥劍。②閃避; 避免; 搪塞; 避開(質問)。He *fences* skillfully on the witness stand. 他在證人席上巧妙地搪塞過去。③保衞; 防禦。④作圍牆。Farmers *fence* with rails. 農夫以柵欄作圍牆。***fence about*** a. 用柵圍住(某地)。b. 預防。to be *fenced about* with penalties. 用處罰來預防。***fence round*** 搪塞; 避開(質問)。to *fence round* the point. 避開問題的要點。***fence with*** 閃避(問題)。

fence·less ['fɛnslɪs; 'fenslis] *adj.* 無圍牆的;無保衞的。—**ness,** *n.*

fenc·er ['fɛnsɚ; 'fensə] *n.* ①舞劍者;鬥劍的人; 劍術教師。②製造或修理籬笆之人。

fence season〖英〗禁獵期。

fence-sit·ter ['fɛns,sɪtɚ; 'fens,sitə] *n.* ①猶豫不決者。②中立者。

fence-strad·dler ['fɛns,strædlɚ; 'fens,strædlə] *n.*〖俗〗兩面討好者。

***fenc·ing** ['fɛnsɪŋ; 'fensiŋ] *n.* ①劍術;鬥劍法。*fencing* master. 劍術教師。②築牆材料。③圍牆(集合稱)。The *fencing* of the farm was in poor repair. 該農場的圍牆失修。④買賣贓物。⑤(對重要問題之)閃避。

fend [fɛnd; fend] *v.t. & v.i.* ①抵擋;抵禦。②謀生; 撫養; 照管。***fend for*** 扶養。***fend for oneself*** 自謀生計;獨立生活。Now that his father is dead he must *fend for himself.* 因爲他父親死了,他必須自謀生活。***fend off*** 擋開;架開;避開(災禍等)。

fend·er ['fɛndɚ; 'fendə] *n.* ①防禦物;防禦者。②(汽車等輪胎上的)擋泥板。③〖英〗(汽車等車頭爲緩和碰撞所裝的)防禦板;擋板。④(防爐炭滾出用的)炭欄;爐圍。⑤(船旁之)防擦索; 護舷材; 護舷墊。

fen·es·tel·la [,fɛnə'stɛlə; ,fenis'telə] *n., pl.* **-lae** [-li; -li:]. ①小窗。②祭壇內放置遺骸之小窗。

fe·nes·trate [fɪ'nɛstret; fi'nestreit] *adj.* ①有孔的。②〖建築〗窗的; 有窗孔的; 多孔的。③〖動物〗有透明斑點的。(亦作 **fenestrated**)

fen·es·tra·tion [,fɛnəs'treʃən; ,fenis'treiʃən] *n.* ①〖建築〗開窗法。②〖外科〗開窗術。(亦作 **fenestration operation**)

fen fire 磷火;鬼火。

Fe·ni·an ['finɪən; 'fi:njən] *n.* 非尼安會之會員(該會目的在使愛爾蘭脫離英國之統治)。—*adj.* 非尼安會之會員的; 非尼安主義的。

fen·land ['fɛnlænd; 'fenlænd] *n.*〖英〗沼地;濕地。

fen·nec, fen·nek ['fɛnɛk; 'fenək] *n.*〖動物〗非洲產之大耳小狐;㹨狐。

fen·nel ['fɛnl; 'fenl] *n.*〖植物〗茴香。***fennel oil*** 茴香油(藥用)。***fennel water*** 茴香液(藥用)。

fen·nel·flow·er ['fɛnl,flauɚ; 'fenl,flauə] *n.*〖植物〗黑種草。

fen·ny ['fɛnɪ; 'feni] *adj.* ①沼澤性的; 多沼地的。②生於沼地的;住於沼地的。

fen·u·greek ['fɛnju,grik; 'fenjugri:k] *n.*〖植物〗葫蘆巴(荳科植物, 其種子作藥用)。

feoff [fɛf; fef] *v.t.* 授與封地;賣封地給…。—*n.* 封地;采邑(=fief).

feoff·ee [fɛf'i; fe'fi:] *n.* 封地受領者;不動產受讓人。

feof·fer, feof·for ['fɛfɚ; 'fefə] *n.* 封采邑者;賜食邑者。

feoff·ment ['fɛfmənt; 'fefmənt] *n.* 封地授與;授與采邑。

FEPC Fair Employment Practices Committee.

-fer〖字尾〗名詞字尾, 表"結(實)者; 產生者"之義, 與形容詞字尾 -ferous 相當。

fe·ral[1] ['fɪrəl; 'fiərəl] *adj.* ①野生的;未馴的。②野蠻的;兇猛的。

fe·ral[2] *adj.* ①致命的。②抑鬱的;悲慘的。

fer-de-lance [fɛrdə'lɑ̃:s; ,fɛədə'lɑ̃:ns] *n.* 熱帶美洲產之大毒蛇。

Fer·di·nand ['fɝdn,ænd; 'fə:dinənd] *n.* 男子名。

fer·e·to·ry ['fɛrə,torɪ; 'feritəri] *n., pl.* **-ries.** ①聖骨箱。②聖骨龕;聖骨龕堂。

fe·ri·al ['fɪrɪəl; 'fiəriəl] *adj.* ①假日的;節日的。②〖宗教〗平日的;週日的(尤指非宗教節日者)。

fe·rine ['fɪraɪn; 'fiərain] *adj.* =**feral**[1].

Fe·rin·ghee [fə'rɪŋgɪ; fə'riŋgi] *n.*〖英印〗歐洲人;(尤指)葡印混血兒。(亦作 **Feringi**)

fer·ment** [*v.* fɚ'mɛnt; fə:'ment *n.* 'fɝmɛnt; 'fə:ment] *v.i.* ①發酵。Fruit juices *ferment* if they are kept a long time. 果汁若放置很久,就會發酵。②激動;紛擾。—*v.t.* ①鼓勵;醞釀。②使發酵。—*n.* ①酵母;發酵劑。Yeast is a *ferment.* 酵素是一種發酵劑。②激動。She was thrown into a *ferment* by his unexpected arrival. 他的突然到來使她激動不已。be in a ferment*** 在騷動中;在激動中。

fer·ment·a·ble [fəˈmɛntəbḷ; fəːˈmentəbəl] *adj.* 可發酵的。—**fer·ment·a·bil·i·ty,** *n.*

fer·men·ta·tion [ˌfɝmɛnˈteʃən; ˌfəːmenˈteiʃən] *n.* ①發酵。②動亂;騷動。

fer·men·ta·tive [fəˈmɛntətɪv; fəˈmentətiv] *adj.* ①促起發酵的。②發酵而產生的。(亦作 **fermentive**)

Fer·mi [ˈfɛrmɪ; ˈfɛəmi] *n.* 費爾米(Enrico, 1901–1954, 義大利籍物理學家, 原子彈發明人之一, 自1939年後移居美國)。

fer·mi·um [ˈfɛrmɪəm; ˈfɛəmiəm] *n.* 〖化〗鐨(放射性元素;符號爲 Fm)。

***fern** [fɝn; fəːn] *n.* 羊齒;羊齒植物(集合稱)。a hillside covered with *fern.* 長滿羊齒植物的山邊。—**like,** *adj.*

fern·er·y [ˈfɝnərɪ; ˈfəːnəri] *n., pl.* **-er·ies.** 羊齒植物之苗圃。

fern·y [ˈfɝnɪ; ˈfəːni] *adj.,* **fern·i·er, fern·i·est.** 羊齒植物的;多羊齒植物的。

fe·ro·cious [fəˈroʃəs; fəˈrouʃəs] *adj.* ①殘忍的;兇猛的。②非常的。—**ness,** *n.*

fe·ro·cious·ly [fəˈroʃəslɪ; fəˈrouʃəsli] *adv.* ①兇猛地。②非常地。

fe·roc·i·ty [fəˈrɑsətɪ; fəˈrɔsiti] *n., pl.* **-ties.** 兇猛;獰惡;殘暴。

-ferous 〖字尾〗表"結(實);產生;含有"之義。

fer·rate [ˈfɛret; ˈfereit] *n.* 〖化〗鐵酸鹽。

fer·re·ous [ˈfɛrɪəs; ˈferiəs] *adj.* ①鐵的;鐵製的;含鐵的。②似鐵的;堅硬的。

fer·ret[1] [ˈfɛrɪt; ˈferit] *n.* ①〖動物〗雪貂;白鼬(用以捕鼠、獵兔等)。②搜索者;偵探。—*v.t.* & *v.i.* ①用雪貂打獵。②搜索;捕獵;偵察。③使痛苦;使煩惱。***ferret about*** 到處搜尋。***ferret for*** 探索。***ferret out*** a. 探出;搜出。b. 從…中趕出。—**er,** *n.*

fer·ret[2] *n.* 絲帶;棉帶(繫物用)。(亦作 **ferreting**)

fer·ri·age [ˈfɛrɪɪdʒ; ˈferiidʒ] *n.* ①擺渡;渡船業;擺渡之設備。②渡費。

fer·ric [ˈfɛrɪk; ˈferik] *adj.* ①鐵的;得自鐵的;含鐵的。②〖化〗三價鐵的。

fer·rif·er·ous [fɛˈrɪfərəs; feˈrifərəs] *adj.* 產鐵的;含鐵的。

Fer·ris wheel [ˈfɛrɪs~; ˈferis~] 阜氏大輪(一種供遊戲之豎立大輪, 輪緣裝有座位供人迴旋)。

fer·rite [ˈfɛraɪt; ˈferait] *n.* 〖化〗鐵酸鹽。sodium *ferrite.* 鐵酸鈉。

ferro- 〖字首〗〖化〗表"含鐵"之義(爲 ferri- 之異體)。

fer·ro·chro·mi·um [ˈfɛroˈkromɪəm; ˌferouˈkroumiəm] *n.* 〖化〗鐵鉻齊。

fer·ro·con·crete [ˌfɛroˈkɑnkrit; ˌferouˈkɔnkriːt] *n.* 鋼筋混凝土;鋼骨水泥。

fer·ro·man·ga·nese [ˌfɛroˈmæŋgəˌnis; ˌferouˈmæŋgəniːs] *n.* 錳鐵齊;錳鐵。

fer·ro·type [ˈfɛroˌtaɪp; ˈferoutaip] *n.* 鐵版照相;鐵版照相法。

fer·rous [ˈfɛrəs; ˈferəs] *adj.* 〖化〗二價鐵的;含二價鐵的。

fer·ru·gi·nous [fɛˈrudʒənəs; feˈruːdʒinəs] *adj.* ①鐵的;含鐵的。②鐵銹色的;紅褐色的。

fer·rule [ˈfɛrəl; ˈferuːl] *n., v.,* **-ruled, -rul·ing.** —*n.* ①金屬箍;金屬包頭。②〖機械〗套圈。—*v.t.* 裝以金屬箍。

fer·ry** [ˈfɛrɪ; ˈferi] *n., pl.* **-ries,** *v.,* **-ried, -ry·ing.** —*n.* ①渡船。②渡口;渡頭。The boatman rowed the traveler over the *ferry.* 船夫帶旅客過渡頭。③飛機輸送制度。—*v.t.* ①以船渡。②用飛機輸送。—*v.i.* ①乘船渡過。②乘飛機飛渡。ferry bridge*** 渡船橋;浮橋;運送列車的渡船。***ferry master*** 經營擺渡事業者。***ferry steamer*** 擺渡汽艇;渡輪。

fer·ry·boat [ˈfɛrɪˌbot; ˈferibout] *n.* 渡船。

fer·ry·man [ˈfɛrɪmən; ˈferimən] *n., pl.* **-men.** 渡船夫;擺渡者。

***fer·tile** [ˈfɝtḷ; ˈfəːtail] *adj.* ①多產的;肥沃的;豐富的。*Fertile* soil produces good crops. 肥沃的土壤產生好的農作物。②能生長的(種子); 能孵的(卵); 受精的;能生育的。Chicks hatch from *fertile* eggs. 小雞自受精卵中孵出。③〖物理〗可(被)變爲分裂材料或物質的。—**ly,** *adv.* —**ness,** *n.*

***fer·til·i·ty** [fɝˈtɪlətɪ; fəːˈtiliti] *n.* ①肥沃;豐饒;豐富。②生產力;生殖力。the *fertility* of soil. 土地生產力。③出生率(爲 mortality 之對)。

fer·ti·li·za·tion [ˌfɝtḷəˈzeʃən; ˌfəːtilaiˈzeiʃən] *n.* ①肥沃;施肥(法)。②〖生物〗受精作用;授精。

fer·ti·lize [ˈfɝtḷˌaɪz; ˈfəːtilaiz] *v.,* **-lized, -liz·ing.** —*v.t.* ①使肥沃;施肥於…。②〖生物〗使受精;使受胎。③充實。—*v.i.* 施肥。

***fer·ti·liz·er** [ˈfɝtḷˌaɪzɚ; ˈfəːtilaizə] *n.* ①肥料。②受精媒介物。③充實他人者。He was not only a very distinguished writer but a *fertilizer* of other talents. 他不僅是個傑出的作家, 並且具有使人獲益的其他才幹。

fer·u·la [ˈfɛrjulə; ˈferulə] *n., pl.* **-lae** [-li; -liː]. ①〖植物〗阿魏草。②=**ferule**[1].

fer·ule[1] [ˈfɛrəl; ˈferuːl] *n., v.,* **-uled, -ul·ing.** —*n.* 教鞭;戒尺。***be under the ferule*** 在(老師)鞭策之下。—*v.t.* 用戒尺懲罰;打…的手心。

fer·ule[2] *n., v.t.,* **-uled, -ul·ing.** =**ferrule.**

fer·ven·cy [ˈfɝvənsɪ; ˈfəːvənsi] *n.* 熱情;熱心;熱烈。

fer·vent [ˈfɝvənt; ˈfəːvənt] *adj.* ①強烈的; 熱情的; 熱烈的。②熱的; 白熱的。—**ness,** *n.*

fer·vent·ly [ˈfɝvəntlɪ; ˈfəːvəntli] *adv.* 熱烈地。

fer·vid [ˈfɝvɪd; ˈfəːvid] *adj.* ①熱情的;激情的;熱烈的。②熾熱的; 灼熱的; 似火的。—**ness,** *n.* —**ly,** *adv.*

***fer·vo(u)r** [ˈfɝvɚ; ˈfəːvə] *n.* ①熱誠;熱心。The patriot's voice trembled from the *fervor* of his emotion. 這位愛國者由於感情熱烈而聲音發抖。②熱;熾熱;白熱。

F.E.S. Fellow of the Entomological (or Ethnological) Society.

fes·cue [ˈfɛskju; ˈfeskjuː] *n.* ①〖植物〗田邊草。②教鞭。

fess, fesse [fɛs; fes] *n.* 〖紋章〗中帶(橫跨盾形之中央)。

-fest 〖字尾〗表"會合; 競賽; 比賽"之義。

fes·ta [ˈfɛstɑ; ˈfestə] 〖義〗*n.* 祝日;祭日;祝宴;節日;假日。

fes·tal [ˈfɛstḷ; ˈfestl] *adj.* ①節日的; 假日的; 祭日的。②快樂的; 歡樂的; 宴樂的。—**ly,** *adv.*

fes·ter [ˈfɛstɚ; ˈfestə] *v.i.* ①生膿; 潰膿。②腐敗;腐爛。③使煩惱。—*v.t.* ①使化膿。②使潰爛。③使煩惱、痛苦。—*n.* 膿瘡;膿疹;潰爛。

***fes·ti·val** [ˈfɛstəvḷ; ˈfestəvəl] *n.* ①節日;節期。②慶祝。Every year the city has a music *festival* in May. 每年五月這城中有一連串的音樂演奏會。③飲宴; 作樂。—*adj.*

節日的; 喜慶的。—ly, adv.

Festival of Lanterns 元宵節;「燈節。」

fes·tive ['fɛstɪv; 'festiv] adj. ①節日的; 歡樂的; 宴樂的。②快樂的。—ness, n. —ly, adv.

fes·tiv·i·ty [fɛs'tɪvətɪ; fes'tiviti] n., pl. -ties. ①歡宴; 作樂。②(pl.) 祝典; 慶祝活動。

fes·toon [fɛs'tun; fes'tu:n] n. ①裝飾之花綵。②垂花雕刻。—v.t. ①飾以花綵。②結綵;作成花綵。

fe·tal ['fitl; 'fi:tl] adj. 胎兒的; 似胎兒「的。(亦作 foetal)」

fetch**[1] [fɛtʃ; fetʃ] v.t. ①取來; 拿來; 接來。*Fetch* a doctor at once. 立刻去請個醫生來。②使出來; 使發生; 使流(淚、血等); 使外出。③售得。These old books won't *fetch* (you) much. 這些舊書賣不到很多錢。④打擊。⑤〖俗〗吸引; 迷惑。The girl's beauty *fetched* him completely. 那女孩的美麗完全把他迷住了。⑥説服〖常 round〗. His argument *fetched* her round. 他的議論説服了她。⑦完成。⑧擊倒;擊斃。I got in another shot and *fetched* him. 我又射了一發而擊倒了他。—v.i. ①攜帶;帶來。②〖航海〗航行;前進;取道;駛。③〖方〗到達;抵達。He *fetched* home after his long ride. 坐了很久的車之後他回到了家。④(獵犬)拾回獵物。fetch about*** 來往移動(=move about);旋轉;籌劃。***fetch and carry*** (***for***) 做雜事;供使役。***fetch away*** (or ***way***) (物)散離;失散(=get loose). ***fetch down*** 打下(射擊物); 使(物價)下落。***fetch headway***〖航海〗開始快速前進。***fetch in*** 拉進(黨內);圍。***fetch out*** 使顯出(光彩等);抽出。***fetch to*** 使甦醒。***fetch up*** a. 停止;停步(=stop). The man *fetched up* at the tavern. 那人在旅店前停下脚步。 b. 趕上(=catch up). c. 扶養。She had to *fetch up* her younger sisters. 她必須扶養她的妹妹們。—n. ①帶來;拿來。②詭計;謀略。「②相同物。」

fetch[2] n. ①活人之魂;人將死時所現之魂。

fetch·ing ['fɛtʃɪŋ; 'fetʃiŋ] adj. 〖俗〗引人的; 嬌媚的; 誘惑的。—ly, adv.

fete, fête [fet; feit] n., v., **fet·ed, fet·ing** or **fêt·ed, fêt·ing.** —n. 慶典; 慶祝;祝宴;節日。***a garden fete***〖美〗園遊會。***fête champêtre***〖法〗野宴會; 戶外宴會。—v.t. ①宴請; 招待。②慶祝。③讚揚; 稱讚。

fete day 節日; 生日; 聖徒之祭日。

fe·tial ['fiʃəl; 'fi:ʃəl] adj. 國際關係的; 外交的。—n.古羅馬由祭司組成的外交團之一員。(亦作 **fecial**)

fe·ti·cide ['fitə,saɪd; 'fi:tisaid] n. 殺胎;墮胎。(亦作 **foeticide**)

fet·id ['fɛtɪd; 'fetid] adj. 臭的; 有惡臭的。—ly, adv. —i·ty, —ness, n.

fe·tish, fe·tich(e) ['fitɪʃ; 'fi:tiʃ] n. ①任何被認爲有神靈之物; 神物。②被盲目崇拜的事物;偶像。***make a*** (***perfect***) ***fetish of*** 盲目崇拜。

fe·tish·ism ['fitɪʃɪzm; 'fi:tiʃizəm] n. ①拜物教。②〖精神病學〗戀物癖;片段戀癖。③盲目崇拜。(亦作 **fetichism**)

fe·tish·ist ['fitɪʃɪst; 'fi:tiʃist] n. ①庶物崇拜者;拜物教徒。②盲目崇拜者。③戀物癖者。(亦作 **fetichist**)

fe·tish·is·tic [,fitɪʃ'ɪstɪk; ,fi:tiʃ'istik] adj. 庶物崇拜的; 迷信的; 拜物教的。(亦作 **fetichistic**)

fet·lock ['fɛt,lɑk; 'fetlɔk] n. ①距毛(馬蹄上之長簇毛)。②球節(生距毛之突起部分)。(亦作 **fetterlock**)

fe·tol·o·gy [fi'tɑlədʒɪ; fi:'tɔlədʒi] n.「胎兒學。」

fe·tor ['fitɚ; 'fi:tə] n. 臭氣;惡臭。(亦作 **foetor**)

fet·ter** ['fɛtɚ; 'fetə] n. ①足械; 脚鐐。②(常 pl.)束縛; 囚禁。World trade free of political *fetters* is necessary. 不爲政治束縛之國際貿易是必需的。be in fetters*** 被鎖上脚鐐;在囚禁中。—v.t. ①加以足械;加以脚鐐。②束縛;限制。We reverence tradition but will not be *fettered* by it. 我們尊敬傳統但不願被它束縛。—er, n. —less, adj.

fet·ter·lock ['fɛtɚ,lɑk; 'fetəlɔk] n. ①=**fetlock.** ②馬腿上之鐐。

fet·tle ['fɛtl; 'fetl] n. (身心之)狀態;情形。***in fine*** (or ***good***) ***fettle*** 精神奕奕;身體健壯。

fe·tus ['fitəs; 'fi:təs] n. 胎兒;胎。(亦「作 **foetus**)」

feu [fju; fju:] n. 〖蘇〗納定額租金之永遠租用(地)。—v.t. 〖蘇〗准永遠租用。

feud[1] [fjud; fju:d] n. ①家族之累世宿仇。②仇恨; 爭執; 夙怨; 不和。***at feud with*** 與…不和; 與…有仇。***deadly feud*** 不共戴天之仇。—v.i. 彼此仇視; 爭鬥; 爭執。

feud[2] n. 封地; 領地;采邑;食邑。

***feu·dal**[1] ['fjudl; 'fju:dl] adj. ①封建的; 封建制度的。the *feudal* age (days, times). 封建時代。②食邑的; 封地的。

feu·dal[2] adj. 仇恨的;宿仇的。

feu·dal·ism ['fjudl,ɪzəm; 'fju:dəlizəm] n. ①封建制度。②寡頭制度。

feu·dal·ist ['fjudlɪst; 'fju:dəlist] n. ①封建論者。②精通封建法之學者。

feu·dal·is·tic [,fjudl'ɪstɪk; ,fju:də'listik] adj.①封建制度的;封建主義的。②傾向封建制度的。

feu·dal·i·ty [fju'dælətɪ; fju:'dæliti] n., pl. -ties. ①封建制度; 封建政體。②封地;采邑。③封建諸侯或貴族(指統治集團)。

feu·dal·i·za·tion [,fjudlə'zeʃən; ,fju:dəlai'zeiʃən] n. 封建化; 使爲領地; 使合封建制度。

feu·dal·ize ['fjudl,aɪz; 'fju:dəlaiz] v.t., -ized, -iz·ing. 使合封建制度。

feu·dal·ly ['fjudlɪ; 'fju:dəli] adv. ①依照封建制度地。②在封建制度之保有權下。

feu·da·to·ry ['fjudə,torɪ; 'fju:dətəri] adj., n., pl. -ries. —adj. 封建的;受封的。—n. ①家臣;諸侯。②領地;采邑。

feu de joie [,fœdə'ʒwɑ; ,fœdə'ʒwɑ:] 〖法〗祝砲(=fire of joy); 爲慶祝而舉之火(=bonfire).

feud·ist[1] ['fjudɪst; 'fju:dist] n. 〖美〗爭執者; 不和者; 有宿仇者。

feud·ist[2] n. 封建法學者。

feuil·le·ton [fœjə'tõ; 'fə:itõ:] 〖法〗n. ①(法國報紙之)文藝欄;文藝批評欄。②文藝欄之作品。

***fe·ver** ['fivɚ; 'fi:və] n. ①熱病; 發燒; 發熱。Has he any *fever?* 他發燒嗎? ②狂熱; 激昂。—v.i. 發熱; 發燒; 患熱病。The malaria victim *fevers* intermittently. 瘧疾患者會間歇地發燒。—v.t. 使發燒; 使發熱; 使興奮。The scorching blast *fevers* the blood. 灼熱的風使血液發熱。—less, adj.

fever blisters 面疱疹。

fe·vered ['fivɚd; 'fi:vəd] adj. ①發燒的;患熱病的。②激動的。

fe·ver·few ['fivɚ,fju; 'fi:vəfju:] n.

〖植物〗小白菊;驅熱菊。 「熱的興奮。」
fever heat ①生病時的高體溫。②狂
***fe·ver·ish** ['fivərɪʃ; 'fiːvəriʃ] *adj.* ①發熱的;熱病的。②狂熱的;熱烈的。③產生熱病的。④由熱病而產生的。⑤不安定的。The condition of the stock market was *feverish.* 股票市場的情況不安定。⑥狂亂的。a wallpaper with a *feverish* contemporary design. 有混亂的現代化圖案之壁紙。⑦悶熱的。The afternoon was *feverish.* 那天下午很悶熱。—**ly,** *adv.* —**ness,** *n.*
fe·ver·ous ['fivərəs; 'fiːvərəs] *adj.* =**feverish.** —**ly,** *adv.*
fe·ver·root ['fivəˌrut; 'fiːvəruːt] *n.* 北美產之忍冬科植物之一種。
fever sore 壞疽性潰瘍;口唇瘡。
fever therapy 〖醫〗發熱療法(用人工方法使人發燒以治病)。 「*n.* 藥用植物。」
fe·ver·weed ['fivəˌwid; 'fiːvəwiːd]
‡**few** [fju; fjuː] *adj.,* **few·er, few·est,** *n.* —*adj.* ①很少的;不多的(不用冠詞 a, =not many). Very *few* people understood what he said.極少人懂得他說的是什麼。②少數的;幾(個);數(個)(與冠詞 a 連用, =some). He has a *few* friends. 他有幾個朋友。***a few more*** 再多幾個。***at*** (***the***) ***fewest*** 至少。***every few minutes*** 每隔幾分鐘。The buses run *every few minutes.* 公共汽車每隔幾分鐘一班。***few and far between*** **a.** 偶一。**b.** 間隔很遠的。***no fewer than*** 不下於;約有(=as many as). There were *no fewer than* 500 people present. 出席的不下五百人。***some few*** 相當多的;一些。***the few*** 少數人。—*n.* 很少的人或物(不用 a);數個人或物(與 a 連用)。Of my friends *few* live in England. 我的朋友中,很少人住在英國。***a good few*** 〖英俗〗相當多的(=quite a large number). ***few or no*** 幾無。***no few*** =**not a few.** ***not a few*** 不少的;許多的。*Not a few* of the members were absent. 有不少會員未到。***only a few*** 只有少數;只有幾個。***quite a few*** 〖美,俗〗相當多的;頗有幾個。*Quite a few* students were absent yesterday. 昨天有相當多的學生缺席。—**ness,** *n.* 〖注意〗(1) **few, a few, fewer** 皆係指"數"的,若指"量"則用 little, a little (或 some), less 代之。(2) **few** 的相對字是 many; little 的相對字是 much. a few 和 a little 的相對字是 none. fewer 和 less 的相對字是 more.
fey [fe; fei] *adj.* 〖蘇,古〗①注定死亡的;瀕死的;臨終的。②發狂的。(亦作 **fay**) —**ness,** *n.*
fez [fɛz; fez] *n., pl.* **fez·zes.** 土耳其氈帽(無邊,紅色,飾有黑纓)。—**zed,** *adj.*
ff. ① and the following. 及其下;及其後。② for tissimo. 〖音樂〗極強;用最強音。③ folios. 對開頁;對摺本。 **F.G.S.** Fellow of the Geological Society. **F.H.** fire hydrant. **f.i.** for instance.
fi·an·cé [ˌfiən'se, fiˌɑn'se, fi'ɑnse; fiː'ɑ̃ːnsei, fi'ɑːnsei] *n.* 未婚夫。
fi·an·cée [ˌfiən'se, fiˌɑn'se, fi'ɑnse; fiː'ɑ̃ːnsei, fi'ɑːnsei] *n.* 未婚妻。
fi·as·co[1] [fɪ'æsko; fiː'æskou] *n., pl.* **-cos, -coes.** 完全失敗;慘敗;結果可笑的行動。
fia·sco[2] ['fjasko; 'fjɑːskou] *n., pl.* **-schi** [-ski; -skiː]. 〖義〗酒瓶。
fi·at ['faɪət; 'faiæt] *n.* ①命令;諭。②認可;許可。***fiat money*** 〖美〗不兌換紙幣。—*v.t.* ①認可。②以命令宣布。
fib[1] [fɪb; fib] *n., v.,* **fibbed, fib·bing.** —*n.* 無關緊要的謊言;小謊。—*v.i.* 撒小謊。
fib[2] *v.t. & v.i.,* **fibbed, fib·bing.** 〖俚〗以拳輕擊。
fib·ber ['fɪbə; 'fibə] *n.* 撒小謊者。
***fi·ber** ['faɪbə; 'faibə] *n.* ①纖維;纖維質。②纖維組織;織地。cloth of coarse *fiber.* 織地粗劣的布。③性情。A man of strong moral *fiber* can resist temptation. 品格堅強的人能抵抗誘惑。④骨氣;力量。His objectivity gave *fiber* to his point of view. 他的客觀性給他的觀點增加力量。⑤本質。⑥〖植物〗鬚根。—**fi·bered,** *adj.* —**less,** *adj.*
fi·ber·board ['faɪbəˌbord; 'faibəbɔːd] *n.* 纖維板。
fi·ber·glass ['faɪbəˌglæs; 'faibəglɑːs] *n.* 纖維玻璃。(亦作 **fiber glass**)
***fi·bre** ['faɪbə; 'faibə] *n.* =**fiber.**
fi·bril ['faɪbrəl; 'faibril] *n.* ①原纖維;纖絲。②〖植物〗根毛。
fi·brin ['faɪbrɪn; 'faibrin] *n.* ①〖生理〗纖維蛋白;纖維素。②〖植物〗麩質。
fi·brin·o·gen [faɪ'brɪnədʒən; fai'brinədʒən] *n.* 纖維蛋白原。—**ic,** *adj.*
fi·brin·ous ['faɪbrɪnəs; 'faibrinəs] *adj.* 有纖維素的。(亦作 **fibrinogenic**)
fi·broid ['faɪbrɔɪd; 'faibrɔid] *adj.* 纖維狀的;纖維性的。—*n.* 〖醫〗纖維肌瘤;類纖維瘤。 「〖生化〗生絲素;絲心蛋白。」
fi·bro·in ['faɪbroɪn; 'faibrouin] *n.*
fi·bro·ma [faɪ'bromə; fai'broumə] *n., pl.* **-mas, -ma·ta** [-mətə; -mətə]. 〖醫〗纖維瘤。—**tous,** *adj.*
fi·brous ['faɪbrəs; 'faibrəs] *adj.* 纖維的;有纖維的;纖維狀的。—**ly,** *adv.* —**ness,** *n.*
fib·ster ['fɪbstə; 'fibstə] *n.* 〖俗〗撒小謊者。
fib·u·la ['fɪbjələ; 'fibjulə] *n., pl.* **-lae** [-ˌli; -liː], **-las.** ①〖解剖〗腓骨。②〖考古〗(古希臘、羅馬之)搭扣;扣針。—**fib·u·lar,** *adj.*
-fic 〖字尾〗表"生產;引起;做"之義。
-fication 〖字尾〗表"作爲或狀態"之名詞字尾,相當於以 **-fy** 爲字尾的動詞。
fich·u ['fɪʃu; 'fiːʃuː] *n.* 三角形披肩。
fick·le ['fɪkl̩; 'fikl] *adj.* 多變的;不專的。*fickle* fortune. 多變的命運。—**ness,** *n.*
fic·tile ['fɪktl̩; 'fiktail] *adj.* ①可塑造的;可塑性的。②塑造的;黏土製的。③陶製的;陶器的。④聽從的;順從的。—*n.* (一件)陶器。
fic·tion** ['fɪkʃən; 'fikʃən] *n.* ①小說。He prefers history to *fiction.* 他對歷史要比小說喜歡些。②想像;虛構;杜撰。③虛構之事;杜撰的故事。We want facts, not *fictions.* 我們需要事實,不要杜撰的故事。④〖法律〗假定;擬制。It is a legal *fiction* that a corporation is a person. 把團體(法人)當做一個人是一種法律上的假設。Fact is stranger than fiction.*** 事實比想像奇怪。
fic·tion·al ['fɪkʃənl̩; 'fikʃənəl] *adj.* 小說的;想像的;虛構的;杜撰的。—**ly,** *adv.*
fic·tion·ist ['fɪkʃənɪst; 'fikʃənist] *n.* 小說家;短篇故事作家。
fic·ti·tious [fɪk'tɪʃəs; fik'tiʃəs] *adj.* ①假的;假定的;虛構的;假想的。②佯裝的;僞裝的。—**ly,** *adv.* —**ness,** *n.*
fictitious person 〖法律〗法人。
fic·tive ['fɪktɪv; 'fiktiv] *adj.* ①能想像創造的;屬於想像創造的。②想像的;虛構的;

無稽的。—**ly**, *adv.*

fid 〔fɪd; fid〕 *n.* ①解繩用之木釘;張纜針。②支撐材;固定材。③〖航海〗支撐中桅之方栓。

fid·dle** 〔'fɪdl; 'fidl〕 *n., v.,* **-dled, -dling.** —*n.* 〖俗〗小提琴。 ***be as fit as a fiddle 精神健旺的。 ***hang up one's fiddle when one comes home*** (在外歡喜)在家則抑鬱。 ***hang up the fiddle*** 隱退;放棄事業。 ***play first fiddle*** 爲首;領頭。 ***play second fiddle*** 居次位;聽人指揮。 ***with a face as long as a fiddle*** 板着臉;面色極爲陰鬱。—*v.t.* ①〖俗〗(用小提琴)演奏。②虛度(光陰)。—*v.i.* ①〖俗〗奏小提琴。②作無益之事;瞎動。The embarrassed boy *fiddled* with his hat. 那感到尷尬的孩子撫弄着他的帽子。 ***fiddle away one's time*** 虛度光陰。

fid·dle-de-dee 〔ˌfɪdlˈdiˈdi; ˈfidldiˈdi:〕 *n. & interj.* 胡說;瞎扯。

fid·dle-fad·dle 〔'fɪdlˌfædl; 'fidlˌfædl〕 *n., interj., v.,* **-fad·dled, -fad·dling.** —*n. & interj.* 〖俗〗胡說;瞎扯。—*v.i.* 大驚小怪;無理取鬧。

fid·dler 〔'fɪdlɚ; 'fidlə〕 *n.* ①彈奏小提琴者。②玩忽者;虛擲光陰者。③一種蟹(螯一大一小)。 ***pay the fiddler*** 承擔後果;負擔玩樂之費用(=to pay the piper)。

fiddler's green 水手們想像中的樂園;經常有醇酒、美人與歌舞的地方。

fid·dle·stick 〔'fɪdlˌstɪk; 'fidlstik〕 *n.* ①拉提琴的弓。②無聊事。③無價值之事或物。

fid·dling 〔'fɪdlɪŋ, 'fɪdlɪŋ; 'fidliŋ〕 *adj.* ①作無謂之事的;瑣細的;無用的;無益的。②演奏提琴的。—*n.* 演奏提琴。

***fi·del·i·ty** 〔faɪ'dɛlətɪ, fə–; fi'deliti, fai–〕 *n., pl.* **-ties.** ①忠貞;忠誠;節操。②盡職。His *fidelity* and industry brought him speedy promotion. 他的盡職與勤勉使他很快獲得晉陞。③精確;正確;翔實。④〖無線電〗傳眞性。

fidelity insurance 忠實保險(因員工不忠實或疏忽而招致損失之保險)。

fidg·et 〔'fɪdʒɪt; 'fidʒit〕 *v.i.* 不停地動;煩躁不安;坐立不安;煩亂。—*v.t.* 使不安;使煩躁。—*n.* ①煩躁不安;侷促不安。②侷促不安的人;坐立不安的人。 ***give one the fidgets*** 使之煩躁不安。

fidg·et·y 〔'fɪdʒɪtɪ; 'fidʒiti〕 *adj.* 侷促不安的;煩亂的;煩躁的。

FIDO 〔'faɪdo; 'faidou〕 *n.* 〖航空〗火焰驅霧法(在機場跑道兩側燃燒液體燃料驅散濕霧以便飛機升降,爲 *F*og *I*nvestigation *D*ispersal *O*perations之略)。

fi·du·cial 〔fɪ'duʃəl, –'dɪu–; fi'dju:ʃjəl〕 *adj.* ①有信仰的;信賴的;信託的。②〖天文,物理〗基準的。—**ly**, *adv.*

fi·du·ci·ar·y 〔fɪ'duʃɪˌɛrɪ; fi'dju:ʃjəri〕 *adj., n., pl.* **-ar·ies.** —*adj.* ①受託的;受託領管的;受託人的;信託的。②信用發行的。—*n.* 信託者。—**fi·du·ci·ar·i·ly**, *adv.*

fie 〔faɪ; fai〕 *interj.* 呸!咄!(表示厭惡、輕蔑、斥責或佯作驚訝的發聲)。

fief 〔fif; fi:f〕 *n.* 領地;封土;采邑。(亦作 **feoff**)

‡field 〔fild; fi:ld〕 *n.* ①田地;田野。Who owns that *field?* 那塊田地爲誰所有?②場地;運動場。a baseball *field.* 棒球場。③產地;(煤、油)田。an oil *field.* 油田。④戰場(=battlefield);戰役;戰爭。⑤界;範圍;領域。That is outside my *field.* 那已超出了我的範圍。⑥〖物理〗場(如力場等)。A magnet has a *field* around it. 磁鐵四周有磁場。⑦視界;視域。⑧一片;茫茫一片。 A *field* of ice surrounds the North pole. 一片冰雪環繞着北極。⑨(畫等的)底;畫面。⑩(電視中的)影面;幕面。⑪活動場;舞臺。⑫參加比賽者的集合稱。⑬比賽中除特別指出者外其他參加者的集合稱。 ***be in the field*** 去從軍;去參戰;去參加運動。 ***fair field and no favor*** 公平無私。 ***hold the field*** 堅守陣地。 ***in one's own field*** 在自己本行內。 ***in the field*** a. 實地。b. 在某一行中。He is known *in the field* as a fine mathematician. 在數學界他是知名的數學家。 ***keep*** (or ***maintain***) ***the field*** 繼續戰鬥;繼續活動。 ***lose the field*** 敗退。 ***play the field*** 〖俗〗與數個異性交遊。 ***take the field*** 開戰;開賽。They *took the field* at dawn. 天一亮他們就打起仗來。—*v.t.* ①〖棒球〗(在外野)接(球)擲還。Well *fielded!* 外野守得好!②送到戰場;送到競賽場。—*v.i.* 〖棒球〗擔任外野手;守備。He *fields* well. 他外野守得很好。

field artillery 〖軍〗野砲;野戰砲兵。

field battery 〖軍〗野砲隊;野戰砲兵;野戰砲列。

field book 測量者或博物學家之筆記本。

field corn 飼料用玉蜀黍。

field day ①運動比賽日。②〖軍〗野外演習日。③有重大事件的日子。④大過其癮的機會;大發威力的機會。

field·er 〔'fildɚ; 'fi:ldə〕 *n.* 〖棒球、板球〗外場員;外野手。

field event 田賽項目(跳高、跳遠等)。

field·fare 〔'fildˌfɛr, –ˌfær; 'fi:ldfɛə〕 *n.* (歐洲產之)一種鶇。

field glass(es) 小型的雙眼望遠鏡。

field goal ①〖橄欖球〗射中可得三分之球。②〖籃球〗比賽時投進得二分之球。

field gun 〖軍〗野砲;野戰砲。

field hockey 曲棍球。

field hospital 野戰醫院。

field house 運動場旁的貯藏室、更衣室等。

field·ing 〔'fildɪŋ; 'fi:ldiŋ〕 *n.* 〖棒球〗守衞。

field magnet 〖物理〗場磁體;場磁鐵;界磁。

field marshal 〖英〗陸軍元帥。

field mouse 田鼠;地鼠。

field officer 陸軍校級軍官。

field of fire (鎗、砲等之)射界。

field of honor 戰場;決鬥場。

field·piece 〔'fildˌpis; 'fi:ldpi:s〕 *n.* 〖軍〗野戰砲(=field gun)。

fields·man 〔'fildzmən; 'fi:ldzmən〕 *n., pl.* **-men.** 〖英,板球〗外場員。

field sport ①戶外運動(如狩獵、釣魚、競技等)。②田賽。

field trip (學生的)實地考察旅行。

field umpire 〖棒球〗壘裁判員。

field·ward(s) 〔'fildwɚd(z); 'fi:ldwəd(z)〕 *adv.* 向原野地。

field work 野外調查工作。

field·work 〔'fildˌwɝk; 'fi:ldwə:k〕 *n.* (戰地臨時築成的)野堡。

fiend** 〔find; fi:nd〕 *n.* ①惡魔;魔鬼。②窮兇極惡的人。③〖俗〗(耽於某種習慣、遊戲的)迷;狂。a dance *fiend.* 舞迷。④鬼才;傑出人才。 ***the Fiend 魔鬼;撒旦。

fiend·ish 〔'findɪʃ; 'fi:ndiʃ〕 *adj.* ①極惡的;兇狠的。②極壞的;極苦的;很討厭的。—**ness**, *n.* —**ly**, *adv.*

***fierce** 〔fɪrs; fiəs〕 *adj.,* **fierc·er, fierc·est.** ①兇猛的;野的。*fierce* animals. 猛獸。②猛烈的;強勁的。a *fierce* storm. 猛烈的暴

風雨。③〖俚〗很壞的; 討厭的。This heat is really *fierce.* 這熱天眞討厭。—**ly,** *adv.* —**ness,** *n.*

fi·e·ri fa·ci·as 〔'faɪə,raɪ'feʃɪ,æs; 'faiərai'feiʃiæs〕〖拉〗執行令狀。

fi·er·i·ly 〔'faɪrɪlɪ; 'faiərili〕 *adv.* 如火地; 熾熱地; 猛烈地; 激忿地。

fi·er·i·ness 〔'faɪrɪnɪs; 'faiərinis〕 *n.* 如火; 熾熱; 猛烈; 暴烈; 火性; 急性。

***fier·y** 〔'faɪrɪ, 'faɪərɪ; 'faiəri〕 *adj.,* **fier·i·er, fier·i·est.** ①火的; 熾熱的; 燃燒的; 如火的。②火紅的。③激情的; 激昂的。a *fiery* speech. 激昂的演說。④火性的; 烈性的(馬)。⑤紅腫的。⑥易着火的; 易燃的。⑦(礦坑等)含有易燃氣體的。⑧刺激的。

fi·es·ta 〔fɪ'ɛstə; fi'estə〕〖西〗 *n.* ①宗教之節日; 聖徒之紀念日。②假日; 祝樂。

fi. fa. fieri facias (拉=see it is done).

fife 〔faɪf; faif〕 *n., v.,* **fifed, fif·ing.** —*n.* 音調尖銳的短笛; 笛子; 橫笛。—*v.t.* & *v.i.* 吹奏橫笛。

fif·er 〔'faɪfə; 'faifə〕 *n.* 吹奏橫笛者; 笛手。

fife rail 〖航海〗(繞桅之)拴索座。

‡fif·teen 〔fɪf'tin, 'fɪf'tin; 'fif'ti:n〕 *n., adj.* 十五; 十五個; 15。*fifteen* years. 十五年。*Fifteen* were found. 找到了十五個。

fif·teen·fold 〔'fɪf,tin'fold; 'fifti:n-'fould〕 *adj.* & *adv.* 十五倍的(地)。

***fif·teenth** 〔fɪf'tinθ; 'fif'ti:nθ〕 *adj.* ①第十五。②十五分之一的。—*n.* ①第十五; 第十五個。the *fifteenth* of the month. 當月十五號。②十五分之一。—**ly,** *adv.*

‡fifth 〔fɪfθ; fifθ〕 *adj.* ①第五的。the *fifth* day. 第五天。②五分之一的。***smite*** **(*a person*)** ***under the fifth rib*** 刺殺第五肋骨的下部; 刺中要害。***the fifth act*** 第五幕; 終幕; 人生的終幕; 晚年; 晚景。—*n.* ①第五。the *fifth* of the month. 當月五號。②五分之一。③〖音樂〗第五度; 五度音程。—*adv.* 排在第五地。

Fifth Avenue 第五街(紐約鬧街)。

fifth column 第五縱隊; 奸細; 間諜。

fifth columnist 第五縱隊分子。

fifth·ly 〔'fɪfθlɪ; 'fifθli〕 *adv.* 第五(地)。

fifth wheel 多餘的事物或人。

***fif·ti·eth** 〔'fɪftɪɪθ; 'fiftiiθ〕 *n., adj.* ①第五十(的)。②五十分之一(的)。one *fiftieth* of the total. 全部的五十分之一。

‡fif·ty 〔'fɪftɪ; 'fifti〕 *n., pl.* **-ties.** ①五十; 五十個。*Fifty* are found. 找到了五十個。②(*pl.*) 五十到五十九之間。a man in his *fifties.* 一個五十幾歲的人。③五十元的鈔票。④口徑 0.50 英寸的鎗。—*adj.* 五十; 五十個; 50。*Fifty* people were found. 找到了五十個人。

fif·ty-fif·ty 〔'fɪftɪ'fɪftɪ; 'fifti'fifti〕 *adj.* & *adv.* 〖俗〗二一添作五; 平分爲二分的(地); 各有二分之一的(地)。***go fifty-fifty*** 平分; 均攤。

fif·ty-first 〔'fɪftɪ'fɝst; 'fifti'fə:st〕 *n., adj.* ①第五十一(的)。②五十一分之一(的)。

fif·ty·fold 〔'fɪftɪ,fold; 'fiftifould〕 *adj.* & *adv.* 五十倍的(地)。

fif·ty-sec·ond 〔'fɪftɪ'sɛkənd; 'fifti-'sekənd〕 *n., adj.* ①第五十二(的)。②五十二分之一(的)。

fif·ty-third 〔'fɪftɪ'θɝd; 'fifti'θə:d〕 *n., adj.* ①第五十三(的)。②五十三分之一(的)。

fig**[1] 〔fɪg; fig〕 *n.* ①〖植物〗無花果; 無花果樹。②些微之量; 瑣屑; 少許。Their opinion wasn't worth a *fig.* 他們的意見毫不足取。③表示輕蔑的手勢。Adam fig*** 香蕉。***A fig for...!*** 甚麼東西! (那) 有甚麼了不起! ***Chinese fig*** 柿。***fig's end*** 無價值的東西。***not to care*** (or ***give***) ***a fig*** (or ***fig's end***) ***for...*** 對…毫不介意; 毫不重視…。I *don't care a fig for* your opinion. 我一點也不重視你的意見。—**gy,** *adj.*

fig[2] *v.,* **figged, fig·ging,** *n.* —*v.t.* 〖俗〗①盛裝〖out〗。to *fig* out a horse. 盛裝一匹馬。②刷新; 修整〖up〗。—*n.* 〖俗〗①盛裝; 服裝。②健康狀況。***in full fig*** 〖俗〗盛裝; 裝備齊全。

fig. ①figure; figures. ②figurative. ③figuratively.

fig·eat·er 〔'fɪg,itə; 'fig,i:tə〕 *n.* 〖美〗「無花果蟲」。

‡fight 〔faɪt; fait〕 *v.,* **fought** 〔fɔt; fɔ:t〕, **fight·ing,** *n.* —*v.t.* ①打(仗); 與…戰爭; 使戰鬥; 抵抗。to *fight* a battle. 打仗。Doctors *fight* disease. 醫生們與疾病作戰。②指揮; 操縱。The captain *fought* his ship well. 這艦長善於指揮他的軍艦作戰。③對…帶來不必要的困難。—*v.i.* 戰爭; 打架; 奮鬥。They were *fighting* (in order) to preserve their independence. 他們爲了維護獨立而戰。***fight against*** (or ***with***) 抵抗; 與…戰。***fight back*** 抵抗; 堵擊。***fight down*** 打敗; 壓服。***fight for*** 爲…而戰。He died *fighting for* his country. 他爲捍衞國家而戰死。***fight hand to hand*** 短兵相接。***fight it out*** 徹底解決; 打出結果; 一決雌雄。***fight*** **(*something*** or ***someone*)** ***off*** 擊退(某人或物)。***fight on*** 繼續作戰。***fight one's way*** 殺出一條血路; 打開一條生路。***fight one's way in life*** (or ***in the world***) 在人生中刻苦奮鬥。***fight shy of*** **a.** 遠離(人); 避(人)。**b.** 避免。***fight to a finish*** 戰到底; 決勝負。***fight together*** 打成一團。***fight tooth and nail*** 徹底地打; 打個够。***fight up against*** 與…力戰苦鬥。***fight with windmills*** (亦作 **tilt at windmills**) 與想像中的對手或幻想中的惡勢力鬥爭。—*n.* ①戰; 戰役; 戰鬥; 打仗。Who won the *fight?* 誰戰勝了? ②爭論; 爭鬥; 激辯。She starts a *fight* every time she phones me. 她每次跟我通電話都要跟我爭論。③戰鬥力; 戰意; 鬥志。④拳擊比賽。The champion had not had a *fight* for over a year. 這拳王已有一年多沒有參加比賽了。***a fight against*** (or ***with***) 抗抵…之戰。***a fight for freedom*** 爲自由而戰。***a free fight*** 戰鬥。***give*** (or ***make***) **(*a*)** ***fight*** 打一仗。***prize fight*** 拳擊。***put up a good fight*** 奮勇戰鬥。***running fight*** 追擊戰。***show fight*** 表示戰意; 反抗。***stand-up fight*** 光明正大的戰鬥。

***fight·er** 〔'faɪtə; 'faitə〕 *n.* ①戰鬥者; 戰士。②職業拳擊家。③戰鬥機。④好鬥之動物。

fight·er-bomb·er 〔'faɪtə'bɑmə; 'faitə'bɔmə〕 *n.* 戰鬥轟炸機。

fighter plane 戰鬥機。

fight·ing** 〔'faɪtɪŋ; 'faitiŋ〕 *n.* 戰事; 開火。Has the *fighting* stopped yet? 戰事已停止了嗎? ***street fighting 巷戰; 街頭戰。—*adj.* ①戰鬥的; 交戰的; 戰爭的。②適於戰鬥的; 適於比賽的。③挑戰性的。Those are *fighting* words. 那些都是挑戰性的話。***fighting chance*** 經過掙扎後成功的機會。***fighting cock*** 鬥雞; 好鬥的男子。***fighting men*** 兵士。***fighting plane*** 戰鬥機。***fight-***

ing power (or *strength*) 戰鬥力。 *fighting spirit* 戰鬥精神;戰鬥意志。 —ly, *adv.*

fig leaf ①無花果之葉。②(裸體雕像等之)陰部覆蓋物; 僅可蔽體之衣服。③權宜之計。④掩飾物。

fig·ment [ˈfɪgmənt; ˈfigmənt] *n.* 想像物;虛構之事;無稽之談。

fig tree 無花果樹。 *under one's vine and fig tree* 安閒地在自己家中。

fig·u·rant [ˈfɪgjəˌrænt; ˈfigjurənt] *n.* ①芭蕾舞舞伶。②跑龍套之臨時演員; 不重要的角色。

fig·u·rante [ˌfɪgjəˈrænt; ˌfigjuˈrɑ̃ːnt] *n.* figurant 之女性。

fig·u·ra·tion [ˌfɪgjəˈreʃən; ˌfigjuˈreiʃən] *n.* ①定形;成形。②形狀;輪廓。③比喩的表現;意匠。④〖音樂〗音形法。

fig·ur·a·tive [ˈfɪgjərətɪv; ˈfigjurətiv] *adj.* ①比喩的; 假借的。②象徵的。③修飾多的;詞藻富麗的;多比喩的。—ness, *n.*

fig·ur·a·tive·ly [ˈfɪgjərətɪvlɪ; ˈfigjurətivli] *adv.* 比喩地;假借地。

‡**fig·ure** [ˈfɪgjə, ˈfɪgə; ˈfigə] *n., v.,* **-ured, -ur·ing.** —*n.* ①數字(尤指阿拉伯數字)。1, 2, 3, 4, etc., are *figures.* 1, 2, 3, 4 等就是數字。②(*pl.*)(以數字)計算。to be poor at *figures.* 拙於計算。③形象;形體; 肖像。She saw dim *figures* moving. 她看見有模糊的人影移動。④圖形;圖解。⑤人物;名人。⑥體態;風度;身裁; 樣子; 相貌。She has a beautiful *figure.* 她有美麗的體態。⑦圖畫。⑧相似;象喩。⑨圖案。⑩價目;價錢。I bought it at a low *figure.* 我買的價錢很便宜。⑪動作所造成的軌跡;輪廓。⑫象徵。The dove is a *figure* of peace. 鴿是和平的象徵。⑬〖文學〗喩; 借喩。 *a figure of fun* 姿態滑稽的人。 *a man of figure* 有聲望的人。 *cut* (or *make*) *a* (*brilliant,* or *conspicuous*) *figure* 露頭角; 放異彩; 惹人注目;給人良好印象。The couple *cut* quite *a figure.* 那一對夫婦相當出風頭。 *cut a fine figure* 儀表甚佳。 *cut a poor* (or *sorry*) *figure* 現窮相;露拙相;露出可憐相;給人不良印象。 *cut no figure* 不足道; 算不得數。 *do figures* 計算。 *double figures* 二位數字 (自10到 99 皆是)。 *go the whole figure* 徹底行動。 *keep one's figure* 保持體態苗條。—*v.t.* ①演算;解 (算學問題)。②〖俗〗想;認爲。He *figured* himself a good candidate. 他認爲自己是個好的候選人。③用數字表示。④用圖表示。⑤加圖案;飾以圖案;加花樣。⑥〖俚〗懂。He *figured* the whole scheme right away. 他立刻懂了整個計畫。—*v.i.* ①出名; 露頭角。②演算。The carpenter was *figuring* on a board with a pencil. 木匠用鉛筆在木板上演算。③〖俚〗有道理;合乎情理。Sure, that *figures.* 那的確有道理。 *figure as* 扮演…角色。 *figure in* 〖俗〗 a. 算入。 b. 參加。 *figure on* a. 料想;估計。 b. 依靠;倚賴。He is a person you can always *figure on* to pay his bills. 他是個在付帳方面永遠靠得住的人。 *figure oneself* 想像。 *figure out* a. 演算出來。*Figure* it *out* and see what it comes. 把它演算出來,看結果得多少。 b. 理解。I can't *figure out* what he was hinting at. 我不能理解他用意何在。 *figure out at* 總計…;合計…。 *figure up* 總計。—fig·ur·er, *n.*

fig·ured [ˈfɪgjəd, ˈfɪgəd; ˈfigəd] *adj.* ①用圖形表示出來的;圖示的;圖解的。②飾有圖案或花紋的。③〖音樂〗華麗的;註有數字來指示和弦的。④多文飾的;文飾富麗的。

fig·ure·head [ˈfɪgjəˌhɛd; ˈfigəhed] *n.* ①船首所飾之雕像;破浪神。②有名無實的首領; 傀儡。

figure skate 花式溜冰者之溜冰鞋。

figure skating 花式溜冰。

fig·u·rine [ˌfɪgjəˈrin; ˈfigjuriːn] *n.* (陶土、金屬等之)小雕像;小塑像。

fig·wort [ˈfɪgˌwɝt; ˈfigwəːt] *n.* 〖植物〗元參科之植物; 玄參。

Fi·ji [ˈfidʒi; fiːˈdʒiː, ˈfiːˈdʒiː] *n.* ①非濟(南太平洋之一國, 首都爲蘇瓦 Suva)。②飛枝羣島之居民。

Fi·ji·an [fiˈdʒiən; fiːˈdʒiːən] *adj.* 飛枝羣島的;其人民、語言或文化的。 —*n.* 飛枝羣島的人;飛枝羣島的語言。

Fiji Islands 飛枝羣島(南太平洋之羣島, 非濟國之一部分)。

fil·a·gree [ˈfɪləˌgri; ˈfiləgriː] *n., adj., v.* =**filigree.**

***fil·a·ment** [ˈfɪləmənt; ˈfiləmənt] *n.* ①絲; 線; 纖維。② (電燈泡中的) 燈絲。③〖植物〗花絲。

fil·a·men·ta·ry [ˌfɪləˈmɛntərɪ; ˌfiləˈmentəri] *adj.* ①絲的; 細線的; 花絲的。②如絲的; 花絲質的。

fil·a·men·tous [ˌfɪləˈmɛntəs; ˌfiləˈmentəs] *adj.* 如絲的; 似線的;纖維所成的;纖維狀的。②多線或絲狀物的。

fi·lar [ˈfaɪlɚ; ˈfailə] *adj.* ①線的; 絲的。

fi·lar·i·a [fɪˈlɛrɪə; fiˈlɛəriə] *n., pl.* **-lar·i·ae** [-ˈlɛrɪˌi; -ˈlɛəriiː].〖醫〗血絲蟲。—**fi·lar·i·al, fi·lar·i·an,** *adj.*

fil·a·ri·a·sis [ˌfɪləˈraɪəsɪs; ˌfiləˈraiəsis] *n.* 絲蟲病。

fil·a·ture [ˈfɪlətʃɚ; ˈfilətʃə] *n.* ①紡絲;抽成線;繅絲。②紡車;紡織機。③繅絲廠。

fil·bert [ˈfɪlbɚt; ˈfilbət] *n.* ①〖植物〗榛樹;榛子。②〖俚〗自認的評論專家。

filch [fɪltʃ; filtʃ] *v.t.* 偸竊 (小量的瑣碎之物);竊取。—**er,** *n.* —**ing·ly,** *adv.*

***file**[1] [faɪl; fail] *n., v.,* **filed, fil·ing.** —*n.* ①文卷櫃; 公文箱 (匣、夾等)。 Put this letter in the main *file.* 將這文件放入文卷總檔中。②案卷;文卷;檔卷。③行列。④〖軍〗縱隊。 *blank file* 〖軍〗缺伍。 *file by file* 一隊一隊; 陸續。 *file clerk* 管檔案者。 (*march*) *in file* 成縱隊(前進)。 *keep on file* 存卷; 歸檔。 *the rank and file* 〖軍〗士兵; (轉爲)常人。 —*v.t.* ①歸檔; 存卷。Those documents were *filed* away years ago. 那些文件在多年以前便已歸檔了。②把…排成縱隊前進。③提出;申請。④〖新聞〗發電報; 發消息。 He *filed* his story from Taipei. 他從臺北發出這則消息。—*v.i.* ①排成單行或列隊行進。The people *filed* out. 人們排隊出去。② 〖美〗登記競選。③申請。He *filed* for a civil-service job. 他申請一個公務員的職位。 *file an information* 起訴;告發。 *file in* 陸續編入。 *file off* 排成縱隊前進。 *file on* (or *upon*) 進入或占據 (無人認領之土地)。—**fil·er,** *n.*

file[2] *n., v.,* **filed, fil·ing.** —*n.* ①銼子; 銼刀。②狡猾的人。 *bite* (or *gnaw*) *a file* 咬不動; 徒勞。 —*v.t.* ①用銼子銼。②修整;精練。 *file one's teeth* 銼牙; 咬牙切齒。—**fil·er,** *n.*

file·fish [ˈfaɪlˌfɪʃ; ˈfailfiʃ] *n., pl.* **-fish, -fish·es.** 魨;鮏魚。

fil·e·mot [ˈfɪləˌmɑt; ˈfilimɔt] *n., adj.* 枯葉色(的);黃褐色(的)。

fi·let [fɪˈle; fiˈlei] 〖法〗 *n.* ①方眼花邊網。②肉片; 魚片 (=fillet).

fil·i·al 〔ˈfɪlɪəl; ˈfiljəl〕 *adj.* 子女的;子女應作的;孝順的。—**i·ty,** —**ness,** *n.* —**ly,** *adv.*

fil·i·ate 〔ˈfɪlɪˌet; ˈfilieit〕 *v.t.,* **-at·ed, -at·ing.** ①判定私生子之父。②〖古〗=**affiliate.**

fil·i·a·tion 〔ˌfɪlɪˈeʃən; ˌfiliˈeiʃən〕 *n.* ①子女對父母之關係。②系統; 由來; 血統。③〖法律〗私生子之父親的鑑定; 收作養子。④分會;分社。⑤關係之考證。

fil·i·beg 〔ˈfɪləˌbɛg; ˈfilibeg〕 *n.* 〖蘇〗=**kilt.**

fil·i·bus·ter 〔ˈfɪləˌbʌstɚ; ˈfilibʌstə〕 *n.* ①〖美〗**a.** 議院中用冗長的演說或其它方法故意阻礙提案之通過的議員。 **b.** 用上述方法故意阻礙提案之通過。②未受本國命令而攻擊他國者;掠奪兵;海盜。—*v.i.* ①〖美〗用冗長的演說或其它方法故意阻礙議案之通過。②未受政府命令而攻擊他國;侵奪;行海盜行爲。 —*v.t.* 用冗長的演說等阻礙。 —**er,** *n.*

fil·i·cide 〔ˈfɪləˌsaɪd; ˈfilisaid〕 *n.* ①殺子女者。②殺子女。

fil·i·gree 〔ˈfɪləˌgri; ˈfiligriː〕 *n.* ①金銀銅絲所纏類似花邊之細工。②任何似花邊之纖巧的圖案或花紋。③過於精緻而不切實用的東西; 易損之物。—*adj.* 飾有金銀絲細工的; 作有金銀絲細工或精美圖案花紋的。—*v.t.* 用金銀細工裝飾。

fil·ing 〔ˈfaɪlɪŋ; ˈfailiŋ〕 *n.* (文件等之)整理彙集;作成檔案。

Fil·i·pine 〔ˈfɪləˌpin; ˈfilipiːn〕 *adj.* = **Philippine.**

Fil·i·pi·nize 〔ˌfɪləˈpinaɪz; ˌfiliˈpiːnaiz〕 *v.t.,* **-nized, -niz·ing.** 菲化;菲律賓化;全部或大部以菲律賓人擔任。

Fil·i·pi·no 〔ˌfɪləˈpino; ˌfiliˈpiːnou〕 *n., pl.* **-nos,** *adj.* —*n.* 菲律賓人。 —*adj.* 菲律賓的。

‡**fill** 〔fɪl; fil〕 *v.t.* ①使滿;填充;塞。*Fill* the hole with sand. 用沙把這洞口填塞起來。②瀰漫;充滿;普及。Smoke *filled* the room. 煙瀰漫那房間。③使滿足;使飽。They *filled* their guest with good food. 他們以美食款待客人。④供應 (貨物)。 A store *fills* orders, prescriptions, etc. 店鋪供應定貨及配藥方等。⑤填 (空); 補 (缺)。⑥任職; 補缺。⑦使鼓脹。—*v.i.* ①滿;充滿。Her eyes *filled* with tears. 她的眼裏充滿了淚。②阻塞。His heart *filled* at the words. 聽到那些話他覺得心中難過。***fill away*** 〖航海〗藉風航行。***fill in* a.** 填寫。 to *fill in* a form (check). 填表格 (支票)。**b.** 填滿。**c.** 補缺; 暫代他人職務。***fill one's place*** 代替。***fill out* a.** 填好。to *fill* a form *out*. 填好一張表格。**b.** 脹滿;膨脹。**c.** 使更完全; 使內容更爲充實。***fill the bill*** 滿足需要;如約完成;適合條件; 合格。***fill up*** 填好; 填滿。to *fill* a paper *up*. 把文件填好;把試卷答好。***fill up time*** 消磨時光。—*n.* ①填塞物; 填料。②盡量;盡性。Eat and drink your *fill*. 盡量吃喝罷。

fill-dike 〔ˈfɪlˌdaɪk; ˈfildaik〕 *n.* 二月間融雪或雨水漲滿溝渠之季節。

fille 〔ˈfijə; ˈfiːjə〕 〖法〗 *n.* ①女兒。②女郎;少女。③老處女。④娼妓。***fille de chambre*** 侍女;貼身丫頭。***fille de joie*** 娼妓。

fill·er 〔ˈfɪlɚ; ˈfilə〕 *n.* ①填裝之人或物。②填塞物。③雪茄煙之煙草部分。④〖新聞〗補白 (資料)。⑤用於填充之器具 (如漏斗等)。

fil·let 〔ˈfɪlɪt; ˈfilit〕 *n.* ①束髮帶; 窄狹的帶子。②肉片; 魚片。—*v.t.* ①以帶束結。②切(魚肉)成片。

fill-in 〔ˈfɪlˌɪn; ˈfilˌin〕 *n.* ①代替之人或物。②摘要。③在等待時間所作之消遣。

fill·ing 〔ˈfɪlɪŋ; ˈfiliŋ〕 *n.* ①供填塞用之物。②(織品的)緯。③填充;充滿;供應。

filling station 汽車加油站。

fil·lip 〔ˈfɪləp; ˈfilip〕 *v.t.* ①以指頭彈。②彈指以投擲;將…彈出去。③激動;振奮;刺激。—*v.i.* 彈指。—*n.* ①彈指; 以指彈擊。②刺激物; 興奮物。③一擊。④不足取之物。***not worth a fillip*** 毫不足取。

fil·lis·ter 〔ˈfɪlɪstɚ; ˈfilistə〕 *n.* ①(嵌鑲玻璃等之)凹槽;槽口。②槽口鉋。

fil·ly 〔ˈfɪlɪ; ˈfili〕 *n., pl.* **-lies.** ①小雌馬;母駒。②〖俗〗活潑的小姑娘;年輕的女子。

***film** 〔fɪlm; film〕 *n.* ①薄膜;表面之一層。②軟片;膠捲。③電影;影片。 a *film* actor. 電影演員。—*v.i.* ①起一層薄膜。②適於上鏡頭。She *films* well. 她很上鏡頭。③拍電影。—*v.t.* ①拍成電影。②拍攝爲電影片。③覆以薄膜。—**like,** *adj.*

film·a·ble 〔ˈfɪlməbl̩; ˈfilməbl〕 *adj.* 可拍成電影的。

film·dom 〔ˈfɪlmdəm; ˈfilmdəm〕 *n.* 電影界。

film·i·ness 〔ˈfɪlmɪnɪs; ˈfilminis〕 *n.* 極薄;輕如薄膜。

film·let 〔ˈfɪlmˌlɛt; ˈfilmlet〕 *n.* 短片。

film maker ①電影製作人;製片家;電影導演。②(照片之)軟片製作者。

film·o·gra·phy 〔ˈfɪlməgræfɪ; ˈfilməgræfi〕 *n.* 討論電影的著作。

film star 電影明星。

film·strip 〔ˈfɪlmˌstrɪp; ˈfilmstrip〕 *n.* 幻燈片之影片。

film·y 〔ˈfɪlmɪ; ˈfilmi〕 *adj.,* **film·i·er, film·i·est.** ①薄膜的; 如薄膜的; 極薄的。②覆有薄膜的;朦朧的;陰霾的。

fi·lose 〔ˈfaɪlos; ˈfailous〕 *adj.* 似線的; 線狀的;有線狀突出物的。

fil·o·selle 〔ˌfɪloˈsɛl; ˌfiləˈsel〕〖法〗*n.* 刺繡用之絲線。

fils 〔fis; fiːs〕 *n., pl.* **fils.** 〖法〗兒子(有時用於姓名後作 Jr. 之義)。Dumas *fils*. 小仲馬。

fil·ter** 〔ˈfɪltɚ; ˈfiltə〕 *n.* ①過濾器。②用以過濾之物; 過濾材料。③〖電〗濾波器; 濾光器;(照相機之)濾光鏡。filter bed*** 濾水池。***filter paper*** 濾紙。—*v.t.* 過濾;濾清。*Filter* out all the dirt before using the water. 在用這水之前先將其中所有污物濾除。—*v.i.* ①滲入。②漏過; 濾過。③透過。Daylight *filtered* through clouds. 日光透過雲層。—**er,** *n.*

fil·ter·a·ble 〔ˈfɪltərəbl̩; ˈfiltərəbl〕 *adj.* ①可過濾的。②〖細菌〗濾過性的。

filter center 資料處理中心;情報整理站。

filter cigarette 濾嘴香煙。

filter tip ①香煙濾嘴。②濾嘴香煙。

filth 〔fɪlθ; filθ〕 *n.* ①骯髒;污物。②醜行;猥褻語;齷齪的想法;猥褻作品。

filth disease 污物病;由不潔而生的疾病。

filth·i·ness 〔ˈfɪlθɪnɪs; ˈfilθinis〕 *n.* 污穢;不潔。

filth·y** 〔ˈfɪlθɪ; ˈfilθi〕 *adj.,* **filth·i·er, filth·i·est.** ①污穢的;不潔的。His clothes are *filthy*. 他的衣服不潔。②醜惡的;卑鄙的。③猥褻的;淫穢的。④〖俚〗充滿的; 豐富的〖常with〗. They are *filthy* with money. 他們腰纏萬貫。be filthy with money*** 富有;飽聚孽財。***filthy pelf*** 造孽錢。—**filth·i·ly,** *adv.*

filthy lucre ①〖蔑〗臭錢。②〖廢〗不義之財;用卑鄙手段得來之財。

fil·tra·ble 〔ˈfɪltrəbl̩; ˈfiltrəbl〕 *adj.* = **filterable.**

fil·trate 〔ˈfɪltret; ˈfiltreit〕 *v.,* **-trat·ed, -trat·ing,** *n.* —*v.t. & v.i.* 過濾; 濾清。—*n.* 濾液;經濾清的水。—**fil·trat·a·ble,** *adj.*

fil·tra·tion 〔fɪlˈtreʃən; filˈtreiʃən〕 *n.*

過濾;濾清。

fim·bri·ate [ˈfɪmbrɪˌet; ˈfimbrieit] *adj., v.,* **-at·ed, -at·ing.** —*adj.* 〖動、植物〗有緣緣的;有鬚毛爲緣的。—*v.t.* 〖紋章〗鑲以窄邊。

***fin** [fɪn; fin] *n., v.,* **finned, fin·ning.** —*n.* ①鰭。②鰭狀物。③〖航空〗(飛機的)安定翼;直尾翼。④〖俚〗美金五元的鈔票。You owe me a *fin.* 你欠我美金五元。—*v.i.* 將鰭露出水面。—*v.t.* 〖機械〗加以鰭、散熱片、突片等。—**less,** *adj.* —**like,** *adj.*

Fin. ①Finland. ②Finnish. **fin.** ①finance. ②financial. ③ad finem (拉 =at the end).

fi·na·gle [fəˈnegl̩; fiˈneigl] *v.,* **-gled, -gling.** —*v.i.* 〖俗〗行騙; 欺詐。—*v.t.* 〖俗〗①欺騙 (某人); 騙取 (某物)。②以計取得。—**fi·na·gler,** *n.*

‡**fi·nal** [ˈfaɪnl̩; ˈfainl] *adj.* ①最後的;最終的。the *final* chapter of a book. 一本書的最後一章。②決定的;確定的。My judgment is *final.* 我的判斷是確定的(不再變更的)。③〖文法〗表示目的的。—*n.* ①(常 *pl.*)大考;期末考試;決賽。She was busily preparing for the *finals.* 她忙於準備大考。②結局;終局。***take one's final(s)***參加大考(或決賽)。

fi·na·le [fɪˈnɑlɪ; fiˈnɑːli] *n.* ①樂曲或戲劇的最後部分;最後一幕;終曲;終場。②終;結局;收尾。

fi·nal·ist [ˈfaɪnl̩ɪst; ˈfainəlist] *n.* (競「爭中之)獲決賽權者。」

fi·nal·i·ty [faɪˈnælətɪ; faiˈnæliti] *n., pl.* **-ties.** ①結局;最後;完結;定局;解決。②最後的事物;最後的行爲、決定、宣告或安排。③〖哲學〗目的論。

fi·nal·ize [ˈfaɪnl̩ˌaɪz; ˈfainəlaiz] *v.,* **-ized, -iz·ing.** —*v.t.* 完成; 作最後決定。—*v.i.* 完成工作或事務。—**fi·nal·i·za·tion,** *n.*

‡**fi·nal·ly** [ˈfaɪnl̩ɪ; ˈfainəli] *adv.* ①最後地;最後一點(=lastly, 演說時用之)。*Finally,* I wish to thank all who cooperated in this important object. 最後我要向所有爲此重要目標協力合作的人道謝。②完全地; 決定地。③最後;終於。

***fi·nance** [fəˈnæns, ˈfaɪnæns; faiˈnæns, fiˈn-, ˈfainæns] *n., v.,* **-nanced, -nanc·ing.** —*n.* ①財政; 財務; 財政學。②(*pl.*)財源;歲入; 基金。The school had to close for lack of *finances.* 那學校因財源短缺而必須關閉。—*v.t.* ①供以經費; 負擔經費。Uncle will *finance* my way through college. 叔父會供我讀完大學。②讓…賒帳。—*v.i.* 掌財政;掌理財務;處理財務。

finance bill 撥款法案。

finance company 貸款公司(尤指貸款供分期付款購物者)。

fi·nan·cial** [fəˈnænʃəl, faɪˈnænʃəl; faiˈnænʃəl, fi-] *adj.* 財政的; 財務的; 金融的。to be in *financial* difficulties. 在財政困難中(卽經費支絀之意)。a *financial* center. 金融中心。financial year*** 〖英〗會計年度 (=〖美〗 fiscal year).

fi·nan·cial·ly [fəˈnænʃəlɪ; faiˈnænʃəli] *adv.* 財政上; 經費上。

fin·an·cier [ˌfɪnənˈsɪr; faiˈnænsiə] *n.* ①財政家;理財家。②資本家;金融業者。—*v.i.* 掌理財務;理財。—*v.t.* 負擔…經費。

fin·back [ˈfɪnˌbæk; ˈfinbæk] *n.* 〖動物〗脊鰭鯨。

finch [fɪntʃ; fintʃ] *n.* 雀科中鳴禽之類;鷽「類(雀、交喙、磧鶸、梅花雀等)。」

‡**find** [faɪnd; faind] *v.,* **found** [faʊnd; faund], **find·ing,** *n.* —*v.t.* ①發現;尋得;找尋。Can you *find* me a good one? 你能替我找一個好的嗎? I *found* him at home. 我發現他在家。②拾得;看見。I *found* this knife in the street. 我在街上拾得這把小刀。③有;得到;利用。Can you *find* time to do this? 你有時間做這件事嗎? ④覺得;感覺;感到。I hope you *found* your bed comfortable. 我希望你感覺你的床很舒適。⑤發覺;探知;獲知;得知。When he woke up, he *found* himself in prison. 當他醒來,他發現自己已入了獄。⑥判定;認定。The judge *found* the prisoner guilty. 法官判定該犯人有罪。⑦達於;自然成爲。Water *finds* its level. 水自然成爲水平面。⑧供給。⑨會使用;恢復使用。Experience helped the young bird to *find* his wings. 經驗使小鳥學會使用牠的兩翼。—*v.i.* ①(法官)達成最後決定。②〖英〗打獵時發現獵物。***find a person in*** (***out, up,*** or ***in bed***)發現某人在家(外出,起床,睡覺)。***find a person out*** 發現某人做錯。***find fault with*** 批評;反對;非難(參看 **fault**)。***find it in one's heart*** 忍心 (主要用於疑問句及否定句)。***find oneself*** 自知;發現自己的能力。***find oneself*** (***a person***) ***in*** 供給;供應。***find one's feet*** **a.** 能站立與走路。**b.** 能獨立行動。***find one's place*** (***in a book***) 翻到(書中)要讀的一頁。***find one's voice*** (or ***tongue***) (因害羞沉默一會兒之後) 開始講話。***find one's way*** 抵達; 到達。Rivers *find their way* to the sea. 諸河均歸海。***find out*** 查出來;揭露;顯示。***find*** (***some, no, not much***) ***pleasure in*** 從…中獲得(得到一些、得不到、得到不多)樂趣;(有一點、不、不太)喜歡…。***find something out*** 尋出究竟。—*n.* ①發現。②發現物。That was a good *find.* 那是一個好的發現。

find·a·ble [ˈfaɪndəbl̩; ˈfaindəbl] *adj.* 可發現的;可找到的。

find·er [ˈfaɪndɚ; ˈfaində] *n.* ①發現者;尋得者; 拾者。②(望遠鏡、顯微鏡或照相機上的) 指導鏡;檢像鏡。***range finder*** 測距器。

fin de siè·cle [fædəˈsjɛkl; fɛːn də ˈsjekl] 〖法〗十九世紀末的; 頹廢的; 委靡的。

***find·ing** [ˈfaɪndɪŋ; ˈfaindiŋ] *n.* ①發現。They are of your own *finding.* 它們是你自己發現的。②發現物;心得。He published his *findings* in scholarly journals. 他在學術性雜誌上發表他的心得。③判決;判定;結論。④(*pl.*) 工匠所備置的工具、器材、零件等。

‡**fine**¹ [faɪn; fain] *adj.,* **fin·er, fin·est,** *adv., v.,* **fined, fin·ing.** —*adj.* ①優美的。What a *fine* view! 多麼美好的景色! ②纖細的; 微小的。The pencil should have a *fine* point. 這鉛筆應有尖而細的端。③純的。*fine* gold. 純金。④(布疋等)細密的;細緻的。⑤精細的;精微的。The law makes *fine* distinctions. 法律作出精微的區別。⑥晴朗的; 清明的。 *fine* weather. 晴天。⑦鋒利的;銳利的。⑧優雅的;雅緻的。*fine* manners. 優雅的風度。⑨(衣服等)漂亮的;華麗的。⑩(健康等)安好的;安康的。I'm feeling *fine.* 我很好。⑪ (文章等)華而不實的;過分虛飾的。⑫美貌的;英俊的。⑬非常的。You make a *fine* mistake if you think so. 如果你這樣想,你便大錯特錯了。⑭(選手等)訓練有素的。***Fine feathers make fine birds.*** 人憑衣裳馬憑鞍。***one*** (***some***) ***fine day*** (***morning***) =***one of these fine days*** 將來有一天。—*adv.* 〖俗〗很好地;優美地。That will suit

me *fine*. 那會適合於我。***cut*** (or ***run***) ***it*** (or ***things***) (***rather***) ***fine*** 給自己不很足够的(時間或空間)。—*v.t.* 使更精美;精鍊;澄清;使純良;使精細;使優雅。—*v.i.* 變精美;變純良;變精細;變優雅;澄清。The weather gradually *fined*. 天氣漸漸地變好。

fine²** *n., v.,* **fined, fin·ing.** —*n.* ①罰鍰;罰金。Club members who were late had to pay a 25-cent *fine*. 遲到的會員必須繳付兩角半的罰鍰。②〖古〗結尾;結束;結局。in fine*** a. 最後。b. 總而言之。—*v.t.* 處以罰鍰;處以罰金。He was *fined* 10 dollars. 他被處罰鍰十元。

fi·ne³ ['fine; 'fi:nei]〖義〗*n.*〖音樂〗終結。

fine arts 美術(包括繪畫、雕刻、建築等)。

fine-cut ['faɪn'kʌt; 'fain'kʌt] *adj.* 細切的(指烟草絲)。—*n.* 烟絲。

fine-draw ['faɪn'drɔ; 'fain'drɔ:] *v.t.,* **-drew, -drawn, -draw·ing.** ①細縫(兩布邊)而不見痕跡;巧縫。②拉細(銅絲等)。③巧妙地引出(推理等);巧妙地說出。

fine-drawn ['faɪn'drɔn; 'fain'drɔ:n] *adj.* ①細縫的。②抽成極細的(銅絲等)。③極巧妙的(推理、論據等)。

fine·grained ['faɪn'grend; 'fain-'greind] *adj.* 有細密紋理的(如木材、皮革等)。

fine·ly ['faɪnlɪ; 'fainli] *adv.* ①佳好地。The house has been *finely* restored. 那房子修復得很好。②細微地。③敏銳地。④優雅地。⑤非常地。

fine·ness ['faɪnnɪs; 'fainnis] *n.* ①佳好;精良。②(金銀飾物、貨幣等之)純度。③細微。④優雅。⑤敏銳。⑥靈敏。

fin·er·y ['faɪnərɪ; 'fainəri] *n., pl.* **-er·ies.** 華麗的衣服、裝飾品等。

fine·spun ['faɪn'spʌn; 'fain'spʌn] *adj.* ①細紡的;纖細的;纖弱的。②不切實際的;微妙的;空想的。

fi·nesse [fə'nɛs; fi'nes] *n., v.,* **-nessed, -ness·ing.** —*n.* ①技巧。②詭謀;策略;權術。③(橋牌戲)偷牌。—*v.i.* ①運用策略;用計。②(橋牌)偸牌。—*v.t.* ①用計策獲致或改變。②(橋牌之)偸(牌)。—**fi·ness·er,** *n.*

‡fin·ger ['fɪŋgə; 'fiŋgə] *n.* ①手指(常將大拇指除外)。My pen slipped out of my *fingers*. 我的鋼筆從我手中滑掉了。②指狀物。③手指之寬度(¾英寸)。④手指之長度(4½英寸)。⑤關係;參與。He seems always to have a *finger* in some magisterial affair. 他好像經常參與一些行政長官的事。***burn one's fingers*** 多管閒事而自尋煩惱。***have a finger in the pie*** a. 參加一分。He *has a finger in* every political *pie*. 他每一項政治事件都要插手。b. 管閒事;干涉。***have*** (***a subject***) ***at one's fingers' ends*** 精通;熟悉(一問題)。***keep*** (or ***have***) ***one's fingers crossed*** 希望成功;祝好運。*Keep your fingers crossed* that I get the job. 你替我祝福讓我弄到這分差事罷。***lay a finger on*** 觸(傷害,打,虐待)。***lay*** (or ***put***) ***one's finger on*** a. 明指;記得。b. 發現;找到。***not lift a finger*** 不作嘗試;不採取任何行動。The house was falling into ruin, but he *wouldn't lift a finger* to repair it. 房屋快要垮了,他却不設法修理。***One's fingers are all thumbs.*** 某人笨拙至極(=One is very clumsy). ***put the finger on***〖俚〗a. 指認(兇手,疑犯等)。b. 指定(被謀殺的對象)。***slip through one's fingers*** 放過;錯過。She let the chance of a lifetime *slip through her fingers*. 她讓一生難得的好機會錯過。***snap one's finger at*** 輕蔑;不予重視。***twist*** (or ***turn***) ***around one's little finger*** 玩弄於股掌之上。—*v.t.* ①以手指摸或試。②偸;竊;順手牽羊。③以手指撥彈(樂器)。④以某種指法彈(一段音樂)。⑤手指般地伸展於。New roads *fingered* once trackless plains. 新公路手指般伸展於曾經是人跡未到的平原。⑥指出;指定。She *fingered* a boy friend as one of the killers. 她指出一個男朋友為兇手之一。⑦〖俚〗祕密監視。We have been *fingering* him for months. 我們祕密監視他已有數月。—*v.i.* ①以指撫摸。②用指彈。③手指般地伸展。Searchlights *fingered* across the black water. 許多探照燈手指似地在黑漆漆的水上縱橫交錯。

finger alphabet 指語字母;手語字母。

finger board ①(小提琴、吉他等頸部的)指板。②(鋼琴或風琴之)鍵盤。

finger bowl (餐桌上盛水供餐後洗指頭用的)洗指碗。

fin·gered ['fɪŋgəd; 'fiŋgəd] *adj.* ①有(某種或某數之)手指的。②因接觸而汚損的。③〖植物〗指狀的;掌狀的。④指彈的;指奏的。

fin·ger·ing¹ ['fɪŋgərɪŋ; 'fiŋgəriŋ] *n.* ①指觸;撫弄。②〖音樂〗指法;指法記號。

fin·ger·ing² *n.* (編織或鈎織用之)細毛線。

finger language 指語;指談;手語。

fin·ger·ling ['fɪŋgəlɪŋ; 'fiŋgəliŋ] *n.* ①極小之物。②長不及指之魚;魚苗。

finger mark 指紋;指痕。(亦作**finger-mark**)

fin·ger·nail ['fɪŋgə,nel; 'fiŋgəneil] *n.*手指甲。

finger plate 指板(門上防止手指汚染之金屬或玻璃板)。

fin·ger·post ['fɪŋgə,post; 'fiŋgəpoust] *n.* ①指標。②指南。

fin·ger·print ['fɪŋgə,prɪnt; 'fiŋgə-print] *n.* 指紋。—*v.t.* 取…之指紋。

fin·ger·stall ['fɪŋgə,stɔl; 'fiŋgə-stɔ:l] *n.* (用於防護受傷手指之)指套。

fin·ger·tip ['fɪŋgə,tɪp; 'fiŋgətip] *n.* ①指尖;指頭。②保護指尖之物。***have ... at one's fingertips*** a. 有…在手頭(即可使用)。b. 與…熟悉;精通。***to one's*** (or ***the***) ***fingertips*** 完全地;充分地。

fin·i·al ['fɪnɪəl, 'faɪnɪəl; 'fainiəl] *n.* ①〖建築〗頂尖。②最高點。

fin·i·cal ['fɪnɪk]; 'finikəl] *adj.* 過於講究細節的;(文體)過分雕琢的;苛求的;吹毛求疵的。—**i·ty,** —**ness,** *n.* —**ly,** *adv.*

fin·ick·ing ['fɪnɪkɪŋ; 'finikiŋ] *adj.* =finical.

fin·ick·y ['fɪnɪkɪ; 'finiki] *adj.* =finical.

fin·i·kin ['fɪnɪkɪn; 'finikin] *adj.* = finical. (亦作 **finnikin**)

fi·nis ['faɪnɪs; 'fainis]〖拉〗*n.*終;完;結束。

‡fin·ish ['fɪnɪʃ; 'finiʃ] *v.t.* ①結束;完成。He didn't *finish* it in time. 他沒有及時把它完成。②用盡;吃完。We have *finished* (=eaten up) all the meat. 我們把所有的肉都吃完了。③〖俚〗毁掉;殺;累死。That long climb almost *finished* me. 爬那麼久幾乎把我累死了。④〖俗〗徹底征服;壓服。My answer *finished* him. 我的回答壓服了他(使他閉口無言)。⑤修飾;使達善美之境。He decided to *finish* his plan more carefully. 他決定對自己的計畫作更細心的修整。⑥作成某種表面。⑦完成…之教育。She was *finished* at an exclusive school. 她在一

所貴族化的學校完成教育。—*v.i.* ①結束；終止。The war hasn't *finished* yet. 戰爭尚未結束。②完成。He didn't *finish* in time. 他沒有及時完成。***finish off*** a. 結束；用完。b. 毀掉；殺死。***finish up*** a. 完成；結束。We *finished* it *up* with a song. 我們以一曲而告結束。b. 用盡。***finish with*** a.完成。b. 斷絕來往；斷絕關係；絕交。—*n.* ①終止；結束。②最後一層塗飾。③完美；嫻雅。***be in at the finish***（獵狐狐死時）最後在場；(喻)目覩(戰鬥等的)最後一幕。

fin·ished 〔ˈfɪnɪʃt; ˈfiniʃt〕 *adj.* ①結束的；終止的；完畢的。②完成的。③加工的；精製的。④高度修飾的；達於善美之境的。⑤多才多藝的；有成就的。⑥已無望的；垮了臺的。

fin·ish·er 〔ˈfɪnɪʃɚ; ˈfiniʃə〕 *n.* ①完成者；完工者；精作匠。②最後決勝負之一擊。

fin·ish·ing 〔ˈfɪnɪʃɪŋ; ˈfiniʃiŋ〕 *adj.* 最後的；結束的。—*n.* ①結尾；完成；完工。②(*pl.*)(建築物中)燈光、鉛管等之裝置。

finish line （賽跑或賽馬等之）終點線。

fi·nite 〔ˈfaɪnaɪt; ˈfainait〕 *adj.* 有限的。

finite verbs 有限式動詞；定動詞(受身、數、時等限定，字形發生變化的動詞)。

fink 〔fɪŋk; fiŋk〕 *n.* 〖美俚〗①通消息者；告密者。②破壞罷工者。—*v.i.* 〖美俚〗告密。

Fin·land 〔ˈfɪnlənd; ˈfinlənd〕 *n.* 芬蘭(北歐一國，首都爲赫爾辛基 Helsinki)。

Finn 〔fɪn; fin〕 *n.* ①芬蘭人。②語言似芬蘭語之民族的人。

fin·nan had·die 〔ˈfɪnənˈhædɪ; ˈfinənˈhædi〕 燻鱈魚。

finnan haddock =**finnan haddie.**

finned 〔fɪnd; find〕 *adj.* 有鰭的。

fin·ner 〔ˈfɪnɚ; ˈfinə〕 *n.* =**finback.**

Finn·ic 〔ˈfɪnɪk; ˈfinik〕 *adj.* 芬蘭人的；芬蘭語的。

Finn·ish 〔ˈfɪnɪʃ; ˈfiniʃ〕 *adj.* 芬蘭的；芬蘭人的；芬蘭語的。—*n.* 芬蘭語。

fin·ny 〔ˈfɪnɪ; ˈfini〕 *adj.* ①有鰭的；多鰭的；鰭狀的。②魚的；多魚的。

fiord 〔fjord, fjɔrd; fjɔːd〕 *n.* 伸入海岸斷崖絕壁間的狹長海灣；狹灣；澳。

***fir** 〔fɝ; fəː〕 *n.* 樅樹；樅木。

‡fire 〔faɪr; ˈfaiə〕 *n., v.,* **fired, fir·ing.** —*n.* ①火。*Fire* burns. 火燃燒。②爐火。Put some coal on the *fire.* 添一點煤在爐火上。③火災；火警。There was a *fire* in the next street last night. 昨夜鄰街上失火了。④(熱、火、亮)似火的東西。⑤熱情；狂熱；興奮。⑥劇痛；高熱；發炎。⑦〖古〗磨難；苦難。⑧砲火。The soldiers advanced under the enemy's *fire.* 兵士們在敵人砲火下前進。***between two fires*** 兩面受敵。***catch*** (or ***take***) ***fire*** 着火。Paper *catches fire* easily. 紙容易着火。***fight fire with fire*** 以火攻火；以其人之道還治其人之身。***go through fire and water*** 赴湯蹈火；冒一切危險。***hang fire*** a. 遲遲不響。b. 動作遲緩。c. 被躭擱。***lay a fire*** 堆起燃料（準備生火)。***make a fire*** 生火(如火爐等)。***miss fire*** a. (鎗砲)打不響。b. 失敗。***on fire*** 着火；失火(在燃燒中)。The house was *on fire.* 房屋失火了。***open fire*** 開火；開鎗射擊。***play with fire*** 玩火；作危險之事。***set fire to*** 放火焚燒；縱火。Who *set fire to* the house? 是誰放火燒房? ***set on fire*** 放火焚燒；縱火 (= set fire to). He *set* the building *on fire.* 他放火燒此建築物。***set the Thames on fire*** 做驚人之事。***take fire*** a. 開始燃燒。b. 被激動；受感召。***There's no smoke without fire.*** 無火不起煙；無風不起浪。***under fire*** a. 在敵人砲火下。b. 遭受嚴厲批評或抨擊。—*v.t.* ①點燃；使燃燒。②加添燃料。③燒…使乾。Bricks are *fired* to make them hard. 燒磚使其變硬。④激起。Stories of adventure *fire* the imagination. 冒險故事激起想像。⑤拋；投；擲。⑥放(鎗)；開(火)。He *fired* his gun. 他放鎗。⑦〖俗〗解職；辭退。—*v.i.* ①燃燒；起火。Damp gunpowder will not *fire.* 潮濕的火藥不會起火。②放鎗；開鎗。The officer ordered his men to *fire.* 軍官命令他的士兵開鎗。③如火般發光。④激動。He *fired* inwardly at these sarcasms. 他對那些譏諷深感憤慨。⑤射擊。⑥管鍋爐；司爐。The ship's firemen went on strike, and there was no one to *fire.* 船上火夫在鬧罷工，以致無人司爐。***fire at*** (or ***on***) 對…開鎗。***fire away*** a. 繼續開鎗 (= continue firing). b. 〖俚〗繼續講下去(如講故事等)或提出問題。The reporters *fired away* at the President. 新聞記者向總統提出一連串問題。***fire off*** 發射(火箭、太空船等)。***fire up*** a. (在鍋爐中等)起火。b. 發怒。c. 發動(機器)。

fire alarm ①火警警報。②火警警報器；「火警警鐘。(略作 **f.a.**)」

fire ant (生在南美及美國東南之)一種毒蟻。

fire apparatus 消防設備。

fire·arm 〔ˈfaɪrˌɑrm; ˈfaiərɑːm〕 *n.* (常 *pl.*)火器；鎗砲(尤指一人可携帶者)；輕武器。

fire·ball 〔ˈfaɪrˌbɔl; ˈfaiəbɔːl〕 *n.* ①似火球之物。②大流星。③燒夷彈。④充滿精力的人物。⑤〖棒球〗快球。

fire·ball·er 〔ˈfaɪrˌbɔlɚ; ˈfaiəˌbɔːlə〕 *n.* 〖棒球〗投快速球取勝之投手。

fire balloon ①藉火焰熱氣上升之氣球。②載有煙火在空中燃放之氣球。

fire bell 失火警鐘；報火警鐘。

fire·bird 〔ˈfaɪrˌbɝd; ˈfaiəbəːd〕 *n.* 金鶺鳥。

fire blight 一種蘋果樹及桃樹病(其花、葉、嫩枝受到一種細菌之侵襲)。

fire·board 〔ˈfaɪrˌbord; ˈfaiəbɔːd〕 *n.* 壁爐遮火板。

fire·boat 消防船。

fire bomb 燒夷彈。

fire·box 〔ˈfaɪrˌbɑks; ˈfaiəbɔks〕 *n.*(機車等之)燃燒室。

fire·brand 〔ˈfaɪrˌbrænd; ˈfaiəbrænd〕 *n.* ①燃燒的木柴；火把。②放火者；煽動者。③精力極其充沛者；非常激烈者。

fire·break 〔ˈfaɪrˌbrek; ˈfaiəbreik〕 *n.* 森林中或草原上之火巷。

fire·brick 〔ˈfaɪrˌbrɪk; ˈfaiəbrik〕 *n.* 耐火磚。

fire brigade 救火隊；消防隊。

fire·bug 〔ˈfaɪrˌbʌg; ˈfaiəbʌg〕 *n.* 〖美俗〗放火犯；縱火犯。

fire clay (用以製坩堝、耐火磚等之)耐火黏土。

fire company ①救火隊；消防隊。②〖英〗火災保險公司。

fire control 〖軍〗射擊控制。

fire·crack·er 〔ˈfaɪrˌkrækɚ; ˈfaiəˌkrækə〕 *n.* 爆竹；鞭砲。

fire-cure 〔ˈfaɪrˌkjuə; ˈfaiəˌkjuə〕 *v.t.,* **-cured, -cur·ing.** 用火燻(烟草等)。

fire·damp 〔ˈfaɪrˌdæmp; ˈfaiədæmp〕 *n.* (礦坑內之)甲烷；坑氣；沼氣；瓦斯。

fire department ①消防隊。②消防隊全體隊員。

fire·dog 〔ˈfaɪrˌdɔg; ˈfaiədɔg〕 *n.* (爐之)薪架。

fire·drake 〔ˈfaɪrˌdrek; ˈfaiədreik〕 *n.* (神話中之)火龍；火蛇。

fire drill 消防訓練；救火演習；消防演習。

fire-eat·er ['faɪr,itə; 'faiər,i:tə] *n.* ①玩吞火把戲者。②好勇鬥狠者; 脾氣火暴易與人吵架者。
fire engine 救火機;水龍;救火車。
fire escape 太平梯;避火梯;爲發生火警時便於逃出建築物之各種設備。
fire extinguisher 滅火器。
fire fighter 〖美〗消防隊員。
***fire·fly** ['faɪr,flaɪ; 'faiə-flai] *n., pl.* **-flies.** 螢火蟲。
fire·guard ['faɪr,gɑrd; 'faiəgɑ:d] *n.* ①爐欄。②火巷。
fire hose 消防水管。
fire·house ['faɪr,haus; 'faiəhaus] *n.* = **fire station.**
fire insurance 火災保險。
fire irons 火爐用具(如火鉗、火箸、火鏟等)。
fire·less ['faɪrlɪs; 'faiəlis] *adj.* ①無火的。②無生氣的。
fireless cooker 一種絕緣之烹調器(加熱後, 使熱度不散失, 以烹調食物); 保溫鍋。
fire·light ['faɪr,laɪt;'faiəlait] *n.* 火光。
fire line ①(森林地帶之)防火線。②火警時火場附近之禁止進入線。
fire·lock ['faɪr,lɑk; 'faiəlɔk] *n.* ①燧發鎗(以燧石發火之舊式鎗)。②燧發鎗兵。
fire main 消防水管。
***fire·man** ['faɪrmən; 'faiəmən] *n., pl.* **-men.** ①救火隊員; 消防隊員。②火伕; 管鍋爐者。③〖鐵路〗蒸氣機車之司爐; 柴油或電動機車司機之助手。
fire·mas·ter ['faɪr,mæstə; 'faiə,mɑ:stə] *n.* 〖英〗消防隊長。
fire office 〖英〗火災保險公司事務所。
fire opal 〖礦〗火蛋白石。
fire pan ①火鏟;火斗。②火缽;火盆。③鎗砲內裝彈藥之處。
***fire·place** ['faɪr,ples; 'faiə-pleis] *n.* 壁爐。
fire·plug ['faɪr,plʌg; 'faiə-plʌg] *n.* 消火栓。
fire point 〖化〗(揮發油的)燃點; 發火點。
fire policy 火災保險單。
fire power 〖軍〗火力。
fire·proof ['faɪr'pruf; 'faiə-pru:f] *adj.* 防火的; 禦火的; 耐火的。—*v.t.* 裝防火設備。
fir·er ['faɪrə; 'faiərə] *n.* ①引火之人;縱火之人。②火夫。③發火者; 射擊者。④發火之物;點火物。⑤發火器;鎗;砲。
fire room (輪船的)鍋爐室。(亦作 **stokehold, stokehole**)
fire sale 火災物品大拍賣。
fire screen 遮火板(置於爐火前防熱及火星者)。
fire ship 縱火艇(裝滿易燃物及爆炸物之船隻, 飄至敵人船陣中引火使之燃燒爆炸)。
***fire·side** ['faɪr,saɪd; 'faiə-said] *n.* ①爐邊。②家庭; 家庭生活。They are fighting in defense of their *firesides.* 他們爲保衛家園而戰。—*adj.* 在火爐邊的。
fire station 消防隊。
fire step 〖軍〗塹壕內供射擊用之踏臺。
fire stick ①燃燒之木棒。②用以磨擦生火之木棒。③(*pl.*)火棒;撿炭棒。
fire·stone ['faɪr,ston; 'faiə-stoun] *n.* ①燧石; 打火石。②耐火石。③爐石。
fire tongs 火鉗。
fire tower 森林火警守望塔。
fire·trap ['faɪr,træp; 'faiə-træp] *n.* ①失火時難以逃出之建築物; 無太平門的建築物。②易失火之建築物。
fire walk =**fire-walking.**
fire-walk·ing ['faɪr,wɔkɪŋ; 'faiə-,wɔ:kiŋ] *n.* 〖宗教〗渡火(一種宗教儀式, 裸足行於灼熱之石上)。
fire wall ①防火壁。②汽車或飛機引擎後面的防火板。
fire·war·den ['faɪr,wɔrdn; 'faiə,wɔ:dn] *n.* 〖美〗消防官員。
fire·wa·ter ['faɪr,wɔtə; 'faiə,wɔ:tə] *n.* 火酒;烈酒(諧語)。
fire·weed ['faɪr,wid; 'faiəwi:d] *n.* 在火燒過之地上易於生長的雜草(如 Jimson weed 等)。
fire·wood ['faɪr,wud; 'faiəwud] *n.* 柴;薪。
***fire·works** ['faɪr,wɜks; 'faiəwə:ks] *n. pl.* ①烟火;放烟火。②激烈爭論。Whenever those two get together, there were sure to be *fireworks.* 無論何時祇要那兩個人碰頭, 便有一場激烈爭論。
fire worship 拜火;拜火教。
fir·ing ['faɪrɪŋ; 'faiəriŋ] *n.* ①焙燒;燒窰。②(用烙鐵)灼炙。③用火;生火;使火。④發砲;發射。⑤燃料;煤;薪。
firing line ①火線; 陣線; 戰線。②火線上的士兵。③(任何活動或職業的)前線。
firing party ①喪禮時之禮砲隊。②執行死刑之射擊隊。(亦作 **firing squad**)
firing step =**fire step.**
fir·kin ['fɜkɪn; 'fə:kin] *n.* ①盛乳酪、豚脂等之小木桶。②容量單位(=¼ barrel).
‡**firm**[1] [fɜm; fə:m] *adj.* ①堅固的;堅硬的。*firm* ground. 堅硬的土地。②牢的; 牢固的; 穩固的。a candle *firm* in its socket. 穩插在燭台孔裏的蠟燭。③堅定的; 堅强的。to look *firm.* 顯得很堅強的樣子。④健康的;健全的。⑤(物價等)穩定的。***be as firm as a rock*** 穩如磐石。***be on firm ground*** 脚跟穩固;立脚點穩固。—*v.t.* 使堅固;使堅定。He reshuffled the cabinet to *firm* his government. 他改組內閣以强化其政府。—*v.i.* ①變堅固; 變堅定。The cheese is *firming.* 奶酪在變硬中。②(物價等)回升。After a long decline, prices are *firming* again. 在長期跌落之後, 物價又回升。—*adv.* 堅定地。to stand *firm.* 堅定不屈。to hold *firm* to one's beliefs. 堅持一己之信仰。
firm[2] *n.* 商店; 公司。
fir·ma·ment ['fɜməmənt; 'fə:məmənt] *n.* (the-)(常*sing.*)蒼天;穹蒼。—**al,** *adj.*
fir·man ['fɜmən; fə:'mɑ:n] *n., pl.* **-mans.** 勅令;聖旨。
***firm·ly** ['fɜmlɪ; 'fə:mli] *adv.* 堅定地;堅固地; 堅强地; 强硬地。The enemy is *firmly* entrenched along the northern border. 敵人頑强地沿北面邊界掘壕據守。
***firm·ness** ['fɜmnɪs; 'fə:mnis] *n.* 堅定; 堅固; 堅强; 强硬。
firm·ware ['fɜm,wɛr; 'fə:mwɛə] *n.* 〖電腦〗堅體(界於硬體及軟體間的電腦構成部分)。
firn [fɪrn; fiən] *n.* 粒雪;冰雪;冰河上的半凍雪。
fir·ry ['fɜɪ; 'fə:ri] *adj.* 樅樹的;以樅木作成的;樅樹繁茂的。
‡**first** [fɜst; fə:st] *adj.* ①第一的;最先的。Who was the *first* man to fly across the Atlantic? 誰是第一個飛越大西洋的人? the *first* two (three, etc.). 最先的二個(三個等)。②最重要的; 首要的。③最微小的。I haven't the *first* idea of what you mean. 我一點不懂你的意思。④〖音樂〗最高音的;唱最高音的。***at first hand*** 直接地。***at first sight*** (or *view*)一見之下。to fall in

love *at first sight*. 一見鍾情。**first floor**(英國或歐洲的)二樓(＝美國的 second floor). **first thing** 立即。I'll call on you *first thing* when I arrive. 我一到便拜訪你。**in the first place** 首先。**the first thing in the morning** 一大早。—*n.* ①第一個;(月之)一日。the *first* of May. 五月一日。②(比賽中之)冠軍;首名。③開始;起首。④(*pl.*)上等(第一流品質)的東西;上品。**at first** 最初;起初;當初。*At first* I didn't know what to make of it. 起初我搞不清那是怎麼回事。**first of all** 首先;最重要者。**from first to last** 自始至終。**from the first** 從開始起。—*adv.* ①首先地;最初地。*First,* I wish to consider the economic problem. 首先我想考慮經濟問題。②寧願。I'll go to jail *first.* 我寧願進牢。**first and last** 總而言之;畢竟。*First and last,* it is important to know oneself. 總而言之,認識自己是重要的。**first off** 馬上;立刻。**first or last** 時候不定但總會;遲早不免。〖注意〗**first** 與數目連用時, first 應置於數目的前邊。For tomorrow I want you to do the *first* six problems. 我要你明天做爲首的六個問題。

first aid 急救(在醫生未到前,對傷患者的緊急救護)。

first-aid [ˈfɝstˈed; ˈfəːstˈeid] *adj.* 急救的;急救用的。a *first-aid* kit. 急救箱。

first base ①〖棒球〗第一壘;一壘手。②第一階段;進入成功之門的第一步。

first baseman 〖棒球〗一壘手。

first-born [ˈfɝstˈbɔrn; ˈfəːstbɔːn] *adj.* 最先出生的;年最長的。—*n.* 長子;長女。

first cause ①第一原因;最根本的原因。②原動力。

first class 第一流;第一級。

***first-class** [ˈfɝstˈklæs; ˈfəːstˈklɑːs] *adj.* 頭等的(車廂、房間、艙位等);上等的。—*adv.* ①乘頭等車、船等(旅行)。②〖俗〗很好。

first·com·er [ˈfɝstˌkʌmɚ; ˈfəːstˌkʌmə] *n.* 最先來者;最先到者。

first cousin 堂(表)兄弟姐妹。

first day 星期日。

first-day cover [ˈfɝstˈde～; ˈfəːstˈdei～] 〖集郵〗首日封。

first family ①美國最早移民後裔之家族。②總統(尤指美國總統)家族。

first finger 食指。

first fruits ①一季中最先成熟的果實;初結果實;第一次收成。②〖喻〗初次收益。

first-gen·er·a·tion [ˈfɝstˌdʒɛnəˈreʃən; ˈfəːstˌdʒenəˈreiʃən] *adj.* 歸化爲美國人的;出生在美國的(指父母來自外國者)。

first-hand, first·hand [ˈfɝstˈhænd; ˈfəːstˈhænd] *adj.* 直接的;第一手的。—*adv.* 直接地。

first lady 〖美〗總統夫人;第一夫人;一國元首的夫人。

first-line [ˈfɝstˈlaɪn; ˈfəːstˈlain] *adj.* ①隨時可參加戰鬥的。②最重要的。

first·ling [ˈfɝstlɪŋ; ˈfəːstliŋ] *n.* ①(一類事物中之)最先者。②初產品;最初之結果。③〖動物〗最初生出之幼兒。

first·ly [ˈfɝstlɪ; ˈfəːstli] *adv.* 第一;最初;首先地。

first name (一個人的姓名中之) 名。

first night (戲劇等之)首演。

first-night·er [ˌfɝstˈnaɪtɚ; ˈfəːstˈnaitə] *n.* 經常看第一夜開演的戲的人;搶頭場的人。

first offender 初犯者。

first-rate [ˈfɝsˈtret; ˈfəːstˈreit] *adj.* ①第一流的;最佳的。②〖俗〗很好的;極佳的。—*adv.* 〖俗〗很好地;極佳地。

first run (影片之)首輪放映。

first-run [ˈfɝstˈrʌn; ˈfəːstˈrʌn] *adj.* ①首輪的(影片)。②專映首輪影片的。

first water 最佳品質;最高等級。

firth [fɝθ; fəːθ] *n.* (尤指蘇格蘭境內之)窄狹的海灣;(江、河)入海口。(亦作 **frith**)

fisc [fɪsk; fisk] *n.* 國庫。

***fis·cal** [ˈfɪskl̩; ˈfiskəl] *adj.* 財政的;會計的。*fiscal* year. 會計年度。—*n.* 某些國家的檢察官。—**ly,** *adv.*

Fi·scher[1] [ˈfɪʃɚ; ˈfiʃə] *n.* 費施爾(Emil, 1852–1919, 德國化學家, 曾獲 1902 年諾貝爾化學獎)。

Fi·scher[2] *n.* 費施爾 (Hans, 1881–1945, 德國化學家, 曾獲1930年諾貝爾化學獎)。

‡**fish** [fɪʃ; fiʃ] *n., pl.* **fish·es** or (集合稱) **fish,** *v.*—*n.* ①魚;魚類。*Fishes* swim. 魚游水。②魚肉。Do you like *fish?* 你愛吃魚嗎? ③〖俚〗人。a dull *fish.* 笨漢。④〖工程〗魚尾板。**drink like a fish** 牛飲。**feel like a fish out of water** 覺得侷促不安;覺得如魚出水。**make fish of one and flesh** (or **fowl**) **of another** 對兩人有差別待遇。**other fish to fry** 別的事要做。—*v.i.* ①釣魚;捕魚。to go *fishing.* 出外釣魚。②探求〖for〗. to *fish* for information. 探聽消息。③(河流等) 適於釣魚。This stream *fishes* well. 這條溪有很多魚可釣。④企圖以詐術取得。—*v.t.* ①釣(魚);在…中釣(魚);捕(魚)。②尋出;拖出。He *fished* the map from the back of the drawer. 他從抽屜後面把地圖尋出。**fish in troubled waters** 混水摸魚;趁火打刼。**fish or cut bait** 決定行動方針; 決定取捨。**fish out** 捕盡…中的魚。〖注意〗(1) **fish** 之複數式有二。如指許多條魚時, 則用 fish. 如指許多種類的魚時, 則用 fishes. (2)作②義解時, 不用複數。

fish·a·ble [ˈfɪʃəbl̩; ˈfiʃəbl] *adj.* ①適於釣魚的; 有魚可釣的。②(河流等) 可在裏面合法捕魚的。

fish ball 炸魚丸子。(亦作 **fish cake**)

fish·bolt [ˈfɪʃˌbolt; ˈfiʃboult] *n.* 〖鐵路〗魚尾板螺栓; 軌條螺栓。

fish·bowl [ˈfɪʃˌbol; ˈfiʃboul] *n.* ①金魚缸。②毫無遮蔽之物。

fish culture 養魚;養魚法。

***fish·er** [ˈfɪʃɚ; ˈfiʃə] *n.* ①漁人;漁翁;漁船(＝fisherman). ②以魚爲食之獸。③〖動物〗食魚鼬。④食魚鼬之褐色皮。

fish·er·boat [ˈfɪʃɚˌbot; ˈfiʃəbout] *n.* 漁舟、漁船。

fish·er·folk [ˈfɪʃɚˌfok; ˈfiʃəfouk] *n. pl.* 漁民。

***fish·er·man** [ˈfɪʃəmən; ˈfiʃəmən] *n., pl.* **-men.** ①漁人;漁夫。②漁船。

fish·er·y [ˈfɪʃərɪ; ˈfiʃəri] *n., pl.* **-er·ies.** ①漁場。②漁業。

Fish·es [ˈfɪʃɪz; ˈfiʃiz] *n. pl.*＝**Pisces.**

fish·eye [ˈfɪʃˌaɪ; ˈfiʃˌai] *n.* ①切得過薄而光澤較差的寶石。②懷疑的凝視。③〖攝影〗廣照鏡;魚眼。

fish farm 養魚場。

fish fork ①裝卸魚類之叉。②食魚叉。

fish fry ①以炸魚爲主要食品之野餐。②油炸魚。

fish globe 金魚缽; 養魚用之圓玻璃缸。

fish glue 魚膠。

fish hawk 鶚。

fish·hook [ˈfɪʃˌhuk, ˈfɪʃuk; ˈfiʃhuk] *n.* 釣魚鉤。

***fish·ing** [ˈfɪʃɪŋ; ˈfiʃiŋ] *n.* ①捕魚; 釣魚。②漁場;捕魚的地方。③捕魚權。*fishing* *banks* 海中之淺水漁場。 *fishing boat* 漁船。*fishing float* 上面有小棚之捕魚木筏。 *fishing ground* 漁場。 *fishing line* 釣絲。*fishing net* 漁網。*fishing rod* 釣竿。 *fishing smack* 深海捕魚之小船。 *fishing tackle* 釣具。*fishing worm* 作釣餌用之蟲。

fish joint 〖鐵路〗魚尾接口。

fish kettle 煮魚鍋。

fish knife 食魚刀。

fish·like 〔'fɪʃ,laɪk; 'fiʃlaik〕 *adj.* ①似魚的;魚臭的。②冷淡的;冷血動物的。

fish·line 〔'fɪʃ,laɪn; 'fiʃlain〕 *n.* 釣線;釣綸;釣絲。

fish meal 乾魚粉(作肥料或飼料用)。

fish·mon·ger 〔'fɪʃ,mʌŋgɚ; 'fiʃ,mʌŋgə〕 *n.* 〖英〗魚商;魚販。

fish·plate 〔'fɪʃ,plet; 'fiʃpleit〕 *n.* (鐵軌之)魚尾板。

fish pole 釣魚竿。

fish·pond 〔'fɪʃ,pɑnd; 'fiʃpɔnd〕 *n.* ①養魚池。②〖諧〗海。

fish·pot 〔'fɪʃ,pɑt; 'fiʃpɔt〕 *n.* 捕捉魚蝦之籃狀網罟;捕魚籠。

fish slice 切魚之濶刀。

fish-sound 〔'fɪʃ,saund; 'fiʃsaund〕 *n.* 魚鰾。

fish spear 魚叉。

fish story 〖俗〗誇張荒誕的故事;大話;狂言。

fish·tail 〔'fɪʃ,tel; 'fiʃteil〕 *v.i.* 〖俗〗(使機尾部左右搖擺而)減緩飛機速度;向左右擺動船身而前進。—*n.* 魚尾;魚尾形之物。—*adj.* 魚尾形的;動作似魚尾的。

fish·wife 〔'fɪʃ,waɪf; 'fiʃwaif〕 *n., pl.* **-wives.** ①女魚販。②說話粗野的女人;悍婦。

fish·worm 〔'fɪʃ,wɝm; 'fiʃwə:m〕 *n.* 蚯蚓或其他作魚餌用之蟲。

fish·y 〔'fɪʃɪ; 'fiʃi〕 *adj.,* **fish·i·er, fish·i·est.** ①魚腥味的;似魚的。②魚的。③多魚的。④〖俗〗可疑的;難信的。⑤無表情的;無光澤的;呆滯的。—**fish·i·ness,** *n.*

fish·y·back·ing 〔'fɪʃɪ,bækɪŋ; 'fiʃi,bækiŋ〕 *n.* 用平底船、渡船或類似的船隻運送滿載貨物之卡車。(亦作 **fishback**)

fisk 〔fɪsk; fisk〕 *n.* =**fisc.**

fis·sile 〔'fɪsl̩; 'fisail〕 *adj.* ①可分裂的;易分裂的。②可產生核子分裂的。

fis·sil·i·ty 〔fɪ'sɪlətɪ; fi'siliti〕 *n.* 可裂性;易裂性。

fis·sion 〔'fɪʃən; 'fiʃən〕 *n.* ①分裂。②〖生物〗分裂生殖法。③〖物理〗原子核分裂。—*v.t.* 使發生原子核分裂。—*v.i.* 經過原子核分裂。

fis·sion·a·ble 〔'fɪʃənəbl̩; 'fiʃənəbl〕 *adj.* 可分裂的(特指原子核)。 *fissionable material* 〖物理〗原子核可裂性物質。—*n.* 原子核可分裂性物質。

fission bomb 因原子核分裂作用而獲得威力的原子彈。

fis·sip·a·rous 〔fɪ'sɪpərəs; fi'sipərəs〕 *adj.* ①〖生物〗分裂生殖的。②分裂的;有分裂之傾向的。 —**ly,** *adv.* —**ness,** *n.*

fis·si·ped 〔'fɪsɪpɛd; 'fisiped〕 *adj.* 足趾分裂的。 —*n.* 裂趾類動物。

fis·sure 〔'fɪʃɚ; 'fiʃə〕 *n., v.,* **-sured, -sur·ing.** —*n.* ①裂縫。②裂開;分裂。—*v.t.* 使裂開;使生裂縫。—*v.i.* 裂開;分裂。

***fist** 〔fɪst; fist〕 *n.* ①拳;拳頭。②〖俗〗手。Give me your *fist.* 和我握手吧。③〖俗〗筆跡;手寫物。You wrote an exquisite *fist.* 你寫得一手好字。④〖印刷〗手形指標。*close-fisted* (or *tight-fisted*) 手緊的;吝嗇的。—*v.t.* ①將(手)握成拳頭。②緊握。

fist·fight 〔'fɪst,faɪt; 'fistfait〕 *n.* 打架。

fist·ful 〔'fɪstful; 'fistful〕 *n.* ①一撮;一把。②一批;一套。

fist·ic 〔'fɪstɪk; 'fistik〕 *adj.* 〖俗〗鬥拳的;拳擊的。

fist·i·cuff 〔'fɪstɪ,kʌf; 'fistikʌf〕 *n.* ①一拳;一掌。②(*pl.*) 互毆;亂鬥;拳擊比賽;鬥拳。to come to *fisticuffs.* 互毆。③(*pl.*)拳擊術。 —*v.t.* & *v.i.* 以拳打擊。 —**er,** *n.*

fist law 暴力主義。

fis·tu·la 〔'fɪstʃulə; 'fistjulə〕 *n., pl.* **-las, -lae** 〔-,li; -li:〕. 管;管狀器官。②〖醫〗瘻管;瘺。

fis·tu·lous 〔'fɪstʃuləs; 'fistjuləs〕 *adj.* ①管狀的;中空的。②〖醫〗瘻管的。(亦作 **fistular**)

‡**fit**[1] 〔fɪt; fit〕 *v.,* **fit·ted, fit·ting,** *adj.,* **fit·ter, fit·test,** *n., adv.* —*v.i.* ①合適;合宜。Your clothes *fit* well. 你的衣服很合身。②準備妥善;預備。 —*v.t.* ①適合於。This key doesn't *fit* the lock. 這把鑰匙不合這個鎖。②安裝;裝備。 Father *fitted* new seat covers on our car. 父親在我們的車座上安了新套。③爲…安裝或裝備(某物)。to *fit* a store with counters. 爲店舖設置櫃枱。④使適應。 Military training *fits* men for long marches. 軍事訓練使人適於長途行軍。 *fit* (*something*) *in* 裝配好;湊配。*fit in with* 相合。*fit* (*something*) *on* a. 試穿。 I am going to have my new coat *fitted on.* 我要去試穿新外衣。 b. 置…於原處。 Can you *fit* the lid *on?* 你能把蓋子蓋好嗎? *fit out* 裝備好;裝備齊全。*fit up* 裝置起來;設備。The house is *fitted up* with electric light. 這房屋裝好了電燈。—*adj.* ①合適的;適宜的。 That man is not *fit* for the position. 那個人不適合於那一位置。②對的;適當的。③準備妥當的;合宜的。*fit* for active service. 準備服兵役。④〖俗〗幾乎要;就快要。⑤健康的。I hope you're feeling quite *fit.* 我希望你覺得很好。*fit to be tied* 氣得要命。*fit to kill* 極度地。 She was dressed up *fit to kill.* 她打扮得花枝招展。—*n.* ①適合;適宜。the *fit* of a coat. 外衣的合身。②適合之物。The coat is a good *fit.* 這衣服很合身。 —*adv.* 僅見於下列語中之習慣用法。*see* (or *think*) *fit* 決定。He didn't *think fit* to do what I suggested. 他決定不做我所建議的事。—**ness,** *n.*

***fit**[2] *n.* ①(病)發作;一陣(脾氣等)。a *fit* of coughing. 一陣咳嗽。 in a *fit* of anger. 在盛怒之下。a *fit* of epilepsy. 癲癇發作。②(作某事情的)一段短時間;一陣。 *by fits and starts* 一陣陣地;不規則地。 *give* (*a person*) *a fit* (or *fits*) 〖俗〗作某事而使(某人)大吃一驚或大怒。*have a fit* 〖俗〗大吃一驚;大怒。*throw a fit* 〖俚〗大發雷霆;極爲興奮或緊張。*when the fit is on one* 當某人有興致時;興之所至。

fit[3] *n.* ①歌;歌謠。②歌或歌謠之一節。

fitch 〔fɪtʃ; fitʃ〕 *n.* ①〖動物〗(歐洲產之)臭貓。②臭貓之毛皮。(亦作 **fitchet, fitchew**)

fitch brush 用臭貓之毛或豬毛做的小畫筆。

fit·ful 〔'fɪtfəl; 'fitful〕 *adj.* 斷斷續續的;一陣陣的。—**ly,** *adv.* —**ness,** *n.*

fit·ly 〔'fɪtlɪ; 'fitli〕 *adv.* ①適當地;合宜地。②適時地。

fit·ment 〔'fɪtmənt; 'fitmənt〕 *n.* ①設備;裝備。②(*pl.*)用具;傢具(=fittings).

fit·out 〔'fɪt,aut; 'fit,aut〕 *n.* 裝備;(旅行之)準備。

fit·ter 〔'fɪtɚ; 'fitə〕 *n.* ①適合者;裝配者。②爲人試樣之裁縫。③(*pl.*) 破片;碎片。

fit·ting [ˈfɪtɪŋ; ˈfitiŋ] *adj.* 適當的。—*n.* ①(衣服之) 試穿。②裝備;補給。③(*pl.*) 傢具。—**ness,** *n.*

fit·ting·ly [ˈfɪtɪŋlɪ; ˈfitiŋli] *adv.* 適合地; 適當地。

fit·up [ˈfɪtˌʌp; ˈfitˌʌp] *n.* 〖戲劇〗臨時舞臺。

fitz [fɪts; fits] *n.* 兒子(現多用作若干姓氏之字首, 如: Fitzgerald 意卽 Gerald 之子)。

‡five [faɪv; faiv] *n.* ①五;5。②五人籃球隊。③五個一組之物。—*adj.* 五個。

five-and-dime [ˈfaɪvənˈdaɪm; ˈfaivənˈdaim] *n.* 〖美俗〗廉價商店。(亦作 **five-and-ten**)

five-by-five [ˈfaɪvbaɪˈfaɪv; ˈfaivbaiˈfaiv] *adj.* 〖俚〗矮胖的。

five-fin·ger [ˈfaɪvˌfɪŋgɚ; ˈfaivˌfiŋgə] *n.* ①葉或花呈五瓣狀之植物。②〖動物〗海盤車; 星魚。

five·fold [ˈfaɪvˈfold; ˈfaivˈfould] *adj.* & *adv.* 五倍的(地); 五重的(地); 有五個部分的(地)。

five percenter 〖美〗替公司取得政府合同以換取百分之五之酬金者。

fiv·er [ˈfaɪvɚ; ˈfaivə] *n.* 〖俚〗①美國之五元鈔票。②英國之五鎊鈔票。

fives [faɪvz; faivz] *n.* 〖英〗一種球戲(類似 handball).

five·star [ˈfaɪvˈstɑr; ˈfaivˈstɑː] *adj.* ①五星的。a *fivestar* admiral. 五星海軍上將。②最高級的;第一流的。

‡fix [fɪks; fiks] *v.,* **fixed** or **fixt, fix·ing,** *n.* —*v.t.* ①使穩固; 使固定; 縛緊; 釘牢。to *fix* a picture on the wall. 把圖畫釘在牆上。to *fix* facts in one's mind. 將事實牢記心頭。②歸(咎);委過;寄(希望)於。to *fix* the blame on a person. 委過某人。③安排; 決定; 確定。to *fix* a date for a meeting. 決定開會日期。④整理; 整頓; 準備;修理。to *fix* one's hair. 梳理頭髮。⑤注視; 專心於。to *fix* one's mind on something. 專心於某物。⑥引致;吸引;導致。This unusual sight *fixed* his attention. 這個不平凡景色吸引住他的注意力。⑦使(顏色等)持久不變。⑧使(一情勢或地位)利於己而不利於敵方。⑨懲罰; 處罰。⑩報仇。⑪將(氮)製成混合物(如炸藥、肥料等)。⑫〖攝影〗定(影)。⑬選擇;決定。⑭作弊;賄賂。⑮〖俗〗報復;處罰。⑯〖俗〗將動物去勢。⑰供給。⑱將(細菌)殺死並保存以供顯微鏡觀察。—*v.i.* ①固定;穩固。②安定。③準備。I'm *fixing* to go hunting. 我準備去打獵。④定居。***fix on*** (or ***upon***)決定;選擇。***fix up*** **a.** 預備;安排。**b.** 修理。We have our house *fixed up.* 我們的房子修好了。**c.** 和解;解決。to *fix up* a quarrel. 解決爭端。**d.** 打扮停當。—*n.* ①困境。to be in a *fix.* 處於困境。②定方位。③〖俚〗**a.** 打嗎啡針或海洛英。**b.** 嗎啡或海洛英注射之量。④〖俚〗賄賂。—**a·ble,** *adj.*

fix·ate [ˈfɪkset; ˈfikseit] *v.,* **-at·ed, -at·ing.** —*v.t.* ①使固定以成習慣。②注意。—*v.i.* ①固定。②建立密切關係; 堅持一項行動或目標。

fix·a·tion [fɪksˈeʃən; fikˈseiʃən] *n.* ①固定;決定;裝置。②影像之定色。③病態的固執或偏激。④氮的固定法。

fix·a·tive [ˈfɪksətɪv; ˈfiksətiv] *adj.* 固定的;防止褪色的。—*n.* 固定劑;〖攝影〗定影劑。

fix·a·ture [ˈfɪksətʃɚ; ˈfiksətʃə] *n.* 髮膠。

***fixed** [fɪkst; fikst] *adj.* ①固定的; 不變的;一定的。 a *fixed* income. 固定的收入。*fixed* prices. 定價。②〖俗〗事先祕密決定的;預定的;買通的。a *fixed* horse race. 預定勝負的馬賽。③不揮發的。④僵硬的;直挺挺的。She stood *fixed* in horror. 她嚇得站在那兒一動也不動。—**ly,** *adv.*

fixed charge 〖會計〗固定費用(卽經常開支)。

fixed cost 〖會計〗固定成本。

fixed deposit 定期存款。

fixed idea 〖醫〗固定觀念,固定妄想(無法擺脫的思想或幻想,常爲瘋狂之病癥)。

fix·ed·ness [ˈfɪksɪdnɪs; ˈfiksidnis] *n.* 固定;不變;凝固性;不揮發性。

fixed oil 不揮發油。

fixed star 恆星。

fix·er [ˈfɪksɚ; ˈfiksə] *n.* ①使固定之人或物。②〖美俚〗仲介人;替犯人行賄說情的人;比賽前買通一方放水的人。③〖攝影〗定影劑。

fix·ing [ˈfɪksɪŋ; ˈfiksiŋ] *n.* ①固定。②整理;修理。③(*pl.*)〖美俗〗設備;設施;裝飾品。***fixing solution*** 〖攝影〗定影液。

fix·i·ty [ˈfɪksətɪ; ˈfiksiti] *n., pl.* **-ties.** ①固定(性);永久(性)。②固着性之物。

fixt [fɪkst; fikst] *v.* 〖詩〗pt. & pp. of **fix.**

***fix·ture** [ˈfɪkstʃɚ; ˈfikstʃə] *n.* ①裝置物;(尤指)房屋之附屬裝置。 electric-light *fixtures.* 電燈裝置。②固定一職之人。③預先規定日期的運動項目;運動會。 football and baseball *fixtures.* 預定日期的足球賽及棒球賽。④〖機械〗固定裝置。

fiz, fizz [fɪz; fiz] *v.,* **fizzed, fiz·zing,** *n.* —*v.i.* 作嘶嘶聲。—*n.* ①嘶嘶聲。②有泡沫的飲料(如汽水)。

fiz·zle [ˈfɪzl̩; ˈfizl] *v.,* **-zled, -zling,** *n.* —*v.i.* ①發微弱的嘶嘶聲。②〖俗〗失敗。***fizzle out*** 結果失敗。—*n.* ①嘶嘶聲。②〖俗〗失敗。

fizz·y [ˈfɪzɪ; ˈfizi] *adj.,* **fizz·i·er, fizz·i·est.** 嘶嘶聲的; 泡沫騰湧的。

fjord [fjord; fjɔːd] *n.* =**fiord.**

Fl 化學元素 fluorine之符號。(亦作 **F**)

Fl. ①Flanders. ②Flemish. **fl.** ①floor. ②florin. ③flourished. ④flower. ⑤fluid. ⑥flute. **Fla.** Florida.

flab·ber·gast [ˈflæbɚˌgæst; ˈflæbəgɑːst] *v.t.* 〖俗〗使大吃一驚;使目瞪口呆。

flab·by [ˈflæbɪ; ˈflæbi] *adj.,* **-bi·er, -bi·est.** ①鬆軟的;弱的。②肌肉鬆弛的。③薄弱的;缺乏道德力量的。—**flab·bi·ly,** *adv.* —**flab·bi·ness,** *n.*

fla·bel·late [fləˈbɛlet; fləˈbeleit] *adj.* 〖動、植物〗扇狀的。(亦作 **flabelliform**)

flac·cid [ˈflæksɪd; ˈflæksid] *adj.* 軟弱的; 鬆弛的; 沒氣力的。 —**ly,** *adv.* —**i·ty,** —**ness,** *n.*

flack [flæk; flæk] *n.* 〖俚〗宣傳員; 廣告業務員。

fla·con [flaˈkɔ̃; flaˈkɔ̃] 〖法〗*n.* (裝香水等之)有塞小瓶;長頸細口瓶。

‡flag¹ [flæg; flæg] *n., v.,* **flagged, flag·ging.**—*n.* ①旗;旗幟;國旗。the national *flag.* 國旗。the red *flag.* 紅旗(危險信號旗)。the white *flag.* 白旗(投降標記)。②(狗、鹿等之)茸尾。③旗狀物。④電視攝影機前擋光之布。⑤(*pl.*) 鳥羽;鳥腿下半之茸毛。⑥報頭(印刷報名處);報頭所印刷之報名。***strike the flag*** or ***strike one's flag*** **a.** (船長之)解職。**b.** 投降;罷手。—*v.t.* ①打旗號;打旗語; 打手勢〖有時 down〗. to *flag* down a taxi. 打手勢讓計程車停下來。②懸旗點綴。The streets are *flagged* to celebrate our victory. 街上懸旗慶祝我們的勝利。③搖旗或旗狀物以誘陷(獵物)。—**ger,** *n.*

flag[2] *n.* 菖蒲;香蒲;其葉或花。

flag[3] *n.* (鋪路用之)大石板。

flag[4] *v.i.*, **flagged, flag·ging.** ①消沉;衰退; 疲弱。②枯萎。

flag-boat ['flæg,bot; 'flægbout] *n.* (賽船時之)標識船。

flag captain 旗艦艦長。

Flag Day ①〖美〗國旗紀念日(六月十四日)。②(f- d-)〖英〗售旗募捐日。

flag·el·lant ['flædʒələnt;'flædʒilənt] *n.* 鞭笞者;(尤指因宗教紀律而)自笞者。—*adj.* ①鞭笞的;自笞的。②嚴厲批評的。

flag·el·late[1] ['flædʒə,let; 'flædʒeleit] *v.t.*, **-lat·ed, -lat·ing.** 鞭打;鞭笞。—**flag·el·la·tion,** *n.*

flag·el·late[2] *adj.* ①〖生物〗生有鞭毛的;生有匍匐莖的。②鞭索形的。—*n.* 鞭毛蟲。

flag·el·lat·ed ['flædʒə,letɪd; 'flædʒeleitid] *adj.* =**flagellate[2].**

fla·gel·li·form [flə'dʒɛlɪ,fɔrm; flə'dʒelifɔ:m] *adj.* 〖生物〗鞭索形的;鞭毛狀的。

fla·gel·lum [flə'dʒɛləm; flə'dʒeləm] *n.*, *pl.* **-lums, -la** [-lə; -lə]. ①鞭子。②〖生物〗鞭節;鞭毛。③〖植物〗匍匐莖。

flag·eo·let [,flædʒə'lɛt; ,flædʒə'let] *n.* 哨笛(一種管樂器)。

flag·ging[1] ['flægɪŋ; 'flægiŋ] *n.* ①鋪砌用之石板(集合稱)。②石板鋪砌之道路。

flag·ging[2] *adj.* 萎弱的; 萎垂的;弛減的;失興趣的。—**ly,** *adv.*

fla·gi·tious [flə'dʒɪʃəs; flə'dʒiʃəs] *adj.* 罪大惡極的;無恥的; 可惡的。—**ly,** *adv.*

flag·man ['flægmən; 'flægmən] *n.*, *pl.* **-men.** ①執旗者;旗手。②信號旗手。

flag of convenience 〖航海〗船隻所懸其登記國之國旗(非船主本國之國旗)。

flag officer ①海軍將官。②艦隊司令。

flag of truce 休戰旗(表投降或求和)。

flag·on ['flægən; 'flægən] *n.* ①具有把手、壺蓋之細頸壺。②大肚酒壺。③此種壺中所盛之液體(如酒等)。

flag·pole ['flæg,pol; 'flægpoul] *n.* 旗竿。

fla·gran·cy ['flegrənsɪ; 'fleigrənsi] *n.* 惡極; 罪惡昭彰。(亦作 **flagrance**)

fla·grant ['flegrənt; 'fleigrənt] *adj.* ①窮兇極惡的。②至爲明顯的。—**ly,** *adv.*

flag·ship ['flæg,ʃɪp; 'flægʃip] *n.* ①旗艦。②船公司所有船隻中之最大或最佳者。③航空公司所有客機中之最大或最豪華者。

flag·staff ['flæg,stæf; 'flægstɑ:f] *n.* 旗杆。

flag station (or **stop**) 祇在打信號時火車始停之車站。

flag·stone ['flæg,ston; 'flægstoun] *n.* ①(鋪路用的)大石板。②易分裂爲片狀之堅硬岩石。③(*pl.*) 用大石板鋪的路。

flag-wav·ing ['flæg,wevɪŋ; 'flæg,weiviŋ] *n.* ①揮舞國旗以激起愛國心(尤指過於做作者)。②任何類似之行動。—**flag-wav·er,** *n.*

flail [flel; fleil] *n.* 連枷(舊式打穀具)。—*v.t.* 用連枷打;敲擊。

flair [flɛr; flɛə] *n.* ①敏銳的覺察力、鑑別力或眼光。②天賦;本領。

flak [flæk; flæk] *n.* ①高射砲火。②高射砲。(亦作 **flack**)

·**flake[1]** [flek; fleik] *n.*, *v.*, **flaked, flak·ing.** —*n.* ①薄片;雪片。*flakes* of snow. 雪片。②薄薄一片或一層。*flakes* of rust. 一層層的銹。—*v.i.* 成片剝落(如石塊);成片降下(如雪片)。—*v.t.* ①使成片剝落。Men of the Stone Age *flaked* stones to make tools. 石器時代的人削石爲器。②以薄片遮蓋。

flake[2] *n.* 晒魚架;網棚。

flake out 〖俚〗睡着;打瞌睡。

flake white 〖繪畫〗清鉛粉。

flak jacket 防彈衣;防彈背心。

flak·y ['flekɪ; 'fleiki] *adj.*, **flak·i·er, flak·i·est.** ①由一片一片構成的; 成片的;成層的。②易成片剝落的;易破碎成薄片的。

flam [flæm; flæm] *n.*, *v.*, **flammed, flam·ming.** —*n.* 謊; 詐欺; 虛僞; 虛構。—*v.t.* & *v.i.* 欺騙;詐僞。

flam·beau ['flæmbo; 'flæmbou] *n.*, *pl.* **-beaux** [-boz; -bouz], **-beaus.** ①火炬。②彩飾之大燭臺。

flam·boy·ance [flæm'bɔɪəns;flæm'bɔiəns] *n.* 燦爛;艷麗;華麗。(亦作 **flamboyancy**)

flam·boy·ant [flæm'bɔɪənt; flæm'bɔiənt] *adj.* ①燦爛的;如火的。②神氣活現的。③波狀的;火焰式的。④誇張的;虛飾的。***flamboyant architecture*** 火焰式建築(十五、六世紀流行於法國,以用焰形或波狀曲線爲其特色)。—**ly,** *adv.* —**ism,** *n.*

:**flame** [flem; fleim] *n.*, *v.*, **flamed, flam·ing.** —*n.* ①火焰; 火舌; 燃燒。The house was in *flames* (=on fire). 房子失火了。②似火之物或狀況。③耀目之光亮或顏色。the *flames* of sunset. 火焰似的落霞。④強烈之情感;情焰;熱情。a *flame* of anger. 怒火。⑤〖俗〗愛人。She's an old *flame* of mine. 她是我的舊情人。***burst into flame(s)*** 發火;燃燒。***commit to the flames*** 付之一炬;焚毀。—*v.i.* ①焚燒。The fire *flamed* in the hearth. 火在爐中焚燒。②變得(紅)如火焰。③激動; 面紅。He *flamed* with anger. 他大怒而面紅。④發出亮光;照耀。Her eyes *flamed* with rage. 她雙眼發出憤怒之光。***flame out*** (噴氣引擎)突然熄火。***flame up*** (*out* or *with*) 迸發。—*v.t.* ①在火焰中燒。②用火焰傳遞消息。—**less,** *adj.* —**like,** *adj.*

flame color 鮮明之橘紅色。

fla·men ['flemɛn; 'fleimen] *n.*, *pl.* **fla·mens, fla·mi·nes** ['flæmə,niz;'flæmini:z]. (古羅馬之)祭司。

fla·men·co [flə'mɛŋko; flə'meŋkou] 〖西班牙〗*n.* ①西班牙的吉卜賽舞蹈;其舞曲。②西班牙裔吉卜賽人;其風俗。

flame·out, flame-out ['flem,aut; 'fleimaut] *n.* 〖航空〗熄火(噴氣引擎因突然熄火而失去效用)。

flame projector =**flame thrower.**

flame·proof ['flem,pruf;'fleimpru:f] *adj.* 防火的。

flame-re·sist·ant ['flemrɪ,zɪstənt; 'fleimri,zistənt] *adj.* 抗火的; 耐火的。

flame thrower 〖軍〗噴火器;火焰噴射器。

flame tree 鳳凰木。

flam·ing ['flemɪŋ; 'fleimiŋ] *adj.* ①燃燒的;有火焰的。②火紅的; 火色的。*flaming* poppies. 火紅色的罌粟花。③燃燒似的;溽暑的。a *flaming* August. 炎熱的八月。④熱烈的; 激情的。*flaming* eyes. 冒火的眼睛。*flaming* youth. 熱情的青年時期。⑤誇張的;渲染的。a *flaming* picture. 誇張的圖畫。—**ly,** *adv.*

fla·min·go [flə'mɪŋgo; flə'miŋgou] *n.*, *pl.* **-gos, -goes.** 紅鶴;火鶴。

flam·ma·ble ['flæməbl; 'flæməbl] *adj.* 可著火的; 易燃燒的。

flam·y ['flemɪ; 'fleimi] *adj.*, **flam·i·er,**

flam·i·est. 火焰的；似火焰的；燃燒的。

flan [flæn; flæn] *n.* ①含有乳酪、水果等之餡餅。②已成錢幣形但尚未上印模之金屬塊。③製造錢幣之金屬。

Flan·ders [ˈflændəz; ˈflɑːndəz] *n.* 法蘭德斯(昔歐洲北海沿岸一國家，今爲比利時之東、西法蘭德斯兩省及法國北部一部分)。

flâ·neur [flɑˈnœr; flɑːˈnəː] 〖法〗 *n.* 懶惰的人；終日閒蕩的人。

flange [flændʒ; flændʒ] *n., v.,* **flanged, flang·ing.** —*n.* 輪緣；凸緣。—*v.t.* 裝以凸緣。

flank [flæŋk; flæŋk] *n.* ①腰窩(肋骨與臀部間之部分)。②從腰窩部分割下的牛肉。③(山或建築物等之)一側。④〖軍〗側翼。to attack the left *flank.* 攻擊左翼。⑤大腿之外側。—*v.t.* ①立於…之側；在…之側。High buildings *flanked* the alley. 巷之兩側高屋聳立。②側面攻擊。We were *flanked* by the enemy. 我們遭敵人的側面攻擊。③繞過…之側。④保衛側翼。⑤以船側朝浪。—*v.i.* 占領側翼陣地。

flank·er [ˈflæŋkə; ˈflæŋkə] *n.* ①位於側邊之人或物。②〖軍〗側翼部隊；側衞。③〖築城〗側面之堡壘或砲臺。

flank speed (船之)全速。

***flan·nel** [ˈflænl; ˈflænl] *n.* ①法蘭絨。②棉織法蘭絨；絨布。③抹擦用的法蘭絨布塊。④(*pl.*)法蘭絨製的衣服(尤指褲子、內衣)。—*adj.* 用法蘭絨做的。—*v.t.* 以法蘭絨包或擦。

flan·nel(l)ed [ˈflænld; ˈflænld] *adj.* 穿法蘭絨衣或長褲的。

flan·nel·et(te) [ˌflænlˈɛt; ˌflænlˈet] *n.*柔軟棉織法蘭絨。

flan·nel·ly [ˈflænlɪ; ˈflænli] *adj.* ①法蘭絨做成的；似法蘭絨的。②口齒不清楚的。

***flap** [flæp; flæp] *v.,* **flapped, flap·ping,** *n.* —*v.i.* ①撲拍；飄動；吹動。A sail (flag, etc.) *flaps* in the wind. 帆(旗等)在風中飄動。②鼓翼；鼓翼而飛。③以寬而有彈性之物擊打。—*v.t.* ①使飄動。②鼓(翼)。③拍打；拍擊。to *flap* flies away (*or* off). 拍擊蚊蠅使去。—*n.* ①拍打；撲拍。②拍擊聲。③邊緣；口蓋(口袋蓋，信封塗膠之口蓋等)；活邊(如圓桌周邊可放下成爲方桌之活邊)。the *flap* of a pocket. 口袋蓋。④〖航空〗(飛機的)襟翼。⑤包書紙摺進封面之部分。⑥〖俚〗 **a.** 神經質的興奮或激動。**b.** 緊急狀況。⑦〖外科〗尚未完全從身體割下準備作移植用的皮膚或肌肉。

flap·doo·dle [ˈflæpˌdudl; ˈflæpˌduːdl] *n.* 〖俗〗胡說。

flap-eared [ˈflæpˌɪrd; ˈflæpˌiəd] *adj.* 耳朵下垂的。

flap·jack [ˈflæpˌdʒæk; ˈflæpdʒæk] *n.* 烙餅；大薄煎餅。

flap·per [ˈflæpə; ˈflæpə] *n.* ①拍者；拍子；拍擊具。②寬平之垂下物；口袋蓋；摺桌的活邊。③剛能飛之雛鳥。④〖俗〗(第一次大戰後)服裝奇異舉止輕浮之少女。⑤〖俚〗手。

flare** [flɛr; flɛə] *v.,* **flared, flar·ing,** *n.* —*v.i.* ①閃耀；閃光。②(裙等)向外展開。—*v.t.* ①以光發信號。The rockets *flared* a warning. 火箭發出閃光警告。②顯著地表露或呈現。③使…向外逐漸展開。flare up*** (or *out*) **a.** 驟然震怒。**b.** 突然爆發。—*n.* ①閃光；閃耀。②閃光信號；照明彈。The wrecked ship was burning *flares* to attract attention. 遇難船正燃起閃光信號以引他人注意。③突然爆發；突發。④(裙等的)展開部分。⑤展開之物。

flare·back [ˈflɛrˌbæk; ˈflɛəbæk] *n.* ①砲尾焰。②短暫而未預料之再出現。

flare bomb 〖軍〗閃光彈；照明彈。

flare-path [ˈflɛrˌpæθ; ˈflɛə-pɑːθ] *n.* 夜間飛行用之照明跑道。

flare-up [ˈflɛrˌʌp; ˈflɛəˈʌp] *n.* ①(火焰、光等之)驟發；驟燃；驟熾。②〖俗〗暴怒。③已平靜後之突然爆發。

flar·ing [ˈflɛrɪŋ; ˈflɛəriŋ] *adj.* ①閃光的；燃燒的；閃耀的。②華麗的；虛華的。③形式漸向外張的。 —**ly,** *adv.*

‡**flash**[1] [flæʃ; flæʃ] *n.* ①閃光；閃爍；閃現。a *flash* of lightning. 閃電。②瞬息；一刻。in a *flash.* 瞬間。③〖美〗簡短新聞電報。④一瞬的感覺；忽現的意念。a *flash* of hope. 忽現的一縷希望。⑤手電筒。⑥庸俗之華麗。⑦炸彈等所引起之短暫火焰或高熱。 ***a flash in the pan*** 曇花一現；虎頭蛇尾。—*v.i.* ①閃光；閃爍。The lightning *flashed* across the sky. 閃電閃過天空。②忽現；疾速馳過。③掠過；突然出現(心頭)。The idea *flashed* into (*or* through) his mind. 這念頭忽然閃過他的心頭。④〖俗〗亮相。⑤突然行動。⑥突然發怒。to *flash* out at a stupid remark. 爲一句愚蠢的話而發怒。—*v.t.* ①突然而短促地發出(光或火)；似閃光一般急促地發出。to *flash* a signal. 用閃光發出信號。②發出(訊號、電訊等)。to *flash* news across the world by radio. 用無線電迅速地把消息傳到全世界。③〖俗〗賣弄；誇示。He *flashed* a roll of money. 他拿出一疊鈔票誇示一下。—*adj.* 閃亮的；閃光的。

flash[2] *n.* ①瀉水池。②河中淺灘前之水閘(聚水以便行舟者)。③盜賊所用之隱語；黑話。

flash[3] *adj.* ①俗艷的；贋造的；價廉的。②穿戴虛華之僞飾品的；鄙俗虛飾的。③〖俚〗第一流的；時髦的。④盜賊輩的；與下流社會有關的。⑤機智的；狡猾的。⑥突然而短暫的。

flash·back [ˈflæʃˌbæk; ˈflæʃbæk] *n.* ①〖電影〗倒敍(穿插往事之畫面)。②(故事、小說等之)插敍。

flash·board [ˈflæʃˌbord; ˈflæʃbɔːd] *n.* 插板；閘板；堰板。

flash bulb (照相的)閃光燈泡。

flash burn (原子彈等熱放射造成的)閃光灼傷。

flash card (敎學用)閃視卡片。

flash·cube [ˈflæʃˌkjub; ˈflæʃkjuːb] *n.* 〖攝影〗立方形閃光燈泡。

flash·er [ˈflæʃə; ˈflæʃə] *n.* ①炫耀者；虛飾者；閃耀之物。②使燈光忽明忽滅之裝置。③燈光忽明忽滅之燈塔或浮標。

flash fire 突然而猛烈之火災。

flash flood 急驟之山洪。

flash gun 〖攝影〗閃光槍(一種能同時使閃光燈發光及攝機快門操作的裝置)。

flash·ing [ˈflæʃɪŋ; ˈflæʃiŋ] *n.* ①閃爍；閃耀。②水道中水流的驟漲。③禦水板。—*adj.* 閃亮的；閃爍的。—**ly,** *adv.*

flash lamp (攝影用之)閃光燈。

flash·light [ˈflæʃˌlaɪt; ˈflæʃlait] *n.* ①燈塔閃光燈。②〖美〗手電筒。③(攝影)閃光燈；鎂光燈。

flash point 〖化〗發火點。(亦作 **flashing point**)

flash tube 〖攝影〗 閃光燈泡。

flash·y [ˈflæʃɪ; ˈflæʃi] *adj.,* **flash·i·er, flash·i·est.** ①閃耀的；僅炫耀一時的。②浮華的。③無味的。—**flash·i·ly,** *adv.*

***flask** [flæsk; flɑːsk] *n.* ①任何瓶狀容器；細頸瓶；燒瓶。②(口袋中可攜帶之)扁玻璃瓶或金屬瓶。③盛沙等之盒或框(如鑄造廠做模型用者)。

flask·et [ˈflæskɪt, ˈflɑs-; ˈflɑːskit] *n.* 小細頸瓶；小燒瓶。

‡**flat** [flæt; flæt] *adj.,* **flat·ter, flat·test,**

adv., n., v., **flat·ted, flat·ting.** —*adj.* ①平坦的;平直的。The floor is quite *flat.* 這地板十分平整。②淺的;薄的;扁的。③斷然的;絕對的。a *flat* refusal. 斷然的拒絕。④平淡無味的;無生氣的。Life seemed *flat* to him. 生活在他看來好像是無味的。⑤單調的;無變化的。to color the walls a *flat* tint. 把牆漆成單調的顏色。⑥平臥地上的;倒下的。He knocked the man *flat.* 他把那人打倒在地上。⑦平掛的。a picture that hangs *flat* against the wall. 平掛牆上的一幅畫。⑧〖音樂〗降半音的。B *flat.* 降B調。⑨低沉的。⑩洩了氣的;無空氣的。a *flat* tire. 沒有氣的車胎。⑪暗淡無光的;暗晦的。a *flat* yellow. 暗晦的黃色。⑫彈道低的。⑬(帆)緊的。⑭(畫)無縱深或立體感的。⑮(酒、食物等)走味的。⑯聲調無變化的。a *flat* delivery of the speech. 聲調無變化的演講。⑰(食物烹調)未加香料的。*flat* cooking. 不加香料的烹調。⑱(笑話或言談)不着邊際的。⑲(市場)蕭條的;不景氣的。⑳固定的。***be flat on one's back*** 臥病。***that's flat*** 說一不二(=I mean it). —*adv.* ①〖音樂〗降半音地。②平直地;臥倒地。He was lying *flat* on his back. 他平直地仰臥着。③斷然地;絕對地。to go *flat* against orders. 斷然抗命。④〖財政〗無(利)息。***fall flat*** **a.** 直挺挺地跌倒。**b.** 變成索然寡味。**c.** 徹底失敗。***flat out*** 以最快速度或最大努力。—*n.* ①平的東西;平的部分。②平底船。③淺盒;淺箱;淺籃。④〖美〗沼地;淺沼。⑤無頂篷的鐵路運貨車。⑥〖音樂〗降半音的符號(*b*);降半音。⑦〖俗〗氣不足的輪胎。⑧平地;平原。⑨一層樓房裏幾間屋子所構成的一個居住單位。⑩(戲臺上的)背景屏。⑪笨人。⑫平地賽馬。⑬(*pl.*)女人之平底鞋。—*v.t.* 使平。—*v.i.* 變平。—**ly,** *adv.* —**ness,** *n.*

flat·boat [ˈflætˌbot; ˈflætbout] *n.* (淺水河道上航用的)平底船。

flat·car [ˈflætˌkɑr; ˈflætkɑː] *n.* 〖美俗〗無頂篷或無邊板之鐵路運貨車;平臺型運貨車。

flat·fish [ˈflætˌfɪʃ; ˈflætfiʃ] *n., pl.* **-fish·es, -fish.** 比目魚。

flat·foot [ˈflætˌfut; ˈflætfut] *n.* ①平蹠足;扁平足。②有扁平足之人。③〖俚〗警察(尤指有固定巡區者)。④〖俚〗水手。

flat-foot·ed [ˈflætˈfutɪd; ˈflætˈfutid] *adj.* ①有畸形扁平足的。②〖俗〗決然的;堅定的;屹立不動的;直截了當的。③未準備的。***catch one flat-footed*** 〖俗〗出其不意;使驚奇。—*adv.* 斷然地。

flat·i·ron [ˈflætˌaɪən; ˈflætˌaiən] *n.* 熨斗。

flat·let [ˈflætlɪt; ˈflætlit] *n.* 〖英〗小公寓。

flat-nosed [ˈflætˈnozd; ˈflætˈnouzd] *adj.* 塌鼻子的。

flat-out [ˈflætˌaut; ˈflætˈaut] *adj.* ①最高速度的。②絕對的;不折不扣的。

flat race 平地賽跑;無障礙的賽跑(尤指賽馬)。(亦作 **flat racing**)

flat silver 鍍銀或銀製食器。

flat·ten** [ˈflætn̩; ˈflætn] *v.t.* ①使平。②打倒;摧毀。—*v.i.* ①變平。②倒下;屈服。flatten out*** **a.** 使平;變平。**b.** (飛機俯衝後或上升後)取水平姿式;使(飛機)取水平姿式。

flat·ter** [ˈflætɚ; ˈflætə] *v.t.* ①諂媚;阿諛;奉承。②(圖書等)美於(眞實,眞容)。The picture *flatters* her. 這照片比她本來面目美。③慇懃取悅。I feel *flattered* by your invitation. 受你的邀請,我覺得受寵若驚。④妄想。flatter oneself*** 自以爲;對自己估計過高。—*v.i.* 奉承;諂媚。—**er,** *n.*

flat·ter·ing [ˈflætərɪŋ; ˈflætəriŋ] *adj.* ①諂媚的。②描寫美過其實的。③令人喜愛的。④似有望的。

***flat·ter·y** [ˈflætərɪ; ˈflætəri] *n., pl.* **-ter·ies.** 阿諛之詞;諂媚。Don't be deceived by her *flatteries.* 勿被她的諂媚所騙。

flat tire 走了氣的車胎。

flat·tish [ˈflætɪʃ; ˈflætiʃ] *adj.* 略平的;稍單調的;稍淺薄的。

flat·top [ˈflætˌtɑp; ˈflættɔp] *n.* ①〖俚〗航空母艦。②頂部扁平之物。(亦作 **flat-top**)

flat·u·lence [ˈflætʃələns; ˈflætjuləns] *n.* ①腸胃氣脹。②空虛;浮誇;虛張聲勢。(亦作 **flatulency**)

flat·u·lent [ˈflætʃələnt; ˈflætjulənt] *adj.* ①(患)腸胃氣脹的。②引起腸胃氣脹的(食物)。③空虛的;浮誇的;虛張聲勢的。

fla·tus [ˈfletəs; ˈfleitəs] *n., pl.* **-tus·es.** ①氣息;一陣之風。②腸胃氣。

flat·ware [ˈflætˌwɛr; ˈflætwɛə] *n.* 扁平之餐桌用具(如刀、叉、匙、或碟、盤等)。

flat·ways [ˈflætˌwez; ˈflætweiz] *adv.* =**flatwise.**

flat·wise [ˈflætˌwaɪz; ˈflætwaiz] *adv.* 扁平地;平放地。

flat·work [ˈflætˌwɝk; ˈflætwəːk] *n.* 通常用機械方法熨燙的毛巾、床單、衣服等。

flat·worm [ˈflætˌwɝm; ˈflætwəːm] *n.* 扁形蟲(如條蟲、肝蛭等)。

flaunt [flɔnt; flɔːnt] *v.i.* ①昂首闊步地走;炫耀。②飄蕩。—*v.t.* ①炫耀。②藐視。—*n.* 炫耀;藐視。

flaunt·y [ˈflɔntɪ; ˈflɔːnti] *adj.* 炫耀的;誇示的。

flau·tist [ˈflɔtɪst; ˈflɔːtist] *n.* 吹笛者(=flutist).

fla·ves·cent [fləˈvɛsənt; fləˈvesənt] *adj.* 黃的;變成淡黃色的。

fla·vin(e) [ˈflevɪn; ˈfleivin] *n.* 〖化〗①黃素。②解黃素;四羥黃酮醇。

***fla·vo(u)r** [ˈflevɚ; ˈfleivə] *n.* ①滋味;味道。Chocolate and vanilla have different *flavors.* 巧克力與香草精,其味各不相同。②調味料;香料;佐料。③特點;特別的風味。④芳香;香味。—*v.t.* ①調味。to *flavor* soup with onions. 加洋蔥於湯以美其味。②使具有特殊的風味。—**ful,** *adj.*

fla·vo(u)r·ing [ˈflevrɪŋ; ˈfleivəriŋ] *n.* 調味品。

fla·vo(u)r·less [ˈflevəlɪs; ˈfleivəlis] *adj.* 無滋味的;無趣味的。

fla·vo(u)r·ous [ˈflevərəs; ˈfleivərəs] *adj.* 有風味的;有香氣的;有趣味的。

***flaw**[1] [flɔ; flɔː] *n.* ①裂縫;裂紋。A *flaw* in the dish caused it to break. 盤子上的一條裂紋使它破裂了。②缺陷;瑕疵。—*v.t.* 使有裂縫;使有瑕疵。—*v.i.* 有裂縫;有瑕疵。

flaw[2] *n.* 突起之一陣暴風(通常夾有雨或雪)。

flaw·less [ˈflɔlɪs; ˈflɔːlis] *adj.* 毫無瑕疵的;完美的;完善的。—**ly,** *adv.* —**ness,** *n.*

***flax** [flæks; flæks] *n.* ①亞麻。②亞麻纖維;亞麻紗。

flax·en [ˈflæksn̩; ˈflæksn] *adj.* ①亞麻織的。②淺黃色的。

flax·seed [ˈflæksˌsid, ˈflækˌsid; ˈflækssiːd, ˈflæksiːd] *n.* 亞麻仁;亞麻子。

flax·y [ˈflæksɪ; ˈflæksi] *adj.* =**flaxen.**

flay [fle; flei] *v.t.* ①剝…的皮。②嚴責;苛評。③刼奪;掠奪。—**er,** *n.*

flea** [fli; fliː] *n.* 跳蚤。a flea in one's ear*** **a.** 責備;刺耳的話;譏諷。**b.** 暗示;密告。

flea·bag [ˈfliˌbæg; ˈfliːbæg] *n.* 〖俚〗①牀。②睡袋。③破舊之旅館。④任何低級破舊之場所。⑤長滿跳蚤的狗。⑥劣等的馬。

flea·bane [ˈfliˌben; ˈfliːbein] *n.* 一種

紫菀科之植物。
flea beetle 一種善跳之甲蟲。
flea·bite [ˋfli,baɪt; ˈfli:bait] *n.* ①蚤咬；蚤咬之紅斑。②小傷痛。③少；微量。
flea-bit·ten [ˋfli,bɪtn; ˈfli:ˌbitn] *adj.* ①被蚤咬的；受蚤騷擾的。②淡色之上有褐色斑點或條紋的(指馬之毛色而言)。
fleam [flim; fli:m] *n.* 〖外科〗刺血針。
flèche [flɛʃ; fleiʃ] 〖法〗 *n.* ①矢。②〖築城〗凸角堡。③〖建築〗(教堂)尖塔；尖閣。
fleck [flɛk; flek] *n.* ①點；斑點。②小粒；微粒。—*v.t.* 飾以斑點。
flecked [flɛkt; flekt] *adj.* 有斑點的；有汚點的。
fleck·er [ˋflɛkɚ; ˈflekə] *v.t.* =**fleck.**
flec·tion [ˋflɛkʃən; ˈflekʃən] *n.* ①彎曲；屈曲。②彎曲之部分；彎。③〖解剖〗屈；屈曲。④〖文法〗語形變化。
fled [flɛd; fled] *v.* pt. & pp. of **flee.**
fledge [flɛdʒ; fledʒ] *v.*, **fledged, fledg·ing.** —*v.t.* 養育(雛鳥，以待其羽毛長成)。—*v.i.* 生羽毛。
fledged [flɛdʒd; fledʒd] *adj.* ①初生羽毛的；剛會飛的(雛鳥)。②具有成熟之徵象的。
fledge·less [ˋflɛdʒlɪs; ˈfledʒlis] *adj.* 尙未長羽毛的；尙未完全成熟的。
fledg(e)·ling [ˋflɛdʒlɪŋ; ˈfledʒliŋ] *n.* ①剛生羽毛的雛。②年輕無經驗的人。
***flee** [fli; fli:] *v.*, **fled** [flɛd; fled], **flee·ing.** —*v.i.* ①逃走；逃跑；逃避。The enemy *fled* before our troops. 敵軍見我軍即逃。②飛馳而過；過去；消逝。The smile *fled* from his face. 他臉上的笑容消失了。—*v.t.* 避開；逃避。He *fled* the country. 他逃離祖國。
***fleece** [flis; fli:s] *n.*, *v.*, **fleeced, fleec·ing.** —*n.* ①羊毛。②一次剪下的羊毛。③似羊毛之物。a *fleece* of hair. 蓬鬆捲髮。—*v.t.* ①剪(羊)毛。②作點點或片片之點綴於。a sky *fleeced* with clouds. 點綴着羊毛般白雲的天空。③騙取(錢財等)；詐欺；强奪。to *fleece* a man of his money. 騙取某人的錢財。
fleec·y [ˋflisɪ; ˈfli:si] *adj.*, **fleec·i·er, fleec·i·est.** ①羊毛一般的；柔而白的。②被有羊毛的。③羊毛製的。
fleer [flɪr; fliə] *v.t.* & *v.i.* 獰笑；揶揄；嘲弄。—*n.* 冷嘲。—**ing·ly,** *adv.*
fleet**[1] [flit; fli:t] *n.* ①艦隊。②任何一隊同航行的船；船隊。③一隊(飛機、汽車等)。Admiral of the Fleet*** 海軍元帥(五星上將)。
***fleet**[2] *adj.* ①快速的。a *fleet* horse. 快馬。②〖詩〗瞬息即逝的。—*v.i.* ①疾馳；飛逝。②變換位置。—*v.t.* ①使(時間)飛逝。②〖航海〗使…之位置變動。—**ly,** *adv.* —**ness,** *n.*
fleet[3] *n.* 〖英〗港；灣；小河(今僅用於方言或地名中)。***the Fleet*** 昔日倫敦之一監獄。
fleet admiral ①〖美〗五星海軍上將。②〖英〗海軍總司令。
fleet·ing [ˋflitɪŋ; ˈfli:tiŋ] *adj.* 疾逝的；飛馳的；短暫的。—**ly,** *adv.*
Fleet Street 倫敦之符立德街，爲報館集中地(現多用以表示英國報業界)。
Flem. Flemish. (亦作 **Flem**)
Flem·ing[1] [ˋflɛmɪŋ; ˈflemiŋ] *n.* ①Flanders 人。②荷蘭裔系的比利時人。
Flem·ing[2] *n.* 佛來明 (Sir Alexander, 1881–1955, 英國細菌學家，於 1929 年發現盤尼西林，1945年獲諾貝爾醫學獎)。
Flem·ish [ˋflɛmɪʃ; ˈflemiʃ] *adj.* Flanders 的；Flanders 人的；Flanders 語的。—*n.* Flanders 人；Flanders 語。
flense [flɛns; flenz] *v.t.*, **flensed, flens·ing.** 剝取(鯨、海豹等)之脂肪或皮；剝取(脂肪或皮)。(亦作 **flench**)
‡**flesh** [flɛʃ; fleʃ] *n.* ①肉；肌肉。②肉類(食物)；食肉。Lions and tigers are *flesh*-eating animals. 獅與虎是食肉動物。③肉體；軀殼。The spirit is willing but the *flesh* is weak. 心有餘而力不足。④嫡親；骨肉。⑤人性惡之一面；肉慾；淫慾。the sins of the *flesh.* 肉慾之罪。⑥人類。⑦一切生物。⑧白人皮膚之顏色；略帶黃色之粉白色。⑨果肉；菜蔬的鮮嫩部分。***flesh and blood*** 血肉之軀。***go the way of all flesh*** 死。***have*** (or ***demand***) ***one's pound of flesh*** 索債。***in the flesh*** **a.** 本人。It was quite a thrill to see a real movie star *in the flesh.* 看見眞的電影明星本人，是一件十分令人興奮的事。**b.** 活生生的。***lose flesh*** 變瘦；消瘦。***make a person's flesh creep*** 使某人毛骨悚然。***one's own flesh and blood*** 子女；親屬。***put on flesh*** 長肥；發胖。—*v.t.* ①揷(刀、劍)入於肉中；刺。②以肉餵(鷹等)。③激起(怒氣)；惹起(流血等)。④予…以眞實感〖常out〗. The playwright *fleshed* out his characters. 劇作家將他的人物寫得栩栩如生。⑤(製革時)將皮上之肉刮去。—*v.i.* 〖俗〗發胖。
flesh-and-blood [ˋflɛʃənˋblʌd; ˈfleʃənˈblʌd] *adj.* 確有其人的；眞實的。
flesh·er [ˋflɛʃɚ; ˈfleʃə] *n.* 屠夫；屠刀；販肉者；肉店。
flesh fly 大麻蠅；食肉蠅(其幼蟲以腐肉爲食)。
flesh·i·ness [ˋflɛʃɪnɪs; ˈfleʃinis] *n.* 肉質；多肉；肥胖。
flesh·ings [ˋflɛʃɪŋz; ˈfleʃiŋz] *n. pl.* ①(江湖藝人等所穿之)肉色緊身衣。②〖製革〗從生皮上刮下的肉及其他不潔物(用以製膠者)。
flesh·less [ˋflɛʃlɪs; ˈfleʃlis] *adj.* 瘦的；憔悴的。
flesh·ly [ˋflɛʃlɪ; ˈfleʃli] *adj.* 肉體的；肉慾的；塵世間的；放蕩的。—**flesh·li·ness,** *n.*
flesh·pot [ˋflɛʃ,pɑt; ˈfleʃpɔt] *n.* ①煮肉鍋；盛肉之容器。②(*pl.*)美食；逸樂；奢侈。③(*pl.*)售美食之店；奢侈逸樂之場合。
flesh wound 皮肉傷；輕傷。
flesh·y [ˋflɛʃɪ; ˈfleʃi] *adj.*, **flesh·i·er, flesh·i·est.** ①多肉的；肥胖的。②肉的；似肉的。③多果肉的。
fleur-de-lis [,flɝdəˋli, -ˋlis; ˌflə:dəˈli:, -ˈli:s] *n., pl.* **fleurs-de-lis** [,flɝdəˋliz; ˌflə:dəˈli:z]. ①〖植物〗鳶尾。②鳶尾花形之紋章；百合花形之紋章。
‡**flew** [flu; flu:] *v.* pt. of **fly**[1].
flews [fluz; flu:z] *n. pl.* 犬之上唇鬆垂部分。
flex [flɛks; fleks] *v.t.* & *v.i.* 彎曲；褶曲。—*n.* ①彎曲；褶曲。②=**flexibility.** ③〖俚〗鬆緊帶。
flex. flexible.
flex·i·bil·i·ty [,flɛksəˋbɪlətɪ; ˌfleksəˈbiliti] *n.* 易曲性；柔軔性；適應性。
***flex·i·ble** [ˋflɛksəbl; ˈfleksəbl, -sib-] *adj.* ①易彎曲的；柔順的。Leather, rubber, and wire are *flexible.* 皮革，橡皮和電線都是可彎曲的。②易適應的；可修改的；有伸縮性的。a *flexible* mind. 易適應的頭腦。③易操縱的；易屈服的；易說服的。—**ness,** *n.* —**flex·i·bly,** *adv.*
flex·ile [ˋflɛksɪl; ˈfleksil] *adj.* =**flexible.**
flex·ion [ˋflɛkʃən; ˈflekʃən] *n.* =**flection.**
flex·or [ˋflɛksɚ; ˈfleksə] *n.* 〖解剖〗屈肌。
flex·u·os·i·ty [,flɛkʃuˋɑsətɪ; ˌflekʃuˈɔsiti] *n., pl.* **-ties.** ①彎曲性；彎曲之狀；蜿

蜒曲折。②彎;彎曲部分。

flex·u·ous [ˈflɛkʃuəs, ˈflɛksju-; ˈflekʃuəs, ˈfleksju-] *adj.* ①屈曲的;彎曲的;蜿蜒的。②動搖不定的。③〖植物〗鋸齒狀的;波狀的。

flex·ure [ˈflɛkʃɚ; ˈflekʃə] *n.* ①屈曲;彎曲。②屈曲部分;褶曲。

flib·ber·ti·gib·bet [ˈflɪbətɪˌdʒɪbɪt; ˈflibətiˈdʒibit] *n.* 輕浮之人;多話之人(通常指女人)。—**y**, *adj.*

flick[1] [flɪk; flik] *n.* ①輕擊;輕彈;輕打。②輕擊聲;輕彈聲。③條痕;斑跡;點。—*v.t.* ①輕擊;輕彈;輕拂。②用…作輕擊;投擲。—*v.i.* 撲拍;輕快地振動。

flick[2] *n.* (常 *pl.*)〖英俚〗影片;電影。

*__flick·er__ [ˈflɪkɚ; ˈflikə] *v.i.* ①(火光)搖曳;閃爍不定;明滅不定。The firelight *flickered* on the walls. 爐光在壁上搖曳不定。②輕快顫動;輕快振動。—*n.* ①搖曳閃動的火光。②閃光;火花。③輕快的動作。④短暫之出現;閃動。a weak *flicker* of hope. 希望的微弱閃動。⑤〖美〗金翼啄木鳥。⑥(常 *pl.*) =**flick**[2]. —**y**, *adj.*

flick·er·ing·ly [ˈflɪkərɪŋlɪ; ˈflikəriŋli] *adv.* 閃爍地;搖曳地;撲動地。

flick knife 〖英〗彈簧刀。

fli·er [ˈflaɪɚ; ˈflaiə] *n.* ①飛行者(人或物)。②飛行家。③特快車;特快船。④〖俚〗冒險的買賣;(非本行內的)投機。⑤一種小傳單。⑥〖俗〗如飛之跳躍。⑦機器運轉極速之部分。

‡**flight** [flaɪt; flait] *n.* ①飛行;飛翔。to study the *flight* of birds. 研究鳥的飛翔。②乘飛機旅行;航空;航程。to make a successful *flight*. 作順利的飛行。③飛機之飛行班次。④飛行隊;鳥羣。a *flight* of six birds. 六隻飛鳥。⑤〖美〗(包括兩架以上飛機的)飛行小隊。⑥疾速行動。the *flight* of an arrow. 箭的飛馳。⑦升高。⑧一段(階梯);一重(樓梯)。a *flight* of steps. 一段階梯。⑨逃逸;逃亡。a *flight* of capital. 資金的流出。⑩奔放;煥發。a *flight* of the imagination.想像的奔放。⑪遠距離射箭所用的輕箭;該箭所飛之距離。***in the first flight*** 占首要地位;領頭。***put to flight*** 使逃走;擊退;驅散。***take*** (***to***) ***flight*** 逃走。—*v.i.* (鳥)成隊飛行。—*v.t.* ①射擊(飛鳥)。②將羽毛裝在箭上。

flight bag 旅行袋(乘飛機時用的)。

flight control ①飛行管制。②飛行管制系統。③飛行管制室。④駕駛員控制飛機運動的系統。⑤若干飛機內之儀器艙。

flight deck ①航空母艦之飛行甲板。②

flight feather 鳥翅及尾部之硬桿羽毛。

flight·less [ˈflaɪtlɪs; ˈflaitlis] *adj.*不能飛的。

flight number 飛機班次。

flight pay 〖美空軍〗飛行津貼;空勤加給。

flight strip 簡易飛機場(緊急時用)。

flight-test [ˈflaɪtˌtɛst; ˈflaittest] *v.t.* 將(飛機)試飛。

flight·y [ˈflaɪtɪ; ˈflaiti] *adj.*, **flight·i·er, flight·i·est.** ①好作奇思怪想的;輕浮的;神經微有錯亂的。②不負責任的。③迅速的。—**flight·i·ly**, *adv.* —**flight·i·ness**, *n.*

flim·flam [ˈflɪmˌflæm; ˈflimflæm] *n.*, *adj.*, *v.*, **-flammed, -flam·ming.** —*n.* ①胡說;無聊之言。②欺騙;下流手段。—*adj.* ①無聊的;無意義的。②欺騙的。—*v.t.* 〖俗〗騙(人)錢財;詐騙。—**mer**, *n.*

flim·sy [ˈflɪmzɪ; ˈflimzi] *adj.*, **-si·er, -si·est**, *n.*, *pl.* **-sies.** —*adj.*弱的;脆弱的;無力的。Tissue paper is *flimsy*. 紗紙是脆弱的。—*n.* ①(新聞記者用的)一種薄紙。②(寫於這種薄紙上的)新聞稿。—**flim·si·ly**, *adv.* —**flim·si·ness**, *n.*

flinch [flɪntʃ; flintʃ] *v.i.* 畏縮;退縮。—*v.t.* 從…退縮。—*n.* 畏縮;退縮。—**er**, *n.* —**ing·ly**, *adv.*

flin·ders [ˈflɪndɚz; ˈflindəz] *n. pl.* 破片;碎片。to break into *flinders*. 破碎。

*__fling__ [flɪŋ; fliŋ] *v.*, **flung** [flʌŋ; flʌŋ], **fling·ing**, *n.* —*v.t.* ①投;擲;拋;摔。to *fling* a stone at a dog. 投擲石塊打狗。to *fling* one's clothes on. 將衣急忙穿上。②强投。to *fling* him into jail. 將他下獄。③突然而迅速地派遣。to *fling* fresh troops into a battle. 將生力軍迅速派至戰場。④突然而迅速地說話。⑤推翻。⑥放棄;遺棄。—*v.i.* ①急行;衝(進或出)。to *fling* out of a room. 衝出房間。②暴燥地衝踢。③謾罵〖常 out〗. ***fling caution to the wind*** 置勸告於不顧;鹵莽從事。—*n.* ①投;擲;拋。②恣情放肆的時間。He had his *fling* when he was young; now he must work. 他在年輕時恣情放縱,現在他必須工作了。③一種活潑的蘇格蘭舞。④急衝;衝踢。***have*** (or ***take***) ***a fling at*** a. 試圖。b. 嘲弄;譏笑。***in full fling*** 正進行在高潮中。—**er**, *n.*

*__flint__ [flɪnt; flint] *n.* ①打火石;燧石。②堅硬之物。She must have a heart of *flint*. 她定有一副鐵石心腸。—*v.t.* 裝打火石;給予燧石。—**like**, *adj.*

flint glass 鉛玻璃(用製鏡頭等)。

flint-heart·ed [ˈflɪntˈhɑrtɪd; ˈflintˈhɑːtid] *adj.* 鐵石心腸的。

flint·lock [ˈflɪntˌlɑk; ˈflintlɔk] *n.* ①燧發槍機。②燧發槍。

flint·y [ˈflɪntɪ; ˈflinti] *adj.*, **flint·i·er, flint·i·est.** ①燧石質的;含燧石的。②極堅硬的;殘忍的。—**flint·i·ness**, *n.*

flip[1] [flɪp; flip] *v.*, **flipped, flip·ping**, *n.*, *adj.*, **flip·per, flip·pest.** —*v.t.* ①(以指)彈拋;彈投;輕彈。②捻擲(硬幣等)。③猝然跳動;突然拉動。She *flipped* her fan shut. 她猛然合上了她的扇子。—*v.i.* ①輕擊;輕打。②猝然跳動;彈動。③〖俚〗興奮欲狂。***flip up*** 投擲錢幣以決定機會。—*n.* ①輕彈;彈去;輕打。②跳動;突然的抽動。③跳水時空中翻身。—*adj.* 〖俗〗言語輕佻的;不客氣的;無禮的。

flip[2] *n.* 一種飲料(加糖、香料等於啤酒或蘋果酒等製成)。

flip-flap [ˈflɪpˌflæp; ˈflipflæp] *n.*, *adv.*, *v.*, **-flapped, -flap·ping.** —*n.* ①〖俚〗一種手足輪替觸地的翻觔斗。②一種煙火;爆竹。③噼啪聲。—*adv.* 連續噼啪作聲地。—*v.i.* 噼噼啪啪地動搖。

flip-flop [ˈflɪpˌflɑp; ˈflipflɔp] *n.*, *adv.*, *v.*, **-flopped, -flop·ping.** —*n.* ①朝後翻的觔斗。②噼啪聲。—*adv.* 發出噼啪聲地。—*v.i.* ①朝後翻觔斗。②搖擺。

flip·pan·cy [ˈflɪpənsɪ; ˈflipənsi] *n.*, *pl.* **-cies.** 言語尖刻;不客氣;無禮;輕率。

flip·pant [ˈflɪpənt; ˈflipənt] *adj.* 言語尖刻的;不客氣的;輕率的。—**ly**, *adv.*

flip·per [ˈflɪpɚ; ˈflipə] *n.* ①(海豹、企鵝、海龜等之)類若鰭狀之肢(用以游泳)。②游泳者套在足上的鰭狀橡皮肢。③〖俚〗手。

flip side 〖俚〗唱片之反面(常爲次要之面)。

*__flirt__ [flɝt; fləːt] *v.i.* ①賣弄風情;調情取樂。She *flirts* with every handsome man she meets. 她和所遇到的每個美男子調情。②玩弄;以(某種思想)自娛。He *flirted* with the idea of going to Europe. 他以

去歐洲的遐想自娛。③來回迅速移動。 —*v.t.* ①急揮。She *flirted* her fan. 她急速揮動她的扇子。②急投；急擲。—*n.* ①調情者；賣弄風騷者。②搖動；擺動。

flir·ta·tion 〔flɝˈteʃən; fləːˈteiʃən〕 *n.* ①調情；無誠意的戀愛。②輕浮的戀愛。③(以某種思想)自娛。

flir·ta·tious 〔flɝˈteʃəs; fləːˈteiʃəs〕 *adj.* ①喜調情的；輕浮的。②關於調情或輕浮之戀愛的。—**ly,** *adv.*

***flit** 〔flɪt; flit〕 *v.,* **flit·ted, flit·ting,** *n.* —*v.i.* ①飛躍；輕而快地飛。A humming-bird *flitted* by. 一隻蜂鳥輕快地飛過。②掠過。—*v.t.* 〖蘇、英方〗悄悄搬家；遷居；偷偷溜走(如爲逃債)。—*n.* ①輕快的動作。②飛躍；飛掠。③〖俚〗男子同性戀者。

flitch 〔flɪtʃ; flitʃ〕 *n.* ①醃猪脇肉。②比目魚肉片。③細長的小木板；條板；桁板。

flitch beam 〖建築〗合梁。

flite 〔flaɪt; flait〕 *v.,* **flit·ed, flit·ing,** *n.* —*v.i.* & *v.t.* 〖古,方〗①與(人)爭吵。②斥責。—*n.* 〖古,方〗爭吵；爭論。(亦作 **flyte**)

flit·ter¹ 〔ˈflɪtɚ; ˈflitə〕 *v.i.* & *v.t.* 〖方〗鼓翼飛翔；輕快地移動；翩翩而飛。

flit·ter² *n.* ①飛翔者。②裝飾用的金屬碎片。

fliv·ver 〔ˈflɪvɚ; ˈflivə〕 *n.* ①〖俚〗小而廉價之汽車、飛機等。②〖諧〗汽車。③〖俚〗蹩脚貨。—*v.i.* 〖俚〗失敗。

‡float 〔flot; flout〕 *v.i.* ①漂；浮。Wood *floats* on water. 木浮於水上。②船漂行；漂流；浮動。③步履輕快而優美地走動。She *floated* down the stairs. 她從樓梯飄然地走下來。④傳播。⑤無牽無掛。⑥東飄西蕩。to *float* from place to place. 到處遊蕩。⑦猶豫不決〖常 between〗。⑧對世事不關心。to *float* through life. 一生悠哉遊哉地度過。—*v.t.* ①使漂流；使漂動。②創設(公司)。to *float* a new business company. 創設一個新公司。③發行(公債)。to *float* a loan. 發行公債。④淹沒；氾濫。⑤使平滑。—*n.* ①浮物；漂流物；船；筏。②遊行車。③劇院中之脚燈。④釣魚線上之浮標；浮子。⑤魚鰾。⑥(水車上的)蹼板；(輪船上的)輪翼。⑦(調節流水量的)浮球。⑧(飛機身下的)浮筒。⑨(泥水匠用的)塗牆板。

float·a·ble 〔ˈflotəbl; ˈfloutəbl〕 *adj.* 可浮起的；可航行的。

float·age 〔ˈflotɪdʒ; ˈfloutidʒ〕 *n.* 「=**flotage.**」

float·a·tion 〔floˈteʃən; flouˈteiʃən〕 *n.* 〖英〗=**flotation.**

float bridge (供船裝卸貨物用之)浮橋。

float·er 〔ˈflotɚ; ˈfloutə〕 *n.* ①漂浮者；漂浮物。②〖俗〗經常變換住地、職業等之人；流浪工人。③〖美〗不固定投票給某黨派之選民(尤指可賄買者)。④〖美〗在同一次選舉中於多處作非法投票之人(通常爲受雇者)。⑤〖俚〗警察限令某人離開城鎮的命令。⑥(亦作 **floating policy**) 移動財產之保險。

float·ing 〔ˈflotɪŋ; ˈfloutiŋ〕 *adj.* 漂浮的；移動的；流動的。

floating anchor 海錨；浮錨。

floating bridge 浮橋。

floating capital 浮動資本。

floating debt 浮動債務；短期債務。

floating dock 浮船塢。

floating island ①浮島。②覆有蛋白或奶油之乳蛋羹。

floating light ①燈船。②裝有燈火「之救生圈。」

floating population 流動人口。

floating ribs 〖解剖〗浮肋。

floating stock 〖商〗流動股票。

floating vote 不固定支持某黨派之投票。

float·plane 〔ˈflot,plen; ˈflout,plein〕 「*n.* 水上飛機。」

float·stone 〔ˈflot,ston; ˈfloutstoun〕 *n.* ①〖礦〗浮石。②墁匠之磨石。

floc·cose 〔ˈflɑkos; ˈflɔkous〕 *adj.* ①羊毛狀的；有柔毛叢的；飛絮狀的。②〖植物〗(覆)有叢毛的。

floc·cu·late 〔ˈflɑkjə,let; ˈflɔkjuleit〕 *v.t.* & *v.i.,* **-lat·ed, -lat·ing.** 凝聚；凝集。—**floc·cu·la·tion,** *n.*

floc·cu·lence 〔ˈflɑkjələns; ˈflɔkjuləns〕 *n.* ①毛狀；叢毛狀。②成叢狀。

floc·cu·lent 〔ˈflɑkjələnt; ˈflɔkjulənt〕 *adj.* ①毛狀的；叢毛狀的。②含有柔毛的。③(昆蟲等)覆有柔毛質的。—**ly,** *adv.*

floc·cu·lus 〔ˈflɑkjələs; ˈflɔkjuləs〕 *n., pl.* **-li** 〔-laɪ; -lai〕. ①毛狀物。②〖解剖〗(小腦之)小葉。③〖天文〗譜斑(日周圍之雲狀物)。

flock**¹ 〔flɑk; flɔk〕 *n.* ①羊羣；獸羣；鳥羣。*flocks* and herds. 羊羣和牛羣；牛羊家畜。②人羣；羣衆。People came in *flocks* to see the new bridge. 人們成羣結隊地來參觀新橋。③同一教會之教徒。flower of the flock*** 家中最好的孩子。—*v.i.* 成羣結隊而行；羣集。Sheep usually *flock* together. 羊通常是成羣的。

flock² *n.* ①一叢羊毛。②塡充椅墊、枕頭的毛或棉絮。

flock·bed 〔ˈflɑk,bɛd; ˈflɔkbed〕 *n.* 「鋪有內充毛絨之床褥的床。」

flock·pa·per 〔ˈflɑk,pepɚ; ˈflɔkpeipə〕 *n.* (裱壁用之)毛面紙。

flock·y 〔ˈflɑkɪ; ˈflɔki〕 *adj.,* **flock·i·er, flock·i·est.** ①似毛叢的；羊毛狀的。②覆以羊毛或毛狀物的。

floe 〔flo; flou〕 *n.* ①海面所結之一片浮冰。②此種大片浮冰破裂而成之到處飄浮的冰塊。

flog 〔flɑg; flɔg〕 *v.t.,* **flogged, flog·ging.** ①重打；鞭笞。②〖英俗〗努力銷售。***flog a dead horse*** 徒勞；枉費心機。

flog·ging 〔ˈflɑgɪŋ; ˈflɔgiŋ〕 *n.* 重笞；「鞭打。」

‡flood 〔flʌd; flʌd〕 *n.* ①洪水；氾濫；水災。②大量之水；海；洋；湖；河。③漲潮；湧流海岸之潮水(與 ebb 相對)。The tide is at the *flood.* 潮水正漲。④奔放；狂流；流如注。a *flood* of tears. 淚流如注。a *flood* of words. 滔滔的言辭。a *flood* of people. 人潮。a *flood* of light. 一片光明。***flood plain*** (河邊之)沖積平原。***flood tide*** 正漲之潮；漲潮。***in flood*** (河流等)氾濫。***the Flood*** 聖經所述 Noah 時代的大洪水。—*v.t.* ①氾濫；淹沒。The meadows were *flooded.* 草地被洪水淹沒。②注滿；使氾濫。rivers *flooded* by heavy rainstorms. 因豪雨而氾濫的河流。③壓倒；湧滿。The rich man was *flooded* with requests for money. 那富翁被無數人請求捐款。④以巨光燈照耀。⑤燃料大量流入(汽化器)。—*v.i.* ①氾濫。②湧進。Applications *flooded* in. 申請書大量湧來。③如洪水般流瀉。Sunlight *flooded* into the room. 陽光流瀉進室內。④(馬達)汽化器內燃料太多。⑤月經過多；血崩。***flood out*** 被洪水迫使離開。

flood control 防洪。

flood·gate 〔ˈflʌd,get; ˈflʌdgeit〕 *n.* ①水門；水閘；防潮門。②控制任何流口或通道之物；出口。

flood·ing 〔ˈflʌdɪŋ; ˈflʌdiŋ〕 *n.* ①氾「濫。②血崩；產崩。」

flood·light 〔ˈflʌd,laɪt; ˈflʌdlait〕 *n.* ①

巨光燈;水銀燈。②巨光燈發出之强光。—*v.t.* 以巨光燈照耀。

flood·lit [ˈflʌdlɪt; ˈflʌdlit] *adj.* 巨光燈照耀的。

flood·mark [ˈflʌdˌmɑrk; ˈflʌdmɑːk] *n.* 滿潮標誌;高水標。

flood·wa·ter [ˈflʌdˌwɔtɚ; ˈflʌdˌwɔːtə] *n.* 洪水。

‡**floor** [flor, flɔr; flɔː, flɔə] *n.* ①地板;室內的地面。to sit on the *floor*. 坐在地上。②樓層。ground *floor*.〖英〗底層;一樓。first *floor*.〖美〗底層;一樓;〖英〗二樓。③底部。④〖英〗議會中之議員席;〖美〗發言權。⑤交易所。⑥〖俗〗(價格、量等的)最低標準。***have the floor*** (會議中)輪到發言;有發言權。***mop*** (or ***wipe***) ***the floor with***〖俚〗徹底擊敗。***take the floor*** (在會議中)發言。—*v.t.* ①鋪設地板於。The carpenters began to *floor* the room. 木匠開始鋪房間地板。②打倒。I *floored* him with a blow. 我一擊把他打倒。③〖俗〗難倒;使困惑。④〖俗〗擊敗。***be floored*** 被問題難倒。

floor·age [ˈflorɪdʒ; ˈflɔːridʒ] *n.* ①地板面積(常以平方英尺爲單位)。②做地板之材料。

floor·board [ˈflorˌbord; ˈflɔːbɔːd] *n.* ①一塊地板。②汽車底部(尤指駕駛間之底部)。—*v.t.*〖俗〗將汽車油門踏到底。

floor·cloth [ˈflorˌklɔθ; ˈflɔːklɔθ] *n.* ①鋪地板的漆布。②擦地板之拭布。

floor·er [ˈflorɚ; ˈflɔːrə] *n.* ①鋪地板的人。②擊人倒地之人或物。③〖俗〗難題;難事。

floor·ing [ˈflorɪŋ; ˈflɔːriŋ] *n.* ①地板;地板的集合稱。②做地板的材料。

floor lamp (置於地板上的)座燈;落地燈。

floor leader〖美〗議會中的政黨領袖。

floor manager ①政黨提名大會中候選人之助選員。②旅館百貨公司等, 主管每一層業務之經理。

floor plan 建築物之平面圖。

floor price 最低價格。

floor show (夜總會等中之)歌舞表演。

floor space 房間或房屋面積;建坪。

floor·walk·er [ˈflorˌwɔkɚ; ˈflɔːˌwɔːkə] *n.*〖美〗大百貨公司中之巡視人(其職務爲引導顧客、戒備竊賊、監督店員)。(亦作 **floor walker**)

floo·zy, floo·zie [ˈfluzɪ; ˈfluːzi] *n.*, *pl.* **-zies.**〖美俚〗放蕩之女子。

flop [flɑp; flɔp] *v.*, **flopped, flop·ping,** *n.*, *adv.* —*v.i.* ①跳動。②猛落。③突然改變立場〖常 over〗。④〖俗〗失敗。—*v.t.* ①笨拙地拋下。②笨拙地撲擊。③將(照相底片等)翻過來使左右易位。—*n.* ①笨重的落下;突然落下之聲音。②〖俗〗大失敗。The show was a *flop*. 這次表演是個大失敗。③=**flophouse.** —*adv.* 突然而落地。

flop·house [ˈflɑpˌhaus; ˈflɔphaus] *n.* ①〖美俚〗廉賤之旅社。②〖俗〗監獄。

flop·o·ver [ˈflɑpˌovɚ; ˈflɔpˌouvə] *n.*〖電視〗畫面不斷地上下移動(因收視之干擾或調整不當而起)。

flop·per [ˈflɑpɚ; ˈflɔpə] *n.* ①羽毛未豐的小鳥。②叛徒;變節者。③〖美俚〗露宿街頭的行乞者。

flop·py [ˈflɑpɪ; ˈflɔpi] *adj.*, **-pi·er, -pi·est.**〖俗〗勢將塌落的;鬆懈的;下垂的。

•**flo·ra** [ˈflorə, ˈflɔrə; ˈflɔːrə] *n.*, *pl.* **flo·ras, flo·rae** [ˈflori; ˈflɔːriː]. ①(某區域、某時代的)植物;植物區系(集合稱)。②某區系之植物誌。③(F-)〖羅馬神話〗花神。

flo·ral [ˈflorəl; ˈflɔːrəl] *adj.* ①花的;如花的;由花製成的。②(F-)花神(Flora)的。

Flor·ence [ˈflɔrəns, ˈflɑr-; ˈflɔrəns] *n.* 佛羅倫斯(義大利中部一城市)。

Flor·en·tine [ˈflɔrənˌtin; ˈflɔrəntain] *adj.* 義大利佛羅倫斯城的。—*n.* 佛羅倫斯人。

flo·res·cence [floˈrɛsn̩s; flɔːˈresns, floˈr-] *n.* ①開花;開花期。②全盛期;繁榮期。

flo·res·cent [floˈrɛsn̩t; flɔːˈresnt, floˈr-] *adj.* 開花的。

flo·ret [ˈflorɪt; ˈflɔːrit] *n.* ①小花。②〖植物〗(菊科植物之)小筒花。

flo·ri·cul·ture [ˈflorɪˌkʌltʃɚ; ˈflɔːrikʌltʃə] *n.* 栽培花卉;花藝。—**flo·ri·cul·tur·al,** *adj.*

flo·ri·cul·tur·ist [ˌflorɪˈkʌltʃərɪst; ˌflɔːriˈkʌltʃərist] *n.* 花卉栽培家;花匠。

flor·id [ˈflɔrɪd, ˈflɑrɪd; ˈflɔrid] *adj.* ①顏色鮮麗的; 鮮紅的。②華美的; 燦麗的。③(藝術方面的)多文飾的; 華麗的。—**ly,** *adv.*

Flor·i·da [ˈflɔrədə; ˈflɔridə] *n.* 佛羅里達(美國東南部之一州,首府爲塔拉哈西 Tallahassee)。***Florida Strait*** 佛羅里達海峽。

flo·rid·i·ty [fləˈrɪdətɪ; fləˈriditi] *n.* 鮮麗;鮮紅;華美;燦爛。

flo·rif·er·ous [floˈrɪfərəs; flɔːˈrifərəs] *adj.* 開花的; 多花的。

flor·in [ˈflɔrɪn; ˈflɔrin] *n.* ①一種英國銀幣(值二先令)。② 1252 年發行於 Florence 之一種金幣。③歐洲國家在不同時代所用的金幣或銀幣。

flo·rist [ˈflorɪst; ˈflɔrist] *n.* 花匠;經營花卉業者;花店。

flo·ris·tics [floˈrɪstɪks; flɔˈristiks] *n.* 植物地理學(植物的地理分布之研究)。

flo·ru·it [ˈflorʊɪt; ˈflɔːruit]〖拉〗*n.* 其全盛時期爲…(=he or she flourished, 某人之生死日期不詳時用之:略作 fl., flor., 例如 fl. 1736–1760)。

floss [flɔs; flɔs] *n.* ①(絲棉樹所產的)棉質纖維。②(刺繡用的)絲線。③絲線狀的東西(如玉蜀黍鬚)。④蠶繭外層的粗絲。—**er,** *n.*

floss silk (刺繡用之)散絲;粗絲;絲棉。

floss·y [ˈflɑsɪ; ˈflɔsi] *adj.*, **floss·i·er, floss·i·est.** ①絲絨的;絨毛的;似絨線的;柔軟的。②〖美俚〗艷麗的;時髦的。

flo·tage [ˈflotɪdʒ; ˈfloutidʒ] *n.* ①漂浮;浮力。②〖俗〗漂流物。③(江、河面上之)船、筏等。④(船身之)吃水線以上之部分。(亦作 **floatage**)

flo·ta·tion [floˈteʃən; flouˈteiʃən] *n.* ①漂浮。②(商業的)開創;發軔;設立。③(公司債的)發行;發售。④〖物理〗浮;浮力。⑤浮體學。⑥〖礦〗浮漂選礦法。

flotation gear (飛機在水面降落用之)浮筒起落架;飄浮裝備。

flo·ta·tive [ˈflotətɪv; ˈfloutətiv] *adj.* 浮力的;能漂浮的。(亦作 **floatative**)

flo·til·la [floˈtɪlə; flouˈtilə] *n.* 小型艦艇組成之艦隊;艇隊。

flot·sam [ˈflɑtsəm; ˈflɔtsəm] *n.* 漂浮於海上之遇難船的殘骸或其船貨(別於 jetsam)。***flotsam and jetsam*** **a.** 被發現漂浮於海上或被浪打到岸上之遇難船之殘骸或其船貨。**b.** 各種各樣的瑣事;無價值之事物。**c.** 漂流者;流浪者;游民。(亦作 **flotsan**)

flounce¹ [flauns; flauns] *n.*, *v.*, **flounced, flounc·ing.** —*n.* 衣裙上的荷葉邊裝飾。—*v.t.* 飾以荷葉邊。

flounce² *v.*, **flounced, flounc·ing,** *n.* —*v.i.* ①(因憤怒、傲慢、不耐煩等)離去;盛怒而去;拂袖而去。②急動;急轉。—*n.* ①(因憤怒或不耐煩而作之)身體扭轉;盛怒或不耐煩之舉動;拂袖。②急動;急轉。

flounc·ing ['flaʊnsɪŋ; 'flaunsiŋ] *n.* ①衣裙材料;裙褶料。②衣裙上之荷葉邊裝飾。
floun·der[1] ['flaʊndɚ; 'flaundə] *v.i.* ①掙扎; 深陷〖常 about, along, in, on, through〗。②笨拙而錯亂地說或做。—*n.* ①掙扎;輾轉。②錯亂而笨拙的行動。
floun·der[2] *n., pl.* **-ders, -der.** 比目魚類。
floun·der·ing·ly ['flaʊndərɪŋlɪ; 'flaundəriŋli] *adv.* 掙扎地;顛躓地。
‡**flour** [flaʊr; 'flauə] *n.* ①麪粉; 穀類之粉。②粉末; 碎粉。—*v.t.* ①研成粉末。②覆以麪粉;撒以粉末。
*__flour·ish__ ['flɝɪʃ; 'flʌriʃ] *v.i.* ①茂盛;興隆。Their business seemed to *flourish.* 他們的生意似乎很興隆。②盛行;享盛名。③(手臂等)揮動;擺動。④炫耀。—*v.t.* ①揮舞;搖(旗)。②炫耀;虛飾。③以顏色或花紋等裝飾。④寫花體字作裝飾。—*n.* ①搖動;揮舞。He went away with a *flourish* of his hat. 他揮帽而去。②花體字;修飾的詞藻;華麗的文體。③〖音樂〗有震顫音的花腔。④炫耀;誇示。—**er,** *n.*
flour·ish·ing ['flɝɪʃɪŋ; 'flʌriʃiŋ] *adj.* ①繁茂的。②昌盛的;興隆的。—**ly,** *adv.*
flour mill ①磨粉機。②麪粉廠。
flour·y ['flaʊrɪ; 'flauəri] *adj.* ①麪粉的;似麪粉的;麪粉狀的。②蓋有麪粉的。
flout [flaʊt; flaut] *v.t.* 嘲弄;藐視;輕視。—*v.i.* 嘲弄;侮慢。—*n.* 嘲弄;侮慢;輕視。
‡**flow** [flo; flou] *v.i.* ①流動; 流洩。The tears *flowed* from her eyes. 淚從她眼裏流出。②暢流; 流利。*flowing* verse. 流利的詩。③飄懸; 垂下。a *flowing* tie. 飄懸的領帶。④來自; 爲…之結果。Wealth *flows* from industry and economy. 財富由勤儉而來。⑤盈滿;溢出;氾濫。The river *flowed* over its banks. 這河氾濫。⑥流入;(潮)漲。The tide *flows* twice in twenty-four hours. 二十四小時中潮水兩次高漲。⑦來月經(尤指多量地)。⑧川流不息。A constant stream of persons *flowed* by. 不斷的人羣川流不息地經過。—*v.t.* ①使流。②淹沒。—*n.* ①流動;流出。a constant *flow* from a spring. 自泉中經常流出的水。②奔流; 湧流。a *flow* of angry words. 一陣怒話。③流量。④漲潮。the ebb and *flow* of the sea. 海潮的漲落。⑤潮流;溪流;流水。⑥月經。⑦氾濫。the *flows* of the Nile. 尼羅河的氾濫。
flow·age ['floɪdʒ; 'flouidʒ] *n.* ①流動;溢出;氾濫。②流出物;溢出之液體。
flow chart 流程圖; 流路表(表示公文、人員、物質、裝備等流動情況的圖表)。(亦作 **flow sheet, flowsheet**)
‡**flow·er** ['flaʊɚ; 'flauə] *n.* ①花;花卉。The trees were all in *flower.* 這些樹都在開花。②精華; 精粹。the *flower* of the nation's youth. 一個國家中最優秀的青年。③盛時; 壯年; 青春。the *flower* of life. 人生的青年時代。④(*pl.*)〖化〗華(卽昇華後所留下的微屑)。⑤花狀裝飾物。***flower of the flock*** 家中最好的孩子。***flower show*** 花展。***flowers of speech*** 文飾;修詞用語。***in flower*** 開花中。***in full flower*** 成就之最高峯。—*v.i.* ①開花。Most fruit trees *flower* in the spring. 大多數的果樹在春天開花。②旺盛。③成熟; 發展。Ideas *flower* under favorable conditions. 在良好環境下思想容易發展。—*v.t.* ①飾以花。②使開花。—**ed,** *adj.*
flow·er·bed ['flaʊɚˌbɛd; 'flauəbed] *n.* 花床;花壇。(亦作 **flower bed**)
flower children (or **people**) 嬉皮(因身上常佩花故名)。
flow·er-de-luce ['flaʊrdɪ'lus; 'flauədi'lu:s] *n.* 〖植物〗鳶尾花。
flow·er·et ['flaʊrɪt; 'flauərit] *n.* 小花。
flower girl ①結婚時持花之女童。②〖英〗賣花女。
flow·er·i·ness ['flaʊərɪnɪs; 'flauərinis] *n.* ①多花; 似花。②絢麗。
flow·er·ing ['flaʊərɪŋ; 'flauəriŋ] *adj.* 有花的; 開顯花的。—*n.* ①開花; 成熟。②飾以花。③花狀物;花飾。
flow·er·let ['flaʊrlɪt; 'flauəlit] *n.* 小花。
flower piece 花卉繪畫。
flow·er·pot ['flaʊrˌpɑt; 'flauəpɔt] *n.* 花盆;花缽。
flowers of sulfur 〖化〗硫華。
flower vase 花瓶。
*__flow·er·y__ ['flaʊrɪ, 'flaʊərɪ; 'flauəri] *adj.,* **-er·i·er, -er·i·est.** ①多花的。②絢麗的(文辭)。*flowery* language. 絢麗的文辭。
flow·ing ['floɪŋ; 'flouiŋ] *adj.* ①流動的。②如流的;流暢的。③垂下的;飄垂的。④上漲的(潮); 溢出的。—**ly,** *adv.* —**ness,** *n.*
‡**flown** [flon; floun] *v.* pp. of **fly**[1].
flow·sheet ['floˌʃit; 'flouʃi:t] *n.* =**flow chart.** (亦作 **flow sheet**)
fl. oz. fluid ounce(s). **F.L.S.** Fellow of the Linn(a)ean Society.
flu [flu; flu:] *n.* 〖俗〗=**influenza.**
flub [flʌb; flʌb] *v.,* **flubbed, flub·bing,** *n.* —*v.t.* 做錯;弄糟。—*n.* 錯誤;不佳的表現。
fluc·tu·ant ['flʌktʃuənt; 'flʌktʃuənt] *adj.* ①波動的; 不穩定的。②呈波狀移動的。
fluc·tu·ate ['flʌktʃuˌet; 'flʌktjueit] *v.,* **-at·ed, -at·ing.** —*v.i.*①上下移動;徘徊。②不規則地不斷變動。—*v.t.* 使波動;使變動。
fluc·tu·a·tion [ˌflʌktʃu'eʃən; ˌflʌktju'eiʃən] *n.* ①往復移動; 上下移動; (波浪等的)升降;徘徊。②不規則的變動; 不停的變動;波動。
flue[1] [flu; flu:] *n.* ①(煙囱的)通煙道。②(暖器之)通氣管。③風琴管。④(風琴管的)氣孔。
flue[2] *n.* 絨毛; 毛屑。
flue[3] *n.* 漁網。(亦作 **flew**)
flue[4] *n.* =**flu.**
flu·en·cy ['fluənsɪ; 'flu(:)ənsi] *n.* ①流暢;流利。②流暢的演說;流暢的寫作。
*__flu·ent__ ['fluənt; 'flu(:)ənt] *adj.* ①流利的;流暢的。②寫作或說話流利的。
flu·ent·ly ['fluəntlɪ; 'flu(:)əntli] *adv.* 流利地;流暢地。
flue·y ['fluɪ; 'flu:i] *adj.* 如絨毛的;有絨毛的。
fluff [flʌf; flʌf] *n.* ①軟毛; 柔毛; 絨毛。②鬆軟的絨毛團、塵塊、或髮球。③〖俚〗(戲劇、廣播等中) 臺詞或廣播內容的誤讀。—*v.t.* ①使鬆散;使鬆軟。②〖俚〗讀錯(臺詞、廣播內容等)。—*v.i.* ①變得鬆軟如絨毛。②〖俚〗讀錯(臺詞、廣播內容等)。③輕飄飄地行動或浮動。
fluff·y ['flʌfɪ; 'flʌfi] *adj.,* **fluff·i·er, fluff·i·est.** ①鬆軟如絨毛的。②覆有絨毛的。—**fluff·i·ness,** *n.* —**fluff·i·ly,** *adv.*
*__flu·id__ ['fluɪd; 'flu(:)id] *n.* 流體(包括液體和氣體)。—*adj.* ①流動的; 流質的。②不固定的;易改變的。—**ly,** *adv.* —**ness,** *n.*
flu·id·ics [flu'ɪdɪks; flu:'idiks] *n. pl.* (作 *sing.* 解)應用流體力學。
flu·id·i·fy [flu'ɪdəˌfaɪ; flu(:)'idifai]

v.t., **-fied, -fy·ing.** 液化。
flu·id·i·ty [fluˈɪdətɪ; flu(ː)ˈiditi] *n.* ①流動性;流質;液態。②不固定;易變(性)。
fluid ounce 一種液量單位(=1/16品脫)。
fluke[1] [fluk; fluːk] *n., v.,* **fluked, fluk·ing.** —*n.* 〖俚〗①(撞球戲等中之)僥倖的一擊;倖中。②僥倖。—*v.i.* 〖俚〗作倖中的一擊;僥倖擊中。—*v.t.* 僥倖擊中;倖得。
fluke[2] *n.* ①錨爪;錨鈎。②鯨尾的裂片。
fluke[3] *n.* ①蛭;肝蛭。②比目魚類。
fluk·(e)y [ˈflukɪ; ˈfluːki] *adj.,* **fluk·i·er, fluk·i·est.** 〖俚〗①倖中的。②不定的。
flume [flum; fluːm] *n., v.,* **flumed, flum·ing.** —*n.* ①峽溝;溪澗。②引水溝;人工水道。—*v.t.* ①由水道輸送(木材等)。②由引水溝使(河等)轉向。
flum·mer·y [ˈflʌmərɪ; ˈflʌməri] *n., pl.* **-mer·ies.** ①柔軟易食之食物;(尤指) **a.** 燕麥粥。 **b.** 膠質狀甜食。②假慇懃;諛詞。
flum·mox [ˈflʌməks; ˈflʌməks] *v.t.* 〖俚〗使狼狽;使窘困;使混亂;使失措。
flump [flʌmp; flʌmp] *n.* 猛然置放;突落;砰然聲。—*v.t. & v.i.* 猛然置放;砰然墮落。
flung [flʌŋ; flʌŋ] *v.* pt. & pp. of **fling.**
flunk [flʌŋk; flʌŋk] *v.t.* 〖美俗〗①考試(某科)不及格。②開除(不及格的學生)。③給以不及格。④使失敗。—*v.i.* 〖美俗〗①考試不及格。②放棄;撤退;(因考試不及格而)被退學〖out〗。—*n.* 〖美俗〗不及格;失敗。
flunk·ee [flʌŋˈki; flʌŋˈkiː] *n.* 因考試不及格或工作表現不佳而遭開除者。
flunk·(e)y [ˈflʌŋkɪ; ˈflʌŋki] *n., pl.* **flunk·ies, flunk·eys.** ①〖蔑〗著制服的男僕人;男僕;隨從。②諂媚者。
flunk·(e)y·ism [ˈflʌŋkɪˌɪzəm; ˈflʌŋkiizəm] *n.* 奴顏婢膝;趨炎附勢;卑鄙;諂媚。
flu·or [ˈfluɚ; ˈflu(ː)ɔː] *n.* 〖礦〗氟石。
flu·o·resce [ˌfluəˈrɛs; fluəˈres] *v.i.,* **-resced, -resc·ing.** 發螢光。
flu·o·res·ce·in [ˌfluəˈrɛsɪɪn; ˌfluːəˈresiin] *n.* 〖化〗螢光黃。
flu·o·res·cence [ˌfluəˈrɛsn̩s; ˌfluəˈresns] *n.* ①〖理化〗螢光;螢光性。②發螢光。
flu·o·res·cent [ˌfluəˈrɛsn̩t; ˌfluəˈresnt] *adj.* 螢光的。 ***fluorescent lamp*** 螢光燈;日光燈。 ***fluorescent light*** 螢光。
flu·or·ic [fluˈɔrɪk; flu(ː)ˈɔrik] *adj.* ①〖化〗氟的;氟素性的。②〖礦〗氟石的。
fluor·i·date [ˈfluərəˌdet; ˈfluərideit] *v.t.,* **-dat·ed, -dat·ing.** 在(飲水)中加少量之氟(以防兒童蛀齒)。—**fluor·i·da·tion,** *n.*
flu·o·ride [ˈfluəˌraɪd; ˈfluəraid, -rid] *n.* 氟化物。(亦作 **fluorid**)
flu·or·i·dize [ˈfluərəˌdaɪz; ˈfluərədaiz] *v.t.,* **-dized, -diz·ing.** 〖牙科〗塗氟於(牙齒以防蛀齒)。
flu·o·rin(e) [ˈfluəˌrin; ˈfluəriːn] *n.* 〖化〗氟(一種元素, 符號爲 F)。
fluor·i·nate [ˈfluərəˌnet; ˈfluəraneit] *v.t.,* **-nat·ed, -nat·ing.** ①=**fluoridate.** ②〖化〗使與氟化合。
flu·o·rite [ˈfluəˌraɪt; ˈfluərait] *n.* 〖礦〗氟石。
flu·o·ro·scope [ˈflurəˌskop; ˈfluərəskoup] *n.* 〖醫〗螢光屏;螢光鏡;X 光影屏。
flu·o·ros·co·py [ˌfluərˈɑskəpɪ; ˌfluərˈɔskəpi] *n.* 〖醫〗影屏檢查法;X 光透視法。
flu·or·spar [ˈfluɚˌspar; ˈfluəspɑː] *n.* 〖礦〗氟石(=fluorite). (亦作 **fluor spar**)
flur·ry [ˈflɝɪ; ˈflʌri] *n., pl.* **-ries,** *v.,* **-ried, -ry·ing.** —*n.* ①一陣疾風。②一陣驟雨;驟然下降的一陣雪。③突然的興奮;激動;恐慌;困惑;擾亂。—*v.t.* 使激動;使迷惑;使恐慌。
flush**[1] [flʌʃ; flʌʃ] *v.i.* ①(臉)發紅;現紅色;發紅光。As he spoke to her she *flushed* (up). 當他和她講話時,她臉發紅。②激流;泛溢。③〖植物〗發芽。—*v.t.* ①使(臉)發紅。Exercise *flushed* his face. 運動使他臉發紅。②沖洗;沖刷。③排水。④使興奮。The team was *flushed* with its first victory. 這隊因初次勝利而感興奮。—*n.* ①面紅;紅光。②激流;泛溢。③旺盛;活力。the first *flush* of youth. 青年的活力初現。④茂盛;茂生。⑤一陣熱之感覺。 ***flush toilet 抽水馬桶。
***flush**[2] *adj.* ①齊平的;同高的。②富裕的;豐足的;很多的。The rich man was always *flush* with money. 那個富翁經常帶着很多錢。③揮霍的;浪費的。④繁榮的。⑤發紅的。*flush* with health. 健康而面色紅潤。⑥直截的;正面的。⑦活力充沛的。⑧滿盈的;氾濫的。The reservoir was *flush.* 水庫裏裝滿着水。—*adv.* ①齊平地。②直截地;正面地。The fighter hit him *flush* on his nose. 那拳師正好打中他的鼻子。—*v.t.* 使齊平。
flush[3] *v.i.* 突然驚起;突然飛起。—*v.t.* ①使驚起。②〖美俗〗從隱藏處露出;挖出。—*n.* ①驚起。②受驚而突然飛起之鳥。—**er,** *n.*
flush[4] *n.* 〖牌戲〗同花;清一色。
flush gate 水庫或壩上之溢洪道、水門等排水裝置。
flus·ter [ˈflʌstɚ; ˈflʌstə] *v.t.* 使慌亂;使興奮。—*v.i.* 緊張不安;迷惘。—*n.* 慌亂;興奮。 ***be all in a fluster*** 一陣慌亂;狼狽不堪。
***flute** [flut; fluːt] *n., v.,* **flut·ed, flut·ing.** —*n.* ①笛;橫笛。to play on a *flute.* 吹笛。②長凹槽。—*v.t.* ①用笛子吹出(曲調等)。②在(柱等上面)刻成凹槽。—*v.i.* 吹笛子。
flut·ed [ˈflutɪd; ˈfluːtid] *adj.* ①有凹槽的。②(聲音)清楚而柔和的;似笛音的。
flut·ing [ˈflutɪŋ; ˈfluːtiŋ] *n.* ①吹笛;笛聲。②柱面上所刻之凹槽飾紋;凹槽。③刻凹槽。
flut·ist [ˈflutɪst; ˈfluːtist] *n.* 吹笛人。(亦作 **flautist**)
flut·ter** [ˈflʌtɚ; ˈflʌtə] *v.i.* ①擺動;飄動。②鼓翼;拍翅。The birds *fluttered* in the trees. 鳥在樹林中鼓翼而飛。③煩躁不安地動。She *fluttered* about the room anxiously. 她焦慮不安地在房內走來走去。④急跳;顫動。Her heart *fluttered.* 她的心急跳。⑤心煩意亂。⑥微弱而不規則地跳動。—*v.t.* ①使心亂。②(鳥)鼓(翼)。③使擺動。—*n.* ①擺動。②鼓翼。③煩擾;心亂。She immediately fell into a *flutter.* 她立刻變得焦躁不安。④=**flutter kick.** ***be in a flutter 心緒不寧。—**y,** *adj.*
flutter kick 游泳者膝部保持不動,僅用小腿上下擊水之泳法。
flut·y [ˈflutɪ; ˈfluːti] *adj.,* **flut·i·er, flut·i·est.** 笛聲的;似笛聲的;清亮的(聲音)。
flu·vi·al [ˈfluvɪəl; ˈfluːvjəl] *adj.* ①河的;河川的。②河流作用的;河成的。③棲於河中的;生於河中的。(亦作 **fluviatile**)
flux [flʌks; flʌks] *n.* ①流;流動。②不斷的改變;變遷。to be in a state of *flux* and reflux. 不斷地消長;不斷地變遷。③不正常的流血;溢出液;痢。④鎔接劑;助熔劑。⑤(液體、熱的)流動率;通量。—*v.t.* ①使瀉;清瀉;放血。②鎔接;鎔化。—*v.i.* ①潮漲;流出。②鎔接;鎔化。③改變。

flux·ion [ˈflʌkʃən; ˈflʌkʃən] *n.* ①流動;溢出。②不斷的變化。③排出物;溢出物。④充血。⑤〖數學〗流數。

flux·ion·al [ˈflʌkʃənl; ˈflʌkʃənl] *adj.* ①流動性的。②〖數學〗流數的。(亦作 **fluxionary**)

fluxional analysis (or **calculus**)〖數學〗流數術(卽微積分學)。

fly[1] [flaɪ; flai] *v.*, **flew** [flu; flu:], **flown** [flon; floun], **fly·ing**, *n.* —*v.i.* ①飛;空中航行。Birds *fly*. 鳥飛。②飛奔;飛馳。Time *flies*. 時間飛馳(光陰似箭)。③逃走。④隨風飄揚;飄揚。Flags were *flying* on every mast. 旗子在每根旗桿上飄揚。⑤〖棒球〗打高飛球。⑥突然而迅速之變動。The door *flew* open. 門突然開了。—*v.t.* ①使飛;放(紙鳶);懸(旗)。to *fly* a kite. 放紙鳶。②逃亡。to *fly* the country. 逃出國境。③駕駛(飛機、飛船)。④空運。We will *fly* the merchandise to Boston. 我們將把貨物空運到波士頓。⑤逃避。***fly a kite***〖俚〗滾開! ***fly at*** 猛烈攻擊。***fly high***; ***fly at high game*** 有大志;野心很大。***fly in pieces*** 摔成碎片。***fly in the face of*** 大膽反抗。***fly into a rage*** (or ***a temper***) 狂怒。***fly off*** 突然離去;逃脫。***fly off the handle*** 無朕兆而突然激動或大怒。***fly out*** a.〖棒球等〗因擊高飛球而被接殺出局。b. 突然發脾氣。***fly to arms*** 迅速武裝備戰。***let fly*** a. 射;拋;擲。b. 斥;怒斥。***make the feathers*** (or ***dust***) ***fly*** 惹起爭吵。***make the money fly*** 揮霍無度。***send a person flying*** 驅逐某人。***send things flying*** 四處亂拋東西。—*n.* ①衣服上蓋鈕釦的遮蓋。②帳篷門簾。③〖英〗輕便馬車。④〖棒球〗高飛球。⑤(*pl.*) 舞臺上之空間。⑥飛行。⑦飛行路線。⑧旗子的水平長度;與旗竿接觸之一邊相平行的旗邊。⑨=**flywheel.** ⑩=**flyleaf.** ***on the fly*** a. 匆忙地。b. 在飛行中;尙未着陸。

fly[2] *n.*, *pl.* **flies.** ①蒼蠅。②(包括蒼蠅、蚊、蚋等之) 兩翼類昆蟲。③任何有透明翼之昆蟲(如蜉蝣)。④(有翼、絲、金線等)蟲形釣魚鉤。***a fly on a wheel*** 自負之人。***break a fly on a wheel*** 殺鷄用牛刀;小題大作。***fly in the ointment***毀滅或減低他物價值的小東西;瑕疵。***no flies on***〖俚〗機警的;聰明的;不易受騙的。

fly[3] *adj.* 〖英俚〗伶俐的;活潑的;敏捷的;聰明的。

fly·a·way [ˈflaɪəˌwe; ˈflaiəwei] *adj.* ①隨風飄動的。②輕浮的;不定的。—*n.* ①逃走者。②輕浮之人。

fly ball 〖棒球〗高飛球。(亦作 **fly**)

fly·blow [ˈflaɪˌblo; ˈflaiblou] *n.*, *v.*, **-blew, -blown, -blow·ing.** —*n.* 蠅卵;蛆。—*v.t.* ①產蠅卵於(肉等)中。②使玷染;玷汚。

fly·blown [ˈflaɪˌblon; ˈflaibloun] *adj.* ①生了蛆的。②弄髒的。

fly·boat [ˈflaɪˌbot; ˈflaibout] *n.* 快艇。

fly book 釣者收藏蟲形釣魚鉤之盒。

fly·boy [ˈflaɪˌbɔɪ; ˈflaibɔi] *n.* 〖美俚〗美國空軍人員;飛行員。

fly-by [ˈflaɪˌbaɪ; ˈflaibai] *n.* =**flyover.**

fly-by-night [ˈflaɪbaɪˌnaɪt; ˈflaibaiˌnait] *adj.* ①不可信任的。②短暫的。—*n.* 〖俚〗①夜間潛逃之欠債者。②不可信任之人。

fly·catch·er [ˈflaɪˌkætʃɚ; ˈflaiˌkætʃə] *n.* ①捕食昆蟲的鳥。②誘捕蠅、蟲之植物;捕蠅草。③捕蠅器。

fly·er [ˈflaɪɚ; ˈflaiə] *n.* =**flier.**

fly-fish [ˈflaɪˌfɪʃ; ˈflaiˌfiʃ] *v.i.* 以蟲(形)餌釣魚。—**er,** *n.*

fly-fish·ing [ˈflaɪˌfɪʃɪŋ; ˈflaiˌfiʃiŋ] *n.* 以蟲(形)餌釣魚。

fly·flap [ˈflaɪˌflæp; ˈflaiˌflæp] *n.* 撲蠅器;蠅拍。

*__fly·ing__ [ˈflaɪɪŋ; ˈflaiiŋ] *adj.* ①飛的;飛行中的。②飄揚的。a *flying* banner. 飄揚的旗幟。③迅速移動的。④匆忙的。⑤飛快的。⑥匆促的;短暫的。a *flying* visit. 短時的訪問。⑦逃亡的。They pursued the *flying* enemy. 他們追趕逃走的敵人。—*n.* 飛行。

flying boat 水上飛機;飛艇。

flying bomb 自導飛彈。

flying bridge 浮橋;艦橋。

flying buttress 〖建築〗拱柱;飛支柱。

flying colors ①臨風招展的旗幟。②勝利;成功。

flying column 游擊隊;別動隊。

flying field 〖美〗小飛機場。

flying fish 飛魚。

flying fox 大蝙蝠(以果爲食)。

flying jump 急行跳高。

flying machine 飛機;飛船。

fly·ing-off [ˈflaɪɪŋˌɔf; ˈflaiiŋˌɔ:f] *n.* 〖航空〗起飛;離陸;離艦。

flying saucer (or **disk**) 飛碟。

flying squad (警察及工商界等處理緊急事件之)機動小組。

flying squadron 游擊艦隊。

flying squirrel 飛鼠。

flying start 有力之開始。

fly·leaf [ˈflaɪˌlif; ˈflaili:f] *n.*, *pl.* **-leaves.** 蝴蝶頁(書前或書後的空白頁)。

fly·man [ˈflaɪmən; ˈflaimən] *n.*, *pl.* **-men.** ①〖英〗輕便馬車之御者。②〖戲劇〗藏於舞臺上空管理布景的人。

fly net 防蠅網(披於馬身者); 防蠅、蚊等之窗紗、網帳等。

fly·o·ver [ˈflaɪˌovɚ; ˈflaiˌouvə] *n.* ①慶典時飛機編隊低空飛行。②轟炸機從假想目標上空之通過。③〖英〗公路上之陸橋。

fly·pa·per [ˈflaɪˌpepɚ; ˈflaiˌpeipə] *n.* 捕蠅紙。

fly·past [ˈflaɪˌpæst; ˈflaipɑ:st] *n.* (閱兵之)空中分列式。

fly sheet ①廣告傳單;傳單。②(摺疊成小册子之)用法說明單。

fly·speck [ˈflaɪˌspɛk; ˈflaispek] *n.* ①蠅糞斑。②小斑;汚點。—*v.t.* 汚以小斑。

fly swatter 蒼蠅拍。

flyte [flaɪt; flait] *v.*, **flyt·ed, flyt·ing,** *n.* =**flite.**

fly·trap [ˈflaɪˌtræp; ˈflaitræp] *n.* ①捕蠅器。②捕蠅草。

fly·way [ˈflaɪˌwe; ˈflaiwei] *n.* 候鳥遷棲所經之路徑。

fly·weight [ˈflaɪˌwet; ˈflaiweit] *n.* 蠅量級之鬥拳者(體重在112磅以下)。

fly·wheel [ˈflaɪˌhwil; ˈflaiwi:l] *n.* 〖機械〗(控制速度的)整速輪;飛輪。

FM frequency modulation. 調頻。

F.M. ①〖美軍〗 field manual. ②field marshal. ③frequency modulation. ④Foreign Mission. **Fm** 化學元素 fermium 之符號。 **fm.** ①fathom. ②from. **f.m.** 〖處方〗做成混合劑。 **F.M.S.** Federated Malay States. **fn.** footnote.

F number 〖攝影〗焦距比數。

fo. folio. **F.O.** ①field officer. ②陸軍校級軍官(亦作 **f.o.**)。 ③Foreign Office. 外交部。 **FOA, F.O.A.** Foreign Operations Administration.

foal [fol; foul] *n.* 馬仔;小馬;驢仔;小驢。***in*** (or ***with***) ***foal*** (雌馬) 懷孕。—*v.t.* 產

(小馬)。—*v.i.* (馬、驢等)生仔。

foal·y [ˈfolɪ; ˈfouli] *adj.* (雌馬)懷孕的。

foam** [fom; foum] *n.* ①水沫; 泡沫。The *foam* is made by waves breaking on the shore. 泡沫是由海浪衝擊岸上所造成的。②〖詩〗海。—*v.i.* 起泡;(口)流泡沫。a *foaming* glass of beer. 一杯起滿泡沫的啤酒。—*v.t.* 使起泡沫。foam at the mouth*** 暴怒;震怒。

foam rubber 泡沫乳膠;海綿乳膠。

foam·y [ˈfomɪ; ˈfoumi] *adj.*, **foam·i·er, foam·i·est.** ①覆有泡沫的;起泡沫的。②由泡沫所成的。③如泡沫的。—**foam·i·ly,** *adv.*

fob[1] [fɑb; fɔb] *n.* ①(男褲上之)錶袋。②露於錶袋外的短錶鍊。③此等錶鍊端之飾物。

fob[2] *v.t.*, **fobbed, fob·bing.** 欺騙;混騙。***fob off*** 騙人;以騙術脫手(贋品或劣貨)。

f.o.b., F.O.B. free on board.

fo·cal [ˈfokl̩; ˈfoukəl] *adj.* 焦點的;與焦點有關的。

fo·cal·ize [ˈfokl̩ˌaɪz; ˈfoukəlaiz] *v.t.* & *v.i.*, **-ized, -iz·ing.** ①使集於焦點;集於一點。②〖醫〗限局。—**fo·cal·i·za·tion,** *n.*

focal plane 〖光〗焦平面。

focal point 焦點。

fo'c's'le [ˈfoksl̩, ˈfouksl] *n.* =**forecastle.**

fo·cus** [ˈfokəs; ˈfoukəs] *n.*, *pl.* **-cus·es** or **-ci** [-saɪ; -sai], *v.*, **-cused, -cus·ing.** —*n.* ①〖物理〗焦點。②焦距。A near-sighted eye has a shorter *focus* than a normal eye. 一隻近視眼比一隻正常眼睛有較短的焦距。③配光; 對光。④(問題等之) 中心點; 焦點。a *focus* of trouble between nations. 國際糾紛的焦點。⑤震央。⑥〖醫〗病竈。in focus*** 清晰。***out of focus*** 模糊不清。—*v.t.* ①集中於焦點;集成焦點。②調節(鏡頭、眼睛等); 定…的焦點。to *focus* the lens of a microscope. 定顯微鏡的焦點。③集中。to *focus* one's attention on... 集中注意力於…之上。—*v.i.* 集中於焦點;調節眼睛。

***fod·der** [ˈfɑdɚ; ˈfɔdə] *n.* ①秣;馬(牛)料; 草料。②無價值之人。—*v.t.* 喂以草料。

***foe** [fo; fou] *n.* ①仇敵; 敵人。②敵手;對手。a political *foe.* 政敵。③反對者。a *foe* to progress. 阻止進步者。④有害物。

foehn [fen, fœn; fein, fœn] *n.* 〖氣象〗焚風(吹入山谷之乾燥熱風)。

foe·man [ˈfomən; ˈfoumən] *n.*, *pl.* **-men.** 〖古,詩〗敵兵;敵人。

foe·tal [ˈfitl̩; ˈfiːtl] *adj.* =**fetal.**

foe·ti·cide [ˈfitəˌsaɪd; ˈfiːtisaid] *n.* =**feticide.**

foe·tus [ˈfitəs; ˈfiːtəs] *n.* 胎;胎兒。

***fog**[1] [fɑg, fɔg; fɔg] *n.*, *v.*, **fogged, fog·ging.** —*n.* ①霧。*Fog* is the sailor's greatest enemy. 霧是水手最大的敵人。②困惑;迷惑。He was in a *fog.* 他如墜五里霧中。③(照相底片上)不清楚之處;朦朧。—*v.t.* ①(霧)籠罩;使朦朧。Something *fogged* our photographs. 我們的照片很模糊。②使困惑。③〖美俚〗快而有力地投(球)。—*v.i.* ①爲霧所籠罩。②〖照相〗變得模糊。

fog[2] *n.*, *v.*, **fogged, fog·ging.** —*n.* ①刈後再生之草。②(冬季原野上之)枯草。③〖方〗苔。—*v.t.* ①讓草高高地立在(地上)。②將牛羊等放在割後重長之草地上吃草。

fog bank (由遠處望見的)霧層。

fog·bound [ˈfɑgˌbaund; ˈfɔgbaund] *adj.* ①〖航海〗爲濃霧所阻而無法航行的(船)。②爲濃霧所包圍的;籠罩着濃霧的。

fog·bow [ˈfɑgˌbo; ˈfɔgbou] *n.* 霧虹。

fo·gey [ˈfogɪ; ˈfougi] *n.*, *pl.* **-geys.** =**fogy.**

***fog·gy** [ˈfɑgɪ, ˈfɔgɪ; ˈfɔgi] *adj.*, **-gi·er, -gi·est.** ①有濃霧的;霧深的。a *foggy* night 霧夜。②模糊的; 朦朧的; 困惑的。He has only a *foggy* idea of it. 他對那件事只有模糊的觀念。—**fog·gi·ly,** *adv.* —**fog·gi·ness,** *n.*

fog·horn [ˈfɑgˌhɔrn; ˈfɔghɔːn] *n.* ①霧號(在霧中警告船隻的號角)。②粗嗄的聲音。

fo·gle [ˈfogəl; ˈfougəl] *n.* 〖俚〗絲質手帕或圍巾。

fog-sig·nal [ˈfɑgˌsɪgnl̩; ˈfɔgˌsignl] *n.* 〖英〗起霧警告信號(置於鐵軌上者)。

fo·gy [ˈfogɪ; ˈfougi] *n.*, *pl.* **-gies.** 守舊者; 老頑固; 落伍者 (前面常用 old 形容)。—**ish,** *adj.* 「*n.* 守舊主義;古板行爲。

fo·gy·ism [ˈfogɪˌɪzəm; ˈfougiizəm]

föhn [fen; fein] 〖德〗 *n.* =**foehn.**

foi·ble [ˈfɔɪbl̩; ˈfɔibl] *n.* ①弱點;小缺點。②劍身自中央至尖端之部分。

foil[1] [fɔɪl; fɔil] *v.t.* 打敗;阻止。

***foil**[2] *n.* ①箔。②烘托; 襯托。The green pillow was a *foil* for Jenny's red hair. 綠色枕頭正好是珍妮的紅髮的烘托。③陪襯之下使他人相得益彰者。④〖建築〗葉形飾。⑤襯托在寶石下的薄金屬片。⑥氣墊船。—*v.t.* ①以箔包裹或襯托。②烘托;襯托。

foil[3] *n.* ①鈍頭劍 (練習劍術時用)。②(*pl.*) 鈍頭劍劍術。「飾物的。

foiled [fɔɪld; fɔild] *adj.* 〖建築〗有葉狀

foist [fɔɪst; fɔist] *v.t.* ①蒙騙;騙售;混騙。②偷偷插入;混入。

fol. ①folio. ②followed. ③following. ④〖處方〗一葉 (=a leaf).

:fold [fold; fould] *v.t.* ①摺疊。He *folded* the paper in two and put it away. 他把紙對摺,然後放到一邊。②抱 (膀臂)。③擁抱;摟抱;緊抱。He *folded* the child in his arms. 他緊抱這孩子在懷中。④籠罩; 包圍。London was *folded* in fog. 倫敦爲濃霧所籠罩。⑤關(羊)入欄。The sheep are *folded* for the night. 羊被關入欄中過夜。⑥包起。to *fold* something in paper. 用紙將某物包起。⑦終止;結束。⑧(打紙牌時)將牌面朝下放在桌上表示不參加。***fold down*** 將 (書頁)摺起。***fold up*** **a.** 摺疊起來。**b.** 歇業;關閉。**c.** 崩潰。—*v.i.* ①摺疊。②(戲劇等)因生意不好而停止演出。The show will *fold* after Saturday night's performance. 星期六晚間演出後該劇就要停止演出了。③將牌面朝下放在桌上表示不參加。—*n.* ①摺層; 摺縫。She kept her handkerchief in a *fold* of her dress. 她把手帕放於衣服的摺層中。②羊欄。③同一欄中之羊羣。④教會; 一個教會的教徒。⑤山谷;山坳。⑥蛇或繩之一捲。***return to the fold*** 回老家;回歸教會。

-fold 〖字尾〗表"倍;重"之義。「**faltboat.**

fold·boat [ˈfoldˌbot; ˈfouldbout] *n.* =

fold·er [ˈfoldɚ; ˈfouldə] *n.* ①摺疊者; 摺疊器。②硬紙夾。③摺疊的小冊子。

fol·de·rol [ˈfɑldəˌrɑl; ˈfɔldərɔl] *n.* =**falderal.**

fold·ing[1] [ˈfoldɪŋ; ˈfouldiŋ] *n.* 摺疊;摺痕。—*adj.* 摺疊的; 有摺痕的。***a folding bed*** 可摺合之床。***a folding chair*** 可摺合之椅子。***a folding fan*** 摺扇。***a folding screen*** 屏風。***a folding stool*** 可摺合之凳子。***folding doors*** 疊門;雙扇門。

fold·ing² *n.* ①(於墾殖地等)圈養羊羣。②羊圈之堆肥。

fo·li·a·ceous 〔ˌfolɪ'eʃəs; ˌfouli'eiʃəs〕 *adj.* ①葉的; 葉狀的。②有葉的; 有葉狀器官的。③由葉狀薄層組成的(如某些之岩石)。

***fo·li·age** 〔'folɪɪdʒ; 'fouliidʒ〕 *n.* ①樹或植物的葉子之集合稱。*foliage* plant. 以樹葉供人觀賞的植物。②葉或花形飾物。

fo·li·ar 〔'folɪə; 'fouliə〕 *adj.* 葉的; 似葉的;葉質的;葉狀的。

fo·li·ate 〔*adj.* 'folɪɪt; 'fouliit *v.* 'folɪˌet; 'foulieit〕 *adj., v.*, **-at·ed, -at·ing.** —*adj.* ①有葉的; 覆有葉的。②葉狀的。③有葉狀裝飾的。 —*v.i.* ①生葉; 發葉。②分成薄片。—*v.t.* ①打成薄片; 做成箔。②〖建築〗飾以葉形飾。③敷金屬箔爲底。④將(書)葉編號。

fo·li·a·tion 〔ˌfolɪ'eʃən; ˌfouli'eiʃən〕 *n.* ①生葉;發葉。②〖建築〗花葉形裝飾。③葉(集合稱)。④製箔; 敷箔。⑤(書籍等之)葉數或其編號。⑥(礦物、岩石等之)剝離成層; 剝理。⑦將玻璃後面塗水銀使成鏡子。

fo·lic acid 〔'folɪk～; 'foulik～〕〖生化〗葉酸;維他命 Bc.

fo·li·o 〔'folɪˌo; 'fouliou〕 *n., pl.* **-li·os,** *adj., v.* —*n.* ①(書本等之)對開張;對摺紙(成兩葉或四頁者)。②對摺本; 對開本(高度超過十一英寸者)。③〖印刷〗頁碼。④(單面標頁碼的書以或原稿之)一頁。⑤〖簿記〗總帳中左右相對兩頁記一頁碼的一頁。***in folio*** 最大開本的。—*adj.* 最大開本的; 對摺本的。—*v.t.* 記頁碼於(一頁上)。

fo·li·ole 〔'folɪˌol;'foulioul〕 *n.* ①〖植物〗小葉。②〖動物〗小葉狀器官。

fo·li·ose 〔'folɪos;'foulious〕 *adj.* 〖植物〗葉子茂盛的;多葉的。(亦作 **folious**)

fo·li·um 〔'folɪəm; 'fouliəm〕 *n., pl.* **-li·a** 〔-lɪə; -liə〕, **-li·ums.** ①(岩石之) 薄層。②張;葉。

‡folk 〔fok; fouk〕 *n., pl.* **folk** or **folks,** *adj.* —*n.* ①(常 *pl.*)(作 *pl.* 解)人們; 世人。*Folks* say there wasn't much rain last summer. 人們說去年夏天雨水不太多。②民族;種族。③(*pl.*) 〖俗〗家人; (某人之)父母。the old *folks* at home. 家中的老人。the young *folks.* 兒女;孩子們。④(常 *pl.*)(作 *pl.* 解) 某一階層或某一類的人。town *folk.* 城裏人。poor *folks.* 窮人。***just folks***〖俗〗樸質無華的人; 古道熱腸的人。—*adj.* 民間的; 民俗的;相傳的。

folk custom 民習;民俗。

folk dance 民間舞;土風舞。

folk etymology ①文字之通俗變化(例如 cole slaw 變爲 cold slaw)。②通俗而不準確之字源。(亦作 **popular etymology**)

folk·lore 〔'fokˌlor; 'fouk-lɔː〕 *n.* ①民間傳說;民俗。②民俗學。

folk music 民間音樂。

folk-rock 〔'fokˌrɑk;'fouk-rɔk〕 *n.* 帶民歌色彩的搖滾樂曲。

folk song 民歌;民謠。

folk·sy 〔'foksɪ; 'fouksi〕 *adj.*, **-si·er, -si·est.** 〖美俗〗①民間的; 人民的。②友善的; 好交際的; 隨便的。—**folk·si·ly,** *adv.* —**folk·si·ness,** *n.*

folk tale 民間故事; 民間傳說。(亦作 **folk story**)

folk·way 〔'fokˌwe; 'foukwei〕 *n.* 傳統之習俗;民風。

fol·li·cle 〔'fɑlɪkl; 'fɔlikl〕 *n.* ①〖植物〗蓇葖。②〖解剖〗濾泡;濾囊。

fol·lic·u·lar 〔fə'lɪkjələ; fə'likjulə〕 *adj.* ①〖植物〗蓇葖的。②〖解剖〗濾泡的; 濾囊的;毛囊的。③〖醫〗起自濾泡的;小泡性的。

‡fol·low 〔'fɑlo; 'fɔlou〕 *v.t.* ①跟隨;跟在後。Night *follows* day. 夜繼晝之後。②由…而起;爲…之結果。Misery *follows* war. 窮困由戰爭而起。③沿行; 循(路)。to *follow* a road. 沿路而行。④從事(某種職業); 經營。What profession do you *follow?* 你從事何種職業?⑤能聽懂;跟得上。to *follow* a speech. 聽懂演說。⑥遵循; 仿效; 合於。to *follow* the directions (teachings) of ... 遵從…的指導(教訓)。⑦注視;注意;看清。⑧追趕。The dog *followed* the fox. 獵狗追趕狐狸。⑨繼承。He will *follow* his father as manager of the business. 他將繼承其父爲這公司經理。⑩爭取; 追求。He *follows* fame. 他求名。⑪追隨;服從。We *follow* our president. 我們追隨總統。—*v.i.* ①跟隨。Go on ahead and I'll *follow.* 你在前面走,我就跟來。②密切注意;發生興趣。French politics are too complicated for me to *follow.* 法國政治太複雜,我弄不清楚。③繼之而來。If you eat too much candy, a stomach ache will *follow.* 如果你吃太多糖果,胃痛會繼之而生。④力求上進。***as follows*** 如下。He wrote *as follows.* 他所寫如下。***follow one's bent*** 隨自己的天性。***follow out (a plan, etc.)*** 徹底實行(計畫等)。***follow suit*** 照樣行事。***follow the example of...*** 仿照…的榜樣。***follow the fashion*** 合於時尚;趕時髦。***follow through*** 貫徹到底。***follow (something) up*** **a.** 乘;趁。**b.** 貫徹到底。**c.** 緊隨不捨。—*n.* 追隨;跟蹤。

***fol·low·er** 〔'fɑloə; 'fɔlouə〕 *n.* ①跟隨者。②隨員。③門徒; 信徒。④夥伴。Robin Hood and his *followers.* 羅賓漢及其夥伴們。⑤僕人。⑥〖俗〗追求女人者。

‡fol·low·ing 〔'fɑləwɪŋ; 'fɔlouiŋ〕 *n.* 擁護者;崇拜者;徒衆。The man has a large *following.* 此人擁有大批的黨羽。***the following*** 如下; 下列。I need *the following:* eggs, sugar, butter, and milk. 我需要下列各物: 蛋、糖、牛油及牛奶。—*adj.* 下列的; 其次的。the *following* sentences. 下列的句子。the *following* day. 次日。—*prep.* 隨後;接着。*Following* the lecture tea served. 演講後茶會開始。

fol·low-on 〔'fɑloˌɑn; 'fɔlou'ɔn〕 *n.* 隨後發生之事物; 繼任者。—*adj.* 後繼的; 隨後來的。

follow shot 〖電影,電視〗隨事物之移動所攝取之鏡頭。

fol·low-the-lead·er 〔ˌfɑloðə'lidə; ˌfɔlouðə'liːdə〕 *n.* 一種兒童遊戲, 參加者須模仿領導人之一舉一動。 —*adj.* 模仿的。(亦作 **follow-my-leader**)

fol·low-through 〔'fɑloˌθru;'fɔlou-'θruː〕 *n.* ①〖運動〗完成動作(如擊球,於擊中球後之繼續動作)。②發展或趨勢等之繼續。

fol·low-up 〔'fɑloˌʌp, 'fɑləˌwʌp; 'fɔ-louʌp〕 *n.* ①緊接之事件;接連行動;緊隨。②對可能之顧客再度訪問或寫信以推銷貨品。③〖新聞〗進一步之報導; 主要消息之花邊新聞。—*adj.* 續行的;再度的。

***fol·ly** 〔'fɑlɪ; 'fɔli〕 *n., pl.* **-lies.** ①愚笨;愚蠢。It is *folly* to eat too much. 吃得過多乃是愚蠢。②愚行;荒唐事。"You are too old for such *follies,*" said Mother. 母親說,"你這樣大了,不應再做這種荒唐事"。③吃虧上當之事。④(*pl.*)一種輕鬆歌舞劇。

fo·ment 〔fo'mɛnt; fou'ment〕 *v.t.* ①

煽動。②以熱水洗；以熱布敷(傷口、創口、痛處)。—**a·tion,** —**er,** *n.*

*__fond__ [fand; fɔnd] *adj.* ①愛；嗜好；喜歡(恆用於 be fond of 一片語中)。He is very *fond* of his mother. 他非常愛他的母親。②愛憐的；慈愛的。③癡愛的；溺愛的。④渴望的。

fon·dant ['fandənt; 'fɔndənt] *n.* 一種軟糖(尤指用作其他糖果之糖心者)。

fon·dle ['fandl; 'fɔndl] *v.,* **fon·dled, fon·dling.** —*v.t.* 撫弄；撫愛。—*v.i.* (以態度、言語、撫摸)表示撫愛。—**fon·dler,** *n.*

fond·ling ['fandlıŋ; 'fɔndliŋ] *n.* ①被鍾愛、或溺愛之人或動物。②〖英方〗笨瓜。

*__fond·ly__ ['fandlı; 'fɔndli] *adv.* ①喜愛地；情深地。②輕信地；天眞地。He *fondly* believed that all man were his friends. 他輕信所有的人都是他的朋友。③〖古〗愚蠢地。

*__fond·ness__ ['fandnıs; 'fɔndnis, 'fɔnnis] *n.* 溺愛；鍾愛；嗜好。to have a *fondness* for.... 嗜好…。

fon·du ['fandu; 'fɔndu:] *adj., n., pl.* **-dus.** —*adj.* ①混合的；變柔的。②溶解的。—*n.* 芭蕾舞者着力腿之徐徐彎曲。

fon·due ['fandu; 'fɔndu:] *n.* 一種乾酪、鷄蛋等調製之食品。—*adj.* (亦作 **fondu**) 溶解的。

font [fant; fɔnt] *n.* ①〖宗教〗盛聖水之洗禮盆；聖水盆。②〖古〗泉；泉源。③來源；原始；開始。④(英亦作 **fount**) 一套字體相同之活字。

fon·tal ['fantl; 'fɔntl] *adj.* 泉水的；來源的；泉源的。

fon·ta·nel(le) [ˌfantə'nɛl; ˌfɔntə'nel] *n.* ①〖解剖〗顖門；囟。②〖廢〗排膿口。

‡**food** [fud; fu:d] *n.* ①食物；食料。We should soon die without *food* and drink. 若沒有食物和飲料，我們不久就會死的。②養料；滋養品。Milk is a valuable *food.* 牛奶是一種有價值的滋養品。③精神食糧；材料；資料。*food* for thought.值得思考之事。***food controller*** 戰爭時統制食糧的官員。

food stamp 美國聯邦政府發給貧民之糧票。

food·stuff ['fudˌstʌf; 'fu:dstʌf] *n.* 食品；食料；糧食。

‡**fool**[1] [ful; fu:l] *n.* ①愚人；獃子。That man is a *fool.* 那人是一個愚人。②(昔日國王豢養的)弄臣；小丑。③受騙者。④縱情者(前面常用現在分詞)。***All Fool's Day*** 萬愚節(四月一日)。***be a fool for one's pains*** 做徒勞無功的事。***be nobody's fool*** 機智的；聰明的。***be no fool*** 不傻；聰明。***make a fool of*** 愚弄；欺騙。***play*** (or ***act***) ***the fool*** 裝傻；詼諧。—*v.i.* ①戲謔；開玩笑。It's time for you to stop *fooling.* 是你停止開玩笑的時候了。②愚笨地玩弄。③無所事事；虛擲光陰。Stop *fooling* about! 不要再浪費光陰。—*v.t.* 愚弄；欺騙。You can't *fool* me any longer. 你再也不能欺騙我了。***fool around*** 〖美俗〗a. 優遊；嬉戲；不務正業；虛度光陰。b. 調戲。***fool away*** 〖俗〗浪費；虛擲。***fool with*** 〖俗〗笨拙地把玩；不小心地玩弄。—*adj.* 〖俗〗=**foolish; silly.**

fool[2] *n.* 果醬及乳油所製之食品。

fool duck 〖美〗紅鴨。

fool·er·y ['fulərı; 'fu:ləri] *n., pl.* **-er·ies.** 愚蠢的言行或想法。

fool·har·dy ['fulˌhardı; 'fu:lˌha:di] *adj.,* **-di·er, -di·est.** 有勇無謀的；魯莽的。—**fool·har·di·ly,** *adv.* —**fool·har·di·ness,** *n.*

fool hen 〖美〗松鷄。

*__fool·ish__ ['fulıʃ; 'fu:liʃ] *adj.* 愚蠢的；不智的；可笑的。How *foolish!* 多麼愚蠢啊！—**ly,** *adv.* —**ness,** *n.*

fool·proof ['ful'pruf; 'fu:l-pru:f] *adj.* ①愚人也能的。②極簡單的。③萬無一失的。

fools·cap ['fulzˌkæp; 'fu:lzkæp] *n.* ①(丑角所戴的)錐形帽(亦作 **fool's cap**)。②大頁紙(寬爲12或13½英寸，長15到17英寸)。

fool's gold 鐵礦或黃銅礦。

fool's paradise 幻想的幸福；空想。

‡**foot** [fut; fut] *n., pl.* **feet** [fit; fi:t], *v.* —*n.* ①足；脚。A dog has four *feet.* 一隻狗有四足。②呎；英尺(=12 inches)。③底部；基部。④(鞋、襪的)足部。⑤步兵。horse and *foot.* 騎兵與步兵。⑥〖詩〗音步。⑦步行。swift of *foot.* 走路很快。⑧床或墳墓之下端。Put the blanket at the *foot* of the bed. 將毯子放在床上的脚頭。⑨一系列之最後一個。⑩(*pl.*) a. 渣滓；沉澱物。b. 戲臺下方的照明燈。(***go***) ***at a foot's pace*** 用步行速度(走路)；常步。***be on one's feet*** a. 站起(講演)。b. 病愈；復元。c. 經濟獨立；自立。***carry*** (***a person***) ***off his feet*** a. 將某人捲(擧)起(如强風)。b. 使興奮；使狂喜；使雀躍；使歡騰。***fall*** (or ***land***) ***on one's feet*** 幸運；運道好。After he was fired, he *fell on his feet* and found a better job. 他被開革後，運氣很好，找到一分更好的工作。***feet first*** a. 脚先。We plunged into the river *feet first.* 我們跳進河中，脚先下水。b. (亦作 **feet foremost**) 死了。***get off on the right*** (or ***wrong***) ***foot*** 開始進行順利(不順利)。***keep one's feet*** 不跌倒(如行走於冰上時)。***on foot*** a. 徒步；步行。b. 進行中。***put one's best foot forward*** a. 盡最大努力。b. 給人良好印象。c. 儘量快走或快跑。***put one's foot down*** a. 下決心並堅定地去做。b. 反對。***put one's foot in*** (or ***into***) ***it*** 多管閒事惹出麻煩；犯難堪的錯誤。***put one's foot in one's mouth*** =**put one's foot in** (*or* **into**) **it.** ***set foot on*** (or ***in***) 踏上；進入(用在否定句中)。Never *set foot on* our property again! 永遠不要再踏上我們的土地。***set on foot*** 開始；發動。***set*** (***a person or thing***) ***on his*** (or ***its***) ***feet*** 使(某人或物)自立。***sit at one's feet*** 受業於某人；景仰效法某人。***stand on one's own feet*** 自食其力；自力；獨立。***under foot*** a. 阻礙；妨礙。b. 在掌握中；屈服。***with one foot in the grave*** 垂死。—*v.i.* ①步行(常與 it 連用)。The last train has gone, and we'll have to *foot* it. 末班火車已開，我們只好步行了。②跳舞。③(船等)移動。④結算〖up〗。The various items *foot* up to $50. 這些數目加起來總共五十元。—*v.t.* ①步行。②做(襪子的)足部。③加；結算。④〖俗〗付(帳)。⑤跳舞。⑥以爪捕捉(如鷹)。⑦建立。***foot up*** a. 累積。b. 加；結算。The waiter *footed up* our bill. 侍者替我們算帳。

foot·age ['futıdʒ; 'futidʒ] *n.* ①英尺數；以英尺計算之長度。②影片之連續鏡頭。

foot-and-mouth disease ['futn̩'mauθ~; ˌfutn'mauθ~] 口蹄疫；口蹄病(牛、羊、豬等的傳染病)。

*__foot·ball__ ['futˌbɔl; 'futbɔ:l] *n.* ①橄欖球運動；橄欖球戲。Do you like playing *football?* 你喜歡玩橄欖球嗎？②橄欖球。③〖英〗=**soccer.**④〖英〗每隊十五人之橄欖球戲。

foot·ball·er ['futˌbɔlɚ; 'futˌbɔ:lə] *n.* 足球隊員；橄欖球隊員。(亦作 **footballist**)

foot·bath ['futˌbæθ; 'futba:θ] *n.* 濯足；

濯足具;洗脚盆。

foot-bind·ing ['fʊt,baɪndɪŋ; 'fut-,baindiŋ] *n.* 中國古時婦女之纏足。

foot·board ['fʊt,bord; 'futbɔːd] *n.* ①踏足板;踏臺。②床之靠足一端的豎板。

foot·boy ['fʊt,bɔɪ; 'futbɔi] *n.* 小僕;小廝。

foot brake 脚刹車。

foot·bridge ['fʊt,brɪdʒ; 'futbridʒ] *n.* (只供人行,不准車輛通行之)小橋;窄橋。

foot-can·dle ['fʊt'kændl; 'fut'kændl] *n.* 呎燭光(標準燭光一英尺距離之照度,爲照度單位)。

foot·cloth ['fʊt,klɔθ; 'futklɔθ] *n., pl.* **-cloths.** ①地氈。②馬之披衫。

foot·ed ['fʊtɪd;'futid] *adj.* 有…脚的(常用於組成複合字,如: four-*footed* animal).

foot·er ['fʊtɚ; 'futə] *n.* ①步行者;徒步者。②有某高度或長度之人或物(常用於組成複合字,如:six-*footer*).

foot·fall ['fʊt,fɔl; 'futfɔːl] *n.* 脚步;脚步聲。

foot fault 〖網球〗足部失誤(發球時踩線、越線或躍起之犯規)。

foot·gear ['fʊt,gɪr; 'futgiə] *n.* 覆足之物(如鞋、襪等)。

foot·hill ['fʊt,hɪl; 'futhil] *n.* 大山或大山脈山麓之小丘。

foot·hold ['fʊt,hold; 'futhould] *n.* ①着足點;立足點。②鞏固的立足點;根據地。

***foot·ing** ['fʊtɪŋ; 'futiŋ] *n.* ①立穩;立穩脚跟。He lost his *footing* and fell. 他失足而跌倒。②立足點。③地位;關係;狀態。The army is on a war *footing*. 軍隊在備戰狀態中。④結算;加。⑤結算之總數。⑥足部之動作;走路;跳舞。⑦入會費;執業費。⑧鞋或襪之足部。⑨編織襪之足部。

foot·le ['fʊtl; 'fuːtl] *v.*, **-led, -ling,** *n., adj.* —*v.i.* 〖俚〗說傻話;作傻事。—*n.* 〖俚〗愚蠢而無意義之談;愚行。—*adj.* 〖俚〗愚蠢的。

foot·less ['fʊtlɪs; 'futlis] *adj.* ①無足的。②無基礎的;無實質的。③〖俗〗笨拙的;無效率的。④〖詩〗人跡未到的。

foot·lights ['fʊt,laɪts; 'futlaits] *n. pl.* 舞臺上的脚燈。***appear before the footlights*** 登臺獻藝。***be behind the footlights*** 在臺下(觀劇)。***smell of the footlights*** 演員的氣味。***the footlights*** 演戲之職業;舞臺;劇院。

foot·ling ['fʊtlɪŋ; 'fuːtliŋ] *adj.* 〖俗〗愚蠢的;傻的。

foot·lock·er ['fʊt,lɑkɚ; 'fut,lɔkə] *n.* 士兵存放私人物件之小箱。

foot-loose ['fʊt,lus; 'futluːs] *adj.* 自由自在的。

foot·man ['fʊtmən; 'futmən] *n., pl.* **-men.** ①侍者;閽者;隨從。②步兵。③火爐前烘物之金屬架。

foot·mark ['fʊt,mɑrk; 'futmɑːk] *n.* 脚印;足跡。

foot·note ['fʊt,not; 'futnout] *n., v.,* **-not·ed, -not·ing.** —*n.* 註脚;附註(印在頁底的註解)。—*v.t.* 加註脚。

foot·pace ['fʊt,pes; 'futpeis] *n.* ①常步;徐步。②臺階;高臺。③樓梯平臺。

foot·pad ['fʊt,pæd; 'futpæd] *n.* (大道上的)徒步刼盜(別於 highwayman 騎馬刼盜)。

foot passenger 步行者。

foot·path ['fʊt,pæθ; 'futpɑːθ] *n.* 小徑;小路;步行道。

foot·plate ['fʊt,plet; 'futpleit] *n.* ①馬車踏脚板。②火車司機及司爐所立之平臺。

foot-pound ['fʊt'paʊnd; 'fut'paund] *n.* 〖物理〗呎磅(能之單位,使一磅重之物升高一英尺所需之能)。

foot·print ['fʊt,prɪnt; 'futprint] *n.* 足跡;脚印。—*v.t.* 在…上印上脚印。

foot race 競走;賽跑。

foot·rest ['fʊt,rɛst; 'fut-rest] *n.* 脚凳。

foot·rope ['fʊt,rop;'fut-roup] *n.* 〖航海〗①帆之下緣索。②捲帆時水手立足之纜索。

foot rule 十二英寸長之尺。

foot·sie ['fʊtsi; 'futsiː] *n.* 〖俗〗調戲;偷情。***play footsie with*** a. 調戲;偷情。b. (尤指政治上之)秘密合作或結盟。

foot soldier 步兵。

foot·sore ['fʊt,sor; 'futsɔː] *adj.* 脚痛的(尤指因走路過多而致的)。

foot·stalk ['fʊt,stɔk; 'futstɔːk] *n.* ①〖植物〗葉柄;毛梗。②〖動物〗肉莖。

foot·step** ['fʊt,stɛp; 'futstep] *n.* ①脚步。②脚步聲。③步度。④足跡。⑤階梯。follow in one's footsteps*** 效法某人。

foot·stone ['fʊt,ston; 'futstoun] *n.* ①墓脚之臺石。②基石。

foot·stool ['fʊt,stul; 'futstuːl] *n.* 脚凳。

foot·sure ['fʊt,ʃʊr;'fut-ʃuə] *adj.* 〖英〗脚根穩的。

foot-ton ['fʊt'tʌn; 'fut'tʌn] *n.* 呎噸(能之單位,將一噸重物舉高一英尺所需之能)。

foot warmer 溫足裝置;脚爐。

foot·way ['fʊt,we; 'futwei] *n.* ①步行小徑。②〖英〗人行道。

foot·wear ['fʊt,wɛr;'futwɛə] *n.* 穿在脚上之物(如鞋、靴等,主爲商人之用語)。

foot·work ['fʊt,wɝk; 'futwəːk] *n.* ①(拳擊、跳舞、角力等中之)步法;腿功。②跑腿的工作。③巧妙的策略運用。

foo·zle ['fuzl; 'fuːzl] *v.*, **-zled, -zling,** *n.* —*v.t. & v.i.* 笨拙地做;把事情搞糟;笨擊。—*n.* ①笨拙之行爲;笨拙之一擊(高爾夫球)。②〖俗〗笨拙者;容易受騙者。

fop [fɑp; fɔp] *n.* 紈袴子;花花公子。

fop·ling ['fɑplɪŋ; 'fɔpliŋ] *n.* 小紈袴子。

fop·per·y ['fɑpərɪ; 'fɔpəri] *n., pl.* **-per·ies.** ①紈袴子之行爲、服飾、形跡等。②愚事;矯飾之物。

fop·pish ['fɑpɪʃ; 'fɔpiʃ] *adj.* ①紈袴子的;適合於紈袴子的。②空虛的;愚笨的;矯飾的。—**ly,** *adv.* —**ness,** *n.*

‡for [fɔr, fɚ; fɔː, fə] *prep.* ①向;對;爲。Sea air is good *for* the health. 海上的空氣對健康有益。②給;與;適於。I bought it *for* you. 這個是買給你的。③以…爲目的地;開往…的。to leave *for* New York. 啓程到紐約去。the train *for* San Francisco. 開往舊金山的火車。④交換;替代;代表。I sold the horse *for* $10. 我把馬賣了十塊錢。⑤因爲;爲了。He was punished *for* stealing. 他因偷竊而受處罰。⑥贊成;支持。Are you against it or *for* it? 你對此事是反對呢還是贊成?⑦作爲;當作。It was built *for* (= as) a pleasure boat. 這船建作遊艇之用。⑧就…而論;雖然。⑨經過(多少時間或距離)(注意 for 常被省略)。We stayed (*for*) three days. 我們逗留了三天。⑩若要(僅用於下列句式中)。It is impossible *for* me to go. 要我去是不可能的。⑪希望;渴望;貪求。We longed *for* home. 我們渴望回家。⑫喜歡;尊敬。⑬表示對比。*For* one enemy he has a hundred friends. 他有一敵而有百友(敵友之比爲一比一百)。⑭對…特別敏感。He has an eye *for* beauty. 他能鑑賞美。⑮尋找。She is hunting *for* her cat. 她正在找她的貓。⑯是。They know it *for* a fact.他們知道那是事實。***as for***至於。***ask for***

懇求;探詢。*be in for* 免不掉;定要受罰。If you break the school windows, you'll *be in for* trouble! 你如打破了學校中的窗子,你一定會惹出麻煩! *be out for* 有做…之意向。*but for* 如無;如非。*But for* your help, I should have failed. 如非你的幫助,我恐已失敗。*care for* 喜歡;照料。*for all I know* 就我所知。He may be in Africa *for all I know*. 就我所知,他可能在非洲。*for all that* 儘管如此;雖然這樣。*for all the world (like)* 的確。*for certain* 的確;確實。*for ever (and ever)* 永遠地。*for fear (that)* 以免;因恐。*for fear of* 因恐。*for life* 終生。*for the nonce* 暫時。*for the present* 暫時地。*for the sake of; for somebody's sake* 爲了…的緣故。*for the time being* 暫時(=for the present). *for (one) to* (某人)要、該、或須(作某事)。It is time *for us to* go. 我們現在該走了。*for want (or lack) of* 因缺乏…的緣故。*For want of* money, he could not go abroad. 因爲缺錢,他不能去外國。*look for* 找尋。*Oh, for ....* 但願有…! *Oh, for* a fine day! 但願有一個晴天! *once for all* 最後地; 祇此一次。*take (someone) for* 認某人爲。*wait for* 等候。*word for word* 逐字地;一字一字地。—*conj.* 因;因爲。He felt no fear, *for* he was a brave man. 他不感覺害怕,因他是一個勇士。〖注意〗 **for** 用作連接詞,以連接兩個對等子句 (coördinate clauses)時,通常須以一逗點(,)分開之,如無逗點分開,易被誤爲介系詞。

for- 〖字首〗表"離去;禁止;不究;過度;强烈"之義。

for·age [ˈfɔrɪdʒ, ˈfɑr-; ˈfɔridʒ] *n., v.,* **-aged, -ag·ing.** —*n.* ①牛馬之飼料。②搜尋糧食。③搜尋芻秣。④搶掠。—*v.i.* ①搜尋糧草。②搜尋〖for, about〗。—*v.t.* ①從…處獲得或取到糧食。②蹂躪;刼掠。③供以糧草;飼。④搜尋。—**for·ag·er,** *n.*

forage cap 〖英〗步兵便帽。

foraging party 糧草徵發隊。

fo·ra·men [foˈremən; fouˈreimən] *n., pl.* **-ram·i·na** [-ˈræmənə; -ˈræmənə]. 〖解剖, 動、植物〗孔;小孔;胚孔。

fo·ram·i·nate [fəˈræmɪnɪt; fəˈræminit] *adj.* 〖罕〗有小孔的。(亦作**foraminous**)

fo·ram·i·nat·ed [fəˈræmɪˌnetɪd; fəˈræmineitid] *adj.* =**foraminate.**

fo·ram·i·nif·er·a [fəˌræməˈnɪfərə; fəˌræmiˈnifərə] *n. pl.* 〖動物〗有孔蟲類。

for·as·much [ˌfɔrəzˈmʌtʃ; fərəzˈmʌtʃ] *conj.* (=considering that; since) 鑒於;因爲;既然〖as〗。

for·ay [ˈfɔre; ˈfɔrei] *n.* ①侵掠;蹂躪。②突襲。—*v.t. & v.i.* 侵掠; 蹂躪; 刼掠。

for·bade [fəˈbæd; fəˈbeid, fɔːˈb-, -ˈbæd] *v.* pt. of **forbid.** (亦作 **forbad**)

***for·bear**[1] [fɔrˈbɛr; fɔːˈbɛə] *v.t. & v.i.,* **-bore, -borne, -bear·ing.** ①自制;避免。He *forbore* to hit back, because the other boy was smaller. 他不予還手,因爲另外那個孩子較小。②忍住;容忍。—**er,** *n.*

for·bear[2] [ˈfɔrˌbɛr; ˈfɔːbɛə] *n.*=**forebear.**

for·bear·ance [fɔrˈbɛrəns; fɔːˈbɛərəns] *n.* ①抑制。②耐性; 自制。③〖法律〗債務清償期之延緩。④放棄執行某些權利。

***for·bid** [fəˈbɪd; fəˈbid, fɔːˈb-] *v.t.,* **-bade** or **-bad, -bid·den** or **bid, -bid·ding.** ①禁止;不許。The teacher *forbade* us to leave our seats. 老師不准我們離開座位。②命令離開;拒絕進入。I *forbid* you the house. 我拒絕你到家裏來。③阻止。God *forbid!* 但願上帝阻止(這事發生)! ④逐出;趕出。He is *forbidden* in Taipei. 他被逐出臺北。*God forbid that....* 但願上帝不許(某事)發生。—**der,** *n.*

***for·bid·den** [fəˈbɪdn̩; fəˈbidn, fɔːˈb-] *adj.* ①被禁的。Eve ate the *forbidden* fruit. 夏娃食了禁果。②〖物理〗禁戒的。—**ly,** *adv.* —**ness,** *n.*

for·bid·ding [fəˈbɪdɪŋ; fəˈbidiŋ] *adj.* ①形勢險惡的。②冷峻的。

for·bore [fɔrˈbor, fə-; fɔːˈbɔː, -ˈbɔə] *v.* pt. of **forbear**[1].

for·borne [fɔrˈborn; fɔːˈbɔːn] *v.* pp. of **forbear**[1].

for·by(e) [fɔrˈbaɪ; fɔːˈbai] *adv., prep.* 〖蘇, 古〗①貼近;貼近而過。②其他;此外。

‡**force**[1] [fors, fɔrs; fɔːs] *n., v.,* **forced, forc·ing.** —*n.* ①力; 力量; 暴力(不可用複數)。He didn't use much *force.* 他沒有用多大力量。②感情的力量; 道德的力量。He lacks *force* and determination. 他缺乏意志力和果斷力。③影響力; 說服力;控制力; 生動。He writes with *force.* 他寫得生動有力。④自然力。⑤勢力; 權力。These liberals represent a *force* in national affairs. 這些自由分子在政治上代表一種勢力。⑥(常 *pl.*) 部隊;組織;實力;武力。⑦法律上之效力;實施。The law remains in *force.* 這法令仍有效。⑧意義。I saw the *force* of your remarks. 我明白你評語中的意義。⑨〖物理〗力。*by force* 以武力; 以强力。*by force of* 藉…之力。*come (or go) into force* 生效(指法律或章程等)。*in force* a. 在有效期間; 在施行中。This rule is no longer *in force.* 這條規則現已失效。b. 以壓倒之勢。They attacked *in force.* 他們以壓倒之勢攻擊了。*put into force* 實施; 實行。—*v.t.* ①强迫; 迫使。They were *forced* to leave the town. 他們被迫離開此城。②突破; 强行。③强奪; 强取。④用特殊方法使生長。⑤迫使(人或動物)做最大之努力。⑥攻克。They *forced* the town after a long seige. 他們將該鎮長期包圍後終於將它攻克。⑦用暴力; 加壓力。*force one's hand* 逼某人表示意向; 逼某人採取行動。—**a·ble,** *adj.* —**less,** *adj.* —**forc·er,** *n.*

force[2] *n.* 〖英北部〗瀑布。

forced [forst; fɔːst] *adj.* 不得已的;强迫的; 勉强的。a *forced* landing. (飛機) 被迫降落。a *forced* march. 强行軍。

forc·ed·ly [ˈforsɪdlɪ; ˈfɔːsidli] *adv.* 强迫地;勉强地;不得已。

force-feed [ˈforsˈfid; ˈfɔːsˈfiːd] *v.t.,* **-fed, -feed·ing.** ①强迫…飲食。②强迫…接受。

force·ful [ˈforsfəl; ˈfɔːsful] *adj.* 堅强的;强有力的;有效的。—**ly,** *adv.*

force ma·jeure [forsmaˈʒœr; fɔːsmaˈʒœr] 〖法〗①優勢。②〖法律〗不可抗力。

force·meat [ˈforsˌmit; ˈfɔːsmiːt] *n.* 加佐料之細切肉;五香碎肉。

force-out [ˈforsˌaʊt; ˈfɔːs-aut] *n.* 〖棒球〗封殺。

for·ceps [ˈfɔrsəps; ˈfɔːseps] *n., pl.* **-ceps, -ci·pes** [-səˌpiz; -sipiːz]. (醫生用的) 鉗子;鑷子。—**like, for·cip·i·al,** *adj.*

force pump 壓水唧筒。

for·ci·ble [ˈforsəbl̩; ˈfɔːsəbl] *adj.* ①有力的; 能感動或說服的。②强行的。—**for·ci·bil·i·ty,** *n.* —**for·ci·bly,** *adv.*

Ford¹ [ford; fɔːd] *n.* 福特(Henry, 1863–1947, 美國汽車製造者)。

Ford² *n.* 福特 (Gerald Rudolph, 1913–, 於1973–1974任美國副總統, 1974–1977 任美國第三十八任總統)。

ford [ford; fɔːd] *n.* 水淺可涉處; 淺灘。—*v.t.* 涉水;涉過 (淺灘等)。—**a·ble,** *adj.*

for·do [fɔr'du; fɔː'duː] *v.t.*, **-did, -done.** 〖古〗①殺;毀;挫。②使疲倦。(亦作 **foredo**)

for·done [fɔr'dʌn; fɔː'dʌn] *adj.* 〖古〗筋疲力竭的。(亦作 **foredone**)

fore¹ [for; fɔː] *adj.* ①在前部的;向前面的;在船首的。②(地點、時間、順序、階級等)在前的。—*adv.* 在前地;向前地;在船首地。***fore and aft*** 首尾;前後;全船。—*n.* 前部;首;(船之) 前檣。***to the fore*** **a.** 居領導地位;在顯著位置。to come *to the fore.* 站在領導地位。**b.** 在手邊;現成。**c.** 尙在人間。—*prep., conj.* (亦作 **'fore**) 〖方〗=**before.**

fore² *interj.* (高爾夫球) 對在前者警告使防被球擊之叫聲。

fore- 〖字首〗表"位置之前;時間之前"之義。

fore-and-aft ['forənd'æft; 'fɔːrənd-'ɑːft] *adj.* 〖航海〗自船首至船尾的;縱的;縱置的。—*adv.* 在船首與船尾地(=fore).

fore·arm¹ ['for,ɑrm; 'fɔːrɑːm] *n.* 前臂(肘至腕間之部分)。

fore·arm² [for'ɑrm; fɔːr'ɑːm] *v.t.* 預先武裝;警備;預備;準備攻擊(常用於被動式)。

fore·bear ['for,bɛr; 'fɔːbɛə] *n.* (常 *pl.*)祖先。(亦作 **forbear**)

fore·bode [for'bod; fɔː'boud] *v.*, **-bod·ed, -bod·ing.** —*v.t.* ①預示;預兆(尤指不祥之事)。②預感(不祥之事)。—*v.i.* ①預言。②有預感。—**fore·bod·er,** —**ment,** *n.*

fore·bod·ing [for'bodɪŋ; fɔː'boudiŋ] *n.* ①預言;警告。②預感。—*adj.* (凶事之)預兆的。—**ly,** *adv.* —**ness,** *n.*

fore·brain ['for,bren; 'fɔːbrein] *n.* 〖解剖〗前腦。

fore·cab·in ['for,kæbɪn; 'fɔː,kæbin] *n.* 船首之客艙(通常爲二等艙);船首室。

fore·cast [*v.* for'kæst; 'fɔː-kɑːst, fɔː'k-, 'fɔə-k-, fɔə'k- *n.* 'for,kæst; 'fɔː-kɑːst] *v.*, **-cast** or **-cast·ed, -cast·ing,** *n.* —*v.t.* ①預言;預測。Cooler weather is *forecast* for tomorrow. 明天天氣預報較爲涼爽。②事先安排; 預見。—*n.* ①預言; 預告; 預測。②事先的安排;先見之明。③預兆。Summer styles are often a *forecast* of autumn fashions. 夏裝的款式常常是秋裝的預兆。—**a·ble,** *adj.* —**er,** *n.*

fore·cas·tle ['foksl; 'fouksl] *n.* ①前檣前之上甲板。②(商船的) 水手艙 (以前在船首部分)。(亦作 **fo'c's'le, fo'c'sle**)

fore·close [for'kloz; fɔː'klouz] *v.t.* & *v.i.*, **-closed, -clos·ing.** ①拒絕;阻止。②取消抵押品之贖回權。③取得專有權。④提早關閉、解決或回答。—**fore·clos·a·ble,** *adj.*

fore·clo·sure [for'kloʒə; fɔː'klouʒə] *n.* ①拒斥。②〖法律〗抵押品贖取權之取消。

fore·court ['for,kort; 'fɔː-kɔːt] *n.* ①(建築物之) 前庭。②〖網球〗球場近網之半部。③〖籃球〗球場接近進攻之籃框的部分。

fore·done [for'dʌn; fɔː'dʌn] *adj.* 〖古〗=**fordone.**

fore·doom [*v.* for'dum; fɔː'duːm *n.* 'for,dum; 'fɔːduːm] *v.t.* 事先注定(常用於被動式)。—*n.* 預定之命運。

***fore·fa·ther** ['for,fɑðə; 'fɔː,fɑːðə] *n.* 祖先;祖宗。—**ly,** *adj.*

Forefathers' Day 〖美〗清教徒登陸美洲紀念日(十二月二十二日)。

fore·fend [for'fɛnd; fɔː'fend] *adj.* =**forfend.**

***fore·fin·ger** ['for,fɪŋgə; 'fɔː,fiŋgə] *n.* 食指。

fore·foot ['for,fut; 'fɔː-fut] *n., pl.* **-feet.** ①四足動物的前足。②船龍骨的前端。

fore·front ['for,frʌnt; 'fɔː-frʌnt] *n.* (the–)最前部; 最前線; 最活動之中心;最重要的地方。

fore·gath·er [for'gæðə; fɔː'gæðə] *v.i.* =**forgather.**

fore·gift ['for,gɪft, ; 'fɔː-gift] *n.* 〖法律〗承租者預付之租金。

fore·go [for'go; fɔː'gou] *v.t.*, **-went, -gone, -go·ing.** ①在…之前;前行;先行。②棄絕; 棄去 (=forgo). —**er,** *n.*

fore·go·ing [for'go·ɪŋ; fɔː'gouiŋ] *adj.* 前面的;前述的。

fore·gone [for'gɔn; fɔː'gɔn] *adj.* ①先前的;過去的。②預知的;既知的。—*v.* pp. of **forego.** —**ness,** *n.*

foregone conclusion ①不可避免的結果; 不容懷疑的東西; 事前可獲知之事實。②遽下之結論;武斷。

fore·ground ['for,graund; 'fɔːgraund] *n.* ①前景 (如景物、圖畫等最靠近觀察者之部分)。②最受人注意之地位。

fore·hand ['for,hænd; 'fɔːhænd] *adj.* ①前面的; 居前的。②〖網球〗正擊的。③預先做的; 預付的。—*n.* ①正擊; 順擊。②馬身之前部。③有利地位;優勢。—*adv.* 〖網球〗正擊地;順擊地。

fore·hand·ed ['for'hændɪd; 'fɔː-'hændid] *adj.* ①〖網球〗正擊的。②隨機應變的。③謹慎的;節儉的。④富裕的。—*adv.* 〖網球〗正擊地;順擊地。—**ly,** *adv.*

***fore·head** ['fɑrɪd, 'for,hɛd; 'fɔrid, 'fɔːhed] *n.* ①前額。②前部。

:for·eign ['fɔrɪn, 'fɑrɪn; 'fɔrin] *adj.* ①外國的; 外來的; 對外的; 外交的。*foreign* policy. 外交政策。②本身所無的;不適宜的;無關連的。Sitting still is *foreign* to a boy's nature. 靜靜坐着不是男孩的本性。③〖醫〗外來的; 異質的。④外地的。⑤〖法律〗(美國某州之) 管轄外的。⑥本身以外的。a statement supported by *foreign* testimony. 由外來的證詞所支持的聲明。⑦陌生的。—*adv.* (僅用於下列片語中) ***go foreign*** 〖航海〗**a.** 在從事對外貿易的船上當船員。**b.** 航行於外國水域的。***sell foreign*** 〖航海〗將船隻售給外國船主。—**ly,** *adv.* —**ness,** *n.*

foreign affairs 外交事務;國際關係。

foreign aid 外援。

foreign bill 國外匯票。

for·eign-born ['fɔrɪn'bɔrn; 'fɔrin-'bɔːn] *adj.* 生於國外的。

foreign correspondent (新聞機構之)國外特派員。

***for·eign·er** ['fɔrɪnə, 'fɑrɪnə; 'fɔrinə] *n.* ①外國人。How many *foreigners* are there in this town? 此城有多少外國人? ②外國船。③〖俗〗外地人。

foreign exchange ①國際匯兌。②外國匯票之集合稱;外匯。

for·eign-flag ['fɔrɪn,flæg; 'fɔrinflæg] *adj.* ①(飛機、船隻等) 登記在外國的。②〖美〗(船隻之)掛外國旗的。

foreign goods 舶來品;外國貨。

foreign legion ①外國志願軍。②(F-

L-) 法國之外籍兵團。 「國外之傳教機構。」

foreign mission ①外國使節館。②

foreign office ①(F- O-)〖英〗外交部(略作 **F.O.**)。②政府機構中負責外交事務之部門(通常指內閣組織中之外交部)。

foreign press 外國報紙(集合稱)。

Foreign Service 美國國務院之一部門, 負責駐外使節之派遣及訓練。

foreign settlers 外僑。

fore·judge 〔for'dʒʌdʒ; fɔː'dʒʌdʒ〕 *v.t.*, **-judged, -judg·ing.** 預斷;推斷;臆斷。

fore·know 〔for'no; fɔː'nou〕 *v.t.*, **-knew, -known, -know·ing.** 預知。—**ing·ly,** *adv.* —**a·ble,** *adj.* —**er,** *n.*

fore·knowl·edge 〔'for,nalɪdʒ; 'fɔː-'nɔlidʒ, fɔː'n-〕 *n.* 預知;先知。

for·el 〔'farəl; 'fɔrəl〕 *n.* ①(書籍封面用之)一種羊皮紙。②書盒。(亦作 **forrel**)

fore·land 〔'forlənd; 'fɔːlənd〕 *n.* ①岬;崎;海角。②沿海地區。

fore·leg 〔'for,lɛg; 'fɔːleg〕 *n.* 獸的前腿。

fore·lock[1] 〔'for,lak; 'fɔːlɔk〕 *n.* 垂於或堆於前額之髮;馬額上之長毛。 ***seize*** (or ***take***) ***time by the forelock*** 把握時機;動作敏捷;作事先計畫。

fore·lock[2] *n.* 栓;楔。—*v.t.* 以栓、楔固定。

*__fore·man__ 〔'formən; 'fɔːmən〕 *n., pl.* **-men.** ①工頭;領班。②陪審團之主席。

fore·mast 〔'for,mæst; 'fɔːmaːst〕 *n.* 船的前檣。

*__fore·most__ 〔'for,most, 'fɔr-, -məst; 'fɔːmoust, 'fɔə-, -məst〕 *adj.* 最先的;第一的;首要的。He is our *foremost* poet. 他是我國最重要的詩人。—*adv.* 最前。 ***first and foremost*** 首先;第一。 「名;教名。」

fore·name 〔'for,nem; 'fɔːneim〕 *n.*

*__fore·noon__ 〔'for,nun, 'fɔr-; 'fɔːnuːn, 'fɔə-〕 *n.* 午前;上午。—*adj.* 午前的;上午的。

fo·ren·sic 〔fə'rɛnsɪk; fə'rensik〕 *adj.* ①屬於或適於法庭的;法庭的。②討論的;辯論的。—*n.* (*pl.*)(作 *sing.* or *pl.* 解)(美國學校中之)辯論練習;辯論課程。

forensic medicine 法醫學。

fore·or·dain 〔,forɔr'den; 'fɔːrɔː-'dein〕 *v.t.* ①預先注定;注定命運。②預先任命(聖職)。—**ment,** *n.*

fore·or·di·na·tion 〔,forɔrdn̩'eʃən; ,fɔːrɔːdi'neiʃən〕 *n.* ①預定命運; 注定;宿命。②預先任命(聖職)。

fore·part 〔'for,part; 'fɔːpaːt〕 *n.* 前部;最前部。 「動物之)前蹄。」

fore·paw 〔'for,pɔ; 'fɔːpɔː〕 *n.* (四足

fore·peak 〔'for,pik; 'fɔːpiːk〕 *n.* 〖航海〗船首艙。

fore·quar·ter 〔'for,kwɔrtɚ; 'fɔː-,kwɔːtə〕 *n.* (牛、羊、猪等的)一側之前半部。

fore·reach 〔for'ritʃ; fɔː'riːtʃ〕 *v.t.* & *v.i.* 〖航海〗追過(他船);駛過;超越。

fore·run 〔for'rʌn; fɔː'rʌn〕 *v.t.*, **-ran, -run, -run·ning.** 〖罕, 古〗①預告;預示。②爲…之先驅;在…前。③跑在前面。④超越。

fore·run·ner 〔'for,rʌnɚ; 'fɔː,rʌnə〕 *n.* ①前鋒;先驅。②預兆。③祖先。 ***the Forerunner*** 施洗約翰。

fore·said 〔'for,sɛd; 'fɔːsed〕 *adj.* 上述的;前述的。 「前檣主帆。」

fore·sail 〔'for,sel; 'fɔːseil〕 *n.* 〖航海〗

*__fore·see__ 〔for'si, fɔr-; fɔː'siː, fɔə-〕 *v.t.*, **-saw** 〔-'sɔ; -'sɔː〕, **-seen** 〔-'sin; -'siːn〕, **-see·ing.** 先見;預知。 to *foresee* trouble. 預知有困難。—*v.i.* 先見;預知。—**fore·s**[er], *n.*

fore·see·a·ble 〔for'siəbl̩; fɔː'siːəb[le]〕 *adj.* 可預知的;能預測的。—**fore·see·a·bl**[y], *adv.* —**fore·see·a·bil·i·ty,** *n.*

fore·shad·ow 〔for'ʃædo; fɔː'ʃædo[u]〕 *v.t.* 預示;預兆。—*n.* 預兆。—**er,** *n.*

fore·shank 〔'for,ʃæŋk; 'fɔːʃæŋk〕 牛前腿上部之肉。

fore·sheet 〔'for,ʃit; 'fɔː-ʃiːt〕 *n.* ①〖[航]海〗前桅帆之帆脚索。②(*pl.*)敞式船艇之前部(亦作 **headsheet**)

fore·shore 〔'for,ʃor; 'fɔː-ʃɔː〕 *n.* ①[漲]潮則淹, 退潮則現之岸;(高潮線與低潮線之[間]的)海浦。②渚;海灘。

fore·short·en 〔for'ʃɔrtn̩; fɔː'ʃɔːtn〕 *v.t.* ①〖美術〗立體構圖中因表示遠近而縮小。②省略;節要;縮短。

fore·show 〔for'ʃo; fɔː'ʃou〕 *v.t.*, **-showed, -shown, -show·ing.** 預示;預兆。

*__fore·sight__ 〔'for,saɪt; 'fɔː-sait〕 *n.* ①先見之明;遠見。②向前看; 前瞻; 遠瞻未來。③(槍上之)前端準星。

fore·sight·ed 〔'for,saɪtɪd; 'fɔː,saitid〕 *adj.* 有先見之明的。—**ness,** *n.*

fore·skin 〔'for,skɪn; 'fɔː-skin〕 *n.* 包皮。

‡**for·est** 〔'fɔrɪst, 'far-; 'fɔrist〕 *n.* ①[森]林;森林地帶。*forest* preserve. 保護林。②森林中之樹。③(如森林中樹木)林立之物。④〖英法律〗國王狩獵之御林。—*adj.* 森林的;[在]森林中的。*forest* dwellers.居住森林中的人。—*v.t.* 植樹於;使成林。—**al,** *adj.* —**less,** *ad[j.]*

fore·stall 〔for'stɔl; fɔː'stɔːl〕 *v.t.* ①[先]採取行動以預防或阻止。②占先一步; 先…着; 先發制人。③壟斷 (市場等); 囤積居奇。—**er,** —**ment,** *n.*

for·est·a·tion 〔,fɔrɪs'teʃən; ,fɔris'teiʃən〕 *n.* 造林;植林(法)。 「前桅支索。」

fore·stay 〔'for,ste; 'fɔːstei〕 *n.* 〖造船〗

for·est·ed 〔'fɔrəstɪd; 'fɔrəstid〕 *ad[j.]* 樹木叢生的;爲森林所廣被的。

for·est·er 〔'fɔrɪstɚ; 'fɔristə〕 *n.* ①[保]林人員;林務官。②居住於森林地帶的人或獸。③森林學者。④灰色大袋鼠。⑤斑蛾。

forest reserve 〖美〗保存林;保護林

for·est·ry 〔'fɔrɪstrɪ; 'fɔristri〕 *n.* ①森林學。②林政;林業。③造林法;山林管理法。④〖罕〗森林地。

fore·taste 〔*n.* 'for,test; 'fɔː-teist, 'fɔə- *v.* for'test; fɔː'teist〕 *n., v.,* **-tast·ed, -tast·ing.** —*n.* 預嘗;先試;預先獲得的經驗。—*v.t.* 預嘗;先試;預先獲得經驗。

*__fore·tell__ 〔for'tɛl, fɔr-; fɔː'tel, fɔə-〕 *v.t.* & *v.i.*, **-told, -tell·ing.** 預言; 預測。Who can *foretell* what a baby will d[o] next? 誰能預言嬰孩的次一動作? —**a·ble,** *adj.* —**er,** *n.*

fore·thought 〔'for,θɔt; 'fɔː-θɔːt〕 *n.* ①事先的盤算;預籌。②預謀;存心。

fore·thought·ful 〔for'θɔtfəl; fɔː'θɔːtful〕 *adj.* 有遠慮的;有遠見的。

fore·time 〔'for,taɪm; 'fɔːtaim〕 *n.* 往昔。

fore·to·ken 〔*n.* 'for,tokən; 'fɔː,toukən *v.* for'tokən; fɔː'toukən〕 *n.* 預兆;徵候。—*v.t.* 預兆;預示。

fore-tooth 〔'for,tuθ; 'fɔːtuːθ〕 *n., pl.* **-teeth.** 前齒;門齒。

fore·top 〔'for,tap; 'fɔː-tɔp〕 *n.* ①〖航海〗前檣之平臺;前檣樓。②(馬等之)額毛。③額前覆蓋之髮;劉海。

fore-top·gal·lant [ˌfortəˈgælənt; ˌfɔːtəˈgælənt] *adj.* 【航海】前桅之上桅的(自桅座數起之第三段)。

fore-top·mast [forˈtɑpˌmæst; ˈfɔː-tɔpmɑːst] *n.* 【航海】前桅之中桅(自桅座數起之第二段)。

fore-top·sail [forˈtɑpˌsel; ˈfɔː-tɔpseil] *n.* 【航海】前桅之中桅之帆。

:for·ev·er [fəˈɛvə; fəˈrevə] *adv.* ①永遠地;無盡地。to go away *forever.* 永遠離開。②繼續地;不斷地。He's *forever* complaining. 他不斷地埋怨。***forever and a day*** 永遠地。***forever and aye*** (文學) 永遠地。***forever and ever*** 永遠地。

for·ev·er·more [fəˌɛvəˈmor; fəˌrevəˈmɔː] *adv.* 永遠 (forever 之强勢語)。

fore·warn [forˈwɔrn; fɔːˈwɔːn] *v.t.* 預先警告。

fore·went [forˈwɛnt; fɔːˈwent] *v.* pt. of **forego.**

fore·wom·an [ˈforˌwumən; ˈfɔːˌwumən] *n., pl.* **-wom·en.** ①女工頭。②女陪審長。

fore·word [ˈforˌwɜd; ˈfɔːwəːd] *n.* 前言;引言;序。

fore·yard [ˈforˌjɑrd; ˈfɔːjɑːd] *n.* (船) 前桅最下部的帆桁。

***for·feit** [ˈfɔrfɪt; ˈfɔːfit] *v.t.* (因被沒收而)喪失(所有權);(因過失、犯罪等而)喪失(職位、生命);(因過勞而)喪失(健康)。He *forfeited* his life by his careless driving. 他因駕駛不慎而喪生。—*n.* ①喪失物;沒收物。②罰鍰;處罰。③違約罰金。—*adj.* 喪失的;沒收的。His lands and titles were *forfeit.* 他的土地與爵位均已喪失(被剝奪)。

for·feit·a·ble [ˈfɔrfɪtəbḷ; ˈfɔːfitəbl] *adj.* 可沒收的。

for·feit·er [ˈfɔrfɪtə; ˈfɔːfitə] *n.* 受沒收處分者;因犯罪而喪失職位的人。

for·fei·ture [ˈfɔrfɪtʃə; ˈfɔːfitʃə] *n.* ①(權利、名譽等)喪失;沒收。②沒收物;罰金。

for·fend [forˈfɛnd; fɔːˈfend] *v.t.* ①【美】防護;保護。②【古】禁止;阻止。(亦作 **forefend**)

for·gath·er [fɔrˈgæðə; fɔːˈgæðə] *v.i.* ①相遇;集合。②偶遇;不期而遇。③交往【with】。

for·gave [fəˈgev; fəˈgeiv] *v.* pt. of **forgive.**

***forge**[1] [fordʒ; fɔːdʒ] *n., v.,* **forged, forg·ing.** —*n.* ①鍛鐵場;鐵工廠;鐵匠鋪。②熔爐;鍛鐵爐。—*v.t.* ①(鐵匠)打(鐵);錘鍊成。The smith soon *forged* three shoes for the horse. 那鐵匠不久便給這馬打了三隻蹄鐵。②僞造(文書、簽字等)。③做出;設計(計畫等)。④編(假故事或謊話等)。—*v.i.* ①鍛鐵。②僞造文書。—**a·ble,** *adj.* —**forg·er,** *n.*

forge[2] *v.i.,* **forged, forg·ing.** ①徐緩推進【常 ahead】。②隨波前進。

for·ger·y [ˈfɔrdʒərɪ; ˈfɔːdʒəri] *n., pl.* **-ger·ies.** ①僞造;僞造文書。②僞造物。

:for·get [fəˈgɛt; fəˈget] *v.,* **-got** or **-gat, -got·ten** or **-got, -get·ting.** —*v.t.* 忘記;遺忘;忽略;忽視。I have *forgotten* your name. 我忘了你的名字。—*v.i.* 忘記;忘却。***forget oneself*** **a.** 失態;忘形。You are *forgetting yourself!* 你忘形了! **b.** 忘我;大公無私。**c.** 心不在焉。**d.** 無知覺。

for·get·ful [fəˈgɛtfəl; fəˈgetful] *adj.* ①健忘的;不留心的。②【古】使遺忘的。***be forgetful of*** 不注意。The hotel *is forgetful of* the comfort of its guests. 這旅館不注意客人的舒適。—**ly,** *adv.* —**ness,** *n.*

for·get-me-not [fəˈgɛtmɪˌnɑt; fəˈgetminɔt] *n.* 【植物】琉璃草;勿忘草。

for·get·ta·ble [fəˈgɛtəbḷ; fəˈgetəbl] *adj.* 可忘記的。—**ness,** *n.*

forg·ing [ˈfɔrdʒɪŋ; ˈfɔːdʒiŋ] *n.* ①鍛鍊;鍛鍊物。②(馬奔跑時)後腿之蹄鐵擊傷前腿。—*adj.* 鍛鍊的;鍛造的。

for·giv·a·ble [fəˈgɪvəbḷ; fəˈgivəbl] *adj.* 可寬恕的;可原諒的。

***for·give** [fəˈgɪv; fəˈgiv] *v.,* **-gave, -giv·en, -giv·ing.** —*v.t.* ①原諒;寬恕;赦免。They *forgave* their enemies. 他們寬恕他們的敵人。②寬免;放棄追索。—*v.i.* 原諒;寬恕。He is not a man who *forgives* easily. 他不是一個輕易寬恕人的人。—**for·giv·er,** *n.*

for·giv·en [fəˈgɪvən; fəˈgivn] *v.* pp. of **forgive.**

for·give·ness [fəˈgɪvnɪs; fəˈgivnis] *n.* ①寬恕;原諒。②寬仁之心。③寬減。

for·giv·ing [fəˈgɪvɪŋ; fəˈgiviŋ] *adj.* 寬恕的;寬仁的;慈悲的。—**ness,** *n.* —**ly,** *adv.*

for·go [fɔrˈgo; fɔːˈgou] *v.t.,* **-went, -gone, -go·ing.** 棄絕;拋棄;放棄。(亦作 **forego**) —**er,** *n.*

:for·got [fəˈgɑt; fəˈgɔt] *v.* pt. & pp. of **forget.**

:for·got·ten [fəˈgɑtn̩; fəˈgɔtn] *v.* pp. of **forget.**

for·int [ˈfɔrɪnt; ˈfɔːrint] *n.* 匈牙利的貨幣單位。

fork** [fɔrk; fɔːk] *n.* ①叉;肉叉。knife and *fork.* 刀叉(食具)。②草叉;耙(農具)。③似叉之物;分岔。④分叉處。⑤【美】河川之主要支流。a tuning fork*** 【物理】音叉。—*v.t.* ①以叉叉(物)。②使分岔。③【西洋棋】以一子同時攻對方之二子。—*v.i.* 成叉形;分岔。Here the river *forks.* 河在此處分岔。***fork out*** (***over,*** or ***up***) 【俗】交出;付出。—**less,** *adj.* —**like,** *adj.*

forked [fɔrkt; fɔːkt] *adj.* ①有叉的;叉狀的。②多曲折線條的;之字形的。③模稜兩可的;不誠實的;說謊的。—**ly,** *adv.* —**ness,** *n.*

fork lift 堆高機。

fork-lift truck [ˈfɔrkˌlɪft~; ˈfɔːk-lift~] 裝有堆高機之車輛。

fork·y [ˈfɔrkɪ; ˈfɔːki] *adj.,* **fork·i·er, fork·i·est.** =**forked.**

***for·lorn** [fəˈlɔrn; fəˈlɔːn] *adj.* ①孤零的;孤寂無伴的。One seems *forlorn* without friends. 一個人沒有朋友就顯得孤零。②不幸的;可憐的;絕望的。③被遺棄的【有時 of】。④失去的;喪失的【常 of】. —**ly,** *adv.* —**ness,** *n.*

forlorn hope ①絕少成功希望的計畫。②危險或孤注一擲的計畫。③負有很危險任務的一羣士兵(如敢死隊、突擊隊等)。

:form [fɔrm; fɔːm] *n.* ①形狀;外貌;輪廓;人形;形體。What he saw seemed to have the *form* of a man. 他所見的東西好像是有人的形狀。②形式;形態;姿態。These are two different *forms* of the same thing. 這些是同一事物的兩種不同的形式。③方式;制度。④禮節;表面形式;手續;程序。Shaking hands is a *form.* 握手是一種禮節。⑤表格。Please fill in this *form.* 請塡寫此表格。⑥(英國學校裏的)班;級。⑦模子;模型;假人;假模特兒。a dressmaker's *form.* 裁縫店的假模特兒。⑧做事的方式;態度;方法。⑨種類。Heat, light, and electricity are *forms* of energy. 熱、火、電是不同種的"能"。⑩身心的健康情況。Athletes exercise to keep in *form.* 運動員練習以保

持續峯狀態。⑪長凳。⑫〖印刷〗板。⑬〖文法〗型;式。⑭文件;公文程式。⑮〖結晶〗面式。**good** (or **bad**) **form** (不)合乎禮儀的舉動。—*v.t.* ①構造;作成;變成。Water *forms* ice when it freezes. 水凍結時就變成冰。②養成。③排列。The soldiers *formed* themselves into lines. 這些士兵排成隊伍。④組織。We *formed* a club. 我們組織一個俱樂部。—*v.i.* 形成。—**a·bil·i·ty,** *n.* —**a·ble,** *adj.* —**a·bly,** *adv.*

-form 〖字尾〗表"有…的形式"之義。

***for·mal** [ˈfɔrml; ˈfɔːməl] *adj.* ①正式的;傳統的;禮儀的。a *formal* call. 正式的拜訪。*formal* dress. 禮服。②合式的;合法的。A contract is a *formal* agreement. 合同就是一種合法的協議。③形式的;形式上的(對內容而言)。—**ness,** *n.*

form·al·de·hyde [fɔrˈmældəˌhaɪd; fɔːˈmældihaid] *n.* 〖化〗甲醛。

for·ma·lin [ˈfɔrməlɪn; ˈfɔːməlin] *n.* 甲醛液(用以消毒、殺菌、除臭等);福馬林。

for·mal·ism [ˈfɔrmlˌɪzəm; ˈfɔːməlizəm] *n.* 形式主義;拘泥虛禮。—**for·mal·is·tic,** *adj.*

for·mal·ist [ˈfɔmlɪst; ˈfɔːməlist] *n.* 形式主義(論)者;拘泥虛禮之人。

for·mal·i·ty [fɔrˈmælətɪ; fɔːˈmæliti] *n., pl.* **-ties.** ①禮節;儀式。②形式的拘泥;禮節的嚴守。③拘束。④規定的秩序或程式。⑤形式或禮貌上該做的事。 ***go through due formalities*** 經正式的手續。 ***without formality*** 不拘形式。

for·mal·ize [ˈfɔrmlˌaɪz; ˈfɔːməlaiz] *v.,* **-ized, -iz·ing.** —*v.t.* ①使正式;正式化;形式化;使合禮儀。②賦以定形;使成形。—*v.i.* 正式化;合禮儀。—**for·mal·i·za·tion, for·mal·iz·er,** *n.*

***for·mal·ly** [ˈfɔrməlɪ; ˈfɔːməli] *adv.* ①正式地。They *formally* announced their engagement. 他們正式宣告訂婚。②就形式而言。

for·mat [ˈfɔrmæt; ˈfɔːmæt, -mɑː] 〖法〗*n.* ①書刊之版式。②任何事之構成、格式、計畫、形態等。

for·mate [ˈfɔrmet; ˈfɔːmeit] *n.* 〖化〗蟻酸鹽。

***for·ma·tion** [fɔrˈmeʃən; fɔːˈmeiʃən] *n.* ①構成;組成。②編組;隊形。troops in battle *formation.* 成戰鬥隊形的軍隊。③構成物。④〖地質〗岩層;層。—**al·ly,** *adv.* —**al,** *adj.*

form·a·tive [ˈfɔrmətɪv; ˈfɔːmətiv] *adj.* ①使成形的;造型的。②形成的;發展的。③〖文法〗構成字的。—*n.* 〖文法〗①構成字之要素(如字首、字尾等)。②含有此等字素之字。—**ly,** *adv.* —**ness,** *n.*

forme [fɔrm; fɔːm] *n.* 〖英〗〖印刷〗版(=form).

‡for·mer¹ [ˈfɔrmɚ; ˈfɔːmə] *adj.* ①前者(為 latter 之對)。②往昔的;早先的。in *former* times. 往昔。③早期的。④前一個的。Our *former* process was too costly. 我們的上一個製造方法成本過高。⑤前任的。

form·er² *n.* ①組成者(物);構成者(物);創造者。②模型;鑄型。

***for·mer·ly** [ˈfɔrmɚlɪ; ˈfɔːməli] *adv.* 先前;從前。

for·mic [ˈfɔrmɪk; ˈfɔːmik] *adj.* ①〖化〗蟻酸的。②螞蟻的。

for·mi·cate [ˈfɔrmɪˌket; ˈfɔːmikeit] *v.i.,* **-cat·ed, -cat·ing.** 似螞蟻般爬動;爬滿了螞蟻。

***for·mi·da·ble** [ˈfɔrmɪdəbl; ˈfɔːmidəbl, fɔːˈmid-] *adj.* ①可畏懼的;難以克服的。a *formidable* task. 艱難的工作。②龐大的;可敬畏的。He has a *formidable* knowledge of history. 他有豐富的歷史知識。③强大的;強力的。—**for·mi·da·bly,** *adv.* —**for·mi·da·bil·i·ty,** *n.*

form·less [ˈfɔrmlɪs; ˈfɔːmlis] *adj.* ①無形狀的;無形式的;不成形狀(形式)的。②無規定形式的;無一定形式的。—**ly,** *adv.*

form letter 格式函件(內容一致而可以寄給許多不同的人的信函)。

form master 英國學校的班級導師。

***For·mo·sa** [fɔrˈmosə; fɔːˈmousə, -ouzə] *n.* 臺灣(正式名稱為 Taiwan).

For·mo·san [fɔrˈmosən; fɔːˈmousən] *adj.* 臺灣的;臺灣高山族的;臺灣高山族語的。—*n.* 臺灣高山族;臺灣高山族語。

***for·mu·la** [ˈfɔrmjələ; ˈfɔːmjulə] *n., pl.* **-las, -lae** [-ˌli; -liː]. ①客套語(如How do you do? Excuse me. Thank you. 等);(法律文件或宗教儀式所用之)套語。②〖數學〗公式。③〖化學〗分子式。The *formula* for water is H_2O. 水的分子式為 H_2O. ④製法(=recipe). ⑤〖醫〗處方;藥方。⑥做事之定規。⑦常套;俗套。⑧牛奶、糖與水混合的嬰兒食品。⑨教義之正式聲明。—*adj.* 根據公式的;俗套的。

for·mu·lar·ize [ˈfɔrmjələˌraɪz; ˈfɔːmjuləraiz] *v.t.,* **-ized, -iz·ing.** =**formulate.** —**for·mu·lar·i·za·tion,** *n.*

for·mu·la·ry [ˈfɔrmjəˌlɛrɪ; ˈfɔːmjuləri] *adj., n.,* **-ries.** —*adj.* 公式的;規定的。—*n.* ①套語集。②公式集;法式書。③公式;定式。④藥方書;藥方表。⑤(宗教之)儀式書。

for·mu·late [ˈfɔrmjəˌlet; ˈfɔːmjuleit] *v.t.,* **-lat·ed, -lat·ing.** ①用公式表示。②有系統地陳述。③設計或規劃(方法、制度等)。

for·mu·la·tion [ˌfɔrmjəˈleʃən; ˌfɔːmjuˈleiʃən] *n.* ①有系統而確切的陳述或說明。②化成公式的說明。③設計;規劃。

for·mu·lism [ˈfɔrmjəˌlɪzəm; ˈfɔːmjulizəm] *n.* ①公式主義。②公式之系統。—**for·mu·lis·tic,** *adj.*

for·mu·list [ˈfɔrmjəlɪst; ˈfɔːmjulist] *n.* 公式主義者。

for·mu·lize [ˈfɔrmjəˌlaɪz; ˈfɔːmjulaiz] *v.t.,* **-lized, -liz·ing.** =**formulate.** —**for·mu·li·za·tion, for·mu·liz·er,** *n.*

for·ni·cate¹ [ˈfɔrnəˌket; ˈfɔːnikeit] *v.i.,* **-cat·ed, -cat·ing.** (未婚男女與異性)通姦;和姦。—**for·ni·ca·tor,** *n.*

for·ni·cate² *adj.* 彎曲的。(亦作 **fornicated**)

for·ni·ca·tion [ˌfɔrnɪˈkeʃən; ˌfɔːniˈkeiʃən] *n.* ①私通;和姦。②〖聖經〗通姦;宿娼;亂倫;偶像崇拜。

for·ni·ca·trix [ˌfɔrnɪˈketrɪks; ˌfɔːniˈkeitriks] *n., pl.* **-ca·tri·ces** [-kəˈtraɪsiz; -kəˈtraisiːz]. 與人通姦或和姦的女子。

for·ra·der [ˈfɔrədɚ; ˈfɔrədə] *adv.* 〖方〗更向前地。

for·rel [ˈfɑrəl; ˈfɔrəl] *n.* =**forel.**

***for·sake** [fɚˈsek; fəˈseik] *v.t.,* **-sook, -sak·en, -sak·ing.** ①遺棄;背棄;棄絕。She has *forsaken* her old friends. 她背棄了她的老友。②放棄;革除。—**for·sak·er,** *n.*

for·sak·en [fɚˈsekən; fəˈseikən] *v.* pp. of **forsake.** —*adj.* 被棄的;孤獨的。

for·sook [fɚˈsʊk; fəˈsuk] *v.* pt. of **forsake.**

for·sooth [fɚˈsuθ; fəˈsuːθ] *adv.* 〖古〗確實;實在;的確。

for·swear [fɔrˈswɛr; fɔːˈswɛə] *v.,* **-swore, -sworn, -swear·ing.** —*v.t.* ①誓

絕;戒絕;放棄。②背(誓)。③背信。—*v.i.* 作僞誓(與 oneself 連用)。—**er,** *n.*

for·swore [fɔr'swor; fɔː'swɔː] *v.* pt. of **forswear.**

for·sworn [fɔr'sworn; fɔː'swɔːn] *v.* pp. of **forswear.** —*adj.* (作)僞誓的。

for·syth·i·a [fə'sɪθɪə; fɔː'saiθjə] *n.* 〖植物〗連翹。

fort** [fort; fɔːt] *n.* ①堡壘;砲臺。②〖北美〗易貨站。hold the fort*** **a.** 防禦(對批評之)辯護。**b.** 維持現狀。They are *holding the fort* in our absence. 當我們不在時他們爲我們維持現狀(代理我們的工作)。—*v.t.* 築城防禦。

for·ta·lice ['fɔrtəlɪs; 'fɔːtəlis] *n.* ①小堡;外堡。②〖古〗要塞;堡壘。

for·te[1] ['fɔrtɪ; 'fɔːti] 〖義〗 *adj.* & *adv.* 〖音樂〗强音的(地)(略作 **f.**). —*n.* 一段强音的樂章。

forte[2] [fort; fɔːt] *n.* ①長處;擅長。②劍「身之最强部分。」

‡**forth** [forθ, fɔrθ; fɔːθ] *adv.* ①向前。②(自…)以後。③出外;離。④露出;出現。The sun came *forth* from behind the cloud. 太陽從雲後露出來。***and so forth*** 等等。***back and forth*** 來回地;前後地。***bring forth*** 產生;導致。***call forth*** 喚起。***put forth*** (草木)發(芽);生(葉)。

forth·com·ing ['forθ'kʌmɪŋ; fɔːθ'kʌmiŋ] *adj.* ①卽將出現的。The *forthcoming* week will be busy. 下週將甚忙。②卽將來到的;需要時卽可供給的;現成的。③友善的;好商量的。—*n.* 出現。

forth·right [ˌforθ'raɪt; ˌfɔːθ'rait] *adj.* ①坦白的;直率的。②直接的。—*adv.* (亦作 **forthrightly**) ①一往直前地。②立卽地。③直率地。—*n.* 〖古〗直路。—**ly,** *adv.* —**ness,** *n.*

forth·rights [ˌforθ'raɪts; ˌfɔːθ'raits] 「*adv.* = **forthright.**」

forth·with [forθ'wɪθ; 'fɔːθ'wiθ] *adv.* 立刻;不猶豫地;不延遲地。

***for·ti·eth** ['fɔrtɪɪθ; 'fɔːtiiθ] *n., adj.* ①第四十(的)。②四十分之一(的)。

for·ti·fi·a·ble ['fɔrtəˌfaɪəbl; 'fɔːtifaiəbl] *adj.* ①可使鞏固的。②可設防的。

***for·ti·fi·ca·tion** [ˌfɔrtəfə'keʃən; ˌfɔːtifi'keiʃən] *n.* ①築城;設防。②(常 *pl.*)防禦工事。③碉堡;堡壘;要塞。④加維他命或礦物質於食物中。⑤加强。the *fortification* of wine with alcohol. 將酒精加入酒中使酒力加强。

for·ti·fi·er ['fɔrtəˌfaɪə; 'fɔːtifaiə] *n.* ①築城家。②使鞏固之人或物。③〖諧〗補劑;酒。

***for·ti·fy** ['fɔrtəˌfaɪ; 'fɔːtifai] *v.,* **-fied, -fy·ing.** —*v.t.* ①加强。②設防;防衞。③加以滋養料(=enrich). ④增長心理上或道德上的力量。⑤證實;確定。He marshaled the facts to *fortify* his accusation. 他列舉事實以證實他的指控。⑥加酒精於葡萄酒等。—*v.i.* 設立防禦工事。

for·tis·si·mo [fɔr'tɪsəˌmo; fɔː'tisimou] 〖義〗 *adj.* & *adv.* 〖音樂〗最强的(地);最强音的(地)。(略作 **ff.**)

for·ti·tude ['fɔrtəˌtjud; 'fɔːtitjuːd] *n.* 堅忍;剛毅。

for·ti·tu·di·nous [ˌfɔrtə'tjudɪnəs; ˌfɔːti'tjuːdinəs] *adj.* 堅忍的;不屈不撓的。

***fort·night** ['fɔrtnaɪt, -nɪt; 'fɔːtnait] *n.* 兩禮拜;兩星期。a *fortnight's* holiday. 兩禮拜的假期。

fort·night·ly ['fɔrtˌnaɪtlɪ; 'fɔːtˌnaitli] *adj.* ①二週一次的。②隔週發行的。—*adv.* 二週一次地;隔週地。—*n.* 雙週刊。

For·tran, FORTRAN ['fɔrˌtræn; 'fɔːtræn] *n.* 〖電腦〗公式翻譯程式(爲 Formula Translator 之略)。

***for·tress** ['fɔrtrɪs; 'fɔːtris] *n.* ①堡壘。②安全處所。—*v.t.* 以堡壘防守。They *fortressed* the town against the anticipated flood. 他們加强了那個城市的防水措施以防預期來臨的水災。—**like,** *adj.*

for·tu·i·tism [fɔr'tjuəˌtɪzəm; fɔː'tju(ː)itizəm] *n.* 〖哲學〗偶然說;偶然論。

for·tu·i·tist [fɔr'tjuətɪst; fɔː'tju(ː)itist] *n.* 偶然論者。

for·tu·i·tous [fɔr'tjuətəs; fɔː'tju(ː)itəs] *adj.* ①偶然的;意外的。②幸運的。—**ly,** *adv.* —**ness,** *n.*

for·tu·i·ty [fɔr'tjuətɪ; fɔː'tju(ː)iti] *n., pl.* **-ties.** ①偶然性;偶然或意外之事實。②偶然;機緣。③偶然之事故;意外之災害。

***for·tu·nate** ['fɔrtʃənɪt; 'fɔːtʃnit, -tʃn̩it, -tʃənit] *adj.* ①幸運的;幸福的。You are a *fortunate* man. 你是一個幸運的人。②帶來幸運的。a *fortunate* star. 吉星;福星。—**ly,** *adv.* —**ness,** *n.*

‡**for·tune** ['fɔrtʃən; 'fɔːtʃən] *n., v.,* **-tuned, -tun·ing.** —*n.* ①財富;產業。②運氣;幸運。*Fortune* was against us; we lost. 我們運氣不好,因而失敗。③命運;機會。What will be our *fortune?* 我們未來命運如何?④(F-)擬人化的命運。Perhaps Dame *Fortune* will smile on our venture. 也許命運女神會向我們的事業微笑。⑤〖古〗女財主。***make a fortune*** 致富;發財。You'll *make a fortune* out of it. 你將要以此而發財。***seek one's fortune*** 尋出路;碰運氣。***tell a person's fortune*** 算命。She has had her *fortune told.* 她請人給她算過命了。***try one's fortune*** 碰運氣。—*v.t.* 〖古〗帶幸運給某人或某事。—*v.i.* 偶然發生。—**less,** *adj.*

fortune hunter 想與富人結婚者。

for·tune·tell·er ['fɔrtʃənˌtɛlə; 'fɔːtʃənˌtelə] *n.* 算命者;賣卜者;看相者。

for·tune·tell·ing ['fɔrtʃənˌtɛlɪŋ; 'fɔːtʃənˌteliŋ] *n., adj.* 算命(的);占卜(的)。

‡**for·ty** ['fɔrtɪ; 'fɔːti] *n., pl.* **-ties,** *adj.* —*n.*四十;四十個;40。a man of *forty.* 四十歲的人。the *forties.* 四十年代。—*adj.* 四十。

for·ty-eighth ['fɔrtɪ'etθ; 'fɔːti'eitθ] *n., adj.* 第四十八(的);四十八分之一(的)。

for·ty-fifth ['fɔrtɪ'fɪfθ; 'fɔːti'fifθ] *n., adj.* 第四十五(的);四十五分之一(的)。

for·ty-five ['fɔrtɪ'faɪv; 'fɔːti'faiv] *n.* ①四十五轉的唱片。②〖美俗〗四十五口徑手槍。

for·ty·fold ['fɔrtɪˌfold; 'fɔːtifould] 「*adj.* & *adv.* 四十倍的(地)。」

for·ty·ish ['fɔrtɪʃ; 'fɔːtiʃ] *adj.* 大約四十的;大約四十歲的。

for·ty-nine ['fɔrtɪ'naɪn; 'fɔːti'nain] *n., adj.* 四十九;四十九個;49。

for·ty-nin·er [ˌfɔrtɪ'naɪnə; ˌfɔːti'nainə] *n.* 〖美〗1849年往 California 採掘黃金之冒險者。

fo·rum ['forəm, 'fɔrəm; 'fɔːrəm] *n., pl.* **fo·rums, fo·ra** ['forə; 'fɔːrə]. ①古羅馬的市場與公共集會地。②討論會。③法庭。the *forum* of conscience. 良心的裁判。

‡**for·ward** ['fɔrwəd; 'fɔːwəd] *adv.* ①繼續向前;向前面(=forwards). to go *forward.* 走向前。from this time *forward.* 從

此以後。*Forward!*（口令）前進！②朝飛機或輪船之首端地。***backward(s) and forward(s)*** 來來去去地；前後地（=to and fro）。***look forward to*** 期待；希望。I am *looking forward to* the holidays. 我期待着假期。—*adj.* ①向前的；前部的。②早的；先的；早熟的。A child of four years that can read is *forward* for his age. 四歲的孩子能讀書，以其年齡而論是早熟的。③迅速的；敏捷的。④鹵莽的；大膽的。⑤進步的。⑥急切的；熱心的。to be *forward* to help others. 熱心助人。⑦〖商〗未來的；預定的。*forward* prices. 預約價目。—*v.t.* ①轉遞；轉寄。Please *forward* my mail to my new address. 請將我的信件轉到我的新住址。②助長；促進。He *forwarded* his friend's plan. 他曾協助朋友的計畫。—*n.*（足球等隊員的）前鋒。—**ly,** *adv.* —**ness,** *n.*

forward delivery 〖商〗定期交貨；「來日交貨。」

for·ward·er [ˈfɔrwədə; ˈfɔːwədə] *n.* ①促進者；助成者。②運送者；運輸(業)者。

forwarding agent 運輸(業)者。

forward quotation 〖商〗期貨報價。

for·wards [ˈfɔrwədz; ˈfɔːwədz] *adv.* 「=**forward.**」

for·wea·ried [fɔrˈwɪrɪd; fɔːˈwiərid] *adj.* =**forworn.**

for·went [fɔrˈwɛnt; fɔːˈwent] *v.* pt. 「of **forgo.**」

for·worn [fɔrˈworn; fɔːˈwɔːn] *adj.* 〖古〗筋疲力竭的；破爛的。(亦作 **foreworn**)

fos·sa [ˈfɑsə; ˈfɔsə] *n., pl.* **-sae** [-si; -siː]. 〖解剖〗(骨骼等中之)窩；凹穴。

fosse [fɑs; fɔs] *n.* ①〖築城〗護城河；壕。②壕溝；溝渠。③〖解剖〗=**fossa.**

fos·sick [ˈfɑsɪk; ˈfɔsik] *v.i.* 〖澳〗①〖採礦〗從廢礦中尋求黃金。②翻尋；探求。—*v.t.* 〖澳〗搜尋；採掘。—**er,** *n.*

***fos·sil** [ˈfɑsl̩; ˈfɔsl, -sil] *n.* ①化石。②老頑固；古物。—*adj.* ①成化石的；有化石特性的。②從土中掘出的。③陳腐的。*fossil* ideas. 陳腐的思想。—**like,** *adj.*

fos·sil·if·er·ous [ˌfɑsəˈlɪfərəs; ˌfɔsiˈlifərəs] *adj.* 含有化石的。

fos·sil·ize [ˈfɑsl̩ˌaɪz; ˈfɔsilaiz] *v.t.* & *v.i.,* **-ized, -iz·ing.** ①變成化石；使成化石。②變成古板或頑固；使變成古板或頑固。③使變成死物或過去之物。④〖俗〗尋找化石。

fos·so·ri·al [fɑˈsorɪəl; fɔˈsɔːriəl] *adj.* 〖動物〗①掘地的。②適於掘地的。

Fos·ter [ˈfɔstɚ; ˈfɔstə] *n.* 福斯特(Stephen Collins, 1826–1864, 美國作曲家)。

***fos·ter** [ˈfɔstɚ; ˈfɔstə] *v.t.* ①養育；撫育；看護。②心懷；存心。③鼓勵；助長。Ignorance *fosters* superstition. 無知助長迷信。④〖英〗將小孩委託養父母家。⑤〖廢〗飼；餵。—*n.* 〖廢〗養父(母)。—*adj.* 養育的；收養的。

fos·ter·age [ˈfɔstərɪdʒ; ˈfɔstəridʒ] *n.* ①養育；寄養；收養。②養子身分。③勉勵；助長。

foster care 孤兒、不良少年等在公共機構或私人家庭裏所受之照顧。

fos·ter·er [ˈfɑstərɚ; ˈfɔstərə] *n.* ①養父或養母。②鼓勵或助長之人或事物。③保護者；後臺；靠山。

foster home 養父母之家。

fos·ter·ling [ˈfɔstəlɪŋ; ˈfɔstəliŋ] *n.* 養子(女)。

fos·ter-moth·er [ˈfɔstəˈmʌðɚ; ˈfɔstəˈmʌðə] *n.* 〖英〗保育器。—*v.t.* 將…作爲養母奉養。

foster parent 養父或養母。

fos·tress [ˈfɑstrɪs; ˈfɔstris] *n.* 養母；保姆。

fought [fɔt; fɔːt] *v.* pt. & pp. of **fight.**

foul** [faul; faul] *adj.* ①污穢的；惡臭的；味惡的。a *foul* smell. 惡臭的氣味。Open the windows, and let out the *foul* air. 請打開窗子，讓污濁的空氣流出去。②邪惡的；不正的；不光明的(fair 之對)。③碰撞的。④(繩等)糾纏着的。⑤阻塞的；塡塞住的。⑥(船等)底部覆有海藻、貝殼等的。⑦險惡的；逆的；暴風雨的。*Foul* weather delayed the ship. 壞天氣使船耽擱。⑧討厭的；叫人發嘔的。⑨泥濘的。⑩(草稿等)錯誤百出的；更改甚多的。⑪不公平的；違規的。⑫(言語)粗俗的；瀆神的。—*v.t.* ①使污穢；使臭。Factory chimneys *foul* the air with smoke. 工廠的烟囱所冒之烟使空氣污濁。②(船)碰撞(船)。③與…糾纏。The rope *fouled* the anchor chain. 繩與錨鏈糾纏在一起。④(競技)對…犯規。⑤使污塞；阻塞。Grease *fouled* the drain. 油污阻塞住排水管。⑥用海藻等遮覆(船底)。—*v.i.* ①變髒。②(船)碰撞。③糾結；纏；塞住。④(競技)犯規。⑤〖棒球〗打球出線外。foul out*** **a.** 〖棒球〗因擊出之界外球被接住而出局。**b.** 〖籃球〗犯滿離場。***foul up*** 〖美俗〗弄糟；搞壞。—*n.* ①(競技)犯規。②〖美，棒球〗界外球。③相撞；糾纏。—*adv.* 碰撞地；爭執不和地。***fall*** (***go,*** or ***run***) ***foul of*** **a.** 與…爭執不和；(船與船)互撞。**b.** 與…衝突。**c.** 攻擊。

fou·lard [fuˈlɑrd; fuːˈlɑːd] 〖法〗*n.* ①一種軟薄花綢。②此綢所製之領帶等。

foul ball 〖棒球〗界外球。 「毛織品。」

fou·lé [fuˈle; fuːˈlei] 〖法〗*n.* 一種女用

foul line ①〖棒球〗界線(本壘至第一壘或第三壘間的直線及其延長線)。②〖籃球〗邊線。

foul·ly [ˈfaullɪ, ˈfaulɪ; ˈfaulli, ˈfauli] *adv.* ①污穢地。②邪惡地。③討人厭地。

foul·mouthed [ˈfaulˈmauðd; ˈfaulˈmauðd] *adj.* 口出惡言的；出言不遜的；出言粗俗的。(亦作 **foul-spoken, foul-tongued**)

foul·ness [ˈfaulnɪs; ˈfaulnis] *n.* ①污穢。②不潔之物。③邪惡。

foul play ①犯規。②欺詐；暴行。

foul shot 〖籃球〗①罰球。②罰球所得之一分。 「混亂；一團糟。②(機器之)故障。」

foul-up [ˈfaulˌʌp; ˈfaulˌʌp] *n.* 〖俗〗①

fou·mart [ˈfumɑrt; ˈfuːmɑːt] *n.* 〖動物〗歐洲臭貓。 「**find.**」

‡found[1] [faund; faund] *v.* pt. & pp. of

found[2] *adj.* 〖英〗不另加費供應的(如對房客等)；已包括在價款、租金內的(通常放在句子的後面)。—*n.* 〖英〗不另加費供應的東西(如給傭人的膳食)。

***found**[3] *v.t.* 建立；創設；以…爲基礎。—*v.i.* ①以…爲根據〖常 on, upon〗. ②以…爲意見之根據〖常 on, upon〗.

found[4] *v.t.* ①鎔(金屬)於模型中。②鑄造。

‡foun·da·tion [faunˈdeʃən; faunˈdeiʃən] *n.* ①基礎；根基；根據。The rumor has no *foundation.* 謠言無根據。②基金；基金會。the Carnegie *Foundation.* 卡內基基金會。③建設；建立(如城鎭、教會、學校等)。The *foundation* of the Republic of China was in 1911. 中華民國的建立是在1911年。④= **foundation garment.** ⑤粉底。—**ar·y,** —**al,** *adj.* —**al·ly,** *adv.*

foun·da·tion·er [faunˈdeʃənɚ; faunˈdeiʃn̩ə] *n.* 〖英〗領受獎學金之學生。

foundation garment 女人之內衣

如腰帶、緊身搭等。

foundation school 由捐助基金所創立之學校。

foundation stone ①基石。②基礎；基本原理；根基。

***found·er**[1] 〔ˈfaundɚ; ˈfaundə〕 *n.* 建立者；創設者。*founder's* shares. (公司的)發起人股。

***foun·der**[2] *v.i.* ①進水而沉沒。②跌倒；跌跛。③崩潰；失敗。④因過食而生病。 A pet may *founder* if fed improperly. 寵愛的動物(如狗、貓等)如飼餵不當會生病的。 —*v.t.* ①使(馬)跌跛。②使進水而沉沒。 —*n.* 驢馬等足部發炎。

found·er[3] *n.* 鎔金屬品之人；鑄造者。

founding father 開國者；創立人。

found·ling 〔ˈfaundlɪŋ; ˈfaundliŋ〕 *n.* 棄兒；棄嬰。

foundling hospital 育嬰堂；棄兒養育院。

found·ress 〔ˈfaundrɛs; ˈfaundris〕 *n.* ①女創立者。②寄贈基金之女人。

found·ry 〔ˈfaundrɪ; ˈfaundri〕 *n., pl.* **-ries.** ①鑄造工廠。②鑄造。③鑄造之成品。④鑄造法。

fount[1] 〔faunt; faunt〕 *n.* ①源泉。②根源；來源。

fount[2] *n.* 〖英、印刷〗字體、大小均一樣之一套活字。(亦作 **font**)

***foun·tain** 〔ˈfauntn̩, -tɪn; ˈfauntin〕 *n.* ①噴泉；噴水池。②泉源；源流。③(街頭或學校中的)飲水處。④本源；出處。⑤(鋼筆等的)貯墨器。⑥(在餐館內)出售蘇打水、冰淇淋等的櫃臺(=soda fountain)。 —*v.i.* (水之)噴灑。 —**ed,** —**like,** *adj.* —**less,** *adj.*

foun·tain·head 〔ˈfauntn̩ˌhɛd; ˈfauntinˈhed〕 *n.* ①水源；源頭。②本源；根源。

fountain pen 鋼筆；自來水筆。

‡**four** 〔for, fɔr; fɔː, fɔə〕 *n., adj.* 四；四個；4。 ***on all fours*** 匍匐着；爬着。

four·bag·ger 〔ˈforˈbægɚ; ˈfɔːˈbægə〕 *n.* 〖棒球，俚〗全壘打。

four·flush·er 〔ˈforˌflʌʃɚ; ˈfɔːˌflʌʃə〕 *n.* ①〖撲克〗虛稱有一手同花牌者；偷雞者。②〖俚〗吹嘘者；虛張聲勢者。

four·fold 〔ˈforˈfold; ˈfɔː-fould〕 *adj.* ①四倍的。②四重的；四摺的。 —*adv.* 四倍地；四重地；四摺地。

four-foot·ed 〔ˈforˈfutɪd; ˈfɔːˈfutid〕 *adj.* 有四足的。

four-hand·ed 〔ˈforˈhændɪd; ˈfɔːˈhændid〕 *adj.* ①有四手的。②供四人玩的(遊戲等)。③〖音樂〗供二人演奏的(如鋼琴二重奏)。

Four-H club, 4-H club 〔ˈforˌetʃ～; ˈfɔːrˈeitʃ～〕 四健會(美國農業部主持之"四健運動"的機構，其目的爲推進農民的教育與社交生活，四個 H 卽 head, hands, heart 及 health 之略)。

Fou·ri·er·ism 〔ˈfurɪəˌrɪzəm; ˈfuriərizəm〕 *n.* (法國社會主義者傅立葉氏 F. M. C. Fourier 所倡之)社會共產主義。

four-in-hand 〔ˈforɪnˌhænd; ˈfɔːrinˈhænd〕 *n.* ①打活結之領帶。②由一人御駛而駕四馬的車。③同駕一輛馬車的四匹馬。 —*adj.* four-in-hand 的。

four-o'clock 〔ˈforəˌklak; ˈfɔːrəˌklɔk〕 *n.* ①〖植物〗紫茉莉。②澳洲食蜜鳥。

four·pence 〔ˈforpəns; ˈfɔːpəns〕 *n.* 四辨士；價值四辨士之英國銀幣。

four·pen·ny 〔ˈforˌpɛnɪ; ˈfɔːpəni〕 *n.* =**fourpence.** —*adj.* 值四辨士的。

four-post·er 〔ˈforˈpostɚ; ˈfɔːˈpoustə〕 *n.* ①四柱的床。②四桅的帆船。

four·score 〔ˈforˈskor; ˈfɔːˈskɔː〕 *n., adj.* 八十；80。

four·some 〔ˈforsəm; ˈfɔːsəm〕 *n.* ①四人的一組。②〖運動〗**a.** (每邊兩人的)四人對抗賽；雙打。**b.** 與賽的四人。 ***a mixed foursome*** (男女)混合四人對抗賽；男女混合雙打。 —*adj.* 四人一組的；由四人組成的。

four·square 〔ˈforˈskwɛr; ˈfɔːˈskwɛə〕 *adj.* ①四方的；正方的。②坦白的；率直的。③堅定的；不妥協的。 —*adv.* 不含混其詞地；正直地。 —*n.* 正方形。 —**ly,** *adv.* —**ness,** *n.*

‡**four·teen** 〔ˈforˈtin, ˈfɔr-; ˈfɔːˈtiːn〕 *n., adj.* 十四；十四個；14。

***four·teenth** 〔ˈforˈtinθ, ˈfɔr-; ˈfɔːˈtiːnθ〕 *n., adj.* ①第十四(的)；第十四個(的)。②十四分之一(的)。

‡**fourth** 〔forθ, fɔrθ; fɔːθ, fɔəθ〕 *adj.* 第四的；第四個的；四分之一的。 —*n.* ①第四。②四分之一。③〖音樂〗第四度音(程)。④(the F-) =**the Fourth of July.**

fourth dimension 第四度空間(除長、闊、高三度外之第四度空間，卽時間)。

Fourth Estate, fourth estate 第四階級(指新聞界)。

fourth·ly 〔ˈforθlɪ; ˈfɔːθli〕 *adv.* 第四。

Fourth of July 七月四日(美國1776年獨立紀念日)。

four-wheel·er 〔ˈforˈhwilɚ; ˈfɔːˈwiːlə〕 *n.* ①〖英〗四輪馬車。②四輪車輛。

***fowl** 〔faul; faul〕 *n., pl.* **fowls** or **fowl,** *v.* —*n.* ①禽；鳥。 the *fowls* of the air. 飛禽。②家禽；鷄。③禽肉；鷄肉(食物)。 —*v.i.* 獵野禽。

Fowl·er 〔ˈfaulɚ; ˈfaulə〕 *n.* 福勒(Henry Watson, 1858–1933, 英國辭典編纂者)。

fowl·er 〔ˈfaulɚ; ˈfaulə〕 *n.* 捕鳥者；獵野禽者。

fowl·ing 〔ˈfaulɪŋ; ˈfauliŋ〕 *n.* 捕鳥；獵野禽。

fowling piece 鳥鎗；獵鎗。

fowl-run 〔ˈfaulˌrʌn; ˈfaulrʌn〕 *n.* 〖英〗養鷄場。

‡**fox** 〔fɑks; fɔks〕 *n.* ①狐。②狐皮。③狡猾的人。 —*v.t.* & *v.i.* ①〖俗〗用狡計；欺詐。②(使)變色；褪色。③(啤酒)變酸。④獵狐。

fox brush 狐尾。

fox earth 狐穴。

foxed 〔fɑkst; fɔkst〕 *adj.* ①變酸的(如啤酒)。②汚損的；變色的(如舊書)。③被詐欺的。④修理過的(如鞋)。⑤酒醉的。

fox·glove 〔ˈfɑksˌglʌv; ˈfɔksglʌv〕 *n.* 〖植物〗指頂花。

fox·hole 〔ˈfɑksˌhol; ˈfɔkshoul〕 *n.* 〖軍〗散兵坑。

fox·hound 〔ˈfɑksˌhaund; ˈfɔkshaund〕 *n.* 狐猩(獵狐用的一種獵犬)。

fox-hunt 〔ˈfɑksˌhʌnt; ˈfɔkshʌnt〕 *v.i.* 獵狐。 —**er,** *n.*

fox·i·ness 〔ˈfɑksɪnɪs; ˈfɔksinis〕 *n.* 狐性；狡猾。

fox·tail 〔ˈfɑksˌtel; ˈfɔksteil〕 *n.* ①狐尾。②〖植物〗狐尾草。

fox terrier 一種獵狐小狗(現多飼作玩物)。

fox trot ①狐步舞。②狐步舞曲。③(騎馬中)一種小跑步法(由快步改爲慢步時用)。

fox-trot 〔ˈfɑksˌtrɑt; ˈfɔkstrɔt〕 *v.i.,* **-trot·ted, -trot·ting.** ①(馬)走 fox trot 步。②跳狐步舞。

fox·y 〔ˈfɑksɪ; ˈfɔksi〕 *adj.,* **fox·i·er, fox·i·est.** ①如狐的；狡猾的。②紅褐色的；有褐或黃色斑點的(如舊書等)。③損壞的；殘缺的。④變色的。⑤酸的(啤酒、酒等)。

foy·er 〔ˈfɔɪɚ; ˈfɔiei〕 *n., pl.* **-ers.** ①(戲院、旅館或公寓等門口內的)休憩處。②(門口

內的)走廊。

fp. 〖音樂〗forte-piano. **F.P.** ①field punishment. ②fireplug. ③foot-pound. **f.p.** ①fireplug. ②foot-pound. ③〖音樂〗forte-piano. ④freezing point. ⑤fully paid. **fpm** feet per minute. (亦作 **ft/min**) **f.p.s.** ①feet per second. ②foot-pound-second. ③frames per second. **Fr** 化學元素 francium 之符號。**Fr.** ①Father. ②*pl.* **Fr., Frs.** franc. ③France. ④frater. ⑤French. ⑥Friar. ⑦Friday. **fr.** franc; from; fragment.

Fra, fra [frɑ; frɑː] *n.* 天主教修道士之稱號。

fra·cas ['frekəs; 'frækɑː] *n., pl.* **-es.** 吵鬧;喧嚷;打鬧;騷動;打架。

frac·tion** ['frækʃən; 'frækʃən] *n.* ①部分;片;微量。Only a *fraction* of the regiment returned alive. 該團僅極少數人生還。②〖數學〗分數。complex *fraction.* 繁分數。③分裂;破碎。a fraction of a second*** 頃刻。—*v.t.* ①使成爲部分(分數)。②分餾。

frac·tion·al ['frækʃənḷ; 'frækʃənḷ] *adj.* ①分數的。②極小的;極少的;瑣屑的。③〖化〗分段的;分別的。

fractional currency 輔幣。

frac·tion·al·ism ['frækʃənḷˌɪzəm; 'frækʃənəlizəm] *n.* 分裂主義或政策。

frac·tion·ar·y ['frækʃənˌɛrɪ; 'frækʃənəri] *adj.* =**fractional.**

frac·tion·ate ['frækʃənˌet; 'frækʃəneit] *v.t.,* **-at·ed, -at·ing.** 〖化〗①將…分餾。②用分餾法取得。

frac·tion·a·tion [ˌfrækʃən'eʃən; ˌfrækʃən'eiʃən] *n.*〖化〗分餾(法);分別(法)。

frac·tion·ize ['frækʃənˌaɪz; 'frækʃənaiz] *v.t.* & *v.i.,* **-ized, -iz·ing.** 分爲碎片;化爲分數。

frac·tious ['frækʃəs; 'frækʃəs] *adj.* 乖張的;易怒的;性情暴戾的;難駕馭的;倔强的。—**ly,** *adv.* —**ness,** *n.*

***frac·ture** ['fræktʃɚ; 'fræktʃə] *n., v.,* **-tured, -tur·ing.** —*n.* ①破口;裂縫。The *fracture* on the foundation is widening. 屋基上的裂口正在擴大中。②斷折;破碎。③〖外科〗挫傷;骨折。④〖礦〗斷口。—*v.t.* 折斷;破碎。He fell from a tree and *fractured* his leg. 他從樹上跌下,跌斷了腿。—*v.i.* 折斷;破碎。—**frac·tur·a·ble, frac·tur·al,** *adj.*

frae [fre; frei] *prep., adv.* 〖蘇〗=**from.**

frae·num ['frinəm; 'friːnəm] *n., pl.* **-na** [-nə; -nə]. 〖解剖,動物〗=**frenum.**

***frag·ile** ['frædʒəl; 'frædʒail,-dʒil] *adj.* ①易碎的;脆的。Be careful; that thin glass is *fragile.* 當心,那薄玻璃是易碎的。②不實在的;缺少力量的。—**ly,** *adv.* —**ness,** *n.*

fra·gil·i·ty [fræ'dʒɪlətɪ; frə'dʒiliti] *n.* 脆弱性;虛弱;易壞。

***frag·ment** ['frægmənt; 'frægmənt] *n.* 碎片;斷片;破片。Try to put the *fragments* of a broken vase together. 試將一破花瓶的碎片再拼爲整瓶。—*v.i.* 成爲碎片。The chair *fragmented* under his weight. 在他的體重下,椅子破碎了。—*v.t.* 打碎;打破。The vase was *fragmented* in shipment. 花瓶在運送途中被打碎了。

frag·men·tal [fræg'mɛntḷ; fræg'mentl] *adj.* ①=**fragmentary.** ②〖地質〗碎屑質的;斷岩的。—**ly,** *adv.*

frag·men·tar·y ['frægmənˌtɛrɪ; 'frægməntəri] *adj.* 殘破不全的;片斷的;不完整的;不連接的。

frag·men·ta·tion [ˌfrægmən'teʃən; ˌfrægmən'teiʃən] *n.* ①破碎;殘破。②崩潰。③(砲彈等之)爆裂。

***fra·grance** ['fregrəns; 'freigrəns] *n.* 香味;香氣。the *fragrance* after showers. 雨後的清香。

***fra·gran·cy** ['fregrənsɪ; 'freigrənsi] *n., pl.* **-cies.** =**fragrance.**

***fra·grant** ['fregrənt; 'freigrənt] *adj.* 芳香的;馥郁的;愉快的。*fragrant* tea. 香茶。*fragrant* memories. 愉快的回憶。—**ly,** *adv.* —**ness,** *n.*

***frail**[1] [frel; freil] *adj.* ①脆弱的;不堅實的;不鞏固的。a *frail* child. 脆弱的小孩。②意志薄弱的;易墮落的;易受誘惑的。③操守不堅的;淫蕩的。—**ness,** *n.*

frail[2] ①燈心草所編之簍(用以裝無花果、葡萄乾等)。②一簍葡萄乾等之重量(通常爲 50 或75磅)。

frail·ly ['frellɪ; 'freilli] *adv.* 脆弱地;不堅實地。

***frail·ty** ['freltɪ; 'freilti] *n., pl.* **-ties.** ①脆弱。②意志薄弱;易受誘惑之性質。③品德上的缺點;過失。He loved her in spite of her little *frailties.* 雖然她品德上有小小的缺點,他還是愛她。

fraise [frez; freiz] *n.* ①〖築城〗寨柵。②十六世紀時着於頸際之襞襟。

F.R.A.M. Fellow of the Royal Academy of Music.

fram·b(o)e·si·a [fræm'biʒɪə; fræm'biːʒiə] *n.* 〖醫〗印度痘(一種皮膚傳染病)。

‡frame [frem; freim] *n., v.,* **framed, fram·ing.** —*n.* ①骨架;架子。②身體;體格。He has a strong *frame.* 他的體格很强。③框架。④構造;組織。⑤心境;心情。He is in an unhappy *frame* of mind. 他心境不佳。⑥〖電影〗軟片中的一個畫面。⑦(滾球戲的)一回。⑧(電視中的)像;形像。⑨〖俗〗棒球之一局。—*v.t.* ①構造;組織;設計。His lips could not *frame* the words. 他說不出話來。②給…裝框。③〖美〗陷害;誣陷。The prisoner claimed that he had been *framed* by his enemies. 犯人聲稱他是被仇人陷害的。—*v.i.* 發展;進行;有成功希望。

frame house 木架屋;木造居屋。

fram·er ['fremɚ; 'freimə] *n.* ①組成者;計劃者;設計者。②裝框者。

frame saw 框鋸(緊裝於框上之鋸)。

frame-up ['fremˌʌp; 'freim'ʌp] *n.* 〖俗〗①陰謀詭計。②誣陷之計。

***frame·work** ['fremˌwɝk; 'freimwəːk] *n.* ①骨架;支架。②組織;體制。the *framework* of society. 社會的組織。③果樹之枝。—*v.t.* 在(果樹上)接枝。

fram·ing ['fremɪŋ; 'freimiŋ] *n.* ①結構;組織。②構想;策劃;設計。③骨架;體制;結構物。

***franc** [fræŋk; fræŋk] *n.* 法郎(錢幣名,通用於法國、比利時及瑞士)。

‡France[1] [fræns; frɑːns] *n.* 法國;法蘭西(西歐一國,首都爲巴黎 Paris).

France[2] [fræns; frɑ̃s] *n.* 法朗士 (Anatole, 1844–1924, 法國小說家及諷刺家,曾獲1921年諾貝爾文學獎)。

Fran·ces ['frænsɪs; 'frɑːnsis] *n.* 女子名(暱稱 Fran, Fannie, Fanny).

fran·chise ['fræntʃaɪz; 'fræntʃaiz] *n.* ①政府特許之權;特權。②特權區。③選舉權;參政權。④經銷權。⑤有經銷權之地區。⑥免除賦稅負擔之特權。⑦〖廢〗免除受刑之特權。—*v.t.* ①賦與特權。②賦與市民權;賦與選舉權。—**fran·chis·al**, *adj.* —**ment**, *n.*

fran·chi·see [ˌfræntʃaɪˈzi; ˌfræntʃaiˈziː] *n.* 經公司授權而設立零售店或分號的人。

fran·chis·er [ˈfræntʃaɪzɚ; ˈfræntʃaizə] *n.* 經銷商;代銷商。

Fran·cis [ˈfrænsɪs; ˈfrɑːnsis] *n.* ①男子名。②聖芳濟 (Saint, 全名 Francis of Assisi, 1181? -1226, 義大利修士, 曾建立聖芳濟修會)。

Fran·cis·can [frænˈsɪskən; frænˈsiskən] *adj.* 天主教聖芳濟修會的。—*n.* 聖芳濟修會的修道士。

fran·ci·um [ˈfrænsɪəm; ˈfrænsiəm] *n.* 〖化〗鍅(元素名, 符號為 Fr)。

Franck [frɑŋk; frɑːŋk] *n.* 佛朗克 (James, 1882-1964, 出生德國之美國物理學家, 1925年獲諾貝爾獎)。

Fran·co [ˈfrɑŋko; ˈfrɑːŋkou] *n.* 佛朗哥(Francisco, 1892-1975, 西班牙將軍, 1939-1975為元首)。—**ism**, —**ist**, *n.*

Fran·co-A·mer·i·can [ˈfræŋkoəˈmɛrəkən; ˈfræŋkouəˈmerikən] *n.* 法美血統。—*adj.* 法美的。

fran·co·lin [ˈfræŋkəlɪn; ˈfræŋkoulin] *n.* 鷓鴣。

Fran·co·phil(e) [ˈfræŋkəˌfaɪl; ˈfrɑːŋkəfail] *adj.* 崇拜法國的;親法的。—*n.* 崇拜法國者;親法分子。

franc-ti·reur [ˌfrɑ̃ˌtiˈrœr; ˌfrɑ̃ːˌtiːˈrœr] *n.*, *pl.* **francs-ti·reurs.** (法國陸軍之)非正規之狙擊兵。

fran·gi·bil·i·ty [ˌfrændʒəˈbɪlətɪ; ˌfrændʒiˈbiliti] *n.* 易碎性;脆弱性。

fran·gi·ble [ˈfrændʒəbl̩; ˈfrændʒibl] *adj.* 易碎的;易破的;脆弱的。—**ness**, *n.*

fran·gi·pane [ˈfrændʒəˌpen; ˈfrændʒipein] *n.* ①一種乳油與杏仁所製之烟餅。②=**frangipani.**

fran·gi·pan·i [ˌfrændʒɪˈpænɪ; ˌfrændʒiˈpæni] *n.*, *pl.* **-pan·is**, **-pan·i.** ①〖植物〗赤素馨。②赤素馨花所製之香水。(亦作 **frangipanni**)

Frank[1] [fræŋk; fræŋk] *n.* ①日耳曼民族之法蘭克人。②(地中海及愛琴海東海岸國家所稱之)西歐人或居民。

Frank[2] *n.* 佛蘭克(Glenn, 1887-1940, 美國教育家)。

Frank[3] *n.* 男子名。

frank** [fræŋk; fræŋk] *adj.* ①坦白的;率直的;老實的。a *frank* look. 率直的表情。②明白的;無掩飾的。be perfectly frank with you*** 老實對你說(句中挿語)。—*v.t.* ①免費寄送(信件等)。②免費運送(某人等)。③取得免費。④使能自由出入。⑤使(某人)來去自如;便利(某人)交際。A sizable inheritance will *frank* you faster than anything else. 一筆可觀的遺產將比其他東西更能使你便於交際。—*n.* ①免費遞送的簽字式。②免費遞送的權利。③免費遞送的信件、包裹等。—**a·bil·i·ty**, —**er**, *n.* —**a·ble**, *adj.*

Frank·en·stein [ˈfræŋkənˌstaɪn; ˈfræŋkənstain] *n.* ①Mary Shelly 所著 *Frankenstein* 中之男主角名。②作法自斃者。③Frankenstein 所創之怪物。④危及創造者之物。

frank·furt·er [ˈfræŋkfɚtɚ; ˈfræŋkfətə] *n.* 一種牛肉及猪肉所製之微紅色臘腸。(亦作 **frankforter**)

frank·in·cense [ˈfræŋkɪnˌsɛns; ˈfræŋkinsens] *n.* 乳香(主要用於供奉神祇)。

Frank·ish [ˈfræŋkɪʃ; ˈfræŋkiʃ] *adj.* ①日耳曼民族之法蘭克人的;其語言或文化的。②西歐人的。—*n.* 日耳曼民族之法蘭克語。

Frank·lin[1] [ˈfræŋklɪn; ˈfræŋklin] *n.* 富蘭克林 (Benjamin, 1706-1790, 美國政治家、著作家和發明家)。—**i·an**, *adj.*, *n.*

Frank·lin[2] *n.* 佛蘭克林(Sir John, 1786-1847, 英國北極探險家)。

frank·lin [ˈfræŋklɪn; ˈfræŋklin] *n.* ①(十四及十五世紀英格蘭非出身於貴族之)中等階級小地主。②〖英〗擁有土地之富農。

***frank·ly** [ˈfræŋklɪ; ˈfræŋkli] *adv.* 坦白地;率直地;明白地。*Frankly* (speaking), I don't like him. 坦白地說, 我不喜歡他。

***frank·ness** [ˈfræŋknɪs; ˈfræŋknis] *n.* 坦白;率直;明白。

frank·pledge [ˈfræŋkˌplɛdʒ; ˈfræŋkpledʒ] *n.* 〖英史〗①十家互保制。②十家互保制中之一家。

***fran·tic** [ˈfræntɪk; ˈfræntik] *adj.* ①似發狂的;狂亂的;激昂的。*frantic* cries for help. 狂呼求救。②〖古〗發瘋的。—**ness**, *n.* —**al·ly**, —**ly**, *adv.*

frap [fræp; fræp] *v.t.*, **frapped**, **frap·ping.** ①〖航海〗(用索等)縛緊。②拉緊(索)。

frap·pé [fræˈpe; fræˈpei] *adj.* 冰的;凍的。wine *frappé.* 冰凍過的酒。—*n.* 冰凍飲料。

F.R.A.S. Fellow of the Royal Astronomical Society.

frat [fræt; fræt] *n.* 〖俗〗(=fraternity) 大學男生聯誼社;兄弟會。

fra·ter·nal [frəˈtɝnl̩; frəˈtəːnl] *adj.* ①兄弟的;如兄弟的;友愛的。②兄弟會的;互助的。③孿生子的;同胞性的 (為 identical "同胚性的"之對)。—**ism**, *n.* —**ly**, *adv.*

***fra·ter·ni·ty** [frəˈtɝnətɪ; frəˈtəːniti] *n.*, *pl.* **-ties.** ①博愛。②團體;同行;同業的人。the medical *fraternity.* 醫界同人。③兄弟會(美國男學生中的一種組織)。④〖天主教〗俗人(僧侶之對)所組織之宗教或慈善團體。

fraternity house (美國大學) 兄弟會會所。

frat·er·ni·za·tion [ˌfrætɚnɪˈzeʃən; ˌfrætənaiˈzeiʃən] *n.* 視如兄弟;親睦;親善。

frat·er·nize [ˈfrætɚˌnaɪz; ˈfrætənaiz] *v.*, **-nized**, **-niz·ing.** —*v.i.* ①結交如兄弟;親善;友善地交往。②(在占領敵國領土期間, 對其國民)友善。③〖俗〗(士兵)與敵人發生性行為。—*v.t.* 〖罕〗使親善。—**frat·er·niz·er**, *n.*

frat·ri·cid·al [ˌfrætrəˈsaɪdl̩; ˌfreitriˈsaidl] *adj.* 殺害兄弟或姐妹的;殺害親屬或同胞的。

frat·ri·cide [ˈfrætrəˌsaɪd; ˈfreitrisaid] *n.* ①殺害兄弟或姊妹者。②殺害兄弟或姊妹的行為。

Frau [frau; frau] *n.*, *pl.* **Fraus**, **Frauen** [ˈfrauən; ˈfrauən]. 〖德〗①太太 (=Mrs.). ②(亦作 **frau**)太太;夫人;妻。

***fraud** [frɔd; frɔːd] *n.* ①詐欺;欺騙。②詐欺的行為;騙人的事或人。The so-called specific was a *fraud.* 所謂的特效藥原是騙人的東西。—**ful**, *adj.* —**ful·ly**, *adv.*

fraud·u·lent [ˈfrɔdʒələnt; ˈfrɔːdjulənt] *adj.* ①詭詐的;不誠實的。②藉以欺騙的。③騙取的。—**ly**, *adv.* —**fraud·u·lence**, **fraud·u·len·cy**, *n.*

fraught [frɔt; frɔːt] *adj.* ①充滿;滿載〖常 with〗。②〖古〗裝載;滿載。—*n.* 〖蘇〗(船上之)載貨。

Fräu·lein [ˈfrɔɪlaɪn; ˈfrɔilain] *n.*, *pl.* **Fräu·leins**, **Fräu·lein.** 〖德〗①小姐 (=

Miss). ②(f-)小姐;未婚女子。

frax·i·nel·la [ˌfræksɪˈnɛlə; ˌfræksiˈnelə] *n.* 〖植物〗白蘚。

fray[1] [fre; frei] *n.* ①吵鬧;喧嘩。②爭吵;衝突。

fray[2] *v.t.* ①磨損;磨破。②磨去;磨擦。③擾亂;使煩惱。—*v.i.* 被磨損;被磨破;破爛。—*n.* (衣服、布料)磨破之處。 **—ed·ness,** *n.*

fraz·zle [ˈfræzl;ˈfræzl] *v.,* **-zled, -zling,** *n.* —*v.t.* & *v.i.* 〖俗〗①擦損;(使)破爛。②(使)疲憊。—*n.* 〖俗〗①擦損;破爛。②疲憊。

FRB, F.R.B. ①Federal Reserve Bank. 聯邦準備銀行。②Federal Reserve Board. **FRC** Federal Radio Commission. **F.R.C.P.** Fellow of the Royal College of Physicians.

freak[1] [frik; fri:k] *n.* ①畸形物。②異想天開。③風向之突變。④朝三暮四;反覆無常。***freak of nature*** 造化的惡作劇;天生的畸形。***out of mere freak*** 只由於一時高興。—*adj.* 畸形的;怪誕的。—*v.i.* 作輕浮之事;作古怪行徑。**—ful,** *adj.*

freak[2] *v.t.* 〖詩〗加以斑點;飾以條紋;飾以彩色。—*n.* 〖詩〗彩色之斑紋或條紋。

freak·ish [ˈfrikɪʃ; ˈfri:kiʃ] *adj.* 怪異的;荒誕的。**—ness,** *n.* **—ly,** *adv.*

freak-out [ˈfrikˌaut; ˈfri:k-aut] *n.* 〖俚〗①由吸毒引起的幻覺。②以吸毒逃避現實。

·**freck·le** [ˈfrɛkl̩; ˈfrekl] *n., v.,* **-led, -ling.** —*n.* ①雀斑;痣。②小斑點。*Freckles* of paint spattered on the floor. 油漆細點濺上了地板。—*v.t.* 使生雀斑。Her face was *freckled* all over. 她的臉長滿了雀斑。—*v.i.* 生雀斑;生斑點。 **—freck·led,** *adj.* **—d·ness,** *n.*

freck·ly [ˈfrɛkl̩ɪ; ˈfrekl̩i] *adj.,* **-li·er, -li·est.** 多雀斑的;多小斑點的。

Fred [frɛd; fred] *n.* 男子名(Frederick之暱稱)。

Fred·er·ick [ˈfrɛdrɪk; ˈfredrik] *n.* 男子名。

:**free** [fri; fri:] *adj.,* **fre·er, fre·est,** *adv., v.,* **freed, free·ing.** —*adj.* ①自由的;無約束的。 All men are now *free* in America. 在美國現在人人都是自由的。②不忙的;空閑的。Are you *free?* 你現在有空嗎?③隨便的;無拘束的。You are *free* to do what you like. 你可以隨便做你所喜歡的事。④免費的。All the books were given away *free*. 所有的書都免費贈送了。⑤明白的;直率的。I am *free* to confess. 我直率的招認。⑥免稅的。⑦慷慨的;不吝嗇的。He is *free* with (*or* of) his money. 他用錢豪爽。⑧豐富的;充足的。⑨不拘泥於規則或形式的;隨意的。⑩奔放的;任性的;放縱的。⑪〖化〗游離的。Oxygen exists *free* in air. 氧游離於空氣中。⑫流利的;流暢的;優美的。⑬在場者均參加的。⑭懸空的;未固定的。⑮(石頭)易刻的;(土地)易於耕種的。⑯不用動力而運動的。⑰可自由進入並使用的〖常 of〗. ***free and clear*** 〖法律〗沒有義務或牽連的。***free and easy*** 不拘禮儀的;自由的。***free from*** (or ***of***) **a.** 無…的。**b.** 免…的;無…之憂的。***free hand*** 處理上之完全自由。I gave her a *free hand* in arranging the party. 我給她完全自由去籌劃宴會的事。***free of*** 離開。***free with*** 大方的;不吝嗇的。He is *free with* his tongue. 他隨口亂講。***make free with*** 隨意使用;對…隨便。***set free*** 釋放。***with a free hand*** 大方地;慷慨地。—*adv.* ①免費地。②自由地;隨意地;無拘束地。—*v.t.* ①使自由;釋放。②使免除。③澄清;辯明。He will have to *free* himself of this charge of stealing. 他將必須辯白此竊盜的控訴。**—ly,** *adv.* **—ness,** *n.*

free alongside ship =**f. a. s.** (亦作 **free alongside vessel**)

free·bie [ˈfribi; ˈfri:bi:] *n.* 〖主美俚〗不化錢的東西。(亦作 **freebee**)

free·board [ˈfriˌbord; ˈfri:ˌbɔ:d] *n.* ①〖造船〗乾舷(自吃水線與船舷間之部分)。②(船舶之)吃水線上之船身。③汽車底盤與地面間之距離。

free·boot·er [ˈfriˌbutɚ; ˈfri:ˌbu:tə] *n.* 海盜;流寇;山賊。

free·born [ˈfriˌbɔrn; ˈfri:ˈbɔ:n] *adj.* ①生而自由的。②自由民的(不是奴隸的)。

free delivery 免費郵遞。

freed·man [ˈfridmən; ˈfri:dmæn] *n., pl.* **-men.** 解脫奴隸身分而得自由的人。

:**free·dom** [ˈfridəm; ˈfri:dəm] *n.* ①自由;自由權。He was given his *freedom*. 他得到了他的自由。②使用的自由;自由使用權。 We give a guest the *freedom* of our home. 我們讓賓客自由使用我們的住宅。③不羈;奔放;磊落;率直。④動作優美;優游閒適。⑤豁免權或特權(如城市所有之)。⑥免除。*freedom* from taxation. 免稅權。⑦享受民權。⑧放縱的言語或行動。***four freedoms*** 四大自由,即:*freedom* of speech, 言論自由;*freedom* of worship, 信仰自由;*freedom* from want, 不虞匱乏之自由;*freedom* from fear, 免於恐懼之自由, 爲美故總統羅斯福(Franklin D. Roosevelt) 1941 年所提倡。

freedom fighter 自由鬥士。

freedom of the city 榮譽市民權。

freedom of the press 新聞自由。

freedom of the seas 〖國際法〗公海自由。

freedom ride 〖美〗自由乘車(運動)(反對種族隔離的黑人及白人故意乘公共汽車到實施種族隔離的各州表示抗議所做的旅行)。

freedom rider 參加自由乘車運動者。

freed·wom·an [ˈfridˌwumən; ˈfri:dˌwumən] *n., pl.* **-wom·en.** 解脫奴隸身分而得自由之婦女。

free-for-all [ˈfrifəˈɔl; ˈfri:fərˈɔ:l] *n.* ①可自由參加之競賽(爭)。②混戰;混鬥。—*adj.* 對任何人公開的。

free form 〖美〗自由形態(用於藝術作品的一種不對稱, 非直線的形態)。

free-form [ˈfriˌfɔrm; ˈfri:fɔ:m] *adj.* 自由形態的。

free goods ①免稅之進口貨品。②空氣或水等不需成本之貨物。

free hand 全權;無拘束。

free·hand [ˈfriˌhænd; ˈfri:hænd] *adj.* & *adv.* 手畫的(地)。

free·hand·ed [ˈfriˈhændɪd; ˈfri:ˈhændid] *adj.* ①慷慨的;好施與的。②不受拘束的。 **—ly,** *adv.* **—ness,** *n.*

free-heart·ed [ˈfriˈhɑrtɪd; ˈfri:ˈhɑ:tid] *adj.* ①輕鬆的;無憂無慮的。②慷慨的。③坦白的。 **—ly,** *adv.* **—ness,** *n.*

free·hold [ˈfriˌhold; ˈfri:hould] *n.* ①(終身或世襲之)不動產。 ②上述不動產之保有。—*adj.* 保有 freehold 的。**—er,** *n.*

free lance ①(自由賣作品給任何顧買者的)著作家、藝術家等。②有自主立場的人。③爲自己所選擇的某種事業或主張而奮鬥或工作的人。④中古時期之傭兵。

free-lance [ˈfriˈlæns; ˈfri:ˈlɑ:ns] *v.,* **-lanced, -lanc·ing,** *adj., adv.* —*v.i.* 做 free lance 的作家;藝術家。—*adj.* & *adv.*

free lance 的(地)。—**free-lanc·er**, *n.*

free list 〖美〗海關免稅品。

free liver 好吃喝的人。

free love 自由性愛;自由性愛主義。

free-lov·ism [ˌfriˈlʌvɪzəm; ˌfriː-ˈlʌvizəm] *n.* =**free love.**

free·man [ˈfrimən; ˈfriːmæn] *n., pl.* **-men.** ①自由人; 自由民。②公民;享有所有公民權的人。

free·mar·tin [ˈfriˌmɑrtɪn; ˈfriːˌmɑː-tin] *n.*〖動物〗與公牛攣生而無生殖力之母牛。

Free·ma·son [ˈfriˌmesn̩; ˈfriːˌmeisn] *n.* ①共濟會(一國際性的祕密互助團體)之會員。②(f-)中世紀時歐洲有祕密組織之石匠。

Free·ma·son·ry [ˈfriˌmesn̩rɪ; ˈfriː-ˌmeisnri] *n.* ①共濟會之主義、制度等。②共濟會之會員。③(f-)同病相憐。

free port ①自由港。②無稅港。

free press 不受政府控制的出版物。

free rider 非工會會員但享受工會活動成果的工人。

free·si·a [ˈfriʒɪə, -zɪə; ˈfriːʒiə, -ziə] *n.* 「(南非洲產)鳶尾科植物。」

free-spend·er [ˈfriˈspɛndɚ; ˈfriː-ˈspendə] *n.* 揮金如土者。

free-spo·ken [ˈfriˈspokən; ˈfriː-ˈspoukən] *adj.* 坦白的;直言的。—**ly**, *adv.* —**ness**, *n.*

free·stone [ˈfriˌston; ˈfriː-stoun] *n.* ①砂石;石灰石。②肉與核容易分開的果子(尤指桃、李)。—*adj.* 果肉與核容易分開的。

free·style [ˈfriˌstaɪl; ˈfriːˌstail] *n.* 〖游泳〗自由式。

free-swim·ming [ˈfriˈswɪmɪŋ; ˈfriːˈswimiŋ] *adj.* 〖動物〗可自由游泳的。

free·think·er [ˈfriˈθɪŋkɚ; ˈfriːˈθiŋ-kə] *n.* (尤指在宗教上)自由思想者。—**free-think·ing**, *n., adj.*

free thought 自由宗教思想。

free-tongued [ˈfriˈtʌŋd; ˈfriːˈtʌŋd] *adj.* 說話沒遮攔的。

free trade 自由貿易。

free·trad·er [ˈfriˌtredɚ; ˈfriːˌtreidə] *n.* 提倡自由貿易者。(亦作 **free trader**)

free-trad·ing [ˈfriˈtredɪŋ; ˈfriːˈtrei-diŋ] *adj.* 贊成自由貿易的。

free verse 自由詩體(不守傳統的格律)。

free·way [ˈfriˌwe; ˈfriːˌwei] *n.* 高速公路。

free·wheel [ˈfriˈhwil; ˈfriːˈwiːl] *n.* ①(腳踏車後輪中軸上之)飛輪。②(汽車的)活輪。—*v.i.* ①(車輛等)滑行。②自由自在,輕鬆愉快地活動〖常 about, through, around〗。

free·will [ˈfriˈwɪl; ˈfriːˈwil] *adj.* ①出於自動的; 自願的; 志願的。②〖神學、哲學〗自由意志說的。

freeze** [friz; friːz] *v.,* **froze** [froz; frouz], **froz·en** [ˈfrozn̩; ˈfrouzn], **freez-ing,** *n.* —*v.i.* ①結冰;凍結。②凍傷;凍斃。③(因恐怖等而)僵硬;呆住。His face *froze* with terror. 他的臉因恐怖而無人色。④凍冷;酷寒。⑤感覺凍冷;感覺酷寒。I'm *freezing*. 我感覺酷寒。⑥(因冷而)固着;緊縮。⑦(釘子、螺絲等因生銹而)緊着。⑧突然停止。Fear made him *freeze* in his tracks. 恐懼使他突然停止前進。⑨慌張。A good driver does not *freeze* in an emergency. 良好的汽車駕駛人在緊急狀況時不慌張。—*v.t.* ①使凍結;使結冰。The pond has *frozen* over. 水池結凍了。②使冰冷。③冷藏(食物)。④以冰凍使固着;凍結。⑤使凍傷或凍斃。⑥使僵硬;使發呆。⑦使沮喪。⑧〖俗〗限定(價格);固定(職業)。⑨封存(存款)。⑩〖外科〗凝凍(以人工方法使不感痛苦或使機能緩慢)。freeze one's blood*** 使驚惶;使戰慄。***freeze on to*** (or ***onto***)〖俗〗緊執;緊握;固着。***freeze out*** 〖俗〗逼走;去掉;攆走。***freeze over*** 爲冰所封。***make one's blood freeze*** 使惶恐;使戰慄。—*n.* ①凍結;結冰。②冰凍期;嚴寒時期。③凍結(政府限制物價、生產等)。The government will put a *freeze* on new construction. 政府將實施禁建。—**freez·a·ble,** *adj.*

freez·er [ˈfrizɚ; ˈfriːzə] *n.* ①製冰機。②冷藏器;冰箱。

freez·ing [ˈfrizɪŋ; ˈfriːziŋ] *adj.* ①冰凍的;在冰點下的; 寒冷的。②冷淡的。—*n.* 冰凍;冷凍(作用)。—**ly,** *adv.*

***freight** [fret; freit] *n.* ①貨物(特指裝載於車船上者)。②運費。*freight* paid. 運費付訖。③運貨; 運輸。④運貨火車或船。He sent the box by *freight*. 他把箱子用火車(或船)運去。⑤負擔;重負。—*v.t.* ①裝貨於。They *freighted* the boat with bananas. 他們把香蕉裝載在船上了。②運輸(貨物)。to *freight* goods. 運貨。③使負重;使苦惱。—**less,** *adj.*

freight·age [ˈfretɪdʒ; ˈfreitidʒ] *n.* ①運費。②運送之貨物。③運貨;貨物運輸。

freight agent 運貨代理商。

freight car 運貨車廂;卡車。

freight·er [ˈfretɚ; ˈfreitə] *n.* ①〖美〗貨船;載貨飛機;運輸機。②運貨人。③貨主。

freight house 〖美〗貨運倉庫。

freight ton 貨運噸(因貨而變者)。

freight train 貨運列車。

‡**French** [frɛntʃ; frentʃ] *adj.* 法國的;法國人的;法語的;法屬的。—*n.* 法語。—*v.t.* (常 f-) 做法國菜。***the French*** 法國人(集合稱)。—**ly,** *adv.* —**ness,** *n.*

French·i·fy [ˈfrɛntʃəˌfaɪ; ˈfrentʃifai] *v.t. & v.i.,* **-fied, -fy·ing.** (使)法國化。(亦作 **frenchify**)

French kiss =**soul kiss.**

French-kiss [ˈfrɛntʃˌkɪs; ˈfrentʃˈkis] *v.t. & v.i.* =**soul-kiss.**

***French·man** [ˈfrɛntʃmən; ˈfrentʃ-mən] *n., pl.* **-men.** ①法國人;法國男子。②法國船。

French Revolution 法國大革命「(1789–1799)。」

French window 落地窗。

French·wom·an [ˈfrɛntʃˌwumən; ˈfrentʃˌwumən] *n., pl.* **-wom·en.** 法國女人或女居民。

French·y [ˈfrɛntʃɪ; ˈfrentʃi] *adj.,* **French-i·er, French·i·est,** *n., pl.* **French·ies.** —*adj.* 〖俗〗似法國人的;法國風的。—*n.*〖俗〗法國人。—**French·i·ly,** *adv.* —**French·i-ness,** *n.*

fre·net·ic [frəˈnɛtɪk; frəˈnetik] *adj.* ①如狂的。②瘋癲的。—*n.* 發狂者。(亦作 **phrenetic**) —**al·ly,** *adv.*

fre·num [ˈfrinəm; ˈfriːnəm] *n., pl.* **-na** [-nə; -nə]. 〖解剖, 動物〗繫帶。(亦作 **fraenum**)

fren·zied [ˈfrɛnzɪd; ˈfrenzid] *adj.* 激怒的;瘋狂的。(亦作 **phrensied**) —**ly,** *adv.*

fren·zy [ˈfrɛnzɪ; ˈfrenzi] *n., pl.* **-zies.** *v.,* **-zied, -zy·ing.** —*n.* 暴怒; 狂亂。 in a *frenzy* of despair. 因絕望而狂亂。—*v.t.* 使瘋狂;使憤怒。(亦作 **phrensy**)

Fre·on [ˈfriɑn; ˈfriːɔn] *n.* 〖商標名〗二

氯二氟代甲烷(電冰箱的冷凍劑)。

freq. ①frequent. ②frequentative. ③frequently. ④frequency.

fre·quence ['frikwəns; 'friːkwəns] *n.* =**frequency.**

fre·quen·cy ['frikwənsɪ; 'friːkwənsi] *n., pl.* **-cies.** ①頻仍;時常發生。②〖電〗周率。③〖數學〗頻率。

*__fre·quent__ [*adj.* 'frikwənt; 'friːkwənt *v.* frɪ'kwɛnt; fri'kwent] *adj.* ①時常的;屢次的。 He is a *frequent* visitor. 他是一個常來的客人。②隔着短距離的。—*v.t.* 常去;常在。He no longer *frequents* bars. 他不再去酒吧間了。—**a·ble,** *adj.* —**ness,** *n.*

fre·quen·ta·tion [ˌfrikwən'teʃən; ˌfriːkwen'teiʃən] *n.* 常往;屢訪。

fre·quen·ta·tive [frɪ'kwɛntətɪv; fri'kwentətiv] *adj.* 反覆的。—*n.* 〖文法〗反覆動詞(如 prickle 是 prick 的反覆動詞)。

fre·quent·er [frɪ'kwɛntɚ; fri'kwentə] *n.* 經常來往或照顧之人;常客。

‡**fre·quent·ly** ['frikwəntlɪ; 'friːkwəntli] *adv.* 時常地;屢次地。It happens *frequently*. 這事時常發生。

fres·co ['frɛsko; 'freskou] *n., pl.* **-coes** or **-cos,** *v.,* **-coed, -co·ing.**—*n.* ①作壁畫;壁畫法。②壁畫。*in fresco* 用壁畫法。—*v.t.* 用壁畫法畫。—**er,** *n.*

‡**fresh** [frɛʃ; freʃ] *adj.* ①新鮮的;新做的。This meat is not very *fresh*. 這肉不太新鮮。②涼爽的; 清新的。③新奇的; 重新的。I'd like to see something *fresh*. 我倒願意看看新奇的事。④淡的; 不是鹹的。⑤活潑的; 有生氣的。I feel quite *fresh*. 我覺得精神爽快。⑥健壯的; 年輕的。He looked as *fresh* as a boy after his vacation. 他度過假期以後看上去像少年一樣健康。⑦無經驗的。⑧鮮艷的。⑨新到的; 剛出來的。⑩〖俚〗鹵莽的;厚顏的; 無理的。⑪更多的。⑫(母牛之)剛生小牛的。—*n.* 一段涼爽清新的時間。—*adv.* 最近地; 新近地; 剛剛。 The eggs are *fresh* laid. 這些蛋是剛下的。—**ly,** *adv.* —**ness,** *n.*

fresh-air ['frɛʃ'ɛr; 'freʃ'ɛə] *adj.* 戶外的;戶外生活的。

fresh·en ['frɛʃən; 'freʃn] *v.t.* ①使新鮮;使有生氣。②去…之鹽分;使變淡。③使清新;使涼爽。—*v.i.* ①變爲新鮮。②成爲淡水。③變清新; 變涼爽。④產犢。⑤(風)變强。⑥盥洗打扮。—**er,** *n.*

fresh·et ['frɛʃɪt; 'freʃit] *n.* ①因暴雨或融雪所造成的洪水。②入海的淡水溪流。

fresh·man ['frɛʃmən; 'freʃmən] *n., pl.* **-men** [-mən; -mən], *adj.* —*n.* ①大學或高級中學一年級學生。②新手;初學者。—*adj.* 一年級生的;開始的;無經驗的。—**ship,** *n.*

fresh-run ['frɛʃˌrʌn; 'freʃˌrʌn] *adj.* 由海新入河川的(魚)。

fresh water ①淡水。②湖水; 河水; 池水。

fresh-wa·ter ['frɛʃˌwɔtɚ; 'freʃˌwɔːtə] *adj.* ①淡水的; 生於淡水的。②未慣於航海的。③無經驗的;技巧未純熟的。④〖美〗不著名的或小的。

*__fret__[1] [frɛt; fret] *v.,* **fret·ted, fret·ting,** *n.*—*v.i.* ①煩躁;激怒。What are you *fretting* about? 你在煩躁甚麼? ②腐蝕。③侵蝕。④受磨損; 受侵蝕〖常 away〗。Limestone slowly *frets* away under pounding by the wind and rain. 風吹雨打下石灰石慢慢地磨損了。⑤激動(如水等)。—*v.t.* ①磨擦;擦損;侵蝕。②使煩躁;折磨。You are *fretting* yourself needlessly. 你在不必要地折磨你自己。③使起皺紋。*fret away* 損耗;損傷。—*n.* ①焦急;煩躁。②侵蝕;磨損。③侵蝕或磨損之處。—**ter,** *n.*

fret[2] *n., v.,* **fret·ted, fret·ting.** —*n.* 格子細工。—*v.t.* 飾以格子細工。 —**less,** *adj.*

fret[3] *n., v.,* **fret·ted, fret·ting.** —*n.* (琵琶等絃樂器上之) 品、柱、橋、馬。—*v.t.* 裝以品、柱、橋、馬。—**less,** *adj.*

fret·ful ['frɛtfəl; 'fretful] *adj.* 易忿怒的;焦急的;煩躁的。(亦作 **fretsome**)—**ly,** *adv.* —**ness,** *n.*

fret saw 細工鋸。

fret·ted[1] ['frɛtɪd; 'fretid] *adj.* 有格子紋的;格子細工的。

fret·ted[2] *adj.* ①腐蝕的; 耗損的。②躁急的;煩悶的。

fret·work ['frɛtˌwɝk; 'fretwəːk] *n.* 浮凸細工;格子細工。

Freud [frɔɪd; frɔid] *n.* 佛洛伊德 (Sigmund, 1856–1939, 奧國心理分析及精神病學家)。

Freud·i·an ['frɔɪdɪən; 'frɔidiən, -jən] *adj.* 佛洛伊德 (Freud) 的;佛洛伊德之精神分析學派的。 —*n.* 佛洛伊德精神分析學派之信守者。—**ism,** *n.*

F.R.G.S. Fellow of the Royal Geographical Society. **Fri.** Friday.

fri·a·bil·i·ty [ˌfraɪə'bɪlətɪ; ˌfraiə'biliti] *n.* 易(粉)碎性; 脆弱。

fri·a·ble ['fraɪəbl̩; 'fraiəbl] *adj.* 脆的;易碎的。—**ness,** *n.*

fri·ar ['fraɪɚ; 'fraiə] *n.* (天主教的)修道士;修道僧。

fri·ar·y ['fraɪərɪ; 'fraiəri] *n., pl.* **-ar·ies,** *adj.* —*n.* 〖羅馬天主教〗①修道院;寺院。②教團;修道會。—*adj.* ①修道士的;似修道士的。②教團的;修道會的。

F.R.I.B.A. Fellow of the Royal Institute of British Architects.

frib·ble ['frɪbl̩; 'fribl] *adj., n., v.,* **-bled, -bling.** —*adj.* 無價值的; 不重要的;瑣碎的。—*n.* ①浪費時間之人;不務正業者。②瑣碎之事;無足輕重之事物。 —*v.i.* 浪費時光;作無謂之事;輕狂;戲弄。 —*v.t.* 浪費; 無謂地耗費〖常 away〗.—**frib·bler,** *n.*

fric·an·deau [ˌfrɪkən'do; 'frikəndou] *n., pl.* **-deaus, -deaux** [-'doz; -douz]. 用醬汁醃的或燉的肉類 (尤指小牛肉)。(亦作 **fricando**)

fric·as·see [ˌfrɪkə'si; ˌfrikə'siː] *n., v.,* **-seed, -see·ing.** —*n.* 一種食品(以細切之鷄肉或小牛肉,燉於肉汁及醬汁中而製成)。—*v.t.* 把(肉類)調製爲上述食品。

fric·a·tive ['frɪkətɪv; 'frikətiv] *adj.* 摩擦的; 由摩擦而產生的。*fricative* consonants. 摩擦子音。—*n.* 〖語音〗摩擦音。

*__fric·tion__ ['frɪkʃən; 'frikʃən] *n.* ①摩擦。Matches are lighted by *friction*. 火柴由摩擦而着火。②衝突; 不和。 There is some *friction* in the group. 在這團體中有一點摩擦。—**less,** *adj.* —**less·ly,** *adv.*

fric·tion·al ['frɪkʃənəl; 'frikʃənl] *adj.* 摩擦的;由摩擦而生的。—**ly,** *adv.*

‡**Fri·day** ['fraɪdɪ; 'fraidi] *n.* ①星期五。②忠僕; 忠誠的隨從 (原指魯濱遜飄流記中之 Friday). *Good Friday* 〖宗教〗耶穌受難節。

fridge [frɪdʒ; fridʒ] *n.* 〖主英,俗〗冰箱(=refrigerator).

fried [fraɪd; fraid] *adj.* ①煎炸的; 油炸的。②〖俚〗醉酒的。—*v.* pt. & pp. of **fry.**

fried·cake ['fraɪdˌkek; 'fraidkeik] *n.* 小煎餅(尤指油煎圈餅)。

‡friend 〔frɛnd; frend〕 *n.* ①朋友;友人;贊助者。He has a large number of *friends.* 他有很多的朋友。He is a *friend* of mine. 他是我的一個朋友。②(F-)基督教教友派信徒。③同胞;屬同一組織的人。***be friends with*** 與…有交情。***make friends again*** 重歸和好。***make friends with*** 與…交友。—*v.t.* 〖罕〗交朋友。

friend at court 有勢力的朋友。

friend·less 〔ˈfrɛndlɪs; ˈfrendlis〕 *adj.* 無朋友的;孤獨無靠的。—**ness,** *n.*

‡friend·ly 〔ˈfrɛndlɪ; ˈfrendli〕 *adj.,* **-li·er, -li·est,** *adv.* —*adj.* ①朋友似的;友善的;親切的。to have *friendly* relations with .... 與…相好。a *friendly* nation. 友邦。He spoke in a *friendly* way. 他說話的態度很親切。②順利的;有利的;幸運的;贊助的。a *friendly* shower. 及時雨。***Friendly Society*** 互助會。—*adv.* 友善地;朋友般地。—**friend·li·ly,** *adv.* —**friend·li·ness,** *n.*

friend of the court 與案件無關而被邀向法官提供意見之第三者。

‡friend·ship 〔ˈfrɛndʃɪp; ˈfrendʃip〕 *n.* 友誼;友情;友善。How long will the *friendship* last? 這友情將可延續好久?

fri·er 〔ˈfraɪɚ; ˈfraiə〕 *n.* =**fryer.**

frieze[1] 〔friz; fri:z〕 *n.* ①(牆等的)橫飾帶(牆頂與天花板間之橫條)。②〖建築〗腰線;腰帶。

frieze[2] *n., v.,* **friezed, friez·ing.** —*n.* 一種厚絨(作外衣用)。—*v.t.* 使(布)上起細毛。

frig·ate 〔ˈfrɪgɪt; ˈfrigit〕 *n.* ①主要爲偵察用之舊式掛帆的快速戰艦。②一種驅逐艦級的反潛艇戰艦。

fright** 〔fraɪt frait〕 *n.* ①驚駭;受驚。What was the cause of his *fright?* 他受驚的原因是甚麼?②〖俗〗奇醜之人;怪物。What a *fright* you look in that silly hat! 你戴上那個好笑的帽子,樣子多麼醜怪呀! ***get (or ***have***) ***a fright*** 受驚;吃驚。***give somebody a fright*** 使某人吃一驚。***take fright at*** 因…而吃驚。—*v.t.* 使受驚;嚇。

fright·en** 〔ˈfraɪtn̩; ˈfraitn〕 *v.t.* ①恐嚇;使吃驚;使駭怕。The noise *frightened* me. 騷亂聲使我吃驚。②嚇走〖常 away, off〗. —*v.i.* 吃驚。She *frightens* easily. 她膽子小。be frightened of*** 害怕。***be frightened out of one's life*** 嚇得要死。***frighten somebody into doing something*** 用恐嚇手段逼使某人作某事。***frighten somebody out of doing something*** 使某人嚇得不敢做某事。—**a·ble,** *adj.* —**er,** *n.* —**ing·ly,** *adv.*

fright·ened 〔ˈfraɪtn̩d; ˈfraitnd〕 *adj.* ①受驚的;受恐嚇的。②駭怕的〖of〗. ***be frightened at*** 受…驚駭。—**ly,** *adv.*

***fright·ful** 〔ˈfraɪtfəl; ˈfraitful〕 *adj.* ①可怕的;令人毛骨悚然的。②醜的;驚人的;駭人聽聞的。③〖俗〗討厭的;不愉快的。④〖俗〗極大的;非常的。It was a *frightful* storm. 那是一次極大的風暴。—**ly,** *adv.* —**ness,** *n.*

frig·id 〔ˈfrɪdʒɪd; ˈfridʒid〕 *adj.* ①嚴寒的。②冷淡的;無情的;呆板的。③(女人之)性冷感的。④缺乏想像力或情感的。—**ly,** *adv.* —**ness,** *n.*

Frig·id·aire 〔ˌfrɪdʒɪˈdɛr; ˌfridʒiˈdɛə〕 *n.* 〖商標名〗電冰箱。

fri·gid·i·ty 〔frɪˈdʒɪdətɪ; friˈdʒiditi〕 *n.* ①嚴寒;冷淡;無情;呆板。②性冷感。

fri·jol, fri·jole 〔ˈfrihol; ˈfri:houl〕 *n., pl.* **-joles** 〔-holz; -houlz〕. 菜豆;豆(特指墨西哥及美國西南部所產者)。

frill 〔frɪl; fril〕 *n.* ①(衣飾的)縐邊。②(常 *pl.*)〖美俗〗矯飾;裝模作樣。③鳥或動物頭部周圍的綣毛。④累贅或多餘之物。⑤〖照相〗膠片的邊皺。***put on one's frills*** 擺架子;裝腔作勢。—*v.t.* 鑲縐邊於;使在邊緣起皺紋。—*v.i.* 膠片的邊起縐紋。—**er,** *n.* —**y,** *adj.*

frill·ing 〔ˈfrɪlɪŋ; ˈfriliŋ〕 *n.* 縐邊。

***fringe** 〔frɪndʒ; frindʒ〕 *n., v.,* **fringed, fring·ing,** *adj.* —*n.* ①(地毯等之)鬚邊;綫。②如鬚邊之物(如前額之垂髮)。A *fringe* of hair hung over her forehead. 一抹垂髮(劉海)垂懸在她的前額上。③(如森林)最外之邊緣。④邊;緣;端。—*v.t.* 鑲…以邊。The river is *fringed* with trees. 河之兩邊有樹。—*adj.* ①邊界的;邊緣的。②次要的;額外的。—**less,** *adj.* —**like,** *adj.*

fring·y 〔ˈfrɪndʒɪ; ˈfrindʒi〕 *adj.* 似綫的;以綫爲飾的。

frip·per·y 〔ˈfrɪpərɪ; ˈfripəri〕 *n., pl.* **-per·ies.** ①賤價(質劣)而虛華的服飾。②誇示;矯飾;裝腔作勢。③瑣屑不值錢的東西。

fris·bee, fris·by 〔ˈfrɪzbi; ˈfrizbi:〕 *n.* ①飛盤(一種遊戲)。②(F-)其商標名。

Fris·co 〔ˈfrɪsko; ˈfriskou〕 *n.* 〖俗〗=**San Fransisco.**

fri·sette 〔frɪˈzɛt; friˈzet〕 *n.* 婦女額前之鬈髮;髮纓。

frisk 〔frɪsk; frisk〕 *v.i.* 歡躍;雀躍。—*v.t.* ①雀躍;歡躍;高興地搖動。②〖俚〗遍身搜查。③〖俚〗扒竊。—*n.* 雀躍;歡欣鼓舞。—**er,** *n.* —**ing·ly,** *adv.*

fris·ket 〔ˈfrɪskɪt; ˈfriskit〕 *n.* 〖印刷〗挾紙框。

frisk·y 〔ˈfrɪskɪ; ˈfriski〕 *adj.,* **frisk·i·er, frisk·i·est.** 好跳躍的;嬉戲的;活潑的。—**frisk·i·ly,** *adv.* —**frisk·i·ness,** *n.*

frit 〔frɪt; frit〕 *n., v.,* **frit·ted, frit·ting.** —*n.* ①半鎔之玻璃原料。②半鎔之人工軟瓷原料。—*v.t.* & *v.i.* 加熱調製(玻璃原料);使成半鎔之玻璃或軟瓷原料。(亦作 **fritt**)

frit fly 歐洲產之一種損害穀類之小蠅。

frith 〔frɪθ; friθ〕 *n.* (狹窄的)海灣;(江、河)入海口。(亦作 **firth**)

frit·il·lar·y 〔ˈfrɪtl̩ˌɛrɪ; friˈtiləri〕 *n., pl.* **-lar·ies.** ①〖植物〗貝母。②〖動物〗翅色斑駁之一類蝴蝶。

frit·ter[1] 〔ˈfrɪtɚ; ˈfritə〕 *v.t.* ①慢慢消耗;浪費〖away〗. ②切碎;撕碎。—*v.i.* ①縮小;萎縮〖away〗. ②成碎片。—*n.* 碎片;屑。—**er,** *n.*

frit·ter[2] *n.* (以果肉等爲餡的)油炸餅。

Fritz 〔frɪts; frits〕 *n.* 〖俚〗①德國兵(通常爲輕蔑語)。②德國砲彈、飛機、潛艇等。

friv·ol 〔ˈfrɪvl̩; ˈfrivəl〕 *v.,* **-ol(l)ed, -ol(l)ing.** —*v.i.* 〖俗〗兒戲;輕舉妄動;浪費時光。—*v.t.* 〖俗〗徒費;浪費〖away〗. —**er,** *n.*

fri·vol·i·ty 〔frɪˈvɑlətɪ; friˈvɔliti〕 *n., pl.* **-ties.** ①輕浮;妄動。②輕浮的言語或舉動。

friv·o·lous 〔ˈfrɪvələs; ˈfrivələs, -vləs〕 *adj.* ①輕浮的;妄動的。②無價值的;不重要的。③輕浮的;輕薄的。—**ly,** *adv.* —**ness,** *n.*

friz 〔frɪz; friz〕 *v.,* **frizzed, friz·zing,** *n., pl.* **friz·zes.** —*v.t.* & *v.i.* ①(使)成鬈髮。②(使)成毛團。—*n.* ①鬈曲;鬈縮。②鬈縮之物;鬈髮。—**er,** *n.*

fri·zette 〔frɪˈzɛt; friˈzet〕 *n.* =**fri·sette.**

frizz[1] 〔frɪz; friz〕 *v., n.* =**friz.**

frizz[2] *v.t.* & *v.i.,* **frizzed, frizz·ing.** 作唧唧聲而煎炸。

friz·zle[1] 〔ˈfrɪzl̩; ˈfrizl〕 *v.,* **friz·zled, friz·zling,** *n.* —*v.t.* & *v.i.* (使)鬈曲。

—*n.* 鬈髮；鬈曲。—**friz·zler,** *n.*

friz·zle² *v.,* **friz·zled, friz·zling,** *n.* —*v.i.* (烹煎時)發嘶嘶聲。—*v.t.* 烹煎到發嘶嘶聲。—*n.* (烹煎時所發的)嘶嘶聲。

friz·zly 〔ˈfrɪzl̩ɪ; ˈfrizl̩i〕 *adj.,* **-zli·er, -zli·est.** 有鬈髮的；鬈曲的。

friz·zy 〔ˈfrɪzɪ; ˈfrizi〕 *adj.,* **-zi·er, -zi·est.** ＝**frizzly.** —**friz·zi·ly,** *adv.* —**friz·zi·ness,** *n.*

fro** 〔fro; frou〕 *adv.* 回；返；復（僅用於下列成語中）。to and fro*** 來回地；往返地。walking *to and fro.* 走來走去。

***frock** 〔frak; frɔk〕 *n.* ①長袍；罩袍；工人穿的外袍；僧袍。②教士之職位或權力。—*v.t.* ①供以長袍；穿以長袍。②使爲僧；授以聖職。—**less,** *adj.*

frock coat (男子所著之雙排鈕扣，長及膝部之)常禮服。

frog** 〔frag; frɔg〕 *n., v.,* **frogged, frog·ging.** —*n.* ①蛙。②〖鐵道〗轍叉。③馬蹄軟甲。④(紡錠形的)飾扣。⑤(F-)〖鄙〗法國人。⑥吊劍帶。⑦挿花用的有刺小鐵塊；劍山。a frog in the*** (or ***one's***) ***throat*** 喉頭因不適而微帶嘶啞。—*v.i.* 捕蛙。—**like,** *adj.*

frog·eat·er 〔ˈfrag͵itɚ; ˈfrɔg͵i:tə〕 *n.* ①食蛙之人。②(F-)〖鄙〗法國人。

frog·fish 〔ˈfrag͵fɪʃ; ˈfrɔgfiʃ〕 *n., pl.* **-fish, -fish·es.** ①躄魚科之魚。②琵琶魚。

frog·gy 〔ˈfragɪ; ˈfrɔgi〕 *adj.,* **-gi·er, -gi·est,** *n., pl.* **-gies.** —*adj.* 蛙的；多蛙的；似蛙的。—*n.* ①蛙(小兒語)。②(F-)〖俚〗法國人。—**frog·gi·ness,** *n.*

frog·man 〔ˈfragmən, ˈfrɔg-; ˈfrɔgmən〕 *n., pl.* **-men.** 蛙人（爲軍事偵察或水底障礙物之爆破而潛入水中者）；潛水夫。

frog-march 〔ˈfrag͵martʃ; ˈfrɔgma:tʃ〕 *v.t., n.* 蛙式抬運（由四人各執頑强囚犯之一肢，令其俯伏而抬運之)。

frol·ic 〔ˈfralɪk; ˈfrɔlik〕 *n., v.,* **-icked, -ick·ing,** *adj.* —*n.* ①嬉戲；作樂。②歡樂聚會。—*v.i.* 嬉戲；作樂。—*adj.* 嬉戲的；作樂的。

frol·ic·some 〔ˈfralɪksəm; ˈfrɔliksəm〕 *adj.* 嬉戲的；作樂的。—**ly,** *adv.* —**ness,** *n.*

‡**from** 〔fram, frʌm, frəm; frɔm, frəm, frm〕 *prep.* ①從；自；由（表行動之起點）。*from* top to bottom. 從頂到底。②由（何處）；從（表來源、根源等）。Where does he come *from?* 他是那裡人？③距；離〖常away〗。It is three miles (away) *from* the town. 距城裏有三英里遠。④因；因爲(尤指疾病等)。to suffer *from* a cold. 患傷風。⑤以免；防止。to save something *from* damage. 保護某物以免受損。⑥與（表比較、區別等）。I cannot tell one *from* the other. 我分辨不清這個與那個。⑦根據；依照。to judge *from* appearances. 根據外表判斷。⑧又(表反覆動作)。*from* time to time. 時時；有時。

frond 〔frand; frɔnd〕 *n.* ①(羊齒植物、棕櫚等的)複葉。②(海草、地衣等的)葉狀體。—**ed,** *adj.* —**less,** *adj.*

frond·age 〔ˈfrandɪdʒ; ˈfrɔndidʒ〕 *n.* 「葉(集合稱)。

fron·dose 〔fran'dos; frɔn'dous〕 *adj.* ①〖詩,古〗有葉的；多葉的。②葉狀體的；葉狀的。

‡**front** 〔frʌnt; frʌnt〕 *n.* ①前部；前面；正面；開頭。There is a picture in the *front* of the book. 在書的卷頭有一幅挿畫。②前線；前方；戰地。③（政治或經濟鬥爭中的）陣線。④(河邊、街邊的)土地；濱。⑤容貌；模樣。⑥架子；傲氣。The clerk has the most outrageous *front.* 那個職員有一付最可惡的臭架子。⑦〖俗〗（聘來作號召的）名譽領袖。⑧額。⑨臉。⑩厚顏；厚臉皮。⑪面臨街道等的地產界線。⑫〖俗〗作爲掩護的事物；幌子。That store was a *front* for foreign agent. 那一家店是外國間諜的幌子。⑬階級、地位、財富等之外表。⑭戴在胸口的東西。⑮〖戲院〗**a.** 大廳。**b.** 辦事處。**c.** 舞臺之前部。⑯〖氣象〗鋒。***change front*** 改變方向。***come to the front*** 出風頭；出名。***in front*** 在前面。Mr. Smith was *in front.* 史密斯先生在前面。***in front of*** 在…的前面。***out front*** **a.** 門口外。He's waiting *out front.* 他在門外等。**b.** (競賽等)領先。**c.** 〖戲院〗在表演中。***put a bold front on*** (***a situation***) 大膽面對(局面)。***put up a front*** 擺場面。***show*** (or ***present***) ***a bold front*** 顯出大膽的樣子。—*adj.* ①前面的；正面的。②〖語音〗前舌面的。—*v.t.* ①面向；朝對。The house *fronts* the sea. 此屋面朝海。②在…之前面。③面對；對抗；反抗；不懼。to *front* danger. 不怕危險。④作…之正面。⑤領導樂隊。—*v.i.* ①面對(某方向)。Most houses *front* on the street. 大多數房屋都是面對街道。②爲…作掩護。—*adv.* 向前地。Eyes *front!* 向前看！

front·age 〔ˈfrʌntɪdʒ; ˈfrʌntidʒ〕 *n.* ①前面。②(建築物等)前面或正面的長度。③(建築物等的)朝向。④對街或對河之地。⑤建築物與街或河之間的空間。

fron·tal 〔ˈfrʌntl; ˈfrʌntl〕 *adj.* ①前面的；正面的。②額的；前額的。—*n.* ①前額骨。②建築物之正面。③套在額上的帶或裝飾品。—**ly,** *adv.*

***fron·tier** 〔frʌnˈtɪr, franˈ-, ˈfrʌntɪr, ˈfran-; ˈfrʌntjə, ˈfrɔn-, -tiə〕 *n.* ①邊境；邊界；邊疆。②（常 *pl.*）未開發的領域。the *frontiers* of science. 科學尙待研究之領域。③〖數學〗邊界；界。—*adj.* 邊界的；國境的。*frontier* spirit. 〖美〗拓荒精神。—**less,** *adj.* —**like,** *adj.*

fron·tiers·man 〔frʌnˈtɪrzmən; frʌnˈtjəzmən〕 *n., pl.* **-men.** 住於邊疆的人；拓荒者。

fron·tis·piece 〔ˈfrʌntɪs͵pis; ˈfrʌntispi:s〕 *n., v.,* **-pieced, -piec·ing.** —*n.* ①卷頭挿畫。②〖建築〗(門窗頂上的)三角楣飾。—*v.t.* ①在(書)上加卷頭挿畫。②將…畫在卷頭挿畫中。

front·less 〔ˈfrʌntlɪs; ˈfrʌntlis〕 *adj.* 〖古〗無恥的。—**ly,** *adv.* —**ness,** *n.*

front·let 〔ˈfrʌntlɪt; ˈfrʌntlit〕 *n.* ①額飾。②(鳥、獸等之)前額部。

front man ①代表人。②掩護者。

front matter 正文以前之資料。

front-page 〔ˈfrʌntˈpedʒ; ˈfrʌntˈpeidʒ〕 *adj., v.,* **-paged, -pag·ing.** —*adj.* (宜於)報紙第一版的；重要的。—*v.t.* 刊載於報紙之第一版。

frore 〔fror; frɔ:〕 *adv.* 〖古、詩〗凍結的；嚴寒的。

***frost** 〔frɔst, frast; frɔst, frɔ:st〕 *n.* ①冰凍；嚴寒；冰點以下的溫度。②寒天；嚴寒的天氣。③霜。The grass was covered with *frost.* 草上蓋滿了霜。④冷淡；冷酷。⑤〖俚〗失敗。The entertainment was a *frost.* 這餘興節目完全失敗。⑥〖俗〗(友誼之)冷漠。—*v.t.* ①覆以霜（或似霜之物）。The cook *frosted* the cake with a mixture of sugar and whites of eggs. 廚師以糖混和蛋白覆於蛋糕上。②(被霜)損害；凍死。—*v.i.* ①結霜；結冰〖up, over〗。I think the water pipes have *frosted* up. 我想水管已經結冰了。②(油漆等)表面凝成似霜物。

—less, *adj.* —like, *adj.*

frost·bite ['frɔst,baɪt; 'frɔstbait] *n.*, *v.*, **-bit** [-,bɪt; -bit], **-bit·ten**, **-bit·ing.** —*n.* 凍傷；凍瘡。—*v.t.* 凍傷。

frost·bit·ten ['frɔst,bɪtn̩; 'frɔst,bitn] *adj.* 凍傷的。—*v.* pp. of **frostbite.**

frost·ed ['frɔstɪd; 'frɔstid] *adj.* ①(降)霜的。②冰凍的。③凍傷的。④覆以糖霜的。⑤表面呈霜狀的；閃光的（玻璃）。⑥冷酷的。⑦冰淇淋做的(餅或飲料等)。⑧快凍的。—*n.* 濃飲料(牛乳、糖漿、冰淇淋做成)。

frost·fish ['frɔst,fɪʃ; 'frɔːstfiʃ] *n.*, *pl.* **-fish·es, -fish.** (北美產的)一種小鱈魚。

frost·i·ly ['frɔstəlɪ; 'frɔstili] *adv.* 冷峻地。

frost·i·ness ['frɔstɪnɪs; 'frɔstinis] *n.* ①酷寒。②冷峻；無情。

frost·ing ['frɔstɪŋ; 'frɔstiŋ] *n.* ①糖霜(用覆糕餅表面)。②(玻璃等的)無光澤面。

frost·work ['frɔst,wɝk; 'frɔst-wəːk] *n.* ①(玻璃窗等上的)霜花。②霜花紋細工。

***frost·y** ['frɔstɪ, 'frɑstɪ; 'frɔsti, 'frɔːsti] *adj.*, **frost·i·er, frost·i·est.** ①寒冷的。*frosty* weather. 寒冷的天氣。②覆有霜的。The glass is *frosty*. 那玻璃上覆有霜。③覆有似霜之物的。④冷淡的；無情的。⑤似霜的；灰白的。⑥(似)老年的；頭髮灰白的。

froth [frɔθ; frɔθ] *n.* ①泡沫。②輕浮的事物；淺見；空談。—*v.i.* 起泡沫；發泡沫。—*v.t.* 覆以泡沫；使起泡沫。—**er**, *n.*

froth-blow·er ['frɔθ,bloɚ; 'frɔːθ-,blouə] *n.* 〖英〗愛喝啤酒的人。

froth·y ['frɔθɪ; 'frɔθi] *adj.*, **froth·i·er, froth·i·est.** ①泡沫的；似泡沫的；起泡沫的。②輕浮的；淺薄的；空虛的。—**froth·i·ly**, *adv.* —**froth·i·ness**, *n.*

frou·frou ['fru,fru; 'fruː-fruː] *n.* ①(行動時衣裙所發的)沙沙聲。②女裝之裝飾品。

frow [frau; frau] *n.* ①荷蘭或德國之婦女。②婦人；妻子。

fro·ward ['froɚd; 'frouəd] *adj.* 剛愎的；頑固的；倔强的。—**ly**, *adv.* —**ness**, *n.*

***frown** [fraun; fraun] *n.* 顰眉；蹙額；不悅。There was a deep *frown* on his face. 他的額頭深深皺着。—*v.i.* 顰眉；蹙額；不悅〖常 on, upon〗. Don't *frown* at me like that. 不要那樣對我蹙眉。—*v.t.* 蹙額表示；顰眉責之。She *frowned* her disapproval. 她蹙眉表示不贊許。—**er**, *n.* —**ing·ly**, *adv.*

frowst [fraust; fraust] *v.i.* 〖英〗懶懶地在屋內坐臥；懶坐。

frowst·y ['fraustɪ; 'frausti] *adj.*, **frowst·i·er, frowst·i·est.** 〖英俗〗有霉味的；有惡臭的。—**frowst·i·ly**, *adv.* —**frowst·i·ness**, *n.*

frowz·y ['frauzɪ; 'frauzi] *adj.*, **frowz·i·er, frowz·i·est.** ①不整潔的；汚穢的；懶散的。②臭的；難聞的。(亦作 **frouzy, frousy, frowsy**) —**frowz·i·ly**, *adv.* —**frowz·i·ness**, *n.*

froze [froz; frouz] *v.* pt. of **freeze.**

***fro·zen** ['frozn̩; 'frouzn] *v.* pp. of **freeze.** —*adj.* ①結冰的；覆以冰的。a *frozen* river. 結了冰的河。②極冷的。③凍殭的；凍死的。④因凍結而塞住的。⑤冷酷無情的。⑥驚呆了的。⑦〖美〗(事實、眞理)不可推翻的；不容否認的。⑧(物價、資產等)凍結的。—**ly**, *adv.* —**ness**, *n.*

F.R.S. Fellow of the Royal Society.

frs. francs. **frt.** freight.

fruc·ti·fi·ca·tion [,frʌktəfə'keʃən; ,frʌktifi'keiʃən] *n.* ①結果實。②果實。③結果實的器官。

fruc·ti·fy ['frʌktə,faɪ; 'frʌktifai] *v.*, **-fied, -fy·ing.** —*v.i.* 結果實。—*v.t.* 使(植物)結果實；使(土地)肥沃。

fruc·tose ['frʌktos; 'frʌktous] *n.* 〖化〗果糖($C_6H_{12}O_6$)。(亦作 **fruit sugar**)

fruc·tu·ous ['frʌktʃuəs; 'frʌktjuəs] *adj.* 肥沃的；生產的；有利的。—**ly**, *adv.* —**ness**, *n.*

***fru·gal** ['frugl̩; 'fruːgəl] *adj.* 節儉的；節省的；節約的。He ate a *frugal* supper of bread and milk. 他吃了一頓僅有麪包和牛奶的節儉晚餐。—**ly**, *adv.* —**ness**, *n.*

fru·gal·i·ty [fru'gælətɪ; fruː'gæliti] *n.* 節儉；節約；儉省。

fru·giv·o·rous [fru'dʒɪvərəs; fruː-'dʒivərəs] *adj.* 〖動物〗(常)食果實的。

‡fruit [frut; fruːt] *n.* ①水果；果類。We get a lot of *fruits* from South Africa. 我們從南非運來很多種的水果。He does not eat much *fruit*. 他不大吃水果。②植物之實；果實。③任何人類可用的植物的產物（如穀類、棉花、水果等)。④成果；收獲；結果。I hope your hard work will bear *fruit*. 我希望你的辛勤工作會產生好的結果。⑤〖俚〗同性戀者。***fruit of the body*** (***loins*** or ***womb***) 子女。—*v.i.* & *v.t.* 結果實；使結果實。This tree *fruits* well. 這棵樹結的果實甚多。〖注意〗**fruit** 作集合名詞時，不用複數。**fruits** 指許多不同種類的水果。

fruit·age ['frutɪdʒ; 'fruːtidʒ] *n.* ①結實。②果實(集合稱)。③產物；結果；成果。

fruit·ar·i·an [fru'tɛrɪən; fruː'tɛə-riən] *n.* 常食果實的人；果食主義者。

fruit cake 攙有乾果的糕餅；水果蛋糕。

fruit·er ['frutɚ; 'fruːtə] *n.* ①裝運水果的船。②種果樹者。③果樹。

fruit·er·er ['frutərɚ; 'fruːtərə] *n.* 〖主英〗①水果商；青果商。②裝運水果的船。

fruit fly 果蠅(其幼蟲以果實爲食)。

***fruit·ful** ['frutfəl; 'fruːtful] *adj.* ①多實的；多產的；肥沃的。②有收獲的；有利的。A successful plan is *fruitful*. 成功的計畫是會產生好結果的。—**ly**, *adv.* —**ness**, *n.*

fru·i·tion [fru'ɪʃən; fruː'iʃən] *n.* ①實現；完成；成果。②享受；享成。③結果實。

***fruit·less** ['frutlɪs; 'fruːtlis] *adj.* ①無結果的；徒勞的；無用的。②不毛的；不結實的。—**ly**, *adv.* —**ness**, *n.*

fruit machine 〖英〗吃角子老虎(一種賭具)。

fruit piece 果實的靜物畫(雕刻)。

fruit·y ['frutɪ; 'fruːti] *adj.*, **fruit·i·er, fruit·i·est.** ①水果的；(味道)像水果的。②味醇的。③宏亮的(聲音等)。④〖俚〗有趣味的；耐人尋味的(故事、談話等)。⑤〖俚〗瘋的。⑥〖俚〗同性戀的。—**fruit·i·ness**, *n.*

fru·men·ta·ceous [,frumɛn'teʃəs; ,fruːmen'teiʃəs] *adj.* 似穀物的；以穀物製的。

fru·men·ty ['frumәntɪ; 'fruːmənti] *n.* (加香料、牛奶等煮成的)麥粥。(亦作 **fro-menty**)

frump [frʌmp; frʌmp] *n.* ①衣衫不整潔、乖戾守舊的女人。②(*pl.*)〖英方〗慍怒；乖戾。

frump·ish ['frʌmpɪʃ; 'frʌmpiʃ] *adj.* 衣衫不整潔而有時乖戾的；乖戾守舊的。—**ly**, *adv.* —**ness**, *n.*

frump·y ['frʌmpɪ; 'frʌmpi] *adj.*, **frump·i·er, frump·i·est.** =**frumpish.** —**frump·i·ly**, *adv.* —**frump·i·ness**, *n.*

***frus·trate** [ˈfrʌstret; frʌsˈtreit, ˈfrʌstreit] *v.*, **-trat·ed, -trat·ing,** *adj.* —*v.t.* 破壞;使無效;挫敗。The great artist had never been *frustrated* in his ambition to paint. 這位偉大的藝術家在其繪畫的希望中從未受到過挫折。—*v.i.* 挫敗。His trouble is that he *frustrates* much too easily. 他的毛病是他很容易感到挫敗。—*adj.*〖古〗失意的。—**frus·trat·er,** *n.* —**frus·trat·ing·ly,** *adv.* —**frus·tra·tive,** *adj.*

frus·tra·tion [frʌsˈtreʃən; frʌsˈtreiʃən] *n.* 挫折;頓挫;失敗;無效;破壞。

frus·tule [ˈfrʌstʃul; ˈfrʌstʃul] *n.*〖植物〗硅藻之硅酸殼。

frus·tum [ˈfrʌstəm; ˈfrʌstəm] *n., pl.* **-tums, -ta** [-tə; -tə].〖幾何〗截頭體;墩;臺。

fru·tes·cent [fruˈtɛsn̩t; fruːˈtesnt] *adj.*〖植物〗灌木性的;變成灌木的;似灌木的。

fru·ti·cose [ˈfrutəˌkos; ˈfruːtikous] *adj.* 灌木狀的;灌木的。

***fry¹** [fraɪ; frai] *v.*, **fried, fry·ing,** *n., pl.* **fries.** —*v.t.* & *v.i.* 油煎;油炸。to *fry* ham. 油炸火腿。—*n.* ①油炸食物。②〖美〗備有油炸食物的戶外活動。

fry² *n., pl.* **fry.** ①魚苗。②魚苗羣;羣居的動物。③小東西;小生物;孩子。***small fry*** **a.** 小孩子。**b.** 不重要的人或物。

fry·er, fri·er [ˈfraɪɚ; ˈfraiə] *n.* ①油炸食品的人。②煎鍋;炸鍋。③適於油炸之食物。

frying pan** 煎鍋;油炸鍋。out of the frying pan into the fire*** 每況愈下;愈弄愈糟(=from bad to worse).

F.S. Field Service. **ft.** ①feet. ②foot. ③fort. ④fortification. **FTC** Federal Trade Commission. **fth(m).** fathom.

fub·sy [ˈfʌbzɪ; ˈfʌbzi] *adj.*, **fub·si·er, fub·si·est.**〖英方〗肥胖的;臃腫的。

fuch·sia [ˈfjuʃə; ˈfjuːʃə] *n.* ①(F-)吊鐘花屬。②紫紅色。—*adj.* 紫紅色的。

fuch·sin, fuch·sine [ˈfuksɪn; ˈfuksin] *n.*〖化〗一品紅;洋紅(染料)。

fu·ci [ˈfjusaɪ; ˈfjuːsai] *n.* pl. of **fucus.**

fu·cus [ˈfjukəs; ˈfjuːkəs] *n., pl.* **fu·cus·es, fu·ci.** ①〖植物〗黑角菜屬之海藻。②顏料;染料。

fud·dle [ˈfʌdl̩; ˈfʌdl] *v.*, **-dled, -dling,** *n.* —*v.t.* ①灌醉;使爛醉。②使糊塗。—*v.i.* 淺酌(烈酒等)。—*n.* ①爛醉。②糊塗;一團糟。—**fud·dler,** *n.*

fud·dy-dud·dy [ˈfʌdɪˌdʌdɪ; ˈfʌdiˌdʌdi] *n., pl.* **-dud·dies,** *adj.* —*n.*〖俚〗①嘮叨難纏的人。②古板的人;守舊的人。—*adj.* ①守舊的;舊式的。②吹毛求疵的。

fudge [fʌdʒ; fʌdʒ] *n., v.*, **fudged, fudg·ing,** *interj.* —*n.* ①由糖、牛奶、奶油等混做的軟糖。②虛構的故事;胡言。③〖美〗報紙中挿入的最後消息。—*v.t.* ①彌縫;補綴。②敷衍了事。—*v.i.* ①胡說八道。②欺騙〖常on〗。③規避(責任);食言。—*interj.* 胡說!廢話!

fu·el** [ˈfjuəl; fjuəl, fjoəl, fjuil, ˈfjuːəl] *n., v.*, **-el(l)ed, -el·(l)ing.** —*n.* ①燃料。②刺激物。His insults were *fuel* to her hatred. 他的侮辱更加强她的恨。add fuel to the flames*** 火上加油(喻使怒上加怒,恨上加恨等)。—*v.t.* ①加燃料於;加油於。②作爲原動力。The pool-building boom is *fueled* by many things. 游泳池大量興建是由許多因素促成的。—*v.i.* 加油;加燃料。—(l)er, *n.*

fuel cell 直接轉變燃料與氧化劑之化學能爲電能的裝置。

fuel oil 燃料油。

fug [fʌg; fʌg] *n., v.*, **fugged, fug·ging.** —*n.*〖俗〗①(換氣不良之)氣悶的狀態。②(室隅、桌下等處的)灰塵;垃圾。—*v.i.* 待在悶熱室中。

fu·ga·cious [fjuˈgeʃəs; fjuːˈgeiʃəs] *adj.* ①難捉摸的;易逃走的;疾逝的;暫時的。②〖植物〗易逝的;早謝的。—**ly,** *adv.* —**fu·gac·i·ty, —ness,** *n.*

-fuge〖字尾〗表"驅逐;逃走"之義。如: refuge.

fug·gy [ˈfʌgɪ; ˈfʌgi] *adj.*, **fug·gi·er, fug·gi·est.**〖俗〗①悶的;不通氣的。②好逗留在悶室中的。

***fu·gi·tive** [ˈfjudʒətɪv; ˈfjuːdʒitiv] *n.* ①逃亡者;亡命徒。The murderer became a *fugitive* from justice. 這個殺人犯變成一個逃犯。②短暫或不可捉摸之物。—*adj.* ①逃亡的。②瞬時卽逝的。*fugitive* colors. 易褪的顏色。③卽興的。*fugitive* verses. 卽興詩。④流浪的;巡廻的。⑤(花朶等)易謝的。

fu·gle [ˈfjugl̩; ˈfjuːgl] *v.i.*, **fu·gled, fu·gling.**〖俗〗①做嚮導;示範。②作信號。

fu·gle·man [ˈfjugl̩mən; ˈfjuːglmæn] *n., pl.* **-men.** ①〖軍〗示範兵。②模範;指導者。

fugue [fjug; fjuːg] *n.*〖音樂〗遁走曲(在一個樂曲中,有一個或一個以上之主題或旋律在不同部分重複演奏者)。—**fu·guist,** *n.*

Fu·ji [ˈfudʒɪ, ˈfju-; ˈfuːdʒiː] *n.* 富士山(在日本本州中南境)。

Fu·kien [ˈfuˈkjɛn; ˈfuːˈkjen] *n.* 福建(中國東南之一省,省會福州 Foochow).

-ful〖字尾〗表"充滿…的;具有…特性的;易於…的"之義。如: beautiful, forgetful.

Ful·bright [ˈfulˌbraɪt; ˈfulbrait] *n.* ①傅爾布萊特(James William, 1905–, 美國政壇人物)。②〖俗〗Fulbright Act 之獎學金。③獲得 Fulbright 獎學金者。

Fulbright Act 1946 年美國國會通過之法案,以出售剩餘物資之款派遣美國留學生到海外進修或選送外國學生到美國進修。

ful·crum [ˈfʌlkrəm; ˈfʌlkrəm] *n., pl.* **-crums** or **-cra** [-krə; -krə], *v.* —*n.*〖機械〗槓桿支點。—*v.t.* ①裝上槓桿支點。②使成爲槓桿支點。

***ful·fil(l)** [fulˈfɪl; fulˈfil] *v.t.*, **-filled, -fill·ing.** ①實踐(諾言);應驗(預言);完成(任務)。②盡;履行(責任、義務等)。to *fulfil* a duty. 盡職。③滿足;令滿意。④充分發展潛在能力(通常作反身用法)。

ful·fil(l)·ment [fulˈfɪlmənt; fulˈfilmənt] *n.* ①(義務、職務等的)履行;(契約、條件、命令等的)實行;實踐。②(願望、期待、預言等的)實現;滿足。

ful·gent [ˈfʌldʒənt; ˈfʌldʒənt] *adj.*〖詩〗燦爛的;輝耀的。

ful·gu·rate [ˈfʌlgjəˌret; ˈfʌlgjuəreit] *v.*, **-rat·ed, -rat·ing.** —*v.i.* 閃爍;閃現(如閃光)。—*v.t.*〖醫〗電擊;電灼。

ful·gu·rite [ˈfʌlgjəˌraɪt; ˈfʌlgjurait] *n.* ①〖地質〗閃電岩(砂土、岩山等受閃電打擊而形成之管狀物)。②炸藥之一種。

ful·ham [ˈfuləm; ˈfuləm] *n.*〖俚〗假骰子;欺騙的賭博。(亦作 **fullam, fullom**)

fu·lig·i·nous [fjuˈlɪdʒənəs; fjuːˈlidʒinəs] *adj.* ①(似)煤烟的。②黑褐色的;暗黑的。

‡**full¹** [ful; ful] *adj.* ①滿的;裝滿的。The room was *full* of people. 屋裏充滿了人。②豐富的;有很多的。a lake *full* of fish. 有很多魚的湖。③完全的;充足的。*full* pay. 全薪。④寬鬆的(衣服)。Please make this coat a little *fuller* across the back. 請把

這件外衣的背部做寬鬆些。⑤宏亮清晰的(聲音)。⑥豐滿的。⑦同父母的。*full* brothers. 同胞兄弟。⑧(酒等)濃郁的。⑨滿帆的。⑩十足的。a *full* scholar. 不折不扣的學者。⑪到極限的。*full* colonel. 上校。***at full length*** 伸直的;詳細的。***full of*** **a.** 充滿。**b.** 爲…全部占有。 *—adv.* 完全地;端正地。The blow hit him *full* in the face. 這一擊正中在他的臉上。***full many*** 很多。***full well*** 很好。*—v.i.* (月亮)變圓。*—n.* 最高或最充分的境界,狀態。***at full*** 全部地;徹底地。***at the full*** 在到達最高點或最充分狀態時。***in full*** 完全地;不省略地。***to the full*** 完全地。to enjoy oneself *to the full.* 盡情享樂。

full² *v.t.* 蒸洗(毛織品)。*—v.i.* (毛織品)質地變密。

full·back [ˈfulˌbæk; ˈfulbæk] *n.* 〖足球〗後衞。

full binding (書卷之)全皮裝釘。

full blast 〖俗〗以最高速度或最大能力;大規模展開。

full blood ①純血種的人或動物。②與父母雙方均有關係之親戚。

full-blood·ed [ˈfulˈblʌdɪd; ˈfulˈblʌdid] *adj.* ①純血種的。②多血質的;有精神的。

full-blown [ˈfulˈblon; ˈfulˈbloun] *adj.* ①盛開的。②成熟的。③(帆等)張滿的。

full-bod·ied [ˈfulˈbɑdɪd; ˈfulˈbɔdid] *adj.* ①(人)肥的。②(酒等)濃郁而强烈的。

full-bot·tomed [ˈfulˈbɑtəmd; ˈfulˈbɔtəmd] *adj.* ①(假髮)底部儘量張開的。②底寬的,裝載量多的(船)。

full dress ①〖軍〗全裝;禮服。②大禮服;(尤指)正式的晚禮服。

full-dress [ˈfulˈdrɛs; ˈfulˈdres] *adj.* ①穿禮服的。②正式的。③全力以赴的;盡所有的。④詳盡的。

full·er [ˈfulɚ; ˈfulə] *n.* 漿洗布疋者;漂布者。***fuller's earth*** 漂布泥;漂白土。

full·er·y [ˈfulərɪ; ˈfuləri] *n., pl.* **-er·ies.** 漂布工場。

full-faced [ˈfulˈfest; ˈfulˈfeist] *adj.* ①圓臉的;面頰豐滿的;(月等)圓圓的。②向正面的。③〖印刷〗粗體鉛字的。

full-fash·ioned [ˈfulˈfæʃənd; ˈfulˈfæʃənd] *adj.* (長襪等)編織完全合脚的。(亦作 **fully-fashioned**)

full-fledged [ˈfulˈflɛdʒd; ˈfulˈfledʒd] *adj.* ①羽毛長全的(鳥)。②發育完全的;有充分資格的。

full-grown [ˈfulˈgron; ˈfulˈgroun] *adj.* 成熟的;成長的。

full·heart·ed [ˈfulˈhɑrtɪd; ˈfulˈhɑːtid] *adj.* ①勇氣百倍的;嘔心血的。②熱心的。

full house ①大客滿;客滿的戲院。②〖牌戲〗有三張相同及另兩張相同之一手牌。

full-length [ˈfulˈlɛŋθ; ˈfulˈleŋθ] *adj.* ①全長的;等身的。②(小說等)足本的;未縮短的。*—n.* 全身像。*—adv.* 全長地;等身地。

full mark 滿分。

full moon 圓月;滿月;(一月之)月圓期。

full-mouthed [ˈfulˌmauðd; ˈfulˌmauðd] *adj.* ①吵鬧的。②(牛等)牙齒長全的。

***full·ness** [ˈfulnɪs; ˈfulnis] *n.* ①充滿;滿;完全;十分;豐滿。in its *fullness.* 十分地;盡情地。in the *fullness* of time. 時機成熟時;在預定之時。②肥滿。③(色、音等的)豐滿;豐富。④發脹。(亦作 **fulness**)

full powered (船隻之)全靠引擎的;全機動的(無需帆的)。

full professor (正)教授。

full sail ①(船之)全帆。②全帆張滿地。③很快地;强力地。

full-scale [ˈfulˈskel; ˈfulˈskeil] *adj.* ①照原尺寸的。②全部的;完全的。

full sentence 完整句子。

full-size [ˈfulˈsaɪz; ˈfulˈsaiz] *adj.* ①完全長大的。②全長的;全身的。③照原尺寸的。(亦作 **full-sized**)

full speed 全速(地)。

full stop 句點。

full swing 全力活動;自由活動;活動的高潮。

full time 全時間;專任。

full-time [ˈfulˈtaɪm; ˈfulˈtaim] *adj.* 〖美〗全時間的;專任的。

full-tim·er [ˈfulˈtaɪmɚ; ˈfulˈtaimə] *n.* 〖英〗全讀生(爲 half-timer 之對)。

:ful·ly [ˈfulɪ; ˈfuli] *adv.* ①完全地;全部地。Was he *fully* satisfied? 他完全滿意嗎? ②充足地;十分地。*fully* equipped. 裝備齊全。

ful·mi·nant [ˈfʌlmənənt; ˈfʌlminənt] *adj.* ①爆鳴性的;嚴詞譴責的;突然發生而嚴重的。②〖醫〗急性的。

ful·mi·nate [ˈfʌlməˌnet; ˈfʌlmineit] *v.,* **-nat·ed, -nat·ing,** *n. —v.i.* ①猛烈攻擊;嚴詞譴責〖常 against〗。②大怒;怒喝。③猛烈爆發。④(疾病)突然爆發。*—v.t.* ①使…起猛烈爆發。②嚴詞譴責。*—n.* 〖化〗有高度爆炸力之化合物;雷粉。②雷酸鹽。

fulminating powder 〖化〗①爆炸粉。②雷酸鹽。

ful·mi·na·tion [ˌfʌlməˈneʃən; ˌfʌlmiˈneiʃən] *n.* ①抨擊。②猛烈的爆發。

ful·mi·na·to·ry [ˈfʌlmənəˌtorɪ; ˈfʌlminətəri] *adj.* 雷鳴的;爆鳴的;怒斥的。

ful·min·ic [fʌlˈmɪnɪk; fʌlˈminik] *adj.* ①高度爆炸性的;不穩定的。②〖化〗雷酸的。

fulminic acid 〖化〗雷酸。

ful·some [ˈfulsəm; ˈfulsəm] *adj.* 過度的(諂媚、稱讚等);令人作嘔的。*fulsome* praise. 言不由衷的讚美。**—ly,** *adv.*

ful·vous [ˈfʌlvəs; ˈfʌlvəs] *adj.* 黃褐色的。

fu·ma·role [ˈfjuməˌrol; ˈfjuːməroul] *n.* (火山的)噴氣孔;噴煙孔。

fu·ma·to·ry [ˈfjuməˌtorɪ; ˈfjuːmətəri] *adj., n.,* **-to·ries.** 燻烟的。*—n.* 燻蒸所。

***fum·ble** [ˈfʌmbl; ˈfʌmbl] *v.,* **-bled, -bling,** *n. —v.i.* ①摸索;搜尋。He *fumbled* about in his pockets for the ticket. 他在口袋裏摸索着找票。②(運動時)失球;漏接球。③做事笨手笨脚。*—v.t.* ①拙笨地處理。②(運動時)失(球);漏接(球)。③(演員等)漏(詞)。*—n.* ①摸索;搜尋。②拙笨的處理。③失球;運球、傳球等失當。**—fum·bler,** *n.*

***fume** [fjum; fjuːm] *n., v.,* **fumed, fum·ing.** *—n.* ①(常*pl.*)(有害的、氣味難聞而强烈的)烟、氣體、汽等。The strong *fumes* of the acid nearly choked him. 這種酸的强烈臭氣幾乎使他窒息。②一陣忿憤或不安。in a *fume* of impatience. 在一陣不耐煩中。*—v.i.* ①發散出臭氣;發出烟氣。He *fumed* with brandy. 他發出白蘭地的酒味。②忿怒;發怒。*—v.t.* ①(以烟等)燻。*fumed* oak. 被烟燻黑的橡木。②發出燻煙。

fu·mi·gate [ˈfjuməˌget; ˈfjuːmigeit] *v.t.,* **-gat·ed, -gat·ing.** 以烟燻消毒;燻。**—fu·mi·ga·tion,** *n.*

fu·mi·ga·tor [ˈfjuməˌgetɚ; ˈfjuːmigeitə] *n.* ①烟燻消毒的人或物。②(消毒、燻香等用之)烟燻器。

fu·mi·to·ry [ˈfjuməˌtorɪ; ˈfjuːmətəri] *n., pl.* **-to·ries.** 〖植物〗延胡索屬之植物。

fum·y [ˈfjumɪ; ˈfjuːmi] *adj.,* **fum·i·er,**

fum·i·est. ①多烟的;發烟的。②烟狀的;像蒸氣的。

‡fun [fʌn; fʌn] *n.* ①戲鬧;玩笑;樂趣。We had a lot of *fun.* 我們玩得很熱鬧。②有趣的人或事。Sailing a boat is great *fun.* 划船是一件極有趣的事。***have fun*** 高興;開心。***in*** (or ***for***) ***fun*** 玩笑地;非認眞地。I said it only *in fun.* 我說這話不過玩笑而已。***like fun*** 〖俗〗決不;靠不住地。***make fun of*** 嘲弄;開玩笑。***out of fun*** 開玩笑。***poke fun at*** =make fun of. —*v.i.* 〖俗〗開玩笑;取笑。—*adj.* ①玩笑的;有趣的。②奇妙的;奇幻的。

fu·nam·bu·list [fjuˈnæmbjulɪst; fjuːˈnæmbjulist] *n.* 走繩索賣藝者。

***func·tion** [ˈfʌŋkʃən; ˈfʌŋkʃən] *n.* ①作用;機能;官能。The *function* of the eye is to see. 眼的功能是看。②特殊目標或用途;功能。③責任;職責;職權。You must not exceed your *functions.* 你絕不可越權。④祝典;典禮;正式集會。⑤〖數學〗函數。⑥與其他因素有密切關係之事。Price is a *function* of supply and demand. 供求決定物價。—*v.i.* 擔任工作;有效用。Mary *functioned* as teacher. 瑪麗擔任教師的職務。

func·tion·al [ˈfʌŋkʃənl; ˈfʌŋkʃənl] *adj.* ①官能的;機能的;關於機能的。*functional* disease. 官能病。②職務上的;職掌上的。③〖數學〗函數的。④以實用爲着眼而設計的。*functional* furniture. 實用的傢具。⑤有多種用途的;可改變用途的。⑥可以使用的;可操作的。—*n.* 〖數學〗汎函數。—**ly,** *adv.*

functional illiterate 職務性文盲(知識不足應付其職務上之需要者)。

func·tion·al·ism [ˈfʌŋkʃənlˌɪzəm; ˈfʌŋkʃənlizm] *n.* (建築等的)實用主義。

func·tion·ar·y [ˈfʌŋkʃənˌɛrɪ; ˈfʌŋkʃn̩əri] *n., pl.* **-ar·ies,** *adj.* —*n.* 官員;官吏;公務員。—*adj.* 職務上的。

function word 句中表示關係或文法意義之字(介系詞、連接詞、助動詞屬之)。

***fund** [fʌnd; fʌnd] *n.* ①專款;基金。a relief *fund.* 救濟基金。②貯藏;貯藏之量。③(*pl.*)金錢;財源;現款。in *funds.* 有錢。out of *funds.* 缺錢。—*v.t.* ①儲蓄(一筆錢)以備付息。②爲…備基金。③將(公債)由短期改爲長期。④將…列爲專款或基金;存放;收集。

fun·da·ment [ˈfʌndəmənt; ˈfʌndəmənt] *n.* ①根本;基本原理。②臀部。③肛門。

***fun·da·men·tal** [ˌfʌndəˈmɛntl; ˌfʌndəˈmentl] *adj.* ①基本的;根本的;初階的;重要的。the *fundamental* rules of grammar. 文法的基本規則。②〖音樂〗基礎音的;原音的。—*n.* ①基本原理;基本法則。②〖音樂〗基音;原音。③〖物理〗基諧波。—**ly,** *adv.*

fun·da·men·tal·ism [ˌfʌndəˈmɛntlˌɪzəm; ˌfʌndəˈmentəlizəm] *n.* 基督教基本主義(絕對相信聖經之記載而排斥進化論)。—**fun·da·men·tal·ist,** *n., adj.*

fun·da·men·tal·i·ty [ˌfʌndəmɛnˈtælɪtɪ; ˌfʌndəmenˈtæliti] *n.* 基本性;重要性;根本。

fundamental unit 〖物理〗基本單位。

funded debt 固定負債;長期債款。

fund·hold·er [ˈfʌndˌholdɚ; ˈfʌndˌhouldə] *n.* 〖英〗公債所有人。

fund·rais·ing [ˈfʌndˌrezɪŋ; ˈfʌndˌreiziŋ] *n.* 籌款;募款。—*adj.* 籌款的;募款的。

fun·dus [ˈfʌndəs; ˈfʌndəs] *n., pl.* **-di** [-daɪ; -dai]. 〖解剖〗(胃、子宮等的)底;底部。

fu·ner·al** [ˈfjunərəl; ˈfjuːnərəl] *n.* 葬禮;喪禮。The admiral was given a state *funeral.* 這位海軍上將被授以國葬。be one's funeral*** 〖俗〗對某人有不愉快的結局;某人必須解決之事。Let him worry—it's *his funeral!* 讓他煩惱吧——這事須由他自行解決。—*adj.* 送殯的;適於喪禮的。

funeral home 殯儀館。(亦作**funeral chapel, funeral church, funeral parlor, funeral residence, mortuary**)

fu·ner·ar·y [ˈfjunəˌrɛrɪ; ˈfjuːnərəri] *adj.* 葬禮的;埋葬的。

fu·ne·re·al [fjuˈnɪrɪəl; fju(ː)ˈniəriəl] *adj.* ①喪禮的;似葬禮的。②陰森的;憂鬱的。

fu·nest [fjuˈnɛst; fjuːˈnest] *adj.* 凶惡的;致命的;不吉的;造成災禍的。

fun fair 〖主英〗娛樂場;兒童樂園。

fun·fest [ˈfʌnˈfɛst; ˈfʌnˈfest] *n.* 同樂會;娛樂會。

fun·gi [ˈfʌndʒaɪ; ˈfʌŋgai] *n.* pl. of **fungus.**

fun·gi·ble [ˈfʌndʒəbl̩; ˈfʌndʒibl] *adj.* 〖法律〗代替的;可代替的。—*n.* 〖法律〗代替物。

fun·gi·cide [ˈfʌndʒəˌsaɪd; ˈfʌndʒisaid] *n.* 殺黴菌劑。

fun·gi·form [ˈfʌndʒɪˌfɔrm; ˈfʌndʒifɔːm] *adj.* 黴菌狀的。

fun·gin [ˈfʌndʒɪn; ˈfʌndʒin] *n.* 黴菌素;黴菌纖維素。

fun·go [ˈfʌŋgo; ˈfʌŋgou] *n.* 〖棒球〗獨自將球擲起以棒擊打之練習法。

fun·goid [ˈfʌŋgɔɪd; ˈfʌŋgɔid] *adj.* 黴菌狀的;黴菌性的;蕈樣的。—*n.* 黴菌。

fun·gous [ˈfʌŋgəs; ˈfʌŋgəs] *adj.* ①黴菌的;如黴菌的;黴菌引致的。②倏生倏滅的。

fun·gus [ˈfʌŋgəs; ˈfʌŋgəs] *n., pl.* **fun·gi** or **fun·gus·es,** *adj.* —*n.* ①蕈類;黴菌。②黴菌狀腫;贅肉。③長得很快的東西。—*adj.* 黴菌的;黴菌狀的。(亦作 **fungal**)

fu·ni·cle [ˈfjunɪkl̩; ˈfjuːnikl] *n.* 〖植物〗細索;纖維。

fu·nic·u·lar [fjuˈnɪkjələ; fjuːˈnikjulə] *adj.* ①繩索的;懸於繩索上的。②臍帶的。—*n.* 纜車。

funicular railway 纜車。

fu·nic·u·lus [fjuˈnɪkjələs; fjuːˈnikjuləs] *n., pl.* **-u·li** [-jəˌlaɪ; -julai]. ①細索;纖維。②〖解剖〗臍帶;精絲。③〖植物〗胚珠柄。

fu·ni·form [ˈfjunəfɔrm; ˈfjuːnifɔːm] *adj.* 繩狀的;帶狀的。

funk¹ [fʌŋk; fʌŋk] *n.* 〖俗〗①恐懼;怯懦。②懦夫。***funk hole*** 〖美俗〗隱藏處;安全處。—*v.t.* ①恐懼;畏懼。②恐嚇。—*v.i.* 畏縮。

funk² *n.* 强烈而難聞之氣味(尤指烟)。—*v.t.* ①向…噴烟;以烟擾亂。②吸(烟斗)。—*v.i.* 抽烟;吸烟。

funked [fʌŋkt; fʌŋkt] *adj.* 〖美南方〗(烟草之)發霉的。

funk·y [ˈfʌŋkɪ; ˈfʌŋki] *adj.,* **funk·i·er, funk·i·est.** ①〖俗〗恐懼的;怯懦的。②〖俗〗臭的;有臭味的。—**funk·i·ness,** *n.*

fun·nel [ˈfʌnl̩; ˈfʌnl] *n., v.,* **-nel(l)ed, -nel·(l)ing.** —*n.* ①漏斗。②(汽船、火車等的)烟囱。③漏斗形的東西。④通氣道;通烟道。—*v.i.* 通過漏斗。—*v.t.* 集中。

fun·nel(l)ed [ˈfʌnl̩d; ˈfʌnld] *adj.* ①有漏斗的;漏斗狀的。②有(…個)烟囱的。a two-*funneled* steamer. 兩個烟囱的輪船。

fun·nel·form [ˈfʌnl̩ˌfɔrm; ˈfʌnlfɔːm] *adj.* 〖植物〗漏斗狀的。

fun·nies [ˈfʌnɪz; ˈfʌniz] *n. pl.* 〖美〗連環圖畫;漫畫欄。

fun·ni·ment [ˈfʌnɪmənt; ˈfʌnimənt] *n.* 滑稽;笑談。

‡fun·ny [ˈfʌnɪ; ˈfʌni] *adj.*, **-ni·er, -ni·est,** *n., pl.* **-nies.** —*adj.* ①有趣的;好玩的。What a *funny* story! 多麼有趣的故事啊! ②奇特的; 難以了解的。He has a *funny* temper. 他有奇特的性情。③可疑的;不光明的。④無禮的; 粗野的。Don't get *funny* with me, young man! 在我面前休得放肆,小伙子! —*n.* 笑話;趣事。—**fun·ni·ly,** *adv.*

funny business 〖俚〗不道德的行爲。

fun·ny·man [ˈfʌnɪˌmæn; ˈfʌnimæn] *n., pl.* **-men.** 諧角;好幽默的人。

funny money 〖美加俗〗①投資於不健全或不實際之事業的金錢。②不穩定的錢; 取不回來的錢。

funny paper 報紙上刊載連環圖畫、猜字遊戲等文字之版。

fun·ster [ˈfʌnstɚ; ˈfʌnstə] *n.* 故意逗人笑的人。

‡fur [fɝ; fəː] *n., v.,* **furred, fur·ring,** *adj.* —*n.* ①獸皮之軟毛;毛皮。②(*pl.*)毛皮衣。She was wearing very expensive *furs.* 她穿着非常昂貴的皮衣。③舌苔。A sick person often has *fur* on his tongue. 一個病人舌上常常有苔。***fur and feather*** 可獵的禽獸(如野兔等)。***make the fur fly*** **a.** 惹是非; 造亂子; 吵架。**b.** 趕快地做。She was late and *made the fur fly* in her rush to get out. 她遲了所以匆匆忙忙地趕着出去。***stroke a person's fur the wrong way*** 激怒某人。***the fur fly*** **a.** 東西被打破、打壞、亂丟。**b.** 事情很快做好。Boy, did *the fur fly* when she worked. 乖乖,她做起事來眞快! —*v.t.* ①覆以毛皮;襯以毛皮;裝以毛皮。②覆舌苔等。—*adj.* 毛皮的。*fur* rug. 毛皮地毯。

fur. ①furlong(s). ②further.

fur-bear·er [ˈfɝˌbɛrɚ; ˈfəːˌbɛərə] *n.* ①生毛之動物。②皮毛有商業價值之動物。

fur·be·low [ˈfɝblˌo; ˈfəːbilou] *n.* ①(女服的) 裙褶; 裙飾。②(*pl.*)俗麗的裝飾。—*v.t.* 加以俗麗的裝飾。

fur·bish [ˈfɝbɪʃ; ˈfəːbiʃ] *v.t.* ①擦亮; 磨光 〖up〗。②刷新;重溫。

fur·cate [*v.* ˈfɝket; ˈfəːkeit, fəːˈk- *adj.* ˈfɝket; ˈfəːkeit] *adj., v.,* **fur·cat·ed, fur·cat·ing.** —*adj.* 分叉的。—*v.i.* 分叉;分歧。—**fur·ca·tion,** *n.*

fur farm 爲取毛皮而養獸的牧場。

fur farming 爲取毛皮而養獸。

fur·fur [ˈfɝfɚ; ˈfəːfə] *n., pl.* **fur·fur·es.** ①皮屑。②(*pl.*)皮屑之小片。

fur·fu·ra·ceous [ˌfɝfjuˈreʃəs; ˌfəːfjuəˈreiʃəs] *adj.* ①似糠的。②鱗狀的。

fu·ri·ous** [ˈfjurɪəs; ˈfjuəriəs, ˈfjoər-, ˈfjɔər-, ˈfjɔːr-] *adj.* ①狂怒的;狂暴的;猛烈的。②(工作行動等) 非常努力而速度快的。His *furious* activity put us all to shame. 他的孜孜不倦使我們大家赧顏。fast and furious*** 極快的。—**ly,** *adv.* —**ness,** *n.*

furl [fɝl; fəːl] *v.t.* 捲起; 疊起。to *furl* a flag (an umbrella). 疊好一面旗(一把傘)。—*v.i.* 收疊;捲起。—*n.* 收疊。

furl. furlough.

fur·long [ˈfɝlɔŋ; ˈfəːlɔŋ] *n.* 長度名(一英里的八分之一)。

fur·lough [ˈfɝlo; ˈfəːlou] *n.* ①休假(尤指軍人及在外國工作的官員之休假)。②暫時或永久解雇的鐵路工人。—*v.t.* ①准假; 給假。②暫時或永久解雇。

fur·me·ty [ˈfɝmətɪ; ˈfəːməti] *n.* =**frumenty.**

fur·nace** [ˈfɝnɪs; ˈfəːnis] *n.* ①火爐;鎔爐。②極熱的地方。③嚴苛的試煉;磨煉。the *furnace* of affliction. 苦難的磨煉。(be***) ***tried in the furnace*** 受過磨煉;飽經風霜。—*v.t.* 將金屬在鎔爐裏加熱。

fur·nace·man [ˈfɝnɪsˌmæn; ˈfəːnismən] *n., pl.* **-men.** 照顧鎔爐之工人。

‡fur·nish [ˈfɝnɪʃ; ˈfəːniʃ] *v.t.* ①供給〖常 with〗。to *furnish* a library with books. 供給圖書館書籍。②陳設;布置(房間)。The house is well *furnished.* 這房屋內布置得很好。—**er,** *n.*

fur·nish·ing [ˈfɝnɪʃɪŋ; ˈfəːniʃiŋ] *n.* ①供給物。②(*pl.*)傢具;室內陳設品。③(*pl.*)〖美〗服飾品。

‡fur·ni·ture [ˈfɝnɪtʃɚ; ˈfəːnitʃə] *n.* ①傢具。a piece (*or* an article) of *furniture.* 一件傢具。Beds, chairs, tables, and desks are *furniture.* 床、椅、桌及書桌皆是傢具。②設備品;必需品。③〖印刷〗排版時夾在鉛字之間的襯托木條或鉛條。

fu·ror [ˈfjurɔr; ˈfjuərɔː] *n.* ①熱烈的稱羨; 熱狂; 風靡。to make (*or* create) a *furor.* (書籍、劇本等)風靡一時。②狂怒。

fu·ro·re [ˈfjuror; for ① fjuəˈrɔːri, for ② fuˈrɔːri] *n.* ①=**furor.** ②〖音樂〗激情;熱情。

fur piece ①皮領。②皮披肩。

furred [fɝd; fəːd] *adj.* ①毛皮的。②毛皮做的。③穿毛皮衣的。④有舌苔的。

fur·ri·er[1] [ˈfɝɪɚ; ˈfʌriə] *n.* 皮貨商;做或修理毛皮外衣的人。

fur·ri·er[2] *adj.* furry 之比較級。

fur·ri·er·y [ˈfɝɪərɪ; ˈfʌriəri] *n., pl.* **-er·ies.** ①毛皮類(集合稱)。②皮貨業; 修理皮貨者之業務。

fur·ring [ˈfɝɪŋ; ˈfəːriŋ] *n.* ①(衣類的) 毛皮裝飾; 毛皮襯裏。②舌苔。③ (水壺上的) 水垢。

***fur·row** [ˈfɝo; ˈfʌrou] *n.* ①畦;犂溝。②車轍; 輪溝。Heavy trucks made deep *furrows* in the muddy road. 重貨車在泥路上壓成深深的輪溝。③(臉上的) 皺紋。—*v.t.* ①犂;耕。②使起皺紋。—*v.i.* ①做畦。②發生皺紋。His brow *furrowed* in deep thought. 他皺了眉頭在沉思。

fur·ry [ˈfɝɪ; ˈfəːri] *adj.,* **-ri·er, -ri·est.** ①被有毛皮的; 如毛皮的。②毛皮製的。③襯有毛皮的;毛皮鑲邊的。④有舌苔的。⑤柔軟的。

fur seal 〖動物〗海狗(一名膃肭獸)。

‡fur·ther [ˈfɝðɚ; ˈfəːðə] compar. *adj. & adv.* of **far** with superl. **fur·thest,** *v.* —*adj.* ①較遠的; 更遠的。the *further* end of the village. 村子較遠的盡頭。②另外的; 添加的; 更多的。Have you any *further* need of me? (此外)你還需要我(幫你甚麼忙)嗎? —*adv.* ①較遠地; 更進一步地。It's not *further* than a mile from here. 從這裏走去,不超過一英里遠。②此外;並且。***be further continued*** 待續。***I'll see you further first.*** 我絕不贊成(此處 further 爲 in hell 的婉轉語)。—*v.t.* 促進;增進;贊助。

fur·ther·ance [ˈfɝðərəns; ˈfəːðərəns] *n.* 促進;推廣;提高。

***fur·ther·more** [ˈfɝðɚˌmor, -ˌmɔr; ˈfəːðəˈmɔː, -ˈmɔə] *adv.* 再者; 此外。*Furthermore,* he left orders not to be disturbed. 此外,他下令不得打擾他。

fur·ther·most [ˈfɝðɚˌmost; ˈfəːðəmoust] *adj.* 最遠的。

***fur·thest** [ˈfɝðɪst; ˈfəːðist] *adj. & adv.* superl. of **far** with **fur·ther** as compar. I hope to return in a week at *furthest.* 我希望最遲一星期可以歸來。

fur·tive ['fɝtɪv; 'fəːtiv] *adj.* ①偷偷的；祕密做的。②賊頭賊腦的；狡猾的。—**ly,** *adv.*

fu·run·cle ['fjurʌŋkḷ; 'fjuərʌŋkl] *n.* 【醫】癤瘡；疔瘡。

fu·ry** ['fjurɪ; 'fjuəri, 'fjoər–, 'fjɔər–, 'fjɔːr–] *n., pl.* **-ries.** ①憤怒；憤激。She was in one of her wild *furies.* 她在一陣憤怒中。②狂暴；猛烈。③狂怒的人（尤指女人)。He found himself married to a jealous *fury.* 他發現他娶了個善妬的潑婦。④(F–)【希臘神話】復仇女神。like fury*** 猛烈地；强烈地。

furze [fɝz; fəːz] *n.* 【植物】金雀花。

furz·y ['fɝzɪ; 'fəːzi] *adj.* **furz·i·er, furz·i·est.** 多金雀花的；似金雀花的。

fus·ces·cent [fʌ'sɛsənt; fʌ'sesənt] *adj.* 微帶暗褐色的。

fus·cous ['fʌskəs; 'fʌskəs] *adj.* 暗褐「色的。」

***fuse** [fjuz; fjuːz] *n., v.,* **fused, fus·ing.** —*n.* ①【電】保險絲。②導火線；導火管。—*v.t.* ①融觸；使融合。Copper and zinc are *fused* to make brass. 銅與鋅被融於一起而製成黃銅。②結合一起；合併。—*v.i.* ①融化。②結合。③【英】燒斷保險絲。

fu·see [fju'zi; fjuː'ziː] *n.* ①耐風火柴。②信管。③【獸醫】(馬脚的）骨腫。④【鐵路】紅色閃光信號（危險信號)。

fu·se·lage ['fjuzḷɪdʒ, ˌfjuzḷ'ɑʒ; 'fjuːzilɑːʒ] *n.* 飛機機身；機身骨架。

fusel oil 【化】雜醇油（酒精發酵副產品)。

Fu·shun ['fu'ʃun; 'fuː'ʃun] *n.* 撫順（在中國遼寧省東北部，以產煤著稱)。

fu·si·bil·i·ty [ˌfjuzə'bɪlətɪ; ˌfjuːzə'biliti] *n.* ①熔性。②熔度。

fu·si·ble ['fjuzəbḷ; 'fjuːzəbl] *adj.* 易熔解的；可熔解的；易熔性的。

fu·si·form ['fjuzəˌfɔrm; 'fjuːzəfɔːm] *adj.* 【生物】紡錘狀的。

fu·sil[1] ['fjuzḷ; 'fjuːzil] *adj.* ①被熔解的。②熔鑄而製成的。(亦作 **fusile**)

fu·sil[2] *n.* 燧石鎗；燧發鎗（用火石引發的舊式長鎗)。

fu·sil·ier, fu·sil·eer [ˌfjuzḷ'ɪr; ˌfjuːzi'liə] *n.* ①燧石鎗手。②(*pl.*) 燧石鎗團。

fu·sil·lade [ˌfjuzḷ'ed; ˌfjuːzi'leid] *n., v.,* **-lad·ed, -lad·ing.** —*n.* ①鎗砲的齊射；猛射；連發。②(比喻）連續急發。—*v.t.* 以齊射或連發砲攻擊或擊落。

fu·sion** ['fjuʒən; 'fjuːʒən] *n.* ①融解；融合。②聯合；結合。a *fusion* of interests. 利益的結合。③融合一起的東西。④【物理】核子融合。⑤【眼科】雙像併合。heat of fusion*** 融解熱。***point of fusion*** 融解點。

fusion bomb 氫彈（=hydrogen bomb).

fu·sion·ist ['fjuʒənɪst; 'fjuːʒənist] *n.* 聯合論者。—*adj.* 聯合論（者)的。

***fuss** [fʌs; fʌs] *n.* ①無謂紛擾；小題大做。to make a great *fuss* about trifles. 因細故而大事紛擾。to get into a *fuss.* 急躁；焦急。②愛小題大做的人。—*v.i.* 無謂紛擾；小題大做。Don't *fuss* over the children so much. 不要過於爲孩子們擔心。—*v.t.* 煩擾。

fuss and feathers 誇耀；誇示。

fuss·budg·et ['fʌsˌbʌdʒɪt; 'fʌsˌbʌdʒit] *n.* 愛挑剔的人。(亦作 **fusspot**)

fuss·y ['fʌsɪ; 'fʌsi] *adj.,* **fuss·i·er, fuss·i·est.** ①愛挑剔的；難以取悅的。②整潔的；漂亮的。③繁瑣的；需要特別注意的。—**fuss·i·ly,** *adv.* —**fuss·i·ness,** *n.*

fus·tian ['fʌstʃən, 'fʌstjən; 'fʌstiən, –tjən] *n.* ①(歐洲於中世紀流行的）麻紗布；麻紗布衣。②浮誇而無價值的話。—*adj.* ①麻紗布做的。②浮誇的；無價值的。

fus·tic ['fʌstɪk; 'fʌstik] *n.* ①【植物】佛提樹（桑科樹)。②由該樹所提煉之黃色染料。

fus·ti·gate ['fʌstəˌget; 'fʌstigeit] *v.t.,* **-gat·ed, -gat·ing.** ①棒打；以棍打。②抨擊；批抨。—**fus·ti·ga·tion,** *n.*

fust·y ['fʌstɪ; 'fʌsti] *adj.,* **fust·i·er, fust·i·est.** ①腐臭的。②舊式的；保守的；頑固的。—**fust·i·ness,** *n.*

fu·su·ma ['fusumɑ; 'fuːsuːmɑː] *n.* 日「式房屋之拉門。」

***fu·tile** ['fjutḷ, –tɪl; 'fjuːtail] *adj.* ①徒勞的；無益的；無用的。He's a *futile* sort of person. 他是一個無大用的人。②不重要的；瑣細的。③爲瑣事而忙的。a *futile* life. 庸碌的一生。—**ly,** *adv.*

fu·til·i·tar·i·an [ˌfjutɪlə'tɛrɪən; fjuːˌtili'tɛəriən] *adj.* 悲觀主義的。—*n.* 悲觀主義者。

fu·til·i·ty [fju'tɪlətɪ; fjuː'tiliti] *n., pl.* **-ties.** ①無用；無益；無效；徒勞。②不重要的事。

fut·tock ['fʌtək; 'fʌtək] *n.* 【造船】複肋材。

futtock shrouds 【造船】連接上下「桅之鐵索；自下桅登桅樓之鐵索梯。」

‡**fu·ture** ['fjutʃɚ; 'fjuːtʃə] *n.* ①將來；未來；前途。Our *future* seems very uncertain. 我們的前途似難預測。②(*pl.*)期貨。to deal in *futures.* 期貨買賣。③【文法】未來時間；未來式。***for the future; in (the) future*** 今後；在將來。*For the future,* try to live a better life. 從此以後，努力向好路上走。***in the near future*** 在不久的將來。—*adj.* 將來的；未來的。

fu·ture·less ['fjutʃəlɪs; 'fjuːtʃəlis] *adj.* 前途無望的；不作未來打算的。

future life 來生；來世。

future perfect 【文法】未來完成式。

future shock 未來之震盪（因社會之加速改變而引起的緊張、迷惘等反常現象)。

future tense 【文法】未來式。

fu·tur·ism ['fjutʃɚˌɪzəm; 'fjuːtʃərizəm] *n.* 未來派（1910 年發源於義大利之文學、藝術、音樂等方面反對因襲傳統之新主義)。(亦作 **Futurism**)

fu·tur·ist ['fjutʃərɪst; 'fjuːtʃərist] *n.* ①未來派藝術家或作家。②【神學】未來信徒（相信聖經中預言會實現者)。—*adj.* 未來派的；未來派作家或藝術家的；未來信徒的。(亦作 **Futurist**) —**ic,** *adj.*

fu·tu·ri·ty [fju'turətɪ; fjuː'tjuəriti] *n., pl.* **-ri·ties.** ①未來。②未來之狀態（事件)。③後世之人。④來生。

fu·tur·ol·o·gy [ˌfjutʃə'rɑlədʒɪ; ˌfjuːtʃər'ɔlədʒi] *n.* 前瞻學（研究及預測科學未來之發展及對社會之影響)。

fuze [fjuz; fjuːz] *n.* =**fuse.**

fu·zee [fju'zi; fjuː'ziː] =**fusee.**

fuzz [fʌz; fʌz] *n.* ①絨毛；細毛；碎毛。②【美，俚】**a.** 警官；刑警。**b.** 警察。—*v.t.* 使成絨毛狀；覆以絨毛。***fuzz up*** 弄亂。—*v.i.* ①變成絨毛狀；覆有絨毛。②作絨毛狀飛散。

fuzz·ball ['fʌzˌbɔl; 'fʌzbɔːl] *n.* 馬勃菌；牛屎菌（=puffball).

fuzz·y ['fʌzɪ; 'fʌzi] *adj.,* **fuzz·i·er, fuzz·i·est.** ①絨毛的。②似絨毛的。③被以絨毛的。④朦朧的；模糊的。—**fuzz·i·ness,** *n.*

fuzz·y-head·ed ['fʌzɪ'hɛdɪd; 'fʌzi'hedid] *adj.* ①頭腦不清楚的。②頭暈的。

fwd. forward. **FY** fiscal year.
-fy 〖字尾〗用以形成動詞,表: ①使化成,如: liquefy. ②使有, 如: glorify. ③變成, 如: emulsify.
fyke 〔faɪk; faik〕 *n.* 一種袋形魚網。
fyl·fot 〔ˈfɪlfɑt; ˈfilfɔt〕 *n.* 卐字形。
F.Z.S., F.Z.S.L. Fellow of the Zoological Society, London.

G

G or **g** 〔dʒi; dʒiː〕 *n., pl.* **G's** or **g's** 〔dʒiz; dʒiːz〕. ①英文字母之第七個字母。②〖音樂〗C 長調的第五音。③ G 字形之物。④〖電〗高斯 (=gauss). ⑤〖心理〗一般智能。⑥德國人(語、文)。⑦(評分)好 (表 good; 相當於 B, 乙等)。⑧〖俚〗一千元 (Grand 之簡稱)。⑨中世紀羅馬數字之 400。⑩〖電〗電導。⑪公克。⑫〖物理〗重力 (=gravity).
G ① German. ② Gulf. **G.** gravity.
g. ①gram. ②guinea. ③gauge. ④genitive. ⑤gender. ⑥general. ⑦generally. ⑧going back to. ⑨gold. ⑩grain; grains. ⑪〖足球〗guard. ⑫gun. **GA, G.A.** ①General Assembly. ②General Agent. ③General of the Army. ④General Average. **Ga** 化學元素 gallium 之符號。 **Ga.** Georgia.
gab 〔gæb; gæb〕 *n., v.,* **gabbed, gabbing.** —*n.* 〖俗〗空談;饒舌。to have the gift of (the) *gab.* 有口才。to blow the *gab.* 洩露祕密;告密。Stop (*or* Stow) your *gab.* 別講廢話! 閉嘴! —*v.i.* 空談;喋喋不休。
gab·ar·dine 〔ˈgæbəˌdin, ˌgæbəˈdin; ˈgæbədiːn, ˌgæbəˈdiːn〕 *n.* =**gaberdine.**
gab·bies 〔ˈgæbɪz; ˈgæbiz〕 *n. pl.* 〖美俚〗有聲電影 (=talkies).
gab·ble 〔ˈgæbl̩; ˈgæbl〕 *v.,* **-bled, -bling,** *n.* —*v.i.* & *v.t.* ①急促而不清楚地說出。②嘈囋。—*n.* 饒舌;急促而無意義的話。
gab·by 〔ˈgæbɪ; ˈgæbi〕 *adj.,* **gab·bi·er, gab·bi·est.** 饒舌的。
gab·er·dine 〔ˌgæbəˈdin; ˌgæbəˈdiːn〕 *n.* ①軋別丁(布料)。②長而鬆的袍子。
gab·fest 〔ˈgæbfɛst; ˈgæbfest〕 *n.* 〖美俗〗冗長的空談。
ga·bi·on 〔ˈgebɪən; ˈgeibiən〕 *n.* ①(防禦工事之)泥籃;泥籮。②(築河堤等之)石籃;石籮。
ga·bi·on·ade 〔ˌgebɪənˈed; ˌgeibiəˈneid〕 *n.* 石框堤;蛇籠堤。
ga·ble 〔ˈgebl̩; ˈgeibl〕 *n.* (尖頂屋兩端之)山形牆。
ga·bled 〔ˈgebl̩d; ˈgeibld〕 *adj.* 有山形牆的。
gable roof 人字(山)形屋頂。
ga·blet 〔ˈgeblɪt; ˈgeiblit〕 *n.* 小山形牆。
gable window 山形牆之窗。
Ga·bon 〔ˌgaˈbɔ̃; ˌgaˈbɔ̃ː〕 *n.* 加彭(非洲中部一共和國, 首都 Libreville). (亦作**Gabun**)
Gab·o·nese 〔ˌgæbəˈniz; ˌgæbəˈniːz〕 *adj., n., pl.* **-nese.** —*adj.* 加彭的;加彭人的;加彭語的。—*n.* 加彭人。
Ga·bri·el 〔ˈgebrɪəl; ˈgeibriəl〕 *n.* ①男子名。②〖聖經〗加百列 (七大天使之一, 上帝的使者)。
ga·by 〔ˈgebɪ; ˈgeibi〕 *n., pl.* **ga·bies.** 〖俗〗愚人;呆子;蠢物。
gad[1] 〔gæd; gæd〕 *v.,* **gad·ded, gadding,** *n.* —*v.i.* 閒逛; 遊蕩; 閒遊。—*n.* 閒逛;遊蕩。*on* (or *upon*) *the gad* 遊蕩着。
gad[2] *n., v.,* **gad·ded, gad·ding.** —*n.* ①(趕牲畜用之)刺棒。②尖頭棒;鑿。—*v.t.* 〖採礦〗以 gad 鑿碎或弄鬆。
Gad 〔gæd; gæd〕 *interj.* 〖俗〗 God 之婉轉語, 一種較溫和的咒語。(亦作 **gad**)
gad·a·bout 〔ˈgædəˌbaut; ˈgædəbaut〕 *n.* 〖俗〗遊蕩者;好閒逛者。—*adj.* 好遊蕩的。
gad·bee 〔ˈgædˌbi; ˈgædbiː〕 *n.* 牛虻。
gad·di 〔gədˈdi; gədˈdiː〕 *n.* 〖英印〗①(君主坐席的)墊子。②王座;王位。
gad·fly 〔ˈgædˌflaɪ; ˈgædflai〕 *n., pl.* **-flies.** ①牛虻。②令人討厭的人。
gadg·et 〔ˈgædʒɪt; ˈgædʒit〕 *n.* 〖俗〗設計精巧的小機械。
gadg·e·teer 〔ˌgædʒəˈtɪə; ˌgædʒiˈtiə〕 *n.* 發明或喜歡精巧小機械的人。
ga·doid 〔ˈgedɔɪd; ˈgeidɔid〕 *adj.* 鱈科的。—*n.* 鱈科之魚。
gad·o·lin·i·um 〔ˌgædəˈlɪnɪəm; ˌgædəˈliniəm〕 *n.* 〖化〗釓(稀土族元素, 符號 Gd).
Gael 〔gel; geil〕 *n.* 蓋爾人(蘇格蘭高地及愛爾蘭之 Celt 人)。
Gael·ic 〔ˈgelɪk; ˈgeilik〕 *adj.* 蓋爾人的。—*n.* 蓋爾語。
gaff[1] 〔gæf; gæf〕 *n.* ①大魚鈎;大魚叉。②(縱帆上緣的)斜桁。③鬥鷄之鐵距。④電線工人爬桿時綑在腿上的鐵鈎。***stand the gaff*** 〖俚〗忍受痛苦或懲罰而屹然不動。***throw a gaff into*** 〖俚〗打斷;擾亂。—*v.t.* ①以大鈎拖(魚)。②〖俚〗欺騙。
gaff[2] *n.* 〖英俚〗低級的娛樂場所 (通常稱爲 penny gaff). —*v.i.* 賭博 (尤指小賭博)。
gaffe 〔gæf; gæf〕 *n.* 過失;失態;謬誤。
gaf·fer 〔ˈgæfə; ˈgæfə〕 *n.* ①老人;(尤指)鄉下老頭(常爲輕蔑或諧語)。②〖英〗a. 工頭;領班。b. 〖俚〗父親。③〖愛〗年輕小伙子;孩子。④玻璃工人(指負責吹玻璃之工頭)。
gaff-top·sail 〔ˌgæfˈtɑpˌsel; ˌgæfˈtɔpseil〕 *n.* 中桅帆(通常爲三角形)。
gag 〔gæg; gæg〕 *n., v.,* **gagged, gagging.** —*n.* ①箝口具。②置於口中使之張開不閉之物。③官方的壓制言論自由。④〖俗〗演員加的額外的話或動作 (以逗觀衆發笑者); 插科打諢。—*v.t.* ①塞物於口使不能聲張。②將張口器置口中使保持不閉。③壓制言論自由。④令人作嘔。—*v.i.* ①作嘔。②〖俗〗插科打諢。
ga·ga 〔ˈgɑgɑ; ˈgɑːgɑː〕 *adj.* 〖美俗〗①天眞的; 愚蠢的。②非常起勁的; 瘋狂的。***go gaga*** 瘋狂的;狂熱的。—*n.* 低級的觀衆。
gage[1] 〔gedʒ; geidʒ〕 *n., v.,* **gaged, gaging.** —*n.* ①象徵挑戰之物 (如投擲手套等); 挑戰。②抵押物。—*v.t.* 〖古〗以(某物)做擔保。
gage[2] *n., v.t.* =**gauge.**
gag·er 〔ˈgedʒə; ˈgeidʒə〕 *n.* =**gauger.**
gag·ger·y 〔ˈgægərɪ; ˈgægəri〕 *n.* 開玩笑;插科打諢。
gag·gle 〔ˈgægl̩; ˈgægl〕 *n., v.,* **gaggled, gag·gling.** —*n.* 〖方〗①鵝羣。②一羣女人(輕蔑語)。③鵝叫聲。—*v.i.* (鵝)咯咯叫。—*v.t.* 咯咯地說出或發出。
gag law (or **rule**) 〖俗〗限制言論之法律;言論箝制令。
gag line 簡短之滑稽文字。
gag·man 〔ˈgægˌmæn; ˈgægmæn〕 *n., pl.* **-men.** ①爲演員寫笑料的人。(亦作 **gagwriter**) ②〖俚〗編笑話者。
gag·ster 〔ˈgægstə; ˈgægstə〕 *n.* ① =**gagman.**
ˈgai·e·ty 〔ˈgeətɪ; ˈgeiəti, ˈgeiiti〕 *n., pl.* **-ties.** ①歡樂的精神; 歡樂的氣象。Her

G

gaiety helped the party. 她的歡樂精神助使宴會成功。②(*pl.*)樂事。③華麗(服飾等)。

***gai·ly** [ˈgelɪ; ˈgeili] *adv.* ①歡樂地。②華麗地。She was *gaily* dressed. 她穿著華麗。

:gain [gen; gein] *v.t.* ①得到; 獲得。 to *gain* experience as one grows older. 隨着年齡增長而獲得經驗。②到達(尤指經過一番努力); 抵達。 The swimmer *gained* the shore. 游泳者抵達岸上。③獲勝。The stronger army *gained* the battle. 較强的軍隊打了勝仗。④獲益; 進步; 增加。My watch *gains* three minutes a day. 我的錶每天快三分鐘。—*v.i.* ①增進; 進步。She is *gaining* in weight. 她的體重正增加中。②得利; 獲益。He has obviously *gained* by the change. 這一改變對他顯然有益。 ***gain ground*** 進步; 得勢。 ***gain on*** (or ***upon***) **a.** 接近; 追及; 趕上。 **b.** 跑得快於。 **c.** 侵蝕。 ***gain over*** (***somebody***) 說服(某人)。 ***gain strength*** 恢復體力。 ***gain time*** 拖延時間;節省時間。—*n.* ①獲得之物;利益。No pains, no *gains*. 不辛勞, 無所獲。②增加; 增添。③獲取財富。 to be blinded by the love of *gain*. 利令智昏。④(*pl.*) 贏餘;利潤。⑤收音機、唱機、擴音機等之音量調節器。

gain·er [ˈgenɚ; ˈgeinə] *n.* ①獲得者; 獲利者;勝利者。②一種花式跳水。

gain·ful [ˈgenfəl; ˈgeinful] *adj.* 有利益的;有報酬的。—**ly,** *adv.*

gain·ings [ˈgenɪŋz; ˈgeiniŋz] *n. pl.* 獲得物; 所得; 收入; 收益; 獎品; 獎金。

gain·less [ˈgenlɪs; ˈgeinlis] *adj.* 無利益的;不划算的。

gain·ly [ˈgenlɪ; ˈgeinli] *adj.* ①(態度、動作等)輕捷的;優美的。②〖方〗合適的。

gain·say [genˈse; geinˈsei] *v.*, **-said** or **-sayed, -say·ing,** *n.*—*v.t.* 否認(主用於否定語中)。She is a fine woman—that nobody can *gainsay*. 她是個好女人——無人能否認。—*n.* 否認;矛盾。

gainst, 'gainst [gɛnst; genst] *prep., conj.* 〖詩〗 =**against.**

***gait** [get; geit] *n.* 步態;步法。He has a lame *gait* because of an injured foot. 他因一足受傷而跛行。—*v.t.* ①教馬走步法。②讓馬、狗等走路以觀察其步法、體態等。

gait·ed [ˈgetɪd; ˈgeitid] *adj.* 某種步態的 (多用於複合詞)。 slow-*gaited.* 慢步的。

gai·ter [ˈgetɚ; ˈgeitə] *n.* ①綁腿。②兩側均可鬆緊而無帶的鞋。③長統橡膠鞋。

gal [gæl; gæl] *n.* 〖俚〗 =**girl.**

Gal. Galatians. **gal.** gallon(s).

ga·la [ˈgelə; ˈgɑːlə] *n.* 節日;慶祝;特別娛樂。—*adj.* 節日的;快樂的;慶祝的。

ga·lac·ta·gogue [gəˈlæktəˌgɔg; gəˈlæktəgɔg] *adj.* 〖醫〗催奶的;催奶劑的。—*n.* 催奶劑。

ga·lac·tic [gəˈlæktɪk; gəˈlæktik] *adj.* ①(得自)乳汁的。②〖天文〗天河的;銀河的。

ga·lac·toid [gəˈlæktɔɪd; gəˈlæktɔid] *adj.* 似乳的;乳狀的。

Gal·a·had [ˈgæləˌhæd; ˈgæləhæd] *n.* ①加拉哈特(亞瑟王之圓桌武士之一, 因其忠潔與高貴而尋獲聖盤)。②忠潔、高貴的人。

gal·an·tine [ˈgælənˌtin; ˈgælәntiːn] *n.* 一種冷菜(犢、鷄等之肉, 去骨紮緊煮熟後冷食者)。(亦作 **galatine**)

ga·lan·ty show [gəˈlæntɪ～; gəˈlænti～] (以剪紙之圖像所映演之) 影子戲。

gal·a·te·a [ˌgæləˈtiə; ˌgæləˈtiə] *n.* 一種上等之棉布(通常有藍色條紋, 製衣用, 得名自一英國軍艦)。

Ga·la·tia [gəˈleʃə; gəˈleiʃiə] *n.* 加拉太(小亞細亞中部之一古國名)。

Ga·la·tian [gəˈleʃən; gəˈleiʃən] *adj.* 加拉太的;加拉太人的。—*n.* 加拉太人。

Ga·la·tians [gəˈleʃənz; gəˈleiʃiənz] *n.* (新約聖經中之)加拉太書。

gal·ax·y [ˈgæləksɪ; ˈgæləksi] *n., pl.* **-ax·ies.** ①(G-)天河;銀河。②類似銀河的星羣。③一羣顯赫的人。a *galaxy* of talent. 一羣才子。④一列燦麗奪目之物。

gal·ba·num [ˈgælbənəm; ˈgælbənəm] *n.* 白松香。

gal coal 適於製煤氣用之煤炭。

***gale**[1] [gel; geil] *n.* ①大風; 狂風。Hundreds of trees were blown down in the *gale*. 數百株樹在狂風中被吹倒了。②〖氣象〗每小時速度達 32 到 63 英里之風。③〖詩〗微風; 柔風。④一陣 (鬧聲)。 *gales* of laughter. 陣陣笑聲。

gale[2] *n.* 〖植物〗楊梅科之灌木。

gale[3] *n.* 〖英〗定期償付之租金、利息等。

ga·le·ate [ˈgelɪˌet; ˈgeilieit] *adj.* ①戴盔的。②〖動、植物〗有盔狀體的。③盔形的。

ga·lee·ny [gəˈlinɪ; gəˈliːni] *n., pl.* **-nies.** 〖英方〗珠鷄 (=guinea fowl).

Ga·len [ˈgelən; ˈgeilin] *n.* ①伽林 (Claudius, 130?–?200, 古希臘名醫及有關醫術之作家)。②〖謔〗醫生;郎中;草藥醫生。

ga·le·na [gəˈlinə; gəˈliːnə] *n.* 〖礦〗方鉛礦 (PbS).

Ga·len·ic, ga·len·ic [gəˈlɛnɪk; gəˈlenik] *adj.* 古希臘名醫 Galen 的; 其醫術的。*Galenic* pharmacy. 草本製劑; 草藥。

ga·le·nite [gəˈlinaɪt; gəˈliːnait] *n.* =**galena.**

ga·le·ro [gɑˈlɛro; gɑːˈlerou] 〖義〗 *n.* 「樞機主教之寬邊紅帽。」

Gal·i·le·an[1] [ˌgæləˈliən; ˌgæliˈliːən] *adj.* 加利利的。—*n.* 加利利人。 ***the Galilean*** 基督 (因在 Galilee 長大, 故名)。

Gal·i·le·an[2] *adj.* 伽利略 (Galileo) 的。

Gal·i·lee [ˈgæləˌli; ˈgæliliː] *n.* 加利利 (Palestine 北部一地區)。

Gal·i·le·o [ˌgæləˈlio; ˌgæliˈleiou] *n.* 伽利略(全名 Galileo Gililei, 1564–1642, 義大利物理及天文學家)。

gal·in·gale [ˈgælɪnˌgel; ˈgæliŋgeil] *n.* 〖植物〗英國產之一種香根莎草。

gal·i·ot [ˈgælɪət; ˈgæliət] *n.* 〖航海〗①(昔地中海上)帆槳並用的小快艇。②輕快的荷蘭貨船。(亦作 **galliot**)

gal·(l)i·pot [ˈgælɪˌpɑt; ˈgælipɔt] *n.* 「一種松脂。」

gall**[1] [gɔl; gɔːl] *n.* ①膽汁; 膽囊。②任何苦的東西;苦味。③怨恨。④〖美俗〗厚顏無恥; 大膽。to have the *gall* to do... 竟有臉皮做…。 ***dip one's pen in gall 心懷怨恨地寫。 ***gall and wormwood*** 深的怨恨;惡毒。

gall[2] *n.* ①磨擦的傷。②令人煩惱之物。③煩惱。—*v.t.* ①磨傷。②使煩惱; 屈辱。 —*v.i.* 磨傷。

gall[3] *n.* 樹癭(因蟲害而生於植物之葉、莖或根上之瘤);五倍子;沒食子。

gal·lant** [ˈgælənt; ˈgælənt, gəˈlænt] *adj.* ①英勇的;勇敢的。a *gallant* soldier. 英勇的兵。②莊嚴的; 壯麗的。 a *gallant* sight. 壯麗的景色。③(對女人)慇懃的。He was very *gallant* at the ball. 他在舞會中對女人頗獻慇懃。④關於愛情的。 —*n.* ①勇敢的人。②時髦的人。③ (對女人) 獻慇懃者。④情人; 愛人。 ***play the gallant 求

愛;調戲。—*v.t.* (對女人)獻慇懃; 向(女人)求婚;追求。—*v.i.* 獻慇懃。**—ly,** *adv.*

gal·lant·ry ['gæləntrɪ; 'gæləntri] *n., pl.* **-ries.** ①勇敢;豪俠。②(對女人) 極端慇懃。

gall bladder 膽囊;苦膽。

gal·le·ass, gal·li·ass ['gælɪˌæs; 'gæliæs] *n.* (十六、七世紀時行於地中海之)三桅軍艦。(亦作 **galeas, galeass**)

gal·le·on ['gælɪən; 'gæliən] *n.* (十五、六世紀西班牙人的) 大型帆船。

gal·ler·y** ['gælərɪ, -lrɪ; 'gæləri] *n., pl.* **-ler·ies.** ①走廊。②(戲院、教堂等中的)最高樓座。③(最高樓座的)觀衆;聽衆。④(一般的)觀衆;聽衆。⑤美術陳列館;畫廊。⑥(議會等的)旁聽者;(高爾夫球賽的)觀衆。⑦陳列的藝術品。⑧(作攝影室、打靶等用的)大房間。bring down the gallery*** 博得滿堂采。***play to the gallery*** 〖俗〗以迎合低級趣味的手段獲取一般人的稱讚。

gallery hit (play or **shot)** 球賽中爲討好觀衆而作的表演性動作。

***gal·ley** ['gælɪ; 'gæli] *n., pl.* **-leys.** ①(昔日用帆與長槳的)狹長之船。②大型划船。③軍艦上之廚房。④〖印刷〗長方活字盤。

galley proof 〖印刷〗字盤內排就之活字所印之校樣。

galley slave ①船役奴隸(囚徒)。②做苦工的人。

gal·ley-west ['gælɪ'wɛst; 'gæli'west] *adv.*〖俗〗徹底地;粉碎地。to knock his opponent *galley-west.* 將他的敵手徹底擊敗。

gall·fly ['gɔlˌflaɪ; 'gɔːlflai] *n., pl.* **-flies.** 五倍子蟲;沒食子蜂。

gal·liard ['gæljəd; 'gæljəd] *n.* (流行於十六、十七世紀時之)一種活潑輕快的雙人舞。

Gal·lic ['gælɪk; 'gælik] *adj.* ①高盧(Gaul)的;高盧人 (the Gauls) 的。②法蘭西的。

gal·lic ['gælɪk; 'gælik] *adj.* 沒食子性的; 五倍子的;蟲癭的。***gallic acid*** 〖化〗沒食子酸 ($C_6H_2(OH)_3CO_2H$).

Gal·li·can ['gælɪkən; 'gælikən] *adj.* ①=**Gallic.** ②法國天主教的。③〖宗教〗1870 年以前法國天主教會中主張限制教皇權力之一派的。④法國的。—*n.* 法國天主教徒;主張限制教皇權力者。

Gal·li·can·ism ['gælɪkəˌnɪzəm; 'gælikənizəm] *n.* 〖宗教〗加利亞主義(法國天主教會 1682 年宣布教皇權力應有限制之原則)。

Gal·li·ce ['gæləsi; 'gælisi(:)] *adv.* 用法語;以法國式。(亦作 **gallice**)

Gal·li·cism ['gæləˌsɪzəm; 'gælisizəm] *n.* ①法語特有的語法。②另一語言中的法語成語或字句。③法國的習俗、思考方式等。(亦作 **gallicism**)

Gal·li·cize ['gæləˌsaɪz; 'gælisaiz] *v.t.* & *v.i.,* **-cized, -ciz·ing.** (使)法國化(指思想、語言等方面而言)。(亦作 **gallicize**)

gal·li·mau·fry [ˌgælə'mɔfrɪ; ˌgæli'mɔːfri] *n., pl.* **-fries.** 雜亂混合物; 雜燴;雜湊食品。

gal·li·na·cean [ˌgælə'neʃən; ˌgæli'neiʃən] *n.* 鶉鷄類之鳥(鷄、雉、鶉等)。

gal·li·na·ceous [ˌgælə'neʃəs; ˌgæli'neiʃəs] *adj.* ①(關於)家禽的。②鶉鷄類的。

gall·ing ['gɔlɪŋ; 'gɔːliŋ] *adj.* 令人苦惱的;可恨的;難堪的;令人生氣的。

gal·li·nip·per ['gæləˌnɪpɚ; 'gæliˌnipə] *n.* 〖俗〗大蚊子;任何咬人之昆蟲。

gal·li·nule ['gæləˌnjul; 'gælinjuːl] *n.* 鷂類的水鳥;鷂。

Gal·li·o ['gælɪo; 'gæliou] *n.* ①迦流(亞該亞之方伯, 拒絕干涉宗教問題:見新約使徒行傳18章)。②不管職務以外之事的人。

gal·li·ot ['gælɪət; 'gæliət] *n.* =**galiot.**

gal·li·pot¹ ['gæləˌpɑt; 'gælipɔt] *n.* ①陶製的藥罐。②〖俗〗草藥商人;藥劑師。

gal·li·pot² *n.* =**galipot.**

gal·li·um ['gælɪəm; 'gæliəm] *n.* 〖化〗鎵(化學元素之一, 符號 Ga).

gal·li·vant ['gæləˌvænt; ˌgæli'vænt] *v.i.* 閒逛;與異性遊蕩。(亦作 **galavant**)

gall-less ['gɔllɪs; 'gɔːllis] *adj.* ①無膽汁的;無膽囊的。②心中不懷怨恨的;不易生氣的。

gall·nut ['gɔlˌnʌt; 'gɔːlnʌt] *n.* 五倍子;沒食子。

Gallo- 〖字首〗表 "Gaul 的; 法國的; 法…的"之義。*Gallo*-Briton. 法英的。a *Gallo*-American. 法系(親法)美人。

Gal·lo·ma·ni·a [ˌgælə'menɪə; ˌgælə'meiniə] *n.* 醉心於法國;法蘭西狂。

***gal·lon** ['gælən; 'gælən] *n.* (液體量名)加侖(=4 quarts;美加侖等於 3.7853 公升; 英加侖等於 4.546 公升)。

gal·lon·age ['gælənɪdʒ; 'gælənidʒ] *n.* 加侖量。

gal·loon [gə'lun; gə'luːn] *n.* (常含有金、銀、絲的棉、毛、緞等的)細帶;縧帶;金銀帶;金銀絲花邊。

***gal·lop** ['gæləp; 'gæləp] *n.* (馬等) 疾馳; 飛奔。 He rode away at full *gallop* (*or* at a *gallop*). 他騎馬疾馳而去。—*v.i.* ①騎快馬。He *galloped* off at full speed. 他騎馬飛馳而去。②倉促而做;匆匆地做。to *gallop* through one's work. 匆匆將工作做完。③飛馳(如人或時間)。 —*v.t.* 使(馬)飛馳。 to *gallop* a horse. 使馬飛馳。

gal·lo·pade [ˌgælə'ped; ˌgælə'peid] *n.* 一種活潑的匈牙利舞;其舞曲。(亦作 **galopade**)

Gal·lo·phile ['gæləˌfaɪl; 'gæləfail] *n.* 愛好法國的人;親法者。(亦作 **Gallophil**)

Gal·loph·il·ism [gə'lɑfəlɪzəm; gə'lɔfəlizəm] *n.* 親法;愛法。

Gal·lo·phobe ['gæləˌfob; 'gæləfoub] *n.* 憎惡法國的人;恐法病者。

Gal·lo·pho·bi·a [ˌgælə'fobɪə; ˌgælə'foubiə] *n.* 憎惡法國;恐法病。

gal·lop·ing ['gæləpɪŋ; 'gæləpiŋ] *adj.* ①飛馳的。②(如疾病之) 快速發展的。*galloping* consumption. 奔馬癆;百日癆。

Gal·lo·way ['gæləˌwe; 'gæləwei] *n.* ①加羅韋(蘇格蘭西南端之一地區, 牛馬之名產地)。②(常 g-) 加羅韋原產的一種馬。③(常 g-) 加羅韋種的食用牛。

gal·lows ['gæloz, -əz; 'gælouz] *n., pl.* **-lows·es** or **-lows,** *adj.* —*n.* ①絞架。to send a man to the *gallows.* 處人以絞刑。②絞刑。a crime deserving of the *gallows.* 應處絞刑的罪行。***cheat the gallows*** 逃過絞刑;逃過死刑。***come to the gallows*** 上絞架;被絞死。 ***gallows bird*** 〖俗〗該處絞刑的人。***gallows tree*** 絞架;絞首臺。***have the gallows in one's face*** 看上去像被宣判絞刑似的。—*adj.* 〖俚〗①罪該被絞死的;罪大惡極的。②野性難馴的。③好極了;棒極了。

gall·stone ['gɔlˌston; 'gɔːlstoun] *n.* 〖醫〗膽石。

Gal·lup ['gæləp; 'gæləp] *n.* 蓋洛普 (George Horace, 1901–, 美統計學家, 蓋洛普民意測驗之創始人)。—*v.i.* & *v.t.* (g-)作民意測驗;作民意調查。

Gal·lup poll ['gæləp'pol; 'gæləp-

ˈpoul]〖美〗蓋洛普民意測驗。

gal·lus [ˈgæləs; ˈgæləs] *n., adj., adv.*〖英方〗=**gallows.**

ga·loot, gal·loot [gəˈlut; gəˈluːt] *n.*〖俚〗愚蠢的人;蠢貨;獃子。

gal·op [ˈgæləp; ˈgæləp] *n.* 流行於19世紀的一種²/₄拍之活潑舞蹈;其舞曲。—*v.i.* 跳galop 舞。(亦作 **gallopade, galopade**)

ga·lore [gəˈlor; gəˈlɔː] *adv.* 豐富地;很多地。

ga·losh(e) [gəˈlɑʃ; gəˈlɔʃ] *n.*(常 *pl.*)膠質套鞋。(亦作 **galoche, golosh**)

gals. gallons.

ga·lumph [gəˈlʌmf; gəˈlʌmf] *v.i.* ①昂首闊步;意氣揚揚地走(Lewis Carroll 創造的字, =gallop+triumph)。② =**gallop.**

gal·van·ic [gælˈvænɪk; gælˈvænik] *adj.* ①以化學作用產生電流的。②(比喻)如被電擊的;震驚的。 ***galvanic battery*** 電池。***galvanic cell*** 電池。

gal·va·nism [ˈgælvəˌnɪzəm; ˈgælvənizəm] *n.* ①由化學作用產生的電。②〖醫〗電療。

gal·va·nize [ˈgælvəˌnaɪz; ˈgælvənaiz] *v.t.*, **-nized, -niz·ing.** ①將電流應用於。②鍍鋅於(鋼鐵)以防生銹。③(比喻)使驚起;使驚跳;激勵。④〖醫〗用電療以刺激(肌肉或神經)。—**gal·va·ni·za·tion,** *n.*

galvanized iron 塗鋅鐵;白鐵。

galvano- 〖字首〗表"以化學作用產生電流的"之義。

gal·va·nog·ra·phy [ˌgælvəˈnɑgrəfɪ; ˌgælvəˈnɔgrəfi] *n.* 電氣製版術。

gal·va·nom·e·ter [ˌgælvəˈnɑmətɚ; ˌgælvəˈnɔmitə] *n.* 電流計。

gal·va·nom·e·try [ˌgælvəˈnɑmətrɪ; ˌgælvəˈnɔmitri] *n.* 電流測定(法)。

gal·va·no·plas·tics [ˌgælvənoˈplæstɪks; ˌgælvənouˈplæstiks] *n.*(作 *sing.* 解) =**galvanoplasty.**

gal·va·no·plas·ty [ˈgælvənəˌplæstɪ; ˈgælvənəˌplæsti] *n.* 電版術;電鍍法。—**gal·va·no·plas·tic,** *adj.* —**gal·van·o·plas·ti·cal·ly,** *adv.*

gal·va·no·scope [gælˈvænəˌskop; gælˈvænəskoup] *n.* 電流檢查器。

gam¹ [gæm; gæm] *n., v.,* **gammed, gam·ming.** —*n.* ①鯨魚羣。②(海上捕鯨船間)社交性訪問;交歡。③(一般的)社交訪問;交際。—*v.i.* ①(尤指在海上)作社交訪問。②(鯨魚)結集成羣;聚攏。—*v.t.*(尤指在海上)社交性訪問;與…交際。

gam² *n.*〖俚〗腿(尤指女人漂亮的腿)。

gam·bade [gæmˈbed; gæmˈbeid] *n.* ①(馬的)跳躍。②惡作劇。③(常 *pl.*)繫於鞍旁用以代鐙之長靴。(亦作 **gambado**)

Gam·bi·a [ˈgæmbɪə; ˈgæmbiə] *n.* ①甘比亞河(在非洲西部)。②(The ~)甘比亞(非洲西部沿岸一國,首都班竹 Banjul)。—**Gam·bi·an,** *adj., n.*

gam·bier [ˈgæmˌbɪr; ˈgæmbiə] *n.* 檳榔膏(用爲止血、收斂劑、製皮、染料等)。(亦作 **gambir**)

gam·bit [ˈgæmbɪt; ˈgæmbit] *n.* ①下棋開局時犧牲一個棋子以取優勢的一着棋。②任何爲取得優勢的策略或活動。

***gam·ble** [ˈgæmbl̩; ˈgæmbl] *v.,* **-bled, -bling,** *n.* —*v.i.* ①賭博。to *gamble* at cards. 賭紙牌。②打賭。to *gamble* on the result of a race. 對比賽之結果打賭。③孤注一擲;冒大險。He lost his fortune *gambling* on the stock exchange. 他因買賣股票喪失了他的財產。—*v.t.* ①賭輸〖常 away〗. He has *gambled* away half his wealth. 他賭博輸去了半數財產。②打賭。—*n.* 冒險;冒險的事業。

gam·bler [ˈgæmblɚ; ˈgæmblə] *n.* 聚賭者;賭徒(尤指以賭爲生者)。***take a gambler's chance*** 一賭輸贏;試試運氣。

gam·bling [ˈgæmblɪŋ; ˈgæmbliŋ] *n.* 賭博。***gambling hell*** (or ***house***) 賭窟;賭場。***gambling table*** 賭桌。

gam·boge [gæmˈbodʒ; gæmˈbuːʒ] *n.* ①籐黃;雌黃(一種褐色的樹脂,用於醫藥、顏料)。②雌黃(黃色顏料)。

gam·bol [ˈgæmbl̩; ˈgæmbəl] *v.,* **-bol(l)ed, bol·(l)ing,** *n.* —*v.i.* 歡跳;雀躍。—*n.*歡躍;歡跳。

gam·brel [ˈgæmbrəl; ˈgæmbrəl] *n.* ①(獸類,特指馬之)後腳踝關節。②(屠夫用以掛肉的)馬脚狀鐵鉤。

‡game¹ [gem; geim] *n., adj.,* **gam·er, gam·est,** *v.,* **gamed, gam·ing.** —*n.* ①遊戲;比賽。to play a *game* of tennis. 打一場網球。②遊戲器具;體育用品。This shop sells *games*. 這家店舖經售體育用品。③(*pl.*)競技會;運動會。the Olympic *Games*. 奧林匹克運動會。④一場(球賽等);一局。to win four *games* in the first set. 初賽勝四場。⑤(比賽中之)積分;得分。At the end of the first period the *game* was 6 to 3 in our favor. 上半場比賽完畢,結果爲 6 比 3,我方領先。⑥比賽之方法或技巧。His *game* of chess is improving. 他的棋藝日有進步。⑦謀畫;策略。He tried to trick us, but we saw through his *game*. 他圖欺騙我們,但我們窺破了他的詭計。⑧獵物(集合稱)。⑨野獸或野禽之肉。⑩受人欺侮、迫害等之對象。⑪〖俗〗行業。***be on*** (***off***) ***one's game*** 玩得好(不好)。***big game*** 大獵物(如獅、虎、象等)。***fly at higher game*** 有野心;有大志。***have the game in one's hands*** 有把握獲勝。***make game of*** 取笑;戲弄。***play a winning game*** 可望成功。***play the game***(遊戲中)照規矩做;(轉爲)正直誠實。—*adj.* ①與狩獵法等有關的。②勇敢的;有膽量的。Are you *game* to swim across the river? 你有膽量游過這河嗎? ***die game*** **a.** 勇敢地爭鬥而後死。**b.** 奮鬥到底。—*v.t.* 賭輸〖常 away〗. —*v.i.* 賭博。

game² *adj.*〖俗〗受傷的;跛的;無用的。「a *game* leg. 一隻跛腿。」

game·cock [ˈgemˌkɑk; ˈgeimkɔk] *n.* ①鬥雞。②勇敢有生氣之人。

game fowl ①獵鳥;獵禽。②鬥雞。

game·keep·er [ˈgemˌkipɚ; ˈgeimˌkiːpə] *n.* 獵場看守人。

game law(s) 漁獵法。

game·less [ˈgemlɪs; ˈgeimlis] *adj.*「無獵物的。」

game license 狩獵許可證。

game·ly [ˈgemlɪ; ˈgeimli] *adv.*(如鬥雞般)不屈不撓地;勇敢地。

game·ness [ˈgemnɪs; ˈgeimnis] *n.* 勇敢;不屈不撓;不認輸。

game of chance 靠運氣而不靠技巧的遊戲,如輪盤戲。「遊戲,如西洋棋。」

game of skill 靠技巧而不靠運氣的「遊戲,如西洋棋。」

game plan〖美〗策略。

game room 娛樂室(尤指供桌上遊戲者);遊戲室。

games·man·ship [ˈgemzmənˌʃɪp;

ˈgeimzmənʃip] *n.* 競賽時使用雖不光明但並非犯規之方法。
game·some [ˈgemsəm; ˈgeimsəm] *adj.* 好戲謔的;好玩的;好作樂的。
game·ster [ˈgemstɚ; ˈgeimstə] *n.* ①賭徒; 賭棍。②體育比賽中之不屈不撓者。
gam·ete [ˈgæmit; ˈgæmiːt] *n.* 〖生物〗接合體; 配偶子。
game tenant 爲取得在他人產業上之「漁獵權而付租金者。」
ga·me·to·phyte [gəˈmito,faɪt; gəˈmiːtoufait] *n.* 〖植物〗配偶體。
gam·in [ˈgæmɪn; ˈgæmin] *n.* ①街頭流浪兒。②活潑有生氣者。—*adj.* ①街頭流浪兒的。②活潑的;有生氣的。
gam·ine [gæˈmin; ˈgæmiːn] *n., pl.* **gam·ines.** 〖法〗①樂觀而好動的女孩子。②調皮的女孩。③無人管教之女孩。
gam·ing [ˈgemɪŋ; ˈgeimiŋ] *n.* 賭博。a *gaming* table. 賭桌。
gam·ma [ˈgæmə; ˈgæmə] *n.* ①希臘字母之第三字母(Γ, γ)(相當於英文字母G, g). ②(一系列中)列爲第三者的符號。③= **microgram.** ④〖物理〗咖馬(地磁場强度單位)。⑤〖英〗學校班級(分爲三級)中最差之一級。
gam·ma·di·on [gəˈmedɪən; gəˈmeidiən] *n., pl.* **-di·a** [-dɪə; -diə]. 由四個大寫的希臘字母 Gamma (Γ) 自同一中心向四方放射而構成之圖形(尤指成卐形者)。
gamma rays 〖物理〗γ 射線。
gam·mer [ˈgæmɚ; ˈgæmə] *n.* 老嫗;老媼;(尤指)鄉下老太婆。
gam·mon[1] [ˈgæmən; ˈgæmən] *n.* 〖俗〗胡說; 誆騙; 欺詐。That is all *gammon.* 那全是胡說。—*v.i.* 〖俗〗①胡說。②裝胡塗。—*v.t.* 〖俗〗誆騙。—*interj.* 〖俗〗胡說!
gam·mon[2] *n.* ①醃豬脇肉的下部。②燻腿;臘腿。—*v.t.* 醃(臘肉)。
gam·mon[3] *n.* 西洋雙陸遊戲之全勝(卽在敵手未棄一子前所獲之勝利)。
gamo- 〖字首〗表"兩性聯合;合併;結合"「等義。」
gam·o·gen·e·sis [,gæməˈdʒɛnɪsɪs; ,gæməˈdʒenisis] *n.* 〖生物〗兩性生殖。
gam·o·ma·ni·a [,gæməˈmenɪə; ,gæməˈmeiniə] *n.* 〖醫〗求偶癖。
gam·o·pet·al·ous [,gæməˈpɛtələs; ,gæməˈpetələs] *adj.* 〖植物〗花瓣相連的。
gam·o·sep·a·lous [,gæməˈsɛpələs; ,gæməˈsepələs] *adj.* 〖植物〗花萼相連的。
gamp [gæmp; gæmp] *n.* 〖英俗〗大傘。
gam·ut [ˈgæmət; ˈgæmət] *n.* ①〖音樂〗**a.** 全音階。**b.** 音域。**c.** 譜表。②整個範圍。
gam·y [ˈgemɪ; ˈgeimi] *adj.,* **gam·i·er, gam·i·est.** ①(森林等) 多獵物的。②有活力的;勇敢的。③有野獸、野禽之氣味的。④有濃烈之味道的。⑤〖俚〗稍稍不正當的。
gan·der [ˈgændɚ; ˈgændə] *n.* ①雄鵝。②蠢物; 笨人。③〖俚〗長久的注視。*take a gander* 〖俚〗看一下。—*v.i.* 〖俚〗看一看。
Gan·dhi [ˈgandɪ; ˈgændiː] *n.* ①甘地 (Mohandas K., 1869–1948, 印度政治、社會和宗教領袖)。②甘地夫人(Indira, 1917–, 印度總理 1966–1977, 係尼赫魯之女)。
Gan·dhi·ism [ˈgændɪ,ɪzəm; ˈgændiizəm] *n.* 甘地主義; 消極抵抗主義。(亦作 **Gandhism**)
***gang**[1] [gæŋ; gæŋ] *n.* ①羣; 隊。a *gang* of slaves. 一隊奴隸。②幫(尤指專作惡事者)。a *gang* of thieves. 一幫盜賊。③一組; 一套(工具、機械等)。—*v.t.* 〖俗〗①組成幫。②成羣地攻擊。—*v.i.* 聯合在一起。The boys *ganged* together. 那些男孩組成一個幫。*gang up on* 聯合對付(某人或某國)。
gang[2] *v.i.* 〖蘇〗去; 行走。to *gang* one's ain (=own) gait. 按照自己的意思行事。
gang·board [ˈgæŋ,bord; ˈgæŋbɔːd] *n.* =**gangplank.**
gang·bust·er [ˈgæŋ,bʌstɚ; ˈgæŋbʌstə] *n.* 〖俗〗掃蕩流氓組織之執法人員。
gang·er [ˈgæŋɚ; ˈgæŋə] *n.* ①工頭。②跑得快的馬。③〖方〗步行者。
Gan·ges [ˈgændʒiz; ˈgændʒiːz] *n.* 恆河(在印度北境)。—**Gan·get·ic,** *adj.*
gang·land [ˈgæŋ,lænd; ˈgæŋlænd] *n.* 〖俗〗盜匪充斥的街區;黑社會。
gan·gle [ˈgæŋgḷ; ˈgæŋgl] *v.i.,* **-gled, -gling.** 行動蹣跚。
gang·lead·er [ˈgæŋ,lidɚ; ˈgæŋ,liːdə] 「*n.* 黑社會頭子。」
gang·like [ˈgæŋ,laɪk; ˈgæŋlaik] *adj.* 如流氓的。*ganglike* behavior. 流氓行爲。
gan·gling [ˈgæŋglɪŋ; ˈgæŋgliŋ] *adj.* 〖俗〗(身體) 瘦長的。
gan·gli·on [ˈgæŋglɪən; ˈgæŋgliən] *n., pl.* **-gli·a** [-glɪə; -gliə], **-gli·ons.** ①神經中樞;神經節。②力量、活動、興趣等之中心。
gang·ly [ˈgæŋglɪ; ˈgæŋgli] *adj.* =**gangling.**
gang·plank [ˈgæŋ,plæŋk; ˈgæŋplæŋk] *n.* (輪船之) 跳板。(亦作 **brow, gangway**)
gang plow (or **plough**) ①有數個犁頭之犁。②結合犁(數犁結合在一起者)。
gan·grene [ˈgæŋgrin, gæŋˈgrin; ˈgæŋgriːn] *n., v.,* **-grened, -gren·ing.** —*n.* 壞疽。—*v.t.* 使生疽;使腐化。—*v.i.* 生疽。—**gan·gre·nous,** *adj.*
***gang·ster** [ˈgæŋstɚ; ˈgæŋstə] *n.* 〖美俗〗歹徒;匪盜。a *gangster* film. 匪盜影片。
gang·ster·dom [ˈgæŋstɚdəm; ˈgæŋstədəm] *n.* ①黑社會。②匪盜或其行爲。
gang·ster·ism [ˈgæŋstɚ,rɪzəm; ˈgæŋstərizəm] *n.* 歹徒及其犯罪行爲;犯罪。
gangue [gæŋ; gæŋ] *n.* 〖礦〗礦皮; 脈石。(亦作 **gang**)
gang-up [ˈgæŋ,ʌp; ˈgæŋʌp] *n.* 〖美俗〗聯合在一起(對付某人或某國);攻擊。
gang war 流氓集團間因爭地盤而起的「打鬥。」
gang·way [ˈgæŋ,we; ˈgæŋwei] *n.* ①〖英〗(戲院、音樂廳中兩排座位間的)通道(美國作 aisle). ②(置於船與岸間的)跳板。③船上的通道。—*interj.* 讓路!躲開!
gan·net [ˈgænɪt; ˈgænit] *n.* 塘鵝。
gan·oid [ˈgænɔɪd; ˈgænɔid] *n.* 硬鱗魚。—*adj.* ①(魚鱗)光滑的;珐瑯質的;有硬鱗的。②硬鱗魚類的。
gant·let[1] [ˈgæntlɪt; ˈgæntlit] *n.* ①夾鞭刑(古刑罰, 排人成二列, 犯人行走其間, 由列隊者鞭打)。②交叉的兩條鐵路重疊之一段。*run the gantlet* **a.** 受夾鞭刑。**b.** 受雙方夾擊。—*v.t.* 鋪(鐵軌)使交叉的兩條鐵路重疊爲一。(亦作 **gauntlet**)
gant·let[2] *n.* =**gauntlet**[1].
gan·try [ˈgæntrɪ; ˈgæntri] *n., pl.* **-tries.** ①桶架。②(高架移動起重機之)構臺; 高架移動起重機。③(鐵路上支持信號裝置的) 跨線橋。(亦作 **gauntry**)
Gan·y·mede [ˈgænə,mid; ˈgænimiːd] *n.* ①〖希臘神話〗Zeus 帶去爲衆神司酒的美少年。②木星最大的衞星。
***gaol** [dʒel; dʒeil] *n.* 〖英〗=**jail.**—**gaol-er,** *n.*
gaol·bird [ˈdʒel,bɝd; ˈdʒeilbəːd] *n.*

G

〖英俗〗囚犯。

gaol-break 〔ˈdʒelˌbrek; ˈdʒeilbreik〕 *n.* 〖英俗〗越獄。

gap** 〔gæp; gæp〕 *n., v.*, **gapped, gap·ping.** —*n.* ①縫隙;缺口;漏洞。We must see that there is no *gap* in our defenses. 注意不要讓我們的防線有漏洞。②間斷;空白。③意見、個性等之差異。a wide *gap* between the views of two statesmen. 兩位政治家政見之歧異。④山間窄徑;山凹。fill*** (***stop,*** or ***supply***) ***a gap*** 補充所缺之物;補缺。***open a gap*** 開一缺口;予以機會。—*v.t.* 造成縫隙;打開缺口。

gape** 〔gep; geip〕 *v.*, **gaped, gap·ing,** *n.* —*v.i.* ①裂開。A deep hole in the earth *gaped* before us. 在我們面前的地上裂開着一深坑。②張嘴;張嘴注視。He *gaped* and yawned. 他張口打呵欠。—*n.* ①裂口;裂隙。②張嘴;打呵欠。③張嘴凝望。④〖動物〗嘴張開時之寬度。 ***the gapes **a.** 一陣呵欠。**b.** (家禽或鳥類之)張嘴病。

gape·worm 〔ˈgepˌwɝm; ˈgeipˌwəːm〕 *n.* 呵欠蟲(寄生於稚禽氣管中,爲張嘴病病因)。

gar 〔gar; gaː〕 *n.* =**garfish.**

G.A.R. Grand Army of the Republic.

***ga·rage** 〔gəˈraʒ, gəˈradʒ, ˈgæradʒ; ˈgæraːʒ, -ridʒ, ˈgæraːdʒ〕 *n., v.*, **-raged, -rag·ing.** —*n.* 汽車間;修車廠。—*v.t.* 置於汽車間中;送入修車廠。He *garages* his car near the railroad station. 他將汽車放在靠近火車站的一個停車房裏。

ga·rage·man 〔gəˈraʒmæn; ˈgæraːʒmən〕 *n., pl.* **-men.** 〖英〗汽車技工。

G

garage sale 家庭舊貨出售(常在賣主家停車房裏進行)。(亦作**tag sale, yard sale**)

Garand rifle 伽蘭德半自動步鎗(口徑爲 0.30 英寸,亦稱 M-1, 美陸軍第二次世界大戰及韓戰中之標準步槍)。

garb 〔garb; gaːb〕 *n.* ①裝束;打扮。 a man in clerical *garb*. 一個裝束像牧師的人。②衣服。③外表;外觀。 —*v.t.* 穿衣;打扮(通常用於反身代名詞前或在被動式中)。to *garb* oneself in.... 穿…的服裝。to *garb* oneself as a sailor. 打扮成一個水手。

gar·bage 〔ˈgarbɪdʒ; ˈgaːbidʒ〕 *n.* ①廚房的剩飯殘羹。②無價值的東西。③〖俚〗多餘而無必要的東西。④浮游於太空的已失去作用之人造衛星或火箭。***garbage can*** 垃圾箱。***garbage truck*** 垃圾車。

gar·ble 〔ˈgarbl̩; ˈgaːbl〕 *v.*, **-bled, -bling,** *n.* —*v.t.* ①竄改;曲解。a *garbled* text. 竄改過的版本。②無意中使(文字、電稿等)混亂或不清楚。—*n.* ①竄改;曲解。②被竄改的句子。

gar·çon 〔ˌgarˈsɔ̃; ˌgarˈsɔ̃〕 〖法〗 *n.* ①餐廳侍者。②少年。③男僕。④未婚男子。

:gar·den 〔ˈgardn̩; ˈgaːdn〕 *n.* ①花園;菜圃;果園。What a beautiful *garden!* 多麼美麗的花園啊! ②(常 *pl.*) 公園。 botanical *garden(s)*. 植物園。—*v.i.* 栽培花木;從事園藝。Some people *garden* for pleasure. 有些人種植花木以爲娛樂。—*v.t.* 造園。—*adj.* ①種於花園中的。*garden* plants. 栽培園中的植物。②普通的。***lead one up the garden path*** 〖俗〗帶入歧途;欺騙;哄。

***gar·den·er** 〔ˈgardnə, ˈgardn̩ə; ˈgaː-dnə〕 *n.* 園丁;花匠;園藝家。

gar·den·esque 〔ˌgardəˈnɛsk; ˌgaː-dəˈnesk〕 *adj.* 花園一般的。

gar·de·ni·a 〔garˈdinɪə; gaːˈdiːniə〕 *n.* 〖植物〗梔子屬;梔子花。

***gar·den·ing** 〔ˈgardn̩ɪŋ; ˈgaːdniŋ〕 *n.* 園藝。He is very fond of *gardening.* 他非常愛好園藝。

gar·den·ize 〔ˈgardn̩ˌaɪz; ˈgaːdənaiz〕 *v.*, **-ized, -iz·ing.** —*v.t.* 使花園化。to *gardenize* a public square. 將一個廣場花園化。—*v.i.* 當園丁;照料花園。

Garden of Eden ①(聖經中)亞當與夏娃所住之伊甸樂園。②無罪;無辜。

garden party 園遊會。

gar·den-va·ri·e·ty 〔ˈgardn̩vəˌraɪətɪ; ˈgaːdnvəˌraiəti〕 *adj.* 普通的。

gare·fowl 〔ˈgɛrˌfaul; ˈgɛəfaul〕 *n., pl.* **-fowls,** (集合稱) **-fowl.** 大海燕。

gar·fish 〔ˈgarˌfɪʃ; ˈgaːfiʃ〕 *n., pl.* **-fish, -fish·es.** 長嘴硬鱗魚。

Gar·gan·tu·an 〔garˈgæntʃuən; gaː-ˈgæntjuən〕 *adj.* 龐大的;巨大的。(亦作 **gargantuan**)

gar·get 〔ˈgargɪt; ˈgaːgit〕 *n.* 〖獸醫〗①(牛、豬等之)咽喉腫瘍。②(牛羊之)乳房炎。

gar·gle 〔ˈgargl̩; ˈgaːgl〕 *v.*, **-gled, -gling,** *n.* —*v.t. & v.i.* 以含漱劑漱(喉)。—*n.* 含漱劑(用以漱口之藥水)。—**gar·gler,** *n.*

gar·goyle 〔ˈgargɔɪl; ˈgaːgɔil〕 *n.* 〖建築〗承霤口;筧嘴。

Gar·i·bal·di 〔ˌgærəˈbɔldɪ; ˌgæriˈbɔːl-di〕 *n.* 加里波的(Giuseppe, 1807–1882, 義大利愛國者及將軍)。—**an,** *adj., n.*

gar·ish 〔ˈgɛrɪʃ, ˈgærɪʃ; ˈgɛəriʃ〕 *adj.* 炫耀的;虛飾的;俗美的。—**ly,** *adv.*

gar·land 〔ˈgarlənd; ˈgaːlənd〕 *n.* ①花圈。②類似花圈之裝飾品。③詩歌選粹。—*v.t.* ①飾以花圈。②做成花圈。—**less,** *adj.*

gar·lic 〔ˈgarlɪk; ˈgaːlik〕 *n.* 蒜;蒜頭。—*adj.* ①有蒜味的。②以蒜調味的。 *garlic* salt. 大蒜鹽。

gar·lick·y 〔ˈgarlɪkɪ; ˈgaːliki〕 *adj.* ①有蒜臭味的。②食大蒜的;如大蒜的。

***gar·ment** 〔ˈgarmənt; ˈgaːmənt〕 *n.* ①衣服;任何外衣。②外表。—*v.t.* 使穿衣服。a lovely lady *garmented* in silk. 穿着綢衣的可愛女人。

gar·ner 〔ˈgarnə; ˈgaːnə〕 *v.t.* ①收藏;儲藏。②獲取;取得。—*n.* ①穀倉;倉庫。②所收藏的東西。

gar·net 〔ˈgarnɪt; ˈgaːnit〕 *n.* ①〖礦〗石榴子石。②深紅色。—*adj.* 暗紅色的;深紅色的。

gar·nish 〔ˈgarnɪʃ; ˈgaːniʃ〕 *n.* ①食物上的裝飾。②裝飾品。③〖俚〗工頭或老囚犯向新進之工人或囚犯所勒索的金錢。—*v.t.* ①加裝飾。②在食物上加添調味料。 to *garnish* fish with slices of lemon. 用檸檬片添加在一盤魚上。

gar·nish·ee 〔ˌgarnɪˈʃi; ˌgaːniˈʃiː〕 *n., v.*, **-nish·eed, -nish·ee·ing.** —*n.* 〖法律〗第三債務人(代被告保管其財產並接到法庭扣押令於訟案未決期間不得處分所代保管之財產者)。—*v.t.* 〖法律〗①(以扣押令)扣押(債務人的財產)。②命令(第三債務人)在訴訟期間不得處分所保管之被告之財產。

gar·nish·ment 〔ˈgarnɪʃmənt; ˈgaː-niʃmənt〕 *n.* ①裝飾。②〖法律〗(關於某案件對當事人以外之第三者的)傳票。③(發給第三債務人的)扣押令。

gar·nish·ry 〔ˈgarnɪʃrɪ; ˈgaːniʃri〕 *n., pl.* **-ries.** 裝飾品;裝飾。

gar·ni·ture 〔ˈgarnɪtʃə; ˈgaːnitʃə〕 *n.* ①裝飾(物)。②傢具裝備。③衣裳;服飾。

ga·rotte 〔gəˈrat; gəˈrɔt〕 *n., v.t.*

=**garrote.**

gar·ret [ˈgærɪt; ˈgærət, -rit] *n.* 頂閣; 閣樓。a poor poet living in a *garret.* 一位住在閣樓上的窮詩人。

gar·ret·eer [ˌgærəˈtɪr; ˌgærəˈtiə] *n.* 住閣樓的人;(特指)窮作家或藝術家。

gar·ri·son [ˈgærəsn̩; ˈgærisn] *n.* ①衞戍部隊; 要塞防守隊。②要塞; 衞戍地。—*v.t.* 屯兵;鎮守。to *garrison* troops in the city. 令軍隊鎮守此城。

gar·rot(t)e [gəˈrot; gəˈrɔt] *n., v.,* **-rot·(t)ed, -rot·(t)ing.** —*n.* ①西班牙的一種絞刑。②此種絞刑所用的鐵環。③突擊時用以絞殺敵人哨兵之繩子或皮帶。④(如行刼時所施之)扼人咽喉使之失去抵抗力; 勒殺。—*v.t.* ①處以上述之絞刑; 絞死。②勒人咽喉使失去抵抗力(以便行刼)。③勒殺搶刼。—**gar·rot·(t)er,** *n.*

gar·ru·li·ty [gəˈrulətɪ; gæˈruːliti] *n.* 愛說閒話;多嘴。

gar·ru·lous [ˈgærələs; ˈgæruləs] *adj.* 愛說閒話的;多嘴的。

gar·ter [ˈgɑrtɚ; ˈgɑːtə] *n.* ①襪帶。②扣襯衫袖子的帶子。③【英】**a.** Order of the Garter 之徽章。**b.** Order of the Garter 之勳位。**c.** (G-)=**Order of the Garter.** **d.**(常G-)有此勳位的人。***garter belt*** 婦女用的一種寬腰帶。***Order of the Garter*** 嘉德勳位(英國歷史最久的最高勳位)。

garth [gɑrθ; gɑːθ] *n.* 捕魚用的壩或堰。

Gar·y [ˈgɛrɪ; ˈgɛəri] *n.* 蓋瑞(美國 Indiana 西北部之一城市,世界青少棒賽場地)。

gas [gæs; gæs] *n., pl.* **gas·es,** *v.,* **gassed, gas·sing.** —*n.* ①氣體; 瓦斯。Air is a mixture of *gases.* 空氣是許多氣體的混合物。②煤氣; 毒氣。to turn on (off) the *gas.* 扭開(關掉)煤氣。③笑氣(牙醫用做麻醉劑, 即 N_2O)。④【美俗】汽油。⑤【俗】空談; 瞎吹牛。⑥【俚】**a.** 有趣的人或事。The party was an absolute *gas,* and we loved it. 那次派對眞是好玩, 我們喜歡它。**b.** 給某人很大影響的人或事。***step on the gas*** 【俚】**a.** 踩汽車的加速器。**b.** 加緊;匆忙。—*v.t.* ①供以煤氣。②以煤氣處理。③【俗】加汽油。④以毒氣攻擊;以毒氣殺害。⑤用瓦斯將(紗、線、或紡織物之)多餘纖維燒掉。⑥【俚】胡說。⑦【俚】使開心。—*v.i.* ①【俚】空談; 閒扯。②發散氣體。***gas up*** 加油。

gas·bag [ˈgæsˌbæg; ˈgæsbæg] *n.* ①(飛艇、飛船等之) 蓄氣囊。②【美俚】廢話連篇者;愛瞎吹者。

gas bomb 毒氣(炸)彈。

gas burner ①煤氣爐。②煤氣噴嘴。

gas chamber 用毒氣處決死囚的房間。

Gas·con [ˈgæskən; ˈgæskən] *n.* ①(法國) Gascony 人(以好吹噓聞名)。②(g-)好吹噓者。—*adj.* ①Gascony (人)的。②好吹噓的。—**ism,** *n.*

gas·con·ade [ˌgæskənˈed; ˌgæskəˈneid] *n., v.,* **-con·ad·ed, -con·ad·ing.** —*n.* 誇口;吹噓;吹牛。—*v.i.* 誇口;吹噓;吹牛。

gas·e·i·ty [gæsˈiətɪ; gæsˈiːiti] *n.* 氣體;氣態。

gas·e·lier [ˌgæsəˈlɪr; ˌgæsəˈliə] *n.* (吊在天花板之)瓦斯花燈。

***gas·e·ous** [ˈgæsɪəs; ˈgeizjəs, ˈgæz-, ˈgeis-, ˈgæs-, -zjəs] *adj.* ①氣體的; 似氣體的;氣體狀態的。a *gaseous* mixture. 氣體混合物。②【俗】不可靠的;不具體的。

gas fitter 煤氣匠。

gash [gæʃ; gæʃ] *n.* 縱深的創傷或切痕。—*v.t.* 深傷;深切。

gas helmet 防毒盔;防毒帽。

gas·hold·er [ˈgæsˌholdɚ; ˈgæsˌhouldə] *n.* 裝瓦斯之容器(通常爲圓桶形的)。

gas·house [ˈgæsˌhaus; ˈgæshaus] *n.* 煤氣廠(=gasworks)。

gas·i·form [ˈgæsəˌfɔrm; ˈgæsifɔːm] *adj.* 氣狀的。

gas·i·fy [ˈgæsəˌfaɪ; ˈgæsifai] *v.t.* & *v.i.,* **-fied, -fy·ing.** (使) 氣化。—**gas·i·fi·ca·tion,** *n.*

gas·ket [ˈgæskɪt; ˈgæskit] *n.* ①【航海】束帆索。②(用橡膠、蔴辮、金屬、紙等所製, 裝於活塞周圍或鐵管接通處以免漏氣等的) 圈形或帶形填塞物。

gas·light [ˈgæsˌlaɪt; ˈgæslait] *n.* ①煤氣燈光。②煤氣燈。

gas log (煤氣暖爐用的)圓材狀燃管。

gas·man [ˈgæsˌmæn; ˈgæsmæn] *n., pl.* **-men.** ①煤氣公司劃表人 (派往各用戶劃定煤氣使用量的公司職員)。②煤氣工人。③【採礦】礦坑中檢查通風狀況以防沼氣爆炸的人。

gas mask 防毒面具。

gas meter 煤氣表。***lie like a gas meter*** 亂扯謊。

gas·o·gene [ˈgæsəˌdʒin; ˈgæsədʒiːn] *n.* 輕便之蘇打水製造機。

gas·o·lier [ˌgæsəˈlɪə; ˌgæsəˈliə] *n.* =**gaselier.**

***gas·o·line, gas·o·lene** [ˈgæsl̩ˌin, ˌgæsl̩ˈin; ˈgæsəliːn, -soul-] *n.* 【美】汽油(英國稱爲 petrol)。

gas·om·e·ter [gæsˈɑmətɚ; gæˈsɔmitə] *n.* ①煤氣計量表。②煤氣槽;蓄氣器。

gas oven 煤氣爐。

gasp** [gæsp, gɑsp; gɑːsp] *v.i.* ①喘息;喘氣。He was *gasping* for breath. 他喘息着。②渴望;渴求【常 for, after】。—*v.t.* 喘氣而語【常 out, away, forth】。to *gasp* out a few words. 喘着氣說出了幾個字。gasp one's last*** 死。—*n.* 喘息;喘氣。***at one's (the) last gasp*** 即將氣絕;將死;奄奄一息。*At his last gasp* he confessed to the murder. 將要氣絕時, 他承認了殺人。***to the last gasp*** 直到死時。—**ing·ly,** *adv.*

gasp·er [ˈgæspɚ, ˈgɑspɚ; ˈgɑːspə] *n.* ①喘息者;喘氣者。②【英俚】低廉的香煙。

gas pipe 煤氣管。

gas range 煤氣爐灶。

gas·sing [ˈgæsɪŋ; ˈgæsiŋ] *n.* ①【紡織】以煤氣燒去布等之細毛。②毒氣攻擊;毒氣戰。③【俚】瞎聊天;閒聊。④(電解時之)氣體之放出。

gas station 加油站。

gas stove (炊事用)煤氣爐。

gas·sy [ˈgæsɪ; ˈgæsi] *adj.,* **-si·er, -si·est.** ①氣體的;像氣體的;充滿氣體的。②【俗】誇張的;空談的。③腸胃氣脹的。

gas tank ①貯藏煤氣或汽油的槽。②汽車之油箱。

gas·ter·o·pod [ˈgæstərəˌpɑd; ˈgæstərəpɔd] *n., adj.* =**gastropod.**

gas·tight [ˈgæsˈtaɪt; ˈgæsˈtait] *adj.* ①不漏氣的。②在一定壓力下某種氣體打不進的。

gas·tral·gi·a [gæsˈtrældʒɪə; gæsˈtrældʒiə] *n.* 【醫】胃痛。

gas·tric [ˈgæstrɪk; ˈgæstrik] *adj.* 胃的; 胃部的。***gastric juice*** 胃液。***gastric ulcer*** 胃潰瘍。

gas·tri·tis [gæsˈtraɪtɪs; gæsˈtraitis] *n.* 胃炎;(特指)胃黏膜炎。

gastro- 【字首】表"胃、腹"之義。

gas·tro·en·ter·i·tis [ˌgæstroˌɛntəˈraɪtɪs; ˌgæstrouˌentəˈraitis] *n.* 【醫】腸胃炎。

gas·tro·en·ter·ol·o·gy [ˌgæstroˌɛntəˈrɑlədʒɪ; ˌgæstrouˌentəˈrɔlədʒi] *n.* 胃腸學;胃腸病學。

gas·trol·o·gy 〔gæs'trɑlədʒɪ; gæs'trɔlədʒi〕 *n.* ①〖醫〗胃(病)學。②烹飪學(幽默語)。—**gas·trol·o·gist,** *n.*
gas·tro·nome 〔'gæstrə,nɑm; 'gæstrənoum〕 *n.* =**gastronomer.**
gas·tron·o·mer 〔gæs'trɑnəmɚ; gæs'trɔnəmə〕 *n.* 美食家。
gas·tro·nom·ic 〔,gæstrə'nɑmɪk; ,gæstrə'nɔmik〕 *adj.* 美食學的;烹飪學的。
gas·tro·nom·i·cal 〔,gæstrə'nɑmɪkl; ,gæstrə'nɔmikəl〕 *adj.* =**gastronomic.** —**ly,** *adv.*
gas·tron·o·mist 〔gæs'trɑnəmɪst; gæs'trɔnəmist〕 *n.* =**gastronomer.**
gas·tron·o·my 〔gæs'trɑnəmɪ; gæs'trɔnəmi〕 *n.* 美食法;美食學。
gas·tro·pod 〔'gæstrə,pɑd; 'gæstrəpɔd〕 *n.* 〖動物〗腹足類動物(如蝸牛等)。—*adj.* (亦作 **gastropodous**) 腹足類動物的。
gas·trop·to·sis 〔,gæstrɑp'tosɪs; ,gæstrɔp'tousis〕 *n.* 〖醫〗胃下垂。
gas·tro·scope 〔'gæstrə,skop; 'gæstrəskoup〕 *n.* 〖醫〗胃窺器;胃窺鏡。
gas·tros·co·py 〔gæs'trɑskəpɪ; gæs'trɔskəpi〕 *n.* 胃鏡檢法。
gas·tru·la 〔'gæstrulə; 'gæstrulə〕 *n., pl.* **-las, -lae** 〔-,li; -liː〕. 〖生物〗胚囊;原腸胚;蛹囊。—**gas·tru·lar,** *adj.*
gas·work·er 〔'gæs,wɝkɚ; 'gæs,wəːkə〕 *n.* 煤氣廠工人。
gas·works 〔'gæs,wɝks; 'gæswəːks〕 *n. pl.* (作 *sing.* 解)煤氣廠。
gat[1] 〔gæt; gæt〕 *n.* 〖俚〗手鎗。
gat[2] *v.* 〖古〗pt. of **get.**
G
‡**gate**[1] 〔get; geit〕 *n., v.,* **gat·ed, gat·ing.** —*n.* ①圍牆門;籬笆門;大門。He jumped over the *gate* into the field. 他跳過大門跑進田野。②大門口。③水門;水閘。④運動會、展覽會等的觀衆數。There was a *gate* of thousands. 觀衆數以千計。⑤運動會、展覽會的門票收入。The two teams divided a *gate* of $3250. 兩隊平分 3250 元之售票收入。⑥牌樓。⑦入口。⑧欄杆(鐵路或公路上的)。⑨門徑。Hard work is the *gate* to success. 努力工作是成功之門徑。***at the gate of death*** 臨死亡之門;將死。***get the gate*** 被解僱;被開除;被趕走。***give (a person) the gate*** 〖俚〗開革(某人)。I guess his girl has *given him the gate.* 我猜他被他的女友甩掉了。—*v.t.*〖英〗(大學處罰學生)使禁足。
「爲或動作。」
gate[2] *n.* 〖古〗①小徑。②〖方言〗習慣性行
gate bill 〖英〗(Oxford, Cambridge 大學)學生逾時返校之紀錄,或此項罰款。
gate-crash 〔'get,kræʃ; 'geitkræʃ〕 *v.t. & v.i.* 〖俚〗未經邀請或購票而入場。
gate crasher 未受邀請而參加舞會、茶會或其他集會的人;看白戲者。
gate·house 〔'get,haus; 'geithaus〕 *n.* ①傳達室。②閘門。
「*n.* 看門者;門房。」
gate·keep·er 〔'get,kipɚ; 'geit,kiːpə〕
gate-leg table 〔'get,lɛg~; 'geit,leg~〕 活動桌子(可摺疊者)。(亦作 **gate-legged table**)
gate money (運動、展覽會、音樂會等之)入場費;入場費收入。
「下客之區域。」
gate position 機場中指定飛機載客、
gate·post 〔'get,post; 'geitpoust〕 *n.* 大門的門柱。***between you and me and the gatepost*** 極祕密的;嚴守祕密的。

***gate·way** 〔'get,we; 'geit-wei〕 *n.* ①大門口。②大門口上方之建築物。③通路。④方法;手段。a *gateway* to success. 到達成功之路。
‡**gath·er** 〔'gæðɚ; 'gæðə〕 *v.t.* ①集合;聚集。He soon *gathered* a crowd round him. 他不久便聚合了一羣人在他的周圍。②採集;收拾。to *gather* flowers (fruit, shells, etc.). 採集花(果、貝殼等)。③漸增。The train *gathered* speed as it left the station. 火車離站時增加速度。④推斷;結論;了解。What did you *gather* from his statement? 你推想他那聲明的意思是甚麼? ⑤打摺;摺皺。a skirt *gathered* at the waist. 腰部打摺的裙子。⑥吸引;喚起注意。A good football game always *gathers* a crowd. 一場好的足球賽總能吸引觀衆。⑦圍繞在或吸引到某人或某物。⑧選擇。⑨鼓起勇氣,努力等〖常 up〗。He *gathered* up his strength for the hard job. 他拿出力量來做艱難的工作。—*v.i.* ①聚集;集合。A crowd *gathered* round him. 一羣人聚攏在他周圍。②增加;漸增;積累。The dusk is *gathering.* 暮色漸濃。③蹙眉。④化膿。***be gathered to one's fathers*** 死;被埋葬(=die). ***gather breath*** a. 停下來休息或思索。b. 呼吸;喘一口氣。***gather oneself together*** 振起精神。***gather speed*** 逐漸加快(指運動體而言)。***gather the brows*** 蹙眉。—*n.* ①集合;聚集。②(*pl.*)衣服之褶。③收集之數量(如收成等)。
***gath·er·ing** 〔'gæðrɪŋ; 'gæðəriŋ〕 *n.* ①集合;集結;聚集。②集結一起的人;會議。③收集一起的東西。④膿瘡。⑤衣服之褶。
gathering coal 火種。(使火終夜不息的大煤塊)。
「禁足處分。」
gat·ing 〔'getɪŋ; 'geitiŋ〕 *n.* 英國大學之
Gat·ling gun 〔'gætlɪŋ~; 'gætliŋ~〕 *n.* 格林式機關鎗。
GATT, G.A.T.T. General Agreement on Tariffs and Trade.
gauche 〔goʃ; gouʃ〕 *adj.* 笨拙的;粗魯的;無社交手腕的。
gau·che·rie 〔,goʃə'ri, 'goʃə,ri; 'gouʃəri(ː)〕 *n., pl.* **-ries.** ①笨拙;無手腕。②笨拙的舉動。
Gau·cho, gau·cho 〔'gautʃo; 'gautʃou〕 *n., pl.* **-chos.** 高楚人;高楚牧人(南美西班牙人與印第安人之混血種族)。
gaud 〔gɔd; gɔːd〕 *n.* ①俗麗之裝飾品。②(*pl.*)俗麗的儀式或誇示。
gaud·er·y 〔'gɔdərɪ; 'gɔːdəri〕 *n., pl.* **-ries.** ①俗麗之裝飾品(尤指首飾)。②誇示。
gaud·y 〔'gɔdɪ; 'gɔːdi〕 *adj.,* **gaud·i·er, gaud·i·est.** 俗麗的。—**gaud·i·ly,** *adv.*
gauf·fer 〔'gɔfɚ, 'gɑfɚ; 'gɔːfə, 'gɔfə〕 *n., v.t.* =**goffer.**
gauge** 〔gedʒ; geidʒ〕 *n., v.,* **gauged, gaug·ing.** —*n.* ①標準度量;標準計。②計量器。a steam *gauge.* 蒸氣壓力計。③(鐵道)兩軌間之距離;軌幅。④估計與判斷的方法;估量;判斷。⑤形狀大小;容量;範圍。⑥航行中之船對另外之船與風的關係位置。take the gauge of*** 度量;計量。to *take the gauge of* a man's ability. 估量某人之能力。—*v.t.* ①精確計量。to *gauge* the rainfall. 計量雨量。②估計;估量。to *gauge* a person's strength. 估量一人的體力。③使合乎標準。④劃分。⑤鑿或琢磨(磚石等)使其大小形狀一致。(亦作 **gage**)
gaug·er 〔'gedʒɚ; 'geidʒə〕 *n.* ①度量的

人；度量物；計量者(器)。②(須繳消費稅之飲料之)量器檢查官；收稅官。(亦作 **gager**)
gauging rod (收稅官用之)檢量竿。
Gau·guin [ˌgoˈgɛ̃; ˌgouˈgɛ̃] *n.* 高更 (Eugene Henri Paul, 1848–1903, 法國畫家)。
Gaul [gɔl; gɔːl] *n.* ①高盧(歐洲西部一古國)。②(用 Celtic 語的)高盧人。③法國人。
Gaul·ish [ˈgɔlɪʃ; ˈgɔːliʃ] *adj.* 高盧的；高盧人的；高盧語的。—*n.* 古高盧之語言。
Gaull·ism [ˈgolɪzəm, ˈgɔ-; ˈgoulizəm] *n.* 法國戴高樂之政治主張。
Gaull·ist [ˈgolɪst, ˈgɔ-; ˈgoulist, ˈgɔː-] *n.* ①戴高樂之支持者。②第二次大戰期間在納粹占領下從事反抗運動的法國人。
***gaunt** [gɔnt, gɑnt; gɔːnt] *adj.* ①憔悴的；骨瘦如柴的。a *gaunt* figure. 枯瘦的身軀。②荒涼的。a *gaunt* hillside. 荒涼不毛的山坡。
gaunt·let[1] [ˈgɔntlɪt, ˈgɑnt-; ˈgɔːntlit] *n.* ①(騎士戴的)鐵手套。②寬口粗大的手套。***take up the gauntlet*** a. 接受挑戰。b. 表示無畏。***throw down the gauntlet*** 挑戰。
gaunt·let[2] *n.* =**gantlet**[1].
gaun·try [ˈgɔntrɪ; ˈgɔːntri] *n.*, *pl.* **-tries.** =**gantry.**
gauss [gaus; gaus] *n.*【物理】高斯(磁感「應或磁場强度單位)。」
Gau·ta·ma [ˈgautəmə; ˈgautəmə] *n.* 喬答摩(釋迦牟尼, 563?–?483 B.C., 之初名, 印度哲學家, 佛教創始者)。
***gauze** [gɔz; gɔːz] *n.* ①薄紗；棉紗。②【醫】紗布。③薄霧。—**like,** *adj.*
gauz·y [ˈgɔzɪ; ˈgɔːzi] *adj.*, **gauz·i·er, gauz·i·est.** 如紗的；如煙霧的；薄的；透明的。a *gauzy* mist. 薄霧。
‡**gave** [gev; geiv] *v.* pt. of **give.**
gav·el [ˈgævl̩; ˈgævl] *n.*, *v.*, **-el(l)ed, -el·(l)ing.** —*n.* (法官等所用之)小木槌；議事槌。—*v.t.* 藉敲議事槌代替議事程序而做成(裁決)或使(會議)進行。—*v.i.* 擊議事槌。Governor Green *gaveled* for attention. 葛林州長擊議事槌使(與會者)注意。***gavel down*** 擊議事槌表示否決。
gav·el·kind [ˈgævl̩ˌkaɪnd; ˈgævlkaind] *n.*【英法律】男子對未立遺囑之死者之財產予以平均繼承之制度或習慣。
ga·vot(te) [gəˈvɑt; gəˈvɔt] *n.* ①甘伏舞(法國舊式舞蹈)。②甘伏舞曲。
Ga·wain [ˈgɑwɪn; ˈgɑːwein] *n.* (亞瑟王傳說)加文(圓桌武士之一, 亞瑟王之侄)。
gawk [gɔk; gɔːk] *n.* 呆子；笨拙的人。—*v.i.*【俗】做笨拙的舉動；呆視。
gawk·y [ˈgɔkɪ; ˈgɔːki] *adj.*, **gawk·i·er, gawk·i·est.** 拙笨的；蠢的。—**gawk·i·ly,** *adv.*
‡**gay** [ge; gei] *adj.*, **gay·er, gay·est.** *n.* —*adj.* ①歡欣的。the *gay* voices of young children. 小孩們歡欣的聲音。②五光十色的；輕快的。*gay* colors. 繽紛之彩色。③放蕩的；淫佚的。to lead a *gay* life. 過放蕩的生活。④衣着華麗的。⑤【美俚】同性戀的。⑥【美俚】放肆的；無禮的。—*n.*【美俚】同性戀者。
gay dog【俚】縱情逸樂者；追逐聲色者。
gay·e·ty [ˈgeətɪ; ˈgeiəti] *n.*, *pl.* **-ties.** =**gaiety.**
***gay·ly** [ˈgelɪ; ˈgeili] *adv.* =**gaily.**
gay science 詩的藝術。
gaz. ①gazette. ②gazetteer.
‡**gaze** [gez; geiz] *v.*, **gazed, gaz·ing,** *n.* —*v.i.* 凝視；注視〖at, on, upon〗. What are you *gazing* at? 你在凝視甚麼? She *gazed* upon him in bewilderment. 她茫然凝視着他。—*n.* 凝視；注視。—**less,** *adj.* —**gaz·er,** *n.* —**gaz·ing·ly,** *adv.*
ga·ze·bo [gəˈzibo; gəˈziːbou] *n.*, *pl.* **-bos, -boes.** 露臺；陽臺；涼亭。
ga·zelle [gəˈzɛl; gəˈzel] *n.*, *pl.* **-zelles, -zelle.**【動物】瞪羚(產於北非及亞洲)。
ga·zette [gəˈzɛt; gəˈzet] *n.*, *v.*, **-zet·ted, -zet·ting.** —*n.* ①報紙(主要用爲報刊名稱)。②政府之公報。—*v.t.* 刊載於公報上；宣布(常用於被動式)。
gaz·et·teer [ˌgæzəˈtɪr; ˌgæziˈtiə] *n.* ①地名辭典。②政府公報發行官。—*v.t.* 在地名辭典中對…作地理描述。
gaz·o·gene [ˈgæzəˌdʒin; ˈgæzədʒiːn] *n.* =**gasogene.**
G.B. Great Britain. **G.B.S.** George Bernard Shaw. **G.C.D., g.c.d., gcd** greatest common divisor.
GCE, G.C.E. General Certificate of Education. **G.C.F., g.c.f.** greatest common factor. **GCI**【軍】ground controlled interception. 地面管制攔截系統(用以追踪或攔截不明航空器之雷達設備)。
G clef【音樂】高音部譜表記號(即𝄞)。
G.C.M., g.c.m. greatest common measure. **GCR** ground controlled radar. **Gd** 化學元素 gadolinium 之符號。
GDP gross domestic product. **gds.** goods.
gear** [gɪr; giə] *n.* ①齒輪；齒輪裝置；聯動機。*gear* wheel. 齒輪。②機器的運轉靈活。③工具；道具。fishing *gear.* 釣魚具。④馬具。⑤能搬運的私人財物(如衣物等)。⑥甲冑與武器。in gear*** 機器靈活；無毛病。A car cannot go unless it is *in gear.* 一部車子若聯動機不聯好便不能開行。***in*** (or ***into***) ***high gear*** 進入最高速度, 活動或效率。***out of gear*** a. 機器不靈；出了毛病。b. 與馬達分開。***shift gears*** a. 換檔。b. 改變態度或方法以適應新情勢。—*v.t.* ①以齒輪連起。②開動；發動(機器)。to *gear* up (down) a car. 開快(慢)車。③裝上齒輪；安裝機器等。④增加；使爲…而服務。The steel industry was *geared* to the needs of war. 鋼鐵工業爲滿足戰爭需要而增加產量。—*v.i.* ①配搭活動；運動靈活。②準備；安排；計劃。
gear·box [ˈgɪrˌbɑks; ˈgiəbɔks] *n.* ①齒輪箱(匣)。②(傳動裝置中之)變速箱。
gear case ①齒輪匣(保持滑油及防止灰塵者)。②脚踏車飛輪及鏈條外之保護外殼。
gear·ing [ˈgɪrɪŋ; ˈgiəriŋ] *n.* ①裝置齒輪。②傳動；聯動。in (out of) *gearing.* 在(不在)傳動。③傳動裝置；齒輪裝置。
gear·shift [ˈgɪrˌʃɪft; ˈgiəˌʃift] *n.* 操縱桿；齒輪轉換裝置。
geck·o [ˈgɛko; ˈgekou] *n.*, *pl.* **-os, -oes.**【動物】壁虎類；守宮科之動物。
gee[1] [dʒi; dʒiː] *n.*【英俚】馬(兒語作「**gee-gee**)。」
gee[2] *interj.*, *v.*, **geed, gee·ing.** —*interj.* ①(馭牛、馬聲)向右轉。②向前走；快一點〖常 up〗. —*v.t.* & *v.i.* ①向右轉。②閃避。
gee[3] *interj.* 表示驚奇強調等的感歎語。*Gee,* that's great! 噫！那眞棒！
geese [gis; giːs] *n.* pl. of **goose.**
gee-string [ˈdʒiˌstrɪŋ; ˈdʒiːstriŋ] *n.*【俗】袴布；遮羞布。(亦作 **G-string**)
gee·zer [ˈgizɚ; ˈgiːzə] *n.*【俚】古怪的老人；老頭兒；(罕指)老太婆。
Ge·hen·na [gɪˈhɛnə, gə-; giˈhenə] *n.* ①【聖經】Jerusalem 附近之 Hinnom 谷。②【新約聖經】地獄。③苦難之地。

Gei·ger counter ['gaɪgə~; 'gaigə~] 蓋氏計算器(用以測量放射作用及測驗宇宙線質點等)。「放射性微粒;輻射。」

Gei·gers ['gaɪgəz;'gaigəz] *n. pl.*〖俗〗

gei·sha ['geʃə; 'geiʃə] *n., pl.* **-sha, -shas.** (日本之)藝妓。(亦作 **geisha girl**)

Geiss·ler tube ['gaɪslə~;'gaislə~] 蓋斯勒管(眞空放電之實驗用眞空管)。

Geist [gaɪst; gaist]〖德〗*n.* 精神;時代精神。

gel [dʒɛl; dʒel] *n., v.,* **gelled, gel·ling.** —*n.*〖理化〗凝膠;膠滯體;乳膠體。—*v.i.* 膠化;成凝膠狀。

gel·a·tin(e) ['dʒɛlətn,-tɪn;ˌdʒeləˈti:n] *n.* ①膠;動物膠;骨膠。②植物膠。***explosive gelatin*** 爆發性硝酸甘油化合物。***gelatin paper***〖照相〗亞膠紙。***gelatin plate***〖照相〗乾板。

ge·lat·i·nize [dʒɪ'lætəˌnaɪz; dʒi'lætinaiz] *v.,* **-nized, -niz·ing.** —*v.i.* 成爲膠狀。—*v.t.* ①使成爲膠狀。②塗以膠質。

ge·lat·i·nous [dʒə'lætənəs; dʒi'lætinəs] *adj.* ①膠質的;含膠的。②膠狀的。

ge·la·tion [dʒɛl'eʃən; dʒe'leiʃən] *n.* ①凍結。②〖理化〗凝膠作用。

geld[1] [gɛld; geld] *v.t.,* **geld·ed** or **gelt, geld·ing.** ①閹割;去(馬等)之勢;去卵巢。②取去(重要部分);使弱。

geld[2] *n.*〖英史〗(古代英國地主對君主所納之)稅;貢賦。(亦作 **gelt, gheld**)

geld·ing ['gɛldɪŋ; 'geldiŋ] *n.* ①去勢的馬。②閹人;太監。

gel·id ['dʒɛlɪd; 'dʒelid] *adj.* ①似冰的;冰冷的;極寒冷的。②(性質、態度等)冷漠的。

gel·ig·nite ['dʒɛlɪgˌnaɪt; 'dʒelignait] *n.* 一種含有硝化甘油之炸藥。

gelt [gɛlt; gelt] *v.* pt. & pp. of **geld**[1].

*__gem__ [dʒɛm; dʒem] *n., v.,* **gemmed, gem·ming.** *adj.* —*n.* ①珠寶;寶石。②精華;佳作;珍貴之物。the *gem* of the collection of curios, foreign stamps, paintings. 所蒐集之古董、外國郵票、繪畫中的精華部分。③被尊敬或喜愛的人。④〖印刷〗四磅因鉛字。—*v.t.* ①飾以寶石;似飾有寶石。The night sky is *gemmed* with stars. 夜空點綴着晶瑩星光。②開採寶石;探勘寶石。—*adj.*〖珠寶〗最高品質的。

Ge·ma·ra [gə'mɑrɑ; ge'mɑ:rə] *n.* 猶太教的經典 Talmud 中的註釋篇。

gem·i·nate [*v.* 'dʒɛməˌnet;'dʒemineit *adj.* 'dʒɛmənɪt; 'dʒeminit] *v.,* **-nat·ed, -nat·ing,** *adj.* —*v.t.* & *v.i.* (使)成雙;(使)成對。—*adj.* (亦作 **geminated**)〖動、植物〗(葉)雙生的;成雙的;成對的。

gem·i·na·tion [ˌdʒɛmə'neʃən; ˌdʒemi'neiʃən] *n.* ①重複。②〖語音〗原爲單音之子音之重複發音。③〖文法〗子音字母之重複。

Gem·i·ni ['dʒɛməˌnaɪ; 'dʒeminai] *n. pl.*〖天文〗①雙子座。②雙子宮。③〖美〗雙子星太空船。

gem·ma ['dʒɛmə; 'dʒemə] *n., pl.* **-mae** [-mi; -mi:].〖生物〗①無性芽;子芽;芽。②芽體;分芽子。

gem·mate ['dʒɛmet; 'dʒemeit] *adj., v.,* **-mat·ed, -mat·ing.** —*adj.*〖生物〗有芽的;發芽生殖的。—*v.i.* 有芽;生芽;發芽生殖。

gem·ma·tion [dʒɛm'eʃən; dʒe'meiʃən] *n.*〖生物〗①發芽;無性芽生殖;芽之排列法。②細胞發芽。

gem·mip·a·rous [dʒɛm'ɪpərəs; dʒe'mipərəs] *adj.*〖生物〗發芽的;由芽生殖的。

gem·mule ['dʒɛmjul; 'dʒemju:l] *n.*〖生物〗小芽;小芽體。

gems·bok ['gɛmzbɑk; 'gemzbɔk] *n., pl.* **-boks, -bok.** (南非產之)大羚羊。(亦作 **gemsbuck**)「*n.* 適於作爲飾物的寶石。」

gem·stone ['dʒɛmˌston;'dʒemstoun]

gem-stud·ded ['dʒɛmˌstʌdɪd;'dʒemˌstʌdid] *adj.* 鑲滿寶石的。

gen [dʒɛn; dʒen] *n., v.,* **genned, gen·ning.** —*n.*〖英,軍俚〗情報;一般布告。—*v.t.* 供給內幕消息。「Geneva.」

Gen. ①〖軍〗General. ②Genesis. ③

gen. ①gender. ②general. ③genitive. ④genus.

-gen〖字尾〗表"生;被生"之義。

gen·darme ['ʒɑndɑrm; 'ʒɑ̃dɑ:m] *n., pl.* **-darmes** [-dɑrmz; -dɑ:mz].〖法〗①憲兵。②歐洲某些國家的警察。

gen·dar·me·rie [ˌʒɑ̃darmə'ri; ˌʒɑ̃dɑ:mə'ri:]〖法〗*n.* 憲兵隊;憲兵警察(集合稱)。(亦作 **gendarmery**)

*__gen·der__ ['dʒɛndə; 'dʒendə] *n.* ①〖文法〗性。②〖俗〗性別。the female *gender.* 女性。③〖文法〗(1)**masculine gender.** 陽性。(2)**feminine gender.** 陰性。(3)**common gender.** 通性。(4)**neuter gender.** 中性。

gene [dʒin; dʒi:n] *n.*〖生物〗遺傳因子。

ge·ne·a·log·i·cal [ˌdʒinɪə'lɑdʒɪk]; ˌdʒi:niə'lɔdʒikəl] *adj.* 宗譜的;家系的。a *genealogical* tree. 家系圖。(亦作 **genealogic**) **—ly,** *adv.*

ge·ne·al·o·gist [ˌdʒɛnɪ'ælədʒɪst; ˌdʒi:ni'ælədʒist] *n.* 系譜學者;系譜家。

ge·ne·al·o·gy [ˌdʒinɪ'ælədʒɪ; ˌdʒi:ni'ælədʒi] *n., pl.* **-gies.** ①宗譜;系譜;家系。②裔系。③家系學;系圖學。

gen·er·a ['dʒɛnərə; 'dʒenərə] *n.* pl. of **genus.** 「bəl] *adj.* 可產生的。」

gen·er·a·ble ['dʒɛnərəb]; 'dʒenərə-

‡**gen·er·al** ['dʒɛnərəl; 'dʒenərəl] *adj.* ①普遍的;大衆的。A government takes care of the *general* welfare. 政府負責大衆的福利。②總括的;一般的;普通的。the *general* plan (idea, etc.). 一般的計畫(概念等)。She referred to her trip in a *general* way. 她只是概括的敍述其旅行。③首席的;階級最高的(用於官銜之後)。the postmaster *general.* 郵務部長。④〖醫〗(麻醉之)全身的。*general* anesthetics. 全身麻醉劑。***as a general rule*** 照例地;通常。—*n.* ①大體;一般。②〖美〗陸軍二級上將;將軍;上將。*General* William. 威廉將軍。③將官;帶兵官。Napoleon was a great *general.* 拿破崙是一位偉大的將領。④一般的事實、觀念、原則或敍述。⑤〖宗教〗修道會長。***in general*** 就大體而論。—*v.t.* 指揮;作…之將軍。〖注意〗(1)美國陸軍:*General* of the Army. 一級上將(俗稱五星上將)。*General.* 二級上將。Lieutenant *General.* 中將。Major *General.* 少將。Brigadier *General.* 准將。(2)美國空軍:*General* of the Air Force. 一級上將。二級以下與陸軍同。

General Assembly ①(美國若干州的)州議會。②(聯合國的)會員大會。③聯合國大會。「事法庭。」

general court-martial 最高軍

general election 大選。

general headquarters〖美陸軍〗總司令部。(略作 GHQ)

gen·er·al·is·si·mo [ˌdʒɛnərəlˈɪsəˌmo; ˌdʒenərəˈlisimou] *n., pl.* **-mos.** ①大元帥；最高統帥；委員長。②(某些國家中的)軍團司令。

gen·er·al·ist [ˈdʒɛnərəlɪst; ˈdʒenərəlist] *n.* 通曉各方面知識技能的人；通才。

gen·er·al·i·ty [ˌdʒɛnəˈrælətɪ; ˌdʒenəˈræliti] *n., pl.* **-ties.** ①概論；概說；通則；通論。I wish you would come down from *generalities* to particulars. 我希望你別談大概而談細節。②(the-)多數；大部分。③一般性；通性；普遍性。

gen·er·al·i·za·tion [ˌdʒɛnərələˈzeʃən; ˌdʒenərəlaiˈzeiʃən] *n.* ①概括；一概而論。②概括的論述；一般的法則。

gen·er·al·ize [ˈdʒɛnərəlˌaɪz; ˈdʒenərəlaiz] *v.i.* & *v.t.*, **-ized, -iz·ing.** ①歸納；概括；綜合；做出結論。②概括地說。③推廣。

gen·er·al·ly [ˈdʒɛnərəlɪ; ˈdʒenərəli] *adv.* ①通常。He *generally* comes here on Tuesdays. 他通常禮拜二來這裏。②概括地；一般地。*generally* speaking. 一般言之。③普遍地；廣泛地。It was once *generally* believed that the earth was flat. 從前大家都普遍地相信地球是扁平的。

gen·er·al·ship [ˈdʒɛnərəlˌʃɪp; ˈdʒenərəlʃip] *n.* ①將才。②指揮、管理、或領導之才幹。③將官職位、身分、階級、任期、或權力。

gen·er·ate [ˈdʒɛnəˌret; ˈdʒenəreit] *v.t.*, **-at·ed, -at·ing.** ①產生；使發生；造成。②創造。③養育(後代)。④【數學】動點成(線)；動線成(面)；動面成(立體)。***generating station*** (or ***plant***)發電廠。

*__gen·er·a·tion__ [ˌdʒɛnəˈreʃən; ˌdʒenəˈreiʃən] *n.* ①同時代的人(集合稱)；一代人。the present *generation.* 現在的一代人。②代(約三十年)。a *generation* ago. 一代以前。③(家族中之)一代；一世。④產生；發生。the *generation* of steam. 蒸汽的產生。⑤生育後裔；養育後代。⑥同一時期之產物(尤指產品之舊式者)。The new computers are much better in performance than the previous *generation.* 新的電子計算機較以前的產品在性能方面好得多。

generation gap 代溝(兩代之間在思想、態度等各方面的差距)。

gen·er·a·tive [ˈdʒɛnəˌretɪv; ˈdʒenərətiv] *adj.* ①生產的；有生產力的。②生殖的；有生殖力的。a *generative* cell. 生殖細胞。

gen·er·a·tor [ˈdʒɛnəˌretə; ˈdʒenəreitə] *n.* ①發電機。②產生蒸汽或煤氣的機器。③生產者；製造者；生殖者。

gen·er·a·trix [ˌdʒɛnəˈretrɪks; ˌdʒenəˈreitriks] *n., pl.* **gen·er·a·tri·ces** [ˌdʒɛnərəˈtraɪsiz; ˌdʒenərəˈtraisiːz]. ①【數學】母量(生出線、面、立體的母點、母線、母面)。②基體；母體。③發電機。

ge·ner·ic [dʒəˈnɛrɪk; dʒiˈnerik] *adj.* ①【生物】屬的；類的。②一般的；普通的；非特殊的。(亦作 **generical**)

*__gen·er·os·i·ty__ [ˌdʒɛnəˈrɑsətɪ; ˌdʒenəˈrɔsiti] *n., pl.* **-ties.** ①慷慨。His *generosity* to the poor is well known. 他對窮人之慷慨爲人所熟知。②寬大；大度。③(常 *pl.*)慷慨或寬大的行爲。We thanked him for his *generosities.* 我們對他的慷慨行爲表示感謝。

*__gen·er·ous__ [ˈdʒɛnərəs; ˈdʒenərəs] *adj.* ①具有高貴者之氣質的；有雅量的；大度的；寬大的；高潔的。a *generous* spirit. 高潔之精神。②慷慨的；大方的；不吝嗇的。a *generous* giver (contributor). 慷慨的給予者(捐助者)。③大量的；豐富的；充分的。④肥沃的。⑤氣味濃郁的。⑥濃的；濃厚的。**—ly,** *adv.*

Gen·e·sis [ˈdʒɛnəsɪs; ˈdʒenisis] *n.* 創世紀(舊約的首卷)。

gen·e·sis [ˈdʒɛnəsɪs; ˈdʒenisis] *n., pl.* **-ses** [-ˌsiz; -siːz]. 根源；創造；發生；誕生。

gen·et [ˈdʒɛnɪt; ˈdʒenit] *n.* (非洲、南歐、西亞產之)獛；其毛皮。(亦作 **genette**)

ge·net·ic [dʒəˈnɛtɪk; dʒiˈnetik] *adj.* ①遺傳學的。②發生的；發生論的；起源的。(亦作 **genetical**) **—al·ly,** *adv.*

ge·net·i·cist [dʒəˈnɛtəsɪst; dʒiˈnetisist] *n.* 遺傳學者。

ge·net·ics [dʒəˈnɛtɪks; dʒiˈnetiks] *n.* (作 *sing.* 解)【生物】遺傳學；發生學。

Ge·ne·va [dʒəˈnivə; dʒiˈniːvə] *n.* 日內瓦(瑞士西南部城市)。

ge·ne·va [dʒəˈnivə; dʒiˈniːvə] *n.*一種荷蘭杜松子酒。

Geneva Convention 【軍】日內瓦協定(成立於1864年，有關俘虜或傷兵之處理)。

Ge·ne·van [dʒəˈnivən; dʒiˈniːvən] *adj.* ①日內瓦(人)的。②喀爾文(Calvin)教派的。*Genevan* theory. 喀爾文派神學。**—*n.*** ①日內瓦人。②喀爾文教派之信徒。

Gen·e·vese [ˌdʒɛnəˈviz; ˌdʒenəˈviːz] *adj., n., sing.* & *pl.* **=Genevan.**

Gen·ghis Khan [ˈdʒɛn·gɪzˈkɑn; ˈdʒeŋgisˈkɑːn] 成吉思汗 (1162–1227, 中國元太祖)。(亦作 **Jenghis Khan, Jenghiz Khan**)

*__gen·ial__[1] [ˈdʒinjəl; ˈdʒiːnjəl, -niəl] *adj.* ①愉快的；和藹的；慇懃的。a man with a *genial* character. 一個有和藹性格的人。②幫助滋長的；和暖的。*genial* sunshine. 和煦的陽光。a *genial* climate. 和暖的氣候。③天才的。**—ly,** *adv.*

ge·ni·al[2] [dʒɪˈnaɪəl; dʒiˈnaiəl] *adj.* 【解剖，動物】頤的；顎的。

ge·ni·al·i·ty [ˌdʒinɪˈælətɪ; ˌdʒiːniˈæliti] *n.* 懇切；和藹；愉快；誠懇。

ge·nic·u·late [dʒəˈnɪkjəlɪt; dʒəˈnikjulit] *adj.* ①有膝狀關節的。②彎成膝狀的。(亦作 **geniculated**)

ge·nie [ˈdʒinɪ; ˈdʒiːni] *n., pl.* **ge·ni·i.** 【回教神話】神怪。

ge·ni·i [ˈdʒinɪˌaɪ; ˈdʒiːniai] *n.* pl. of **genius** or **genie.**

ge·nis·ta [dʒɪˈnɪstə; dʒiˈnistə] *n.* 【植物】豆科之一屬。

gen·i·tal [ˈdʒɛnətl̩; ˈdʒenitl] *adj.* 生殖的；生殖器的。

gen·i·ti·val [ˌdʒɛnəˈtaɪvl̩; ˌdʒeniˈtaivəl] *adj.* 【文法】屬格的；屬格形的。

gen·i·tive [ˈdʒɛnətɪv; ˈdʒenitiv] *adj.* 【文法】所有位的；所有格的。**—*n.*** 所有位；所有格。***the genitive case*** 所有格。

*__gen·ius__ [ˈdʒinjəs; ˈdʒiːnjəs] *n., pl.* **-ius·es** for ①, ②, ③, ④, ⑤, **ge·ni·i** [ˈdʒinɪˌaɪ; ˈdʒiːniai] for ⑥. ①天才；天賦。men of *genius.* 有天才的人。②天才者；才子。Einstein was a mathematical *genius.* 愛因斯坦是一個數學天才。③才能；強烈的性向。a *genius* for acting. 演劇的才能。④一個人、民族、時代、語言等之特質或精神。⑤影響他人的人。⑥精靈；守護神。

genius lo·ci [~ˈlosaɪ; ~ˈlousai] ①一個地方的守護神。②一個地方的風氣或特色。

Gen·o·a [ˈdʒɛnəwə, dʒəˈnoə; ˈdʒenouə, dʒəˈnouə] *n.* 熱那亞(義大利西北部海港)。

gen·o·cide [ˈdʒɛnəˌsaɪd; ˈdʒenəsaid] *n.* (對人種、國民等有計畫的)集團大屠殺；種族滅絕。

Gen·o·ese 〔ˌdʒɛnəˈwiz; ˌdʒenouˈiːz〕 *adj.* 熱那亞(Genoa)的;熱那亞人的。—*n.* 熱那亞人。(亦作 **Genovese**)

gen·o·type 〔ˈdʒɛnoˌtaɪp; ˈdʒenoutaip〕 *n.* ①【生物】因子型;遺傳型。②有共通遺傳型之個體羣。

gen·re 〔ˈʒɑnrə; ʒɑ̃ːr〕【法】 *n.* ①類;型;式樣。②風俗畫;(日本之) 浮世繪 (=genre painting). —*adj.*【藝術】風俗畫的。

gens 〔dʒɛnz; dʒenz〕 *n., pl.* **gen·tes** 〔ˈdʒɛntiz; ˈdʒentiːz〕.【古羅馬】同祖先之一族;氏族。

gen·seng 〔ˈdʒɛnˈsɛŋ; ˈdʒenˈseŋ〕 *n.* =**ginseng.**

gent 〔dʒɛnt; dʒent〕 *n.*【俚】①紳士;男子(諧語)。②(*pl.*)男廁所。(亦作 **Gent**)

gen·teel 〔dʒɛnˈtil; dʒenˈtiːl〕 *adj.* ①上流社會的。②有禮貌的;有教養的;嫻雅的。③裝做貴族的;假裝爲紳士的。to live in *genteel* poverty. 過窮而擺闊人架子的生活。—**ly,** *adv.*

gen·teel·ism 〔dʒɛnˈtilɪzəm; dʒenˈtiːlizəm〕 *n.* 婉曲語。"Limb" is a *genteelism* for "leg." "Limb" 是 "leg" 的婉曲語。

gen·tian 〔ˈdʒɛnʃən; ˈdʒenʃiən〕 *n.*【植物】龍膽屬植物。

Gen·tile, gen·tile 〔ˈdʒɛntaɪl; ˈdʒentail〕 *n.* ①非猶太人。②異教徒;基督教徒(以別於猶太教徒)。③【美】非 Mormon 教友。—*adj.* ①非猶太人的。②異教徒的。③非 Mormon 教的。④【文法】表示國籍的。⑤種族的;民族的。

gen·tile·dom 〔ˈdʒɛntaɪldəm; ˈdʒentaildəm〕 *n.* (猶太人眼中的) 外邦人的世界;異教徒。

gen·til·i·ty 〔dʒɛnˈtɪlətɪ; dʒenˈtiliti〕 *n., pl.* **-ties.** ①高貴的出身或身分。②優美儀態。③文雅風度。④(the-)(*pl.*)假裝文雅。

:gen·tle 〔ˈdʒɛntḷ; ˈdʒentl〕 *adj.,* **-tler, -tlest.** *v.,* **-tled, -tling.** —*adj.* ①溫和的;溫柔的;和善的;溫馴的;易控制的。the *gentle* sex. 婦女;女性。a *gentle* wind. 和風。②文雅的;高尚的;彬彬有禮的;清白的;出身名門的。a man of *gentle* birth. 身世清白的人。③輕輕的;低聲的。a *gentle* smile. 輕盈的笑。④有資格戴紋章的。—*v.t.* ①馴馭。to *gentle* a colt. 馴馭一匹小馬。②撫慰。③使溫和。④輕打。⑤封爲貴族。—**ness,** *n.*

gen·tle·folk(s) 〔ˈdʒɛntḷˌfok(s); ˈdʒentlfouk(s)〕 *n. pl.* 出身名門者;上流人士。

:gen·tle·man 〔ˈdʒɛntḷmən; ˈdʒentlmən〕 *n., pl.* **-men.** ①上流人;紳士;君子。a true *gentleman.* 溫厚的君子。②可敬之人;有教養者。③先生(普通對男子的尊稱)。Ladies and *Gentlemen*: 諸位先生諸位女士:④人;男人。Who's the *gentleman* in the corner? 在牆角的那個人是誰? ⑤有錢有地位無需工作以謀生的人。⑥貴族之侍從。⑦美國參院或衆院的男議員。***the gentleman in black*** 魔鬼。

gen·tle·man-at-arms 〔ˈdʒɛntḷmənətˈɑrmz; ˈdʒentlmənətˈɑːmz〕 *n., pl.* **gen·tle·men-at-arms.** (於重大儀式中陪伴英王之) 四十侍衞之一。

gen·tle·man·like 〔ˈdʒɛntḷmənˌlaɪk; ˈdʒentlmənlaik〕 *adj.* (似)紳士的;舉止高雅的;不愧爲紳士的;風度好的;有禮貌的。

gen·tle·man·ly 〔ˈdʒɛntḷmənlɪ; ˈdʒentlmənli〕 *adj.* 紳士的;不愧爲紳士的。

gen·tle·man·ship 〔ˈdʒɛntḷmənˌʃɪp; ˈdʒentlmənʃip〕 *n.*【罕】紳士之身分(品格)。

gen·tle·wom·an 〔ˈdʒɛntḷˌwumən; ˈdʒentlˌwumən〕 *n., pl.* **-wom·en.** ①貴婦淑女;有地位之婦女。②有教養之婦女;女士。③(貴婦之)女侍。④美國參院或衆院之女議員。—**like,** *adj.* —**ly,** *adv.*

***gen·tly** 〔ˈdʒɛntlɪ; ˈdʒentli〕 *adv.* ①輕輕地;小心地。Hold it *gently.* 小心地拿住它。②逐漸地。The road sloped *gently* to the sea. 此路逐漸向海邊傾斜下去。

gen·tly-born 〔ˌdʒɛntlɪˈbɔrn; ˌdʒentliˈbɔːn〕 *adj.* 紳士出身的;書香門第的。

gen·try 〔ˈdʒɛntrɪ; ˈdʒentri〕 *n.* ①紳士;上流社會人士(尤指英國之僅次於貴族者)。②(作 *pl.* 解) 某一階級或社團的人們。the newspaper *gentry.* 新聞界人士。③可享紋章的平民 (尤指大地主)。④紳士之身分、地位。

gen·u·flect 〔ˈdʒɛnjuˌflɛkt; ˈdʒenjuːflekt〕 *v.i.* ①屈膝;跪拜。②作卑躬屈膝態。

gen·u·flec·tion, gen·u·flex·ion 〔ˌdʒɛnjuˈflɛkʃən; ˌdʒenju(ː)ˈflekʃən〕 *n.* 跪拜。

***gen·u·ine** 〔ˈdʒɛnjuɪn; ˈdʒenjuin〕 *adj.* ①眞正的;非僞造的。a *genuine* pearl. 眞珍珠。②眞實的;非僞裝的。*genuine* sorrow. 眞實的傷感。③誠懇的。a *genuine* person. 誠懇的人。④純種的。—**ly,** *adv.*

ge·nus 〔ˈdʒinəs; ˈdʒiːnəs〕 *n., pl.* **gen·er·a, ge·nus·es.** ①種;類;屬。②【生物】屬。③【邏輯】類概念。***the genus Homo*** 人類。

Geo. George.

geo-【字首】表"地球;土地;地面"之義。

ge·o·bi·ol·o·gy 〔ˌdʒiobaɪˈɑlədʒɪ; ˌdʒiːoubaiˈɔlədʒi〕 *n.* 地理生物學。

ge·o·cen·tric 〔ˌdʒioˈsɛntrɪk; ˌdʒiːouˈsentrik〕 *adj.* ①以地球爲中心的;地球中心的。②由地球中心所見或測量的。the *geocentric* latitude. 地心緯度。(亦作 **geocentrical**) —**al·ly,** *adv.*

ge·o·cen·tri·cism 〔ˌdʒioˈsɛntrɪsɪzəm; ˌdʒiːouˈsentrisizm〕 *n.* 地球中心說。

ge·o·chem·is·try 〔ˌdʒioˈkɛmɪstrɪ; ˌdʒiːouˈkemistri〕 *n.* 地質化學。—**ge·o·chem·ist,** *n.* —**ge·o·chem·i·cal,** *adj.*

ge·o·chro·nol·o·gy 〔ˌdʒiokrəˈnɑlədʒɪ; ˌdʒiːoukrəˈnɔlədʒi〕 *n.* 地質紀年學。

geod. ①geodesy. ②geodetic.

ge·ode 〔ˈdʒiod; ˈdʒiːoud〕 *n.*【地質】晶腺(晶簇之一種)。

ge·o·des·ic 〔ˌdʒiəˈdɛsɪk; ˌdʒiːouˈdesik〕 *adj.* (亦作 **geodesical**)【數學】測地學的;用測地學測定的;短程的。—*n.* 測地線;短程線。

ge·od·e·sy 〔dʒiˈɑdəsɪ; dʒiːˈɔdisi〕 *n.* 大地測量學(爲應用數學中之一支, 硏究並測定地球形狀及龐大的部分地表, 或精確定出在地面上之點)。(亦作 **geodetics**)

ge·o·det·ic 〔ˌdʒiəˈdɛtɪk; ˌdʒiːəˈdetik〕 *adj.* 用測地學測定的; 測地學的。(亦作 **geodetical**)

geog. ①geographer. ②geographic. ③geographical. ④geography.

ge·og·no·sy 〔dʒɪˈɑgnəsɪ; dʒiˈɔgnəsi〕 *n.* 地球構造學。

ge·og·ra·pher 〔dʒiˈɑgrəfɚ; dʒiˈɔgrəfə〕 *n.* 地理學家。

ge·o·graph·ic 〔ˌdʒiəˈgræfɪk; dʒiəˈgræfik〕 *adj.* 地理的;地理學的。*geographic* features. 地勢。*geographic* latitude. 地理緯度。

ge·o·graph·i·cal 〔ˌdʒiəˈgræfɪkḷ; dʒiəˈgræfikəl〕 *adj.* =**geographic.**

***ge·og·ra·phy** 〔dʒiˈɑgrəfɪ; dʒiˈɔgrəfi, ˈdʒiɔg-〕 *n., pl.* **-phies.** ①地理;地理學。

the *geography* of Europe. 歐洲地理。②地形。The *geography* of New England. 新英格蘭之地形。③地理書。

geol. ①geologic. ②geological. ③geologist. ④geology.

ge·o·log·ic [ˌdʒiəˈlɑdʒɪk; dʒiəˈlɔdʒik] *adj.*地質學的。(亦作**geological**)—**al·ly,** *adv.*

ge·ol·o·gist [dʒɪˈɑlədʒɪst; dʒiˈɔlədʒist] *n.* 研究地質之學者;地質學家。

ge·ol·o·gize [dʒɪˈɑləˌdʒaɪz; dʒiˈɔlədʒaiz] *v.,* **-gized, -giz·ing.** —*v.i.* 研究地質學;蒐集地質學的標本。—*v.t.* 做(某地方)的地質調查;將…作地質上的研究。

ge·ol·o·gy [dʒiˈɑlədʒɪ; dʒiˈɔlədʒi] *n., pl.* **-gies.** ①地質學。②有關地質學的書。③某一地區之地質概況。the *geology* of North America. 北美地質概況。

geom. ①geometry. ②geometric(al).

ge·o·man·cy [ˈdʒiəˌmænsɪ; ˈdʒiːəˌmænsi] *n.* 土占;地卜(抓沙撒地, 按其所成形象以斷吉凶)。

ge·om·e·ter [dʒiˈɑmətə; dʒiˈɔmitə] *n.*①幾何學家。②尺蠖。

ge·o·met·ric [ˌdʒiəˈmɛtrɪk; dʒiəˈmetrik] *adj.* ①幾何的;幾何學的。②整齊而有系統的。—**al·ly,** *adv.*

ge·o·met·ri·cal [ˌdʒiəˈmɛtrɪkl; dʒiəˈmetrikəl] *adj.* =**geometric.**

ge·o·me·tri·cian [ˌdʒiəmə ˈtrɪʃən; ˌdʒioumeˈtriʃən] *n.* 幾何學家。

geometric mean 幾何平均數;等比中項。

geometric progression 幾何級數。

ge·om·e·trid [dʒiˈɑmətrɪd; dʒiˈɔmitrid] *adj.* 尺蠖科的。—*n.* 尺蠖蛾(其幼蟲即爲尺蠖)。

ge·om·e·trize [dʒiˈɑməˌtraɪz; dʒiˈɔmitraiz] *v.,* **-trized, -triz·ing.** —*v.i.* 研究幾何學;依幾何原理(或方法)處理。—*v.t.* 使化爲幾何圖形;使合於幾何原理。

ge·om·e·try** [dʒiˈɑmətrɪ; dʒiˈɔmitri, ˈdʒjɔm–, ˈdʒɔm–] *n., pl.* **-tries.** 幾何學。a *geometry* book. 幾何學書。analytic geometry*** 解析幾何學。***Euclidean geometry*** 歐氏幾何學。***non-Euclidean geometry*** 非歐氏幾何學。***plane geometry*** 平面幾何學。***solid geometry*** 立體幾何學。***spherical geometry*** 球面幾何學。

ge·oph·a·gy [dʒiˈɑfədʒɪ; dʒiːˈɔfədʒi] *n.* 食土(精神病的病徵, 或因饑荒地區缺糧之故)。(亦作 **geophagia, geophagism**)

ge·o·phys·i·cal [ˌdʒioˈfɪzɪkl; ˈdʒi(ː)ouˈfizikl] *adj.* 地球物理學(上)的。—**ly,** *adv.*

ge·o·phys·i·cist [ˌdʒioˈfɪzɪsɪst; ˌdʒiːouˈfizisist] *n.* 地球物理學家。

ge·o·phys·ics [ˌdʒioˈfɪzɪks; ˌdʒiːouˈfiziks] *n.* (作 *sing.* 解)地球物理學。

ge·o·phyte [ˈdʒiəˌfaɪt; ˈdʒiːəfait] *n.* 〖植物〗在地面下發芽的植物。

ge·o·pol·i·tic [ˌdʒioˈpɑlətɪk; ˌdʒiːouˈpɔlitik] *adj.* 地緣政治學的。

ge·o·po·lit·i·cal [ˌdʒiəpəˈlɪtɪkl; ˌdʒiːəpəˈlitikl] *adj.* =**geopolitic.**

ge·o·pol·i·ti·cian [ˌdʒioˌpɑləˈtɪʃən; ˌdʒiːouˌpɔliˈtiʃən] *n.* 地緣政治學者。

ge·o·pol·i·tics [ˌdʒioˈpɑlətɪks; ˌdʒiːouˈpɔlitiks] *n.* ①地緣政治學(研究地理與政治間之關係之科學)。②納粹德國之膨脹論(認爲領土應視經濟和政治需要而擴張)。

ge·o·pol·i·tist [ˌdʒioˈpɑlətɪst; ˌdʒiːouˈpɔlitist] *n.* =**geopolitician.**

ge·o·ram·a [ˌdʒiəˈrɑmə; ˌdʒiːəˈrɑːmə] *n.* 內面繪有世界地圖之空心大圓球(人立於內部看圖)。

George [dʒɔrdʒ; dʒɔːdʒ] *n.* ①英國的守護神。②〖英俚〗飛機上之自動駕駛儀。③〖英俚〗刻有 St. George 像的硬幣。④男子名。***By George!*** **a.** 表驚愕之嘆詞。**b.**(發誓語)的確! ***St. George's Day*** 守護神日(四月二十三日)。

geor·gette [dʒɔrˈdʒɛt; dʒɔːˈdʒet] *n.* 一種透明細薄縐紗。(亦作 **georgette crepe**)

Geor·gia [ˈdʒɔrdʒə, -dʒjə; ˈdʒɔːdʒjə, -dʒiə] *n.* ①喬治亞(美國南部之一州, 首府亞特蘭大 Atlanta)。②喬治亞(蘇聯高加索南部之一共和國, 全名 Georgian Soviet Socialist Republic, 首府 Jiflis)。

Geor·gi·an [ˈdʒɔrdʒən; ˈdʒɔːdʒjən] *adj.* ①英國王 George 一世至四世 (1714–1830)的。②英國國王 George 一世至四世之時期的。③該時期中之建築、藝術或裝飾之形式的。④蘇聯喬治亞共和國的;喬治亞人民、語言的或其文化的。⑤美國喬治亞州的。⑥英王 George 五世的。—*n.* ①美國喬治亞州居民。②外高加索的語言。③英王 George 時之建築、藝術或裝飾形式。

geor·gic [ˈdʒɔrdʒɪk; ˈdʒɔːdʒik] *adj.* 農業的;田園的。—*n.* 田園詩。***the Georgics*** 羅馬詩人 Virgil 所作之農事詩。

ge·o·stat·ic [ˌdʒiəˈstætɪk; ˌdʒiːəˈstætik] *adj.* 〖土木〗地壓的;土壓的;可以支持土壓的。

ge·o·stat·ics [ˌdʒiəˈstætɪks; ˌdʒiːəˈstætiks] *n.* 〖物理〗剛體靜力學。

ge·o·strat·e·gy [ˌdʒioˈstrætədʒɪ; ˌdʒiːouˈstrætidʒi] *n.* 與戰略有關之地緣政治學。

ge·o·stroph·ic [ˌdʒiəˈstrɑfɪk; ˌdʒiːəˈstrɔfik] *adj.* 〖氣象〗因地球自轉而起之風的;地轉(地球之自轉)的。

ge·o·ther·mom·e·ter [ˌdʒioθəˈmɑmətə; ˌdʒiːouθəˈmɔmitə] *n.* 地溫計。

ge·o·trop·ic [ˌdʒiəˈtrɑpɪk; ˌdʒiːəˈtrɔpik] *adj.* 〖生物〗屈地性的;關於屈地性的;受屈地性影響的;有屈地性的。

ge·ot·ro·pism [dʒiˈɑtrəˌpɪzəm; dʒiːˈɔtrəpizəm] *n.* 〖生物〗屈地性。

Ger. ①German. ②Germanic. ③Germany. **ger.** ①gerund. ②gerundive.

Ger·ald [ˈdʒɛrəld; ˈdʒerəld] *n.* 男子名。

ge·ra·ni·um [dʒəˈrenɪəm; dʒiˈreinjəm] *n.* 〖植物〗①牻牛兒。②天竺葵。③鮮紅色。

ger·fal·con [ˈdʒɝˌfɔlkən, -ˌfɔkən; ˈdʒəːˌfɔːlkən, -ˌfɔːkən] *n.* 〖動物〗白隼(產於歐洲寒帶地方的大鷹)。(亦作 **gyrfalcon**)

ger·i·at·ric [ˌdʒɛrɪˈætrɪk; ˌdʒeriˈætrik] *adj.* 老人病科的; 老人的。

ger·i·at·rics [ˌdʒɛrɪˈætrɪks; ˌdʒeriˈætriks] *n.* (作 *sing.* 解) 老人病科;老人醫學。—**ger·i·a·tri·cian, ger·i·at·rist,** *n.*

***germ** [dʒɝm; dʒəːm] *n.* ①細菌;病菌。Is this milk free from *germ?* 這奶沒有病菌嗎? ②種子;芽;胚。③原始; 根源。the *germ* of life. 生命的根源。

Germ. German; Germany.

‡Ger·man [ˈdʒɝmən; ˈdʒəːmən] *n.* ①德國人。②德語;德文。—*adj.* 德國的;德國人的;德語的。

ger·man [ˈdʒɝmən; ˈdʒəːmən] *adj.* ①關係密切的 (=germane). ②同父母的。③同祖父母的;同外祖父母的。

German Democratic Republic 德意志民主共和國(東德之正式名稱)。
ger·man·der [dʒəˈmændɚ; dʒəːˈmændə] *n.* 〖植物〗石蠶屬之植物。
ger·mane [dʒɝˈmen; dʒəːˈmein] *adj.* 有密切關係的; 恰當的。
Ger·man·ic [dʒɝˈmænɪk; dʒəːˈmænik] *adj.* ①德國的。②日耳曼民族的。
Ger·man·ism [ˈdʒɝmənˌɪzəm; ˈdʒəːmənizəm] *n.*①日耳曼精神;德國人特性。②德語語調。③親德;醉心德國。
Ger·man·ist [ˈdʒɝmənɪst; ˈdʒəːmənist] *n.* 研究德國人的生活、語言、文學的學者或專家;德國專家。
ger·ma·ni·um [dʒɝˈmenɪəm; dʒəːˈmeiniəm] *n.* 〖化〗鍺(稀金屬元素, 符號Ge)。
Ger·man·ize [ˈdʒɝməˌnaɪz; ˈdʒəːmənaiz] *v.,* **-ized, -iz·ing.** —*v.t.* ①使德國化。②譯爲德語。 —*v.i.* 採用德國人之方法、習慣等;德國化。—**Ger·man·i·za·tion,** *n.*
Ger·man·o·phile [dʒɝˈmænəˌfaɪl; dʒəːˈmænəfail] *n.* 親德(者);德國崇拜(者)。—*adj.* 親德的;崇拜德國的。
Ger·ma·no·pho·bi·a [ˌdʒɝmənəˈfobɪə; ˌdʒəːmənəˈfoubiə] *n.* 厭惡德國;恐德病。
‡Ger·ma·ny [ˈdʒɝmənɪ; ˈdʒəːməni] *n.* 德國;德意志(歐洲中北部之一國家, 1945 年德國被分成四占領區, 分別由法、英、蘇聯、美四國所占領, 1949年法、英、美三占領區合組成西德, West Germany, 以波昂 Bonn 爲首都, 蘇聯占領區組成東德, East Germany, 以東柏林 East Berlin 爲首都)。
germ bomb 細菌炸彈。
germ carrier 帶菌者。
ger·men [ˈdʒɝmɪn; ˈdʒəːmin] *n., pl.* **-mens, -mi·na** [-mɪnə; -minə]. =**germ** (現僅用於比喻)。
germ·free [ˈdʒɝmˌfri; ˈdʒəːmˈfriː, -friː] *adj.* ①無菌的。②(實驗用動物)在無菌狀態下出生, 長大的。
ger·mi·cid·al [ˌdʒɝməˈsaɪdl̩; ˌdʒəːmiˈsaidl] *adj.* 殺菌的;有殺菌力的。
ger·mi·cide [ˈdʒɝməˌsaɪd; ˈdʒəːmisaid] *n.* 殺菌劑;殺菌物。
ger·mi·cul·ture [ˈdʒɝməˌkʌltʃɚ; ˈdʒəːmiˌkʌltʃə] *n.* 細菌培養。
ger·mi·nal [ˈdʒɝmənl̩; ˈdʒəːminl] *adj.* ①幼芽的; 胚種的。the *germinal* cell. 胚種細胞。②細菌的;菌狀的。③原始的;初期的。
germinal disk 〖胚胎〗胚盤。
germinal vesicle 〖胚胎〗胚核。
ger·mi·nant [ˈdʒɝmənənt; ˈdʒəːminənt] *adj.* 萌芽的;開始發達的;有成長力的。
ger·mi·nate [ˈdʒɝməˌnet; ˈdʒəːmineit] *v.,* **-nat·ed, -nat·ing.** —*v.i.* 發芽;發育。Seeds *germinate* in the spring. 種子在春季發芽。—*v.t.* ①使發芽。②創造;使發生;使產生。
ger·mi·na·tion [ˌdʒɝməˈneʃən; ˌdʒəːmiˈneiʃən] *n.* 萌芽;發育。
ger·mi·na·tive [ˈdʒɝməˌnetɪv; ˈdʒəːminətiv] *adj.* 發芽的; 可萌發的; 有生長力的。
germ·proof [ˈdʒɝmˌpruf; ˈdʒəːmpruːf] *adj.* 抗菌的。
germ theory ①細菌病源論。②生命由細胞發展論。
ger·on·toc·ra·cy [ˌdʒɛrənˈtɑkrəsɪ; ˌdʒerənˈtɔkrəsi] *n., pl.* **-cies.** ①老年人統治;老人政治。②老年人組織之統治機構。
ger·on·tol·o·gy [ˌdʒɛrənˈtɑlədʒɪ; ˌdʒerənˈtɔlədʒi] *n.* 老人醫學。 —**ge·ron·to·log·i·cal,** *adj.* —**ger·on·tol·o·gist,**
ger·ry·man·der [ˈgɛrɪˌmændɚ; ˈdʒerimændə] *v.t.* & *v.i.* ①〖美〗〖政治〗 己黨之利益擅自改劃(州、郡等之選區)。② 公平地操縱;竄改以獲非分之利益。—*n.* 爲 黨之利益所作之選區的擅自改畫。
ger·trude [ˈgɝtrud; ˈgəːtruːd] *n.* 兒外衣(棉製, 兩肩釘有鈕扣)。
***ger·und** [ˈdʒɛrənd, -ʌnd; ˈdʒerənd, -rʌnd] *n.* 〖文法〗動名詞 (即 v.+ing 作 詞用者, 如 seeing, believing)。
gerund grinder 〖俗〗①拉丁文法 師。②學究; 腐儒。
ge·run·di·al [dʒəˈrʌndɪəl; dʒəˈrʌndiəl] *adj.* ①動名詞的。②作動名詞用的。
ge·run·dive [dʒəˈrʌndɪv; dʒiˈrʌndiv] *adj.* 動名詞的。—*n.* 〖拉〗動詞狀形容詞。
ges·so [ˈdʒɛso; ˈdʒesou] *n.* (雕刻、繪 用之) 石膏 (粉)。
gest(e) [dʒɛst; dʒest] *n.* ①冒險故事; 功故事。②冒險;武功;功績。
Ge·stalt [gəˈʃtɑlt; gəˈʃtɑːlt] *n., p* **-stalt·en** [-ˈʃtɑltən; -ˈʃtɑːltən]. 〖德〗〖 理〗形態 (經驗之統一的全體)。***Gestalt psychology*** 形態心理學; 格式塔心理學。
Ge·sta·po [gəˈstɑpo; gesˈtɑːpou] 蓋世太保(納粹德國之祕密警察)。
ges·tate [ˈdʒɛstet; ˈdʒesteit] *v.t.* & *v.i.* **-tat·ed, -tat·ing.** ①懷孕;孕育。②醞釀(畫);在腦海中形成。
ges·ta·tion [dʒɛsˈteʃən; dʒesˈteiʃən] *n.* ①懷孕。the *gestation* period. 懷孕期。②(計畫在腦中的)孕育;形成;發展。
ges·tic·u·lar [dʒɛsˈtɪkjəlɚ; dʒesˈtikjulə] *adj.* 表情或達意之動作的。
ges·tic·u·late [dʒɛsˈtɪkjəˌlet; dʒesˈtikjuleit] *v.,* **-lat·ed, -lat·ing.** —*v.i.* 做 情或達意的動作或姿態。—*v.t.* 以動作表達。
ges·tic·u·la·tion [ˌdʒɛstɪkjəˈleʃən; dʒesˌtikjuˈleiʃən] *n.* 表情或達意的動作; 手勢;姿態。
ges·tic·u·la·tive [dʒɛsˈtɪkjəˌletɪv; dʒesˈtikjulətiv] *adj.* 做姿態 (手勢)的;以 勢或姿態表示的;指手畫脚的。—**ly,** *adv.*
ges·tic·u·la·to·ry [dʒɛsˈtɪkjələˌtorɪ; dʒesˈtikjuleitəri] *adj.* =**gesticulative.**
***ges·ture** [ˈdʒɛstʃɚ; ˈdʒestʃə] *n., v.,* **-tured, -tur·ing.** —*n.* ①手勢;表情;姿勢 to make a friendly *gesture.* 作友善的手 勢。②姿態; 表示。His resignation wa merely a *gesture.* 他的辭職只是一種姿態。—*v.i.* 作手勢。 —*v.t.* 以手勢來表達。 She *gestured* her intention of joining them by waving from the balcony. 她從陽臺 上揮手示意她要參加他們。
‡get [gɛt; get] *v.,* **got, got** or **got·ten get·ting,** *n.* —*v.t.* ①得到; 獲得; 收到。Where did you *get* the money? 你從哪 裏弄到的錢? ②得(病); 患(病)。I have *got* a bad cold. 我得了重感冒。③取;索。I am going to *get* my hat from the other room. 我從另一間房內取來我的帽子。④購 買;定購。Will you *get* one for me? 你願 意替我購買一件嗎?⑤使;令。I am going to *get* (=have) my hair cut. 我要去理髮。⑥說服;促使。We *got* him to speak. 我 們叫他講話。⑦弄;搞;放;置;搬;移。Try to *get* these things out of the way. 設法 把這些東西都移開。I want to *get* these

chairs upstairs. 我想把這些椅子搬到樓上去。⑧穿〖on〗. The coat was so small that he couldn't *get* it on. 這件衣服太小,他穿不上。⑨瞭解;明白。I don't *get* what you mean. 我不明白你的意思是甚麼。⑩使困惑;難住。This problem *gets* me. 這問題把我難住了。⑪準備;做。Jane helped her mother *get* dinner. Jane 幫忙他母親做飯。⑫生產;生育(通常指動物)。I had rather adopt a child than *get* it. 我寧願收養一個孩子而不願生孩子。⑬射中;擊中。The bullet *got* the soldier in the arm. 子彈打中那兵的臂。⑭〖俗〗殺;殺死。It *got* them in the end. 那終於弄死他們。⑮捉住;捕獲。The police *got* the thief. 警察把賊抓住。⑯使…有孕。to *get* a woman with child. 使一女人有孕。 —*v.i.* ①變成;變得;成爲(=become)(常與形容詞的比較級連用)。It is *getting* colder. 天氣漸漸變冷了。②回到;去到;達到;抵達(=go, come, etc.). Can we *get* to the station in time? 我們能够及時趕到車站嗎? Your letter *got* here yesterday. 你的信昨天到了這兒(昨天收到你的信)。***get about*** a. 行動。He *gets about* quickly. 他行動快。b. 走動。c. 旅行。He *gets about* a great deal. 他常旅行。d. 散播。***get above oneself*** 自視很高;自傲。***get abroad*** 散傳;傳播;流布。***get across*** a. 使人了解。He was unable to *get across* to the group what he meant. 他無法使大家了解他的意思。b. 成功。c. 使渡過;使橫過。d. 說服。***get after*** a. 責罵。b. 敦促。***get ahead*** 前進;成功;長進。He *got ahead* by sheer determination. 他完全靠毅力成功。***get ahead of*** 超過;勝過。***get along*** a. 進展。How are you *getting along?* 您好嗎? b. 相處。They *get along* well together. 他們相處甚好。c. 走;離開。It's time for me to *get along*. 是我該走的時候了。d. 成功;繁榮。e. 度日;過活。We can't *get along* without money. 沒有錢我們無法度日。***get along in years*** 變老;老了。***get along with*** a. 與人相處。He doesn't *get along with* anybody in the office. 他與辦公室裏任何人都合不來。b. 進步。c. 滾開。*Get along with* you! 滾蛋!胡說! ***get around*** a. 走動(=get about). b. 規避。c. 傳播。d. 征服;影響;說服;哄騙;得寵於。***get around to*** 找到時間做;注意及。***get at*** a. 得到。b. 意指。What are you *getting at?* 你意何所指? c. 了解;發現。d. 賄賂。***get away*** a. 逃脫。b. 出發旅行;開始度假。***get (a thing) away*** 移動(某物);移去。***get away with*** 逃避懲罰。***get back*** a. 回來。b. 取回。c. 〖俚〗報仇〖常at〗。***get behind*** a. (在工作、功課等方面)落後。b. 支持;贊助。***get by*** a. 躲過。b. 勉強及格。c. 通過;走過。***get down*** a. 取下。Go to the cupboard and *get down* the jam. 到櫃櫥去把果醬取下來。b. 下來。c. 吞下。d. 使疲倦;使無精神。***get down to (one's work)*** 靜下心(工作)。***get even with*** 〖俗〗報復。I'll *get even with* him sooner or later. 我遲早要向他報復。***get going*** a. 開始。It's past seven—we must *get going*. 過七點了——我們必須開始了。b. 趕緊;加快。If we don't *get going*, we'll never arrive in time. 如果我們不趕緊,我們將無法及時到達。***get his (hers, yours, etc.)*** 受其應受之獎賞或懲罰。***get hold of*** 〖俗〗得到;找到;把握住。Can you *get hold of* the manager? 你能找到經理嗎? I'll explain, and you'll *get hold of* the idea. 我一加解釋,你就可把握住這個概念了。***get home*** a. 到家。b. 中肯;被了解。That remark *got home*. 那個評論中肯。***get (a person) home*** 送(某人)回家。He's drunk; we'd better *get him home*. 他醉了,我們最好送他回家。***get in*** a. 進入。b. 回家。At what time did he *get in?* 他甚麼時候回家的? c. 加入。d. 進站;到達。What time does the train from Taipei *get in?* 從臺北來的火車何時進站? e. 進貨。f. 當選。g. 收割。The farmers were busy *getting in* the crops. 農夫們正忙於收割莊稼。h. 收回(借款)。i. 牽涉。***get into*** a. 穿起。b. 使醉;(酒)衝(頭)。The whisky *got into* his head. 威士忌使他頭暈腦脹。c. 相信;認爲。d. 發現;學會。You'll soon *get into* the way of doing it. 你會立刻學會如何做。e. 控制。***get in with*** 與…交往;參加;加入。***get it*** a. 受責;受罰。b. 瞭解;懂得。This is just between us, *get it?* 這件事不可讓第三者知道,你懂得嗎? ***get next to*** 變成與…熟識。***get off*** a. 下去;下車。b. 脫下。c. 付郵。*Get* this letter *off* by the first post. 把這封信交第一班郵遞寄出去。d. 起身;動身。e. 開始。He couldn't *get off* to sleep. 他不能入睡。f. 獲釋;被原諒;不受處罰。g. 講(笑話)。h. 講演。i. 送走。j. 使入睡。She *got* the baby *off* (to sleep) at last. 她最後總算把嬰兒哄睡着了。***get off on the wrong foot*** 作了錯誤的開端;一開始就給人壞印象;出師不利。***get off to a flying start*** 成功地開始;一開始卽順利;出師先捷。***get on*** a. 進步。You are *getting on* nicely with your English. 你的英文進步很順利。b. 痊癒。She was very ill, but she is now *getting on* nicely. 她的病很重,但是她現在大見痊癒。c. 登上;騎上;爬上。I *get on* the train every morning at 7:30. 我每天早晨七點半上火車。d. 相處。They *get on* very well together. 他們相處甚好。e. 成功;繁榮。He's sure to *get on* in life. 他一定會成功。f. 變老;老了。g. 接近;邁進(常用進行式)。He's *getting on* for seventy. 他近七十歲了。h. 使進步。He's very good at *getting* his pupils *on*. 他善於督促學生進步。***get one's hand in*** 熟練;習慣。***get one's own back on (a person)*** 向(某人)報復;報仇。***get one's second wind*** 重獲精力;重新鼓起精神。***get on in years*** =**get along in years.** ***get on one's nerves*** 使人受刺激而感到不安。Turn off that radio; it's *getting on my nerves*. 關上收音機罷,它使我精神不安。***get on the ball*** 注意;留心;警惕。***get out*** a. 下車。b. 洩露出去。c. 出版。***get out of*** a. 放棄;棄絕。You should *get out of* that bad habit. 你應該棄絕那壞習慣。b. 使說出;得自。I could *get* nothing *out of* him. 我不能使他說出任何消息。c. 躲閃;避免。He decided to *get out of* attending school. 他決定不去上學(逃學)。***get over*** a. 恢復;痊癒。It took me a long time to *get over* my cold. 過了好久,我的傷風才好。b. 趨訪。I'll try to *get over* to see you sometime next week. 下星期我得空就去拜訪你。c. 躲開。d. 克服。Here is a difficulty for you to *get over*. 這裏有一樁困難要你克

服。e. 越過。f. 做完;完成。g.〖俗〗成功。h. 使清晰易解。*get rid of* 去掉。We shall be glad to *get rid of* him. 擺脫掉他,我們將很高興。*get round* =get around. *get set* 準備。*get someone's goat* 煩擾某人;激怒某人。That constant hammering *got his goat*. 那連續不斷的鎚打聲擾亂了他。*get something down cold* 深知某事物;牢記某事物。*get something over with* 做完。*get there*〖俗〗成功。*get through* a. 完成。b. 及格。Did you *get through* the exam? 你考試及格了嗎? c. 抵達。I started as soon as your message *got through* to me. 一接到你的信我就立刻開始了。d. 通過。e. 用盡。*get to* a. 開始;着手。We must *get to* work. 我們必須開始工作。b.〖美俚〗賄賂(某人)。c. 接觸。d. 造成印象。*get together* a. 聚首。b. 聚集;積聚。c.〖俗〗達成協議。*get* (*a thing*) *under* a. 控制。b. 鎮服。*get up* a. 起床。I shall *get up* at seven o'clock tomorrow. 我明天要在七點起床。*Get* the children *up*. 叫孩子們起床。b. 準備;籌劃。c. 艶裝;穿起。d. 起來。e. 唸到;讀到。f. 追及;勝過。g. 變强;增加速度。h. 鼓勵;激勵。i. 獲悉。j. 清洗。*get up out of the wrong side of the bed* 情緒不佳;不愉快。*have got*〖俗〗a. 有(=have). *Have* you *got* a newspaper? 你有報紙嗎? b. 必須;得;該(與不定詞連用)。I *have got* to go to the doctor's. 我得看病去。—*n.* ①動物的後代;後裔。②難接的回球(如網球)。③生殖。④〖英俚〗a. 私生子。b. 贏利;薪資。What's your week's *get?* 你的週薪多少?〖注意〗今日英語趨勢,口語上常用 get 作爲被動式助動詞以代替 be, 使語氣加强: We all *got* punished. 我們全體被罰。

get·at·a·ble 〔gɛt'ætəbḷ; get'ætəbl〕 *adj.* 可達到的;易接近的;可得到的。

get·a·way 〔'gɛtə͵we; 'getəwei〕 *n.*〖俗〗①逃走;逃亡。②起跑;開始(賽跑)。

Geth·sem·a·ne 〔gɛθ'sɛmənɪ; geθ'seməni〕 *n.*〖聖經〗客西馬尼 (Jerusalem 附近之一花園,耶穌被出賣被捕之地)。

get-out 〔'gɛt͵aut; 'getaut〕 *n.* ①〖商〗虧盈兩相抵。②〖英〗躲避困難或窮局的手段。③〖美俗〗退路;下場的手段。*as all get-out* 最;極。

get-rich-quick 〔'gɛt 'rɪtʃ 'kwɪk; 'get-ritʃ'kwik〕 *adj.*〖美〗(利用別人的投機心理而想)一攫千金的;投機致富的。

get-to·geth·er 〔'gɛttu͵gɛðə; 'gettu͵geðə〕 *n.*〖美俗〗①非正式的社交集會;聯歡會。②會議。

get-tough 〔'gɛt'tʌf; 'get'tʌf〕 *adj.* (遇到困難時)採取强硬手段的。

Get·tys·burg 〔'gɛtɪz͵bɝg; 'getizbə:g〕 *n.* 蓋茨堡(美國 Pennsylvania 州南部之一鎭,南北戰爭時南軍於1863年7月 1–3日於該處被北軍擊敗)。*Gettysburg Address* 林肯於1863年11月19日在 Gettysburg 所作闡述民主主義精神之演說。

get·up 〔'gɛt͵ʌp; 'getʌp〕 *n.*〖俗〗①(書的)裝訂形式。②服式;裝束。③外觀;外表。

Ge·um 〔'dʒiəm; 'dʒi:əm〕 *n.*〖植物〗①水楊梅屬。②(g-) 水楊梅屬植物;水楊梅。

gew·gaw 〔'gjugɔ; 'gju:gɔ:〕 *n.* 華麗而無價值之物;小擺飾;玩具。—*adj.* 虛華而無價值的。(亦作 **geegaw**)

gey·ser 〔'gaɪzə, 'gaɪsə *for*①, 'gizə *for* ②; 'gaizə *for* ①,'gi:zə *for* ②〕 *n.* ①間歇泉。②〖英〗熱水鍋爐。—**al,** —**ic,** *adj.*

gey·ser·ite 〔'gaɪzə͵raɪt; 'gaizərait〕 *n.*〖礦〗矽華。

G-force 〔'dʒi͵fors; 'dʒi:fɔ:s〕 *n.* 地心吸力對人或物所產生之力;火箭或飛機速度改變時人體之反應力。

Gha·na 〔'gɑnə; 'gɑ:nə〕 *n.* 迦納 (非洲西部一國家, 首都阿克拉 Accra). —**ian, Gha·nan, Gha·ni·an,** *n., adj.*

ghar·ri, ghar·ry 〔'gærɪ;'gæri〕 *n., pl.* **-ries.**〖印度〗馬車;出租馬車。

***ghast·ly** 〔'gæstlɪ, 'gɑst-; 'gɑ:stli〕 *adj.,* **-li·er, -li·est,** *adv.* —*adj.* ①可怕的;可怖的。Murder is a *ghastly* crime. 殺人是可怕的罪行。②面色慘白的;面如死人的。③〖俗〗驚人的。a *ghastly* failure. 驚人的失敗;大失敗。④很壞的;令人不快的。—*adv.*(亦作**ghastlily, ghastily**) 可怖地;慘白地。—**ghastli·ness,** *n.*

ghat, ghaut 〔gɔt;gɔ:t〕〖印度〗*n.* ①山路。②山脈。③(爲船靠岸、水浴等而設的) 河邊的石階。*burning ghat* 河邊的火葬場。

gha·zi 〔'gɑzi; 'gɑ:zi:〕 *n., pl.* **-zis.** ①回教徒之士兵 (尤指與非回教徒作戰者)。②(G-) 土耳其給凱旋歸來的蘇丹或將軍的封號。

ghee 〔gi; gi:〕〖印度〗*n.* (水牛的) 奶油(烹飪用)。

gher·kin 〔'gɝkɪn; 'gə:kin〕 *n.* 小胡瓜;未熟之黃瓜。

ghet·to 〔'gɛto; 'getou〕 *n., pl.* **-tos, -toes.** ①(城市中)猶太人之居住區。②城市中任何民族聚居的區域。③〖美〗城市中黑人, 波多黎各人或其他少數民族聚居的區域。

Ghib·el·line 〔'gɪbḷɪn; 'gibilain〕 *n.* 吉伯林黨員。*the Ghibellines* 吉伯林黨;保皇黨(中古神聖羅馬帝國中反抗教皇黨而擁護德國皇帝之黨派)。—*adj.* 吉伯林黨的。

***ghost** 〔gost; goust〕 *n.* ①鬼;靈魂。Do you like *ghost* stories? 你喜歡鬼故事嗎? ②一些;一絲;一點。not the *ghost* of a chance. 一點機會也沒有;一點希望也沒有。③〖攝影〗假像。④血影細胞。*give up the ghost*〖古〗死。*the ghost walks* 發餉之日(原爲戲院中俚語)。This is the day *the ghost walks.* 今天是發餉日。*the Holy Ghost*〖宗教〗聖靈。—*v.t.* ①爲人代筆。②(鬼) 出沒。—*v.i.* 做 *ghost* writer; 爲人代筆。—*adj.* 僻遠的。—**i·ly,** *adv.*

ghost·like 〔'gost͵laɪk; 'goustlaik〕 *adj. & adv.* 似幽靈的(地);似鬼怪的(地);可怖的(地)。

ghost·ly 〔'gostlɪ;'goustli〕 *adj.,* **-li·er, -li·est.** ①似鬼的; 鬼狀的。②精神的; 宗教的。—**ghost·li·ness,** *n.*

ghost·write 〔'gost͵raɪt;'goust-rait〕 *v.t. & v.i.,* **-wrote, -writ·ing.** 爲人代筆。

ghost writer 爲人代筆的作者。(亦作 **ghostwriter**)

ghoul 〔gul; gu:l, gaul〕 *n.* ①(東方神話中的) 食屍鬼。②盜屍的人。③有令人憎懼或特殊習性的人。

ghoul·ish 〔'gulɪʃ; 'gu:liʃ, 'gauliʃ〕 *adj.* 食屍鬼似的;殘忍的;可怖的。

GHQ, G.H.Q. General Headquarters.

ghyll 〔gɪl; gil〕 *n.* 峽谷;谿。

G.I., GI 〔'dʒi'aɪ; 'dʒi:'ai〕 *adj., n., pl.* **G.I.'s, GI's or GIs,** *v.,* **GI'd, GI'ing.** —*adj.* ①美國陸軍的; 由美國陸軍補給部所發出的 (Government Issue 之縮寫)。②〖俗〗服從規定的;標準的。—*n.*〖俗〗美國兵。*GI*

Jane 美國女兵。*GI Joe* 美國大兵。—*v.t.* 爲檢閱而打掃。—*v.i.* 遵守軍中規定,習慣。

G.I. ①galvanized iron. ②gastrointestinal. ③ general issue. ④government issue. **Gi** gilbert; gilberts. **gi.** gill; gills.

‡gi·ant [ˈdʒaɪənt; ˈdʒaiənt] *n.* ①巨人;大力士; 偉人。②巨大的怪物。—*adj.* 龐大的;巨大的。a *giant* cabbage. 一棵巨大的捲心菜。—**like,** *adj.*

gi·ant·ess [ˈdʒaɪəntɪs; ˈdʒaiəntis] *n.* 「女巨人。」

gi·ant·ism [ˈdʒaɪəntɪzm; ˈdʒaiəntizm] *n.* 〖醫〗頎長病;巨大畸形。

giant powder 一種炸山用的炸藥。

giaour [dʒaur; ˈdʒauə] *n.* 邪教徒;異教徒(回教徒對基督徒的蔑稱)。

gib¹ [gɪb; gib] *n., v.,* **gibbed, gib·bing.** —*n.* ①產卵期後之雄鮭魚下顎之鉤狀彎曲。②凹字楔;凹字榫。—*v.t.* 用凹字楔結牢。

gib² *n.* 貓之暱稱;(特指經去勢之)雄貓。

Gib. Gibraltar.

gib·ber [ˈdʒɪbɚ, ˈgɪbɚ; ˈdʒibə] *v.i.* & *v.t.* 嘰哩呱啦而言;喋喋而言。—*n.* 嘰哩呱啦之言語。

gib·ber·ish [ˈdʒɪbərɪʃ, ˈgɪb-; ˈgibəriʃ, ˈdʒib-] *n.* 快而不清的言語;亂語。

gib·bet [ˈdʒɪbɪt; ˈdʒibit] *n., v.,* **-bet·ed, -bet·ing.** —*n.* 絞架;絞臺。—*v.t.* ①吊於絞架上。②公開侮辱或嘲弄。③絞死。

Gib·bon [ˈgɪbən; ˈgibən] *n.* 吉朋(Edward, 1737–1794, 英國歷史家)。

gib·bon [ˈgɪbən; ˈgibən] *n.* 長臂猿(特指東南亞及東印度者)。

gib·bos·i·ty [gɪˈbɑsətɪ; giˈbɔsiti] *n., pl.* **-ties.** ①凸圓;凸彎曲。②圓形凸出;隆起。③駝背。

gib·bous [ˈgɪbəs; ˈgibəs] *adj.* ①圓形凸出的;凸狀的;隆起的。②(月等天體在半月後)滿月前之形狀的;凸圓(大於半圓)的。③駝背的;佝僂的。(亦作 **gibbose**)

gibe [dʒaɪb; dʒaib] *v.,* **gibed, gib·ing,** *n.* —*v.i.* & *v.t.* 譏笑;嘲弄。—*n.* 嘲弄;辱罵。(亦作 **jibe**) —**gib·ing·ly,** *adv.*

gib·er [ˈdʒaɪbɚ; ˈdʒaibə] *n.* 嘲笑者。

gib·ing [ˈdʒaɪbɪŋ; ˈdʒaibiŋ] *adj.* 譏刺的;諷嘲的。—**ly,** *adv.*

gib·lets [ˈdʒɪblɪts; ˈdʒiblits] *n. pl.* 禽類內臟等之雜碎;鷄、鴨、鵝的雜碎。

Gi·bral·tar [dʒɪbˈrɔltɚ; dʒiˈbrɔːltə] *n.* ①直布羅陀(西班牙南端之地區,爲英國之殖民地及要塞)。②(作普通名詞用)堅固的要塞;牢不可破之地。***the Strait of Gibraltar*** 直布羅陀海峽。

gi·bus [ˈdʒaɪbəs; ˈdʒaibəs, ˈdʒib-] *n., pl.* **-bus·es.** 一種可摺疊之綢質高帽。(亦作 **gibus hat**)

gid·dy** [ˈgɪdɪ; ˈgidi] *adj.,* **-di·er, -di·est,** *v.,* **-died, -dy·ing.** —*adj.* ①頭暈的;眩暈的。It makes me *giddy* to turn round quickly. 轉得太快使我頭暈。②使人頭暈的。to look down from a *giddy* height. 從一個令人頭暈的高處往下看。③輕佻的。④無聊的。play*** (or ***act***) ***the giddy goat*** 〖俗〗做傻事。—*v.t.* & *v.i.* (使)頭暈。—**gid·di·ly,** *adv.* —**gid·di·ness,** *n.*

gid·dy-go-round [ˈgɪdɪgoˌraund; ˈgidigouˌraund] *n.* 〖英〗轉盤;廻轉木馬(=merry-go-round).

Gide [ʒid; ʒiːd] *n.* 紀德(André, 1869–1951, 法國小說家、批評家及散文家, 1947年得諾貝爾獎)。

Gid·e·on [ˈgɪdɪən; ˈgidiən] *n.* 〖聖經〗「基甸(以色列之英雄)。」

‡gift [gɪft; gift] *n.* ①禮物。birthday and Christmas *gifts.* 生日和聖誕禮物。②贈予。The house came to him by *gift* from an uncle. 這房子是他的一個伯父的贈予。③贈予之權利。④天才;天賦;天資。to have a *gift* for poetry. 有詩的天才。a person of many *gifts.* 多才多藝者。***by gift*** 贈送地。***gift of gab*** 口才;雄辯之才。—*v.t.* 賦與(才能)(常用被動式)。We are all *gifted* with a conscience. 我們大家皆生而具有良心。—**less,** *adj.*

gift book 寄贈書;贈閱本。

gift certificate (百貨公司等之)禮券。

***gift·ed** [ˈgɪftɪd; ˈgiftid] *adj.* 有天才的。a *gifted* musician. 有天才的音樂家。—**ly,** *adv.* —**ness,** *n.*

gig¹ [gɪg; gig] *n., v.,* **gigged, gig·ging.** —*n.* ①二輪單馬車。②(大船上之)輕便小艇。③旋轉的東西;陀螺。—*v.i.* 乘坐二輪單馬車。

gig² *n., v.,* **gigged, gig·ging.** —*n.* 魚叉。—*v.t.* & *v.i.* 以魚叉捉(魚)。

giga- 〖字首〗表"十億"之義。

***gi·gan·tic** [dʒaɪˈgæntɪk; dʒaiˈgæntik] *adj.* 巨大的;龐大的;似巨人的。He has a *gigantic* appetite and eats *gigantic* meals. 他有很大的食量,能吃很多的食物。—**al·ly,** *adv.* —**ism,** —**ness,** *n.*

***gig·gle** [ˈgɪgl̩; ˈgigl] *n., v.,* **-gled, -gling.** —*n.* 傻笑。—*v.i.* 格格地笑。The girls *giggled.* 女孩子們格格地笑。

gig·gly [ˈgɪglɪ; ˈgigli] *adj.,* **-gli·er, -gli·est.** 好傻笑的;格格而笑的。

gig·man [ˈgɪgmən; ˈgigmən] *n., pl.* **-men.** ①有二輪馬車之人。②庸俗的人。

gig·o·lo [ˈdʒɪgəˌlo; ˈdʒigəlou] *n., pl.* **-los.** ①職業的男舞伴;婦女之男伴。②靠女子贍養之男人;吃軟飯之人。

gig·ot [ˈdʒɪgət; ˈdʒigət] *n.* ①(食用之)羊腿。②羊腿形袖子。

Gi·la monster [ˈhilə~; ˈhiːlə~] (美國 New Mexico 州, Arizona 州等之沙漠地方的)大毒蜥蜴。

gil·bert [ˈgɪlbɚt; ˈgilbət] *n.* 〖電〗吉伯(磁通勢 magnetomotive force 的單位)。

Gil·ber·ti·an [gɪlˈbɝtɪən; gilˈbəːtjən] *adj.* ①吉柏特 (Sir William Schwenck Gilbert, 1836–1911, 英國喜劇作家)的。②有吉柏特之輕鬆歌劇作風的;滑稽的。

gild¹** [gɪld; gild] *v.t.,* **gild·ed** or **gilt, gild·ing.** ①鍍金;給…鍍金。②虛飾;文飾。gild the pill*** 給藥丸鍍金;(引喻)虛飾外觀。***gild the refined gold*** 作多餘之事。

gild² *n.* =**guild.**

gild·ed [ˈgɪldɪd; ˈgildid] *adj.* ①貼金箔的;塗金(粉)的;鍍金的;塗成金色的。*gilded* spurs. 金馬刺。②富有的;富豪的。*gilded* youth. 大少爺;紈袴子弟。

Gilded Chamber 〖英〗上院。

gild·ing [ˈgɪldɪŋ; ˈgildiŋ] *n.* ①鍍金;塗金。②鍍金或塗金之材料(如金粉等)。③(對不愉快事實等之)表面的裝飾;粉飾。④外表。

***gill¹** [gɪl; gil] *n.* ①鰓。②(*pl.*)〖植物〗菌鰓;菌褶。③(*pl.*)頤邊肉;顎下肉。to look rosy (blue) about the *gills.* 呈健康(虛弱)之色。to turn red in the *gills.* 發怒。④家禽頸下之垂肉。—*v.t.* ①用刺網捕魚。②洗(魚)。③除去(菌鰓)。—**ed,** *adj.*

gill² [dʒɪl; dʒil] *n.* 液量名(=$^{1}/_{4}$ pint).

gill³ 〔dʒɪl; dʒil〕 *n.* 少女；愛人。(亦作 **jill**)
gill⁴ 〔gɪl; gil〕 *n.* (樹木繁盛的)峽谷；(峽谷中的)溪流。(亦作 **ghyll**)
gil·lie, gil·ly 〔ˈgɪlɪ; ˈgili〕 *n., pl.* **-lies.** ①(昔蘇格蘭高地之)酋長之從僕。②(蘇格蘭高地之)獵人之從僕。③一種婦女運動鞋。
gill net (捕魚用之)刺網。
gill-net 〔ˈgɪlˌnɛt; ˈgilnet〕 *v.t. & v.i.,* **-net·ted, -net·ting.** 用刺網捕魚。
gil·ly·flow·er 〔ˈdʒɪlɪˌflauə; ˈdʒiliˌflauə〕 *n.* 紫羅蘭。
***gilt¹** 〔gɪlt; gilt〕 *v.* pt. & pp. of **gild.** —*n.* ①(鍍於他物上之)鍍金。The *gilt* is coming off this frame. 這框子上的鍍金在逐漸脫落。②表面的裝飾；無深度的修飾。—*adj.* 鍍(燙)金的。a book with a *gilt* top. 頂端燙金的書。
gilt² *n.* 幼母豬。
gilt-edged 〔ˈgɪltˈɛdʒd; ˈgilt-edʒd〕 *adj.* ①邊緣塗金的；(紙、書籍等)金邊的。②(證券等)上等的。③極佳的。(亦作 **gilt-edge**)
gim·bals 〔ˈdʒɪmbl̩z; ˈdʒimbəlz〕 *n. pl.* (羅盤針的)平衡圈環。
gim·crack 〔ˈdʒɪmˌkræk; ˈdʒimkræk〕 *n.* 虛華而無用之物；玩物。—*adj.* ①虛華而無用的。②草率製成的。(亦作 **jimcrack**)
gim·let 〔ˈgɪmlɪt; ˈgimlit〕 *n.* 螺絲錐；鑽子。eyes like *gimlets.* 銳利的眼。—*v.t.* 以鑽子鑽(孔)。
gimlet eye 銳眼。
gim·mick 〔ˈgɪmɪk; ˈgimik〕 *n.* 〖美俚〗①(魔術師等之)祕密裝置。②巧妙的小機械；新發明之物件。③噱頭。
gimp 〔gɪmp; gimp〕 *n.* 絨絲帶；棉帶(有時以金屬絲為心織成)。
***gin¹** 〔dʒɪn; dʒin〕 *n.* 杜松子酒。
gin² *n., v.,* **ginned, gin·ning.** —*n.* ①軋棉機。②舉或拉重物之裝置(如絞盤等)。③陷阱。—*v.t.* ①析出(棉花之籽)。②誘陷。
gin·ge·li 〔ˈdʒɪndʒəlɪ; ˈdʒindʒəli〕 *n., pl.* **-lis.** =**gingili.**
gin·gel·ly 〔ˈdʒɪndʒəlɪ; ˈdʒindʒəli〕 *n., pl.* **-lies.** =**gingili.**
***gin·ger** 〔ˈdʒɪndʒə; ˈdʒindʒə〕 *n.* ①薑。②〖俗〗活潑；精力；元氣。There is no *ginger* in him. 他沒有精神。③淡赤黃色。—*adj.* 淡赤黃色的。—*v.t.* ①使活潑；使有生氣〖up〗. to *ginger* up a performance. 使表演生動活潑。②以薑佐…之味。
ginger ale (or **beer**) 薑汁汽水。
***gin·ger·bread** 〔ˈdʒɪndʒəˌbrɛd; ˈdʒindʒəbred〕 *n.* ①薑餅。②好看而無實質之物；俗艷而無用的飾物。—*adj.* 好看而不值錢的；俗艷而無用的；虛華的。
gin·ger·ly 〔ˈdʒɪndʒəlɪ; ˈdʒindʒəli〕 *adj. & adv.* 極度小心謹慎的(地)。(亦作 **ginger**)
gin·ger·nut 〔ˈdʒɪndʒəˌnʌt; ˈdʒindʒənʌt〕 *n.* 薑汁餅乾。(亦作 **gingerbread nut**)
ginger pop =**ginger ale.**
gin·ger·race 〔ˈdʒɪndʒəˌres; ˈdʒindʒəreis〕 *n.* 生薑之根。(亦作 **ginger root**)
gin·ger·snap 〔ˈdʒɪndʒəˌsnæp; ˈdʒindʒəsnæp〕 *n.* 一種以杜松子酒作香料，加糖漿的薄脆餅乾。
gin·ger·y 〔ˈdʒɪndʒərɪ; ˈdʒindʒəri〕 *adj.* ①薑的；有薑味的；辛辣的。②薑色(赤黃色)的。③活潑的；精力充沛的。
ging·ham 〔ˈgɪŋəm; ˈgiŋəm〕 *n.* 有條紋或方格紋的棉布。—*adj.* 有條紋或方格紋之棉布所製的。
gin·gi·li 〔ˈdʒɪndʒəlɪ; ˈdʒindʒəli〕 *n., pl.* **-lis.** ①芝蔴(樹)。②芝蔴籽。③芝蔴油。
gin·gi·val 〔dʒɪnˈdʒaɪvl̩, ˈdʒɪndʒəvl̩; dʒinˈdʒaivəl〕 *adj.* ①齒齦的。②〖語音〗齒齦的；齒槽的。—*n.* 〖語音〗齒齦音；齒槽音。
ging·ko, gink·go 〔ˈgɪŋko, ˈdʒɪ-; ˈgiŋkou〕 *n., pl.* **-koes, -goes.** 銀杏；白果樹。
gink 〔gɪŋk; giŋk〕 *n.* 〖美俚〗傢伙；人。
gin·ner 〔ˈdʒɪnə; ˈdʒinə〕 *n.* 軋棉工人。
gin·seng 〔ˈdʒɪnsɛŋ; ˈdʒinseŋ〕 *n.* ①人參；高麗參。②人參之根(中國人用之作藥物)。
Gin·za, the 〔ˈgɪnzə; ˈginzə〕 *n.* 銀座(東京之街道，以夜總會、酒吧等而聞名)。
Gio·con·da, La 〔dʒoˈkɑndə, dʒoˈkondɑ; dʒouˈkɔndə, dʒouˈkoundɑː〕〖義〗 *n.* =**Mona Lisa.**
gip·po 〔ˈdʒɪpo; ˈdʒipou〕 *n.* 〖軍俚〗菜湯；肉湯；燉肉。
***Gip·sy** 〔ˈdʒɪpsɪ; ˈdʒipsi〕 *n., pl.* **-sies,** *adj.* =**Gypsy.**
***gi·raffe** 〔dʒəˈræf, -ˈrɑf; dʒiˈrɑːf, -ˈræf〕 *n.* 長頸鹿。
gir·an·dole 〔ˈdʒɪrənˌdol; ˈdʒirəndoul〕 *n.* ①多枝燭架。②旋轉煙火。③旋轉噴水。④大寶石周圍有小寶石裝飾的垂飾或耳飾。
gir·a·sol 〔ˈdʒɪrəˌsɑl; ˈdʒirəsɔl〕 *n.* 〖礦〗火蛋白石。(亦作 **girasole**)
***gird¹** 〔gɝd; gəːd〕 *v.,* **girt** or **gird·ed, gird·ing.** —*v.t.* ①以帶束緊；束縛。to *gird* the waist with a sash. 以飾帶束腰。②繫以帶；配以帶。③佩帶。④圍繞；圍起。a sea-*girt* isle. 海中小島。⑤賦予；給予。to be *girt* with supreme power. 被賦予最高權力。⑥準備從事〖常 up〗. to *gird* up one's loins. 鼓起勇氣；磨劍以待。—*v.i.* 磨劍以待。He *girded* for a rough fight. 他磨劍以待更艱苦的戰鬥。
gird² *n.* 冷笑；譏誚。—*v.i.* 嘲弄；譏誚〖at〗. —*v.t.* 嘲弄；譏誚。
gird·er 〔ˈgɝdə; ˈgəːdə〕 *n.* 桁；樑。
***gir·dle¹** 〔ˈgɝdl̩; ˈgəːdl〕 *n., v.,* **-dled, -dling.** —*n.* ①帶子；腰帶。②圍繞物；似帶狀物。a *girdle* of green fields round a town. 圍繞於城市周圍的一片綠野。③〖解剖〗帶；環狀骨。*have* (or *hold*) *under one's girdle* 控制；使服從。—*v.t.* ①以帶束縛；圍繞。Wide roads *girdle* the city. 很寬的路圍繞着這城市。②在…周圍繞行。a satellite *girdling* the moon. 繞月飛行的人造衛星。③將(樹皮)刮掉一圈。
gir·dle² *n.* 〖蘇〗烘餅用的淺鍋。(亦作 **griddle**)
gir·dle·cake 〔ˈgɝdl̩ˌkek, ˈgɪrdl̩-; ˈgəːdlkeik〕 *n.* 〖蘇〗用淺鍋烘製之餅。(亦作 **griddlecake**)
‡girl 〔gɝl; gəːl〕 *n.* ①女孩。②少女；青年女子。③女僕；女傭。They have a new *girl* to do the housework. 他們雇了一個新女傭做家事。④女職員。a shop (office) *girl.* 女店(職)員。⑤〖俗〗愛人 (=sweetheart). He took his *girl* to the movies last night. 昨晚他帶他女友去看電影。⑥〖俗〗女人(不拘年齡)。⑦女兒。He sent his *girl* to a fashionable school. 他將女兒送至一所時髦的學校。
girl Friday 忠實能幹的女祕書、女僕等。
girl friend ①女朋友。②(男人之)情人。
girl·hood 〔ˈgɝlhud; ˈgəːlhud〕 *n.* ①少女時代。in her *girlhood.* 在她的少女時代。②女子們；婦女界；女流。
girl·ie 〔ˈgɝlɪ; ˈgəːli〕 *n.* ①(對少女之暱稱)妞兒；姑娘。②〖俚〗娼妓。—*adj.* 以暴露的女郎為號召的。
girl·ish 〔ˈgɝlɪʃ; ˈgəːliʃ〕 *adj.* ①女子的。②似女孩子的(男孩)。③適於女子的。—**ly,** *adv.* —**ness,** *n.*
girl scout 女童子軍隊員。

Gi·ronde [dʒɪˈrand; dʒiˈrɔnd] *n.* 吉倫泰黨(1791–1793, 法國大革命時期之穩健的共和主義的政黨)。

Gi·ron·dist [dʒəˈrandɪst; dʒiˈrɔndist] *n.* 吉倫泰黨員。—*adj.* 吉倫泰黨的。

girt¹ [gɜt; gəːt] *v.* pt. & pp. of **gird¹**. —*adj.* 〖航海〗(船停泊時) 栓得很牢不會因風或浪而動盪的。

girt² *v.t.* ①圍以帶;繫以帶。②(以帶尺)量測(樹之周圍)。—*v.i.* (樹身) 周長。—*n.* ①周圍之長度。②繫馬鞍之肚帶。

girth [gɜθ; gəːθ] *n.* ①(馬等之)肚帶; 繫帶。②周圍; 周量。—*v.t.* ①以帶束繫。②圍繞。—*v.i.* 量周長。

gist [dʒɪst; dʒist] *n.* ①(the–) (*sing.*)要旨;要領;梗概。②〖法律〗訴訟主因。

git·tern [ˈgɪtən; ˈgitəːn] *n.* 類似吉他的古樂器。

give [gɪv; giv] *v.*, **gave, giv·en, giv·ing,** *n.* —*v.t.* ①給予; 贈予。My brother *gave* me his watch. 我哥哥把他的錶送給我。②付給; 花去; 報償。How much did you *give* for the cow? 這隻牛你花多少錢買的? ③供給;開藥給(病人)。to *give* medicine to a patient. 給一病人開藥。④交付;委託;讓渡;讓給。to *give* one's daughter in marriage. 以女妻人; 嫁女兒。⑤將(名譽、地位、任務等) 授予;賦予。to *give* a person an important post. 給某人一重要位置。⑥給予(祝福、鼓勵、保證等)。to *give* a person one's blessing. 祝福某人。⑦傾心於; 獻身於; 致力於。to *give* one's mind (*or* attention) to.... 注意…; 傾全心於…。⑧懲罰;課以。to *give* a man six months' hard labor. 處罰某人做六個月苦工。⑨設(筵);開(會);上演;演出。to *give* a dinner. 設筵。to *give* a garden party. 開園遊會。to *give* a play. 上演一劇。⑩傳染。You've *given* me your cold. 你把感冒傳染給我了。⑪激起;煽動;挑動。His speech *gave* them offense. 他的演說激怒了他們。⑫產生;產出。Cows *give* milk. 母牛產牛奶。⑬做;動(身體方面的動作)。to *give* a guess. 猜一猜。⑭發出(聲、光、熱)。The sun *gives* lights. 太陽發出光。⑮傳布;發表;宣布;聲明。to *give* one's opinion. 發表意見。⑯舉出;舉示;示出;載入。to *give* examples. 舉例。⑰指定;規定。*Give* yourself an hour to get there. 限於一小時到那裏。⑱描寫。to *give* the scenery of a place. 描寫一個地方的景色。⑲讓步; 允許; 使能做。to *give* a person to understand. 使某人了解。⑳俯視;可見。The window *gives* the lake. 隔窗可見湖。㉑假定;假設(主要用過去分詞)。*Given* health, the thing can be done. 如果身體健康,這件事就能做。㉒選擇。*Give* me liberty, or *give* me death. 不自由毋寧死。㉓乾杯祝賀。I *give* you the King. 為國王乾杯。㉔希望;但願。I *give* you joy. 願你快樂。㉕歸於。The pamphlet is *given* to his pen. 那本小冊子是出自他的手筆。㉖犧牲。He gallantly *gave* his life for his country. 他英勇地為國捐軀。㉗為…把電話接到…。He asked central to *give* him the long-distance operator. 他請總機把電話接到長途臺接線員。㉘使…懷孕; 使…產子。He *gave* her five children in five years of marriage. 他結婚五年,使太太生了五個孩子。㉙替…生子(後面與間接受詞連用)。She *gave* him a handsome son. 她替他生了一個漂亮的兒子。㉚介紹。Ladies and gentlemen, I *give* you the Governor of New York. 諸位, 我請紐約州州長和諸位見面。—*v.i.* ①贈給;捐贈;布施。It is more blessed to *give* than to receive. 施比受更為有福。②(對壓力之) 不能支撐; 彎曲;塌陷。The army never *gives.* 此軍永不退卻。③(氣候) 變溫暖;(冰霜等) 溶解。④通往; 通到。a road which *gives* on to the highway. 通到公路的一條路。⑤適應; 順應。He *gave* to the motion of the horse. 他順應馬身之動作。⑥發生。You poor academics don't know what *gives* in the rough-and-tumble. 你們這些可憐的讀書人不知道社會上實際競爭的實況。***give about*** **a.** 分配。**b.** 流布;傳播。***give again*** 歸還。***give a good account of oneself*** 作優異(英勇)之表現。***give and take*** 互相遷就。***give a person the cold shoulder*** 以冷淡的態度待人。***give away*** **a.** 贈送;捐贈。He has *given away* all his money. 他把所有的錢都贈送掉了。**b.** 犧牲; 失掉。**c.** 背叛;暴露;洩露。**d.** 頒發。**e.** 把新娘的手放在新郎手中, 表示她將受新郎照顧。The bride was *given away* by her father. 新娘的父親將她交給新郎。***give a wide berth to*** 避免。***give back*** **a.** 送還; 交還; 歸還。**b.** 後退。***give battle*** 作堅決的抵抗。***give birth to*** **a.** 生孩子。Mrs. Chang *gave birth to* her second child this morning. 張太太今早生了她第二個孩子。**b.** 導致; 造成。***give cause*** 給予…之理由。His failure at school *gave* his father *cause* to feel bitterly disappointed. 他在學校成績不佳使他父親大為失望。***give chase*** 追。***give currency to*** 傳播。***give down*** (牛等) 使奶流出。***give forth*** 發出。***give ground*** 敗退;讓步。***give in*** **a.** 屈服;投降 (=yield or surrender). Don't *give in* while you stand and see. 你一息尚存時, 勿投降。**b.** 塌陷。**c.** 同意。**d.** 公開宣布。***give (something) in*** 呈交;遞交 (=deliver). You must *give in* your examination papers now. 你們現在必須交試卷了。***give it to*** 〖俗〗處罰; 責備。***give off*** 發生;放出。***give one a piece of your mind*** 責難;詬罵。***give one a ring*** 〖俗〗打電話給某人。***give one his head*** 讓某人自由發展。***give oneself out to be*** (or ***as***) 自稱為。***give oneself to*** 專心致力於;沾染。*Give yourself to* study. 努力讀書罷。***give one the go-by*** 不理睬。***give one to understand*** 使人了解。***give out*** **a.** 用完;用盡 (=become used up). Our food supply at last *gave out.* 我們的食物終於用完了。**b.** 疲倦。**c.** 分發。**d.** 公布; 宣布。**e.** 發出。***give over*** **a.** 停止。**b.** 交給; 交付;交出。**c.** 停止做。**d.** 放棄。**e.** 縱於。***give place to*** 讓位。***give rise to*** 引起。***give someone a hand*** **a.** 援助。**b.** 贊許; 稱贊。***give someone the gate*** 解雇; 放棄。***give someone the slip*** 溜走。***give thanks*** 作感恩祈禱。***give the gun*** **a.** 加大(引擎之) 油門。**b.** 加速。***give the lie to*** **a.** 指責撒謊。**b.** 證明為不眞實。***give up*** **a.** 停止。**b.** 戒除。**c.** 投降。**d.** 自首。**e.** 放棄。**f.** 讓給。***give vent to*** 發洩。***give voice*** 引吭高歌。***give way*** **a.** 退後。**b.** 坍塌。**c.** 失效; 屈服; 讓步。**d.** 為…所代替。—*n.* ①彈性; 彈力。There is no *give* in a stone floor. 石頭地面沒有彈力。②(精神、性格等) 適應性。③給予。

give-and-take [ˈgɪvənˈtek; ˈgivənˈteik] *n.* ①有取有予；公平交易。②互相遷就；讓步。—*adj.* 有取有予的；互相遷就的。

give·a·way [ˈgɪvəˌwe; ˈgivəwei] *n.* 〖俗〗①(無意的)洩漏。②(推銷貨物之)贈品；免費樣品。③〖無線電，電視〗(表演問答節目得獎者的)贈獎節目。—*adj.* 〖俗〗①大廉賣的。②〖無線電，電視〗有獎的(問答節目)。

‡giv·en [ˈgɪvən; ˈgivn] *v.* pp. of **give.** —*adj.* ①約定的；指定的。②慣於；沉溺於；癖好。③設若；假使。④贈予的。⑤(公文)899日執行及交出的。—*n.* (推理過程中之)已知事物。

given name 敎名；名(對姓而言)。

***giv·er** [ˈgɪvɚ; ˈgivə] *n.* 給與者；施贈者。God loves a cheerful *giver*.神愛樂善好施〔者。〕

giv·ing [ˈgɪvɪŋ; ˈgiviŋ] *n.* 贈品。

giz·zard [ˈgɪzɚd; ˈgizəd] *n.* ①(鳥之)沙囊；第二胃(即眞胃)。②〖俗〗喉嚨。③〖俗〗(人之)胃。***fret one's gizzard*** 苦惱；自苦。***stick in one's gizzard*** 無味；不合胃口；不滿意。

Gjel·le·rup [ˈgɛlərup; ˈgelərup] *n.* 葢萊羅普 (Karl, 1857–1919, 丹麥小說家，曾獲1917年諾貝爾文學獎)。

Gk. Greek. **Gl** 化學元素 glucinum 之〔符號。〕

gla·brous [ˈglebrəs; ˈgleibrəs] *adj.* 〖生物〗無毛的；平滑的；光禿的。

gla·cé [glæˈse; ˈglæsei] 〖法〗 *adj.* ①(布、皮等)光滑的。②(糕餅)覆有糖霜的。③凍結的；冷凍的。

gla·cial [ˈgleʃəl; ˈgleisjəl] *adj.* ①冰的；冰河的；冰河期的。the *glacial* period (era). 冰河期。②〖化〗結晶狀的。③似冰的；極冷的；冷淡的。—**ly,** *adv.*

glacial acetic acid 〖化〗冰醋酸。

glacial epoch 〖地質〗冰河時代。

gla·cial·ist [ˈgleʃəlɪst; ˈgleiʃəlist] *n.* 冰河學者。

gla·ci·ate [ˈgleʃɪˌet; ˈgleiʃieit] *v.,* **-at·ed, -at·ing.** —*v.t.* ①使結成冰；使凍結。②使覆以冰。③〖地質〗使受冰河作用。—*v.i.* 爲冰所覆。—**gla·ci·a·tion,** *n.*

***gla·cier** [ˈgleʃɚ; ˈglæsjə, ˈgleis-] *n.* 冰河。—**ed,** *adj.*

gla·ci·ol·o·gy [ˌglesɪˈɑlədʒɪ; ˌgleisiˈɔlədʒi] *n.* ①冰河學。②冰河造成的地理特徵。

gla·cis [ˈglesɪs; ˈglæsis] *n.* ①緩斜坡；徐坡。②〖築城〗(城前的)斜堤。③緩衝地區。④戰場。

‡glad [glæd; glæd] *adj.,* **glad·der, glad·dest.** ①高興的；歡喜的 (僅作 predicate adjective 用)。I feel very *glad* about it. 我對此事感覺非常高興。I'm *glad* to hear of it. 聞知此事，我甚覺高興。②使人歡樂的；佳(音)。Have you heard the *glad* news? 你聽到好消息了嗎？③情願的。I'll be *glad* to do you a favor. 我願意幫你一個忙。④晴朗的。a *glad* spring morning. 晴朗的春天早晨。

glad·den [ˈglædn̩; ˈglædn] *v.t.* 使快樂；使興奮。

***glade** [gled; gleid] *n.* ①森林中的小空〔地。②一片蓋有草的沼澤低地。〕

glad eye 〖俗〗媚眼；秋波。

glad hand 〖俗〗(由衷的或矯飾的)熱烈〔歡迎。〕

glad-hand [ˈglædˌhænd; ˈglædhænd] *v.i.* & *v.t.* 〖俗〗①熱烈地歡迎。②虛情假意地歡迎。

glad·i·a·tor [ˈglædɪˌetɚ; ˈglædieitə] *n.* ①古羅馬公開表演之格鬥者。②精於辯論或格鬪之人。③職業拳擊手。—**i·al,** *adj.*

glad·i·o·lus [ˌglædɪˈoləs; ˌglædiˈouləs] *n., pl.* **-li** [-laɪ; -lai] or **-lus·es.** 〖植物〗劍蘭。(亦作 **gladiola**)

***glad·ly** [ˈglædlɪ; ˈglædli] *adv.* 高興地；歡喜地；樂意地。I would *gladly* come, but I have no time. 我很願來，但我沒有時間。

***glad·ness** [ˈglædnɪs; ˈglædnis] *n.* 歡樂；歡喜；喜悅。

glad rags 〖俚〗考究的衣服(尤指晚禮服)。

glad·some [ˈglædsəm; ˈglædsəm] *adj.* ①高興的；快樂的。②可喜的；令人愉快的。—**ly,** *adv.* —**ness,** *n.*

Glad·stone[1] [ˈglædˌston; ˈglædstən] *n.* 內有二座的四輪遊覽馬車。

Glad·stone[2] *n.* 格萊斯頓 (William Ewart, 1809–1898, 英國政治家，於1868–94年間四任英國首相)。

glair(e) [glɛr; glɛə] *n.* ①(用於釉光或粘漿的)蛋白。②(蛋白製的)釉光；釉漿(用於裝訂書本等)。③蛋白狀物質。—*v.t.* 塗以蛋白。

glair·e·ous [ˈglɛrɪəs; ˈglɛəriəs] *adj.* =**glairy.**

glair·y [ˈglɛrɪ; ˈglɛəri] *adj.* ①蛋白狀的；蛋白狀黏質的。②塗有蛋白的。—**glair·i·ness,** *n.*

glaive, glave [glev; gleiv] *n.* 〖古〗〔劍；(特指)闊劍。〕

glam·or·ize [ˈglæməraɪz; ˈglæməraiz] *v.t.* ①使有魅力。②使光榮；讚美。(亦作 **glamourize**)

glam·or·ous [ˈglæmərəs; ˈglæmərəs] *adj.* ①富有魅力的；迷人的。②刺激性的；冒險性的。—**ly,** *adv.* —**ness,** *n.*

glam·our [ˈglæmɚ; ˈglæmə] *n.* 魅力；魔力；神奇的景色。***cast a glamour over*** 迷惑。***glamour boy*** (or ***girl***) 特別漂亮而衣着入時的男(女)。

‡glance[1] [glæns, glɑns; glɑːns] *n., v.,* **glanced, glanc·ing.** —*n.* ①一瞥；一見。to take a *glance* of the newspaper. 匆匆地看看報紙。②閃耀；閃光。the *glance* of spears in the sunlight. 槍頭在陽光中的閃光。③一滑；迅速而迂曲的運動。④約略的敍述。—*v.i.* ①匆匆地一看；略略地一看。He *glanced* up and saw me. 他抬頭一看，看見了我。②閃耀；閃光。Their helmets *glanced* in the sun. 他們的鋼盔在陽光中閃耀。③擦過。The arrow *glanced* off his armor. 箭頭擦過他的甲胄。④約略地提到。This newspaper article *glanced* at our relations with Japan. 這篇報紙論文略略地提到了我們對日本的關係。—*v.t.* ①瞥閃。to *glance* one's eye over. 瀏覽；匆匆閱過。②瞥見。The man *glanced* the burglar climbing out of the window. 那人瞥見小偷從窗戶爬出來。③反光。④使擦過。⑤〖廢〗約略提及；暗示。

glance[2] *n.* 〖礦〗輝礦類。

glancing angle 〖光學〗掠射角。

gland**[1] [glænd; glænd] *n.* 〖解剖〗腺。lachrymal gland*** 淚腺。***lymphatic gland*** 淋巴腺。***salivary gland*** 唾腺。***thyroid gland*** 甲狀腺。

gland[2] *n.* 〖機械〗塡函蓋 (壓榨塡料的壓〔蓋)。〕

glan·dered [ˈglændɚd; ˈglændəd] *adj.* (尤指馬)患鼻疽的。

glan·ders [ˈglændɚz; ˈglændəz] *n.* 〔馬鼻疽；鼻疽。〕

glan·du·lar [ˈglændʒəlɚ; ˈglændjulə] *adj.* ①腺的；似腺的；有腺的。②本性的；本能的；天生的。③性的。—**ly,** *adv.*

***glare**[1] [glɛr; glɛə] *n., v.,* **glared, glar·ing.** —*n.* ①刺目的强光；强烈的閃光。②怒目而

視。to look at someone with an angry *glare*. 對某人怒目而視。③炫目；耀目。—*v.i.* ①發出强光；閃耀。②怒視。He *glared* at me like a bull at a red rag. 他對我怒目而視，好似（鬥牛時）牛對紅布的怒視一樣。—*v.t.* ①以怒視表示。to *glare* defiance at each other. 彼此以怒目表示不屈服。②炫示。

glare² *n.* (冰等的)光滑的表面。—*adj.* 光滑而發亮的；似鏡面的。

glar·ing ['glɛrɪŋ; 'glɛəriŋ] *adj.* ①閃耀的；耀目的。②怒視的；虎視的。③顯著的；昭彰的。—**ly**, *adv.* —**ness**, *n.*

glar·y ['glɛrɪ; 'glɛəri] *adj.*, **glar·i·er**, **glar·i·est.** ①眩目的；閃耀的。②〖美〗(冰等)極光滑的。

Glas·gow ['glæsgo, 'glæsko, 'glɑ–; 'glɑːsgou] *n.* 格拉斯哥（蘇格蘭的最大都市及主要港口）。—**Glas·we·gi·an**, *n.*, *adj.*

glass** [glæs, glɑs; glɑːs] *n.* ①玻璃。*Glass* breaks easily. 玻璃易於破碎。②玻璃杯；酒杯；一杯之量。a *glass* of water. 一杯水。③鏡子。a looking *glass*. 面鏡。④玻璃製品。I want a new *glass* for my watch. 我需要一個新的玻璃錶面。⑤晴雨表。The *glass* (=barometer) is falling. 晴雨表在下降。⑥望遠鏡。⑦(*pl.*)眼鏡。Where are my *glasses?* 我的眼鏡在那裏？ ***see (or ***view***) ***something through rose-colored glasses*** 過分樂觀。—*v.t.* ①裝以玻璃；嵌以玻璃。to *glass* a window. 窗上裝玻璃。②反射；反映。The flowers *glass* themselves in the pool. 花映於池中。③密封於玻璃容器中。*glassed* fruits. 密封於玻璃容器中之水果。④使有(玻璃狀的)呆板光面；使鈍滯。Boredom *glassed* his eyes. 厭倦使他的眼睛鈍滯無光。⑤用望遠鏡等觀察。We went out that afternoon and *glassed* the country from the hills. 那天下午我們走到郊外，從山上用望遠鏡欣賞鄉間景色。—*v.i.* 呈玻璃狀；顯得光滑如鏡。The river is *glassing* in a breathless calm. 河水在無風的寧靜中顯得光滑如鏡。—*adj.* 玻璃製的。a *glass* eye. 假眼。

glass blower 吹玻璃工人；吹玻璃器。

glass blowing ①吹製玻璃；玻璃器製造。②玻璃器吹製術。

glass eye ①玻璃製義眼。②(鳥)畫眉的一種。③鱸的一種。

glass·ful ['glæs,ful, 'glɑs–; 'glɑːsful] *n.*, *pl.* **-fuls.** 一杯之量。

glass·house ['glæs,haus; 'glɑːshaus] *n.* ①暖房。②玻璃廠。

glass·i·fy ['glæsə,faɪ; 'glɑːsifai] *v.*, **-fied, -fy·ing.** —*v.t.* 以玻璃覆蓋或包圍。—*v.i.* 成爲玻璃或像玻璃。

glass·i·ly ['glæsɪlɪ; 'glɑːsili] *adv.* ①目光遲鈍地。He eyed me *glassily*. 他目光遲鈍地看着我。②似玻璃地。

glass·ine ['glæsin; 'glɑːsiːn] *n.* 半透明玻璃紙。

glass·i·ness ['glæsɪnɪs; 'glɑːsinis] *n.* 玻璃質；玻璃狀。

glass·mak·ing ['glæs,mekɪŋ; 'glɑːs-,meikiŋ] *n.* 玻璃（器皿）製造術。—**glass·mak·er**, *n.*

glass·ware ['glæs,wɛr; 'glɑːs–wɛə] *n.* 玻璃器皿（集合稱）。

glass wool 玻璃絨；玻璃綿。

glass·work ['glæs,wɝk; 'glɑːs–wəːk] *n.* ①玻璃（器）製造（業）。②玻璃製品；玻璃器類。③玻璃之嵌裝。④(*pl.*)(作 *sing.* 解)玻璃廠；玻璃工場。—**er**, *n.*

glass·wort ['glæs,wɝt; 'glɑːs–wəːt] *n.* 岡羊栖菜屬之植物（歐洲產，昔日自其燒成的灰提取製造玻璃用的蘇打灰）。

glass·y ['glæsɪ, 'glɑsɪ; 'glɑːsi] *adj.*, **glass·i·er, glass·i·est.** ①似玻璃的。②遲鈍的(目光等)。③堅定的。④尖銳的；刺耳的。

glass·y-eyed ['glæsɪ,aɪd, 'glɑs–; 'glɑːsiaid] *adj.* 表情呆滯的；目光遲鈍的。

Glau·ber's salt(s) ['glaubəz~; 'glaubəz~] 〖化〗芒硝；硫酸鈉 ($Na_2SO_4 \cdot 10H_2O$)。(亦作 **Glauber salt(s)**)

glau·co·ma [glɔ'komə; glɔː'koumə] *n.* 〖醫〗綠內障；青光眼。

glau·co·ma·tous [glɔ'komətəs; glɔː'koumətəs] *adj.* 青光眼的；綠內障的。

glau·cous ['glɔkəs; 'glɔːkəs] *adj.* ①綠灰色的；淡藍綠色的。②〖植物〗(葡萄、李等)有霜的；覆有白粉的。—**ness**, *n.*

***glaze** [glez; gleiz] *v.*, **glazed, glaz·ing,** *n.* —*v.t.* ①裝玻璃；罩以玻璃。to *glaze* a window. 給窗子裝上玻璃。②上釉。to *glaze* pottery. 給陶器上釉。③使鈍滯。His eyes were *glazed* in pain. 他的眼睛因痛苦而眼力鈍滯。④使…表面光滑。to *glaze* metal surfaces. 使金屬表面光滑。—*v.i.* ①變成爲光滑。②(眼力)變鈍滯。—*n.* ①釉。②覆罩的一層。a *glaze* of ice on the walk. 路上的一層冰。

glazed [glezd; gleizd] *adj.* ①似玻璃的；光滑的。②裝有玻璃的。③上過釉的。④鈍滯的(目光等)。

glaz·er ['glezɚ; 'gleizə] *n.* 瓷器上釉工人；加光工人；光布工人；軋光機。

gla·zier ['gleʒɚ; 'gleizjə] *n.* ①裝玻璃工人。Is your father a *glazier?* 〖諧〗你父親是裝玻璃的嗎？(你怎麼可以擋着人家的視線呢？) ②瓷器上釉工人；光布工人。***glazier's diamond*** 劃玻璃用的鑽石；玻璃刀。

gla·zier·y ['gleʒərɪ; 'gleiʒəri] *n.* 玻璃工人之工作；裝玻璃。

glaz·ing ['glezɪŋ; 'gleiziŋ] *n.* ①鑲嵌玻璃的工作。②(嵌於窗、框的)玻璃。③上釉；加光。④釉藥；光滑劑。⑤上釉的表面；加光面。

glaz·y ['glezɪ; 'gleizi] *adj.*, **glaz·i·er, glaz·i·est.** ①如玻璃的。②上過釉的；光滑的。③(目光)呆滯的。—**glaz·i·ness**, *n.*

***gleam** [glim; gliːm] *n.* ①微弱的閃光；一絲光線。the *gleam* of a distant lighthouse. 遠處燈塔的閃光。②瞬息的一現。—*v.i.* ①隱約閃光；閃爍。Light *gleamed* in the east. 光亮在東方閃爍着。②忽現；突現。Courage *gleamed* in his eye. 他的眼裏突現勇氣。—*v.t.* 隱約地閃現。

gleam·y ['glimɪ; 'gliːmi] *adj.*, **gleam·i·er, gleami·est.** ①發光的；閃爍的；(光、色)朦朧的。②下小雨而出太陽的。

glean [glin; gliːn] *v.t.* ①拾取(遺穗)；自(稻田)拾殘餘的膹穗。to *glean* corn. 拾殘餘的膹穀。②收集。to *glean* news. 搜集消息。—*v.i.* 拾膹穗。②收集。

glean·er ['glinɚ; 'gliːnə] *n.* 拾穗的人；零碎物蒐集者。

glean·ing ['glinɪŋ; 'gliːniŋ] *n.* ①拾遺穗；殘餘物之收拾。②(常 *pl.*) 所拾得之遺穗；收集得之殘遺物；蒐集物；拾遺。

glebe [glib; gliːb] *n.* ①〖詩〗土；土壤；耕地；田地。②教會所屬田地；聖職領耕地。

glee [gli; gliː] *n.* ①歡樂；高興。full of *glee.* 高興之至。in high *glee.* 高興之至。②三部或四部合唱曲(通常無伴奏)。

glee club 合唱團；合唱俱樂部。

glee·ful ['glifəl; 'gliːful] *adj.* 歡喜的；

極高興(開心)的;快樂的。

glee·man ['glimən; 'gli:mən] *n., pl.* **-men.** 〖古〗吟遊詩人;到處流浪的樂師。

gleep [glip; gli:p] *n.* 〖物理〗實驗用原子爐之一種。

glee·some ['glisəm; 'gli:səm] *adj.* 〖古〗=**gleeful.**

gleet [glit; gli:t] *n.* ①〖醫〗慢性尿道炎;後淋。②〖獸醫〗慢性鼻腔炎。—*v.i.* 流稀薄液體。

glen [glɛn; glen] *n.* 峽谷;幽谷。

glen·gar·ry [glɛn'gærɪ; glen'gæri] *n., pl.* **-ries.** (蘇格蘭高地人的)船型便帽。(亦作 **Glengarry**)

gle·noid ['glinɔɪd; 'glinɔid] *adj.* 〖解剖〗(有)淺窩的;(有)關節窩的。

glib [glɪb; glib] *adj.,* **glib·ber, glib·best.** ①口齒伶俐的;油腔滑調的。②(動作、態度等)敏捷的。③從容的。—**ly,** *adv.*

glide** [glaɪd; glaid] *v.,* **glid·ed, glid·ing,** *n.* —*v.i.* ①滑翔;滑動。②溜走。The thief *glided* out of the room. 賊溜出房間。The years *glided* past. 年華逝去。—*v.t.* ①使滑動。②乘滑翔機橫越。to *glide* the Atlantic. 乘滑翔機橫渡大西洋。glide into*** 從某一狀態逐漸轉變爲另一狀態。—*n.* ①滑動;滑走;滑步。②〖音樂〗滑唱(奏)。③〖語音〗漸變;滑過。④流水。to fish in the *glides* of stream. 在溪流中釣魚。

glide path 〖航空〗①滑降臺。②滑降航道。

***glid·er** ['glaɪdɚ; 'glaidə] *n.* ①滑翔機。②滑行的人或物。*glider* bomb. 滑翔式炸彈。

glide vehicle 有翼飛彈(進入大氣層後可作長距離滑翔飛行)。

glid·ing ['glaɪdɪŋ; 'glaidiŋ] *adj.* 似滑行的;滑的;流暢的。—*n.* 滑動;滑翔。—**ly,** *adv.*

glim [glɪm; glim] *n.* 〖俚〗①燈火;燈光;蠟燭。to douse the *glim.* 熄燈。②微弱的跡象。There was not a *glim* of hope. 一點希望也沒有。③眼睛。

glim·mer** ['glɪmɚ; 'glimə] *n.* ①微光;一絲光線。②隱約的一瞥。a *glimmer* of hope. 一線希望。—*v.i.* ①發微光。lights *glimmering* in the distance. 遠處微弱的燈光。②朦朧出現。go glimmering*** 逐漸消失。Hopes for a good crop *went glimmering* in the drought. 旱災期中豐收的希望逐漸消失了。

glim·mer·ing ['glɪmərɪŋ; 'glimərin] *n.* ①微光;一絲光線。②隱約的一瞥。—*adj.* 微弱地發光的。—**ly,** *adv.*

***glimpse** [glɪmps; glimps] *n., v.,* **glimpsed, glimps·ing.** —*n.* ①一瞥。to get (*or* catch) a *glimpse* of something from the window of a train. 由火車窗中瞥見某物。②一閃。—*v.t.* 瞥見;看一眼。I *glimpsed* her dress as she went by. 當她走過時我瞥見她的衣服。—*v.i.* ①投以一瞥。②閃爍不定;發微光。—**glimps·er,** *n.*

***glint** [glɪnt; glint] *v.i.* ①閃耀;閃閃發光。to *glint* in the sun. 在太陽照耀下閃閃發光。②(箭矢)疾進;飛馳。—*v.t.* 閃耀;反映。The sword *glinted* back the sun's rays. 刀反映陽光閃閃發亮。—*n.* 閃爍;閃光。the *glint* of sunshine. 閃爍之陽光。

gli·o·ma [glaɪ'omə; glai'oumə] *n., pl.* **-ma·ta** [-mətə; -mətə]. 〖醫〗神經膠質瘤。

glis·sade [glɪ'sad; gli'sa:d] *n., v.,* **-sad·ed, -sad·ing.** —*n.* ①(登山者沿覆雪斜坡之)滑降。②(芭蕾舞中之)滑步。—*v.i.* ①滑降。②跳滑步;作滑步。③滑行。

glis·san·do [glɪ'sando; gli'sa:ndou] *n., pl.* **-di** [di; di:], *adj.* —*n.* 〖音樂〗滑奏;滑音;滑唱。—*adj.* 滑奏的;滑音的;滑唱的。

***glis·ten** ['glɪsn̩; 'glisn] *v.i.* 閃爍;輝耀。eyes *glistening* with tears. 閃耀着淚水的眼睛。The lake *glistens* in the moonlight. 湖水在月光下閃亮。—*n.* 閃爍;閃光。

glis·ter ['glɪstɚ; 'glistə] *v.i., n.* 〖古〗= **glitter.**

glitch [glɪtʃ; glitʃ] *n.* 〖美俚〗突然故障。

***glit·ter** ['glɪtɚ; 'glitə] *v.i.* 閃爍;輝耀;燦爛。a rich lady *glittering* with jewels. 滿身珠寶燦爛的富婦。—*v.t.* ①使閃爍;使輝耀。brilliant stars *glittering* the sky. 亮晶晶的星星使天空閃亮。②飾以發亮的東西。—*n.* ①閃爍;輝耀;燦爛。②發亮的東西(集合稱)。a neckline trimmed with *glitter.* 有燦爛裝飾的衣領口。

glit·ter·y ['glɪtərɪ; 'glitəri] *adj.* 閃爍的;燦爛的。

gloam [glom; gloum] *v.i.* 〖蘇〗成薄暗;暗下來;變朦朧。—*n.* 〖詩〗黃昏;薄暮。

gloam·ing ['glomɪŋ; 'gloumiŋ] *n.* (the–) (*sing.*)黃昏;薄暮。in the *gloaming* of one's life. 在晚年。

gloat [glot; glout] *v.i.* ①專心地凝視;幸災樂禍地看或想;貪婪地逼視;垂涎〖常over〗. to *gloat* over another's misfortunes. 幸災樂禍地看別人的不幸。②滿足;竊喜。—*n.* 沾沾自喜。—**er,** *n.*

glob [glɑb; glɔb] *n.* ①水珠。②(可塑性物質的)一團;一堆。

glob·al ['globl̩; 'gloubəl] *adj.* ①球形的。②全球的;全世界的。a *global* war. 全球性戰爭。③全部的;全體的;全盤的。—**ly,** *adv.*

glo·bate ['globet; 'gloubeit] *adj.* 球形的;球狀的。

***globe** [glob; gloub] *n., v.,* **globed, glob·ing.** —*n.* ①球;球狀物。②(常 the–)地球。He journeys over much of the *globe.* 他廣遊世界。③地球儀。④星球。—*v.t.* & *v.i.* (使)成球形。

globe·fish ['glob,fɪʃ; 'gloubfiʃ] *n., pl.* **-fish, -fish·es.** 魚虎;河豚。

globe·flow·er ['glob,flauɚ; 'gloub,flauə] *n.* 〖植物〗金梅草。

globe-trot ['glob,trɑt; 'gloubtrɔt] *v.i.,* **-trot·ted, -trot·ting.** 周遊世界。

globe·trot·ter ['glob,trɑtɚ; 'gloub,trɔtə] *n.* 遊歷世界者;世界觀光旅行家。

globe-trot·ting ['glob,trɑtɪŋ; 'gloub,trɔtiŋ] *adj.* 遊歷世界的。—*n.* 環球旅行。

glo·bose ['globos; 'gloubous] *adj.* 球狀的;圓形的。—**ly,** *adv.*

glo·bos·i·ty [glo'bɑsətɪ; glou'bɔsiti] *n.* 球形;球狀。

glob·u·lar ['glɑbjələ; 'glɔbjulə] *adj.* ①球狀的;圓的。②由小球做成的。③完整的。***globular chart*** 球面射影地圖。***globular projection*** (地圖繪製的)球面投影法。

globular sailing 〖航海〗大圈航法。

glob·ule ['glɑbjul; 'glɔbju:l] *n.* 極小的球體或一滴。

glob·u·let ['glɑbjulɪt; 'glɔbjulit] *n.* 極小的一滴。

glob·u·lin ['glɑbjəlɪn; 'glɔbjulin] *n.* 〖生化〗血球素;球蛋白。

glock·en·spiel ['glɑkən,spil; 'glɔkənspi:l] *n.* 〖音樂〗①鐵琴。②有可發鐘聲的金屬製圓筒管的鍵盤樂器。③鐘組樂器。

glom [glɑm; glɔm] *v.,* **glommed, glom·ming,** *n.* —*v.t.* 〖俚〗①偷。②抓。③看;瞪。—*n.* 〖俚〗一瞥。

glom·er·ate ['glɑmərɪt; 'glɔmərit] *adj.* 集合成球狀的;密集成簇的。

glom·er·a·tion [ˌglɑməˈreʃən; ˌglɔməˈreiʃən] *n.* 密集成球狀;集成物。

glom·er·ule [ˈglɑməˌrul; ˈglɔməru:l] *n.* ①〖植物〗團繖花。②〖解剖〗腎臟之絲球體。—**glo·mer·u·lar,** *adj.*

***gloom** [glum; glu:m] *n.* ①幽暗;黑暗。The future seemed filled with *gloom.* 未來似乎充滿了黑暗。②憂鬱;愁眉不展。What can we do to chase her *gloom* away? 我們有何辦法解除她的憂鬱呢?—*v.i.* ①變暗;變朦朧; 變憂鬱。 ②現愁容; 呈不豫之色。—*v.t.* 使暗;使朦朧;使憂鬱。

***gloom·y** [ˈglumɪ;ˈglu:mi] *adj.,* **gloom·i·er, gloom·i·est.** ①幽暗的;黑暗的。②愁苦的; 抑鬱的; 悲觀的。to feel *gloomy* about the future of a warring world. 對於戰亂的世界之未來感到悲觀。 ③令人沮喪的; 使氣餒的。 *gloomy* prospects. 令人沮喪的展望。—**gloom·i·ness,** *n.* —**gloom·i·ly,** *adv.*

Glo·ri·a [ˈglorɪə; ˈglɔ:riə] *n.* ①榮耀頌歌;頌樂。②(g-) 上述之曲。③(g-) 圓光;光輪。④(g-)絲毛合織的有光布。

glo·ri·fi·ca·tion [ˌglorəfəˈkeʃən, ˌglɔr-; ˌglɔ:rifiˈkeiʃən] *n.* ①對神之讚美; 頌榮。 ②頌歌; 讚歌。 ③稱讚; 讚美。the *glorification* of labor. 勞動之讚美。④〖俗〗祝賀;慶祝。

glo·ri·fy [ˈgloraˌfaɪ, ˈglɔr-; ˈglɔ:rifai] *v.t.,* **-fied, -fy·ing.** ①加榮耀於;使光榮。②讚美; 崇拜 (上帝)。We sing hymns to *glorify* God. 我們唱聖詩讚美上帝。③使更美; 使更壯麗。Sunset *glorified* the valley. 夕陽使山谷生色。—**glo·ri·fi·er,** *n.*

glo·ri·ole [ˈglorɪˌol; ˈglɔ:rioul] *n.* 圓光;光輪。

***glo·ri·ous** [ˈglorɪəs, ˈglɔr-; ˈglɔ:riəs] *adj.* ①光榮的。a *glorious* victory. 光榮的勝利。②輝煌燦爛的; 可稱頌的。a *glorious* sunset. 光輝燦爛的落日。③〖俗〗爽快的; 宜人的。 What *glorious* weather! 多麼宜人的天氣啊! —**ness,** *n.* —**ly,** *adv.*

‡**glo·ry** [ˈglorɪ, ˈglɔrɪ; ˈglɔ:ri] *n., pl.* **-ries,** *v.,* **-ried, -ry·ing,** *interj.* —*n.* ①光榮。Scientific achievement may bring greater *glory* than fighting. 科學成就也許比戰爭會帶來更大的榮耀。②光榮的成就; 可誇耀的事物。③光輝;壯麗。the *glory* of a sunset. 落日的光輝。④輝煌;昌盛;偉大。⑤天堂;天國。⑥讚美;讚頌;榮耀。*Glory* to God in the highest! 榮耀歸於天上的上帝!⑦(神像等的)光輪。***go to glory*** 〖俗〗死。***in one's glory*** 〖俗〗得意;開心。***send to glory*** 〖俗〗殺死。—*v.i.* 自豪; 歡樂; 得意。 to *glory* in one's strength. 以其强壯而自豪。—*interj.* (亦作 **glory be**) 表示驚奇、高興等的感歎詞。

glory hole ①(玻璃熔解爐之)爐口。②〖俗〗放雜亂東西的房間、抽屜等。③〖航海〗司爐或管事之房間。④船尾之貯藏室。

gloss[1] [glɔs; glɔs] *n.* ①(表面的) 平滑光澤。②光滑的表面。③虛飾; 虛僞。—*v.t.* ①使光滑;加光澤於。②掩飾〖over〗。—*v.i.* 發光亮;發光澤。

gloss[2] *n.* ①解釋; 註釋。②字彙; 語彙。③加於行間的不同文字的譯文。④曲解。 —*v.t.* ①爲…加註解。②在字彙中加 (字)。 ③曲解; 詭辯〖常 over〗。—*v.i.* 作解釋;加註。

gloss. glossary.

glos·sa [ˈglɑsə; ˈglɔsə] *n., pl.* **-sae** [-si; -si:] or **-sas.** 〖解剖〗舌。 —**glos·sal,** *adj.*

glos·sar·i·al [glɑˈsɛrɪəl; glɔˈsɛəriəl] *adj.* 字彙的; 辭典的。

glos·sa·rist [ˈglɑsərɪst; ˈglɔsərist] *n.* 字彙編纂(或註解)者; 辭典編纂者。

glos·sa·ry [ˈglɑsərɪ, ˈglɔs-; ˈglɔsəri] *n., pl.* **-ries.** 字彙;(特殊的或專門的)辭典。

glos·se·mat·ics [ˌglɑsɪˈmætɪks; ˌglɔsiˈmætiks] *n.* (作*sing.* 解)言理學(丹麥語言學家 Hjelmslev 等所倡導)。

glos·si·tis [glɑˈsaɪtɪs; glɔˈsaitis] *n.* 〖醫〗舌炎。

glos·sog·ra·pher [glɑˈsɑgrəfə; glɔˈsɔgrəfə] *n.* 註釋者;註解者。

glos·so·la·li·a [ˌglɑsoˈlelɪə; ˌglɔsouˈleiliə] *n.* 〖醫〗言語不清。

***gloss·y** [ˈglɔsɪ; ˈglɔsi] *adj.,* **gloss·i·er, gloss·i·est.** ①平滑的;有光澤的。The seat of a pair of serge trousers may get *glossy.* 一條嗶嘰褲的襠部可能變爲光滑。②似是而非的。a *glossy* deceit. 似是而非的欺騙。—**gloss·i·ly,** *adv.* —**gloss·i·ness,** *n.*

glot·tal [ˈglɑtl; ˈglɔtl] *adj.* ①〖解剖〗聲門的;喉門的。②〖語音〗自聲門發出的。*glottal* stop. 聲門閉鎖音。 —**glot·tic,** *adj.*

glot·tis [ˈglɑtɪs; ˈglɔtis] *n.* 喉門;聲門。

‡**glove** [glʌv; glʌv] *n., v.,* **gloved, glov·ing.** —*n.* ①手套。a pair of *gloves.* 一付手套。②拳擊手套;棒球手套。***be hand and*** (or ***in***) ***glove*** …非常親密;合作。***fit like a glove*** 恰合。***handle with gloves*** 溫和地對待; 小心對付。 ***handle with kid gloves*** 參看 **kid gloves.** ***handle without gloves*** 粗暴地對待;嚴酷對待。***put on the gloves*** 〖俗〗作拳擊比賽。***take off the gloves to*** (***a person***) 認眞地爭辯或打鬥。***take up the glove*** 應戰。***throw down the glove*** 挑戰。—*v.t.* ①戴以手套。②作…之手套。

glove fight (用手套的)拳擊。

glove·man [ˈglʌvˌmæn; ˈglʌvmæn] *n., pl.* **-men** [-mən; -mən]. 〖棒球〗外野手。

glov·er [ˈglʌvə; ˈglʌvə] *n.* 製造手套者;手套商。

‡**glow** [glo; glou] *n.* ①赤熱; 白熱。②光輝;輝耀。the *glow* of the sky at sunset. 落日時天空的光輝。③熱情; 紅光煥發。 the *glow* of health on his cheeks. 兩頰紅光煥發。in a *glow* of enthusiasm. 熱心如炙。④熱心的表情。a *glow* of interest or excitement. 臉上興趣濃厚或興奮的表情。—*v.i.* ①發紅光;熾燃;紅似火。 woods and forests that *glow* with autumn tints. 染着秋日紅色似火的森林。②紅光煥發。*glowing* with health. 容光煥發。③表現熱心;生氣蓬勃。to *glow* with pride. 得意揚揚。

glow·er [ˈglauə; ˈglauə] *v.i.* 怒目而視; 皺眉〖at〗。The fighters *glowered* at each other. 鬥士們怒目注視對方。—*n.* 怒目;皺眉。—**ing·ly,** *adv.*

glow·ing [ˈgloɪŋ; ˈglouiŋ] *adj.* ①熾熱的;赤熱的。②光輝的;燦爛的。③容光煥發的。④熱心的; 生氣勃勃的。⑤有利的; 讚揚的。***paint in glowing colors*** 作生動的敍述;熱烈地讚賞。—**ly,** *adv.*

glow·worm [ˈgloˌwɜm; ˈglouwə:m] *n.* 螢火蟲。

glox·in·i·a [glɑkˈsɪnɪə; glɔkˈsinjə] *n.* 〖植物〗大岩桐。

gloze [gloz; glouz] *v.,* **glozed, gloz·ing.** —*v.t.* ①(原指)註釋;解釋。②掩飾〖常 over〗。—*v.i.* 〖古〗①作註釋。②諂媚。

glu·cide [ˈgluˌsaɪd; ˈglu:said] *n.* 糖精; 甜精。

glu·cin·i·um [gluˈsɪnɪəm; glu:ˈsiniəm] *n.* =**glucinum.**

glu·ci·num 〔glu'saɪnəm; gluː'sainəm〕 *n.* 〖化〗鋊（爲 beryllium 之舊稱, 係一種金屬元素, 符號 Gl）. 「糖。」

glu·cose 〔'glukos; 'gluːkous〕 *n.* 葡萄

glu·co·side 〔'glukə,saɪd; 'gluːkəsaid〕 *n.* 〖化〗糖原質; 葡萄糖苷。

***glue** 〔glu; gluː〕 *n., v.,* **glued, glu·ing.** —*n.* ①膠。to fasten with *glue.* 用膠黏起。②有膠般黏性之物。—*v.t.* ①黏。to *glue* something on again. 把某件東西又黏起來。②固着; 黏附; 使不移動。He *glues* his eyes to the show window. 他目不轉睛地看着櫥窗。③塗以膠水〖有時 up〗.

glue·pot 〔'glu,pɑt; 'gluː-pɔt〕 *n.* 熔膠鍋。

glue-snif·fing 〔'glu,snɪfɪŋ; 'gluː,snifiŋ〕 *n.* ①强力膠癮。②吸强力膠（過癮）。

glue·y 〔'gluɪ; 'gluːi〕 *adj.,* **-i·er, -i·est.** 膠質的; 膠狀的; 塗膠的; 塗滿膠水的; 黏性的。

glum 〔glʌm; glʌm〕 *adj.,* **glum·mer, glum·mest.** 陰鬱的; 沉默的; 怏怏不樂的。—**ly,** *adv.* —**ness,** *n.* 「莖衣。」

glume 〔glum; gluːm〕 *n.* 〖植物〗穇穎;

glut 〔glʌt; glʌt〕 *v.,* **glut·ted, glut·ting,** *n.* —*v.t.* ①使充滿; 使吃飽; 過分地吃。The boys *glutted* themselves with cake. 孩子們吃糕點過了量。②過多地供應。③阻塞。—*v.i.* 吃得過飽。—*n.* ①充足之量; 大量。②過多的供應; 充斥。

glu·ta·mine 〔'glutəmin; 'gluːtəmiːn〕 *n.* 〖化〗麩酸胺; 穀氨基醯胺。

glu·ten 〔'glutn̩; 'gluːtən〕 *n.* 麪筋; 麩質。

glu·te·nous 〔'glutn̩əs; 'gluːtnəs〕 *adj.* ①似麪筋的。②含大量麪筋的。

glu·te·us 〔glu'tiəs; gluː'tiːəs〕 *n., pl.* **-te·i** 〔-'tiaɪ; -'tiːai〕. 〖解剖〗臀筋; 臀肌。

glu·ti·nos·i·ty 〔,glutə'nɑsətɪ; ,gluːti'nɔsiti〕 *n.* 黏性; 黏凝。

glu·ti·nous 〔'glutɪnəs; 'gluːtinəs〕 *adj.* 黏的; 膠質的。*glutinous rice* 糯米。

glut·ton¹ 〔'glʌtn̩; 'glʌtn〕 *n.* 貪食者; 貪多者。He is a *glutton* for work. 他是一個工作不倦的人。

glut·ton² *n.* 〖動物〗狼獾。

glut·ton·ize 〔'glʌtn̩,aɪz; 'glʌtn̩aiz〕 *v.i. & v.t.,* **-ized, -iz·ing.** 暴食; 貪食。

glut·ton·ous 〔'glʌtn̩əs; 'glʌtn̩əs〕 *adj.* ①貪吃的; 饕餮的。②貪心的; 不知足的。to be *gluttonous* of....貪…。—**ly,** *adv.* —**ness,** *n.*

glut·ton·y 〔'glʌtn̩ɪ; 'glʌtn̩i〕 *n., pl.* **-ton·ies.** 暴食; 貪食。 「甘油; 丙三醇。」

glyc·er·in(e) 〔'glɪsrɪn; 'glisərin〕 *n.*

glyc·er·in·ate 〔'glɪsərɪnet; 'glisərineit〕 *v.,* **-at·ed, -at·ing,** *n.* —*v.t.* 以甘油處理; 混合以甘油。—*n.* 甘油酸鹽類。

glyc·er·ol 〔'glɪsə,rol, -,rɑl; 'glisərɔl〕 *n.* 〖化〗甘油。 「〖化〗甘油基的。」

glyc·er·yl 〔'glɪsə,rɪl; 'glisəril〕 *adj.*

gly·cine 〔'glaɪsin; glai'siːn〕 *n.* 〖化〗糖膠; 氨基乙酸; 氨基醋酸。

gly·co·gen 〔'glaɪkədʒən; 'glikoudʒen〕 *n.* 〖生化〗肝糖; 動物澱粉。

gly·co·gen·e·sis 〔,glaɪkə'dʒenəsɪs; ,glaikə'dʒenisis〕 *n.* 〖生化〗動物澱粉生成; 牲粉生成。（亦作 **glycogeny**） 「醇。」

gly·col 〔'glaɪkol; 'glaikɔl〕 *n.* 〖化〗乙二

gly·co·su·ri·a 〔,glaɪko'sjʊrɪə; ,glaikou'sjuəriə〕 *n.* 〖醫〗糖尿病之一種。

glyp·tic 〔'glɪptɪk; 'gliptik〕 *adj.* （寶石）雕刻的。—*n.* 雕刻。 「石雕刻術。」

glyp·tics 〔'glɪptɪks; 'gliptiks〕 *n.* 寶

glyp·tog·ra·phy 〔glɪp'tɑgrəfɪ; glip'tɔgrəfi〕 *n.* 寶石雕刻術(學)。—**glyp·tog·ra·pher,** *n.* —**glyp·to·graph·ic,** *adj.*

G.M. ① general manager. ② Grand Marshal. ③ Grand Master.

gm. gram(s).

G-man 〔'dʒi,mæn; 'dʒiːmæn〕 *n., pl.* **G-men.** 美國聯邦調查局的特務人員。

Gmc. Germanic. (亦作 **Gmc**)

G.M.T. Greenwich Mean Time. 世界標準時; 格林威治時間。

gnarl 〔nɑrl; nɑːl〕 *n.* 木節; 木瘤。—*v.t.* 扭曲; 撓捻; 使成結。—*v.i.* 形成節瘤。

gnarled 〔nɑrld; nɑːld〕 *adj.* ①多瘤節的; 粗糙的。②飽經風霜的(面容); 性格乖戾的; 拗脾氣的。 「**gnarl·i·est.** =**gnarled.**」

gnarl·y 〔'nɑrlɪ; 'nɑːli〕 *adj.,* **gnarl·i·er,**

gnash 〔næʃ; næʃ〕 *v.t. & v.i.* 咬（牙）; 切（齒）。***gnash the teeth*** 咬牙切齒。—*n.* 咬牙切齒。

gnat** 〔næt; næt〕 *n.* ①蚋。②〖英〗蚊。strain at a gnat*** 遲疑於瑣碎事物。***strain at a gnat and swallow a camel*** 斤斤於小事, 對大事反持無所謂的態度。 「頜的。」

gnath·ic 〔'næθɪk; 'næθik〕 *adj.* 顎的;

***gnaw** 〔nɔ; nɔː〕 *v.t. & v.i.,* **gnawed, gnawed** or **gnawn, gnaw·ing.** ①咬; 齧; 噬。The dog was *gnawing* (at) a bone. 狗在啃骨頭。②咬成。A rat can *gnaw* a hole through wood. 老鼠能咬穿木頭成洞。③侵蝕; 損壞。The acid *gnaws* at the metal. 酸類會侵蝕金屬。④使苦惱; 使痛苦; 折磨。fear and anxiety *gnawing* (at) her heart. 折磨着她心的恐懼和焦慮。—**a·ble,** *adj.* 「壞者。②齧齒動物。」

gnaw·er 〔'nɔɚ; 'nɔːə〕 *n.* ①齧者; 蝕

gnaw·ing 〔'nɔɪŋ; 'nɔːiŋ〕 *n.* ①齧; 咬。②(常 *pl.*) 似被咬、齧般的痛; 陣痛。—*adj.* 齧的; 咬的。—**ly,** *adv.*

gneiss 〔naɪs; nais〕 *n.* 〖地質〗片麻巖。

gnome¹ 〔nom; noum〕 *n.* 傳說中居於地下保護珍藏之小神; 地精。

gno·me² 〔nom, 'no,mi; 'noumiː〕 *n., pl.* **gnomes** or **gno·mae** 〔'no,mi; 'noumiː〕. 格言。 「言的; 箴言的。②格言作者的。」

gno·mic 〔'nomɪk; 'noumik〕 *adj.* ①格

gnom·ish 〔'nomɪʃ; 'noumiʃ〕 *adj.* 似地精的。 「言作者。」

gno·mist 〔'nomɪst; 'noumist〕 *n.* 格

gno·mol·o·gy 〔no'mɑlədʒɪ; nou'mɔlədʒi〕 *n., pl.* **-gies.** 格言集; 箴言集。

gno·mon 〔'nomɑn; 'noumɔn〕 *n.* ①日晷儀; 日規。②日規的指時針。③〖數學〗折磬形（自平行四邊形之一角, 除去一相似形所餘之形)。 「感; 神祕的直覺。」

gno·sis 〔'nosɪs; 'nousis〕 *n.* 直覺; 靈

Gnos·tic 〔'nɑstɪk; 'nɔstik〕 *adj.* 諾斯替教的。—*n.* 諾斯替教徒。

gnos·tic 〔'nɑstɪk; 'nɔstik〕 *adj.* ①知識的; 關於知識的。②有知識的。（亦作 **gnostical**)

Gnos·ti·cism 〔'nɑstə,sɪzəm; 'nɔstisizəm〕 *n.* 諾斯替教（尊重某種靈的直覺的初期基督教之一派)。 「duct.」

GNP, G.N.P. gross national pro-

gnu 〔nu; nuː〕 *n., pl.* **gnus, gnu.** 南非產似牛的一種大羚羊。

‡go¹ 〔go; gou〕 *v.,* **went, gone, go·ing,** *n., pl.* **goes,** *interj., adj.* —*v.i.* ①行走; 去。to *go* to London (the station). 到倫敦(車站)去。to *go* by train (air, sea).

乘火車(飛機,海船)而行。to *go* the shortest way. 走捷徑。to *go* on a journey (visit). 作旅行(訪問)。to *go* swimming (hunting, fishing, shooting). 出外游泳(狩獵,釣魚,射擊)。to *go* to school (church, bed, sea). 上學(做禮拜,就寢,當水手)去。The train was *going* (at) fifty miles an hour. 這火車正以每小時五十英里的速度行駛。The prime minister decided to *go* to the country. 首相決定舉行一次普選。②離去;消失;過去。It is time to *go*. 是離去的時候了。His sight is *going*. 他的目力逐漸衰弱。War must *go* (=be got rid of)! 戰爭必須消除! Be *gone!* 走開! Get you *gone!* 走開!滾開! Vacation *goes* quickly. 假期過得很快。③通;達;延及。This road *goes* to London. 這條路通倫敦。The coat won't *go* round him—it's too small. 這件衣不合他的身——它太小了。His memory does not *go* back that far. 他記不起那麼久遠的事。④傾向;有助於。That *goes* to prove that.... 那可以證明…。⑤結果;結局;終於;成功。The play *went* very well. 這齣戲甚爲成功。How are things *going?* 一切情形怎樣? Jones knows how to make things *go*. 鍾斯很會辦事。⑥歸其所有;歸其管轄;歸於。The first prize *goes* to you. 第一獎歸你所得。⑦習慣於;過慣…之生活;有…之習慣;經常處於。Some savages always *go* naked. 有些野蠻人過慣裸體生活。He *went* in fear of his life. 他經常恐懼喪失生命。to *go* hungry. 經常挨餓。⑧變;逐漸。to *go* bad 變壞。to *go* out of date. 變爲陳舊;漸被廢棄。He's *gone* blind. 他已經變瞎了。⑨開始;開動。Here *goes!* 開始! ⑩判決;裁定。The case *went* against him. 這案判決他敗訴。The case *went* in his favor. 這案判決他勝訴。⑪聽從指揮或指導;依…下判斷。It's a good rule to *go* by. 這是應該遵循的良規。We have no evidence to *go* upon. 我們沒有證據以資判斷。⑫迎合;趕上。We must *go* with the times (tide). 我們必須趕上時代(迎合潮流)。⑬坍塌;折斷;跌落;生病;失敗。He's far *gone*. 他的病況嚴重。⑭活動;運行;工作。The clock does not *go* well. 這鐘走得不準。to *go* by steam (electricity, etc.). 用蒸汽(電等)發動。⑮作…舉動;發出…聲音;作…姿勢。Bang *went* the gun! 轟然砲響! It has just *gone* six. 時鐘剛剛敲過六點。⑯裝進;納入;被包容。This letter won't *go* into this small envelope. 這信裝不進這小信封。⑰出賣;賣給。The painting *goes* to the highest bidder. 這幅畫賣給出價最高者。⑱賣得;以…價錢出售。The house *went* very cheap. 這房子賣得很便宜。⑲有某種說法;有某些字句或調子。The story *goes* that.... 故事是這樣的…。as the saying *goes*. 常言道。This is how the song *goes* (=is sung). 這就是這歌曲的唱法。I'm not quite sure how the words *go*. 我不大記得那些字句是怎樣的。⑳流通;通用;通行;流傳。American banknotes *go* anywhere. 美國的鈔票到處都通用。㉑稱爲;叫做;冒(名)。He *goes* by the name of Dick. 他名叫狄克。She *went* under a false name. 她用假名。㉒至某種程度。That's *going* too far. 那(說得、做得)太過分了。㉓被除去;被廢棄;被花費;被失去;死。All his money *goes* on books. 他所有的錢都花在書籍上。His wife *went* first. 他的妻子先死。㉔將;要。It's *going* to rain. 快要下雨了。㉕有;備有(只用其現在分詞形式)。There's sure to be some sort of dinner *going*. 一定會備有某種晚餐。㉖照一般水準。He's a good actor, as actors *go* nowadays. 照目前一般水準而論,他是一個好演員。㉗〖俗〗用以加强否定命令式的語氣。Don't *go* and make a fool of yourself. 不要把你自己弄成一個傻瓜。㉘招惹;惹來。Don't *go* to any trouble. 不要招惹麻煩。㉙起訴;訴諸;控訴。to *go* to court. 訴諸法庭。㉚損壞;發生故障。The engine in the old car finally *went*. 這輛老汽車的引擎終於壞了。㉛歸屬;應置於。This book *goes* on the top shelf. 這本書應置於頂層書架上的。Where is this table to *go?* 這桌子應置於何處? *—v.t.* ①賭;打賭。I will *go* you a shilling. 我要和你打賭一先令。②〖俗〗忍耐;忍受。I can't *go* tea. 我不喝茶。***as things*** (or ***people***) ***go*** 就一般情形而言。***dead and gone*** 已死去。***get going*** 開始。***go about*** **a.** 忙於;着手;作。*Go about* your business. 去做你自己的事。**b.** 來去移動;走來走去;四處走動。**c.** (謠言等)流傳。**d.** 轉身;轉向。***go after*** 追求。to *go after* fame. 追求名譽;爲名。***go against*** 反對;相反;不利於。It *goes against* my principles. 這與我的主張相反。***go ahead*** **a.** 不猶豫地向前進;做下去。**b.** 進步;成功;勝過對方。He's *going ahead* fast. 他進步很快。***go aloft*** 〖俚〗死。***go along*** 進行;進步。***go along with*** **a.** 陪伴。**b.** 贊成;同意。***Go along with you!*** 滾你的! 去你的! 別胡說啦! ***go and*** (考慮欠週地;不幸地;愚昧地)竟然做…。She had to *go and* lose her gloves at the theater. 她(不幸地)竟在戲院中丟了手套。***go around*** **a.** 四處走動;走來走去。**b.** 供應。**c.** 常與…在一起〖with〗。***go astray*** 迷途。***go at*** **a.** 衝向;突擊;打擊。**b.** 精力充沛地開始(進行)…。to *go at* one's work with a will. 抱着決心,精力充沛地繼續做其工作。***go away*** 離去。***go back*** **a.** 回去。**b.** 過盛時;走下坡。**c.** 回溯;追溯。***go back of*** 〖俗〗調查;查究。***go back on*** (or ***upon***) 違背(諾言等);背棄;食(言)。***go bad*** 變壞;腐敗;變酸。***go before*** 走在前面。***go behind*** **a.** 調查眞相;調查內幕。**b.** 虧本。***go between*** 作中間人;作媒人;調停;斡旋。***go beyond*** 超出;超過。***go by*** **a.** 過去;逝。**b.** 受指導;遵照;依循。Don't *go by* what she says. 別聽她的。**c.** 受…所控制。**d.** 稱爲;名叫;叫做。***go down*** **a.** (船)沉沒。**b.** (日)落;(月)下。**c.** 吞下。**d.** 受歡迎;被公認、相信或讚許。**e.** 被記得;永垂不朽。**f.** 繼續不斷;延續。**g.** (風、海浪等)平息;平靜。**h.** (物價)下降;跌落。**i.** 被推翻;被征服;屈服。**j.** (英牛津與劍橋兩大學用語)離開大學;退學。**k.** 降下;下斜。**l.** 承受失敗。***go down on one's knees*** 跪;屈膝。***Go easy!*** 輕鬆一點! 慢一點! ***go far*** 著名;成名;揚名。***go for*** **a.** 想得到;延請。**b.** 讚許;贊助;支持。**c.** 被認爲。All my work *went for* nothing. 我一切的工作都歸於零。**d.** 襲擊。***go for a walk*** (***ride, swim, etc.***) 去散步(騎馬、游泳等)。***go for broke*** 〖俚〗盡力而爲;孤注一擲。***go forth*** 公布;宣布。***go forward*** 前進;進展;進步。***go halves*** (or ***shares***) 平分;分攤。***go hard with*** 遭遇困難。***go in*** **a.** 進入;放入。**b.** (日、月、星辰等)被雲所遮蓋。**c.** (板球戲等)開始一局比賽。***go in for*** **a.** 愛好;

嗜好（=take an interest in)。**b.** 參加（=take part in)。***Going, going, gone!***（拍賣時用語）要賣了，要賣了，賣掉了！***go into*** **a.** 考慮；討論。Why *go into* that matter now? 為甚麼現在要討論那件事情？**b.** 從事。**c.** 進入；加入；納入。**d.** 調查；查究。**e.** 穿着。**f.** 變為；發作。***go in with*** 入股；聯合。***go off*** **a.** 爆炸；（鎗、爆竹等）響（=explode)。The firecracker *went off* with a bang. 爆竹啪一聲響了。**b.** 離去；（劇本中）下場；離開劇臺。**c.** 突發；突然說出或作出。**d.** 發生。**e.** 變壞；降低品質。**f.** 完成；演出。The performance *went off* very well. 這表演甚佳。**g.** 逃走。**h.**（貨物）銷售；售出。***go off one's head*** 〖俗〗變蠢；變瘋；行為愚笨。***go on*** **a.** 繼續；持久。*Go on* with your work. 繼續你的工作。**b.** 過去；消逝。**c.** 接着。**d.** 發生。What's *going on* here? 這裏發生甚麼事？**e.** 穿進；戴進。**f.**〖板球〗投球。**g.** 上臺；出場。**h.** 繼續某種舉動。**i.** 受支持；受資助；受救濟。***go (on) a journey (voyage, visit, trip, etc.)*** 去旅行（航海、拜訪、遠足等)。***go on for*** 接近；將近（常用進行式)。He's *going on for* fifty. 他年近五十。***go (one) better*** 勝過；超越；出價高於。***go out*** **a.** 熄滅（=stop burning)。**b.** 離開。**c.** 參加社交活動；交際。**d.** 離職；退休；下臺。**e.** 過時；不流行。**f.**（婦女）離家工作。**g.** 出國；到外國去。**h.**（年）終了。**i.**（心）同情；憐憫。Her heart *went out* to the poor orphan child. 她的心同情這個可憐的孤兒。**j.**（工人）罷工。***go out of fashion*** 過時；不時髦。***go out of office*** 失去政權。***go out of one's mind*** 發瘋。***go out of print*** 絕版。***go over*** **a.** 視察；查看；複習（=inspect, review)。**b.** 橫過；越過。**c.** 投靠；背叛自己的政黨或宗教等。**d.** 成功。***go round*** **a.** 足够分配。**b.** 繞道；走彎路。**c.** 拜訪。***go straight*** 過誠實的生活。***go strong*** 無老態。***go the way of all flesh*** 死。***go the whole hog*** 做事徹底。***go through*** **a.** 審閱；查閱（=examine)。I will *go through* your papers. 我將審閱你們的卷子。**b.** 忍受；經歷。**c.** 舉行；參加。**d.** 做完；耗盡；至…之盡頭。**e.**（書）銷售；售完。**f.** 被接納；被認可。***go through with*** 完成。***go to*** **a.** 總共。Twelve inches *go to* one foot. 十二英寸總共為一英尺。**b.** 有助於；促成。***go together*** **a.** 相配；調和。**b.** 可能共存。**c.** 經常作伴；形影不離（如情侶般)。***go to it*** 〖俗〗立刻開始。***go to pieces*** **a.** 破碎；瓦解。**b.** 身體衰弱。**c.** 神經錯亂。***go to (the) pot*** 變壞；粉碎；崩潰。***go to seed*** **a.**（花）結子；結實。**b.** 體格或智力變弱。***go to war (with or against)*** 訴諸戰爭；（與…）宣戰。***go under*** **a.** 淹沒；沉沒。**b.** 失敗；破滅；被毀滅。***go up*** **a.**（物價）上升；高漲。**b.** 爆炸；爆發。**c.** 蓋建。**d.** 毀壞。**e.**（英國牛津及劍橋兩大學用語）進入大學；入學。**f.** 增加。***go with*** **a.** 配合；調和。This color does not *go with* that. 這顏色同那顏色不調和。**b.** 陪伴；同意。**c.** 屬於；連同。***go without*** 沒有。***go without saying*** 不待言。It *goes without saying* that....（某事）自不待言。***let go*** **a.** 鬆手；放鬆。Please *let go* of my arm. 請放開我的手臂。**b.** 釋放。**c.** 解雇。**d.** 忘記；放棄；拋棄。***let go with*** 盡情說；縱情叫喊。***let oneself go*** 發脾氣；任性。***so far as it goes*** 就目前的情形而論。***to go*** **a.** 剩下；尚有。**b.**〖俗〗（食物）非在出賣地附近消費。coffee and doughnuts *to go*. 買了帶回去吃的咖啡和油煎圈餅。—*n.* ①去；進行。the come and *go* of the seasons. 四季的來與去。②〖俗〗精神；精力。He still has plenty of *go* in him. 他尚有足够的精力。③〖俗〗事態；事件。It's a queer *go*. 這是一件奇怪的事。④〖俗〗時尚；時髦；流行式樣。⑤〖俗〗嘗試；機會。Let's have a *go* at it. 讓我們試一試；給我們一個機會。⑥成功的事；勝利。⑦協定；交易。Thirty dollars? It's a *go*. 三十元？成交了。⑧〖俗〗（拳擊）比賽。the main *go*. 主要比賽。***all*** (or ***quite***) ***the go*** 流行；時髦。***from the word 'go'*** 從頭；一開始。He's been against the plan *from the word 'go'*. 他一開始便反對那計畫。***no go*** 〖俗〗不行；不要；沒有用；無價值。We tried to get there by noon, but it was *no go*. 我們想辦法中午以前到達那裏，可是沒有用。***on the go*** 〖俗〗活動；活躍；忙碌。—*interj.*（賽跑）起步的號令。On your mark! Get set! *Go!* 各就各位！預備！起！—*adj.*〖美〗①預備好的；齊備的。②功能精確的。〖注意〗(1)**go and** 是非正式的加重語氣用語：*Go and* try it yourself. 你自己去試試看（無實際動作之意)。(2)**go** 與不定詞連用，有加强語氣的作用。俗語中可省略不定詞的 to，如：He finally had to *go* ask for a raise. 他終於不得不去請求加薪。

go²〖日〗*n.* 圍棋。（亦作 Go)

G.O., g.o. ①general office. ②general order.

go·a 〔'goə; 'gouə〕 *n.* 西藏產的一種羚羊。

goad 〔god; goud〕 *n.* ①（驅畜用之）刺棒。②刺激物。—*v.t.* 刺激；驅迫。Hunger *goaded* him to steal a loaf of bread. 饑餓驅迫他偷一塊麪包。

go-a·head 〔'goə,hɛd; 'gouəhed〕 *adj.* ①前進的。②〖俗〗進取的；積極的；有冒險精神的。—*n.*〖俗〗①前進；進步；前進的命令或信號。②有進取心的人；有冒險精神的人。

***goal** 〔gol; goul〕 *n.* ①（賽跑之）終點。②（足球等）球門。③攻球門。④中一球；得一分。to score (kick, get) a *goal*. 得（踢，獲）一分。⑤守門員；門將。⑥目標；鵠的。one's *goal* in life. 生活的目標。—**less,** *adj.*

goal·ie, goal·ee 〔'golɪ; 'gouli〕 *n.*〖俗〗=**goalkeeper.**

goal·keep·er 〔'gol,kipə; 'goul,ki:pə〕 *n.*〖足球等〗守門員。（亦作 **goaltender**)

goal line 〖橄欖球等〗決勝線。

goal post 〖足球等〗球門柱。

goal tending 〖籃球〗趁球快進入對方籃筐時違規將其打出。

go-as-you-please 〔'goəzju'pliz; 'gouəzju'pli:z〕 *adj.* ①漫無計畫的。②不受拘束的；隨心所欲的；隨便的。

:goat 〔got; gout〕 *n., pl.* **goats** or **goat.** ①山羊。②〖美俚〗代人受過者；替罪的人。He was always made the *goat* when someone was needed to take the blame. 每當有人必須受責時他常被迫代人受過。③〖俚〗色鬼。***get one's goat*** 〖美俚〗使人發怒或煩躁。***separate the sheep from the goats*** 將好人與壞人分開。—**like,** *adj.*

goat·ee 〔go'ti; gou'ti:〕 *n.* 山羊鬍鬚。

goat·herd 〔'got,hɝd; 'gouthə:d〕 *n.* 牧養山羊者；牧羊人。

goat·ish 〔'gotɪʃ; 'goutiʃ〕 *adj.* ①似山羊的。②淫亂的；好色的。（亦作 **goaty**) —**ly,** *adv.* —**ness,** *n.*

goat·skin 〔'got,skɪn; 'gout-skin〕 *n.* 羊皮；羊皮革。

goat·suck·er ['got,sʌkə; 'gout,sʌkə] *n.* 蚊母鳥;歐夜鷹。

gob[1] [gɑb; gɔb] *n.* 〖俚〗美國水兵。

gob[2] *n.* ①〖俗〗塊;團。a *gob* of butter. 一塊奶油。②〖採礦〗塡塞材料。③(*pl.*)〖俗〗大量。*gobs* of money. 很多錢。

gob[3] *n.* 〖俚〗嘴。

go·bang [go'bæŋ; gou'bæŋ] *n.* (用圍棋盤下的)五子棋。

Go·bat [,go'ba; ,gɔː'ba] *n.* 高巴(Charles Albert, 1843–1914, 瑞士政治家, 曾獲 1902 年諾貝爾和平獎)。

gob·bet ['gɑbɛt; 'gɔbit] *n.* ①小片;(生肉的)一塊;一口。②(原文或樂曲)的一段。

gob·ble[1] ['gɑbl; 'gɔbl] *v.t.* & *v.i.*, **-bled, -bling.** 大吃; 狼吞虎嚥。He doesn't eat, he simply *gobbles*. 他不是在吃，他是在吞。***gobble up*** 〖俗〗貪取;急攫。We *gobbled up* the enemy. 我們把敵人全部殲滅了。

gob·ble[2] *v.*, **-bled, -bling,** *n.* —*v.i.* 作咯咯聲(如火鷄)。—*v.t.* 咯咯地發出。—*n.* 咯咯聲。

gob·ble·de·gook, gob·ble·dy·gook ['gɑbldɪ,guk; 'gɔbldiguk] *n.* 〖美俚〗冗長的官樣文章。

gob·bler[1] ['gɑblə; 'gɔblə] *n.* 雄火鷄。

gob·bler[2] *n.* 狼吞虎嚥的人。

Gob·e·lin ['gɑbəlɪn; 'goubəlin] *adj.* (似)高布林織的。*Gobelin* blue. 暗青綠色。the *Gobelin* tapestry. 高布林織掛毛氈(巴黎高布林工廠所製之室內裝飾用花紋織品)。

go-be·tween ['gobə,twin; 'gou-bi,twiːn] *n.* 居間人; 中人; 從中斡旋者; 媒人。

gob·let ['gɑblɪt; 'gɔblit] *n.* ①高脚玻璃杯。②〖古〗盃。

gob·lin ['gɑblɪn; 'gɔblin] *n.* 惡鬼; 小妖精。

go·by ['gobɪ; 'goubi] *n., pl.* **-bies, -by.** 鰕虎魚;鰻。

go-by ['go,baɪ; 'goubai] *n.* 〖俗〗不理;忽視。to give one (a person or thing) the *go-by*. 視同陌路;置之不顧。

go·cart ['go,kɑrt; 'gou-kɑːt] *n.* ①(嬰兒)推車。②(嬰兒)習步車。③一種車身很低的單人遊戲車, 最高時速爲60英里。

‡**God** [gɑd; gɔd] *n., v.,* **god·ded, god·ding,** *interj.* —*n.* ①上帝。Pray to *God*. 向上帝祈禱。*God* help you! 願上帝助你! ②(g-)神;男神。Neptune was the *god* of the sea. (羅馬神話) Neptune 是海神。③(g-) 偶像; 神像。④(g-) 受尊崇的人或物。a (little) tin *god*. 過分受尊崇的官員。to make a *god* of one's belly. 尊崇自己的肚子(重視飲食)。***the gods*** **a.** 戲院中的樓座。**b.** 戲院中樓座的觀衆。—*v.t.* (g-)奉爲神聖; 崇拜。—*interj.* 表示失望、懷疑、絕望、厭煩等的感歎詞。*God*, there she goes singing off key again! 我的老天哪, 她又唱走調了!

God-aw·ful ['gɑd'ɔfəl; 'gɔd'ɔːfəl] *adj.* 〖俗〗(有時用 g-) 非常可怖(震驚)的。

god·child ['gɑd,tʃaɪld; 'gɔdtʃaild] *n., pl.* **-chil·dren.** 敎子;敎女。

god·damn ['gɑd'dæm; 'gɔd'dæm] *interj.* 〖俗〗用以表示任何强烈之感情(常與 it 連用)。—*n.* ①用"goddamn"作强調或發誓。②無價值之物。not to give a good *god-damn*. 不理睬。—*adj.* & *adv.* =**goddamned.** —*v.t.* & *v.i.* 用 goddamn 罵、發誓、强調等。

god·damned ['gɑd'dæmd; 'gɔd'dæmd] *adj.* (常略作 **goddamn, goddam**)該死的; 壞透了的。—*adv.* ① (常用最高級 god-damnedest) 最難相處;最難應付;極爲複雜或特別。②=**damned.**

god·daugh·ter ['gɑd,dɔtə; 'gɔd-,dɔːtə] *n.* 敎女。

***god·dess** ['gɑdɪs; 'gɔdis] *n.* ①女神。Venus was a *goddess* worshiped by the Romans. 維納斯是羅馬人所崇拜的女神。②絕代美女。—**ship,** —**hood,** *n.*

go·det [,go'dɛ; ,gou'de] 〖法〗*n.* 女人裙後所附三角布片(用以顯示褶紋)。

go-dev·il ['go,dɛvl; 'gou,devl] *n.* 〖美〗油管通潔器。②木材運搬橇。

***god·fa·ther** ['gɑd,fɑðə; 'gɔd,fɑːðə] *n.* ①敎父。②保護者;監護者。—*v.t.* 作…之敎父。—**ly,** *adv.*

God-fear·er ['gɑd,fɪrə; 'gɔd,fiərə] *n.* 敬畏上帝者。

God-fear·ing ['gɑd,fɪrɪŋ; 'gɔd,fiəriŋ] *adj.* 敬畏上帝的;虔敬的。

God·for·sak·en ['gɑdfə'sekən; 'gɔd-fə,seikn] *adj.* ①見棄於神的;罪惡的。②〖俗〗荒蕪的; 悽慘的。③可憐的; 被忽視的。(亦作 **godforsaken**)

God-giv·en ['gɑd,gɪvən; 'gɔd,givən] *adj.* ①神賜的。②絕好的; 受歡迎的;適宜的。(有時作 **god-given**)

God·head ['gɑdhɛd; 'gɔdhed] *n.* ①上帝。②(g-) 神性; 神格。③〖罕〗(g-) 神;女神。

god·hood ['gɑdhud; 'gɔdhud] *n.* 神格;神性。

Go·di·va [gə'daɪvə; gə'daivə] *n.* 哥黛娃(十一世紀時英國貴婦, 相傳曾爲民請命而裸體乘馬通過 Coventry)。

god·less ['gɑdlɪs; 'gɔdlis] *adj.* ①無神的;不信有神存在的。②不信神的。③邪惡的。—**ly,** *adv.* —**ness,** *n.*

god·like ['gɑd,laɪk; 'gɔdlaik] *adj.* 如神的;尊嚴的。—**ness,** *n.*

god·li·ness ['gɑdlɪnɪs; 'gɔdlinis] *n.* 神聖;虔敬。

god·ly ['gɑdlɪ; 'gɔdli] *adj.,* **-li·er, -li·est.** ①虔誠的;敬拜神的。the *godly*. 善男信女。②正當的。to run a *godly* race. 按上帝意旨規規矩矩過日子。—**god·li·ly,** *adv.*

God-man ['gɑd,mæn; 'gɔd'mæn] *n.* 神人;(尤指)耶穌基督。

***god·moth·er** ['gɑd,mʌðə; 'gɔd,mʌ-ðə] *n.* 敎母。—*v.t.* 作…之敎母。

go·down [go'daun; 'goudaun] *n.* (遠東地區之)倉庫;棧房。

god·par·ent ['gɑd,pɛrənt; 'gɔd,pɛə-rənt] *n.* 敎父或敎母。

God's acre 墳場;公墓。

God's country ①風景秀麗, 物產豐富之區。②家鄉。

god·send ['gɑd,sɛnd; 'gɔdsend] *n.* 意外獲得的心愛物;天賜之物。

god·ship ['gɑdʃɪp; 'gɔdʃip] *n.* =**god-hood.**

god·son ['gɑd,sʌn; 'gɔdsʌn] *n.* 敎子。

God·speed ['gɑd,spid; 'gɔd'spiːd] *n.* 成功;幸運。

God's plenty 非常豐富之量。

God·ward ['gɑdwəd; 'gɔdwəd] *adv.* & *adj.* ①向神(的);對神(的)。②有關神(的)。

God·wards ['gɑdwədz; 'gɔdwədz] *adv.* =**Godward.**

god·wit ['gɑdwɪt; 'gɔdwit] *n.* 〖動物〗鷸科之長嘴涉水禽。

go·er ['goə; 'gouə] *n.* ①去的人;出席者。②行人; 路人; 去的東西;動的東西;轉動之物;鐘錶; 車; 馬。comers and *goers*. 來來往往的人。a good (poor, slow) *goer*. 健步(遲步)的人;快(慢)馬;好(不好)的鐘。

Goe·the ['getɪ; 'gəːtə] *n.* 歌德(Johann Wolfgang von, 1749–1832, 德國文學家)。

—an, *adj.*, *n.*

gof·fer ['gɑfə, 'gɔfə; 'goufə] *v.t.* 加褶皺 (於布等)。—*n.* ①(爲衣服裝飾之) 皺褶; 襞。②壓褶皺之具。(亦作 **gauffer**)

go-get·ter ['go'gɛtə; 'gou'getə] *n.* 〖俚〗積極能幹的人; 積極進取的人; 老手。—**go-get·ting**, *adj.*

gog·gle ['gɑgl; 'gɔgl] *n.*, *v.*, **-gled**, **-gling**, *adj.* —*n.*(*pl.*)護目鏡。—*v.i.* & *v.t.* ①瞪(眼); 睜視; 轉動(眼睛)。②〖俗〗用魚叉捕魚。—*adj.* 睜視的; 圓睜的; 眼球凸出的。

gog·gle-box ['gɑgl̩,bɑks; 'gɔglbɔks] *n.* 〖英俚〗電視機。

Gogh [go; gou] *n.* 梵谷 (Vincent van, 1853–1890, 荷蘭後期印象派畫家)。

gog·let ['gɑglɪt; 'gɔglit] *n.* 冷水瓶。(亦作 **guglet, gurglet**)

go-go ['go,go; 'gou,gou] *adj.* ①阿哥哥舞的。②跳阿哥哥舞者的。③跳阿哥哥舞的夜總會的。

go-go fund 用於股票投機的資本。

‡**go·ing** ['goɪŋ; 'gouiŋ] *n.* ①離去; 離開。His *going* was unexpected. 他的離去是意外的。②道路的狀況; 行走的情況。The *going* is hard over this rough mountain road. 在這崎嶇的山路上行走頗爲吃力。③(行駛或工作的)速度或方法。For a train, 70 miles an hour is good *going*. 以火車而論, 每小時七十英里是很快的速度。④進度; 進步。good *going* toward the presidency. 當總統的希望甚佳(頗有進展)。⑤(*pl.*) 行爲; 舉止; 風度。—*adj.* ①進行中的; 運轉的。The clock is *going*. 鐘在走。②活動的; 存在的。a *going* business (*or* concern). 在營業中的商店。③目前的; 現在的。What is the *going* price of farmland in Ohio? 俄亥俄州的農地時價若干? ***be going to*** 將要; 就要; 正打算。Do you think it *is going to* rain? 你以爲就要下雨麼? ***going and coming*** 進退維谷的。***going away*** a. 〖運動〗領先甚多。The champion won the bout *going away*. 拳王以壓倒性優勢贏得這場比賽。b. 〖賽馬〗迅速超前。***going on*** 將近; 幾乎。

go·ing-o·ver ['goɪŋ'ovə; 'gouiŋ'ouvə] *n.*, *pl.* **go·ings-o·ver.** ①調查; 核對。②苛斥。③痛打; 毒打。

goings on ①行爲; 舉止; 品行(常與such, strange 連用)。a person's strange *goings on*. 一個人的奇怪行爲。②事件。

goi·tre, goi·ter ['gɔɪtə; 'gɔitə] *n.* 〖醫〗甲狀腺腫。—**goi·trous**, *adj.*

goi·trog·e·nous [gɔɪ'trɑdʒənəs; gɔi'trɔdʒənəs] *adj.* 造成甲狀腺腫的。

Gol·con·da [gɑl'kɑndə; gɔl'kɔndə] *n.* ①葛康達(印度古都, 16 世紀以其財富及金剛石切割術聞名)。②(常 g-)大富源; 寶庫。

‡**gold** [gold; gould] *n.* ①金; 黃金。②錢財。③金幣。④貴重華麗之物。a heart of *gold*. 高貴的心。⑤金黃色。the red and *gold* of the autumn woods. 秋季樹林中紅色和金黃色的景色。—*adj.* ①金製的; 金的。*gold* coin (watch). 金幣(錶)。②金黃色的。③用金子付的。

gold·beat·er ['gold,bitə; 'gould,bi:tə] *n.* 金箔工人。

gold·beat·ing ['gold,bitɪŋ; 'gould,bi:tiŋ] *n.* 製金箔。(亦作**gold beating**)

gold brick ①〖美俗〗假金磚; 假金條。②〖美俗〗假物。③〖美軍俚〗藉故逃避工作者; 吊兒郎當者。(亦作 **goldbrick**)

gold-brick ['gold,brɪk; 'gould,brik] *v.i.* 〖軍俚〗逃避勤務; 裝病。—*v.t.* 〖美俚〗欺詐; 詐騙。—*n.* 裝病躲懶者。—**er**, *n.*

gold·bug ['gold,bʌg; 'gouldbʌg] *n.* 金甲蟲。

Gold Coast ①黃金海岸(西非海岸之一地區, 現爲 Ghana 國土之一部分)。②〖美俗〗高級住宅區。

gold digger ①掘金者。②〖俗〗以色爲餌騙取男人金錢的女人。

gold dust 粉狀金; 金屑。

‡**gold·en** ['goldn̩; 'gouldən] *adj.* ①金製的(通常用 gold)。②金色的。*golden* hair. 金色的頭髮。③含金的; 產金的。④興隆的; 昌盛的。⑤可貴的; 重要的。a *golden* opportunity. 好機會。⑥有才幹的; 事業蒸蒸日上的。the *golden* girl of Broadway. 百老匯的一個有才幹的女演員。⑦柔和而響亮的。a *golden* voice. 響亮圓潤的嗓音。⑧〖俚〗有錢的; 小康的。If I can raise a hundred dollars more, I'll be *golden*. 我如果能再弄到一百塊錢, 我的日子就好過了。***the golden age*** 黃金時代。***the golden rule*** 金科玉律。—**ly**, *adv.* —**ness**, *n.*

golden boy 〖俗〗有才幹者; 前途極有希望者。

golden calf 金錢; 物質財富。

golden carp 金魚。

gold·en·eye ['goldən,aɪ; 'gouldənai] *n.*, *pl.* **-eyes, -eye.** 白頰鳧。

Golden Fleece 〖希臘神話〗(英雄 Jason 率 Argonauts 至 Colchis 尋找的) 金羊毛。

Golden Gate 金門灣 (連接太平洋與美國舊金山灣之海峽)。

golden goose 傳說中每日下一金蛋之鵝, 後爲其貪得之主人所殺。

golden mean ①中庸之道。②＝**golden section.**

golden opinions 稱道; 讚賞。

gold·en·rod ['goldn̩,rɑd; 'gouldənrɔd] *n.* 〖植物〗紫菀科植物; 秋麒麟草。

gold·en·seal ['goldən,sil; 'gouldənsi:l] *n.* 〖植物〗金印章; 北義黃連(可作藥用)。

golden section 〖美術〗黃金分割 (即矩形短邊與長邊之比例等於長邊與長短二邊和之比例)。

Golden State 美國加利福尼亞州之別稱。

golden wedding 金婚(結婚五十周年紀念)。

gold fever 採金熱。

gold field 採金區; 金鑛區; 金田。

gold-filled ['gold'fɪld; 'gould'fild] *adj.* 包金的; (牙齒)塡金的。

gold·finch ['gold,fɪntʃ; 'gouldfintʃ] *n.* 金翅雀; 小碛鷚。

***gold·fish** ['gold,fɪʃ; 'gouldfiʃ] *n.*, *pl.* **-fish·es** or **-fish.** ①金魚。②〖俚〗鮭罐頭。

gold foil (牙科用)金箔。

gold·i·locks ['goldɪ,lɑks; 'gouldilɔks] *n.*, *pl.* **-locks.** ①(作 *sing.* 解) 金髮的人。②(作 *sing.* or *pl.* 解) 歐洲毛莨。③(作 *sing.* or *pl.* 解) 金鳳花。(亦作 **goldylocks**)

gold lace 金線帶。

gold leaf 金箔。

gold mine ①金礦; 金山。②〖俗〗大富源; 大財源。③寶庫; 源泉。

gold plate 金器(集合稱)。

gold reserve 黃金準備金之存量。

gold rush 湧向新採金地之人潮。

***gold·smith** ['gold,smɪθ; 'gouldsmiθ] *n.* 金匠。

Gold·smith ['gold,smɪθ; 'gouldsmiθ] *n.* 哥德斯密 (Oliver, 1728–1774, 愛爾蘭的詩人、劇作家、散文家及小說家)。

gold standard 〖經濟〗金本位(制)。

gold stick 〖英〗①國家大典等時替國王執金色之杖的宮內官。②其金色之杖。

***golf** 〔gɑlf, gɔlf; gɔlf〕 *n.* 高爾夫球戲。—*v.i.* 打高爾夫球。

golf club ①高爾夫球棒。②高爾夫俱「樂部。」

golf course (or **links**) 高爾夫球場;灼球場。

golf·er 〔'gɑlfɚ; 'gɔlfə〕 *n.* 玩高爾夫球「者。」

golf widow 高爾夫球迷(被丢在家中)的妻子。

Gol·gi 〔'gɔldʒɪ; 'gɔːldʒi〕 *n.* 高爾基(Camillo, 1844–1926, 義大利解剖學家及病理學家, 曾獲1906年諾貝爾生理及醫學奬)。

Gol·go·tha 〔'gɑlgəθə; 'gɔlgəθə〕 *n.* ①各各他(基督被釘於十字架之地)。②(g-)墓地。③(g-)受難之地;殉教(犧牲)之地。

Go·li·ath 〔gə'laɪəθ; gə'laiəθ, gou'l-〕 *n.* ①聖經所載被大衞殺死之巨人。②(g-) 巨人;大亨;異常重要之事物。

gol·li·wog(g) 〔'gɑlɪˌwɑg; 'gɔliwɔg〕 *n.* ①黑面、烱眼、豎髮、奇裝之玩偶。②奇異醜陋之人。

gol·ly 〔'gɑlɪ; 'gɔli〕 *interj.* 表驚異之聲「(God 之變體, 又作 by golly).」

go·losh(e) 〔gə'lɑʃ; gə'lɔʃ〕 *n.* =galosh(e).

go·lup·tious 〔gə'lʌpʃəs; gə'lʌpʃəs〕「*adj.* 〖俚, 諧〗可口的;好吃的。」

G.O.M. 〖英〗 the Grand Old Man (W. E. Gladstone 的綽號)。

Go·mor·rah, Go·mor·rha 〔gə'mɑrə; gə'mɔrə〕 *n.* ①〖聖經〗蛾摩拉(因其居民罪惡重大與其鄰市 Sodom 同被神毀滅之一古城, 見舊約創世記19章24節)。②罪惡之城。

gon·ad 〔'gɑnæd; 'gɔnæd〕 *n.* 〖解剖〗性腺;生殖腺。—**al,** —**i·al,** —**ic,** *adj.*

gon·a·do·trop·ic 〔ˌgɑnədo'trɑpɪk; ˌgɔnədou'trɔpik〕 *adj.* 親生殖腺的; 向生殖腺的。

gon·do·la 〔'gɑndələ; 'gɔndələ〕 *n.* ①威尼斯運河中航行之平底輕舟。②〖美〗平底船。③〖美〗無蓋貨車車廂。④(飛船等之) 吊船;吊籃。

gon·do·lier 〔ˌgɑndə'lɪr; ˌgɔndə'liə〕「*n.* gondola 之船夫。」

‡gone 〔gɔn; gɔn, gɔːn〕 *v.* pp. of **go.** —*adj.* ①離去的。②失去的;無望的。a *gone* case. 無可救藥的情形。③死去的。④〖美〗用完的;耗盡的。It's all *gone.* 完全用完了。⑤失敗的;毀壞了的。One plane was reported missing, and we all thought that it was *gone.* 一架飛機據報失蹤, 我們大家均認爲它已毀壞了。⑥弱的;昏眩的。a *gone* feeling. 昏眩的感覺。⑦過去的。⑧懷孕的。⑨〖俚〗特出的;異常優秀的。***far gone*** **a.** 深入;深陷。**b.** 筋疲力竭的。**c.** 瀕臨死亡的。***gone on*** 〖俗〗與…相愛。He is (dead) *gone on* the girl. 他被這女孩弄得神魂顚倒。***real gone*** 〖俚〗好極了;棒。—**ness,** *n.*

gon·er 〔'gɑnɚ; 'gɔnə〕 *n.* 〖俗〗即將滅亡之人或物; 無可救藥者; 臨死者。That man is a *goner.* 那個人是無望了。

gon·fa·lon 〔'gɑnfələn, -lɑn; 'gɔnfələn〕 *n.* 旒旗(中世紀義大利所用的旗章)。

gon·fa·lon·ier 〔ˌgɑnfələ'nɪr; ˌgɔnfələ'niə〕 *n.* ①(旒) 旗手。②(中古義大利都市國家的)行政長官。

gong 〔gɔŋ; gɔŋ〕 *n.* ①銅鑼。②鈴盅。

go·ni·om·e·ter 〔ˌgonɪ'ɑmɪtɚ; ˌgouni'ɔmitə〕 *n.* 測角器。

go·ni·om·e·try 〔ˌgonɪ'ɑmɪtrɪ; ˌgouni'ɔmitri〕 *n.* 測角術。

gon·na 〔'gɔnə; 'gɔːnə〕 *v.* 〖方, 美俚〗「=**going to.**」

gon·o·coc·cus 〔ˌgɑnə'kɑkəs; ˌgɔnə'kɔkəs〕 *n., pl.* **-coc·ci** 〔-'kɑksaɪ; -'kɔksai〕. 淋菌。

gon·or·rh(o)e·a 〔ˌgɑnə'riə; ˌgɔnə'riːə〕 *n.* 〖醫〗淋病。

goo 〔gu; guː〕 *n.* 〖美俚〗黏性體。

goo·ber 〔'gubɚ, 'gʊbɚ; 'guːbə〕 *n.* 〖美南部〗落花生。(亦作 **goober pea**)

‡good 〔gʊd; gud〕 *adj.,* **bet·ter, best,** *n., interj, adv.* —*adj.* ①美好的;優良的;上等的。This is a *good* knife. 這是一把好刀。I've found a *good* house. 我發現了一幢好房子。*good* looks. 美貌。②有禮的。*good* manners. 禮貌。③適意的; 愉快的。to have a *good* (=pleasant) time. 玩得很快樂。④有益的;宜於。Milk is *good* for children. 牛奶對於小孩有益。Is this *good* to eat (drink, etc.)? 這適宜於吃(喝等)嗎? ⑤滿足的; 充分的;很。to have a *good* drink. 喝得很痛快。⑥善良的; 有德的。He's a very *good* man. 他是一個非常善良的人。⑦負責的; 忠實的; 循規蹈矩的。Try to be a *good* boy. 努力做個循規蹈矩的孩子。⑧慈善的;和善的。He is very *good* to the poor. 他對窮人很慈善。⑨通達的; 老練的; 勝任的。He is very *good* at French. 他精通法文。⑩新鮮的;純良的。This meat is not very *good.* 這肉不太新鮮。⑪强健的; 有力的。We're *good* for another five miles. 我們還有氣力再走五英里路。⑫有趣的。a *good* story. 有趣的故事。a *good* joke. 有趣的笑話。⑬眞正的; 不假的。I cannot tell *good* bills from the forged ones. 我不能辨别眞鈔和這些僞鈔。⑭有教養的。She has a *good* background. 她出身良好。⑮價值相當的。Two thousand stamps are *good* for one coffeepot. 集滿兩千張印花可換一隻咖啡壺。⑯親密的。He is a *good* friend of mine. 他是我的密友。⑰合適的。a *good* day for fishing. 釣魚的好天氣。⑱安全的; 靠得住的。a *good* investment. 安全的投資。***a good deal*** 很多; …得多; …得很。***a good many*** 很多的; 非常多的。***as good as*** 幾乎等於; 實際上。***be good for nothing*** 一無所長;毫無用處。***feel good*** 感覺健康舒適或得意洋洋。***good evening*** 晚安(晚間見面時之用語)。***good for*** **a.** 適於。**b.** 能支付。**c.** 值得。***good morning*** (***afternoon, day***) 早(午, 日)安。***good night*** 晚安(晚間分别時或就寢時之用語)。***hold good*** 有效。***in good faith*** 眞誠地;實在地。***in good health*** 健康的。***in good repair*** 勤修的;修理完整的。***in good spirits*** 高興的; 興緻勃勃的。***in good taste*** 風格高尙的。***in good time*** 早到地; 準時地。***make good*** **a.** 修補。The carpenter will *make good* the broken chair. 木匠會把破椅子修好。**b.** 成功。**c.** 恢復名譽。The young man has learned a lesson, and will *make good.* 那青年已受了教訓, 會改過自新的。**d.** 賠補; 償付。**e.** 履行;實現。The convicts *made good* their getaway. 囚犯們實現了他們的逃亡計畫。**f.** 證明;證實。***no good*** 〖俗〗**a.** 毫無用處。**b.** 毫無價值。***the good and the bad*** 善與惡;善者與惡者。—*n.* ①善行;道德。to do *good.* 行善。②利益; 好處; 幸福。I am telling you this for your *good.* 我告訴你這件事是爲你好。What's the *good* of doing that? 那樣做有甚麼益處? ③好人;善人。***come to no good*** 結果失敗。***do somebody good*** 對某人有益。***for good*** (***and***

all）永久地。He says he is leaving the country *for good.* 他說他此次離國將不再回來。***to the good*** **a.** 在有利的一方；作爲盈利；作純益。We were $5 *to the good.* 我們賺了五元。**b.** 有益；有好處。—*interj.*（表滿意、愉快、同意等）好的！—*adv.*〖俗〗=**well.** ***good and***〖俗〗很；極；非常。This soup is *good and* hot. 這湯很熱。〖注意〗**good, well** 均表好。good 是形容詞；well 或爲形容詞，或爲副詞，如：I feel *good.* 和 I feel *well.* 兩句中，good 和 well 均爲常用的形容詞，但各有不同的含義，good 指身體上實際感覺健康舒暢，well 僅指未病的狀態。

Good Book 聖經。

:good-by(e)〔gud'baɪ; gud'bai, 'gud-'bai〕*interj., n., pl.* **-by(e)s.** 再會；再見。I must say *good-by.* 我必須告辭了。

good cheer ①興高采烈；勇氣。②宴遊行樂。③美酒佳餚。

good-fel·low·ship〔ˌgud'fɛloʃɪp; ˌgud'felouʃip〕*n.* 親交；親睦。（亦作 **good-fellowhood**）

good-for-noth·ing〔'gudfə'nʌθɪŋ; 'gudfəˌnʌθiŋ〕*adj.* 無益的；無用的。—*n.* 無用之人。

good-heart·ed〔'gud'hartɪd; 'gud-'hɑːtid〕*adj.* 仁慈的；體諒的；寬厚的。（亦作 **goodhearted**）—**ly,** *adv.* —**ness,** *n.*

Good Hope, Cape of 好望角（南非共和國西南端）。

good humor 高興的情緒。

good-hu·mo(u)red〔gud'jumərd; 'gud'hjuːməd〕*adj.* 高興的；愉快的；和善的。

good·ish〔'gudɪʃ; 'gudiʃ〕*adj.* ①尙好的；差强人意的。②（數量、大小等）相當的。

good Joe〖俗〗古道熱腸者；好好先生。

good life ①正直的生活。②享受的生活。

***good-look·ing**〔'gud'lukɪŋ; 'gud-'lukiŋ〕*adj.* 貌美的；漂亮的。

good looks 漂亮；標緻。

good·ly〔'gudlɪ; 'gudli〕*adj.,* **-li·er, -li·est.** ①適意的；優良的。②漂亮的；美觀的。③頗多的；相當大的。a *goodly* sum of money. 相當大的一筆錢。—**good·li·ness,** *n.*

good·man〔'gudmən; 'gudmən〕*n., pl.* **-men.**〖古，方〗家長；戶主；丈夫。

***good-na·tured**〔'gud'netʃərd; 'gud-'neitʃəd〕*adj.* 和藹的；和善的；溫厚的。a *good-natured* man. 和善的人。—**ly,** *adv.* —**ness,** *n.*

good-neigh·bor〔'gud'nebər; 'gud-'neibə〕*adj.* 睦鄰的。

good·ness**〔'gudnɪs; 'gudnis〕*n.* ①良；善；佳。*goodness* of heart. 心地良善。②仁慈。Have the *goodness* to shut the door. 請將門關上。③美德；長處；精華。—*interj.*（表驚訝等）天呀！For goodness'*** (or ***God's***) ***sake!*** 務請；千萬。***Goodness knows!*** 天曉得！***Goodness me!*** (or ***Goodness gracious!***)（表驚訝等）啊呀！天呀！***Thank goodness!*** 謝天謝地！***wish to goodness*** 極其願望。

goods**〔gudz; gudz〕*n. pl.* ①貨物（不與數目字連用）。He buys and sells leather *goods.* 他買賣皮貨。②財產；所有物。③〖美〗布料；布。④〖美俚〗工具；必需品。⑤〖英〗貨運。a *goods* train. 運貨火車。a *goods* agent. 貨運代理人。catch with the goods*** **a.** 追回被竊物。**b.** 行竊時捕之。***deliver the goods*** **a.** 交貨；履行契約。**b.**〖俚〗克盡責任。***get*** (or ***have***) ***the goods on*** 發見或知道…之缺點。***goods and chattels***〖法律〗有體動產。

good-sized〔'gud'saɪzd; 'gud'saizd〕*adj.* 大型的。

good speed 佳運；成功。

good-tem·pered〔'gud 'tempərd; 'gud'tempəd〕*adj.* 好脾氣的；溫和的。

good·wife〔'gudˌwaɪf; 'gudwaif〕*n., pl.* **-wives.** 女主人；主婦。

***good will** ①善意；親切；親善。②自願；欣然之同意。③商譽；信譽。（亦作 **goodwill**）

***good-will**〔'gud'wɪl; 'gud'wil〕*adj.* 友好的；親善的。a *good-will* tour. 友好訪問。a *good-will* ambassador. 親善大使。

good·y¹〔'gudɪ; 'gudi〕*n., pl.* **good·ies,** *adj., interj.* —*n.*〖俗〗（常 *pl.*）好吃之物；糖果；餅。—*adj.*〖俗〗僞善的；假道學的。—*interj.*〖俗〗好呀！

good·y² *n., pl.* **good·ies.** ①身分低微之老婦。②對此等老婦之稱呼。*Goody* Smith. 史密斯老太婆。

good·y-good·y〔'gudɪ'gudɪ; 'gudi-'gudi〕*adj., n., pl.* **-good·ies.** —*adj.* =**goody¹.** —*n.* 道學先生；僞善者；好好先生。

goo·ey〔'guɪ; 'guːi〕*adj.,* **goo·i·er, goo·i·est.**〖美俚〗①膠黏的。②黏而甜的。—*n.*〖美俚〗黏的東西；糖蜜。

goof〔guf; guːf〕*n., pl.* **goofs.** *v.,* **goofed, goof·ing.** —*n.*〖俚〗①呆子。②失誤。—*v.t.* 搞壞；弄糟〖常 up〗。—*v.i.* ①犯錯。②打發時間〖常 off, around〗。***goof off***〖俚〗浪費時間。***goof up***〖俚〗犯錯。

go-off〔'goˌɔf; 'gouˌɔːf〕*n.*〖俗〗出發；着手；開始。

goof-off〔'gufˌɔf; 'guːfˌɔːf〕*n.* 推卸責任者。

goof·y〔'gufɪ; 'guːfi〕*adj.,* **goof·i·er, goof·i·est.**〖俚〗愚蠢的；可笑的。—**goof·i·ness,** *n.*

goo·gly〔'guglɪ; 'guːgli〕*n.*〖曲棍球、板球戲〗曲球。

goo·gol〔'gugal; 'guːgɔl〕*n.* 一後面帶一百個零的數目（常以10^{100}表示）。

gook〔guk; guk〕*n.*〖美軍俚，蔑〗菲律賓人、韓國人、日本人等。

goon〔gun; guːn〕*n.*〖俚〗①笨人。②暴徒（尤指受雇破壞罷工或恫嚇工廠者）。

goos·an·der〔gus'ændər; guː'sændə〕*n.*〖動物〗秋沙鴨。

goose**〔gus; guːs〕*n., pl.* **geese**〔gis; giːs〕for ①—④, **gooses** for ⑤. ①鵝。a drove of *geese.* 一羣鵝。②雌鵝。③鵝肉。④傻瓜；笨伯。⑤（裁縫用有長曲柄的）熨斗。All his geese are swans.*** 他喜歡誇大。***be unable to say "bo" to a goose*** 極爲膽小。***cook one's goose*** **a.** 澆冷水；毀人的希望、計畫等。**b.** 徹底毀滅一個人的機會。***kill the goose that lays the golden eggs*** 斷絕財源。***the goose hangs high*** 前途有望。—*v.t.*〖俚〗①觸（人）肛門使驚。②（開車時）作不平均的加油。

goose·ber·ry〔'gusˌbɛrɪ; 'guzbəri〕*n., pl.* **-ries.** 醋栗。

goose egg ①〖俚〗零分。②〖俗〗頭上被擊或碰撞而起的腫瘤。

goose flesh 小疙瘩；雞皮疙瘩。（亦作 **gooseflesh, goose bumps, goose pimples, goose skin**）

goose·foot〔'gusˌfut; 'guːsfut〕*n., pl.* **-foots.**〖植物〗藜屬植物。

goose·gog〔'gusˌgag; 'guːsgɔg〕*n.*〖英方〗=**goose-berry.**

goose grass〖植物〗豬殃殃。

goose·herd〔'gusˌhɜd; 'guːshəːd〕*n.* 飼鵝者。

goose·neck ['gus,nɛk; 'gu:snek] *n.* 曲如鵝頸之物。

gooseneck lamp 有活動曲莖可自由調整之臺燈。

goose pimples(or **skin**) = **goose flesh.**

goose-step ['gus,stɛp; 'gu:sstep] *v.i.* 〖俗〗①正步走。②按上方命令行動。

goose step 〖軍〗正步(彎膝蓋伸直腿走的步法)。

goos·ey, goos·ie ['gusɪ; 'gu:si] *n.* 〖兒語〗鵝;呆子。

goos·y ['gusɪ; 'gu:si] *adj.*, **goos·i·er, goos·i·est.** ①像鵝的; 愚蠢的。②〖俚〗易受驚的;膽怯的;神經質的。

G.O.P. or **GOP** Grand Old Party. 美國的共和黨(the Republican Party).

go·pher ['gofɚ; 'goufə] *n.* ①囊頰獸(北美產之掘地齧齒動物)。②一種地鼠。③(G-) 美國 Minnesota 州居民。

gopher ball 〖棒球俚〗被擊中而成爲全壘打的球。

go·pher·wood ['gofɚ,wud; 'goufə-wud] *n.* 〖聖經〗製造 Noah 方舟所用之木材。(亦作 **gopher**)

go·ral ['gorəl; 'gourəl] *n.* (喜馬拉雅山產之)斑羚。

gor·cock ['gɔr,kɑk; 'gɔ:kɔk] *n.* 〖蘇〗雄赤松鷄。

Gor·di·an knot ['gɔrdɪən~; 'gɔ:-djən~] ①〖希臘神話〗 Phrygia 王 Gordius 之難結(按神諭能解之者,即可爲亞細亞王,後亞歷山大以劍砍斷之)。 ②難題。 ***cut the Gordian knot*** 用强硬手段解決難事。

gore[1] [gor, gɔr; gɔ:, gɔə] *n.* 血塊;淤血;凝血。

gore[2] *v.t.*, **gored, gor·ing.** (獸等)用角抵死。

gore[3] *n.*, *v.*, **gored, gor·ing.** —*n.* ①長三角形布;衽;襠。②三角地帶。—*v.t.* 縫以長三角布。

*__gorge__ [gɔrdʒ; gɔ:dʒ] *n.*, *v.*, **gorged, gorg·ing.** —*n.* ①隘路; 峽。 the Yangtse *Gorges*. 長江三峽。②嚥下物。③胃內之物。④厭惡;憎恨;憤懣。⑤〖築城〗背面的出入口。⑥狹道的阻塞物。 An ice *gorge* blocked the river. 冰塊塞住河道。 ***make one's gorge rise*** 使厭惡;使煩厭;使作嘔。 The cruelty of war *made his gorge rise.* 戰爭的殘暴使他痛惡萬分。 —*v.t.* ①塞飽。 to be *gorged* with food. 胡亂地吃飽。②狼吞虎嚥。—*v.i.* 亂吃至飽;貪食。

*__gor·geous__ ['gɔrdʒəs; 'gɔ:dʒəs] *adj.* ①華麗的; 燦爛的; 輝煌的。 a *gorgeous* sunset. 光輝燦爛的落日。②〖俚〗爽快的;令人滿意的。 *gorgeous* weather. 宜人的天氣。 —**ly,** *adv.* —**ness,** *n.*

gor·get ['gɔrdʒɪt; 'gɔ:dʒit] *n.* ①頸甲;護喉。②昔婦女用護肩布。③衣領。④導引器(去結石的外科手術器)。

gorget patch (軍服之)領章。

gor·gi·o ['gɔrdʒɪo; 'gɔ:dʒiou] *n.*, *pl.* **-os.** (吉普賽語) 非吉普賽人。—*adj.* 非吉普賽人的。

Gor·gon ['gɔrgən; 'gɔ:gən] *n.* ①〖希臘神話〗蛇髮女怪。② (g-) 醜陋可怕之女人。

Gor·go·ni·an [gɔr'gonɪən; gɔ:'gou-niən] *adj.* (似) Gorgon 的; 令人恐怖的。

gor·gon·ize ['gɔrgən,aɪz; 'gɔ:gənaiz] *v.t.*, **-ized, -iz·ing.** (如 Gorgon般) 睨視使化成石;以可怖的臉孔睨視。

Gor·gon·zo·la [,gɔrgən'zolə; ,gɔ:gən-'zoulə] 〖義〗 *n.*羊乳製的上等乾酪。

gor·hen ['gɔr,hɛn; 'gɔ:hen] *n.* 雌赤松鷄。

go·ril·la [gə'rɪlə; gə'rilə, gu'r-] *n.* ①大猩猩。②醜陋而粗暴之人。③〖俚〗流氓。

gor·mand ['gɔrmənd; 'gɔ:mənd] *n.* = **gourmand.**

gor·mand·ize ['gɔrmən,daɪz; 'gɔ:-məndaiz] *v.*, **-ized, -iz·ing,** *n.* —*v.i.* & *v.t.* 大食;拚命吃。 —*n.* 〖罕〗貪食;美食之癖好。—**gor·mand·iz·er,** *n.*

go-round ['go,raund; 'gouraund] *n.* 〖美俗〗①爭論激烈的會議, ②表演;輪班。③周遊一遍。

gorse [gɔrs; gɔ:s] *n.* 〖植物〗(=furze) 金雀花。—**gors·y,** *adj.*

gor·y ['gorɪ, 'gɔrɪ; 'gɔ:ri] *adj.*, **gor·i·er, gor·i·est.** ①染血的; 血腥的。②流血的;殘酷的。③不愉快的。 ***gory talk*** 〖美俗〗大話。

gosh [gɑʃ; gɔʃ] *interj.* 表示驚愕之歎詞;婉和的誓語。

gos·hawk ['gɑs,hɔk; 'gɔshɔ:k] *n.* 蒼鷹。

Go·shen ['goʃən; 'gouʃən] *n.* ①〖聖經〗歌珊地(出埃及以前以色列人所居住之埃及北部之肥沃牧羊地)。②豐饒樂土。

gos·ling ['gɑzlɪŋ; 'gɔzliŋ] *n.* ①小鵝。②愚蠢而無經驗的人。

go-slow ['go,slo; 'gou'slou] *n.* 〖俗〗①運動進行、變動等有意的趨緩。②有意緩慢之政策。③〖英〗減產;減慢。

*__gos·pel__ ['gɑspl; 'gɔspəl, -pel] *n.* ①福音。②(G-) 新約四福音書之一。 the *Gospel* according to St. John(Matthew, Mark, Luke). 約翰(馬太,馬可,路加)福音。③〖俗〗信仰;主義。 the *gospel* of health. 對健康之信仰;健康主義。④眞理。⑤黑人的一種宗教音樂(爲靈歌、布魯士及爵士樂之綜合型態)。 ***gospel truth*** 絕對眞理。 ***take as gospel*** 相信爲絕對眞理。

gos·pel·(l)er ['gɑsplɚ; 'gɔspələ] *n.* ①聖餐時讀福音者。②傳福音者。 hot *gospeler.* 熱烈宣傳者。

gospel shop 〖蔑〗美以美會教堂。

gospel side 神壇之北面。

Gos·plan [gɑs'plæn; gɔs'plæn] *n.* (蘇聯之)國家計畫委員會。

gos·sa·mer ['gɑsəmɚ; 'gɔsəmə] *n.* ①蛛絲;游絲。 ②薄紗。 ③輕而薄的防水布或衣。—*adj.* 如游絲的;極輕而薄的;纖細的。

gos·sa·mer·y ['gɑsəmərɪ; 'gɔsəmə-ri] *adj.* 似蛛絲的;似薄紗的;輕而薄的。

*__gos·sip__ ['gɑsəp; 'gɔsip] *n.*, *v.*, **-siped, -sip·ing.** —*n.* ①閒話;閒談。 She is too fond of *gossip.* 她太喜歡說閒話。②慣於閒談之人。③輕鬆的文字或談話。④〖古〗教父;教母。⑤〖古〗朋友。—*v.i.* 說閒話;論人是非;散播謠言。 —**er,** *n.* —**ing·ly,** *adv.*

gos·sip·mon·ger ['gɑsɪp,mʌŋgɚ; 'gɔsip,mʌŋgə] *n.* 散布謠言者; 饒舌者。

gos·sip·y ['gɑsəpɪ; 'gɔsipi] *adj.* ①喜饒舌的。②漫談式的。—**gos·sip·i·ness,** *n.*

gos·soon [gɑ'sun; gɔ'su:n] *n.* 〖愛〗少年;小僮;僮僕。

:**got** [gɑt; gɔt] *v.* pt. & pp. of **get.**

Goth [gɑθ; gɔθ] *n.* ①哥德人。②野蠻人;粗人。

Goth., goth. Gothic.

Goth·am ['gɑtəm *for*①, 'gɑθəm *for*②; 'goutəm *for*①, 'gouθəm *for*②] *n.* ①哥譚鎭;愚人村(英國童話中之一鄉村, 相傳其居民均甚爲愚蠢)。②紐約市之俗稱。

Goth·am·ite ['gɑtəm,aɪt *for*①, 'gɑθ-əm,aɪt *for*②; 'goutəmait *for*①, 'gouθə-mait *for* ②] *n.* ①哥譚村之居民; 呆子。②〖謔〗紐約市人。

***Goth·ic** [ˈgɑθɪk; ˈgɔθik] *n.* ①哥德式的建築。②哥德語。③〖印刷〗哥德體活字。—*adj.* ①〖建築〗哥德式的。②哥德人的;哥德語的。③未開化的; 野蠻的。④中世紀的。⑤〖印刷〗哥德體的。 **—al·ly,** *adv.*

Goth·i·cism [ˈgɑθəˌsɪzəm; ˈgɔθisizəm] *n.* ①〖建築〗哥德式模倣;哥德式傾向。②野蠻;粗野。③哥德語法。

go-to-meet·ing [ˈgotuˈmitɪŋ; ˈgou-tuˈmi:tiŋ] *adj.* 外出用的;赴會穿的。

***got·ten** [ˈgɑtn̩; ˈgɔtn] *v.* pp. of **get.**

got-up [ˈgɑtˈʌp; ˈgɔtˈʌp] *adj.* 修飾的;做作的;人工的;假的。 a *got-up* affair. 做成的把戲。—*n.* 〖俗〗一步登天的人;暴發戶。

gouache [gwɑʃ; guˈɑ:ʃ] 〖法〗 *n.* 〖美術〗樹膠水彩畫;其畫法;其顏料。

Gou·da [ˈgaʊdə; ˈgaudə] *n.* 一種荷蘭乾酪。

gouge [gaʊdʒ; gaudʒ] *n., v.,* **gouged, goug·ing.** —*n.* ①半圓鑿。②半圓鑿所鑿的槽或孔。③〖俗〗詐欺。④〖俗〗騙子。—*v.t.* ①(用半圓鑿)鑿。②挖;挖出。③〖俗〗詐欺。

Gou·lard [guˈlɑrd; gu:ˈlɑ:d] *n.* 〖醫〗稀鉛醋液(一種洗滌水)。

gou·lash [ˈgulæʃ; ˈgu:læʃ] *n.* 一種由菜、牛肉等合煮而成且有辣味的食品。

gourd [gord; guəd] *n.* ①葫蘆。②結葫蘆的植物。③葫蘆製的瓶、盌等。④南瓜屬植物。Spanish *gourd.* 南瓜。 sponge (*or* towel) *gourd.* 絲瓜。 white *gourd.* 冬瓜。⑤葫蘆形的細頸瓶。

gourde [gurd; guəd] *n.* 海地之貨幣名。

gour·mand [ˈgurmənd; ˈguəmənd] *n.* 美食者;饕餮者。(亦作 **gormand**)

gour·mand·ism [ˈgurməndɪzm̩; ˈguəməndizm] *n.* 美食主義。

gour·mand·ize [ˈgurmənˌdaɪz; ˈguə-məndaiz] *v.t.* & *v.i.,* **-ized, -iz·ing.** ①狼吞虎嚥地吃東西。②縱情於美食。

gour·mand·iz·er [ˈgurmənˌdaɪzɚ; ˈguəmənˌdaizə] *n.* 縱情美食者。

gour·met [ˈgurme; ˈguəmei] *n.* 能品評及精選美酒、美食的人。

gout [gaut; gaut] *n.* ①〖醫〗痛風。②〖古、詩〗(血的)凝塊;滴。

goût [gu; gu:] 〖法〗 *n.* 味;味覺;趣味;鑑賞力。

gout·y [ˈgautɪ; ˈgauti] *adj.,* **gout·i·er, gout·i·est.** ①痛風的。②患痛風的;易患痛風的。③(因痛風而)腫起的。**—gout·i·ly,** *adv.* **—gout·i·ness,** *n.*

Gov. Governor.

gov. ①government. ②governor.

***gov·ern** [ˈgʌvɚn; ˈgʌvən] *v.t.* ①統治;治理;管理。Who *governs* this country? 誰統治這個國家? ②控制;抑制;約束。You should *govern* your temper. 你應該抑制你的脾氣。③支配;影響;左右。the motives *governing* a person's decision. 支配一個人的主意的動機。④規定;規則。the principles *governing* a case. 處理某一事件的原則。⑤〖文法〗需用(某一語態或格);限定(某字)應用於某一格或語態。—*v.i.* ①統治;執行。Who are the men who really *govern* in this country? 誰是這國的眞正統治者? ②有決定性之影響力。

gov·ern·a·ble [ˈgʌvɚnəbl̩; ˈgʌvənəbl] *adj.* 可統治的;可控制的。

gov·ern·ance [ˈgʌvɚnəns; ˈgʌvə-nəns] *n.* ①統治;統御;統轄;支配;管理。②統治方式;管理法。

gov·ern·ess [ˈgʌvənɪs; ˈgʌvənis] *n.* ①女家庭教師。②女統治者。—*v.t.* & *v.i.* 作女家庭教師;作保姆。

gov·ern·ing [ˈgʌvənɪŋ; ˈgʌvəniŋ] *adj.* 統治的; 管理的; 有統治權或管理權的。the *governing* body of a school(college, hospital). 學校(學院、醫院)的主管團體。

‡gov·ern·ment [ˈgʌvɚnmənt; ˈgʌvən-mənt] *n.* ①管轄;統治。under the *government* of.... 在…統治之下。②政府; 內閣。a *government* official. 官吏。a *government* office. 官廳。③政體。republican *government.* 共和政體。④政權; 統治權。⑤管轄區域;縣;州;省;國。⑥管理; 支配。⑦〖文法〗需用;需要;限定;限用。

gov·ern·men·tal [ˌgʌvɚnˈmɛntl̩; ˌgʌvənˈmentl] *adj.* 政府的; 管轄的; 政治(上)的;統治的。

government bond 公債。

‡gov·er·nor [ˈgʌvɚnɚ, ˈgʌvnɚ, ˈgʌvɚ-nɚ; ˈgʌvənə] *n.* ①統治者;管理者。②〖美〗州長。③省主席。④總督。⑤(俱樂部、社團、機關之) 幹事; 理事。⑥ (機械) 調速機。⑦〖英俚〗 父親。 ***governor-general*** 總督。**—ship,** *n.*

govt., Govt. ①government. ②Government.

gow·an [ˈgauən; ˈgauən] *n.* 〖蘇〗 延命菊; 田野間白色或黃色之花。

gowk [gauk; gauk] *n.* 〖蘇〗 ①郭公鳥。②呆子;蠢貨。

gown** [gaun; gaun] *n.* ①女人所穿之長服。an evening *gown.* (女人之)晚禮服。②(法官、敎士、律師、學人等所穿之) 長服。③晨衣;睡衣。④大學的教師或學生;大學中一分子。take the gown*** 受聖職。—*v.t.* & *v.i.* (使)穿着長服。

gowns·man [ˈgaunzmən; ˈgaunz-mən] *n., pl.* **-men.** 職業上穿長袍 (gown) 者(如法官、律師、大學敎授等)。

goy [gɔɪ; gɔi] *n., pl.* **goy·im** [ˈgɔɪɪm; ˈgɔiim], **goys.** 非猶太人;異邦人;異教徒。(亦作 **goi**)

G.P. ①general practitioner. ②Gloria Patri (拉=Glory to the Father). ③Graduate in Pharmacy. ④Grand Prix. **gp.** group. **GPO, G.P.O.** ①General Post Office. ② Government Printing Office. **Gr.** ①Grade. ②Grecian. ③Greece. ④Greek. ⑤gross. ⑥〖英〗 gunner. **gr.** ①gram(s). ②grain(s).

Graaf·i·an follicle [ˈgrɑfɪən~; ˈgrɑ:fiən~] 〖解剖〗(卵巢內)格拉夫氏卵胞。

grab** [græb; græb] *n., v.,* **grabbed, grab·bing.** —*n.* ①突攫; 抓握。to make a *grab* at a rope. 抓握住繩子。②被抓握之物。③〖機械〗攫取機;起重鈎。have the grab on*** 〖英俚〗占上風; 占便宜。 ***up for grabs*** 〖美俗〗努力者得之。—*v.t.* ①急抓;搶。The dog *grabbed* the meat and ran. 狗搶了肉就跑。②奪。 I did the work but he *grabbed* the credit. 我作了工作而他奪去了功勞。 ③逮捕。 ④匆匆忙忙地上車。—*v.i.* 急抓;搶奪。**—ba·ble,** *adj.*

grab bag 〖美俗〗 ①摸彩袋 (袋中放置許多不同的物品, 購者付出一定額之錢後, 即可在袋中任摸取一物)。②任何雜湊或聚會。

grab bar 與牆平行之扶手。

grab·ber [ˈgræbɚ; ˈgræbə] *n.* ①强奪者; 强取者。②貪心漢。

grab·ble [ˈgræbl̩; ˈgræbl] *v.,* **-bled, -bling.** —*v.i.* ①摸索。②匍匐; 爬。—*v.t.* 攫取;握住。

‡grace [gres; greis] *n., v.,* **graced,**

grac·ing. —*n.* ①優雅;溫文。She danced with *grace.* 她舞步優雅。②善意;恩賜;仁慈。an act of *grace.* 仁慈的行爲。③(上帝的)恩典;慈悲。By the *Grace* of God. 藉上帝的慈悲。④食前或食後的簡短感恩祈禱。to say (a) *grace.* 作簡短感恩祈禱。⑤(G-)閣下;夫人(對公爵、公爵夫人、大主教等之尊稱)。His (Her, Your) *Grace* (=He, She, You). 閣下;夫人。⑥緩期;寬限。⑦謙和;厚道;美德。⑧(G-) (*pl.*)〖希臘神話〗掌管美麗、溫雅的三女神。⑨〖音樂〗裝飾音。***be in a person's good*** (or ***bad***) ***graces*** 受某人之寵愛(憎惡)。***days of grace*** (法定的或習慣的)滙票等付款的寬限日期。***fall from grace*** 失寵。***have the grace*** 表現正義感;有雅量。***with bad grace*** 不願意地;勉强地。***with good grace*** 願意地;欣然地。—*v.t.* ①增光;增色;使增光榮。Her character is *graced* with every virtue. 她的品格秉具一切的美德。②〖音樂〗加裝飾音。③使更美麗;點綴。Many trees and flowers *grace* the landscape. 許多的樹和花使風景更爲美麗。

***grace·ful** [ˈgresfəl; ˈgreisful] *adj.* 優雅的;合度的。a *graceful* dancer. 優美的舞者。a *graceful* letter of thanks. 得體的謝函。—**ness,** *n.* —**ly,** *adv.*

grace·less [ˈgreslɪs; ˈgreislis] *adj.* ①不美的。②不雅的;粗野的。③邪惡的。④爲神所棄的;墮落的。—**ly,** *adv.* —**ness,** *n.*

grace note(s) 〖音樂〗裝飾音;花音。

grac·ile [ˈgræsl̩;ˈgræsl] *adj.* ①細薄的;纖弱的。②纖細優美的;苗條而高貴的。

gra·cious** [ˈgreʃəs; ˈgreiʃəs] *adj.* ①親切的;仁慈的;和藹的(常指皇族人士,如:His gracious Majesty). She welcomed her guests in a *gracious* manner. 她態度親切地歡迎客人。②優裕的;舒適的;雅緻的。—*interj.* (表驚駭等) 天啊! ***Good gracious! (or ***Gracious me!*** or ***Gracious goodness!***) 天啊! —**ly,** *adv.* —**ness,** *n.*

grack·le [ˈgrækl̩; ˈgrækl] *n.* 白頭翁科之鳥。

grad [græd; græd] *n.* 〖俗〗畢業生(=graduate).

grad. ①graduate. ②graduated.

gra·date [ˈgredet; grəˈdeit] *v.,* **-dat·ed, -dat·ing.** —*v.i.* (色等)逐漸轉變。—*v.t.* ①使(色彩)逐漸轉變。②依等級或次序排列。

gra·da·tion [greˈdeʃən; grəˈdeiʃən] *n.* ①(狀態、性質、程度等之)漸變。②(常 *pl.*)次序;等級;階級區別。③顏色之漸變。④定次序;分等級。—**al,** *adj.* —**al·ly,** *adv.*

grade** [gred; greid] *n., v.,* **grad·ed, grad·ing.** —*n.* ①〖美〗班;年級。②階級;等級。This pupil has a high *grade* of intelligence. 這個學生有很高的智力。③同級或同等之人或事物。④(美國學校) 分數;成績;等第。⑤〖美〗道路之傾斜;傾斜度。⑥雜交種動物(尤指與優秀品種交配而生者)。at grade*** 在同一水平面上。***down grade*** **a.** 下坡;往下走。**b.** 變壞。***make the grade*** **a.** 上坡。**b.** 克服困難;成功。***on the up*** (or ***down***) ***grade*** 上升(下降);盛(衰)。***the grades*** 〖美俗〗小學。***up grade*** **a.** 上坡;往上走。**b.** 變好。***up to grade*** 夠標準。This shipment is not *up to grade.* 這批貨物不夠標準。—*v.t.* ①分級;分等;歸類。②〖美〗批分數於(試卷等);定成績。The teacher *graded* the papers. 教師評閱試卷。③〖美〗使近於水平(如建築基地等)。④將(劣種家畜)與優良品種交配。—*v.i.* ①屬於某等(級)。②漸變;漸近。Red *grades* into orange. 紅色逐漸趨於橙色。

grade crossing 〖美〗(公路與鐵路或鐵路與鐵路之)平面交叉;平交道。

grade·less [ˈgredlɪs; ˈgreidlis] *adj.* 無坡度的。

grad·er [ˈgredɚ; ˈgreidə] *n.* ①分等級之人;分類機。②〖美〗…年級生。a fourth *grader.* 四年級生。③〖土木〗平地機。④評分者。

grade(d) school 〖美〗小學;初等學校。

grade separation 不在同一水平面上的道路之立體交叉。

gra·di·ent [ˈgredɪənt; ˈgreidjənt] *n.* ①(鐵路、公路等之)斜率;坡度。②(溫度、氣壓等之)升降率;表示此升降率之曲線。③(道路等之)有坡度的部分;斜坡。—*adj.* ①漸傾的;傾斜的。②〖動物〗能步行的。

gra·di·ent·er [ˈgredɪəntɚ;ˈgreidjəntə] *n.* 傾斜測定器。

gra·din [ˈgredɪn; ˈgreidin] *n.* ①階梯形座席之一列。②祭壇後方置蠟燭或花之台。

gra·dine [greˈdin;greiˈdiːn] *n.* =**gradin.**

grad·ing [ˈgredɪŋ; ˈgreidiŋ] *n.* ①分等級;分階段。②〖土木〗平地面;緩和坡度。

***grad·u·al**[1] [ˈgrædʒuəl; ˈgrædjuəl, -dʒuəl] *adj.* ①逐漸的;漸次的。the *gradual* increase in the cost of living. 生活費用逐漸增高。②坡度不大的。a gradual slope. 傾斜度不大的山坡。—**ness,** *n.* —**ly,** *adv.*

grad·u·al[2] *n.*〖天主教〗①彌撒聖祭時在書簡與福音書之朗讀間,由司祭與聖歌隊所唱之應答歌。②(聖歌隊用)彌撒聖歌集。

grad·u·al·ism [ˈgrædʒuəˌlɪzəm; ˈgrædjuəlizəm] *n.* 漸進主義;按步就班主義。—**grad·u·al·is·tic,** *adj.*—**grad·u·al·ist,** *n.*

***grad·u·ate** [*v.* ˈgrædʒuˌet; ˈgrædjueit *n., adj.* ˈgrædʒuɪt; ˈgrædjuit, -djueit] *v.,* **-at·ed, -at·ing,** *n., adj.* —*v.i.* ①畢業;得學位。He *graduated* at Oxford. 他畢業於牛津大學。②漸變。—*v.t.* ①〖美〗授與學位;准予畢業。The university *graduated* 350 students last year. 該大學去年畢業學生350人。②刻度於(表、計、尺等)。a ruler *graduated* in inches. 刻度爲英寸之尺。③定等級。—*n.* ①畢業生;得學位者(在英國專指大學畢業生)。high school *graduates.* 〖美〗高中畢業生。②有刻度的容器;分度器。—*adj.* ①已得學士學位的;研究院的。*graduate* courses. 研究院裏的學科。②(鳥尾)最長的羽毛位於中央的。〖注意〗**to be graduated from** 的用法已漸淘汰,現在多用 to graduate from.

grad·u·a·ted [ˈgrædʒuˌetɪd;ˈgrædjueitid] *adj.* ①按程度排列的。②有刻度的。③(鳥尾)最長的羽毛位於中央的。④(稅率)累進的。

graduate school (大學之)研究院;研究所。

graduate student 研究生。

***grad·u·a·tion** [ˌgrædʒuˈeʃən; ˌgrædjuˈeiʃən] *n.* ①畢業;得學位。What will you do after *graduation?* 你畢業以後將作何事?②畢業式;授予學位典禮。③度;分畫;分度。④分等;分階級。⑤(*pl.*)表經緯度或數量等的線。〖注意〗畢業式英國稱 **speech-day.**

grad·u·a·tor [ˈgrædʒuˌetɚ; ˈgrædjueitə] *n.* ①分(量器等之)度之人。②分度器。

gra·dus [ˈgredəs; ˈgrædəs] *n.*①寫拉丁文詩用之韻律辭典。②(音樂之)由淺至深之練習曲集。

Grae·cism 〔ˈgrisɪzm; ˈgriːsizm〕 *n.* =**Grecism.**

Grae·cize 〔ˈgrisaɪz; ˈgriːsaiz〕 *v.t.* & *v.i.*, **-cized, -ciz·ing.** 〖主英〗=**Grecize.**

Graeco- 〖字首〗=**Greco-.**

graf·fi·to 〔grəˈfito; grəˈfiːtou〕 *n., pl.* **-ti** 〔-ti; -tiː〕. 〖考古〗粗刻；粗畫(古羅馬等古蹟柱上或壁上亂刻之畫或文字)。

***graft**[1] 〔græft, grɑft; grɑːft〕 *v.t.* ①接枝。to *graft* a shoot from a good apple tree in (into, on, *or* upon) an old tree. 將優良品種的蘋果樹的嫩枝接到一株老樹上去。②用接枝法改良。③〖外科〗移植(皮膚等)。④使融合。—*v.i.* ①接枝。②行移植皮膚手術。—*n.* ①(接枝用的)嫩枝。②接枝。③〖外科〗(皮膚等之)移植。

***graft**[2] *n.* 〖美俗〗①貪汚。②貪汚的方法。③貪汚所得。④〖英俚〗職業。—*v.t.* & *v.i.* 〖美俗〗貪汚。

graft·age 〔ˈgræftɪdʒ; ˈgrɑːftidʒ〕 *n.* 接枝法。

graft·er 〔ˈgræftɚ; ˈgrɑːftə〕 *n.* ①接枝之人。②〖美俗〗瀆職公務員；貪官汚吏；騙子。

graft hybrid 由接枝而成之交配種植物，兼具兩者之特性者。

gra·ham 〔ˈgreəm; ˈgreiəm〕 *adj.* 用全麥粉做的。—*n.* 全麥麪包。

Grail 〔grel; greil〕 *n.* 聖杯(耶穌於最後晚餐時所用者)。

grail[1] 〔grel; greil〕 *n.* ①製梳者之銼。②=**gravel.**

grail[2] *n.* =**gradual**[2].

‡grain 〔gren; grein〕 *n.* ①穀粒；穀類；穀物(在英國通常稱爲 corn)。②粒；顆粒。*grains* of sand (gold, salt, etc.). 沙(金、鹽等)粒。③最小的重量單位 (=0.0648 gram, 來自一麥粒之重)。④珍珠之重量單位 (=¼克拉)。⑤少許；微量。⑥木紋；石紋；紋。⑦天性；脾氣。two brothers of different *grain.* 個性不同的兩兄弟。⑧皮革之糙面。⑨結晶狀態。boiled to the *grain.* 煮至結晶狀態。⑩〖火箭〗固體燃料之單位。***against the*** (or ***one's***) ***grain*** 違反本性、興趣等。Shouting always went *against her grain.* 高聲喊叫是她最不願意做的事。***in grain*** **a.** 染進纖維中的；染得不褪色的。**b.** 本性的；徹底的；眞正的。***with a grain of salt*** 帶有保留。You should take his promise *with a grain of salt.* 你不可全信他的允諾。—*v.t.*①作成細粒。②模倣木紋、石紋等而畫；漆成紋理。③除去(皮)之毛；使(革等)表面粗糙。④餵以穀類。—*v.i.* 成爲細粒。—**less,** *adj.*

grain alcohol 乙醇；酒精。

grained 〔grend; greind〕 *adj.* ①(木、石等)有紋理的。②粗糙的。③(獸皮)已經去毛的。④成顆粒狀的。⑤具有某種特質的。—**ness,** *n.*

grain·field 〔ˈgren,fild; ˈgreinfiːld〕 *n.* 種穀類之田地。

grain·ing 〔ˈgrenɪŋ; ˈgreiniŋ〕 *n.* ①木紋漆畫法。②木料或大理石等之紋理。

grains 〔grenz; greinz〕 *n. pl.* (常作*sing.* 解)魚叉。

grain·y 〔ˈgrenɪ; ˈgreini〕 *adj.*, **grain·i·er, grain·i·est.** ①粒狀的；多粒的。②木紋狀的。③(照片、底片等)呈顆粒狀的。

Gral·la·to·res 〔,grælәˈtoriz; ,grælәˈtɔːriːz〕 *n. pl.* 〖動物〗涉禽類。

gral·la·to·ri·al 〔,grælәˈtorɪәl; ,grælәˈtɔːriәl〕 *adj.* 〖動物〗涉禽類的。

***gram**[1] 〔græm; græm〕 *n.* 克；公分。(英亦作 **gramme**)

gram[2] *n.* 〖植物〗雞豆(在東方用作人畜的食料)。

gram. ①grammar. ②grammatical.

-gram 〖字尾〗①表"寫成之物；畫成之物"之義之名詞字尾，如：telegram. ②表"…克或公分"之義之名詞字尾，如：kilogram.

gra·ma 〔ˈgrɑmә; ˈgrɑːmә〕 *n.* 〖植物〗美國西部之一種牧草。(亦作 **grama grass**)

gram·a·ry(e) 〔ˈgræmәrɪ; ˈgræmәri〕 *n.* 〖古〗魔術。

gram atom 〖化〗克原子。

gra·mer·cy 〔grәˈmɝsɪ; grәˈmәːsi〕 *interj.* 〖古〗①多謝！謝謝您！②表驚異之嘆詞。

gram·i·na·ceous 〔,gremɪˈneʃәs; ,greimiˈneiʃәs〕 *adj.* 禾本的；草的；似草的。

gra·min·e·ous 〔grәˈmɪnɪәs; greiˈminiәs〕 *adj.* ①〖植物〗禾本科的。②草的；似草的。

gram·ma·logue 〔ˈgræmә,lɔg; ˈgræmәlɔg〕 *n.* ①(速記等中之)用一語標、記號或符號所代表的字。②(=logogram)標語。

gram·mar** 〔ˈgræmɚ; ˈgræmә〕 *n.* ①文法；文法規則。to study English *grammar.* 研究英文文法。②文法書。③措辭；語法。④基本規則。*grammar* of politics. 政治學要義。grammar school*** 〖美〗初級中學；〖英〗以拉丁文、希臘文爲主科之中學。

gram·mar·i·an 〔grәˈmɛrɪәn; grәˈmɛәriәn〕 *n.* 文法家；文法學者。

gram·mat·i·cal 〔grәˈmætɪkl; grәˈmætikәl〕 *adj.* ①文法的。②合乎文法的。—**ly,** *adv.* —**i·ty,** —**ness,** *n.*

***gramme** 〔græm; græm〕 *n.* 〖英〗=**gram**[1].

gram-mo·lec·u·lar 〔ˈgræmәˈlɛkjәlɚ; ˈgræmәˈlekjulә〕 *adj.* (含)克分子的。

Gram·my 〔ˈgræmɪ; ˈgræmi〕 *n., pl.* **-mys, -mies.** 金唱片(由美國國家錄音藝術科學學院，每年頒給行銷一百萬張以上唱片的歌星)。

***gram·o·phone** 〔ˈgræmәfon; ˈgræmәfoun〕 *n.* 留聲機(在美國 phonograph 一字較爲常用)。—**gram·o·phon·ic,** *adj.*

gram·pus 〔ˈgræmpәs; ˈgræmpәs〕 *n.* ①一種大海豚；鯱。②一種有齒的小鯨；逆戟鯨。③〖俗〗呼吸粗沉的人。

gran·a·ry 〔ˈgrænәrɪ; ˈgrænәri〕 *n., pl.* **-ries.** ①穀倉。②穀產豐富的地區。

‡grand 〔grænd; grænd〕 *adj.* ①雄偉的；壯麗的；堂皇的。He lives in a *grand* house. 他住在一所富麗堂皇的房子裏。②顯赫的；高貴的。*grand* music. 高尙音樂。③最高級的。*grand* duke. 大公。④主要的。⑤總計的。*grand* total. 總計。⑥〖俗〗完美的；無疵的。to have a *grand* time. 玩得很痛快。⑦自負的；神氣活現的。Jane is awfully *grand* since her husband got promoted. 珍自從她丈夫晉級後便神氣活現。⑧大規模的；盛大的。a *grand* welcome party. 盛大的歡迎會。⑨受尊敬的。a *grand* old man. 長者。⑩(親屬名稱中)上溯或下降二代的；相隔二輩之關係的。—*n.* ①=**grand piano.** ②〖美俗〗一千元。—**ly,** *adv.* —**ness,** *n.*

gran·dad 〔ˈgræn,dæd; ˈgrændæd〕 *n.* 〖俗〗=**granddad.**

gran·dam 〔ˈgrændәm; ˈgrændæm〕 *n.* 〖古〗①祖母。②老太婆。

grand·aunt 〔ˈgrændˈænt; ˈgrændɑːnt〕 *n.* 祖父(祖母、外祖父、外祖母)的姐妹；姑婆；姨婆；舅婆。

Grand Bank(s) 大灘(在紐芬蘭東南，世界最大漁場之一)。

Grand Canyon 大峽谷(在美國Ari-zona 州北部)。

grand·child ['grænd,tʃaɪld; 'grænd-tʃaild] *n., pl.* **-chil·dren** [-,tʃɪldrən; -,tʃildrən] 孫子;孫女;外孫;外孫女。

grand·dad, grand-dad ['græn-,dæd; 'grændæd] *n.* 祖父;外祖父;爺爺;阿公(暱語或兒語)。

grand·daugh·ter ['grænd,dɔtɚ; 'grænd,dɔːtə] *n.* 孫女;外孫女。

grand·du·cal [,grænd'djukəl; 'grænd-'djuːkəl] *adj.* 大公的;大公國的。

grand duchess ①大公夫人。②與大公階級相等之貴婦。③俄國沙皇時代之公主。

grand duchy 大公國。

grand duke ①大公。②俄國沙皇時代之太子。

gran·dee [græn'di; græn'diː] *n.* ①大公。②(葡、西二國之)貴族。③顯貴之人。

grande toi·lette [,grɑ̃dtɔɪ'lɛt; ,grɑ̃dtɔi'let] 〖法〗禮服。

***gran·deur** ['grændʒɚ; 'grændʒə] *n.* 偉大;高貴;莊嚴;富麗堂皇。The *grandeur* of Niagara Falls is most impressive. 尼加拉瀑布景色極爲壯觀。

‡**grand·fa·ther** ['grænd,fɑðɚ; 'grænd-,fɑːðə] *n.* ①祖父;外祖父。②祖先。③始祖;創始者。

grand·fa·ther·ly ['græn,fɑðɚlɪ; 'grænd,fɑːðəli] *adj.* ①祖父的;似祖父的。②慈祥的;縱容的。

grand finale (音樂會、表演等之)終場演奏。

gran·dil·o·quence [græn'dɪlə-kwəns; græn'diləkwəns] *n.* 冠冕堂皇之措詞;誇張的表現。

gran·dil·o·quent [græn'dɪləkwənt; græn'diləkwənt] *adj.* 詞藻浮華的;誇大的。(亦作 **grandiloquous**) **—ly,** *adv.*

gran·di·ose ['grændɪ,os; 'grændious] *adj.* ①宏偉的;崇高的;富麗堂皇的。②虛華的;浮華的(文體)。**—gran·di·os·i·ty,** *n.*

gran·dio·so [,grændi'oso; ,grændiː-'ousou] *adj.* 〖音樂〗威風堂堂的。

grand jury 大陪審團。

grand larceny 〖法律〗大竊盜罪。

***grand·ma** ['grændmɑ; 'grænmɑː] *n.* 〖俗〗 =**grandmother.**

***grand·ma(m)·ma** ['græn,mɑmə, 'grænd-,-mə,mɑ; 'græn,mɑːmə, 'grænd-, -mə,mɑː] *n.* 〖俗〗 =**grandmother.**

grand march 開舞會時賓客繞場一周之儀式。

grand master ①高段棋手之尊號。②在任何方面有特殊成就者。

‡**grand·moth·er** ['grænd,mʌðɚ; 'grænd,mʌðə] *n.* ①祖母;外祖母。②女祖先。

grand·moth·er·ly ['grænd,mʌðɚ-lɪ; 'grænd,mʌðəli] *adj.* ①(似)祖母的。②慈祥的;溺愛的。③好管閒事的;好小題大做的。

grand·neph·ew ['græn'nɛfju; 'græn-,nevjuː] *n.* 姪孫;姪外孫。

grand·niece ['græn'nis, 'grænd-; 'grænniːs, 'grænd-] *n.* 姪孫女;姪外孫女。

grand old man (任何方面之)元老。

Grand Old Party 美國共和黨。

grand opera 〖音樂〗大歌劇。

***grand·pa** ['grændpɑ, 'grænpɑ, 'græm-pɑ; 'grændpɑː, 'grænpɑː, 'græmpɑː] *n.* 〖俗〗 =**grandfather.**

***grand·pa·pa** ['græn,pɑpə; 'grænd-pə,pɑː] *n.* 〖俗〗 =**grandfather.**

grand·par·ent ['grænd,pɛrənt; 'grænd,pɛərənt] *n.* 祖父或祖母;外祖父或外祖母。

grand piano 平臺型鋼琴。

Grand Prix [grɑ̃'pri; grɑ̃'priː] *pl.* **Grand Prix, Grands Prix, Grand Prixes** [grɑ̃'pri; grɑ̃'priː] ①國際長途大賽車。②(g- p-) 〖法〗最高獎;第一特獎。

grand-scale ['grænd'skel; 'grænd-'skeil] *adj.* 大規模的;盛大的。

grand·sire ['græn,saɪr; 'græn,saiə] *n.* 〖古〗①祖父;祖先。②老人。

grand slam ①〖橋牌〗大滿貫。②〖棒球〗滿壘時之全壘打。③〖運動〗在一個季節中的全部主要比賽中獲勝。

***grand·son** ['grænd,sʌn; 'grændsʌn] *n.* 孫子;外孫。

grand·stand ['græn,stænd; 'grænd-stænd] *n., v.,* **-stand·ed, -stand·ing,** *adj.* —*n.* ①正面觀衆席;大看臺。②坐在正面觀衆席上之觀衆。—*v.i.* 〖俗〗賣弄以求觀衆喝彩。—*adj.* ①正面觀衆席的。②位置最適宜的;一覽無遺的。③取悅觀衆的;賣弄的。**—er,** *n.*

grandstand play 〖俗〗①(在棒球賽等中)爲討好觀衆的技巧的賣弄。②任何做作的舉動。

grand tour 遍遊歐洲大陸。(昔英貴族認係教育子弟所必需) ***make the grand tour of*** 遍遊。

grand·un·cle ['grænd'ʌŋkl̩; 'grænd-,ʌŋkl] *n.* 父或母之 uncle.

grange [grendʒ; greindʒ] *n.* ①農場。②〖英〗農莊。③(G-) 〖美〗農人協進會之地方分支機構。

grang·er ['grendʒɚ; 'greindʒə] *n.* ①大農場的管理員。②〖美〗農人。③(G-) 〖美〗農人協進會會員。

grang·er·ize ['grendʒə,raɪz; 'grein-dʒəraiz] *v.t.,* **-ized, -iz·ing.** ①將自其他書刊剪取之插圖插入(一書)。②自…剪取插圖。

gra·nif·er·ous [grə'nɪfərəs; grə-'nifərəs] *adj.* 生穀粒的;結粒狀之實的。

***gran·ite** ['grænɪt; 'grænit] *n.* ①花崗石;花崗岩。②硬度、耐久性等可與花崗石相比之物。a heart of *granite.* 鐵石心腸。

gran·ite·ware ['grænɪt,wɛr; 'græ-nit,wɛə] *n.* ①花崗石花紋的琺瑯鐵器。②花崗石花紋的陶器。

gra·nit·ic [grə'nɪtɪk, græ-; græ'nitik] *adj.* ①花崗石的;似花崗岩的。②堅硬的。

gra·niv·o·rous [grə'nɪvərəs; grə-'nivərəs] *adj.* 食穀的;以種子爲食的。

gran·ny, gran·nie ['grænɪ; 'græ-ni] *n., pl.* **-nies.** 〖俗〗①祖母;奶奶。②老太婆。③老乳母。④(亦作 **granny knot, granny's knot**) 祖母結(一種繩結,係平結之末端錯誤地交叉而成)。

‡**grant** [grænt; grɑːnt] *v.t.* ①允許;答應;准。to *grant* a request (a favor). 答應一項請求。②承認;姑認。to *grant* the truth of what someone says. 承認某人所說的話是眞的。③授與(權利等);讓與(財產);租與;賜。***take for granted*** (=accept as true) 視爲當然;認定是實。He spoke English so well that I *took* it *for granted* that he was an American. 他講英文講得好極了,因此我認爲他是個美國人。—*n.* ①允許;答應;授與;讓與。②授與之物;獎助金;贈款。**—a·ble,** *adj.* **—er,** *n.* **—ed·ly,** *adv.*

gran·tee [græn'ti; grɑːn'tiː] *n.* 〖法律〗受讓人;受補助者。

grant-in-aid ['græntɪn'ed; 'grɑːnt-in'eid] *n., pl.* **grants-in-aid.** ①(中央對地方政府之)補助金。②獎學金;教育補助金。

grant·or ['grænta; grɑːn'tɔː] *n.* 〖法律〗授予者;讓渡人。
gran·u·lar ['grænjələ;'grænjulə] *adj.* 粒的;含顆粒的;生粒的;粒狀的。—**i·ty,** *n.*
gran·u·late ['grænjəˌlet; 'grænjuleit] *v.,* **-lat·ed, -lat·ing.** —*v.t.* ①使成粒狀。*granulated* sugar. 砂糖。②使(皮膚表面)生小粒;使生肉芽。—*v.i.* ①成粒狀。②形成肉芽。—**gran·u·la·tion, gran·u·lat·er, gran·u·lat·or,** *n.* —**gran·u·la·tive,** *adj.*
gran·ule ['grænjul; 'grænjuːl] *n.* ①小粒。②粒狀物。
gran·u·lose ['grænjəˌlos; 'grænjulous] *n.* 〖化〗澱粉粒質。—*adj.* 粒狀的。
***grape** [grep;greip] *n.* ①葡萄。a cluster of *grapes.* 一簇葡萄。②葡萄樹。③葡萄汁;葡萄酒。④深紫紅色。
grape-bran·dy ['grepˌbrændɪ; 'greipˌbrændi] *n.* 葡萄白蘭地。
grape·fruit ['grepˌfrut; 'greipfruːt] *n.* ①柚子。②柚樹。
grap·er·y ['grepərɪ; 'greipəri] *n., pl.* **-er·ies.** 葡萄園;葡萄栽培室。
grape·shot ['grepˌʃɑt; 'greipʃɔt] *n.* 葡萄彈(大砲用之一種散彈)。
grape·stone ['grepˌston; 'greipstoun] *n.* 葡萄核;葡萄子。
grape sugar 葡萄糖。
grape·vine ['grepˌvaɪn; 'greipvain] *n.* ①葡萄藤;葡萄樹。②〖美俗〗(祕密消息或謠言之)不脛而走。③〖美俗〗謠言。
graph[1] [græf; græf] *n.* 曲線圖。—*v.t.* 畫(曲線圖);以曲線圖表示(方程式或函數)。
graph[2] *n.* 〖英〗膠版。—*v.t.* 以膠版印刷。
-graph 〖字尾〗①表"書寫、描繪、記錄等用之器具"之義,如:phonograph. ②表"所寫之物;圖畫"之義,如:autograph.
-grapher 〖字尾〗表"書寫者;描繪者;記錄者"之義的名詞字尾,如:stenographer.
graph·ic ['græfɪk; 'græfik] *adj.* ①生動的。②圖表的。③(繪圖雕版等)平面的。④書寫的;文字的。(亦作 **graphical**) —**al·ly,** —**ly,** *adv.* —**al·ness,** —**ness,** *n.*
graphic arts ①製版木刻等平面藝術。②繪畫、印刷藝術。
graph·ics ['græfɪks; 'græfiks] *n.* ①(作 *sing.* 解)製圖法;製圖學。②(作 *sing.* 解)圖表算法。③(作 *pl.*解)=**graphic arts**①。
graph·ite ['græfaɪt;'græfait] *n.* 石墨。—**gra·phit·ic,** *adj.*
graph·ol·o·gy [græ'fɑlədʒɪ; græ'fɔlədʒi] *n.* 筆跡學;(特指)筆相學。
graph·o·type ['græfəˌtaɪp; 'græfətaip] *n.* 白堊版;白堊凸版(術)。
graph paper 方格紙;坐標紙。
-graphy 〖字尾〗①表"畫法;書法;紀錄法"之義之名詞字尾,如:calligraphy. ②表"記述之物;學術上之記述"之義,如:biography.
grap·nel ['græpnəl; 'græpnəl] *n.* ①爪鉤;鉤錨。②小錨。(亦作 **graplin**)
grap·ple ['græpl; 'græpl] *v.,* **grap·pled, grap·pling,** *n.* —*v.t.* 抓住;捉牢;鉤住。—*v.i.* ①用爪鉤尋找或抓物。②格鬥;揪打。—*n.* ①抓緊;揪打。②爪鉤;鉤竿。
grappling iron (or **hook**) 爪鉤;鉤錨。
grap·y ['grepɪ; 'greipi] *adj.,* **grap·i·er, grap·i·est.** 葡萄(狀)的;(味等)似葡萄的。
grasp** [græsp; grɑːsp] *v.t.* ①緊握;抓住;把持。②領會;瞭解。to *grasp* an argument. 瞭解議論。—*v.i.* 做抓之企圖或動作〖常at, for〗. a drowning man *grasping* at straws. 企圖抓住草的行將溺斃者。grasp at* a.** 欲抓取;攫取;貪欲。A person who *grasps at* too much may lose everything. 貪得無厭的人,很可能毫無所得。**b.** 殷切地接受。—*n.* ①緊握;把握;把握力。②(能力等所及之)範圍。He has an excellent position within his *grasp.* 他有一個可垂手而得的好職位。③控制力;控制。④瞭解。⑤瞭解力。—**a·ble,** *adj.* —**less,** *adj.*
grasp·ing ['græspɪŋ; 'grɑːspiŋ] *adj.* ①抓的;把握住的。②貪婪的。—**ness,** *n.* —**ly,** *adv.*
:grass [græs; grɑːs] *n.* ①青草;草。②草地;草原;牧場。③禾本植物(如穀類、甘蔗等)。④〖俚〗大麻煙。***at grass* a.** 在牧場上。**b.** 空閑;無所事事。***go to grass* a.** 去牧場;休息。**b.** 退休。Many men lack a sense of purpose after they have *gone to grass.* 許多人在退休以後就失去了生活的意義。***not to let the grass grow under one's feet*** 及時行動;勿懈怠。***put* (*send,* or *turn*) *out to grass* a.** 將牲畜放到牧場去。**b.**〖俗〗開除;强迫退休。—*v.t.* ①用草覆蓋;使長草。②使吃草;牧。—*v.i.* ①被草所覆蓋。②吃草。
grass hand ①(中文或日文之)草書。②〖英俚〗〖印刷〗臨時排字工人。
***grass·hop·per** ['græsˌhɑpə; 'grɑːsˌhɔpə] *n.* ①蚱蜢。②小型偵察機。③一種用降落傘空投的自動天氣紀錄報告儀。
grass·land ['græsˌlænd; 'grɑːs-lænd] *n.* 牧場;草原;草原地帶。
grass·plot ['græsˌplɑt; 'grɑːs'plɔt] *n.* 草坪。
grass roots ①農村地區。②一般人民。③基礎;根源。
grass-roots ['græs'ruts;'grɑːs'ruːts] *adj.* 〖俗〗①民間的;一般民衆的。②鄉村的;農村的。(亦作 **grass-root**)
grass snake (沼澤中之)無毒小蛇。
grass widow 離婚或與夫分居之女子。
grass-wid·owed ['græs'wɪdod; 'grɑːs'widoud] *adj.* 與丈夫分居的。
grass widower 離婚或與妻分居之男子。
***grass·y** ['græsɪ; 'grɑːsi] *adj.,* **grass·i·er, grass·i·est.** ①草的;由草組成的。②多草的;草深的;草茂盛的。a *grassy* lawn. 草深的草地。③似草的;草色的。
***grate**[1] [gret; greit] *n., v.,* **grat·ed, grat·ing.** —*n.* ①壁爐之鐵欄;爐架。②門窗之鐵柵欄。③壁爐。—*v.t.* 加築鐵柵欄於。to *grate* a window. 加鐵柵欄於窗戶。
***grate**[2] *v.,* **grat·ed, grat·ing,** *n.* —*v.i.* ①發生不愉快的影響。His rude manners *grate* on me. 他的粗率無禮使我很不愉快。②磨擦發聲。③刺耳。—*v.t.* ①使發磨擦聲;軋。to *grate* one hard substance against (upon, *or* on) another. 使一堅硬物與另一堅硬物磨擦發聲。②擦碎;磨損。③刺激;打擾。—*n.* 刺耳之磨擦聲。
***grate·ful** ['gretfəl; 'greitful] *adj.* ①感謝的;感激的。He was *grateful* for all you did. 他對你的一切幫助甚表感激。②致謝意的。③受歡迎的;討喜歡的;爽快的。A breeze is *grateful* on a hot day. 輕風在熱天是受歡迎的。—**ness,** *n.* —**ly,** *adv.*
grat·er ['gretə; 'greitə] *n.* ①磨碎(擦碎)東西的人。②磨碎(擦碎)東西的工具;擦子;鋰刀。③裝鐵柵欄的人。
grat·i·cule ['grætɪkjul; 'grætikjuːl]

n. ①分成小方格以便複製的圖形。②光學儀器中目鏡上之分度。

grat·i·fi·ca·tion 〔ˌgrætəfəˈkeʃən; ˌgrætifiˈkeiʃən〕 *n.* ①滿足。②喜悅；滿足感。③使滿足(喜悅)之事物。④報酬；賞錢。

***grat·i·fy** 〔ˈgrætəˌfaɪ; ˈgrætifai〕 *v.t.*, **-fied, -fy·ing.** ①使高興。We were *gratified* to learn that you had passed the examination. 我們很高興獲悉你已考試及格。②使滿足。③〖古〗賞與；報酬；行賄。

grat·i·fy·ing 〔ˈgrætəˌfaɪɪŋ; ˈgrætiˌfaiiŋ〕 *adj.* 悅人的；使人滿足的。—**ly,** *adv.*

gra·tin 〔ˈgrætn̩; ˈgrætɛ̃ːŋ〕〖法〗*n.* 〖烹飪〗某種菜餚上的焦殼；該種菜餚。

grat·ing¹ 〔ˈgretɪŋ; ˈgreitiŋ〕 *n.* ①門窗之柵欄。②〖物理〗光柵。

grat·ing² *adj.* ①使生刺耳之音的。②聲音刺耳的。③討厭的。—**ly,** *adv.*

gra·tis 〔ˈgretɪs; ˈgreitis〕 *adv.* 免費地。—*adj.*免費的。Entrance is *gratis.* 免費入場。

***grat·i·tude** 〔ˈgrætəˌtjud; ˈgrætitjuːd〕 *n.* 感謝；感激。I can hardly express my *gratitude* to you for your help. 對於你的幫助，我很難表達我的感激。

gra·tu·i·tous 〔grəˈtjuətəs; grəˈtju(ː)itəs〕 *adj.* ①沒有報酬的；免費的。②無故的。③〖法律〗贈予的。④天然生產的。—**ly,** *adv.*

gra·tu·i·ty 〔grəˈtjuətɪ; grəˈtju(ː)iti〕 *n., pl.* **-ties.** ①報酬；小帳。②禮物；軍人退伍時的獎金；退役慰勞金。

grat·u·late 〔ˈgrætʃʊˌlet; ˈgrætʃuleit〕 *v.,* **grat·u·lat·ed, grat·u·lat·ing.** —*v.t.* 〖古〗歡迎；祝；賀；對…表示喜悅。—*v.i.* 表示欣喜。—**grat·u·la·to·ry,** *adj.*

gra·va·men 〔grəˈvemɛn; grəˈveimen〕 *n., pl.* **-va·mi·na** 〔-ˈvæmɪnə; -ˈvæminə〕, **-mens.** ①訴苦；苦情。②〖法律〗(訴訟、起訴、陳情等之)最重要點。

‡**grave¹** 〔grev; greiv〕 *n.* ①坟墓；墓碑。②死地。a watery *grave.* 水葬；葬身水中。③死。***as secret as the grave*** 絕對祕密。***beyond the grave*** 死後；在陰間。***dread the grave*** 怕死。***find one's grave in*** (*a place*) 死於(某處)。***have one foot in the grave*** 老得快要死了；離死不遠。***in one's grave*** 已死。***make someone turn in his grave*** 做死者不願做的事或說死者不願聽的話。***on this side of the grave*** 在人世間；活着。***to one's grave*** 至死。***turn over in one's grave*** 死不瞑目。

***grave²** *adj.,* **grav·er, grav·est,** *n.* —*adj.* ①莊重的；嚴肅的。a *grave* ceremony. 隆重的儀式。②嚴重的；重大的。③陰暗的；陰沉的。④〖語音〗**a.** 低沉的；抑音的；鈍音的。**b.** 有抑音符(ˋ)(如 belovèd)的。—*n.* 抑音；抑音符。—**ly,** *adv.* —**ness,** *n.*

grave³ *v.t.,* **graved, graved** or **grav·en, grav·ing.** ①雕刻；刻鏤。②留下深刻印象；銘記。

grave⁴ *v.t.,* **graved, grav·ing.** 〖航海〗「清除(船底)並塗以瀝青。」

gra·ve⁵ 〔ˈgrɑve; ˈgrɑːve〕〖義〗*adj.* 〖音樂〗①緩慢的；莊嚴的。②(音)低的。—*adv.* ①緩慢而莊嚴地。②低沉地。

grave·clothes 〔ˈgrevˌkloðz; ˈgreivklouðz〕 *n. pl.* 壽衣。

grave·dig·ger 〔ˈgrevˌdɪgɚ; ˈgreivˌdigə〕 *n.* ①挖墳坑者。②一種甲蟲。

***grav·el** 〔ˈgrævl̩; ˈgrævəl〕 *n., v.,* **-el(l)ed, -el·(l)ing,** *adj.* —*n.* ①碎石。②腎砂；尿砂。③結砂病。—*v.t.* ①鋪碎石於(道路)。②使困惑；使苦惱。③使船擱淺。④〖俗〗使不安。—*adj.* 粗糙的；刺耳的。

grav·el-blind 〔ˈgrævl̩ˌblaɪnd; ˈgrævəlblaind〕 *adj.* 幾乎完全盲目的。

grav·el·ly 〔ˈgrævəlɪ; ˈgrævəli〕 *adj.* ①碎石的；多碎石的；碎石構成的；似碎石的。②沙啞的。

gravel road 碎石路。

grav·el·stone 〔ˈgrævl̩ˌston; ˈgrævəlstoun〕 *n.* 碎石。

grav·en 〔ˈgrevən; ˈgreivən〕 *adj.* ①雕刻的。②銘記的。—*v.* pp. of **grave³**.

graven image ①塑像。②偶像；偽神。

grav·er 〔ˈgrevɚ; ˈgreivə〕 *n.* ①雕刻刀。②雕刻師；(尤指)刻石匠。

grave·rob·ber 〔ˈgrevˌrɑbɚ; ˈgreivˌrɔbə〕 *n.* ①盜墓者。②偷屍供醫學解剖者。(亦作 **grave robber**)

Graves' disease 〖醫〗突眼性甲狀腺腫。

grave·stone 〔ˈgrevˌston; ˈgreivstoun〕 *n.* 墓碑。

grave·yard 〔ˈgrevˌjɑrd; ˈgreivjɑːd〕 *n.* ①墓地；墳場。②棄置廢物之場所。

graveyard shift (or **watch**) 〖採礦〗第三班工作；大夜班(自午夜至翌晨8時)。

grav·id 〔ˈgrævɪd; ˈgrævid〕 *adj.* 妊娠的；懷孕的。—**i·ty,** *n.*

gra·vim·e·ter 〔grəˈvɪmətɚ; grəˈvimətə〕 *n.* =**gravity meter.**

grav·i·tate 〔ˈgrævəˌtet; ˈgræviteit〕 *v.i.,* **-tat·ed, -tat·ing.** ①由引力而移動；吸引。②沉澱。③向一方移動的趨向；傾至一方。④被吸引〖常 to, toward〗。

grav·i·ta·tion** 〔ˌgrævəˈteʃən; ˌgræviˈteiʃən〕 *n.* ①地球或其他天體之吸力作用。②因吸力而發生之移動或動向。③沉澱；下降。④向某方移動之傾向。the *gravitation* of population to the cities. 人口向城市移動的傾向。universal gravitation*** 萬有引力。—**al, grav·i·ta·tive,** *adj.*

grav·i·tom·e·ter 〔ˌgrævəˈtɑmətɚ; ˌgrævəˈtɔmətə〕 *n.* 比重計；比重測量計。

grav·i·ty** 〔ˈgrævətɪ; ˈgræviti〕 *n., pl.* **-ties.** ①地心吸力。②萬有引力。Newton's law of *gravity.* 牛頓的萬有引力定律。③重；重力。He balanced the long pole at its center of *gravity.* 他把長竿放在重心處，使之平衡。④嚴肅；莊重。⑤嚴重；重大。⑥音調的低沉；低抑。specific gravity*** 比重。

gravity meter 重差計；比重計。

gra·vure 〔ˈgrevjər; ˈgreivjə〕 *n.* ① =**photogravure.** ②照像版；影印版。

***gra·vy** 〔ˈgrevɪ; ˈgreivi〕 *n., pl.* **-vies.** ①肉湯。②用肉湯調製的濃汁。

gravy boat 盛調味汁之(船形)器皿。

‡**gray** 〔gre; grei〕 *n.* ①灰色。②灰布；灰色衣服。③灰色馬。④灰色東西。⑤着灰衣之人。—*adj.* ①灰色的。The sky is *gray* on a dull, cloudy day. 在陰沉有雲的日子裏，天空是灰色的。②有灰髮的；有白髮的。He is growing *gray.* 他鬢髮漸白。③年老的；成熟的。④舊的；古老的。⑤陰沉的；陰慘的。The future looks *gray.* 未來似乎是灰色的。⑥位於分界線上的；在二者之間的。—*v.t.* & *v.i.* 使成灰色；變灰色。—**ly,** *adv.*

gray·beard 〔ˈgreˌbɪrd; ˈgreibiəd〕 *n.* 鬍鬚半白的老人；老人。(亦作 **greybeard**)

gray-head·ed 〔ˈgreˈhɛdɪd; ˈgreiˈhedid〕 *adj.* ①頭髮半白的。②老年的。③舊的。(亦作 **grey-headed**)

gray·ish 〔ˈgreɪʃ; ˈgreiiʃ〕 *adj.* 淺灰色

的;微帶灰色的。

Gray Lady *pl.* **Gray Ladies.** 醫院中之紅十字會志願婦女工作者。

gray·lag ['greˌlæg; 'greilæg] *n.* (歐洲之普通)灰色雁。(亦作 **greylag**)

gray·ling ['grelɪŋ; 'greiliŋ] *n.* ①鱒類。②數種灰色或褐色之蝶類。

gray·ly ['grelɪ; 'greili] *adv.* 灰色地;薄暗地。(亦作 **greyly**)

gray market 稀有貨物之祕密買賣而未至公然犯法程度者(以別於黑市買賣)。

gray matter ①〖解剖〗灰白質。②〖俗〗智慧;頭腦。

gray mullet 烏魚。

gray·ness ['grenɪs, -nɛs; 'greinis] *n.* 灰色;陰暗。(亦作 **greyness**)

gray·wacke ['greˌwæk; 'greiwæk] *n.* 〖地質〗硬砂岩。(亦作 **greywacke**)

*__graze__[1] [grez; greiz] *v.*, **grazed, graz·ing,** *n.* —*v.i.* ①吃青草。②放牧。—*v.t.* 放牧;用以放牧。to *graze* cattle. 放牛。—*n.* 放牧。—**graz·a·ble, —a·ble,** *adj.*

graze[2] *v.t.* ①磨擦。②擦傷皮膚。—*v.i.* (經過時)輕擦。—*n.* ①磨擦;輕觸。②擦傷。

graz·er ['grezə; 'greizə] *n.* ①在牧場食草之牲畜。②放牧者。

gra·zier ['greʒə; 'greizjə] *n.* 畜牧者;養畜者。

graz·ing ['grezɪŋ; 'greiziŋ] *n.* 放牧。

gra·zio·so [grɑ'tsjoso; grɑ:'tsjousou] 〖義〗*adj.* & *adv.* 〖音樂〗優美的(地);典雅的(地)。

Gr. Br., Gr. Brit. Great Britain.

GRE graduate record examination.

*__grease__ [*n.* gris; gri:s *v.* griz, gris; gri:z, gri:s] *n.*, *v.*, **greased, greas·ing.** —*n.* ①油;脂肪。②〖狩獵〗獵物的肥胖;狩獵季節。③已剪下但尚未清滌的羊毛。—*v.t.* ①塗以油脂。Many Indians *greased* their bodies. 許多印第安人在身上塗油脂。②塗油使轉動靈活。③〖俚〗賄賂。***grease a person's hand*** (or ***palm***) 賄賂某人。

grease cup 機械軸承上盛潤滑油之杯狀物。

grease gun (加潤滑油用的)黃油槍。

grease monkey 〖俚〗修理汽車或飛機之技工。

grease paint (演員化妝用之)油彩。

grease·proof ['grisˌpruf; 'gri:s-pru:f] *adj.* 不吸收油脂的。

greas·er ['grisə; 'gri:sə] *n.* ①(車輛、機械之)搽油工人(或器具)。②〖美俚〗油腔滑調的人。③(輪船的)火夫長。④〖美俚、蔑〗墨西哥人;西班牙系美國人。⑤〖俗〗鳴叫的鵝。

grease·wood ['grisˌwud; 'gri:s-wud] *n.* 〖植物〗美國西部產之一種堅硬、多刺灌木。

greas·y ['grisɪ; 'gri:si] *adj.*, **greas·i·er, greas·i·est.** ①含油脂的;油膩的。②塗有油脂的。③似油脂的;潤滑的。—**greas·i·ly,** *adv.* —**greas·i·ness,** *n.*

‡**great** [gret; greit] *adj.* ①巨大的。②非常的;很;極。That fellow is a *great* talker. 那個人極爲健談。③高貴的;慷慨的;地位高的。④大的。We heard a *great* noise. 我們聽見一聲巨響。⑤著名的;偉大的。Beethoven was a *great* musician. 貝多芬是一個大音樂家。⑥夙喜的。That is a *great* habit of his. 那是他夙喜的習慣。⑦親密的;要好的。He is a *great* friend of mine. 他是我的一個很要好的朋友。⑧〖俗〗很好的;很快活的。We had a *great* time at the party. 我們在宴會中很快樂。⑨衆多的。⑩特出的;盛大的。⑪重要的。⑫主要的。⑬流行的。⑭長一輩的或小一輩的。*great-grandfather.* 曾祖父。⑮〖俗〗擅長的;精明的。He is *great* on the subject. 他精於此道。***a great deal of*** 很多的(用於不可數的名詞前)。***a great many*** 許多的;很多的(用於可數的名詞前)。***a great number of*** 很多的(用於可數的名詞前)。***have a great*** (or ***good***) ***mind to*** 極想;極欲。I *have a great mind to* write to him. 我極想寫信給他。—*adv.* 〖俗〗順利地;得意地。Things have been going *great* for him the last few months. 過去數月來他一切都很順利。—*n.* 重要人物;偉大人物。She is one of the theater's *greats.* 她是偉大的演員之一。

great-aunt ['gret'ænt; 'greit'ɑ:nt] *n.* =**grandaunt.**

Great Bear 〖天文〗大熊星座。

Great Britain 英國;大不列顛(包括England, Scotland 和 Wales).

great·coat ['gretˌkot; 'greit'kout] *n.* 〖主英〗大衣;外套(美國多用 overcoat).

great·er ['gretə; 'greitə] *adj.* 包括市區及郊區的。

greatest common divisor 〖數學〗最大公約數;最大公因子。

great-grand·child [ˌgret'grændˌtʃaɪld; 'greit'græn-tʃaild] *n.*, *pl.* **-chil·dren.** (外)曾孫;(外)曾孫女。

great-grand·daugh·ter [ˌgret'grændˌdɔtə; 'greit'grænˌdɔ:tə] *n.* (外)曾孫女。

great-grand·fa·ther [ˌgret'grændˌfɑðə; 'greit'grændˌfɑ:ðə] *n.* (外)曾祖父。

great-grand·moth·er [ˌgret'grændˌmʌðə; 'greit'grænˌmʌðə] *n.* (外)曾祖母。

great-grand·par·ent [ˌgret'grændˌpɛrənt; 'greit'grændˌpɛərənt] *n.* (外)曾祖父或(外)曾祖母。

great-grand·son [ˌgret'grændˌsʌn; 'greit'grænsʌn] *n.* (外)曾孫。

great gross 大籮(12籮,或144打)。

great-heart·ed ['gret'hɑrtɪd; 'greit'hɑ:tid] *adj.* ①豪爽的;寬大的;慷慨的;高貴的。②勇敢的;有活力的。

Great Lakes 大湖(在美國與加拿大間)。

‡**great·ly** ['gretlɪ; 'greitli] *adv.* 很;極;非常。He was *greatly* surprised. 他非常吃驚。〖注意〗(1) **very** 通常與形容詞連用,如:*very* ill. (2) **much** 通常與動詞的過去分詞連用,如:*much* pleased. 此外,亦與形容詞的比較級連用,如:*much* better. (3) **greatly** 僅可與動詞之過去分詞連用,如:*greatly* delighted.

great-neph·ew ['gret'nɛfju; 'greit'nefju:] *n.* =**grandnephew.**

*__great·ness__ ['gretnɪs; 'greitnis] *n.* ①大;巨大;廣大。②偉大;卓越;著名;重要;高貴。③大量;大度。

great-niece ['gret'nis; 'greit'ni:s] *n.* =**grandniece.**

great power 强國;大國。

Great Salt Lake 大鹽湖(在美國Utah 州之北部)。

great seal ①國璽。②(G- S-)〖英〗國璽大臣;國璽大臣之職位。

great-un·cle ['gret'ʌŋkl; 'greit'ʌŋkl] *n.* =**granduncle.**

Great Wall (of China) (中國之)萬里長城。

Great War 第一次世界大戰(自1914至1918年)。
greaves[1] 〔grivz; gri:vz〕 *n. pl.* 溶脂「之渣滓;油渣。」
greaves[2] *n. pl.* 脛甲;護脛。
grebe 〔grib; gri:b〕 *n.* 鸊鷉。
Gre·cian 〔ˈgriʃən; ˈgri:ʃən〕 *adj.* 希臘的。—*n.* ①希臘人。②精通希臘語的人。〖注意〗作形容詞及名詞①解時, **Greek** 較常用。
Grecian nose 懸膽鼻。
Gre·cism 〔ˈgrisɪzm̩; ˈgri:sizm〕 *n.* ①希臘成語;希臘語風。②希臘文化精神;希臘藝術精神。(亦作 **Graecism**)
Gre·cize 〔ˈgrisaɪz; ˈgri:saiz〕 *v.*, **-cized, -ciz·ing.** —*v.t.* ①使希臘化。②譯爲希臘語。—*v.i.* 變爲希臘式;摹擬希臘語風、習俗等。(亦作 **Graecize**)
Greco- 〖字首〗表"希臘"之義。
Gre·co-Ro·man 〔ˌgrikoˈromən; ˌgri:kouˈroumən〕 *adj.* 希臘羅馬的;受希臘羅馬影響的。
·**Greece** 〔gris; gri:s〕 *n.* 希臘(歐洲南部一國家,首都雅典 Athens).
greed 〔grid; gri:d〕 *n.* 貪慾;貪婪。
·**greed·y** 〔ˈgridɪ; ˈgri:di〕 *adj.*, **greed·i·er, greed·i·est.** ①貪婪的;貪得的。to be *greedy* for gold. 貪財。②貪食的。—**greed·i·ly,** *adv.* —**greed·i·ness,** *n.*
‡**Greek** 〔grik; gri:k〕 *adj.* 希臘的;希臘人的;希臘語的。—*n.* ①希臘人。②希臘文;希臘語。③無法了解之語文等。It's *Greek* to me. 這我不懂。④希臘正教之教徒。
Greek cross 四臂長度相等的十字架。
Greek (Orthodox) Church 希臘正教。
‡**green** 〔grin; gri:n〕 *n.* ①綠色;青色。②綠色衣服。③綠色顏料;綠色染料。a picture in *greens* and blues. 用藍綠兩主色所繪之圖畫。④草地;草原。⑤〖高爾夫〗 **a.** 果嶺;穴週場地。**b.** 高爾夫球場。⑥(*pl.*) 結綵用之綠色帶葉樹枝。⑦(*pl.*) 青菜。***the Green*** 代表愛爾蘭共和國之顏色。—*adj.* ①綠色的。②長滿綠草的。A "*green* Christmas" means that the ground is not white with snow. "綠色耶誕"的意思就是說地上沒有白雪。③覆有生長之樹木、草、葉等的。④充滿精力的。*green* old age. 老而益壯。⑤未成熟的。⑥嫉妒的;臉發青的。⑦沒有訓練的;沒有經驗的;易受騙的。a boy who is still *green* to his job. 對其職務尚無經驗之小夥子。⑧新的。a *green* wound. 新傷口。⑨(肉類)未煮熟的;生的。⑩用綠色蔬菜做的。***be*** (or ***turn***) ***green with envy*** (or ***jealousy***) 心中充滿嫉妒。—*v.i.* & *v.t.* (使)成爲綠色。Our lawn grass does not *green* up until the middle of May. 我們草坪上的草要到五月中才變綠(才長好)。—**ness,** *n.*
green·back 〔ˈgrinˌbæk; ˈgri:nbæk〕 *n.* 〖美俗〗美鈔。
green·belt 〔ˈgrinˌbelt; ˈgri:nˈbelt〕 *n.* ①圍繞社區之公園綠地。②柔道家在第二年訓練時由柔道協會所頒授的綠帶。
green-blind 〔ˈgrin ˈblaɪnd; ˈgri:nˈblaind〕 *adj.* 綠色色盲的。
green·bri·er 〔ˈgrinˌbraɪɚ; ˈgri:nˌbraiə〕 *n.* 〖植物〗牛尾菜屬植物。
green card 綠卡(在美國居留的許可證)。
green corn 作蔬菜食用的玉蜀黍穗。
green·er·y 〔ˈgrinərɪ; ˈgri:nəri〕 *n., pl.* **-er·ies.** ①青葱的草木或葉。②裝飾用的綠樹枝葉。③暖房;溫室。
green-eyed 〔ˈgrinˌaɪd; ˈgri:naid〕 *adj.* ①綠眼的;碧眼的。②妒嫉的;不信任的。
green-eyed monster 妒嫉。
green·finch 〔ˈgrinˌfɪntʃ; ˈgri:nfintʃ〕 *n.* ①鶯(歐洲產)。②美國 Texas 產之麻雀。
green fingers〖英俗〗=**green thumb.**
green·fly 〔ˈgrinflaɪ; ˈgri:nflai〕 *n.* 綠色蚜蟲。
green·gage 〔ˈgrinˈgedʒ; ˈgri:ngeidʒ〕 「*n.* 〖植物〗青梅。」
green·gro·cer 〔ˈgrinˌgrosɚ; ˈgri:nˌgrousə〕 *n.* 〖英〗賣蔬菜及水果的零售商或店。
green·gro·cer·y 〔ˈgrinˌgrosərɪ; ˈgri:nˌgrousəri〕 *n., pl.* **-cer·ies.** 〖英〗①蔬菜業;水果業。②蔬菜店;水果店。③(*pl.*)蔬菜類;水果類。
green·heart 〔ˈgrinˌhɑrt; ˈgri:nhɑ:t〕 *n.* (西印度及南美產之)綠心木;其木材。
green·horn 〔ˈgrinˌhɔrn; ˈgri:nhɔ:n〕 *n.* 〖俗〗①無經驗的人。②易受騙的人;愚蠢的人。③移民新來者。—**ism,** *n.*
green·house 〔ˈgrinˌhaus; ˈgri:nhaus〕 *n.* ①溫室;花房。②〖俚〗飛機上(轟炸員之)玻璃隔開的小間。
greenhouse effect 溫室效果。
green·ing 〔ˈgrinɪŋ; ˈgri:niŋ〕 *n.* 綠皮蘋果。
green·ish 〔ˈgrinɪʃ; ˈgri:niʃ〕 *adj.* 淺綠「色的;帶綠色的。」
green-keep·er 〔ˈgrinˌkipɚ; ˈgri:nˌki:pə〕 *n.* 高爾夫球場管理人。
Green·land 〔ˈgrinlənd; ˈgri:nlənd〕 *n.* 格陵蘭(北美洲東北部之一島, 屬丹麥)。—**er,** *n.* —**ic,** *adj., n.* —**ish,** *adj.*
green light ①交通號誌之綠色燈光。②〖俗〗核准;許可;授權。
green·ly 〔ˈgrinlɪ; ˈgri:nli〕 *adv.* ①綠色地。②新鮮地;無經驗地;愚蠢地。③生意盎然地。
green manure ①〖農業〗綠肥。②尚「未經過腐爛之肥料。」
green·ness 〔ˈgrinnɪs; ˈgri:nnis〕 *n.* ①綠。②草木;綠地。③不成熟;無經驗;年輕。④輕信;天眞。
green pepper 青辣椒。
green power 綠權(金錢的力量)。
green revolution 綠色革命(使低度開發國家農作物增產,其經濟因而有革命性之改革)。
green·room 〔ˈgrinˌrum; ˈgri:nru(:)m〕 *n.* (劇場之)演員休息室;後臺。
green·sand 〔ˈgrinˌsænd; ˈgri:nsænd〕 「*n.* 綠砂。」
green·shank 〔ˈgrinˌʃæŋk; ˈgri:nʃæŋk〕 *n.* 青足鷸。
green·sick 〔ˈgrinˌsɪk; ˈgri:nsik〕 *adj.* 「患萎黃病的。」
green·sick·ness 〔ˈgrinˌsɪknɪs; ˈgri:nsiknis〕 *n.* 〖醫〗萎黃病;綠色貧血。(亦「作 **chlorosis**)」
green soap 軟肥皂。
green·stone 〔ˈgrinˌston; ˈgri:nstoun〕 *n.* 綠岩。
green·stuff 〔ˈgrinˌstʌf; ˈgri:nˌstʌf〕 *n.* 〖美俗〗蔬菜。(英亦作 **greenstuffs**)
green·sward 〔ˈgrinˌswɔrd; ˈgri:nswɔ:d〕 *n.* 青草;生有青草之土層;草皮。
green tea 綠茶。
green thumb ①栽植花卉、植物等之特殊能力。②對園藝之愛好。
Green·wich 〔ˈgrɪnɪdʒ; ˈgrinidʒ, ˈgren-,-itʃ〕 *n.* 格林威治(英國國立天文臺所在地)。
Greenwich (Mean) Time 世「界標準時。」
Green·wich Village 〔ˈgrɛnɪtʃ~; ˈgrenitʃ~〕格林威治村(在美國 New York 市 Manhattan 區,爲藝術家、作家、嬉皮等集

居之地)。 「n. 青葱的森林。}
green·wood ['grin,wud; 'gri:nwud]
green·y ['grinɪ; 'gri:ni] *adj.* 【俗】= greenish. —*n.* =greenhorn.
‡**greet** [grit; gri:t] *v.t.* ①致候;致敬;打招呼。②歡迎;接受。His speech was *greeted* with cheers. 他的演說受到熱烈的喝采。③映入眼簾。When we reached the top of the hill, a magnificent view of the sea *greeted* us. 當我們抵達山頂時,一片壯麗的海景映入眼簾。—**er,** *n.*
***greet·ing** ['gritɪŋ; 'gri:tiŋ] *n.* ①問候;祝賀;致敬歡迎。②(*pl.*)某一特殊節日之祝賀。Christmas *greetings.* 耶誕節之祝賀。—**ly,** *adv.* —**less,** *adj.*
gre·gar·i·ous [grɪ'gɛrɪəs; gre'gɛəriəs] *adj.* ①羣居的。②合羣的。③社交的;愛交際的。④一羣的;羣衆的。—**ly,** *adv.*
Gre·go·ri·an [grɛ'gorɪən; gre'gɔ:riən] *adj.* 教皇 Gregory (Pope Gregory I, 540?–604; Pope Gregory XIII, 1572–85)的。
Gregorian calendar 格里高里曆(即今各國通行之曆法, 每年 365日, 閏年爲366日, 每四年一閏)。 「(爲天主教聖歌)。}
Gregorian chant 格里高里聖歌
Greg·o·ry ['grɛgərɪ; 'gregəri] *n.* 男子名。 「要成分爲大黃 rhubarb).}
Gregory's powder 【藥】瀉劑 (主
grem·lin ['grɛmlɪn; 'gremlin] *n.* (想像中與飛機駕駛員搗亂的)小鬼;小妖精。
grem·mie, grem·my ['grɛmɪ; 'gremi] *n., pl.* **grem·mies.** 【美俚】(因不熟練而)笨手笨脚的衝浪板運動者。
gre·nade [grɪ'ned; gri'neid] *n.* ①【軍】手榴彈。②裝有化學藥物等之圓玻璃瓶。
gren·a·dier [,grɛnə'dɪr; ,grenə'diə] *n.* ①手榴彈兵。②身軀特別高大的步兵。③英軍近衞軍步兵聯隊中之士兵。—**i·al,** *adj.* —**ly,** *adv.* —**ship,** *n.*
gren·a·dine[1] [,grɛnə'din; ,grenə'di:n] *n.* 一種用絲、毛等織的薄紗。 「漿。}
gren·a·dine[2] *n.* 一種用石榴汁製的糖
Gresh·am's law (or **theorem**) ['grɛʃəmz~; 'greʃəmz~] 【經濟】葛氏定律(劣幣驅逐良幣之法則)。
gres·so·ri·al [grɛ'sorɪəl; gre'sɔəriəl] *adj.* 【動物】(鳥、昆蟲等之足)適於步行的。
‡**grew** [gru; gru:] *v.* pt. of **grow.**
grew·some ['grusəm; 'gru:səm] *adj.* =**gruesome.**
‡**grey** [gre; grei] *n., adj., v.* =**gray.** 【注意】**grey** 及 **gray** 讀音相同。grey 爲英國拼法, gray 爲美國拼法。
grey·cing ['gresɪŋ; 'greisiŋ] *n.* 【英俗】greyhound racing 之略。
grey·hound** ['gre,haund; 'greihaund] *n.* ①【動物】靈緹(一種獵犬)。②快船。③(G-)美國灰狗巴士。greyhound racing*** (以電兔引誘的)跑狗;賽狗。(亦作 **grayhound**)
grid [grɪd; grid] *n.* ①鐵柵;格子。②(蓄電池中的)鉛板。③【電】眞空管中之柵極。④地圖、空中照相等上面的座標方格。⑤橄欖球場。⑥ =**grillage.** —*adj.* 【俚】橄欖球的。
grid circuit 【電】柵極電路。
grid·dle ['grɪdl; 'gridl] *n., v.,* **-dled, -dling.** —*n.* ①(煎餅用的) 淺鍋。②(選鑛用的)鑛篩。 —*v.t.* ①以淺鍋煎炙。②以鑛篩選(鑛)。 「keik] *n.* 薄餅。}
grid·dle·cake ['grɪdl,kek; 'gridl-
grid·i·ron ['grɪd,aɪən; 'grid,aiən] *n.* ①鐵格架;焙器。②任何似格架之物。③【美】橄欖球場。④ 舞臺上方用以操縱懸掛之布景等的裝置。
grid leak 【電】柵漏電阻。
grief** [grif; gri:f] *n.* ①悲傷;憂愁。②可憂之事; 傷心事。His failure to live a good life was a great *grief* to his parents. 他之不務正業是他父母的一大傷心事。bring...to grief*** 使遭受困難;使失敗。***come to grief*** 遭受困難;失敗。Their marriage *came to grief* after only two years. 他們結婚才兩年便鬧房失和。 —**less,** *adj.* —**less·ness,** *n.* —**ful,** *adj.*
grief-strick·en ['grif,strɪkən; 'gri:f,strikən] *adj.* 極度悲傷的。
***griev·ance** ['grivəns; 'gri:vəns] *n.* 苦況; 委屈; 寃情。
***grieve** [griv; gri:v] *v.,* **grieved, griev·ing.** —*v.i.* 悲傷;傷心; 傷懷。We must all *grieve* at (for, *or* over) the death of such a great man. 對這樣一位偉人之死, 我們大家必感悲傷。—*v.t.* 使傷心; 使悲傷。It *grieves* me to think.... 想及…卽感悲傷。—**griev·er,** *n.* —**griev·ing·ly,** *adv.*
***griev·ous** ['grivəs; 'gri:vəs] *adj.* ①難受的;痛苦的。*grievous* pain. 難受的痛苦。②嚴重的; 極惡的。 Wasting food when people are starving is a *grievous* wrong. 在別人挨餓時浪費食物是一種嚴重的罪惡。③悲慘的。④充滿悲傷的; 表示悲傷的。⑤造成極大的肉體痛苦的。—**ness,** *n.* —**ly,** *adv.*
grif·fin[1] ['grɪfɪn; 'grifin] *n.* 【希臘神話】半獅半鷲之怪獸。(亦作 **gryphon**) 「生手。}
grif·fin[2] *n.* 新來(印度或東方)之歐洲人;
grif·fon[1] ['grɪfən; 'grifən] *n.* ① = **griffin**[1]. ② = **griffon vulture.**
grif·fon[2] *n.* ①一種粗毛的荷蘭小狗。②一種粗毛的獵狗。
griffon vulture 大禿鷹。 「騙子。}
grift·er ['grɪftɚ; 'griftə] *n.* 【美俚】
grig [grɪg; grig] *n.* 【方】①蟋蟀;蚱蜢。②小鰻。③精力充沛的人。***merry*** (or ***lively***) ***as a grig*** 活潑高興的;極快活的。
Gri·gnard [,gri'njar; ,gri:'nja:] *n.* 格雷尼亞 (Victor, 1871–1934, 法國化學家, 曾獲1912年諾貝爾獎)。
grill[1] [grɪl; gril] *n.* ①烤架。②燒烤食品。③(亦作 **grillroom**)烤肉店。④燒烤。—*v.t. & v.i.* ①炙;燒;烤。②嚴加拷問。③對…用火刑。
grill[2] *n., v.t.* =**grille.**
gril·lage ['grɪlɪdʒ; 'grilidʒ] *n.* 格床(在鬆軟地上支持建築物底部的木製格架)。(亦作 **grid**)
grille [grɪl; gril] *n.* ①鐵柵; 鐵欄。②鐵格子窗。③郵票上小圓點組成之長方形圖案。—*v.t.* ①裝鐵柵或鐵格子窗。②在(郵票)上印小圓點組成之長方形圖案。—**grilled,** *adj.*
grille·work ['grɪl,wɝk; 'grilwə:k] *n.* =**grillwork.** 「*n.* 烤肉房;烤肉館。}
grill·room ['grɪl,rum; 'grilru(:)m]
grill·work ['grɪl,wɝk; 'gril,wə:k] *n.* 格子形圖案; 花格形裝置。
grilse [grɪls; grils] *n., pl.* **grils·es, grilse.** 從海中初次回到河裏來的幼鮭。
***grim** [grɪm; grim] *adj.,* **grim·mer, grim·mest.** ①冷酷的; 嚴厲的。 a *grim* expression. 冷酷的表情。②倔强的;不屈的。③猙獰的; 陰森的; 殘忍的。④可怕的。He made *grim* jokes about death and ghosts. 他講了些有關死與鬼的令人毛骨悚然的笑話。—**ly,** *adv.* —**ness,** *n.*

gri·mace [grɪˈmes; griˈmeis] *n., v.,* **-maced, -mac·ing.** —*n.* ①面部的歪扭。②鬼臉。③獰笑。 —*v.i.* 扮鬼臉。

gri·mal·kin [grɪˈmælkɪn; griˈmælkin] *n.* ①貓;(特指)老母貓。②惡毒的老婦。

grime [graɪm; graim] *n., v.,* **grimed, grim·ing.** —*n.* ①汚穢。②(道德上的)汚點。—*v.t.* 使汚濁;使覆有汚穢物。

Grimm's law [grɪmz~; grimz~] 【語言】格利姆法則(日耳曼語系之子音變化法則)。

grim·y [ˈgraɪmɪ; ˈgraimi] *adj.,* **grim·i·er, grim·i·est.** 汚穢的;極髒的。

grin** [grɪn; grin] *v.,* **grinned, grin·ning,** *n.* —*v.i.* 露齒;露齒而笑(表示高興、輕蔑或滿足)。He was *grinning* with delight. 他高興得露齒而笑。—*v.t.* 以露齒笑表示。He *grinned* his delight. 他露齒笑表示高興。grin and bear it*** 逆來順受。—*n.* 露齒;露齒笑;裂口笑。—**ner,** *n.* —**ning·ly,** *adv.*

***grind** [graɪnd; graind] *v.,* **ground** [graʊnd; graund], **grind·ing,** *n.* —*v.t.* ①磨碎(成粉)。to *grind* something to powder. 將某物磨成粉。②磨尖;磨光;磨損;折磨。people who are *ground* down by poverty. 受窮苦折磨的人們。③磨擦;旋轉而磨擦。④廻轉;轉動(磨機等)。to *grind* out some verses. 搜索枯腸作成數句詩。⑤【俗】(教師)嚴令學生用功;灌輸。—*v.i.* ①磨;擦。②【俗】刻苦用功【常 away】。to *grind* away at English studies. 用苦功研讀英文。③可磨;受磨。This wheat *grinds* well. 這種小麥易磨成粉。—*n.* ①碾;磨;搗;擂。②苦工作;重功課。③下苦功讀書的學生。④【俚】(跳舞時之)扭屁股。—**a·ble,** *adj.*

grind·er [ˈgraɪndɚ; ˈgraində] *n.* ①研磨者。②磨器。③臼齒。④(*pl.*)【俗】牙齒。

grind·er·y [ˈgraɪndərɪ; ˈgraindəri] *n., pl.* **-ies.** ①磨礪器具之處。②【英】皮革匠之原料、用具等。

grind·ing [ˈgraɪndɪŋ; ˈgraindiŋ] *n.* 碾磨;製粉;摩擦。—*adj.* ①磨的。②費事的;無聊的。③壓迫的。④疼痛難挨的;苦惱的。—**ly,** *adv.*

grind·stone [ˈgraɪndˌston; ˈgraindstoun] *n.* 砥石;磨刀石。***hold*** (***keep,*** or ***put***) ***one's nose to the grindstone*** 不得休息地勉强勞動。

grin·go [ˈgrɪŋgo; ˈgriŋgou] *n., pl.* **-gos.** 外國人;(中南美人蔑稱)英國人或美國人。

grip** [grɪp; grip] *n., v.,* **gripped** or **gript, grip·ping.** —*n.* ①緊握;抓握物;握力。to let go one's *grip* on a branch. 鬆開所握之枝條。②把手;柄。③特殊方式之握手。④【美】手提箱;手提包。⑤控制。to have the power in one's *grip*. 大權在握。⑥了解。⑦劇痛。⑧流行性感冒。⑨【美俚】舞臺工作人員(尤指換布景者)。come to grips*** a. 揪扭;肉搏。b. 認眞地處理。We'll *come to grips* with the problem very soon. 我們將很快處理這個問題。c. 直接面對。—*v.t.* ①抓緊。②吸住(注意力)。to *grip* the attention of one's audience. 吸引住聽衆的注意力。—*v.i.* 抓緊;抱住。—**less,** *adj.*

gripe [graɪp; graip] *v.,* **griped, grip·ing,** *n.* —*v.t.* ①抓住;控制。②使腸疼痛。③【俚】煩擾。—*v.i.* ①抓牢。②感覺腸疼痛。③【美俗】發怨言。—*n.* ①抓住;掌握。②【俚】怨言。③(*pl.*)腸疼痛;腹疼痛。④支配;主宰。⑤痛苦。⑥把;柄。

grippe [grɪp; grip] *n.* 【俗】流行性感冒。(亦作 **grip**)

grip·per [ˈgrɪpɚ; ˈgripə] *n.* 握住者;(各種)挾握之器具。

grip·ping [ˈgrɪpɪŋ; ˈgripiŋ] *adj.* 握住的;引起注意的。

grip·sack [ˈgrɪpˌsæk; ˈgripsæk] *n.* 旅行袋;手提包。

gript [grɪpt; gript] *n.* 【古】pt. & pp. of **grip.**

gri·saille [grɪˈzel; griˈzeil] *n.* 純以灰色畫法(裝飾用);(玻璃等上之)純灰色畫。

gri·sette [grɪˈzɛt; griˈzet] *n.* (法國之)女工;女店員。

gris·kin [ˈgrɪskɪn; ˈgriskin] *n.* 【英】猪腰瘦肉。

gris·ly [ˈgrɪzlɪ; ˈgrizli] *adj.,* **-li·er, -li·est.** 可怕的;猙獰的。

grist [grɪst; grist] *n.* ①預備磨粉的穀物;一次所磨之穀物或粉。②【美俗】多量;很多。***All is grist that comes to one's mill.*** 事事盤算巨細無遺。***bring grist to the mill*** 獲利。***grist to*** (or ***for***) ***one's mill*** 有利。

gris·tle [ˈgrɪsl̩; ˈgrisl] *n.* 軟骨。

gris·tly [ˈgrɪslɪ; ˈgrisḷi] *adj.,* **-tli·er, -tli·est.** (似)軟骨的。

grist·mill [ˈgrɪstˌmɪl; ˈgristmil] *n.* 磨粉廠;磨坊。

grit** [grɪt; grit] *n., v.,* **grit·ted, grit·ting.** —*n.* ①砂礫。I've got a bit of *grit* in my shoe. 我的鞋子裏面弄砂石進去了。②粗砂石。③勇氣。put a little grit in the machine*** 使行動受到妨礙。—*v.t.* ①軋轢而磨。②覆以砂礫。—*v.i.* 發軋軋之聲。

grits [grɪts; grits] *n.* (作 *sing.* or *pl.* 解)①粗碾去殼的小麥。②【美】粗碾玉蜀黍。

grit·ty [ˈgrɪtɪ; ˈgriti] *adj.,* **-ti·er, -ti·est.** ①有砂的;像砂的。②【俗】有勇氣的;有膽子的。—**grit·ti·ness,** *n.* —**grit·ti·ly,** *adv.*

griz·zle[1] [ˈgrɪzl̩; ˈgrizl] *v.,* **griz·zled, griz·zling,** *adj., n.* —*v.i.* & *v.t.* (使髮)變成灰色。—*adj.* 灰色的。—*n.* ①灰色。②灰色(假)髮。③灰色動物(尤指馬)。

griz·zle[2] *n., v.* 【英俗】—*n.* 訴苦的人。—*v.i.* ①露齒作笑狀。②訴苦。

griz·zled [ˈgrɪzl̩d; ˈgrizld] *adj.* 灰色的(髮)。

griz·zly [ˈgrɪzlɪ; ˈgrizli] *adj.,* **-zli·er, -zli·est,** *n., pl.* **-zlies.** —*adj.* 帶灰色的;灰色(髮)的。—*n.* 灰熊。

grm. gram. **gro.** gross (12打)。

***groan** [gron; groun] *n.* ①呻吟;嘆息。②表示諷嘲、不贊成等的低沉的聲音。—*v.i.* ①呻吟。The wounded man lay there *groaning*. 受傷者躺在那裏呻吟着。②負擔過重。③受苦;受折磨。The people are still *groaning* under injustice. 人們仍然在不公平之下受折磨。—*v.t.* 噓(某人);呻吟表示;哼着說。The speaker was *groaned* down by the audience. 演講人被聽衆噓下臺來。—**er,** *n.* —**ing·ly,** *adv.*

groat [grot; grout] *n.* ①(1351–1662年間)英國4辨士銀幣。②極小的款額。

groats [grots; grouts] *n. pl.* 粗碾去殼的穀。

***gro·cer** [ˈgrosɚ; ˈgrousə] *n.* 食品雜貨商;家庭用品商。

***gro·cer·y** [ˈgrosərɪ; ˈgrousəri] *n., pl.* **-cer·ies.** ①食品雜貨店(業);家庭用品商店(業)。②(*pl.*)食品雜貨;家庭用品。③【美俚】酒吧。

grog [grɑg; grɔg] *n.* ①烈酒與水之混合飲料。②烈酒。

grog blossom 【俗】(因飲酒而引起的)鼻尖紅斑。

grog·ger·y [ˈgrɑgərɪ; ˈgrɔgəri] *n., pl.* **-ger·ies.** 【英】酒店;低級酒吧。

grog·gy [ˈgrɑgɪ; ˈgrɔgi] *adj.,* **-gi·er, -gi·est.** 【俗】①不穩的。②無力的。③酒醉的。

—grog·gi·ly, *adv.* —grog·gi·ness, *n.*

grog·ram [ˈgrɑgrəm; ˈgrɔgrəm] *n.* 一種絲毛合織物;此種織物製成之衣服。

grog·shop [ˈgrɑg,ʃɑp; ˈgrɔgʃɔp] *n.* 〖英〗酒店。

groin [grɔɪn; grɔin] *n.* ①鼠蹊。②〖建築〗穹稜。③〖水利工程〗丁壩。—*v.t.* ①使成稜建。②建築丁壩。

grom·met [ˈgrɑmɪt; ˈgrɔmit] *n.* ①金屬孔眼。②索環。

***groom** [grum; grum, gru:m] *n.* ①馬夫。②新郎。③英國宮中的侍從官。④〖古〗男僕。—*v.t.* ①餵(馬);看(馬);洗刷。②整飾。Keep yourself well *groomed.* 把你自己弄整潔些。③〖美〗推荐;培植(候選人)。—**er,** *n.* —**ish,** *adj.* —**ish·ly,** *adv.*

grooms·man [ˈgrumzmən; ˈgrumzmən] *n., pl.* **-men.** 男儐相。〖注意〗男儐相有數人時, 其最主要者稱 best man.

groove** [gruv; gru:v] *n., v.,* **grooved, groov·ing.** —*n.* ①溝;槽; 凹線。 Wheels leave *grooves* in a dirt road. 車輪在土路上留下了凹痕。②固定的方式;習慣。 ***in the groove 〖俚〗 **a.** 〖音樂〗流暢而用高度技巧演奏。 **b.** 完美的(地)。 **c.** 合時。 —*v.t.* ①挖溝槽於。 The sink shelf is *grooved* so that the water will run off. 洗池上有溝槽, 爲的是讓水流走。②〖俚〗灌唱片。③〖棒球〗將(球)投得使打擊手容易擊中。

groov·y [ˈgruvɪ; ˈgru:vi] *adj.,* **groov·i·er, groov·i·est.** ①溝的;槽的。②〖俗〗千篇一律的;偏狹的。③〖俚〗順利的;圓滿的。

***grope** [grop; group] *v.,* **groped, grop·ing,** *n.* —*v.i.* 摸索;盲目尋求。The detectives *groped* for some clue to the murder. 偵探們摸索着尋找謀殺案的線索。—*v.t.* 摸索(路)。—*n.* 摸索。—**grop·er,** *n.* —**grop·ing,** *adj.* —**grop·ing·ly,** *adv.*

gros·beak [ˈgros,bik; ˈgrousbi:k] *n.* 蠟嘴鳥。

gro·schen [ˈgroʃən; ˈgrouʃən, ˈgrɔʃ-] *n.* ①昔德國小銀幣。②〖俗〗德國小鎳幣 (10 pfennigs).

gros·grain [ˈgro,gren; ˈgrougrein] *n.* 粗紋綢。

gross** [gros; grous] *adj., n., pl.* **gross·es** for ①, **gross** for ②, *v.* —*adj.* ①總共的。 *gross* receipts (income). 全部的收入。②未打折扣的。 *gross* profit. 毛利。③重大的。④粗鄙的。⑤肥大的。⑥濃密的。—*n.* ①總數;總量。②籮;十二打 (12 dozen). ***in (the) gross **a.** 大體上;一般地;總括地。 **b.** 躉售;批發 (=wholesale). —*v.t.* 總共賺得。—**ly,** *adv.* —**ness,** *n.*

gross national product 〖經濟〗國民生產毛額; 國民總生產額。

gross ton 長噸 (2,240磅)。

gross weight 總重;毛重。

grot [grɑt; grɔt] *n.* 〖詩〗=**grotto.**

***gro·tesque** [groˈtɛsk; grouˈtesk] *adj.* ①醜怪的。②古怪的; 可笑的。 The monkey's *grotesque* antics made the children laugh. 猴子的古怪動作使得兒童大笑。—*n.* 怪異的圖畫、雕刻、畫像等。 —**ly,** *adv.* —**ness,** *n.*

gro·tes·que·rie, gro·tes·que·ry [groˈtɛskərɪ; grouˈteskəri] *n., pl.* **-ries.** ①怪誕事物或作品(集合稱)。②怪誕。

grot·to [ˈgrɑto; ˈgrɔtou] *n., pl.* **-toes, -tos.** ①巖穴。②(人造避暑用的)洞室。

grot·ty [ˈgrɑtɪ; ˈgrɔti] *adj.,* **-ti·er, -ti·est.** 〖英俚〗吝嗇的;小氣的;脾氣壞的。

grouch [grautʃ; grautʃ] *v.i.* 〖俗〗惱怒。—*n.* 〖俗〗①惱怒的人。②怒氣;不滿。

grouch·y [ˈgrautʃɪ; ˈgrautʃi] *adj.,* **grouch·i·er, grouch·i·est.** 〖俗〗惱怒的;不悅的; 心有不平的。—**grouch·i·ly,** *adv.*

:ground¹ [graund; graund] *n.* ①地;土地; 泥土; 土壤。②地面。 It fell to the *ground.* 它落到地面上了。③戰場; 房屋四周的空地;地基。④(常 *pl.*) 根據;理由。What *grounds* have you for thinking that...?你有甚麼根據認爲…? ⑤背景(=background); 底子。The cloth has a blue pattern on a white *ground.* 那布爲白地藍花紋。⑥(*pl.*) 渣滓;沉澱。⑦〖無線電〗接地。⑧(*pl.*)基礎;根基。⑨底;湖底。***above*** (or ***below***) ***ground*** 活 (死) 的。***break ground*** **a.** 挖;犂。 **b.** 破土;動工。 **c.** 做準備工作。 ***cover ground*** **a.** 走過某些路程;走遍某些地區。 **b.** 旅行。 **c.** 論及;提到。 ***cut the ground from under someone*** (or ***one's feet***) 先發制人;揭露計畫。 ***fall to the ground*** 墜地;失敗。 ***from the ground up*** **a.** 完全地;徹底地。 The professor knew his subject *from the ground up.* 教授對於他講的題目徹底了解。 **b.** 從最基本開始而逐漸上升。 ***gain ground*** **a.** 前進;進步。 **b.** 流行;流傳;得勢。 ***get off the ground*** 〖俗〗開始行動; 有進展。 ***give ground*** 撤退;屈降。 ***hold one's ground*** 堅持立場;不稍讓步。 ***lose (one's) ground*** 落伍;失勢;衰退。 ***on one's own ground*** 在自己最熟悉的方面或情況下。 ***on the ground of*** 因爲。 ***on the ground that*** 因爲。 ***run into the ground*** 〖俗〗過分; 過度; 誇張。 ***shift one's ground*** 改變立場;採不同論點。 ***stand one's ground*** 堅持立場; 不稍讓步。 ***suit down to the ground*** 〖俗〗完全滿意。 ***take ground*** 占領陣地。—*adj.* 土地的;地面上的。—*v.t.* ①放在地上。to *ground* arms. 放下武器。②使(船)觸礁;使擱淺。③建立於鞏固之基礎上。The theory is well *grounded.* 這學說的基礎很穩固。④教以基本知識; 打基礎。⑤給以背景;加底子。⑥使(電線等)接地。—*v.i.* (船)觸礁;擱淺。 The boat *grounded* in shallow water. 船在淺水擱淺。

ground² *v.* pt. & pp. of **grind.**

ground·age [ˈgraundɪdʒ; ˈgraundidʒ] *n.* 〖主英〗(船舶)進港費;停泊費。

ground bait 投餌。

ground control (機場之)地面管制。

ground control(led) approach 〖航空〗地面控制進場。

ground controller (機場之)飛行管制員。

ground crew 〖美〗(修護飛機的)地勤人員。

ground·er [ˈgraundɚ; ˈgraundə] *n.* 〖棒球〗滾地球。

ground floor ①〖英〗一樓。②〖美俗〗在買賣中最有利的地位或關係。③事業之開始。

ground game 〖英〗地面之獵物。

ground glass ①毛玻璃。②玻璃粉。

ground hog (美國產之)土撥鼠。

ground-hog day 〖美〗 =**Candlemas** (2月2日)。

ground hostess 地勤小姐。

ground·ing [ˈgraundɪŋ; ˈgraundiŋ] *n.* ①〖電〗接地。②基礎。③(染色的) 底色。

ground ivy 〖植物〗連錢草。

ground-launched [ˈgraund,lɔntʃt; ˈgraund,lɔ:ntʃt] *adj.* 由地面發射的。

ground·less [ˈgraundlɪs; ˈgraundlis] *adj.* 無根據的；無理由的。 —**ly,** *adv.* —**ness,** *n.*

ground·ling ['graundlɪŋ; 'graundliŋ] *n.* ①靠近地面的植物或動物。 ②水底的魚類。③在地面工作或生活之人員。④趣味低級之觀衆或讀者。—*adj.* 卑俗的；低級的。

ground note 〖音樂〗基音；主音。

ground·nut ['graund,nʌt; 'graundnʌt] *n.* ①落花生類的植物。②落花生。

ground pine 歐洲產薄荷屬草本植物。

ground plan ①一層房屋的設計圖；平面圖。②初步的或根本的計畫。

ground rent (建築物之)地租。

ground rule ①〖運動〗體育場或體育館之運動規章。②基本規則。

ground·sel ['graunsl; 'graunsl] *n.* ①〖植物〗橐吾屬之雜草。②=**groundsill.**

ground·sill ['graundsɪl; 'graundsil] *n.* 基礎木材；基礎。(亦作 **groundsel**)

ground speed 〖航空〗地速（航空器速度對地之水平分速，略作 **G. S.**）.（亦作 **groundspeed**）

ground swell ①(由遠處暴風雨或地震所引起的)巨浪。②數量、程度、力量等之巨幅增加。

ground-to-air ['graundtu'ɛr; 'graundtu'ɛə] *adj.* 地對空的。

ground-to-ground ['graundtu'graund; 'graundtu'graund] *adj.* 地對地的。

ground water 地下水。

ground wire 〖電〗地線；接地線。

ground·work ['graund,wɝk; 'graundwə:k] *n.* 基礎；根基。

ground zero (炸彈的)着地點；原子彈「爆炸的中心地區。

‡group [grup; gru:p] *n.* ①組；羣；集團；團體。People were standing about in small *groups.* 人們三五成羣地散立着。②種類。Wheat, rye, and oats belong to the grain *group.* 小麥、裸麥及燕麥都屬穀類。③空軍大隊。④〖化〗基；根。⑤〖數學〗羣。—*v.t.* & *v.i.* ①聚合；成羣。The children *grouped* (themselves) round the hero. 孩子們圍在英雄的四周。②分類。

group·er ['grupɚ; 'gru:pə] *n., pl.* **-ers, -er.** 暖海中鱸科之魚。

group·ie ['grupɪ; 'gru:pi] *n.* 〖俚〗搖滾「樂團女歌迷。

group insurance 團體保險。

***grouse**[1] [graus; graus] *n., pl.* **grouse.** 松鷄。

grouse[2] *v.,* **groused, grous·ing,** *n.* —*v.i.* 〖俚〗鳴不平；埋怨。—*n.* 〖俚〗①牢騷；不平之鳴。②發牢騷的人。

grout[1] [graut; graut] *n.* ①(填縫隙用的)水泥漿。②(牆壁、天花板等之)最後一層細灰泥。③(*pl.*)=**groats.** ④(*pl.*)〖英〗渣；糟粕。—*v.t.* 用水泥漿填塞；粉飾。

grout[2] *v.t.* & *v.i.* (猪等)以鼻掘(土)。

***grove** [grov; grouv] *n.* 叢樹；小樹林。—**groved,** *adj.* —**less,** *adj.*

grov·el ['grɑvl; 'grɔvl] *v.i.,* **-el(l)ed, -el·(l)ing.** ①五體投地；匍匐。②卑躬屈節。③以享受卑劣的事物爲樂。***grovel in the dust*** (or ***dirt***) 匍匐於地；搖尾乞憐。—**er,** *n.* —**ing,** *adj.* —**ing·ly,** *adv.*

‡grow [gro; grou] *v.,* **grew, grown, grow·ing.** —*v.i.* ①生長；發育。②增長；長大；長長。How quickly she is *growing!* 她長得多麼快啊！③變成；逐漸。He is *growing* old. 他漸老了。***grow into*** **a.** 長得够大。He'll *grow into* his brother's suits before long. 他不久便長大得可以穿他哥哥的衣服了。**b.** 變得成熟或有經驗。***grow on*** (or ***upon***) 對…逐漸增加效力或影響。The habit *grew on* me. 我漸漸染上該習慣。***grow out of*** **a.** 長得太高大。**b.** 由…而來。The plan *grew out of* a casual conversation. 這個計畫肇始於一次隨便的談話。***grow up*** **a.** 長大；成人。**b.** 崛起。New cities *grow up* in the desert. 城市在沙漠中崛起了。—*v.t.* ①種植；栽培。Farmers *grow* rice. 農夫種稻。②留；蓄。to *grow* a beard. 留鬍鬚。③發展；形成。

grow·er ['groɚ; 'grouə] *n.* ①種植者；栽培者。②生長物；植物。

grow·ing ['groɪŋ; 'grouiŋ] *n.* 成長；發育；發達；栽培。—*adj.* ①生長的。②隨發育而生的。③適於(促進)成長的。④發育期中的。a *growing* child. 發育期中的孩子。⑤(大小、體積、强度等)增加中的。—**ly,** *adv.*

growing pains ①青少年期之情感上的失去平衡。②兒童或少年期的一種關節痛。③任何新事物初期或舊事物因發展過速而面臨的困難。Taipei is a city beset by *growing pains.* 臺北市因發展過速而面臨許多難題。

***growl** [graul; graul] *v.i.* (犬等)作低吠聲〖at〗；咆哮；鳴不平；隆隆作響。The dog was angry and *growled* at me. 那狗發怒向我咆哮。—*v.t.* 咆哮着說〖out〗. He *growled* (out) his disapproval. 他怒聲提出反對。—*n.* 怒吠聲；怨言；不平；咆哮聲；隆隆聲。He answered the question with a *growl.* 他以咆哮來回答這問題。

growl·er ['graulɚ; 'graulə] *n.* ①咆哮者；鳴不平者。②〖英俚〗(昔)四輪馬車。③〖美俚〗(昔)盛啤酒容器。④小冰山。

‡grown [gron; groun] *v.* pp. of **grow.** —*adj.* ①發育完成的；成年的。a *grown* man. 成人。②長滿某物的。

***grown-up** [*adj.* 'gron'ʌp; 'grounʌp *n.* 'gron,ʌp; 'grounʌp, 'groun'ʌp] *adj.* 成年的；成熟的；適於成年人的。—*n.* 成年人；大人。There were no *grown-ups* there, only children. 那裏沒有大人，祇有小孩。

‡growth [groθ; grouθ] *n.* ①生長；發展。Childhood is a period of rapid *growth.* 幼年是生長迅速的時期。②生長物。③生長或發育之量。④〖醫〗腫瘤。Cancer causes a *growth.* 癌症引起腫瘤。⑤栽培；培養。Are these apples of foreign *growth?* 這些蘋果是外國產的麼？⑥增加；擴張。the *growth* of population. 人口的增加。⑦來源。⑧演進；演變。***evil growth*** 弊病；惡病。

growth ring 〖植物〗年輪。（亦作 **annul ring**）

groyne [grɔɪn; grɔin] *n., v.,* **groyned, groyn·ing.** —*n.* 〖土木〗防砂堤。—*v.t.* 築防砂堤於(海灘)。

grub [grʌb; grʌb] *n., v.,* **grubbed, grub·bing.** —*n.* ①蠐螬；蛆。②〖俚〗食物。③服賤役者；窮文人。④骯髒的人。⑤〖板球〗滾入之球。⑥墾地中留下之殘根。—*v.i.* ①拱；掘；挖。The pigs were *grubbing* about among the trees. 豬在樹叢間到處亂拱。②作苦工。③〖俚〗吃。④尋找；搜索。⑤仔細研究。—*v.t.* ①掘出；挖出土地中之(根等)。He was in the garden *grubbing* up weeds. 他在園裏除草。②〖俚〗餵；供以食物。

grub·ber ['grʌbɚ; 'grʌbə] *n.* 挖者；挖樹根的苦力；勤勞之人；用以挖掘的工具。

grub·by ['grʌbɪ; 'grʌbi] *adj.,* **-bi·er, -bi·est.** ①汚穢的；不潔的。②爲蠐螬擾害的。③〖方〗矮小的。④卑鄙的；可恥的。

grub·stake ('grʌbˌstek; 'grʌbsteik) *n., v.,* **-staked, -stak·ing.** —*n.* 〖美西部〗①(以分其所獲爲條件)供給採礦者之金錢或物品。②資助金。—*v.t.* 〖俗〗供以上述之金錢或用品;資助(採礦者等)。—**grub·stak·er,** *n.*

Grub Street ①倫敦街名(即今Milton Street; 昔寒士集居之地)。②寒士(集合稱)。

***grudge** (grʌdʒ; grʌdʒ) *n., v.,* **grudged, grudg·ing.** —*n.* 遺恨; 惡意; 怨恨。He bears me *grudge.* 他對我有怨恨。—*v.t.* ①嫉妒。He *grudged* my prize. 他嫉妒我的獲獎。②吝惜;吝嗇。—*v.i.* 懷恨;心懷不滿。—**grudg·er,** *n.*

grudg·ing ('grʌdʒɪŋ; 'grʌdʒiŋ) *adj.* ①吝嗇的。②惡意的。③不願的。—**ly,** *adv.*

gru·el ('gruəl; gruəl) *v.,* **-el(l)ed, -el(l)ing,** *n.* —*v.t.* ①使筋疲力竭。②嚴詰;嚴懲。—*n.* 粥。***have*** (or ***get***) ***one's gruel*** 〖俗〗受重罰。—**gru·el·(l)er,** *n.*

gru·el·(l)ing ('gruəlɪŋ; 'gruəliŋ) *adj.* 令人筋疲力竭的; 嚴厲的; 激烈的。—*n.* ①懲罰。②令人筋疲力竭之工作。③疲勞審問。—**ly,** *adv.*

grue·some ('grusəm; 'gru:səm) *adj.* ①令人毛骨悚然的。②討厭的。—**ly,** *adv.* —**ness,** *n.*

gruff (grʌf; grʌf) *adj.* ①(聲音)粗嗄的;沙啞的。②(行爲或態度)粗暴的;粗率的。(亦作 **gruffy**) —**ish,** *adj.* —**ly,** *adv.* —**ness,** *n.*

***grum·ble** ('grʌmbl; 'grʌmbl) *v.,* **-bled, -bling,** *n.* —*v.i.* ①喃喃訴苦;發怨言;鳴不平。to *grumble* at (about, *or* over) one's food. 埋怨食物不好。②隆隆作響;(雷)鳴。—*v.t.* 喃喃地說出;埋怨地道出。to *grumble* (out) an answer. 喃喃作答。—*n.* ①怨言。That fellow is full of *grumbles.* 那傢伙滿腹牢騷。②隆隆聲; 雷聲。—**grum·bler,** *n.* —**grum·bly,** *adj.*

grum·bling ('grʌmblɪŋ; 'grʌmbliŋ) *adj.* ①喃喃鳴不平的; 出怨言的。②疼痛的。—**ly,** *adv.*

grume (grum; gru:m) *n.* ①〖醫〗血塊;凝血。②任何似血之液體。

gru·mous ('grumos; 'gru:mous) *adj.* ①〖植物〗由聚團顆粒而成的。②〖醫〗似血塊(凝血)的;(血)凝固的。

grump·y ('grʌmpɪ; 'grʌmpi) *adj.,* **grump·i·er, grump·i·est.** 性情乖戾的。

Grun·dy, Mrs. ('grʌndɪ; 'grʌndi) *n.* ①心胸狹窄、愛挑剔他人者。②社會上對某人行爲道德之詆議。

Grun·dy·ism ('grʌndɪˌɪzəm; 'grʌndiizm) *n.* 褊狹而愚昧的拘泥習俗;顧忌體面。

***grunt** (grʌnt; grʌnt) *n.* ①(猪等)咕嚕聲; 輕微喉聲。②火魚。—*v.i.* (猪等)發低沉的咕嚕聲。—*v.t.* 以低沉的咕嚕聲說出; 發(怨言)。The sullen boy *grunted* his apology. 那發着脾氣的孩子咕嚕着賠不是。—**ing·ly,** *adv.*

grunt·er ('grʌntɚ; 'grʌntə) *n.* ①作喉鳴之動物或人;鳴不平者。②猪。③火魚。

Gru·yère (cheese) (gru'jɛr; 'gru:jɛə) *n.* 一種瑞士乾酪。

gr. wt. gross weight.

gryph·on ('grɪfən; 'grifən) *n.* =**griffin**[1].

gs. guineas. **G.S., g.s.** ①General Secretary. ②Girl Scouts. ③Grand Scribe. ④Grand Secretary. ⑤General Service. ⑥General Staff. ⑦ground speed. **G.S.A.** Girl Scouts of America.

G-string ('dʒistrɪŋ; 'dʒi:striŋ) *n.* ①〖音樂〗(小提琴之) G 弦。②(圍下體之)遮羞布。

G-suit (太空人等所穿之)重力衣。

gt. ①gilt. ②great. ③〖處方〗一滴(=drop). **Gt. Br(it).** Great Britain.

G.T.C., g.t.c. ①good till cancel(l)ed 〖商〗未取消前仍有效。②good till countermanded. 〖商〗未撤回前仍有效。

gua·cha·ro ('gwatʃaro; 'gwa:tʃa:rou) *n., pl.* **-ros, -roes.** (南美產)大怪鴟。

guai·a·cum, guai·o·cum ('gwaɪəkəm; 'gwaiəkəm) *n.* 〖植物〗①癒瘡木(熱帶美洲產)。②癒瘡木脂。

Guam (gwam; gwa:m) *n.* 關島(位於西太平洋,屬美國)。

gua·na·co (gwa'nako; gwa:'na:kou) *n., pl.* **-cos.** 〖動物〗(南美 Andes 山地產之)栗色駱馬。

gua·no ('gwano; 'gwa:nou) *n., pl.* **-nos,** *v.* —*n.* ①海鳥糞;鳥糞石。②用魚製的人造肥料。③人造氮肥。—*v.t.* 施肥於。

guar. guaranteed.

gua·ra·ni (ˌgwara'ni; ˌgwa:ra:'ni:) *n., pl.* **-ni, -nis.** 巴拉圭的貨幣單位。

***guar·an·tee** (ˌgærən'ti; ˌgærən'ti:) *n., v.,* **-teed, -tee·ing.** —*n.* ①擔保;保證。②擔保人;保證人。to stand *guarantee* for. 作…之保證人。③接受保證的人。④保證書。⑤〖法律〗抵押品; 抵押物。What *guarantee* can you offer? 你能拿出甚麼做抵押? ⑥任何可資保證之事物。—*v.t.* 保證;擔保。This clock is *guaranteed* for one year. 此鐘保用一年。His insurance *guaranteed* him against money loss in case of fire. 他的保險保證他在火災時不受金錢上的損失。

guar·an·tor ('gærəntɚ; ˌgærən'tɔ:) *n.* 保證人;擔保人。

***guar·an·ty** ('gærəntɪ; 'gærənti) *n., pl.* **-ties,** *v.,* **-tied, -ty·ing.** —*n.* ①保證;擔保。②所作之保證; 作爲保證之物。—*v.t.* 保證; 擔保。

‡**guard** (gard; ga:d) *v.t.* ①保守; 保衞; 保護。②看守; 看管。③當心。*Guard* your tongue. 當心不可亂說話。—*v.i.* 預防; 提防〖against〗. to *guard* against disease. 預防疾病。—*n.* ①守衞者;防衞物。②警戒。Be on your *guard* against pickpockets. 謹防扒手。③(爲防護主力所派出之)部隊。the advanced (rear) *guard.* 前(後)衞。④(監獄的)看守(人員)。⑤管車人。⑥禁衞軍;御林軍。the *Guards.* 禁衞軍團;警衞團。⑦(劍術、拳擊的)防禦姿勢;防衞術。⑧(籃球、足球之)衞;後衞。***keep guard*** 放哨;守望。***mount guard*** 上班放哨;去站崗。***off guard*** **a.** 不當班。**b.** 不備;疏忽。***off one's guard*** 疏忽;不提防。He struck me while I was *off my guard.* 他乘我不備打我。***on guard*** **a.** 當班;值班。**b.** 警戒;準備防禦。***on one's guard*** 警戒着。***put*** (or ***set***) ***a person on his guard*** 使某人提防。***relieve guard*** 換班;接班。***row the guard*** 用小船巡衞軍艦周圍。***run the guard*** 偷過哨兵線。***stand guard over*** 看守。The dog *stood guard over* his wounded master. 狗看守着牠受傷的主人。***stand*** (or ***lie***) ***upon one's guard*** 警戒;提防。

guard-boat ('gardˌbot; 'ga:dbout) *n.* 巡邏艇;監視船。

guard-book ('gardˌbuk; 'ga:dbuk) *n.* 爲防夾物過多裂開而在背脊附加細長紙片或布片之簿子。

guard·ed ['gardɪd; 'gɑːdid] *adj.* ①安全的。②謹愼的。③有人防守的。 —**ly,** *adv.* —**ness,** *n.*
guard·er ['gardə; 'gɑːdə] *n.* 看守「者;衛兵;護衛。
guard·house ['gard,haus;'gɑːdhaus] *n.* ①禁閉室。②衛兵室。
guard·i·an ['gardɪən; 'gɑːdjən, -diən] *n.* ①(法定)監護人。②保護人; 監守人。—*adj.* 保護的。***guardian angel***護守天神。
guard·i·an·ship ['gardɪən,ʃɪp; 'gɑːdjənʃip] *n.* 監護人之地位、責任或權力;保護;監護。「儀仗隊。(亦作 **honor guard**)
guard of honor ①儀隊。②(喪儀用)
guard·rail ['gard,rel; 'gɑːdreil] *n.* ①〖鐵路〗護輪之軌條。②(樓梯等之)護欄。
guard ring 戒指扣(防另一戒指脫落者)。
guard·room['gard,rum;'gɑːdru(ː)m] *n.* ①衛兵室;哨亭。②禁閉室。
guard ship (港內)警備艦;哨艦。
guards·man ['gardzmən; 'gɑːdzmən] *n., pl.* **-men.** ①衛兵。②〖美〗(屬於州的)國民兵之一員。③〖英〗皇家禁衛軍步兵團之一員。
Gua·te·ma·la [,gwɑtə'mɑlə; ,gwæti'mɑːlə] *n.* 瓜地馬拉(國名,位於中美洲,首都 瓜地馬拉 Guatemala City)。—**Gua·te·ma·lan,** *adj., n.* 「(樹或果)。
gua·va ['gwɑvə; 'gwɑːvə] *n.* 番石榴
gua·yu·le [,gwɑ'jule; gwɑː'julei] *n.* 〖植物〗①(熱帶美洲產之)膠樹。②該樹之膠。
gu·ber·na·to·ri·al [,gjubənə'torɪəl; ,gjuːbənə'touriəl] *adj.* 〖美〗州長的。
gudg·eon[1] ['gʌdʒən; 'gʌdʒən] *n.* ①〖動物〗白楊魚(常被用爲餌)。②鰷魚。③易受騙之人。④誘餌;誘惑物。—*v.t.* 欺騙。
gudg·eon[2] *n.* ①輪軸。②穿軸之孔。③將兩塊石頭相連之金屬竿。
guel·der-rose ['gɛldə,roz; 'geldərouz] *n.* 〖植物〗雪球。
Guelph, Guelf [gwɛlf; gwelf] *n.* (12-15 世紀義大利之) 敎皇黨員。—**ic,** *adj.*
guer·don ['gɜdn̩; 'gəːdən] *n., v.t.* 〖詩〗報酬。
gue(r)·ril·la [gə'rɪlə; gə'rilə] *n.* ①游擊隊隊員;(常 *pl.*) 游擊隊。②游擊戰。—*adj.* 游擊的; 游擊隊的。
Guern·sey ['gɜnzɪ; 'gəːnzi] *n.* ①根西島(英吉利海峽羣島之一島)。②(此島所產之)根西乳牛。
guern·sey ['gɜnzɪ; 'gəːnzi] *n., pl.* **-seys.** 水手穿的一種厚毛衣。
‡guess [gɛs; ges] *v.t.* ①猜度;臆測;推量。*Guess* what I have in my hand. 猜我手中有甚麼東西。②〖美俗〗想; 相信 (=think, believe). I *guess* it's going to rain. 我想要下雨了。—*v.i.* 猜; 猜想; 猜測。It was too important to *guess* about. 這事太重要了不能胡猜。***guess at*** 猜着。I can't even *guess at* her age. 我甚至連她的年紀也猜不着。***keep (one) guessing*** 不明說;讓人猜。—*n.* 猜測; 臆測。I'll allow you three *guesses.* 我將讓你猜三次。***at a guess*** 依推測;憑估計。***by guess*** 由估計;未經精確計算。—**a·ble,** *adj.* —**er,** *n.* —**ing·ly,** *adv.*
guess·ti·mate [*v.* 'gɛstə,met; 'gestəmeit *n.* 'gɛstəmɪt;'gestəmit] *v.,* **-mat·ed, -mat·ing,** *n.* 〖俚〗—*v.i. & v.t.* 估計;猜測。—*n.* 估計所得之結果。(亦作 **guesti·mate**) 「*n.* 所作之猜測;臆測;臆斷。
guess·work ['gɛs,wɜk; 'ges-wəːk]
‡guest [gɛst; gest] *n.* ①客人;來賓。We are expecting *guests* to dinner. 我們在等候着客人進餐。②旅客; 宿客。 paying *guest.* 宿客。—**less,** *adj.*
guest·cham·ber ['gɛst,tʃembə; 'gest,tʃeimbə] *n.* (公共建築物中之)客房。(亦作 **guest room**) 「**guesthouse**)
guest house 上等旅舍;賓館。(亦作
guest-night ['gɛst,naɪt; 'gestnait] *n.* (學校、俱樂部等)招待賓客之夜晚。
guff [gʌf; gʌf] *n.* ①〖俚〗胡言; 廢話。②〖俚〗反辯。③〖蘇〗突來的一陣風。
guf·faw [gʌ'fɔ; gʌ'fɔː] *n.* 哄笑;大笑;捧腹。—*v.i.* 捧腹大笑;哄笑。
gug·gle ['gʌgl̩;'gʌgl] *v.i., n.* =**gurgle.**
Gui·a·na [gɪ'ænə; gai'ænə] *n.* 圭亞那(南美洲東北部一地區,分屬荷、法兩國)。
guid·a·ble ['gaɪdəbl̩; 'gaidəbl] *adj.* 可引導的;可指導的。
***guid·ance** ['gaɪdn̩s; 'gaidəns] *n.* ①指導;領導;嚮導。under competent *guidance.* 在適當的指導之下。②〖航空〗(無人駕駛的)導航。
‡guide [gaɪd; gaid] *v.,* **guid·ed, guid·ing,** *n.* —*v.t.* ①引導;指導;領導。The President skillfully *guided* the country through a difficult period. 總統英明地領導國家度過難關。②處理; 督導; 支配;管理。—*n.* ①引導者; 嚮導。②指南。 a *Guide* to English Grammar. 英文文法指南。③〖機械〗導桿;導體;引導機。④路標。⑤〖軍〗標兵。—**guid·ing·ly,** *adv.* —**less,** *adj.*
guide·board ['gaɪd,bord;'gaidbɔːd] *n.* 路標;路牌。 「旅行指南。
guide·book ['gaɪd,buk;'gaidbuk] *n.*
guided missile 電導飛彈。
guide·line ['gaɪd,laɪn; 'gaidlain] *n.* ①指導方針。②指示方向用的繩或物。
guide·post ['gaɪd,post; 'gaidpoust] *n.* 路標;指路牌。
guide rope ①導繩 (保持重物穩定或調度其方向)。②〖航空〗(汽球之) 調節繩。
guide word 引導字。
gui·don ['gaɪdn̩; 'gaidən] *n.* ①(原指)騎兵隊之三角旗; 其旗手。②〖美陸軍〗(爲部隊標幟之) 部隊旗; 其旗手。
guild [gɪld; gild] *n.* ①互助會; 協會。②(中世紀之) 同業公會; 基爾特。(亦作 **gild**)
guil·der ['gɪldə; 'gildə] *n.* ①基爾德(荷蘭錢幣單位)。②荷蘭銀幣名 (值一個基爾德)。③舊荷蘭、德國或奧國之金幣或銀幣名。(亦作 **gulden, gilder**)
guild·hall ['gɪld'hɔl; 'gild'hɔːl] *n.* ①(公會集會用的) 會館;公所。②〖英〗市政廳。(亦作 **gildhall**)
guilds·man ['gɪldzmən; 'gildzmən] *n., pl.* **-men.** 同業公會會員。
guild socialism 基爾特社會主義(主張產業國有而由工會管理)。
guile [gaɪl; gail] *n.* 狡計; 詐術; 騙術。—**ful,** *adj.* —**ful·ly,** *adv.*
guile·less ['gaɪllɪs; 'gaillis] *adj.* 不狡猾的;誠實的;坦白的。—**ly,** *adv.* —**ness,** *n.*
Guil·laume [,gi'jom; ,giː'joum] *n.* 吉永 (Charles Edouard, 1861-1938, 生於瑞士之法國物理學家, 獲 1920 年諾貝爾物理獎)。
guil·le·mot ['gɪlə,mɑt; 'gilimɔt] *n.* 海鳩。 「繩形飾。
guil·loche [gɪ'loʃ; gi'louʃ] *n.* 〖建築〗
guil·lo·tine ['gɪlə,tin; 'gilətiːn, ,gilə-

ˈtiːn〕 *n.* ①斷頭臺。②切紙機。③(外科用)環狀刀。④〖英〗=**cloture.** —*v.t.* ①在斷頭臺上斬首。②切(紙)。③割除(扁桃腺)。④〖英〗對(某一議案)終結辯論而付表決。

***guilt**〔gɪlt; gilt〕*n.* ①罪; 罪行; 罪狀。The evidence proved his *guilt.* 證據證明了他的罪狀。②內疚。

***guilt·less**〔ˈgɪltlɪs; ˈgiltlis〕*adj.* ①無罪的; 無辜的。The prisoner was proved *guiltless* and released. 這犯人被判無罪, 並獲釋放。②無知的;無經驗的〖of〗. —**ly,** *adv.* —**ness,** *n.*

***guilt·y**〔ˈgɪltɪ; ˈgilti〕*adj.,* **guilt·i·er, guilt·i·est.** ①有罪的;犯罪的。You have been *guilty* of a serious blunder. 你犯了一個大錯。②自覺有罪的; 心虛的。—**guilt·i·ly,** *adv.* —**guilt·i·ness,** *n.*

guimpe〔gɪmp; gimp〕*n.* (與圍裙或背心裙配穿的)一種襯衫。

***Guin·ea**〔ˈgɪnɪ; ˈgini〕*n.* 幾內亞(西非之一共和國, 首都康那克立 Conakry). —**Guin·e·an,** *adj.*

***guin·ea**〔ˈgɪnɪ; ˈgini〕*n.* ①昔英國金幣名。②〖動物〗珠鷄。③〖俚〗打雜工人。

Guin·ea-Bis·sau〔ˈgɪnɪbɪˈsau; ˈginibiˈsau〕*n.* 幾內亞比索(西非之一國, 首都比索 Bissau).

guinea fowl 珠鷄。

guinea hen ①珠鷄。②雌珠鷄。

guinea pig ①〖動物〗天竺鼠; 荷蘭猪。②供作實驗或觀察之人或物。

gui·pure〔gɪˈpjur; giˈpjuːə〕*n.* 一種花邊。

guise〔gaɪz; gaiz〕*n., v.,* **guised, guis·ing.** —*n.* ①裝束;打扮。②外貌;外表。③假裝。under the *guise* of friendship. 僞裝友善。—*v.t.* 穿着; 打扮。

***gui·tar**〔gɪˈtɑr; giˈtɑː〕*n.* 吉他;六絃琴。

gui·tar·ist〔gɪˈtɑrɪst; giˈtɑːrist〕*n.* 彈奏吉他者。

gulch〔gʌltʃ; gʌlʃ〕*n.* 〖美〗峽谷;深谷。

gul·den〔ˈguldən; ˈguldən〕*n., pl.* **-dens, -den.** ①=**guilder.** ②德奧兩國以前之金銀幣。

gules〔gjulz; gjuːlz〕*n., adj.* 〖紋章〗紅色(的)。

***gulf**〔gʌlf; gʌlf〕*n.* ①海灣。the *Gulf* of Mexico. 墨西哥灣。②深淵。③隔閡。④漩渦;漩流。⑤裂罅;深坑。*the gulf below* 地獄。—**like,** —**y,** *adj.*

Gulf States 美國瀕墨西哥灣諸州。

Gulf Stream 墨西哥灣流。

gulf·weed〔ˈgʌlfˌwid; ˈgʌlfwiːd〕*n.* 〖植物〗馬尾藻屬。

gull¹〔gʌl; gʌl〕*n.* 鷗。

gull² *n.* 易受人愚弄之人。—*v.t.* 欺騙。

Gul·lah〔ˈgʌlə; ˈgʌlə〕*n.* ①美國 Georgia, South Carolina 兩州海邊之黑人。②其方言。

gul·let〔ˈgʌlɪt; ˈgʌlit〕*n.* ①食道。②咽喉。③海峽。④峽谷。

gul·li·bil·i·ty〔ˌgʌləˈbɪlətɪ; ˌgʌliˈbiliti〕*n.* 易受欺騙的性格。(亦作 **gullability**)

gul·li·ble〔ˈgʌləbḷ; ˈgʌləbl〕*adj.* 易受欺騙的。(亦作 **gullable**) —**gul·li·bly,** *adv.*

Gul·li·ver's Travels〔ˈgʌlɪvəz~; ˈgʌlivəz~〕格利佛遊記(英國 Jonathan Swift 作)。

Gull·strand〔ˈgʌlstrand; ˈgʌlstraːnd〕*n.* 格爾斯特蘭(Allvar, 1862–1930, 瑞典眼科醫師, 曾獲 1911 年諾貝爾醫學獎)。

gul·ly〔ˈgʌlɪ; ˈgʌli〕*n., pl.* **gul·lies,** *v.,* **-lied, -ly·ing.** —*n.* (亦作 **gulley**) ①溪谷。②(爲流水沖成的)溝渠。—*v.t.* ①開溝。②(由流水而)沖成水溝。

***gulp**〔gʌlp; gʌlp〕*v.t.* ①吞飲; 狼吞虎嚥。②抑制(嗚咽);忍氣。to *gulp* down a sob 飲泣吞聲。—*v.i.* 嗆。—*n.* ①吞。②一次吞飲之量。—**er,** *n.* —**ing·ly,** *adv.* —**y,** *adj.*

***gum¹**〔gʌm; gʌm〕*n., v.,* **gummed, gum·ming.** —*n.* ①樹膠;樹脂。②〖美〗口香糖。③橡皮。④橡皮樹;橡膠樹。⑤(*pl.*)橡皮鞋; 橡皮套鞋。⑥郵票背面信封口上之膠質。*sweet gum* 蘇合香。—*v.t.* ①塗以樹膠;以樹膠黏合。②使有黏性。His pocket was all *gummed* up with candy. 他的衣袋全被糖弄黏了。—*v.i.* ①分泌樹膠。②變成黏的。*gum up the works* 〖俚〗把事情弄糟。

gum² *n.* (常*pl.*)齒齦。

gum·bo〔ˈgʌmbo; ˈgʌmbou〕*n., pl.* **-bos.** ①秋葵; 秋葵莢。②加秋葵莢之(鷄肉)湯。③(美西部)一種細黏土。

gum·boil〔ˈgʌmˌbɔɪl; ˈgʌmbɔil〕*n.* 〖醫〗齦膿腫。

gum·drop〔ˈgʌmˌdrɑp; ˈgʌmdrɔp〕*n.* 樹膠丸。

gum elastic 彈性樹膠。

gum·ma〔ˈgʌmə; ˈgʌmə〕*n., pl.* **-ma·ta**〔-mətə; -mətə〕, **-mas.** 〖醫〗(第三期梅毒之)樹膠腫;梅毒瘤。—**tous,** *adj.*

gum·my〔ˈgʌmɪ; ˈgʌmi〕*adj.,* **gum·mi·er, gum·mi·est.** ①樹膠(性)的;黏性的。②塗有樹膠的。③分泌樹膠液的。④腫脹的。

gump·tion〔ˈgʌmpʃən; ˈgʌmpʃən〕*n.* 〖俗〗①常識; 好的判斷力; 實幹的才力。②創業精神。③勇氣。

gum resin 樹膠脂(樹膠與樹脂之混合物)。

gum·shoe〔ˈgʌmˈʃu; ˈgʌmˈʃuː〕*n., adj., v.,* **-shoed, -shoe·ing.** —*n.* ①〖俗〗橡膠套鞋。②(*pl.*)膠底靴。③〖俚〗潛行者; 偵探;警探。—*adj.* 〖美俚〗潛行的;偷偷摸摸的。—*v.i.* 〖美俚〗潛行;偵察。

gum tree 產樹膠之樹。*up a gum tree* 〖美〗進退兩難。

gum·wood〔ˈgʌmˌwud; ˈgʌmwud〕*n.* 橡膠樹的木材。

‡gun〔gʌn; gʌn〕*n., v.,* **gunned, gun·ning.** —*n.* ①鎗; 砲。an air *gun.* 氣鎗。②似鎗或砲之物。③(鳴鎗或砲的)信號;敬禮。*as sure as a gun* 無疑; 的確。*be made like a gun* 造得結實。*blow great guns* (風)狂吹; 起大風。*carry too many* (or *the biggest*) *guns* (議論競賽中)穩操勝算。*give it the gun* 〖俚〗使某事物開始或加速。*give something the gun* 〖俚〗使某事物加速; 發動。*go great guns* 〖俚〗迅速有效地做。*great gun* 〖俗〗名人; 偉人; 高級將官。*Great guns!* 〖俗〗啊呀! 完了! 糟了! *jump the gun* a. 賽跑時不等鳴鎗而搶先。b. 作任何過早行動。*spike one's guns* 使無能爲力; 擊敗。*stick to one's guns* 堅守立場。—*v.i.* 放鎗;發砲;用鎗狩獵。He went *gunning* for rabbits. 他打兔子去了。—*v.t.* ①〖俗〗開鎗射擊(人)。②〖俚〗開(飛機發動機)的節流瓣以加快速度。*gun for* a. 搜尋;追趕;用鎗獵…。b. 力求; 爭取。

gun·boat〔ˈgʌnˌbot; ˈgʌnbout〕*n.* 砲艇;砲艦。

gunboat diplomacy 武力外交。

gun carriage 砲架。

gun·cot·ton〔ˈgʌnˌkatṇ; ˈgʌnˌkɔtn〕*n.* 火藥棉。

gun crew 船上之鎗砲手。

gun·dog〔ˈgʌnˌdɔg; ˈgʌndɔg〕*n.* 獵犬。(亦作 **gun dog**)

gun·fight〔ˈgʌnfaɪt; ˈgʌnfait〕*n.* 鎗戰。

gun·fire〔ˈgʌnˌfaɪr; ˈgʌnˌfaiə〕*n.* 砲火;砲轟。

gun·flint〔ˈgʌnˈflɪnt; ˈgʌnflint〕*n.* 燧發鎗中之打火石。

gun harpoon (用砲射出的)捕鯨叉。

gun·lock [ˈgʌn͵lɑk; ˈgʌnlɔk] *n.* 鎗機。

gun·mak·er [ˈgʌn͵mekɚ; ˈgʌn͵meikə] *n.* 製造鎗枝之個人或工廠。

gun·man [ˈgʌn͵mæn; ˈgʌnmən] *n., pl.* **-men.** 〖美〗①持鎗搶刼及殺人者。②携鎗者。③製造鎗枝者。—**ship,** *n.*

gun metal ①砲銅;靑銅。②暗灰色。

gun·nel¹ [ˈgʌnl̩; ˈgʌnl̩] *n.* =**gunwale.**

gun·nel² *n.* 鳚魚之一種。

gun·ner [ˈgʌnɚ; ˈgʌnə] *n.* ①砲手。②(軍艦之)鎗砲官。③帶鎗獵人。***gunner's daughter*** 水手被鞭打時綁在上面的大砲。to be married(*or* kiss)the *gunner's daughter.* 被綁在大砲上鞭打。

gun·ner·y [ˈgʌnərɪ; ˈgʌnəri] *n.* ①砲術;砲學;造砲學。②鎗砲射擊法。③鎗砲之總稱。

gun·ning [ˈgʌnɪŋ; ˈgʌniŋ] *n.* 鎗獵;鎗獵法。to go *gunning.* 去打獵。

gun·ny [ˈgʌnɪ; ˈgʌni] *n., pl.* **gun·nies.** ①粗麻布。②麻布袋。

gunny bag (or **sack**) 麻布袋。

gun pit ①掩護砲及砲兵之土坑。②砲座;砲位。

gun·point [ˈgʌn͵pɔɪnt; ˈgʌnpɔint] *n.* 鎗口。***at gunpoint*** 在鎗口威脅下。The robbers made him open the safe *at gunpoint.* 强盜們用鎗對着他逼他開保險箱。

***gun·pow·der** [ˈgʌn͵paudɚ; ˈgʌn͵paudə] *n.* ①火藥。②一種綠茶。

gun·rack [ˈgʌn͵ræk; ˈgʌnræk] *n.* 牆上之鎗架。

gun room ①軍械室。②〖英〗(軍艦之)下級軍官室。

gun·run·ning [ˈgʌn͵rʌnɪŋ; ˈgʌn͵rʌniŋ] *n.* 私運軍火。—**gun·run·ner,** *n.*

gun·ship [ˈgʌn͵ʃɪp; ˈgʌn-ʃip] *n.* 武裝直昇機。

gun·shot [ˈgʌn͵ʃɑt; ˈgʌn-ʃɔt] *n.* ①(鎗砲內射出之)砲彈。②射擊鎗聲。We heard *gunshots.* 我們聽到鎗聲。③鎗或砲之射程。

gun-shy [ˈgʌn͵ʃaɪ; ˈgʌn-ʃai] *adj.* 爲鎗砲聲所嚇壞了的(獵犬或馬)。

gun·sight [ˈgʌn͵saɪt; ˈgʌn-sait] *n.* 準星。

gun·smith [ˈgʌn͵smɪθ; ˈgʌn-smiθ] *n.* 造鎗匠;修鎗匠;鎗砲工人。

gun·stock [ˈgʌn͵stɑk; ˈgʌn-stɔk] *n.* 鎗托;鎗柄。

Gun·ter [ˈgʌntɚ; ˈgʌntə] *n.* ①甘特(Edmund, 1581–1626, 英國數學家)。②(g-) =**Gunter's scale.** ***according to Gunter*** 〖美〗精確地;正確地。

Gunter's chain 甘特氏測鍊。

Gunter's scale 甘特氏比例尺(用於測量及航海)。

gun·wale [ˈgʌnl̩; ˈgʌnl̩] *n.* 船舷的上緣。

gup·py [ˈgʌpɪ; ˈgʌpi] *n., pl.* **-pies.** (西印度羣島產之)一種胎生小魚。

gur·gi·ta·tion [͵gɝdʒəˈteʃən; ͵gəːdʒəˈteiʃən] *n.* 液體的沸騰;洶湧;旋洄之狀。

gur·gle [ˈgɝgl̩; ˈgəːgl] *v.,* **-gled, -gling,** *n.* —*v.i.* ①潺潺而流。②作汩汩聲。③(喉嚨)作咯咯聲。—*v.t.* ①使發潺潺聲。②作咯咯聲。—*n.* 潺潺聲。

Gur·kha [ˈgurkə; ˈguəkə] *n.* 廓爾喀族(尼泊爾之一勇猛種族)。

gur·nard [ˈgɝnəd; ˈgəːnəd] *n., pl.* **-nards, -nard.** 魴鮄。

gur·net [ˈgɝnɪt; ˈgəːnit] *n., pl.* **-nets, -net.** =**gurnard.**

gur·ry [ˈgʌrɪ; ˈgʌri] *n., pl.* **-ries.** 〖印〗小寨。

gu·ru [ˈguru; ˈguruː] *n.* ①(印度之)教派之領袖;宗教師。②(印度宗教師穿的)外袍。③出類拔萃的人物。④專家或權威。

***gush** [gʌʃ; gʌʃ] *v.i.* ①湧出;傾流;傾瀉。oil *gushing* from a well. 從油井中湧出的油。②感情奔流;滔滔不絕地說或寫。young girls who *gush* over handsome film stars. 熱心地談論漂亮電影明星的女孩子。—*v.t.* 湧出;傾瀉。—*n.* ①湧出;傾出。a *gush* of blood. 血湧流出來。②滔滔不絕的話。

gush·er [ˈgʌʃɚ; ˈgʌʃə] *n.* ①油井。②滔滔不絕地說話者;亂動感情者。

gush·ing [ˈgʌʃɪŋ; ˈgʌʃiŋ] *adj.* ①湧出的;噴出的。②感情橫溢的。

gush·y [ˈgʌʃɪ; ˈgʌʃi] *adj.,* **gush·i·er, gush·i·est.** =**gushing.**

gus·set [ˈgʌsɪt; ˈgʌsit] *n.* ①(插接於衣物手套中以加强或撐大用的)三角片;衽;襠。②〖機械〗隅板;角板。③古代甲胄膝肘彎曲連接處之金屬板片。—*v.t.* 接以三角片。

gus·sy [ˈgʌsɪ; ˈgʌsi] *v.t. & v.i.,* **gussied,gus·sy·ing.** 〖美俚〗過分打扮;過分修飾〔up〕。(亦作 **gussie**)

***gust**¹ [gʌst; gʌst] *n.* ①突然一陣;陣風;陣雨。a *gust* of wind 一陣狂風。②一陣。a *gust* of anger. 一陣發怒。

gust² *n.* 〖古, 詩〗①味;風味。the *gust* of novelty. 新鮮的風味。②嘗味。—*v.t.* 〖蘇〗嘗味。

gus·ta·tion [gʌsˈteʃən; gʌsˈteiʃən] *n.* 嘗味;味覺。

gus·ta·to·ry [ˈgʌstə͵torɪ,–͵tɔrɪ; ˈgʌstətəri] *adj.* 嘗味的; 味覺的。a *gustatory* nerve. 味覺神經。

gustatory bud (or **corpuscle**) 〖解剖〗(舌面之)味蕾。

gus·to [ˈgʌsto; ˈgʌstou] *n., pl.* **-tos.** ①興味;趣味;享樂。②(個人的)愛好;癖好;嗜愛。③藝術的風格。

gust·y [ˈgʌstɪ; ˈgʌsti] *adj.,* **gust·i·er, gust·i·est.** ①(風、雨等)陣陣的;颳風的。②(音響、笑等)突發的。③空洞的。④熱烈的;有活力的。⑤〖主蘇〗美味的;可口的。

gut [gʌt; gʌt] *n., v.,* **gut·ted, gut·ting.** —*n.* ①(*pl.*)腸;內臟。②(*pl.*)〖俚〗勇氣。a man with plenty of *guts.* 有很大膽量的人。③(*pl.*)內容。④腸線(用做提琴絃及網球拍、外科手術等)。⑤蠶腹中的絲囊。⑥狹溝;隘口。—*v.t.* ①取出內臟。②掠奪或破壞…之內部。Fire *gutted* the building and left only the brick wall standing. 大火燒毀這座房子的內部,只留磚牆頹立。

Gu·ten·berg [ˈgutn̩͵bɝg; ˈguːtnbəːg] *n.* 古騰堡(Johann, 1398?–1468, 德國活字印刷發明人)。***Gutenberg Bible*** 1456 年以前在 Mainz 印的第一本用活字印刷的拉丁文聖經,據傳爲古騰堡所印。

gut·ta [ˈgʌtə; ˈgʌtə] *n., pl.* **gut·tae** [ˈgʌti; ˈgʌtiː]. ①〖醫〗點;滴;量滴。②〖建築〗雨珠飾。

gut·ta-per·cha [ˈgʌtəˈpɝtʃə; ˈgʌtəˈpəːtʃə] *n.* 馬來樹膠(用於補牙或作絕緣體)。

gut·tate [ˈgʌtet; ˈgʌteit] *adj.* 〖生物〗有點滴狀斑點的; 點滴狀的; 含點滴的。(亦作 **guttated**)

***gut·ter** [ˈgʌtɚ; ˈgʌtə] *n.* ①(街道旁的)排水溝; 陰溝。②(沿屋簷裝設的)承霤; 導水溝。③溝;槽。④貧民區;貧民窟;貧困的生活。to rise from the *gutter.* 從下層社會中掙扎出來。⑤書本相對頁面之內側在中央所合成之空白。⑥整聯郵票相連處之空白。⑦保齡球道兩旁之槽。—*v.t.* ①於…挖溝。②爲…裝導水槽。—*v.i.* ①融流(蠟燭的融化流下)。②成

槽;成流。

gutter child =**guttersnipe.**

gut·ter·man (ˈgʌtəmən; ˈgʌtəmən) *n., pl.* **-men.** ①賣便宜貨的小販。②清除陰溝的人。

gut·ter·snipe (ˈgʌtəˌsnaɪp; ˈgʌtəsnaip) *n.* 〖俗〗街頭貧兒;無賴童子。

gut·tle (ˈgʌtl̩; ˈgʌtl) *v.t. & v.i.,* **-tled, -tling.** 貪食;大嚼。—**gut·tler,** *n.*

gut·tur·al (ˈgʌtərəl; ˈgʌtərəl) *adj.* ①喉的; 咽喉的。②自喉間發出的; 粗啞的。The man spoke in a *guttural* voice. 這個人以粗啞的聲音講話。③〖語音〗發自舌後與軟腭間的。—*n.* 舌後音;軟腭音(如 g, k 是)。

gut·tur·al·ize (ˈgʌtərəlˌaɪz; ˈgʌtərəlaiz) *v.t.,* **-ized, -iz·ing.** ①以喉發音;用喉音講。②〖語音〗喉音化。

gut·ty (ˈgʌtɪ; ˈgʌti) *n.* 〖高爾夫〗馬來樹膠製成之球。

*__guy__[1] (gaɪ; gai) *n., v.,* **guyed, guy·ing.** —*n.* ①形狀古怪的人;稻草人。②〖美俗〗(= fellow)人; 傢伙。Who is that *guy?* 那個傢伙是誰? ***give the guy to*** 〖英俚〗逃過(某人)。—*v.t.* 〖俗〗挖苦;嘲弄;揶揄。

guy[2] *n., v.,* **guyed, guy·ing.** —*n.* 支索;張索;拉線。—*v.t.* 用支索撐住。

Guy·a·na (gaɪˈænə; gaiˈænə) *n.* 蓋亞那(南美北部一國, 首都喬治市 Georgetown).

guz·zle (ˈgʌzl̩; ˈgʌzl) *v.,* **-zled, -zling,** *n.* —*v.i. & v.t.* ①狂飲;豪飲。—*n.* ①酒。②縱飲。

gybe (dʒaɪb; dʒaib) *v.i. & v.t.,* **gybed, gyb·ing,** *n.* 〖航海〗=**jibe.**

*__gym__ (dʒɪm; dʒim) *n.* 〖俗〗①體育館。②體育(學科)。***gym shoe*** 球鞋;運動鞋。***gym suit*** 運動衣。

gym. gymnasium; gymnastics.

gym·kha·na, gym·ka·na (dʒɪmˈkɑnə; dʒimˈkɑːnə) *n.* 運動會(場)。

*__gym·na·si·um__ (dʒɪmˈnezɪəm; dʒimˈneiziəm) *n., pl.* **-si·ums** or **-si·a** (-zɪə; -ziə). ①健身房;體育館。②(G-)德國大學預科學校。—**gym·na·si·al,** *adj.*

gym·nast (ˈdʒɪmnæst; ˈdʒimnæst) *n.* 體育家;健身運動家。

*__gym·nas·tic__ (dʒɪmˈnæstɪk; dʒimˈnæstik) *adj.* 體操的;體育的。

*__gym·nas·tics__ (dʒɪmˈnæstɪks; dʒimˈnæstiks) *n.* ①(作 *pl.* 解)體操。②(作 *sing.* 解)健身術。

gym·nos·o·phist (dʒɪmˈnɑsəfɪst; dʒimˈnɔsəfist) *n.* 古印度之隱逸哲學家(衣着極少, 甚至全裸, 修神祕主義與禁慾主義)。

gym·no·sperm (ˈdʒɪmnəˌspɝm; ˈdʒimnəspəːm) *n.* 〖植物〗裸子植物。

gym·no·sper·mous (ˌdʒɪmnəˈspɝməs; ˌdʒimnəˈspəːməs) *adj.* 〖植物〗裸子植物的。

gymp (gɪmp; gimp) *n.* =**gimp.**

gyn·ae·ce·um (ˌdʒɪnɪˈsiəm; ˌdʒainiˈsiːəm) *n., pl.* **-ce·a** (-ˈsiə; -ˈsiːə). ①〖植物〗=**gynoecium.** ②(古希臘、羅馬)婦女用房間。

gyn·ae·coc·ra·cy (ˌdʒɪnɪˈkɑkrəsɪ; ˌdʒiniˈkɔkrəsi) *n.* =**gynecocracy.**

gy·nae·col·o·gy (ˌdʒaɪnɪˈkɑlədʒɪ; ˌgainiˈkɔlədʒi) *n.* =**gynecology.**

gy·nan·drous (dʒɪˈnændrəs; dʒiˈnændrəs) *adj.* 〖植物〗雌雄蕊合生的;雌雄合體的。

gyn·e·coc·ra·cy (ˌdʒɪnɪˈkɑkrəsɪ; ˌdʒiniˈkɔkrəsi) *n.* 婦女統治。

gy·ne·co·log·ic (ˌgaɪnɪkəˈlɑdʒɪk; ˌgainəkəˈlɔdʒik) *adj.* 婦科醫學的。

gy·ne·co·log·i·cal (ˌdʒaɪnɪkəˈlɑdʒɪkl̩; ˌgainəkəˈlɔdʒəkəl) *adj.* =**gynecologic.**

gy·ne·col·o·gist (ˌdʒaɪnɪˈkɑlədʒɪst; ˌgainiˈkɔlədʒist) *n.* 婦科醫生。

gy·ne·col·o·gy (ˌdʒaɪnɪˈkɑlədʒɪ; ˌgainiˈkɔlədʒi) *n.* 〖醫〗婦科醫學。

gyn·oc·ra·cy (dʒɪˈnɑkrəsɪ; dʒiːˈnɔkrəsi) *n.* =**gynecocracy.**

gy·noe·ci·um (dʒɪˈnisɪəm; dʒiˈnisiəm) *n., pl.* **-ci·a** (-sɪə; -siə). 〖植物〗(花之)雌蕊;雌器官。

gyp[1] (dʒɪp; dʒip) *n.* 〖英〗(大學之)校工。

gyp[2] *n., v.,* **gypped, gyp·ping.** —*n.* 〖俚〗①欺騙。②騙子。③ =**gypsy.** —*v.t. & v.i.* 〖俚〗欺騙;騙取。

gyps (dʒɪps; dʒips) *n.* =**gypsum.**

gyp·se·ous (ˈdʒɪpsɪəs; ˈdʒipsiəs) *adj.* 石膏(質)的;似石膏的;含石膏的。

gyp·soph·i·la (dʒɪpˈsɑfɪlə; dʒipˈsɔfilə) *n.* 瞿麥屬植物。

gyp·sum (ˈdʒɪpsəm; ˈdʒipsəm) *n.* 〖礦〗石膏 ($CaSO_4 \cdot 2H_2O$).

*__Gyp·sy__ (ˈdʒɪpsɪ; ˈdʒipsi) *n., pl.* **-sies,** *adj., v.,* **-sied, -sy·ing.** —*n.* ①(亦作 g-)吉普賽人。②吉普賽語。③(g-) 似吉普賽人的人;流浪者。④(g-) 自任騎師與訓練者的賽馬馬主。—*adj.* (g-)吉普賽人的;似吉普賽人的。a *gypsy* girl. 吉普賽女郎。*gypsy* music. 吉普賽音樂。—*v.i.* (g-)流浪;過吉普賽式生活。a glorious place for *gypsying.* 流浪的好去處。(亦作 **Gipsy, gipsy**)

gy·rate (*adj.* ˈdʒaɪret; ˈdʒaiərit *v.* ˈdʒaɪret; ˌdʒaiəˈreit) *adj., v.,* **-rat·ed, -rat·ing.** —*adj.* ①〖植物〗渦狀的。②盤旋的;螺旋形的;纏繞的;圓形的。—*v.i.* 廻旋;旋轉。A top *gyrates.* 陀螺旋轉。

gy·ra·tion (dʒaɪˈreʃən; ˌdʒaiəˈreiʃən) *n.* 廻旋;旋轉。

gy·ra·to·ry (ˈdʒaɪrəˌtorɪ; ˈdʒaiərətəri) *adj.* 廻旋的;旋轉(運動)的。

gyre (dʒaɪr; dʒaiə) *n.* ①旋轉運動; 廻旋。②旋轉體;環;旋風。

gy·rene (dʒaɪˈrin; dʒaiəˈriːn) *n.* 〖美軍俚〗海軍陸戰隊隊員(蔑稱)。

gyr·fal·con (ˈdʒɝˌfɔlkən; ˈdʒəːˌfɔlkən) *n.* =**gerfalcon.**

gy·ro (ˈdʒaɪro; ˈdʒaiərou) *n., pl.* **-ros.** ①=**gyroscope.** ②=**gyrocompass.**

gyro- 〖字首〗表"環;輪;螺旋"之義。

gy·ro·com·pass (ˈdʒaɪroˌkʌmpəs; ˈdʒaiərouˌkʌmpəs) *n.* 廻轉儀羅盤; 環動羅盤。

gy·ro·graph (ˈdʒaɪrəˌgræf; ˈdʒaiərəgræf) *n.* 測轉器;轉速器。

gy·roi·dal (dʒaɪˈrɔɪdəl; dʒaiəˈrɔidəl) *adj.* 螺旋形的;廻旋的。

gy·ro·pi·lot (ˈdʒaɪrəˌpaɪlət; ˈdʒaiərəˌpailət) *n.* 〖航空〗自動駕駛儀。

gy·ro·plane (ˈdʒaɪrəˌplen; ˈdʒaiərəˌplein) *n.* =**autogiro.**

gy·ro·scope (ˈdʒaɪrəˌskop; ˈgaiərəskoup) *n.* 廻轉機;環動儀;方向陀螺儀。—**gy·ro·scop·ics,** *n.* —**gy·ro·scop·ic,** *adj.*

gy·ro·sta·bi·liz·er (ˌdʒaɪrəˈstebəˌlaɪzɚ; ˌdʒaiərəˈsteibəˌlaizə) *n.* 廻轉穩定器(減低船或飛機的動搖之裝置)。

gy·rus (ˈdʒaɪrəs; ˈdʒaiərəs) *n., pl.* **gy·ri** (ˈdʒaɪraɪ; ˈdʒaiərai). 〖解剖〗大腦之廻轉;腦回。

gyve (dʒaɪv; dʒaiv) *n., v.,* **gyved, gyv·ing.** —*n.* (常 *pl.*) 足械;脚鐐。—*v.t.* 上脚鐐。

H

H or **h** [etʃ; eitʃ] *n., pl.* **H's** or **h's** [ˈetʃɪz; ˈeitʃiz]. ①英文字母之第八個字母。②代表一系列中第八的符號。

H [etʃ; eitʃ] *n.* ①H 形物。②(中世紀羅馬數字之)200。③〖化〗氫(hydrogen)之符號。—*adj.* H形的。

H., h. ①harbor. ②hard. ③hardness. ④heavy sea. ⑤height. ⑥hence. ⑦high. ⑧hour(s). ⑨hundred. ⑩husband. ⑪〖音樂〗horns.

***ha** [hɑ; hɑː] *interj.* 哈;噫(表示驚異、快樂、懷疑、勝利等所發出的聲音)。

ha. hectare(s).

Hab·ak·kuk [ˈhæbəˌkʌk; ˈhæbəkək] *n.* ①哈巴谷(紀元前七世紀的希伯來之先知)。②〖聖經〗(略作 **Hab.**) 哈巴谷書。

ha·ba·ne·ra [ˌhɑbəˈnɛrə; ˌhɑːbəˈnɛərə] *n.* 哈巴奈拉舞(起源於古巴之慢速西班牙舞);其舞曲。

ha·be·as cor·pus [ˈhebɪəsˈkɔrpəs; ˈheibjəsˈkɔːpəs] 〖法律〗人身保護令(被拘捕的人須於一定時間內移送法院處理之命令)。

Ha·ber [ˈhɑbɚ; ˈhɑːbə] *n.* 哈勃(Fritz, 1868–1934, 德國化學家, 獲 1918 年諾貝爾化學獎)。

hab·er·dash·er [ˈhæbɚˌdæʃɚ; ˈhæbədæʃə] *n.* ①〖美〗男子服飾經售商。②經售零星服飾雜貨之商人。

hab·er·dash·er·y [ˈhæbɚˌdæʃərɪ; ˈhæbədæʃəri] *n., pl.* **-er·ies.** ①〖英〗服飾雜貨商店。②〖美〗男子服飾(店);此種店內所售之物。

hab·er·geon [ˈhæbɚdʒən; ˈhæbədʒən] 「*n.* 〖史〗短鱗鎧;無袖之鎧甲。」

ha·bil·i·ment [həˈbɪləmənt; həˈbiliment] *n.* ①(*pl.*) 服裝; 衣著。②一件衣服。③(*pl.*)裝備;設施。

ha·bil·i·tate [həˈbɪləˌtet; həˈbiliteit] *v.,* **-tat·ed, -tat·ing.** —*v.i.* 取得資格(如在大學教書之資格)。—*v.t.* ①〖美西部〗以資金及必需品供給(礦場)。②給…穿衣。

‡hab·it [ˈhæbɪt; ˈhæbit] *n.* ①習慣;習性。Some people say that smoking is a bad *habit.* 有人說吸煙是一種壞習慣。②(和尚所穿的)法服;衣服。a monk's *habit.* 僧袍; 法衣。③女子騎馬裝。④神性;體質;心境。The runner was of lean *habit.* 那賽跑的人體質很瘦。⑤(動植物的)習性。The woodbine is of a twining *habit.* 忍冬有盤纏的習性。***be in*** (or ***have***) ***the*** (or ***a***) ***habit of....*** 有…的習慣;有…的脾氣。***break off a habit*** 革除習慣。***form good habits*** 養成好習慣。***get*** (or ***fall***) ***into the habit of*** (後接 gerund) 養成…之習慣。 ***habit of body*** 體質。***habit of mind*** 性情;癖性。—*v.t.* 裝扮;穿(法衣)。

hab·it·a·ble [ˈhæbɪtəbl̩; ˈhæbitəbl] *adj.* 可居住的; 適於居住的。The house is no longer *habitable.* 這房子已不再適於居住。—**hab·it·a·bil·i·ty,** *n.* —**hab·it·a·bly,** *adv.*

hab·it·ant [ˈhæbətənt; ˈhæbitənt] *n.* ①住民; 居住者。②加拿大或美國 Louisiana 州之法國住民(特指農民)。

hab·i·tat [ˈhæbəˌtæt; ˈhæbitæt] *n.* ①(動植物的)產地; 棲息地。②居留地。③海底科學研究船。

***hab·i·ta·tion** [ˌhæbəˈteʃən; ˌhæbiˈteiʃən] *n.* ①居住。These slums are not fit for human *habitation.* 這些貧民窟不適於人居住。②住所。On these vast plains there was not a single human *habitation.* 在這些大平原上,沒有一處人的住所。

hab·it-form·ing [ˈhæbɪtˌfɔrmɪŋ; ˈhæbitˌfɔːmiŋ] *adj.* (藥物等)易於上癮的。Wine and cigarette are *habit-forming.* 煙酒易於上癮。

***ha·bit·u·al** [həˈbɪtʃuəl; həˈbitjuəl, hæˈb-, -tʃuəl] *adj.* ①習慣的;慣於所作的。a *habitual* liar. 慣於說謊者。②慣常的;通常的。to sit down in one's *habitual* seat. 坐在其慣常所坐的座位上。③日常的;平常的。—**ly,** *adv.* —**ness,** *n.*

ha·bit·u·ate [həˈbɪtʃuˌet; həˈbitjueit, hæˈb-, -tʃueit] *v.t.,* **-at·ed, -at·ing.** ①使習慣於(常爲反身用法)。to *habituate* oneself to hard work (getting up early, a cold climate). 使自己慣於艱苦的工作(早起, 寒冷的氣候)。 ②〖美俗〗常至; 常往。—**ha·bit·u·a·tion,** *n.*

hab·i·tude [ˈhæbəˌtjud; ˈhæbitjuːd] *n.* ①習慣;習癖;習性。②性質;氣質;體質。

ha·bit·u·é [həˈbɪtʃuˌe; həˈbitjuei] 〖法〗 *n.* 常客。

ha·chure [hæˈʃur; hæˈʃjuə] *n., v.,* **-chured, -chur·ing.** —*n.* ①表示陰影之平行線;影線。②(以平行線表示之)陰影。③(*pl.*) 蓑狀線(地圖上表示土地起伏者)。—*v.t.* 以蓑狀線表示;以影線表示。

ha·ci·en·da [ˌhɑsɪˈɛndə; ˌhæsiˈendə] 〖西班牙、美洲〗 *n.*大田莊; 農場; 牧場; 工場。

hack**[1] [hæk; hæk] *v.t.* ①斧劈;亂砍。Tom *hacked* the box apart with the dull ax. 湯姆用那把鈍的斧頭把盒子劈開。②以鋤破(地)。③(足球賽時)猛踢(對方球員)之脛。④(籃球賽時)打(對方持球球員)之臂。⑤支解;隨意刪改。The editor *hacked* the story to bits. 編輯將那篇報導刪改得面目全非。⑥大量削減。The Senate *hacked* the budget almost in half. 參議院將預算幾乎削減了一半。—*v.i.* ①亂砍。②乾咳。③故意踢對方球員之脛。hack around*** 〖美俚〗遊蕩;尋樂。—*n.* ①亂砍; 亂劈。②砍劈用之工具(如斧、鋤)。③(用鋤、斧等砍劈之)裂口;裂痕。④乾咳。⑤脛部被踢之傷口。⑥說話中的猶豫。

hack[2] *n.* ①〖美〗出租馬車。②〖俗〗出租汽車。③〖英〗出租之馬。④乘用之馬。⑤服賤役者。⑥受雇傭之文人。⑦以賺錢爲目的之劣等藝術家。—*v.t.* ①出租(馬等)。②因久用使之破敝。③雇用(文人)。④賣文。He *hacked* out articles for cheap magazines. 他替低級的雜誌寫文章。⑤使變成陳腔濫調。—*v.i.* ①乘租賃的馬或馬車出遊。②〖俗〗駕駛出租汽車。—*adj.* ①出租的; 受雇的。②受雇的人所作的。③陳腐的;破的;陳舊的。

hack[3] *n.* ①(磚、魚、乳酪等之) 晾棚。②飼草架。—*v.t.* 放在晾棚晾乾。

hack·a·more [ˈhækəˌmor; ˈhækəˌmɔː] *n.* 〖美西部〗(馴馬用之)繮繩。

hack·ber·ry [ˈhækˌbɛrɪ; ˈhækberi] *n., pl.* **-ries.** (美國) 朴樹;朴子;朴樹木材。

hack·le[1] [ˈhækl̩; ˈhækl] *n., v.,* **-led, -ling.** —*n.* ①麻梳。②雄鷄等頸部的細長羽毛。③蠅鉤(釣魚用之人造假蠅)。④(*pl.*) 狗

後頸部之毛。***with one's hackles up*** 擺着要鬥的姿勢；發怒。—*v.t.* ①梳(麻等)。②加羽毛於(蠅鉤)。

hack·le² *v.t.* & *v.i.*, **-led, -ling.** 亂砍；亂劈；亂切。

hack·man [ˈhækmən; ˈhækmən] *n.*, *pl.* **-men.** 〖美〗(出租馬車的)車夫。

hack·ma·tack [ˈhækməˌtæk; ˈhækmətæk] *n.* 〖植物〗①(美國產之)落葉松。②杜松。③落葉松之木材；杜松之木材。

hack·ney [ˈhæknɪ; ˈhækni] *n.*, *pl.* **-neys,** *adj.*, *v.*, **-neyed, -ney·ing.** —*n.* ①騎乘之馬。②出租之馬車。③操賤役者。—*adj.* ①受雇的。②陳腐的；陳舊的。*hackney* expression. 陳腐的語句。—*v.t.* ①常常使用。②使陳腐。③出租。

hackney carriage (or **coach**) ①出租之馬車。②(兩馬拉的)四輪(六座)馬車。

hack·neyed [ˈhæknɪd; ˈhæknid] *adj.* 陳腐的；陳舊的；平凡的。

hack·saw [ˈhækˌsɔ; ˈhæksɔː] *n.* (鋸金屬用的)鋼鋸。(亦作 **hack saw**)

hack·work [ˈhækˌwɝk; ˈhækwəːk] *n.* 劣等作品(尤指文學作品)。

:had [hæd; hæd] *v.* pt. & pp. of **have.** ***be had*** 受騙；上當；被利用。***had as good*** (***do***) (如此)也好；(那樣做)較好。***had better*** (or ***best***) ***do*** 最好…。***had rather do*** 還是…的好。〖注意〗**had better, had rather.** 意爲最好…；還是…的好。had better 是一個常用的習慣語，用於勸解或間接命令。在一般非正式的用法中，通常把 had 略去：If he asks you to do it, you *better* do it. 假如他要求你做，你最好就做了吧。had rather, would rather 皆用於表示偏愛、嗜好。後者尤爲正式。

had·dock [ˈhædək; ˈhædək] *n.*, *pl.* **-dock, -docks.** 黑線鱈。

Ha·des [ˈhediz; ˈheidiːz] *n.* ①〖希臘神話〗冥府；黃泉。②(亦作 **Pluto, Dis**) 冥王；閻王。③ (h-)〖俗〗地獄。

hadj·i [ˈhædʒi; ˈhædʒi(ː)] *n.*, *pl.* **-is.** ①赴麥加朝聖過的回教徒。②近東各地曾赴耶路撒冷朝聖之基督徒。(亦作 **hajji**)

***had·n't** [ˈhædn̩t; ˈhædnt] =**had not.**

hadst [hædst; hædst] *v.* 〖古〗 have 之第二人稱、單數、過去式。

hae·mal [ˈhiməl; ˈhiːməl] *adj.* =**hemal.**

hae·mat·ic [hiˈmætɪk; hiːˈmætik] *adj.*, *n.* =**hematic.**

haem·a·tin [ˈhɛmətɪn; ˈhemətin] *n.* =**hematin.** —**haem·a·tin·ic,** *adj.*

haem·a·tite [ˈhɛməˌtaɪt; ˈhemətait] *n.* =**hematite.** —**haem·a·tit·ic,** *adj.*

hae·ma·tu·ri·a [ˌhiməˈtjurɪə; ˌhiːməˈtjuəriə] *n.* =**hematuria.**

hae·mo·glo·bin [ˌhiməˈglobɪn; ˌhiːmouˈgloubin] *n.* =**hemoglobin.**

hae·mo·phil·i·a [ˌhiməˈfɪlɪə; ˌhiːmouˈfiliə] *n.* =**hemophilia.**

haem·or·rhage [ˈhɛmrɪdʒ; ˈheməridʒ] *n.* =**hemorrhage.**

haem·or·rhoid(s) [ˈhɛməˌrɔɪd(z); ˈhemərɔid(z)] *n.* =**hemorrhoid(s).**

ha·fiz [ˈhɑfɪz; ˈhɑːfiz] *n.* 能背誦全部可蘭經之回教徒的尊稱。

haf·ni·um [ˈhæfnɪəm; ˈhæfniəm] *n.* 〖化〗鉿(一種四價金屬元素，符號 Hf)。

haft [hæft; hɑːft] *n.* 刀柄；劍柄。—*v.t.* 裝柄於(刀劍等)。

hag¹ [hæg; hæg] *n.* ①老醜婆；巫婆；女巫。②〖動物〗穿口盞類動物；醜魚。

hag² *v.t.* 〖蘇，英方〗砍；伐(木)。—*n.* ①伐木。②將要砍伐之林區。③伐下之樹木。④挖去泥炭後之垂直邊緣。⑤沼地；沼地中之硬地。

hag·ber·ry [ˈhægˌbɛrɪ; ˈhægberi] *n.* =**hackberry.**

hag·fish [ˈhægˌfɪʃ; ˈhægfiʃ] *n.*, *pl.* **-fish·es, -fish.** 醜魚。

Hag·ga·i [ˈhægɪˌaɪ; ˈhægeiai] *n.* 〖聖經〗①哈基(希伯來之一先知)。②(舊約中之)哈基書(略作 **Hag**)。

***hag·gard** [ˈhægəd; ˈhægəd] *adj.* ①憔悴的；形容枯槁的。②野性的(特指鷹)。*haggard* hawks. 野鷹。—*n.* 羽毛剛豐滿即被捕獲之鷹。—**ness,** *n.*

hag·gis [ˈhægɪs; ˈhægis] *n.* 〖蘇〗將羊之心、肺、肝等內臟和燕麥粉同煮成之食物。

hag·gish [ˈhægɪʃ; ˈhægiʃ] *adj.* (似)巫婆的；似老醜婆的；老而醜的。

hag·gle [ˈhægl̩; ˈhægl] *v.*, **-gled, -gling,** *n.* —*v.t.* 亂砍；粗切。—*v.i.* ①爭論。②討價還價〖about, over〗。—*n.* ①講價。②爭論。③亂砍；粗切。

hagi- 〖字首〗 **hagio-** 之異體。

hag·i·arch·y [ˈhægɪˌɑrkɪ; ˈhægiɑːki] *n.*, *pl.* **-ies.** 聖人政治；聖徒之階級組織。

hagio- 〖字首〗表"聖人的；神聖的"之義。

Hag·i·og·ra·pha [ˌhægɪˈɑgrəfə; ˌhægiˈɔgrəfə] *n. pl.* (舊約聖經中)預言書與律法以外之部分。

hag·i·og·ra·pher [ˌhægɪˈɑgrəfɚ; ˌhægiˈɔgrəfə] *n.* ① Hagiographa 作者之一。②神聖作家。③聖徒傳作者。(亦作 **hagiographist**)

hag·i·og·ra·phy [ˌhægɪˈɑgrəfɪ; ˌhægiˈɔgrəfi] *n.* 聖徒傳；聖徒言行錄。

hag·i·ol·o·gy [ˌhægɪˈɑlədʒɪ; ˌhægiˈɔlədʒi] *n.*, *pl.* **-gies.** ①聖徒(傳)研究。②聖徒傳；聖徒言行錄。③聖徒名錄。

hag·rid·den [ˈhægˌrɪdn̩; ˈhægˌridn] *adj.* 受夢魘侵擾的；被恐怖等心理所騷擾的。

Hague, The [heg; heig] *n.* 海牙(荷蘭之行政首都，爲國際法庭所在地)。

hah [hɑ; hɑː] *interj.* =**ha.**

ha-ha¹ [ˌhɑˈhɑ; hɑ(ː)ˈhɑː] *interj.* 哈哈！—*n.* 哈哈(笑聲)。

ha-ha² [ˈhɑˌhɑ; ˈhɑ(ː)hɑ] *n.* (設於環繞花園或公園的溝中之)低籬笆；低牆垣。

Hahn [hɑn; hɑːn] *n.* 哈恩 (Otto, 1879–1968, 德國理化學家，獲1944年諾貝爾化學獎)。

haik, haick [haɪk; haik] *n.* 阿拉伯人披於身上作爲外衣之長方毛布或棉布。

hail¹** [hel; heil] *v.t.* ①向…歡呼；致敬。They *hailed* him (as) King. 他們高呼擁戴他爲王。②招呼；呼叫。Let's *hail* a taxi, shall we? 我們叫輛出租汽車好嗎？—*v.i.* 招呼；來(指船)。hail from*** 來自 (=come from). Where does the ship *hail from?* 這隻船來自何地(意指其原屬何港)？—*n.* ①歡呼；致敬。②呼喊；招呼。***within hail*** 在可以招呼的距離以內。—*interj.* 〖詩〗歡呼或致賀之聲。*Hail* to the winner! 勝者萬歲！***Hail Mary!*** 萬福瑪利亞！

***hail²** *n.* ①雹；冰雹。②(如雹之)一陣。a *hail* of bullets. 一陣鎗彈。—*v.i.* ①下雹。It *hailed* during the night. 夜間下了雹。②(如雹般地)落下。—*v.t.* 猛烈地撒下、投下或傾下。to *hail* blows on someone. 打擊(咒罵等)像雹般落在某人身上。

hail fellow (well met) ①非常親密的；極要好的；太隨便的〖with〗。②親友；密友；嘻嘻哈哈的朋友。(亦作 **hail-fellow**)

hail·stone [ˈhelˌston; ˈheil-stoun] *n.* (一粒)冰雹。
hail·storm [ˈhelˌstɔrm; ˈheil-stɔːm] 「*n.* 降雹。」
hain't [hent; heint] 〖方〗=**have** (**has**) **not.**
hair [hɛr; hɛə] *n.* ①髮;毛;獸毛。He had his *hair* cut. 他理了髮。That man has red *hair*. 那個人頭髮是紅的。②毛狀物。③〖植物〗茸毛。④極小的空間;極微。a *hair's* breadth. 一髮之差。to be not worth a *hair*. 一錢不值。***a hair of the dog*** (***that bit one***) 用以攻毒的毒;用以解宿醉的酒。***by the turn of a hair*** 差一點兒;險些兒;幾乎。***comb a person's hair for him*** 申斥某人。***do up one's hair*** 梳頭。***get in one's hair*** 〖俗〗觸怒;激怒;使發躁。***get one by the short hairs*** 支配人;操縱人。***keep one's hair on*** 〖俗〗保持鎮靜;別興奮。***let one's hair down*** 〖俚〗**a.** 使生氣;惹怒。**b.** 隨意;不拘謹。He finally *let his hair down* and actually cracked a joke. 他終於變得態度隨便,並且說了一個笑話。**c.** 實說;直言無隱。***lose one's hair*** **a.** 落髮(變成禿頭)。**b.**〖俗〗發怒;發脾氣。***make one's hair stand on end*** 使人毛髮悚然。***not turn a hair*** 絲毫不為所動;毫不疲倦。***split hairs*** 作極細微的分析;作過分的挑剔。***tear one's hair*** (***out***) (悲傷或激怒之餘) 扯頭髮。***to*** (***the turn of***) ***a hair*** 完全一樣;絲毫不差。You've described him *to a hair*. 你已將他描繪得絲毫不差。—*adj.* 毛髮製的;保護毛髮的。
hair·breadth [ˈhɛrˌbrɛdθ; ˈhɛə-bredθ] *adj.* 間不容髮的。a *hairbreadth* escape. 死裏逃生。—*n.* 間不容髮;極狹;極短之距離。to escape death by a *hairbreadth*. 死裏逃生;間不容髮。(亦作 **hairsbreadth, hair's-breadth**)
hair·brush [ˈhɛrˌbrʌʃ; ˈhɛə-brʌʃ] 「*n.* 髮刷;毛刷。」
hair·cloth [ˈhɛrˌklɔθ; ˈhɛə-klɔθ] *n.* 毛布(馬鬃與駱駝毛合織成的布)。
hair·curl·ing [ˈhɛrˌkɜlɪŋ; ˈhɛəˌkəː-liŋ] *adj.* =**hair-raising.**
hair·cut [ˈhɛrˌkʌt; ˈhɛə-kʌt] *n.* ①理髮。②男子髮型。
hair·do [ˈhɛrˌdu; ˈhɛə-duː] *n., pl.* **-dos.** ①女人的髮式。②做頭髮(指女人頭髮)。
hair·dress [hɛrˌdrɛs; ˈhɛədres] *n.* 女人的髮式。—*v.i.* (女人)做頭髮。
hair·dress·er [ˈhɛrˌdrɛsɚ; ˈhɛəˌdresə] *n.* (專給女子理髮之)理髮匠;美容師。〖注意〗專給男子理髮修面者稱為 **barber.**
hair·dress·ing [ˈhɛrˌdrɛsɪŋ; ˈhɛəˌdresiŋ] *n.* 美容業。
hair dye 染毛劑;染髮劑。
hair grip 〖英〗髮夾。
hair·i·ness [ˈhɛrɪnɪs; ˈhɛərinis] *n.* 有毛;多毛;毛髮狀。 「無髮的;禿頂的。」
hair·less [ˈhɛrlɪs; ˈhɛəlis] *adj.* 無毛的;
hair·like [ˈhɛrˌlaɪk; ˈhɛəlaik] *adj.* 似毛的;極細的。
hair·line [ˈhɛrˌlaɪn; ˈhɛəlain] *n.* ①用(馬等之)毛製的線或細索。②頭部生髮部分之輪廓。③(書畫或印刷中之) 極細之線。***to a hairline*** 精密地。—*adj.* 很窄的;很近似的;差別極微的。
hair net 髮網。
hair oil 髮油。 「=**toupee.**」
hair·piece [ˈhɛrˌpis; ˈhɛəpiːs] *n.*
hair·pin [ˈhɛrˌpɪn; ˈhɛəpin] *n.* 夾髮針。—*adj.* (道路) U形急轉彎的。***a hairpin bend*** (道路之) U形急彎。

hair-rais·er [ˈhɛrˌrezɚ; ˈhɛəˌreizə] *n.* 〖俗〗驚人之故事;令人毛骨悚然之經歷。
hair-rais·ing [ˈhɛrˌrezɪŋ; ˈhɛəˌreiziŋ] *adj.* 〖俗〗令人毛骨悚然的。—**ly,** *adv.*
hair ribbon 飾髮用之緞帶。
hair's-breadth [ˈhɛrzˈbrɛdθ; ˈhɛəz-bredθ] *n., adj.* =**hairbreadth.**
hair shirt (苦行者所着之) 粗毛布襯衣。
hair space 〖印刷〗字與字間之最小間隔。
hair·split·ter [ˈhɛrˌsplɪtɚ; ˈhɛəˌsplitə] *n.* 吹毛求疵者;作不必要之區別者。
hair·split·ting [ˈhɛrˌsplɪtɪŋ; ˈhɛəˌsplitiŋ] *n.* 辨別過細;析理太細。—*adj.* 辨別過細的;析理太細的。*hairsplitting* habits. 吹毛求疵的習慣。
hair spray 髮膠。
hair·spring [ˈhɛrˌsprɪŋ; ˈhɛə-spriŋ] *n.* 游絲(鐘錶內的一種渦狀細發條)。
hair·streak [ˈhɛrˌstrik; ˈhɛə-striːk] *n.* (翅上有細紋的) 毛紋蝶。
hair stroke (印刷或書寫的)細線。
hair·style [ˈhɛrˌstaɪl; ˈhɛə-stail] *n.* 髮型。 「的理髮師。」
hair stylist 髮型專家;為婦女做頭髮
hair trigger (鎗之) 微力扳機;有此種扳機之手鎗。
hair-trig·ger [ˈhɛrˈtrɪgɚ; ˈhɛəˈtrigə] *adj.* 容易觸發的;一觸即發的。a *hair-trigger* temper. 火爆脾氣。
hair·weav·ing [ˈhɛrˌwivɪŋ; ˈhɛəˌwiːviŋ] *n.* 頭髮或假髮的移植。
***hair·y** [ˈhɛrɪ; ˈhɛəri] *adj.,* **hair·i·er, hair·i·est.** ①長有毛的;多毛的。a *hairy* body. 多毛的身體。②如毛的;毛狀的。③毛製的。
Hai·ti [ˈhetɪ; ˈheiti] *n.* ①海地(黑人共和國,位於西印度羣島中,首都為太子港 Port-au-Prince)。②=**Hispaniola.**
Hai·ti·an [ˈhetɪən; ˈheitiən] *adj.* 海地的;海地人的。—*n.* 海地人。 「=**hadji.**」
haj·ji [ˈhædʒi; ˈhædʒiː] *n., pl.* **haj·jis**
hake [hek; heik] *n., pl.* **hakes, hake.** 鱈魚;鱈魚類之魚。
ha·kim[1] [hɑˈkɪm; hɑːˈkim] *n.* (回教國家之)學者;醫生。(亦作 **hakeem**)
ha·kim[2] [ˈhɑkɪm; ˈhɑːkim] *n.* (回教國家之)統治者;法官。
Hal [hæl; hæl] *n.* Henry 之暱稱。
Hal. ①Halifax. ②〖化〗halogen.
ha·la·la [həˈlɑlə; həˈlɑːlə] 〖阿拉伯〗 *n., pl.* **ha·la·la, ha·la·las.** 哈拉拉(沙烏地阿拉伯的貨幣單位)。(亦作 **halalah**)
ha·la·tion [heˈleʃən; həˈleiʃən] *n.* 〖攝影〗照相底片上顯現之光輪狀暈。
hal·berd [ˈhælbɚd; ˈhælbə(ː)d] *n.* 戟(古兵器)。(亦作 **halbert**) **—ier,** *n.*
hal·cy·on [ˈhælsɪən; ˈhælsiən] *n.* 翠鳥;魚狗。—*adj.* ①平靜的;太平的。②翠鳥的。③富足的;興盛的。④快樂的;無憂無慮的。(亦作 **halcyonian, halcyonic**)
halcyon days ①多至前後十四天風平浪靜的日子。②太平日子;安樂平靜的日子。
***hale**[1] [hel; heil] *adj.,* **hal·er, hal·est.** 强壯的;矍鑠的。He's ninety, but still *hale* and hearty. 他九十歲了,但仍健壯。
hale[2] *v.t.,* **haled, hal·ing.** 猛拉;拖曳。—**hal·er,** *n.* 「壯;矍鑠。」
hale·ness [ˈhelnɪs; ˈheilnis] *n.* 健
‡**half** [hæf, hɑf; hɑːf] *n., pl.* **halves,** *adj., adv.* —*n.* ①半;一半。(The) *half* of

six is three. 六的一半是三。②(球戲中之)半場時間; 半時。③二幾乎相等部分之一。Your *half* is bigger than mine. 你的一半比我的大。④〖美俗〗五角。⑤〖棒球〗半局。***better half*** 妻子。***by half*** 大大地; 非常地。***by halves*** a. 不完全。b. 不熱心。***cry halves*** 要求一半。***do*** (***something***) ***by halves*** 半途而廢;有始無終。***not*** (***the***) ***half of*** 僅其次要者; 僅小部分。***see with half an eye*** 一看就明白。—*adj.* ①半個的;一半的。*half* an hour (*or* a *half* hour). 半小時。②不完全的; 有一半無一半的。A *half* truth is often no better than a lie. 半眞半假的話不見得比說謊要好。—*adv.* ①一半地;部分地。He was *half* asleep. 他半睡着。②差不多;幾乎。The beggar was *half* dead from hunger. 那乞丐已餓得半死。***go halves with*** (***a person***) ***in*** (***a thing***) 與(某人)平分(某物)。***not half*** 壓根兒不;毫不;極小的程度。〖注意〗**half a** 是一般的說法,比較正式的用法是 **a half.**

half-and-half [ˈhæfn̩ˈhæf; ˈhɑːfəndˈhɑːf] *adj.* ①兩者各半的。②兩者兼有的。—*adv.* 等量地;各半地。—*n.* ①兩者各半之混合物。②(黑啤酒與烈啤酒各半的)混合啤酒。③混雜物。④〖俚〗(白人與黑人之)混血兒。

half·back [ˈhæf,bæk; ˈhɑːfˈbæk] *n.* (足球)中衛。

half-baked [ˈhæfˈbekt; ˈhɑːfˈbeikt] *adj.* ①半熟的。②缺乏經驗的。③無事實根據的。④不完全的。⑤〖俗〗古怪的;瘋狂的。

half binding 半革裝訂。

half blood 半血親(同父異母或同母異父)的關係。

half-blood [ˈhæf,blʌd; ˈhɑːfblʌd] *n.* ①半血親的兄弟、姊妹。②混血兒。—**ed,** *adj.*

half-boiled [ˈhæfˈbɔɪld; ˈhɑːfˈbɔild] *adj.* 半熟的;半沸的。

half boot 半長統靴。

half-bound [ˈhæfˈbaund; ˈhɑːfˈbaund] *adj.* 半革裝釘的。

half-bred [ˈhæf,brɛd; ˈhɑːfbred] *adj.* ①雜種的。②無教養的。

half-breed [ˈhæf,brid; ˈhɑːfbriːd] *n.* ①混血兒;混合種。②白人與印第安人之混血兒。—*adj.* 白人與印第安人之混血兒的。

half brother 同母異父或同父異母兄弟。

half-caste [ˈhæf,kæst; ˈhɑːfkɑːst] *n.* ①混血兒。②歐亞混血兒(特指歐洲人和印度人或回教徒結合而生者)。—*adj.* 混血的;歐亞混血兒的。

half cock 鎗機半引而不能擊發之位置。***go off*** (***at***) ***half cock*** (or ***go off half-cocked***) a. 過早射擊。b. 〖俗〗未經詳細考慮便做或說。

half-cock [ˈhæfˈkɑk; ˈhɑːfˈkɔk] *v.t.* 「將鎗機半引。」

half-cocked [ˈhæfˈkɑkt; ˈhɑːfˈkɔkt] *adj.* ①鎗機半引的。②未充分考慮或準備的。

half-con·so·nant [ˈhæfˈkɑnsənənt; ˈhɑːfˈkɔnsənənt] *n., adj.* 半子音(的)。

half-cooked [ˈhæfˈkukt; ˈhɑːfˈkukt] *adj.* 半煮的;半熟的。

half crown ①英國銀幣名。②二先令六辨士之值。(亦作**half dollar**)

half dollar (美、加)半元銀幣。

half-done [ˈhæfˈdʌn; ˈhɑːfˈdʌn] *adj.* ①半完成的。②半熟的。

half eagle (美國昔時之)五元金幣。

half gainer 一種跳水姿勢(跳水者面朝外,在空中翻半個觔斗,下水時頭朝下,面對跳板)。

half-har·dy [ˈhæfˈhardɪ; ˈhɑːfˈhɑːdi] *adj.* (植物)半耐寒性的。

half-heart·ed [ˈhæfˈhartɪd; ˈhɑːfˈhɑːtid] *adj.* 不熱心的;無興趣的;無決心的;無精神的。—**ly,** *adv.* —**ness,** *n.*

half hitch 〖航海〗半結(繩結之一種)。

half holiday 半日休假(下午或包括下午與晚間)。

half hose 半長統襪。

half-hour [ˈhæfˈaur; ˈhɑːfˈauə] *n. adj.* 半小時(的)。—**ly,** *adj., adv.*

half-length [ˈhæfˈlɛŋθ; ˈhɑːfˈleŋθ] *adj.* 半身的;半身像的。—*n.* 半身像。

half-life [ˈhæf,laɪf; ˈhɑːflaif] *n.* 〖核子物理〗半衰期(放射性物質的原子之半數衰變所需時間)。

half-mast [ˈhæfˈmæst; ˈhɑːfˈmɑːst] *n.* (下)半旗。—*v.t.* 下半旗。

half measure 姑息手段; 權宜辦法。

half moon ①半月。②半月形; 半月形物;〖築城〗半月堡。(亦作 **halfmoon, half moon**)

half mourning 半喪服;着半喪服期。

half nelson 〖摔角〗扼頸之一種。***get a half nelson on*** 把…完全壓住。

half note 〖音樂〗半音符; 二分音符。

half pay ①半薪。②〖英〗軍官退休或半退休時所領的核減薪水。

half-pay [ˈhæfˈpe; ˈhɑːfˈpei] *adj.* 支「半薪的;休職的。」

***half·pen·ny** [ˈhepnɪ, ˈhepənɪ; ˈheipni, ˈheipəni] *n., pl.* **half·pen·nies** or **half·pence,** *adj.* —*n.* ①半辨士銅幣。Can you give me two *halfpennies* for this penny? 你能給我兩個半辨士銅幣換我這個辨士嗎? ②半辨士之值。three *halfpence.* 一辨士半。—*adj.* ①半辨士的。a *halfpenny* stamp. 一張半辨士的郵票。②瑣細的;微不足道的。

half·pen·ny·worth [ˈhepənɪ,wɝθ; ˈheipəniwəːθ] *n.* 值半辨士之物;微量之物。

half pint ①半品脫。②〖俗〗矮子。③〖俚〗無足輕重之人。

half-price [ˈhæfˈpraɪs; ˈhɑːfˈprais] *adv.* 半價。Children (admitted) *half-price.* 兒童半價優待(半票)。

half-seas over [ˈhæfsiz~; ˈhɑːfsiːz~] ①〖航海〗半途的。②(任何事之)半途的。③〖俗〗半醉的。

half sister 同父異母或同母異父姊妹。

half sole (鞋底之)前掌。

half-sole [ˈhæfˈsol; ˈhɑːfˈsoul] *v.t.* 加前掌於(鞋底)。

half sovereign 英國值十先令的金幣。

half step 〖音樂〗半音。

half-tim·bered [ˈhæfˈtɪmbəd; ˈhɑːfˈtimbəd] *adj.* (房屋)木架間塗以灰泥造成的。

half time ①半工半薪;半日工作。②(球賽)半場;休息時間。

half-tim·er [ˈhæf,taɪmə; ˈhɑːf,taimə] *n.* ①作半工者。②〖英〗半工半讀的學童。

half tint 中色;半濃淡色。

half title 書籍第一頁之書名或章名。

half-tone [ˈhæf,ton; ˈhɑːftoun] *n.* ①(書報上所用有濃淡色的)網版圖。②〖美術〗(間於深淺色之間的)半調色;間色。③〖音樂〗半音。—*adj.* 網版的; 半調色的。

half-track [ˈhæf,træk; ˈhɑːftræk] *n.* 〖軍〗①半履帶車。②裝於前輪或後輪之履帶。

half-truth [ˈhæf,truθ; ˈhɑːf-truːθ] *n.* 含片面眞理或部分眞實的話。

half volley (網球、足球等)球剛起地所作之一擊(踢)。

half-vol·ley [ˈhæfˈvɑlɪ; ˈhɑːfˈvɔli]

v.t. & *v.i.* 〖網球、板球〗於球甫將跳起時擊出。
half·way ['hæf'we; 'hɑːf'wei] *adv.* 半路地。*halfway* home. 在回家的半途中。**go** (or **meet**) **halfway** 妥協;向…讓步。—*adj.* ①在中途的。②不徹底的;部分的。
halfway house ①兩地間中途歇脚之小客棧。②任何路程之中途地點。③折中辦法。
half-wit ['hæf,wɪt; 'hɑːfwit] *n.* ①魯鈍者;愚蠢者。②意志薄弱的人。
half-wit·ted ['hæf'wɪtɪd; 'hɑːf'witid] *adj.* 遲鈍的;白癡的;愚蠢的。—**ly,** *adv.*
half-year·ly ['hæf'jɪrlɪ; 'hɑːf'jəːli] *adv.* & *adj.* 每半年(的)。
hal·i·but ['hæləbət; 'hælibət] *n., pl.* **-buts, -but.** 大比目魚。
hal·ide ['hælaɪd; 'hælaid] *n.* 〖化〗鹵素化物。—*adj.* 鹵素的。(亦作 **halid**)
hal·i·dom ['hælɪdəm; 'hælidəm] *n.* 〖古〗聖物;聖寶。**by my halidom** 誓必。
hal·i·dome ['hælɪ,dom; 'hælidoum] *n.* =**halidom.**
hal·ite ['hælaɪt; 'hælait] *n.* 岩鹽。
hal·i·to·sis [,hælə'tosɪs; ,hæli'tousis] *n.* 〖醫〗口臭。
***hall** [hɔl; hɔːl] *n.* ①〖美〗通道;走廊。②(靠近門口之)走廊;門廳。Leave your hat and coat in the *hall.* 把你帽子和上衣放在門口走廊裏。③會堂。a dance *hall.* 跳舞廳。④辦公室;衙門。city *hall.* 市政廳。⑤(大學裏的)宿舍;演講廳等。a *hall* of residence. 大學的宿舍。⑥〖英〗(地主的)府第。
hal·le·lu·jah, hal·le·lu·iah [,hælə'lujə; ,hæli'luːjə] *interj.* 哈利路亞(讚美上帝語)。—*n.* 讚美詩。(亦作 **alleluia**)
Hal·ley ['hælɪ; 'hæli] *n.* 哈雷(Edmund, 1656–1742, 英國天文學家)。
Halley's comet 〖天文〗哈雷彗星。
hal·liard ['hæljəd; 'hæljəd] *n.* =**halyard.**
hall·mark ['hɔl,mark; 'hɔːlmɑːk] *n.* ①(金銀的)純度檢驗證明印記。②純正之證明。③品質的證明。—*v.t.* 加刻純度檢驗證明印記。
hal·lo [hə'lo; hə'lou] *interj., n., pl.* **-los,** *v.,* **-loed, -lo·ing.** —*interj., n.* ①喂!②啊!—*v.i.* & *v.t.* ①招呼(某人);喊住(某人)。②作 hallo 之聲嗾使獵犬前進。③歡呼。(亦作 **hollo, holla, halloa, holloa, hillo, hilloa, hullo**)
Hall of Fame ①紐約市之美國歷史名人紀念祠。②(亦作 **hall of fame**)某一行業或學術界傑出人物之集合稱。
***hal·loo** [hə'lu; hə'luː] *interj., n., pl.* **-loos,** *v.,* **-looed, -loo·ing.**—*interj., n.* 呼叫;大聲喊叫(尤指引人注意或狩獵時嗾犬者)。—*v.t.* & *v.i.* 招呼;喊叫。(亦作 **hallow**)
***hal·low** ['hælo; 'hælou] *v.t.* ①使神聖。ground *hallowed* by sacred memories. 因神聖之記憶而成爲神聖化的土地。②視爲神聖而崇敬。*Hallowed* be thy name. 我等願爾名見聖(天主經中一句)。
hal·lowed ['hælod; 'hæloud] *adj.* ①神聖化的。②神聖的。*hallowed* ground. 神聖的土地;墓地。
Hal·low·een, Hal·low·e'en [,hælo'in, ,hɑl-; 'hælou'iːn, ,hælou'iːn] *n.* 萬聖節前夕(即十月三十一日之夜)。
Hal·low·mas ['hælo,mæs; 'hælou-mæs] *n.* 萬聖節(十一月一日)。
Hall·statt ['hɔlstæt; 'hælstæt] *adj.* 初期鐵器時代的(出自奧地利地名)。

hal·lu·ci·nate [hə'lusn,et; hə'luːsi-neit] *v.,* **-nat·ed, -nat·ing.**—*v.t.* 引起幻覺;使有幻覺。—*v.i.* 發生幻覺。—**hal·lu·ci·na·to·ry, hal·luc·i·na·tive,** *adj.*
hal·lu·ci·na·tion [hə,lusn'eʃən; hə-,luːsi'neiʃən] *n.* ①幻覺。②幻覺中所看見之物或聽見之聲音。
hall·way ['hɔl,we; 'hɔːlwei] *n.* 走廊;玄關。
hal·ma ['hælmə; 'hælmə] *n.* 一種跳棋(棋盤有 256 目)。
ha·lo ['helo; 'heilou] *n., pl.* **-los** or **-loes,** *v.,* **-loed, -lo·ing.** —*n.* ①(日月的)暈輪;光圈。②(神像等頭上所畫之)光環。③(圍繞着一個理想人物或有價值之物的)榮光;榮耀。④〖解剖〗乳頭周圍之乳輪。—*v.i.* 成暈輪。—*v.t.* 環以光輪。
hal·o·gen ['hælədʒən; 'hælədʒən] *n.* 〖化〗鹵素。
hal·oid ['hælɔɪd; 'hælɔid] *adj.* 〖化〗鹵素的。—*n.* 鹵素之金屬鹽。
***halt**[1] [hɔlt; hɔːlt] *v.i.* 立定;停止行進。The troops *halted* for a rest. 這軍隊停止行進;休息片刻。—*v.t.* 使立定;使停止前進。—*n.* ①立定;停止行進。The train came to a *halt.* 火車停車。②(火車停留的)小站;電車站。**call a halt** 命令停止。The officer *called a halt.* 軍官呼令立定。—*interj.* 立定!站住!
halt[2] *v.i.* ①猶豫;躊躇。to *halt* between two opinions. 躊躇於兩種意見之間。②囁嚅而言。③(韻文等)有缺點。—*adj.* 跛的;蹣跚的。
hal·ter[1] ['hɔltɚ; 'hɔːltə] *n.* ①韁繩。②絞首用繩索。③吊死。④婦女之袒肩露背胸衣。—*v.t.* ①以韁繩縛繫。②以繩吊縊。
hal·ter[2] *n.* 猶豫者;說話囁嚅者;使停止者。
hal·ter·break ['hɔltɚ,brek; 'hɔːltə-breik] *v.t.* 馴服(小馬等)使帶絡頭。
halt·ing ['hɔltɪŋ; 'hɔːltiŋ] *adj.* ①跛的;有缺陷的。②躊躇的;曖昧的。—**ly,** *adv.*
halve [hæv; hɑːv] *v.t.* **halved, halv·ing.** ①二等分;分享。to *halve* an apple. 把一蘋果分成兩分。②減半。③〖高爾夫〗與敵方以同樣桿數完成(一洞或一次比賽)。④〖木工〗將(兩木)各刳去厚度之半而接合。
halves [hævz; hɑːvz] *n.* pl. of **half.** **go halves** 平均分配。
hal·yard ['hæljəd; 'hæljəd] *n.* 帆、旗等的升降索。(亦作 **halliard**)
***ham** [hæm; hæm] *n., v.,* **hammed, ham-ming.** —*n.* ①火腿。a slice of *ham.* 一片火腿。②(獸類之)大腿。③膕;腿彎。④(*pl.*)臀部。⑤〖俚〗笨拙的演員。⑥〖俚〗表演過火(者)。⑦〖俚〗業餘無線電務員。**squat on one's hams** 蹲下。—*v.i.* & *v.t.* 〖俚〗表演不佳;表演過火。**ham it up** 〖俚〗表演過火;作過火之表演。
ham·a·dry·ad [,hæmə'draɪəd; ,hæmə-'drai-əd] *n., pl.* **-ads, -ades.** ①〖希臘神話〗樹神。②印度產之一種毒蛇。
ha·mal [hə'mɑl; hə'mɑːl] *n.* ①(東方國家之)搬夫;挑夫;輿夫。②(印度之)家僕。(亦作 **hammal, hamaul, hummaul**)
Ham·burg ['hæmbɝg; 'hæmbəːg] *n.* 漢堡(德國西北部城市)。
ham·burg·er ['hæmbɝgɚ; 'hæmbəː-gə] *n.* ①=**hamburg steak.** ②夾牛肉餅的三明治。③攪碎的牛肉。
hamburg steak 漢堡牛肉餅(碎牛肉煎成的餅)。
hames [hemz; heimz] *n. pl.* 馬軛。
ham-fist·ed ['hæm,fɪstɪd; 'hæm,fistid] *adj.* 拳頭大的;笨拙的。(亦作 **ham-handed**)

Ham·ite [ˈhæmaɪt; ˈhæmait] *n.* ①哈姆人(傳爲 Noah 次子, Ham 之後裔)。②(非洲)哈姆族人。

Ham·it·ic [hæmˈɪtɪk; hæˈmitik] *adj.* Ham 的;哈姆族(語)的。—*n.* 哈姆語。

Ham·let [ˈhæmlɪt; ˈhæmlit] *n.* ①哈姆雷特(莎士比亞作四大悲劇之一)。②哈姆雷特(該劇中之主人公名)。(略作 **Haml.**)

***ham·let** [ˈhæmlɪt; ˈhæmlit] *n.* ①小村。②鄉村中一小片房子。

ham·mer** [ˈhæmɚ; ˈhæmə] *n.* ①鎚(如釘鎚等);鐵鎚。②(拍賣者手中所持之)木槌。③〖樂〗琴鎚。④似鎚之物;當作鎚用之物。⑤〖運動〗鏈球。⑥〖解剖〗鎚骨。bring*** (or ***send***) ***to the hammer*** 拿去拍賣。***come*** (or ***go***) ***under the hammer*** 被拍賣掉。The old house and the furniture in it *went under the hammer.* 那幢老屋及裏面的傢具被拍賣掉了。***hammer and tongs*** 〖俗〗拚命;竭力。—*v.t.* ①鎚打;鎚成(某形狀)。to *hammer* nails into a piece of wood. 將釘子釘進一塊木頭裏。②釘〖常 down, up〗。③用鍾和釘拼合〖常 together〗。④用力敲打〖常 out〗. to *hammer* a home run. 用力擊出一個全壘打。⑤努力或費力地工作〖常out, together〗. to *hammer* out an agreement. 努力達成協議。⑥努力使終止。⑦辯論時提出(有力的理由、論點等)(常與 home 連用)。—*v.i.* ①鎚打;敲打。②埋頭工作〖常 away〗. He *hammered* away at his speech for hours. 他化了幾小時修改他的講稿。③重申;一再强調〖常 away〗. The teacher *hammered* away at the multiplication tables. 老師一再朗讀乘法表。***hammer*** (***away***) ***at*** **a.** 苦心研究;下苦功。**b.** 一再强調。***hammer out*** **a.** 用鎚打成器;用鎚打平;用鎚打掉。**b.** 用力去完成;用心去想通或說明。

ham·mer·cloth [ˈhæmɚˌklɔθ; ˈhæməkləθ] *n.* (馬車之)車夫座位上之布篷。

ham·mer·head [ˈhæmɚˌhɛd; ˈhæmə-hed] *n.* ①錘頭。②撞木鮫。③鯉屬小海魚。

hammer lock 摔角時將對手之臂反轉從背後向上扭折的動作。

ham·mer·smith [ˈhæmɚˌsmɪθ; ˈhæməsmiθ] *n.* 鍛工。

hammer throw 〖田徑〗擲鏈球。

***ham·mock** [ˈhæmək; ˈhæmək] *n.* 吊牀。

hammock chair 可折疊的帆布躺椅。

Ham·mond organ [ˈhæmənd~; ˈhæmənd~] 〖商標名〗一種電子琴。

ham·my[1] [ˈhæmɪ; ˈhæmi] *adj.*, **-mi·er, -mi·est.** 〖俚〗過分的;誇張的。

ham·my[2] *adj.*, **-mi·er, -mi·est.** 似火腿的。

***ham·per**[1] [ˈhæmpɚ; ˈhæmpə] *v.t.* 使不能行動自如;妨礙;阻礙;困累。He has been *hampered* by poverty. 他爲貧窮所困累。—*n.* ①足械。②(船上的)不可缺少而又礙事的船具(如繩索等)。

ham·per[2] *n.* 有蓋大籃(尤指裝食物者)。a picnic *hamper.* 野餐時用的籃子。

ham·shack·le [ˈhæmˌʃækl; ˈhæmˌʃækl] *v.t.*, **-led, -ling.** ①將(牛、馬等的)頭與前足縛在一起使不能動。②束縛;抑制。

ham·ster [ˈhæmstɚ; ˈhæmstə] *n.* (歐洲、亞洲產之)一種大鼠。

ham·string [ˈhæmˌstrɪŋ; ˈhæm-striŋ] *n.*, *v.*, **-strung** or **-stringed, -string·ing.** —*n.* 〖解剖〗腿筋。—*v.t.* ①斷腿筋使之殘廢。②使殘廢;使跛。③使無效;破壞。

Ham·sun [ˈhɑmsun; ˈhɑːmsun] *n.* 哈姆孫 (Knut, 1859–1952, 挪威小說家, 曾獲1920年諾貝爾文學獎)。

ham·u·lus [ˈhæmjuləs; ˈhæmjuləs] *n.* *pl.* **-li** [-ˌlaɪ; -lai]. 〖解剖, 動物〗鉤狀突起;鉤。

‡hand [hænd; hænd] *n.* ①手;掌。Hold out your right *hand.* 伸出你的右手。②(猴子的)脚;(高級脊椎動物的)前脚。③如手之物(如鐘錶之針)。The *hands* of a clock or watch show the time. 鐘或錶之針指示時間。④勞工;雇工。a farm *hand.* 農場的雇工。⑤(常 *pl.*) 掌握;處理;控制。We are in the *hands* of God. 我們都在上帝的掌握之中。⑥方面;方向。At her left *hand* stood two men. 在她的左邊站着兩個男人。⑦關係;參與。He had no *hand* in the matter. 他跟這件事毫無關係。⑧來源;出處。⑨筆跡;書法。He writes in a clear *hand.* 他的書法寫得很清楚。⑩簽名。to set one's *hand* to a document. 在文件上簽字。⑪技巧;手法;才能。The artist's work showed a master's *hand.* 那藝術家的作品表現出名家的手筆。⑫行家;巧匠;能手。⑬拍手喝采。The crowd gave the winner a big *hand.* 羣衆對得勝者大喝其采。⑭婚約。He offered her his *hands.* 他向她求婚。⑮一手寬(約四英寸,量馬之高度用)。⑯〖牌戲〗一手牌;競賽之一盤;玩牌者。⑰水手。All *hands* on deck! 全體水手上甲板。⑱人(就能力而言)。He was a poor *hand* running a business. 他不善於做生意。⑲(商談中之)地位。an action to strengthen one's *hand.* 加强自己(談判)地位的一步驟。⑳幫助。Give him a *hand.* 幫助他一下。㉑一束煙草;一束香蕉。㉒〖羅馬法〗丈夫對妻之控制權。***a bird in the hand*** 掌中物。***a good*** (***poor***) ***hand at*** 巧(拙)於。***at first*** (***second***) ***hand*** 直(間)接。She heard the story *at second hand.* 她間接聽得此事。***at hand*** **a.** 近處;在手邊。The examinations are *at hand.* 考試卽將舉行。**b.** 準備好了的。***at one's hand*** 由某人之手;憑某人之手。***at the hand***(***s***) ***of*** 被;受。They suffered *at the hands of* their stepfather. 他們備受繼父虐待(吃盡繼父的苦頭)。***bear*** (***give,*** or ***lend***) ***a hand*** 干與〖in〗;幫助〖with〗. Please *lend a hand with* the baggage. 請幫忙搬動行李。***bind*** (***a person***) ***hand and foot*** 使(某人)完全無能或不克活動。***by hand*** 手工做的;用手。Was this made *by hand?* 這是手工做的嗎? ***by the hands of*** 經…之手。***change hands*** (財產等)換主人;易手。***clean hands*** 無辜;淸白。***come to hand*** 收到;找着。***eat*** (or ***feed***) ***out of one's hand*** 〖喩〗順從;易對付;易管理。***fight hand to hand*** 短兵相接;肉搏。***free hand*** 自由;不受限制。***from hand to hand*** 用手傳遞;從甲手到乙手。***from hand to mouth*** 僅够糊口;毫無積蓄。***gain the upper hand of*** 占優勢。***get a big hand*** 大受喝采;大受歡迎。***go hand in hand with*** 與…齊步;以…的同等速率前進。***hand and foot*** 手脚一齊;完全;盡力。***hand and*** (or ***in***) ***glove with*** 跟…很親密。***hand in hand*** **a.** 手牽手地。They walked away *hand in hand.* 他們攜手離去。**b.** 共同地。***hand over hand*** (or ***fist***) (如爬繩般)雙手交互地攀登;〖喩〗進展快速。***hands down*** 不費力;輕而易擧地。***Hands off!*** 不許動手!不要干涉! ***Hands up!*** **a.** 擧起你的手(作爲投降等的象徵)! **b.** 擧手表示同意或準備回答問題。***hand to hand*** 接近。***have one's*** (or ***a***) ***hand***

in 干與;熟習。**have one's hands full** 事忙;無法分身;盡力而爲。I *have my hands full.* 我事忙。**in hand** a. 在控制下。b. 擁有;保有。c. 工作已經着手;正在進行。**join hands** a. 結成同夥;成爲夥伴。b. 結婚。**lay hands on** a. 攫;取;拿。b. 抓住;逮捕。c. 襲擊;危害。d. 按手祝福(某人)。**off hand** 馬上;立卽。**off one's hands** a. 不在某人掌握中;脫手。b. 責任完成。**on all hands** (從)四方八面;一致。**on hand** a. 現有。b. 在近處。c. 準備。d. 〖美〗出席。**on one's hands** 在某人監督或掌握中;在手中。**on the one hand** 一方面。**on the other hand** 他方面。**out of hand** a. 卽時。b. 難控制。**shake hands with someone** 與某人握手。**tie one's hands** 束縛;使某人無能爲力。**try one's hand at** 試作。**wash one's hands of** 洗手不幹;拒絕對…負責。**with a heavy** (or **iron**) **hand** 壓制地;用鐵腕。—*v.t.* ①交給;傳遞。He *handed* me the book. 他將書交給了我。②扶持;以手助。**hand down** a. 傳遞。to *hand down* to posterity. 傳給後代。b. 宣布。**hand in** 提出;遞進;繳交。**hand out** 分給;交給;給。**hand over** 給他人;移交;讓與。—*adj.* 手的;手用的;手製的。

hand·bag [ˈhændˌbæg, ˈhæn-; ˈhændbæg] *n.* ①女用手提包。②小旅行袋。

hand baggage 手提行李。

hand·ball [ˈhændˌbɔl; ˈhændbɔːl] *n.* 手球(用手將球擊向牆壁讓對方去接的球戲)。

hand·bar·row [ˈhændˌbæro; ˈhændˌbærou] *n.* ①手推車。②擔架。

hand·bell [ˈhændˌbɛl; ˈhændbel] *n.* 手搖鈴。

hand·bill [ˈhændˌbɪl; ˈhændbil] *n.* 傳單。

hand·book [ˈhændˌbuk; ˈhændbuk] *n.* ①手册;便覽。②旅行指南。③(賽馬的)彩票簿;賭帳。④賭場。

hand·breadth [ˈhændˌbrɛdθ; ˈhændbredθ] *n.* 掌幅;掌幅尺(約4英寸)。

hand·car [ˈhændˌkar; ˈhændkaː] *n.* 〖美〗(鐵道路線檢查或工人交通用之)手搖車。

hand·cart [ˈhændˌkart; ˈhændkaːt] *n.* 手推(拉)車。

hand·clasp [ˈhændˈklæsp; ˈhændˈklæsp] *n.* 二人或二人以上之握手(表示歡迎、分手等)。

hand·cuff [ˈhændˌkʌf; ˈhændkʌf] *n., pl.* **-cuffs**, *v.* —*n.* (常 *pl.*)手銬。—*v.t.* 加手銬於…。

hand drill 手鑽。

hand·ed [ˈhændɪd; ˈhændid] *adj.* ①有手的。②使用或具有某種手的(常用於組成複合字,如 left-*handed* 等)。③由幾個人組成的(如 three-*handed* bridge. 三人打的橋牌)。

hand·ed·ness [ˈhændɪdnɪs; ˈhændidnis] *n.* 用右手或左手的習慣。

Han·del [ˈhændl; ˈhændl] *n.* 韓德爾(George Frederick, 1685–1759, 德國作曲家)。

hand·fast [ˈhændˌfæst; ˈhændfaːst] *v.t.* 〖古〗①使訂婚;使結婚。②緊握。—*adj.* 〖古〗①吝嗇的。②訂了婚的;已結婚的。—*n.* 〖古〗①緊握。②握手爲約。③合約;(尤指)婚約。—**ing**, *n.*

*__hand·ful__ [ˈhændˌful, ˈhæn-; ˈhændful, ˈhæn-] *n., pl.* **-fuls.** ①一撮;一把。a *handful* of clay. 一把泥土。②少數(人或物)。Only a *handful* of people came to the meeting. 只有少數人到會。③〖俗〗可厭之人;難控制之人;棘手之事。That young boy of hers is quite a *handful.* 她的那個小兒子是一個極難管束的孩子。

hand gallop (馬)慢跑。

hand glass ①有柄之手鏡。②(閱讀時執於手中之)放大鏡。③(保護植物幼苗用之)玻璃框。

hand grenade ①手榴彈。②(手擲的)滅火瓶。

hand·grip [ˈhændˌgrɪp; ˈhændgrip] *n.* ①握手。②握柄。③(*pl.*)扭打;格鬥。

hand·hold [ˈhændˌhold; ˈhændhould] *n.* ①把握;掌握。②把手;把柄。

*__hand·i·cap__ [ˈhændɪˌkæp; ˈhændikæp] *n., v.,* **-capped, -cap·ping.** —*n.* ①〖運動〗(優劣懸殊者作比賽時,所給予優者之)障礙。②〖運動〗使用障礙之比賽。③障礙;困難。Poor eyesight is a *handicap* to a student. 視力不好是學生的障礙。—*v.t.* ①加障礙於(比賽者)。②使受障礙。③根據過去比賽紀錄預測(優勝者)。④賭比賽之優勝者。

hand·i·capped [ˈhændɪˌkæpt; ˈhændikæpt] *adj.* ①身體有缺陷的。②智力不足的。③〖運動〗在不利情形下比賽的。

hand·i·cap·per [ˈhændɪˌkæpɚ; ˈhændiˌkæpə] *n.* (賽馬等時)加障礙於優勢者以求機會平均的人。

hand·i·craft [ˈhændɪˌkræft; ˈhændikraːft] *n.* ①手工;手藝。②需要手工技藝的行業(如製陶、木工等)。③手工藝品。

hand·i·crafts·man [ˈhændɪˌkræftsmən; ˈhændiˌkraːftsmən] *n., pl.* **-men.** 手藝人;工匠。

Hand·ie-Talk·ie [ˈhændɪˌtɔkɪ; ˈhændiˌtɔːki] *n.* 〖商標名〗一種可隨身携帶的小型輕便無線電報或電話機。

hand·i·ly [ˈhændɪlɪ; ˈhændili] *adv.* ①方便地。②靈巧地;熟練地。③容易地。

hand·i·ness [ˈhændɪnɪs; ˈhændinis] *n.* 靈巧;敏捷。

hand in glove 親密地。(亦作 **hand and glove**)

hand·i·work [ˈhændɪˌwɝk; ˈhændiwəːk] *n.* ①手工。②手工藝品;自製物品。③行爲的後果。

*__hand·ker·chief__ [ˈhæŋkɚtʃɪf, -ˌtʃif; ˈhæŋkətʃif] *n.* ①手帕;手絹;手巾。a pocket *handkerchief.* 手帕。②頭巾;圍巾。a neck *handkerchief.* 圍巾。**throw the handkerchief to** 〖遊戲〗拋手巾催(某人)追趕自己;〖喩〗暗示心意。

hand language (啞巴的)手語;指語。

‡**han·dle** [ˈhændl; ˈhændl] *n., v.,* **-dled, -dling.** —*n.* ①柄;把手。We carry a bucket by the *handle.* 我們握着把手提桶。②可乘之機;口實。Don't let your conduct give any *handle* for gossip. 不要讓你的行爲有任何落給別人閒談的話柄。③〖俗〗名字;頭銜。④(賽馬或賽狗)賭注的總和。⑤織物予人之感覺。**fly off the handle** 發怒;激動。—*v.t.* ①以手觸動;持;執;搬。You shouldn't *handle* books with dirty hands. 你不可用髒手拿書。②管理;指揮。An officer must know how to *handle* men. 一個軍官必須懂得怎樣指揮士兵。③對付;對待。The speaker was roughly *handled* by the mob. 演講者受了羣衆的侮辱。④〖美〗經銷;買賣。This shop does not *handle* foreign goods. 這個商店不經銷外國貨。⑤討論(題目)。The poem *handles* the problems of love and death. 這首詩討論有關愛與死的問題。—*v.i.* 操作;舉動;行動。This car *handles* easily. 這輛車很靈活。—**han·dled,** *adj.*

handle bar ①(脚踏車之)把手。②〖俗〗長八字鬍。

H

han·dler ['hændlɚ; 'hændlə] *n.* ①處理者;操作者;指揮者。②陶器工人。③(拳師、摔角者等之)經理人;教練;副手。④(鬥犬或馬等之)訓練者。

hand line 手執之釣絲。(亦作 **handline**)

han·dling ['hændlɪŋ; 'hændliŋ] *n.* ①以手觸摸、執握、利用。②管理;處理。③筆法;畫法。④裝柄。

hand loom 〖英〗手搖紡織機。(亦作 **handloom**)

hand·made ['hænd'med; 'hænd'meid] *adj.* 手工做的(對機器做的而言)。*handmade* shoes. 手工做的鞋。

hand·maid ['hænd,med; 'hændmeid] *n.* ①女僕;婢女。②受制於他物之事物。(亦作 **handmaiden**)

hand-me-down ['hænmɪ,daun; 'hænmidaun] *adj.* 〖俚〗①現成的;便宜的。②舊的。*hand-me-down* garments. 舊衣服。—*n.* 〖俚〗舊衣服;現成衣服。

hand organ 一種大型手風琴。

hand·out ['hænd,aut; 'hændaut] *n.* ①(給登門求乞者的)施捨物品。②(免費奉送的)廣告物品。③政府或商店等送給報社發表的新聞。④傳單。

hand·o·ver ['hænd,ovɚ; 'hænd,ouvə] *n.* 移交。

hand-pick ['hænd'pɪk; 'hænd'pik] *v.t.* ①用手摘;用手撿。②親自仔細挑選。③(為達某種目的而)挑選。

hand-picked ['hænd'pɪkt; 'hænd'pikt] *adj.* ①手摘的(指果實、蔬菜等)。②精選的。③特選的(尤指非公正的選擇)。

hand puppet 手指操縱的木偶。

hand·rail ['hænd,rel; 'hændreil] *n.* 扶手;欄干。

hand·saw ['hænd,sɔ; 'hænd'sɔː] *n.* 手鋸。

hand's-breadth, hands-breadth ['hændz,brɛdθ; 'hændzbredθ] *n.* =**handbreadth.**

hands-down ['hændz'daun; 'hændz'daun] *adj.* ①容易的。②毫無疑問的。

hand·sel ['hænsl; 'hænsl] *n., v.,* **-sel(l)ed, -sel·(l)ing.** —*n.* ①賀禮;新年禮物;新郎給新娘的禮物。②第一次付款;第一筆生意所得之款。③初試;初嘗。—*v.t.* ①致送賀儀與…。②首先使用或嘗試。③為…舉行開幕典禮。(亦作 **hansel**)

hand·set ['hænd'set; 'hænd'set] *n., v.,* **-set, -set·ting,** *adj.* —*n.* (電話送話器與受話器在一起的)聽筒。—*v.t.* 用手排(鉛字)。—*adj.* ①(鉛字)手排的。②(書籍等)用手排鉛字印刷的。

hand·shake ['hænd,ʃek; 'hændʃeik] *n.* 握手。—*v.i.* 握手。—*v.t.* 一面握手一面向(沿)…走。

hands-off ['hændz'ɔf; 'hændz'ɔːf] *adj.* 袖手旁觀的;不干預的。*hands-off* policy. 不干涉政策。

:hand·some ['hænsəm; 'hænsəm] *adj.,* **-som·er, -som·est.** ①美觀的;漂亮的;美貌的。He's a *handsome* fellow. 他是一個漂亮的男子。②相當大的。a *handsome* sum of money. 一筆相當大的款項。③慷慨的;大方的。a *handsome* gift. 大方的禮物。④〖俗〗優美的;合宜的。⑤熟練的;得體的。a *handsome* speech. 一篇得體的演說。***Handsome is that*** (or ***as***) ***handsome does.*** 慷慨大方始為美。—**ly,** *adv.* —**ness,** *n.*

hand·spike ['hæn,spaɪk; 'hænspaik] *n.* ①木梃(粗木棍)。②〖軍〗瞄準棍。

hand·spring ['hæn,sprɪŋ; 'hænspriŋ] *n.* 豎蜻蜓;翻觔斗。

hand·stamp ['hænd,stæmp; 'hændstæmp] *n.* ①以手操作的打印器。②以手蓋的印記或戳記(如郵戳)。—*v.t.* ①以手蓋印於…。②用打印器蓋上(印記或戳記)。

hand·stand ['hænd,stænd; 'hænstænd] *n.* 倒立;豎蜻蜓。

hand-to-hand ['hændtə'hænd; 'hændtə'hænd] *adj.* 交手的;肉搏的;白刃戰的。

hand-to-mouth ['hændtə'mauθ; 'hændtə'mauθ] *adj.* & *adv.* ①無隔宿之糧的(地)。②不慮將來的(地);不儉省的(地)。

hand truck 小手推車。

hand·work ['hænd,wɝk; 'hændwəːk] *n.* 手工;精細工藝。

hand·wo·ven ['hænd'wovən; 'hænd'wouvən] *adj.* 用手織機編織的。

hand·writ·ing ['hænd,raɪtɪŋ; 'hænd,raitiŋ] *n.* 筆跡;書法;筆風;手寫物。***handwriting on the wall*** 災禍之預兆。

hand·y** ['hændɪ; 'hændi] *adj.,* **hand·i·er, hand·i·est.** ①便利的。A good tool box is a *handy* thing to have in any house. 一個好的工具箱是任何家庭所應具備的一種方便的東西。②手熟的;敏捷的。③易於駕馭的。It is quite a *handy* little sailing boat. 這是一艘十分易於操縱的小帆船。④在手邊的;容易取得的。come in handy*** 遲早會有用處。

hand·y-dand·y ['hændɪ,dændɪ; 'hændi'dændi] *n.* 猜對方那一手中握有東西的遊戲。

hand·y·man ['hændɪ,mæn; 'hændimæn] *n., pl.* **-men.** ①受雇做雜事的人。②〖俗〗水兵。

:hang [hæŋ; hæŋ] *v.,* **hung** or **hanged, hang·ing,** *n.* —*v.t.* ①懸;掛;吊。*Hang* your hat up. 把你的帽子掛起來。②絞死。The murderer was caught and *hanged.* 兇手被捕獲絞死了。③釘十字架處死。④懸掛以點綴之。The walls were *hung* with pictures. 牆上掛有許多圖畫。⑤垂(首)。He *hung* his head in shame. 他羞愧的垂着頭。⑥固定於適當的角度。⑦貼(紙等)在牆上。⑧拖延(時間)。⑨懸擱。⑩起綽號。⑪陳列。The gallery *hung* his paintings in a small corner. 畫廊將他的畫放在一個小角落陳列。⑫附加。⑬(將門用鉸鏈)裝在門框上。⑭一種較輕的咀咒 (=damn). I'll be *hanged* if I do. 我才不幹哩!—*v.i.* ①懸;掛;吊。The picture was *hanging* on the wall. 此畫掛在牆上。②吊死。③附着;纏住。He *hung* by her side, unwilling to leave. 他纏着她,捨不得離開。④視…而定。His future *hangs* on the outcome of their discussion. 他的前途要看他們討論的結果而定。⑤徘徊。⑥猶豫不決;躊躇。⑦上十字架。⑧擱置。⑨飄浮在空中。Fog *hung* over the city. 該城被霧籠罩。⑩負荷;擺不脫。guilt that *hangs* on his conscience. 他良心上擺不脫的內疚。⑪注意;思考〖常 on, upon〗. They *hung* on his every word. 他們留心他所說的每一句話。⑫被陳列。His works *hang* in most major museums. 他的作品被陳列在多數大博物館中。⑬意見不一致(如陪審團)。⑭合身。⑮〖俗〗閒蕩。to *hang* about a place. 在某處閒蕩。***hang about*** (or ***around***) **a.** 留在近旁;在附近。**b.** 閒呆着。He's too fond of *hanging about* at street corners. 他非常喜愛在街角處閒呆着。***hang back*** 躊躇不前；退縮。When the officer asked for volunteers, not one soldier *hung back.* 那位軍官徵求志願擔任某任務時，沒有一位兵士退縮。***hang by a hair*** (or ***single thread***) 千鈞一髮。***hang fire*** (槍等)發火慢；〖喩〗(事情)懸擱；耽擱時間。***hang in the balance*** 岌岌可危。***Hang it!*** 該死的；他媽的(煩惱的咒語)！***hang on*** **a.** 緊抱。**b.** 不願讓(人等)走開、停下、或離去。**c.** 堅持。**d.** 依恃；斜靠。**e.** 仔細地考慮或聽。**f.** 視…而定。***hang one on*** 〖俚〗 **a.** 拳擊；打。**b.** 爛醉如泥。***hang out*** **a.** 前靠；伸出身體。Don't *hang out* of the window; you may fall. 不要把身子伸出窗外，你可能會摔下去。**b.** 掛在外面。**c.** 〖俚〗居住；停留。***hang over*** **a.** 接近。**b.** 威脅；逼近。**c.** 擱置。***hang together*** **a.** (人等)團結一致。If we all *hang together,* we can succeed in our plan. 如果我們大家團結一致；我們可按計畫成功。**b.** (物等)和諧一致。***hang up*** **a.** 放在鈎、栓等上面；掛；吊。**b.** 掛斷電話。**c.** 中止。The plan has been *hung up.* 該計畫已被擱置。***hang wall paper*** 糊壁紙。***let things go hang*** 〖俗〗不在乎事情；漠不關心。—*n.* ①懸；掛；吊；掛樣；垂下狀態。She changed the *hang* of her skirt. 她改變了她的裙子的樣子。②〖美俗〗用法；作法；訣竅。③〖美俗〗意義；意念。④一點點。not care a *hang.* 毫不在乎。〖注意〗在正式英語中，**hang** 作"絞死"解時，其變化爲 hang, hanged. 作其他意義解時，其變化爲 hang, hung, hung.

hang·ar [ˈhæŋɚ; ˈhæŋə] *n.* ①飛機庫。②棚廠。(英亦作 **hangarage**)

hang·ar-deck [ˈhæŋɚˌdɛk; ˈhæŋədek] *n.* 航空母艦上之機庫甲板。

hang·bird [ˈhæŋˌbɝd; ˈhæŋbəːd] *n.* 懸巢鳥(在樹枝上懸巢的鳥，如金鶯、燕雀等)。

hang·dog [ˈhæŋˌdɔg; ˈhæŋdɔg] *adj.* ①低賤的。②鬼鬼祟祟的。—*n.* 卑賤的人。

hang·er [ˈhæŋɚ; ˈhæŋə] *n.* ①懸掛者。②掛物之工具或機械。③掛物之鉤或環。④一種短刀。⑤〖俚〗球賽中輕而易舉之得分。⑥執行絞刑之劊子手。

hang·er-on [ˈhæŋɚˈɑn; ˈhæŋərˈɔn] *n., pl.* **hang·ers-on.** 依附者；食客；隨從者。

hang·fire [ˈhæŋˌfaɪr; ˈhæŋfaiə] *n.* 由於引線故障而起的炸藥之延時爆炸。

***hang·ing** [ˈhæŋɪŋ; ˈhæŋiŋ] *n.* ①絞死；絞刑。There were three *hangings* last month. 上月有三宗絞刑。②懸掛；垂掛。③(常 *pl.*)(窗帘、門簾、幔帳等)懸掛物。—*adj.* ①應處絞刑的。a *hanging* crime (*or* matter). 應處絞刑的罪。②意欲判以絞刑的。③懸掛的。④傾斜的。⑤位於高處或斜坡上的。⑥沮喪的；鬱鬱不樂的。

hang·man [ˈhæŋmən; ˈhæŋmən] *n., pl.* **-men.** 絞刑吏；劊子手。

hang·nail [ˈhæŋˌnel; ˈhæŋneil] *n.* 指甲根上的肉刺；逆臚。

hang·out [ˈhæŋˌaut; ˈhæŋˈaut] *n.* 〖美俚〗①(流氓等之)住處。②一個人常去之處。

hang·o·ver [ˈhæŋˌovɚ; ˈhæŋˌouvə] *n.* ①殘遺物。②〖美俚〗宿醒(酒醒後之殘餘影響)。—*adj.* 殘餘效力的。(亦作 **hang-over**)

hang·up [ˈhæŋˌʌp; ˈhæŋʌp] *n.* 〖俚〗①心理的或情緒的問題。②令人煩惱的難題。

hank [hæŋk; hæŋk] *n.* ①一束；一捲(絲等)。②漢克(長度單位名)。③(船帆上的)金屬環；木環。—*v.t.* (將帆)在環上扣緊。

han·ker [ˈhæŋkɚ; ˈhæŋkə] *v.i.* 渴望；切望(與after, for 或不定詞連用)。

han·ker·ing [ˈhæŋkərɪŋ; ˈhæŋkəriŋ] *n.* 熱望；渴望；切望；眷戀。—*adj.* 熱望的；切望的；眷戀的。—**ly,** *adv.*

han·kie [ˈhæŋkɪ; ˈhæŋki] *n.* 〖俗〗=**handkerchief.**

Han·kow [ˈhænˈkau; hænˈkau] *n.* 漢口(中國長江中游之一大都市)。

han·ky [ˈhæŋkɪ; ˈhæŋki] *n.* 〖兒語〗=**handkerchief.**

han·ky-pan·ky [ˈhæŋkɪˈpæŋkɪ; ˈhæŋkiˈpæŋki] *n.* 〖俗〗①幻術；戲法。②騙術；不道德的行爲。③戲言；輕佻之行爲。***play hanky-panky with*** 欺瞞；瞞騙。

Han·ni·bal [ˈhænəbl̩; ˈhænibəl] *n.* 漢尼巴(247–183 B.C., 迦太基大將，曾對抗羅馬及侵入義大利)。

Ha·noi [hɑˈnɔɪ; hɑːˈnɔi] *n.* 河內。

Han·o·ver [ˈhænovɚ; ˈhænəvə] *n.* ①漢諾威(昔普魯士之一省)。②德國西北部一城市。③英國漢諾威王朝(自喬治一世到維多利亞)。—**i·an,** *adj., n.*

Hans [hæns, -z; hæns, -z] *n.* ①德文及荷文中男子名 Johannes (卽英文 John) 之省略。②〖俗〗德國人；荷蘭人。

Han·sard [ˈhænsɚd; ˈhænsəd] *n.* 英國國會議事錄。

Han·sard·ize [ˈhænsɚˌdaɪz; ˈhænsədaiz] *v.t.* 〖英〗引用議事錄提醒(國會議員之)矛盾。

hanse [hæns; hæns] *n.* 〖史〗①(中世紀北歐之)商人公會。②商人公會之入會費。③(H-) =**Hanseatic League.**

Han·se·at·ic League [ˌhænsɪˈætɪk (-zɪ-)~; ˌhænsiˈætik (-zi-)~] 漢撒同盟(14–15 世紀北歐商業都市之政治及商業同盟)。

han·sel [ˈhænsl̩; ˈhænsl] *n., v.,* **-sel(l)ed, -sel·(l)ing.** =**handsel.**

Han·sen's disease [ˈhænsənz~; ˈhænsənz~] 麻瘋病。

han·som [ˈhænsəm; ˈhænsəm] *n.* 一馬二輪有蓋雙座小馬車(御者座位高踞車後者)。

hap [hæp; hæp] *n., v.,* **happed, hap·ping.** —*n.* ①意外事件。②幸運。***by good hap*** 幸運。—*v.i.* 偶然發生。

hap·ax le·go·me·non [ˈhæpæksl ɪˈgɑmənɑn; ˈhæpækslіˈgɔmənɔn] *pl.* **hap·ax le·go·me·na** [-nə; -nə]. 〖希〗在正式文件或公文中只出現一次的文字或成語。

hap·haz·ard [*n.*ˈhæpˌhæzɚd; ˈhæpˌhæzəd *adj.* & *adv.* ˌhæpˈhæzɚd; ˌhæpˈhæzəd] *n.* 偶然；偶然事件；隨便。—*adj.* 偶然的；隨便的。a *haphazard* remark. 隨口而出的話。—*adv.* 偶然地；隨便地。—**ly,** *adv.* —**ness,** *n.*

hap·less [ˈhæplɪs; ˈhæplis] *adj.* 不幸的；倒霉的。—**ly,** *adv.* —**ness,** *n.*

hap·log·ra·phy [hæpˈlɑgrəfɪ; hæpˈlɔgrəfi] *n.* 重複之字或字母之脫漏(如：philology 誤作 philogy 之類)。

hap·lol·o·gy [hæpˈlɑlədʒɪ; hæpˈlɔlədʒi] *n.* 〖語音〗重複音省略(如：papa 略作 pa；humblely 略作 humbly)。

hap·ly [ˈhæplɪ; ˈhæpli] *adv.* 〖古〗偶然地；或許。

ha'p'orth [ˈhepəθ; ˈheipəθ] *n.* 〖俗〗=**halfpennyworth.**

‡hap·pen [ˈhæpən; ˈhæpən] *v.i.* ①發生；偶然發生。Accidents will *happen.* 意外之事總要發生。②偶然；偶而；恰巧。I *happened* to be out when he called. 他來訪我, 恰巧我出去了。**happen in with** 偶然和…碰見。**happen on** 遇見; 偶然發現。**happen to one** 臨身; 臨頭。

***hap·pen·ing** ['hæpənɪŋ; 'hæpəniŋ] *n.* 事件; 意外的事件。These *happenings* must now be described more fully. 這些事件現在必須報導詳細一點。

hap·pen·stance ['hæpn͵stæns; 'hæpənstæns] *n.* 〖美俗〗意外的事情; 偶然的事件。—*adj.* 偶然的; 意外的。

***hap·pi·ly** ['hæpɪlɪ; 'hæpili] *adv.* ①快樂地; 高興地。The children were playing *happily* in the garden. 孩子們在花園裏很快樂地玩耍。②幸運地; 幸而。③適當地; 技巧地。

:hap·pi·ness ['hæpɪnɪs; 'hæpinis] *n.* ①快樂; 幸福。His promotion brought him *happiness*. 他由於升級而感到愉快。②幸運。③適當。

:hap·py ['hæpɪ; 'hæpi] *adj.*, **hap·pi·er, hap·pi·est.** ①高興的; 愉快的; 滿足的; 快樂的。The story has a *happy* ending. 這小說有一個快樂的結局。②幸福的; 幸運的。by a *happy* chance. 運氣好; 湊巧。③適當的; 成功的。That word is not a *happy* one. 那個字不恰當。④喜歡的(常用在複合字中)。a trigger-*happy* gangster. 一個動不動就開槍的歹徒。**as happy as the day is long** =**as happy as a king.** 非常快樂; 非常幸福。**happy land** 樂土。**hit** (or **strike**) **the happy mean** 採取中庸之道。

hap·py-go-luck·y ['hæpɪ͵go'lʌkɪ; 'hæpigou'lʌki] *adj.* 快樂的; 聽天由命的; 隨遇而安的。to go through life in a *happy-go-lucky* fashion. 以聽天由命的方式度日。

happy landing 一路順風; 旅途愉快。

Haps·burg ['hæpsbɝg; 'hæpsbəːg] *n.* 哈布斯堡皇族(爲歐洲著名之家族, 於1276–1918年間統治奧國; 1516年, Charles I, 至1700年統治西班牙; 1438–1806年間統治神聖羅馬帝國)。(亦作 **Habsburg**)

ha·ra-ki·ri ['hɑrə'kɪrɪ, 'hærə–; 'hærə'kiri] 〖日〗*n.* 切腹自殺; 剖腹。(亦作 **hari-kari**)

ha·rangue [hə'ræŋ; hə'ræŋ] *n., v.,* **-rangued, -rangu·ing.** —*n.* ①大聲疾呼的演說。②長篇的高談闊論。②猛烈的口頭攻擊。—*v.t.* 向…作大聲疾呼演說。—*v.i.* 高談闊論。

har·ass ['hærəs, hə'ræs; 'hærəs] *v.t.* ①侵擾; 襲擊。②使困苦; 使煩惱。

har·ass·ment ['hærəsmənt; 'hærəsmənt] *n.* ①侵擾。②煩惱; 困苦。③使煩惱之事物。

Har·bin ['hɑr'bin; 'hɑː'bin] *n.* 哈爾濱「(中國東北之一都市)。」

har·bin·ger ['hɑrbɪndʒɚ; 'hɑːbindʒə] *n.* ①先驅; 先鋒。②先兆; 預兆。③(爲國王、部隊等作住宿招待等而派之)前站人員。—*v.t.* 作先鋒; 預兆。

:har·bo(u)r ['hɑrbɚ; 'hɑːbə] *n.* ①港。②避難所。The old inn was a *harbor* for tired travelers. 那家老旅館是疲乏的旅客之避難所。—*v.t.* ①庇護; 藏匿。You may be punished if you *harbor* an escaped criminal or a spy. 你若藏匿逃犯或間諜, 你是會受懲罰的。②懷藏(惡意等)。to *harbor* evil thoughts. 心懷惡意。—*v.i.* 躲藏; 潛伏; 停泊。「*n.* 避難; 保護; (船之)避難所。」

har·bor·age ['hɑrbərɪdʒ; 'hɑːbəridʒ]

harbor dues (船舶之)入港稅; 碇泊費。

har·bor·less ['hɑrbəlɪs; 'hɑːbəlis] *adj.* 無港的; 無避難所的; 無宿處的。

harbor master 港務長。

:hard [hɑrd; hɑːd] *adj.* ①堅硬的 (soft的相對字)。Stone is very *hard*. 石頭是非常堅硬的。②結實的; 堅固的。a *hard* knot. 堅固的繩結。③嚴重的; 嚴厲的。a *hard* blow. 重擊。④辛苦的; 艱難的。*hard* work. 辛苦的工作。⑤刻苦的; 堅忍的。a *hard* worker. 堅忍的工作者。⑥難堪的; 不悅的。a *hard* face. 不悅人的面孔。⑦强烈的; 狂暴的。*hard* drinking. 狂飲。⑧無情的。a *hard* heart. 無情的心。⑨含有抵銷肥皂作用之無機鹽的。*hard* water. 硬水。⑩〖美〗含酒精成分多的。*hard* liquor. 烈酒。⑪〖語音〗硬的; 不濁的。⑫無法忍受的。*hard* luck. 運氣不好。⑬艱苦的。the *hard* times of the Depression. 經濟不景氣時的艱苦生活。⑭無法否認的。*hard* facts. 無法否認的事實。⑮嚴格的。a *hard* master. 嚴師。⑯含有敵意的; 不友善的。*hard* feelings. 敵意。⑰界線分明的; 不妥協的。a *hard* line. 堅決的立場。⑱現實的; 不帶感情成分的。a *hard*, practical man. 現實而講實際的人。⑲名譽不佳的; 惡性難改的。a *hard* character. 惡性難改的人。⑳有足够準備金的。㉑現款的。*hard* cash. 現款。㉒(織物)光滑的。㉓(太空船之着落)撞毀的。a *hard* landing on the moon. 在月球上着陸撞毀。㉔(飛彈)可從地下發射室發射的。㉕〖軍〗設於地下可抗拒核子爆炸的。㉖(火箭)着地時速度在每小時100英里至300英里之間的。**a hard nut to crack** (喻)難解決的問題。**as hard as brick** 實在硬; 硬得很。**as hard as nails** a. 身體結實的; 强健的。b. 無憐憫心的; 硬心腸的。**at hard edge** 拚命; 認眞; 拚命搏鬥。**be hard on** (or **upon**) 虐待; 難堪。**be hard up** (**for money**) 手頭兒緊; 缺錢; 窮困。**hard and fast** 嚴格的; 不許變動的; 牢不可破的。**hard of hearing** 略聾; 重聽。**hard up** 〖俗〗需款孔亟; 非常需要某物。The country is *hard up* for technicians and doctors. 該國非常需要技術人員和醫生。**have a hard time of it** 受難; 受苦; 遭殃。—*adv.* ①努力地; 辛苦地; 强烈地。They tried *hard* to succeed. 他們努力工作以期成功。It is raining *hard*. 雨下得很大。He worked very *hard*. 他工作得很辛勤。②堅硬地; 堅固地。③堅牢地; 緊地。④難堪地; 苛虐地。⑤猛烈地; 竭力地。⑥接近地; 緊隨地。⑦非常地; 極。⑧聚精會神地。⑨深深受感動地。⑩立刻; 馬上。⑪用力地; 困難地。to breathe *hard*. 呼吸困難。**be hard put to it** 極端困難; 正爲難; 不知所措。**go hard with** 受苦; 受窘。**hard by** 近傍。**hard over** 〖航海〗儘量靠一邊。**look** (**gaze**, or **stare**) **hard at** 盯。**run** (**a person**) **hard** 逼近(某人)。

hard-and-fast ['hɑrdən'fæst; 'hɑːdn'fɑːst] *adj.* 不可觸犯的; 非遵守不可的。

hard·back ['hɑrdbæk; 'hɑːdbæk] *n.* 硬封面的書。

hard·bake ['hɑrd͵bek; 'hɑːdbeik] *n.* 〖英〗以砂糖或糖蜜與杏仁製成之點心。

hard·ball ['hɑrd͵bɔl; 'hɑːdbɔːl] *n.* 硬式棒球。

hard-bit·ten ['hɑrd'bɪtn̩; 'hɑːd'bitn] *adj.* 不屈服的; 倔强的; 頑强的。*hard-bitten* soldiers. 抗敵不屈的兵士。

hard·board ['hɑrd͵bord; 'hɑːdbɔːd] *n.* 〖建築〗高壓板。

hard-boil [ˈhardˈbɔɪl; ˈhaːdˈbɔil] *v.t.* 煮(蛋)至硬。

hard-boiled [ˈhardˈbɔɪld; ˈhaːdˈbɔild] *adj.* ①煮硬了的(蛋)。②〖俗〗頑强的;冷酷無情的。③理智的。④〖俚〗硬挺的(如帽子或襯衫)。 「*adj.* 辛苦得到的。」

hard·bought [ˈhard,bɔt; ˈhaːdbɔːt]

hard cash ①硬幣。②現款。

hard coal 無烟煤。

hard copy 淸稿。

hard core ①黨派中之核心中堅分子。②社會中拒絕改變而難以應付之集團。

hard-core [ˈhard,kor; ˈhaːdkouə] *adj.* ①核心分子的;中堅分子的。②明顯的;不掩藏的。

hard court 混凝土或柏油鋪的網球場。

hard·cov·er [ˈhardˈkʌvɚ; ˈhaːdˈkʌvə] *n.* 精裝書。—*adj.* 精裝書的;用硬封面裝訂的。

hard drug 毒品。

hard-earned [ˈhardˈɝnd; ˈhaːdˈəːnd] *adj.* 辛苦得到的;憑血汗掙得的。

*__hard·en__ [ˈhardn̩; ˈhaːdn] *v.t.* ①使堅强;使堅固。to *harden* the heart. 硬着心腸。②鍛鍊;使剛毅。to *harden* the body. 鍛鍊身體。③〖軍〗加强(軍事設施)以防原子彈攻擊。—*v.i.* ①變硬;變堅强。②成爲無情;堅定。③漲價。④(市場)穩定。When the speculators withdrew from the market the prices *hardened.* 當投機者從市場撤退時,物價穩下來了。*harden off* 使(植物、苗、枝等)受冷而變强。 「①硬化。②硬化劑。」

hard·en·ing [ˈhardn̩ɪŋ; ˈhaːdniŋ] *n.*

hard-fa·vo(u)red [ˈhardˈfevɚd; ˈhaːdˈfeivəd] *adj.* 面貌嚴厲的;面貌難看的。(亦作 **hard-featured**)

hard-fist·ed [ˈhardˈfɪstɪd; ˈhaːdˈfistid] *adj.* ①有結實之雙手的;有臂力的。②吝嗇的;自私的。③殘酷的。(亦作 **hardfisted**)

hard goods 耐用商品(如汽車、傢具、家庭電器等)。 「(北美產)類繡線菊之灌木。」

hard·hack [ˈhard,hæk; ˈhaːdhæk] *n.*

hard·hand·ed [ˈhardˈhændɪd; ˈhaːdˈhændid] *adj.* ①因勞動而手粗硬的。②手段强硬的;苛刻的。(亦作 **hard-handed**)

hard·hat [ˈhard,hæt; ˈhaːdhæt] *n.* ①(工人戴的)安全帽;頭盔。②建築工人。③〖美〗直言的保守分子;極端的愛國分子。

hard·head [ˈhard,hɛd; ˈhaːdhed] *n.* 講求實際的人;不感情用事的人。

hard-head·ed [ˈhardˈhɛdɪd; ˈhaːdˈhedid] *adj.* ①精明的;冷靜的。②實際的;不流於空想的。③頑固的。

hard-heart·ed [ˈhardˈhartɪd; ˈhaːdˈhaːtid] *adj.* 硬心腸的;無情的。

hard-hit·ting [ˈhardˈhɪtɪŋ; ˈhaːdˈhitiŋ] *adj.* 能用力打擊的;用力打擊的。

har·di·hood [ˈhardɪ,hud; ˈhaːdihud] *n.* ①大膽;剛毅。②蠻勇;厚顏。③健壯。

har·di·ly [ˈhardḷɪ; ˈhaːdili] *adv.* ①大膽地;剛毅地。②魯莽地。③耐勞刻苦地。

har·di·ness [ˈhardɪnɪs; ˈhaːdinis] *n.* ①强壯;耐勞;堅强。②大膽;厚顏。

hard knocks 〖美俗〗挫折;艱苦。

hard labor 勞役;苦役。

hard line 死硬路線(尤指政治方面一成不變的態度)。 「主張採用强硬政策的。」

hard-line [ˈhard,laɪn; ˈhaːdlain] *adj.*

hard-lin·er [ˈhardˈlaɪnɚ; ˈhaːdˈlainə] *n.* 〖俗〗主張採取强硬行動者;不妥協者。

‡**hard·ly** [ˈhardlɪ; ˈhaːdli] *adv.* ①幾乎不;大概不。I could *hardly* understand him. 我不大能懂他的意思。②剛剛;恰好(與 when 連用)。He had *hardly* reached there when it began to snow. 他剛一到達那裏,就下雪了。③努力地;刻苦地。money *hardly* earned. 辛苦賺來的錢。④嚴厲的;刻薄的。to deal *hardly* with a person. 待人苛刻。***hardly ever*** 很少。***think*** (or ***speak***) ***hardly of*** 把…想得(說得)很壞。 「人造寶石。」

hard mass ①冒充寶石用的硬玻璃。②

hard money ①可與黃金或其他貴金屬兌換的貨幣。②以平衡支付或運出黃金來維持外匯率不變的貨幣。③銀行緊縮信用、提高利率及其他限制投資政策下的貨幣。

hard·mouthed [ˈhardˈmauðd; ˈhaːdˈmauðd] *adj.* ①(馬等)不易駕御的。②頑强的。③言語粗暴的。

*__hard·ness__ [ˈhardnɪs; ˈhaːdnis] *n.* ①堅硬;硬度。②困難;難解。③嚴厲;冷酷;無情。④飛彈基地能抵禦核子攻擊的能力。

hard news 政治、外交等重要新聞。

hard-nosed [ˈhard,nozd; ˈhaːdnouzd] *adj.* =**hard-headed.**

hard-of-hear·ing [ˈhardəvˈhɪrɪŋ; ˈhaːdəvˈhiəriŋ] *adj.* 不良於聽的;重聽的。

hard·pan [ˈhard,pæn; ˈhaːdpæn] *n.* 〖美〗①(軟土下面的)硬質地質。②堅固的基礎;實質。to get down to *hardpan.* 討論基本問題。③最低點。

hard-pressed [ˈhardˈprɛst; ˈhaːdˈprest] *adj.* ①受强烈之壓力的;受緊壓的。②財政緊迫的。 「(亦作 **hurds**)」

hards [hardz; haːdz] *n.pl.* 麻屑;毛屑。

hard sauce 在牛油中加砂糖、香料,製成的乳脂狀調味品(澆在布丁、餅之類的上面)。

hard science 基本科學(諸如物理、化學、生物、地質、天文等學)。 「說服工作。」

hard sell ①積極的推銷技術。②困難的

hard-sell [ˈhardˈsɛl; ˈhaːdˈsel] *adj., v.,* **-sold, -sell·ing.** —*adj.* 有力而積極的。—*v.t.* 積極推銷。

hard-set [ˈhardˈsɛt; ˈhaːdˈset] *adj.* ①在困難中的。②變堅固的。③將要孵化的(蛋)。④堅決的;頑固的。⑤空腹的;飢餓的。

hard-shell [ˈhard,ʃɛl; ˈhaːdʃel] *adj.* ①有硬殼的。②〖美俗〗頑固的;不妥協的。(亦作 **hard-shelled**)

*__hard·ship__ [ˈhardʃɪp; ˈhaːdʃip] *n.* 困苦;艱難;辛苦。to bear *hardship* without complaint. 苦而不怨。 「飛彈發射基地。」

hard site 建築在地下,可防原子彈攻擊的

hard·stand [ˈhard,stænd; ˈhaːdstænd] *n.* 可停放車輛、飛機等的堅硬地面。

hard·tack [ˈhard,tæk; ˈhaːdˈtæk] *n.* 無鹽的硬餅乾(作海員船上乾糧或軍用口糧)。

hard·top, hard-top [ˈhard,tap; ˈhaːdtɔp] *n.* ①室內電影院。②有固定金屬頂篷,窗與窗間無支柱之汽車。

*__hard·ware__ [ˈhard,wɛr; ˈhaːd-wɛə] *n.* ①五金器具。to deal in *hardware.* 做五金生意。②軍火、武器等。③電子計算機、核子反應器等的零件。④(用於飛彈、飛機等中的)機器、零件。⑤〖電腦〗硬體;硬具。

hard·wood [ˈhard,wud; ˈhaːd-wud] *n.* ①硬木(如橡木、桃花心木、烏木)。②闊葉樹;非針葉樹。③闊葉樹之木材。—*adj.* 硬木的;硬木製成的。

hard·work·ing [ˈhard,wɝkɪŋ; ˈhaːd,wəːkiŋ] *adj.* 苦幹的;不辭辛勞的。

Har·dy [ˈhardɪ; ˈhaːdi] *n.* 哈代(Thomas, 1840–1928, 英國詩人及小說家)。

***har·dy** ['hardɪ; 'ha:di] *adj.*, **-di·er, -di·est.** ①强壯的。②需要膽量與勇敢的。*Hardy* sports are now in vogue. 需要膽量的運動現在很時髦。③耐寒的(植物)。④魯莽的;輕率的。a *hardy* assertion. 輕率的斷語。⑤能吃苦耐勞的。

hare** [hɛr; hɛə] *n., pl.* **hares** or **hare,** *v.* —*n.* 野兎。 ***as mad as a March hare 狂若三月之兎。***hare and hounds*** 撒紙追逐遊戲。***make a hare of a man*** 騙人。***run with the hare and hunt with the hounds*** 兩面討好。 —*v.i.* 〖主英〗快跑。

hare·bell ['hɛr,bɛl; 'hɛəbel] *n.* 〖植物〗山小菜;藍鈴花。(蘇亦作 **bluebell**)

hare·brained ['hɛr'brend; 'hɛə-'breind] *adj.* 輕率的;粗心的。

hare·lip ['hɛr'lɪp; 'hɛə'lip] *n.* 兎唇。 —**ped,** *adj.*

har·em ['hɛrəm; 'hɛərem] *n.* ①(回教徒之)閨房。②(妻、妾、女僕等)女眷。③爲一個雄動物所控制之許多雌動物。

har·i·cot ['hærɪ,ko; 'hærikou] *n.*①扁豆;扁豆莢。②蔬菜燉羊肉。

haricot bean 扁豆。

hark [hark; ha:k] *v.i.* 聽(常用於命令語句)。*Hark!* 聽!—*v.t.* 〖古〗聽。***hark after*** 追隨。***Hark away*** (or ***forward***)*!* (嗾狗)去!跑! ***hark back*** **a.** (獵犬)循原路而返以求嗅跡。**b.** 復原;歸還;舊事重提。

har·le·quin ['harləkwɪn; 'ha:likwin] *n.* ①(常 H-)一種趣劇或啞劇中的諧角。②丑角。—*adj.* ①滑稽的;可笑的。②斑色的。③雜湊的。

har·le·quin·ade [,harləkwɪn'ed; ,ha:likwi'neid] *n.* ①(戲劇中,尤指啞劇中)以丑角爲主的一幕;丑角戲。②諧謔;滑稽。

har·lot ['harlət; 'ha:lət] *n.* 妓女。 —*adj.* 妓女的。

har·lot·ry ['harlətrɪ; 'ha:lətri] *n.* ①賣淫行爲。②淫婦;娼妓(罵女人語)。

:harm [harm; ha:m] *n.* 傷害; 損害; 害處。to do somebody *harm* (*or* do *harm* to somebody). 於某人有害; 爲害某人。There is no *harm* in doing that. 那樣做並無害處。***Harm set, harm get.*** 害人反害己。 —*v.t.* 傷害;損害;有害於。

har·mat·tan [,harmə'tæn; ,ha:mə-'tæn] *n.* (12—2月間自 Sahara 地區向非洲西海岸吹的) 含塵砂熱風。

***harm·ful** ['harmfəl; 'ha:mful] *adj.* 有害的。*harmful* plants. 有害的植物。—**ly,** *adv.* —**ness,** *n.*

***harm·less** ['harmlɪs; 'ha:mlis] *adj.* ①無害處的;無損害的。It's quite a *harmless* habit. 那完全是一個於人無害的習慣。②無辜的; 無惡意的。—**ly,** *adv.* —**ness,** *n.*

har·mon·ic [har'manɪk; ha:'mɔnik] *adj.*(亦作 **harmonical**)①調和的; 和諧的。② 〖音樂〗和音的。***harmonic conjugates*** 〖數學〗調和共軛素。 ***harmonic function*** 〖數學〗調和函數。 ***harmonic mean*** 〖數學〗調和中項。***harmonic progression*** 〖數學〗調和級數。***harmonic proportion*** 〖數學〗調和比例。***harmonic tones*** 〖音樂〗陪音;和音。—*n.* ① 〖音樂〗陪音;和音。②〖數學〗調和函數。 —**al·ly,** *adv.*

har·mon·i·ca[har'manɪkə; ha:'mɔnikə] *n.* 口琴。(亦作 **mouth organ**)

har·mon·ics [har'manɪks; ha:'mɔniks] *n.* 〖音樂〗和聲學。

***har·mo·ni·ous** [har'monɪəs; ha:'mounjəs, -niəs] *adj.* ①協調的; 調和的。*harmonious* colors. 調和的色彩。②和睦的。*harmonious* neighbors. 和睦的鄰居。③音調和諧的;悅耳的。—**ly,** *adv.*

har·mo·nist ['harmənɪst; 'ha:mənist] *n.* ①和聲學者;對和聲有特長的作曲家。②詩人。③四福音書之對照研究者。④使某事物調和或一致的人。

har·mo·ni·um [har'monɪəm; ha:'mounjəm, -niəm] *n.* 小風琴。

har·mo·nize ['harmə,naɪz; 'ha:mənaiz] *v.*, **-nized, -niz·ing.**—*v.t.* ①使調和;使一致。②〖音樂〗加調和音(使成諧調)。—*v.i.* ①和諧;一致;諧調;相稱;調和。②和諧地演奏或唱。—**har·mo·ni·za·tion,** *n.*

***har·mo·ny** ['harmənɪ; 'ha:məni] *n., pl.* **-nies.** ①協調; 調和。the *harmony* of color in nature. 大自然界的色彩的協調。②和睦; 和平共處。They worked in perfect *harmony*. 他們合作無間。③〖音樂〗和聲; 和聲學。He is a master of melody and *harmony*. 他是一個精於旋律與和聲的人。④對同一題目的不同敍述中的相同之處;一致點。

har·ness** ['harnɪs; 'ha:nis] *n.* ①馬具。②降落傘繫在身體上的繩子。③牽小孩走路使不會摔倒的繩帶等。④〖古〗甲冑。 ***die in harness 殉職。 ***in harness*** **a.** 在從事經常的工作中;在工作中。 After his illness he longed to get back *in harness*. 他病後渴望重新回到他的工作崗位上去。 **b.** 在同等地位合作。 ***work*** (or ***run***) ***in harness*** 共同工作。—*v.t.* ①束以馬具; 駕(馬)於車。to *harness* a horse to a carriage. 駕馬於車(使之工作)。②利用(水、瀑布等)使產生動力。③控制;駕御。④〖古〗披甲冑於;穿(甲冑)。

harp** [harp; ha:p] *n.* ①豎琴。②豎琴形之物。③(H-)〖天文〗天琴座。④〖美俚〗愛爾蘭人。—*v.i.* ①彈豎琴。②不停地說 〖on, upon〗. ***harp on 反覆申說; 囉囉唻唻。 to *harp on* the glories of a former day. 反覆述說往昔光榮事蹟。

har·per ['harpɚ; 'ha:pə] *n.* 彈豎琴者;豎琴師。 「琴者(尤指職業豎琴師)。

harp·ist ['harpɪst; 'ha:pist] *n.* 彈豎

har·poon [har'pun; ha:'pu:n] *n.* 魹;魚叉。 —*v.t.* 以魚叉投射(魚)。

harpoon gun 發射魚叉之砲;捕鯨砲。

harp·si·chord ['harpsɪ,kɔrd; 'ha:psikɔ:d] *n.* 大鍵琴 (鋼琴的前身,盛行於十六、十七、十八世紀)。

Har·py ['harpɪ; 'ha:pi] *n., pl.* **-pies.** ①〖希臘神話〗首及身似女人,而翅膀、尾巴及爪似鳥之怪物。②(h-) 殘酷貪婪之人。③(h-) 一種美洲熱帶地方之短翼鷹; 角鷹 (=harpy eagle).

har·que·bus(e) ['harkwɪbəs; 'ha:kwibəs] *n., pl.* **-bus·es.** 火繩槍。

har·ri·dan ['hærədən; 'hæridən] *n.* 年老色衰之娼妓;惡婦;醜婆。

har·ri·er ['hærɪɚ; 'hæriə] *n.* ①獵兎狗。②(*pl.*) 獵兎的人與狗。③越野賽跑者。④一種掠吃小動物之鷹。⑤掠奪者;蹂躪者。

Har·ris tweed ['hærɪs~; 'hæris~] 手織粗呢(蘇格蘭 Harris 島產)。

har·row ['hæro; 'hærou] *n.* 耙。***under the harrow*** 受苦;遭難。—*v.t.* ①耙掘。②傷害;使傷心。③使不舒適;使受痛苦。—*v.i.*

受耙。「*adj.* 悲慘的；痛心的；傷心的。」
har·row·ing 〔'hærəwɪŋ; 'hærouiŋ〕
***har·ry** 〔'hærɪ; 'hæri〕 *v.*, **-ried, -ry·ing,** *n.*—*v.t.* ①掠奪；蹂躪。②使受痛苦；使苦惱。③不斷地襲擊以困擾之。—*v.i.* 作擾亂性之攻擊；掠奪。—*n.* 掠奪；襲擊；困擾。
***harsh** 〔harʃ; hɑːʃ〕 *adj.* ①粗糙的；刺耳的；刺目的。a *harsh* voice. 刺耳的聲音。②嚴厲的；苛刻的。a *harsh* judge (judgment, punishment). 嚴厲的法官(審判、懲罰)。③殘酷的；無情的。a *harsh* man. 一個無情的人。④崎嶇不平的。a *harsh* coast. 崎嶇的海岸。⑤(味道)澀口的。—**ly,** *adv.* —**ness,** *n.*
hart 〔hart; hɑːt〕 *n., pl.* **harts, hart.** 雄鹿(尤指五歲以上之雄紅鹿)。
har·tal 〔har'tal; 'hɑːtɑːl, -təl〕 *n.* (印度甘地派之)杯葛運動；(印度國民運動者對英國貨之)抵制運動。
har·te·beest 〔'hartə,bist; 'hɑːtibiːst〕 *n., pl.* **-beest, -beests.** (南非產之)大羚羊。(亦作 **hartbeest**)
harts·horn 〔'harts,hɔrn; 'hɑːtshɔːn〕 *n.* ①雄鹿之角。②鹿角精(昔自雄鹿角採取之碳酸銨)。「tʌŋ〕 *n.* 〖植物〗一種羊齒植物。」
hart's-tongue 〔'harts,tʌŋ; 'hɑːts-
har·um-scar·um 〔'hɛrəm'skɛrəm; 'hɛərəm'skɛərəm〕 *adj.* 輕率的；冒失的；鹵莽的；狂妄的。—*adv.* 輕率地；鹵莽地。—*n.* ①輕率漢；冒失鬼。②粗率的行爲。
Har·vard 〔'harvəd; 'hɑːvəd〕 *n.* 美國哈佛大學(在Massachusetts州 Cambridge, 哈佛學院創立於1636年，爲美國最早之學院)。
***har·vest** 〔'harvɪst; 'hɑːvist〕 *n.* ①收穫；收穫量；收穫物。②收穫期。③成果；結果。to reap the *harvest* of one's hard work. 收得辛勤工作的成果。—*v.t.* ①收割；收穫。②定時殺死(受保護之劣質野生動物)以免擁擠。—*v.i.* 收割。
harvest bug (mite, or **tick)** 秋蚲(於秋天收穫期困擾農民的一種沙蚤)。
har·vest·er 〔'harvɪstə; 'hɑːvistə〕 *n.* ①收穫者。②收割機。
harvest fly 秋蟬；(鳴於收穫期之)蟬。
harvest home ①收穫終結。②慶祝收穫節。③收穫節所唱之歌。
har·vest·man 〔'harvɪstmən; 'hɑːvistmən〕 *n.* ①收割者。②長脚蜘蛛。
harvest moon 秋分前後之滿月。
harvest mouse 一種歐洲產的小鼠，築窩於穀莖叢間。「*n.* 收穫；收割；收割物。」
har·vest·ry 〔'harvɪstrɪ; 'hɑːvistri〕
‡**has** 〔hæz; hæz〕 *v.* have 的第三人稱，單數，現在式，直說法。
has-been 〔'hæz,bɪn; 'hæzbin〕 *n.* 〖俗〗過時代的人或物；曾經紅過的人。
ha·sen·pfef·fer 〔'hazən,(p)fɛfə; 'hɑːzən,(p)fefə〕 *n.* 加香料燜製之鹽漬兔肉。
hash 〔hæʃ; hæʃ〕 *n.* ①熟肉末炒馬鈴薯泥。②混雜；混雜物。③亂七八糟。***make a hash of*** 弄糟。***settle a person's hash*** 使服貼；使啞口無言；使屈服而不再找麻煩。—*v.t.* ①切細。②〖俗〗弄成亂七八糟。③徹底討論或檢討。***hash over*** 〖俚〗重行討論；檢討。
hash·eesh, hash·ish 〔'hæʃiʃ; 'hæʃiːʃ〕 *n.* 印度大麻葉製造的一種麻醉藥。
hash house 〖美俚〗經濟小吃店。
hash mark 〖美軍俚〗作服役年資識別而縫在制服左袖上的斜布條(每條代表三年)。
hash-sling·er 〔'hæʃ,slɪŋə; 'hæʃ,sliŋə〕 *n.* 〖俚〗hash house 的男女侍者。
has·let 〔'hæslɪt; 'heizlit〕 *n.* (猪等之)臟腑；肚雜。(亦作 **harslet**)
‡**has·n't** 〔'hæznt; 'hæznt〕 =**has not.**
hasp 〔hæsp; hɑːsp〕 *n.* ①門窗、箱子等之鐵釦。②一束紗或線。—*v.t.* 用鐵釦扣上。
has·sle 〔'hæsl; 'hæsl〕 *n., v.*, **-sled, -sling.** —*n.* (亦作 **hassel**) 〖俗〗(激烈的)爭論或爭吵。—*v.t.* 〖美俚〗虐待；騷擾。
has·sock 〔'hæsək; 'hæsək〕 *n.* ①膝墊(祈禱時跪用)。②一種有墊子的矮脚凳。③草叢。
hast 〔hæst; hæst〕 *v.* 〖古〗have 之第二人稱，單數，現在式，直說法。"Thou hast" 意爲 "you have".「〖植物〗戟狀的。」
has·tate 〔'hæstet; 'hæsteit〕 *adj.*
haste** 〔hest; heist〕 *n., v.*, **hast·ed, hast·ing.** —*n.* 匆忙；急忙。He went off in great *haste.* 他匆匆離去。Haste makes waste.*** =**More haste, less speed.** 欲速則不達；忙中有錯。***in haste*** **a.** 匆忙地。**b.** 草率地。***make haste*** 急忙；匆忙。—*v.t.* & *v.i.* =**hasten.**
***has·ten** 〔'hesn; 'heisn〕 *v.t.* 催促；促進。—*v.i.* 趕快；急行。to *hasten* away. 急忙離去。
***hast·i·ly** 〔'hestlɪ; 'heistili〕 *adv.* ①匆忙地。②草率地。She had married *hastily,* and as *hastily* grown weary of her choice. 她草草結婚，並很快地對她所選擇的丈夫發生厭惡。
***hast·y** 〔'hestɪ; 'heisti〕 *adj.*, **hast·i·er, hast·i·est.** ①匆匆的；急忙的。a *hasty* visit. 匆匆的訪問。②草率的；率爾的。③易怒的；壞脾氣的。④生氣或心情不好時所說的或所作的。⑤短暫的。a *hasty* glance. 短暫的一瞥。—**hast·i·ness,** *n.*
‡**hat** 〔hæt; hæt〕 *n., v.*, **hat·ted, hat·ting.** —*n.* ①帽(通常指有邊者，以別於無邊的 bonnet, cap等)。②天主教紅衣主教所戴的紅帽。③紅衣主教的職位與職務。***hat in hand*** 恭謹；謙和。***My hat!*** 〖俚〗唉呀(表驚訝等的驚嘆句)！***send*** (or ***pass***) ***round the hat*** 募捐。***take off one's hat to*** 對…表示敬意。***talk through one's hat*** 〖俚〗說大話；吹牛。***toss*** (or ***throw***) ***one's hat in the ring*** 參加比賽；(尤指)參加競選。***under one's hat*** 〖俚〗獨自地；祕密地。—*v.t.* 戴帽子。The lady was beautifully gowned and *hatted.* 那婦人穿漂亮的衣服，戴美麗的帽子。
hat·band 〔'hæt,bænd; 'hætbænd〕 *n.* ①帽子的緞帶。②帽上服喪之黑帶。
hat-block 〔'hæt,blak; 'hætblɔk〕 *n.* 帽子之木型。
hat·box 〔'hæt,baks; 'hætbɔks〕 *n.* 帽盒。
***hatch**[1] 〔hætʃ; hætʃ〕 *v.t.* ①孵(卵)；孵(雛)。to *hatch* eggs. 孵卵。②陰謀；圖謀。to *hatch* a plot. 暗中圖謀。③計畫；安排。—*v.i.* 可孵出小鷄；(小鷄)被孵出。Three chickens *hatched* today. 三隻小鷄今天孵出來了。—*n.* ①孵。②一窩所孵之雛。
hatch**[2] *n.* ①艙口；艙門。②地板或天花板上之開口。③艙口蓋；地窖蓋。④水門；閘。⑤(上下開合門的)下半扇門。⑥〖俚〗喉嚨。under hatches*** 在甲板下；被關着。
hatch[3] *n.* 影線(表示陰影之細密平行線條或交叉線條)。—*v.t.* 在…上畫或雕刻影線。
hat·check girl 〔'hæt,tʃɛk～; 'hættʃek～〕 飯店、夜總會等的衣帽間女服務生。
hatch·er·y 〔'hætʃərɪ; 'hætʃəri〕 *n., pl.* **-er·ies.** 孵卵所；魚卵孵化所。
hatch·et** 〔'hætʃɪt; 'hætʃit〕 *n.* ①手斧；斧頭。②(北美印第安人的)戰斧；鉞。bury***

the hatchet (or *tomahawk*) 修睦;媾和。*dig up* (or *take up*) *the hatchet* 開戰。*throw the helve after the hatchet* 吃了虧又吃虧;陪了夫人又折兵。

hatchet face 瘦削之臉。

hatchet man 〖俗〗①職業兇手。②破壞他人(尤指候選人)名譽的作家或演說者。③替上司做惡人的人。

hatch·et·y [ˈhætʃətɪ; ˈhætʃəti] *adj.* ①斧狀的。②瘦削的。

hatch·ing [ˈhætʃɪŋ; ˈhætʃiŋ] *n.* (細平行線形成的)陰影;影線;影線法。

hatch·ment [ˈhætʃmənt; ˈhætʃmənt] *n.* 忌中紋標(方形黑框中畫死者之紋章者,揭於門前或墓前)。

hatch·way [ˈhætʃˌwe; ˈhætʃwei] *n.* ①艙口。②地板口;屋頂口;地窖口。

‡**hate** [het; heit] *v.*, **hat·ed, hat·ing,** *n.* —*v.t.* ①憎惡;憎恨。My cat *hates* dogs. 我的貓恨狗。②不喜歡。I *hate* to trouble you (*or* I *hate* troubling you). 我不喜歡麻煩你。—*v.i.* 憎恨。She *hated* easily. 她容易對人懷恨。—*n.* ①憎恨;憎惡。He was filled with *hate* for his enemy. 他對敵人滿懷憎恨。②被憎恨之物。Snakes are her special *hate.* 蛇是她特別憎恨的東西。

*__hate·ful__ [ˈhetfəl; ˈheitful] *adj.* ①可惡的;可恨的。②表示憎惡的。*hateful* glances. 表示憎惡的目光。—**ly,** *adv.* —**ness,** *n.*

hat·er [ˈhetɚ; ˈheitə] *n.* 懷恨者。

hat·ful [ˈhætfʊl; ˈhætful] *n., pl.* **-fuls.** ①一帽所裝之量。②很多。I mean to earn a *hatful* of money. 我打算賺許多錢。

hath [hæθ; hæθ] *v.* 〖古〗有(=has).

hat·less [ˈhætlɪs; ˈhætlis] *adj.* 不戴帽的;無帽的。

hat·pin [ˈhætˌpɪn; ˈhætpin] *n.* (女帽之)帽針。

hat·rack [ˈhætˌræk; ˈhæt-ræk] *n.* 帽架。

*__ha·tred__ [ˈhetrɪd; ˈheitrid] *n.* 憎恨;仇恨;憎惡。He looked at me with *hatred* in his eyes. 他以憎恨的目光望着我。

hat·ter [ˈhætɚ; ˈhætə] *n.* 製帽人;帽商。*as mad as a hatter* 極瘋狂;狂怒。

hat tree 立式衣帽架。

hau·berk [ˈhɔbɝk; ˈhɔːbəːk] *n.* 鱗鎧;鎖子鎧(中古時代所用)。

*__haugh·ty__ [ˈhɔtɪ; ˈhɔːti] *adj.*, **-ti·er, -ti·est.** 傲慢的;驕傲的;不遜的。a *haughty* smile. 驕傲的微笑。—**haugh·ti·ly,** *adv.* —**haugh·ti·ness,** *n.*

*__haul__ [hɔl; hɔːl] *v.t.* ①拖;拉;曳。②運輸。③使降下〖常 down〗. to *haul* down the flag. 降旗。④逮捕而押至法庭等〖常 before, in, to, into〗. —*v.i.* ①拖;拉;曳。②改變方向。The wind *hauled* around to the east. 風向轉往東。*haul a person over the coals* 向某人吹毛求疵;嚴責某人。*haul down one's flag* (or *colors*) 投降。*haul off* a. 將船開駛。b. 撤退;縮手準備出擊。*haul on* (or *to*) *the wind* 駛往迎風方向。*haul up* a. 改轉航路。b. 使船轉為迎風前進。c. 帶到上司面前受斥責。d. 停止。The boats *hauled up* at the pier. 船在碼頭停泊。—*n.* ①用力拖拉。②拖拉的距離。a long *haul.* 長距離的拖拉。③所拖拉之量(尤指一網所打之魚);努力的結果;收穫。a good *haul* of fish. 一滿網之魚。*long haul* a. 長時間。b. 長距離。c. 船隻被拉上岸作較長期之修理、貯藏等。*short haul* a. 短時間。b. 短距離。c. 船隻被拉上岸作短期之修理、貯藏等。

haul·age [ˈhɔlɪdʒ; ˈhɔːlidʒ] *n.* 拖曳;索引力;(貨物之)搬運;(貨物之)運費。

haul·er [ˈhɔlɚ; ˈhɔːlə] *n.* 拖曳者;貨運馬車夫;(坑內)礦箱搬運者。(英亦作 **haulier**)

haulm [hɔm; hɔːm] *n.* ①(草等之)莖。②〖英〗豆稭;麥稈(集合稱)。(亦作 **halm**)

haunch [hɔntʃ, hantʃ; hɔːntʃ] *n.* ①腰;臀部。②(動物之)腰部。③〖建築〗拱腰。*squat* (or *sit*) *on one's haunches* 蹲(坐)下。

*__haunt__ [hɔnt, hant; hɔːnt] *v.t.* ①常到;常至;(鬼)出沒。This old castle is said to be *haunted.* 這座古堡據說有鬼。②縈繞於心。Memories of his youth *haunted* the old man. 這老人常想起青年時代。③常與…為伍。—*v.i.* ①常去或停留某處。②(鬼)出沒。—*n.* ①(常 *pl.*)常到的地方。to revisit the *haunts* of one's schooldays. 重遊學生時代所常到的地方。②〖方〗鬼。

haunt·ed [ˈhɔntɪd; ˈhɔːntid] *adj.* ①鬼常出沒的;鬼作祟的。a *haunted* house. 鬼屋。②縈繞於懷的。③煩擾的;困惑的。

haunt·ing [ˈhɔntɪŋ; ˈhɔːntiŋ] *adj.* 常浮現於腦海中的;不易忘懷的。a *haunting* melody. 常常想起來的調子。—*n.* 常到;常去;(鬼等之)出沒;縈繞於懷。

Haupt·mann [ˈhauptmən, ˈhauptmɑn; ˈhauptmən, ˈhauptmɑːn] *n.* 霍普特曼(Gerhart, 1862–1946, 德國劇作家、小說家及詩人,曾獲1912年諾貝爾文學獎)。

haust. 〖處方〗一口(=a draught).

haut·boy [ˈhobɔɪ; ˈoubɔi] *n.* =**oboe.** —**ist,** *n.*

haute cou·ture [ˌotkuˈtuɚ; ˌoutkuːˈtuə] 〖法〗①(製銷新款式的)高級服裝店。②高級服裝設計師。③新流行服裝款式。

haute cui·sine [ˌotkwiˈzin; ˌoutkwiːˈziːn] 〖法〗①高級烹調術。②名菜佳餚。

haute é·cole [ˌoteˈkɔl; ˌouteiˈkɔːl] 〖法〗高等馬術。

hau·teur [hoˈtɝ, o-; ouˈtəː, ˈoutəː] *n.* 傲慢;擺架子。

haut monde [oˈmɔ̃d; ouˈmɔ̃d] 〖法〗上流社會(=high society).

Ha·van·a [həˈvænə; həˈvænə] *n.* ①哈瓦那(古巴首都)。②哈瓦那雪茄煙。

‡**have** [hæv; hæv] *v.*, **had, hav·ing,** *aux. v., n.* —*v.t.* ①有;包括有。I *have* a house in the country. 我在鄉間有一幢房屋。②令;使。*Have* him shut the door. 叫他把門關上。③必須;不得不(與 infinitive 連用)。Men *have* to eat. 人必須吃東西。④獲得;取用;吃;喝。Will you *have* another cup of tea? 你要再喝一杯茶嗎? ⑤有(指抽象的事物);表現。I *have* no fear. 我無恐懼。⑥享受;經歷。Did you *have* a pleasant time? 你過得快樂嗎? ⑦進行;作。to *have* a talk with him. 和他作一次談話。Let me *have* a look (a try, etc.) (=Let me look, etc.). 讓我看一看(試一試等)。⑧允許;准;忍耐(多用否定式)。He won't *have* any noise while he is reading. 當他讀書時,他不許有鬧聲。⑨說;宣稱;認為。So gossip *has* it. 傳說如此。⑩記憶;牢記。He *has* the directions in mind. 他將命令牢記在心。⑪懂;通曉。He *has* no Latin. 他不懂拉丁文。⑫心存;蓄懷。I *have* your idea now. 現在我明白你的意思了。⑬生;生產。She is going to *have* a baby. 她要生小孩了。⑭有(指人與人之間的某種關係)。She *has* three brothers. 她有三個弟兄。⑮〖俗〗戰勝;使迷惑;打敗。He *had* me in that argument. 在那次辯論中,他戰勝了我。

⑯欺騙；瞞。⑰邀請；招待。We *had* John over for dinner last Saturday. 上星期六我們邀請了約翰一同吃晚飯。⑱表示；表現。*Have* pity on him! 可憐可憐他吧！***had better*** (or ***best***) 應該；最好。***had rather*** (or ***sooner***) 寧願。***have and (to) hold*** 保有。***have a person up*** 使某人出庭而受到控訴(常用於被動式中)。***have at (a person)*** 攻擊(某人)。***Have done!*** (=Stop!) 算了吧！***have got*** 〖英俗〗有 (=have). ***have had it*** 〖俚〗a. 厭了；够了；膩了。b. 失敗；失去昔日威風。c. 獲得最後一次表現的機會而未能善加利用。d. 不再流行。***have it*** a. 勝過。The ayes *had it*. 贊成者占多數。b. 打；懲罰(參看 Let him have it!)。***have it coming*** 〖俗〗活該；應得。***have it in for*** 〖俗〗懷恨。***have it on (a person)*** 勝過(某人)。***have it out***(打仗)打出個結果；(辯論)辯出個結果。***have it out with someone*** 同某人去理論。***Have it your own way!*** 隨你的便吧(拒絕進一步討論或辯論時用之)。***have nothing on*** 並不較…强。Kerensky thought Napoleon *had nothing on* him. 克倫斯基認爲拿破崙並不比他强。***have nothing to do with*** 與…無關。This *has nothing to do with* you. 這個與你無關。***have on*** a. 穿(衣)；戴(帽)。b. 有…安排或計畫。What do you *have on* for tomorrow night? 你明天晚上有何計畫？***have to do with*** a. 與…有關。This *has* something *to do with* you. 它與你有關。b. 爲…的伴侶、夥友、或朋友；與…交往。***Let him have it!*** a. 〖俗〗懲罰他！b. 坦白告訴他你對他的看法。—*aux. v.* 用以形成完成時態。I *have* finished it. 我做完了。—*n.* ①〖俚〗騙子。②(常 *pl.*) 有產者；富人。the *haves* and have-nots. 富人與窮人。〖注意〗**Have you...?** 與 **Do you have...?** 在英國前者問目前特殊的事例，後者則問通常的習慣。但在美國趨勢是一律不用 Have you...? 而用 Do you have...?

have·lock ['hævlɑk; 'hævlɔk, -lək] *n.* 覆於軍帽上將頸後及兩頰遮住的遮陽布。

ha·ven ['hevən; 'heivn] *n.* ①港口；避風港。②避難所；安息所。—*v.t.* ①安置(船舶)於港中。②給予避難安息之所；庇護。

have-not ['hævˌnɑt; 'hævnɔt] *n.* 〖俗〗窮人；貧窮或缺乏資源之國家。

:have·n't ['hævn̩t; 'hævnt] = **have not.**

ha·ver ['hevɚ; 'heivə] 〖蘇〗 *v.i.* 說廢話。—*n.* (*pl.*) 多嘴；廢話。

hav·er·sack ['hævɚˌsæk; 'hævəsæk] *n.* 行軍糧袋；乾糧袋。

hav·ing ['hæviŋ; 'hæviŋ] *n.* ①所有；持有。②所有物；財產。③(常 *pl.*) 〖蘇〗行爲；態度。

hav·oc ['hævək; 'hævək] *n.* 大破壞；蹂躪；毀壞。The earthquake caused terrible *havoc*. 那次地震造成了可怕的毀壞。***play havoc with*** (or ***among***); ***make havoc of*** 大肆破壞。

haw[1] [hɔ; hɔː] *n.* ①山楂；山楂之實。②籬；園地；庭園。

haw[2] *interj., n.* 呵(話頓住時的發聲)；支吾聲；囁嚅聲。—*v.i.* 言語支吾；囁嚅。

haw[3] *n.* ①〖獸醫〗(馬、犬等之)瞬膜。②(常 *pl.*) 瞬膜炎。

haw[4] *interj.* 〖美〗豁(叱馬使向左轉之叫聲)。—*v.t.* 使(馬)向左轉。—*v.i.* (馬)向左轉。

Ha·wai·i [hə'wɑijə; hɑː'waiiː, hə'w-, -'wɑːiː] *n.* ①夏威夷(美國之一州，首府火奴魯魯Honolulu)。②夏威夷羣島(=Hawaiian Islands)。③夏威夷島。

Ha·wai·ian [hə'waɪən; hɑː'waii-ən, hə'w-, -'waijən] *adj.* 夏威夷的。—*n.* 夏威夷人；夏威夷語。

Hawaiian Islands 夏威夷羣島(構成美國夏威夷州之一羣島嶼)。

haw·finch ['hɔˌfɪntʃ; 'hɔːfintʃ] *n.* 歐洲產之蠟嘴鳥。

haw-haw ['hɔ'hɔ; 'hɔː'hɔː] *interj., n.* 哈哈。—*v.i.* 哈哈大笑；縱聲高笑。

***hawk**[1] [hɔk; hɔːk] *n.* ①鷹。②類若鷹的食肉鳥；禿鷹；鳶。③掠奪他人的人。④鷹派(主戰分子)。—*v.i.* 以鷹獵鳥。

hawk[2] *v.t.* ①沿街叫賣。②散播。—*v.i.* 做小販。

hawk[3] *v.i.* 大聲清喉嚨。—*n.* 清喉嚨時的聲音。

hawk[4] *n.* (泥水匠用之)圬板；盛漿鏝板。

hawk·er ['hɔkɚ; 'hɔːkə] *n.* ①放鷹者；以鷹行獵者。②沿街叫賣之小販。

hawk-eyed ['hɔkˌaɪd; 'hɔːk-aid] *adj.* 目力甚强的；目光銳敏的。

hawk·ish ['hɔkɪʃ; 'hɔːkiʃ] *adj.* ①似鷹的。②好戰的；主戰的。

hawk moth 天蛾科之蛾。

hawk nose 鷹鉤鼻。

hawks·bill ['hɔksˌbɪl; 'hɔːksbil] *n.* (熱帶海中之)一種小龜；玳瑁。

hawk·shaw ['hɔkˌʃɔ; 'hɔːkʃɔː] *n.* 偵探。(亦作 **Hawkshaw**)

hawk·weed ['hɔkˌwid; 'hɔːkwiːd] *n.* ①水蘭屬之植物。②菊科或紫菀科之植物。

Haworth [hɑrθ; hɑːθ] *n.* 哈爾斯 (Sir Walter Norman, 1883–1950, 英國化學家，曾獲1937年諾貝爾化學獎)。

hawse [hɔz, hɔs; hɔːz] *n.* 〖航海〗①錨鏈孔之部分。②錨鏈孔。③船首與錨間之水平距離。④停泊時船首前兩錨鏈之狀態。

hawse·hole ['hɔzˌhol, -'hɔs-; 'hɔːz-houl] *n.* 〖航海〗錨鏈孔(在船首兩側之孔)。***come in through*** (or ***at***) ***the hawseholes*** 從水手出身。

haw·ser ['hɔzɚ, 'hɔsɚ; 'hɔːzə] *n.* 大纜；大鐵索；錨鏈。

***haw·thorn** ['hɔˌθɔrn; 'hɔːθɔːn] *n.* 〖植物〗山楂。

Haw·thorne ['hɔˌθɔrn; 'hɔːθɔːn] *n.* 霍桑 (Nathaniel, 1804–1864, 美國作家)。

hay**[1] [he; hei] *n.* ①乾草；秣。②〖俚〗少量之錢。hit the hay*** 〖俚〗上床。***look for a needle in a bundle of hay*** 草綑中找針(做沒把握的事)。***make hay*** a. 準備草秣。b. 弄亂。c. 把握時機。***make hay of*** 使無效；弄亂。***Make hay while the sun shines.*** 把握時機。—*v.t.* ①製成乾草。②供給乾草。—*v.i.* 製乾草。

hay[2] *n.* 一種古老的鄉村舞蹈。

hay·cock ['heˌkɑk; 'heikɔk] *n.* 田野中之圓錐形乾草堆。

Hay·dn ['haɪdn̩, 'hedn̩; 'haidn] *n.* 海頓 (Franz Joseph, 1732–1809, 奧國作曲家)。

hay fever 乾草熱；花粉熱(過敏症)。

hay·field ['heˌfild; 'heifiːld] *n.* 牧草場。

hay·fork ['heˌfɔrk; 'heifɔːk] *n.* 乾草叉。

hay·loft ['heˌlɔft; 'heilɔft, -lɔːft] *n.* 馬廐或穀倉中盛乾草的地方。

hay·mak·er ['heˌmekɚ; 'heiˌmeikə] *n.* ①製乾草之人；火力乾草機。②〖俚〗〖拳擊〗擊倒對手之一擊。

hay·mow ['heˌmau; 'heimau] *n.* 乾草堆；乾草棚。

hay·rack ['heˌræk; 'heiræk] *n.* ①餵牛馬時用的乾草架。②牛車上的乾草架。③裝

有乾草架的牛車。

hay·rick 〔ˈheˌrɪk; ˈheirik〕 *n.* 戶外的乾草堆。(亦作 **haystack**)

hay·seed 〔ˈheˌsid; ˈheisiːd〕 *n.* ①(乾草中的)草種子。②乾草屑。③〖美俚〗鄉巴佬;村夫(略帶輕蔑語)。「*n.* 〖美俗〗鄉巴佬。」

hay·shak·er 〔ˈheˌʃekɚ; ˈheiˌʃeikə〕

hay·stack 〔ˈheˌstæk; ˈheistæk〕 *n.* 大乾草堆(在戶外者)。***look for a needle in a haystack*** 做沒有希望的事;海底撈針。

hay tedder 晒草機。

hay·wire 〔ˈheˌwaɪr; ˈheiˌwaiə〕 *n.* 〖美〗綑乾草用之鉛絲;自乾草束取去乾草後之糾結雜亂的鉛絲。—*adj.* 〖美俚〗①糾結雜亂的;混亂的。②瘋狂的;興奮的;失去控制的。

haz·ard** 〔ˈhæzɚd; ˈhæzəd〕 *n.* ①冒險;危險。a life full of *hazards.* 充滿冒險的一生。②未知數。③意外事件。to meet at *hazard.* 偶然相遇。④高爾夫球場上的障礙物。⑤一種擲骰子戲。at all hazards*** 不顧任何危險。—*v.t.* 賭;冒…的危險 to *hazard* a remark (guess). 冒險而批評(猜測)。

haz·ard·ous 〔ˈhæzɚdəs; ˈhæzədəs〕 *adj.* 危險的;冒險的。a *hazardous* investment. 一項冒險的投資。—**ly,** *adv.*

***haze¹** 〔hez; heiz〕 *n.* ①薄霧;陰霾;暈。②(思想等之)模糊不清。a *haze* of misunderstanding. 因不了解而致認識不清。

haze² *v.t.* 戲弄(大學新生)。

***ha·zel** 〔ˈhezl̩; ˈheizl〕 *n.* ①榛。②榛實(=hazelnut). ③榛木。④榛木手杖。⑤淡褐色(尤指眼睛的)。—*adj.* ①榛的;榛木的。②淡褐色的。「*n.* 榛實。」

ha·zel·nut 〔ˈhezl̩nət,-ˌnʌt; ˈheizlnʌt〕

haz·ing 〔ˈhezɪŋ; ˈheiziŋ〕 *n.* ①被欺侮。②〖航海〗罰做苦工。③罰做苦工之時間。

ha·zy 〔ˈhezɪ; ˈheizi〕 *adj.,* **ha·zi·er, ha·zi·est.** ①有薄霧的;暈的。②模糊的;朦朧的。—**ha·zi·ly,** *adv.* —**ha·zi·ness,** *n.*

HB, H.B. ①halfback. ②(鉛筆) hard black. ③heavy bombardment. **Hb.** 〖生化〗hemoglobin. **H.B.M.** His *or* Her Britannic Majesty.

H-bomb 〔ˈetʃˌbɑm; ˈeitʃbɔm〕 *n.* 氫彈。

H.C. House of Commons. **H.C.F., h.c.f.** highest common factor. 最大公約數。 **h.c.l.** 〖俗〗high cost of living. **hd.** ①hand. ②head. **hdkf.** handkerchief. **hdqrs.** headquarters.

HE high explosive. 高性能炸藥。

He 化學元素 helium 之符號。

:he 〔hi; hiː〕 *pron., pl.* **they,** *n., adj.* —*pron.* 他;彼(第三人稱,單數,主格)。*He* is here. 他在這裏。***He who....***(文學或古典用法)凡是…的人。***It is he who....***(文學或古典用法)…的是他。It is *he* who is to blame. 應負其咎的是他。—*n.* 男孩;男人;雄獸。—*adj.* 〖俗〗(植物或雌性動物)很大的;很强壯的;完美的。

H.E. ①His Eminence. ②His Excellency. ③high explosive.

:head 〔hɛd; hed〕 *n., pl.* **heads** or (for ⑧) **head,** *adj., v.* —*n.* ①人的頭;頭部。to bow one's *head.* 低頭。②動物的頭。Better be the *head* of an ass than the tail of a horse. 〖諺〗寧爲驢頭不爲馬尾;寧爲鷄口毋爲牛後。③任何物件的頂端。the *head* of a mountain. 山頂。④任何東西的最前端部分。the *head* of a procession. 遊行行列的排頭。⑤主要人物;領袖;首長。the *head* of a college. 學院院長。⑥領袖的地位;主要的權威;領導;命令;指導。to be at the *head* of a business. 擔任一個公司的經理。⑦人。Kings and queens are crowned *heads.* 國王與皇后是被加冕的人。⑧(牲畜等之)頭數。Ten cows are ten *head* of cattle 十頭牛卽爲十頭家畜。⑨圓如頭的東西。a *head* of cabbage. 一顆包心菜。⑩〖植物〗穗;頭狀花;花冠。a clover *head.* 苜蓿花。⑪〖醫〗瘡、丘疹等的膿包。The boil has come to a *head.* 那瘡子的頭已經熟了。⑫工具的鎚擊或切割部分。the *head* of a hammer. 鎚頭。⑬(鼓等)一端所蒙的皮。⑭桶的任何一端。⑮理解力;智力;才智。The old man has a wise *head.* 那老人非常有智謀。Two *heads* are better than one. 三個臭皮匠勝過諸葛亮。⑯要點;要旨;題目。⑰危機;極點;結論。⑱逐漸獲得的力量。As more people joined, the movement gathered *head.* 因爲有更多人參加,這一運動得到了新的力量。⑲(蒸汽、水等的)壓力;落差;水源高度。a *head* of water driving turbine. 推動渦輪的水壓。⑳水源地;發源地。the *head* of the Nile. 尼羅河的發源地。the *head* of a bay. 海灣頭。㉑泡沫;渣滓。the *head* on a glass of ale. 一杯麥酒上的泡沫。㉒(*pl.*)錢幣上有人像的一面。*Heads* or tails? (擲錢時)要人頭,還是背面? ㉓(*pl.*)〖釀酒〗剛發酵時所產生之酒精。㉔標題。㉕(船上之)廁所。***an old head on young shoulders*** 年輕人的智慧;年輕而有見識的人;少年老成。***be unable to make head or tail of it*** 一點兒都不明白。***by the head*** a. 船首較船尾吃水深的。b. 微醉的。***by the head and ears*** 强迫地。***come to a head*** a. 化膿。b. 趨於危險;到達高潮。***down by the head*** 船首較船尾吃水深的。***eat one's head off*** a. 吃得太多。b. 不值得耗於所吃的;(馬)能吃不能做。***fall head first*** (or ***foremost***) 突然頭朝下地跌倒。***from head to foot*** 從頭到脚;全身。***give one his head*** 讓某人隨意而爲。***go to one's head*** a. 影響某人思想。b. 使眩暈;使激動;使醉。c. 使自負。***hang*** (or ***hide***) ***one's head*** a. 垂頭喪氣。b. 感到可恥。***head and shoulders*** 相當地;可觀的。As an orator he stood *head and shoulders* above his contemporaries. 他是當時最傑出的演說家。***head first*** (or ***foremost***) a. 頭先;頭在前。b. 匆忙地。***head over heels*** a. 翻觔斗;頭朝下。b. 慌慌張張地;急促地。c. 完全地;徹底地。*head over heels* in debt (love). 深陷於債務(戀愛)中。***hold one's head high*** 趾高氣揚。***keep one's head*** 不爲激動;保持冷靜的態度。***keep one's head above water*** a. 保持浮起。b. 避免失敗、損害、打擊、死亡等。c. 〖喩〗不欠債。***lay heads together*** 集議。***light in the head*** a. 暈頭暈腦的。b. 愚蠢的。c. 瘋狂的。***lose one's head*** (=get excited)失去理智;情感衝動。***make head*** 往前擠;前進。***make head against*** 成功地抵制。***on*** (or ***upon***) ***one's head*** 歸於某人之責任;落在肩上。*On your head* be it. 你應負責。***out of*** (or ***off***) ***one's head*** 〖俗〗a. 大爲激動。b. 神經錯亂;瘋顚。c. 置之腦後;不想。***out of one's own head*** 自出心裁;出於自己的主意。***over head and ears*** a. 淹沒。b. 深陷。***over one's head*** a. 超過某人的理解力。b. 未與人商量;不關照。It was done *over my head.* 該事是未和我商量做成的。***over the heads of other persons*** 越級。***put a thing*** (***idea, etc.***) ***out of***

one's head 不再想某事(觀念等);放棄;使某人忘掉某物。***put heads together*** **a.** 商議;會談。**b.** 圖謀;計畫。***put (an idea) into a person's head*** 提示(觀念)給某人;使想起。***shake one's head*** 搖頭(表示不同意)。***shake one's head at*** 對…搖頭(表示懷疑或不贊成)。***take (something) into one's head*** **a.** 相信。**b.** 計畫;意欲。***talk a person's head off*** 談得使某人生厭。***talk over a person's head (over the heads of an audience)*** 談得使某人(聽衆)不懂。***turn one's head*** **a.** 影響思想。**b.** 使眩暈;使激動。**c.** 使自負。—*adj.* ①在頭部的;在頂端的;在前部的。②自前面來的。③爲首的;領頭的。—*v.t.* ①爲首;領頭;在最前端。to *head* a revolt (*or* rebellion). 領導叛亂。②使面向…(而行)。to *head* a boat toward the shore. 使船向岸邊行駛。③主持;領導。to *head* a business. 領導一項業務。④勝過;超越。to *head* all records. 打破一切記錄。⑤以頭撞、擊、觸。to *head* the ball. (在足球中)以頭頂球。⑥供…頂端;裝以頭。to *head* a pin. 做針的頭。⑦砍下(動物)的頭。to *head* a hen. 切下鷄的頭。⑧剪掉(樹)的頭。—*v.i.* ①向某處或方向走去。to *head* south. 向南走去。②長出頂;長出頭。The cabbages are *heading* up nicely. 捲心菜長得很好。③達到危險階段。④〖美〗(河等)發源〖in, from〗. ***head off*** **a.** 走到前邊而引導或攔回。**b.** 阻止;防止。to *head off* a quarrel. 防止口角發生。***head up*** 指揮;當主管。

***head·ache** [ˈhɛdˌek; ˈhedeik] *n.* ①頭痛。to suffer from *headache(s)*. 患頭痛。②〖美〗令人頭痛的事物或情勢。The question was giving the Government a very bad *headache*. 這問題使政府大爲頭痛。

head·ach·y [ˈhɛdˌekɪ; ˈhedeiki] *adj.* ①頭痛的。②令人頭痛的。

head·band [ˈhɛdˌbænd; ˈhedbænd] *n.* ①(繞着頭的)束髮帶。②〖印刷〗印於頁首或章首之飾帶。③〖裝訂〗書脊內部上下的布帶。

head·board [ˈhɛdˌbord; ˈhedbɔːd] *n.* 任何物體前部或上端之板(如床頭板)。

head·cheese [ˈhɛdˌtʃiz; ˈhedtʃiːz] *n.* 〖美〗猪頭糕(以猪或犢之頭、足等切碎煮成)。

head·cloth [ˈhɛdˌklɔθ, -ˌklɑθ; ˈhedˌklɔːθ] *n.* 包頭巾。

head cold 傷風。

head count 清點人數。

head-count·er [ˈhɛdˌkauntɚ; ˈhedˌkauntə] *n.* 民意測驗家。

head·dress [ˈhɛdˌdrɛs; ˈheddres] *n.* ①首飾;頭巾。②頭髮之梳式。

-headed 〖字尾〗表"頭…的;…頭的"之義。如:long-*headed*, clear-*headed*.

head·er [ˈhɛdɚ; ˈhedə] *n.* ①爲釘、針等物加頭的人或機器。②一種收割機。③露頭磚。④兩長樑間之橫樑。⑤〖俗〗倒栽;倒落。to take a *header* into a swimming pool. 倒栽入游泳池。⑥〖足球〗以頭頂球。

head-fal·sie [ˈhɛdˌfɔlsɪ; ˈhedˌfɔːlsi] *n.* 〖俚〗假髮。

head fast 〖航海〗船首纜。(亦作 **head-fast**)

head·first [ˈhɛdˈfɝst; ˈhedˈfəːst] *adv.* ①頭向前地。②不顧前後地;急忙忙地;輕舉妄動地。(亦作 **headforemost**)

head·frame [ˈhɛdˌfrem; ˈhedfreim] *n.* 礦坑入口處裝起重機等之支架。

head gate 總水門;閘門。

head·gear [ˈhɛdˌgɪr; ˈhedgiə] *n.* ①馬首之裝具。②戴在頭上之物;頭飾;帽子。

head·hunt [ˈhɛdˌhʌnt; ˈhedˌhʌnt] *n.* ①野蠻人獵人頭之出征。②〖俚〗爲公司羅致高級職員。—*v.t. & v.i.* ①外出獵人頭。②〖俚〗爲公司羅致(高級職員)。

head·hunt·er [ˈhɛdˌhʌntɚ; ˈhedˌhʌntə] *n.* ①獵取人頭之野蠻人。②〖俚〗爲公司羅致高級職員者。

head·ing [ˈhɛdɪŋ; ˈhediŋ] *n.* ①作頭部用之材料(如桶等頂端之木板)。②標題;標題字;題目。③〖航海〗船頭的方向。④〖航空〗飛行方向。⑤〖採礦〗橫坑道;橫坑道之端。

head·lamp [ˈhɛdˌlæmp; ˈhedˌlæmp] *n.* ①=**headlight.** ②礦工戴在額前的照明燈。(亦作 **head lamp**)

head·land [ˈhɛdlənd; ˈhedlənd] *n.* ①岬;崎。②畦頭未耕之地。

head·less [ˈhɛdlɪs; ˈhedlis] *adj.* ①無頭的。②無首領的。③愚笨的;無知的。

***head·light** [ˈhɛdˌlaɪt; ˈhedlait] *n.* 〖美〗(汽車、火車、電車等頭部之)前燈。

head·line** [ˈhɛdˌlaɪn; ˈhedlain] *n., v.,* **-lined, -lin·ing.** —*n.* 〖美〗①報紙雜誌上的標題;大字標出的重要標題。②(*pl.*)風頭;宣揚。to go into *headlines.* 大出風頭。make headlines*** 受到宣揚。—*v.t.* ①爲…做標題。②包括於標題中。③宣揚。

head·lin·er [ˈhɛdˌlaɪnɚ; ˈhedˌlainə] *n.* ①寫新聞標題的編輯。②掛頭牌之演員。

head·lock [ˈhɛdˌlɑk; ˈhedlɔk] *n.* 〖摔角〗將對手之頭緊挾於腋下之一種摔角法。

***head·long** [ˈhɛdˌlɔŋ; ˈhedlɔŋ] *adv.* ①頭先地;頭向前地。②急速而用力地。to rush *headlong* into the crowd. 匆忙而用力地擠進人堆裏去。③輕率地;鹵莽地。—*adj.* ①頭先的;頭向前的。a *headlong* fall. 頭先着地的摔了一交。②匆促而用力的。③輕率的。a *headlong* leader. 有勇無謀的領袖。

head louse 頭蝨。

head·man [ˈhɛdmən, ˈhɛdˌmæn; ˈhedmæn, ˈhedmən] *n., pl.* **-men.** ①(部族等之)頭目;酋長;首領。②工頭;領班。

head·mas·ter [ˈhɛdˈmæstɚ, -ˈmɑs-; ˈhedˈmɑːstə] *n.* (中學或小學)校長。(亦作 **head master**)〖注意〗校長英作**headmaster,** 美作 **principal.**

head·mis·tress [ˈhɛdˈmɪstrɪs; ˈhedˈmistris] *n.* 女校長。

head money ①人頭稅。②(捕獲俘虜或犯人之)懸賞金。③(移民之)入國稅。

head·most [ˈhɛdˌmost; ˈhedmoust] *adj.* 領先的;最先的;最前面的。

head-note [ˈhɛdˌnot; ˈhednout] *n.* 眉批。

head office 總公司;總行;總局。

head-on [ˈhɛdˈɑn, -ˈɔn; ˈhedˈɔn] *adj.* ①頭向前的;正面的。a *head-on* collision. 正面相撞。②輕率的。—*adv.* ①頭向前地;正面地。②輕率地。

head·phones [ˈhɛdˌfonz; ˈhedfounz] *n. pl.* (收話機之)聽筒;〖無線電〗耳機。

head·piece [ˈhɛdˌpis; ˈhedpiːs] *n.* ①胄;盔。②頭巾;帽子。③耳機。④頭;智力;理解。⑤書籍一章或一頁上裝飾之圖樣。

head pin ①保齡球戲中之先頭之瓶。②〖俚〗最重要之人。(亦作 **headpin**)

head·quar·ter [ˈhɛdˈkwɔrtɚ, -ˌkw-; ˈhedˈkwɔːtə] *v.i. & v.t.* 以…作總部;設總公司於…。The new company will *headquarter* in New York. 新公司總部將設於紐約。

***head·quar·ters** [ˈhɛdˈkwɔrtɚz,

–ˌkwɔr–; ˈhedˈkwɔːtəz] *n.* (作*pl.* or *sing.* 解) ①總部;司令部。general *headquarters.* 總司令部。②大本營;總辦公處;總署。③總部的全體人員。
head·rest [ˈhɛdˌrɛst; ˈhedrest] *n.* 靠頭之物(如理髮椅端之頭枕)。
heads [hɛdz; hedz] *adj.* (硬幣)正面朝上的。
head·set [ˈhɛdˌsɛt; ˈhedset] *n.* =**headphones.**
head·ship [ˈhɛdʃɪp; ˈhedʃip] *n.* ①首領之職權;指導者之地位。②〖英〗校長之職位。
heads·man [ˈhɛdzmən; ˈhedzmən] *n., pl.* **-men.** ①劊子手。②〖英〗〖礦冶〗搬運工人。③捕鯨船指揮;首領。
heads or tails ①擲銅板猜正反面之遊戲。②以上述方法解決問題。
head·spring [ˈhɛdˌsprɪŋ; ˈhedspriŋ] *n.* ①(河流之)水源。②起源;源泉。
head·stall [ˈhɛdˌstɔl; ˈhedstɔːl] *n.* 絡頭(馬具)。
head·stand [ˈhɛdˌstænd; ˈhedstænd] *n.* 倒立;豎蜻蜓。
head start 領先;先起步。
head·stock [ˈhɛdˌstɑk; ˈhedstɔk] *n.* 〖機械〗(車牀等之)軸承(臺)。
head·stone [ˈhɛdˌston; ˈhedstoun] *n.* ①墓碑。②基石;礎石。
head·strong [ˈhɛdˌstrɔŋ; ˈhedstrɔŋ] *adj.* 頑固的;剛愎的;倔强的;任性的。
heads-up [ˈhɛdzˈʌp; ˈhedzˈʌp] *adj.* 〖俗〗機警的;足智多謀的。
head tax 人頭稅。
head-to-head [ˈhɛdtəˈhɛd; ˈhedtəˈhed] *adj.* 〖美〗近距離戰的。
head-to-toe [ˈhɛdtəˈto; ˈhedtəˈtou] *adj.* 〖俗〗從頭到脚的;徹底的。
head voice 頭音;頭腔共鳴而發之高音。
head·wait·er [ˈhɛdˈwetə; ˈhedˈweitə] *n.* 餐館等之侍者管理員;大班。
head·wa·ters [ˈhɛdˌwɔtəz; ˈhedˌwɔːtəz] *n. pl.* 河源;上游。
head·way [ˈhɛdˌwe; ˈhedwei] *n.* ①前進;行進。②進步;成功。③同向而行的車輛、船隻間的距離(時數或里數)。trains running on ten-minute *headway.* 隔十分鐘開出一列的火車。④〖建築〗高空(地板至天花板的垂直距離)。
head wind (自船首吹來的)逆風。(亦作 **headwind**)
head word ①標題字。②〖文法〗主要語;被修飾語(對修飾語而言)。
head·work [ˈhɛdˌwɝk; ˈhedwəːk] *n.* ①勞心的工作;腦力(精神)勞動;思想。②〖建築〗(拱頭石等上的)雕刻的動物頭裝飾。
head·y [ˈhɛdɪ; ˈhedi] *adj.,* **head·i·er, head·i·est.** ①任性的;頑固的;性急的。②易使人醉的;易使人迷惑的。③令人興奮的。④〖俗〗有腦筋的;有判斷力的。⑤破壞性的。
***heal** [hil; hiːl] *v.t.* ①治愈;使復原。Though the wound is cured, it is not *healed.* 此傷口雖經治療,但尚未痊癒。②和解;平息。to *heal* a quarrel. 和解糾紛。—*v.i.* 痊癒;復原。—**er,** *n.*
heal-all [ˈhilˌɔl; ˈhiːl-ɔːl] *n.* 萬靈藥。
‡**health** [hɛlθ; helθ] *n.* ①健康;身體的狀況(好或壞)。Fresh air and exercise are good for the *health.* 新鮮空氣與運動有益於健康。②使人健康的力量。There is *health* in the sunshine. 日光使人健康。③蓬勃;繁榮。economic *health.* 經濟的蓬勃。***drink a health to*** 舉杯祝…健康。We all *drank a health to* the bride. 我們都舉杯祝新娘健康。*public health* 公共衞生。
***health·ful** [ˈhɛlθfəl; ˈhelθful] *adj.* 於健康有益的;衞生的。*healthful* exercise. 健身運動。—**ly,** *adv.* —**ness,** *n.*
health insurance 健康保險。
health officer 衞生人員。
health resort (避暑、避寒的)休養地。
***health·y** [ˈhɛlθɪ; ˈhelθi] *adj.,* **health·i·er, health·i·est.** ①健康的;健壯的。②表示健康的。a *healthy* appearance. 健康的外表。③有益於健康的;衞生的。*healthy* readings for the young people. 有益青年身心之讀物。—**health·i·ness,** *n.* —**health·i·ly,** *adv.*
heap** [hip; hiːp] *n.* ①堆。a *heap* of books. 一堆書。②許多;大量。It did me a *heap* of good to see old friends. 見到老朋友使我非常快樂。③〖俚〗汽車(尤指舊車)。be struck*** (or ***knocked***) ***all of a heap*** 〖俗〗嚇成一團;搞得一團糟。***heaps of*** 大量的;極多的。He has *heaps of* money. 他有極多的錢。***heaps of times*** 時常地;常常地。—*v.t.* ①堆積。*Heap* the sand up. 將沙堆起來。②累積〖up〗. ③大量賜給;濫給。④大量裝載。—*v.i.* 形成堆。—**y,** *adj.*
heaps [hips; hiːps] *adv.* 〖俗〗很;非常地。
‡**hear** [hɪr; hiə] *v.,* **heard** [hɝd; həːd], **hear·ing.** —*v.t.* ①聽見;聽到(聲音)。We listened but could *hear* nothing. 我們注意靜聽,但甚麼也聽不見。②聞知;聽說。I've *heard* the story before. 我從前曾聽過這故事。③(=listen to) 傾聽。to *hear* a person's explanation. 傾聽某人的解釋。④審問。Which judge will *hear* the case? 那位法官審問這案件? ⑤聽從;允許;應允。Lord, *hear* my prayer. 主啊,請俯允我的禱告! —*v.i.* ①得到消息;接到信〖from, about, of〗. I *hear* (=receive a letter) from Mr. Smith every week. 我每週都接到史密斯先生的信。②聽覺。She doesn't (=can't) *hear* very well. 她的聽覺不大好。***Hear! Hear!*** (喝采的聲音)好哇! 好哇! ***hear out*** 聽完;聽到底。***will not hear of it*** 不許;不予考慮;不贊同。I *won't hear of* such a thing! 我不贊同此事! 〖注意〗**hear, listen** 均指聽,聞。hear 指耳朵聽聲音的自然活動。listen 指主動聽一聲音,並求了解。
‡**heard** [hɝd; həːd] *v.* pt. & pp. of **hear.**
***hear·er** [ˈhɪrə; ˈhiərə] *n.* 聽者;聽衆。
hear·ing** [ˈhɪrɪŋ; ˈhiəriŋ] *n.* ①聽;聽力;聽覺。Her *hearing* is not very good. 她的聽覺不大好(卽有點聾)。②聽訟;調查庭;審問。③發言的機會。Give us a *hearing.* 給我們發言的機會;好好聽我們的話。④聽力所及的距離。to talk freely in the *hearing* of others. 在別人能聽得見的範圍內暢言無忌。give somebody a hearing*** 聽某人申述理由等。***hard of hearing*** (=deaf)耳聾。***in the hearing of*** 在…可聽見的範圍之內。***out of hearing*** 聽不見的。***within hearing*** 在可以聽見的距離以內。
hearing aid 助聽器。
heark·en [ˈhɑrkən; ˈhɑːkən] *v.i.* 聽;傾聽。—*v.t.* 〖古〗聽。(亦作 **harken**)
hear·say [ˈhɪrˌse; ˈhiəsei] *n.* 風聞;謠傳;道聽途說。I don't believe it; it's merely *hearsay.* 我不相信;它僅是一種謠傳罷了。—*adj.* 風聞的;謠傳的。
hearsay evidence 〖法律〗非直接證據;根據傳說的證據。
hearse [hɝs; həːs] *n.* ①柩車;靈車。②〖古〗棺架;棺臺。

‡heart (hɑrt; hɑːt) *n.* ①心；心臟。He has a weak *heart.* 他的心臟很衰弱。②心腸；衷心；心情；愛心；元氣；膽力；精神；熱誠。He has a very kind *heart.* 他的心腸很慈悲。③中心；內部。to get to the *heart* of the subject. 深刻地了解這一問題；抓住這問題的中心。④心形物。⑤被寵愛的人；受讚美之人。sweetheart. 情人；愛人。⑥橋牌上的紅心。⑦(*pl.*) 一套紅心牌；玩牌者要去掉紅心的一種牌戲。***after one's own heart*** 正如己之所願；正合己意；正投所好。***at heart*** **a.** 在思想與感情深處。**b.** 眞正地。***break the heart of somebody*** (or ***break somebody's heart***) 使某人傷心。***by heart*** 由記憶地；從記憶地。***do one's heart good*** 使喜歡。***eat one's heart out*** 深覺憂傷。***from one's heart*** 眞誠地；懇摯地。***from the bottom of one's heart*** 眞誠地；從心底地。***get to the heart of*** 發現…的祕密或隱意。***have a change of heart*** 改變主意。***have a heart*** 慈悲；同情。***have at heart*** 將…牢記在心。***have one's heart in one's boots*** (or ***mouth***) 深爲驚恐；嚇一跳。***have one's heart in the right place*** 懷好意；懷善意。***have the heart*** **a.** 有勇氣(做某事)。**b.** (在否定語態中) 心腸狠得足以(做某事)。***heart and soul*** 全心全力地。***in one's heart of hearts*** 在思想或感情深處。***lose heart*** 灰心；喪氣。***lose one's heart to somebody*** (=fall in love with somebody) 傾心於某人。***near one's heart*** (or ***close to one's heart***) 對某人有價值或有趣的；懷念的。***set one's heart against*** 極力反對。***set one's heart at ease*** (or ***rest***) 安心。***set one's heart on some object*** 渴望獲得某物。***take heart*** 振起精神；鼓起勇氣。***take*** (or ***lay***) ***to heart*** **a.** 認眞；介意。**b.** 傷心。***to one's heart's content*** 儘量；縱情。The children played in the snow *to their heart's content.* 孩子們在雪地上縱情遊戲。***wear one's heart on one's sleeve*** 開誠布公。***with all one's heart*** 誠懇地；欣然地。—*v.t.* 將…記在心中。to *heart* a warning. 將警告記在心中。

heart·ache (ˈhɑrtˌek; ˈhɑːt-eik) *n.* 傷心；悲痛。

heart attack 心臟病發作。

heart·beat (ˈhɑrtˌbit; ˈhɑːtbiːt) *n.* 心搏動。

heart·break (ˈhɑrtˌbrek; ˈhɑːtbreik) *n.* 傷心；悲痛；斷腸；心碎。

heart·break·ing (ˈhɑrtˌbrekɪŋ; ˈhɑːtˌbreikiŋ) *adj.* ①傷心的；令人悲痛的。②〖俗〗無聊的；令人厭煩的。—**ly,** *adv.*

heart·bro·ken (ˈhɑrtˌbrokən; ˈhɑːtˌbroukən) *adj.* 悲痛的；傷心的；斷腸的。—**ly,** *adv.* —**ness,** *n.*

heart·burn (ˈhɑrtˌbɜn; ˈhɑːtbəːn) *n.* ①〖醫〗胃痛；胃灼熱。②不平；仇恨；嫉妒。

heart·burn·ing (ˈhɑrtˌbɜnɪŋ; ˈhɑːtˌbəːniŋ) *n., adj.* 不平(的)；嫉妒(的)。

heart disease 心臟病。

heart·ed (ˈhɑrtɪd; ˈhɑːtid) *adj.* 有…之心的；呈…心情的 (常用於複合字中)。sad-*hearted.* 憂心的。

heart·en (ˈhɑrtn̩; ˈhɑːtn) *v.t.* 鼓勵；激勵；使振作。

heart failure 心臟衰弱。

heart·felt (ˈhɑrtˌfɛlt; ˈhɑːtfelt) *adj.* 銘心的；至誠的。

heart-free (ˈhɑrtˌfri; ˈhɑːtfriː) *adj.* 不爲愛情所束縛的。Rose is still *heart-free.* 露絲尚未墜入情網。

***hearth** (hɑrθ; hɑːθ) *n.* ①爐牀。②家庭；爐邊。The soldiers longed for their own *hearths.* 士兵們思家。③鎔爐床。

hearth·rug (ˈhɑrθˌrʌg; ˈhɑːθrʌg) *n.* 爐邊地毯。—*adj.* ①家庭的。②如爐邊地毯的。

hearth·side (ˈhɑrθˌsaɪd; ˈhɑːθsaid) *n.* ①爐邊。②家庭。

hearth·stone (ˈhɑrθˌston; ˈhɑːθstoun) *n.* ①爐底石。②家庭；爐邊。

***heart·i·ly** (ˈhɑrtɪlɪ; ˈhɑːtili) *adv.* ①誠懇地。②有好胃口地；痛快地。to eat *heartily.* 吃得很痛快。③完全地；十分地。to be *heartily* glad. 十分高興。

heart·land (ˈhɑrtˌlænd; ˈhɑːtlænd) *n.* ①心臟地帶 (經濟上、軍事上均能自立，非常堅固之地域)。②重要地區。

heart·less (ˈhɑrtlɪs; ˈhɑːtlis) *adj.* ①無情的。②無勇氣的；不熱心的。—**ly,** *adv.* —**ness,** *n.*

heart-lung machine (ˈhɑrtˈlʌŋ~; ˈhɑːtˈlʌŋ~) 心肺機 (心臟手術臨時代替病人心肺的機器)。

heart murmur 〖醫〗心雜音。

heart-rend·ing (ˈhɑrtˌrɛndɪŋ; ˈhɑːtˌrendiŋ) *adj.* 悲慘的；傷心的；心碎的。—**ly,** *adv.*

hearts·ease, heart's-ease (ˈhɑrtsˌiz; ˈhɑːts-iːz) *n.* ①心平氣和。②〖植物〗三色菫。

heart·sick (ˈhɑrtˌsɪk; ˈhɑːt-sik) *adj.* 悲痛的；苦惱的；不樂的。

heart·sore (ˈhɑrtˌsor; ˈhɑːt-sɔː) *n.* 悲痛；憂傷。—*adj.* 悲痛的；憂傷的。

heart-strick·en (ˈhɑrtˌstrɪkn̩; ˈhɑːtˌstrikn) *adj.* 悲痛欲絕的。(亦作 **heart-struck**) —**ly,** *adv.*

heart·strings (ˈhɑrtˌstrɪŋz; ˈhɑːtstriŋz) *n. pl.* 深情；心弦。***break one's heartstrings*** 使傷心。***pull at one's heartstrings*** 打動心弦。

heart·throb (ˈhɑrtˌθrab; ˈhɑːtθrɔb) *n.* ①心跳。②熱情。③愛人。

heart-to-heart (ˈhɑrttəˈhɑrt; ˈhɑːttəˈhɑːt) *adj.* 坦率的；老老實實的。

heart-whole (ˈhɑrtˈhol; ˈhɑːtˈhoul) *adj.* ①不爲愛情所動的；情竇未開的。②誠實的；堅毅的。—**ness,** *n.*

heart·wood (ˈhɑrtˌwud; ˈhɑːtwud) *n.* (樹木之) 心材。

***heart·y** (ˈhɑrtɪ; ˈhɑːti) *adj.,* **heart·i·er, heart·i·est,** *n., pl.* **heart·ies.** —*adj.* ①誠懇的；熱烈的；友善的。a *hearty* welcome. 竭誠的歡迎。②健旺的；強健的。③豐盛的；旺盛的；食量大的。a *hearty* appetite. 旺盛的食慾。④有精神的；豪爽的。⑤有力的。⑥(土壤) 肥沃的。—*n.* 水手同伴；勇敢的好同志。My *hearties!* 〖航海〗夥伴們！—**heart·i·ness,** *n.*

‡heat (hit; hiːt) *n.* ①熱；熱力。the *heat* of the sun (fire, etc.). 太陽(火等)的熱力。②熱度；溫度。③熱天；暑天。We can't work in the *heat.* 我們在暑天裏不能工作。④高潮；最激烈的階段。in the *heat* of the fight. 在戰事最激烈時。⑤(賽跑) 賽一次。preliminary (*or* trial) *heats.* 初賽。the final *heat.* 決賽。⑥溫暖；暖氣。to enjoy the *heat.* 享受溫暖。⑦〖物理〗熱。radiant *heat.* 輻射熱。⑧〖俗〗壓力；強制；蹂躪。⑨(臉上的) 發熱。⑩一舉；一次的努力。He did a piece of painting at a single *heat.* 他一舉而完成一幅畫。

⑪(尤指雌性)動物之交尾期;交尾期之性慾。in (*or* on) *heat*. 在交尾期中。⑫濃烈之香味。⑬熱情;感情激動。to speak with considerable *heat*. 相當激昂地講話。⑭〖美俚〗警察。***a dead heat*** (競賽中)並列名位。—*v.i.* ①發熱。Water *heats* slowly. 水是慢慢變熱的。②激昂。—*v.t.* ①使發熱。The room is *heated* by stove. 這房間以火爐取暖。②激動。Smith was *heated* with passion. 史密斯甚爲激昂。③使沸騰。

heat·ed [ˈhitɪd; ˈhiːtid] *adj.* ①熱的;加熱的。②激動的;激烈的。*heated* discussion. 激烈的討論。

heat energy 熱能。

***heat·er** [ˈhitɚ; ˈhiːtə] *n.* ①火爐;暖氣設備;加熱器。a gas-*heater*. 暖氣爐。②加熱之人。③〖俚〗手鎗;左輪鎗。

heat exchange 熱之傳遞。

heat exhaustion 〖醫〗中暑衰竭。

heath [hiθ; hiːθ] *n.* ①〖植物〗石南屬的常青灌木;石南樹叢。②叢生石南的荒地。***one's native heath*** 某人的故鄉。

heath cock 雄黑松鷄。

***hea·then** [ˈhiðən; ˈhiːðən] *n., pl.* **-thens** or **-then,** *adj.* —*n.* ①不信聖經中所說之上帝者;不信基督教、猶太教或回教者;異教徒。②壞人;粗野的人。—*adj.* 不信基督教、猶太教、或回教的;異教的。*heathen* customs. 異教社會的風俗。

hea·then·dom [ˈhiðəndəm; ˈhiːðəndəm] *n.* ①異教世界;異教徒(集合稱)。②異教;邪教;異端。

hea·then·ish [ˈhiðənɪʃ; ˈhiːðəniʃ] *adj.* ①異教徒的;不信基督教的。②野蠻的;未開化的。—**ly,** *adv.* —**ness,** *n.*

hea·then·ism [ˈhiðənˌɪzəm; ˈhiːðənizəm] *n.* ①異教(之教義);邪教;異端;偶像崇拜。②野蠻;蠻風。

hea·then·ize [ˈhiðənˌaɪz; ˈhiːðənaiz] *v.t.* & *v.i.,* **-ized, -iz·ing.** (使)成爲異教徒;(使)異教化。

heath·er [ˈhɛðɚ; ˈheðə] *n.* 石南屬的植物;石南。***set the heather on fire*** 煽動;火上加油。***take to the heather*** 〖蘇〗做土匪。—*adj.* 顏色或外觀似石南的。

heather mixture 雜色毛呢。

heath·er·y [ˈhɛðərɪ; ˈheðəri] *adj.* ①(似)石南的。②石南叢生的。(亦作 **heathy**)

heath·y [ˈhiθɪ; ˈhiːθi] *adj.,* **heath·i·er, heath·i·est.** (似)石南的;石南叢生的;多荒野的。

heat·ing [ˈhitɪŋ; ˈhiːtiŋ] *adj.* 使生熱的;使溫暖的。a *heating* apparatus (*or* system). 暖氣裝置。—*n.* 暖氣(裝置);加熱。

heating pad 取暖用的小電毯。

heat lightning 無雷聲之閃電。

heat-re·sist·ant [ˈhitrɪˌzɪstənt; ˈhiːtriˌzistənt] *adj.* 耐熱的;抗熱的。

heat·ron·ic [hitˈrɑnɪk; hiːtˈrɔnik] *adj.* (在塑模時,塑膠原料)以高周波加熱處理的。

heat shield (火箭鼻部之)熱屏。

heat spot ①痣;雀斑。②皮膚上之熱覺點。

heat·stroke [ˈhitˌstrok; ˈhiːt-strouk] *n.* 中暑。

heat-treat [ˈhitˌtrit; ˈhiːt-triːt] *v.t.* 以加熱處理(金屬等)以期產生預定的性質。

heat wave ①熱浪。②炎熱期;酷暑季。

heave** [hiv; hiːv] *v.,* **heaved** or (航海用) **hove, heav·ing,** *n.* —*v.t.* ①用力舉起。②拋;投;擲。to *heave* a brick through a window. 將磚自窗中拋出。③發出(歎聲等)。to *heave* a sigh (groan). 發出一聲歎息(呻吟)。④使隆起;使凸起。The wind *heaves* the waves. 風吹水起浪。⑤〖航海〗移至某種位置或方向。*Heave* up the anchor! 起錨!⑥嘔吐。⑦拉起(繩子、鏈、電纜等)。—*v.i.* ①拖;拉;曳〖on, at〗. They *heaved* on the rope. 他們拖着繩子。②(波濤等)洶湧;起伏。Waves *heave* in a storm. 在暴風雨中波浪洶湧。③喘息。④要嘔吐;嘔吐。⑤凸起;凸出。⑥移動;向一個方向前行。The ship *hove* alongside (out of the harbor). 船靠着碼頭(駛出港口)。Heave ho*** (or ***away***)! 用力拉(水手拉錨時的呼聲)! ***heave in sight*** (船)駛入視線內。***heave to*** 使船停駛;停止。—*n.* ①舉;拋。②起伏。the *heave* of the sea. 海濤的起伏。③(*pl.*)(作 *sing.* 解)馬的喘息症。—**less,** *adj.*

‡**heav·en** [ˈhɛvən; ˈhevn] *n.* ①(基督教所指的)天堂;天國。to be in *heaven*. 歸西天(卽死了)。②任何想像中的極樂世界。③(H-)上帝(=God);天。It was the will of *Heaven*. 那是天意。*Heaven* forbid! 天不容! Good *Heavens!* 天啊! Thank *Heaven* you were not killed. 感謝蒼天,你沒有被殺。④(常 *pl.*)天空;空際。the starry *heavens*. 星空。***move heaven and earth*** 竭盡全力。

heav·en-born [ˈhɛvənˌbɔrn; ˈhevnbɔːn] *adj.* ①天生的;天賦的;神賦與的。②自天降的。③(諷刺語)有特殊天才的。

***heav·en·ly** [ˈhɛvənlɪ; ˈhevnli] *adj.* ①天國的;神聖的。our *heavenly* Father. 我們的天父。②如天堂的。③天空的;太空的。*heavenly* bodies. 天體。④〖俗〗卓越的;超絕的。a *heavenly* voice. 美妙的聲音。—**heav·en·li·ness,** *n.*

heav·en·ly-mind·ed [ˈhɛvn̩lɪˈmaɪndɪd; ˈhevnliˈmaindid] *adj.* 信心極深的;虔誠的;篤信的。—**ness,** *n.*

heav·en·ward [ˈhɛvənwɚd; ˈhevnwəd] *adj.* & *adv.* 向天空的(地);向天國的(地)。

heav·en·wards [ˈhɛvənwɚdz; ˈhevnwədz] *adv.* 向天空地;向天國地。

heav·er [ˈhivɚ; ˈhiːvə] *n.* ①擧者;挑夫;擧物之裝置。②〖航海〗(捲繩用之)槓桿。

***heav·i·ly** [ˈhɛvɪlɪ; ˈhevili] *adv.* ①很重地;很;極。He suffered *heavily*. 他極爲痛苦。②沮喪地;憂鬱地;沉重緩慢地。③稠密地。*heavily* wooded area. 樹木很密的地區。

heav·i·ness [ˈhɛvɪnɪs; ˈhevinis] *n.* ①重;重量。②遲鈍;不活潑;疲倦。③笨拙。④沉重的心情;哀愁。

Heav·i·side layer [ˈhɛvɪˌsaɪd~; ˈhevisaid~] 電離層(於地面約 100 公里之高度處反射電波之氣層)。

‡**heav·y** [ˈhɛvɪ; ˈhevi] *adj.,* **heav·i·er, heav·i·est,** *n., pl.* **heav·ies,** *adv.* —*adj.* ①重的;沉重的;較重的。The box is too *heavy*. 這箱子太重了。②較大的;大的。*heavy* rain. 大雨。③難堪的;苛刻的。*heavy* taxes. 苛稅。④難應付的;難處理的。A *heavy* road is hard to travel over. 崎嶇的路難行。⑤嚴重的;重大的。a *heavy* offense. 重罪。⑥深邃的。⑦壓垂的;載滿的。eyes *heavy* with sleep. 睡意極濃的眼。⑧憂愁的;令人沮喪的;心情沉重的。a *heavy* heart. 沉重的心情。⑨陰沉的;多雲的。a *heavy* sky. 陰沉的天。⑩稠的;厚的;粗的。a *heavy* line. 粗線條。⑪遲緩的;笨拙的;不雅觀的。⑫沉悶的;

無生氣的。*heavy* reading. 沉悶的讀物。⑬聲音高而悶的。the *heavy* roar of cannon. 大砲的隆隆聲。⑭〖軍〗**a.** 重武裝的。**b.** 巨型的。⑮懷孕的。a woman *heavy* with child. 孕婦。⑯思想遲鈍的(人); 講話不流利的(人)。⑰未發好的。*heavy* bread. 未發好的麪包。⑱〖化〗重的。*heavy* hydrogen. 重氫 (符號爲 H^2 或 D)。⑲過量的。a *heavy* smoker. 吸烟過量者。—*n.* ①沉重的東西。②〖俗〗劇中的惡棍; 反派角色。③〖軍〗重武器。④〖俚〗重量級拳擊手。⑤〖俚〗小偷; 强盜。⑥〖衝浪運動〗巨浪。—*adv.* 沉重地(=heavily). ***hang heavy*** 慢慢地毫無趣味地過去。We *hang heavy* on our hands. 我們發現時間眞不易度過。

heav·y-armed [ˈhɛvɪˈɑrmd; ˈheviˈɑːmd] *adj.* 重裝甲的; 有重兵器裝備的。

heavy artillery 〖軍〗①重砲。②〖美〗口徑在 155mm以上之重砲。

heavy bomber 重轟炸機。

heav·y-du·ty [ˈhɛvɪˈdjutɪ; ˈhveiˈdjuːti] *adj.* ①耐用的; 爲載重、爬山等而設計的。*heavy-duty* tires. 載重輪胎; 加强車胎。②重稅的。

heav·y-foot·ed [ˈhɛvɪˈfutɪd; ˈheviˈfutid] *adj.* 笨拙的。

heav·y-hand·ed [ˈhɛvɪˈhændɪd; ˈheviˈhændid] *adj.* ①拙劣的。②暴虐的。—**ly,** *adv.* —**ness,** *n.*

heav·y-heart·ed [ˈhɛvɪˈhɑrtɪd; ˈheviˈhɑːtid] *adj.* 心情沉重的; 悲哀的; 抑鬱的。

heavy industry 重工業。

heav·y-lad·en [ˈhɛvɪˈledn̩; ˈheviˈleidn] *adj.* ①負重的。②心情沉重的。

heavy metal ①重金屬。②重砲。③强敵。

heavy oil 重油。

heav·y-set [ˈhɛvɪˈsɛt; ˈheviˈset] *adj.* 體格魁偉的; 健壯的。

heavy spar 〖礦〗重晶石; 重晶礦。

heavy water 〖化〗重水(分子式爲D_2O)。

heav·y·weight [ˈhɛvɪˌwet; ˈheviweit] *n.* ①重量級拳擊家 (體重在 175 磅以上者)。②超過平均重量的人或物。③〖俗〗聰明的人; 重要的人; 說話有力量的人。***light heavyweight*** 輕重量級拳擊家 (175 磅與 158 磅之間)。—*adj.* ①重的。②特別厚重的。③〖拳擊〗重量級的。④(馬等)載重高達205磅的。

Heb. ①Hebrew. ②Hebrews.

heb·do·mad [ˈhɛbdəˌmæd; ˈhebdəmæd] *n.* 七日; 一週。

heb·dom·a·dal [hɛbˈdɑmədl̩; hebˈdɔmədl] *adj.* 一週的; 七日的; 每七日的。

He·be [ˈhibɪ; ˈhiːbi(ː)] *n.* 〖希臘神話〗青春女神。

heb·e·tate [ˈhɛbɪˌtet; ˈhebiteit] *v.,* **-tat·ed, -tat·ing,** *adj.* —*v.t.* & *v.i.* (使)變遲鈍; (使)變愚蠢。—*adj.* ①遲鈍的; 愚蠢的。②〖植物〗尖端柔鈍的。—**heb·e·ta·tion,** *n.*

heb·e·tude [ˈhɛbɪˌtjud; ˈhebitjuːd] *n.* 遲鈍; 愚蠢; 昏迷狀態。

He·bra·ic [hiˈbre·ɪk; hi(ː)ˈbreiik] *adj.* 希伯來人的; 希伯來語的。

He·bra·ism [ˈhibrɪˌɪzəm; ˈhiːbreiizəm] *n.* ①希伯來語風(習俗等)。②猶太教。

He·bra·ist [ˈhibrɪɪst, ˈhiːbreiist] *n.* 希伯來語言學(文學)家; 希伯來學者; 希伯來思想之人; 猶太教信徒。

He·bra·is·tic [ˌhibrɪˈɪstɪk; ˌhiːbreiˈistik] *adj.* 希伯來(習俗, 語風, 學者)的。

He·bra·ize [ˈhibrɪˌaɪz; ˈhiːbreiaiz] *v.,* **-ized, -iz·ing.** —*v.t.* 以希伯來語陳述; 使成希伯來語風。—*v.i.* 希伯來(語)化; 採取希伯來式的行動或思想。

***He·brew** [ˈhibru; ˈhiːbruː] *n.* ①希伯來人。②希伯來語文。—*adj.* 希伯來人的; 希伯來語文的。〖注意〗在美國 **Hebrew** 卽指猶太人 (Jew)。

Hebrew calendar 猶太曆。

He·brews [ˈhibruz; ˈhiːbruːz] *n.* 〖聖經〗希伯來書(新約中的一篇)。

Hec·a·te [ˈhɛkətɪ; ˈhekəti(ː)] *n.* 〖希臘神話〗司月、地、冥世、魔法之女神。

hec·a·tomb [ˈhɛkəˌtom; ˈhekətoum] *n.* ①大屠殺。②(古希臘羅馬之) 一次百牛的大祭祀。③大量。

heck[1] [hɛk; hek] *n.* 〖蘇, 北英〗①(家畜之) 飼草架。②格子 (擋魚用)。***be*** (*or* ***live***) ***at heck and manger*** 過優裕的生活。

heck[2] *n.* 〖俗,方〗地獄(hell 之委婉稱)。—*interj.* 〖俗,方〗畜生(表示憤怒等)!

heck·le [ˈhɛkl; ˈhekl] *v.,* **-led, -ling,** *n.* —*v.t.* ①(以難題)詰問(演說者); 使困惱。②(以麻梳) 梳理 (麻等)。—*n.* 麻梳。

heck·ler [ˈhɛklɚ; ˈheklə] *n.* 以難題詰問演說者的搗蛋分子。

hec·tare [ˈhɛktɛr; ˈhektɑː] *n.* 公頃 (面積之單位, =1萬平方公尺)。(略作 **ha**)

hec·tic [ˈhɛktɪk; ˈhektik] *adj.* ①發紅的。②發熱的; 發燒的。③〖俗〗興奮的; 緊張忙碌的。④有肺病跡象的。—*n.* ①臉紅。②高熱; 熱病。③患肺癆病者。

hecto- 〖字首〗表"一百"之義。

hectog. hectogram(me).

hec·to·gram(me) [ˈhɛktəˌgræm; ˈhektougræm] *n.* 兡; 百公分; 公兩。(亦作 **hektogram**)

hec·to·graph [ˈhɛktəˌgræf; ˈhektougrɑːf] *n.* 膠版(印刷用)。—*v.t.* 以膠版印刷。

hectol. hectoliter.

hec·to·li·ter, hec·to·li·tre [ˈhɛktəˌlitɚ; ˈhektouˌliːtə] *n.* 公石; 百公升。

hectom. hectometer.

***hec·to·me·ter, hec·to·me·tre** [ˈhɛktəˌmitɚ; ˈhektouˌmiːtə] *n.* 粨; 公引 (=100公尺)。

Hec·tor [ˈhɛktɚ; ˈhektə] *n.* 赫脫 (Homer 史詩 Iliad 中 Troy 戰爭之勇士)。

hec·tor [ˈhɛktɚ; ˈhektə] *n.* 暴徒; 威嚇者; 作威作福者。—*v.i.* & *v.t.* 威嚇; 凌辱; 作威作福。

he'd [hid; hiːd] =**he had, he would** or **he should.**

hed·dle [ˈhɛdl̩; ˈhedl] *n., v.,* **-dled, -dling.** —*n.* 〖紡織〗綜絖; 通線具。—*v.t.* 把(線)通過綜絖孔。

hedge** [hɛdʒ; hedʒ] *n., v.,* **hedged, hedg·ing.** —*n.* ①灌木樹籬。②障壁或界限。a *hedge* of stones. 石子圍牆。③保護或防禦之方法或工具。④賭博或做生意時之預留地步或採取對策以防徹底失敗。be on the hedge; sit on*** (***both sides of***) ***the hedge*** 取兩面態度; 騎牆。***come down on the wrong side of the hedge*** (狩獵時) 打錯主意。***dead hedge*** (樹枝等編成之)樹籬。***not grow on every hedge*** 稀少。***off a hedge*** 公然竊取。***quickset hedge*** 樹籬。***take a sheet off a hedge*** 公然竊取。—*v.t.* ①圍以樹籬; 以樹籬隔開。to *hedge* a field. 栽植灌木於田地四周; 圍禁。②包圍; 圍困; 限制。③做兩面投機以防損失; (賭博中) 兩方下注。④閃避問題。The President *hedged* the question of tax relief. 總統對減稅問

題避不作答。⑤受到…之保護。—*v.i.* ①圍樹籬;修籬笆。②隱藏;潛藏。③兩方下注。④閃爍其詞;廻避。

hedge·hog [ˈhɛdʒˌhɑg; ˈhedʒhɔg] *n.* ①美洲豪猪。②猬。③〖軍〗拒馬等之障礙物(通常以帶刺鐵網爲之)。

hedge·hop [ˈhɛdʒˌhɑp; ˈhedʒhɔp] *v.i.*, **-hopped, -hop·ping.** 〖美俚〗(飛機)超低空飛行(如作噴射殺蟲劑等)。

hedge marriage ①祕密結婚。②不合法之結婚。

hedge·row [ˈhɛdʒˌro; ˈhedʒrou] *n.* 灌木樹籬。

hedge school (昔愛爾蘭之)露天學校。

hedge sparrow 籬雀。

he·don·ic [hiˈdɑnɪk; hiːˈdɔnik] *adj.* ①快樂的。②唯樂說(論)的。③快樂主義(者)的。

he·don·ism [ˈhidn̩ˌɪzəm; ˈhiːdənizəm] *n.* ①快樂主義。②〖心理〗唯樂說。

he·don·ist [ˈhidnɪst; ˈhiːdənist] *n.* ①享樂主義者。②尋求快樂者;過着享樂生活的人。—*adj.* =**hedonistic.**

he·do·nis·tic [ˌhidəˈnɪstɪk; ˌhiːdəˈnistik] *adj.* ①享樂主義(者)的;快樂主義(者)的。②享樂的;過着享樂生活的;放縱的。

hee·bie-jee·bies [ˈhibɪˈdʒibɪz; ˈhiːbiˈdʒiːbiz] *n.* (作 *pl.* 解)〖俚〗神經過敏;緊張;悒鬱。

***heed** [hid; hiːd] *v.t.* 注意到;留心到。—*v.i.* 注意;留意。—*n.* 注意;留心。to give *heed* to a warning. 注意一項警告。—**er,** *n.*

heed·ful [ˈhidfəl; ˈhiːdful] *adj.* 注意的;留心的;謹愼的。—**ly,** *adv.* —**ness,** *n.*

***heed·less** [ˈhidlɪs; ˈhiːdlis] *adj.* 不注意的;不留心的;不謹愼的。to be *heedless* of others. 不留意他人。—**ly,** *adv.* —**ness,** *n.*

hee·haw [ˈhiˌhɔ; ˈhiːˈhɔː] *v.i.* ①驢叫。②大笑;傻笑。—*n.* ①驢叫聲。②狂笑;傻笑。

‡heel¹ [hil; hiːl] *n.* ①踵;足跟。②鞋或襪的踵部。③鞋或靴的後跟。④獸類相當於人踵部的後腿部分;有蹄的飛節;馬的後足。⑤船的後部;龍骨的後端;桅的下部。⑥像踵的東西。⑦殘餘部分;後部。***at (one's) heel (s)*** 緊接後邊的。***come to heel*** **a.** (狗)緊跟於主人之後。**b.**馴服。***down at the heel(s)*** 鞋後跟穿破的;襤褸的;邋遢的。***drag one's heels*** **a.** 故意延宕;有意躭擱。**b.** 勉强同意。***head over heels*** (or ***heels over head***) **a.** 顚倒;倒轉;匆忙。**b.** 完全。***kick*** (or ***cool***) ***one's heels*** 等候;久候。***kick up one's heels*** 歡欣;興奮(尤指重獲自由之樂)。***lay by the heel(s)*** **a.** 囚禁。**b.** 獲得勝利;使無效。***on (upon) the heels of*** 緊接而來。***out at heel(s)*** 襪跟穿破的;衣衫襤褸的。***show a clean pair of heels*** = **show one's heels to** 逃脫;將追捕者摔在後面。***take to one's heels*** 逃走。***to heel*** **a.** 緊隨在後。**b.** 在控制之下;被征服。***turn on one's heel(s)*** 急轉身。***under the heel of*** 在…的蹂躪之下。—*v.t.* ①補鞋跟。to sole and *heel* a pair of shoes. 補一雙鞋之鞋底及鞋跟。②尾隨。③以鞋後跟踏(地板等)。④〖俗〗給(錢等)予某人。⑤以高爾夫球棒之底部擊(球)。—*v.i.* ①尾隨而行。②跳舞時按節拍以後跟踏地。***heel in*** 暫時以土包覆植物之根部。

heel² *v.i.* (船)傾向一邊。—*v.t.* 使(船)傾向一邊。—*n.* 傾側。

heel³ *n.* 〖俗〗卑鄙之徒。

heel-and-toe [ˈhilənˈto; ˈhiːlənˈtou] *adj.* 前足踵落地後,後足踵始離地的(步法)。

heel·ball [ˈhilˌbɔl; ˈhiːlbɔːl] *n.* ①踵之底部。②蜜蠟與油烟混合之墨。

heeled [hild; hiːld] *adj.* ①有後踵的。high-*heeled.* 高跟的。②〖美俚〗**a.** 有錢的;富有的。well-*heeled* travelers. 有錢的旅客。**b.** 帶手鎗的。

heel·er [ˈhilɚ; ˈhiːlə] *n.* ①上鞋跟者;修鞋跟者。②〖美俗〗(政客的)部下;食客。

heel·ing [ˈhilɪŋ; ˈhiːliŋ] *n.* 〖航海〗(船的)傾斜。

heel·tap [ˈhilˌtæp; ˈhiːltæp] *n.* ①鞋跟上另加之皮。②(杯中)殘酒。***No heeltaps!*** 乾杯!

heft [hɛft; heft] *n.* ①重量;重。②大部分;主要部分。—*v.t.* ①掂(持物而估其重量)。②舉起。

heft·y [ˈhɛftɪ; ˈhefti] *adj.*, **-i·er, -i·est.** 〖俗〗大的;强壯的;重的。a *hefty* fellow. 一個健壯的人。

He·gel [ˈhegl̩; ˈheigl] *n.* 黑格爾(Georg Wilhelm Friedrich, 1770-1831, 德國哲學家)。

He·ge·li·an [heˈgelɪən; heiˈgiːljən] *adj.* 黑格爾(哲學)的。—*n.* 黑格爾派哲學家;黑格爾之門徒。

heg·e·mon·ic [ˌhɛdʒəˈmɑnɪk; ˌhiːgiˈmɔnik] *adj.* 支配的;掌霸權的;指導的;優越的。(亦作 **hegemonical**)

he·gem·o·ny [hiˈdʒɛmənɪ; hi(ː)ˈgeməni] *n.*, *pl.* **-nies.** 領導權;霸權;盟主權。

he·gi·ra [hiˈdʒaɪrə; ˈhedʒirə] *n.* ①(常 H-) 紀元622年, Mohammed 自 Mecca 至 Medina 之逃走。②(常 H-) 回教紀元(卽紀元 622 年)。③離開;逃避。(亦作 **hejira, hijra, hijrah**)

heif·er [ˈhɛfɚ; ˈhefə] *n.* ①三歲以下之小母牛。②年輕女子。

heigh [he, haɪ; hei] *interj.* 嗨!(引人注意、質問、鼓舞、或表示高興等之呼喊聲)。

heigh-ho [ˈheˈho; ˈheiˈhou] *interj.* 嗨嗬(表示疲倦、失望、驚悸等之呼聲)。

‡height [haɪt; hait] *n.* ①高;高度。the *height* of a mountain. 山之高度。②身高。He is six feet in *height.* 他有六英尺高。③(常 *pl.*)高地;山岡。on the mountain *heights.* 在山岡上。④頂點;極度。⑤〖古〗社會上之高貴地位。(亦作 **hight**)

***height·en** [ˈhaɪtn̩; ˈhaitn] *v.t.* ①增高;提高;加高。to *heighten* an effect. 提高效能。②增進;增强。③加强(色彩);誇張。—*v.i.* ①增高。Day by day the structure *heightened.* 建築物逐日增高。②增加;提高。

Hei·lung·kiang [ˈheˈlʊŋdʒɪˈɑŋ; ˈheiˈluŋˈdʒjaːŋ] *n.* 黑龍江(**a.** 中國東北與俄國間之界河。**b.**中國東北之一省,省會爲北安市, Peian)。

hei·nous [ˈhenəs; ˈheinəs] *adj.* 極惡的;可憎的;可恨的。—**ly,** *adv.* —**ness,** *n.*

***heir** [ɛr; ɛə] *n.* 嗣子;繼承人。to fall *heir* to one's father's bad temper. 繼承了父親的壞脾氣的人。—*v.t.* 〖方〗繼承。

heir apparent *pl.* **heirs apparent.** ①法定繼承人。②繼承某地位已成定局的人。

heir at law *pl.* **heirs at law.** 當然繼承人。

heir·ess [ˈɛrɪs; ˈɛəris] *n.* 女繼承人。

heir·less [ˈɛrlɪs; ˈɛəlis] *adj.* 無繼承人的;無嗣的。

heir·loom [ˈɛrˌlum; ˈɛəluːm] *n.* 傳家寶;祖傳物。

heir presumptive *pl.* **heirs presumptive.** 雖爲繼承人但其繼承權可因近親之出生而消失的人。

heist (haɪst; haist) 〖美俚〗 *v.t. & v.i.* 搶;偷。—*n.* 盜竊。—**er,** *n.* 「**tare.**」

hek·tare (ˈhɛktɛr; ˈhektɑː) *n.* =**hec-**

Hel (hel; hel) *n.* 〖北歐神話〗①陰間之女神。②陰間。(亦作 **Hela**)

‡**held** (hɛld; held) *v.* pt. & pp. of **hold.**

Hel·en (ˈhɛlɪn; ˈhelin) *n.* 〖希臘神話〗 Zeus 與 Leda 所生之女(因被 Paris 所拐而引起 Troy 戰爭)。

he·li·a·cal (hɪˈlaɪəkl; hi(ː)ˈlaiəkəl) *adj.* 〖天文〗 太陽的; 與太陽同方向並與太陽(幾乎) 同時出沒的。(亦作 **heliac**)

He·li·an·thus (ˌhilɪˈænθəs; ˌhiːliˈænθəs) *n., pl.* **-thus·es.** 〖植物〗 ①向日葵屬。②(h-) 向日葵屬之任一種植物;向日葵。

hel·i·borne (ˈhɛlɪˌborn; ˈhelibɔːn) *adj.* 以直升機運送或完成的。

hel·i·cal (ˈhɛlɪkl; ˈhelikl) *adj.* 螺旋形的。

hel·i·coid (ˈhɛlɪˌkɔɪd; ˈhelikɔid) *adj.* 螺旋形(狀)的。—*n.* 〖幾何〗螺旋體;螺旋面。—**al,** *adj.* —**al·ly,** *adv.* 「利空低音大號。」

hel·i·con (ˈhɛlɪˌkɑn; ˈhelikən) *n.* 海

Hel·i·con (ˈhɛlɪˌkɑn; ˈhelikən) *n.* ①赫利孔山(在希臘南部, 相傳是 Apollo 與 Muses 所居之山)。②詩思之源泉。

hel·i·cop·ter (ˈhɛlɪˌkɑptɚ, ˈhi-; ˈhelikɔptə) *n.* 直升飛機。 —*v.i. & v.t.* 乘坐直升飛機。

hel·i·lift (ˈhɛlɪˌlɪft; ˈhelilift) *v.t.* 以直升機運輸 (尤指在緊急時)。 「**heli-.**」

helio- 〖字首〗表"太陽"之義。母音前爲

he·li·o·cen·tric (ˌhilɪoˈsɛntrɪk; ˌhiːliouˈsentrik) *adj.* 〖天文〗以太陽爲中心的。(亦作**heliocentrical**)—**al·ly,** *adv.*—**i·ty,** *n.*

He·li·o·chrome (ˈhilɪoˌkrom; ˈhiːlioukroum) *n.* 〖商標名〗 天然色照片。

he·li·o·gram (ˈhilɪəˌgræm; ˈhiːliəgræm) *n.* 日光反射信號。

he·li·o·graph (ˈhilɪəˌgræf; ˈhiːliougrɑːf) *n.* ①日光反射信號機。②太陽照像機(昔攝太陽照片用)。③日光儀; 感光日照計。—*v.t. & v.i.* 以日光反射信號機通訊。

he·li·og·ra·phy (ˌhilɪˈɑgrəfɪ; ˌhiːliˈɔgrəfi) *n.* ①〖天文〗 太陽面學。②照相製版法。③日光反射信號法。

he·li·o·gra·vure (ˌhilɪəgrəˈvjur; ˈhiːliougrəˈvjuə) *n.* 凹版照相(術)。

he·li·om·e·ter (ˌhilɪˈɑmətɚ; ˌhiːliˈɔmitə) *n.* 太陽儀。

He·li·os (ˈhilɪˌɑs; ˈhiːliɔs) *n.* 〖希臘神話〗 赫利阿斯 (Hyperion 與 Thia 之子, Phaëthon 之父,太陽之神)。(亦作 **Helius**)

he·li·o·scope (ˈhilɪəˌskop; ˈhiːliəskoup) *n.* 觀日望遠鏡。

he·li·o·stat (ˈhilɪəˌstæt; ˈhiːlioustæt) *n.* 日光反射器;向日鏡。

he·li·o·ther·a·py (ˌhilɪoˈθɛrəpɪ; ˌhiːliouˈθerəpi) *n.* 〖醫〗 日光療法。

he·li·o·trope (ˈhiljəˌtrop; ˈheljətroup) *n.* ①〖植物〗 天芥菜屬植物。 ②淡紫色。③〖礦〗 血玉髓;血石。—*adj.* 淡紫色的。

he·li·o·trop·ic (ˌhilɪəˈtrɑpɪk; ˌheljəˈtrɔpik) *adj.* 〖植物〗 向日性的。

he·li·ot·ro·pism (ˌhilɪˈɑtrəpɪzm; ˌhiːliˈɔtrəpizəm) *n.* 〖植物〗向日性。

he·li·o·type (ˈhilɪəˌtaɪp; ˈhiːliətaip) *n., v.,* **-typed, -typ·ing.** —*n.* ①膠版印製之圖畫。②膠版印刷。③珂羅版。—*v.t.* 膠版印製。 「**heliport.**」

hel·i·pad (ˈhɛləˌpæd; ˈhelipæd) *n.* =

hel·i·port (ˈhɛləˌport; ˈhelipɔːt) *n.* 直升機機場 (常爲屋頂)。

he·li·um (ˈhilɪəm; ˈhiːljəm) *n.* 氦 (化學元素, 符號爲 He)。

he·lix (ˈhilɪks; ˈhiːliks) *n., pl.* **he·lix·es, hel·i·ces** (ˈhɛlɪˌsiz; ˈhelisiːz). ①螺旋; 螺旋形之物。②〖解剖〗耳輪。③〖建築〗(柱頭之) 渦卷。④〖數學〗 螺旋; 螺旋線。⑤(H-) 〖動物〗蝸牛屬。⑥蝸牛。

hell** (hɛl; hel) *n.* ①地獄;冥府。②邪惡的地方。 a gambling *hell.* 賭博場。③苦境; 難境。④地獄中的人。⑤用以表示憤怒、煩惱、驚訝。Go to *hell!* 滾蛋! 該死! What the *hell* are you doing? 你到底在搞甚麼? ⑥引起痛苦之事(尤指挨罵)。⑦裁縫放碎布的容器。 ***be hell on 〖俚〗 **a.** 苛刻於。**b.** 有害於。***get*** (or ***catch***) ***hell*** 〖俚〗挨罵。***hell of a*** 〖俚〗 **a.** 很壞的; 很難的。**b.** 不平常的;重要的。**c.** 很多。**d.** 很。 ***make one's life a hell*** 使生活成爲地獄般的苦境。 ***play hell with*** 〖俚〗 盲目地處理; 加害。 ***raise hell*** 〖俚〗 **a.** 狂歡。 **b.** 大吵大鬧;極力反對。 ***suffer hell on earth*** 忍受人間之苦。

he'll (hil; hiːl) ①=**he will.** ②=**he shall.**

Hel·las (ˈhɛləs; ˈhelæs) *n.* 希臘(古名)。

hell·bend·er (ˈhɛlˌbɛndɚ; ˈhelˌbendə) *n.* ①(北美產之) 大鯢魚。②〖俚〗 **a.** 長時間之鬧飲。 **b.** 酒醉喧鬧之人。**c.** 魯莽之人。

hell·bent (ˈhɛlˌbɛnt; ˈhelbent) *adj.* 〖美俚〗①熱心的;堅決的〖for, on〗。②開快車的。

hell·box (ˈhɛlˌbɑks; ˈhelbɔks) *n.* 〖印刷〗廢鉛字箱。

hell·cat (ˈhɛlˌkæt; ˈhelkæt) *n.* ①凶惡的婦人;悍婦。②巫婆;女妖。 「物〗蒜藜蘆。」

hel·le·bore (ˈhɛləˌbor; ˈhelibɔː) *n.* 〖植

Hel·lene (ˈhɛlin; ˈheliːn) *n.* 希臘人。

Hel·len·ic (hɛˈlɛnɪk; heˈliːnik) *adj.* 希臘的; 古希臘之歷史、語言或文化的。—*n.* ①包括希臘語的印歐語系。②古希臘語。

Hel·len·ism (ˈhɛlɪnˌɪzəm; ˈhelinizəm) *n.* ①古希臘文化或理想;希臘精神。②古希臘風格(指語言、思想等)。③希臘文明。

Hel·len·ist (ˈhɛlɪnɪst; ˈhelinist) *n.* ①採用希臘語(風)之非希臘人。②古代希臘文化、語言、文學、制度研究者。

hell-fire, hell·fire (ˈhɛlˈfaɪr; ˈhelˈfaiə) *n.* ①地獄之火。②地獄之懲罰。

hell·gra(m)·mite (ˈhɛlgrəˌmaɪt; ˈhelgrəmait) *n.* 美洲產之翅蟲之幼蟲 (用作魚餌)。 「*n.* 地獄之犬;凶惡之人。」

hell·hound (ˈhɛlˌhaund; ˈhelhaund)

hel·lion (ˈhɛljən; ˈheljən) *n.* 〖俗〗①地獄裏的人;應該下地獄的人;惡人。②潑婦。

hell·ish (ˈhɛlɪʃ; ˈheliʃ) *adj.* ①(來自)地獄的。②兇惡的。③〖俗〗令人討厭的。

***hel·lo** (həˈlo; hʌˈlou) *interj., v.,* **-loed, -lo·ing,** *n., pl.* **-los.** —*interj.* 喂! 哈囉! —*v.i. & v.t.* 向人呼"喂!" —*n.* 表示歡迎或驚訝的呼聲; 引人注意的呼聲。(亦作 **hullo**)

hello girl 〖美俗〗女電話接線生。

hell·u·va (ˈhɛləvə; ˈheləvə) 〖主美俚〗 *adv.* 很; 非常。—*adj.* ①非常困難的; 不愉快的;很壞的;腐敗的。②了不起的;傑出的。

***helm**¹ (hɛlm; helm) *n.* ①舵;舵柄;駕駛盤。②樞機。 the *helm* of state. 國家的樞機(即一國之政府)。③〖氣象〗山頭雲。—*v.t.* 駕駛;掌舵。—**less,** *adj.* 「(或配備)鋼盔。」

helm² 〖古,詩〗 *n.* =**helmet.** —*v.t.* 戴

helm cloud 〖氣象〗山頭雲。

***hel·met** (ˈhɛlmɪt; ˈhelmit) *n.* 盔;鋼盔。

Soldiers wear steel *helmets*; firemen wear leather *helmets*. 兵士們戴鋼盔，消防隊員戴皮盔。

hel·minth ['hɛlmɪnθ; 'helminθ] *n.* 寄生蟲；腸蟲；蛔蟲。

hel·min·thic [hɛl'mɪnθɪk; hel'minθik] *adj.* ①腸蟲的；蛔蟲的；寄生蟲的。②驅腸蟲的；殺腸蟲的。—*n.* 驅腸蟲劑；殺腸蟲劑。

helms·man ['hɛlmzmən; 'helmzmən] *n.*, *pl.* **-men.** 舵手。

helm wind 【氣象】山頭風。

Hel·ot ['hɛlət; 'helət] *n.* ①古斯巴達的農奴。②(h-) 奴隸；農奴。

hel·ot·ism ['hɛlət,ɪzəm; 'helətizəm] *n.* (斯巴達)農奴制度；農奴身分。

hel·ot·ry ['hɛlətrɪ; 'helətri] *n.* ①農奴；奴隸（集合稱）。②農奴(奴隸)制度；農奴(奴隸)之境遇。

:help [hɛlp; help] *v.t.* ①幫助；幫忙；援助；攙扶。Please *help* me. 請幫助我。②資助；賙濟；接濟。③(餐席上)奉(菜等)。Let me *help* you to some more meat. 讓我再給你一點肉吧。④減輕；減緩。This medicine will *help* your cough. 這種藥會減輕你的咳嗽。⑤阻止；避免(常與can, can't 連用)。I can't *help* thinking that he is still alive. 我不能不認爲他尚活着。⑥促進；助長。to *help* digestion. 促進消化。—*v.i.* ①幫助；援助；救助。That doesn't *help* much. 那沒有甚麼用處。②開飯；上菜。***help but*** 避免；不。She couldn't *help but* plague her husband. 她無法不使她丈夫頭痛(她天生是一個找丈夫麻煩的女人)。***help oneself to*** **a.** 自取(所需)。*Help* yourself to all you wish. 你要甚麼就拿甚麼好了。**b.** 擅取；侵占。***help out*** 協助；協助完成。***So help me God!*** 我在說實話；我敢對天發誓！—*n.* ①幫助；救助；救濟。Thank you for your kind *help*. 謝謝你的惠助。②幫助者；助手；助力。You were a great *help* to me. 你是我的得力助手。③【美】僕人；佣人。a lady *help*. 女僕。④補救辦法；防止辦法。⑤一人一分之食物。—**er,** *n.*

·help·ful ['hɛlpfəl; 'helpful] *adj.* 有幫助的；有益的；有用的。You've been very *helpful*. 你(給我們)幫了很多忙。—**ly,** *adv.* —**ness,** *n.*

help·ing ['hɛlpɪŋ; 'helpiŋ] *n.* ①輔助；援助。②(食物的)一分；一客。three *helpings* of meat and vegetables. 三客肉與蔬菜。—*adj.* 輔助的；幫助的。

helping hand 幫助；援助；援手。

·help·less ['hɛlplɪs; 'helplis] *adj.* ①無依無靠的；無助的；不能自立的。②迷惑的；混亂的。He looked at her with a *helpless* expression on his face. 他以迷惑的表情看着她。

·help·less·ly ['hɛlplɪslɪ; 'helplisli] *adv.* 孤零無依地；無助地。She looked round *helplessly*. 她無助地向四周張望。

help·less·ness ['hɛlplɪsnɪs; 'helplisnis] *n.* 無助。

help·mate ['hɛlp,met; 'helpmeit] *n.* ①助手；伴侶。②配偶。

help·meet ['hɛlp,mit; 'helpmi:t] *n.* ＝**helpmate.**

Hel·sin·ki ['hɛlsɪŋkɪ; 'helsiŋki] *n.* 赫爾辛基(芬蘭, Finland 的首都)。

hel·ter-skel·ter ['hɛltə'skɛltə; 'heltə'skeltə] *adv.* 手忙脚亂地；慌張地。—*adj.* 倉皇的；慌張的。—*n.* 慌張；狼狽。

helve [hɛlv; helv] *n.*, *v.*, **helved, helv·ing.** —*n.* 工具之柄；(尤指) 斧柄。—*v.t.* 裝柄於…。—**helv·er,** *n.*

Hel·ve·tia [hɛl'viʃə; hel'vi:ʃiə] *n.* ①赫爾維希亞(古羅馬時代之阿爾卑斯山地之一區；今爲瑞士之西部及北部地區)。②【詩】瑞士(拉丁名＝Switzerland)。

Hel·ve·tian [hɛl'viʃən; hel'vi:ʃiən] *adj.* 赫爾維希亞(人)的；瑞士的。—*n.* 赫爾維希亞人；瑞士人。

·hem[1] [hɛm; hem] *n.*, *v.*, **hemmed, hem·ming.** —*n.* ①衣服邊緣。②邊緣。the *hem* of the sea. 海邊。—*v.t.* ①縫…的邊。②包圍；關閉【常 in, about, around】。to *hem* out. 閉門不納。

hem[2] *interj.*, *n.*, *v.*, **hemmed, hem·ming.** —*interj.* 哼(表示懷疑或引人注意)。—*n.* 哼聲。—*v.i.* 發哼聲；(講演時)停頓；遲疑。***hem and haw*** 避免作正面的答覆。

he·ma·chrome ['himə,krom; 'hi:məkroum] *n.* 【醫】血紅素；血色質。

he·mal ['himəl; 'hi:məl] *adj.* 血的；血管的。(亦作 **hematal, haemal**)

he-man ['hi'mæn; 'hi:'mæn] *n.*, *pl.* **-men.** 【俗】有男性魅力的男人；雄壯的男人。

he·ma·tem·e·sis [,himə'tɛməsɪs; ,hi:mə'teməsis] *n.* 【醫】吐血；嘔血；咯血。

he·mat·ic [hi'mætɪk; hi:'mætik] *adj.* ①血的；血色的；多血的。②對血液起作用或效驗的。—*n.* 淨血藥。

hem·a·tin(e) ['hɛmətɪn; 'hemətin] *n.* ①蘇木紅。②血質。③血黑質。

hem·a·tite ['hɛmə,taɪt; 'hemətait] *n.* 【礦】赤鐵礦 (Fe_2O_3)。

hem·a·to·cyte ['hɛmato,saɪt; 'hemətousait] *n.* 血球；血細胞。

he·ma·tol·o·gy [,hɛmə'tɑlədʒɪ; ,hemə'tɔlədʒi] *n.* 血液學。

he·ma·tu·ri·a [,himə'tjurɪə; ,hi:mə'tju:riə] *n.* 【醫】血尿；血尿症。

heme [him; hi:m] *n.* 血質；血基質。

hemi- 【字首】表"半"之義。

hem·i·cra·ni·a [,hɛmɪ'krenɪə; ,hemi'kreiniə] *n.* 【醫】偏頭痛。

hem·i·cy·cle ['hɛmə,saɪkl; 'hemi,saikl] *n.* ①半圓(形)。②半圓形之建築物、房間、鬥技場、牆壁等。

Hem·ing·way ['hɛmɪŋ,we; 'hemiŋwei] *n.* 海明威 (Ernest, 1899–1961, 美國小說家, 1954年得諾貝爾獎)。

hem·i·ple·gi·a [,hɛmɪ'plidʒɪə; ,hemi'pli:dʒiə] *n.* 【醫】半身不遂；偏癱。

He·mip·ter·a [hɪ'mɪptərə; hi'miptərə] *n. pl.* 【動物】半翅類(如臭蟲、蟬等)。—**he·mip·ter·al, he·mip·ter·ous,** *adj.*

·hem·i·sphere ['hɛməs,fɪr; 'hemisfiə] *n.* ①半球；地球的半面。②【解剖】大腦半球。

hem·i·spher·ic [,hɛmə'sfɛrɪk; ,hemi'sferik] *adj.* ①半(地)球的。②半球狀的。

hem·i·spher·i·cal [,hɛmə'sfɛrəkl; ,hemi'sferikəl] *adj.* ＝**hemispheric.** —**ly,** *adv.*

hem·i·stich ['hɛmə,stɪk; 'hemistik] *n.* 【詩學】①由 cesura 分開之半行。②不完全之詩行。

hem·line ['hɛmlaɪn; 'hemlain] *n.* 上衣, 裙之底緣。

·hem·lock ['hɛmlɑk; 'hemlɔk] *n.* ①胡蘿蔔科毒草。②該毒草提鍊之毒藥。③【美】鐵杉。④鐵杉木。

hemo- 【字首】表"血"之義。(亦作 **hem-, haem-, haemo-**)

he·mo·di·a·lyz·er [,himo'daɪə,laɪzə; ,hi:mou'daiə,laizə] *n.* 人造腎。

he·mo·glo·bin [ˌhiməˈglobɪn; ˌhiːmouˈgloubin] *n.* 血紅蛋白;血紅素。

he·mo·phil·i·a [ˌhiməˈfɪlɪə; ˌhiːmouˈfiliə] *n.* 〖醫〗血友症;出血不止症。

hem·or·rhage [ˈhɛmərɪdʒ; ˈheməridʒ] *n., v.,* **-rhaged, -rhag·ing.** —*n.* 出血; 溢血。—*v.i.* 出血(尤指大量之出血)。—**hem·or·rhag·ic,** *adj.*

hem·or·rhoid(s) [ˈhɛməˌrɔɪd(z); ˈheməroid(z)] *n.* 〖醫〗痔。

hemp [hɛmp; hemp] *n.* ①大麻。②大麻纖維。③大麻製之麻醉劑。—**like,** *adj.*

hemp·en [ˈhɛmpən; ˈhempən] *adj.* 大麻製的;似大麻的。

hem·stitch [ˈhɛmˌstɪtʃ; ˈhemstitʃ] *v.t.* (於布等之邊緣上)結垂綫。—*n.* ①垂綫。②編結垂綫的針法。—**er,** *n.*

:hen [hɛn; hen] *n.* ①母雞。*Hens* lay eggs. 母雞生蛋。②雌鳥; 雌。③〖俗〗女人(尤指好管閒事的); 長舌婦。 ***be like a hen with one chicken*** =**be like a hen on a hot girdle.** 大驚小怪。 ***sell one's hens on a rainy day*** 不會做生意。—**like,** *adj.*

hen·bane [ˈhɛnˌben; ˈhenbein] *n.* 一種茄科之毒草;自此毒草提取之毒。

:hence [hɛns; hens] *adv.* ①因此; 所以; 故。It is very late; *hence* you must go to bed. 時間已很晚,因此你必須去睡覺了。②從此時;從此地。③從此世;從此生。After a long, hard life they were taken *hence.* 過了一個長又辛苦的一生後,他們死了。—*interj.* 滾開! *Hence!* 滾開! *Hence* with him! 把他帶走! ***hence with*** 拿走。〖注意〗 **hence** 作"因此"解,係較正式的用語,通常則用 therefore, consequently 等字。

***hence·forth** [ˌhɛnsˈforθ; ˈhensˈfɔːθ] *adv.* 自此以後;從今以後;今後。

***hence·for·ward** [ˈhɛnsˈfɔrwəd; ˈhensˈfɔːwəd] *adv.* =**henceforth.**

hench·man [ˈhɛntʃmən; ˈhentʃmən] *n., pl.* **-men.** ①親信。②忠實的追隨者。③走狗。

hen·coop [ˈhɛnˌkup; ˈhenkuːp] *n.* 雞塒;飼養家禽的欄棚。

hendeca- 〖字首〗表"十一"之義。

hen·dec·a·syl·lab·ic [ˌhɛndɛkəsɪˈlæbɪk; ˈhendekəsiˈlæbik] *adj.* 含有十一音節的。—*n.* 十一音節的一行詩。

hen·dec·a·syl·la·ble [ˌhɛndɛkəˈsɪləbl; ˈhendekəˌsiləbl] *n.* 十一音節的一行詩或字。

hen·di·a·dys [hɛnˈdaɪədɪs; henˈdaiədis] *n.* 〖修辭〗重名法(用 and 連接兩名詞以代替一名詞及一形容詞之修辭法,如: death and honor =honorable death).

hen·e·quen, hen·e·quin [ˈhɛnəkɪn; ˈhenəkin] *n.* (墨西哥產)龍舌蘭之一種;其纖維。

hen harrier (產於歐洲的) 灰色鷲。

hen-heart·ed [ˈhɛnˌhɑrtɪd; ˈhenˌhaːtid] *adj.* 膽小的;怯懦的。

hen·house [ˈhɛnˌhaus; ˈhenhaus] *n., pl.* **-hous·es.** 鷄塒。

Hen·ley [ˈhɛnlɪ; ˈhenli] *n.* 亨利國際賽船大會 (自 1839 年以來每年在英國 Henley-on-Thames 舉行)。

hen·na [ˈhɛnə; ˈhenə] *n., adj., v.,* **-naed, -na·ing.** —*n.* ①指甲花 (亞熱帶灌木)。②(取自指甲花的)深橘紅色顏料(染頭髮等)。③紅褐色。—*adj.* 紅褐色的。—*v.t.* 以此顏料染。

hen·ner·y [ˈhɛnərɪ; ˈhenəri] *n., pl.* **-ner·ies.** 養鷄場。

hen·o·the·ism [ˈhɛnəθɪɪzm; ˈhenəθiizm] *n.* 擇一神教(自多數神中特選一神而敬奉之,但不否認其他諸神之存在)。

hen party 〖俗〗女人的聚會。

hen·peck [ˈhɛnˌpɛk; ˈhenpek] *v.t.* 駕馭(丈夫);對(丈夫)嘮嗦。

hen·pecked [ˈhɛnˌpɛkt; ˈhenpekt] *adj.* 懼內的;怕老婆的。

Hen·ri·et·ta [ˌhɛnrɪˈɛtə; ˌhenriˈetə] *n.* 女子名。

hen·roost [ˈhɛnˌrust; ˈhenruːst] *n.* 塒;鷄窩。

Hen·ry [ˈhɛnrɪ; ˈhenri] *n.* 男子名。

hep¹ [hɛp; hep] *adj.* 〖美俚〗通曉…的;知悉…的〖常 to〗。

hep² [hʌt, hʌp; hʌt, hʌp] *interj.* 齊步走時喊叫之"一,二"口令。

hep·a·rin [ˈhɛpərɪn; ˈheparin] *n.* 〖生化〗肝素;肝磷脂(肝臟中含有多量的防止血液凝固之物質)。 —**oid,** *adj.*

he·pat·ic [hɪˈpætɪk; hiˈpætik] *adj.* ①肝臟的。②肝臟色的。③〖植物〗地錢類的。—*n.* ①治肝病之藥。②地錢。

he·pat·i·ca [hɪˈpætɪkə; hiˈpætikə] *n., pl.* **-cas, -cae** [-ˌsi; -siː]. 〖植物〗地錢屬植物;地錢。

hep·a·ti·tis [ˌhɛpəˈtaɪtɪs; ˌhepəˈtaitis] *n.* 〖醫〗肝炎。

hep·cat [ˈhɛpˌkæt; ˈhepkæt] *n.* 〖俚〗爵士音樂之大師;愛好爵士音樂者。

Hep·ple·white [ˈhɛplˌhwaɪt; ˈheplwait] *n.* ①海普懷特 (George, ?-1786, 英國傢具設計家)。②海普懷特式傢具。—*adj.* 海普懷特式的(傢具)。

hepta- 〖字首〗表"七"之義(在母音前作 **hept-**).

hep·ta·chord [ˈhɛptəˌkɔrd; ˈheptəkɔːd] *n.* ①七弦琴。②〖音樂〗七音音階。

hep·tad [ˈhɛptæd; ˈheptæd] *n.* ①七;七個之一組。②〖化〗七價之基; 七價元素。

hep·ta·gon [ˈhɛptəˌgɑn; ˈheptəgən] *n.* 七角形;七邊形。—**al,** *adj.*

hep·ta·he·dron [ˌhɛptəˈhidrən; ˈheptəˈhedrən] *n., pl.* **-drons, -dra** [-drə; -drə]. 七面體。

hep·tam·e·ter [hɛpˈtæmətə; hepˈtæmitə] *n.* 七音步之詩行。—*adj.* 含七音步的。—**hep·ta·met·ri·cal,** *adj.*

hep·tar·chy [ˈhɛptɑrkɪ; ˈheptaːki] *n., pl.* **-chies.** ①七頭政治。②(常 H-)〖英史〗(449-828 Anglo-Saxon 時代之) 七王國。③七盟邦。

Hep·ta·teuch [ˈhɛptəˌtjuk; ˈheptətjuːk] *n.* 舊約聖經之開首七卷。

hep·tode [ˈhɛptod; ˈheptoud] *n.* 〖電〗七極眞空管。

:her [hɝ; həː, əː, hə, ə] *pron.* the objective case of **she.** 她;伊。I like *her.* 我喜歡她。—*adj.* the possessive form of **she.** 她的;伊的。*Her* father is dead. 她的父親死了。

her. ①heraldic. ②heraldry.

He·ra [ˈhirə; ˈhiːrə] *n.* 〖希臘神話〗Zeus 之妹及妻,司婦女與婚嫁之女神(相當於羅馬神話之 Juno).

***her·ald** [ˈhɛrəld; ˈherəld] *n.* ①傳令官。②使者;報信者。③司紋章的官。④先驅;前鋒。In England the cuckoo is a *herald* of spring. 在英國杜鵑鳥是春的預兆。⑤(古代)戰時代表國王之使節。—*v.t.* 預報; 宣布。The newspaper *heralded* the arrival of the army. 報紙宣布大軍的到達。

he·ral·dic [hɛˈrældɪk; heˈrældik, hiˈr-] *adj.* ①傳令(官)的;司紋章之官的。②紋章的;紋章學的。**—al·ly,** *adv.*
her·ald·ry [ˈhɛrəldrɪ; ˈherəldri] *n., pl.* **-ries.** ①紋章學。②紋章圖樣學。③紋章之總稱。**—her·ald·ist,** *n.*
***herb** [ɝb, hɝb; həːb] *n.* ①草;藥草;香草。a *herb* garden. 藥草園。②〖古〗=**herbage.** **—like, —y,** *adj.*
her·ba·ceous [hɝˈbeʃəs; həːˈbeiʃəs] *adj.* ①草本植物的。②像葉的;綠的。③種有草本植物的。 **—ly,** *adv.*
herb·age [ˈɝbɪdʒ, ˈhɝ-; ˈhəːbidʒ] *n.* ①草本植物之集合稱;草(尤指牧草)。②草本植物之多汁的莖與綠葉。③〖法律〗(在他人土地上之)牧畜權。
herb·al [ˈhɝbl, ˈɝbl; ˈhəːbəl] *adj.* 草本的;草本的。—*n.* 植物誌。
herb·al·ist [ˈhɝblɪst, ˈɝbl-; ˈhəːbəlist] *n.* ①植物學家;草本學家。②採集草本植物的人;植物採集者。③種植或賣草藥者;草藥商。④草藥醫生。
her·bar·i·a [hɝˈbɛrɪə; həːˈbɛəriə] *n.* pl. of **herbarium.**
her·bar·i·um [hɝˈbɛrɪəm; həːˈbɛəriəm] *n., pl.* **-i·ums, -i·a.** ①臘葉植物標本。②植物標本簿(箱、室、館)。
herb doctor 草藥醫生。
Her·bert [ˈhɝbɚt; ˈhəːbət] *n.* 赫伯特(George, 1593–1633, 英國牧師、詩人)。
herb·i·cide [ˈhɝbəˌsaɪd; ˈhəːbisaid] *n.* 除草藥。**—her·bi·cid·al,** *adj.*
her·biv·o·rous [hɝˈbɪvərəs; həːˈbivərəs] *adj.* 草食的。
her·bo·rize [ˈhɝbəˌraɪz; ˈhəːbəraiz] *v.,* **-rized, -riz·ing.** —*v.i.* 〖古〗採集植物。
herb-tea [ˈhɝbˌti; ˈhəːbtiː] *n.* 〖英〗湯藥;藥湯。
herb-wa·ter [ˈhɝbˌwɔtɚ; ˈhəːbˌwɔːtə] *n.* =**herb-tea.**
her·cu·le·an [hɝˈkjulɪən; ˌhəːkjuˈliːən] *adj.* ①體力極大的;極魁梧的。②極艱鉅的;需大力氣的。③(H-) Hercules 的。
Her·cu·les [ˈhɝkjəˌliz; ˈhəːkjuliːz] *n.* ①海克力斯(希臘神話中的大力士)。②〖天文〗武仙座。(亦作 **Heracles, Herakles**)
Hercules beetle (蟲)大金龜子。
Her·cu·les'-club [ˈhɝkjəˌlizklʌb; ˈhəːkjuliːzklʌb] *n.* 〖植物〗山椒類。
Hercules powder 礦山用炸藥之一種。
herd** [hɝd; həːd] *n.* ①獸羣。a *herd* of cows. 一羣牛。②〖蔑〗人羣;普通人;羣衆。③牧人(多用於復合字中)。ride herd on*** 控制;管束。***the herd*** 羣衆。—*v.t.* ①使成羣;放牧(牛羊等)。②領一羣人至某地。The teacher *herded* the children into the classroom. 老師把小孩們領進課室裏。—*v.i.* 成羣;羣集。People *herded* together like cattle. 人們像牛一般羣聚一起。
herd·book [ˈhɝdˌbuk; ˈhəːdˈbuk] *n.* (牛、羊等之)血統簿。
herd·er [ˈhɝdɚ; ˈhəːdə] *n.* 牧牛羣或羊羣的人。
herd instinct 〖心理〗成羣本能。
herds·man [ˈhɝdzmən; ˈhəːdzmən] *n., pl.* **-men.** ①牧者;牧人。②(H-)〖天文〗=**Boötes.**
He·re [ˈhiri; ˈhiːriː] *n.* =**Hera.**
‡here [hɪr; hiə, hjəː] *adv.* ①在這裏;向這裏。I live *here.* 我住在這裏。②現在;這時。*Here* he stopped reading and looked up. 這時他停止看書,抬頭看看。③今世。④用以喚起他人注意之詞。Look *here!* (呼人注意之詞)喂!⑤正考慮中。The matter *here* is of grave concern to us all. 正被考慮中之事對我們有重大影響。***here and now*** 現在;立刻;馬上。***here and there*** 到處;處處。***here below*** 在世界上;今世。***here goes*** 〖俗〗表示自己將做出大膽或不愉快事的決心。***Here's a health (luck) to you!*** (敬酒時用語)祝你健康(幸運)! ***here, there and everywhere*** 到處。***neither here nor there*** 不重要的;不切題的;離題。—*n.* ①這裏;此處(與介系詞連用)。over *here.* 在我這裏;在我這邊。②此生;今生。***the here and now*** 目前。—*interj.* ①(喚人注意之詞)喂!②(點名時之答語)到!有!〖注意〗**here** 常用於以下的倒裝句法: *Here's* the book you're looking for. 這就是你正在找的書。*Here* you are. 你所要的東西在這裏了。*Here* it is! 我找到它了,這裏就是! *Here* we are. 我們終於到達了(目的地)。*Here* he comes! (正在找他)他來了!
here·a·bout(s) [ˌhɪrəˈbaut(s); ˈhiərəˌbaut(s)] *adv.* 附近;在這一帶。
***here·af·ter** [hɪrˈæftɚ, -ˈaf-; hiərˈɑːftə, hjəːr-] *adv.* ①此後;將來。I shall be careful *hereafter.* 我此後將小心。②來世。—*n.* ①將來。②來世。
here·at [hɪrˈæt; hiərˈæt] *adv.* ①〖廢〗在此地。②此時。③因此。
here·by [hɪrˈbaɪ; ˈhiəˈbai, ˈhjəːˈb-] *adv.* 由此;藉此。Notice is *hereby* given that....爲布告事;特此通告(通告用語)。
he·red·i·ta·ble [həˈrɛdətəbl; hiˈreditəbl] *adj.* =**heritable.** **—he·red·i·ta·bil·i·ty,** *n.*
her·e·dit·a·ment [ˌhɛrəˈdɪtəmənt; ˌheriˈditəmənt] *n.* 〖法律〗可繼承之財產。
***he·red·i·tar·y** [həˈrɛdəˌtɛrɪ; hiˈreditəri] *adj.* ①世襲的。②遺傳的。③〖數學〗傳襲類的。**—he·red·i·tar·i·ly,** *adv.*
he·red·i·tism [həˈrɛdɪtɪzm; hiˈreditizm] *n.* 遺傳論。
he·red·i·tist [həˈrɛdətɪst; hiˈreditist] *n.* 遺傳論者。
he·red·i·ty [həˈrɛdətɪ; hiˈrediti] *n., pl.* **-ties.** ①遺傳。②遺傳性。③得自祖先的身心特性。
Her·e·ford [ˈhɛrəfɚd; ˈherifəd] *n.* ①赫里福(英格蘭 Herefordshire 之首府)。②赫里福種之牛(紅毛白斑之食用牛)。—*adj.* 赫里福種的。
here·from [hɪrˈfrɑm; hiəˈfrɔm] *adv.* 從此;由此。
***here·in** [hɪrˈɪn; ˈhiərˈin, ˈhjəːr-] *adv.* ①在此處。*Herein* is love. 這其間有情愛。②如此;鑒於。
here·in·af·ter [ˌhɪrɪnˈæftɚ; ˈhiərinˈɑːftə] *adv.* 在下;在下文中。... *hereinafter* called Buyer. …以下稱買方。
here·in·be·fore [ˌhɪrɪnbɪˈfor; ˈhiərinbiˈfɔː] *adv.* 在上;上文中;在前條。
here·in·to [hɪrˈɪntu; hiərˈintuː] *adv.* 到這裏面;此中。
here·of [hɪrˈɑv; hiərˈɔv] *adv.* 於此;關於此點。
here·on [hɪrˈɑn; ˈhiərˈɔn] *adv.* =**hereupon.**
here's [hɪrz; hiəz] =**here is.** ***here's to*** 敬祝健康、快樂、成功等。*Here's to* you! 敬祝健康。
he·re·si·arch [hɪˈrisɪɑrk; heˈriːziɑːk] *n.* 異教之創始者;邪教之首領。
her·e·sy [ˈhɛrəsɪ; ˈherəsi] *n., pl.* **-sies.** ①異端邪說;異教。to fall into *heresy.* 陷於旁門左道中。②信或持異端邪說。

her·e·tic [ˈhɛrətɪk; ˈherətik, -rit-] *n.* 持異端邪說者;異教徒。—*adj.* =**heretical.**

he·ret·i·cal [həˈrɛtɪkḷ; hiˈretikəl] *adj.* 異端邪說的;信異端邪說的。—**ly,** *adv.* —**ness,** *n.* 「(=to this).」

here·to [hɪrˈtu; ˈhiəˈtuː] *adv.* 至此

***here·to·fore** [ˌhɪrtəˈfor, -ˈfɔr; ˈhiətu-ˈfɔː, ˈhjəː-, -ˈfɔə] *adv.* 直到此時; 此時以前 (=hitherto). 「*adv.* =**hereto.**」

here·un·to [ˌhɪrʌnˈtu; ˈhiərʌnˈtuː]

here·up·on [ˌhɪrəˈpɑn; ˈhiərəˈpɔn] *adv.* ①於此。②隨後;隨即。

here·with [hɪrˈwɪθ; ˈhiəˈwið] *adv.* ①同此;附此。②因此;藉此。 「繼承稅。」

her·i·ot [ˈhɛrɪət; ˈheriət] *n.*【英】借地

her·it·a·ble [ˈhɛrətəbḷ; ˈheritəbl] *adj.* ①可繼承的。②可遺傳的。—**her·it·a·bil·i·ty,** *n.* —**her·it·a·bly,** *adv.*

***her·it·age** [ˈhɛrətɪdʒ; ˈheritidʒ] *n.* ①遺產。②繼承物; 祖先遺留下之事物(如特性、文化、傳統等)。We Chinese have a great cultural *heritage.* 我們中國人有偉大的文化遺產。③天賦的命運; 與生俱來的權利。Poverty was his *heritage.* 他生於貧窮之家。④【聖經】上帝之選民;以色列人。

her·i·tor [ˈhɛrətɚ; ˈheritə] *n.* 繼承人; 嗣子。(女性爲 **heritress**)

her·maph·ro·dite [hɚˈmæfrəˌdaɪt; həːˈmæfrədait] *n.* ①兩性體; 兩性動物; 兩性花。②陰陽人。③具有兩種相反性格的人。④(亦作 **hermaphrodite brig**) 有前桅橫帆與後桅橫帆之二桅帆船。—*adj.* 兩性體的; 陰陽人的;具有相反性格的。

her·maph·ro·dit·ic [hɚˌmæfrəˈdɪtɪk; həːˌmæfrəˈditik] *adj.* 具有男女兩性的;雌雄同體的。(亦作 **hermaphroditical, hermaphroditish**)

her·maph·ro·dit·ism [hɚˈmæfrədaɪˌtɪzəm; həːˈmæfrədaitizm] *n.* 雌雄同體;兼具兩性。(亦作 **hermaphrodism**)

her·me·neu·tic [ˌhɚmənˈjutɪk; ˌhəːmənˈjuːtik] *adj.* (特指聖經之)解釋(學)的;釋經學的。(亦作 **hermeneutical**)

her·me·neu·tics [ˌhɚmənˈjutɪks; ˌhəːmənˈjuːtiks] *n.* (作 *sing.*解)解釋學;聖經註解學。

Her·mes [ˈhɚmiz; ˈhəːmiːz] *n.*【希臘神話】漢密士(司道路、科學、發明、口才、幸運等之神;爲 Zeus 及其他衆神之使者)。

her·met·ic [hɚˈmɛtɪk; həːˈmetik] *adj.* ①密封的;不漏氣的。②鍊金術的。

her·met·i·cal [hɚˈmɛtɪkḷ; həːˈmetikl] *adj.* =**hermetic.** —**ly,** *adv.*

***her·mit** [ˈhɚmɪt; ˈhəːmit] *n.* ①修仙者; 隱士;隱居者。②一種蜂雀。③含有胡桃、葡萄乾等的小甜餅。—**ic,** —**i·cal,** —**ish,** *adj.*

her·mit·age [ˈhɚmɪtɪdʒ; ˈhəːmitidʒ] *n.* ①隱居之所。②(H-) 產於法國東南部的一種酒。③(H-) 在列寧格勒之一博物館(原爲 Catherine II 之宮殿)。

hermit crab 寄生蟹。

hern [hɚn; həːn] *n.*【古,方】=**heron.**

her·ni·a [ˈhɚnɪə; ˈhəːnjə] *n., pl.* **-ni·as, -ni·ae** [-nɪˌi; -niiː].【醫】脫腸;疝氣;突逸。—**her·ni·al,** *adj.*

‡**he·ro** [ˈhɪro; ˈhiərou, ˈhjəːr-] *n., pl.* **-roes.** ①英雄;勇士;豪傑。②(小說、戲劇、史詩等中之)男主角。③超越常人者;神人;半神。④一種大型三明治; 做這種三明治用的麪包。—**like,** *adj.*

Her·od [ˈhɛrəd; ˈherəd] *n.* 希律王(73?–4 B. C., 猶太之王,在位期間37–4 B. C., 以殘虐聞名,見馬太福音第二章)。

He·rod·o·tus [həˈrɑdətəs; heˈrɔdətəs] *n.* 希羅多德(紀元前第五世紀希臘歷史學家,被稱爲史學家之父)。

he·ro·ic** [hɪˈro·ɪk; hiˈrouik, heˈr-, həˈr-] *adj.* ①英勇的;英雄式的。②有關英雄或英勇事蹟的。The *Iliad* and the *Odyssey* are *heroic* poems. "伊利亞德"與"奧德賽"是講述英雄事蹟的詩篇。③特大的; 較眞的爲大的。④英雄故事詩的。⑤採取大膽或極端辦法的。⑥(文體等)崇高的; 壯麗雄偉的。heroic couplet*** 英雄雙行體(詩)。—*n.* ①英雄故事詩。②(*pl.*) **a.** 咬文嚼字; 文縐縐的用語。**b.** 裝腔作勢的辭句、感情或行爲。**c.** 英雄體詩。—**ness,** —**i·ty,** *n.*

he·ro·i·cal [hɪˈro·ɪkḷ; hiˈrouikəl] *adj.* =**heroic.** —**ly,** *adv.* 「英;嗎啡精。」

her·o·in [ˈhɛro·ɪn; ˈherouin] *n.* 海洛

***her·o·ine** [ˈhɛro·ɪn; ˈherouin] *n.* ①女英雄;女傑。②(小說、戲劇、史詩等的)女主角。

***her·o·ism** [ˈhɛroˌɪzəm; ˈherouizəm] *n.* ①英勇;英豪;英雄氣概。②豪俠的行爲;勇敢的事蹟。His returning into the burning building was true *heroism.* 他的回到正在起火的房子是眞正的勇敢行爲。

***her·on** [ˈhɛrən; ˈherən] *n.* 蒼鷺。

her·on·ry [ˈhɛrənrɪ; ˈherənri] *n., pl.* **-ries.** 蒼鷺結集孵卵之處。

hero worship 英雄崇拜。

he·ro-wor·ship [ˈhɪroˌwɝʃɪp; ˈhiərouˌwəːʃip] *n., v.,* **-ship(p)ed, -ship(p)ing.** —*v.t.* 崇拜。—*n.* =**hero worship.**

hero worshipper 英雄崇拜者。(亦作 **hero-worshiper, hero-worshipper**)

her·pes [ˈhɝpiz; ˈhəːpiːz] *n.*【醫】疱疹。

her·pe·tol·o·gy [ˌhɝpəˈtɑlədʒɪ; ˌhəːpəˈtɔlədʒi] *n.* 爬蟲類與兩棲類動物學。

Herr [hɛr; hɛə] *n., pl.* **Her·ren** [ˈhɛrən; ˈhɛərən].【德】①先生;君;閣下。②紳士。

Her·ren·volk [ˈhɛrənˌfɔlk; ˈherənfɔlk]【德】*n.* 優越民族(納粹時代德人之自稱)。

her·ring** [ˈhɛrɪŋ; ˈheriŋ] *n., pl.* **-rings, -ring.** 鯡;青魚。packed as close as herrings*** 緊密;擠得像(罐頭內的)沙丁魚一般。

her·ring·bone [ˈhɛrɪŋˌbon; ˈheriŋboun] *n.* ①鯡魚骨。②人字形。③【滑雪】踏著雪橇以人字形步法上坡。—*adj.* 鯡魚骨狀的;人字形的。 「西洋)。」

herring pond【英諧】大洋(特指北大

‡**hers** [hɝz; həːz] *pron.* ①她的(所有物)。Is that his or *hers?* 那個是他的還是她的? ②屬於她的。This money is *hers.* 這筆錢是屬於她的。

‡**her·self** [həˈsɛlf; həːˈself, həˈs-, əːˈs-, əˈs-] *pron.* ①她自己(her 的反身代名詞)。She hurt *herself* very badly. 她傷了自己,傷得很重。②(她)親自; (她)本人(用以加強語勢)。She *herself* told me the news. 這消息是她親自告訴我的。③正常 (= her real self). She's not *herself* today. 她今天與平時不同(失常)。***(all) by herself*** **a.** 獨力; 自行。**b.** 單獨; 孤獨。Does her mother let her go out (*all*) *by herself?* 她母親讓她獨自一人出去嗎?

Hertz·i·an waves [ˈhɛrtsɪən(ˈhɝt-)~; ˈhəːtsiən~] 電磁波。

***he's** [hiz; hiːz] =**he is** 或 **he has.**

hes·i·tance [ˈhɛzətəns; ˈhezitəns] *n.*

=hesitancy.

hes·i·tan·cy ['hɛzətənsɪ; 'hezitənsi] *n., pl.* -cies. 猶豫不決;躊躇;懷疑。

hes·i·tant ['hɛzətənt; 'hezitənt] *adj.* ①猶豫的; 躊躇的; 懷疑的。②吞吞吐吐的。—ly, *adv.*

***hes·i·tate** ['hɛzə,tet; 'heziteit] *v.i.*, **-tat·ed, -tat·ing.** ①猶豫;躊躇;遲疑。He's still *hesitating* about joining the expedition. 他對於參加這探險隊仍猶豫不決。②不欲;不願。He *hesitated* to take such a big risk. 他不願冒這樣大的危險。③停頓。I *hesitated* before reciting the next line. 朗誦下一行之前我停頓了。④支吾其辭。Embarrassment caused the speaker to *hesitate.* 困窘使演講人吞吞吐吐。—**hes·i·tat·er, hes·i·ta·tor,** *n.*

hes·i·tat·ing·ly ['hɛzə,tetɪŋlɪ;'heziteitiŋli] *adv.* 言語支吾地;吞吞吐吐地。

***hes·i·ta·tion** [,hɛzə'teʃən; ,hezi'teiʃən] *n.* ①躊躇;疑慮; 遲疑。His *hesitation* cost him the championship. 猶豫使他失去了冠軍。②停頓。③言語支吾。*hesitation* in his speech. 他言談中的支吾。④不願意。

hes·i·ta·tive ['hɛzə,tetɪv; 'heziteitiv] *adj.* 猶豫的;遲疑的。—**ly,** *adv.*

Hes·pe·ri·an [hɛs'pɪrɪən;hes'piəriən] *adj.* ①Hesperia 的; 西國的。②西方的。③〖詩〗Hesperides 的。—*n.*〖罕〗西國之人;西方之居民。

Hes·per·i·des [hɛs'pɛrə,diz; hes'peridiːz] *n. pl.*〖希臘神話〗①(作 *pl.*解)看守金蘋果園之三至七個仙女。②(作 *sing.* 解)金蘋果園。

Hes·per·us ['hɛspərəs; 'hespərəs] *n.* 黃昏星;長庚星;金星。(亦作 **Hesper**)

Hess [hɛs; hes] *n.* 希斯(Victor Franz, 1883–1964, 出生奧國之美國物理學家, 1936 年得諾貝爾物理獎)。

Hes·se ['hɛsɪ;'hesi] *n.* 赫塞(Hermann, 1877–1962, 德國詩人及小說家, 1946 年獲諾貝爾獎)。

Hes·sian ['hɛʃən; 'heʃən] *adj.* 德國赫斯州 (Hesse) 的; 赫斯州人的。—*n.* ①赫斯人。②〖美〗(美國獨立戰爭時英國所雇用之) Hesse 傭兵。③傭兵; 可用金錢雇用的人。④ (h-)一種粗麻布。⑤(*pl.*) =**Hessian boots.**

Hessian boots 德國 Hesse 州士兵穿的前有飾縫的長靴。

Hessian fly 麥蠅(似蚊, 爲麥之害蟲)。

hest [hɛst; hest] *n.*〖古〗=**behest.**

he·tae·ra [hɪ'tɪrə;hi'tiərə] *n., pl.* **-rae** [-ri; -riː]. ①(古希臘之)妾;妓女;藝妓。②利用美色獲取財富或社會地位之女子。

he·tae·rism [hɪ'tɪrɪzm̩; hi'tiərizm] *n.* ①(公然之) 蓄妾。②(古代或原始社會之)雜婚。(亦作 **hetairism**)

he·tai·ra [hɪ'taɪrə; hi'taiərə] *n., pl.* **-rai** [-raɪ; -rai]. =**hetaera.**

he·tai·rism [hɪ'taɪrɪzm̩; hi'taiərizm] *n.* =**hetaerism.**

hetero-〖字首〗表"其他; 不同" 之義(母音之前作 **heter-**).

het·er·o·clite ['hɛtərə,klaɪt; 'hetərouklait] *adj.*(亦作 **heteroclitic, heteroclitical**) ①(特指字尾變化)不規則的。②不正常的;畸形的。—*n.* ①〖文法〗不規則名詞或動詞等。②〖罕〗反常之事物;畸形之人或物。

het·er·o·cy·clic [,hɛtərə'saɪklɪk; ,hetərə'saiklik] *adj.* 〖化〗①雜環族化合物的。②此種化學的。

het·er·o·dox ['hɛtərə,dɑks; 'hetərədɔks] *adj.* 非正統的;異端的;左道的;信仰異端邪說的(爲 orthodox 之對)。

het·er·o·dox·y ['hɛtərə,dɑksɪ; 'hetərədɔksi] *n., pl.* **-dox·ies.** 異端邪說。

het·er·o·dyne ['hɛtərə,daɪn; 'hetərədain] *adj., n., v.,* **-dyned, -dyn·ing.** —*adj.*〖無線電〗外差式的。—*n.*〖無線電〗外差。 —*v.t.* & *v.i.* 產生外差效果。

het·er·og·a·mous [,hɛtə'rɑgəməs; ,hetə'rɔgəməs] *adj.* ①〖生物〗異形配子的;依異形配偶子生殖的; 世代交替的。②〖植物〗生(兩種)異性花的。

het·er·o·ge·ne·i·ty [,hɛtərədʒə'niətɪ; ,hetəroudʒi'niːiti] *n.* ①異種;異質。②異類混合;異成分。

het·er·o·ge·ne·ous [,hɛtərə'dʒinɪəs; 'hetərou'dʒiːnjəs] *adj.* ①不同類的;龐雜的。②由不同種類之物構成的;混雜的。

het·er·o·gen·e·sis [,hɛtərə'dʒɛnɪsɪs; ,hetərou'dʒenisis] *n.* 〖生物〗①異形生殖;異代生殖。②自然發生。③(有性生殖與無性生殖之)世代交替。

het·er·o·lo·gy [,hɛtə'rɑlədʒɪ; ,hetə'rɔlədʒi] *n.* 異種性;異質性;相異性。

het·er·o·mor·phic [,hɛtərə'mɔrfɪk; ,hetərə'mɔːfik] *adj.* ①〖生物〗異形的; 變形的。②(蟲)完全變態的。

het·er·on·o·my [,hɛtə'rɑnəmɪ; ,hetə'rɔnəmi] *n.* 他律;他律性。

het·er·o·nym ['hɛtərə,nɪm;'hetərənim] *n.* 同拼法異音異義之字(例如: wind 可作"風"解,讀如 [wɪnd; wind]; 又可作"纏繞"解,讀如 [waɪnd; waind])。

het·er·o·sex·u·al [,hɛtərə'sɛkʃuəl; ,hetərə'sekʃuəl] *adj.*〖生物〗異性的;異性愛的。—*n.*異性戀之人(爲 homosexual 之對)。

het·er·o·sex·u·al·i·ty [,hɛtərə,sɛkʃu'ælətɪ; ,hetərə,sekʃu'æliti] *n.* 異性愛。

het·er·o·tax·y ['hɛtərə,tæksɪ; 'hetərə,tæksi] *n.* ①〖醫〗內臟變位。②〖地質〗地層變位。(亦作 **heterotaxia, heterotaxis**)

het·er·o·zy·gote [,hɛtərə'zaɪgot; ,hetərə'zaigout] *n.*〖生物〗異基因合子。

het·man ['hɛtmən; 'hetmən] *n., pl.* **-mans.** ①(昔)波蘭司令官。②哥薩克人酋長。

Het·ty ['hɛtɪ; 'heti] *n.* 女子名。

heu·ris·tic [hju'rɪstɪk; hjuə'ristik] *adj.* 使學生自行發現的;啓發式的。—*n.* (*pl.*) 啓發式教學法。—**al·ly,** *adv.*

Hev·e·sy ['hɛvɛʃɪ; 'heveʃi] *n.* 海威希 (George de, 1885–1966, 匈牙利化學家, 1943 年獲諾貝爾獎)。

***hew** [hju; hjuː] *v.,* **hewed, hewed** or **hewn, hew·ing.**—*v.t.*①砍;劈。to *hew* out a career for oneself. 自行艱苦地創出一番事業。②砍成;將…削成某形狀。to *hew* logs into beams. 將木材削成桁樑。—*v.i.* ①砍;削。He *hewed* vigorously each time. 他每次都用力地砍。②奉行; 遵守〖常 to〗。—**a·ble,** *adj.*

hew·er ['hjuə; 'hjuːə] *n.* ①砍伐者;劈削(木、石等)者。②採煤夫;採礦夫。

hex [hɛks; heks] *v.t.*〖美方〗蠱惑; 使着魔。—*n.* ①〖美方〗女巫; 巫醫。②〖美方〗魔法; 蠱惑。③〖美俗〗不吉利的東西。—**er,** *n.*

hexa-〖字首〗表"六"之義(母音前作**hex-**).

hex·a·chord ['hɛksə,kɔrd; 'heksəkɔːd] *n.*〖音樂〗六聲音階。

hex·ad ['hɛksæd; 'heksæd] *n.* ①六之

數。②六之羣;六個之一組。③〖化〗六價元素。

hex·a·gon 〔ˈhɛksəˌgɑn; ˈheksəgən〕 *n.* 六角形;六邊形。—**al,** *adj.* —**al·ly,** *adv.*

hex·a·gram 〔ˈhɛksəˌgræm; ˈheksəgræm〕 *n.* 六角星形;六線形(✡)。

hex·a·he·dron 〔ˌhɛksəˈhidrən; ˈheksəˈhedrən〕 *n., pl.* **-drons, -dra** 〔-drə; -drə〕. 六面體。

hex·am·e·ter 〔hɛksˈæmətɚ; hekˈsæmitə〕 *adj.* 六音步之詩的。—*n.* 六音步的詩行。

hex·an·gu·lar 〔hɛksˈæŋgjəlɚ; heksˈæŋgjulə〕 *adj.* (有)六角的。 —**ly,** *adv.*

hex·a·pod 〔ˈhɛksəˌpɑd; ˈheksəpɔd〕 *adj.* (有)六足的。—*n.* 六足類;昆蟲。

Hex·a·teuch 〔ˈhɛksəˌtjuk; ˈheksətjuːk〕 *n.* (舊約聖經開始之)六卷書。

***hey** 〔he; hei〕 *interj.* (招呼人使之注意之聲)喂! *Hey!* Stop! 喂!止步!

hey·day 〔ˈheˌde; ˈheidei〕 *n.* ①盛年;壯年; 全盛時期。 ②〖罕〗興高采烈。(亦作 **heydey**)

Hey·se 〔ˈhaɪzə; ˈhaizə〕 *n.* 海策 (Paul Johann Ludwig von, 1830–1914, 德國小說家、劇作家及詩人,曾獲1910年諾貝爾文學獎)。

HF, H.F. 〖無線電〗 high frequency. 高頻率;短波。 **Hf** 化學元素 hafnium 之符號。 **hf.** half. **HG** ①High German. ②〖英〗 Home Guard. **Hg** 化學元素 hydrargyrum (=mercury) 之符號。 **hg.** ①hectogram(s). ②heliogram. **H.G.** ①High German. ②His (*or* Her) Grace. ③Horse Guards. ④Holy Ghost. **HH** double hard. **H.H.** ①His (*or* Her) Highness. 殿下。② His Holiness (the Pope). 宗座;陛下(對教皇尊敬語)。 **hhd.** hogshead(s).

H-hour 〔ˈetʃˌaur; ˈeitʃ-auə〕 *n.* 〖軍〗攻擊開始時刻。

hi 〔haɪ; hai〕 *interj.* (引人注意或打招呼之聲)喂!

H.I. Hawaiian Islands.

hi·a·tus 〔haɪˈetəs; haiˈeitəs〕 *n., pl.* **-tus·es, -tus.** ①空隙; 裂縫。②(文章中的)脫漏。 ③兩相接元音間之稍停或間歇(如co-operation)。④裂孔(骨骼等中的裂縫)。

hi·ber·nal 〔haɪˈbɝnl; haiˈbəːnl〕 *adj.* 冬日的; 寒冷的。

hi·ber·nate 〔ˈhaɪbɚˌnet; ˈhaibəneit〕 *v.i.,* **-nat·ed, -nat·ing.** ①冬眠;蟄伏。②過冬; 避寒。③退隱。 —**hi·ber·na·tor,** *n.*

hi·ber·na·tion 〔ˌhaɪbɚˈneʃən; ˌhaibəːˈneiʃən〕 *n.* ①冬眠;冬眠期。 ②避寒;過冬。③退隱。

Hi·ber·ni·a 〔haɪˈbɝnɪə; haiˈbəːniə〕 *n.* 〖詩〗愛爾蘭(=Ireland, 拉丁名)。

Hi·ber·ni·an 〔haɪˈbɝnɪən; haiˈbəːniən〕 *adj.* 愛爾蘭(人)的。—*n.* 愛爾蘭人。

Hi·ber·ni·cism 〔haɪˈbɝnəˌsɪzəm; haiˈbəːnisizəm〕 *n.* 愛爾蘭人之特性、習俗、慣用語法等。(亦作 **Hibernianism**)

hi·bis·cus 〔haɪˈbɪskəs; haiˈbiskəs〕 *n.* 〖植物〗芙蓉。

hic·cup, hic·cough 〔ˈhɪkʌp; ˈhikʌp〕 *n., v.,* **-cuped** or **-cupped, -cup·ing** or **-cup·ping.** —*n.* 打嗝;呃逆。—*v.i.* 打嗝;打呃。—*v.t.* 打嗝發出。

hic ja·cet 〔hɪkˈdʒesɛt; hikˈdʒeiset〕 〖拉〗①(墓碑之開始二字) 永眠於此 (=here lies). ②墓碑;墓誌銘。

hick 〔hɪk; hik〕 *n.* 〖俗〗鄉下人; 農夫;質樸的人; 土頭土腦的人。—*adj.* 〖俗〗 鄉下人的;鄉下的;鄉鄙的;粗俗的。

hick·ey 〔ˈhɪkɪ; ˈhiki〕 *n., pl.* **-eys.** ①叫不出名字或忘了名字的機器、裝置。②〖俚〗面皰。

hick·o·ry 〔ˈhɪkərɪ, ˈhɪkrɪ; ˈhikəri〕 *n., pl.* **-ries.** ①北美產之山胡桃樹。②山胡桃木。

hid 〔hɪd; hid〕 *v.* pt. & pp. of **hide**[1].

hi·dal·go 〔hɪˈdælgo; hiˈdælgou〕 *n., pl.* **-gos.** 西班牙之紳士。

hid·den 〔ˈhɪdn̩; ˈhidn〕 *v.* pp. of **hide**[1]. —*adj.* 隱藏的;祕密的。

hidden tax 間接稅(正稅以外的捐稅)。

‡**hide**[1] 〔haɪd; haid〕 *v.,* **hid, hid·den** or **hid, hid·ing,** *n.* —*v.t.* ①藏;躲避。 Where did you *hide* it? 你把它藏在哪裏?②遮蔽;遮掩。 The sun was *hidden* by the clouds. 太陽爲雲所遮。③保密;隱瞞。 I have nothing to *hide.* 我沒有甚麼可隱瞞的。 —*v.i.* 躲藏;走避。 You had better *hide.* 你最好躲藏起來。 ***hide out*** 躲避;隱藏。 After breaking out of jail, he *hid out* in a deserted farmhouse. 他越獄後在一幢無人居住的農舍裏躲藏。—*n.* 〖英〗獵人或觀察野獸者隱藏之所。—**hid·a·ble,** *adj.*—**hid·er,** *n.*

hide[2] *n., v.,* **hid·ed, hid·ing.** —*n.* ①獸皮。②〖俗〗(人的)皮膚。③〖俗〗 安全;福利。 ***hide nor*** (or ***or***) ***hair*** 跡象; 痕跡。 ***neither hide nor hair*** 甚麼也沒有。 ***save one's hide*** 逃避懲罰。 ***tan one's hide*** 打某人一頓。—*v.t.* ①〖俗〗 打;鞭笞。②以獸皮覆蓋繩子(以保護之)。 —**less,** *adj.*

hide[3] *n.* 英國昔日之地積單位 (約相當於80–120英畝不等)。

hide-and-seek 〔ˈhaɪdn̩ˈsik; ˈhaidnˈsiːk〕 *n.* 捉迷藏。(亦作 **hide-and-go-seek**)

hide·a·way 〔ˈhaɪdəˌwe; ˈhaidəwei〕 *n.* ①退隱的地方。 ②逃避的地方; 隱匿的地方。—*adj.* 隱藏的; 掩蔽的。

hide·bound 〔ˈhaɪdˌbaund; ˈhaidbaund〕 *adj.* ①皮包骨的(指動物言)。②心地狹窄而固執的; 頑固的。③保守的; 守舊的。 —**ness,** *n.*

***hid·e·ous** 〔ˈhɪdɪəs; ˈhidiəs〕 *adj.* 醜惡的; 可憎的; 可怕的; 龐大的。 a *hideous* crime. 極惡之罪。—**ly,** *adv.* —**ness,** *n.*

hide·out 〔ˈhaɪdˌaut; ˈhaidaut〕 *n.* 〖俗〗(罪犯之) 隱匿之所; 隱藏。

hid·ing[1] 〔ˈhaɪdɪŋ; ˈhaidiŋ〕 *n.* ①躲藏。②藏匿處。

hid·ing[2] *n.* 〖俗〗鞭打。

hie 〔haɪ; hai〕 *v.,* **hied, hie·ing** or **hy·ing.** —*v.i.* 快走;疾走。—*v.t.* 使快走;催促;嗾使。

hi·er·arch 〔ˈhaɪəˌrɑrk; ˈhaiərɑːk〕 *n.* ①教主;主教。②高僧。 ③高位有權威的人。

hi·er·ar·chy 〔ˈhaɪəˌrɑrkɪ; ˈhaiərɑːki〕 *n., pl.* **-chies.** ①聖秩制度; 教階組織。②階級組織。③科學之分類 (如門、綱、目、科、屬、種等);層系。 —**hi·er·ar·chi·cal, hi·er·ar·chic,** *adj.* —**hi·er·ar·chi·cal·ly,** *adv.*

hi·er·at·ic 〔ˌhaɪəˈrætɪk; ˌhaiəˈrætik〕 *adj.* ①(亦作 **hieratical**) 聖職的; 僧侶的。②供神聖用途的; 僧侶用的。③古埃及僧侶所用之一種象形文字的。 —*n.* 古埃及僧侶用之象形文字。—**al·ly,** *adv.*

hi·er·o·glyph 〔ˈhaɪərəˌglɪf; ˈhaiərouglif〕 *n.* ①象形文字。②象形文字寫的文章。③神祕的符號。④難理解的文字。

hi·er·o·glyph·ic 〔ˌhaɪərəˈglɪfɪk; ˌhaiərouˈglifik〕 *adj.* ①(古埃及) 象形文字的。②有神祕意義的; 象徵的。③(字) 潦草難

解的。—*n.* ①(古埃及之)象形文字;圖畫文字。②(常*pl.*)象形文字的文章。③祕密文字;密語。④(*pl.*)潦草難解的文字、數字等。

hi·er·o·glyph·i·cal 〔ˌhaɪərəˈglɪfɪkl, ˌhaɪrə-;ˌhaiərouˈglifikəl, -rəˈg-〕*adj.* =**hieroglyphic.** —**ly,** *adv.*

hi·er·o·phant 〔ˈhaɪərəˌfænt; ˈhaiərəfænt〕 *n.*①解釋宗教上之祕義者。②(古希臘等之)神祕儀式之祭司。

hi-fi 〔ˈhaɪˈfaɪ;ˈhaiˈfai〕〖俗〗*adj.* =**high-fidelity.** —*n.* ①=**high fidelity.** ②具高度傳眞性之收音機、電唱機或其他播音設備。

hig·gle 〔ˈhɪgl; ˈhigl〕 *v.i.,* **-gled,-gling.** ①討價還價。②爭論。(亦作 **haggle**)

hig·gle·dy-pig·gle·dy 〔ˈhɪgldɪˈpɪgldɪ; ˈhigldiˈpigldi〕 *adv.* 雜亂無章地;紊亂地。—*adj.* 混亂的。—*n.* 雜亂;紊亂;混亂。

:high 〔haɪ; hai〕 *adj.* ①高的; 高大的。That's a very *high* tower. 那是一座很高的塔。②高級的; 高等的; 高尚的。 a *high* purpose. 高尚的目標。③(=very great)極大的。I have a *high* opinion of that man. 我極重視那人(卽極器重他)。④尖銳的(聲音、嗓子)。She spoke in a *high* voice. 她講話的聲音很尖。 ⑤超乎尋常的。 ⑥主要的; 重要的。⑦價昂的。Strawberries are *high* in winter. 多天草莓昂貴。⑧達於最高點的。 ⑨略微敗壞的; 略有臭味的。 This meat has rather a *high* flavor. 這肉有敗壞的味道。⑩傲慢的。⑪〖俗〗帶有酒意的;酩酊的。He was so *high* he couldn't stand up. 他醉得站不起來。⑫嚴重的。 ⑬興高采烈的。 He was in *high* spirits. 他很高興。⑭奢侈的。 They have indulged in *high* living for years. 他們過奢侈的生活已有多年。⑮遙遠的。⑯極端的。⑰高地的;內陸區的。 ***be high on*** 特別喜歡。 ***be on one's high horse; ride the high horse*** 顯得盛氣凌人。 ***high and low*** 高低貴賤的(人們)。 ***the Most High*** 〖聖經〗上帝。 ***with a high hand*** 傲慢地;用高壓手段地。 —*adv.* ①高; 高度地。 The eagle flies *high.* 鷹飛得很高。②奢侈地。 They have always lived *high.* 他們生活一向奢侈。 ***fly high*** **a.** 有高超的理想、計畫、希望、雄心等。**b.** 高興得飄飄然。 His stories began to sell, and he was *flying high.* 他的小說開始暢銷,他高興得飄飄欲仙。 ***high and dry*** **a.** (船) 擱淺。**b.** 孤獨無助。Her date left her *high and dry.* 和她約會的男友爽約了(使她孤單單地空等)。 ***high and low*** 到處。 ***run high*** (海)起風浪;(情緒)激昂。 Popular feeling (*or* passions)ran *high.* 羣情激昂。 —*n.* ①高地。②高氣壓區域。③齒輪產生最高速度之組合。④〖俗〗最高紀錄。Inflationary pressures sent the cost of living to a new *high.* 通貨膨脹的壓力使得生活費用達到了一個新的最高紀錄。⑤〖俗〗中學。 ***on high*** **a.** 高高在上; 在天空中。**b.** 在天堂中。〖注意〗**high, tall** 均作"較一般爲高"解。high 常指物(但不指人)之高: *High* hills surround the valley. 高峯圍繞着山谷。tall 可指人亦可指物: He is a *tall* man. 他是個高個子。

high-and-might·y 〔ˈhaɪənˈmaɪtɪ; ˈhaiənˈmaiti〕 *adj.* 驕傲的;盛氣凌人的。

high-an·gle 〔ˈhaɪˌæŋgl; ˈhaiˌæŋgl〕 *adj.* 高角度的。 *high-angle* gun. 高角砲。

high·ball 〔ˈhaɪˌbɔl; ˈhaibɔːl〕 *n.* ①混有冰、汽水或薑汁的威士忌或其他烈酒。②〖鐵路〗**a.** 使火車開動的手勢或以燈火做的信號。**b.** 使火車全速行進的信號。—*v.i.* 〖俚〗(火車等) 全速行進。 —*v.t.* 給(火車司機) 做信號使其開始行進。

high·bind·er 〔ˈhaɪˌbaɪndɚ; ˈhaiˌbaində〕 *n.* 〖美俚〗①華人區內黑社會中之黨羽(常被雇用去詐財或殺人)。②惡徒;流氓。③騙徒。④不老實的政治領袖;政客。

high-blood·ed 〔ˈhaɪˈblʌdɪd; ˈhaiˈblʌdid〕 *adj.* 血統純正的;出身高貴的。

high blower 奔馳時呼吸聲甚大之馬。

high-blown 〔ˈhaɪˌblon; ˈhai-bloun〕 *adj.* 誇張的; 自負的。

high·born 〔ˈhaɪˌbɔrn;ˈhaibɔːn〕 *adj.* 出身名門的; 出身高貴的。

high·boy 〔ˈhaɪˌbɔɪ;ˈhaibɔi〕 *n.*〖美〗有足之高屜櫃。

high·bred 〔ˈhaɪˌbrɛd; ˈhai-bred〕 *adj.* ①出身名門的;出身高貴的。②血統純正的;純種的。③教養良好的。

high·brow 〔ˈhaɪˌbraʊ; ˈhai-brau〕 *n.* 〖俚〗有高深學問的人;自炫博學的人。—*adj.* 〖俚〗有高深學問的;自炫博學的。 —**ism,** *n.*

high-browed 〔ˈhaɪˌbraʊd; ˈhaiˈbraud〕 *adj.* ①高額頭的。②(似)有教養的;(似)有高深學問的。

high·chair 〔ˈhaɪˌtʃɛr; ˈhai-tʃɛə〕 *n.* 小孩吃飯時所用之高脚椅子。

high-class 〔ˈhaɪˈklæs; ˈhaiˈklɑːs〕 *adj.* 高級的;上流的;上等的。

high-col·ored 〔ˈhaɪˈkʌlɚd; ˈhaiˈkʌləd〕 *adj.* ①色彩强烈的;鮮明的。②紅的;櫻紅色的。③誇張的。

high day 節日。

high-def·i·ni·tion 〔ˈhaɪˌdɛfəˈnɪʃən; ˈhaiˌdefiˈniʃən〕 *adj.* 〖電視〗畫面很鮮明的。

higher criticism 研究聖經之一部門。

higher education 高等教育。

high·er-up 〔ˈhaɪɚˈʌp; ˈhaiərˈʌp〕 *n.* 〖美俗〗職位或地位較高的人。(亦作**high-up**)

high·fa·lu·tin 〔ˌhaɪfəˈlutn̩; ˈhaifəˈluːtin〕 *n.* 〖俗〗誇張的話。—*adj.* 〖俗〗誇張的; 驕傲的; 虛飾的。(亦作 **highfalutin', hifalutin, hifalutin', highfaluting**)

high-fed 〔ˈhaɪˈfɛd; ˈhaiˈfed〕 *adj.* 養尊處優的。

high fidelity (收音機、電唱機之)高度傳眞性。

high-fi·del·i·ty 〔ˈhaɪfəˈdɛlətɪ; ˈhaifiˈdeliti〕 *adj.* 高度傳眞的。

high·fli·er, high·fly·er〔ˈhaɪˌflaɪɚ; ˈhaiˈflai-ə〕 *n.* ①高飛之鳥(蝴蝶、人)。②抱負極高之人;自命不凡的人;野心家。③〖英史〗(17-18世紀之)高教會派之人;保守黨員。

high-flown 〔ˈhaɪˈflon; ˈhaiˈfloun〕 *adj.* ①高尚的;崇高的。②過甚其詞的;虛飾的。

high·fly·ing 〔ˈhaɪˈflaɪɪŋ; ˈhaiˈflaiiŋ〕 *adj.* ①高飛的;高空飛行的。②抱負(過)高的;(過分)野心的;誇張的。

high frequency 〖無線電〗高頻率(數)(3-30 megacycles).

high-grade 〔ˈhaɪˈgred; ˈhaiˈgreid〕 *adj.* ①高級的; 高等的(指品質而言)。②(礦石等) 含量豐富的。

high-hand·ed 〔ˈhaɪˈhændɪd; ˈhaiˈhændid〕 *adj.* 專橫的;橫暴的; 高壓的。(亦作 **highhanded**) —**ly,** *adv.* —**ness,** *n.*

high-hat 〔ˈhaɪˌhæt; ˈhaihæt〕 *v.,* **-hatted, -hat·ting,** *adj., n.* —*v.t.* 〖俚〗擺架子;對人驕傲; 冷待;以勢利相待。—*adj.* 〖俚〗①擺架子的;驕傲的;勢利的。②時髦的;漂亮的。—*n.* 〖俚〗 勢利之徒。

high-heart·ed 〔ˈhaɪˈhɑrtɪd; ˈhai-

ˈhɑːtid] *adj.* 有精神的;勇敢的;果敢剛毅的。—**ly,** *adv.* —**ness,** *n.*

high horse 驕傲的態度或脾氣;藐視的態度。

high hurdles 〖田徑〗高欄。

high iron 〖俚〗①幹線路軌。②快車路軌。

high·jack [ˈhaɪˌdʒæk; ˈhaidʒæk] *v.t.* 〖美俗〗=**hijack.** —**er,** *n.*

high jump 跳高。

high jumper 跳高者。

high-key [ˈhaɪˈki; ˈhaiˈkiː] *adj.* (相片)單調的;缺少色調對比的。

high-keyed [ˈhaɪˈkid; ˈhaiˈkiːd] *adj.* ①調子高的。②敏感的;有精神的;緊張的。③(繪畫)顏色鮮亮或單純的。

***high·land** [ˈhaɪlənd; ˈhailənd] *n.* ①高地。②(*pl.*) 丘陵地帶。—*adj.* 高地的;丘陵地帶的。

high·land·er [ˈhaɪləndɚ; ˈhailəndə] *n.* ①高地人。②(H-) 蘇格蘭高地人。

high-lev·el [ˈhaɪˈlɛvəl; ˈhaiˈlevəl] *adj.* ①高階層的。②高級的。③高空的。

high·light [ˈhaɪˌlaɪt; ˈhailait] *v.* **-light·ed, -light·ing,** *n.* —*v.t.* ①〖繪畫,攝影〗投强光使顯著。②使顯著;使精彩;强調。—*n.* =**high light.**

high light ①〖繪畫,攝影〗最光亮之部分。②(新聞、節目等之)最精彩之場面;最有趣之事件;最重要之點;最顯著之部分。

high-liv·ing [ˈhaɪˈlɪvɪŋ; ˈhaiˈliviŋ] *adj.* 生活豪華的。

high-low [ˈhaɪˌlo; ˈhailou] *n.* 有帶之皮靴(高及足踝者)。

‡**high·ly** [ˈhaɪlɪ; ˈhaili] *adv.* ①高度地;有利地;高貴地。He spoke very *highly* of her. 他極讚揚她。②很;極。a *highly* amusing film. 極有趣的影片。③高價地。a *highly* paid official. 薪俸優厚之官吏。

high-mind·ed [ˈhaɪˈmaɪndɪd; ˈhaiˈmaindid] *adj.* ①品格高尚的;慷慨的。②〖罕〗高傲的。—**ly,** *adv.* —**ness,** *n.*

high-muck-a-muck [ˈhaɪˌmʌkəˈmʌk; ˈhaiˌmʌkəˈmʌk] *n.* 〖美俚〗要人;自以爲了不起的人。(亦作 **high-muckety-muck**)

***high·ness** [ˈhaɪnɪs; ˈhainis] *n.* ①高;高度;高尚。②(H-) 大人;閣下;殿下(對皇族的尊稱)。Her (His, Your) *Highness.* 大人;閣下;殿下(用以避免說She, He, You)。

high noon ①中午。②極點;最高峯。

high-oc·tane [ˈhaɪˈɑkten; ˈhaiˈɔktein] *adj.* ①(汽油)含辛烷數很高的。②有生氣的;强有力的;鼓勵的。

high-pitched [ˈhaɪˈpɪtʃt; ˈhaiˈpitʃt] *adj.* ①聲調高的;聲音尖銳的。②高傲的。③坡度大的。④感情衝動的。

high-pres·sure [ˈhaɪˈprɛʃɚ; ˈhaiˈpreʃə] *adj., v.,* **-sured, -sur·ing.** —*adj.* ①高壓的。②〖氣象〗高氣壓的。③强迫的;急迫的。—*v.t.* 〖俗〗强迫;施以壓力。

high-rank·ing [ˈhaɪˌræŋkɪŋ; ˈhaiˌræŋkiŋ] *adj.* 高級官員的;高階層的。

high rise 多層建築物。

high-ris·er [ˈhaɪˈraɪzɚ; ˈhaiˌraizə] *n.* 單人雙人兩用活動牀。

high·road [ˈhaɪˈrod; ˈhaiˈroud] *n.* ①大道;公路。②直接而容易的方法;捷徑。

high school 〖美〗中學。

high seas ①外洋;外海。②(the-)公海(在領海以外之海面)。

high-sound·ing [ˈhaɪˈsaundɪŋ; ˈhaiˈsaundiŋ] *adj.* (文體、頭銜等)派頭大的;誇張的;招搖的。

high-speed [ˈhaɪˌspid; ˈhai-spiːd] *adj.* 高速度的。*high-speed* computers. 高速計算機。

high-spir·it·ed [ˈhaɪˌspɪrɪtɪd; ˈhaiˈspiritid] *adj.* ①高傲的;趾高氣揚的。②勇敢的。③烈性的。—**ly,** *adv.* —**ness,** *n.*

high spirits 快樂;歡欣。

high-strung [ˈhaɪˈstrʌŋ; ˈhaiˈstrʌŋ] *adj.* ①敏感的;易激動的;神經過敏的;緊張的。②高調的。③繃緊的。

high-style [ˈhaɪˈstaɪl; ˈhai-stail] *adj.* 最新款式的;最時髦的。

hight [haɪt; hait] *adj.* 〖古,詩〗稱爲 (= named, called). —*v.t.* 〖蘇〗①承諾;約定。②〖古〗命令。

high table 英國大學中院長導師等的較高餐桌,常有美酒佳餚。*eat* (or *dine*) *at high table* 〖英〗享受山珍海味。

high·tail [ˈhaɪˌtel; ˈhaiteil] *v.i.* 〖俗〗匆忙地走開(尤指爲避某人或某事)。*hightail it* 跑去;急走。

high·teen [ˈhaɪˈtin; ˈhaiˈtiːn] 〖俗〗 *adj.* 十八、九歲的。—*n.* 十八、九歲的少年。

high-ten·sion [ˈhaɪ ˈtɛnʃən; ˈhaiˈtenʃən] *adj.* 〖電〗高壓的。

high-test [ˈhaɪˈtɛst; ˈhaiˈtest] *adj.* ①經嚴格試驗的。②(汽油)沸點低的。

high tide ①高潮。②高潮時間。③最高點。

high time ①正是時候(再遲就爲時已晚);早該。It is *high time* he found a job. 他早該找到一分工作了。②〖俗〗一段狂歡享樂時間;飲酒作樂。

high-toned [ˈhaɪˈtond; ˈhaiˈtound] *adj.* ①調子高的。②高潔的;高尚的。③〖美〗過分高尚的;曲高和寡的。④〖美俗〗漂亮的;時髦的。(亦作 **high-tone**)

high treason 叛國;叛逆罪。

high-up [ˈhaɪˈʌp; ˈhaiˈʌp] *adj., n., pl.* **-ups.** —*adj.* 高級的;高位的。—*n.* 高級(高位)人員。

***high·way** [ˈhaɪˌwe; ˈhaiwei] *n.* ①大道;公路。ocean *highways.* 航路。②直截的途徑。a *highway* to success. 成功之大道。

high·way·man [ˈhaɪˌwemən; ˈhaiweimən] *n., pl.* **-men.** 攔路搶刼者;强盜。

H.I.H. His (*or* Her) Imperial Highness.

hi·jack [ˈhaɪˌdʒæk; ˈhaidʒæk] *v.t.* & *v.i.* 〖美俗〗刼奪(飛機);刼持(運輸中之貨物,特指違禁或走私物品)。The plane was *hijacked* soon after it took off. 此飛機起飛後不久卽遭刼持。

hi·jack·er [ˈhaɪˌdʒækɚ; ˈhaiˌdʒækə] *n.* 〖美俗〗强盜;刼持犯;刼機者。

***hike** [haɪk; haik] *v.,* **hiked, hik·ing,** *n.* —*v.i.* ①〖俗〗徒步旅行;遠足;行軍。②舉高;升高〖常 up〗. —*v.t.* ①突然地移動、拉高或舉起。②使高漲。to *hike* gas rates. 提高煤氣價格。—*n.* ①徒步旅行;遠足。The soldiers were trained to take long *hikes.* 士兵受訓作長途步行。②升起。

hik·er [ˈhaɪkɚ; ˈhaikə] *n.* 〖俗〗徒步旅行者。

***hik·ing** [ˈhaɪkɪŋ; ˈhaikiŋ] *n.* 〖俗〗徒步旅行。

hi·lar·i·ous [həˈlɛrɪəs; hiˈlɛəriəs] *adj.* ①高興的;熱鬧的。②有趣的;妙的。—**ly,** *adv.* —**ness,** *n.*

hi·lar·i·ty [həˈlærətɪ; hiˈlæriti] *n.* 歡樂;熱鬧。

hil·ding [ˈhɪldɪŋ; ˈhildiŋ] *adj.* 〖古〗卑鄙的。—*n.* 〖古〗卑鄙的人。

Hill [hɪl; hil] *n.* 希爾 (Archibald Vivian, 1886–, 英國生理學家, 1922年獲諾貝爾醫學獎)。

:hill [hɪl; hil] *n.* ①小山;丘陵;岡巒。②小土堆。③根上堆有泥土之植物。④坡路。This old jalopy won't make it up the next *hill*. 這部老爺車會爬不上下一個斜坡。⑤〖俚〗(棒球場之)壘。***go over the hill*** **a.**〖俚〗逃獄。**b.** (軍中之)擅離所屬部隊。**c.** 突然或偷偷地離開。Rumor has it that her husband has *gone over the hill*. 謠傳她丈夫偷偷地離開了。***over the hill*** **a.** 過了危機。The new tax program is now *over the hill*. 新的稅法已渡過了危機。**b.** 過了有效時期或高峯。***the Hill*** 美國國會 (=Capitol Hill). —*v.t.* ①堆土堆於根上。②作成土堆或小丘。—**er,** *n.*

hill·bil·ly [ˈhɪlˌbɪlɪ; ˈhilˌbili] *n., pl.* **-lies,** *adj.* —*n.*〖美俗〗①南部山林地帶之人;山地人。②山地民謠。—*adj.* 山地的。

hill·ock [ˈhɪlək; ˈhilək] *n.* 小丘。—**ed,** —**y,** *adj.*

***hill·side** [ˈhɪlˌsaɪd; ˈhilˈsaid] *n.* 山坡。

***hill·top** [ˈhɪlˌtɑp; ˈhilˈtɔp] *n., v.,* **-topped, -top·ping.** —*n.* 山頂;山巓。—*v.i.* 騎馬、徒步或坐車獵狐。—**per,** *n.*

hill·y [ˈhɪlɪ; ˈhili] *adj.,* **hill·i·er, hill·i·est.** ①多小山的。②如小山的。③高峻的。—**hill·i·ness,** *n.*

hilt [hɪlt; hilt] *n.* (劍或刀等的)柄。***hilt to hilt*** 一人對一人之戰。(***up***) ***to the hilt*** 完全地; 徹底地。—*v.t.* 加柄於。—**ed,** *adj.* —**less,** *adj.*

hi·lum [ˈhaɪləm; ˈhailəm] *n., pl.* **hi·la** [ˈhaɪlə; ˈhailə]. ①〖植物〗(種子之)臍。②(澱粉粒之)核;粒心。③〖解剖〗(內臟之血管、神經等出入之)門。

:him [hɪm; him] *pron.* objective case of **he.** 他;彼。I lent *him* the books. 我把那些書借給他了。

H.I.M. His(*or* Her) Imperial Majesty. 「聖上;陛下。」

Him·a·la·yan [hɪˈmɑljən; ˌhiməˈleiən] *adj.* 喜馬拉雅山脈(產)的。

Him·a·la·yas [hɪˈmɑləjəz; ˌhiməˈleiəz] *n. pl.* (the–) 喜馬拉雅山脈。(亦作 **the Himalaya, Himalaya Mountains**)

:him·self [hɪmˈsɛlf; himˈself] *pron.* ①他自己(him 的反身代名詞)。He will hurt *himself* if he doesn't take care. 他若不小心,他會傷着他自己的。He ought to be ashamed of *himself*. 他應當自覺羞愧。②(他) 親自 (用以加強語勢)。He *himself* says so (*or* He says so *himself*). 他本人如此說。③健康;正常。He felt like *himself* again. 他感到復原了。***beside himself*** 神經錯亂;瘋顛。He was *beside himself* with grief. 他因悲傷而神經錯亂。(***all***) ***by himself*** **a.** 獨力;自行。Can he do it (*all*) *by himself* or will he get somebody else to do it? 他能自做,還是將找別人做? **b.** 單獨;孤獨。Wasn't he afraid to go there *by himself?* 他不怕獨自一人到那裏去嗎?

Hi·na·ya·na [ˌhɪnəˈjɑnə; ˌhinəˈjɑːnə] *n.*〖佛〗小乘。

hind¹** [haɪnd; haind] *adj.,* **hind·er, hind·most** or **hind·er·most.** 在後的;後部的。the *hind* wheels of a cart. 車的後輪。on one's hind legs*** 採取堅決或獨立的立場。

hind² *n., pl.* **hinds, hind.** 三歲或三歲以上的雌性紅鹿。

hind³ *n.* ①〖古〗農夫;鄉下人。②〖蘇,北英〗熟練的農人;農場管理人。

Hind. ①Hindu. ②Hindustan. ③Hindustani.

hind·brain [ˈhaɪndˌbren; ˈhaindbrein] *n.*〖解剖〗後腦。

***hin·der¹** [ˈhɪndɚ; ˈhində] *v.t.* 妨礙; 阻止。Don't *hinder* me. 不要阻礙我。—*v.i.* 成爲阻礙。Help out; don't *hinder*. 幫幫忙;不要礙事。—**er,** *n.* —**ing·ly,** *adv.*

hind·er² [ˈhaɪndɚ; ˈhaində] *adj.* 後面的;後邊的;後部的。

hind·er·most [ˈhaɪndɚˌmost; ˈhaindəmoust] *adj.*〖廢〗=**hindmost.**

Hin·di [ˈhɪndi; ˈhinˈdiː] *adj.* 北印度的。—*n.* 北印度語。

hind·most [ˈhaɪndˌmost; ˈhaindmoust] *adj.* 最後方的;最靠近後方的;最後的。

Hin·doo [ˈhɪndu; ˈhinˈduː] *n., adj.* =**Hindu.**

hind·quar·ter [ˈhaɪndˈkwɔrtɚ; ˈhaindˈkwɔːtə] *n.* ①(牛、羊肉等之)後臀及腿。②尾部;後端。

hin·drance [ˈhɪndrəns; ˈhindrəns] *n.* ①妨礙;阻礙。②妨礙之人或物;阻礙物。

hind·sight [ˈhaɪndˌsaɪt; ˈhaindsait] *n.* ①〖軍〗(鎗等之)照門。②〖諧〗事後聰明。***knock*** (or ***kick***) ***the hindsight out*** (or ***off***)〖美俗〗完全打垮;粉碎。

Hin·du [ˈhɪndu; ˈhinˈduː] *n.* 印度人;印度教教徒。—*adj.* 印度(人、語文)的;印度教的。(亦作 **Hindoo**)

Hin·du-Ar·a·bic numerals [ˈhɪnduˈærəbɪk~; ˈhinduːˈærəbik~] 阿拉伯數字。(亦作 **Arabic numerals**)

Hin·du·ism [ˈhɪnduˌɪzəm; ˈhinduːizəm] *n.* 印度教。(亦作 **Hindooism**)

Hin·du·stan [ˌhɪnduˈstæn; ˌhinduˈstɑn] *n.* ①印度斯坦(指印度北部)。②印度斯坦(指 Deccan 高原以北)。③印度(共和國)。

Hin·du·sta·ni [ˌhɪnduˈstænɪ; ˌhinduˈstɑːni] *adj.* 印度的; 印度人的; 印度語的。—*n.* 印度之普通語言。(亦作 **Hindoostani, Hindostani**)

hinge** [hɪndʒ; hindʒ] *n., v.,* **hinged, hing·ing.** —*n.* ①鉸鏈;關鍵;樞紐。②似鉸鏈之物;關節。③依仗之物; 主旨; 重要之點。off the hinges*** (身體) 活動不靈的;(精神)錯亂的。—*v.t.* ①裝以鉸鏈。②使依靠。He *hinged* his action on future sales. 他以將來銷售量爲他行動的準繩。—*v.i.* ①依鉸鏈而轉動。②以…爲轉移。Everything *hinges* on what he decides. 一切皆以他的決定爲轉移。—**hinged,** —**like,** *adj.* —**less,** *adj.* —**hing·er,** *n.*

hin·ny¹ [ˈhɪnɪ; ˈhini] *n., pl.* **-nies.** 駃。

hin·ny² *v.i.,* **-nied, -ny·ing.** (馬)嘶。

hi·no·ki cypress [hɪˈnokɪ~; hiˈnouki~] 檜木。

***hint** [hɪnt; hint] *n.* ①暗示; 提示。A black cloud gave a *hint* of a coming storm. 一片黑雲預示將有暴風雨。②少量;少許。③〖廢〗場合;機會。—*v.t.* 暗示;示意。He *hinted* that he might be late. 他曾暗示他可能遲到。—*v.i.* 暗示;示意〖at〗。I *hinted* at his imprudence. 我曾暗示他的不謹慎。—**er,** *n.* —**ing·ly,** *adv.*

hin·ter·land [ˈhɪntɚˌlænd; ˈhintəlænd] *n.* ①海岸之後方地區;內地。②(常*pl.*)偏僻地區;背地。③港口之腹地。

hip¹** [hɪp; hip] *n., interj., v.,* **hipped, hip·ping.** —*n.* 臀;股。to stand with one's hands on one's *hips*. 兩手叉腰而立。have*** (***get***, or ***take***) (***a person***) ***on the hip*** 制伏(某人);制勝(某人)。***on*** (or ***upon***) ***the hip***蒙受不利;處於不利地位。***smite hip and thigh*** 無情地攻打(舊約士師記,第十五章第八節)。—*interj.* 歡呼之聲,如: Hip, hip, hurrah! —*v.t.* 傷(家畜等之)臀部。—**less,** *adj.* —**like,** *adj.*

hip[2] *n.* 玫瑰花的荚。

hip[3] *adj.* 〖俚〗內行的;知曉最新觀念、消息、發展的。—*n.* 〖美俚〗對新的及時髦的東西之了解或注意。

hip[4] *n.* =**hyp** (hypochondria).

hip bath 坐浴。

hip·bone [ˈhɪpˌbon; ˈhipboun] *n.* 〖解剖〗臀骨;無名骨;髖骨。(亦作 **hip bone**)

hipe [haɪp; haip] *n., v.,* **hiped, hip·ing.** —*n.* 〖摔角〗抱投。—*v.t.* & *v.i.* 〖摔角〗將(對手)抱起投擲。—**hip·er,** *n.*

hipped[1] [hɪpt; hipt] *adj.* ①有(某種之)股的;臀部…的。②股關節脫節的。

hipped[2] *adj.* ①〖俗〗被(…)迷住的;熱心於…的〖on〗。②〖俗〗抑鬱的。③〖俗〗被激怒的。

hip·pie [ˈhipɪ; ˈhi:pi] *n., pl.* **-pies.** 嬉皮。(英亦作 **hippy**)

hip·pie·dom [ˈhipɪdəm; ˈhi:pidəm] *n.* 嬉皮世界。(亦作 **hipdom**)

hip·pish [ˈhɪpɪʃ; ˈhipiʃ] *adj.* 〖英〗〖俗〗有點抑鬱的;無精打彩的。

hip·po [ˈhɪpo; ˈhipou] *n., pl.* **-pos.** 〖俗〗河馬。

hip·po·cam·pus [ˌhɪpəˈkæmpəs; ˌhipəˈkæmpəs] *n., pl.* **-pi** [-paɪ; -pai]. ①〖希臘、羅馬神話〗海怪(拖海神之車的馬頭魚尾怪獸)。②海馬。③〖解剖〗(腦中之)海馬趾。

hip·po·cras [ˈhɪpəˌkræs; ˈhipəkræs] *n.* 香料藥酒(興奮劑或滋補飲料)。

Hip·poc·ra·tes [hɪˈpɑkrəˌtiz; hiˈpɔkrəti:z] *n.* 希波克拉底 (460?-?377 B. C., 希臘醫生,有醫藥之父之稱)。—**Hip·po·crat·ic, Hi·po·crat·i·cal,** *adj.*

Hip·po·crat·ic oath [ˌhɪpəˈkrætɪk~; ˌhipouˈkrætik~] 新開業醫生所立之誓約(傳爲Hippocrates 所訂)。

Hip·po·crene [ˈhɪpəˌkrin; ˌhipoˈkri:ni:] *n.* ①〖希臘神話〗Helicon 山之靈泉。②詩之靈感。—**Hip·po·cre·ni·an,** *adj.*

hip·po·drome [ˈhɪpəˌdrom; ˈhipədroum] *n.* ①(古希臘、羅馬之)跑馬場、競技場。②馬戲場。—**hip·po·drom·ic,** *adj.*

hip·po·griff, hip·po·gryph [ˈhɪpəˌgrɪf; ˈhipəgrif] *n.* (神話中)半馬半鷲之怪物。

hip·po·pot·a·mus [ˌhɪpəˈpɑtəməs; ˌhipəˈpɔtəməs] *n., pl.* **-mus·es, -mi** [-ˌmaɪ; -mai]. 河馬。(略作 **hippo**)

hip·py [ˈhɪpɪ; ˈhipi] *adj.,* **-pi·er, -pi·est.** 臀部大的。

hip·py·ism, hip·pie·ism [ˈhɪpɪˌɪzəm; ˈhipiizəm] *n.* 奉行嬉皮思想及言行。

hip roof 〖建築〗前後及兩側均爲斜面之屋頂。

hip·ster [ˈhɪpstɚ; ˈhipstə] *n.* 〖俚〗①爵士音樂迷。②=**beatnik.**

hir·a·ble [ˈhaɪrəbl; ˈhaiərəbl] *adj.* 可雇用的;可租賃的。(亦作 **hireable**)

hir·cine [ˈhɝsaɪn; ˈhə:sain] *adj.* ①(似)山羊的。②有山羊臭的。③好色的。

‡hire [haɪr; ˈhaiə] *v.,* **hired, hir·ing,** *n.* —*v.t.* ①雇;請。②租;雇。***hire on*** 找到職業。***hire out*** 出租。He makes a living by *hiring out* horses. 他靠出租馬匹爲生。—*n.* 工資;租金;租用。***for hire*** 爲臨時雇用的;出租的。to work *for hire.* 做臨時雇工。This car is *for hire.* 這輛車是出租的。***on hire*** 出租的。He has horses *on hire.* 他有馬出租。〖注意〗租房屋或田地,須用 rent,但租屋若屬臨時性的,也可用hire. 如:to *hire* a hall for an evening. 租會堂用一晚。

hire·ling [ˈhaɪrlɪŋ; ˈhaiəliŋ] *n.* ①專爲金錢之工作者。②受雇而工作者。—*adj.* 被雇傭的;專爲金錢的。

hire-pur·chase [ˈhaɪrˈpɝtʃəs; ˈhaiəˈpə:tʃəs] *n.* 〖英〗①分期付款。②用分期付款所購之物。—*adj.* 分期付款的。

hir·er [ˈhaɪrɚ; ˈhaiərə] *n.* 雇主;雇用者。

hiring hall 碼頭工人候職廳。

Hir·o·shi·ma [ˈhiroˈʃimɑ; hiˈrɔʃimə] *n.* 廣島(日本本州西南岸城市,1945年8月6日爲美國原子彈所襲擊)。

hir·sute [ˈhɝsut; ˈhə:sju:t] *adj.* ①多毛的。②〖動、植物〗有鬃毛的。③毛的;毛質的。—**ness,** *n.*

‡his [hɪz, ɪz; hiz, iz] *pron.* possessive case of **he,** *adj.* —*pron.* 他的(所有物)。That book is *his,* not mine. 那書是他的,不是我的。—*adj.* 他的。Is that *his* own idea? 那是他自己的意思嗎?

His·pan·io·la [ˌhɪspənˈjolə; ˌhispənˈjoulə] *n.* 希斯盤紐拉島(西印度羣島中之一島,爲多明尼加與海地二國所在地,舊名Haiti, Hayti).

his·pid [ˈhɪspɪd; ˈhispid] *adj.* 〖動、植物〗有鬃毛的;多剛毛的。—**i·ty,** *n.*

***hiss** [hɪs; his] *v.i.* ①發嘶嘶聲。The snake raised its head and *hissed.* 此蛇抬起頭來並發出嘶嘶聲。②發噓聲表示憎惡或反對。—*v.t.* ①以噓聲說明或表示。②發噓聲表示憎惡或反對。③以噓聲迫使或逐走。—*n.* 嘶嘶聲;嗤嗤聲。—**er,** *n.* —**ing·ly,** *adv.*

hiss·ing [ˈhɪsɪŋ; ˈhisiŋ] *n.* ①發嘶嘶之聲。②嘶嘶聲。

hist [hɪst; hist] *interj.* 噓! —*v.t.* 發出"噓"聲。

hist. ①histology. ②historian. ③historical. ④history.

his·ta·mine [ˈhɪstəˌmin; ˈhistəmi:n] *n.* 〖化〗組織胺(身體組織在過敏性反應中放出的一種白結晶體的毒素,能減低血壓,刺激胃液分泌)。—**his·ta·min·ic,** *adj.*

his·tol·o·gy [hɪsˈtɑlədʒɪ; hisˈtɔlədʒi] *n.* ①組織學。②(尤指微生物之)組織構造。

***his·to·ri·an** [hɪsˈtorɪən; hisˈtɔ:riən] *n.* 歷史學家。

***his·tor·ic** [hɪsˈtɔrɪk; hisˈtɔrik] *adj.* ①歷史上著名的;有歷史性的。*historic* times. 有歷史記載的時期。②=**historical.**

***his·tor·i·cal** [hɪsˈtɔrɪkl, -ˈtɑrɪkl; hisˈtɔrikəl, is-] *adj.* ①歷史上的;眞實的。*historical* events and people. 歷史上的眞實事件和人物。②依據歷史的。③有關歷史的。④=**historic.** —**ly,** *adv.* —**ness,** *n.*

his·to·ric·i·ty [ˌhɪstəˈrɪsətɪ; ˌhistəˈrisiti] *n.* 史實性;歷史的根據。

his·to·ried [ˈhɪstərɪd; ˈhistərid] *adj.* 有歷史的;史上所載的;有來由的。

his·to·ri·og·ra·pher [ˌhɪstorɪˈɑgrəfɚ; ˌhistɔ:riˈɔgrəfə] *n.* ①歷史家。②史料編纂者。—**ship,** *n.*

his·to·ri·og·ra·phy [hɪsˌtorɪˈɑgrəfɪ; ˌhistɔ:riˈɔgrəfi] *n., pl.* **-phies.** ①史料編纂(法)。②史料。③史評。④正史。

‡his·to·ry [ˈhɪstrɪ, ˈhɪstərɪ; ˈhistəri, -tri] *n., pl.* **-ries.** ①歷史。the *history* of England. 英國史。②沿革;過去。a house with a strange *history*. 有一段奇史的家屋。③對所發生之事的述說。④歷史學。⑤史劇。Shakespeare's comedies, *histories*, and tragedies. 莎士比亞的喜劇、史劇和悲劇。⑥可決定未來之重大事件、行動或思想。⑦充滿重大或不平常事件之過去。a ship with a *history*. 有光榮過去（歷史）的船。***ancient history*** 上古史（自遠古至 A.D. 476 年）。***become history*** 成爲歷史題材。***make history*** 創造歷史。***medieval history*** 中古史(自 A.D. 476 至 1453 年)。***modern history*** 近世史（自 1453 年以後至現代）。***natural history*** 博物學。

his·tri·on·ic [ˌhɪstrɪ'ɑnɪk; ˌhistri'ɔnik] *adj.* ①演員的; 演劇的。②做戲的; 假扮的。③面部肌肉的。（亦作 **histrionical**）**—al·ly,** *adv.*

his·tri·on·ics [ˌhɪstrɪ'ɑnɪks; ˌhistri'ɔniks] *n.*（作 *sing.* or *pl.* 解）①演戲。②做作。

his·tri·o·nism ['hɪstrɪəˌnɪzəm; 'histriənizəm] *n.* 演技。

‡hit [hɪt; hit] *v.,* **hit, hit·ting,** *n.* **—***v.t.* ①擊中;打中。The stone *hit* the window. 石頭擊中窗子。②打;擊。He *hit* me on the head. 他打我的頭。③碰撞。I *hit* my head on (*or* against) the wall. 我的頭碰到了牆。④〖美俗〗到達。⑤攻擊; 抨擊。The reviews *hit* the new play. 報章評論攻擊該新劇。⑥打擊;使受創。The stockbroker was hard *hit* by the fall in stocks. 股票經紀人因股票跌價而受了重大的打擊。⑦嚴厲或有效地攻擊〖常 out〗. The speech *hits* out at warmongering. 這篇演說對煽動戰爭之行爲大加撻伐。⑧請求;要求。He *hit* me for a loan. 他向我提出借錢的要求。⑨達到。Prices are expected to *hit* a new high. 物價預期將漲到新高峯。⑩出現;登載。When will this report *hit* the papers? 這篇報導幾時可見報? ⑪找到; 發現。⑫猜中。You have *hit* it! 你猜對了! ⑬表現成功;精確製造。⑭出發;上路。Let's *hit* the road. 我們上路吧。⑮受影響。We were all *hit* by the depression. 我們都受到不景氣的影響。**—***v.i.* ①打;打擊。②推動內燃機之汽缸的活塞。***hit below the belt*** 以不合規矩的手段攻擊。***hit home*** 說話搔着癢處。***hit it off*** 〖俗〗相處甚善;相合。***hit off*** **a.** 模仿。**b.** 巧妙地表示出。***hit on*** (or ***upon***) **a.** 無意中遇見;到達。**b.** 偶然發現;忽然想起;猜中。to *hit on* a plan for making money. 忽然想起一個賺錢的方法。***hit the ceiling*** 大爲生氣。***hit the high spots*** **a.** 上街;上夜總會。We will *hit the high spots* when you come to town. 等你到城裏來時我們將一道上街去玩。**b.** 做事馬虎;隨隨便便。***hit the nail on the head*** 說話中肯;一語道破。***hit the spot*** 滿足某一需要。I was dying of thirst, and that coca-cola just *hit the spot*. 我正渴得要死，那瓶可口可樂正好滿足需要。**—***n.* ①打;擊。②攻擊; 抨擊。③〖棒球〗安打。④有效的文字表現。We savored the barbed *hits* in his reply. 我們對他答覆裏的那些帶刺的語句很欣賞。⑤(嘗試、演出等之)成功。Your play will surely become a *hit*. 你的劇本一定會成功。⑥〖俚〗注射毒品(尤指海洛英)。***hit or miss*** 隨便;馬虎。The paint job had been done *hit or miss*. 這件油漆的工作做得很馬虎。**—less,** *adj.* **—ta·ble,** *adj.* **—ter,** *n.*

hit-and-run ['hɪtn̩'rʌn; 'hitn'rʌn] *adj.* ①撞倒行人就逃走的(如汽車等)。②打了人就跑的。**—ner,** *n.*

hit-and-run play 〖棒球〗打帶跑戰術;擊球跑壘戰術。

hit batsman 〖棒球〗被對方投手投球擊中而獲得保送上一壘的打擊手。

˙hitch [hɪtʃ; hitʃ] *v.t.* ①急動; 猛拉。He *hitched* his chair nearer to the fire. 他將椅子拉近火爐。②繫住;拴住;鉤住。③套…於車上。The farmer *hitched* up his team and drove to town. 那農夫將各馬匹與車套好後，即驅車上城去。④搭便車。⑤〖俚〗結婚。They got *hitched* in 1931. 他們於1931年結婚。⑥被…掛住或鉤住。**—***v.i.* ①被繫住; 被拉住。Her dress *hitched* on a nail. 她的衣襟被釘掛住了。②跛行。***hitch up*** 將（牲畜）套車。**—***n.* ①急動; 猛拉。The sailor gave his trousers a *hitch*. 那水手拉了一拉他的褲子。②連接;接頭;栓子。③跛行。④障礙;阻礙。Everything went off without a *hitch*. 一切情形進行順利。⑤(暫時栓物用的）結。⑥〖軍俚〗服役期間。

hitch·hike ['hɪtʃˌhaɪk; 'hitʃhaik] *v.,* **-hiked, -hik·ing,** *n.* **—***v.i.* 沿途搭乘別人便車以旅行。**—***n.* 沿途搭乘別人便車的旅行。**—hitch·hik·er,** *n.*

hith·er ['hɪðɚ; 'hiðə] *adv.* 到此處。to come *hither*. 到此處來。***hither and thither*** 到處。***hither and yon*** 從此到彼(尤指較遠處);到處。He looked *hither and yon* for the coin. 他到處找那枚硬幣。**—***adj.* 在這邊的。on the *hither* side of sixty. 不到六十歲。

hith·er·most ['hɪðɚˌmost; 'hiðəmoust] *adj.* 沿此方向最近處的。

˙hith·er·to [ˌhɪðɚ'tu; 'hiðə'tuː] *adv.* 迄今; 至今。a fact *hitherto* unknown. 迄今無人知道的事實。

hith·er·ward(s) ['hɪðɚwɚd(z); 'hiðəwəd(z)] *adv.* 〖古,罕〗 =**hither.**

Hit·ler ['hɪtlɚ; 'hitlə] *n.* 希特勒(Adolf, 1889–1945, 納粹黨魁，於 1933–45 任德國總理)。**—i·an,** *adj.*

Hit·ler·ism ['hɪtlɚˌɪzəm; 'hitlərizəm] *n.* 希特勒主義(德國之國家社會主義)。

Hit·ler·ist ['hɪtlɚˌɪst; 'hitlərist] *n.* =**Hitlerite.**

Hit·ler·ite ['hɪtlɚˌaɪt; 'hitlərait] *n.* 希特勒主義者。**—***adj.* 希特勒主義(者)的;納粹黨的。

hit-or-miss ['hɪtɚ'mɪs; 'hitə'mis] *adj.* 隨便的;偶然的;聽天由命的。

hit parade 流行歌曲或唱片目錄。

hit·ter ['hɪtɚ; 'hitə] *n.* ①〖棒球〗打擊手。②打擊之物或人。

Hit·tite ['hɪtaɪt; 'hitait] *n.* 希泰族(小亞細亞的古代民族)。**—***adj.* 希泰族(語)的。

˙hive [haɪv; haiv] *n., v.,* **hived, hiv·ing.** **—***n.* ①蜂房。②羣居一起之蜜蜂。③鬧市;鬧區; 鬧地。④一大羣麕集的人。⑤似蜂房的事物。**—***v.t.* ①置(蜂)於蜂房中。②儲藏(蜜)於蜂房中。③儲藏以供日後應用。**—***v.i.* ①進入蜂房。②如蜂一般地集居於一處。***hive off*** 〖主英〗**a.** 脫離（組織等)。**b.** 消滅。**—less,** *adj.* **—like,** *adj.*

hives [haɪvz; haivz] *n.* 〖醫〗蕁麻疹。

H.J. here lies (拉 =hic jacet). **hl.** hectoliter(s). **H.L.** House of Lords. **hm.** hectometer(s).

h'm [həm; həm] *interj.* hem 或 hum 之略。

H.M. His (*or* Her) Majesty. **Ho** 化學元素 holmium 之符號。**H.O.** ①Head Office. ②Home Office.

˙ho(a) [ho; hou] *interj.* ①表示嘲笑、喜悅、

或驚愕之聲。②引起注意之聲。What *ho!* 甚麼！Westward *ho!* 向西去啊！③呼牛馬停止之聲。(亦作 **whoa**)

hoar 〔hor; hɔː〕 *adj.* ①灰白的。②灰白頭髮的；年老的。③鋪滿白霜的。—*n.* ①灰白；灰白色。②白髮。③白霜。

***hoard** 〔hord, hɔrd; hɔːd, hɔəd〕 *v.i.* 貯藏金錢、貨物等。—*v.t.* 聚藏。A squirrel *hoards* nuts for the winter. 松鼠聚藏堅果過冬。—*n.* 貯藏物。

hoard·er 〔ˈhordə; ˈhɔːdə〕 *n.* 囤積者；聚藏者。

hoard·ing 〔ˈhordɪŋ; ˈhɔːdiŋ〕 *n.* ①貯藏。②(*pl.*) 貯藏物。③招貼板；廣告牌。④(工地四周的) 板垣；圍籬。

hoar·frost 〔ˈhor,frɔst; ˈhɔːˈfrɔst〕 *n.* 白霜。

hoar·hound 〔ˈhor,haund; ˈhɔːhaund〕 *n.* =**horehound.**

hoar·i·ness 〔ˈhorɪnɪs; ˈhɔːrinis〕 *n.* ①(毛髮之)灰白；有白髮。②古老。

***hoarse** 〔hors; hɔːs, hɔəs〕 *adj.*, **hoars·er, hoars·est.** ①嘶啞的；粗嗄的。a *hoarse* voice. 粗嗄的聲音。②發嘶啞聲的；聲音粗嗄的。—**ly,** *adv.* —**ness,** *n.*

hoar·stone 〔ˈhor,ston; ˈhɔːstoun〕 *n.* 〖英〗①(自太古存在的)界石。②(歷史性或傳說中的)古石。

hoar·y 〔ˈhorɪ; ˈhɔːri〕 *adj.*, **hoar·i·er, hoar·i·est.** ①灰白的；鬚髮斑白的。②古代的。—**hoar·i·ly,** *adv.* —**hoar·i·ness,** *n.*

hoax 〔hoks; houks〕 *n.* ①惡作劇。②騙局。—*v.t.* 用騙局欺詐。They *hoaxed* him out of his money. 他們騙去他的錢。—**er,** *n.*

hob 〔hab; hɔb〕 *n.* ①火爐後面或旁邊之架子。②丟鐵圈之釘(一種遊戲用)。③妖魔；鬼(=hobgoblin)。④〖俗〗惡作劇；破壞。⑤鄉下佬。***play*** (or ***raise***) ***hob with*** 搗亂。—**like,** *adj.*

hob·ba·de·hoy 〔ˈhabədɪˈhɔɪ; ˈhɔbədiˈhɔi〕 *n.* =**hobbledehoy.**

Hobbes 〔habz; hɔbz〕 *n.* 霍布士(Thomas, 1588–1679, 英國哲學家)。

hob·ble 〔ˈhabl̩; ˈhɔbl〕 *v.*, **-bled, -bling,** *n.* —*v.i.* ①蹣跚。②跛行。③韻律不完全的(詩歌)。—*v.t.* ①使跛行。②將(馬)腿綑縛以阻其行動。③妨礙；阻止。—*n.* ①跛行。②束縛馬腿用的繩或帶。③困境；困難。

hob·ble·de·hoy 〔ˈhabldɪˈhɔɪ; ˈhɔbldiˈhɔi〕 *n.* ①青年人。②蠢笨之青年人。

hob·by**[1] 〔ˈhabɪ; ˈhɔbi〕 *n.*, *pl.* **-bies.** ①嗜好；別好；癖。Gardening, collecting postage stamps or old swords are hobbies. 種植花木、集郵或集古劍皆是嗜好。②=**hobbyhorse.** ***ride a hobby (or ***hobbyhorse***) 費太多時間或精神於一種嗜好上。—**ist,** *n.* —**less,** *adj.*

hob·by[2] *n.*, *pl.* **-bies.** 一種小鷹。

hob·by·horse 〔ˈhabɪ,hɔrs; ˈhɔbihɔːs〕 *n.* ①(兒童玩具) **a.** 木馬。**b.** 搖馬。**c.** 旋轉木馬。②化裝舞會中附於跳舞者腰際之馬形物。

hob·gob·lin 〔ˈhab,gablɪn; ˈhɔb,gɔblin〕 *n.* 妖魔；惡鬼。

hob·nail 〔ˈhab,nel; ˈhɔbneil〕 *n.* (釘於鞋跟之)平頭釘。—*v.t.* 釘以平頭釘。

hob·nob 〔ˈhab,nab; ˈhɔbnɔb〕 *v.*, **-nobbed, -nob·bing,** *n.*, *adv.* —*v.i.* ①交好；親睦〖常 with〗。②共飲；碰杯。—*n.* 共飲。—*adv.* 隨意地；不留意地。

ho·bo 〔ˈhobo; ˈhoubou〕 *n.*, *pl.* **-bos, -boes,** *v.*, **-boed, -bo·ing.** —*n.* 〖美〗①游民；流氓。②流動工人。—*v.i.* 過流浪生涯。

Hob·son's choice 〔ˈhabsənz～; ˈhɔbsnz～〕 不容挑選(即對所提供之物祇可接受或拒絕)。

hock[1] 〔hak; hɔk〕 *n.* (馬牛等的) 後脚踝關節。—*v.t.* 割斷膕腱使成殘廢。

hock[2] *n.* 德國萊茵河地區所產之白葡萄酒。

hock[3] *n.*, *v.t.* 〖美俚〗典當；典質。***in hock*** **a.** 在他處作抵押。**b.** 欠債。***out of hock*** **a.** 已贖出(抵押物)。**b.** 已不欠債。—**er,** *n.*

***hock·ey** 〔ˈhakɪ; ˈhɔki〕 *n.* 曲棍球。

hockey stick 曲棍(曲棍球具)。

ho·cus 〔ˈhokəs; ˈhoukəs〕 *v.*, **-cus(s)ed, -cus·(s)ing,** *n.* —*v.t.* ①欺騙。②加麻醉劑於(飲料)中；使麻醉。—*n.* 加麻醉劑之飲料；蒙汗藥酒。

ho·cus-po·cus 〔ˈhokəsˈpokəs; ˈhoukəsˈpoukəs〕 *n.*, *v.*, **-cus(s)ed, -cus·(s)ing.** —*n.* ①變戲法時所用之無意義的話；咒語。②戲法；魔術。③詭計；欺騙。—*v.t.* & *v.i.* 欺騙。

hod 〔had; hɔd〕 *n.* ①搬運磚瓦灰泥等物之工具(有一長柄，並可放於肩上)。②煤斗。

hod carrier 瓦匠之助手(用 hod 搬運磚瓦、灰泥給水泥匠者)。(亦作 **hodman**)

hod·den 〔ˈhadn̩; ˈhɔdn〕 *n.* 〖蘇〗本色羊毛粗呢。—*adj.* 羊毛粗呢的。(亦作 **hoddin**)

hodge 〔hadʒ; hɔdʒ〕 *n.* 〖主英〗農場工人；鄉下人。(亦作 **Hodge**)

hodge·podge 〔ˈhadʒ,padʒ; ˈhɔdʒpɔdʒ〕 *n.* 混雜物；雜食 (=hotchpotch)。

Hodg·kin's disease 〔ˈhadʒkɪnz～; ˈhɔdʒkinz～〕 何杰金氏病(一種癌症)。

hod·man 〔ˈhadmən; ˈhɔdmən〕 *n.*, *pl.* **-men.** ①=**hod carrier.** ②苦工。

hod·om·e·ter 〔haˈdamɪtə; hɔˈdɔmitə〕 *n.* (汽車等之)路程計；里程計。

***hoe** 〔ho; hou〕 *n.*, *v.*, **hoed, hoe·ing.** —*n.* 鋤頭。—*v.t.* & *v.i.* 鋤；掘。to *hoe* up weeds. 鋤草。—**ho·er,** *n.* —**like,** *adj.*

hoe·cake 〔ˈho,kek; ˈhoukeik〕 *n.* 〖美〗玉米餅。

hoe·down 〔ˈho,daun; ˈhoudaun〕 *n.* ①一種公共舞會。②上述舞會之鄉間音樂。

hog** 〔hag; hɔg〕 *n.*, *v.*, **hogged, hog·ging.** —*n.* ①猪；長成的猪。②〖俗〗自私者；貪婪者；骯髒者。③〖英方〗**a.** 未剪過毛的一歲綿羊。**b.** 自上述羊剪下的羊毛。**c.** 其他家畜，如未滿一歲的閹牛。④〖鐵路俚〗火車頭。⑤木材切碎機。go (the) whole hog*** 盡力而爲之。***live*** (or ***eat***) ***high off the hog*** 〖俗〗富裕。***live high on the hog*** 生活奢侈。***make a hog of oneself*** 貪食。—*v.t.* ①〖美俚〗貪取。②彎背(如猪狀)。③切成木片。—**like,** *adj.*

hog·back 〔ˈhag,bæk; ˈhɔgbæk〕 *n.* 〖地理〗豚脊丘；峻銳的山脊。—**hog-backed,** *adj.*

hog cholera 猪霍亂。

hog·fish 〔ˈhag,fɪʃ; ˈhɔgfiʃ〕 *n.*, *pl.* **-fish, -fish·es.** 西印度羣島附近之一種食用海魚。

hog·ger·y 〔ˈhagərɪ; ˈhɔgəri〕 *n.*, *pl.* **-ger·ies.** ①養猪場。②猪(集合稱)。③(猪一樣的)汚穢、貪婪的行爲。

hog·get 〔ˈhagɪt; ˈhɔgit〕 *n.* 〖方〗①兩歲的雄猪。②一歲之羊或駒。

hog·gish 〔ˈhagɪʃ; ˈhɔgiʃ〕 *adj.* ①似猪的；自私的；貪婪的。②汚穢的；不潔的。—**ly,** *adv.* —**ness,** *n.*

hog·ma·nay 〔,hagməˈne; ˈhɔgmənei〕 *n.* 〖蘇，北英〗①除夕日。②(孩子們所得之)年節禮物。③孩子們之挨家要年禮。(亦作 **hagmenay, hagmane, hogmenay, hogmane**)

hog·nose snake 〔ˈhag,noz～; ˈhɔg,nouz～〕 北美產之一種無毒蛇。(亦作 **hog-**

nose)
hogs·head 〔ˈhɑgzˌhɛd; ˈhɔgzhed〕 *n.* ①可容100至140加命之大桶。②液量單位(合63加命)。
hog·wash 〔ˈhɑgˌwɑʃ; ˈhɔg-wɔʃ〕 *n.* ①猪食;殘湯剩菜。②空洞的話或文章;劣作。
hoick(s) 〔hɔɪk(s); hɔik(s)〕 *interj.* 激勵獵犬之聲。—*v.i.* & *v.t.* 激勵獵犬跑快。
hoi·den 〔ˈhɔɪdn̩; ˈhɔidn〕 *n., adj., v.i.* =**hoyden.** —**ish,** *adj.*
hoi(c)k 〔hɔɪk; hɔik〕 *v.t.* & *v.i.* (使)(飛機)急劇上升。
hoi pol·loi 〔ˈhɔɪpəˈlɔɪ; ˈhɔipəˈlɔi〕〖希〗(常 the-)民衆;百姓;烏合之衆。
***hoist** 〔hɔɪst; hɔist〕 *v.t.* 升高;升起;舉起。to *hoist* a flag (sail). 升旗(帆)。—*n.* ①升高;舉起。②起重機。an ammunition *hoist.* (兵艦上的)彈藥起卸機。③〖俗〗推動。④旗和帆在旗桿或帆桅上之高度。⑤在旗桿上所做之信號。—**er,** *n.*
hoi·ty-toi·ty 〔ˈhɔɪtɪˈtɔɪtɪ; ˈhɔitiˈtɔiti〕 *adj.* ①輕佻的;浮誇的。②易怒的;傲慢的。—*n.* ①輕佻的行爲。②傲慢;蠻橫。—*interj.* (表驚訝或藐視之聲) 嗳喲! (亦作 **highty-tighty**)
ho·key-po·key 〔ˈhokɪˈpokɪ; ˈhouki-ˈpouki〕 *n.* 〖俗〗①戲法;欺騙。②(沿街叫賣的)廉價冰淇淋。(亦作 **hoky-poky**)
Ho·kiang 〔ˈhʌˈdʒjɑŋ; ˈhʌˈdʒjɑːŋ〕 *n.* 合江(中國東北之一省,省會爲佳木斯, Kiamusze).
ho·kum 〔ˈhokəm; ˈhoukəm〕 *n.* 〖俚〗①無聊話;討人歡喜的話。②(戲劇中)討人高興或令人流淚的慣用手法;噱頭。
‡hold[1] 〔hold; hould〕 *v.,* **held** or 〖古〗 **hold·en, hold·ing,** *n.* —*v.t.* ①握住;拿住。*Hold* him tight or else he will move (fall, run away, etc.). 把他抓緊,不然他就會動(跌倒,逃跑等)。②使固定不動;按住。He will *hold* the paper steady while you draw. 你畫時他會按住紙。③支撐;托住不墜。He *held* his head in his hands. 他以手托住頭。④握有;持;抱。He was *holding* a book in his hands. 他手中持有一書。⑤維持。This wall is not strong enough to *hold* pictures. 這牆不够堅實,不能掛圖畫。⑥容納;裝。The room could *hold* fifty people. 該房間可容五十人。⑦掌握;保持;固執。⑧舉行;開(會)。⑨堅守。*Hold* the fort. 堅守堡壘。⑩法庭裁決。The court *holds* him guilty. 法院判決他有罪。⑪抑制;約束。⑫信仰;堅信。People once *held* that the world was flat. 從前人們相信地球是平的。⑬守信;守約。He *held* his promise. 他守信不渝。⑭占有。⑮保留。⑯扣留。The police *held* him at the station house. 警察將他扣押在派出所裏。⑰妨礙;阻止。Fear *held* him from acting. 恐懼使他不採取行動。⑱認爲;評價。We *held* her best of all the applicants. 我們認爲她是求職者中之最佳者。⑲瞄準;對準。He *held* a gun on the prisoner. 他將鎗對着戰俘。—*v.i.* ①停留;維持;抑制。The soldiers *held* back for a short time. 士兵們停了一會兒未動。②屹立不壞。The dike *held* during the flood. 堤壩在洪水中屹立不壞。③堅守。He *held* to his promise. 他堅守諾言。④有效。The rule *holds* in all cases. 這規則在各種情形之下均有效。⑤繼續。The weather *held* warm. 天氣繼續暖和。⑥保持。***hold aloof*** 置身事外。***hold back*** **a.** 克制。**b.** 抵擋。**c.** 隱而不宣。**d.** 保有;扣留。He *held back* ten dollars. 他扣下了十元。***hold down*** **a.** 壓制壓住。**b.** 〖俚〗保有。to *hold down* a job. 保有一分工作。***hold forth*** **a.** 演說;說教;長篇大論地講。**b.** 給予;提議。***hold good*** 有效。For how long will your offer *hold good*. 你的提議能有效多久? ***hold in*** **a.** 壓抑。**b.** 忍耐;忍住。***hold off*** **a.** 使離開;使不接近。His cold manner *holds* people *off*. 他冷淡的態度使人不敢親近。**b.** 抵抗。**c.** 延緩。***hold on*** **a.** 等候。**b.** 抓住。*Hold on* to my hand tightly while we cross this street. 我們過街時要抓緊我的手。**c.** 支持。**d.**〖俗〗停止。*Hold on* now! That isn't what I meant at all. 住口!那根本不是我的意思。***hold one's ground*** (or ***one's own***) 堅持自己地位或立場;不讓步。Our troops *held their ground* bravely. 我們的軍隊勇敢地堅守陣地。***hold one's horses*** 少安毋躁。***hold one's peace*** 保持靜默。***hold one's tongue*** 住嘴。"*Hold your tongue!*" cried my mother, and I said no more. 母親喊"住嘴!"我就不再說了。***hold one to something*** 堅持令…履行諾言。They promised him a partnership, and I am sure he will *hold them to it.* 他們承允他入夥,我想他會堅持要他們履行諾言。***hold out*** **a.** 伸出。He was *holding* his arms *out.* 他將兩臂伸出。**b.** 給予。**c.** 拖延;延續。**d.** 支持。**e.**〖俚〗不使發生。**f.** 維持。Will the food *hold out*? 糧食能維持下去嗎? **g.**〖俚〗扣壓;保留。He was suspected of *holding out* important information. 他有扣壓重要消息的嫌疑。***hold out on*** 隱瞞。***hold over*** **a.** 展期;延擱。The matter was *held over* until the next meeting. 這事將延至下次會議。**b.** 逾期延續。**c.** 保存。Please *hold over* the rest of the goods. 請保存其餘貨物。***hold still*** 靜止不動。It is hard for a child to *hold still* while being photographed. 小孩照像時而靜止不動是很難的。***hold the bag*** 受害。***hold*** **(*things*)** ***together*** 使(某物)聯合在一起;使團結。Love of country *holds* the nation *together.* 愛國心使全國人民團結一致。***hold true*** 適用。***hold up*** **a.**〖美〗攔路搶刼。Thieves *held* him *up* in the park and took his wallet. 強盜在公園裏搶了他的錢包。**b.** 使停滯。**c.** 經久。**d.** 展覽;提出。**e.** 擁護;支持。**f.** 停止。They *held up* at the gate. 他們在大門口停住。**g.** 保持地位或現狀。***hold water*** 眞實的;有效的。His account of the robbery won't *hold water.* 他對搶刼案的陳述是不眞實的。***hold with*** **a.** 同意;贊成。I don't *hold with* his pessimistic views. 我不同意他悲觀的看法。**b.** 原諒。I won't *hold with* such lawless acts. 我不能原諒這種目無法紀的行動。—*n.* ①把握;把持力。I can't keep *hold* of it; it's too slippery. 我握不住它,它太滑了。②支持物。③掌握;把持。A habit has a *hold* on you. 習慣可以左右你。④擒拿法。⑤〖音樂〗音之持續。⑥監牢。⑦〖古〗堡壘。⑧預約。⑨〖火箭〗發射前之意外耽延。***get hold of*** 獲得;取得。***lay*** (or ***take***) ***hold of*** **a.** 抓住。**b.** 控制。***no hold(s) barred*** 毫無限制;行動完全自由。There were *no holds barred* when the enemies met in combat. 仇人打仗時拚一個你死我活。***take hold*** 生根;依戀。It's hard for

him to *take hold* in the new place. 他不容易在這個新地方永久居留下來。—**a·ble,** *adj.*

hold² *n.* (船之)貨艙;船艙。

hold·all ['hold,ɔl; 'houldɔːl] *n.* ①旅行用之大帆布袋。②放雜物的大袋。

hold·back ['hold,bæk; 'houldbæk] *n.* ①(馬車之)抑車鉤。②妨礙;箝制;阻止。③抑制之物。④扣壓。⑤不願作承諾之人。—*adj.* 沒有進步的;落後的。

hold·en ['holdən; 'houldən] *v.* 〖古〗pp. of **hold.**

***hold·er** ['holdɚ; 'houldə] *n.* ①持有人;所有人。②支持物。③票據持有人。a share *holder*; a stock *holder.* 股票持有人;股東。—**ship,** *n.*

hold·fast ['hold,fæst; 'houldfɑːst] *n.* ①緊纏;緊握。②緊握之物;把持之物(如鉤、箝等)。③〖植物〗吸盤。

hold·ing ['holdɪŋ; 'houldiŋ] *n.* ①土地。②(*pl.*)(股票、債券等)財產。③(運動中)以手或臂所作之阻擋犯規。

holding company 擁有其他公司之股權,而能控制各該公司的公司。

hold·out ['hold,aut; 'houldaut] *n.* ①伸出;給予;延續。②伸出、給予、延續的事物。③欲取得優厚條件而拖延簽約者。④拒絕參加團體活動的人。⑤堅强據點。

hold·o·ver ['hold,ovɚ; 'hould,ouvə] *n.* ①從上一時代遺留下來的人或事。②大部分同事已去職後仍留在原職的人。③檔期已屆而仍繼續上映或上演的電影或戲。

hold·up ['hold,ʌp; 'houldʌp] *n.* ①〖美俗〗攔路搶刼。②(交通之)阻塞。③〖俗〗被敲竹槓。④卡車或旅行車後門的掛鉤。

‡hole [hol; houl] *n., v.,* **holed, hol·ing.** —*n.* ①洞;孔;穴。These roads are full of *holes.* 這些路滿是坑窪。②狹小、黑暗而卑陋的居所。What a wretched little *hole* he lives in! 他住在多麼可憐的一間小屋裡啊! ③〖俗〗瑕疵;缺點。There is a *hole* in your argument. 你的辯論中有一個缺點(漏洞)。④〖俗〗難於脫身之處境;窘境。⑤(高爾夫球場上之)洞。⑥(高爾夫球場上)自球座至洞之距離。⑦小海灣;小港。⑧監獄中之隔離囚房。***a hole in the wall*** 簡陋的居所或工作環境。Their first shop was *a real hole in the wall.* 他們的第一家店眞是簡陋。***a square peg in a round hole*** 方枘圓鑿(喻人不稱其位)。***burn a hole in one's pocket*** 使人浪費金錢。His inheritance was *burning a hole in his pocket.* 他所繼承的遺產正促使他濫用金錢。***in the hole*** a. 欠債。b. (紙牌) 牌面朝下。***like a rat in a hole*** 如洞中之鼠;如甕中之鼈(不能脫身)。***make a hole in*** 挖一個洞;費去一大筆錢。The hospital bills have *made a* large *hole in* my savings. 住院費使我動用了積蓄中的一大部分。***pick holes in*** 對…吹毛求疵。***put (a person) in a hole*** 置(人)於困境。—*v.t.* ①鑽(洞);打(洞);鑿(洞)。②(打高爾夫球)入洞。***hole out*** 打高爾夫球入洞。***hole up*** a. 入洞過冬。b. 隱居或藏匿一段時期。—**less,** *adj.* 〖注意〗hole 及 cavity 均作"洞穴"解。hole 係常用的字,指任何物體中之"開口""穿孔"或"洞穴"。cavity 主要爲科學或專門用語,祇指堅硬物體上之洞穴,通常表面有開口可見。

hole-and-cor·ner ['holən'kɔrnɚ; 'houlən(d)'kɔːnə] *adj.* ①〖俗〗祕密的;偷偷的。②瑣碎的;無趣的。(亦作**hole-in-corner**)

hole·proof ['hol,pruf; 'houlpruːf] *adj.* ①(衣服之)不會破洞的。②(法律之)沒有漏洞的。

hole·y ['holɪ; 'houli] *adj.* 有孔的;多孔的。

hol·i·but ['hɑləbət; 'hɔlibət] *n., pl.* **-but, -buts.** =**halibut.**

‡hol·i·day ['hɑlə,de; 'hɔlidei] *n.* ①假日;節日。Sunday is a *holiday.* 禮拜天是假日。②(常 *pl.*) 假期。When do the *holidays* begin? 假期何時開始? ③宗教上的節日。④油漆時漏漆的地方。***on (a) holiday*** 在假期中。Mr. Smith is away *on holiday* at present. 史密斯先生目前正在度假。***take (or have) a holiday*** 休假。—*adj.* 適於假期的;歡忭的。—*v.i.* 〖英〗度假。The star is *holidaying* in London. 該明星正在倫敦度假。

hol·i·day·mak·er ['hɑləde,mekɚ; 'hɔlədi,meikə] *n.* 〖英〗於休假日出去郊遊者;行樂者;趣味低級而喧噪的遊客。

ho·li·ly ['holɪlɪ; 'houlili] *adv.* ①虔誠地。②神聖地;淸淨地。

ho·li·ness ['holɪnɪs; 'houlinis] *n.* 神聖。***His*** (or ***Your***) ***Holiness*** (對敎皇的尊稱)敎皇陛下;宗座。

hol·la ['hɑlə; 'hɔlə] *interj., n., pl.* **-las,** *v.t. & v.i.,* **-laed, -la·ing.** =**hollo.**

***Hol·land** ['hɑlənd; 'hɔlənd] *n.* 荷蘭 (the Netherlands 的舊稱)。

hol·lan·daise (sauce) [,hɑlən'dez; ,hɔlən'deiz] *n.* 荷蘭酸辣醬(以蛋黃、牛油、檸檬汁或醋等製成)。

Hol·land·er ['hɑləndɚ; 'hɔləndə] *n.* ①荷蘭人。②荷蘭船。③〖造紙〗漂打機。

hol·ler ['hɑlɚ; 'hɔlə] 〖美俚〗*v.t. & v.i.* 呼喊;叫喊。—*n.* holler 之叫聲。

hol·lo ['hɑlo; 'hɔlou] *interj., n., pl.* **-los,** *v.,* **-loed, -lo·ing.** —*interj.* 喂! —*n.* hollo 之叫聲。—*v.t. & v.i.* ①叫 hollo;喂喂地叫。②叱喊(獵犬)。(亦作 **holloa**)

‡hol·low ['hɑlo; 'hɔlou] *adj.* ①空的;中空的。②凹陷的。③呆滯的;沉重的。④空虛的。a *hollow* victory. 空虛的勝利。⑤虛僞的;假的。*hollow* words (sympathy, promises). 虛僞的言語(同情,許諾)。⑥饑餓的;空腹的。—*n.* ①洞;孔;穴。a *hollow* in the ground. 地上的洞。②山谷。—*v.t.* 使成空洞〖常out〗. The river banks were *hollowed* out by rushing water. 河岸爲流水所沖刷而成空洞。—*v.i.* 形成空洞。—*adv.* 〖俗〗徹底地。***beat all hollow*** a. 毒打。b. 使(他人)相形見絀;徹底擊敗。His performance *beat* the others *all hollow.* 他的表現使別人相形見絀。—**ness,** *n.* —**ly,** *adv.*

hol·low-eyed ['hɑlo,aɪd; 'hɔlouaid] *adj.* 凹眼的。

hol·low·heart·ed ['hɑlo'hɑrtɪd; 'hɔlou'hɑːtid] *adj.* (心地)不誠實的;虛僞的。—**ness,** *n.*

hol·ly ['hɑlɪ; 'hɔli] *n., pl.* **-lies.** ①冬青類。②(耶誕節裝飾用之)樹葉及果實。

hol·ly·hock ['hɑlɪ,hɑk; 'hɔlihɔk] *n.* 〖植物〗蜀葵。

Hol·ly·wood ['hɑlɪ,wud; 'hɔliwud] *n.*好萊塢(在洛杉磯 Los Angeles 市,爲美國電影工業中心)。—**ite,** —**er,** *n.*

Hol·ly·wood·i·an ['hɑlɪ,wudɪən; 'hɔli,wudiən] *n.* ①好萊塢電影工作者。②好萊塢人。—*adj.* ①電影事業的;表面上的;無內容的。②好萊塢的。

Hol·ly·woo·dish ['hɑlɪ,wudɪʃ; 'hɔli,wudiʃ] *adj.* 好萊塢的;好萊塢電影事業的;不實際的。

holm [hom; houm] *n.* ①(河或湖中之)小島。②河邊低地。

Holmes 〔homz; houmz〕 *n.* 福爾摩斯 (Sherlock, 英國 Sir Arshur Conan Doyle 所著偵探小說中之名探)。
hol·mi·um 〔'holmɪəm; 'houlmiəm〕 *n.* 〖化〗鈥(稀土族金屬元素之一,符號 Ho)。
hol·o·caust 〔'hɑlə,kɔst; 'hɔləkɔːst〕 *n.* ①燔祭(燒全獸的祭禮)。②(人或獸之)全部焚燬。③大規模之毀滅。—**al,** —**ic,** *adj.*
hol·o·graph 〔'hɑlə,græf; 'hɔləgrɑːf〕 *n.* ①(全文)親筆。②親筆文書。—*adj.* 親筆的。—**ic,** —**i·cal,** *adj.*
hol·o·graph·ic will〔,hɑlə'græfɪk~; ,hɔlə'græfik~〕〖法律〗親筆遺書。
hol·o·phote 〔'hɑlə,fot; 'hɔləfout〕 *n.* (燈臺等燈光之)全光反射裝置;全反射鏡。
hol·o·thu·ri·an 〔,hɑlə'θjurɪən; ,hɔlə'θjuːriən〕 *adj.* 〖動物〗沙噀類的。—*n.* 沙噀類之動物。(亦作 **holothurioid**)
holp 〔holp; houlp〕 *v.* 〖古〗pt. of **help.**
hol·pen 〔'holpən; 'houlpən〕 *v.* 〖古〗pp. of **help.**
Hol·stein 〔'holstaɪn; 'hɔlstain〕 *n.* 荷蘭北部 Holstein 種乳牛。
hol·ster 〔'holstɚ; 'houlstə〕 *n.* 手鎗皮套。—*v.t.* 將…放入皮套。—**ed,** *adj.*
holt 〔holt; hoult〕 *n.* ①種樹之小丘。②森林;森林地。
‡**ho·ly** 〔'holɪ; 'houli〕 *adj.,* **-li·er, -li·est,** *n., pl.* **-lies.** —*adj.* ①神賜的;神聖的。*holy* water. 聖水。②聖潔的;至善的。to live a *holy* life. 過聖潔的生活。③宗教的。*holy* rites. 宗教儀式。④可怕的;可畏的。***a holy terror*** 可怕的人;淘氣的孩子。***holy bread*** 聖餐禮所使用之麪包。***holy cats*** 〖俚〗表示驚奇、驚訝、惶惑等的感嘆詞。***Holy Communion*** 聖餐禮。***the Holy City*** 聖城(卽耶路撒冷);天堂。***the Holy Father*** 敎皇。***the Holy Roman Empire*** 神聖羅馬帝國。***the Holy Rood*** **a.** 耶穌釘死於其上之十字架。**b.** 十字架。***the Holy Saturday*** 復活節前之星期六。***the Holy Scripture*** 聖經。***the Holy Spirit*** (or ***Ghost***)聖靈。***the Holy Thursday*** **a.** 復活節前之星期四。**b.** 復活節後之第四十天;耶穌升天日。***the Holy Week*** 復活節之前一週。***the Holy Writ*** 聖經。—*n.* 聖地。the *Holy* of Holies. (猶太敎敎堂中)至聖之地。〖注意〗**holy** 與 **sacred** 均作"神聖的"解。holy 着重於內在含有一種神聖之本質,使之值得崇拜。sacred 則着重於"由於將某物奉獻給宗敎之用途而獲得之神聖性",且使之值得崇敬:God is *holy.* 上帝是神聖的。Churches are *sacred.* 敎堂是神聖的。
Holy Alliance 〖史〗神聖同盟 (1815 年俄、奧、普締結於巴黎)。
ho·ly·day 〔'holɪ,de; 'houlidei〕 *n.* 宗敎之祭日;聖日。(亦作 **holy day**)
Holy Grail 聖杯或碟(據傳爲耶穌於最後晚餐所用者)。
Holy Land 聖地(卽巴勒斯坦)。
holy of holies ①最神聖的地方。②猶太敎寺廟之內殿。
holy orders 聖職;牧師任命式。
Holy Place ①聖所。②聖殿;大殿。
ho·ly·stone 〔'holɪ,ston; 'houlistoun〕 *n., v.,* **-stoned, -ston·ing.** —*n.* (磨甲板之)磨石。—*v.t. & v.i.* 用磨石磨。
Holy Trinity 三位一體。
•**hom·age** 〔'hɑmɪdʒ, 'ɑm-; 'hɔmidʒ〕 *n.* ①效忠;臣服。to do (*or* pay) *homage* to. 向…效忠或臣服。②尊崇;敬意。to pay *homage* to the genius of Shakespeare. 向莎士比亞的天才表示敬意。③(封建制度之)主僕關係。④表(封建)主僕關係之事物。
hom·bre 〔'ɔmbre; 'ɔːmbrei〕〖西〗*n.* 男人 (=man, fellow)。
Hom·burg 〔'hɑmbɝg; 'hɔmbəːg〕 *n.* ①杭堡帽(男用窄邊凹頂之氈帽)。②類似之女用氈帽。(亦作 **homburg**)
‡**home** 〔hom; houm〕 *n., adv., adj., v.,* **homed, hom·ing.** —*n.* ①家; 家庭;家園。I shall be glad to see the old *home* once more. 我將樂於再見老家一次。②家;家鄉;祖國。Every man went back to his *home.* 人人都回家去了。③庇護所; 避難所。④動物或植物之棲息或生長地。⑤產地;會集之處。Paris is the *home* of women's fashions. 巴黎是婦女時裝會集之處。⑥〖棒球〗本壘。⑦徑賽跑道之終點。⑧墳墓。***at home*** **a.** 在家裏。Is anybody *at home?* 有人在家嗎? **b.** 無拘束;舒適;安詳。Please make yourself *at home.* 請不要客氣;請勿拘禮。**c.** 接見客人;會客。When is he *at home?* 他何時在家? **d.** (球賽等) 在本地或本隊球場舉行。***be at home in*** 熟習;精通。He *is* quite *at home in* modern history. 他精通近代史。***not at home to*** 不會(客)。Mrs. Smith is *not at home to* anyone except relatives. 史密斯太太不會客,但親戚除外。—*adv.* ①在家;到家;向家(=at, to, *or* toward home)。When shall we be *home?* 我們何時可以回到家? ②中的地; 恰中地。 to strike *home.* 恰中目標。③深入地。to drive a nail *home.* 將釘完全打進去。***bring home*** 弄清楚;强調。***see one home*** 送某人回家。***write home about*** 特加評論。The town was nothing to *write home about.* 這城沒有甚麼值得一提的。 —*adj.* ①家的; 家庭內的。 ②國內的; 本國的。 *home* affairs. 內政。*home* industries. 國內工業。③中的的;有效的。***be home free*** 穩操勝算;遙遙領先。to *be home free* in a national election. 在全國性選舉中遙遙領先。 —*v.i.* ①回家。②成家。③(導向飛彈、飛機等)向目標前進〖常 in, on〗。***home in on*** (火箭)藉導航系統飛向 (目標)。—*v.t.* ①送返家。②供以家。③用自動儀引導…至機場、目標等。〖注意〗**home** 含有"家庭之溫暖及情感";而 **house** 僅指房屋而已。但在房產廣告等中,亦常用 home 以代替 house,蓋欲取其親切之意。
home base 〖棒球〗本壘。
home·bod·y 〔'hom,bɑdɪ; 'houm,bɔdi〕 *n., pl.* **-bod·ies.** 娛樂或工作都在家裏的人。
home-born 〔'hom,bɔrn; 'houmbɔːn〕 *adj.* 本國生的;內地生的;土產的;土著的。
home-bound 〔'hom,baund; 'houm-baund〕 *adj.* 回家的。(亦作 **homebound**)
home·bred 〔'hom'brɛd; 'houm'bred〕 *adj.* ①在家裏(國內)長大的;家內飼養的; 國產的。②乏敎養的;不懂世故的;粗野的。
home-brew 〔'hom'bru; 'houm'bruː〕 *n.* 自釀之飲料(啤酒等)。
home-brewed 〔'hom'brud; 'houm-'bruːd〕 *adj.* 自釀的。—*n.* 自釀酒。
home·com·ing〔'hom,kʌmɪŋ; 'houm-,kʌmiŋ〕 *n.* ①歸家;歸國。②大學每年一度之校友集會。—**home·com·er,** *n.*
Home Department〖英〗內政部。
home economics 家政學。
home·felt 〔'hom,fɛlt; 'houmfelt〕 *adj.* 深切地感到的;內在的;內心的;祕密的。
home front (戰爭時)後方(指支援戰事

之平民)。

home-grown ['hom'gron; 'houm-'groun] *adj.* (水果、蔬菜等) 自家種植的。

home guard 鄉團;民團。

home-keep·ing ['hom,kipɪŋ;'houm-,ki:piŋ] *adj.* 不離開家的;不喜歡外出的。

home·land ['hom,lænd; 'houmlænd] *n.* 祖國;故鄉。

home·less ['homlɪs; 'houmlis] *adj.* 無家可歸的。—**ly**, *adv.* —**ness**, *n.*

home·like ['hom,laɪk; 'houmlaik] *adj.* 如在家的; 友好的; 熟悉的; 舒適的。—**ness**, *n.*

***home·ly** ['homlɪ; 'houmli] *adj.*, **-li·er**, **-li·est.** ①家常的。②樸素的。③〖美〗不漂亮的。a *homely* girl. 一個不漂亮的女孩。④似家的; 令人思家的。⑤友善的。—**home-li·ness**, *n.*

***home·made** ['hom'med;'houm'meid] *adj.* ①家製的; 自製的。②本國製造的。I prefer a *homemade* car to one of those foreign models. 我寧要一部國產車而不要那些外國車。

home·mak·er ['hom,mekɚ;'houm-,meikə] *n.*〖美〗主婦; 女管家。

home·mak·ing['hom,mekɪŋ;'houm-,meikiŋ] *n.* 管家。—*adj.* 管家的。

Home Minister 〖英〗內政大臣。

Home Office 〖英〗內政部。

home office 總公司。

ho·me·o·path['homɪə,pæθ;'houmiə-pæθ] *n.* 同種療法醫師;順勢療法醫師。(亦作 **homoeopath**)

ho·me·o·path·ic [,homɪə'pæθɪk; ,houmiə'pæθik] *adj.* 同種療法(論)的;順勢療法(論)的。(亦作 **homoeopathic**)

ho·me·op·a·thist [,homɪ'ɑpəθɪst; ,houmi'ɔpəθist] *n.* =**homeopath.** (亦作 **homoeopathist**)

ho·me·op·a·thy [,homɪ'ɑpəθɪ;,hou-mi'ɔpəθi] *n.* 同種療法(用與該病原體同性質之其他病原體治療之方法, 爲 allopathy 之對)。(亦作 **homoeopathy**)

home·own·er ['hom,onɚ; 'houm-,ounə] *n.* 房主;房屋所有者。

home·place ['hom,ples; 'houmpleis] *n.* 出生地;祖籍。

home plate 〖棒球〗=**home base.**

Ho·mer ['homɚ; 'houmə] *n.* 荷馬 (古希臘詩人,約生於西元前九世紀左右)。

hom·er ['homɚ; 'houmə] *n.*〖俗〗①〖棒球〗=**home run.** ② =**homing pigeon.** —*v.i.* 擊出全壘打。

Ho·mer·ic [ho'mɛrɪk; hou'merik] *adj.* ①荷馬或荷馬之詩的。②荷馬風格的。

Homeric laughter 不能抑制地大聲發笑;縱聲大笑。

home·room ['hom,rum; 'houmrum] *n.* 固定供同一班學生上課用之教室。

home rule 地方自治。

home ruler 提倡地方自治者。

home run 〖棒球〗全壘打。

Home Secretary 〖英〗內政部長。

***home·sick** ['hom,sɪk; 'houm-sik] *adj.* 思家的;害懷鄉病的。 —**ness**, *n.*

home·site ['hom,saɪt; 'houmsait] *n.* ①住宅基地。②家;房屋。

home·spun['hom,spʌn;'houm-spʌn] *adj.* ①家裏織的。②樸素的;簡陋的;粗野的。—*n.* ①手織物。②一種鬆疏而堅韌之毛織物。

***home·stead** ['hom,stɛd;'houm-sted, -stid] *n.* ①〖美〗家園; 田園。②美國或英國政府給予開墾者之土地。 —*v.t.* & *v.i.* 在…定居。Pioneers *homesteaded* the valley. 墾荒者在山谷定居下來。

home·stead·er ['hom,stɛdɚ;'houm-stedə] *n.* ①homestead 之所有者。②承領美國或英國政府放領之公地者。

homestead law 有關公地放領之法律。

home stretch ①(賽馬或賽跑) 最後之直線賽程。②任何工作之最後部分。

home study 函授 (課程)。

home·town ['hom'taun;'houm'taun] *n.* 家鄉。—*adj.* 家鄉的。

***home·ward** ['homwɚd; 'houmwəd] *adv.* (亦作 **homewards**) 向家而(行)。*homeward* bound. 回航的。—*adj.* 歸家的;回國的。on a *homeward* course. 在歸家的途中。

***home·work** ['hom,wɝk; 'houmwə:k] *n.* ①在家裏做的工作 (尤指替工廠所做者)。②課外應預習或練習的功課;家庭作業。

home·work·er['hom'wɝkɚ;'houm-'wə:kə] *n.* 家裏的傭人(如女傭、園丁等)。

home·y ['homɪ; 'houmi] *adj.*, **home-i·er, home·i·est.** 〖俗〗如家的;安適的;友善的。(亦作 **homy**) —**ness, hom·i·ness**, *n.*

hom·i·cid·al [,hɑmə'saɪdl; ,hɔmi-'saidl] *adj.* ①殺人(犯)的。②有殺人癖好的。

hom·i·cide ['hɑmə,saɪd; 'hɔmisaid] *n.* ①殺人者。②殺人。

hom·i·let·ic [,hɑmə'lɛtɪk;,hɔmi'letik] *adj.* 說教術的;說教的;講道的;教訓的。(亦作 **homiletical**) —**al·ly**, *adv.*

hom·i·let·ics [,hɑmə'lɛtɪks; ,hɔmi-'letiks] *n.* (作 *sing.* 解) 說教術。

hom·i·ly ['hɑmlɪ;'hɔmili] *n.*, *pl.* **-lies.** ①講道。②枯燥之道德講演或寫作。

hom·ing ['homɪŋ; 'houmiŋ] *adj.* 歸家的;能識歸路的;思家的。

homing device 使飛機或飛彈自動飛向目標之裝置。

homing pigeon 傳信鴿。

hom·i·ny ['hɑmənɪ; 'hɔmini] *n.* 玉米糝。

hom·ish ['homɪʃ; 'houmiʃ] *adj.* = **homey.**

Ho·mo ['homo;'houmou] *n.*, *pl.* **Hom-i·nes** ['hɑmə,niz; 'hɔməni:z].〖拉〗①人屬(靈長類之一屬)。②(h-) 人。

ho·mo ['homo; 'houmou] *n.*, *pl.* **-mos.** 〖俚〗=**homosexual.**

homo- 〖字首〗表"相同"之義。

ho·mo·cen·tric [,homə'sɛntrɪk; ,houmə'sentrik] *adj.* 同心的;共心的。(亦作 **homocentrical**)

ho·moe·o·path ['homɪə,pæθ; 'hou-mjəpæθ] *n.* =**homeopath.**

ho·mog·a·my [ho'mɑgəmɪ; hou-'mɔgəmi] *n.* ①〖植物〗具同種、同性花。②〖植物〗雌雄蕊之同時成熟。③〖生物〗同子生殖。

ho·mo·ge·ne·i·ty [,homədʒə'niətɪ; ,hɔmodʒe'ni:iti] *n.* ①同種;同質;同性。②均質;均一。(亦作 **homogeneousness**)

ho·mo·ge·ne·ous [,homə'dʒinɪəs; ,hɔmə'dʒi:niəs] *adj.* ①同類的; 相似的。②以類似成分所組成的。③〖數學〗齊次的。④〖物理〗均等性的;均質的;等質的。—**ly**, *adv.*

ho·mo·gen·e·sis [,homə'dʒɛnəsɪs; ,hɔmə'dʒenəsis] *n.* 〖生物〗同形生殖 (爲 heterogenesis 之對)。

ho·mog·e·nize [ho'mɑdʒə,naɪz;hou-'mɔdʒənaiz] *v.t.*, **-nized, -niz·ing.** 使性

質相同；使均質；使調勻。

ho·mog·e·nous 〔hə'madʒənəs; hə'mɔdʒənəs〕 *adj.* 〖生物〗①構造相同的。②同類的；相似的。③同形質的。

hom·o·graph 〔'hamə,græf; 'hɔməgrɑːf〕 *n.* 同形異義字（例如 fair, 市集，與 fair, 美的）。 **—ic,** *adj.*

ho·mol·o·gate 〔hə'malə,get; hə'mɔləgeit〕 *v.,* **-gat·ed, -gat·ing.** —*v.t.* 〖法律〗贊同；確認；許可。—*v.i.* 同意。**—ho·mol·o·ga·tion,** *n.*

ho·mol·o·gize 〔hə'malə,dʒaɪz; hə'mɔlədʒaiz〕 *v.,* **-gized, -giz·ing.** —*v.t.* 使成相同；使成對應。—*v.i.* 相同；一致；對應。**—ho·mol·o·giz·er,** *n.*

ho·mol·o·gous 〔ho'maləgəs; hɔ'mɔləgəs〕 *adj.* ①相同的；對應的。②〖化〗同族的。③〖生物〗對應的；異形同原的(器官)。

hom·o·logue 〔'hamə,lɔg; 'hɔməlɔg〕 *n.* ①同系物；對應物。②〖生物〗同原器官；對應器官。③〖化〗同族體。

ho·mol·o·gy 〔ho'malədʒɪ; hɔ'mɔlədʒi〕 *n.* ①相同(關係)；對應。②〖生物〗(器官之)相同。③〖化〗(化合物之)同族關係。

hom·o·nym 〔'hamə,nɪm; 'hɔmənim〕 *n.* ①同音異義字（如 meat 與 meet）。②同名之人。**—i·ty,** *n.*

hom·o·nym·ic 〔,hamə'nɪmɪk; ,hɔmə'nimik〕 *adj.* ①同音異義字的。②同名的。

ho·mon·y·mous 〔ho'manəməs; hɔ'mɔniməs〕 *adj.* ①同名的。②同音異義（字）的。③意義曖昧的。**—ly,** *adv.*

hom·o·phone 〔'hamə,fon; 'hɔməfoun〕 *n.* ①同音之字母或音標(如 cork 一字中 c 與 k 爲 homophones)。②同音異義字。

hom·o·phon·ic 〔,hamə'fanɪk; ,hɔmə'fɔnik〕 *adj.* ①同音的；同音異義的。②〖音樂〗齊唱的；齊奏的。

ho·moph·o·nous 〔ho'mafənəs; hɔ'mɔfənəs〕 *adj.* 發音相同的；同音的。

ho·moph·o·ny 〔ho'mafənɪ; hɔ'mɔfəni〕 *n.* ①同音異義。②〖音樂〗齊唱；齊奏。

ho·mop·ter·ous 〔ho'maptərəs; hou'mɔptərəs〕 *adj.* 〖動物〗同翅類的(蟬等)。

ho·mo·sex·u·al 〔,homə'sɛkʃuəl; 'houmou'seksjuəl〕 *adj.* ①同性戀的。②同性的。—*n.* 同性戀者。

ho·mo·sex·u·al·i·ty 〔,homə,sɛkʃu'ælətɪ; 'houmouseksju'æliti〕 *n.* 〖精神分析〗同性戀；同性性慾。

ho·mo·zy·gote 〔,homə'zaɪgot; ,houmə'zaigout〕 *n.* 〖生物〗純合子；同型結合體。

ho·mun·cle 〔ho'mʌŋkḷ; hou'mʌŋkl〕 *n.* =**homuncule.**

ho·mun·cule 〔ho'mʌŋkjul; hou'mʌŋkjuːl〕 *n.* 矮人；侏儒。

ho·mun·cu·lus 〔ho'mʌŋkjələs; hou'mʌŋkjuləs〕 *n., pl.* **-li** 〔-,laɪ; -lai〕. ①矮人；侏儒。②(人之)胎兒。③(示範解剖用之)人體模型。 **—ho·mun·cu·lar,** *adj.*

hom·y 〔'homɪ; 'houmi〕 *adj.* =**homey.**

hon 〔hʌn; hʌn〕 *n.* 〖俗〗(常 H-) 親愛的人；情人（爲 honey 之縮寫）。

Hon. Honorable.

Ho·nan 〔'ho'næn; 'hou'næn〕 *n.* 河南(中國中部之一省，省會爲開封，Kaifeng)。

Hon·du·ras 〔han'durəs; hɔn'djuərəs〕 *n.* 宏都拉斯（國名，位於中美洲北部，首都爲特古西加帕 Tegucigalpa)。

hone 〔hon; houn〕 *n., v.,* **honed, hon·ing.** —*n.* ①細磨刀石。②磨孔用的機械工具。—*v.t.* ①（在細磨刀石上）磨。②磨孔以放大之。

‡hon·est 〔'anɪst; 'ɔnist〕 *adj.* ①誠實的；忠實的。He has an *honest* face. 他有一副誠實的面孔。②坦白的；直率的。He was perfectly *honest* in telling me the story. 他完全坦白地告訴我這事。③未攙雜的；純淨的；眞的。④以正當手段獲得的。⑤令人尊敬的。⑥可靠的；眞實的。⑦樸實的；未加裝飾的。⑧〖古〗貞潔的。 **—ness,** *n.*

honest in·jun 〔~'ɪndʒən; ~'indʒən〕 〖俗〗眞實地；老實地。

Honest John ①〖美〗誠實約翰火箭。②〖俗〗a. 誠實人。 b. 容易受騙的老實人。

***hon·est·ly** 〔'anɪstlɪ; 'ɔnistli〕 *adv.* 誠實地；坦白地；正當地。Did you get it *honestly?* 你取之正當嗎？—*interj.* (表示埋怨、疑惑、生氣)。 *Honestly!* I want to finish this work and you keep interrupting. 眞是！我想把這事做完，而你老是來打擾。

***hon·es·ty** 〔'anɪstɪ; 'ɔnisti〕 *n., pl.* **-ties.** ①誠實；公正；正直。 *Honesty* is the best policy. 誠實爲最上策。②〖古〗貞潔。

‡hon·ey 〔'hʌnɪ; 'hʌni〕 *n., pl.* **-eys,** *adj., v.,* **hon·eyed** or **hon·ied, hon·ey·ing.** —*n.* ①蜂蜜。②甜蜜。③愛人。—*adj.* 甜蜜的；親愛的。—*v.t.* 加蜜；甜言蜜語地說出。—*v.i.* 說甜言蜜語〖常 up〗。She got where she did by *honeying* up to the boss. 她所以能爬到現在這個位子是靠她向老闆灌迷湯的工夫。**—ful, —like,** *adj.* **—less,** *adj.*

hon·ey·bee 〔'hʌnɪ,bi; 'hʌnibiː〕 *n.* 蜜蜂。

hon·ey·comb 〔'hʌnɪ,kom; 'hʌnikoum〕 *n.* ①蜂巢；蜂房。②似蜂巢之物。—*adj.* 似蜂巢的。—*v.t.* ①作許多小洞於。The rock was *honeycombed* with passages. 岩石上有許多蜂窩狀的小孔。②滲透至各部分。—*v.i.* 作成蜂巢形。

hon·ey·dew 〔'hʌnɪ,dju; 'hʌnidjuː〕 *n.* ①樹蜜。②蚜蟲分泌之甜蜜。③=**honeydew melon.** ④一種加有甜味之煙草。**—ed,** *adj.*

honeydew melon 蜜瓜（一種青皮綠瓤之甜瓜)。

hon·eyed 〔'hʌnɪd; 'hʌnid〕 *adj.* ①甜的。②多蜂蜜的。③甜如蜂蜜的；阿諛的。**—ly,** *adv.* **—ness,** *n.*

***hon·ey·moon** 〔'hʌnɪ,mun; 'hʌnimuːn〕 *n.* ①蜜月(即結婚後的第一個月)；蜜月假期。They are on their *honeymoon.* 他們在度蜜月。②任何和諧的期間。③初期和諧的新關係。The *honeymoon* between Congress and the President was over. 國會與新總統的和諧關係已過去了。—*v.i.* 度蜜月〖常 in, at〗。They will *honeymoon* in Scotland. 他們將在蘇格蘭度蜜月。**—er,** *n.*

hon·ey·suck·le 〔'hʌnɪ,sʌkḷ; 'hʌni,sʌkl〕 *n.* 〖植物〗忍冬；金銀花。

hon·ey·sweet 〔'hʌnɪ,swit; 'hʌniswiːt〕 *adj.* 甜如蜜的。

hon·ey-tongued 〔'hʌnɪ,tʌŋd; 'hʌnitʌŋd〕 *adj.* 嘴巧的；善辯的；會說話的。

Hong Kong 〔'haŋ'kaŋ; hɔŋ'kɔŋ, 'hɔŋ'k-〕 香港(在珠江口外，原爲中國土地，1842年割讓與英)。（亦作 **Hongkong**）

hon·ied 〔'hʌnɪd; 'hʌnid〕 *adj.* =**honeyed.**

honk 〔hɔŋk; hɔːŋk〕 *n.* ①雁鳴。②如雁鳴的聲音。—*v.t.* & *v.i.* 作類似雁鳴之聲；按(如汽車喇叭)。**—er,** *n.*

honk·y, honk·ie [ˈhaŋkɪ; ˈhɔŋki] *n., pl.* **honk·ies.**〖美俚〗〖蔑〗白種人。

honk·y-tonk [ˈhaŋkɪˌtaŋk; ˈhɔŋki-tɔŋk] *n.*〖美俚〗下等酒館、夜總會或舞廳。—*adj.* ①下等酒館、夜總會或舞廳的。②有很多此種酒館的。

Hon·o·lu·lu [ˌhanəˈlulə; ˌhɔnəˈluːluː] *n.* 檀香山;火奴魯魯(夏威夷州首府)。

‡**hon·or** [ˈanə; ˈɔnə] *n.* ①名譽;信用。It was greatly to his *honor* that he refused the reward. 他之拒絕酬勞使他獲得極大的榮譽。②尊敬; 敬重。③(H-) 閣下(對於法官、市長之尊稱)。His *Honor* the Judge. 法官閣下。Yes, Your *Honor.* 是,閣下。④被引以為榮之人或物。He is an *honor* to his country. 他是全國引以為榮的人。⑤(*pl.*) **a.** 光榮; 榮譽。to do the *honors.* 盡主人之誼; 款待。**b.** 為優等學生開的高級課程。⑥榮幸。May I have the *honor* of your company at dinner? 敬備非酌,恭請光臨。⑦尊敬之行為;敬禮;致敬。funeral *honors.* 葬禮。⑧榮譽感;是非感;節義;廉恥心;自尊心; 道義。⑨階級; 官銜; 高位。Knighthood is an *honor.* 武士是一種階級。⑩貞節;貞操。***an affair of honor*** 決鬥。***an honors degree*** 優等學位(應考科目較普通學位專門者)。***be bound in honor to do something*** 道義上應作某事。***birthday honors*** 祝壽儀式。***debt of honor*** 法律上不能追索的,但道義上及名譽上應清還之債務;信用欠款;賭債。***do a person the honor of...*** 給予某人…之榮幸(客套語)。Will you *do me the honor of* dining with me this evening? 今晚敬備非酌,恭候光臨。***do honor to*** **a.** 尊敬;敬重。**b.** 使…為之增光。Such good children would *do honor to* any mother. 品行這麼優良的孩子可使任何母親為之增光。***do the honors*** 擔任主人之角色。Father *did the honors* at the family Thanksgiving dinner. 在家庭的感恩節晚餐上父親擔任主人角色(替別人切肉、添菜等工作)。***guard of honor*** =**honor guard.** ***have the honor of*** (or ***to***)... 有…之榮幸(客套語)。May I *have the honor of* doing so? 我能作這事嗎? I *have the honor to* inform you that.... 敬此奉告。***in honor of*** 尊敬;表敬意於; 紀念。***maid of honor*** **a.** 宮女。**b.**〖美〗女儐相。***military honor*** 戰功; 戰績。***military honors*** 軍葬禮。***pledge one's honor*** (= give one's word of honor) 以名譽擔保。***save one's honor*** 保全體面。***the honors list*** 受勛者名單。***the honors of war*** 給予戰敗軍隊之恩惠(如准其保留武器、旗幟等)。***the last (funeral) honors*** 葬禮。***upon*** (or ***on***) ***one's honor*** 憑良心說話或作事。We were *on our honor* not to cheat on the exam. 我們考試不作弊是對自己良心負責。***win honor in battle*** 立戰功。—*v.t.* ①尊敬;使榮耀。*Honor* the King. 致敬吾王。②承認;如期支付。to *honor* a check. 如期支付支票。—*adj.* 光榮的;榮譽的。—**er,** *n.* —**less,** *adj.*

***hon·or·a·ble** [ˈanərəbl̩; ˈɔnərəbl] *adj.* ①誠實的; 正直的。many years of *honorable* work. 多年忠實的工作。②榮譽的;體面的; 光榮的。an *honorable* duty. 光榮的職位。③值得光榮的; 值得尊敬的; 高尚的。④表示尊敬的。*honorable* burial. 光榮的葬禮。⑤有爵位的;地位高的。⑥(H-) 加於人名前之敬稱語(略作 **Hon.**)。—**ness,** *n.* —**hon·or·a·bly,** *adv.*〖注意〗**honorable** 用以尊稱政要名人如國會議員、法官、州長、市長等時,應作大寫,通常於其前加 the. 如: The *Honorable* Alfred Vandenberg. 稱呼上,如名字用縮寫時, honorable 一字也可縮寫。如: The *Hon.* T. E. Dewey.

honorable discharge〖美軍〗①光榮服役期滿後之退役。②此種退役證書。

honorable mention 頒給比賽中未獲大獎的優良作品之獎狀。

hon·o·rar·i·um [ˌanəˈrɛrɪəm; ˌɔnəˈrɛəriəm] *n., pl.* **-rar·i·ums, -rar·i·a** [-ˈrɛrɪə; -ˈrɛəriə]. 酬勞金;謝禮(習慣上或禮貌上未便定價錢者)。

hon·or·ar·y [ˈanəˌrɛrɪ; ˈɔnərəri] *adj.* ①榮譽的。②名譽的(無報酬及正式職責的)。an *honorary* degree. 名譽學位。③道義上的(債務等,即無法律上之强制力者)。*honorary* debts. 雖無法律强制力但道義上須償還的債。

honor bright 以人格保證; 眞的。

hon·or·ee [ˌanəˈri; ˌɔnəˈriː] *n.*〖美〗①受獎者;受勳者。②(宴會等之)主賓。

honor guard =**guard of honor.**

hon·or·if·ic [ˌanəˈrɪfɪk; ˌɔnəˈrifik] *adj.* (亦作 **honorifical**) 尊敬的;尊稱的。—*n.* ①尊稱(如 Doctor, Professor, Rt., Hon. 等)。②(東方語言,尤以中文及日文中的) 尊稱; 敬語。如:貴(姓)大(名);令(郎)。—**al·ly,** *adv.*

ho·no·ris cau·sa [haˈnɔrɪsˈkɔzə; hɔˈnɔːrisˈkɔːzə]〖拉〗為了名譽(=for the sake of honor).

honor roll ①中小學優等學生名單。②對社會有功或為國捐軀之人的名單。

honors list 指定接受表揚人員之名單。

‡**hon·our** [ˈanə; ˈɔnə] *n.*〖英〗=**honor.**

hooch [hutʃ; huːtʃ] *n.*〖美俚〗酒;(特指)私酒。(亦作 **hootch**)

***hood**[1] [hud; hud] *n.* ①頭巾;兜帽。②任何形狀與用途類似頭巾之物。③汽車引擎上之覆蓋。④〖放鷹術〗鷹的頭罩(當鷹不在捕獵時)。⑤學位服(如學士袍、碩士袍等)上之後垂布(用以辨別學位之高低)。—*v.t.* 以頭巾遮蓋。—**less,** *adj.* —**like,** *adj.*

hood[2] *n.*〖美俚〗流氓;地痞。

-hood〖字尾〗①加於人、生物之名詞形成含"性質;狀態;階級;身分;境遇"之義的名詞,如: childhood. ②加於形容詞造成表示"狀態"之名詞,如: falsehood. ③造成"…團體; …界; …社會"之義的集合名詞,如: priesthood.

hood·ed [ˈhudɪd; ˈhudid] *adj.* ①戴頭巾的。②覆有頭巾狀之物的。③〖植物〗頭巾狀的。④〖動物〗有頭巾狀之羽毛的; 有冠頂的。

hood·ie [ˈhudɪ; ˈhudi] *n.* 戴冠烏鴉。

hood·lum [ˈhudləm; ˈhuːdləm] *n.*〖美俚〗流氓;不良少年;惡漢。—**ish,** *adj.*

hood·man-blind [ˈhudmənˌblaɪnd; ˈhudmənblaind] *n.*〖古〗捉迷藏遊戲。

hoo·doo [ˈhudu; ˈhuːduː] *n., pl.* **-doos,** *v., adj.* —*n.* ① =**voodoo.** ②〖俗〗不吉利之人(或物);倒楣鬼;瘟神。③〖俗〗倒楣;歹運。④〖地質〗奇形怪石(因侵蝕而形成者)。—*v.t.*〖俗〗使倒楣;使不幸。—*adj.*〖俗〗不幸的; 倒楣的。—**ism,** *n.*

hood·wink [ˈhudˌwɪŋk; ˈhudwiŋk] *v.t.* ①蒙混;欺騙。②蔽目。③遮蓋;藏匿。

hoo·ey [ˈhuɪ; ˈhuːi] *interj.*〖美俚〗胡說! —*n.*〖美俚〗瞎話; 夢話; 無聊的老套; 胡鬧。

***hoof** [huf, huf; huːf] *n., pl.* **hoofs** or **hooves,** *v.* —*n.* ①(馬、牛、羊、豬等之)蹄。②(馬、牛、羊、豬等之)足。③〖諧〗(人之)脚。

④〖方〗有蹄之動物。***on the hoof***(指家畜)活着。***under the hoof*** 備受蹂躪。—*v.t.* 〖俚〗走;步行(常與 it 連用)。Let's *hoof* it to the supermarket. 我們步行到超級市場去罷。—*v.i.* ①〖俗〗走;行走;步行。②〖俚〗跳舞。—**less,** *adj.* —**like,** *adj.*

hoof·beat [ˈhʊfˌbit, ˈhuf–; ˈhuːfbiːt] *n.* 蹄聲。

hoofed [huft; huːft] *adj.* ①有(…之)蹄的。②蹄狀的;蹄形的。

hoof·er [ˈhʊfɚ; ˈhuːfə] *n.* ①〖方〗徒步旅行者。②〖俚〗跳木屐舞或踢躂舞的職業舞女。

hook** [hʊk; huk] *n.* ① 鉤;釣鉤。a fish-*hook.* 釣魚鉤。②鐮刀;彎刀。③急遽的彎曲。④地岬;地角;鉤狀岬。⑤投球所成之曲線。⑥〖拳擊〗鉤拳。⑦(高爾夫球之)左曲球。⑧〖音樂〗符鉤。⑨(*pl.*)〖俚〗手;指。by hook or (by) crook*** 用各種方法;不擇手段。***get*** (or ***give***) ***the hook*** 丟掉差事。***hook, line, and sinker***〖俗〗完全;一齊。***off the hook***〖俚〗**a.** 脫離困境。**b.** 沒有義務。***on one's own hook*** 獨立。***on the hook***〖俚〗**a.** 受約束。**b.** 拖延;敷延。—*v.t.* ①掛(物)於鉤上;用鉤鉤住。Please *hook* my dress for me. 請將我的衣服掛到衣鉤上。②用鉤釣(魚)。③彎成鉤形。④〖美俗〗偷竊。⑤以計捕捉;欺騙;詐取。to *hook* a husband. 釣金龜婿。⑥鉤射(球)。⑦(高爾夫球戲中)擊(球)使向左彎。⑧〖拳擊〗用鉤拳打。—*v.i.* ①彎曲如鉤;彎曲。②用鉤鉤住。Does the dress *hook* at the back or at the side? 這件衣服是在背面還是在側面用扣鉤扣住? ③(魚)上鉤。***hook it***〖俚〗逃去。***hook up*** **a.** 用鉤鉤住或鉤緊。**b.** 裝(收音機、電話等)。—**like,** *adj.*

hook·a(h) [ˈhʊkə; ˈhukə] *n.* 水烟筒。

hooked [hʊkt; hukt] *adj.* ①鉤狀的;鉤曲的。②有鉤(形物)的。③〖俚〗**a.** 有毒癮的。**b.** 對(某事)有癮的;着迷的。④〖俚〗結了婚的。

hook·er [ˈhʊkɚ; ˈhukə] *n.*〖航海〗①荷蘭之雙桅帆船。②愛爾蘭海岸之單桅漁船。③船(蔑稱或暱稱)。

hook·nose [ˈhʊkˌnoz; ˈhuknouz] *n.* 鷹鉤鼻。

hook-nosed [ˈhʊkˌnozd; ˈhuknouzd] *adj.* 鷹鉤鼻的。

hook·up [ˈhʊkˌʌp; ˈhukʌp] *n.* ①〖無線電〗聯播;轉播。a nationwide TV *hookup.* 全國性電視聯播。②〖電〗線路(圖);接線(圖)。③〖俗〗(政黨或政府間的)聯盟。④連接;接合。

hook·worm [ˈhʊkˌwɝm; ˈhukwəːm] *n.* ①十二指腸蟲;鉤蟲。②十二指腸蟲病。

hook·y[1] [ˈhʊkɪ; ˈhuki] *adj.,* **hook·i·er, hook·i·est.** 鉤形的;有鉤的;多鉤的。

hook·y[2] *n.*〖俚〗逃學(僅用於 to play *hooky* 片語中)。(亦作 **hookey**)

hoo·li·gan [ˈhulɪgən; ˈhuːligən] *n.*〖俗〗流氓;歹徒;不良少年。—*adj.* 流氓的。

***hoop**[1] [hʊp, hup; huːp] *n.* ①(桶等之)箍。②鐵環(兒童玩具)。③昔時婦女襯裙襬用之籐圈。④槌球戲之弓形小門。⑤任何圈狀物。⑥戒指圍繞手指之部分。⑦〖籃球俗〗**a.** 籃圈。**b.** 籃筐(包括網)。—*v.t.* ①加箍於(桶等)。②包圍;擁抱。—**like,** *adj.*

hoop[2] *v.i.* 呼喊。—*n.* ①呼喊。②百日咳之咳聲。

hoop·er [ˈhupɚ; ˈhuːpə] *n.* 箍桶匠;桶匠。

Hooper rating 美國統計學家 Claude E. Hooper 創設之電視、廣播節目分等法。

hooping cough〖醫〗百日咳。(亦作 **whooping cough**)

hoop iron (桶等之)鐵箍。

hoop·la [ˈhuplɑ; ˈhuːplɑː] *n.* ①投環戲。②不着邊際或故意混淆視聽的宣傳。

hoo·poe [ˈhupu; ˈhuːpuː] *n.* 戴勝(一種顏色鮮艷的鳥,有長而尖銳的喙及扇形冠)。

hoop skirt ①用彈性環狀物張開之女裙。②=**hoop**[1]③.

hoos(e)·gow [ˈhusgaʊ; ˈhuːsgau] *n.*〖美俚〗監獄。

Hoo·sier [ˈhuʒɚ; ˈhuːʒə] *n.* ①〖美〗印第安納州人之綽號。②(常 h-)〖俚〗粗人;鄉巴佬。—*adj.* 印第安納州的。

hoot[1] [hut; huːt] *n.* ①梟叫聲。②表示反對或輕蔑之叫囂。③汽笛、汽車喇叭、霧笛、警報等聲音。④最少的關心、興趣或考慮;一點點。***not care a hoot*** 毫不在乎。***not worth a hoot*** 毫無價值。—*v.i.* ①梟叫。②作梟叫。③叫囂(表示輕蔑或反對)。④〖英〗按汽車喇叭。—*v.t.* ①叫囂(表示輕蔑或反對)。②以叫囂驅逐。

hoot[2] *interj.*〖蘇,北英〗表示不耐煩、不滿意、反對、厭惡等的聲音。

hoot·er [ˈhutɚ; ˈhuːtə] *n.* ①叫囂之人。②(唬唬叫的)梟。③汽笛;警笛;(汽車)喇叭。

hoove [huv; huːv] *n.* (家畜之)鼓脹症。

Hoo·ver [ˈhuvɚ; ˈhuːvə] *n.* ①胡佛(Herbert Clark, 1874–1964, 美國第31任總統1929–33)。②胡佛(John Edgar, 1895–1972,美國犯罪學家及聯邦調查局F.B.I.局長)。

hop**[1] [hɑp; hɔp] *v.,* **hopped, hop·ping,** *n.* —*v.i.* ①跳躍(指人時爲單足向前跳,指動物時爲兩足齊向前跳,如鳥、蛙、袋鼠等)。Sparrows were *hopping* about on the lawn. 麻雀在草地上到處跳躍。②〖俗〗跳舞。③飛行;做短程旅行。④〖俗〗(飛機)起飛。—*v.t.* ①跳過;躍過。to *hop* a ditch. 躍過一溝。②跳上(移動中的車輛)。③〖俗〗乘坐飛機飛過。hop off*** (飛機)起飛。—*n.* ①跳躍。②〖俗〗飛機之一次飛行。③〖俗〗舞會。④〖俗〗跳舞;舞蹈。⑤短程旅行。⑥球的反跳。***hop and jump***〖美俚〗短距離。***hop, skip, and jump*** (田賽)三級跳遠。

hop[2] *n., v.,* **hopped, hop·ping.** —*n.* ①蛇麻草;忽布。②(*pl.*)蛇麻子;忽布花;酒花(使啤酒帶苦味之原料)。③〖俚〗鴉片。—*v.t.* 加蛇麻子於(啤酒)以調味。—*v.i.* 摘蛇麻子。***hop up***〖美俚〗**a.** 以痲醉劑痲醉。**b.** 刺激;使興奮。**c.** 加强。

Hope [hop; houp] *n.* 鮑伯·霍伯(Bob, Leslie Townes, 1903–, 英國出生之美國喜劇演員)。

‡hope [hop; houp] *n., v.,* **hoped, hop·ing.** —*n.* 希望;所希望之事物;信心。His *hopes* were disappointed. 他的希望未能實現。While there is life there is *hope.* 有生命卽有希望。***past*** (or ***beyond***) ***hope*** 無望的;不會成功的;無可救藥的。—*v.t.* & *v.i.* 希望;期望。I *hope* to see you soon. 我希望不久能見到你。***hope against hope*** 存萬一的希望;絕望中仍抱希望。***hope for*** 希望得到。

hope chest〖美俗〗嫁妝箱。

***hope·ful** [ˈhopfəl; ˈhoupful] *adj.* 有希望的;抱樂觀的;懷希望的。The future does not seem very *hopeful.* 前途似不樂觀。—*n.* 有希望之人;有前途之人。a young *hopeful.* 有希望的年輕人。—**ness,** *n.*

hope·ful·ly [ˈhopfəlɪ; ˈhoupfuli] *adv.* ①抱着希望地。②如果順利的話。

Ho·pei [ˈhoˈpe; ˈhouˈpei] *n.* 河北(中國北部之一省,省會爲保定, Paoting)。(亦作 **Hopeh**)

***hope·less** [ˈhoplɪs; ˈhouplis] *adj.* ①無希望的;絕望的。a *hopeless* illness. 絕症。②毫無辦法的;辦不到的。—**ly,** *adv.*

hop·head [ˈhɑpˌhɛd; ˈhɔphed] *n.* 〖俚〗有毒癮的人。

hop·lite [ˈhɑplaɪt; ˈhɔplait] *n.* (古希臘之) 重甲步兵。

hop-o'-my-thumb [ˈhɑpəmaɪˈθʌm; ˈhɔpəmiˈθʌm] *n.* 矮人; 侏儒。

hopped-up [ˈhɑptˈʌp; ˈhɔptˈʌp] *adj.* 〖美俚〗①興奮的; 過分激動的。②引擎經過加強的。③麻醉的; 經過刺激的。

hop·per¹ [ˈhɑpə; ˈhɔpə] *n.* ①跳躍者; 跳躍物。②蚱蜢或其他跳躍之昆蟲。③(碾米機、煤爐等的) 漏斗。④〖澳〗袋鼠。⑤廁所。

hop·per² *n.* 蛇麻子摘取者(機)。

hopper car 一種裝運煤炭、石子等之卡車(車底可傾斜以卸下所載之物)。

hopper dredge 一種自動挖泥機。

hop·ple [ˈhɑpl̩; ˈhɔpl] *v.*, **-pled, -pling,** *n.* —*v.t.* ①縛(牛、馬)之兩足。②拘束。—*n.* (牛、馬等之)足械。

hop·scotch [ˈhɑpˌskɑtʃ; ˈhɔpskɔtʃ] *n.* 跳房子(兒童遊戲)。—*v.i.* 到處旅行、走動。

hor. ①horizon. ②horizontal. ③horology.

Hor·ace [ˈhɑrɪs; ˈhɔrəs] *n.* 賀瑞斯(65–8 B.C., 原名 Quintus Horatius Flaccus, 羅馬詩人及諷刺家)。

ho·ra·ry [ˈhorərɪ; ˈhɔːrəri] *adj.* ①時間(上)的。②每小時的。③繼續一小時的。

Ho·ra·tian [həˈreʃən; həˈreiʃiən] *adj.* 詩人 Horace 的; Horace 風格的。

horde [hord; hɔːd] *n.*, *v.*, **horded, hord·ing.** —*n.* ①羣衆; 大羣。②遊牧部落。—*v.i.* 成羣; 成部落而居。

hore·hound [ˈhorˌhaund; ˈhɔːhaund] *n.* 〖植物〗(原產歐洲之)野生苦汁薄荷。(亦作 **hoarhound**)

***ho·ri·zon** [həˈraɪzn̩; həˈraizn, huˈr–, əˈr–, uˈr–] *n.* ①地平線。The sun sank below the *horizon.* 太陽沉到地平線下去了。②(常 *pl.*) (思想、經驗、興趣、觀察力等)限度; 範圍; 眼界。*extend the horizon of knowledge* 擴大知識之範圍。

***hor·i·zon·tal** [ˌhɑrəˈzɑntl̩; ˌhɔriˈzɔntl] *adj.* ①與地平線平行的; 水平的; 橫的(爲 vertical 之對)。a *horizontal* line. 水平線。②平的; 平坦的。③依水平方向放置、行動、動作的。④只包含製造中一階段的; 只包括某一羣人或某一行業的。a *horizontal* union. 同業公會。⑤地位相等之職務或人員的。—*n.* 水平線; 水平面; 水平方面; 橫的位置。*out of the horizontal* 不成水平的。—**ly,** *adv.*

horizontal bar 單槓。

horizontal integration 商業上之同業合併。

hor·mone [ˈhɔrmon; ˈhɔːmoun] *n.* 荷爾蒙 (人體內能影響某種器官作用之內分泌)。

‡**horn** [hɔrn; hɔːn] *n.* ①(牛羊等頭上所生之) 角。②鹿角; 犄角。③(其他動物的) 觸角。④角質; 角製之物。a knife with a handle of *horn.* 角柄小刀。⑤挖空獸角而成之容器。a drinking *horn.* 角製杯。⑥號角; 喇叭。⑦示警之裝置; 汽笛。a fog *horn.* 霧笛。⑧似角之物。⑨新月之鈎尖。⑩(常 *pl.*) 妻與人通姦之丈夫頭上所長的想像的角; 綠帽子。⑪〖俚〗擴音器。⑫(the –) 〖美俚〗電話。*blow one's own horn* 〖俗〗自誇; 吹牛; 自吹自擂。*draw* (or *pull*) *in one's horns* 縮頭; 不再熱心活動。*English horn* 英國管(樂器)。*French horn* 法國號(樂器)。*lock horns* 爭執; 衝突。*on the horns of a dilemma* 處於進退維谷之境。*take the bull by the horns* 不畏艱險; 勇往直前。—*adj.* 角製的; 角質的。—*v.t.* ①用角觸; 用角刺或傷害。②使(丈夫) 當王八(即偷漢子)。*horn in* 干涉; 闖入。

horn·beam [ˈhɔrnˌbim; ˈhɔːnbiːm] *n.* 〖植物〗角木 (北美產 birch 一類的樹)。

horn·bill [ˈhɔrnˌbɪl; ˈhɔːnbil] *n.* (亞洲南部產之)犀鳥。

horn·blende [ˈhɔrnˌblɛnd; ˈhɔːnblend] *n.* 〖礦〗角閃石。

horn·book [ˈhɔrnˌbuk; ˈhɔːnbuk] *n.* ①角帖書。②初學入門書。

horned [hɔrnd; ˈhɔːnid, hɔːnd] *adj.* 有角的; 有角形突起的。*horned owl* 鴟鵂。*horned toad* 一種小的食蟲蜴。

hor·net [ˈhɔrnɪt; ˈhɔːnit] *n.* 大黃蜂。*arouse* (or *stir up*) *a hornets' nest* 四處樹敵。*bring a hornets' nest about one's ears* 招惹麻煩。

horn·i·ness [ˈhɔrnɪnɪs; ˈhɔːninis] *n.* 角質; 硬質; 堅硬。

horn·less [ˈhɔrnlɪs; ˈhɔːnlis] *adj.* ①無角的。②無喇叭的。

horn·pipe [ˈhɔrnˌpaɪp; ˈhɔːnpaip] *n.* ①角笛舞(昔流行於水手中)。②其舞曲。③角笛。

horn pout (美國東部產之)角鯰。

horn pox 〖醫〗水痘。

horn·stone [ˈhɔrnˌston; ˈhɔːnstoun] *n.* 〖礦〗角石; 黑硅石。

horn·swog·gle [ˈhɔrnˌswɑgl̩; ˈhɔːnˌswɔgl] *v.t.*, **-gled, -gling.** 〖俚〗欺騙。

horn·work [ˈhɔrnˌwɝk; ˈhɔːn–wəːk] *n.* ①角細工; 角製品。②〖築城〗角堡。

horn·worm [ˈhɔrnˌwɝm; ˈhɔːn–wəːm] *n.* 天蛾之幼虫(尾端有一尾角)。

horn·wort [ˈhɔrnˌwɝt; ˈhɔːn–wəːt] *n.* 〖植物〗金魚藻。

horn·y [ˈhɔrnɪ; ˈhɔːni] *adj.*, **horn·i·er, horn·i·est.** ①角的; 角質的。the *horny* coat of the eye. 眼角膜。②有角的。③堅硬如角的。④〖俚〗淫亂的。—**horn·i·ness,** *n.*

horol. horology.

hor·o·loge [ˈhɔrəˌlodʒ; ˈhɔrəlɔdʒ] *n.* 時計; 時辰儀; 鐘錶。

ho·rol·o·ger [hoˈrɑlədʒə; hɔˈrɔlədʒə] *n.* ①鐘錶製造者或商人。②鐘錶專家。(亦作 **horologist**)

hor·o·log·ic [ˌhɑrəˈlɑdʒɪk; ˌhɔrəˈlɔdʒik, ˌhɔːr–] *adj.* ①鐘錶的。②鐘錶學的。

ho·rol·o·gy [hoˈrɑlədʒɪ; hɔˈrɔlədʒi, hɔːˈr–] *n.* ①鐘錶學; 鐘錶製造法。②測時法。

hor·o·scope [ˈhɔrəˌskop; ˈhɔrəskoup] *n.* ①占星術。②算命所用之天宮圖。to cast a *horoscope.* 造命運圖; 算命。

hor·o·scop·ic [ˌhɔrəˈskɑpɪk; ˌhɔːrəˈskɔpik] *adj.* 占星術的; 天宮圖的。(亦作 **horoscopical**)

ho·ros·co·py [hoˈrɑskəpɪ; hɔˈrɔskəpi] *n.* ①占星(術)。②(天宮圖之)諸星之配置; 出生時之天體位置。

hor·ren·dous [hoˈrɛndəs; hɔˈrendəs] *adj.* 可怖的; 驚人的。

hor·rent [ˈhɔrənt; ˈhɔrənt] *adj.* (剛毛似地) 豎立的。

***hor·ri·ble** [ˈhɑrəbl̩; ˈhɔrəbl, –rib–] *adj.* ①可怕的; 可怖的。a *horrible* murder. 可怕的謀殺。②〖俗〗極可憎的; 極可厭的。

***hor·ri·bly** [ˈhɔrəblɪ; ˈhɔrəbli] *adv.* ①可怕地; 令人毛骨悚然地。②〖俗〗非常; 分外。

***hor·rid** [ˈhɔrɪd, ˈhɑr–; ˈhɔrid] *adj.* ①可怕的; 可怖的。②〖俗〗極可厭的。What a *horrid* nuisance! 眞討厭! —**ly,** *adv.* —**ness,** *n.*

***hor·rif·ic** [hɔˈrɪfɪk; hɔˈrifik] *adj.* 令人毛骨悚然的; 可怖的。

hor·ri·fied [ˈhɔrəˌfaɪd; ˈhɔrifaid] *adj.* ①驚悸的;驚駭的。②帶有恐怖感的。

***hor·ri·fy** [ˈhɔrəˌfaɪ, ˈhɑr-; ˈhɔrifai] *v.t.*, **-fied, -fy·ing.** ①嚇;使恐怖;使戰慄。②驚駭。

***hor·ror** [ˈhɑrə; ˈhɔrə] *n.* ①恐怖;戰慄。She fled in *horror.* 她嚇跑了。②極度憎惡。③〖俗〗慘狀;慘事。the *horrors* of modern warfare. 現代戰爭之慘狀。④恐怖之原因。⑤〖俗〗極壞或極討厭之物。⑥(the -)(*pl.*)〖俚〗a. 極度的抑鬱。b. 震顫譫妄。—*interj.* 表示輕微的氣餒、驚訝、失望等之感歎詞。

hor·ror-strick·en [ˈhɑrəˌstrɪkən; ˈhɔrəˌstrikən] *adj.* 驚恐的;戰慄的。(亦作 **horror-struck**)

hors [ɔr; ɔː] 〖法〗*adv.*, *prep.* 在外;在…之外(=outside, out, out of).

hors con·cours [ɔrkɔŋˈkur; ɔːkɔːŋˈkur] 〖法〗審查外的;非比賽的。

hors de combat [ˈɔrdəˈkɑmbɑ; ˈhɔːdəˈkɔ̃ːmbɑː] 〖法〗失去戰鬥力的。

hors d'oeu·vre [ɔrˈdœvrə; ɔːˈdəːvr] *pl.*, **hors d'oeu·vre, hors d'oeu·vres** [ɔrˈdœvrə; ɔːˈdəːvr]. 〖法〗前菜(正菜前所上之開胃小菜)。

‡horse [hɔrs; hɔːs] *n.*, *pl.* **hors·es** or **horse,** *v.*, **horsed, hors·ing,** *adj.* —*n.* ①馬;發育完全之雄馬。②騎兵。*horse* and foot. 騎兵和步兵。③三脚架。a clothes *horse.* 烘衣架;晒衣架。④(健身用之)木馬。⑤馬屬之動物,如驢、騾等。⑥〖謔〗人;傢伙。⑦〖俚〗馬力(=horsepower). ⑧〖美俚〗學生考試或背書時用以作弊的小條子。⑨〖棋戲〗〖俗〗馬(=knight). ⑩〖航海〗一種索環。⑪〖美俚〗海洛因。***a horse of another*** (or ***a different***) ***color*** 完全是另一回事。***back the wrong horse*** 判斷錯誤;支持失敗者。***eat*** (***work***) ***like a horse*** 大吃(努力工作)。***flog*** (or ***beat***) ***a dead horse*** 枉費精力;企圖將已經討論過而揚棄的舊事重提。***from the horse's mouth*** 〖俚〗來自可靠的來源;有權威。***hold one's horses*** 鎮靜;不衝動。***look a gift horse in the mouth*** 受人禮物而細察其優劣(因由馬齒可知其年齡故云)。***mount*** (***ride*** or ***be on***) ***the high horse*** 趾高氣揚;態度高傲。***put the cart before the horse*** 倒因爲果;本末倒置。***To horse!*** (口令)上馬!—*v.t.* ①供以馬。②置於馬上。③置於背上。④取笑;揶揄。⑤迫使工作。⑥〖古〗使(某人)仰臥(以鞭打)。—*v.i.* ①騎馬。②(母馬之)欲交配。③〖鄙〗性交。***horse around*** 〖俚〗鬼混。—*adj.* ①馬的。②騎馬的。③很大的。

***horse·back** [ˈhɔrsˌbæk; ˈhɔːsbæk] *n.* 馬背。He is on *horseback.* 他騎在馬上。—*adv.* 在馬背上。—*adj.* 〖美俗〗未多加考慮而作的。

horse bean (作爲馬飼料之)蠶豆。

horse block (乘馬或下馬用之)踏臺。

horse box ①〖英〗載馬用鐵路貨車。②〖英,謔〗教堂之長椅席。③(船上之)馬檻。

horse·break·er [ˈhɔrsˌbrekə; ˈhɔːsˌbreikə] *n.* 馴馬師。

horse·car [ˈhɔrsˌkɑr; ˈhɔːskɑː] *n.* 〖美〗①馬拉的街車。②載馬之車輛。

horse chestnut 〖植物〗七葉樹;七葉樹之實。

horse·cloth [ˈhɔrsˌklɔθ; ˈhɔːsklɔθ] *n.*, *pl.* **-cloths.** 馬衣;馬被。

horse collar 馬之頸圈。

horse coper 馬商;馬販。

horse doctor 馬醫;獸醫;鐵蹄工。

horse-faced [ˈhɔrsˌfest; ˈhɔːsfeist] *adj.* 馬面的;長面的。

horse·flesh [ˈhɔrsˌflɛʃ; ˈhɔːsfleʃ] *n.* ①馬肉。②馬(集合稱)。

horse·fly [ˈhɔrsˌflaɪ; ˈhɔːsflai] *n.*, *pl.* **-flies.** 馬蠅;虻。

horse gear 馬具;馬力裝置。

Horse Guards ①騎兵護衞隊。②英國禁衞軍之騎兵旅。

horse·hair [ˈhɔrsˌhɛr; ˈhɔːshɛə] *n.* ①馬鬃;馬尾毛。②馬鬃所織的織物。—*adj.* 馬鬃織成的;覆以馬鬃布的;塡有馬鬃的。

horse·hide [ˈhɔrsˌhaɪd; ˈhɔːshaid] *n.* ①馬之生皮;馬革。②〖俚〗棒球。—*adj.* 用馬革做的。

horse latitudes (北大西洋之)無風帶。

horse·laugh [ˈhɔrsˌlæf; ˈhɔːslɑːf] *n.* 呵呵大笑;癡笑。—*v.i.* 呵呵大笑。

horse·leech [ˈhɔrsˌlitʃ; ˈhɔːsliːtʃ] *n.* ①(歐洲產之)馬蝗。②貪欲者;榨取者。

horse·less [ˈhɔrslɪs; ˈhɔːslis] *adj.* ①無馬的。②(馬車)不用馬的;自行推進的。

horse mackerel 竹筴魚。

***horse·man** [ˈhɔrsmən; ˈhɔːsmən] *n.*, *pl.* **-men.** ①騎馬者。②騎兵。③善騎者;馬術師。④養馬者。

horse·man·ship [ˈhɔrsmənˌʃɪp; ˈhɔːsmənʃip] *n.* 馬術。

horse marine ①(想像中之)騎馬水兵。②騎馬執行陸上勤務的水兵或水手;執行船上任務的騎兵。③用非所長者;外行。

horse opera 〖美俚〗西部武俠片;西部片;西部廣播(電視)連續劇。

horse pistol 馬上用之大型短槍。

horse·play [ˈhɔrsˌple; ˈhɔːs-plei] *n.* 粗鄙的娛樂;喧鬧的取笑;惡作劇。

horse·play·er [ˈhɔrsˌpler; ˈhɔːsˌpleiə] *n.* 慣賭馬的人。

horse·pond [ˈhɔrsˌpɑnd; ˈhɔːs-pɔnd] *n.* 供馬沐浴或飲水之小池。

***horse·pow·er** [ˈhɔrsˌpauə; ˈhɔːsˌpauə] *n.* 馬力(動力單位,一匹馬力 = 550 呎磅/秒)。

horse·pow·er-hour [ˈhɔrsˌpauəˈaur; ˈhɔːsˌpauərˌauə] *n.* 馬力小時。

horse race 賽馬。

horse·rad·ish [ˈhɔrsˌrædɪʃ; ˈhɔːsˌrædiʃ] *n.* ①〖植物〗辣菜。②辣菜根製調味品。

horse sense 〖俗〗(粗淺實用之)常識。

***horse·shoe** [ˈhɔrʃˌʃu, ˈhɔrs-; ˈhɔːʃʃuː, ˈhɔːsʃuː] *n.*, *v.*, **-shoed, -shoe·ing,** *adj.* —*n.* ①蹄鐵。②U形物。③(*pl.*)(作 *sing.* 解)擲蹄鐵遊戲。—*v.t.* 裝蹄鐵於(馬)。—*adj.* 蹄鐵形的;U 形的。a *horseshoe* bend in the river. 河川的U字形彎曲。

horseshoe magnet 馬蹄形磁鐵。

horse·tail [ˈhɔrsˌtel; ˈhɔːs-teil] *n.* ①馬尾。②(昔土耳其作爲軍旗、總督旗之)馬尾。③〖植物〗木賊屬之植物。

horse·whip [ˈhɔrsˌhwɪp; ˈhɔːs-wip] *n.*, *v.*, **-whipped, -whip·ping.** —*n.* 馬鞭。—*v.t.* 笞以馬鞭。

horse·wom·an [ˈhɔrsˌwumən; ˈhɔːsˌwumən] *n.*, *pl.* **-wom·en.** 女騎師。

horse wrangler 〖美〗牧場中趕牲畜的工人。

hor. som. at bedtime.〖處方〗睡覺時。

hors·y [ˈhɔrsɪ; ˈhɔːsi] *adj.*, **hors·i·er, hors·i·est.** ①馬的;似馬的;馬性的。②好馬的;愛賽馬的。③對馬或馬賽熟悉的。④〖俚〗大而笨拙的。(亦作 **horsey**) —**hors·i·ness,** *n.*

hort. ①horticultural. ②horticulture.
hor·ta·tion 〔hɔrˈteʃən; hɔːˈteiʃən〕 *n.* 勸告;督促;勸勉;激勵。
hor·ta·to·ry 〔ˈhɔrtəˌtorɪ; ˈhɔːtətəri〕 *adj.* 督促的;勸告的。(亦作 **hortative**)
hor·ti·cul·tur·al 〔ˌhɔrtɪˈkʌltʃərəl; ˌhɔːtiˈkʌltʃərəl〕 *adj.* 園藝的;園藝學的。
hor·ti·cul·ture 〔ˈhɔrtɪˌkʌltʃɚ; ˈhɔːtiˌkʌltʃə〕 *n.* 園藝;園藝學。
hor·ti·cul·tur·ist 〔ˌhɔrtɪˈkʌltʃərɪst; ˌhɔːtiˈkʌltʃərist〕 *n.* 園藝學家。
hor·tus sic·cus 〔ˈhɔrtəsˈsɪkəs; ˈhɔːtəsˈsikəs〕 〖拉〗植物壓乾標本(集)。
hor. un. spatio at the end of one hour. 〖處方〗一小時後。
Hos. Hosea.
ho·san·na 〔hoˈzænə; houˈzænə〕 *interj., n., pl.* **-nas,** *v.,* **-naed, -na·ing.** —*interj.* 和撒那(讚美上帝之語)。—*n.* 讚美(上帝)之聲。—*v.t.* 稱讚。
***hose** 〔hoz; houz〕 *n., pl.* for ① & ②**hose,** 〖古〗 **hosen,** for ③**hoses,** *v.,* **hosed, hos·ing.** —*n.* ①長統襪。②昔日男用緊身褲(由腰部至腳趾)。③運輸液體所用之軟管(如救火車上之水管、橡皮管等)。a fire *hose.* 救火水管。—*v.t.* ①以軟水管輸水浸澆。②〖加、俚〗 **a.** 欺騙。**b.** 打敗。
Ho·se·a 〔hoˈziə; houˈziə〕 *n.* ①何西阿(紀元前八世紀之希伯來先知)。②(舊約聖經之)何西阿書。(略作 **Hos.**)
hose-tops 〔ˈhoztɑps; ˈhouztɔps〕 *n. pl.* 〖蘇〗無足部之長統襪。
ho·sier 〔ˈhoʒɚ; ˈhouʒə〕 *n.* 襪商。
ho·sier·y 〔ˈhoʒərɪ; ˈhouʒəri〕 *n.* ①襪類。②襪業。
hosp. hospital.
hos·pice 〔ˈhɑspɪs; ˈhɔspis〕 *n.* ①(旅客住之)招待所(尤指僧侶所設者)。②救濟院。
***hos·pi·ta·ble** 〔ˈhɑspɪtəbl̩; ˈhɔspitəbl〕 *adj.* ①善於款待客人的;招待慇懃的。a *hospitable* man. 善於款待客人的人。②寬容的。③不固執己見的〖常 to〗. He is *hospitable* to new ideas. 他願接受新思想。—**hos·pi·ta·bly,** *adv.*
‡**hos·pi·tal** 〔ˈhɑspɪtl̩; ˈhɔspitl〕 *n.* ①醫院。He's still in *hospital.* 他還在醫院裏。②(用於專門名詞中)慈善組織。③可携帶之物的修理廠。violin *hospital.* 小提琴修理店。
hos·pi·tal·(l)er 〔ˈhɑspɪtl̩ɚ; ˈhɔspitlə〕 *n.* ①住院者。②(H-)中世紀時照料貧病者之慈善團體之團員。③某些倫敦醫院的傳教士。④在醫院照料貧病者之宗教團體的團員。
hos·pi·tal·ism 〔ˈhɑspɪtl̩ɪzm̩; ˈhɔspitlizm〕 *n.* ①醫院制度。②(特指由於醫院設備不良之)不衞生狀態。③由上述狀態引起的對住院病患之心理或生理影響。④住孤兒院而產生的心理或生理影響。
***hos·pi·tal·i·ty** 〔ˌhɑspɪˈtælətɪ; ˌhɔspiˈtæliti〕 *n., pl.* **-ties.** 好客;款待;慇懃。to partake of *hospitality.* 受人款待;受人厚遇。
hos·pi·tal·i·za·tion 〔ˌhɑspɪtl̩əˈzeʃən; ˌhɔspitəlaiˈzeiʃən〕 *n.* ①入院;入院治療。②〖俗〗醫療保險。③住院期間。
hospitalization insurance 醫療保險。
hos·pi·tal·ize 〔ˈhɑspɪtl̩ˌaɪz; ˈhɔspitlaiz〕 *v.t.,* **-ized, -iz·ing.** 使入院;送入醫院;允其住院;使習慣於醫院。
hospital ship 醫院船。
hospital train 醫院列車。
host**[1] 〔host; houst〕 *n.* ①主人(對賓客而言)。As Mr. Smith was away, Tom, the eldest son, acted as *host* at the dinner party. 史密斯先生不在家,長子湯姆便擔任宴會中的主人。②旅館主人。③寄生物之宿主;寄主;主木。reckon without one's host*** 忽略困難之處;忽略計畫失敗之可能性;獨斷計算。—*v.t.* ①作東。He hosted a reception for new members. 他爲新會員舉行了一次酒會。②款待。
***host**[2] *n.* ①極多;大羣。②軍隊。③天體。
hos·tage 〔ˈhɑstɪdʒ; ˈhɔstidʒ〕 *n., v.,* **-taged, -tag·ing.** —*n.* ①人質;作抵押品的人。The bandits kept one of their prisoners as a *hostage.* 土匪將所擄的人中留一作爲人質。②抵押;抵押品。***give hostages to fortune*** 擁有可能喪失之人或物(如妻兒、珠寶等)。—*v.t.* 做爲人質。
host cell 爲寄生物所寄生之細胞。
hos·tel 〔ˈhɑstl̩; ˈhɔstəl〕 *n.* ①旅社;招待所(特指爲青年所設而不以營利爲目的者)。a Y. M. C. A. *hostel.* 青年會寄宿舍。②〖英〗大學之學生宿舍。—*v.i.* & *v.t.* ①宿於招待所或旅社。②開招待所;開旅社。
hos·tel·(l)er 〔ˈhɑstl̩ɚ; ˈhɔstələ〕 *n.* ①寄宿生。②住 hostel 的人。
hos·tel·ry 〔ˈhɑstl̩rɪ; ˈhɔstəlri〕 *n., pl.* **-ries.** 〖古〗旅館;客棧。
***host·ess** 〔ˈhostɪs; ˈhoustis〕 *n.* ①女主人。②旅館女主人。③作東道之女人。④(客機之)空中小姐。⑤(餐廳、火車、巴士等之)服務小姐。⑥職業舞女。—*v.t.* 在…作女主人。
***hos·tile** 〔ˈhɑstɪl; ˈhɔstail〕 *adj.* ①敵方的。the *hostile* army. 敵軍。②懷敵意的。—*n.* ①敵人。②〖美史〗對白人含敵意之印第安人。
***hos·til·i·ty** 〔hɑsˈtɪlətɪ; hɔsˈtiliti〕 *n., pl.* **-ties.** ①敵意;敵對。feelings of *hostility.* 敵對的情緒。②戰爭狀態。③反對;反抗;抵抗。They carry on mad *hostility* against all established institutions. 他們對一切現行制度進行瘋狂之反對。④(*pl.*)戰爭;戰鬥。
hos·tler 〔ˈhɑslɚ; ˈɔslə〕 *n.* ①馬夫;旅館馬夫。②在調車場或機車廠中調動火車頭者。(亦作 **ostler**)
host of heaven 日月星辰;天體。
‡**hot** 〔hɑt; hɔt〕 *adj.,* **hot·ter, hot·test,** *adv., v.,* **hot·ted, hot·ting.** —*adj.* ①熱的;灼熱的。a *hot* day. 熱天。Running makes me *hot.* 跑路使我感覺很熱。②辛辣的。Pepper is *hot.* 胡椒是辣的。③激動的;激烈的。a *hot* temper. 暴燥脾氣。④興趣濃厚的;熱心的;熱烈的;渴望的。⑤新的;新鮮的;强烈的。⑥逼近的;緊迫的。in *hot* pursuit. 緊追;逼近。⑦有放射性的。⑧爵士音樂的。⑨〖俚〗以不法手段得來的。*hot* goods. 贓物;贓貯。⑩好色的。⑪〖俚〗大膽而技巧的。a *hot* pilot. 大膽而技高的飛行員。⑫正在流行的;很受歡迎的;銷路好的。Frank Sinatra was the *hottest* singer of the 1940's. 佛蘭克辛那屈是1940年代最紅的歌星。⑬〖俚〗很幸運的。The cards are *hot* for me tonight. 今晚我的牌運很好。⑭可笑的;滑稽的。That's a *hot* one! 那眞是滑稽透頂!⑮〖遊戲〗接近所尋找之事物或回答的。⑯〖俚〗很有趣的;聳人聽聞的。a *hot* news story. 聳人聽聞的消息。⑰〖俚〗(車輛之)可開得很快的。a *hot* new jet plane. 一架新的快速噴射機。⑱可以做得很快或很好的。Finish writing that story while you're still *hot.* 當你正起勁的時候把那篇東西寫完。⑲高壓電線的。a *hot*

wire. 高壓電線。⑳通電的。***hot and hot*** (食物) 起鍋後馬上就吃的。***in hot blood*** 激昂。***in hot haste*** 火急。***make a place too hot for*** (***a person***) 逼(某人)離開某地;使(某人)無法逗留某地。***make it hot for*** 使…感覺不好受;使…人覺得麻煩。—*adv.* ①熱狀地;熱烈地。②趁熱。The dish is served *hot.* 這道菜要趁熱吃。***blow hot and cold*** (意見或態度)反覆無常。***get it hot*** 被痛罵。***Give it him hot!*** 〖俗〗對他予以斥責。—*v.t.* & *v.i.* 〖英俗〗溫熱〖常up〗。***hot it up*** 〖俚〗享樂;使熱烈起來。***hot up*** **a.** 加熱;加溫。**b.** 〖主英〗裝飾;使熱鬧。

hot air 〖俚〗空話;大話;誇張之辭。

hot-air [ˈhatˌɛr; ˈhɔtɛə] *adj.* 熱(暖)氣的。

hot atom 熱原子(具有放射核的原子)。

hot·bed [ˈhatˌbɛd; ˈhɔtbed] *n.* ①溫床。②極易於滋長(惡事)之環境。

hot·blood [ˈhatˌblʌd; ˈhɔtblʌd] *n.* 易激動者;情感强烈者;輕擧妄動者。

hot-blood·ed [ˈhatˈblʌdɪd; ˈhɔtˈblʌ-did] *adj.* ①易怒的。②輕率的。③情感强烈的;熱切的。

hot·box [ˈhatˌbaks; ˈhɔtbɔks] *n.*(鐵路車輛之)過熱軸承箱。

hot cake (在淺鍋上煎的)薄餅。***sell*** (or ***go***) ***like hot cakes*** 〖俗〗現蒸熱賣;暢銷。

hot·cha [ˈhatʃa; ˈhaːtʃaː] *interj.* 表示贊同、高興等之感歎詞,現常爲滑稽用法。

Hotch·kiss [ˈhatʃkɪs; ˈhɔtʃkis] *n.*哈乞開斯重機槍。

hotch·pot [ˈhatʃˌpat; ˈhɔtʃpɔt] *n.* ①〖法律〗財產混同(爲遺產之平均分配將所有財產合併)。②=**hotchpotch.**

hotch·potch [ˈhatʃˌpatʃ; ˈhɔtʃpɔtʃ] *n.* ①雜煮;雜燴。②混雜物。③〖法律〗=**hotchpot.**

hot corner 〖棒球俚〗靠近第三壘的內野手之守備位置。

hot dog①=**frankfurter.**②熱狗(夾香腸之小麪包)。③〖美俚〗善於表演絕技之運動員。

‡**ho·tel** [hoˈtɛl; houˈtel, ouˈt-] *n.* 旅館;旅社。He is stopping in the *hotel.* 他住在旅館裏。

Ho·tel *n.* 通訊電碼,代表字母H.

hô·tel de ville [ˌoˈtɛldəˈvil; ˌouˈtel dəˈviːl] 〖法〗市政廳。

hô·tel Dieu [ˌoˌtɛlˈdjɜ; ˌouˌtelˈdjəː] 〖法〗醫院。

ho·tel·ier [ˌhotəˈlɪr; ˌhoutəˈliə] *n.* 旅館經理或老闆。(亦作 **hotelkeeper**)

hot·foot [ˈhatˌfut; ˈhɔtfut] *n.*, *pl.* **-foots,** *adv.*, *v.* —*n.* ①將火柴偸偸地插進他人鞋底與上皮之間,然後點之使燃的惡作劇。②心靈的刺激。—*adv.* 〖俗〗飛速地;急忙地。—*v.i.* 〖俗〗趕忙;急忙。

hot·head [ˈhatˌhɛd; ˈhɔthed] *n.*暴躁之人;性急之人。

hot·head·ed [ˈhatˈhɛdɪd; ˈhɔtˈhedid] *adj.* ①烈性的;易怒的。②急躁的;鹵莽的。(亦作 **hot-brained**)

hot·house [ˈhatˌhaus; ˈhɔthaus] *n.* 溫室;暖房。—*adj.* ①溫室的(植物等)。②過分保護的;人工的;纖弱的。

hot issue 上市後不久價格猛漲之股票。

hot line 熱線(兩政府首腦間隨時保持暢通以應付緊急情況之直接電話線)。

hot·ly [ˈhatlɪ; ˈhɔtli] *adv.* ①暑熱地;熱地。②熱心地;猛烈地。③發怒地。

hot·ness [ˈhatnɪs; ˈhɔtnis] *n.* ①熱;暑熱。②熱心;熱烈。③激怒;易怒。

hot pack 〖醫〗熱敷。

hot pants 熱褲。

hot plate ①輕便電爐。②餐廳出售的熱食。③保溫盤。④火爐上的扁平烤盤。

hot pot 與馬鈴薯合燉之牛、羊肉。

hot potato 〖俗〗困境;不易應付之局面。

hot-press [ˈhatˌprɛs; ˈhɔtpres] *n.* (紙之)加熱壓平機。—*v.t.* 加熱壓平。

hot rod ①換裝强力馬達的舊車。②馬力强大設備簡單之汽車。

hot seat 〖俚〗①電椅。②不舒服或尷尬的局面。

hot-short [ˈhatˈʃɔrt; ˈhɔtˈʃɔːt] *adj.* (指金屬達鍛造溫度)有熱脆性的。

hot·shot [ˈhatˌʃat; ˈhɔt-ʃɔt] *adj.* 〖俚〗①很成功又主動的。②誇示技巧的。③不停的。—*n.* ①有專技者;藝高自負者。②消防隊員。

hot spring 溫泉。

hot·spur [ˈhatˌspɜ; ˈhɔtspəː] *n.* 性急的人。—*adj.* 性急的。

hot stuff 〖俚〗①很有趣或很可稱道的人或事。②好色的人。③大膽的;轟動的。

hot-tem·pered [ˈhatˈtɛmpəd; ˈhɔt-ˈtempəd] *adj.* 性急的;暴躁的;易怒的。

Hot·ten·tot [ˈhatn̩ˌtat; ˈhɔtntɔt] *n.* ①南非一蠻族土人。②Hottentot 語。③無教化者;智能低下者。—*adj.* Hottentot 人或其語言的。

hot·ter [ˈhatə; ˈhɔtə] *v.i.* 〖蘇,北英〗①上下震動。②口吃。

hot war 熱戰;交戰。

hot water〖俗〗困境。

hot-water bag 熱水袋。(亦作 **hot-water bottle**)

hough [hak; hɔk] *n.* 〖英〗=**hock**[1]. —*v.t.* 〖蘇〗割去腿筋使殘廢。—*v.i.* 〖英方,廢〗乾咳。

hound** [haund; haund] *n.* ①獵犬。a pack of *hounds.* 一羣獵犬。②任何狗。③可鄙的人。④〖俗〗迷於某事的人。follow the hounds*** 帶一羣獵犬狩獵。***ride to hounds*** = **follow the hounds.** —*v.t.* ①用獵犬狩獵。②追捕。③嗾使;激勵。to *hound* a dog at quarry. 嗾使獵犬追捕獵物。

hound's-tongue [ˈhaundzˌtʌŋ; ˈhaundztʌŋ] *n.* 〖植物〗大琉璃草屬之野草。

‡**hour** [aur; auə] *n.* ①小時;鐘頭。There are 24 *hours* in a day. 一日有二十四小時。②時期;時間。the happiest *hours* of my life. 我一生中最快樂的時期。③時刻;鐘點。The clock struck the *hour.* 鐘已報時。④固定的時間。office *hours.* 辦公時間。⑤短的時期。⑥一節課;堂。⑦經度十五度。⑧(*pl.*) **a.** 工作、辦公、上課等時間。**b.** 起居作息時間。**c.** 天主教祈禱及禮拜時間(每天七次)。**d.** 此種祈禱或禮拜。**e.** 〖希臘神話〗司季節、秩序、正義、和平等之女神。⑨一小時所行的距離。The town is an *hour* from here. 市鎮距此有一小時之路。***after hours*** 下班以後。***at the eleventh hour***在最後時刻。***in an evil hour*** 在不祥或不利的時間。***keep bad*** (or ***late***) ***hours*** 晚睡晚起;遲出遲歸。***keep good*** (or ***early***) ***hours*** 早睡早起;早出早歸。***of the hour*** 現時的。***one's*** (***last***) ***hour*** **a.** 死亡之時刻。**b.** 任何緊要關頭。***the small hours*** 清晨時間。—*adj.* 時間的。〖注意〗鐘點的寫法。有上下文時,尤其在正式文體中,用文字書寫,如: four o'clock.四點鐘。在非正式文體中,則寫作: at 4 p. m. 在下午四點鐘。just after 9 a. m. 剛在上午九點鐘以後。from 10 to 12. 自十點至十二點。

hour·glass [ˈaurˌglæs; ˈauə-glaːs] *n.* 滴漏;更漏。

hour hand 時針;短針。

hou·ri [ˈhurɪ; ˈhuri] *n.*, *pl.* **-ris.** 〖回教〗天堂之美女。

hour·ly [ˈaurlɪ; ˈauəli] *adv.* ①每小時。②常常。③隨時地。—*adj.* ①以小時計的。②

每小時一次的。③時常的。④經常的。

:house 〔*n.* haus; haus *v.* hauz; hauz〕 *n.*, *pl.* **hous·es** 〔ˋhauzɪz; ˈhauziz〕, *v.*, **housed, hous·ing,** *adj.* —*n.* ①房屋;住宅。My *house* is quite small. 我的房子很小。②居住一屋中的人;家庭;家族。③住處;住所;家。④容納任何東西之房屋;倉房。an engine *house.* 機器房。⑤議會中之一院。the *House* of Representatives. (美國國會之)衆議院。the *Houses* of Parliament. (英國)國會之兩院。⑥議會一院之會所。⑦商號。⑧戲院;娛樂場所。⑨觀衆;聽衆。A large *house* heard the singer. 許多聽衆聽這歌唱家唱歌。⑩貴族或王室之家族;王朝。He was a prince of the *house* of David. 他是大衞王皇族中的王子。***a house of ill fame*** (***repute***) 妓院;妓女戶。***be in possession of the House*** 有發言權。***be in the House*** 任下院議員。***bring down the house*** 受到盛大鼓掌喝采。***clean house*** **a.** 整理房屋。**b.** 排除不良分子。***house and home*** 家;家庭(强意語)。***house of refuge*** 貧民(難民)收容所;養育院。***keep a good house*** 過着豐衣足食的生活;厚待客人。***keep house*** **a.** 成家。**b.** 料理家事、家務。**c.** (與…)住同一房屋〖with〗. ***keep open house*** 隨時歡迎客人來臨。***keep the*** (or ***one's***) ***house*** 居家不外出。***like a house afire*** (or ***on fire***) 〖俚〗盛;快。***make*** (or ***keep***) ***a House*** 湊足(維持)下院之定員。***on the house*** 免費地;由公家或業主支付地。***play house*** (兒童)辦家家酒。***put*** (or ***set***) ***one's house in order*** **a.** 整頓事務。**b.** 改過;修身。—*v.t.* ①供給房屋。②供給住所。③貯藏(物品)。—*v.i.* 居住。—*adj.* ①有關房屋的。②適合於房屋的。

house-a·gent 〔ˋhaus,edʒənt: ˈhaus-ˌeidʒənt〕 *n.* 〖英〗房地產經紀人。

house arrest 軟禁。

house·boat 〔ˋhaus,bot; ˈhausbout〕 *n.* 船宅(供居住之船隻)。

house·break 〔ˋhaus,brek; ˈhaus-breik〕 *v.t.*, **-broke, -brok·en, -break·ing.** 訓練(貓、狗等)使其不在屋內便溺或使其在某一規定地方便溺。

house·break·er 〔ˋhaus,brekɚ; ˈhaus-ˌbreikə〕 *n.* ①(尤指白日)侵入家宅圖謀不軌者;强盜。②〖英〗**a.** 拆屋人(=〖美〗house-wrecker). **b.** 購買即將拆除房屋中之門窗等作爲古董出售者;拆屋前購買房屋中仍可使用之材料者。

house·break·ing 〔ˋhaus ,brekɪŋ; ˈhausˌbreikiŋ〕 *n.* ①侵入家宅行竊。②〖英〗房屋拆除。

house·bro·ken 〔ˋhaus,brokən; ˈhausˌbroukən〕 *adj.* 訓練成習慣良好的(貓、狗等)。(亦作 **house-trained**)

house car 〖鐵路〗加蓋之貨車廂。

house·clean 〔ˋhaus,klin; ˈhausklìːn〕 *v.t.* 清潔房屋。—*v.i.* 做清潔房屋工作。

house coat ①婦女家居長衣。②=**dressing gown.**

house dog 家犬。

house·dress 〔ˋhaus,drɛs; ˈhausdres〕 *n.*家常便服。

house duty 房捐;家屋稅。

house finding agency 房屋經紀業。

house flag (船上之)公司旗;船主旗。

house-flan·nel 〔ˋhaus,flænl; ˈhaus-ˌflænl〕 *n.* (擦地板等用之)粗絨布。

house·fly 〔ˋhaus,flaɪ; ˈhausflai〕 *n.*, *pl.* **-flies.** 蒼蠅;家蠅。

house·ful 〔ˋhaus,ful; ˈhausful〕 *n.*, *pl.* **-fuls.** 滿屋。

:house·hold 〔ˋhaus,hold,-,old; ˈhaus-hould〕 *n.* ①家庭;家屬;家眷(有時連用人也包括在內)。②家事;家務。③王室;皇族。the Royal *Household.* 王室。—*adj.* ①家庭的;家務的。*household* affairs. 家務;家事。②普通的;家常的。③王室的。*household* cavalry. 護衞國王之騎兵隊。

house·hold·er 〔ˋhaus,holdɚ; ˈhaus-ˌhouldə〕 *n.* ①房主;住屋者。②家長;戶長。

household troops 御林軍。

household word 家喻戶曉之字、名字等。

house·keep 〔ˋhaus,kip; ˈhauski:p〕 *v.i.*, **-kept, -keep·ing.** 管家。

***house·keep·er** 〔ˋhaus,kipɚ; ˈhaus-ˌki:pə〕 *n.* ①主婦。②女管家。③(旅館、醫院等之)女傭頭(管理打掃工人者)。

***house·keep·ing** 〔ˋhaus,kipɪŋ; ˈhaus-ˌki:piŋ〕 *n.* ①家事;家政;家庭經濟。②管家。③工商機構財產及設備之管理及保養。

house·leek 〔ˋhaus,lik; ˈhaus-li:k〕 *n.* 〖植物〗石蓮花。

house·less 〔ˋhauslɪs; ˈhauslis〕 *adj.* 無家的;無家可歸的。

house·lights 〔ˋhaus,laɪts; ˈhauslaits〕 *n. pl.* 戲院或講堂內觀衆席之照明燈光。

house·maid 〔ˋhaus,med; ˈhaus-meid〕 *n.* 女用人;女僕。

house·man 〔ˋhausmən; ˈhausmən〕 *n.*, *pl.* **-men.** ①男用人;男僕。②保鏢。③賭場中代表莊家的人。

house·mas·ter 〔ˋhaus,mæstɚ; ˈhaus-ˌmɑ:stə〕 *n.* ①戶長;家長。②(男校之)舍監。

house·mis·tress 〔ˋhaus,mɪstrɪs; ˈhausˌmistris〕 *n.* ①女主人;主婦。②(女校之)女舍監。

house·moth·er 〔ˋhaus,mʌðɚ; ˈhaus-ˌmʌðə〕 *n.* 女舍監;(宿舍等之)女管理員。

house of cards 不實在或快要崩潰的構造或計畫。

House of Commons 英國國會下院。

house of detention 看守所。

house of God 教會;教堂。

House of Lords 英國國會上院。

house party ①連續數日之家中大宴會。②此種宴會之全體賓客。

house·phone 〔ˋhaus,fon; ˈhausfoun〕 *n.*內線電話。

house physician 駐院(內科)醫師。

house plant 室內盆栽植物。

house·room 〔ˋhaus,rum; ˈhausrum〕 *n.* ①(房屋)住人或放東西的地方。②住宿。

house surgeon 駐院(外科)醫師。

house-to-house 〔ˋhaustəˋhaus; ˈhaus-təˈhaus〕 *adj.* 挨戶的;逐戶的。

house·top 〔ˋhaus,tɑp; ˈhaus-tɔp〕 *n.* 屋頂;房頂。***cry*** (***publish,*** or ***shout***) ***from the housetop***(***s***) 公開宣揚。

house trailer 可供居住之拖車。

house·wares 〔ˋhaus,wɛrz; ˈhaus-ˌwɛəz〕 *n. pl.* 家庭用具(如厨具等)。

house·warm·ing 〔ˋhaus,wɔrmɪŋ; ˈhausˌwɔ:miŋ〕 *n.* 遷入新居之慶宴;喬遷宴。

***house·wife** 〔ˋhaus,waɪf; ˈhaus-waif〕 *n.*, *pl.* **-wives.** 主婦。She's a bad *housewife.* 她不善做主婦。

house·wife·ly 〔ˋhaus,waɪflɪ; ˈhaus-ˌwaifli〕 *adj.* 主婦似的;節儉的;會當家的。

house·wif·er·y 〔ˋhaus,waɪfrɪ, ˋhʌzɪfrɪ; ˈhauswaifəri, ˈhʌzifri〕 *n.* 家政;家事;家務。a *housewifery* school. 家政學校。

***house·work** ['haus,wɜk; 'haus-wə:k] *n.* 家事;家務。

house·wreck·er ['haus,rɛkə; 'haus,rekə] *n.* 拆屋人。

hous·ing[1] ['hauzɪŋ; 'hauziŋ] *n.* ①供給住宅。②房屋; 住宅(集合稱)。 a *housing* shortage. 房荒。③袒護; 遮蔽; 避難(所)。④〖機械〗(支持機械某部分之)框;架構。⑤〖航海〗檣脚。⑥置放立像的壁龕。

hous·ing[2] *n.* ①馬衣。②(*pl.*)馬飾物。

Hous·ton ['hjustən; 'hju:stən] *n.* 休斯頓(美國 Texas 州東南部之一海港)。

Hou·yhn·hnm [hu'ɪnəm; 'huihnəm] *n.* 通人性之馬(見 Swift 所著之 "Gulliver's Travels").

hove [hov; houv] *v.* pt. and pp. of **heave.**

hov·el ['hʌvl; 'hɔvəl] *n.*, *v.*, **-el(l)ed, -el·(l)ing.** —*n.* ①簡陋小屋;茅舍。②牛舍;雜物室。—*v.t.* 納入棚舍中。

hov·el·(l)er ['hʌvlə; 'hɔvḷə] *n.*無執照之領港者。

***hov·er** ['hʌvə, 'hɑvə; 'hɔvə, 'hʌv-] *v.i.* ①翱翔;盤旋。②守在近旁;不遠去。③搖曳不定。The sick man *hovered* between life and death. 那病人命在旦夕。—**ing·ly,** *adv.*

Hov·er·craft ['hʌvə,kræft; 'hɔvə-krɑ:ft] *n.* 〖商標名〗氣墊船(車)。

hovering act 〖國際法〗①禁止船隻在領海內逗留的法律。②規定領海外之外國船應受檢查之法律。

‡**how** [hau; hau] *adv.* ①怎樣; 如何 (=in what manner). *How* shall I do it? 我怎樣做? I don't know *how* to do it. 我不知道怎樣做。②怎樣;如何(=by what means). I don't know *how* to explain it. 我不知道該怎樣解釋。③身體怎樣(=in what state of health). *How* are you? 你好嗎? *How* do you do? 你好嗎? (注意:How are you? 限用於熟人之間: How do you do? 主要用於初次見面的朋友之間, 比較正式)。④如何; 怎樣(用於詢人意見等)。*How* do you like it? 你喜不喜歡它? ⑤多少;好多(=to what extent). *How* old is he? 他的年紀有多大? ⑥多麼; 何等(用於驚歎句中)。*How* kind of you! 你多麼客氣啊! *How* well she sings! 她唱得多麼好聽啊! ⑦價錢多少(= at what price). *How* do you sell these apples? 你的這些蘋果怎麼賣? ⑧爲甚麼;爲何(=for what reason; why). *How* is it you are late? 你爲甚麼遲到?⑨何種速度(=at what rate). *How* long will it take to do the job? 做這件工作要花多少時間? ⑩何種狀態(=in what condition). *How* do I look? 我看起來怎麼樣? ***And how!***〖俗〗當然。Am I happy? *And how!* 我快樂嗎? 當然! ***How about....***(=What is your opinion concerning....) 你覺得怎樣? ***How come?***〖俗〗(爲 How does [did] it come that 之略。) 爲何? *How come* you never visit us any more? 你爲何不再來看我們?***how else*** 別的有甚麼(辦法等); 此外如何。***How now?*** 這是甚麼意思? ***how often*** 次數多少。***How so?*** 爲甚麼是這樣? ***How then?*** 這是甚麼意思? —*n.* 方法; 方式。the *how* and why of it. 此事之方法及理由。

how·be·it [hau'biɪt; 'hau'bi:it] *adv.* 雖然如此;然而。—*conj.*〖古〗雖然;無論如何。

how·dah ['haudə; 'haudə] *n.* 象輿;象轎(象背所置之座)。(亦作 **houdah**)

how-do-you-do ['haudəju'du; 'hau-dju'du:, -djə'd-, -di'd-, -dʒu'd-] *n.*〖俗〗困境;令人爲難的立場。Here's a pretty (*or* nice) *how-do-you-do.* 這糟了;這就難了。(亦作 **how-d'ye-do**)

how·e'er [hau'ɛr; hau'ɛə] *conj., adv.* =**however.**

‡**how·ev·er** [hau'ɛvə; hau'evə] *adv.* ①無論如何 (=no matter how). *However* we do it, it will be wrong. 我們無論怎樣做,都是錯的。②以何種方法;怎樣。*However* did you manage to get there? 你究竟用何種方法到達那裏呢? —*conj.* 然而; 可是。Later, *however,* he made up his mind to go. 可是後來,他仍然決定去了。

how·itz·er ['hauɪtsə; 'hauitsə] *n.* 榴彈砲;曲射砲。

howl** [haul; haul] *v.i.* ①(犬、狼等) 吠;嗥;咆哮。②怒號;哀號。The wind *howled* through the trees. 風在林間怒號。③高聲叫囂。—*v.t.* ①以吼叫迫使。The angry mob *howled* the speaker off the platform. 憤怒的羣衆將演說者吼下臺。②吼叫。howl down***以吼叫聲使他人所說的話聽不見。—*n.* ①嗥叫;呼號。the *howls* of a dog. 犬的叫聲。②哀號;怒吼。a *howl* of pain. 痛苦的哀號。③輕蔑、嘲弄等之吼叫。④喊;大叫。

howl·er ['haulə; 'haulə] *n.* ①號叫之人或發出號叫聲之物。②中南美所產之吼猴。③〖俚〗愚蠢可笑的錯誤。

howl·et ['haulɪt; 'haulit] *n.* 〖古〗梟。

howl·ing ['haulɪŋ; 'hauliŋ] *adj.* ①吠的; 嗥的;咆哮的。②淒涼的;荒僻的。③〖俚〗非常的;極端的。

how·so·ev·er [,hauso'ɛvə; ,hausou'evə] *adv.* =**however.**

hoy[1] [hɔɪ; hɔi] *n.* 沿海航行的單桅船;小船。

hoy[2] *interj.* 嗬!喂!(呼船或趕牲畜之聲)。—*n.* "hoy" 之呼聲。

hoy·den ['hɔɪdn̩; 'hɔidn] *n.* 頑皮、喧鬧的女孩。—*adj.* 頑皮而喧鬧的; 粗野的。—*v.i.* 擧止粗野;喧鬧。(亦作 **hoiden**)

hoy·den·ish ['hɔɪdn̩ɪʃ; 'hɔidniʃ] *adj.* 頑皮女孩似的;喧鬧的;粗野的。

Hoyle [hɔɪl; hɔil] *n.* ①霍愛爾 (Edmond, 1672–1769, 英國紙牌遊戲書之著者)。②霍愛爾所著之紙牌遊戲書。***according to Hoyle*** **a.** 照霍愛爾所定之規則(的)。**b.** 規規矩矩地(的); 公正地(的)。

HP, H.P., hp, h.p. horsepower.

H.P. ①〖電〗high power. ②high pressure. ③high priest.

H.Q., Hq., h.q. Headquarters.

hr. ①hour. ②hours.

H.R. ①Home Rule. ②House of Representatives.

H.R.H. His (*or* Her) Royal Highness. 殿下。

hrs. hours.

H.S. ①High School. ②〖英〗Home Secretary.

h.s. ①in this sense. ②at bedtime.〖處方〗就寢時。

H.S.H. His (*or* Her) Serene Highness.

Hsing·an ['ʃɪŋ'ɑn; 'ʃiŋ'ɑ:n] *n.* 興安(中國東北之一省,省會爲呼倫, Hulun 或海拉爾, Hailar).

H. S. M. His (Her) Serene Majesty.

ht. ①height. ②heat.

hub[1] [hʌb; hʌb] *n.* ①輪軸。②中心。***the Hub*** 美國波士頓之別稱。

hub[2] *n.* 〖俗〗丈夫 (husband 之略稱)。

hub·ba hub·ba ['hʌbə'hʌbə; 'hʌbə-'hʌbə] 〖俚〗表示贊同、熱心的感嘆詞,尤指第二次大戰期中美國士兵看到少女時發出之聲。

hub·ble ['hʌbl̩; 'hʌbl] *n.* ①〖美方〗小瘤。②〖蘇,北英〗**a.** 堆。**b.** 喧囂。

hub·ble-bub·ble ['hʌbl̩,bʌbl̩; 'hʌbl-,bʌbl] *n.* ①一種水烟管。②起水泡的聲音; 哇啦哇啦(講話聲); 吵鬧聲。

hub·bly ['hʌblɪ; 'hʌbli] *adj.* 〖美方〗多瘤的;凹凸不平的。

hub·bub ['hʌbʌb; 'hʌbʌb] *n.* 嘈雜;喧囂;騷嚷。

hub·by ['hʌbɪ; 'hʌbi] *n., pl.* **hub·bies.** 〖俗〗丈夫(暱稱)。

huck·a·back ['hʌkə,bæk; 'hʌkəbæk] *n.* 一種粗麻布或棉布(作臉巾用)。

huck·le·ber·ry ['hʌkl̩,bɛrɪ; 'hʌklbəri] *n., pl.* **-ries.** 越橘;越橘樹。—*adj.* 越橘的;用越橘做的。

huck·le·bone ['hʌkl̩,bon; 'hʌklboun] *n.* 〖解剖〗①臀骨;無名骨。②踝骨;距骨。

huck·ster ['hʌkstɚ; 'hʌkstə] *n.* ①叫賣販;零售商。②惟利是圖之商人。③〖美俗〗廣告業者。④使用引人注目的方法銷售貨品或達到目的的人。—*v.t. & v.i.* ①叫賣;負販。②講價;還價。—**ism,** *n.*

HUD [hʌd; hʌd] *n.* 〖美〗住宅及都市開發部(爲 Department of *H*ousing and *U*rban *D*evelopment 之略)。

hud·dle** ['hʌdl̩; 'hʌdl] *v.,* **-dled, -dling,** *n.* —*v.i.* ①擠成一團;縮成一團。The children *huddled* together for warmth. 孩子們擠成一團以取暖。②〖橄欖球〗賽前球員列隊(等候開賽訊號)。③商量;交換意見;決定。—*v.t.* ①使成一團。The cat *huddled* itself on the cushion. 貓將身子縮成一團睡在椅墊上。②匆忙或胡亂地作(事)、穿(衣)等。③匆忙混亂地催趕或推塞。He *huddled* the children into the automobile. 他急急忙忙地把小孩推進汽車裏。huddle on*** 匆忙而草率地穿(衣)。—*n.* ①一堆;一團。②混亂;雜亂。③〖橄欖球〗賽前球員之列隊。④祕密的會談。The delegates have been in a *huddle* for two hours. 代表們已密談兩小時。***go into a huddle*** 祕密會商;密談。—**hud·dler,** *n.*

Hu·di·bras·tic [,hjudɪ'bræstɪk; ,hju:di'bræstik] *adj.* 似 (Samuel Butler所寫諷刺詩)Hudibras 的;諷刺而滑稽的。

Hud·son[1] ['hʌdsn̩; 'hʌdsn] *n.* 哈得孫河(在美國 New York 州東部)。

Hud·son[2] *n.* 哈得孫(Henry, 1576–1611, 英國航海家, Hudson 河及 Hudson 灣之發現者)。

Hudson Bay 哈得孫灣(在加拿大北部)。

Hu·é [hju'e; hju'ei] *n.* 順化(越南中部之一海港)。

***hue**[1] [hju; hju:] *n.* 顏色;色度;色彩。the *hues* of the rainbow. 虹之色彩。

hue[2] *n.* 喊叫聲。

hue and cry ①追捕罪犯之喊叫。②此種追捕。③高聲喧嚷;叫囂之反對或責難。

huff [hʌf; hʌf] *n.* 發怒;憤怒。to get into a *huff*. 發怒。—*v.t.* ①開罪;使怒。②脅迫;非禮待之。—*v.i.* ①怒;憤。②〖英方〗吹;噴。

huff·ish ['hʌfɪʃ; 'hʌfiʃ] *adj.* 惱怒的;性急的;脾氣暴躁的。

huff·y ['hʌfɪ; 'hʌfi] *adj.,* **huff·i·er, huff·i·est.** ①惱怒的;被激怒的。②易怒的;暴躁的。—**huff·i·ly,** *adv.* —**huff·i·ness,** *n.*

hug** [hʌg; hʌg] *v.,* **hugged, hug·ging,** *n.* —*v.t.* ①緊抱;擁抱。The girl was *hugging* her doll. 那女孩緊抱着她的洋娃娃。②堅持;固執。③保持靠近。hug oneself*** 竊喜;深自慶幸。—*v.i.* 靠緊;接近。—*n.* 緊抱;擁抱。The little girl gave her mother a big *hug*. 那小女孩緊抱她母親。

‡**huge** [hjudʒ; hju:dʒ] *adj.,* **hug·er, hug·est.** 極大的;巨大的;無限的。a *huge* animal. 巨大的動物。—**ly,** *adv.* —**ness,** *n.*

huge·ous ['hjudʒəs; 'hju:dʒəs] *adj.* 〖俗、謔〗=huge.

hug·ga·ble ['hʌgəbl̩; 'hʌgəbəl] *adj.* 逗人愛的;使人想擁抱的。

hug·ger-mug·ger ['hʌgɚ,mʌgɚ; 'hʌgə,mʌgə] *n.* 雜亂;混亂。—*adj. & adv.* ①祕密的(地)。②雜亂的(地);混亂的(地)。—*v.t.* 隱密;密而不宣。—*v.i.* 祕密行動。

hug·ger-mug·ger·y ['hʌgɚ,mʌgrɪ; 'hʌgə,mʌgəri] *n., pl.* **-ger·ies.** ①混亂;雜亂。②祕密。

hug-me-tight ['hʌgmə,taɪt; 'hʌgmətait] *n.* 〖美〗一種編織之緊身上衣(有時無袖)。

Hu·go ['hjugo; 'hju:gou] *n.* 雨果(Victor Marie, 1802–85, 法國詩人、小說家及劇作家)。

Hu·gue·not ['hjugə,nɑt; 'hju:gənɔt] *n.* (十六、七世紀間之)法國新教徒。

huh [hʌ; hʌ] *interj.* 哼! 哈! (表驚異、輕蔑、疑問等)。

hula hoop 呼拉圈(一種套在身上扭腰旋轉用的塑膠圈)。

hu·la-hu·la ['hulə'hulə; 'hu:lə'hu:lə] *n.* 草裙舞(一種夏威夷土風舞)。(亦作 **hula**)

hula skirt ①夏威夷土人的草裙。②模倣草裙之裙子。

hulk [hʌlk; hʌlk] *n.* ①廢船。②監獄船。③笨大之船。④笨大之人或物。—*v.i.* 變龐大〖常 up〗。

hulk·ing ['hʌlkɪŋ; 'hʌlkiŋ] *adj.* 笨大的;笨重的。

Hull [hʌl; hʌl] *n.* 赫爾 (Cordell, 1871–1955, 美國政治家, 1933–44 任國務卿, 1945 年諾貝爾和平獎得主)。

***hull**[1] [hʌl; hʌl] *n.* ①殼;莢;皮。②果托。③覆被物。—*v.t.* 去殼;去皮。to *hull* berries. 剝漿果皮。—**er,** *n.*

hull[2] *n.* 船身;(水上飛機之)機身;(飛艇之)艇身。***hull down*** (船)在遠際,船身隱於水平線下僅見檣帆的。***hull up*** (船)近得可見船身的。—*v.t.* 以魚雷等轟擊(船)之船身。—*v.i.* 漂流。—**hull-less,** *adj.*

hul·la·ba·loo ['hʌləbə,lu; ,hʌləbə'lu:] *n.* 喧囂;嘈聲;騷擾。(亦作 **hullaballoo**)

***hul·lo** [hə'lo; 'hʌ'lou, hʌ'lou] *interj., n., pl.* **-los,** *v.,* **-loed, -lo·ing.** —*interj.* 喂!哈囉!(表驚訝、引起注意及電話招呼聲)。—*n.* 喂聲;招呼用之呼喊聲。—*v.i.* 呼"喂";喊。—*v.t.* 以"喂"招呼;喊。(英亦作 **hulloa**)

***hum**[1] [hʌm; hʌm] *v.,* **hummed, humming,** *n., interj.* —*v.i.* ①作營營聲;作嗡嗡聲。The sewing machine *hums* busily. 縫紉機忙碌地軋軋響着。②閉唇低唱;(在喉間)發出 m 聲(以示懷疑、不滿)。She is always *humming* to herself. 她老是自己低聲哼唱。③〖俗〗忙碌;活躍起來。The new manager soon made things *hum*. 這新經理不久便使一切活躍起來了。—*v.t.* ①閉口低唱。②低唱而使…。to *hum* a child to sleep. 低唱而使嬰孩睡覺。③〖英俚〗發出臭味(如臭汗等)。—*n.* ①營營聲;閉口低唱。②(表示不滿、猶豫等之)m聲。—*interj.* 哼;哦(似m聲,用以表示猶豫、不滿等)。

hum[2] *n., v.t.,* **hummed, hum·ming.** 〖俗〗欺瞞;詐欺。

‡**hu·man** ['hjumən; 'hju:mən] *adj.* ①人物的;人類的(對動物或上帝而言)。a *human* being. 人。*human* nature. 人性。He is more *human* than his brother. 他比他兄弟更富人情味。②似人類的。③與人類有關的。*human* affairs. 與人類有關之事。④有同情心的。—*n.* 人;人類。—**like,** *adj.* —**ness,** *n.*

***hu·mane** [hju'men; hju:'mein] *adj.*

①仁愛的; 慈悲的; 人道的。a man of *humane* character. 仁者;古道熱腸者。②人文的; 高尙的; 文雅的。 *humane* studies (*or* learning). 人文學科。—**ly,** *adv.* —**ness,** *n.*

humane society (常 H- S-)促進仁慈的社會團體,尤指愛護動物之社團。

hu·man·ics [hju'mænɪks; hju:'mæniks] *n.* (作 *sing.* 解)人類學。

***hu·man·ism** ['hjumən,ɪzəm; 'hju:mənizm] *n.* ①人性;人情; 人道。②人文主義;人本主義。③人文學;古典文化之研究。

hu·man·ist ['hjumənɪst; 'hju:mənist] *n.* ①人文主義者。②人文學者;古典文化學者。

hu·man·is·tic [,hjumən'ɪstɪk; ,hju:mə'nistik] *adj.* ①人性的;人情的;人道的。②人文學者的。③人文主義的。

hu·man·i·tar·i·an[hju,mænə'tɛrɪən; hju:,mæni'tɛəriən] *n.* ①人道主義者; 慈善家; 博愛者。②基督凡人論者。—*adj.* ①人道主義的;慈善的;博愛的。②基督凡人論者的。

hu·man·i·tar·i·an·ism[hju,mænə'tɛrɪənɪzəm; hju:,mæni'tɛəriənizəm] *n.* ①人道主義;博愛主義。②〖宗教〗基督凡人論。

hu·man·i·ty** [hju'mænətɪ; hju:'mæniti] *n., pl.* **-ties.** ①人類。 Advances in science help all *humanity.* 科學的進步有助於全人類。②人性。③人道;仁慈。an act of *humanity.* 仁慈的行爲。the humanities*** **a.** 希臘拉丁語言文學。**b.** 人文學科(包括語言、文學、哲學、藝術等)。

hu·man·ize ['hjumə,naɪz; 'hju:mənaiz] *v.,* **-ized, -iz·ing.** —*v.t.* ①教化;感化。②使成爲人; 賦予人性。 —*v.i.* 成爲人; 變爲有人性。 —**hu·man·i·za·tion,** *n.*

hu·man·kind ['hjumən,kaɪnd; 'hju:mən'kaind] *n.* 人類(集合稱)。

hu·man·ly ['hjumənlɪ; 'hju:mənli] *adv.* ①像人地; 用(於)人情; 用人力。②在人力或學識之範圍內; 依人類之經驗或知識。*humanly* speaking. 從人的立場來說。

***hum·ble** ['hʌmbl; 'hʌmbl] *adj.,* **-bler, -blest,** *v.,* **-bled, -bling.** —*adj.* ①卑下的;微賤的。a man of *humble* birth. 出身微賤之人。②謙遜的;謙恭的。 a *humble* attitude. 謙遜的態度。③低的;矮的;小的。—*v.t.* 使卑下;抑低;挫(他人的銳氣等)。to *humble* one's enemies. 挫敵人的銳氣。—**ness,** *n.* —**hum·bly,** *adv.*

humble pie ①(昔於狩獵後給僕人吃的)鹿等動物之內臟做的餡餅。②屈辱;丟臉。***eat humble pie*** 忍受恥辱;低聲下氣地賠不是。

hum·bug ['hʌm,bʌg; 'hʌmbʌg] *n., v.,* **-bugged, -bug·ging,** *interj.* —*n.* ①欺詐;誘騙;詐僞之言行。②吹牛的人;騙子;詐欺者。③空洞的話。 —*v.t.* 欺騙;瞞騙。 —*v.i.* 行騙。—*interj.* 胡說!瞎扯!

hum·bug·ger·y['hʌm,bʌgərɪ; 'hʌm,bʌgəri] *n., pl.* **-ger·ies.** 欺騙;欺瞞;詐騙。

hum·drum ['hʌm,drʌm; 'hʌmdrʌm] *adj.* 單調的;乏味的;平凡的。—*n.* ①單調;日常事務。②單調乏味之言談; 無聊話。③庸俗之人。

hu·mer·al['hjumərəl; 'hju:mərəl] *adj.* ①肩的;肩部的。②〖解剖、動物〗上膊部的。

hu·mer·us ['hjumərəs; 'hju:mərəs] *n., pl.* **-mer·i** [-mə,raɪ; -mərai]. 〖解剖、動物〗上膊骨;肱骨。

hu·mid ['hjumɪd; 'hju:mid] *adj.* 潮濕的; 濕潤的。—**ly,** *adv.* —**ness,** *n.*

hu·mid·i·fi·er [hju'mɪdə,faɪr; hju:'midi,faiə] *n.* 濕潤機。

hu·mid·i·fy [hju'mɪdə,faɪ; hju:'midifai] *v.t.,* **-fied, -fy·ing.** 使(空氣等)濕潤;使潮濕。—**hu·mid·i·fi·ca·tion,** *n.*

hu·mid·i·ty [hju'mɪdətɪ; hju:'miditi] *n.* ①潮濕; 濕氣。②濕度。relative *humidity.* 相對濕度。

hu·mi·dor ['hjumɪ,dɔr; 'hju:midɔ:] *n.* ①保濕裝置(使菸草貯藏室或箱保持適當之濕度者)。②(有此種裝置之)菸草貯藏室(箱)。

***hu·mil·i·ate** [hju'mɪlɪ,et; hju:'milieit] *v.t.,* **-at·ed, -at·ing.** 使丟臉; 貶抑;屈辱。to *humiliate* oneself. 丟臉;丟人。

hu·mil·i·at·ing [hju'mɪlɪ,etɪŋ; hju:'mili,eitiŋ] *adj.* 貶抑的;屈辱的;恥辱的。

***hu·mil·i·a·tion** [hju,mɪlɪ'eʃən; hju:,mili'eiʃən, ,hju:mili'ei-] *n.* 丟臉; 抑貶;屈辱; 謙卑。The manner of his reception was a *humiliation* to him. 他受接待之狀況對他是一種恥辱。

***hu·mil·i·ty** [hju'mɪlətɪ; hju:'militi] *n., pl.* **-ties.** ①謙遜;謙恭;謙卑。②(*pl.*)謙恭之行爲。

hum·mel ['hʌml; 'hʌml] *adj.* 〖蘇〗①(牛、鹿等)無角的。②無芒的(穀);無穀針的。—*v.t.* 除去(大麥)的芒刺。

hum·ming ['hʌmɪŋ; 'hʌmiŋ] *adj.* ①作嗡嗡等聲的;閉唇低唱的。②〖俗〗活潑的;活躍的。Business is *humming.* 生意很旺盛。③〖俗〗猛烈的;强的;重的。④〖俗〗起泡的。—*n.* 嗡嗡聲;閉唇低唱。

hum·ming·bird ['hʌmɪŋ,bɝd; 'hʌmiŋbə:d] *n.* (美洲產之)蜂雀。

humming top 發響聲之陀螺。

hum·mock ['hʌmək; 'hʌmək] *n.* ①圓丘; 圓岡。②(冰原上之)冰丘。

hum·mock·y ['hʌməkɪ; 'hʌməki] *adj.* 有圓丘的;似圓丘的。

hu·mo(u)r** ['hjumɚ, 'ju-; 'hju:mə, 'ju:-] *n.* ①幽默;詼諧;滑稽。The story is full of *humor.* 這故事很幽默。②幽默感。a man of *humor.* 有幽默感的人; 幽默家。③幽默的言詞或文章。④心情;心境。Success puts you in a good *humor.* 成功使人高興。⑤幻想;遐想。⑥體液。⑦(*pl.*)有趣的節目。*humors* of the occasion. 那個場合的有趣節目。 ***out of humor 不悅;生氣。 ***sense of humor*** 幽默感。 to have a good *sense of humor.* 很有幽默感。—*v.t.* ①縱容;聽任;遷就。 It isn't wise to *humor* a small child. 縱容小孩是不智的。②適應; 順應。You can't force the lock; you must *humor* it. 你不應用死力開那把鎖; 你應該順着它。 —**less,** *adj.*

hu·mor·al ['hjumərəl; 'hju:mərəl] *adj.* 〖醫〗體液的;由體液引起的。

hu·mor·esque [,hjumə'rɛsk; ,hju:mə'resk] *n.* 〖音樂〗 諧謔曲。

hu·mo(u)r·ist ['hjumərɪst; 'hju:mərist] *n.* ①富幽默感者;詼諧者。②幽默作家。

hu·mo(u)r·is·tic [,hjumə'rɪstɪk; ,hju:mə'ristik] *adj.* 滑稽的;滑稽作家的。

***hu·mo(u)r·ous** ['hjumərəs, 'ju-; 'hju:mərəs, 'ju:-] *adj.* 富幽默感的; 滑稽的。a *humorous* writer. 幽默作家。—**ly,** *adv.* —**ness,** *n.*

hu·mo(u)r·some['hjumɚsəm; 'hju:məsəm] *adj.* ①情緒不定的;易怒的。②滑稽的。

***hump** [hʌmp; hʌmp] *n.* ①圓形之隆起物;(駝)峯;(人身上之)瘤;隆肉。Some camels have two *humps* on their backs. 有些駱駝背上有雙峯。②圓丘;岡。③〖英〗(the-)憂鬱;情緒低落。*over the hump* 克服難關;脫離困境。—*v.t.* ①使隆起成圓丘形;駝(背)。The cat *humped* her back when she saw the dog. 那貓見了狗就弓起她的背。②〖美俚〗使(自己)努力;奮發。*Hump* yourselves now. 你們現在要努力。③〖俚、鄙〗與(女人)性交。—*v.i.* 〖美俚〗努力;奮發。

hump·back 〔'hʌmp,bæk; 'hʌmpbæk〕 *n.* ①駝背。②駝背之人;駝子。③座頭鯨。

hump·backed 〔'hʌmp,bækt; 'hʌmpbækt〕 *adj.* 駝背的;傴僂的。

humped 〔hʌmpt; hʌmpt〕 *adj.* 有肉瘤(隆肉)的。 「疑惑、不滿聲)。

humph 〔hʌmf; hʌmf〕 *interj.* 哼!(表

Hum·phrey 〔'hʌmfrɪ; 'hʌmfri〕 *n.* 男子名。

hump·ty-dump·ty 〔'hʌmptɪ'dʌmptɪ; 'hʌmpti'dʌmpti〕 *adj.* 矮胖的;短粗的。

humpty dumpty 矮胖之人(典出於一兒歌,其主角爲蛋狀之人)。

hump·y 〔'hʌmpɪ; 'hʌmpi〕 *adj.* 有瘤的;有隆肉的;多瘤的。

hu·mus 〔'hjuməs; 'hju:məs〕 *n.* 腐植土。

Hun 〔hʌn; hʌn〕 *n.* ①(第四、五世紀蹂躪歐洲的)匈奴人。②(引申爲)破壞者;野蠻人。③〖俗、蔑〗德國兵(用於第一、二次世界大戰時)。

Hun. ①Hungarian. ②Hungary.

Hu·nan 〔'hu'nɑn; 'hu:'nɑ:n〕 *n.* 湖南(中國中南部之一省,省會長沙, Changsha).

***hunch** 〔hʌntʃ; hʌntʃ〕 *n.* ①圓形之隆起物;肉峯;瘤。②(餅等之)厚片;塊。③〖美俗〗預感;疑心。to have a *hunch* that something is going to happen. 預感有甚麼事將要發生。—*v.t.* 彎(背);聳(肩)。—*v.i.* ①前進。②彎腰駝背。 「bæk〕 *n.* 駝背人。

hunch·back 〔'hʌntʃ,bæk; 'hʌntʃ-

hunch·backed 〔'hʌntʃ,bækt; 'hʌntʃbækt〕 *adj.* 駝背的。 「有隆起物的。

hunch·y 〔'hʌntʃɪ; 'hʌntʃi〕 *adj.* 駝背的;

‡**hun·dred** 〔'hʌndrəd; 'hʌndrəd〕 *n.*, *adj.* ①百;百個。two *hundred* and five. 二百零五。②〖美俚〗百元鈔票。③〖英俚〗百鎊鈔票。④〖數學〗=**hundred's place.** ***have one hundred and one things to do*** 〖俗〗有很多事情要做。〖注意〗**hundred** 之前若有其他表數之形容詞, 則 hundred 不加 s; 但若欲表"甚多"而又無其他確定的數字冠於其前則用 hundreds of. 如: *Hundreds of* people were present. 出席的人數以百計。

hun·dred·fold 〔'hʌndrəd,fold; 'hʌndrədfould〕 *adj.*, *adv.*, *n.* 百倍;百重。

hun·dred-per·cent 〔'hʌndrədpə'sɛnt; 'hʌndrədpə'sent〕 *adj.* & *adv.* 百分之百的(地);完全的(地);徹底的(地)。

hun·dred-per·cent·er 〔'hʌndrədpə'sɛntə; 'hʌndrədpə'sentə〕 *n.* 狂熱的愛國者。 「百位。

hundred's place 〖數學〗(數字之)

***hun·dredth** 〔'hʌndrədθ; 'hʌndrədθ〕 *n.*, *adj.* ①第一百個(的)。②百分之一(的)。

hun·dred·weight 〔'hʌndrəd,wet; 'hʌndrədweit〕 *n.*, *pl.* **-weights, -weight.** 衡量名(英爲112磅,美爲 100 磅,略作 **cwt.**).

Hundred Years' War 百年戰爭(1337 至 1453年的英法戰爭)。

hung 〔hʌŋ; hʌŋ〕 *v.* pt. and pp. of **hang.** ***hung on*** 〖俗〗很感興趣的。***hung over*** 宿醉的。***hung up*** **a.** 〖俚〗(棒球或壘球跑壘者)陷於兩壘之間有被殺出局之危險。**b.** 因遭遇困難而逗留。

Hung. ①Hungarian. ②Hungary.

Hun·gar·i·an 〔hʌŋ'gɛrɪən; hʌŋ'gɛəriən〕 *adj.* ①匈牙利的。②匈牙利人的;匈牙利語的。—*n.* ①匈牙利人。②匈牙利語文。

***Hun·ga·ry** 〔'hʌŋgərɪ; 'hʌŋgəri〕 *n.* 匈牙利(中歐國名,首都布達佩斯 Budapest).

hun·ger** 〔'hʌŋgə; 'hʌŋgə〕 *n.* ①饑餓。to feel *hunger.* 感覺饑餓。②渴望;慾望。a *hunger* for kindness. 渴望得到恩惠。hunger cure*** 饑餓療法。—*v.i.* ①餓;覺餓。②渴望;極想〖for, after〗。—*v.t.* 使饑餓。

hunger strike 絕食示威(貫徹要求之一種手段)。

hung·o·ver 〔'hʌŋ'ovə; 'hʌŋ'ouvə〕 *adj.* 〖美俚〗①感到宿醉的。②如宿醉般難過的。

‡**hun·gry** 〔'hʌŋgrɪ; 'hʌŋgri〕 *adj.*, **-gri·er, -gri·est.** ①饑餓的。I'm *hungry*—what time is dinner? 我餓了—何時進餐? ②顯出饑餓的。③使饑餓的。④渴望的〖for〗。to be *hungry* for knowledge. 渴望求知。⑤貧乏的。⑥饑饉的;荒年的。*hungry* times. 饑荒年代。***go hungry*** 挨餓。—**hun·gri·ly,** *adv.* —**hun·gri·ness,** *n.*

hunk 〔hʌŋk; hʌŋk〕 *n.* 〖俗〗大塊;厚片。

hun·ker 〔'hʌŋkə; 'hʌŋkə〕 *v.i.* 蹲下。—*n.* 僅見於下列習慣用語。on one's *hunkers.* 〖蘇〗蹲着。 「卑鄙的人;守財奴。

hunks 〔hʌŋks; hʌŋks〕 *n. sing.* or *pl.*

hunk·y-do·ry 〔,hʌŋkɪ'dorɪ; ,hʌŋki'douri〕 *adj.* 〖俗〗令人滿意的;相當好的。

Hun·nish 〔'hʌnɪʃ; 'hʌniʃ〕 *adj.* ①匈奴的;似匈奴的。②破壞的;野蠻的。

‡**hunt** 〔hʌnt; hʌnt〕 *v.t.* ①狩獵。②在(某地區)狩獵;搜索(某地區)中之獵物。to *hunt* the county. 在這郡中狩獵。③用(馬、狗等)狩獵。④追尋;尋求〖常 up, out〗。⑤捕捉;追逐〖常 from, down〗。They *hunted* him down and strung him up. 他們把他捉住然後將他綑起來。—*v.i.* ①狩獵。Wolves *hunt* in packs. 狼成羣獵食。②尋求〖for, after〗。They *hunted* high and low for the missing will. 他們四處尋找那遺失的遺囑。③遍索;仔細搜索。***hunt down*** 追捕或尋找,不達目的不休。***hunt up*** 仔細尋找。—*n.* ①狩獵;打獵。to have a good *hunt.* 做一次很滿意的狩獵。②追尋;搜索。③獵人會;狩獵隊。④被搜索或狩獵的地區。 「字方法。

hunt and peck 看一個鍵按一下的打

***hunt·er** 〔'hʌntə; 'hʌntə〕 *n.* ①狩獵者;獵人。The Red Indians used to be clever *hunters* and fishers. 印第安人以前是聰明的獵人和漁夫。②獵馬;獵犬。③獵錶;雙蓋錶。④尋找某物的人。a fortune *hunter.* 淘金者。

hunter's moon 仲秋後之第一個滿月。

hunt·ing 〔'hʌntɪŋ; 'hʌntiŋ〕 *n.* 狩獵(尤指獵狐);探尋;追求。—*adj.* 狩獵的。

hunting box 獵舍。 「蓋的)錶殼。

hunting case (附有保護錶面玻璃之

hunting crop 狩獵用之鞭。

hunting horn 獵人用的號角。

hunting watch 狩獵用之錶;雙蓋錶。

hunt·ress 〔'hʌntrɛs, -trɪs; 'hʌntris〕 *n.* ①女獵人;女獵神(Diana). ②母獵馬。

***hunts·man** 〔'hʌntsmən; 'hʌntsmən〕 *n.*, *pl.* **-men.** 〖英〗①獵人。②管獵犬者。

Hu·peh, Hu·pei 〔'hu'pe; 'hu:'pei〕 *n.* 湖北(中國中部之一省,省會武昌, Wuchang).

hur·dle [ˈhɝdl; ˈhəːdl] *n., v.,* **-dled, -dling.** ①(跳欄、賽跑、或賽馬時置於跑道上的)欄。②(*pl.*)(作*sing.*解)跳欄賽跑。the high (low) *hurdles.* 高(低)欄賽跑。③障礙;困難。④臨時圍欄;疏籬。⑤昔日用以拖載犯人至刑場之雪橇狀囚車。—*v.t.* ①跳越;跳過。②克服(困難、障礙等)。③圍以臨時圍欄。—*v.i.* 躍欄或其他障礙。—**hur·dler,** *n.*

hurdle race 障礙競走;跳欄賽跑。

hur·dy-gur·dy [ˈhɝdɪˌgɝdɪ; ˈhəːdiˌgəːdi] *n., pl.* **-dies.** 絞絃琴;古代四絃琴。

***hurl** [hɝl; həːl] *v.t.* ①用力投擲。They *hurled* themselves at the enemy. 他們向敵人猛撲。②激烈地說出;憤慨地說出。③丟下;推翻。—*v.i.* ①用力投擲。②〖俚〗(壘球中)投球。—*n.* 用力或猛烈的投擲。

hurl·er [ˈhɝlɚ; ˈhəːlə] *n.* ①投擲者。②〖棒球〗〖俚〗投手。

hurl·y-burl·y [ˈhɝlɪˌbɝlɪ; ˈhəːliˌbəːli] *n., pl.* **-burl·ies,** *adj.* —*n.* 騷擾;喧囂。—*adj.* 騷擾的;喧囂的;混亂的。

Hu·ron, Lake [ˈhjʊrən; ˈhjuərən] *n.* 休倫湖(爲美國加拿大間五大湖之一)。

***hur·rah** [həˈrɔ; huˈrɑː] *interj., n.* ①歡呼聲;讚賞的呼聲。*Hurrah* for the King! 吾王萬歲!②歡樂;鋪張;騷動。—*v.i.* 歡呼;呼hurrah. We *hurrah* when we see the soldiers go by. 我們看到士兵經過時向他們歡呼。—*v.t.* 以歡呼迎接;以歡呼鼓勵。(亦作**hurray, hooray, hoorah**)

***hur·ri·cane** [ˈhɝɪˌken; ˈhʌrikən, -kin] *n.* ①颶風;暴風;暴風雨。②(怒氣或其他强烈情感的)暴發。a *hurricane* of applause. 掌聲雷動。

hurricane deck (內河船上的)上層甲板。

hur·ri·cane-force wind [ˈhɝɪˌkenˌfɔrsˌwɪnd; ˈhʌrikənˌfɔːsˌwind] 颶風級風力(時速73英里以上之風)。

hurricane lamp 馬燈;防風燈。

hurricane lantern 防風燈籠。

hur·ri·coon [ˈhɝəkun; ˈhəːrəkuːn] *n.* 偵察颶風用的測候汽球。

***hur·ried** [ˈhɝɪd; ˈhʌrid] *adj.* 匆忙的;草率的。a *hurried* meal. 一頓匆忙的飯。—**ly,** *adv.* —**ness,** *n.*

***hur·ried·ly** [ˈhɝɪdlɪ; ˈhʌridli] *adv.* 匆忙地;草率地。

hur·ri·er [ˈhɝɪr; ˈhʌriə] *n.* 做事匆忙者。

‡hur·ry [ˈhɝɪ; ˈhʌri] *v.,* **-ried, -ry·ing,** *n., pl.* **-ries.** —*v.i.* 匆忙;慌張;趕快。Don't *hurry*—there's plenty of time. 不要忙——時間還多着哩。*Hurry* up! You'll be late. 趕快!你要遲到了。—*v.t.* ①催促;驅趕。We *hurried* them off. 我們趕快把他們送走了。Can you *hurry* up the dinner? 你能叫他們快點開飯嗎?②匆匆移開或拿走。He *hurried* his book out of sight when the teacher appeared. 老師來到時,他趕快將書藏起來。—*n.* ①匆忙;慌張。Don't go yet—there's no *hurry.* 還不要去——不必匆忙。②匆忙之行動。In her *hurry,* she dropped the eggs. 她在匆忙中將蛋掉到地上去了。*in a hurry* **a.** 匆忙地;匆促地。Why are you *in* such *a hurry?* 你爲甚麼這樣匆忙?**b.**〖俗〗容易地。**c.**〖俗〗願意地。I shall not ask him to dinner again *in a hurry.* 我不願再請他吃飯。

hurry call 緊急呼救。

hur·ry-scur·ry, hur·ry-skur·ry [ˈhɝɪˈskɝɪ; ˈhʌriˈskʌri] *adv., adj., n., v.,* **-ried, -ry·ing.** —*adv.* 慌忙地;急迫地;倉猝地。—*adj.* 慌張的;倉猝的。—*n.* 慌張;倉皇。—*v.i.* 倉皇前進;倉猝行事。

hurst [hɝst; həːst] *n.* ①小林;叢林;有小林的山崗。②〖蘇〗沙洲。

‡hurt [hɝt; həːt] *v.,* **hurt, hurt·ing,** *n., adj.* —*v.t.* ①使疼痛;傷害。Did you *hurt* yourself? 你受傷了嗎? I won't *hurt* you. 我不會傷害你。②使苦惱;使傷心。I was rather *hurt* by what they said about me. 他們對我的批評,使我相當傷心。③損害;有不良影響。Another glass won't *hurt* you. 再來一杯對你不會有害。④損傷;損害。—*v.i.* 疼痛;使痛;有害。My shoe is too tight; it *hurts.* 我的鞋太緊了,使我脚很痛。—*n.* ①疼痛;傷害。②創傷;傷口。It was a severe *hurt* to his pride. 那對他的自尊是一個嚴重的創傷。③損害;不良影響。—*adj.* ①受傷的。The *hurt* child was taken to the hospital. 受傷的小孩被送進醫院。②傷感情的。③看樣子受了委曲的。Take that *hurt* look off your face! 不要擺出一付受欺侮的面孔。④損壞的。

hurt·ful [ˈhɝtfəl; ˈhəːtful] *adj.* 有害的;造成損害的。—**ly,** *adv.* —**ness,** *n.*

hur·tle [ˈhɝtl; ˈhəːtl] *v.,* **-tled, -tling,** *n.* —*v.i.* ①碰撞;衝擊。②急動;突進。③反響;鳴響。—*v.t.* 使猛撞;使衝撞。—*n.* 猛撞;衝撞。

hurt·less [ˈhɝtlɪs; ˈhəːtlis] *adj.*①不加害的;無害的。②沒受傷的。—**ly,** *adv.*

‡hus·band [ˈhʌzbənd; ˈhʌzbənd] *n.* ①丈夫。They are *husband* and wife. 他們是夫婦。②節儉的經理人。③〖英〗經理人。—*v.t.* ①節用;節儉。②使(某女子)結婚。

hus·band·age [ˈhʌzbəndɪdʒ; ˈhʌzbəndidʒ] *n.* 商船主付與其船務代表之酬金。

hus·band·man [ˈhʌzbəndmən; ˈhʌzbəndmən] *n., pl.* **-men.** 農夫。

hus·band·ry [ˈhʌzbəndrɪ; ˈhʌzbəndri] *n.* ①耕種;務農。②處理自己事務;節用。③小心處理;家政;節儉。

***hush** [hʌʃ; hʌʃ] *v.t.* ①使肅靜;發"噓"聲而使安靜。②緩和;使平靜;催眠。to *hush* a baby to sleep. 使嬰孩安靜而睡。*hush up* **a.** 隱瞞;隱祕不宣。**b.**〖俗〗使肅靜。—*v.i.* 肅靜;緘默。The wind has *hushed.* 風已靜止。—*n.* 肅靜;安靜。in the *hush* of night. 在靜悄悄的夜晚。—*interj.* 肅靜!不要吵!

hush·a·by [ˈhʌʃəˌbaɪ; ˈhʌʃəbai] *interj., v.,* **-bied, -by·ing.** —*interj.* 哄幼兒入睡之聲。—*v.t.* 唱搖籃歌使入睡。

hush-hush [ˈhʌʃˌhʌʃ; ˈhʌʃˈhʌʃ] *adj.* 祕密的;暗中進行的。—*n.* 祕密的事。—*v.t.* ①封鎖(新聞等)。②隱密;抹殺。

Hu Shih [ˈhuˈʃɪr; ˈhuːˈʃir] 胡適(1891–1962,中國哲學家及作家)。

hush money (塞嘴的)賄賂;遮羞費。

***husk** [hʌsk; hʌsk] *n.* ①(果物或穀類的)外殼;皮;莢。②皮;殼(無價值之物)。—*v.t.* ①剝…的皮或殼。②用粗嗄聲音講話。He *husked* out his orders. 他用粗嗄的聲音發號施令。—*v.i.* (聲音)變爲粗嗄。—**er,** *n.*

husk·ing [ˈhʌskɪŋ; ˈhʌskiŋ] *n.* ①剝玉蜀黍殼的工作。②剝玉蜀黍殼的集會。

***husk·y¹** [ˈhʌskɪ; ˈhʌski] *adj.,* **husk·i·er, husk·i·est,** *n., pl.* **husk·ies.** —*adj.* ①殼的;多殼的;有殼的;似殼的。②(聲音)有些沙啞的;嗄聲的。a *husky* cough. 乾咳。③〖俗〗壯碩的。He's a fine, *husky* fellow. 他是一個很壯的人。—*n.*〖美俗〗强壯結實之人。—**husk·i·ly,** *adv.* —**husk·i·ness,** *n.*

husk·y[2] *n., pl.* **husk·ies.** ①愛斯基摩犬。②一種拉雪車的狗(亦作 **Siberian Husky**). ③〖加〗a. 愛斯基摩人。b. 愛斯基摩方言。—*adj.* 〖加〗愛斯基摩的。(亦作 **Husky**)

hus·sar [hʊ'zɑr; hu'zɑː] *n.* ①輕騎兵。②第十五世紀時之匈牙利輕騎兵。

hus·sy ['hʌsɪ, 'hʌzɪ; 'hʌsi, 'hʌzi] *n., pl.* **-sies.** ①賤婦。②輕佻或粗野之女子。

hus·tings ['hʌstɪŋz; 'hʌstiŋz] *n.* (作 *sing.* or *pl.* 解)〖英〗①國會議員候選人發表政見之講臺。②任何發表競選演說之講臺。③選舉程序。

***hus·tle** ['hʌsl̩; 'hʌsl] *v.,* **-tled, -tling,** *n.* —*v.i.* ①〖俗〗趕忙着做; 有力地工作。Come on, now! *Hustle!* 不要浪費時間! 快把工作做好! ②擁擠; 推擁而進。③〖俗〗生意或賺錢方面表現很積極。④〖俚〗a. 以不正當的方法賺錢。b. (妓女)拉客。—*v.t.* ①驅趕; 驅逐。The police *hustled* the tramps out of town. 警察驅逐游民離開城鎮。②猛推; 亂擠。③催促。I don't want to *hustle* you into a decision. 我不擬催促你作快速決定。④强迫(某人)買或做事。⑤以積極或不正當的方法獲得金錢。⑥强索金錢。⑦以高壓手段推銷或向(某地)下工夫。⑧强賣。to *hustle* souvenirs. 强賣土產品。⑨〖俚〗騙賭。⑩〖俚〗欺騙。They *hustled* him out of his savings. 他們把他的儲蓄騙走了。—*n.* ①〖俗〗急遽之活動; 奮發; 努力。②亂擠; 推擁。The railway station was a scene of *hustle* and bustle. 火車站是擁擠喧嚷之所。③急忙。④〖俚〗騙人使其上當的勾當。

hus·tler ['hʌslɚ; 'hʌslə] *n.* ①猛推亂擠的人。②〖俗〗精力極爲旺盛者; 做事極端積極者。③〖俚〗騙徒。④〖俚〗妓女。

***hut** [hʌt; hʌt] *n., v.,* **hut·ted, hut·ting.** —*n.* ①簡陋的小屋; 茅舍。②〖軍〗臨時軍營。—*v.t.* 供應小屋。—*v.i.* 住小屋。

hutch [hʌtʃ; hʌtʃ] *n.* ①養小動物之圈欄(尤指兔箱)。②茅屋; 小舍。③箱。④(麪包店之)和麪鉢; 捏鉢。⑤〖採礦〗洗礦槽; 礦石搬運車。

hut circle 〖考古〗環狀之石塊或泥土(爲史前居民之遺跡)。

hut·ment ['hʌtmənt; 'hʌtmənt] *n.* ①臨時營房。②在臨時營房住宿。

Hux·ley[1] ['hʌkslɪ; 'hʌksli] *n.* 赫胥黎 (Thomas Henry, 1825–1895, 英國生物學家)。

Hux·ley[2] *n.* 赫胥黎(Aldous Leonard, 1894–1963, J. S. Huxley 之弟, 英國小說家、詩人及散文家)。

huz·za [hə'zɑ, hʊ'zɑ; hu'zɑː, hʌ'zɑː] *interj., n., pl.* **-zas,** *v.,* **-zaed, -za·ing.** —*interj.* 表大喜、讚許、歡呼等之聲。—*n.* "huzza" 聲。—*v.i.* 發 "huzza" 聲。—*v.t.* 向…歡呼。(亦作 **huzzah**)

H.V., h.v. high voltage.

Hwai [hwaɪ; hwai] *n.* 淮河(在中國河南、安徽兩省境內)。

hwan [hwɑn, wɑn; hwɑːn, wɑːn] *n., pl.* **hwan.** 元(韓國貨幣單位)。(亦作 **won**)

Hwang Hai ['hwɑŋ'haɪ; 'hwɑːŋ'hai] 黃海(中國與韓國間之一海灣)。(亦作 **Yellow Sea**)

Hwang Ho ['hwɑŋ'ho; 'hwɑːŋ'hou] 黃河。(亦作 **Hwangho, Yellow River**)

Hwang Pu ['hwɑŋ'pu; 'hwɑːŋ'puː] 黃埔(在中國廣州, 爲黃埔軍校所在地)。

H.W.M. high-water mark.

hwy. highway.

hy·a·cinth ['haɪə,sɪnθ; 'haiəsinθ] *n.* ①〖植物〗風信子; 洋水仙; 水葫蘆。②〖礦〗紅鋯英石(紅風信子石)。

hy·a·cin·thine [,haɪə'sɪnθɪn, -θaɪn; ,haiə'sinθain] *adj.* ①風信子的; 似風信子的。②飾以風信子的。

Hy·ads ['haɪædz; 'haiædz] *n. pl.* ①〖希臘神話〗Atlas 之七個女兒, 死後化爲星。②〖天文〗金牛座中之五星羣。(亦作 **Hyades**)

hy·a·line ['haɪəlɪn; 'haiəlin] *adj.* 玻璃狀的; 似水晶的; 透明的。—*n.* 似玻璃般透明之物; 平穩似鏡之海; 碧空。

hy·a·lite ['haɪə,laɪt; 'haiəlait] *n.* 〖礦〗玉滴石; 玻璃蛋白石。

hy·a·loid ['haɪə,lɔɪd; 'haiəlɔid] *adj.* 〖解剖〗玻璃狀的; 透明的。—*n.* 〖解剖〗(眼球的)玻璃狀膜。

hy·a·lu·ron·ic acid [,haɪəlʊ'rɑnɪk~; ,haiəlu'rɔnik~] 〖生化〗琉璃醣炭基酸。

hy·a·lu·ron·i·dase [,haɪəlʊ'rɑnədes; ,haiəlu'rɔnideis] *n.* 〖生化〗琉璃醣炭基酸酶。

***hy·brid** ['haɪbrɪd; 'haibrid] *n.* ①雜種; 混血兒。②混成之物; 混合語。—*adj.* 雜種的; 混成之物的; 混合語的。a *hybrid* animal. 雜種動物(如騾等)。

hy·brid·ist ['haɪbrɪdɪst; 'haibridist] *n.* 雜種繁殖者。

hy·brid·i·ty [haɪ'brɪdətɪ; hai'briditi] *n.* 混血; 雜種; 雜交(現象)。(亦作 **hybridism**)

hy·brid·i·za·tion [,haɪbrɪdə'zeʃən; ,haibridai'zeiʃən] *n.* (異種)雜交; 配種。

hy·brid·ize ['haɪbrɪd,aɪz; 'haibridaiz] *v.,* **-ized, -iz·ing.** —*v.t.* 使雜交; 使成混合物。—*v.t.* 產生雜種; 成爲混合之物。

hybrid vigor 雜種優勢。

hyd. ①hydraulics. ②hydrostatics.

hy·da·tid ['haɪdətɪd; 'haidətid] *n.* 〖醫〗①胞囊; 泡。②水泡腫; 水泡狀胎塊。—*adj.* 胞囊的。(亦作 **hydatidinous**)

Hyde Park (倫敦之)海德公園。

hy·dra ['haɪdrə; 'haidrə] *n., pl.* **-dras, -drae** [-dri; -driː]. ①(H-)〖希臘神話〗九頭怪蛇(斬去一頭立生二頭之怪蛇, 後爲 Hercules 所殺)。②難根除之禍害; 大患。③〖動物〗水螅。④〖天文〗長蛇座。

hy·dran·gea [haɪ'drendʒə; hai'dreindʒə] *n.* 繡球花。

hy·drant ['haɪdrənt; 'haidrənt] *n.* 給水龍頭; 消火栓。

hy·drate ['haɪdret; 'haidreit] *n., v.,* **-drat·ed, -drat·ing.** —*n.* 水化物; 氫氧化物。—*v.t.* & *v.i.* (使)成水化物。

hy·dra·tion [haɪ'dreʃən; hai'dreiʃən] *n.* 水化(作用)。

hy·drau·lic [haɪ'drɔlɪk; hai'drɔːlik] *adj.* ①水力的; 水力學的。a *hydraulic* lift. 水力昇降機。②用水發動的; 水壓的。a *hydraulic* press. 水壓機。*hydraulic* power plant. 水力發電廠。③水硬的。*hydraulic* cement. 水硬水泥。—**al·ly,** *adv.*

hy·drau·lics [haɪ'drɔlɪks; hai'drɔːliks] *n.* (作 *sing.* 解)水力學。

hy·dra·zide ['haɪdrə,zaɪd; 'haidrəzaid] *n.* 醯肼; 癆得治(一種肺病特效藥)。

hy·dric ['haɪdrɪk; 'haidrik] *adj.* 〖化〗氫的; 含氫的。

-hydric 〖字尾〗表 "氫的; 含氫" 之義。

hy·drid(e) ['haɪdraɪd; 'haidraid] *n.* 〖化〗氫化物。

hy·dri·od·ic acid [,haɪdrɪ'ɑdɪk~; ,haidri'ɔdik~] 〖化〗氫碘酸。

hy·dro ['haɪdro; 'haidrou] *n., pl.* **-dros.** ①〖英俗〗水療院; 水療旅館(=hydropathic). ②〖俗〗水上飛機(=hydroplane).

③〖美俗〗(=hydraulic power)水力。④水力發電所(=hydroelectric power plant). —*adj.* 水力發電的。

hy·dro·car·bon [ˌhaɪdroˈkɑrbən; ˈhaidrouˈkɑːbən] *n.* 炭氫化合物。

hy·dro·cele [ˈhaɪdrəˌsil; ˈhaidrəsiːl] *n.* 〖醫〗積水。

hy·dro·ceph·a·lus [ˌhaɪdrəˈsɛfələs; ˈhaidrouˈsefələs] *n.* 〖醫〗腦水腫;腦積水。(亦作 **hydrocephaly**)

hy·dro·chlo·ric acid [ˌhaɪdrəˈklorɪk～; ˈhaidrəˈklɔrik～] 鹽酸 (HCl).

hy·dro·chlo·ride [ˌhaɪdrəˈkloraɪd; ˌhaidrəˈklouraid] *n.* 〖化〗氫氯化物。

hy·dro·cor·ti·sone [ˌhaɪdroˈkɔrtəson; ˌhaidrəˈkɔːtisoun] *n.* ①〖生化〗氫羥腎上腺皮質素。②〖藥〗氫化可體松。

hy·dro·cy·an·ic acid [ˌhaɪdrosaɪˈænɪk～; ˌhaidrousaiˈænik～] 〖化〗氫氰酸 (HCN).

hy·dro·dy·nam·ic [ˌhaɪdrodaɪˈnæmɪk; ˈhaidroudaiˈnæmik] *adj.* 水力的;流體動力的;水動力學的;流體動力學的。

hy·dro·dy·nam·ics [ˌhaɪdrodaɪˈnæmɪks; ˈhaidroudaiˈnæmiks] *n.*(作*sing.*解)水動力學;水力學;流體動力學。(亦作 **hydromechanics**)

hy·dro·e·lec·tric [ˌhaɪdroɪˈlɛktrɪk; ˌhaidrouiˈlektrik] *adj.* 水電的;水力發電的。

hy·dro·e·lec·tric·i·ty [ˌhaɪdroɪˌlɛkˈtrɪsətɪ; ˌhaidrouiˌlekˈtrisiti] *n.* 水力電。

hy·dro·flu·or·ic acid [ˌhaɪdrəfluˈɑrɪk～; ˌhaidrəfluːˈɔrik～] 氟氫酸 (HF).

hy·dro·foil [ˈhaɪdroˌfɔɪl; ˈhaidrəˌfɔil] *n.* ①水翼船。②(水翼船上的)水翼。

hy·dro·gen** [ˈhaɪdrədʒən, -dʒɪn; ˈhaidridʒən, -drədʒən, -drədʒin] *n.* 〖化〗氫 (H). ***hydrogen bomb 氫彈(略作 **H-bomb**).

hy·dro·gen·ate [ˈhaɪdrədʒənˌet; ˈhaidrədʒəneit] *v.t.*, **-at·ed, -at·ing.** 使與氫化合;使含氫。—**hy·dro·gen·a·tion,** *n.*

hy·drog·e·nous [haɪˈdrɑdʒənəs; haiˈdrɔdʒinəs] *adj.* 氫的;含氫的;含水的。

hydrogen peroxide 〖化〗過氧化氫(H_2O_2)。

hydrogen sulfide 〖化〗硫化氫(H_2S).

hy·dro·graph [ˈhaɪdrəˌgræf; ˈhaidrəgrɑːf] *n.* 自記水位計;水位圖。

hy·drog·ra·pher [haɪˈdrɑgrəfɚ; haiˈdrɔgrəfə] *n.* 水道學者;水道測量家。

hy·dro·graph·ic survey [ˌhaɪdrəˈgræfɪk～; ˌhaidrəˈgræfik～] 水形測量。

hy·drog·ra·phy [haɪˈdrɑgrəfɪ; haiˈdrɔgrəfi] *n.* 水道學;水道測量學。

hy·droid [ˈhaɪdrɔɪd; ˈhaidrɔid] *adj.* 水螅蟲的;水螅類的;似水螅的。—*n.*水螅類動物。

hy·dro·ki·net·ics [ˌhaɪdrəkɪˈnɛtɪks; ˌhaidrəkiˈnetiks] *n.* (作 *sing.* 解) 〖物理〗流體動力學。(亦作 **hydrodynamics**)

hy·drol·o·gist [haɪˈdrɑlədʒɪst; haiˈdrɔlədʒist] *n.* 水文學者。

hy·drol·o·gy [haɪˈdrɑlədʒɪ; haiˈdrɔlədʒi] *n.* 水文學(研究陸地上之水的性質、現象及分布)。(亦作 **hydrogeology**)

hy·drol·y·sis [haɪˈdrɑləsɪs; haiˈdrɔlisis] *n.*, *pl.* **-ses** [-ˌsiz; -siːz]. 〖化〗加水分解。

hy·dro·lyze [ˈhaɪdrəˌlaɪz; ˈhaidrəlaiz] *v.t.* & *v.i.*, **-lyzed, -lyz·ing.** 〖化〗(使)加水分解。

hy·dro·me·chan·ics [ˌhaɪdromɪˈkænɪks; ˈhaidroumiˈkæniks] *n.*(作 *sing.* 解) 流體力學。

hy·dro·me·te·or [ˌhaɪdrəˈmitɪɚ; ˌhaidrəˈmiːtiə] *n.* 〖氣象〗水象(大氣中水汽因凝結或昇華之任何產物,如雨、雪、雹等)。

hy·drom·e·ter [haɪˈdrɑmətɚ; haiˈdrɔmitə] *n.* 液體比重計。

hy·drom·e·try [haɪˈdrɑmətrɪ; haiˈdrɔmitri] *n.* 液體比重測定(法)。

hy·dro·path·ic [ˌhaɪdrəˈpæθɪk; ˌhaidrəˈpæθik] *adj.* 水療法的。—*n.* 〖英俗〗水療院。

hy·drop·a·thy [haɪˈdrɑpəθɪ; haiˈdrɔpəθi] *n.* 〖醫〗水療法。

hy·dro·phane [ˈhaɪdrəˌfen; ˈhaidrəfein] *n.* 水蛋白石。

hy·dro·pho·bi·a [ˌhaɪdrəˈfobɪə; ˌhaidrəˈfoubjə] *n.* 〖醫〗狂犬症;恐水症。

hy·dro·pho·bic [ˌhaɪdrəˈfobɪk; ˌhaidrəˈfoubik] *adj.* 狂犬症的;恐水症的;患恐水症的。

hy·dro·phone [ˈhaɪdrəˌfon; ˈhaidrəfoun] *n.* ①水聽器。②水管測漏儀。③〖醫〗水診器。

hy·dro·phyte [ˈhaɪdrəˌfaɪt; ˈhaidrəfait] *n.* 水生植物。

hy·dro·plane [ˈhaɪdrəˌplen; ˈhaidrouplein] *n.*, *v.*, **-planed, -plan·ing.** —*n.* (亦作 **hydroairplane**) ①水上滑行艇。②水上飛機。③(潛艇之)水平舵。—*v.i.* ①水上滑行。②乘坐水上飛機。

hy·dro·pon·ic [ˌhaɪdrəˈpɑnɪk; ˌhaidrəˈpɔnik] *adj.* 水耕的;水耕法的。

hy·dro·pon·ics [ˌhaɪdrəˈpɑnɪks; ˌhaidrəˈpɔniks] *n.* (作 *sing.* 解)水耕法。

hy·drop·o·nist [haɪˈdrɑpənɪst; haiˈdrɔpənist] *n.* 水耕農業經營者。

hy·dro·pow·er [ˈhaɪdroˌpauɚ; ˈhaidrouˌpauə] *n.* 用水力發電所產生之電。

hy·drop·sy [ˈhaɪdrɑpsɪ; ˈhaidrɔpsi] *n.* 〖醫〗 =**dropsy.**

hy·dro·qui·none [ˌhaɪdrokwɪˈnon; ˈhaidroukwiˈnoun] *n.* 〖化〗對苯二酚(一種顯影劑)。(亦作 **hydroquinol, quinol**)

hy·dro·scope [ˈhaɪdrəˌskop; ˈhaidrəskoup] *n.* 水中鏡。

hy·dro·ski [ˈhaɪdroski; ˈhaidrouskiː] *n.*, *pl.* **-skis, -ski.** (飛機的)起降滑板。

hy·dro·sol [ˈhaɪdrəˌsɑl; ˈhaidrəsɔl] *n.* 〖化〗水溶膠。(亦作 **hydrosole**)

hy·dro·sphere [ˈhaɪdrəˌsfɪr; ˈhaidrəsfiə] *n.* ①大氣中之水氣。②(地球之)水界。

hy·dro·stat [ˈhaɪdrəˌstæt; ˈhaidroustæt] *n.* ①水位計。②汽鍋控制器。

hy·dro·stat·ic [ˌhaɪdrəˈstætɪk; ˌhaidrouˈstætik] *adj.* 流體靜力學的;靜水學的。

hy·dro·stat·i·cal [ˌhaɪdrəˈstætɪkl; ˌhaidrouˈstætikəl] *adj.* =**hydrostatic.**

hydrostatic press 水壓機。

hy·dro·stat·ics [ˌhaɪdrəˈstætɪks; ˌhaidrouˈstætiks] *n.* (作 *sing.* 解)流體靜力學;靜水學。

hy·dro·sul·fate [ˌhaɪdrəˈsʌlfet; ˌhaidrəˈsʌlfeit] *n.* 〖化〗酸性硫酸鹽。

hy·dro·tax·is [ˌhaɪdrəˈtæksɪs; ˌhaidrəˈtæksis] *n.* 〖生物〗趨水性。

hy·dro·ther·a·py [ˌhaɪdrəˈθɛrəpɪ; ˌhaidrəˈθerəpi] *n.* 水療法。

hy·drot·ro·pism [haɪˈdrɑtrəˌpɪzəm; haiˈdrɔtrəpizəm] *n.* 〖植物〗向水性;背水性。

hy·drous [ˈhaɪdrəs; ˈhaidrəs] *adj.* ①

含水的。②含氫的。

hy·drox·id(e) 〔haɪˈdrɑksaɪd; haiˈdrɔksaid〕 *n.* 〖化〗氫氧化物。

hy·drox·yl 〔haɪˈdrɑksɪl; haiˈdrɔksil〕 *n., adj.* 〖化〗氫氧基(的);羥基(的)。

hydroxyl group〖化〗氫氧基化合物。

Hy·dro·zo·a 〔ˌhaɪdrəˈzoə; ˌhaidrəˈzouə〕 *n. pl.* 〖動物〗水螅水母類。

hy·dro·zo·an 〔ˌhaɪdrəˈzoən; ˌhaidrəˈzouən〕 *adj.* 水螅水母類的。—*n.* 水螅水母類的動物。

Hy·drus 〔ˈhaɪdrəs; ˈhaidrəs〕 *n., gen.* **-dri** 〔-draɪ; -drai〕. 〖天文〗水蛇座。

hy·e·na 〔haɪˈinə; haiˈiːnə〕 *n.* 〖動物〗土狼;鬣狗。(亦作 **hyaena**)

hy·e·noid 〔haɪˈinɔɪd; haiˈiːnɔid〕 *adj.* 似土狼的。(亦作 **hyeniform**)

hy·e·tol·o·gy 〔ˌhaɪɪˈtɑlədʒɪ; ˌhaiiˈtɔlədʒi〕 *n.* 研究雨、雪、雹等之氣象學。

Hy·ge·ia 〔haɪˈdʒiə; haiˈdʒi(ː)ə〕 *n.* 〖希臘神話〗司健康之女神。

hy·ge·ian 〔haɪˈdʒiən; haiˈdʒi(ː)ən〕 *adj.* ①健康的;衞生的。②(H-) 健康女神的。—*n.* 傳授或提倡衞生者。

hy·giene 〔ˈhaɪdʒin, ˈhaɪdʒɪˌin; ˈhaidʒiːn〕 *n.* 衞生學;保健法。(亦作**hygienics**)

hy·gi·en·ic 〔ˌhaɪdʒɪˈɛnɪk; haiˈdʒiːnik〕 *adj.* ①衞生的;保健的。②衞生學的。(亦作 **hygienical**)

hy·gi·en·ics 〔ˌhaɪdʒɪˈɛnɪks; haiˈdʒiːniks〕 *n.* (作 *sing.* 解)衞生學。

hy·gi·en·ist 〔ˈhaɪdʒɪənɪst; ˈhaidʒiənist〕 *n.* 衞生學者。(亦作 **hygeist, hygieist**)

hy·grol·o·gy 〔haɪˈgrɑlədʒɪ; haiˈgrɔlədʒi〕 *n.* 濕度學。

hy·grom·e·ter 〔haɪˈgrɑmətɚ; haiˈgrɔmitə〕 *n.* 濕度計。

hy·gro·met·ric 〔ˌhaɪgrəˈmɛtrɪk; ˌhaigrouˈmetrik〕 *adj.* ①濕度測定法的。②易吸收濕氣的;對濕氣很敏感的。

hy·grom·e·try 〔haɪˈgrɑmətrɪ; haiˈgrɔmitri〕 *n.* 濕度測定(法)。

hy·gro·scope 〔ˈhaɪgrəˌskop; ˈhaigrəskoup〕 *n.* 〖物理〗驗濕器。

hy·gro·scop·ic 〔ˌhaɪgrəˈskɑpɪk; ˌhaigrəˈskɔpik〕 *adj.* ①驗濕器的;用驗濕器可驗出的。②易濕的;吸濕性的。

Hyk·sos 〔ˈhɪksos; ˈhiksɔs〕 *n. pl.* 自紀元前18世紀至16世紀統治埃及之王朝。(亦作 **Shepherd Kings**)

hy·la 〔ˈhaɪlə; ˈhailə〕 *n.* 〖動物〗雨蛙。

hy·lo·the·ism 〔ˈhaɪləθiˌɪzəm; ˈhailəθiːizəm〕 *n.* 物質宇宙卽神論;汎神論。

hy·lo·zo·ism 〔ˌhaɪləˈzoɪzəm; ˌhailəˈzouizəm〕 *n.* 萬物均有生命之主張;生命與物質不可分離之學說。

Hy·men 〔ˈhaɪmən; ˈhaimen〕 *n.* 〖希臘神話〗婚姻之神。(亦作 **Hymenaeus**)

hy·men 〔ˈhaɪmən; ˈhaimen〕 *n.* 處女膜。

hy·me·ne·al 〔ˌhaɪməˈniəl; ˌhaimeˈni(ː)əl〕 *adj.* 婚姻的;結婚的。—*n.* 婚禮頌歌。

Hy·me·nop·ter·a 〔ˌhaɪməˈnɑptərə; ˌhaiməˈnɔptərə〕 *n. pl.* 〖昆蟲學〗膜翅類。

hy·me·nop·ter·ous 〔ˌhaɪməˈnɑptərəs; ˌhaiməˈnɔptərəs〕 *adj.* 〖昆蟲學〗膜翅類的。

hy·men·ot·o·my 〔ˌhaɪməˈnɑtəmɪ; ˌhaiməˈnɔtəmi〕 *n., pl.* **-mies.** 〖外科〗①處女膜切開術。②膜切開術。

hymn 〔hɪm; him〕 *n.* ①讚美詩;聖歌。②讚美;稱讚。—*v.t.* & *v.i.* 唱讚美詩讚美;唱讚美歌。

hym·nal 〔ˈhɪmnəl; ˈhimnəl〕 *n.* 讚美詩集。—*adj.* 讚美詩的。

hymn·book 〔ˈhɪmˌbuk; ˈhimbuk〕 *n.* 讚美詩集;聖歌集。

hym·nist 〔ˈhɪmnɪst; ˈhimnist〕 *n.* 讚美詩(聖歌)作者。

hym·no·dy 〔ˈhɪmnədɪ; ˈhimnədi〕 *n.* ①讚美詩之歌唱。②讚美詩(聖歌)學。③讚美詩;聖歌(集合稱)。—**hym·no·dist,** *n.*

hym·nog·ra·pher 〔hɪmˈnɑgrəfɚ; himˈnɔgrəfə〕 *n.* 讚美詩學者;讚美詩作者。(亦作 **hymnologist**)

hym·nol·o·gy 〔hɪmˈnɑlədʒɪ; himˈnɔlədʒi〕 *n.* ①讚美詩學。②讚美詩(集合稱)。③讚美詩之編製。

hy·oid 〔ˈhaɪɔɪd; ˈhaiɔid〕 *adj.* 〖解剖〗U 字形的;舌骨的。(亦作 **hyoidal, hyoidean**) —*n.* 舌骨。

hy·os·cine 〔ˈhaɪəˌsin; ˈhaiəsiːn〕 *n.* 〖化〗亥俄辛;莨菪鹼。

hyp 〔hɪp; hip〕 *n.* 〖古〗(常 *pl.*)=**hypochondria.** (亦作 **hip**)

hyp·a·cu·sia 〔ˌhɪpəˈkjuʒə; ˌhipəˈkjuːʒə〕 *n.* 聽覺不全。

hyp·al·ge·si·a 〔ˌhɪpælˈdʒizɪə; ˌhipælˈdʒiːziə〕 *n.* 〖醫〗痛覺減退;痛覺遲鈍。(亦作 **hypalgia**)

hy·pal·la·ge 〔hɪˈpælədʒi; haiˈpæləgi(ː)〕 *n.* 〖修辭、文法〗代換法(如apply water to the wound 換爲 apply the wound to water)。

hype 〔haɪp; haip〕 *n., v.,* **hyped, hyping.** —*n.* ①=**hypodermic.** ②吸毒成癮者。③廣告。④欺騙; 騙局。 —*v.t.* ①(用刺激針劑)强行刺激。②使熱烈起來〖up〗。

hyper- 〖字首〗表"超過的;超越的;過度的;非常的"之義(爲 hypo- 之對)。

hy·per·a·cid·i·ty 〔ˌhaɪpərəˈsɪdətɪ; ˌhaipərəˈsiditi〕 *n.* 〖醫〗胃酸過多症。

hy·per·a·cu·sis 〔ˌhaɪpərəˈkjusɪs; ˌhaipərəˈkjuːsis〕 *n.* 〖醫〗聽覺過敏。(亦作 **hyperacousia, hyperacusia**)

hy·per·aes·the·sia 〔ˌhaɪpərɛsˈθiʒə; ˌhaipəresˈθiːʒə〕 *n.* 〖醫〗感覺過敏;知覺過敏。

hy·per·al·ge·si·a 〔ˌhaɪpərælˈdʒizɪə; ˌhaipərælˈdʒiːziə〕 *n.* 〖醫〗痛覺過敏。(亦作 **hyperalgesis, hyperalgia**)

hy·per·bo·la 〔haɪˈpɝbələ; haiˈpəːbələ〕 *n.* 〖數學〗雙曲線。

hy·per·bo·le 〔haɪˈpɝbəˌli; haiˈpəːbəliː〕 *n.* 〖修辭〗誇張法。

hy·per·bol·ic 〔ˌhaɪpɚˈbɑlɪk; ˌhaipəˈbɔlik〕 *adj.* ①誇張的。②雙曲線的。(亦作 **hyperbolical**)

hy·per·bo·re·an 〔ˌhaɪpɚˈborɪən; ˌhaipəˈbɔːriən〕 *adj.* ①極北的。②酷寒的。③(H-)北方淨土之人的。—*n.*①(H-)〖希臘神話〗北方淨土之民。②〖俗〗極北之人;北方人。

hy·per·con·scious 〔ˌhaɪpɚˈkɑnʃəs; ˌhaipəˈkɔnʃəs〕 *adj.* 强烈意識的;知覺過敏的。

hy·per·cor·rect 〔ˌhaɪpɚkəˈrɛkt; ˌhaipəkəˈrekt〕 *adj.* ①過分正確的; 吹毛求疵的。②〖語文〗矯枉過正的。

hy·per·crit·ic 〔ˌhaɪpɚˈkrɪtɪk; ˈhaipəːˈkritik〕 *n.* 嚴酷的批評家。

hy·per·crit·i·cal 〔ˌhaɪpɚˈkrɪtɪkl; ˈhaipəːˈkritikəl〕 *adj.* 酷評的;苛求的;吹毛求疵的。

hy·per·crit·i·cism 〔ˌhaɪpɚˈkrɪtəˌsɪzəm; ˈhaipəˈkritisizəm〕 *n.* 酷評;苛求;吹毛求疵。

hy·per·cy·the·mi·a [ˌhaɪpəsaɪˈθimɪə; ˌhaipəsaiˈθiːmiə] *n.* 〖醫〗紅血球過多。

hy·per·cy·to·sis [ˌhaɪpəsaɪˈtosɪs; ˌhaipəsaiˈtousis] *n.* 白血球過多症。

hy·per·fo·cal distance [ˈhaɪpəˈfokəl～; ˈhaipəˈfoukəl～] 〖攝影〗最近的照像距離。

hy·per·gly·ce·mi·a [ˌhaɪpəglaɪˈsimɪə; ˌhaipəglaiˈsiːmiə] *n.* 〖醫〗多糖血;血糖過多症。(亦作 **hyperglycaemia**)

hy·per·hi·dro·sis [ˌhaɪpəhɪˈdrosɪs; ˌhaipəhiˈdrousis] *n.* 〖生理〗多汗症。(亦作 **hyperidrosis**)

hy·per·ker·a·to·sis [ˌhaɪpəˌkɛrəˈtosɪs; ˌhaipəˌkerəˈtousis] *n.* 〖醫〗角化過度;表皮角化病。

hy·per·leu·co·cy·to·sis [ˌhaɪpəˌlukosaɪˈtosɪs; ˌhaipəˌluːkousaiˈtousis] *n.* 〖醫〗白血球過多症。(亦作 **hyperleukocytosis**)

hy·per·mar·ket [ˈhaɪpəˌmarkɪt; ˈhaipəmɑːkit] *n.* 〖英〗(通常設在郊外的)大規模超級市場。

hy·per·met·ri·cal [ˌhaɪpəˈmɛtrɪkl; ˌhaipəˈmetrikəl] *adj.* 〖詩〗詩行末尾音節過多的。(亦作 **hypermetric**)

hy·per·me·tro·pi·a [ˌhaɪpəmɪˈtropɪə; ˌhaipəmiˈtroupiə] *n.* 〖醫〗遠視。(亦作 **hypermetropy, hyperopia**) —**hy·per·me·trop·ic,** *adj.* [ˈɔpik] *adj.* 遠視的。

hy·per·op·ic [ˌhaɪpəˈɑpɪk; ˌhaipər-]

hy·per·phys·i·cal [ˌhaɪpəˈfɪzɪkl; ˌhaipəˈfizikl] *adj.* 超自然的;超物質的。

hy·per·pi·e·sia [ˌhaɪpəpaɪˈiʒə; ˌhaipəpaiˈiːʒə] *n.* 〖醫〗血壓過高;原發性血壓過高病。

hy·per·pi·et·ic [ˌhaɪpəpaɪˈɛtɪk; ˌhaipəpaiˈetik] *adj.* 〖醫〗血壓過高的;原發性血壓過高的。—*n.* 上述病之病患。

hy·per·sen·si·tive [ˌhaɪpəˈsɛnsətɪv; ˈhaipəˈsensitiv] *adj.* ①過度敏感的。②〖醫〗神經過敏的;過敏症的;過敏性的。—**ness, hy·per·sen·si·tiv·i·ty,** *n.*

hy·per·son·ic [ˌhaɪpəˈsɑnɪk; ˌhaipəˈsɔnik] *adj.* 〖物理〗超音速的(音速之約5倍以上的)。

hy·per·ten·sion [ˈhaɪpəˈtɛnʃən; ˌhaipəˈtenʃən] *n.* ①張力過度;壓力過大。②〖醫〗**a.** 高血壓。**b.** (由於高血壓而致之)過度緊張、頭暈、目眩等。

hy·per·ten·sive [ˌhaɪpəˈtɛnsɪv; ˌhaipəˈtensiv] *adj.* 高血壓的。—*n.* 患高血壓的人。

hy·per·thy·roid [ˌhaɪpəˈθaɪrɔɪd; ˌhaipəˈθairɔid] *adj.* ①甲狀腺(機能)亢進的。②激越的;亢進的。—*n.* ①機能亢進的甲狀腺。②機能亢進甲狀腺患者。

hy·per·thy·roid·ism [ˌhaɪpəˈθaɪrɔɪdˌɪzəm; ˌhaipəˈθairɔidizəm] *n.* 〖醫〗甲狀腺(機能)亢進;其病徵。

hy·per·tro·phy [haɪˈpɜtrəfɪ; haiˈpəːtrəfi] *n., pl.* **-phies,** *v.,* **-phied, -phy·ing.** —*n.* 〖醫,植物〗肥大;肥腫。—*v.t.* & *v.i.* (使)肥大。

hy·pe·thral [hɪˈpiθrəl; hiˈpiːθrəl] *adj.* (古典建築)全部或部分露天的。(亦作 **hypaethral**)

***hy·phen** [ˈhaɪfən; ˈhaifən] *n.* 連字號(-)。—*v.t.* 以連字號(-)連接。〖文法〗 **hyphen**的用途大別有三:⑴連接一複合字(compound word)的各部分,如: four-footed 四足的。⑵表示一單字中音節的畫分法。⑶於抄寫或印刷文字一行之末尾,表示該單字之一部被移至次一行。〖注意〗關於複合字中連號的使用,美國式寫法,避用連字號,英國式法,喜用連字號。玆以 gas 合成的複合字爲例:

〖美〗	〖英〗
gas burner	gas-burner
gas engine	gas-engine

hy·phen·ate [ˈhaɪfənˌet; ˈhaifənei… *v.,* **-at·ed, -at·ing,** *n., adj.* —*v.t.* 以 hyphe… 連接。 —*n.* 歸化的美國公民。 —*adj.* hyphen 連接的。—**hy·phen·a·tion,** *n.*

hy·phen·at·ed [ˈhaɪfənˌetɪd; ˈha… fəneitid] *adj.* ①以短橫連接的。②〖譏〗關… 歸化之美國人的。「化之美國人。

hyphenated American 〖美〗歸…

hy·phen·ism [ˈhaɪfənɪzəm; ˈhaifən… izəm] *n.* 歸化爲美國者之精神或作風。

hyp·na·gog·ic [ˌhɪpnəˈgɑdʒɪk; ˌhip… nəˈgɔdʒik] *adj.* ①催眠的。②〖心理〗睡眠… 發生的。 [ˈgɔg] *n.* 催眠劑。

hyp·na·gogue [ˈhɪpnəˈgɑg; ˈhipnə-

hyp·no·gen·e·sis [ˌhɪpnoˈdʒɛnəsɪs; ˌhipnouˈdʒenəsis] *n.* 催眠。—**hyp·no·ge·net·ic,** *adj.* [ˈnɔlədʒi] *n.* 催眠學。

hyp·nol·o·gy [hɪpˈnɑlədʒɪ; hip-

hyp·no·sis [hɪpˈnosɪs; hipˈnousis] *n.* *pl.* **-no·ses** [-ˈnosiz; -ˈnousiːz]. ①催眠狀態。②催眠術。

hyp·no·ther·a·py [ˌhɪpnoˈθɛrəpɪ; ˌhipnouˈθerəpi] *n.* 催眠療法。

hyp·not·ic [hɪpˈnɑtɪk; hipˈnɔtik] *adj.* ①催眠的;催眠術的。②易於催眠的。③使睡眠的。—*n.* ①被催眠之人;易受催眠之人。②催眠藥;催眠術。—**al·ly,** *adv.*

hyp·no·tism [ˈhɪpnəˌtɪzəm; ˈhipnətizəm] *n.* ①催眠術。②催眠。③催眠狀態。

hyp·no·tist [ˈhɪpnətɪst; ˈhipnətist] *n.* 施催眠術者。

hyp·no·tize [ˈhɪpnəˌtaɪz; ˈhipnətaiz] *v.t.,* **-tized, -tiz·ing.** ①施催眠術。②〖俗〗使着迷;使恍惚。(亦作 **hypnotise**)

hy·po[1] [ˈhaɪpo; ˈhaipou] *n.* 〖化〗低亞硫酸鈉 (sodium hyposulphite 之簡稱,洗相片時作定影之用)。

hy·po[2] *n.* ①〖俗〗皮下注射;皮下注射藥。②〖俚〗憂鬱症;憂鬱症患者。③〖俚〗刺激。

hypo- 〖字首〗表下列諸義:①在下,如: hypodermic 皮下的。②低於(指程度);次於。③〖化〗次(如: hypophosphite 次磷酸鹽)

hy·po·ba·rop·a·thy [ˌhaɪpobəˈrɑpəθɪ; ˌhaipoubəˈrɔpəθi] *n.* 〖醫〗低氣壓病。

hy·po·blast [ˈhaɪpəˌblæst; ˈhaipəblæst] *n.* 內胚層;內胚葉;下胚葉。

hy·po·caust [ˈhɪpəˌkɔst; ˈhipəkɔːst] *n.* (古羅馬)熱氣炕。

hy·po·chlo·rite [ˌhaɪpəˈklɔraɪt; ˌhaipəˈklɔːrait] *n.* 〖化〗次氯酸鹽。

hy·po·chlo·rous acid [ˌhaɪpəˈklorəs～; ˌhaipəˈklourəs～] 〖化〗次氯酸。

hy·po·chon·dri·a [ˌhaɪpəˈkɑndrɪə; ˌhaipouˈkɔndriə] *n.* 〖精神病〗憂鬱症;臆想病。(亦作 **hypochondriasis**)

hy·po·chon·dri·ac [ˌhaɪpəˈkɑndrɪˌæk; ˌhaipouˈkɔndriæk] *adj.* (亦作 **hypochondriacal**)患憂鬱症的。—*n.* 憂鬱症患者。

hy·poc·o·rism [haɪˈpɑkərɪzm; haiˈpɔkərizəm] *n.* ①暱稱。②使用暱稱。③嬰兒語之模仿。

hy·po·co·ris·tic [ˌhɪpəkəˈrɪstɪk;

ˌhipəkəˈristik] *adj.* 表示親愛的；暱稱的。—*n.* 暱稱。

hy·po·cot·yl [ˌhaɪpəˈkɑtḷ; ˌhaipəˈkɔtil] *n.* 〖植物〗胚軸。

hy·poc·ri·sy [hɪˈpɑkrəsɪ; hiˈpɔkrəsi] *n., pl.* **-sies.** 僞善；矯飾。

hyp·o·crite [ˈhɪpəˌkrɪt; ˈhipəkrit, -puk-] *n.* 僞君子。to play the *hypocrite*. 作僞君子。

hyp·o·crit·i·cal [ˌhɪpəˈkrɪtɪkḷ; ˌhipəˈkritikəl] *adj.* 僞善的；矯飾的。—**ly,** *adv.*

hy·po·derm [ˈhaɪpəˌdɝm; ˈhaipədəːm] *n.* 〖動物〗皮下結締組織；皮下。—**al,** *adj.*

hy·po·der·mic [ˌhaɪpəˈdɝmɪk; ˌhaipəˈdəːmik] *adj.* ①皮下注射的。a *hypodermic* injection. 皮下注射。②皮下的。—*n.* ①皮下注射器。②皮下注射藥。—**al·ly,** *adv.*

hy·po·der·mis [ˌhaɪpəˈdɝmɪs; ˌhaipəˈdəːmis] *n.* 〖動物〗下皮。

hy·po·func·tion [ˌhaɪpoˈfʌŋkʃən; ˌhaipouˈfʌŋkʃən] *n.* 機能減退；官能不足。

hy·po·gas·tric [ˌhaɪpəˈgæstrɪk; ˌhaipəˈgæstrik] *adj.* 〖解剖〗胃下的；下腹部的。

hyp·o·gene [ˈhɪpəˌdʒin; ˈhipədʒiːn] *adj.* 地面下形成的。

hy·po·gen·e·sis [ˌhaɪpəˈdʒɛnəsɪs; ˌhaipəˈdʒenisis] *n.* 〖醫〗發育不全。

hy·po·ge·ous [ˌhaɪpəˈdʒiəs; ˌhaipəˈdʒiːəs] *adj.* ①地下的。②〖植物〗長在或留在地下的。

hyp·o·ge·um [ˌhɪpəˈdʒiəm; ˌhipəˈdʒiːəm] *n.* 地下室；地窖。

hy·po·gly·ce·mi·a [ˌhaɪpoglaɪˈsimɪə; ˌhaipouglaiˈsiːmiə] *n.* 〖醫〗低糖血；血糖缺乏。(亦作 **hypoglycaemia**)

hy·po·lith·ic [ˌhaɪpəˈlɪθɪk; ˌhaipəˈliθik] *adj.* (植物之)長在岩石下的。

hy·pom·ne·sia [ˌhaɪpəmˈniʒə; ˌhaipəmˈniːʒə] *n.* 〖醫〗記憶力減退。(亦作 **hypomnesis**)

hy·po·phos·phate [ˌhaɪpəˈfɑsfet; ˌhaipouˈfɔsfeit] *n.* 〖化〗次磷酸鹽或酯。

hy·po·phos·phite [ˌhaɪpəˈfɑsfaɪt; ˌhaipəˈfɔsfait] *n.* 〖化〗次磷酸鹽。

hy·po·phos·phor·ous acid [ˌhaɪpəˈfɑsfərəs~; ˌhaipəˈfɔsfərəs~] 次磷酸。

hy·poph·y·sis [haɪˈpɑfəsɪs; haiˈpɔfəsis] *n., pl.* **-ses** [-ˌsiz; -siːz]. 〖解剖〗腦下垂體。

hy·po·pla·sia [ˌhaɪpəˈpleʒə; ˌhaipəˈpleiʒə] *n.* 〖醫,植物〗發育不全。(亦作 **hypoplasty**)

hy·po·sen·si·tize [ˌhaɪpəˈsɛnsəˌtaɪz; ˌhaipəˈsensitaiz] *v.t.,* **-tized, -tiz·ing.** 使(某人)不對某些藥物過敏。

hy·po·spray [ˈhaɪpoˌspre; ˈhaipousprei] *n.* 無針注射器。

hy·pos·ta·sis [haɪˈpɑstəsɪs; haiˈpɔstəsis] *n., pl.* **-ses** [-ˌsiz; -siːz]. ①〖哲學〗基礎；本質；實在。②〖神學〗三位一體之一。③〖醫〗**a.** 血液下沉症；墜積性充血。**b.** 沉渣；沉澱。

hy·po·stat·ic [ˌhaɪpəˈstætɪk; ˌhaipəˈstætik] *adj.* ①〖哲學〗本質的；實在的。②〖神學〗位格的。*hypostatic* union. 基督之位格的結合(神人合一)。③〖醫〗血液下沉的；墜積性的。④〖生物〗(遺傳因子)劣性的；弱性的。(亦作 **hypostatical**)

hy·pos·ta·tize [haɪˈpɑstəˌtaɪz; haiˈpɔstətaiz] *v.t.,* **-tized, -tiz·ing.** 使具體化；視爲實體；視爲實在。

hy·po·style [ˈhɪpəˌstaɪl; ˈhaipoustail] *adj.* 〖建築〗多柱式的。—*n.* 多柱式建築。

hy·po·sul·fite, hy·po·sul·phite [ˌhaɪpəˈsʌlfaɪt; ˌhaipouˈsʌlfait] *n.* 〖化〗①次亞硫酸鹽。②硫代硫酸鈉；大蘇打。

hy·po·sul·fur·ous [ˌhaɪpəˈsʌlfərəs; ˌhaipəsʌlˈfjurəs] *adj.* 〖化〗低亞硫酸的。(亦作 **hyposulphurous**)

hyposulfurous acid 〖化〗低亞硫酸。

hy·po·tax·is [ˌhaɪpəˈtæksɪs; ˌhaipouˈtæksis] *n.* 〖文法〗附屬關係；附屬結構(如附屬子句等)。—**hy·po·tac·tic,** *adj.*

hy·po·ten·sion [ˌhaɪpəˈtɛnʃən; ˌhaipəˈtenʃən] *n.* 〖醫〗低壓；低血壓。

hy·po·ten·sive [ˌhaɪpoˈtɛnsɪv; ˌhaipouˈtensiv] *adj.* 〖醫〗低血壓的；引起低血壓的。—*n.* ①低血壓病患。②低血壓劑。

hy·pot·e·nuse [haɪˈpɑtṇˌjus; haiˈpɔtinjuːz] *n.* 〖數學〗(直角三角形之)斜邊。

hy·po·thal·a·mus [ˌhaɪpəˈθæləməs; ˌhaipəˈθæləməs] *n., pl.* **-mi** [-maɪ; -mai]. 〖解剖〗視丘下部。

hy·poth·ec [haɪˈpɑθɛk; haiˈpɔθek] *n.* 〖法律〗抵押權；擔保權。

hy·poth·e·car·y [haɪˈpɑθəˌkɛrɪ; haiˈpɔθəkeri] *adj.* ①抵押權的。②以抵押取得的。

hy·poth·e·cate [haɪˈpɑθəˌket; haiˈpɔθikeit] *v.t.,* **-cat·ed, -cat·ing.** 抵押。—**hy·poth·e·ca·tion,** *n.*

hy·poth·e·nuse [haɪˈpɑθəˌnus; haiˈpɔθənuːs] *n.* =**hypotenuse.**

hy·po·ther·mi·a [ˌhaɪpəˈθɝmɪə; ˌhaipəˈθəːmiə] *n.* 〖醫〗體溫過低。

hy·poth·e·sis [haɪˈpɑθəsɪs; haiˈpɔθisis] *n., pl.* **-ses** [-ˌsiz; -siːz]. (科學上的)假設；學說。

hy·poth·e·size [haɪˈpɑθəˌsaɪz; haiˈpɔθisaiz] *v.,* **-sized, -siz·ing.** —*v.i.* 假設。—*v.t.* 作爲假設。

hy·po·thet·ic [ˌhaɪpəˈθɛtɪk; ˌhaipouˈθetik] *adj.* ①假說的；假定的。②好作臆測的。(亦作 **hypothetical**)

hy·po·thet·i·cal·ly [ˌhaɪpəˈθɛtɪkḷɪ; ˌhaipouˈθetikəli] *adv.* 假想地；假定地。

hy·po·thy·roid·ism [ˌhaɪpəˈθaɪrɔɪdˌɪzəm; ˌhaipəˈθairɔidizəm] *n.* 〖醫〗甲狀腺機能減退。

hy·po·ty·po·sis [ˌhaɪpətaɪˈposɪs; ˌhaipətaiˈpousis] *n.* 〖修辭〗生動的描述。

hyp·sog·ra·phy [hɪpˈsɑgrəfɪ; hipˈsɔgrəfi] *n.* 測高學；測高法。

hyp·som·e·ter [hɪpˈsɑmɪtɚ; hipˈsɔmitə] *n.* 測高計。

hyp·som·e·try [hɪpˈsɑmətrɪ; hipˈsɔmitri] *n.* 測高法。

hy·rax [ˈhaɪræks; ˈhaiəræks] *n., pl.* **-es, -ra·ces** [-rəˌsiz; -rəsiːz]. 〖動物〗蹄兔。

hy·son [ˈhaɪsṇ; ˈhaisn] *n.* 熙春茶(綠茶之一種)。

hy-spy [ˈhaɪˌspaɪ; ˈhaispai] *n.* 一種捉迷藏遊戲。(亦作 **I spy**)

hys·sop [ˈhɪsəp; ˈhisəp] *n.* ①〖植物〗牛膝草。②〖聖經〗祓禊木。

hys·ter·ec·to·my [ˌhɪstəˈrɛktəmɪ; ˌhistəˈrektəmi] *n., pl.* **-mies.** 〖外科〗子宮切除(術)。

hys·ter·e·sis [ˌhɪstəˈrisɪs; ˌhistəˈriːsis] *n.* 〖物理〗滯後現象；滯後作用。

hys·te·ri·a [hɪsˈtɪrɪə; hisˈtiəriə] *n.* ①歇斯的里症；癔病。②無理由的過度興奮。

hys·ter·ic [hɪsˈtɛrɪk; hisˈterik] *adj.*

=hysterical. —*n.* ①(常 *pl.*)歇斯的里之發作。to go off (*or* into) *hysterics*. 發歇斯的里。②發狂。③易發歇斯的里之人。

*__hys·ter·i·cal__ 〔hɪsˈtɛrɪkl; hisˈterikəl〕 *adj.* ①患歇斯的里症的;(情緒)過度狂烈的;不可抑制的。②非常可笑的。Oh, that joke is *hysterical*. 啊! 那個笑話眞令人捧腹。(亦作 **hysteric**) —**ly,** *adv.*

hys·ter·ics 〔hɪsˈtɛrɪks; hisˈteriks〕 *n. pl.* (作 *sing.* or *pl.* 解)歇斯的里症的發作;發狂。

hys·ter·i·tis 〔ˌhɪstəˈraɪtɪs; ˌhistəˈraitis〕 *n.* 〖醫〗子宮炎。(亦作 **metritis**)

hys·ter·ol·o·gy 〔ˌhɪstəˈrɑlədʒɪ; ˌhistəˈrɔlədʒi〕 *n.* 〖醫〗子宮學。

hys·ter·on prot·er·on 〔ˈhɪstəˌrɑnˈprɑtəˌrɑn; ˈhistərɔnˈprɔtərɔn〕〖希〗①〖修辭〗倒置法;逆序法(如 I die, I faint, I fail)。②〖邏輯〗倒逆論法。

hys·ter·ot·o·my 〔ˌhɪstəˈrɑtəmɪ; ˌhistəˈrɔtəmi〕 *n., pl.* **-mies.** 〖外科〗子宮切開(術)。

I

I or **i** 〔aɪ; ai〕 *n., pl.* **I's** or **Is, i's** or **is** 〔aɪz; aiz〕. ①英文字母之第九個字母。②羅馬數字的 1 (如III=3; IX=9)。

‡**I** *pron., pl.* **we.** 我(第一人稱,單數,主格)。*I*'m coming. 我來了。It is *I*. 是我(僅見於寫作中,口語則用 It's me)。

I 化學元素 iodine 之符號。

I. ①Idaho. ②Island. ③Islands. ④Isle. ⑤Isles. ⑥Israel. ⑦Israeli. **i.** ①interest. ②intransitive. ③island. **Ia.** Iowa. **I.A.A.F.** International Amateur Athletic Federation. **IAEA** International Atomic Energy Agency.

-ial 〖字尾〗=**-al** (形容詞及名詞字尾)。

i·amb 〔ˈaɪæmb; ˈaiæmb〕 *n.* =**iambus.**

i·am·bic 〔aɪˈæmbɪk; aiˈæmbik〕 *n.* ①(詩律之)抑揚格。②(常*pl.*)抑揚格詩。③抑揚格詩之一行。—*adj.* 抑揚格的;用抑揚格寫的。

i·am·bus 〔aɪˈæmbəs; aiˈæmbəs〕 *n., pl.* **-bi** 〔-baɪ; -bai〕,**-bus·es.** 〖韻律〗短長格;抑揚格。

-ian 〖字尾〗=**-an** (名詞及形容詞字尾)。

iar·o·vize 〔ˈjɑrəˌvaɪz; ˈjɑːrəvaiz〕 *v.t.*, **-vized, -viz·ing.** (用人工方法)使(植物)提早開花結實。(亦作 **jarovize**)

IARU International Amateur Radio Union. **IATA, I.A.T.A.** International Air Transport Association.

ib. ibidem. **IBC** International Boxing Club. **I.B.E, IBE** International Bureau of Education. 國際教育局。

I·be·ri·a 〔aɪˈbɪrɪə; aiˈbiəriə〕 *n.* ①伊比利半島(包括西班牙及葡萄牙兩國之一大半島)。②伊比利(高加索山脈南方古代之一地區,卽今蘇聯之 Georgia)。

I·be·ri·an 〔aɪˈbɪrɪən; aiˈbiəriən〕 *adj.* ①伊比利(半島)的。②伊比利人的。—*n.*①古伊比利人。②古伊比利語。

Iberian Peninsula 伊比利半島(在歐洲西南部,卽西、葡二國所在地)。

i·bex 〔ˈaɪbɛks; ˈaibeks〕 *n., pl.* **i·bex·es, ib·i·ces** 〔ˈɪbɪˌsiz; ˈibisiːz〕. 有大角之野生山羊。

ibid. ibidem.

i·bi·dem 〔ɪˈbaɪdɛm; iˈbaidem〕〖拉〗*adv.* 在(前面所引用之)同一書(章、頁、處)中;同上;同前。(略作 **ib.** 或 **ibid.**)

i·bis 〔ˈaɪbɪs; ˈaibis〕 *n., pl.* **i·bis·es, i·bis.** 朱鷺。***the sacred ibis*** 古埃及之靈鳥。

-ible 〖字尾〗**-able** 之異體,如: edible.

IBM, I.B.M. ①intercontinental ballistic missile. ②International Business Machines.

I·bo 〔ˈibo; ˈiːbou〕 *n., pl.* **I·bos, I·bo.** ①伊波族(非洲一黑人種族)。②此族人之語言。(亦作 **Igbo**)

IBRD International Bank for Reconstruction and Development. 國際復興開發銀行,又稱世界銀行。

Ib·sen 〔ˈɪbsn; ˈibsn〕 *n.* 易卜生(Henrik, 1828–1906,挪威之劇作家及詩人)。—**ism,** *n.*

-ic 〖字尾〗①表"…的;似…的;關於…的;屬於…的"之義之形容詞字尾。②〖化〗表較 -ous 多原子價之形容詞字尾,如: ferric. ③-ic 之形容詞字尾之名詞轉用,如: public.

I.C. 〖拉〗 Iesus Christus (=Jesus Christ). **i.c.**〖處方〗在兩餐之間(=between meals). **ICA** 國際合作總署 (=International Cooperation Administration).

-ical 〖字尾〗①表"…的;似…的; 關於…的"之義, 並自 -ic 字尾之名詞造成形容詞, 如: musical. ②自-ic 之形容詞造成另一形容詞, 如: comical.

ICAO International Civil Aviation Organization.

I·car·i·an 〔ɪˈkɛrɪən; aiˈkɛəriən〕 *adj.* (似) Icarus 的;膽大妄爲的;雄心過大的。

I·ca·rus 〔ˈɪkərəs; ˈaikərəs〕 *n.* 〖希臘神話〗伊卡爾斯 (Daedalus 之子,以用蠟與羽毛造成之翼逃出 Crete 島, 因過分接近太陽,其翼卒爲所融,墮海而死)。

ICBM, I.C.B.M. intercontinental ballistic missile. **I.C.C., ICC** ①International Control Commission. ②Interstate Commerce Commission.

‡**ice** 〔aɪs; ais〕 *n., v.,* **iced, ic·ing,** *adj.* —*n.* ①冰。Is the *ice* thick enough for skating? 這冰厚得可以在上面溜冰嗎? ②冰糕(用果汁加糖製的, 似冰淇淋而無牛奶等)。③糖與蛋白混製的覆於糕點上的一層糖霜 (=icing)。④冰水或果汁等做成冰屑加以糖及香料之食物。⑤矜持。⑥〖俚〗金鋼鑽。⑦〖俚〗非法營利機構主持人付給警察的保護費。⑧〖俚〗戲票黃牛付給戲院經理的賄賂。***break the ice*** **a.** 破除矜持;開始(融洽)。**b.** 着手做(應小心的事情)。 ***cut no ice*** 無甚價値; 無影響; 嚇不倒。 His father's position *cuts no ice* with me. 他父親的地位在我看來沒有甚麼了不起。 ***on ice*** **a.** 〖俚〗成功或實現的機會很大。 The contract is *on ice*. 契約簽訂的希望很大。 **b.** 在拘禁中; 無活動。**c.** 擱置; 暫緩。 Let's put that topic *on ice* for the moment. 我們暫且不要討論這個問題。 ***on thin ice*** 在危險或困難的境況中。—*v.t.* ①冰凍; 冷藏。*iced* water. 冰水。②使結冰。The pond was *iced* over. 池水結冰了。③加糖衣於(糕點)上。—*v.i.* ①結冰。The fish is *icing* in the refrigerator. 魚在冰箱中結冰。②被冰覆蓋〖常 up〗。—*adj.* 冰的。

Ice. ①Iceland. ②Icelandic.

ice age 〖地質〗冰河時代。

ice ax(e) (登山用)碎冰斧。

ce bag (or **pack**) 冰袋(消腫或減痛用)。
ce belt 沿破冰船之吃水線裝的厚甲。
ce·berg ['aɪs,bɝg; 'aisbəːg] *n.* ①冰山。②〖俗〗冷峻的人。***the tip of the iceberg*** 表面的東西;某事物的一小部分。
ce·blink ['aɪs,blɪŋk; 'aisbliŋk] *n.* 冰映光(因冰原之反映而出現於地平線者)。(亦作 **blink**)
ce·boat ['aɪs,bot; 'aisbout] *n.* ①冰上滑行的船。②破冰船。
ce·boat·ing ['aɪs,botɪŋ; 'ais,boutiŋ] *n.* 駕駛 iceboat 之運動。
ce·bound ['aɪs,baund; 'aisbaund] *adj.* ①冰封的(海港、河流等)。②凍結於冰中而不能行駛的(船等)。
ce·box ['aɪs,bɑks; 'aisbɔks] *n.* ①〖美〗冰箱。②〖俚〗監獄內之單人囚房。
ce·break·er ['aɪs,brekɚ; 'ais,breikə] *n.* ①破冰船。②碎冰堆;碎冰機。
ce·cap ['aɪs,kæp; 'ais-kæp] *n.* ①(高山等上之)常積不消之冰。②冰枕。
ce-cold ['aɪs'kold; 'ais'kould] *adj.* ①冰冷的。②冷若冰霜的;無感情的。
ce cream 冰淇淋。
ce-cream ['aɪs'krim; 'ais'kriːm] *adj.* 冰淇淋的。
ce-cream cone ①盛冰淇淋之圓錐形筒(可食)。②冰淇淋捲。
ce-cream soda 冰淇淋蘇打。
ce cube 小冰塊(如冰箱中所做的)。
ced [aɪst; aist] *adj.* ①覆以冰的;含冰的;冰凍的。②覆有糖霜的。
ce·fall ['aɪs,fɔl; 'aisfɔːl] *n.* ①冰崩。②冰瀑。③懸在崖上之冰塊。
ce field 冰原(漂浮於海面之大塊冰層)。
ce fishing 冰上挖洞釣魚。
ce floe (海上之)浮冰。
ce fog 冰霧。(亦作 **frozen fog, pogonip**)
ce foot 寒帶地區海岸之冰牆。
ce-free ['aɪs'fri; 'ais'friː] *adj.* ①不冰凍的;無冰封的。②無冰的。
ce hockey 冰球戲。
ce·house ['aɪs,haus; 'aishaus] *n.* ①冰庫。②(愛斯基摩人之)冰屋。③製冰廠。
Ice·land ['aɪslənd; 'aislənd] *n.* 冰島(北大西洋中之一共和國,首都雷克雅未克 Reykjavik)。
Ice·land·er ['aɪs,lændɚ; 'aisləndə] *n.* 冰島人。
Ice·lan·dic [aɪs'lændɪk; ais'lændik] *adj.* 冰島的。—*n.* 冰島語。
Iceland spar 冰洲石(方解石之一種)。
ce-lol·ly ['aɪs,lɑlɪ; 'ais,lɔli] *n., pl.* **-lies.** 〖英〗冰棒。
ce machine 製冰機。
ce·man ['aɪs,mæn; 'aismæn] *n., pl.* **-men.** ①〖美〗送冰人;售冰人。②善於在冰上行動者。③溜冰場上之冰地管理員。
ce pack ①(海中的)浮冰羣。②(醫療用)冰袋。
ce pick (碎冰用之)冰鋤。
ce pitcher 冰水壺。
ce plant 製冰廠。
ce point 冰點。
ce run 春天或初夏時河冰之迅速解凍。
ce sheet (長久覆蓋於陸地的)大冰原。
ce show 溜冰表演。
ce-skate ['aɪs,sket; 'aisskeit] *v.i.,* **-skat·ed, -skat·ing.** 溜冰;滑冰。—**ice-skat·ing,** *n.*
ce skate ①(附於鞋上溜冰用的)冰刀。②溜冰鞋。
ce storm 〖氣象〗冰暴。
ce tongs 夾冰塊之鉗子。
ice tray 冰箱中結冰塊用的金屬盤。
ice water ①(經冰凍冷的)冰水。②(由冰融解而成的)冰水。
I.C.F.T.U. International Confederation of Free Trade Unions.
I Ching ['i'dʒɪŋ; 'iː'dʒiŋ] 〖中〗*n.* 易經。(亦作 **Book of Changes**)
ich·neu·mon [ɪk'njumən; ik'njuːmən] *n.* ①貓鼬(產於非洲,食鱷卵)。②姬蜂。
ich·no·graph ['ɪknə,græf; 'iknəgrɑːf] *n.* 〖製圖〗平面圖。
ich·nog·ra·phy [ɪk'nɑgrəfɪ; ik'nɔgrəfi] *n.* 〖製圖〗平面圖法。
i·chor ['aɪkɔr; 'aikɔː] *n.* ①〖希臘、羅馬神話〗流動於諸神血管中之靈液。②〖醫〗膿水;敗液。
ichthyo- 〖字首〗表"魚"之義(母音前作 **ichthy-**)。
ich·thy·oid ['ɪkθɪ,ɔɪd; 'ikθiɔid] *adj.* (亦作 **ichthyoidal**)魚形的;魚狀的;似魚的。—*n.* 〖古動物〗任何似魚的脊椎動物。
ich·thy·ol ['ɪkθɪ,ol; 'ikθioul] *n.* 〖藥〗魚油精;魚石脂(皮膚病外用藥)。
ich·thy·ol·o·gy [,ɪkθɪ'ɑlədʒɪ; ,ikθi'ɔlədʒi] *n.* 魚類學。—**ich·thy·ol·o·gist,** *n.*
ich·thy·oph·a·gous [,ɪkθɪ'ɑfəgəs; ,ikθi'ɔfəgəs] *adj.* 食魚的;以魚爲食的。
ich·thy·o·saur ['ɪkθɪə,sɔr; 'ikθiəsɔː] *n.* 〖古生物〗魚龍(一種魚形爬蟲類動物)。
ich·thy·o·sau·rus [,ɪkθɪə'sɔrəs; ,ikθiə'sɔːrəs] *n., pl.* **-sau·ri** [-'sɔraɪ; -'sɔːrai], **-sau·rus·es.** =**ichthyosaur.**
ich·thy·o·sis [,ɪkθɪ'osɪs; ,ikθi'ousis] *n.* 〖醫〗魚鱗癬。
-ician 〖字尾〗表"精於或從事某學術之人"之義,如: mathematician, musician, politician.
i·ci·cle ['aɪsɪkl; 'aisikl] *n.* (垂於屋簷等處的)冰柱;垂冰。
i·ci·ly ['aɪslɪ; 'aisili] *adv.* 如冰地;冰冷地。
i·ci·ness ['aɪsɪnɪs; 'aisinis] *n.* 冰冷;冷淡;冷酷。
ic·ing ['aɪsɪŋ; 'aisiŋ] *n.* ①覆於糕點上的一層糖衣。②〖氣象〗結冰;積冰。
ICJ International Court of Justice.
ick·y ['ɪkɪ; 'iki] *adj.,* **ick·i·er, ick·i·est.** 〖俚〗①討厭的(尤指因太嗲或多愁善感而言)。②樸素的;老實的;保守的。③黏的。
i·con ['aɪkɑn; 'aikɔn] *n., pl.* **i·cons, i·co·nes.** ①(希臘教會所崇拜的)聖像。②畫像;偶像。③〖邏輯〗表示相似或相同之符號。(亦作 **ikon, eikon**) —**ic,** *adj.*
i·con·o·clasm [aɪ'kɑnə,klæzəm; ai'kɔnəklæzəm] *n.* 聖(畫)像破壞;偶像破壞;迷信之破除。
i·con·o·clast [aɪ'kɑnə,klæst; ai'kɔnəklæst] *n.* ①反對崇拜偶像者。②破除傳統或迷信者。
i·con·o·clas·tic [aɪ,kɑnə'klæstɪk; ai,kɔnə'klæstik] *adj.* 破壞偶像的;破除迷信的。
i·co·nog·ra·phy [,aɪkən'ɑgrəfɪ; ,aikɔ'nɔgrəfi] *n.* ①圖像學;肖像研究(尤指對某一人畫像的研究)。②圖像畫法。
i·co·nol·a·try [,aɪkə'nɑlətrɪ; ,aikə'nɔlətri] *n.* 偶像崇拜。—**i·co·nol·a·ter,** *n.*
i·co·nom·a·chy [,aɪkə'nɑməkɪ; ,aikə'nɔməki] *n.* 對偶像之敵視。
i·con·o·phile [aɪ'kɑnəfaɪl; ai'kɔnəfail] *n.* 圖畫、雕刻等之愛好者或鑑賞家。
i·con·o·scope [aɪ'kɑnə,skop; ai'kɔnəskoup] *n.* 〖電視〗映像管。
i·co·sa·he·dron [,aɪkosə'hidrən;

ˌaikəsəˈhedrən〕 *n.*, *pl.*-**drons,-dra**〔-drə; -drə〕.【幾何】二十面體。

ICRC International Committee of the Red Cross.

-ics【字尾】造成"…學; …術"之義之名詞。【注意】**-ics** 作學術、科學之名稱時作單數解, 如: Mathematics *deals* with number. 指具體的活動現象時常作複數解, 如:His mathematics *are* weak. 若干可作單數或複數解者如: Politics *is* (*are*) fascinating.

ic·ter·ic〔ɪkˈtɛrɪk; ikˈterik〕*adj.*(亦作 **icterical**)【醫】①(患)黃疸的。②醫治黃疸用的。—*n.* 黃疸之藥。

ic·ter·us〔ˈɪktərəs; ˈiktərəs〕*n.*【醫】「黃疸。」

ic·tus〔ˈɪktəs; ˈiktəs〕*n.*, *pl.* **-tus·es, -tus.** ①【韻律】强音; 揚音。②【醫】搏動; 發作。*ictus* solis. 日射病; 中暑。*ictus* sanguinis. 中風。*ictus* cordis. 心的搏跳。

***i·cy**〔ˈaɪsɪ; ˈaisi〕*adj.*, **i·ci·er, i·ci·est.** ①似冰的; 極冷的; 滑溜的。*icy* cold. 冰冷。②多冰的; 覆蓋着冰的。③冰的。④冷淡的; 不熱烈的。an *icy* welcome. 冷淡的歡迎。

id[1]〔ɪd; id〕*n.*【生物】遺傳基質(細胞原形質之單位)。

id[2] *n.*【精神分析】(the-) 本能衝動(人類精神之潛在部分, 係 libido 積貯之所, 及本能活動力之源泉)。

I'd〔aɪd; aid〕I should, I would, 或 I 「had 之縮寫。」

Id. Idaho. **id.**【拉】idem (=the same).

I.D. ①identification. ②identity. ③Industrial Division. ④Infantry Division. ⑤Intelligence Department. **i.d.** inside diameter. **IDA** International Development Association. **Ida.** Idaho.

I·da·ho〔ˈaɪdəˌho; ˈaidəhou〕*n.* 愛達荷(美國西北部之一州, 其首府爲 Boise). —**an**, *n.*, *adj.*

I.D. card identity card. (亦作 ID 「card)」

-ide【字尾】名詞字尾, 用於化合物之名稱中, 如: carbide, chloride.

‡i·de·a〔aɪˈdiə, -ˈdɪə; aiˈdiə〕*n.* ①主意; 意見; 辦法; 計策。That's a good *idea*. 那是個好辦法。②感覺; 印像。I have an *idea* that he will come today. 我認爲他今天會來。③思想; 概念。④計畫; 企圖。the *idea* of becoming an engineer. 想當工程師的計畫。⑤幻想。***force one's ideas on somebody*** 勉强某人接受自己的意見。***form an idea of something*** 對於某事構成一種概念。***get ideas into one's head*** 存幻想; 抱空想; 希望獲得不能得到之物。***the young idea*** 小孩的想法。—**less**, *adj.*【注意】**idea** 後面如用動詞, 應作: *idea* of+gerund. 如: They got the happy *idea* of *climbing* the hill. 他們想到爬山的好主意。不作: They got the happy *idea to climb* the hill.

i·de·a·is·tic〔aɪˌdɪəˈɪstɪk; aiˌdiəˈistik〕*adj.* 觀念的(尤指其抽象或象徵性的)。

***i·de·al**〔aɪˈdiəl, aɪˈdil, aɪˈdɪəl; aiˈdiəl, -ˈdiːəl, -ˈdiːl〕*n.* ①理想。to realize one's *ideal*. 實現某人的理想。②理想的事物或人。③無法實現之理想。④最後目標(尤指高尙的目標)。—*adj.* ①理想的; 完美的。It was an *ideal* day for a picnic. 那是出外野餐的理想的日子。②空想的; 想像中的。

i·de·al·ism〔aɪˈdiəlˌɪzəm; aiˈdiəlizəm〕*n.* ①唯心論; 理想主義。②合於個人理想的生活態度。③文藝上注重想像的一種創作, 常表現出與事實不符的美妙境界。

i·de·al·ist〔aɪˈdɪəlɪst; aiˈdiəlist〕*n.* 理想主義者; 追求理想而不顧實際的人。

i·de·al·is·tic〔ˌaɪdiəlˈɪstɪk; aiˌdiəˈlistik〕*adj.* 高尙理想的; 理想主義的; 不切實際的。(亦作 **idealistical**)

i·de·al·is·ti·cal·ly〔ˌaɪdiəlˈɪstɪklɪ, ˌaidiəˈlistikli〕*adv.* 理想上; 不切實際地。

i·de·al·i·ty〔ˌaɪdɪˈælətɪ; ˌaidiˈæliti〕*n.*, *pl.* **-ties.** ①觀念性。②理想的事物。③理想力; 想像力。

i·de·al·i·za·tion〔aɪˌdiələˈzeʃən; aɪˌdiəlaiˈzeiʃən〕*n.* 理想化; 理想化之事物。

i·de·al·ize〔aɪˈdiəlˌaɪz; aiˈdiəlaiz〕*v.t.* **-ized, -iz·ing.** 將…理想化。—*v.i.* 理想化; 形成理想。

i·de·al·ly〔aɪˈdiəlɪ; aiˈdiəli〕*adv.* ①按照理想地; 完美地。②在觀念上; 在理論上。

idea man (在商業機構中)提供新構想、新花樣的人。

idea of reference【精神病】以爲他人的言行均針對自己而發之疑心病。

i·de·ate〔*n.* aɪˈdiɪt; aiˈdiːit *v.* aɪˈdiet; aiˈdiːeit〕*v.*, **-at·ed, -at·ing**, *n.* —*v.t.* 將…觀念化; 想像。—*v.i.* 形成觀念; 想像。—*n.*【哲學】與觀念相應之實在。

i·de·a·tion〔ˌaɪdɪˈeʃən; ˌaidiˈeiʃən〕*n.* 觀念作用; 觀念化。

i·dée fixe〔ˈideˈfiks; ˈiːdeiˈfiːks〕【法】固定觀念; 對一事之偏執。

i·dem〔ˈaɪdɛm; ˈaidem〕【拉】*pron.*, *adj.* 同上(的); 同字(的); 同著者(的); 同書(的)。(略作 **id.**)

i·den·tic〔aɪˈdɛntɪk; aiˈdentik〕*adj.* ①=**identical.** ②【外交】(文書)同文的; (行動)同步驟的。*identic* note. 同文通牒。

***i·den·ti·cal**〔aɪˈdɛntɪkl; aiˈdentikəl〕*adj.* ①同一的; 絲毫不差的。Both events happened on the *identical* day. 兩件事發生在同一天。②完全相同的。That is the *identical* pen I lost. 那和我所遺失的筆完全相同。③完全符合的; 完全一致的。—**ly**, *adv.*

identical equation【數學】恒等式

identical twins 同性雙胎; 同卵雙胎

i·den·ti·fi·ca·tion〔aɪˌdɛntəfəˈkeʃən; aiˌdentifiˈkeiʃən〕*n.* ①認明; 證明。②證件。③鑑定; 確認。

identification card 身分證。

identification tag 美軍官兵套在頸上的金屬牌, 上刻有佩帶者之軍籍號碼和姓名

***i·den·ti·fy**〔aɪˈdɛntəˌfaɪ; aiˈdentifai〕*v.*, **-fied, -fy·ing.** —*v.t.* ①認明; 認出; 鑑定。Could you *identify* your umbrella? 你能認出你的傘嗎? ②作認明或識別之方法。③認爲係同一的。④使有關係; 聯合; 參與。He refused to *identify* himself with such policy. 他拒絕參與此一政策。—*v.i.* 與他人融爲一體; 打成一片。

i·den·ti·ty〔aɪˈdɛntətɪ; aiˈdentiti〕*n.*, *pl.* **-ties.** ①本人; 本身; 本體。The writer concealed his *identity*. 作者隱匿其眞實姓名。②絕對相似; 同一性質。③同一。mistaken (*or* false) *identity*. 錯認爲同一人。④相同; 一致。

identity card 身分證。(亦作 ID 「**card, I.D. card**)」

identity crisis 自覺危險期(男女在發育期間的困惱時期)。

id·e·o·gram〔ˈɪdɪəˌgræm; ˈidiougræm〕*n.* ①表意文字。②記號, 如: 7, =, & 等。

id·e·o·graph〔ˈɪdɪəˌgræf; ˈidiougrɑːf〕*n.* =**ideogram.**

id·e·o·graph·ic〔ˌɪdɪəˈgræfɪk; ˌidi

ou'græfik] *adj.* ①表意文字的；表意的。②記號的。(亦作 **ideographical**)

id·e·og·ra·phy [ˌɪdɪ'ɑgrəfɪ; ˌidi'ɔgrəfi] *n.* ①表意文字之使用；表意文字法。②表意文字學。③使用記號。

i·de·o·log·i·cal [ˌaɪdɪə'lɑdʒɪkl; ˌaidiə'lɔdʒikəl] *adj.* 觀念學的；意識形態的。

i·de·ol·o·gist [ˌaɪdɪ'ɑlədʒɪst; ˌaidi'ɔlədʒist] *n.* ①觀念學家；觀念論者。②理論家；空想家；理想家。③提倡某觀念的人。

i·de·ol·o·gy [ˌaɪdɪ'ɑlədʒɪ; ˌaidi'ɔlədʒi] *n., pl.* **-gies.** 意識；意識形態；觀念學。

ides [aɪdz; aidz] *n. pl.* (作 *sing.* or *pl.* 解) 古羅馬曆三、五、七、十各月之十五日；其他各月分之十三日。

id est [ˌɪd'ɛst; ˌid'est] 〖拉〗卽；換言之(=that is, 通常略作 i.e.).

id·i·o·cy ['ɪdɪəsɪ; 'idiəsi] *n., pl.* **-cies.** ①白癡。②極愚蠢的行爲。

id·i·o·glos·si·a [ˌɪdɪə'glɑsɪə; ˌidiə'glɔːsiə] *n.* ①一己的語言(如小孩們所發明，而只在他們之間通行的)；自我語法。②言語不清楚之一種病態。

id·i·o·graph ['ɪdɪəˌgræf; 'idiəgrɑːf] *n.* 特別的記號；簽名；私章；商標。

id·i·o·lect ['ɪdɪəˌlɛkt; 'idiəlekt] *n.* 〖語言〗個人語言(帶有個人發音、語彙及文法等特點之語言)。

id·i·om ['ɪdɪəm; 'idiəm, 'idjəm] *n.* ①習語；成語；慣用語法(如："How do you do?" "I have caught cold." 等是)。②方言。③某一民族之特別語法。④音樂、藝術等個人表現之風格；格調；筆調。

id·i·o·mat·ic [ˌɪdɪə'mætɪk; ˌidiə'mætik] *adj.* ①慣用的；合於習慣用法的；通順的。*idiomatic* phrases. 習慣語；成語。②表現某一語言特性的；具有某一語言特性的。(亦作 **idiomatical**) **—al·ly,** *adv.*

id·i·op·a·thy [ˌɪdɪ'ɑpəθɪ; ˌidi'ɔpəθi] *n.* 〖醫〗自發症；原發病；特發病(非由他病引起者)。**—id·i·o·path·ic,** *adj.*

id·i·o·syn·cra·sy [ˌɪdɪə'sɪnkrəsɪ; ˌidiə'siŋkrəsi] *n., pl.* **-sies.** ①個人心理之特點；癖性。②特異之體質。③(對某些藥物、食物之)敏感。(亦作 **idiosyncracy**)

id·i·o·syn·crat·ic [ˌɪdɪosɪn'krætɪk; ˌidiəsin'krætik] *adj.* 特癖的；特性的；特質的；由於特質所致的。

id·i·ot ['ɪdɪət; 'idiət, 'idjət] *n.* ①白癡。②極蠢之人。"I've left my umbrella in the train. What an *idiot* I am!" "我把傘丟在火車上了，我眞是一個糊塗蟲啊！"

idiot card 〖電視〗提示卡。(亦作 **cue card**)

id·i·ot·ic [ˌɪdɪ'ɑtɪk; ˌidi'ɔtik] *adj.* 白癡的；極愚的。

id·i·ot·i·cal·ly [ˌɪdɪ'ɑtɪkḷɪ; ˌidi'ɔtikəli] *adv.* ①極愚地。②…得不像話；…得荒唐。It is *idiotically* cheap. 這便宜得不像話。

id·i·ot·ize ['ɪdɪətˌaɪz; 'idiətaiz] *v.t.,* **-ized, -iz·ing.** 使愚蠢；使成白痴。

idiot savant *pl.* **idiot savants.** 〖心理〗具有特殊技能而心智不健全者。

i·dle ['aɪdḷ; 'aidl] *adj.,* **i·dler, i·dlest,** *v.,* **i·dled, i·dling,** *n.*—*adj.*①不作事的；停頓的；閒散的。When men cannot find employment they are *idle*. 當人們找不到工作，他們就是閒散的。②懶惰的。③無用的；無益的。Don't listen to *idle* tales. 不要聽無益的閒話。④無因的；無由的。*idle* rumors. 無根據的謠言。—*v.i.* ①遊手好閒；不作事。Don't *idle* about. 不要遊手好閒。②浪費時間；虛擲時光。③(機器)慢慢轉動或發動而不發出力量。The windmill *idled* in the breeze. 風車在微風中慢慢轉動。—*v.t.* ①浪費；虛擲。Don't *idle* away your time. 不要浪費光陰。②使(機器)慢慢轉動而不發出力量。③使停止工作。—*n.* (引擎之)慢轉動。**—i·dly,** *adv.*

***i·dle·ness** ['aɪdḷnɪs; 'aidlnis] *n.* ①懶惰；閒散；安逸。*Idleness* is the parent of all vice. 〖諺〗懶惰爲萬惡之源。②失業(狀態)；賦閒。③無益；白費。

idle pulley 〖機械〗游滑車；游輪。

i·dler ['aɪdlɚ; 'aidlə] *n.* ①懶惰者；遊手好閒者；遊民。②〖機械〗=**idle wheel.** ③〖機械〗=**idle pulley.**

idle wheel 〖機械〗惰輪；遊輪。

I·do ['ido; 'iːdou] *n.* 伊多語 (Jespersen 等將 Esperanto 簡化而成的一種世界語)。

***i·dol** ['aɪdḷ; 'aidl] *n.* ①偶像；神像。②〖聖經〗邪神；假神。③寵愛物；崇拜物。Don't make an *idol* of wealth. 不要崇拜錢財。④幻想。⑤謬論。

i·dol·a·ter [aɪ'dɑlətɚ; ai'dɔlətə] *n.* ①偶像崇拜者。②(對某人或某物的)崇拜者。

i·dol·a·tress [aɪ'dɑlətrɪs; ai'dɔlətris] *n.* idolater 之女性。

i·dol·a·trize [aɪ'dɑləˌtraɪz; ai'dɔlətraiz] *v.,* **-trized, -triz·ing.** —*v.t.* 奉爲神聖。—*v.i.* 崇拜偶像。

i·dol·a·trous [aɪ'dɑlətrəs; ai'dɔlətrəs] *adj.* ①崇拜偶像的。②過分尊崇的。③盲目崇拜的。

i·dol·a·try [aɪ'dɑlətrɪ; ai'dɔlətri] *n., pl.* **-tries.** ①偶像崇拜。②過度崇信。③崇拜之事物。

i·dol·ism ['aɪdḷɪzṃ; 'aidəlizəm] *n.* ①=**idolatry.** ②謬見；謬誤的推理。

i·dol·i·za·tion [ˌaɪdḷə'zeʃən; ˌaidəlai'zeiʃən] *n.* 偶像化；盲目的崇拜；醉心。

i·dol·ize ['aɪdḷˌaɪz; 'aidəlaiz] *v.t.,* **-ized, -iz·ing.** ①偶像化；奉爲神聖。②過度崇拜或讚揚。

idols of the cave 由偏見而生的謬論或錯覺；偏見。

idols of the theater 由傳統信仰或技術而生的謬見。

idols of the tribe 由於人之本性或人類社會組織而生的謬見。

IDP International Driving Permit.

i·dyl, i·dyll ['aɪdḷ; 'idil] *n.* ①田園詩；牧歌；卽景詩。②簡單而美妙可作詩詠嘆之情景；田園風景。

i·dyl(l)·ist ['aɪdɪlɪst; 'aidilist] *n.* 田園詩人；牧歌作者。

i·dyl·lic [aɪ'dɪlɪk; ai'dilik] *adj.* ①適於抒情詩的。②簡單而美妙的。

-ie 〖字尾〗表"小"之義 (常含鍾愛、親暱等意味)，如：Annie, birdie.

IE. Indo-European.

I.E. ①Indo-European. ②Industrial Engineer.

i.e. 〖拉〗id est (=that is; that is to say). 卽；就是。〖注意〗**i. e.** 現僅用於論文及參考書中，通常以 that is 代替之。

‡if [ɪf; if] *conj.* ①假使；假設；倘若。**a.** 指現在時間：*If* you wish, I will help you. 假使你希望，我願意幫助你。**b.** 指將來時間：*If* he comes, I will tell him. 假使他來了，我一定告訴他。**c.** 指過去時間：*If* I had known, I might have gone. 假使我早知道，我可能已經去了。②〖俗〗縱令；卽使。*If* he is little, he is strong. 他雖小，但很强壯。③何時(=

whenever). *If* I feel any doubt, I inquire. 我一有疑惑就問。④是否(=whether). I wonder *if* he is at home. 我不知道他是否在家。⑤與否定式連用，表示驚異或憎惡。And *if* he didn't try to knock me down! 令人可驚的是他竟欲把我打倒！ ***as if*** 好像；彷彿。He talks *as if* he were tired. 他談話的神態彷彿他已疲倦不堪。***even if*** 縱令；即使。We shall go, *even if* it rains. 縱使下雨，我們也要去。***if any*** 若有的話。***if anything*** 或許甚至。*If anything* you ought to apologize. 你或許甚至應該道歉。***if it were not for*** 若不是…的話。*If it were not for* your help, I would have died. 要不是你救我，我一定死掉了。***if necessary*** 如果必要；在必要時。***if only*** 若…那就好了；我多麼希望…啊！ *If only* I knew! (or *If* I *only* knew!) 假若我知道那就好了！ ***if possible*** 如果可能的話。***if so be that*** 如果；假使。***if you please*** (or ***will***) **a.** 請。**b.** 如何(徵詢他人意見)。***what if*** **a.** 算甚麼；又何妨。*What if* I fail! 我失敗算甚麼！ **b.** 怎麼辦；如何才好。*What if* you should fail! 你如果失敗，怎麼辦！ —*n.* ①假設。②條件。③不確定性。The future is full of *ifs.* 未來太不可靠。〖注意〗在正式用法中，if 用於表示情況或條件，不能與 or 連用。

IFC International Finance Corporation. 國際金融機構。

if·fy [ˈɪfɪ; ˈifi] *adj.* 〖俗〗未定的；未確實的；可疑的。

I.F.S. Irish Free State.

IFTU International Federation of Trade Unions.

I.G. ①Indo-Germanic. ②Inspector General.

ig·loo [ˈɪglu; ˈiglu:] *n., pl.* **ig·loos.** ①愛斯基摩人用雪塊砌成的圓頂小舍。②海豹在冰層呼吸孔上方之雪中所挖的洞。③〖軍〗貯存火箭或其他彈藥之圓頂倉庫。(亦作 **iglu**)

ig·ne·ous [ˈɪgnɪəs; ˈigniəs] *adj.* ①火的；火熱的。②〖地質〗火成的。*igneous* rock. 火成岩。

ig·nes·cent [ɪgˈnɛsn̩t; igˈnesnt] *adj.* ①受鋼鐵敲擊則發火花的(石頭等)。②突然燃起的。—*n.* 發火(花)之物質。

ig·nes fat·u·i [ˈɪgnizˈfætʃuˌaɪ; ˈigni:zˈfætjuai] 〖拉〗pl. of **ignis fatuus.**

ig·nis fat·u·us [ˈɪgnɪsˈfætʃuəs; ˈignisˈfætjuəs] 〖拉〗①燐火；鬼火。②引人入迷途的東西；不切實際的計畫或目標。

ig·nit·a·ble, ig·nit·i·ble [ɪgˈnaɪtəbl̩; igˈnaitəbl] *adj.* 易發火的；可燃性的。

ig·nite [ɪgˈnaɪt; igˈnait] *v.*, **-nit·ed, -nit·ing.** —*v.t.* ①使發火；使燃燒。②使灼熱；使發赤熱之光。③煽動；激動。—*v.i.* 發火；着火；開始燃燒。

ig·ni·tion [ɪgˈnɪʃən; igˈniʃən] *n.* ①點火；發火；燃燒。②(內燃機內的)發火裝置。***ignition charge*** 導火藥。***ignition point*** 〖物理〗燃點。***ignition wire*** 點火線。

ig·no·ble [ɪgˈnobl̩; igˈnoubl] *adj.* ①卑鄙的；下流的。To betray a friend is *ignoble.* 背棄朋友是爲人所不齒的(事)。②出身低微的。③不光榮的；不名譽的。④品質低劣的。—**ig·no·bly,** *adv.* —**ness,** *n.*

ig·no·min·i·ous [ˌɪgnəˈmɪnɪəs; ˌignəˈminiəs] *adj.* 可恥的；不名譽的；可鄙的；屈辱的。—**ly,** *adv.*

ig·no·min·y [ˈɪgnəˌmɪnɪ; ˈignəmini] *n., pl.* **-min·ies.** ①羞恥；不名譽。②醜行；可恥的行爲；墮落的行爲。

ig·no·ra·mus [ˌɪgnəˈreməs; ˌign ˈreiməs] *n., pl.* **-mus·es.** 無知的人。

***ig·no·rance** [ˈɪgnərəns; ˈignəran *n.* 無知；不知。If he did wrong, it w from (*or* through) *ignorance.* 假若他做了，那是由於無知。to live in a state *ignorance.* 生活在渾渾噩噩之中。

***ig·no·rant** [ˈɪgnərənt; ˈignərənt] *a* ①無知識的；未受教育的。②不知道的；不明的。He was *ignorant* of the fact. 他不道這事實。③無知所造成的。④顯示無知的。天眞的。⑥原始的；幼稚的。—**ly,** *adv.* 〖注 **ignorant, illiterate, uneducated** 均表知的。ignorant 指缺乏一般知識，有時指乏某一科目之知識。illiterate 指不能讀或即文盲的。uneducated 指未在學校或從本上獲得有系統的訓練或學識，即未受教育的

***ig·nore** [ɪgˈnor, -ˈnɔr; igˈnɔ:, -ˈnɔə] **-nored, -nor·ing.** 不理睬；忽視。to *ign* rude remarks. 不理睬無理的批評。

ig·no·tum per ig·no·ti·us [ɪ ˈnotəm pɝ ɪgˈnoʃɪəs; igˈnoutəm pə: ˈnouʃiəs] 〖拉〗以所更不知者來解釋所不知 (=the unknown through the mo unknown).

ig·nuts [ˈɪgnʌts; ˈignʌts] *n. pl.* 〖美俚〗笨人

I-go [ˈiˈgo; ˈi:ˈgou] *n.* 圍棋。(亦作 **go**

i·gua·na [ɪˈgwɑnə; iˈgwɑ:nə] *n.* 〖動 鬣蜥蜴(美洲熱帶地方所產之一種大蜥蜴)。

I.H.P., i.h.p. indicated horsepowe

ih·ram [iˈrɑm; i:ˈrɑ:m] *n.* 回教徒往加朝聖者所着之服裝(包括兩塊白棉布，一塊在腰部，另一塊披於左肩)。

IHS 希臘文耶穌 "ΙΗΣΟΥΣ" 一字之略。

I.H.S. ①Iesus Hominum Salvator (=Jesus, Savior of Men 人類之救主耶穌 ②In Hoc Signo [Vinces] (拉=in [by] th sign [thou shalt conquer] 憑此符號汝得勝)。③In Hoc [Cruce] Salus (拉=in th [cross] is salvation 賴此十字架而得救)。

Ike [aɪk; aik] *n.* 艾森豪(Dwight Dav Eisenhower) 之暱稱。

i·ke·ba·na [ˈikɛˈbɑnɑ; ˈi:keˈbɑ:nɑ:] 〖日〗*n.* 插花

i·kon [ˈaɪkɑn; ˈaikɔn] *n.* =**icon.**

Il 化學元素 illinium 之符號。

il- 〖字首〗 **in-** 之異體(用於 "l" 前)。

il·e·ac [ˈɪlɪˌæk; ˈiliæk] *adj.* ①廻腸的 ②腸塞痃痛的。

il·e·um [ˈɪlɪəm; ˈiliəm] *n.* 〖解剖〗廻腸

il·e·us [ˈɪlɪəs; ˈiliəs] *n.* 〖醫〗腸塞痃痛

i·lex [ˈaɪlɛks; ˈaileks] *n., pl.* **i·lex·e** 〖植物〗①(I-)冬青屬。②冬青屬植物；冬青

I·li [ˈiˈli; ˈi:ˈli:] *n.* ①伊犂河(發源於中新疆省西北部)。②伊犂(在新疆省，即今之定縣)。

il·i·ac [ˈɪlɪˌæk; ˈiliæk] *adj.* 腸骨的；廻腸的。

Il·i·ad [ˈɪlɪəd; ˈiliəd] *n.* 伊里亞德(希著名史詩，相傳爲荷馬 Homer 所作)。

il·i·um [ˈɪlɪəm; ˈiliəm] *n., pl.* **il·i·a** [ˈɪlɪ ˈiliə]. 〖解剖〗腸骨；髂骨。

ilk [ɪlk; ilk] *adj.* 〖廢〗同一的；相同的。—*n.* 〖俗〗家族；種；類。he and his *ilk.* 與他的家人。***of that ilk*** **a.** 同名的。**b.** 種的；同類的。

‡ill [ɪl; il] *adj.*, **worse** [wɝs; wə:s], **wor** [wɝst; wə:st], *n., adv.* —*adj.* ①生病的 He has been *ill* for a long time. 他已了很久。②邪惡的；惡劣的。an *ill* deed. 惡的行爲。*ill* will. 惡意。*ill* temper (humor). 壞脾氣。*ill* repute (*or* fame).

名;聲名狼藉。*ill* news. 壞消息。③不順利的;不幸的。an *ill* wind 逆風。④不仁慈的;嚴酷的;殘忍的。⑤不佳的;有缺點的。⑥無技巧的;無效率的。***ill off*** 過得不好。***Ill weeds grow apace.*** 〖諺〗莠草生長得快;(喩)有害之物生長或傳播得快。***It's an ill wind that blows nobody any good.*** 〖諺〗無人得到好處的風,可就眞是壞風(意謂:世上沒有對人人皆不利之事)。—***n.*** ①疾病。②惡事;傷害。He spoke no *ill* of them. 他並沒有說他們的壞話。③不幸。Poverty is an *ill*. 貧窮乃一不幸。***take ill*** 對…生氣;爲…冒犯。—***adv.*** ①惡地;有害地。It *ill* becomes you to criticize him. 你不應批評他。②不利地;不幸地。to fare *ill*. 運氣不佳。③嚴酷地;殘忍地。④困難地;幾乎不能地。We could *ill* afford the time and money. 我們無力負擔所需的時間和金錢。〖注意〗 **ill** 作"生病的"解時,不用於名詞前。若說"生病的人"則須作 sick man. 又 We visited the sick. 我們訪問病人。"the sick" 係指醫院中的全體病人。在此不可用 "the *ill*".

I'll 〔aɪl; ail〕 ①=**I shall.** ②= **I will.**

Ill. Illinois. **ill.** ①illustrated. ②illustration. ③illustrator. ④most illustrious.

ill-ad·vised 〔ˈɪlədˈvaɪzd; ˈilədˈvaizd〕 *adj.* 欠考慮的;愚蠢的。—**ly,** *adv.*

ill-af·fect·ed 〔ˈɪləˈfɛktɪd; ˈiləˈfektid〕 *adj.* 有惡意的;不平的;不服的。

il·la·tion 〔ɪˈleʃən; iˈleiʃən〕 *n.* 推理;推論;推定。

il·la·tive 〔ɪˈletɪv; iˈleitiv〕 *adj.* 推論的;推斷的。*illative* conjunctions.〖文法〗推論連接詞(如 then, therefore, so 等)。—**ly,** *adv.*

ill-be·ing 〔ˈɪlˈbiɪŋ; ˈilˈbiːiŋ〕 *n.* 惡劣之狀態;不幸;不健康。

ill-bod·ing 〔ˈɪlˈbodɪŋ; ˈilˈboudiŋ〕 *adj.* 不吉的;不祥的。

ill-bred 〔ˈɪlˈbrɛd; ˈilˈbred〕 *adj.* 教養不良的;粗野的;無禮的。

ill breeding 教養不良;粗野;無禮。

ill-come 〔ˈɪlˌkʌm; ˈilkʌm〕 *adj.* 不受歡迎的。

ill-con·di·tioned 〔ˈɪlkənˈdɪʃənd; ˈilkənˈdiʃənd〕 *adj.* ①性惡的;壞心地的;壞脾氣的。②情況不佳的;惡性的。

ill-con·sid·ered 〔ˈɪlkənˈsɪdɚd; ˈilkənˈsidəd〕 *adj.* 考慮欠周的;不智的;不宜的。

ill-de·fined 〔ˈɪldɪˈfaɪnd; ˈildiˈfaind〕 *adj.* (界限等)不清楚的; 不確切的;欠明確的。

ill-dis·posed 〔ˈɪldɪsˈpozd; ˈildisˈpouzd〕 *adj.* ①懷惡意的;有敵意的。②不利的;不贊成的。

***il·le·gal** 〔ɪˈligl̩; iˈliːgəl〕 *adj.* ①不合法的;違法的;犯法的。②不合規定的。—**ly,** *adv.*

il·le·gal·i·ty 〔ˌɪliˈgælətɪ; ˌiliːˈgæliti〕 *n., pl.* **-ties.** ①非法;犯規。②非法行爲。

il·le·gal·ize 〔ɪˈligl̩ˌaɪz; iˈliːgəlaiz〕 *v.t.,* **-ized, -iz·ing.** 使成爲非法;使違法。

il·leg·i·bil·i·ty 〔ɪˌlɛdʒəˈbɪlətɪ; iˌledʒiˈbiliti〕 *n.* 模糊不清;不可辨識。

il·leg·i·ble 〔ɪˈlɛdʒəbl̩; iˈledʒəbl〕 *adj.* (字跡)難讀的; 難認的。—**il·leg·i·bly,** *adv.*

il·le·git·i·ma·cy 〔ˌɪlɪˈdʒɪtəməsɪ; ˌiliˈdʒitiməsi〕 *n., pl.* **-cies.** ①不法; 違法。②私生;庶出。③不合理。

il·le·git·i·mate 〔ˌɪlɪˈdʒɪtəmɪt; ˌiliˈdʒitimit〕 *adj., v.,* **-mat·ed, -mat·ing.** —*adj.* ①非婚生的;私生的。②不合法的;不合規則的。③不合理論的; 不合條理的。—*v.t.* ①使不合法;使成私生子。②宣布爲不合法。

il·le·git·i·ma·tion 〔ˌɪlɪˌdʒɪtəˈmeʃən; ˌiliˌdʒitiˈmeiʃən〕 *n.* 宣告(認定)違法;私生子之宣告。

ill fame 惡名。

ill-fat·ed 〔ˈɪlˈfetɪd; ˈilˈfeitid〕 *adj.* ①苦命的;命途多舛的。②不幸的;不吉的。

ill-fa·vored 〔ˈɪlˈfevɚd; ˈilˈfeivəd〕 *adj.* ①難看的(人或臉色)。②令人不快的。

ill-fed 〔ˈɪlˌfɛd; ˈilˈfed〕 *adj.* 營養不良的。

ill-fit·ted 〔ˈɪlˈfɪtɪd; ˈilˈfitid〕 *adj.* 不適宜的。

ill-found·ed 〔ˈɪlˈfaʊndɪd; ˈilˈfaundid〕 *adj.* 缺乏根據的;無正當理由的。

ill-got·ten 〔ˈɪlˈgɑtn̩; ˈilˈgɔtn〕 *adj.* 來路不正的;以卑汚或不光明的手段得來的。

ill health 不健康。

ill-hu·mo(u)r 〔ˈɪlˈhjumɚ; ˈilˈhjuːmə〕 *n.* 惡劣的情緒; 壞脾氣。(亦作 **ill humor**)

ill-hu·mored 〔ˈɪlˈhjumɚd; ˈilˈhjuːməd〕 *adj.* 壞脾氣的;性情惡劣的。

il·lib·er·al 〔ɪˈlɪbərəl; iˈlibərəl〕 *adj.* ①氣度狹隘的;不開明的。②吝嗇的。③鄙俗的;無教養的。—**ly,** *adv.*

il·lib·er·al·i·ty 〔ɪˌlɪbəˈrælətɪ; iˌlibəˈræliti〕 *n.* ①吝嗇;氣度狹小。②鄙俗。

il·lic·it 〔ɪˈlɪsɪt; iˈlisit〕 *adj.* 法所不許的;被禁止的;不適宜的。the *illicit* sale of drugs. 毒品的私賣。—**ly,** *adv.*

il·lim·it·a·ble 〔ɪˈlɪmɪtəbl̩; iˈlimitəbl〕 *adj.* 無限的;無極的; 無窮的。—*n.* 無窮之事物。—**il·lim·it·a·bly,** *adv.*

il·lin·i·um 〔ɪˈlɪnɪəm; iˈliniəm〕 *n.* 〖化〗鉯(稀土族元素之一, 現稱 promethium).

Il·li·nois 〔ˌɪləˈnɔɪ; ˌiliˈnɔi〕 *n., pl.* **-nois.** ①伊利諾(美國中西部之一州, 首府爲春田 Springfield). ②伊利諾河。③伊利諾人。

il·lit·er·a·cy 〔ɪˈlɪtərəsɪ; iˈlitərəsi〕 *n., pl.* **-cies.** ①文盲。②無教育;無學識。③因無教育或學識而於說或寫中所犯的錯誤。

il·lit·er·ate 〔ɪˈlɪtərɪt; iˈlitərit〕 *adj.* ①不能讀寫的;目不識丁的。②知識淺陋的;缺乏教育的。an *illiterate* letter. 一封文詞不通的信。③未開化的;沒有文化的。—*n.* 文盲;目不識丁者。—**ness,** *n.*

ill-judged 〔ˈɪlˈdʒʌdʒd; ˈilˈdʒʌdʒd〕 *adj.* 不明智的;愚昧的;魯莽的; 不合時宜的。

ill-kempt 〔ˈɪlˈkɛmpt; ˈilˈkempt〕 *adj.* 不整潔的;未梳理的。

ill-look·ing 〔ˈɪlˈlʊkɪŋ; ˈilˈlukiŋ〕 *adj.* ①(相貌)醜的; 面目可憎的。②樣子可怕的。

ill-man·nered 〔ˈɪlˈmænɚd; ˈilˈmænəd〕 *adj.* 無禮貌的;不客氣的;粗野的。

ill nature 性情乖張;居心惡毒。

ill-na·tured 〔ˈɪlˈnetʃɚd; ˈilˈneitʃəd〕 *adj.* 性情惡劣的;根性不良的; 居心惡毒的;乖張的。—**ly,** *adv.*

***ill·ness** 〔ˈɪlnɪs; ˈilnis〕 *n.* 不健康; 疾病(爲 health 之對)。He is suffering from a serious *illness.* 他患着嚴重的病。

il·log·i·cal 〔ɪˈlɑdʒɪkl̩; iˈlɔdʒikəl〕 *adj.* ①不合邏輯的。②不合常理的。—**ly,** *adv.*

il·log·i·cal·i·ty 〔ɪˌlɑdʒɪˈkælətɪ; iˌlɔdʒiˈkæliti〕 *n.* ①不合邏輯;不合理;矛盾。②不合邏輯之事;不合理之事。

ill-o·mened 〔ˈɪlˈomɪnd; ˈilˈoumend〕 *adj.* 惡兆的;不吉的;惡運的。

ill-sort·ed 〔ˈɪlˈsɔrtɪd; ˈilˈsɔːtid〕 *adj.* 不相配的。

ill-spent 〔ˈɪlˈspɛnt; ˈilˈspent〕 *adj.* 使用不當的;浪費的。

ill-starred 〔ˈɪlˈstɑrd; ˈilˈstɑːd〕 *adj.* 命運壞的;倒霉的。

ill-suit·ed 〔ˈɪlˈsutɪd; ˈilˈsjuːtid〕 *adj.* 不合適的。

ill temper 壞脾氣;性情乖戾。
ill-tem·pered [ˈɪlˈtɛmpəd; ˈilˈtempəd] *adj.* 壞脾氣的;易怒的;暴躁的。
illth [ɪlθ; ilθ] *n.* 貧乏。
ill-timed [ˈɪlˈtaɪmd; ˈilˈtaimd] *adj.* 不合時宜的。
ill-treat [ˌɪlˈtrit; ˈilˈtriːt] *v.t.* 虐待;苛待;傷害。
ill turn ①不仁的、懷敵意的或惡毒的行爲。②(健康、財富等之)衰落。
il·lume [ɪˈlum; iˈluːm] *v.t.*, **-lumed, -lum·ing.** 〖詩〗=**illuminate.**
il·lu·mi·na·ble [ɪˈlumənəbl̩; iˈljuːmənəbl] *adj.* 可以照明的;可啓迪的;可解釋的。
il·lu·mi·nant [ɪˈlumənənt; iˈljuːminənt] *adj.* 發光的。—*n.* 發光體;發光物(石油、瓦斯、電燈等)。
***il·lu·mi·nate** [ɪˈluməˌnet; iˈljuːmineit] *v.t.*, **-nat·ed, -nat·ing.** ①(以燈光)照明;照亮。a poorly *illuminated* room. 燈光不明的房間。②闡釋;說明。Our interesting teacher could *illuminate* almost any subject we studied. 我們那位風趣的教師幾乎能闡釋我們所學的每一門課。③以燈裝飾(街道、房屋等)以示慶祝。The streets were *illuminated* for the celebration. 街道張掛燈火以示慶祝。④以金、銀、鮮艷顏色、插畫、圖案等裝飾(書籍、字母等)。⑤啓迪;啓蒙;啓發;教化。⑥顯揚;使顯赫。
il·lu·mi·na·ti [ɪˌlumɪˈnetaɪ; iˌluːmiˈnɑːti] *n. pl., sing.* **-na·to** [-ˈneto; -ˈnɑːtou], or **-na·tus** [-ˈnetəs; -ˈnɑːtəs]. 先覺者;自稱先覺者。
***il·lu·mi·na·tion** [ɪˌluməˈneʃən; iˌljuːmiˈneiʃən] *n.* ①照明;照亮。②光亮;亮度。③闡釋;說明。④以燈火裝飾;張掛燈火;燈飾。⑤以金、銀、彩色、圖畫、圖案裝飾書籍及字母。⑥啓蒙;啓迪;啓發;教化。She found great *illumination* in the lecture. 她從那演講得到很大的啓發。
il·lu·mi·na·tive [ɪˈluməˌnetɪv; iˈljuːminətiv] *adj.* 照明的;啓發的。
il·lu·mi·na·tor [ɪˈluməˌnetɚ; iˈljuːmineitə] *n.* ①照明之人;照明器;照耀物;啓發者。②作書稿彩飾之人。
il·lu·mine [ɪˈlumɪn; iˈljuːmin] *v.t.*, **-mined, -min·ing.** ①(以燈光)照亮;照明。A smile often *illumines* a homely face. 笑容常可使醜者產生一點媚力。②啓蒙;啓發。
illus. ①illustrated. ②illustration.
ill-us·age [ˈɪlˈjusɪdʒ; ˈilˈjuːzidʒ] *n.* 虐待;苛待。
ill-use [*v.* ˈɪlˈjuz; ˈilˈjuːz *n.* ˈɪlˈjus; ˈilˈjuːs] *v.*, **-used, -us·ing,** *n.* —*v.t.* ①虐待。②妄用;濫用。—*n.* ①虐待(=ill-usage)。②濫用;妄用。
***il·lu·sion** [ɪˈljuʒən; iˈluːʒən, iˈljuː-] *n.* ①幻影;幻象。②錯覺;幻想。an *illusion* of wealth. 對財富的幻想。③錯誤的印象或概念。④(婦女覆面用之)絲質薄面紗。
il·lu·sion·al [ɪˈluʒənəl; iˈluːʒənəl] *adj.* 錯覺的;虛幻的;幻想的。
il·lu·sion·ism [ɪˈluʒənˌɪzəm; iˈluːʒənizəm] *n.* 迷妄論;幻想說(認人世爲幻影)。
il·lu·sion·ist [ɪˈluʒənɪst; iˈluːʒənist] *n.* ①迷妄論者。②易發生幻覺的人;陷入錯覺的人。③魔術家。
il·lu·sion·less [ɪˈluʒənlɪs; iˈluːʒənlis] *adj.* 無幻覺的。
il·lu·sive [ɪˈlusɪv; iˈluːsiv] *adj.* 虛幻的;迷惑的;欺騙的。—**ly,** *adv.* —**ness,** *n.*
il·lu·so·ry [ɪˈlusərɪ; iˈluːsəri] *adj.* 虛幻的。
illust. ①illustrated. ②illustration.
***il·lus·trate** [ˈɪləstret, ɪˈlʌstret; ˈiləstreit] *v.*, **-trat·ed, -trat·ing.** —*v.t.* ①舉例說明。②(在教科書等內)插圖;作圖解。a well-*illustrated* textbook. 一本插圖很豐富的教科書。—*v.i.* 舉例說明;提出例證。The speaker said he would endeavor to *illustrate.* 演講人說他將盡力舉例說明。
il·lus·trat·ed [ˈɪləstretɪd; ˈiləstreitid] *adj.* 有插圖的。—*n.* 〖英〗有插圖的報章雜誌。
***il·lus·tra·tion** [ɪˌləsˈtreʃən; ˌiləsˈtreiʃən] *n.* ①插圖;圖解。②例證;實例。He gave an *illustration* of what he meant. 他對所說的話給與例證。③舉例說明。
il·lus·tra·tive [ɪˈlʌstrətɪv, ˈɪləsˌtretɪv; ˈiləstreitiv] *adj.* 闡釋的;說明的。
il·lus·tra·tor [ˈɪləsˌtretɚ; ˈiləstreitə] *n.* ①畫插圖者。②用以說明之事物。
il·lus·tri·ous [ɪˈlʌstrɪəs; iˈlʌstriəs] *adj.* ①著名的;顯赫的;傑出的。Washington and Lincoln are *illustrious* Americans. 華盛頓與林肯是著名的美國人。②光榮的。—**ly,** *adv.* —**ness,** *n.*
ill will 惡意;敵意;憎惡。
ill-wish·er [ˈɪlˈwɪʃɚ; ˈilˈwiʃə] *n.* 幸災樂禍者;希望他人不幸者。
ILO, I.L.O. International Labor Organization (*or* Office).
‡**I'm** [aɪm; aim] =**I am.**
im- 〖字首〗**in-** 之異體(用於 b, m, p 等之前),如: immoral.
***im·age** [ˈɪmɪdʒ; ˈimidʒ] *n., v.*, **-aged, -ag·ing.** —*n.* ①像;肖像;影子。She saw her *image* in the mirror. 她看見鏡中她的影子。②塑像;石像。③形象;象喩。Poetry often contains *images.* 詩中常含有意象。④心像;概念;想像。⑤化身。As a civil servant, he is the *image* of conscientiousness. 做爲公僕,他是負責作風的化身。—*v.t.* ①造…之肖像;作…之像。②想像出。I couldn't *image* what my friends were doing at home. 我不能想像出我的朋友在家裏做甚麼事。③反映;照出。④描繪;以象喩描寫。The novelist finely *images* the hero. 小說家很精緻地描寫書中的英雄。
im·age-build·ing [ˈɪmɪdʒˌbɪldɪŋ; ˈimidʒˌbildiŋ] *n.* 威望之建立(以宣傳及廣告在大衆面前創造或維持有利印象)。
im·age·ry [ˈɪmɪdʒrɪ; ˈimidʒəri] *n., pl.* **-ries.** ①心象;意象;想像物。②象喩;比喩;直喩。Poetry contains *imagery.* 詩歌中有比喩。③像;雕像(集合稱)。
i·mag·i·na·ble [ɪˈmædʒɪnəbl̩; iˈmædʒinəbl] *adj.* 可想像的;可能的。to try every means *imaginable.* 試用一切可能的方法。—**i·mag·i·na·bly,** *adv.*
i·mag·i·nal [ɪˈmædʒənəl; iˈmædʒinəl] *adj.* 〖昆蟲學〗①成蟲的。②形狀如成蟲的。
***i·mag·i·nar·y** [ɪˈmædʒəˌnɛrɪ; iˈmædʒinəri] *adj.* 想像的;假想的;虛構的。Fairies are *imaginary.* 小仙子是虛構的。
***i·mag·i·na·tion** [ɪˌmædʒəˈneʃən; iˌmædʒiˈneiʃən] *n.* ①想像;幻想;幻覺。②想像力。He has a very strong *imagination.* 他有很強的想像力。
***i·mag·i·na·tive** [ɪˈmædʒəˌnetɪv; iˈmædʒinətiv] *adj.* ①富於想像的。②想像的。③幻想的;虛構的。Fairy tales are *imag-*

inative. 神仙故事都是虛構的。—**ly,** *adv.*

‡**i·mag·ine** 〔ɪ'mædʒɪn; i'mædʒin〕 *v.*, **-ined, -in·ing.** —*v.t.* ①想像;幻想。We can hardly *imagine* life without electricity. 我們難於想像出沒有電時的生活情形。②假想;猜想。I cannot *imagine* what you mean. 我猜不出你的意思。③想;以爲;認爲;相信。She *imagined* someone was watching her. 她以爲有人在看着她。—*v.i.* ①猜測;假定。②想像;幻想。

im·ag·ism 〔'ɪmɪdʒɪzəm; 'imidʒizəm〕 *n.* 〖文學〗意像主義(1912年前後英美現代詩之一派,主題與形式方面擺脫因襲之風,取材於現代生活,注重心像的明瞭表現)。

im·ag·ist 〔'ɪmədʒɪst; 'imidʒist〕 *n.* 意像主義者。—*adj.* 意像主義(者)的。

i·ma·go 〔ɪ'mego; i'meigou〕 *n.*, *pl.* **-goes, -gi·nes** 〔-dʒɪ,niz; -dʒiniːz〕. ①(蝶、蛾等之)成蟲期;成蟲。②〖精神分析〗成像(幼年時形成後一直保存未變的所愛之人之理想化的概念)。

i·mam 〔ɪ'mɑm; i'mɑːm〕 *n.* ①(回教之)祭司;導師。②(I-)回教領袖之稱號。(亦作 **imaum**)

im·bal·ance 〔ɪm'bæləns; im'bæləns〕 *n.* ①不平衡;不安定。②〖醫〗(內分泌等之)不均衡。

im·be·cile 〔'ɪmbəsl; 'imbisiːl〕 *n.* ①心智能力極低者(近乎白癡)。②極愚蠢的人。—*adj.* ①低能的。②極愚蠢的。

im·be·cil·ic 〔,ɪmbə'sɪlɪk; ,imbi'silik〕 *adj.* 極愚蠢的。

im·be·cil·i·ty 〔,ɪmbə'sɪlətɪ; ,imbi'siliti〕 *n.*, *pl.* **-ties.** ①低能。②愚蠢;頑鈍。③極愚之言行。

im·bed 〔ɪm'bɛd; im'bed〕 *v.t.*, **-bed·ded, -bed·ding.** =**embed.**

im·bibe 〔ɪm'baɪb; im'baib〕 *v.*, **-bibed, -bib·ing.** —*v.t.* ①飲。②吸入;吸取。③(心智活動的)吸收;接受;習染。to *imbibe* ideas (knowledge, etc.). 吸收思想(知識等)。—*v.i.* ①飲酒。②吸入。

im·bri·cate 〔*v.* 'ɪmbrɪ,ket; 'imbrikeit *adj.* 'ɪmbrɪkɪt, -,ket; 'imbrikit〕 *adj.*, *v.*, **-cat·ed, -cat·ing.** —*adj.* (亦作 **imbricated**) 覆瓦狀的; 重疊的; 鱗狀的。—*v.t.* & *v.i.* (葉、鱗等)作瓦狀疊覆;(使)作覆瓦狀;(使)成鱗狀。

im·bri·ca·tion 〔,ɪmbrɪ'keʃən; ,imbri'keiʃən〕 *n.* 疊覆; 鱗狀(裝飾); 覆瓦狀(構造)。

im·bro·glio 〔ɪm'broljo; im'brouliou〕 *n.*, *pl.* **-glios.** ①糾紛; 糾葛。②複雜困難的情勢;意見紛歧。③(戲劇等)錯綜複雜的情節。

im·brue 〔ɪm'bru; im'bruː〕 *v.i.*, **-brued, -bru·ing.** (以血等)染汚;浸染。

im·brute 〔ɪm'brut; im'bruːt〕 *v.t.* & *v.i.*, **-brut·ed, -brut·ing.** (使)墮畜道;(使)變野蠻。

im·bue 〔ɪm'bju; im'bjuː〕 *v.t.*, **-bued, -bu·ing.** ①灌輸;影響。He is *imbued* with new ideas. 他深受新思想的影響。②浸染。

im·burse 〔ɪm'bɝs; im'bəːs〕 *v.t.*, **-bursed, -burs·ing.** ①放入皮夾中;貯存。②支付; 退還(款項)。

IMCO Inter-Governmental Maritime Consultative Organization. 政府間海事協議機構。 **IMF, I.M.F.** International Monetary Fund. **imit.** ①imitation. ②imitative.

im·i·ta·bil·i·ty 〔,ɪmɪtə'bɪlətɪ; ,imitə'biliti〕 *n.* 可模仿;模仿之可能性。

im·i·ta·ble 〔'ɪmɪtəbl; 'imitəbl〕 *adj.* 可模仿的。

***im·i·tate** 〔'ɪmə,tet; 'imiteit〕 *v.t.*, **-tat·ed, -tat·ing.** ①模仿;仿效;效法。The little boy *imitated* his father. 這小男孩模仿他的父親。②學; 模擬; 假裝。③假充;冒充。Wood is often painted to *imitate* stone. 木頭常塗油漆假充石頭。

im·i·ta·tion** 〔,ɪmə'teʃən; ,imi'teiʃən〕 *n.* ①模仿; 仿效; 效法。We learn many things by *imitation.* 我們由模仿學習許多事物。②模擬。in imitation of*** 模仿; 仿效; 效法;模擬。—*adj.* 假造的;冒充的。*imitation* pearls (leather). 人造珍珠(皮革)。

im·i·ta·tive 〔'ɪmə,tetɪv; 'imitətiv〕 *adj.* ①喜模仿的。Monkeys are *imitative.* 猴子喜歡模仿他人。②模仿的; 模擬的。③假的; 僞造的。***imitative arts*** 模仿藝術(指繪畫、雕刻等)。***imitative music*** 擬聲音樂(模仿禽獸或自然界聲音之音樂)。***imitative words*** 形聲字;擬聲字(如 bang, whiz 等)。—**ly,** *adv.*

im·i·ta·tor 〔'ɪmə,tetɚ; 'imiteitə〕 *n.* 模仿者。

im·mac·u·la·cy 〔ɪ'mækjələsɪ; i'mækjuləsi〕 *n.* 清淨;純潔;純正;無瑕。

im·mac·u·late 〔ɪ'mækjəlɪt; i'mækjulit〕 *adj.* ①潔淨的; 無瑕的。②純潔的; 無罪的。③純色的;無雜色的。—**ly,** *adv.*

Immaculate Conception 聖靈懷胎(天主教義所稱聖母瑪利亞之懷胎)。

im·ma·nence 〔'ɪmənəns; 'imənəns〕 *n.* ①內在;內涵。②〖神學〗(神)在宇宙內之內在(性)或普遍存在(性)。(亦作 **immanency**)

im·ma·nent 〔'ɪmənənt; 'imənənt〕 *adj.* ①〖哲學〗內在的;內涵的。②〖神學〗(神)內在於宇宙的。

Im·man·u·el[1] 〔ɪ'mænjuəl; i'mænjuəl〕 *n.* 男子名。

Im·man·u·el[2] *n.* 以馬內利(救主基督之別稱;其希伯來文原義爲 God with us).

im·ma·te·ri·al 〔,ɪmə'tɪrɪəl; ,imə'tiəriəl〕 *adj.* ①不重要的。②非物質的;精神的。

im·ma·te·ri·al·ism 〔,ɪmə'tɪrɪəl,ɪzəm; ,imə'tiəriəlizəm〕 *n.* 〖哲學〗非物質主義;唯心論。

im·ma·te·ri·al·i·ty 〔,ɪmmə,tɪrɪ'ælətɪ; 'imə,tiəri'æliti〕 *n.*, *pl.* **-ties.** ①非物質性;非實體性; 非重要性。②非物質(無實體)之物。③不重要。

im·ma·te·ri·al·ize 〔,ɪmmə'tɪrɪəl,aɪz; ,imə'tiəriəlaiz〕 *v.t.*, **-ized, -iz·ing.** 使成非物質;使歸無形。

im·ma·ture 〔,ɪmə'tjʊr; ,imə'tjuə〕 *adj.* ①未成熟的; 發育未完全的; 發展未完全的。②〖地質〗受輕度侵蝕的。

im·ma·tu·ri·ty 〔,ɪmə'tjʊrətɪ; ,imə'tjuəriti〕 *n.* ①未成熟; 未發育。②未成熟的行爲。

im·meas·ur·a·bil·i·ty 〔ɪ,mɛʒərə'bɪlətɪ; i,meʒərə'biliti〕 *n.* 不可測度;無量;無限。

im·meas·ur·a·ble 〔ɪ'mɛʒərəbl; i'meʒərəbl〕 *adj.* 不能衡量的; 無限的。an *immeasurable* abyss. 無底深淵。—**im·meas·ur·a·bly,** *adv.*

im·me·di·a·cy 〔ɪ'midɪəsɪ; i'miːdiəsi〕 *n.*, *pl.* **-cies.** ①直接; 立刻; 鄰近;目前。②(*pl.*)目前之需要。

‡**im·me·di·ate** 〔ɪ'midɪɪt; i'miːdjət〕

adj. ①立即的; 即刻的。to take *immediate* action. 採取緊急行動。②直接的。*immediate* contact. 直接接觸。③最接近的。one's *immediate* family. 近親屬(如父、母、兄弟、姊妹等)。④近的;鄰近的。the *immediate* neighborhood. 近鄰。⑤與目前有關的。our *immediate* plans. 我們目前的計畫。

‡**im·me·di·ate·ly**〔ɪ'midɪɪtlɪ;i'mi:djətli〕*adv.* ①立即; 即刻; 緊; 剛。He arrived *immediately* after I left. 我離開之後，他緊接着就到。②直接地。 The two objects are *immediately* contiguous. 那兩個東西緊接在一起。—*conj.* …之後馬上。*Immediately* his intentions are understood, he may leave. 他的目的被了解之後他會馬上離開。

im·med·i·ca·ble〔ɪ'mɛdəkəbl;i'medikəbl〕*adj.* 無法治療的; 不可挽救的; 不可救藥的。

***im·me·mo·ri·al**〔ˌɪmə'morɪəl; ˌimi'mɔ:riəl〕*adj.* 太古的;極古的;人所不能記憶的。from time *immemorial.* 從太古起。

***im·mense**〔ɪ'mɛns; i'mens〕*adj.* ①極廣大的;無邊的;無量的。an *immense* body of water. 一片汪洋。②〖俚〗非常好的;好極的。—*n.* 無際;無量;無限。 the dark *immense* of air. 無邊無際之黑暗天空。—**ly,** *adv.*

im·men·si·ty〔ɪ'mɛnsətɪ; i'mensiti〕*n., pl.* **-ties.** ①無際;無量;無限;無邊。②巨大之物;無邊之物;無際的空間;無盡的生存。

im·merge〔ɪ'mɝdʒ; i'mə:dʒ〕*v.,* **-merged, -merg·ing.** —*v.i.* 浸;沉入。—*v.t.* 浸漬;沉入;沒入。

im·merse〔ɪ'mɝs;i'mə:s〕*v.t.,* **-mersed, -mers·ing.** ①浸入。②陷於。to be *immersed* in debt. 陷於債務中。 ③沉溺於。④給…施洗禮。

im·mer·sion〔ɪ'mɝʃən; i'mə:ʃən〕*n.* ①浸入;沉入。②浸禮; 洗禮。③沉溺; 專心。

immersion heater 沉浸在水中的電熱水器。

im·me·thod·i·cal〔ˌɪmmɪ'θɑdɪkl; ˌimi'θɔdikəl〕*adj.* 無秩序的;不規則的;不成體系的;紊亂的。

***im·mi·grant**〔'ɪməgrənt, -ˌgrænt; 'imigrənt〕*n.* (自外國移入的) 移民。 Canada has many *immigrants* from Europe. 加拿大有許多自歐洲移入的移民。—*adj.* (自外國)移入的。

im·mi·grate〔'ɪməˌgret; 'imigreit〕*v.i.* & *v.t.,* **-grat·ed, -grat·ing.** 自外國移來;移居入境。

***im·mi·gra·tion**〔ˌɪmə'greʃən; ˌimi'greiʃən〕*n.* ①(自外地) 移居入境。②外來的移民(集合稱)。the *immigration* of 1940. 1940 年入境的移民。

im·mi·gra·tor〔'ɪməˌgretɚ; 'iməgreitə〕*n.* (自外地)移民入境者。

im·mi·nence〔'ɪmənəns; 'iminəns〕*n.* ①即將來臨; 逼近。②即將來臨之事物; 緊迫的危險或禍患。(亦作 **imminency**)

***im·mi·nent**〔'ɪmənənt; 'iminənt〕*adj.* ①即將來臨的;逼近的。He was faced with *imminent* death. 他面臨逼在眼前的死亡。②朝前突出的。 —**ly,** *adv.*

im·mis·ci·ble〔ɪ'mɪsəbl; i'misəbl〕*adj.* 不融和的;難混合的〖with〗。

im·mis·sion〔ɪ'mɪʃən; i'miʃən〕*n.* 注入;注射。

im·mit·i·ga·ble〔ɪ'mɪtəgəbl; i'mitigəbl〕*adj.* 不能減輕的;不可和緩的;不能寬恕的。

im·mix·ture〔ɪm'mɪkstʃɚ;i'mikstʃə〕*n.* ①混合;混和。②被捲入。

im·mo·bile〔ɪ'mobl; i'moubail〕*adj.* ①不能(被)移動的。②不動的;不變的;靜止的。

im·mo·bil·i·ty〔ˌɪmo'bɪlətɪ; ˌimou'biliti〕*n.* 不動(之狀態或性質);固定;靜止。

im·mo·bi·lize〔ɪ'moblˌaɪz; i'moubilaiz〕*v.t.,* **-lized, -liz·ing.** ①固定; 使不動。②使 (軍隊等) 不能動員。 Our planes were *immobilized* by bad weather. 我們的飛機因惡劣的天氣而無法出動。③停止 (貨幣)流通。—**im·mo·bi·li·za·tion,** *n.*

im·mod·er·ate〔ɪ'mɑdərɪt; i'mɔdərit〕 *adj.* 無節制的;太多的;極端的。 —**ly,** *adv.* —**ness,** *n.*

im·mod·er·a·tion〔ɪmˌmɑdə'reʃən; 'iˌmɔdə'reiʃən〕*n.* 無節制;過度;極端。

im·mod·est〔ɪ'mɑdɪst; i'mɔdist〕*adj.* ①粗魯的; 無禮的。②厚顏無恥的。③無節制的;過度的。④放肆的;不貞的。—**ly,** *adv.*

im·mod·es·ty〔ɪ'mɑdɪstɪ; i'mɔdisti〕*n.* ①無禮;粗暴。②無節制;過度。③不貞;不正當的行爲。

im·mo·late〔'ɪməˌlet; 'imouleit〕*v.t.,* **-lat·ed, -lat·ing.** ①犧牲。②爲祭神而用火燒死;以…爲犧牲。

im·mo·la·tion〔ˌɪmə'leʃən; ˌimou'leiʃən〕*n.* 犧牲。

im·mo·la·tor〔'ɪməˌletɚ; 'imouleitə〕*n.* 供犧牲的人;奉獻犧牲者。

im·mor·al〔ɪ'mɔrəl; i'mɔrəl〕*adj.* ①不道德的; 邪惡的。 Lying and stealing are *immoral.* 說謊與偸竊是不道德的。②淫蕩的;不貞的。—**ly,** *adv.*

im·mo·ral·i·ty〔ˌɪmə'rælətɪ; ˌimə'ræliti〕*n., pl.* **-ties.** ①不道德;罪惡。②淫蕩;不貞。③不道德的行爲;淫蕩的行爲。

***im·mor·tal**〔ɪ'mɔrtl; i'mɔ:tl〕*adj.* ①不死的;永遠的。A man's body dies, but his soul may be *immortal.* 一個人的肉體死去，但其靈魂可能不死。②神祇的; 神聖的; 與神祇有關的。③永遠被人記得的; 聲名永垂不朽的。The fame of Homer should be *immortal.* 荷馬的名譽該是不朽的了。—*n.* ①(the～) (*pl.*) 神祇(尤指古希臘羅馬的神祇)。②不朽的人物。 Shakespeare is one of the *immortals.* 莎士比亞是不朽的人物之一。

immortal hand〖橋牌〗無法被擊敗的一手牌。

***im·mor·tal·i·ty**〔ˌɪmɔr'tælətɪ; ˌimɔ:'tæliti〕*n.* ①不朽;不朽或不死的性質。②不朽的聲名; 不朽的行爲。 He has achieved *immortality.* 他已獲得永垂不朽的聲名。

im·mor·tal·i·za·tion〔ɪˌmɔrtəlaɪ'zeʃən; iˌmɔ:təlai'zeiʃən〕*n.* 不朽;不滅;永存。

im·mor·tal·ize〔ɪ'mɔrtlˌaɪz; i'mɔ:təlaiz〕*v.t.,* **-ized, -iz·ing.** ①使不朽;使永存。②使得不朽之名。

im·mor·tal·ly〔ɪ'mɔrtəlɪ; i'mɔ:təli〕*adv.* ①永遠;永久;常年地。②〖俗〗無限地;非常。

im·mor·telle〔ˌɪmɔr'tɛl; ˌimɔ:'tel〕*n.* 〖植物〗山鼠麴草。

im·mov·a·bil·i·ty〔ɪˌmuvə'bɪlətɪ; iˌmu:və'biliti〕*n.* 固定(性);不動(性)。

im·mov·a·ble〔ɪ'muvəbl; i'mu:vəbl〕*adj.* ①不可移動的; 固定的; 不動的。②堅定不移的。③不動的。④不受感動的;無感情的。—*n.* (*pl.*) 不動產。

im·mov·a·bly〔ɪ'muvəblɪ; i'mu:vəbli〕*adv.* 不動地。

im·mune〔ɪ'mjun; i'mju:n〕*adj.* ①免

除的;被豁免的(如免付捐稅等)。②免疫的(如由種痘等的結果)。to be *immune* from smallpox as the result of vaccination. 由於種痘的結果而不受天花的傳染。

immune body 免疫體;抗體。

im·mu·ni·ty 〔ɪˈmjunətɪ; iˈmju:niti〕 *n., pl.* **-ties.** ①免疫;免疫性。②(捐稅、義務等的)免除。③安全;安全性。

im·mu·ni·za·tion 〔ˌɪmjunəˈzeʃən; ˌimju(:)naiˈzeiʃən〕 *n.* 成不感性;免疫作用;免疫法。

im·mu·nize 〔ˈɪmjəˌnaɪz; ˈimju:naiz〕 *v.t.* 使免疫。

im·mu·nol·o·gy 〔ˌɪmjəˈnɑlədʒɪ; ˌimjuˈnɔlədʒi〕 *n.* 免疫學;疾病預防學。

im·mure 〔ɪˈmjur; iˈmjuə〕 *v.t.*, **-mured, -mur·ing.** 幽禁;囚禁。—**ment,** *n.*

im·mu·ta·ble 〔ɪˈmjutəbl̩; iˈmju:təbl〕 *adj.* 不變的;不易的。—**im·mu·ta·bil·i·ty,** *n.* —**im·mu·ta·bly,** *adv.*

imp[1] 〔ɪmp; imp〕 *n.* ①小鬼。②頑童。

imp[2] *v.t.*, **imped, imp·ing.** ①〖古〗添翼於。②〖古〗修補;增添。③以羽毛修補(鷹翼)。

imp. ①imperative. ②imperfect. ③imperial. ④import. ⑤imported. ⑥imprimatur (拉 = let it be printed).

im·pact 〔*n.* ˈɪmpækt; ˈimpækt *v.* ɪmˈpækt; imˈpækt〕 *n.* ①衝突;撞擊。②撞擊力;震擊力。③影響。—*v.t.* ①塡裝;擠入;壓緊。②擊中。—*v.i.* ①撞擊。②發生影響。

im·pact·ed 〔ɪmˈpæktɪd; imˈpæktid〕 *adj.* ①壓緊的。②〖醫〗陷在顎骨中長不出的(牙齒);嵌入的。③〖美〗(某地區內因居民陡增,公共設施需要增加而造成之)財務負擔沉重的。

im·pac·tion 〔ɪmˈpækʃən; imˈpækʃən〕 *n.* ①裝緊;壓緊。②〖醫〗嵌入;阻塞。

im·pair 〔ɪmˈpɛr; imˈpɛə〕 *v.t.* 損害;傷害。to *impair* one's health. 損害其健康。

im·pair·ment 〔ɪmˈpɛrmənt; imˈpɛəmənt〕 *n.* 損傷;損失。

im·pale 〔ɪmˈpel; imˈpeil〕 *v.t.*, **-paled, -pal·ing.** ①以尖物刺住或刺穿。②處以刺刑。③圍以木樁;以籬圍住。④使…感覺無可奈何。(亦作 **empale**) —**ment,** *n.*

im·pal·pa·ble 〔ɪmˈpælpəbl̩; imˈpælpəbl〕*adj.* ①無法感觸到的。②難理解的。—**im·pal·pa·bil·i·ty,** *n.* —**im·pal·pa·bly,** *adv.*

im·pan·el 〔ɪmˈpænl̩; imˈpænl〕 *v.t.*, **-el(l)ed, -el·(l)ing.** ①列名派充爲陪審員。②從名單中選陪審員。③列…名單。(亦作 **empanel**) —**ment,** *n.*

im·par·a·dise 〔ɪmˈpærəˌdaɪs; imˈpærədais〕 *v.t.*, **-dised, -dis·ing.** ①置於樂園中;使享至福。②使樂園化;使成爲福地。

im·par·i·ty 〔ɪmˈpærətɪ; imˈpæriti〕 *n.* 不同;不等;差異。

im·park 〔ɪmˈpɑrk; imˈpɑ:k〕 *v.t.* 放(動物)於獵苑;圍(林地等)作獵苑。—**a·tion,** *n.*

***im·part** 〔ɪmˈpɑrt; imˈpɑ:t〕 *v.t.* ①分給;傳授。A teacher *imparts* knowledge to her pupils. 教師傳授知識給她的學生。②通知;告知。to *impart* a secret to someone. 告知某人一項祕密。—**a·ble,** *adj.*

***im·par·tial** 〔ɪmˈpɑrʃəl; imˈpɑ:ʃəl〕 *adj.* 公平的;不偏不倚的。Law shall be uniform and *impartial.* 法律應該一視同仁而不偏不倚。—**ly,** *adv.*

im·par·ti·al·i·ty 〔ˌɪmpɑrˈʃælətɪ; ˈimˌpɑ:ʃiˈæliti〕 *n.* 公平;無私。

im·part·i·ble 〔ɪmˈpɑrtəbl̩; imˈpɑ:tibl〕 *adj.* (土地等)不可分的。

im·pass·a·bil·i·ty 〔ˌɪmpæsəˈbɪlətɪ; ˈimˌpɑ:səˈbiliti〕 *n.* 不能通行或通過。We were stopped by the complete *impassability* of the road. 我們因路完全不通而停下來。

im·pass·a·ble 〔ɪmˈpæsəbl̩; imˈpɑ:səbl〕 *adj.* ①不能通行或通過的。②無法流通或傳布的。—**im·pass·a·bly,** *adv.* —**ness,** *n.*

im·passe 〔ɪmˈpæs; æmˈpɑ:s〕〖法〗 *n.* ①僵局。②死路;死巷。

im·pas·si·bil·i·ty 〔ɪmˌpæsəˈbɪlətɪ; imˌpæsiˈbiliti〕 *n.* ①無痛感。②麻木;泰然自若。③冷淡;無動於衷。

im·pas·si·ble 〔ɪmˈpæsəbl̩; imˈpæsəbl〕 *adj.* ①不感覺痛苦的。②麻木的;泰然自若的。③無動於衷的;不動感情的。—**ness,** *n.*

im·pas·sion 〔ɪmˈpæʃən; imˈpæʃən〕 *v.t.* 使感動;使感激。

im·pas·sioned 〔ɪmˈpæʃənd; imˈpæʃənd〕 *adj.* 充滿熱情的;感奮的;慷慨激昂的。

im·pas·sive 〔ɪmˈpæsɪv; imˈpæsiv〕 *adj.* ①不動感情的;鎭靜的。②麻木的;無知覺的。③不能傷害的。④不動的;靜止的。—**ness,** *n.*

im·pas·sive·ly 〔ɪmˈpæsɪvlɪ; imˈpæsivli〕 *adv.* 鎭靜地;不動感情地。

im·pas·siv·i·ty 〔ˌɪmpæˈsɪvətɪ; ˌimpæˈsiviti〕 *n.* 無感覺;冷淡;冷靜;泰然自若。

im·paste 〔ɪmˈpest; imˈpeist〕 *v.t.*, **-past·ed, -past·ing.** ①用漿糊封牢。②使成糊狀。③〖繪畫〗厚塗彩色。

im·pas·to 〔ɪmˈpɑsto; imˈpɑ:stou〕 *n.* 〖繪畫〗厚塗(畫法);厚塗的顏料。

***im·pa·tience** 〔ɪmˈpeʃəns; imˈpeiʃəns〕 *n.* ①性急;暴躁。He has a keen *impatience* with the dull. 他對於遲鈍的人極不耐煩。②難耐;難忍。*impatience* of hypocrisy. 對於僞善之不能忍耐。③焦急。

im·pa·tient** 〔ɪmˈpeʃənt; imˈpeiʃənt〕 *adj.* ①不耐煩;不能忍受。Jim is *impatient* with his little sister. 吉姆對他的小妹妹實在不耐煩。②焦急。The horses were *impatient* to start in the race. 馬急着要開始競賽。③表示不耐煩的。impatient of*** 不能忍受;忍不住;討厭。—**ly,** *adv.*

im·pawn 〔ɪmˈpɔn; imˈpɔ:n〕 *v.t.* ①質押;典當。②立誓擔保。

im·peach 〔ɪmˈpitʃ; imˈpi:tʃ〕 *v.t.* ①非難;挑剔;指摘。②控告;控訴。③檢舉;彈劾。—*n.* =**impeachment.**

im·peach·a·ble 〔ɪmˈpitʃəbl; imˈpi:tʃəbl〕 *adj.* 應彈劾的;可檢舉的;可告發的。

im·peach·ment 〔ɪmˈpitʃmənt; imˈpi:tʃmənt〕 *n.* 非難;指摘;檢舉;彈劾。

im·pearl 〔ɪmˈpɝl; imˈpə:l〕 *v.t.* 〖詩〗①使成珍珠狀。②綴以珍珠。

im·pec·ca·bil·i·ty 〔ɪmˌpɛkəˈbɪlətɪ; imˌpekəˈbiliti〕 *n.* 無過;無罪;無瑕疵;完善。

im·pec·ca·ble 〔ɪmˈpɛkəbl̩; imˈpekəbl〕 *adj.* 無瑕疵的;完善的;純潔的。—*n.* 完善、純潔、無罪的人。

im·pe·cu·ni·os·i·ty 〔ˌɪmpɪˌkjunɪˈɑsətɪ; ˌimpiˌkju:niˈɔsiti〕 *n.* 無錢;貧窮。

im·pe·cu·ni·ous 〔ˌɪmpɪˈkjunɪəs; ˌimpiˈkju:njəs〕 *adj.* 貧窮的;無錢的。

im·ped·ance 〔ɪmˈpidn̩s; imˈpi:dəns〕 *n.* 〖電〗阻抗(於交流電中電壓對電流之比,相當於直流電之電阻)。

im·pede 〔ɪmˈpid; imˈpi:d〕 *v.t.*, **-ped·ed, -ped·ing.** 妨礙;阻礙。

im·ped·i·ment 〔ɪmˈpɛdəmənt; im-

I

ˈpedimənt〕 *n.* ①妨礙; 阻礙; 妨礙物。②結巴;口吃。*throw impediments in the way* 阻礙進行。

im·ped·i·men·ta 〔ˌɪmpɛdəˈmɛntə; imˌpediˈmentə〕 *n. pl.* ①妨礙物; (旅行時之)累贅;(特指)行李。②〖軍〗輜重。③〖法律〗障礙;阻礙。

im·ped·i·men·tal 〔ɪmˌpɛdəˈmɛntl̩; imˌpediˈmentl〕 *adj.* 妨礙的。

***im·pel** 〔ɪmˈpɛl; imˈpel〕 *v.t.*, **-pelled, -pel·ling.** ①推進。②逼迫; 驅使。Hunger *impelled* the lazy man to work. 饑餓驅使那懶人工作。

im·pel·lent 〔ɪmˈpɛlənt; imˈpelənt〕 *adj.* 推進的;强迫的; 驅使的。—*n.* 推進力。

im·pel·ler 〔ɪmˈpɛlɚ; imˈpelə〕 *n.* ①推進物; 推進者。②〖機械〗(渦輪、電扇等之)葉輪。

im·pend 〔ɪmˈpɛnd; imˈpend〕 *v.t.* ①迫近;逼近。②懸空;懸掛。

im·pend·ence 〔ɪmˈpɛndəns; imˈpendəns〕 *n.* 臨頭;迫切;急迫。(亦作 **impendency**)

im·pend·ent 〔ɪmˈpɛndənt; imˈpendənt〕 *adj.* =**impending.**

im·pend·ing 〔ɪmˈpɛndɪŋ; imˈpendiŋ〕 *adj.* ①可能就要發生的。②即將舉行的。③懸在上面的。

im·pen·e·tra·bil·i·ty 〔ˌɪmpɛnətrəˈbɪlətɪ; imˌpenitrəˈbiliti〕 *n.* ①不可入;不能貫穿。②〖物理〗不可入性。③不可測知; 不可解。④無情;冷酷。

im·pen·e·tra·ble 〔ɪmˈpɛnətrəbl̩; imˈpenitrəbl〕 *adj.* ①不能穿過的; 不能進入的。②不接納(外來思想、影響等)的。③不可理解的; 難以探究的。④〖物理〗不可入的。—**im·pen·e·tra·bly,** *adv.*

im·pen·e·trate 〔ɪmˈpɛnɪˌtret; imˈpenitreit〕 *v.t.*, **-trat·ed, -trat·ing.** 透入;穿入;浸透。

im·pen·i·tent 〔ɪmˈpɛnətənt; imˈpenitənt〕 *adj.* 無悔意的;不悔悟的。—**im·pen·i·tence, im·pen·i·ten·cy,** *n.* —**ly,** *adv.*

imper. imperative.

im·per·a·ti·val 〔ɪmˌpɛrəˈtaɪvəl; imˌperəˈtaivəl〕 *adj.* 〖文法〗祈使語氣的。

***im·per·a·tive** 〔ɪmˈpɛrətɪv; imˈperətiv〕 *adj.* ①急需的;必要的。It is *imperative* that we should have a strong air force. 我們急需要有強大的空軍。②命令式的; 令人必須服從的。an *imperative* tone. 命令式的語調。③〖文法〗祈使法的。the *imperative* mood. 祈使法;祈使語氣。—*n.* ①命令; 誡命。②〖文法〗祈使法 (=imperative mood). ③規則。④需要。—**ly,** *adv.* —**ness,** *n.*

im·pe·ra·tor 〔ˌɪmpəˈretɚ; ˌimpəˈreitə〕 *n.* 〖羅馬史〗①凱旋將軍;大將軍(對戰勝將軍之稱號)。②元首;皇帝。

im·per·cep·ti·bil·i·ty 〔ˌɪmpɚˌsɛptəˈbɪlətɪ; ˈim-pəˌseptəˈbiliti〕 *n.* 細微; 目所不見;心所不覺。

im·per·cep·ti·ble 〔ˌɪmpɚˈsɛptəbl̩; ˌimpəˈseptəbl〕 *adj.* ①不能感覺到的。②微小的。—**ness,** *n.* —**im·per·cep·ti·bly,** *adv.*

im·per·cep·tive 〔ˌɪmpɚˈsɛptɪv; ˌimpəˈseptiv〕 *adj.* 無感受的;不感覺的。

im·per·cip·i·ent 〔ˌɪmpɚˈsɪpɪənt; ˌimpəˈsipiənt〕 *adj.* =**imperceptive.**

imperf. ①imperfect. ②imperforate(d).

***im·per·fect** 〔ɪmˈpɝfɪkt; imˈpəːfikt〕 *adj.* ①不完全的; 有缺點的。an *imperfect* husband. 有缺點的丈夫。②〖文法〗未完了時的; 半過去的。*imperfect* tense.〖文法〗未完了時式;半過去式(表示過去進行或過去習慣的時式)。—*n.* 未完了時式動詞; 半過去式動詞(英文中無此時式,但有was studying及used to study, 與其他語言之未完了時式相似)。—**ly,** *adv.* —**ness,** *n.*

im·per·fec·tion 〔ˌɪmpɚˈfɛkʃən; ˌimpəˈfekʃən〕 *n.* ①不完善;不完全。②缺點。

im·per·fo·rate 〔ɪmˈpɝfərɪt; imˈpəːfərit〕 *adj.* ①無孔的。②(郵票)無齒孔的。③〖解剖〗無正常之開口的。—*n.* 無齒孔之郵票。

***im·pe·ri·al** 〔ɪmˈpɪrɪəl; imˈpiəriəl〕 *adj.* ①帝國的; 皇帝的; 至尊的。His *Imperial* Majesty. 國王陛下;皇上。②宗主國的;宗主權的。③壯麗的; 堂皇的。the *imperial* hyacinth. 壯麗的洋水仙。④宏大的; 質地最優的。⑤英國度量衡制的。—*n.* ①皇帝髭(蓄於下唇下面之小鬚)。②一種紙的尺度(美制23×31英寸,英制22×30英寸)。—**ly,** *adv.*

imperial gallon 英國(法定)加侖(約等於 1.2美國加侖)。(略作 **imp. gal.**)

im·pe·ri·al·ism 〔ɪmˈpɪrɪəlˌɪzəm; imˈpiəriəlizəm〕 *n.* ①帝國主義。②霸業。

im·pe·ri·al·ist 〔ɪmˈpɪrɪəlɪst; imˈpiəriəlist〕 *n.* 帝國主義者。—*adj.* 帝國主義的。

im·pe·ri·al·is·tic 〔ɪmˌpɪrɪəlˈɪstɪk; imˌpiəriəˈlistik〕 *adj.* ①帝國主義的。②支持帝國主義的。—**al·ly,** *adv.*

Imperial Valley 帝王谷(美國 California 州東南部之一灌溉農業區域)。

im·per·il 〔ɪmˈpɛrəl; imˈperil〕 *v.t.*, **-il(l)ed, -il·(l)ing.** 使陷於危險中;危及。

***im·pe·ri·ous** 〔ɪmˈpɪrɪəs; imˈpiəriəs〕 *adj.* ①傲慢的;專橫的。an *imperious* gesture. 一副蠻橫姿態。②迫切的; 緊急的。*imperious* want. 迫切的需要。—**ness,** *n.*

im·pe·ri·ous·ly 〔ɪmˈpɪrɪəslɪ; imˈpiəriəsli〕 *adv.* 專橫地。

im·per·ish·a·bil·i·ty 〔ˌɪmpɛrɪʃəˈbɪlətɪ; imˌperiʃəˈbiliti〕 *n.* 不滅;不朽;永恒。

im·per·ish·a·ble 〔ɪmˈpɛrɪʃəbl̩; imˈperiʃəbl〕 *adj.* 不滅的; 不朽的; 不會被遺忘的; 永恒的。—**im·per·ish·a·bly,** *adv.* —**ness,** *n.*

im·pe·ri·um 〔ɪmˈpɪrɪəm; imˈpiəriəm〕 *n.*, *pl.* **-ri·a** 〔-rɪə; -riə〕. ①統帥權;最高統治權;帝權。②〖法律〗司法權;絕對權;主權。

im·per·ma·nence 〔ɪmˈpɝmənəns; imˈpəːmənəns〕 *n.* =**impermanency.**

im·per·ma·nen·cy 〔ɪmˈpɝmənənsɪ; imˈpəːmənənsi〕 *n.* 非永久;非永續性;無常。

im·per·ma·nent 〔ɪmˈpɝmənənt; imˈpəːmənənt〕 *adj.* 非永久的。—**ly,** *adv.*

im·per·me·a·ble 〔ɪmˈpɝmɪəbl̩; imˈpəːmjəbl〕 *adj.* 不能貫穿的;不透(水等)的; 無浸透性的。—**im·per·me·a·bil·i·ty,** *n.*

im·per·son·al 〔ɪmˈpɝsn̩l; imˈpəːsənl〕 *adj.* ①一般人稱的; 非指某一特殊人稱的。②無人格的;不具人格的。③〖文法〗無人稱的;無主的。④客觀的。—**ly,** *adv.*

im·per·son·al·i·ty 〔ˌɪmpɝsn̩ˈælətɪ; imˌpəːsəˈnæliti〕 *n.* ①客觀。②無人格; 不具人格。③一般性。④無人格性之事物。

im·per·son·ate 〔*v.* ɪmˈpɝsn̩ˌet; imˈpəːsəneit *adj.* ɪmˈpɝsn̩ɪt; imˈpəːsnit〕 *v.*, **-at·ed, -at·ing,** *adj.* —*v.t.* ①扮演;飾。②模仿; 模擬。③人格化; 代表; 爲…之典型。—*adj.* 具有人格的。—**im·per·son·a·tor,** *n.*

im·per·son·a·tion 〔ˌɪmpɝsn̩ˈeʃən; imˌpəːsəˈneiʃən〕 *n.* 扮演;模擬。

im·per·ti·nence [ɪm'pɝtn̩əns; im'pəːtinəns] *n.* ①無禮；鹵莽。②無禮的行爲；鹵莽的話。③無禮的人；冒失鬼。④不切題；不相干。(亦作 **impertinency**)

im·per·ti·nent [ɪm'pɝtn̩ənt; im'pəːtinənt] *adj.* ①無禮的；粗暴的。②不切題的；不相干的。

im·per·ti·nent·ly [ɪm'pɝtn̩əntlɪ; im'pəːtinəntli] *adv.* 無禮地；冒昧地。

im·per·turb·a·bil·i·ty [ˌɪmpɚˌtɝbə'bɪlətɪ; 'im-pə(ː)ˌtəːbə'biliti] *n.* 冷靜；沉着；鎮定。

im·per·turb·a·ble [ˌɪmpɚ'tɝbəbl̩; ˌim-pə(ː)'təːbəbl] *adj.* 鎮靜的；沉靜的；不易激動的。

im·per·turb·a·bly [ˌɪmpɚ'tɝbəblɪ; ˌim-pə(ː)'təːbəbli] *adv.* 鎮靜地；泰然自若地。

im·per·tur·ba·tion [ˌɪmpɝtə'beʃən; ˌimpə(ː)tə'beiʃən] *n.* 沉着；冷靜。

im·per·vi·a·ble [ɪm'pɝvɪəbl̩; im'pəːviəbl] *adj.* =**impervious.**

im·per·vi·ous [ɪm'pɝvɪəs; im'pəːvjəs] *adj.* ①不能透過的；不能滲透的。②不受影響的；不爲所動的。—**ly,** *adv.*—**ness,** *n.*

im·pe·ti·go [ˌɪmpɪ'taɪgo; ˌimpi'taigou] *n.* 【醫】小膿疱疹。

im·pe·trate ['ɪmpəˌtret; 'impətreit] *v.t.*, **-trat·ed, -trat·ing.** ①懇求。②以懇求獲得。

im·pet·u·os·i·ty [ˌɪmpɛtʃu'ɑsətɪ; imˌpetju'ɔsiti] *n., pl.* **-ties.** ①猛烈；激烈；熱烈。②激烈之動作或感情。

im·pet·u·ous [ɪm'pɛtʃuəs; im'petjuəs] *adj.* ①猛烈的；奔騰的。②輕舉妄動的；衝動的。Children are usually more *impetuous* than old people. 孩子們常比老年人衝動。—**ness,** *n.*

im·pet·u·ous·ly [ɪm'pɛtʃuəslɪ; im'petʃuəsli] *adv.* 奔騰地；猛烈地；衝動地。

im·pe·tus ['ɪmpətəs; 'impitəs] *n., pl.* **-tus·es.** ①衝力。②推動力；原動力；刺激。

imp. gal. imperial gallon.

im·pi ['ɪmpɪ; 'impi] *n., pl.* **im·pies.** 【南非】Kaffir 族之武裝大部隊。

im·pi·e·ty [ɪm'paɪətɪ; im'paiəti] *n., pl.* **-ties.** ①(對上帝) 不信；不敬；邪惡。②不恭；不尊敬；不孝順。③不恭敬或不虔敬的言行。

im·pinge [ɪm'pɪndʒ; im'pindʒ] *v.t.*, **-pinged, -ping·ing.** ①打擊；衝擊。②侵害；侵犯。③影響。

im·pinge·ment [ɪm'pɪndʒmənt; im'pindʒmənt] *n.* 影響。

im·pi·ous ['ɪmpɪəs; 'impiəs] *adj.* (對上帝)不信的；不虔敬的；邪惡的；瀆聖的；不恭的；不孝順的。—**ly,** *adv.*

imp·ish ['ɪmpɪʃ; 'impiʃ] *adj.* 像小鬼的；頑皮的；惡作劇的。

im·pla·ca·bil·i·ty [ˌɪmplekə'bɪlətɪ; imˌplækə'biliti] *n.* ①難和解；難撫慰。②深仇；殘忍。

im·pla·ca·ble [ɪm'plekəbl̩; im'plækəbl] *adj.* 難和解的；難平息的。—**im·pla·ca·bly,** *adv.* —**ness,** *n.*

im·plant [ɪm'plænt; im'plɑːnt] *v.t.* ①灌輸；注入。②嵌入。③【醫】移植。④種植；培植。—*n.* 【醫】①移植的活體素。②內有放射性物質以嵌入器官或體素內俾治療癌症之小管。

im·plan·ta·tion [ˌɪmplæn'teʃən; ˌim-plɑːn'teiʃən] *n.* ①種植；培植；移植。②教；灌輸；鼓吹。③(牙齒之) 嵌入。④【醫】(藥品等之)皮下注入；皮下插入。⑤【醫】(腫瘤細胞等之)轉移。

im·plau·si·ble [ɪm'plɔzəbl̩; im'plɔːzəbl] *adj.* 不似眞實的；難於相信的。

***im·ple·ment** [*n.* 'ɪmpləmənt; 'impliмənt *v.* 'ɪmpləˌmɛnt; 'impliment] *n.* 工具；器具。farm *implements.* 農具。—*v.t.* ①(以工具)供給。②實現；完成。③使生效；實施；執行。to *implement* an order. 執行一項命令。

im·ple·men·tal [ˌɪmplə'mɛntl̩; ˌimpli'mentl] *adj.* 工具的；作手段的；有幫助的。

im·ple·men·ta·tion [ˌɪmpləmɛn'teʃən; ˌimplimen'teiʃən] *n.* ①履行；完成；實行。②供給工具。

im·ple·tion [ɪm'pliʃən; im'pliːʃən] *n.* ①充滿；充實。②充滿之物。

im·pli·cate ['ɪmplɪˌket; 'implikeit] *v.*, **-cat·ed, -cat·ing,** *adj.* —*v.t.* ①牽連；涉及。②暗示。③使糾纏；使糾結。—*adj.* 暗示的。

im·pli·ca·tion [ˌɪmplɪ'keʃən; ˌimpli'keiʃən] *n.* ①含意；含蓄。②暗示。③牽連；糾纏。

im·pli·ca·tive [ɪm'plɪkətɪv; im'plikətiv] *adj.* ①有含蓄的；有言外之意的；暗示的。②牽連的。

im·plic·it [ɪm'plɪsɪt; im'plisit] *adj.* ①暗含的；含蓄的。②絕對的；盲從的；毫不懷疑的；不問理由的。③幾乎整個包括在內的。—**ly,** *adv.*

im·plied [ɪm'plaɪd; im'plaid] *adj.* 含蓄的；暗示的；言外的。

im·plied·ly [ɪm'plaɪdlɪ; im'plaidli] *adv.* 不言而喻地；言外地。

***im·plore** [ɪm'plor, -'plɔr; im'plɔː] *v.*, **-plored, -plor·ing.** —*v.t.* 懇求；哀求；苦求。to *implore* a judge for mercy. 懇求法官的憐憫。—*v.i.* 懇求；哀求。She wished he would stop begging and *imploring.* 她但願他不再苦苦哀求。

im·plor·ing [ɪm'plorɪŋ; im'plɔːriŋ] *adj.* 哀懇的；切求的。—**ly,** *adv.*

im·plo·sion [ɪm'ploʒən; im'plouʒən] *n.* ①向內破裂。②【語音】內破裂；閉壓 (如發 p、t、k 等子音時)。

***im·ply** [ɪm'plaɪ; im'plai] *v.t.*, **-plied, -ply·ing.** ①暗示；暗指；意含；含…的意思。Silence sometimes *implies* consent. 沉默有時意含應允。②包含；必須具備。③意指；認爲。You *imply* that I am not telling the truth. 你的意思認爲我說的不是實話。

im·po ['ɪmpo; 'impou] *n.* 【英俚】罰做作業 (imposition 之略)。

im·pol·der, em·pol·der [ɪm'poldɚ; im'pouldə] *v.t.* 開發(海埔新生地)。

im·po·lite [ˌɪmpə'laɪt; ˌim-pə'lait] *adj.* 不客氣的；無禮貌的；粗魯的。—**ness,** *n.*

im·po·lite·ly [ˌɪmpə'laɪtlɪ; ˌim-pə'laitli] *adv.* 不客氣地；無禮貌地。to behave *impolitely.* 行爲不客氣。

im·pol·i·tic [ɪm'pɑlətɪk; im'pɔlitik] *adj.* 失策的；不智的；不利的；不得宜的。—**ly,** *adv.* —**ness,** *n.*

im·pon·der·a·bil·i·ty [ɪmˌpɑndərə'bɪlətɪ; imˌpɔndərə'biliti] *n.* 不可稱量；極輕微。

im·pon·der·a·ble [ɪm'pɑndərəbl̩; im'pɔndərəbl] *adj.* ①不可稱量的；極輕的。②無法衡量的。—*n.* ①【物理】不可稱量之物 (指光、熱等)。②(*pl.*)不可計量或估價之物。

***im·port** [*v.* ɪm'port, -'pɔrt; im'pɔːt *n.* 'ɪmport, -pɔrt; 'impɔːt] *v.t.* ①輸入；進

口。America *imports* raw silk from Japan. 美國自日本輸入生絲。②意含;含…的意思。What does this news *import?* 此項消息有何意義? —*v.i.* 重要;有重大關係。—*n.* ①(常 *pl.*) 輸入品;進口貨。*Imports* exceeded exports in value last year. 去年輸入品的價值超出輸出品。②輸入;進口。③意義;涵義。What is the *import* of his remarks? 他的話的涵義是甚麼? ④重要性。

im·port·a·ble [ɪmˈportəbl̩; imˈpɔːtəbl] *adj.* 可輸入的;可進口的。—**im·port·a·bil·i·ty,** *n.*

‡im·por·tance [ɪmˈpɔrtn̩s; imˈpɔːtəns] *n.* 重要;重要性。Do you realize the *importance* of this question? 你了解這個問題的重要性嗎? a person of *importance.* 重要的人。He spoke with an air of *importance.* 他說話時露出了不起的神氣。

‡im·por·tant [ɪmˈpɔrtn̩t; imˈpɔːtənt] *adj.* ①重要的;重大的;要緊的。This matter is very *important.* 這事非常重要。②位尊的;顯要的。A prime minister is a very *important* man. 首相是一個很顯要的人物。③自尊自大的;驕傲的。An *important* little man rushed around giving orders. 一個自尊自大的小人物東奔西跑發布命令。④大額的;大量的。He spent *important* money on a small gem for his wife. 他花大筆錢買一小小的寶石給太太。—**ly,** *adv.*

im·por·ta·tion [ˌɪmporˈteʃən; ˌimpɔːˈteiʃən] *n.* ①輸入;進口。②輸入品;進口貨。

im·port·er [ɪmˈportɚ; imˈpɔːtə] *n.* 「輸入者;進口商。」

import exchange 進口外匯。

im·por·tu·nate [ɪmˈpɔrtʃənɪt; imˈpɔːtjunit] *adj.* ①堅決請求的;纏擾不休的。②急切的;緊急的。③討厭的。—**ly,** *adv.*

im·por·tune [ˌɪmpɚˈtjun; imˈpɔːtjuːn] *v.,* **-tuned, -tun·ing.** —*v.t.* 强求;不斷請求;煩瀆。—*v.i.* 做迫切請求。

im·por·tu·ni·ty [ˌɪmpɚˈtjunətɪ; ˌimpɔːˈtjuːniti] *n., pl.* **-ties.** ①强求;堅請;煩瀆。②(*pl.*)不斷的請求;堅決的請求。

***im·pose** [ɪmˈpoz; imˈpouz] *v.,* **-posed, -pos·ing.** —*v.t.* ①課(稅);加(負擔、懲罰)於。New duties were *imposed* on wines and spirits. 酒類被加徵新稅。②强欲;强使。You shouldn't *impose* yourself (*or* your company) on people who don't want you. 你不應當勉强與不需要你的人在一起。③騙使他人買受(贋品等)。④〖宗敎〗按(手)於其上以行堅振禮或任命聖職禮。⑤〖印刷〗整版;裝版。—*v.i.* 利用;欺騙。*impose on* (or *upon*) **a.** 占…的便宜;利用。**b.** 欺騙。**c.** 强(人)所難;打擾。

***im·pos·ing** [ɪmˈpozɪŋ; imˈpouziŋ] *adj.* ①壯麗的;堂皇的。The Capitol at Washington, D. C., is an *imposing* building. 位於華盛頓的國會會堂是一座堂皇宏偉的建築物。②偉大的;威風凜凜的;令人羨慕的;難忘的。an *imposing* old lady. 一位儀容莊重的老婦人。—**ly,** *adv.*

im·po·si·tion [ˌɪmpəˈzɪʃən; ˌimpəˈziʃən] *n.* ①(稅等之)徵;課。②徵稅;課稅。③苛捐雜稅。④科罰;懲罰;負擔。⑤欺騙;欺詐。⑥占便宜;利用。⑦(宗敎上的)按手禮。⑧〖印刷〗整版。

***im·pos·si·bil·i·ty** [ɪmˌpɑsəˈbɪlətɪ; imˌpɔsəˈbiliti] *n., pl.,* **-ties.** 不可能;不可能之事。Don't expect me to do *impossibilities!* 不要希望我做不可能的事!

‡im·pos·si·ble [ɪmˈpɑsəbl̩; imˈpɔsəbl] *adj.* ①不可能的;於理不通的。What an *impossible* story! 多麼不可能的事啊! ②做不到的。Few things are *impossible.* 很少有事情是做不到的。③不容易的;很難的。It's *impossible* for me to get there by ten o'clock. 要我十點鐘到達那裏是不易辦到的。④令人無法忍受的。an *impossible* person. 令人無法忍受的人。—*n.* 不可能;不可能之事。His statement is in the nature of an *impossible.* 他的言論屬於不可能的範圍。

im·pos·si·bly [ɪmˈpɑsəblɪ; imˈpɔsibli] *adv.* 不可能地;難以相信地。

im·post¹ [ˈɪmpost; ˈimpoust] *n.* ①進口稅;關稅。②稅;貢賦。—*v.t.* 分(進口貨)之種類以決定其稅額。

im·post² *n.* 〖建築〗支撐拱門之柱頭。

im·pos·tor, im·pos·ter [ɪmˈpɑstɚ; imˈpɔstə] *n.* (冒充某人或某種地位以欺詐別人的)騙子。

im·pos·ture [ɪmˈpɑstʃɚ; imˈpɔstʃə] *n.* ①欺騙;蒙騙。②欺騙行爲;蒙騙行爲。

im·pot [ˈɪmpɑt; ˈimpɔt] *n.* 〖英俚〗= **impo.**

im·po·tence [ˈɪmpətəns; ˈimpətəns] *n.* ①無能;無助;虛弱。②〖醫〗陽萎;腎虛。

im·po·ten·cy [ˈɪmpətənsɪ; ˈimpətənsi] *n.* =**impotence.**

im·po·tent [ˈɪmpətənt; ˈimpətənt] *adj.* ①無行動能力的;無能的;虛弱的。②無效力的;無力量的;無助的。③陽萎的;不能性交的。—**ly,** *adv.* —**ness,** *n.*

im·pound [ɪmˈpaund; imˈpaund] *v.t.* ①(將獸類)關於欄中。②扣留;收押;保管。③聚集(水)。—**a·ble,** *adj.*

im·pov·er·ish [ɪmˈpɑvərɪʃ; imˈpɔvəriʃ] *v.t.* ①使成赤貧。②耗盡(地力);使(土壤)貧瘠。③用盡;竭盡。(亦作 **empoverish**)

im·pov·er·ish·ment [ɪmˈpɑvərɪʃmənt; imˈpɔvəriʃmənt] *n.* ①赤貧;貧窮;貧乏;貧瘠。②致使貧乏或貧瘠之事物。

im·pow·er [ɪmˈpauɚ; imˈpauə] *v.t.* =**empower.**

im·prac·ti·ca·bil·i·ty [ɪmˌpræktɪkəˈbɪlətɪ; imˌpræktikəˈbiliti] *n., pl.* **-ties.** ①不能實行;不切實際;不能實行之事。②不堪用;難馭;固執。

im·prac·ti·ca·ble [ɪmˈpræktɪkəbl̩; imˈpræktikəbl] *adj.* ①不能實行的;不切實際的。②難駕馭的。③不能用的。—**im·prac·ti·ca·bly,** *adv.* —**ness,** *n.*

im·prac·ti·cal [ɪmˈpræktɪkl̩; imˈpræktikəl] *adj.* 不合實際的;不能實行的。

im·prac·ti·cal·i·ty [ɪmˌpræktɪˈkælətɪ; imˌpræktiˈkæliti] *n., pl.* **-ties.** ①不實際性;不能實行。②不切實際之事。

im·pre·cate [ˈɪmprɪˌket; ˈimprikeit] *v.t.,* **-cat·ed, -cat·ing.** 詛咒;祈求天降禍於。

im·pre·ca·tion [ˌɪmprɪˈkeʃən; ˌimpriˈkeiʃən] *n.* ①詛咒;咒語。②祈求。

im·pre·ca·to·ry [ˈɪmprɪkəˌtorɪ; ˈimprikeitəri] *adj.* 詛咒的。

im·pre·ci·sion [ˌɪmprɪˈsɪʒən; ˌimpriˈsiʒən] *n.* 不正確;不精確。

im·preg [ˈɪmprɛg; ˈimpreg] *n.* 經合成樹脂處理的合板。

im·preg·na·ble¹ [ɪmˈprɛgnəbl̩; imˈpregnəbl] *adj.* 不能攻破的;難攻取的;鞏固的。—**im·preg·na·bil·i·ty,** *n.*

im·preg·na·ble² *adj.* (卵)可以受精的;可以受孕的。

im·preg·nate 〔*v.* ɪm'prɛgnet; 'impregneit, im'preg- *adj.* ɪm'prɛgnɪt; im'pregnit, -neit〕 *v.*, **-nat·ed, -nat·ing,** *adj.* —*v.t.* ①使懷孕;使受胎。②〖生物〗授精;使結實。③使充滿;使飽和。④灌輸;注入。—*adj.* ①懷孕的。②飽和的;充滿的。

im·preg·na·tion 〔ˌɪmprɛg'neʃən; ˌimpreg'neiʃən〕 *n.* ①受胎;懷孕;授精;飽和;充滿;注入;灌輸。②使懷孕(飽和、充滿等)之物。

im·pre·sa·ri·o 〔ˌɪmprɪ'sɑrɪˌo; ˌimpre'sɑːriou〕 *n., pl.* **-ri·os.** ①(歌劇團或音樂團的)經理人。②(音樂家等的)私人經理人、教師或訓練者。③戲劇等的製作人。

im·pre·scrip·ti·ble 〔ˌɪmprɪ'skrɪptəbl̩; ˌimpri'skriptibl〕 *adj.* 〖法律〗不受法律及慣例之支配的;不可侵犯的;絕對的。

***im·press¹** 〔*v.* ɪm'prɛs; im'pres *n.* 'ɪmprɛs; 'impres〕 *v.t.* ①使得深刻印象。A hero *impresses* us with his courage. 一個英雄以其勇敢使我們得到深刻的印象。②給以影響;使感動。The book did not *impress* me at all. 這本書完全沒有使我感動的地方。③銘記;印入記憶。④蓋印於;蓋(印)。to *impress* wax with a seal. 用印蓋在火漆上。⑤傳遞(動力)。—*v.i.* 引人注目;給人以深刻印象。—*n.* ①印象;印記;記號;特徵。An author leaves the *impress* of his personality on what he writes. 作者於其著作中留下他的性格的特徵。②刻銘;蓋印。③表記;徽章。

im·press² *v.t.* ①强迫(男人)服兵役。to *impress* seamen. 徵海員服役。②徵用。③引用;利用。④積極說服。—*n.* 强迫徵集。

im·press·i·bil·i·ty 〔ˌɪmprɛsə'bɪlətɪ; imˌpresi'biliti〕 *n.* 易感動;感受性。

im·press·i·ble 〔ɪm'prɛsəbl̩; im'presəbl〕 *adj.* 易感動的;感受性强的;敏感的。

***im·pres·sion** 〔ɪm'prɛʃən; im'preʃən〕 *n.* ①印象;效果。His speech made a strong *impression* on the audience. 他的演說給聽衆一個深刻的印象。②意念;概念。I was under the *impression* that you were out of town. 在我的意念中認爲你下鄉去了(卽我以爲你已不在城裏了)。③印;印痕。The thief had left an *impression* of his foot in the garden. 小偸在花園中留下一個脚印。④蓋印;銘刻。a firm *impression* of the seal on the wax. 封蠟上的固印。⑤(書籍)一版所印之總數;一版(卽原版再印刷一次)。⑥印成的一册;一本。⑦(印刷的)壓力。as light an *impression* as practicable. (印刷時)能辦到的最輕壓力。

im·pres·sion·a·ble 〔ɪm'prɛʃənəbl̩; im'preʃənabl〕 *adj.* ①易受感動的;敏感的;易受影響的。②可加印圖樣或文字的。—**im·pres·sion·a·bil·i·ty,** *n.*

im·pres·sion·ism 〔ɪm'prɛʃənˌɪzəm; im'preʃənizəm〕 *n.* 〖繪畫,文學,音樂〗印象主義;印象派;印象主義作風。

im·pres·sion·ist 〔ɪm'prɛʃənɪst; im'preʃənist〕 *n.* 印象主義者;印象派之藝術家。—*adj.* 印象主義的;印象派的。

im·pres·sion·is·tic 〔ɪmˌprɛʃən'ɪstɪk; imˌpreʃə'nistik〕 *adj.* 印象主義的;印象派的;引起泛泛印象的。

***im·pres·sive** 〔ɪm'prɛsɪv; im'presiv〕 *adj.* 感人的;留給人深刻印象的。

im·pres·sive·ly 〔ɪm'prɛsɪvlɪ; im'presivli〕 *adv.* 令人難忘地;令人注目地。

im·press·ment 〔ɪm'prɛsmənt; im'presmənt〕 *n.* 强迫徵兵;徵用。the *impressment* of private property. 私有財產之徵用。

im·prest 〔'ɪmprɛst; 'imprest〕 *n.* 預付之款;訂金。

im·pri·ma·tur 〔ˌɪmprɪ'metɚ; ˌimpri'meitə〕 *n.* ①(特指天主敎之)出版許可。②准許;許可;讚許。

im·pri·mis 〔ɪm'praɪmɪs; im'praimis〕 〖拉〗 *adv.* 第一;首先(=in the first place).

im·print 〔*n.*'ɪmprɪnt; 'im-print *v.* ɪm'prɪnt; im'print〕 *n.* ①印跡;痕跡。②印象;印記。③書封底或內封面上所印的出版者姓名、出版時間與地點、印刷者的姓名等。—*v.t.* 蓋印於;印刻。

***im·pris·on** 〔ɪm'prɪzn̩; im'prizn〕 *v.t.* ①下獄;禁錮;收押。For what offence was he *imprisoned?* 他因何罪而下獄?②拘束;限制;關閉。a bird *imprisoned* in a cage. 關在籠中之鳥。

***im·pris·on·ment** 〔ɪm'prɪzn̩mənt; im'priznmənt〕 *n.* ①監禁;禁錮;下獄。②入獄;坐牢。

im·prob·a·bil·i·ty 〔ɪmˌprɑbə'bɪlətɪ; imˌprɔbə'biliti〕 *n., pl.* **-ties.** 未必然;無或然性;未必有之事。

im·prob·a·ble 〔ɪm'prɑbəbl̩; im'prɔbəbl〕 *adj.* 未必然的;似不可信的。—**im·prob·a·bly,** *adv.*

im·pro·bi·ty 〔ɪm'probətɪ; im'proubiti〕 *n.* 不誠實;邪惡。

im·promp·tu 〔ɪm'prɑmptu; im'prɔmptjuː〕 *adj.* 未事先準備的;臨時的;卽席的。—*adv.* 卽席地;臨時地。—*n.* 卽席演說;卽席演出;卽席之作。

***im·prop·er** 〔ɪm'prɑpɚ; im'prɔpə〕 *adj.* ①不合適的;不適當的。That bright dress is *improper* for a funeral. 那件顏色鮮艷的衣服不適合葬禮時穿。②錯誤的;不標準的。*Improper* treatment of the disease may cause the death of the patient. 錯誤治療可使病人致死。③不道德的;下流的。—**ly,** *adv.*

improper fraction 〖數學〗假分數。

im·pro·pri·ate 〔ɪm'proprɪˌet; im'prouprieit〕 *v.t.,* **-at·ed, -at·ing.** 〖英國敎會法〗將(敎會財產)移交俗人。—**im·pro·pri·a·tion,** *n.*

im·pro·pri·a·tor 〔ɪm'proprɪˌetɚ; im'prouprieitə〕 *n.* 將敎會財產移作個人財產之俗人。

im·pro·pri·e·ty 〔ˌɪmprə'praɪətɪ; ˌimprə'praiəti〕 *n., pl.* **-ties.** ①不適當;不正當。②不正當的行爲。③錯誤的語詞等。

im·prov·a·bil·i·ty 〔ɪmˌpruvə'bɪlətɪ; imˌpruːvə'biliti〕 *n.* 改善之可能性;可改善。

im·prov·a·ble 〔ɪm'pruvəbl̩; im'pruːvəbl〕 *adj.* 可改良的;可改善的。—**im·prov·a·bly,** *adv.*

‡**im·prove** 〔ɪm'pruv; im'pruːv〕 *v.,* **-proved, -prov·ing.** —*v.t.* ①改良;改善;增進。It isn't quite good enough; I want to *improve* it. 那還不够好,我還想加以改良。②利用。to *improve* one's time. 善用時間。③增高(土地、財產)的價值。to *improve* a lot by building on it. 在一塊地上建起房屋以增其價值。—*v.i.* ①改良;改善;進步。I hope the weather will *improve.* 我希望天氣會變好。②漲價。The price of cotton *improves.* 棉價漲。*improve on* (or

upon) 改良；改進。This can hardly be *improved on.* 這幾乎是無可再改進的了。

***im·prove·ment** [ɪmˈpruvmənt; imˈpruːvmənt] *n.* ①改良；改善；進步。There is room for *improvement.* 尙有改進的餘地。②改進之處；進步之處。③利用。the *improvement* of an opportunity. 利用一機會。④(土地、不動產等)價值之提高。⑤爲提高土地、不動產等之價值而增加的建築或設施等。⑥二者相形之下顯得較好之人或事物。

im·prov·er [ɪmˈpruvɚ; imˈpruːvə] *n.* ①改善者；改良者；改良之物。②只爲習藝不取工資之學徒。

im·prov·i·dence [ɪmˈprɑvədəns; imˈprɔvidəns] *n.* ①缺乏遠見；不顧未來。②不事積蓄；不節儉。

im·prov·i·dent [ɪmˈprɑvədənt; imˈprɔvidənt] *adj.* ①無遠見的；不顧未來的。②不事積蓄的；無節儉習慣的。

im·pro·vi·sa·tion [ˌɪmprəvaɪˈzeʃən; ˌimprəvaiˈzeiʃən] *n.* ①卽席而作。②卽席而作之事物。—**al,** *adj.*

im·prov·i·sa·tor [ɪmˈprɑvəˌzetɚ; imˈprɔvizeitə] *n.* 卽興詩人；卽興作曲家；卽席演奏家。

im·prov·i·sa·to·re [ɪmˌprɑvɪzəˈtorɪ; imˌprɔvizəˈtɔːri] *n., pl.* **-to·ri** [-ˈtorɪ; -ˈtɔːri]. 〖義〗=**improvisator.**

im·prov·i·sa·to·ri·al [ɪmˌprɑvɪzəˈtorɪəl; imˌprɔvizəˈtɔːriəl] *adj.*①卽席的；卽興的。②卽興詩人的；卽席演奏家的。

im·pro·vi·sa·to·ry [ɪmˈprɑvəzəˌtorɪ; ˌimprəˈvaizətəri] *adj.* =**improvisatorial.**

im·pro·vise [ˈɪmprəˌvaɪz; ˈimprəvaiz] *v.,* **-vised, -vis·ing.** —*v.t.* & *v.i.* ①卽席而作。②臨時製作。—**im·pro·vis·er,** *n.*

im·pru·dence [ɪmˈprudn̩s; imˈpruːdəns] *n.* ①輕率；不謹愼。②輕率的行爲。

im·pru·dent [ɪmˈprudn̩t; imˈpruːdənt] *adj.* 不謹愼的；輕率的；不加思慮的。—**ly,** *adv.*

im·pu·dence [ˈɪmpjədəns; ˈimpjudəns] *n.* ①鹵莽；厚顏；卑鄙。②冒失的行爲。

***im·pu·dent** [ˈɪmpjədənt; ˈimpjudənt] *adj.* 鹵莽的；厚顏的；卑鄙的。—**ly,** *adv.*

im·pu·dic·i·ty [ˌɪmpjəˈdɪsətɪ; ˌimpjuˈdisiti] *n.* 無恥；淫褻。

im·pugn [ɪmˈpjun; imˈpjuːn] *v.t.* 指責；駁斥。

im·pugn·a·ble [ɪmˈpjunəbl̩; imˈpjuːnəbl] *adj.* 可非難的；可指責的；可駁斥的。

im·pugn·ment [ɪmˈpjunmənt; imˈpjuːnmənt] *n.* 攻擊；非難；駁斥；指責。

***im·pulse** [ˈɪmpʌls; ˈimpʌls] *n.* ①刺激；推動；推進。to give an *impulse* to trade. 促進貿易。②情感的衝動；突然的慾望。a man of *impulse.* 感情易衝動之人。③〖物理〗衝；衝力；衝量。④〖電〗脈衝。⑤〖生理〗衝動；興奮。

im·pul·sion [ɪmˈpʌlʃən; imˈpʌlʃən] *n.* ①驅使。②衝動；激動。③刺激；推動力。

im·pul·sive [ɪmˈpʌlsɪv; imˈpʌlsiv] *adj.* ①爲突然的感情所驅使的；易衝動的。②有推動力的；推進的。③激動的；刺激性的。—**ness,** *n.*

im·pul·sive·ly [ɪmˈpʌlsɪvlɪ; imˈpʌlsivli] *adv.* 衝動地。

im·pu·ni·ty [ɪmˈpjunətɪ; imˈpjuːniti] *n.* (懲罰、損失、傷害等之) 免除。***with impunity*** 不受懲罰地；無慮地；無妨地。You cannot do this *with impunity.* 你不能夠做這事而免受罰(你做這事必受罰)。

im·pure [ɪmˈpjur; imˈpjuə] *adj.* ①髒的；不純潔的。②同他物相混雜的。③不道德的；淫猥的。④(顏色、音調、式樣)複雜的。⑤不慣用的；不合文法的。—**ly,** *adv.* —**ness,** *n.*

im·pu·ri·ty [ɪmˈpjurətɪ; imˈpjuəriti] *n., pl.* **-ties.** ①不純；不潔。②不道德；淫猥。③(*pl.*)雜質；不純之物；不潔之物。

im·put·a·bil·i·ty [ɪmˌpjutəˈbɪlətɪ; imˌpjuːtəˈbiliti] *n.* 可歸罪；可使負責。

im·put·a·ble [ɪmˈpjutəbl̩; imˈpjuːtəbl] *adj.* 可歸罪的；可使負責的。

im·pu·ta·tion [ˌɪmpjuˈteʃən; ˌimpju(ː)ˈteiʃən] *n.*①歸咎；歸罪。②責難；汚名。

im·put·a·tive [ɪmˈpjutətɪv; imˈpjuːtətiv] *adj.* ①可歸罪於…的〖to〗. ②歸咎的；好責難的。—**ly,** *adv.*

im·pute [ɪmˈpjut; imˈpjuːt] *v.t.,* **-put·ed, -put·ing.** 歸罪於；歸咎於；諉於。

In 化學元素 indium 之符號。

‡in [ɪn; in] *prep.* ①在…內；在…中(表示場所與方向)。There is a pencil *in* the box. 匣中有一枝鉛筆。②進；入(=into). Put it *in* your pocket. 把它放進你的口袋裏。③在(環境)下；在(情況)下。to sit *in* the sun (sunshine). 坐在陽光中。④用。to write *in* ink. 用墨水寫。⑤在…方面；對於。to believe *in* God. 相信上帝。⑥在(時間)以內；過(若干時間)。*in* January. 在一月裏。*in* the morning (afternoon, evening). 在早晨(下午，晚間)。⑦(與 gerund 連用，中文譯法不定)。to spend one's time *in* reading. 把時間用於讀書。⑧ in 除以上各定義及用法外，尙有無數習慣用法，玆分爲六大類列後：A. 指明地點者：*in* church (prison, school, etc.). 在教堂(監獄、學校等)中。***in front*** (***of***) 在前面，在…之前。***in one's way*** 妨礙某人。***in the middle*** (***of***)在中間；在…的中間。***in the north*** (***south, etc.***) (***of***) 在北方(南方等)；在…的北方(南方等)。***in the way*** (***of***) 妨礙；有礙於。B. 指明狀態或原因者：*in* color (white, black, etc.). 彩色的(白色的、黑色的等) The name was painted *in* red. 名字是漆爲紅色的。***in a hurry*** 匆忙的。***in common*** (***with***) 共同地；與…共同。***in company*** (***with***) 一同；和…一同。***in fun*** (=jokingly) 玩笑地。***in hundreds*** (***thousands, etc.***) 成百(千等)地。***in one's own interest*** 爲自己的利益。***in public*** (***private***) 公開(祕密)地。***in some way or other*** 無論如何。***in the name of*** 藉…之名。***in the open*** 在戶外。***in this*** (***that, the right, etc.***)***way***這樣地(那樣地、正確地等)。***in time*** (***for***) 及時；趕上。***in twos and threes*** 三三兩兩地。C. 指明狀態或情況者：***in a difficulty*** (or ***in difficulties***) 在困境中。***in danger*** (***safety***) 在危險(安全)中。***in debt*** 負債。***in good*** (***bad***) ***health*** (不)健康的。***in love*** (***with***) 戀愛；與…在戀愛。***in need*** (***of***) 窮困；缺乏。***in*** (***good, proper***) ***order*** 整齊的；可使用的。***in the dark*** (***light***) 在黑暗(光明)中；被隱瞞而不知情。***in the distance*** 在遠方。***in use*** 在使用中。D. 構成一般副詞短語者：***in addition*** (***to***) 加上；加於…之上；…之外。***in all*** 總計；總共。***in any case*** 無論如何。***in a sense*** 有幾分；在某種意義上。***in comparison*** (***with***) 比較起來；和…比較起來。***in fact*** 事實上。***in name*** 在名義上。***in one word*** 一言以蔽之。***in***

other words 換言之。*in particular* 特別地。*in short* 簡而言之。*in the beginning* 在當初; 在開始。*in the end* 最後。*in the first* (*second, last*) *place* 第一(第二、最後一)點。*in the same way* 同樣地。E. 構成複合介系詞者: *in case of* 倘使; 若遇…時。*in honor of* 紀念; 爲表示對…之敬意。*in place of* 代替。*in spite of* 雖然;不管;縱使。*in the hands of* 在…手中。*in the way of* (=such as) 關於; 就。*in time of* 若遇…時。*in view of* 鑒於; 由…觀之。*in want of* 需要。F. 構成複合連接詞者: *in case* 假如。*in so far as* (=in the degree that) 就…而論。*in such a way that* (+ a clause) 如此…以致。*in that* (=because; since) 因爲。*in the way...* (=in which) 像…一樣地。He doesn't do it *in the way* (in which) I like. 他不是照我所喜歡的樣子做的。—*adv.* ①在家; 在辦公室。Is anybody *in?* 有人在家嗎? The Labor Party was *in.* 工黨執政。②(火)未熄滅;還在燒着。Is the fire *in?* 火還在燒着嗎? ③(車、船)到達; 抵站; 靠碼頭。Is the train (boat) *in?* 火車(船)到了嗎? ④上市。Strawberries are now *in.* 草莓正當時令。⑤與其他動詞連用, 其意義約可分七大類: A. 進; 入。*make one's way in* 向裏邊走去。B. 不出去;(留)在家裏。*stay* (*keep*) *in* 留(守)在家裏。C. 拜訪。*call in* 拜訪。*drop in* 偶然過訪。D. 向內部;向裏面。E. 穿入; 穿進。*give in* (=yield) 投降; 認輸; 屈服。*join in* (=participate) 加入。*set in* 嵌入。F. 與 find 或 follow 連用: My friend went *in* and I followed him *in.* 我的朋友進去,我就跟着他進去。G. 與其他及物動詞連用: Somebody pushed me *in.* 有人把我推了進去。*in for* 注定;一定得到或遇到。*in for* a whale of one hour's entertainment. 定可嘗到一小時美妙的娛樂消遣。*in for it* a. 鐵定要做。b. 定會倒楣;定會挨罵。He will be *in for it* if he doesn't get home on time. 他如果不及時回家定會倒楣。*in with* 與…友善; 與…熟悉。—*adj.* ①內的; 在內的。an *in* patient. 住院病人(爲 out patient 之對)。②進來的。the *in* train. 進站的火車。③當權的;執政的。a member of the *in* party. 執政黨黨員。—*n.* ①執政黨; 政府黨。②內情; 細節。to know all the *ins* and outs of a problem (situation, etc.). 熟悉一問題(情況等)的原委。③(道路的)曲折。the *ins* and outs of a road. 道路之彎彎曲曲。④〖俗〗入口。⑤有權者。⑥權勢; 勢力。to enjoy some sort of *in.* 享受某種權勢。*the ins and the outs* 執政黨與在野黨。〖注意〗**in** 指明所在處, 係靜止的狀態。**into** 表示進入,係動的狀態。但 in 亦常用作 into 的意思,尤以口語爲然。

in. inch; inches.

in- 〖字首〗①表"否定"之義。②表"into; against; toward"之義。

***in·a·bil·i·ty** [ˌɪnəˈbɪlətɪ; ˌinəˈbiliti] *n.* 無能力; 無才能; 無力量。*inability* to help (stand, pay). 不能幫助(站立,付錢)。

in ab·sen·tia [ˌɪnæbˈsɛnʃɪə; in æbˈsenʃiə] 〖拉〗(=in (one's) absence) 不在; 缺席。to be awarded a degree *in absentia.* 未在現場接受學位。

in·ac·ces·si·bil·i·ty [ˌɪnækˌsɛsəˈbɪlətɪ; ˈinækˌsesəˈbiliti] *n.* 令人無法接近、到達、獲得等之狀況或性質。

in·ac·ces·si·ble [ˌɪnəkˈsɛsəbl̩; ˌinækˈsesəbl] *adj.* ①不能進入的。②難達到的。③難得到的;不能得到的。④不能親近的;不能與之會晤的。⑤難懂的;難解的。—**in·ac·ces·si·bly,** *adv.* —**ness,** *n.*

in·ac·cu·ra·cy [ɪnˈækjərəsɪ; inˈækjurəsi] *n., pl.* **-cies.** ①不精確。②錯誤。

in·ac·cu·rate [ɪnˈækjərɪt; inˈækjurit] *adj.* 不準確的;有錯誤的。—**ness,** *n.* —**ly,** *adv.*

in·ac·tion [ɪnˈækʃən; inˈækʃən] *n.* 「不活動;懶散;怠惰。」

***in·ac·tive** [ɪnˈæktɪv; inˈæktiv] *adj.* ①不活動的; 不活潑的; 懶惰的。forced by illness to lead an *inactive* life. 因病而被迫過着不活動的生活。②停止活動的;停止的; 停業的。an *inactive* machine. 停止活動的機器。③非現役的(軍人、軍人名册等)。④交易甚少的。—**ly,** *adv.*

in·ac·tiv·i·ty [ˌɪnækˈtɪvətɪ; ˌinækˈtiviti] *n.* ①不活動狀態;不活動;靜止。②閒散;不工作;怠惰。

in·a·dapt·a·bil·i·ty [ˌɪnəˌdæptəˈbɪlətɪ; ˌinəˌdæptəˈbiliti] *n.* 不適應性。

in·a·dapt·a·ble [ˌɪnəˈdæptəbl̩; ˌinəˈdæptəbl] *adj.* 不能適應的。

in·ad·e·qua·cy [ɪnˈædəkwəsɪ; inˈædikwəsi] *n.* ①不充分; 不完全。②不適當;不合格;無力;無能。

***in·ad·e·quate** [ɪnˈædəkwɪt; inˈædikwit] *adj.* 不充分的; 不適當的; 不合格的; 不勝任的。*inadequate* preparation for an examination. 對於一考試的不充分的準備。—**ly,** *adv.* —**ness,** *n.*

in·ad·mis·si·bil·i·ty [ˌɪnədˌmɪsəˈbɪlətɪ; ˈinədˌmisəˈbiliti] *n.* 不可承認、容許或採納之性質。

in·ad·mis·si·ble [ˌɪnədˈmɪsəbl̩; ˌinədˈmisəbl] *adj.* ①不能承認的。②不可容許的。

in·ad·vert·ence [ˌɪnədˈvɝtn̩s; ˌinədˈvəːtəns] *n.* ①不注意;粗心。②疏忽。

in·ad·vert·en·cy [ˌɪnədˈvɝtn̩sɪ; ˌinədˈvəːtənsi] *n., pl.* **-cies.** =**inadvertence.**

in·ad·vert·ent [ˌɪnədˈvɝtn̩t; ˌinədˈvəːtənt] *adj.* ①不注意的;粗心的;疏忽的。②非有意的;因疏忽所致的。—**ly,** *adv.*

in·ad·vis·a·ble [ˌɪnədˈvaɪzəbl̩; ˌinədˈvaizəbl] *adj.* 不妥的;失策的;不智的。

in·al·ien·a·ble [ɪnˈeljənəbl̩; inˈeiljənəbl] *adj.* 不能讓與的;不可剝奪的。

in·al·ter·a·ble [ɪnˈɔltərəbl̩; inˈɔːltərəbl] *adj.* 不可變動的;不能變更的;不易的。

in·am·o·ra·ta [ɪnˌæməˈrɑtə; inˌæməˈrɑːtə] *n., pl.* **-tas.** 〖義〗情婦;姘婦;情人。

in·am·o·ra·to [ɪnˌæmoˈrɑto; inˌæməˈrɑːtou] *n., pl.* **-tos.** 〖義〗情郎;姘夫;情人。

in-and-in [ˈɪnəndˈɪn; ˈinəndˈin] *adj. & adv.* 出自同血統的(地); 近親交配的(地)。

in·ane [ɪnˈen; iˈnein] *adj.* ①愚蠢的。②無意義的。③空的; 空虛的。—*n.* 空虛之物; 太空;太虛。

in·an·i·mate [ɪnˈænəmɪt; inˈænimit] *adj.* ①無生命的。②無生氣的; 單調的; 死氣沉沉的。—**in·an·i·ma·tion,** *n.*

in·a·ni·tion [ˌɪnəˈnɪʃən; ˌinəˈniʃən] *n.* ①空;無內容。②身體衰弱;不能吸收營養。

in·an·i·ty [ɪnˈænətɪ; iˈnæniti] *n., pl.* **-ties.** ①愚蠢; 無意義。②無意義或糊塗的行爲、言語等。③空;空虛。

in·ap·peas·a·ble [ˌɪnəˈpizəbl̩; ˌinəˈpiːzəbl] *adj.* 不可和緩的;難勸解的;難使鎮

靜的;無法滿足的。
in·ap·pli·ca·bil·i·ty 〔ˌɪnæplɪkəˈbɪlətɪ; ˈinˌæplikəˈbiliti〕 *n.* 不適用。
in·ap·pli·ca·ble 〔ɪnˈæplɪkəbl̩; inˈæplikəbl〕 *adj.* 不適用的; 不能適用的。
in·ap·po·site 〔ɪnˈæpəzɪt; inˈæpəzit〕 *adj.* 不適合的;不適宜的;不相稱的。—**ly,** *adv.*
in·ap·pre·ci·a·ble 〔ˌɪnəˈpriʃɪəbl̩; ˌinəˈpriːʃəbl〕 *adj.* 不值得考慮的; 毫無價值的;微不足道的。—**in·ap·pre·ci·a·bly,** *adv.*
in·ap·pre·ci·a·tion 〔ˌɪnəˌpriʃɪˈeʃən; ˌinəˌpriːʃiˈeiʃən〕 *n.* 不能認識眞價; 缺乏鑑賞力。
in·ap·pre·ci·a·tive 〔ˌɪnəˈpriʃɪˌetɪv; ˌinəˈpriːʃieitiv〕 *adj.* 不能作正當評價的; 不解眞趣的; 無鑑賞力的 〖of〗.
in·ap·pre·hen·si·ble 〔ˌɪnæprɪˈhɛnsəbl̩; ˌinæpriˈhensibl〕 *adj.* 不可理解的;難了解的。
in·ap·pre·hen·sive 〔ˌɪnæprɪˈhɛnsɪv; ˌinæpriˈhensiv〕 *adj.* ①無理解力的;不覺察的 〖of〗. ②不掛慮的;不知危險的。
in·ap·proach·a·ble 〔ˌɪnəˈprotʃəbl̩; ˌinəˈproutʃəbl〕 *adj.* ①不可接近的; 難於接近的。②無敵的;無匹的。
in·ap·pro·pri·ate 〔ˌɪnəˈproprɪɪt; ˌinəˈproupriit〕 *adj.* 不合宜的;不適合的;不當的。
in·apt 〔ɪnˈæpt; inˈæpt〕 *adj.* ①不適宜的;不合適的。②笨拙的。
in·ap·ti·tude 〔ɪnˈæptəˌtjud; inˈæptitjuːd〕 *n.* ①不適宜。②笨拙。
in·arch 〔ɪnˈɑrtʃ; inˈɑːtʃ〕 *v.t.* 〖園藝〗接(枝)。
in·arm 〔ɪnˈɑrm; inˈɑːm〕 *v.t.* 抱; 擁抱。
in·ar·tic·u·late 〔ˌɪnɑrˈtɪkjəlɪt; ˌinɑːˈtikjulit〕 *adj.* ①發音不清楚的; 說話不清楚的。②不能說話的; 不能以言語表達思想的; 啞的。③不善於辭令的。④無關節的。—**ly,** *adv.* —**ness,** *n.*
in·ar·ti·fi·cial 〔ɪnˌɑrtəˈfɪʃəl; ˌinɑːtiˈfiʃəl〕 *adj.* ①不加人工的;自然的。②拙劣的;無技巧的。③天眞的;單純的。
in·ar·tis·tic 〔ˌɪnɑrˈtɪstɪk; ˌinɑːˈtistik〕 *adj.*①非藝術的。②不懂藝術的;無高尙趣味的。
***in·as·much** 〔ˌɪnəzˈmʌtʃ; ˌinəzˈmʌtʃ〕 *adv.* 因…之故; 既 (與 as 連用=since, because, 係文學用字)。*Inasmuch* as the debtor has no property, I abandoned the claim. 債務人既無財產,我乃放棄債權。
in·at·ten·tion 〔ˌɪnəˈtɛnʃən; ˌinəˈtenʃən〕 *n.* ①不注意;粗心。②疏忽的行為。
in·at·ten·tive 〔ˌɪnəˈtɛntɪv; ˌinəˈtentiv〕 *adj.* 不注意的;疏忽的。—**ly,** *adv.*
in·au·di·bil·i·ty 〔ˌɪnɔdəˈbɪlətɪ; inˌɔːdəˈbiliti〕 *n.* 不能聽到;聽不見。
in·au·di·ble 〔ɪnˈɔdəbl̩; inˈɔːdəbl〕 *adj.* 聽不見的;不能被聽見的。—**in·au·di·bly,** *adv.*
in·au·gu·ral 〔ɪnˈɔgjərəl; iˈnɔːgjurəl〕 *adj.* ①就職的; 就任的。②開幕的;落成的;成立的。—*n.* ①就職演說。②就職典禮。
in·au·gu·rate 〔ɪnˈɔgjəˌret; iˈnɔːgjureit〕 *v.t.,* **-rat·ed, -rat·ing.** ①舉行就職典禮;使就任。to *inaugurate* a president. 舉行總統就職典禮。②開創; 創始。to *inaugurate* a new era. 開創一新紀元。③為…舉行開幕式或落成典禮。to *inaugurate* a new bridge. 舉行新橋落成典禮。
in·au·gu·ra·tion 〔ɪnˌɔgjəˈreʃən; iˌnɔːgjuˈreiʃən〕 *n.* ①就職; 就職典禮。the *inauguration* of the President. 總統之就職。②開創;創始。③開幕式;開幕。
Inauguration Day (美國總統之)就職日(即每隔四年的元月二十日)。
in·au·gu·ra·tor 〔ɪnˈɔgjəˌretɚ; iˈnɔːgjureitə〕 *n.* ①創始者。②舉行就職禮者。
in·aus·pi·cious 〔ˌɪnɔˈspɪʃəs; ˌinɔːsˈpiʃəs〕 *adj.* 不幸的;不利的;不祥的;凶兆的。
in-be·tween 〔ˌɪnbɪˈtwin; ˌinbiˈtwiːn〕 *n.* 介乎中間的事物。—*adj.* 介乎中間的。
in·board 〔ˈɪnˌbord; ˈinbɔːd〕 *adj.* & *adv.* ①〖航海〗在船內(的);在船艙中部(的)。②〖機械〗向內側(的)。—*n.* 推進機位於船體內的艇。
in·born 〔ɪnˈbɔrn; ˈinˈbɔːn〕 *adj.* ①天生的;天賦的。②遺傳的。
in·bound 〔ˈɪnˈbaund; ˈinbaund〕 *adj.* 開向本國的;歸航的。
in·breathe 〔ɪnˈbrið; ˈinˈbriːð〕 *v.t.,* **in·breathed, in·breath·ing.** ①吸入; 吸收。②鼓吹;感召;予以靈感。
in·bred 〔ɪnˈbrɛd; ˈinˈbred〕 *adj.* ①天生的。②近親繁殖的。
in·breed 〔ɪnˈbrid; ˈinˈbriːd〕 *v.t.,* **in·bred, in·breed·ing.** ①使生於內部; 內生。②使同族或近親繁殖。
in·breed·ing 〔ˈɪnˌbridɪŋ; ˈinˈbriːdiŋ〕 *n.* 〖生物〗近親交配。
in·built 〔ˈɪnˌbɪlt; ˈinbilt〕 *adj.* 裝置於(機器)內部的。
inc. ①inclosure. (信函內的)附件。②(亦作 **Inc.**) incorporated. 用於商店名稱之後,表示其爲公司組織。③including. ④included. ⑤inclusive. ⑥increase.
In·ca 〔ˈɪŋkə; ˈiŋkə〕 *n.* ①印加族人。the *Incas.* 印加族(昔居於南美秘魯 Andes 山脈地方之印第安族土人)。②印加皇帝或其家族中之一人。—**ic,** *adj.* —**In·can,** *n.,* *adj.*
In·ca·bloc 〔ˈɪŋkəblɑk; ˈiŋkəblɔk〕 *n.* 〖商標名〗(手錶的)防震裝置。
in·cal·cu·la·bil·i·ty 〔ˌɪnkælkjələˈbɪlətɪ; inˌkælkjuləˈbiliti〕 *n., pl.* **-ties.** ①不可勝數;無量。②難預測;不可靠。③不可勝數的東西;難預測的東西。
in·cal·cu·la·ble 〔ɪnˈkælkjələbl̩; inˈkælkjuləbl〕 *adj.* ①不可數的; 無數的。②預料不到的;難預測的。③不定的;不可靠的。—**in·cal·cu·la·bly,** *adv.*
In·ca·les·cent 〔ˌɪnkəˈlɛsənt; ˌinkəˈlesənt〕 *adj.* 變熱的;溫度漸增的。
in·can·desce 〔ˌɪnkənˈdɛs; ˌinkənˈdes〕 *v.i.* & *v.t.,* **-desced, -desc·ing.** (使)白熱化。
in·can·des·cence 〔ˌɪnkənˈdɛsn̩s; ˌinkənˈdesns〕 *n.* 白熱。
in·can·des·cent 〔ˌɪnkənˈdɛsn̩t; ˌinkənˈdesnt〕 *adj.* ①赤熱的;白熱的。an *incandescent* lamp. 白熱燈。②極亮的。③傑出的。
in·can·ta·tion 〔ˌɪnkænˈteʃən; ˌinkænˈteiʃən〕 *n.* ①咒語; 咒文。②魔法。③念咒。④口頭禪。⑤(掩飾內容貧乏之)冗語。
in·ca·pa·bil·i·ty 〔ˌɪnkepəˈbɪlətɪ; inˌkeipəˈbiliti〕 *n.* 無能;不勝任;無力。
in·ca·pa·ble** 〔ɪnˈkepəbl̩; inˈkeipəbl〕 *adj.* 無能力的;不能的。An employer cannot afford to hire *incapable* workers. 一個雇主不能出錢雇用沒有能力的工人。 ***incapable of **a.** 無能力或無權力做; 不會。An idiot is *incapable* of learning. 白癡不能學習。**b.** 不容許。This house is *incapable* of repair. 這房子無法修理。**c.** 法律上無資格做。—*n.* 完全無能力者。
in·ca·pac·i·tate 〔ˌɪnkəˈpæsəˌtet; ˌinkəˈpæsiteit〕 *v.t.,* **-tat·ed, -tat·ing.**

①使不能；使不適於。②〖法律〗褫奪資格。—**in·ca·pac·i·ta·tion**, *n.*

in·ca·pac·i·ty 〔ˌɪnkəˈpæsətɪ; ˌinkəˈpæsiti〕 *n.*, *pl.* **-ties.** ①無能力；不適任。②〖法律〗資格之褫奪；無資格。

in·car·cer·ate 〔ɪnˈkarsəˌret; inˈkaːsəreit〕 *v.*, **-at·ed, -at·ing,** *adj.* —*v.t.* 監禁；下獄。

in·car·cer·a·tion 〔ɪnˌkarsəˈreʃən; inˌkaːsəˈreiʃən〕 *n.* 監禁；下獄；入獄。

in·car·na·dine 〔ɪnˈkarnəˌdaɪn; inˈkaːnədain〕 *adj.*, *n.*, *v.*, **-dined, -din·ing.** —*adj.* ①肉色的；淡紅的。②紅的；血紅色的。—*n.* 肉色；深紅；血紅色。—*v.t.* 染成血紅色；使成肉色或淡紅色。

in·car·nate 〔*adj.* ɪnˈkarnɪt; inˈkaːnit *v.* ɪnˈkarnet; ˈinkaːneit〕 *adj.*, *v.*, **-nat·ed, -nat·ing.** —*adj.* ①具有肉體的；成爲人形的；化身的。②淡紅色的(花卉)。—*v.t.* ①使有具體形式；賦以形體。②使具體化；實現。③爲…的典範；總括。

in·car·na·tion 〔ˌɪnkarˈneʃən; ˌinkaːˈneiʃən〕 *n.* ①具體化；化身。②(神靈的)化爲人身。***the Incarnation*** 耶穌之爲神性與人性的聯合；基督之化爲人。

in·case 〔ɪnˈkes; inˈkeis〕 *v.t.*, **-cased, -cas·ing.** ①裝入匣內；裝入箱內。②包裹；包住。(亦作 **encase**)

in·case·ment 〔ɪnˈkesmənt; inˈkeismənt〕 *n.* ①裝箱。②箱；袋；包裹物。

in·cau·tious 〔ɪnˈkɔʃəs; inˈkɔːʃəs〕 *adj.* 不注意的；不謹愼的；鹵莽的。

in·cen·di·a·rism 〔ɪnˈsɛndɪəˌrɪzəm; inˈsendjərizəm〕 *n.* ①縱火。②煽動變亂。

in·cen·di·ar·y 〔ɪnˈsɛndɪˌɛrɪ; inˈsendjəri〕 *adj.*, *n.*, *pl.* **-ar·ies.** —*adj.* ①縱火的；放火的。②煽動的；煽惑的。③引起燃燒的。—*n.* ①縱火者；放火者。②煽動者；煽惑者。③燃燒彈。

in·cen·dive 〔ɪnˈsɛndɪv; inˈsendiv〕 *adj.* 會引起燃燒的；易燃的。

in·cense[1] 〔ˈɪnsɛns; ˈinsens〕 *n.* ①供神所焚燒的香。②(由上項香所發之)烟或香氣。③任何香氣。—*v.t.* ①敬香；上香。②加香味；用香水。—*v.i.* 敬香；上香。

in·cense[2] 〔ɪnˈsɛns; inˈsens〕 *v.t.*, **-censed, -cens·ing.** 激怒；激動。

in·cen·so·ry 〔ˈɪnsɛnˌsorɪ; ˈinsensəri〕 *n.*, *pl.* **-ries.** 香爐。

in·cen·tive 〔ɪnˈsɛntɪv; inˈsentiv〕 *n.* 刺激；鼓勵；動機。He hasn't much *incentive* (*or* many *incentives*) to work hard. 他沒有努力工作的動機。—*adj.* 激勵的；誘發的；刺激的。an *incentive* speech. 激勵的演說。

in·cep·tion 〔ɪnˈsɛpʃən; inˈsepʃən〕 *n.* 開始；開端。

in·cep·tive 〔ɪnˈsɛptɪv; inˈseptiv〕 *adj.* ①開始的；起初的。②〖文法〗表示動作或狀態開始的；表始的(主指希臘文、拉丁文之動詞)。—*n.* 〖文法〗表始動詞。

in·cep·tor 〔ɪnˈsɛptɚ; inˈseptə〕 *n.* ①(在 Cambridge 大學)卽將接受學位之人。②開始者；初學者。

in·cer·ti·tude 〔ɪnˈsɝtəˌtjud; inˈsəːtitjuːd〕 *n.* ①不確實；不定；疑惑。②不安定；不安全；不可靠。

***in·ces·sant** 〔ɪnˈsɛsn̩t; inˈsesnt〕 *adj.* 不絕的；不斷的；無盡的。The *incessant* noise of whistles kept me awake all night. 不斷的汽笛聲使我整夜未能入睡。—**ness**, *n.*

in·ces·sant·ly 〔ɪnˈsɛsn̩tlɪ; inˈsesntli〕 *adv.* 不斷地；不絕地。

in·cest 〔ˈɪnsɛst; ˈinsest〕 *n.* 亂倫；血族相姦。

in·ces·tu·ous 〔ɪnˈsɛstʃuəs; inˈsestjuəs〕 *adj.* 亂倫的；犯亂倫罪的。

‡**inch**[1] 〔ɪntʃ; intʃ〕 *n.* ①吋；英寸(=1/12英尺)。She is five feet six *inches.* 她身長五英尺六英寸。②些微；絲毫。He escaped death by an *inch.* 他死裏逃生。③(*pl.*) 身高。His legs are too long for his *inches.* 對他的身高而言，他的腿太長了。***by inches*** 逐漸地；一點一點地。He's dying *by inches.* 他已氣息奄奄。***every inch*** 完全地；徹頭徹尾地。He is *every inch* a soldier. 他是一個十足的軍人。***inch by inch*** 漸漸地；一步一步地。***to an inch*** 精確地；準確地。***within an inch of*** 幾乎。He came *within an inch of* being struck by the falling tile. 他差一點就被落下的瓦打着了。—*v.i.* 慢慢前進；慢慢移動。They were *inching* along the slippery ridge. 他們在滑溜溜的山脊上慢慢前進。—*v.t.* 慢慢推進。It was *inching* the U. S. into a war that did not have to be fought. 它在慢慢地將美國推進不必打的戰爭之中。***inch along*** 慢慢前進；蠕蠕而行。***inch one's way forward*** 慢慢前進；蠕蠕而行。

inch[2] *n.* 〖蘇，愛〗島；小島。

inch·meal 〔ˈɪntʃˌmil; ˈintʃmiːl〕 *adv.* 一英寸一英寸地；漸漸。(亦作 **by inchmeal**)

in·cho·ate 〔ɪnˈko·ɪt; ˈinkoueit〕 *adj.* 剛開始的；早期的；不完全的；未發展的。

in·cho·a·tion 〔ˌɪnkoˈeʃən; ˌinkouˈeiʃən〕 *n.* 發端；開始；初期。

in·cho·a·tive 〔ɪnˈkoətɪv; ˈinkoueitiv〕 *adj.* ①〖罕〗=**inchoate.** ②〖文法〗=**inceptive.** —*n.* 〖文法〗=**inceptive.**

inch·worm 〔ˈɪntʃˌwɝm; ˈintʃwəːm〕 *n.* 尺蠖(=measuring worm).

in·ci·dence 〔ˈɪnsədəns; ˈinsidəns〕 *n.* ①落下；落下之方向；影響。②影響的範圍；勢力範圍。③〖幾何〗部分的對等(如兩形的對等線、點等)。④投射；入射；投射的方向。

***in·ci·dent** 〔ˈɪnsədənt; ˈinsidənt〕 *n.* ①事件；事變。Frontier *incidents* have been common on the border. 邊界事件在邊境上是常發生的。②(小說、戲劇、詩中的)事件；揷曲。③人們不願正確敍述的事件(如叛變、戰爭等)。④附帶的事物。—*adj.* ①易於發生的。the dangers *incident* to the life of an aviator. 飛行家所易遭遇之危險。②附帶的。③當然有關的；必然相連的。④入射的。*incident* angle. 入射角。⑤外來的。attacks by *incident* forces. 外敵之攻擊。

in·ci·den·tal 〔ˌɪnsəˈdɛntl̩; ˌinsiˈdentl〕 *adj.* ①隨帶的；附屬的；難免的。②偶然的；臨時的。—*n.* ①偶然的事；小事。②(*pl.*)臨時費用；雜項。

***in·ci·den·tal·ly** 〔ˌɪnsəˈdɛntl̩ɪ; ˌinsiˈdentəli〕 *adv.* ①附帶地；偶然地；不意地。In this discussion grave questions were *incidentally* brought up. 在這討論中嚴重問題附帶地被提到。②讓我順便一提。Fred said, *incidentally*, that he had had no dinner. 讓我順便一提，Fred 說他沒有吃過晚飯。

in·cin·er·ate 〔ɪnˈsɪnəˌret; inˈsinəreit〕 *v.*, **-at·ed, -at·ing.** —*v.t.* ①燒成灰②焚化；火葬。—*v.i.* 燒成灰。—**in·cin·er·a·tion**, *n.*

in·cin·er·a·tor 〔ɪnˈsɪnəˌretə; inˈsinəreitə〕 *n.* 焚化者;焚化爐;火葬爐。

in·cip·i·ence 〔ɪnˈsɪpɪəns; inˈsipiəns〕 *n.* 初;始;早期。

in·cip·i·en·cy 〔ɪnˈsɪpɪənsɪ; inˈsipiənsi〕 *n.* =**incipience.**

in·cip·i·ent 〔ɪnˈsɪpɪənt; inˈsipiənt〕 *adj.* 剛開始的; 初期的。

in·cise 〔ɪnˈsaɪz; inˈsaiz〕 *v.t.*, **-cised, -cis·ing.** ①切;割;切開。②刻;雕。

in·ci·sion 〔ɪnˈsɪʒən; inˈsiʒən〕 *n.* ①切口。②割切。③尖刻性。④邊緣之鋸齒狀缺口。

in·ci·sive 〔ɪnˈsaɪsɪv; inˈsaisiv〕 *adj.* ①鋒利的。②尖刻的。③門牙的。

in·ci·sive·ly 〔ɪnˈsaɪsɪvlɪ; inˈsaisivli〕 *adv.* 鋒利地;尖刻地。

in·ci·sor 〔ɪnˈsaɪzɚ; inˈsaizə〕 *n.* 前齒;門牙。

in·ci·ta·tion 〔ˌɪnsaɪˈteʃən; ˌinsaiˈteiʃən〕 *n.* =**incitement.**

in·cite 〔ɪnˈsaɪt; inˈsait〕 *v.t.*, **-cit·ed, -cit·ing.** 引起;激動;鼓動。—**in·cit·er,** *n.*

in·cite·ment 〔ɪnˈsaɪtmənt; inˈsaitmənt〕 *n.* ①激勵物;鼓勵物;煽動物。②激勵;鼓勵;煽動。

in·ci·vil·i·ty 〔ˌɪnsəˈvɪlətɪ; ˌinsiˈviliti〕 *n., pl.* **-ties.** ①粗魯; 無禮。②粗魯的行動;無禮的舉動。

in·ci·vism 〔ˈɪnsɪvɪzm̩; ˈinsivizəm〕 *n.* 無愛國心; 對公益事無興趣。

incl. ①inclosure. ②including. ③inclusive.

in·clem·en·cy 〔ɪnˈklɛmənsɪ; inˈklemənsi〕 *n., pl.* **-cies.** ①(天氣和氣候的)嚴酷;(風雨的)狂暴。②殘酷無情。

in·clem·ent 〔ɪnˈklɛmənt; inˈklemənt〕 *adj.* ①嚴寒的;有狂風暴雨的。②殘酷的。

in·clin·a·ble 〔ɪnˈklaɪnəbl̩; inˈklainəbl〕 *adj.* ①傾向於…的;意欲…的。②有利於…的;對…有好感的。③可傾斜的。

***in·cli·na·tion** 〔ˌɪnkləˈneʃən; ˌinkliˈneiʃən〕 *n.* ①傾向。②意願; 愛好。③傾斜(度)。④〖數學〗傾度;傾角。⑤傾斜面。

in·cline** 〔*v.* ɪnˈklaɪn; inˈklain *n.* ˈɪnklaɪn, ɪnˈklaɪn; inˈklain, ˈinklain〕 *v.*, **-clined, -clin·ing,** *n.* —*v.i.* ①愛好;性近;傾向。Dogs *incline* toward meat as a food. 狗愛以肉爲食。②傾斜;傾。He *inclined* toward the speaker to hear more clearly. 他傾身向那講話者以便聽得更清楚些。—*v.t.* ①使傾向;使心願。*Incline* your hearts to obey God's laws. 傾心服從上帝的律法。②使低;使彎;使前傾。③使相信。incline one's ear*** 樂聽;傾聽。—*n.* 傾斜;傾斜面。

in·clined 〔ɪnˈklaɪnd; inˈklaind〕 *adj.* ①欲;喜好。②傾斜的。③方向與他物成角度的。

in·clin·ing 〔ɪnˈklaɪnɪŋ; inˈklainiŋ〕 *n.* 趨向;傾向;個性。

in·cli·nom·e·ter 〔ˌɪnklɪˈnɑmətɚ; ˌinkliˈnɔmitə〕 *n.* 傾斜計;傾角計。

***in·close** 〔ɪnˈkloz; inˈklouz〕 *v.t.* =**enclose.**

in·clo·sure 〔ɪnˈkloʒɚ; inˈklouʒə〕 *n.* 〔=**enclosure.**〕

‡in·clude 〔ɪnˈklud; inˈkluːd〕 *v.t.*, **-clud·ed, -clud·ing.** ①包括;包含;連…算在內。There are ten of us in the house, *including* the four servants. 我們共有十人在屋內,包括四個僕人。②把…包括在(某事物)之內。He *included* a sum for tips in his estimate of expenses. 他將小費包括在費用的估計中。

in·clud·ed 〔ɪnˈkludɪd; inˈkluːdid〕 *adj.* ①被包入的;包括在內的。②〖植物〗(雌蕊或雄蕊)不生出於花冠之外的。

in·clu·sion 〔ɪnˈkluʒən; inˈkluːʒən〕 *n.* ①包括。②包含的東西。③〖生物〗原形質中浮游的小顆粒。④〖礦〗結晶中含有的異體物。

in·clu·sive 〔ɪnˈklusɪv; inˈkluːsiv〕 *adj.* ①包括的; 包含的〖常 of〗. ②包括一切的。***inclusive of*** 包括…在內。—**ly,** *adv.*

in·co·er·ci·ble 〔ˌɪnkoˈɝsəbl̩; ˌinkouˈəːsibl〕 *adj.* ①不可壓制的。②〖物理〗不能用壓力使之液化的。

in·cog 〔ɪnˈkɑg; inˈkɔg〕 *adj., adv., n.* 〖俗〗=**incognito** or **incognita.**

in·cog·i·ta·ble 〔ɪnˈkɑdʒətəbl̩; inˈkɔdʒətəbl〕 *adj.* 無法想像的;不可理解的。

in·cog·ni·to 〔ɪnˈkɑgnɪˌto; inˈkɔgnitou〕 *adj., adv., n., pl.* **-tos.** —*adj.* 隱姓埋名的;微行的;化名的。—*adv.* 隱姓埋名地; 化名或假冒身分地;微行地。—*n.* ①隱姓埋名者;微行者。②隱姓埋名或僞裝的狀態與情況。

in·cog·ni·zance 〔ɪnˈkɑgnɪzəns; inˈkɔgnizəns〕 *n.* 不知;不識。

in·cog·ni·zant 〔ɪnˈkɑgnɪzənt; inˈkɔgnizənt〕 *adj.* 不知的; 不覺察的〖of〗.

in·co·her·ence 〔ˌɪnkoˈhɪrəns; ˌinkouˈhiərəns〕 *n.* ①無邏輯的聯貫。②無聯貫的思想與言語。③不黏附。

in·co·her·ent 〔ˌɪnkoˈhɪrənt; ˌinkouˈhiərənt〕 *adj.* ①(思想等)無條理的;無邏輯的。②(人之)不能清楚講話或表達思想的;語無倫次的。③不黏附的;鬆散的。④不團結的;不和諧的。⑤不協調的。⑥性質不同的。

in·co·he·sive 〔ˌɪnkoˈhisɪv; ˌinkouˈhiːsiv〕 *adj.* 鬆散的; 分散的。

in·com·bus·ti·bil·i·ty 〔ˌɪnkəmˌbʌstəˈbɪlətɪ; ˈinkəmˌbʌstəˈbiliti〕 *n.* 不燃性。

in·com·bus·ti·ble 〔ˌɪnkəmˈbʌstəbl̩; ˌinkəmˈbʌstəbl〕 *adj.* 不能燃燒的;防火的。—*n.* 不能燃燒之物。

***in·come** 〔ˈɪnˌkʌm, ˈɪŋˌkʌm; ˈinkəm, ˈiŋk-,-kʌm〕*n.* 收入;所得(指由產業、商業、勞動等所獲的報酬)。The government tax on *income* is called *income* tax. 政府對於(個人)收入所課的稅稱爲所得稅。—**less,** *adj.*

in·com·er 〔ˈɪnˌkʌmɚ; ˈinˌkʌmə〕 *n.*①進來者;新進者;新任者; 接任者。②〖主英方〗移民。③〖狩獵〗向獵者飛來之野鷄、野鴨等。

income tax 所得稅。***income tax return*** (*or* report). 所得稅申報表。

in·com·ing 〔ˈɪnˌkʌmɪŋ; ˈinˌkʌmiŋ〕 *adj.* ①進來的。②新來的。③繼任的;新任的。④收益的。⑤(時間)即將開始的。—*n.* ①進來;到來。②進來之物;新來之物。

in·com·men·su·ra·bil·i·ty 〔ˌɪnkəˌmɛnʃərəˈbɪlətɪ; ˈinkəˌmenʃərəˈbiliti〕 *n.* ①不能比較 (因無共同單位等)。②〖數學〗不能通約。

in·com·men·su·ra·ble 〔ˌɪnkəˈmɛnʃərəbl̩; ˌinkəˈmenʃərəbl〕 *adj.* ①不能用同一標準計量的;不能比較的。②〖數學〗無公約量的;不能通約的;無理的。 —*n.* 不能通約之數或量;不能用同一標準計量之物。

in·com·men·su·rate 〔ˌɪnkəˈmɛnʃərɪt; ˌinkəˈmenʃərit〕 *adj.* ①不成比例的;不相稱的; 不足的。②不能比較的。

in·com·mode 〔ˌɪnkəˈmod; ˌinkəˈmoud〕 *v.t.*, **-mod·ed, -mod·ing.** ①使感覺不便;使感到不適。②擾亂;妨礙。

in·com·mo·di·ous 〔ˌɪnkəˈmodɪəs; ˌinkəˈmoudiəs〕 *adj.* ①不寬敞的。②不舒服的; 不方便的。

in·com·mu·ni·ca·bil·i·ty 〔ˌɪnkəˌmjunɪkəˈbɪlətɪ; ˌinkəˌmju:nikəˈbiliti〕 *n.* 不能傳達;難通;失去連絡。

in·com·mu·ni·ca·ble 〔ˌɪnkəˈmjunɪkəbl̩; ˌinkəˈmju:nikəbl〕 *adj.* ①不能聯絡的;不能以言語表達的。②沉默的。

in·com·mu·ni·ca·do 〔ˌɪnkəˌmjunɪˈkado; ˌinkəˌmju:niˈka:dou〕 *adj.* 被禁止與外界接觸的;被單獨監禁的。

in·com·mu·ni·ca·tive 〔ˌɪnkəˈmjunəˌketɪv; ˌinkəˈmju:nikətiv〕 *adj.* 沉默寡言的;不愛說話的;不愛交際的。

in·com·mut·a·ble 〔ˌɪnkəˈmjutəbl̩; ˌinkəˈmju:təbl〕 *adj.* 不能交換的; 不能變換的;不變的;不能改變的。

in·com·pact 〔ˌɪnkəmˈpækt; ˌinkəmˈpækt〕 *adj.* 不緊密的;不簡潔的;散漫的。

in·com·pa·ra·ble 〔ɪnˈkampərəbl̩; inˈkɔmpərəbl〕 *adj.* ①舉世無雙的。*incomparable* beauty. 舉世無雙的美。②不能比較的; 不適於比較的〖常 with, to〗。

in·com·pat·i·bil·i·ty 〔ˌɪnkəmˌpætəˈbɪlətɪ; ˈinkəmˌpætəˈbiliti〕 *n.*, *pl.*-ties. ①不能和諧共存;不能兩立;不相投合; 矛盾。②(*pl.*)不能相容的特點。

in·com·pat·i·ble 〔ˌɪnkəmˈpætəbl̩; ˌinkəmˈpætəbl〕 *adj.* ①不能兩立的;不能和諧共存的; 矛盾的。 Cats and dogs are *incompatible*. 貓和狗是不能共處的。②〖邏輯〗不能同時成立的(兩個以上的命題)。③〖醫〗不能同時並服的(藥品)。—*n.* ①(常 *pl.*)不能和諧共存的人或物。②不能同時並服之藥。③(*pl.*)〖邏輯〗不能同時屬於一物的兩種以上特性。—**in·com·pat·i·bly**, *adv.*

in·com·pe·tence 〔ɪnˈkampətəns; inˈkɔmpitəns〕 *n.* ①無能力;不勝任。②〖法律〗無資格。③〖醫〗機能不全。

in·com·pe·ten·cy 〔ɪnˈkampətənsɪ; inˈkɔmpitənsi〕 *n.* ① = **incompetence.** ②(*pl.*)無能的表現或行爲。

in·com·pe·tent 〔ɪnˈkampətənt; inˈkɔmpitənt〕 *adj.* ①無能力的;不能勝任的。He is *incompetent* to teach English (for teaching English; as an English teacher). 他沒有教英語(做英語教員) 的能力。②不合格的; 沒有資格的。③法律上無效的。④〖醫〗機能不全的。 —*n.* ①無能力者; 不能勝任者。②無法定之資格者。—**ly**, *adv.*

in·com·plete 〔ˌɪnkəmˈplit; ˌinkəmˈpli:t〕 *adj.* 不完全的;不足的。—**ness**, *n.*

in·com·plete·ly 〔ˌɪnkəmˈplitlɪ; ˌinkəmˈpli:tli〕 *adv.* 不完全地。

in·com·ple·tion 〔ˌɪnkəmˈpliʃən; ˌinkəmˈpli:ʃən〕 *n.* 不完全;不完備;未完成。

in·com·pli·ant 〔ˌɪnkəmˈplaɪənt; ˌinkəmˈplaiənt〕 *adj.* ①不服從的;不讓步的。②不柔軟的;不能彎曲的;不能變化的。

in·com·pre·hen·si·bil·i·ty 〔ˌɪnkamprɪˌhensəˈbɪlətɪ; inˌkɔmprihensəˈbiliti〕 *n.* 不可理解; 不可思議。

in·com·pre·hen·si·ble 〔ˌɪnkamprɪˈhensəbl̩; inˌkɔmpriˈhensəbl〕 *adj.* 不能理解的;不可思議的。to be *incomprehensible* to ordinary minds. 非普通人所能理解者。—**ness**, *n.* —**in·com·pre·hen·si·bly**, *adv.*

in·com·pre·hen·sive 〔ˌɪnkamprɪˈhɛnsɪv; inˌkɔmpriˈhensiv〕 *adj.* ①不了解的;無理解力的。②範圍狹窄的。

in·com·press·i·ble 〔ˌɪnkəmˈprɛsəbl̩; ˌinkəmˈpresəbl〕 *adj.* 不能壓縮的;堅硬的。—**in·com·press·i·bil·i·ty**, *n.*

in·com·put·a·ble 〔ˌɪnkəmˈpjutəbl̩; ˌinkəmˈpju:təbl〕 *adj.* 不能計算的;難數的。

in·con·ceiv·a·bil·i·ty 〔ˌɪnkənˌsivəˈbɪlətɪ; ˈinkənˌsi:vəˈbiliti〕 *n.* 不能想像;不可思議。

in·con·ceiv·a·ble 〔ˌɪnkənˈsivəbl̩; ˌinkənˈsi:vəbl〕 *adj.* ①不可思議的; 不可想像的。②〖俗〗難以令人相信的; 非凡的。—**in·con·ceiv·a·bly**, *adv.*

in·con·clu·sive 〔ˌɪnkənˈklusɪv; ˌinkənˈklu:siv〕 *adj.* ①(證據、論據、討論、行動等)非決定性的;不確定的;不能使人信服的。②不得要領的;不能產生明確效果的。—**ly**, *adv.*

in·con·den·sa·ble 〔ˌɪnkənˈdɛnsəbl̩; ˌinkənˈdensəbl〕 *adj.* 不可凝縮的。

in·con·dite 〔ɪnˈkandɪt; inˈkɔndit〕 *adj.* ①胡亂拼湊成的;拙劣的(文學作品)。②未經精製的; 粗糙的。

in·con·form·i·ty 〔ˌɪnkənˈfɔrmətɪ; ˌinkənˈfɔ:miti〕 *n.* 不一致; 不適合;不遵從。

in·con·gru·i·ty 〔ˌɪnkaŋˈgruətɪ; ˌinkɔŋˈgru:iti〕 *n.*, *pl.* -ties. ①不合適; 不相稱。②不和諧。③不協調之物;不相稱之物。

in·con·gru·ous 〔ɪnˈkaŋgruəs; inˈkɔŋgruəs〕 *adj.* ①不合適的;不適宜的;不相稱的。A fur coat is *incongruous* with a bathing suit. 皮大衣和游泳衣是不相稱的。②不和諧的; 不協調的; 不一致的。③前後不一致的;有矛盾的。an *incongruous* story. 前後不一致的故事。—**ly**, *adv.* —**ness**, *n.*

in·con·nect·ed 〔ˌɪnkənˈnɛktɪd; ˌinkənˈnektid〕 *adj.* 不相干的;彼此無關係的。

in·con·sec·u·tive 〔ˌɪnkənˈsɛkjətɪv; ˌinkənˈsekjutiv〕 *adj.* 不連續的; 無連絡的;前後不一貫的。

in·con·se·quence 〔ɪnˈkansəˌkwɛns; inˈkɔnsikwəns〕 *n.* ①不合邏輯;不合理; 矛盾。②不切題; 不連貫。

in·con·se·quent 〔ɪnˈkansəˌkwɛnt; inˈkɔnsikwənt〕 *adj.* ①不合邏輯的;邏輯上無聯繫的。②不切題的;不合理的。③不連貫的。④不重要的;無價值的。⑤不配合的;不調和的。

in·con·se·quen·tial 〔ˌɪnkansəˈkwɛnʃəl; ˌinkɔnsiˈkwenʃəl〕 *adj.* ①不重要的; 繁瑣的。②不合邏輯的; 前後無關連的;不切題的(=inconsequent).

in·con·sid·er·a·ble 〔ˌɪnkənˈsɪdərəbl̩; ˌinkənˈsidərəbl〕 *adj.* 不值得考慮的;不重要的;微末的。

in·con·sid·er·ate 〔ˌɪnkənˈsɪdərɪt; ˌinkənˈsidərit〕 *adj.* ①不顧及他人(權利、感情等)的;不體恤他人的。 It was *inconsiderate* of him to forget. 他不顧慮別人,把事情忘了。②行動輕率的; 不加思慮的。③未經愼重考慮的。 —**ly**, *adv.* —**ness**, *n.*

in·con·sist·en·cy 〔ˌɪnkənˈsɪstənsɪ; ˌinkənˈsistənsi〕 *n.*, *pl.* -cies. ①不一致。②前後矛盾。③不一致或矛盾之事物或行爲。

in·con·sist·ent 〔ˌɪnkənˈsɪstənt; ˌinkənˈsistənt〕 *adj.* ①前後不一致的; 矛盾的;不合的。His account of what happened was *inconsistent*. 他對於發生事件的敍述,前後互相矛盾。②不協調的; 不一律的。③無定見的;多變的。 —**ly**, *adv.*

in·con·sol·a·ble 〔ˌɪnkənˈsoləbl̩; ˌinkənˈsouləbl〕 *adj.* 不能慰藉的; 傷心的。*inconsolable* grief. 無法安慰的憂傷。—**in·con·sol·a·bly**, *adv.*

in·con·so·nance 〔ɪnˈkansənəns;

in'kɔnsənəns] *n.* (聲音、行動、思想等之)不調和;不和諧。

in·con·so·nant [ɪn'kɑnsənənt; in'kɔnsənənt] *adj.* 不調和的;不和諧的; 不一致的。

in·con·spic·u·ous [ˌɪnkən'spɪkjuəs; ˌinkən'spikjuəs] *adj.* ①不引人注意的; 不太顯眼的。The woman's dress was an *inconspicuous* gray. 那女人的服裝是一種不顯眼的灰色。②〖植物〗小而色淡的(花)。

in·con·stan·cy [ɪn'kɑnstənsɪ; in'kɔnstənsi] *n.* 易變;無常;輕浮。

in·con·stant [ɪn'kɑnstənt; in'kɔnstənt] *adj.* ①無常的; 多變的; 無定向的。②不專的; 輕浮的。an *inconstant* lover. 愛情不專者。

in·con·sum·a·ble [ˌɪnkən'sjuməbl̩; ˌinkən'sju:məbl] *adj.* 燒不盡的;用不盡的;非消耗性的。

in·con·test·a·ble [ˌɪnkən'tɛstəbl̩; ˌinkən'testəbl] *adj.* 無可置辯的; 不容置疑的。—**in·con·test·a·bly,** *adv.*

in·con·ti·nence [ɪn'kɑntənəns; in'kɔntinəns] *n.* ①不能自制; 不停止; 無力控制。②不貞;縱慾。③〖醫〗大小便失禁。

in·con·ti·nent [ɪn'kɑntənənt; in'kɔntinənt] *adj.* ①不能自制的;不停的;無力控制的。②不貞的;淫亂的;縱慾的。③〖醫〗失禁的。④不能抑制的;不能制止的〖of〗. —*adv.* 立刻;馬上。 —**ly,** *adv.*

in·con·tro·vert·i·ble [ˌɪnkɑntrə'vɝtəbl̩; 'inkɔntrə'və:təbl] *adj.* 無爭辯餘地的;無疑問的;明確的。—**in·con·tro·vert·i·bil·i·ty,** —**ness,** *n.* —**in·con·tro·vert·i·bly,** *adv.*

in·con·ven·ience** [ˌɪnkən'vinjəns; ˌinkən'vi:njəns] *n.,v.,-ienced, -ienc·ing.** —*n.* (亦作 **inconveniency**) ①不便;困難。I was put to great *inconvenience.* 我感受到極大的不便。It is no *inconvenience* to me. 這對我並無不便。②不便之事;困難之事。—*v.t.* 使感不便;使感困難。I hope I do not *inconvenience* you. 希望我不會給你許多不便。

***in·con·ven·ient** [ˌɪnkən'vinjənt; ˌinkən'vi:njənt] *adj.* 不便的; 有困難的。If (it is) not *inconvenient* to you, I should like to call on you this evening. 若對你沒有不方便的話, 我想在今天晚上來拜訪你。You have come at a very *inconvenient* time. 你來得最不適時。—**ness,** *n.* —**ly,** *adv.*

in·con·vert·i·ble [ˌɪnkən'vɝtəbl̩; ˌinkən'və:təbl] *adj.* 不能兌換的(紙幣); 不能變換的。—**in·con·vert·i·bil·i·ty,** *n.* —**in·con·ver·ti·bly,** *adv.*

in·con·vin·ci·ble [ˌɪnkən'vɪnsəbl̩; ˌinkən'vinsəbl] *adj.* 無法使人信服的。

incor., incorp. incorporated.

***in·cor·po·rate**[1] [*v.* ɪn'kɔrpəˌret; in'kɔ:pəreit, iŋ'k– *adj.* ɪn'kɔrpərɪt; in'kɔ:pərit, iŋ'k–] *v.,* **-rat·ed, -rat·ing,** *adj.* —*v.t.* ①合併;併入;編入。Your suggestions will be *incorporated* in the plan. 你的建議將被編入這計畫中。②組成公司。③具體表現。to *incorporate* one's thoughts in an article. 在一篇文章中把思想具體表現出來。④混合。to *incorporate* a chemical substance with others. 把一種化學物質同他種化學物質混合。—*v.i.* ①合併;結合。The firm *incorporated* with others. 這公司與別家合併了。②組成法人。They will *incorporate* as soon as they have a little more capital. 他們一有更多資本時便要組成法人。—*adj.* ①合併的;併入的。②公司組織的。③具體化的。the doctrines *incorporate* in scriptural writings. 經典中所表現的教條。—**in·cor·po·ra·tive,** *adj.*

in·cor·po·rate[2] *adj.* =**incorporeal.**

in·cor·po·ra·tion [ɪnˌkɔrpə'reʃən; inˌkɔ:pə'reiʃən] *n.* ①編入;結合。②團體組織;法人;公司。

in·cor·po·ra·tor [ɪn'kɔrpəˌretɚ; in'kɔ:pəreitə] *n.* ①組合者;聯合者。②〖美〗社員;基本社員。

in·cor·po·re·al [ˌɪnkɔr'porɪəl; ˌinkɔ:'pɔ:riəl] *adj.* ①非物質的;無形體的;精神的。②無形物的。③〖法律〗無形的。—**i·ty,** *n.* —**ly,** *adv.*

incorr. incorrect.

in·cor·rect [ˌɪnkə'rɛkt; ˌinkə'rekt] *adj.* ①不正確的; 錯誤的。②不適當的; 不合宜的。—**ly,** *adv.* —**ness,** *n.*

in·cor·ri·gi·bil·i·ty [ˌɪnkɔrɪdʒə'bɪlətɪ; inˌkɔridʒə'biliti] *n.* 不能矯正;難悛改;難控制;固執。

in·cor·ri·gi·ble [ɪn'kɔrɪdʒəbl̩; in'kɔridʒəbl] *adj.* ①積習難改的;根深蒂固的。②固執的; 任性的; 不能控制的。③難以處理的;難以修整的。—*n.* 積習難改之人或動物。—**ness,** *n.* —**in·cor·ri·gi·bly,** *adv.*

in·cor·rupt [ˌɪnkə'rʌpt; ˌinkə'rʌpt] *adj.* ①不腐敗的。②無錯誤的; 無瑕疵的; 純粹的。③清廉的; 方正的; 不能收買的。—**ly,** *adv.* —**ness,** *n.*

in·cor·rupt·i·ble [ˌɪnkə'rʌptəbl̩; ˌinkə'rʌptəbl] *adj.* ①廉潔的; 不貪污受賄的。②不腐朽的。—**in·cor·rupt·i·bil·i·ty,** *n.* —**in·cor·rupt·i·bly,** *adv.*

in·cor·rup·tion [ˌɪnkə'rʌpʃən; ˌinkə'rʌpʃən] *n.* 〖古〗不腐敗;清廉;方正。

incr. ①increased. ②increasing.

in·creas·a·ble [ɪn'krisəbl̩; in'kri:səbl] *adj.* 可增加的;可加大的。

‡**in·crease** [*v.* ɪn'kris; in'kri:s, iŋ'k– *n.* 'ɪnkris,'ɪŋk–; 'inkri:s,'iŋ–k–] *v.,***-creased, -creas·ing,** *n.* —*v.i.* 增加;增多;增大。His vanity *increased* with years. 他的虛榮心隨年齡而增高。—*v.t.* 增加;加大。This feeling *increased* her happiness. 這種感覺增加了她的幸福。 —*n.* ①增長; 增加; 增進。 an *increase* of warmth (coldness, money, work, etc.). 熱(冷、錢、工作等)的增加。There was a steady *increase* in population. 人口在不斷增加中。②增加額;增加量。③生產物; 利益。 ④農作物。The earth yields her *increase.* 大地生產農作物。***on the increase*** 在增加中 (=increasing). Crime in our big cities is ***on the increase.*** 在我們的大城市裏犯罪正在增加中。

in·creas·ing [ɪn'krisɪŋ; in'kri:siŋ] *adj.* 日益增多的;越來越多的。

***in·creas·ing·ly** [ɪn'krisɪŋlɪ; in'kri:siŋli] *adv.* 逐漸地; 漸增地。The work is getting *increasingly* difficult. 工作越來越困難了。

in·cred·i·bil·i·ty [ˌɪnkrɛdə'bɪlətɪ; inˌkredi'biliti] *n., pl.* **-ties.** ①不可信; 難信;可疑。②不可信之事物。

***in·cred·i·ble** [ɪn'krɛdəbl̩; in'kredəbl] *adj.* 難以置信的;可疑的。The hero fought with *incredible* bravery. 那個英雄以令人難以相信的勇氣作戰。—**ness,** *n.* —**in·cred·i-**

bly, *adv.* 〔kri'dju:liti〕 *n.* 不信;懷疑。

in·cre·du·li·ty 〔ˌɪnkrə'djulətɪ; ˌin-〕

in·cred·u·lous 〔ɪn'krɛdʒələs; in'kredjuləs〕 *adj.* 不肯輕信的; 不相信的。—**ness,** *n.* —**ly,** *adv.*

in·cre·ment〔'ɪnkrəmənt;'inkrimənt〕 *n.* ①增加; 生長; 增加之過程。unearned *increment.* (地價的) 自然增值。②增加數量; 增收。③盈餘。④〖數學〗增量。—**al,** *adj.*

in·cre·tion 〔ɪn'kriʃən; in'kri:ʃən〕 *n.* 內分泌;內分泌物。

in·crim·i·nate 〔ɪn'krɪməˌnet; in'krimineit〕 *v.t.,* **-nat·ed, -nat·ing.** ①牽累。②控告。—**in·crim·i·na·tor,** *n.*

in·crim·i·na·to·ry 〔ɪn'krɪmənəˌtorɪ; in'kriminətəri〕 *adj.* 連累的;控告的;使負罪的。

in·crust 〔ɪn'krʌst; in'krʌst〕 *v.t.* ①覆以硬殼;包以皮;在…表面上形成一層外殼。②鑲嵌;鍍。—*v.i.* 形成外殼。—**ant,** *adj.,n.*

in·crus·ta·tion 〔ˌɪnkrʌs'teʃən; ˌinkrʌs'teiʃən〕 *n.* ①覆以外皮;外皮;皮殼。②礦滓;水垢;疤。③〖建築〗表面裝飾;鑲嵌物。

in·cu·bate 〔'ɪnkjəˌbet; 'inkjubeit〕 *v.,* **-bat·ed, -bat·ing.** —*v.t.* ①鳥孵(卵);人工孵(卵)。②籌策(計畫)。③保育(早產嬰兒)。④培養(細菌)。—*v.i.* ①孵卵。②形成。

in·cu·ba·tion 〔ˌɪnkjə'beʃən; ˌinkju'beiʃən〕 *n.* ①孵卵;孵雛。②疾病的潛伏期。③沉思。—**al,** *adj.*

in·cu·ba·tive 〔'ɪnkjəˌbetɪv; 'inkjubeitiv〕 *adj.* ①孵化的。②潛伏(期)的。

in·cu·ba·tor〔'ɪnkjəˌbetɚ;'inkjubeitə〕 *n.* ①孵卵器;孵雛器。②早產嬰兒保育器。

in·cu·ba·to·ry 〔ɪn'kjubəˌtorɪ; 'inkjubeitəri〕 *adj.* =**incubative.**

in·cu·bus 〔'ɪnkjəbəs;'inkjubəs〕 *n., pl.* **-bus·es, -bi** 〔-ˌbaɪ; -bai〕. ①壓在熟睡者身上的魔鬼。②夢魘。③像惡夢般壓迫着人的事物;負擔。

in·cul·cate 〔ɪn'kʌlket, 'ɪnkʌlˌket; 'inkʌlkeit, in'k-〕 *v.t.,* **-cat·ed, -cat·ing.** 諄諄教誨; 三番五次地重述以深深印刻於(心)〖常 in, on, upon〗. Week after week she *inculcated* good manners in her pupils. 她一週又一週地把良好的禮節反覆灌輸給她的學生。—**in·cul·ca·tor,** *n.*

in·cul·ca·tion 〔ˌɪnkʌl'keʃən; ˌinkʌl'keiʃən〕 *n.* 諄諄教誨;教導;受教誨。

in·cul·pate 〔ɪn'kʌlpet,'ɪnkʌlˌpet;'inkʌlpeit,in'k-〕 *v.t.,* **-pat·ed, -pat·ing.** ①控告;歸罪;指責。②使成有罪;連累。

in·cul·pa·tion 〔ˌɪnkʌl'peʃən; ˌinkʌl'peiʃən〕 *n.*①控告;歸罪;連累。②非難;譴責。

in·cul·pa·to·ry 〔ɪn'kʌlpəˌtorɪ; in'kʌlpətəri〕 *adj.* 歸罪的; 諉罪的; 牽連的。

in·cum·ben·cy 〔ɪn'kʌmbənsɪ; in'kʌmbənsi〕 *n., pl.* **-cies.** ①憑依。②職責;義務。③(牧師等的)在職;任期。

in·cum·bent 〔ɪn'kʌmbənt; in'kʌmbənt〕 *adj.* ①躺臥的;憑依的。②使負有義務的。It is *incumbent* upon (*or* on) you to warn them. 你有警告他們的責任。③現任的; 在職的。④〖詩〗危急的。—*n.* ①在職者;在職的牧師。②居住者;房客。

in·cum·ber 〔ɪn'kʌmbɚ; in'kʌmbə〕 *v.t.* =**encumber.**

in·cu·nab·u·la 〔ˌɪnkju'næbjələ; ˌinkju'næbjulə〕 *n. pl., sing.* **-lum** 〔-ləm; -ləm〕. ①初期;早期。②紀元 1500年以前印行之書籍;古版本。

in·cu·nab·u·lar 〔ˌɪnkju'næbjəlɚ; ˌinkju'næbjulə〕 *adj.* 最早期的。

***in·cur** 〔ɪn'kɝ;in'kə:, iŋ'k-〕*v.t.,* **-curred, -cur·ring.** ①遭遇; 陷於。to *incur* debts. 陷於債務中; 負債。②招致; 蒙受; 惹起。to *incur* hatred. 招致仇恨。

in·cur·a·ble 〔ɪn'kjurəbḷ; in'kjuərəbl〕 *adj.* 不能治療的; 無可救藥的; 不能改正的。—*n.* 患不治之症者。—**in·cur·a·bil·i·ty,** *n.*

in·cur·a·bly 〔ɪn'kjurəblɪ; in'kjuərəbli〕 *adv.* 無可救藥地。

in·cu·ri·os·i·ty 〔ˌɪnkjurɪ'ɑsətɪ; inˌkjuəri'ɔsiti〕 *n.* 無好奇心;不關心。

in·cu·ri·ous 〔ɪn'kjurɪəs; in'kjuəriəs〕 *adj.* 無好奇心的;不注意的;不關心的。②無味的;平淡無奇的。a not *incurious* anecdote. 相當有趣的軼事。—**ly,** *adv.* —**ness,** *n.*

in·cur·rence 〔ɪn'kɝəns; in'kə:rəns〕 *n.* 招致;惹起。

in·cur·sion 〔ɪn'kɝʒən, -ʃən; in'kə:ʃən〕 *n.* ①入侵;侵犯;襲擊。②進入;流入。

in·cur·sive 〔ɪn'kɝsɪv; in'kə:siv〕 *adj.* 入侵的;來犯的;襲擊的;流入的。

in·cur·vate 〔*v.* ɪn'kɝvet; 'inkə:veit *adj.* ɪn'kɝvɪt; 'inkə:veit〕 *adj., v.,* **-vat·ed, -vat·ing.** —*adj.* 彎曲的; 內曲的。—*v.t.* & *v.i.* (使)曲;(使)屈曲;(使)內曲。

in·cur·va·tion 〔ˌɪnkɝ'veʃən; ˌinkə:'veiʃən〕 *n.* ①彎曲;內曲。②屈身;鞠躬。

in·curve[1] 〔'ɪnˌkɝv; 'in'kə:v〕 *n.* ①內曲;彎曲。②〖棒球〗內曲球。

in·curve[2] 〔ɪn'kɝv;'in'kə:v〕*v.t. & v.i.,* **-curved, -curv·ing.** 彎曲;(使)內曲。

in·cus 〔'ɪŋkəs; 'iŋkəs〕 *n., pl.* **in·cu·des** 〔ɪn'kjudiz;in'kju:di:z〕. 〖解剖〗砧骨(中耳之一小骨)。

in·cuse 〔ɪn'kjuz; in'kju:z〕 *adj.* 打印的; 鑄印的。—*n.* (貨幣等之)印鑄之花紋。

Ind 〔ɪnd; ind〕 *n.* 〖詩, 古〗= **India.**

Ind. ①India. ②Indian. ③Indiana. ④Indies. **in d.** daily. 〖處方〗每日。

Ind. E. Industrial Engineer.

in·debt·ed 〔ɪn'dɛtɪd; in'detid〕 *adj.* ①負債的。to be *indebted* to a person for a large sum. 欠某人一大筆款。②(因受恩惠而)感激的。I am greatly *indebted* to you for your kindness. 我非常感激你的恩惠。

in·debt·ed·ness 〔ɪn'dɛtɪdnɪs; in'detidnis〕 *n.* ①受恩惠。②所欠之款。③債務之集合稱。

in·de·cen·cy 〔ɪn'disṇsɪ; in'di:snsi〕 *n., pl.* **-cies.** ①不禮貌;粗野;猥褻;下流。②粗魯的言行;猥褻的事物。

in·de·cent 〔ɪn'disṇt; in'di:snt〕 *adj.* ①不禮貌的。②不道德的;猥褻的。—**ly,** *adv.*

in·de·cid·u·ous 〔ˌɪndɪ'sɪdʒuəs; ˌindi'sidjuəs〕 *adj.* 〖植物〗不落葉的;常綠的。

in·de·ci·pher·a·ble 〔ˌɪndɪ'saɪfrəbḷ; ˌindi'saifərəbl〕 *adj.* ①不可辨識的; 辨讀不出的。②(密碼)譯不出來的。

in·de·ci·sion 〔ˌɪndɪ'sɪʒən;ˌindi'siʒən〕 *n.* 缺乏決心;猶豫不決;優柔寡斷。

in·de·ci·sive 〔ˌɪndɪ'saɪsɪv; ˌindi'saisiv〕 *adj.* ①無決定性的。②優柔寡斷的。③不明確的。—**ly,** *adv.* —**ness,** *n.*

in·de·clin·a·ble 〔ˌɪndɪ'klaɪnəbḷ; ˌindi'klainəbl〕 *adj.* 〖文法〗字尾不變化的。—*n.* 字尾不變化之字;不變化詞。

in·dec·o·rous 〔ɪn'dɛkərəs; in'dekərəs] *adj.* 不適宜的；不雅的；失禮的。—**ly**, *adv.* —**ness**, *n.*

in·de·co·rum [ˌɪndɪ'korəm; ˌindi'kɔːrəm] *n.* ①無禮儀；不適當；不雅。②不適當的舉止、言談等。

‡**in·deed** [ɪn'did; in'diːd] *adv.* ①的確；實在(表示贊同對方的意見)。It is *indeed* very good. 那的確很好。Yes, *indeed* (or *Indeed*, yes). 的確是的。No, *indeed* (or *Indeed*, no). 的確不。②眞正；的確(表示自己確定的意見)。There are *indeed* exceptions to this rule. 這規則的確有許多例外。③實在；的確(用以加强 very 等字的語氣)。Thank you very much *indeed*. 實在非常感謝你。—*interj.* 眞的！的確！(表同意、驚異或反語等。) "He spoke to me about you." "*Indeed!*" "他曾對我談起你。""眞的！"(表驚訝的口吻。)

indef. indefinite.

in·de·fat·i·ga·bil·i·ty [ˌɪndɪˌfætɪgə'bɪlətɪ; ˌindiˌfætigə'biliti] *n.* 不疲倦；不屈不撓。

in·de·fat·i·ga·ble [ˌɪndɪ'fætɪgəbl̩; ˌindi'fætigəbl] *adj.* 不疲倦的；不屈不撓的。—**in·de·fat·i·ga·bly**, *adv.* —**ness**, *n.*

in·de·fea·si·bil·i·ty [ˌɪndɪˌfizə'bɪlətɪ; 'indiˌfiːzə'biliti] *n.* 不能廢除。

in·de·fea·si·ble [ˌɪndɪ'fizəbl̩; ˌindi'fiːzəbl] *adj.* 不能取消的；不能廢止的。—**in·de·fea·si·bly**, *adv.*

in·de·fect·i·ble [ˌɪndɪ'fɛktəbl̩; ˌindi'fektəbl] *adj.* 不至缺損的；不至失敗的；不朽的；無缺點的。—**in·de·fect·i·bly**, *adv.*

in·de·fec·tive [ˌɪndɪ'fɛktɪv; ˌindi'fektiv] *adj.* 無缺點的；無瑕疵的。

in·de·fen·si·bil·i·ty [ˌɪndɪˌfɛnsə'bɪlətɪ; 'indiˌfensə'biliti] *n.* 不能防守；難以防禦；不能辯護。

in·de·fen·si·ble [ˌɪndɪ'fɛnsəbl̩; ˌindi'fensəbl] *adj.* ①不能防守的。②無法辯護的。—**in·de·fen·si·bly**, *adv.*

in·de·fin·a·ble [ˌɪndɪ'faɪnəbl̩; ˌindi'fainəbl] *adj.* ①難下定義的；難描寫或解釋清楚的。②難確定的；不明確的。—*n.* 難描寫的人或物。—**in·de·fin·a·bly**, *adv.* —**ness**, *n.*

***in·def·i·nite** [ɪn'dɛfənɪt; in'definit] *adj.* ①不確定的；模糊的。He gave me an *indefinite* answer. 他給我一個含糊的答覆。②無限制的；無限期的。He has been sentenced to an *indefinite* prison term. 他被判無期徒刑。③〖數學〗不定的。*indefinite* integral. 不定積分。④〖文法〗不定的。—**ly**, *adv.* —**ness**, *n.*

indefinite article 〖文法〗不定冠詞(卽 a 或 an).

indefinite pronoun 〖文法〗不定代名詞(如 some, any, somebody 等)。

in·de·flec·ti·ble [ˌɪndɪ'flɛktəbl̩; ˌindi'flektəbl] *adj.* 不屈不撓的。

in·de·his·cent [ˌɪndɪ'hɪsn̩t; ˌindi'hisənt] *adj.* 〖植物〗(果實等)成熟時不裂開的。—**in·de·his·cence**, *n.*

in·de·lib·er·ate [ˌɪndɪ'lɪbərɪt; ˌindi'libərit] *adj.* 未經考慮的；無意的。

in·del·i·bil·i·ty [ˌɪndɛlə'bɪlətɪ; inˌdeli'biliti] *n.* 不能消除；難刪；難忘。

in·del·i·ble [ɪn'dɛləbl̩; in'delibl] *adj.* ①難擦掉的。②不能洗雪的；永恒的；不可磨滅的；難忘的。—**in·del·i·bly**, *adv.*

in·del·i·ca·cy [ɪn'dɛləkəsɪ; in'delikəsi] *n.*, *pl.* **-cies.** ①不精緻；粗糙。②不適當或下流之舉止、言詞等。

in·del·i·cate [ɪn'dɛləkət; in'delikit] *adj.* ①不精緻的；粗糙的。②不適當的；粗野的。—**ly**, *adv.* —**ness**, *n.*

in·dem·ni·fi·ca·tion [ɪnˌdɛmnəfə'keʃən; inˌdemnifi'keiʃən] *n.* ①賠償。②賠償物；賠償金。

in·dem·ni·fy [ɪn'dɛmnəˌfaɪ; in'demnifai] *v.t.*, **-fied, -fy·ing.** ①賠償；償付；付還。②使安全；使免受傷害、損失等；保險。—**in·dem·ni·fi·er**, *n.*

in·dem·ni·ty [ɪn'dɛmnətɪ; in'demniti] *n.*, *pl.* **-ties.** ①(對於損害或損失之)賠償；賠款。②(對於損害或損失之)保險。

in·de·mon·stra·ble [ɪn'dɛmənstrəbl̩; in'demənstrəbl] *adj.* 不能證明的；難以表明的。

in·dent [*v.* ɪn'dɛnt; in'dent *n.* ɪn'dɛnt, 'ɪndɛnt; 'indent, in'd-] *v.t.* ①切割(邊緣)使成鋸齒狀。②以不規則之騎縫分割(契約)。③製作(契約)之複本。④以契約束縛。⑤(特指一段文字的首行)縮進排印(或書寫)。⑥使成凹凸不齊之曲線。⑦定購；向…定貨。⑧留凹痕於…。—*v.i.* ①形成鋸齒狀邊緣。②訂立契約。③縮進排印或書寫。④起凹痕。—*n.* ①缺口；鋸齒狀缺痕。②契約。③縮印(或縮進書寫)之一行或段落；縮印所留的空位。④訂貨單；徵用命令。an *indent* for goods. 貨品訂購單；徵用物資命令。—**er**, *n.*

in·den·ta·tion [ˌɪndɛn'teʃən; ˌinden'teiʃən] *n.* ①成犬牙交錯狀。②一段文字第一行開始之空格。③缺口；凹入處。④海岸線上之凹進處。

in·dent·ed [ɪn'dɛntɪd; in'dentid] *adj.* ①鋸齒狀的。②(印刷、原稿等)從邊上向內縮進排印的。③受契約約束的；契約勞工的。

in·den·tion [ɪn'dɛnʃən; in'denʃən] *n.* ①(印刷、原稿等之)行首縮進；行首空格。②＝**indentation.**

in·den·ture [ɪn'dɛntʃɚ; in'dentʃə] *n.*, *v.*, **-tured, -tur·ing.** —*n.* ①契約；合同。②服務契約；學徒契約。③正式的名單；清單。④成犬牙交錯狀。***take up*** (or ***be out of***) ***one's indentures*** 服務期滿。—*v.i.* 以契約束縛。

in·den·ture·ship [ɪn'dɛntʃɚˌʃɪp; in'dentʃəʃip] *n.* 服務契約期間；學徒契約期間。

in·de·pend·ence** [ˌɪndɪ'pɛndəns; ˌindi'pendəns] *n.* 獨立；自立；自主。When you begin to earn money you can live a life of *independence*. 當你開始賺錢時，你就可以過獨立的生活了。Independence Day*** 美國獨立紀念日(七月四日，紀念1776年七月四日通過獨立宣言)。

in·de·pend·en·cy [ˌɪndɪ'pɛndənsɪ; ˌindi'pendənsi] *n.*, *pl.* **-cies.** ①獨立國。②獨立。

‡**in·de·pend·ent** [ˌɪndɪ'pɛndənt; ˌindi'pendənt] *adj.* ①獨立的；自立的；不依賴他人的。The Republic of China is an *independent* country. 中華民國是一個獨立的國家。②(脫離…而)獨立的；(與…)無關的〖of〗. If you earn a good salary, you can be *independent* of your parents. 假若你所獲薪俸不低，你就能離開你的父母而獨立。③自主的；不受他人控制的；不須接受他人幫助的；自由的；自尊心强的。Modern young women are getting more and more *independent*. 現代的年輕婦女們越來越自由了。④有足够的錢生活而不需要任何工作的。He has an *independent* income. 他有一分不必工作而能維持生活的收入。⑤〖數學〗獨立的。*independent* equation. 獨立方程(式)。—*n.* ①〖政治〗中

立派;無黨派者。One third of the voters classify themselves as *independents*. 三分之一的投票人將自己歸類爲無黨無派者。②有獨立思想的人;自立的人。

independent clause 〖文法〗獨立子句。(亦作 **main clause** 或 **principal clause**)

in·de·pend·ent·ly** [ˌɪndɪˈpɛndəntlɪ; ˌindiˈpendəntli] *adv.* 自立地; 獨立地。to live *independently*. 過自立生活。independently of*** 與…無關。

in-depth [ˈɪnˌdɛpθ; ˈindepθ] *adj.* 深入「討論的。」

in·de·scrib·a·bil·i·ty [ˌɪndɪˌskraɪbəˈbɪlətɪ; ˌindisˌkraibəˈbiliti] *n.* 不可名狀;難以形容。

in·de·scrib·a·ble [ˌɪndɪˈskraɪbəbl̩; ˌindisˈkraibəbl] *adj.* 難以形容的; 不可名狀的。—*n.* 難以形容之事物;難以描寫之事物。—**in·de·scrib·a·bly,** *adv.*

in·de·struct·i·bil·i·ty [ˌɪndɪˌstrʌktəˈbɪlətɪ; ˈindisˌtrʌktəˈbiliti] *n.* 不可破壞;不滅。

in·de·struct·i·ble [ˌɪndɪˈstrʌktəbl̩; ˌindisˈtrʌktəbl] *adj.* 不能毀滅的。—**in·de·struct·i·bly,** *adv.* —**ness,** *n.*

in·de·ter·mi·na·ble [ˌɪndɪˈtɝmɪnəbl̩; ˌindiˈtəːminəbl] *adj.* 不能確定的;難決定的; 無法解決的。—*n.* 無法解決的問題; 難確定之點。—**in·de·ter·mi·na·bly,** *adv.*

in·de·ter·mi·nate [ˌɪndɪˈtɝmənɪt; ˌindiˈtəːminit] *adj.* ①不確定的;未決定的;猶豫不決的。②含糊的; 模糊的。③〖數學〗(量) 不定的。④〖植物〗無限的。—**ly,** *adv.* —**ness, in·de·ter·mi·na·cy,** *n.*

indeterminate sentence 刑事案中之不確定刑期, 視犯者在獄行爲而定。

in·de·ter·mi·na·tion [ˌɪndɪˌtɝməˈneʃən; ˈindiˌtəːmiˈneiʃən] *n.* ①不定;不確定。②不果斷;優柔寡斷。

in·de·ter·min·ism [ˌɪndɪˈtɝmənˌɪzəm; ˌindiˈtəːminizəm] *n.*〖哲學〗非定命論;非預定論;自由意志論。

***in·dex** [ˈɪndɛks; ˈindeks] *n., pl.* **-dex·es, -di·ces,** *v.* —*n.* ①索引。②標記; 表徵;指標。Manner of walking gives an *index* to one's character. 行路的姿態是人的性格的表徵。③食指。④指針。A dial or scale usually has an *index*. 一個日規或磅秤常有指度針。⑤〖數學〗指數。⑥指數。*index* of living. 生活指數。a price *index*. 物價指數。 —*v.t.* ①給…編索引; 編入索引中。②指示出; 指出。 Wrinkles *index* advancing age. 皺紋表示着年歲在增加。③將…列爲禁書。④調整收入、待遇以配合生活指數所反映之物價變動。—**er,** *n.* —**i·cal,** *adj.*

Index Ex·pur·ga·to·ri·us [~ɛkˌspɝgəˈtɔrɪəs; ~eksˌpəːgəˈtɔːriəs]〖拉〗(昔天主教會之)禁書目錄。

index finger 食指。

index number 〖數學〗指數;〖統計〗(物價、工資、人口等之)指數。

index of refraction 〖數學〗折射「率。」

‡In·di·a [ˈɪndɪə; ˈindjə] *n.* 印度(國名, 位於亞洲南部, 首都新德里 New Delhi)。

India ink ①墨。②墨汁。

In·di·a·man [ˈɪndɪəmən; ˈindjəmən] *n., pl.* **-men.**(昔東印度公司的)印度貿易船。

‡In·di·an [ˈɪndɪən; ˈindjən] *n.* ①〖美〗印第安人;印第安語。②印度人;東印度羣島人。—*adj.* ①〖美〗印第安人的。②印度的;東印度羣島的。

In·di·an·a [ˌɪndɪˈænə; ˌindiˈænə] *n.* 印第安納(美國中西部之一州, 首府爲 Indianapolis)。—**In·di·an·i·an,** *n., adj.*

Indian agency 〖美〗印第安事務所。

Indian agent 〖美〗代表政府處理印第安人事務之官員。

Indian bread 玉蜀黍粉製之麪包。

Indian club 瓶狀之木棒(體操用具)。

Indian corn ①玉蜀黍。②玉蜀黍植物。

Indian file 單行縱隊。

Indian gift 〖美俗〗期待還禮所送的禮「物。」

Indian giver 〖美俗〗期待還禮而送禮的人; 把禮物送人後又索回者。

Indian hemp 印度大麻。

In·di·an·ize [ˈɪndɪənˌaɪz; ˈindiənaiz] *v.t.,* **-ized, -iz·ing.** 使 Indian 化。

Indian meal 玉蜀黍粉;玉米粥。

Indian Ocean 印度洋。

Indian sign ①印第安人所使用之信號、標記等。②顯示有印第安人存在之跡象。③魔術; 魔力。***have*** (or ***put***) ***the Indian sign on*** **a.** 使無助;擊敗; 征服。**b.** 使着迷。

Indian summer ①(深秋、初冬之)小陽春。②(老年之)回春期。

Indian wrestling 角力(尤指二人以手相交, 以肘置桌, 力將對方之手壓至桌面之角力)。

India paper ①聖經紙。②中國等地拓「印版畫所用之紙。」

India rubber, india rubber 彈性橡皮;天然橡膠;(擦鉛筆字用的)橡皮。

In·dic [ˈɪndɪk; ˈindik] *adj.* 印度(人)的;印度語(系)的。

indic. ①indicating. ②indicative.

in·di·cant [ˈɪndɪkənt; ˈindikənt] *adj.* 表示的;指示的。—*n.* ①指示物。②〖醫〗病徵。

‡in·di·cate [ˈɪndəˌket; ˈindikeit] *v.t.,* **-cat·ed, -cat·ing.** ①指示;指出。 A thermometer *indicates* temperature. 溫度計指示溫度。 ②顯示; 象徵。 Fever *indicates* sickness. 身體發熱象徵有病。③表示需要…作爲治療。The symptom *indicates* strict dieting. 這徵候表示需要嚴格的選定飲食。④說;表示。 —**in·di·cat·a·ble,** *adj.*

***in·di·ca·tion** [ˌɪndəˈkeʃən; ˌindiˈkeiʃən] *n.* ①指示; 指標; 象徵; 預兆。 Did he give you any *indication* of his feelings? 關於他的感想, 他曾對你作任何透露嗎? ②(各種計器的)度數之指示。③〖醫〗病的徵示。

***in·dic·a·tive** [ɪnˈdɪkətɪv; inˈdikətiv] *adj.* 指示的;表示的;象徵的〖of〗。Is a high forehead always *indicative* of great mental power? 前額高是否就表示智慧高? —*n.*〖文法〗①直陳法。②直陳法動詞。〖文法〗**the indicative mood.** 直陳法。

in·di·ca·tor [ˈɪndəˌketɚ; ˈindikeitə] *n.* ①指示者;指示物。②指示器;指示針;指壓器。③指示劑。

in·di·ca·to·ry [ˈɪndəkəˌtorɪ; inˈdikətəri] *adj.* 指示的;表示的。「of **index.**」

in·di·ces [ˈɪndəˌsiz; ˈindisiːz] *n.* pl.

in·di·ci·a [ɪnˈdɪʃɪə; inˈdiʃiə] *n. pl., sing.* **-di·ci·um** [-ˈdɪʃɪəm; -ˈdiʃiəm]. ①指標;標記。②〖美〗(代替郵票之)郵戳;作廢之戳記。

in·di·cial [ɪnˈdɪʃəl; inˈdiʃəl] *adj.* ①表示的;顯示的。②(如)指標或食指的。

in·dict [ɪnˈdaɪt; inˈdait] *v.t.*〖法律〗控訴; 控告; 起訴。 to *indict* a person for riot (*or* as a rioter *or* on a charge of rioting). 控告人以暴亂罪。—**er,** —**or,** *n.*

in·dict·a·ble [ɪn'daɪtəbl; in'daitəbl] *adj.* 可提起公訴的；可以控告的。an *indictable* offence. 刑事罪。 —**in·dict·a·bly,** *adv.*

in·dict·ee [,ɪndaɪ'ti; ,indai'ti:] *n.* 〔法律〕被起訴者；被告。

in·dic·tion [ɪn'dɪkʃən; in'dikʃən] *n.* ①羅馬皇帝每隔十五年規定財產價值之宣布(作爲課稅基礎)。②根據此種宣布而徵之稅。③宣布；詔示。

in·dict·ment [ɪn'daɪtmənt; in'daitmənt] *n.* ①起訴；提起公訴。to bring in an *indictment*. 提起公訴。②控告；告發。**bill of** ***indictment*** 起訴書。

In·dies ['ɪndɪz; 'indiz] *n.* (the-)①(作*pl.*解)東印度羣島(=the East Indies). ②(作*pl.*解)西印度羣島(=the West Indies). ③(作 *sing.* 解)東印度羣島、印度及印度支那。

***in·dif·fer·ence** [ɪn'dɪfərəns; in'difərəns] *n.* ①無興趣；不重視；漠不關心。He treated my request with *indifference.* 他對我的請求不予重視。②不重要；無足輕重。Success or failure should not be a matter of *indifference* to you. 成敗對於你不應該是一件無足輕重的事。

in·dif·fer·en·cy [ɪn'dɪfərənsɪ; in'difərənsi] *n.* =**indifference.**

***in·dif·fer·ent** [ɪn'dɪfərənt; in'difərənt] *adj.* ①不感興趣的；漠不關心的。How can you be so *indifferent* to the sufferings of these children? 你對這些孩子們的苦難怎能如此漠不關心？②沒有關係的；無重要性的。The time for starting is *indifferent* to me. 開始的時間對我是沒有關係的。③平常的；不好不壞的。His English is *indifferent.* 他的英文平常。④相當壞的。He's a very *indifferent* (=rather bad) player. 他是一個演技相當差的角色。⑤中立的；不偏不倚的。⑥〔物理〕中性的。⑦非必要的。—*n.* ①對政治或宗教漠不關心的人。②漠不關心的行爲。—**ly,** *adv.*

in·dif·fer·ent·ism [ɪn'dɪfərəntɪzm; in'difərəntizəm] *n.* ①(對眞僞、善惡等之)冷淡主義；傍觀主義；冷淡。②〔宗教〕信教無差別論。—**in·dif·fer·ent·ist,** *n.*

in·di·gence ['ɪndədʒəns; 'indidʒəns] *n.* ①貧窮；困乏。②窮人。

in·di·gene ['ɪndə,dʒin; 'indidʒi:n] *n.* 土人；當地人；土生(當地)之動物或植物。

in·dig·e·nous [ɪn'dɪdʒənəs; in'didʒinəs] *adj.* ①土產的；本地所產的。②生而俱有的；天生的；固有的。—**ly,** *adv.*

in·di·gent ['ɪndədʒənt; 'indidʒənt] *adj.* ①貧窮的；貧乏的。②缺乏的；全無的〔of〕. to be *indigent* of. 全無…。—**ly,** *adv.*

in·di·gest·ed [,ɪndə'dʒɛstɪd; ,indi'dʒestid] *adj.* ①未消化的。②未整理的；無次序的；雜亂的；粗率的。③未詳加考慮的。

in·di·gest·i·bil·i·ty [,ɪndə,dʒɛstə'bɪlətɪ; 'indi,dʒestə'biliti] *n.* 不消化；難理解。

in·di·gest·i·ble [,ɪndə'dʒɛstəbl; ,indi'dʒestəbl] *adj.* ①不能消化的；難消化的。②難理解的；難接受的。③不愉快的。

in·di·ges·tion [,ɪndə'dʒɛstʃən; ,indi'dʒestʃən] *n.* 消化不良症；未被消化的狀態。

in·di·ges·tive [,ɪndə'dʒɛstɪv; ,indi'dʒestiv] *adj.* 消化不良的。

in·dig·nant [ɪn'dɪgnənt; in'dignənt] *adj.* 憤慨的；不平的〔at (an action), over (a matter), with (a person)〕. to be *indignant* with a cruel man. 對殘忍的人憤憤不平。to be *indignant* at a false accusation. 對誣告憤憤不平。

in·dig·nant·ly [ɪn'dɪgnəntlɪ; in'dignəntli] *adv.* 憤怒地；憤慨地。

***in·dig·na·tion** [,ɪndɪg'neʃən; ,indig'neiʃən] *n.* 憤怒；憤慨；義憤。

indignation meeting 公憤示威大會。

in·dig·ni·ty [ɪn'dɪgnətɪ; in'digniti] *n., pl.* **-ties.** 輕蔑；侮辱；有傷尊嚴。

***in·di·go** ['ɪndɪ,go; 'indigou] *n., pl.* **-gos, -goes,** *adj.* —*n.*①靛青；藍靛。②產靛之豌豆科植物。③紫藍色。—*adj.* 紫藍色的。

indigo blue 藍靛；紫藍色(=indigo).

indigo bunting 美國東部的一種雀類之鳥(雄者紫藍色)。(亦作 **indigo bird**)

in·dig·o·tin [ɪn'dɪgətɪn; in'digətin] *n.* 〖化〗藍靛；靛精 ($C_{16}H_{10}N_2O_2$)。

***in·di·rect** [,ɪndə'rɛkt; ,indi'rekt] *adj.* ①間接的；迂廻的。②非直接相關的；次要的。an *indirect* result. 間接結果；次要結果。③兜圈子的；不着邊際的；不得要領的。to make an *indirect* reference to a person. 暗指某人。④不誠實的；欺騙的。*indirect* methods. 騙人的方法；不正當的手段。—**ly,** *adv.* —**ness,** *n.* 〖文法〗(1) **indirect quotation.** 間接引句，亦稱 **indirect speech.** 卽重述他人的話而不保留原句中之人稱、時間等。(2)**indirect object.** 間接受詞。

indirect cost 間接成本。

in·di·rec·tion [,ɪndə'rɛkʃən; ,indi'rekʃən] *n.* ①間接的行動(方法)。②不誠實；欺騙。③無目標。

indirect lighting 反射或分散照明(以避免刺眼或陰影)。

indirect tax 間接稅。

in·dis·cern·i·ble [,ɪndɪ'zɝnəbl,-'sɝn-; ,indi'sə:nəbl] *adj.* 不能識別的；難辨認的；看不見的。—*n.* 不能識別的事物。—**in·dis·cern·i·bly,** *adv.*

in·dis·ci·pline [ɪn'dɪsəplɪn; in'disiplin] *n.* 訓練不足；無紀律；無秩序。

in·dis·creet [,ɪndɪ'skrit; ,indis'kri:t] *adj.* 不穩重的；不審愼的；輕率的。—**ly,** *adv.*

in·dis·crete [,ɪndɪ'skrit, ɪn'dɪskrit; indi'skri:t] *adj.* 未分開的；密合的。

in·dis·cre·tion [,ɪndɪ'skrɛʃən; ,indis'kreʃən] *n.* ①不謹愼；鹵莽；輕率。②不審愼的言行。 —**ar·y,** *adj.*

in·dis·crim·i·nate [,ɪndɪ'skrɪmənɪt; ,indis'kriminit] *adj.* ①紊亂的；雜亂的。②不辨善惡的；不分皂白的。③無偏袒的。—**ly,** *adv.*

in·dis·crim·i·na·tion [,ɪndɪ,skrɪmə'neʃən; 'indis,krimi'neiʃən] *n.* 無差別；無區別。

***in·dis·pen·sa·ble** [,ɪndɪ'spɛnsəbl; ,indis'pensəbl] *adj.* ①不可缺少的；絕對必要的。Air, food, and water are *indispensable* to life. 空氣、食物和水，對於生命是缺一不可的。②不能避免的。—*n.* 不可缺少之物。clothing and food and other *indispensables.* 衣服和食物以及其他不可或缺之物。—**in·dis·pen·sa·bil·i·ty,** —**ness,** *n.*

in·dis·pen·sa·bly [,ɪndɪ'spɛnsəblɪ; ,indis'pensəbli] *adv.* 不能缺少地。

in·dis·pose [,ɪndɪ'spoz; ,indis'pouz] *v.t.* ①使不適合；使不合格。②使不願意；使嫌惡。③使微感不適。

in·dis·posed [,ɪndɪ'spozd; ,indis'pouzd] *adj.* ①不願意的；嫌惡的。②微感不適的。to be *indisposed* with a cold. 因傷

風而微感不適。

in·dis·po·si·tion [ˌɪndɪspəˈzɪʃən; ˌindispəˈziʃən] *n.* ①微恙；不適。②不願；不欲；嫌惡〖to, towards〗. an *indisposition* to (do) the work. 對這工作的嫌惡。

in·dis·put·a·ble [ˌɪndɪˈspjutəbl; ˈindisˈpjuːtəbl] *adj.* 不容置辯的；無容懷疑的；明白的；確實的。—**in·dis·put·a·bil·i·ty,** *n.* —**in·dis·put·a·bly,** *adv.*

in·dis·so·cia·ble [ˌɪndɪˈsoʃəbl; ˌindiˈsouʃəbl] *adj.* 不能分離的。

in·dis·sol·u·bil·i·ty [ˌɪndɪˌsɑljəˈbɪlətɪ; ˈindiˌsɔljuˈbiliti] *n.* 不可分解；不能溶解；不能廢棄。

in·dis·sol·u·ble [ˌɪndɪˈsɑljəbl; ˌindiˈsɔljubl] *adj.* ①不可分解的(物質)。②不能溶解的。③永遠不變的；堅固的；固定的。④永遠有效的。—**in·dis·sol·u·bly,** *adv.*

in·dis·tinct [ˌɪndɪˈstɪŋkt; ˌindisˈtiŋkt] *adj.* ①不清楚的；模糊的。②不能分開的；無明確定義的。—**ly,** *adv.* —**ness,** *n.*

in·dis·tinc·tive [ˌɪndɪsˈtɪŋktɪv; ˌindisˈtiŋktiv] *adj.* 無特色的；無差別的；不顯著的。—**ly,** *adv.* —**ness,** *n.*

in·dis·tin·guish·a·ble [ˌɪndɪsˈtɪŋgwɪʃəbl; ˌindisˈtiŋgwiʃəbl] *adj.* 不能區別的；不能辨別的。—**in·dis·tin·guish·a·bly,** *adv.*

in·dite [ɪnˈdaɪt; inˈdait] *v.t.,* **-dit·ed, -dit·ing.** 著作；撰寫。

in·di·um [ˈɪndɪəm; ˈindiəm] *n.* 〖化〗銦(稀金屬元素之一；符號 In).

in·di·vert·i·ble [ˌɪndəˈvɝtəbl; ˌindaiˈvəːtibl] *adj.* 難令轉向的；難令分心的。—**in·di·vert·i·bly,** *adv.*

‡**in·di·vid·u·al** [ˌɪndəˈvɪdʒuəl; ˌindiˈvidjuəl] *n.* ①個人；個體。②人。a rather odd *individual*. 一個頗爲奇特的人。—*adj.* ①個別的；單獨的；特別的。A teacher cannot give *individual* attention to each pupil if his class is large. 如果班上的人數衆多，教師便不能個別地注意到每一個學生。②獨特的；有特性的。an *individual* style of speaking. 講話的獨特風格。③供一人用的。*individual* saltcellars. (餐桌上)每隻祇供一人用的盛鹽碟。

in·di·vid·u·al·ism [ˌɪndəˈvɪdʒuəlˌɪzəm; ˌindiˈvidjuəlizəm] *n.* ①個人主義。②利己主義。③個體；個性。

in·di·vid·u·al·ist [ˌɪndəˈvɪdʒuəlɪst; ˌindiˈvidjuəlist] *n.* ①個人生活而不欲與他人合作者。②個人主義者；擁護個人主義的人。

in·di·vid·u·al·is·tic [ˌɪndəˌvɪdʒuəlˈɪstɪk; ˌindiˌvidjuəˈlistik] *adj.* 個人主義的；利己主義的。—**al·ly,** *adv.*

***in·di·vid·u·al·i·ty** [ˌɪndəˌvɪdʒuˈælətɪ; ˌindiˌvidjuˈæliti] *n., pl.* **-ties.** ①個性；個人的人格。a man of marked *individuality*. 一個有特異個性的人。②個體狀態；獨立存在。③(*pl.*) 特質；特徵。④個人利益。⑤個人；個體。

in·di·vid·u·al·ize [ˌɪndəˈvɪdʒuəlˌaɪz; ˌindiˈvidjuəlaiz] *v.t.,* **-ized, -iz·ing.** ①使有個性；使具個性；使特殊化。This school *individualizes* its course of study. 這學校有特殊的課程。②個別地加以考慮；個別地加以列舉。③詳細敍述。④置於個人之手中。—**in·di·vid·u·al·i·za·tion,** *n.*

in·di·vid·u·al·ly [ˌɪndəˈvɪdʒuəlɪ; ˌindiˈvidjuəli] *adv.* ①個別地；單獨地。②個人地。③明確地。

in·di·vid·u·ate [ˌɪndəˈvɪdʒuˌet; ˌindiˈvidjueit] *v.t.,* **-at·ed, -at·ing.** 使個體化；賦以個性。

in·di·vid·u·a·tion [ˌɪndəˌvɪdʒuˈeʃən; ˈindiˌvidjuˈeiʃən] *n.* ①個體化；個性化。②以個體存在之狀態。

in·di·vis·i·bil·i·ty [ˌɪndəˌvɪzəˈbɪlətɪ; ˈindiˌviziˈbiliti] *n.* ①不可分性。②〖數學〗不能整除。

in·di·vis·i·ble [ˌɪndəˈvɪzəbl; ˌindiˈvizəbl] *adj.* ①不能分割的；不能分裂的。②〖數學〗不能整除的。—*n.* 不能分割之物；不能整除之數。—**ness,** *n.* —**in·di·vis·i·bly,** *adv.*

Indo- 〖字首〗表"印度的；印度人的；印度與…的" 之義。

In·do·chi·na [ˈɪndoˈtʃaɪnə; ˈindouˈtʃainə] *n.* ①中南半島。②前法屬印度支那。

In·do-Chi·nese [ˈɪndotʃaɪˈniz; ˈindou-tʃaiˈniːz] *adj., n., pl.* **-nese.** —*adj.* ①中南半島的；中南半島之民族或其語言的。②印度支那語系的。—*n.*中南半島人；印度支那人。

in·doc·ile [ɪnˈdɑsl; inˈdousail] *adj.* 難教的；難制馭的；不聽命的；不順從的。

in·do·cil·i·ty [ˌɪndoˈsɪlətɪ; ˌindouˈsiliti] *n.* 難教；難制馭；不順從。

in·doc·tri·nate [ɪnˈdɑktrɪnˌet; inˈdɔktrineit] *v.t.,* **-nat·ed, -nat·ing.** ①灌輸學說、信仰或主義；施以思想訓練。②教導。

in·doc·tri·na·tion [ɪnˌdɑktrɪˈneʃən; inˌdɔktriˈneiʃən] *n.* 教導；教化；(思想、主義等之)灌輸。—**al,** *adj.*

In·do-Eu·ro·pe·an [ˌɪndəˌjurəˈpiən; ˈindouˌjuərəˈpiːən] *adj.* ①印歐的。②印歐語系的。—*n.* ①印歐語系。②使用印歐語的人。

In·do-Ger·man·ic [ˌɪndodʒɝˈmænɪk; ˈindoudʒəːˈmænik] *adj., n.* =**Indo-European.**

in·do·lence [ˈɪndələns; ˈindələns] *n.* 懶惰；怠惰。

in·do·lent [ˈɪndələnt; ˈindələnt] *adj.* ①懶惰的；怠惰的。②〖醫〗不痛的。③〖醫〗頑性的。—**ly,** *adv.*

in·dom·i·ta·ble [ɪnˈdɑmətəbl; inˈdɔmitəbl] *adj.* 不能征服的；不屈不撓的。—**in·dom·i·ta·bly,** *adv.*

In·do·ne·sia [ˌɪndoˈniʃə; ˌindouˈniːzjə] *n.* ①馬來羣島。②印尼共和國(首都爲雅加達, Jakarta).

In·do·ne·sian [ˌɪndoˈniʃən; ˌindouˈniːzjən] *adj.* 印尼人的；印尼語的；印尼共和國的。—*n.* ①印尼人。②印尼語。

***in·door** [ˈɪnˌdor; ˈindɔː] *adj.* 戶內的；室內的(爲 outdoor 之對)。*indoor* games. 室內遊戲。

***in·doors** [ˈɪnˈdorz; ˈinˈdɔːz] *adv.* 在戶內；入戶內(爲 outdoors 之對)。You stay too much *indoors*. 你在戶內的時候太多了。

in·dor·sa·tion [ˌɪndɔrˈseʃən; ˌindɔːˈseiʃən] *n.* 〖英〗=**endorsement.**

in·dorse [ɪnˈdɔrs; inˈdɔːs] *v.t.* =**endorse.** —**in·dors·a·ble,** *adj.*

in·dorse·ment [ɪnˈdɔrsmənt; inˈdɔːsmənt] *n.* =**endorsement.**

in·dors·er, in·dors·or [ɪnˈdɔrsɚ; inˈdɔːsə] *n.* =**endorser.**

in·draft, in·draught [ˈɪnˌdræft; ˈindrɑːft] *n.* ①吸入；吸入物。②流入；內流。

in·draw·ing [ˈɪnˌdrɔɪŋ; ˈinˌdrɔːiŋ] *n.* 吸入；引入。—*adj.* 吸入的；引入的。

in·drawn [ˈɪnˈdrɔn; ˈinˈdrɔːn] *adj.* 內

向的。an aloof, *indrawn* man. 冷漠而內向的人。

in·du·bi·ta·bil·i·ty 〔ɪnˌdjubɪtəˈbɪlətɪ; inˌdju:bitəˈbiliti〕 *n.* 不容置疑。

in·du·bi·ta·ble 〔ɪnˈdjubɪtəbl; inˈdju:bitəbl〕 *adj.* 不容置疑的;不容置辯的;無疑的;明確的。—**ness,** *n.*

in·du·bi·ta·bly 〔ɪnˈdjubɪtəblɪ; inˈdju:bitəbli〕 *adv.* 不容置疑地;無疑地。

***in·duce** 〔ɪnˈdjus; inˈdju:s〕 *v.t.,* **-duced, -duc·ing.** ①引誘; 說服。What *induced* you to do such a foolish thing? 是甚麼引誘你作這樣的傻事? ②招致; 惹起。Some drugs *induce* sleep. 有些藥物使人入睡。③感應。*induced* current. 感應電流。④歸納。—**in·duc·er,** *n.* —**in·duc·i·ble,** *adj.*

induced drag 〖航空〗誘導阻力。

in·duce·ment 〔ɪnˈdjusmənt; inˈdju:smənt〕 *n.* ①勸誘;誘導。②引誘物;刺激;動機。

in·duct 〔ɪnˈdʌkt; inˈdʌkt〕 *v.t.* ①使正式就任; 使正式就職。②引入(處所、座位);介紹。 to *induct* a person into a seat. 引一個人入座。③〖美〗徵召入伍。④使正式加入(會社等)。⑤歸納。—**or,** *n.*

in·duct·ance 〔ɪnˈdʌktəns; inˈdʌktəns〕 *n.* 〖電〗①電感; 感應; 感應係數。②誘導子;感應器。

in·duct·ee 〔ˌɪndʌkˈti; ˌindʌkˈti:〕 *n.* ①就任者。②〖美〗應召入伍之兵。

in·duc·tile 〔ɪnˈdʌktl; inˈdʌktail〕 *adj.* 無伸縮性的; 無延性的; 無柔軟性的; 不順從的。—**in·duc·til·i·ty,** *n.*

in·duc·tion 〔ɪnˈdʌkʃən; inˈdʌkʃən〕 *n.* ①〖電〗感應;誘導。②〖邏輯〗歸納法。③歸納法所得之法則或理論。④就職式; 聖職就任式。⑤引入(座位);介紹。⑥導致;引起。

induction center 〖美〗徵兵中心。

induction coil 〖電〗感應圈。

in·duc·tive 〔ɪnˈdʌktɪv; inˈdʌktiv〕 *adj.* ①歸納的; 根據歸納法的。an *inductive* method. 歸納法。②感應的;誘導的。③誘人的;動人的;感人的。④緒論的;入門的。—**ly,** *adv.* —**ness,** *n.*

in·duc·tiv·i·ty 〔ˌɪndʌkˈtɪvətɪ; ˌindʌkˈtiviti〕 *n.* ①誘導性;感應性;誘導力。②〖電〗誘導率;電介質常數。

in·duc·tor 〔ɪnˈdʌktɚ; inˈdʌktə〕 *n.* ①授職者;聖職授與者。②〖電〗誘導子;感應器。③〖化〗感應物質;誘導質。

in·due 〔ɪnˈdju; inˈdju:〕 *v.t.* =**endue.**

***in·dulge** 〔ɪnˈdʌldʒ; inˈdʌldʒ〕 *v.,* **-dulged, -dulg·ing.** —*v.t.* ①放任;縱容。He *indulges* his children too much. 他太放縱他的孩子們。to *indulge* oneself in eating and drinking. 縱情於吃喝上。②遷就。③〖天主教〗赦免;恕罪;賦予特權。—*v.i.* 縱情;任意;耽溺。He *indulges* in tobacco. 他吸煙無度。—**in·dulg·er,** *n.* —**in·dulg·ing·ly,** *adv.*

***in·dul·gence** 〔ɪnˈdʌldʒəns; inˈdʌldʒəns〕 *n.* ①放任;恣縱;耽溺〖in〗. Constant *indulgence* in bad habits brought about his ruin. 經常耽溺於惡習導致他的毀滅。②所耽溺之事;嗜好。③恩惠;特權。④〖天主教〗免罪;赦免。⑤縱容;遷就。to treat a child with *indulgence.* 以縱容對待孩子。

in·dul·gent 〔ɪnˈdʌldʒənt; inˈdʌldʒənt〕 *adj.* ①放任的; 縱容的; 溺愛的。②寬大的〖to〗. to be *indulgent* to. 對…寬大的。

in·dul·gent·ly 〔ɪnˈdʌldʒəntlɪ; inˈdʌldʒəntli〕 *adv.* 縱容地;寬容地。

in·du·rate 〔*v.* ˈɪndjʊˌret; ˈindjuəreit *adj.* ˈɪndjʊrɪt; ˈindjuəreit〕 *v.,* **-rat·ed, -rat·ing,** *adj.* —*v.t.* ①使堅硬。②使無情;使無感覺或頑固。③使習慣於。to *indurate* oneself to privation and suffering. 使自己能吃苦耐勞。④使建立;使變爲永久。—*v.i.* ①硬化;變硬。②建立;變爲永久性。—*adj.* 硬化的;無情的;無感覺的。

in·du·ra·tion 〔ˌɪndjʊˈreʃən; ˌindjuəˈreiʃən〕 *n.* ①硬化;硬化之部分。②狠心;頑固;無人情。③〖醫〗硬結。

in·du·ra·tive 〔ˈɪndjʊˌretɪv; ˈindjuərətiv〕 *adj.* (使)硬固的; 硬化性的; 頑固的。

In·dus 〔ˈɪndəs; ˈindəs〕 *n.* ①〖天文〗印第安座;南天星座。②印度河(在印度西北部)。

indus. ①industrial. ②industry.

***in·dus·tri·al** 〔ɪnˈdʌstrɪəl; inˈdʌstriəl〕 *adj.* ①工業的;實業的。the *industrial* areas of a country. 一國之工業區。an *industrial* school. 工業學校。*industrial* chemistry. 工業化學。②產業工人的;有關產業工人的。—*n.* ①工業(尤指製造業)之雇員。②從事工業之公司。③工業產品。④(*pl.*) 工業公司所發行之股票及債券。—**ly,** *adv.*

industrial arts 工藝(尤指學校中之「工藝科目」)。

industrial design 工業設計。

industrial disease 工業病 (因從事某種工業生產而引起的特有疾病)。

industrial insurance 產業工人人壽保險。(亦作 **industrial life insurance**)

in·dus·tri·al·ism 〔ɪnˈdʌstrɪəlˌɪzəm; inˈdʌstriəlizəm〕 *n.* 工業主義;產業主義;工業制度;工業社會。

in·dus·tri·al·ist 〔ɪnˈdʌstrɪəlɪst; inˈdʌstriəlist〕 *n.* ①產業主義者; 工業家;實業家;企業家。②產業勞工。

in·dus·tri·al·i·za·tion 〔ɪnˌdʌstrɪələˈzeʃən, -aɪˈz-; inˌdʌstriəlaiˈzeiʃən〕 *n.* 工業化;產業化。

in·dus·tri·al·ize 〔ɪnˈdʌstrɪəlˌaɪz; inˈdʌstriəlaiz〕 *v.,* **-ized, -iz·ing.** —*v.t.* ①使工業化。②將…組成企業。—*v.i.* 工業化。

industrial park 工業區。

industrial psychology 工業心「理學」。

industrial relations 勞資關係。

industrial revolution 工業革命; 產業革命(即因機器的發明所引起的社會變遷,尤指十八世紀末十九世紀初發生於英國者)。

industrial union 工會。(亦作 **vertical union**)

***in·dus·tri·ous** 〔ɪnˈdʌstrɪəs; inˈdʌstriəs〕 *adj.* 勤勉的;奮發的。—**ly,** *adv.* —**ness,** *n.*

‡**in·dus·try** 〔ˈɪndəstrɪ; ˈindəstri〕 *n.,* *pl.* **-tries.** ①勤勉;孜孜不倦。His success was due to his *industry* and thrift. 他的成功係由於他的勤儉。②工業;實業;製造業。the cotton and woolen *industries.* 棉毛工業。heavy (light) *industry.* 重(輕)工業。the tourist *industry.* 觀光事業。domestic *industry.* 家庭工業。

in·dwell 〔ɪnˈdwɛl; ˈinˈdwel〕 *v.,* **-dwelt, -dwell·ing.** —*v.t.* ①居住。②鼓動;激勵;占有。—*v.i.* ①居住〖常 in〗. ②占有;充塞。—**er,** *n.*

in·dwell·ing 〔ɪnˈdwɛlɪŋ; ˈinˈdweliŋ〕 「*adj.* (導管等)留在體內的。」

-ine 〖字尾〗①表"似…的; 關於…的; …性質的"之義之形容詞字尾, 如: feminine. ②用作科學名詞, 或自專有名詞造成的形容詞字尾, 如: Byzantine. ③〖化〗鹽基、元素之名, 或造成化學用語之字尾，如：iodine. ④表"技術、處理、行動" 等之抽象名詞字尾，如：famine. ⑤女性形之名詞字尾，如：heroine.

in·e·bri·ant [ɪnˈibrɪənt; inˈiːbriənt] *adj.* 醉人的；麻醉的。—*n.* 麻醉劑。

in·e·bri·ate [*v.* ɪnˈibrɪˌet; iˈniːbrieit *n., adj.* ɪnˈibrɪɪt; iˈniːbriit] *v.*, **-at·ed, -at·ing,** *n., adj.* —*v.t.* ①使醉。②激勵；鼓舞。—*n.* 酒徒；醉漢(尤指常醉者)。—*adj.* 大醉的；酩酊的(=inebriated).

in·e·bri·a·tion [ɪnˌibrɪˈeʃən; iˌniːbriˈeiʃən] *n.* 醉；酩酊。

in·e·bri·e·ty [ˌɪnɪˈbraɪətɪ; ˌiniˈbraiəti] *n.* 醉；酩酊。

in·ed·i·ble [ɪnˈɛdəbl̩; inˈedibl] *adj.* 不可食的；不宜食用的。—**in·ed·i·bil·i·ty,** *n.*

in·ed·it·ed [ɪnˈɛdɪtɪd; inˈeditid] *adj.* 未編輯的；未刊行的；未出版的；未經校訂的。

in·ed·u·ca·ble [ɪnˈɛdʒəkəbl; inˈedʒukəbl] *adj.* 不能教育的；無法造就的。

in·ef·fa·ble [ɪnˈɛfəbl̩; inˈefəbl] *adj.* ①言語難以形容的。②不應說出的。—**in·ef·fa·bly,** *adv.* —**ness, in·ef·fa·bil·i·ty,** *n.*

in·ef·face·a·ble [ˌɪnəˈfesəbl̩; ˌiniˈfeisəbl] *adj.* 不可磨滅的；不能消除的；不能洗刷的。—**in·ef·face·a·bly,** *adv.* —**in·ef·face·a·bil·i·ty,** *n.*

in·ef·fec·tive [ˌɪnəˈfɛktɪv; ˌiniˈfektiv] *adj.* ①無效的；用處小的。②無能力的；不能幹的。③缺乏藝術效果的。—**ly,** *adv.* —**ness,** *n.*

in·ef·fec·tu·al [ˌɪnəˈfɛktʃʊəl; ˌiniˈfektjuəl] *adj.* ①無效果的；無用的；無益的；不能產生預期效果的。②無力的；無法施展的。—*n.* 無用的人；無一技之長者。—**ly,** *adv.* —**i·ty,** —**ness,** *n.*

in·ef·fi·ca·cious [ˌɪnɛfəˈkeʃəs; ˌinefiˈkeiʃəs] *adj.* 無效的。—**ly,** *adv.* —**ness, in·ef·fi·cac·i·ty,** *n.*

in·ef·fi·ca·cy [ɪnˈɛfəkəsɪ; inˈefikəsi] *n.* 無效果；無效能；無效力。*inefficacy* of laws in preventing crime. 法律對於防範犯罪之無效果。

in·ef·fi·cien·cy [ˌɪnəˈfɪʃənsɪ; ˌiniˈfiʃənsi] *n.* ①無效率。②無能。③效率很低的行爲。

in·ef·fi·cient [ˌɪnəˈfɪʃənt; ˌiniˈfiʃənt] *adj.* ①效率很低的。②無能的；不能幹的。—**ly,** *adv.*

in·e·las·tic [ˌɪnɪˈlæstɪk; ˌiniˈlæstik] *adj.* ①無彈性的；無彈力的。②無伸縮性的；無適應性的。

in·e·las·tic·i·ty [ˌɪnɪlæsˈtɪsətɪ; ˌinilæsˈtisiti] *n.* 無彈性；無韌性；無伸縮性；不能通融性。

in·el·e·gance [ɪnˈɛləgəns; inˈeligəns] *n.* ①不優雅；粗野。②不優雅之事物。

in·el·e·gan·cy [ɪnˈɛləgənsɪ; inˈeləgənsi] *n., pl.* **-cies.** =**inelegance.**

in·el·e·gant [ɪnˈɛləgənt; inˈeligənt] *adj.* 不優美的；不雅緻的；粗俗的。—**ly,** *adv.*

in·el·i·gi·bil·i·ty [ˌɪnɛlɪdʒəˈbɪlətɪ; inˌelidʒəˈbiliti] *n.* 無資格；不合格。

in·el·i·gi·ble [ɪnˈɛlɪdʒəbl̩; inˈelidʒəbl] *adj.* ①沒有資格的；不合格的。②不適當的；不妥當的。—*n.* 無資格者；不合格者。—**ness,** *n.* —**in·el·i·gi·bly,** *adv.*

in·el·o·quent [ɪnˈɛləkwənt; inˈeləkwənt] *adj.* 不善辯的；無辯才的。—**in·el·o·quence,** *n.* —**ly,** *adv.*

in·e·luc·ta·ble [ˌɪnɪˈlʌktəbl; ˌiniˈlʌktəbl] *adj.* 難免的；無可如何的；不能抵抗的。*ineluctable* facts of human existence. 人生之中種種無可如何的事實。—**in·e·luc·ta·bly,** *adv.* —**in·e·luc·ta·bil·i·ty,** *n.*

in·ept [ɪnˈɛpt; iˈnept] *adj.* ①不合適的；不相宜的。②可笑的；愚蠢的。③拙笨的；無效率的。—**ly,** *adv.* —**ness,** *n.*

in·ept·i·tude [ɪnˈɛptəˌtjud; iˈneptitjuːd] *n.* ①不適宜；愚蠢。②愚蠢的言行。

in·e·qual·i·ty [ˌɪnɪˈkwɑlətɪ; ˌini(ː)ˈkwɔliti] *n., pl.* **-ties.** ①不平等；不平均。②不平處；不規則處；不齊整處。③〖數學〗不等式(如 a>b).

in·eq·ui·ta·ble [ɪnˈɛkwɪtəbl̩; inˈekwitəbl] *adj.* 不公平的；不公正的。—**in·eq·ui·ta·bly,** *adv.* —**ness,** *n.*

in·eq·ui·ty [ɪnˈɛkwɪtɪ; inˈekwiti] *n., pl.* **-ties.** ①不公平；不公正。②不公平的事件；不公正的實例。

in·e·rad·i·ca·ble [ˌɪnɪˈrædɪkəbl; ˌiniˈrædikəbl] *adj.* 根深蒂固的；不能根絕的。—**ness,** *n.* —**in·e·rad·i·ca·bly,** *adv.*

in·e·ras·a·ble [ˌɪnɪˈresəbl̩; ˌiniˈreisəbl] *adj.* 不能抹去的；擦不掉的。

in·er·ra·ble [ɪnˈɛrəbl̩; inˈerəbl] *adj.* 不可能失誤的；無誤的；確實的。

in·er·rant [ɪnˈɛrənt; inˈerənt] *adj.* 無錯誤的。

in·ert [ɪnˈɝt; iˈnəːt] *adj.* ①無行動能力的；無生命的。②不活潑的；懶惰的；遲鈍的。③〖化〗不起化學作用的；惰性的。—**ly,** *adv.*

in·er·tia [ɪnˈɝʃə; iˈnəːʃjə] *n.* ①不活動；遲鈍。②〖物理〗惰性；慣性；慣量。law of *inertia.* 慣性定律。—**in·er·tial,** *adj.*

inertial guidance (or **navigation**)(機、船、飛彈等之)慣性導航。

in·ert·ness [ɪnˈɝtnɪs; inˈəːtnis] *n.* 不活潑；遲鈍。

in·es·cap·a·ble [ˌɪnəˈskepəbl; ˌinisˈkeipəbl] *adj.* 無法逃避的；免不了的；不可避免的。—**in·es·cap·a·bly,** *adv.* —**in·es·cap·a·bil·i·ty,** *n.*

in·es·sen·tial [ˌɪnəˈsɛnʃəl; ˈiniˈsenʃəl] *adj.* 不要緊的；非必要的；可無的；不重要的。—*n.* 非必要之事物。

in·es·ti·ma·ble [ɪnˈɛstəməbl̩; inˈestiməbl] *adj.* 不能估計的；無價的。—**in·es·ti·ma·bly,** *adv.*

in·ev·i·ta·bil·i·ty [ˌɪnɛvətəˈbɪlətɪ; inˌevitəˈbiliti] *n.* 不可避免；必然性。

***in·ev·i·ta·ble** [ɪnˈɛvətəbl̩; inˈevitəbl] *adj.* 一定發生的；不可避免的。Death is *inevitable.* 死是不可避免的。—**in·ev·i·ta·bly,** *adv.*

in·ex·act [ˌɪnɪgˈzækt; ˌinigˈzækt] *adj.* 不精確的；不正確的。—**ly,** *adv.* —**ness,** *n.*

in·ex·act·i·tude [ˌɪnɪgˈzæktəˌtjud; ˌinigˈzæktitjuːd] *n.* 不正確；不精密。

in·ex·cus·a·ble [ˌɪnɪkˈskjuzəbl̩; ˌiniksˈkjuːzəbl] *adj.* 無可辯解的；不能原諒的。—**in·ex·cus·a·bly,** *adv.*

in·ex·haust·i·ble [ˌɪnɪgˈzɔstəbl̩; ˌinigˈzɔːstəbl] *adj.* ①無窮盡的；取之不盡用之不竭的。②不倦的。—**in·ex·haust·i·bil·i·ty,** —**ness,** *n.* —**in·ex·haust·i·bly,** *adv.*

in·ex·ist·ent [ˌɪnɪgˈzɪstənt; ˌinigˈzistənt] *adj.* ①不存在的。②內在的。

in·ex·o·ra·bil·i·ty [ɪnˌɛksərəˈbɪlətɪ; inˌeksərəˈbiliti] *n.* 嚴密性；無情。

in·ex·o·ra·ble [ɪnˈɛksərəbl; inˈeksərəbl] *adj.* ①無情的；殘酷的。②不爲所動的；堅決不動的；不能改變的。—**in·ex·o·ra·bly,** *adv.*

in·ex·pe·di·ent [ˌɪnɪkˈspidɪənt; ˌiniksˈpiːdjənt] *adj.* 不合權宜的;不合宜的;失策的;不聰明的。—**in·ex·pe·di·ence, in·ex·pe·di·en·cy,** *n.* —**ly,** *adv.*

***in·ex·pen·sive** [ˌɪnɪkˈspɛnsɪv; ˌiniksˈpensiv] *adj.* 價廉的;不貴重的。—**ly,** *adv.* —**ness,** *n.*

in·ex·pe·ri·ence [ˌɪnɪkˈspɪrɪəns; ˌiniksˈpiəriəns] *n.* 無經驗;缺乏經驗。

***in·ex·pe·ri·enced** [ˌɪnɪkˈspɪrɪənst; ˌiniksˈpiəriənst] *adj.* 無經驗的; 缺乏經驗的。He was *inexperienced* in business. 他對於商業無經驗。

in·ex·pert [ˌɪnɪkˈspɝt; ˌiniksˈpəːt] *adj.* 技術不精的;不熟練的。—**ly,** *adv.* —**ness,** *n.*

in·ex·pi·a·ble [ɪnˈɛkspɪəbl; inˈekspiəbl] *adj.* ①不能抵償的;不能贖的。②不能平息的(盛怒);壓不住的(感情)。

in·ex·pi·ate [ɪnˈɛkspɪˌet; inˈekspieit] *adj.* 未抵償的;(罪)未贖的。

in·ex·plain·a·ble [ˌɪnɪkˈsplenəbl; ˌiniksˈpleinəbl] *adj.* 無法解釋的;不能說明的。

in·ex·pli·ca·bil·i·ty [ɪnˌɛksplɪkəˈbɪlətɪ; inˌeksplikəˈbiliti] *n.* 不能說明性;不可解釋;神祕性。

in·ex·pli·ca·ble [ɪnˈɛksplɪkəbl; inˈeksplikəbl] *adj.* 不可解釋的; 不能理解的;神祕的。—**in·ex·pli·ca·bly,** *adv.* —**ness,** *n.*

in·ex·plic·it [ˌɪnɪkˈsplɪsɪt; ˌiniksˈplisit] *adj.* 不明白的;不明確的;沒說清楚的;含糊的。—**ly,** *adv.* —**ness,** *n.*

in·ex·press·i·ble [ˌɪnɪkˈsprɛsəbl; ˌiniksˈpresəbl] *adj.* 不可表達的; 難以形容的; 說不出的。—*n.* ①不能以言語表達之事物。②(*pl.*)〖俗〗褲子。—**in·ex·press·i·bil·i·ty,** *n.* —**in·ex·press·i·bly,** *adv.*

in·ex·pres·sive [ˌɪnɪkˈsprɛsɪv; ˌiniksˈpresiv] *adj.* 無表情的;無意義的;呆滯的;沉默的。—**ly,** *adv.* —**ness,** *n.*

in·ex·pug·na·ble [ˌɪnɪkˈspʌgnəbl; ˌiniksˈpʌgnəbl] *adj.* 難攻陷的(城堡、軍隊等);難征服的; 難推翻的(議論等)。—**in·ex·pug·na·bly,** *adv.* —**ness,** *n.*

in·ex·ten·si·ble [ˌɪnɪkˈstɛnsəbl; ˌiniksˈtensəbl] *adj.* 不可擴張的;不能伸展的。

in·ex·tin·guish·a·ble [ˌɪnɪkˈstɪŋgwɪʃəbl; ˌiniksˈtiŋgwiʃəbl] *adj.* 不能撲滅的;無法抑制的。—**in·ex·tin·guish·a·bly,** *adv.*

in·ex·tir·pa·ble [ˌɪnɪkˈstɝpəbl; ˌiniksˈtəːpəbl] *adj.* 不能消滅的; 無法除去的。

in·ex·tri·ca·ble [ɪnˈɛkstrɪkəbl; inˈekstrikəbl] *adj.* ①不能解脫的; 不能擺脫的。②糾纏的。③不能解決的; 複雜的。—**in·ex·tri·ca·bly,** *adv.* —**ness,** *n.*

inf. ①infantry. ②inferior. ③infield. ④infielder. ⑤infinitive. ⑥infinity. ⑦infirmary. ⑧information. ⑨below; after. ⑩〖處方〗a. infuse. b. infusion. **in f.** in the end; finally.

in·fall [ˈɪnˌfɔl; ˈinfɔːl] *n.* ①入侵。②塌陷;崩陷。③(水庫、運河等之)進水口。

in·fal·li·bil·i·ty [ɪnˌfæləˈbɪlətɪ; inˌfæləˈbiliti] *n.* 絕無謬誤;絕對可靠性。

in·fal·li·ble [ɪnˈfæləbl; inˈfæləbl] *adj.* ①永遠不會錯的; 絕無謬誤的(人)。②絕對可靠的; 絕對無疑的; 絕對確實的。③必然的。—*n.* 絕無謬誤的人或事物。

in·fal·li·bly [ɪnˈfæləblɪ; inˈfæləbli] *adv.* 必然地;絕對地。

***in·fa·mous** [ˈɪnfəməs; ˈinfəməs] *adj.* ①無恥的;罪大惡極的。②不名譽的;聲名狼藉的。*infamous* behavior. 不名譽的行爲。—**ly,** *adv.* —**ness,** *n.*

in·fa·my [ˈɪnfəmɪ; ˈinfəmi] *n., pl.* **-mies.** ①不名譽;醜名;可恥。②可恥的行爲。

***in·fan·cy** [ˈɪnfənsɪ; ˈinfənsi] *n., pl.* **-cies.** ①幼年;幼稚期。from *infancy* to old age. 從幼年到老年。②初期; 未發達階段。Flying is no longer in its *infancy.* 飛行已非初期階段了。③〖法律〗未成年。

***in·fant** [ˈɪnfənt; ˈinfənt] *n.* ①嬰兒;幼兒。②法定未成年者(卽未滿二十一歲)。—*adj.* ①嬰兒的; 幼年的。*infant* voices. 童音。②初期的; 幼稚時期的。*infant* industries. 幼稚時期的工業。③未成年的。—**hood,** *n.* —**like,** *adj.*

in·fan·ta [ɪnˈfæntə; inˈfæntə] *n.* ①(西班牙或葡萄牙之)公主。②infante 之妻。

in·fan·te [inˈfænte; inˈfænti] *n.* (西班牙或葡萄牙之)王子;親王。

in·fan·ti·cid·al [ɪnˈfæntəˌsaɪdəl; inˈfæntiˌsaidl] *adj.* 殺嬰的。

in·fan·ti·cide [ɪnˈfæntəˌsaɪd; inˈfæntisaid] *n.* ①殺嬰。②犯殺嬰罪者; 殺嬰者。

in·fan·tile [ˈɪnfənˌtaɪl; ˈinfəntail] *adj.* ①嬰兒的。*infantile* mortality. 嬰兒死亡率。②似嬰兒的;幼稚的。③初期的;發端的。—**in·fan·til·i·ty,** *n.*

infantile paralysis 小兒痲痺症。

in·fan·ti·lism [ɪnˈfæntəlɪzm; inˈfæntilizəm] *n.* ①〖醫〗幼稚病;幼稚型(至成年期仍保有幼兒之特性)。②幼稚;不成熟。

in·fan·tine [ˈɪnfənˌtaɪn; ˈinfəntain] *adj.* 嬰兒的;似幼兒的;幼稚的。

***in·fan·try** [ˈɪnfəntrɪ; ˈinfəntri] *n.* ①步兵(集合稱)。an *infantry* regiment. 一個步兵團。②步兵團。the 8th *infantry.* 第八步兵團。

in·fan·try·man [ˈɪnfəntrɪmən; ˈinfəntrimən] *n., pl.* **-men.** 步兵。

infant(s') school 幼兒學校(合辦幼稚園及日間托兒所的學校)。

in·fat·u·ate [ɪnˈfætʃʊˌet; inˈfætjueit] *v.,* **-at·ed, -at·ing,** *adj., n.* —*v.t.* ①使愚蠢;使糊塗。②使糊塗或極端的熱情(主要用過去分詞)。to be *infatuated* with pride. 驕傲沖昏了頭。③迷戀。—*adj.* 沉醉的;迷戀的。—*n.* 迷戀者。

in·fat·u·at·ed [ɪnˈfætʃʊˌetɪd; inˈfætjueitid] *adj.* 昏頭昏腦的;入迷的;跟(女人等)打得火熱的。—**ly,** *adv.*

in·fat·u·a·tion [ɪnˌfætʃʊˈeʃən; inˌfætjuˈeiʃən] *n.* ①迷惑;受惑。②迷戀;醉心。

in·fea·si·ble [ɪnˈfizəbl; inˈfiːzəbl] *adj.* 不能實行的;行不通的。—**in·fea·si·bil·i·ty,** *n.*

***in·fect** [ɪnˈfɛkt; inˈfekt] *v.t.* ①傳染;傳播(病菌)於。to *infect* a wound (drinking water, etc.) with disease germs. 傳播病菌於傷口(飲水等)。②影響;使受感染。—*v.i.* 受感染。—**or,** *n.*

in·fect·ant [ɪnˈfɛktənt; inˈfektənt] *adj.* 傳染的;傳播的。—*n.* 傳播劑;媒體。

***in·fec·tion** [ɪnˈfɛkʃən; inˈfekʃən] *n.* ①傳染;感染。Air, water, clothing, and insects are all means of *infection.* 空氣、水、衣服及昆蟲都是傳染疾病的媒體(媒介)。②傳染或感染之源。③傳染病。④(流行於社會的)影響;情緒;思想。⑤道德上的汚染。

***in·fec·tious** [ɪnˈfɛkʃəs; inˈfekʃəs] *adj.* ①傳染的; 有傳染性的。Measles is an *infectious* disease. 痲疹是一種傳染病。②易傳染的;易傳播的。③能使成爲非法的;能導致充公的。—**ly,** *adv.* —**ness,** *n.*

in·fec·tive [ɪnˈfɛktɪv; inˈfektiv] *adj.* 傳染性的; 易傳染的。—**ness, in·fec·tiv·i·ty,** *n.*

in·fec·tor [ɪnˈfɛktɚ; inˈfektə] *n.* 傳播者;傳染者。

in·fe·cund [ɪnˈfikənd; inˈfiːkənd] *adj.* 不結實的;不生子的;不毛的。

in·fe·lic·i·tous [ˌɪnfəˈlɪsətəs; ˌinfiˈlisitəs] *adj.* ①不幸的;不快樂的。②不適當的;不貼切的(辭句等)。—**ly,** *adv.* —**ness,** *n.*

in·fe·lic·i·ty [ˌɪnfəˈlɪsətɪ; ˌinfiˈlisiti] *n., pl.* **-ties.** ①不幸。②不適當;不剴切。③不貼切的辭句;不適當的行爲。

in·fer [ɪnˈfɝ; inˈfəː] *v.,* **-ferred, -fer·ring.** —*v.t.* ①推論出;推斷出;推知。to *infer* an unknown fact from a known fact. 從已知的事實推斷出未知的事實。②暗指;意含。Ragged clothing *infers* poverty. 破爛服裝暗示貧窮。—*v.i.* 推論;推斷;推知。—**rer,** *n.*

in·fer·a·ble [ɪnˈfɝəbl̩; inˈfəːrəbl] *adj.* 可推論的;可推知的。(亦作 **inferrible**) —**in·fer·a·bly,** *adv.*

in·fer·ence [ˈɪnfərəns; ˈinfərəns] *n.* 推斷;推論。to draw an *inference* from... 由…而推得一論斷。

in·fer·en·tial [ˌɪnfəˈrɛnʃəl; ˌinfəˈrenʃəl] *adj.* 推論(上)的;根據推理的。—**ly,** *adv.*

in·fe·ri·or** [ɪnˈfɪrɪɚ; inˈfiəriə] *adj.* ①下級的; 初等的;較低的。an *inferior* court (of law). 初等法院。an *inferior* officer. 下級軍官。②次等的;較劣的。This cloth is *inferior* to real silk. 這布次於眞絲。③〖植物〗下生的; 下位的。④〖印刷〗在鉛字線下的(如 H_2SO_4 中之 2 與 4)。inferior to*** a. (階級)較低的。b. (品質) 較差的。—*n.* ①部下; 屬員; 晚輩。A good leader gets on well with *inferiors.* 一個好的領袖能與部屬相處得很好。②低劣之物; 劣品。—**ly,** *adv.*

inferior goods 因消費者收入增高而銷售量減低的貨物。

in·fe·ri·or·i·ty [ɪnˌfɪrɪˈɑrətɪ; inˌfiəriˈɔriti] *n.* 初等; 下級; 低劣。***inferiority complex*** 自卑感;自卑心理;自卑情結。

in·fer·nal [ɪnˈfɝnl̩, -nəl; inˈfəːnl] *adj.* ①地獄的; 冥府的。the *infernal* regions. 地獄。②地獄般的;惡魔般的;殘酷的。an *infernal* deed. 殘暴的行爲。③〖俗〗可憎的;可惡的。—**i·ty,** *n.* —**ly,** *adv.*

infernal machine 定時炸彈; 僞裝的炸彈。

in·fer·no [ɪnˈfɝno; inˈfəːnou] *n., pl.* **-nos.** ①地獄。②地獄般可怖的地方或景物。

in·fer·tile [ɪnˈfɝtl̩; inˈfəːtail] *adj.* 不肥沃的;貧瘠的;不毛的;不能生殖的。*infertile* soil. 不毛之土。—**in·fer·til·i·ty,** *n.*

in·fest [ɪnˈfɛst; inˈfest] *v.t.* 擾亂;騷擾;蹂躪;羣居於;包圍。The house is *infested* with rats. 家中受鼠擾害。—**er,** *n.*

in·fes·ta·tion [ˌɪnfɛsˈteʃən; ˌinfesˈteiʃən] *n.* 蹂躪;騷擾;橫行;蔓延。

in·fi·del [ˈɪnfədl̩; ˈinfidəl] *n.* ①無信仰者。②不信基督教者。—*adj.* 不信教的;異教的。

in·fi·del·i·ty [ˌɪnfəˈdɛlətɪ; ˌinfiˈdeliti] *n., pl.* **-ties.** ①無宗教信仰。②不信基督教。③(夫婦間的)不忠實;不貞。④不信;背信。⑤不忠實的行爲;不貞的行爲。⑥不傳眞;不正確。

in·field [ˈɪnˌfild; ˈinfiːld] *n.* ①農家周圍的耕地; 內田。②〖棒球、板球〗內野; 內野手(集合稱)。③賽馬場或田徑場爲跑道所包圍的部分。

in·field·er [ˈɪnˌfildɚ; ˈinˌfiːldə] *n.* 〖棒球、板球〗內野手。

in·fight·ing [ˈɪnˌfaɪtɪŋ; ˈinˌfaitiŋ] *n.* ①近接戰; 肉搏戰。②局外人所不知的敵對團體或個人間之鬥爭。③羣鬥。

in·fil·trate [ɪnˈfɪltret; inˈfiltreit] *v.,* **-trat·ed, -trat·ing,** *n.* —*v.t.* ①滲透; 透入。②滲過;透過; 突破(陣線)。—*v.i.* 浸透;浸潤。—*n.* 滲透物; 滲入物。—**in·fil·tra·tive,** *adj.* —**in·fil·tra·tor,** *n.*

in·fil·tra·tion [ˌɪnfɪlˈtreʃən; ˌinfilˈtreiʃən] *n.* ①滲透。②滲透物。③滲透戰術。

in·fil·tree [ˌɪnfɪlˈtri; ˌinfilˈtriː] *n.* 以滲透方式入境者。

infin. infinitive.

in·fi·nite** [ˈɪnfənɪt; ˈinfinit] *adj.* ①無限的;無窮的。②極大的。Teaching little children takes *infinite* patience. 教導幼兒須有極大的耐心。the Infinite*** 上帝(=God). ***the infinite*** 太空;穹蒼。—*n.* 無窮數。an *infinite* of possibilities. 可能性之無限多。

in·fi·nite·ly [ˈɪnfənɪtlɪ; ˈinfinitli] *adv.* 無限地; 無窮地。

in·fin·i·tes·i·mal [ˌɪnfɪnəˈtɛsəml̩; ˌinfiniˈtesiməl] *adj.* ①無限小的; 極微的。②〖數學〗無限小的。—*n.* 無限小;極微之量。—**ly,** *adv.* —**ness,** —**i·ty,** *n.*

infinitesimal calculus 〖數學〗微積分。

in·fin·i·ti·val [ˌɪnfɪnəˈtaɪvl̩; inˌfiniˈtaivəl] *adj.* 〖文法〗不定詞的。—**ly,** *adv.*

***in·fin·i·tive** [ɪnˈfɪnətɪv; inˈfinitiv] *n.* 〖文法〗不定詞(動詞的一種形式,不受身、數等限制)。不定詞的主要用法有六種:①作名詞用: *To love* our country is our first duty. 愛國是我們的第一義務。②作形容詞用: There is no house *to let.* 沒有出租的房子。③作副詞用: They came *to play.* 他們來玩。④獨立的用法: *To tell* you the truth, I don't want *to marry* her. 告訴你老實話, 我並不想和她結婚。⑤在若干動詞如: feel, hear, see, let, watch, have, make 之後, 若需要 infinitive 做受詞補足語時, 習慣不用 "to". I made him *go.* 我使他去的。⑥動詞片語的一部分: He will *do* most of the work. 他將做大部分工作。—*adj.* 〖文法〗不定詞的。*infinitive* phrase. 不定詞片語。〖注意〗 **help** 之後用 "to" 或不用 "to" 均可: *Help* him (*to*) finish the job. 幫他把這工作完成。

in·fin·i·tude [ɪnˈfɪnəˌtjud; inˈfinitjuːd] *n.* ①無限。②無限的數量、範圍等。

in·fin·i·ty [ɪnˈfɪnətɪ; inˈfiniti] *n., pl.* **-ties.** ①無窮; 無盡。②無限大的距離、空間、時間、數量等。③〖數學〗無限大; 無窮。④無邊;無量。***to infinity*** 無窮盡。

in·firm [ɪnˈfɝm; inˈfəːm] *adj.* ①虛弱的;殘廢的。②意志薄弱的;猶疑不定的。③不堅固的; 不穩固的。—*v.t.* 使動搖; 使不鞏固; 使無效。—**a·ble,** *adj.* —**ly,** *adv.* —**ness,** *n.*

in·fir·ma·ry [ɪnˈfɝmərɪ; inˈfəːməri] *n., pl.* **-ries.** ①療養所。②醫院(尤指機關、學校等所附設者)。

in·fir·mi·ty [ɪnˈfɝmətɪ; inˈfəːmiti] *n., pl.* **-ties.** ①虛弱;萎弱;殘廢。②疾病。③(心理或性格上的)弱點。

in·fix [*v.* ɪnˈfɪks; inˈfiks *n.* ˈɪnˌfɪks; ˈinfiks] *v.t.* ①固定;揷入;嵌入。②教導;注入;灌輸;深印。③〖文法〗揷(字腰)於一字的中間。—*n.* 〖文法〗字腰(揷入於一字中, 其作用與字首、字尾同: 例如阿拉伯文 iq-ta-riba 中之 -ta-.

infl. influence(d).

***in·flame** [ɪnˈflem; inˈfleim] *v.,* **-flamed,**

-flam·ing. —*v.t.* ①激動;激起。He was *inflamed* with lust (anger). 他慾(怒)火中燒。②使紅;使熱;使腫;使發炎。—*v.i.* ①變激動;激昂。②紅腫;發炎。③着火。—**in-flam·er,** *n.* —**in·flam·ing·ly,** *adv.*

in·flam·ma·bil·i·ty [ɪnˌflæməˈbɪlətɪ; inˌflæməˈbiliti] *n.* ①易燃性;燃燒性。②易興奮;易怒。

in·flam·ma·ble [ɪnˈflæməbl̩; inˈflæməbl] *adj.* ①易燃的;易着火的。②易激動的;易怒的。—*n.* 易燃之物。—**in·flam·ma·bly,** *adv.* —**ness,** *n.*

in·flam·ma·tion [ˌɪnfləˈmeʃən; ˌinfləˈmeiʃən] *n.* ①發炎;炎症。②(身體上)發炎部分;發炎之處。③憤怒;激昂。

in·flam·ma·to·ry [ɪnˈflæməˌtorɪ; inˈflæmətəri] *adj.* ①有刺激性的;有煽動性的。②發炎的;引起炎症的;有發炎現象的。*inflammatory fever*〖醫〗炎症熱。—**in·flam·ma·to·ri·ly,** *adv.*

in·flate [ɪnˈflet; inˈfleit] *v.,* **-flat·ed, -flat·ing.** —*v.t.* ①(灌入氣體)使脹大。②使得意洋洋。③使(通貨)膨脹;使(物價)騰貴。—*v.i.* ①膨脹。②得意。—**in·flat·ed,** *adj.*

***in·fla·tion** [ɪnˈfleʃən; inˈfleiʃən] *n.* ①脹大;膨大。②誇張。*inflation* of language. 誇大其詞。③通貨膨脹。④(由於通貨膨脹所造成的)物價騰貴。

in·fla·tion·ar·y [ɪnˈfleʃənˌɛrɪ; inˈfleiʃənəri] *adj.* ①使膨脹的;有膨脹性的。②通貨膨脹的。

inflationary spiral 惡性通貨膨脹。

in·fla·tion·ism [ɪnˈfleʃənˌɪzəm; inˈfleiʃənizəm] *n.* 通貨膨脹政策。

in·fla·tion·ist [ɪnˈfleʃənɪst; inˈfleiʃənist] *n.* 通貨膨脹論者。

in·flect [ɪnˈflɛkt; inˈflekt] *v.t.* ①改變(聲音)的音調。②〖文法〗變字形。③使彎曲;使屈折(常指向內彎曲)。—*v.i.*發生文法變化。—**ed·ness,** —**or,** *n.*

in·flec·tion [ɪnˈflɛkʃən; inˈflekʃən] *n.* ①音調變化。②〖文法〗變化;語尾變化。③彎曲;曲折。④彎曲之處。—**less,** *adj.*

in·flec·tion·al [ɪnˈflɛkʃənl̩; inˈflekʃənəl] *adj.* ①彎曲的;曲折的。②有字尾變化的;表字尾變化的。

inflectional language 有字尾變化的語文。

in·flec·tive [ɪnˈflɛktɪv; inˈflektiv] *adj.* ①彎曲的;反曲的;可使彎曲的。②〖文法〗有字尾變化的。

in·flex·i·bil·i·ty [ɪnˌflɛksəˈbɪlətɪ; inˌfleksəˈbiliti] *n.* 不屈(性);不撓(性);剛强;執拗。

in·flex·i·ble [ɪnˈflɛksəbl̩; inˈfleksəbl] *adj.* ①堅定的;强硬的;不屈的。②不可變的;不可更易的。③不易彎曲的。—**in·flex·i·bly,** *adv.* —**ness,** *n.*

in·flex·ion [ɪnˈflɛkʃən; inˈflekʃən] *n.* =**inflection.** —**al,** *adj.* —**less,** *adj.*

***in·flict** [ɪnˈflɪkt; inˈflikt] *v.t.* ①予以;加(害)。to *inflict* a blow (wound, etc.) on someone. 予人以打擊(傷害等)。②使受;使負擔(痛苦等)。The judge *inflicted* the death penalty on the criminal. 法官處該罪犯以死刑。

in·flic·tion [ɪnˈflɪkʃən; inˈflikʃən] *n.* ①傷害;打擊。②(所受的)痛苦;負擔;刑罰。

in·flo·res·cence [ˌɪnfloˈrɛsn̩s; ˌinflɔːˈresns] *n.* ①開花。②〖植物〗花序;花簇。③花(集合稱)。④(一朵)花。

in·flo·res·cent [ˌɪnfloˈrɛsn̩t; ˌinflɔːˈresnt] *adj.* 正開花的。

in·flow [ˈɪnˌflo; ˈin-flou] *n.* ①流入;輸入。②流入物。

‡in·flu·ence [ˈɪnfluəns; ˈinfluəns] *n., v.,* **-enced, -enc·ing.** —*n.* ①影響;感化力〖on〗. Many a woman has had a civilizing *influence* on her husband. 許多女人對於她的丈夫都有一種影響力。②權力;勢力。Will you exercise your *influence* on my behalf? 你願意使用你的權力給我幫忙嗎? ③予以影響者;有勢力者。He's an *influence* for good in the town. 他是城裏影響人爲善的一個人。④〖電〗感應;靜電影響。—*v.t.* ①影響;改變。The weather *influences* crops. 天氣影響農作物。②促使採取某種行動。Outside factors *influenced* him to resign. 外來因素促使他辭職。③加酒於(飲料)。—**a·ble,** *adj.* —**in·flu·enc·er,** *n.*

in·flu·ent [ˈɪnfluənt; ˈinfluənt] *adj.* 流入的。—*n.* ①流進另一河流之河;支流。②對本地生物平衡有重要關係之動植物。

***in·flu·en·tial** [ˌɪnfluˈɛnʃəl; ˌinfluˈenʃəl] *adj.* ①有影響的;有勢力的。*influential* politicians. 有勢力的政客。②運用勢力的;造成結果的。—*n.* 有影響力的人物。—**ly,** *adv.*

***in·flu·en·za** [ˌɪnfluˈɛnzə; ˌinfluˈenzə] *n.* 流行性感冒。(亦作 **flu**)

in·flux [ˈɪnˌflʌks; ˈinflʌks] *n.* ①流入;注入。②河流之會合處。③灌輸。—**ion,** *n.*

in·fold [ɪnˈfold; inˈfould] *v.t.* ①包裹;封入。②擁抱;緊抱。(亦作 **enfold**) —**er,** —**ment,** *n.*

‡in·form [ɪnˈfɔrm; inˈfɔːm] *v.t.* ①通知;報告。Has he been *informed* of his father's death yet? 把他父親的死訊通知他了沒有? ②使感受;賦與活力。Breath *informs* the body. 呼吸使身體有活力。—*v.i.* ①告發;訴寃。One thief *informed* against the others. 一個賊告發其他的賊。②供給知識。In theory news *informs* while advertising sells. 原則上新聞的作用在供應知識,而廣告的作用在出售商品。

***in·for·mal** [ɪnˈfɔrml̩; inˈfɔːməl] *adj.* ①非正式的;不拘禮儀的。an *informal* visit. 非正式的訪問。②俗用的;通俗的(字、詞等)。*informal* English. 俗用英語。

in·for·mal·i·ty [ˌɪnfɔrˈmælətɪ; ˌinfɔːˈmæliti] *n., pl.* **-ties.** ①非正式;不拘禮儀;簡便。②非正式的行爲。

in·for·ma·lize [ɪnˈfɔrməlˌaɪz; inˈfɔːməlaiz] *v.t.,* **-ized, -iz·ing.** 使不拘形式。

in·for·mal·ly [ɪnˈfɔrml̩ɪ; inˈfɔːməli] *adv.* 非正式地;不拘形式地。

in·form·ant [ɪnˈfɔrmənt; inˈfɔːmənt] *n.* ①通知者;報告者;告密者。②講本國語以供外國人學習或研究者;語料供應人。

‡in·for·ma·tion [ˌɪnfəˈmeʃən; ˌinfəˈmeiʃən] *n.* ①消息;情報〖about, on〗. Can you give me any *information* about (*or* on) this matter? 關於此事,你能供給我甚麼消息麼? ②知識;見聞。A dictionary gives *information* about words. 字典供給字的知識。③報告;通知。This guidebook is for the *information* of travelers. 這本旅行指南是供旅客閱覽的。④〖法律〗告發;告訴。to lay *information* against a person. 告發某人。⑤詢問處;服務臺。

information agency 新聞處;新聞發布室。

in·for·ma·tion·al [ˌɪnfəˈmeʃənəl; ˌinfəˈmeiʃənəl] *adj.* 新聞的;情報的;供消

息的;供資料的;見聞的;密告的。
Information Bureau 新聞局。
in·form·a·tive [ɪnˈfɔrmətɪv; inˈfɔːmətiv] *adj.* 供給知識(情報)的;有益的;有教育價值的。—**ly,** *adv.* —**ness,** *n.*
in·formed [ɪnˈfɔrmd; inˈfɔːmd] *adj.* 有知識的; 見聞廣的; 精明的; 消息靈通的。a well-*informed* man. 消息靈通的人。
in·form·er [ɪnˈfɔrmɚ; inˈfɔːmə] *n.* ①控告者;告發者;告密者。②通知者;報告者。
in·for·mi·da·ble [ɪnˈfɔrmədəbl̩; inˈfɔːmidəbl] *adj.* 不可怕的;不足畏的。
in·fra [ˈɪnfrə; ˈinfrə] 〖拉〗 *adv.* 在下;以下(指書之前後)。See *infra*, p. 40. 參看以下第四十頁。
in·fract [ɪnˈfrækt; inˈfrækt] *v.t.* 破壞;侵犯;違反(法律、權利等)。—**or,** *n.*
in·frac·tion [ɪnˈfrækʃən; inˈfrækʃən] *n.* ①違犯;犯法;違反。②不全骨折(斷骨位置未移動者)。
infra dig 〖拉〗〖俗〗 =**infra dignitatem.**
in·fra dig·ni·ta·tem [ˈɪnfrəˌdɪgnəˈtetəm; ˈinfrəˌdigniˈteitəm] 〖拉〗 (=beneath one's dignity)有失身分;有失體面。
in·fran·gi·ble [ɪnˈfrændʒəbl̩; inˈfrændʒibl] *adj.* ①不能破壞的;不能分離的(原子等)。②不能侵犯的;不可違背的。
in·fra·red [ˌɪnfrəˈrɛd; ˈinfrəˈred] *adj.* 〖物理〗紅外線 (infrared rays) 的。*infrared* photography. 紅外線攝影術。—*n.* 紅外線。
infrared rays 紅外線。
in·fra·son·ic [ˌɪnfrəˈsɑnɪk; ˌinfrəˈsonik] *adj.* (聲波)頻率低於聽覺範圍的。
in·fra·struc·ture [ˈɪnfrəˌstrʌktʃɚ; ˈinfrəˌstrʌktʃə] *n.* ①基礎;基本設施。②北大西洋公約組織之永久性軍事設施。
in·fre·quence [ɪnˈfrikwəns; inˈfriːkwəns] *n.* =**infrequency.**
in·fre·quen·cy [ɪnˈfrikwənsɪ; inˈfriːkwənsi] *n.* 稀罕; 罕見。
in·fre·quent [ɪnˈfrikwənt; inˈfriːkwənt] *adj.* ①稀少的; 罕見的。an *infrequent* visitor. 稀客。②稀疏的。—**ly,** *adv.*
in·fringe [ɪnˈfrɪndʒ; inˈfrindʒ] *v.,* **-fringed, -fring·ing.** —*v.t.* 侵犯; 侵害; 違背。—*v.i.* 侵犯;侵害 〖on, upon〗.
in·fringe·ment [ɪnˈfrɪndʒmənt; inˈfrindʒmənt] *n.* ①違反;觸犯。②侵害;侵犯。
in·fruc·tu·ous [ɪnˈfrʌktʃuəs; inˈfrʌktjuəs] *adj.* ①不結實的; 不毛的。②無益的;無用的。
in·fu·ri·ate [*adj.* ɪnˈfjurɪɪt; inˈfjuərieit *v.* ɪnˈfjurɪˌet; inˈfjuərieit] *v.,* **-at·ed, -at·ing,** *adj.* —*v.t.* 激怒; 使狂怒。 to be *infuriated* at. 對…極爲憤怒。—*adj.* 狂怒的。—**ly,** *adv.* —**in·fu·ri·a·tion,** *n.*
in·fuse [ɪnˈfjuz; inˈfjuːz] *v.,* **-fused, -fus·ing.** —*v.t.* ①注入;灌輸。②感召;鼓舞。The soldiers were *infused* with his courage. 兵士們爲其勇氣所鼓舞。③浸;泡製。—*v.i.* 泡出味道。—**in·fus·er,** *n.*
in·fu·si·ble[1] [ɪnˈfjuzəbl̩; inˈfjuːzəbl] *adj.* 不溶解(性)的。—**ness,** *n.*
in·fu·si·ble[2] *adj.* 可注入的。
in·fu·sion [ɪnˈfjuʒən; inˈfjuːʒən] *n.* ①注入;灌輸。②注入物;混入物。③泡製成的浸劑、湯、茶等。④〖醫〗輸血或輸鹽水等; 被輸之血或鹽水等。
in·fu·sive [ɪnˈfjusɪv; inˈfjuːsiv] *adj.* 「浸透的。
In·fu·so·ri·a [ˌɪnfjuˈsorɪə; ˌinfjuˈsɔːriə] *n. pl.* 〖動物〗纖毛蟲類;滴蟲類。
in·fu·so·ri·al [ˌɪnfjuˈsorɪəl; ˌinfjuˈsɔːriəl] *adj.* (含)纖毛蟲的;(含)滴蟲的。
in·fu·so·ri·an [ˌɪnfjuˈsorɪən; ˌinfjuˈsɔːriən] *adj.* =**infusorial.** —*n.* 纖毛蟲;滴蟲。
-ing 〖字尾〗加於原形動詞之後造成動名詞及現在分詞。
in·gath·er [ɪnˈgæðɚ; inˈgæðə] *v.i.* & *v.t.* 收集;收割;採集。
in·gath·er·ing [ˈɪnˌgæðrɪŋ; ˈinˌgæðəriŋ] *n.* ①收穫;收集。②收穫物;收集物。—*adj.* 收集的;聚集的。
in·gem·i·nate [ɪnˈdʒɛməˌnet; inˈdʒemineit] *v.t.,* **-nat·ed, -nat·ing.** (爲強調語氣而)重復;反復;反復地講。
***in·gen·ious** [ɪnˈdʒinjəs; inˈdʒiːnjəs] *adj.* ①智巧的; 有發明天才的; 敏捷的; 靈敏的。an *ingenious* mind. 靈敏的頭腦。②設計精巧的(機械等)。This mousetrap is an *ingenious* device. 這捕鼠器是一件精巧的裝置。—**ly,** *adv.* —**ness,** *n.* 〖注意〗 **ingenious, ingenuous.** ingenious 指智巧的;靈敏的。ingenuous 指直率的;誠懇的;樸實的。
in·gé·nue [æʒeˈny; ˌɛ̃ːʒeiˈnjuː] *n., pl.* **-nues** [-ny, -njuz; -ny, -njuːz], *adj.* 〖法〗 —*n.* ①天眞無邪的女子。②戲劇中演此種角色之女演員。③經驗不足者。—*adj.* 天眞的。
***in·ge·nu·i·ty** [ˌɪndʒəˈnuətɪ; ˌindʒiˈnjuːiti] *n., pl.* **-ties.** ①智巧; 善發明或設計之才; 創造力。The boy showed *ingenuity* in making toys. 那男孩在玩具製作上表現了智巧。②精巧的裝置或機器。
in·gen·u·ous [ɪnˈdʒɛnjuəs; inˈdʒenjuəs] *adj.* ①坦白的;老實的。②誠樸的;天眞的。an *ingenuous* smile. 天眞的微笑。—**ly,** *adv.* —**ness,** *n.*
in·ger·ence [ˈɪndʒərəns; ˈindʒərəns] *n.* 干涉;侵犯。
in·gest [ɪnˈdʒɛst; inˈdʒest] *v.t.* ①〖生理〗嚥下;攝取(食物等)於體內。②吸收。
in·ges·tion [ɪnˈdʒɛstʃən; inˈdʒestʃən] *n.* 取入;嚥入;攝取。
in·gle [ˈɪŋgl̩; ˈiŋgl] *n.* 〖蘇〗①爐中之火。②壁爐。
in·gle·nook [ˈɪŋgl̩ˌnuk; ˈinglnuk] *n.* 爐邊;爐隅。
in·glo·ri·ous [ɪnˈglorɪəs; inˈglɔːriəs] *adj.* ①不名譽的; 羞辱的。②不出名的; 沒沒無聞的。—**ly,** *adv.* —**ness,** *n.*
in·go·ing [ˈɪnˌgoɪŋ; ˈinˌgouiŋ] *n., adj.* 進來(的);就任(的)。
in·got [ˈɪŋgət; ˈiŋgət] *n.* (金、銀、鋼等之)條或塊;錠。
in·graft [ɪnˈgræft; inˈgrɑːft] *v.t.* =**engraft.**
in·grain [*v., adj.* ɪnˈgren; ˈinˈgrein *n.* ˈɪnˌgren; ˈinˈgrein] *v.t.* ①生染(卽先染色而後織造);深染。②(習慣等)使根深蒂固。—*adj.* ①生染的; 深染的。②天生的;根深蒂固的。—*n.* ①生染羊毛、棉紗等。②天生的性格。
in·grained [ɪnˈgrend; inˈgreind] *adj.* ①生染的; 深染的。②根深蒂固的; 天生的。—**ly,** *adv.* —**ness,** *n.*
in·grate [ˈɪngret; inˈgreit] *n.* 忘恩負義的人。—*adj.* 〖古〗忘恩負義的。
in·gra·ti·ate [ɪnˈgreʃɪˌet; inˈgreiʃieit] *v.t.,* **-at·ed, -at·ing.** 逢迎;討好(與反身代名詞連用)。***ingratiate oneself with*** 迎合。—**in·gra·ti·a·tion,** *n.*
in·gra·ti·at·ing [ɪnˈgreʃɪˌetɪŋ; inˈgreiʃieitiŋ] *adj.* ①巴結的;逢迎的;討好的;拍馬屁的。②吸引人的;迷人的。—**ly,** *adv.*
in·gra·ti·a·to·ry [ɪnˈgreʃɪəˌtorɪ; in-

ˈgreiʃiətəri] *adj.* 目的在討好的。

in·grat·i·tude [ɪnˈgrætəˌtjud; inˈgrætitjuːd] *n.* 忘恩負義。

in·gre·di·ent [ɪnˈgridɪənt; inˈgriːdjənt] *n.* (混合物的)成分;組成分子。

in·gress [ˈɪngrɛs; ˈingres] *n.* ①進入。②准許進入;入場權(爲 egress 之對)。③入口。—**ive,** *adj.*

in-group [ˈɪnˌgrup; ˈingruːp] *n.* 〖社會〗內羣;內集團;圈內(爲 out-group之對)。

in·grow·ing [ˈɪnˌgroɪŋ; ˈinˌgrouiŋ] *adj.* ①生在內面的;向內生的。②生入肉中的。

in·grown [ˈɪnˌgron; ˈingroun] *adj.* ①生入內部的;向內生的;天性的。②(指甲等)向肉內生長的。

in·growth [ˈɪnˌgroθ; ˈingrouθ] *n.* 向內生長;向內生長物。

in·gui·nal [ˈɪŋgwɪnl; ˈiŋgwinl] *adj.* 〖解剖〗鼠蹊部的;腹股溝的。

in·gulf [ɪnˈgʌlf; inˈgʌlf] *v.t.* =**engulf.**

in·gur·gi·tate [ɪnˈgɝdʒəˌtet; inˈgəːdʒiteit] *v.t.* & *v.i.,* **-tat·ed, -tat·ing.** ①大口吞嚥;大口喝。②捲入。

***in·hab·it** [ɪnˈhæbɪt; inˈhæbit] *v.t.* 居住於;占據。Fish *inhabit* the sea. 魚棲於海中。—*v.i.* 〖古〗居;住。—**er,** —**or,** *n.*

in·hab·it·a·ble [ɪnˈhæbɪtəbl; inˈhæbitəbl] *adj.* ①可居住的。②適於居住的。

in·hab·it·an·cy [ɪnˈhæbətənsɪ; inˈhæbitənsi] *n., pl.* **-cies.** ①居住。②住所;家。(亦作 **inhabitance**)

***in·hab·it·ant** [ɪnˈhæbətənt; inˈhæbitənt] *n.* 居民;居住者。an *inhabitant* of the town. 城裏人。

in·hab·i·ta·tion [ɪnˌhæbəˈteʃən; inˌhæbiˈteiʃən] *n.* 居住;棲息。

in·hal·ant [ɪnˈhelənt; inˈheilənt] *adj.* 吸入(用)的。—*n.* 吸入孔;吸入器;吸入藥。

in·ha·la·tion [ˌɪnhəˈleʃən; ˌinhəˈleiʃən] *n.* 吸入;吸入物;吸入藥。

in·hale [ɪnˈhel; inˈheil] *v.,* **-haled, -hal·ing,** *n.* —*v.t.* 吸入;把…吸進肺裏。to *inhale* air. 吸入空氣。—*v.i.* 吸。—*n.* 一吸。

in·hal·er [ɪnˈhelɚ; inˈheilə] *n.* 吸入器;吸入者;空氣濾過器。

in·har·mon·ic [ˌɪnhɑrˈmɑnɪk; ˌinhɑːˈmɔnik] *adj.* 不協調的;不和諧(音)的。

in·har·mo·ni·ous [ˌɪnhɑrˈmonɪəs; ˌinhɑːˈmounjəs] *adj.* 不和諧的;不一致的;不協調的。—**ly,** *adv.* —**ness,** *n.*

in·here [ɪnˈhɪr; inˈhiə] *v.i.,* **-hered, -her·ing.** ①(性質等)存在;固有;具有。②(權利等)屬。③(意義)含有。

in·her·ence [ɪnˈhɪrəns; inˈhiərəns] *n.* ①固有;具有;生得;天賦。②〖哲學〗(屬性於實體之)內屬。

in·her·en·cy [ɪnˈhɪrənsɪ; inˈhiərənsi] *n., pl.* **-cies.** ①固有;天賦。②固有(天賦)之性質;與生俱來的東西;固有物。

***in·her·ent** [ɪnˈhɪrənt; inˈhiərənt] *adj.* 固有的;與生俱來的。—**ly,** *adv.*

***in·her·it** [ɪnˈhɛrɪt; inˈherit] *v.t.* ①繼承。The eldest son will *inherit* the title. 長子將繼承爵位。②由遺傳而得。③繼承…之爵位及財產。A son *inherits* his father. 兒子繼承他父親的爵位及財產。—*v.i.* ①繼承。A son *inherits* from his father. 兒子繼承父親。②接受遺傳的力量、特點等。

in·her·it·a·ble [ɪnˈhɛrətəbl; inˈheritəbl] *adj.* ①可以繼承的;會遺傳的。②有繼承資格的。

***in·her·it·ance** [ɪnˈhɛrətəns; inˈheritəns] *n.* ①繼承。to receive something by *inheritance.* 由繼承而得到某物。②遺傳。③繼承權。④繼承物;遺產;遺留物。Good health is a fine *inheritance.* 健康是一種良好的遺傳物。

inheritance tax 〖法律〗遺產稅。

in·her·it·ed [ɪnˈhɛrətɪd; inˈheritid] *adj.* 遺傳的;繼承的。

in·her·i·tor [ɪnˈhɛrətɚ; inˈheritə] *n.* (遺產)繼承人。

in·her·i·tress [ɪnˈhɛrətrɪs; inˈheritris] *n.* =**inheritrix.**

in·her·i·trix [ɪnˈhɛrətrɪks; inˈheritriks] *n., pl.* **-trix·es, in·her·i·tri·ces** [ɪnˌhɛrɪˈtraɪsiz; inˌheriˈtraisiːz]. 女性繼承人。

in·he·sion [ɪnˈhiʒən; inˈhiːʒən] *n.* =**inherence.**

in·hib·it [ɪnˈhɪbɪt; inˈhibit] *v.t.* ①抑制。②禁止。to *inhibit* someone from doing something. 禁止某人做某事。

in·hi·bi·tion [ˌɪnhɪˈbɪʃən; ˌinhiˈbiʃən] *n.* ①抑制;抑制力。②禁止。③化學反應之停止或減速。

in·hib·i·to·ry [ɪnˈhɪbəˌtorɪ; inˈhibitəri] *adj.* 禁止的;抑制的。(亦作**inhibitive**)

in·hos·pi·ta·ble [ɪnˈhɑspɪtəbl; inˈhɔspitəbl] *adj.* ①冷淡的;不親切待客的。②荒涼的;不毛的;無遮蓋的。—**in·hos·pi·ta·bly,** *adv.*

in·hos·pi·tal·i·ty [ˌɪnhɑspəˈtælətɪ; ˈinˌhɔspiˈtæliti] *n.* 不善款待;冷淡;不親切。

in-house [ˈɪnˌhaus; ˈinˌhaus] *adj.* 機構、集團等內部的。

in·hu·man [ɪnˈhjumən; inˈhjuːmən] *adj.* ①無情的;殘忍的;無人性的。②不適合人類的。③非人類的。④超人的。—**ly,** *adv.*

in·hu·mane [ˌɪnhjuˈmen; ˌinhjuːˈmein] *adj.* 不近人情的;薄情的;不人道的。

in·hu·man·i·ty [ˌɪnhjuˈmænətɪ; ˌinhjuːˈmæniti] *n., pl.* **-ties.** ①殘暴;無人性;不人道。②殘暴無人性之行爲。

in·hu·man·ize [ɪnˈhjumənˌaɪz; inˈhjuːmənaiz] *v.t.,* **-ized, -iz·ing.** 使殘酷;使無人性。

in·hu·ma·tion [ˌɪnhjuˈmeʃən; ˌinhjuːˈmeiʃən] *n.* 埋葬;土葬。

in·hume [ɪnˈhjum; inˈhjuːm] *v.t.,* **-humed, -hum·ing.** 埋葬;土葬。

in·hu·mor·ous [ɪnˈhjumərəs; inˈhjuːmərəs] *adj.* 不幽默的;不滑稽的。

in·im·i·cal [ɪnˈɪmɪkl; iˈnimikəl] *adj.* ①不友善的;有敵意的。②不利的;有害的;抵觸的。—**ly,** *adv.*

in·im·i·ta·ble [ɪnˈɪmətəbl; iˈnimitəbl] *adj.* ①無法模仿的。②無比的;無雙的。—**in·im·i·ta·bly,** *adv.*

in·iq·ui·tous [ɪˈnɪkwətəs; iˈnikwitəs] *adj.* ①極爲不公的;不公平的。②邪惡的。—**ly,** *adv.*

in·iq·ui·ty [ɪˈnɪkwətɪ; iˈnikwiti] *n., pl.* **-ties.** ①極度之不公平;不法;邪惡。②邪惡或不公、不法、不義之行爲。

init. ①initial. ②initio(拉=at the beginning).

***i·ni·tial** [ɪˈnɪʃəl; iˈniʃəl] *adj., n., v.,* **-tial(l)ed, -tial·(l)ing.** —*adj.* 最初的;開始的。the *initial* letter of a word. 一字開始的字母。—*n.* ①(一字的)起首字母。②(*pl.*)姓名起首字母。G.B.S. are the *initials* for George Bernard Shaw. 蕭伯納姓名的起首字母是 G. B. S. —*v.t.* 簽姓名起首字母於。—**ly,** *adv.*

i·ni·ti·ate[1] [ɪˈnɪʃɪˌet; iˈniʃieit] *v.t.*, **-at·ed, -at·ing.** ①創始;發起。②以正式儀式介紹加入。③引(人)入某種學科的知識;教以初步。

i·ni·ti·ate[2] [ɪˈnɪʃɪɪt; iˈniʃiit] *n.* 由正式儀式被介紹加入的人;被引入某種學科之知識的人;被教以入門知識的人。—*adj.* ①由正式儀式被介紹加入的。②被引入某種科學之知識的;有入門知識的;創始的;初期的。

i·ni·ti·a·tion [ɪˌnɪʃɪˈeʃən; iˌniʃiˈeiʃən] *n.* ①創始;發起。②正式加入(社團等)。*initiation* fee. (俱樂部等之)入會費。③入會式;入社式。④入門。⑤(對某種學問或事情之)內行知識。

***i·ni·ti·a·tive** [ɪˈnɪʃɪˌetɪv; iˈniʃiətiv] *n.* ①初步;起首;主動。to take the *initiative* in making acquaintances. 主動交友。②主動力;進取的精神。③創制權。④優先權。—*adj.* 自發的。

i·ni·ti·a·tor [ɪˈnɪʃɪˌetɚ; iˈniʃieitə] *n.* 創始者;發起人;教導者;傳授者。

i·ni·ti·a·to·ry [ɪˈnɪʃɪəˌtorɪ; iˈniʃiətəri] *adj.* ①起始的;初步的;入門的。②入會(黨)的;入社的。

i·ni·ti·o [ɪˈnɪʃɪo; iˈniʃiou] 〖拉〗 *adv.* 在(書之頁、章等)之開頭;在卷首;起初(=at the beginning).

in·ject [ɪnˈdʒɛkt; inˈdʒekt] *v.t.* ①注射。②投入;加入。③注入;灌入。

in·jec·tion [ɪnˈdʒɛkʃən; inˈdʒekʃən] *n.* ①注射;注入。②加入;混入。③注射之物;注射劑;針藥。Penicillin is an effective *injection*. 盤尼西林是一種有效的注射藥。④〖醫〗充血。⑤將衞星射入軌道之作業。

in·jec·tor [ɪnˈdʒɛktɚ; inˈdʒektə] *n.* ①注射者。②注射器。③〖機械〗噴射給水器。

in·ju·di·cious [ˌɪndʒuˈdɪʃəs; ˌindʒuːˈdiʃəs] *adj.* 欠考慮的;不智的。**—ly,** *adv.*

in·junct [ɪnˈdʒʌŋkt; inˈdʒʌŋkt] *v.t.* 〖俗〗=**enjoin.**

in·junc·tion [ɪnˈdʒʌŋkʃən; inˈdʒʌŋkʃən] *n.* ①命令;訓諭。John obeyed his mother's *injunction* to hurry straight home. 約翰遵奉母諭卽刻兼程返家。②〖法律〗禁止令;强制令。

in·jur·ant [ˈɪndʒərənt; ˈindʒərənt] *n.* 傷害物。

***in·jure** [ˈɪndʒɚ; ˈindʒə] *v.t.*, **-jured, -jur·ing.** ①傷害;損害。In the railroad accident 300 people were *injured*. 在該次火車失事中有三百人受傷。②傷(感情);使冤屈。You have an *injured* look. 你像是受了冤屈的樣子。**—in·jur·er,** *n.*

in·jured [ˈɪndʒɚd; ˈindʒəd] *adj.* ①受損害的;受傷害的。the *injured*. 受傷者。②受委曲的;生氣的。

***in·ju·ri·ous** [ɪnˈdʒurɪəs; inˈdʒuəriəs] *adj.* ①有害的。habits that are *injurious* to health. 有害於健康的習慣。②不公平的;誹謗的。**—ly,** *adv.* **—ness,** *n.*

***in·ju·ry** [ˈɪndʒərɪ; ˈindʒəri] *n.*, *pl.* **-ries.** ①傷害;損害;損毀。②冤屈;屈辱。I take it as a personal *injury*. 我認爲這是對個人的侮辱。

***in·jus·tice** [ɪnˈdʒʌstɪs; inˈdʒʌstis] *n.* ①不公正;不公平;不講道義。*Injustice* is inevitable in war. 戰爭中不公正是無法避免的。②不公正的行爲;不義的行爲。

‡ink [ɪŋk; iŋk] *n.* ①墨水;油墨。to write a letter in *ink*. 用墨水寫信。②(烏賊等的)墨汁。—*v.t.* ①塗墨水於;以墨水沾汚。②以墨水劃掉〖out〗. He *inked* out many lines. 他用墨水劃掉很多行。③簽(合約)。He readily *inked* the contract. 他很樂意地在合同上簽了字。—*v.i.* 加墨水。to *ink* in a drawing. 加墨水於圖畫(指原鉛筆畫稿)。

ink bag (烏賊等之)墨囊。

ink bottle 墨水瓶。

ink·er [ˈɪŋkɚ; ˈiŋkə] *n.* ①〖印刷〗墨棒;墨滾。②〖電信〗受信印字機。③塗墨者;用墨者。

ink eraser 退墨水用之橡皮、藥水、刀子等。

ink·fish [ˈɪŋkˌfɪʃ; ˈiŋkfiʃ] *n.* 烏賊;墨魚。

ink·horn [ˈɪŋkˌhɔrn; ˈiŋkhɔːn] *n.* 昔之角質墨水壺。—*adj.* 賣弄學問的;學究氣的。

ink·i·ness [ˈɪŋkɪnɪs; ˈiŋkinis] *n.* ①黑;墨黑。②塗有墨水;墨水汚染。

ink·ling [ˈɪŋklɪŋ; ˈiŋkliŋ] *n.* ①略知;微覺。to have (get, *or* give) an *inkling* of. 略有所知。②暗示。③〖方〗極小的聲音。I could not hear an *inkling* of his breathing. 他的聲息我一點也聽不到。

ink·sling·er [ˈɪŋkˌslɪŋɚ; ˈiŋkˌsliŋə] *n.* 〖俚〗作家。

ink·sling·ing [ˈɪŋkˌslɪŋɪŋ; ˈiŋkˌsliŋiŋ] *n.* 〖俚〗寫作。

***ink·stand** [ˈɪŋkˌstænd; ˈiŋkstænd] *n.* ①墨水瓶架(並可架筆者)。②墨水壺;墨水瓶。

ink·stone [ˈɪŋkˌston; ˈiŋkstoun] *n.* ①硯。②綠礬。

ink-wash [ˈɪŋkˌwɑʃ; ˈiŋkwɔʃ] *adj.* 用稀釋墨水畫的。an *ink-wash* drawing. 一張淡墨畫。

ink·well [ˈɪŋkˌwɛl; ˈiŋkwel] *n.* 墨水池。

ink·y [ˈɪŋkɪ; ˈiŋki] *adj.*, **ink·i·er, ink·i·est.** ①如墨的;黑的。*inky* darkness. 墨黑;漆黑。②染有墨水的;用墨水寫的。③墨水的。④含墨水的。

in·laid [ˈɪnˌled; ˈinˈleid] *adj.* ①嵌入的;鑲嵌的。*inlaid* work. 鑲嵌細工。②有嵌花裝飾的。—*v.* pt. & pp. of **inlay.**

***in·land** [*adj.* ˈɪnlənd; ˈinlənd *n.* ˈɪnˌlænd, ˈɪnlənd; ˈinlənd *adv.* ˈɪnˌlænd, ˈɪnlənd; inˈlænd, ˈinˈlænd] *adj.* ①內陸的;內地的。an *inland* sea. 內(陸)海。②國內的;非外國的。*inland* trade. 國內貿易。—*n.* (一國之)內地;腹地。—*adv.* 在內地;向內地。

in·land·er [ˈɪnləndɚ; ˈinləndə] *n.* 內地人。

Inland Sea, the 瀨戶內海(在日本本州之南)。

in-law [ˈɪnˌlɔ; ˈinlɔː] *n.* 〖俗〗姻親。

in·law [ɪnˈlɔ; inˈlɔː] *v.t.* 〖法律〗恢復(犯人之)法律權益。

in·lay [*v.* ɪnˈle; ˈinˈlei *n.* ˈɪnˌle; ˈinlei] *v.*, **-laid, -lay·ing,** *n.*, *pl.* **-lays.** —*v.t.* 鑲;嵌。—*n.* ①鑲嵌物。②牙中所鑲之金或瓷。③鑲嵌圖案。

in·lay·er [ˈɪnˌleɚ; ˈinˌleiə] *n.* 鑲嵌匠;鑲嵌物。

in·let [*n.* ˈɪnˌlɛt; ˈinlet *v.* ɪnˈlɛt; ˈinlet] *n.*, *v.*, **-let, -let·ting.** —*n.* ①海口;港;灣。②通路;入口。oil *inlets*. 潤滑油門。air *inlet*. 氣門。③挿入之物。④准許;放進。—*v.t.* 挿入;放進。

in loc. cit. in loco citato(拉=in the place cited).

in·look [ˈɪnˌluk; ˈinluk] *n.* 內省;向內看。

in·lot [ˈɪnlɑt; ˈinlɔt] *n.* 一塊土地之中間部分。

in·ly [ˈɪnlɪ; ˈinli] *adv.* 〖詩〗①在內;在心中。②深深地;由衷地;親密地。

in·mate [ˈɪnmet; ˈinmeit] *n.* ①同屋居住者。②監牢、醫院、救濟院等所收容之人。

be the inmate of one's heart 常留在某人心中。

in me·mo·ri·am [ˌɪnməˈmorɪˌæm; in miˈmɔːriæm] 〖拉〗①爲紀念…;爲弔悼…(=in memory of). ②追悼之詩(文)。

in·most [ˈɪnˌmost; ˈinmoust] *adj.* ①最內部的;最深處的。②祕藏於心中的;最奧祕的。one's *inmost* thought. 心底的打算。

inn** [ɪn; in] *n.* ①旅館;客棧。②酒館;酒店。 ***the Inns of Court (倫敦)四法學院。〖注意〗 **inn** 特指開設於鄉間或公路旁者,設備比較簡陋。**hotel** 開設於都市,建築現代化,設備亦較華貴。

inn·age [ˈɪnɪdʒ; ˈinidʒ] *n.* ①飛機於飛行結束後油箱中之賸油。②貨櫃經運達收貨人手中時櫃中賸餘的貨物。

in·nards [ˈɪnɚdz; ˈinədz] *n. pl.* 〖方〗①內臟。②(物之)內部。

in·nate [ɪˈnet, ɪnˈnet; ˈiˈneit] *adj.* 生來的;天賦的;固有的。 **—ly,** *adv.* **—ness,** *n.*

in·nav·i·ga·ble [ɪˈnævəgəbl̩; iˈnævəgəbl] *adj.* 不能航行的;不通航的。

***in·ner** [ˈɪnɚ; ˈinə] *adj.* 內部的;內在的;內心的。the *inner* life. 精神生活。

inner circle 核心集團(權力中心周圍的一群人士)。

in·ner-di·rect·ed [ˈɪnɚdəˈrɛktɪd; ˈinədiˈrektid] *adj.* 言行由個人之價值觀決定的。**—ness,** *n.*

inner ear 內耳。

Inner Mongolia 內蒙古。

in·ner·most [ˈɪnɚmost; ˈinəmoust] *adj.* 最內的;最中心的;最深入的。**—n.** 最深處;最內部。

in·ner·spring [ˈɪnɚˌsprɪŋ; ˈinəspriŋ] *adj.* 藏有彈簧的。 *innerspring* mattress. 彈簧牀墊。

inner tube (車之)內胎。

in·ner·vate [ɪˈnɝvet, ˈɪnɚˌvet; ˈinəːveit, iˈnəːveit] *v.t.,* **-vat·ed, -vat·ing.** 〖生理〗①使神經分布於…。②促使(神經或器官等)活動。

in·ner·va·tion [ˌɪnɚˈveʃən; ˌinəːˈveiʃən] *n.* ①〖生理〗(器官之)神經支配。②〖解剖〗神經分布;神經感覺。

inn·hold·er [ˈɪnˌholdɚ; ˈinˌhouldə] *n.* =**innkeeper.**

***in·ning** [ˈɪnɪŋ; ˈiniŋ] *n.* ①〖棒球〗一局。②執政時期;當權。He has had a good long *inning*. 他已當權甚久。③活躍的機會或時期。④(*pl.*)海埔新生地。⑤墳築沼澤地。⑥收割農作物。〖注意〗 在英國用複數形 innings, 但仍作單數解。

inn·keep·er [ˈɪnˌkipɚ; ˈinˌkiːpə] *n.* 旅館主人。

***in·no·cence** [ˈɪnəsn̩s; ˈinəsns] *n.* ①無罪;淸白。The accused man proved his *innocence* of the crime. 被告經證實無罪。②天眞無邪;率直。③無知;愚笨。④一種藍色小花;矢車菊等。

in·no·cen·cy [ˈɪnəsn̩sɪ; ˈinəsnsi] *n.* ①=**innocence** (一至三義)。②天眞行爲。*innocencies* of childhood. 兒童時期的天眞行爲。

***in·no·cent** [ˈɪnəsn̩t; ˈinəsnt] *adj.* ①無罪的。Is he guilty or *innocent* of the crime? 他有罪還是無罪? ②天眞無邪的;不懂事的。③無害處的。④無知的;愚昧的。Don't be so *innocent* as to believe everything you hear. 不要太愚昧而相信你所聽到的每一件事情。⑤缺乏;無〖of〗. windows *innocent* of glass. 沒有玻璃的窗子。**—n.** ①無罪的人;天眞無邪的人。②無知的人。**—ly,** *adv.*

in·noc·u·ous [ɪˈnɑkjuəs; iˈnɔkjuəs] *adj.* ①無害的;無毒的。②不會刺激人的。③乏味的。**—ly,** *adv.* **—ness,** *n.*

in·nom·i·nate [ɪˈnɑmənɪt; iˈnɔminit] *adj.* ①無名的。the *innominate* bone. 〖解剖〗無名骨;髖骨。②匿名的;不知名的。

in·no·vate [ˈɪnəˌvet; ˈinouveit] *v.,* **-vat·ed, -vat·ing.** **—***v.i.* ①改革〖on, upon, in〗. **—***v.t.* 發明;創始。

in·no·va·tion [ˌɪnəˈveʃən; ˌinouˈveiʃən] *n.* ①改革之處。②改革。

in·no·va·tion·al [ˌɪnəˈveʃənl̩; ˌinouˈveiʃənl] *adj.* 革新的;創始的。

in·no·va·tion·ist [ˌɪnəˈveʃənɪst; ˌinouˈveiʃənist] *n.* 主張革新者。

in·no·va·tor [ˈɪnəˌvetɚ; ˈinouveitə] *n.* 革新者;創始者。

in·no·va·to·ry [ˈɪnəˌvetərɪ; ˈinouveitəri] *adj.* 革新的;革新主義的。

in·nox·ious [ɪˈnɑkʃəs; iˈnɔkʃəs] *adj.* 無害的;無毒的。

in·nu·en·do [ˌɪnjuˈɛndo; ˌinjuˈendou] *n., pl.* **-does.** ①暗指;影射。②間接誹謗;諷刺。③〖法律〗(訴訟狀中之)註釋。

***in·nu·mer·a·ble** [ɪˈnjumərəbl̩, ɪnˈnju–; iˈnjuːmərəbl] *adj.* 無數的。He has given *innumerable* excuses for being late. 他說了無數遲到的理由。**—in·nu·mer·a·bly,** *adv.*

in·nu·tri·ent [ɪˈnjutrɪənt; iˈnjuːtriənt] *adj.* 不營養的;缺乏滋養的。

in·nu·tri·tion [ˌɪnjuˈtrɪʃən; ˌinjuːˈtriʃən] *n.* 營養不良。

in·nu·tri·tious [ˌɪnjuˈtrɪʃəs; ˌinjuːˈtriʃəs] *adj.* 養分甚少的;營養不良的。

in·ob·serv·ance [ˌɪnəbˈzɝvəns; ˌinəbˈzəːvəns] *n.* ①不注意;玩忽;怠慢。②(對規則、祭典等之)不遵守;忽視。

in·ob·tru·sive [ˌɪnəbˈtrusɪv; ˌinəbˈtruːsiv] *adj.* 不冒失的;不莽撞的。

in·oc·cu·pa·tion [ˌɪnɑkjəˈpeʃən; ˈinˌɔkjuˈpeiʃən] *n.* 無職業。

in·oc·u·lant [ɪnˈɑkjələnt; iˈnɔkjulənt] *n.* 所接種之物(如痘苗)。

in·oc·u·late [ɪnˈɑkjəˌlet; iˈnɔkjuleit] *v.t. & v.i.,* **-lat·ed, -lat·ing.** ①以細菌或病菌注射預防。to be *inoculated* against smallpox. 種牛痘(預防天花)。②攙入。③注入;灌輸(頭腦中)。

in·oc·u·la·tion [ɪnˌɑkjəˈleʃən; iˌnɔkjuˈleiʃən] *n.* ①接種疫苗;種痘;預防注射。②置細菌等於泥土或培養基中。③接芽;接木。④灌輸。

in·oc·u·la·tor [ɪnˈɑkjəˌletɚ; iˈnɔkjuleitə] *n.* 接木者;接種者;種苗者;種痘醫生;接種物;注射物。

in·o·dor·ous [ɪnˈodərəs; inˈoudərəs] *adj.* 無臭的。

in·of·fen·sive [ˌɪnəˈfɛnsɪv; ˌinəˈfensiv] *adj.* 無害的;無礙的;不令人討厭的。

in·of·fi·cial [ˌɪnəˈfɪʃəl; ˌinəˈfiʃəl] *adj.* 非官方的;非正式的。

in·of·fi·cious [ˌɪnəˈfɪʃəs; ˌinəˈfiʃəs] *adj.* ①無職務的;無用的;無效的。②〖法律〗不盡道德義務的;不近人情的。

in·op·er·a·ble [ɪnˈɑpərəbl̩; inˈɔpərəbl] *adj.* ①〖外科〗不能動手術的。②不能實行的;不能操作的。

in·op·er·a·tive [ɪnˈɑpəˌretɪv; inˈɔpərətiv] *adj.* 不能使用的;無效的;無益的。

in·op·por·tune [ˌɪnɑpɚˈtjun, ɪnˌɑp–; inˈɔpətjuːn] *adj.* 不合時宜的;不適合的。

—ly, *adv.*
in·or·di·nate [ɪn'ɔrdṇɪt; i'nɔːdinit] *adj.* ①未經控制的;無節制的;放肆的。②過度的。③不規則的。
in·or·di·nate·ly [ɪn'ɔrdṇɪtlɪ; i'nɔː-dinitli] *adv.* 過度地。
in·or·gan·ic [ˌɪnɔr'gænɪk; ˌinɔː'gænik] *adj.* ①不含有動植物有機體的組織的。②〖化〗無機的。*inorganic* chemistry. 無機化學。③非由動植物之活動產生的;無生物的。
in·or·gan·i·za·tion [ɪnˌɔrgənə'zeʃən; inˌɔːgənai'zeiʃən] *n.* 無組織。
in·or·gan·ized [ɪn'ɔrgənaɪzd; in'ɔː-gənaizd] *adj.* 無組織的。
in·or·nate [ˌɪnɔr'net; ˌinɔː'neit] *adj.* 「無華麗裝飾的。
in·os·cu·late [ɪn'ɑskjəˌlet; i'nɔskju-leit] *v.t.* & *v.i.*, **-lat·ed, -lat·ing.** ①(使)(血管等)接合;吻合。②使(纖維等)纏合。③(使)結合。
in·os·cu·la·tion [ɪnˌɑskjə'leʃən; iˌnɔskju'leiʃən] *n.* 接合;吻合;結合;纏合。
in·ox·i·dized [ɪn'ɑksədaɪzd; in'ɔksə-daizd] *adj.* 未經氧化的。
in par·vo [ɪn'parvo; in'paːvou] 〖拉〗小型的 (=in miniature).
in·pa·tient ['ɪnˌpeʃənt; 'inˌpeiʃənt] *n.* 住院病人(爲 outpatient 之對)。
in·phase ['ɪnˌfez; 'infeiz] *adj.* 〖電流〗同相的;同位相的。
in-plant ['ɪn'plænt; 'in'plaːnt] *adj.* 「工廠中實地的。
in·pour [*n.* 'ɪnˌpor; 'inpɔː *v.* ɪn'por; in'pɔː] *n.* 湧入;流入。 —*v.i.* & *v.t.* 湧進;流入。
in·pour·ing ['ɪnˌporɪŋ; 'inˌpɔːriŋ] *n.*注入;流入;增加。 a great *inpouring* of mail. 郵件之大批湧到。 —*adj.* 流入的; 注入的。
in·put ['ɪnˌput; 'in-put] *n.*, *v.*, **-put-ted, -put·ting.** —*n.* ①置入之物或量。②〖機械,電〗輸入(量)。③〖電腦〗輸入(將資料轉移至電腦計算機內的步驟)。④〖蘇,北英〗捐款。—*v.t.* & *v.i.*〖電腦〗輸入。
in·quest ['ɪnkwɛst; 'inkwest] *n.* ①審訊;偵訊;驗屍。②參加審訊之陪審員之集合稱。③調查。***coroner's inquest*** 驗屍。***Great*** (or ***Last***) ***Inquest*** 最後審判 (=Last Judgement).
in·qui·e·tude [ɪn'kwaɪəˌtjud; in-'kwaiətjuːd] *n.* ①(身心之)不安;動搖。②(*pl.*)焦慮。occupied by a thousand *inquietudes.* 極爲焦慮不安的。
in·qui·line ['ɪnkwəlaɪn, -lɪn; 'inkwə-lain, -lin] *n.* 〖動物〗寄生動物。—*adj.* 生活在別的動物之巢或殼內的。
***in·quire** [ɪn'kwaɪr; in'kwaiə] *v.t.* & *v.i.* =**enquire.** —**in·quir·er,** *n.*
in·quir·ing [ɪn'kwaɪrɪŋ; in'kwaiə-riŋ] *adj.* 愛追究的;好奇的;懷疑的;探詢的。—ly, *adv.*
***in·quir·y** [ɪn'kwaɪrɪ, 'ɪnkwərɪ; in-'kwaiəri] *n.* =**enquiry.**
in·quis·ite [ɪn'kwɪzɪt; in'kwizit] *v.t.*, **-it·ed, -it·ing.** 審訊;調查。
in·qui·si·tion [ˌɪnkwə'zɪʃən; ˌinkwi-'ziʃən] *n.* ①調查;研討。②〖法律〗調查;審訊。③(I-)〖羅馬天主教〗宗教裁判所(=the Holy Office);宗教裁判。
in·qui·si·tion·al [ˌɪnkwə'zɪʃənḷ; ˌinkwi'ziʃənḷ] *adj.* ①調查的。②宗教裁判所的。
in·quis·i·tive [ɪn'kwɪzətɪv; in'kwi-zitiv] *adj.* ①好奇的; 好問的。 She was a bit *inquisitive,* as girls are. 她有點好奇,就像所有女孩們一樣。②好管閒事的。—**ly,** *adv.* —**ness,** *n.*
in·quis·i·tor [ɪn'kwɪzətɚ; in'kwizitə] *n.* ①調查者;審訊者。② (I-) 宗教裁判官。
in·quis·i·to·ri·al [ɪnˌkwɪzə'torɪəl; inˌkwizi'tɔːriəl] *adj.* ①(似)宗教裁判所(官)的。②追究的;愛盤根究底的;過分好奇的。
in re [ɪn'ri; in'riː] 〖拉〗關於 (=in the matter of).
I.N.R.I. Iesus Nazarenus, Rex Iudaeo-rum (拉=Jesus of Nazareth, King of the Jews).
in·road ['ɪnˌrod; 'inroud] *n.* ①攻擊;襲擊。②(常 *pl.*) 損害; 侵蝕; 花費。 ***make an inroad on*** (or ***upon***) 侵犯。 ***make inroads into*** 侵入。***make inroads on*** (or ***upon***) 侵蝕。—*v.i.* 進犯。
in·root·ed ['ɪnˌrutɪd; 'inˌruːtid] *adj.* 根深蒂固的。
in·rush ['ɪnˌrʌʃ; 'inrʌʃ] *n.* 湧入;侵入;來襲;流入。
in·rush·ing ['ɪnˌrʌʃɪŋ; 'inˌrʌʃiŋ] *adj.* 大批湧進的。
INS, I.N.S. 〖美〗International News Service (1958 年與 UP 合併成 UPI).
ins. ①inches. ②insurance. ③insulated. ④inspector. ⑤inscribed.
in·sal·i·vate [ɪn'sæləˌvet; in'sæli-veit] *v.t.*, **-vat·ed, -vat·ing.** 使(食物)與唾液混合。
in·sal·i·va·tion [ɪnˌsælə'veʃən; inˌsæli'veiʃən] *n.* 〖生理〗混涎作用。
in·sa·lu·bri·ous [ˌɪnsə'lubrɪəs; ˌinsə'ljuːbriəs] *adj.* 有害身體的;不宜於健康的(氣候、土地等);不衞生的。
in·sa·lu·bri·ty [ˌɪnsə'lubrətɪ; ˌinsə'ljuːbriti] *n.* 不衞生;不健康。
***in·sane** [ɪn'sen; in'sein] *adj.* ①患精神病的;瘋狂的。②爲瘋人設的。an *insane* asylum. 瘋人院。 ③極愚蠢的; 毫無見識的。—**ness,** *n.*
in·sane·ly [ɪn'senlɪ; in'seinli] *adv.* 「瘋狂地。
in·san·i·tar·y [ɪn'sænəˌtɛrɪ; in'sæni-təri] *adj.* 不衞生的;有害健康的。
in·san·i·ta·tion [ɪnˌsænɪ'teʃən; inˌsæni'teiʃən] *n.* 不清潔;不衞生。
***in·san·i·ty** [ɪn'sænətɪ; in'sæniti] *n.*, *pl.* **-ties.** ①瘋狂; 精神錯亂。 *insanity* of grandeur. 誇大妄想狂。②極愚;愚頑。adolescent *insanity.* 青春期癡呆; 單一性癡呆。③瘋狂之事;愚不可及之事。
in·sa·tia·bil·i·ty [ɪnˌseʃɪə'bɪlətɪ; inˌseiʃiə'biliti] *n.* 貪慾;不知足。
in·sa·tia·ble [ɪn'seʃɪəbḷ; in'seiʃiəbl] *adj.* 無饜的;不知足的;貪的。
in·sa·tia·bly [ɪn'seʃɪəblɪ; in'seiʃiəbli] *adv.* 不知足地;無饜地。
in·sa·ti·ate [ɪn'seʃɪɪt; in'seiʃiit] *adj.* 「無饜的。
in·scape ['ɪnˌskep; 'inskeip] *n.* 內景;內部景象。
in·scribe** [ɪn'skraɪb; in'skraib] *v.t.*, **-scribed, -scrib·ing.** ①題記; 刻銘。②題獻。This book I *inscribed* to.... 這本書獻給…。③登記; 列入名單。④深刻於; 銘記於。My father's words are *inscribed* in my memory. 我父親的話深刻在我的記憶中。⑤〖幾何〗使內接。⑥〖英〗買或賣股票。inscribed stock*** 記名股票。
inscribed circle 內接圓。
***in·scrip·tion** [ɪn'skrɪpʃən; in'skrip-

ʃən] *n.* ①題名; 題字; 碑銘。A monument usually has an *inscription* on it. 紀念碑上通常是有碑銘的。②(書中的)題獻; 獻詞。

in·scrip·tion·less [ɪnˈskrɪpʃənlɪs; inˈskripʃənlis] *adj.* 無碑銘的; 無題字的。

in·scrip·tive [ɪnˈskrɪptɪv; inˈskriptiv] *adj.* 銘的;銘刻的;題字的;碑銘的。

in·scru·ta·bil·i·ty [ɪnˌskrutəˈbɪlətɪ; inˌskruːtəˈbiliti] *n., pl.* **-ties.** ①不可測度; 不可了解;不可思議。②不可思議之事物。

in·scru·ta·ble [ɪnˈskrutəbl̩; inˈskruːtəbl] *adj.* ①不可了解的;不可思議的;不可測度的。②不能透視的。—**in·scru·ta·bly,** *adv.*

***in·sect** [ˈɪnsɛkt; ˈinsekt] *n.* ①昆蟲。Flies, mosquitoes, and gnats are *insects.* 蠅、蚊、蚋皆係昆蟲。②卑鄙的人。—*adj.* 昆蟲的;像昆蟲的;殺昆蟲的。

in·sec·tar·i·um [ˌɪnsɛkˈtɛrɪəm; ˌinsekˈtɛəriəm] *n., pl.* **-i·a** [-ɪə; -iə]. ①昆蟲飼養所; 昆蟲館。②所飼養之昆蟲。(亦作 **insectary**)

in·sec·ti·cid·al [ɪnˌsɛktəˈsaɪdl̩; in-ˈsektisaidəl] *adj.* 殺蟲的。

in·sec·ti·cide [ɪnˈsɛktəˌsaɪd; inˈsektisaid] *n.* 殺蟲劑。

in·sec·tile [ɪnˈsɛktl̩; inˈsektil] *adj.* ①昆蟲的;似昆蟲的。②由昆蟲組成的。

in·sec·ti·vize [ɪnˈsɛktəvaɪz; inˈsektivaiz] *v.t.,* **-vized, -viz·ing.** 施行高壓手段;使人民過蟲蟻生活。

in·sec·ti·vore [ɪnˈsɛktəˌvor; inˈsektivɔː] *n.* 食蟲動物;食蟲植物。

in·sec·tiv·o·rous [ˌɪnsɛkˈtɪvərəs; ˌinsekˈtivərəs] *adj.* 食蟲的; 食蟲動物(植物)的。

in·sec·tol·o·gy [ˌɪnsɛkˈtɑlədʒɪ; ˌin-sekˈtɔlədʒi] *n.* 昆蟲學。

insect powder 除蟲粉。

in·se·cure [ˌɪnsɪˈkjur; ˌin-siˈkjuə] *adj.* ①不安全的; 有危險的。②不可靠的; 不堅固的。—**ly,** *adv.*

in·se·cu·ri·ty [ˌɪnsɪˈkjurətɪ; ˌin-siˈkjuəriti] *n., pl.* **-ties.** ①不安全;不可靠。②不安全的事物。

in·sem·i·nate [ɪnˈsɛməˌnet; inˈsemineit] *v.t.,* **-nat·ed, -nat·ing.** ①播種於;種植。②(特指用人工方法)使受精;使懷孕。

in·sem·i·na·tion [ɪnˌsɛməˈneʃən; inˌsemiˈneiʃən] *n.* 播種;受精;受胎。artificial *insemination.* 人工受精。

in·sen·sate [ɪnˈsɛnset,-sɪt; inˈsenseit] *adj.* ①無感覺的。②無情的;無理性的。*insensate* rage. 無理的暴怒。③愚鈍的。

in·sen·si·bil·i·ty [ˌɪnsɛnsəˈbɪlətɪ; inˌsensəˈbiliti] *n., pl.* **-ties.** ①無感情。②無知覺。

***in·sen·si·ble** [ɪnˈsɛnsəbl̩; inˈsensəbl] *adj.* ①無感覺力的;不能感覺或察覺的。When your hands are frozen, they become *insensible.* 當你的手凍僵的時候,它們就沒知覺了。②不知的。We are not *insensible* of your kindness. 我們並非不知你的好意。③不省人事的;昏迷的。④不易被感覺到的。The room grew cold by *insensible* degrees. 這房間不知不覺地慢慢地冷下來。⑤非物質的。—**in·sen·si·bly,** *adv.*

in·sen·si·tive [ɪnˈsɛnsətɪv; inˈsensitiv] *adj.* ①無感覺的;無感覺力的。*insensitive* to light. 對光沒有感覺。②感覺遲鈍的。

in·sen·ti·ent [ɪnˈsɛnʃɪənt; inˈsenʃənt] *adj.* 無知覺的; 無感覺的;無生命的;無情的。

in·sep·a·ra·bil·i·ty [ɪnˌsɛpərəˈbɪlətɪ; inˌsepərəˈbiliti] *n.* 不可分(離)性。

***in·sep·a·ra·ble** [ɪnˈsɛpərəbl̩; inˈsepərəbl] *adj.* 不能分離的。—*n.* (常 *pl.*)不能分離的人或物;密友。—**in·sep·a·ra·bly,** *adv.*

***in·sert** [ɪnˈsɝt; inˈsəːt] *v.t.* 插入;嵌入;刊入。to *insert* a key in a lock. 插鑰匙於鎖中。—*n.* 嵌入的東西; 插入的東西。The newspaper had an *insert* of several pages of pictures. 該報紙有數頁插圖。

in·ser·tion [ɪnˈsɝʃən; inˈsəːʃən] *n.* ①插入; 刊入。②插入物; 刊入物。③(衣服接縫處之)飾帶;花邊。④=**injection**⑤.

in-ser·vice [ˈɪnˈsɝvɪs; ˈinˈsəːvis] *adj.* ①在職的。②從工作中學得的。

in·set [*v.* ɪnˈsɛt; ˈinˈset *n.* ˈɪnˌsɛt; ˈinset] *v.,* **-set, -set·ting,** *n.* —*v.t.* 插入;添入;填入;嵌入。—*n.* 插入物; 添入物; 填入物;嵌入物(如插在較大圖畫、地圖等中之小幅圖畫、地圖等)。

in·shoot [ˈɪnˌʃut; ˈinʃuːt] *n.* 〖棒球〗「投手所投之內曲球。」

in·shore [*adj.* ˈɪnˌʃor; ˈinˈʃɔː *adv.* ˈɪnˈʃor; ˈinˈʃɔː] *adj.* 向海岸的; 近海岸的。*inshore* fishing. 近海漁業。—*adv.* 向海岸。*inshore of* 更接近海岸。

‡**in·side** [*n., adj., adv.* ˈɪnˈsaɪd; ˈinˈsaid *prep.* ɪnˈsaɪd; ˈinˈsaid] *n.* ①內部;內面;內側。Let me see the *inside* of it. 讓我看看它的內部。②(*pl.*)內臟。③內幕;局中。Only someone on the *inside* could have told. 只有知道內幕的人才會洩漏。④〖俚〗內幕消息。⑤〖印刷〗一張紙上印着第二頁的一邊。⑥(跑道等之)內圈。The horse came up fast on the *inside.* 那匹馬從內線跑道上很快地趕上來。—*adj.* ①內部的; 靠內面的。*inside* trouble. 腸胃病。②爲局中人所知或所做的; 祕密的。③〖俚〗潛伏某機關團體中作奸細的; 內線的。④戶內的。—*adv.* 在裏面; 在內部;在戶內。Shall we go *inside* or outside? 我們是到裏面去呢還是到外面去? ***inside of*** 在(某時間或空間)之內。Our car broke down again *inside of* a mile. 我們的車在一英里之內又拋了錨。***inside out*** **a.** 翻轉地;裏在外地。He was wearing his coat *inside out.* 他把衣服反穿着。**b.** 完全地;徹底地。He knew his trade *inside out.* 他對他的行業瞭如指掌。—*prep.* ①在…裏面; 在內。The nut is *inside* the shell. 果實在殼裏。②在…結束以前。He answered *inside* an hour. 他在一小時以內就回答了。〖注意〗**inside of** 爲俗語中表時間所常用的重複前置詞: He'll be back *inside of* an hour. 他將在一小時內回來。較正式的習慣語用 within: He will return *within* an hour.

inside job 內賊所爲之案件。

in·sid·er [ɪnˈsaɪdɚ; ˈinˈsaidə] *n.* ①內部的人; 團員; 會員。②〖俗〗熟知內幕的人;局中人。③〖俗〗享有某種便利的人。

inside track ①(跑道的)內圈。②〖俗〗有利; 優先。to have (*or* to be on) the *inside track.* 跑內圈;處於有利的地位。

in·sid·i·ous [ɪnˈsɪdɪəs; inˈsidiəs] *adj.* ①狡猾的;詭詐的; 陰險的。*insidious* wiles. 奸計。②伺隙而乘的;暗中活動的。the *insidious* approach of age. 不知不覺的日漸年老。—**ly,** *adv.*

***in·sight** [ˈɪnˌsaɪt; ˈinsait] *n.* ①洞察力; 窺察力; 見識。a man of *insight.* 有洞察力的人;有見識的人。②洞察;窺察。

in·sight·ful [ˈɪnˌsaɪtful; ˈinsaitful] *adj.* 富於洞察力的。

in·sig·ne [ɪnˈsɪgni; inˈsigniː] *n.* sing. of **insignia.**

in·sig·ni·a [ɪnˈsɪgnɪə; inˈsigniə] *n.* pl. of **insigne.** 徽章;勳章;標幟。〖注意〗 **insignia** 雖爲複數形,但常用作單數,如 His *insignia* is a cross. 他的徽章是一個十字。有將 insignias 當 insignia 複數的用法,如The PX sold all sorts of *insignias.* 該福利社有各種徽章出售。但嚴格說來,把 insignia 作單數用是錯的,因此,過去罕爲人用的單數形 insigne, 現在其常用度又已漸增。

in·sig·nif·i·cance [ˌɪnsɪgˈnɪfəkəns; ˌinsigˈnifikəns] *n.* ①無重要性。②無意義。

in·sig·nif·i·can·cy [ˌɪnsɪgˈnɪfəkənsɪ; ˌinsigˈnifikənsi] *n., pl.* **-cies.** ①=**insignificance.** ②無關重要(無意義)之事物。

***in·sig·nif·i·cant** [ˌɪnsɪgˈnɪfəkənt; ˌinsigˈnifikənt] *adj.* 無關重要的;無意義的;無用的。Forget this *insignificant* quarrel. 忘了這場無意義的吵架吧。—*n.* 無關重要的字、事物或人。—**ly,** *adv.*

in·sin·cere [ˌɪnsɪnˈsɪr; ˌinsinˈsiə] *adj.* 不誠懇的;無誠意的;不誠實的。—**ly,** *adv.*

in·sin·cer·i·ty [ˌɪnsɪnˈsɛrətɪ; ˌinsinˈseriti] *n., pl.* **-ties.** ①無誠意; 虛僞。②虛僞之言行。

in·sin·u·ate [ɪnˈsɪnjuˌet; inˈsinjueit] *v.t.,* **-at·ed, -at·ing.** ①暗指; 暗示。②以間接紆曲方式使進入(與反身代名詞連用)。to *insinuate* oneself into a person's favor. 紆曲求寵。③緩慢而細心地驅進。

in·sin·u·at·ing [ɪnˈsɪnjuˌetɪŋ; inˈsinjueitiŋ] *adj.* ①曲意奉承的;巧妙巴結的;獻媚的。②徐入的;暗入的。③暗示的。—**ly,** *adv.*

in·sin·u·a·tion [ɪnˌsɪnjuˈeʃən; inˌsinjuˈeiʃən] *n.* ①暗示;暗指。②間接諷刺。③紆曲而進;紆曲求寵。④討人歡心的言行。

in·sin·u·a·tive [ɪnˈsɪnjuˌetɪv; inˈsinjueitiv] *adj.* ①討人歡心的;巧妙巴結的。②暗示的;暗指的。③間接諷刺的;暗諷的。

in·sip·id [ɪnˈsɪpɪd; inˈsipid] *adj.* ①沒有味道的; 淡而無味的。②乏味的; 缺乏風味的;枯燥的;不精采的。—**ly,** *adv.* —**ness,** *n.*

in·si·pid·i·ty [ˌɪnsɪˈpɪdətɪ; ˌinsiˈpiditi] *n., pl.* **-ties.** ①沒有味道;沒有趣味。②沒有味道或趣味的東西。

in·sip·i·ence [ɪnˈsɪpɪəns; inˈsipiəns] *n.* 愚笨;不智。

‡in·sist [ɪnˈsɪst; inˈsist] *v.i.* 堅持;力言;强調〖on, upon〗. I *insist* on being there. 我堅持要在那裏。—*v.t.* 堅持;强調。I *insist* that you shall be there. 我堅持要你在那裏。

in·sist·ence [ɪnˈsɪstəns; inˈsistəns] *n.* 堅持;强調。

in·sist·en·cy [ɪnˈsɪstənsɪ; inˈsistənsi] *n., pl.* **-cies.** ①=**insistence.** ②顯著或緊急之事。

in·sist·ent [ɪnˈsɪstənt; inˈsistənt] *adj.* ①堅持的〖on〗. In spite of the rain he was *insistent* on going out. 不顧天雨, 他堅持要外出。②顯著的;緊急的。—**ly,** *adv.*

in·si·ti·tious [ˌɪnsɪˈtɪʃəs; ˌinsiˈtiʃəs] *adj.* 插進的;從外部引來的。

in·snare [ɪnˈsnɛr; inˈsnɛə] *v.t.,* **in·snared, in·snar·ing.** =**ensnare.**

in·so·bri·e·ty [ˌɪnsəˈbraɪətɪ; ˌinsouˈbraiəti] *n.* 不節制;暴飲;酗酒。

in·so·cia·ble [ɪnˈsoʃəbl̩; inˈsouʃəbl] *adj.* 不善交際的;不愛社交的。

in·so·far [ˌɪnsoˈfɑr; ˌinsouˈfɑː] *adv.* 至…程度;在…的範圍;只要…(常與 as 連用)。*Insofar* as I can say now, I shall come. 目前我祇能說,我將會來。(亦作 **in so far**)

in·so·late [ˈɪnsoˌlet; ˈinsouleit] *v.t.,* **-lat·ed, -lat·ing.** 曝於陽光中曬乾或漂白。

in·so·la·tion [ˌɪnsoˈleʃən; ˌinsouˈleiʃən] *n.* ①日曝;曬乾;日光浴。②〖醫〗中暑;日射病。③〖氣象〗日照(率)。

in·sole [ˈɪnˌsol; ˈinsoul] *n.* (鞋靴的)內底;軟墊。

in·so·lence [ˈɪnsələns; ˈinsələns] *n.* ①粗野;無禮。②粗野無禮的言行;侮辱。

***in·so·lent** [ˈɪnsələnt; ˈinsələnt, -sul-] *adj.* 粗野的; 無禮的; 侮慢的。"Shut up!" the *insolent* boy said to his father. "住嘴!" 那個無禮的孩子對他父親說。—*n.* 侮慢無禮的人。—**ly,** *adv.*

in·sol·u·ble [ɪnˈsɑljəbl̩; inˈsɔljubl] *adj.* ①不能溶解的。②不能解決的; 難以解釋的。—**in·sol·u·bil·i·ty,** *n.*

in·solv·a·ble [ɪnˈsɑlvəbl̩; inˈsɔlvəbl] *adj.* 不能解決的;無法解答的。

in·sol·ven·cy [ɪnˈsɑlvənsɪ; inˈsɔlvənsi] *n., pl.* **-cies.** 無力償付債務;破產。

in·sol·vent [ɪnˈsɑlvənt; inˈsɔlvənt] *adj.* 無力償付債務的;破產的。—*n.* 破產者。

in·som·ni·a [ɪnˈsɑmnɪə; inˈsɔmniə] *n.* 失眠;失眠症。

in·som·ni·ac [ɪnˈsɑmnɪæk; inˈsɔmniæk] *n.* 失眠症患者。—*adj.* ①患失眠的。②導致失眠的。

in·so·much [ˌɪnsəˈmʌtʃ; ˌinsouˈmʌtʃ] *adv.* 至如此程度;就此程度而言。He worked very fast, *insomuch* that he was through in an hour. 他工作得很快, 在一小時之內便做完了。***insomuch as* a.** 由於;因爲。**b.** 到…的程度。

in·sou·ci·ance [ɪnˈsusɪəns; inˈsuːsjəns] 〖法〗*n.* 不注意;漫不經心;無憂無慮。

in·sou·ci·ant [ɪnˈsusɪənt; inˈsuːsjənt] 〖法〗*adj.* 不注意的;漫不經心的;無憂無慮的。

in·span [ɪnˈspæn; inˈspæn] *v.t. & v.i.,* **-spanned, -span·ning.** 〖南非〗套牛馬於(車);駕軛於(牛馬)。

***in·spect** [ɪnˈspɛkt; inˈspekt] *v.t.* ①檢查;檢閱;審查。to *inspect* food (goods, etc.). 檢查食物(貨物等)。②調查;視察;巡察。

***in·spec·tion** [ɪnˈspɛkʃən; inˈspekʃən] *n.* 調查;檢查;視察;檢閱。a house-to-house *inspection.* 挨戶檢查。

in·spec·tive [ɪnˈspɛktɪv; inˈspektiv] *adj.* ①注意的; 留神的。②視察的;調查的。

***in·spec·tor** [ɪnˈspɛktɚ; insˈpektə] *n.* ①檢查員; 視察員; 巡視員。②檢閱官。③(警察的)巡官。—**al,** *adj.*

in·spec·tor·ate [ɪnˈspɛktərɪt; inˈspektərit] *n.* ①inspector 之職責或管區。②檢查員、視察員、巡視員等之集合稱;視察團。

inspector general *pl.* **inspectors general.** ①檢查長;視查長。②〖美軍〗(I- G-)監察局局長;督察署署長(由少將任之)。

in·spec·tor·ship [ɪnˈspɛktɚˌʃɪp; inˈspektəʃip] *n.* inspector 之職位或任期。

in·spir·a·ble [ɪnˈspaɪrəbl̩; inˈspaiərəbl] *adj.* 可被感動的;可影響的;可授意的。

***in·spi·ra·tion** [ˌɪnspəˈreʃən; ˌinspəˈreiʃən, -spiˈr-] *n.* ①靈感; 啓示。Poets and artists often draw their *inspiration* from nature. 詩人與藝術家往往由自然得到靈感。②靈機; 靈悟。③鼓勵者; 激勵之事物。His wife was a constant *inspiration* to him. 他的太太對他是一個經常的鼓勵者。④

激動;感化。⑤指示;授意。⑥神的感召。⑦吸入;吸氣。

in·spi·ra·tion·al [ˌɪnspəˈreʃənl; ˌinspəˈreiʃənl] *adj.* ①靈感的;關於靈感的。②給與靈感的;有鼓舞力的。③受靈感影響的;由靈感的。

in·spi·ra·tion·ist [ˌɪnspəˈreʃənɪst; ˌinspəˈreiʃənist] *n.* 靈感論者。

in·spi·ra·tor [ˈɪnspəˌretɚ; ˈinspəreitə] *n.* 〖機械〗(蒸氣機之) 吸入器;注入器。

in·spir·a·to·ry [ɪnˈspaɪrəˌtorɪ; inˈspaiərətəri] *adj.* 吸氣的;吸入的。

˙in·spire [ɪnˈspaɪr; inˈspaiə] *v.*, **-spired, -spir·ing.** —*v.t.* ①使感動; 鼓舞。 The speaker *inspired* the crowd. 演說者感動了羣衆。②激發;激起。③影響。His sly ways *inspire* me with distrust. 他的狡詐態度使我不信任他。④授意;教唆。⑤予以神召;使受神的感召。⑥賜給靈感。⑦促成;造成;導致。⑧吸入(空氣)。—*v.i.* ①給與靈感。②吸入空氣。

in·spired [ɪnˈspaɪrd; inˈspaiəd] *adj.* ①吸入的。②受到靈感的; 受神啓示的。③受(有勢力者等)指使的;授意的。

in·spir·ing [ɪnˈspaɪrɪŋ; inˈspaiəriŋ] *adj.* 灌輸…的;鼓舞的;激勵的。

in·spir·it [ɪnˈspɪrɪt; inˈspirit] *v.t.* 鼓舞;激勵;鼓勵。

in·spis·sate [ɪnˈspɪset; inˈspiseit] *v.t.* & *v.i.*, **-sat·ed, -sat·ing.** (由蒸發等)濃縮;濃化。

in·spis·sa·tion [ˌɪnspɪˈseʃən; ˌinspiˈseiʃən] *n.* 濃縮;變濃厚;濃化。

Inst. ①Institute. ②Institution. **inst.** ①instant. 本月。②instructor. ③instrument. 〖注意〗 **inst.** 作"本月"解, 在現代商業書信中已很少使用。

in·sta·bil·i·ty [ˌɪnstəˈbɪlətɪ; ˌinstəˈbiliti] *n.* 不穩固;不穩定;變遷無常。

in·sta·ble [ɪnˈstebl̩; inˈsteibl] *adj.* 不穩定的;變化無常的。

˙in·stal(l) [ɪnˈstɔl; inˈstɔːl] *v.t.*, **-stalled, -stall·ing.** ①(以正式儀式)使就職。to *install* a person in an office. 使一人就任一職位。②安置。③裝設。

in·stal·la·tion [ˌɪnstəˈleʃən; ˌinstəˈleiʃən] *n.* ①就任;就職;安置。②裝設;裝置。③裝置物;所裝設的機器。④軍事設施(包括人員、裝備及建築物等)。

˙in·stall·ment [ɪnˈstɔlmənt; inˈstɔːlmənt] *n.* ①就職。②裝設。the *installment* of electric lights in a house. 屋內裝電燈。③安頓。④分期付款〖in, by, on〗. to buy a motorcar and pay for it by monthly *installments* of £20. 購一輛汽車, 按每月二十鎊分期付款。⑤連載。a story that appears in *installments.* 連續刊載之小說。⑥分批。***installment plan*** 分期付款辦法 (英亦作 **hire-purchase**). (亦作 **instalment**)

:in·stance [ˈɪnstəns; ˈinstəns] *n.*, *v.*, **-stanced, -stanc·ing.** —*n.* ①實例;例證。This is only one *instance* out of many. 這不過是許多例證中之一。②階段; 步驟。③請求; 建議。④訴訟程序。a court of the first *instance.* 預審庭。***at the instance of*** 應…的請求或建議。I come here *at the instance of* Dr. Jekyll. 我乃應 Jekyll 博士的請求而來。***for instance*** 例如。***in the first instance*** 首先;第一。—*v.t.* 引以爲例;示例證明。—*v.i.* 獲得例證。It *instances* in a great author. 這可以從一位大作家的作品裏獲得例證。

in·stan·cy [ˈɪnstənsɪ; ˈinstənsi] *n.* 强迫;堅求;緊急;迫切。

:in·stant [ˈɪnstənt; ˈinstənt] *n.* ①瞬間;頃刻;刹那;此刻。I went that *instant.* 我立即去了。②〖俗〗不需多加烹調即可食用的食物或飲料(如咖啡精等)。***on the instant*** 立刻;立即。***the instant (that)*** 一經…(立即)。I told you *the instant* I knew. 我一經知道,立刻告訴了你。—*adj.* ①立刻的;卽時的。to sentence a man to *instant* death. 判決將某人立即處死。②緊急的;迫切的。to be in *instant* need of help. 急需幫助。③本月的(略作 **inst.**). the 10th *instant.* 本月十日。

in·stan·tan·é [ˌɛ̃stanˈtane; ˌɛ̃stanˈtɑːnei] 〖法〗*n.* ①〖照相〗快照。②速寫;短評。

in·stan·ta·ne·ous [ˌɪnstənˈtenɪəs; ˌinstənˈteinjəs] *adj.* ①卽時的;瞬息卽逝的。②卽時做成的;卽時發生的。an *instantaneous* photograph. 拍攝後立卽可取之照片;快照。—**ly,** *adv.* —**ness,** *n.*

instant coffee 咖啡精。

in·stan·ter [ɪnˈstæntɚ; inˈstæntə] *adv.* 立卽; 卽刻。

˙in·stant·ly [ˈɪnstəntlɪ; ˈinstəntli] *adv.* 立卽地; 立刻地。He was *instantly* killed. 他立卽被殺死。

in·stan·to·graph [ɪnˈstæntəˌgræf; inˈstæntəgrɑːf] *n.* 快照;速取照相。

instant tea 茶精。

in·state [ɪnˈstet; inˈsteit] *v.t.*, **-stat·ed, -stat·ing.** 置於某一地位、職位、銜位等之上。

in·stau·ra·tion [ˌɪnstɔˈreʃən; ˌinstɔːˈreiʃən] *n.* 恢復;復興;復舊;修理。

in·stau·ra·tor [ˈɪnstɔˌretɚ; ˈinstɔːreitə] *n.* 恢復者;復舊者;改良者。

:in·stead [ɪnˈstɛd; inˈsted] *adv.* 代替;更換。If you cannot go, let him go *instead.* 如果你不能去, 讓他替你去。***instead of*** 代替。I will go *instead of* you. 我代你去。

in·step [ˈɪnˌstɛp; ˈin-step] *n.* ①足背;跗。②鞋襪等的足背部分。③馬之後腿踝關節與骹關節之間的向前部分。

in·sti·gate [ˈɪnstəˌget; ˈinstigeit] *v.t.*, **-gat·ed, -gat·ing.** 鼓動; 煽動; 教唆。 to *instigate* someone to commit a crime. 教唆某人犯罪。

in·sti·ga·tion [ˌɪnstəˈgeʃən; ˌinstiˈgeiʃən] *n.* 鼓動;煽動;教唆。***at the instigation of*** 受…的鼓動或教唆。

in·sti·ga·tor [ˈɪnstəˌgetɚ; ˈinstigeitə] *n.* 教唆者;鼓動者;煽動者。(亦作**instigant**)

in·stil [ɪnˈstɪl; inˈstil] *v.t.* =**instill.**

in·still [ɪnˈstɪl; inˈstil] *v.t.*, **-stilled, -still·ing.** ①逐漸灌輸。to *instill* ideas into a person's mind. 將觀念灌輸入某人的心中。②徐徐滴入。

in·stil·la·tion [ˌɪnstɪˈleʃən; ˌinstiˈleiʃən] *n.* ①滴下;滴注。②逐漸灌輸。③滴注物。

in·stil·la·tor [ˈɪnstɪˌletɚ; ˈinstileitə] *n.* 滴管;滴注器。

in·stil·ment [ɪnˈstɪlmənt; inˈstilmənt] *n.* ①逐漸灌輸。②徐徐滴入; 滴注。(亦作 **instillment**)

˙in·stinct¹ [ˈɪnstɪŋkt; ˈinstiŋkt] *n.* ①本能;直覺。Birds learn to fly by *instinct.* 鳥學飛係由本能。We sometimes act on *instinct.* 我們有時由直覺而行動。②天性;天才。

˙in·stinct² [ɪnˈstɪŋkt; inˈstiŋkt] *adj.* 充滿的〖with〗. The picture is *instinct* with life and beauty. 這幅畫充滿生命與美。

˙in·stinc·tive [ɪnˈstɪŋktɪv; inˈstiŋktiv]

adj. 本能的; 天生的; 直覺的。Climbing is *instinctive* in monkeys. 爬高是猴子的本能。—**ly,** *adv.*

***in·sti·tute** [ˈɪnstəˌtjut; ˈinstitjuːt] *v.,* **-tut·ed, -tut·ing,** *n.* —*v.t.* ①創立; 設立; 制定。to *institute* laws. 制定法律。②開始; 着手。The police *instituted* an inquiry into the causes of the accident. 警方開始調查肇禍原因。③授以聖職; 任命。—*n.* ①會; 社; 學會; 學院; 硏究所; 講習會。an art *institute.* 藝術學院。②會館; 會址。③原則; 規則; 習俗。④(*pl.*) 初級法律教科書。

***in·sti·tu·tion** [ˌɪnstəˈtjuʃən; ˌinstiˈtjuːʃən] *n.* ①社會或教育事業機構(如教會、學校、醫院等)。②慣例; 風俗; 制度。Giving presents on Christmas is an *institution.* 耶誕節送禮是一種風俗。③創立; 設立; 制定。④法規; 法律。⑤會; 社; 院。⑥〖俗〗知名之士; 著名人物。He was one of the *institutions* of the place. 他是當地知名人物之一。⑦〖宗敎〗聖職任命。

in·sti·tu·tion·al [ˌɪnstəˈtjuʃənl̩; ˌinstiˈtjuːʃənl] *adj.* ①設立的; 制度的。②(宗敎等)制度化的; 組織化的; 以社會(慈善)事業爲特色的。③學會的; 協會的; 敎育機構的。④法律的; 習俗的。⑤〖美〗〖廣告〗非爲眼前推銷的; 爲建立永久信譽的。⑥爲大衆使用而缺少變化的。

in·sti·tu·tion·al·ize [ˌɪnstəˈtjuʃənl̩ˌaɪz; ˌinstiˈtjuːʃənəlaiz] *v.t.,* **-ized, -iz·ing.** ①使制度化或習俗化。②使在學院中生長或訓練。③使(精神病患者)住院。

in·sti·tu·tion·ar·y [ˌɪnstəˈtjuʃənˌɛrɪ; ˌinstiˈtjuːʃənəri] *adj.* ①學會的; 協會的; 敎育機構的; 學院的。②設立的; 制定的。③授聖職的。

in·sti·tu·tor [ˈɪnstəˌtjutɚ; ˈinstitjuːtə] *n.* ①制定者; 設立者; 創建者。②〖英國國敎〗聖職任命者。(亦作 **instituter**)

in-store [ˈɪnˈstor; ˈinˈstɔː] *adj.* 在店內發生的。

in·stream·ing [ˈɪnˌstrimɪŋ; ˈinˌstriːmiŋ] *n.* 內流; 流入; 湧進。—*adj.* 內流的; 湧進的。

***in·struct** [ɪnˈstrʌkt; inˈstrʌkt] *v.t.* ①敎; 授; 指導。to *instruct* a class in history. 敎授一班歷史。②下命令與; 指令。Have you been *instructed* when to start? 你已奉令何時出發否? ③通知。—**ed,** *adj.*

***in·struc·tion** [ɪnˈstrʌkʃən; inˈstrʌkʃən] *n.* ①敎授; 敎育; 敎導。to give *instruction* in English. 敎授英語。②(*pl.*) 指令; 命令。to give a person strict *instructions* to arrive early. 嚴令某人及早到達。

in·struc·tion·al [ɪnˈstrʌkʃənl̩; inˈstrʌkʃənl] *adj.* 敎授的; 敎育的; 敎訓的。(亦作 **instructionary**)

instructional television 〖美〗閉路電視敎學節目。(略作 **ITV**)

***in·struc·tive** [ɪnˈstrʌktɪv; inˈstrʌktiv] *adj.* 敎訓的; 有益的; 供給知識的。*instructive* lessons. 有益的敎訓。A trip around the world is an *instructive* experience. 環球旅行是一種能夠增長見聞的經驗。—**ly,** *adv.*

***in·struc·tor** [ɪnˈstrʌktɚ; inˈstrʌktə] *n.* ①敎師。②〖美〗大學講師。③(對於某種科目或問題的)指導書。

in·struc·tress [ɪnˈstrʌktrɪs; inˈstrʌktris] *n.* instructor 之女性。

***in·stru·ment** [ˈɪnstrəmənt; ˈinstrumənt, -trəm-] *n.* ①工具; 手段; 方法; 傀儡。Literature is one of the most powerful *instruments* for forming character. 文學爲修養人格最有力的工具之一。②器械; 器具; 儀器。③樂器。stringed (wind) *instruments.* 絃(管)樂器。④法定文件(如證券、合同等)。—*v.t.* ①裝以儀器。to *instrument* a space capsule. 將儀器裝在太空艙裏。②編樂譜; 改編爲管絃樂。—*adj.* 〖航空〗藉儀器導航的。*instrument* flying. 藉儀器導航的飛行。

in·stru·men·tal [ˌɪnstrəˈmɛntl̩; ˌinstruˈmentl] *adj.* ①有功用的; 有幫助的。Mr. Hill was *instrumental* in finding a job for George. 爲 George 找工作, Hill 先生出了力。②用樂器演奏的; 供樂器演奏而作的。③工具的; 器具的; 用器具做成的。*instrumental* drawing. 器械畫。*instrumental* errors. 儀器差。—*n.* 〖音樂〗爲樂器演奏而譜的樂曲。—**ly,** *adv.*

in·stru·men·tal·ist [ˌɪnstrəˈmɛntl̩ɪst; ˌinstruˈmentəlist] *n.* 樂器演奏者。

in·stru·men·tal·i·ty [ˌɪnstrəmɛnˈtælətɪ; ˌinstrumenˈtæliti] *n., pl.* **-ties.** ①工具; 媒介; 助力。②執行部門。***by*** (or ***through***) ***the instrumentality of*** 以…爲方法; 藉…。

in·stru·men·ta·tion [ˌɪnstrəmɛnˈteʃən; ˌinstrumenˈteiʃən] *n.* ①〖音樂〗管絃樂法; 樂器演奏(法)。②器具之使用。③〖罕〗手段; 媒介。④〖醫〗器械應用; 器械療法。

instrument board (or **panel**) 儀表板。

in·stru·ment·ed [ˈɪnstrəˌmɛntɪd; ˈinstrumentid] *adj.* 裝有儀器導航的。

instrument flight 儀器飛行。

instrument flying 儀器飛行法。

instrument landing 儀器着陸。

in·sub·or·di·nate [ˌɪnsəˈbɔrdn̩ɪt; ˌinsəˈbɔːdnit] *adj.* 犯上的; 不服從的。—*n.* 犯上者; 不服從的人。—**ly,** *adv.*

in·sub·or·di·na·tion [ˌɪnsəˌbɔrdn̩ˈeʃən; ˈinsəˌbɔːdiˈneiʃən] *n.* 不服從; 不順從; 違抗行爲; 犯上。

in·sub·stan·tial [ˌɪnsəbˈstænʃəl; ˌinsəbˈstænʃəl] *adj.* ①脆弱的; 薄弱的; 纖弱的。②非眞實的; 想像的; 不實在的。

in·suf·fer·a·ble [ɪnˈsʌfrəbl̩; inˈsʌfərəbl] *adj.* 不可忍受的; 難堪的; 難受的。—**in·suf·fer·a·bly,** *adv.*

in·suf·fi·cien·cy [ˌɪnsəˈfɪʃənsɪ; ˌinsəˈfiʃənsi] *n.* 太少; 缺乏; 不充足。(亦作 **insufficience**)

***in·suf·fi·cient** [ˌɪnsəˈfɪʃənt; ˌinsəˈfiʃənt] *adj.* ①不充足的; 不够的。②不能勝任的; 能力不足的。—**ly,** *adv.*

in·suf·flate [ɪnˈsʌflet, ˈɪnsəˌflet; inˈsʌfleit, ˈinsəfleit] *v.t.,* **-flat·ed, -flat·ing.** ①〖醫〗將(空氣、藥品等)吹入體內。②吹入; 散布(消毒藥等)。③對(受洗者)吹氣。

in·su·lar [ˈɪnsəlɚ; ˈinsjulə] *adj.* ①島嶼的; 島民的。②居於島上的; 位於島上的。③形成一島的; 孤立如島嶼的。④胸襟褊狹的。*insular* prejudices. 褊狹之見。

in·su·lar·ism [ˈɪnsələrɪzm̩; ˈinsjulərizəm] *n.* ①島國特性。②褊狹; 胸襟狹窄。

in·su·lar·i·ty [ˌɪnsəˈlærətɪ; ˌinsjuˈlæriti] *n.* ①島性; 島上生活狀態。②褊狹; 偏頗。

in·su·late [ˈɪnsəˌlet; ˈinsjuleit] *v.t.,* **-lat·ed, -lat·ing.** ①使(電、熱、聲等)與外界絕緣。②隔離; 使孤立。

in·su·la·tion [ˌɪnsəˈleʃən; ˌinsjuˈleiʃən] *n.* ①隔離;孤立。②〖電〗絕緣;絕緣體;絕緣材料。

in·su·la·tor [ˈɪnsəˌletɚ; ˈinsjuleitə] *n.* ①〖電〗絕緣體;絕緣物。②隔離者;隔絕物。

in·su·lin [ˈɪnsəlɪn; ˈinsjulin] *n.* ①胰島素(胰臟分泌之一種荷爾蒙)。②(I-)一種含有胰島素之藥品(治糖尿病)的商標名。

in·su·lin·ize [ˈɪnsələnaɪz; ˈinsjulinaiz] *v.t.*, **-ized, -iz·ing.** 用胰島素治療。

***in·sult** [*v.* ɪnˈsʌlt; inˈsʌlt *n.* ˈɪnsʌlt; ˈinsʌlt] *v.t.* ①侮辱;侮慢;對…無禮。②刺激;攻擊。Harsh noises *insulted* our ears. 鬧聲刺耳。—*v.i.* 〖古〗傲慢無禮。—*n.* 侮辱;侮慢;無禮。

in·sult·ing [ɪnˈsʌltɪŋ; inˈsʌltiŋ] *adj.* 侮辱的;無禮的;失禮的。—**ly,** *adv.*

in·su·per·a·bil·i·ty [ɪnˌsupərəˈbɪlətɪ; inˌsjuːpərəˈbiliti] *n.* 不能制勝;不能超越。

in·su·per·a·ble [ɪnˈsupərəbl; inˈsjuːpərəbl] *adj.* 不能超越的;不能克服的。—**in·su·per·a·bly,** *adv.*

in·sup·port·a·ble [ˌɪnsəˈportəbl; ˌin-səˈpɔːtəbl] *adj.* ①難堪的;不能忍受的。②無理的;無法支持的。

in·sup·press·i·ble [ˌɪnsəˈprɛsəbl; ˌin-səˈpresəbl] *adj.* 不能抑制的;不能壓服的;不能阻止的。

in·sur·a·ble [ɪnˈʃurəbl; inˈʃuərəbl] *adj.* 可保險的。

in·sur·ance** [ɪnˈʃurəns; inˈʃuərəns] *n.* ①保險。②保險業。③保險金額;保險額。When her husband died, she received $2,000 *insurance.* 她丈夫死後,她得到二千元的保險金額。④保險費(=premium)。⑤保證。fire insurance*** 火災保險;火險。***insurance agent*** 保險經紀人。***insurance company*** 保險公司。***insurance policy*** 保險單。〖注意〗保險。美作 **insurance.** 英作 **assurance.**

in·sur·ant [ɪnˈʃurənt; inˈʃuərənt] *n.* 被保險者;投保者。

***in·sure** [ɪnˈʃur; inˈʃuə] *v.t.*, **-sured, -sur·ing.** ①使確實。Check your work to *insure* its accuracy. 檢查你的工作以求其絕對精確。②保證;確保。③保險。④投保各種保險。Was he *insured* at the time of the accident? 他在遭遇意外時,是否曾投保壽險?

in·sured [ɪnˈʃurd; inˈʃuəd] *adj.* 加入保險的。—*n.* 被保險者;保戶。

in·sur·er [ɪnˈʃurɚ; inˈʃuərə] *n.* ①保險業者;保險公司。②被保險者;投保者。③保險外務員。④保險或保護之事物。

in·sur·gence [ɪnˈsɝdʒəns; inˈsəːdʒəns] *n.* 暴動;叛亂。

in·sur·gen·cy [ɪnˈsɝdʒənsɪ; inˈsəːdʒənsi] *n.* =**insurgence.**

in·sur·gent [ɪnˈsɝdʒənt; inˈsəːdʒənt] *n.* ①起事者;暴動者;叛徒。②〖美〗叛黨者。—*adj.* ①起事的;暴動的;叛亂的。②向前湧進的;衝擊的。

in·sur·mount·a·ble [ˌɪnsɚˈmauntəbl; ˌinsəˈmauntəbl] *adj.* 難越過的;不能克服的。

in·sur·rec·tion [ˌɪnsəˈrɛkʃən; ˌinsəˈrekʃən] *n.* 起義;暴動;叛亂。—**al,** *adj.*

in·sur·rec·tion·ar·y [ˌɪnsəˈrɛkʃənˌɛrɪ; ˌinsəˈrekʃənəri] *adj., n., pl.* **-ar·ies.** —*adj.* 暴動的;參加叛亂的;從事叛亂的。—*n.* 暴動者;叛徒。

in·sur·rec·tion·ist [ˌɪnsəˈrɛkʃənɪst; ˌinsəˈrekʃənist] *n.* 暴動者;造反者;叛亂者。

in·sur·rec·tion·ize [ˌɪnsəˈrɛkʃənˌaɪz; ˌinsəˈrekʃənaiz] *v.t.*, **-ized, -iz·ing.** ①使(某一國家)發生叛亂。②促使(個人或團體)從事叛亂。

in·sus·cep·ti·bil·i·ty [ˌɪnsəˌsɛptəˈbɪlətɪ; ˈin-səˌseptəˈbiliti] *n.* 無感覺;無感受性。

in·sus·cep·ti·ble [ˌɪnsəˈsɛptəbl; ˌin-səˈseptəbl] *adj.* ①不受…的〖of〗。②不爲…所動的;不受感動的;無感覺的〖to〗。

int. ①interest. ②interim. ③interior. ④interjection. ⑤internal. ⑥international. ⑦interpreter. ⑧interval. ⑨intransitive.

in·tact [ɪnˈtækt; inˈtækt] *adj.* ①未觸動的;未受傷的;完整的。The money was returned *intact* by its finder. 錢原封未動地被拾者送還。②未受影響的;未減少的。③未經閹割的。④處女膜完整的;處女的。

in·tagl·iat·ed [ɪnˈtæljetɪd; inˈtæljeitid] *adj.* 凹刻的;凹雕的。

in·tagl·io [ɪnˈtæljo; inˈtaːliou] *n., pl.* **-tagl·ios, -ta·gli** [-ˈtɑljɪ;-ˈtaːlji], *v.* —*n.* ①凹刻;凹紋。②凹刻雕刻物(寶石)。—*v.t.* 施以凹紋;凹雕;刻(花紋)於表面。

in·take [ˈɪnˌtek; ˈin-teik] *n.* ①(水、氣體流入溝、管等之)入口;引入口。②引入。③引入之物。④引入之量。⑤收斂;縮小。⑥〖採礦〗通風孔。

in·tan·gi·ble [ɪnˈtændʒəbl; inˈtændʒəbl] *adj.* ①不能觸摸的;無實體的。②難弄明白的;模糊的。—*n.* 無實體之物;不可捉摸之物。—**in·tan·gi·bil·i·ty,** *n.* —**in·tan·gi·bly,** *adv.*

in·tar·sist [ɪnˈtɑrsɪst; inˈtaːsist] *n.* 木工鑲嵌匠。

in·te·ger [ˈɪntədʒɚ; ˈintidʒə] *n.* ①整數。②本身完整之物;完全的東西。

in·te·gral [ˈɪntəgrəl; ˈintigrəl] *adj.* ①構成整體所必需的;必要的;主要的。②〖數學〗整數的;積分的。③完整的;整個的。—*n.* ①整體;完整物。②〖數學〗整數;積分。

in·te·gral·i·ty [ˌɪntəˈgrælətɪ; ˌintiˈgræliti] *n.* 完全;圓滿;無缺。

in·te·grant [ˈɪntəgrənt; ˈintigrənt] *adj.* 構成整體的;成分的;要素的;不可缺少的。—*n.* 成分;要素。

in·te·grate [ˈɪntəˌgret; ˈintigreit] *v.*, **-grat·ed, -grat·ing.** —*v.t.* ①使成完全之物;使完全。②合(部分)成一整體;合而爲一。③表示…之總數或平均值。④〖數學〗求…之積分。⑤取消種族隔離;使各種族機會平等。—*v.i.* 種族融和;同化。

in·te·grat·ed [ˈɪntəˌgretɪd; ˈintigreitid] *adj.* ①無種族界線的。②綜合各方面使整體和諧的。③結構配合適宜的。

integrated circuit 積體電路(略作 IC)。(亦作 **microcircuit, monolithic circuit**)

in·te·gra·tion [ˌɪntəˈgreʃən; ˌintiˈgreiʃən] *n.* ①成爲整體;完成;集成。②〖數學〗積分法。③〖心理〗(人格的)統合;融合。

in·te·gra·tion·ist [ˌɪntəˈgreʃənɪst; ˌintiˈgreiʃənist] *n.* 〖美〗主張種族平等者;擁護取消種族隔離者。

in·te·gra·tor [ˈɪntəˌgretɚ; ˈintigreitə] *n.* ①完成(集成、統合)之人或物。②〖數學〗積分儀;求積器。

in·teg·ri·ty [ɪnˈtɛgrətɪ; inˈtegriti] *n.* ①誠篤;正直;廉正。a man of *integrity.* 正直之人。②完整;無缺。

in·teg·u·ment [ɪnˈtɛgjəmənt; inˈtegjumənt] *n.* 皮膚;外殼;外皮。

in·teg·u·men·ta·ry [ɪn͵tɛgjəˈmɛntərɪ; in͵teguˈmentəri] *adj.* ①外皮的。②皮膚的。③外殼的。

***in·tel·lect** [ˈɪntl͵ɛkt; ˈintilekt] *n.* ①理解力;思維能力;悟力;智力。*Intellect* distinguishes man from the animals. 智力使人異於動物。②聰明;大智;超越的智慧。③(作 *sing.* or *pl.* 解) 知識分子(集合稱)。the *intellect*(*s*) of the age. 當代的知識分子。

in·tel·lec·tion [͵ɪntlˈɛkʃən; ͵intiˈlekʃən] *n.* ①思維(作用);思考。②概念;觀念;理解。

in·tel·lec·tive [͵ɪntlˈɛktɪv; ͵intiˈlektiv] *adj.* ①智力的;理性的。②有智力的;聰明的。

***in·tel·lec·tu·al** [͵ɪntlˈɛktʃuəl; ͵intiˈlektjuəl] *adj.* ①智力的。*intellectual* faculties. 智力;智能。②需用智慧的。③有智力的;聰明的。④理智的。—*n.* ①有知識者;知識分子。②憑理智做事者。 —**ly,** *adv.*

in·tel·lec·tu·al·ism [͵ɪntlˈɛktʃuəl͵ɪzəm; ͵intiˈlektjuəlizəm] *n.* ①對理智之偏重;理智的傾向;獻身於知識的追求。②〖哲學〗主知主義;理智主義。

in·tel·lec·tu·al·ist [͵ɪntlˈɛktʃuəlɪst; ͵intiˈlektjuəlist] *n.* ①偏重理智者。②〖哲學〗主知主義者;理智主義者。

in·tel·lec·tu·al·i·ty [͵ɪntl͵ɛktʃuˈælətɪ; ˈinti͵lektjuˈæliti] *n., pl.* **-ties.** ①理智;智力;聰明。②傑出的知識分子。

in·tel·lec·tu·al·ize [͵ɪntlˈɛktʃuəl͵aɪz; ͵intiˈlektjuəlaiz] *v.,* **-ized, -iz·ing.** —*v.t.* 賦與理性;使變為有理智;使有智慧。—*v.i.* 訴諸智力;思考;推理。

***in·tel·li·gence** [ɪnˈtɛlədʒəns; inˈtelidʒəns] *n.* ①智力;才智;穎才。a boy who shows very little *intelligence.* 一個缺乏智力之男孩。②情報;消息。③情報人員。④情報交換。⑤(I-)神;靈。the Supreme *Intelligence.* 上帝。

intelligence agent 間諜;情報人員。

intelligence department (or **bureau**) 情報局;情報部。

intelligence officer 情報官。

intelligence quotient 智力商數;智商(略作 IQ)。

in·tel·li·genc·er [ɪnˈtɛlədʒənsə; inˈtelidʒənsə] *n.* ①通報者;情報員。②偵探;間諜。

intelligence test 智力測驗。(亦作「**achievement test**」)

***in·tel·li·gent** [ɪnˈtɛlədʒənt; inˈtelidʒənt] *adj.* 有才智的;伶俐的;聰明的。an *intelligent* reply. 巧妙的答覆。—**ly,** *adv.*

in·tel·li·gent·si·a [ɪn͵tɛləˈdʒɛntsɪə, -ˈgɛnt-; in͵teliˈdʒentsiə, -ˈgent-] *n. pl.* (常 the-)知識階級;知識分子(集合稱)。

in·tel·li·gi·bil·i·ty [ɪn͵tɛlɪdʒəˈbɪlətɪ; in͵telidʒəˈbiliti] *n., pl.* **-ties.** ①可理解性;明瞭。②可理解之事物。

in·tel·li·gi·ble [ɪnˈtɛlɪdʒəbl; inˈtelidʒəbl] *adj.* 可理解的;易領悟的;淸晰的。to make oneself *intelligible.* 使自己的思想(言語等)為人所了解。—**in·tel·li·gi·bly,** *adv.*

In·tel·sat [ˈɪntɛl͵sæt; ˈintelsæt] *n.* 國際通信衞星組織 (*In*ternational *Tel*ecommunications *Sat*ellite [Consortium]).

in·tem·per·ance [ɪnˈtɛmpərəns; inˈtempərəns] *n.* ①無節制;過度;放縱。②飲酒過度。③無節制之行動。

in·tem·per·ate [ɪnˈtɛmpərɪt; inˈtempərit] *adj.* ①無節制的;過度的;放縱的;狂妄的。②飲酒過度的。③酷烈的(氣候等)。

‡**in·tend** [ɪnˈtɛnd; inˈtend] *v.t.* ①意欲;意指;存心。I *intended* to leave the next day. 我本欲於次日卽離去。②設計;計畫。This book is *intended* for beginners. 本書係為初學者而編。③(字、聲明、專有名詞等)表示。—*v.i.* 有目的或企圖。

in·tend·ance [ɪnˈtɛndəns; inˈtendəns] *n.* ①監督;管理。②管理部。

intendance officer 〖軍〗主計官。

in·tend·an·cy [ɪnˈtɛndənsɪ; inˈtendənsi] *n., pl.* **-cies.** ①intendant 之職位或管區。②監督官;管理官(集合稱)。③(西班牙殖民地等之)行政區。

in·tend·ant [ɪnˈtɛndənt; inˈtendənt] *n.* (法國、西班牙等之)監督官;管理官;(西班牙殖民地等之)地方行政長官。

in·tend·ed [ɪnˈtɛndɪd; inˈtendid] *adj.* ①有計畫的;故意的。②未來的;未婚的。—*n.* 〖俗〗未婚夫(妻)。

***in·tense** [ɪnˈtɛns; inˈtens] *adj.* ①非常的;强烈的;劇烈的。*intense* pain (heat, etc.). 劇烈的疼痛(暑熱等)。②緊張的。③熱情的;趨於極端的。④熱烈的;熱心的。⑤易於動感情的。an *intense* person. 感情豐富的人。—**ly,** *adv.*

in·ten·si·fi·ca·tion [ɪn͵tɛnsəfəˈkeʃən; in͵tensifiˈkeiʃən] *n.* ①加强;增强;强化。②〖攝影〗加强明暗度。

in·ten·si·fy [ɪnˈtɛnsə͵faɪ; inˈtensifai] *v.,* **-fied, -fy·ing.** —*v.t.* ①使强烈。to *intensify* colors. 加强色彩。②〖攝影〗加强明暗度。—*v.i.* 變强烈;增强。—**in·ten·si·fi·er,** *n.*

in·ten·sion [ɪnˈtɛnʃən; inˈtenʃən] *n.* ①(精神上的)緊張;努力。②强烈;激烈。③强度;强化。④〖邏輯〗內涵(為 extension 之對)。⑤決心。

***in·ten·si·ty** [ɪnˈtɛnsətɪ; inˈtensiti, -sət-] *n., pl.* **-ties.** ①劇烈;强烈。②緊張。③熱烈;熱情。He spoke with great *intensity.* 他講話極為激昂。④(電、熱、光、聲等之)强度。

intensity of illumination 照明度。

in·ten·sive [ɪnˈtɛnsɪv; inˈtensiv] *adj.* ①精深的;透徹的。*intensive* reading. 精讀。②密集的;集中的。③增强的。④〖農業〗密集栽培的;集約栽培的。*intensive* agriculture. 密集農業。*intensive* culture. 密集耕作。⑤〖文法〗加强的;增强語氣的。⑥〖醫〗漸進的。—*n.* ①使增强的東西。②增强語氣的字、字首等。—**ly,** *adv.*

intensive care unit 全天候緊急醫療小組。

in·tent** [ɪnˈtɛnt; inˈtent] *n.* ①意旨;意向(主要為法律用語)。②目的;計畫。③意義。What is the *intent* of that sentence? 那句話的意思是甚麼? ***to all intents and purposes 實際上(=practically). The revised edition is *to all intents and purposes* a new book. 這修訂版實際上是一本新書了。***with good*** (***evil***) ***intent*** 好(惡)意地。—*adj.* ①專心的;專注的。I hope you are *intent* on doing your best. 我希望你專心盡力。②熱心的。③決心的。 —**ly,** *adv.*

***in·ten·tion** [ɪnˈtɛnʃən; inˈtenʃən] *n.* ①意旨;意向;目的;意圖。Good acts are better than good *intentions.* 好的行動比好的意向更好。②意義。③〖哲學〗概念;觀念。④

〖醫〗癒合。to heal by (the) first (second) *intention*. 直(間)接癒合。⑤(*pl.*) 結婚的意向。What are your *intentions* with regard to her? 你有沒有同她結婚的意思?

in·ten·tion·al [ɪnˈtɛnʃənl; inˈtenʃənl] *adj.* ①有意的;故意的。②目的的;企圖的。—**ly**, *adv.*

in·ter [ɪnˈtɝ; inˈtəː] *v.t.*, **-terred, -ter·ring.** 埋;葬。

inter- 〖字首〗①表"在一起; 交互"之義。②表"在…之間"之義。③表"在(多數)之中; 在(一羣)中"之義。

in·ter·act[1] [ˌɪntɚˈækt; ˌintərˈækt] *v.i.* 交互作用;互相影響;相制;交感。

in·ter·act[2] [ˈɪntɚˌækt; ˈintərækt] *n.* =**entr'acte.**

in·ter·ac·tion [ˌɪntɚˈækʃən; ˌintərˈækʃən] *n.* 交互作用;互相影響;相制;交感。

in·ter·ac·tive [ˌɪntɚˈæktɪv; ˌintərˈæktiv] *adj.* 交互作用的;互相影響的。

in·ter a·li·a [ˈɪntɚˈelɪə; ˈintərˈeiliə] 〖拉〗和其他事物(=among other things).

in·ter a·li·os [ˈɪntɚˈelɪˌos; ˈintərˈeiliousʃ] 〖拉〗和其他人(=among other persons).

in·ter-A·mer·i·can [ˌɪntərəˈmɛrɪkən; ˌintərəˈmerikən] *adj.* 美洲大陸(各國)間的。

in·ter·a·tom·ic [ˌɪntərəˈtɑmɪk; ˌintərəˈtɔmik] *adj.* 各原子間的。

in·ter·blend [ˌɪntɚˈblɛnd; ˈintəˈblend] *v.t.* & *v.i.*, **-blend·ed** or **-blent, -blend·ing.** 混合;相混;攙雜。

in·ter·bor·ough [ˈɪntɚˌbɝo; ˈintəˈbʌrə] *adj.* 自治區間的。

in·ter·breed [ˌɪntɚˈbrid; ˈintəˈbriːd] *v.t.* & *v.i.*, **-bred, -breed·ing.** ①(使)混種;雜交繁殖;生育雜種。②(使)同族通婚。

in·ter·ca·lar·y [ɪnˈtɝkəˌlɛrɪ; inˈtəːkələri] *adj.* ①閏的。an *intercalary* day. 閏日(2月29日)。an *intercalary* month. 閏月(二月)。an *intercalary* year. 閏年。②插入的。

in·ter·ca·late [ɪnˈtɝkəˌlet; inˈtəːkəleit] *v.t.*, **-lat·ed, -lat·ing.** ①加添(日、月等)於曆中;閏。②挿入;添入於中間。

in·ter·ca·la·tion [ɪnˌtɝkəˈleʃən; inˌtəːkəˈleiʃən] *n.* ①置閏。②挿入。③挿入之物。

in·ter·cede [ˌɪntɚˈsid; ˌintəˈsiːd] *v.i.*, **-ced·ed, -ced·ing.** ①代爲懇求;代爲求情;說人情。to *intercede* with the governor for a condemned man. 替犯人在州長面前說情。②從中調停。

in·ter·cel·lu·lar [ˌɪntɚˈsɛljələ; ˌintəˈseljulə] *adj.* 細胞間的。

***in·ter·cept** [*n.* ˈɪntɚˌsɛpt; ˈintəsept *v.* ˌɪntɚˈsɛpt; ˌintəˈsept] *v.t.* ①中途攔截。②竊聽;竊讀;截獲。We *intercepted* the enemy's battle plan. 我們截獲了敵軍的作戰計畫。③截斷(自來水、電力等)。④阻止。to *intercept* the flight of a criminal. 阻止一罪犯的逃跑。⑤〖數學〗截切;截取。—*n.* ①截取;截奪;妨礙。②〖數學〗截距。*intercept form* 截距式;截部式。—**in·ter·cep·tion,** *n.*

in·ter·cep·tive [ˌɪntɚˈsɛptɪv; ˌintəˈseptiv] *adj.* 遮斷的;攔截的;阻止的。

in·ter·cep·tor [ˌɪntɚˈsɛptɚ; ˌintəˈseptə] *n.* ①攔截者;阻止者;障礙物。②〖軍〗攔截機。

in·ter·ces·sion [ˌɪntɚˈsɛʃən; ˌintəˈseʃən] *n.* 從中調停;仲裁;說項;代爲求情;代禱。to make an *intercession* to A for B. 爲B向A說項。

in·ter·ces·sor [ˌɪntɚˈsɛsɚ; ˌintəˈsesə] *n.* 調停者;代求者;調解人。

in·ter·ces·so·ry [ˌɪntɚˈsɛsərɪ; ˌintəˈsesəri] *adj.* 調停的; 調解的。an *intercessory* prayer. 〖宗教〗代禱。

***in·ter·change** [*v.* ˌɪntɚˈtʃendʒ; ˌintəˈtʃeindʒ *n.* ˈɪntɚˌtʃendʒ; ˈintətʃeindʒ] *v.*, **-changed, -chang·ing,** *n.* —*v.t.* ①交換;互換。to *interchange* gifts. 交換禮物。②輪換;交替。—*v.i.* ①互換。②交替;輪換。—*n.* ①交換;互換。②輪換; 交替。an *interchange* of hard work with rest. 辛勞工作與休息之輪換。③立體交叉道。

in·ter·change·a·bil·i·ty [ˌɪntɚˌtʃendʒəˈbɪlətɪ; ˈintəˌtʃeindʒəˈbiliti] *n.* 可交換(交替)性。

in·ter·change·a·ble [ˌɪntɚˈtʃendʒəbl; ˌintəˈtʃeindʒəbl] *adj.* ①可互相交換的。②可替換的。—**in·ter·change·a·bly,** *adv.*

in·ter·cit·y [ˌɪntɚˈsɪtɪ; ˌintəˈsiti] *adj.* 城市之間的。

in·ter·class [ˈɪntɚˈklæs; ˈintəˈklɑːs] *adj.* 班級間的; 班際的。

in·ter·col·le·giate [ˌɪntɚkəˈlidʒɪɪt; ˈintəkəˈliːdʒiit] *adj.* 大學(學院)之間的。

in·ter·co·lo·ni·al [ˌɪntɚkəˈlonɪəl; ˈintəkəˈlounjəl] *adj.* 殖民地間的。

in·ter·co·lum·nar [ˌɪntɚkəˈlʌmnɚ; ˌintəkəˈlʌmnə] *adj.* 〖建築〗柱間的。

in·ter·co·lum·ni·a·tion [ˌɪntɚkəˌlʌmnɪˈeʃən; ˌintəkəˌlʌmniˈeiʃən] *n.* 〖建築〗柱間; 柱間距離定比。

in·ter·com [ˈɪntɚˌkɑm; ˈintəkɔm] *n.* 〖俚〗(飛機、房屋等內連絡用的)對講機(爲intercommunication system之略)。

in·ter·com·mu·ni·cate [ˌɪntɚkəˈmjunəˌket; ˌintəkəˈmjuːnikeit] *v.*, **-cat·ed, -cat·ing.** —*v.t.* 相通;互通;互相連絡。—*v.i.* ①互通消息。②(房間等)相通。—**in·ter·com·mu·ni·ca·tion,** *n.*

in·ter·com·mun·ion [ˌɪntɚkəˈmjunjən; ˌintəkəˈmjuːnjən] *n.* ①互相交通;交際;來往。②各教會間之互相交往。

in·ter·com·mu·ni·ty [ˌɪntɚkəˈmjunətɪ; ˌintəkəˈmjuːniti] *n.* 共通性;共有。—*adj.* 各社區之間的。

in·ter·con·nect [ˌɪntɚkəˈnɛkt; ˈintəkəˈnekt] *v.t.* & *v.i.*(使)互相連接(連絡)。—**in·ter·con·nec·tion,** *n.*

in·ter·con·ti·nen·tal [ˌɪntɚˌkɑntəˈnɛntəl; ˌintəˌkɔntəˈnentəl] *adj.* 大陸間的;洲際的。an *intercontinental* ballistic missile. 洲際彈道飛彈。

in·ter·cos·tal [ˌɪntɚˈkɑstl; ˌintəˈkɔstl] *adj.* ①〖解剖〗肋間的; 生於肋間的。②〖植物〗位於葉脈間的。—*n.* 肋間肌(部分)。

***in·ter·course** [ˈɪntɚˌkors, -ˌkɔrs; ˈintəkɔːs, -kɔəs] *n.* ①交往; 交際; 交通。to hold (have) *intercourse* with friends. 同朋友們交往。②(思想、感情、精神等的)交通;交流。③交媾。sexual *intercourse.* 性交。④中斷期間。

in·ter·crop [ˌɪntɚˈkrɑp; ˌintəˈkrɔp] *v.*, **-cropped, -crop·ping,** *n.* —*v.i.* & *v.t.* 作物之間作。—*n.* ①間作之作物。②間行種植。

in·ter·cur·rent [ˌɪntɚˈkɝənt; ˌintəˈkʌrənt] *adj.* ①起於中間的;中間的。②〖醫〗間發的; 併發的。

in·ter·de·nom·i·na·tion·al 〔ˌɪntədɪˌnɑməˈneʃənl̩; ˌintədiˌnɔmiˈneiʃənl̩〕 *adj.* 宗派間的。

in·ter·den·tal 〔ˌɪntəˈdɛntl; ˌintə(ː)ˈdentl〕 *adj.* ①在牙齒之間的。②〖語音〗將舌尖放在上下牙間而發音的。

in·ter·de·part·men·tal 〔ˌɪntədɪˌpɑrtˈmɛntl; ˌintədiˌpɑːtˈmentl〕 *adj.* 各部(局、廳、系)間的。

in·ter·de·pend 〔ˌɪntədɪˈpɛnd; ˌintədiˈpend〕 *v.i.* 互相依賴。

in·ter·de·pend·ence 〔ˌɪntədɪˈpɛndəns; ˌintədiˈpendəns〕 *n.* 相倚; 互賴。(亦作 **interdependency**)

in·ter·de·pend·ent 〔ˌɪntədɪˈpɛndənt; ˈintədiˈpendənt〕 *adj.* 相倚的;互賴的。—**ly,** *adv.*

in·ter·dict 〔*n.* ˈɪntəˌdɪkt; ˈintədikt *v.* ˌɪntəˈdɪkt; ˌintəˈdikt〕 *v.t.* ①禁止。②限制。③〖宗教〗停止…之教權。—*n.* ①禁止;禁令。②〖宗教〗停止教權。

in·ter·dic·tion 〔ˌɪntəˈdɪkʃən; ˌintəˈdikʃən〕 *n.* ①禁止;禁制;停止。②〖宗教〗停止教權。③〖法律〗禁治產。④〖軍〗對敵軍陣地、交通補給線之持續轟炸。

in·ter·dic·to·ry 〔ˌɪntəˈdɪktərɪ; ˌintəˈdiktəri〕 *adj.* 禁止的;禁制的。(亦作 **interdictive**)

‡**in·ter·est** 〔ˈɪntərɪst, ˈɪntrɪst; ˈintrist, ˈintərest〕 *n.* ①興趣;趣味;愛好;關心。He examined the machine with great *interest*. 他很有興趣地檢查機器。②刺激起興趣的力量。A dull book lacks *interest*. 一本枯燥的書缺乏趣味。③所愛好之事物;嗜好。He has two great *interests* in life: music and painting. 他一生有兩大愛好:音樂與繪畫。④股份; 所有權。to have an *interest* in a business. 在某商店中有股份。⑤(常 *pl.*) 利益;利害。to look after one's own *interests*. 祇顧自己的利益。It is (to) your *interest* to go. 去對你有利。⑥利息;利潤。⑦影響力;勢力;控制力。⑧(*pl.*) 夥伴;利害相關者;業者。the moneyed *interests*. 金融業者。⑨附加物;額外之物。She returned our favor with *interest*. 她加重地報答我們的恩惠。⑩利害關係。Everything goes by *interest* nowadays. 當今一切都是利害關係。⑪重要性。***in the interest(s) of*** 爲…計;爲對…有利。***take (an) interest in*** 愛好;熱心;關心。He *takes a* great *interest in* history. 他很愛好歷史。—*v.t.* ①使感興趣;使熱心。Politics *interests* me very much. 政治使我很感興趣。②與…有關係。The fight for peace *interests* all nations. 爲和平而奮鬥與所有的國家都有關係。

***in·ter·est·ed** 〔ˈɪntərɪstɪd, ˈɪntrɪstɪd; ˈintristid, ˈintərestid〕 *adj.* ①感興趣的。He did not seem at all *interested* in the subject. 他對這題目似乎一點也不感覺興趣。②表現出興趣的。③不公平的;偏私的;自私的。an *interested* witness. 偏心的證人。④有利害關係的; 有股份的。the *interested* party. 有利害關係的一方。—**ly,** *adv.*〖注意〗**interested** 有兩個意思相反的字。uninterested 意爲不感興趣的; disinterested 指公正不阿的,不偏不倚的。

‡**in·ter·est·ing** 〔ˈɪntərɪstɪŋ, ˈɪntrɪstɪŋ; ˈintristiŋ, ˈintərestiŋ〕 *adj.* 令人發生興趣的;有趣味的。It's very *interesting*. 那是很有趣的。***be in an interesting condition*** (*situation* or *state*) 懷孕。—**ly,** *adv.*

***in·ter·fere** 〔ˌɪntəˈfɪr; ˌintəˈfiə〕 *v.i.*, **-fered, -fer·ing.** ①衝突; 抵觸; 妨害〖常 with〗. You mustn't let pleasure *interfere* with business. 你不可讓玩樂妨礙事業。②干涉;干預〖常 with, in〗. That woman is always *interfering* in other people's affairs. 那婦人總是愛管別人的閒事。③仲裁;調停。④〖物理〗(光波、音波、電波等)干擾。⑤〖運動〗犯規妨礙對方球員。⑥〖法律〗聲稱已在他人之先作過同樣之發明。

***in·ter·fer·ence** 〔ˌɪntəˈfɪrəns; ˌintəˈfiərəns〕 *n.* ①衝突;干涉。We will stop *interference* from outside. 我們將阻止外來干預。②(無線電)干擾。③〖物理〗(光波、音波等的) 干擾。④〖運動〗犯規妨礙對方球員。

in·ter·fer·ing 〔ˌɪntəˈfɪrɪŋ; ˌintəˈfiəriŋ〕 *adj.* ①干涉的; 愛多管閒事的。②干擾的;抵觸的。

in·ter·fer·om·e·ter 〔ˌɪntəfɪˈrɑmətə; ˌintəfiəˈrɔmitə〕 *n.* 〖物理〗干涉計。

in·ter·flow 〔ˌɪntəˈflo; ˌintəˈflou〕 *v.i.* 混流;合流;混合。—*n.* 混流;混合。

in·ter·flu·ent 〔ɪnˈtɜfluənt; inˈtəːfluənt〕 *adj.* 互相流入的;混合的;流於中間的。

in·ter·fuse 〔ˌɪntəˈfjuz; ˌintəˈfjuːz〕 *v.*, **-fused, -fus·ing.** —*v.t.* ①充滿; 散布; 滲入; 瀰漫。②使融合; 使混合。 —*v.i.* 混合; 融合。 —**in·ter·fu·sion,** *n.*

in·ter·gla·cial 〔ˌɪntəˈgleʃəl; ˈintəˈgleisjəl〕 *adj.* 〖地質〗二冰河期間的。

in·ter·im 〔ˈɪntərɪm; ˈintərim〕 *n.* 中間時期;過渡時間;暫時;臨時。***in the interim*** 在其間;在其時。—*adj.* 過渡時期的; 臨時的; 暫時的。—*adv.* 於其時;於此際。

***in·te·ri·or** 〔ɪnˈtɪrɪə; inˈtiəriə〕 *n.* ①內部; 內面。The *interior* of the house was beautifully decorated. 這房子的內部裝飾得非常漂亮。②內政。the Department of the *Interior* of the U.S.A. 美國的內政部(在英國稱爲 Home Office). ③(一國之)內地; 腹地。④室內圖; 屋內圖。—*adj.* ①在內的;內部的。*interior* decorators. 室內裝潢家。*interior* decoration. 室內裝飾。②內地的。③內政的; 國內的。the *interior* trade. 國內貿易。④祕密的。an *interior* cabinet. 祕室。⑤〖數學〗內的。*interior* angle. 內角。⑥精神的;心靈的。—**ly,** *adv.*

in·ter·is·land 〔ˌɪntəˈaɪlənd; ˌintəˈailənd〕 *adj.* 島與島之間的。

interj. interjection.

in·ter·ja·cent 〔ˌɪntəˈdʒesənt; ˌintəˈdʒeisənt〕 *adj.* 在中間的; 介在的;居間的。

in·ter·ject 〔ˌɪntəˈdʒɛkt; ˌintəˈdʒekt〕 *v.t.* 投入其間;突然插入;插入(語詞等)。

***in·ter·jec·tion** 〔ˌɪntəˈdʒɛkʃən; ˌintəˈdʒekʃən〕 *n.* ①感歎詞。②(語詞之) 插入。③插入之語詞。

in·ter·jec·tion·al 〔ˌɪntəˈdʒɛkʃənl̩; ˌintəˈdʒekʃənl̩〕 *adj.* ①叫聲的;感嘆的;感嘆詞的。②插入的;插句的。

in·ter·jec·tion·al·ize 〔ˌɪntəˈdʒɛkʃənlˌaɪz; ˌintəˈdʒekʃənəlaiz〕 *v.t.*, **-ized, -iz·ing.** 使變爲感歎詞。

in·ter·join 〔ˌɪntəˈdʒɔɪn; ˌintəˈdʒɔin〕 *v.t.* & *v.i.* 連接;互相連結。

in·ter·knit 〔ˌɪntəˈnɪt; ˌintəˈnit〕 *v.t.*, **-knit·ted** or **-knit, -knit·ting.** 編合;纏繞。

in·ter·lace 〔ˌɪntəˈles; ˌintəˈleis〕 *v.*, **-laced, -lac·ing.** —*v.t.* ①編織;編結。②交

織;交錯;組合。—*v.i.* 交織;交錯。

in·ter·lan·guage 〔ˈɪntəˌlæŋgwɪdʒ; ˈintəˌlæŋgwidʒ〕 *n.* 國際語。

in·ter·lard 〔ˌɪntəˈlɑrd; ˌintəˈlɑːd〕 *v.t.* 使有變化;混入;點綴;使雜有。

in·ter·lay 〔ˌɪntəˈle; ˌintəˈlei〕 *v.t.*, **-laid, -lay·ing.** ①挿入中間。②挿於中間點綴〖常 with〗. to *interlay* silver with gold. 以金飾銀。

in·ter·leaf 〔ˈɪntəˌlif; ˈintəliːf〕 *n., pl.* **-leaves.** ①挿頁;挿入之空白紙。②此等空白紙上之批注。

in·ter·leave 〔ˌɪntəˈliv; ˌintəˈliːv〕 *v.t.,* **-leaved, -leav·ing.** 挿以空白紙。

in·ter·line[1] 〔*v.* ˌɪntəˈlaɪn; ˌintəˈlain *n.* ˈɪntəˌlaɪn; ˈintəˌlain〕 *v.,* **-lined, -lin·ing,** *n.*— *v.t.* ①挿(字等)於行間。②寫、印於行間。to *interline* English and Chinese. 隔行書寫(或印刷)英文和中文。—*n.* 挿入之行。

in·ter·line[2] 〔ˌɪntəˈlaɪn; ˌintəˈlain〕 *v.t.,* **-lined, -lin·ing.**(衣服面裏之間)加襯層。

in·ter·lin·e·al 〔ˌɪntəˈlɪnɪəl; ˌintəˈliniəl〕 *adj.* ①隔行排列的。②挿於行間的。

in·ter·lin·e·ar 〔ˌɪntəˈlɪnɪə; ˌintəˈliniə〕 *adj.* ①挿於行間的。②含有相間排列之兩種文字或譯文的。

in·ter·lin·e·a·tion 〔ˌɪntəˌlɪnɪˈeʃən; ˈintəˌliniˈeiʃən〕 *n.* 書(印) 於行間; 書(印) 於行間之詞句。

in·ter·lin·ing 〔ˈɪntəˌlaɪnɪŋ; ˈintəˌlainiŋ〕 *n.* (衣服面裏間之)加襯層。

in·ter·link 〔*v.* ˌɪntəˈlɪŋk; ˌintəˈliŋk *n.* ˈɪntəˌlɪŋk; ˈintə(ː)ˌliŋk〕 *v.t.* 環接;使連鎖。—*n.* 連環;連鎖。

in·ter·lock 〔ˌɪntəˈlɑk; ˌintəˈlɔk〕 *v.i.* 結合; 連結; 互鎖。—*v.t.* 連繫; 結合; 使互連鎖。 ***interlocking director*** 兼任主任。 ***interlocking mechanism*** 聯鎖機構。 ***interlocking signals*** 〖鐵道〗聯動式信號; 連鎖信號。

in·ter·lo·cu·tion 〔ˌɪntələˈkjuʃən; ˌintəlouˈkjuːʃən〕 *n.* 對話; 會談。

in·ter·loc·u·tor 〔ˌɪntəˈlɑkjətə; ˌintəˈlɔkjutə〕 *n.* ①談話者;對話者。②(吟唱班中之)問話者。

in·ter·loc·u·to·ry 〔ˌɪntəˈlɑkjəˌtorɪ; ˌintəˈlɔkjutəri〕 *adj.* ①對話的; 對話體的。②〖法律〗中間(判決)的。③挿入主題的。

in·ter·lope 〔ˌɪntəˈlop; ˌintəˈloup〕 *v.i.,* **-loped, -lop·ing.** ①無執照營業。②干涉他人之事;闖入;妨礙。

in·ter·lop·er 〔ˌɪntəˈlopə; ˌintəˈloupə〕 *n.* ①私商。②闖入者; 妨礙者; 干涉他人之事者。

in·ter·lude 〔ˈɪntəˌlud; ˈintəluːd〕 *n., v.,* **-lud·ed, -lud·ing.** —*n.* ①塡補二事件間之事物;中間時間;間隔之時間。②歌調各段間之過門;節目間之挿樂;挿曲;幕間音樂。③(多幕劇之)幕間節目; 幕間表演。—*v.i.* 干擾;干涉。—*v.t.* 打斷;挿嘴。

in·ter·lu·nar 〔ˌɪntəˈlunə; ˌintəˈluːnə〕 *adj.* 不見月之期間的。

in·ter·mar·riage 〔ˌɪntəˈmærɪdʒ; ˌintəˈmæridʒ〕 *n.* ①異族結婚;不同階級間的通婚。②近親結婚;血族結婚。③通婚。

in·ter·mar·ry 〔ˌɪntəˈmærɪ; ˈintəˈmæri〕 *v.i.,* **-ried, -ry·ing.** ① (兩不同家族、種族或階級間)由於通婚而結合。②近親結婚。③通婚。

in·ter·med·dle 〔ˌɪntəˈmɛdl̩; ˌintəˈmedl〕 *v.i.* 干涉;管閒事 〖in, with〗. He often *intermeddles* with my affairs. 他常干預我的事。

in·ter·me·di·a 〔ˌɪntəˈmidɪə; ˌintəˈmiːdiə〕 *n.* pl. of **intermedium.**

in·ter·me·di·ar·y 〔ˌɪntəˈmidɪˌɛrɪ; ˌintəˈmiːdjəri〕 *n., pl.* **-ar·ies,** *adj.* —*n.* 中人;居間者;斡旋者;媒介物;媒人。through the *intermediary* of.... 經由…之手。—*adj.* ①居間的;斡旋的;媒介的。②中間的;過渡的。

***in·ter·me·di·ate**[1] 〔ˌɪntəˈmidɪɪt; ˌintəˈmiːdjət〕 *adj.* ①中間的;中級的。Gray is *intermediate* between black and white. 灰色是介於黑色與白色之間的。②中間人的;居間的。—*n.* ①中間物; 居間物。②中間人;調停者。③〖美〗中型轎車。—**ly,** *adv.*

***in·ter·me·di·ate**[2] 〔ˌɪntəˈmidɪˌet; ˌintəˈmiːdieit〕 *v.i.* 作中人;干預。

intermediate frequency 〖電〗「中頻。」

intermediate range ballistic missile 中程彈道飛彈(射程在800至1,500海里之內)。

in·ter·me·di·a·tion 〔ˌɪntəˌmidɪˈeʃən; ˌintəˌmiːdiˈeiʃən〕 *n.* 居間;調停;調解。

in·ter·me·di·a·tor 〔ˌɪntəˈmidɪˌetə; ˌintəˈmiːdieitə〕 *n.* 居間者;調停者;仲裁人。

in·ter·me·di·um 〔ˌɪntəˈmidɪəm; ˌintəˈmiːdiəm〕 *n., pl.* **-di·a, -di·ums.** 中間物;媒介物。

in·ter·ment 〔ɪnˈtɝmənt; inˈtəːmənt〕 「*n.* 埋葬。」

in·ter·mez·zo 〔ˌɪntəˈmɛtso; ˌintəˈmetsou〕 *n., pl.* **-zos, -zi** 〔-sɪ; -si〕. ①挿劇;挿曲;幕間演出。②間奏曲。

in·ter·mi·gra·tion 〔ˌɪntəmaɪˈgreʃən; ˌintəmaiˈgreiʃən〕 *n.* 相互移民。

in·ter·mi·na·ble 〔ɪnˈtɝmɪnəbl̩; inˈtəːminəbl〕 *adj.* 無終止的;冗長的。 —**in·ter·mi·na·bly,** *adv.*

in·ter·min·gle 〔ˌɪntəˈmɪŋgl̩; ˌintəˈmiŋgl〕 *v.t.* & *v.i.,* **-gled, -gling.** 混合;交融;攙雜。

in·ter·mis·sion 〔ˌɪntəˈmɪʃən; ˌintəˈmiʃən〕 *n.* ①活動暫停之時;休息時間;間歇。②暫停; 中止;中斷。The rain continued all day without *intermission.* 雨整天不停地繼續下。

in·ter·mit 〔ˌɪntəˈmɪt; ˌintəˈmit〕 *v.t.* & *v.i.,* **-mit·ted, -mit·ting.** 暫停;中止;間斷;間歇。

in·ter·mit·tence 〔ˌɪntəˈmɪtn̩s; ˌintəˈmitəns〕 *n.* 斷續;間歇。(亦作 **intermittency**)

in·ter·mit·tent 〔ˌɪntəˈmɪtn̩t; ˌintəˈmitənt〕 *adj.* 斷續的;間歇的。*intermittent* fever. 〖醫〗間歇熱。—**ly,** *adv.*

in·ter·mix 〔ˌɪntəˈmɪks; ˌintəˈmiks〕 *v.t.* & *v.i.* 混合;混雜;交雜;融合。

in·ter·mix·ture 〔ˌɪntəˈmɪkstʃə; ˌintəˈmikstʃə〕 *n.* ①混合。②混合物。

in·tern[1] 〔ɪnˈtɝn; inˈtəːn〕 *v.t.* (在一定區域內)拘留;禁閉。

in·tern[2] 〔ˈɪntɝn; ˈintəːn〕 *n.* (亦作 **interne**) 〖美〗住院見習醫生。—*v.i.* 任住院見習醫生。

***in·ter·nal** 〔ɪnˈtɝnl̩; inˈtəːnl〕 *adj.* ①內在的;內部的(爲external之對)。He suffered *internal* injuries in the accident. 他在此次意外事件中受了內傷。②內服的。 *internal* remedies. 內服藥。③國內的;內政的。 *internal* trade (revenue, etc.). 國內貿易 (稅收等)。④主觀的;精神的;心靈的。⑤內在的;本

質上的。—*n.* ①(*pl.*)內臟。②精神;靈魂。—**ly,** *adv.*
internal-combustion engine 內燃機。
in·ter·nal·i·ty [ˌɪntɚˈnælətɪ; ˌintəˈnæliti] *n.* 內在;內在性。
in·ter·nal·ize [ɪnˈtɝnlaɪz; inˈtəːnəlaiz] *v.t.,* **-ized, -iz·ing.** ①壓制(感情)。②使適應(新文化、習俗等)。③予…以主觀特性。
internal medicine 內科醫學。
internal revenue 除關稅外之一切稅收。
internal screw 陰螺釘。
internal secretion 〖生理〗內分泌。
*__in·ter·na·tion·al__ [ˌɪntɚˈnæʃənl; ˌintəˈnæʃənl] *adj.* 國際的。*international* trade (market, conference, etc.). 國際貿易(市場,會議等)。—*n.* ①(I-)國際社會主義者與國際共產主義者之組織。②〖英〗國際運動競賽;參加是項競賽者。③僑居國外者。—**ly,** *adv.*
international candle 國際燭光(光之强度單位)。
International Certificate of Vaccination 國際預防接種證明書,俗稱黃皮書 (Yellow Book).
International Civil Aviation Organization 國際民航組織。(略作 I. C. A. O.)
International Court of Justice 國際法庭。
international date line 國際換日線。
International Energy Agency 國際能源總署。
In·ter·na·tio·nale [ˌɪntɚˌnæʃəˈnɑl; ˌintənæʃəˈnɑːl] 〖法〗 *n.* 國際歌 (1871年在法國初次演唱的革命歌曲)。
in·ter·na·tion·al·ism [ˌɪntɚˈnæʃənlˌɪzəm; ˌintəˈnæʃnəlizəm] *n.* 國際主義。
in·ter·na·tion·al·ist [ˌɪntɚˈnæʃənlɪst; ˌintəˈnæʃənəlist] *n.* ①國際法學者;通曉國際關係者。②國際主義者。—*adj.* 贊成國際主義的。
in·ter·na·tion·al·i·ty [ˌɪntɚˌnæʃəˈnælətɪ; ˌintəˌnæʃəˈnæliti] *n.* 國際性。
in·ter·na·tion·al·i·za·tion [ˌɪntɚˌnæʃənləˈzeʃən; ˈintəˌnæʃənəlaiˈzeiʃən] *n.* 國際化;國際共管。
in·ter·na·tion·al·ize [ˌɪntɚˈnæʃənlˌaɪz; ˌintəˈnæʃnəlaiz] *v.t.,* **-ized, -iz·ing.** 國際化;使歸數國共管。
International Labor Organization 國際勞工組織。(略作 I.L.O.)
international law 國際法;國際公法。
International Monetary Fund 國際貨幣基金會。
International Phonetic Alphabet 國際音標。(略作 IPA)
International Refugee Organization 國際難民組織。(略作I.R.O.)
in·terne [ˈɪntɝn; ˈintəːn] *n.* =**intern**².
in·ter·ne·cine [ˌɪntɚˈnisɪn; ˌintəˈniːsain] *adj.* ①互相毀滅的; 兩敗俱傷的。②致命的;毀滅的。(亦作 **internecive**)
in·tern·ee [ˌɪntɝˈni; ˌintəːˈniː] *n.* (戰爭中被視爲俘虜或敵僑而)被拘留者。
in·tern·ist [ɪnˈtɝnɪst; inˈtəːnist] *n.* 〖醫〗內科醫師。
in·tern·ment [ɪnˈtɝnmənt; inˈtəːnmənt] *n.* 拘留; 禁閉。 an *internment* camp. 〖英〗俘虜(或敵國人民)拘留所(=〖美〗detention camp).
in·ter nos [ˈɪntɚˈnos; ˈintəˈnous] 〖拉〗這話祇在我們之間講;祕密的(=between ourselves).
in·tern·ship [ˈɪntɝnˌʃɪp; ˈintəːnʃip] *n.* 實習醫生之職位或服務期限。
in·ter·nun·ci·o [ˌɪntɚˈnʌnʃɪˌo; ˌintəˈnʌnʃiou] *n., pl.* **-os.** ①羅馬教皇之代理聖使。②使者。
in·ter·o·ce·an·ic [ˌɪntɚˌoʃɪˈænɪk; ˈintərˌouʃiˈænik] *adj.* 兩大海洋間的。
in·ter·pel·late [ˌɪntɚˈpɛlet, ɪnˈtɝpɪˌlet; inˈtəːpeleit] *v.t.,* **-lat·ed, -lat·ing.** (議會中議員向政府官員)質詢。
in·ter·pel·la·tion [ˌɪntəpɛˈleʃən; inˌtəːpeˈleiʃən] *n.* 質詢;質問。
in·ter·pel·la·tor [ˌɪntəpɛˈletɚ; ˌintəpeˈleitə] *n.* (議會之) 質詢者;提出質詢之議員。
in·ter·pen·e·trate [ˌɪntɚˈpɛnəˌtret; ˌintəˈpenitreit] *v.t.* & *v.i.,* **-trat·ed, -trat·ing.** 滲透;貫通;穿通。—**in·ter·pen·e·tra·tion,** *n.*
in·ter·phone [ˈɪntɚˌfon; ˈintəfoun] *n.* (船、飛機等之)內部電話;對講機。
in·ter·plan·e·tar·y [ˌɪntɚˈplænəˌtɛrɪ; ˌintəˈplænitəri] *adj.* 〖天文〗行星間的;在行星間的;太陽系內的。
in·ter·play [ˈɪntɚˌple; ˈintəˈplei] *n.* 相互作用; 作用及反作用。—*v.i.* 交互作用;相互影響。
in·ter·plead [ˌɪntɚˈplid; ˌintəˈpliːd] *v.i.* 〖法律〗(爲確定與第三人有關之爭執而)相互訴訟。
in·ter·po·late [ɪnˈtɝpəˌlet; inˈtəːpouleit] *v.t.* & *v.i.,* **-lat·ed, -lat·ing.** ①加入字句以竄改(書等)。②添進(字句等)。③〖數學〗在級數中插入(中項)。
in·ter·po·la·tion [ɪnˌtɝpəˈleʃən; inˌtəːpouˈleiʃən] *n.* ①挿入;添加;竄改。②添入物;添入之字句。
in·ter·pos·al [ˌɪntɚˈpozl; ˌintəˈpouzl] *n.* =**interposition.**
*__in·ter·pose__ [ˌɪntɚˈpoz; ˌintəˈpouz] *v.,* **-posed, -pos·ing.** —*v.t.* ①置於…之間;使介入。②提出以爲妨害或阻礙。 He *interposed* his authority. 他以權勢來阻撓。③挿入(話語)以打斷談話;提出(異議)。to *interpose* an objection. 提出異議。—*v.i.* ①介於二者間;挿入。to *interpose* in a dispute. 介入爭吵。②仲裁;調停。to *interpose* between two persons who are quarreling. 調停兩個正在吵架的人。③挿嘴;干涉。—**in·ter·pos·a·ble,** *adj.* —**in·ter·pos·al, in·ter·pos·er,** *n.*
in·ter·po·si·tion [ˌɪntəpəˈzɪʃən; inˌtə(ː)pəˈziʃən] *n.* ①置於中間; 挿入; 調停;妨害; 干涉。②挿入物。③〖美〗主張州政府可反對侵犯其主權之任何聯邦法令的學說。
*__in·ter·pret__ [ɪnˈtɝprɪt; inˈtəːprit] *v.t.* ①解釋; 闡明。 to *interpret* a dream. 圓夢。②演出;演奏。to *interpret* the role of Hamlet. 演出哈姆雷特這個角色。③了解;認爲。 We *interpreted* his silence as a refusal. 我們認爲他的沉默卽是拒絕。④口頭翻譯;通譯。—*v.i.* ①通譯。②解說;闡釋。
in·ter·pret·a·ble [ɪnˈtɝprɪtəbl; inˈtəːpritəbl] *adj.* 可解釋的;可通譯的。
*__in·ter·pre·ta·tion__ [ɪnˌtɝprɪˈteʃən; inˌtəːpriˈteiʃən] *n.* ①解釋;解說。different *interpretations* of the same facts. 對於同一事實之不同的解釋。②演出; 演奏。The

newspapers praised the actor's *interpretation* of Hamlet. 各報對該演員之飾演哈姆雷特加以讚揚。③翻譯;通譯。

in·ter·pre·ta·tive 〔ɪnˈtɝprɪˌtetɪv; inˈtəːpritətiv〕 *adj.* ①解釋的;說明的;用以解釋的。②因翻譯而造成的。③需要媒體表現之藝術(如音樂需演奏者及戲劇需演員)的。

***in·ter·pret·er** 〔ɪnˈtɝprɪtɚ; inˈtəːpritə〕 *n.* ①解釋者。②通譯員;翻譯員(特指口頭翻譯並以爲職業者)。

in·ter·punc·tion 〔ˌɪntɚˈpʌŋkʃən; ˌintəˈpʌŋkʃən〕 *n.* ①標點。②標點符號。

in·ter·ra·cial 〔ˌɪntɚˈreʃəl; ˌintəˈreiʃjəl〕 *adj.* 各種族間的;包括各種族的。

in·ter·reg·num 〔ˌɪntɚˈrɛgnəm; ˌintəˈregnəm〕 *n., pl.* **-nums, -na** 〔-nə;-nə〕. ①舊統治者政權結束而繼任者未就任之空隙狀態;空位期。②國家中無正常統治者的時期。③休止時間;中間期。

in·ter·re·late 〔ˌɪntərɪˈlet; ˌintəriˈleit〕 *v.t.* & *v.i.*, **-lat·ed, -lat·ing.** (使)相互關連。

in·ter·re·lat·ed 〔ˌɪntərɪˈletɪd; ˌintəriˈleitid〕 *adj.* 互相關連的;相關的。

in·ter·re·la·tion 〔ˌɪntərɪˈleʃən; ˈintəriˈleiʃən〕 *n.* 相互關係。

interrog. ①interrogation. ②interrogatively.

in·ter·ro·gate 〔ɪnˈtɛrəˌget; inˈterəgeit〕 *v.*, **-gat·ed, -gat·ing.** —*v.t.* 訊問;審問;詳問。The lawyer took two hours to *interrogate* the witness. 律師費兩小時的時間訊問證人。—*v.i.* 提出一連串問題。

***in·ter·ro·ga·tion** 〔ɪnˌtɛrəˈgeʃən; inˌterəˈgeiʃən〕 *n.* ①詰問;訊問;審問。②被審訊。He seemed shaken after his *interrogation*. 他被審訊後似乎驚惶不已。③問題。④問號"?"。

***in·ter·rog·a·tive** 〔ˌɪntəˈrɑgətɪv; ˌintəˈrɔgətiv〕 *adj.* ①疑惑的。an *interrogative* look (glance, etc.). 疑惑的樣子(目光等)。②問句的;疑問的。an *interrogative* sentence. 疑問句。—*n.* 疑問詞;疑問字(指疑問代名詞,疑問副詞等而言)。"Who", "why", and "what" are *interrogatives*. Who, why, 和 what 是疑問字。—**ly,** *adv.* 〖文法〗(1) **Interrogative pronoun.** 疑問代名詞。(2) **Interrogative adverb.** 疑問副詞。(3) **Interrogative sentence.** 疑問句。

in·ter·ro·ga·tor 〔ɪnˈtɛrəˌgetɚ; inˈterəgeitə〕 *n.* 訊問者;質詢者。

in·ter·rog·a·to·ry 〔ˌɪntəˈrɑgəˌtorɪ; ˌintəˈrɔgətəri〕 *adj., n., pl.* **-ries.** —*adj.* 疑問的;質問的;表疑問的。—*n.* ①疑問;質問;詢問。②〖法律〗書面質詢。

***in·ter·rupt** 〔ˌɪntəˈrʌpt; ˌintəˈrʌpt〕 *v.t.* ①打斷(談話、工作、休息等);打擾。Don't *interrupt* me when I'm busy. 在我忙着的時候,不要來打擾我。②遮斷;妨礙。to *interrupt* a view. 遮斷視線。③使中斷。The war *interrupted* the flow of commerce between the two countries. 戰爭使這兩國的通商中斷了。—*v.i.* 打斷;插嘴。—**ive,** *adj.*

in·ter·rupt·ed 〔ˌɪntəˈrʌptɪd; ˌintəˈrʌptid〕 *adj.* ①被打斷的;被打擾的;中斷的。②〖植物〗不對稱的;不規律的。—**ly,** *adv.*

in·ter·rupt·er, in·ter·rupt·or 〔ˌɪntəˈrʌptɚ; ˌintəˈrʌptə〕 *n.* ①遮斷者(物);阻礙者(物);插嘴的人。②〖電〗斷續器;斷流器。

in·ter·rupt·i·ble 〔ˌɪntəˈrʌptəbḷ; ˌintəˈrʌptibl〕 *adj.* 可被打斷的;可中斷的。

***in·ter·rup·tion** 〔ˌɪntəˈrʌpʃən; ˌintəˈrʌpʃən〕 *n.* ①打岔;阻斷;中斷。without *interruption*. 毫無間斷地。②使中斷之事物;打岔的事。Numerous *interruptions* have prevented me from finishing the work. 無數打岔的事使我未能將此工作完成。

in·ter·scho·las·tic 〔ˌɪntɚskəˈlæstɪk; ˌintəskəˈlæstik〕 *adj.* (中、小學之)校際的。

in·ter·sect 〔ˌɪntəˈsɛkt; ˌintəˈsekt〕 *v.t.* ①貫穿。②相交。—*v.i.* 交叉。

in·ter·sec·tant 〔ˌɪntəˈsɛktənt; ˌintəˈsektənt〕 *adj.* 相交的;交叉的。

in·ter·sec·tion 〔ˌɪntəˈsɛkʃən; ˌintəˈsekʃən〕 *n.* ①交叉點。②交叉。③〖幾何〗交點;交叉線。—**al,** *adj.*

in·ter·space 〔*n.* ˈɪntɚˌspes; ˈintəspeis *v.* ˌɪntɚˈspes; ˈintəˈspeis〕 *n., v.,* **-spaced, -spac·ing.** —*n.* (時間或場所之)中間的空間;空隙;間隔。—*v.t.* ①留間隔或空間於…之間。②占…之空間。

in·ter·sperse 〔ˌɪntəˈspɝs; ˌintəˈspəːs〕 *v.t.,* **-spersed, -spers·ing.** ①點綴。②散置;散布。—**in·ter·sper·sion,** *n.*

in·ter·state 〔ˌɪntəˈstet; ˌintəˈsteit〕 *adj.* (美國之)州與州間的;州際的。

in·ter·stel·lar 〔ˌɪntəˈstɛlɚ; ˈintəˈstelə〕 *adj.* 星球與星球間的;星際的。

in·ter·stice 〔ɪnˈtɝstɪs; inˈtəːstis〕 *n., pl.* **-sti·ces.** 細口;小縫;空隙;罅隙。

in·ter·sti·tial 〔ˌɪntəˈstɪʃəl; ˌintəˈstiʃəl〕 *adj.* ①空隙的;生於空隙內的;形成空隙的。②〖解剖〗在細胞組織之間的;間質性的。

in·ter·tex·ture 〔ˌɪntəˈtɛkstʃɚ; ˌintəˈtekstʃə〕 *n.* ①組合;編織;組織。②編織物。

in·ter·twine 〔ˌɪntəˈtwaɪn; ˌintəˈtwain〕 *v.t.* & *v.i.*, **-twined, -twin·ing.** 糾纏;纏繞;編結。to *intertwine* flowers in a garland. 將花編結成花圈。

in·ter·twist 〔*n.* ˈɪntɚˌtwɪst; ˈintəˌtwist *v.* ˌɪntɚˈtwɪst; ˌintəˈtwist〕 *n., v.t., v.i.* 絞合;搓合;撚合。

in·ter·ur·ban 〔ˌɪntɚˈɝbən; ˌintəˈəːbən〕 *adj.* 城市間的;市鎮間的。

in·ter·val** 〔ˈɪntɚvḷ; ˈintəvəl〕 *n.* ①中間時間(常指休息、休止、或間隔之時間)。the *interval* between two acts of a play. 戲劇兩幕之間隔時間。②間歇;(很短的)時間;期間。trains and trams leaving at short *intervals*. 每隔很短的時間就開出的火車及電車。③間隔;距離。④〖音樂〗音程。at intervals*** **a.** (=now and then) 時時。**b.** (=here and there) 處處。

in·ter·vale 〔ˈɪntɚˌvel; ˈintəveil〕 *n.* 〖美、加〗(丘陵間或沿河岸之)低地。(亦作 **interval(e) land**)

***in·ter·vene** 〔ˌɪntəˈvin; ˌintəˈviːn〕 *v.i.*, **-vened, -ven·ing.** ①挿入;介於其間。A week *intervenes* between Christmas and New Year's Day. 聖誕節與元旦之間相距一禮拜。②干涉;調停。The President *intervened* in the strike. 總統出面調停罷工事件。③〖法律〗(第三者)參加訴訟。④衝突;阻撓。⑤於…之間發生。

in·ter·ven·tion 〔ˌɪntəˈvɛnʃən; ˌintəˈvenʃən〕 *n.* ①仲裁;調停。*intervention* in a dispute. 調停爭端。②(大國對小國內政的)干涉。armed *intervention*. 武力干涉。③介入之物,事件,或時間。

in·ter·ven·tion·ist 〔ˌɪntəˈvɛnʃənɪst;

ˌintəˈvenʃənist] *n.* (他國)內政干涉論者。—*adj.* 干涉主義的;干涉主義者的。

***in·ter·view** [ˈɪntəˌvju; ˈintəvjuː] *n.* ①接見;會見。an *interview* with a manager for a job. 謁見經理求職。②(新聞記者的)訪問。to refuse to give any *interviews* to journalists. 拒絕接見新聞記者。③(報章雜誌上發表的)訪問記。—*v.t.* 接見;會見;會談。to *interview* a manager for a job. 謁見經理求職。**—er,** *n.*

in·ter·view·ee [ˌɪntəvjuˈi; ˌintəvjuːˈiː] *n.* 被接見者;被訪問者。

in·ter·volve [ˌɪntəˈvɑlv; ˌintəˈvɔlv] *v.t. & v.i.*, **-volved, -volv·ing.** ①互捲;捲合。②互相牽連。

in·ter·weave [ˌɪntəˈwiv; ˌintəˈwiːv] *v.*, **-wove** or **-weaved, -wo·ven** or **-wove** or **-weaved, -weav·ing,** *n.* —*v.t. & v.i.* ①交織;織合。②混合;緊接。—*n.* 混合;交織。

in·tes·ta·cy [ɪnˈtɛstəsɪ; inˈtestəsi] *n.* 無遺囑死亡。

in·tes·tate [ɪnˈtɛstet; inˈtestit] *adj.* ①未留遺囑的。②未按遺囑處分的。—*n.* 未留遺囑之死者。

in·tes·ti·nal [ɪnˈtɛstɪnḷ; inˈtestinḷ] *adj.* 腸的;在腸內的。

in·tes·tine [ɪnˈtɛstɪn; inˈtestin] *n.* ①腸。②大腸。③小腸。—*adj.* 國內的;內部的。

in·thral(l) [ɪnˈθrɔl; inˈθrɔːl] *v.t.* = **enthrall.**

in·throne [ɪnˈθron; inˈθroun] *v.t.* = **enthrone.**

***in·ti·ma·cy** [ˈɪntəməsɪ; ˈintiməsi] *n.*, *pl.* **-cies.** ①親密;親近。②親密的行動(如吻或撫摸等)。She allowed him to hold her hand, but forbade him any *intimacies.* 她讓他握她的手,但不許他有過於親密的行動。③熟稔;熟悉。④(房間等)舒適感。The *intimacy* of the room was enhanced by its warm colors. 該房間溫暖的色澤更增加它的舒適感。⑤祕密;隱私。

***in·ti·mate**[1] [ˈɪntəmɪt; ˈintimit] *adj.* ①親密的;親近的。an *intimate* friend. 密友;至友。②內心的;心底的。one's *intimate* feelings (thoughts, etc.). 其內心的感情(思想等)。③私人的;祕密的。an *intimate* diary. 私人日記。④本質的。the *intimate* structure of matter. 物質的本質構造。⑤熟稔的;精湛的。an *intimate* knowledge of Greek philosophy. 對希臘哲學的熟稔的知識。⑥詳細的。⑦令人有賓至如歸之感的。an *intimate* café. 一個令人有賓至如歸之感的咖啡館。⑧性關係的。—*n.* 密友;知己。**—ly,** *adv.*

in·ti·mate[2] [ˈɪntəˌmet; ˈintimeit] *v.t.*, **-mat·ed, -mat·ing.** ①暗示;暗指。to *intimate* disapproval of a plan. 暗示對一計畫之不贊成。②宣布;通知。

in·ti·ma·tion [ˌɪntəˈmeʃən; ˌintiˈmeiʃən] *n.* ①暗示;暗指。A frown is often an *intimation* of disapproval. 皺眉頭通常是不贊許的暗示。②宣布;通知。

in·tim·i·date [ɪnˈtɪməˌdet; inˈtimideit] *v.t.*, **-dat·ed, -dat·ing.** ①恐嚇;使畏懼。②脅迫;威迫。

in·tim·i·da·tion [ɪnˌtɪməˈdeʃən; inˌtimiˈdeiʃən] *n.* 恐嚇;恫嚇;脅迫。

in·tim·i·da·tor [ɪnˈtɪməˌdetə; inˈtimideitə] *n.* 威嚇者;脅迫者。

in·tinc·tion [ɪnˈtɪŋkʃən; inˈtiŋkʃən] *n.* 〖宗教〗麪包蘸酒(以兼備聖餐之二要素)。

in·ti·tle [ɪnˈtaɪtḷ; inˈtaitl] *v.t.* = **entitle.**

‡**in·to** [ˈɪntu, ˈɪntʊ; ˈintu, ˈintuː, ˈintə] *prep.* ①進入…之內;深入…之中。to go *into* the house. 進入房屋內。②成爲(…之狀況)。The house is divided *into* ten rooms. 該屋分爲十個房間。③〖數學〗除。2 *into* 20 equals 10. 2 除 20 等於 10。

***in·tol·er·a·ble** [ɪnˈtɑlərəbḷ; inˈtɔlərəbl] *adj.* 難耐的;受不了的;無法忍受的。*intolerable* heat (insolence). 無法忍受的熱度(侮辱)。**—in·tol·er·a·bil·i·ty,** *n.* **—in·tol·er·a·bly,** *adv.*

in·tol·er·ance [ɪnˈtɑlərəns; inˈtɔlərəns] *n.* ①不容異說;偏執。②不能忍耐;不寬容。

in·tol·er·ant [ɪnˈtɑlərənt; inˈtɔlərənt] *adj.* ①不容有異說的;偏執的(尤指宗教方面而言)。②不能忍耐的;不寬容的〖of〗。

in·tomb [ɪnˈtum; inˈtuːm] *v.t.* = **entomb.**

in·to·nate [ˈɪntoˌnet; ˈintouneit] *v.t. & v.i.*, **-nat·ed, -nat·ing.** ① = **intone.** ②以某種聲調說或唱。

***in·to·na·tion** [ˌɪntoˈneʃən; ˌintouˈneiʃən] *n.* ①誦讀;朗誦;唱。the *intonation* of a psalm. 聖歌的誦讀。②(語言之)語調;音調。English *intonation* is not hard to learn. 英語語調不難學習。③〖音樂〗調音。

in·tone [ɪnˈton; inˈtoun] *v.*, **-toned, -ton·ing.** —*v.t.* ①發音調;抑揚其聲。a well-*intoned* delivery. 聲調良好的致詞。②唱;吟誦。—*v.i.* ①吟誦。②〖音樂〗發音。

In·tour·ist [ɪnˈtʊrɪst; ˈintuərist] *n.* 蘇聯之官方旅行社,其服務對象爲外國遊客。—*adj.* Intourist 主辦的或供給的。

in·tox·i·cant [ɪnˈtɑksəkənt; inˈtɔksikənt] *n.* ①酒精飲料。②麻醉劑(如鴉片)。—*adj.* 醉人的;使醉的。

***in·tox·i·cate** [ɪnˈtɑksəˌket; inˈtɔksikeit] *v.*, **-cat·ed, -cat·ing.** —*v.t.* ①使醉。Alcohol *intoxicates* people. 酒能醉人。②使太興奮。to be *intoxicated* with (*or* by) success. 因成功而陶醉。—*v.i.* 醉人。Wine has the power to *intoxicate.* 酒能醉人。

in·tox·i·cat·ed [ɪnˈtɑksəˌketɪd; inˈtɔksikeitid] *adj.* ①醉酒的。②興奮的;似醉的。

in·tox·i·cat·ing [ɪnˈtɑksəˌketɪŋ; inˈtɔksəkeitiŋ] *adj.* ①能使人醉的。Whiskey is an *intoxicating* liquor. 威士忌是能醉人的酒。②(酒類)蒸餾的。③令人興奮的。

in·tox·i·ca·tion [ɪnˌtɑksəˈkeʃən; inˌtɔksiˈkeiʃən] *n.* ①醉。②極度興奮。③〖醫〗中毒。

intr. ①intransitive. ②introduce. ③introduced. ④introducing. ⑤introduction. ⑥introductory.

intra- 〖字首〗表"在內"之義。

in·trac·ta·ble [ɪnˈtræktəbḷ; inˈtræktəbl] *adj.* 難駕馭的;難處理的;倔强的;頑梗的。an *intractable* child. 不聽話的小孩;頑童。—*n.* 難駕馭之人。**—in·trac·ta·bil·i·ty, —ness,** *n.* **—in·trac·ta·bly,** *adv.*

in·tra·dos [ɪnˈtredɑs; inˈtreidɔs] *n.* 〖建築〗穹窿之內面;拱之下面;內弧面。

in·tra·mu·ral [ˌɪntrəˈmjʊrəl; ˈintrəˈmjuərəl] *adj.* ①同一大學的;(大學)校內的;內部的。②城市內的;建築物內的。③〖解剖〗臟器壁內的;壁間的。

in·tra·na·tion·al [ˌɪntrəˈnæʃənḷ; ˌintrəˈnæʃənḷ] *adj.* 國內的。

intrans. intransitive.

in·tran·si·gence [ɪnˈtrænsədʒəns;

in'trænsidʒəns] *n.* 不讓步;不妥協;强硬。

in·tran·si·gen·cy [ɪn'trænsədʒənsɪ; in'trænsidʒənsi] *n.* =**intransigence.**

in·tran·si·gent [ɪn'trænsədʒənt;in'trænsidʒənt] *adj.* 不妥協的; 不讓步的。—*n.* 不妥協的人;强硬分子(尤指政治上的)。

***in·tran·si·tive** [ɪn'trænsətɪv; in'trænsitiv] *adj.* 不及物的(動詞)。—*n.* 不及物動詞。—**ly,** *adv.* 〖文法〗 **intransitive verb** 不及物動詞, 即無直接受詞之動詞。如: be, rise 等是。

in·trant ['ɪntrənt; 'intrənt] *n.* 加入者; 入會者; 入學者。—*adj.* 進來的;加入的。

in·tra·state [ˌɪntrə'stet; ˌintrə'steit] *adj.* 〖美〗州內的。

in·tra·u·ter·ine device [ˌɪntrə'jutərɪn～; ˌintrə'ju:tərin～] 子宮內避孕裝置。

in·tra·ve·nous [ˌɪntrə'vinəs;ˌintrə'vi:nəs]*adj.* 〖醫〗①靜脈內的。②靜脈注射的。

in·treat [ɪn'trit; in'tri:t] *v.t. & v.i.* =**entreat.**

in·trench [ɪn'trɛntʃ; in'trentʃ] *v.t. & v.i.* =**entrench.**

in·trep·id [ɪn'trɛpɪd; in'trepid] *adj.* 「無畏的;勇猛的。」

in·tre·pid·i·ty [ˌɪntrə'pɪdətɪ; ˌintrə'piditi] *n.* 勇猛;剛勇;無畏;大膽。

in·tri·ca·cy ['ɪntrəkəsɪ; 'intrikəsi] *n., pl.* **-cies.** ①紛亂;錯綜。②紛繁的部分;糾纏不清的事物。

***in·tri·cate** ['ɪntrəkɪt; 'intrikit] *adj.* ①錯綜複雜的; 糾纏不清的; 頭緒紛繁的。an *intricate* knot. 糾纏不清的結。②難懂的。an *intricate* design. 難懂的設計。—**ly,** *adv.*

in·tri·g(u)ant ['ɪntrəgənt; 'intrigənt] *n.* 陰謀家;私通者;姦夫。

in·tri·g(u)ante [ˌɪntrə'gænt; ˌintri'gænt] *n.* 女陰謀家;淫婦。

***in·trigue** [*n.* ɪn'trig, 'ɪntrig; in'tri:g, 'intri:g *v.* ɪn'trig;in'tri:g] *n., v.,* **-trigued, -tri·guing.** —*n.* ①陰謀;密謀。The royal palace was filled with *intrigue*. 皇宮內充滿了勾心鬥角。②私通; 風流艷事。③錯綜複雜的劇情。—*v.i.* ①設陰謀;密謀〖against〗. to *intrigue* against one's friends. 設陰謀以陷害其友。②私通〖with〗. to *intrigue* with a woman. 同一女人私通。—*v.t.* ①激起…的好奇和興趣; 吸引。 an *intriguing* item of news. 一條極吸引人的新聞。②使困惑。I am *intrigued* by this event. 這次事件使我大惑不解。

in·trin·sic [ɪn'trɪnsɪk; in'trinsik] *adj.* ①本身的;實質的;固有的。the *intrinsic* value of a coin. 一錢幣之實際價值。②〖解剖〗本體內的;本質內的。

in·trin·si·cal [ɪn'trɪnsɪkḷ; in'trinsikəl] *adj.* =**intrinsic.** —**ly,** *adv.*

in·tro ['ɪntro; 'introu] *n., pl.* **-tros.** 〖美俚〗①社交場合之介紹。②爵士樂之序曲。

intro- 〖字首〗表"向內;在內"之義。

intro., introd. ①introduce. ②introduced. ③introducing. ④introduction. ⑤introductory.

:in·tro·duce [ˌɪntrə'djus;ˌintrə'dju:s] *v.t.,* **-duced, -duc·ing.** ①納入;引入;傳入。to *introduce* a story into the conversation. 引一段故事於會話中。②插入。to *introduce* a tube into the throat. 挿一管於喉間。③提倡; 採用。to *introduce* a new word. 採用一新字。④介紹相識;推薦;介紹。The chairman *introduced* the speaker to the audience. 主席將演說者介紹給聽衆。⑤提出;貢獻。to *introduce* a question for debate. 提出一問題以供討論。to *introduce* a bill into Congress. 向國會提出一法案。⑥使認識;使熟悉。I *introduce* my country cousin to the city by showing him the sights. 我領着我的鄉下親戚參觀城市中的一切名勝, 使他熟悉這城市的情形。⑦爲…之始;引導。Relative pronouns *introduce* adjective clauses.關係代名詞引出形容詞子句。⑧引進(外來物)。Many fruits and vegetables have been *introduced* into Taiwan in recent years. 近年來臺灣已引進了多種水果和蔬菜。

in·tro·duc·er [ɪnˌtrə'djusɚ; ˌintrə'dju:sə] *n.* 介紹人;推薦人; 輸入者;創始者;提出者;誘導者。

***in·tro·duc·tion** [ˌɪntrə'dʌkʃən; ˌintrə'dʌkʃən] *n.* ①介紹; 推薦。a letter of *introduction*. 介紹信。②輸入;傳入。foreign words of recent *introduction*. 新近傳入之外國字。③採用;使用。④被採用之物。Radios are a later *introduction* than telephones. 無線電的使用比電話遲。⑤初步; 入門。*An Introduction to Greek Grammar*. "希臘文法初步"。⑥引言;緒論;總論。

in·tro·duc·to·ry [ˌɪntrə'dʌktərɪ; ˌintrə'dʌktəri] *adj.* 介紹的; 導引的; 初步的; 開端的。*introductory* address. 介紹辭; 開會辭。

in·tro·it [ɪn'tro·ɪt; 'intrɔit] *n.* ①〖天主教〗入祭文 (祭司昇壇時所唱之讚美詩等)。②〖英國國教〗聖餐式前所唱的歌。

in·tro·mis·sion [ˌɪntrə'mɪʃən; ˌintrou'miʃən] *n.* ①挿入;送入。②准入;入場(加入)許可。

in·tro·mit [ˌɪntrə'mɪt; ˌintrou'mit] *v.t.,* **-mit·ted, -mit·ting.** ①使入內;挿入;送入。②准入;許入。

in·trorse [ɪn'trɔrs; in'trɔ:s] *adj.* 〖植物〗向內的;內曲的 (爲 extrorse 之對)。

in·tro·spect [ˌɪntrə'spɛkt; ˌintrou'spekt] *v.i. & v.t.* 內省;自省;反省。

in·tro·spec·tion [ˌɪntrə'spɛkʃən; ˌintrou'spekʃən] *n.* 內省;自省;反省。

in·tro·spec·tive [ˌɪntrə'spɛktɪv; ˌintrou'spektiv] *adj.* 內省的; 好內省的。*introspective method* 〖心理〗內省法。—**ly,** *adv.* —**ness,** *n.*

in·tro·ver·sion [ˌɪntrə'vɝʃən; ˌintrou'və:ʃən] *n.* ①向內; 內曲。②(器官等之)內向;內曲;內轉;內傾。③〖心理〗內向性。

in·tro·vert [*v.* ˌɪntrə'vɝt; ˌintrou'və:t *n.* 'ɪntrəˌvɝt; 'introuvə:t] *v.t.* ①使內向; 使內省。②使向內彎曲。—*v.i.* 成爲內向者。—*n.* ①個性內傾者;慣於自省之人。②〖俗〗怕羞者。

***in·trude** [ɪn'trud; in'tru:d] *v.,* **-trud·ed, -trud·ing.** —*v.i.* ①闖入;侵擾〖upon〗. to *intrude* upon a person's privacy. 闖入某人的私室。—*v.t.* ①强使他人採納。to *intrude* one's views upon others. 强使他人採納己見。②强擠入。③〖地質〗迸入。—**in·trud·er,** *n.*

***in·tru·sion** [ɪn'truʒən; in'tru:ʒən] *n.* ①闖入; 侵擾。②闖入或侵擾之事例。to be angry at numerous *intrusions* on one's privacy. 因屢屢被人侵擾其清靜生活而發怒。③强使他人採納。④〖地質〗岩石的迸入。

in·tru·sive [ɪn'trusɪv; in'tru:siv] *adj.* ①闖入的;打擾的。②〖地質〗迸入的。③〖語音〗插入的。—**ly,** *adv.*

***in·trust** [ɪn'trʌst; in'trʌst] *v.t.* =**entrust.**

in·tu·bate ['ɪntjuˌbet; 'intjubeit] *v.t.,* **-bat·ed, -bat·ing.** 〖醫〗插管入(咽喉等)。—**in·tu·ba·tion,** *n.*

in·tu·it ['ɪntjuɪt; 'intju(:)it] *v.t.* & *v.i.* 直覺;直觀;由直覺或直觀獲知。

in·tu·i·tion [ˌɪntju'ɪʃən; ˌintju(:)'iʃən] *n.* ①直覺;直觀。to know something by *intuition.* 靠直覺而知某事物。②直覺知識;直觀眞理。③直覺力。—**less,** *adj.*

in·tu·i·tion·al [ˌɪntju'ɪʃənl̩; ˌintju(:)-'iʃənəl] *adj.* 直觀的;直覺的;有直觀力的;基於直覺的。

in·tu·i·tion·al·ism [ˌɪntju'ɪʃənl̩ˌɪzəm; ˌintju'iʃənəlizm] *n.* =**intuitionism.**

in·tu·i·tion·ism [ˌɪntju'ɪʃənɪzm̩; ˌin-tju'iʃənizm] *n.* ①〖倫理〗直覺說。②〖哲學〗直覺主義;直觀主義。

in·tu·i·tive [ɪn'tjuɪtɪv; in'tju(:)itiv] *adj.* ①直覺的;具有直覺的。Are women more *intuitive* than men? 女人較男人更具有直覺嗎? ②由直覺而得的。③可以靠直覺得知的。—**ly,** *adv.* —**ness,** *n.*

in·tu·i·tiv·ism [ɪn'tjuətɪvɪzm̩; in-'tju(:)itivizm] *n.* ①〖倫理〗直覺說。②直觀;直覺力。

in·tu·mes·cence [ˌɪntju'mɛsn̩s; ˌin-tju(:)'mesəns] *n.* ①膨脹;腫大;沸騰。②膨脹物;疙瘩;膨大部;隆起。

in·tu·mes·cent [ˌɪntju'mɛsn̩t; ˌin-tju(:)'mesənt] *adj.* 腫起的;膨脹的。

in·tus·sus·cep·tion [ˌɪntəssə'sɛp-ʃən; ˌintəssə'sepʃən] *n.* ①〖生理〗攝取;營養作用。②〖醫〗腸管鉗入;腸套疊。③(思想等之)吸收;攝取;同化。

in·unc·tion [ɪn'ʌŋkʃən; in'ʌŋkʃən] *n.* ①塗油。②〖醫〗塗油或軟膏。③軟膏。

in·un·date ['ɪnənˌdet; 'inʌndeit] *v.t.,* **-dat·ed, -dat·ing.** 淹沒;氾濫;使充滿。a place *inundated* with visitors. 遊客擁擠的地方。

in·un·da·tion [ˌɪnən'deʃən; ˌinʌn-'deiʃən] *n.* 淹沒;氾濫;洪水。

in·ur·bane [ˌɪnɝ'ben; ˌinə:'bein] *adj.* 粗野的;不禮貌的。—**in·ur·ban·i·ty,** *n.*

in·ure [ɪn'jur; i'njuə] *v.,* **-ured, -ur-ing.** —*v.t.* 鍛鍊;使堅强;使慣於。—*v.i.* ①生效;有效力;適用。②有助益。(亦作 **enure**) —**ment,** *n.*

in·urn [ɪn'ɝn; in'ə:n] *v.t.* ①置(骨灰)於缸內。②埋葬。

in·u·tile [ɪn'jutɪl; in'ju(:)til] *adj.* 無用的;無益的。

in·u·til·i·ty [ˌɪnju'tɪlətɪ; ˌinju(:)'tiliti] *n., pl.* **-ties.** ①無益;無用。②無用之人(物)。

inv. ①invented. ②invention. ③inventor. ④inventory. ⑤invoice.

***in·vade** [ɪn'ved; in'veid] *v.t.,* **-vad·ed, -vad·ing.** ①侵犯;侵略。Soldiers *invaded* the country. 有軍隊侵犯該國。②擁入;强入。My house was *invaded* by a crowd of visitors. 我的屋裏擠滿一羣訪客。③遍布;充滿。④侵害;干擾。to *invade* another person's rights. 侵害他人之權益。—*v.i.* 侵略;侵犯。—**in·vad·er,** *n.*

***in·va·lid**[1] ['ɪnvəlɪd; ˌinvə'li:d, 'invəli:d] *n.* ①病人;殘廢者;病弱者。an asylum for *invalids.* 傷殘療養院。②因傷殘而退役之陸海軍士兵。—*adj.* ①有病的;殘廢的。a home of rest for *invalid* soldiers. 傷(病)兵之休息所。②供殘病者用的。—*v.t.* ①(因殘病而)使退役。②使虛弱;使病;使殘廢。—*v.i.* ①成爲病人或殘廢者。②因傷殘或生病而退役。

in·val·id[2] [ɪn'vælɪd; in'vælid] *adj.* 無效的;作廢的(爲 valid 之對)。—**ly,** *adv.*

in·val·i·date [ɪn'væləˌdet; in'væli-deit] *v.t.,* **-dat·ed, -dat·ing.** 使無效;使無價值;使作廢。—**in·val·i·da·tion,** *n.*

in·va·lid·ism ['ɪnvəlɪdˌɪzəm; 'invəli-dizəm] *n.* 久病;虛弱(之狀態);慢性衰弱病。

in·va·lid·i·ty [ˌɪnvə'lɪdətɪ; ˌinvə'liditi] *n.* ①無效;無力。②=**invalidism.**

***in·val·u·a·ble** [ɪn'væljəbl̩; in'væ-ljuəbl] *adj.* 無價的;價值高到無法衡量的。—**in·val·u·a·bly,** *adv.*

In·var [ɪn'vɑr; in'vɑ:] *n.* 〖商標名〗不變鋼(鎳 36%,鐵 64%之合金,膨脹係數極小)。

in·var·i·a·bil·i·ty [ɪnˌvɛrɪə'bɪlətɪ; inˌvɛəriə'biliti] *n.* 不變;不易;不變性。

in·var·i·a·ble [ɪn'vɛrɪəbl̩; in'vɛəriə-bl] *adj.* ①不變的;不易的。②〖數學〗常數的。—*n.* ①不變的東西。②〖數學〗常數。

***in·var·i·a·bly** [ɪn'vɛrɪəblɪ; in'vɛəriə-bli] *adv.* 不變地;一定地。Spring *invariably* follows winter. 春天一定跟着冬天來。

***in·va·sion** [ɪn'veʒən; in'veiʒən] *n.* 侵犯;侵入;侵害。the *invasion* of an enemy. 敵人之侵犯。

in·va·sive [ɪn'vesɪv; in'veisiv] *adj.* 侵入的;侵略的。*invasive* war. 侵略戰爭。

in·vec·tive [ɪn'vɛktɪv; in'vektiv] *n.* ①痛罵;大罵;猛烈抨擊。speeches filled with *invective.* 帶有猛烈抨擊的言詞。②(*pl.*)咒語;罵人話。—*adj.* 痛斥的;大罵的。

in·veigh [ɪn've; in'vei] *v.i.* 猛烈抨擊;痛罵〖against〗。

in·vei·gle [ɪn'vigl̩; in'vi:gl] *v.t.,* **-gled, -gling.** 誘騙;誘惑;誘陷。

in·vei·gle·ment [ɪn'viglmənt; in-'vi:glmənt] *n.* 誆騙;勾引;籠絡;誘陷;誘惑。

***in·vent** [ɪn'vɛnt; in'vent] *v.t.* ①發明;創作。Who *invented* the steam engine? 誰發明了蒸汽機? ②虛構;杜撰(謊言等)。What explanation (excuse) can we *invent?* 我們能假造出甚麼解釋(辯解)呢? —*v.i.* 創作;創造。

in·vent·er [ɪn'vɛntɚ; in'ventə] *n.* =**inventor.**

***in·ven·tion** [ɪn'vɛnʃən; in'venʃən] *n.* ①發明;發明物。It's a most useful *invention.* 那是一項非常有用的發明。②發明之才;創作能力;虛構杜撰的能力。③虛構的故事。Newspapers are full of *inventions.* 報上充滿編造的故事。

in·ven·tive [ɪn'vɛntɪv; in'ventiv] *adj.* ①有發明才智的;善於創造的。②發明的。③顯示出創造力的。—**ly,** *adv.* —**ness,** *n.*

***in·ven·tor** [ɪn'vɛntɚ; in'ventə] *n.* 發明家;發明者。Edison was a famous *inventor.* 愛迪生是一個著名的發明家。

in·ven·to·ry ['ɪnvənˌtorɪ; 'invəntri] *n., pl.* **-to·ries,** *v.,* **-to·ried, -to·ry·ing.** —*n.* ①詳細目錄;財產目錄;存貨清單。an *inventory* of household furniture. 家具目錄。②清單上開列之貨品;存貨。③任何詳細記載。④存貨之總值。⑤清單目錄等之編製。—*v.t.* 編列詳細目錄;列入詳細目錄;清點存貨。Some stores *inventory* their stock once a month. 有些商店每月清點存貨一次。

in·ve·rac·i·ty 〔ˌɪnvəˈræsətɪ; ˌinvəˈræsiti〕 *n.*, *pl.* **-ties.** 不誠實;虛僞;謊言。

in·ver·ness 〔ˌɪnvəˈnɛs; ˌinvəˈnes〕 *n.* ①一種附有可以卸除之長披肩的外衣。②其披肩。(亦作 **Inverness cape**)

in·verse 〔ɪnˈvɝs; inˈvəːs〕 *adj.*, *n.*, *v.*, **-versed, -vers·ing.** —*adj.* (位置、方向等)倒轉的;逆的;反的。—*n.* ①倒轉狀態。②倒轉之物。③相反之物。Evil is the *inverse* of good. 惡爲善之反。—*v.t.* 使顚倒;使倒轉。—**ly,** *adv.*

in·ver·sion 〔ɪnˈvɝʃən; inˈvəːʃən〕 *n.* ①倒轉;倒置;反轉。②倒轉物; 反轉物; 倒置物。③〖修辭〗倒裝法。④〖數學〗反演變換。⑤〖音樂〗(和音、音程、對位音、主題的)轉回。⑥〖化〗轉化。⑦〖氣象〗海拔愈高溫度愈高之反現象。⑧〖醫〗倒錯。sexual *inversion.* 性慾倒錯;性慾反向。⑨〖電〗由直流轉變爲交流。

in·ver·sive 〔ɪnˈvɝsɪv; inˈvəːsiv〕 *adj.* 顚倒的;逆的;使倒轉的;使轉換的。

in·vert** 〔*v.* ɪnˈvɝt; inˈvəːt *n.* ˈɪnvɝt; ˈinvəːt〕 *v.t.* ①上下顚倒;倒轉。to *invert* a glass. 倒轉酒杯。②前後倒置; 轉換。③〖音樂〗轉回。inverted commas*** (=quotation marks)〖英〗引號(如' '或" "是)。—*n.* ①顚倒之物。②同性戀者。③圖案顚倒印刷之稀有郵票。

in·vert·ase 〔ɪnˈvɝtes; inˈvəːteis〕 *n.* 〖化〗轉化酶。

in·ver·te·brate 〔ɪnˈvɝtəbrɪt; inˈvəːtibrit〕 *adj.* ①無脊椎的;無脊椎動物的。②不堅定的;意志薄弱的。—*n.* ①無脊椎動物。②意志薄弱者。

***in·vest** 〔ɪnˈvɛst; inˈvest〕 *v.t.* ①投(資)。to *invest* one's money in stocks and shares. 投資於股票。②花費。to *invest* large sums in books. 在書籍上花大筆金錢。③籠罩; 包圍。④授權給。⑤(以正式儀式)使就職。⑥充滿某種特點。Goodness *invests* his every action. 他的一舉一動都出諸善意。⑦賦予。⑧使穿着。Spring *invests* the trees with leaves. 春天使樹木長葉子。—*v.i.* ①投資。Learn to *invest* wisely. 學習聰明地投資。②〖俗〗購買。to *invest* in a new hat. 買一頂新帽子。

***in·ves·ti·gate** 〔ɪnˈvɛstəˌget; inˈvestigeit〕 *v.t.* & *v.i.*, **-gat·ed, -gat·ing.** 調查;研究。to *investigate* a crime. 調查犯罪。—**in·ves·ti·ga·tor,** *n.*

***in·ves·ti·ga·tion** 〔ɪnˌvɛstəˈgeʃən; inˌvestiˈgeiʃən〕 *n.* 調查; 研究。the subject under *investigation.* 在調查中之問題。

in·ves·ti·ga·tive 〔ɪnˈvɛstəˌgetɪv; inˈvestigeitiv〕 *adj.* ①調查的;審查的; 研究的。②好研究的; 愛調查的。(亦作 **investigatory**)

in·ves·ti·ture 〔ɪnˈvɛstətʃɚ; inˈvestitʃə〕 *n.* ①敍任;敍爵;敍任式;敍爵式。②被服;遮蓋物。

***in·vest·ment** 〔ɪnˈvɛstmənt; inˈvestmənt〕 *n.* ①投資。By careful *investment* of his capital, he obtained a good income. 因其穩妥之投資, 他獲得了很好的收入。②投入之資本。 wise and profitable *investments.* 穩妥而獲利的投資。③可獲利的東西。④正式就職;正式授權。⑤被覆物;包覆物。⑥圍攻。⑦鐵工廠中做模型用的一種耐火物質。

investment bank 投資銀行。

investment company 投資(信託)公司。

in·ves·tor 〔ɪnˈvɛstɚ; inˈvestə〕 *n.* 投資者。

in·vet·er·a·cy 〔ɪnˈvɛtərəsɪ; inˈvetərəsi〕 *n.*, *pl.* **-cies.** ①(習性等之)根深蒂固;(感情或疾病等之)頑固。②積習;宿怨;痼疾。

in·vet·er·ate 〔ɪnˈvɛtərɪt; inˈvetərit〕 *adj.* ①習慣已深的;成嗜癖的。an *inveterate* smoker. 老煙客。②根深蒂固的; 難改的。—**ly,** *adv.*

in·vid·i·ous 〔ɪnˈvɪdɪəs; inˈvidiəs〕 *adj.* ①招嫉妬的; 惹人惡感的。②易招怨恨的。③分畛域的;分討厭或不平之差別的。—**ly,** *adv.*

in·vig·i·late 〔ɪnˈvɪdʒəˌlet; inˈvidʒileit〕 *v.i.*, **-lat·ed. -lat·ing.** ①〖英〗(筆試場)監考。②監視。

in·vig·or·ate 〔ɪnˈvɪgəˌret; inˈvigəreit〕 *v.t.*, **-at·ed, -at·ing.** 使强壯;鼓舞。Exercise and good books *invigorate* the body and mind. 運動與好書使身心健康。

in·vig·or·at·ing 〔ɪnˈvɪgəˌretɪŋ; inˈvigəreitiŋ〕 *adj.* ①增加精神的; 鼓舞的; 激勵的。②爽快的。

in·vig·or·a·tion 〔ɪnˌvɪgəˈreʃən; inˌvigəˈreiʃən〕 *n.* 鼓舞;激勵。

in·vig·or·a·tive 〔ɪnˈvɪgəˌretɪv; inˈvigəreitiv〕 *adj.* 增加精神的;使身心爽快的;激勵的。

in·vig·or·a·tor 〔ɪnˈvɪgəˌretɚ; inˈvigəreitə〕 *n.* ①增加精神之人(物)。②刺激物;强壯劑。

in·vin·ci·ble 〔ɪnˈvɪnsəbl̩; inˈvinsəbl〕 *adj.* 不可征服的;難以克服的。 an *invincible* army. 所向無敵之軍隊。 —**in·vin·ci·bil·i·ty,** *n.* —**in·vin·ci·bly,** *adv.*

in·vi·o·la·ble 〔ɪnˈvaɪələbl̩; inˈvaiələbl〕 *adj.* ①不可褻瀆的; 神聖的。②無法加以傷害的;無法侵犯的。③無法破壞的。—**in·vi·o·la·bil·i·ty,** *n.* —**in·vi·o·la·bly,** *adv.*

in·vi·o·late 〔ɪnˈvaɪəlɪt; inˈvaiəlit〕 *adj.* 未受侵犯的;未被破壞的;未被褻瀆的。

in·vis·i·bil·i·ty 〔ˌɪnvɪzəˈbɪlətɪ; inˌvizəˈbiliti〕 *n.* 不可見;看不見。

***in·vis·i·ble** 〔ɪnˈvɪzəbl̩; inˈvizəbl〕 *adj.* ①不可見的; 看不見的。 Many stars are *invisible* without a telescope. 許多星辰不用望遠鏡便看不見。②無從覺察的。 *invisible* differences. 無從覺察的區別。③大衆所不知曉的。④無形的。 —*n.* ①看不見的人或物。②(the-)靈界;幽冥世界。③(the I-)上帝。—**in·vis·i·bly,** *adv.*

***in·vi·ta·tion** 〔ˌɪnvəˈteʃən; ˌinviˈteiʃən〕 *n.* ①邀請; 招待。 Thank you for your kind *invitation.* 謝謝你的盛意邀請。②請柬;請帖。to send out *invitations* to a dinner party. 發出宴客請帖。③引誘; 鼓勵。④建議。⑤挑逗;激怒。—*adj.* 〖運動〗邀請的。an *invitation* match. 邀請賽。

‡in·vite 〔*v.* ɪnˈvaɪt; inˈvait *n.* ˈɪnvaɪt; ˈinvait〕 *v.*, **-vit·ed, -vit·ing,** *n.* —*v.t.* ①邀請。 I *invited* him to my house. 我邀請他到我家裏。②請求; 懇請。 He *invited* our opinion of his work. 他請求我們對他的工作表示意見。③招致; 引起。 The letter *invited* some question. 這信引起了某種問題。④引誘;誘惑。The cool water of the lake *invited* us to swim. 清涼的湖水引起我們游泳的興趣。 —*v.i.* ①邀請。②引誘。—*n.* 〖俗〗=**invitation.**

in·vit·ing 〔ɪnˈvaɪtɪŋ; inˈvaitiŋ〕 *adj.* 誘惑人的; 動人心目的。an *inviting* spot. 引人入勝的地點。

in·vo·ca·tion 〔ˌɪnvəˈkeʃən; ˌinvou-

ˈkeiʃən] *n.* ①祈禱。②(以法術)召鬼。③召鬼所念之咒語。

in·voc·a·to·ry [ɪnˈvɑkəˌtorɪ; inˈvɔkətəri] *adj.* 求神救助的。

in·voice [ˈɪnvɔɪs; ˈinvɔis] *n., v.,* **-voiced, -voic·ing.** —*n.* 〖商〗①發票;發貨單。②發票上所列之貨物。—*v.t.* ①開發票;開列帳單。②開發票給。

in·voke [ɪnˈvok; inˈvouk] *v.t.,* **-voked, -vok·ing.** ①求(神)保護、賜福、啓示、幫助等;祈求;求助於。②懇求;乞求;迫切地需求。③以法術召(鬼)。

in·vo·lu·cre [ˈɪnvəˌlukɚ; ˈinvəluːkə] *n.* ①〖解剖〗皮膜;外膜。②〖植物〗總苞。

in·vol·un·tar·y [ɪnˈvɑlənˌtɛrɪ; inˈvɔləntəri] *adj.* ①非本意的;非由己意的。②無意的;無心的。*involuntary* homicide. 過失殺人。③不隨意的;本能的。Breathing is mainly *involuntary*. 呼吸大抵是自然而然的。 —**in·vol·un·tar·i·ly,** *adv.*

in·vo·lute [ˈɪnvəˌljut; ˈinvəluːt] *adj.* ①紛亂的;複雜的。②〖植物〗(葉等)內捲的;內旋的。③〖動物〗捲成螺狀的;回旋的。—*n.* 〖幾何〗漸伸線;漸開線。

in·vo·lu·tion [ˌɪnvəˈluʃən; ˌinvəˈluːʃən] *n.* ①捲入;包入。②捲入(包入)之物。③複雜;錯亂。④〖文法〗複雜句。⑤〖數學〗冪方;乘方;乘法。⑥〖生物〗退化(爲 evolution 之對)。⑦〖醫〗(產後子宮等之)退縮;子宮內轉。⑧復舊。

***in·volve** [ɪnˈvɑlv; inˈvɔlv] *v.t.,* **-volved, -volv·ing.** ①包括。Housekeeping *involves* cooking, washing dishes, sweeping, and cleaning. 家務包括烹飪、洗碟、打掃及洗刷。②影響;牽涉;拖累。③使陷於。One foolish mistake can *involve* you in a good deal of trouble. 一次愚昧的錯誤可使你陷於極大的麻煩。④使糾纏;使變複雜。A sentence that is *involved* is hard to understand. 複雜的句子難懂。⑤潛心於;專心於。⑥包圍;包裹。Clouds *involved* the hilltop. 雲繞山巔。⑦盤繞;包;捲;纏。⑧〖數學〗自乘;乘方。to *involve* (a number) to the fifth power. (把某數)乘五次方。

in·volve·ment [ɪnˈvɑlvmənt; inˈvɔlvmənt] *n.* ①捲入;連累;帶累。②(事務的)紛繁;爲難;(財政)困難。③包含;含蓄。

in·vul·ner·a·bil·i·ty [ˌɪnvʌlnərəˈbɪlətɪ; inˌvʌlnərəˈbiliti] *n.* 不能傷害;刀鎗不入;不能攻破;無懈可擊。

in·vul·ner·a·ble [ɪnˈvʌlnərəbḷ; inˈvʌlnərəbl] *adj.* ①不能傷害的。Achilles was *invulnerable* except for his heel. Achilles 除了脚踵部分外,是不會受傷害的。②無懈可擊的。

***in·ward** [ˈɪnwɚd; ˈinwəd] *adj.* ①內在的;內心的(爲outward之對)。*inward* happiness. 精神的快樂。②向內的;向中心的。an *inward* curve. 向內的弧線。③內陸的。④本來具有的。⑤體內的。⑥祕密的;隱私的。⑦(聲音等之)不清楚的。⑧精神上的。—*adv.* =**inwards.**

in·ward·ly [ˈɪnwɚdlɪ; ˈinwədli] *adv.* ①在內;在內部。②向內地。③內心方面(爲 outwardly 之對)。④暗自地;小聲地。

in·ward·ness [ˈɪnwɚdnɪs; ˈinwədnis] *n.* ①本質;眞義。②心性;靈性。③誠意。

in·wards [ˈɪnwɚdz; ˈinwədz] *adv.* ①向內地;向內部地(爲 outwards 之對)。②向內心地;向心靈地。—*n. pl.* 〖俗〗①內部;內臟。②〖英〗進口貨或進口稅。

in·weave [ɪnˈwiv; ˈinˈwiːv] *v.t.,* **in·wove** or **in·weaved, in·wo·ven** or **in·wove** or **in·weaved, in·weav·ing.** 織進;交織;織成。

in·wrought [ɪnˈrɔt; ˈinˈrɔːt] *adj.* ①(花型、圖案等)織入的;繡入的。②(織物等)繡有(花型)的。③密合的;混淆的。

I/O input/output. 〖電腦〗輸入或輸出。

Io 化學元素 ionium 之符號。

IOC International Olympic Committee.

i·o·did [ˈaɪədɪd; ˈaiədid] *n.* 〖化〗=**iodide.**

i·o·dide [ˈaɪəˌdaɪd; ˈaiədaid] *n.* 〖化〗碘化物。

i·o·din [ˈaɪədɪn; ˈaiədin] *n.* 〖化〗=**iodine.**

i·o·dine [ˈaɪəˌdaɪn; ˈaiədiːn] *n.* ①〖化〗碘。②酒碘。*tincture of iodine* 碘劑;碘酒。

i·o·dize [ˈaɪəˌdaɪz; ˈaiədaiz] *v.t.,* **-dized, -diz·ing.** 以碘處理;加碘於…。

i·o·do·form [aɪˈodəˌfɔrm; aiˈɔdəfɔːm] *n.* 〖化〗三碘化甲烷 (CHI_3)。

i·on [ˈaɪən; ˈaiən] *n.* 〖物理〗離子;游子。

-ion 〖字尾〗由拉丁系動詞作成表"動作;狀態"或"人;物"等之名詞,如:fashion, inflation, mission, question, region.

I·o·ni·a [aɪˈonɪə; aiˈounjə] *n.* 愛奧尼亞(小亞細亞海岸古地名,包括附近諸島嶼)。

I·o·ni·an [aɪˈonɪən; aiˈounjən] *adj.* ①愛奧尼亞(人)的。②〖建築〗愛奧尼亞式的。—*n.* 愛奧尼亞人。

I·on·ic [aɪˈɑnɪk; aiˈɔnik] *adj.* ①Ionia (人)的。②〖建築〗Ionia 式的(其特徵爲柱頭帶渦卷形裝飾)。③〖韻律〗Ionia 音步的。④Ionia 語的。—*n.* ①Ionia 語。②Ionia音步;以此寫成之詩。③(i-)〖印刷〗一種活字體。

i·on·ic [aɪˈɑnɪk; aiˈɔnik] *adj.* 〖物理〗離子的;含離子的。

i·o·ni·um [aɪˈonɪəm; aiˈouniəm] *n.* 〖化〗鐖(放射性釷的同位素,符號 Io)。

i·on·i·za·tion [ˌaɪənəˈzeʃən; ˌaiənaiˈzeiʃən] *n.* 〖物理〗離子化;電離。

i·on·ize [ˈaɪənˌaɪz; ˈaiənaiz] *v.t.* & *v.i.,* **-ized, -iz·ing.** (使)分解成離子;電離。

i·on·o·sphere [aɪˈɑnəˌsfɪr; aiˈɔnəsfiə] *n.* 〖物理〗①電離層(大氣層之一部分,位於地球上空約25英里處,中含自由電荷質點,能反射無線電波)。②電離圈(電離層之圈)。

i·o·ta [aɪˈotə; aiˈoutə] *n.* ①希臘字母的第九個字母(I, ι)。②些微;一點。

I.O.U., IOU 借據(尤指非正式之借據,源出 I owe you. 我欠你;玆借到)。*IOU* $50. John Smith. 玆借到五十元。約翰史密斯(簽名)。

I·o·wa [ˈaɪəwə; ˈaiouə] *n.* ①愛阿華(美國中西部之一州,首府 Des Moines)。②愛阿華河(自 Iowa 北境流入 Mississippi 河)。

IPA, I.P.A. ①International Phonetic Alphabet. ②International Phonetic Association. ③International Press Association.

ip·e·cac [ˈɪpɪˌkæk; ˈipikæk] *n.* =**ipecacuanha.**

ip·e·cac·u·an·ha [ˌɪpɪˌkækjuˈænə; ˌipikækjuˈænə] *n.* ①吐根樹。②〖藥〗吐根(吐劑或瀉劑)。

I.P.R. Institute of Pacific Relations.

IQ, I.Q. intelligence quotient. 智商。

i.q. idem quod (拉=the same as).

Ir Irish. **Ir** 化學元素 iridium 之符號。

ir- 〖字首〗=**in-** (用於以 r 開始之字)。

i·ra·de [ɪˈrɑdɪ; iːˈrɑːdi] *n.* 土耳其皇帝或回教國王之勅令。

I·rak [i'rɑk; i'rɑːk] *n.* =**Iraq.**

I·ran [aɪ'ræn, i'rɑn; i'rɑːn] *n.* 伊朗(國名,位於亞洲西南部,首都德黑蘭 Teheran).

I·ra·ni·an [aɪ'renɪən; i'reinjən] *adj.* 伊朗的; 伊朗人的; 伊朗語系的。—*n.* 伊朗人; 伊朗語。

I·raq [i'rɑk; i'rɑːk] *n.* 伊拉克 (國名,位於亞洲西南部,阿拉伯半島之北端,首都巴格達 Bagdad). (亦作 **Irak**)

I·ra·qi [ɪ'rɑkɪ; i'rɑːki] *n., pl.* **-qis,** *adj.* —*n.* ①伊拉克人。②伊拉克語。—*adj.* 伊拉克的;伊拉克人或其語言的。(亦作 **Iraki**)

i·ras·ci·ble [aɪ'ræsəbl̩; i'ræsibl] *adj.* ①易怒的;暴躁的。②發怒的;有怒容的。—**i·ras·ci·bil·i·ty,** *n.*

i·rate ['aɪret; ai'reit] *adj.* 發怒的;生氣的。—**ly,** *adv.*

IRBM, I.R.B.M. Intermediate Range Ballistic Missile. 中程彈道飛彈。

IRC ① International Red Cross. 國際紅十字會。 ② International Rescue Committee.

ire [aɪr; 'aiə] *n.* 忿怒; 怒氣。

Ire. Ireland.

ire·ful ['aɪrfəl; 'aiəful] *adj.* 忿怒的;發怒的。

***Ire·land** ['aɪrlənd; 'aiələnd] *n.* 愛爾蘭 (不列顛羣島中之一島, 分爲北愛爾蘭 Northern Ireland 及愛爾蘭自由邦 Irish Free State, 北愛爾蘭爲不列顛聯合王國之一部,首府爲 Belfast,愛爾蘭自由邦自 1922年爲獨立國, 1949 年成爲愛爾蘭共和國 Republic of Ireland, 首都都伯林 Dublin).

I·re·ne[1] [aɪ'rini; ai'riːni] *n.* 〖希臘神話〗和平之女神(Zeus 與 Themis 之女)。

I·re·ne[2] [aɪ'rin; ai'riːni, ai'riːn] *n.* 女子名。(亦作 **Irena, Irina**)

i·re·nic [aɪ'rɛnɪk; ai'riːnik] *adj.* 和平的; 促進和平的。

i·re·ni·cal [aɪ'rɛnɪkl̩; ai'riːnikəl] *adj.* =**irenic.**

i·ren·i·con [aɪ'rɛnɪkɑn; ai'riːnikɔn] *n.* =**eirenicon.**

i·ri·da·ceous [ˌaɪrɪ'deʃəs; ˌaiəri'deiʃəs] *adj.* 〖植物〗鳶尾科的。

ir·i·des·cent [ˌɪrə'dɛsn̩t; ˌiri'desnt] *adj.* 呈虹色的; 現暈光的。—*n.* 虹色的衣料或其他物質。—**ir·i·des·cence,** *n.*

i·rid·i·um [aɪ'rɪdɪəm; ai'ridiəm] *n.* 〖化〗銥(金屬元素, 符號爲 Ir)。

***i·ris** ['aɪrɪs; 'aiəris] *n., pl.* **-es, ir·i·des** ['aɪrɪˌdiz; 'airidiːz]. ①(眼球的)虹膜。②鳶尾屬植物;其花。③(I-)〖希臘神話〗彩虹之女神。

***I·rish** ['aɪrɪʃ; 'aiəriʃ] *adj.* 愛爾蘭的; 愛爾蘭人的; 愛爾蘭語的。 —*n.* ①愛爾蘭人。②愛爾蘭語。③愛爾蘭人所講的英語。〖注意〗Irish 指全體愛爾蘭人,作複數解。The *Irish* are hospitable. 愛爾蘭人均好客。一個愛爾蘭人稱 Irishman.

I·rish·er ['aɪrɪʃɚ; 'aiəriʃə] *n.* 愛爾蘭人;愛爾蘭系的人。

I·rish·ism ['aɪrɪʃɪzm̩; 'aiəriʃizəm] *n.* 愛爾蘭習俗; 愛爾蘭語特色。(亦作 **Iricism**)

I·rish·man ['aɪrɪʃmən; 'aiəriʃmən] *n., pl.* **-men.** 愛爾蘭人。

I·rish·wom·an ['aɪrɪʃˌwumən; 'aiəriʃˌwumən] *n., pl.* **-wom·en.** 愛爾蘭女人。

i·ri·tis [aɪ'raɪtɪs; aiə'raitis] *n.* 〖醫〗虹膜炎。

irk [ɝk; əːk] *v.t.* 令厭煩; 使苦惱。

irk·some ['ɝksəm; 'əːksəm] *adj.* 令人厭煩的;令人苦惱的。

IRO, I.R.O. International Refugee Organization.

‡**i·ron** ['aɪən; 'aiən] *n.* ①鐵。②鐵器。③熨斗。④ (*pl.*) 鐐銬。 to put a man in *irons.* 加以鐐銬。⑤(鐵似的)毅力; 堅定不移的意志。men of *iron.* 鐵漢; 意志堅強的人; 無情漢。⑥〖高爾夫〗鐵頭球棒。⑦〖俚〗手槍。⑧烙鐵。⑨魚叉。⑩含鐵質之補藥。⑪鉋刃。 ***as hard as iron*** 堅似鐵的。 ***cast iron*** 鑄鐵。 ***have too many irons in the fire*** 同時要辦的事務太多; 經營的事業過多。 ***irons in the fire*** 待辦之事; 工作。 ***pig iron*** 鑄鐵; 銑鐵。 ***rule with a rod of iron*** (or ***with an iron hand***) 行苛政;施高壓政策。 ***strike while the iron is hot*** 打鐵趁熱; 趁好機會。 ***wrought iron*** 鍛鐵。—*adj.* ①鐵製的。 *iron* gates. 鐵門。②似鐵的; 堅強的。 an *iron* will. 不屈的意志。③苛刻的; 殘酷的。 ***the iron hand of fate*** 命運之鐵腕。 —*v.t.* ①熨燙 (衣服等)。 to *iron* a shirt. 燙襯衫。②裝以鐵; 用鐵鋪蓋。—*v.i.* 燙衣服。 ***iron out*** 〖俗〗**a.** 燙衣服。**b.** 燙衣服將縐紋除去。**c.** 消除 (困難、歧見等)。The problem should have been *ironed out* months ago. 這問題幾個月前就該解決的。

Iron Age ①〖考古〗鐵器時代(繼 Stone Age, Bronze Age 之時代)。② (i- a-) 〖希臘神話〗黑鐵時代(繼 golden age, silver age 及 bronze age 之世界最後而最墮落、最黑暗的時代)。

i·ron·bound ['aɪənˌbaund; 'aiənbaund] *adj.* ①鐵封的;鐵包的。②堅固的;不可變動的。③爲懸崖峭壁所封的;險阻的。

i·ron·clad ['aɪən'klæd; 'aiənklæd] *adj.* ①裝有鐵甲的; 裝甲的。②嚴格的; 硬性的。—*n.* 裝甲艦(十九世紀中葉與末年使用之舊式木造裝甲艦)。

iron curtain 鐵幕 (指共黨國家似與外界有一鐵幕相隔)。

i·ron·er ['aɪənɚ; 'aiənə] *n.* 作熨燙的人或物。

i·ron·fist·ed ['aɪən'fɪstɪd; 'aiən'fistid] *adj.* ①無情的。②吝嗇的。

i·ron-found·ry ['aɪənˌfaundrɪ; 'aiənˌfaundri] *n.* 鑄鐵所; 製鐵所。

i·ron-gray, i·ron-grey ['aɪən'gre; 'aiən'grei] *adj.* 鐵灰色的。

iron hand 鐵腕(喻堅強嚴厲的手段)。

i·ron·hand·ed ['aɪən'hændɪd; 'aiən'hændid] *adj.* 鐵腕的;嚴厲的。 —**ly,** *adv.* —**ness,** *n.*

i·ron-heart·ed ['aɪən'hɑrtɪd; 'aiən'hɑːtid] *adj.* 鐵石心腸的。

iron horse 〖俗〗①機關車;火車頭。②腳踏車;三輪車。

i·ron·ic [aɪ'rɑnɪk; ai'rɔnik] *adj.* = **ironical.**

i·ron·i·cal [aɪ'rɑnɪkl̩; ai'rɔnikəl] *adj.* ①(用反語以)譏諷的; 幽默的。②反常的; 出乎意料的。③愛用反語的。—**ly,** *adv.*

i·ron·ing ['aɪənɪŋ; 'aiəniŋ] *n.* ①熨平。②〖俗〗已熨平或待熨之衣服。

ironing board 熨衣板。

i·ro·nist ['aɪrənɪst; 'airənist] *n.* 用反語者;諷刺家。

iron lung 鐵肺 (一種人工呼吸儀器)。

i·ron·mas·ter ['aɪənˌmæstɚ; 'aiənˌmɑːstə] *n.* 鐵工廠廠長;製鐵業者。

iron mo(u)ld 鐵銹痕;墨跡。

i·ron-mo(u)ld ['aɪənˌmold; 'aiənmould] *v.t.* & *v.i.* 沾到銹痕或墨跡。

i·ron·mon·ger ['aɪənˌmʌŋgɚ; 'aiənˌmʌŋgə] *n.* 〖英〗五金商;鐵器商。

i·ron·mon·ger·y ['aɪənˌmʌŋgərɪ; 'aiənˌmʌŋgəri] *n., pl.* **-ger·ies.** 〖英〗①鐵器類。②鐵器店;五金店。③鐵器業。

iron ration 野戰口糧。
i·ron·side ['aɪən,saɪd; 'aiən-said] *n.* ①剛毅果決之人。②(I-) 英王 Edmund 二世之綽號。③(I-)(*pl.*) a. (作 *sing.* 解) Oliver Cromwell 之綽號。b. (Oliver Cromwell 所屬之)鐵騎兵(團)。④(*pl.*)(作 *sing.* 解)裝甲軍艦。
i·ron·smith ['aɪən,smɪθ; 'aiənsmiθ] *n.* 鐵匠；鐵工。
i·ron·stone ['aɪən,ston; 'aiən-stoun] 「*n.*鐵礦石；鐵礦。」
i·ron·ware ['aɪən,wɛr; 'aiənwɛə] *n.* 鐵器；五金。
i·ron·weed ['aɪən,wid; 'aiənwi:d] 「*n.*〖植物〗紫菀屬之草。」
i·ron-willed ['aɪən,wɪld; 'aiənwild] *n.* 意志堅强的。
i·ron·wood ['aɪən,wud; 'aiənwud] *n.* 各種木質極爲堅實之樹；其木材。
i·ron·work ['aɪən,wɝk; 'aiənwə:k] *n.* 鐵製之物。
i·ron·work·er ['aɪən,wɝkə; 'aiən,wə:kə] *n.* ①鐵匠。②(造橋等之)鋼架工匠。
i·ron·works ['aɪən,wɝks; 'aiənwə:ks] *n. pl.* or *sing.* 鐵工廠；鍊鐵廠。
i·ron·y[1] ['aɪənɪ; 'aiəni] *adj.* 鐵的；含鐵的；似鐵的。
i·ro·ny**[2] ['aɪrənɪ; 'aiərəni] *n., pl.* **-nies.** ①〖修辭〗反語法(例如某人做了一件極愚的事，而你却反說"How clever!" "多聰明啊！")。②嘲弄；諷刺；反常之事；出乎意料之事。It was the *irony* of fate that the great cancer doctor died of cancer himself. 偉大的癌症醫師自己死於癌症，乃是命運的嘲弄。③裝傻。Socratic irony*** 假裝愚昧而使對方困惑；裝傻愚弄對方。
Ir·o·quoi·an [,ɪrə'kwɔɪən; ,irə'kwɔiən] *adj.* Iroquois 人的；Iroquois 語的。—*n.* Iroquois 人；Iroquois 語(集合稱)。
Ir·o·quois ['ɪrə,kwɔɪ; 'irəkwɔi] *n. pl.* or *sing.* 依洛郭亦族之人(昔居住於 New York 州之北美印第安人之一族，性强悍好戰，文化程度頗高)。—*adj.* 該族之人的；其部落的。
ir·ra·di·ance [ɪ'redɪəns; i'reidiəns] *n.* ①發光；光輝；燦爛。②〖物理〗光滲；照光；輻照。(亦作 **irradiation, irradiancy**)
ir·ra·di·ant [ɪ'redɪənt; i'reidiənt] *adj.* 發光的；照耀的；燦爛的。
ir·ra·di·ate [ɪ'redɪ,et; i'reidieit] *v.,* **-at·ed, -at·ing.** —*v.t.* ①照射；照耀；發出；射出。②啓發；啓迪。③使發光；使生輝。④用紫外線或放射線處理。—*v.i.* 發光；照耀。—*adj.* 光亮的；發光的。
ir·ra·di·a·tion [ɪ,redɪ'eʃən; i,reidi'eiʃən] *n.* ①發光；照射。②光；光線。③頴悟；領悟；啓迪。④〖光學〗光滲；眩視(在黑暗背景前，發光體顯得較實物爲大之現象)。
ir·ra·tion·al [ɪ'ræʃənḷ; i'ræʃənl] *adj.* ①不合理的；無理性的。②愚蠢的；愚妄的。It is *irrational* to be afraid of the number 13. 怕13這個數字是愚笨的。③〖數學〗無理的。—*n.*〖數學〗無理數。—**ly,** *adv.* —**ness,** *n.*
ir·ra·tion·al·i·ty [ɪ,ræʃə'nælətɪ; i,ræʃə'næliti] *n., pl.* **-ties.** ①不合理；無理性；不明理；無知。②不合理之事。
ir·ra·tion·al·ize [ɪ'ræʃənḷ,aɪz; i'ræʃənlaiz] *v.t.,* **-ized, -iz·ing.** 使失去理性；使不合理。
ir·re·claim·a·ble [,ɪrɪ'kleməbḷ; ,iri'kleiməbl] *adj.* 不能收回的；不能回復的；不能矯正的；不能開墾的。
ir·rec·on·cil·a·ble [ɪ'rɛkən,saɪləbḷ; i'rekənsailəbl] *adj.* ①不能和解的；不能妥協的。②不能相容的；矛盾的。—*n.* ①(政治上的)不妥協者。②(*pl.*)衝突的觀念、信仰等。—**ir·rec·on·cil·a·bil·i·ty,** *n.*
ir·re·cov·er·a·ble [,ɪrɪ'kʌvərəbḷ; ,iri'kʌvərəbl] *adj.* ①不能挽回的。②不能治療的；不能補救的。③收不回來的。
ir·re·cu·sa·ble [,ɪrɪ'kjuzəbḷ; ,iri'kju:zəbl] *adj.* 無法反對的；無法拒絕的。
ir·re·deem·a·ble [,ɪrɪ'diməbḷ; ,iri'di:məbl] *adj.* ①不能收回的(政府公債等)。②不能兌現的(紙幣)。③不能挽救的；不能恢復的。
ir·re·den·tism [,ɪrɪ'dɛntɪzṃ; ,iri'dentizəm] *n.* ①(I-)義大利民族統一主義。②民族統一主義。
ir·re·den·tist [,ɪrɪ'dɛntɪst; ,iri'dentist] *n.* ①(I-) 義大利民族統一黨員(1878年創立之義大利一政黨之黨員，該黨主張將使用義大利語而由外人統治之區域併合於義大利)。②民族統一派之人。—*adj.* 民族統一黨的；民族統一主義的。
ir·re·duc·i·ble [,ɪrɪ'djusəbḷ; ,iri'dju:səbl] *adj.* ①不能減縮的。②難歸復於(所期望的狀態等)的。
ir·ref·ra·ga·ble [ɪ'rɛfrəgəbḷ; i'refrəgəbl] *adj.* 不可辯駁的；無爭論之餘地的；不可否認的；頑梗的。
ir·re·fran·gi·ble [,ɪrɪ'frændʒəbḷ; ,iri'frændʒəbl] *adj.* ①不可違反的(法律等)。②〖光學〗不可屈折的。
ir·ref·u·ta·bil·i·ty [ɪ,rɛfjutə'bɪlətɪ; i,refjutə'biliti] *n.* 不能反駁；不能爭辯。
ir·ref·u·ta·ble [ɪ'rɛfjutəbḷ; i'refjutəbl] *adj.* 不能反駁的；不能辯駁的。
irreg. ①irregular. ②irregularly.
***ir·reg·u·lar** [ɪ'rɛgjələ; i'regjulə, 'i'r-] *adj.* ①不規則的；不合常規的。*irregular* troops. 非正規軍。②不整齊的；不一致的；不平坦的。a coast with an *irregular* outline. 不整齊之海岸線。③〖文法〗變化不規則的(動詞等)。④不合法的；不合道德的。*irregular* behavior. 不合乎道德的行爲。⑤不合規格的。—*n.* ①非正規軍；游擊隊。②不合規格之物品。—**ly,** *adv.*
ir·reg·u·lar·i·ty [,ɪrɛgjə'lærətɪ; i,regju'læriti] *n., pl.* **-ties.** ①不規則；不均勻；不對稱。②違法；不道德。③不規則之事物或變化；違法行爲。④不合規格之事物。
ir·rel·a·tive [ɪ'rɛlətɪv; i'relətiv] *adj.* ①無(親戚)關係的。②不適當的；不切題的。
ir·rel·e·vance [ɪ'rɛləvəns; i'relivəns] *n.* ①無關聯；離題。②無關聯的事物。
ir·rel·e·van·cy [ɪ'rɛləvənsɪ; i'relivənsi] *n., pl.* **-cies.** =**irrelevance.**
ir·rel·e·vant [ɪ'rɛləvənt; i'relivənt] *adj.* ①不相關的；離題的。②〖法律〗與本案無關的(證據)。
ir·re·li·gion [,ɪrɪ'lɪdʒən; ,iri'lidʒən] *n.* 無宗教；無信仰；反宗教。
ir·re·li·gious [,ɪrɪ'lɪdʒəs; ,iri'lidʒəs] *adj.* ①無宗教的；無宗教信仰的。②反宗教的；不敬神的。
ir·re·me·di·a·ble [,ɪrɪ'midɪəbḷ; ,iri'mi:diəbl] *adj.* 不能補救的；無可救藥的。
ir·re·mov·a·ble [,ɪrɪ'muvəbḷ; ,iri'mu:vəbl] *adj.* 不能移動的；不能除去的；不能撤免的。
ir·rep·a·ra·ble [ɪ'rɛpərəbḷ; i'repərəbl] *adj.* ①不能修補的。②不能挽回的。—**ir·rep-**

a·ra·bly, *adv.*

ir·re·pa·tri·a·ble 〔ˌɪrɪˈpetrɪəbl̩; ˌiriˈpætriəbl〕 *n.* (因政治理由)不能遣還故國者。

ir·re·place·a·ble 〔ˌɪrɪˈplesəbl̩; ˌiriˈpleisəbl〕 *adj.* 不能替換的; 不能代替的。

ir·re·press·i·ble 〔ˌɪrɪˈprɛsəbl̩; ˌiriˈpresəbl〕 *adj.* 不能壓服的; 不能抑制的。—**ir·re·press·i·bil·i·ty,** *n.* —**ir·re·press·i·bly,** *adv.*

ir·re·proach·a·ble 〔ˌɪrɪˈprotʃəbl̩; ˌiriˈproutʃəbl〕 *adj.* 無可責難的; 無過失的。—**ir·re·proach·a·bly,** *adv.*

ir·re·sist·i·bil·i·ty 〔ˌɪrɪˌzɪstəˈbɪlətɪ; ˈiriˌzistəˈbiliti〕 *n.* 不可抵抗;不可壓制; 不可反駁。

***ir·re·sist·i·ble** 〔ˌɪrɪˈzɪstəbl̩, ˌɪrrɪ–; ˌiriˈzistəbl, ˈiriˈz–, –tib–〕 *adj.* ①不可抵抗的。②不能壓制的。③極為誘惑人的。④不能反駁的。—**ir·re·sist·i·bly,** *adv.*

ir·res·o·lu·ble 〔ɪˈrɛzəljəbl̩; iˈrezəljubl〕 *adj.* 無法解決或解釋的。

ir·res·o·lute 〔ɪˈrɛzəˌlut; iˈrezəluːt〕 *adj.* 無決斷的;猶豫不決的。

ir·res·o·lu·tion 〔ˌɪrɛzəˈluʃən; iˌrezəˈluːʃən〕 *n.* 優柔寡斷; 躊躇不定。

ir·re·solv·a·ble 〔ˌɪrɪˈzɑlvəbl̩; ˌiriˈzɔlvəbl〕 *adj.* ①不可分解 (分離、分析)的。②不能解決的。

ir·re·spec·tive 〔ˌɪrɪˈspɛktɪv; ˌirisˈpektiv〕 *adj.* 不顧的;不論的;不拘的。

ir·re·spon·si·bil·i·ty 〔ˌɪrɪˌspɑnsəˈbɪlətɪ; ˈirisˌpɔnsəˈbiliti〕 *n.* ①不負責任; 無責任。②無責任感。

ir·re·spon·si·ble 〔ˌɪrɪˈspɑnsəbl̩; ˌirisˈpɔnsəbl〕*adj.* ①不須負責任的;無責任感的。*irresponsible* behavior. 無責任感的行爲。

ir·re·spon·sive 〔ˌɪrɪˈspɑnsɪv; ˌirisˈpɔnsiv〕 *adj.* 無反應的;不起感應的〖to〗.

ir·re·ten·tion 〔ˌɪrɪˈtɛnʃən; ˌiriˈtenʃən〕 *n.* 不能保持;無保持力;不能牢記。

ir·re·ten·tive 〔ˌɪrɪˈtɛntɪv; ˌiriˈtentiv〕 *adj.* 不能保持的; 無保持力的; 無記憶力的。

ir·re·trace·a·ble 〔ˌɪrɪˈtresəbl̩; ˌiriˈtreisəbl〕 *adj.* 不能復原的; 不可挽回的; 不可探源的;不可回顧的。

ir·re·triev·a·ble 〔ˌɪrɪˈtrivəbl̩; ˌiriˈtriːvəbl〕 *adj.* 不能恢復的; 不能復原的; 不能補救的。—**ir·re·triev·a·bly,** *adv.*

ir·rev·er·ence 〔ɪˈrɛvərəns;iˈrevərəns〕 *n.* ①不恭;不敬。②不敬的言行。③不受尊敬。

ir·rev·er·ent 〔ɪˈrɛvərənt; iˈrevərənt〕 *adj.* 不敬的;不恭的。—**ly,** *adv.*

ir·re·vers·i·ble 〔ˌɪrɪˈvɝsəbl̩;ˌiriˈvəːsəbl〕 *adj.* ①不能倒逆的;不能反轉的。②不能取消的;不能變更的。—**ir·re·vers·i·bil·i·ty,** *n.*

ir·rev·o·ca·ble 〔ɪˈrɛvəkəbl̩; iˈrevəkəbl〕 *adj.* ①不能撤回的; 不能取消的; 最後的。②不能喚回的。*irrevocable* yesterday. 不能喚回的昨天。—**ir·rev·o·ca·bil·i·ty,** *n.* —**ir·rev·o·ca·bly,** *adv.*

ir·ri·ga·ble 〔ˈɪrɪgəbl̩; ˈirigəbl〕 *adj.* 可灌溉的(土地等)。

ir·ri·gate 〔ˈɪrəˌget; ˈirigeit〕 *v.,* **-gat·ed, -gat·ing.** —*v.t.* ①灌溉 (農田等)。②〖醫〗注洗;沖洗(傷口等)。③使潮濕。 —*v.i.* ①灌溉農田。②沖洗傷口。

***ir·ri·ga·tion** 〔ˌɪrəˈgeʃən; ˌiriˈgeiʃən〕 *n.* ①灌溉。②〖醫〗注洗術;沖洗。

ir·ri·ga·tor 〔ˈɪrəˌgetɚ; ˈirigeitə〕 *n.* ①灌溉者;水車。②〖外科〗灌注器;注洗器。

ir·ri·ta·bil·i·ty 〔ˌɪrətəˈbɪlətɪ; ˌiritəˈbiliti〕 *n., pl.* **-ties.** ①易怒; 不能忍耐; 暴躁。②過敏反應;腫痛;發炎。③〖生物〗刺激感受性;激應性。

ir·ri·ta·ble 〔ˈɪrətəbl̩; ˈiritəbl〕 *adj.* ①易怒的;性急的。②過敏的。③易感受刺激的。—**ir·ri·ta·bly,** *adv.*

ir·ri·tan·cy 〔ˈɪrətənsɪ; ˈiritənsi〕 *n., pl.* **-cies.** ①煩悶;發怒;懊惱。②使煩悶之事物;刺激;刺激物。

ir·ri·tant 〔ˈɪrətənt; ˈiritənt〕 *adj.* 有刺激性的。—*n.* 刺激物;刺激劑。

***ir·ri·tate** 〔ˈɪrəˌtet; ˈiriteit〕 *v.,* **-tat·ed, -tat·ing.** —*v.t.* ①激怒;擾。Flies *irritate* horses. 蒼蠅擾馬。②使感不適;使過敏。The thick smoke *irritated* my eyes. 濃煙使我的眼睛感覺不適。③刺激。—*v.i.* 使發怒;使發脾氣。

ir·ri·tat·ed 〔ˈɪrəˌtetɪd; ˈiriteitid〕 *adj.* ①發怒的;不耐煩的。②(身體之某部分) 受刺激而不適的。

ir·ri·tat·ing 〔ˈɪrəˌtetɪŋ; ˈiriteitiŋ〕 *adj.* 刺激的;使憤怒的;氣人的;惱人的。an *irritating* reply. 氣人的回答。

***ir·ri·ta·tion** 〔ˌɪrəˈteʃən; ˌiriˈteiʃən〕 *n.* ①刺激;激怒;觸怒。②發怒;苦惱;煩躁。③〖生理,醫〗刺激;興奮;反應過敏。muscular *irritation* causing contraction. 使發生收縮作用之筋肉刺激。④刺激物;令人煩惱之事物。

ir·ri·ta·tive 〔ˈɪrəˌtetɪv; ˈiriteitiv〕 *adj.* ①刺激性的。②〖醫〗由刺激所引起的;刺激的。

ir·rupt 〔ɪˈrʌpt; iˈrʌpt〕 *v.i.* ①突然衝入。②(一羣人)突然從事於暴力行爲。③動物之因死亡率降低而突然增加。

ir·rup·tion 〔ɪˈrʌpʃən; iˈrʌpʃən〕 *n.* 「入侵;入寇。」

ir·rup·tive 〔ɪˈrʌptɪv; iˈrʌptiv〕 *adj.* ①突入的;衝入的;侵入的。②〖地質〗穿入的。

Ir·ving 〔ˈɝvɪŋ; ˈəːviŋ〕 *n.* 歐文 (Washington, 1783–1859, 美國散文家、小說家及歷史家)。

‡is 〔ɪz, z, s, ; iz, z, s〕 *v.* be 的第三人稱, 單數, 現在, 直說法。 ***as is*** 〖俗〗照原樣;照現在的樣子。We bought the table *as is.* 我們買的時候這張桌子就是這個樣子。

Is. ①Isaiah. ②Island. ③isle. **is.** ①island. ②isle. **Isa.** Isaiah.

I·saac[1] 〔ˈaɪzək; ˈaizək, –zik〕 *n.* 男子名。

I·saac[2] *n.* 〖聖經〗以撒 (希伯來之族長, Abraham 與 Sarah 之子, Jacob 之父, 參看舊約創世紀21章3節)。

I·sa·ian 〔aɪˈzeən; aiˈzaiən〕 *adj.* ①以賽亞的。②以賽亞書的。(亦作 **Isaianic**)

Is·car·i·ot 〔ɪsˈkærɪət; isˈkæriət〕 *n.* ①以色加略 (出賣耶穌者 Judas 之姓)。②賣友者; 背信者。

is·chi·um 〔ˈɪskɪəm; ˈiskiəm〕 *n., pl.* **is·chi·a** 〔ˈɪskɪə; ˈiskiə〕.〖解剖〗坐骨。

-ise 〖字尾〗 ①名詞字尾, 如: exercise, franchise. ②〖英〗＝**-ize.**

-ish 〖字尾〗表下列諸義之形容詞字尾: ①(附於國民、人種之名稱後)表"…的;屬於…的; …性的"之義, 如:English. ②表"似…的;有…性質的"之義, 如:boyish. ③表"稍…的;頗…的"之義, 如:thinnish. ④〖俗〗表 "約…的 (時刻、年齡)"之義, 如: a sixtyish, white-haired gentleman. 一個六十開外的白髮紳士。

Ish·ma·el 〔ˈɪʃmɪəl; ˈiʃmeiəl〕 *n.* ①〖聖經〗以實瑪利 (Abraham 與其侍女 Hagar 所生之子, 參看舊約創世紀16章12節)。②被社

會唾棄者;社會之敵。

Ish·ma·el·ite [ˈɪʃməlˌaɪt; ˈiʃmiəlait] *n.* ①Ishmael 之後裔。②被社會唾棄者。

i·sin·glass [ˈaɪzɪŋˌglæs; ˈaiziŋglɑːs] *n.* ①魚膠。②〖礦〗雲母。

I·sis [ˈaɪsɪs; ˈaisis] *n.* 〖埃及神話〗愛色斯(司豐饒之女神)。

isl. *pl.* **isls.** ①island. ②isle.

Is·lam [ˈɪsləm; ˈizlɑːm] *n.* ①伊斯蘭教;回教。②回教徒(集合稱)。③回教國。

Is·lam·ism [ˈɪsləmɪzəm; ˈizləmizəm] *n.* ①回教;伊斯蘭教。②回教之教義、習俗等。

Is·lam·ite [ˈɪsləmˌaɪt; ˈizləmait] *n., adj.* 回教徒(的)。

Is·lam·it·ic [ˌɪsləˈmɪtɪk; ˌizləˈmitik] *adj.* 伊斯蘭的;回教(徒)的。(亦作 **Islamic**)

‡**is·land** [ˈaɪlənd; ˈailənd] *n.* ①島;島嶼。Taiwan is an *island.* 臺灣是一個島。②似島之物。safety *island.* (街市之)安全島。③(主力艦或航空母艦右舷的)甲板室;艦臺等。***Island of Saints*** 聖人島(愛爾蘭的別名)。***island platform*** 〖鐵路〗上下兩線並用,立於鐵路中的月臺。—*v.t.* ①使變成島。②以島點綴。③置於島上;孤立。

is·land·er [ˈaɪləndɚ; ˈailəndə] *n.* 島民。

isle** [aɪl; ail] *n.* 島;嶼(詩中用語)。The British Isles*** 不列顛羣島(包括大不列顛、愛爾蘭及其附近島嶼)。—*v.t.* ①使成爲島嶼。②置於島嶼上。

is·let [ˈaɪlɪt; ˈailit] *n.* 小島;小島嶼。

ism [ˈɪzəm; ˈizəm] *n.* 主義;學說;制度;論。This is the age of *isms.* 這是一個充滿各種主義的時代。

-ism 〖字尾〗造成與用**-ize**結尾動詞相當之名詞:①表"行爲;實行"之義, 如: baptism. ②表"因...過度而致病"之義, 如:alcoholism. ③表"體系;主義; 制度" 之義, 如: Calvinism. ④表"特性;特徵"之義, 如:Americanism. ⑤表"實例;例證"之義, 如 colloquialism.

‡**is·n't** [ˈɪznt, ˈɪzn; ˈiznt, ˈizn] =**is not.** It *isn't* mine. 那不是我的。「(母音前作 **is-**)」

iso- 〖字首〗表"相等(的);相同(的)"之義。

i·so·bar [ˈaɪsəˌbɑr; ˈaisoubɑː] *n.* ①〖氣象〗等壓線(在地圖上所畫表示氣壓相等之線)。②〖理化〗同量素。

i·so·bar·ic [ˌaɪsəˈbærɪk; ˌaisouˈbærik] *adj.* ①表示等壓的。②同量素的。

i·so·chro·mat·ic [ˌaɪsəkroˈmætɪk; ˌaisoukrouˈmætik] *adj.* ①〖光學〗等色的。②〖照相〗=**orthochromatic.**

i·soch·ro·nous [aɪˈsɑkrənəs; aiˈsɔkrənəs] *adj.* 等時(性)的。

i·so·cli·nal [ˌaɪsəˈklaɪnl; ˌaisəˈklainl] *adj.* ①〖磁學〗等俯角的;等傾角的。②〖地質〗等傾斜的(指褶曲之地層言)。

i·soc·ra·cy [aɪˈsɑkrəsɪ; aiˈsɔkrəsi] *n., pl.* **-cies.** 平等參政權;平等參政制度。

i·so·crat·ic [ˌaɪsəˈkrætɪk; ˌaisəˈkrætik] *adj.* 平等參政權的;平等參政制度的。

i·so·dy·nam·ic [ˌaɪsədaɪˈnæmɪk; ˌaisədaiˈnæmik] *adj.*(亦作 **isodynamical**)〖磁學〗等(磁)力的。—*n.* 等磁力線。

i·so·gloss [ˈaɪsəˌglɑs; ˈaisouglɔs] *n.* 〖語言〗等語線(語言地圖上區分語言特徵不同地域的線)。

i·so·gon·ic [ˌaɪsəˈgɑnɪk; ˌaisəˈgɔnik] *adj.* 〖磁學〗等偏角的。—*n.* 等偏(角)線;等方位角線。

***i·so·late** [ˈaɪslˌet, ˈɪs-; ˈaisəleit, -sol-] *v.t.*, **-lat·ed, -lat·ing.** ①使隔離;使孤立。When a person has an infectious disease, he is usually *isolated.* 當某人患傳染病時, 他通常被隔離起來。②〖化〗分解;使游離。A chemist can *isolate* the oxygen from the hydrogen in water. 化學家能將水中之氧與氫分解。—*adj.* 孤立的;隔離的。

i·so·lat·ed [ˈaɪslˌetɪd; ˈaisəleitid] *adj.* ①孤立的。②〖數學〗孤立。—**ly,** *adv.*

i·so·la·tion [ˌaɪslˈeʃən; ˌaisəˈleiʃən] *n.* 隔離;孤立;游離。

i·so·la·tion·ism [ˌaɪslˈeʃənɪzm; ˌaisəˈleiʃənizm] *n.* (政治或經濟上之)孤立主義。

i·so·la·tion·ist [ˌaɪslˈeʃənɪst; ˌaisəˈleiʃənist] *n.* 孤立主義者。

i·so·la·tive [ˈaɪslˌetɪv; ˈaisələtiv] *adj.* ①傾向於孤立的。②〖語言〗成爲孤立性的。***isolative change*** (音韻的)孤立性變化。

i·so·la·tor [ˈaɪslˌetɚ; ˈaisəleitə] *n.* ①隔離之人或物。②〖電〗絕緣體。

i·so·mer [ˈaɪsəmɚ; ˈaisəmə] *n.* 〖化〗同質異構物;同分異構物。

i·so·mer·ic [ˌaɪsəˈmɛrɪk; ˌaisouˈmerik] *adj.* 〖化〗同質異構的;同分異構的。

i·som·er·ism [aɪˈsɑməˌrɪzəm; aiˈsɔmərizəm] *n.* 〖化〗同質異構;同分異構。

i·som·er·ous [aɪˈsɑmərəs; aiˈsɔmərəs] *adj.* ①〖植物〗(花等)各部分均由同數構成的;等數的。②〖動物〗(昆蟲之脚等)均有同數之節的。③〖化〗同質異構的;同分異構的。

i·so·met·ric [ˌaɪsəˈmɛtrɪk; ˌaisouˈmetrik] *adj.* ①等大的;等積的;等角的。②〖結晶〗等軸晶的。

i·so·met·ri·cal [ˌaɪsəˈmɛtrɪkl; ˌaisouˈmetrikəl] *adj.* =**isometric.** —**ly,** *adv.*

isometric exercise 鍛鍊肌肉運動(如以手推牆之運動)。

i·so·met·rics [ˌaɪsəˈmɛtrɪks; ˌaisəˈmetriks] *n.* =**isometric exercise.**

i·so·mor·phic [ˌaɪsəˈmɔrfɪk; ˌaisouˈmɔːfik] *adj.* ①〖化〗同形的;同構的。②〖生物, 礦〗異種同形的;異質同形的。

i·so·mor·phism [ˌaɪsəˈmɔrfɪzm; ˌaisouˈmɔːfizəm] *n.* ①〖生物〗異種同形。②〖化, 礦〗異質同形;類質同像;同形性。

i·so·mor·phous [ˌaɪsəˈmɔrfəs; ˌaisouˈmɔːfəs] *adj.* 〖化, 結晶〗類質同像的;異種同形的。*isomorphous* crystal. 同形晶體。

i·so·oc·tane [ˌaɪsəˈɑkten; ˌaisouˈɔktein] *n.* 〖化〗異辛烷(用以判斷汽油耐爆性標準的一種碳氫化合物)。

i·so·pod [ˈaɪsəˌpɑd; ˈaisəpɔd] *n.* 〖動物〗等足類動物。—*adj.* 等足的;等足類的。

i·sos·ce·les [aɪˈsɑslˌiz; aiˈsɔsiliːz] *adj.* 二等邊的;等腰的(三角形)。

i·so·seis·mal [ˌaɪsəˈsaɪzml; ˌaisəˈsaizml] *adj.* 〖地震〗等震的;等震線的。—*n.* 等震線。

i·sos·ta·sy [aɪˈsɑstəsɪ; aiˈsɔstəsi] *n.* 〖地質〗(地殼之)均衡。(亦作 **isostacy**)

i·so·stat·ic [ˌaɪsəˈstætɪk; ˌaisəˈstætik] *adj.* 均衡(說)的。

i·so·therm [ˈaɪsəˌθɝm; ˈaisouθəːm] *n.* 等溫線(在地圖上所畫表示溫度相等之線)。

i·so·ther·mal [ˌaɪsəˈθɝml; ˌaisouˈθəːməl] *adj.* 〖氣象, 理化〗表示等溫的;等溫(線)的。—*n.* 等溫線。

i·so·tope [ˈaɪsəˌtop; ˈaisoutoup] *n.* 〖化〗同位素(原子序相同原子量相異之元素)。

i·so·trop·ic [ˌaɪsəˈtrɑpɪk; ˌaisouˈtrɔpik] *adj.* 〖物理〗等方性的;各向同性的。

i·so·type [ˈaɪsəˌtaɪp; ˈaisətaip] *n.* 代表某一數量或事實的圖表、圖畫或記號。

I-spy [ˈaɪspaɪ; ˈaispai] *n.*〖主英〗= **hide-and-seek.**

Is·ra·el [ˈɪzrɪəl; ˈizreiəl, -riəl] *n.* ①以色列(新興國名,原爲巴勒斯坦之一部,於 1948 年 5 月 15日宣布爲猶太國家,首都爲耶路撒冷 Jerusalem)。②猶太人。③以色列(位於巴勒斯坦北部之古國)。④〖聖經〗Jacob 的別名(創世紀32章28節)。

Is·rae·li [ɪzˈrelɪ; izˈreili] *n., pl.* **-lis, -li,** *adj.* —*n.* 以色列人; 猶太人。—*adj.* 以色列(人)的; 猶太(人)的。

Is·ra·el·ite [ˈɪzrɪəlˌaɪt; ˈizriəlait] *n.*以色列人;猶太人;希伯來人。—*adj.* 以色列人的。

is·su·ance [ˈɪʃuəns; ˈisjuːəns] *n.* ①發給;配給。an *issuance* of rations. 食糧之配給。②發行;發布。

‡**is·sue** [ˈɪʃʊ, ˈɪʃju; ˈisjuː, ˈiʃuː, ˈiʃjuː] *v.,* **-sued, -su·ing,** *n.* —*v.t.* ①發行。The government *issues* stamps. 政府發行印花稅票(或郵票)。②發刊;印行。—*v.i.* ①冒出;流出。Smoke *issues* from the chimney. 煙自煙囱中冒出。②結果。③發出;出。④得…結果。⑤生;出生。⑥發刊;印行;出版。—*n.* ①發行。the *issue* of a newspaper (a new coinage). 報紙(新貨幣)之發行。②(雜誌之)期。Have you read the latest *issue* of the *Time* magazine? 你看過最近一期的"時代"雜誌嗎?③發出。the *issue* of an order. 命令之發出。④流出。an *issue* of blood from the nose. 鼻中出血。⑤出口。⑥結果;後果。⑦問題。the *issues* of a political campaign. 關於競選運動之諸問題。⑧子孫; 後代。***at issue*** **a.** 爭論中的;待決的; 待討論的。The matter really *at issue* was whether he or his brother was to be the boss of the company. 眞正的爭執點是他和他的弟弟誰該當該公司的老板。**b.** 意見不一致。***in the issue*** 結局。 ***join issue with*** 對…持異議;與…爭辯。 ***make an issue (of)*** 挑起爭辯或討論。 ***take issue*** 不同意; 不同。—**is·su·a·ble,** *adj.* —**is·su·er,** *n.*

-ist〖字尾〗①形成以 **-ize** 結尾之動詞之"動作者,"如: antagonist, rhapsodist. ②表"(主義、慣例等之) 信奉者; 支持者," 如: Buddhist, imperialist. ③表"從事(特殊研究、職業等)者,"如: dentist, pianist.

Is·tan·bul [ˌɪstɑnˈbul; ˌistænˈbuːl] *n.* 伊斯坦堡(土耳其名,舊稱君士坦丁堡,爲土耳其歐洲部分之一城市)。(亦作 **Stambul, Stamboul**)

isth·mi·an [ˈɪsmɪən; ˈisθmiən] *adj.* ①地峽的。②(I-)巴拿馬地峽的。the *Isthmian* Canal. 巴拿馬運河。③(I-) 科林斯地峽的。***Isthmian games*** 科林斯地峽運動大會(隔年舉行一次海神 Poseidon 之祭典,爲古希臘四大競技會之一)。—*n.* 地峽的居民。

•**isth·mus** [ˈɪsməs; ˈisməs, -sθm-, -stm-] *n., pl.* **-mus·es, -mi** [-maɪ; -mai]. ①地峽。 the *Isthmus* of Panama. 巴拿馬地峽。②〖解剖〗峽部。 the *isthmus* of the throat. 咽峽。

is·tle [ˈɪstlɪ; ˈistli] *n.* 若干熱帶美洲植物之纖維(爲製繩、網、地毯等之原料)。

‡**it** [ɪt; it] *pron., pl.* **they.** ①它; 牠(第三人稱,單數,中性, 主格及受格; 可指無生物,動物,有時亦指很小的小孩)。 Please go and get my book; *it* is on the table; can't you see *it?* 請去把我的書拿來,就在桌上,你看不見嗎? Where is the dog? *It* is in the other room. 狗在哪裏? 牠在另一間房裏。Look at the poor little child; *it* has just fallen down. 看那可憐的小孩,它剛剛跌倒。② (=that, this) 那個; 這個。What is that? *It* (=That) is my book. 那是甚麼? 那是我的書。Who is that? *It* (=That) is my friend. 那是誰?那是我的朋友。③作無人稱動詞及無人稱結構之主詞,多指自然現象、時間與距離。*It* is raining (snowing, etc.). 正下雨(下雪等)。*It* happens that I received the letter this morning. 我今天早晨趕巧接到這信。 *It's* rather warm today. 今天相當暖。 *It's* five o'clock. 五點鐘了。*It* is 20 miles to (from) London. 到(從)倫敦去(來)有二十英里遠。④置於句首做假主詞, 以代替後述較長之短語或子句。 *It* doesn't seem right that he should do it. 他這樣做似乎不對。⑤用作動詞的含糊的受詞。 He lorded *it* over us. 他對我們逞威風。 ⑥作以述詞所分開之關係代名詞的前述詞。*It* was a blue car that passed. 過去的是一輛藍轎車。***be with it***〖俚〗**a.** 注意的;機警的。**b.** 瞭解或欣賞。***get with it***〖俚〗提起興趣來;振作起來。***have it***〖俚〗**a.** 美麗動人。**b.** 愛某人。**c.** 有能力;技巧的;有才幹。 ***have it one's own way*** 堅持自己的意見。***keep at it*** (= continue doing something) 繼續做某事而不中輟。

It., Ital. ①Italian. ②Italic. ③Italy.

ITA〖英〗Independent Television Authority. **ital.** italic; italics.

‡**I·tal·ian** [ɪˈtæljən; iˈtæljən] *adj.* 義大利的;義大利人的;義大利語的。 —*n.* ①義大利人。②義大利語文。

I·tal·ian·ism [ɪˈtæljənɪzm̩; iˈtæljənizəm] *n.* ①義大利風格。②義大利氣質。③義大利語特色。④對義大利之偏好;親義主義。

I·tal·ian·ize [ɪˈtæljənˌaɪz; iˈtæljənaiz] *v.i.* & *v.t.,* **-ized, -iz·ing.** (使)有義大利風格;義大利化。

i·tal·ic [ɪˈtælɪk; iˈtælik] *adj.* ①用義大利體(卽斜體) 字印刷的。②(I-) 古代義大利的;古義大利人的;古義大利語的。—*n.* (常 *pl.*) 義大利體字;斜體字(字母或數字)。

i·tal·i·cize [ɪˈtæləˌsaɪz; iˈtælisaiz] *v.t.,* **-cized, -ciz·ing.** ①(用義大利體)印刷。Examples in grammar books are often *italicized*. 文法書中的例子常用斜體字印刷。②在字下畫橫線以表示斜體。

‡**It·a·ly** [ˈɪtlɪ; ˈitəli, ˈitli] *n.* 義大利 (國名,位於南歐地中海岸,首都羅馬 Rome).

ITC International Trade Charter. 國際貿易憲章。

itch [ɪtʃ; itʃ] *n.* ①癢。②疥癬。to suffer from the *itch*. 患疥癬。③渴望; 渴想。to have an *itch* for money. 渴想發財。—*v.i.* ①發癢。Scratch yourself if you *itch*. 你若癢就搔好了。②渴望; 渴想。 He was *itching* for the lesson to end. 他渴望着功課完畢。 —*v.t.* ①使發癢。This wool shirt *itches* my back. 這件羊毛衫使我背上發癢。②使煩擾;使不悅。

itch·ing [ˈɪtʃɪŋ; ˈitʃiŋ] *n.* 癢;渴望。 to have an *itching* for...,渴望…。—*adj.* ①癢的;渴望着的。to have an *itching* ear. 想聽閒話。②貪財的;貪得的。***have an itching palm*** 貪財。

itch mite 疥蟲。

itch·y [ˈɪtʃɪ; ˈitʃi] *adj.,* **itch·i·er, itch-**

i·est. ①癢的;生疥癬的。②渴望的。

-ite〖字尾〗形容詞及名詞字尾。①表"與…有關係者; 自…來的人; …之信奉者"之義, 如: Darwinite, Israelite. ②學術用語。**a.**岩石、礦物之名稱, 如: dolomite. **b.** 化石之名稱, 如: ammonite. **c.** 鹽類之名稱, 如: sulphite. **d.** 炸藥之名稱, 如: dynamite. **e.** 商品之名稱, 如: ebonite.

***i·tem** ['aɪtəm; 'aitem, -təm, -tim] *n.* ①條;款;項目。 the first *item* on a program. 節目中之第一項。②一條新聞。 Are there any interesting *items* (of news) in the paper this morning? 今晨報紙上有甚麼有趣的新聞嗎? *—adv.* 又; 同樣地; 亦(列舉項目時用語)。

i·tem·ize ['aɪtəm,aɪz; 'aitemaiz] *v.t.*, **-ized, -iz·ing.** 詳列;縷列。**—i·tem·i·za·tion, i·tem·iz·er,** *n.*

it·er·ate ['ɪtə,ret; 'itəreit] *v.t.*, **-at·ed, -at·ing.** 重複;重做;重述。

it·er·a·tion [,ɪtə'reʃən; ,itə'reiʃən] *n.* ①重做;重述。②重做的事物; 重述的話。

it·er·a·tive ['ɪtə,retɪv; 'itərətiv] *adj.* ①反覆的;重做的。②〖文法〗表反覆的(動詞)。

ITF International Trade Fair. 國際促進貿易展覽會。

I·thu·ri·el [ɪ'θjurɪəl; i'θjuəriəl] *n.* Milton 所著"失樂園"中一天使之名。

i·tin·er·a·cy [aɪ'tɪnərəsɪ; ai'tinərəsi] *n.* =**itinerancy.**

i·tin·er·an·cy [aɪ'tɪnərənsɪ; i'tinərənsi] *n.*①巡廻;遊歷。②巡廻傳教會;巡廻法官團。③巡廻工作;外勤公務。

i·tin·er·ant [aɪ'tɪnərənt; i'tinərənt] *adj.* ①巡廻的。②(臨時工人) 飄蕩的; 流動的。 *—n.* ①巡廻工作者。②時而工作時而飄蕩的人。**—ly,** *adv.*

i·tin·er·ar·y [aɪ'tɪnə,rɛrɪ; ai'tinərəri] *n., pl.* **-ar·ies,** *adj.* *—n.* ①旅行路線; 旅行計畫。②旅行日誌。③旅行指南。*—adj.* ①巡廻的。②旅行的;旅程的。

i·tin·er·ate [aɪ'tɪnə,ret; i'tinəreit] *v.i.*, **-at·ed, -at·ing.** ①巡廻;遊歷。②巡廻傳教;巡廻審判。

i·tin·er·a·tion [aɪ,tɪnə'reʃən; i,tinə'reiʃən] *n.*=**itinerancy.**

-itis〖字尾〗表"炎症"之義, 如: bronchitis.

it'll ['ɪtl̩; 'itl] ①=**it will.** ②=**it shall.**

ITO International Trade Organization.

‡its [ɪts; its] *pron.*, possessive of **it,** *adj.* 它的;牠的(it的所有格)。The dog wagged *its* tail. 那狗搖牠的尾巴。

‡it's [ɪts; its] ①=**it is.** ②=**it has.**

‡it·self [ɪt'sɛlf; it'self] *pron.* ①(它) 本身 (用以加強前面名詞的語勢)。 The land *itself* is worth more than the old house. 這地皮本身比那舊房子還要值錢些。②它自己(it 的反身代名詞)。 That dog is always stretching (scratching, etc.) *itself*. 這狗總是伸懶腰(抓癢等)。③正常狀態。After much tender care, the puppy was soon *itself* again. 經過悉心調治後, 小狗很快地復原了。 ***(all) by itself*** **a.** 自行;單獨地(= without help). **b.** 單獨 (= alone). The house stands *(all) by itself*. 這房子孤零零地獨立着。 ***in itself*** 就其本身而論; 本質上。***of itself*** 自行。The light went out *of itself*. 燈光自行熄滅。〖注意〗**by itself** (自行)指不藉外界助力。**of itself** (自行)指不受外界影響。

I.T.T.C. International Telephone and Telegraph Corporation. **I.T.T.F.** International Table Tennis Federation.

it·ty-bit·ty ['ɪtɪ'bɪtɪ; 'iti'biti] *adj.* 〖兒語〗小的。(亦作 **itsy-bitsy**)

ITU International Telecommunication Union.

-ity〖字尾〗表"狀態;特性"之抽象名詞字尾, 如: calamity, majority, probity.

IUD intrauterine device. 子宮內避孕裝置。

-ium〖字尾〗①拉丁語之中性形容詞字尾, 如: medium. ②金屬元素之名稱字尾, 如: sodium.

IV intravenous(ly).

I·van ['aɪvən; 'aivən] *n.* 男子名。

‡I've [aɪv; aiv] =**I have.**

-ive〖字尾〗表"有…傾向的;有…性質的"之義之形容詞字尾, 如: aggressive, extensive.

i·vied ['aɪvɪd; 'aivid] *adj.* 長滿常春藤的; 爬滿常春藤的。

***i·vo·ry** ['aɪvərɪ; 'aivəri] *n., pl.* **-ries,** *adj.* *—n.* ①象牙; 象牙質。②似象牙之質。③乳白色。④(*pl.*)〖俚〗**a.** 鋼琴的鍵盤。**b.** 骰子。**c.** 撞球的球。**d.** 牙齒。 *—adj.* ①象牙製的。②象牙質的; 似象牙質的。③乳白色的。 **—like,** *adj.*

Ivory Coast 象牙海岸 (非洲西部之一共和國, 首都阿必尚 Abidjan).

ivory nut 象牙棕櫚之實。

ivory palm 象牙棕櫚樹。

ivory tower ①象牙之塔(與世隔絕之夢想境界)。 ②對實務或俗事之冷漠態度。

i·vor·y-white ['aɪvərɪ'hwaɪt; 'aivəri'wait] *adj.* 象牙色的;乳白色的。

***i·vy** ['aɪvɪ; 'aivi] *n., pl.* **-vies.** ①常春藤。②類似常春藤之植物。 **—like,** *adj.*

Ivy League ①美國東部若干歷史悠久名望素著之大學或大學學生的。②較保守或高雅的。 ③美國東北部八個著名大學 (Yale, Harvard, Princeton, Columbia, Dartmouth, Cornell, Pennsylvania, Brown)之聯合運動組織。④屬於該組織之大學或其師生。

IWA(C) International Whaling Agreement (Convention). 國際捕鯨協定(會議)。

i·wis [ɪ'wɪs; i'wis] *adv.*〖古〗的確;實在(=certainly). (亦作 **ywis**)

I.W.W. Industrial Workers of the World. **IX, I.X.** Jesus Christ.

ix·i·a ['ɪksɪə; 'iksiə] *n.*〖植物〗鳶尾屬之植物。

iz·ard ['ɪzəd; 'izəd] *n.* (Pyrenees 山產之)羚羊。

-ize, -ise〖字尾〗動詞字尾。①表"使變成…(狀態); 使…化; 以…處理" 之義之及物動詞, 如: Americanize, civilize. ②表"採取…行動;變成…(狀態);…化"之義之不及物動詞, 如: apologize, materialize.

Iz·ves·ti·a [ɪz'vɛstɪə; iz'vestiə] *n.* 消息報(蘇聯政府機關報)。

iz·zard ['ɪzəd; 'izəd] *n.*〖古,方〗字母 Z. from A to *izzard*. 自A至Z; 自始至終;全部。

J

J or j [dʒe; dʒei] *n., pl.* **J's or j's** [dʒez; dʒeiz]. ①英文字母之第十個字母。②以英文字母 J 所代表之聲音, 如: judge, rajah. ③J狀物。④(在某些序列中的)第十個。

J. ①James. ②Journal. ③Judge. ④Justice.

J/A Joint Account.

JAA Japan Asia Airways. 日本亞細亞航空公司。

jab [dʒæb; dʒæb] *v.*, **jabbed, jab·bing,** *n.* —*v.t. & v.i.* 刺;戳;猛碰。—*n.* ①刺;戳。②〖俗〗皮下注射。(亦作 **job**) —**bing·ly,** *adv.*

jab·ber [ˈdʒæbɚ; ˈdʒæbə] *v.t. & v.i.* ①急言; 快而含糊地說。②信口閑談。—*n.* 含糊不清的話或聲音; 無聊的閑談。—**er,** *n.* —**ing·ly,** *adv.*

jab·ber·wock·y [ˈdʒæbɚˌwɑkɪ; ˈdʒæbəˌwɔki] *n.*, *pl.* **-wock·ies,** *adj.* —*n.* ①無意義的話。②無意義的文章。—*adj.* 無意義的;空洞的。(亦作 **Jabberwock, Jabberwocky**)

ja·bot [ʒæˈbo; ˈʒæbou] *n.* (女服胸部之)摺縐花邊。

ja·cinth [ˈdʒesɪnθ; ˈdʒæsinθ] *n.* 〖礦〗①紅鋯英石;紅風信子石。②帶紅的橙色。

jack** [dʒæk; dʒæk] *n.* ①男子; 少年; 常人。②起重機;千斤頂。③(紙牌) 畫有王宮僕人之牌(介於十點與王后之間)。④艦首所懸表示國籍或信號之旗。⑤(常 J-)水手;水兵。⑥(常 J-)雜工。⑦〖英〗保齡球戲用以瞄準之小球。⑧烤肉夾。⑨公驢。⑩北美洲西部的一種大野兔。⑪〖電〗插座。⑫〖俚〗錢。⑬伐木工人。⑭時鐘之人形鐘錘。⑮ =**jacklight.** ***before one can say Jack Robinson 立時;快地。I'll be back *before you can say Jack Robinson.* 我一會就回來。***every man jack*** = **everyone.** ***Jack in office*** 作威作福的小官;擺官架子的人。***Jack of all trades*** 博而不精之人。—*v.t.* 抬起;提醒。***jack up*** **a.** 用起重工具抬起。**b.**〖俗〗提高(價目、工資等)。**c.**〖俗〗提醒某人之責任。

jack-a-dan·dy [ˌdʒækəˈdændɪ; ˌdʒækəˈdændi] *n.*, *pl.* **-dies.** 花花公子; 紈袴子。—**ism,** *n.*

jack·al [ˈdʒækɔl; ˈdʒækɔːl] *n.* ①〖動〗胡狼。②卑鄙之人;走狗。

jack·a·napes [ˈdʒækəˌneps; ˈdʒækəneips] *n.* ①頑皮的兒童。②自負之人。③〖古〗猴; 猿。

jack·ass [ˈdʒækˌæs; ˈdʒækæs] *n.* ①公驢。②愚蠢的人。—**er·y,** —**ism,** —**ness,** *n.*

jack·boot [ˈdʒækˌbut; ˈdʒækbuːt] *n.* (過膝的)長統靴。

jack·daw [ˈdʒækˌdɔ; ˈdʒækdɔː] *n.* 〖鳥〗穴烏。

jack·et** [ˈdʒækɪt; ˈdʒækit] *n.* ①短外衣;夾克。②書籍的包皮紙;鍋爐的水箱。③馬鈴薯的皮。④穿在上身的任何衣着。⑤保護性外套。⑥唱片的外套。⑦公文卷宗。dust a person's jacket*** 打人。—*v.t.* ①穿以短外衣;包以書皮。②〖俗〗打;擊;拍。—**ed,** —**like,** *adj.* —**less,** *adj.*

jack·ham·mer [ˈdʒækˌhæmɚ; ˈdʒækˌhæmə] *n.* 一種用壓縮空氣操作的輕便鑽(在岩石上鑽孔用者)。

jack-in-a-box [ˈdʒækɪnəˌbɑks; ˈdʒækinəbɔks] *n.*, *pl.* **-box·es.** ①=**jack-in-the-box.** ②〖植物〗(熱帶產之)蓮葉桐。

jack-in-the-box [ˈdʒækɪnðəˌbɑks; ˈdʒækinðəbɔks] *n.* 打開盒蓋即跳出一個小人的玩具。(亦作 **jack-in-a-box**)

Jack-in-the-green [ˈdʒækɪnðəˌgrin; ˈdʒækinðəgriːn] *n.* 〖英〗五朔節(May Day) 遊戲中頭與手被置入用青葉遮蓋着的金字塔形框內之男子或小孩。

jack-in-the-pul·pit [ˈdʒækɪnðəˈpʊlpɪt; ˈdʒækinðəˈpulpit] *n.*, *pl.* **-pul·pits.** 〖植物〗(北美產之)黃花菖蒲。

jack·knife [ˈdʒækˌnaɪf; ˈdʒæknaif] *n.*, *pl.* **-knives.** ①〖美〗較大型的摺合小刀;水手刀。②鏢刀式跳水。

jack·leg [ˈdʒækˌlɛg; ˈdʒækleg] *n.* 〖俚〗惡訟師;用不正當手段執行業務之自由職業者。

jack·light [ˈdʒækˌlaɪt; ˈdʒækˌlait] *n.* (漁獵用) 手提油燈。—*v.t.* 用燈光漁獵。

jack-of-all-trades [ˌdʒækəvˈɔlˌtredz; ˈdʒækəvˈɔːl-treidz] *n.*, *pl.* **jacks-of-all-trades.** (有時 J-) 萬能先生;萬事通 (尤指手工靈活者)。(亦作 **jack of all trades**)

jack-o'-lan·tern [ˈdʒækəˌlæntən; ˈdʒækəˌlæntən] *n.* ①十月三十一日萬聖節前夕用的雕成人面狀的空心南瓜燈。②像上述南瓜燈之人造燈。③鬼火;磷火。

jack plane 粗鉋。

jack pot ①〖牌戲〗(撲克戲中) 須俟有人持有一對 jack 或更佳之牌時方可開始下注之一種累積賭注。②任何累積賭注或大獎。③〖俗〗任何企業中所可能獲得之最大利益。***hit the jack pot*** 〖俚〗得到驚人的成功;有突然的好運。(亦作 **jackpot**)

jack·pud·ding [ˈdʒækˈpʊdɪŋ; ˈdʒækˈpudiŋ] *n.* 〖古〗小丑;滑稽之人。

jack rabbit (北美洲產之)長腿長耳兔。

jack·screw [ˈdʒækˌskru; ˈdʒækskruː] *n.* 螺旋起重機;起重螺絲。

jack·snipe [ˈdʒækˌsnaɪp; ˈdʒæksnaip] *n.* ①歐、亞洲產之小鷸鷸。②美洲產之小千鳥。

jack staff 〖航海〗艦(船)首旗竿(懸掛該船所屬國之國旗者)。

jack·stone [ˈdʒækˌston; ˈdʒækstoun] *n.* ①(遊戲用之)小石;小金屬塊。②(*pl.*)(作 *sing.* 解)一種拋小石或小金屬塊之遊戲。

jack·straw [ˈdʒækˌstrɔ; ˈdʒækstrɔː] *n.* ①稻草人。② **a.** (*pl.*) (作 *sing.* 解) 一種將多數之草、木片或骨片雜亂擲於桌上一次揀起一根,不得觸動其他之遊戲。**b.** 上述遊戲所用之草、木片、骨片等。③小人物。

jack-tar [ˈdʒækˈtɑr; ˈdʒækˈtɑː] *n.* 〖俗〗水兵;水手。(亦作 **Jack Tar**)

jack towel 兩端連接,掛在滾筒上用以擦手之長毛巾。

Ja·cob[1] [ˈdʒekəb; ˈdʒeikəb] *n.* 男子名。

Ja·cob[2] *n.* 〖聖經〗雅各 (Issac 之次子, 猶太人之祖先, 參看創世紀25章24–34節)。

Ja·cob[3] *n.* 雅各 (François, 1920–, 法國遺傳學家, 曾獲1965年諾貝爾醫學獎)。

Jac·o·be·an [ˌdʒækəˈbiən; ˌdʒækəˈbiːən] *adj.* 英王 James I (1603–25) 時代的。—*n.* 詹姆斯一世時代的作家、政治家等。

Jac·o·bin [ˈdʒækəbɪn; ˈdʒækəbin] *n.* ①法國大革命時代之激進民主主義者。②激進派;過激黨員。③〖宗教〗Dominican 派之修道僧。—**ic,** —**i·cal,** *adj.* —**i·cal·ly,** *adv.*

Jac·o·bin·ism [ˈdʒækəbɪnɪzəm; ˈdʒækəbinizəm] *n.* ①法國大革命期中 Jacobin 黨人之政治主張。②激進主義。

Jac·o·bite [ˈdʒækəˌbaɪt; ˈdʒækəbait] *n.* 英王 James II (1688年被迫遜位) 之擁護者。—**ly,** *adv.*

ja·co·bus [dʒəˈkobəs; dʒəˈkoubəs] *n.*, *pl.* **-bus·es.** 英王 James 一世時代之金幣名。

jac·o·net [ˈdʒækəˌnɛt; ˈdʒækənet] *n.* ①一種薄的白棉布。②一種單面光澤染色棉布。

Jacque·mi·not [ˈdʒækmɪˌno; ˈdʒækminou] *n.* 四季開花的深紅色雜種薔薇。

Jac·que·rie [ʒakˈri; ʒakˈriː] 〖法〗 *n.* ① (1357–58年法國之) 農民暴動。②(j-)農民

暴動。

jac·ti·ta·tion [ˌdʒæktɪˈteʃən; ˌdʒækˈtiˈteiʃən] *n.* ①吹牛。②〖法律〗詐稱。③〖醫〗煩躁;翻騰;輾轉不寧。

jade[1] [dʒed; dʒeid] *n.* ①翡翠;硬玉;玉。②玉製飾物。③翡翠色;綠色。—*adj.* 綠的;玉色的。 **—like,** *adj.*

jade[2] *n., v.,* **jad·ed, jad·ing.**—*n.* ①瘦馬;老馬;駑馬。②〖謔〗女人。 ***the lying jade*** 謠言(擬人稱)。 —*v.t.* ①使疲倦。②使乏味;使厭膩。—*v.i.* 變疲倦;變疲憊。**—jad·ish,** *adj.* **—jad·ish·ly,** *adv.* **—jad·ish·ness,** *n.*

jad·ed [ˈdʒedɪd; ˈdʒeidid] *adj.* ①疲憊不堪的。②厭倦的。**—ly,** *adv.* **—ness,** *n.*

jade·ite [ˈdʒedaɪt; ˈdʒeidait] *n.* 〖礦〗硬玉;翡翠;玉。

jae·ger [ˈjegɚ; ˈjeigə] *n.* ①純羊毛織物。②海鷗類海鳥。③昔奧國或德國軍中之槍手。④獵人。(亦作 **jager, jäger, yager**)

jag[1] [dʒæg; dʒæg] *n., v.,* **jagged, jag·ging.** —*n.* (邊緣或表面上)尖銳的突出;鋸齒形缺刻。—*v.t.* 使成鋸齒狀。

jag[2] *n.* ①〖方〗小量載荷(木材、乾草等)。②〖美俚〗令人爛醉之酒量;酩酊。③〖美俚〗縱飲;痛飲;狂飲。④〖蘇,英北部〗皮袋。

JAG, J.A.G. Judge Advocate General.

jag·ged [ˈdʒægɪd; ˈdʒægid] *adj.* 不整齊的;有鋸齒形之邊的。**—ly,** *adv.* **—ness,** *n.*

jag·gy [ˈdʒægɪ; ˈdʒægi] *adj.,* **-gi·er, -gi·est.** =**jagged.**

jag·uar [ˈdʒægwɑr, ˈdʒægjuˌɑr; ˈdʒægjuə, -gwə] *n.* 〖動物〗一種美洲虎。

Jah [dʒɑ; dʒɑː] *n.* =**Jehovah.**

Jah·ve(h) [ˈjɑve; ˈjɑːvei] *n.*=**Jehovah.**

jai a·lai, jai·a·lai [haɪ ɑˈlaɪ; hai ɑːˈlai] 〖西〗盛行於拉丁美洲之一種手球遊戲。

***jail** [dʒel; dʒeil] *n.* ①監牢;牢獄。three years in *jail*. 在獄中三年。②(犯人候審或犯小罪者之)拘留所。—*v.t.* 下獄;監禁。**—less,** *adj.* **—like,** *adj.* 〖注意〗**jail** 英國拼爲 **gaol,** 拼法不同但讀音相同。

jail·bird [ˈdʒelˌbɝd; ˈdʒeilbəːd] *n.* ①〖俗〗犯人;囚犯。②常犯法的人。

jail·break [ˈdʒelˌbrek; ˈdʒeilbreik] *n.* 越獄。

jail·er, jail·or [ˈdʒelɚ; ˈdʒeilə] *n.* 獄卒;看守。(英亦作 **gaoler**)

Jain [dʒaɪn; dʒain] *n.* 〖宗教〗耆那教徒。—*adj.* 耆那教(徒)的。(亦作**Jaina, Jainist**)

Jain·ism [ˈdʒaɪnɪzəm; ˈdʒainizəm] *n.* 〖宗教〗耆那教(紀元前六世紀起於印度)。

Ja·kar·ta [dʒəˈkɑrtə; dʒəˈkɑːtə] *n.* 雅加達(印尼共和國之首都)。(亦作 **Djakarta**)

jake [dʒek; dʒeik] *n.* ①〖美俗〗鄉下佬;無經驗的人。②〖美俚〗錢;現金。③〖美俚〗用 Jamaica 生薑提製成之一種酒。 —*adj.* 〖美俚〗好的;對的;上等的;令人滿意的。

JAL Japan Air Lines.

jal·ap [ˈdʒæləp; ˈdʒæləp] *n.* ①〖植物〗(墨西哥產之)一種塊根牽牛。②瀉根(上述植物之塊根,用作瀉藥)。**—ic,** *adj.*

ja(l)·lop·y [dʒəˈlɑpɪ; dʒəˈlɔpi] *n., pl.* **-lop·ies.** 〖俚〗破舊的汽車(飛機)。

jal·ou·sie [ˌʒæluˈzi; ˈʒæluːziː] *n.* 百葉窗。 **—jal·ou·sied,** *adj.*

jam[1]** [dʒæm; dʒæm] *v.,* **jammed, jam·ming,** *n.* —*v.t.* ①壓緊;擠緊。②夾傷;擠傷。to *jam* one's fingers in the door. 將手指擠在門縫中軋傷了。③推開;擠。④塞滿;塞入。⑤使(機械等)發生故障。⑥〖無線電〗干擾(信號)。 —*v.i.* ①(機械等) 發生故障。②擁塞。They *jammed* into the elevator. 他們擠進電梯裏。 ***be jammed for time 匆匆忙忙。 ***be jammed in*** 〖俗〗陷入窘境。 ***be jammed with*** (***people***) 擠滿了(人)。 ***get jammed*** 擠得動不得。—*n.* ①擁擠之人羣;堆積之物。②〖美俗〗困難;障礙。He got himself into a *jam* with the tax people. 他和稅務人員間發生了困難(稅務人員認爲他有謊報、欠稅等情事)。③妨礙;擁擠。

jam[2] *n.* 果醬。**—like, —my,** *adj.*

Jam. ①Jamaica. ②〖聖經〗James.

Ja·mai·ca [dʒəˈmekə; dʒəˈmeikə] *n.* ①牙買加(西印度羣島中之一島,首都爲京斯敦 Kingston)。②牙買加甜酒。**—Ja·mai·can,** *adj., n.*

jamb(e) [dʒæm; dʒæm] *n.* (門、窗、壁爐等之)側柱。

jam·bo·ree [ˌdʒæmbəˈri; ˌdʒæmbəˈriː] *n.* ①〖美俗〗喧鬧之宴會或娛樂。②童軍大會。③(政黨等之)大會。

James [dʒemz; dʒeimz] *n.* ①男子名。②〖聖經〗雅各書。

jam-pack [ˈdʒæmˈpæk; ˈdʒæmˈpæk] *v.t.* 塞滿。

jam-packed [ˈdʒæmˈpækt; ˈdʒæmˈpækt] *adj.* 〖美俗〗塞緊的;擠得透不過氣的。

jams [dʒæmz; dʒæmz] *n. pl.* pajamas 之縮寫字。

Jan. January.

Jane [dʒen; dʒein] *n.* ①女子名。②(j-)〖美俚,蔑〗女人。a G. I. *Jane*. 女兵。

jan·gle [ˈdʒæŋgl̩; ˈdʒæŋgl] *v.,* **-gled, -gling,** *n.* —*v.i.* ①(鈴)亂響。②爭吵。—*v.t.* ①亂搖(鈴)使發刺耳之聲。②爭論。③刺激;使不安。—*n.* ①噪音;亂吵。②口角。**—jan·gler,** *n.* **—jan·gly,** *adj.*

jan·i·tor [ˈdʒænətɚ; ˈdʒænitə] *n.* 管門者;照管一座樓房或辦公室之工友。 **—i·al,** *adj.* **—ship,** *n.*

jan·i·tress [ˈdʒænətrɪs; ˈdʒænitris] *n.* janitor 之女性。

Jan·i·zar·y [ˈdʒænəˌzɛrɪ; ˈdʒænizəri] *n., pl.* **-zar·ies.** ①古土耳其王之近衞步兵。②土耳其兵。③壓迫者之爪牙。(亦作 **janizary, Janissary, janissary**)

Jan·sen·ism [ˈdʒænsn̩ɪzəm; ˈdʒænsn̩izəm] *n.* Jansen 派之教義(17世紀荷蘭神學家 Jansen 主倡之教義)。

‡Jan·u·ar·y [ˈdʒænjuˌɛrɪ; ˈdʒænjuəri] *n., pl.* **-ar·ies.** 正月。

Ja·nus [ˈdʒenəs; ˈdʒeinəs] *n.* 〖羅馬神話〗門神。

Ja·nus-faced [ˈdʒenəsˌfest; ˈdʒeinəsfeist] *adj.* ①有兩副面孔的(如羅馬門神 Janus)。②有兩種對比性質的。③欺詐的。④看到或覺察兩種相反方面的。

Jap [dʒæp; dʒæp] *adj., n.* 〖俗、蔑〗 Japanese.

Jap. ①Japan. ②Japanese.

‡Ja·pan [dʒəˈpæn, dʒæ-; dʒəˈpæn] *n.* 日本(國名,位於亞洲東部,首都爲東京 Tokyo). (亦作 **Nihon, Nippon**)

ja·pan [dʒəˈpæn; dʒəˈpæn] *n., v.,* **-panned, -pan·ning.** —*n.* 漆;漆器。—*v.t.* 漆以日本漆。**—ner,** *n.*

Japan, Sea of 日本海。

Japan Current, the 日本海流;黑潮(太平洋暖流之一)。(亦作 **Japan Stream, Kuroshio, Black Stream**)

‡Jap·a·nese [ˌdʒæpəˈniz; ˌdʒæpəˈniːz, ˈdʒæpəˈniːz] *adj., n., pl.* **-nese.** —*adj.* 日本的;日本人的;日本語文的。—*n.* ①日本人。②日語;日文。

Jap·a·nesque [ˌdʒæpəˈnɛsk; ˌdʒæpəˈnesk] *adj.* 日本式(風味、作風)的。—*n.* 日本式的事物。

J

Jap·a·nize ['dʒæpə,naɪz; 'dʒæpənaiz] *v.t.* & *v.i.*, **-nized, -niz·ing.** (使)日本化。

Jap·a·nol·o·gy [,dʒæpə'nɑlədʒɪ; ,dʒæpə'nɔlədʒi] *n.* 日本(事物)研究;日本學。

Ja·pan·o·phile [dʒə'pænə,faɪl; dʒə'pænəfail] *n.* 崇拜日本者;親日者。

jape [dʒep; dʒeip] *n., v.*, **japed, jap·ing.** —*n.* 戲謔;嘲弄;愚弄。 —*v.t.* & *v.i.* 戲謔;嘲弄;愚弄。 —**jap·er,** —**r·y,** *n.* —**jap·ing·ly,** *adv.*

Ja·pon·ic [dʒə'pɑnɪk; dʒə'pɔnik] *adj.* 關於日本的;日本特有的;日本風尚的。

ja·pon·i·ca [dʒə'pɑnɪkə; dʒə'pɔnikə] *n.*〖植物〗日本產的植物(如山茶等)。

***jar**[1] [dʒɑr; dʒɑː] *n.* ①大口瓶。②一瓶之量。a *jar* of strawberry jam. 一瓶草莓醬。

***jar**[2] *n., v.*, **jarred, jar·ring.** —*n.* ①搖撼;震動。②軋轢聲。③衝突;不和。④刺激;激動。—*v.t.* ①震驚;震動。Your heavy footsteps *jar* my table. 你那沈重的脚步聲使我的桌子震動。②使作軋轢聲。③激動。The children's screams *jar* my nerves. 孩子們的尖叫聲使我神經不安。 —*v.i.* ①衝突;不諧。Our opinions *jar*. 我們的意見相衝突。②作軋轢聲。③震動。The window *jarred* in the frame. 窗在框中震動。④激動。 —**ring·ly,** *adv.*

jar[3] *n.* 旋轉。***on the jar*** (門)半開半掩。

jar·di·niere [,dʒɑrdṇ'ɪr; ,ʒɑːdi'njɛə] *n.* (裝飾用之) 花盆;花架。

jar·gon ['dʒɑrgən; 'dʒɑːgən] *n.* ①某一行業或學科專用的術語。②難懂的話。③寫得極壞的英文;洋涇濱英文;多用怪癖字的語言。④喋喋不休的閒談。—*v.i.* ①說行話。②閒談。

jar·go·nel(le) [,dʒɑrgə'nɛl; ,dʒɑːgə'nel] *n.*〖植物〗一種早熟之梨。

jarl [jɑrl; jɑːl] *n.*〖史〗(古代北歐之)酋長;貴族。—**dom,** *n.*

jar·o·vize ['jɑrə,vaɪz; 'jɑːrəvaiz] *v.t.*, **-vized, -viz·ing.** 使(植物)早熟。(亦作 **iarovize, yarovize**)

jar·ring ['dʒɑrɪŋ; 'dʒɑːriŋ] *n.* ①震動。②不睦;衝突。—*adj.* ①粗糙刺耳的。②衝突的;不睦的。—**ly,** *adv.*

jar·vey ['dʒɑrvɪ; 'dʒɑːvi] *n., pl.* **jar·veys.**〖英俚〗(出租馬車之) 車夫。(亦作 **jarvie, jarvy**)

Jas.〖聖經〗James.

jas·min(e) ['dʒæsmɪn; 'dʒæsmin] *n.* ①〖植物〗茉莉。②淺黃色。(亦作 **jessamine**)

Ja·son ['dʒesṇ; 'dʒeisn] *n.*〖希臘神話〗吉生(Aeson 之子, Medea 之夫, 率領 Argonauts 前往 Colchis 國尋得金羊毛)。

jas·per ['dʒæspɚ; 'dʒæspə] *n.* ①不透明有色之半寶石;碧石。②〖聖經〗碧玉。③1775年左右 Wedgwood 所發明的一種細陶器。

Ja·ta·ka ['dʒɑtəkə; 'dʒɑːtəkə] *n.* 闍陀伽本生經(講述佛陀前生之故事之經典)。

ja·to ['dʒeto; 'dʒeitou] *n., pl.* **-tos.** 靠噴射之起飛(爲 *j*et *a*ssisted *t*ake-*o*ff 之略)。

jato unit 起飛補助火箭。

jaun·dice ['dʒɔndɪs; 'dʒɔːndis] *n., v.*, **-diced, -dic·ing.** —*n.* ①黃疸病。②因猜疑、嫉妬而生之偏見。 —*v.t.* ①使患黃疸病。②使懷偏見;使猜忌。

jaunt [dʒɔnt; dʒɔːnt] *v.i.* 遠足;遊覽。—*n.* 遠足;遊覽。—**ing·ly,** *adv.*

jaunting car 愛爾蘭的一種雙輪馬車。

jaun·ty ['dʒɔntɪ; 'dʒɔːnti] *adj.*, **-ti·er, -ti·est.** ①活潑的。②漂亮時髦的。③洋洋得意的;很氣派的。—**jaun·ti·ly,** *adv.* —**jaun·ti·ness,** *n.*

Ja·va ['dʒɑvə; 'dʒɑːvə] *n.* ①爪哇(南洋羣島之一,今屬印尼)。②爪哇及其附近島嶼所產之咖啡。③(常 j-)〖美俚〗咖啡。

Java man〖人類〗爪哇猿人(1891年於爪哇發現其化石)。(亦作 **Pithecanthropus**)

Jav·a·nese [,dʒævə'niz; ,dʒɑːvə'niːz] *adj., n., pl.* **-nese.** —*adj.* 爪哇的;爪哇人的;爪哇語的。—*n.* 爪哇人;爪哇語。

jave·lin ['dʒævlɪn; 'dʒævlin] *n.* ①標槍。②擲標槍之運動項目。—*v.t.* 擲標槍。

jaw** [dʒɔ; dʒɔː] *n.* ①顎;顎。Hold your *jaw!* 別多講! ②(*pl.*) 口;山谷或海峽之狹口。③工作鉗等之一邊。④〖俗〗喋喋不休;斥責。into*** (or ***out of***) ***the jaws of death*** 陷入(脫離)生死之憂。***lantern jaws*** 瘦長的嘴臉。***wag one's*** (or ***the***) ***jaws*** 聒噪不休。—*v.i.*〖俚〗①嘮叨;閑談。②責罵;漫罵。—*v.t.*〖俚〗教訓;責罵。—**less,** *adj.*

jaw·bone ['dʒɔ'bon; 'dʒɔːboun] *n.* ①頷骨;顎骨;牙床骨。②下顎骨。

jaw·bon·ing ['dʒɔ,bonɪŋ; 'dʒɔː,bouniŋ] *n.*〖美俚〗有影響力人士如州長等向工會或財經界領袖所發的指示。

jaw·break·er ['dʒɔ,brekɚ; 'dʒɔː,breikə] *n.*〖俚〗①非常難讀的字。②硬糖果。③(亦作 **jaw crusher**) 壓碎礦石之機器。

***jay** [dʒe; dʒei] *n.* ①〖動物〗樫鳥。②〖俚〗愛講話的笨伯;刺刺不休者。

Jay·hawk·er ['dʒe,hɔkɚ; 'dʒei,hɔːkə] *n.* ①美國 Kansas 州人或居民之綽號。②(有時 j-)〖美俚〗內戰期中 Missouri 與 Kansas 二州之廢奴主義者的游擊隊士兵。

jay·walk ['dʒe,wɔk; 'dʒeiwɔːk] *v.i.*〖俗〗不遵守交通規則而穿越馬路。—**er,** *n.*

***jazz** [dʒæz; dʒæz] *n.* ①爵士樂。②爵士舞。③狂噪。This is the age of *jazz*. 這是狂噪的時代。④〖俚〗活潑;熱鬧。⑤〖俚〗誇張的話。—*adj.* 爵士音樂的;似爵士樂的。*jazz* music. 爵士音樂。—*v.t.* ①奏(樂曲)成爵士音樂。②〖俚〗使有活力〖常 up〗。—*v.i.* ①跳爵士舞。②快活地行動〖常 up〗。—**er,** *n.*

jazz band 爵士樂隊。

jazz buff 爵士樂迷。

jazz·man ['dʒæz,mæn; 'dʒæzmæn] *n., pl.* **-men.** 爵士音樂家。

jazz·nik ['dʒæznɪk; 'dʒæznik] *n.*〖美俚〗=**jazz buff.**

jazz singer 爵士歌唱家。

jazz·y ['dʒæzɪ; 'dʒæzi] *adj.*, **jazz·i·er, jazz·i·est.** ①爵士樂的。②活潑的。—**jazz·i·ly,** *adv.* —**jazz·i·ness,** *n.*

J.C. ①Jesus Christ. ②Julius Caesar. ③jurisconsult. **J.C.D.** ①Juris Canonici Doctor (拉=Doctor of Canon Law). ②Juris Civilis Doctor (拉 = Doctor of Civil Law). **JCS, J.C.S.** Joint Chiefs of Staff. **jct., jctn.** junction. **JD** ①juvenile delinquency. ②juvenile delinquent. **Je.** June.

***jeal·ous** ['dʒɛləs; 'dʒeləs] *adj.* ①嫉妒的;妒忌的。Why is he so *jealous?* 他爲甚麼如此妒忌? ②妒羨的;羨慕的。He is *jealous* of his sister. 他妒羨他的姊妹。③注意的;愛惜的。④忠實的;審愼的。The dog was a *jealous* guardian of the child. 這狗是這小孩子的謹愼的守衞。⑤不可不信的;須絕對忠實的。The Lord thy God is a *jealous* God. 主,你的神,乃是一個不可不信的神。—**ly,** *adv.* —**ness,** *n.*

jeal·ous·y 〔dʒɛləsɪ; ˈdʒeləsi〕 *n.*, *pl.* **-ous·ies.** ①嫉妒;妒忌。What is the reason for his *jealousy?* 他所以妒忌的理由是甚麼? ②小心翼翼的維護(某事);珍視。

jean 〔dʒin, dʒen; dʒein〕 *n.* ①斜紋布。②(*pl.*) a. 斜紋布工作服。b.〖俚〗褲子;牛仔褲。

jeep 〔dʒip; dʒiːp〕 *n.* ①吉普車。②輕型偵察機。③護航母艦。—*v.i.* 乘吉普車。

jeep·load 〔ˈdʒipˌlod; ˈdʒiːp–loud〕 *n.* 一吉普車所裝之數或量。

jeep·ney 〔ˈdʒipnɪ; ˈdʒiːpni〕 *n.*, *pl.* **-neys, -nies.** 菲律賓之小型巴士。

***jeer** 〔dʒɪr; dʒiə〕 *v.i.* & *v.t.* ①嘲弄;揶揄;戲弄〖at〗。Do not *jeer* at the mistakes or misfortunes of others. 不要嘲笑別人的錯誤或不幸。②以嘲笑驅走〖off〗。—*n.* 嘲笑;嘲弄;譏評。—**er,** *n.*

jeer·ing·ly 〔ˈdʒɪrɪŋlɪ; ˈdʒiəriŋli〕 *adv.* 「嘲弄地;揶揄地。」

Jef·fer·son 〔ˈdʒɛfəsn; ˈdʒefəsn〕 *n.* 傑佛遜 (Thomas, 1743–1826, 於1801–09年任美國第三任總統)。

Jef·fer·so·ni·an 〔ˌdʒɛfəˈsonɪən; ˌdʒefəˈsouniən〕 *adj.* Thomas Jefferson 的;其民主作風或政治主張的。—*n.* Jefferson 之崇拜者。—**ism,** *n.*

je·had 〔dʒɪˈhad; dʒiˈhɑːd〕 *n.* =**jihad.**

Je·hol 〔dʒəˈhol; dʒəˈhoul〕 *n.* 熱河(中國東北之一省,省會爲承德 Chengteh).

Je·ho·vah 〔dʒɪˈhovə; dʒiˈhouvə〕 *n.* 耶和華(舊約聖經中對上帝的稱呼)。

Je·hu 〔ˈdʒihju; ˈdʒiːhjuː〕 *n.* ①〖聖經〗耶戶(紀元前九世紀猶太之先知)。②〖聖經〗耶和(以色列第10代之王)。③(j–)〖謔〗開快車者。④(j–)〖俚〗任何開車者。

je·june 〔dʒɪˈdʒun; dʒiˈdʒuːn〕 *adj.* ①空洞的。②缺乏營養的。③枯燥無味的。④不成熟的。—**ly,** *adv.* —**ness, je·ju·ni·ty,** *n.*

je·ju·num 〔dʒɪˈdʒunəm; dʒiˈdʒuːnəm〕 *n.* 〖解剖〗空腸;小腸中段。

Je·kyll, Dr. 〔ˈdʒikl̩; ˈdʒiːkil〕 *n.* 吉柯醫生 (Robert Louis Stevenson 之名著 *Dr. Jekyll and Mr. Hyde* 中之主角, 服用自配之藥可使自己在原來之善良紳士與凶暴殘忍之 Mr. Hyde 間往復蛻變)。

jell 〔dʒɛl; dʒel〕 *v.i.* 〖美俗〗①變成冷凍。②(計畫、意見等)固定。—*v.t.* 使成凍子;使凝固。—*n.* 〖俗〗=**jelly.**

jel·lied 〔ˈdʒɛlɪd; ˈdʒelid〕 *adj.* ①成冷凍的。②塗凍子的;摻入凍子的。—**ness,** *n.*

jel·li·fy 〔ˈdʒɛləˌfaɪ; ˈdʒelifai〕 *v.t.* & *v.i.*, **-fied, -fy·ing.** ①(使)成冷凍。②(使)變成膠狀。—**jel·li·fi·ca·tion,** *n.*

jel·lo 〔ˈdʒɛlo; ˈdʒelou〕 *n.* 一種作甜食用的凍狀食品。

***jel·ly** 〔ˈdʒɛlɪ; ˈdʒeli〕 *n.*, *pl.* **-lies,** *v.*, **-lied, -ly·ing,** *adj.* —*n.* ①凍子(煮肉或果汁而成的食品,凍變透明,熱則融化)。②似凍子之物。—*v.i.* 成凍子。—*v.t.* ①使成凍子。②塗凍子於…上。—*adj.* 含凍子的;用凍子做的。—**like,** *adj.*

jel·ly·fish 〔ˈdʒɛlɪˌfɪʃ; ˈdʒelifiʃ〕 *n.*, *pl.* **-fish·es, -fish.** 水母;海蜇。

jem·my 〔ˈdʒɛmɪ; ˈdʒemi〕 *n.*, *pl.* **-mies,** *v.*, **-mied, -my·ing.** —*n.*〖英俚〗①=**jimmy.** ②燒羊頭。③大衣。—*v.t.* =**jimmy.**

je ne sais quoi 〔ʒənəˌseˈkwa; ʒənəˌseiˈkwa〕〖法〗①我不知是甚麼 (=I don't know what). ②難於描述的事物。

jen·net 〔ˈdʒɛnɪt; ˈdʒenit〕 *n.* ①(西班牙種之)小馬。②雌驢。(亦作 **genet**)

jen·ny 〔ˈdʒɛnɪ; ˈdʒeni〕 *n.*, *pl.* **-nies.** ①一種(同時可紡幾條線之)舊式紡紗機。②某些動物之雌性者(用於複合語,如 *jenny* ass 等)。

jeop·ard 〔ˈdʒɛpəd; ˈdʒepəd〕 *v.t.* = **jeopardize.**

jeop·ard·ize 〔ˈdʒɛpədˌaɪz; ˈdʒepədaiz〕 *v.t.*, **-ized, -iz·ing.** 使瀕於險境;冒…之危險。

jeop·ard·y 〔ˈdʒɛpədɪ; ˈdʒepədi〕 *n.*, *pl.* **-dies.** 危險;危難。

Jeph·thah 〔ˈdʒɛfθə; ˈdʒefθə〕 *n.* 〖聖經〗以色列的士師(舊約士師記 11–14 章)。

Jer. ①〖聖經〗Jeremiah. ② Jeremy. ③ Jersey.

jer·bo·a 〔dʒəˈboə; dʒəːˈbouə〕 *n.*〖動物〗(亞、非洲產之)跳鼠。

jer·e·mi·ad 〔ˌdʒɛrəˈmaɪæd; ˌdʒeriˈmaiæd〕 *n.* 悲歎;哀歎;悲傷的故事;哀史。

Jer·e·mi·ah 〔ˌdʒɛrəˈmaɪə; ˌdʒeriˈmaiə〕 *n.* ①〖聖經〗耶利米(希伯來一先知)。②〖聖經〗舊約中之耶利米書。③斥責惡行及預言罪惡者。

Jer·i·cho 〔ˈdʒɛrəˌko; ˈdʒerikou〕 *n.* ① Palestine 之一古城。②遙遠的地方。***Go to Jericho!*** 滾開!

jerk**[1] 〔dʒɝk; dʒəːk〕 *n.* ①急拉;急停;急動。The car stopped with a *jerk*. 車子頓然停止。②肌肉的痙攣。③〖俚〗未經世故的人;愚笨的人。get a jerk on***〖俗〗趕(工作);趕快弄。***in a jerk*** 立刻。***physical jerks***〖俗〗體操;運動。—*v.t.* ①急拉;急推;急拋。②抽水。③〖俗〗在冰果店供應冰淇淋、蘇打水等。—*v.i.* ①急動;連續急動而行;急停。The door *jerked* open. 門突然開了。②結結巴巴的說。She *jerked* along through her story. 她結結巴巴地把話講完。③〖俗〗在冰果店作服務生。—**er,** *n.* —**ing·ly,** *adv.*

jerk[2] *v.t.* 乾製(肉,牛肉)。—*n.* (牛)肉乾。

jer·kin 〔ˈdʒɝkɪn; ˈdʒəːkin〕 *n.* ①(十六、十七世紀時男人穿的)短皮上衣。②女子之背心。

jerk·wa·ter 〔ˈdʒɝkˌwɔtə; ˈdʒəːkˌwɔːtə〕 *n.* 支線專用之火車。—*adj.* ①支線的。②〖俗〗小的;不重要的。

jerk·y 〔ˈdʒɝkɪ; ˈdʒəːki〕 *adj.*, **jerk·i·er, jerk·i·est.** ①急動的;急停的;痙攣性的。②〖俚〗愚笨可笑的。—**jerk·i·ly,** *adv.* —**jerk·i·ness,** *n.*

Jer·o·bo·am 〔ˌdʒɛrəˈboəm; ˌdʒerəˈbouəm〕 *n.*〖聖經〗①耶羅波安(以色列第一代之王)。②耶羅波安(以色列一富有之王)。③(j–) 可裝約⅘加侖之酒瓶;此等酒瓶中所裝之物。

jer·ry 〔ˈdʒɛrɪ; ˈdʒeri〕 *n.*, *pl.* **-ries,** *adj.* —*n.* ①〖俚〗剪布機。②〖俚〗 鎚擊的嘈聲。③〖英俚〗啤酒店。④〖英俚〗便器。⑤〖美俚〗鐵路工人。⑥〖英俚〗圓硬氈帽。⑦偷工減料的營造商。⑧〖英俚〗德國人;德國兵。—*adj.* ①偷工減料的。②〖俚〗覺知的;知曉的。

jer·ry-build 〔ˈdʒɛrɪˌbɪld; ˈdʒeribild〕 *v.t.*, **-built, -build·ing.** 偷工減料地建造。

jer·ry-build·er 〔ˈdʒɛrɪˌbɪldə; ˈdʒeriˌbildə〕 *n.* 偷工減料的營造商。

jer·ry-build·ing 〔ˈdʒɛrɪˌbɪldɪŋ; ˈdʒeriˌbildiŋ〕 *n.* 偷工減料的建築工程。

jer·ry-built 〔ˈdʒɛrɪˌbɪlt; ˈdʒeribilt〕 *adj.* ①(建築物)偷工減料的。②(計畫、組織等)匆匆地或雜亂無章地發展成的。

jer·ry·man·der 〔ˈdʒɛrɪˌmændə; ˈdʒeriˌmændə〕 *v.t.*, *n.* =**gerrymander.**

***Jer·sey** 〔ˈdʒɝzɪ; ˈdʒəːzi〕 *n.*, *pl.* **-seys.** ①澤西(法國海岸附近之英屬島嶼)。②澤西產之乳牛。③=**New Jersey.** ④(j–)(女用)緊身內衣。⑤(j–) 緊身套頭衫。⑥(j–) 一種(由

J

棉、毛、絲等織成的)衣料。

*Je·ru·sa·lem [dʒə'rusələm; dʒə'ru:sələm] n. 耶路撒冷 (以色列的首都)。

jess [dʒɛs; dʒes] n. (繫鷹足之)足帶。—v.t. 繫以足帶。(亦作 jesse)

jes·sa·mine ['dʒɛsəmɪn; 'dʒesəmin] n. =jasmin(e).

Jes·se ['dʒɛsɪ; 'dʒesi] n. ①男子名。②〖聖經〗耶西 (David 之父)。(亦作 Jessie)

*jest [dʒɛst; dʒest] n. ①笑話;玩笑;滑稽。②嘲弄。to make a *jest* of a person. 愚弄人。③嘲笑的對象;笑柄。a standing *jest*. 經常爲人嘲笑的對象。***in jest*** 不認眞地。Many a true word is spoken *in jest*. 戲言中常含有眞理。—*v.i.* ①講笑話;開玩笑〖常 with〗. Please don't *jest* with me. 請你不要跟我開玩笑。②取笑〖常 at〗. —*v.t.* 嘲笑;嘲弄。—ful, *adj.*

jest·book ['dʒɛst,bʊk; 'dʒestbuk] n. 「笑話集。」

jest·er ['dʒɛstɚ; 'dʒestə] n. 小丑;弄臣。

Je·su ['dʒizju; 'dʒi:zju:] n. 〖詩〗=Jesus.

Jes·u·it ['dʒɛʒuɪt; 'dʒezjuit] n. ①耶穌會會員。②(j-) 陰謀家; 虛僞者(反耶穌會者稱該會會員的蔑視之詞)。—*adj.* ①耶穌會會員的。②(j-) 狡猾的;虛僞的。—ic, —i·cal, —ist, *adj.* —i·cal·ly, *adv.*

Jes·u·it·ism ['dʒɛʒuɪt,ɪzəm; 'dʒezjuitizəm] n. ①耶穌會教義、習慣、組織等。②(j-) 狡獪; 陰險。③(j-) 雙關語; 模稜兩可之遁辭。

Jes·u·it·ry ['dʒɛʒuɪtrɪ; 'dʒezjuitri] n. 「=Jesuitism.」

*Je·sus ['dʒizəs; 'dʒi:zəs] n. ①耶穌 (亦作 Jesus Christ). ②上帝。***Company*** (or ***Society***) ***of Jesus*** 耶穌會。—*interj.* 表誓言或强烈的懷疑、喪膽、敬畏、失望、痛苦等。

Jesus freak 〖美俚〗(常 J-F-)狂信耶穌的人。

*jet¹ [dʒɛt; dʒet] n., v., jet·ted, jet·ting, *adj.* —*n.*①噴射;噴出。②噴射口。③噴射機(=jet plane). ④噴出物。—*v.i.* & *v.t.* ①迸出;射出。Water *jetted* from the broken pipe. 水從破裂的管中噴出來。②乘坐噴射機。③迅速地移動或旅行。—*adj.* ①噴射的;噴射機的。②噴射推進的。③用噴射機的。④迅速的。—ting·ly, *adv.*

jet² n. ①〖礦〗黑玉。②漆黑。—*adj.* ①黑玉所製的。②漆黑的。

jet age 噴射機時代。

jet black 黑玉色;漆黑。

jet-black ['dʒɛt'blæk; 'dʒet'blæk] *adj.* 黑玉色的;漆黑的。

jet·boat ['dʒɛt,bot; 'dʒetbout] n. 噴「汽船。」

jet·borne ['dʒɛt,born; 'dʒetbɔ:n] *adj.* 由噴射機運載或運輸的。

jet engine 噴射機引擎。(亦作 jet 「motor)」

jet fighter 噴射戰鬥機。

jet-hop ['dʒɛt,hɑp; 'dʒethɔp] *v.i.* 乘噴射機至各地旅行。

jet·lin·er ['dʒɛt,laɪnɚ; 'dʒet,lainə] 「n. 噴射客機。」

jet plane 噴射式飛機。

jet·port ['dʒɛt,pɔrt; 'dʒetpɔ:t] n. 噴「射機機場。」

jet-pro·pelled ['dʒɛtprə'pɛld; 'dʒet-prə'peld] *adj.* 噴射推進式的。

jet·sam ['dʒɛtsəm; 'dʒetsəm] n. ①船舶遇難時爲減輕負擔而拋棄之貨物。②被拋棄之物。③〖喻〗命運多舛之人。(亦作 jetsom)

jet set 乘噴射機遊玩的上流社會人物們。(亦作 jet-set)

jet stream ①噴射氣流。②火箭或噴射「引擎之廢氣。」

jet·ti·son ['dʒɛtəsn̩; 'dʒetisn] *v.t.* ①(船或飛機遇難時)向船(機)外投棄(貨物)。②投棄;除去;放棄。③〖紙牌俚〗丟掉不要之牌。—*n.* ①(船或飛機遇難時) 向船(機)外拋貨。②向船或飛機外拋棄之貨物。—a·ble, *adj.*

jet transport 噴射運輸機。

jet·ty¹ ['dʒɛtɪ; 'dʒeti] n., *pl.* -ties, *v.* -tied, -ty·ing. —*n.* ①防波堤。②碼頭。—*v.t.* 使建築物之上部突出。

jet·ty² *adj.*①黑玉製的。②似黑玉的;烏黑的。

jeu [ʒɛ; ʒə:(ʒφ)] n., *pl.* jeux [ʒɛ; ʒə:(ʒφ)] 〖法〗娛樂;遊戲。

jeu d'es·prit [ʒφdɛs'pri; ʒφdes'pri:] 「〖法〗警句;妙語。」

*Jew [dʒu, dʒɪu; dʒu:] n. ①猶太人。②〖俗〗高利貸者; 守財奴。③信猶太教者;希伯來人。***go to the Jews*** 往放債者去借債。—*adj.* 猶太人的; 屬於猶太人的; 有猶太人特性的。—*v.t.* (j-)〖鄙〗欺騙;殺價。

Jew-bait·ing ['dʒu,betɪŋ; 'dʒu:,beitiŋ] n. 虐待 (迫害、排斥) 猶太人。—Jew bait·er, *n.*

*jew·el ['dʒuəl, 'dʒɪuəl; 'dʒu:əl, dʒuəl, dʒu:l, 'dʒu:il] n., v., -el(l)ed, -el·(l)ing —*n.* ①珠寶。②珠寶飾物。③貴重的物或人。④錶中之寶石。⑤似珠寶之物 (如星星、露珠等)。—*v.t.* 嵌以珠寶; 飾以珠寶。God has *jeweled* the sky with stars. 造物主在天上飾以星星。—like, *adj.*

jew·el·er ['dʒuələ; 'dʒu:ələ] n. ①珠寶商。②鐘錶商;鐘錶匠。(英亦作 jeweller)

jew·el·ler·y ['dʒuəlrɪ; 'dʒu:əlri] n. 〖英〗=jewelry.

*jew·el·ry ['dʒuəlrɪ; 'dʒu:əlri, 'dʒuəl-] n. 珠寶之集合稱;鑲嵌有寶石之飾物。

jew·el·weed ['dʒuəl,wid; 'dʒu:əlwi:d] n. 〖植物〗(北美產之)水金鳳。

Jew·ess ['dʒuɪs; 'dʒu:is] n. 〖蔑〗猶太女人。

jew·fish ['dʒu,fɪʃ; 'dʒu:fiʃ] n., *pl.* 「-fish, -fish·es. 大海鱸。」

*Jew·ish ['dʒuɪʃ, 'dʒɪuɪʃ; 'dʒu:iʃ] *adj.* 猶太的; 猶太人的; 似猶太人的。***Jewish calendar*** 猶太曆(自3761 B. C. 算起, 相傳是年爲創世之年)。***Jewish Law*** 猶太法 (摩西十誡)。—*n.* 意第緒語 (=Yiddish). —ly, *adv.* —ness, *n.*

Jew·ry ['dʒurɪ; 'dʒuəri] n., *pl.* -ries. ①猶太人之總稱;猶太民族。②猶太人居住區;猶太(人)街。③羅馬人統治之南巴勒斯坦的一部分區域 (=Judea).

Jew's-harp, Jews'-harp ['dʒuz,hɑrp; 'dʒu:z'hɑ:p] n. 單簧口琴(由一鋼舌圈以鐵框構成, 啣於牙間, 以指撥而發聲)。

Jez·e·bel ['dʒɛzəbl̩; 'dʒezəbl] n. ①〖聖經〗猶太王 Ahab 之妻。②蕩婦;悍婦。

JFK John Fitzgerald Kennedy.

jib¹ [dʒɪb; dʒib] n. ①(前檣支索的)船首三角帆。②起重機之鐵臂。***cut off one's jib*** 打斷他人談話。***the cut of one's jib***〖俗〗相貌; 風采; 裝束。—*adj.* 船首三角帆的。

jib² v., jibbed, jib·bing, n. —*v.i.* ①側行或後退而不前進;逡巡不前。②震驚或畏葸。—*v.t.* (船變方向時) 轉移,移動(帆、帆桁等)。—*n.* 逡巡不前之馬或其他動物。

jib·ber ['dʒɪbɚ; 'dʒibə] n. 拒向前走之馬; 躊躇不前的人。

jib boom 〖航海〗第二斜桅。

jibe¹ [dʒaɪb; dʒaib] v., jibed, jib·ing, n. —*v.t.* & *v.i.* ①嘲弄;諷罵〖常 at〗. ②〖美俗〗同意;與…相和諧。—*n.* 嘲弄;諷罵。

jibe² v., jibed, jib·ing, n. —*v.i.* ①〖航海〗(因風向或船首方向改變縱帆或其下桁) 自

一舷移至他舷。②〖航海〗改變船首方向使帆移至他舷。 —*v.t.* 改變（帆）之方向。—*n.* 帆之方向之改變。(亦作 **gybe**)

jiff [dʒɪf; dʒif] *n.* =**jiffy.**

jif·fy [ˈdʒɪfɪ; ˈdʒifi] *n.*〖俗〗一瞬間。Wait half a *jiffy*. 等一下。 ***in a jiffy*** 馬上；即刻。

jig [dʒɪg; dʒig] *n., v.,* **jigged, jig·ging.** —*n.* ①捷格舞（一種急迫輕快的舞蹈）。to dance a *jig*. 跳一支捷格舞。②捷格舞曲。③特種魚鈎(尤指適於冰下釣魚者)。④篩。⑤〖蔑〗黑人。⑥〖俚〗詭計；玩笑。 ***in jig time*** 〖俗〗馬上。 ***jig cut*** 〖美〗很深的傷痕。 ***jig water*** 〖美〗酒。 ***on the jig*** 戰戰兢兢地。 ***the jig is up*** 一切都完了(無望了)。—*v.t.* ①跳（捷格舞）。②搖。 —*v.i.* ①作輕快之跳舞。②蹦跳。③用 jig 魚鈎釣魚。④用礦篩搖篩。—**like,** —**ish,** *adj.*

jig·ger [ˈdʒɪgɚ; ˈdʒigə] *n.* ①跳捷格舞的人。②(洋酒的)計量杯(通常爲$1\frac{1}{2}$盎司)；一計量杯的酒量。③〖俗〗新玩意兒；新發明。④〖撞球〗球棒架子。⑤一種特製魚鈎。⑥〖高爾夫〗一種頭小的鐵製高爾夫球棒。⑦(製陶器用的)車床臺。⑧染布機。⑨(倉庫用的)小起重機。⑩〖採礦〗篩礦者；篩礦器。⑪〖航海〗a. 一種小絞轆。b. 一種補助帆。c. 有該帆的小船。d. =**jigger mast.** ⑫〖電信〗振動變壓器。

jig·gered [ˈdʒɪgɚd; ˈdʒigəd] *adj.* damned 之婉轉語。

jigger mast ①(四桅船之）最後桅。②小船船尾用以張小帆之短桅。

jig·gle [ˈdʒɪgl̩; ˈdʒigl] *v.,* **-gled, -gling,** *n.* —*v.t.* & *v.i.* 上下或左右急速移動。—*n.* 上下或左右急速移動。—**jig·gly,** *adj.*

jig·saw [ˈdʒɪgˌsɔ; ˈdʒigsɔː] *n., v.,* **-sawed, -sawed** or **-sawn, -saw·ing,** *adj.* —*n.* 鋼絲鋸；鏤花鋸；一種豎鋸。—*v.t.* 用鋼絲鋸鋸。—*adj.* 用鋼絲鋸鋸成的。

ji·had [dʒɪˈhad; dʒiˈhaːd] *n.* ①(回教徒之）聖戰。②(爲擁護或反對主義等之）鬥爭或運動。(亦作 **jehad**)

Jill [dʒɪl; dʒil] *n.* ①女子名。②(常 j-)少女；情人。

jilt [dʒɪlt; dʒilt] *v.t.* 遺棄；拋棄（情人）。—*n.* 拋棄戀人的女子。—**er,** *n.*

Jim [dʒɪm; dʒim] *n.* 男子名(James 之暱稱)。

Jim Crow 〖美俚〗①老烏（對黑人之蔑稱）。②對黑人之不平等待遇；種族分離。

Jim-Crow, jim-crow [ˈdʒɪmˈkro; ˈdʒimˈkrou] *adj.* 黑人的；歧視黑人的；隔離黑人的。—*v.t.* 歧視(黑人)。

Jim Crow·ism [ˈdʒɪmˈkroɪzəm; ˈdʒimˈkrouizəm] ①黑白（人）分離作法或政策。②反黑人的情緒。

jim·jams [ˈdʒɪmˌdʒæmz; ˈdʒimdʒæmz] *n. pl.* ①〖俚〗〖醫〗(酒精中毒之)震顫性狂譫症。②〖俚〗心神不定；神經過敏。③〖俗〗怪癖。

jim·my [ˈdʒɪmɪ; ˈdʒimi] *n., pl.* **-mies,** *v.,* **-mied, -my·ing.** —*n.* (盜賊用之）撬門棒。—*v.t.* 撬開(門、窗等)。(亦作 **jemmy**)

Jim·son weed [ˈdʒɪmsn̩ˌwid; ˈdʒimsnwiːd] 一種茄科毒草。(亦作**jimson weed**)

***jin·gle** [ˈdʒɪŋgl̩; ˈdʒiŋgl] *v.,* **-gled, -gling,** *n.* —*v.i.* ①作玎璫聲。The bells *jingled*. 鐘在玎璫響。②(詩句)充滿簡單的韻及重覆字句。③作玎璫聲而行走。④押韻。—*v.t.* 使作玎璫聲。He *jingled* the keys. 他把鑰匙弄得玎璫響。—*n.* ①玎璫聲。②聲韻鏗鏘之詩篇。③一種二輪馬車。—**jin·gler,** *n.* —**jin·gling·ly,** *adv.*

jin·gly [ˈdʒɪŋglɪ; ˈdʒiŋgli] *adj.* 發玎璫聲的。

jin·go [ˈdʒɪŋgo; ˈdʒiŋgou] *n., pl.* **-goes,** *adj.* —*n.* 侵略主義者；極端之愛國主義者；主戰論者。***by*** (***the living***) ***jingo!*** 誓必；一定。I know you can do it, *by jingo!* 我知道你能做到，準不會錯！—*adj.* 侵略主義的；侵略性的。

jin·go·ism [ˈdʒɪŋgoˌɪzəm; ˈdʒiŋgouizəm] *n.* 侵略主義；强硬之外交政策。—**jin·go·ist,** *n.*

jin·go·is·tic [ˌdʒɪŋgoˈɪstɪk; ˌdʒiŋgouˈistik] *adj.* 侵略主義的。(亦作 **jingoish**)

jink [dʒɪŋk; dʒiŋk] *v.i.* ①急轉。②躲開。—*n.* ①〖蘇〗急轉；閃避。②(*pl.*)喧嚷；狂歡。

jin·ni, jin·nee [dʒɪˈni; dʒiˈniː] *n., pl.* **jinn** [dʒɪn; dʒin].〖回教神話〗神靈；靈魔。(亦作 **djin, djinn, djinni, jin**)

jin·rik·i·sha, jin·rick·sha [dʒɪnˈrɪkʃə; dʒinˈrikʃə]〖日〗*n.* 人力車；黃包車。(亦作 **jinrickshaw, jinriksha, rickshaw, ricksha**)

jinx [dʒɪŋks; dʒiŋks] *n.* 〖美俚〗不祥之人(物)。—*v.t.*〖美俚〗①使倒楣。②煞風景。

jit·ney [ˈdʒɪtnɪ; ˈdʒitni] *n., pl.* **-neys.** 〖美俚〗①五分；五分鎳幣。②五分錢一次的公共汽車；中型公車。***jitney circuit*** 〖美〗郊外的廉價戲。***jitney dance*** 〖美〗五分錢跳一次的公開舞會。

jit·ter [ˈdʒɪtɚ; ˈdʒitə] *v.i.* 〖美俚〗神經過敏；心神不定；動作緊張。—*v.t.* 神經質地說出或作。—*n.* (*pl.*) (常 the-)〖俚〗神經質；神經過敏。

jit·ter·bug [ˈdʒɪtɚˌbʌg; ˈdʒitəbʌg] *n., v.,* **-bugged, -bug·ging.** —*n.* ①〖俚〗搖滾音樂狂；熱門音樂迷。②一種交際舞。—*v.i.* 〖俚〗似搖滾音樂狂地跳；狂舞。

jit·ter·y [ˈdʒɪtərɪ; ˈdʒitəri] *adj.*〖美俚〗神經過敏的；戰戰兢兢的。—**jit·ter·i·ness,** *n.*

jive [dʒaɪv; dʒaiv] *n., v.,* **jived, jiv·ing.** —*n.* 〖俚〗①搖滾樂。②搖滾樂者之術語。③無意義的或欺騙的話。—*v.i.* ①奏搖滾樂。②隨搖滾樂起舞。—*v.t.* 欺騙(某人)。

JJ., jj. ①Judges. ②Justices. **Jno.** John. **Jo.** Joel.

jo(e) [dʒo; dʒou] *n., pl.* **joes.** 〖蘇, 英北部〗愛人；情人。

Joan of Arc [ˈdʒonəvˈark; ˈdʒounəvˈɑːk] 聖女貞德 (Saint, 1412–1431, 法國民族女英雄, 後被燒死, 1920年尊爲聖女)。(法文作 **Jeanne d'Arc**)

Job [dʒob; dʒoub] *n.* ①男子名。②〖聖經〗約伯(希伯來之族長)。③(舊約中之)約伯記。

‡**job¹** [dʒab; dʒɔb] *n., v.,* **jobbed, job·bing,** *adj.* —*n.* ①一件工作。Dick had the *job* of painting the boat. 狄克要替這條小船上油漆。②須做的事情；應盡之責。③〖美俗〗職位；工作；職業。He has a *job* as a teacher. 他得到一個教員的職位。④包工；散工。⑤〖俗〗事件；事情。⑥(假公濟私的) 營利事業。⑦〖俚〗盜竊或其他犯罪行爲。⑧〖俚〗人或事（尤指引起注意者)。I like that blonde *job* in the red dress. 我喜歡那個穿紅衣服的金髮妞兒。⑨〖印刷〗零星印刷工作。***on the job*** 〖俚〗盡職的；盡責的。—*v.t.* ①購買（大量貨物）以分售零售商；買賣；經紀；租賃。②分包(工作)給人。③假公濟私。④開革。His party *jobbed* him. 他的黨開革了他。⑤欺騙。They *jobbed* him out of his property. 他們騙走了他的財產。—*v.i.* ①做散工。②作經紀。③假公濟私。—*adj.* ①包工的；臨時雇用的。②大宗的。

job² *v.,* **jobbed, job·bing,** *n.* =**jab.**

J

job action〖美〗在工作崗位上所作(以代替罷工)的鬥爭。
job analysis 職務分析。
jo·ba·tion [dʒoˈbeʃən; dʒouˈbeiʃən] *n.* 〖俗〗斥責;冗長之訓誡。
job·ber [ˈdʒabɚ; ˈdʒɔbə] *n.* ①〖英〗股票經紀人。②批發商。③做散工者。④假公濟私者。
job·ber·y [ˈdʒabərɪ; ˈdʒɔbəri] *n.* 假公濟私;瀆職行爲;官商勾結;貪污舞弊。
job·hold·er [ˈdʒabˌholdɚ; ˈdʒɔbˌhouldə] *n.* ①有一定職業的人。②〖美〗政府職員。
job·less [ˈdʒablɪs; ˈdʒɔblis] *adj.* ①無業的。②失業的。—*n.* (常 the-)(作 *pl.* 解)失業者。—**ness,** *n.*
job lot (廉價)整批出售的貨物。
job printer 承印零碎印刷的印刷商。
job work 零碎印刷。
Jock [dʒak; dʒɔk] *n.* ①〖俚〗蘇格蘭人;蘇格蘭兵。②〖蘇, 北英〗a. John 之暱稱。b. 鄉下小伙子。
jock[1] [dʒak; dʒɔk] *n.* 〖俗〗賽馬的騎師。
jock[2] *n.* ①=**jockstrap.** ②〖俚〗運動員。
jock·ey [ˈdʒakɪ; ˈdʒɔki] *n., pl.* **-eys,** *v.,* **-eyed, -ey·ing.** —*n.* ①賽馬的騎師;騎手。②〖俗〗駕駛或指揮(飛機或汽車)的人。***Jockey Club*** 賽馬俱樂部(尤指英國之 Newmarket 的)。—*v.t.* & *v.i.* ①(在賽馬會中)騎(馬)。②欺騙; 瞞。③運用手段(以謀職位或利益)。④〖俗〗駕駛(飛機或汽車)。—**like,** —**ish,** *adj.* —**ism,** —**ship,** *n.*
jock·o [ˈdʒako; ˈdʒɔkou] *n., pl.* **-os.** ①〖動物〗=**chimpanzee.** ②猴子(暱稱)。
jock·strap [ˈdʒakˌstræp; ˈdʒɔk-stræp] *n.* (運動員所穿之)鬆緊內褲。(亦作**athletic supporter**)
jo·cose [dʒoˈkos; dʒəˈkous] *adj.* 詼諧的;滑稽的。—**ly,** *adv.* —**ness, jo·cos·i·ty,** *n.*
joc·u·lar [ˈdʒakjəlɚ; ˈdʒɔkjulə] *adj.* 滑稽的;詼諧的。—**ly,** *adv.*
joc·u·lar·i·ty [ˌdʒakjəˈlærətɪ; ˌdʒɔkjuˈlæriti] *n., pl.* **-ties.** 滑稽;詼諧。
joc·und [ˈdʒakənd; ˈdʒɔkənd] *adj.* 歡樂的;高興的。—**ly,** *adv.*
jo·cun·di·ty [dʒoˈkʌndətɪ; dʒouˈkʌnditi] *n.* 歡樂;高興;快活。
jodh·purs [ˈdʒadpɚz; ˈdʒɔdpəz] *n. pl.* 馬褲。
Joe [dʒo; dʒou] *n.* ①男子名。②〖美俗〗兵。③(常 j-)〖俚〗傢伙。***not for Joe*** 〖英俚〗絕非…;絕不…。
joe [dʒo; dʒou] *n.* 〖蘇〗=**jo.**
Jo·el [ˈdʒoəl; ˈdʒouel] *n.* 〖聖經〗①約珥(希伯來預言家)。②約珥書(舊約之一卷)。
joe-pye weed [ˌdʒoˈpaɪ~; ˌdʒouˈpai~] (美國產之)紫花;紫菀草。
jo·ey [ˈdʒoɪ; ˈdʒoui] *n., pl.* **-eys.** 〖澳〗幼獸;(尤指)小袋鼠。
jog[1] [dʒag; dʒɔg] *v.,* **jogged, jog·ging,** *n.* —*v.t.* ①推動;輕搖;輕撞。②喚起(記憶);使憶起; 提醒。③使上下顛動。④使(馬)維持慢步行走。⑤將(一疊大小相同的紙張)搡齊。—*v.i.* 搖盪前進; 踱踱前進; 沉重緩慢而行;徐行。—*n.* ①輕推; 搖動。②慢步。③暗示。—**ger,** *n.*
jog[2] *n.* 〖美〗(線或面之)凸出或凹入部分(尤指成直角者)。
jog·ging [ˈdʒagɪŋ; ˈdʒɔgiŋ] *n.* 慢跑運動。
jog·gle[1] [ˈdʒagl̩; ˈdʒɔgl] *v.,* **-gled, -gling,** *n.*—*v.t.* & *v.i.* ①輕搖; 震動; 輕推。②搖曳而行〖on, along〗. —*n.* 搖動;震動;搖曳的行進。—**jog·gler,** *n.*
jog·gle[2] *n.* 〖建築〗嚙合;榫。—*v.t.* 使嚙合;榫接。
jog trot ①緩步。②例行事務;徐緩之辦事態度。
Jo·han·nine [dʒəˈhænɪn; dʒəˈhænin] *adj.* 〖聖經〗使徒約翰的;約翰福音書的。
Jo·han·nis·ber·ger [dʒəˈhænɪsˌbɝgɚ; dʒəˈhænisˌbəːgə] *n.* 一種白葡萄酒。
John [dʒan; dʒɔn] *n.* ①男子名。②(新約)約翰福音。③約翰(耶穌的門徒)。④施洗約翰。
john [dʒan; dʒɔn] *n.* 〖俚〗厠所。
John Bull ①英國人。②典型的英國人。
John Company 英國東印度公司。
John Doe [~do; ~dou] ①某甲(法律或正式文件上所用之假定之人)。②張三(無名的普通市民)。
John Do·ry [~ˈdorɪ; ~ˈdɔːri] *pl.* **John Do·rys.** 魴(一種海魚)。(亦作 **John Doree**)
John Han·cock [~ˈhænkak; ~ˈhæn-kɔk]〖美俗〗親筆簽字。
john·ny [ˈdʒanɪ; ˈdʒɔni] *n.* ①(J-)男子名(John 之俗稱)。②任何男子或男童;漢子;傢伙。③花花公子;紈袴子。
john·ny·cake [ˈdʒanɪˌkek; ˈdʒɔnikeik] *n.* 〖美〗一種玉蜀黍粉製成之餅。
John·ny-jump-up [ˈdʒanɪdʒʌmp-ˌʌp; ˈdʒɔnidʒʌmpˌʌp] *n.* 〖植物〗①紫羅蘭。②〖美〗野生三色紫羅蘭。
Johnny Raw 生手;新兵。
John o' Groat's (House) [ˈdʒan-əˈgrots; ˈdʒɔnəˈgrouts] 蘇格蘭之最北端。***from John o' Groat's to Land's End*** 從英國之極北到極南;在全英國。
John·son[1] [ˈdʒansn̩; ˈdʒɔnsn] *n.* 約翰生 (Andrew, 1808–1875, 美國第十七任總統, 任期 1865–69)。
John·son[2] 約翰生 (Samuel, 1709–1784, 世稱 Dr. Johnson, 英國辭典編纂者及作家)。
John·son[3] *n.* 詹森 (Lyndon Baines, 1908–1973, 1963–1969任美國第三十六任總統)。
John·son·ese [ˌdʒansn̩ˈiz; ˌdʒɔnsəˈniːz] *n.* ①Samuel Johnson 的文體。②似 Samuel Johnson 之誇張的文體。—*adj.* Johnson 派的(文體)。
John·so·ni·an [dʒanˈsonɪən; dʒɔnˈsounjən] *adj.* (似) Samuel Johnson 或其作品的;誇張的。—*n.* Samuel Johnson之摹仿者、崇拜者或研究者。—**ism,** *n.* —**ly,** *adv.*
John the Baptist 〖聖經〗施洗約翰(聖經中預報耶穌來臨並以水施洗禮者)。
joie de vi·vre [ʒwadəˈvivr; ʒwadəˈviːvr] 〖法〗生活樂趣(=joy of living).
‡join [dʒɔɪn; dʒɔin] *v.t.* ①連接; 接合; 結合; 聯合。②會合; 交接。The brook *joins* the river. 溪與河會合。③使締交;使聯姻。④回;歸。⑤加入;參加。⑥伴;隨同。I'll *join* you later. 過些時我將隨同你一起。⑦接近;毗連。His farm *joins* mine. 他的田地毗連着我的田地。⑧用直線或曲線連結。⑨會戰;交戰。The opposing armies *joined* battle in the valley. 敵對兩軍在山谷中交戰。—*v.i.* ①加入; 參加。②聯合。③伴隨; 一同。Will you *join* with me in buying a present for her? 你可同我聯合給她買一件禮物嗎?④毗連。⑤從軍〖常up〗. He *joined* up to fight for his country. 他從軍爲國而戰。***join battle*** 交戰;會戰。***join forces*** (***with***)(與)合作;聯合行動。***join issue*** 討論;妥協;共同起訴。***join the colors*** 服兵役。***join the*** (***great*** or ***silent***) ***majority*** 死。***join up*** 〖俗〗入伍; 從軍。—*n.* 連接處; 接縫處。

—a•ble, *adj.* 〖注意〗 join 本意卽爲接合在一起, 其後不可再加 together.

join·der 〔ˈdʒɔɪndɚ; ˈdʒɔində〕 *n.* ①連合;接合。②〖法律〗聯合訴訟;共同訴訟。

join·er 〔ˈdʒɔɪnɚ; ˈdʒɔinə〕 *n.* ①聯合者;接合物。②細工木匠。③〖俗〗加入許多俱樂部及社團的人。

join·er·y 〔ˈdʒɔɪnərɪ; ˈdʒɔinəri〕 *n.* ①細木匠業;細木工。②細木工的製品。

joint** 〔dʒɔɪnt; dʒɔint〕 *n.* ①連接物; 連接處。②〖解剖〗關節。The man is getting old and his *joints* are stiff. 這人漸漸老了, 關節也硬化了。③大塊(肉)。④接合;聯接(之狀態)。a perfect *joint*. 完全接合。⑤(樹之枝幹上的) 附根; 節疤(藉以生枝發葉者)。⑥〖俚〗下流場所。 ⑦〖俚〗含有大麻煙的香煙。 ***out of joint **a.** 脫節;脫臼。**b.** 不吉利。**c.** 不相稱;不合適。***put a person's nose out of joint*** 奪愛;破壞;擾亂。—*v.t.* ①(用連接物)接合。②自關節切斷;分節。Please *joint* this chicken before sending it. 把這隻鷄送去以前, 先自關節處切斷。—*v.i.* 接合。—*adj.* ①共同的;連合的。*joint* efforts. 共同的努力。②共有的;共享的。*joint* owners. 共有者。

joint account 兩人共有之銀行戶頭。

Joint Chiefs of Staff 〖美〗參謀首長聯席會議。

Joint Commission on Rural Reconstruction 農復會。(略作 JCRR)

joint committee 上下兩院所共組之委員會。

joint·ed 〔ˈdʒɔɪntɪd; ˈdʒɔintid〕 *adj.* 接合的;有接縫的;有關節的。—**ly,** *adv.* —**ness,** *n.*

joint·er 〔ˈdʒɔɪntɚ; ˈdʒɔintə〕 *n.* ①接合之人或物。②接合之器具(如石工用的塗縫鏝, 木工用的長鉋等)。

joint family 數代同堂之大家庭。

jointing rule 〖石工〗接縫規;榫規。

joint·less 〔ˈdʒɔɪntlɪs; ˈdʒɔintlis〕 *adj.* ①無接縫的; 無關節的; 無接合部的。②僵硬的;不能彎曲的。

joint·ly 〔ˈdʒɔɪntlɪ; ˈdʒɔintli〕 *adv.* 聯合地;連帶地。

joint resolution 上下兩院之共同決議。

joint·ress 〔ˈdʒɔɪntrɪs; ˈdʒɔintris〕 *n.* 〖法律〗(有 jointure 繼承權之)女性。

joint return 夫妻所得稅之共同申報。

joint session 上下兩院之聯席會議。

joint stock 合資;合股。

joint-stock 〔ˈdʒɔɪntˈstɑk; ˈdʒɔint-stɔk〕 *adj.* 合資的;股份組織的。

joint-stock company 股份公司。(亦作 **joint-stock corporation**)

joint stool 摺凳。

join·ture 〔ˈdʒɔɪntʃɚ; ˈdʒɔintʃə〕 *n., v.,* **-tured, -tur·ing.** 〖法律〗 —*n.* 寡婦所得產(夫生前指定由妻繼承之財產)。 —*v.t.* 劃定寡婦所得產給(妻子)。—**join·tured,** *adj.*

joist 〔dʒɔɪst, dʒɔɪs; dʒɔist〕 *n.* 托梁;小桁;欄柵。—*v.t.* 裝小桁;架托梁。—**ed,** *adj.*

joke** 〔dʒok; dʒouk〕 *n., v.,* **joked, jok·ing.** —*n.* ①笑話;玩笑;幽默。That was a good *joke*. 那是一個好笑話。②笑柄;取笑之人物;取笑之對象。③開玩笑的話;戲言。④過於容易的事。The test was a *joke* to the whole class. 全班都認爲那次測驗題目太容易。a practical joke*** 惡作劇。***have joke (with somebody)*** (與人)開玩笑。***in joke*** 玩笑地; 不認眞地。***make a joke about something*** 把某事當做兒戲; 不認眞作。***no joke*** 不是兒戲;重要的事。***play a joke on somebody*** 捉弄人。***see a joke*** 識幽默。***take a joke*** 經得起開玩笑。 ***the best of the joke*** 笑話的重點。 ***the joke of the town (village, etc.)*** 笑柄;最有趣的人(事、物)。—*v.i.* 說笑話; 開玩笑。 He's always *joking*. 他老是說笑話。—*v.t.* ①取笑;愚弄。②以說笑話取得。The comedian *joked* coins from the audience. 小丑說笑話以賺得聽衆的硬幣。—**less,** *adj.*

jok·er 〔ˈdʒokɚ; ˈdʒoukə〕 *n.* ①愛講笑話者;滑稽角色;詼諧者。②〖英俚〗人;傢伙。③〖美〗意圖淆亂本意, 使法案歸於無效而插入之含混語句。④(紙牌中可當任何點數用的一張)飛牌; 百搭。⑤取巧。⑥隱伏而未被發覺之困難。⑦〖俚〗自以爲聰明而令人討厭的人。

jok·ing 〔ˈdʒokɪŋ; ˈdʒoukiŋ〕 *adj.* 戲謔的;打趣的;(當着)開玩笑的。—**ly,** *adv.*

jok·y 〔ˈdʒokɪ; ˈdʒouki〕 *adj.,* **jok·i·er, jok·i·est.** 〖俗〗滑稽的;詼諧的;好笑的。

Jo·liot-Cu·rie[1] 〔ˌʒoˈljoˌkyˈri; ˌʒɔːˈliou-ˌkyˈriː〕 *n.* 若利歐居里(Frédéric, 1900–1958, 法國物理學家, 曾獲1935年諾貝爾化學獎)。

Jo·liot-Cu·rie[2] *n.* 若利歐居里 (Iréne, 1897–1956, Marie 及 Pierre Curie 之女, 法國物理學家, 曾獲1935年諾貝爾化學獎)。

jol·li·fi·ca·tion 〔ˌdʒɑləfəˈkeʃən; ˌdʒɔ-lifiˈkeiʃən〕 *n.* 歡宴;作樂;歡樂時日。

jol·li·fy 〔ˈdʒɑləˌfaɪ; ˈdʒɔlifai〕 *v.,* **-fied, -fy·ing.** —*v.t.* 〖俗〗使愉快; 使高興。—*v.i.* 飲酒作樂;歡樂。

jol·li·ly 〔ˈdʒɑləlɪ; ˈdʒɔləli〕 *adv.* 歡樂地。

jol·li·ty 〔ˈdʒɑlɪtɪ; ˈdʒɔliti〕 *n., pl.* **-ties.** 快樂;歡樂;歡宴;喜慶。

***jol·ly** 〔ˈdʒɑlɪ; ˈdʒɔli〕 *adj.,* **-li·er, -li·est,** *adv., v.,* **-lied, -ly·ing,** *n.* —*adj.* ①高興的;愉快的;歡樂的。②宜人的;爽快的。We are having *jolly* weather. 天氣很宜人。③〖英俗〗**a.** 很;非常。**b.** 微醉。④大的。—*adv.* 〖英俗〗極;很;非常。—*v.t.* & *v.i.* 〖俗〗恭維; 捧; 奉承。—*n.* 〖俗〗①恭維;奉承。②作樂。

jolly boat 大船上所携帶的小艇。(亦作 **jolly-boat**)

Jolly Roger 海盜旗(骷髏旗)。

***jolt** 〔dʒolt; dʒoult〕 *v.t.* 搖動;使顚簸。—*v.i.* 顚簸而行;搖動;震盪。—*n.* ①顚簸;搖動。②震驚。③令人震驚之事。The news was a *jolt* to me. 那件消息令我震驚。④未料到的拒絕或失敗。⑤〖俚〗徒刑。⑥〖俚〗麻醉藥之注射。⑦任何東西之可提神的分量。 —**er,** *n.* —**ing·ly,** *adv.*

jolt·er·head 〔ˈdʒoltɚˌhɛd; ˈdʒoultəhed〕 *n.* 笨大的頭;笨人;呆子。—**ed,** *adj.*

jolt·y 〔ˈdʒoltɪ; ˈdʒoulti〕 *adj.,* **jolt·i·er, jolt·i·est.** 〖俗〗搖動的。—**jolt·i·ness,** *n.*

Jo·nah 〔ˈdʒonə; ˈdʒounə〕 *n.* ①〖聖經〗約拿(希伯來的先知)。②約拿書(舊約聖經之一卷)。③不祥的人物。(亦作 **Jonas**)

Jon·a·than 〔ˈdʒɑnəθən; ˈdʒɔnəθən〕 *n.* ①美國人(尤指新英格蘭人)。②〖聖經〗約拿單(Saul 之子, David 之友)。③男子名。④(美國產之)一種秋熟蘋果。

Jones 〔dʒonz; dʒounz〕 *n.* 仲斯(Daniel, 1881–1968, 英國語音學家)。

jon·gleur 〔ˈdʒɑŋglɚ; ʒɔːŋˈgləː〕 〖法〗*n.* (中世紀)吟遊詩人。

jon·quil 〔ˈdʒɑŋkwɪl; ˈdʒɔŋkwil〕 *n.* 〖植物〗長壽花;黃水仙。

Jor·dan 〔ˈdʒɔrdn; ˈdʒɔːdn〕 *n.* 約旦(**a.** 亞洲西南部之一國, 其首都爲阿曼 Amman。**b.** 巴勒斯坦境內之一河流, 流入死海)。

J

Jordan almond (西班牙產)約旦杏。

jo·rum [ˈdʒorəm; ˈdʒɔːrəm] *n.* ①大盃；大酒盅。②一大盃酒。

Jos. ①Joseph. ②Josephine. ③Josiah.

Jo·seph [ˈdʒozəf; ˈdʒouzif] *n.* ①〖聖經〗約瑟(Jacob 之愛子,後爲埃及之長官)。②〖聖經〗聖母瑪利亞之丈夫。③男子名。④(j-) 十八世紀婦人之長大衣。

josh [dʒaʃ; dʒɔʃ] *n.* 〖美俚〗戲謔；揶揄。—*v.t. & v.i.* 〖美俚〗揶揄；戲弄；(無惡意地)開玩笑。—**er,** *n.*

Josh. 〖聖經〗 Joshua.

Josh·u·a [ˈdʒaʃuə; ˈdʒɔʃwə] *n.* ①男子名。②〖聖經〗約書亞 (繼承 Moses 爲以色列民族之領導者)。③約書亞書 (舊約之一卷)。

jos·kin [ˈdʒaskɪn; ˈdʒɔskin] *n.* 〖俚〗村夫；蠢漢；鄉下佬。

joss [dʒas; dʒɔs] *n.* ①(中國之) 神像；菩薩。②〖俗〗好運；機會。

joss·er [ˈdʒasə; ˈdʒɔsə] *n.* 〖英俚〗呆子；「笨伯；老漢。」

joss house (中國的)神廟。

joss stick (中國祭神用之)香。

***jos·tle** [ˈdʒasl; ˈdʒɔsl] *v.,* **-tled, -tling,** *n.* —*v.t.* 推擠。I was *jostled* by the crowd. 我爲羣衆所擠。—*v.i.* ①推擠 (如在人羣中) 〖常with, against〗. He *jostled* against the crowd. 他在人羣中擠。②〖美俚〗扒竊。③(與某人或某事)並存。④競爭。—*n.* 擁擠；推撞。(亦作 **justle**) —**ment, jos·tler,** *n.*

jot [dʒat; dʒɔt] *n., v.,* **jot·ted, jot·ting.** —*n.* 些微；少量。***jot or tittle*** 些微。***not a jot*** 一點也不。—*v.t.* 匆匆而記；略記〖down〗.

Joule [dʒaul; dʒuːl] *n.* ①焦耳 (James Prescott, 1818–1889, 英國物理學家)。②(j-) 〖物理〗焦耳(電能之實用單位＝10^7 爾格)。

jounce [dʒauns; dʒauns] *v.,* **jounced, jounc·ing,** *n.* —*v.t. & v.i.* (上下)震動；搖撼；顚簸。—*n.* 震動；搖撼；顚簸。

jour. ①journal. ②journeyman.

‡jour·nal [ˈdʒɝnl; ˈdʒəːnl] *n.* ①日誌；日記。②報紙；雜誌。the *Ladies' Home Journal.* "婦女家庭雜誌"。③流水帳。④〖機械〗軸頸。—**ar·y,** —**ish,** *adj.*

jour·nal·ese [ˌdʒɝnlˈiz; ˌdʒəːnəˈliːz] *n.* 新聞文體。—*adj.* 新聞文體的。

***jour·nal·ism** [ˈdʒɝnlˌɪzəm; ˈdʒəːnəlizəm] *n.* ①新聞學；新聞業。②報章雜誌(集合稱)。③報章雜誌上之文章。

***jour·nal·ist** [ˈdʒɝnlɪst; ˈdʒəːnəlist] *n.* ①新聞記者；新聞工作者。②記日記者。

jour·nal·is·tic [ˌdʒɝnlˈɪstɪk; ˌdʒəːnəˈlistik] *adj.* 新聞事業的；新聞工作者的；新聞文字的；新聞雜誌特有的。

jour·nal·ize [ˈdʒɝnlˌaɪz; ˈdʒəːnəlaiz] *v.,* **-ized, -iz·ing.** —*v.t.* ①載入日記。②〖簿記〗載入日記簿。—*v.i.* ①記日記。②從事報章雜誌事業。—**jour·nal·i·za·tion, jour·nal·iz·er,** *n.*

‡jour·ney [ˈdʒɝnɪ; ˈdʒəːni] *n., pl.* **-neys,** *v.,* **-neyed, -ney·ing.** —*n.* 旅行；旅程。I wish you a safe *journey.* 祝你一路平安。***break one's journey (at)*** 中途逗留。We *broke our journey at* Japan for one night. 我們中途在日本停留了一夜。—*v.i.* 旅行。—**er,** *n.*

jour·ney·man [ˈdʒɝnɪmən; ˈdʒəːnimən] *n., pl.* **-men.** ①熟練工人。②(學徒滿期的)職工。

jour·ney·work [ˈdʒɝnɪˌwɝk; ˈdʒəːniwəːk] *n.* ①短工；散工。②無聊的工作。

joust [dʒʌst; dʒaust] *n.* ①(騎士)馬上之長槍比武。②(*pl.*)比賽；競技。—*v.i.* ①馬上用長槍比武。②策劃。(亦作 **just**)

Jove [dʒov; dʒouv] *n.* ①＝**Jupiter.** ②〖詩〗木星。***by Jove!*** **a.** 表驚異、快樂或加重語氣之歎詞。**b.** 發誓用語。

jo·vi·al [ˈdʒovɪəl; ˈdʒouvjəl] *adj.* ①天性快活的；和氣的；快樂的。②(J-) Jove 的。—**i·ty,** *n.* —**ly,** *adv.*

Jo·vi·an [ˈdʒovɪən; ˈdʒouviən] *adj.* ①Jove 的；Jove 似的；威風凜凜的。②木星(Jupiter) 的。—**ly,** *adv.*

jowl [dʒaul; dʒaul] *n.* ①下顎；顎。②頰。③胖人下顎之垂肉。④魚頭。⑤(家畜的)喉部垂肉。***cheek by jowl*** 極爲接近的。

‡joy [dʒɔɪ; dʒɔi] *n.* ①歡喜；快樂；高興。He was filled with *joy.* 他充滿歡喜。②使人快樂之事物；樂事。***for joy*** 由於快樂或高興而 (做某事)。***to the joy of*** 令…極爲快樂，高興。—*v.i.* 歡樂；欣喜；愉快。—*v.t.* 使快樂；致賀。

joy·bells [ˈdʒɔɪˌbɛlz; ˈdʒɔibelz] *n. pl.* 「(教堂之)喜鐘；祝鐘。」

Joyce¹ [dʒɔɪs; dʒɔis] *n.* 女子名。

Joyce² *n.* 喬伊斯 (James, 1882–1941, 愛爾蘭作家)。

***joy·ful** [ˈdʒɔɪfəl; ˈdʒɔiful] *adj.* ①歡喜的；快樂的；高興的。②令人歡樂高興的。*joyful news.* 令人歡欣的消息。③表示高興的。—**ness,** *n.* —**ly,** *adv.*

joy·less [ˈdʒɔɪlɪs; ˈdʒɔilis] *adj.* ①不令人喜悅的；不足樂的。②無歡樂的；悲愁的。—**ly,** *adv.* —**ness,** *n.*

***joy·ous** [ˈdʒɔɪəs; ˈdʒɔiəs] *adj.* 快樂的；高興的。—**ly,** *adv.* —**ness,** *n.* 〖注意〗**joyous** 指快樂的性情或氣質。**joyful** 指因某事而快樂或歡樂。

joy-ride [ˈdʒɔɪˌraɪd; ˈdʒɔiraid] *v.i.* 〖俗〗駕車兜風。—**joy-rid·er,** *n.*

joy stick 〖俚〗(飛機之)駕駛桿；操縱桿。

JP jet propulsion. **J.P.** Justice of the Peace. **Jr., jr.** ①Journal. ②Junior. **J.T.C.** Junior Training Corps.

Ju. June.

Juan Car·los [wanˈkarlos; wɑːnˈkɑːlɔːs] *n.* 卡洛斯(Juan Carlos Alfonso Victor Maria de Borbón y Borbón,1938– 1975年佛朗哥去世，即位爲西班牙國王)。

ju·bi·lance [ˈdʒubləns; ˈdʒuːbiləns] *n.* 歡喜；欣喜；喜悅。(亦作 **jubilancy**)

ju·bi·lant [ˈdʒublənt; ˈdʒuːbilənt] *adj.* 歡呼的；喜洋洋的；(令人) 喜悅的。—**ly,** *adv.*

Ju·bi·la·te [ˌdʒubəˈleti; ˌdʒuːbiˈlɑːti] *n.* ①〖聖經〗詩篇第一百篇；其樂曲。②〖天主教〗復活節後之第三禮拜日。

ju·bi·late [ˈdʒublˌet; ˈdʒuːbileit] *v.i.,* **-lat·ed, -lat·ing.** ①歡呼；歡唱。②歡欣慶祝。—**ju·bi·la·to·ry,** *adj.*

ju·bi·la·tion [ˌdʒublˈeʃən; ˌdʒuːbiˈleiʃən] *n.* ①歡呼；喜悅。②歡欣慶祝。

ju·bi·lee [ˈdʒublˌi; ˈdʒuːbiliː] *n.* ①猶太之五十年節。②歡騰；狂歡節。③二十五或五十周年紀念。④天主教之大赦年。***ordinary jubilees*** 羅馬天主教會每二十五年一次之大赦年。

Jud. ①Judges. ②Judith. ③ Judicial.

Ju·dae·a [dʒuˈdiə; dʒuːˈdiə] *n.* ＝**Judea.** —**Ju·dae·an,** *adj., n.*

Ju·dah [ˈdʒudə; ˈdʒuːdə] *n.*〖聖經〗猶太 (**a.** Jacob 之第四子。**b.** 其後裔。**c.** 古巴勒斯坦南部之一王國)。

Ju·da·ic [dʒu'deɪk; dʒuː'deiik] *adj.* 猶太人(民族)的;猶太人習俗(文化)的;猶太教的。(亦作 **Judaical**) —**al·ly,** *adv.*

Ju·da·ism ['dʒudɪ,ɪzəm; 'dʒuːdeiizəm] *n.* ①猶太教。②猶太主義;信奉猶太教;遵奉猶太人之習俗、規律等。③猶太人(集合稱)。

Ju·da·ize ['dʒudɪ,aɪz; 'dʒuːdeiaiz] *v.t. & v.i.,* **-ized, -iz·ing.** (使)成猶太式;(使)猶太化;(使)皈依猶太教。—**Ju·da·i·za·tion, Ju·da·iz·er,** *n.*

Ju·das ['dʒudəs; 'dʒuːdəs] *n.* ①聖經中之猶大(即出賣耶穌者)。②出賣朋友的人。③(常 j-)門戶上小孔(以窺探外面者)。—*adj.* 引誘其他動物到屠宰場之引誘物的。—**like,** *adj.*

Judas tree 〖植物〗洋蘇木。

jud·der ['dʒʌdə; 'dʒʌdə] *v.i., n.* 戰慄。

Jude [dʒud; dʒuːd] *n.* 〖聖經〗①耶穌的十二門徒之一。②猶大書(新約之一卷)。③猶大書之作者。

Ju·de·a [dʒu'diə; dʒuː'diə] *n.* 昔羅馬統治的南Palestine 之一部分。(亦作 **Judaea**)

Judg. 〖聖經〗Judges.

judge [dʒʌdʒ; dʒʌdʒ] *n., v.,* **judged, judg·ing.** —*n.* ①司法官;推事;審判官。The *judge* was very kind.這法官很仁慈。②裁判者。③鑑識家。He is a good *judge* of horses. 他是一個很會鑑賞馬的人。④士師(古以色列的統治者)。—*v.t.* ①審判。God will *judge* all men. 上帝將審判一切人。②裁判;判斷;評判。I can't *judge* whether he was right or wrong. 我不能斷定他是對是錯。③鑑定;識別。Who is going to *judge* the horses? 誰來鑑定這些馬? ④想;認為。We *judged* it better to start at once. 我們認為立刻出發較好。⑤批評;譴責。Who can *judge* another? 誰能批評他人? —*v.i.* ①當法官;審判。②判斷;估計。**judge by** (or **from**) 由…觀之;由…看來。*Judging from* (or *by*) what you say, he ought to succeed. 由你的話看來,他應該會成功。 —**a·ble,** *adj.* —**judg·er,** *n.*

judge advocate *pl.* **judge advocates.** 〖軍〗軍法官;檢察官。

Judge Advocate General *pl.* **Judge Advocate Generals** 或 **Judge Advocates General.** 〖軍〗軍法處長;軍法局長。

judge-made ['dʒʌdʒ,med; 'dʒʌdʒmeid] *adj.* 法官制定的。

judge-made law 〖法律〗判例法。

Judg·es ['dʒʌdʒɪz; 'dʒʌdʒiz] *n.*(作 *sing.* 解)〖聖經〗士師記(舊約之一卷)。

judge·ship ['dʒʌdʒʃɪp; 'dʒʌdʒʃip] *n.* judge 之地位、職權或任期。

judg(e)·mat·ic [dʒʌdʒ'mætɪk; dʒʌdʒ'mætik] *adj.* 〖俗〗考慮周到的;有良好判斷力的;聰敏的。—**al·ly,** *adv.*

judge·mat·i·cal [dʒʌdʒ'mætɪkḷ; dʒʌdʒ'mætikl] *n.* =**judgematic.**

***judg(e)·ment** ['dʒʌdʒmənt; 'dʒʌdʒmənt] *n.* ①審判;判決。The *judgment* was against him. 判決於他不利。②判斷力。③判斷;意見。It was a bad plan in his *judgment.* 依他判斷,這是個不妥的計畫。④天譴;報應。⑤批評;責難。**the** (**Day of**) **Judgment** (基督教所謂的)最後審判日;世界末日。—**al,** *adj.*

Judgment Day, judgment day 〖神學〗世界末日;最後審判日。

judgment debt 經法院裁定之債務。

judgment seat 推事席;審判官席;法庭。

ju·di·ca·to·ry ['dʒudɪkə,torɪ; 'dʒuːdikətəri] *adj., n., pl.* **-ries.** —*adj.* 裁判的;司法的。—*n.* ①裁判所;法庭。②司法行政;法院(集合稱)。

ju·di·ca·ture ['dʒudɪkətʃə; 'dʒuːdikətʃə] *n.* ①司法行政。②司法權。③法官或法院之管轄區。④司法官的集合稱。⑤法院;司法部。***The Supreme Court of Judicature*** 英國高等法院。

***ju·di·cial** [dʒu'dɪʃəl; dʒuː'diʃəl] *adj.* ①法庭的;法官的;司法的。a *judicial* assembly. 法庭。*judicial* murder. 法庭所作不公平之死刑判決。②公平的;公正的。a man with a *judicial* mind. 內心公正的人。③法官或法院裁決的。—**ly,** *adv.* —**ness,** *n.*

judicial proceedings 審判程序;訴訟手續。

judicial separation 經法院裁定的夫妻分居。(亦作 **limited divorce**)

Judicial Yuan (中國之)司法院。

ju·di·ci·ar·y [dʒu'dɪʃɪ,ɛrɪ; dʒuː'diʃiəri] *n., pl.* **-ar·ies,** *adj.* —*n.* ①司法部;司法制度。②司法官(集合稱)。—*adj.* 司法的;法院的;法官的。—**ju·di·ci·ar·i·ly,** *adv.*

ju·di·cious [dʒu'dɪʃəs; dʒuː'diʃəs] *adj.* 賢明的;深思遠慮的。—**ly,** *adv.* —**ness,** *n.*

ju·do ['dʒudo; 'dʒuːdou] 〖日〗*n.* 柔道(舊稱 jujitsu). —*adj.* 柔道的。—**ist,** *n.*

***jug**[1] [dʒʌg; dʒʌg] *n., v.,* **jugged, jug·ging.** —*n.* ①壺;細頸瓶。A *jug* usually has a spout or a narrow neck, and a handle. 壺通常有壺嘴或細頸及瓶耳。②壺中之物。③〖俚〗監牢。④〖俚〗內燃機之汽化器。—*v.t.* ①〖俚〗關進監牢。②裝入壺中。③在土鍋中燉肉。

jug[2] *n., v.,* **jugged, jug·ging.** —*n.* 夜鶯之鳴聲;唧唧聲。—*v.i.* 發出唧唧聲。

Jug·ger·naut ['dʒʌgə,nɔt; 'dʒʌgənɔːt] *n.* ①(印度教的) Krishna 神像(亦作 **Jagannath**). ②(j-) 誘人盲目崇信而為之犧牲之習俗、制度、信仰等。

jug·gins ['dʒʌgɪnz; 'dʒʌginz] *n., pl.* **-gins·es.** 〖俚〗容易受騙的人;愚人。

jug·gle ['dʒʌgḷ; 'dʒʌgl] *v.,* **-gled, -gling,** *n.* —*v.t.* ①變(戲法);耍(把戲)。②騙取。③竄改。④似漏接後又抓住。⑤思考。—*v.i.* ①變戲法;耍把戲。②欺瞞;騙。—*n.* ①變把戲;魔術。②騙術。—**jug·gling·ly,** *adv.*

jug·gler ['dʒʌglə; 'dʒʌglə] *n.* 變戲法者;行騙者。***a juggler with words*** 詭辯家。

jug·gler·y ['dʒʌglərɪ; 'dʒʌgləri] *n., pl.* **-ies.** ①戲法;幻術。②詐欺。

Ju·go·slav, Ju·go-Slav ['jugo-slav; 'juːgou'slɑːv] *n., adj.* =**Yugoslav.** —**ic,** *adj.* —**i·a,** *n.*

jug·u·lar ['dʒʌgjələ; 'dʒʌgjulə] *adj.* ①頸部的;喉部的。②頸靜脈的。③〖動物〗喉下胸前有腹鰭的。—*n.* 〖解剖〗頸靜脈。

jug·u·late ['dʒugjə,let; 'dʒuːgjuleit] *v.t.,* **-lat·ed, -lat·ing.** ①斷…之喉;切斷…之頸靜脈;殺。②〖醫〗用嚴厲的手段止住(疾病);陡止;頓挫。

juice** [dʒus; dʒuːs] *n., v.,* **juiced, juic·ing.** —*n.* ①汁;液。②〖美俚〗酒。③(*pl.*)體液。④〖美俚〗電。⑤〖俚〗汽油。⑥精華;活力。He might be an old man, but he's still got the *juice* of life. 他雖是個老人,但是他依舊精力充沛。the digestive juices*** 消化液。—*v.t.* 〖俗〗擠出汁來。**juice up a.** 加強;加速。**b.** 加油。**c.** 使刺激;使有大場面。

J

They *juiced up* the movie by adding some battle scenes. 他們加了些戰爭鏡頭把電影弄得刺激些。—**juiced,** *adj.* —**less,** *adj.*

juice·head [ˈdʒusˌhɛd; ˈdʒu:shed] *n.* 〖美俚〗經常飲酒的人。

juic·er [ˈdʒusɚ; ˈdʒu:sə] *n.* ①果汁機；搾汁機。②電影，電視或舞臺劇的燈光技師。

***juic·y** [ˈdʒusɪ; ˈdʒu:si] *adj.*, **-i·er,-i·est.** ①多汁液的。②有趣的(尤指稍不道德的)；生動的。—**juic·i·ly,** *adv.* —**juic·i·ness,** *n.*

ju·jit·su [dʒuˈdʒɪtsu; dʒu:ˈdʒitsu:] 〖日〗 *n.* 柔術 (judo 之舊稱)。(亦作 **jiujitsu, jiujutsu** 或 **jujutsu**)

ju·ju [ˈdʒudʒu; ˈdʒu:dʒu:] *n.* ①(西非土著之)符咒；護符。②其魔力。③(施用上物時之)禁忌。—**ism,** —**ist,** *n.*

ju·jube [ˈdʒudʒub; ˈdʒu:dʒu:b] *n.* ①〖植物〗棗樹；棗實。②棗形或棗味之糖果。

juke·box [ˈdʒukˌbɑks; ˈdʒu:kbɔks] *n.* 自動點唱機。—*adj.* 自動點唱機的。(亦作**juke**)

juke joint 〖美俚〗鄉間小酒店；(有jukebox的)小舞廳。(亦作 **jook joint, jook**)

Jukes [dʒuks; dʒu:ks] *n. pl.* 疾病、犯罪及貧窮數代相傳的紐約家庭。

Jul. ①Jules. ②Julius. ③July.

ju·lep [ˈdʒulɪp; ˈdʒu:lep] *n.* ①〖美〗一種白蘭地或威士忌加糖、冰及薄荷等之混合飲料。②用以調和藥物之糖水。

Jul·ian [ˈdʒuljən; ˈdʒu:ljən] *n.* ①男子名。②朱利安 (A.D. 331–363, 羅馬皇帝 A.D. 361–363, 稱爲 Julian the Apostate). —*adj.* Julius Caesar 的。

Julian calendar 羅馬儒略曆 (凱撒大帝於紀元前 46 年所創, 以 365 日爲一年, 每四年一閏, 閏年爲 366 日)。

ju·li·enne [ˌdʒulɪˈɛn; ˌdʒu:liˈen] *n.* 配以菜片(絲)之清湯。—*adj.* 切成絲或片的(蔬菜等)。

Ju·li·et[1] [ˈdʒulijət; ˈdʒu:ljət] *n.* ①女子名。②朱麗葉 (Shakespeare 所作 *Romeo and Juliet* 中之女主角)。

Ju·li·et[2] *n.* 通訊電碼, 代表字母J.

Jul·ius Cae·sar [ˈdʒuljəsˈsizɚ; ˈdʒu:ljəsˈsi:zə] ①參看 **Caesar.** ②莎翁一悲劇名。

:Ju·ly [dʒuˈlaɪ; dʒu(:)ˈlai] *n., pl.* **-lies.** 七月。

jum·bal [ˈdʒʌmbl; ˈdʒʌmbl] *n.* =**jumble**[2].

jum·ble[1] [ˈdʒʌmbl; ˈdʒʌmbl] *v.,* **-bled, -bling,** *n.* —*v.t.* 混合；混雜。—*v.i.* 混雜；亂成一團。—*n.* ①一團；一堆。②雜亂。—**ment, jum·bler,** *n.* —**jum·bling·ly,** *adv.*

jum·ble[2] *n.* 一種環形的小甜餅。

jumble sale 〖英〗=**rummage sale.**

jum·bly [ˈdʒʌmblɪ; ˈdʒʌmbli] *adj.* 〖罕〗混雜的。

jum·bo [ˈdʒʌmbo; ˈdʒʌmbou] *n., pl.* **-bos,** *adj.* —*n.* ①粗大難看之物；巨漢；巨獸。②=**jumbo jet.** —*adj.* 粗大的；巨大的。

jumbo jet 巨無霸噴射客機(波音747噴射機屬之)。

:jump [dʒʌmp; dʒʌmp] *v.i.* ①跳；躍。This horse can't *jump.* 這馬不能跳。②猛跳；驚跳。My heart *jumped* when I heard the news. 我聽到這消息, 心立刻跳起來。③突升。Prices *jumped.* 物價突漲。④〖俗〗趕忙服從。⑤〖俚〗充滿着活動。The whole town is *jumping* with excitement. 全城充滿着興奮的活動。⑥開始某事, 戰役, 攻擊等(尤指大規模者)。⑦越過(不經中間步驟)。to *jump* to a conclusion. 遽下結論。⑧突然改變。The traffic light *jumpe*[d] from green to red. 交通指揮燈由綠燈突[然變]爲紅燈。⑨毫無目的地從一處至另一處；徘徊[。]⑩省略(字、數目等)。This typewriter *jumps* and needs repairing. 這個打字[機]會跳(字), 需要修理。⑪從飛機上跳傘。⑫[活]力充沛地開始某事〖常in, into〗. He *jumpe*[d] into the discussion right away. 他立[刻]加入討論。⑬快速升級。—*v.t.* ①使跳。②[跳]過；躍過。③(西洋棋中) 跳過而吃 (對方之[棋]子)。④〖俚〗逃亡。⑤漏掉；略去。⑥欺騙。([7)]〖美俚〗跳上(火車)。⑧跳級；越級。⑨使越[級]上升。The college *jumped* him fro[m] instructor to full professor. 該大學[把]他從講師一下升爲正教授。⑩時間未到而先[開]始。Our car *jumped* the red light an[d] collided with a truck. 我們的車闖紅燈[而]撞上了一部卡車。⑪突然增加。The stor[e] *jumped* its prices to offset heavy ex[penditures]. 那家店突然加價以便彌補很大[的]開銷。⑫(如由埋伏)突然攻擊。***jump aboar***[***d***] (or ***on board***)加入已進行中的活動。***jum***[***p***] ***a claim*** 强占他人(地產等之)產權。***jum***[***p***] ***all over someone*** 〖俚〗譴責或批評某人。***jump at*** 欣然接受。***jump down some***[***one's***] ***one's throat*** 責罵某人。***jump in*** (o[r] ***into***) ***with both feet*** 熱心地, 快速地加入[。] ***jump ship*** 水手棄船逃亡。***jump th***[***e***] ***rails*** (or ***track***) (火車等) 出軌。***jum***[***p***] ***upon*** (or ***on***) 責罰；突擊。—*n.* ①跳；躍。The *jump* was a very difficult one[.] 這一跳是很難的。②驚跳。③突升；突增。④[跳]躍之距離。⑤應跳越之物。⑥跳躍比賽。[⑦](西洋棋中)吃對方棋子之一着。⑧(*pl.*)〖俗[俚]〗神經緊張；憂慮；焦灼。***have*** (or ***get***) ***th***[***e***] ***jump on*** 〖俚〗占優勢；勝過。***high*** (***broad***) ***jump*** 跳高(遠)。***on the jump*** 匆匆忙忙[。] ***pole jump*** (=pole vault) 撐竿跳高。—**a**[**-**]**ble,** *adj.* —**ing·ly,** *adv.*

jump area 指定敵後傘兵着陸區。

jump ball 〖籃球〗跳球。

jump belt 綑在身上的小型火箭引擎, 能使人跳過障礙或作短距離之飛行。(亦作 **jump rocket**)

jumped-up [ˈdʒʌmptˌʌp; ˈdʒʌmptˌʌp] *adj.* ①出身低微的。②新興的。

jump·er[1] [ˈdʒʌmpɚ; ˈdʒʌmpə] *n.* ①跳躍者；跳的選手。②一種滑冰、滑雪等用之橇。③鐘錶之掣子。④接續器(臨時導電用)。⑤送貨卡車上遞送包裹之人。⑥〖礦〗(上下跳動以鑽孔之)鑽孔機。***jumper wire*** 〖電〗跨接線。

jump·er[2] *n.* ①工裝。②短掛。③(穿於 blouse 外面的)一種無袖長衣。④附有頭巾之皮毛外套。⑤(*pl.*)小孩的遊戲衣。

jump·ing [ˈdʒʌmpɪŋ; ˈdʒʌmpiŋ] *n., adj.* 跳躍(的)。

jumping bean 跳豆(一種墨西哥樹的種子, 因裏面寄生小蛾幼蟲, 故會跳動)。

jumping jack 跳娃娃(玩具)。

jump·ing-off place [ˈdʒʌmpɪŋˈɔf～; ˈdʒʌmpiŋˈɔ:f～] ①路程的終點。②偏僻的地方。③(財力、能力等之)極限。④起點；出發點。

jump·mas·ter [ˈdʒʌmpˌmæstɚ; ˈdʒʌmpˌmɑ:stə] *n.* 指導傘兵或他人跳傘者。

jump-off [ˈdʒʌmpˌɔf; ˈdʒʌmpˌɔ:f] *n.* ①開始；發動。②起點。③發動競賽或軍事攻擊之地點。④馬跳躍比賽之決賽。

jump pass 〖籃球、橄欖球〗跳起傳球。

jump rope 跳繩遊戲；此遊戲用的繩。

jump seat (汽車上之)活動或摺疊椅。

J

jump shot 〖籃球〗跳躍投籃。
jump suit ①跳傘衣。②似跳傘衣之便服。
jump·y [ˈdʒʌmpɪ; ˈdʒʌmpi] *adj.*, **jump·i·er, jump·i·est.** ①跳動的;痙攣的。②神經質的。—**jump·i·ly,** *adv.* —**jump·i·ness,** *n.*
Jun. ①June. ②Junior. **junc.** junction.
jun·co [ˈdʒʌŋko; ˈdʒʌŋkou] *n., pl.* **-cos.** 磧弱(一種小鳥)。
***junc·tion** [ˈdʒʌŋkʃən; ˈdʒʌŋkʃən] *n.* ①聯絡;連接。Our two armies hope to make a *junction.* 我們兩軍希望會師。②(河流之)會合處;(鐵路等之)交叉點。—**al,** *adj.*
junc·ture [ˈdʒʌŋktʃɚ; ˈdʒʌŋktʃə] *n.* ①時刻;時際。②接合點;接縫。③接合;連合。④時機;危機。⑤〖語音〗相鄰音節之連合(如 night rate 讀成 nitrate 等)。
:June [dʒun; dʒuːn] *n.* 六月。
Jung·frau, the [ˈjuŋˌfrau; ˈjuŋfrau] *n.* 少女峯(Alps 山脈之高峯,在瑞士西南部)。
***jun·gle** [ˈdʒʌŋgl; ˈdʒʌŋgl] *n.* ①叢林;叢林地帶。②藪地;藪沼。③〖美俚〗流浪者之宿營地。④一堆雜亂之物。⑤令人迷惘之事。a *jungle* of legal double-talk. 一堆令人不解的法律上之模稜兩可的言論。⑥暴力與爲生存而鬥爭的場合。⑦激烈的競爭場合。the advertising *jungle.* 廣告業的激烈競爭。—**jun·gled,** *adj.*
jungle fever 叢林熱(一種惡性瘧疾)。
Jun·gle·gym [ˈdʒʌŋglˈdʒɪm; ˈdʒʌŋglˈdʒim] *n.* 〖商標名〗遊樂場所供兒童爬的立體方格鐵架。
jun·gly [ˈdʒʌŋglɪ; ˈdʒʌŋgli] *adj.*, **-gli·er, -gli·est.** (似)叢林的;居住在叢林中的。
***jun·ior** [ˈdʒunjɚ; ˈdʒuːnjə] *adj.* ①年少的;年幼的。John Brown, *Junior.* 小約翰·布朗(即約翰·布朗的兒子)。②下級的;職位低的。③(四年制中學或大學)三年級生的。④日期較後的;遲於。⑤資淺的。—*n.* ①年少者。②職位低者。③〖美〗(四年制中學或大學)三年級學生。④〖俗〗對冒昧的年輕人的稱呼。Look, *junior,* I didn't ask your opinion. 喂,小伙子,我並沒有徵求你的意見啊!
junior college (二年制)專科學校。
junior high school 初級中學。
jun·ior·i·ty [dʒunˈjɔrətɪ; ˌdʒuːniˈɔriti] *n.* 後輩;晚輩;少年;後進。
ju·ni·per [ˈdʒunəpɚ; ˈdʒuːnipə] *n.* 〖植物〗杜松。*oil of juniper* 杜松油(可作藥)。
junk[1] [dʒʌŋk; dʒʌŋk] *n.* ①破爛物。②〖俚〗垃圾。③不值錢的東西;便宜貨。④〖航海〗古時海員所帶之乾鹹肉。*junk price* 賠本價錢;極便宜的價錢。—*v.t.* 〖俚〗當作廢物;丢掉。
junk[2] *n.* 中國大帆船。
junk[3] *n.* 〖俗〗毒品(尤指海洛因)。
Jun·ker [ˈjuŋkɚ; ˈjuŋkə] 〖德〗 *n.* ①德國的年輕貴族;(高傲的)普魯士貴族。②保持特權的貴族。(亦作 **junker**) —**ish,** *adj.*
jun·ker [ˈdʒʌŋkɚ; ˈdʒʌŋkə] *n.* ①吸食痲藥者。②破汽車。
jun·ket [ˈdʒʌŋkɪt; ˈdʒʌŋkit] *n.* ①凍奶食品;乳酪。②宴會;野宴。③遊覽。④立法機關委員會之訪查旅行。⑤以公款支付之遊覽。—*v.i.* 遊覽;郊外野宴(尤指支付公款者)。—*v.t.* 以遊宴款待。—**eer,** —**ter,** *n.*
junk·ie [ˈdʒʌŋkɪ; ˈdʒʌŋki] *n.* 〖俗〗①有毒癮者;烟毒犯。②舊貨商。
junk jewelry 廉價首飾。
junk mail 〖俗〗由廠家寄出的商業廣告信。
junk·man [ˈdʒʌŋkˌmæn; ˈdʒʌŋkmæn] *n., pl.* **-men.** 買賣破舊爛物者;舊貨商。
junk shop 舊貨店。
Ju·no [ˈdʒuno; ˈdʒuːnou] *n., pl.* **-nos.** ①〖羅馬神話〗羅馬女神(Jupiter 之妻,專司婚姻及生育,相當於希臘女神 Hera)。②貴婦人。③女子名。
junr. junior.
jun·ta [ˈdʒʌntə; ˈdʒʌntə] *n.* ①會議(特指西班牙或拉丁美洲的立法或行政機構)。②祕密結社。③(控制政黨的)私黨。④執政團(尤指政變後合法政府尙未成立時統治一國者)。
jun·to [ˈdʒʌnto; ˈdʒʌntou] *n., pl.* **-tos.** (政治性之)祕密會議;祕密結社;私黨。
Ju·pi·ter [ˈdʒupətɚ; ˈdʒuːpitə] *n.* ①〖羅馬神話〗羅馬主神。②〖天文〗木星。③〖美〗一種中程彈道飛彈之名。
Ju·ra [ˈdʒurə; ˈdʒuərə] *n.* ①〖地質〗侏羅紀。②侏羅紀之岩石。
ju·ral [ˈdʒurəl; ˈdʒuərəl] *adj.* ①法律上的。②關於權利、義務的。—**ly,** *adv.*
Ju·ras·sic [dʒuˈræsɪk; dʒuəˈræsik] *adj.* 〖地質〗侏羅紀的。—*n.* =**Jura.**
ju·rat [ˈdʒuræt; ˈdʒuəræt] *n.* 〖法律〗宣誓書末尾之宣誓場所、日期、地點及監誓人姓名之記載。
ju·ra·tion [dʒuˈreʃən; dʒuəˈreiʃən] *n.* 宣誓;監誓。
ju·ra·to·ry [ˈdʒurəˌtɔrɪ; ˈdʒuərətəri] *adj.* 宣誓的。
ju·rid·i·cal [dʒuˈrɪdɪkl̩; dʒuəˈridikəl] *adj.* 審判上的;司法上的;法律上的;法學上的。(亦作 **juridic**) —**ly,** *adv.*
juridical association 社團法人。
juridical days 開庭日期。
juridical person 法人。
ju·ris·con·sult [ˌdʒurɪskənˈsʌlt; ˌdʒuəriskənˈsʌlt] *n.* 法學者;(特指)國際法或民法學者。
***ju·ris·dic·tion** [ˌdʒurɪsˈdɪkʃən; ˌdʒuərisˈdikʃən] *n.* ①司法權;裁判權。②管轄權。It doesn't lie within my *jurisdiction* to set you free. 我無權將你開釋。③管轄區域。④權力;控制;管轄。—**ju·ris·dic·tive,** *adj.*
ju·ris·dic·tion·al [ˌdʒurɪsˈdɪkʃənl̩; ˌdʒuərisˈdikʃənl̩] *adj.* ①司法權的;裁判權的。②管轄權的;管轄區的。③權限的;權力的;管轄的。—**ly,** *adv.*
ju·ris·pru·dence [ˌdʒurɪsˈprudn̩s; ˈdʒuərisˌpruːdəns] *n.* ①〖法律〗法理學;法律哲學。②法律體系。③法律之一部門(如民法、刑法等)。④〖民法〗法院之裁定(尤指覆判)。*comparative jurisprudence* 比較法學。*medical jurisprudence* 法醫學。
ju·ris·pru·dent [ˌdʒurɪsˈprudn̩t; ˌdʒuərisˈpruːdənt] *adj.* 精通法律的;專攻法學的。—*n.* 法理學者;法學家。
ju·ris·pru·den·tial [ˌdʒurɪspruˈdenʃəl; ˌdʒuərispruːˈdenʃəl] *adj.* 法學上的;法理學上的。—**ly,** *adv.*
ju·rist [ˈdʒurɪst; ˈdʒuərist] *n.* ①法律學者;法理學家;法學權威。②法學作家。
ju·ris·tic [dʒuˈrɪstɪk; dʒuəˈristik] *adj.* ①法學者的;法科的;法學的。②法律上的。a *juristic* act. 法律行爲。(亦作 **juristical**) —**al·ly,** *adv.*
ju·ror [ˈdʒurɚ; ˈdʒuərə] *n.* ①陪審團之一員。②審查委員;評判員。③宣誓人。
***ju·ry**[1] [ˈdʒurɪ; ˈdʒuəri, ˈdʒoər-] *n., pl.* **-ries.** ①陪審團。②(比賽等之)評判委員會。*grand jury* 大陪審團(由12人至23人組成,審查控罪,並於獲得充分證據時提出起訴)。*petty* (or *petit*) *jury* 小陪審團(由12人組成,在法庭中審判案件)。—**less,** *adj.*

J

ju·ry² *adj.* 〖航海〗應急的;臨時的。
jury box 陪審團席。
ju·ry·man [ˈdʒurɪmən; ˈdʒuərimən] *n., pl.* **-men.** 陪審團之一員。
jury mast 〖航海〗應急桅。
ju·ry-pack·ing [ˈdʒurɪˌpækɪŋ; ˈdʒuəriˌpækiŋ] *n.* (律師) 非法影響陪審團之作法(使對某案有利)。
ju·ry·wom·an [ˈdʒurɪˌwumən; ˈdʒuəriˌwumən] *n., pl.* **-wom·en.** 女陪審員(juryman 之女性)。
jus [dʒʌs; dʒʌs] *n., pl.* **ju·ra** [ˈdʒurə; ˈdʒuərə]. 〖拉〗①法律;法。②法律權利(權力)。
jus·sive [ˈdʒʌsɪv; ˈdʒʌsiv] *adj.* 〖文法〗表示命令的。—*n.* 命令字、形態、或語態(此語態祇限於 Semitic 語言)。
‡**just¹** [dʒʌst; dʒʌst] *adj.* ①公平的;正直的。a *just* price. 公平的價格。He's a very *just* man. 他是一個很正直的人。②合法的; 正當的。③應當的;應得的。You have received a *just* reward. 你已得到應得的報酬。④確實的;精確的。⑤允當的。a *just* opinion. 允當的意見。⑥有正當理由的。⑦恰當的。⑧眞正的;直的。
‡**just²** *adv.* ①正好; 剛巧。 That is *just* what I think. 那正是我所想的。②幾乎不;僅僅地。③正要;正欲。We're *just* off. 我們正要離去。④剛才; 方才; 剛剛。I have *just* seen him. 我剛才看見他。⑤請(較 please 爲隨便)。*Just* shut the door. 請關門。⑥(試)…看! *Just* listen! 聽聽看!⑦〖俗〗十分;頗;眞正。⑧祇不過是; 僅…而已。He is *just* an ordinary man. 他祇是一個普通人。⑨接近地。See the picture *just* above. 請看正上面的那張畫。***just about*** 正是…附近。***just now*** a. 剛才。b. 此刻。***just so*** 正是如此;對極了。***just then*** 正當那時。
just³ *n., v.i.* =**joust.**
‡**jus·tice** [ˈdʒʌstɪs; ˈdʒʌstis] *n.* ①正義;公道; 公理。②公平; 合理。③公平處理;公平待遇。I hope you will receive *justice.* 我希望你會得到公平處理。④法律的制裁;審判。⑤法官。⑥保安官(=justice of the peace). ***bring to justice*** 使歸案受審。 The murderer was *brought to justice.* 兇手已歸案受審。***do justice to*** a. 公平對待。b. 賞識;欣賞。***do oneself justice*** 盡量發揮能力;作優良表現。***have a sense of justice*** 具有正義感。***justice of the peace*** 保安官;地方執法官。—**less,** *adj.* —**like,** *adj.*
jus·tice·ship [ˈdʒʌstɪsˌʃɪp; ˈdʒʌstisʃip] *n.* 法官之職權、地位或任期。
jus·ti·ci·ar [dʒʌsˈtɪʃɪɚ; dʒʌsˈtiʃiɑː] *n.* 〖英史〗(Norman 王朝及 Plantagenet 王朝初期之)最高司法官。—**ship,** *n.*
jus·ti·ci·ar·y [dʒʌsˈtɪʃɪˌɛrɪ; dʒʌsˈtiʃiəri] *n., pl.* **-ar·ies.** ①=**justiciar.** ②司法官;(尤指) 高等法院法官。—*adj.* 司法上的。
jus·ti·fi·a·bil·i·ty [ˌdʒʌstəˌfaɪəˈbɪlətɪ; ˌdʒʌstiˌfaiəˈbiliti] *n.* 可辯明; 可辯解性; 有理;正當。
jus·ti·fi·a·ble [ˈdʒʌstəˌfaɪəbl̩; ˈdʒʌstifaiəbl] *adj.* 可能辯明白的;有理由的。—**jus·ti·fi·a·bly,** *adv.* —**ness,** *n.*
***jus·ti·fi·ca·tion** [ˌdʒʌstəfəˈkeʃən; ˌdʒʌstifiˈkeiʃən] *n.* ①辯護;辯明。②理由;口實。③〖神學〗不因罪惡而受譴責; 釋罪。④〖印刷〗整版。
jus·ti·fi·ca·tive [ˈdʒʌstəfəˌketɪv; ˈdʒʌstifikeitiv] *adj.* =**justificatory.**
jus·ti·fi·ca·to·ry [ˈdʒʌstəfəˌketərɪ; ˈdʒʌstifikeitəri] *adj.* 辯護的;辯明的。
jus·ti·fi·er [ˈdʒʌstəˌfaɪɚ; ˈdʒʌstifaiə] *n.* ①證明者;辯明者; 證明物; 辯明物。②〖印刷〗整版工人。
‡**jus·ti·fy** [ˈdʒʌstəˌfaɪ; ˈdʒʌstifai] *v.,* **-fied, -fy·ing.** —*v.t.* ①證明爲正當或應該;替…辯護。②證明確有其事。③認爲無罪。④將(鉛字各行)排成適當長度。—*v.i.* ①〖法律〗證明所做之事爲正當行爲。②〖印刷〗(鉛字各行長度)正合適。—**ing·ly,** *adv.*
Jus·tin·i·an I [dʒʌsˈtɪnɪən; dʒʌsˈtiniən] 查士丁尼一世(483–565, the Great, 東羅馬皇帝, 在位期間 527–565)。
Justinian Code 東羅馬皇帝Justinian一世時所編纂之法典。
jus·tle [ˈdʒʌsl̩; ˈdʒʌsl] *v., n.* =**jostle.**
***just·ly** [ˈdʒʌstlɪ; ˈdʒʌstli] *adv.* ①公正地;正當地;公平地。②有正當理由地; 理由充分地。③正確地。
just·ness [ˈdʒʌstnɪs; ˈdʒʌstnis] *n.* 公平;公正;正直;正當;正確;精確。
***jut** [dʒʌt; dʒʌt] *v.,* **jut·ted, jut·ting,** *n.* —*v.i.* 突出; 伸出; 凸出。—*n.* 突出部分; 尖端。—**ting·ly,** *adv.*
Jute [dʒut; dʒuːt] *n.* ①朱特人。②(*pl.*) 朱特族 (第五世紀時侵入英國東南部之日耳曼民族)。—**Jut·ish,** *adj.*
jute [dʒut; dʒuːt] *n.* 〖植物〗黃麻; 黃麻的纖維。—*adj.* 黃麻的。—**like,** *adj.*
ju·ve·nes·cence [ˌdʒuvəˈnɛsn̩s; ˌdʒuːviˈnesns] *n.* 返老還童;變年輕。
ju·ve·nes·cent [ˌdʒuvəˈnɛsn̩t; ˌdʒuːviˈnesnt] *adj.* ①達靑年期的; 年輕的。②看來年輕的。③有返老還童作用的。
***ju·ve·nile** [ˈdʒuvənl̩; ˈdʒuːvinail] *adj.* ①幼年的; 少年的。②適於少年的。③不成熟的。—*n.* ①年少者。②少年讀物。③演少年的演員。④剛會飛的鳥。—**ly,** *adv.* —**ness,** *n.*
juvenile officer 主管少年犯罪的警官。
ju·ve·ni·li·a [ˌdʒuvɪˈnɪlɪə; ˌdʒuːviˈniliə] *n. pl.* 少年時代之作品(集)。
ju·ve·nil·i·ty [ˌdʒuvəˈnɪlətɪ; ˌdʒuːviˈniliti] *n., pl.* **-ties.** ①少年;年輕。②少年男女(集合稱)。③(*pl.*)少年或童年之言行。
jux·ta·pose [ˌdʒʌkstəˈpoz; ˈdʒʌkstəpouz] *v.t.,* **-posed, -pos·ing.** 並列;並置。
jux·ta·po·si·tion [ˌdʒʌkstəpəˈzɪʃən; ˌdʒʌkstəpəˈziʃən] *n.* 並置; 並列; 毗連。

K

K or **k** [ke; kei] *n., pl.* **K's** or **Ks** [kez; keiz]. ①第十一個英文字母。②〖化〗鉀(potassium)。③K 所代表之聲音。④一序列中之第十一個。⑤中世紀羅馬數字代表250。
K ①Kaiser. ②〖西洋棋〗 king. ③化學元素 potassium 之符號。
K., k. ①karat(carat).②kilo.③kilogram. ④king. ⑤knight. ⑥kopeck(s). ⑦krona; kronor. ⑧krone; kronen; kroner. ⑨〖電〗 capacity. ⑩〖航海〗 knot.
Kaa·ba [ˈkɑbə; ˈkɑːbə] *n.* 建於麥加 (Mecca) 之回教大寺院中的石造聖堂。(亦作

Caaba)

kab·(b)a·la ['kæbələ; kə'bɑːlə] *n.* =cab(b)ala.

Ka·bul ['kɑbul; 'kɔːbul] *n.* 喀布爾(阿富汗之首都)。

ka·di ['kɑdɪ; 'kɑːdi] *n.* =**cadi.**

kaf·fee·klatsch ['kɔfɪˌklʌtʃ; 'kɔːfiˌklʌtʃ] *n., pl.* **-klätsche** [-ˌklɛtʃə; -ˌkletʃə], **-klatsch·es.** 咖啡聚會(非正式的聚會,有咖啡、點心招待)。(亦作 **coffee klatsch**)

Kaf·(f)ir ['kæfɚ; 'kæfə] *n.* ①左道者(回敎徒給非回敎徒的稱呼)。②南非洲Bantu族之一種黑人; Kaffir 語。③(*pl.*) 南非洲礦山股份。***Kafir Circus*** (or ***market***) 南非礦山股票市場。(亦作 **Caffre**)

kaf·tan ['kæftən; 'kæftən] *n.* =**caftan.**

kai·ak ['kaɪæk; 'kaiæk] *n.* =**kayak.**

Kai·feng ['kaɪ'fʌŋ; 'kai'fʌŋ] *n.* 開封(中國河南省之省會)。

kail [kel; keil] *n.* =**kale.**

kai·ser ['kaɪzɚ; 'kaizə] *n.* ①皇帝。②德國皇帝之尊稱 (1871–1918)。③奧國皇帝之尊稱 (1804–1918)。④神聖羅馬帝國皇帝之尊稱 (962–1806)。⑤行使絕對權威的人;獨裁者。

KAL Korean Air Lines. 大韓航空公司。

ka·lash·ni·kov [kə'lɑʃnɪˌkɔf; kə'lɑːʃniˌkɔːf] *n.* 俄製衝鋒鎗。

kale [kel; keil] *n.* ①無頭甘藍。②〖蘇〗蔬菜;菜湯。③〖美俗〗現錢。(亦作 **kail**)

ka·lei·do·scope [kə'laɪdəˌskop; kə'laidəskoup] *n.* ①萬花筒。②不斷改變之事物。

ka·lei·do·scop·ic [kəˌlaɪdə'skɑpɪk; kəˌlaidə'skɔpik] *adj.* 千變萬化的;萬花筒的。

ka·lei·do·scop·i·cal [kəˌlaɪdə'skɑpɪkḷ; kəˌlaidə'skɔpikəl] *adj.* =**kaleidoscopic.** **—ly,** *adv.*

kal·ends ['kælɪndz; 'kælendz] *n. pl.* =**calends.**

Ka·le·va·la [ˌkɑlɪ'vɑlə; 'kɑːleˌvɑːlɑː] *n.* (Elias Lönnrot 十九世紀初所集古詩、神話、英雄事蹟等而編成之)芬蘭民族史詩。

kale·yard ['kelˌjɑrd; 'keiljɑːd] *n.* 〖蘇〗菜園。(亦作 **kailyard**)

ka·li·um ['kelɪəm; 'keiliəm] *n.* 〖化〗鉀(=potassium, 符號 K)。

kal·mi·a ['kælmɪə; 'kælmiə] *n.* 〖植物〗美國石南科。

ka·long ['kɑlɑŋ; 'kɑːlɑːŋ] *n.* 〖動物〗(馬來羣島產之)大蝙蝠。

kal·pa ['kælpə; 'kælpə] 〖梵〗 *n.* 刼(世界自創造至毀滅之四十三億二千萬年)。

kal·so·mine ['kælsəˌmaɪn; 'kælsəmain] *n., v.t.,* **-mined, -min·ing.** =**calcimine.** **—kal·so·min·er,** *n.*

Ka·ma·ku·ra [ˌkɑmɑ'kurɑ; ˌkɑːmɑː'kurɑː] *n.* 鎌倉(日本本州一城市,有大佛像)。

Kam·chat·ka [kæm'tʃætkə; kæm'tʃætkə] *n.* 堪察加半島(在蘇俄亞洲之東北部)。**—Kam·chat·kan,** *adj., n.*

Ka·mer·lingh On·nes ['kɑmɚlɪŋ'ɔnəs; 'kɑməliŋ'ɔːnəs] 卡麥令翁奈(Heike, 1853–1926,荷蘭人,曾獲1913年諾貝爾物理獎)。

ka·mi·ka·ze [ˌkɑmɪ'kɑzɪ; ˌkɑːmi'kɑːzi] 〖日〗 *n.* 神風(第二次世界大戰中駕駛飛機撞擊敵艦的肉彈戰術);此種戰術之飛機或駕駛員。**—*adj.*** 神風特攻隊的。

kamp·tu·li·con [kæmp'tjulɪkɑn; kæmp'tjuːlikɔn] *n.* 橡皮地毯。

Kan. Kansas.

Ka·nak·a [kə'nækə; kə'nækə] *n.* ①夏威夷土人。②南太平洋島上的土人。

***kan·ga·roo** [ˌkæŋgə'ru; ˌkæŋgə'ruː] *n., pl.* **-roos** or **-roo.** 袋鼠。**—like,** *adj.*

Kan·san ['kænzən; 'kænzən] *adj.* 美國 Kansas 州的。**—*n.*** Kansas 人。

Kan·sas ['kænzəs; 'kænzəs] *n.* ①堪薩斯(美國中部之一州,首府 Topeka)。②堪薩斯河(自 Kansas 州東北部流入 Missouri 河)。

Kan·su ['kæn'su; 'kæn'suː] *n.* 甘肅(中國西北之一省,省會蘭州, Lanchow)。

Kant [kænt; kænt] *n.* 康德(Immanuel, 1724–1804,德國哲學家)。

Kant·i·an ['kæntɪən; 'kæntiən] *adj.* 康德的;康德哲學的;康德學派的。**—*n.*** 康德派的學者。

Kant·ism ['kæntɪzəm; 'kæntizəm] *n.* 康德哲學。

Kant·ist ['kæntɪst; 'kæntist] *n.* 康德學派之哲學家。

Kao·hsiung ['gau'ʃjuŋ; 'gau'ʃjuŋ] *n.* 高雄(中國臺灣省西南部之一海港)。

Kaohsiung Export Processing Zone 高雄加工出口區。

ka·o·li·ang [ˌkɑolɪ'æŋ; ˌkɑːouli'æŋ] 〖中〗 *n.* 高粱;高粱酒。

ka·o·lin(e) ['keəlɪn; 'keiolin] *n.* 高嶺土(中國江西省景德鎮之白陶土)。***kaolin porcelain*** 高嶺瓷器。**—ka·o·lin·ic,** *adj.*

Ka·pell·meis·ter [kɑ'pɛlˌmaɪstɚ; kɑː'pelˌmaistə] *n., pl.* **-ter.** 〖德〗(合唱團、管絃樂團等之)指揮。

ka·pok ['kepɑk; 'keipɔk] *n.* 木棉花;木絲棉。

kap·pa ['kæpə; 'kæpə] *n.* 希臘字母之第十字 (K, κ)。

ka·put, ka·putt [kə'put; kə'puːt] *adj.* 〖俗〗被毀壞的;完蛋的;被擊敗的。

Ka·ra·chi [kə'rɑtʃɪ; kə'rɑːtʃi] *n.* 喀拉蚩(巴基斯坦一城市)。

kar·a·kul(e) ['kærəkʌl; 'kærəkʌl] *n.* (蘇聯 Uzbek 共和國產之)一種羔羊;其毛皮。

kar·at ['kærət; 'kærət] *n.* =**carat.**

ka·ra·te [kɑ'rɑte; kɑː'rɑːtei] 〖日〗 *n.* 空手道(一種類似中國拳術之自衛術)。

kar·ma ['kɑrmə; 'kɑːmə] *n.* ①〖印度敎〗羯磨;業。②〖佛敎〗因果報應;因緣。③命運;宿緣;宿命。**—kar·mic,** *adj.*

ka(r)·roo [kə'ru; kə'ruː] *n., pl.* **-roos.** (南非洲之)乾燥臺地。

kart [kɑrt; kɑːt] *n.* (特指賽車用之)小型汽車。

kar·tel ['kɑrtəl; 'kɑːtəl] *n.* (南非牛車中之)木床。

kar·tell ['kɑrtɛl; 'kɑːtel] *n.* =**cartel.**

kart·ing ['kɑrtɪŋ; 'kɑːtiŋ] *n.* 駕駛 kart 的競賽。

kar·y·o·plasm ['kærɪəˌplæzəm; 'kæriəplæzəm] *n.* 〖生物〗核質;核漿。**—ic, —at·ic,** *adj.*

Kas·bah ['kɑzbɑ; 'kæzbə] *n.* 阿爾及爾之古老土人區。(亦作 **Casbah**)

Kash·mir [kæʃ'mɪr; kæʃ'miə] *n.* ①喀什米爾(印度西北部)。②(k-)=**cashmere.**

kat·a·bat·ic [ˌkætə'bætɪk; ˌkætə'bætik] *adj.* 〖氣象〗(風、氣流等)下降的;因下降氣流所致的(爲 anabatic 之對)。

ka·tab·o·lism [kə'tæbəlɪzṃ; kə'tæbəlizm] *n.* =**catabolism.** **—kat·a·bol·ic,** *adj.* **—kat·a·bol·i·cal·ly,** *adv.*

Kate [ket; keit] *n.* 女子名(Katherine, Catherine 之暱稱)。

Kath·a·rine, Kath·er·ine ['kæθrɪn; 'kæθrin] *n.* 女子名(=Catherine)。

kat·i·on ['kætˌaɪən; 'kætaiən] *n.* 〖化〗=**cation.**

K

ka·ty·did ['ketɪ,dɪd; 'keitidid] *n.* (美洲產)螽斯科之昆蟲。

kau·ri ['kaurɪ; 'kauəri] *n., pl.* **-ris.** ①(紐西蘭產之)一種高的松樹。②其木材。③其樹脂。

kau·ry ['kaurɪ; 'kauəri] *n., pl.* **-ries.** =**kauri.**

ka·va ['kɑvə; 'kɑːvə] *n.* ①〖植物〗Polynesia 產的一種灌木。②其根所製的飲料。

kay·ak ['kaɪæk; 'kaiæk] *n.* ①愛斯基摩人用的皮船。②以其他材料作的類似愛斯基摩人皮船的小船,用於各種競賽。(亦作**kaiak, kyak, kyack**)

kay·o ['ke'o; 'kei'ou] *n., pl.* **kay·os,** *v.t.,* **-oed, -o·ing.** 〖美俚〗〖拳擊〗擊倒(=K.O., knockout 之縮寫)。

Ka·zak(h)·stan [,kɑzak'stɑn; ,kɑː-zɑːk'stɑːn] *n.* 哈薩克(蘇聯中亞境內共和國之一, 首府爲 Alma-Ata)。(全名作 **Kazak Soviet Socialist Republic**)

K.B. ①King's Bench.②Knight Bachelor.

K.B.E., KBE Knight Commander of the British Empire. **K.C.** ①King's College (London). ②Knight Commander. ③King's Counsel. ④Knights of Columbus. **K.C.B.** Knight Commander of the Bath. **K.C.M.G.** Knight Commander of the Order of St. Michael and St. George. **K.C.V.O.** Knight Commander of the (Royal) Victorian Order.

ke·a ['keə; 'keiə] *n.* (紐西蘭產之)食肉鸚鵡。

Keats [kits; kiːts] *n.* 濟慈(John, 1795–1821, 英國詩人)。**—i·an,** *adj.*

keck [kɛk; kek] *v.i.* ①想吐;作嘔。②表示或感覺厭惡。③(鳥)格格叫。

kedge [kɛdʒ; kedʒ] *v.,* **kedged, kedg·ing,** *n.* —*v.t.* 〖航海〗收拋在船前方的小錨之錨鍊以使(船)前移。—*v.i.* 〖航海〗①投錨以移動船舶。②(船)由於小錨之使用而移動。—*n.* (亦作 **kedge anchor**)〖航海〗小錨。

kedg·er·ee, kedj·er·ee ['kɛdʒə-,ri; ,kedʒə'riː] *n.* 〖東印度〗(有鷄蛋、葱、豆等之)燴飯。

keel**[1] [kil; kiːl] *n.* ①〖船〗龍骨; 船脊骨。false *keel.* 副龍骨。②〖詩〗船。③龍骨狀之物。④飛機、飛艇之龍骨。⑤〖植物〗龍骨瓣。on an even keel*** 平穩的; 平放的。 —*v.t.* ①裝以龍骨。②使傾覆。—*v.i.* 傾覆。 ***keel over*** **a.** 傾覆。**b.** 倒; 暈倒。**c.** 突然翻倒。**—less,** *adj.*

keel[2] *n.* ①平底運煤船。②此船所裝之煤量。③秤煤的單位, 等於 47,488 磅或 21.2 長噸。

keel·age ['kilɪdʒ; 'kiːlidʒ] *n.* (船之)入港稅。

keel·block ['kil,blɑk; 'kiːlblɔk] *n.* 〖造船〗龍骨臺。

keel·boat ['kil,bot; 'kiːlbout] *n.* 〖美〗(美國西部用之)運貨船。

keel·haul ['kil,hɔl; 'kiːlhɔːl] *v.t.* ①將(人)用繩子拖過船底(爲一種刑罰)。②嚴責。(亦作 **keelhale, keeldrag, keelrake**)

keel·less ['killɪs; 'kiːllis] *adj.* ①〖航海〗無龍骨的。②(鳥)無龍骨突起的。

keel line 〖航海〗(船之)首尾線。

keel·son ['kɛlsn̩; 'kelsn] *n.* 〖造船〗內龍骨;底材。

***keen**[1] [kin; kiːn] *adj.* ①鋒利的;銳利的。②尖銳的;刺人的;刻骨的;尖刻的。③銳敏的;敏捷的。④聰明的;智慧的。⑤深深感覺的(情感等)。⑥熱心的;渴望的(常與 about, for 或不定詞連用)。She is really *keen* about the trip. 她渴望能成行。⑦熱烈的;激烈的。⑧〖俚〗了不起的;好的;偉大的。 ⑨强烈的。**—ly,** *adv.* **—ness,** *n.*

keen[2] *n.* 〖愛〗①慟哭死者。②哀哭;輓歌。—*v.t.* & *v.i.* 〖愛〗慟哭(死者);爲死者而慟哭。

keen·er ['kinə; 'kiːnə] *n.* 〖愛〗哭喪人(尤指職業之哭喪女人)。

keen-set ['kin'sɛt; 'kiːn'set] *adj.* 饑餓的;渴望的〖for〗。

keen-wit·ted ['kin'wɪtɪd; 'kiːn'witid] *adj.* 機智敏銳的。

‡keep [kip; kiːp] *v.,* **kept** [kɛpt; kept], **keep·ing,** *n.* —*v.t.* ①保存;保持;保留。*Keep* it for yourself. 你自己保存起來罷。②保藏;收藏。③保守(祕密等)。④經售; 經銷。Do you *keep* (=sell) postcards? 你們經售明信片嗎? ⑤養護;維持;生活。He has a wife and family to *keep.* 他有妻室兒女要養活。⑥管理;經理;經營。to *keep* shop. 經營商店。⑦遵守;履行。⑧保持(狀態、活動等)。⑨防止;預防〖from〗。What shall I do to *keep* this from getting dirty? 我該怎樣防止這東西染污? ⑩慶祝;紀念。⑪保護;保衞。⑫餵; 飼養。 She *keeps* chickens. 她飼養鷄。⑬抑制;忍住。⑭保持有用的狀態。⑮保管;照顧。She *keeps* my dog when I travel. 我出門旅行時她替我照顧狗。⑯蓄(妾);金屋藏(嬌)。⑰保持在原位。 Please *keep* your seats. 請不要離開你們的座位。⑱保持(職位)。He *kept* the job. 他保住了他的差事。⑲繼續遵循。—*v.i.* ①保持;維持(原狀)。The weather is *keeping* dry. 天氣保持着乾燥。②能保存;能持久不壞。The butter *kept* in the icebox. 那牛油放在冰箱內能經久不壞。③積留原處。④遠離;不接觸〖常 away, back, off, out〗。*Keep* off the grass. 請勿踐踏草地。⑤約束;抑制。try to *keep* from smiling. 忍住不笑。***keep an eye on*** 照料;照應;照管。***keep at*** 堅持;不要放棄。***keep back*** **a.** 阻住;擋住。The dikes *kept back* the flood-waters. 堤防使洪水不致氾濫。**b.** 遠離。**c.** 拒絕洩露。 ***keep goal*** (足球)守門。 ***keep good time***(鐘、錶)時間走得準確。***keep hold of*** 把握;緊握。***keep (something) in mind*** 記住;不要忘記。***keep in touch with*** 與…保持聯繫。***keep in with***〖俗〗與…保持友誼。***keep it up*** 照目前的情形繼續下去。***keep on (doing something)*** 繼續(做某事);不斷。***keep on at (a person)*** 追問(某人); 謾罵(某人)。***keep one's hand*** (or ***eye***) ***in*** 繼續練習以免荒廢。***keep one's head*** 保持冷靜;不受激動。***keep one's temper*** 抑制住怒氣。***keep tab*** (or ***keep tabs***) ***on*** 參看 **tab.** ***keep to*** **a.** 遵奉;遵照。She *keeps to* the rules. 她遵守規則。**b.** 局限。*Keep to* the right (left). (標語) 行人靠右 (左)。***keep to oneself*** **a.** 不與他人交往。**b.** 保守祕密。***keep track of*** 參看 **track.** ***keep (something) under*** 控制; 壓制。 ***keep up*** **a.** 保持; 繼續下去。*Keep up* your courage. 不要氣餒。**b.** 保存。**c.** 使浮起;支撐不倒下。**d.** 不落後。**e.** 忍受;忍耐。 ***keep up appearances*** 裝面子;擺闊。 ***keep up on*** (or ***with***) 繼續注意。 ***keep up with*** 保持與…同樣的速度;趕得上。 —*n.* ①生計;生活之所需(食糧和住所)。②砲臺或城堡的最堅實部分。 ***for keeps*** **a.** 歸優勝者所有的。**b.** 〖俗〗永久地;永遠地。**c.** 認眞的;不是鬧着玩的。 ***in good keep*** 情況良好; 在良好狀態中 (=in good condition).

***keep·er** ['kipə; 'kiːpə] *n.* ①看守人;監

護人。Am I my brother's *keeper?* 我是我弟弟的監護人嗎？②管理人。③遵守人。④扣住他物使之固定的東西。⑤耐貯藏之物（如水果等）。⑥達到法定重量的魚(釣者釣到後可保留者)。—**less,** *adj.* —**ship,** *n.*

keeper hook 戲院中扣牢門窗等用的"S" 形鉤子。

keep·ing [ˈkipɪŋ; ˈkiːpiŋ] *n.* ①保管；保護；管理。 The valuables are in safe *keeping.* 貴重物品都保管得很安全。②養；飼。③慶祝；紀念。④一致；協調。A good man's actions are in *keeping* with his promises. 一個正直人的言行是一致的。⑤保存。

keep·sake [ˈkipˌsek; ˈkiːpseik] *n.* 紀念物；贈品。

keg [kɛg; keg] *n.* ①小桶（容量通常在十加侖以下)。②稱釘子的衡量名,等於 100磅。

Kel·ler [ˈkɛlɚ; ˈkelə] *n.* 海倫凱勒(Helen Adams, 1880–1968, 美國盲啞女作家)。

Kel·logg [ˈkɛlɑg; ˈkelɔg] *n.* 凱洛格 (Frank Billings, 1856–1937, 美國政治家, 1925–29 爲國務卿, 1929 年獲諾貝爾和平獎)。

ke·loid [ˈkilɔɪd; ˈkiːlɔid] *n.* 〖醫〗蟹狀腫。(亦作 **cheloid**) —**al,** *adj.*

kelp [kɛlp; kelp] *n.* ①一種大海藻；海帶之屬。②海草灰。

kel·pie [ˈkɛlpɪ; ˈkelpi] *n.* 〖蘇格蘭傳說〗馬形水鬼(致人溺死或警告人們將溺死)。

kel·py [ˈkɛlpɪ; ˈkelpi] *n.* =**kelpie.**

kel·son [ˈkɛlsn̩; ˈkelsn] *n.* =**keelson.**

Kelt [kɛlt; kelt] *n.* =**Celt.**

Kelt·ic [ˈkɛltɪk; ˈkeltik] *n., adj.* =**Celtic.** —**al·ly,** *adv.*

kemp [kɛmp; kemp] *n.* (羊毛中揀出的)粗毛。—**y,** *adj.*

ken [kɛn; ken] *n., v.,* **kenned** or **kent, ken·ning.** —*n.* ①眼界；視界。②知識範圍；領悟；見地。 What happens on Mars is beyond our *ken.* 火星上發生的事情我們無法知道。 —*v.t.* ①看；認識。②〖古、蘇〗相識；知道。③〖法律〗承認繼承。 —*v.i.* 曉得；認識；知道。

Ken. Kentucky.

Ken·ne·dy [ˈkɛnədɪ; ˈkenidi] *n.* ①甘廼廸 (John Fitzgerald, 1917–1963, 美國政治家，於 1961–63 任美國第三十五任總統)。②甘廼廸 (Robert Francis, 1925–1968, 美國政治領袖，John Fitzgerald 之弟)。

Kennedy, Cape *n.* 甘廼廸角（在美國 Florida 州東部, 爲火箭試驗中心所在地)。

***ken·nel**[1] [ˈkɛnl̩; ˈkenl] *n., v.,* **-nel(l)ed, -nel·(l)ing.** —*n.* ①狗舍。②(*pl.*) 飼狗場。③狗羣。④不佳的住處。 —*v.t.* 置於狗舍；畜養於狗舍中。—*v.i.* 宿於狗舍。

ken·nel[2] *n.* 溝渠；陽溝。

ke·no [ˈkino; ˈkiːnou] *n.* 一種似 lotto 之賭博。

Kent [kɛnt; kent] *n.* ①肯特（英格蘭東南部之一州)。②Britain 島東南部之古代 Angles 人所建之王國。—**ish,** *adj.*

kent·ledge [ˈkɛntlɛdʒ; ˈkentledʒ] *n.* 〖航海〗壓艙用之鐵塊。

Ken·tuck·i·an [kənˈtʌkɪən; kenˈtʌkiən] *adj.* Kentucky 州的。—*n.* Kentucky人。

Ken·tuck·y [kənˈtʌkɪ; kenˈtʌki] *n.* 肯塔基(美國之一州, 首府爲 Frankfort)。

Ken·ya [ˈkɛnjə; ˈkiːnjə] *n.* 肯亞共和國 (在非州東部, 原爲英國直轄殖民地, 首府 Nairobi).

kep·i [ˈkɛpɪ; ˈkepi] *n., pl.* **kep·is.** 〖法〗法國之平頂軍帽。

‡kept [kɛpt; kept] *v.* pt. & pp. of **keep.** —*adj.* 被人供養的。 a *kept* woman. 姘婦；情婦。

ke·ram·ics [kɪˈræmɪks; kiˈræmiks] *n. pl.* =**ceramics.**

ker·a·tin [ˈkɛrətɪn; ˈkerətin] *n.* 〖化〗角質素。(亦作 **ceratin**)

ker·a·tose [ˈkɛrəˌtos; ˈkerətous] *adj.* 角質的。—*n.* (海綿類之)角質纖維。

***kerb** [kɝb; kəːb] *n.* 〖英〗(街頭的)邊石；井欄石 (=curb).

kerb market =**kerbstone market.**

kerb·stone [ˈkɝbˌston; ˈkəːbstoun] *n.* 邊石；欄石 (=curbstone).

kerbstone market 交易所外之有價證券市場；場外交易。

ker·chief [ˈkɝtʃɪf; ˈkəːtʃif] *n.* ①(昔婦人的)頭巾。②手帕(=handkerchief).

ker·chiefed [ˈkɝtʃɪft; ˈkəːtʃift] *adj.* 包着頭巾的。(亦作 **kerchieft**)

kerf [kɝf; kəːf] *n.* ①(鋸或斧之)切痕；鋸口。②鋸下或砍下之物。③切斷。—*v.t.* (在木材上)用鋸子鋸口。(亦作 **curf**)

ker·mes [ˈkɝmiz; ˈkəːmiz] *n.* ①雌胭脂蟲之乾燥屍體(用作紅色染料)；洋紅。②(此蟲所棲之)一種橡樹(亦作 **kermes oak**). ③(亦作 **kermes mineral**) 〖化〗無定形三硫化銻；紅安礦。

ker·mess [ˈkɝmɪs; ˈkəːmis] *n.* ①(荷、比等國之)每年一次之大市集。②〖美〗熱鬧的義賣市。(亦作 **kirmess, kermis**)

kern[1] [kɝn; kəːn] *n.* 〖印刷〗鉛字上下突出部分。—*v.t.* 〖印刷〗使鉛字上下突出。

kern[2]**, kerne** [kɝn; kəːn] *n.* ①〖史〗(愛爾蘭、蘇格蘭之)輕武裝步兵。②愛爾蘭農夫。

***ker·nel** [ˈkɝnl̩; ˈkəːnl] *n., v.,* **-nel(l)ed, -nel·(l)ing.** —*n.* ①核；仁。②穀粒；麥粒。③中心；要點。—*v.t.* 包在核內。

***ker·o·sene** [ˈkɛrəˌsin, ˌkɛrəˈsin; ˈkerəsiːn] *n.* 〖美〗煤油；火油。(亦作**kerosine**)

Ker·ry [ˈkɛrɪ; ˈkeri] *n., pl.* **-ries.** 愛爾蘭西南部 Kerry 州所產的小種黑色乳牛。

ker·sey [ˈkɝzɪ; ˈkəːzi] *n., pl.* **-seys.** ①平滑有棱的薄絨布。②(*pl.*) 此種布做的褲子。

ker·sey·mere [ˈkɝzɪmɪr; ˈkəːzimiə] *n.* =**cashmere, cassimere.**

kes·trel [ˈkɛstrəl; ˈkestrəl] *n.* (鳥)茶隼。

ketch [kɛtʃ; ketʃ] *n.* 〖航海〗①一種有大小二桅之帆船。②一種雙桅小船。***bomb ketch*** (初期海軍的)臼砲艦。

ketch·up [ˈkɛtʃəp; ˈketʃəp] *n.* 蕃茄醬。(亦作 **catsup, catchup**)

ke·tone [ˈkiton; ˈkiːtoun] *n.* 〖化〗酮類。

ket·tle** [ˈkɛtl̩; ˈketl] *n.* ①壺；罐；鍋。②茶壺；開水壺 (=teakettle). A watched *kettle* never boils. 看着的茶壺永遠不開(喻性急無用)。③ = **kettledrum.** ***kettle of fish **a.** 爲難的處境；一團糟。**b.** 情況；正考慮中之事。

ket·tle·drum [ˈkɛtl̩ˌdrʌm; ˈketldrʌm] *n.* 定音鼓。

kev·el [ˈkɛvəl; ˈkevəl] *n.* 〖航海〗盤繩栓；纜耳。(亦作 **cavel, cavil, kevil**)

Kew [kju; kjuː] *n.* 倫敦西郊之一村鎮(爲著名植物園之所在地)。

kew·pie [ˈkjupɪ; ˈkjuːpi] *n.* ①塑膠或賽璐珞製之洋娃娃。②(K-) 其商標名。

‡key[1] [ki; kiː] *n., pl.* **keys,** *adj., v.,* **keyed, key·ing.** —*n.* ①鑰匙。②解答；答案。③解答之書；題解。④地理上的要衝；門戶。⑤(鋼琴、打字機等的) 鍵。⑥〖音樂〗調；主調音。⑦聲調；音調；格調；風格。⑧栓；楔。⑨(上發條等用之) 鑰匙。⑩重要或必要之人或物。⑪(*pl.*) 精神上的權威。***all in the same key*** 單調

地。*in a minor key* 傷感地。*power of the keys* 教皇在宗教問題的權威。—*adj.* 最主要的;基礎的;機要的。—*v.t.* ①調音。②使帶有…語調。③〖繪畫〗使有某種色調或色彩。④以栓或楔使牢固。⑤鎖。⑥予以鑰匙。*key up* a. 提高勇氣和精神;激勵。The coach *keyed up* the team for the big game. 教練在大賽前激勵他的球隊。 b. 提高音調。

key² *n.* 低島;暗礁。

key·board [ˈkiˌbord; ˈkiːbɔːd] *n.* (鋼琴或打字機的) 鍵盤。—*v.t.* 以鍵盤輸入資料。

key bugle 一種有鍵之喇叭。

key·hole [ˈkiˌhol; ˈkiːhoul] *n.* (鎖上的) 鑰孔。—*adj.* ①很祕密的(如得自偷窺而來的);內幕的。②偷偷打聽的。

key industry 國家之基本工業 (如鋼鐵工業、煤礦工業等)。

key·less [ˈkilɪs; ˈkiːlis] *adj.* ①無鑰匙的;無鍵的。②以轉柄上發條的時計。

Keynes [kenz; keinz] *n.* 凱因斯(John Maynard, 1883–1946, 英國經濟學家)。—**i·an,** *adj., n.* —**i·an·ism,** *n.*

key·note [ˈkiˌnot; ˈkiːnout] *n., v.,* **-not·ed, -not·ing.** —*n.* ①〖音樂〗主音;主調音。②主旨;要義。③(政黨等之)施政方針。—*v.t.* ①(政黨等)發表施政方針演說。②〖音樂〗彈出主調音。

key·not·er [ˈkiˈnotɚ; ˈkiːˈnoutə] *n.* 〖美俗〗發表政策演說者。

key punch 打卡機;打孔機。

key·punch [ˈkiˌpʌntʃ; ˈkiːpʌntʃ] *v.t.* (在卡片或紙帶上)打孔。 **—er,** *n.*

key ring 鑰匙環。

key·stone [ˈkiˌston; ˈkiː-stoun] *n.* ①〖建築〗楔石;拱心石。②要旨;根本原理。

key word ①可解答某字、某句或某段文字意義之字。②解答或編成暗號之關鍵語。

kg kilogram(s). **kg.** ①keg(s). ②kilogram(s). **K.G.** Knight of the Garter.

khad·dar [ˈkʌdɚ; ˈkʌdə] *n.* 〖印度〗手「織棉布。」

khak·i [ˈkakɪ; ˈkaːki] *n., pl.* **khak·is,** *adj.* —*n.* ①土黃色。②黃色卡其布。③(常 *pl.*)卡其布的制服;卡其褲。—*adj.* 土黃色的;卡其布料的。

kha·lif [kəˈlif; kaːˈliːf] *n.* =**caliph.**

kha·li·fa [kəˈlifə; kaːˈliːfə] *n.* =**khalif.**

kham·sin [ˈkæmsɪn; ˈkæmsin] *n.* 〖氣象〗非洲熱風 (每年三、四、五月間由撒哈拉沙漠吹至埃及之東南風)。(亦作 **kamseen, kamsin**)

khan¹ [kan; kaːn] *n.* ①可汗;汗 (韃靼與蒙古民族對國王、皇帝的稱呼)。②(中亞細亞、阿富汗等地)酋長或官吏之稱號。

khan² *n.* 商隊宿店(商賈停宿之簡陋旅社)。

khan·ate [ˈkanet; ˈkaːneit] *n.* ①汗國(可汗, khan, 之領地)。②可汗之地位(任期)。

khe·dive [kəˈdiv; kiˈdiːv] *n.* 土耳其在埃及之總督稱號(1867–1914, 當埃及獨立以前)。

khi [kaɪ; kai] *n.* 希臘字母之第22字(Χ, χ).

Khing·an [ˈʃɪŋˈan; ˈʃiŋˈaːn] *n.* 興安嶺(在中國東北境)。

Khmer [kmɛr; kmɛə] *n.* ①高棉 (中南半島之一國, 首都爲金邊 Pnom Penh, 原名柬埔寨 Cambodia). ②高棉人。③高棉語。

Khrush·chev [xruʃˈtʃɔf; xruʃˈtʃɔːf] *n.* 赫魯雪夫 (Nikita Sergeyevich, 1894–1971, 蘇聯共黨首領, 1958–1964任總理)。

Ki. 〖聖經〗The Book of Kings.

KIA killed in action. 陣亡。

Kiang·si [dʒɪˈɑŋˈsi; dʒiˈaːŋˈsiː] *n.* 江西(中國東南部之一省, 省會南昌Nanchang)。

Kiang·su [ˈkjæŋˈsu; ˈkjæŋˈsuː] *n.* 江蘇(中國東部之一省, 省會鎮江 Chinkiang)。

Kiao·chow Bay [ˈkjauˈtʃau～; ˈkjauˈtʃau～] 膠州灣。

kib·butz [kɪˈbuts; kiˈbuts] *n., pl.* **-but·zim** [-buˈtsim; -buˈtsiːm]. (以色列) 集體農場。

kibe [kaɪb; kaib] *n.* (足之) 凍瘡;皸。to gall (*or* tread on) a person's *kibes.* (喻)傷某人的感情。

kib·itz [ˈkɪbɪts; ˈkibits] *v.t.* 〖美俗〗①從背後看別人玩紙牌。②(尤指看牌人) 亂多嘴多管閒事。

kib·itz·er [ˈkɪbɪtsɚ; ˈkibitsə] *n.,* 〖美俗〗①從背後看別人玩紙牌者。②(尤指於看牌時)多管閒事的人;貢獻不必要意見的人。③他人工作時或討論正事時開玩笑的人。

ki·bosh [ˈkaɪbɑʃ; ˈkaibɔʃ] *n.*〖俚〗夢話胡說。*put the kibosh on* 〖俚〗使無效;阻止;挫敗;制服。

:kick [kɪk; kik] *v.t.* ①踢;蹴。The horse *kicked* the boy. 那馬踢那男孩。②踢中;踢贏。③使汽車加速。He *kicked* his car into high gear. 他使汽車速度加快。④(鎗砲等)後坐。—*v.i.* ①踢;(馬) 踢跳。The child was screaming and *kicking.* 那孩子亂叫亂踢。②(鎗發射時的) 後坐。This old gun *kicks* badly. 這枝老鎗後坐得厲害。③〖俗〗埋怨;反對;反抗。④活躍。He is still around and *kicking.* 他還保持很活躍。*kick about* 經常來往各地。*kick around* 〖俚〗a. 虐待(他人)。b. 討論或考慮 (建議、計畫等)。 c. 時常遷居或更換工作。*kick back* a. 〖俗〗突然後退。b. 〖俚〗付回扣; 行賄。c. 〖俚〗退還贓物或贓款。*kick in* a. 付款。b. 死亡。 *kick off* a. (足球比賽) 開球。b. 〖俚〗死。c. 〖俚〗發起; 領頭; 開始。*kick one's heels* 無益的等待;白費時間。*kick out* 開除。*kick over* 〖俗〗(內燃機) 開始着火。 *kick the bucket* 死。 *kick the habit* 戒絕烟酒等之癮頭。*kick up* a. 〖俚〗開始;引起。b. 踢起。*kick up a dust* (*a fuss,* or *a row*) 惹亂子; 找麻煩。 *kick up one's heels* 尋歡作樂。*kick upstairs* 明升暗降。—*n.* ①踢。The bruise was caused by a *kick.* 這傷痕是腳踢的。②踢的力量或脾氣。③(足球) 球員。He's a good *kick.* 他很會踢球。④〖美俚〗興致; 狂熱。⑤〖俗〗刺激; 力氣。He has no *kick* left. 他沒有力氣 (抵抗)了。This wine has no *kick.* 這酒不够勁。⑥(鎗發射時的)後坐力。⑦抱怨;反對。⑧強烈而短暫的嗜好。⑨袋。⑩〖英俚〗六辨士。*a kick in one's gallop* 〖俗〗輕率;游移。*for kicks* 〖俚〗爲了興趣。*get a kick out of* 覺得有味。*get more kicks than halfpence* 得不償失。*get the kick* 〖俚〗被解雇。

kick·back [ˈkɪkˌbæk; ˈkikbæk] *n.* ①〖美俗〗強烈的反應。②〖俚〗贓贓之退回。③〖美俗〗折頭;佣金。④回扣。

kick·ball [ˈkɪkˌbɔl; ˈkikbɔːl] *n.* 兒童踢球戲(類似棒球, 但不以棒打, 而以腳踢)。

kick·board [ˈkɪkˌbord; ˈkikbɔːd] *n.* 練習游泳踢腳時支撐雙臂的木板。

kick·er [ˈkɪkɚ; ˈkikə] *n.* ①難馴服之馬(好踢人者)。②頑固者。③叛黨者。④混合飲料中之酒的成分。⑤原動力。⑥〖俚〗遊艇之輔助馬達。⑦(報紙等)大標題上面用顯著鉛字排的較短之標題。

kicking strap (用以防馬踢人之)兜帶。

kick·off ['kɪk,ɔf; 'kik'ɔ:f] *n.* ①〖足球〗(比賽開始時之)開球。②事情之開始。the campaign *kickoff*. 競選之開始。—*adj.* 作爲開頭的。

kick·shaw ['kɪkʃɔ; 'kikʃɔ:] *n.* ①怪講究的菜。②無用的裝飾;無用之物;玩具。(亦作 **kickshaws**)

kick·stand ['kɪk,stænd; 'kikstænd] *n.*脚踏車或摩托車後輪上可放下或收起的支架柱(停車時用)。

kick starter (引擎的)脚發動板。(亦作 **kick start**)

kick·up ['kɪk,ʌp; 'kik'ʌp] *n.* ①向上踢。②〖俗〗騷動。

kid[1] [kɪd; kid] *n., v.,* **kid·ded, kid·ding.** ①小山羊。②小山羊肉。③小山羊皮所製之革。④(*pl.*) 小山羊皮所製之手套或鞋。⑤〖俗〗小孩。 a *kid* sister. 小妹妹。 —*v.i.* & *v.t.* 產小山羊。—**like,** *adj.*

kid[2] *v.t.* & *v.i.,* **kid·ded, kid·ding.** 〖俗〗①逗,哄騙。Don't *kid* me! 不要騙我! ②嘲弄;開玩笑。No *kidding.* 並非開玩笑。

kid[3] *n.* 盛食物給水手之小木桶。

Kid·der·min·ster ['kɪdɚ,mɪnstɚ; 'kidə,minstə] *n.* (英國 Kidderminster 市產之)一種毛絨編織之地毯。

kid·die car ['kɪdɪ~; 'kidi~] ①小孩玩的三輪脚踏車。②小三輪車。(亦作 **kiddy car**)

kid·dy ['kɪdɪ; 'kidi] *n., pl.* **-dies.** 〖俗〗小孩。(亦作 **kiddie**)

kid-glove ['kɪd'glʌv; 'kid'glʌv] *adj.* ①戴羔皮手套的。②過分斯文的;過分講究的。

kid-gloved ['kɪd'glʌvd; 'kid'glʌvd] *adj.* 〖俗〗小心的;仔細的;體諒的。

kid gloves 羔皮手套。 ***handle with kid gloves*** 〖俗〗小心謹愼的應付。

kid·nap ['kɪdnæp; 'kidnæp] *v.t.,* **-nap(p)ed, -nap·(p)ing.** ①誘拐(兒童)。②綁架;勒贖。—**(p)er,** *n.*

***kid·ney** ['kɪdnɪ; 'kidni] *n., pl.* **-neys.** ①腎。②腰子(作食用)。③個性;天性;性格;脾氣。④種;類。

kidney bean 菜豆。

kidney stone 〖醫〗腎結石。

kid·skin ['kɪd,skɪn; 'kidskin] *n.* 羔(羊)皮(製鞋、手套用)。—*adj.* 羔羊皮製的。

kid stuff ①適合於小孩的事物。②簡單容易的事。

kil·der·kin ['kɪldɚkɪn; 'kildəkin] *n.* ①(16–18 加侖之)中桶。②同上之液量單位名(=2 firkins)。

kill**[1] [kɪl; kil] *v.t.* ①殺;宰;使死。The blow *killed* him. 這一擊致他於死。②破壞;摧毀;扼殺。③使(議案等)不能通過;阻擱。to *kill* a bill in Parliament. 使法案在國會中不能通過。④取消;删去(字、項目等)。⑤抵消;中和(色彩)。One color may *kill* another near it. 一種顏色可中和其近旁的顏色的色彩。⑥〖俗〗壓制;制服。⑦消遣;排遣;打發。⑧浪費(時間)。⑨徹底征服。That giggle of hers *kills* me. 她的笑聲使我爲之傾倒。⑩使(聲音)減低或消失。⑪使精疲力竭。The long hike *killed* us. 那長途跋涉把我們累死了。⑫使機器引擎等停止運轉。⑬〖網球〗殺(球)。⑭完全消耗;用完。—*v.i.* ①殺;殺害。 Thou shalt not *kill!* 你不可殺人! ②被殺。③產生不可抗拒的效果。 She was dressed to *kill.* 她打扮得花枝招展,目的在使人拜倒她的石榴裙下。 ***kill off a. 徹底毁滅;屠殺。The invaders *killed off* all the inhabitants of the town. 侵略者將全城居民殺光。b.〖俚〗消除。 ***kill time*** 消磨時間。 ***kill two birds with one stone*** 一舉兩得;一箭雙鵰。 ***kill with kindness*** 過於熱心助人反而害人。—*n.* ①殺;宰。②(獵獲的)動物。There was a plentiful *kill.* 獵獲的動物甚豐。

kill[2] *n.* 〖美方〗水道;溪;河。

kill·dee ['kɪl,di; 'kildi:] *n.* =**killdeer.**

kill·deer ['kɪl,dɪr; 'kildiə] *n.* (北美產之)小水鳥。

kill·er ['kɪlɚ; 'kilə] *n.* ①殺生者(指人、動物或物);殺人者(尤指職業兇手)。②=**killer whale.** ③郵戳。④做郵戳之裝置。⑤〖俚〗具有很大的影響力的人或事物。

killer boat 捕鯨船。

kill·er-dill·er ['kɪlɚ'dɪlɚ; 'kilə'dilə] *n.* 〖俚〗非常之人或事。

killer whale 大海豚。

kill·ing ['kɪlɪŋ; 'kiliŋ] *adj.* ①殺害的;致死的。②〖俗〗極迷人的;迷魂蕩魄的。③令人疲憊的。④〖俗〗笑死人的;非常可笑的。—*n.* ①謀殺;殺戮。②一次行獵所得之獵物總和。③〖俗〗大發利市(尤指股票投機)。—**ly,** *adv.*

kill-joy ['kɪl,dʒɔɪ; 'kildʒɔi] *adj.* 煞風景的;掃興的。—*n.* 掃興之人;煞風景。

kill-time ['kɪl,taɪm; 'kiltaim] *adj., n.* 消磨時間的(事)。

kiln [kɪl, kɪln; kiln, kil] *n.* 窰;爐。—*v.t.* 於窰內燒或焙。

kiln-dry ['kɪl,draɪ; 'kildrai] *v.t.,* **-dried, -dry·ing.** 置於窰中烘乾。

ki·lo ['kɪlo; 'ki:lou] *n., pl.* **ki·los.** ①公斤(=kilogram)。②公里(=kilometer)。

Ki·lo *n.* 通訊電碼,代表字母 K.

kilo. ①kilogram. ②kilometer.

kilo- 〖字首〗表"千"之義。

kil·o·cal·o·rie ['kɪlə,kælərɪ; 'kilə,kæləri] *n.* 〖物理〗大卡(熱量單位,等於1,000卡)。(亦作 **kilogram calorie**)

kil·o·cy·cle ['kɪlə,saɪkl; 'kilə,saikl] *n.* 〖電〗千周;千周率。

***kil·o·gram(me)** ['kɪlə,græm; 'kilə-græm, -loug-] *n.* 公斤(= 2.2046 磅)。

kil·o·gram-me·ter, kil·o·gram-me·tre ['kɪlə,græm'mitɚ; 'kilə,græm-'mi:tə] *n.* 〖物理〗千克米(功之單位)。

kil·o·hertz ['kɪlə,hɝts; 'kiləhə:ts] *n.* 〖電〗千赫。

***kil·o·li·ter, kil·o·li·tre** ['kɪlə,litɚ; 'kilə,li:tə] *n.* 公秉;千公升 (=264.17加侖, 35.31 立方英尺,或一立方公尺)。

***kil·o·me·ter, kil·o·me·tre** ['kɪlə,mitɚ; 'kilə,mi:tə] *n.* 公里 (=1,000 公尺; 3,280.8 英尺)。

kil·o·met·ric [,kɪlə'mɛtrɪk; ,kilə'metrik] *adj.* =**kilometrical.**

kil·o·met·ri·cal [,kɪlə'mɛtrɪkl; ,kilə'metrikəl] *adj.* 公里的;以公里標示的;以公里衡量的。

kil·o·ton ['kɪlə,tʌn; 'kilətʌn] *n.* ①千噸。②相當於千噸 TNT 之爆炸力。

kil·o·volt ['kɪlə,volt; 'kiləvoult] *n.* 〖電〗千伏特(電壓之單位)。

kil·o·watt ['kɪlə,wɑt; 'kiləwɔt] *n.* 〖電〗瓩 (=1,000 watts)。

kil·o·watt-hour ['kɪlə,wɑt'aʊr; 'kilə,wɔt'auə] *n.* 〖電〗千瓦特時(能、電力單位,俗稱"度")。

kilt [kɪlt; kilt] *n.* (蘇格蘭高地男子所着之)褶疊短裙。—*v.t.* 打褶;撩起。—**like,** *adj.*

kilt·ed [ˈkɪltɪd; ˈkiltid] *adj.* ①穿褶疊短裙的。②打褶的。

kil·ter [ˈkɪltɚ; ˈkiltə] *n.* 〖美俗〗(身心等的)良好狀態。

kilt·ie, kilt·y [ˈkɪltɪ; ˈkilti] *n., pl.* **kilt·ies.** ①穿裙子(kilt)者。②蘇格蘭高地(穿裙子的)士兵。

ki·mo·no [kəˈmonə; kiˈmounə] *n., pl.* **-nos.** ①日本之和服。②婦女所着寬大之晨衣。

kin** [kɪn; kin] *n.* ①家族;親戚。②親戚關係。What *kin* is she to you? 她與你是甚麼親戚關係? ③性質相似之物;地位職業等相似之人。next of kin*** 最近親。***of kin*** 有親屬關係。—*adj.* ①有親屬關係的。②性質類似的。

-kin 〖字尾〗表"小"之義,如: lambkin, manikin.

kin·chin [ˈkɪntʃən; ˈkintʃən] *n.* 〖俚〗小孩(=child)(盜賊隱語)。

‡**kind¹** [kaɪnd; kaind] *adj.* ①慈愛的;親切的;和藹的。a *kind* mother. 慈愛的母親。②仁慈的;溫和的。It was *kind* of you to help us. 承蒙惠助,不勝感激。③宜人的。*kind* weather. 宜人的天氣。

‡**kind²** *n.* ①種;類;屬。②性質。to differ in degree but not in *kind*. 是程度不同,非性質不同。***after one's*** (or ***its***) ***kind*** 〖古〗依其本性。***in kind*** **a.** 以貨(代錢)。to pay *in kind*. 付給貨物(代替付錢)。**b.** 同樣地。to repay insolence *in kind*. 以無禮報無禮。**c.** 實質上;特質上。***kind of*** 〖俗〗有一點;有幾分(作副詞用)。He looks *kind of* pale after his illness. 他病後面色有點蒼白。***nothing of the kind*** 絕無其事。***of a kind*** **a.** 同類的。**b.** 品質極低劣的。***something of the kind*** 類似的事物。

kind·a, kind·er [ˈkaɪndɚ; ˈkaində] *adv.* 〖俗〗有一點;有幾分(=kind of).

kin·der·gar·ten [ˈkɪndɚˌgartn̩; ˈkindəˌgɑːtn] *n.* 幼稚園。〖注意〗此字最後音節中字母"t"非"d",因係沿用德文拼法。

kin·der·gart·ner, kin·der·gar·ten·er [ˈkɪndɚˌgartnɚ; ˈkindəˌgɑːtnə] *n.* ①幼稚園教師;保姆。②幼稚園兒童;幼生。

kind-heart·ed [ˈkaɪndˈhartɪd; ˈkaindˈhɑːtid] *adj.* 好心腸的;仁慈的。—**ly,** *adv.*

***kin·dle** [ˈkɪndl; ˈkindl] *v.,* **-dled, -dling.** —*v.t.* ①燃起;使着火。The spark *kindled* the dry wood. 星火燃着乾木。②使發紅光。③引起;激起。④使明亮。—*v.i.* ①燃燒;着火。This wood is too wet to *kindle*. 這木柴太濕不易燃燒。②顯出興奮激動的情態。Her eyes *kindled* with excitement. 她的兩眼顯出興奮的神色。

kind·li·ness [ˈkaɪndlɪnɪs; ˈkaindlinis] *n.* ①親切;和善。②和藹或親切的行為。③(氣候的)溫和;爽快。

kin·dling [ˈkɪndlɪŋ; ˈkindliŋ] *n.* ①點燃;點火。②(情緒之)激怒。③引火之易燃物。

‡**kind·ly** [ˈkaɪndlɪ; ˈkaindli] *adj.,* **-li·er, -li·est,** *adv.* —*adj.* ①和藹的;溫和的;親切的。*kindly* faces. 和藹的面孔。②爽快的;宜人的。③(土壤之對作物)有利的。—*adv.* ①和善地;溫和地;親切地。He spoke very *kindly*. 他說話非常親切。②誠懇地;至誠地。③請(=please). Would you *kindly* close the door? 請關上門好嗎? ***take kindly to*** 欣然接受;泰然處之。

kind·ness** [ˈkaɪndnɪs; ˈkaindnis] *n.* ①仁慈;親切;和藹。②仁慈的行為。He has done (*or* shown) me many *kindnesses*. 他幫了我不少忙。③友善的感覺;喜愛。out of kindness*** 出於仁慈;好心。

***kin·dred** [ˈkɪndrɪd; ˈkindrid] *n.* ①家族;親戚(集合稱)。Most of his *kindred* are still living in Ireland. 他的大部分親屬現仍住在愛爾蘭。②家族關係;親戚關係。③相似。—*adj.* ①同宗的;同族的。②同源的;同系的。③類似的;同類的。

kin·dred·ship [ˈkɪndrɪdʃɪp; ˈkindridʃip] *n.* 血親關係;親戚關係;家族關係。

kine [kaɪn; kain] *n. pl.* 〖古〗牛;雌牛(=cows).

kin·e·ma [ˈkɪnəmə; ˈkinimə] *n.* 電影;電影院(=cinema).

kin·e·mat·ic [ˌkɪnəˈmætɪk; ˌkainiˈmætik] *adj.* 〖物理〗運動的;運動學(上)的。

kin·e·mat·ics [ˌkɪnəˈmætɪks; ˌkainiˈmætiks] *n.* (作 *sing.* 解)〖物理〗運動學。

kin·e·mat·o·graph [ˌkɪnəˈmætəˌgræf; ˌkainiˈmætəgrɑːf] *n., v.t., v.i.* =**cinematograph.**

kin·e·scope [ˈkɪnɪˌskop; ˈkiniskoup] *n.* ①(電視機之)影像放映眞空管。②(電視)錄像。—*v.t.* (電視)錄像。

ki·ne·si·ol·o·gy [kɪˌnisɪˈɑlədʒɪ; kiˌniːsiˈɔlədʒi] *n.* 人體運動學。

kin·es·thet·ic [ˌkɪnɪsˈθɛtɪk; ˌkainisˈθetik] *adj.* 運動覺的;肌感覺的。

ki·net·ic [kɪˈnɛtɪk; kaiˈnetik] *adj.* ①〖物理〗運動的;引起運動的。②由運動而起的。***kinetic energy*** 〖物理〗動能。

kinetic art 活動藝術(指可用機械力驅動活動部分的雕塑等)。

ki·net·ics [kɪˈnɛtɪks; kaiˈnetiks] *n.* (作 *sing.* 解)〖物理〗動力學。

kin·folk(s) [ˈkɪnˌfok(s); ˈkinfouk(s)] *n. pl.* 〖方〗=**kinsfolk(s).**

King [kɪŋ; kiŋ] *n.* 金恩(Martin Luther, 1929–1968, 美國黑人民權運動領袖, 1964年獲諾貝爾和平獎)。

‡**king** [kɪŋ; kiŋ] *n.* ①君王;君主。the *King* of England. 英國國王。②〖美俗〗(某一界的)巨子;大王。an oil *king*. 石油大王。③最高者。*king* of beasts. 獅(萬獸之王)。④(棋子中的)王;將。⑤(紙牌中的)老K. ⑥(K-)上帝;基督。King of kings. 耶穌基督。—*v.t.* 使成為君主。—*v.i.* ①君臨。②扮演國王;行為高傲如國王(常與 it 連用)。—*adj.* 最重要的;最大的。

King-at-Arms [ˈkɪŋətˈarmz; ˈkiŋətˈɑːmz] *n.* =**King-of-Arms.**

king·bird [ˈkɪŋˌbɝd; ˈkiŋbəːd] *n.* ①(北美產)必勝鳥。②極樂鳥之一種。

king·bolt [ˈkɪŋˌbolt; ˈkiŋboult] *n.* ①(連結前軸與車身之)中樞梢。②〖建築〗大鐵桿。③〖機械〗大螺釘。

king crab 〖動物〗鱟(=horseshoe crab).

king·craft [ˈkɪŋˌkræft; ˈkiŋ-krɑːft] *n.* (國王的)治國之術;王道。

king·cup [ˈkɪŋˌkʌp; ˈkiŋkʌp] *n.* ① =**buttercup.** ②〖英方〗=**marsh marigold.**

‡**king·dom** [ˈkɪŋdəm; ˈkiŋdəm] *n.* ①王國。the *kingdom* of England. 英格蘭王國。②國度;領域;範圍。③自然三界之一。the animal (vegetable, mineral) *kingdom*. 動物(植物、礦物)界。④神之王國。

kingdom come 〖俗〗來世;天國。

king·fish [ˈkɪŋˌfɪʃ; ˈkiŋfiʃ] *n., pl.* **-fish, -fish·es.** ① **a.** (北美、澳洲產之)王魚。**b.**

一種似 drumfish 之食用魚。c. =Spanish mackerel. ②〖俗〗(社會上某界之)巨子; 領導人物;首腦。

king·fish·er 〔ˈkɪŋˌfɪʃɚ; ˈkiŋˌfiʃə〕 *n.* 魚狗(一種水鳥, 因其啄魚爲食故名); 翠鳥。

king·hood 〔ˈkɪŋhud; ˈkiŋhud〕 *n.* 國王之位。

King James Version =Authorized Version.

King Lear 李爾王(莎翁四大悲劇之一; 其主角)。

king·let 〔ˈkɪŋlɪt; ˈkiŋlit〕 *n.* ①小王; ②金冠鷦鷯。

*__king·ly__ 〔ˈkɪŋlɪ; ˈkiŋli〕 *adj.*, **-li·er, -li·est,** *adv.* —*adj.* ①王的;國王的。②適於君王的。③儼若君王的;高貴的。—*adv.* 君王地;儼若君王地。—**king·li·ness,** *n.*

king·mak·er 〔ˈkɪŋˌmekɚ; ˈkiŋˌmeikə〕 *n.*有足够的權威或影響力而能選擇國王或其他公職人員者。

King-of-Arms, king-of-arms 〔ˌkɪŋəvˈɑrmz; ˌkiŋəvˈɑːmz〕 *n., pl.* **Kings-of-Arms.** 〖英〗紋章院長。

king of beasts 獅。

king of birds 鷹。

King of Kings ①萬王之王(耶穌基督)。②(古代東方諸國之)皇帝。(亦作 **King of kings**)

king of terrors 死。

king of the forest 橡樹。

king·pin 〔ˈkɪŋˌpɪn; ˈkiŋ-pin〕 *n.* ①〖俗〗主腦之人或物。②〖俗〗制度中之支柱。③(保齡球之)中央瓶。—*adj.* 〖俗〗重要的;突出的。

king post 〖建築〗中柱;雄柱。

King's (or **Queen's**) **Bench** 參看 **bench.**

King's (or **Queen's**) **Counsel** 〖英〗王室顧問律師。

King's (or **Queen's**) **English, the** 標準英語。

king's highway 〖英〗公路; 主要道路。

king·ship 〔ˈkɪŋʃɪp; ˈkiŋʃip〕 *n.* 王位; 王權;王之尊嚴;王之統治。

king-size 〔ˈkɪŋˌsaɪz; ˈkiŋsaiz〕 *adj.* 〖美俗〗特大的。

king-sized 〔ˈkɪŋˌsaɪzd; ˈkiŋˌsaizd〕 *adj.* =**king-size.**

king snake 〖動物〗(美國南部所產之)一種無毒大蛇。

king's ransom 大量之金錢;高價。

king's weather 〖俗〗好天氣。

king truss 〖建築〗有中柱之桁構;主構架。

kink 〔kɪŋk; kiŋk〕 *n.* ①(線、繩、索等之)紐結;糾纏。②頸、背等處之痙攣。③〖俗〗神經混亂;怪想;幻想;奇癖。④(阻礙機器或計畫的)缺陷。—*v.t.* 使糾結;使絞。—*v.i.* 打結;糾纏。

kin·ka·jou 〔ˈkɪŋkəˌdʒu; ˈkiŋkədʒuː〕 *n.* 〖動物〗蜜熊(中南美產的夜行性小獸)。

kink·y 〔ˈkɪŋkɪ; ˈkiŋki〕 *adj.*, **kink·i·er, kink·i·est.** ①糾結的;(頭髮等)捲縮的。②〖美俗〗古怪的;乖僻的。

kin·less 〔ˈkɪnlɪs; ˈkinlis〕 *adj.* 無親屬的;無親戚的。

ki·no 〔ˈkino; ˈkiːnou〕 *n., pl.* **-nos.** =**keno.**

kins·folk(s) 〔ˈkɪnzˌfok(s); ˈkinzfouk(s)〕 *n. pl.* 親戚;血族。(亦作 **kinfolk**)

kin·ship 〔ˈkɪnʃɪp; ˈkinʃip〕 *n.* ①家族關係;血族關係。

kins·man 〔ˈkɪnzmən; ˈkinzmən〕 *n., pl.* **-men.** 親屬; 親戚(指男性者, 女性者爲 **kinswoman**).

kins·wom·an 〔ˈkɪnzˌwumən; ˈkinzˌwumən〕 *n., pl.* **-wom·en.** (女性之)血族; (女性之)親戚。

ki·osk 〔kɪˈɑsk; ˈkiːɔsk〕 *n.* ①土耳其式之涼亭。②公共電話亭;報攤;音樂臺。

kip¹ 〔kɪp; kip〕 *n.* 小獸皮(牛犢、羊羔等之生皮)。

kip² *n.* 〖俚〗寄宿舍;客棧;床。

kip·per 〔ˈkɪpɚ; ˈkipə〕 *v.t.* 鹽醃而曬乾或燻製。—*n.* ①產卵季中或季後之雄鮭。②鮭魚乾。③〖俚〗人;年輕人;兒童。

Kir·ghiz 〔kɪrˈgiz; ˈkəːgiz〕 *n., pl.* **-ghiz, -ghiz·es.** ①吉爾吉斯人(中西亞之一蒙古族之人)。②吉爾吉斯語。

Kir·giz 〔kɪrˈgiz; ˈkəːgiːz〕 *n.* 吉爾吉斯(蘇聯中亞之一共和國, 首府 Frunze).

Ki·rin 〔ˈkiˈrɪn; ˈkiːˈrin〕 *n.* 吉林(中國東北之一省, 省會吉林市 Kirin).

kirk 〔kɝk; kəːk〕 *n.* 〖蘇〗①教會;禮拜堂。②教會的信徒。***the Kirk*** 〖英〗蘇格蘭(長老)教會。

kirk·man 〔ˈkɝkmən; ˈkəːkmən〕 *n., pl.* **-men.** ①蘇格蘭教會之信徒。②〖蘇〗教士;僧侶。

kir·mess 〔ˈkɝmɪs; ˈkəːmis〕 *n.* =**kermess.**

kirsch·was·ser 〔ˈkɪrʃˌvɑsɚ; ˈkiəʃˌvɑːsə〕 *n.* 櫻桃酒。

kir·tle 〔ˈkɝtl; ˈkəːtl〕 *n.* 〖古〗①(男用)短上衣。②(女用)短裙;襯裙;長袍。

kis·met 〔ˈkɪzmɛt; ˈkismet〕 *n.* 命運;天命。(亦作 **kismat**) —**ic,** *adj.*

‡**kiss** 〔kɪs; kis〕 *v.t.* ①吻;和…接吻。②輕拂。A soft wind *kissed* the tree tops. 輕風拂弄樹梢。③藉吻使消失。to *kiss* away tears. 一吻而使悲傷消盡。***kiss hands*** (大臣等被授任時)吻君王的手。***kiss the book*** (or ***the Bible***)在法庭上吻聖書而宣誓。***kiss the dust*** (or ***ground***) 受辱; 被殺。***kiss the rod*** 受處罰。—*v.i.* ①吻; 接吻。②藉吻表示感情。***kiss off*** 不在乎;拒絕;不顧。—*n.* ①吻; 接吻。②輕拂。③一種糖果。④以蛋白砂糖做成的一種蛋糕。

kiss·er 〔ˈkɪsɚ; ˈkisə〕 *n.* ①接吻的人。②〖俚〗嘴;嘴唇;臉。

kissing bug ①各種在面、唇等部吮血之有毒昆蟲。②好接吻的人;欲接吻的衝動。

kissing crust 〖俗〗烤麪包時兩麪包相鄰接處之軟皮。

Kis·sin·ger 〔ˈkɪsɪndʒɚ; ˈkisindʒə〕 *n.* 季辛吉(Henry, 1923–, 原籍德國之美國政治學家, 爲尼克森之國策顧問, 1973–1977 任國務卿, 曾獲1973年諾貝爾和平獎)。

kissing gate 〖英方〗(一次僅容一人通過之)U形或V形旋轉的小門。

kissing kin ①可以接吻來寒暄的親戚, 如:堂兄弟姐妹等;近親。②〖俚〗相處和諧的人或事。

kiss-in-the-ring 〔ˈkɪsɪnðəˈrɪŋ; ˈkisinðəˈriŋ〕 *n.* 接吻遊戲(若干人圍成環狀, 一人持手帕繞環而行, 其將手帕擲於某人之後即跑, 某人拾手帕即追。擲手帕者在未跑至拾手帕者所遺空位之前, 若被拾手帕者追及, 則將被拾手帕者親吻)。

kiss-me-quick 〔ˈkɪsmɪˈkwɪk; ˈkismiˈkwik〕 *n.* ①〖植物〗野生三色堇。②戴於頭後的無緣軟帽。③鬢。

kiss-of-life 〔ˈkɪsəvˈlaɪf; ˈkisəvˈlaif〕 *adj.* 〖英〗口對口的。*kiss-of-life* respiration treatment. 口對口的人工呼吸法。

kit 〔kɪt;kit〕 *n., v.,* **kit·ted, kit·ting.** —*n.* ①(兵士或水手之除武器以外的)裝備。*kit* inspection. 裝備檢查。②個人之行裝。③一組工具。④一套運動用具。golfing (skiing) *kit.* 高爾夫(滑雪)用具。⑤工具箱; 用具箱。⑥木桶。⑦〖俗〗一組、一套、一羣(人或物)。⑧小貓(kitten 之縮寫)。***kit and caboodle*** (or *boodle*)〖俗〗全部人員或東西（常與 whole 連用)。—*v.t.*〖主英〗裝備。

Kit-cat [ˈkɪtˌkæt; ˈkitkæt] *n.* ①1703–20年在倫敦的 Whig 黨員、文人等所組織之俱樂部（=Kit-cat Club).②該俱樂部之會員。③半身畫像。—*adj.* ①該俱樂部的。②(亦作 **kit-cat**) 半身(畫像)的。

‡**kitch·en** [ˈkɪtʃɪn, -ən; ˈkitʃin, -tʃən] *n.* ①厨房。②炊具；厨房用具。—*adj.* ①厨房的。②在厨房工作的。*kitchen* help. 厨房幫手。③(語言之)粗俗的;不雅的。

kitchen cabinet ①〖美俗〗(政府首長之)智囊團。②厨房內的餐具櫃。

kitch·en·er [ˈkɪtʃɪnɚ; ˈkitʃinə] *n.* ①厨子;(尤指寺院之)厨司。②〖英〗厨竈。

kitch·en·ette, kitch·en·et [ˌkɪtʃɪnˈɛt; ˌkitʃiˈnet] *n.* (公寓等之)小厨房；室內厨房。

kitchen garden 產品供自用之菜圃;菓果園。

kitch·en·maid [ˈkɪtʃɪnˌmed; ˈkitʃin-meid] *n.* 厨師之助手;燒飯女工。

kitchen midden 〖考古〗貝塚。

kitchen physic ①美好豐盛之食物。②〖諧〗(給與病人之)滋養食品。

kitchen police 〖軍〗①炊事兵（集合稱)。②炊事勤務。③因犯小錯而被罰到厨房做工的士兵。(略作 **K. P.**)

kitchen stuff ①炊事材料（蔬菜等)。②厨房之剩屑。

kitch·en·ware [ˈkɪtʃɪnˌwɛr; ˈkitʃin-ˌwɛə] *n.* 厨房用具(如壺、鍋、罐等)。

***kite** [kaɪt; kait] *n., v.,* **kit·ed, kit·ing.** —*n.* ①風箏;紙鳶。to fly a *kite.* 放風箏。②〖動物〗鳶。③任何高而輕的帆。④〖商〗爲舉債而開的支票。⑤〖俚〗第二次世界大戰期中使用的任何飛機。—*v.i.* 像風箏一樣飛；輕快地移動。

kite balloon (or **sausage**) 繫留氣球(供軍事上觀測之用)。

kith [kɪθ; kiθ] *n.* 朋友；鄰人（現僅用於 *kith and kin* 中,意爲“親友”，今更作狹義之“親戚”解)。

kitsch [kɪtʃ; kitʃ] *n.* 投大衆所好的無美學價值的藝術或文學。

***kit·ten** [ˈkɪtn̩; ˈkitn] *n.* 小貓。*have a kitten* (or *kittens*)〖俚〗煩惱；心煩意亂。—*v.t.* & *v.i.* ①生(小貓)。②賣弄風情。

kit·ten·ish [ˈkɪtn̩ɪʃ; ˈkitn̩iʃ] *adj.* ①似小貓的;頑皮的。②頑皮姑娘的;搔首弄姿的。—**ly,** *adv.* —**ness,** *n.*

kit·ti·wake [ˈkɪtɪˌwek; ˈkitiweik] *n., pl.* **-wake, -wakes.** 三指鷗(後趾甚短，產於北極海及北大西洋)。

kit·tle [ˈkɪtl̩; ˈkitl] *adj.,* **-tler, -tlest,** *v.,* **-tled, -tling.** ①〖蘇、北英〗發癢的;難駕御的；煩惱的。②冒險的；不確定的。—*v.t.*〖英方〗①抓癢；用湯匙攪拌。②以甜言蜜語取悅(某人)。③使迷惑。

K

kit·ty [ˈkɪtɪ; ˈkiti] *n., pl.* **-ties.** ①(兒語或暱稱)小貓。②賭錢時之抽頭錢。③賭注;下注。④一次發牌後所賸的牌（由叫牌最高者用之)。⑤儲蓄(尤指小額集存者)。

ki·wi [ˈkiwɪ; ˈki:wi] *n.* ①鷸鴕(=apteryx，產於紐西蘭，長嘴無翅)。②〖英空軍俗〗地勤人員。

K.K.K., KKK Ku Klux Klan.

kl., kl kiloliter(s).

Klan [klæn; klæn] *n.* =**Ku Klux Klan.**

Klans·man [ˈklænzmən; ˈklænzmən] *n., pl.* **-men.** 三K黨員。

klax·on [ˈklæksən; ˈklæksən] *n.* (常 K-)〖商標名〗①一種汽車喇叭。②一種作警報用的喇叭。

klep·to·ma·ni·a [ˌklɛptəˈmenɪə; ˌkleptouˈmeiniə] *n.* 竊盜狂。(亦作**clepto-mania**)

klep·to·ma·ni·ac [ˌklɛptəˈmenɪˌæk; ˌkleptouˈmeiniæk] *n.* 有竊盜狂的人。(亦作 **cleptomaniac**)

klieg (or **kleig**) **light** 强烈弧光燈(拍攝電影用者)。

KLM Koninklijke Luchtroat Maatschappij (荷=Royal Dutch Airlines).

kloof [kluf; klu:f]〖南非〗*n.* 峽谷。

klys·tron [ˈklaɪstrɑn; ˈklaistrɔn] *n.* 〖電信〗速調電子管;速度調制電子管;調速管。

km. ①kilometer(s). ②kingdom.

knack [næk; næk] *n.* ①(由練習而得之)技巧;竅門;能力。②習慣;慣技。③首飾;玩具;瑣屑之物。④東西破裂的尖銳聲音。

knack·er [ˈnækɚ; ˈnækə] *n.* ①〖英〗屠宰廢馬商人。②收買廢屋、廢船者。③〖方〗老病無用的家畜(尤指馬)。

knack·y [ˈnækɪ; ˈnæki] *adj.,* **knack-i·er, knack·i·est.** 熟練的；巧妙的；有技巧的。

knag [næg; næg] *n.* ①木節；木瘤。②(掛物用之)木釘。

knag·gy [ˈnægɪ; ˈnægi] *adj.,* **-gi·er, -gi·est.** ①多節(瘤)的;粗糙的。②脾氣躁的。

knap[1] [næp; næp] *n.* 〖方〗小山頂;小山。

knap[2] *v.,* **knapped, knap·ping,** *n.* —*v.t.* & *v.i.* 〖方〗①折斷；搗碎。②敲；打。③咬。—*n.* 〖方〗敲;打;搗擊。

knap·per [ˈnæpɚ; ˈnæpə] *n.* ①搗碎的人。②(長柄的)碎石鎚。

knap·sack [ˈnæpˌsæk; ˈnæpsæk] *n.* (帆布或皮製的)背包。

knap·weed [ˈnæpˌwid; ˈnæpwi:d] *n.*〖植物〗矢車菊。

knar [nɑr; nɑ:] *n.* 木節;木瘤。

***knave** [nev; neiv] *n.* ①騙子；詭計多端的人。②〖紙牌〗=**jack**③.

knav·er·y [ˈnevərɪ; ˈneivəri] *n., pl.* **-er·ies.** ①惡行;奸詐；奸猾。②欺詐的行爲。

knav·ish [ˈnevɪʃ; ˈneiviʃ] *adj.* 奸詐的；不誠實的。—**ly,** *adv.*

***knead** [nid; ni:d] *v.t.* ①揉(土、麪等)。A baker *kneads* dough. 麪包師揉麪團。②按摩。③捏製;塑造。

knead·ing trough [ˈnidɪŋ~; ˈni:-diŋ~] 揉麪槽;揉麪鉢。

‡**knee** [ni; ni:] *n.* ①膝;膝頭。②似膝之物；褲之膝部。*bring a person to his knees* 使某人屈膝；迫使屈服。*go on one's knees* 跪下;祈禱。*on the knees of the gods* 非人所能控制地。—*v.t.* ①用膝蓋碰或打。②向…下跪(如表示尊敬等)。③膝行。

knee action ①汽車前輪的緩衝方式。②機器接合處之有限度彎曲以利取下零件。

knee breeches 長及膝蓋的短袴。

knee·cap [ˈniˌkæp; ˈni:-kæp] *n.* ①膝蓋骨。②護膝。

knee-deep [ˈniˈdip; ˈni:ˈdi:p] *adj.* 深及膝的;深可沒膝的。

knee-high [ˈniˈhaɪ; ˈni:ˈhai] *adj.* 高及膝的。*knee-high to a grasshopper* 很短的。

knee·hole [ˈniˌhol; ˈni:houl] *n.* (寫字桌等下方之)容膝處。

knee jerk 〖醫〗膝反射。

knee-jerk [ˈniˌdʒɝk; ˈni:dʒə:k] *adj.* 本能反應的(如膝反射等)。

knee joint ①膝關節。②〖機械〗肘接。

***kneel** [nil; ni:l] *v.i.,* **knelt** or **kneeled, kneel·ing.** ①跪下。He *knelt* down to pick up his hat. 他跪下拾取帽子。②跪着。—*n.*

跪的動作或姿態。
knee·pad [ˈniˌpæd; ˈniːpæd] *n.* (籃球隊員等用之)護膝棉墊。
knee·pan [ˈniˌpæn; ˈniːpæn] *n.* 膝蓋骨。
knee-slap·per [ˈniˌslæpɚ; ˈniːˌslæpə] *n.* 〖美〗令人捧腹大笑的笑話。
knee swell (or **stop**) (風琴之)增音器。
*__knell__ [nɛl; nel] *n.* ①鐘聲(特指喪鐘、葬鐘等)。②凶兆；不吉之兆。③哀傷的聲音。—*v.i.* ①發出喪鐘聲。②發出哀傷的、凶兆的或警告的聲音。—*v.t.* 以鐘聲宣布或召集。
knelt [nɛlt; nelt] *v.* pt. & pp. of **kneel.**
Knes·set, knes·set [ˈknɛsɛt; ˈkneset] *n.* 以色列之國會。
knew [nju, nu; njuː] *v.* pt. of **know.**
Knick·er·bock·er [ˈnɪkɚˌbɑkɚ; ˈnikəbɔkə] *n.* ①在紐約之荷蘭人後裔。②居住在紐約之人。③(k-)(*pl.*) =**knickers.**
knick·ers [ˈnɪkɚz; ˈnikəz] *n. pl.* (女用)半短內褲;(男用)燈籠短褲。
knick·knack [ˈnɪkˌnæk; ˈniknæk] *n.* 小傢具；小裝飾品；小衣飾；小古董。(亦作 **nicknack**)
knick·knack·er·y [ˈnɪkˌnækərɪ; ˈniknækəri] *n.* =**knicknacks** (集合稱)。
knick·nack [ˈnɪkˌnæk; ˈniknæk] *n.* =**knickknack.**
‡**knife** [naɪf; naif] *n.*, *pl.* **knives,** *v.*, **knifed, knif·ing.** —*n.* ①有柄的小刀。②工具或機械中切斷時用的刃部。***before you can say knife*** 非常突然地;忽然。***get one's knife into a person*** 對某人作無情的攻擊。***under the knife*** 在被施行外科手術中。***war to the knife*** 血戰。—*v.t.* ①(用小刀)切割。②〖美俚〗圖用陰險手段擊敗。—*v.i.* 如刀割般地分開或行走。
knife·board [ˈnaɪfˌbord; ˈnaifbɔːd] *n.* ①磨刀板。②〖英〗公共汽車頂上之座位。
knife edge ①刀刃。②〖機械〗刃狀物(如天平之支點等)。
knife-edged [ˈnaɪfˌɛdʒd; ˈnaif-edʒd] *adj.* 刀刃般利的。
knife grinder 磨刀匠;磨刀石。
knife-ma·chine [ˈnaɪfməˌʃin; ˈnaif-məˌʃiːn] *n.* 磨刀機。
knife·point [ˈnaɪfˌpɔɪnt; ˈnaifpɔint] *n.* 刀尖。***at knifepoint*** 在威脅下；在刀尖脅迫下。
knife rest ①餐桌上之刀叉臺。②〖軍〗=**cheval-de-frise.**
knife switch 〖電〗閘刀開關。
‡**knight** [naɪt; nait] *n.* ①(中古時的)騎士;武士;騎俠。②爵士(凡被封爲爵士者,其姓名皆冠以 Sir 之頭銜)。③衞護某一貴婦之男子。④各種政治、社交、慈善團體的會員。⑤(獻身主義的)勇士;義人。⑥〖諧〗專門人材;專家。⑦〖西洋棋〗有馬頭的棋子。—*v.t.* 授以爵位。He was *knighted* for his war services. 他因戰功而被封爲爵士。
knight·age [ˈnaɪtɪdʒ; ˈnaitidʒ] *n.* 爵士團;爵士姓名錄。
knight bachelor 勳位最低之爵士。
knight-er·rant [ˈnaɪtˈɛrənt; ˈnaitˈerənt] *n., pl.* **knights-er·rant.** 遊俠騎士。
knight-er·rant·ry [ˈnaɪtˈɛrəntrɪ; ˈnaitˈerəntri] *n., pl.* **-ries.** 騎士作風；俠義行爲。
knight·hood [ˈnaɪtˌhud; ˈnaithud] *n.* ①爵士的地位或身分。②騎士的任務。③騎士的資格或身分。④騎士(集合稱)。
knight·ly [ˈnaɪtlɪ; ˈnaitli] *adj.* 武士的;勇敢的;慷慨的;謙恭的;俠義的。***knightly*** valor. 俠義的勇氣。—*adv.* 行爲如騎士地;英勇地;慷慨地;謙恭地。
Knights of Columbus, the 美國天主教之一慈善組織。
*__knit__ [nɪt; nit] *v.*, **knit·ted** or **knit, knit·ting,** *n.* —*v.t.* ①編織;編結。Mother is *knitting* a sweater. 母親正在編結毛線衫。②皺起;皺眉。to *knit* one's brows. 皺眉頭。③黏合。④將(碎片)拼合。⑤結合一起。—*v.i.* ①編織毛線。②長合(如碎骨)。A broken bone *knits.* 碎骨長合。③如眉般皺起;皺眉。—*n.* ①編織之線。②編織之衣服。
knit·ted [ˈnɪtɪd; ˈnitid] *adj.* 編織的(如衣料等)。
knit·ter [ˈnɪtɚ; ˈnitə] *n.* 編織人;編織機。
knit·ting [ˈnɪtɪŋ; ˈnitiŋ] *n.* ①編織；編結。②編織物。
knitting machine 針織機。
knitting needle 編織毛線所用的長針。
‡**knives** [naɪvz; naivz] *n.* pl. of **knife.**
*__knob__ [nɑb; nɔb] *n., v.,* **knobbed, knob·bing.** —*n.* ①節；瘤;球塊。②圓形或球形的門柄；抽屜柄。③圓形山；圓丘。④〖俚〗頭。—*v.t.* ①在…上生節或長瘤。②裝以門柄；裝以把手。③(琢石時)將(多餘石塊)敲掉。—**like,** *adj.*
knob·ble [ˈnɑbl̩; ˈnɔbl] *n.* 小瘤;小節;痣;小圓塊。
knob·by [ˈnɑbɪ; ˈnɔbi] *adj.,* **knob·bi·er, knob·bi·est.** ①多節的；多瘤的；瘤狀的。②〖美〗多丘陵的;丘陵性的;崎嶇的。
knob·ker·rie [ˈnɑbˌkɛrɪ; ˈnɔbˌkeəri] *n.* (南非土人用作武器的)圓頭棒。(亦作 **knobkery**)
knob·stick [ˈnɑbˌstɪk; ˈnɔbstik] *n.* ①=**knobkerrie.** ②〖英〗在罷工期中工作之工人;未加入工會之工人。
‡**knock** [nɑk; nɔk] *v.t.* ①打擊；敲；撞；碰；碰倒。He *knocked* him on the head. 他打他的頭。②〖英俗〗使感驚訝。What *knocks* me is his impudence! 使我深爲驚訝的是他的厚顏無恥！③〖美俗〗吹毛求疵；找碴兒。—*v.i.* ①敲擊。②(機器)發出如敲擊之聲。The engine is *knocking.* 那引擎發出爆震響聲。③互撞;發抖。④敲門。⑤〖俗〗攻擊;批評；抨擊；吹毛求疵。***knock about*** (or ***around***) a. 〖俗〗流浪;漂泊。b. 遊手好閒。c. 虐待。***knock against*** 偶然遇到。***knock down*** a. (拍賣時)賣(給出價最高者)。The picture was *knocked down* to me at an auction. 這幅畫在拍賣中賣給我了。b. 迫使減價。c. (將汽車、機器等)拆散;拆零(以便裝運)。d. 擊倒；打倒；撞倒。e. 拆毀；拆除。These old buildings will be *knocked down.* 這些舊房子將被拆除。f. 〖俚〗盜用雇主之錢。g. 〖俚〗取得(薪金或學位)。h. (風)使船傾斜。***knock it off*** 〖俚〗停止！不要吵！(通常用以喝止爭吵、打架或爭執)。***knock off*** 〖俗〗a. 下班。b. 即席做成；匆匆做成。He *knocks off* a poem. 他即席賦詩。c. 減價。to *knock off* 10 cents from the price. 減價一角。d. 收拾。e. 殺害；謀殺。f. 死。g. 解除;免除。h. 打敗。i. 搶刼。***knock on*** a. 敲擊。to *knock on* a window. 敲擊窗門。b. 結束。***knock on wood*** a. 敲擊木器以避凶。b. 希望災禍不會發生。***knock (oneself) out*** 做得筋疲力盡。***knock out*** a. 〖拳擊〗擊倒(使昏);打敗。Joe *knocked* him *out* with one punch. 喬一拳將他擊昏。b. 磕出(烟斗)中的烟灰。c. 使異常吃驚；嚇倒。d. 〖俚〗立刻有效地提出。e. 破壞。***knock out of the***

box〖棒球〗連連擊中對方投手投出的球，迫使該投手被調出場。**knock over** a. 打倒(人或事物)；打翻。b. 震驚；嚇呆。c. 搶刼。**knock together** a. 拼攏；湊成。b. 相碰；相撞。c. (以一物)敲擊(另一物)。**knock up** a. 向上擊。b. 以敲門喚醒。c. 使疲倦。d. 匆匆做成；草草造成。e. 損壞。The children *knocked up* the new table. 孩子們將新桌子弄壞了。f. 傷害。g.〖俚〗使懷孕。—*n.* ①打；擊；敲。②敲門；敲門聲。③爆聲。④〖英俚〗拍賣時彼此勾結出低價的商人集團；有此種行爲發生之拍賣。

knock·a·bout [ˈnɑkəˌbaut; ˈnɔkəbaut] *adj.* ①粗暴的；騷亂的；喧鬧的。②(衣服等)粗牢的。③胡鬧的。④無目的的；東飄西蕩的。—*n.* ①一種單桅小帆船。②鬧劇。③〖澳〗流動的農場幫工。

knock·down [ˈnɑkˌdaun; ˈnɔkˈdaun] *adj.* ①打倒的；銳不可當的。②折疊式的(如床等可拆開裝合者)。③(價格之)壓低的；減至最低的。—*n.* ①擊倒；壓倒。②打倒他人的一擊。③可拆散之傢具。④〖美俚〗介紹。⑤減價；減少。⑥船在强風中沉沒。

knock·er [ˈnɑkɚ; ˈnɔkə] *n.* ①敲門者；來客。②〖英〗挨戶推銷的售貨員。③門鎚；門環。④〖俗〗吹毛求疵者。⑤〖俚、鄙〗女人乳房。**on the knocker**〖英俚〗挨戶訪問；挨戶售貨。

knock·ing [ˈnɑkɪŋ; ˈnɔkiŋ] *n.* 爆震音；機械故障的聲音。

knock-knee [ˈnɑkˌni; ˈnɔkniː] *n.* ①羅圈腿；兩腿向內彎曲。②(*pl.*)向內彎曲的腿之膝部。

knock-kneed [ˈnɑkˌnid; ˈnɔkniːd] *adj.* 兩腿向內彎曲的。

knock·out [ˈnɑkˌaut; ˈnɔkaut] *n.* ①(拳擊)擊昏；打敗。②(使對方被擊昏之)一擊。③〖美俗〗漂亮的人；引人之物。④盒子、箱子等可輕易拿開的一塊(可拿開以取裏面之東西)。—*adj.* ①擊昏的。②壓倒性的。

***knoll**¹ [nol; noul] *n.* 小山；小丘；丘頂。

knoll² *v.t., v.i., n.*〖英方，古〗=**knell.**

knop [nɑp; nɔp] *n.* ①圓形把手；鈕子；拉手。②〖建築〗蕾形裝飾；頂華。

***knot**¹ [nɑt; nɔt] *n., v.,* **knot·ted, knot·ting.** —*n.* ①(繩、索等結成的)結；結節。to tie a rope in a *knot* (*or* to tie a *knot* in a rope). 將繩打一結；繩上打一結。②(以絲帶等結成的)蝴蝶結。③羣；簇。A *knot* of people stood talking outside the door. 一羣人站在門外談天。④木頭上的節瘤。⑤硬塊。⑥婚姻結合。⑦困難；糾紛。⑧要點。⑨浬；海里(記船之時速的單位)。a vessel of 35 *knots.* 時速35海里之船。**tie oneself (up) in** (or **into**) **knots** 陷入困難中；陷於糾紛中。**tie the knot**〖俗〗結婚。They will *tie the knot* in November. 他們將在十一月結婚。—*v.t.* ①結；包紮。②使結合；使糾結。③打結成(縫)。—*v.i.* ①打結。②糾纏；糾結。③形成硬塊。④打結成縫。—**like,** *adj.*

K

knot² *n.* 鷸類之一種涉禽。

knot·grass [ˈnɑtˌgræs; ˈnɔtgrɑːs] *n.*〖植物〗一種野草(開小藍花)；萹蓄。

knot·hole [ˈnɑtˌhol; ˈnɔthoul] *n.* (木材上之)節孔。

knot·ted [ˈnɑtɪd; ˈnɔtid] *adj.* ①有節的；多節的；多結的。②糾纏的；困難的。

knot·ty [ˈnɑtɪ; ˈnɔti] *adj.,* **-ti·er, -ti·est.** ①(木材)多節的；(繩索)多結的。②使人困惑的；困難的。—**knot·ti·ness,** *n.*

knot·work [ˈnɑtˌwɝk; ˈnɔtwəːk] *n.* 編結細工；縫飾。

knout [naut; naut] *n.* 木柄皮鞭(俄國昔日刑具之一種)。—*v.t.* 鞭打。

‡**know** [no; nou] *v.,* **knew, known, know·ing,** *n.* —*v.t.* ①知道；懂得；了解。②認識；熟識；認出。I've *known* him since he was a child. 從他小時候起，我就認識他。③經歷；嘗受。He has *known* better days. 他曾享受過優裕的日子(意謂並非一生窮困)。④辨識出；分別出。⑤對…有研究；精通。He *knows* literature. 他對文學很有研究。⑥記牢。to *know* a lesson. 將一課記牢。—*v.i.* 知道；懂得；了解。I'm not guessing; I really *know.* 我不是猜測，我真地知道。**be known as** 以…著稱；聞名。**be known to** 爲…所熟知。**know about** (or **of**) a. 懂得；知道。b. 聽別人說過。**know better (than to)** 知道(某事)是不對的；不會愚到如此程度。You ought to have *known better.* 你應該早就知道(這是不對的)。**know how to do** (=be able to do) 會；能够。**know one's own business; know what's what; know a thing** (or **move**) **or two; know the ropes** 精明能幹。**know somebody by name** 僅知其名(尚未謀面)。**know somebody by sight** 僅識其面貌(不知其名)。**know this from that** 辨得清楚。to *know* good *from* evil. 辨善惡。**make oneself known** 自我介紹。—*n.* 知曉；知識(僅見於下一習慣語中)。**in the know**〖俗〗熟悉內幕消息。

know·a·ble [ˈnoəbl̩; ˈnouəbl] *adj.* ①可知的；可發現的；可理解的。②容易相識的；易於接近的(人)。—*n.* 可知之事；可理解之事物。

know-all [ˈnoˌɔl; ˈnouˌɔːl] *n.*〖俗〗=**know-it-all.**

know-how [ˈnoˌhau; ˈnouhau] *n.* 知識；技能；方法；祕訣。the *know-how* of the atomic bomb. 原子彈之製造方法(技術)。

***know·ing** [ˈnoɪŋ; ˈnouiŋ] *adj.* ①有學問的；博學的。a *knowing* scholar. 博學之士。②聰穎的；機警的。a *knowing* dog. 機警的狗。③自以爲無所不知的。④心照不宣的。—*n.* 知識；知曉。**There is no knowing....** 不可能知道。*There's no knowing* when we shall meet again. 不知何時我們始能再會面。

know·ing·ly [ˈnoɪŋlɪ; ˈnouiŋli] *adv.* ①心照不宣地。②故意地；有意地。

know-it-all [ˈnoɪtˌɔl; ˈnouitˌɔːl] *n.*〖俗〗學識淵博的人；裝出無所不知的人；萬事通。—*adj.* 自以爲了不起的；自大的。

‡**knowl·edge** [ˈnɑlɪdʒ; ˈnɔlidʒ] *n.* ①知識；學識；學問。*Knowledge* is power. 知識即是力量。②知曉；了解。A baby has no *knowledge* of good and evil. 嬰兒不了解善惡。③熟悉；認識。He has a good *knowledge* of London. 他對倫敦的情形很熟悉。**come to one's knowledge** 爲某人獲悉。**to one's certain knowledge** 某人確知。He had *to my certain knowledge* been forced to act in that way. 我確知他是被迫那樣做的。**to one's knowledge** a. 確知。b. (與否定詞連用)就某人所知。**to the best of my knowledge** (=as far as I know) 據我所知；就我所知而論。**without the knowledge of** 連…都不知道。

knowl·edge·a·ble [ˈnɑlɪdʒəbl; ˈnɔlidʒəbl] *adj.*〖俗〗(對某一問題)有豐富知識的；博識的。(亦作 **knowledgable**)

‡**known** [non; noun] *v.* pp. of **know.** —*adj.* 已知的。

know-noth·ing [ˈnoˌnʌθɪŋ; ˈnou-

ˌnʌθiŋ] *n.* ①無知之人。②不可知論者。—*adj.* ①一無所知的;無知的。②不可知論的。

knt. knight.

knuck·le** [ˈnʌkḷ; ˈnʌkl] *n.*, *v.*, **-led, -ling.** —*n.* ①指關節;指節。to give a boy a rap over (*or* on) the *knuckles.* 輕敲一個孩子的指節,以示呵責。②(做食物用的)動物的蹄爪。③(*pl.*)(戴於指節上做武器用的)鐵拳頭。—*v.t.* & *v.i.* 以指節打(壓、擦);(打彈子時)把指節放於地上。knuckle down*** **a.** 專心工作;下決心工作。**b.** (亦作 **knuckle under**)屈服;讓步。

knuckle ball 〖棒球〗一種很不容易擊中的慢速度變化球。

knuckle bone ①(人之)指節骨。②(獸之)膝節骨。③(*pl.*)用羊之膝節骨之骨片所作的一種遊戲。(亦作 **knucklebone**)

knuck·le-dust·er [ˈnʌkḷˌdʌstɚ; ˈnʌklˌdʌstə] *n.* (金屬製之)指節環(打架時用之)。(亦作 **brass knuckles**)

knur, knurr [nɝ; nəː] *n.* ①(木之)結節;硬瘤。②(球戲用之)木球。

knurl [nɝl; nəːl] *n.* ①(木之)結節。②(金屬表面之)小粒;小隆起;(硬幣邊緣上之)刻痕;壓花紋。③〖蘇〗矮壯的人。—*v.t.* 在…邊緣上壓花紋或刻痕。(亦作 **nurl**) **—y,** *adj.*

KO, K.O., k.o. 〖拳擊〗knockout.

ko·a·la [kəˈɑlə; kouˈɑːlə] *n.* 〖動物〗(澳洲產之)無尾熊(袋熊類,有背子爬樹的習性)。

ko·bold [ˈkobɑld; ˈkoubould] *n.* 〖德國傳說〗①(入家宅中惡作劇或予人幫助的)小精靈。②(居於礦坑內等之)小妖精;地靈。

Koch [kox; kɔːx] *n.* 考克 (Robert, 1843–1910, 德國醫生及細菌學家, 1905 年得諾貝爾獎)。

ko·dak [ˈkodæk; ˈkoudæk] *n.*, *v.*, **-daked, -dak·ing.** —*n.* (K-) 柯達牌小型手提照相機。—*v.t.* & *v.i.* 用上述照相機照(相)。

K. of C. Knight(s) of Columbus.

Koh·i·noor [ˌkoɪˈnur; ˈkouinuə] *n.* ①英王室所藏之一顆 106 克拉之印度產大鑽石。②(k-)任何上等的大鑽石。③最美麗或最寶貴之物。

kohl [kol; koul] *n.* 東方婦女所用之一種化妝墨。

kohl·ra·bi [ˈkolˈrabɪ; ˈkoulˈrɑːbi] *n.*, *pl.* **-bies.** 〖植物〗一種可供食用之球莖甘藍。

ko·la [ˈkolə; ˈkoulə] *n.* 〖植物〗①=**kola nut.** ②可樂樹(熱帶非洲、西印度羣島、巴西等產)。(亦作 **cola**)

kola nut 可樂子(含咖啡精甚多)。

ko·lin·sky [kəˈlɪnskɪ; kəˈlinski] *n.* ①〖動物〗(亞洲產之)貂;西伯利亞貂。②(西伯利亞)貂皮。

kol·khoz [kɑlˈkɔz; kəlˈkɔːz] 〖俄〗 *n.* 集體農場。(亦作 **kolhoz, kolkhos**)

Kom·in·tern [ˈkɑmɪnˌtɝn; ˈkɔminˌtəːn] *n.* =**Comintern.**

koo·doo [ˈkudu; ˈkuːduː] *n.* =**kudu.**

kook·y [ˈkukɪ; ˈkuːki] *adj.*, **kook·i·er, kook·i·est.** 〖俚〗①乖僻的;怪人的;笨蛋的。②瘋子的。(亦作 **kookie**)

ko·pe(c)k [ˈkopɛk; ˈkoupek] *n.* =**copeck.**

kop·je [ˈkɑpɪ; ˈkɔpi] 〖南非〗*n.* 小山;丘。

Ko·ran [koˈran; kɔˈrɑːn] *n.* 可蘭經(回教的經典)。(亦作 **Quran**) **—ic,** *adj.*

***Ko·re·a** [koˈriə; kəˈriə, kɔˈr-] *n.* 韓國(第二次世界大戰以後分爲南韓與北韓)。

***Ko·re·an** [koˈriən; kəˈriən, kɔˈr-] *adj.* 韓國的;韓國人的;韓國語文的。—*n.* ①韓國人。②韓國語文。

Korean War 韓戰(北韓、中共與南韓、聯合國之戰爭,自 1950 年6月25日至1953年7月27日)。

ko·sher [ˈkoʃɚ; ˈkouʃə] *adj.* ①〖猶太教〗經正式處理的;衞生合法的;清淨的(食物等);販賣或使用合法之衞生食物的(商店、家庭等)。②〖美俚〗合適的;眞正的。***keep kosher*** 遵守猶太食物衞生。—*n.* 〖俗〗合法之衞生食物。—*v.t.* 使衞生合法。(亦作 **kasher**)

kot·wal [ˈkotwɑl; ˈkoutwɑːl] *n.* 〖英印〗(都市之)警察局長;都市長官。(亦作 **cotwal**)

kou·mis(s), kou·myss [ˈkumɪs; ˈkuːmis] *n.* =**kumiss.**

kour·bash, koor·bash [ˈkurbæʃ; ˈkuəbæʃ] *n.* =**kurbash.**

Kow·loon [kauˈlun; ˈkauˈluːn] *n.* ①九龍(香港對面之一半島)。②九龍港埠。

kow·tow [kauˈtau; ˈkauˈtau] *v.i.* ①磕頭(係中文之譯音)。②恭服;順從。—*n.* 磕頭。(亦作 **kotow**)

KP, K.P. Kitchen Police. **K.P.** ①Knight of the Order of St. Patrick. ②Knights of Pythias. **Kr** 化學元素 krypton 之符號。 **kr.** ① kreutzer. ② krona. ③ krone. ④kronen. ⑤kroner. ⑥ kronor. ⑦króna. ⑧krónur.

kraal [krɑl; krɑːl] *n.* (亦作**craal**) ①南非土人之小村莊。②牛羊之圍欄;牛羊之棚舍。—*v.t.* 圍在圍欄之中。

kraft [kræft; kræft] *n.* 牛皮紙。

krait [kraɪt; krait] *n.* (印度等地產之)一種毒蛇。

kra·ken [ˈkrɑkən; ˈkrɑːkən] *n.* (常K-)〖挪威傳說〗海怪。

Kraut [kraut; kraut] *n.* 〖蔑〗(常 k-) 德國人。

Krem·lin [ˈkrɛmlɪn; ˈkremlin] *n.* ①蘇聯政府之行政部門(尤指其外交部)。②(the-)克里姆林宮(在莫斯科,係蘇聯政府的中樞辦公所在)。③(k-) 任何俄國城市的城堡。

Krem·lin·ol·o·gy [ˌkrɛmlɪnˈɑlədʒɪ; ˌkremlinˈɔlədʒi] *n.* 蘇聯政治之研究(尤指其外交政策)。(亦作 **Sovietology**). **—Krem·lin·ol·o·gist,** *n.*

kre·o·sote [ˈkriəˌsot; ˈkriːəsout] *n.* **=creosote.**

kreu(t)·zer [ˈkrɔɪtsɚ; ˈkrɔitsə] *n.* 昔德、奧之銅幣 (與 farthing 等值)。

krieg·spiel [ˈkrigˌspil; ˈkriːgspiːl] 〖德〗 *n.* 兵棋 (一種盤上戰爭演習,用作戰術教學)。

krim·mer [ˈkrɪmɚ; ˈkrimə] *n.* 克里米亞區產的一種灰羊皮。(亦作 **crimmer**)

kris [kris; kriːs] *n.* =**creese.**

Krish·na [ˈkrɪʃnə; ˈkriʃnə] *n.* 〖印度神話〗 Vishnu 之第八化身。

Kriss Krin·gle [ˈkrɪsˈkrɪŋḷ; ˈkrisˈkriŋgl] =**Santa Claus.**

kro·na [ˈkronə; ˈkrounə] *n.*, *pl.* **-nor** [-nɔr; -nɔː]. 瑞典及冰島之貨幣單位 (相當於丹麥及挪威之 krone)。

kro·ne^{1} [ˈkronɛ; ˈkroune] *n.*, *pl.* **-ner** [-nɛr; -nɛə]. 丹麥、挪威之貨幣單位。

kro·ne^{2} [ˈkronə; ˈkrounə] *n.*, *pl.* **-nen** [-nən; -nən]. ①昔德國金幣。②昔奧地利金幣。

Kroo [kru; kruː] *n.* 克魯族(西非 Liberia 沿岸之黑人種族); 克魯人。—*adj.* 克魯族(人)的。

Kroo·man [ˈkrumən; ˈkruːmən] *n.*, *pl.* **-men.** =**Kroo.**

krul·ler [ˈkrʌlɚ; ˈkrʌlə] *n.* =**cruller.**

kryp·ton [ˈkrɪptɑn; ˈkriptɔn] *n.* 〖化〗氪 (一種稀有氣體元素, 符號 Kr)。

Kt, Kt. 〖西洋棋〗 knight. **kt.** ①karat, carat. ②kiloton. ③knot. **K.T.** ①Knight of the Thistle. ②Knight(s) Templar.

Kua·la Lum·pur ['kwɑlə'lumpur; ˌkwɑːlə'lumpuə] 吉隆坡(馬來西亞 Selangor 邦及馬來西亞聯邦之首府)。

Ku·blai Khan ['kjublaɪ'kɑn; 'kublai'kɑːn] 忽必烈汗 (1216–1294, 中國元朝開國者, 卽元世祖)。

ku·dos ['kjudɑs; 'kjuːdɔs] *n.* 〖俗〗光榮; 聲譽; 聲望; 稱讚。

ku·du ['kudu; 'kuːduː] *n.* 〖動物〗(南非產之)紐角鹿。(亦作 **koodoo**)

Kuhn [kun; kuːn] *n.* 古恩 (Richard, 1900–1967, 德國化學家, 獲 1938 年諾貝爾化學獎, 但因納粹反對而未領)。

Ku-Klux, Ku·klux ['kjuˌklʌks; 'kjuːˌklʌks] *n.* ① = **Ku Klux Klan.** ② 三K黨黨員。

Ku Klux·er ['kju'klʌksɚ; 'kjuː-'klʌksə] 三K黨員。

Ku Klux·ism [~'klʌksɪzəm; ~'klʌksizəm] 三K黨的主張, 作風, 作法。(亦作 **Ku Kluxery**)

Ku Klux Klan ['kjuˌklʌks'klæn; 'kjuː-klʌks'klæn] 〖美〗三K黨 (a. 內戰後於南方成立之祕密團體, 以重建及保持白人優越地位爲宗旨。b. 1915 年由生於美國之白人新教徒組成之祕密團體, 以反舊教徒、猶太人、黑人及東方人爲宗旨)。(略作 **K.K.K.**)(亦作 **Ku Klux**)

kuk·ri ['kukrɪ; 'kukri] 〖印度〗*n.* Gurkha 人所用之一種彎刀。

ku·lak [ku'lɑk; kuː'lɑːk] 〖俄〗*n.* ①剝削貧農之富農。②自耕農。

Kul·tur ['kultur; kul'tuə] 〖德〗*n.* ①(一民族或一時代之)文化。②〖蔑〗德國文化。

Kul·tur·kampf [kul'turˌkɑmpf; kul'tuːəˌkɑːmpf] 〖德〗*n.* 文化鬥爭 (1872–1886間德皇政府與羅馬天主敎會間關於敎育權及敎職任命權之爭)。

Ku·lun ['ku'lun; 'kuː'luːn] *n.* 庫倫 (Ulan Bator 之中文名)。

ku·miss, ku·mys ['kumɪs; 'kuːmis] *n.* ①乳酒 (昔韃靼人以馬乳或駱駝乳釀成之酒)。②(今歐美人以牛乳釀製之)牛乳酒。(亦作 **Koumis**)

küm·mel ['kɪml̩; 'kuməl] *n.* 欽梅爾酒 (以小茴香或葛縷子等調味釀成, 波羅的海東岸之名產)。

kum·quat ['kʌmkwɑt; 'kʌmkwɔt] *n.* 金橘; 金橘樹。(亦作 **cumquat**)

kung fu 功夫; 中國武術; 中國功夫。

Kun·ming ['kun'mɪŋ; 'kun'miŋ] *n.* 昆明(中國雲南省省會)。

Kuo·min·tang ['kwomɪn'tæŋ; 'kwoumin'tæŋ] *n.* (中國的)國民黨。

kur·bash ['kurbæʃ; 'kuəbæʃ] *n.* (昔時土耳其、埃及等地用爲刑具之)皮鞭。—*v.t.* 用皮鞭打; 鞭笞。(亦作 **kourbash**)

Kurd [kɝd; kəːd] *n.* 庫德人 (主要居於 Kurdistan 之遊牧回敎徒)。

Ku·ril(e) Islands ['kurɪl (-ril)~; 'kuːril(-riːl)~] 千島羣島(在日本之東北)。

Kur·saal ['kurˌzɑl; 'kuəzɑːl] 〖德〗*n.*, *pl.* **-sä·le** [-ˌzelə; -ˌzeilə]. (海水浴場、溫泉等之)大娛樂廳。

Ku·wait [ku'wet; ku'weit] *n.* 科威特 (亞洲西南部一國在波斯灣之西北隅, 於1961年獨立, 其首都爲 Al Kuwait)。(亦作 **Koweit**)

Ku·wai·ti [ku'wetɪ; ku'weiti] *n.* 科威特人。—*adj.* 科威特的; 科威特人的。

KV, kv kilovolt(s).

kvas(s) [kvæs, kvɑs; kvæs, kvɑːs] 〖俄〗*n.* (俄製之)裸麥啤酒; 淡啤酒。(亦作 **quass**)

kw. kilowatt.

Kwang·chow ['gwɑŋ'dʒo; 'gwɑːŋ-'dʒou] *n.* 廣州(中國廣東省省會, 亦作 **Canton**)

Kwang·si ['kwæŋ'si; 'gwɑːŋ'siː] *n.* 廣西(中國南部之一省, 省會桂林, Kweilin)。

Kwang·tung ['kwæŋ'tʌŋ; 'gwɑːŋ-duŋ] *n.* 廣東 (中國南部之一省, 省會廣州, Canton 或 Kwangchow)。

Kwan-yin ['kwɑn'jɪn; 'kwɑːn'jin] 〖中〗*n.* 觀音菩薩。(亦作 **Kuan Yin**)

Kwei·chow ['gwe'dʒo; 'gwei'dʒou] *n.* 貴州(中國南部一省, 省會貴陽, Kweiyang)。

K.W.H., KWh, kwh, kwhr Kilowatt-hour.

Ky. Kentucky.

ky·lin ['kilɪn; 'kiːlin] 〖中〗*n.* 麒麟。

ky·loe ['kaɪlo; 'kailou] *n.* 蘇格蘭高地產之長角種小牛。

ky·mo·graph ['kaɪməˌgræf; 'kaiməgrɑːf] *n.* 〖醫〗波動曲線記錄器 (記錄脈搏、鼓動、呼吸及發音等)。

Kyr·i·e e·le·i·son ['kɪrɪˌi ə'leəsn̩; 'kiriˌiːə'leiəsn̩] 〖希〗啓應禱文; 啓應禱告 (= Lord, have mercy. 上主, 求祢垂憐! 希臘正敎及天主敎會用爲彌撒的起頭句, 英國國敎會用爲聖餐禮中及對十誡之應答句)。

L

L or l [ɛl; el] *n.*, *pl.* **L's, Ls, l's, ls** [ɛlz; elz]. ①英文字母之第十二個字母。②羅馬數字的50 (如: CL=150, XL=40, LV=55)。③ (L) L形之物; 建築物在一端作直角伸出之側翼。

L. ①Lady. ②Lake. ③Late. ④Latin. ⑤law. ⑥latitude. ⑦left. ⑧liber(拉=book). ⑨Liberal. ⑩London. ⑪Lord. ⑫Low. ⑬large. ⑭lempira(s). ⑮leu; lei. ⑯lev; leva. ⑰Licentiate. ⑱lira. ⑲place (拉=locus). ⑳stage left. ㉑lumen.

l. ①land. ②latitude. ③law. ④leaf. ⑤league. ⑥left. ⑦length. ⑧line. ⑨link. ⑩lira. ⑪liras. ⑫liter. ⑬large. ⑭lumen.

La 〖化〗元素 lanthanum 之符號。

la[1] [lɑ; lɑː] *n.* 〖音樂〗全音階長音階的第六音。

la[2] [lɔ, lɑ; lɔː] *interj* 〖古, 方〗看! 看哪! 呀! 啊呀! (表强意或驚訝之聲)。

La. Louisiana.

L.A. ①Latin America. ②Law Agent. ③ Legislative Assembly. ④ Library Association. ⑤ Local Authority. ⑥Local Agent. ⑦〖美俗〗Los Angeles.

L/A Letter of Authorization.

laa·ger ['lɑgɚ; 'lɑːgə] 〖南非〗*n.* 〖軍〗(以車輛圍成以爲防衞之) 臨時陣營; 車陣。—*v.t.* 將(車輛) 布成車陣。—*v.i.* 布車陣; 宿營於車陣中。(亦作 **lager**)

Lab. ①Laborite. ②Labrador.

lab [læb; læb] *n.* 〖俗〗= **laboratory.**

lab·e·fac·tion [ˌlæbɪ'fækʃən; ˌlæbi'fækʃən] *n.* 動搖; 衰弱; 沒落; 頹廢。

***la·bel** ['lebl̩; 'leibl] *n.*, *v.*, **-beled, -bel·ing.** —*n.* ①標籤; 籤條。to put *labels* on one's luggage. 加標籤於行李上。②(用以描述某人、某事物或思想的) 短片語。 —*v.t.* ①

貼標籤於。②指爲；稱爲。to *label* a man a liar. 指某人爲撒謊者。

la·bel·lum [lə'bɛləm; lə'beləm] *n., pl.* **-bel·la** [-'bɛlə; -'belə]. 〖植物〗唇形瓣。

la·bi·al ['lebɪəl; 'leibjəl] *adj.* 唇的。*labial* sounds. 唇音(如：b, p, m 等)。—*n.*唇音。

la·bi·al·ism ['lebɪəl,ɪzəm; 'leibiəlizm] *n.* 〖語音〗①唇音之特性。②發唇音之傾向(尤指發音上之缺點言)。

la·bi·al·ize ['lebɪəl,aɪz; 'leibiəlaiz] *v.t.*, **-ized, -iz·ing.** 〖語音〗用唇發出(聲音)；唇音化；以圓唇形發(母音)。

la·bi·ate ['lebɪ,et; 'leibieit] *adj.* ①〖動物〗(形狀、機能等)似唇的；唇狀的；有唇狀物的。②〖植物〗有唇狀物的；唇狀的；唇形花冠的。

la·bile ['lebḷ; 'leibḷ] *adj.* 〖理化〗不安定的；易起化學變化的；易變的；不穩的。

la·bi·o·den·tal [,lebɪo'dɛntḷ; 'leibiou'dentḷ] *adj.* 〖語音〗唇齒(音)的。—*n.* 唇齒音(如 f, v 等)。

la·bi·um ['lebɪəm; 'leibiəm] *n., pl.* **la·bi·a.** ①唇；唇形器官。②(*pl.*) 陰唇。③〖蟲〗下唇。④〖植物〗(唇形花冠之)下唇瓣。

‡**la·bo(u)r** ['lebɚ; 'leibə] *n.* ①勞動；勞作。②工作；一件件的工作(尤指困難的工作)。③勞工；勞動階級。skilled and unskilled *labor*. 有特殊技術與無特殊技術之勞工。④分娩；陣痛。a woman in *labor*. 在分娩中的婦女。—*v.i.* ①勞動；勞作。to *labor* in the field. 在田間操作。②緩慢顚簸而行。The ship *labored* through the heavy seas. 此船在風浪濤濤的海上緩慢而顚簸地航行。③分娩；陣痛。④詳細說明；拖長。—*v.t.* ①仔細地分析解釋。②使疲倦。Don't *labor* the reader with unnecessary detail. 不要用不必要的細節使讀者疲倦。③開(礦)。***labor under*** 受…的不利影響；爲…所支配。

***lab·o·ra·to·ry** ['læbrə,torɪ; lə'bɔrətəri, 'læbərə-] *n., pl.* **-ries,** *adj.* —*n.* ①科學實驗室(尤指化學方面者，略作 **lab**)。②化學物品、藥品、炸彈等製造廠。—*adj.* 科學實驗室的；實驗技術的。

laboratory school 附屬於大學以訓練實習教師之學校。

labor camp ①勞工營。②農場流動幫工的臨時住處。

Labor Day 〖美〗勞工節(九月的第一個禮拜一)。

la·bo(u)red ['lebɚd; 'leibəd] *adj.* ①緩慢的；困難的。②不流暢的；矯揉造作的。

***la·bo(u)r·er** ['lebərɚ; 'leibərə] *n.* ①勞動者。②勞工；苦力。

Labor Exchange ①勞力交換(按照所花勞力之分量，不以貨幣爲媒介之產品與產品的直接交換)。②職業介紹所。

la·bo(u)r·ing ['lebərɪŋ; 'leibəriŋ] *n.* ①勞動；操勞；辛勞的工作。②〖蘇〗農場。—*adj.* ①從事於勞動的。②困苦的；辛勞的；痛苦的。③因生產而痛苦的。④(船)劇烈顚簸的。

***la·bo·ri·ous** [lə'borɪəs; lə'bɔːriəs] *adj.* ①費力的；艱難的。a *laborious* task. 艱苦的工作。②努力的；勤勞的。③具見苦心的；不流利的。*laborious* style (speech). 不流利的文體(演說)。—**ly,** *adv.* —**ness,** *n.*

la·bo(u)r·ite ['lebə,raɪt; 'leibərait] *n.* ①勞工黨員或其擁護者；勞工主義者。②(常 L-) 工黨黨員(尤指英國工黨黨員)。

labor market 勞動市場。

labor of love 甘心情願做的工作(或爲喜愛該工作本身或爲所愛者而做)。

Labor Party 勞工黨；工黨。

la·bor-sav·ing ['lebɚ,sevɪŋ; 'leibə,seiviŋ] *adj.* 省力的；節省人力的。a *labor-saving* device. 省力的器械。

labor turnover ①勞工周轉(某一時期中，如一年或一月中，雇主所雇以替換因故離職工人之新工人人數)。②勞工周轉率(此種替換新工與全部工人數所成之比率)。

labor union 工會。

Labour Party (英國之)工黨。

Lab·ra·dor ['læbrə,dɔr; 'læbrədɔː] *n.* 拉布拉多(**a.** 北美洲東北部之一半島，包括加拿大的紐芬蘭及拉布拉多省。**b.** 該半島之東部，紐芬蘭之一部分)。

la·brum ['lebrəm; 'leibrəm] *n., pl.* **la·bra** ['lebrə; 'leibrə]. ①唇；唇狀邊緣；唇狀物。②〖動物〗**a.** (昆蟲等之)上唇；外唇。**b.** (單殼軟體動物之)殼外緣。

la·bur·num [lə'bɝnəm; lə'bəːnəm] *n.* 〖植物〗金鏈花(一種豌豆科有毒灌木)。

lab·y·rinth ['læbə,rɪnθ; 'læbərinθ] *n.* ①迷宮。②複雜難解的事物。③錯綜複雜的安排、配置等。④複雜的關係或情況。⑤(L-)〖希臘神話〗Daedalus 爲克里底王 Minos 所建的迷宮。⑥〖解剖〗內耳。⑦〖解剖〗迷路。

lab·y·rin·thi·an [,læbə'rɪnθɪən; ,læbə'rinθiən] *adj.* =**labyrinthine.**

lab·y·rin·thic [,læbə'rɪnθɪk; ,læbə'rinθik] *adj.* =**labyrinthine.** —**lab·y·rin·thi·cal·ly,** *adv.*

lab·y·rin·thine [,læbə'rɪnθɪn; ,læbə'rinθain] *adj.* ①迷宮的；迷路的。②複雜難解之事物的。③錯綜複雜的；難懂的；迷惑的。

lac¹ [læk; læk] *n.* 〖英印〗①十萬。②十萬羅比(rupee)。③任何巨大的數目；無數。(亦作 **lakh**)

lac² *n.* 蟲膠(亞洲南部一種介殼科昆蟲分泌於樹上的似樹脂之物質，可作漆或染料用)；蟲膠漆；蟲膠染料。

lace** [les; leis] *n., v.,* **laced, lac·ing.** —*n.* ①緞帶；絲帶；花邊；飾帶；飾邊。a dress trimmed with *lace*. 飾花邊的服裝。②帶(如 shoe-laces 鞋帶等)。③加在食物或飲料中的少量酒。—*v.t.* ①以帶結。to *lace* (up) one's shoes. 結起鞋帶。②飾以花邊。③(以胸衣)束腰〖up〗。④編結。⑤加上條紋；畫上條紋。⑥〖俗〗鞭打。⑦攙酒於(飲料)。He took his coffee *laced* with brandy. 他喝加白蘭地酒的咖啡。⑧混合。—*v.i.* 結帶子；用帶結。lace into*** **a.** 打擊。**b.** 嚴厲批評。The teacher *laced into* his students for not studying. 老師因學生不用功而罵他們。

lac·er·ate ['læsə,ret; 'læsəreit] *v.,* **-at·ed, -at·ing,** *adj.* —*v.t.* ①撕裂；劃破。The bear's claws *lacerated* his flesh. 那熊的爪子把他的肉劃破了。②傷害(情感等)；使傷心。—*adj.* ①撕裂的；劃破的。②〖植物〗有缺裂邊緣的(葉)。

lac·er·a·tion [,læsə'reʃən; ,læsə'reiʃən] *n.* ①撕裂；暴力損裂。②破口；裂傷。③苦惱；痛苦。

lace·wing ['les,wɪŋ; 'leis,wiŋ] *n.* 草蜻蛉。

lace·work ['les,wɝk; 'leis,wəːk] *n.* 花邊；花邊細工。

lach·es ['lætʃɪz; 'lætʃiz] *n.* (作*sing.*解)〖法律〗(履行義務或主張權利之)怠慢；懈怠。

lach·ry·mal ['lækrəmḷ; 'lækriməl] *adj.* ①眼淚的；生淚的。②哭泣的。***the lachrymal glands*** 淚腺。—*n.* ①(*pl.*) 淚分泌器官；淚腺。②=**lachrymatory.** (亦作 **lacrimal**)

lach·ry·ma·to·ry 〔ˈlækrəməˌtorı; ˈlækrimətəri〕 *adj., n., pl.* **-ries.** —*adj.* 眼淚的;催淚的。—*n.*〖考古〗淚壺(發現於古羅馬人墓中之細頸小瓶,據考證爲盛悲悼者眼淚之用者)。(亦作 **lacrimatory**)

lach·ry·mose 〔ˈlækrəˌmos; ˈlækrimous〕 *adj.* ①悲慘的;令人落淚的。②悲哀的;好流淚的。(亦作 **lacrimose**)

lac·ing 〔ˈlesıŋ; ˈleisiŋ〕 *n.* ①飾花邊;結紐帶。②紐;帶;鞋帶。③花邊裝飾;(制服上鑲滾之)金或銀辮帶。④〖俗〗鞭打;笞。⑤攙在食物或飲料的少量酒。

la·cin·i·ate 〔ləˈsınıˌet; ləˈsinieit〕 *adj.* ①有綫(邊)的。②〖動、植物〗有細長裂片的;鋸齒狀的。

:lack 〔læk; læk〕 *v.t.* ①缺乏;沒有。A coward *lacks* courage. 怯懦者缺乏勇氣。②短少。The vote *lacks* three of being a majority. 投票結果尙少三票方能構成多數。—*v.i.* 缺乏;無。Money was *lacking* for the plan. 這計畫尙缺經費。***lack in*** 在(某方面)缺少或不足。—*n.* ①缺乏;無。*Lack* of rest made her tired. 缺乏休息使她疲倦。②缺乏的東西。***for lack of*** 因缺少(某物)。***supply the lack*** 供給所缺乏之物。

lack·a·dai·si·cal 〔ˌlækəˈdezıkl; ˌlækəˈdeizikəl〕 *adj.* ①懶散的;沒精打采的;感傷的。②懶惰的。

lack·a·day 〔ˈlækəˌde; ˈlækədei〕 *interj.* 〖古〗悲哉!哀哉!噫!(表悲哀、驚異、悔恨等之驚嘆語)。

lack·er 〔ˈlækɚ; ˈlækə〕 *n., v.* =**lacquer.**

lack·ey 〔ˈlækı; ˈlæki〕 *n., pl.* **-eys,** *v.,* **-eyed, -ey·ing.** —*n.* ①男僕;跟班。②卑躬屈膝者。—*v.t. & v.i.* ①作跟班;伺候。②俯耳聽命(於)。(亦作 **lacquey**)

lack·lus·ter, lack·lus·tre 〔ˈlækˌlʌstɚ; ˈlækˌlʌstə〕 *adj.* 無光澤的;黯淡的。

la·con·ic 〔ləˈkɑnık; ləˈkɔnik〕 *adj.* 簡潔的;簡明的。(亦作 **laconical**) —**al·ly,** *adv.*

la·con·i·cism 〔ləˈkɑnəsızəm; ləˈkɔnisizəm〕 *n.* =**laconism.**

lac·o·nism 〔ˈlækənızəm; ˈlækənizəm〕 *n.* ①(語句之)簡潔。②簡潔之語句。

lac·quer 〔ˈlækɚ; ˈlækə〕 *n.* ①漆。②(中國、日本等地產之)天然漆。③漆器(=lacquer ware)。—*v.t.* 塗漆於。(亦作 **lacker**) —**er,** *n.*

lac·quey 〔ˈlækı; ˈlæki〕 *n., pl.* **-queys,** *v.t.,* **-queyed, -quey·ing.** =**lackey.**

lac·ri·mal, lac·ry·mal 〔ˈlækrıml; ˈlækriml〕 *adj.* =**lachrymal.**

la·crosse 〔ləˈkrɔs; ləˈkrɔs〕 *n.* 長曲棍球(一種球戲,在加拿大通行,兩隊各十人,以長柄球拍擊球,使入對方之球門)。

lac·ta·ry 〔ˈlæktərı; ˈlæktəri〕 *adj., n., pl.* **-ries.** —*adj.* 〖罕〗乳的;乳狀的。—*n.* 牛乳房。

lac·tase 〔ˈlæktes; ˈlækteis〕 *n.* 〖生化〗乳糖酶(分解乳糖之酵素)。

lac·tate 〔ˈlæktet; ˈlækteit〕 *v.,* **-tat·ed, -tat·ing,** *n.* —*v.i.* ①分泌乳;生乳。②哺乳;授乳。—*n.* 〖化〗乳酸鹽。

L

lac·ta·tion 〔lækˈteʃən; lækˈteiʃən〕 *n.* ①乳之分泌;生乳。②哺乳;授乳。③生乳期;授乳期。

lac·te·al 〔ˈlæktıəl; ˈlæktiəl〕 *adj.* ①乳的;乳汁的;乳狀的。②〖解剖〗輸送(輸入)乳糜的。—*n.* 〖解剖〗乳糜管。

lac·te·ous 〔ˈlæktıəs; ˈlæktiəs〕 *adj.* ①〖古〗乳的;似乳的;乳白色的。②〖解剖〗=**lacteal.**

lac·tes·cence 〔lækˈtɛsəns; lækˈtesəns〕 *n.* ①乳(狀)化。②乳汁狀;乳汁色;乳狀液。③〖植物、蟲〗乳狀液之分泌。

lac·tes·cent 〔lækˈtɛsənt; lækˈtesənt〕 *adj.* ①成爲乳狀的;乳狀的。②〖昆蟲〗分泌乳狀液體的。

lac·tic 〔ˈlæktık; ˈlæktik〕 *adj.* 乳的;由乳而來的(尤指酸乳)。

lactic acid 〖化〗乳酸。

lac·tif·er·ous 〔lækˈtıfərəs; lækˈtifərəs〕 *adj.* ①出乳汁的。②〖解剖〗輸送乳汁的。③〖植物〗輸送乳狀液的;生乳液的。

lac·to·ba·cil·lus 〔ˌlæktobəˈsıləs; ˌlæktoubəˈsiləs〕 *n., pl.* **-cil·li** 〔-ˈsılaı; -ˈsilai〕. 〖細菌〗乳桿菌屬。

lac·to·fla·vin 〔ˌlæktoˈflevın; ˌlæktouˈfleivin〕 *n.* =**riboflavin.**

lac·tom·e·ter 〔lækˈtɑmətɚ; lækˈtɔmitə〕 *n.* 驗乳計;乳汁比重計。

lac·tose 〔ˈlæktos; ˈlæktous〕 *n.* 〖化〗乳糖。

la·cu·na 〔ləˈkjunə; ləˈkjuːnə〕 *n., pl.* **-nae** 〔-ni; -niː〕, **-nas.** ①孔;窩;凹。②空隙;裂口。③闕文;脫漏;空白。④〖植物〗體素間之空隙。

la·cus·trine 〔ləˈkʌstrın; ləˈkʌstrin〕 *adj.* ①湖的;湖水的;湖上的。②生活在湖上的。③〖生物〗棲居於湖中的。

lac·y 〔ˈlesı; ˈleisi〕 *adj.,* **lac·i·er, lac·i·est.** 絲或緞帶的;有花邊的;帶狀的。

:lad 〔læd; læd〕 *n.* ①少年;青年。the *lads* of the village. 村中的青年們。②老友(暱稱)。my *lads.* 我的老朋友們。③〖俗〗人。

·lad·der 〔ˈlædɚ; ˈlædə〕 *n.* ①梯。②進身的階梯;立身成名的步驟。the *ladder* of fame. 成名的步驟。③(襪子上因脫線而成的)梯形裂縫;抽絲。④類似梯之物。***get one's foot on the ladder*** 著手;開始。***get up*** (or ***mount***) ***a ladder*** 〖俗〗上絞架;被絞死。***kick down*** (or ***away***) ***the ladder*** 過河拆橋。—*v.t.* ①爬梯。②裝設梯子。to *ladder* a water tower. 在水塔上架梯子。③〖主英〗使(襪子)抽絲。—*v.i.* ①襪子抽絲。②成名;走紅。He *laddered* to the top of his profession. 他爬上他行業的最高峯。

ladder back 梯狀椅背(椅背直柱間有橫檔)。

lad·die 〔ˈlædı; ˈlædi〕 *n.* 〖蘇〗少年;年輕人;小哥;老兄(親密的招呼語)。

lade 〔led; leid〕 *v.,* **lad·ed, lad·en** or **lad·ed, lad·ing.** —*v.t.* ①裝載。to *lade* a ship with cargo. 以貨物裝載於船上。②加負擔於。trees *laden* with fruit. 結滿果子的樹。③以杓汲取。—*v.i.* ①載貨;裝載。②以杓汲取液體。

·lad·en 〔ˈledn; ˈleidn〕 *adj.* 載滿的;充滿的。a mind *laden* with grief. 充滿憂傷的心。—*v.* pp. of **lade.**

la-di-da 〔ˌlɑdıˈdɑ; ˈlɑːdiˈdɑː〕 *n., adj.* 〖俚〗裝模作樣的(人)。—*interj.* 對裝模作樣的人所發的嘲笑聲。—*v.i.* 裝腔作勢。(亦作 **la-de-da, lah-di-dah**)

lad·ing 〔ˈledıŋ; ˈleidiŋ〕 *n.* ①裝載。②所裝載的貨物。***bill of lading*** 提貨單;提單。

la·dle 〔ˈledl; ˈleidl〕 *n., v.,* **-dled, -dling.** —*n.* 長柄杓。—*v.t.* ①以杓舀取;掬之以杓〖out〗。②給予;贈送〖out〗。

la·dle·ful 〔ˈledlˌful; ˈleidlful〕 *n., pl.* **-fuls.** 一滿杓之量。

:la·dy 〔ˈledı; ˈleidi〕 *n., pl.* **-dies.** ①家庭的主婦;(有地位者的)妻子;夫人。officers and their *ladies.* 軍官們和他們的夫人。②

貴婦;淑女(身分高,有教養,氣質好的婦女)。③任何婦人。④情婦;戀人。⑤妻子。⑥(L-)〖英〗夫人(與 Lord 相對)。*Our Lady* 聖母瑪麗亞。—*adj.* 女性的。a *lady* doctor (clerk, etc.). 女醫生(職員等)。—**ish,** *adj.*

Lady Bountiful 慷慨的女慈善家。

la·dy·bug [ˈledɪˌbʌg; ˈleidibʌg] *n.* 瓢蟲。(亦作 **ladybird**)

lady chair 兩人互握對方之手而形成的座位。

Lady Chapel 大教堂中的聖母堂(或稱玫瑰堂)。

Lady Day 報喜節(三月二十五日,天使 Gabriel 告知 Mary 將爲耶穌之母)。

la·dy·fin·ger [ˈledɪˌfɪŋgɚ; ˈleidiˌfiŋgə] *n.* 〖美〗一種指狀之小鬆脆餅。

la·dy·hood [ˈledɪˌhʊd; ˈleidihud] *n.* ①貴婦、淑女之身分或品格。②貴婦、淑女之集合稱 (=ladies).

lady in waiting 女王或公主之侍女;宮女。(亦作 **lady-in-waiting**)

la·dy-kill·er [ˈledɪˌkɪlɚ; ˈleidiˌkilə] *n.* 〖俚〗使女性一見鍾情之男子。

la·dy·like [ˈledɪˌlaɪk; ˈleidilaik] *adj.* ①風度雍容如貴婦的。②適於貴婦身分的。③貞淑的;溫雅的。

la·dy·love [ˈledɪˌlʌv; ˈleidilʌv] *n.* 愛人;情人(指女性);情婦。

la·dy·ship [ˈledɪˌʃɪp; ˈleidiʃip] *n.* ①貴婦的階級或地位。②夫人(對貴族夫人的尊稱)。Your *Ladyship*. 夫人(對談話之對方的稱呼)。

lady's maid 專管貴婦衣著及化妝之女僕。

la·dy's-slip·per [ˈledɪzˌslɪpɚ; ˈleidizˌslipə] *n.* 〖植物〗①鬼督郵。②〖美〗鳳仙花。

la·dy's-smock [ˈledɪzˌsmɑk; ˈleidizsmɔk] *n.* =**cuckooflower.** (亦作 **lady smock**)

LAFTA Latin America Free Trade Association.

‡lag¹ [læg; læg] *v.,* **lagged, lag·ging,** *n., adj.* —*v.i.* ①慢慢地走;落後〖常 behind〗. The lame child *lagged* behind. 跛足的孩子落在後面。②未充分發展。③逗留;延遲。④慢慢地減少。Interest *lags* in such matters. 對這類事的興趣慢慢地消失了。—*n.* ①落後;遲。②落後的人。—*adj.* ①遲的。②慢的。③最後的。

lag² *n.* 〖俗〗①犯罪的人;囚徒。②徒刑。—*v.t.* 〖俚〗①監禁(囚牢)。②逮捕。

lag³ *n., v.,* **lagged, lag·ging.** —*n.* ①桶板。②〖機械〗(被覆汽鍋等之)套板。—*v.t.* 覆以套板。

lag·an [ˈlægən; ˈlægən] *n.* 〖法律〗(海船失事時,繫有辨識物主浮標的)投入海中之貨物。(亦作 **lagend, ligan**)

la·ger [ˈlɑgɚ; ˈlɑːgə] *n.* (亦作 **lager beer**) 一種啤酒(釀成後通常儲藏之時間爲六星期至六個月)。—*v.t.* 釀製此種啤酒。

lag·gard [ˈlægɚd; ˈlægəd] *adj.* 緩慢的;落後的;落伍的。—*n.* 行動緩慢或落後者。

lag·ging¹ [ˈlægɪŋ; ˈlægiŋ] *n.* ①〖機械〗加被覆物;(汽缸等之)被覆物。②〖建築〗拱模撐(建造中之圓拱的支撐物)。

lag·ging² *n.* 落後;徐動;遲滯。—*adj.* 拖延的;欲前不前的;緩慢的。—**ly,** *adv.*

la·gn(i)appe [lænˈjæp; lænˈjæp] *n.* 〖美方〗(交易時附送給顧客之)小贈品。

la·goon [ləˈgun; ləˈguːn] *n.* ①與面積較大之河湖相接之池或小湖。②中有沙堤與海相隔之淺水。③環形珊瑚島中之海水;礁湖。(亦作 **lagune**)

la·gune [ləˈgun; ləˈguːn] *n.* =**lagoon.**

la·ic [ˈleɪk; ˈleiik] *n.* 常人;世俗之人(別於任聖職者而言)。—*adj.* 常人的;世俗之人的。

la·i·cal [ˈleɪkl; ˈleiikəl] *adj.* =**laic.**

laid [led; leid] *v.* pt. & pp. of **lay¹.** —*adj.* 有緊密平行線痕跡的(如水印)。***laid up*** a. 貯藏的;留作未來用的。b. 臥病的;臥床不起的。c. (船隻)除役後停泊安全處所的。

laid paper 有平行水印格子之紙張。

‡lain [len; lein] *v.* pp. of **lie².**

lair [lɛr; lɛə] *n.* ①野獸的巢穴。The tiger retired to its *lair.* 那老虎退回其洞穴中。②盜賊的藏身地。③〖英〗牛舍。—*v.i.* 去巢穴;在巢穴中休息;有巢穴。—*v.t.* 供以巢穴;置於巢穴中;做爲巢穴用。

laird [lɛrd; lɛəd] *n.* 〖蘇〗地主(尤指富裕者)。

lais·sez faire, lais·ser faire [ˌlɛseˈfɛr; ˈleiseiˈfɛə] ①放任政策。②自由競爭。

la·i·ty [ˈleətɪ, ˈleɪtɪ; ˈleiiti] *n., pl.* **-ties.** ①俗人(別於僧侶、教士而言)。②外行人;門外漢(別於專家或專門職業者而言)。

‡lake¹ [lek; leik] *n.* 湖;湖水。The *lake* teems with fish. 此湖產魚甚豐。

lake² *n.* ①一種深紅色的顏料。②深紅色。

Lake Country (or **District**) 英格蘭西北部的湖泊區。

lake dweller 史前期居住在湖上架屋中的人。

lake dwelling 史前期在湖上的木架屋。

lake·front [ˈlekˌfrʌnt; ˈleikfrʌnt] *n.* 湖邊平地。

lake herring (北美產)湖鯡。

lake·let [ˈleklɪt; ˈleiklit] *n.* 小湖。

Lake poets 湖邊詩人(19世紀初居於英格蘭 Lake District 之 Wordsworth, Coleridge, Southey 等)。

lake·side [ˈlekˌsaɪd; ˈleiksaid] *n.* 湖邊。

lake trout 北美湖中所產的灰鱒魚。

lakh [læk; lɑːk, læk] *n.* 〖英印〗①十萬。②十萬盧比 (rupee). ③無數。(亦作 **lac**)

Lal·lan [ˈlælən; ˈlælən] *n., adj.* 蘇格蘭低地(的)。

lal·la·tion [læˈleʃən; læˈleiʃən] *n.* 〖語音〗將 r 發成似 l 之音。

lam¹ [læm; læm] *v.,* **lammed, lam·ming.** —*v.t.* 〖俚〗(以鞭等)打;毆打;笞。—*v.i.* 打;鞭笞〖常 out, into〗.

lam² *n., v.,* **lammed, lam·ming.** —*n.* 〖俚〗避罪逃亡;脫逃。***be on the lam*** 在逃;逃亡中。***take it on the lam*** 急遽逃走;拔腳脫逃。—*v.i.* 〖俚〗逃跑;急遽逃亡;脫逃。

Lam. 〖聖經〗Lamentations.

la·ma¹ [ˈlɑmə; ˈlɑːmə] *n.* 喇嘛僧。***Grand*** (or ***Dalai***) ***Lama*** 達賴喇嘛。***Panchen Lama*** 班禪喇嘛。

la·ma² *n.* =**llama.**

La·ma·ism [ˈlɑməɪzəm; ˈlɑːməizəm] *n.* 喇嘛教。

La·ma·ist [ˈlɑməɪst; ˈlɑːməist] *n.* 喇嘛教徒。

La·ma·ite [ˈlɑməˌaɪt; ˈlɑːməait] *n.* =**Lamaist.**

La·marck [ˌlaˈmark; ˌlaˈmɑːk] *n.* 拉馬克 (Chevalier de, 1744–1829, 法國博物學家)。—**i·an,** *adj., n.*

la·ma·ser·y [ˈlɑməˌsɛrɪ; ˈlɑːməsəri] *n., pl.* **-ser·ies.** 喇嘛寺院。

Lamb [læm; læm] *n.* 蘭姆 (Charles, 1775–1834, 英國散文家及批評家)。

‡lamb [læm; læm] *n.* ①小羊;羔羊。as gentle as a *lamb.* 十分馴良。②羔羊肉。roast *lamb.* 烤羊肉。③年幼而天眞無邪之人。***like a lamb*** a. 溫順地;膽怯地。b. 易受欺地。***the Lamb*** 耶穌基督。—*v.i.* 生小羊。

lam·bast(e) [læmˈbest; læmˈbeist]

v.t., **-bast·ed, -bast·ing.** 〖俚〗①痛打；鞭打。②嚴厲責罵。

lamb·da [ˈlæmdə; ˈlæmdə] *n.* ①希臘字母之第11字(Λ, λ)。②〖醫〗人字縫尖。

lamb·da·cism [ˈlæmdəsɪzəm; ˈlæmdəsizm] *n.* ①1字(音)之使用過多。②將[r]發成[l]音之傾向。

lam·ben·cy [ˈlæmbənsɪ; ˈlæmbənsi] *n.*, *pl.* **-cies.** ①(火焰、光等之)輕輕搖曳；閃爍。②(天空、眼等之)柔和的光輝。③(機智等之)輕妙。④發柔和之光者。

lam·bent [ˈlæmbənt; ˈlæmbənt] *adj.* ①(火、光)輕輕搖曳的。②溫柔而光明的；閃爍的。③輕妙的。

lamb·kin [ˈlæmkɪn; ˈlæmkin] *n.* ①小羊。②對年輕人或幼兒之暱稱。

lamb·ling [ˈlæmlɪŋ; ˈlæmliŋ] *n.* = **lambkin.**

Lamb of God 〖聖經〗耶穌(上帝的羔羊，以喻基督爲贖世人之罪獻身作獻祭之犧牲，見約翰福音1章29節)。

lam·bre·quin [ˈlæmbrəˌkɪn; ˈlæmbəkin] *n.* ①〖美〗(門、窗等上部之)垂幃。②中世紀時代鋼盔上的布外罩。

lamb·skin [ˈlæmˌskɪn; ˈlæm-skin] *n.* 羊羔皮；羊皮紙。

***lame** [lem; leim] *adj.*, **lam·er, lam·est,** *v.*, **lamed, lam·ing.** —*adj.* ①跛足的。He is *lame* of one leg. 他跛一脚。②僵痛的。a *lame* back. 僵痛的背。③理由不充足的。④不完全的；不完美的。—*v.i.* 變跛；跛行。—*v.t.* 使跛；使成殘廢。The accident *lamed* him for life. 這意外使他終身成爲殘廢。—**ly,** *adv.* —**ness,** *n.*

la·mé [læˈme, lɑ-; lɑːˈmei] 〖法〗*n.* 金屬絲織物(用於婦女晚禮服、聖袍等)。

lame duck ①再競選失敗的現任國會議員(尤指衆院議員)。②無能之人；無用之物(如廢船等)。③投機者；(尤指)股票市場中無能履行契約義務者。④不能再競選連任的總統。

la·mel·la [ləˈmɛlə; ləˈmelə] *n.*, *pl.* **-lae** [-li; -liː], **-las.** (尤指骨或體素之)薄板；薄片；薄葉；薄層；菌褶。—**la·mel·lar,** *adj.*

lam·el·late [ˈlæməˌlet, ləˈmɛlet; ˈlæməleit] *adj.* ①薄板的；薄層的；由薄片或薄層構成的。②平坦的；平板狀的。

***la·ment** [ləˈmɛnt; ləˈment] *v.t.* ①哀悼；悲傷；慟哭。to *lament* the death of a friend. 哀悼朋友的死。③悔恨；惋惜。—*v.i.* 悲傷；慟哭；哀悼。Why does she *lament?* 她爲何悲傷？—*n.* ①悲傷；哀悼；慟哭。②哀歌；輓詩。③悔恨；遺憾；惋惜。

***lam·en·ta·ble** [ˈlæməntəbl; ˈlæməntəbl] *adj.* ①可悲的；悲慘的；令人悔恨的；令人惋惜的。a *lamentable* accident. 一件悲慘的意外事件。②悲哀的；哀傷的。a *lamentable* cry. 悲哀的哭聲。③(表示輕蔑)可憐的；低劣的。—**lam·en·ta·bly,** *adv.*

***lam·en·ta·tion** [ˌlæmənˈteʃən; ˌlæmenˈteiʃən, -mən-] *n.* ①哀傷；哀痛；慟哭。②(L-)(*pl.*)(作*sing.*解)舊約中的耶利米哀歌。

la·ment·ed [ləˈmɛntɪd; ləˈmentid] *adj.* ①被惋惜的；被悼念的。②遺憾的；可惜的。

la·mi·a [ˈlemɪə; ˈleimiə] *n.*, *pl.* **-as, -mi·ae** [-mɪˌi; -miiː]. ①〖希臘、羅馬神話〗女首蛇身之妖魔。②妖婦；女妖。

lam·i·na [ˈlæmənə; ˈlæminə] *n.*, *pl.* **-nae** [-ˌni; -niː], **-nas.** ①(金屬、骨、動植物體素、岩石等之)薄板；薄片；薄層；薄膜。②〖植物〗葉片；葉身。③〖解剖〗板；層。

lam·i·nal [ˈlæmɪnl; ˈlæminəl] *adj.* 由薄板(薄片)組成的；成薄層的；鱗片(薄片)狀的。

lam·i·nar [ˈlæmɪnɚ; ˈlæminə] *adj.* ①成薄層的。②流線的。

lam·i·nate [*v.* ˈlæməˌnet; ˈlæmineit *adj.* ˈlæmənɪt, -ˌnet; ˈlæminit] *v.*, **-nat·ed, -nat·ing,** *adj.* —*v.t.* ①錘打或輾壓(金屬)成薄板；作成薄片。②切成薄板；分成薄片。③覆以薄板。④疊合薄片作成。⑤粘合(薄片)。—*v.i.* 成爲薄板或薄片。—*adj.* 由薄片組成的；薄板(薄片)狀的。—**lam·i·na·tion,** *n.*

lam·i·nat·ed [ˈlæməˌnetɪd; ˈlæmineitid] *adj.* 薄板(薄片)狀的；由薄層組成的。*laminated* wood. 疊合木材。

Lam·mas [ˈlæməs; ˈlæməs] *n.* 收穫節(天主教節日之一，在八月一日)。(亦作 **Lammas Day**)

‡**lamp** [læmp; læmp] *n.* ①燈。an electric (oil) *lamp.* 電(油)燈。②任何似燈之物。the *lamps* of heaven. 天上星辰。③(*pl.*)〖俗〗眼睛。***smell of the lamp*** 有下過苦工的痕跡。His dissertation *smells of the lamp.* 他的論文有下過工夫的痕跡。—*v.t.* 〖俚〗看。

lamp·black [ˈlæmpˌblæk; ˈlæmp-blæk] *n.* 燈之煤烟。—*v.t.* 覆以燈之煤烟。

lamp chimney (煤油燈之)燈罩。

lam·pi·on [ˈlæmpɪən; ˈlæmpiən] *n.* (有彩色玻璃罩之)小油燈。

lamp·light [ˈlæmpˌlaɪt; ˈlæmp-lait] *n.* 燈光。

lamp·light·er [ˈlæmpˌlaɪtɚ; ˈlæmpˌlaitə] *n.* ①點燃街燈之燈夫。②點燈之物(如火把、紙撚等)。

lamp·lit [ˈlæmpˌlɪt; ˈlæmp-lit] *adj.* 被燈光照明的。

lam·poon [læmˈpun; læmˈpuːn] *n.* 諷嘲之文章。—*v.t.* 以詩、文攻擊或譏諷。—**er,** —**ist,** *n.*

lam·poon·er·y [læmˈpunərɪ; læmˈpuːnəri] *n.*, *pl.* **-er·ies.** ①寫諷嘲文章。②諷嘲的精神或性質。

lamp·post [ˈlæmpˌpost; ˈlæmppoust] *n.* 街燈柱。

lam·prey [ˈlæmprɪ; ˈlæmpri] *n.*, *pl.* **-preys.** 〖動物〗八目鰻。

lamp·shade [ˈlæmpˌʃed; ˈlæmpʃeid] *n.* 燈罩。

lamp·wick [ˈlæmpwɪk; ˈlæmpwik] *n.* 燈心。

Lan·ca·shire [ˈlæŋkəˌʃɪr; ˈlæŋkəʃiə] *n.* 蘭開夏(英國西北部一郡名，以棉產出名)。

Lan·cas·ter [ˈlæŋkəstɚ; ˈlæŋkəstə] *n.* 卡斯忒皇室(1399-1461 之英國王室)。

Lan·cas·tri·an [læŋˈkæstrɪən; læŋˈkæstriən] *adj.* ①Lancashire 或 Lancaster 的。②〖英史〗Lancaster 皇室的。—*n.* ①Lancashire 或 Lancaster 之人。②〖英史〗Lancaster 皇室之人；(尤指於薔薇戰爭期間)擁護 Lancaster 皇室的人。

lance** [læns, lɑns; lɑːns] *n.*, *v.*, **lanced, lanc·ing.** —*n.* ①輕騎兵所持之長矛。②戰士(特指執矛騎馬者)。③似鎗矛之工具(如魚叉等)。④刺胳針。break lance with*** 交鋒；激辯。—*v.t.* ①以鎗矛攻擊。②以刺胳針刺破或切開。to *lance* a boil (abscess). 刺破一個水泡(膿瘡)。—*v.i.* 衝進。

lance corporal 〖英軍〗代理下士之上等兵(薪餉並不增加)。

lance·let [ˈlænslɪt; ˈlɑːnslit] *n.* 蛞蝓魚。

lan·ce·o·late [ˈlænsɪəlɪt; ˈlɑːnsiəlit] *adj.* ①鎗尖形的。*lanceolate* prism. 鎗尖形稜柱。②〖植物〗披針狀的(葉)。

lanc·er [ˈlænsɚ; ˈlɑːnsə] *n.* ①鎗騎兵。②(*pl.*)(作 *sing.* 解)方塊舞(quadrille)之一種；其舞曲。

lance sergeant 〖英軍〗代理中士職務之下士;代理中士。

lan·cet [ˈlænsɪt; ˈlɑːnsit] *n.* ①〖外科〗刺胳針;披針(兩面開口之小尖刀);刺血針。②尖頂拱(=lancet arch)。③頂呈尖拱狀的窗戶(=lancet window)。

lance·wood [ˈlænsˌwud; ˈlɑːnswud] *n.* (熱帶美洲產之)一種堅韌的木材(用以製鎗柄、弓、車軸等);任何產此種木材之樹。

lan·ci·nate [ˈlænsənet; ˈlænsineit] *v.t.*, **-nat·ed, -nat·ing.** 刺;戳。—**lan·ci·nat·ing**, *adj.*

lan·ci·na·tion [ˌlænsəˈneʃən; ˌlænsiˈneiʃən] *n.* 劇烈而穿刺的痛。

‡land [lænd; lænd] *n.* ①陸地(對海空而言)。We came in sight of *land*. 我們望見了陸地(指航行於海上時)。②土地;田地。Farmers work on the *land*. 農人在農田中工作。③國土;國度;國家。He has visited many different *lands*. 他遊歷了許多不同的國家。④地產;(私有的)田地。These *lands* belong to my brother. 這些田地爲我的哥哥所有。***by land*** 由陸路(旅行)。Are you going *by land* or by sea? 你將由陸路還是由海路去? ***come to land*** (船)抵岸;(飛機)着陸。***go on the land*** 做莊稼;務農。***reach land*** 登岸。—*v.t.* ①使(飛機)降落;使着陸。The pilot *landed* the airplane. 駕駛員將飛機降落。②(自船上)卸下。③(飛機)使降落;(船舶)卸下(客、貨)。④〖俗〗得到;獲得。to *land* a job. 獲得一個工作。⑤使處於(某種環境中)。to be *landed* in great difficulties. 處於極大的困難中。⑥擊;打。to *land* a person a blow in the eye. 在某人眼睛上打一拳。—*v.i.* ①登岸;着陸。We *landed* at Southampton. 我們在南安普敦登岸。②(罪犯等)落網。The thief *landed* in jail. 該竊賊被捕入獄了。③(終於)到達。***land on*** 責罵;責備。***land*** (or ***fall***) ***on one's feet*** 處於危險境地中而倖獲安全。***land up*** 以陸地阻塞或環繞。

land agency ①地產買賣經紀業務。②土地管理(處)。

land agent ①地產買賣經紀人或公司。②公有土地管理官員。③〖英〗地產管理人。

lan·dau [ˈlændɔ; ˈlændɔː] *n.* ①一種四輪有頂篷之馬車(其頂篷分爲兩半,可各自放下者)。②頂篷分爲兩半可各自放下之轎式汽車。

lan·dau·let(te) [ˌlændɔˈlɛt; ˌlændɔːˈlet] *n.* ①小型之 landau 馬車(一人乘坐之四輪馬車)。②小型之 landau 轎式汽車(其頂篷之後部可摺下)。

land bank ①土地銀行(以輔助不動產交易爲營業方針之銀行)。②〖英〗以前以不動產作發行基金之銀行。

land breeze 日落後由陸地吹向海的風。

L and D ①loans and discount. ②loss and damage.

land·ed [ˈlændɪd; ˈlændid] *adj.* ①擁有土地的。a *landed* proprietor. 地主;土地占有人。②由田地等構成的(指財產)。

land·fall [ˈlændˌfɔl; ˈlændfɔːl] *n.* ①〖航空、航海〗接近陸地;着陸。②〖航海〗看到陸地;所看到的陸地。③因所有人之死亡而產權突然移轉之地產。④山崩。

land·form [ˈlændˌfɔrm; ˈlændfɔːm] *n.* 地面形象。

land-grab·ber [ˈlændˌgræbɚ; ˈlændˌgræbə] *n.* 侵占土地者。

land grant 〖美〗政府撥給大學或鐵路等之土地。

land·grave [ˈlændˌgrev; ˈlændgreiv] *n.* ①(12世紀德國)有領地管轄權的伯爵。②(帝制時代德國)某些王子之稱號。

land·gra·vine [ˈlændgrəˌvin; ˈlændgrəviːn] *n.* ①landgrave 之妻。②女性之 landgrave.

land·hold·er [ˈlændˌholdɚ; ˈlændˌhouldə] *n.* 地主;持有土地者。

land hunger 貪得土地慾;領土擴張慾。

***land·ing** [ˈlændɪŋ; ˈlændiŋ] *n.* ①登陸;上岸;(飛機)着陸。②(船等)卸貨處;碼頭。③樓梯頂端的走廊;樓梯階段間的駐脚台。④魚類之大量捕獲。

landing craft 登陸艇。

landing field 飛機起落場。

landing gear 起落架(飛機機身下之滑行輪或浮艇,於陸上或水面升降用之)。

landing net 袋網;手網(盛釣起之魚者)。

landing party 登陸先頭部隊。

landing place ①(飛機之)降陸場;埠頭。②=**landing.**

landing stage 棧橋(架於水上或浮於水上供人貨起落者)。

landing strip 起落地帶(供飛機升降用之狹長形跑道)。

landing system 飛機着陸之導航設施。

land-job·ber [ˈlændˌdʒɑbɚ; ˈlændˌdʒɔbə] *n.* 土地投機商人;地產經紀人。

***land·la·dy** [ˈlændˌledɪ, ˈlænˌledɪ; ˈlænˌleidi, -ndˌl-] *n., pl.* **-dies.** ①女房東;女地主。②旅舍、寄宿舍等之女主人。

land law(s) 土地法。

land·less [ˈlændlɪs; ˈlændlis] *adj.* ①無地產的;無土地的;無陸地的。②不見陸地的。

land·line [ˈlændˌlaɪn; ˈlændlain] *n.* 敷設在地面上或埋在地下的通信電線。

land·locked [ˈlændˌlɑkt; ˈlændlɔkt] *adj.* ①完全爲陸地所包圍或幾乎包圍的(港口、海灣等)。②生活在與海水隔絕之水中的。

***land·lord** [ˈlændˌlɔrd, ˈlæn-; ˈlænlɔːd, -ndl-] *n.* ①房東;地主。②旅舍等之主人。

land·lub·ber [ˈlændˌlʌbɚ; ˈlændˌlʌbə] *n.* 〖航海〗新水手;不慣於航海者(輕蔑語)。

***land·mark** [ˈlændˌmɑrk, ˈlæn-; ˈlændmɑːk, ˈlænm-] *n.* ①顯而易見的目標;陸標。The church on the hilltop was a well-known *landmark*. 山頂上的教堂是一個著名的陸標。②(歷史上劃時代的)重要事件。The invention of the printing press was a *landmark* in the progress of civilization. 印刷機的發明是文化發展史上一件劃時代的事情。③界石;界標。④傳統的教理。

land·mass [ˈlændˌmæs; ˈlændmæs] *n.* 大塊陸地。(亦作 **land mass**)

land mine 〖軍〗地雷。

land·oc·ra·cy [lændˈɑkrəsɪ; lændˈɔkrəsi] *n.* 〖謔〗有地產的人們;大地主階級。

land·o·crat [ˈlændokræt; ˈlændoukræt] *n.* 〖謔〗地主階級者。

land office 國有土地管理局。

land of milk and honey ①極肥沃豐饒的土地。②主的恩賜。(亦作 **Land of Milk and Honey**)

Land of Promise 天國。(亦作 **promised land**)

***land·own·er** [ˈlændˌonɚ; ˈlændˌounə] *n.* 地主;擁有土地者。

land·own·er·ship [ˈlændˌonɚʃɪp; ˈlændˌounəʃip] *n.* 土地所有權。

land·own·ing [ˈlændˌonɪŋ; ˈlændˌouniŋ] *adj.* ①擁有土地的。②有關土地所有權的。—*n.* 作爲地主。

land-poor [ˈlændˈpur; ˈlændˈpuə] *adj.* 〖俗〗擁有(許多)土地卻(因稅捐高而)窮困的。

land reform 土地改革。

***land·scape** ['lænskep, 'lænd-; 'lænskeip, -nds-] *n.*, *v.*, **-scaped, -scap·ing.** —*n.* ①(陸上)風景；山水。a *landscape* of snow. 雪景。②山水風景畫。—*v.t.* 使美化；使風景宜人。The park is *landscaped*. 公園美化了。—*v.i.* 作庭園設計師。

landscape architect 造園技師；景色美化設計家。

landscape architecture 都市美化設計術。

landscape gardener 庭園設計師；造園家。

landscape gardening 庭園之設計或監造；造園法。

landscape painter 風景畫家。

land·scap·er ['læn,skepə; 'læn,skeipə] *n.* 造園家；庭園設計師。

land·scap·ist ['lænskepɪst; 'lænskeipist] *n.* ①=**landscape painter.** ②=**landscape architect** (or **gardener**).

Lands End, Land's End 地角(在英格蘭之西南端)。

land shark ①碼頭上之騙子。②=**landgrabber.**

land·slide ['lænd,slaɪd; 'lændslaid] *n.* ①山崩。②因崩裂所滑下的山石。③〖美〗(一政黨或候選人所得的)壓倒性多數票；大勝利。—*v.i.* ①如山崩似的塌下。②在選舉中以壓倒性多數獲勝。

land·slip ['lænd,slɪp; 'lændslip] *n.* 〖英〗山崩。

lands·man[1] ['lændzmən; 'lændzmən] *n.*, *pl.* **-men.** ①(亦作 **landman**) 陸居者；陸上工作者。②初次航海之水手。

lands·man[2] ['lɑntsmən; 'lɑːntsmən] *n.*, *pl.* (英) **-leit** [-laɪt; -lait], (猶太語) **-men.** ①同胞。②猶太同胞。

Land·sturm ['lɑnt,ʃturm; 'lɑːntʃtuəm] *n.* (瑞士、德國等之)總動員；國民軍。

land tax 土地稅；地租。

land·ward ['lændwəd; 'lændwəd] *adv.* (亦作 **landwards**) 向陸地地。—*adj.* 面向陸地的。

Land·wehr ['lɑnt,ver; 'lændveiə] 〖德〗*n.* (德國、瑞士、奧地利之)後備軍。

land wind 自陸地吹向海面之風。

***lane** [len; lein] *n.* ①小路；小徑。the country *lanes* in England. 英國的鄉村小道。②〖美〗(公路上用白線標出的)單行道。③(城市中的)小巷；衚；弄。④(船或飛機的)航路。⑤賽跑跑道的一行。⑥保齡球道。

Lang·muir ['læŋmjur; 'læŋmjuə] *n.* 蘭穆爾(Irving, 1881–1967, 美國化學家, 1932 年曾獲諾貝爾化學獎)。

lang·syne ['læŋ'saɪn; 'læŋ'sain] *adv.*, *n.* 〖蘇〗許久以前。

‡lan·guage ['læŋgwɪdʒ; 'læŋgwidʒ] *n.* ①語言；文字。Animals do not possess *language*. 動物沒有語言文字。②一個國家或民族的語言文字。the *languages* of Europe. 歐洲之各種語文。③語調；措辭。bad *language*. 粗話。④其他表情達意的方法。finger *language*. 手語。⑤術語。technical *language*. 專門術語。⑥語言學。⑦特殊的表達方式。⑧態度；立場。He just doesn't speak my *language*. 他和我所持立場不同。

L

language laboratory 電化語言教室。

langue d'oc [lɑ̃g'dɔk; ,lɑ̃g'dɔːk] 〖法〗①中世紀法國南部之方言(參看 **langue d'oïl**)。②現代 Provence 語。

langue d'o·ïl [lɑ̃g'dɔ̈il(dɔ̈ːj); ,lɑ̃gdɔː'iːl] 〖法〗①中世紀法國北部之方言(參看 **langue d'oc**)。②現代法語。

lan·guid ['læŋgwɪd; 'læŋgwid] *adj.* ①精神不振的；軟弱無力的。A hot, sticky day makes a person *languid*. 悶熱的天氣使人精神不振。②毫無興趣的；漠不關心的。③不活潑的；停滯的；遲緩的。a *languid* market. 蕭條的市場。④不起效用的；無生氣的。a *languid* style. 無生氣的文體。—**ly,** *adv.* —**ness,** *n.*

***lan·guish** ['læŋgwɪʃ; 'læŋgwiʃ] *v.i.* ①變得衰弱無力；凋萎；憔悴。The flowers *languished* from lack of water. 花因缺水而凋萎。②渴望；苦思。She *languished* for home. 她苦思家鄉。③面呈愁思傷感或脈脈含情之色。④受苦；受折磨；呻吟。⑤鬆弛；鬆懈。⑥減低；減少。—*n.* ①愁思傷感或親切溫柔之色。②憔悴。

lan·guish·ing ['læŋgwɪʃɪŋ; 'læŋgwiʃiŋ] *adj.* ①衰弱下去的；漸漸變弱的。②憔悴的。③渴念的；脈脈含情的。She gave the young man a *languishing* look. 她向那青年作脈脈含情的一瞥。④纏綿的；拖延的。

lan·guish·ment ['læŋgwɪʃmənt; 'læŋgwiʃmənt] *n.* ①衰弱；憔悴。②脈脈含情的表情。

lan·guor ['læŋgə; 'læŋgə] *n.* ①無精力；衰弱；倦怠。A long illness causes *languor*. 長期患病造成虛弱。②無興趣；沒精打采；漠不關心。③柔情。④不活潑；遲緩；停滯。⑤(氣壓的)沉悶；靜止。

lan·guor·ous ['læŋgərəs; 'læŋgərəs] *adj.* ①倦怠的；無力的；鬱悶的。②令人倦怠的；令人無力的。—**ly,** *adv.*

lan·gur [lʌŋ'gur; lʌŋ'guə] *n.* 亞洲產的一種長尾猴，以樹葉、果實等爲食。(亦作 **leaf monkey**)

lan·iard ['lænjəd; 'lænjəd] *n.* =**lanyard.**

lank [læŋk; læŋk] *adj.* ①瘦長的；細長的。②(指毛髮)平直的；無鬈曲或波浪狀的。

lank·i·ly ['læŋkɪlɪ; 'læŋkili] *adv.* 以瘦長形式地。

lank·y ['læŋkɪ; 'læŋki] *adj.*, **lank·i·er, lank·i·est.** 瘦長的；細長的。—**lank·i·ness,** *n.*

lan·o·lin(e) ['lænəlɪn; 'lænəlin] *n.* 〖化〗羊毛脂(製藥膏用)。

lan·sign ['læn,saɪn; 'lænsain] *n.* 〖語意學〗代表一種事物或觀念的一個字或音等。

lans·que·net ['lænskə,nɛt; 'lɑːnskinet] *n.* ①(16–17世紀德國之)雇傭兵。②一種紙牌遊戲。

***lan·tern** ['læntən; 'læntən] *n.* ①燈籠；提燈。like a *lantern* in the dark. 如黑暗中的明燈。②燈塔上的燈火室。③〖建築〗頂塔；天窗。④幻燈。—*v.t.* 供以燈火；配以燈火。to *lantern* a fishing boat. 給漁船配燈。

lantern fly 白蠟蟲(產於南美)。

lantern jaw 瘦削的下巴。

lan·tern-jawed ['læntən,dʒɔd; 'læntəndʒɔːd] *adj.* 下巴瘦削的；臉形瘦長的。

lantern pin·ion [~'pɪnjən; ~'pinjən] 燈形輪(輪周裝與軸平行之柱形小棒以代齒輪)。(亦作 **lantern wheel**)

lantern slide 幻燈片。

lan·tha·num ['lænθənəm; 'lænθənəm] *n.* 〖化〗鑭(一種金屬元素，符號 La)。

lan·yard ['lænjəd; 'lænjəd] *n.* ①(發砲用的)拉火索。②舟上繫物之短索。③水手套在頸上，以懸小刀或哨子等的繩索(=knife lanyard)。(亦作 **laniard**)

La·oc·o·ön [le'ɑkə,wɑn; lei'ɔkouən] *n.* ①〖希臘神話〗Troy 城 Apollo 神殿之一

祭司。②與困難勇敢奮鬥者。

La·od·i·ce·a 〔ˌleədəˈsiə; ˌleioudiˈsiə〕 *n.* 敍利亞西北一海港,今名 Latakia.

La·od·i·ce·an 〔leˌɑdɪˈsiən; ˌleioudiˈsiən〕 *adj.* ① Laodicea 的。②不熱心的;(尤指)對宗教冷淡的。—*n.* ①Laodicea人。②(對宗教、政治等)不熱心的人;冷淡的人。

Laos 〔lauz; lauz〕 *n.* 寮國(中南半島之一王國,首都永珍, Vientiane).

La·o·tian 〔leˈoʃən; leiˈouʃən〕 *n.* 寮國人。—*adj.* 寮國的。

Lao-tzu, Lao-tse, Lao-tze 〔ˈlauˈdzʌ; ˈlɑːouˈtsei〕 *n.* 老子 (604?–?531 B.C., 中國哲學家)。

lap**[1] 〔læp; læp〕 *n.* ①人坐下時腰至兩膝部分。The mother had the baby on her *lap.* 母親把孩子放在腿上。②(坐下時)腰至兩膝部分的衣裙。③衣裙的邊緣;用以兜盛東西時的裙子之前部。④(任何東西)休息或養育之處。⑤環境;境遇。Everything falls into his *lap.* 他處於順境。⑥控制範圍。I'm going to drop the whole thing in your *lap.* 我將把整個事情交給你。in Fortune's lap*** 幸運;好運。

***lap**[2] *v.*, **lapped, lap·ping,** *n.* —*v.i.* ①重疊;層疊。Shingles on a roof *lap.* 屋頂板是層疊的。②延伸。③包圍。④跑完全程。—*v.t.* ①包裹。to *lap* a bandage around the wrist. 用綳帶將手腕包起來。②領先(其他賽跑者)一圈。③跑完。He *lapped* the course in 3 minutes 8 seconds. 他以三分八秒跑完全程。④使重疊。—*n.* ①重疊;重疊部分。The front *lap* of a winter coat should be at least 6 inches wide. 多季外套前擺重疊部分至少應有六英寸寬。②賽跑中之一圈。③〖建築〗搭接。

lap**[3] *v.*, **lapped, lap·ping,** *n.* —*v.t.* ①舐;舐食。Cats and dogs *lap* water. 貓狗舐水。②欣然接受。③輕拍;輕擊。The sea *laps* the base of the cliff. 海水輕拍斷崖的底部。lap up*** **a.**〖俗〗熱烈地接受。**b.** 吃或喝。The cat *lapped up* the milk and looked for more. 貓喝完了奶還想再喝一些。—*v.i.* ①輕拍;輕擊。Little waves *lapped* against the boat. 碎浪輕拍小舟。②舐。—*n.* ①舐。②被舐之物;被舐之量。③給狗吃的流體食物。④〖俚〗流質食品;淡酒;飲料。⑤輕拍聲;輕擊聲。

lap·a·rot·o·my 〔ˌlæpəˈrɑtəmɪ; ˌlæpəˈrɔtəmi〕 *n., pl.* **-mies.**〖外科〗剖腹手術;開腹術。

lap·board 〔ˈlæpˌbord; ˈlæpbɔːd〕 *n.* 圓板(置於膝上用以代替桌子之薄板)。

lap dissolve 〖電影、電視〗溶;化(即一場面逐漸消失,另一場面逐漸引入)。

lap dog 膝狗;巴兒狗(常被置於膝上撫弄的小狗)。(亦作 **lapdog**)

la·pel 〔ləˈpel; ləˈpel〕 *n.*西服上身的翻領。

lapel mike 可夾在口袋或衣襟上的小型麥克風。

lap·ful 〔ˈlæpˌful; ˈlæpful〕 *n., pl.* **-fuls.** 滿膝;滿兜。

lap·i·dar·i·an 〔ˌlæpəˈdɛrɪən; ˌlæpiˈdɛəriən〕 *adj.* ①刻在石上的;碑文的。②有碑文之風格的。

lap·i·dar·y 〔ˈlæpəˌdɛrɪ; ˈlæpidəri〕 *adj., n., pl.* **-dar·ies.** —*adj.* ①雕刻寶石的;玉細工的。②刻在石上的;碑文的;適於碑銘的。*lapidary* inscriptions. 碑文。—*n.*①寶石匠。②寶石鑑定家;寶石收藏家;寶石商。③玉細工;寶石雕刻。

lap·i·date 〔ˈlæpəˌdet; ˈlæpideit〕 *v.t.,* **-dat·ed, -dat·ing.** ①以石投擊。②投石擊死。

lap·i·da·tion 〔ˌlæpəˈdeʃən; ˌlæpiˈdeiʃən〕 *n.* 以石投擊;投石擊死。

lap·in 〔ˈlæpɪn; ˈlæpin〕〖法〗 *n.* 兔子;其毛皮。

lap·is laz·u·li 〔ˈlæpɪsˈlæzjəlaɪ; ˌlæpisˈlæzjulai〕 ①〖礦〗青金石;璧琉璃。②天藍色。

lap joint 〖建築〗搭接;搭接榫;接搭縫;疊接。

Lap·land 〔ˈlæpˌlænd; ˈlæplænd〕 *n.* 拉布蘭(北歐地名,包括挪威、瑞典、芬蘭之北部及蘇聯西北部 Kola 半島之一地區)。

Lap·land·er 〔ˈlæpˌlændə; ˈlæplændə〕 *n.* 拉布蘭人。

Lapp 〔læp; læp〕 *n.* 拉布蘭人;拉布蘭語。

lap·pet 〔ˈlæpɪt; ˈlæpit〕 *n.* ①(衣、帽等之)垂下部分;垂飾。②衣襟。③(肉、膜等之)垂下部分;(火鷄之)肉垂;耳朵。

***lapse** 〔læps; læps〕 *n., v.,* **lapsed, laps·ing.** —*n.* ①失誤;差錯;筆誤。a *lapse* of the tongue. 失言。②過失;小疵。a moral *lapse.* 道德上的過失。③流逝;經過。the *lapse* of time. 時間的流逝。④〖法律〗(特權等的)消滅;終止;失效。⑤倒退;墮落。⑥消失;廢止。⑦〖保險〗因不交保險費而使保險失效。⑧逐漸傾倒、流逝、滑過等動作。—*v.i.* ①過失。②失誤;失足。to *lapse* into bad habits. 不愼養成壞習慣。③消滅;終止;失效。④塌陷。The house *lapsed* into ruin. 那房屋塌陷成一片廢墟。⑤滑過;流過。⑥背教;離宗叛道。⑦消逝。⑧消失;廢止。—*v.t.* 使終止;廢止。

lapse rate 〖氣象〗(與高度成比例的)氣溫遞減率;直減率。

lap·sus 〔ˈlæpsəs; ˈlæpsəs〕〖拉〗 *n.* 失誤。

lapsus cal·a·mi 〔~ˈkæləˌmaɪ; ~ˈkæləmai〕〖拉〗筆誤(=a slip of the pen).

lapsus lin·guae 〔~ˈlɪŋgwi; ~ˈliŋgwiː〕〖拉〗失言(=a slip of the tongue).

lap time 游泳比賽一次來回所需之時間。

La·pu·ta 〔ləˈpjutə; ləˈpjuːtə〕 *n.* Swift 作 *Gulliver's Travels* 中之一飛行的浮島(其居民富幻想不務實際)。

lap·wing 〔ˈlæpˌwɪŋ; ˈlæpwiŋ〕 *n.* 田鳧。

LARA Licensed Agency for Relief of Asia.

lar·board 〔ˈlɑrbəd; ˈlɑːbəd〕 *n.* 左舷(用於古代航海術中,今易爲 port, 爲 starboard 之對)。—*adj.* 左舷的;向左舷的;在左舷的。

lar·ce·ner 〔ˈlɑrsn̩ə; ˈlɑːsinə〕 *n.* =**larcenist.**

lar·ce·nist 〔ˈlɑrsn̩ɪst; ˈlɑːsinist〕 *n.* 竊盜;竊盜犯。

lar·ce·nous 〔ˈlɑrsənəs; ˈlɑːsinəs〕 *adj.* ①竊盜的;似竊盜的。②犯竊盜罪的;好偸竊的。

lar·ce·ny 〔ˈlɑrsn̩ɪ; ˈlɑːsni〕 *n., pl.* **-nies.** 〖法律〗竊盜;竊盜罪。

larch 〔lɑrtʃ; lɑːtʃ〕 *n.* ①落葉松。②落葉松之木材。

***lard** 〔lɑrd; lɑːd〕 *n.* 豬油。—*v.t.* ①加豬油。②於烹調之前塞或覆鹹肉或醃肉於(牛、鷄等瘦肉之中或之上)。③夾雜;點綴(文章、演說等)。a speech *larded* with technical terms. 夾雜專門術語的演說。

lar·da·ceous 〔lɑrˈdeʃəs; lɑːˈdeiʃəs〕 *adj.* ①豬油的;似豬油的。②〖生化〗澱粉樣的。

lard·er 〔ˈlɑrdə; ˈlɑːdə〕 *n.* ①食物貯藏室。②家用食料。

lard oil 由豬油提煉出之油(供作滑潤油及燈油之用)。

lard·y 〔ˈlɑrdɪ; ˈlɑːdi〕 *adj.,* **lard·i·er, lard·i·est.** ①豬油的;似豬油的。②含多量豬油的;多脂的。③肥胖的。

lar·dy-dar·dy ['lardɪ'dardɪ; 'lɑːdi'dɑːdi] *adj.* 〖俗〗裝腔作勢的；過於矯飾的。

la·res ['leriz; 'leəriːz] *n., sing.* **lar.** (古羅馬之)家神；社稷神。

lares and pe·na·tes [~~pə'netiz; ~~pə'neitiːz] ①(古羅馬之)家神。②(寶貴的)家財；傳家寶。

‡**large** [lardʒ; lɑːdʒ] *adj.*, **larg·er, larg·est,** *n., adv.* —*adj.* ①大的；巨大的。a *large* house. 大房子。②廣濶的；廣博的；無限制的。③大規模的；大量的。④寬大的；慷慨的。a *large* heart. 寬厚的心胸。⑤誇大的；誇張的。⑥〖航海〗順風的。—*n.* 僅見於下列成語中的習慣用法。 ***at large*** **a.** 自由的。**b.** 詳細地；長篇大論地；冗長地。**c.** 一般的；整個的。**d.** 隨便地；拉雜地；零亂地。arrangements made *at large*. 隨便的安排。**e.** 代表一州或一區的。***in (the) large*** 大規模地；廣義地。—*adv.* ①誇大地；自誇地。to talk *large*. 誇大。②順風地。a ship sailing *large*. 順風而駛的船。***by and large*** (=on the whole) 整個地；大體而論。

large·heart·ed ['lardʒ'hartɪd; 'lɑːdʒ'hɑːtid] *adj.* 寬宏大量的；慈悲心腸的。

large intestine 〖解剖〗大腸。

‡**large·ly** ['lardʒlɪ; 'lɑːdʒli] *adv.* ①大量地；很多地。to drink *largely*. 大量地飲酒。②大半地；主要地。It is *largely* a matter of conjecture. 那大半係屬猜測。

large-mind·ed ['lardʒ'maɪndɪd; 'lɑːdʒ'maindid] *adj.* 寬大的；度量大的。

large·ness ['lardʒnɪs; 'lɑːdʒnis] *n.* ①巨大；廣大。②寬大。③偉大。④廣博。

large-scale ['lardʒ'skel; 'lɑːdʒ'skeil] *adj.* ①大規模的；範圍大的；大批的。*large-scale* preparations for war. 大規模的備戰。②大比例尺的(地圖)。

lar·gess(e) ['lardʒɪs; 'lɑːdʒes] *n.* ①慷慨的贈與；豐厚的禮物。②慷慨幫助(尤指長輩給予晚輩者)。③固有性質。

lar·ghet·to [lar'geto; lɑː'getou] *adj., adv., n., pl.* **-tos.** —*adj. & adv.* 〖音樂〗稍緩慢的(地)；甚緩板的(地)。—*n.* 稍緩慢的樂曲或樂章。

larg·ish ['lardʒɪʃ; 'lɑːdʒiʃ] *adj.* 頗大的。

lar·go ['largo; 'lɑːgou] *adv., adj., n., pl.* **-gos.** —*adv. & adj.* 〖音樂〗極緩慢地(的)；最緩板地(的)。—*n.* 極緩慢的樂曲或樂章。

lar·i·at ['lærɪət; 'læriət] *n.* ①繫繩(用以繫食草中之馬等)。② =**lasso.** —*v.t.* ①以繫繩繫住。②=**lasso.**

•**lark**¹ [lark; lɑːk] *n.* ①雲雀；百靈鳥。to be as happy as a *lark*. 十分快樂。②一種灰黃色。③詩人；歌手。—*v.i.* 獵捕雲雀。

lark² *n.* 〖俗〗①嬉戲；歡樂。②頑皮的行動。—*v.i.* ①玩樂；自娛。②做出頑皮的行動。③(獵狐者)作不必要的躍馬。

lark·spur ['lark,spɝ; 'lɑːk-spəː] *n.* 〖植物〗飛燕草。

lark·y ['larkɪ; 'lɑːki] *adj.*, **lark·i·er, lark·i·est.** 〖俗〗嬉戲的；好耍鬧的。

lar·ri·gan ['lærɪgən; 'lærigən] *n.* 〖美〗油皮靴(伐木工人等用之長統鞋)。

lar·ri·kin ['lærə,kɪn; 'lærikin] *n.* 無賴；流氓；不良少年。—*adj.* 粗暴的；無賴的。

lar·rup ['lærəp; 'lærəp] *v.t.* 〖俗〗①擊打；鞭打；笞。②徹底擊敗。

•**lar·va** ['larvə; 'lɑːvə] *n., pl.* **-vae.** ①(昆蟲的)幼蟲。②幼態時期之動物(如未變成青蛙之蝌蚪)。The tadpole is the *larva* of the frog. 蝌蚪是青蛙的幼蟲。③(*pl.*)惡鬼。

lar·vae ['larvi; 'lɑːviː] *n.* pl. of **larva.**

lar·val ['larvəl; 'lɑːvəl] *adj.* ①幼蟲的；幼蟲時期的；幼態時期的。②未成熟的；發展未全的；在發展初期的。

la·ryn·ge·al [lə'rɪndʒɪəl; ,lærin'dʒiːəl] *adj.* ①喉頭的；在喉頭附近的。②治療喉頭用的。

lar·yn·gi·tis [,lærɪn'dʒaɪtɪs; ,lærin'dʒaitis] *n.* 喉炎。

la·ryn·go·scope [lə'rɪŋgə,skop; lə'riŋgəskoup] *n.* 〖外科〗喉頭鏡。

lar·yn·got·o·my [,lærɪŋ'gɑtəmɪ; ,læriŋ'gɔtəmi] *n.* 〖外科〗喉頭切開術。

lar·ynx ['lærɪŋks; 'læriŋks] *n., pl.* **la·ryn·ges** [lə'rɪndʒiz; lə'rindʒiːz], **lar·ynx·es.** 喉頭(包括聲帶)。

las·car ['læskɚ; 'læskə] *n.* ①(歐洲船上之)東印度水手。②(英國陸軍中之)東印度砲手。

las·civ·i·ous [lə'sɪvɪəs; lə'siviəs] *adj.* ①淫亂的；好色的。②有挑逗性的；猥褻的。—**ly,** *adv.* —**ness,** *n.*

lase [lez; leiz] *v.i.*, **lased, las·ing.** 〖光學〗(晶體)適於作雷射之用；發出雷射光。

la·ser ['lezɚ; 'leizə] *n.* 〖物理〗雷射(爲 *l*ight *a*mplification by *s*timulated *e*mission of *r*adiation 之略)。

•**lash**¹ [læʃ; læʃ] *n.* ①鞭上皮條部分。The whip was 20 feet long from butt to *lash*. 那皮鞭從握柄之一端到皮條末端有20英尺長。②鞭撻。③睫毛(=eyelash)。④打擊；譏刺；譏罵。⑤責打。⑥鞭子。⑦拍打。the *lash* of a north wind. 北風的拍打。—*v.t.* ①鞭撻；鞭策；打。to *lash* a horse across the back with a whip. 以鞭打馬背。②前後揮動或打擊。③諷刺；抨擊。④激動；煽動。The speaker *lashed* his listeners into a fury. 講演者煽動聽衆，使之憤怒。⑤大量生產；大量印製。—*v.i.* ①擺動。The lion's tail *lashed* back and forth. 獅尾前後擺動。②拍打；抽打。③急動；猛衝；猛然攻擊。④譏刺；譏罵。The author *lashes* out at Fascism. 作者譏罵法西斯主義。***lash out*** **a.** 鞭撻；打擊；攻擊。**b.** 責備；責罵；諷刺。**c.** 突然做；突然行動。**d.** 作過分的動作或暴烈的行爲。

•**lash**² *v.t.* 縛；束；綑；紮。to *lash* two things together. 將兩物縛在一起。

lash³ *n.* 將裝貨的駁船直接運上大船之一種海運系統。(亦作 **LASH**)

lash·er ['læʃɚ; 'læʃə] *n.* ①鞭打者；申斥者。②〖英方〗堰；自堰流下之水。③繫索。

lash·ing ['læʃɪŋ; 'læʃiŋ] *n.* ①鞭打。②叱責。③綁縛；綁縛的繩子。④(*pl.*)〖俗〗很多；大量〖常 of〗。

lash-up ['læʃ,ʌp; 'læʃʌp] *adj., n.* 臨時做成的(東西)。

•**lass** [læs; læs] *n.* ①少女；女孩。②愛人；情婦。the young hero of the story and his *lass*. 故事中的年輕男主角及其愛人。③〖蘇〗女僕。

las·sie ['læsɪ; 'læsi] *n.* 〖蘇〗①小姑娘；少女。②愛人(指女性)。

las·si·tude ['læsə,tjud; 'læsitjuːd] *n.* 疲乏；倦怠；懶散。

las·so ['læso; 'læsou] *n., pl.* **-sos** or **-soes,** *v.,* **-soed, -so·ing.** —*n.* 套索；一端有活結之繩索(用以擲出套牛、馬者)。—*v.t.* 以活結套索擲捕(牛、馬)。

‡**last**¹ [læst, lɑst; lɑːst] *adj.* ①最後的；末尾的(爲 first 之對)。the *last* house in the street. 街頭最末的一棟房子。②最末的(指時間的順序)。the *last* day in the year.

一年的最後一天。③昨（晚）；上（週等）；去（年）。*last* night. 昨晚。in January *last*. 在去年一月裏。④唯一的；最後的。This will be your *last* chance (*last* day here). 這將是你最後一次機會了(在此最後的一天)。⑤最近的（指過去時間）。the *last* news I heard. 我所聽到的最近的消息。⑥最不可能的；最不適的。He's the *last* man I want to see. 他是我最不願見的一個人。⑦最大的；極端的。a paper of *last* importance. 最重要的一篇文件。⑧臨終的。his *last* hours. 他臨終的幾小時。⑨決定性的；結論的。the *last* word in the argument. 爭論的裁決。⑩單獨的（與 every 連用藉以加强語氣）。every *last* square inch of good land. 好土地的每一平方英寸。***last of all*** 最後。—*adv.* ①最後地；最末地。Who spoke *last?* 誰最後講話？②最近一次地。When did you *last* see him? 你最近一次是甚麼時候看見他？—*n.* 最後之人或事物。the *last* of the Stuart kings. 斯圖亞特王室的最後一王。***at last***（＝in the end; after a long delay）終於；到底。*At last!* 達到目的時之感嘆語。***at long last***（經過重重困難或不愉快的經歷之後）終於。***breathe*** (or ***gasp***) ***one's last*** 死。***see the last of*** a. 不再看見。b. 送…的終。***to the last*** 至終；始終；到底。

last²** *v.i.* ①延續；持續。The storm *lasted* three days. 暴風雨延續了三天。②支持；持久。If my health *lasts*, I will try to finish it. 假使我的健康能支持的話，我就要努力把它完成。③維持。How many days will our food *last?* 我們的食糧可維持多少天？—*v.t.* ①安然度過；生還〖常 out〗。②繼續滿足…之需要。It will *last* you a lifetime. 這將滿足你終生的需要。last out*** 維持過去；度過。Will this coal *last out* the winter? 這點煤可把多天維持過去嗎？

last³ *n.* 鞋楦（修鞋或製鞋用）。***stick to one's last*** 堅守自己的崗位；只管自己的事。—*v.t.* 固定於鞋楦。

last⁴ *n.* ①一種重量單位（約等於 4000 磅）。②一種容量單位（約等於10夸脫）。

last day, the 最後審判日。

last ditch 〖美〗最後防線。

last-ditch 〔ˈlæstˈdɪtʃ; ˈlɑːstˈditʃ〕 *adj.* 最後防線上的；不再後退的。

las·tex 〔ˈlæstɛks; ˈlæsteks〕 *n.* ①橡皮線；鬆緊線（一種有彈性之紗線）。②(L-) 此種橡皮線之商標名。

***last·ing** 〔ˈlæstɪŋ, ˈlɑs-; ˈlɑːstiŋ〕 *adj.* 持久的；永恒的；永久的。People are hoping for a *lasting* peace. 人們在希望有永久的和平。

Last Judgment （世界末日之）最後審判。

***last·ly** 〔ˈlæstlɪ, ˈlɑst-; ˈlɑːstli〕 *adv.* 最後地；最後一點。

last-min·ute 〔ˈlæstˈmɪnɪt; ˈlɑːstˈminit〕 *adj.* （某事發生以前）最後一刻的；最後關頭的。

Last Supper （耶穌與其使徒之）最後晚餐。

last word ①（結束爭論的）最後一句話。②最後決定權。③定論。④最進步的型式；最新發明。⑤〖俗〗好得無以復加的事物。

Lat. Latin. **lat.** latitude.

latch** 〔lætʃ; lætʃ〕 *n.* ①門閂。②小彈簧鎖；閂鎖。on the latch*** 祇栓着門閂，但沒有上鎖。—*v.t.* 以門栓（門等）。—*v.i.* ①栓。②抓住〖on, upon〗。③〖俗〗得到〖on, upon〗。④〖俗〗了解〖on, upon〗。

latch·key 〔ˈlætʃˌki; ˈlætʃkiː〕 *n.* 門鎖鑰匙；彈簧鎖鑰匙。

latch·string 〔ˈlætʃˌstrɪŋ; ˈlætʃstriŋ〕 *n.* 栓鎖帶。***hang out*** (or ***draw in***) ***the latchstring for*** 許（不許）…自由出入家裏。

‡late 〔let; leit〕 *adj.,* **lat·er** or **lat·ter, lat·est** or **last,** *adv.,* **lat·er, lat·est** or **last.** —*adj.* ①遲的；晚的。He was *late* for dinner. 他沒有趕上吃飯。②在後的；將盡的；末期的。the *late* eighteenth century. 十八世紀末葉。③近來的；近時的；新近的。the *latest* news. 最近的消息。④亡故的；已故的。the *late* King. 故王；先王。⑤已辭職的；前任的。the *late* prime minister. 卸職的內閣總理。***at*** (***the***) ***latest*** 最遲。***of late*** (＝lately) 近來。I've been rather ill *of late.* 近來我的身體很不好。—*adv.* ①遲；晚。He got here five minutes *late.* 他到這裏遲了五分鐘。②近來地；新近地。I saw him as *late* as yesterday. 我昨天還看見他。③以前；先前。John Smith, *late* of Boston. 以前在波士頓的約翰・史密斯。***better late than never*** 亡羊補牢（永不爲遲）。***later on*** 後來；過些時。***sooner or later*** 遲早；總有一天。—**ness,** *n.*

late·com·er 〔ˈletˌkʌmɚ; ˈleitˌkʌmə〕 *n.* 晚來者；新進者。

la·teen 〔læˈtin; ləˈtiːn〕 *adj.* 〖航海〗大三角帆的。—*n.* ①大三角帆。②有大三角帆之船。

la·teen-rigged 〔læˈtinˌrɪgd; læˈtiːnrigd〕 *adj.* 有大三角帆的。

lateen sail 大三角帆。

***late·ly** 〔ˈletlɪ; ˈleitli〕 *adv.* 近來；最近。I haven't seen him *lately.* 我近來未曾見到他。

lat·en 〔ˈletn̩; ˈleitn〕 *v.t.* & *v.i.* (使)遲。

la·ten·cy 〔ˈletn̩sɪ; ˈleitənsi〕 *n.* 隱伏；潛伏；潛在。

***la·tent** 〔ˈletn̩t; ˈleitənt〕 *adj.* 潛在的；潛伏性的；隱藏的；不易被覺察的。*latent* disease germs. 潛伏性的病菌。—**ly,** *adv.*

***lat·er** 〔ˈletɚ; ˈleitə〕 *adj.* comp. of **late.** 更遲的；更後的。—*adv.* 後來；稍後；隨後。I will see you *later.* 稍後再見。

***lat·er·al** 〔ˈlætərəl; ˈlætərəl〕 *adj.* 旁邊的；側面的。—*n.* ①側部；側生枝。②側路；支線。—**ly,** *adv.*

lateral pass 〖橄欖球〗（幾與決勝線平行的）側向傳球。

Lat·er·an 〔ˈlætərən; ˈlætərən〕 *n.* ①（羅馬）拉特蘭大聖堂（天主教堂中居最高位）。②拉特蘭宮（昔教皇宮殿，現改爲博物館）。

lat·er·ite 〔ˈlætəˌraɪt; ˈlætərait〕 *n.* 〖礦〗紅土（鐵礬土之氫氧化物）。

lat·est** 〔ˈletɪst; ˈleitist〕 *adj.* sup. of **late.** ①最遲的；最晚的。②最近的；最新的。the *latest* fashion. 最新型。—*adv.* 最遲地；最近地。at*** (***the***) ***latest*** 最遲；最晚。Be at the airport at 7 o'clock *at the latest.* 最遲七點鐘到飛機場。***the latest*** a. 最近情況。b. 最新發展；最近模型。This is *the latest* in phonographs. 這是最新型的留聲機。

la·tex 〔ˈletɛks; ˈleiteks〕 *n., pl.* **lat·i·ces** 〔ˈlætəˌsiz; ˈlætisiːz〕, **la·tex·es.** （植物之）乳液（如橡膠樹、罌粟花等之漿汁）。

lath 〔læθ, lɑθ; lɑːθ〕 *n., pl.* **laths,** *v.* —*n.* ①板條。②代替板條之有孔金屬板或網。③用板條作成之物。***as thin as a lath*** 骨瘦如柴。—*v.t.* 覆以板條。

lathe 〔leð; leið〕 *n., v.,* **lathed, lath·ing.** —*n.* ①車床。②旋盤；鏇床。***drill lathe*** 鑽孔車床。***screw-cutting lathe*** 螺絲車床。

—*v.t.* 以車床旋削。

lath·er [ˈlæðɚ; ˈlɑːðə] *n.* ①肥皂泡沫。②(馬等之)汗沫。③焦急。—*v.t.* ①塗以肥皂泡沫。②〖俗〗用力鞭打。③使緊張;使焦急〖常 up〗. —*v.i.* ①(肥皂水)起泡。②(馬等)身上冒沫狀之汗。

lath·er·y [ˈlæðərɪ; ˈlɑːðəri] *adj.* ①覆滿泡沫的;會起泡沫的。②非實質的;空虛的。

la·thi [ˈlɑti; ˈlɑːtiː] *n.* (印度)套於竹竿中的鐵棒(尤指警察用的)。

lath·ing [ˈlæθɪŋ; ˈlɑːθiŋ] *n.* ①覆以板條;釘板條。②供塗灰泥之板條骨架; 木條(集合稱)。③用板條等作成之物。

lath·work [ˈlæθˌwɝk; ˈlɑːθwəːk] *n.* 「=lathing.」

lath·y [ˈlæθɪ; ˈlɑːθi] *adj.*, **lath·i·er, lath·i·est.** 似板條的;細長的;瘦長的。

‡Lat·in [ˈlætɪn; ˈlætin] *n.* ①拉丁文。②拉丁民族之人(義大利人、法國人、西班牙人、葡萄牙人、羅馬尼亞人等)。③南美洲人。to group *Latins* on one side and North Americans on the other. 將南美洲人視爲一集團,而北美洲人爲另一集團。④古羅馬人。⑤羅馬天主教徒。—*adj.* ①拉丁文的。*Latin* grammar. 拉丁文法。②用拉丁文寫作的。a *Latin* verse. 一首拉丁詩。③拉丁民族的。the *Latin* countries. 拉丁民族諸國。④有拉丁民族之特色的。He is very *Latin* in temperament. 他的脾氣有拉丁民族之特色。⑤古羅馬的;古羅馬人的。⑥羅馬天主教徒的。

Latin America 拉丁美洲(即南美洲、中美洲、墨西哥、及西印度羣島等地)。

Lat·in-A·mer·i·can [ˈlætn̩əˈmɛrɪkən; ˈlætinəˈmerikən] *adj.* 拉丁美洲(人)的。—*n.* 拉丁美洲人。

Latin Church 羅馬天主教。

Lat·in·ism [ˈlætn̩ˌɪzəm; ˈlætinizəm] *n.* ①拉丁語風;拉丁語法。②拉丁民族作風。

Lat·in·ist [ˈlætn̩ɪst; ˈlætinist] *n.* 拉丁語學者。

La·tin·i·ty [læˈtɪnətɪ; ləˈtiniti] *n.* ①拉丁語之使用。②拉丁語法; 拉丁語風。③拉丁語之知識。④拉丁民族之特色。

Lat·in·ize [ˈlætn̩ˌaɪz; ˈlætinaiz] *v.*, **-ized, -iz·ing.** —*v.t.* ①使成拉丁語風;使拉丁語化; 譯爲拉丁語。②使成古代羅馬(拉丁)風式;使拉丁化。③使合於天主教之教義、儀式等。④將…音譯成拉丁字母。—*v.i.* 用拉丁語。

Latin Quarter (巴黎 Seine 河南岸,學者及藝術家薈集之)拉丁地區。

lat·ish [ˈletɪʃ; ˈleitiʃ] *adj.* & *adv.* 稍遲; 「稍後。」

·lat·i·tude [ˈlætəˌtjud; ˈlætitjuːd] *n.* ①緯度; 緯線。thirty degrees of *latitude* north of the equator. 北緯三十度。②某緯度之地區。high *latitudes.* 高緯度地區(距離赤道很遠的地區)。③行動的餘地;範圍;自由。***north*** (***south***) ***latitude*** 北(南)緯。***warm*** (***cold***) ***latitudes*** 熱(寒)帶地區。

lat·i·tu·di·nal [ˌlætəˈtjudənl̩; ˌlætiˈtjuːdinl] *adj.* 緯度的。

lat·i·tu·di·nar·i·an [ˌlætəˌtjudn̩ˈɛrɪən; ˈlætiˌtjuːdiˈnɛəriən] *adj.* 自由主義的; 寬容的; 不拘泥於教條的。—*n.* 自由主義者; 不拘泥於教條者。

lat·i·tu·di·nar·i·an·ism [ˌlætəˌtjudəˈnɛrɪəˌnɪzəm; ˈlætiˌtjuːdiˈnɛəriənizəm] *n.* (特指宗教上的)自由主義。

la·trine [ləˈtrin; ləˈtriːn] *n.* 廁所(尤指兵營或營地中者)。

lat·ten [ˈlætn̩; ˈlætən] *n.* ①黃銅薄片。「②錫板;薄金屬板。」

‡lat·ter [ˈlætɚ; ˈlætə] *adj.* ①後者。Of these two men the former is dead and the *latter* still alive. 這兩人中,前者已死,後者還活着。②(時間上)較後的。the *latter* half of the year. 下半年。

lat·ter-day [ˈlætɚˈde; ˈlætəˈdei] *adj.* ①近代的;當今的。②後期的;後來的。

Latter-day Saint 〖美〗摩門(Mormon)教徒。

lat·ter·ly [ˈlætəlɪ; ˈlætəli] *adv.* ①最「近地;目前地。②後來。」

lat·tice [ˈlætɪs; ˈlætis] *n.*, *v.*, **-ticed, -tic·ing.** —*n.* (窗等的)格子。—*v.t.* ①做成格子式樣。②裝格子於。

lat·tice·work [ˈlætɪsˌwɝk; ˈlætiswəːk] *n.* ①格子細工。②格子(集合稱)。

Lat·vi·a [ˈlætvɪə; ˈlætviə] *n.* 拉脫維亞(原爲波羅的海沿岸小國, 1940 年爲蘇聯兼併,正式名稱爲 Latvian Soviet Socialist Republic, 首都爲里加 Riga)。

Lat·vi·an [ˈlætvɪən; ˈlætviən] *adj.* ①拉脫維亞的;拉脫維亞人的。②拉脫維亞語的。—*n.* ①拉脫維亞人。②拉脫維亞語。

lau·an [ˈluˌɑn; ˈluːˌɑːn] *n.* 〖植物〗柳安木。

laud [lɔd; lɔːd] *v.t.* 褒獎; 讚美。to *laud* a person to the skies. 對某人極口稱頌。—*n.* ①褒獎;讚美。②讚美詩;頌歌。③(常 L-)(*pl.*)(作 *sing.* or *pl.* 解)清晨所作之宗教讚課。

laud·a·ble [ˈlɔdəbl̩; ˈlɔːdəbl] *adj.* 值得讚美的; 值得褒獎的。 —**laud·a·bly,** *adv.* —**laud·a·bil·i·ty,** *n.*

lau·da·num [ˈlɔdn̩əm; ˈlɔdnəm] *n.* 鴉片酊; 鴉片丁幾(鴉片溶於酒精,作止痛劑或毒藥用)。

lau·da·tion [lɔˈdeʃən; lɔːˈdeiʃən] *n.* 「讚美;頌揚。」

laud·a·to·ry [ˈlɔdəˌtorɪ; ˈlɔːdətəri] *adj.* 讚賞的;褒揚的。

‡laugh [læf, lɑf; lɑːf] *v.i.* 笑。It's not a matter to *laugh* about. 這不是一件好笑的事。—*v.t.* ①(藉笑)使消除〖away, off〗. He *laughed* away my fears. 他一笑使我的恐懼全消。②以笑表示。to *laugh* a reply. 以笑作答。③笑至於。 to *laugh* oneself into convulsion. 笑得前仰後合。***He laughs best who laughs last.*** 別高興得太早。***laugh at*** (=make fun of) **a.** 笑;嘲笑; 嘲弄。Don't *laugh at* her. 不要嘲笑她。**b.** 一笑置之。to *laugh at* difficulties. 對困難一笑置之。**c.** 雖覺可笑但帶有同情心。***laugh in one's face*** 公開侮辱某人; 當面嘲笑某人。***laugh in one's sleeve*** 竊喜; 暗暗高興。***laugh off*** 一笑置之(參看 *v.t.* ①)。***laugh on the wrong*** (or ***other***) ***side of one's mouth*** 〖俗〗煩惱; 憂愁; 失望; 幾乎要哭出來。***laugh out of court*** 一笑置之。***laugh over*** 笑着談論。We all *laughed over* the letter—it was very amusing. 我們讀這信時都笑了—信寫得很有趣。—*n.* ①笑。We all had a good *laugh* about it. 我們對這個都笑得够了。②笑柄。③(*pl.*)娛樂。simply for *laughs.* 只爲了娛樂。***break into a laugh*** 忽然笑起來。***have the last laugh on*** 表面上似乎失敗但獲得最後的勝利或成功。***raise a laugh*** 引人發笑。

laugh·a·ble [ˈlæfəbl̩; ˈlɑːfəbl] *adj.* 可笑的; 有趣的。a *laughable* error. 可笑的錯誤。

laugh·a·bly [ˈlæfəblɪ; ˈlɑːfəbli] *adv.* 「可笑。」

laugh·ing [ˈlæfɪŋ; ˈlɑːfiŋ] *adj.* ①帶笑的;笑容滿面的。②可笑的;令人發噱的。—*n.* 笑(的動作)。—**ly,** *adv.*

laughing gas 〖化〗笑氣(卽N_2O)。

laughing jackass 笑魚狗(一種澳洲產之鳥,其鳴聲似人笑聲)。

laugh·ing·stock [ˈlæfɪŋˌstɑk; ˈlɑː-fiŋ-stɔk] *n.* 笑柄;受人嘲笑者。

laugh·ter** [ˈlæftɚ, ˈlɑf-; ˈlɑːftə] *n.* ①笑。I heard sounds of *laughter* in the next room. 我聽見隔壁房間裏笑的聲音。②笑聲。Their *laughter* made him angry. 他們的笑聲使他生氣。burst into laughter*** 不禁而笑;失聲而笑。***roar with laughter*** 哄然大笑。

launch** [lɔntʃ, lɑntʃ; lɔːntʃ, lɔːnʃ, lɑːntʃ, lɑːnʃ] *v.t.* ①使(船)入水;行入水式。to *launch* a ship. 使船入水。②使(飛機)升空;發射(飛彈等)。to *launch* a plane from an aircraft carrier. 使飛機自航空母艦升空。③使(某人)從事。to *launch* a young man into business. 使一青年入實業界。④開辦;創辦。⑤發動。to *launch* an attack. 發動攻擊。⑥投;擲。—*v.i.* 開始;着手。He used the money to *launch* into a new business. 他利用這筆錢開始從事一新的行業。launch (out) into*** 狂熱於;熱心於。***launch out*** 開始;着手。—*n.* ①入水;入水式。the *launch* of a new liner. 新郵輪的入水。②軍艦所帶的大艇。③遊艇。

launch·ing [ˈlɔntʃɪŋ; ˈlɔːntʃiŋ] *n.* ①開辦或創辦(之行動)。②發射(之行動)。

launching pad 火箭或飛彈發射台。

launching platform ①火箭或飛彈發射台。②火箭或飛彈發射場。

launch vehicle 推動太空船、人造衛星等進入軌道的火箭。

laun·der [ˈlɔndɚ; ˈlɔːndə] *v.t.* 洗熨(衣服等)。—*v.i.* ①經洗。②洗熨衣服。—*n.* 洗鑛槽。

laun·der·ette [ˌlɔndəˈrɛt; ˌlɔːndə-ˈret] *n.* =**laundromat.**

laun·dress [ˈlɔndrɪs; ˈlɔːndris] *n.* 洗衣婦。

laun·dro·mat [ˈlɔndrəmæt; ˈlɔːndrə-mæt] *n.* ①(營業性)自動洗衣場。②論磅收費的洗衣店。

***laun·dry** [ˈlɔndrɪ, ˈlɑn-; ˈlɔːndri] *n., pl.* **-dries.** ①洗衣房;洗衣店。Send these shirts to the *laundry*. 將這些襯衫送到洗衣店去。②〖俗〗所洗或送洗的衣服(集合稱)。Has the *laundry* come back yet? 洗的衣服送回來了嗎?

laun·dry·man [ˈlɔndrɪmən; ˈlɔːn-drimən] *n., pl.* **-men.** ①洗衣匠。②洗衣店所雇取送衣服者。

laun·dry·wom·an [ˈlɔndrɪˌwumən; ˈlɔːndriˌwumən] *n., pl.* **-wom·en.** 洗衣婦。

lau·re·ate [*n., adj.,* ˈlɔrɪɪt; ˈlɔːriit *v.,* ˈlɔrɪˌet; ˈlɔːrieit] *n.* ①桂冠詩人(=poet laureate)。②任何贏得榮譽者。Nobel *laureate* in physics. 諾貝爾物理學獎得獎人。③稱讚者;讚美者。—*adj.* ①戴桂冠的。②有名的。—*v.t.* ①任命桂冠詩人。②使戴月桂以示尊榮。

lau·re·ate·ship [ˈlɔrɪɪtˌʃɪp; ˈlɔːriit-ʃip] *n.* 桂冠詩人之地位或任期。

lau·rel** [ˈlɔrəl, ˈlɑr-; ˈlɔrəl] *n.* ①月桂樹。②桂樹葉。a *laurel* wreath. 桂冠。③(*pl.*)光榮;榮譽。④(*pl.*)勝利。look to one's laurels*** 愛惜名譽;保持紀錄。***rest on one's laurels*** 對既得之榮譽感到滿足。***win*** (or ***gain***) ***laurels*** 博得榮譽。—*v.t.* 戴桂冠。

***la·va** [ˈlɑvə, ˈlævə; ˈlɑːvə] *n.* ①(火山流出的)熔岩;岩漿。②(由熔岩凝結成的)火山岩。

la·va·bo [ləˈvebo; ləˈveibou] *n., pl.* **-boes, -bos.** 〖天主教〗①洗手式(彌撒聖祭時奉獻後祭司之洗手儀式)。②洗手式時所唱之詩篇(卽詩篇26章6–12節)。③(洗手式用的)手巾或水缽。④(修道院中之)洗手室。

la·va·lier(e) [ˌlævəˈlɪr; ˌlævəˈliə] *n.* 綴有寶石之環狀首飾。(亦作 **lavallière**)

lav·a·to·ry [ˈlævəˌtorɪ; ˈlævətəri] *n., pl.* **-ries.** ①盥洗室。②廁所;便所。③臉盆;洗手缸。

lave [lev; leiv] *v.,* **laved, lav·ing.** —*v.t.* ①〖詩〗洗濯;洗浴。②(河水)向着…慢慢流動;沖洗。③汲取;倒出;以杓舀出。—*v.i.* 〖詩〗洗;沐浴;沖洗。

***lav·en·der** [ˈlævəndɚ; ˈlævində] *n.* ①歐薄荷;薰衣草。②歐薄荷之乾花乾葉(用以薰衣物者,使免爲蠹蟲所蝕)。③淡紫色。—*adj.* 淡紫色的。—*v.i.* 以歐薄荷薰(衣物)。

la·ver[1] [ˈlevɚ; ˈleivə] *n.* ①〖聖經〗(猶太人神殿中之)洗盆(僧侶洗手足用)。②洗禮盆;洗禮用水。

la·ver[2] *n.* 〖植物〗(供食用之)紫菜。

***lav·ish** [ˈlævɪʃ; ˈlæviʃ] *adj.* ①豐富的;過多的;過度的。*lavish* praise. 過度的稱頌。②過度慷慨的;濫用的;浪費的。to be *lavish* with money. 浪費金錢。—*v.t.* 浪費;濫用。to *lavish* care and affection on one's children. 對孩子過度溺愛。—**ment,** *n.*

***lav·ish·ly** [ˈlævɪʃlɪ; ˈlæviʃli] *adv.* 浪費地;豐富地。Both volumes are *lavishly* illustrated. 兩册均有豐富插圖。

‡law[1] [lɔ; lɔː] *n.* ①法律。That is against the *law*. 那事是違法的。②法律之一條。③法律之推行;法治。to maintain *law* and order. 維持法治與社會秩序。④法律系統。courts of *law*. 法院。⑤特殊的法規。criminal *law*. 刑法。⑥法則;原則。the *law* of supply and demand. 供求原則。⑦法學;法律學。My brother is studying *law*. 我的弟弟在研讀法學。⑧法律業。to enter *law*. 開始從事法律工作。⑨訴訟。⑩規則。the *laws* of hospitality. 待客之道。⑪定律。the *law* of gravitation. 萬有引力定律。⑫戒律;規律。⑬數學定理。***go to law*** 訴諸法律;提起訴訟。***lay down the law*** **a.** 下令(指必須服從者)。**b.** 申斥;斥責。**c.** 權威地說。***Necessity knows no law.*** 需要之前無法律(有必要時,就顧不得是否合法了)。***take the law into one's own hands*** 私行治罪或保衞自己的權益。***the Law*** 舊約聖經;摩西律。—*v.t.* 〖主方〗控告。

law[2] *interj.* 〖卑〗噯呀!不得了!(表驚異)

law-a·bid·ing [ˈlɔəˌbaɪdɪŋ; ˈlɔːəˌbaidiŋ] *adj.* 守法的;安分守己的;守秩序的。*law-abiding* people. 守法的良民。

law·break·er [ˈlɔˌbrekɚ; ˈlɔːˌbreikə] *n.* 犯法者;罪犯。

law·break·ing [ˈlɔˌbrekɪŋ; ˈlɔːˌbrei-kiŋ] *n., adj.* 犯法(的);違法(的)。

law clerk 律師助手。

law court 法庭(=court of law)。

***law·ful** [ˈlɔfəl; ˈlɔːful] *adj.* ①合法的;法律所許可的。*lawful* business. 法律准許的營業。②法定的。to reach *lawful* age. 達到法定年齡。③依法的。*lawful* arrest. 依法的逮捕。④守法的。—**ly,** *adv.* —**ness,** *n.*

law·giv·er [ˈlɔˌgɪvɚ; ˈlɔːˌgivə] *n.* 立法者;制定法律者。

law·less [ˈlɔlɪs; ˈlɔːlis] *adj.* ①沒有法律的;法律無法實行的。②目無法紀的;違法的。

③難管訓的。—ly, *adv.* —ness, *n.*

law·mak·er 〔ˈlɔˌmekɚ; ˈlɔːˌmeikə〕 *n.* 立法者;立法機關的一員。

law·mak·ing 〔ˈlɔˌmekɪŋ; ˈlɔːˌmeikiŋ〕 *n., adj.* 立法(的)。

***lawn**[1] 〔lɔn; lɔːn〕 *n.* ①(經人工修整而點綴於房屋周圍的)草地。②(網球等的)球場。a tennis *lawn.* 網球場。

lawn[2] *n.* 一種薄麻布(用以製作女服,主教法衣袖子);主教之職權。

lawn mower 割草機。

lawn swing 兒童玩的相向鞦韆。

lawn tennis 網球(尤指需要草地球場者)。

lawn·y[1] 〔ˈlɔnɪ; ˈlɔːni〕 *adj.* ①〖罕〗草地多的。②似草地的。

lawn·y[2] *adj.* (似)薄麻布的。

law of conservation of energy 〖物理〗能量不滅律。

law of conservation of mass 〖物理〗質量不滅律。

law of conservation of matter 〖物理〗物質不滅律。

law officer ①司法官(英國特指檢察總長及次長)。②執法人員。

law of gravitation 〖物理〗萬有引力定律。

law of nations 國際(公)法。

law of reflection 〖物理〗反射定律(光之反射角等於入射角)。

law of sines 〖數學〗正弦定律。

law of tangents 〖數學〗正切定律。

Law·rence[1] 〔ˈlɔrəns; ˈlɔrəns〕 *n.* 男子名。

Law·rence[2] *n.* 勞倫斯(David Herbert, 1885–1930, 英國小說家、詩人)。

Law·rence[3] *n.* 勞倫斯(Thomas Edward, 1888–1935, 世稱 Lawrence of Arabia, 英國考古學家、軍人及作家)。

law·suit 〔ˈlɔˌsut; ˈlɔː-sjuːt〕 *n.* 訴訟;訟案。

***law·yer** 〔ˈlɔjɚ; ˈlɔːjə〕 *n.* 律師。a *lawyer* by profession. 職業律師。

lax 〔læks; læks〕 *adj.* ①鬆弛的;散漫的。②放鬆的。③不嚴謹的;馬馬虎虎的。④放縱的;不檢點的。⑤不明確的;模糊的。⑥腹瀉的;拉痢的。⑦〖植物〗散開的。⑧〖語音〗放鬆有關各部肌肉發出的(母音)。—*n.* 放鬆肌肉所發的母音。—ly, *adv.*

lax·a·tion 〔lækˈseʃən; lækˈseiʃən〕 *n.* ①放鬆;使鬆弛。②鬆弛;鬆懈。③通便劑。

lax·a·tive 〔ˈlæksətɪv; ˈlæksətiv〕 *adj.* ①通便的。②未被抑制的。—*n.* 通便劑。

lax·i·ty 〔ˈlæksətɪ; ˈlæksiti〕 *n.* ①(道德、行為等之)不嚴謹;放縱。②不明確;曖昧。③鬆弛。

‡**lay**[1] 〔le; lei〕 *v.,* **laid** 〔led; leid〕, **lay·ing** 〔ˈle·ɪŋ; ˈleiiŋ〕, *n.* —*v.t.* ①置放;橫置;鋪設。He *laid* his hand on my shoulder. 他將他的手放在我的肩上。②使。They *laid* the land waste. 他們將該地區夷為平地。③產(卵)。Hens *lay* eggs. 母鷄生蛋。④撲滅;消除;驅除。The rain has *laid* the dust. 雨已使灰塵不揚。What can we do to *lay* his doubts? 我們能有甚麼辦法消除他的疑惑? ⑤準備;鋪設;布置。to *lay* the table. 擺設餐桌(準備吃飯)。⑥提出;陳述。to *lay* facts before a committee. 向委員會提陳事實。⑦課(稅);下(令)。to *lay* heavy taxes on tea and coffee. 對茶和咖啡課以重稅。⑧以…為背景(常用被動語態)。The scene of the story is *laid* in London. 這故事以倫敦為背景。⑨覆蓋;塗(顏料等)。to *lay* a floor with a carpet. 以地毯鋪於地板上。⑩打;擊。to *lay* blows on a person. 打擊某人。⑪打(賭);賭注。I *lay* 10 dollars that he will not come. 我賭十塊錢,他不會來。⑫砌。to *lay* bricks. 砌磚。⑬設計;安排。⑭歸咎;委諸於。to *lay* the blame for something on somebody. 將某事之罪責歸於某人。⑮鋪平;擺平。to *lay* the nap of cloth. 將布擺平。⑯埋葬。They *laid* him to rest. 他們將他埋葬。⑰置於某一情況下。The failure of his crops *laid* him in debt. 歉收使他負債。⑱搓(繩)。⑲〖俚〗與…發生肉體關係。—*v.i.* ①產卵。The hens don't *lay* in this cold weather. 在這寒冷的天氣中,這些鷄不會產卵。②打賭;賭注。③努力從事。to *lay* to one's work. 努力工作。④計劃。to *lay* for a chance to escape. 計劃如何逃脫。***lay aboard*** (從前海戰時)沿(敵艦)停泊俾攀登之。***lay about*** 向四面揮打。***lay a course*** 按計畫進行。***lay a finger on*** 傷害。Don't dare to *lay a finger on* her! 不可傷害她! ***lay aside*** **a.** 貯藏;儲蓄。to *lay aside* money for one's old age. 儲蓄金錢以備老年之用。**b.** 推置一邊;棄置。He *laid* his book *aside* to listen. 他將書推置一邊而注意傾聽。**c.** 拋棄;革除。to *lay aside* old habits. 革除舊習慣。**d.** =**lay up.** ***lay a snare*** (***a trap,*** or ***an ambush***) 設圈套;設陷穽。***lay away*** **a.** 留作後用。**b.** 埋葬。They *laid* him *away* in the tomb. 他們將他葬在墳墓裏。***lay bare*** 露出;揭開。to *lay* one's heart *bare.* 傾訴衷曲。***lay (fast) by the heels*** 逮捕監禁。The police will soon *lay* the thief *by the heels.* 警察不久將逮捕這竊賊下獄。***lay claim*** 宣稱有權;提出要求。The prince *laid claim* to the throne. 王子宣稱有權繼承王位。***lay down*** **a.** 使躺下。*Lay* the baby *down* gently. 將嬰孩輕輕放下(使躺着)。**b.** 藏(酒於地窖中)。**c.** 放棄;犧牲。to *lay down* one's life. 捐軀。**d.** 賭(錢)。**e.** 計劃;設計。**f.** 規定(規則、原則等)。to *lay* something *down* as a maxim. 將某語定為座右銘。**g.** 栽植;墾殖(土地)為牧場。***lay eyes on*** (=catch sight of) 看見。***lay for*** 準備伏擊。***lay hands on*** (or ***upon***) **a.** 攫取;破壞;傷害。He keeps everything he can *lay* his *hands on.* 凡能攫取到手的東西,他均持之不放。**b.** 尋獲;找到。**c.** 捕;逮捕。**d.** 〖宗教〗行按手禮;祝聖(使成教士或主教)。***lay hold of*** 抓住。*Lay hold of* that rope and pull. 抓住那根繩子用力拉。***lay in*** 貯藏。***lay it on; lay it on thick; lay it on with a trowel*** 〖俗〗誇張;過甚其辭。***lay low*** 使倒下。The blow *laid* him *low.* 這一擊把他打倒了。***lay off*** **a.** 駛(船)離(岸或他船)。**b.** 〖美〗暫時解雇。*lay off* workmen during a business depression. 商業蕭條期間將工人暫時解雇。**c.** 休息。The doctor told her to *lay off* for a week. 醫生告訴她須休息一禮拜。***lay on*** **a.** 猛(打)。**b.** 塗;敷。**c.** 裝(水管、煤氣管等)。Gas and water are *laid on.* 煤氣管與水管皆已裝好。***lay oneself out*** 盡力;用盡苦心。***lay one's finger on*** 指出(毛病等)。***lay one's hopes on*** (=place confidence in) 深信;信任;指望;寄託希望於。***lay on the line*** **a.** 籌足(款項)。**b.** 無條件地發表或提出(聲明、建議等)。***lay open*** **a.** 揭發。to *lay open* plots. 揭發陰謀。**b.** 使曝露。to *lay open* a wound. 曝露傷口。**c.** 使破傷;傷及。***lay out*** **a.** 打開備用。to *lay*

out one's evening clothes. 取出晚禮服待穿。b. 出現;呈現。c. 準備埋葬。d. 〖俗〗擊倒;擊昏。e. 用(錢)。f. 計劃;設計。well-*laid out* streets and avenues. 設計很好的街道和馬路。***lay over*** a. 〖俚〗優於;勝過。It *lays over* anything of the kind. 這勝過任何同類的事物。b. 擱置;擱延。***lay siege to*** 包圍;圍攻(=besiege). to *lay siege to* a castle. 圍攻堡壘。***lay stress*** (***weight***, or ***emphasis***) ***on*** 強調…的重要。***lay to*** a. 努力工作。He was told to get a shovel and *lay to* with the others. 他被命令拿起鏟子與別人一起努力工作。b. 減少船的搖動。c. 將船駛進船塢或其他安全地帶。d. 猛烈攻打。***lay to*** (or ***at***) ***a person's door*** 委(過)於某人;歸咎;歸罪。***lay to heart*** 愼重考慮;牢記。***lay to rest*** 使安息;安葬。***lay*** (***a person***) ***under a necessity*** 使不得不;迫使。***lay*** (***a person***) ***under contribution*** 強使(某人)捐助。***lay up*** a. 貯藏。to *lay up* stores (goods, etc.). 貯藏必需品(貨物等)。b. 使(船)入船塢。to *lay up* a ship for repairs. 使船入船塢修理。c. 臥床(用被動語態)。***lay*** (***the land***) ***waste*** 使成一片荒涼;夷爲平地。—*n.* ①方位;位置;地形;地勢。the *lay* of the ground. 那塊地的地形。②價格。③產卵之狀態或行動。④捕魚歸來後分給船員的紅利。⑤〖俚〗a. 性交。b. 姘頭。***lay of the land*** 所面對之局勢。

‡lay² *v.* pt. of lie².

lay³ *adj.* ①普通平民的;凡俗的(對牧師、僧侶而言)。a *lay* sermon. 凡俗身分者所作的講道。②非屬於專門職業的(對律師、醫師等而言);外行的。*lay* vocabulary. 非專門性辭彙。

lay⁴ *n.* ①短抒情詩(尤指能唱者)。②歌。

lay-by [ˈleˌbaɪ; ˈleibai] *n.* 〖英〗①幹道旁邊之停車修理區。②河道中停泊駁船之處。

lay days ①(船舶之)載貨或卸貨期間;停泊期間。②〖航海〗(出港之)遲延日數。

***lay·er** [ˈleɚ;lɛə, ˈleiə] *n.* ①一層。a *layer* of clay. 一層泥土。②賭錢者。③產卵雞。④放置者。⑤〖園藝〗壓條;用壓條法分出的植物。⑥編繩機。—*v.t.* 以壓條培植(新植物)。—*v.i.* 分層堆積或凝集。

layer cake 〖美〗夾心蛋糕。

lay·ette [leˈɛt; leiˈet] *n.* 新生嬰兒所用之全套衣物(包括衣服、被褥、雜物等)。

lay figure ①(美術家或商店的)人體模型;人體木像。②傀儡似的人物;無用的人。

lay·ing [ˈleɪŋ; ˈleiiŋ] *n.* ①置放;布置;鋪設。②(繩之)撚法。③最初所塗底層。④(砲之)瞄準。⑤一次孵的蛋。

***lay·man** [ˈlemən;ˈleimən] *n., pl.* **-men.** ①門外漢;外行人(對專家而言)。Where the law is concerned, I am only a *layman*. 談到法律,我不過是個門外漢。②俗人(對教士而言)。

lay·off [ˈleˌɔf; ˈleiɔːf] *n.* ①臨時解雇。②失業時期。③休息;中止活動。

lay·out [ˈleˌaut; ˈleiaut] *n.* ①〖美〗設計;布置。②呈現;陳列。③設計之物。④一套工具。⑤布置之環境。

lay·o·ver [ˈleˌovɚ; ˈleiˌouvə] *n.* 〖美〗中途停留。

lay shaft 〖機械〗副軸。

lay-up [ˈleˌʌp; ˈleiʌp] *n.* ①〖籃球〗籃板球。②架船作修理;船在不使用時之貯藏。

laz·a·ret, laz·a·rette [ˌlæzəˈrɛt; ˌlæzəˈret] *n.* =**lazaretto.**

laz·a·ret·to [ˌlæzəˈrɛto; ˌlæzəˈretou] *n., pl.* **-tos.** ①傳染病院;(尤指)痲瘋病院。②檢疫所;檢疫船。③〖航海〗(近船尾的)食糧貯藏室。

lazar house 痲瘋病院。

Laz·a·rus [ˈlæzərəs; ˈlæzərəs] *n.* ①〖聖經〗拉撒路(一患癩病的乞丐,在世間受盡苦難,死後進天堂)。②〖聖經〗Mary 與 Martha 之兄(耶穌使之復活者)。③(l-)患癩病或其他可怕疾病之乞丐。***Lazarus and Dives*** 貧者與富者。

laze [lez;leiz] *v.,* **lazed, laz·ing,** *n.* —*v.i.* 懶散;怠惰。—*v.t.* 懶惰地打發(時光)〖away〗。—*n.* 懶惰中打發時間的狀態;閒散;懶散。

***la·zi·ly** [ˈlezɪlɪ; ˈleizili] *adv.* 懶洋洋地。He stretched his arms *lazily*. 他懶洋洋地伸欠胳臂。

la·zi·ness [ˈlezɪnɪs; ˈleizinis] *n.* 懶惰;怠惰。He was punished for his *laziness*. 他因懶惰而受懲罰。

***la·zy** [ˈlezɪ; ˈleizi] *adj.,* **-zi·er, -zi·est.** ①懶惰的;怠惰的。He's a *lazy* fellow. 他是一個懶人。②緩慢的;不活潑的。a *lazy* walk. 緩慢的散步。③令人懶惰的。*lazy* summer day. 令人懶惰的夏天。④不直立的。—**la·zi·ly,** *adv.* —**la·zi·ness,** *n.*

la·zy·back [ˈlezɪˌbæk; ˈleizibæk] *n.* 車內座椅所附的靠背。

la·zy·bones [ˈlezɪˌbonz; ˈleizibounz] *n.* (常作 *sing.* 解)〖俗〗懶人;懶骨頭。(亦作 **lazybone**)

lazy Susan (置於餐桌中央便於取食之)大轉盤。

lazy tongs 惰鉗(用以夾取遠處之物者)。

laz·za·ro·ne [ˌlæzəˈrone; ˌlæzəˈrounei] *n., pl.* **-ni** [-nɪ;-ni]. (Naples 之)無家惰民;乞丐;叫化子;癟三。

lb. *pl.* **lbs., lb.** ①(L.) libra (=pound). ②librae (=pounds). **LC** 〖美海軍〗landing craft. **L.C.** ①Library of Congress. ②Lord Chamberlain. ③Lord Chancellor. ④Lower Canada. **l.c.** ①(=L. loco citato) in the place cited. ②(=lower case) in small letters, not capital letters. ③left center. ④letter of credit. **L/C, l/c** letter of credit. **L.C.C.** London City (*or* County) Council. **L.C.D., l.c.d.** 〖數學〗lowest common denominator. **L.C.F., l.c.f.** 〖數學〗lowest common factor. **L.C.J.** 〖英〗Lord Chief Justice. **L.C.M., l.c.m.** 〖數學〗lowest common multiple. **Ld.** ①Limited. ②Lord. **L.D.** ①Lady Day. ②Laus Deo (拉 =Praise be to God). ③Litterarum Doctor (拉=Doctor of Letters).

lea [li;liː] *n.* 〖詩〗草原;牧場。—*adj.* (土地)未耕種的。

leach [litʃ; liːtʃ] *v.t.* ①過濾(水等)。②將(礦石、木皮等)浸於濾水中。③濾取(可溶物質)。—*v.i.* 過濾;經過濾而分離。—*n.* ①過濾。②濾器。③濾劑;濾液。—**a·ble,** *adj.*

‡lead¹ [lid;liːd] *v.,* **led, lead·ing,** *n., adj.* —*v.t.* ①引導;嚮導。to *lead* a blind man. 引導一盲人。②牽引。to *lead* a horse. 牽馬(與騎馬相對)。③領導;率領。The expedition was *led* by Mr. Smith. 這探險隊係由史密斯先生領導。④過(生活)。to *lead* a busy (happy, an idle) life. 過忙碌(快樂、閒散)的生活。⑤居首;爲第一名。He *leads* his class. 他是班上的第一名。⑥導引(水、蒸汽等)。⑦影響;使。Such actions *lead* us to distrust him. 如此的行爲使我們不信任他。⑧引領出(牌)。—*v.i.* ①領導;率領;帶隊。Who is going to *lead*? 由誰領導? ②做嚮導;領路。*Lead*, I will follow. 你領路,我跟着來。③通;至;達。Where does this road *lead* (to)?這條路通那裏?④(比賽中)領先。Which horse was *leading?* 哪一匹馬領先? ⑤被帶領。⑥居首。He *leads* in mathematics. 他的數學最好。⑦出牌;首先打出。⑧(拳擊中)首擊;試擊對方。**lead astray** 引入歧途。Our guide *led* us *astray*. 我們的嚮導把我們領入歧途。**lead by the nose** 牽着鼻子走;完全掌握。She *leads* her husband *by the nose*. 她完全控制着她丈夫。**lead off** a. 開始;率先(=begin). b.〖棒球〗打第一棒;擔任第一棒打擊手。**lead on** 使誤入歧途;使誤解。He *led* me *on* to think that he loved me. 他使我誤以爲他愛我。**lead one a dance** (or **chase**) 令人焦急;使陷入困難。She *led* her boy friend *a* fine *dance*. 她使她男友焦急得坐立不安。**lead out** a. 開始。b. 將舞伴帶至舞池起舞。**lead the way** 引路;帶路。**lead up to** 漸次提及;鋪路。These reforms *led up to* the establishment of a republic. 這些改革給共和國之建立鋪好道路。—*n.* ①領導;指導;榜樣。②領導地位。to take the *lead.* 領先。③領先之程度。He had a *lead* of 3 yards in the race. 在那次賽跑中,他領先三碼。④(紙牌戲中之)出牌權。Whose *lead* is it? 輪到誰先出牌?⑤領先者;領導者。⑥〖劇〗主角;主要演員。⑦(狗等頸上所拴以便人牽引用的)皮帶。⑧指示;指標。⑨〖礦〗礦脈。⑩冰間水路。⑪導電體。⑫〖拳擊〗擊向對方之一擊。⑬〖新聞〗新聞報告的第一段;頭條新聞。⑭跑壘員準備跑壘而離壘的姿勢。—*adj.* ①領頭的。②最重要的。the *lead* article in this month's issue. 這期月刊最重要的文章。③〖棒球〗(跑壘員)最接近得分的。

***lead²** [lɛd; led] *n.* ①鉛。*Lead* is a heavy metal. 鉛是重金屬。②(測水深用的)鉛錘。③(鉛筆中的)鉛心。④鎗彈。⑤〖印刷〗鉛條。⑥(*pl.*)(鋪屋頂用的)鉛板。⑦(*pl.*)裝玻璃之鉛質框架。**black lead** 黑鉛;石墨。**red lead** 赤鉛;鉛丹。**white lead** 炭酸鉛;鉛粉。—*adj.* ①鉛製的。②含鉛的。—*v.t.* ①以鉛接合;以鉛沉壓。②〖印刷〗塞鉛條於(活字)的行間。③上含有鉛的釉於(陶器)。④以鉛處理;使與鉛混和。*leaded* zinc. 含鉛的鋅。—*v.i.* 被鉛覆蓋或阻塞。A gun barrel may *lead.* 鎗管可能被鉛所阻塞。

lead·en [ˈlɛdn̩; ˈledn] *adj.* ①鉛製的;鉛做的。②鉛色的;淺黑色的。③沉重的;難動的。④沉悶的。⑤憂鬱的;意志消沉的。⑥低級的;低賤的。his golden tact and *leaden* taste. 他可貴的機智和低級的趣味。—*v.t.* 使沉重;使不活潑。

***lead·er** [ˈlidɚ; ˈliːdə] *n.* ①領袖;指揮者。the *leader* of a choir. 歌詠隊的指揮。②(報紙的)社論。③馬車之先導馬。The whips cracked, the *leaders* capered, and away we rattled. 鞭子噼啪地響,領頭的馬奔跑起來,我們的車嘎嘎地駛了過去。④(釣絲上的)蚊鉤。⑤吸引顧客之廉價品。a loss *leader.* (貨物之)犧牲品。⑥(*pl.*)〖印刷〗(用以指示之)點線或虛線。⑦主要辯護人。⑧(自莖端或大枝所發出的)最長大的嫩枝。⑨腱;肌肉。⑩試探性的問話。⑪居首之事物。⑫屋頂導水管。⑬膠卷或錄音帶開始之空白部分。

lead·er·ette [ˌlidəˈrɛt; ˌliːdəˈret] *n.* 〖英〗(報紙、刊物之)短篇社論;短評。

***lead·er·ship** [ˈlidɚʃɪp; ˈliːdəʃip] *n.* ①領導地位;領導權。②領導能力。There was no *leadership* in him. 他沒有領導能力。③領導階層。The party *leadership* ignored the dispute. 黨的領導階層忽視了那爭論。

lead-free [ˈlɛdˈfri; ˈledˈfriː] *adj.* 無鉛的。*lead-free* gasoline. 無鉛汽油。

lead·in [ˈlidˌɪn; ˈliːdˈin] *n.* ①〖無線電〗引入線(自天線接至接收機之線)。②連接戶外輸電線與室內電表之電線。③用以引起興趣之事物。④序言;介紹辭。—*adj.*〖無線電〗引入的。(亦作 **lead-in**)

‡**lead·ing¹** [ˈlidɪŋ; ˈliːdiŋ] *adj.* 領導的;指導的;主要的;在前的。the *leading* topics of the hour. 目前的主要論題。—*n.* ①領導;指導。The king entrusted the *leading* of the army to the earl. 國王將軍隊交給伯爵指揮。②疏導。They proposed a *leading* of excess water to arid lands. 他們提議將過量的水疏導至乾燥地區。

lead·ing² [ˈlɛdɪŋ; ˈlediŋ] *n.* ①鉛細工;鉛之覆蓋物;鉛框。②〖英〗(蓋屋頂用之)鉛板。③〖印刷〗鉛條。④鉛條;鉛板(集合稱)。

leading article ①報紙的社論。②報紙上的最重要消息;頭條新聞。(亦作 **leader**)

leading case 〖法律〗成爲判例之案件。

leading edge ①〖航空〗翼或螺旋槳之前緣。②〖航海〗最先着風之帆緣。

leading lady 〖劇〗女主角。

leading light 重要人物;領導人物。

leading man 〖劇〗男主角。

leading question 對答案有暗示性的問題。

leading rein (牽馬等之)韁繩;牽繩。

leading strings ①幼兒學步時所用之扶手索。②(尤指過分或控制性之)領導;拘束。to be in *leading strings.* 過分依賴別人;受人操縱;被牽制。

leading tone (or **note**)〖音樂〗音階中之第七音;導音。

lead line [lɛd~; led~]〖航海〗測深索;鉛條。

lead·off [ˈlidˌɔf; ˈliːdˈɔːf] *n.* ①開始;着手;最初之一手。②〖拳擊〗開賽之第一擊。③〖棒球〗第一棒打擊手。—*adj.* (亦作 **lead-off**) 起頭的;最先的。

lead pencil [lɛd~; led~] (石墨)鉛筆。

lead-pipe cinch [ˈlɛdˌpaɪp~; ˈledpaip~]〖俚〗①極容易之事。②無疑之事。

lead poisoning [lɛd~; led~]〖醫〗鉛中毒;鉛毒症。

leads·man [ˈlɛdzmən; ˈledzmən] *n., pl.* **-men.**〖航海〗測鉛手;海洋測深水夫。

lead time [lid~; liːd~] ①產品設計與實際生產間相隔之時間。②要求之提出至交貨所隔之時間。

lead-up [ˈlidʌp; ˈliːdʌp] *n.* 準備階段或步驟。

lead·work [ˈlɛdˌwɝk; ˈledwəːk] *n.* 鉛細工。

lead·y [ˈlɛdɪ; ˈledi] *adj.,* **lead·i·er, lead·i·est.** 似鉛的;含鉛的。

***leaf** [lif; liːf] *n., pl.* **leaves,** *v.* —*n.* ①樹葉;草葉。He was hidden by the *leaves.* 他爲樹葉遮住。②(書的)一張;一葉(即兩面或兩頁, two pages). There is a *leaf* missing in this book. 這本書裏差一葉。③花瓣。④(金屬)箔。gold *leaf* 金箔。⑤(活邊桌之)活邊。⑥門扇;扉。**in leaf** 生滿葉的;綠葉滿枝的。The trees will soon be *in leaf.* 樹木不久都要綠葉滿枝了。**take a leaf out of** (or **from**) **one's book** 仿傚某人;依樣畫葫蘆。**turn over a new leaf** 改過自新。—*v.i.* ①(樹)生葉。The trees *leaf* out in the spring. 樹在春季生葉。②翻書頁〖常 through〗。—*v.t.* 翻(書等)的頁。

leaf·age [ˈlifɪdʒ; ˈliːfidʒ] *n.* 葉(集合稱)。

leaf bud 〖植物〗葉芽;嫩葉。

L

leafed [lift; liːft] *adj.* 有葉子的。
leaf fat (腰子周圍之)猪油。
leaf lard 板油(由 leaf fat 煉出之最佳的猪油)。
leaf·less [ˈliflɪs; ˈliːflis] *adj.* 無葉的;不生葉的。
ˈ**leaf·let** [ˈliflɪt; ˈliːflit] *n.* ①小葉。②傳單;散葉印刷品;摺叠的印刷品。advertising *leaflets.* 廣告傳單。—*v.i.* 散發傳單、說明書等。
leaf·mold 腐葉土。
leaf·stalk [ˈlifˌstɔk; ˈliːfstɔːk] *n.* 〖植物〗葉柄。
ˈ**leaf·y** [ˈlifɪ; ˈliːfi] *adj.,* **leaf·i·er, leaf·i·est.** ①多葉的;葉叢密的。a *leafy* shrub. 多葉的樹叢。②葉狀的。—**leaf·i·ness,** *n.*
:**league**[1] [lig; liːg] *n., v.,* **leagued, lea·guing.**—*n.*①聯盟;同盟。*Leagues* are commonly made for mutual defense. 同盟通常是爲了共同防禦而締結。②同盟中之會員或國家之集合稱。③〖美〗棒球聯合會。④種類。He is a bit out of your *league.* 他是有一點跟你們格格不入。*in league* 聯合的;聯盟的。*the League* =the League of Nations. —*v.t.* 組聯盟或同盟。
league[2] *n.* 里格(長度名,約等於三英里)。
League of Nations 國際聯盟。
lea·guer[1] [ˈligɚ; ˈliːgə] *n.* 聯盟之加盟員(團體、國);盟國;入盟者。
lea·guer[2] *n.* 〖古〗圍攻;圍攻之軍隊;圍軍的陣營。
Le·ah [ˈliə; ˈliːə] *n.* ①女子名。②〖聖經〗利亞(雅各之原配:參看創世記29章16–30節)。
ˈ**leak** [lik; liːk] *n.* ①漏洞;漏隙;漏處;隙。a *leak* in the roof. 屋頂的漏雨處。②漏出之物;漏出量。③逃逸之方法。④逃逸。⑤〖俗〗小便。⑥漏電。—*v.i.* ①漏;(水、光等經由洞、隙)流入或洩出。The ship was *leaking* badly. 這船漏得厲害。②洩漏〖out〗. The news has *leaked* out. 消息洩漏出去了。—*v.t.* ①漏;使(水、氣體、光等)流入或洩出。That pipe *leaks* gas. 那管子漏氣。②洩漏。
leak·age [ˈlikɪdʒ; ˈliːkidʒ] *n.* ①漏;漏泄。②漏泄物。③漏泄量。④(祕密等的)洩漏。
leakage current 〖電〗漏失之電流。
leak·i·ness [ˈlikɪnɪs; ˈliːkinis] *n.* 漏雨;漏氣。
leak·proof [ˈlikˌpruf; ˈliːkpruːf] *adj.* 不會漏的;防漏的。
leak·y [ˈlikɪ; ˈliːki] *adj.,* **leak·i·er, leak·i·est.** 漏的;有漏隙的。
leal [lil; liːl] *adj.* 〖詩,蘇〗忠實的;信實的。*the land of the leal* 天國。
ˈ**lean**[1] [lin; liːn] *v.,* **leaned** or **leant, lean·ing,** *n.* —*v.i.* ①傾斜;傾側。②凭;靠。*Lean* on my arm. 靠在我的臂上。③傾身。to *lean* forward (back). 傾身向前(後)。to *lean* over a fence. 傾身於籬笆上;將身子伸過籬笆。④依賴;依靠。to *lean* on a friend's advice. 依賴朋友的建議。⑤傾向;偏。—*v.t.* 使傾斜;使倚凭。to *lean* a ladder against a wall. 將梯靠於牆上。*lean over backward* 〖俗〗 **a.** 矯枉過正。**b.** 盡最大努力。—*n.* 傾斜。*on the lean* 傾斜。
ˈ**lean**[2] *adj.* ①瘠瘦的;瘦的。*lean* meat. 瘦肉;筋肉。②不豐富的;歉收的;貧乏的。*lean* years. 歉收之年。a *lean* diet. 粗食。③稀薄的。④緊湊的。—*n.* 瘦肉。—*v.t.* 使消瘦。He had been *leaned* out by his illness. 他因生病而消瘦。—**ness,** *n.*
lean·ing [ˈlinɪŋ; ˈliːniŋ] *n.* ①傾斜。②傾向;嗜好;偏好。—*adj.* 傾斜的。
Leaning Tower of Pisa, the (義大利)比薩斜塔。
lean limbed 四肢瘦長的。
leant [lɛnt; lent] *v.* pt. & pp. of **lean.**
lean-to [ˈlinˌtu; ˈliːntuː] *adj., n., pl.* **-tos.** —*adj.* (屋頂)單傾斜面的;一面緊靠牆或房屋的。—*n.* ①祇有一斜面屋頂之屋。②此等屋之屋頂。
:**leap** [lip; liːp] *n., v.,* **leaped** or **leapt** [lɛpt, lipt; lept, liːpt], **leap·ing.** —*n.* ①跳;躍。The horse took the *leap* with great ease. 那匹馬輕易地躍過。②被跳過之物。③一躍之距離。a *leap* of 10 feet. 十英尺的一跳。④劇增。a *leap* of over 117 percent. 百分之一百十七以上的劇增。*a leap in the dark* 在黑暗中的跳;冒險。*by leaps and bounds* 躍進地;迅速地。Their business has grown *by leaps and bounds.* 他們的營業發展迅速。—*v.i.* ①跳;躍;猛衝。He *leapt* on his enemy with a knife in his hand. 他手持小刀向他的仇敵衝過去。②急速進步;飛躍。*leap out of one's skin* 大喜;大驚。*Look before you leap.* 三思而後行。—*v.t.* ①跳過;躍過。②使跳過;使躍過。to *leap* a horse over a hedge. 縱馬躍過樹籬。
leap day 閏日(二月二十九日)。(亦作 **leap-year day**)
leap·er [ˈlipɚ; ˈliːpə] *n.* 跳的人(馬);跳躍的東西。
leap·frog [ˈlipˌfrɑg, -ˌfrɔg; ˈliːpfrɔg] *n., v.,* **-frogged, -frog·ging.** —*n.* ①跳蛙遊戲;跳背遊戲(一人彎背站立,讓另一人跳過)。②跳蛙式前進。—*v.i.* ①作跳蛙式前進。②彼此忽前忽後地行進。—*v.t.* ①互相增進。②閃過;跳過;越過。
leap·ing [ˈlipɪŋ; ˈliːpiŋ] *n.* 跳躍(之行動)。—*adj.* ①跳躍的;跳躍而行的。②用於跳躍的。a *leaping* board. 跳板。
leap year 閏年。
leap-year [ˈlipˌjɪɚ; ˈliːp-jəː] *adj.* 閏年的。
Lear [lɪr; liə] *n.* 莎翁戲劇中的李爾王(King Lear).
:**learn** [lɝn; ləːn] *v.,* **learned** or **learnt** [lɝnt; ləːnt], **learn·ing.** —*v.t.* ①學習;學。He is *learning* French now. 他現在正在學法文。②學會;(由學而)懂得。Have you *learned* your lessons? 你的功課都學會了嗎? ③聞及;獲悉。We have not yet *learned* whether he arrived safely. 我們尙未獲悉他是否安全到達。④〖俗〗教。He *learned* me how to play chess. 他教我(如何)下棋。—*v.i.* ①學;學習。He *learns* very quickly. 他學得很快。②聞;聞悉〖of〗. to *learn* of an accident. 聞悉意外事件。*learn by heart* 默誦;默記。to *learn* a poem *by heart.* 默誦一篇詩。
learn·a·ble [ˈlɝnəbl̩; ˈləːnəbl] *adj.* 可學的;可習得的。
ˈ**learn·ed** [ˈlɝnɪd; ˈləːnid] *adj.* ①有學問的;博學的。He's a very *learned* man. 他是一個很有學問的人。②學術性的。a *learned* periodical. 學術性刊物。③有經驗的;顯示有見聞的。He was *learned* in the ways of the world. 他精通世務。—**ly,** *adv.* —**ness,** *n.* 〖注意〗**learned** (*adj.*) 中 -ed 之 e 要發音,而 **learned** (pt. & pp.) 字尾內的"e"不發音。
learned profession 需要學問的職業。
learn·er [ˈlɝnɚ; ˈləːnə] *n.* 學習者;初學者。
ˈ**learn·ing** [ˈlɝnɪŋ; ˈləːniŋ] *n.* ①學問;學識;學術。a man of great *learning.* 學識豐富的人。②學習。
:**learnt** [lɝnt; ləːnt] *v.* pt. & pp. of **learn.**

L

leas·a·ble ['lisəbl; 'li:səbl] *adj.* 可出租的。

lease** [lis; li:s] *n., v.,* **leased, leas·ing.** —*n.* 租;租期;租約。We hold the land by (*or* on) *lease.* 我們租得這塊地。 ***a new lease of (or ***on***) ***life*** 由於健康恢復或煩惱解除而重新開始的生活。 Plastic surgery has given many persons *a new lease on life.* 整形外科給許多(有殘缺的)人帶來新生活。 —*v.t.* ①租得。②租出。 He *leased* his home for the summer. 他將房子出租了一個夏季。 —*v.i.* 出租。

lease·back ['lis,bæk; 'li:sbæk] *n.* 反租(房屋、土地等轉讓後由新業主長期租給原業主使用之安排)。(亦作 **sale and leaseback**)

lease·hold ['lis,hold; 'li:should] *n.* ①租賃權。②租用之土地或建築物。—*adj.* 租得的。

lease·hold·er ['lis,holdə; 'li:s-,houldə] *n.* 土地租用人。

lease-lend ['lis'lɛnd; 'li:s'lend] *n., v.t.,* **-lent, -lend·ing,** *adj.* 〖主英〗=**lend-lease.**

leash [liʃ; li:ʃ] *n.* (牽狗等所用的) 皮帶。 ***hold*** (or ***have***) ***in leash*** 控制。 ***slip the leash*** 脫去束縛。 ***strain at the leash*** 焦急地等待獲得允許做某事。 —*v.t.* ①以皮帶束縛。②加以抑制。

‡least [list; li:st] *adj.* 最小的;最少的;最不重要的。The *least* bit of dirt in a watch may make it stop. 錶中最少量的污物都可能使它停止不走。 ***not the least*** 一點也沒有。You *haven't the least* chance of success. 你連一點成功的機會都沒有。 —*n.* 最少;最小;最少量。 That's the (very) *least* of it. 那是最不重要的一點。 ***at*** (***the***) ***least*** 至少。 You should read one book a month *at least.* 你至少應該每月讀一本書。 ***least of all*** 最不(應該); 尤其不。 He liked that book *least of all.* 他最不喜歡那本書。 ***not in the least*** 一點也不 (= not at all). This book is *not in the least* difficult. 這本書一點也不難讀。 ***The least said the better.*** 說得愈少愈好;最好不說。 ***to say the least of it*** 至少可以如此說(尚且不說其他)。 —*adv.* 最少; 最不; 最沒有。 the *least* interesting. 最沒有趣味的。

least common multiple 〖數學〗最小公倍數。(略作 **L. C. M.**)

least·wise ['list,waɪz; 'li:stwaiz] *adv.* 〖俗〗至少;無論如何。(亦作 **leastways**)

‡leath·er ['lɛðə; 'leðə] *n.* ①皮革。 The book is bound in *leather.* 此書係用皮面裝訂。②皮革製品。③狗耳朶下垂之部分。④馬鐙皮帶。 —*adj.* 皮革製的; 皮的。 *Leather* gloves are stronger than cotton gloves. 皮手套比棉手套結實。—*v.t.* ①覆以皮革。②〖俗〗以皮鞭打; 鞭笞。 I'd like to *leather* him black and blue. 我要把他揍得青一塊紫一塊的。

leath·er·back ['lɛðə,bæk; 'leðə:-bæk] *n.* 赤道區之大海龜, 體重有時達一噸。

leather cloth 皮布; 防水布。(亦作 **leathercoat**)

leath·er·craft ['lɛðə,kræft; 'leðə-kra:ft] *n.* ①皮製工藝品。②皮革手工之技巧。

leath·er·ette [,lɛðə'rɛt; ,leðə'ret] *n.* 假皮;人造皮。

leath·er·head ['lɛðə,hɛd; 'leðəhed] *n.* ①〖俚〗笨蛋。②(澳洲產之) 一種禿頭鳥。

leath·er-lunged ['lɛðə'lʌŋd; 'leðə'lʌŋd] *adj.* 大嗓門的。

leath·ern ['lɛðən; 'leðən] *adj.* ①革的;革製的。②似革的。

leath·er·neck ['lɛðə,nɛk; 'leðənek] *n.* 〖俚〗美海軍陸戰隊員。

leath·er·oid ['lɛðə,rɔɪd; 'leðərɔid] *n* 〖商標名〗(L-)假皮;人造皮;假皮紙(用以製皮包等)。 —*adj.* 假皮製成的; 人造皮的。

leather paper 假皮紙。

leath·er·work ['lɛðə,wɜk; 'leðə-wə:k] *n.* ①皮革裝潢。②皮革製品。—**er,** *n*

leath·er·y ['lɛðərɪ; 'leðəri] *adj.* 似革的;堅韌的;粗糙的。

‡leave¹ [liv; li:v] *v.,* **left** [lɛft; left], **leav·ing.** —*v.t.* ①留置;置放。 *Leave* the book on the table. 將書留放在桌子上。②遺置;忘記。I've *left* my things at home. 我把我的東西忘記在家裏了。 ③讓; 聽任。 *Leave* things as they are. 一切聽其自然。④離開;離別;辭去。 When did you *leave* London? 你甚麼時候離開倫敦的? ⑤(死後)遺留。He *left* his house to his brother. 他將他的房子遺留給他的兄弟。⑥付託;委託;依賴。All right, *leave* the matter to me. 好的,這事交給我辦罷。⑦剩餘。 Six from nine *leaves* three. 九減六餘三。⑧走過;經過。⑨遺棄。⑩留下。 The wound *left* a scar. 那傷口留下一個疤。⑪放棄或停止。He *left* drinking nearly two years. 他差不多有兩年未喝酒。⑫省略;遺漏; 不提〖常 off, out〗. to *leave* out information in a report. 報告中有些資料未提及。—*v.i.* ①出發;啓程;往;赴〖for〗. We're *leaving* for Canada soon. 我們不久就要到加拿大去。②停止〖off〗. Has the rain *left* off yet? 雨是否已經停止? ③離去。We *leave* tonight. 我們今晚走。 ***leave alone*** 別管;別干涉;別攪擾。 *Leave* that box *alone.* 別管那箱子。 ***leave behind*** 忘記携帶; 遺落; 棄置。Oh dear! The bag has been *left behind.* 哦! 袋子忘記帶了。 ***leave behind one*** 丟棄。 I've *left* my dirty clothes *behind me.* 我已將我的髒衣服丟棄了。 ***leave go of*** 放手;放掉。 ***leave hold of*** =leave go of. ***leave off*** **a.** 脫去(衣服)。It's hot today—I think I'll *leave off* my coat. 今天天氣很熱,我想我要脫去我的上衣。 **b.** 戒除 (習慣);停止;放棄。*Leave off* your bad habits. 戒除你的壞習慣。 ***leave out*** 遺漏;忽略;省略。 ***leave*** (***a matter***) ***over*** 拖延(一事)。 ***leave over*** 剩餘。There was nothing *left over.* 沒有一點東西剩餘下來。 ***leave room*** (or ***place***) ***for*** 留出空位讓給。 ***leave school*** 畢業。 Has your brother *left school* yet? 你的兄弟畢業了嗎? ***leave somebody to himself*** (or ***his own devices***)不管他;讓他隨便行動。 ***leave word*** (***with somebody***)(***for something***) 留言;留信。

leave²** *n.* ①許可;同意。 You have my *leave* to do what you like. 我允許你自由活動。 ②請假; 准假; 假期。 to ask for *leave.* 請假。a six months' *leave.* 六個月的假。③離開;告別。 to take one's *leave.* 告別。 ***leave of absence 休假。 ***on leave*** 告假中;休假中。 ***take leave of*** 向…告別。 ***take leave of one's senses*** 發狂。 Have you *taken leave of your senses?*你發狂了嗎?

leave³ *v.i.,* **leaved, leav·ing.** 長葉;生葉。

leave·break·er ['liv,brekə; 'li:v-,breikə] *n.* 〖軍〗休假終了尚未歸艦之水兵。

leaved [livd; liːvd] *adj.* ①有葉的;(有)…葉的。 a narrow-*leaved* tree. 狹葉樹。 ②(門等)…扇的。a two-*leaved* screen. 二折屏風。

leav·en [ˈlɛvən; ˈlevən] *n.* ①酵;酵母。②(瀰漫社會的)影響力;潛在勢力。③氣味;色彩。—*v.t.* ①混以酵母;使發酵。②影響;感化;使逐漸改變。

leav·er [ˈlivɚ; ˈliːvə] *n.* ①離開者。②〖英〗退學者(尤指退學覓職者)。

leaves [livz; liːvz] *n.* pl. of **leaf.**

leave-tak·ing [ˈlivˌtekɪŋ; ˈliːvˌteikiŋ] *n.* 告別;道別。

leav·ings [ˈlivɪŋz; ˈliːviŋz] *n. pl.* 渣滓;糟粕;殘餘。

Leb·a·non [ˈlɛbənən; ˈlebənən] *n.* 黎巴嫩(國名,位於地中海東岸,巴勒斯坦北部,首都貝魯特 Beirut). —**Leb·a·nese,** *adj., n.*

Le·bens·raum [ˈlebənsˌraum; ˈleibənsraum] 〖德〗 *n.* ①生存空間(德國納粹理論中認爲滿足一國生存所需資源的領土)。②生活、生長或活動所需之空間。③行動之自由。(亦作 **lebensraum**)

lech·er [ˈlɛtʃɚ; ˈletʃə] *n.* 好色之徒;色情狂者。—*v.i.* 耽於色情。

lech·er·ous [ˈlɛtʃərəs; ˈletʃərəs] *adj.* ①好色的;淫蕩的。②邪淫的;誘人起淫思的。

lech·er·y [ˈlɛtʃərɪ; ˈletʃəri] *n.* ①好色;淫蕩;縱慾。②好色的行爲;淫蕩的行爲。

lec·i·thin [ˈlɛsəθɪn; ˈlesiθin] *n.* 〖生化〗磷脂;蛋黃素(含於腦、神經體素、卵黃、及植物種子等之中)。

lec·tern [ˈlɛktən; ˈlektəːn] *n.* ①教堂中的讀經台。②桌面傾斜的講台。

lec·tion [ˈlɛkʃən; ˈlekʃən] *n.* ①(一特定版本中某章句之)本文;讀法。②〖宗教〗(禮拜儀式中選讀之)聖句;日課。

lec·tion·ar·y [ˈlɛkʃənˌɛrɪ; ˈlekʃənəri] *n., pl.* **-ar·ies.** 〖宗教〗聖句集;日課表。

lec·tor [ˈlɛktɚ; ˈlektə] *n.* 大學講師。

lec·tor·ate [ˈlɛktərɪt; ˈlektərit] *n.* 大學講師職位。

lec·ture [ˈlɛktʃɚ; ˈlektʃə] *n., v.,* **-tured, -tur·ing.** —*n.* ①演講(特指有教育和學術性者)。*lectures* on Greek philosophy. 希臘哲學演講。②教訓;訓誡;譴責。 —*v.i.* 演講;開演講課。 —*v.t.* ①對…演講。 He was *lecturing* a group of tourists. 他對著一羣旅客演講。②訓誡;責罵。

lec·tur·er [ˈlɛktʃərɚ; ˈlektʃərə] *n.* ①講演人;講課人。He is the best *lecturer* on the campus. 他是那校園內講課講得最好的。②(英國等大學的)講師。③訓誡者。

lec·ture·ship [ˈlɛktʃɚˌʃɪp; ˈlektʃəʃip] *n.* 講師之職位。

lecture theater 階梯式教室。

led [lɛd; led] *v.* pt. & pp. of **lead**¹. —*adj.* 被領導的;受控制的。

ledge [lɛdʒ; ledʒ] *n.* ①(牆壁等)突出之狹長部分。 a window *ledge.* 窗枱。②岩石面之突出部分。 a *ledge* of rock on the side of a cliff. 峭壁邊上突出的石頭。③(距海岸不太遠的)暗礁。④礦層;礦脈。

ledg·er [ˈlɛdʒɚ; ˈledʒə] *n.* ①〖簿記〗總帳。②〖建築〗(修建或油漆房屋時,外層所架設之竹、木架子上的)橫板。③(釣魚時)投置水中之餌。④蓋於墓上之大石板。—*adj.* 不動的;固定的。

ledger bait 底餌(固定於一處的釣魚餌,通常放在水底)。

ledger line 附有底餌之釣絲。

Lee [li; liː] *n.* 男子名。

lee [li; liː] *n.* ①庇蔭;庇蔭處。②避風處。③〖航海〗風吹向處;下風處。—*adj.* ①避風的。the *lee* side of a ship. 一隻船的下風之一邊。②下風處的。

lee·board [ˈliˌbord; ˈliːbɔːd] *n.* 〖航海〗下風板(附在平底船兩側,防止船向下風方向漂流)。

leech [litʃ; liːtʃ] *n.* ①〖動物〗水蛭。②榨取他人利益者;食客。③〖古〗醫生。④〖醫〗一種抽血的器具。⑤〖航海〗縱帆之外緣。 ***stick like a leech*** 緊緊附着而不離。—*v.t.* ①〖古〗醫治。②抽…的血;用水蛭吸…的血。 —*v.i.* 緊緊附着。

leek [lik; liːk] *n.* 〖植物〗韮。 ***eat the leek*** 忍氣吞聲。 ***not worth a leek*** 一文不值。

Lee Kuan Yew [ˈliˈkwɑnˈjau; ˈliːˈkwɑːnˈjau] 李光耀(1923–, 新加坡政治領袖,自1959年任總理)。

leer [lɪr; liə] *n.* ①秋波;媚眼;睨視。②含惡意或淫意的一瞥。 —*v.i.* 送秋波;使媚眼;含惡意或淫意地睨視。 —*v.t.* 以(目)相挑。 ***leer one's eyes at*** 向…送秋波。

leer·y [ˈlɪrɪ; ˈliəri] *adj.,* **leer·i·er, leer·i·est.** ①送秋波的;使媚眼的;睨視的。②〖俚〗提防的;多疑的〖of〗。③〖俚〗狡猾的;機敏的。

lees [liz; liːz] *n. pl.* 沉於杯底的殘渣。 ***drink*** (or ***drain***) ***a cup to the lees*** 乾杯;歷盡辛酸。

lee shore 下風頭之海岸(對航行中之帆船爲一大威脅)。 ***on a lee shore*** 在困難或危險中。

Lee Tsung-dao [ˈliˈdʒʌŋˈdau; ˈliːˈdʒʌŋˈdau] 李政道(1926–, 歸化美國之中國科學家,與楊振寧因在基本物理學定律"對等性之觀念"上之理論研究而共同獲得1957年之諾貝爾物理獎)。

lee·ward [ˈliwɚd; ˈliːwəd] *adj.* 在下風方向的。—*adv.* 向下風地。 —*n.* 在下風的一側。on the *leeward.* 在下風之方向。

lee·way [ˈliˌwe; ˈliːwei] *n.* ①〖航海〗風壓(船隻或飛機被風吹向下風處而離航線);風壓差;風壓角。②時間之損失;落後。to make up *leeway.* 脫出逆境。③〖俗〗活動的餘地;充裕之時間。④選擇之餘地;改變之餘地。

‡left¹ [lɛft; left] *adj.* ①在左的;左方的;左側的(爲 right 之對)。Not many people can write with the *left* hand. 沒有多少人能用左手寫字。②左翼的;左傾的;急進的。 —*n.* ①左方;左側。Come and sit on my *left.* 來坐到我的左邊。②急進派。③〖拳擊〗用左手的一擊;左拳。He knocked out his opponent with a fast *left.* 他用快速的左拳擊倒了他的對手。***the Left*** 左派。—*adv.* ①在(向)左邊。to turn *left.* 向左轉。②左傾地。

‡left² *v.* pt. & pp. of **leave**¹. ***get left*** 〖俚〗 **a.** 競爭中被丢在後面;落後。 **b.** 失望。

left-face [ˈlɛftˈfes; ˈleftˈfeis] *v.i.,* **-faced, -fac·ing.** 作向左轉的動作。

left field 〖棒球〗左外野。 ***out in left field*** 〖俚〗完全錯誤。

left fielder 〖棒球〗左外野手。

left-foot·ed [ˈlɛftˈfutɪd; ˈleftˈfutid] *adj.* ①左脚較强的。②笨拙的;不自然的。

left-hand [ˈlɛftˈhænd; ˈlefthænd] *adj.* ①左方的。②左手的;用左手的。③不自然的;勉强的;不合條理的。④不合法的。

left-hand·ed [ˈlɛftˈhændɪd; ˈleftˈhændid] *adj.* ①慣用左手的;拙笨的。That man is *left-handed.* 那個人是慣用左手的。

②用左手做的。③左旋的；反時鐘方向的。④無誠意的；可疑的。*a left-handed compliment* 口是心非的恭維話；帶有諷刺意味的恭維話。—*adv.* ①用左手。The ball was pitched *left-handed*. 球被用左手投出。②朝左邊；朝反時鐘方向。

left-handed marriage 貴族男子與平民之婚姻；門戶不相當之結婚。

left-hand·er 〔ˈlɛftˈhændɚ; ˈleftˈhændə〕 *n.* ①慣用左手的人；由左手操用的東西。②〖棒球〗左手投球手。③〖拳擊〗左手之擊打；左拳。

left·ish 〔ˈlɛftɪʃ; ˈleftiʃ〕 *adj.* 左派的；左翼的。

left·ism 〔ˈlɛftɪzm̩; ˈleftizəm〕 *n.* 左翼主義（政治上之過激思想、行動等）。（亦作 Leftism）

left·ist 〔ˈlɛftɪst; ˈleftist〕 *n.* ①左派議員；左派的人；社會主義者。②左撇子。—*adj.* 左派的；左翼的；過激的。

left-lug·gage 〔ˈlɛftˈlʌgɪdʒ; ˈleftˈlʌgidʒ〕 *n.* 〖英〗存放之行李。

left-luggage office 行李房。

left-off 〔ˈlɛftˈɔf; ˈleftˈɔːf〕 *adj.* 捨棄的；不用的；脫掉的。

left·o·ver 〔ˈlɛftˌovɚ; ˈleftˌouvə〕 *adj.* 殘餘的；賸下的。—*n.* 剩餘物；剩飯。

left·ward 〔ˈlɛftwɚd; ˈleftwəd〕 *adv.* & *adj.* 在左方(的)；向左(的)。

left·wards 〔ˈlɛftwɚdz; ˈleftwədz〕 *adv.* =**leftward.**

left wing ①(政治上之)左翼(政黨)；急進派。②(各種球類運動中之)左翼(隊員)。

left-wing 〔ˈlɛftˌwɪŋ; ˈleftwiŋ〕 *adj.* 左翼的；急進的。

left·wing·er 〔ˈlɛftˈwɪŋɚ; ˈleftˈwiŋə〕 *n.* ①(球類運動之)左翼隊員。②=**leftist.**

left·y 〔ˈlɛftɪ; ˈlefti〕 *n., pl.* **left·ies.** ①〖美俚〗慣用左手的人；左撇子（常用作綽號)。②〖棒球〗左手投手。③(英國常指)左派人士或社會主義者。

‡**leg** 〔lɛg; leg〕 *n., v.,* **legged, leg·ging.** —*n.* ①腿；足。A man has two *legs*; a dog has four. 人有兩腿；狗有四腿。②衣物的腿部。③(桌、椅等的)腿；脚。the *legs* of a chair. 椅腿。④旅行中的一段路程。the first *leg* of a round-the-world flight. 環球飛行之第一段路程。⑤(三角形之)腰。⑥(船)搶風直駛之一段航程。⑦接力賽中每人所負責的距離。⑧屈膝禮（一腿後退另一腿彎曲而行之禮)。***be all legs***（指人）長得過高而細瘦。***feel*** (or ***find***) ***one's legs***（指嬰孩）能立；能行走。***give a person a leg up*** 扶人上馬；(轉爲）助人克服困難。***have not a leg to stand on***（對自己的行動)無理由可申述。***on one's hind legs***〖諧〗=**on one's legs.** ***on one's last*** (or ***its***) ***legs*** 將死；將失敗；黔驢技窮。He looked like he was *on his last legs*. 他看來好像要死了。***on one's legs*** 起立(作演說等)；(病後)能行動的。***pull a person's leg*** a. 開玩笑。b. 欺騙；愚弄。***set a person on his legs*** 使某人恢復健康；使某人事業繁榮。***shake a leg***〖俗〗跳舞。***stand on one's own legs*** 自立；不依賴人。***stretch one's legs***（久坐之後）出外散步。***take to one's legs*** 逃逸。***talk the hind leg(s) off a donkey*** (***dog,*** or ***horse***)〖美俗〗喋喋不休。***walk a man off his legs*** 使某人走得疲倦。—*v.i.*〖俗〗走；跑(常與 it 連用)。We couldn't get a ride so we had to *leg* it. 我們搭不上車，祇得走路。***leg up*** 扶（人）上馬。

leg·a·cy 〔ˈlɛgəsɪ; ˈlegəsi〕 *n., pl.* **-cies** ①〖法〗遺產；遺贈物。②祖先傳下來的東西；遺物。Books are the *legacies* that a great genius leaves to mankind. 書籍是偉大天才留給人類的遺物。

legacy duty (or **tax**) 遺產稅。

***le·gal** 〔ˈligl̩; ˈliːgəl〕 *adj.* ①法律的；法律上的。to take *legal* action. 提起訴訟。②法定的。③律師的。④法律承認的；合法的。

legal age 法定年齡。

legal cap 〖美〗(律師用之)長形格子紙。

legal holiday 法定假日。

le·gal·ism 〔ˈligl̩ˌɪzəm; ˈliːgəlizəm〕 *n.* ①(極端的)守法主義；合法主義。②〖神學〗律法尊重主義(靠善行得救的學說)。③法律術語(尤指空洞無內容者)。④(L-)(中國哲學中之)法家思想。

le·gal·ist 〔ˈligəlɪst; ˈliːgəlist〕 *n.* ①守法主義者。②法律專家。③〖神學〗律法尊重主義者。④(L-)(中國哲學中之)法家。

le·gal·is·tic 〔ˌligl̩ˈɪstɪk; ˌliːgəˈlistik〕 *adj.* 守法主義的；律法尊重主義的。

le·gal·i·ty 〔lɪˈgælətɪ; liːˈgæliti〕 *n., pl.* **-ties.** ①合法性；正當。②墨守法規。③〖神學〗對於行善而非對於神恩之依賴。

le·gal·i·za·tion 〔ˌligl̩əˈzeʃən; ˌliːgəlaiˈzeiʃən〕 *n.* 合法化。

le·gal·ize 〔ˈligl̩ˌaɪz; ˈliːgəlaiz〕 *v.t.,* **-ized, -iz·ing.** 法定；使合法化；法律認可。

***le·gal·ly** 〔ˈliglɪ; ˈliːgəli〕 *adv.* 在法律上；從法律的觀點。*Legally* she had no claim to the estate. 在法律上她對那筆財產沒有要求的權利。

legal name ①依法登記之姓名。②依法登記之公司行號或團體名稱。

legal representative 法定代理人。

legal reserve (銀行之)法定準備金。

legal right 合法權利。

legal separation (夫婦)法律上之分居。

legal tender 〖法律〗法定貨幣。

legal weight 貨物之實重。

leg art 〖美俚〗以大腿曲線美爲主題之照片；裸體或半裸體照片；大腿藝術。

leg·a·tar·y 〔ˈlɛgəˌtɛrɪ; ˈlegətəri〕 *adj.* 遺產的；遺贈的。—*n.* =**legatee.**

leg·ate[1] 〔ˈlɛgɪt; ˈlegit〕 *n.* ①羅馬教皇的使節。②使節；使者。③(古羅馬之)副將；副總督。

le·gate[2] 〔lɪˈget; liˈgeit〕 *v.t.,* **-gat·ed, -gat·ing.** 遺贈。

leg·a·tee 〔ˌlɛgəˈti; ˌlegəˈtiː〕 *n.* 受遺產者；受遺贈者。

leg·a·tine 〔ˈlɛgətɪn; ˈlegətain〕 *adj.* 教皇使節的；使節的；公使的；大使的。

le·ga·tion 〔lɪˈgeʃən; liˈgeiʃən〕 *n.* ①公使館全體人員。②公使館。③公使之職權。④公使之派遣。⑤公使之任務。

le·ga·to 〔lɪˈgato; leˈgɑːtou〕〖義〗*adj.* & *adv.*〖音樂〗圓滑的(地)。

le·ga·tor 〔lɪˈgetɚ; liˈgeitə〕 *n.* 〖法律〗①遺贈人。②立遺囑人。

leg bail 〖俚〗逃獄；逃亡。to give *leg bail.* 逃亡。

leg bye 〖板球〗因球打中擊球人而得之分。

***leg·end** 〔ˈlɛdʒənd; ˈledʒənd〕 *n.* ①傳奇；稗史。②傳奇文學。Some cartoons are good enough to become *legend*. 有些漫畫好得可以成爲傳奇文學。③傳奇性人物。He became a *legend* in his own time. 他成了他那個時代的傳奇性人物。④(錢幣或獎章上的）刻字。⑤(繪畫、地圖等的)說明；圖例。—**ist,** *n.*

leg·end·ar·y 〔ˈlɛdʒəndˌɛrɪ; ˈledʒəndəri〕 *adj.* 傳奇的；野史的。—*n.* ①傳奇故事

書；傳奇故事集。②傳奇文學作家。 —**leg·end·ar·i·ly,** *adv.*

leg·end·ry ['lɛdʒəndrɪ; 'ledʒəndri] *n.* 傳說(集合稱)；傳奇文學。

leg·er·de·main [ˌlɛdʒədɪ'men; 'ledʒədə'mein] *n.* ①手法；(魔術家之)戲法；障眼法。②詐術。③詭辯。

-legged 〖字尾〗表 "有…腿的"之義，如：a four-*legged* animal. 四足動物。

leg·gings ['lɛgɪŋz; 'legiŋz] *n. pl.* 護脛；裹腿；綁腿。

leg guard 護膝(尤指冰上曲棍球等所用的)。

leg·gy ['lɛgɪ; 'legi] *adj.* ①長腿的。②腿長得很難看的。③莖細長的(樹等)。④暴露大腿的。

Leg·horn ['lɛgˌhɔrn; 'leg'hɔːn *for* ① 'lɛgən; le'gɔːn *for* ② 'lɛgən; 'leghɔːn *for* ③] *n.* ①來亨(義大利西部一港埠)。②(偶作 l-)來亨鷄。③(l-)來亨產的一種草；該草編的闊邊平頂草帽。

leg·i·bil·i·ty [ˌlɛdʒə'bɪlətɪ; ˌledʒə'biliti] *n.* 易讀；易認。

leg·i·ble ['lɛdʒəbl; 'ledʒəbl] *adj.* ①(字跡等)易認識的；易讀的；清楚的。②可看出的；可辨認的。—**leg·i·bly,** *adv.*

*__le·gion__ ['lidʒən; 'liːdʒən] *n.* ①古羅馬之軍團(約由三千至六千人組成，其中約有三百至七百爲騎兵)。②軍事性或半軍事性之單位。③聲勢浩大之武裝人員；軍隊。④衆多的人或物。He has a *legion* of devoted followers. 他有衆多的忠實信徒。*__the Legion__* **a.** 美國退伍軍人協會(＝the American Legion). **b.** 法國之外籍兵團。

le·gion·ar·y ['lidʒənˌɛrɪ; 'liːdʒənəri] *adj., n., pl.* **-ar·ies.** —*adj.* 軍團的；組成軍團的。—*n.* ①古羅馬軍團中之一分子。②英國退伍軍人協會會員。

le·gioned ['lidʒənd; 'liːdʒənd] *adj.* 組成軍團的。

Le·gion·naire [ˌlidʒən'ɛr; ˌliːdʒə'nɛə] *n.* ①〖美〗退伍軍人協會會員。②法國外籍兵團團員。③(l-)＝**legionary.**

Legion of Merit 美國之功勳勳章，由總統頒給美國或盟國之有功人員。

leg-i·ron ['lɛgˌaɪən; 'legˌaiən] *n.* 足鐐。(亦作 **leg iron**)

leg·is·late ['lɛdʒɪsˌlet; 'ledʒisleit] *v.,* **-lat·ed, -lat·ing.** —*v.i.* 制定法律；立法。to *legislate* against gambling. 立法禁止賭博。—*v.t.* 立法迫使；立法創造。The council *legislated* him out of office. 議會立法革除他的職務。

*__leg·is·la·tion__ [ˌlɛdʒɪs'leʃən; ˌledʒis'leiʃən] *n.* ①立法；制定法律。The major function of Congress is *legislation.* 國會的主要權責是立法。②法律。

*__leg·is·la·tive__ ['lɛdʒɪsˌletɪv; 'ledʒislətiv, -leit-] *adj.* ①關於立法的。②有權制定法律的；立法的。a *legislative* body. 立法機構。③法律規定的。—*n.* 立法機構。

Legislative Assembly (某些國家)兩院制立法機構之下院。

Legislative Council (某些國家)兩院制立法機構之上院。

leg·is·la·tive·ly ['lɛdʒɪsˌletɪvlɪ; 'ledʒisleitivli] *adv.* 以立法的方式；在立法方面；以立法者身分。

Legislative Yuan (中國的)立法院。

leg·is·la·tor ['lɛdʒɪsˌletɚ; 'ledʒisleitə] *n.* 制定法律者；議員；立法委員。

*__leg·is·la·ture__ ['lɛdʒɪsˌletʃɚ; 'ledʒisleitʃə] *n.* 立法機關；議會(如英國的 Parliament, 美國的 Congress). The *legislature* in every state except Nebraska is a bicameral body. 除 Nebraska 外，每州的立法機關都是兩院制。

le·gist ['lidʒɪst; 'liːdʒist] *n.* ①法律學者；精通法律者。②(L-)(中國古代哲學之)法家(＝Legalists).

le·git [lə'dʒɪt; lə'dʒit] *n.* 〖俚〗＝**legitimate drama.** —*adj.* 〖俚〗＝**legitimate.**

le·git·i·ma·cy [lɪ'dʒɪtəməsɪ; li'dʒitiməsi] *n.* ①合法性；正當。②嫡出；正統。

*__le·git·i·mate__[1] [lɪ'dʒɪtəmɪt; li'dʒitimit] *adj.* ①合法的；正當的。②正式婚生的；嫡出的。a *legitimate* child. 嫡出子。③理由充足的；合理的。a *legitimate* reason for being absent from school. 缺課之充足的理由。④合乎一般標準的。⑤根據繼承權準則的。⑥合理的；合乎邏輯的。⑦眞正的。⑧舞臺的。—*n.* (the-) ＝**legitimate drama** (or **stage**).

*__le·git·i·mate__[2] [lɪ'dʒɪtəˌmet; li'dʒitimeit] *v.t.* ①使合法；認爲正當。It was *legitimated* by the majority of the voters. 這事被大多數投票者認爲正當。②立爲嫡嗣。

legitimate drama ①專門適用於舞臺之戲劇(不適用於作電影劇本)。②文藝性之戲劇(別於歌舞雜耍等)。

le·git·i·mate·ly [lɪ'dʒɪtəmɪtlɪ; li'dʒitimitli] *adv.* 正當地；合理地；合法地。

legitimate stage (or **theater**) 舞臺戲劇。

le·git·i·ma·tion [lɪˌdʒɪtə'meʃən; liˌdʒiti'meiʃən] *n.* ①(使)合法；認爲正當。②認爲嫡出；立嫡。

le·git·i·ma·tize [lɪ'dʒɪtəməˌtaɪz; li'dʒitimətaiz] *v.t.,* **-tized, -tiz·ing.** ＝**legitimate**[2].

le·git·i·mism [lɪ'dʒɪtəmɪzm; li'dʒitimizəm] *n.* 正統主義。

le·git·i·mist [lɪ'dʒɪtəmɪst; li'dʒitimist] *n.* (王位繼承的)正統主義者。—*adj.* 正統主義的。

le·git·i·mi·za·tion [lɪˌdʒɪtəmɪ'zeʃən; liˌdʒitimai'zeiʃən] *n.* ＝**legitimation.**

le·git·i·mize [lɪ'dʒɪtəˌmaɪz; li'dʒitimaiz] *v.t.,* **-mized, -miz·ing.** ＝**legitimate**[2].

leg·man ['lɛgmən; 'legmən] *n., pl.* **-men.** 〖美〗①通訊記者；外勤記者；訪員。②爲專欄作家奔走蒐集資料的助理員。

leg-of-mut·ton ['lɛgə'mʌtn̩; 'legəv'mʌtn] *adj.* 羊腿形的；一端寬一端窄的。(亦作 **leg-o'-mutton**)

leg·pull ['lɛgˌpul; 'legpul] *n.* 〖俚〗惡作劇；愚弄。

leg-rest ['lɛgrɛst; 'legrest] *n.* (病人用的)脚凳。

leg·room ['lɛgˌrum; 'legruːm] *n.* (座位前)伸脚之餘地。

leg show 暴露大腿的表演。

leg·ume ['lɛgjum; 'legjuːm] *n.* ①莢豆。②豆莢。③(作爲蔬菜的)豆類。

le·gu·men [lɪ'gjumən; li'gjuːmən] *n., pl.* **-mi·na** [-mɪnə; -minə]. ＝**legume.**

le·gu·min [lɪ'gjumɪn; li'gjuːmin] *n.* 〖生化〗豆類蛋白質；豆球朊。

le·gu·mi·nous [lɪ'gjumənəs; li'gjuːminəs] *adj.* ①豆的；似豆的；生豆的。②豆科的。

leg work 〖俗〗走路；跑腿(如外勤記者等)。(亦作 **legwork**)

lehr [lɪr; liə] *n.* 玻璃鍛燒爐。

le·hu·a [lɪ'huɑ; lei'huːɑː] *n.* (夏威夷及太平洋諸島嶼產)桃金孃樹；其木材；其花。

lei [le;ˈleii] *n.* (夏威夷人戴在頸上的)花圈。
Leib·nitz [ˈlaɪbnɪts; ˈlaibnits] *n.* 萊布尼玆 (Gottfried Wilhelm von, 1646–1716, 德國哲學家及數學家)。 「以魚叉刺(魚)。」
leis·ter [ˈlistə; ˈliːstə] *n.* 魚叉。—*v.t.*
lei·sure** [ˈliʒə, ˈlɛʒə; ˈleʒə] *n.* ①空閒; 閒暇。I have not a moment's *leisure.* 我沒有一點空閒。②自在; 不勉强。at leisure*** **a.** 在閒暇中的;閒暇的。I am quite *at leisure.* 我十分空閒。**b.** 慢慢地; 不匆忙地。**c.** 失業。***at one's leisure*** 當其空閒的時候。Please do it *at your leisure.* 請你在閒暇時做一下。—*adj.* ①空閒的; 閒暇的。*leisure* time. 閒暇的時間。②有空閒的。the *leisure* class. 有閒階級。③(衣服)閒暇時穿的。
lei·sured [ˈliʒɚd; ˈleʒəd] *adj.* ①有空暇的。②不慌不忙的;從容不迫的。
***lei·sure·ly** [ˈliʒəlɪ, ˈlɛʒəlɪ; ˈleʒəli] *adv.* 不匆忙地; 悠閒地。to work *leisurely.* 悠閒地工作。—*adj.* 不匆忙的; 審愼的。*leisurely* movements. 不慌不忙的動作。—**lei·sure·li·ness,** *n.* 「*adj.* 空閒的;有閒暇的。」
lei·sure-time[ˈliʒəˈtaɪm;ˈleʒəˈtaim]
leit·mo·tif, leit·mo·tiv [ˈlaɪtmoˌtif; ˈlaitmouˌtiːf] *n.* ①〖音樂〗示導動機; 主樂旨。②反覆出現的主題;主旨;中心思想。
LEM Lunar Excursion Module. 太空船之登月艙。 「情人;情夫;(尤指)情婦。」
lem·an [ˈlɛmən; ˈlemən] *n.* 〖古〗愛人;
lem·ma [ˈlɛmə; ˈlemə] *n., pl.* **-ma·ta** [-mətə; -mətə], **-mas.** ①輔助定理;輔助命題。②(文章、議論等之)主題。③(字典等之)標題字。 「(北極地方產)旅鼠。」
lem·ming [ˈlɛmɪŋ; ˈlemiŋ] *n.* 〖動物〗
***lem·on** [ˈlɛmən; ˈlemən] *n.* ①檸檬;檸檬樹。②檸檬色; 淡黃色。③〖俚〗令人討厭之物;無價值之物。He found he had created a *lemon.* 他發覺他所創造的是一種沒有甚麼價值的東西。—*adj.* ①檸檬色的; 淡黃色的。The winter afternoon glowed with a hazy *lemon* light. 淡黃色的光朦朧地照着那多天的下午。②檸檬味的。*lemon* tea. 檸檬茶。 「*n.* 檸檬水。」
***lem·on·ade** [ˌlɛmənˈed; ˌleməˈneid]
lemon drop 檸檬糖。 「蘇打水)。」
lemon squash 〖英〗檸檬水(檸檬汁加
lemon squeezer 檸檬榨汁器。
le·mur [ˈlimɚ; ˈliːmə] *n.* 〖動物〗(Madagascar 島產之)狐猴。
Le·nard [ˈlenɑrt; ˈleinɑːt] *n.* 雷納特 (Philipp, 1862–1947, 德國物理學家, 曾獲1905年諾貝爾物理獎)。
:lend [lɛnd; lend] *v.,* **lent, lend·ing.** —*v.t.* ①借出;借與。Please *lend* me five dollars. 請借給我五塊錢。②貸(款)。Banks *lend* money and charge interest. 銀行貸款取息。③增添。A becoming dress *lends* charm to a girl. 合身的衣服能使女性增益其美。④提供。⑤使(自己或本身)適合於。***lend itself to*** 適合。***lend oneself to*** 幫助;協助;參與。—*v.i.* 貸款。
lend·er [ˈlɛndɚ; ˈlendə] *n.* 借錢予人者。
lend·ing [ˈlɛndɪŋ; ˈlendiŋ] *n.* ①借出; 貸與。②借出或借入之物。
lending library 收費出租書籍的圖書館;租書店。(亦作 **circulating library, rental library**)
lend-lease [ˈlɛndˈlis; ˈlendˈliːs] *n., adj., v.,* **-leased, -leas·ing.** —*n.* 資援(二次大戰時美國通過租借法案, Lend-Lease Act, 對盟國所作的物資、武器援助)。—*adj.* (根據)租借法案的。—*v.t.* 根據租借法案予以資援。
Lend-Lease Act 租借法案(美國國會於1941年3月授權總統對盟國援助之法案)。
:length [lɛŋkθ, lɛŋθ; leŋθ, leŋkθ] *n.* ①長; 長度。What is the *length* of the story? 這故事有多長? ②時間;期間。③一段; 一截。④(紙牌遊戲中) 超過平均數之紙牌數。He had *length* in trumps. 他有超過平均數的王牌。⑤船或馬等的長度(競賽時作長度的單位)。The horse won by two *lengths.* 此馬以二馬的身長獲勝。***at full length***全身伸展地。***at length*** **a.** 最後;終於。*At length* he came to understand it. 最後他才了解了。 **b.** 時間很長地;詳盡地。***go (to) any length(s), go all lengths*** 盡一切所能爲。***in length*** 在長度上; 長。***keep at arm's length*** 避免與人太親近。
***length·en** [ˈlɛŋkθən, ˈlɛŋθ–; ˈleŋθən, –ŋkθ–] *v.t.* 使長; 放長; 加長。Ask the tailor to *lengthen* this skirt. 要裁縫將此裙放長。—*v.i.* 漸長;變長。 「作 **L.O.A.**)。」
length over all 〖航海〗船之全長(略
length·ways [ˈlɛŋkθˌwez; ˈleŋθweiz] *adv.* & *adj.* =**lengthwise.**
length·wise [ˈlɛŋkθˌwaɪz; ˈleŋθwaiz] *adv.* & *adj.* 縱長地(的)。
length·y [ˈlɛŋkθɪ; ˈleŋθi] *adj.,* **length·i·er, length·i·est.** ①(演說、寫作、文體等之)冗長的;長而乏味的。②〖俗〗高的(指人言)。—**length·i·ness,** *n.* —**length·i·ly,** *adv.*
le·ni·ence [ˈliniəns; ˈliːnjəns] *n.* =**leniency.**
le·ni·en·cy [ˈliniənsɪ;ˈliːnjənsi] *n., pl.* **-cies.** ①寬大;仁慈;厚道。②仁慈寬大的行動。
le·ni·ent [ˈliniənt;ˈliːnjənt] *adj.* 寬大的; 慈悲爲懷的;溫和的;(刑罰)輕的。—**ly,** *adv.*
Len·in [ˈlɛnɪn; ˈlenin] *n.* 列寧 (Nikolai, 1870–1924,俄國共產黨領袖,建立蘇維埃政府)。
Len·in·grad [ˈlɛnɪngræd;ˈleningrɑːd] *n.* 列寧格勒(蘇聯西北部一城市,原名 St. Petersburg)。
Len·in·ism [ˈlɛnɪnɪzm; ˈleninizəm] *n.* 列寧主義(主張無產階級獨裁)。
Len·in·ist [ˈlɛnɪnɪst; ˈleninist] *n.* 列寧主義者。—*adj.* 列寧主義的; 列寧的。
Len·in·ite [ˈlɛnɪnˌaɪt; ˈleninait] *adj., n.* =**Leninist.**
le·nis [ˈlinɪs; ˈleinis] *adj., n., pl.* **le·nes** [ˈliniz; ˈleineiz]. 〖語音〗—*adj.* 發音時不費力的。—*n.* 發音較不費力之子音。
len·i·tive [ˈlɛnətɪv; ˈlenitiv] *adj.* ①鎭痛的;緩和的。②緩和精神痛苦的。—*n.* 〖醫〗鎭痛劑;緩和劑;緩瀉劑。
len·i·ty [ˈlɛnətɪ; ˈleniti] *n.* ①富於慈悲心;寬厚;寬恕。②寬厚之行爲。
***lens** [lɛnz; lenz] *n., pl.* **lens·es.** ①透鏡;(望遠鏡、顯微鏡、照相機等的)鏡頭。②眼睛中之水晶體。③觀察之媒介。This artist is the *lens* through which the 16th century can be examined and understood. 這藝術家是我們可藉以觀察並了解十六世紀的媒介。 「**-men.** 〖俗〗攝影師。」
lens·man [ˈlɛnzmən;ˈlenzmən] *n., pl.*
Lent [lɛnt; lent] *n.* 封齋期; 四旬齋(自聖灰日起至復活節前夕之四十個週日, 爲紀念耶穌在荒野禁食)。
:lent [lɛnt; lent] *v.* pt. & pp. of **lend.**
Lent·en [ˈlɛntən; ˈlentən] *adj.* ①封齋期的;適於封齋期的。②(l-) 貧乏的; 陰鬱的;

不開朗的。

len·tic·u·lar [lɛnˈtɪkjələ; lenˈtikjulə] *adj.* ①(凸)透鏡狀的; 扁豆狀的; 雙凸的。②〖光學〗小透鏡的。③(眼球之)水晶體的。—*n.* 雙凸透鏡。

len·ti·form [ˈlɛntəˌfɔrm; ˈlentifɔːm] *adj.* =**lenticular.**

len·ti·go [lɛnˈtaɪgo; lenˈtaigou] *n., pl.* **-tig·i·nes** [-ˈtɪdʒəˌniz; -ˈtidʒəniːz]. 〖醫〗小痣; 雀斑; 面皰。

len·til [ˈlɛntl; ˈlentil] *n.* 〖植物〗扁豆。***sea lentil*** 馬尾藻。

len·tisk [ˈlɛntɪsk; ˈlentisk] *n.* 〖植物〗乳香樹 (=mastic).

Lent lily 〖植物〗水仙。

len·to [ˈlɛnto; ˈlentou] 〖義〗 *adj. & adv.* 〖音樂〗緩慢的(地)。

len·toid [ˈlɛntɔɪd; ˈlentɔid] *adj.* 形似透鏡的。—*n.* 形似透鏡之物。

Le·o [ˈlio; ˈliːou] *n.* ①男子名。②〖天文〗獅子座。③〖天文〗獅子宮(黃道之第五宮)。

Le·o·nar·do da Vin·ci [ˌliəˈnɑrdodəˈvɪntʃi; ˌliːəˈnɑːdoudəˈvintʃiː] 達文西(1452–1519, 義大利畫家、雕刻家、建築家及工程師)。

le·o·nine [ˈliəˌnaɪn; ˈliːənain] *adj.* ①獅的; 似獅的。②威風凜凜的; 勇猛的。③(L-)羅馬教皇 Leo 的。

leonine partnership (賺錢分利「賠本不認帳的)合夥。

le·on·ti·a·sis [ˌliənˈtaɪəsɪs; ˌliːɔnˈtaiəsis] *n., pl.* **-ses** [-siz; -siːz]. 〖醫〗獅面(一種痲瘋病)。

***leop·ard** [ˈlɛpəd; ˈlepəd] *n.* 豹。Can the *leopard* change his spots? 難道豹會改變他的斑點嗎?(喻, 本性難移。)

leopard cat 豹貓(一種有斑點的野貓)。

leop·ard·ess [ˈlɛpədɪs; ˈlepədis] *n.* 母豹。

leopard frog 產於北美與中美的一種「有斑點的青蛙。

le·o·tard [ˈliətɑrd; ˈliːətɑːd] *n.* ①練習舞蹈、特技表演等時所穿之緊身運動衣。②(*pl.*)舞蹈家及特技表演者所穿之緊身褲。

lep·er [ˈlɛpə; ˈlepə] *n.* 痲瘋病患者。

leper house 痲瘋病院。

le·pid·o·lite [ləˈpɪdəˌlaɪt; liˈpidoulait] *n.* 〖礦〗鱗雲母。

lep·i·dop·ter·ist [ˌlɛpəˈdɑptərɪst; ˌlepiˈdɔptərist] *n.* 研究飛蛾、蝴蝶等之專家; 飛蛾蝴蝶等之收集者。

lep·i·dop·ter·ous [ˌlɛpəˈdɑptərəs; ˌlepiˈdɔptərəs] *adj.* 鱗翅類的。(亦作 **lepidopteral**)

lep·o·rine [ˈlɛpəˌraɪn; ˈlepərain] *adj.* 「野兔的; 似野兔的。

lep·ra [ˈlɛprə; ˈleprə] *n.* 〖醫〗痲瘋病 (=leprosy).

lep·re·chaun [ˈlɛprəˌkɔn; ˈleprəkɔːn] *n.* 〖愛爾蘭傳說〗妖精(常顯形爲矮小老人, 告訴人寶藏之所在)。

lep·rol·o·gy [lɛpˈrɑlədʒɪ; lepˈrɔlədʒi] *n.* 痲瘋病理學。

lep·ro·sar·i·um [ˌlɛprəˈsɛrɪəm; ˌleprəˈsɛəriəm] *n., pl.* **-sar·i·ums, -sar·i·a** [-ˈsɛrɪə; -ˈsɛəriə]. ①痲瘋病院; 痲瘋病療養所。②痲瘋病人隔離區。

lep·ro·sy [ˈlɛprəsɪ; ˈleprəsi] *n.* ①痲瘋病。②腐敗; 墮落。

lep·rot·ic [lɛpˈrɑtɪk; lepˈrɔtik] *adj.* 痲「瘋的; 痲瘋所引起的。

lep·rous [ˈlɛprəs; ˈleprəs] *adj.* ①(患)痲瘋病的。②鱗狀的。

lep·to·dac·tyl [ˌlɛptəˈdæktl; ˌleptəˈdæktil] *adj.* (鳥)有細長的腳趾的。

Les·bi·an [ˈlɛzbɪən; ˈlezbiən] *adj.* ①Lesbos (希臘之一島)的。②(女性)同性戀的。③色情的。—*n.*(女性)同性戀者。

Les·bi·an·ism [ˈlɛzbɪənɪzm; ˈlezbiənizəm] *n.* 女性間的同性戀(關係)。

Lesbian love (女性間之)同性戀。

lese majesty [liz~; liːz~] 〖法律〗冒犯君主之罪; 不敬罪; 大逆罪。(亦作 **leze majesty**)

le·sion [ˈliʒən; ˈliːʒən] *n.* ①傷害; 損害。②〖醫〗(機能或組織上或器官上之)損害。

Le·so·tho [ləˈsoto; ləˈsoutou] *n.* 賴索托(非洲南部一王國, 首都 Maseru).

‡**less** [lɛs; les] *adj.* ①較小的; 較少的。*Less* noise, please! 請不要大聲吵鬧! ②(年紀、職位、重要性等)較小的。***nothing less than*** 至少; 等於。—*adv.* ①較小; 不及; 較差。He is *less* clever than his brother. 他不及他的兄弟聰明。②較少; 不如。He should speak *less* and listen more. 他應該少說多聽。***(not) any the less*** 不減; 依然。***less and less*** 越來越小(少)地。There is *less and less* trouble every day. 麻煩一天比一天少。***less than*** 決不; 毫不。***more or less*** 或多或少; 多少有點。***none the less*** a. 一點也不減少。b. 仍然。***still less*** 更不。—*n.* 較少(或小)之量或額。I hope to see *less* of that in future. 我希望將來少看到一點那樣的事。***the less*** a. 較小者。b. 較不重要的人。—*prep.* 不足; 減除。〖注意〗**less** 較少的, 指"量"。**fewer** 較少的, 指"數"。

-less 〖字尾〗表"無; 缺; 不能; 不"之義。

les·see [lɛsˈi; leˈsiː] *n.* 賃借人; 承租人。

***less·en** [ˈlɛsn; ˈlesn] *v.t.* ①使小; 減少; 減輕。This circumstance *lessens* the danger. 這環境會減少危險。②輕視; 藐視; 抹煞。—*v.i.* 變小; 變少; 收縮。

les·sened [ˈlɛsnd; ˈlesnd] *adj.* 減少的; 縮小的; 減輕的。

les·sen·ing [ˈlɛsnɪŋ; ˈlesniŋ] *n.* 減輕; 變小; 減少。—*adj.* 減少中的; 減輕中的。

***less·er** [ˈlɛsə; ˈlesə] *adj.* 較少的; 較小的; 次要的。*lesser* rivers. 較小的河流。〖注意〗**less** 與 **lesser** 皆係 **little** 的比較級, less 指數量, 而 lesser 指價值或重要性。

Lesser Bear, the 〖天文〗小熊座(=Ursa Minor).

Lesser Dog, the 〖天文〗小天狗座。

less·ness [ˈlɛsnɪs; ˈlesnis] *n.* =**inferiority.**

‡**les·son** [ˈlɛsn; ˈlesn] *n.* ①功課; 課業; 課程; 一課。How long does the *lesson* last? 這課要上好久? ②教訓; 譴責。You should teach him a *lesson.* 你該好好地斥責他一頓。③(在禮拜儀式中誦讀的)一段聖經。***give lessons*** 教課; 授課; 教授。***learn one's lesson*** (從經驗中)獲取教訓。***take*** (or ***have***) ***lessons*** 受課; 學習。—*v.t.* ①教。②教訓; 斥責。I'll *lesson* you, you madman. 我要教訓你, 你這個瘋子。

les·sor [ˈlɛsɔr; leˈsɔː] *n.* 出租人; 地主。

***lest** [lɛst; lest] *conj.* ①以免; 因恐。Be careful *lest* you fail. 小心以免失敗。②=**that** (用於表示恐懼、危險等字之後)。

‡**let**¹ [lɛt; let] *v.,* **let, let·ting,** *n.* —*v.t.* ①讓; 允許。She is *letting* her hair grow. 她正把頭髮留長。②解散; 放開; 釋放。She *let* down her hair. 她鬆下她的頭髮。③讓(表示間接的命令)。*Let's* (=Shall we) go. 我們去吧。④出租。⑤認爲; 假設。*Let* the two lines be parallel. 假設此兩線相平行。—*v.i.* 被出租。That house *lets* for $80

a month. 那棟房子以每月八十元出租。***let alone*** a. 別管; 別干涉; 別攪擾。b. 更不必說;遑論。***let a man (friend, etc.) down*** 使某人(朋友等)失望。***let a person down easily*** (or ***gently***) 寬宏對待某人; 避免羞辱某人。***let be*** 別找麻煩; 別干預。***let by*** 讓過去。*Let* me *by*, please. 請讓一讓。***let down*** a. 放下;鬆下。b. 慢下來。c. 使失望。d. 羞辱。***let drive (at)*** 瞄擊; 放(槍等)。***let drop*** a. 說出; 吐出。b. 使停止; 擱置。***let fall*** a. 使跌倒; 丟下。b. 說出;吐出。***let fly*** a. 飛擲。b. 發出。***let go*** 放掉。He *let go* the ladder and jumped. 他推開梯子跳下來。***let go of*** 放手; 放掉。***let in*** a. 捲入(麻煩)。It could still *let* us *in* for trouble. 這仍可能使我們捲入麻煩中。b. 容許(某人)知道或參加 (某事)。I'll *let* you *in* on it. 我將容許你參與此事。***let into*** a. 嵌入。b. 告知。***let know*** 告訴;通知。***let loose*** 放;解開。to *let loose* a torrent of invective. 破口大罵。***let off*** a. 放(槍砲)。b. 了事;算數;使免受刑罰;釋放。*Let* him *off* with a fine. 讓他罰款了事。c. 讓…離去。***let on*** 〖俗〗 a. 洩露(祕密等)。Don't you *let on* I wasn't there. 別讓人知道我沒在那裏。b. 假裝;使信。***let one have it*** 〖俗〗向某人猛烈攻擊、射擊或斥責。***let oneself go*** 儘量發洩情感(熱情、失望等)。***let out*** a. 租出去。to *let out* horses by the day. 按日出租馬匹。b. 放出;洩出。c. 放寬;放大(衣服)。d. 〖俗〗解雇; 解職; 開除; 釋放。e. (學校) 放學;(戲院)散場。***let out at*** 向…猛擊、猛踢等;(喩)猛烈地攻訐。***let (something) pass*** 忽視; 不加重視。***let slip*** 無意中洩露。***let the cat out of the bag*** 洩露祕密。***let up*** 〖俗〗停止。The rain is *letting up*. 雨要停了。***let up on*** 〖俗〗從寬發落;原諒。—*n.* 出租;租出。

let² *v.*, **let·ted, let·ting,** *n.* —*v.t.* 〖古〗阻礙; 阻撓; 妨礙。 —*n.* ①阻礙; 妨礙。②(網球等發球時) 球的碰網。***without let or hindrance*** 毫無阻礙。

-let 〖字尾〗①表"小"之義。如: ringlet 小環, streamlet 小河。②表(身體上所佩帶之)小飾物。如: anklet 脚環, armlet 臂環。

let-a·lone [ˈlɛtəˈlon; ˈletəˈloun] *adj.* 放任(主義)的。

letch [lɛtʃ; letʃ] *n.* 〖俚〗①渴望。②情慾。

let·down [ˈlɛtˌdaun; ˈletˈdaun] *n.* ①減少;減退;弛緩。②〖俗〗失望。③(飛機)降落前之減低高度。—*adj.* ①氣餒的。②飛機降落前減低高度的。

le·thal [ˈliθəl; ˈli:θəl] *adj.* ①致命的;致死的。②毀滅性的。

lethal chamber ①毒氣行刑室。②(如使用致命氣體的)動物無痛屠宰場。

le·thal·i·ty [lɪˈθælətɪ; liˈθæliti] *n.* 致命性;毀滅性。

le·thar·gic [lɪˈθɑrdʒɪk; leˈθɑ:dʒik] *adj.* ①昏睡的;使人昏昏欲睡的。②昏睡症的;患昏睡症的;懶散的。③遲滯的;不活潑的。

leth·ar·gy [ˈlɛθədʒɪ; ˈleθədʒi] *n.*, *pl.* -gies. ①昏睡;昏睡病。②無力氣; 無興趣;怠倦。③冷淡;不關心。

Le·the [ˈliθi; ˈli:θi:] *n.* ①〖希臘神話〗遺忘川(冥府中一河流, 死者飲其水, 則忘盡前生之事)。②忘却;遺忘。—**an,** *adj.*

let-off [ˈlɛtɔf; ˈletɔ:f] *n.* ①免除;免罰。②〖運動〗得分機會之疏忽;罰對方出局機會之錯過。

‡let's [lɛts, lɛs; lets] =**let us.**

Lett [lɛt; let] *n.* ①列特族之人(居於波羅的海東岸)。②列特語。

‡let·ter¹ [ˈlɛtə; ˈletə] *n.* ①字母。②書信;函。a business *letter.* 商業信函。③正式證書;許可證;特權狀。④正確之用字;字義。He kept the *letter* of a law but not the spirit. 他保持了法律的條文,但沒有保持其精神。⑤(*pl.*) a. 文學。a man of *letters.* 文人;文學家。b. 文學知識;文學修養。c. 寫作生涯。⑥鉛字。⑦鉛字之一種字體。⑧美國大學贈與校內優秀運動員之一種榮譽(以校名之第一字母爲其象徵)。***to the letter*** (做)到每一細節。We followed his instructions *to the letter.* 我們絲毫不差地遵從他的指示。—*v.t.* ①寫字母於。②將…刻成字母。—*v.i.* 獲得大學優秀運動員之榮譽。

let·ter² *n.* 出租人。

letter balance 秤信件重量之秤。

letter board 排字版。

letter bomb 書信炸彈。

letter book 信件謄錄簿。

let·ter-bound [ˈlɛtəˌbaund; ˈletəbaund] *adj.* 拘泥於字句的。

letter box 〖英〗信箱 (=mailbox).

letter card 〖英〗封緘信片;郵簡。

letter carrier 〖美〗郵差。

letter drop (郵局或郵車之)受信口。

let·tered [ˈlɛtəd; ˈletəd] *adj.* ①受過教育的。②有學問的;博學的。③有文學修養的。④印有字母的;印有文字的。

letter file 信夾。

let·ter·form [ˈlɛtəˌfɔrm; ˈletəfɔ:m] *n.* ①(活字的)字體。②信紙;信箋。

let·ter·gram [ˈlɛtəˌgræm; ˈletəgræm] *n.* 書信電報;減價電報;間送電報(投遞較慢而費用較低)。

let·ter·head [ˈlɛtəˌhɛd; ˈletəhed] *n.* ①印在信紙上的銜頭。②有銜的信紙。

let·ter·ing [ˈlɛtərɪŋ; ˈletəriŋ] *n.* ①(書寫、雕刻之)文字。②文字之書寫、揚印或雕刻。

let·ter·man [ˈlɛtəˌmæn; ˈletəmən] *n.*, *pl.* -men. 美國大學裏受贈校名第一字母之榮譽的優秀運動員。

letter of advice 〖商〗(送貨等的)通知書。

letter of attorney 委任狀。

letter of credence =**letters of credence.**

letter of credit 信用狀。

letter of intent 合同之草約。

letter paper 信紙。

let·ter-per·fect [ˈlɛtəˈpɝfɪkt; ˈletəˈpə:fikt] *adj.* ①完全記住(功課或臺詞)的。②(校對等)無訛的。

let·ter·press [ˈlɛtəˌprɛs; ˈletəpres] *n.* 印刷物中的文字部分(以別於插圖部分)。

letter press 複印器。

letter sheet 郵簡;信箋。

letters of credence 國書;信任狀。

letters patent 〖法律〗專利特許證。

letter stamp 郵戳。

let·ter·weight [ˈlɛtəˌwet; ˈletəweit] *n.* ①=**paperweight.** ②=**letter balance.**

letter writer ①寫信人。②尺牘。③書信複印器。

Let·tic [ˈlɛtɪk; ˈletik] *adj.*①列特(Lett)族的。②列特語的。—*n.* 列特語(=Lettish).

let·ting [ˈlɛtɪŋ; ˈletiŋ] *n.* 〖主英〗租金。

Let·tish [ˈlɛtɪʃ; ˈletiʃ] *adj.* 列特 (Lett) 人的;列特族的;列特語的。—*n.* 列特語。

•let·tuce [ˈlɛtɪs, -əs; ˈletis] *n.* ①類似萵苣之一種青菜,可生食者。②〖俚〗鈔票;美鈔。

He collected quite a handful of *lettuce*. 他收集了一大把鈔票。

let·up [ˈlɛtˌʌp; ˈletʌp] *n.*【美俗】停止;中止;弛緩。

le·u [ˈlɛu; ˈleu] *n., pl.* **lei** [le; lei]. 羅馬尼亞之銀幣(=100 bani). (亦作 **ley**)

leu·cine [ˈlusin; ˈluːsiːn] *n.*【生化】亮氨酸;白氨基酸。

leu·co·cyte [ˈljukəˌsaɪt; ˈljuːkəsait] *n.*【生理】白血球。

leu·co·cy·th(a)e·mi·a [ˌlukosaɪˈθimɪə; ˌluːkousaiˈθiːmiə] *n.*【醫】=**leukemia.**

leu·co·pe·ni·a [ˌlukəˈpinɪə; ˌluːkəˈpiːniə] *n.*【醫】白血球減少症。(亦作 **leukopenia**)

leu·co·plast [ˈljukəˌplæst; ˈljuːkəplæst] *n.*【植物】白色體;無色體。

leu·cor·rh(o)e·a [ˌljukəˈriə; ˌljuːkəˈriːə] *n.*【醫】白帶。(亦作 **leukorrhea**)

leu·cot·o·my [luˈkɑtəmɪ; luːˈkɔtəmi] *n.*【醫】額葉白質切除術。(亦作 **leukotomy**)

leu·k(a)e·mi·a [ljəˈkimɪə; ljuːˈkiːmiə] *n.*【醫】白血球過多症;血癌。

leu·k(a)e·mic [ljəˈkimɪk; ljuːˈkiːmik] *adj.*【醫】白血球過多症的;血癌的。

leu·k(a)e·moid [ljəˈkimɔɪd; ljuˈkiːmɔid] *adj.* 似白血球過多症的;似血癌的。

lev [lɛf; lef] *n., pl.* **le·va** [ˈlɛvə; ˈlevə]. 保加利亞的一種金幣單位。

Lev. Leviticus.

Le·vant [ləˈvænt; liˈvænt] *n.* ①地中海東部及愛琴海沿岸的國家和島嶼。②(l-)(山羊皮製之)上等摩洛哥紋皮(特用於裝訂書籍者)。③(l-)(起於地中海的)强烈的東風。

le·vant [ləˈvænt; liˈvænt] *v.i.*【英】(爲賴債等而)逃亡;逃匿;溜掉。

le·vant·er¹ [ləˈvæntɚ; liˈvæntə] *n.* ①(地中海特有的)强烈東風。②(L-) =**Levantine.**

le·vant·er² *n.*【英】逃亡者;逃債者;因逃債而出走的人。

Le·van·tine [ləˈvæntɪn, ˈlɛvənˌtaɪn; ˈlevəntain] *adj.* 屬於或有關 Levant 的。—*n.* ①Levant 之居民。②Levant 之船隻。

Levant mo·roc·co [~ məˈrɑko; ~məˈrɔkou] =**Levant** ②.

lev·ee¹ [ˈlɛvɪ; ˈlevi, ləˈviː] *n., v.,* **-eed, -ee·ing.** —*n.* ①(美國的)防洪堤。②碼頭。—*v.t.* 築防洪堤於。

lev·ee² [ləˈvi; ˈlevi] *n.* ①接見會(君主或其他顯要人物於早晨起牀後立即舉行者)。②【美】總統或其他高級官員所舉行之招待會。③【英】(宮廷的)午朝(下午二、三時召開,限男子)。

‡lev·el [ˈlɛvḷ; ˈlevl] *adj., n., v.,* **-el(l)ed, -el·(l)ing,** *adv.* —*adj.* ①平的;水平的;平坦的;齊平的。②平衡的;健全的。③平等的。Those children want to be *level* with adults. 那些孩子們要與成人平等。④平穩的。⑤平板的;單調的。⑥勢均力敵的。The race was clearly *level*. 那賽跑顯然勢均力敵。⑦公正的;公平的。⑧均勻的。***do one's level best*** 盡一切可能;盡最大努力。—*n.* ①平面;水平面;水平線。How high are we above sea *level?* 我們高出海平面有多少?②高度。③水平儀(一種測量儀器)。④水平儀之測量。⑤平等之地位或情況。⑥(社會、道德、知識上的)標準。⑦水平的狀態。⑧階層;階級。⑨程度。***find one's own level*** 找到與自己身分、才幹等相當的人或適當的位置。***on the level***【俗】誠實的;直率的。—*v.t.* ①使平;使成水平;拆毀。②舉(鎗)瞄準。③使同等;使相同。Death *levels* all men. 死使一切人皆平等。④針對(某話、意向等)。—*v.i.* ①(拿武器)瞄準;對準【at】。②變成平等;變平。③均勻分散或分布。④坦白說話。***level off*** (or ***out***) **a.** 刮平;整平。**b.** 停止增加。**c.**【航空】(飛機於上升或下降後)作水平飛行。***level with***【俚】對…說實話。—*adv.* 水平地;平衡地。

level crossing【英】=**grade crossing.**

lev·el·(l)er [ˈlɛvḷə; ˈlevələ] *n.* ①使成水平的人(物)。②平等主義者;平等論者。

lev·el-head·ed [ˈlɛvḷˈhɛdɪd; ˈlevlˈhedid] *adj.* 穩健的;頭腦清晰的;明智的。

lev·el·(l)ing [ˈlɛvḷɪŋ; ˈlevəliŋ] *n.* ①使平;使平坦。②【測量】抄平;水平測量;高低測量。③平等運動。④【語言】(字形變化之)單純化。

leveling rod (**pole** or **staff**) (測量用之)準尺。

lev·el·ly [ˈlɛvḷɪ; ˈlevəli] *adv.* ①平地;水平地。②無感情地;無動於衷地。

lev·el·man [ˈlɛvḷmən; ˈlevlmən] *n., pl.* **-men.** 水平儀器操作員。

·lev·er [ˈlɛvɚ, ˈlivɚ; ˈliːvə] *n.* ①槓桿。②任何作用似槓桿之物。③(用以達到目的之)工具。④(機械之)手桿。gearshift *lever.* (汽車之)排擋桿。—*v.t.* 以槓桿移動;撬開。—*v.i.* 使用槓桿。The worker is *levering* at the rock. 工人用槓桿移動巖石。

lev·er·age [ˈlɛvərɪdʒ; ˈliːvəridʒ] *n.* ①槓桿作用。②使用槓桿所獲的利益或力量;槓桿率。③(達到某目的之)手段;力量;影響。④爲達到某目的而使用的手段或力量之效果。

lever arm【物理】桿臂。

lev·er·et [ˈlɛvərɪt; ˈlevərit] *n.* 未足歲之小野兔。

lev·i·a·ble [ˈlɛvɪəbl; ˈleviəbl] *adj.* ①可課稅的(貨物)。②可課的(稅)。

le·vi·a·than [lɪˈvaɪəθən; liˈvaiəθən] *n.* ①【聖經】巨大海獸(認係指爬蟲或鯨魚)。②任何巨大之物(如巨艦等)。③巨大之海生動物(如鯨魚等)。④(亦作 **Leviathan state**)(L-)獨裁國家;專制政權。—*adj.* 極大的;龐大的。

lev·i·gate [ˈlɛvəˌget; ˈlevigeit] *v.,* **-gat·ed, -gat·ing,** *adj.* —*v.t.* ①粉碎;研細。②使光滑;磨光。—*adj.* 光滑的。—**lev·i·ga·tion,** *n.*

lev·in [ˈlɛvɪn; ˈlevin] *n.*【古】閃電。

le·vis [ˈlivaɪz; ˈliːvaiz] *n. pl.*【美】①(在接縫處加强縫製之)藍色緊身工作褲;牛仔褲。②(L-)(亦作 **Levi's**)其商標名。

lev·i·tate [ˈlɛvəˌtet; ˈleviteit] *v.,* **-tat·ed, -tat·ing.** —*v.i.* 輕浮;浮於空氣中。—*v.t.*【罕】使浮於空氣中。

lev·i·ta·tion [ˌlɛvəˈteʃən; ˌleviˈteiʃən] *n.* ①輕浮;浮起。②藉魔術使身體浮於空中。

Le·vite [ˈlivaɪt; ˈliːvait] *n.*【聖經】利未人。

Le·vit·i·cal [ləˈvɪtɪkḷ; liˈvitikəl] *adj.* ①利未人的。②【聖經】利未記的;利未記中之律法的。

Levitical degrees 聖經利未記律法中規定之不能結婚的親屬關係。

Le·vit·i·cus [ləˈvɪtɪkəs; liˈvitikəs] *n.* 利未記(舊約聖經之第三書)。

lev·i·ty [ˈlɛvətɪ; ˈleviti] *n., pl.* **-ties.** ①輕率;輕浮;浮躁。②輕率的舉動。③不穩定;善變。

le·vo·ro·ta·tion [ˌlivoroˈteʃən; ˌliːvourouˈteiʃən] *n.* 左旋轉;反時鐘旋轉;左旋。

lev·u·lose [ˈlɛvjəˌlos; ˈlevjulous] *n.*【化】左旋糖;果糖。

lev·y [ˈlɛvɪ; ˈlevi] *v.,* **lev·ied, lev·y·ing,** *n., pl.* **lev·ies.** —*v.t.* ①征稅。The government *levies* taxes for national expenses.

政府爲國家的費用而征稅。②徵集。③發動(戰爭);作(戰)。to *levy* war on a nation. 向一國開戰。—*v.i.* ①扣押。②仰賴。—*n.* ①徵稅;徵集。capital *levy*. 資本課稅。②徵集之錢;徵集之人。

lev·y·ist [ˈlɛvɪɪst; ˈleviist] *n.* 主張沒收資本者。

lewd [lud; luːd] *adj.* 淫蕩的;猥褻的;不貞潔的;好色的。—**ly,** *adv.* —**ness,** *n.*

lewd·ster [ˈludstɚ; ˈluːdstə] *n.* 好色者。

Lew·is [ˈljuɪs; ˈluːis] *n.* 劉易斯(Sinclair, 1885–1951, 美國小說家, 曾獲1930年諾貝爾文學獎)。

lew·is [ˈljuɪs; ˈluːis] *n.* 鳩尾起重器;吊楔。(亦作 **lewisson**)

Lewis (machine) gun 劉易斯式輕機槍(美國人 I. N. Lewis 上校所發明者)。

lew·is·ite [ˈluɪsˌaɪt; ˈljuːisait] *n.* 〖化〗路易毒氣;糜爛性毒氣;氯乙烯二氯胂。

lex [lɛks; leks] *n., pl.* **le·ges** [ˈlidʒiz; ˈliːdʒiːz].〖拉〗法;法律。

lex. lexicon.

lex·i·cal [ˈlɛksɪkḷ; ˈleksikəl] *adj.* ①語句的;語彙的。②辭書的;辭典的; 字典(編輯)的。—**ly,** *adv.*

lexicog. ①lexicographer. ②lexicographical. ③lexicography.

lex·i·cog·ra·pher [ˌlɛksəˈkɑgrəfɚ; ˌleksiˈkɔgrəfə] *n.* 辭典編纂人。(亦作 **lexicographist**)

lex·i·co·graph·ic [ˌlɛksəkəˈgræfɪk; ˌleksikouˈgræfik] *adj.* 辭典編纂(術)的。(亦作 **lexicographical**)

lex·i·cog·ra·phy [ˌlɛksəˈkɑgrəfɪ; ˌleksiˈkɔgrəfi] *n.* 辭典編纂;辭典編纂法。

lex·i·col·o·gy [ˌlɛksɪˈkɑlədʒɪ; ˌleksiˈkɔlədʒi] *n.* 辭彙學。

lex·i·con [ˈlɛksɪkən; ˈleksikən] *n., pl.* **lex·i·ca** [ˈlɛksɪkə; ˈleksikə], **lex·i·cons.** ①字典(尤指希臘語、希伯來語、拉丁語及阿拉伯語者)。②專門字典。③字彙。

Ley·den jar [ˈlaɪdṇ~; ˈlaidn~]〖電〗萊頓瓶。

lf. 〖棒球〗left field(er).

L.F., LF, l.f. 〖無線電〗低頻率;長波(爲 low frequency 之略)。

L.G., LG., LG ①Life Guards. ②Low German.

L/G Letter of Guarantee.

l.g., lg. 〖足球〗left guard.

Lha·sa [ˈlɑsə; ˈlɑːsə] *n.* 拉薩 (西藏之首府)。

L. H. D. Litterarum Humaniorum Doctor (拉=Doctor of the Humanities).

Li 化學元素 lithium 之符號。

li[1] [li; liː]〖中〗*n., pl.* **li.** 里(約等於$^1/_3$英里)。

li[2] 〖中〗 *n.* 禮。

li·a·bil·i·ty [ˌlaɪəˈbɪlətɪ; ˌlaiəˈbiliti] *n., pl.* **-ties.** ①有義務;應該。*liability* for a debt. 負擔債務。②易患;易染。③(*pl.*) 債務(爲 assets 之對)。④不利;缺點。

liability insurance 責任保險。

liability limit 責任保險最高保險額。

***li·a·ble** [ˈlaɪəbḷ; ˈlaiəbl] *adj.* ①可能遭受的。Glass is *liable* to break. 玻璃易被打破。②易患的; 易陷的。All men are *liable* to make mistakes. 人皆易犯錯誤。③應負責的;有責任的。④有義務的。Citizens are liable to certain duties. 公民須盡若干義務。⑤受控制的。

li·aise [lɪˈez; liˈeiz] *v.i.,* **li·aised, li·ais·ing.** ①連絡〖with, between〗。② 當連絡官。

li·ai·son [ˌlieˈzɔ̃; li(ː)ˈeizɔ̃ːŋ] *n.* ①聯絡。②男女間之曖昧。③連音 (指法語中一字不發音之子音字尾與其次一字之母音字首的連結發音者)。④〖烹飪〗變稠作料(如放在湯裏的太白粉、蛋等物)。*liaison officer* 連絡官。

li·a·na [lɪˈɑnə; liˈɑːnə] *n.* (熱帶) 葛類植物。

liang [ljɑŋ; ljɑːŋ] *n., pl.* **liang, liangs.** (中國之)兩(16兩爲一斤)。

li·a·nous [lɪˈɑnəs; liˈɑːnəs] *adj.* 如葛的;籐狀的。

Liao·ning [ˈljauˈnɪŋ; ˈljauˈniŋ] *n.* 遼寧(中國東北部之一省,省會爲瀋陽, Mukden 或 Shenyang).

Liao·pei [ˈljauˈbe; ˈljauˈbei] *n.* 遼北(中國東北部之一省,省會爲遼源,Liaoyüan) (亦作 **Liaopeh**)

Liao·tung Peninsula [ˈljauˈduŋ~ ˈljauˈduŋ~] 遼東半島(在中國東北部)。

***li·ar** [ˈlaɪɚ; ˈlaiə] *n.* 說謊者。A successful *liar* should have a good memory. 成功的說謊者應有很好的記憶力。

Li·as [ˈlaɪəs; ˈlaiəs] *n.* ①〖地質〗黑侏羅(爲侏羅系中之一部)。②(l-) (英國西南部地方產之)青色石灰岩。

Lib, lib [lɪb; lib] *n.* (尤指婦女) 解放運動。—*adj.* 與婦女解放運動有關的。

li·bate [ˈlaɪbet; ˈlaibeit] *v.t.* 向…祭酒。—*v.i.* ①傾酒於地以祭神。②〖諧〗喝酒。

li·ba·tion [laɪˈbeʃən; laiˈbeiʃən] *n.* ①傾酒或油於地(或牲品上)以祭神。②祭神之酒或油;奠酒。③〖諧〗一杯酒。

Lib. Cong.〖美〗Library of Congress.

li·bel [ˈlaɪbḷ; ˈlaibəl] *n., v.,* **-bel(l)ed -bel·(l)ing.** —*n.* ①誹謗人之文字、言詞或圖畫等。②誹謗罪。③誹謗或譏諷之東西。④誹謗; 中傷。⑤〖法律〗原告之訴狀。—*v.t.* ①寫或印文字誹謗。②誹謗;中傷。③〖法律〗起訴。

li·bel·(l)ant [ˈlaɪbḷənt; ˈlaibələnt] *n.* ①〖法律〗(宗教或海事法庭之)告訴人; 原告。②=**libeler.**

li·bel·(l)ee [ˌlaɪbəˈli; ˌlaibəˈliː] *n.* 〖法律〗(宗教或海事法庭之)被告。

li·bel·(l)er [ˈlaɪbələ; ˈlaibələ] *n.* =**libel(l)ist.**

li·bel·(l)ist [ˈlaɪbəlɪst; ˈlaibəlist] *n.* 中傷者;誹謗者。

li·bel·(l)ous [ˈlaɪbələs; ˈlaibələs] *adj.* 誹謗性的。

***lib·er·al** [ˈlɪbərəl; ˈlibərəl] *adj.* ①慷慨的;大方的。a *liberal* giver. 慷慨的施捨者。②豐富的;充分的。③寬厚的; 大度的; 無偏見的。④自由主義(主張民主制度與社會改革)的。⑤傳意的;不拘泥於字句的。a *liberal* translation. 意譯。⑥文理科的。⑦不受約束的;無拘束的。⑧大的。⑨不嚴格的;放縱的。—*n.* ①自由主義者(與 conservative 相對)。②(L-) 自由黨黨員。

liberal arts 文理科 (包括藝術、自然科學、社會科學、及人文學科, 與實用科學相對)。

liberal education 非專科教育;通才教育。

lib·er·al·ism [ˈlɪbərəlˌɪzəm; ˈlibərəlizəm] *n.* ①(規範行爲、態度等之)自由理念。②(政治、經濟、社會等之)自由主義;改進主義;進步主義。③(有時 L-)自由黨之政治原則。④現代基督教推翻一切教會之傳統教條、儀式而設法符合科學原則之傾向。—**lib·er·al·ist,** *n.*

lib·er·al·is·tic [ˌlɪbərəˈlɪstɪk; ˌlibərəˈlistik] *adj.* 自由主義的。

lib·er·al·i·ty [ˌlɪbəˈrælətɪ; ˌlibəˈræliti] *n., pl.* **-ties.** ①慷慨好施。②豐厚的禮物或賜予物。③心胸寬大;公平無私;無偏見。④自由主義。

lib·er·al·i·za·tion [ˌlɪbərəlaɪˈzeʃən; ˌlibərəlaiˈzeiʃən] *n.* 自由主義化; 寬大。

lib·er·al·ize [ˈlɪbərəlˌaɪz; ˈlibərəlaiz]

v.t. & v.i., **-ized, -iz•ing.** ①(使) 自由主義化;使心胸寬大;變成寬厚。②(使) 自由化;打破傳統。

lib•er•al•ly [ˈlɪbərəlɪ; ˈlibərəli] *adv.* ①慷慨地。②自由地;開通地。③豐富地。

Liberal Party (英國之)自由黨。

lib•er•ate [ˈlɪbəˌret; ˈlibəreit] *v.t.,* **-at-ed, -at•ing.** ①釋放;使獲自由;解放;解救。to *liberate* slaves. 解放奴隸。②〖化〗使(物質)游離。③〖俚〗偷。④消除社會的各種偏見(現尤指性別的偏見)。

lib•er•a•tion [ˌlɪbəˈreʃən; ˌlibəˈreiʃən] *n.* ①釋放;解放。②〖化〗游離。

lib•er•a•tive [ˈlɪbəˌretɪv; ˈlibəreitiv] *adj.* 解放的;贊成解放的。

lib•er•a•tor [ˈlɪbəˌretɚ; ˈlibəreitə] *n.* 釋放者;解放者。

Li•be•ri•a [laɪˈbɪrɪə; laiˈbiəriə] *n.* 賴比瑞亞(非洲西部之一國, 其首都爲蒙羅維亞, Monrovia). —**Li•be•ri•an,** *adj., n.*

lib•er•tar•i•an [ˌlɪbɚˈtɛrɪən; ˌlibəˈtɛə-riən] *adj.* ①自由意志論的。②主張(思想、行動等之)自由的; 自由論的。—*n.* 自由論者。

li•ber•ti•cide [lɪˈbɝtəˌsaɪd; liˈbəːti-said] *n.* ①破壞自由。②破壞自由者。—*adj.* 破壞自由的。

lib•er•tine [ˈlɪbɚˌtin; ˈlibətain] *n.* ①放蕩者;淫蕩者。②宗教上的自由思想者;懷疑論者。—*adj.* ①放蕩的;佚樂的;淫蕩的。②自由思想的。③道德律廢棄論的。

lib•er•tin•ism [ˈlɪbɚtɪnˌɪzəm; ˈlibə-tinizəm] *n.* ①放縱;淫蕩。②(宗教上的) 自由思想。

lib•er•ty [ˈlɪbɚtɪ; ˈlibəti] *n., pl.* **-ties.** ①自由。②自由權。*liberty* of conscience. 信仰自由。*liberty* of speech. 言論自由。③失禮; 冒昧。④(給予水手、船員等)上岸的許可; 准假。⑤使用或留住權。⑥政府給予之權利或特權。⑦自由活動的範圍。⑧自由女神像。***at liberty*** **a.** 空閒的;閒暇的。When shall you be *at liberty?* 你何時有空閒? **b.** 失業。***be at liberty to*** **(*do*)** 被允許; 可隨意。I *am* not *at liberty to tell* you. 我不可隨意告訴你。***set at liberty*** 釋放。***take liberties*** **(*with*)** 太隨便; 冒昧。You mustn't *take liberties with* a woman. 你不可對女人太隨便。

Liberty Bell 自由鐘(1776 年美國宣言獨立時所鳴之鐘)。

liberty bond 〖美〗第一次世界大戰時美國所發行之戰時公債。

liberty cap 自由帽(昔日爲已獲自由的奴隸所戴之無沿帽, 今作自由之表徵)。

liberty day 〖航海〗獲准上陸日。

Liberty Island 自由島(在紐約灣內, 自由神像在此島上, 昔稱 Bedloe's Island).

liberty man 〖航海〗獲准上陸之海員。

liberty of the press 出版自由。

Liberty Ship 自由輪(美國於二次大戰中大批建造之一種商船, 每艘載重約11,000噸)。

li•bid•i•nal [lɪˈbɪdn̩əl; liˈbidənəl] *adj.* 求生之本能或力量的。

li•bid•i•nous [lɪˈbɪdn̩əs; liˈbidinəs] *adj.*①好色的;淫蕩的。②〖精神分析〗libido的。

li•bi•do [lɪˈbaɪdo; liˈbiːdou] *n.* ①〖精神分析〗本能的衝動;生命力。②性衝動;性慾。

Li•bra [ˈlaɪbrə; ˈlaibrə] *n.* 〖天文〗①天秤座。②天秤宮(黃道之第七宮)。

li•bra[ˈlaɪbrə; ˈlaibrə] *n., pl.* **-brae** [-bri; -briː]. ①磅(重量單位, 略作**lb.**). ②鎊(英幣單位, 略作 £).

***li•brar•i•an** [laɪˈbrɛrɪən; laiˈbrɛəriən] *n.* 圖書館員;圖書館長;圖書室主任。

‡li•brar•y [ˈlaɪˌbrɛrɪ, -brərɪ; ˈlaibrəri] *n., pl.* **-brar•ies.** ①圖書館;圖書室。②文庫;叢書。The Everyman's *Library.* 人人文庫。③藏書。④書房。***free library*** 免費借書之圖書館。***lending library*** 書可借出之圖書館(通常需收費)。***reference library*** 參考圖書館(書不可借出者)。

library binding ①書籍之結實的布封面。②布裝書之印行。

library card 借書證。(亦作 **borrower's card**)

library edition 精裝本(適於圖書館陳列保藏之版本)。

Library of Congress 美國國會圖書館。

Library of Congress classification 美國國會圖書館書目分類法(以二十六字母加上阿拉伯數字爲編號)。

library science 圖書館(管理)學。

li•bra•tion [laɪˈbreʃən; laiˈbreiʃən] *n.* ①均衡。②緩慢的來回擺動。③〖天文〗(月等之) 天平動。

li•bret•tist [lɪˈbrɛtɪst; liˈbretist] *n.* 歌劇、樂劇等之劇本作者; 歌詞作者。

li•bret•to [lɪˈbrɛto; liˈbretou] *n., pl.* **-tos, -ti** [-tɪ; -ti]. ①歌劇或其他歌曲之詞。②歌劇劇本。

Lib•y•a [ˈlɪbɪə; ˈlibiə] *n.* 利比亞 (北非之一國, 1969年改制共和, 正式名稱爲 Libyan Arab Republic, 首都爲的黎波里, Tripoli).

lice [laɪs; lais] *n.* pl. of **louse.**

***li•cense, li•cence** [ˈlaɪsn̩s; ˈlaisəns] *n., v.,* **-censed** or **-cenced, -cens•ing** or **-cenc•ing.** —*n.* ①特許;許可。②執照;特許證。a driving *license.* 駕駛執照。a *license* to practise as a doctor. 醫師開業執照。③放肆; 放縱。④(文學、美術等的)破格;不按格律。poetic *license.* 詩中(文法、字序、音律等) 之破格。 —*v.t.* 許可; 特許。to *license* a doctor to practise medicine. 許可醫生行醫。—**less,** *adj.*

licensed premises 〖英〗特許賣烟酒的餐館。

li•cen•see, li•cen•cee [ˌlaɪsn̩ˈsi; ˌlaisənˈsiː] *n.* 執照持有者。

license plate 汽車牌照。

li•cens•er, li•cenc•er [ˈlaɪsn̩sɚ; ˈlaisənsə] *n.* 有權批准執照的人; 頒發執照者;許可者。

li•cen•sor [ˈlaɪsn̩sɚ; ˈlaisənsə] *n.* 〖法律〗=**licenser.**

li•cen•ti•ate [laɪˈsɛnʃɪɪt; laiˈsenʃiit] *n.* ①(專門職業之)有開業資格者;領得開業執照者。②(歐洲大陸之大學所頒之)學士與博士之間的學位。③(長老教會之)有資格而未就任之牧師。—**ship,** *n.*

li•cen•tious [laɪˈsɛnʃəs; laiˈsenʃəs] *adj.* ①放蕩不拘的; 淫佚的。②放縱的; 無法無天的;不守法則的。③〖罕〗(文法、文體等規則之) 破格的。 —**ly,** *adv.* —**ness,** *n.*

li•chee [ˈlitʃi; ˈliːtʃiː] *n.* =**litchi.**

li•chen [ˈlaɪkɪn, -kən; ˈlaikən] *n.* ①〖植物〗青苔; 地衣。②〖醫〗苔癬; 匐行疹。

li•chen•ous [ˈlaɪkɪnəs; ˈlaikinəs] *adj.* 青苔的;長滿了青苔的。

lich gate [lɪtʃ~; litʃ~] 教堂墓地前面有頂蓋的門(棺木可放置於此以待神父或牧師來臨)。(亦作 **lych gate**)

lic•it [ˈlɪsɪt; ˈlisit] *adj.* 合法的;正當的。a *licit* transaction. 合法的交易。

***lick** [lɪk; lik] *v.t.* ①以舌舐;舐。The cat

was *licking* its paws. 貓舐爪。②(火)捲燒；(浪)沖洗。③〖俗〗打擊；戰勝；征服。④〖俗〗揍一頓。—*v.i.* ①(浪)沖洗。②(火)捲燒。***lick into shape*** 整頓；使具規模。***lick one's chops*** 因期待好事而沾沾自喜。***lick one's lips*** 垂涎；滿足。***lick one's wounds*** 求復元；生聚教訓；重整旗鼓。***lick someone's boots*** 拍某人的馬屁。He refused to *lick the boss's boots* to get a pay raise. 他不肯爲加薪而對上司拍馬屁。***lick the dust*** 被擊倒；被殺。***lick up*** (or ***off***) 舐盡；舐掉。—*n.* ①舐。②極少之量；少許。③〖俗〗打；擊。He hit the board a hard *lick*. 他重打板子一下。④有天然鹽而獸類常往舐食之處。⑤〖俗〗(動作、努力等之)一下。⑥〖俗〗速度。***a lick and a promise*** a. 馬虎的洗擦。b. 敷衍。

lick·er·ish 〔ˈlɪkərɪʃ; ˈlikəriʃ〕 *adj.* ①美味的。②貪饞的；貪吃好食的。③貪婪的；渴望的；淫慾的。(亦作 **liquorish**) **—ly,** *adv.*

lick·e·ty-split 〔ˈlɪkətɪˈsplɪt; ˈlikitiˈsplit〕 *adj.* & *adv.* 〖俗〗急速的(地)。(亦作 **lickety-cut**)

lick·ing 〔ˈlɪkɪŋ; ˈlikiŋ〕 *n.* ①舐。②〖俗〗擊打；擊敗。③挫折。 —*adv.* 非常。

Lick Observatory 美國 California 州 Hamilton 山頂上的天文臺。

lick·spit·tle 〔ˈlɪkˌspɪtl̩; ˈlikspitl〕 *n.*, *v.*, **-spit·tled, -spit·tling.** —*n.* 諂諛者；奉承者。—*v.t.* & *v.i.* 諂諛；奉承。

lic·o·rice 〔ˈlɪkərɪs; ˈlikəris〕 *n.* ①〖植物〗甘草(歐洲一種開小藍花之豆科植物)。②甘草根；甘草汁(製藥用)。③加甘草汁之糖果。(亦作 **liquorice**)

lic·tor 〔ˈlɪktɚ; ˈliktə〕 *n.* 古羅馬持束棒爲長官清道並協助處罰罪犯之小吏。

lid** 〔lɪd; lid〕 *n.* ①蓋。the *lid* of a box. 箱蓋。②眼瞼(=eyelid)。③〖俚〗帽子。④禁止；管制。blow the lid off*** 〖俚〗暴露；揭開內幕。***flip one's lid*** 〖美俚〗興奮；激動；失去情緒上的控制。 —*v.t.* ①加蓋於。②閉；關。She *lidded* her eyes. 她閉上眼睛。

lid·less 〔ˈlɪdlɪs; ˈlidlis〕 *adj.* ①無蓋的。②無眼瞼的。③〖詩〗不需睡覺的；永遠醒着的。

Li·do 〔ˈlido; ˈliːdou〕 *n.* ①里度(義大利 Venice 附近之一小島，爲一近代化之海濱浴場)。②(l-)任何豪華的海濱遊樂場。

lie**[1] 〔laɪ; lai〕 *n.*, *v.*, **lied, ly·ing.** —*n.* ①謊言；欺人之談。②虛僞之行爲。His pose of humility was a *lie*. 他謙恭的樣子是虛僞的。③對謊言或虛僞之指控。 She threw the *lie* in his face. 她當着他的面指控他撒謊。act a lie*** 作欺騙的行爲。***a white lie*** 沒有惡意的謊言。***give a person the lie*** 責某人撒謊。They *gave each other the lie* in a brawl. 他們在鬥毆中互控對方撒謊。***give the lie to*** (***something***) a. 證實(某事)爲虛僞；反駁。b. 反駁；控以說謊。—*v.i.* ①撒謊。You're *lying!* 你撒謊！ Don't *lie* to me! 不要對我撒謊！②作假。③作不正確表示。That thermometer must be *lying*. 那溫度計必定不準確。 —*v.t.* 以謊言使。 to *lie* oneself out of a difficulty. 撒謊以求擺脫困難。***lie in one's throat*** (or ***teeth***) 說大謊。

‡**lie**[2] *v.*, **lay, lain, ly·ing,** *n.* —*v.i.* ①臥；躺。The dog was *lying* on the ground. 犬臥地上。②在(某種狀態中或某處)。His money *lay* idle in the bank. 他的錢閒擱在銀行裏。③位於；在。 Ireland *lies* to the west of England. 愛爾蘭位於英格蘭之西。④存在。 The cure *lies* in education. 挽救之道在於教育。⑤(死人)葬(在)；長眠地下。⑥〖古〗過夜；住宿。⑦〖法律〗成立；可獲准。The appeal will not *lie*. 該控訴不能成立。 ***as far as in me lies*** 就我能力所及。***find out how the land lies*** 注意事情究竟如何。 ***Let sleeping dogs lie.*** 不必多找麻煩；不必討論可引起麻煩之問題。 ***lie back*** a. 倚靠椅背等而仰臥。b. 停止忙碌；休息。***lie by*** a. 休息。 I must *lie by* for a day or two. 我必須休息一兩天。 b. 未被使用。***lie down on the job*** 偷懶。 ***lie down under*** 未抗議或抵抗(侮辱等)；甘受(侮辱等)。***lie in*** a. 睡懶覺。b. (產婦)待產。The time had come for her to *lie in*. 她生產的時候已經到了。***lie low*** a. 被征服；被制服。b. 藏身。***lie off*** (船)離岸(或其他船隻)不遠。***lie over*** 擱延。***lie to*** (船)逆風時幾乎不能前進。***lie up*** a. 臥床不起；不出門。b. (船)停在船塢；不使用。***lie with*** a. 爲…之職責。b. 與…發生肉體關係。***take lying down*** 甘心屈服或忍受。I refuse to *take* such an insult *lying down*. 我絕不忍受這樣的侮辱。—*n.* ①(僅 *sing.*)位置；方向；形勢。 the *lie* of the land. 地勢。②動物常出沒之所。③〖英〗一臥；一躺。

lie-a·bed 〔ˈlaɪəˌbɛd; ˈlai-əbed〕 *n.* 〖俗〗睡懶覺者；遲起床者。

Lie·der·kranz 〔ˈlidɚˌkrɑnts; ˈliːdəkrɑːnts〕 〖德〗 *n.* ①一組歌曲。②男聲合唱團。③一種具有强烈香味之乳酪；其商標。

lie detector 測謊器。

lie-down 〔ˈlaɪˌdaʊn; ˈlaidaun〕 *n.* 〖主英〗小睡；午睡。

lief 〔lif; liːf〕 *adv.* 喜悅地；自願地。***would*** (or ***had***) ***as lief*** 甘願；情願。Frankly, I'd just *as lief* stay. 坦白地說，我願意留下來。—*adj.* ①寶貴的；珍愛的。②自願的。**—ly,** *adv.*

liege 〔lidʒ; liːdʒ〕 *n.* ①主上；君王。②臣僕。—*adj.* ①(封建制度中)君主的；君王的。②臣僕的。③有主僕關係的。④忠實的。

liege·man 〔ˈlidʒmən; ˈliːdʒmæn〕 *n.*, *pl.* **-men.** ①(封建制度下之)家臣。②忠實的部下。

lie-in 〔ˈlaɪˌɪn; ˈlaiin〕 *n.* ①(早上的)懶覺。②躺地示威(多人躺在公路或公共場所等以示威或抗議)。

lien 〔lin; liən〕 *n.* 〖法律〗留置權；質權；抵押權。

lieu 〔lu; ljuː〕 *n.* 場所(僅用於下列成語中)。 ***in lieu of*** 代替(=instead of). He gave us an I.O.U. *in lieu of* cash. 他以一張欠條代替現金給我們。

Lieut. Lieutenant.

lieu·ten·an·cy 〔luˈtɛnənsɪ; lefˈtenənsi〕 *n.*, *pl.* **-cies.** lieutenant 之階級、職權或任期。

lieu·ten·ant** 〔luˈtɛnənt, lɪu-, lɛf-; lefˈtenənt, leˈt-〕 *n.* ①代理上級官者；副官。②陸軍中尉，少尉。③海軍上尉，中尉。④助理人員；助手。 He was the President's intimate friend and most trusted *lieutenant*. 他是總統親近的友人，也是最受信任的助手。first lieutenant*** 〖美〗(陸軍、空軍或海軍陸戰隊之)中尉。***lieutenant colonel*** 〖美〗陸軍中校；空軍中校。***lieutenant commander*** 〖美〗海軍少校。***lieutenant general*** 〖美〗陸軍中將；空軍中將。***lieutenant governor*** 〖美〗副州長；〖英〗副總督。***lieutenant junior grade*** 〖美〗海軍中尉。***second lieutenant*** 〖美〗(陸軍、空軍或海軍陸戰隊之)少尉。**—ship,** *n.*

life** [laɪf; laif] *n., pl.* **lives** [laɪvz; laivz], *adj.* —*n.* ①生命;性命。How did *life* begin? 生命是怎樣開始的? ②壽命。③一生; 終身。④生活。⑤傳記;言行錄。He has written a *life* of Shakespeare. 他著了一部莎士比亞傳。⑥精神;生氣; 活力。Put more *life* into your work. 工作時要有精神。⑦人; 活的人。Five *lives* were lost. 五人失蹤。⑧存在之時間。⑨生物(集合稱)。⑩力量或生氣等之來源。He was the *life* (and soul) of the party. 他是那聚會的靈魂。⑪社交活動;社交生涯。⑫(死裏逃生後的)新生命;新機會。⑬生涯。He was fighting for his political *life*. 他正在爲自己的政治生涯奮鬥。⑭終身徒刑; 無期徒刑。⑮實物(非模型或圖片)。⑯〖保險〗可能長壽的人;壽險對象。⑰力;動力;彈力。⑱活的狀態; 活動的狀態。The engine coughed into *life*. 引擎突突幾聲後發動了。⑲人生。After all, *life* is worth living. 人生畢竟是值得過的。a good*** (***bad***) ***life***〖保險〗(不)可能活到平均壽命的人。***a matter of life and death*** 生死問題;嚴重的事情。***as large*** (or ***big***) ***as life*** **a.** 與活的一樣大。a statue *as large as life*. 如眞人一般大的雕像。**b.** 親自; 不可能錯誤; 毋容置疑。There he stood, *as large as life*. 那裏站着的就是他本人。***bring to life*** 使蘇醒;使復活。***come to life*** (***again***) **a.** 蘇醒。**b.** 表現生氣或活力。**c.** 栩栩如生。***expectation of life***(人壽保險中)某一年齡的人可能活的平均壽命。***for life*** 終身。***for one's*** (***dear,*** or ***very***) ***life*** 爲了保全性命;拚命。***for the life of me*** 要我的命也…;打死我也…;無論如何也…。***from life*** 根據實物。***future*** (***eternal, everlasting***) ***life*** 來生(永生)。***give one's life*** 捐軀;獻身。***have the time of one's life***〖俗〗享受着一生中前所未有的快樂。***in life*** 一生中。***lose one's life*** 喪失生命; 喪生; 死。***not on your life***〖俗〗絕對不。Will I stand for such a thing? *Not on your life!* 我會贊成這種事嗎? 絕對不! ***on your life*** 無論如何(要);絕對(要)。Obey them *on your life*. 無論如何要服從他們。***run for dear*** (or ***one's***) ***life*** 逃命。***see life*** 得到生活經驗; 閱歷世事。***take one's life in one's hands*** 故意冒生命的危險。***take one's own life*** 自殺。***take somebody's life*** 殺死某人。***the life*** 逼眞;活龍活現;栩栩如生。***the other life*** 來生;來世。***this life*** 今生;此生;今世。***true to life*** 與事實相符;與實際生活相同。—*adj.* ①生命的。②終身的。③人壽保險的。

life-and-death [ˈlaɪfənˈdɛθ; ˈlaifənˈdeθ] *adj.* 有關生死的; 決定生死的。(亦作 **life-or-death**)

life annuity 終身年金。

life arrow 海難救生用的繩索投射箭。

life assurance〖英〗人壽保險(=life insurance).

life belt 救生帶;浮帶。

life·blood [ˈlaɪfˌblʌd; ˈlaifblʌd] *n.* ①保持生命所必需的血液。②任何事物的主要部分或原動力。

life·boat [ˈlaɪfˌbot; ˈlaifbout] *n.* 海上救生船;救生艇。

life·boat·man [ˈlaɪfˌbotmən; ˈlaifˌboutmən] *n., pl.* **-men.** 救生艇上人員。

life breath 生氣。

life buoy 救生圈;救生袋。

life car 海難救生用的防水乘具。

life company 人壽保險公司。

life craft 救生艇。

life cycle〖生物〗生活環(自最初卵之受精起而至再生殖下一代之循環)。

life expectancy 平均壽命 (=expectation of life).

life-force [ˈlaɪfˌfɔrs; ˈlaiffɔːs] *n.* 生命力。

life-form [ˈlaɪfˌfɔrm; ˈlaiffɔːm] *n.* 生物。

life·ful [ˈlaɪffəl; ˈlaifful] *adj.* ①充滿生氣的。②賦予生命的。

life-giv·ing [ˈlaɪfˌgɪvɪŋ; ˈlaifˌgiviŋ] *adj.* 賦與生命的;增加生氣的;提神的;鼓舞的。

Life Guards〖英〗御林軍騎兵團。

life·guard [ˈlaɪfˌgɑrd; ˈlaifgɑːd] *n.* ①游泳場之救生人員。②〖英〗英王侍衞。—*v.t.* 保衞。—*v.i.* 擔任救生人員的工作。

life gun 救生繩具投射機。

life history ①〖生物〗生活史(生物自初生, 卽卵或胞子, 至成熟之生活過程)。②〖生物〗=**life cycle.** ③〖社會〗個人生活史。

life insurance ①人壽保險。②(保險公司付給之)人壽保險金。③(保險人付給保險公司之)人壽保險費。④人壽保險與遺產保險之合稱。

life jacket 救生衣。

***life·less** [ˈlaɪflɪs; ˈlaiflis] *adj.* ①無生命的。②死的。③無趣味的; 枯燥無味的。a *lifeless* performance. 死氣沉沉的表演。④失去知覺的。⑤無生物的。⑥(食物)無營養的。—**ly,** *adv.*

life·like [ˈlaɪfˌlaɪk; ˈlaif-laik] *adj.* ①生動的;栩栩如生的。②(圖畫等)維妙維肖的。—**ness,** *n.*

life line ①救生索(從岸上拋到船上或拋給將溺的人的索; 繫於救生衣上之索等); (喻義) 似救生索之物。②繫於潛水人員作升降用或發信號用之繩索。③(手相) 生命線。④〖航海〗重要之航線。⑤〖商〗生命線。⑥轉運物資至某一地點之唯一途徑。

life·long [ˈlaɪfˈlɔŋ; ˈlaif-lɔŋ] *adj.* 終身的;畢生的。

life net (火災時之)救生網。

life office 人壽保險業; 人壽保險公司之辦事處。

life peer 止於一身之貴族(子孫不能承襲)。

life preserver ①〖美〗救生工具(如衣、帶、圈等)。②〖英〗防身用之短棒(其一端塡以金屬)。

lif·er [ˈlaɪfɚ; ˈlaifə] *n.*〖俚〗被處無期徒刑者。

life raft 救生艇。

life ring 救生圈。

life·sav·er [ˈlaɪfˌsevɚ; ˈlaifˌseivə] *n.* ①救命者;救命恩人。②(浴場等之)救生隊員。③〖俚〗使人免於困難的人(物)。

life·sav·ing [ˈlaɪfˌsevɪŋ; ˈlaifˌseiviŋ] *adj.* 救生(用)的;救難(用)的; 救溺的。—*n.* 救命;救溺。

life sciences 生物科學(包括動物學、植物學、生物化學、生物物理學、微生物學等)。

life scientist 生物科學家。

life sentence 無期徒刑之判決。

life-size [ˈlaɪfˈsaɪz; ˈlaifˈsaiz] *adj.* 與實物大小一樣的。(亦作 **life-sized**)

life span 壽命 (生物可能的最長生命)。

life·spring [ˈlaɪfˌsprɪŋ; ˈlaifspriŋ] *n.* 生命的源泉。

life tenure 終生職。

life·time** [ˈlaɪfˌtaɪm; ˈlaiftaim] *n.* ①一生;終身。②有生之日。My grandfather saw many changes during his *lifetime*. 我祖父在世時看到許多改變。the chance of a lifetime*** 終身不再的機會。—*adj.* 終身的。

life vest 救生衣。

life·work [ˈlaɪfˈwɝk; ˈlaifˈwəːk] *n.* 終身事業。

LIFO last in, first out. 後進先出。

‡lift [lɪft;lift] *v.t.* ①舉起;抬起;搬起。This box is too heavy for me to *lift*. 這箱太重,我搬不起。②(自土中)掘出。③晉升;擢升。④提高。⑤〖俗〗撿起;偸。⑥〖美〗償付;贖。⑦使向上突出。⑧解除(禁令等)。⑨抄襲。⑩帶;運送。—*v.i.* ①升高。The huge airliner *lifted* from the airport. 大客機從機場起飛。②被舉起;被推起。The window won't *lift*. 這窗戶不能推起。③(霧等)消散。The mist began to *lift*. 霧開始消散。④向上突出。***lift one's hand against*** 〖俗〗威脅。***lift up one's eyes*** 抬頭;向上看。***lift up one's voice*** 高呼。—*n.* ①高舉;舉起。②所舉的高度。③幫助;助手。Give me a *lift* with this job. 幫我做這件事。④〖英〗電梯。⑤(鞋跟)皮之一層。⑥高地。⑦一次搬起或運起之量。⑧以車帶人之行動。⑨進步;增進。⑩抬起的狀態;舉起的狀態。⑪有系統之運輸。They moved 1332 troops in a single *lift*. 他們一次運輸1332人的部隊。⑫一次印出之一堆(紙張)。***give a person a lift*** 讓某人搭乘自己的汽車;幫助某人。—**a·ble,** *adj.* 〖注意〗電梯 **lift** 爲英語, **elevator** 爲美語。

lift·boy [ˈlɪftˌbɔɪ; ˈliftbɔi] *n.* 〖英〗電梯管理員。

lift bridge 升降橋(船舶通過時,橋面可開啓者)。

lift capacity 空運能力。

lift·man [ˈlɪftmən; ˈliftmæn] *n., pl.* **-men.** 〖英〗電梯司機 (=elevator operator).

lift-off [ˈlɪftˌɔf; ˈliftɔːf] *n.* 升空; 發射(尤指火箭或直升機)。

lift pump 抽水機。

lig·a·ment [ˈlɪgəmənt; ˈligəmənt] *n.,* ①〖解剖〗韌帶;紐帶;連帶筋肉、骨骼、器官之韌帶。②紐;帶。

li·gate [ˈlaɪget; ˈlaigeit] *v.t.,* **-gat·ed, -gat·ing.** 〖外科〗結紮。

li·ga·tion [laɪˈgeʃən; laiˈgeiʃən] *n.* ①〖外科〗結紮。②被結紮之狀態。③縫合線;結紮繩。④結紮處。

lig·a·ture [ˈlɪgəˌtʃʊr; ˈligətʃuə] *n., v.,* **-tured, -tur·ing.** —*n.* ①綁縛之物;結合之物(如繃帶、繩)等。②〖外科〗縫合線;縛線。③縛;綁。④〖音樂〗連結線。⑤〖印刷〗連字(如Æ, *ffl* 等)。⑥〖印刷〗啣接二字之短畫。—*v.t.* 綁;縛;結紮。

li·geance [ˈlaɪdʒəns; ˈlaidʒəns] *n.* 忠;效忠(如臣之對君,人民之對政府等)。

li·ger [ˈlaɪgɚ; ˈlaigə] *n.* 雄獅與雌虎交配而生之雜交種。

‡light[1] [laɪt; lait] *n., adj., v.,* **light·ed** or **lit, light·ing.** —*n.* ①光;光線;光亮。②發光物(如燈); 引火物(如火柴)。Put a *light* to the fire. 將火點着。③火(=fire)。④光源。A tall building cuts off our *light*. 一座高的建築物擋住我們的光。⑤照明;光度。⑥光明之處。*light* and shade. 明與暗。⑦白天;日間。⑧天明;破曉。⑨使光線進入之物(如窗戶等)。⑩了解;明白。We need more *light* on this subject. 對此事我們須有更多的了解。⑪見解;事實的眞相。⑫顯赫人物;典範人物。Dr. Sun Yat-sen is one of the *lights* of history. 孫中山博士是歷史上著名人物之一。⑬同意。⑭目光;臉上的光彩。The *light* died out of her eyes. 她眼中的光彩消失了(她顯得失望和沮喪)。⑮交通燈光號誌。⑯日光。⑰眞理。⑱衆人之耳目。⑲〖古〗視力。⑳燈塔。㉑(*pl.*)一個人所有的知識能力與思想能力等。***according to one's lights*** 儘量依據某人自己之意見、所知及良心。***by the light of nature*** 由於天分。***hide one's light under a bushel*** 埋沒自己的才幹。***in a good***(or ***bad***) ***light*** **a.** (不)容易看清的。Hang the picture *in a good light*. 把那圖畫掛在容易看清楚的地方。**b.** 從好(或壞)的觀點。***in the light of*** 從…的觀點。***see the light*** (***of the day***) **a.** 出生。**b.** 公開;公諸於世。**c.** 得到正確的觀念。***shed*** (or ***throw***) ***light on*** 對…加以說明;使人明白。***stand in a person's light*** 遮住某人的光;阻礙某人成功或進步之機會。***stand in one's own light*** 遮住自己的光線;使自己名譽受損。***strike a light*** 點火;點燈。***the light of one's countenance*** 允許;同意。***the light of one's eye*** 某人所鍾愛者。—*adj.* ①光明的;明亮的。This is quite a *light* room. 這是一間光線充足的房間。②淺色的;淡色的。③容光煥發的。*lighter* than his brother. 比他兄(弟)更爲容光煥發。—*v.t.* ①點燃。Shall I *light* the lamp? 我需將燈點着嗎?②供給光線;使光明。Electricity *lights* our houses. 電使我們的房屋光明。③使容光煥發。④使發光。His style is *lighted* up with flashes of wit. 他的文體以其所顯示的機智而光芒萬丈。⑤以燈引路。—*v.i.* ①變亮;轉爲光亮。②着火。③容光煥發。***light up*** 點燈;照亮。〖注意〗**lighted, lit.** 此兩形式無論作過去式或過去分詞,均係正確用法。lighted 用作形容詞或過去分詞的情形較爲普遍。lit 則用作過去式之情形較多。

light[2]** *adj.* ①輕的。②分量輕的(就體積論)。a *light* metal. 輕金屬。③輕捷的;靈活的。④輕微的。a *light* wind. 和風。⑤愉快的;高興的。⑥輕浮的;輕率的。⑦軟性的;通俗的。*light* literature. 通俗文學。*light* music. 輕音樂。⑧輕巧的。a *light* bridge. 便橋。⑨不重要的;微小的。⑩多孔的;含沙的。a *light* soil. 含沙的土。⑪味淡的;酒精成分不多的。⑫易消化的。⑬輕裝備的。*light* cavalry. 輕騎兵。⑭小規模的。*light* industries. 輕工業。⑮輕音的(音節)。⑯頭暈的。⑰載貨很少的;未載貨的。⑱(武器等)小型的;小口徑的。⑲淫蕩的;人盡可夫的。⑳易變的。as light as air*** (***a feather***) 輕如空氣(鴻毛)。***light fingers*** **a.** 手指靈活。**b.** 善於偸竊。***light hand*** **a.** 手的靈巧。**b.** (待人接物)手段高妙。***light in the head*** **a.** 頭暈的。**b.** 愚蠢的。**c.** 失去理智的;瘋狂的。***make light of*** 低估;輕視。—*adv.* ①輕輕地;容易地。②不帶貨地。***get off light*** 〖俗〗逃過了嚴厲的懲罰。***Light come, light go.*** 〖諺〗(指金錢)易來易去。

light[3] *v.i.,* **light·ed** or **lit, light·ing.** ①(自馬上)下來。He *lighted* from his horse. 他下馬。②(鳥等)棲止。A bird *lighted* on the branch. 一鳥棲息於此枝上。③偶遇。④突然落下。***light into*** 〖俚〗**a.** 攻擊。**b.** 責備。***light out*** 〖俚〗突然離去;迅速離開。

light-armed [ˈlaɪtˈɑrmd; ˈlaitˈɑːmd] *adj.* 僅持輕武器的;輕裝備的。

light bulb 燈泡。

light-col·ored [ˈlaɪtˈkʌlɚd; ˈlait-ˈkʌləd] *adj.* 顏色淺的;不黑的。

***light·en[1]** [ˈlaɪtn̩; ˈlaitn] *v.t.* ①使光明。②使淡。—*v.i.* ①變成光明;變亮。The eastern sky *lightened*. 東方的天空亮了。②閃電。

***light·en[2]** *v.t.* ①減輕;使輕。②使輕鬆;使愉快。—*v.i.* ①變輕。Censorship has *lightened* somewhat. 檢查有些變鬆了。②變愉快。

light·en·ing [ˈlaɪtnɪŋ; ˈlaitniŋ] *n.* 〖醫〗孕腹輕鬆(懷孕末期子宮之落進骨盆,其結果爲孕婦腹部形狀改變及呼吸較易)。

light·er[1] [ˈlaɪtɚ; ˈlaitə] *n.* ①點火的人

或物。②打火機。

light·er² *n.* 駁船。—*v.t.* 以駁船運(貨)。

light·er·age ['laɪtərɪdʒ; 'laitəridʒ] *n.*①駁運。②駁運費。

light·er·man ['laɪtəmən; 'laitəmən] *n., pl.* **-men.** 駁船夫；駁船船戶。

light·er-than-air ['laɪtəðən'ɛr; 'laitəðən'ɛə] *adj.* 〖航空〗①比空氣輕的(飛船等)。②氣球的；飛船的。

light·face ['laɪt,fes; 'laitfeis] *n.* 一種細體鉛字。—*adj.* (鉛字)線條很細的。

light·fast ['laɪt,fæst; 'laitfɑ:st] *adj.* 不因光而褪色的。

light-fin·gered ['laɪt'fɪŋgəd; 'lait,fiŋgəd] *adj.* ①善偷竊的。②手指靈巧的。

light-foot ['laɪt,fut; 'laitfut] *adj.* 脚步輕捷的。

light-foot·ed['laɪt'futɪd; 'lait'futid] *adj.* 脚快的；脚步輕捷的。

light-hand·ed ['laɪt'hændɪd; 'lait,hændid] *adj.* ①(工場、船上等)人手不够的。②空手的；手中持物少的。③(手段等)輕妙的；手工靈巧的。

light-head·ed ['laɪt'hɛdɪd; 'lait'hedid] *adj.* ①頭昏眼花的；神志顚狂的。②三心兩意的；輕率的。③輕浮的。—**ly,** *adv.*

light-heart·ed ['laɪt'hɑrtɪd; 'lait'hɑ:tid] *adj.* 無憂無慮的；愉快的。

light·heart·ed·ly ['laɪt'hɑrtɪdlɪ; 'lait'hɑ:tidli] *adv.* 輕鬆愉快地。

light heavyweight 重乙級(選手體重於拳擊在161–175磅, 於摔角在176–191磅, 於舉重在168–180磅者)。

light-horse·man ['laɪt,hɔrsmən; 'lait'hɔ:smən] *n., pl.* **-men.** 輕騎兵。

***light·house** ['laɪt,haus; 'laithaus] *n.* 燈塔。

light·ing ['laɪtɪŋ; 'laitiŋ] *n.* ①點燈；點火。②(繪畫中)光線的明暗。③舞臺照明法；舞臺燈光(集合稱)。④照明。

***light·ly** ['laɪtlɪ; 'laitli] *adv.* ①輕微地；輕輕地。He was punished *lightly.* 他受輕微的懲罰。②稍微地；微少地。③飄忽地。④輕快地。⑤快樂地；(心情)輕鬆地。⑥漠不關心地；輕蔑地。⑦輕率地。⑧輕易地。*Lightly* come, *lightly* go. (指金錢)易來易去。

light-mind·ed ['laɪt'maɪndɪd; 'lait'maindid] *adj.* 輕浮的；輕率的；浮躁的。

light·ness¹ ['laɪtnɪs; 'laitnis] *n.* ①明亮；光亮。②(色彩等之)淡薄。

light·ness² *n.* ①輕。②敏捷；靈活。③(心情之)輕快；愉快。④輕率；輕薄；輕浮。⑤柔和；溫和。⑥優雅。

light·ning** ['laɪtnɪŋ; 'laitniŋ] *n.* 閃電。like lightning*** 像閃電一般。***with lightning speed*** =like lightning. —*v.i.* 閃電。It *lightninged* terribly last night. 昨晚閃電閃得很厲害。

lightning ar·rest·er [~ə'rɛstə; ~ə'restə] 〖電〗(裝於無線電等上之)避雷器。

lightning bug (or **beetle**) 〖美〗螢火蟲(=firefly).

lightning rod (or **conductor**) ①避雷針。②用以避免攻擊之事物。

light-o'-love ['laɪtə'lʌv; 'laitə'lʌv] *n.* ①輕佻的女人；蕩婦。②妓女。

light·proof ['laɪt'pruf; 'laitpru:f] *adj.* 防光的。

lights [laɪts; laits] *n. pl.* (家畜類之)肺臟(餵犬、貓之食物)。

light·ship ['laɪt,ʃɪp; 'lait-ʃip] *n.* 燈塔船；信號船。

light-skirts ['laɪt,skɜts; 'lait-skə:ts] *n.* 蕩婦；淫婦。

light·some¹ ['laɪtsəm; 'laitsəm] *adj.* 光亮的；輝耀的。

light·some² *adj.* ①活潑的；輕巧的。②愉快的；歡樂的。③輕浮的；瑣細的。—**ly,** *adv.*

light-struck ['laɪt,strʌk; 'laitstrʌk] *adj.* (膠捲)意外曝光的。

light·tight ['laɪt,taɪt; 'lait'tait] *adj.* 防光的。

light trap ①(通往暗房的)遮光通路。②捕蟲燈。

light wave 〖物理〗光波。

light·weight ['laɪt'wet; 'lait-weit] *n.* ①標準重量以下的人。②〖俗〗無能之人；不重要之人。③輕量級拳擊家或其他選手(體重在127至135磅之間)。—*adj.* ①〖拳擊〗輕量級的。②特輕的。③不重要的；輕鬆性的。

light·wood ['laɪt,wud; 'lait-wud] *n.* ①起火柴。②易燃之木材。

light-year ['laɪt'jɪr; 'lait'jə:] *n.* 光年(光在一年內所行的距離, 用作星球間距離的單位, 約 6,000,000,000,000英里)。

lig·ne·ous ['lɪgnɪəs; 'ligniəs] *adj.* 〖植物〗木的；似木的；木質的。

lig·ni·fi·ca·tion [,lɪgnəfɪ'keʃən; ,lignifi'keiʃən] *n.* 木質化。

lig·nin ['lɪgnɪn; 'lignin] *n.* 〖化〗木質。

lig·nite ['lɪgnaɪt; 'lignait] *n.* 〖礦〗褐炭。

lig·num vi·tae ['lɪgnəm'vaɪtɪ; 'lignəm'vaiti:] 〖植物〗(熱帶美洲產)癒瘡木。

lig·u·late['lɪgju,lɪt;'ligjulit] *adj.* 〖植物〗舌狀的；有舌狀花冠的。(亦作 **ligulated**)

lig·ule ['lɪgjul; 'ligju:l] *n.* 〖植物〗小舌片；舌狀片；舌狀花冠。

lik·a·ble ['laɪkəbl̩; 'laikəbl] *adj.* 可愛的；可喜的；有人望的。—**lik·a·bil·i·ty,** *n.*

‡like¹ [laɪk; laik] *prep., adj.,* (poetic) **lik·er, lik·est,** *adv., n., conj., v.,* **liked, lik·ing.** —*prep.* ①像；似；如。He saw a number of small hard things *like* stones. 他看見一些像石頭一樣小而堅硬的東西。②依照；如同；像。Do it *like* this. 照這樣做。③代表着…之特徵。It was *like* him to remember us at Christmas. 像他這種人在聖誕節會記起我們的。***like a book*** **a.** 用辭拘謹。He talks *like a book.* 他說話用辭拘謹。**b.** 瞭如指掌。***like anything*** 〖俗〗非常；極其。***nothing like*** 差得甚遠。***something like*** 差不多；幾乎。It cost me *something like* $500. 那差不多花了我五百元。—*adj.* ①同樣的；相似的。They are as *like* as two peas. 他們相似極了。②可能會；像要。It looks *like* rain. 好像要下雨。③適於；高興於。I feel *like* working. 我現在覺得很願意工作。***Like father like son.*** 有其父必有其子。—*adv.* ①〖俗〗或有可能地。*Like* enough it will rain. 很可能會下雨。②同樣地。③〖古〗相等地。④與…相同地。***(as) like as not*** 很可能。***like crazy*** 〖俚〗瘋狂地。—*n.* 相似的人或事物。***and the like*** 等等；及其同類者(=and so forth). He studies music, painting, *and the like.* 他研究音樂、繪畫等等。***the like*** (or ***likes***) ***of*** **a.** 類似之人或物；相等之人或物。**b.** 性質相同之物。—*conj.* 〖俗〗像；似；如。He looks *like* he will get the job. 他看來好像會得到那工作。—*v.t.* 〖廢〗比較。—*v.i.* 〖方〗接近；近乎。

‡like² *v.,* **liked, lik·ing,** *n.* —*v.t.* ①喜歡；愛好。Do you *like* fish? 你喜歡魚嗎？②欲；想；願意(與 should, would 連用)。I should *like* to stay here (go out). 我想留在這裏

(出去)。③特別喜歡;最愛。④適合…的健康。I like lobster but it does not *like* me. 我喜歡吃龍蝦,但它不宜於我的健康。⑤感覺。—*v.i.* 覺得喜歡。Take whichever you *like*. 你隨便選那一個都可以。***as you like*** 自由;隨便;如你所好。You can do *as you like*. 你可自由行動。—*n.* (*pl.*) 愛好;嗜好。〖注意〗(1) like 之後用 gerund 或 infinitive 均可, 如: I *like* reading. 我喜歡讀書。I *like* to read in bed. 我喜歡躺在床上讀書。(2)**like, love**不能互換。like 意爲"喜歡",並不表示强烈之感情:I *like* books. 我喜歡書。love 着重於强烈之情感,親密之依戀:She *loves* her mother. 她愛她的母親。

-like 〖字尾〗①像。wolflike. 像狼一般的。②有…特徵的。childlike. 小孩似的。③適於…。businesslike. 適於公事的;一本正經的。

like·a·ble [ˈlaɪkəbl̩; ˈlaikəbl] *adj.* = **likable.** 「*n.* 可能性。」

like·li·hood [ˈlaɪklɪˌhud; ˈlaiklihud]

‡like·ly [ˈlaɪklɪ; ˈlaikli] *adj.*, **-li·er, -li·est,** *adv.* —*adj.* ①有可能的。He isn't *likely* to come now; it's too late. 這時他不會來了,時間已經太晚了。②合適的; 如所期望的。Is there a *likely* place to fish? 有適合釣魚的地方嗎? ③前途有望的。—*adv.* 或許; 或有可能地。—**like·li·ness,** *n.*

like-mind·ed [ˈlaɪkˈmaɪndɪd; ˈlaikˈmaindid] *adj.* 同心的;同志的;同意見的;志趣相同的。—**ly,** *adv.* 「—*v.i.* 像;似。」

lik·en [ˈlaɪkən; ˈlaikən] *v.t.* 比喻爲。

•like·ness [ˈlaɪknɪs; ˈlaiknis] *n.* ①相像;相似。I cannot see much *likeness* between them. 我看不出他們之間有多少相似。②相似之點。③相似物; 肖像; 照相。④容貌;相貌。***in the likeness of*** 外貌似。Jupiter appeared *in the likeness of* a swan. Jupiter神以天鵝的樣子出現。

•like·wise [ˈlaɪkˌwaɪz; ˈlaik-waiz] *adv.* ①同樣地;照樣地。②也;亦。Mary must go home now, and Nell *likewise*. 瑪麗現在要回家,奈爾也要回去。—*conj.* 且;亦。

•lik·ing [ˈlaɪkɪŋ; ˈlaikiŋ] *n.* 愛好;嗜好。The tea is not to my *liking*. 這茶不合我的胃口。***on liking*** 以喜歡爲條件。

•li·lac [ˈlaɪlək; ˈlailək] *n.* ①紫丁香花。a bunch of *lilac*. 一束紫丁香花。②淡紫色;淡紫紅色。—*adj.* 淡紫色的;淡紫紅色的。

lil·i·a·ceous [ˌlɪlɪˈeʃəs; ˌliliˈeiʃəs] *adj.* ①百合的;似百合的。②〖植物〗百合科的。

Lil·li·put [ˈlɪləˌpʌt; ˈlilipʌt] *n.* 小人國(Swift 著 *Gulliver's Travels* 中所想像之一國家,其人民約六英寸高)。—*adj.* 特小的。

Lil·li·pu·tian [ˌlɪləˈpjuʃən; ˌliliˈpjuːʃiən] *adj.* ①小人國 (Lilliput) 的。②非常(矮)小的。③心地狹窄的。—*n.* ①Lilliput人。②侏儒。③心地狹窄的人;小人。

lilt [lɪlt; lilt] *n.* ①輕快之旋律或節拍。②節律輕快的歌曲。③輕快活潑之動作。—*v.t.* & *v.i.* ①輕快地唱或奏。②輕快地動。

•lil·y [ˈlɪlɪ; ˈlili] *n.*, *pl.* **lil·ies,** *adj.* —*n.* 百合;百合花。***Chinese sacred lily*** 水仙。***Easter lilies*** 白百合。***lilies and roses*** 美貌;美容。***tiger lilies*** 紅百合。***water lilies*** 睡蓮。—*adj.* 潔白的; 純白色的;純潔的;可愛的。my lady's lily hand. 我愛人的潔白的手。 「*adj.* 膽小的;怯儒的。」

lil·y-liv·ered [ˈlɪlɪˈlɪvəd; ˈliliˌlivəd]

lily of the valley *pl.* **lilies of the valley.** 〖植物〗鈴蘭。

lily pad 〖美〗(浮於水上的)睡蓮之葉。

lil·y-white [ˈlɪlɪˈhwaɪt; ˈliliˈhwait] *adj.* ①如百合般白的;潔白的。②清白的;無瑕疵的。③(L-)〖美〗Lily-white 黨的。—*n.* (L-) 美國南部共和黨中排斥黑人主張全白人主義之一派的黨員。 「首都)。」

Li·ma¹ [ˈlimə; ˈliːmə] *n.* 利瑪 (秘魯之

Li·ma² *n.* 通訊電碼,代表字母L.

Li·ma bean [ˈlaɪmə~; ˈlaimə~] 〖植物〗頓馬豆(綠白色扁豆)。(亦作 **lima bean**)

•limb¹ [lɪm; lim] *n.* ①(四)肢; 手足。He lost a *limb* in the battle. 他在戰爭中失去一肢。②樹的大枝。③(某物之)分支或後裔。④惡作劇之年輕人;頑皮的小孩。***be torn limb from limb*** 被碎屍。***escape with life and limb*** 逃出而未受大傷害。***limb from limb*** 完全分開的。***out on a limb*** 在不能後退的危險狀態。—*v.t.* 切斷…之手足。—**less,** *adj.*

limb² *n.* ①〖天文〗(日、月等之)邊緣。②〖機械〗分度圈 (四分儀等之刻度部分)。③〖植物〗邊緣;葉邊。

lim·ber¹ [ˈlɪmbɚ; ˈlimbə] *n.* 〖兵學〗(砲)前車(通常由二輪、一軸、一杆、一彈箱、一座位構成)。—*v.t.* & *v.i.* 裝(砲)於前車上〖常up〗。

lim·ber² *adj.* ①柔軟的; 易曲的。②靈活的。—*v.i.* & *v.t.* 使(自身) 變柔軟靈活〖常up〗。—**ness,** *n.* 「或排水槽。」

lim·ber³ *n.* (常*pl.*)〖航海〗船上之排水孔

lim·bo [ˈlɪmbo; ˈlimbou] *n.* ①地獄邊緣之一地區(爲未受洗而死亡之嬰兒或耶穌降臨以前死亡之善良人所暫時棲止之處)。②安置被遺棄之人或物的地方; 丟棄廢物之所。③監牢;拘留所。④困境。⑤(兩種不同狀態之)中間狀態。 「官;執法人員。」

limb of the law 警察、律師、或法

Lim·burg·er [ˈlɪmbɝgɚ; ˈlimbəːgə] *n.* 林堡乾酪(產於比利時 Limburg,氣味濃烈)。

•lime¹ [laɪm; laim] *n.*, *v.*, **limed, lim·ing.** —*n.* ①石灰。②(=birdlime)塗在樹枝上以捕鳥之黏性物質; 黏鳥膠。—*v.t.* ①以石灰處理。②塗黏鳥膠於 (樹枝等)。The birds would find the twigs *limed* for them. 小鳥會發覺樹枝上塗了黏膠以捕捉它們。③以黏鳥膠捕(鳥)。

lime² *n.* 菩提樹。

lime³ *n.* ①一種極像檸檬之芸香科樹; 萊姆樹。②萊姆果(可作調味或藥用)。

lime·ade [ˌlaɪmˈed; ˌlaimˈeid] *n.* 一種用萊姆果、糖及水調和的飲料。

lime burn·er [ˈlaɪmˌbɝnɚ; ˈlaimˌbəːnə] 燒(製)石灰者。(亦作 **limeburner**)

lime juice 柚汁;萊姆果汁。

lime-juic·er [ˈlaɪmˌdʒusɚ; ˈlaimˌdʒuːsə] *n.* 〖美, 水手俚語〗①英國水兵(因英艦上水兵均强迫服 lime 果汁以防壞血症,故稱)。②英國船隻。 「灰窖。」

lime·kiln [ˈlaɪmˌkɪl; ˈlaimkiln] *n.* 石

lime·light [ˈlaɪmˌlaɪt; ˈlaimlait] *n.* ①聚光燈;水銀燈(舞臺上照明某一角色或目標之用)。②聚光燈射在舞臺上的光;舞臺上聚光燈所照的部分。③衆目注視的中心。***be fond of the limelight*** 愛引人注意; 愛出風頭。***be in the limelight*** **a.** 被聚光燈所照明。**b.** 爲衆目所視;引萬人注視。

li·men [ˈlaɪmɛn; ˈlaimen] *n.*, *pl.* **li·mens, lim·i·na** [ˈlɪmənə; ˈlimənə]. 〖心理〗閾(意識之界限);刺激閾(引起感覺所需之神經刺激之最小限度)。

lim·er·ick [ˈlɪmərɪk; ˈlimərik] *n.*一種五行滑稽詩(1,2,5 行押一韻,3,4 行押一韻)。

•lime·stone [ˈlaɪmˌston; ˈlaimstoun]

n. 石灰石。
lime tree 菩提樹。
lime twig ①塗黏鳥膠的樹枝。②陷阱。
lime·wa·ter [ˈlaɪmˌwɔtə; ˈlaimˌwɔːtə] *n.* ①石灰水。②含磷酸鈣或炭酸鈣很多的水。
lim·ey [ˈlaɪmɪ; ˈlaimi] *n.* 〖美俚〗①英國兵；英國水兵。②英國人。③英國船。—*adj.* ①英國的。②=**limy.**
lim·i·nal [ˈlɪmɪnl; ˈliminl] *adj.* 〖心理〗閾的；刺激閾的。
‡lim·it [ˈlɪmɪt; ˈlimit] *n.* ①界限；邊界。As we grow older, we learn the *limits* of our abilities. 當我們年齡漸長，我們便了解自己能力的限度。②〖數學〗極限。③(the-)(球賽、拳擊賽等之)全場。Although he went the *limit*, he lost the fight on points. 雖然他賽畢全場，但因得分較少而輸掉那場拳賽。④(*pl.*)疆界；領土。***the limit*** 〖俚〗忍受的極限。That's *the limit!* 那已是極限了！***within limits*** 在限度內地。***without limit*** 無限地。—*v.t.* ①定界限於…；限制；限定。Membership is *limited* to women. 會員限於婦女。②〖法律〗確定；確切指派。—**a·ble,** *adj.*
***lim·i·ta·tion** [ˌlɪməˈteʃən; ˌlimiˈteiʃən] *n.* ①缺陷；環境的限制。He knows his *limitations.* 他自知他的缺陷。②限制。③(法律)有效時期。④限額。The import *limitation* has reduced to $100 per person. 進口限額已減少到每人一百美元。
lim·i·ta·tive [ˈlɪməˌtetɪv; ˈlimiteitiv] *adj.* 限制的；限定的。
***lim·it·ed** [ˈlɪmɪtɪd; ˈlimitid] *adj.* ①有限制的。②有限的；狹窄的；少的。The accommodation of the hall is very *limited.* 會場的可容人數很有限。③〖美〗(火車、汽車等)乘客有定額的；特別的。④〖政治〗被(憲法)限制的；立憲制的。*limited* government. 立憲政治。⑤(公司)有限責任的。—*n.* 〖美〗特別快車(指火車、汽車等)。—**ly,** *adv.* —**ness,** *n.*
limited company 有限責任公司。
limited divorce 夫妻分居。
limited edition (書籍)限額發行之一版。
limited monarchy 君主立憲政體。
limited policy 有限賠償保險證明書。
limited war 有限度戰爭。
lim·it·less [ˈlɪmɪtlɪs; ˈlimitlis] *adj.* 無界限的；無限制的。—**ly,** *adv.* —**ness,** *n.*
limn [lɪm; lim] *v.t.* ①描；畫。②描寫；描述。
lim·nol·o·gy [lɪmˈnɑlədʒɪ; limˈnɔlədʒi] *n.* 湖沼學；淡水生物學。
lim·o·nene [ˈlɪməˌnin; ˈliməniːn] *n.* 〖化〗檸檬油精 ($C_{10}H_{16}$)。
li·mo·nite [ˈlaɪməˌnaɪt; ˈlaimənait] *n.* 〖礦〗褐鐵礦 ($2Fe_2O_3 \cdot 3H_2O$)。
lim·ou·sine [ˈlɪməˌzin; ˈlimu(ː)ziːn] *n.* ①轎車型之汽車。②接送旅客於機場與市區間之小型巴士。
limousine liberal 〖美〗富有的自由分子。
limp¹ [lɪmp; limp] *adj.* ①柔軟的；易曲的。②無力的；軟弱的。—**ly,** *adv.* —**ness,** *n.*
***limp²** *v.i.* ①跛行。The wounded soldier *limped* off the battlefield. 負傷之兵士跛行着離開戰場。②(詩歌等)做壞；錯用音律。His verse *limps.* 他的詩錯用了音律。③勉強航行或飛行。—*n.* (通常前加不定冠詞)跛行。
lim·pet [ˈlɪmpɪt; ˈlimpit] *n.* ①〖動物〗蝛(貝之一種)。②堅守某一職位之人；堅隨旁人的人。
lim·pid [ˈlɪmpɪd; ˈlimpid] *adj.* ①清澈的；透明的。②明晰的；清楚的。③平穩無事的。—**ness,** *n.*
lim·pid·i·ty [lɪmˈpɪdətɪ; limˈpiditi] *n.* ①清澈；透明。②明晰；清楚。
lim·pid·ly [ˈlɪmpɪdlɪ; ˈlimpidli] *adv.* 清澈地；明晰地。
lim·y [ˈlaɪmɪ; ˈlaimi] *adj.*, **lim·i·er, lim·i·est.** ①石灰的；石灰狀的；含石灰的。②塗有黏鳥膠的。—**lim·i·ness,** *n.*
lin. ①lineal. ②linear.
lin·a·ble [ˈlaɪnəbl; ˈlainəbl] *adj.* 成直線排列的。(亦作 **lineable**)
lin·age [ˈlaɪnɪdʒ; ˈlainidʒ] *n.* ①排成一列(一直線)。②(原稿等之)行數。③按行數付的稿費。
linch·pin [ˈlɪntʃˌpɪn; ˈlintʃpin] *n.* ①(軸端之)輪轄；制輪楔。②樞紐；關鍵。
Lin·coln [ˈlɪŋkən; ˈliŋkən] *n.* 林肯(Abraham, 1809-1865, 美國第十六任總統，以解放黑奴著稱於世)。
Lincoln's Birthday 林肯誕辰紀念日(二月十二日，為美國許多州之法定節日)。(亦作 **Lincoln Day**)
lin·dane [ˈlɪnˌden; ˈlindein] *n.* 農藥之一種。
Lind·bergh [ˈlɪnbɜg; ˈlindbəːg] *n.* 林白(Charles Augustus, 1902-1974,美國飛行家，於 1927 年首次完成橫渡大西洋不着陸飛行)。
lin·den [ˈlɪndən; ˈlindən] *n.* 菩提樹。
‡line¹ [laɪn; lain] *n., v.,* **lined, lin·ing.** —*n.* ①直線；線。②線條；筆劃。③繩；索；(電)線。The storm blew the *lines* down. 暴風雨將電線吹落了。④排；列。a long *line* of trees (hills, etc.). 一長列樹(小山等)。⑤(臉上的)皺紋。His face was covered with deep *lines* of care. 他的臉上滿是愁苦的皺紋。⑥(印刷物之)一行。⑦短簡；短函。Drop me a few *lines* letting me know how you are. 請惠我數行，告訴我你的近況。⑧運輸線路；運輸公司。a steamship *line.* 輪船公司。⑨(球場等的)場線。Did the ball cross the *line?* 球過線了嗎？⑩行業；本行。That's not my *line.* 那不是我的本行。⑪貨品之一種。⑫〖數學〗線。⑬(*pl.*)輪廓；外貌。a ship of fine *lines.* 外貌美觀的船。⑭(*pl.*)結構設計。two books written on the same *lines.* 結構(梗概)相同之兩本書。⑮邊界。the *line* between Texas and Mexico. 德克薩斯州與墨西哥的邊界。⑯一連串有關之人或事物。⑰家族；家系。⑱行程；方向。⑲行動、行為、思想之方向。⑳最前線之戰壕或其他防禦工事。㉑(*pl.*)(兵士之)雙行。㉒部隊或船隻之並列。㉓軍隊或艦隊之戰備布署。㉔鐵軌。They blew out the main *line.* 他們炸毀了主線鐵軌。㉕(*pl.*)(劇本中演員之)臺詞。㉖五線譜中之一線。㉗(*pl.*)命運。㉘(*pl.*)韁繩。㉙一英寸之十二分之一。㉚(常 the-)赤道。㉛概略的了解。He tried to get a *line* on his brother's plans. 他想辦法對他兄(弟)的計畫獲得概略的了解。㉜詩句；詩節；詩篇。***all along the line*** 在每一方面；到處。to be successful *all along the line.* 在每一方面都成功。***bring (a person) into line*** 使(某人)同意或合作。***come into line (with)*** (與…)同意；合作。***down the line*** 完全；從頭到尾。They are prepared to back the President *down the line.* 他們準備擁護總統到底。***draw the*** (or ***a***) ***line*** 加限制；止於。They would *draw the line* at murder. 他們止於謀殺(除了殺人以外幹別的犯法勾當都可以)。***form into line*** (軍隊等)排成隊；整隊。***get*** (or ***have***) ***a line on*** 〖俗〗得到有關…的消息。***go up in one's lines*** (英國為

go up on one's lines) 忘記臺詞。***go up the line*** 到前線去。***Hard lines!*** 眞倒霉! ***hold the line*** 維持現狀。***in line*** **a.** 排成隊。The boys were standing *in line*. 男孩子們排成隊站着。**b.** 同意。He is *in line* with our previous policy. 他同意我們先前的辦法。**c.** 準備就緒。**d.** 按順序。He is next *in line*. 按順序下一個該輪到他。***in line for*** 即將可得;即將可達;即將輪到。He is *in line for* a promotion. 他即可晉升。***in line of duty*** 執行職務中。A policeman met his death *in line of duty*. 一個警察因公殉職。***keep in line with*** 保持與…一致。***lay it on the line*** 把事情坦白說出。***line abreast*** (海軍)艦隊並列前進。***line astern*** 艦隊縱列前進。***Line engaged!*** =***Line busy!*** (電話線路)有人講話。***marriage lines*** 結婚證書。***on a line*** **a.** 平;沒有高低;在一條線上。**b.** 直飛地(擊球)。***on the line*** **a.** 在兩者之中;兩者皆非。**b.** 暴露在危險中。**c.** 立即。**d.** 爲妓女。She lost her job and went *on the line*. 她失了業而淪爲妓女。***out of line*** **a.** 不同意;不和諧。**b.** 行爲不檢。**c.** 不妥當;不合適。***party line*** **a.** 黨的路線。**b.** 〖美〗幾家共用的電話線路。***read between the lines*** 領會言外之意。***take*** (or ***keep to***) ***one's own line*** 單獨行動。***the line*** **a.** 赤道。**b.** 正規軍;戰鬥兵;戰鬥艦。***toe the line*** **a.** 服從教訓;接受命令;接納一政黨之思想、計畫等。**b.** 負責;盡忠職守。—*v.t.* ①畫線於。②使生皺紋。③排成隊伍或行列。Cars were *lined* up along the road for a mile. 汽車在街上排起一英里長的行列。④〖棒球〗(打擊手)使(擊出的球)直飛。—*v.i.* ①排隊;成行;成列。The troops *lined* up and marched away. 軍隊排隊開走了。②相鄰接。Their lands *lined* on the brook. 他們的土地在小溪處相接。③〖棒球〗擊出直飛球。The batter *lined* to the first baseman. 打擊手向一壘手擊出直飛球。***line off*** 分爲行;分爲列。to *line* several columns *off*. 分出若干行。***line out*** **a.** 〖棒球〗擊出直飛球而被接殺。He *lined out* to the shortstop. 他擊出直飛球而被遊擊手接殺。**b.** 逐行讀出或唱出讓人重複。

line² *v.t.*, **lined, lin·ing.** ①襯裏於(衣服)。②塡;裝。③當做襯裏。***line one's purse*** (or ***pocket***) 以錢裝入私囊(尤指不應得之錢)。

line·a·ble [ˈlaɪnəbl; ˈlainəbl] *adj.* =**linable.**

lin·e·age¹ [ˈlɪnɪɪdʒ; ˈliniidʒ] *n.* ①血統;系統。②世系;家系。③傳統。

line·age² [ˈlaɪnɪdʒ; ˈlainidʒ] *n.* =**linage.**

lin·e·al [ˈlɪnɪəl; ˈliniəl] *adj.* ①直系的;正統的;嫡系的。②世襲的;繼承的。③線的;直線的。④長度的 (=linear).

lin·e·al·ly [ˈlɪnɪəlɪ; ˈliniəli] *adv.* 成直系地。

lin·e·a·ment [ˈlɪnɪəmənt; ˈliniəmənt] *n.* (常*pl.*) ①外貌;輪廓。②特徵。—*v.t.* 作成;形成。

lin·e·ar [ˈlɪnɪə; ˈliniə] *adj.* ①線的;直線的。②線做成的;線之使用的。③在一直線的;整列的。④長度的;有關長度的。⑤線狀的;細長的。⑥〖數學〗一次的;線性的。⑦在座標上成直線的;成正比例的。—**ly,** *adv.* —**i·ty,** *n.*

linear measure 長度。

lin·e·a·tion [ˌlɪnɪˈeʃən; ˌliniˈeiʃən] *n.* ①畫線;以線分劃。②線;輪廓。③線的排列。④(詩或散文之)分行。

line drawing 線畫(如鋼筆畫、鉛筆畫等)。

line engraving ①線雕(法)。②線雕銅版。③線雕銅版畫。

line·man [ˈlaɪnmən; ˈlainmən] *n., pl.* **-men.** ①電報、電話線架設或保養工。②(足球)前鋒。③(鐵路)巡道員。④(測量)執線手。

lin·en** [ˈlɪnɪn, -ən; ˈlinin] *n.* ①亞麻布;亞麻線。②亞麻布衣衫等(包括桌布、餐巾、床單、毛巾、襯衫等)。The house had a good stock of *linens*. 那一家備有很多亞麻布織物。wash one's dirty linen in public*** 向外宣揚家醜。—*adj.* 亞麻布製的。

linen draper 〖英〗布商。

line of credit 〖商〗信用貸款之限額。

line of fire 彈道。

line of force 〖物理〗力線;磁力線;電力線。

line of Life (手掌上之)生命線。

line of sight ①視線(自眼睛至目標間之直線)。②雷達天線之直線電波。

line of succession ①家系;族系。②繼任之次序。

***lin·er¹** [ˈlaɪnɚ; ˈlainə] *n.* ①〖美〗(輪船公司的)班輪;(航空公司的)班機。an Atlantic *liner*. 航行大西洋的定期班輪。an air-*liner*. 定期班機。②劃線者。

lin·er² *n.* ①加襯裏者。②襯裏物。③〖機械〗(防止機器磨損用的)襯墊;襯圈。

lines·man [ˈlaɪnzmən; ˈlainzmən] *n., pl.* **-men.** ①電報、電話線之架設或保護工人。②(鐵路之)巡道員。③(球賽等之)巡邊員;司線員。④(足球之)前鋒。

line-up [ˈlaɪnˌʌp; ˈlainʌp] *n.* ①陣列;陣容。②排列成行或陣之人或物。③運動員之排列;配置。④人民或公司等爲謀共同福利彼此間的組織;人民團體;公會。(亦作 **lineup**)

ling¹ [lɪŋ; liŋ] *n., pl.* **ling, lings.** 一種似鱈之魚。

ling² *n.* 〖植物〗石南。

-ling 〖字尾〗①附於名詞後表"小"之義(常含有輕蔑之意),如: duckling. ②表"屬於…之人或物;與…有關者"之義,如:hireling.

lin·ger** [ˈlɪŋgɚ; ˈliŋgə] *v.i.* ①逗留;徘徊;留戀。②遲緩。to *linger* over one's work. 工作遲緩。③(疾病)纏綿。④漫步。to *linger* homeward. 漫步回家。—*v.t.* 苟延(殘生);浪費(光陰)〖常 away, out〗. ***linger on (人)苟延殘喘;(習俗)歷久猶存。—**er,** *n.*

lin·ge·rie [ˈlænʒəˌri; ˈlɛ̃:nʒəri:] *n.* ①女用內衣(尤指由亞麻或絲製成之好品質者)。②一般亞麻布製品。

lin·go [ˈlɪŋgo; ˈliŋgou] *n., pl.* **-goes.** 〖諧、蔑〗①外國語言。②古怪之詞句。③特殊行業、團體等所使用之術語;專門術語。

lin·gua fran·ca [ˈlɪŋgwə ˈfræŋkə; ˈliŋgwəˈfræŋkə] ①一種混合語言(大部分爲義大利語組成,拉丁民族與阿拉伯人、土耳其人、希臘人等相處時使用之)。②任何混合國際語言(如商人所用的洋涇濱英語之類)。

lin·gual [ˈlɪŋgwəl; ˈliŋgwəl] *adj.* ①舌的。②語言的。③〖語音〗舌音的。—*n.* 〖語音〗舌音(字)(t, d, th, s, n, l, r)。—**ly,** *adv.*

Lin·gua·phone [ˈlɪŋgwəˌfon; ˈliŋgwəfoun] *n.* 〖商標名〗靈格風(學習語言用之唱片)。

lin·gui·form [ˈlɪŋgwɪˌfɔrm; ˈliŋgwifɔ:m] *adj.* 舌狀的。

lin·guist [ˈlɪŋgwɪst; ˈliŋgwist] *n.* ①語言學家。②通好幾種外國語文者。

lin·guist·er [ˈlɪŋgwɪstɚ; ˈliŋgwistə] *n.* 〖美〗=**interpreter.**

lin·guis·tic [lɪŋˈgwɪstɪk; liŋˈgwistik] *adj.* ①語言上的。②語言學上的。

lin·guis·ti·cal [lɪŋˈgwɪstɪkl; liŋˈgwistikl] *adj.* =**linguistic.** —**ly,** *adv.*

linguistic form 〖語言〗任何有含義的語言單位(如句、片語、字、字尾等)。
lin·guis·tics [lɪŋˈgwɪstɪks; liŋˈgwistiks] *n. pl.* (作 *sing.* 解)語言學。
lin·gu·late [ˈlɪŋgjuˌlet; ˈliŋgjuleit] *adj.* 舌狀的。(亦作 **lingulated**)
lin·i·ment [ˈlɪnəmənt; ˈlinimənt] *n.* 軟膏;塗敷藥。
*__lin·ing__ [ˈlaɪnɪŋ; ˈlainiŋ] *n.* ①(衣的)襯裏。an overcoat with a fur *lining.* 毛皮裏大衣;皮大衣。②加襯裏。***Every cloud has a silver lining.*** 禍中有福;否極泰來。
*__link¹__ [lɪŋk; liŋk] *n.* ①環; 鏈環。②連結物; 連鎖物; 一環。③(常 *pl.*)襯衫之活袖扣。④英國之長度名(等於 7.92 英寸)。—*v.t.* ①連結; 環接; 連繫。②挽(臂)。—*v.i.* 連結; 環接。The new company *linked* with several older ones in self-protection. 那家新公司與幾家較老的公司聯合以保護自己。—**a·ble,** *adj.* —**er,** *n.*
link² *n.* 火炬。
link·age [ˈlɪŋkɪdʒ; ˈliŋkidʒ] *n.* ①聯合; 連鎖。②〖機械〗傳桿裝置。③〖電〗鎖交;通匝。④〖生物〗接合;關聯;連鎖遺傳。
link·boy [ˈlɪŋkˌbɔɪ; ˈliŋkbɔi] *n.* =**link-man.**
linked-club [ˈlɪŋktˈklʌb; ˈliŋktˈklʌb] *n.* 三節棍。
linking verb 〖文法〗連繫動詞, 亦稱綴系動詞(爲不及物動詞之一種, 不需受詞 object, 却必需補語 complement, 如:be, become, seem 等)。(亦作 **link verb**)
link·man [ˈlɪŋkmən; ˈliŋkmən] *n., pl.* **-men.** 持火炬者(昔受雇執火把爲行人照明走黑路者)。
links [lɪŋks; liŋks] *n. pl.* ①草地;(尤指)近海岸之沙丘。②高爾夫球場。
Link trainer (陸上)林克式訓練機(受訓者坐於機艙內操縱全機, 情形逼眞, 一如在空中然)。
linn [lɪn; lin] *n.* 〖蘇〗①瀑布。②(瀑布下之)潭。③谿谷;絕壁。
Linn. ①Linnaeus. ②Linn(a)ean.
Lin·n(a)e·an [lɪˈniən; liˈniːən] *adj.* 林奈的;林奈式(植物分類法)的。
lin·net [ˈlɪnɪt; ˈlinit] *n.* 紅雀。
li·no [ˈlaɪno; ˈlainou] *n., pl.* **-nos.** 〖俗〗①=**linoleum.** ②=**lynotype.** ③=**lynotypist.**
li·no·le·um [lɪˈnolɪəm; liˈnouljəm] *n.* ①油氈;油布(一種地板布, 以帆布爲底, 上塗軟木屑及氧化亞麻仁油之混合物)。②任何類此之地板布。
Lin·o·type [ˈlaɪnəˌtaɪp; ˈlainətaip] *n.* 〖印刷〗①〖商標名〗鑄造排字機(將一行活字鑄爲一條者)。②(l-)此等排字機鑄出的鉛板。—*v.t.* (l-) 用鑄造排字機排(字、文稿)。—*v.i.* (l-)操作鑄造排字機。—**lin·o·typ·er,** —**lin·o·typ·ist,** *n.*
lin·seed [ˈlɪnˌsid; ˈlinsiːd] *n.* 亞麻仁;亞麻子。
linseed cake 亞麻仁餅(用作家畜之飼料)。
linseed meal 亞麻仁粉。
linseed oil 亞麻仁油;亞麻子油。
lin·sey-wool·sey [ˈlɪnzɪˈwʊlzɪ; ˈlinziˈwulzi] *n., pl.* **-wool·seys.** 棉毛織品;麻毛織品。
lin·stock [ˈlɪnˌstɑk; ˈlinstɔk] *n.* 〖史〗火繩桿(昔用於燃點放火砲)。
lint [lɪnt; lint] *n.* ①軟布; 絨布。②棉毛織物上掉下來的柳絮狀纖維。③生棉。—*v.i.* (布等)留柳絮狀纖維於物上。—**less,** *adj.*
lin·tel [ˈlɪntl̩; ˈlintl] *n.* 〖建築〗(門或窗上之)橫木;楣石。
lint·er [ˈlɪntɚ; ˈlintə] *n.* ①(*pl.*)棉毛(第一次軋後仍附於棉子上者)。②軋(棉)毛機。

lin·y [ˈlaɪnɪ; ˈlaini] *adj.,* **lin·i·er, lin·i·est.** ①似線的; 細的。②劃線的; 多線的; 多條痕的。
Lin Yu·tang [ˈlɪnjuˈtæŋ; ˈlinjuːˈtɑːŋ] 林語堂(1895–1976, 中國作家、語言學家)。
‡**Li·on** [ˈlaɪən; ˈlaiən] *n.* ①〖天文〗獅子星; 獅子座。②國際獅子會會員。
‡**li·on** [ˈlaɪən; ˈlaiən] *n.* ①獅。②異常勇猛的人。③名人。***as brave as a lion*** 勇猛如獅。***as strong as a lion*** 强壯如獅。***beard the lion in his den*** 入虎穴取虎子; 奮勇迫敵。***lion in the way*** (or ***path***) 危險的障礙。The indecisive man always sees a *lion in the way.* 優柔寡斷的人在他眼前經常有危險的障礙。***put one's head into the lion's mouth*** 置身險境。***the lion's share*** 最大或最好的部分。***twist the lion's tail*** 激怒英國;向英國挑釁。
li·on·ess [ˈlaɪənɪs; ˈlaiənis] *n.* 雌獅。
li·on·et [ˈlaɪənˌɛt; ˈlaiənit] *n.* 小獅。
li·on·heart·ed [ˈlaɪənˈhɑrtɪd; ˈlaiənˌhɑːtid] *adj.* 勇猛(如獅)的; 大膽的。—**ness,** *n.* —**ly,** *adv.*
lion hunter ①獵獅人。②〖英〗巴結名人者。
li·on·ize [ˈlaɪənˌaɪz; ˈlaiənaiz] *v.t.* 把(某人)視爲名人。—*v.i.* 巴結名人;攀龍附鳳。—**li·on·i·za·tion, li·on·iz·er,** *n.*
li·on·like [ˈlaɪənˌlaɪk; ˈlaiənlaik] *adj.* 獅子般的。
‡**lip** [lɪp; lip] *n., adj., v.,* **lipped, lip·ping.** —*n.* ①唇。②(常 *pl.*)口。She refused to open her *lips.* 她拒絕開口(說話)。③〖解剖〗唇狀構造。④(器皿等的)邊;緣;口。⑤樂器之嘴。⑥吹奏管樂器時吹奏者的唇舌位置。⑦〖俚〗冒失的說話。None of your *lip.* 不要冒失地說話。***bite one's lip*** (or ***tongue***)咬唇(表示困惑);忍笑;抑制一種情感的表示。***button one's lip*** 〖俚〗不開口; 拒絕洩密。***curl one's lip*** 撇嘴(表示輕蔑、嫌惡等)。***hang on a person's lips*** 傾聽某人的每一言一字。***keep a stiff upper lip*** 鼓勇;不害怕;不氣餒。—*adj.* ①口頭的;不誠實的;假做的。*lip* worship. 口頭崇拜。②用雙唇發音的。—*v.t.* ①以嘴唇碰。②輕輕說出。I heard my name most fondly *lipped.* 我聽到我的名字被深情地輕輕說出。③〖詩〗接吻。④擊高爾夫球使之觸及洞緣而不掉進去。—*v.i.* 用嘴唇吹奏樂器。—**less,** *adj.* —**like,** *adj.*
li·pase [ˈlaɪpes; ˈlaipeis] *n.* 〖生化〗脂肪分解酵素; 脂酶。
lip-deep [ˈlɪpˈdip; ˈlipˈdiːp] *adj.* 表面上的;膚淺的;空口的;無誠意的。
lip language 唇語(與聾者通話用之)。
lip microphone 連接嘴唇的擴音器。
Li Po [ˈliˈbɔ; ˈliːˈbɔː] 李白(字太白, 700?–762, 中國唐代詩人)。(亦作 **Li Pai**)
li·po·ma [lɪˈpomə; liˈpoumə] *n., pl.* **-ma·ta** [-mətə; -mətə], **-mas.** 〖醫〗脂肪腫; 脂肪瘤。
lip-read [ˈlɪpˌrid; ˈlip-riːd] *v.,* **-read, -read·ing.** —*v.t.* 以唇讀法了解。—*v.i.* 運用唇讀法。
lip-read·er [ˈlɪpˌridɚ; ˈlipˌriːdə] *n.* 唇讀者。
lip reading 唇讀法(聾子以觀察人發聲時之口形而學語之方法)。
lip salve ①唇用藥膏。②諛詞;奉承。
lip service 口惠;空口的應酬話。
lip·stick [ˈlɪpˌstɪk; ˈlip-stik] *n.* 〖美〗口紅;唇膏。
lip-wor·ship [ˈlɪpˈwɝʃəp; ˈlipˈwəː-ʃip] *n.* 口是心非的崇拜。

lip-wor·ship·er [ˈlɪpˈwɝʃəpɚ; ˈlip-ˈwəːʃipə] *n.* 口是心非的崇拜者。
liq. ①liquid. ②liquor. ③〖處方〗solution.
li·quate [ˈlaɪkwet; ˈlaikweit] *v.*, **-quat·ed, -quat·ing.** —*v.t.* ① 熔;熔解。②〖冶金〗熔析。—*v.i.* 〖冶金〗被熔析。—**li·qua·tion,** *n.*
liq·ue·fac·tion [ˌlɪkwɪˈfækʃən; ˌlikwiˈfækʃən] *n.* 液化;熔解。
liq·ue·fy [ˈlɪkwəˌfaɪ; ˈlikwifai] *v.t.* & *v.i.*, **-fied, -fy·ing.** (使)液化;熔解。—**liq·ue·fi·a·ble,** *adj.* —**liq·ue·fi·er,** *n.*
li·ques·cence [lɪˈkwɛsəns, -n̩s; liˈkwesns] *n.* 液化;融化。(亦作 **liquescency**) —**li·ques·cent,** *adj.*
li·queur [lɪˈkɝ, lɪˈkjʊr; liˈkjuə] *n.* 一種含有强烈酒精及香味之甜酒。
***liq·uid** [ˈlɪkwɪd; ˈlikwid] *n.* ①液體。Air is a fluid but not a *liquid*; water is both a fluid and a *liquid*. 空氣是流體不是液體,水是流體也是液體。②流音(卽 l, r 是)。—*adj.* ①液體的;稀的。②清澈的;明亮的;透明的。*liquid* eyes. 明亮的眼睛。③清脆的;柔和的。④不定的;易變的。*liquid* opinions. 不定的意見。⑤〖商〗易變賣的。*liquid* assets. 流動資產(卽易賣爲現金者)。⑥充滿淚水的。Sorrow made the eyes of many grow *liquid*. 悲傷使許多人淚水盈眶。⑦(動作)柔軟的。—**ness,** *n.* 〖注意〗 **liquid** 與 **fluid** 不同。liquid 指液體。fluid 指流體,卽液體與氣體。
liquid air 液體空氣。
liq·ui·date [ˈlɪkwɪˌdet; ˈlikwideit] *v.*, **-dat·ed, -dat·ing.** —*v.t.* ①償付(債務);淸償。②清算;清理(公司、企業的)帳目。③清除;消滅。④殺戮;清算。⑤變賣。—*v.i.* 清理債務。
liq·ui·da·tion [ˌlɪkwɪˈdeʃən; ˌlikwiˈdeiʃən] *n.* ①清算;清理。②清除;整肅;消滅。***go into liquidation*** 破產。
liq·ui·da·tor [ˈlɪkwɪˌdetɚ; ˈlikwideitə] *n.* 清算人;(公司等之)帳目清理人。
liquid fire (噴火武器噴出之)燃燒液。
liq·uid-fu·eled [ˈlɪkwɪdˈfjuəld; ˈlikwidˈfjuəld] *adj.* (火箭、飛彈等)用液體燃料推進的。
liquid glass 水玻璃(工業上用作保藏或防火之塗料)。(亦作 **water glass**)
li·quid·i·ty [lɪˈkwɪdətɪ; liˈkwiditi] *n.* ①流動性。②(音等之)流暢;清脆;明亮。③流動資產。④〖商〗資產變賣能力;資產折現力。
liq·uid·ize [ˈlɪkwəˌdaɪz; ˈlikwidaiz] *v.t.*, **-ized, -iz·ing.** 使成流動體;使液化。
liquid measure 液量(如 4 gills=1 pint, 2 pints=1 quart, 4quarts=1 gallon).
liquid oxygen 液化氧。(亦作 **lox**)
liquid propellant 火箭之液體燃料。
liquid rocket 用液體燃料推進的火箭。
liq·uor** [ˈlɪkɚ; ˈlikə] *n.* ①酒類。spirituous *liquor*. 烈酒(如白蘭地、威士忌等)。②酒。brandy and other *liquors*. 白蘭地及其他的酒。③滷汁;液體。Pickles are put up in salty *liquor*. 醃菜是放在鹽中滷的。④藥湯(溶有藥物的水)。in liquor*** 醉。Men *in liquor* must be handled differently. 對酒醉的人必須用不同的對待法。—*v.t.* 灌以酒〖常 up〗。—*v.i.* 喝酒〖常 up〗。—**y,** *adj.*
liq·uo·rice [ˈlɪkərɪs; ˈlikəris] *n.* 甘草。
liq·uor·ish [ˈlɪkərɪʃ; ˈlikəriʃ] *adj.* ①=**lickerish.** ②嗜酒的。③帶有酒味的。—*n.* 〖方〗甘草。—**ly,** *adv.* —**ness,** *n.*
li·ra [ˈlɪrə, ˈlɪrɑ; ˈliərə] *n.*, *pl.* **li·re** [ˈlɪre; ˈlirei], **li·ras.** 里拉(a. 義大利貨幣名; b. 土耳其貨幣名)。
Lis·bon [ˈlɪzbən; ˈlizbən] *n.* 里斯本(葡萄牙首都)。
lisle [laɪl; lail] *n.* ①里耳線(一種堅韌的棉線)。②里耳線之編織物(長襪、手套等)。
lisp [lɪsp; lisp] *n.* ①口齒不清(尤指將 s, z 發作 [θ;θ]、[ð;ð])。②口齒不清之字音。—*v.i.* ①將 s, z 發作 [θ;θ]、[ð;ð]。②發音口齒不清;似小孩地說話。—*v.t.* 口齒不清或如小孩地發出(聲音);口齒不清地說。—**er,** *n.*
lisp·ing [ˈlɪspɪŋ; ˈlispiŋ] *n.* (幼兒等之)口齒不清的發音。—*adj.* 口齒不清的;咬舌的。—**ly,** *adv.*
lis·som [ˈlɪsəm; ˈlisəm] *adj.*=**lissome.**
lis·some [ˈlɪsəm; ˈlisəm] *adj.* ①柔軟的。②輕快的;敏捷的。
‡**list**[1] [lɪst; list] *n.* ①目錄;一覽表;册;單;簿。His name stands first on the *list*. 他的名字列第一。②批發商之開價 (=*list* price)。③證券交易所所經營之股票的完整記載。***the active*** (***retired***) ***list*** 常備(退)役名册。***the free list*** a.(戲院等的)免票名單。b. (進口)免稅貨物表。—*v.t.* ①列於表上。to *list* a person's name. 將某人名字列於表上。②列成一表;造册;編目錄。to *list* all one's books. 將某人所有的書編一目錄。③列舉。*List* five reasons why you enjoyed the book. 列舉五個理由說明你爲何喜歡那本書。④將…列爲…(與as連用)。He *lists* himself as a political liberal. 他將自己列爲政治上的自由主義者。—*v.i.* ①〖罕〗應徵;徵募。②被列入目錄定價出售。The wrench alone *lists* at $3. 僅是螺旋鉗一樣售價就要三元。
list[2] *n.* (船)傾側。—*v.i.* (船)傾側。—*v.t.* 使傾側。
list[3] *v.t.* & *v.i.* 〖古,詩〗聽。
list[4] *v.i.* 〖古〗願意;高興。—*n.* 〖古〗願望。
list[5] *n.* ①(織物等之)緣;織邊。②細長的(布)片。③(動物體上的)有色條紋。④(頭髮的)分開部分。⑤境界。⑥〖美〗田壟。⑦(*pl.*)(競技場的)柵;競技場。—*v.t.* ①鑲布邊於…。②〖美〗起壟於…。③將…作條紋排列。
‡**lis·ten** [ˈlɪsn̩; ˈlisn] *v.i.* ①傾聽;注意聽。He was *listening* to the music. 他正在聽音樂。②聽從;服從。Don't *listen* to him — he's a very foolish fellow. 不要聽他的話——他是一個大傻瓜。③〖俚〗聽起來似乎。It doesn't *listen* right. 這聽起來似乎不對。***listen in*** a. 聽(收音機)廣播。I was *listening in* on the radio. 我正在聽(收音機)廣播。b. 聽他人在電話上講話。
lis·ten·a·ble [ˈlɪsn̩əbl; ˈlisnəbl] *adj.* 值得一聽的。
***lis·ten·er** [ˈlɪsn̩ɚ, ˈlɪsnɚ; ˈlisn̩ə] *n.* ①聽者。②聽衆之一。*Listeners* wrote in to congratulate the radio actor on his performance. 聽衆寫信恭賀那廣播演員的演技。
lis·ten·er-in [ˈlɪsn̩ɚˈɪn; ˈlisn̩ərˈin] *n.* 無線電收聽者。
listening post ①〖軍〗偵察敵方軍事行動之聽音哨。②情報站。
list·er [ˈlɪstɚ; ˈlistə] *n.* 〖美〗起壟機(一種農具)。
Lis·ter·ism [ˈlɪstərɪzəm; ˈlistərizəm] *n.* 〖醫〗石炭酸消毒法;李斯德氏法。
Lis·ter·ize [ˈlɪstəˌraɪz; ˈlistəraiz] *v.t.*, **-ized, -iz·ing.** 用李斯德氏法處理;用石炭酸消毒。
list·less [ˈlɪstlɪs; ˈlistlis] *adj.* ①沒精打采的;倦怠的。②漠不關心的;冷漠的;不留心的。—**ness,** *n.*
list·less·ly [ˈlɪstlɪslɪ; ˈlistlisli] *adv.* 無

精打采地；漠不關心地。「商之開價。

list price〖商〗價目表所列之價格；批發

lit [lɪt; lit] *v.* pt. & pp. of **light**[1] and **light**[3].

lit·a·ny [ˈlɪtṇɪ; ˈlitəni] *n., pl.* **-nies.** 〖宗教〗連禱。*The Litany* (禱告中之)連禱文。「(亦作 **lichee**)

li·tchi [ˈlitʃi; ˈliːtʃiː] *n.* 荔枝；荔枝樹。

Lit. D. Lit(t)erarum Doctor (拉=Doctor of Literature).

-lite〖字尾〗表"石"之義(用於礦物或化石之名稱中)，如：cryolite.

•**li·ter, li·tre** [ˈlitɚ; ˈliːtə] *n.* 竔；公升。

lit·er·a·cy [ˈlɪtərəsɪ; ˈlitərəsi] *n.* 有閱讀書寫之能力。

lit·(t)e·rae hu·ma·ni·o·res [ˈlɪtərihjuˌmænɪˈoriz; ˈlitəriːhjuˌmæni ˈouriːz]〖拉〗人文學(尤指古典文學之研究)。

•**lit·er·al** [ˈlɪtərəl; ˈlitərəl] *adj.* ①完全依照原文或原本的；逐字的(翻譯)；精確的。*literal* translation. 直譯。②求實際的；無理想的。He has rather a *literal* mind. 他具有相當實際的頭腦。③實實在在的；一點不誇張的；忠實的；翔實的。④字母的。a *literal* error. 字母錯誤；排字錯誤。⑤文字上的；字面上的。The distress signal SOS has no *literal* meaning. 求救信號 SOS 在字面上並沒有甚麼意義。—*n.* 排字錯誤。

lit·er·al·ism [ˈlɪtərəlˌɪzəm; ˈlitərəlizəm] *n.* ①拘泥字義之傾向。②直譯主義。③〖文藝〗徹底的寫實主義；直寫主義。—**lit·er·al·is·tic,** *adj.* —**lit·er·al·is·ti·cal·ly,** *adv.* 「*n.* 拘泥字義者。

lit·er·al·ist [ˈlɪtərəlɪst; ˈlitərəlist]

lit·er·al·ize [ˈlɪtərəˌlaɪz; ˈlitərəlaiz] *v.t.,* **-ized, -iz·ing.** ①照字義解釋。②直譯。

•**lit·er·al·ly** [ˈlɪtərəlɪ; ˈlitərəli] *adv.* ①逐字地；嚴格地；按字面地。②實在地；不誇張地。The children were *literally* starving. 孩子們的確是在挨餓。

•**lit·er·ar·y** [ˈlɪtəˌrɛrɪ; ˈlitərəri] *adj.* ①文學的；著作的。For a long period of time Latin was the *literary* language of Italy. 有很長一段時期，拉丁語是義大利之文學語言。②精通文學的。—**lit·er·ar·i·ly,** *adv.* —**lit·er·ar·i·ness,** *n.*

lit·er·ate [ˈlɪtərɪt; ˈlitərit] *adj.* ①能閱讀及寫作的。②受過教育的；精通文學的。—*n.* ①能閱讀及寫作之人。②學者；文士。

lit·e·ra·ti [ˌlɪtəˈretaɪ; ˌlitəˈreitai]〖拉〗*n.* pl. of **literatus.** 文人；學者；文學界。

lit·e·ra·tim [ˌlɪtəˈretɪm; ˌlitəˈreitim]〖拉〗*adv.* 逐字地；照字義。

•**lit·er·a·ture** [ˈlɪtərətʃɚ; ˈlitəritʃə] *n.* ①文學。*Literature* stands related to man as science stands to nature. 文學之於人的關係正如科學之於自然。②文獻；著作。③著作生涯。④文學之研究。I shall take *literature* and mathematics this spring. 今年春天我要修文學及數學。⑤〖俗〗任何印刷品；說明書。⑥音樂作品。

literature search 文獻調查。

lit·e·ra·tus [ˌlɪtəˈretəs; ˌlitəˈreitəs]〖拉〗*n.* sing. of **literati.**

lith-〖字首〗表"石"之義。「氧化鉛。

lith·arge [ˈlɪθɑrdʒ; ˈliθɑːdʒ] *n.*〖化〗

lithe [laɪð; laið] *adj.,* **lith·er, lith·est.** 柔軟的；易彎的。—**ly,** *adv.* —**ness,** *n.*

lithe·some [ˈlaɪðsəm; ˈlaiðsəm] *adj.* =**lithe.** —**ness,** *n.*

lith·i·a [ˈlɪθɪə; ˈliθiə] *n.* ①〖醫〗結石(病)。②〖化〗氧化鋰。

lith·ic [ˈlɪθɪk; ˈliθik] *adj.* ①石的。*lithic* debris. 石礫堆。②〖醫〗結石的；膀胱結石的。③〖化〗鋰的。「**-fied, -fy·ing.**(使)石化。

lith·i·fy [ˈlɪθəˌfaɪ; ˈliθifai] *v.t. & v.i.,*

lith·i·um [ˈlɪθɪəm; ˈliθiəm] *n.*〖化〗鋰(金屬元素之最輕者，符號 Li).

lith·o·graph [ˈlɪθəˌgræf; ˈliθəgrɑːf] *n.*石印品；石版畫。—*v.t. & v.i.* 石印；以石版印刷。—**er,** *n.*

lith·o·graph·ic [ˌlɪθəˈgræfɪk; ˌliθəˈgræfik] *adj.* 石版印刷的；石版印刷術的。

li·thog·ra·phy [lɪˈθɑgrəfɪ; liˈθɔgrəfi] *n.* ①石版印刷術。②鋁或鋅版印刷術(指以此等金屬版代替石版者)。

li·thol·o·gy [lɪˈθɑlədʒɪ; liˈθɔlədʒi] *n.* ①巖石學。②〖醫〗結石學。③(岩石或岩層之)岩石學上的特性。

lith·o·print [ˈlɪθəˌprɪnt; ˈliθəprint] *v.t. & v.i.* 用石版印刷。—*n.* 石版印刷品。—**er,** *n.* 「*n.* 巖石圈；地殼。

lith·o·sphere [ˈlɪθəˌsfɪr; ˈliθəsfiə]

li·thot·o·my [lɪˈθɑtəmɪ; liˈθɔtəmi] *n.*〖外科〗膀胱結石割治術；截石術。

Lith·u·a·ni·a [ˌlɪθjuˈenɪə; ˌliθjuːˈeinjə] *n.* 立陶宛(波羅的海沿岸小國，現在蘇聯控制下，首都爲Vilna).—**Lith·u·a·ni·an,** *adj., n.*

Lit. Hum. Literae Humaniores (拉=more humane studies). 「訴訟的。

lit·i·ga·ble [ˈlɪtɪgəbl; ˈlitigəbl] *adj.* 可

lit·i·gant [ˈlɪtəgənt; ˈlitigənt] *n.* 訴訟當事人。*the parties litigant* 訴訟當事人。—*adj.* 訴訟的；好爭訟的。

lit·i·gate [ˈlɪtəˌget; ˈlitigeit] *v.,* **-gat·ed, -gat·ing.** —*v.t.* ①訴訟。②爭論。—*v.i.* 訴訟。—**lit·i·ga·tor,** *n.*

lit·i·ga·tion [ˌlɪtəˈgeʃən; ˌlitiˈgeiʃən] *n.* ①訴訟；起訴。②〖古〗爭論。

li·ti·gious [lɪˈtɪdʒɪəs; liˈtidʒəs] *adj.* ①好訟的。②可訴訟的；可爭的。③訴訟的。—**ly,** *adv.* —**li·ti·gi·os·i·ty,** —**ness,** *n.*

lit·mus [ˈlɪtməs; ˈlitməs] *n.* 石蕊色素(取自地衣類之一種青色染料)；草藍。***litmus paper*** 石蕊試紙(用以試驗酸性或鹼性者，遇鹼呈藍色，遇酸呈紅色)。

li·to·tes [ˈlaɪtəˌtiz; ˈlaitoutiːz] *n.*①〖修辭〗間接肯定法；曲言法(以反面否定代替肯定，如 no easy 代替 very difficult, not bad 代替 very good等)。②曲言法的辭句。

•**lit·ter** [ˈlɪtɚ; ˈlitə] *n.* ①(用後散置的)雜物；垃圾。Always pick up your *litter* after a picnic. 野餐後務須將一切雜物收拾起來。②雜亂；零亂。③(豬、狗等)一胎所生的小豬小狗；一窩。a *litter* of puppies. 一窩小狗。④豬窩；狗窩。⑤擔架；舁床(抬病人或受傷者用)。⑥轎；輿。⑦(森林中地上之)爛葉。***be in litter*** (豬、狗等)臨產。***in a litter*** (房間等)亂七八糟；混亂。—*v.t.* ①使雜亂；使零亂。②產(小動物)。Wolves *littered* their young in the deserted farmhouses. 狼在荒廢的農舍中生下小狼。③用稻草等爲(動物)作床；用草鋪(狗、豬等)的窩〖常down〗. —*v.i.* ①亂丟雜物。Don't *litter.* 勿亂丟雜物。②(動物)生產。The cat had *littered* in the closet. 貓在壁櫥中生產了。

lit·te·ra·teur [ˌlɪtərəˈtɝ; ˌlitərəˈtəː] *n.* 文學家；文人。

litter bag〖美〗塑膠垃圾袋。

lit·ter·bug [ˈlɪtɚˌbʌg; ˈlitəbʌg] *v.i.,*

n. 破壞清潔(者); 隨地丟棄廢物(者)。

lit·ter·y 〔ˈlɪtərɪ; ˈlitəri〕 *adj.* ①草薦的。②滿是稻草的。③散亂的;雜亂的。

‡lit·tle 〔ˈlɪtl; ˈlitl〕 *adj.*, **less** or **less·er, least**; or **lit·tler, lit·tlest,** *adv.*, **less, least,** *n.* —*adj.* ①小的 (爲 big 之對)。What a pretty *little* house! 多麼小巧玲瓏的房子啊! ②短的。Come a *little* way with me. 與我同走短短一程路。③很少的;些微的 (不用冠詞"a"有"幾乎沒有"或"實際等於沒有" 之意。爲 much 之對)。I see very *little* of him. 我很少見到他。④少許的;少量的;一些 (須與冠詞 a 連用)。⑤瑣細的;無聊的; 不重要的。Why do you come to me with every *little* difficulty? 你爲甚麼有一點小麻煩便來找我?⑥胸襟狹小的;氣量小的。⑦可愛的;可憐的。Bless your *little* heart! 祝福你可愛的心腸。⑧好玩的;有趣的。What *little* game are you up to now? 你們玩甚麼有趣的遊戲啊? ⑨卑鄙的。I know all about your *little* scheme. 我看穿了你卑鄙的詭計。⑩小規模的。⑪位置不重要的; 無影響力的;卑微的。Tax reductions help the *little* fellow. 減稅以蘇民困。⑫微弱的;不强的。***but little*** 祇一點; 幾無。 ***go but a little way to*** 差得遠; 不够。 —*adv.* ①很少(不用冠詞"a"有"幾乎不"之意)。He slept very *little* last night. 他昨晚睡得很少。② 完全不 (=not at all). He *little* knew what trouble he was going to have. 他完全不知道他將遭遇甚麼困難。③稍微地;稍稍地(須與冠詞 a 連用)。That hat is a *little* too small. 那頂帽子有點嫌太小了。 ***little less*** (or ***better***) ***than*** 差不多等於。***little more than*** 不過。That's worth *little more than* a shilling! 那不過值一先令。***little short of*** 幾近於。***not a little*** 相當地 (=considerably). He was *not a little* annoyed when he heard the news. 他聽到這消息時, 他相當地煩惱。—*n.* ①一點點; 少許;些許。②一會兒;短時間;短距離。Please wait a *little.* 請稍等片刻。***in little*** 小規模的。a painting done *in little.* 小規模的油漆工程。***little by little*** 漸漸地;漸次地。***little or nothing*** (=hardly anything) 幾乎沒有甚麼東西。***make little of*** 不重視;輕視。to *make little of* one's troubles. 對某人的困難加以低估。***not a little*** 不少的; 相當多的(=a great deal of). ***think little of*** **a.** 看不起;輕視。**b.** 滿不在乎;不遲疑。

Little America 小美洲(南極探險基地, 位於南極洲鯨魚灣附近, 爲 Richard E. Byrd 少將所創設)。

Little Europe 歐洲共同市場各會員國。

little fellow 〖美俗〗平民;無政治或經濟影響力者;小老百姓。

little finger 小指。

Little Fox 〖天文〗狐狸座(=Vulpecula).

little go 〖英俗〗劍橋大學文學士考試之初試。

Little League 世界少棒聯盟。

little magazine 小型文藝雜誌 (尤指非商業性者)。

little man =**little fellow.**

lit·tle·ness 〔ˈlɪtlnɪs; ˈlitlnis〕 *n.* ①小;少量。②鄙陋;卑劣;氣量狹窄。

little people ①=**fairies.** ②小民;老百姓。

little review 小型文藝批評雜誌。

Little Rock 小巖(美國 Arkansas 州之首府)。

Little Russia 小俄羅斯(指蘇聯歐洲西南部地區, 包括烏克蘭及其鄰近地區)。

Little Russian ①小俄羅斯人。②烏克蘭語 (=Ukrainian).

little theater ①小劇院;適合於小劇院之戲劇。②業餘性之戲劇。

lit·to·ral 〔ˈlɪtərəl; ˈlitərəl〕 *adj.* (沿)海岸的。—*n.* 沿岸地;沿海地區。—**ly,** *adv.*

li·tur·gi·cal 〔lɪˈtɜdʒɪkl; liˈtəːdʒikəl〕 *adj.* 禮拜式的;崇拜儀式的。—**ly,** *adv.*

lit·ur·gy 〔ˈlɪtədʒɪ; ˈlitədʒi〕 *n., pl.* **-gies.** ①禮拜儀式。②禱告文式; 祈禱文。③特種禮拜式。④聖體崇拜式。⑤聖餐儀式 (尤指東方正教者)。

liv·a·ble 〔ˈlɪvəbl; ˈlivəbl〕 *adj.* ①適於居住的; 可住的 (房屋、氣候等)。②適於同住的;可以相處的(人)。③有生活價值的。(亦作 **liveable**) —**ness,** *n.*

‡live[1] 〔lɪv; liv〕 *v.*, **lived, liv·ing.** —*v.i.* ①生;活;生存。He's still *living.* 他尚活着。②繼續活; 繼續生存。 He *lived* to the age of 75. 他活到七十五歲。③生活;過活。They *lived* very happily. 他們生活得很快樂。④居; 住。 Where do you *live?* 你住在何處? ⑤(指無生命之事物) 繼續; 照樣;存留;未被破壞。His memory will always *live.* 他將永遠爲人記得。⑥享受人生;高興地過日子。⑦過有意義的生活。—*v.t.* ①過(某種的生活)。to *live* a happy life. 過快樂的生活。②實踐於生活中; 表現於生活中。 What other men were preaching, he *lived.* 別人用嘴巴所說的, 他却用行動實踐於生活中。 ③全心全力地體驗或享受。(***as sure***) ***as I live*** 極確實。 ***live and let live*** 互相容忍彼此的缺點; 待人寬容如待己。***live by*** 賴…爲生。He *lives by* teaching. 他以教書爲生。 ***live by oneself*** 獨居。***live*** (***something***) ***down*** 改過自新地生活使人忘掉(過去的過失)。to *live down* a scandal. 洗心革面地生活使人忘掉已往的醜行。***live high*** 過奢侈生活。 ***live high off the hog*** 〖俗〗家境優裕。***live in*** 寄宿於工作處。Do your workers *live in* or out? 你的員工們是寄宿店中或是外宿? ***live it up*** 享受人生;過快樂的日子。He *lived it up* with wine and song. 他飲酒高歌盡情地享受人生。***live on*** **a.** 繼續活着 (on 係 adv.). The old people died but the young ones *lived on.* 老人死了, 但年輕人都還繼續活着。**b.** 以…爲食;靠…過活 (on 係 prep.). He *lives* chiefly *on* fruit. 他主要以果實爲食。***live on the cross*** 〖俗〗胡行亂爲地生活。***live on the square*** 規規矩矩生活。***live out*** **a.** 活過(一定時期); 保持壽命。**b.** 不寄宿在工作處。 ***live through*** 活過; 經過…而未死。Will he *live through* the night? 他會活過這一夜嗎? ***live up to*** 依(某種標準)生活;遵從(主義等)行動;實行…。***live well*** **a.** 過好日子。**b.** 過道德的生活;做善人。He died a peaceful death after having *lived well* all his life. 他終其一生不做壞事, 然後在安祥中逝世。***live with*** 接受;忍受。***where one lives*** 〖俚〗要害。The word goes right *where I live.* 這話刺中了我的致命傷。

·live[2] 〔laɪv; laiv〕 *adj.* ①活的; 有生命的。②燒燃的; 熾熱的。*live* coals (embers). 正燃着的煤(餘燼)。③(鎗彈等) 未爆發的; 未用過的。a *live* shell. 實彈; 未用過的砲彈。④(電線)充電的。⑤精力充沛的;活動的。⑥〖美〗目下最爲人所關切的(問題等)。a *live* question. 目下最爲人所關切的問題。⑦〖俗〗最近的; 最新的; 現代的。*live* ideas. 新思想。⑧

動的；發動的。*live* wheels. 轉動的輪子。⑨未掘出的；天然的。*live* metal. 天然的金屬。⑩正用着的。⑪生動的。The portrait is always *live* and spirited. 那畫像總是栩栩如生而神采奕奕。⑫現場傳播的。a *live* TV show. 現場的電視演出。⑬鮮艷的。*live* colors. 鮮艷的顏色。—*adv.* 現場。The race will be telecast *live*. 比賽將有電視現場播出。—**ness,** *n.*

live·a·ble 〔ˈlɪvəbḷ; ˈlivəbl〕 *adj.* =**liv·able. —ness,** *n.*

-lived 〖字尾〗表"…之生命的"之義之形容詞字尾。

live-in 〔ˈlɪvˌɪn; ˈlivin〕 *adj.* 寄宿於工作處的。

***live·li·hood** 〔ˈlaɪvlɪˌhʊd; ˈlaivlihud〕 *n.* 生計；營生。He wrote for a *livelihood*. 他以寫作爲生。

live·li·ly 〔ˈlaɪvlɪlɪ; ˈlaivlili〕 *adv.* ①活潑地；快活地。②有生氣地；靈活地。③鮮艷地；鮮明地。④驚險地。⑤生動地。⑥興奮地。

live·li·ness 〔ˈlaɪvlɪnɪs; ˈlaivlinis〕 *n.* 活潑；鮮明；生動。

live load 〔laɪv~; laiv~〕 〖機械〗活載(荷)；動載(荷)。

live·long 〔ˈlɪvˌlɔŋ, ˈlaɪv-; ˈlivlɔŋ, ˈlaiv-〕 *adj.* (時間)冗長的；長久的。

live·ly** 〔ˈlaɪvlɪ; ˈlaivli〕 *adj.,* **-li·er, -li·est,** *adv., n.* —*adj.* ①活潑的；快活的。She's as *lively* as a kitten. 她快活得像一隻小猫。②鮮明的；鮮麗的。What *lively* colors! 多麼鮮明的色彩！③有生氣的；靈活的。④驚險的。They had a very *lively* time. 他們有一段驚險的經歷。⑤生動的；寫實的。⑥興奮的；刺激的。⑦彈性好的；跳得好的。⑧熱鬧的。⑨熱烈的。⑩(空氣)新鮮的；令人振作的。⑪(船)破浪前進的。make things lively for*** (***a person***) 使(某人)感困難或危險等。—*adv.* ①活潑地。②驚險地。—*n.* 活潑的人。

liv·en 〔ˈlaɪvən; ˈlaivən〕 *v.t.* 注以生命；使奮起；使快活〖常 up〗。How can we *liven* things up? 我們怎樣才能使一切事物有生氣呢？—*v.i.* 變爲活潑有力；現愉快之色〖常up〗。

live oak 〔laɪv~; laiv~〕 ①(美國南部所產之)一種槲樹(其木多作造船之用)。②槲樹類樹木。

live-out 〔ˈlɪvˌaut; ˈlivaut〕 *adj.* 不寄宿於工作處的。

live parking 〔laɪv~; laiv~〕 駕駛人不離開的停車。

liv·er¹** 〔ˈlɪvə; ˈlivə〕 *n.* ①肝臟。②(食物)肝。③肝的病態。The doctor says it's just a touch of *liver*. 醫生說這祇是一點兒肝病。④猪肝色。hot liver*** 多情；熱情。—*adj.* 猪肝色的。—*v.i.* (油漆、墨水)變乾。

liv·er² *n.* ①生活者。My father was a good *liver*. 我的父親是個懂得生活的人。②居民；居住者。

liver extract (治貧血用的)動物肝精。

liv·er·ied 〔ˈlɪvərɪd; ˈlivərid〕 *adj.* 穿制服的。

liv·er·ish 〔ˈlɪvərɪʃ; ˈlivəriʃ〕 *adj.* ①似肝的。②〖俗〗(生)肝病的。③〖俗〗脾氣壞的；乖戾的；暴躁的。

Liv·er·pool 〔ˈlɪvəˌpul; ˈlivəpuːl〕 *n.* 利物浦(英國西部海港)。

Liv·er·pud·li·an 〔ˌlɪvəˈpʌdlɪən; ˌlivəˈpʌdliən〕 *adj., n.* Liverpool 的(市民)。

liv·er·wort 〔ˈlɪvəˌwɝt; ˈlivəwəːt〕 *n.* 〖植物〗苔類之植物；地錢。

liv·er·wurst 〔ˈlɪvəˌwɝst; ˈlivəwəːst〕 *n.* 〖美〗(以肝爲主製成的)臘腸。

liv·er·y** 〔ˈlɪvərɪ; ˈlivəri〕 *n., pl.* **-er·ies,** *adj.* —*n.* ①(昔日封建領主之臣下所穿的)一種特殊制服。②男僕所穿之制服。③(文官或公司行員等所穿之)特殊服裝。④其職工可穿公會會員制服之同業公會；同業公會。⑤特殊之服色、裝束或外貌等。the green *livery* of summer. 夏季之葱綠景色。⑥代人飼馬。⑦〖美〗馬車出租店；馬房。⑧(任何車或船之)出租店。⑨定量飼料；定糧。⑩〖法律〗交割；讓與。in livery*** 穿着制服。***out of livery*** 穿便衣。—*adj.* ①出租的。②爲制服之一部分的。

liv·er·y·man 〔ˈlɪvərɪmən; ˈlivərimən〕 *n., pl.* **-men.** ①同業公會會員(可穿公會之特殊服裝者)。②馬車店或馬房之工作人員。

livery stable 車馬出租所；代人養馬之馬店。

lives 〔laɪvz; laivz〕 *n.* pl. of **life.**

live·stock 〔ˈlaɪvˌstɑk; ˈlaivstɔk〕 *n.* (作*sing.* or *pl.* 解)家畜(如馬、牛、羊、猪等)。

live weight 〔laɪv~; laiv~〕 毛重(牲畜被宰前的重量)。

live wire 〔laɪv~; laiv~〕 ①有電流的電線。②〖俗〗精力充沛的人；很活躍的人。

liv·id 〔ˈlɪvɪd; ˈlivid〕 *adj.* ①鉛色的；土色的；青灰色的。②青黑色的。—**ly,** *adv.* —**ness,** *n.*

li·vid·i·ty 〔lɪˈvɪdətɪ; liˈviditi〕 *n.* 鉛色；土色；(因瘀血而呈)青紫色。

liv·ing** 〔ˈlɪvɪŋ; ˈliviŋ〕 *adj.* ①活的；活在世上的。No man *living* could do better. 當代的人沒有一個能做得比這再好的了。②强烈的；現成的。③現行的；現代的。④栩栩如生的；極似的。He is the *living* image of his father. 他極像他的父親。⑤生活的；生活其間的。⑥够生活的。⑦燃燒的。⑧天然的；未經人工改變的。The road was hewn out of the *living* rock. 那條路是削平天然岩石而成的。⑨實演(非錄音或製成電影)的。⑩令人清爽的；給人以力量的。⑪極；非常；絕對(作强調用)。the living*** 現世的人。He's still in the land of *the living*. 他尙活在人間。***within living memory*** 在當今人的記憶中。—*n.* ①生計；生存。②生活；生涯。③牧師有薪金的職位；教士有給職。—**ly,** *adv.*

living death 死般的情況；陰慘的生活。

liv·ing-in 〔ˈlɪvɪŋˈɪn; ˈliviŋˈin〕 *n.* (被雇者)住在東家。(參看 **living-out**)

living likeness 逼眞的畫像。

liv·ing-out 〔ˈlɪvɪŋˈaut; ˈliviŋˈaut〕 *n.* 通勤(被雇者住在外面)。(參看 **living-in**)

living picture =**tableau vivant.**

***living room** ①起居室；客廳(=parlor *or* sitting room)。②生活空間；居住空間。Surplus populations would demand *living room*. 多出的人口將需要他們的生活空間。

living space 生活空間。

living standard 生活水準。

Liv·ing·stone 〔ˈlɪvɪŋstən; ˈliviŋstən〕 *n.* 李文斯頓(David, 1813–1873, 蘇格蘭之傳教士, 非洲探險家)。

living wage 生活工資(維持合理生活所需要之工資)。

liz·ard 〔ˈlɪzəd; ˈlizəd〕 *n.* ①〖動物〗蜥蜴；石龍子。②〖動物〗守宮；壁虎(=house lizard)。③〖俚〗沉迷於歡樂場中之人。

LL, LL., L.L. ①Late Latin. ②Low Latin.

'll 〖俗〗will 之縮寫(有時亦轉用爲 shall 之縮寫)。I'*ll*. =I will (*or* I shall).

ll. ①lines. ②leaves. ③laws.

lla·ma 〔ˈlɑmə; ˈlɑːmə〕 *n., pl.* **-mas, -ma.** 〖動物〗駱馬(南美產之一種駱駝)。

lla·no 〔ˈlɑno; ˈlɑːnou〕 *n., pl.* **-nos.** (南美 Amazon 河以北之)大草原。

LL.B. Legum Baccalaureus (拉=Bach-

elor of Laws). 「Laws).」
LL.D. Legum Doctor (拉=Doctor of」
Lloyd George [ˈlɔɪdˈdʒɔrdʒ; ˈlɔidˈdʒɔːdʒ] 勞埃喬治 (David, 1863–1945, 英國政治家, 於 1916–22 任首相)。
Lloyd's [lɔɪdz; lɔidz] *n.* 勞埃船舶協會(倫敦一促進商業尤其是海上保險之組織, 由保險業者、商人、船主及經紀人組成)。
Lloyd's Register 登載商船及遊艇之船齡、噸位、分類有關航業消息的一本雜誌, 由一個與Lloyd's有關係的非營利性機構所發行。
LM lunar module. 登月小艇。
LNG, L.N.G. liquefied natural gas. 液化天然煤氣。
***lo** [lo; lou] *interj.* 看呀! 瞧! 注意!
loach [lotʃ; loutʃ] *n., pl.* **loach·es, loach.** 泥鰌。
:load [lod; loud] *n.* ①負擔;負荷(物)。②車等所載之量(用於複合字中)。two truckloads of coal. 兩卡車煤。③〖機械〗載荷;負擔。④(槍砲等的)裝塡火藥;裝彈。⑤〖電〗負荷。⑥(常 *pl.*)很多;大量。⑦〖俚〗酒氣。He came in with a small *load* on. 他來的時候微帶着酒氣。⑧載有貨物的車輛。⑨工作分量。The normal teaching *load* of a full professor is eight hours a week. 正教授正常的授課時數爲每星期八小時。***get a load of*** 〖俚〗聽;注意到。***lay load on*** (or ***upon***) 毆打;責備;攻擊。***lay the load on*** 把罪推給…;嫁罪於…。***loads of*** 很多 (=plenty of, lots of). They have *loads of* money. 他們有很多錢。***take a load off a person's mind*** 使人解除憂慮。—*v.t.* ①裝載;裝貨物於(車、船等)。②堆積於;使負擔。③大量地給與;塡滿。a heart *loaded* with sorrow. 滿懷悲傷的心。④裝彈藥於。*Load* your gun! 裝彈藥! ⑤塡鉛以加重(手杖等)。⑥〖棒球〗使滿壘。The pitcher *loaded* the bases by walking three batters. 那投手以壞球保送對方的三個打擊手上壘。⑦裝膠捲。⑧在畫布上堆砌大量顏料。—*v.i.* ①裝貨;載客。The bus usually *loads* at the side door. 公共汽車通常在側門上客(乘客由側門上車)。②裝子彈。③上車〖常 into〗. The campers *loaded* into the buses. 露營者上了公共汽車。④(船)裝貨;載客。The ship *loaded* with people in only 15 minutes. 該船僅歷時十五分鐘便上滿了客人。***loaded dice*** 被塡鉛使投擲時某一面恒向上之骰子。***load the dice*** **a.** 在骰子內塡鉛。**b.** 作弊;取巧。**c.** 使處於不利(或有利)地位;對結果發生好(或壞)影響。***load up*** 裝貨物於車、船等。Have you finished *loading up* yet? 你已將貨物裝載完了嗎? —*adv.* (*pl.*) 〖俗〗很多;大量。It would help *loads* if you sent money. 你如果寄錢來將大有幫助。
load displacement 〖航海〗載貨排水量(船隻滿載貨物時之排水量)。
load draft 〖航海〗載貨吃水。
load·ed [ˈlodɪd; ˈloudid] *adj.* ①載重的;裝着貨的。②裝有彈藥的。③裝塡着(鉛等)的。④〖美俚〗酒醉的。⑤〖俚〗有錢的。⑥〖俗〗意味深長的;有用意的。
load·er [ˈlodɚ; ˈloudə] *n.* ①裝貨的人;裝彈藥的人。②裝貨機;裝彈器。
load·ing [ˈlodɪŋ; ˈloudiŋ] *n.* ①裝載;(船等)上貨。②貨物;船費。③裝塡;塡藥。④(人壽保險)額外保險費。⑤負荷;載荷。⑥〖電〗加載;加電感。
load limit (車輛之)最大載重量。
load line 〖航海〗(船之)裝貨吃水線。
load·mas·ter [ˈlodˌmæstɚ; ˈloudˌmɑːstə] *n.* (巨型運貨機上的)貨運管理員。
load·om·e·ter [loˈdɑmɪtɚ; louˈdɔmitə] *n.* (測定車重的)地磅。
load-shed·ding [ˈlodˌʃɛdɪŋ; ˈloudˌʃediŋ] *n.* 〖電〗①(工場)用電限制。②電力平均分配。
load·stone [ˈlodˌston; ˈloudstoun] *n.* ①天然磁石。②具有吸引力之東西。(亦作 **lodestone**)
loaf**[1] [lof; louf] *n., pl.* **loaves** [lovz; louvz]. ①一條(麪包)。Half a *loaf* is better than no bread. 半條麪包總勝於無麪包(聊勝於無)。②大塊烤過的食物。③圓錐形糖塊。④塊;團。⑤〖俚〗頭腦。Use your *loaf.* 用你的頭腦。loaf of bread*** 〖俚〗腦筋;頭腦。
loaf[2] *v.i.* 游手好閒;虛擲光陰。—*v.t.* 虛擲;浪費。—*n.* (僅 *sing.*)游蕩;不務正業。
loaf·er [ˈlofɚ; ˈloufə] *n.* 閒蕩者。
loaf sugar ①塊糖。②圓錐形糖塊。
loam [lom; loum] *n.* ①沃土。②壚埴(泥、沙、草等之混合物, 用於製坯、塗牆及塡塞洞穴等)。③〖古〗土地。④〖罕〗黏土。—*v.t.* 以沃土、壚埴等遮蓋或塞阻。
loam·y [ˈlomɪ; ˈloumi] *adj.,* **loam·i·er, loam·i·est.** ①沃土的。②壚埴的;似壚埴的。—**loam·i·ness,** *n.*
***loan** [lon; loun] *n.* ①借;借出;借入。He asked me for a *loan* of five dollars. 他向我借五塊錢。②(公)債。③借出物;貸款。The organization was authorized to make *loans* upon farm commodities. 該機構被授權辦理農產品貸款。—*v.t.* ①〖美〗借(=lend). I *loaned* her the clothes to wear. 我借給她衣服穿。②〖方〗借(=borrow). Can I *loan* a ladder from you for a day or so? 我可以借你的梯子用一兩天嗎? —*v.i.* 供應貸款。〖注意〗**loan** 與 **lend** 均爲借。在英國正式用法中, loan 是名詞, lend 爲動詞。但在美語中, loan 既可作名詞, 亦可作爲動詞。「家借來的展覽品。」
loan collection 在展覽會中自收藏」
lo and behold (表示驚訝的感嘆詞)你看! 「購買所。」
loan office ①貸款處。②當鋪。③公債」
loan shark 〖俗〗放高利貸者。「語。」
loan word 自外國文中借用的字;外來」
loath [loθ; louθ] *adj.* 不願意的;勉强的。The little girl was *loath* to leave her mother. 那小女孩不願離開她的母親。***nothing loath*** 非常樂意;很高興。(亦作 **loth**) —**ness,** *n.*
loathe [loð; louð] *v.t.,* **loathed, loath·ing.** 厭惡;嫌惡。—**loath·er,** *n.*
loath·ing [ˈloðɪŋ; ˈlouðiŋ] *n.* 强烈的憎惡(厭惡)。—*adj.* 憎惡的。—**ly,** *adv.*
loath·ly[1] [ˈloθlɪ; ˈlouθli] *adv.* 〖罕〗不情願地;勉强地。
loath·ly[2] [ˈloðlɪ; ˈlouðli] *adj.* 〖罕〗=**loathsome.** —**loath·li·ness,** *n.*
loath·some [ˈloðsəm; ˈlouðsəm] *adj.* 可厭的;令人作嘔的。—**ness,** *n.*
loaves [lovz; louvz] *n.* pl. of **loaf**[1].
lob [lɑb; lɔb] *n., v.,* **lobbed, lob·bing.** —*n.* ①〖方〗高大而遲鈍之人。②〖動物〗一種沙蠋(=lobworm)。③〖網球〗高(緩)球;高擊送回之球。④〖板球〗低(緩)球;下手緩擊之球。—*v.t.* 向上拋投;向上緩射。—*v.i.* ①笨

重而行〖常 along〗. ②擊緩而高曲之球。③〖澳〗到;達。—**ber,** *n.*

lo·bar [ˈlobɚ; ˈloubə] *adj.* ①〖植物〗(葉之)裂片的。②〖醫〗(肺)葉的。

lo·bate [ˈlobet; ˈloubeit] *adj.* 〖生物〗有裂片的;分裂的。(亦作 **lobated**) —**ly,** *adv.*

lo·ba·tion [loˈbeʃən; louˈbeiʃən] *n.* ①分裂;裂片之形成。②裂片。

***lob·by** [ˈlɑbɪ; ˈlɔbi] *n., pl.* **-bies,** *v.,* **-bied, -by·ing.** —*n.* ①廳;廊;休息室。the *lobby* of a hotel. 旅館的大廳。②(英國下議院,美國參議院中的)民衆接待室。③〖美〗(議院外的)遊說議員者(集合稱)。—*v.t.* ①遊說議員使通過(議案等)。to *lobby* a bill through the Senate. 遊說議員使參議院通過一項議案。②遊說(議員或議會)。—*v.i.* 遊說議員。

lob·by·ism [ˈlɑbɪˌɪzəm; ˈlɔbiizəm] *n.* 〖美〗議院外之遊說;議案通過活動。

lob·by·ist [ˈlɑbɪɪst; ˈlɔbiist] *n.* 〖美〗議院外之遊說者;活動議案通過者。

lob·by·man [ˈlɑbɪmən; ˈlɔbimən] *n., pl.* **-men.** (旅館、戲院等的)休息室服務員。

lobe [lob; loub] *n.* ①耳垂。②〖植物〗裂片;瓣。③〖解剖〗葉。④〖機械〗葉形輪;瓣輪。

lo·bec·to·my [loˈbɛktəmɪ; louˈbektəmi] *n., pl.* **-mies.** 〖外科〗肺葉切除。

lobed [lobd; loubd] *adj.* ①(器官等之)有圓形突出部分的。②瓣狀的。

lobe·let [ˈloblɪt; ˈloublit] *n.* ①〖植物〗小裂片。②〖解剖〗小葉。

lo·bel·ia [loˈbiliə; louˈbiːliə] *n.* 〖植物〗山梗菜屬植物。

lob·lol·ly [ˈlɑblɑlɪ; ˈlɔblɔli] *n., pl.* **-lies.** ①美國南部之一種松樹;其木材。②濃稠之粥。③〖美方〗泥濘。④〖航海俚〗醫藥。

lo·bo [ˈlobo; ˈloubou] *n.* (美國西部之)一種灰色大狼。

lo·bot·o·my [loˈbɑtəmɪ; louˈbɔtəmi] *n.* 〖外科〗腦葉切除手術。(亦作 **leucotomy**)

lob·scouse [ˈlɑbˌskaus; ˈlɔbskaus] *n.* 〖航海〗(肉、蔬菜與餅乾合煮而成的)燉菜。

***lob·ster** [ˈlɑbstɚ; ˈlɔbstə] *n.* ①龍蝦。②龍蝦肉(食物)。—*v.i.* 捕龍蝦。

lob·ster-eyed [ˈlɑbstɚˌaɪd; ˈlɔbstər-aid] *adj.* 眼睛突出的。

lob·ster-joint [ˈlɑbstɚˌdʒɔɪnt; ˈlɔbstə-dʒɔint] *n.* 烟斗或烟管之接頭(可自由裝卸)。

lobster pot 捕龍蝦之陷阱。

lobster shift 後半夜班(自午夜至早晨之班)。(亦作 **dog watch, graveyard shift**)

lobster trick =**lobster shift.**

lob·u·lat·ed [ˈlɑbjəˌletɪd; ˈlɔbjuleitid] *adj.* 由小葉片組成的;分成小裂片的。

lob·ule [ˈlɑbjul; ˈlɔbjuːl] *n.* ①〖解剖〗小裂片;小葉。②耳朶(指耳垂部分)。—**lob·u·lar,** *adj.*

lob·worm [ˈlɑbˌwɝm; ˈlɔbwəːm] *n.* 沙蠶。(亦作 **lugworm**)

‡**lo·cal** [ˈlokl̩; ˈloukəl] *adj.* ①地方的;本地的。②局部的。③每站皆停的(火車)。—*n.* ①慢車。②地方新聞。③(工會等的)支部。The *local* would not agree with the national decision to strike. 工會支部不贊成全國工會總部的罷工決策。④本地人。

local color (文藝中的)地方色彩。

lo·cale [loˈkæl; louˈkɑːl] *n.* (事件等的)現場;場所。

local government ①地方政府。②地方自治(=local self-government). ③地方政治學。

lo·cal·ism [ˈloklˌɪzəm; ˈloukəlizəm] *n.* ①地方性質、地方風俗等。②鄉土偏愛;地方主義;偏狹性。③方言。

***lo·cal·i·ty** [loˈkælətɪ; louˈkæliti] *n., pl.* **-ties.** ①位置;所在地。②地方;區域。③一地方的外貌。④位置性。Every real object has *locality* as one of its attributes. 位置性是所有物體的屬性之一。

lo·cal·ize [ˈloklˌaɪz; ˈloukəlaiz] *v.t.,* **-ized, -iz·ing.** ①使地方化。②使限於局部。—*v.i.* 集於一部分;限於局部。—**lo·cal·i·za·tion,** *n.*

lo·cal·ly [ˈloklɪ; ˈloukəli] *adv.* ①從場所、位置上。②在地方上;局部地。③用地方主義。④在本地。

local option 地方居民所有之決定權(例如酒類應否販賣等)。

local time 當地時間。

local union ①工會地方支部。②地方工會。

‡**lo·cate** [ˈloket, loˈket; louˈkeit] *v.,* **-cat·ed, -cat·ing.** —*v.t.* ①設於。He *located* his new store on Main Street. 他將新店開設於大街上。②測出;尋出…的位置。The general tried to *locate* the enemy's camp. 將軍企圖找出敵軍營地的位置。③指出或說明(某地)的位置。④爲…定位;爲…定界限。He carefully *located* the clock in the exact center of the mantel. 他將時鐘小心地定位在壁爐架上正當中。—*v.i.* 〖美〗定居。He went to New York and *located* there. 他到紐約去就定居在那裏了。***be located*** 位於(=be situated). Rome *is located* in Italy. 羅馬位於義大利。—**lo·cat·a·ble,** *adj.* —**lo·cat·er,** *n.*

***lo·ca·tion** [loˈkeʃən; louˈkeiʃən] *n.* ①定位置。②位置;地方;場所。③(電影的)外景拍攝地。The company is on *location.* 該公司在拍外景。④尋找。She devoted all her time to the *location* of the missing money. 她花掉所有時間去尋找失款。⑤南非共和國劃給土人居住的地方。⑥澳洲的農場。⑦〖美〗劃出界線的土地。—**al,** *adj.* —**al·ly,** *adv.*

loc·a·tive [ˈlɑkətɪv; ˈlɔkətiv] *adj.* 〖文法〗位置格的;表示位置的。—*n.* 〖文法〗位置格。

lo·ca·tor [ˈloketɚ; louˈkeitə] *n.* 〖美〗①測定田地礦場邊界的人。②聽音機。③電波探測器;雷達。

loc. cit. loco citato.

loch [lɑk; lɔk] *n.* 〖蘇〗①湖。②內海;海灣。

‡**lock**¹ [lɑk; lɔk] *n.* ①鎖。The *lock* is broken. 鎖壞了。②槍機。③(運河、船塢等的)水閘。④刹車。For a car of this size the *lock* is excellent. 對於這種大小的車子來說,這刹車要算很好。⑤〖機械〗氣閘。⑥(摔角的)揪扭。***be at lock*** 〖俗〗在困窘中。***lock stepper*** 〖俗〗囚犯。***lock, stock and barrel*** 〖俗〗全部;完全地。***under lock and key*** 安全地鎖着;在鎖着的地方。The documents were *under lock and key.* 那些文件放在鎖着(安全)的地方。—*v.t.* ①關鎖;加鎖於;鎖。*Lock* the door. 鎖門。②深陷於;深藏於。The ship was *locked* in ice. 此船深陷冰中。③挽(臂)。④把…關在外面或裏面。*Lock* up the prisoners. 將犯人關起來。⑤使固住;刹住。⑥用水閘使(船)通過。—*v.i.* ①鎖;關鎖。This door won't *lock.* 這門鎖不住。②(船)通過水閘。The ship *locked* into the new canal. 船通過水閘開進新運河。③連鎖。The sections *lock* into one another. 各部分彼此連鎖在一起。***lock away*** 鎖藏起來。***lock horns*** 鬥爭;爭論。***lock in*** 鎖在房內。***lock off*** 在(運河上)設水閘。***lock on*** a. (雷達天線)固定並追踪飛行目標。b. 用雷達等使飛彈等瞄準目標。***lock out*** a. 停工直至職工接

受雇主的條件(雇主對付罷工的方法)。**b.** 將…鎖在外面。***lock the stable door after the horse has been stolen***〖諺〗亡羊補牢。***lock up*** **a.** 關鎖起來。*Lock* these papers *up*. 把這些文件鎖起來。**b.** 使固定;將…弄緊。**—a·ble,** *adj.*

lock² *n.* ①鬈髮。②(*pl.*)頭髮。③(乾草、羊毛等的)一把;小量。

lock·age ['lɑkɪdʒ; 'lɔkidʒ] *n.* ①(河、運河等由於水閘操作的)水面高度。②水閘通過(用水閘操作使船隻自一水面高度移至另一水面高度)。③水閘通過稅。④水閘之構築;水閘之操作。

lock·box ['lɑk,bɑks; 'lɔkbɔks] *n.* 有鎖的箱子。

lock chain (鎖車輪之)鏈鎖。

Locke [lɑk; lɔk] *n.* 洛克 (John, 1632–1704, 英國哲學家)。

lock·er ['lɑkɚ; 'lɔkə] *n.* ①上鎖之人。②(有鎖之)櫥櫃、抽屜、小室或碗櫥等。***Davy Jones's locker*** 海底;水手的墳墓。***go to*** (or ***be in***) ***Davy Jones's locker*** 溺死於海中。***not a shot in the locker*** 囊空如洗。

lock·et ['lɑkɪt; 'lɔkit] *n.* (懸於項鍊下之)小盒。

lock-in ['lɑk,ɪn; 'lɔkin] *n.* 〖美〗(爲貫徹要求,工人或學生等)占據某場所。

lock·jaw ['lɑk,dʒɔ; 'lɔkdʒɔ:] *n.* 〖醫〗牙關緊閉症;顎攣急;咀嚼筋痙攣。

lock keeper 水閘管理員。

lock·nut ['lɑk,nʌt; 'lɔknʌt] *n.* 鎖緊螺母。

lock-on ['lɑk,ɑn; 'lɔkɔn] *n.* 雷達追蹤。

lock·out ['lɑk,aut; 'lɔkaut] *n.* 停工(雇主爲抵制工人非法要求而休業)。*—adj.* 用以關閉的。

locks·man ['lɑksmən; 'lɔksmən] *n., pl.* **-men.** 水閘管理人。

lock·smith ['lɑk,smɪθ; 'lɔk-smiθ] *n.* 鎖匠。

lock step 密集的步伐。

lock stitch 雙線連鎖縫紉。

lock·up ['lɑk,ʌp; 'lɔkʌp] *n.* ①(學校等之)關門時間。②監禁。③拘留所;監獄。④(資本之)固定;固定資本。⑤〖英俗〗租來的貯藏間或車房。

lock-up ['lɑk,ʌp; 'lɔkʌp] *adj.* 〖英〗上鎖的。

lo·co ['loko; 'loukou] *n.* ①〖植物〗瘋草(=locoweed). ②瘋草症。③〖俚〗染瘋草病的動物;瘋人。*—v.t.* ①以瘋草毒之;使染瘋草病。②〖俚〗使發瘋。*—adj.* 〖俚〗瘋的;精神病的。

lo·co ci·ta·to ['lokosaɪ'teto; 'loukousai'teitou] 〖拉〗在前述之處(=in the place cited).

lo·co·fo·co [,loko'foko; ,loukou'foukou] *n., pl.* **-cos.** ①(L-)〖美史〗(1835年左右之)民主黨急進派;此派之黨員。②(昔)任何美國民主黨黨員。**—ism,** *n.*

lo·co·mo·bile [,lokə'mobɪl; ,loukə'moubi:l] *adj.* 自力推動的;可移動的。*—n.* 自力推動之車輛、機器等。

lo·co·mo·tion [,lokə'moʃən; ,loukə'mouʃən] *n.* ①運動;移動;轉位;運轉。②運動力;移轉力;運轉力。③旅行;交通工具。

***lo·co·mo·tive** [,lokə'motɪv; 'loukə,moutiv, ,loukə'm-] *n.* 火車機車;火車頭。*—adj.* ①移動的;運動的。②自力移動的。③旅行的;好旅行的;常常旅行的。He has lately led a very *locomotive* existence. 他最近常常旅行。④火車頭的。

lo·co·mo·tor [,lokə'motɚ; ,loukə'moutə] *adj.* 移動的;運動的;轉位的。*—n.* 有運動力之人;有移動力之物;移動發動機。

locomotor a·tax·i·a [~ə'tæksɪə; ~ə'tæksiə] 〖醫〗脊髓癆;運動性共濟失調。

lo·co·weed ['loko,wid; 'loukouwi:d] *n.* 〖植物〗瘋草(多產於美國西南部,動物食之則引起瘋草症)。

loc·u·lus ['lɑkjələs; 'lɔkjuləs] *n., pl.* **-li** [-,laɪ; -lai]. ①〖動、植物,解剖〗房;胞。②古墳內之屍室。

lo·cum te·nens ['lokəm'tinɛnz; 'loukəm'ti:nenz] 〖拉〗牧師或醫師之臨時代理人。

lo·cus ['lokəs; 'loukəs] *n., pl.* **lo·ci** ['losaɪ; 'lousai], **lo·ca** ['lokə; 'loukə]. ①場所;位置;所在地。②〖幾何〗軌跡。

lo·cus clas·si·cus ['lokəs'klæsɪkəs; 'loukəs'klæsikəs] *pl.* **lo·ci clas·si·ci** ['losaɪ'klæsɪ,saɪ; 'lousai'klæsisai]. 〖拉〗常被引證之章句(=standard passage).

lo·cus in quo ['lokəs ɪn 'kwo; 'loukəs in 'kwou] 〖拉〗現場(=the place in which).

***lo·cust** ['lokəst; 'loukəst] *n.* ①蝗蟲;蚱蜢。a cloud of *locusts*. 遮蔽天日的大羣蝗蟲。②蟬。③〖植物〗刺槐;刺槐之堅實防朽的木材。**—like,** *adj.*

lo·cu·tion [lo'kjuʃən; lou'kju:ʃən] *n.* 語法;語風;語句;慣用語。

loc·u·to·ry ['lɑkjə,torɪ; 'lɔkjutəri] *n.* (修道院之)談話室。

lode [lod; loud] *n.* ①礦脈。②源;泉源。

lode·star ['lod,stɑr; 'loudstɑ:] *n.* ①指示方向之星。②北極星。③指導原則;目標。(亦作 **loadstar**)

***lodge** [lɑdʒ; lɔdʒ] *v.,* **lodged, lodg·ing,** *n.* *—v.t.* ①供以臨時住宿處。The shipwrecked sailors were *lodged* in the school. 那些遇難的水手臨時住宿學校內。②使擊中;使射於(某處)。③儲藏;存放。④提呈;遞。⑤授(權)於某人或物。⑥監禁。⑦使倒地。A sudden hail had *lodged* the crops. 一陣冰雹將農作物打倒在地上。*—v.i.* ①臨時住宿;寄宿。Where are you *lodging* now? 你現在寄宿在何處?②絆於;固定於。The kite *lodged* in the top of a tree. 風箏絆於樹梢間。③躲藏起來。We found the place where the deer had *lodged*. 我們發現了那隻鹿躲藏的地方。④(草類)倒地。*—n.* ①門房;司閽者室。②(鄉間供遊獵者住宿的)小屋。They had a hunting and fishing *lodge* there. 他們在那裏有狩獵釣魚時可住宿的小屋。③(牛津大學各學院大樓入口處的)小房間。④(祕密會社的)分會;支部。⑥海狸、獺等的巢穴。⑥印第安人之住屋。

lodg·er ['lɑdʒɚ; 'lɔdʒə] *n.* 房客;寄宿者。

lodg·ing** ['lɑdʒɪŋ; 'lɔdʒiŋ] *n.* ①臨時住宿處;寓所。Where can we find (a) *lodging* for the night? 我們今晚能在何處找個住宿處? ②(*pl.*)寄宿舍;公寓。It's cheaper to live in *lodgings* than in a hotel. 住在公寓裏比旅館裏便宜些。③住宿;寄宿。board and lodging*** 附伙食的寄宿。***dry lodging*** 不附伙食的寄宿。***take up one's lodgings*** 決定住處;投宿。

lodging house 出租房間的寄宿舍;公寓。

lodg(e)·ment ['lɑdʒmənt; 'lɔdʒmənt] *n.* ①提出;遞。②住宿。③寓所;臨時住宿所。④貯藏物;沉澱物。⑤〖軍〗占領;占據;從敵軍手中奪來之據點。⑥穩固地位。⑦絆結。

lo·ess ['lo·ɪs, lœs; 'louis] *n.* 〖地質〗黃土。

Loe·wi ['lœvɪ; 'lə:vi] *n.* 羅威 (Otto, 1873–1961, 德國藥學家, 1936年獲諾貝爾醫學獎)。

lo-fi ['lo,faɪ; 'loufai] *adj.* 音響不能傳眞的。

*__loft__ 〔lɔft, lɑft; lɔːft〕 *n.* ①閣樓；頂樓。②廐樓（堆積乾草用者，=hayloft）。③鴿房。④貨倉或商業建築的樓上一層。⑤（講堂、教堂的）樓廂。⑥〖高爾夫〗打球棒端的向後傾斜。⑦〖高爾夫〗高擊。⑧羊毛之伸縮性。—*v.t.* ①〖高爾夫〗打（球）高飛出去。②向上投。③升遷；擢升。He was *lofted* to a new job. 他升遷到新職位。④存放在廐樓上。—*v.i.* ①（物品被擊後）向上飛。②向上投；向上擊。

__loft·er__ 〔ˈlɔftɚ; ˈlɔːftə〕 *n.* 〖高爾夫〗高擊球棒。

__loft·i·ness__ 〔ˈlɔftɪnɪs; ˈlɔːftinis〕 *n.* 高「超；高傲。」

*__loft·y__ 〔ˈlɔftɪ, ˈlɑftɪ; ˈlɔːfti〕 *adj.*, __loft·i·er, loft·i·est.__ ①高的；巍然的。②高超的；高尙的。③高傲的；傲慢的。He had a *lofty* contempt for others. 他對別人態度高傲而帶輕蔑。④高深的。—__loft·i·ly,__ *adv.*

‡__log__[1] 〔lɔg, lɑg; lɔg〕 *n., v.,* __logged, log·ging.__ —*n.* ①（自樹上伐下的）圓形木材；木頭。②航海日誌（=logbook）。③（飛機的）飛行記錄；（機器的）使用記錄。④（船運）測速器。⑤無知覺之物。to sleep like a *log.* 睡得像死人。⑥廣播電臺或電視臺之廣播日誌。***as easy as rolling off a log***（像滾木頭一樣）極容易的。***like a log*** 無知覺的；不能動的。***roll logs for a person*** 替某人吹噓。—*v.i.* 伐木。to *log* for a living. 伐木爲生。—*v.t.* ①伐（木）。They *logged* most of the trees in the area. 他們採伐了該地區的大部分樹木。②記載於航海日誌中。③切（木材）。They *logged* the timber into 7-foot lengths. 他們將那木材切成七英尺長。④採伐（某地區）中的樹木。⑤（船）航行（某距離）。The ship *logged* 100 miles that day. 船在那天航行了100英里。⑥（飛行員等）累積（飛行時數）。They asked the pilot how many hours he had *logged.* 他們問那飛行員累積了多少飛行時數。—__like,__ *adj.*

__log__[2] *n.* =__logarithm.__

__log.__ ①logarithm. ②logic.

__lo·gan·ber·ry__ 〔ˈlogənˌbɛrɪ; ˈlougənbəri〕 *n., pl.* __-ries.__ 洛干漿果；大楊莓（raspberry 與 blackberry 的雜種）。

__log·a·rithm__ 〔ˈlɔgəˌrɪðəm; ˈlɔgəriθəm〕 *n.* 〖數學〗對數。

__log·a·rith·mic__ 〔ˌlɔgəˈrɪðmɪk; ˌlɔgəˈriθmik〕 *adj.* 對數的。（亦作 __logarithmical__）

__log·book__ 〔ˈlɔgˌbʊk; ˈlɔgbuk〕 *n.* ①〖航海、航空〗航海日誌；航空日誌。②旅行雜誌。

__log cabin__ 木造小屋。

__loge__ 〔loʒ; louʒ〕〖法〗 *n.* ①（戲院之）包廂。②（展覽會中之）攤位。

__log·ger__ 〔ˈlɔgɚ; ˈlɔgə〕 *n.* ①鋸木者；伐木者。②將木頭裝上車之機械。③伐木曳引機。

__log·ger·head__ 〔ˈlɔgɚˌhɛd; ˈlɔgəhed〕 *n.* ①蠢人；傻子。②一種大頭海龜；紅海龜。③（北美產之）百勞鳥。④捕鯨船尾叉索捲繞之圓柱。***at loggerheads (with)***（與…）相爭；不和。

__log·gia__ 〔ˈlɑdʒɪə; ˈlɔdʒə〕 *n., pl.* __-gias, log·gie__ 〔ˈlɑddʒe, ˈlɔd-; ˈlɔddʒei〕. 〖建築〗（建築物一側俯臨庭院之）走廊。

__log·ging__ 〔ˈlɔgɪŋ; ˈlɔgiŋ〕 *n.* 伐木；伐木「業。」

__log·i·a__ 〔ˈlɑgɪə; ˈlɔgiə〕 *n. pl., sing.* __log·i·on.__ ①（大宗教家之）箴言集。②（L-）未記載於新約四福音中之基督語錄。

*__log·ic__ 〔ˈlɑdʒɪk; ˈlɔdʒik〕 *n.* ①邏輯；論理學；理則學。He argues with learning and *logic.* 他的辯論既有學問又合邏輯。②理則學書籍。③正確的推理。④推理的方法。At this point our *logic* was at fault. 在這一點上我們推理的方法錯誤。⑤推移。

__-logic, -logical__ 〖字尾〗 __-logy__ 之形容詞形，如：biology — biological.

*__log·i·cal__ 〔ˈlɑdʒɪkl; ˈlɔdʒikəl〕 *adj.* ①邏輯的；合邏輯的。②合理的；始終一致的。③當然的；不足爲奇的。War was the *logical* consequence of these conditions. 在那種情形下戰爭是必然的結果。④能推理的。—__ly,__ *adv.* —__ness,__ *n.*

__log·i·cal·i·ty__ 〔ˌlɑdʒɪˈkælətɪ; ˌlɔdʒiˈkæliti〕 *n.* 合邏輯；合理；論法（推理）之正確。

__logical positivism__ 〖哲學〗邏輯的實證主義（主張藉分析科學所使用之語文，以建立可適於一切科學之語彙，以求科學之統一）。

__lo·gi·cian__ 〔loˈdʒɪʃən; louˈdʒiʃən〕 *n.* 邏輯學家；論理學家；理則學家。

__log·i·cize__ 〔ˈlɑdʒɪˌsaɪz; ˈlɔdʒisaiz〕 *v.,* __-cized, -ciz·ing.__ —*v.t.* 使合乎邏輯。—*v.i.* 運用邏輯。

__log·i·on__ 〔ˈlɑgɪˌɑn; ˈlɔgiɔn〕 *n.* sing. 「of __logia.__」

__lo·gis·tic__ 〔loˈdʒɪstɪk; louˈdʒistik〕 *adj.* ①推理的；邏輯的。②計算的。③〖軍〗後勤學的。

__lo·gis·tics__ 〔loˈdʒɪstɪks; louˈdʒistiks〕 *n.* （作 *sing.* or *pl.* 解）①〖軍〗後勤學。②算術計算術。

__log·jam__ 〔ˈlɔgˌdʒæm; ˈlɔːgdʒæm〕 *n., v.,* __-jammed, -jam·ming.__ —*n.* ①河流中木材之阻塞。②停滯狀態；僵局。③擁擠；大量。—*v.i. & v.t.* ①擁塞；擁擠。②阻礙；妨礙。

__log·o·gram__ 〔ˈlɑgəˌgræm; ˈlɔgougræm〕 *n.* ①語標；字標（如$, 代表 dollar）。②代表一字的字母；略字（例如 c. =cent）。③一種字謎。—__mat·ic,__ *adj.*

__log·o·graph__ 〔ˈlɑgəˌgræf; ˈlɔgougrɑːf〕 *n.* ①語標；字標；略字（=logogram）。②〖罕〗〖印刷〗=__logotype.__

__lo·gom·a·chy__ 〔ləˈgɑməkɪ; ləˈgɔməki〕 *n., pl.* __-chies.__ ①字義之爭。②綴字遊戲。

__Log·os__ 〔ˈlɑgɑs; ˈlɔgɔs〕 *n.* ①〖神學〗（三位一體中第二位的）基督；（神的）道。②（有時l-）〖哲學〗理性（宇宙構成或宇宙秩序之根本原理）。

__log·o·type__ 〔ˈlɑgəˌtaɪp; ˈlɔgoutaip〕 *n.* 〖印刷〗①單語活字（將數字母合鑄成一活字者，如：in, an, the, and 等）。②商標。③報刊之刊頭。（亦作 __logo__）

__log·roll__ 〔ˈlɔgˌrol; ˈlɔgroul〕 *v.t. & v.i.* 〖美〗①合力滾動伐下之木材。②互相幫助。③〖政治〗互相合作使（議案）通過。④（作家等）互相稱讚吹噓。

__log·roll·ing__ 〔ˈlɔgˌrolɪŋ; ˈlɔgˌrouliŋ〕 *n.* 〖美〗①（合力）滾木材。②合作；協力。③〖政治〗（議員等爲使彼此提案通過的）互助。④（作家等的）互相標榜。

__log·wood__ 〔ˈlɔgˌwʊd; ˈlɔgwud〕 *n.* 〖植物〗蘇方樹；蘇方木（產於中美及西印度羣島）。

__lo·gy__ 〔ˈlogɪ; ˈlougi〕 *adj.,* __-gi·er, -gi·est.__ 〖美〗（舉動或頭腦）遲鈍的。—__lo·gi·ly,__ *adv.* —__lo·gi·ness,__ *n.*

__-logy__ 〖字尾〗①表"話；言語；談話"之義，如：eulogy. ②表"…學；…論"之義，如：philology.

*__loin__ 〔lɔɪn; lɔin〕 *n.* ①（常 *pl.*）腰；腰部。②（動物的）腰肉。*loin* of mutton. 羊腰肉。***be a fruit*** (or ***child***) ***of one's loins*** 自己生下的孩子。***be sprung from the loins of*** 係…的後裔。***gird (up) one's loins*** 準備遠行；準備行動。He *girded up his loins* to face his competitor. 他磨礪以須準備面對他的對手。

__loin·cloth__ 〔ˈlɔɪnˌklɔθ; ˈlɔinklɔθ〕 *n.* （野「蠻人用的）纏腰布。」

loir [lɔɪr; lɔiə] *n.* (歐洲產)山鼠。

***loi·ter** [ˈlɔɪtɚ; ˈlɔitə] *v.i.* 逍遙; 閒蕩; 且行且止; 徘徊。to *loiter* on one's way home from school. 從學校邊走邊玩地回家。—*v.t.* 荒廢; 虛度(時光)。—**er,** *n.* —**ing,** *adj.* —**ing·ly,** *adv.*

loll [lɑl; lɔl] *v.i.* ①憑倚; (懶洋洋地)站、坐或躺着。②下垂; 伸出〖out〗。—*v.t.* 任其向外伸出〖out〗。—*n.* 憑倚; 垂伸。

Lol·lard [ˈlɑlɚd; ˈlɔləd] *n.* 〖英宗教史〗14-15世紀 John Wycliffe派之信徒。—**ism,** *n.*

lol·li·pop [ˈlɑlɪˌpɑp; ˈlɔlipɔp] *n.* ①棒棒糖。②糖果。③〖英〗(派人在上學放學時間持以)管制交通, 維護學童過街安全的大圓牌桿。(亦作 **lollypop**)

lol·lop [ˈlɑləp; ˈlɔləp] *v.i.* ①〖俗、方〗懶散而行; 懶洋洋地坐或躺着。②蹦跳地走; 跳躍。—*n.*〖英俗〗懶洋洋的走或坐臥; 跳跳蹦蹦; 跳躍。

Lom·bard [ˈlɑmbɚd, -bɑrd; ˈlɔmbəd, -bɑːd] *n.* ①倫巴底人。②放債者; 銀行家。—*adj.* 倫巴底(人)的。

Lombard Street ①倫巴德街(倫敦一街名, 爲金融中心)。②倫敦金融界; 金融市場。***Lombard Street to a China orange*** 極貴重物與極微賤物之對賭。

Lom·bard·y [ˈlɑmbɚdɪ; ˈlɔmbədi] *n.* 倫巴底(義大利北部之一地區, 昔爲王國)。

Lombardy poplar 一種白楊樹。

Lon., Lond. London.

lon. longitude.

***Lon·don** [ˈlʌndən; ˈlʌndən] *n.* ①倫敦(英國的首都)。②加拿大東南一城市。③倫敦(Jack, 1876–1916, 美國小說家)。

Lon·don·er [ˈlʌndənɚ; ˈlʌndənə] *n.* 倫敦人; 倫敦居民。

Lon·don·esque [ˌlʌndəˈnɛsk; ˌlʌndəˈnesk] *adj.* ①如倫敦的; 倫敦特有的。②傑克倫敦之文體的。

London ivy 倫敦之濃霧; 倫敦之煙霾。

London smoke 灰黑色。

***lone** [lon; loun] *adj.* ①孤寂的(多用於詩中)。a *lone* life. 孤寂的生活。②孤立的; 隔離的。a *lone* house. 一所孤立的房屋。③〖諧〗單身的; 寡居的。

lone hand ①玩牌時, 一個人對抗許多人。②不徵詢他人意見或求助他人而獨行其是者。③單獨採取的行動或立場。

***lone·ly** [ˈlonlɪ; ˈlounli] *adj.,* **-li·er, -li·est.** ①孤單的。a *lonely* traveler. 孤單的旅客。②孤寂的; 寂寞的。She was *lonely* when among strangers. 她在生人羣中甚覺寂寞。③偏僻的; 人煙稀少的; 荒涼的。a *lonely* mountain village. 荒涼的山村。④單獨的; 孤立的。—**lone·li·ness,** *n.*

lonely hearts 〖俚〗急於物色結婚對象的中年男女。

lon·er [ˈlonɚ; ˈlounə] *n.* 〖俗〗①喜歡孤獨的人。He is a *loner*, but his world is filled with friends. 他是一個好孤獨的人, 但他的生活圈裏卻充滿着朋友。②獨立的人。

lone·some** [ˈlonsəm; ˈlounsəm] *adj.,* **-som·er, -som·est.** 孤單寂寞的(較 lonely 凄涼的意味更濃)。*lonesome* surroundings. 孤寂的環境。by*** (or ***on***) ***one's lonesome*** 〖俗〗單獨。She went walking *by her lonesome*. 她獨自去散步。—**ly,** *adv.* —**ness,** *n.*

lone wolf ①〖俗〗a. 喜歡單獨行動者。b. 持與他人不同之意見者。②單獨來往之狼。

‡**long**¹ [lɔŋ, lɑŋ; lɔŋ] *adj.,* **long·er, long·est,** *adv., n.* —*adj.* ①(距離、長度等)長的。②(時間)長的; 長久的。We stayed a *long* time. 我們停留了很久的時間。③冗長的; 拖長的。a *long* novel. 一部冗長的小說。④〖語音〗長音(母音、音節)的。⑤達到遠方的; 延持很久的。a *long* memory. 好記性。⑥費時很久的; 慢的。He's awfully *long* getting here. 他來得很慢。⑦(兩個中)較長的; (數個中)最長的。He must have taken the *long* way home. 他一定是走了較遠的那條路回家。⑧集中的; 注意的; 徹底的。a *long* look at one's past mistakes. 徹底檢討過去的錯誤。⑨在某方面充分的〖on〗。He is *long* on talk but short on action. 他祇說不做。⑩機會不多的。⑪(酒類等)沖淡的。***a long face*** 臉有不豫之色。***a long way*** (or ***distance***) (***off***) 遠。***as broad as it is long*** 長寬都是一樣; 終究是一樣。***at*** (***the***) ***longest*** 最長; 最久; 最多。I can wait only three days *at* (*the*) *longest*. 我最多只能等三天。***be long about it*** 費時甚久(=take a long time to do something). Don't *be long about it*; I'm in a hurry. 不要費時太久, 我是很忙的。***have a long head*** 有先見之明; 敏捷伶俐。***have a long tongue*** 長舌; 饒舌。***have a long wind*** 能跑長跑; 能久辯。***in the long run*** 終久; 終極; 往遠看。*In the long run*, this material will wear better than that. 終久這個料子要比那個料子耐穿。***long clothes*** 襁褓。***long odds*** (打賭時)懸殊比數。***take long views*** 眼光遠大; 有先見之明。***the long arm*** 遠及之力量。—*adv.* 長久地; 長期地。to live *long*. 長生。***how long?*** 多久? *How long* can you stay? 你能停留多久? ***long ago*** 很久以前。***long before*** (***after***) 遠在…之前(後)。I knew Smith *long before* I knew you. 我認識史密斯遠在認識你之前。***long since*** 久已。Bows and arrows have *long since* been out of use. 弓箭久已廢棄不用了。***no longer*** 不再。***so*** (or ***as***) ***long as*** 如果; 只要。You may borrow the book *so long as* you keep it clean. 你可以借這本書, 只要你能保持清潔。—*n.* ①長期間。Will it take *long?* 這事要費很久時間才做得完嗎? ②〖語音〗長母音; 長音節。③長的事物。The signal was two *longs* and a short. 這信號是兩長一短。***before long*** 不久(=soon). I shall be seeing you *before long*. 我不久就可見到你了。***the long and*** (***the***) ***short of it*** 要之; 歸結起來; 總之。

***long**² *v.i.* 渴望; 熱望。People are *longing* for peace. 人們渴望着和平。

long. longitude.

Long Beach 長堤(美國 California 州 Los Angeles 以南之一城市)。

long·bill [ˈlɔŋˌbɪl; ˈlɔŋbil] *n.* 長嘴鳥; (特指)山鷸。

long·boat [ˈlɔŋˌbot; ˈlɔŋbout] *n.* 從商船上最大之艇。

long·bow [ˈlɔŋˌbo; ˈlɔŋbou] *n.* 大弓; 長弓。***draw*** (or ***pull***) ***the longbow*** 說大話; 吹牛。

long·cloth [ˈlɔŋˌklɔθ; ˈlɔŋˌklɔθ] *n.* 一種輕柔的上等棉布。

long distance 〖美〗長途電話; 長途電話局。

long dozen 十三個。(亦作 **baker's dozen**)

long-drawn [ˈlɔŋˈdrɔn; ˈlɔŋˈdrɔːn] *adj.* 久延的; 延長的。(亦作 **long-drawn-out**)

long-eared [ˈlɔŋˌɪrd; ˈlɔŋiəd] *adj.* ①長耳的。②似驢的; 愚鈍的。

lon·ge·ron [ˈlɑndʒərən; ˈlɔndʒərən] 〖法〗*n.* 飛機機體之縱樑。

lon·gev·i·ty [lɑnˈdʒɛvətɪ; lɔnˈdʒeviti] *n.* ①長命;長壽。②壽命。***longevity pay*** 〖美軍〗年功加俸。

Long·fel·low [ˈlɔŋˌfɛlo; ˈlɔŋˌfelou] *n.* 朗非羅 (Henry Wadsworth, 1807–1882, 美國詩人)。

long green 〖美俚〗紙幣;現款 (尤指美鈔)。

long·hair [ˈlɔŋhɛr; ˈlɔŋhɛə] *n.* ①〖俗〗知識分子;(尤指)古典音樂家(樂師或作曲家)。②〖俚〗留長髮者(尤指男性嬉皮)。—*adj.* ①知識分子或古典音樂家等的。②留長髮者的。**—ed,** *adj.*

long·hand [ˈlɔŋˌhænd; ˈlɔŋhænd] *n.* 普通書法(非爲 shorthand或typewriting). —*adj.* 用普通書法寫的。

long haul ①長距離貨運。②持久之困難工作。***for*** (or ***over***) ***the long haul***〖俗〗 終久;終極;往遠看。

long head 機智;遠見。

long-head·ed [ˈlɔŋˌhɛdɪd; ˈlɔŋˈhedid] *adj.* ①銳敏的;有先見之明的。②有長頭的。

long·horn [ˈlɔŋˌhɔrn; ˈlɔŋhɔːn] *n.* ①長角動物;(尤指)長角牛。②〖俚〗(L-) 美國德州佬。③(探測飛機的)音響探測器。④一種重約十二磅之長圓形乳酪。

long·ing [ˈlɔŋɪŋ, ˈlɑŋ-; ˈlɔŋiŋ] *n.* 渴望;熱望。a *longing* for home. 思家;懷念家鄉。—*adj.* 渴望的;熱望的。a *longing* look. 渴望的目光。**—ly,** *adv.*

long·ish [ˈlɔŋɪʃ; ˈlɔŋiʃ] *adj.* 稍長的。

Long Island 長島(在美國 New York 州之東南)。

lon·gi·tude [ˈlɑndʒəˌtjud; ˈlɔndʒitjuːd] *n.* ①經度;經線。②〖諧〗長。(略作 **long.**)

lon·gi·tu·di·nal [ˌlɑndʒəˈtjudn̩l; ˌlɔndʒiˈtjuːdinl] *adj.* ①經度(線)的。②長度的。③縱的。—*n.* 框架中的縱柱。**—ly,** *adv.*

long jump 〖主英〗跳遠。

long-lived [ˈlɔŋˈlaɪvd; ˈlɔŋˈlivd] *adj.* ①長壽的;歷時已久的。②耐用的;耐久的。

long play =**long-playing record.**

long-play·ing record [ˈlɔŋˌpleɪŋ~; ˈlɔŋˌpleiiŋ~] 長時間唱片 (通稱LP唱片, 速度爲每分鐘33⅓轉)。

long-range [ˈlɔŋˌrendʒ; ˈlɔŋˈreindʒ] *adj.* ①長距離的;長射程的。②作久遠之計的。③長期的;久遠的。

long-run [ˈlɔŋˈrʌn; ˈlɔŋˈrʌn] *adj.* ①歷時甚久的。②長久才能兌現的(公債等)。

long·shore [ˈlɔŋˌʃor; ˈlɔŋʃɔː] *adj.* 海岸的;沿岸的;在海岸工作的。

long·shore·man [ˈlɔŋˌʃormən; ˈlɔŋʃɔːmən] *n., pl.* **-men.** ①碼頭裝卸工人。②近海漁夫。③海岸散工。

long-short story [ˈlɑŋˈʃɔrt~; ˈlɔŋˈʃɔːt~] 較一般爲長的短篇小說。

long shot ①〖電影〗遠拍。②大膽的(希望不多的、困難的)事業。③〖俗〗得勝機會甚少的打賭。④成功希望不大的人。⑤贏的希望甚少的賽馬。***not by a long shot*** 決不;幾乎不。

long-sight·ed [ˈlɔŋˈsaɪtɪd; ˈlɔŋˈsaitid] *adj.* ①有遠見的;見識高的;聰明的。②遠視眼的。**—ness,** *n.*

long-stand·ing [ˈlɔŋˈstændɪŋ; ˈlɔŋˈstændiŋ] *adj.* 爲時甚久的; 經年累月的。

long-suf·fer·ing [ˈlɔŋˈsʌfərɪŋ; ˈlɔŋˈsʌfəriŋ] *adj.* 忍受長期痛苦與折磨的。—*n.* 對長期痛苦與折磨的忍受。

long suit ①長牌 (同花居多的一手牌)。②長處;優點。

long-term [ˈlɔŋˌtɝm; ˈlɔŋtəːm] *adj.* ①長期的。a *long-term* credit (*or* loan). 長期貸款。②由擁有半年以上之資產所產生的。

long-time [ˈlɔŋˌtaɪm; ˈlɔŋtaim] *adj.* ①長期的。②耐久的;歷時甚久的。

long·tim·er [ˈlɑŋˌtaɪmɚ; ˈlɔŋˌtaimə] *n.* ①老資格;老手。②長期服刑的囚犯。

Long Tom ①(昔軍艦上用的一種)長射程砲。②(l- t-) 〖英方〗長尾山雀。③(l- t-) 〖軍俚〗大砲 (=cannon).

long ton 長噸 (=2,240 磅)。

long-tongued [ˈlɔŋtʌŋd; ˈlɔŋtʌŋd] *adj.* ①有長舌的。②饒舌的; 喋喋不休的。

long wave 〖無線電〗長波。

long-wind·ed [ˈlɔŋˈwɪndɪd; ˈlɔŋˈwindid] *adj.* ①氣息長的。②冗長的;。

long·wise [ˈlɔŋˌwaɪz; ˈlɔŋwaiz] *adv.* 縱;長。(亦作 **lengthways, longways, lengthwise**)

loo·by [ˈlubɪ; ˈluːbi] *n., pl.* **-bies.** 笨伯;蠢夫。

loo·fah [ˈlufɑ; ˈluːfɑː] *n.* ①〖植物〗絲瓜。②絲瓜絡。

‡look [luk; luk] *v.i.* ①視;看;觀;望〖常at〗. Don't *look* at me. 不要望着我。②面上現…的樣子;看來似乎是。She *looks* very ill. 她面現病重的樣子。③留心;注意;查明白。You must *look* at all the facts. 你必須查明一切事實。④(房屋等) 面向;朝…。Our house *looks* upon a garden. 我們的房屋面朝一所花園。⑤尋找;搜查。⑥有…之趨勢。Conditions *look* toward war. 情勢有走向戰爭之趨勢。—*v.t.* ①尋找;訪問。to *look* a name up in the telephone directory. 在電話簿裏找一個人名。②露出表情。to *look* daggers at a person. 惡狠狠地望着一個人。③注視;看。He couldn't *look* us in the face. 他不能正面注視我們。④露出…的表情。He *looked* his despair. 他臉上露出失望之色。⑤顯出(某種歲數)。She scarcely *looks* her years. 她看起來不若她的年齡老(看起來年輕)。⑥檢查;視察〖常 over〗. He *looked* the place over. 他將那地方檢查一遍。***look about one*** 四下觀看;安排。***look after*** **a.** 照料。Will you *look after* my dog (house, garden, etc.), while I'm away? 我不在家的時候, 請你費心照顧一下我的狗(房子、花園等)好嗎? **b.** 目送。She *looked after* him as he walked toward the railway station. 她目送他走向火車站。**c.** 注意。to *look after* one's own interest. 祇管自己的利益。***look a gift horse in the mouth*** 對所收之贈物挑剔。***look ahead*** 前看;預測;未雨綢繆。***look as if*** 看着像是(後接假設法的子句)。***look at*** **a.** 注視;盯。**b.** (在否定句中, 尤其與will, would 連用時) 拒絕;輕視。He wouldn't *look at* the proposal. 他拒絕這項提議。***look back*** **a.** 回顧;回憶。**b.** (對事業等) 不起勁;畏縮;停止不前。From this time on, he never *looked back.* 從此以後, 他便不斷地進步。***Look before you leap.*** 〖諺〗愼思而後行。***look black*** (***at***...)面有怒色。***look blue*** 現有憂傷不滿之色。***look daggers at*** 怒目而視。***look down upon*** (or ***on***) 瞧不起。***look for*** **a.** 尋找;尋求。**b.** 期望。***look forward to*** 期待;盼望。The children are *looking forward to* the holidays. 孩子們在盼望假期。***look in*** (***on***...) 便道訪問。Won't you *look in* (*on* me) when you're in town? 當你進城時順便來看看我, 好嗎? ***look in the face*** 直視其面; 與相抗衡。***look into*** 調查; 考查;

洞察。The police are *looking into* the past record of the man. 警方正在調查那人過去的紀錄。**look like** 看着像是。He *looks like* a fool. 他看來像傻子。**look on a.** 旁觀。**b.** 看(=look at)。**c.** 和…同看(一本書)〖with〗. May I *look on* with you? 我可以和你同看嗎? **look one's age** 和年齡相稱;顯出如眞正年齡一般老。**look oneself again** 好像恢復(健康)了。**look out** 當心;注意。*Look out!* There's a train coming. 當心!火車來了。**look out for** 注意查看;尋找。I'm *looking out for* mistakes. 我在注意查看有無錯誤。**look over a.** 校閱;看過一遍。He signed the contract without even *looking* it *over*. 他對契約連一眼都沒有看就在上面簽了字。**b.** 忽略;寬恕。**look round** 事前仔細考慮;愼思而後行。Don't make a hurried decision; *look round* well first. 不要急作決定,先好好考慮一番。**look sharp a.** 機警。If you want to get ahead, you must learn to *look sharp*. 你如果想一帆風順,你必須學習機警。**b.** 趕快。**look small** 自慚形穢。We made him *look small*. 我們使他自慚形穢。**look through a.** 透過…看。**b.** 看穿;看破。**c.** 由…看出。His greed *looked through* his eyes. 從他的眼睛裏可看出他的貪婪。**look (a thing) through** 徹底審查。**look to a.** 注意;照顧。**b.** 仰賴。An able young man is ashamed to *look to* others for assistance. 一個能幹的青年人恥於求助於他人。**c.** 預期;期待。**look up a.** 漲價;繁榮。Business conditions are beginning to *look up*. 商業情況開始呈現起色。**b.** 仰視。**look (a person) up** 探訪(某人)。**look (a thing) up** 尋找(某物)。to *look up* a word in a dictionary. 在字典中查一字。**look (a person) up and down** 上上下下打量(某人)。**look up to** 崇敬。Our director is a man whom everyone *looks up to*. 我們的主任是一個大家所崇敬的人。**look upon as** 視爲;認爲。—*n.* ①看;視;望;觀。Let's have a *look* at your dictionary. 讓我們看一看你的字典。②神色;外表;表情。There was an angry *look* in his eye. 他眼中含有怒色。③(*pl.*)容貌。good *looks*. 美貌。④尋求;找。

look·er [ˈlukɚ; ˈlukə] *n.* ①觀者。②〖美俗〗美貌之人。

look·er-in [ˌlukɚˈɪn; ˈlukərˈin] *n., pl.* **look·ers-in.** 看電視者。

look·er-on [ˌlukɚˈɑn; ˈlukərˈɔn] *n., pl.* **look·ers-on.** 旁觀者。

look-in [ˈlukˌɪn; ˈlukˌin] *n.* ①迅速之一瞥。②短暫之拜訪。③(賽馬、遊戲等)勝利的希望! ④〖俚〗(冒險)參加的機會。⑤(足球)給斜向跑至場中央之球員的快傳。

looking glass ①鏡子。②製鏡玻璃。

·look·out [ˈlukˌaut; ˈlukˈaut] *n.* ①注意;守望; 謹防。to keep a good *lookout* for. 注意守望着。②守望者;瞭望臺。③遠景;前途。See those clouds! A poor *lookout* for our picnic! 看那些雲啊!我們野餐的前途不妙! ④應注意的事。That's his own *lookout*. 那是他自己應注意的事。**keep (or take) a sharp lookout for** 小心提防;注意警戒。**on the lookout** 注意;警戒;尋找。

look-see [ˈlukˌsi; ˈlukˌsiː] *n.* 〖俚〗看;巡察;檢視;一瞥。

·loom¹ [lum; luːm] *n.* ①織布機。②織布。—*v.t.* 用織布機織。

·loom² *v.i.* ①隱現;隱約可見。The dark outline of another ship *loomed* (up) through the fog. 另一隻船的黑影在霧中隱約出現。②(危險、憂慮)陰森地臨近;可怖地出現。War *loomed* ahead. 戰爭逼近了。③(即將來臨事件)具體化。—*n.* 在視線不清楚情況下之隱約出現。

loon [lun; luːn] *n.* ①鷿鷉(一種水鳥)。②懶人;愚人;無用的傢伙。③〖美俗〗瘋子。

loon·y [ˈlunɪ; ˈluːni] *adj.*, **loon·i·er, loon·i·est,** *n., pl.,* **loon·ies.** 〖俚〗—*adj.* ①發瘋的。②蠢笨的。—*n.* 狂人;瘋子。

***loop** [lup; luːp] *n.* ①(繩、帶、金屬線等所繞成的)圈;環。He wound the garden hose in *loops* and hung it up. 他將花園澆水的橡皮管捲成環狀然後將它掛起來。②由上述圈、環所構成的花樣。③環狀物。④〖航空〗翻圈飛行;翻觔斗。⑤(鐵路之)環狀側線(=loop line)。⑥(電腦)達最終目標前的一連串重覆之指示。⑦(亦作 **Lippes loop**)(the-)(女性避孕之)子宮裝置;樂普。**knock for a loop** 〖美俚〗**a.** 擊倒。**b.** 駁倒;使無效;破壞。—*v.t.* ①使成圈、環。②以圈、環結。③圍以圈、環。—*v.i.* 自成圈環。**loop the loop** 〖航空〗翻觔斗。

loop·er [ˈlupɚ; ˈluːpə] *n.* ①作圈環之物或人。②〖動物〗尺蠖。③(縫紉機等之)作線環之裝置。④(亦作 **blooper**)〖棒球〗飛出內野範圍稍外的高飛球。

loop·hole [ˈlupˌhol; ˈluːphoul] *n.* ①(牆上供射擊、瞭望的)孔眼;小窗。②逃出口;(法規等的)漏洞。to find a *loophole* in the law 在法律中找到一個漏洞。—*v.t.* 做小窗口。

loop line (鐵路之)環狀側線。

loop-the-loop [ˈlupðəˈlup; ˈluːpðəˈluːp] *n.* ①飛行表演之垂直翻觔斗。②(兒童樂園中之)坐旋轉輪遊戲。

:loose [lus; luːs] *adj.*, **loos·er, loos·est** *v.,* **loosed, loos·ing,** *adv., n.* —*adj.* ①未予束縛的;釋放的。The horse was *loose* in the field. 馬是自由自在地(未加繮繩)在田野間。②寬大的;鬆的;寬的。This coat is too *loose*. 這外套太寬大。③不牢的;不堅固的。*loose* earth. 鬆土。④不精確的;不深入的。a *loose* translation. 不拘泥於原文的翻譯。⑤放蕩的。to lead a *loose* life. 過放蕩的生活。⑥沒有包裝的;散裝的。⑦無拘束的;自由的。a *loose* tongue. 饒舌。⑧(身體)不結實的;樣子難看的。a *loose* frame. 不結實的體格。⑨(動作)隨便的;不準確的。⑩(元素)未化合的。⑪未綑紮的。⑫未運用的。*loose* funds. 未運用的款項。**have a loose tongue** 多話;愛講閒話。**have a screw loose** 腦筋不健全;有點瘋。**ride with a loose rein** 放縱;放鬆繮繩。—*v.t.* ①釋放;解囊;揚帆。to *loose* sails. 揚帆。②放(箭、槍)。to *loose* an arrow. 射箭。—*v.i.* 放槍;赦免;釋纜;開船。—*adv.* 鬆弛地;寬鬆地;無拘束地。**break loose** 掙脫繮繩;逃出樊籠。**cast loose a.** 解開;分開。**b.** 遣走;使自由飄泊。**come loose** (結子)鬆開;(被縛者)得脫。**cut loose a.** 斷絕關係;分開。to *cut loose* from old habits. 根絕舊習慣。**b.** 脫逃;擺脫。**c.** 〖俗〗痛飲;大吃大喝。**d.** 放棄約束;縱情。**let loose a.** 釋放;放任;放縱。**b.** 垮。**play fast and loose** 欺騙;欺詐。**set loose** 釋放;放縱;放走。**turn loose a.** 釋放。**b.** 使自由行動。**work loose** (螺絲釘等)鬆弛。—*n.* 解開;放任;放縱。**give (a) loose to** 放蕩;盡情。**on the loose** 〖俗〗**a.** 自由的;沒限制的。**b.** 歡樂;痛飲;放蕩。**c.** 逃走在外的。—**ly,** *adv.* —**ness,** *n.*

loose-bod·ied ['lus'bɑdɪd; 'lu:s-'bɔdid] *adj.* 寬鬆的(衣服等)。

loose box 放飼場;放飼廐。

loose end ①未扣牢的部分。②事情尙未完成之細節。 ***at loose ends*** (or ***at a loose end***) **a.** 尙未確定之狀態。 **b.** 目前的計畫尙未決定。

loose-fit·ting ['lus'fɪtɪŋ; 'lu:s'fitiŋ] *adj.* (衣服)寬大的;不合身的。

loose-joint·ed ['lus'dʒɔɪntɪd; 'lu:s-'dʒɔintid] *adj.* ①關節(接頭)鬆弛的;構造不結實的。②柔軟的;易曲的;動作輕鬆的。

loose-leaf ['lus,lif; 'lu:s,li:f] *adj.* 活頁的(筆記本等)。

*__loos·en__ ['lusn̩; 'lu:sn] *v.t.* ①使鬆;解(結)。 *Loosen* the screw. 將螺絲釘放鬆。②解除(便祕)。③放寬(限制)。 to *loosen* restrictions on trade. 放寬貿易限制。 —*v.i.* ①鬆弛。 The screw has *loosened*. 螺絲釘鬆了。②放鬆。

loose-prin·ci·pled ['lus'prɪnsəpl̩d; 'lu:s'prinsəpld] *adj.* 缺乏操守的。

loose·strife ['lus,straɪf; 'lu:s,straif] *n.* 【植物】珍珠菜。

loot [lut; lu:t] *n.* ①贓物;掠奪品。②【俚】金錢;資本。 —*v.i.* & *v.t.* 掠奪;搶掠。

lop [lɑp; lɔp] *v.*, **lopped, lop·ping,** *adj.*, *n.* —*v.t.* ①砍;伐;截去(樹枝等);修剪(樹木)。②斬;砍(頭、手、脚等)。③刪除。④使下垂。 —*v.i.* ①砍去樹枝;截移。②無力地垂下;垂掛。③跳躍而行。 —*adj.* 下垂的。 —*n.* ①(樹枝等之)剪除。②砍下之物;剪下之樹枝。③(頭、手、足等之)砍去。④砍下之頭、肢。

lope [lop; loup] *v.*, **loped, lop·ing,** *n.* —*v.i.* ①(兎等之)跳躍而行。②(馬等之)散漫安閒而行;大步慢跑。 —*v.t.* 使(馬)大步慢跑。 —*n.* ①大而安閒的步子。②安閒大步的行走。

lop-eared ['lɑp,ɪrd; 'lɔpiəd] *adj.* (兎等)垂耳的。

lop·sid·ed ['lɑp'saɪdɪd; 'lɔp'saidid] *adj.* (船、建築物等)傾向一方的;不對稱的。 **—ly,** *adv.* **—ness,** *n.*

loq. loquitur.

lo·qua·cious [lo'kweʃəs; lou'kweiʃəs] *adj.* ①多嘴的;好辯的。②(鳥等)喧噪的。

lo·quac·i·ty [lo'kwæsətɪ; lou'kwæsiti] *n.* 饒舌;喧噪;刺刺不休。

lo·quat ['lokwɑt; 'loukwɔt] *n.* 【植物】枇杷;盧橘。

loq·ui·tur ['lɑkwətə; 'lɔkwətə] 【拉】 *v.i.* =**he** (**she** or **it**) **speaks.** (略作 **loq.**)

Lor·an, lor·an ['lɔræn; 'lɔ:ræn] *n.* (爲 *Long Range Navigation* 之縮寫)(船隻或飛機由一旣知電臺所發出之電波以測定其位置之)遠航儀;洛蘭。

‡**lord** [lɔrd; lɔ:d] *n.* ①【英】貴族;領主;上議院議員。 The king and all the great *lords* were present. 國王及所有的權貴要員均曾出席。②(對主教等的尊稱)閣下。 Yes, my *lord*. 是,閣下。③對有爵位的貴族的尊稱(冠於姓氏之前,如 *Lord* Tennyson)。④【詩、謔】丈夫。⑤(L-)上帝;耶穌基督;主。 Praise the *Lord*. 讚美主。 Good *Lord*! (表驚訝或厭煩的感歎語)哦!天啊! ***Lord's Supper*** **a.** (耶穌)最後晚餐。 **b.** 聖體聖事;聖餐。 ***act the lord*** 儼若主人發號施令;擺架子。 ***live like a lord*** 過舒適奢華的生活。 —*v.t.* ①統治。②使成貴族。 —*v.i.* 作威作福。 ***lord it over*** 威凌;逞威風。

Lord Chief Justice 【英】最高法院院長。

lord·ling ['lɔrdlɪŋ; 'lɔ:dliŋ] *n.* 小君主;小貴族;微不足道的貴族。

lord·ly ['lɔrdlɪ; 'lɔ:dli] *adj.*, **-li·er, -li·est.** ①貴族的;堂皇的;高貴的。②傲慢的;高傲的;不可一世的。 **—lord·li·ness,** *n.*

Lord Mayor 【英】大都市之市長。

Lord of Lords 萬王之王(卽基督)。

Lord Provost 【蘇】大都市之市長。

Lord's day, the 主日(卽星期日)。

lord·ship ['lɔrdʃɪp; 'lɔ:dʃip] *n.* ①貴族的地位或階級。②閣下(對貴族的尊稱)。 Your *Lordship*. 閣下。③統治;支配;所有權。

Lord's table, the 聖餐臺;祭壇。

lore [lor; lɔ:] *n.* (特殊的)知識;學問。

Lo·rentz ['lorɛnts; 'lourents] *n.* 勞倫茨(Hendrik Antoon, 1853–1928, 荷蘭物理學家,獲1902年諾貝爾物理獎)。

Lorentz force 作用於帶電質點通過磁場之力量。

lor·gnette [lɔrn'jɛt; lɔ:'njet] *n.* ①長柄眼鏡。②(觀歌劇用的)有柄望遠鏡。

lorn [lɔrn; lɔ:n] *adj.* ①【古】孤單的;寂寞的。②【古】被棄的;敗落的;毀壞的。

lor·ry ['lɔrɪ, 'lɑrɪ; 'lɔri] *n.*, *pl.* **-ries.** ①【英】卡車。②長而低的馬車。③(如礦場鐵路用之)手車。 —*v.t.* 用卡車運輸。

lor·ry-hop ['lɔrɪ,hɑp; 'lɔrihɔp] *n.* 【英】(免費)乘(他人的)卡車旅行。

los·a·ble ['luzəbl̩; 'lu:zəbl] *adj.* 可失去的;易失去的。

Los An·ge·les [lɔs'æŋgələs,-'ændʒə-ləs; lɔs'ændʒili:z] *n.* 洛杉磯(美國加州西南部都市)。

‡**lose** [luz; lu:z] *v.*, **lost** [lɔst; lɔst], **los·ing.** —*v.t.* ①失;失落;遺失。 He *lost* all his money. 他把所有的錢都丢了。②損失;失去。 I'm *losing* my hair. 我在掉頭髮。③輸掉;未能得到。 We *lost* the game. 我們比賽輸了。④喪失(妻、子等);(因死亡等)被剝奪。 He has *lost* his wife. 他喪失其妻。⑤未能趕上(火車等)。 to *lose* a train (the boat, the post, etc.). 未趕上火車(船、郵班等)。⑥浪費。 We have no time to *lose*. 我們沒有時間可浪費了。⑦走入歧途。 Be careful—don't *lose* yourself. 小心——不要走入歧途。⑧沉入;沉醉於(用被動式)。 to be *lost* in thought. 沉思。⑨(用被動語態)滅亡;破壞。 The ship and its crew were *lost*. 那艘船及其船員都覆滅了。⑩使失去。 That one act *lost* him his job. 那行爲使他失去他的職位。⑪(鐘錶)走慢。 My watch *loses* two minutes a day. 我的錶每天慢兩分鐘。⑫不再有。 to *lose* one's fear of the dark. 不再怕黑暗。⑬不再看到或聽到。⑭迷失。 He *lost* his bearings in the strange city. 他在那陌生的城市裏迷失了方向。⑮將…丢在後面;超過。⑯走失。 We *lost* ourselves in the woods. 我們在樹林中走失了。⑰(醫生)未能救活(病人)。⑱(孕婦)因小產而喪失(嬰兒)。 —*v.i.* ①虧損;蒙損害。 I don't care whether I gain or *lose*. 我絕不會患得患失。②失敗;輸。 Our team *lost*. 我們的隊輸了。③(鐘錶)走慢。 Does your watch gain or *lose*? 你的錶快了還是慢了? ④遜色;減低價值、美麗等。 a classic that *loses* in translation. 無法翻譯得好的名著。 ***lose oneself*** **a.** 迷途;迷惑(=to lose one's way)。 **b.** 入迷;迷醉。 He seemed to *lose himself* in thought. 他似乎在沉思中。 ***lose one's head*** 驚慌失措。 ***lose one's heart*** 爲…所迷醉;迷醉於。 ***lose one's place*** (***in a book***) (讀書)忘記了所讀到的地方。 ***lose***

out〖美〗失敗；輸。*lose sight of* 參看 sight. *lose track of* 不知…之所在(去向、近況等)。

los·er 〔ˈluzɚ; ˈluːzə〕 *n.* ①失敗者；輸者。②〖俗〗做事老是做不好的人。③〖俚〗品質不佳的東西。④〖俗〗因犯重罪而判刑者。

los·ing 〔ˈluzɪŋ; ˈluːziŋ〕 *adj.* ①輸的；虧折的。②招致損失的。—*n.* ①失敗。②(*pl.*)(尤指投機、賭博等的)損失；輸掉的賭注。

:loss 〔lɔs; lɔːs〕 *n.* ①損失；遺失；喪失。The *loss* of his money worried him. 他爲損失金錢而憂慮。②損失物；虧損。My *losses* have been very great. 我的損失很大。③未得。The *loss* of the reward discouraged him. 未能得獎使他心灰意冷。④浪費。⑤未能保持。*loss* of speed at high altitude. 在高空失速。*at a loss* a. 虧本。b. 迷惑。*at a loss for* 找不出；窮於(辭令)。I am *at a loss for* words. 我找不出言辭來表達我的意思。*at a loss to* 不能。*gain and loss* 得失。*profit and loss* 盈虧。

loss leader 犧牲品。

:lost 〔lɔst; lɔst, lɔːst〕 *v.* pt. and pp. of **lose.** —*adj.* ①失去的。*lost* friends. 失去的朋友。②遺失的；失落的。③敗的；輸的。a *lost* battle. 敗仗。④毀壞的。a *lost* soul. 受汚辱的靈魂。⑤浪費的。*lost* time. 白費的時間。⑥迷失的。⑦困惑的；迷惑的。a *lost* expression. 迷惑的表情。⑧沉迷的。*lost to* a. 不再爲…所有。b. 不感覺；漠然。*lost upon* 對…無效。My hints were not *lost upon* him. 他懂得我的暗示。

lost cause 失敗的主張；完全無成功希望的運動。

Lost Generation 失落的一代(第一次大戰後對世局表悲觀失望的青年，尤指青年作家、藝術家等)。

:lot¹ 〔lɑt; lɔt〕 *n.* 全部；全體；總量。Take the *lot*; don't leave any behind. 全部拿去，一點都不要留下。*a good* (or *great*) *lot* 大量；許多。*a lot* 很多(修飾動詞)。He works *a lot* at home. 他在家裏做很多工作。Thanks *a lot.* 多謝。*a lot* (*of*) or *lots* (*of*) 許多(的)；很多(的)。(指"數"或"量"均可)。I want (have, saw, etc.) *a lot.* 我要(有、看見等)許多。*lots and lots* (*of*) 許多(的)；很多(的)。〖注意〗**lots** 與 **lots of** 在表示大量或許多時，在正式的英語中是避免應用的。

:lot² *n.* ①籤；鬮。to draw (*or* cast) *lots.* 抽籤；拈鬮(以決定某事)。②抽籤或拈鬮決定法。to choose a person by *lot.* 抽籤以選人。③中籤。The *lot* came to (*or* fell upon) me. 我抽中了。④運氣；命運。He has thrown (*or* cast) in his *lot* with us. 他已決定與我們共甘苦。⑤一塊地。a building *lot.* 一塊建築基地。⑥一堆；一組；一包。a fine *lot* of boys. 一羣好孩子。⑦一批(貨物)。⑧電影攝影場。⑨〖俗〗種類。He is a bad *lot.* 他是個壞人。*a bad lot*〖俗〗惡人。*cast* (or *draw*) *lots* 抽籤(決定)。We *draw lots* to decide who should be captain. 我們抽籤決定誰當隊長。*have no part nor lot in* 無任何關係。*in lots* 分堆；分包；分攤。*It falls to his lot* (or *to him as his lot*) *to* 他命當…；他想不到要…。—*v.t.* 劃分(土地等)；分堆；分組。—*v.i.* 抽籤。

loth 〔loθ; louθ〕 *adj.* =**loath.**

Lo·thar·i·o 〔loˈθɛrɪˌo, -ˈθerɪ-; louˈθɑːriou, -ˈθɛər-〕 *n., pl.* **-os.** 色魔；登徒子(典出 Nicholas Rowe 的劇中人)。

lo·tion 〔ˈloʃən; ˈlouʃən〕 *n.* ①〖藥〗洗劑。②〖俗〗酒。③乳液；化妝水。—*v.t.* 搽面霜。

lot·ter·y 〔ˈlɑtərɪ; ˈlɔtəri〕 *n., pl.* **-ter·ies.** ①彩票或獎券的發行。②碰巧之事；偶然之事。*lottery tickets* 彩票；獎券。*lottery wheel* 搖獎筒；搖獎機。

lot·to 〔ˈlɑto; ˈlɔtou〕 *n.* 一種對號碼遊戲。

lo·tus 〔ˈlotəs; ˈloutəs〕 *n.* ①〖植物〗蓮；荷。②〖植物〗百脈根屬。③〖希臘神話〗落拓棗(據傳食該果後卽做極樂的夢而忘却塵世的痛苦)；忘憂樹。(亦作 **lotos**)

lo·tus-eat·er 〔ˈlotəsˌitɚ; ˈloutəsˌiːtə〕 *n.* 食落拓棗而忘却勞苦的人；貪安逸的人。

lotus land 安樂鄉。

lotus position 蓮花坐姿(雙腿曲疊，雙臂置於膝上，用於瑜珈術)。

:loud 〔laud; laud〕 *adj.* ①高聲的；大聲的。He has a *loud* voice. 他的嗓子很宏亮。②〖俗〗(衣服的花色等)刺眼的；庸俗的。③極度的；不斷的；不休的。to be *loud* in demands. 不斷地需求。④喧吵的；吵鬧的。⑤〖俗〗冒失的；略帶粗俗的。⑥强調的。a *loud* denial. 斷然的否認。⑦氣味難聞的；沖鼻的。—*adv.* 高聲地；大聲地。He laughs too *loud.* 他笑的聲音太大了。—**ly,** *adv.* —**ness,** *n.*

loud·ish 〔ˈlaudɪʃ; ˈlaudiʃ〕 *adj.* 音稍高的。

loud·mouthed 〔ˈlaudˈmauðd; ˈlaudˈmauðd〕 *adj.* 高聲談論的；喧嘩的；吼叫的。

***loud·speak·er** 〔ˈlaudˈspikɚ; ˈlaudˈspiːkə〕 *n.* 擴音器；揚聲器。

lou·is d'or 〔ˌluɪˈdɔr; ˈlu(ː)iˈdɔː〕 法國之一種金幣(相當於20法郎)。

Lou·i·si·an·a 〔ˌluɪzɪˈænə, luˌizɪ-; lu(ː)ˌiːziˈænə, -ˈɑːnə〕 *n.* 路易西安那(美國南部之一州，首府 Baton Rouge)。

***lounge** 〔laundʒ; laundʒ〕 *v.,* **lounged, loung·ing,** *n.* —*v.i.* ①散漫怠惰地打發時間。②懶懶地橫靠或坐着。to *lounge* on a sofa. 斜臥沙發上。③閒蕩；漫步〖about〗. to *lounge* about the door. 閒散過日。—*v.t.* 散漫安閒地度(日)；遊散耗費(光陰)。to *lounge* away one's time. 虛度一生。—*n.* ①臥榻；沙發。②休息室；吸煙室。③懶散；閒逸。④漫步。—**loung·er,** *n.*

lounge car 火車上供乘客休息飲酒用之車廂。

lounge lizard 〖美俚〗女人所喜歡的男人(尤指女人願意倒貼者)。

lounge suit 〖英〗日常所着的西服。

lour 〔laur; ˈlauə〕 *v.i.* ①皺眉頭；作怒相〖at, on, upon〗. ②作陰沉的臉色。③(天氣)呈陰霾昏暗狀。—*n.* ①不悅之色。②陰沉的臉色。③陰霾；昏暗。

louse 〔laus; laus〕 *n., pl.* **lice** 〔laɪs; lais〕, *v.,* **loused, lous·ing.** —*n.* ①蝨。②(動、植物身上的)寄生蟲。③〖俚〗可鄙之人。—*v.t.* 除去蝨子。*louse up*〖俚〗弄糟；搞壞。

lous·y 〔ˈlauzɪ; ˈlauzi〕 *adj.,* **lous·i·er, lous·i·est.** ①多蝨的；生蝨的。②〖俚〗汚穢的；令人作嘔的；卑鄙的。③〖俚〗充分供應的。

lout 〔laut; laut〕 *n.* 粗鄙之人；鄉下佬。

lout·ish 〔ˈlautɪʃ; ˈlautiʃ〕 *adj.* 粗鄙的；鄉下氣的。

lou·ver 〔ˈluvɚ; ˈluːvə〕 *n.* ①(多見於中世紀建築物之)屋頂之天窗。②(採光、通風用之)羽板窗。③(汽車前面的)放熱孔。④(*pl.*)〖建築〗=**louver boards.**

louver boards 〖建築〗(羽板窗等之)羽板。

lov·a·ble, love·a·ble 〔ˈlʌvəbl; ˈlʌvəbl〕 *adj.* 可愛的；惹人愛的。

lov·age 〔ˈlʌvɪdʒ; ˈlʌvidʒ〕 *n.* 獨活草(藥用)。

:love 〔lʌv; lʌv〕 *n., v.,* **loved, lov·ing.**

—*n.* ①愛；親愛。 *love* of (*or* for) one's country. 對國家的愛；愛國心。②愛好；喜好。He has a strong *love* of learning. 他極愛求學。③親屬間的問候。Give my *love* to Mary. 代我向瑪麗致候。④愛人；情人。my *love*. 吾愛(夫婦、愛人間相稱語)。⑤戀愛;愛情。They are in *love*. 他們在戀愛中。⑥〖俗〗愉快的人物;漂亮東西。⑦(上帝的)慈愛;(對上帝的)崇敬。⑧〖運動〗(主網球)零點;零分。*love*-all. 零比零。*love*-forty. 零比四十。a *love* game (*or* set). 輸方零分的比賽。⑨(L-) **a.** Venus. **b.** Cupid. ***fall in love with*** 與…發生戀愛;戀愛。 ***for love*** 娛樂性的;非職業的;不爲錢的。He took care of the poor *for love*. 他爲貧民義務服務。***for the love of*** 爲…的緣故。***give love to*** 請致意;請問候。***have a love of*** 愛;歡喜。***in love with*** 與…在戀愛中。***make love*** **a.** 調情。**b.** 性交。***make love to*** 向…求愛。***no love lost*** 敵意;厭惡。There is *no love lost* between them. 他們互無愛情; 他們互相憎恨。 ***not for love or money*** 任何情形之下均不。—*v.t.* ①愛; 戀愛。 He *loved* his mother very deeply. 他愛母至深。②敬拜。 *Love* God. 敬拜上帝。 ③待以仁愛。 The Bible tells us to *love* all men. 聖經告訴我們要愛一切人。④喜好; 愛好。 —*v.i.* 愛; 墮入情網。He can hate but cannot *love*. 他祇能恨,不能愛。

love affair ①戀愛事件;韻事。②對某種活動之迷戀。

love apple 蕃茄。

love beads 愛珠 (作爲裝飾及兄弟愛表徵而掛在脖子上的彩珠)。

love·bird [ˈlʌvˌbɝd; ˈlʌvbəːd] *n.* ①情鳥 (小鸚鵡類, 產於非洲, 雌雄間極爲恩愛)。②(*pl.*) 愛侶; (尤指) 恩愛夫妻。

love-child [ˈlʌvˌtʃaɪld; ˈlʌvtʃaild] *n.*, *pl.* **love-chil·dren.** 私生子。

love-crossed [ˈlʌvˌkrɔst; ˈlʌvkrɔːst] *adj.* 愛情不順利的;情場失意的。

love feast 〖基督教〗①愛餐(初期基督教徒間爲表示友愛之聚餐)。②(模仿前者的美以美教徒間的)愛餐會。③(爲促進感情之)聚餐。

love game 〖網球〗輸方得零分的比賽。

love-in-a-mist [ˈlʌvɪnəˈmɪst; ˈlʌvinəˈmist] *n.* 〖植物〗黑種草(歐洲產之一種開藍花之毛莨科植物)。

love-in-i·dle·ness [ˈlʌvɪnˈaɪdl̩nɪs; ˈlʌvinˈaidlnis] *n.* 〖植物〗三色堇。

love knot 同心結(用緞帶所打之結,爲愛之表示)。

Love·lace [ˈlʌvˌles; ˈlʌvleis] *n.* 登徒子;色魔(小說人物)。

love·less [ˈlʌvlɪs; ˈlʌvlis] *adj.* ①無愛情的。②獲不到愛的。

love letter 情書。

love-lies-bleed·ing [ˈlʌvlaɪzˈblidɪŋ; ˈlʌvlaizˈbliːdiŋ] *n.* 〖植物〗老槍穀;雁來紅。

love·lock [ˈlʌvˌlɑk; ˈlʌvlɔk] *n.* ①(女人的)嬌髮 (額前的捲髮)。②17-18世紀流行之長及肩部的男性髮型。

love·lorn [ˈlʌvˌlɔrn; ˈlʌvlɔːn] *adj.* 失戀的;無人愛的。

love·ly [ˈlʌvlɪ; ˈlʌvli] *adj.*, **-li·er, -li·est,** *n.*, *adv.* —*adj.* ①可愛的;美麗的。a *lovely* woman. 美麗的女人。②〖俗〗愉快的;有趣的。What a *lovely* joke! 多麼有趣的詼諧! ③內在美的。She is endowed with a *lovely* character. 她富有內在美的性格。—*n.* 〖俗〗美女(尤指女藝人、模特兒等)。She is a *lovely*. 她是個美人。—*adv.* 〖口語〗極佳;妙極。The kids behaved *lovely* today. 今天小孩們非常乖。—**love·li·ness,** *n.*

love-mak·ing [ˈlʌvˌmekɪŋ; ˈlʌvˌmeikiŋ] *n.* ①求婚;調情。②性交。

love match 戀愛結婚;愛情的結合(非爲財富、地位等,而純出於愛的婚姻)。

love-phil·ter [ˈlʌvˈfɪltɚ; ˈlʌvˈfiltə] *n.* =**love potion.**

love potion 春藥。(亦作**love-potion**)

‡**lov·er** [ˈlʌvɚ; ˈlʌvə] *n.* ①愛好者;嗜好者。He's a great *lover* of books. 他是個好學之士。②愛人;情人。③(*pl.*)情侶。

love seat 雙人座椅;鴛鴦椅。

love·sick [ˈlʌvˌsɪk; ˈlʌvsik] *adj.* 害相思病的。—**ness,** *n.*

love song 情歌;戀歌。

love story 愛情小說;愛情故事。

love·struck [ˈlʌvˌstrʌk; ˈlʌvstrʌk] *adj.* 受到愛之强烈感染的。

love-to·ken [ˈlʌvˌtokən; ˈlʌvˌtoukn] *n.* 紀念愛情的餽贈品;愛情紀念品。

***lov·ing** [ˈlʌvɪŋ; ˈlʌviŋ] *adj.* ①親愛的;愛戀的; 鍾情的; 仁慈的。 ②忠誠的。 Our *loving* subjects. 〖詔勅用語〗我的忠良的臣民。③示愛的。to cast *loving* glances. 吊膀子。—**ly,** *adv.*

loving cup 愛杯(有兩個杯柄以便輪飲的大銀酒杯)。

lov·ing-kind·ness [ˈlʌvɪŋˈkaɪndnɪs; ˈlʌviŋˈkaindnis] *n.* 慈愛;仁慈。

‡**low**[1] [lo; lou] *adj.* ①低的; 矮的。 The moon was *low* in the sky. 月亮低掛天邊。②淺的。In summer the river is very *low*. 夏季裏河水非常淺。③低弱的。He spoke in a *low* voice. 他以低弱的聲音講話。④微賤的。a man of *low* birth. 出身微賤的人。⑤消沉的。 to be in *low* spirits. 意志消沉。⑥未開化的;低等的。a *low* organism. 低等生物。⑦下流的。*low* thoughts. 下流思想。⑧虛弱的。a *low* state of health. 不健康。⑨壞的。I have a *low* opinion of his abilities. 我瞧不起他的能力。⑩低級的;粗野的;品格低劣的。*low* company. 品格低劣的朋友。⑪近地平線的。a *low* sun. 近地平線的太陽。⑫近赤道的。*low* latitudes. 低緯度。⑬臥倒在地的;死的。The great man is *low*. 那偉人死了。⑭深的(鞠躬)。a *low* bow. 深鞠躬。⑮〖音樂〗低音的。 a *low* note. 低調。⑯〖語音〗舌位低下的。⑰近時的。⑱含養分甚少的。⑲不够標準的。to receive *low* marks in school. 在學校成績不好。⑳含量不多的。a diet *low* in starches. 含澱粉不高的食物。㉑快告罄的。Our stock of towels is *low*. 我們毛巾的存貨快告罄。㉒粗俗的。entertainment of a *low* sort. 低級娛樂。㉓〖拳擊〗打對方腰帶以下部位的。㉔到底的;最低的。㉕〖棒球〗(投出的球)低於打擊手膝部的。***bring low*** 使虛弱、貧困、或地位降低。***in low water*** 缺乏資金; 缺乏銀錢。—*adv.* ①低下地; 低聲地。 to aim *low*. 目標取得低;取法乎下。②謙卑地。③近地平線地。 The sun sank *low*. 太陽西下接近地平線。④緯度低地。⑤近期地。⑥輸贏小地; 花錢少地。to play *low*. 賭小錢。***lay low*** **a.** 擊倒。**b.** 殺死。to *lay* one's attackers *low*. 擊斃攻擊者。***lie low*** 〖俗〗靜待;藏匿不出。***play it low upon*** 虐待;冷待。—*n.* ①低;低者。②(汽車等所用之)初速。③低氣壓區。④最低點。Many stocks fell to new *lows* after the news broke out. 消息傳出後多種股票跌至最低點。

low[2] *v.i.* (牛)鳴叫。—*n.* 牛鳴。

low·born [ˈloˈbɔrn; ˈlouˈbɔːn] *adj.* 出身低賤的。

low·boy [ˈloˌbɔɪ; ˈloubɔi] *n.* 一種矮腳抽屜櫃。

low·bred [ˈloˈbrɛd; ˈlouˈbred] *adj.* 粗野的;粗俗的。

low·brow [ˈloˈbrau; ˈlouˈbrau]〖俗〗*n.* 對文藝活動不感興趣的人;庸俗之輩。—*adj.* 庸俗的;低級趣味的。

low-browed [ˈloˌbraud; ˈloubraud] *adj.* ①額頭低的;狹額的。②門低的;屋宇陰暗的。

Low Church 低教會派(較輕視聖職之特權、儀式、聖餐等之英國國教會之一派)。

low·class [ˈloˈklæs; ˈlouˈklɑːs] *adj.* 低級的。

low comedy (單憑動作取悅觀衆之)低級喜劇。

low-cost [ˈloˈkɔst; ˈlouˈkɔst] *adj.* 便宜的;成本低的。

Low Countries 北海沿岸之低地國家(今荷、比、盧三國)。

low down =**low-down.**

low-down [ˈloˈdaun; ˈlou-daun] *adj.* 〖俗〗身分卑下的;不誠實的。—*n.*〖俚〗(常 the-) 實情;內幕。

Low·ell [ˈloəl; ˈlouəl] *n.* 羅厄爾(James Russell, 1819–1891, 美國詩人、文藝批評家及外交家)。

:low·er[1] [ˈloə; ˈlouə] *v.t.* ①降下;降低。to *lower* a flag. 降旗。②減低。③使(聲音等)低。to *lower* one's voice. 降低其聲音。④削弱;消減。Poor diet *lowers* resistance to illness. 營養不良的飲食會削弱對於疾病的抵抗力。⑤貶抑。to *lower* a person's pride. 挫某人的驕氣。—*v.i.* 降低;跌落。The stocks *lowered* in value. 股票跌價。—*adj.* & *adv.* comparative of **low.**

low·er[2] [ˈlauə; ˈlauə] *v.i., n.* =**lour.**

lower case 〖印刷〗小字盤;小寫字型。(略作 **l. c.**)

low·er-case [ˈloəˈkes; ˈlouəˈkeis] *adj., v.,* **-cased, -cas·ing.**〖印刷〗—*adj.* ①用小寫字型印的。②小字盤的。—*v.t.* 用小寫字型排印。

lower chamber 國會之下議院;衆議院。

lower classes 下級社會。

low·er·class·man [ˈloəˈklæsmən; ˈlouəˈklɑːsmən] *n., pl.* **-men.** 低年級生。

Lower House 下議院;衆議院。

low·er·ing[1] [ˈlauərɪŋ; ˈlauəriŋ] *adj.* ①昏暗的;風雨欲來的。②蹙眉的;陰沉的。

low·er·ing[2] [ˈloərɪŋ; ˈlouəriŋ] *adj.* ①使卑劣的;下賤的。②減低體力的(食物)。—*n.* 低下;低減。

low·er·most [ˈloəˌmost; ˈlouəmoust] *adj.* 最低的;最下的。

lower world ①陰間。②地球。

low-fre·quen·cy [ˈloˈfrikwənsɪ; ˈlouˈfriːkwənsi] *adj.*〖無線電〗低頻率的;長波的。

low-key [ˈloˈki; ˈlouˈkiː] *adj.* 抑制的;不張揚的。(亦作 **low-keyed**)

·low·land [ˈloˌlænd, -lənd; ˈloulænd, -lənd] *n.* 低地。***the Lowlands*** 蘇格蘭東南部的低地(亦作 **the Lowlands of Scotland**)。—*adj.* 低地的。

low·land·er [ˈlolændə; ˈlouləndə] *n.* ①低地人。②(L-)蘇格蘭低地之人或居民。③住於低地之居民。

low-lev·el [ˈloˈlɛvḷ; ˈlouˈlevl] *adj.* ①低階層的。②低空的。

low·life [ˈloˌlaɪf; ˈloulaif] *n., pl.* **-lifes,** *adj.* —*n.*〖俚〗①卑鄙之人;罪犯。②不道德的人或環境。—*adj.* ①道德沉淪的。②不雅的。

·low·ly [ˈlolɪ; ˈlouli] *adj.,* **-li·er, -li·est,** *adv.* —*adj.* ①位低的。②卑下的;謙卑的。a *lowly* heart. 謙虛之心。—*adv.* ①低賤地。②謙遜地。③低聲地。to converse *lowly.* 低聲談話。④位置低下的。—**low·li·ness,** *n.*

low-ly·ing [ˈloˈlaɪɪŋ; ˈlouˈlaiiŋ] *adj.* ①低窪的;低地的。②低垂的。

low-mind·ed [ˈloˈmaɪndɪd; ˈlouˈmaindid] *adj.* 心地卑劣的;卑鄙的。

low-necked [ˈloˈnɛkt; ˈlouˈnekt] *adj.* (婦女服裝)領口開得很低的。

low·ness [ˈlonɪs; ˈlounis] *n.* 卑賤;粗鄙;低聲;低廉;微弱。

low-num·bered [ˈloˈnʌmbəd; ˈlouˈnʌmbəd] *adj.* 號碼少的。

low-pitched [ˈloˈpɪtʃt; ˈlouˈpitʃt] *adj.* ①低調的;柔和的。②(屋頂等)傾斜緩慢的。③地板與天花板之間很矮的。

low-pres·sure [ˈloˈprɛʃə; ˈlouˈpreʃə] *adj.* ①低壓的。②無刺激性的;平淡的;無力量的。③間接的;巧妙的;有說服力的。

low-rise [ˈloˌraɪs; ˈlourais] *adj.* (建築物)祇有幾層而沒有電梯的。

low-spir·it·ed [ˈloˈspɪrɪtɪd; ˈlouˈspiritid] *adj.* 無精打采的;憂鬱的。

low-ten·sion [ˈloˈtɛnʃən; ˈlouˈtenʃən] *adj.*〖電〗低(電)壓的。

lox[1] [lɑks; lɔks] *n.* 燻鹹鮭魚。

lox[2] *n.* (亦作 **LOX**) 液體氧 (=liquid oxygen). —*v.t.* 爲(火箭)加液體氧。

·loy·al [ˈlɔɪəl, ˈlɔjəl; ˈlɔiəl] *adj.* 忠貞的;忠誠的;忠實的。*loyal* subjects of the king. 王之忠貞的臣民。—**ly,** *adv.*

loy·al·ism [ˈlɔɪəlɪzm; ˈlɔiəlizm] *n.* 忠義;忠節;(特指內亂時之)勤王。

loy·al·ist [ˈlɔɪəlɪst; ˈlɔiəlist] *n.* ①忠臣;忠君愛國者;勤王者。②〖英史〗保皇黨員;保守黨員。③(常 L-)(美國獨立戰爭時)忠於英國者。④(L-)(1936至1939年間西班牙內戰時)忠於共和國者。

·loy·al·ty [ˈlɔɪəltɪ, ˈlɔj-; ˈlɔiəlti] *n., pl.* **-ties.** 忠貞;忠誠;忠實。a man of *loyalty.* 忠貞之士。

loz·enge [ˈlɑzɪndʒ; ˈlɔzindʒ] *n.* ①菱形。②菱形物;菱形餅。③錠劑;錠;藥片(治咳嗽、喉痛等之藥片,初爲菱形,故名)。④(寶石上雕琢的)菱形面。

LP (亦作 **Lp, L-P**) long-playing record. **L.P.** ①Labor Party. ②Lord Provost. **l.p.** ①large paper. ②large post. ③long primer. ④low pressure. **LPG** liquefied petroleum gas. **LSD** (亦作 **LSD-25**) lysergic acid diethylamide. 迷幻藥。**L.S.D. £.s.d., l.s.d.** 〖拉〗①(librae, solidi denarii之略)金鎊、先令、辨士。②金錢、財物。**LST** Landing Ship, Tanks. **l.s.t.** local standard time. **Lt.** Lieutenant. **L.T.** Long Ton. **'lt** ①wilt. ②shalt. **Ltd., ltd.** *Esp. Brit.* limited. **Lu** 〖化〗lutetium 或 lutecium 之符號。

lub·ber [ˈlʌbə; ˈlʌbə] *n.* ①大而蠢笨的人;笨漢。②〖航海〗不熟練之水手;新水手。—*adj.* 笨拙的;愚笨的。—*v.i.* 笨手笨脚地操縱船隻。

lub·ber·ly [ˈlʌbəlɪ; ˈlʌbəli] *adj.* ①笨拙的;愚蠢的。②拙於做航海工作的。—*adv.* 粗笨地;拙劣地。

lubber's hole 〖航海〗檣樓升降口。

lube [lub; luːb] *n.*〖機械〗潤滑油。

lu·bri·cant [ˈlubrɪkənt; ˈluːbrikənt]

n. 潤滑油。—*adj.* 潤滑的。

lu·bri·cate ['lubrɪ͵ket; 'lu:brikeit] *v.*, **-cat·ed, -cat·ing.** —*v.t.* ①使潤滑;加潤滑油。②使順利;對…有幫助。Dinner *lubricates* business. 請客吃飯有助生意之進行。—*v.i.* ①生潤滑作用。②喝醉;喝酒。—**lu·bri·ca·tive,** *adj.*

lu·bri·ca·tion [͵lubrɪ'keʃən; ͵lu:bri'keiʃən] *n.* 潤滑;注油。

lu·bri·ca·tor ['lubrɪ͵ketə; 'lu:brikeitə] *n.* ①潤滑者;注油人。②潤滑料;潤滑油。③潤滑器;注油器。

lu·bric·i·ty [lu'brɪsətɪ; lu:'brisiti] *n.*, *pl.* **-ties.** ①平滑。②(精神的)不安定;動搖;難以捉摸。③淫蕩。④狡猾。

lu·bri·cous ['lubrɪkəs; 'lu:brikəs] *adj.* ①平滑的。②不安定的;不確實的;難以捉摸的。③淫蕩的。

lu·cent ['lusn̩t; 'lu:snt] *adj.* ①光輝的;明亮的。②透明的。

lu·cid ['lusɪd; 'lu:sid] *adj.* ①明白的;易懂的。②神志清明的。③光輝的;明亮的。④清澈的;透明的。—**ly,** *adv.* —**ness,** *n.*

lu·cid·i·ty [lu'sɪdətɪ; lu:'siditi] *n.* ①明白;易懂。②清醒。③光輝;光明。④清澈;明晰。

Lu·ci·fer ['lusəfə; 'lu:sifə] *n.* ①金星(＝Venus);曉星。②〖宗教〗惡魔;撒旦(＝Satan). ***as proud as Lucifer*** 極其傲慢。

lu·cif·er·ous [lu'sɪfərəs; lu:'sifərəs] *adj.* ①發光的;光亮的。②啓發(心智)的。

lu·cite ['lusaɪt; 'lu:sait] *n.* ①一種透明的合成樹脂(用以製飛機之擋風玻璃等)。②(L-)此等物質之商標名。

luck [lʌk; lʌk] *n.* ①機運;運氣。to have good *luck* in one's affairs. 百事順遂。②幸運;佳運;好運。I had the *luck* to find him at home. 我幸好在他家裏找到他。***as luck would have it***... 幸運地;不幸地(視上下文而定)。***down on one's luck*** 〖俗〗不幸的;遭不幸的。***for luck*** 祝福;求福。***in luck*** 幸運。***Just my luck!*** 我總是這樣倒楣! ***out of luck*** 不幸。***worse luck*** 不幸的是;更糟糕的是(用作句中挿語)。—**less,** *adj.*

luck·i·ly ['lʌkɪlɪ; 'lʌkili] *adv.* 幸虧;幸;僥倖;幸運地。*Luckily* I was at home when he called. 他來訪時我幸虧在家。

luck·y ['lʌkɪ; 'lʌki] *adj.*, **luck·i·er, luck·i·est.** ①幸運的;好運的。Some people seem to be always *lucky*. 有些人似乎永遠是幸運的。②偶中的;僥倖的;吉祥的。a *lucky* day. 吉日。***by a lucky chance*** 幸而。***lucky bag*** (or ***dip***) 幸運袋(在義賣會等處裝有價值不等之物,付少數金錢,可隨手摸取者)。***lucky dog*** (or ***beggar***) 幸運兒。***lucky tub*** ＝**lucky bag.** —**luck·i·ness,** *n.*

lu·cra·tive ['lukrətɪv; 'lu:krətiv] *adj.* 可獲利的;有收獲的;待遇好的。—**ly,** *adv.*

lu·cre ['lukə; 'lu:kə] *n.* 利益;財富;利慾(常帶有壞的含意)。

Lu·cre·ti·a [lu'kriʃɪə; lu:'kri:ʃjə] *n.* ①〖羅馬神話〗留克利希亞(羅馬之烈婦,於510 B.C. 被 Tarquinius Sextus 所汚後羞憤自殺, Tarquin 一家因此被逐,遂廢王政改共和)。②貞節之模範。

lu·cu·brate ['lukjʊ͵bret; 'lu:kju(:)breit] *v.i.* & *v.t.*, **-brat·ed, -brat·ing.** ①(特指於燈下或夜間)用功;著作;研究。②作深入研究;思索;刻苦著作。

lu·cu·bra·tion [͵lukjʊ'breʃən; ͵lu:kju(:)'breiʃən] *n.* ①燈下(夜間)的用功;夜間之沉思;燈下之著作。②(常 *pl.*) 學術作品;苦心的作品(幽默用語)。

lu·cu·lent ['lukjʊlənt; 'lu:kju(:)lənt] *adj.* 明晰的;易了解的;鮮明的。

lu·di·crous ['ludɪkrəs; 'lu:dikrəs] *adj.* 滑稽的;可笑的。—**ly,** *adv.* —**ness,** *n.*

lu·es ['luiz; 'lju:iz] *n.* ①疫癘。②梅毒。

luff [lʌf; lʌf] *v.t.* & *v.i.* 轉船首向風行駛;轉船首貼風而駛。—*n.* 〖航海〗①逆風航。②貼風行駛;搶風行駛。③船首兩舷的彎曲部。

lug¹ [lʌg; lʌg] *v.*, **lugged, lug·ging,** *n.* —*v.t.* ①使勁拉;用力拖。②〖俗〗(勉强地)牽入;硬拖入。③(船)在大風中不顧危險將(帆)張滿。—*v.i.* 拉;拖。—*n.* ①强拖;拉曳。②〖動物〗餌蟲;沙蠶(＝lugworm). ③(*pl.*)〖俚〗傲慢態度;裝腔作勢。④〖航海〗斜桁用之橫帆。***put on lugs*** 〖美俚〗擺架子;裝腔作勢。

lug² *n.* ①突出部;突起;突緣。②柄;把手。③〖蘇〗耳;耳朵。④〖俚〗笨人;傻子。

***lug·gage** ['lʌgɪdʒ; 'lʌgidʒ] *n.* 〖英〗行李(在美國稱為 baggage). personal *luggage.* 隨身行李;小件行李。

luggage van 〖英〗行李車。

lug·ger ['lʌgə; 'lʌgə] *n.* 有橫帆之帆船;單桅或雙桅帆船(有斜桁者)。

lug·sail ['lʌg͵sel; 'lʌgseil] *n.* 〖航海〗斜桁用橫帆。

lu·gu·bri·ous [lu'gjubrɪəs; lu:'gju:briəs] *adj.* 悲哀的;鬱鬱不樂的。—**ly,** *adv.*

lug·worm ['lʌg͵wɝm; 'lʌgwə:m] *n.* 〖動物〗沙蠋;沙蟲(用作魚餌)。

Luke [luk; lu:k] *n.* ①〖聖經〗路加(耶穌門徒,路加福音作者)。②路加福音。

luke·warm ['luk'wɔrm; 'lu:k-wɔ:m] *adj.* ①溫熱的。②不熱心的;冷淡的。—**ly,** *adv.*

***lull** [lʌl; lʌl] *v.t.* ①使平靜;使入睡。to *lull* a baby to sleep. (搖搖籃或唱歌)使嬰兒入睡。②釋除;消除。to *lull* a person's fears. 消除一個人之恐懼。③使和緩;使平息。to *lull* pain. 減輕痛苦。—*v.i.* (風等)平息;停息。The wind *lulled*. 風已停息。—*n.* 稍息;稍止;間歇。a *lull* in a storm. 暴風的間歇。

***lull·a·by** ['lʌlə͵baɪ; 'lʌləbai] *n.*, *pl.* **-bies.** ①搖籃曲;催眠曲。②任何輕柔的聲音。

lu·lu ['lulu; 'lu:lu:] *n.* 〖美俚〗①異常之事物;引人注目之人。②給議員之津貼。

lum·ba·go [lʌm'bego; lʌm'beigou] *n.* 〖醫〗腰痛;腰部神經痛;腰肌痛;腰風濕痛。

lum·bar ['lʌmbə; 'lʌmbə] *adj.* 〖解剖〗腰部的;腰的。—*n.* 腰動(靜)脈;腰神經;腰椎。

***lum·ber¹** ['lʌmbə; 'lʌmbə] *n.* ①木材;木料(特指已鋸成板形者)。②破舊傢具;無用雜物。a *lumber* room. 堆舊東西的儲藏室。—*v.t.* ①亂堆;亂積。②砍倒(樹)以備做木料。—*v.i.* 砍倒樹木以做木料。

lum·ber² *v.i.* 笨拙而喧鬧地向前走。—*n.* 隆隆之聲。

lum·ber·er ['lʌmbərə; 'lʌmbərə] *n.* ①〖美,加〗伐木工人。②〖俚〗當鋪老板。③〖俚〗騙子。

lum·ber·ing ['lʌmbərɪŋ; 'lʌmbəriŋ] *n.* 木材業。—*adj.* ①(移動時)笨重的。②移動時發出隆隆之聲的。

lum·ber·jack ['lʌmbə͵dʒæk; 'lʌmbədʒæk] *n.* 〖美〗伐木工人。

lum·ber·man ['lʌmbəmən; 'lʌmbəmən] *n.*, *pl.* **-men.** ①伐木工人;鋸木工人。②木材業者。

lum·ber·mill ['lʌmbə͵mɪl; 'lʌmbəmil] *n.* 鋸木廠。

lum·ber·room ['lʌmbə͵rum; 'lʌmbəru(:)m] *n.* 堆置雜物之房間。

lum·ber·yard ['lʌmbə͵jɑrd; 'lʌmbəjɑ:d] *n.* 堆木材場。

lu·men ['lumɪn; 'lu:min] *n., pl.* **-mens, -mi·na** [-mənə; -mənə]. ①〖物理〗流明(光束的强度單位)。②〖解剖〗(管狀器官之)內腔。③〖植物〗細胞腔。

lu·mi·nance ['lumɪnəns; 'lu:minəns] *n.* 光束之强度。

lu·mi·nar·y ['luməˌnɛrɪ; 'lu:minəri] *n., pl.* **-nar·ies.** ①天體(如日、月等)。②發光體。③先知先覺;導師。④名人。***the great luminary*** 太陽。

lu·mi·nes·cence [ˌluməˈnɛsn̩s; ˌlu:miˈnesns] *n.* 無熱光;冷光;(無熱的)發光。

lu·mi·nes·cent [ˌluməˈnɛsn̩t; ˌlu:miˈnesnt] *adj.* 發冷光的。

lu·mi·nif·er·ous [ˌluməˈnɪfərəs; ˌlu:miˈnifərəs] *adj.* 發光的;發光性的;傳光的。

lu·mi·nos·i·ty [ˌluməˈnɑsətɪ; ˌlu:miˈnɔsiti] *n., pl.* **-ties.** ①光輝; 光度; 光明。②發光物;發光體。③〖物理〗發光度。

***lu·mi·nous** ['lumənəs; 'lu:minəs] *adj.* ①發光的; 有光輝的。The sun and stars are *luminous* bodies. 太陽與星都是發光體。②光亮的; 有光澤的。*luminous* paint. 有光澤的油漆。③明晰的; 易懂的。a *luminous* speaker. 明晰的演說者。④(房間等)光度足够的。

lum·me ['lʌmɪ; 'lʌmi] *interj.* 〖英俚〗(表驚訝的感歎詞)呀!啊!

lum·mox ['lʌməks; 'lʌməks] *n.* 〖美俗〗愚蠢不中用者;笨伯;傻瓜。

lump**[1] [lʌmp; lʌmp] *n.* ①小塊。a *lump* of sugar. 一塊(方)糖。②堆; 團; 大量。Colonel Harding owed him a *lump* of money. 哈定上校欠他一大筆錢。③傷腫; 碰傷。He has a bad *lump* on the forehead. 他的前額傷腫得厲害。④蠢笨的人。⑤〖俗〗大塊頭; 體格高大壯健的人。a brave *lump* of a boy. 一個體格碩大而勇敢的男孩。a lump in the throat*** 如骨鯁在喉。***get*** (or ***take***) ***one's lump*** 獲得或忍受應得或不應得的懲罰、痛苦、批評等。***in the lump*** 全部地;總括地(對分別地而言)。—*v.i.* ①成塊狀。Some kinds of food *lump* when they are cooked. 有些食物一經烹煮即成塊狀。②笨拙地移動。—*v.t.* ①堆成一堆;混在一起(不加分別)。The boys agreed to *lump* the expense of their camping holiday. 那些孩子們商定在露營時所需費用混在一起而不分彼此。②忍耐;忍受。If you don't like it you will have to *lump* it. 你若不喜歡它,你也必須勉强忍耐。③做成塊狀。④使隆起或鼓出成塊狀。—*adj.* ①成塊狀的;成堆的。*lump* sugar. 方糖。②包括一些項目的。***a lump sum*** 一次總付之款。

lump[2] *n.* =lumpfish.

lum·pen ['lumpən; 'lumpən] *adj.* 缺乏階級意識之無產階級的;破落戶的。

lum·pen·pro·le·tar·i·at ['lumpənˌproləˈtɛrɪət; 'lumpənˌprouləˌtɛəriət] *n.* 缺乏階級意識的無產階級。

lump·er ['lʌmpɚ; 'lʌmpə] *n.* ①把東西堆成一堆的人。②碼頭上之脚夫。③〖英俚〗河上的賊。④〖英俚〗民兵。

lump·fish ['lʌmpˌfɪʃ; 'lʌmpfiʃ] *n., pl.* **-fish, -fish·es.** (北大西洋產之)一種海魚。

lump·head ['lʌmpˌhɛd; 'lʌmphed] *n.* 〖俗〗傻瓜;笨人。

lump·ing ['lʌmpɪŋ; 'lʌmpiŋ] *adj.* 〖俗〗大量的;豐富的;笨重的。

lump·ish ['lʌmpɪʃ; 'lʌmpiʃ] *adj.* ①塊狀的。②笨重的。③(身體)矮胖的。④愚蠢的;遲鈍的。

lump·y ['lʌmpɪ; 'lʌmpi] *adj.,* **lump·i·er, lump·i·est.** ①多塊狀物的。②(表面上)多塊狀的。③笨拙的。④波濤洶湧的。

lumpy jaw 〖醫〗頷放線菌病。

Lu·na ['lunə; 'lu:nə] *n.* ①〖羅馬神話〗露娜(月神)。②月(擬人稱)。③(l-)〖煉金〗銀。

lu·na·cy ['lunəsɪ; 'lu:nəsi] *n., pl.* **-cies.** ①月夜夢行症;月夜狂;精神錯亂。②瘋狂的行動;不智之舉。③〖法律〗心神喪失。

luna moth 一種美國產之淡綠色大蛾。

lu·nar ['lunɚ; 'lu:nə] *adj.* ①月的;陰曆的。*lunar* eclipse. 月蝕。②似月亮的;圓形或半月形的。③含銀的;銀的。④蒼白的。

lunar module 登月小艇。

lunar orbit 繞月軌道。

lunar probe ①月球探測。②用作月球探測之太空船。

lunar receiving laboratory 探月回程檢驗所。

lunar trajectory 飛向月球的航線。

lu·nate ['lunet; 'lu:neit] *adj.* (亦作 **lunated**) 新月形的。—*n.* ①〖解剖〗月骨。②〖考古〗半月形之工具。

***lu·na·tic** ['lunəˌtɪk; 'lu:nətik, 'lju:-] *n.* ①瘋人; 癲狂者。②極端愚蠢的人; 大傻瓜。—*adj.* ①瘋癲的。②爲瘋人而設的。③極愚的。a *lunatic* policy. 愚蠢的政策。

lunatic asylum 瘋人院。

lunatic fringe 〖俗〗狂熱者;極端分子。

lu·na·tion [luˈneʃən; lu:ˈneiʃən] *n.* 太陰月; 陰曆一個月(一新月至次一新月之間,約$29^1/_2$日,亦稱 lunar month)。

***lunch** [lʌntʃ; lʌntʃ] *n.* ①午餐。I was at *lunch* when he called. 他來訪時,我正在進午餐。②便餐。—*v.i.* 進午餐。We *lunched* in fashionable restaurants. 我們在上等的飯店午餐。—*v.t.* 供給午餐。

lunch counter 飯館中給客人進餐用的長櫃臺。

***lunch·eon** ['lʌntʃən; 'lʌntʃən] *n.* ①午餐。②午宴(較 lunch 正式)。—*v.i.* 進午餐。

lunch·eon·ette [ˌlʌntʃənˈɛt; ˌlʌntʃəˈnet] *n.* ①便餐。②便餐館。

lun·che·te·ri·a [ˌlʌntʃɪˈtɪrɪə; ˌlʌntʃiˈtiəriə] *n.* 〖美〗(無侍者之)小餐館。

lunch·room ['lʌntʃˌrum; 'lʌntʃrum] *n.* 便餐館。

lune [lun; lu:n] *n.* ①〖幾何〗弓形。②半月形之物。

lu·nette [luˈnɛt; lu:ˈnet] *n.* ①新月形之物或空間(例如斷頭臺上的斷頭孔)。②〖建築〗弧面窗;(圓天花板與牆壁接觸處的)半圓壁。③〖築城〗眼鏡堡。

lung** [lʌŋ; lʌŋ] *n.* ①肺臟;肺。*lung* cancer. 肺癌。He has good *lungs.* 他的肺部健康。②大城市內或附近之廣場; 空曠處。at the top of one's lungs*** 儘量大聲的叫喊。

lunge[1] [lʌndʒ; lʌndʒ] *n., v.,* **lunged, lung·ing.** —*n.* 前衝;刺;戳;擊(如鬥劍及拳鬥等)。—*v.i.* 向前刺; 戳; 擊。—*v.t.* 將…向前伸或刺;使朝前衝。

lunge[2] *n., v.,* **lunged, lung·ing.** —*n.* ①調馬繩(調敎馬匹用之長繩)。②圓形調馬場。—*v.t.* 調敎(馬匹)。—*v.i.* (馬)在一個圈內走動;被調馬繩一端扣住而走動。

lunged [lʌŋd; lʌŋd] *adj.* 有肺的;有…肺的。

lung·er ['lʌŋɚ; 'lʌŋə] *n.* ①〖美俚〗慢性肺病患者(特指結核病人)。②衝刺者。

lung·fish ['lʌŋˌfɪʃ; 'lʌŋfiʃ] *n., pl.* **-fish, -fish·es.** 肺魚。

lung-pow·er ['lʌŋˌpauɚ; 'lʌŋˌpauə] *n.* 發聲力;肺力。

lung sac 〖動物〗肺囊。

lung·wort ['lʌŋˌwɝt; 'lʌŋwə:t] *n.* 〖植物〗兜苔。

lu·ni·form ['lunɪfɔrm; 'lu:nifɔ:m] *adj.* 月狀的;半月狀的。

lu·ni·so·lar [ˌlunɪˈsolɚ; ˌlu:niˈsoulə] *adj.* 月與太陽的;太陰太陽的。

lunk·head [ˈlʌŋkˌhɛd; ˈlʌŋkhed] *n.* 〖美俗〗笨伯;傻瓜。

lu·pin, lu·pine[1] [ˈlupɪn; ˈlu:pin] *n.* 〖植物〗羽扁豆。

lu·pine[2] [ˈlupaɪn; ˈlu:pain] *adj.* ①狼的。②貪吃的;貪婪的。③兇猛的;野蠻的。

lu·pus [ˈlupəs; ˈlu:pəs] *n.* ①〖醫〗狼瘡。②(L-)〖天文〗天狼座。

lurch [lɝtʃ; lə:tʃ] *n.* ①(船等之)突然傾斜;滑向一邊。②(醉漢的)東倒西歪;蹣跚之行動。③困境;進退維谷。④(比賽中)慘敗;一面倒。***leave* (*someone*) *in the lurch*** 使某人陷入困境;棄人於危難之中。—*v.i.* ①突然傾向或滑向一邊。②東倒西歪;蹣跚而行。—*v.t.* 欺瞞;偷竊。

lurch·er [ˈlɝtʃɚ; ˈlə:tʃə] *n.* ①潛行的可疑人物;潛伏的惡漢。②小偷;騙子;間諜;偷獵者。③(偷獵者用的)雜種獵犬。

***lure** [lʊr; ljuə, luə] *n., v.,* **lured, lur·ing.** —*n.* ①引誘;誘惑。the *lure* of the sea. 海的誘惑。②引誘物;誘惑物;餌。the *lures* used by a pretty woman to attract men. 一美女用以吸引男人的誘惑物。—*v.t.* 引誘;誘惑。—**ment,** *n.*

lu·rid [ˈlurɪd; ˈljuərid] *adj.* ①(顏色)深濃的;陰慘的。②可怖的;驚人的。

***lurk** [lɝk; lə:k] *v.i.* ①藏躲;潛伏。Some suspicion still *lurked* in his mind. 他的心裏仍潛藏着懷疑。②偷偷地行走。

lurk·ing-place [ˈlɝkɪŋˌples; ˈlə:kiŋ-pleis] *n.* 〖英〗潛藏的地方。

lus·cious [ˈlʌʃəs; ˈlʌʃəs] *adj.* ①味甘美的;濃郁的。②使人感官愉快的。③過飽的。④使人(讀之)身心愉快的(文章);多寓意的。⑤性感的。—**ly,** *adv.* —**ness,** *n.*

lush[1] [lʌʃ; lʌʃ] *adj.* ①青葱的;嫩綠的;多汁的。②青草茂盛的。③豐富的。④過分裝飾的;誇大其詞的。

lush[2] *n.* 〖俚〗①酒。②醉漢。—*v.t.* & *v.i.* 〖俚〗①飲酒。②給以酒。—*adj.* 〖俚〗酒醉的。

***lust** [lʌst; lʌst] *n.* ①貪慾;色慾;慾望。a man filled with *lust*. 充滿貪慾的人。②熱愛。a *lust* for life. 對生命的熱愛。—*v.i.* ①貪求〖for, after〗。②有强烈之性慾。

***lus·ter**[1], **lus·tre** [ˈlʌstɚ; ˈlʌstə] *n.* ①光彩;光澤;光輝。the *luster* of pearls (silk, porcelain). 眞珠(絲,瓷器)的光彩。②榮譽;光榮。to add *luster* to one's name. 令其聲名增輝。③表面有光澤的瓷器;瓷器光澤的表面。④光亮的棉或毛織物。—*v.t.* ①加一個光澤的表層於。②使發光澤。—*v.i.* 有光澤;發亮。

lust·er[2] *n.* 五年。

lus·ter·ware, lus·tre·ware [ˈlʌstɚˌwɛr; ˈlʌstəwɛə] *n.* 有光澤之陶瓷器。

lust·ful [ˈlʌstfəl; ˈlʌstful] *adj.* ①慾火焚身的;好色的;淫蕩的。②貪得的。

lus·tral [ˈlʌstrəl; ˈlʌstrəl] *adj.* ①清淨的;祓除的。②五年期間的;五年一度的。

lus·trate [ˈlʌstret; ˈlʌstreit] *v.t.,* **-trat·ed, -trat·ing.** (在宗教儀式等中)使(心靈等)清淨;使潔淨。—**lus·tra·tion,** *n.*

lus·tring [ˈlʌstrɪŋ; ˈlʌstriŋ] *n.* 〖美〗一種有光澤之絲織物。

lus·trous [ˈlʌstrəs; ˈlʌstrəs] *adj.* 有光澤的;光亮的。—**ly,** *adv.*

lus·trum [ˈlʌstrəm; ˈlʌstrəm] *n., pl.* **-tra** [-trə; -trə], **-trums.** ①(古羅馬每五年一度的)祓除。②五年間。

lust·y [ˈlʌstɪ; ˈlʌsti] *adj.,* **lust·i·er, lust·i·est.** ①壯健的;精力充沛的。②活潑的;快活的。③豐盛的(餐)。—**lust·i·ly,** *adv.*

lu·ta·nist [ˈlutṇɪst; ˈlu:tnist] *n.* 彈琵琶者。

***lute**[1] [lut; lu:t, lju:t] *n.* 琵琶。

lute[2] *n., v.,* **lut·ed, lut·ing.** —*n.* (密封水管等接合處之)封泥。—*v.t.* 以封泥密封。

lu·te·ci·um [luˈtiʃɪəm; lju:ˈti:ʃiəm] *n.* 〖化〗=**lutetium.**

lute·string [ˈlutˌstrɪŋ; ˈlu:t-striŋ] *n.* 絲帶;有光澤的絲織品。

lu·te·ti·um [luˈtiʃɪəm; lju:ˈti:ʃiəm] *n.* 〖化〗鎦(金屬元素之一,化學符號 Lu).

Lu·ther [ˈluθɚ; ˈlu:θə] *n.* 馬丁路德 (Martin, 1483–1546, 德國神學家,宗教改革的領袖)。

Lu·ther·an [ˈluθərən; ˈlu:θərən] *adj.* ①馬丁路德的。②路德教派的。—*n.* 路德教徒。—**ism,** *n.*

lut·ist [ˈlutɪst; ˈlu:tist] *n.* ①彈奏琵琶者。②琵琶製造者。

lux [lʌks; lʌks] *n., pl.* **lux·es, lu·ces** [ˈlusiz; ˈlu:si:z, ˈlju:-]. 〖光學〗勒克斯(即 meter-candle 米燭光, 照度之國際單位)。

lux·ate [ˈlʌkset; ˈlʌkseit] *v.t.,* **-at·ed, -at·ing.** 使(關節)脫臼 —**lux·a·tion,** *n.*

luxe [lʊks, lʌks; luks, lʌks] 〖法〗 *n.* 上等;奢侈;華美。(參看 **deluxe**)

Lux·em·burg [ˈlʌksəmˌbɝg; ˈlʌksəm-bə:g] *n.* 盧森堡(位於德、法、比之間的一小國,首都爲盧森堡 Luxemburg).

lux·u·ri·ance [lʌgˈʒurɪəns; lʌgˈzjuə-riəns] *n.* ①繁茂;多產;豐富。②(文體的)華麗。(亦作 **luxuriancy**)

lux·u·ri·an·cy [lʌgˈʒurɪənsɪ; lʌgˈzjuə-riənsi] *n.* =**luxuriance.**

lux·u·ri·ant [lʌgˈʒurɪənt, lʌkˈʃur-; lʌgˈzjuəriənt, lʌkˈsjuər-] *adj.* ①繁茂的;叢生的(植物等)。②豐富的。③肥沃的;多產的。④華麗的;絢爛的(文體、美術品等)。a *luxuriant* style. 華麗的文體。—**ly,** *adv.*

lux·u·ri·ate [lʌgˈʒurɪˌet; lʌgˈzjuəri-eit] *v.i.,* **-at·ed, -at·ing.** ①繁茂。②縱情享樂〖in〗。③沉溺於…中。

***lux·u·ri·ous** [lʌgˈʒurɪəs, lʌkˈʃur-; lʌgˈzjuəriəs, lʌkˈsjuər-] *adj.* ①豪華的;奢侈的;豐美的。a *luxurious* hotel. 豪華的旅館。②喜奢華的;放縱的;浪費的。*luxurious* habits. 奢華的習慣。—**ly,** *adv.* —**ness,** *n.*

***lux·u·ry** [ˈlʌkʃərɪ; ˈlʌkʃəri] *n., pl.* **-ries,** *adj.*—*n.*①奢侈;奢華。to live in *luxury*. 生活奢華。②奢侈品。His salary is so low that he can enjoy few *luxuries*. 他的薪水很低,所以不能享受甚麼奢侈品。—*adj.* 奢侈的;豪華的。a *luxury* hotel. 豪華旅館。

luxury tax 奢侈品稅。

Lu·zon [luˈzɑn; lu:ˈzɔn] *n.* 呂宋(非律賓羣島中的最大島)。

l.w.m. low-water mark.

-ly 〖字尾〗①附於形容詞造成副詞。如:boldly. 注意:原字尾爲 -le 者不作 -lely 而作-ly. 如 feebly. ②造成"相似的;有…性質的"之義的形容詞。如:kingly, manly. ③造成表"時間的反覆"之副詞或形容詞。如:hourly, daily.④造成表示"程度"的副詞。如:greatly. ⑤造成表示"方向"的副詞。如:northwardly. ⑥造成表示"次序"的副詞。如:thirdly. ⑦造成表"在某一時間"的副詞。如:recently.

ly·ce·um [laɪˈsiəm; laiˈsiəm] *n.* ①講演廳;講堂;供講學的書院。②〖美〗做公開之學術講演或討論的社團;文學會;演講會。③(L-)

古代希臘學者亞里斯多德教授生徒之處；亞里斯多德哲學及其門徒。
lych gate 〔lɪtʃ~; litʃ~〕 =**lich gate.**
ly·co·pod 〔ˈlaɪkəpɑd; ˈlaikəpɔd〕 *n.* =**lycopodium①.**
ly·co·po·di·um 〔ˌlaɪkəˈpodɪəm; ˌlaikəˈpoudjəm〕 *n.* ①石松科植物。②由某幾種石松科植物之胞子製成的可燃性黃粉。
lydd·ite 〔ˈlɪdaɪt; ˈlidait〕 *n.* 苦味酸炸藥。
Lyd·i·a 〔ˈlɪdɪə; ˈlidiə〕 *n.* 里底亞(小亞細亞西部一古國)。
Lyd·i·an 〔ˈlɪdɪən; ˈlidiən〕 *adj.* ①里底亞的；里底亞人的；里底亞語的。②優柔的；柔媚的；逸樂的；淫蕩的。—*n.*里底亞人；里底亞語。
lye 〔laɪ; lai〕 *n.* 灰汁；灰水；鹼液。
ly·ing-in 〔ˈlaɪɪŋˈɪn; ˈlaiiŋˈin〕 *n.* 臨褥；生產；分娩。—*adj.* 生產的；產科的。a *lying-in* hospital. 產科醫院。
lymph 〔lɪmf; limf〕 *n.* ①〖生理〗淋巴；淋巴液。*lymph* gland. 淋巴腺。②〖醫〗血清。
lym·phat·ic 〔lɪmˈfætɪk; limˈfætik〕 *adj.* ①淋巴的；分泌淋巴的；輸送淋巴的。②淋巴性體質的(肌肉薄弱，臉色蒼白，精神遲鈍等現象)；遲鈍的；軟弱的。—*n.* 淋巴腺；淋巴管。
lymph gland (or **node**) 〖解剖〗淋巴腺；淋巴結。
lym·pho·cyte 〔ˈlɪmfəˌsaɪt; ˈlimfəsait〕 *n.* 〖解剖〗 淋巴球；淋巴細胞。 —**lym·pho·cyt·ic,** *adj.*
lymph·oid 〔ˈlɪmfɔɪd; ˈlimfɔid〕 *adj.* 「=**lymphous.**」
lymph·ous 〔ˈlɪmfəs; ˈlimfəs〕 *adj.* 淋巴的；淋巴腺組織的；淋巴性的；含淋巴的。
lyn·ce·an 〔lɪnˈsiən; linˈsiːən〕 *adj.* ①山貓的；似山貓的。②目光敏銳的。
lynch 〔lɪntʃ; lintʃ〕 *n.* 私刑；私罰。—*v.t.* 加私刑；以私刑處死。—**er,** —**ing,** *n.*
lynch law 私刑。
lynx 〔lɪŋks; liŋks〕 *n., pl.* **lynx·es, lynx.** ①山貓。②(L-)〖天文〗天貓座。—**like,** *adj.*
lynx-eyed 〔ˈlɪŋksˌaɪd; ˈliŋksˌaid〕 *adj.* 目光銳利的。
ly·on·naise 〔ˌlaɪəˈnez; ˌlaiəˈneiz〕 「*adj.* 加洋葱片的。」
Ly·ons 〔ˈlaɪənz, ljõ; ˈlaiənz, ljɔ̃〕 *n.* 里昂(法國東部之一城市，法文作 Lyon)。
Ly·ra 〔ˈlaɪrə; ˈlaiərə〕 *n.* 〖天文〗天琴座。
ly·rate 〔ˈlaɪret; ˈlaiərit〕 *adj.* 七弦琴(lyre)狀的。
lyre 〔laɪr; laiə〕 *n.* 古希臘的七絃琴。
lyre·bird 〔ˈlaɪrˌbɝd; ˈlaiəbəːd〕 *n.* (澳洲產之)琴鳥。
***lyr·ic** 〔ˈlɪrɪk; ˈlirik〕 *n.*①抒情詩。②〖俗〗(常*pl.*)歌詞。③抒情詩人。—*adj.* ①抒情詩的。a *lyric* poet. 抒情詩人。②歌唱的；適於歌唱的。*lyric* drama. 歌劇。③感到興奮的。
lyr·i·cal 〔ˈlɪrɪkḷ; ˈlirikəl〕 *adj.* ①感動的；詩的。②=**lyric.** ③有抒情詩之性質的；有抒情味的。—**ly,** *adv.*
lyr·i·cism 〔ˈlɪrəˌsɪzəm; ˈlirisizəm〕 *n.* ①抒情詩體；抒情詩風格。②情感之抒發。
lyr·i·cist 〔ˈlɪrɪsɪst; ˈlirisist〕*n.* 抒情詩人。
lyr·ist 〔*for* ①ˈlaɪrɪst, ˈlɪr-; ˈlaiərist, ˈlir- *for* ②ˈlɪrɪst; ˈlirist〕 *n.* ①彈奏七弦琴(lyre)者。②抒情詩人；吟唱抒情詩者。
ly·sin 〔ˈlaɪsɪn; ˈlaisin〕 *n.* ①〖生化〗 細胞溶解素。②=**lysine.**
ly·sine 〔ˈlaɪsin; ˈlaisiːn〕 *n.* 〖生化〗離氨酸；二氨基己酸 ($C_6H_{14}N_2O_2$)。
ly·sis 〔ˈlaɪsɪs; ˈlaisis〕 *n.* ①〖醫〗(熱或疾病之) 消散；減退。② 〖生化〗(由於溶解素 lysin 之)細胞破壞；溶解。
-lysis 〖字尾〗表"分解；消散；溶解；毀壞"之義，如: analysis.
ly·sol 〔ˈlaɪsɑl; ˈlaisɔl〕 *n.* 〖醫〗來沙爾「(消毒藥水)。」
lys·sa 〔ˈlɪsə; ˈlisə〕 *n.*〖醫〗狂犬病；恐水病。

M

M or **m** 〔ɛm; em〕 *n., pl.* **M's** or **m's.** ①英文之第十三個字母。②羅馬數字的1,000.
M. ①Majesty. ②Marquis. ③Medicine. ④Medium. ⑤Monday. ⑥midnight. ⑦noon (拉丁文 meridies. A. M. =ante meridiem, before noon. 上午。P. M. = post meridiem, afternoon. 下午)。⑧Monsieur. **m.** ①male. ②manual. ③mark². ④married. ⑤masculine. ⑥mass. ⑦medicine. ⑧meridian. ⑨meridional. ⑩meter. ⑪midnight. ⑫mile(s). ⑬million(s). ⑭minute. ⑮mist. ⑯〖處方〗 mix. ⑰molar. ⑱month.
M'- 〖字首〗=**Mac-.** 如: M'Donald.
'm ①=**am.** 如: I'*m* going. ②=**him.** 如: Show'*m* in. ③ =**madam.** 如: Yes'*m*.
Ma 〖化〗元素 masurium 之符號。
***ma** 〔mɑ; mɑː〕 *n.*〖俗〗媽(爲mamma之略)。
M.A. ①Master of Arts (亦作 **A. M.**). ②Military Academy.
ma'am 〔mæm, mɑm; mæm, mɑːm〕 *n.* 「〖俗〗=**madam.**」
Mac- 〖字首〗冠於愛爾蘭或蘇格蘭姓名之前，表"son of"之義，如: Macdonald, McDonald, M'Donald. (略作 **M'-, Mc-** 或 **M'-**)
ma·ca·bre 〔məˈkɑbɚ; məˈkɑːbə〕 *adj.* ①可怕的。②死之舞蹈的。(亦作 **macaber**)
ma·ca·co 〔məˈkeko; məˈkeikou〕 *n., pl.* **-cos.** 〖動物〗狐猴。
mac·ad·am 〔məˈkædəm; məˈkædəm〕 *n.* ①(鋪路用的) 碎石。②碎石所鋪之路。
mac·ad·am·ize 〔məˈkædəmˌaɪz; məˈkædəmaiz〕 *v.t.,* **-ized, -iz·ing.** 以碎石子鋪築(道路)。
Ma·cao 〔məˈkaʊ; məˈkau〕 *n.* 澳門。
ma·caque 〔məˈkɑk; məˈkɑːk〕 *n.* 〖動物〗 獼猴 (亞洲、非洲產)。
mac·a·ro·ni 〔ˌmækəˈronɪ; ˌmækəˈrouni〕 *n., pl.* **-nis, -nies.** ①通心粉；通心麪。②(英國18世紀)醉心於法國或意大利式之時髦男子。(亦作 **maccaroni**)
mac·a·ron·ic 〔ˌmækəˈrɑnɪk; ˌmækəˈrɔnik〕 *adj.* ①(似)通心粉的。②雅俗混合體的。③混合各種語言的。—*n.* ①(*pl.*) 混合語言(由不同種類的語言合成)。②雅俗混合體之詩或文。
mac·a·roon 〔ˌmækəˈrun; ˌmækəˈruːn〕 *n.* 蛋白杏仁餅乾。
Mac·Ar·thur 〔məkˈɑrθɚ; məˈkɑːθə〕 *n.* 麥克阿瑟 (Douglas, 1880–1964, 美國五星上將)。
Ma·cas·sar (oil) 〔məˈkæsɚ; məˈkæsə〕 *n.* 一種植物性髮油。
Ma·cau·lay 〔məˈkɔlɪ; məˈkɔːli〕 *n.* 麥考萊 (Thomas Babington, 1800–1859, 英國歷史家、評論家、詩人及政治家)。
ma·caw 〔məˈkɔ; məˈkɔː〕 *n.* 金剛鸚䳇。
Mac·beth 〔məkˈbɛθ; məkˈbeθ〕 *n.* ①馬克白(莎士比亞之悲劇)。②馬克白(其主角名)。
Macc. Maccabees.
Mac·ca·bees 〔ˈmækəˌbiz; ˈmækəbiːz〕

n. pl. ①紀元前二世紀猶太愛國者之一族。②聖經僞經 (Apocrypha)之最後二書。

mace[1] 〔mes; meis〕 *n.* ①鎚矛。②權杖；職杖。③持權杖之人。④平頭桿（昔時用以打彈球者)。

mace[2] *n.* 肉豆蔻(一種香料)。

mac·é·doine 〔ˌmæseˈdwɑn; ˌmæseiˈdwɑːn〕 *n.* ①以蔬菜水果混合製成之生菜。②雜樣水果凍。③混合物。

Mac·e·do·ni·a 〔ˌmæsəˈdonɪə; ˌmæsiˈdounjə〕 *n.* ①馬其頓王國（古希臘北部之古王國)。②馬其頓地區(位於南歐)。

Mac·e·do·ni·an 〔ˌmæsəˈdonɪən; ˌmæsiˈdounjən〕 *adj.* 馬其頓的；馬其頓人的；馬其頓語的。—*n.* ①馬其頓人。②馬其頓語。

mac·er·ate 〔ˈmæsəˌret; ˈmæsəreit〕 *v.*, **-at·ed, -at·ing.** —*v.t.* ①浸軟；浸化。②使瘦弱；使憔悴；使痛苦。③折磨；虐待。—*v.i.* ①(因被浸而)變軟。②消瘦。

mac·er·a·tion 〔ˌmæsəˈreʃən; ˌmæsəˈreiʃən〕 *n.* ①浸軟；浸化。②(使) 消瘦；憔悴。③折磨。

Mach 〔mɑk; mɑːk〕 *n.* (有時 m-) = **Mach number.**

mach. ①machine. ②machinery. ③machinist.

ma·chet·e 〔mɑˈtʃete; mɑːˈtʃeitei〕 *n.* (中南美土人用)刀；大刀。

Mach·i·a·vel·(l)i·an 〔ˌmækɪəˈvɛlɪən; ˌmækiəˈveliən〕 *adj.* ①義大利政治家馬基維利的；其政治理論的。②運用權謀的；狡猾的。—*n.* 馬基維利主義的信徒；權謀家；策士。

Mach·i·a·vel·li 〔ˌmækɪəˈvɛlɪ; ˌmækiəˈveli〕 *n.* 馬基維利 (Niccolo de Bernardo, 1469–1527, 義大利政治家及著述家，主張權謀霸術者)。

Mach·i·a·vel·lism 〔ˌmækɪəˈvɛlɪzəm; ˌmækiəˈvelizəm〕 *n.* 馬基維利主義 (爲達政治目的可不擇手段)；權謀霸術。

ma·chin·a·ble 〔məˈʃinəbḷ; məˈʃiːnəbl〕 *adj.* (原料) 可用機器切割的。(亦作 **machineable**)

mach·i·nate 〔ˈmækəˌnet; ˈmækineit〕 *v.i. & v.t.*, **-nat·ed, -nat·ing.** 圖謀（不軌)；陰謀(叛變)。—**mach·i·na·tion, mach·i·na·tor,** *n.*

‡ma·chine 〔məˈʃin; məˈʃiːn〕 *n., v.,* **-chined, -chin·ing.** —*n.* ①機器；機械。Sewing *machines* and washing *machines* make housework easier. 縫紉機與洗衣機使家庭工作減輕。②機械裝置；機械作用。Levers and pulleys are *machines.* 槓桿與滑輪是機械裝置。③汽車。④飛機。⑤〖美〗(操縱政黨之) 核心。the Democratic *machine.* 民主黨核心人物。⑥機械般工作的人。Routine work had turned her into a *machine.* 例常工作已使她變成一個機器人。⑦任何複雜的機構或工作體系。—*v.t.* 以機器製造或完成。The material is easy to *machine.* 這原料易於用機器製造(成品)。

machine gun 機關槍。

ma·chine-gun 〔məˈʃinˌgʌn; məˈʃiːngʌn〕 *v.t.*, **-gunned, -gun·ning.** 以機關槍掃射。

ma·chine-hour 〔məˈʃinˈaur; məˈʃiːnˈauə〕 *n.* 機器工時(以一臺機器作業一小時爲單位，作爲計算成本及工作效率的基準)。

ma·chine·like 〔məˈʃinˌlaɪk; məˈʃiːnlaik〕 *adj.* 像機器一樣準確的。

ma·chine-made 〔məˈʃinˌmed; məˈʃiːnmeid〕 *adj.* ①機器製的。②固定型式的；千篇一律的。

ma·chine·man 〔məˈʃinmən; məˈʃiːnmən〕 *n., pl.* **-men.** 機器操作者。

machine pistol 手提輕機槍。

ma·chine-read·a·ble 〔məˈʃinˌridəbḷ; məˈʃiːnˌriːdəbl〕 *adj.* 可直接以電腦處理的。

‡ma·chin·er·y 〔məˈʃinərɪ; məˈʃiːnəri〕 *n., pl.* **-er·ies.** ①機器；機械 (集合稱)。A factory contains much *machinery.* 一個工廠有許多機器。②機械部分；機械作用。*Machinery* is oiled to keep it running smoothly. 給機械加油使保持運轉圓滑。③組織；機關；團體。legal *machinery.* 司法機構。

machine shop 機械工廠；機械修理店。

machine tool 工作母機；機械用具。

ma·chine-tool 〔məˈʃinˈtul; məˈʃiːnˈtuːl〕 *v.t.* 以機器大量製造。

machine translation 電腦翻譯。

ma·chin·ist 〔məˈʃinɪst; məˈʃiːnist〕 *n.* ①機械師。②機械工人。③修理機械者；製造機械者。

Mach number 馬赫值(卽飛行速度與音速之比例值)。

ma·cho 〔ˈmɑˌtʃo; ˈmɑːtʃou〕 *adj.* 粗獷的。

ma·chree 〔məˈkri; məˈkriː〕 *n.* 〖愛〗吾愛。

mac·in·tosh 〔ˈmækɪnˌtɑʃ; ˈmækintɔʃ〕 *n.* = **mackintosh.**

mack·er·el 〔ˈmækərəl; ˈmækrəl〕 *n., pl.* **-el, -els.** 青花魚；鯖。

mack·i·naw 〔ˈmækəˌnɔ; ˈmækənɔː〕 *n.* 〖美〗= **Mackinaw coat.**

Mackinaw coat 〖美方〗雙排鈕方格紋厚短衣。

mack·in·tosh 〔ˈmækɪnˌtɑʃ; ˈmækintɔʃ〕 *n.* ①橡皮布雨衣。②橡皮布；防水布。③雨衣。(亦作 **macintosh**)

ma·cle 〔ˈmækḷ; ˈmækl〕 *n.* 〖礦〗①(特指鑽石的)雙晶。②(礦物的)斑點。③短空晶石。

Mac·Mil·lan[1] 〔məkˈmɪlən, mæk-; məkˈmilən, mæk-〕 *n.* 麥米倫 (Donald Baxter, 1874–1970, 美國北極探險家)。

Mac·mil·lan[2] *n.* 麥米倫 (Harold, 1894–, 英國政治家, 1957–1963 任首相)。

macr- 〖字首〗= **macro-** (用於母音之前)。

mac·ra·mé 〔ˈmækrəˌme; ˈmækrəmei〕 *n.* (傢具裝飾用之) 絲(線) 結的飾緣；流蘇；花邊。

macro- 〖字首〗表"長的；大的；非常的"之義。(母音前作 **macr-**)

mac·ro·cosm 〔ˈmækrəˌkɑzəm; ˈmækrəkɔzəm〕 *n.* ①大宇宙；大世界。②全範圍。

mac·ro·graph 〔ˈmækrəˌgræf; ˈmækrəgrɑːf〕 *n.* 肉眼圖 (與實物同大或稍大)。

ma·crog·ra·phy 〔məˈkrɑgrəfɪ; məˈkrɔgrəfi〕 *n.* ①肉眼檢查(爲 micrography 之對)。②大形書寫(常爲一種神經病之徵候)。

ma·cron 〔ˈmekrən; ˈmækrɔn〕 *n.* (母音上之)長音記號。

mac·ro·phys·ics 〔ˌmækrəˈfɪzɪks; ˌmækrəˈfiziks〕 *n.* 巨體物理學；巨視物理學 (爲 microphysics 之對)。

mac·ro·scop·ic 〔ˌmækrəˈskɑpɪk; ˌmækrəˈskɔpik〕 *adj.* 肉眼可見的；肉眼上的。

mac·ro·spore 〔ˈmækrəˌspor; ˈmækrəspɔː〕 *n.* 〖植物〗= **megaspore.**

mac·u·la 〔ˈmækjulə; ˈmækjulə〕 *n., pl.* **-lae** 〔-ˌli; -liː〕. ①(太陽及其他天體的) 黑點。②(礦物的)傷疵。③痣。—**mac·u·lar,** *adj.*

mac·u·late 〔*v.* ˈmækjuˌlet; ˈmækjuleit *adj.* ˈmækjulɪt; ˈmækjulit〕 *v.*, **-lat·ed, -lat·ing,** *adj.* —*v.t.* 加以斑點；弄污；使不潔。—*adj.* ①有污點的；有斑點的。②染污的；不潔的。—**mac·u·la·tion,** *n.*

:mad [mæd; mæd] *adj.*, **mad·der, mad·dest,** *n.* —*adj.* ①瘋狂的。His wife went *mad.* 他的妻子瘋了。②(風等)狂暴的;(心緒)狂歡的。a *mad* torrent. 激流。③狂妄的;狂熱的;愚蠢的。What a *mad* thing to do! 一件多麼愚蠢的事啊!④(犬)瘋的。A *mad* dog may bite people. 瘋狗會咬人。⑤〖俗〗憤怒的;生氣的。Don't get *mad* at me! 不要對我發脾氣!⑥極爲愚蠢的;不可理喻的。a *mad* scheme to invade France. 侵犯法國的愚蠢計謀。⑦着了迷的。She is *mad* about him. 她對他着了迷。***be as mad as a March hare*** 狂若三月之兎;完全瘋了。***be mad as a hatter*** 完全瘋狂的。***be mad for*** (or ***after***) ***something*** 渴望。***drive*** (or ***send***) ***a person mad*** 逼人使狂。***like mad*** 猛烈地;强有力地;迅速地。—*n.* 氣頭;氣憤。The last time he had a *mad* on, it lasted for days. 上次他生氣,接連好幾天。

Mad., Madm. Madam.

Mad·a·gas·car [ˌmædəˈgæskɚ; ˌmædəˈgæskə] *n.* 馬達加斯加(非洲東南印度洋中之一島,卽馬拉加西共和國, the Malagasy Republic,首都安塔那那利佛Antananarivo). —**Mad·a·gas·can,** *n., adj.*

***mad·am** [ˈmædəm; ˈmædəm] *n., pl.* **mad·ams, mes·dames.** 女士;夫人(對女子之尊稱)。〖注意〗在書信中 **Madam** 或 **Dear Madam** 可兼指已婚及未婚之女子。

mad·ame [ˈmædəm, maˈdam; ˈmædəm, maˈdam] *n., pl.* **mes·dames.** 法國對婦人之尊稱 (=Mrs.);夫人(在英美對外國已婚女性之稱呼)。(略作 **Mme., Mdme.**)

mad·cap [ˈmædˌkæp; ˈmædkæp] *n.* 鹵莽的人;狂暴的人。—*adj.* 狂妄的;鹵莽的。

mad·den [ˈmædn̩; ˈmædn] *v.t.* ①使瘋狂。②使大怒。—*v.i.* 發瘋;發怒。

mad·den·ing [ˈmædnɪŋ; ˈmædn̩iŋ] *adj.* ①使人發狂的;使人氣極的。②狂怒的;狂暴的。

mad·der [ˈmædɚ; ˈmædə] *n.* ①〖植物〗茜草;洋茜。②茜草根。③茜草染料;赤黃色。—*v.t.* 以茜草染料染色。

mad·ding [ˈmædɪŋ; ˈmædiŋ] *adj.* 〖詩,罕〗①瘋狂的;狂亂的。②令人發狂的。

mad-doc·tor [ˈmædˌdɑktɚ; ˈmædˌdɔktə] *n.* 精神病科醫生。

:made [med; meid] *v.* pt. & pp. of make. —*adj.* ①已製成的;已形成的。②特別準備的。③人工製的。④成功的。He is a *made* man. 他是個成功的人。⑤創造的;揑造的。*made* stories. 揑造的故事。

Ma·dei·ra [məˈdɪrə; məˈdiərə] *n.* ①馬得拉羣島(大西洋中葡萄牙屬島,位於非洲西北部)。②(m-)該地產之白葡萄酒。③馬得拉河(經巴西西部流入 Amazon河)。

mad·e·moi·selle [ˌmædəməˈzɛl; ˌmædəmˈzel] *n., pl.* **mad·e·moi·selles, mes·de·moi·selles** [ˌmædəməˈzɛl; ˌmædəmˈzel]. 法國對未婚女子之尊稱 (=Miss);小姐。(略作 **Mlle., Mdlle.**)

made-to-or·der [ˈmedtuˈɔrdɚ; ˈmeidtuˈɔːdə] *adj.* 定做的;如定做的。

made-up [ˈmedˈʌp; ˈmeidˈʌp] *adj.* ①排成的;排好的。②以化妝品裝飾的。③虛構的。a *made-up* story. 揑造的故事。④決定的;有決心的。

mad·house [ˈmædˌhaus; ˈmædhaus] *n., pl.* **-hous·es** [-ˌhauzɪz; -hauziz]. ①精神病院;瘋人院。②混亂吵鬧的地方。

Mad·i·son [ˈmædəsn̩; ˈmædisn] *n.* 麥廸生(James, 1751–1836, 於 1809–17 任美國第四任總統)。

***mad·ly** [ˈmædlɪ; ˈmædli] *adv.* ①瘋狂地。②猛烈地;狂熱地。③愚蠢地。

mad·man** [ˈmædmən; ˈmædmən] *n., pl.* **-men.** 瘋子;精神病患者。He is next door to (=nearly) a *madman.* 他幾乎快成瘋子。talk like a madman*** 胡說八道。

mad money 〖俚〗①男女約會時女子自帶之零錢(以備萬一與男伴分手後可獨自雇車回家)。②女人準備爲萬一時之零錢。

***mad·ness** [ˈmædnɪs; ˈmædnis] *n.* ①瘋狂。②憤怒。③愚蠢;愚蠢的行爲。It would be *madness* to climb the mountain in such a storm. 在這樣的暴風雨中爬山是愚蠢的行爲。④狂犬病。

Ma·don·na [məˈdɑnə; məˈdɔnə] *n.* ①聖母瑪利亞。②聖母的畫像或雕像。③(m-)義大利人對婦女之尊稱(=madam)。

Ma·dras [məˈdræs; məˈdræs] *n.* ①馬德拉斯省(印度東南部)。②馬德拉斯(爲馬德拉斯省之首府)。③(m-)馬德拉斯布(做花條子襯衫用者)。④(m-)馬德拉斯布所做之手絹。—*adj.* (m-)馬德拉斯布做的。

mad·re·pore [ˈmædrɪˌpor; ˌmædriˈpɔː] *n.* 〖動物〗石蠶(熱帶海洋產之石珊瑚之類)。

Ma·drid [məˈdrɪd; məˈdrid] *n.* 馬德里(西班牙首都)。

mad·ri·gal [ˈmædrɪgl̩; ˈmædrigəl] *n.* ①抒情短詩。②情歌。③〖音樂〗重唱歌曲。④任何歌曲。

mad·wom·an [ˈmædˌwumən; ˈmædˌwumən] *n., pl.* **-wom·en.** 瘋女。

Mae·ce·nas [mɪˈsinəs; mi(ː)ˈsiːnæs] *n.* ①米西奈斯(Gaius Cilnius, 70?–8 B.C., 古代羅馬之政治家及詩人, Horace 及 Virgil 之友)。②富有、慷慨的贊助人;(尤指)文學或藝術之資助人。

mael·strom [ˈmelstrəm; ˈmeilstroum] *n.* ①大旋渦。②感情、思想或情況之大混亂。③(M-)挪威西北部海上危險的大旋渦。

mae·nad [ˈminæd; ˈmiːnæd] *n.* ①〖希臘、羅馬神話〗侍奉酒神 Bacchus 之女祭司。②狂女;狂婦。(亦作 **menad**)

ma·es·to·so [ˌmɑɛsˈtoso; ˌmɑːesˈtouzou] 〖義〗 *adj.* & *adv.* 〖音樂〗莊嚴的(地)。

maes·tro [ˈmaɪstro; mɑːˈestrou] *n., pl.* **-tros, -tri** [-trɪ; -tri]. 〖義〗 ①(音樂之)名家;名作曲家;名指揮家。②(藝術之)名家;大師。③(M-)呼叫上述大師時之尊稱。

Mae·ter·linck [ˈmetɚˌlɪŋk; ˈmeitəliŋk] *n.* 梅特林克 (Maurice, 1862–1947, 比利時人,曾獲 1911 年諾貝爾文學獎)。

Mae West [me~; mei~] 一種救生背心(原係美國女演員之名)。

maf·fick [ˈmæfɪk; ˈmæfik] *v.i., n.* 〖英俗〗歡呼慶祝。

ma·fi·a, maf·fi·a [ˈmɑfɪˌɑ; ˈmɑːfiɑː] *n.* ①(西西里島人之)對法律與政府的敵視。②(M-)黑手黨(義大利人或西西里島人的祕密團體,以復仇、勒索等爲目的)。

ma·fi·o·so [ˌmæfɪˈoso; ˌmæfiˈousou] *n., pl.* **-si** [-si; -siː]. 黑手黨之一分子。

mag. ① magazine. ② magnetism. ③ magnitude.

:mag·a·zine [ˌmægəˈzin, ˈmægəˌzin; ˌmægəˈziːn] *n.* ①雜誌。It is a monthly *magazine.* 此爲月刊。②(城堡或戰艦之)火藥貯藏庫。③火藥庫;軍用倉庫。to explode a *magazine.* 爆炸火藥庫。④(連發鎗之)彈倉;彈夾。⑤照像機中的軟片盒。⑥火爐中的燃料室。⑦倉庫。⑧火藥;軍火。—*v.i.* 貯藏。

Mag·da·len(e) ['mægdəˌlin; 'mægdəlin] *n.* (the-) 抹大拉的瑪利亞(原爲一罪人,後悔罪而得救,聖經路加福音八章二節及七章三十七節)。

mag·da·lene ['mægdəlin; 'mægdəli:n] *n.* ①從良之妓女;改邪歸正之婦女。②妓女收容所;妓女教養所。

M.Ag.Ec. Master of Agricultural Economics.

M.Ag.Ed. Master of Agricultural Education.

Ma·gel·lan [mə'dʒɛlən; mə'gelən] *n.* 麥哲倫 (Ferdinand, 1480?–1521, 葡萄牙之航海家)。

Magellan, Strait of 麥哲倫海峽(在智利南端)。

ma·gen·ta [mə'dʒɛntə; mə'dʒentə] *n.* ①紫紅染料。②紫紅色。—*adj.* 紫紅色的。

mag·got ['mægət; 'mægət] *n.* ①蛆。②狂想。He has a *maggot* in his head. 他想入非非。

mag·got·y ['mægətɪ; 'mægəti] *adj.* ①多蛆的。②懷奇想的;異想天開的。

Ma·gi ['medʒaɪ; 'meidʒai] *n.* pl. of **Ma·gus.** ①〖聖經〗東方賢人 (the three Magi, 馬太福音二章一節及二章七至十三節)。②(m-)(古波斯之)僧侶;術士。③占星家。

Ma·gi·an ['medʒɪən; 'meidʒiən] *adj.* 古波斯之僧侶(階級)的。—*n.* ①古波斯之僧侶。②(m-)魔術師;術士。

***mag·ic** ['mædʒɪk; 'mædʒik] *n.* ①魔術;巫術。The fairy's *magic* changed the brothers into swans. 仙人的魔術使兩兄弟變成天鵝。②魔力;媚力。the *magic* of love. 愛情的魅力。③魔法;變戲法。—*adj.* 魔術的;魔力的;似有魔力的。a *magic* transformation in her appearance. 她的外貌像魔術般地改變。

mag·i·cal ['mædʒɪkl; 'mædʒikəl] *adj.* 魔術的;不可思議的。The effect was *magical.* 其效果是不可思議的。

***ma·gi·cian** [mə'dʒɪʃən; mə'dʒiʃən] *n.* 魔術家;幻術家;術士。

ma·gilp [mə'gɪlp; mə'gilp] *n.* =**megilp.**

Ma·gi·not line ['mæʒəˌno~; 'mæʒinou~] 馬奇諾防線(1925–35 年間法國在德法邊境的防線,後爲德軍所攻破)。

mag·is·te·ri·al [ˌmædʒɪs'tɪrɪəl; ˌmædʒis'tiəriəl] *adj.* ①長官的。②有權威的;長官似的。③公正的。④專橫的。⑤執法者的。

mag·is·tra·cy ['mædʒɪstrəsɪ; 'mædʒistrəsi] *n.* ①magistrate 之職權、地位或任期。②magistrate 之管區。③magistrate 之集合稱。(亦作 **magistrature**)

mag·is·tral ['mædʒɪstrəl; mə'dʒistrəl] *adj.* ①主人的;教師的;有權威的;獨斷的。②特別處方的。③〖碉堡〗主要(防線)的。

***mag·is·trate** ['mædʒɪsˌtret, -trɪt; 'mædʒistrit, -treit] *n.* ①長官;政府中有執行法律權之官吏。The President is the chief *magistrate* of the United States. 總統是美國的最高長官。②法官;推事。

Mag·na C(h)ar·ta ['mægnə'kɑrtə; 'mægnə'kɑ:tə] ①英國大憲章(爲 1215 年英王 John 爲貴族等挾迫而承認之自由特書,是英國憲法的基礎)。②任何保證民權及政治自由之基本憲法。

mag·na·li·um [mæg'nelɪəm; mæg'neiliəm] *n.* 〖化〗鎂鋁(鎂與鋁之合金)。

mag·na·nim·i·ty [ˌmægnə'nɪmətɪ; ˌmægnə'nimiti] *n., pl.* **-ties.** ①高尚;大度;慷慨。②高尚;大度或慷慨的行動。

mag·nan·i·mous [mæg'nænəməs; mæg'nænimәs] *adj.* 心地高尚的;度量寬大的;不卑鄙的。—**ly,** *adv.*

mag·nate ['mægnet; 'mægneit] *n.* ①偉人;巨擘;大企業家。commercial *magnates.* 商業泰斗。②舊波蘭或匈牙利上院議員。

mag·ne·sia [mæg'niʃə; mæg'ni:ʃə] *n.* 〖化〗①氧化鎂;苦土。②含水碳酸鎂(俗稱瀉鹽)。

mag·ne·sian [mæg'niʃən; mæg'ni:ʃən] *adj.* 〖化〗鎂的;含鎂的。

mag·ne·si·um ['mæg'niʃɪəm, -ʒɪəm; mæg'ni:zjəm] *n.* 〖化〗鎂(化學符號爲 Mg)。

***mag·net** ['mægnɪt; 'mægnit] *n.* ①磁鐵;吸鐵石。bar *magnet.* 條形磁鐵。natural *magnet.* 天然磁石。horseshoe *magnet.* 蹄形磁鐵。②有吸引力之人或物。Hawaii is a *magnet* for tourists. 夏威夷是一吸引遊客之處。

***mag·net·ic** [mæg'nɛtɪk; mæg'netik, məg-] *adj.* ①有磁性的。②磁的;磁學的。③能被磁化的;能被磁鐵吸引的。④奪魂的;吸引人的。a *magnetic* smile. 醉人的微笑。⑤地球磁場的。⑥催眠的;催眠引起的。

magnetic detector 磁性檢波器。

magnetic field 〖物理〗①磁場。②磁場中之磁力。

magnetic force 〖物理〗磁力。

magnetic mine 磁性水雷。

magnetic needle 磁針。

magnetic pole 〖物理〗磁極;磁北極。

mag·net·ics [mæg'nɛtɪks; mæg'netiks] *n.* 磁學。

magnetic storm 磁暴(因太陽黑點而起的地磁動亂)。

mag·net·ism ['mægnəˌtɪzəm; 'mægnitizəm] *n.* ①磁質;磁性;磁力。②吸引力;魅力。③〖物理〗磁學。

mag·net·ite ['mægnəˌtaɪt; 'mægnitait] *n.* 〖礦〗磁鐵礦 (Fe_3O_4)。

mag·net·ize ['mægnəˌtaɪz; 'mægnitaiz] *v.,* **-ized, -iz·ing.** —*v.t.* ①使磁化。②吸引;奪魂。—*v.i.* 磁化。—**mag·net·i·za·tion,** *n.*

mag·ne·to [mæg'nito; mæg'ni:tou] *n., pl.* **-tos.** 小型磁石發電機(即 magnetoelectric generator 之簡稱)。

mag·ne·to·e·lec·tric [mægˌnitoɪ'lɛktrɪk; mægˌni:toui'lektrik] *adj.* 磁電的。

mag·ne·to·e·lec·tric·i·ty [mægˌnitoɪˌlɛk'trɪsətɪ; mægˌni:touiˌlek'trisiti] *n.* 磁電。

mag·ne·tom·e·ter [ˌmægnə'tɑmətə; ˌmægnə'tɔmitə] *n.* 〖物理〗磁力針;地磁儀。

mag·ne·tron ['mægnəˌtrɑn; 'mægnitrɔn] *n.* 〖電子〗磁控管(用作雷達發射機之超短波振盪器)。

mag·ni·cide ['mægnɪˌsaɪd; 'mægnisaid] *n.* 謀殺要人。

mag·nif·ic [mæg'nɪfɪk; mæg'nifik] *adj.* 〖古〗①莊嚴的;壯麗的;堂皇的。②誇大其辭的;誇大的。

Mag·nif·i·cat [mæg'nɪfɪˌkæt; mæg'nifikæt] *n.* ①〖天主教〗聖母頌(聖經路加福音1: 46–55 之聖母頌歌)。②(m-)頌歌。

mag·ni·fi·ca·tion [ˌmægnəfə'keʃən; ˌmægnifi'keiʃən] *n.* ①擴大。②〖光學〗倍率。③稱讚。④放大的複製品;放大的影本。

***mag·nif·i·cence** [mæg'nɪfəsn̩s; mæg-

ˈnifisns, məg-] *n.* 華麗; 宏大; 堂皇。the *magnificence* of Versailles. 凡爾賽宮的富麗堂皇。

***mag·nif·i·cent** [mægˈnɪfəsn̩t; mægˈnifisnt, məg-] *adj.* ①華麗的; 壯麗的; 宏大的; 堂皇的。a *magnificent* palace. 壯麗的宮殿。②高尚的; 神聖的。a *magnificent* manner. 高尚的態度。③豐富的; 富裕的。a *magnificent* inheritance. 豐富的遺產。④(M-)偉大的(祇用於人名後, 爲頭銜)。Lorenzo the *Magnificent*. 偉大的羅廉佐。—**ly,** *adv.*

mag·nif·i·co [mægˈnɪfəˌko; mægˈnifikou] *n., pl.* **-coes.** ①〖昔〗威尼斯之貴族。②貴人;貴族;顯要之人。

mag·ni·fi·er [ˈmægnəˌfaɪə; ˈmægnifaiə] *n.* ①放大者; 放大之物。②放大鏡。

***mag·ni·fy** [ˈmægnəˌfaɪ; ˈmægnifai] *v.,* **-fied, -fy·ing.** —*v.t.* ①放大;擴大。We *magnify* objects with a microscope. 我們用顯微鏡放大物體。②誇大;誇張。③强調;加强。—*v.i.* 能放大;有放大的能力。Telescopes and microscopes *magnify*. 望遠鏡和顯微鏡能放大。

magnifying glass 放大鏡。

mag·nil·o·quence [mægˈnɪləkwəns; mægˈniləkwəns] *n.* 誇張; 誇大; 誇張的話; 誇張的文體。

mag·nil·o·quent [mægˈnɪləkwənt; mægˈniləkwənt] *adj.* 誇張的;誇大的。

mag·ni·tude** [ˈmægnəˌtjud; ˈmægnitjuːd] *n.* ①大小; 積; 量; 長(度); 矢長。I want to know the *magnitude* of this angle. 我想知道此角的大小。②重要;重大。③道德上的偉大;寬宏大量。④(星辰的)光度;星等。Stars of the first *magnitude* are the brightest. 第一星等的星辰是最明亮的。⑤〖數學〗數量; 長度; 大小; 矢長。of the first magnitude*** 很重要的; 最重要的; 最嚴重的; 第一流的。an artist *of the first magnitude*. 第一流的藝術家。

mag·no·li·a [mægˈnolɪə; mægˈnouljə] *n.* ①〖植物〗木蘭。②木蘭花。

mag·num [ˈmægnəm; ˈmægnəm] *n.* 大酒瓶 (約裝 2 quarts 或 2.3 公升)。

mag·pie [ˈmægˌpaɪ; ˈmægpai] *n.* ①鵲。②饒舌之人。 「culture.」

M. Agr(ic). 〖美〗 Master of Agri-

mags·man [ˈmægzmən; ˈmægzmən] *n., pl.* **-men.** ①雜誌撰稿人。②〖俚〗騙子。

mag·uey [ˈmægwe; ˈmægwei] *n.* 〖植物〗龍舌蘭。

Ma·gus [ˈmegəs; ˈmeigəs] *n., pl.* **Ma·gi.** ①古波斯之僧侶。②〖聖經〗東方三賢士之一。③(m-)(古代之)占星學家;魔術師。

Mag·yar [ˈmægjɑr; ˈmægjɑː] *n.* ①匈牙利之馬札兒人 (原爲蒙古族)。②馬札兒語; 匈牙利語。—*adj.* ①馬札兒人的;馬札兒語的。②匈牙利人的;匈牙利語的。

ma·ha·ra·ja(h) [ˌmɑhəˈrɑdʒə; ˌmɑːhəˈrɑːdʒə] *n.* (印度之)大君。

ma·ha·ra·nee [ˌmɑhəˈrɑni, məˈhɑˈrɑni; ˌmɑːhəˈrɑːniː] *n.* (印度)大君之妻;女君主。(亦作 **maharani**)

ma·hat·ma [məˈhætmə; məˈhɑːtmə] *n.* (密教之)大善知識;大聖。

Ma·ha·ya·na [ˌmɑhəˈjɑnə; ˌmɑːhəˈjɑːnə] *n.* 〖佛教〗大乘;摩訶衍。

Mah·di [ˈmɑdi; ˈmɑːdi(ː)] *n.* 〖回教〗(將於世界末日降臨的)救世主。

mah-jongg [mɑˈdʒɔŋ; ˈmɑːˈdʒɔŋ] *n.* (中國的)麻將牌戲。to play *mah-jongg*. 搓麻將。—*v.i.* (麻將)和了("和"字讀作"胡")。(亦作 **mah-jong**) 「*n.* =**maulstick.**」

mahl·stick [ˈmɑlˌstɪk; ˈmɔːl-stik]

ma·hog·a·ny** [məˈhɑgənɪ; məˈhɔgəni -gn̩i] *n., pl.* **-nies,** *adj.* —*n.* ①〖植物〗桃花心木; 紅木。②桃花心木製成之傢具。③紅褐色。be under the mahogany*** 醉倒在(桃花心木的)桌下。***put*** (or ***stretch***) ***one's legs under a man's mahogany*** 受人款待。***with one's knees under the mahogany*** 就席; 坐席。—*adj.* ①桃花心木的; 桃花心木製的。②桃花心木色的;紅褐色的。

Ma·hom·et [məˈhɑmɪt; məˈhɔmit] *n.* 穆罕默德 (570?–632, 回教教祖)。(亦作 **Mahomed, Mohammed**)

Ma·hom·et·an [məˈhɑmətən; məˈhɔmitən] *adj., n.* =**Mohammedan.**

Ma·hom·et·an·ism [məˈhɑmətəˌnɪzm̩; məˈhɔmitənizəm] *n.* =**Mohammedanism.** 「馭象者。」

ma·hout [məˈhaut; məˈhaut] *n.* 象奴;

Mah·rat·ta [məˈrætə; məˈrætə] *n.* 馬拉塔人(住於印度西部及中部, 性好戰)。

‡maid [med; meid] *n.* ①少女;處女。②未婚女子。an old *maid*. 老處女。③女僕;婢。

mai·dan [maɪˈdɑn; maiˈdɑːn] *n.* 〖英印〗(用作操場或市場之)廣場。

***maid·en** [ˈmedn̩; ˈmeidn] *n.* ①少女;處女。②蘇格蘭從前之斷頭臺。③未交配之馬。④初次競賽。—*adj.* ①少女的; 處女的。②新鮮的;未試用過的;未墾殖的。*maiden* ground. 處女地。③首次的;初次的。a ship's *maiden* voyage. 船的處女航。④未婚的。a *maiden* aunt. 未婚的姑姑(阿姨)。⑤(馬之)未曾得獎的。⑥(競賽之)祇許未交配之馬參加的。⑦未經過考驗的。

maid·en·hair [ˈmedn̩ˌhɛr; ˈmeidnhɛə] *n.* 〖植物〗過壇龍;石長生;孔雀草。

maidenhair tree 〖植物〗銀杏樹; 公孫樹;白果樹。 「hed] *n.* 處女膜。」

maid·en·head [ˈmedn̩ˌhɛd; ˈmeidn-

maid·en·hood [ˈmedn̩ˌhud; ˈmeidnhud] *n.* ①處女身分。②處女時代。(亦作 **maidhood**) 「處女的;似處女的。」

maid·en·ish [ˈmedn̩ɪʃ; ˈmeidn̩iʃ] *adj.*

maid·en·like [ˈmedn̩ˌlaɪk; ˈmeidnlaik] *adj.* 如處女的;柔順的;嬌羞的;羞澀的。

maid·en·ly [ˈmedn̩lɪ; ˈmeidnli] *adj.* ①如處女的; 柔順的; 嬌羞的。②處女的;少女的。—**maid·en·li·ness,** *n.* 「姓;本姓。」

maiden name 女子婚前之姓; 娘家

maid-in-wait·ing [ˈmedɪnˈwetɪŋ; ˈmeidinˈweitiŋ] *n., pl.* **maids-in-wait·ing.** 侍候后妃或公主之少女 (通常爲出身高貴者); 宮女。 「**in-waiting.**」

maid of honor ①伴娘。②=**maid-**

maid·ser·vant [ˈmedˌsɝvənt; ˈmeidˌsəːvənt] *n.* 女僕人;女傭人。

ma·ieu·tic [meˈjutɪk; meiˈjuːtik] *adj.* ①(蘇格拉底式之)問答法的。②助產術的。

mai·gre [ˈmegɚ; ˈmeigə] *adj.* 〖天主教〗①無肉的;素食的。②齋日的。 「**mayhem.**」

mai·hem [ˈmehɛm; ˈmeihem] *n.* =

‡mail¹ [mel; meil] *n.* ①郵件(集合稱)。I had a lot of *mail* last week. 上星期我接到許多信。②信件。The ship sank and the *mails* were lost. 船沉了,信件全損失了。③郵政。I sent her a letter by air *mail.*

我寄給她一封航空信。④郵船;郵車。—*v.t.* 郵寄。I asked him to *mail* a letter for me. 我請他給我寄一封信。—*adj.* 郵政的;書信的。a *mail* train. 郵件火車。

mail² *n.* 盔甲。***a coat of mail*** 盔甲。***chain mail*** 鎖子甲。—*v.t.* 着盔甲。

mail·a·ble [ˈmeləbl; ˈmeiləbl] *adj.* 〖美〗可以郵寄的。—**mail·a·bil·i·ty,** *n.*

mail·bag [ˈmelˌbæg; ˈmeilbæg] *n.* 郵袋。

mail·boat [ˈmelˌbot; ˈmeilbout] *n.* 〖美〗郵件船。(亦作 **mail boat**)

mail·box [ˈmelˌbɑks; ˈmeilbɔks] *n.* ①(公用)郵筒。②(私人)信箱。(亦作 **postbox**)

mail carrier =**mailman.**

mail cart 郵車。

mail·clad [ˈmelˌklæd; ˈmeilklæd] *adj.* 穿戴盔甲的。

mail clerk 郵務員。

mail coach ①郵件馬車。② =**mail cart.**

mail fraud 利用郵件的欺詐行爲。

mail·ing [ˈmelɪŋ; ˈmeiliŋ] *n.* ①〖美〗郵寄。a *mailing* list. 郵寄名單。②〖蘇〗租用之農場;佃租。

mail·lot [maˈjo; maˈjou] *n., pl.* **mail-lots.** 〖法〗①(舞蹈家、賣藝者、體操專家等用的)緊身衣。②游泳衣(尤指上下連在一起者)。③緊身之編織襯衫。

mail·man [ˈmelˌmæn; ˈmeilmæn] *n., pl.* **-men.** 郵差。

mail order 郵購;函購。

mail-or·der [ˈmelˌɔrdɚ; ˈmeilˌɔːdə] *adj.* 〖美〗郵購制的。*mail-order* business. 郵購業。

mail-order house 郵購商號(以辦理郵購業務爲主的商號)。

mail·plane [ˈmelˌplen; ˈmeilplein] *n.* 郵政專機。

mail·sack [ˈmelˌsæk; ˈmeilsæk] *n.* =**mailbag.**

mail-train [ˈmelˌtren; ˈmeiltrein] *n.* 郵政車箱。

***maim** [mem; meim] *v.t.* 使殘廢;傷害其四肢;使不完整。He was seriously *maimed* in the war. 他在戰爭中受重傷而殘廢。—*n.* ①殘廢;傷殘。②缺陷。

maimed [memd; meimd] *adj.* 殘廢的;四肢不全的;跛的。

‡main¹ [men; mein] *adj.* ①最主要的;最重要的;最大的。the *main* street of a town. 市鎮之大街。②最高度的。to do something by *main* strength (*or* force). 傾全力做某事。—*n.* ①(輸送水及汽油等之)總管;幹線。②〖詩〗海洋。③主要部分。The *main* of their investments was lost in the war. 他們投資的大部分在戰爭中損失了。***in the main*** 就一般而論;大致上。*In the main,* the essay was dull reading. 大體上說來那篇散文枯燥無味。

main² *n.* ①鬥鷄比賽。②擲骰子前所猜的5至9之任意數。③擲骰子;擲骰子所下的賭注。

main drag 〖俚〗主要街道。

Maine [men;mein] *n.*緬因(美國東北部之一州,首府爲奧古斯塔 Augusta, 略作 **Me.**). ***from Maine to California*** 全美國。

main hold 〖航海〗中部船艙;中艙。

***main·land** [ˈmenˌlænd, ˈmenlənd; ˈmeinlənd,-lænd] *n.* 大陸;本土。—**er,** *n.*

main line ①〖英〗(鐵路之)幹線。②〖俚〗**a.** 可將痲醉藥直接注射的身上顯著之血管。**b.** 將痲醉藥直接注入血管。

main·line [ˈmenˌlaɪn; ˈmeinlain] *v.i.,* **-lined, -lin·ing.** 〖俚〗將痲醉藥品(尤指海洛因)直接注入靜脈。

***main·ly** [ˈmenlɪ; ˈmeinli] *adv.* ①主要地。It is *mainly* because of my fault. 這主要是由於我的錯。②大部分。The students in my class are *mainly* girls. 我班上的學生大部分是女生。

main·mast [ˈmenˌmæst; ˈmeinmɑːst] *n.* 〖航海〗主桅;大桅;(獨木舟、小舟之)中桅。

main·sail [ˈmenˌsel; ˈmeinseil] *n.* 〖航海〗大帆;主帆。

main·sheet [ˈmenˌʃit; ˈmeinʃiːt] *n.* 〖航海〗大帆索;主帆索。

main·spring [ˈmenˌsprɪŋ; ˈmeinspriŋ] *n.* ①(鐘錶內的)大發條;主發條。②主要原因;主要動機;主要影響。

main·stay [ˈmenˌste; ˈmeinstei] *n.* ①〖航海〗支持主桅之繩索。②主要的依靠。

main stem 〖俚〗城鎮中之主街。

main·stream [ˈmenˌstrim; ˈmeinstriːm] *n.* ①(傾向、潮流等之)主流。②(河川之)主流。—*adj.* Dixieland 與現代爵士樂間之爵士樂的;搖滾音樂的。

main·street [ˈmenˌstrit; ˈmein-striːt] *v.i.* 〖美、加〗沿大街作競選活動。

***main·tain** [menˈten, mənˈten; menˈtein, mən-, mein-] *v.t.* ①保持;維持。Let's *maintain* peace in the world. 我們來維持世界和平吧。②贍養;供給。He has to *maintain* a family. 他要贍養家室。③堅持;主張;擁護。I *maintain* that military training should be given to all students. 我主張學生全體受軍訓。④保養(機器、道路等)。

main·tain·a·ble [menˈtenəbl; menˈteinəbl] *adj.* ①可保持的;可繼續的。②可維持的;可保存的。③可主張的。

***main·te·nance** [ˈmentənəns,-tɪn-; ˈmeintinəns, -tŋəns] *n.* ①保持;保有。*Maintenance* of quiet is necessary in a hospital. 醫院中須保持安靜。②支持;維持。A government collects taxes to pay for its *maintenance.* 政府抽稅以資維持。③贍養;生活費用。Her job provided a mere *maintenance.* 她的職業剛够餬口。④保養。⑤訴訟的非法援助。

main·top [ˈmenˌtɑp; ˈmeintɔp] *n.* 〖航海〗大桅樓。

main·top·gal·lant [ˈmentɑpˈgælənt; ˈmeintɔpˈgælənt] *n.* 〖航海〗大二接桅。

main·top·mast [ˌmenˈtɑpmæst; ˌmeinˈtɔpmɑːst] *n.* 〖航海〗大一接桅。

main·top·sail [ˌmenˈtɑpsel; ˌmeinˈtɔpseil] *n.* 〖航海〗大一接桅之帆;大中帆。

mai·so(n)·nette [ˌmezɔ̃ˈɛt; ˌmeizəˈnet] *n.* 〖主英〗①小屋。②公寓(尤指私人房屋出租做爲公寓者)。

maize [mez; meiz] *n.* ①玉蜀黍 (=Indian corn). ②黃色。—*adj.* 玉蜀黍色的;黃色的。

Maj. Major.

***ma·jes·tic** [məˈdʒɛstɪk; məˈdʒestik] *adj.* 莊嚴的; 高貴的; 宏大的。the *majestic* Alps. 氣勢宏偉的阿爾卑斯山。 —**al,** *adj.* —**al·ly,** *adv.*

***maj·es·ty** [ˈmædʒɪstɪ, ˈmædʒəstɪ; ˈmædʒisti, -dʒəs-] *n., pl.* **-ties.** ①高貴;莊嚴;威嚴。②最高權力;最高權威。Policemen and judges uphold the *majesty* of the law. 警察與法官維護法律無上的權力。 ③皇室人物;王族。 ④(M-) 陛下。Your (His, Her) *Majesty.* 陛下。

Maj. Gen. Major General.

ma·jol·i·ca [məˈdʒɑlɪkə; məˈjɔlikə] *n.* 原產於義大利之一種陶器。(亦作 **maiolica**)

‡ma·jor [ˈmedʒɚ; ˈmeidʒə] *adj.* ①(爲 minor 之對)較大的; 較多的; 主要的。The

M

major part of the town was ruined. 這城鎭的大部分都已成廢墟。②成年的。③(M-)較爲年長的（同姓學生）。Hobbes *Major* is not of a scientific bent. 年齡較大的Hobbes 對科學不感興趣。—*n.* ①成年人(年屆二十一歲者)。②(陸、空軍)少校。③主修課程;主科。④主修某科目或課程的學生。He is a history *major*. 他是主修歷史的學生。⑤〖音樂〗大調; 長調。The scale of C *major* has neither sharps nor flats. C大調之音階既無升調也無降調。⑥〖邏輯〗大前提。***the majors* =major leagues.** —*v.i.* 〖美〗主修。He *majored* in English. 他主修英文。

ma·jor-do·mo [ˈmedʒəˈdomo; ˈmeidʒəˈdoumou] *n., pl.* **-mos.** ①(王室貴族之)家臣;總管家。②管家;家僕。

major general (陸、空軍)少將。

Ma·jor·i·tar·i·an [ˌmədʒɔrəˈterɪən; ˌmədʒɔriˈtɛəriən] *n.* 〖美〗沉默的大多數(Silent Majority) 中之一員。

:ma·jor·i·ty [məˈdʒɔrətɪ, -dʒɑr-; məˈdʒɔriti, -rət-] *n., pl.* **-ties.** ①多數;大半(爲minority 之對)。The *majority* of people prefer peace to war. 大多數的人喜愛和平而不要戰爭。②(投票)超過之數;所多之票數。He was elected by a large *majority*. 他以大多數票當選。③多數黨。The Democratic Party is the *majority*. 民主黨是多數黨。④法定成年。He will reach his *majority* next year. 他下年將達法定成年。⑤陸、空軍少校之軍階。***join*** (***go***, or ***pass over to***) ***the*** (***great***) ***majority*** 死。

major key 〖音樂〗長調。

major league 〖美〗①二大職業棒球協會之一(指 American League 或 National League)。②第一流的。

major premise 〖邏輯〗大前提。

major scale 〖音樂〗長音階。

major suit 〖牌戲〗(橋牌中之)大牌(卽黑桃與紅心, 以其得分較高)。

ma·jus·cule [məˈdʒʌskjul; məˈdʒʌskjuːl] *n.* 大字(尤指古抄本中者)。—*adj.* 大字的;用大字寫的。

:make [mek; meik] *v.,* **made, mak·ing,** *n.* —*v.t.* ①做; 製造; 造成; 招致; 創造。to *make* a dress (a hat, a coat, etc.). 做一件衣服(一頂帽、一件上衣等)。②致使; 使之; 使做;使看來像。She will *make* him happy. 她將使他快樂。③迫使; 令; 導使。I can't *make* the horse go. 我無法使這馬走動。④成爲。She will *make* him a good wife. 她將成爲他的好妻子。⑤安排;整理。to *make* a fire. 生火。⑥得;賺。He *made* a profit of $500. 他賺了五百元。⑦〖俗〗管理;策動。⑧組成;等於;相等。Two and two *make* four. 二加二得四。⑨猜想; 估計; 計算。I *make* the distance across the river 150 feet. 我估計此河有150英尺寬。⑩到達; 抵。The ship *made* port. 船抵港。⑪走;旅行。The train *makes* 40 miles an hour. 這火車時速爲四十英里。⑫接通(電路)。⑬給與。I wish to *make* him a present. 我希望給他一件禮物。⑭被認爲是; 足够; 足以。One swallow does not *make* a summer. 一燕飛來不能認爲夏季已到。⑮〖俚〗使與之性交;引誘。⑯判斷;解釋〖常 of〗。What do you *make* of it? 你對此作何判斷(你對此有何意見)? ⑰保證成功。⑱發表;說出。to *make* a speech. 發表演說。⑲及時到達。to *make* the first show. 及時到達看第一場演出。⑳〖俗〗趕上(火車、飛機等)。If you hurry, you can *make* the next flight. 你如果趕快, 可以趕上下一次班機。㉑獲得榮譽;列入…。The novel *made* the list of the 50 best books of the year. 這本小說被列爲全年五十本最佳書籍之一。㉒立(契、遺囑等)。to *make* a will. 立遺囑。—*v.i.* ①走動; 進行; 向…移動。②(潮或船底水)漲起。③按指定的做。This toy stove *makes* easily. 這個玩具火爐很容易做。***make a difference*** (***to***) 有關係;重要(= be of importance). It doesn't *make any difference to* me. 這對我毫無關係。***make a fool of*** 愚弄。He *made a fool of* himself. 他自取愚弄(他自取嘲笑)。***make after*** 追求; 追趕。***make against*** 反對;不贊成。***make a go of*** 做成功。***make a hit*** 受歡迎。***make a killing*** 獲暴利。***make a match*** 使訂婚; 使結婚。***make a mistake*** 失誤〖常 in〗。***make a monkey out of*** 捉弄。***make an ass*** (***a fool, a beast***) ***of oneself*** 行動如傻瓜;行動愚蠢。***make a night of it*** 徹夜狂歡。***make a play for*** 想取得。***make a point of*** 强調;認爲重要。***make a scene*** 大鬧一番。***make as if*** (or ***though***) 假裝。***make a train*** 趕火車 (=to catch a train). ***make away with*** **a.** 偸。**b.** 殺死。He *made away with* himself. 他自殺了。**c.** 用完;消耗光。***make believe*** 假裝 (=pretend). ***make*** (***so***) ***bold*** 冒昧;膽敢。***make certain*** 確定;無疑;求出。***make do*** 以現有者爲滿足;將就使用。***make eyes at*** 拋媚眼;吊膀子。***make for*** **a.** 移向;走向。He *made for* the door and tried to escape. 他向門走去, 企圖逃跑。**b.** 傾向;導向。**c.** 攻擊。**d.** 促進;有助於…。***make free with*** 盡情用。***make friends with*** 與…交友;親睦。***make good*** **a.** 賠償。The bank teller *made good* the shortage and was given a light sentence. 該銀行出納員將短少的公款賠出來, 而蒙從輕發落。**b.** 成功。**c.** 實現。***make hay while the sun shines*** 善用有利機會。***make head or tail of*** 徹底了解。***make headway*** 前進;進步。***make it*** 〖俗〗**a.** 達成某項特定目標。to *make it* to the train. 趕上火車。**b.** 成功。***make love to*** 向…求愛。***make merry*** 作樂。***make money*** 賺錢。***make much of*** **a.** 特別强調。**b.** 從…獲得很多利益。***make no bones about*** 坦率而言。***make of*** 獲得結論;推論;解釋。***make off*** **a.** 跑開; 匆匆離開。**b.** 〖航海〗離開海岸。***make off with*** 偸。***make oneself at home*** 覺得如在自己家裏一般; 隨便; 不拘束。***make one's own*** 當作自己的看待。***make one's way*** 往前跑;跑上前;前進。***make or break*** 使成功或失敗。***make or mar*** 使成功或失敗。***make out*** **a.** 做;成功。**b.** 分辨;證明。**c.** 寫(支票、帳目等)。**d.** 了解;解釋。**e.** 假裝。**f.** 湊足;完成 (參看 **make up**)。**g.** 〖美俗〗進展。***make over*** **a.** 更正;修改(衣服等)。**b.** 正式轉讓。***make sense*** 合理。***make sure*** **a.** 確信; 無疑 (=make certain). **b.** 查明;弄清。***make the most*** (or ***best***) ***of*** **a.** 善爲利用 (=take advantage of). He *makes the most of* the little he has. 他善爲利用自己所有的那一點。**b.** 相處。***make time*** **a.** 趕緊。**b.** 以某種特定速度旅行。**c.** 〖俚〗追求女人; 與女人發生愛情。***make up*** **a.** 組成; 形成。The committee is *made up* of seven members. 委員會由七人組成。**b.** 虛構;捏造。**c.** 和解; 復交。**d.**

化妝;化裝;塗脂粉。e. 整理(被褥)。f. 準備;製造。g. 完成。h. 重修;補考。i. 補償;彌補。His intelligence *made up* for his lack of personal charm.他的智慧彌補了他的缺乏容貌之美。***make up for*** 補償;賠償。***make up one's mind*** 決心;拿定主意。***make up to*** 獻媚以得寵。***make way for*** 爲…開路;爲…清街。***make with*** 〖俚〗 a. 運用;操作。Let's *make with* the feet. 我們步行罷。b. 促成;產生。He *makes with* the big ideas, but can't follow through on them. 他老是出大主意,但不能實施。—*n.* ①製造方法。Is this your own *make?* 這是你自己做的嗎? ②樣式;牌子。His shirt is of American *make.* 他的襯衫是美國貨。③性質;性格。④製造之量。⑤接通電路。***on the make*** 〖俗〗 a. 急求成功;急求得益。b. 損人利己以求聞達。c. 增加;前進。d. 野合。〖注意〗(1) **made of** 與 **made from** 用法不同。通常原料被製成物品後仍具原質者,用 **of**: The desk is *made of* wood. 這桌子是木頭做的。已失原質者用 **from**: Paper is *made from* rags. 紙是破布做的。(2)**make** 作 *v.t.* ③解時,其後之不定式略去 **to.** 但在被動式中,則 **to** 不能省。

make-be·lieve [ˈmekbəˌliv; ˈmeikbiˌliːv] *n.* ①假裝;虛構。②假裝者。—*adj.* 假裝的。*make-believe* sleep. 假睡。

make-peace [ˈmekˌpis; ˈmeikpiːs] *n.* =**peacemaker.**

*__mak·er__ [ˈmekɚ; ˈmeikə] *n.* ①製造者(主要用於複合字)。an auto-*maker.* 汽車製造商。②(M-)上帝。our *Maker.* 造物主。③〖法律〗出期票人;立借據人。④(橋牌等)首先開王牌而叫成合約的人;主打的人。***go to*** (or ***meet***) ***one's Maker*** 死。

make·shift [ˈmekˌʃɪft; ˈmeikʃift] *n.* ①暫用代替物。②權宜之計。—*adj.* (亦作 **makeshifty**) ①暫時代替的。②權宜的。

*__make-up__ [ˈmekˌʌp; ˈmeikʌp] *n.* ①天性;性格。②化妝品(脂粉等);化裝。That woman uses too much *make-up.* 那女人塗了太多的脂粉。③組織;組成;組成的方法。④〖印刷〗排版;整版。⑤(報紙的)版面。⑥(演員之)扮相。⑦身體或心理組織。the *make-up* of an athlete. 運動選手的體格。⑧重修;補考。Why didn't you come and take the *make-up* exam? 你爲何不來參加補考? (亦作 **makeup**)

make·weight [ˈmekˌwet; ˈmeikweit] *n.* ①補足重量之物;添補物。②填補缺欠的人或物。

mak·ing [ˈmekɪŋ; ˈmeikiŋ] *n.* ①成功之因素。Early hardships were the *making* of him. 早期的困苦是使他成功的因素。②(*pl.*)所需之材料。the *makings* of a house. 房子所需的材料。③(常 *pl.*)所需之性質。④製成之物。⑤一次所產之量。⑥製作者;製作。⑦構造;組織。⑧(*pl.*)〖美俚〗製香煙用的紙和煙草。***in the making*** 製作中;尚未完成;醞釀中;發展中;成長中。

Mal. ①Malachi. ②Malay. ③Malayan.

mal- 〖字首〗表"壞;錯誤;不好"之義,如:maltreat.

Ma·lac·ca [məˈlækə; məˈlækə] *n.* 麻六甲(前馬來亞聯邦南部之殖民地,又該地之首府)。—**Ma·lac·can,** *adj.*

Malacca, Strait of *n.* 麻六甲海峽(在馬來半島與蘇門達臘間)。

Malacca cane(用棕櫚樹幹做的)麻六甲手杖。

Mal·a·chi [ˈmæləˌkaɪ; ˈmæləkai] *n.* ①瑪拉基(紀元前5世紀猶太之先知)。②瑪拉基書(舊約聖經之一卷)。

mal·a·chite [ˈmæləˌkaɪt; ˈmæləkait] *n.* 〖礦〗孔雀石。

mal·a·co·derm [ˈmæləkədɚm; ˈmæləkədəm] *n.* 〖動物〗軟皮動物;(特指)海葵。

mal·a·col·o·gy [ˌmæləˈkɑlədʒɪ; ˌmæləˈkɔlədʒi] *n.* 〖動物〗軟體動物學。

mal·ad·just·ed [ˌmæləˈdʒʌstɪd; ˈmæləˈdʒʌstid] *adj.* ①處置不善的。②失調的。

mal·ad·just·ment [ˌmæləˈdʒʌstmənt; ˈmæləˈdʒʌstmənt] *n.* 調節不善;整理不善;不適應;失調。

mal·ad·min·is·ter [ˌmælədˈmɪnəstɚ; ˌmælədˈministə] *v.t.* 胡亂處理(公務、政事等);瞎搞;胡搞。

mal·ad·min·is·tra·tion [ˌmælədˌmɪnəˈstreʃən; ˈmælədˌminisˈtreiʃən] *n.* 惡政;亂政;(公務、公事之)處理不善;管理不善;紊亂。

mal·a·droit [ˌmæləˈdrɔɪt; ˌmæləˈdrɔit] *adj.* 笨拙的;拙劣的;愚鈍的。—**ly,** *adv.*

mal·a·dy [ˈmælədɪ; ˈmælədi] *n., pl.* **-dies.** ①疾病。It is a deadly *malady.* 此爲致命之疾。②混亂;道德上之缺點。social *maladies.* 社會上的弊病。

ma·la fi·de [ˈmeləˈfaɪdɪ; ˈmeiləˈfaidi] 〖拉〗不誠實地(的);惡意地(的)(=in bad faith).

Má·la·ga [ˈmæləgə; ˈmæləgə] *n.*馬拉加(西班牙南部之一海港)。

Mal·a·ga [ˈmæləgə; ˈmæləgə] *n.* ①西班牙 Málaga 產之白葡萄酒。②加利福尼亞與西班牙產的一種白葡萄。

Mal·a·gas·y [ˌmæləˈgæsɪ; ˌmæləˈgæsi] *n.* ①馬拉加西共和國(參看 **Madagascar**). ②馬拉加西人;馬達加斯加島人。③馬拉加西語。—*adj.* 馬拉加西人(語)的。

ma·la·gue·na [ˌmæləˈgenjə; ˌmæləˈgeinjə] 〖西班牙〗 *n.* 西班牙 Málaga 的舞蹈;其舞曲。

ma·laise [mæˈlez; mæˈleiz] *n.* (病初發時)不舒服;抑鬱。

ma·la·mute [ˈmɑləˌmjut; ˈmɑːləmjuːt] *n.* 一種阿拉斯加的拖橇犬(體粗壯、呈黑白色)。(亦作 **malemute**)

mal·a·pert [ˈmæləˌpɝt; ˈmæləpəːt] *adj.* 〖古〗無禮的;魯莽的。—*n.* 〖古〗無禮的人;魯莽的人。—**ly,** *adv.* —**ness,** *n.*

Mal·a·prop, Mrs. [ˈmæləˌprɑp; ˈmæləprɔp] *n.* Sheridan 喜劇 *The Rivals* 之劇中人(以其誤用文字著名)。

mal·a·prop·ism [ˈmæləprɑpˌɪzəm; ˈmæləprɔpizəm] *n.* ①字之怪誕的誤用。②被誤用之字。

mal·ap·ro·pos [ˌmælæprəˈpo; ˈmælˈæprəpou] *adv.* & *adj.* 不合時地(的);不適當地(的)。—*n.* 不合時宜。

ma·lar [ˈmelɚ; ˈmeilə] *adj.* 〖解剖〗頰的;顴骨的。—*n.* 顴骨(=malar bone).

*__ma·lar·i·a__ [məˈlɛrɪə; məˈlɛəriə] *n.* ①〖醫〗瘧疾。②瘴氣。—**ma·lar·i·an,** *adj.*

ma·lar·i·al [məˈlɛrɪəl; məˈlɛəriəl] *adj.* ①(患)瘧疾的。②(有)瘴氣的。

ma·lar·i·ol·o·gy [məˌlɛrɪˈɑlədʒɪ; məˌlɛəriˈɔlədʒi] *n.* 瘧疾之研究。

ma·lar·key, ma·lar·ky [məˈlɑrkɪ; məˈlɑːki] *n.* 〖美俚〗無聊話;胡說;夢話。

mal·a·thi·on [ˌmæləˈθaɪɑn; ˌmæləˈθaiɔn] *n.* 馬拉松(一種農藥)。

Ma·la·wi [mɑˈlɑwi; mɑːˈlɑːwiː] *n.* 馬拉威(南非一國,首都 Lilongwe).

Ma·lay [məˈle; məˈlei] *n., adj.* =**Malayan.**

Ma·lay·a [mə'leə; mə'leiə] *n.* ①馬來半島。②馬來聯邦 (Federation of, 首都爲吉隆坡 Kuala Lumpur)。
Ma·lay·an [mə'leən; mə'leiən] *n.* 馬來人(語)。—*adj.* 馬來半島的;馬來人(語)的。
Ma·lay·sia [mə'leʒə; mə'leiʒə] *n.* ①馬來羣島。②馬來西亞(1963年獨立之一聯邦國家,由馬來亞、新加坡、沙撈越、及北婆羅洲聯合組成,首都吉隆坡 Kuala Lumpur;新加坡於1965年退出聯邦而獨立)。
Ma·lay·sian [mə'leʃən; mə'leiʃən] *n.* 馬來西亞人。—*adj.* 馬來西亞(人)的。
mal·con·tent ['mælkən,tɛnt; 'mælkən,tent] *adj.* 不滿的;反抗(時政)的。—*n.* ①不滿者;反叛者。②不滿。
mal de mer [maldə'mɛːr; maldə'mɛːr] 〖法〗暈船。
*__male__ [mel; meil] *n.* 男人;男孩;雄性動物。—*adj.* ①屬於男性或雄性的。a *male* choir. 男聲合唱團。②男性的;雄性的。③〖植物〗有雄蕊的。④〖機械〗陽的。*male* screw. 陽螺釘;陽螺旋。⑤有力的;精力超人的。
male- 〖字首〗=**mal-**.
male chauvinism 過分的男性優越感。
male chau·vin·ist [~'ʃovɪnɪst; ~'ʃouvinist] 表現男性優越感的人。
mal·e·dic·tion [,mælə'dɪkʃən; ,mæli'dikʃən] *n.* ①詛咒。②誹謗。—**mal·e·dic·tive, mal·e·dic·to·ry,** *adj.*
mal·e·fac·tion [,mælə'fækʃən; ,mæli'fækʃən] *n.* 罪行;罪惡;犯罪。
mal·e·fac·tor ['mælə,fæktɚ; 'mælifæktə] *n.* 罪犯;作惡者。
mal·e·fac·tress ['mælə,fæktrɪs; 'mælifæktris] *n.* malefactor 之女性。
ma·lef·ic [mə'lɛfɪk; mə'lefik] *adj.* (魔術或星象)爲害的;有害的;邪惡的。—*n.* 〖占星〗凶星。
ma·lef·i·cence [mə'lɛfəsn̩s; mə'lefisns] *n.* 有害;罪行;惡行。
ma·lef·i·cent [mə'lɛfəsn̩t; mə'lefisnt] *adj.* 有害的;傷害的;邪惡的;罪行的。
ma·lev·o·lence [mə'lɛvələns; mə'levələns] *n.* 惡意;敵意;惡毒;怨恨。
ma·lev·o·lent [mə'lɛvələnt; mə'levələnt] *adj.* 惡意的;惡毒的。—**ly,** *adv.*
mal·fea·sance [,mæl'fizn̩s; mæl'fiːzəns] *n.* ①惡行;惡事。②瀆職。
mal·fea·sant [,mæl'fizn̩t; mæl'fiːzənt] *adj.* ①爲惡的;邪惡的。②不法的;犯罪的。—*n.* 做不法行爲的人。
mal·for·ma·tion [,mælfɔr'meʃən; 'mælfɔː'meiʃən] *n.* 畸形。
mal·formed [mæl'fɔrmd; mæl'fɔːmd] *adj.* 畸形的。
Ma·li ['mɑlɪ; 'mɑːli] *n.* 馬利(非洲西部一共和國,首都 Bamako)。
mal·ic acid ['mælɪk~; 'mælik~] 〖化〗蘋果酸($C_2H_3OH(COOH)_2$)。
*__mal·ice__ ['mælɪs; 'mælis] *n.* ①惡意;惡毒;怨恨。He did it through *malice.* 他做此事出自惡意。②蓄意;預謀。to bear *malice* to (towards) somebody. 對某人懷惡意。
malice aforethought 〖法律〗蓄意(殺人等)。
*__ma·li·cious__ [mə'lɪʃəs; mə'liʃəs] *adj.* 懷惡意的;心毒的。a *malicious* remark. 懷惡意的言語。—**ly,** *adv.* —**ness,** *n.*
ma·lign [mə'laɪn; mə'lain] *v.t.* 詆毀;誹謗。—*adj.* ①邪惡的;有害的。②怨恨的;懷惡意的。③極有害的;致命的。—**ly,** *adv.*
ma·lig·nan·cy [mə'lɪgnənsɪ; mə'lignənsi] *n.* ①(極度之)惡意;敵意;惡毒。②(疾病之)惡性。③不祥。(亦作 **malignance**)
ma·lig·nant [mə'lɪgnənt; mə'lignənt] *adj.* ①懷惡意的;惡毒的。②有害的。③惡性的;致死的。a *malignant* cancer. 惡性癌。—**ly,** *adv.*
ma·lign·er [mə'laɪnɚ; mə'lainə] *n.* 誹謗者;中傷者。
ma·lig·ni·ty [mə'lɪgnətɪ; mə'ligniti] *n., pl.* **-ties.** ①極大之惡意(憎恨)。②(常 *pl.*)惡意之行動、感情等。③(病之)惡性。
ma·lines [mə'lin; mə'liːn] *n.* (女服或面紗用之)一種細絲網。
ma·lin·ger [mə'lɪŋgɚ; mə'liŋgə] *v.i.* 裝病以逃避職務;裝病以獲取救濟物。—**y,** *n.*
ma·lin·ger·er [mə'lɪŋgərɚ; mə'liŋgərə] *n.* 裝病以逃避責任者;裝病之士兵。
ma·lism ['melɪzəm; 'meilizəm] *n.* 現世邪惡優勢說。
mal·i·son ['mæləzn̩; 'mælizn] *n.* ①〖古〗咒詛。②〖英方〗殘酷的人;無情的人。
mall [mɔl; mɔːl] *n.* ①樹蔭路。②pall-mall 遊戲;pall-mall 遊戲之場所;pall-mall 用之木槌。—*v.t.* =**maul.**
mal·lard ['mæləd; 'mæləd] *n., pl.* **-lards, -lard.** 野鴨。
mal·le·a·bil·i·ty [,mælɪə'bɪlətɪ; ,mæliə'biliti] *n.* ①可鍛性;可展性。②適應性。
mal·le·a·ble ['mælɪəbl; 'mæliəbl] *adj.* ①(金屬之)可鍛的;可鎚薄的。②(人性之)能適應的。—**ness,** *n.*
mal·let ['mælɪt; 'mælit] *n.* ①木槌。②(曲棍球或馬球之)球棍。
mal·le·us ['mælɪəs; 'mæliəs] *n., pl.* **-le·i** [-lɪ,aɪ; -liai]. 〖解剖〗(中耳的)鎚骨。
mal·low ['mælo; 'mælou] *n.* 〖植物〗錦葵;錦葵屬植物。
malm·sey ['mɑmzɪ; 'mɑːmzi] *n.* 一種甘芳的白葡萄酒。
mal·nu·tri·tion [,mælnju'trɪʃən; 'mælnju(ː)'triʃən] *n.* 營養不足。
mal·o·dor [mæl'odɚ; mæ'loudə] *n.* 惡臭。
mal·o·dor·ous [mæl'odərəs; mæ'loudərəs] *adj.* 有惡臭的。—**ly,** *adv.* —**ness,** *n.*
mal·po·si·tion [,mælpə'zɪʃən; ,mælpə'ziʃən] *n.* ①位置不正。②〖醫〗胎位不正。
mal·prac·tice [mæl'præktɪs; 'mæl'præktis] *n.* ①〖醫〗不當療法。②瀆職;怠忽職務;不當之行爲。
malt [mɔlt; mɔːlt] *n.* ①麥芽。*malt* liquor. 麥芽酒(啤酒之一種)。*malt* sugar. 麥芽糖。②啤酒。③威士忌。—*v.t.* ①以麥芽釀造。②使成麥芽。—*v.i.* 變成麥芽。
Mal·ta ['mɔltə; 'mɔːltə] *n.* 馬爾他(地中海中之島國,位於西西里之南,首都Valletta)。
Malta fever 〖醫〗馬爾他熱。(亦作**Maltese fever**)
Mal·tese [mɔl'tiz; 'mɔːl'tiːz] *adj.* 馬爾他島的;馬爾他島居民的;馬爾他島語言的。—*n.* ①馬爾他島人或居民。②馬爾他島上所說之阿拉伯方言。③馬爾他島之貓。④馬爾他狗(一種長毛白色小狗重約二至七磅)。
mal·tha ['mælθə; 'mælθə] *n.* 軟瀝青。
malt·house ['mɔlt,haus; 'mɔːlthaus] *n.* 麥芽製造所。
Mal·thus ['mælθəs; 'mælθəs] *n.* 馬爾薩斯 (Thomas Robert, 1766–1834, 英國經濟學家,"人口論"作者)。
Mal·thu·si·an [mæl'θjuzɪən; mæl'θjuːziən] *adj.* 馬爾薩斯人口論的。—*n.* 馬爾薩斯主義者。
mal·thu·si·an·ism [mæl'θjuzɪənɪzm;

mælˈθjuːziənizəm] *n.* 馬爾薩斯主義(學說); 馬爾薩斯人口論。

malt·ose [ˈmɔltos; ˈmɔːltous] *n.* 〖化〗麥芽糖($C_{12}H_{22}O_{11}H_2O$)。

mal·treat [mælˈtrit; mælˈtriːt] *v.t.* 虐待。—**ment,** *n.*

malt·ster [ˈmɔltˌstə; ˈmɔːltstə] *n.* 麥芽製造人或販賣人。

malt·y [ˈmɔltɪ; ˈmɔːlti] *adj.*, **malt·i·er, malt·i·est.** ①(如)麥芽的。②〖謔〗嗜麥芽酒的。③〖俚〗醉的。

mal·va·ceous [mælˈveʃəs; mælˈveiʃəs] *adj.* 〖植物〗錦葵科的。

mal·ver·sa·tion [ˌmælvəˈseʃən; ˌmælvəːˈseiʃən] *n.* (公務員之)不法行爲;貪污;瀆職;受賄。

***ma·ma** [ˈmɑmə; məˈmɑː, ˈmɑːmə] *n.* 媽媽。

mam·bo [ˈmɑmbo; ˈmɑːmbou] *n., pl.* **-bos,** *v.* —*n.* 曼波(舞)。—*v.i.* 跳曼波。

mam·e·luke [ˈmæməˌluk; ˈmæmiluːk] *n.* ①(回教國家之)奴隸。②(M-) 1250-1517統治埃及的軍人之一。

***mam·ma**[1] [ˈmɑmə; məˈmɑː] *n.* ①媽媽。②〖俚〗性感的成熟女人。

mam·ma[2] [ˈmæmə; ˈmæmə] *n., pl.* **mam·mae** [ˈmæmi; ˈmæmiː]. ①乳房。②(作 *pl.* 解)〖氣象〗乳房狀雲。

***mam·mal** [ˈmæml; ˈmæməl] *n.* 哺乳動物。Human beings, horses, dogs, lions, rats, and whales are all *mammals*. 人、馬、狗、獅、鼠及鯨魚都是哺乳動物。

Mam·ma·li·a [mæˈmelɪə; mæˈmeiljə] *n. pl.* 〖動物〗哺乳類;哺乳動物。

mam·ma·li·an [mæˈmelɪən; mæˈmeiljən] *adj.* 哺乳類的。—*n.* 哺乳動物。

mam·mal·o·gy [mæˈmælədʒɪ; mæˈmælədʒi] *n.* 哺乳動物學。—**mam·ma·log·i·cal,** *adj.* —**mam·mal·o·gist,** *n.*

mam·ma·ry [ˈmæmərɪ; ˈmæməri] *adj.* ①乳房的; 乳腺的。the *mammary* gland. 〖解剖〗乳腺。*mammary* cancer. 〖醫〗乳癌。②乳房狀的。

mam·mee [mæˈmi; mæˈmiː] *n.* 〖植物〗馬米樹(熱帶美洲產);其果實。

mam·mif·er·ous [mæˈmɪfərəs; mæˈmifərəs] *adj.* 有乳房的; 哺乳動物的。

mam·mil·la, ma·mil·la [mæˈmɪlə; mæˈmilə] *n., pl.* **-mil·lae** [-ˈmɪli; -ˈmiliː]. 〖解剖〗①乳頭。②乳頭狀器官。

Mam·mon, mam·mon [ˈmæmən; ˈmæmən] *n.* ①財神。②財富(被視爲有壞影響)。③貪財。—**ish,** *adj.*

mam·mon·ism [ˈmæmənɪzm; ˈmæmənizm] *n.* 拜金主義; 金錢萬能主義。

mam·mon·ist [ˈmæmənɪst; ˈmæmənist] *n.* 拜金主義者; 金錢萬能主義者。(亦作 **mammonite**) —**ic,** *adj.*

mam·moth [ˈmæməθ; ˈmæməθ] *n.* 已絕種的一種巨象。—*adj.* 龐大的。

mam·my [ˈmæmɪ; ˈmæmi] *n.* ①媽媽; 母親(小兒語)。②〖美俗〗美國白人所雇用之黑人褓姆(尤指美國南部者)。

‡man [mæn; mæn] *n., pl.* **men,** *v.,* **manned, man·ning,** *interj.* —*n.* ①男子。②人(泛指); 人類。*Man* is mortal. 人皆會死。③男僕; 男雇員; 臣。Like master, like *man*. 有其主必有其僕;有其君必有其臣。④丈夫。*man* and wife. 夫妻。⑤兵士。the officers and *men* of an army. 一軍的軍官與士兵。⑥男子漢;大丈夫。Be a *man!* 要做一個大丈夫(勿失男子氣)! ⑦呼人之辭。Hurry up, *man!* 趕快, 趕快! ⑧一顆棋子。⑨所需的人。If you want a good music teacher, here's your *man*. 如你需要一位良好的音樂教師,這便是你所需的人。⑩人(作複合詞, 如 postman. 郵差等)。***act the man*** 勇敢起來。***as a man*** 從人的觀點而言。***as one man*** 一致。***be one's own man*** **a.** 行動自由;爲所欲爲;自主。 **b.** 身心健全。***man and boy*** 從小到大。***my good man*** 對部下的客氣稱呼。***one's man of business*** 某人的代理人或律師。***the man***〖俚〗老板(尤指黑人說他的白人老板)。***to a man*** 一致;皆;諸(=as one man). They all answered "yes" *to a man*. 衆皆答是。***to the last man*** 一致; 毫無例外。—*v.t.* ①備以人員; 供以人員。We can *man* ten ships. 我們可供人員配備十隻船。②使堅强; 振作精神。to *man* oneself for dangers ahead. 振作精神對付未來的危險。③操作; 看守; 堅守崗位。They need more soldiers to *man* the front. 他們需要更多的兵士來守衛前線。—*interj.* 表示驚訝, 熱衷的感嘆詞。*Man!* Listen to him blow that horn! 棒啊! 聽他喇叭吹得多好!

man. manual.

-man 〖字尾〗①表"…國人;…之居民"之義, 如: Englishman. ②表示職業, 如: clergyman. ③表"船 (ship)" 之義, 如: Indiaman. 〖注意〗**-man** 的複數形爲 **-men,** 通常無論單複數形發音皆爲 [-mən; -mən], 但故意或表特殊意義時, 單數形發音爲 [-mæn; -mæn], 複數形發音爲 [-men; -men].

Man, Isle of [mæn; mæn] *n.* 曼島(在愛爾蘭海中, 屬英)。

man-a·bout-town [ˈmænəbaʊtˈtaʊn; ˈmænəbautˈtaun] *n., pl.* **men-a·bout-town.** 經常出沒於遊樂場所的人。(亦作 **man about town**)

man·a·cle [ˈmænəkl; ˈmænəkl] *n., v.,* **-cled, -cling.** —*n.* ①(常 *pl.*) 手銬。②束縛;約束。—*v.t.* ①上手銬。②束縛;妨礙。

‡man·age [ˈmænɪdʒ; ˈmænidʒ] *v.,* **-aged, -ag·ing.** —*v.t.* ①處理;支配;駕馭。to *manage* a horse (a car, a shop, a business, etc.). 馭馬(駛車, 經理店鋪, 經營事業等)。②完成;達成。We finally *managed* to get there in time. 最後我們及時趕到了。③〖俗〗吃。Can you *manage* another slice of cake? 你能再吃一片餅嗎? —*v.i.* ①辦事;處理事務。We can't *manage* with these poor tools. 我們無法用這些壞工具做工。②生活; 過活。to *manage* on one's income. 靠自己的薪俸生活。③撐住;維持。How will she *manage* with her husband gone? 她丈夫走了她如何維持?

man·age·a·bil·i·ty [ˌmænɪdʒəˈbɪlətɪ; ˌmænidʒəˈbiliti] *n.* ①可管理, 可處理性。②溫順;馴良。

man·age·a·ble [ˈmænɪdʒəbl; ˈmænidʒəbl] *adj.* ①可管理的;可處理的。②溫順的。

***man·age·ment** [ˈmænɪdʒmənt; ˈmænidʒmənt] *n.* ①經營;支配;處理;管理。Bad *management* caused the failure. 經營不善招致失敗。②經理;管理人員。③手段;技巧。④資方(以別於勞工階級)。—**al,** *adj.*

management consultant (公司行號聘請的)業務顧問。

***man·ag·er** [ˈmænɪdʒə; ˈmænidʒə] *n.* ①經理。general *manager*. 總經理。②管理業務者;管家務者(通常均有形容詞置於其前)。My wife is an excellent *manager*. 我太

M

太是個很好的管家。③經紀人。

man·ag·er·ess 〔'mænɪdʒərɪs; 'mænidʒəres〕 *n.* 女經理;女管理人;女幹事。

man·a·ge·ri·al 〔ˌmænə'dʒɪrɪəl; ˌmænə'dʒiəriəl〕 *adj.* ①經理的;管理者的。②經營(上)的;管理(上)的。—**ly,** *adv.*

man·ag·er·ship 〔'mænɪdʒɚˌʃɪp; 'mænidʒəʃip〕 *n.* manager 之職位或權力。

man·ag·ing 〔'mænɪdʒɪŋ; 'mænidʒiŋ〕 *adj.* ①管理的;經營的;主腦的。a *managing* director. 總經理; 常務董事。 a *managing* editor. 總編輯。 ②善經營的。③愛管事的;愛管閒事的。*a managing* woman. 愛管閒事的女人。④節儉的;吝嗇的。

man·a·kin 〔'mænəkɪn; 'mænəkin〕 *n.* ①(中南美產之) 燕雀類小鳥。②=**manikin.**

man-at-arms 〔'mænət'ɑrmz;'mænət'ɑ:mz〕 *n., pl.* **men-at-arms.** ①士兵。②中世紀之重騎兵。

man·a·tee 〔ˌmænə'ti; ˌmænə'ti:〕 *n.* 〖動物〗海牛。

Man·ches·ter 〔'mænˌtʃɛstɚ; 'mæntʃistə〕 *n.* ①曼徹斯特 (英格蘭西北部之一城市,為紡織業中心)。 ②曼徹斯特(美國 New Hampshire 州南部之一城市)。 ③曼徹斯特(美國 Connecticut 州中北部之一城市)。

man·chet 〔'mæntʃɛt; 'mæntʃet〕 *n.* 〖古,英方〗(上等麪粉製成的) 白麪包。

man-child 〔'mænˌtʃaɪld; 'mæntʃaild〕 *n., pl.* **men-chil·dren.** 男孩;兒子。

Man·chu 〔mæn'tʃu; mæn'tʃu:〕 *n.* ① 中國的滿族人。 ② 滿族人所通用之通古斯 (Tungus) 語言。—*adj.* 滿族人(語)的。

Man·chu·ri·a 〔mæn'tʃurɪə; mæn'tʃuəriə〕 *n.* 中國東北部;東北九省。

Man·chu·ri·an 〔mæn'tʃurɪən; mæn'tʃuəriən〕 *adj.* (中國之) 東北九省(人)的。—*n.* 東北(九省)人。

man·ci·ple 〔'mænsəpl; 'mænsipl〕 *n.* (大學、寺院等之) 伙食管理員。

Man·cu·ni·an 〔mæn'kjunɪən; mæŋ'kju:niən〕 *adj.* 英國 Manchester 城的。—*n.* 英國 Manchester 城人。

man·da·mus 〔mæn'deməs; mæn'deiməs〕 *n.* 〖法律〗(上級法院給下級法院或官吏的)執行令;命令書。—*v.t.* 〖俗〗送達上項執行令;以上項執行令威脅。

Man·da·rin 〔'mændərɪn; 'mændərin〕 *n.* ①(m-) 滿清官吏。②中國官話;國語。③(m-)橘。—*adj.* (m-) 官僚的;保守的;知識分子的。

mandarin duck 鴛鴦。

mandarin orange 橘。

man·da·tar·y 〔'mændəˌtɛrɪ; 'mændətəri〕 *n., pl.* **-tar·ies.** ①〖法律〗受託者;代理者。②奉命者;奉旨者。③受任託管之國家。(亦作 **mandatory**)

man·date 〔*n.* 'mændet, -dɪt; 'mændeit, -dit *v.* 'mændet; 'mændeit〕 *n., v.,* **-dat·ed, -dat·ing.** —*n.* ①命令; 訓令。②選民對議員或公職人員之要求或授權。③委託統治權。④委託統治地;託管地。⑤(民法) 委任;委託。—*v.t.* 將(某地)委託統治;託管。

man·da·to·ry 〔'mændəˌtorɪ; 'mændətəri〕 *adj., n., pl.* **-ries.** —*adj.* ①(含有)命令的。②〖法律〗無選擇自由的。③受委託統治的。④强迫性的。—*n.* 受委託統治的國家。

man-day 〔'mæn'de; 'mæn'dei〕 *n., pl.* **man-days.** 一人一天所做之工作量;工作日。

man·di·ble 〔'mændəbl; 'mændibl〕 *n.* 〖解剖, 動物〗①(哺乳動物、魚類等之) 顎;(特指) 下顎;下顎骨。②鳥嘴之上部或下部。③(昆蟲之)大顎。 —**man·dib·u·lar, man·dib·u·late,** *adj.*

man·do·la 〔mæn'dolə; mæn'doulə〕 *n.* =**mandora.**

***man·do·lin, man·do·line** 〔'mændḷˌɪn, ˌmændḷ'ɪn; 'mændəlin, ˌmændə'li:n〕 *n.* 曼陀林 (樂器)。 —**man·do·lin·ist,** *n.*

man·do·ra 〔mæn'dorə; mæn'dourə〕 *n.* 大曼陀林 (樂器之一種)。

man·drag·o·ra 〔mæn'drægərə; mæn'drægərə〕 *n.* =**mandrake.**

man·drake 〔'mændrɪk; 'mændreik〕 *n.* 〖植物〗曼陀羅花(可用以製藥)。

man·drel, man·dril 〔'mændrəl; 'mændrəl〕 *n.* 〖機械〗心軸;心棒;靜軸。

man·drill 〔'mændrɪl; 'mændril〕 *n.* 大狒狒(產於西非洲)。

***mane** 〔men; mein〕 *n.* ①鬃。②長而厚的頭髮。 *make neither mane nor tail of* 完全不知道。—**less,** *adj.*

man-eat·er 〔'mænˌitɚ; 'mænˌi:tə〕 *n.* ①食人動物。②食人之野蠻種族。③一種大鯊魚。

man-eat·ing 〔'mænˌitɪŋ; 'mænˌi:tiŋ〕 *adj.* 食人的。

ma·nège, ma·nege 〔mæ'nɛʒ; mæ'neiʒ〕 *n.* ①訓馬(術); 馬術。 ②受過調教之馬的動作及步調。③馬術學校。

ma·nes 〔'meniz; 'meini:z〕 *n. pl.* ①(古羅馬)祖先之靈魂。② (作 *sing.* 解)亡魂。

***ma·neu·ver** 〔mə'nuvɚ; mə'nu:və〕 *n., v.,* **-vered, -ver·ing.** —*n.* ①(軍隊或艦隊之)調遣;換防。②(*pl.*) 演習。The grand *maneuvers* will be held tomorrow. 大演習將於明日舉行。③策略;巧計。—*v.t.* ①調遣。②計誘。to *maneuver* the enemy into (out of) position. 誘敵深入 (離開) 某地。③操縱。—*v.i.* ①演習。②用計策。A scheming person is always *maneuvering* for some advantage. 一個有陰謀的人總是設計討便宜。(亦作 **manoeuvre**) —**er,** —**a·bil·i·ty,** *n.* —**a·ble,** *adj.*

man Friday ①Defoe 所著 "魯濱遜漂流記"中魯濱遜之忠心僕人。②忠僕;從者。

man·ful 〔'mænfəl; 'mænful〕 *adj.* 剛毅的;決斷的;有丈夫氣的。—**ly,** *adv.*

man·ga·nese 〔'mæŋgəˌnis; ˌmæŋgə'ni:z〕 *n.* 〖化〗錳 (化學符號爲 Mn)。

man·gan·ic 〔mæn'gænɪk; mæŋ'gænik〕 *adj.* 〖化〗(含) 錳的;含三價錳的;錳化合物的。

mange 〔mendʒ; meindʒ〕 *n.* 畜疥;獸疥 (家畜等所患之疥癬)。

man·gel-wur·zel 〔'mæŋgḷ'wɝzḷ; 'mæŋgl'wə:zl〕 *n.* 〖植物〗一種飼牛用的甜菜。(亦作 **mangoldwurzel**)

***man·ger** 〔'mendʒɚ; 'meindʒə〕 *n.* ①牛或馬食草用之槽。 ②〖航海〗船首的擋水板。 *dog in the manger* 狗占馬槽。

man·gle[1] 〔'mæŋgḷ; 'mæŋgl〕 *v.t.,* **-gled, -gling.** ①將(皮肉)撕裂。②(因錯誤而)傷害;損壞。—**man·gler,** *n.*

man·gle[2] *n., v.,* **-gled, -gling.** —*n.* 軋布機;軋光機。—*v.t.* 以軋光機軋光。

man·go 〔'mæŋgo; 'mæŋgou〕 *n., pl.* **-goes, -gos.** 芒果; 芒果樹。

man·gold-wur·zel 〔'mæŋgəld'wɝzḷ; 'mæŋgəld'wə:zl〕 *n.* =**mangel-wurzel.**

man·go·nel 〔'mæŋgəˌnɛl; 'mæŋgənel〕 *n.* (古代之軍用) 拋石機。

man·go·steen 〔'mæŋgəˌstin; 'mæŋgousti:n〕 *n.* 〖植物〗山竹果樹;山竹果。

man·grove 〔'mæŋgrov; 'mæŋgrouv〕

n.〖植物〗紅樹（生於熱帶濕地,皮可製藥）。
man·gy 〔'mendʒɪ; 'meindʒi〕 *adj.*, **-gi·er, -gi·est.** ①患疥癩的。②汚穢的;齷齪的。③下賤的。(亦作 **mangey**)
man·han·dle 〔'mæn,hændl; 'mæn,hændl〕 *v.t.*, **-dled, -dling.** ①粗暴地對付。②〖罕〗以人力轉動或處理(不用機械力)。
man-hat·er 〔'mæn,hetə; 'mæn,heitə〕 *n.* ①憤世嫉俗者。②厭惡男人者。
Man·hat·tan 〔mæn'hætn; mæn'hætən〕 *n.* ①曼哈坦島(爲紐約之一部分)。②曼哈坦區(紐約市之一區,包括曼哈坦島)。③過去居住於曼哈坦島之 Algonquian 印第安人。④曼哈坦雞尾酒。
man·hole 〔'mæn,hol; 'mænhoul〕 *n.* 進人洞;人孔;出入孔;濬孔（如鍋爐、下水道等供修理工人出入之孔穴)。
***man·hood** 〔'mænhud; 'mænhud〕 *n.* ①成年；成人。 He is in the prime of *manhood*. 他正當盛年。②勇氣；剛毅。 He proved his *manhood* in the war. 他在戰時表現了男兒的英勇。③男子之集合稱。the *manhood* of China. 中國男兒。
man-hour 〔'mæn'aur; 'mæn'auə〕 *n.* 人時(一人一小時之工作量)。
man·hunt 〔'mæn,hʌnt; 'mænhʌnt〕 *n.*〖美〗搜索逃犯。(亦作 **man hunt**)
ma·ni·a 〔'menɪə; 'meinjə〕 *n.* ①癲狂；狂亂。②熱中;狂熱。
-mania〖字尾〗表下列諸義：①特殊發狂的形態，如：megalomania. ②瘋狂似的嗜好，如：monomania. ③讚美；醉心，如：Anglomania.
ma·ni·ac 〔'menɪ,æk; 'meiniæk〕 *n.* 瘋子。 a sex *maniac*. 一個色情狂。—*adj.* 癲狂的；狂妄的。
ma·ni·a·cal 〔mə'naɪəkl; mə'naiəkəl〕 *adj.* 發狂的;瘋狂似的。 —**ly,** *adv.*
ma·nic 〔'menɪk; 'meinik〕 *adj.* ①〖精神病〗癲狂的;躁狂的。②似發狂的;狂熱的。
man·ic-de·pres·sive 〔'mænɪkdɪ'prɛsɪv; 'mænikdi'presiv〕 *adj.*〖精神病〗癲狂與抑鬱交替發作的。—*n.* 此病之患者。
Man·i·ch(a)e·an 〔,mænə'kiən; ,mæni'kiːən〕 *adj.* 摩尼敎 (Manicheism) 的;摩尼教徒的。—*n.* 摩尼教徒。
Man·i·chee 〔'mænəki; 'mænikiː〕 *n.* 摩尼教徒。
Man·i·ch(a)e·ism 〔'mænə,kiizəm; 'mæni,kiːizəm〕 *n.* 摩尼教（波斯人 Manes 所創)。
man·i·cure 〔'mænɪ,kjur; 'mænikjuə〕 *v.*, **-cured, -cur·ing,** *n.* —*v.t.* & *v.i.* 修(指甲)。—*n.* ①修指甲。②修指甲者。
man·i·cur·ist 〔'mænɪ,kjurɪst; 'mænikjuərist〕 *n.* 修指甲者(通常爲女人)。
***man·i·fest** 〔'mænə,fɛst; 'mænifest〕 *adj.* 顯然的；明白的。 It is *manifest* at a glance. 此事一目了然。—*v.t.* ①顯示;表示。She *manifested* much willingness to go. 她表示很願意去。②證明。 ③清列(船上所載之貨)；記入載貨單。—*v.i.* (鬼)出現。—*n.* ①(船之)載貨單。②(陸上) 運貨單。③(航空機上)旅客名單。 —**ly,** *adv.*
man·i·fes·tant 〔,mænə'fɛstənt; ,mæni'festənt〕 *n.* 發動或參加示威運動者。
***man·i·fes·ta·tion** 〔,mænəfɛs'teʃən; ,mænifes'teiʃən, -fəs-〕 *n.* ①顯示；表明；證明。②顯示或證明的言行。A brave deed is a *manifestation* of courage. 勇敢行動卽爲英勇之表現。③示威運動。④顯聖；顯靈。
man·i·fes·to 〔,mænə'fɛsto; ,mæni'festou〕 *n.*, *pl.*〖美〗**-toes.**〖英〗**-tos.** *v.*, **-toed, -to·ing.** —*n.* 宣言。—*v.i.* 發表宣言。
***man·i·fold** 〔'mænə,fold; 'mænifould〕 *adj.* ①多種的；繁多的。②有許多部分的；多種形式的。③同時做多種事的;多倍的。*manifold* paper. 複寫紙。a *manifold* writer. 複寫機。—*n.* ①複寫本；繕本。②〖機械〗歧管。③多種。 Marriage is a *manifold* of duties. 結婚含有多種義務。④複寫紙。⑤〖數學〗簇；流形。—*v.t.* ①複寫；繕抄。②繁殖；增多。—**ly,** *adv.* —**ness,** *n.*
man·i·fold·er 〔'mænə,foldə; 'mænifouldə〕 *n.* 複寫機;複印機。
man·(n)i·kin 〔'mænəkɪn; 'mænikin〕 *n.*①侏儒;矮人。②人體解剖模型。③＝**mannequin.**
Ma·nil·a 〔mə'nɪlə; mə'nilə〕 *n.* 馬尼拉（菲律賓首都)。
ma·nil·a *n.* ①馬尼拉麻。②馬尼拉紙。
man in the middle 調停人;調解人。
man·i·oc 〔'mænɪ,ɑk; 'mæniɔk〕 *n.* ＝**cassava.**
man·i·ple 〔'mænəpl; 'mænipl〕 *n.* ①古羅馬之步兵中隊（由 60 人或120人組成)。②〖天主教〗司祭左臂所佩之飾帶。
ma·nip·u·late 〔mə'nɪpjə,let; mə'nipjuleit〕 *v.t.*, **-lat·ed, -lat·ing.** ①操作;使用；善理。②把持;操縱。③竄改;假造。
ma·nip·u·la·tion 〔mə,nɪpju'leʃən; mə,nipju'leiʃən〕 *n.* ①(用手的)操縱;(器具之)使用(法)。②巧妙的操縱。③〖商〗(市場的)操縱。④(帳簿、數字之)竄改。⑤〖外科〗觸診。
ma·nip·u·la·tive 〔mə'nɪpjə,letɪv; mə'nipjuleitiv〕 *adj.* 以手處理的；以手操作的;操縱的。
ma·nip·u·la·tor 〔mə'nɪpjə,letə; mə'nipjuleitə〕 *n.* ①用手操縱者;(器具之)使用者。②(市場之)操縱者。③(帳簿之)竄改者。
ma·nip·u·la·to·ry 〔mə'nɪpjələ,torɪ; mə'nipjulətəri〕 *adj.* ＝**manipulative.**
man·i·to 〔'mænə,to; 'mænitou〕 *n.* 神靈(北美印第安人用語)。(亦作 **manitou**)
man·i·t(o)u 〔'mænətu; 'mɑːnətuː〕 *n.* ＝**manito.**
man jack〖俚〗人。***every man jack*** 每一個人。
***man·kind** 〔mæn'kaɪnd; mæn'kaind *for* ① 'mæn,kaɪnd; 'mænkaind *for* ②〕 *n.* ①人類。 to benefit all *mankind*. 爲全人類謀利益。 ②男子之集合稱；男性。*Mankind* and womankind both like praise. 男人和女人都喜歡被稱讚。
man·like 〔'mæn,laɪk; 'mænlaik〕 *adj.* ①似男人的。②有男人氣質的 (＝ manly).
***man·ly** 〔'mænlɪ; 'mænli〕 *adj.*, **-li·er, -li·est.** ①像男人的;强壯的;爽直的;勇敢的;獨立的;高貴的。 A *manly* man is the noblest work of God. 有男子氣概的男人是上帝最崇高的傑作。②適於男人的。*manly* sports. 適於男子的運動。—**man·li·ness,** *n.*
man-made 〔'mæn,med; 'mæn,meid〕 *adj.* ① 人製造的。②人造的 (別於天然的)。
man·na 〔'mænə; 'mænə〕 *n.* ①〖聖經〗嗎哪(以色列人在荒郊所獲得之天降的食物)。②神賜的食物;安慰之辭;精神上的食物。③梣樹之甘而黏的液汁(可作通便劑)。
manned 〔mænd; mænd〕 *adj.* 有人駕駛的；有人操縱的。
man·ne·quin 〔'mænəkɪn; 'mænikin〕 *n.* ①時裝模特兒。②蠟或木製之人體模型(藝

術家、服裝店所用者)。(亦作 **manikin**)
:man·ner ['mænɚ; 'mænə] *n.* ①做事的方法;事情發生的方式; 樣子。The trouble arose in this *manner*. 亂子是這樣發生的。②態度;擧止。He has an austere *manner*. 他有一副嚴肅的態度。③(*pl.*)禮貌; 風俗;習俗。He has no *manners*. 他無禮貌。④(作 *pl.* 解)種類。⑤(文學、藝術的)風格;文體。her *manner* of singing. 她唱歌的風格。***all manner of*** 各種。We saw *all manner of* birds in the forest. 在森林中我們看見各種各類的鳥。***by all manner of means*** 最確實地;一定。***by no manner of means*** 在任何情況下均不。***in a manner*** 有幾分(= in a way; in some degree). ***in a manner of speaking*** 可謂(=so to speak). He is comparatively intelligent, *in a manner of speaking*. 他可以說是比較聰明。***make one's manners***〖美方〗鞠躬、欠身等以示禮貌。***to the manner born*** 生而習慣之;天生適於某種環境、地位、職業等。a chef *to the manner born*. 一個天生的廚師。
man·nered ['mænɚd; 'mænəd] *adj.* ①有禮貌的。②有某種狀態的(多用於複合語)。③矯飾的;不自然的。
man·ner·ism ['mænə,rɪzəm; 'mænərizəm] *n.* ①獨特之格調、形式等(尤指文學、藝術作品中者)。②奇癖。
man·ner·ist ['mænərɪst; 'mænərist] *n.* ①有習癖者。②過分固守某種風格或方法的作家或藝術家。
man·ner·less ['mænəlɪs; 'mænəlis] *adj.* 無禮貌的。
man·ner·ly ['mænəlɪ; 'mænəli] *adj.* 有禮貌的;客氣的。—*adv.* 有禮貌地;客氣地。
man·nish ['mænɪʃ; 'mæniʃ] *adj.* ①像男人的(女人)。②男人特質的;適於男人的。③學男人樣子的。 **—ly,** *adv.* **—ness,** *n.*
man·ni·tol ['mænə,tol; 'mænitoul] *n.*〖化〗木蜜醇;甘露糖醇。
ma·noeu·vre [mə'nuvɚ; mə'nu:və] *n., v.,* **-vred, -vring.**〖英〗=**maneuver.**
man of affairs 經驗豐富的人。
Man of God ①聖人; 先知。②教士。
man of the world 精於世故者。
man-of-war ['mænəv'wɔr; 'mænəv'wɔ:] *n., pl.* **men-of-war.** 軍艦。**—man-of-war's·man,** *n.*
ma·nom·e·ter [mə'nɑmətɚ; mə'nɔmitə] *n.* ①壓力計;氣壓計。②血壓計。**—man·o·met·ric, man·o·met·ri·cal,** *adj.*
man on horseback 國家面臨危機時以救星姿態出現而獨攬或企圖獨攬大權的人;對民主政府構成威脅的軍事領袖。
man·or ['mænɚ; 'mænə] *n.* ①(封建時代貴族之)采邑。the lord of the *manor*. 莊園領主。②地主之田地。**—i·al,** *adj.*
man·pack ['mæn,pæk; 'mænpæk] *adj.* 單人可携帶的。
man·pow·er ['mæn,pauɚ; 'mæn,pauə] *n.* ①人力。②人力(功之單位,合1/10馬力)。③人數;有效(或所需)人員總數;可動員之人力。(亦作 **man power**)
man·qué [mɑn'ke; mɑ:n'kei]〖法〗*adj.* 未實現的;未成功的;受挫折的。
man·rope ['mæn,rop; 'mænroup] *n.*〖航海〗舷門索(上下船攀扶用)。
man·sard ['mænsɑrd; 'mænsɑ:d] *n.* ①雙重斜坡之四邊形屋頂(=mansard roof)。②雙重斜坡屋頂下之閣樓。
manse [mæns; mæns] *n.* 牧師之住宅。
man·ser·vant ['mæn,sɜvənt; 'mæn,sə:vənt] *n., pl.* **men·ser·vants.** 男僕。
man·shift ['mæn,ʃɪft; 'mænʃift] *n.* (輪班制值班時間內)一人的工作量。
man·sion** ['mænʃən; 'mænʃən] *n.* 大廈; 邸。the Mansion House*** 倫敦市長官邸。〖注意〗公寓,英國叫 **mansions**(常作*pl.*形)。美國叫 **apartment house.**
man-sized ['mæn,saɪzd; 'mænsaizd] *adj.* ①宜於男人的; 形狀大小適合成人的。②成人方能勝任的。③大的。(亦作 **man size, man-size**)
man·slaugh·ter ['mæn,slɔtɚ; 'mæn,slɔ:tə] *n.* ①殺人。②〖法律〗過失殺人。
man·slay·er ['mæn,sleɚ; 'mæn,sleiə] *n.* 殺人者。**—man·slay·ing,** *n.*
man·sue·tude ['mænswɪ,tjud; 'mænswitju:d] *n.* 溫柔;文雅。
man·teau ['mænto; 'mæntou] *n., pl.* **-teaus, -teaux** [-toz, -to; -touz, -tou]. 斗篷;外套。
man·tel ['mæntl̩; 'mæntl] *n.* ①壁爐上部及兩側之裝飾構造。②壁爐上之架子。(亦作 **mantle, mantelpiece, mantlepiece**)
mantel board 壁爐架板。
man·tel·et ['mæntl̩ɛt; 'mæntlet] *n.* ①短外套。②〖軍〗(亦作 **mantlet**)(昔攻城軍隊用的)彈盾。
man·tel·shelf ['mæntl̩,ʃɛlf; 'mæntlʃelf] *n.* 壁爐架。(亦作 **mantelpiece**)
man·tel·tree ['mæntl̩,tri; 'mæntl̩tri:] *n.* 支持壁爐開口之楣。
man·til·la [mæn'tɪlə; mæn'tilə] *n.* 女用頭紗;西班牙及墨西哥婦女用的連披肩之頭紗。
man·tis ['mæntɪs; 'mæntis] *n., pl.* **-tis·es, -tes** [-tiz; -ti:z]. 螳螂。
man·tis·sa [mæn'tɪsə; mæn'tisə] *n.*〖數學〗假數(對數之小數部分)。
***man·tle** ['mæntl̩; 'mæntl] *n., v.,* **-tled, -tling.** —*n.* ①無袖外套; 斗篷。②覆罩之物。The ground had a *mantle* of snow. 地上覆有一層雪。③燃罩(如煤氣燈之白熱罩等)。④=**mantel.** ⑤位於地殼與地球外核心間之地層。 —*v.i.* ①罩; 覆。The whole district *mantled* in loveliest white. 整個地區披上一層可愛的銀白外衣。②臉紅。Her cheeks *mantled*. 她兩頰緋紅。③(鳥翼)伸展。④爲泡沫所覆。—*v.t.* ①(以斗篷)覆蓋。②掩藏。Clouds *mantled* the moon. 雲將月遮住。
man-trap ['mæn,træp; 'mæntræp] *n.*〖英〗①捕人陷穽(用以捕捉侵入私宅者)。②危險地。③罪惡場所(如賭場等)。④〖俗〗富有性感的女人。
man·tu·a ['mæntʃuə; 'mæntjuə] *n.* 女用外套。
manu-〖字首〗表"用手做"之義,如: manuscript.
***man·u·al** ['mænjuəl; 'mænjuəl] *adj.* ①手的;手製的。*manual* labor. 手工。②用手操作的;手工的。③如手册的。—*n.*①手册;袖珍本。a pocket reference *manual*. 袖珍參考書。②風琴鍵盤。③(鎗等之)操典。
man·u·al·ly ['mænjuəlɪ; 'mænjuəli] *adv.* 用手地;手工地。
manual training 手工藝訓練。
man·u·code ['mænju,kod; 'mænjukoud] *n.* 極樂鳥。
man·u·fac·to·ry [,mænjə'fæktərɪ; ,mænju'fæktəri] *n., pl.* **-ries.**〖古〗工廠。
:man·u·fac·ture [,mænjə'fæktʃɚ;

ˌmænjuˈfæktʃə] *v.*, **-tured, -tur·ing,** *n.* —*v.t.* ①製造。It is *manufactured* by machinery (hand). 此係機器 (手工)製。②將(原料)製成用品。The workers *manufacture* rags into paper. 工人將破布造成紙。③捏造; 假造。 A knot of politicians *manufactured* public opinion. 一羣政客假造輿論。④粗製濫造地大量寫 (書)。—*n.* ①製造。It is of home (foreign) *manufacture.* 這是本國(外國)造的。②製造品。Plastic is an important *manufacture.* 塑膠是一種重要的產品。

***man·u·fac·tur·er** [ˌmænjəˈfæktʃərɚ; ˌmænjuˈfæktʃərə] *n.* 製造業者;廠主。

manufacturer's agent 經銷商。

man·u·fac·tur·ing [ˌmænjəˈfæktʃərɪŋ; ˌmænjuˈfæktʃəriŋ] *adj.* 製造(業)的;從事製造業的。a *manufacturing* district. 工業區。—*n.* 製造(業)。

man·u·mis·sion [ˌmænjəˈmɪʃən; ˌmænjuˈmiʃən] *n.* (奴隸之) 解放。

man·u·mit [ˌmænjəˈmɪt; ˌmænjuˈmit] *v.t.*, **mit·ted, -mit·ting.** 解放 (奴隸)。

***ma·nure** [məˈnjur; məˈnjuə] *n., v.*, **-nured, -nur·ing.** —*n.* 肥料。 artificial *manure.* 人造肥。 —*v.t.* 施肥。 to *manure* a garden. 施肥於園中。 **—ma·nur·er,** *n.* **—ma·nu·ri·al,** *adj.*

***man·u·script** [ˈmænjəˌskrɪpt; ˈmænjuskript] *n.*草稿;原稿。The work is already complete in *manuscript.* 著作已脫稿。—*adj.* 手寫的;打字機打出的。**—al,** *adj.*

Manx [mæŋks; mæŋks] *adj.* 曼島(Isle of Man) 的;曼島人(語)的。—*n.* 曼島話。

Manx cat 曼島貓(飼貓之一種,無尾)。

Manx·man [ˈmæŋksmən; ˈmæŋksmən] *n., pl.* **-men.** 曼島之人或居民。

‡**man·y** [ˈmɛnɪ; ˈmeni] *adj.*, **more, most,** *n., pron.* —*adj.* 許多的。 I've been there a good (*or* great) *many* times. 我常常到那裏去。 ***a good many*** 相當多的。 ***a great many*** 很多的。 ***as many*** 同數的;同樣多的。I found six mistakes in *as many* lines. 我在六行中發現六個錯誤。 ***as many again*** 兩倍。 ***be one too many for*** 勝過;優於;壓倒性的; 太多的。 He *was one too many for* you that time. 那次他勝過了你。 ***how many*** 有多少。 ***many a*** (=many). 其後須用單數名詞及動詞。*Many a* student fails to pass in the examination. 許多學生考試不及格。 ***one too many*** **a.** 不需要的;多一個的。That drink was *one too many*. 那杯酒是不必再喝的。 **b.** 礙事。—*n.* 許多。Did *many* come? 來了很多人嗎? ***the many*** 多數人;羣衆。 —*pron.* 多人;多數。*Many* of us disagree with her ideas. 我們之中多人不贊同她的想法。〖注意〗⑴凡可計數的事物,形容其多時用 **many,** 否則用 **much.** ⑵many 與 **innumerable** 都指很多的。many 是常用字。 innumerable 指多得不能或難以數計。

man·y·fold [ˈmɛnɪˌfold; ˈmenifould] *adv.* 許多倍; 大大地。

man·y-head·ed [ˈmɛnɪˈhɛdɪd; ˈmeniˈhedid] *adj.* 多頭的。

man·y-sid·ed [ˈmɛnɪˈsaɪdɪd; ˈmeniˈsaidid] *adj.* ①多邊的。②多方面的; 多才多藝的。a *many-sided* man. 多才多藝的人。

man·za·ni·ta [ˌmænzəˈnitə; ˌmænzəˈniːtə] *n.* (美國西部產之) 石南科灌木。

Ma·o·ri [ˈmaurɪ, ˈmɑrɪ; ˈmauri, ˈmɑːəri] *n.* 毛利人(紐西蘭之土人);毛利語。—*adj.* 毛利人的;毛利語的。

‡**map** [mæp; mæp] *n., v.*, **mapped, mapping.** —*n.* ①地圖。to draw a *map.* 繪製地圖。②天體圖。③似地圖之事物。The old man's face is a *map* of time. 那老年人的臉像一張時間的地圖。④〖俚〗臉。Wipe that smile off that ugly *map* of yours. 把那笑容從你這張醜惡的臉抹去吧。 ***put on the map*** 放在地圖上;爲人所知。—*v.t.* ①繪製…之地圖。②計劃〖out〗。to *map* out a new career.計劃一新事業。**—pa·ble, —like,** *adj.*

***ma·ple** [ˈmepl̩; ˈmeipl] *n.* ①楓。②楓木。③楓糖或楓蜜的香味。**—like,** *adj.*

map·per·y [ˈmæpərɪ; ˈmæpəri] *n.* 地圖繪製。

map·ping [ˈmæpɪŋ; ˈmæpiŋ] *n.* 繪製地圖; 製圖。

Ma·quis [mɑˈki; ˈmɑːkiː] *n., pl.* **-quis,** *adj.* —*n.* ①(m-) 地中海沿岸之灌木叢林地帶。②二次大戰中抵抗德軍之法國游擊隊或其隊員。—*adj.* 法國抗德游擊隊的; 其戰術的。

Ma·qui·sard [mɑkɪˈzɑrd; mɑːkiˈzɑːd] *n.* 二次世界大戰時法國之抗德游擊隊隊員。

mar** [mɑr; mɑː] *v.*, **marred, mar·ring,** *n.* —*v.t.* 損毀;損傷;損其美。Weeds *mar* a garden. 野草損傷花園的美觀。 ***make (or ***mend***) ***or mar*** 不成功便完全失敗。—*n.* 缺點。

Mar. March.

mar. ①marine. ②maritime. ③married.

mar·a·bou [ˈmærəˌbu; ˈmærəbuː] *n.* ①(西非產之)大鸛; (印度產之)禿鸛。②鸛之羽毛;鸛之羽毛製裝飾品。(亦作 **marabout**)

Mar·a·bout [ˈmærəˌbut; ˈmærəbuːt] *n.* ①(北非之) 回教隱士或聖者。②回教隱士或聖者之墓。③(m-) =**marabou.**

ma·ra·ca [məˈrɑkə; məˈrɑːkə] *n.* (南美等處跳舞樂隊用的) 響葫蘆。

mar·a·schi·no [ˌmærəˈskino; ˌmærəsˈkiːnou] *n., pl.* **-nos.** 一種櫻桃酒。

ma·ras·mus [məˈræzməs; məˈræzməs] *n.*〖醫〗衰弱;虛弱。**—ma·ras·mic,** *adj.*

Mar·a·thon [ˈmærəˌθɑn; ˈmærəθən] *n.* 馬拉松(在雅典東北, 490 B.C. 雅典人於此擊敗波斯人,一長跑家帶勝利消息,跑到雅典)。

mar·a·thon [ˈmærəˌθɑn; ˈmærəθən] *n.* ①馬拉松 (26 英里 385 碼之長途賽跑)。②長途賽跑;持久賽跑。③任何持久比賽。***marathon race*** 馬拉松賽跑。—**er,** *n.*

ma·raud [məˈrɔd; məˈrɔːd] *v.t.* 搶掠;刼奪(常用於被動式)。—*v.i.* 奪掠。—**er,** *n.*

mar·a·ve·di [ˌmærəˈvedɪ; ˌmærəˈveidi] *n., pl.* **-dis.** ①(昔西班牙之) Moor 人所用之金幣。②西班牙之古銅幣。

***mar·ble** [ˈmɑrbl̩; ˈmɑːbl] *n., adj., v.*, **-bled, -bling.** —*n.* ①大理石。 The monument is carved in *marble.* 此碑由大理石刻成。②(遊戲中之)石彈。③(*pl.*)(作*sing.*解)石彈戲。④(*pl.*) 一堆蒐集的雕刻品。⑤(*pl.*)〖俚〗普通理智;常識。to lose one's *marbles.* 失去理智。⑥雕刻在大理石上的藝術作品。⑦冷峻無情之事物。 —*adj.* ①大理石的。②似大理石白、硬、涼的。③冷酷無情的。 Some politicians are *marble*. 有些政客心如鐵石。—*v.t.* 使有大理石樣色紋。

mar·ble·heart·ed [ˈmɑrbl̩ˈhɑrtɪd; ˈmɑːblˈhɑːtid] *adj.* 冷酷無情的;心如鐵石的。

mar·ble·ize [ˈmɑrbl̩ˌaɪz; ˈmɑːblaiz] *v.t.*, **-ized, -iz·ing.** 作成大理石之形狀、花紋。

mar·bling [ˈmɑrblɪŋ; ˈmɑːbliŋ] *n.* ①

M

模倣大理石花紋之製作,或其藝術。②模造大理石之外表。

mar·bly ['marblɪ; 'mɑːbli] *adj.*, **-bli·er, -bli·est.** 似大理石的; 冷的; 硬的; 冷酷的;冷淡的。

marc [mark, mar; mɑːk, mar] *n.* (葡萄等之)搾渣;果渣。

mar·ca·site ['markəˌsaɪt; 'mɑːkəsait] *n.* 〖礦〗白鐵礦 (FeS_2)。

Mar·cel [mar'sɛl; mɑː'sel] *n.* 男子名。

:March [martʃ; mɑːtʃ] *n.* 三月。

:march¹ [martʃ; mɑːtʃ] *v.i.* ①以整齊步伐進行。②進軍;行軍。The soldiers *marched* towards Berlin. 軍隊向柏林挺進。③前進; 行進。The procession *marched* along the highway. 行列沿公路而行。—*v.t.* 使前進〖off〗. The policeman *marched* the thief off to jail. 警察押着賊到監牢裏去。—*n.* ①前進; 進軍; 行軍。a *march* past. 分列式。②進行曲。③行程。a *march* of twenty miles. 二十英里的行程。④困難的長途行進。⑤發展;進行。It proved a new era in the *march* of civilization. 在人類文明的過程上闢一新紀元。***on the march*** 在行進中;發展中。Automation is *on the march.* 自動化正發展中。***steal a march on*** **a.** 偸襲敵人。**b.** 着人先鞭;占先;占優勢。

march² *n.* ①(常 *pl.*) 邊界;邊疆。②(the Marches) 英格蘭與蘇格蘭, 或英格蘭與威爾斯間之邊界地帶。—*v.i.* 臨界;毗連。

mar·che·sa [mar'keza; mɑː'keizɑː] *n.*, *pl.*-**se** [-zi; -ziː]. (義大利之) 女侯爵 (相當於 marchioness).

mar·che·se [mar'keze; mɑː'keizei] *n.*, *pl.* **-si** [-zi; -ziː]. (義大利之)侯爵(相當於 marquis).

marching orders 行軍命令。

mar·chion·ess ['marʃənɪs; 'mɑːʃənis] *n.* 侯爵夫人;女侯爵。

march·pane ['martʃˌpen; 'mɑːtʃpein] *n.* 杏仁和糖搗碎作成的餅;杏仁糖。

Mar·co·ni [mar'konɪ; mɑː'kouni] *n.* 馬可尼 (Marchese Guglielmo, 1874–1937, 義大利電機學家, 無線電報發明者, 1909年獲諾貝爾物理獎)。

mar·co·ni [mar'konɪ; mɑː'kouni] *n.*, *v.*, **-nied, -ni·ing.** —*n.* 無線電報。—*v.t.* & *v.i.* 打無線電報。

mar·co·ni·gram [mar'konɪˌgræm; mɑː'kounigræm] *n.* (馬可尼式)無線電報。

Mar·co Po·lo ['marko'polo; 'mɑːkou'poulou] 馬哥孛羅 (1254?–1324? 義大利旅行家, 著有東方見聞錄)。

Mar·di gras ['mardɪ'gra; 'mɑːdi'grɑː] 四旬齋前一日 (在紐奧連、巴黎爲尋樂之日)。

mare¹** [mer; mɛə] *n.* 母馬;母驢。Money makes the mare go.*** 有錢能使鬼推磨。***ride shank's mare*** 徒步。***The gray mare is the better horse.*** 母雞司晨。***win the mare or lose the halter*** 孤注一擲。

ma·re² ['merɪ; 'meəri] *n.*, *pl.* **ma·ri·a** ['marɪə; 'mɑːriə]. ①海。②月球表面的黑暗區(昔認爲海)。

ma·re clau·sum ['meri'klɔsəm; 'meəriː'klɔːsəm] 〖拉〗領海(=closed sea).

Ma·re Im·bri·um ['meri'ɪmbrɪəm; 'meəriː'imbriəm] 雨海 (月球表面第二象限內之黑色平原, 面積約三十四萬平方英里)。

ma·re li·be·rum ['meri'lɪbərəm; 'meəriː'libərəm] 〖拉〗公海 (=free sea).

ma·rem·ma [mə'rɛmə; mə'remə] *n.*, *pl.* **-rem·me** [-'rɛmɪ; -'remi]. ①(義大利西部等之)海岸濕地。②(沼澤地之)瘴氣。

mare's-nest ['mɛrzˌnɛst; 'mɛəznest] *n.* ①似是重要而結果證明爲騙局或毫無價值之發現。②很亂的地方或情況。

mare's-tail ['mɛrzˌtel; 'mɛəzteil] *n.* ①〖植物〗杉葉藻;木賊。②(*pl.*) 馬尾雲。

Ma·re Tranquillitatis ['mare~; 'mɑːrei~] 寧靜海(月球表面第一象限內之低窪處, 人類第一次探月之 Apollo 11號太空人降落處)。(亦作 **Sea of Tranquillity**)

marg. ①margin. ②marginal.

Mar·ga·ret ['margrɪt; 'mɑːgərit] *n.* 女子名。(亦作 **Margaretta, Margarete, Margarette**)

mar·ga·rine ['mardʒəˌrin; ˌmɑːdʒə'riːn] *n.* 人造奶油。(亦作 **margarin**)

mar·ga·rite ['margəraɪt; 'mɑːgərait] *n.* 珍珠雲母。

marge [mardʒ; mɑːdʒ] *n.* ①〖古, 詩〗邊緣 (=margin). ②〖英俗〗=**margarine.**

***mar·gin** ['mardʒɪn; 'mɑːdʒin] *n.* ①邊; 緣。He is on the *margin* of death. 他已接近死亡。②書頁邊之空白。Write down a note on the *margin* of the page. 在頁邊空白處寫上一註解。③盈餘;利潤。a large *margin* of profit. 大量盈利。④餘裕; 餘地。We allow a *margin* of 15 minutes in catching a train. 在趕火車時我們常預留十五分鐘的寬裕時間。⑤(證劵交易所中的)保證金。⑥極限。the *margin* of subsistence. 生活之最低需要。⑦〖經濟〗最低報酬。—*v.t.* ①加邊緣於;留邊緣於;圍繞。②記於書頁邊之空白處。③〖商〗交納保證金。

mar·gin·al ['mardʒɪnl; 'mɑːdʒinl, -əl] *adj.* ①邊緣的; 寫或印於欄外的; 有旁註的。a *marginal* note. 旁註;標註。②限界的; 境界的;邊境的。③邊際的。*marginal* utility. 邊際效用。*marginal* land. 邊際土地。④〖社會〗(未十分同化之移民等)在二文化集團中間而無所適從的。⑤〖商〗勉强能收支平衡的。*marginal* profits. 不虧本程度的收益。⑥最起碼的;最低限度的。*marginal* subsistence. 起碼的生活。**—ly,** *adv.*

mar·gi·na·li·a [ˌmardʒə'nelɪə; ˌmɑːdʒi'neiliə] *n. pl.* 旁註;標註。

marginal man 處於兩種不同文化種族之間而又不屬於其中任何一種之人。

marginal sea 領海。

mar·grave ['margrev; 'mɑːgreiv] *n.* 〖史〗(神聖羅馬帝國之)侯爵;邊境侯爵。

mar·gra·vine ['margrəˌvin; 'mɑːgrəviːn] *n.* 〖史〗margrave 之夫人。

mar·gue·rite [ˌmargə'rit; ˌmɑːgə'riːt] *n.* 〖植物〗延命菊;雛菊。

Ma·ri·a [mə'raɪə; mə'raiə] *n.* 女子名。

ma·ri·age de con·ve·nance [ma'rjaʒ dəkɔ̃v'nɑ̃s; ma'rjaʒ dəˌkɔ̃v'nɑ̃s] 〖法〗權宜結婚;政略結婚 (=marriage of convenience).

Mar·i·an¹ ['mɛrɪən; 'meəriən] *n.* 女子名。

Mar·i·an² *adj.* ①聖母瑪利亞的。②(英國或蘇格蘭女王) Mary 的;其時代的。—*n.*①聖母之信奉者。②蘇格蘭女王 Mary之支持者。

Mar·i·an·a's Trench [ˌmɛrɪ'ænə ~; ˌmeəri'ænə~] 馬里亞納海溝。

mar·i·cul·ture [ˌmærə'kʌltʃə; ˌmærə'kʌltʃə] *n.* 水生動植物的培植(作食物及原料用)。(亦作 **sea farming**)

mar·i·gold ['mærəˌgold; 'mærigould]

n.〖植物〗①金盞草。②金盞草之花。

ma·ri·jua·na, ma·ri·hua·na 〔ˌmɑrɪˈhwɑnə; ˌmɑːriˈhwɑːnə〕 *n.* ①大麻。②其乾葉或乾花(用爲麻醉劑);大麻烟。

ma·ri li·be·rum 〔ˈmɛrɪ ˈlaɪbərəm; ˈmɛəriˈlaibərəm〕〖拉〗公海(=open sea).

ma·rim·ba 〔məˈrɪmbə; məˈrimbə〕 *n.* 馬林巴(木琴之一種)。

ma·ri·na 〔məˈrinə; məˈriːnə〕 *n.* 小船之補給休閒基地;小艇停泊補給站。

mar·i·nade 〔*n.* ˌmærəˈned; ˌmæriˈneid *v.* ˈmærəˌned; ˈmærineid〕 *n., v.,* **-nad·ed, -nad·ing.** —*n.* ①滷汁(醋、葡萄酒、油、香料等之混合汁)。②泡過滷汁的魚、肉等。—*v.t.* =**marinate.**

mar·i·nate 〔ˈmærəˌnet; ˈmærineit〕 *v.t.,* **-nat·ed, -nat·ing.** 浸以滷汁;浸以生菜調味品(French dressing).

ma·rine** 〔məˈrin; məˈriːn〕 *adj.* ①海的;海中的;海中產的。*marine* products. 海產;水產。*marine* cable. 海底電線。②海船的;海軍的。*marine* supplies. 船具。—*n.* ①船隻之集合稱;航海業。merchant *marine.* 商船。②艦隊。③海軍;水兵。④海景;海景畫。⑤〖美〗海軍陸戰隊士兵。Tell that*** (or ***it***) ***to the marines!*** 哪有那樣的事!鬼才相信這話!

marine belt 領海。

Marine Corps 〖美〗海軍陸戰隊。

marine court 海員法庭。

marine insurance 海上保險。

marine law 海上法。

marine policy 海上保險單。

mar·i·ner** 〔ˈmærənɚ; ˈmærinə〕 *n.* ①水手;舟子;船員。②(M-)〖美〗探測火星與金星之無人駕駛太空船。 ***master mariner 商船船長。

mariner's compass 航海羅盤。

marine store ①(*pl.*)船具。②船具店。

Mar·i·ol·a·try 〔ˌmɛrɪˈɑlətrɪ; ˌmɛəriˈɔlətri〕 *n.* ①聖母之崇拜(輕蔑語)。②崇拜女人。

mar·i·o·nette 〔ˌmærɪəˈnɛt; ˌmæriəˈnet〕 *n.* (用線牽動之)木偶。

Mar·i·po·sa lily (or **tulip**) 〔ˌmærəˈposə(-zə)~; ˌmæriˈpousə(-zə)~〕〖植物〗(美國西部及墨西哥產)蝴蝶百合。

mar·ish 〔ˈmærɪʃ; ˈmæriʃ〕 *n., adj.*〖古,詩,方〗沼澤(的)。

Mar·ist 〔ˈmɛrɪst; ˈmɛərist〕 *n.* (天主教之)瑪利亞修道會(Society of Mary)之會友。

mar·i·tal 〔ˈmærətḷ; ˈmæritl〕 *adj.* ①婚姻的。②〖古〗夫的。

mar·i·time 〔ˈmærəˌtaɪm; ˈmæritaim〕 *adj.* ①海上的;近海的。②居於海濱的。③海的。*maritime* law. 海上法。④海員的;航海的。

maritime belt 領海。

Maritime Provinces, the (加拿大之)沿海諸省。

mar·jo·ram 〔ˈmɑrdʒərəm; ˈmɑːdʒərəm〕 *n.*〖植物〗一種唇形科薄荷屬之植物。

Mark[1] 〔mɑrk; mɑːk〕 *n.* 男子名。

Mark[2] *n.* ①馬可福音之作者。②〖聖經〗馬可福音。

‡**mark**[1] 〔mɑrk; mɑːk〕 *n.* ①符號;記號。Put a *mark* on it. 在上面做個記號。②分界線。③標誌;標點;符號。punctuation *marks.* 標點符號。a trade *mark.* 商標。④分數;點數。He gained the full *marks.* 他得了滿分。⑤污點;疤痕;痕跡。He showed me the *mark* of the wound. 他將傷疤指給我看。⑥(不能書自己姓名者之)十字畫押。to make one's *mark* on a document. 在一文件上簽署十字畫押。⑦鵠的;目標。⑧常態;標準。⑨影響;印象。⑩名譽。a man of *mark.* 著名的人。⑪(標價格、品質之)標籤;籤條。a price-*mark.* 價格標籤。⑫(常 M-)〖軍〗表示製造中之軍備之符號,常與數目字連用表示採用之先後,如:M-1 rifle. M-1 式步鎗。⑬被嘲笑、欺騙之對象。He was an easy *mark.* 他容易上當。⑭目標。to aim at the *mark.* 對準目標。⑮特徵。the usual *marks* of a gentleman. 君子的一般特徵。 ***below*** (***up to***) ***the mark*** 低於(達到)標準。 ***beside the mark*** **a.** 未中鵠的。**b.** 未成功;失敗。**c.** 離譜;不相干;風馬牛不相及。 ***bless*** (or ***save***) ***the mark*** (亦作 **God bless the mark! God save the mark!**) 表示不贊同、輕視、不耐煩的感嘆詞。 ***hit the mark*** **a.** 中鵠的;達到目的。**b.** 中肯;得當。 ***make one's mark*** 成功;成名。 ***miss the mark*** 未中鵠的;未成功;失誤。 ***of mark*** 重要的;著名的。 ***on your mark*** (or ***marks***)***!*** 預備!(賽跑時就位之口令)。 ***wide of the mark*** **a.** 離鵠的太遠而未中的。**b.** 不切題的。—*v.t.* ①記分數於;列等級於。②加符號於;做標記於。Two of the pupils were *marked* absent. 兩個學生被記缺席。③顯示;指明。A frown *marked* her displeasure. 蹙眉表示她的不悅。④注意;留心。*Mark* carefully how it is done. 注意怎麼做。⑤加標籤(圖印等)於。The prices of these goods are all clearly *marked* on them. 這些貨物的價格都淸楚地以標籤標明於其上。⑥爲…之特徵;爲…之特色;使顯著。An old castle *marks* the town. 一古堡使此市鎭著稱。—*v.i.* 留心;注意;考慮。 ***mark down*** 減價。 ***mark off*** 以界線隔開。 ***mark out*** 劃線分出。 ***mark out for*** 選出。 ***mark time*** **a.** 原地踏步而不前進。**b.** 躭擱;遷延。 ***mark up*** **a.** 加價;漲價。**b.** 加記號;加符號。

mark[2] *n.* 馬克(德國的貨幣名稱)。

mark·down 〔ˈmɑrkˌdaʊn; ˈmɑːkdaun〕 *n.* ①減價。②價格減低額。—*adj.* 減價的。

marked 〔mɑrkt; mɑːkt〕 *adj.* ①有記號的;有痕跡的。②顯著的;顯赫的。③易辨別的;明顯的。④作爲嫌疑或復仇之對象而受到注視的。—**ness,** *n.*

mark·ed·ly 〔ˈmɑrkɪdlɪ; ˈmɑːkidli〕 *adv.* 顯著地。

mark·er 〔ˈmɑrkɚ; ˈmɑːkə〕 *n.* ①作記號之人或物。②記分員。③書籤。④籌碼。

‡**mar·ket** 〔ˈmɑrkɪt; ˈmɑːkit〕 *n.* ①市場;市集;集日。to go to *market.* 上市;趕集。②市集上的羣衆。③市況;市面。The *market* is dull. 市面蕭條。④食物商店。a meat *market.* 肉店。⑤銷路。The product will find a good *market* in Australia. 產品將在澳洲有好的銷路。⑥推銷地區。the foreign *market.* 國外推銷市場。⑦一般的買賣。His house is in the *market.* 他的房子在出售。⑧需要。There is no *market* for these goods. 對這些貨物無需要。⑨行業。the cotton *market.* 棉業。 ***at the market*** 以時價(買、賣股票等)。 ***be in the market for*** 爲…可能的購買者;想買。I *am in the market for* a motorcycle. 我想買一部摩托車。 ***bring one's eggs*** (or ***hogs***) ***to a bad market*** (or ***to the wrong market***) **a.** 計畫失敗。**b.** 因求援對象錯誤而失敗。 ***find a market*** 有銷路;有需要。 ***glut the market*** 因貨品供應太多而造成無法脫售或大幅跌價。 ***on the market*** 出售中;上市。Fresh asparagus

will be *on the market* this week. 新鮮蘆筍本週將上市。***play the market*** 〖股票〗投機。***price out of the market*** 因售價太高而失去顧客。—*v.i.* 在市集上買賣;交易。to go *marketing*. 到市場上去做買賣。—*v.t.* ①出售。②帶(貨物)到市場出售。—*adj.* 市場的。

mar·ket·a·ble ['markɪtəbl; 'mɑːkitəbl] *adj.* 能賣的; 適於在市場上出售的。—**mar·ket·a·bil·i·ty, —ness,** *n.* —**mar·ket·a·bly,** *adv.*

market analysis 〖商〗市場分析。

market analyst 〖商〗市場分析家。

mar·ket·eer [ˌmarkɪt'ɪr; ˌmɑːkit'iə] *n.* 在市場賣東西的人;市場商人。

mar·ket·er ['markɪtɚ; 'mɑːkitə] *n.* 到市場的人;在市場做買賣的人。

mar·ket·ing ['markɪtɪŋ; 'mɑːkitiŋ] *n.* ①在市場之交易;買賣。to do one's *marketing*. 在市場買東西。②市場商品。

market place ①市集;市場。②商業界。(亦作 **marketplace**)

market price 售價;市價。

market research 市場研究;市場調查。

mark·ing ['markɪŋ; 'mɑːkiŋ] *n.* ①記號;印記;斑點;條紋。②作記號; 記分; 捺印。

marks·man ['marksmən; 'mɑːksmən] *n., pl.* **-men.** 射手;善射者。

marks·man·ship ['marksmənʃɪp; 'mɑːksmənʃip] *n.* 射術。

marks·wom·an ['marksˌwʊmən; 'mɑːksˌwumən] *n., pl.* **-wom·en.** 女射手。

Mark Twain ['mark'twen; 'mɑːk'twein] 馬克吐溫 (1835–1910, 眞名 Samuel Langhorne Clemens, 美國幽默作家)。

mark·up ['markˌʌp; 'mɑːkˌʌp] *n.* ①漲價(額)。②〖商〗售價與成本之差額(比率)。③〖印刷〗載在稿件上的有關排版之詳細指示。

marl [marl; mɑːl] *n.* 石灰泥(做肥料用)。***burning marl*** 灼熱地獄中之受苦。

mar·lin ['marlɪn; 'mɑːlin] *n., pl.* **-lin, -lins.** 馬林魚 (一種身體細長之深海大魚)。

mar·line ['marlɪn; 'mɑːlin] *n.* 〖航海〗繩索;小繩;小索。

mar·line·spike ['marlɪnˌspaɪk; 'mɑːlinspaik] *n.* (海員用的) 穿索針; 解索針。(亦作 **marlinspike, marlingspike**)

marlinespike seamanship 船上編繩、打結等的技術。

marl·ite ['marlaɪt; 'mɑːlait] *n.* 牢泥灰石。—**mar·lit·ic,** *adj.*

marl·y ['marlɪ; 'mɑːli] *adj.*, **marl·i·er, marl·i·est.** 石灰泥的;含石灰泥的; 石灰泥狀的;灰泥質的;多石灰泥的。—**marl·i·ness,** *n.*

mar·ma·lade ['marmlˌed, ˌmarml'ed; 'mɑːməleid] *n.* (橘子或檸檬等製成之)果醬。

mar·mo·re·al [mar'morɪəl; mɑː'mouriəl] *adj.* ①大理石的。②冷的;光滑的;如大理石的。(亦作 **marmorean**) —**ly,** *adv.*

mar·mo·set ['marməˌzɛt; 'mɑːməzet] *n.* (中南美洲所產之)小猴。

mar·mot ['marmət; 'mɑːmət] *n.* 〖動物〗山撥鼠。

mar·o·cain ['mærəken; 'mærəkein] *n.* 一種似綢的絲、毛或棉織物。

ma·roon¹ [mə'run; mə'ruːn] *n.* ①深赤褐色。②紙炮;一種警告或危險的信號煙火。—*adj.* 深赤褐色的。

ma·roon² *v.t.* ①放逐於荒島。②使處於孤獨無助之境。—*v.i.* (美國南方)在外作數日露營。—*n.* ①避居於西印度羣島及荷屬圭亞那之黑奴遺族。②被孤立的人。

mar·plot ['marˌplat; 'mɑːplɔt] *n.* 作無聊之干涉而敗人事者。

Marq. ①Marquess. ②Marquis.

marque [mark; mɑːk] *n.* 報復的掠奪 (僅用於 letters of marque 一語中,戰時持此種"捕拿特許狀"者卽可攻奪敵人商船)。

mar·quee [mar'ki; mɑː'kiː] *n.* ①〖英〗(戶外野餐或花園茶會時用之) 大帳幕。②(戲院等門外之)遮簷。

mar·quess ['markwɪs; 'mɑːkwis] *n.* =**marquis.**

mar·que·try, mar·que·te·rie ['markətrɪ; 'mɑːkitri] *n.* (傢具裝飾之)鑲嵌細工。

***mar·quis** ['markwɪs; 'mɑːkwis] *n., pl.* **-quis·es, -quis.** 侯爵。

mar·quis·ate ['markwɪzɪt; 'mɑːkwizit] *n.* 侯爵之身分、地位或領地。

mar·quise [mar'kiz; mɑː'kiːz] *n.* ①侯爵夫人; 侯爵之遺孀。② (英亦作 **marchioness**)女侯爵。③=**marquee.** ④兩端尖之卵形寶石。

mar·qui·sette [ˌmarkɪ'zɛt; ˌmɑːki'zet] *n.* 一種薄而輕有方形網眼之棉、絲、人造絲或尼龍等之織物。

mar·ram grass ['mærəm~; 'mærəm~] 一種生於海灘之野草。

‡**mar·riage** ['mærɪdʒ; 'mæridʒ] *n.* ①婚姻; 結婚。 Their *marriage* was a very happy one. 他們的婚姻非常美滿。②婚禮。When will the *marriage* take place? 婚禮何時舉行? ③密切連繫;結合。the *marriage* of music and drama in opera. 歌劇中音樂與戲劇的密切結合。 ④商業合併。 This major bank *marriage* is the fourth in less than six months. 這次的銀行合併是不到半年裏發生的第四次。***by marriage*** 由姻親關係。He is my uncle *by marriage*. 他是我的姻叔(伯)父。***give (a daughter) in marriage*** 嫁女。***take (a woman) in marriage*** 娶妻。

mar·riage·a·ble ['mærɪdʒəbl; 'mæridʒəbl] *adj.* 適合結婚的;可結婚的。—**mar·riage·a·bil·i·ty,** *n.*

marriage bed ①新床。②夫婦之關係;夫婦床第間之事。

marriage lines 結婚證書。

marriage of convenience 政略結婚;權宜結婚;有企圖之結婚。

marriage portion 嫁妝。

marriage settlement 婚姻財產之設定。

mar·ried** ['mærɪd; 'mærid] *adj.* ①已結婚的;有夫(妻)的。 They are a *married* couple. 他們是一對夫婦。②婚姻的; 夫妻的。③密切結合一起的。get married*** 結婚。They will soon *get married*. 他們不久就要結婚了。—*n.* ①已婚者。②(*pl.*)夫婦。—**ly,** *adv.*

mar·ron ['mærən; 'mærən] *n.* 栗子(尤指烹飪用者)。

mar·rons gla·cés [ma'rɔ̃gla'se; ma'rɔ̃gla'sei] 〖法〗糖製栗子。

mar·row¹ ['mæro; 'mærou] *n.* ①髓。②精華;核心。③〖英〗食用葫蘆。④力量;活力。⑤富於營養的食物。—**ish,** *adj.*

mar·row² *n.* 〖蘇, 英北部〗①伙伴。②配偶。③同伴。

mar·row·bone ['mæroˌbon; 'mærouboun] *n.* ①含髓之骨 (烹飪用)。 ②(*pl.*)〖諧〗膝。③(*pl.*) =**crossbones.**

mar·row·fat ['mæraˌfæt; 'mæroufæt] *n.* 大豌豆之一種。

mar·row·less ['mærolɪs; 'mæroulis] *adj.* 無髓的。

mar·row·y ['mærəwɪ; 'mæroui] *adj.*

①含髓的;多髓的。②(文章等)簡潔有力的。

‡mar·ry¹ 〔'mæri; 'mæri〕 *v.*, **-ried, -rying.** —*v.t.* ①結婚;娶;嫁。They are now *married.* 他們現在已結婚。②嫁(女)〖常off〗。She has *married* off all her daughters. 她把她的女兒們都嫁出去了。③主持…的婚禮;使正式結爲夫婦。The priest *married* them. 牧師主持他們的婚禮。④使密切結合一起。to *marry* intellect with sensibility. 理智與情感融合一起。—*v.i.* ①結婚。She did not *marry* until forty. 她直到四十歲才結婚。②合併;結合。by that old bridge where the waters *marry.* 在河流會合處的那座老橋梁旁邊。—**mar·ri·er,** *n.*

mar·ry² *interj.* (表驚愕、憤怒等)啊!呀!噯!

***Mars** 〔marz; ma:z〕 *n.* ①〖羅馬神話〗戰神。②戰爭。③火星。

Mar·sa·la 〔mar'sala; ma:'sa:la:〕 *n.* ①馬沙拉(義大利 Sicily 島之一海港)。②馬沙拉葡萄酒(一種淡而甜的白色葡萄酒,原產於義大利 Sicily 島)。

Mar·seil·laise 〔,marsl'ez; ma:sə'leiz〕〖法〗 *n.* 馬賽進行曲(法國國歌)。

Mar·seilles 〔mar'selz; ma:'seilz〕 *n.* 馬賽(法國東南部之一海港)。

***marsh** 〔marʃ; ma:ʃ〕 *n.* 沼澤;濕地。to drain a *marsh.* 排乾沼澤。—*adj.* ①生長在沼澤地帶的。②沼澤的。—**like,** *adj.*

***mar·shal** 〔'marʃəl; 'ma:ʃəl〕 *n., v.,* **-shal(l)ed, -shal·(l)ing.** —*n.* ①官(特指警官)。②高級軍官;元帥。field *marshal.* 〖英〗陸軍元帥。③司儀者;司禮官。④法警。⑤王宮中高級官員。—*v.t.* ①整列;排列。He *marshaled* his facts well. 他把事實列舉得很好。②列隊備戰。③用儀式引導。We were *marshaled* before the king. 我們被引導到國王面前。—*v.i.* 按次序就位。—**(l)er,** *n.*

Mar·shall 〔'marʃəl; 'ma:ʃəl〕 *n.* 馬歇爾 (George Catlett, 1880–1959, 美國將軍及外交家)。

marsh gas 〖化〗沼氣;甲烷(CH_4)。

marsh·land 〔'marʃ,lænd; 'ma:ʃlænd〕 *n.* 沼澤地帶。

marsh mallow 〖植物〗藥蜀葵(其根供藥用或作蜜餞糖果)。

marsh·mal·low 〔'marʃ,mælo; 'ma:ʃ,mælou〕 *n.* ①(原指)蜜餞藥蜀葵根。②一種白色鬆軟之糖果。

marsh marigold 〖植物〗立金花、猿猴草之類的植物。

marsh·y 〔'marʃi; 'ma:ʃi〕 *adj.,* **marsh·i·er, marsh·i·est.** ①軟濕似沼澤的。②多沼澤的。③沼澤的。—**marsh·i·ness,** *n.*

mar·su·pi·al 〔mar'sjupiəl; ma:'sju:piəl〕 *n.* 有袋動物(如袋鼠等是)。—*adj.* 有袋動物的。

mar·su·pi·um 〔mar'sjupiəm; ma:'sju:piəm〕 *n., pl.* **-pi·a** 〔-piə; -piə〕.〖動物〗(有袋類動物之)育兒袋。

mart 〔mart; ma:t〕 *n.* ①市場;商業中心。London and New York are the great *marts* of the world. 倫敦與紐約爲世界的大商業中心。②〖詩,古〗市集。

Mar·tel·lo tower 〔mar'tɛlo~; ma:'telou~〕(海岸防守用的)石造圓形碉堡。

mar·ten 〔'martin; 'ma:tin〕 *n., pl.* **-tens, -ten.** ①貂鼠。②貂皮。

Mar·tha 〔'marθə; 'ma:θə〕 *n.* ①〖聖經〗馬大 (Lazarus 及 Mary 之姊,耶穌之友)。②女子名。③作家庭瑣事及照料俗務的女人。

***mar·tial** 〔'marʃəl; 'ma:ʃəl〕 *adj.* ①戰爭的;軍事的。court *martial.* 軍事法庭。②勇武的;好戰的。a boy of *martial* spirit. 有尙武精神的孩子。③威武的;雄糾糾的;適於戰士的。a *martial* stride. 威武的步伐。—**ly,** *adv.*

martial art 任何一種源自東方而廣泛應用爲運動項目的武藝(如空手道、柔道等)。

martial law 戒嚴令;戒嚴法。

Mar·tian 〔'marʃən; 'ma:ʃiən〕 *adj.* ①火星的。②戰神的。—*n.* 火星人。

Mar·tin 〔'martin; 'ma:tin〕 *n.* ①聖·馬丁 (Saint, 315?–?399, Tours 之主教,法國之守護聖徒)。②男子名。

mar·tin 〔'martin; 'ma:tin〕 *n.* 一種短喙燕。

mar·ti·net 〔,martn̩'ɛt; ,ma:ti'net〕 *n.* 厲行嚴格紀律的人(尤指海陸空軍軍官)。

mar·tin·gale 〔'martn̩,gel; 'ma:tngeil〕 *n.* ①馬頷韁。②〖航海〗固定第二斜桅於下方之索具。

mar·ti·ni 〔mar'tini; ma:'ti:ni〕 *n., pl.* **-nis.** 馬丁尼酒(雞尾酒之一種)。

Mar·tin·mas 〔'martinməs; 'ma:tinməs〕 *n.* 聖馬丁節(十一月十一日)。

mart·let 〔'martlit; 'ma:tlit〕 *n.* ①(歐洲普通的)燕子。②〖紋章〗無足之鳥。

mar·tyr** 〔'martə; 'ma:tə〕 *n.* ①烈士;殉道者;殉教者。*martyrs* to duty. 殉職者。②受難者;受苦者。He was a lifelong *martyr* to rheumatism (asthma). 他終身爲風濕症(氣喘症)患者。③誇大受苦而想贏得同情的人。make a martyr of oneself*** **a.** 犧牲。**b.** 故意做出犧牲的樣子。—*v.t.* ①因其堅守其信仰、主義等而處死。②使成爲烈士。③使受苦;使受難。—**ish,** *adj.* —**ly,** *adv., adj.*

mar·tyr·dom 〔'martədəm; 'ma:tədəm〕 *n.* ①殉道;殉教;殉難。②痛苦;苦難。

mar·tyr·ol·o·gy 〔,martə'ralədʒi; ,ma:tə'rɔlədʒi〕 *n., pl.* **-gies.** 殉教史;殉教者列傳;殉教者名單。

***mar·vel** 〔'marvl; 'ma:vəl〕 *n., v.,* **-vel(l)ed, -vel·(l)ing.** —*n.* 奇異之事物(或景象)。Niagara Falls is one of the great *marvels* in the world. 尼加拉瀑布是世界大奇景之一。—*v.i.* 驚異。We all *marveled* at his success. 我們對他的成功都很感驚異。—*v.t.* 對…感驚異;因…感驚異(與子句連用)。I *marvel* how it can be so. 我驚異於事情怎會如此。—**ment,** *n.*

***mar·vel·(l)ous** 〔'marvləs; 'ma:viləs〕 *adj.* ①奇異的;不平常的。②似不可能的。the *marvelous* events of Greek myth. 似不可能的希臘神話故事。③了不起的;卓越的。That was a *marvelous* show. 那是一場了不起的表演。—**ness,** *n.* —**ly,** *adv.*

mar·vie, mar·vy 〔'marvi; 'ma:vi〕 *interj.* 〖美俚〗表驚奇、讚賞等之感歎語(爲 marvelous 之變體)。

Marx 〔marks; ma:ks〕 *n.* 馬克斯(Karl, 1818–1883, 德國政治經濟學家、哲學家及社會主義者)。

Marx·i·an 〔'marksiən; 'ma:ksjən〕 *adj.* 馬克斯的;馬克斯主義的。—*n.* 馬克斯主義者。

Marx·ism 〔'marksizm̩; 'ma:ksizəm〕 *n.* 馬克斯主義。(亦作 **Marxianism**)

Marx·ist 〔'marksist; 'ma:ksist〕 *n., adj.* =**Marxian.**

Mar·y¹ 〔'mɛri; 'mɛəri〕 *n.* 女子名。

Mar·y² *n.* 〖聖經〗聖母馬利亞(耶穌之母,亦作 **the Virgin Mary, Saint Mary**)。

Mary Jane 〖俚〗=**marijuana.** (亦作 **maryjane**)

Mar·y·land 〔'mɛrələnd; 'mɛərilænd〕

n. 馬里蘭(美國東部大西洋岸之一州, 其首府爲 Annapolis).

Mar·y·land·er [ˈmɛrələndɚ; ˈmɛərilændə] *n.* 馬里蘭州居民。

mar·zi·pan [ˈmɑrzəˌpæn; ˌmɑːziˈpæn] *n.* 杏仁和糖搗成的漿(做餅所用者); 杏仁糖。(亦作 **marchpane**)

MAS Malaysian Airline System. 馬來西亞航空公司。

-mas 〖字尾〗表 "節日; 慶祝" 之義, 如: Christmas.

mas., masc. masculine.

mas·car·a [mæsˈkærə; mæsˈkɑːrə] *n.* 染睫毛(或眉毛)油。

mas·cot [ˈmæskət; ˈmæskət] *n.* 吉祥之人(物)。

***mas·cu·line** [ˈmæskjəlɪn; ˈmɑːskjulin] *adj.* ①男性的。②有丈夫氣的; 雄壯的; 强有力的。③〖文法〗陽性的。*masculine* gender. 陽性。④(女性之)像男人樣的。—*n.* ①〖文法〗陽性。②陽性字; 陽性型式。—**ly,** *adv.* —**ness,** *n.*

masculine ending 〖詩〗陽性行末(行末音節有重音者)。

masculine rhyme 〖詩〗單韻(最後一音重讀之韻, 如 disdain, complain).

mas·cu·lin·ist [ˈmæskjəlɪnɪst; ˈmæskjulinist] *n.* 主張男權至上的人。

mas·cu·lin·i·ty [ˌmæskjəˈlɪnətɪ; ˌmæskjuˈliniti] *n.* 丈夫氣; 剛毅; 雄壯。

ma·ser [ˈmezɚ; ˈmeizə] *n.* 分子增幅器(爲 *m*icrowave *a*mplification by *s*timulated *e*mission of *r*adiation 之略)。

***mash** [mæʃ; mæʃ] *n.* ①用熱水泡的碎麥芽(釀啤酒用)。②一種牛馬等之飼料(由穀物、麥麩、熱水混於一起者)。③任何糊狀物。④〖英俚〗馬鈴薯泥(=mashed potatoes). ⑤〖俚〗a. 調情。b. 調情者; 情人。—*v.t.* ①搗碎使成糊狀。*mashed* potatoes. 馬鈴薯泥。②加熱水於(碎麥芽)。③〖俚〗調情。④〖英俚〗泡(茶)。—*v.i.* 〖俚〗調情。

mash·er [ˈmæʃɚ; ˈmæʃə] *n.* ①將食物搗碎成糊狀之人或器具; 搗碎機。②〖俚〗勾搭陌生女子的男人。

mash·ie [ˈmæʃɪ; ˈmæʃi] *n., pl.* **-ies.** 高爾夫球五號鐵頭球棒。

mashie iron 高爾夫球第四號鐵頭球棒。

mashie niblick 高爾夫球第六號鐵頭球棒。

mash note 〖俗〗短情書。

mash·y [ˈmæʃɪ; ˈmæʃi] *adj.,* **mash·i·er, mash·i·est,** *n.*—*adj.* 磨碎的。—*n.* = **mashie.**

mask** [mæsk, mɑsk; mɑːsk] *n.* ①假面具; 面罩。to wear a *mask*. 戴假面具; 隱其眞情。②戴面具的人。③掩飾; 僞裝。He hid his evil plans under a *mask* of friendship. 他藉友誼之名而掩藏其惡毒之詭計。④化裝舞會。⑤= **masque.** ⑥石膏面像。⑦(狐狸之)頭或臉。⑧面龐或頭像(通常爲奇形怪狀, 作裝飾用者)。⑨防毒面具。⑩有些狗嘴周圍的黑色部分。⑪〖軍〗掩體。⑫積分電路中分子的排列。pull off*** (or ***tear off***) ***one's mask*** 現出其眞面目。***throw off one's mask*** 揭掉假面具; 亮出眞相。***under the mask of*** 在僞裝下; 藉名; 託辭。—*v.t.* ①戴假面具。He is *masked*. 他戴假面具。②掩飾; 僞裝。A smile *masked* his disappointment. 微笑遮掩了他的失望。③掩護; 擋住。④隱藏。—*v.i.* 戴面具; 化裝。—**like,** *adj.*

masked [mæskt; mɑːskt] *adj.* ①帶面具的; 化裝的。a *masked* ball. 化裝舞會。②遮蔽的; 隱蔽的。③〖醫〗隱發的。④〖植物〗(花冠)假面狀的。⑤〖動物〗有面具狀斑紋的(如蛹等)。

mask·er [ˈmæskɚ; ˈmɑːskə] *n.* 帶假面具者; 覆面者; 化裝舞蹈者; 假面劇演員。(亦作 **masquer**)

mask·ing [ˈmæskɪŋ; ˈmɑːskiŋ] *n.* 化裝。

mas·och·ism [ˈmæzəˌkɪzəm; ˈmæzəˌkizəm] *n.* ①〖精神病〗受虐狂(以被異性奴役、虐待或傷害爲樂的一種色情狂)。②自我虐待。③喜好自我虐待。—**mas·och·ist,** *n.* —**mas·och·is·tic,** *adj.*

***ma·son** [ˈmesn̩; ˈmeisn] *n.* ①泥瓦匠。②(M-) 共濟會 (Freemason) 會員。—*v.t.* 用磚瓦砌成或加强。

Ma·son-Dix·on line [ˈmesn̩ˈdɪksn̩ ~; ˈmeisnˈdiksn ~] 美國昔日之南北分界線(界於 Pennsylvania 及 Maryland 二州之間, 亦係蓄奴各州與無奴各州之分界線)。(亦作 **Mason and Dixon('s) line**)

ma·son·ic, Ma·son·ic [məˈsɑnɪk; məˈsɔnik] *adj.* 共濟會的; 共濟會會員的。—**al·ly,** *adv.*

Ma·son·ite [ˈmesn̩ˌaɪt; ˈmeisnait] *n.* 〖商標名〗梅索奈特(絕緣用保溫硬質纖維板)。

Mason jar 有金屬螺蓋的玻璃罐。

ma·son·ry [ˈmesn̩rɪ; ˈmeisnri] *n., pl.* **-ries.** ①泥瓦砌工; 磚造物; 石造物。②泥瓦匠業; 泥瓦匠之技藝。③(M-) **a.** 共濟會之主義或規則。**b.** 共濟會會員集合稱。

masque [mæsk, mɑsk; mɑːsk, mæsk] *n.* ①一種歌舞劇(十六、十七世紀盛行於英國)。②此種歌舞劇劇本。③化裝舞會。(亦作 **mask**)

mas·quer [ˈmæskɚ; ˈmɑːskə] *n.* = **masker.**

mas·quer·ade [ˌmæskəˈred; ˌmæskəˈreid, ˌmɑːs-] *n., v.,* **-ad·ed, -ad·ing.** —*n.* ①化裝舞會。②僞裝。a hypocrite's *masquerade* of virtue. 僞君子的道德假面具。—*v.i.* ①參加化裝舞會。②喬裝; 僞裝。a prince who *masquerades* as a peasant. 一位化裝爲農夫的王子。—**mas·quer·ad·er,** *n.*

Mass, mass [mæs, mɑs; mæs, mɑːs] *n.* ①(天主敎的) 彌撒。to go to *Mass*. 去望彌撒。to say *Mass*. 作彌撒。High *Mass*. 大彌撒(有奏樂、燒香等者)。Low *Mass*. 小彌撒(無奏樂者)。②奠祭。③彌撒曲。

‡mass [mæs; mæs] *n.* ①塊; 團。a *mass* of dough. 一團麪。②大量。*mass* production. 大量生產。The poor fellow was a *mass* of bruises. 那可憐的人遍體鱗傷。③大多數。the *mass* of the people. 大多數的人民。④容積; 面積。the sheer *mass* of an iceberg. 冰山的巨大體積。⑤〖物理〗質量。⑥製藥丸之漿狀體。***in the mass*** 大體而論; 概括而言; 整體地。***the masses*** 勞工階級; 平民。—*v.t.* 使集合。to *mass* troops. 集合軍隊。—*v.i.* 集合。Troops are *massing* on the frontier. 軍隊在邊境集結。—*adj.* ①大規模的。*mass* buying. 大量購買。②羣衆的。*mass* protest. 羣衆的抗議。*mass* meeting. 民衆大會。—**ed·ly,** *adv.*

Mass. Massachusetts.

Mas·sa·chu·setts [ˌmæsəˈtʃusɪts; ˌmæsəˈtʃuːsits] *n.* 麻薩諸塞州(位於美國東部新英格蘭地區, 首府爲波士頓, Boston).

***mas·sa·cre** [ˈmæsəkɚ; ˈmæsəkə] *n., v.,* **-cred, -cring.** —*n.* 大屠殺。the *massacre* of millions during the war. 戰爭期間幾百萬人的大屠殺。—*v.t.* 大屠殺。—**mas·sa·crer,** *n.*

mass action 〖物理〗質量作用。

mas·sage [məˈsɑʒ; ˈmæsɑːʒ] *n., v.,* **-saged, -sag·ing.** —*n.* 按摩; 揉。—*v.t.* 按摩; 揉。—**mas·sag·er,** *n.*

mas·sag·ist [mə'sɑʒɪst; mə'sɑːʒist] *n.* 按摩師。
mass communication (用報紙、無線電、電視等爲工具的)大衆傳播。
mass defect 〖物理〗質量虧損。
mas·sé [mæ'se; mæ'sei] *n.* 〖撞球〗以球桿垂直擊球之法。(亦作 **massé shot**)
mas·seur [mæ'sɝ; mæ'səː] *n., pl.* **-seurs.** 操按摩業之男人;男按摩師。
mas·seuse [mæ'sɝz; mæ'səːz] *n., pl.* **-seus·es.** 按摩女。
mass formation 密集隊形。
mas·si·cot ['mæsɪ͵kɑt; 'mæsikɔt] *n.* 〖化〗黄鉛丹;黄丹(PbO)。(亦作**massicotite**)
mas·sif ['mæsɪf; 'mæsiːf] *n.* 〖地質〗主要山彙;叢山;斷層塊。
mass·i·ness ['mæsɪnɪs; 'mæsinis] *n.* 「堅實;厚重。
***mas·sive** ['mæsɪv; 'mæsiv] *adj.* ①大而重的;大塊的。a *massive* rock. 大塊石頭。②寬大的。a *massive* forehead. 寬大的前額。③堅定的;有力的。④宏偉的;莊嚴的;予人深刻印象的。*massive* erudition. 令人佩服的學識。⑤大量的。—**ly,** *adv.* —**ness, mas·siv·i·ty,** *n.*
mass man 易受大衆傳播工具左右,無個性、無責任感的人。
mass media 大衆傳播工具(無線電、電視、報紙、雜誌等)。
mass number 〖物理〗(原子)質量數。
mass-pro·duce ['mæsprə'djus; 'mæsprə͵djuːs] *v.t.,* **-duced, -duc·ing.** 大量生產。—**mass-pro·duc·er,** *n.*
mass production 大量生產。
mass psychology 羣衆心理(學)。
mass society ①一般社會(尤指地區廣大者,或包括各階層者)。②廣大社會。
mass spectrograph〖物理〗質譜儀。
mass·y ['mæsɪ; 'mæsi] *adj.,* **mass·i·er, mass·i·est.**①巨大的;重的。②實體的;結實的。
mast**[1] [mæst, mɑst; mɑːst] *n.* ①檣;桅。②直立之柱。radio *masts.* 無線電鐵塔。sail before the mast*** 做海員。—*v.t.* 立檣;立柱。
mast[2] *n.* 櫸、槲、栗等之果實(豬之飼料)。
mas·ta·ba(h) ['mæstəbə; 'mæstəbə] *n.*(古埃及側面傾斜而平頂的)石室墳墓;石櫈。
mas·tec·to·my [mæs'tɛktəmɪ; mæs'tektəmi]*n., pl.* **-mies.**〖外科〗乳房切除(術)。
‡**mas·ter** ['mæstɚ, 'mɑs-; 'mɑːstə] *n.* ①主人;指揮者;雇主。I like to be my own *master.* 我願做自己的主人(不願受束縛之意)。②家長。③船長。④男教師;校長。a dancing *master.* 舞師。⑤(冠於少年名字前之尊稱)君;小主人。⑥(精通工藝等之)專家;名家。to make oneself (the) *master* of a language. 使自己精通一種語文。⑦藝術大師;藝術大師所作的畫。⑧碩士。*Master* of Arts. 文學碩士。*Master* of Science. 理學碩士。⑨(the M-) 耶穌。⑩勝利者。⑪法院的書記官。⑫(用來複製普通唱片之)母片。⑬師傅(有資格收學徒的匠人)。⑭母機。⑮用機械複製之物。⑯能控制局勢者;能自由行動者。to be *master* of a situation. 對某種情勢能應付裕如。⑰=**master film.** ***be master in one's own house*** 有權處理自己事務,不受他人干涉。***be master of*** **a.** 精通。**b.** 能自由使用。***be master of oneself*** 自制。***be one's own master*** 自由獨立的。***master and man*** 雇主與工人;主與僕。—*adj.* ①主人的;做主人的。②主要的;爲首的;技藝高超的;支配的。—*v.t.* ①馴伏;遏抑;征服;控制。He can not even *master* his temper. 他甚至不能遏制自己的脾氣。②支使;命令。to *master* a ship's crew. 指揮一船的船員。③精通。Chinese is a difficult language to *master.* 中國話是很難精通的語言。—**hood,** *n.* —**less,** *adj.*
-master 〖字尾〗表"…支桅之船"之義。「a four-*master.* 四桅船。
mas·ter-at-arms['mæstərət'ɑrmz; 'mɑːstərət'ɑːmz]*n.,pl.* **mas·ters-at-arms.** ①〖海軍〗紀律官;糾察長(在軍艦上擔任憲兵任務之海軍士官)。②社團中維持秩序的職員。
master builder ①建築師。②監工。③營造商。
mas·ter·dom ['mæstɚdəm; 'mɑːstədəm] *n.* =**mastery.**
master film 用以沖洗大量照片之底片。
mas·ter·ful ['mæstɚfəl; 'mɑːstəful] *adj.* ①喜權勢的;專橫的。②巧妙的;老練的;有力的。—**ly,** *adv.* —**ness,** *n.*
master hand ①熟練(的技巧)。②名師;名匠;名手;專家。
master key 萬能鑰匙(可以開很多不同鎖的鑰匙)。
mas·ter·ly ['mæstɚlɪ; 'mɑːstəli] *adj.* 巧妙的;精巧的。—*adv.* 精巧地。—**mas·ter·li·ness,** *n.*
master mechanic 技工頭;熟練的技工。
mas·ter·mind['mæstɚ͵maɪnd;'mɑːstəmaind] *n.* 大智之人;(尤指)運籌帷幄的人;指揮者。—*v.t.* 爲(計畫等)之策劃人或指揮者。
master of ceremonies 司禮者;司儀。
***mas·ter·piece** ['mæstɚ͵pis, 'mɑs-; 'mɑːstəpiːs] *n.* ①絕妙之作。a scenic *masterpiece.* 絕景。②傑作;名著。*masterpieces* in English literature. 英國文學名著。
master plan (尤指大建築物的)草圖;總綱。
master's degree 碩士學位。(亦作 **master's**)
master sergeant 〖美陸軍、空軍,海軍陸戰隊〗士官長。
mas·ter·ship ['mæstɚʃɪp; 'mɑːstəʃip] *n.* ①master 之地位、職務、身分、尊嚴等。②控制;支配。③精通。④熟練;純熟之技能或知識。⑤碩士學位。
master stroke 極技巧的行動或收穫。
mas·ter·work ['mæstɚ͵wɝk; 'mɑːstəwəːk] *n.* =**masterpiece.**
master workman ①工頭。②技師。
***mas·ter·y** ['mæstərɪ; 'mɑːstəri] *n., pl.* **-ter·ies.** ①統治權;控制權。②征服;勝利。man's *mastery* over nature. 人類的征服自然。③精通〖of〗。④技巧;知識。
mast·head ['mæst͵hɛd; 'mɑːsthed] *n.* ①桅梢。②桅頂瞭望之人。③報頭。—*v.t.* ①升(旗等)於桅頂。②使登桅頂(對水手之一種處罰)。—*adj.* 在桅梢的。
mas·tic ['mæstɪk; 'mæstik] *n.* ①乳香樹脂(醫藥或洋漆之原料)。②(亦作 **mastic tree**) 乳香樹。③膠泥的一種。④乳香酒(加有乳香的葡萄酒)。⑤淡黃色。
mas·ti·cate ['mæstə͵ket; 'mæstikeit] *v.t.,* **-cat·ed, -cat·ing.** ①咀嚼。②磨爛。—**mas·ti·ca·tion,** *n.*
mas·ti·ca·tor ['mæstə͵ketɚ;'mæstikeitə] *n.* ①咀嚼者。②食物搗碎機;碎肉機。③(*pl.*)〖諧〗牙齒。
mas·ti·ca·to·ry ['mæstəkə͵torɪ; 'mæstikətəri] *adj., n., pl.* **-ries.** —*adj.* 咀嚼的;適於咀嚼的。—*n.* 刺激唾液分泌或產生香氣之咀嚼物(如口香糖等)。
mas·tiff ['mæstɪf; 'mæstif] *n.* 大猛犬(耳及唇均下垂)。

mas·ti·tis [mæs'taɪtɪs; mæs'taitis] *n.* 〖醫〗乳腺炎;乳房炎。

mas·to·don ['mæstə,dɑn; 'mæstədɔn] *n.* ①乳齒象(古代的一種似象之巨獸)。②大人物;偉人。—**ic,** *adj.*

mas·toid ['mæstɔɪd; 'mæstɔid] *adj.* 〖解剖、動物〗①乳頭狀的; 乳房狀的。②(耳後之)乳突骨的; 乳狀突起的。—*n.* ①〖解剖、動物〗乳狀突起。②〖俗〗乳突(骨)炎。

mas·toid·i·tis [,mæstɔɪd'aɪtɪs; ,mæstɔid'aitis] *n.* 〖醫〗乳狀突起炎;乳突炎。

mas·tur·bate ['mæstɚ,bet; 'mæstəbeit] *v.i.* & *v.t.,* **-bat·ed, -bat·ing.** 手淫。—**mas·tur·ba·tor,** *n.*

mas·tur·ba·tion [,mæstɚ'beʃən; ,mæstə'beiʃən] *n.* 手淫。—**al,** *adj.*

ma·su·ri·um [mə'sjʊrɪəm; mə'sjuəriəm] *n.* 〖化〗鎷(金屬元素之一, 符號 Ma, 現改稱 technetium).

mat¹** [mæt; mæt] *n., v.,* **mat·ted, mat·ting.** —*n.* ①蓆; 墊。②(用以墊燈、瓶、盤等之)小墊。③一叢;一團;一簇。a *mat* of weeds. 一叢野草。④編織之物。⑤(角力比賽場之)地板墊。⑥裝咖啡或糖等的蓆袋。go to the mat with*** **a.** 在蓆上與(人)角力。**b.** 與(人)就某一問題爭論。—*v.t.* ①鋪蓆於…上。②纏結。The swimmer's wet hair was all *matted* together. 游泳者的濕頭髮都結在一起了。—*v.i.* 結纏一起。The fur collar *mats* when it gets wet. 皮領子潮濕的時候毛結在一起。—**less,** *adj.*

mat² *adj., n., v.,* **mat·ted, mat·ting.** —*adj.* 無光澤的;暗淡的。—*n.* ①畫或像片的厚襯紙或襯邊。②無光澤的面。—*v.t.* ①使無光澤。②加厚襯紙於(畫或照片的)底下或周圍。

mat³ 〖印刷〗紙型(=matrix).

mat·a·dor ['mætə,dɔr; 'mætədɔː] *n.* ①(鬥牛時屠牛之)鬥牛士。②(M-)〖美〗無人駕駛飛機;鬥牛士飛彈。

:match¹ [mætʃ; mætʃ] *n.* ①火柴。to strike (*or* light) a *match.* 擦燃火柴。safety *matches.* 安全火柴。a box of *matches.*一盒火柴。②點鎗用的火繩。

:match² *n.* ①對手; 相似之人或物; 相配之人或物。The hat is a *match* for the coat. 帽子與外衣很相配。②比賽; 競爭。a basketball *match.* 籃球賽。③配偶;姻緣;婚姻。to make a *match.* 作媒;得偶。—*v.t.* ①相等; 相似; 相調諧。They are equally *matched* in their knowledge of Chinese. 他們在中文的造詣上相等。②相配。The color of the shirt does not *match* that of the coat. 襯衫的顏色與上衣的不配合。③匹配。a well *matched* couple. 一對美滿的夫妻。④相對;匹敵。No one can *match* him in argument. 在辯論上無人可與他相比。⑤使一致。to *match* one's actions to one's beliefs. 使行動與信仰一致。⑥對抗。I *matched* my wit against his strength. 我用我的機智對抗他的力氣。⑦拼湊。⑧結婚。—*v.i.* ①相等;適合。②相配。The colors *match* well. 顏色配得很好。③聯姻;匹配。Let beggars *match* with beggars. 瘸爐配破磨;龍配龍, 鳳配鳳。—**er,** *n.*

match·a·ble ['mætʃəbl; 'mætʃəbl] *adj.* 可匹敵的;相配的。

match·board ['mætʃ,bɔrd; 'mætʃbɔːd] *n.* 〖木工〗假型板。

match·book ['mætʃ,bʊk; 'mætʃbuk] *n.* 小書本型的紙火柴。

match·box ['mætʃ,bɑks; 'mætʃbɔks] *n.* 火柴盒。

match·less ['mætʃlɪs; 'mætʃlis] *adj.* 無比的;無雙的。—**ly,** *adv.* —**ness,** *n.*

match·lock ['mætʃ,lɑk; 'mætʃlɔk] *n.* 火繩槍。

match·mak·er ['mætʃ,mekɚ; 'mætʃ,meikə] *n.* ①媒人。②安排比賽的人。③做火柴的人。

match·mak·ing ['mætʃ,mekɪŋ; 'mætʃ,meikiŋ] *n.* ①火柴製造。②做媒;說媒。③(拳擊、摔角等之)競賽之安排。—*adj.* ①火柴製造(者)的。②做媒的。③安排競賽的。

match play 〖高爾夫〗得分競賽。

match point 〖競賽〗為勝利所必要的最後的(決勝的)一分。

match·stick ['mætʃ,stɪk; 'mætʃstik] *n.* 火柴棒。

match·wood ['mætʃ,wʊd; 'mætʃwud] *n.* 做火柴棒的木材。***make matchwood of*** 粉碎。

***mate¹** [met; meit] *n., v.,* **mat·ed, mat·ing.** —*n.* ①一對或一雙中之一; 單隻(鳥)。Where is the *mate* to this glove? 這副手套的另一隻在哪裏?②配偶;夫或妻。She has been a faithful *mate* to him. 她一直都是他的忠實的妻子。③大副;船員。first *mate.* 大副。second *mate.* 二副。④助手。the surgeon's (cook's) *mate.* 外科醫生(廚子)之助手。⑤伴侶(尤指工人階級的伙伴)。Where are you going, *mate?* 朋友,你去哪兒?—*v.t.* ①結伴。②使結成對;使配對。③使符合;使一致。He didn't *mate* his words with deeds. 他的言行不一致。④結婚。—*v.i.* ①結伴。I will not *mate* with him. 我不願與他爲友。②結婚。③相配對。④交配。Birds *mate* in the spring. 鳥在春天交配。—**ship,** *n.*

mate² 〖棋〗*n., v.t.* 將軍;將。—*interj.* 將!

ma·té, ma·te³ ['mɑte; 'mɑːtei] *n.* ①馬黛茶(樹)(巴拉圭及巴西產)。②馬黛茶樹之葉。(亦作 **Paraguay tea**)

ma·te·lot [,mat'lo; ,mat'lou] 〖法〗*n.* 水手。

ma·ter ['metɚ; 'meitə] *n.* 〖英俗〗母親。

ma·ter·fa·mil·i·as [,metɚfə'mɪlɪ,æs; ,meitəfə'miliæs] 〖拉〗*n.* 母親;主婦。

:ma·te·ri·al [mə'tɪrɪəl; mə'tiəriəl, -'tjəːr-] *n.* ①材料; 布料。building *material.* 建材。dress *material.* 衣料。raw *materials.* 原料。②資料;事實;經驗。③(*pl.*) 工具。writing *materials.* 文房用具。—*adj.* ①物質的;非精神的。the *material* civilization. 物質文明。②身體的;肉體的。*material* comforts (*or* delights). 身體的享樂。③重要的;相關的;有干係的〖常 to〗. Hard work is a *material* factor in success. 勤勞是成功的重要因素。④〖法律〗對案件有決定性影響的。The judge warned the witness not to hold back *material* facts. 法官警告證人不得隱瞞決定性的事實。—**ness,** *n.*

ma·te·ri·al·ism [mə'tɪrɪəl,ɪzəm; mə'tiəriəlizəm] *n.* ①唯物論。②現實主義。

ma·te·ri·al·ist [mə'tɪrɪəlɪst; mə'tiəriəlist] *n.* ①物質主義者;唯物論者。②現實主義者;實利主義者。—*adj.* 物質主義(者)的。

ma·te·ri·al·is·tic [mə,tɪrɪəl'ɪstɪk; mə,tiəriə'listik] *adj.* ①唯物論(者)的。②現實主義(者)的。—**al·ly,** *adv.*

ma·te·ri·al·i·ty [mə,tɪrɪ'ælətɪ; mə,tiəri'æliti] *n., pl.* **-ties.** ①物質性;具體性。②有形物;實體。③〖法律〗重要性;重大。

ma·te·ri·al·ize [mə'tɪrɪəl,aɪz; mə'tiəriəlaiz] *v.,* **-ized, -iz·ing.** —*v.t.* ①使具體化; 賦與實質。②使具實體。③使着重現

實; 使物質化。—*v.i.* ①成爲實體; 具有實體。②實現。 —**ma·te·ri·al·i·za·tion, ma·te·ri·al·iz·er,** *n.*

***ma·te·ri·al·ly** [mə'tɪrɪəlɪ; mə'tiəriəli] *adv.* ①物質上地。②實質上地。③重要地;很大地;頗多地。This matter *materially* influences us. 此事影響我們甚大。

ma·te·ri·a med·i·ca [mə'tɪrɪə'mɛdɪkə; mə'tiəriə'medikə] ①藥品;藥物(集合稱)。②藥物學。

ma·té·ri·el [mə,tɪrɪ'ɛl; mə,tiəri'el] *n.* ①設備; 裝備(以別於人員)。②〖軍〗武器彈藥等補給品。(亦作 **materiel**)

***ma·ter·nal** [mə'tɝnl; mə'tə:nl] *adj.* ①母親的;似母親的。*maternal* love. 母愛。②母系的;母方的。*maternal* grandmother. 外祖母。③從母方繼承的。—**ly,** *adv.*

ma·ter·ni·ty [mə'tɝnətɪ; mə'tə:niti] *n.* 母道; 母性。—*adj.* ①懷孕的; 產婦的。a *maternity* nurse. 助產士。a *maternity* ward. 產科病房。②產後的。

maternity hospital 產科醫院。

mate·y ['metɪ; 'meiti] *adj., n., pl.* **mate·ys.** 〖英俗〗 —*adj.* 友善的; 親密的〖with〗. —*n.* 友伴;至友。

math [mæθ; mæθ] *n.* 〖俗〗=**mathematics.**

math. ①mathematical. ②mathematics.

***math·e·mat·i·cal** [,mæθə'mætɪkl; ,mæθi'mætikəl] *adj.* ①數學的;數學上的。②精確的。The birds flew in a *mathematical* formation. 那些鳥以精確的隊形飛翔。(亦作 **mathematic**) —**ly,** *adv.*

math·e·ma·ti·cian [,mæθəmə'tɪʃən; ,mæθimə'tiʃən] *n.* 數學家。

***math·e·mat·ics** [,mæθə'mætɪks; ,mæθi'mætiks] *n.* (作*sing.* 解)數學。

Ma·til·da, Ma·thil·da [mə'tɪldə; mə'tildə] *n.* 女子名。(亦作 **Matilde**)

mat·in ['mætɪn; 'mætin] *n.* ①晨禱。②晨歌(如鳥叫)。—*adj.* ①晨禱的。②早晨的。

mat·i·nee, mat·i·née [,mætn̩'e; 'mætinei] *n.* 下午所演之戲劇或音樂。

mat·ing ['metɪŋ; 'meitiŋ] *n.* 相配;交配。

mat·ins ['mætɪnz; 'mætinz] *n. pl.* ①〖英〗晨禱。②〖詩〗晨歌(尤指鳥所唱者)。

mat·lo(w) ['mætlo; 'mætlou] *n.* 〖英俚〗水手。

mat·rass ['mætrəs; 'mætrəs] *n.* 〖化〗①細頸圓形燒瓶。②(一端封閉之)小玻璃管;閉管(吹管分析用)。

matri- 〖字首〗表"母"之義, 如: matriarch.

ma·tri·arch ['metrɪ,ɑrk; 'meitriɑ:k] *n.* 女家長; 女族長。—**ma·tri·ar·chal,** *adj.*

ma·tri·ar·chate ['metrɪ,ɑrkɪt; 'meitri,ɑ:kit] *n.* ①由 matriarch 所統治之家庭、家族或部族。②女治(制度);母治。

ma·tri·ar·chy ['metrɪ,ɑrkɪ; 'meitriɑ:ki] *n., pl.* **-ies.** 女家長制度;女族長制;母權制。

ma·tri·ces ['metrɪ,siz; 'meitrisi:z] *n.* pl. of **matrix.**

ma·tri·cid·al [,metrə'saɪdl̩; ,meitri'saidəl] *adj.* ①弒母的;有弒母之傾向的。②弒母者的。

ma·tri·cide ['metrə,saɪd; 'meitrisaid] *n.* 弒母;弒母者。

ma·tric·u·lant [mə'trɪkjələnt; mə'trikjulənt] *n.* (大學之)志願入學者;註册入學者。

ma·tric·u·late [mə'trɪkjə,let; mə'trikjuleit] *v.,* **-lat·ed, -lat·ing,** *n.* —*v.t.* (大學中准許)註册入學。—*v.i.* (大學中)註册入學。—*n.* 已註册之學生。—**ma·tric·u·la·tor,** *n.*

ma·tric·u·la·tion [mə,trɪkjə'leʃən; mə,trikju'leiʃən] *n.* 准許入學;註册。

mat·ri·lin·e·al [,metrɪ'lɪnɪəl; ,meitri'liniəl] *adj.* 母系的;母方的;母系主義的。(亦作 **matrilinear**) —**ly,** *adv.*

mat·ri·mo·ni·al [,mætrə'monɪəl; ,mætri'mounjəl] *adj.* 婚姻的; 夫婦的。—**ly,** *adv.*

mat·ri·mo·ny ['mætrə,monɪ; 'mætriməni] *n., pl.* **-nies.** ①婚姻;結婚。②婚姻生活。③婚禮。④婚姻關係。

ma·trix ['metrɪks; 'meitriks] *n., pl.* **ma·tri·ces, ma·trix·es.** ①(生物)母體。②子宮。③〖生物〗細胞間質。④〖礦〗母岩(含有結晶體礦物質或寶石者)。⑤〖印刷〗字模;紙型。⑥〖數學〗陣;矩陣;母式;眞値表。⑦唱片模子。⑧母體;源始。⑨矩陣電路。

ma·tron ['metrən; 'meitrən] *n.* ①年長之已婚婦女(尤指品格高尙者); 太太。②主婦;(機關、學校中之)褓姆。③女舍監;護士長。

ma·tron·age ['metrənɪdʒ; 'meitrənidʒ] *n.* ①matron 之身分或地位。②matron 之庇護或監督。③matron 之集合稱。

ma·tron·ize ['metrən,aɪz; 'meitrənaiz] *v.,* **-ized, -iz·ing.** —*v.t.*①使似年長婦人。②(matron 般)看護。—*v.i.* 成年長婦人。

ma·tron·ly ['metrənlɪ; 'meitrənli] *adj.* ①主婦的; 似主婦的。②嚴肅的。—*adv.* 主婦似地;如主婦地;嚴肅地。

matron of honor 〖美〗已婚之伴娘。

mat·ro·nym·ic [,mætrə'nɪmɪk; ,mætrə'nimik] *adj.* =**metronymic.**

Ma·tsu ['mætsu; mæ'tsu:, 'mætsu:] *n.* 馬祖(中國福建省海岸外之島嶼)。

Matt. ①Matthew. ②Matthias.

mat·ted[1] ['mætɪd; 'mætid] *adj.* ①鋪有蓆的。②亂成一團的。—**ly,** *adv.* —**ness,** *n.*

mat·ted[2] *adj.* 黯無光彩的。

‡**mat·ter** ['mætɚ; 'mætə] *n.* ①實質;實體(爲 form 之對)。②物質;物體(爲 mind, spirit 之對)。the relation between *matter* and spirit. 精神與物質(心物)之關係。③(書或印刷物之)資料;材料。postal *matter.* 郵件。printed *matter.* 印刷品。reading *matter.* 讀物。④理由;原因;根源。That is his *matter* for complaint. 那正是他抱怨的原因。⑤事實; 事件; 問題。It is a *matter* of life and death. 這事關係生死。⑥數量; 內容。a *matter* of ten minutes. 十分鐘。⑦困難。There seems something the *matter* with him. 他似乎有些困難。What's the *matter* with the machine?這部機器有甚麼毛病?⑧(瘡之)膿。⑨重要事項。⑩重要性。decisions of little *matter.* 無關重要的決定。***a hanging matter*** 吊刑案件(犯人應受吊刑處死)。***a matter of life and death*** 生命交關的事項;要緊的事項。***as a matter of fact*** 事實上;實際上。*As a matter of fact,* he didn't know it either. 事實上他也不知道。***as matters stand*** (or ***as the matter stands***) 照目前狀況。***for that matter*** (or ***for the matter of that***) 就那件事而論。***in the matter of*** 至於。***make matters worse*** 使事態惡劣; 把事情弄糟。***matter of moment*** 重要之事。***no laughing matter*** 正經的事;嚴重的事。***no matter*** **a.** 無論;不管。*no matter* what (where, who, when, how, etc.). 不論甚麼(何地、誰、何時、如何等)。**b.** 不重

要; 無關係。*take matters easy* 對事情泰然處之。—*v.i.* ①關係重要(經常用於疑問句、否定句或假設句中)。It does not *matter* at all. 毫無關係。②化膿。

matter of course 當然發生之事。

mat·ter-of-course [ˈmætərəvˈkɔrs; ˈmætərəvˈkɔːs] *adj.* ①自然會發生的;當然的。②認某事爲當然發生的。

matter of fact 〖法律〗①按證據來判定可靠與否的陳述或言論。②事實。

mat·ter-of-fact [ˈmætərəvˈfækt; ˈmætərəvˈfækt] *adj.* 事實的; 實際的; 平凡的;乏味的。—**ly,** *adv.*

mat·ter·y [ˈmætərɪ; ˈmætəri] *adj.* 多膿的。

Mat·thew [ˈmæθju; ˈmæθjuː] *n.* ①馬太(耶穌十二門徒之一, 馬太福音作者)。②馬太福音。

mat·ting [ˈmætɪŋ; ˈmætiŋ] *n.* ①蔴、草等之編織物(如草蓆、蔴包、蔴袋等)。②蓆之集合稱。③製蓆。④無光澤的表面。

mat·tins [ˈmætṇz; ˈmætinz] *n.* (常作 *sing.* 解)〖英〗晨禱。

mat·tock [ˈmætək; ˈmætək] *n.* 鶴嘴鋤。

***mat·tress** [ˈmætrɪs; ˈmætris] *n.* ①床墊。②彈簧床墊。③混凝土地面。

mat·u·rate [ˈmætʃʊˌret; ˈmætjureit] *v.,* **-rat·ed, -rat·ing.** —*v.i.* ①化膿。②成熟。—*v.t.* ①使化膿。②使成熟。

mat·u·ra·tion [ˌmætʃʊˈreʃən; ˌmætjuˈreiʃən] *n.* ①〖醫〗化膿。②成熟。③〖生物〗配偶子之成熟(期)。—**al,** *adj.*

***ma·ture** [məˈtjʊr; məˈtjuə] *adj., v.,* **-tured, -tur·ing.** —*adj.* ①成熟的。a *mature* age. 成熟的年齡。②熟思的; 審愼考慮過的。a *mature* plan. 熟思的計畫。③(付款等)到期的。a *mature* bill. 到期的支票。—*v.i.* ①成熟。②充分發展。③到期。The bill *matures* today. 支票本日到期。—*v.t.* ①使成熟。His character was *matured* by age. 他的品德因年齡而成熟。②審愼以完成。③使趨於完善。—**ly,** *adv.* —**ment,** —**ness, ma·tur·er,** *n.*

***ma·tu·ri·ty** [məˈtjʊrətɪ; məˈtjuəriti] *n.* ①成熟(果實、人格等)。He reached *maturity* at twenty years. 他在二十歲時達到成年。②完成; 備齊(計畫等)。to bring a plan to *maturity*. 使計畫趨於完備。③(債務、支票等)到期。to pay at *maturity*. 到期付款。

ma·tu·ti·nal [məˈtjutɪnl; ˌmætju(ː)ˈtainl] *adj.* 早晨的;清早的;早的。—**ly,** *adv.*

mat·zo [ˈmɑtso; ˈmɑːtsə] *n.* sing. of **matzos.**

matz·os [ˈmɑtsos; ˈmɑːtsous] *n. pl.* =**matzoth.**

matz·oth [ˈmætsoθ; ˈmɑːtsouθ] *n. pl.* (猶太人逾越節所食之)不加酵粉之麪包。

Maud(e) [mɔd; mɔːd] *n.* 女子名。

maud [mɔd; mɔːd] *n.* ①(蘇格蘭南部之牧羊人所着之)灰色方格毛織披肩。②(此種質料所製之)旅行用毛毯。

maud·lin [ˈmɔdlɪn; ˈmɔːdlin] *adj.* ①易傷感的;愛落淚的。②酒後傷感而落淚的。

Maugham [mɔm; mɔːm] *n.* 毛姆(William Somerset, 1874–1965, 英國小說家及劇作家)。

mau·gre, mau·ger [ˈmɔgə; ˈmɔː-gə] *prep.* 〖古〗不管;雖。

maul [mɔl; mɔːl] *v.t.* ①虐打;傷害。②〖美〗用大槌劈開。—*n.* 大槌。(亦作 **mall**)

maul·ey [ˈmɔlɪ; ˈmɔːli] *n.* 〖俚〗拳;手。

maul·stick [ˈmɔlˌstɪk; ˈmɔːl-stik] *n.* (畫家之)腕木(在垂直之畫面繪細線時執於左手支持右手用)。(亦作 **mahlstick**)

Mau Mau [ˈmaʊˌmaʊ; ˈmauˌmau] *pl.* **Mau Maus, Mau Mau.** 毛毛黨人(1950年代初期成立於 Kenya 的革命黨, 以驅逐白人爲目的)。

maund [mɔnd; mɔːnd] *n.* 印度、伊朗、土耳其等之重量單位。

maun·der [ˈmɔndə; ˈmɔːndə] *v.i.* ①絮聒。②徘徊;迷惘地言行。—**er,** *n.*

maun·dy [ˈmɔndɪ; ˈmɔːndi] *n.* 〖宗教〗①倣基督之故事於 Maundy Thursday 爲貧民洗足之儀式。②=**maundy money.**

maundy money 洗足星期四(Maundy Thursday) 施捨給窮人的硬幣。

Maundy Thursday 洗足星期四; 聖星期四(耶穌受難節之前一日)。

Mau·pas·sant [ˈmopəˌsɑnt; ˈmoupəsɑːnt] *n.* 莫泊桑 (Henri René Albert Guy de, 1850–1893, 法國短篇小說家)。

Mau·rice [ˈmɔrɪs; ˈmɔːris] *n.* 男子名。

Mau·ri·ta·ni·a [ˌmɔrɪˈtenɪə; ˌmɔːriˈteiniə] *n.* 茅利塔尼亞 (西非一國家, 首都那瓦克夏特 Nouakchott).

Mau·ri·ti·us [mɔˈrɪʃɪəs; məˈriʃəs] *n.* 模里西斯 (印度洋中一島國, 首都路易斯港 Port Louis).

Mau·ser [ˈmaʊzə; ˈmauzə] *n.* (有時作 m-) 毛瑟槍。

mau·so·le·um [ˌmɔsəˈliəm; ˌmɔːsəˈliːəm] *n., pl.* **-le·ums, -le·a** [-ˈliə, -ˈliːə]. ①壯麗之墓。②(M-)小亞細亞西南部之華麗陵寢, 爲 Caria 國王 Mausolus 之墳墓。

mauve [mov; mouv] *n.* ①淡紫色。②淡紫色染料。—*adj.* 淡紫色的。

mav·er·ick [ˈmævrɪk; ˈmævrik] *n.* ①(美西部)未打烙印之牛; 離開母牛而迷失的小牛。②〖俗〗持異議者。—*v.i.* 〖美西部〗迷失; 迷途。—*adj.* 不隨俗的;不守成規的。

ma·vis [ˈmevɪs; ˈmeivis] *n.* 〖詩〗(歐洲產的)善鳴的畫眉鳥。

ma·vour·neen, ma·vour·nin [məˈvʊrnin; məˈvuəniːn] *n.* 〖愛〗親愛的(=my darling) (指婦女)。

maw [mɔ; mɔː] *n.* ①(動物之)胃或胃腔; (鳥之)嗉囊。②魚之水泡。③(某些動物之)喉、食道、顎、或口腔。④饑餓或食欲之象徵。

mawk·ish [ˈmɔkɪʃ; ˈmɔːkiʃ] *adj.* ①令人作嘔的。②沒風味的。③傷感的;傷懷的;令人落淚的。—**ly,** *adv.* —**ness,** *n.*

max. maximum.

max·i [ˈmæksi; ˈmæksiː] *n., pl.* **max·is.** 迷嬉裝。

max·il·la [mæksˈɪlə; mækˈsilə] *n., pl.* **-lae** [-li; -liː]. ①〖解剖〗顎;顎骨;上顎。②〖動物〗(節足動物之)下顎肢;小鰓。

max·il·lar·y [ˈmæksəˌlɛrɪ; ˈmæksiləri] *adj., n., pl.* **-lar·ies.** —*adj.* 顎的;顎骨的。—*n.* 顎骨。

Max·im [ˈmæksɪm; ˈmæksim] *n.* 馬克沁重機槍。

***max·im** [ˈmæksɪm; ˈmæksim] *n.* ①格言。a golden *maxim.* 金言。②座右銘。

max·i·mal [ˈmæksəməl; ˈmæksiməl] *adj.* 最大的;最高的。—**ly,** *adv.*

Max·i·mal·ist [ˈmæksəməlɪst; ˈmæksiməlist] *n.* ①(昔俄社會革命黨之)極左分子。②俄共黨員。—**Max·i·mal·ism,** *n.*

max·i·mize [ˈmæksəˌmaɪz; ˈmæksimaiz] *v.,* **-mized, -miz·ing.** —*v.t.* 使達最大或最高限度。—*v.i.* 〖神學〗廣義解釋教義等。

***max·i·mum** [ˈmæksəməm; ˈmæksiməm, -ksm-] *n., pl.* **-mums, -ma** [-mə; -mə], *adj.* —*n.* ①最大量; 最高點。The excitement was at its *maximum*. 興奮到了極點。②〖數學〗極大(值); 最大(值)。—*adj.* 最高的; 最大極限的。The *maximum* score on the test is 100. 考試的滿分爲100。—**ly**, *adv.*

maximum thermometer 最高溫度計。

max·well [ˈmækswɛl; ˈmækswəl] *n.* 〖電〗馬(克士威)(磁束之單位)。(略作 **mx**)

‡May [me; mei] *n.* ①五月。②春;盛年;青春。a young woman in her *May*. 正値青春的少婦。③〖英〗(Cambridge 大學之)五月考試;(the Mays) 五月賽船。④五朔節(May Day) 之慶祝。

‡may[1] [me; mei, me, mi, mə] *aux. v.*, pt. **might** ①可能(多少與 perhaps相當)。It *may* be true. 可能是眞的。②可以(表許可)。*May* I ask you a question? 允許我問你一個問題嗎?③願(表願望或請求)。*May* you be happy! 祝你幸福! *May* you live long. 祝你長壽。④俾可;欲(表目的)。He works hard in order that he *may* succeed. 他勤勉用功以求成功。⑤儘可。You *may* well say so. 你有足够的理由可以如此說。⑥能够;能。

may[2] *n.* 〖植物〗山楂花。—*v.i.* 慶祝五朔節;採五月花。

Ma·ya [ˈmɑjə; ˈmɑːjə] *n.*①馬雅人。the *Mayas*. 馬雅族(中美印第安人之一族)。②馬雅語。—*adj.* 馬雅人(語)的。

Ma·yan [ˈmɑjən; ˈmɑːjən] *adj.* 馬雅人(族)的;馬雅語系的。—*n.* ①馬雅(印第安)人。②馬雅語系(中美印第安之一語系)。

May apple 〖植物〗①鬼臼(北美產)。②其可食之果實。(亦作 **Indian apple**)

‡may·be [ˈmebi, ˈmebɪ; ˈmeibiː, –bi] *adv.*, *n.* 大概;或許。*Maybe* he will come. 或許他會來。There are lots of *maybes* in this glittering promise. 在皇皇承諾中,却有一大堆或許。〖注意〗 **maybe, may be.** maybe 是副詞或名詞。may be 是動詞片語。

May beetle(or **bug**)=**cockchafer.**

May·day [ˈmeˌde; ˈmeidei] *n.* (船或飛機所發之)國際無線電求救信號。

May Day ①五朔節(5月1日擧行的春之祭典)。②國際勞動節。③=**Mayday.**

May·fair [ˈmeˌfɛr; ˈmeifɛə] *n.* 倫敦西端上流社會住宅區; 倫敦社交界。

May·flow·er [ˈmeˌflauə; ˈmeiˌflauə] *n.* ①五月花號船(1620年淸敎徒自英渡美所乘者)。②五月開花之植物;五月花。

May fly ①蜉蝣。②作魚餌用的人造蜉蝣。

may·hap [ˈmeˌhæp, meˈhæp; ˈmeihæp] *adv.* =**perhaps.**

may·hem [ˈmehɛm, ˈmeəm; ˈmeihem, ˈmeiəm] *n.* 〖法律〗重傷害罪(用暴力加於他人在防衞時所必要之部分,手、足、目、齒等的傷害)。(亦作 **maihem**)

May·ing, may·ing [ˈmeɪŋ; ˈmeiiŋ] *n.* 五朔節之慶祝;五朔節的採花。

***may·on·naise** [ˌmeəˈnez; ˌmeiəˈneiz] *n.* 以蛋黃、橄欖油、檸檬汁或醋等混製之醬汁。

***may·or** [ˈmeə; mɛə] *n.* 市長。

may·or·al [ˈmeərəl; ˈmɛərəl] *adj.* 市長的。

may·or·al·ty [ˈmeərəltɪ; ˈmɛərəlti] *n.*, *pl.* **-ties.** ①市長職位。②市長任期。

may·or·ess [ˈmeərɪs; ˈmɛəris] *n.* ①市長夫人;女市長。②〖英〗市長所指定之該市第一夫人(通常爲市長夫人,其女兒或姊妹)。

May·pole [ˈmeˌpol; ˈmei-poul] *n.* ①五月柱(慶祝五朔節時飾有花及彩條之柱)。②個子細長的人。(亦作 **maypole**)

May queen 五月皇后(May Day 所選出之美女)。

May·tide [ˈmeˌtaɪd; ˈmeiˈtaid] *n.* 五月;月之季節;五月。

May·time [ˈmeˌtaɪm; ˈmeitaim] *n.* =**Maytide.**

may tree 〖英〗=**hawthorn.**

maz·a·rine [ˌmæzəˈrin; ˌmæzəˈriːn] *n.* ①深藍色。②〖廢〗深藍色服裝。—*adj.* 深藍色的。

Maz·da·ism, Maz·de·ism [ˈmæzdaɪzm̩; ˈmæzdəizm] *n.* =**Zoroastrianism.**

***maze** [mez; meiz] *n.* ①迷宮。②迷惘;惶惑。He was in such a *maze* that he couldn't speak. 他感到迷惘而說不出話。③混亂。—*v.t.* 〖方〗使迷惘;使混亂。

ma·zu·ma [məˈzumə; məˈzuːmə] *n.* 〖美俚〗金錢。

ma·z(o)ur·ka [məˈzɝkə; məˈzəːkə] *n.* 馬厝卡舞(波蘭之輕快舞蹈);馬厝卡舞曲。

ma·zy [ˈmezɪ; ˈmeizi] *adj.*, **ma·zi·er, ma·zi·est.** 如迷宮般彎彎曲曲的;複雜的。

mb. ①millibar(s). ②millibarn(s).

M.B. ①Medicinae Baccalaureus(〖拉〗=Bachelor of Medicine). ②Musicae Baccalaureus (〖拉〗=Bachelor of Music).

MBS Mutual Broadcasting System(美國四大廣播公司之一)。 **mc** ①megacycle. ②millicurie. ③millicycle.

Mc- 〖字首〗 **Mac-** 之異體。

M.C. ①Master of Ceremonies. ②Member of Congress. ③Military Cross. ④Master Commandant.

Mc·Car·thy·ism [məˈkɑrθɪɪzm̩; məˈkɑːθiizəm] *n.* ①公開指控某人有親共而不忠於(美)國之行爲(由 Joseph R. McCarthy 參議員發動故名)。②政府機構之忠貞調查。

Mc·Coy [məˈkɔɪ; məˈkɔi] *n.* (亦作 **the real McCoy**)〖美俚〗(the–)本人;眞貨。—*adj.* 〖美俚〗本人的;眞貨的。

Mcf one thousand cubic feet.

Mc·In·tosh [ˈmækɪntɑʃ; ˈmækintɔʃ] *n.* 一種成熟於早秋的紅色蘋果;其樹。

M.C.S. Master of Commercial Science. **Md** 化學元素 mendelevium 之符號。**Md.** Maryland. **M.D.** ①Doctor of Medicine (Medicinae Doctor). ②Middle Dutch. ③Medical Department. ④memorandum deposit. **M/d, m/d** ①months' date 或 months after date. 發票日…月後之同日。②memorandum of deposit. 存款單;送款票。**MDAP** Mutual Defense Assistance Program.

M-day [ˈɛmˌde; ˈemˌdei] *n.* 〖美〗動員日(=Mobilization Day).

Mdlle. *pl.* **Mdlles.** Mademoiselle.

Mdm(e). *pl.* **Mdms.** Madam(e).

mdse. merchandise. **Me** 〖化〗methyl 之符號。

‡me [mi; miː, mi] *pron.* ①(I 的受格)我。It's *me*. 〖俗〗是我(=It's I)。②〖俗〗代替 my (用於動名詞構造句)。Did you hear about *me* getting promoted? 你有沒有聽到我晉級的消息? ***take it from me*** 〖俗〗我知道我講的話(我說的話千眞萬確)。

ME, ME., M.E. Middle English.

Me. Maine. **M.E.** ①(常 m.e.) managing editor. ②Master of Education. ③Master of Engineering. ④Mechanical Engineer. ⑤Methodist Episcopal. ⑥Middle English. ⑦Military Engineer. ⑧

Mining Engineer. ⑨Most Excellent.

mead[1] 〔mid; mi:d〕 *n.* 一種以蜜、麥芽、酵素、香料及水等釀成之酒。

mead[2] *n.* 〖詩〗草地。

***mead·ow** 〔ˈmɛdo; ˈmedou〕 *n.* ①草地。We are going to mow the *meadow*. 我們將把這草地上的草割去。②河邊低草地。

meadow lark (北美產之)野雲雀。

mead·ow·sweet 〔ˈmɛdəˌswit; ˈmedou-swi:t〕 *n.* 〖植物〗繡線菊。

mead·ow·y 〔ˈmɛdoɪ; ˈmedoui〕 *adj.* (似)草地的; 多草地的。

mea·ger, mea·gre 〔ˈmigɚ; ˈmi:gə〕 *adj.* ①瘦的。②微薄的; 不足的。*meager* pay. 微薄的薪給。③不詳盡的。—**ly**, *adv.* —**ness**, *n.*

‡**meal**[1] 〔mil; mi:l〕 *n.* ①一餐。We take three *meals* a day. 我們每日吃三餐。②一次吃完之食物。

***meal**[2] *n.* ①(各種穀類所碾之)粗粉。corn *meal*. 玉蜀黍粉(粥)。oatmeal. 麥片(粥)。②(任何碾碎之)粉。

meal·ie, meal·y 〔ˈmilɪ; ˈmi:li〕 *n.*, *pl.* **meal·ies.** 〖南非〗①(*pl.*) 玉蜀黍。②玉蜀黍的穗。

meals on wheels 將熱餐送至年老或殘廢者家中的一種服務。

meal ticket ①餐券。②〖俚〗飯票。③〖俚〗飯碗。④〖俚〗可靠的人; 靠得住的人。

meal·time 〔ˈmilˌtaɪm; ˈmi:l-taim〕 *n.* 通常吃飯之時間。

meal worm 食麪粉或米粉之甲蟲的幼蟲(常用以飼鳥)。

meal·y 〔ˈmilɪ; ˈmi:li〕 *adj.*, **meal·i·er, meal·i·est.** ①似粉的; 粉狀而乾的。②含有粉的; 塗有粉的。③(面貌) 蒼白的。④油嘴滑舌的。

mealy bug 水臘樹蟲(一種葡萄害蟲); (香蕉)粉介殼蟲。

meal·y·mouthed 〔ˈmilɪ ˈmauðd; ˈmi:limauðd〕 *adj.* 不敢直說的; 委婉而言的; 轉彎抹角說的; 甜言蜜語的。—**ly**, *adv.*

‡**mean**[1] 〔min; mi:n〕 *v.*, **meant, mean·ing.** —*v.t.* ①意欲; 打算。I do not *mean* to go. 我不想去。He *means* you no harm. 他無意傷害你。②意謂; 意表。What does this word *mean?* 這一字作何解釋? ③有意義。His words *mean* much. 他的話意味深長。④能引起。This frontier incident probably *means* war. 這邊境事件可能導致戰爭。⑤指定; 計劃。I *mean* you to go. 我決定由你去。⑥有價值; 有重要性。Money *means* everything to him. 金錢對他就是一切。⑦作某種解釋。The word "liberal" *means* many things to many people. "liberal" 這個字的解釋人言人殊。⑧造成某種結果。This bonus *means* that we can take a trip to Florida. 這分紅利可以使我們往佛羅里達去度一次假。⑨註定適於作某種用途。He was *meant* for a soldier. 他天生是一個軍人。—*v.i.* 意欲; 懷意。He *means* well. 他出乎好意。***mean well by*** (or *to*) 對…懷善意。

mean**[2] *adj.* ①(品質、等級)低劣的。He is no *mean* student. 他是個好學生。② (社會地位) 卑賤的; 平庸的。He is a man of *mean* birth. 他出身微賤。③鄙陋的; 襤褸的。④卑鄙的。*mean* thoughts (motives). 卑鄙的思想 (動機)。⑤吝嗇的; 節約的。He has no friends, for he is *mean* about money. 因他吝嗇, 所以沒有朋友。⑥不重要的; 無價值的。⑦〖俗〗自卑的; 慚愧的。to feel *mean*. 自慚形穢。⑧〖俗〗難駕馭的; 難控制的。⑨〖俗〗自私的; 脾氣壞的; 殘酷的。⑩〖俗〗身體不適。I feel *mean* today. 我今天覺得不舒服。⑪〖俚〗優秀的; 好的。He blows a *mean* trumpet. 他吹得一口好喇叭。⑫惱人的。a *mean* cold. 惱人的寒冷。⑬羞恥的。have a mean opinion of*** 輕視; 瞧不起。***no mean*** 很好的。(參看①) ***the great and the mean*** 貴賤上下。

mean**[3] *adj.* 中間的; 中庸的; 平均的。*mean* proportional. 〖數學〗比例中項。*mean* velocity. 平均速度。in the mean time*** (or ***while***) 當其時; 於此際。—*n.* ①(*pl.*) 方法; 工具; 手段。There is (are) no *means* of learning what is happening. 沒有辦法得知正發生着甚麼事。②(*pl.*) 財產; 財富。He is a man of *means*. 他乃富有之人。③中間; 中庸。the golden *mean*. 中庸之道。④(*pl.*)〖數學〗**a.** 平均數。**b.** (比例)中項。***a means to an end*** 達到目的之手段 (方法)。***by all means*** **a.** 必定; 當然。**b.** 竭力; 不惜一切。***by any means*** 不顧一切; 以任何方法。***by fair means or foul*** 用各種方法; 不擇手段。***by means of*** 以; 藉。***by no means*** 決不。He is *by no means* an honest man. 他決不是個誠實人。***by some means or other*** 總得; 無論如何設想辦法。***not by any means*** 一點也不。***ways and means*** 辦法。〖注意〗**means** 作方法、工具、手段解時, 形式是複數, 但在文法上作單數或複數名詞均可。means 當作財富解時, 形式及文法上都是複數。

me·an·der 〔mɪˈændɚ; miˈændə〕 *v.i.* ①蜿蜒而流。②漫遊。③閒談。—*n.* (常 *pl.*) 漫遊; 迂迴之路。—**er**, *n.*

me·an·der·ing 〔mɪˈændrɪŋ; miˈændəriŋ〕 *n.* ①曲折的路。②漫遊; 漫步。③聊天; 漫談。—*adj.* ①蜿蜒而流的。②漫遊的; 散步的。③聊天的; 閒談的。—**ly**, *adv.*

mean·ie 〔ˈminɪ; ˈmi:ni〕 *n.* =**meany.**

***mean·ing** 〔ˈminɪŋ; ˈmi:niŋ〕 *n.* ①意義; 含義。What's the *meaning* of this word? 這字作何解? ②目的。What is the *meaning* of life? 人生的目的是甚麼? —*adj.* 有意義的; 含義深長的。He wore a *meaning* look. 他臉上帶有意義深長的表情。—**ly**, *adv.* —**ness**, *n.*

mean·ing·ful 〔ˈminɪŋfl̩; ˈmi:niŋful〕 *adj.* 意味深長的; 富有意義的。—**ly**, *adv.* —**ness**, *n.*

mean·ing·less 〔ˈminɪŋlɪs; ˈmi:niŋlis〕 *adj.* 無意義的; 無價值的; 無目的的。—**ly**, *adv.* —**ness**, *n.*

mean·ly 〔ˈminlɪ; ˈmi:nli〕 *adv.* ①卑賤地。②吝嗇地。

mean·ness 〔ˈminnɪs; ˈmi:nnis〕 *n.* ①卑賤; 平庸。②卑鄙。③吝嗇。④無價值; 無聊。⑤(品質等之)粗劣。⑥卑劣的行爲。

mean·spir·it·ed 〔ˈminˈspɪrətɪd; ˈmi:nˈspiritid〕 *adj.* 卑鄙的; 心胸狹窄的。

means test ①〖英〗對接受失業救濟之人的收入調查。②對接受救濟之人的財務調查。

meant 〔mɛnt; ment〕 *v.* pt. & pp. of **mean**[1].

***mean·time** 〔ˈminˌtaɪm; ˈmi:nˈtaim, ˈmi:n-taim〕 *n.* 中間的時間; 其時; 此際。He will be back in the *meantime*. 他將於其時歸來。—*adv.* 於其時; 於此際。

***mean·while** 〔ˈminˌhwaɪl; ˈmi:nˈwail, -ˈhw-〕 *adv.*, *n.* =**meantime.**

mean·y 〔ˈminɪ; ˈmi:ni〕 *n.*, *pl.* **mean·ies.** 〖俗〗心地狹窄的惡毒的人。(亦作 **meanie**)

***mea·sles** 〔ˈmizl̩z; ˈmi:zlz〕 *n. pl.* (作 *sing.*

or *pl.* 解)①痲疹。*Measles* is a children's disease. 痲疹是小孩生的病。②風疹(=German measles). ③〖獸醫〗(牛、猪的)包蟲病。④〖獸醫〗包蟲。

mea·sly [ˈmizlɪ; ˈmiːzli] *adj.*, **-sli·er, -sli·est.** ①痲疹的;像痲疹的。②患痲疹的。③〖俚〗無價值的;卑劣的;微不足道的。④(肉中)有條蟲幼蟲的。

meas·ur·a·ble [ˈmɛʒrəbl̩; ˈmeʒərəbl] *adj.* ①可測量的。②適度的。***come within a measurable distance of*** 接近。—**meas·ur·a·bil·i·ty, —ness,** *n.* —**meas·ur·a·bly,** *adv.*

‡meas·ure [ˈmɛʒə; ˈmeʒə] *v.*, **-ured, -ur·ing,** *n.* —*v.t. & v.i.* ①量;計。We *measured* the room. 我們丈量這屋子。②有…之尺度;大小爲…。This room *measures* 30 feet across. 那房間寬 30英尺。③測度;估量;與…比較或競爭。to *measure* a person with one's eye. 打量某人。④取出一定之量〖常 out, off〗. to *measure* out a quantity of medicine. 分出一分藥品。⑤〖詩〗走;去;經過(一段路程)。⑥當作…之衡量標準。⑦調整;改正。*Measure* your needs to your income. 量入爲出。***measure one's length*** 跌倒於地。***measure out*** **a.** 仔細分配。**b.** 計量分配。***measure swords*** 鬥劍;參加決鬥、戰役、辯論等。***measure up*** 有足够的資格;符合標準;合格。—*n.* ①大小;尺寸;分量。waist *measure.* 腰圍尺寸。②丈量。③量度器。A ruler is a *measure.* 尺爲一量器。④量度標準;量度單位。the angular *measure.* 角度。the circular *measure.* 弧度。the cubic (*or* solid) *measure.* 體積;容積。the linear (*or* lineal) *measure.* 長度。long (broad) *measure.* 長(闊)度。*measure* of capacity. 容量。square *measure.* 面積。weights and *measures.* 度量衡。⑤任何賴以比較、估計、判斷之標準。Man is a *measure* of all things. 人是萬物之尺度(判斷標準)。⑥限度。He is angry beyond *measure.* 他極爲震怒。⑦〖詩〗韻律;〖音樂〗拍子;節線;小節。⑧舞。⑨措施;步驟;手段。The government has taken decisive *measures* to preserve order. 政府已採斷然手段以維持治安。⑩議案;法令。The senate passed the new *measure.* 參議院通過該議案。⑪〖數學〗約數。⑫量出之一定量。to drink a *measure.* 喝一定量(之酒)。⑬相當之量。to live with a *measure* of enjoyment. 過着相當安適的生活。⑭合理的規範。⑮地層。***beyond measure*** 非常地;極度地(參看⑥例)。***by measure*** 按尺寸(出賣等)地。***for good measure*** 附加地;另外地。***give full measure*** 盡全力;付出全部;給予足量。***give short measure*** 應盡而未盡全力;偷工減料;給予不足之量。***greatest common measure*** (略作 **GCM**) 最大公約數。***in a measure*** 有點兒;多少。***in great measure*** 大半。***in some measure*** 幾分。***made to measure*** (衣服)定做的。***set measures to*** 加限制於…。***take measures*** 採取行動。***take one's measure*** **a.** 判斷某人之性格。**b.** 量身材。***tread a measure*** 跳舞。***with (without) measures*** 適度(過度)地。—**meas·ur·er,** *n.*

meas·ured [ˈmɛʒəd; ˈmeʒəd] *adj.* ①整齊的(步調)。②有韻律的(語調)。③愼重的(發言)。④適度的;基於標準的。—**ly,** *adv.*

meas·ure·less [ˈmɛʒəlɪs; ˈmeʒəlis] *adj.* 不可量的;無限的;廣大的。

***meas·ure·ment** [ˈmɛʒəmənt; ˈmeʒəmənt] *n.* ①量度方法。Clocks give us a *measurement* of time. 鐘給我們一量度時間的方法。②測量;量度。③測得之量;面積。Its *measurement* is thirty acres. 其面積爲三十英畝。④測量制度。the metrical system of *measurement.* 公制量度。

meas·ur·ing [ˈmɛʒrɪŋ; ˈmeʒəriŋ] *n.*, *adj.* 測定(的);測量(用的)。

measuring worm 尺蠖。

‡meat [mit; miːt] *n.* ①食用之肉。*Meat* will not keep overnight in such hot weather. 肉在這樣熱的天氣中不能過夜。②食物。*meat* and drink. 飲食。③可食之部分。the *meat* of a nut. 核仁。④飯;餐。Say grace before *meat.* 吃飯前要禱告。⑤內容;實質。The book was full of *meat.* 那本書頗有內容。

meat and potatoes 〖俚〗最重要「或最基本的部分。」

meat-and-potatoes [ˈmitənpəˈtetoz; ˈmiːtənpəˈteitouz] *adj.* 〖美俗〗最重要的;基本的。

meat·ball [ˈmitˌbɔl; ˈmiːtbɔːl] *n.* ①肉丸。②〖俚〗笨拙的人;飯桶。③〖美海軍俚〗戰鬥能力優勝旗。

meat offering (古猶太人之麪粉和油做的)祭饌。

meat packing 〖美〗精肉業(屠宰、加「工、冷凍、製罐頭等之業務)。」

meat safe 遮蓋食物之具(如紗罩等)。(亦作 **meat-safe**)

me·a·tus [mɪˈetəs; miˈeitəs] *n.*, *pl.* **-tus·es, -tus.** 〖解剖〗管;道。

meat wagon 〖俚〗(醫院之)救護車。

meat·y [ˈmitɪ; ˈmiːti] *adj.*, **meat·i·er, meat·i·est.** ①肉的;有肉味的。②似肉的。③多肉的。④有內容的;有思想的。

Mec·ca [ˈmɛkə; ˈmekə] *n.* ①(亦作 **Mekka, Mekkah**) 麥加(沙烏地阿拉伯一首邑;爲穆罕默德誕生之地,因而成爲回教之聖地)。②(m-) **a.** 急欲前往遊玩之地。**b.** 聖地;發源地。**c.** 希望之目標。—**Mec·can,** *adj., n.*

mec·ca·no [mɛˈkɑno; meˈkɑːnou] *n.* ①鋼質組合性的玩具。②(M-) 其商標名。

mech. ①mechanical. ②mechanics. ③mechanism.

***me·chan·ic** [məˈkænɪk; miˈkænik] *n.* ①機械士。②修理機械之工人。③〖俚〗郎中(賭博行詐者)。—*adj.* =**mechanical.**

***me·chan·i·cal** [məˈkænɪkl̩; miˈkænikəl] *adj.* ①機械上的。②機械製的。③機械的;無表情的;呆板的。④機械學的。⑤摩擦的。—**ly,** *adv.* —**ness,** *n.*

mechanical drawing 機械畫。

mechanical engineering 機械工程。

mech·a·ni·cian [ˌmɛkəˈnɪʃən; ˌmekəˈniʃən] *n.* 機械(工程)師;機械學者;機工。

me·chan·ics [məˈkænɪks; miˈkæniks] *n.* ①(作 *sing.* 解)力學。②機械學。③(常作 *pl.* 解) 技巧;機械式的技巧。

***mech·a·nism** [ˈmɛkəˌnɪzəm; ˈmekənizəm, -kn̩i-] *n.* ①機械;機械裝置。an ingenious *mechanism.* 精巧的機械。②結構;機構。The bones and muscles are parts of the *mechanism* of the body. 骨骼及肌肉爲身體機構的一部分。③手法;技巧。④〖心理〗機構(一種心智中的安排,可以一定或可預知之方式決定思想、感情或行動)。⑤〖哲學〗機械論。

mech·a·nist [ˈmɛkənɪst; ˈmekənist] *n.*

①〖哲學〗機械論者。②〖罕〗＝**mechanician.**

mech·a·nis·tic 〔ˌmɛkəˈnɪstɪk; ˌmekəˈnistik〕 *adj.* 機械論(者)的;機械學的。

mech·a·ni·za·tion 〔ˌmɛkənəˈzeʃən; ˌmekənaiˈzeiʃən〕 *n.* 機械化(特指陸軍部隊之機械化);機動化。

mech·a·nize 〔ˈmɛkəˌnaɪz; ˈmekənaiz〕 *v.t.*, **-nized, -niz·ing.** ①使機械化。②用機械工作。③以機器代替人或獸。④以裝甲車、戰車等機械裝備(軍隊)。

mechanized unit 機械化部隊。

Med. ①medieval. ②Mediterranean.

med. ①medical. ②medicine. ③medi(a)eval. ④medium.

M. Ed. Master of Education.

med·al** 〔ˈmɛdḷ; ˈmedl〕 *n., v.,* **-al(l)ed, -al·(l)ing.** —*n.* 獎牌;獎章;勳章。He won a *medal.* 他贏得一面獎牌。the reverse of the medal*** 問題的另一面。—*v.t.* 授勳。

med·al(l)ed 〔ˈmɛdḷd; ˈmedld〕 *adj.* 曾受勳獎的;佩帶獎章的。

med·al·(l)ist 〔ˈmɛdḷɪst; ˈmedlist〕 *n.* ①曾受獎牌者。②獎牌設計者;獎牌雕刻者;獎牌匠。③〖高爾夫球〗資格賽中得最低桿數者。

me·dal·lion 〔mɪˈdæljən; miˈdæljən〕 *n.* ①大獎牌。②類似獎牌之設計或裝飾。

medal play 〖高爾夫球〗桿數比賽。(亦作 **stroke play**)

***med·dle** 〔ˈmɛdḷ; ˈmedl〕 *v.i.,* **-dled, -dling.** 干預或擾亂他人的事物。Don't *meddle* in my affairs. 不要干預我的事。—**med·dler,** *n.*

med·dle·some 〔ˈmɛdḷsəm; ˈmedlsəm〕 *adj.* 愛管閒事的;管閒事的。—**ly,** *adv.*

Mede 〔mid; miːd〕 *n.* 米底亞人。***the laws of the Medes and the Persians*** 不能修改之法律。

Me·de·a 〔mɪˈdɪə; miˈdiə〕 *n.* 〖希臘神話〗梅廸亞(幫助 Jason 獲得 Golden Fleece 的女魔師)。

med·e·vac 〔ˈmɛdəˌvæk; ˈmedəvæk〕 *n.* 〖美〗運送傷患的軍用直升機。

Me·di·a 〔ˈmidɪə; ˈmiːdiə〕 *n.* 米底亞(古代之王國,位於今伊朗之西北部,紀元前6–7世紀間最盛)。

me·di·a 〔ˈmidɪə; ˈmiːdiə〕 *n.* pl. of **medium.**

me·di·ae·val 〔ˌmidɪˈivḷ; ˌmediˈiːvəl〕 *adj.* ＝**medieval.**

me·di·al 〔ˈmidɪəl; ˈmiːdiəl〕 *adj.* ①中間的;中央的。②中間子音的。③適中的;普通的。—*n.* 中間字母;中間子音。—**ly,** *adv.*

media mix 同時使用數種媒體(如影片、錄音帶、幻燈片等)的(戲院)演出。

Me·di·an 〔ˈmidɪən; ˈmiːdiən〕 *adj.* 米底亞 (Media) 的;米底亞人的;米底亞語的;米底亞文化的。—*n.* 米底亞人。

me·di·an 〔ˈmidɪən; ˈmiːdiən〕 *adj.* 中間的;中央的;中線的;中間數字的。—*n.* ①中間數字。②〖數學〗中線。

median strip 高級公路中間之安全島(通常指有園藝點綴者)。

me·di·ate 〔*v.* ˈmidɪˌet; ˈmiːdieit *adj.* ˈmidɪɪt; ˈmiːdiit〕 *v.,* **-at·ed, -at·ing,** *adj.* —*v.i.* ①居於中間。②調停;斡旋。—*v.t.* ①居間以促成。②做…之中間者。③促成(結果);轉交(禮物);做(傳遞知識之)媒介。—*adj.* ①中間的。②間接的。—**ly,** *adv.*

me·di·a·tion 〔ˌmidɪˈeʃən; ˌmiːdiˈeiʃən〕 *n.* ①仲裁;調解;斡旋;調停。②〖國際法〗(第三國之)居中調停。

me·di·a·tive 〔ˈmidɪˌetɪv; ˈmiːdieitiv〕 *adj.* 居中的;調解的;斡旋的。

me·di·a·tize 〔ˈmidɪəˌtaɪz; ˈmiːdiətaiz〕 *v.,* **-tized, -tiz·ing.** —*v.t.* ①(大國)兼併(小國);使成附屬。②使成間接。—*v.i.* 居於中間。

me·di·a·tor 〔ˈmidɪˌetɚ; ˈmiːdieitə〕 *n.* ①中人;媒介者。②仲裁者;調解者;調停人;斡旋者;仲裁國。③(the M-)(爲神與人間之中保的)耶穌基督(見新約提摩太前書2章5節)。

me·di·a·to·ri·al 〔ˌmidɪəˈtorɪəl; ˌmiːdiəˈtɔːriəl〕 *adj.* ＝**mediatory.**

me·di·a·to·ry 〔ˈmidɪəˌtorɪ; ˈmiːdiətəri〕 *adj.* 仲裁的;調解的;調停的;斡旋的。(亦作 **mediatorial**)

me·di·a·tress 〔ˈmidɪˌetrɪs; ˈmiːdiˌeitris〕 *n.* 女仲裁人;女調解人。(亦作 **mediatrice; mediatrix).**

med·ic[1] 〔ˈmɛdɪk; ˈmedik〕 *n.* 〖植物〗紫苜蓿。(亦作 **medick**)

med·ic[2] *n.* 〖俗〗①醫生;外科醫生。②醫學院學生;實習醫生。③(戰鬥中作急救工作的)醫務兵。

med·i·ca·ble 〔ˈmɛdɪkəbḷ; ˈmedikəbl〕 *adj.* 可治療的;可醫的。

Med·i·caid, med·i·caid 〔ˈmɛdɪked; ˈmedikeid〕 *n.* 〖美〗(聯邦及州政府共同爲無力負擔醫療費用人民所提供的)醫療津貼方案。

***med·i·cal** 〔ˈmɛdɪkḷ; ˈmedikəl〕 *adj.* ①醫學的;醫術的。*medical* schools. 醫學院。②內科的(爲 surgical 之對)。The hospital has a *medical* ward and a surgical ward. 那醫院有一內科病房與一外科病房。③藥的;醫藥的;治療力的。a *medical* compound. 藥劑。—*n.* 〖俗〗①醫生;醫學院學生。②體格檢查。—**ly,** *adv.*

medical examiner ①驗屍官。②保險公司、工廠等的特約醫師。

medical jurisprudence 法醫學。

me·dic·a·ment 〔məˈdɪkəmənt, ˈmɛdɪkə-; meˈdikəmənt〕 *n.* ①藥;藥劑。②醫療的物質、工具或力量。

Med·i·care, med·i·care 〔ˈmɛdɪˌkɛr; ˈmediˈkɛə〕 *n.* 〖美, 加〗公辦之醫療保險制度。

med·i·cate 〔ˈmɛdɪˌket; ˈmedikeit〕 *v.t.,* **-cat·ed, -cat·ing.** ①以藥物治療。②加藥。

med·i·ca·tion 〔ˌmɛdɪˈkeʃən; ˌmediˈkeiʃən〕 *n.* ①藥物治療。②藥物處理;加藥。③藥物;藥劑;藥。

med·i·ca·tive 〔ˈmɛdəˌketɪv; ˈmedikətiv〕 *adj.* ①藥物治療的;藥性的。②起治療作用的;(藥劑)有效的。

me·dic·i·nal 〔məˈdɪsṇḷ; meˈdisinḷ〕 *adj.* 醫藥的;治療的。(亦作**medicinable**)—**ly,** *adv.*

med·i·cine** 〔ˈmɛdəsṇ; ˈmedsin, -disin〕 *n.* ①藥。Have you been taking much *medicine?* 你已服過很多藥嗎? ②醫學。He is studying *medicine.* 他正在學醫。Doctor of *Medicine.* 醫學博士 (略作 **M.D.**). ③內科。④醫生(行業)。⑤巫術。give someone a dose*** (or ***taste***) ***of his own medicine*** 以牙還牙。***take one's medicine*** 做必須做的事;做不喜歡做的事。—*v.t.* 給…服藥或上藥。

medicine ball 藥球(運動用之大而重之實心皮球,重四至九磅)。

medicine dance 未開化部落之宗教舞,旨在治病。

medicine man ①術士(北美土人所信之會治病與有法術之人)。②1900年以前之成藥推銷員,常以表演招攬顧客。

med·i·co 〔ˈmɛdɪˌko; ˈmedikou〕 *n., pl.* **-cos.** 〖俗〗①醫生;外科醫生。②研究醫學的學生;醫學院學生。

***me·di·e·val** 〔ˌmidɪˈivl̩, ˌmɛd-; ˌmedi-ˈiːvəl, ˌmiːd-〕 *adj.* 中古的;中世紀的;中古風的。(亦作 **mediaeval**) —**ism,** *n.* —**ly,** *adv.*

me·di·e·val·ist 〔ˌmidɪˈivl̩ɪst; ˌmedi-ˈiːvəlist〕 *n.* ①中古研究家; 中古史學者。②(藝術、宗教等之)尊重中古精神者;崇尚中古習慣風尚者。

me·di·e·val·ize 〔ˌmidɪˈivl̩ˌaɪz; ˌmedi-ˈiːvəlaiz〕 *v.t.,* **-ized, -iz·ing.** 使中古化;使遵奉中古的格式、思想等。

Me·di·na 〔məˈdinə; meˈdiːnə〕 *n.* ①麥地那(沙烏地阿拉伯西部之一城市,爲穆罕默德墳墓所在地)。②(m-)(摩洛哥)都市中之阿拉伯人集中區。

me·di·o·cre 〔ˈmidɪˌokɚ, ˌmidɪˈokɚ; ˈmiːdioukə〕 *adj.* 平常的;平凡的。

me·di·oc·ri·ty 〔ˌmidɪˈɑkrətɪ; ˌmiːdi-ˈɔkriti〕 *n., pl.* **-ties.** ①平常; 平凡; 平庸。②平凡的人;平庸之才。③平凡的能力或成就。

Medit. Mediterranean (Sea).

***med·i·tate** 〔ˈmɛdəˌtet; ˈmediteit〕 *v.,* **-tat·ed, -tat·ing.** —*v.t.* 想;考慮。—*v.i.* 冥思;回想。

***med·i·ta·tion** 〔ˌmɛdəˈteʃən; ˌmedi-ˈteiʃən〕 *n.* 沉思; 冥想。He sat alone in *meditation.* 他獨自坐着沉思。

med·i·ta·tive 〔ˈmɛdəˌtetɪv; ˈmeditə-tiv〕 *adj.* ①沉思的; 冥想的。②喜沉思的; 愛冥想的。—**ly,** *adv.*

med·i·ta·tor 〔ˈmɛdɪˌtetɚ; ˈmediteitə〕 *n.* 沉思者;冥想者。

***Med·i·ter·ra·ne·an** 〔ˌmɛdətəˈrenɪən; ˌmeditəˈreinjən, -niən〕 *adj.* ①地中海的;地中海沿岸地區的; 地中海民族的。the *Mediterranean* Sea. 地中海。②(m-)被陸地環繞的。—*n.* ①地中海(=Mediterranean Sea). ②地中海民族(=Mediterranean race).

***me·di·um** 〔ˈmidɪəm; ˈmiːdiəm, -dj-〕 *adj., n., pl.* **-di·ums, -di·a** 〔-dɪə; -diə〕. —*adj.* 中間的;中等的;中庸的。to be of *medium* size. 中等大小。—*n.* ①中間之物。②媒介物;媒體。Newspapers and magazines are important *media* for advertising. 報章雜誌爲廣告的重要媒體。 ③藉以生存之物;賴以寄生之物;環境。Water is the *medium* in which fish can live. 水是魚所藉以生存之物。④〖美〗巫;通靈之人。⑤顏料溶解液。⑥〖醫〗細菌培養基。⑦中型印刷紙張。⑧〖英〗書寫或畫圖紙(17½″×22″)。⑨繪畫之方式。

me·di·um·is·tic 〔ˌmidɪəˈmɪstɪk; ˌmiː-diəˈmistik〕 *adj.* 通靈者的;女巫的;似女巫的。

me·di·um-sized 〔ˈmidɪəmˈsaɪzd; ˈmiːdiəmˈsaizd〕 *adj.* 中型的。

med·lar 〔ˈmɛdlɚ; ˈmedlə〕 *n.* 〖植物〗枸杞;枸杞子。***the Japanese medlar*** 枇杷。

med·ley 〔ˈmɛdlɪ; ˈmedli〕 *n., pl.* **-leys,** *adj., v.* —*n.* ①混合; 混合物。②〖音樂〗混合曲。—*adj.* 混合的。—*v.t.* 混合。

Mé·doc 〔ˈmedɑk, meˈdɑk; ˈmedɔk, me-ˈdɔk〕 *n.* ①法國西南部之一地區(爲葡萄之產地)。②Médoc 產之紅葡萄酒。

Med.Sc.D. Doctor of Medical Science.

Me·du·sa 〔məˈdjusə; miˈdjuːzə〕 *n., pl.* **-sas.** 〖希臘神話〗蛇髮之女妖(視者卽變爲石)。

me·du·sa 〔məˈdjusə; miˈdjuːzə〕 *n., pl.* **-sae** 〔-si; -ziː〕, **-sas.** 〖動物〗水母。

meed 〔mid; miːd〕 *n.* 〖詩〗報酬;褒賞。

***meek** 〔mik; miːk〕 *adj.* ①溫順的;謙和的。②馴服的。—**ly,** *adv.* —**ness,** *n.*

meer·schaum 〔ˈmɪrʃəm, -ʃɔm; ˈmiə-ʃəm〕 *n.* ①〖礦〗海泡石。②海泡石做的煙斗。

‡**meet**[1] 〔mit; miːt〕 *v.,* **met, meet·ing,** *n.* —*v.t.* ①遇; 逢。We *met* her in the street. 我們在街上遇到她。②接合;相交;會合。③迎接;迎戰;應戰。I must go to the station to *meet* my mother. 我必須到車站去接我母親。④引見; 結識。I know him by sight but have never *met* him. 我見面認識他,但從未被人介紹過。⑤付(帳單、債務等)。In order to *meet* his expenses, he had to do extra work at night. 爲了支付開消, 他必須在晚上兼差。⑥接觸。His hands *met* hers. 他的手觸到了她的手。⑦會見。*Meet* me at 1:00. 一點鐘的時候與我見面。⑧滿足; 適合。 to *meet* a person's wish. 滿足某人之願望。⑨對付; 反抗。⑩面對。He *met* her glance with a smile. 他以微笑答報她的顧盼。⑪經驗到;受到。He *met* open scorn before he won fame. 他在贏得盛名之前, 曾歷盡公衆的蔑視。⑫聽到或看到。A strange sight *met* my eyes. 我看到一幕奇景。 ⑬互撞。The two cars *met* each other head-on. 兩車迎頭相撞。—*v.i.* ①相遇。 Their cars *met* on the narrow road. 他們的車子在狹路相遇。②會合; 相交。 the place where the two streets *meet.* 兩街相交之處。③結合;和諧相合。His is a nature in which courage and caution *meet.* 他的性格是勇敢與謹愼的融合。④對付; 反抗。⑤集會。 Congress will *meet* next month. 國會下月將集會。⑥相識。⑦同意。***make both ends meet*** 使收支相抵。***meet somebody halfway*** 妥協;作部分讓步。The owners agreed to *meet the strikers halfway.* 雇主同意向罷工者妥協。***meet (up) with*** **a.** 得到。The plan *met with* approval. 該計畫獲得通過。**b.** 嘗到(經驗)。to *meet with* misfortunes. 遇到苦難。**c.** 偶遇。to *meet with* a friend in the train. 在火車中偶遇一朋友。—*n.* 〖美〗①會; 集會; 運動會(在英國用 meeting). ②集會者。③集會之處。④〖數學〗交集。

meet[2] *adj.* 適宜的;合適的。

‡**meet·ing** 〔ˈmitɪŋ; ˈmiːtiŋ〕 *n.* ①會晤;邂逅。Their *meeting* was a joyful one. 他們的相晤很愉快。②會;集會。 to attend a *meeting.* 到會。③宗教集會。 a prayer *meeting.* 祈禱會。④交會處;會合處。the *meeting* of two rivers. 兩河交會處。⑤決鬥;對抗賽。

meeting house 禮拜堂;教堂;聚會所。

meeting place 會場;聚會所。

meet·ly 〔ˈmitlɪ; ˈmiːtli〕 *adv.* 適當地。

Meg 〔mɛg; meg〕 *n.* ①女子名(Margaret 之暱稱)。②〖蘇,英方〗女人;村姑;粗野的女孩。

meg- 〖字首〗 **mega-** 之異體,用在母音前。

mega- 〖字首〗①表"大"之義: megaphone. 揚聲器。②〖物理〗表"1,000,000倍"之義 (在母音前作 **meg-**).

meg·a·ce·phal·ic 〔ˌmɛgəsəˈfælɪk; ˌmegəsəˈfælik〕 *adj.* ①大頭的。②〖頭蓋測量學〗腦容量大(超過1500立方公分)的。(亦作 **megacephalous**)

meg·a·cu·rie 〔ˌmɛgəˈkjurɪ; ˌmegə-ˈkjuəri〕 *n.* 〖物理〗一百萬居里。(略作 **MCi, Mc**)

meg·a·cy·cle 〔ˈmɛgəˌsaɪkl̩; ˈmegə-ˌsaikl〕 *n.* ①〖物理〗百萬周。②〖無線電〗兆周。

meg·a·jet 〔ˈmɛgədʒɛt; ˈmegədʒet〕 *n.* 超級巨無霸噴射客機。

meg·a·lith 〔ˈmɛgəˌlɪθ; ˈmegəˌliθ〕 *n.* 〖考古〗(古時用於建築物或紀念碑之)巨石。

—ic, *adj.* 「張"之義。

megalo- 〖字首〗表"巨大的;不正常的擴

meg·a·lo·ma·ni·a 〔ˌmɛgələˈmenɪə; ˈmegəlouˈmeinjə〕 *n.* ①〖精神病〗妄想自大狂(患者妄想權勢、財富、尊貴等)。②(對偉大事物之)狂熱。

meg·a·lo·ma·ni·ac 〔ˌmɛgələˈmenɪˌæk; ˈmegəlouˈmeiniæk〕 *n.* 患妄想自大狂之人;誇大狂者。

meg·a·lop·o·lis 〔ˌmɛgəˈlɑpəlɪs; ˌmegəˈlɔpəlis〕 *n.* 大城市(由幾個城市及郊區連成者)。(亦作 **megapolis**)

meg·a·lo·pol·i·tan 〔ˌmɛgəloˈpɑlətn̩; ˌmegəlouˈpɔlitn〕 *adj., n.* 大城市的(居民)。

***meg·a·phone** 〔ˈmɛgəˌfon; ˈmegəfoun〕 *n.* 擴音器(放大聲音的喇叭);傳聲筒。

meg·a·scope 〔ˈmɛgəˌskop; ˈmegəskoup〕 *n.* 〖物理〗顯微鏡幻燈(裝置)。—**meg·a·scop·ic, meg·a·scop·i·cal,** *adj.*

meg·a·spore 〔ˈmɛgəˌspor; ˈmegəspɔː〕 *n.* 〖植物〗大芽胞;大胞子。

meg·a·struc·ture 〔ˌmɛgəˈstrʌktʃɚ; ˌmegəˈstrʌktʃə〕 *n.* 超級大廈。

meg·a·ton 〔ˈmɛgəˌtʌn; ˈmegətʌn〕 *n.* ①100萬噸。②相當於100萬噸 TNT 之爆炸威力(氫彈之單位)。

meg·a·watt 〔ˈmɛgəˌwɑt; ˈmegəwɔt〕 *n.* 〖電〗百萬瓦特。

meg·ger 〔ˈmɛgɚ; ˈmegə〕 *n.* 〖電俚〗測高阻計。

me·gilp 〔məˈgɪlp; məˈgilp〕 *n.* 似凍子之油畫材料。(亦作 **megilph, meguilp**)

meg·ohm 〔ˈmɛgˌom; ˈmegoum〕 *n.* 〖電〗百萬歐姆(電阻之單位,略作 **meg, MΩ**)。

meg·ohm·me·ter 〔ˈmɛgomˌmitɚ; ˈmegoumˌmiːtə〕 *n.* 〖電〗測高阻計。

me·grim 〔ˈmigrɪm; ˈmiːgrim〕 *n.* ①〖醫〗偏頭痛。②(*pl.*)憂鬱;抑鬱。③空想;幻想。④〖獸醫〗(牛、馬之)眩暈。

Mei·ji 〔ˈmedʒɪ; ˈmeidʒi〕 *n.* 明治(日本明治天皇 Mutsuhito 之朝代, 1868–1912)。

mei·o·sis 〔maɪˈosɪs; maiˈousis〕 *n.* ①〖生物〗減數分裂。②=**litotes.**

Meis·ter·sing·er 〔ˈmaɪstɚˌsɪŋɚ; ˈmaistəˌsiŋə〕 〖德〗 *n. sing.* or *pl.* (14–16世紀德國)詩樂會會員。(亦作 **mastersinger**)

Mek·ka 〔ˈmɛkə; ˈmekə〕 *n.* =**Mecca.**

Me·kong 〔ˈmeˈkɑŋ; ˈmeiˈkɔŋ〕 *n.* 湄公河(發源於中國西部,下流入中南半島)。

Mekong Delta 湄公河三角洲。

mel·a·mine 〔ˈmɛləmin; ˈmeləmiːn〕 *n.* 〖化〗三聚氰胺。

mel·an·cho·li·a 〔ˌmɛlənˈkolɪə; ˌmelənˈkouljə〕 *n.* 〖精神病〗憂鬱症。

mel·an·cho·li·ac 〔ˌmɛlənˈkolɪˌæk; ˌmelənˈkouliæk〕 *adj.* 患憂鬱症的。—*n.* 憂鬱症患者。

mel·an·chol·ic 〔ˌmɛlənˈkɑlɪk; ˌmelənˈkɔlik〕 *adj.* ①憂鬱的。②患憂鬱症的;(似)憂鬱症的。—*n.* 憂鬱症患者。

***mel·an·chol·y** 〔ˈmɛlənˌkɑlɪ; ˈmelənkəli, –ləŋk–〕 *n., pl.* **-chol·ies,** *adj.* —*n.* ①憂鬱;悲哀。A *melancholy* seized me on reading this poem. 當讀這首詩時,一陣憂鬱侵襲着我。②沉思;愁思。—*adj.* ①憂鬱的;悲哀的。a *melancholy* mood. 憂鬱的心情。②使人悲傷的;令人不快的。③沉思的;愁思的。

mel·a·nism 〔ˈmɛlənɪzəm; ˈmelənizəm〕 *n.* ①〖人種〗黑性(皮膚、毛髮、眼睛等多黑色素)。②〖醫〗黑色素過多;黑色症;黑變病。

Mel·ba toast 〔ˈmɛlbə～; ˈmelbə～〕 烤脆的麪包片。

Mel·bourne 〔ˈmɛlbən; ˈmelbən〕 *n.* 墨爾缽(澳洲東南部之一城市)。

meld[1] 〔mɛld; meld〕 *v.t.* & *v.i.* (於 pinochle 等牌戲中)宣示牌之分數。—*n.* 得分之宣示;可宣示之配合或分數。

meld[2] *v.t.* & *v.i.* (使)融合;(使)結合。

me·lee, mê·lée 〔meˈle, ˈmele; ˈmelei〕 *n.* ①混戰;白刃戰。②羣毆。

mel·io·rate 〔ˈmiljəˌret; ˈmiːljəreit〕 *v.,* **-rat·ed, -rat·ing.** —*v.t.* 改善;改良。—*v.i.* 變良好。—**mel·io·ra·tion, mel·io·ra·tor,** *n.* —**mel·io·ra·tive,** *adj.*

mel·io·rism 〔ˈmiljərɪzəm; ˈmiːljərizəm〕 *n.* 〖倫理〗改善論;社會改良論;世界改善論。

mel·lif·lu·ence 〔məˈlɪfluəns; məˈlifluəns〕 *n.* 甜蜜;流暢;甜美。

mel·lif·lu·ous 〔məˈlɪfluəs; məˈlifluəs〕 *adj.* 甜蜜的(話、音樂、聲音);流暢的。(亦作 **mellifluent**)

***mel·low** 〔ˈmɛlo; ˈmelou〕 *adj.* ①甜而多汁的;軟熟的。a *mellow* persimmon. 甜而多汁的柿子。②成熟的;醇的。*mellow* wine. 醇酒。③(因年齡與經驗而)圓熟的;熟練的;老練的。*mellow* age. 成熟的年齡。④柔和而豐滿的。a *mellow* color. 悅目的顏色。⑤肥沃的;富饒的。*mellow* soil. 肥沃的土壤。⑥〖俚〗歡樂的;沉醉的。—*v.t.* & *v.i.* 使熟;變熟。Apples *mellow* after they have been picked. 蘋果摘下之後變熟。—**ly,** *adv.* —**ness,** *n.*

me·lo·de·on 〔məˈlodɪən; məˈloudiən〕 *n.* ①脚踏風琴之一種。②手風琴之一種。(亦作 **melodion**)

me·lod·ic 〔məˈlɑdɪk; miˈlɔdik〕 *adj.* 旋律的;和諧的;悅耳的。—**al·ly,** *adv.*

me·lod·ics 〔mɪˈlɑdɪks; meˈlɔdiks〕 *n.* (作*sing.* 解)〖音樂〗旋律學。

me·lo·di·ous 〔məˈlodɪəs; miˈloudjəs〕 *adj.* ①和諧的;音樂的;悅耳的。②產生美音的。—**ly,** *adv.* —**ness,** *n.*

mel·o·dist 〔ˈmɛlədɪst; ˈmelədist〕 *n.* 作曲家;聲樂家。

mel·o·dize 〔ˈmɛləˌdaɪz; ˈmelədaiz〕 *v.,* **-dized, -diz·ing.** —*v.t.* 使成旋律;使…之旋律變美;使和諧;使悅耳。—*v.i.* 作曲;作旋律。

mel·o·dra·ma 〔ˈmɛləˌdrɑmə; ˈmeləˌdrɑːmə〕 *n.* ①鬧劇;通俗劇。②任何誇大刺激之文章或言語。

mel·o·dra·mat·ic 〔ˌmɛlədrəˈmætɪk; ˌmelədrəˈmætik〕 *adj.* 通俗劇的。—*n.* (=melodramatics)通俗劇的寫作;通俗劇作風。—**al·ly,** *adv.*

mel·o·dram·a·tist 〔ˌmɛləˈdræmətɪst; ˌmelouˈdræmətist〕 *n.* 通俗劇作者。

mel·o·dram·a·tize 〔ˌmɛləˈdræməˌtaɪz; ˌmeləˈdræmətaiz〕 *v.t.,* **-tized, -tiz·ing.** ①使通俗劇化。②使(小說等)成通俗劇。

***mel·o·dy** 〔ˈmɛlədɪ; ˈmelədi〕 *n., pl.* **-dies.** ①美的曲子;美的音樂。a master of *melody.* 音律大家。②調子。③主調;曲調。popular Negro *melodies.* 流行的黑人歌曲。

mel·on** 〔ˈmɛlən; ˈmelən〕 *n.* ①瓜。water *melon* (*or* watermelon). 西瓜。②深粉紅色。③〖俚〗額外紅利。cut*** (or ***split***) ***a melon*** 〖俚〗分享額外利潤;分紅利。

mel·on-cut·ting 〔ˈmɛlənˌkʌtɪŋ; ˈmelənˌkʌtiŋ〕 *n.* 〖俚〗利益(等)之分配。

Mel·pom·e·ne 〔mɛlˈpɑmənɪ; melˈpɔmini(ː)〕 *n.* 〖希臘神話〗司悲劇之女神。

melt [mɛlt; melt] *v.*, **melt·ed, melt·ed** or **mol·ten, melt·ing,** *n.* —*v.t.* & *v.i.* ①鎔化;融化。Heat will *melt* iron. 熱將使鐵鎔化。②溶解。Sugar *melts* in tea. 糖在茶中溶解。③逐漸消失。The snow *melted* away. 雪漸化了。④漸混〖常 into〗. In the rainbow one color *melts* into another. 在虹中一種顏色漸漸混入另一種。⑤軟化。Her heart *melted* with pity. 她的心因憐憫而軟化。***melt*** (*something*) ***down*** 鎔毀。—*n.* ①鎔化(作用)。②鎔化物。③鎔化量。

melt·ing [ˈmɛltɪŋ; ˈmeltiŋ] *adj.* ①鎔化的;鎔解的。②(感情、心等)受感動的; 軟化的。③(表情、眼神等)使人感動的; 動人的;使人感傷的。④(音)甜美的;柔和的。

melting point 鎔點。

melting pot 鎔爐(借指同化許多種族、形形色色人物之國家或都市)。America is often called a *melting pot*. 美國常被稱爲鎔爐。***go into the melting pot*** 被改造;變軟;軟化。***put*** (or ***cast***) ***into the melting pot*** 改造;重作。

mel·ton [ˈmɛltn̩; ˈmeltən] *n.* ①墨爾登呢(一種光滑的厚呢,做大衣等用)。②墨爾登呢之大衣。

mem. ①member. ②memento. ③memoir. ④memorandum. ⑤memorial.

‡**mem·ber** [ˈmɛmbɚ; ˈmembə] *n.* ①團體中之一員; 會員; 社員。Every *member* of the family came to the funeral. 家裏所有的人都參加了葬禮。②議員。 a *Member* of Parliament. 英國國會議員。③肢體(特指腿或臂);植物之枝葉等各部分。④組成分子。

member bank 〖美〗聯邦準備銀行之會員銀行。

member of Christ 基督教徒。

Member of Congress 美國衆議院議員。(略作 **M.C.**)

*__mem·ber·ship__ [ˈmɛmbɚˌʃɪp; ˈmembəʃip] *n.* ①會員或社員之資格。An honorary *membership* will be conferred on him. 名譽會員的資格將贈予他。②全體會員;全體社員; 會員數目。 The *membership* is limited to 1,000. 會員人數限於一千。

mem·bra·na·ceous [ˌmɛmbrəˈneʃəs; ˌmembrəˈneiʃəs] *adj.* = **membranous.**

mem·brane [ˈmɛmbren; ˈmembrein] *n.* 膜;薄膜。the mucous *membrane*. 黏膜。

mem·bra·nous [ˈmɛmbrənəs, mɛmˈbre-; memˈbreinəs] *adj.* ①膜的;膜質的;膜狀的;膜性的。②結膜的(病)。(亦作 **membranaceous, membraneous**)

me·men·to [mɪˈmɛnto; miˈmentou] *n., pl.* **-tos** or **-toes.** 紀念品。

*__mem·o__ [ˈmɛmo; ˈmemou] *n., pl.* **mem·os.** 〖俗〗 = **memorandum.**

mem·oir [ˈmɛmwɑr; ˈmemwɑː] *n.* ①研究報告。②傳記。③(*pl.*)回憶錄;自傳。

mé·moire [mɛmˈwɑr; memˈwɑː] 〖法〗 *n.* (外交上之)備忘錄。

mem·oir·ist [ˈmɛmwɑrɪst; ˈmemwɑːrist] *n.* 撰寫回憶錄的人;傳記作家。

mem·o·ra·bil·i·a [ˌmɛmərəˈbɪlɪə; ˌmemərəˈbiliə] *n. pl., sing.* **-rab·i·le** [-ˈræbəli; -ˈræbiliː]. ①大事記。②言行錄。

*__mem·o·ra·ble__ [ˈmɛmərəbl̩; ˈmemərəbl] *adj.* 值得紀念的。a *memorable* day (deed). 值得紀念的日子(事跡)。—*n.* (常 *pl.*) 值得紀念的事物。to record the *memorables* of the past. 將過去值得紀念的事記錄下來。—**mem·o·ra·bly,** *adv.*

mem·o·ran·da [ˌmɛməˈrændə; ˌmeməˈrændə] *n.* pl. of **memorandum.**

*__mem·o·ran·dum__ [ˌmɛməˈrændəm; ˌmeməˈrændəm] *n., pl.* **-dums, -da.** ①備忘錄。to make a *memorandum* of. 記錄…。②便箋;摘要;非正式之記錄。③同一機構內之簽條。④〖法律〗買賣契約書。

*__me·mo·ri·al__ [məˈmorɪəl, -ˈmɔr-; miˈmɔːriəl] *n.* ①紀念物。The college was founded as a *memorial* of Dr. Owen. 這學院是爲紀念歐文博士而創辦的。②(常 *pl.*)歷史記載。③請願書;陳情書;奏摺。—*adj.* ①以資紀念的。a *memorial* service. 追悼會。②記憶的;紀念的。

Memorial Day 〖美〗陣亡將士紀念日。

me·mo·ri·al·ist [məˈmorɪəlɪst; məˈmɔːriəlist] *n.* ①請願者;建議者。②回憶錄(言行錄)作者。

me·mo·ri·al·ize [məˈmorɪəlˌaɪz; miˈmɔːriəlaiz] *v.t.,* **-ized, -iz·ing.** ①紀念。②向…上陳情書。

me·mo·ri·a tech·ni·ca [məˈmɔrɪə ˈtɛknəkə; məˈmɔːriə ˈteknikə] 藉字形或其他方式幫助記憶的方法。

*__mem·o·rize__ [ˈmɛməˌraɪz; ˈmeməraiz] *v.t.,* **-rized, -riz·ing.** ①記於心。He finally *memorized* the poem. 他終於記住了那首詩。②記錄;記下。—**mem·o·ri·za·tion,** *n.*

‡**mem·o·ry** [ˈmɛmərɪ; ˈmeməri] *n., pl.* **-ries.** ①記憶力。Commit the poem to *memory*. 記住這首詩。②記憶; 記憶範圍。within living *memory*. 在今人的記憶內。③記憶之人物或事物。His mother died when he was small; she is only a *memory* to him now. 他的母親死時他尙年幼,現在祇能依稀記得她的容貌。④記得;紀念。⑤記憶所及之時間。This has been the hottest summer within my *memory*. 就我記憶所及這是最熱的一個夏天。⑥死後之名望。He has become a *memory*. 他死後的聲名永垂不朽。⑦將資料貯藏於電腦、影片、錄音帶等的方法。***in memory of*** 紀念。They are going to erect a monument *in memory of* the dead. 他們將豎碑以紀念死者。

memory bank 〖電腦〗記憶銀行;記憶庫。

‡**men** [mɛn; men] *n.* pl. of **man.**

*__men·ace__ [ˈmɛnɪs; ˈmenəs, -nis] *n., v.,* **-aced, -ac·ing.** —*n.* 威脅;脅迫。a *menace* to world peace. 對世界和平之威脅。—*v.t.* & *v.i.* 威嚇; 脅迫。The robber *menaced* him with a revolver. 盜賊用手槍威嚇他。

men·ac·ing [ˈmɛnɪsɪŋ; ˈmenəsiŋ] *adj.* 威脅的;恐嚇的;險惡的;脅迫的。—**ly,** *adv.*

me·nad [ˈminæd; ˈmiːnæd] *n.* = **maenad.** —**ic,** *adj.*

mé·nage, me·nage [meˈnɑʒ; meˈnɑːʒ] *n.* ①家庭。②家政;家事;家務管理。

me·nag·er·ie [məˈnædʒərɪ; miˈnædʒəri] *n.* ①巡迴動物園;動物展覽。②獸欄。③被關在獸欄的各種動物。④各種人物之薈集。

Men·ci·us [ˈmɛnʃɪəs; ˈmenʃiəs] *n.* 孟子 (372?-289 B.C., 中國哲學家)。(亦作 **Meng-tzu, Meng-tse**)

*__mend__ [mɛnd; mend] *v.t.* 修補; 改良; 改正錯誤。to *mend* a road. 修補道路。***mend one's fences*** 〖美俗〗照顧自己選區的政治利益(俾能獲得再提名或再獲選)。—*v.i.* ①恢復健康。The patient is *mending* nicely. 病人大見康復。②改進;進步。—*n.* 改進;改良;

改進之處。*on the mend* 在改善中;恢復健康。 「可修理的;可改善的。」

mend·a·ble ['mɛndəbl̩; 'mendəbl] *adj.*

men·da·cious [mɛn'deʃəs; men'deiʃəs] *adj.* ①好說謊的;不誠實的。②虛假的。

men·dac·i·ty [mɛn'dæsətɪ; men'dæsiti] *n.*, *pl.* **-ties.** ①說謊;說謊的習慣。②謊話;虛僞。

Men·del ['mɛndl̩; 'mendl] *n.* 孟德爾 (Gregor Johann, 1822–1884, 奧國生物學家、遺傳學家)。

Men·de·le·ev [ˌmɛndə'leef; ˌmendə'leief] *n.* 門得列夫 (Dmitri Ivanovich, 1834–1907, 俄國化學家, 元素周期律發明者)。

men·de·le·vi·um [ˌmɛndə'lɪvɪəm; ˌmendə'li:viəm] *n.* 〖化〗一種放射性元素(符號 Mv, 原子序101)。

Men·de·li·an [mɛn'dilɪən; men'di:liən] *adj.* Mendel 的;孟德爾定律的。—*n.* 孟德爾學派之人。

Men·del·ism ['mɛndəlɪzəm; 'mendəlizm] *n.* 孟德爾 (Mendel) 遺傳學說。

Mendel's Law 〖優生〗孟德爾(遺傳)定律。

Men·dels·sohn ['mɛndl̩sn̩; 'mendlsn] *n.* 孟德爾松 (Jakob Ludwig Felix, 1809–1847, 德國作曲家、鋼琴家及音樂指揮)。

mend·er ['mɛndɚ; 'mendə] *n.* 修理者;改善者;改良者。

men·di·can·cy ['mɛndɪkənsɪ; 'mendikənsi] *n.* 乞食(生涯);行乞。

men·di·cant ['mɛndɪkənt; 'mendikənt] *adj.* 行乞的。—*n.* ①乞丐。②托鉢僧。

men·dic·i·ty [mɛn'dɪsətɪ; men'disiti] *n.* =**mendicancy.**

Men·e·la·us [ˌmɛnə'leəs; ˌmeni'leiəs] *n.* 〖希臘神話〗梅納雷阿斯(斯巴達之王, Agamemnon 之弟, Helen 之丈夫)。

men·folk(s) ['mɛnˌfok(s); 'menfouk(s)] *n. pl.* 〖方〗男人們。

men·ha·den [mɛn'hedn̩; men'heidn] *n.*, *pl.* **-den** or **-dens.** 大鯡(多產於美國東海岸)。

me·ni·al ['minɪəl; 'mi:niəl] *adj.* ①屬於僕人的;適於僕人的。②低賤的。③做下賤工作的(人)。—*n.* ①賤僕。②下賤之人。—**ly,** *adv.* 「dʒɪəl] *adj.* 腦膜的;髓膜的。」

me·nin·ge·al [mə'nɪndʒɪəl; mə'nin-

me·nin·ges [mə'nɪndʒiz; mə'nindʒi:z] *n. pl.*, *sing.* **me·ninx** ['minɪŋks; 'mi:niŋks]. 〖解剖〗腦膜;脊膜;髓膜。

men·in·gi·tis [ˌmɛnɪn'dʒaɪtɪs; ˌmenin'dʒaitis] *n.* 〖醫〗腦膜炎。—**men·in·git·ic,** *adj.*

me·nis·cus [mə'nɪskəs; mə'niskəs] *n.*, *pl.* **-nis·ci** [-'nɪsaɪ; -'nisai], **-cus·es.** ①新月形之物。②〖物理〗凹凸透鏡。③〖物理〗彎月面(液柱內液體之凹面或凸面)。

Men·non·ite ['mɛnənˌaɪt; 'menənait] *n.* 孟諾 (Menno) 派教徒 (1523年起於瑞士之基督教新派, 反對嬰兒洗禮、誓約、就公職等)。

men·o·pause ['mɛnəˌpɔz; 'menəpɔ:z] *n.* 〖生理〗停經;經絕期;更年期。「餐桌用的。」

men·sal[1] ['mɛnsl̩; 'mensl] *adj.* 餐桌的;

men·sal[2] *adj.* 每月一次的;每月的。

men·ses ['mɛnsiz; 'mensi:z] *n. pl.* 〖生理〗(作*sing.* or *pl.* 解)月經。

men's room 男廁所。(亦作 **men's lounge, gentleman's lounge, gentleman's room**) 「*n.* pl. of **menstruum.**」

men·stru·a ['mɛnstruə; 'menstruə]

men·stru·al ['mɛnstruəl; 'menstruəl] *adj.* ①每月的;每月一次的。②月經的。

men·stru·ate ['mɛnstruˌet; 'menstrueit] *v.i.*, **-at·ed, -at·ing.** 排出月經;行經。

men·stru·a·tion [ˌmɛnstru'eʃən; ˌmenstru'eiʃən] *n.* 月經;行經;經期。

men·stru·um ['mɛnstruəm; 'menstruəm] *n.*, *pl.* **-ums, -stru·a.** 溶媒;溶劑

men·sur·a·bil·i·ty [ˌmɛnʃurə'bɪlətɪ; ˌmenʃurə'biliti] *n.* 可量性;可測性。

men·sur·a·ble ['mɛnʃurəbl̩; 'menʃurəbl] *adj.* ①可量的;可測的。②〖音樂〗有固定節奏或韻律的;有量的。

men·su·ral ['mɛnʃurəl; 'menʃurəl] *adj.* ①有關度量的。②〖音樂〗有固定節奏或韻律的;有量的。

men·su·ra·tion [ˌmɛnʃə'reʃən; ˌmensjuə'reiʃən] *n.* ①測量;測量術。②測量學

˙**men·tal**[1] ['mɛntl̩; 'mentl] *adj.* ①心理的;智力的。a *mental* disease. 精神病。②智力所爲的。*mental* arithmetic. 心算。③有精神病態的。a *mental* patient. 精神病人。④爲精神病人的。a *mental* hospital. 精神病院。⑤知識階級的。⑥〖俗〗有點不正常的;神經兮兮的。The way she behave you'd think she was *mental.* 從她的舉止你會以爲她神經兮兮的。

men·tal[2] *adj.* 〖解剖〗頦的;顎的。

mental age 〖心理〗智力年齡。

men·tal·ism ['mɛntl̩ˌɪzəm; 'mentlizəm] *n.* ①〖哲〗唯心論之一種。②〖心理〗意識論。③〖語言〗智能論。

men·tal·is·tic [ˌmɛntl̩'ɪstɪk; ˌmentə'listik] *adj.* ①唯心論的。②意識論的。③〖語言〗智能論的。

men·tal·i·ty [mɛn'tælətɪ; men'tæliti] *n.*, *pl.* **-ties.** ①智力。An idiot has a very low *mentality.* 白癡的智力甚低。②心理狀態。abnormal *mentality.* 變態心理。

men·tal·ly ['mɛntl̩ɪ; 'mentəli] *adv.* ①精神上地。②藉智力地。

mental reservation 對某項聲明(所持)之未明言的保留。 「感應。」

mental telepathy 精神感應;心電

men·ta·tion [mɛn'teʃən; men'teiʃən] *n.* 精神作用(機能);心理狀態或過程。

men·thene ['mɛnθin; 'menθi:n] *n.* 〖化〗一烯萜。 「薄荷腦。」

men·thol ['mɛnθol; 'menθɔl] *n.* 〖化〗

men·tho·lat·ed ['mɛnθəˌletɪd; 'menθəleitid] *adj.* ①含有薄荷腦的。②經薄荷腦處理過的。

men·ti·cide ['mɛntəˌsaɪd; 'mentisaid] *n.* 用長期訊問、藥物、或酷刑以改變某人之信念或其價值觀念;精神扼殺;洗腦。

‡**men·tion** ['mɛnʃən; 'menʃən] *v.t.* 提及;述及。I hope you didn't *mention* my name to her. 我希望你沒有向她提到我。*Don't mention it.* 不要客氣。*not to mention; without mentioning* 不算;不待言。—*n.* 陳述;提及。There was no *mention* of it in the papers. 報上未提這件事。*at the mention of* 一說到。*make mention of* 提及 (=mention).

men·tor ['mɛntɚ; 'mentɔ:] *n.* ①賢明忠實的顧問;良師。②(M-)〖希臘神話〗Ulysses 之友, 且爲其子 Telemachus 之師。

˙**men·u** ['mɛnju, 'menju, mə'ny; 'menju:] *n.* ①菜單。②菜;餐館供應顧客之食物。The usual *menu* consists of soup, meat, vegetables and dessert. 通常的菜有湯、肉類、蔬菜和甜食。

me·ow [mɪˈau; miˈau] *n.* 貓叫聲。—*v.i.* (貓)叫。(亦作 **miaow, miaou, miaul**)

M.E.P. Master of Engineering Physics. **M.E.P.A.** Master of Engineering and Public Administration.

Me·phis·to·phe·le·an [ˌmɛfɪstəˈfiliən; ˌmefistəˈfiːliən] *adj.* ① Mephistopheles 的。②惡毒而狡猾的。③譏嘲的。(亦作 **Mephistophelian**)

Meph·i·stoph·e·les [ˌmɛfəˈstɑfəˌliz; ˌmefisˈtɔfiliːz] *n.* 哥德所著"浮士德"中之魔鬼;誘惑者。

me·phit·ic [mɛˈfɪtɪk; meˈfitik] *adj.* ①有惡臭的。②毒氣的;有毒的。(亦作 **mephitical**)

me·phi·tis [mɛˈfaɪtɪs; meˈfaitis] *n.* ①(地中發出的)毒氣。②惡臭。

mer. ①mercury. ②meridian. ③meridional.

mer·can·tile [ˈmɝkənˌtil; ˈməːkəntail] *adj.* 商人的;貿易的;商業的。

mercantile agency 商業徵信所。

mercantile marine 一國商船之集合稱。

mercantile paper 商業流通證券。

mercantile system 重商主義。(亦作 **mercantile doctrine, mercantile theory**)

mer·can·til·ism [ˈmɝkənˌtaɪlɪzm̩; ˈməːkəntailizm] *n.* ①重商主義。②商業主義;商人氣質。

mer·can·til·ist [ˈmɝkənˌtaɪlɪst; ˈməːkəntailist] *n.* 重商主義者。—*adj.* 重商主義的。

Mer·ca·tor's projection [mɝˈketɚz～; məːˈkeitɔːz～] 麥卡脫式投影(以直線繪經緯線之地圖繪法)。

***mer·ce·nar·y** [ˈmɝsn̩ˌɛrɪ; ˈməːsinəri] *adj., n., pl.* **-nar·ies.** —*adj.* 為金錢而工作的;被雇的;圖利的。a *mercenary* soldier. 傭兵。—*n.* ①傭兵。②雇來的人。

mer·cer [ˈmɝsɚ; ˈməːsə] *n.* 〖英〗布商;綢緞商。

mer·cer·ize [ˈmɝsəˌraɪz; ˈməːsəraiz] *v.t.,* **-ized, -iz·ing.** 將(棉紗或布)浸入苛性鹼液中以增其韌性、光澤及染色性。—**mer·cer·i·za·tion,** *n.*

mer·cer·y [ˈmɝsərɪ; ˈməːsəri] *n., pl.* **-cer·ies.** 〖英〗①綢布業;布帛店;綢緞店。②布帛類;綢緞類。

***mer·chan·dise** [ˈmɝtʃənˌdaɪz; ˈməːtʃəndaiz] *n., v.,* **-dised, -dis·ing.** —*n.* ①商品。In order to save the vessel in the storm, they threw the valuable *merchandise* overboard. 為了拯救暴風雨中的船,他們將貴重的商品投入海中。②存貨。—*v.t.* & *v.i.* ①交易;買賣。②展覽商品以吸引顧客。(亦作 **merchandize**)

mer·chan·dis·ing [ˈmɝtʃənˌdaɪzɪŋ; ˈməːtʃəndaiziŋ] *n.* 商品之廣告推銷。

‡**mer·chant** [ˈmɝtʃənt; ˈməːtʃənt] *n.* ①商人;零售商。a wholesale *merchant.* 批發商。②店主。—*adj.* 商業的。a *merchant* vessel. 商船。

mer·chant·a·ble [ˈmɝtʃəntəbl̩; ˈməːtʃəntəbl] *adj.* 適於銷售的;可賣的。

mer·chant·man [ˈmɝtʃəntmən; ˈməːtʃəntmən] *n., pl.* **-men.** 商船。

merchant marine ①商船之集合稱。②服務於商船上之全體人員。

merchant prince 富商。

mer·chant·ry [ˈmɝtʃəntrɪ; ˈməːtʃəntri] *n.* ①商業;商務。②商人(集合稱)。

***mer·ci·ful** [ˈmɝsɪfəl; ˈməːsiful] *adj.* 仁慈的;慈悲的。a *merciful* man. 一位仁慈的人。—**ly,** *adv.*

***mer·ci·less** [ˈmɝsɪlɪs; ˈməːsilis] *adj.* 無慈悲心的;殘忍的。a *merciless* king. 一個暴君。—**ly,** *adv.*

mer·cu·ri·al [mɝˈkjurɪəl; məːˈkjuəriəl] *adj.* ①水銀的;含水銀的。*mercurial* poisoning. 水銀中毒。②活潑的;機智的;多變的。③(M-) 水星的;Mercury 神的。—*n.* 水銀劑;汞劑。

mer·cu·ri·al·ism [mɝˈkjurɪəlɪsm̩; məːˈkjuəriəlizm] *n.* 水銀中毒;汞中毒。

mer·cu·ric [mɝˈkjurɪk; məːˈkjuərik] *adj.* 〖化〗水銀的;含有二價汞的。

mer·cu·ro·chrome [mɝˈkjurəˌkrom; məːˈkjuərəkroum] *n.* 〖藥〗水銀紅藥水;紅溴汞;汞紅質(防腐、殺菌劑)。

mer·cu·rous [mɝˈkjurəs, ˈmɝkjə-; ˈməːkjurəs] *adj.* 〖化〗水銀的;含有一價汞的;亞汞的。

***mer·cu·ry** [ˈmɝkjərɪ; ˈməːkjuri] *n., pl.* **-ries.** ①水銀;汞。②溫度計中之水銀柱。The *mercury* stood at nearly 90°. 溫度計水銀柱滯留於九十度左右(卽溫度在九十度左右)。③(M-) 水星;羅馬神話中之使者或商業之神。④使者;傳信人。⑤(M-) 〖美〗(水星計畫中之)單人太空船。

mer·cu·ry-va·por lamp [ˈmɝkjərɪˈvepɚ～; ˈməːkjuriˈveipə～] 〖電〗汞汽燈;水銀燈。

mer·cy** [ˈmɝsɪ; ˈməːsi] *n., pl.* **-cies.** ①仁慈;慈悲;憐憫。They were treated with *mercy.* 他們受到仁慈的待遇。②天恩;恩惠。We must be thankful for small *mercies.* 我們對於小惠亦當感激。③寬恕。④慈善。at the mercy of*** 任…之處置;在…之掌握中。The boat is *at the mercy of* the wild waves. 小舟逐狂浪而漂流。***have (no, little, some, etc.) mercy on*** 對…有(無、幾乎沒有、有些等)慈悲心。*Have mercy on* us! 請發慈悲!

mercy killing 安死術(=euthanasia).

mercy seat ①〖聖經〗約櫃之金蓋(被視為上帝休息之處)。②上帝的王座。

‡**mere**[1] [mɪr; miə] *adj., superl.* **mer·est.** 祇;不過。It's a *mere* trifle. 那祇是瑣事而已。

mere[2] *n.* 〖詩,方〗小湖;池塘;海洋。

‡**mere·ly** [ˈmɪrlɪ; ˈmiəli] *adv.* 僅;祇(=only). I *merely* asked his name. 我祇問了他的名字。

mer·e·tri·cious [ˌmɛrəˈtrɪʃəs; ˌmeriˈtriʃəs] *adj.* ①金玉其外的;外表美麗的;粉飾的。②俗麗的;浮華的(文體)。③妓女的。

mer·gan·ser [məˈgænsɚ; məːˈgænsə] *n., pl.* **-sers, -ser.** 秋沙鴨。

merge [mɝdʒ; məːdʒ] *v.,* **merged, merg·ing.** —*v.t.* 吞併;兼併;合併。The small banks were *merged* into one large organization. 那些小銀行合併成為一個大的組織。—*v.i.* 吞沒;沒入;消沒。Twilight *merged* into darkness. 黃昏漸漸消沒於黑暗中。

mer·gence [ˈmɝdʒəns; ˈməːdʒəns] *n.* 沒入;消失;吞併;合併。

merg·er [ˈmɝdʒɚ; ˈməːdʒə] *n.* ①(土地、契約、債務等之)合併。②(事業、公司等之)

合併;歸併。③兼併者;吞併者;合併者。

me·rid·i·an 〔məˈrɪdɪən, mɪ–; məˈri-diən〕 *n.* ①子午線;子午圈。②太陽或其他天體所達到的最高點;正午。③頂點;鼎盛期。the *meridian* of life. 壯年。④特殊之位置、場所、境遇、性質。***the magnetic meridian*** 磁極子午線。—*adj.* ①子午線的;子午圈的。the *meridian* altitude. 子午線高度。the *meridian* circle. 子午儀。②正午的。③頂點的;全盛的。*meridian* fame. 最高的名譽。

me·rid·i·o·nal 〔məˈrɪdɪənl; məˈridi-ənl〕 *adj.* ①子午線的。②南歐的;南歐人的;法國南部人的。③南方的;南的。—*n.* 南方的居民;南歐人;法國南部人。

me·ringue 〔məˈræŋ; məˈræŋ〕 *n.* ①蛋白與糖的混合物。②其所製成的糕餅等。

me·ri·no 〔məˈrino; məˈri:nou〕 *n.*, *pl.* **-nos,** *adj.* —*n.* ①麥利諾羊。②麥利諾羊毛。③麥利諾羊毛紡成的線。④麥利諾羊毛布。—*adj.* 由麥利諾羊毛、毛線製成的。

mer·i·stem 〔ˈmɛrɪ,stɛm; ˈmeristem〕 *n.* 〖植物〗分裂組織;分生組織。

mer·it** 〔ˈmɛrɪt; ˈmerit〕 *n.* ①優點;美性;價值;功績;功勳。a man of *merits.* 有功之人。②(*pl.*)(應受懲罰或獎賞之)事實或眞相。the *merits* of a case. 案件之眞情。③(常 *pl.*)本身的條件、長處、才幹等。to treat someone according to his *merits.* 按某人本身的條件(才幹)來對待他。make a merit of*** 將…說成應受讚揚之事。***stand on one's own merits*** 靠自己的長處不受他人庇蔭。—*v.t.* 應得。He certainly *merits* such a reward. 他的確應獲此報酬。

mer·i·to·ri·ous 〔,mɛrəˈtorɪəs; ,meri-ˈtɔ:riəs〕 *adj.* 應受褒賞的;有功的;有價值的;善意的。—**ly,** *adv.* —**ness,** *n.*

merit system (美國文官之)考績制度。

mer·lin 〔ˈmɝlɪn; ˈmə:lin〕 *n.* 鷂隼。

mer·lon 〔ˈmɝlən; ˈmə:lən〕 *n.* 〖築城〗堞;雉堞;(鎗眼與鎗眼間的)凸壁。

mer·maid 〔ˈmɝ,med; ˈmə:meid〕 *n.* ①(雌)人魚;美人魚。②善泳之女人。

mer·man 〔ˈmɝ,mæn; ˈmə:mæn〕 *n.*, *pl.* **-men.** ①(雄)人魚。②善泳之男子。

***mer·ri·ly** 〔ˈmɛrɪlɪ; ˈmerili〕 *adv.* 愉快地;高興地。

***mer·ri·ment** 〔ˈmɛrɪmənt; ˈmerimənt〕 *n.* 歡樂;嬉戲。His *merriment* at the family gathering was more pronounced than ever. 在家庭團聚時他的歡樂較前更明顯。

mer·ri·ness 〔ˈmɛrɪnɪs; ˈmerinis〕 *n.* 快樂;愉快。

‡**mer·ry** 〔ˈmɛrɪ; ˈmeri〕 *adj.*, **-ri·er, -ri·est.** ①嬉樂的;嬉戲的。to make *merry.* 行樂;作樂。②快樂的;愉快的。*Merry* Christmas to you! 祝你耶誕快樂! ***make merry*** **a.** 開…的玩笑;笑謔;揶揄。**b.** 取樂。They were *making merry* in the ballroom. 他們正在舞廳中取樂。

mer·ry-an·drew 〔ˈmɛrɪˈændru; ˈme-riˈændru:〕 *n.* 小丑;丑角。

mer·ry-go-round 〔ˈmɛrɪgo,raund; ˈmerigou,raund〕 *n.* ①旋轉木馬。②迅速之旋轉。

mer·ry·mak·er 〔ˈmɛrɪ,mekɚ; ˈme-ri,meikə〕 *n.* 作樂者;嬉戲者。

mer·ry·mak·ing 〔ˈmɛrɪ,mekɪŋ; ˈmeri,meikiŋ〕 *n.* ①作樂;行樂。②快樂的節日。—*adj.* 快樂的;行樂的。

mer·ry·thought 〔ˈmɛrɪ,θɔt; ˈmeri-θɔ:t〕 *n.* =**wishbone.**

me·sa 〔ˈmesə; ˈmeisə〕 *n.* 高坪;臺地;高臺(多見於美國西南部)。

mé·sal·li·ance 〔meˈzælɪəns; meˈzæ-liəns〕 *n.*, *pl.* **mé·sal·li·anc·es.** 〖法〗和身分低於己者締結之婚姻;非門當戶對的婚姻。

mes·cal 〔mɛsˈkæl; mesˈkæl〕 *n.* ①梅斯卡爾酒(蒸餾龍舌蘭製成者)。②(製梅斯卡爾酒用之)龍舌蘭。

mes·ca·line 〔ˈmɛskəlin; ˈmeskəli:n〕 *n.* 〖藥〗麥司卡林(產生幻覺的一種藥物)。(亦作 **mezcaline**)

mes·dames 〔meˈdɑm; ˈmeidæm〕 *n.* pl. of **madam** or **madame.**

mes·en·ter·y 〔ˈmɛsn̩,tɛrɪ; ˈmesəntəri〕 *n.*, *pl.* **-ter·ies.** 〖解剖〗腸系膜。

mesh** 〔mɛʃ; meʃ〕 *n.* ①網孔;篩孔。This net has half-inch *meshes.* 這個網有半英寸見方的網孔。②(*pl.*)網絲。the *meshes* of a spider's web. 蜘蛛網的絲。to be caught in the *meshes* of the law. 被法網所捕。③網。④〖電〗絡。⑤(*pl.*)陷阱。in mesh*** (齒輪)相嚙合。—*v.t.* ①以網捕捉。②編織(網)。to *mesh* a net. 編網。③(齒輪)嚙合。—*v.i.* ①網捕。②嚙合。

me·shu·ga 〔məˈʃugə; məˈʃugə〕 *adj.* 〖俚〗發瘋的;瘋狂的。(亦作 **meshugga**)

mesh·work 〔ˈmɛʃ,wɝk; ˈmeʃ,wə:k〕 *n.* 網狀組織。

mesh·y 〔ˈmɛʃɪ; ˈmeʃi〕 *adj.*, **mesh·i·er, mesh·i·est.** 網的;網狀的。

me·si·al 〔ˈmizɪəl; ˈmi:ziəl〕 *adj.* 中央的;中間的。

mes·mer·ic 〔mɛsˈmɛrɪk; mezˈmerik〕 *adj.* ①催眠術的;催眠的。②迷人的。

mes·mer·ism 〔ˈmɛsmə,rɪzəm; ˈmez-mərizəm〕 *n.* ①催眠術。②吸引;迷惑。

mes·mer·ist 〔ˈmɛsmərɪst; ˈmezmə-rist〕 *n.* 施催眠術者。

mes·mer·ize 〔ˈmɛsmə,raɪz; ˈmezmə-raiz〕 *v.*, **-ized, -iz·ing.** —*v.t.* ①施以催眠術。②吸引;迷住;迷惑。—*v.i.* 催眠。

mesne 〔min; mi:n〕 *adj.* 〖法律〗中間的。

meso- 〖字首〗表"中間;中央"之義。

mes·o·blast 〔ˈmɛsə,blæst; ˈmesə-,blæst〕 *n.* 〖胚胎、動物〗中胚層;中葉。

mes·o·carp 〔ˈmɛsə,kɑrp; ˈmesəkɑ:p〕 *n.* 〖植物〗中果皮。

mes·o·derm 〔ˈmɛsə,dɝm; ˈmesədə:m〕 *n.* 〖胚胎、動物〗中胚層;中葉。

mes·o·morph 〔ˈmɛsəmɔrf; ˈmesə-mɔ:f〕 *n.* ①善於運動之肌肉組織、骨架等。②天生的運動員。

mes·on 〔ˈmizɑn; ˈmi:zɔn〕 *n.* 〖物理〗介子。

Mes·o·po·ta·mi·a 〔,mɛsəpəˈtemɪə; ,mesəpəˈteimjə〕 *n.* 美索不達米亞(亞洲西南部 Tigris 與 Euphrates 兩河間之地區)。

mes·o·tron 〔ˈmɛsə,trɑn; ˈmesətrɔn〕 *n.* =**meson.**

Mes·o·zo·ic 〔,mɛsəˈzoɪk; ,mesouˈzou-ik〕 *n.* 〖地質〗中生代;中生代岩石。—*adj.* 中生代的;中生代岩石的。

mes·quit(e) 〔mɛsˈkit; mesˈki:t〕 *n.* (北美西南及熱帶美洲產之)一種豆科灌木。

***mess** 〔mɛs; mes〕 *n.* ①骯髒的一堆;雜亂的一團。The room was in a *mess.* 這屋子亂七八糟。②紊亂;困難。You have made a *mess* of the job. 你把這事弄糟了。③共食之人(特指軍中)。④(軍隊共食之)膳餐。The officers are at *mess* now. 軍官們正在用膳。⑤一堆食物;食物之一部分;一分食物。He caught a *mess* of fish. 他捉到了

一些魚。⑥不好看或不好吃的食物。⑦令人不愉快或不順遂之事。⑧流質的食物。⑨〖俗〗生活或事業亂糟糟的人。 —*v.t.* ①汚；使紊亂〖常 up〗. to *mess* up a room. 將屋弄亂。②將（事務等）弄糟。 The late arrival of the train *messed* up all our plans. 火車的誤點把我們所有的計畫都弄糟了。③(軍中)供伙食。 —*v.i.* ①共食；聚餐。They decided to *mess* together. 他們決定在一起用膳。②亂忙。***mess about*** (or ***around***) **a.** 亂忙；窮忙。**b.** 浪費時間；吊兒郎當。**c.** 鬼混。***mess about*** (or ***around***) ***with*** 〖俗〗做手脚；更改。***mess in*** (or ***with***) 管閒事。

‡mes·sage 〔ˈmɛsɪdʒ; ˈmesidʒ〕 *n.* ①消息；音信。 a congratulatory *message*. 賀辭；賀電。②官方之（口頭或文字)報告。the President's *message* to Congress. 總統致國會之咨文。③神示；預言。④(信使之)任務。⑤(電影、戲劇、小說中之）寓意；教訓。The new play is short on humor and long on *message*. 那一部新戲缺少幽默感但寓意深長。 ***go on a message*** (or ***messages***) 出差。 ***send somebody on a message*** 差人報信。 —*v.t.* & *v.i.* 通信；報信；送信。We *messaged* him that everything was going well. 我們通知他一切順利。

mes·sa·line 〔ˌmɛsəˈlin; ˌmesəˈliːn〕 *n.* 一種薄而似緞的柔軟絲織物。

***mes·sen·ger** 〔ˈmɛsn̩dʒɚ; ˈmesindʒə〕 *n.* ①報信者；信差。②先驅；豫兆。Dawn is the *messenger* of day. 破曉乃白晝之先驅。 **—ship,** *n.*

mess hall (軍隊、工廠等之)餐廳。

Mes·si·ah 〔məˈsaɪə; miˈsaiə〕 *n.* ①彌賽亞（猶太人所期待的救主)。②基督。③(被壓迫者所期待的）解救者。④(神曲)彌賽亞。

Mes·si·an·ic 〔ˌmɛsɪˈænɪk; ˌmesiˈænik〕 *adj.* 彌賽亞的；基督的；救主的。

mes·sieurs 〔ˈmɛsɚz; ˈmesəːz〕 *n.* pl. of **monsieur.** ①諸位先生；諸君。② = **gentlemen.**

mess jacket 半正式之男用上衣(通常爲白色，長僅及腰，爲侍者、旅館僕歐之制服)。

mess kit (士兵、露營者在野外所使用之)一套金屬餐具。(亦作 **mess gear**)

mess·mate 〔ˈmɛsˌmet; ˈmesmeit〕 *n.* (陸、海軍中)共食團體中之一員；同食者。

Messrs. Messieurs. (用於姓名之前，爲 Mr. 之複數: *Messrs.* Smith and Jones. 但現偶或亦用於商號名稱之前: *Messrs.* Brown, Hubbell and Company).

mes·suage 〔ˈmɛswɪdʒ; ˈmeswidʒ〕 *n.* 〖法律〗(包括附屬建築物及地皮之)家宅。

mess·y 〔ˈmɛsɪ; ˈmesi〕 *adj.*, **mess·i·er, mess·i·est.** ①雜亂的；汚穢的；紊亂的。②生活紊亂的。**—mess·i·ness,** *n.*

mes·ti·zo 〔mɛsˈtizo; mesˈtiːzou〕 *n., pl.* **-zos, -zoes.** 混血兒（特指西班牙人或葡萄牙人與美洲土人之混血兒)。

‡met 〔mɛt; met〕 *v.* pt. & pp. of **meet¹**.

met. ①metaphor. ②metaphysics. ③meteorological. ④meteorology. ⑤metronome. ⑥metropolitan.

meta- 〖字首〗①表"在其中；在後；共同地；轉變"之義，如: metaphysics. ②〖化〗表"…之聚合體；…之衍生物，脫水而衍生的"之義，如: meta-antimonic. ③表"超越"之義。(母音前作 **met-**)

met·a·bol·ic 〔ˌmɛtəˈbɑlɪk; ˌmetəˈbɔlik〕 *adj.* ①變化的；變形的。②〖生物〗新陳代謝的。

me·tab·o·lism 〔məˈtæbl̩ˌɪzəm; meˈtæbəlizəm〕 *n.* 〖生物〗①新陳代謝。②(昆蟲等之)變態。

me·tab·o·lize 〔məˈtæbl̩ˌaɪz; məˈtæbəlaiz〕 *v.*, **-lized, -liz·ing.** —*v.t.* 〖生物〗使新陳代謝；使變形；使變態。—*v.i.* 經過變形之過程。

me·tab·o·lous 〔məˈtæbələs; məˈtæbələs〕 *adj.* 變化的；變形的。

met·a·car·pal 〔ˌmɛtəˈkɑrpl; ˌmetəˈkɑːpl〕 *adj.* 〖解剖〗掌部的；掌骨的。—*n.* 〖解剖〗掌骨。

met·a·car·pus 〔ˌmɛtəˈkɑrpəs; ˌmetəˈkɑːpəs〕 *n., pl.* **-pi** 〔-paɪ; -pai〕. 〖解剖〗掌部；掌骨；掌。

met·a·cen·ter, met·a·cen·tre 〔ˈmɛtəˌsɛntɚ; ˈmetəˌsentə〕 *n.* 〖物理〗(浮體之)外心點；活中心；定傾中心。

met·a·gal·ax·y 〔ˌmɛtəˈgæləksɪ; ˌmetəˈgæləksi〕 *n., pl.* **-ax·ies.** 〖天文〗全宇宙；全星河系統。

met·age 〔ˈmitɪdʒ; ˈmiːtidʒ〕 *n.* (穀類、煤炭等之)稱量；重量檢驗；檢量費。

met·a·gen·e·sis 〔ˌmɛtəˈdʒɛnəsɪs; ˌmetəˈdʒenəsis〕 *n.* 〖生物〗世代交替。

‡met·al 〔ˈmɛtl̩; ˈmetl〕 *n., adj., v.,* **-al(l)ed, -al·(l)ing.** —*n.* ①金屬。Is it made of wood or of *metal?* 它是木頭製的還是金屬製的? ②〖化〗金屬元素。③鋪路用之碎石、煤屑等。④製玻璃或瓷器的熔漿。⑤質料；本質。Cowards are not made of the same *metal* as heroes. 懦夫與英雄本質不同。⑥(*pl.*)〖英〗鐵路軌道。The train ran off the *metals.* 火車出軌。⑦鑄鉛字用的一種鉛合金。⑧已被排版。—*adj.* 金屬製的。—*v.t.* ①以金屬覆蓋；供應金屬。②〖英〗以碎石鋪路。

met·a·lin·guis·tics 〔ˌmɛtəlɪŋˈgwɪstɪks; ˌmetəliŋˈgwistiks〕 *n.* 後設語言學(研究語言與其他文化因素之關係)。

met·al·ize 〔ˈmɛtl̩ˌaɪz; ˈmetl̩aiz〕 *v.t.*, **-ized, -iz·ing.** ①以金屬處理；覆以金屬；以金屬化合物處理。②使化爲金屬；使金屬化。

***me·tal·lic** 〔məˈtælɪk; miˈtælik, meˈt-, məˈt-〕 *adj.* ①金屬的。*metallic* compounds. 金屬化合物。②似金屬的。a *metallic* voice. 清脆的聲音。③〖化〗(金屬元素)游離的；未與其他元素化合的。④含金屬的；產生金屬的。

met·al·lif·er·ous 〔ˌmɛtl̩ˈɪfərəs; ˌmetəˈlifərəs〕 *adj.* 含金屬的；產金屬的。

met·al·line 〔ˈmɛtlɪn; ˈmetl̩in〕 *adj.* ①金屬的；似金屬的；產金屬的。②含金屬(鹽)的。

met·al·log·ra·phy 〔ˌmɛtl̩ˈɑgrəfɪ; ˌmetəˈlɔgrəfi〕 *n.* ①金屬結構學。②〖印刷〗金屬版術。

met·al·loid 〔ˈmɛtl̩ˌɔɪd; ˈmetəlɔid〕 *adj.* ①似金屬的；金屬質的；金屬狀的。②〖化〗類金屬的。—*n.* 〖化〗類金屬(砒、硅等)。

met·al·lur·gist 〔ˈmɛtl̩ˌɝdʒɪst; meˈtælədʒist〕 *n.* 冶金家。

met·al·lur·gy 〔ˈmɛtl̩ˌɝdʒɪ; meˈtælədʒi〕 *n.* 冶金學；冶金術。**—met·al·lur·gic, met·al·lur·gi·cal,** *adj.*

met·al·work 〔ˈmɛtl̩ˌwɝk; ˈmetlwəːk〕 *n.* ①金屬製成品。②金屬品之製造。

met·al·work·er 〔ˈmɛtl̩ˌwɝkɚ; ˈmetlˌwəːkə〕 *n.* 製金屬品之工人。

met·al·work·ing 〔ˈmɛtl̩ˌwɝkɪŋ; ˈmetlˌwəːkiŋ〕*n.* 金屬品之製造；金工。—*adj.* 製造金屬品的。

met·a·mer 〔ˈmɛtəmɚ; ˈmetəmə〕 *n.*

〖化〗同分異構物;位變異構物。

met·a·mere ['mɛtə,mɪr; 'metəmiə] *n.* 〖動物〗(昆蟲之)體節。

me·tam·er·ism [mɪ'tæmərɪzm; mi'tæmərizm] *n.* ①〖化〗同分異構;位變異構。②〖動物〗由體節構成之狀態。

met·a·mor·phic [,mɛtə'mɔrfɪk; ,metə'mɔːfik] *adj.* ①變化的;變性的;變態的;變形的。②〖地質〗變成的。

met·a·mor·phism [,mɛtə'mɔrfɪzəm; ,metə'mɔːfizm] *n.* ①〖地質〗(岩石之)變成(作用)。②變形;變態(=metamorphosis).

met·a·mor·phose [,mɛtə'mɔrfoz; ,metə'mɔːfouz] *v.*, **-phosed, -phos·ing.** —*v.t.* ①使變形。②使(岩石)發生變成作用。—*v.i.* 變形;發生變態。

met·a·mor·pho·ses [,mɛtə'mɔrfə,siz; ,metə'mɔːfousiːz] *n.* pl. of **metamorphosis.**

met·a·mor·pho·sis [,mɛtə'mɔrfəsɪs; ,metə'mɔːfəsis] *n., pl.* **-ses.** ①蛻變。②變成的形態。③一般的變質;變態。④〖醫〗變形;變態。

met·a·phor ['mɛtəfɚ; 'metəfə] *n.* 隱喻;暗譬。to talk by *metaphor.* 以隱喩談話。

met·a·phor·i·cal [,mɛtə'fɔrɪkl̩; ,metə'fɔrikəl] *adj.* 隱喩的;比喩的。—**ly,** *adv.*

met·a·phrase ['mɛtə,frez; 'metəfreiz] *n., v.,* **-phrased, -phras·ing.** —*n.* 翻譯;直譯(別於 paraphrase). —*v.t.* ①翻譯;直譯。②改變…之文體、措辭等。

met·a·phys·ic [,mɛtə'fɪzɪk; ,metə'fizik] *n.* =**metaphysics.**

met·a·phys·i·cal [,mɛtə'fɪzɪkl̩; ,metə'fizikəl] *adj.* ①形而上學的。②極抽象的;難了解的。③第十七世紀英國以 John Donne 爲首的抽象詩派的。—**ly,** *adv.*

met·a·phy·si·cian [,mɛtəfə'zɪʃən; ,metəfi'ziʃən] *n.* 形而上學家;玄學家;形而上學的理論家。(亦作 **metaphysicist**)

met·a·phys·ics [,mɛtə'fɪzɪks; ,metə'fiziks] *n.* (作 *sing.* 解)形而上學;玄學。

met·a·plasm ['mɛtəplæzm̩; 'metəplæzəm] *n.* ①〖生物〗後含物(細胞中由無生命的、非原生質的物質構成的部分)。②〖文法〗字形變化。

me·tas·ta·sis [mə'tæstəsɪs; mə'tæstəsis] *n., pl.* **-ses** [-,siz; -siːz]. ①〖醫〗(病毒之)遷徙。②〖生物〗新陳代謝。③〖修辭〗(話題之)急轉。

met·a·tar·sal [,mɛtə'tɑrsəl; ,metə'tɑːsəl] *adj.* 〖解剖〗蹠的;蹠骨的。—*n.* 蹠骨。

met·a·tar·sus [,mɛtə'tɑrsəs; ,metə'tɑːsəs] *n., pl.* **-si** [-saɪ; -sai]. ①〖解剖〗蹠;蹠骨。②(蟲)蹠節。③(鳥)自脛骨至趾骨之部分。

me·tath·e·sis [mə'tæθəsɪs; me'tæθəsis] *n., pl.* **-ses** [-,siz; -siːz]. ①〖音韻〗音位(字位)轉變(例如 clapse>clasp). ②〖化〗置換;(由於化學物互相反應的)複分解。③〖醫〗病部轉位。

Met·a·zo·a [,mɛtə'zoə; ,metə'zouə] *n. pl.* 〖動物〗複細胞動物;後生動物。

mete¹ [mit; miːt] *v.t.,* **met·ed, met·ing.** ①分配;分給;給與(賞罰)〖常out〗。②〖詩〗衡量。

mete² *n.* 分界石;境界標;境界線;境界。***metes and bounds*** 〖法律〗境界;區畫。

me·tem·psy·cho·sis [,mɛtəmsaɪ'kosɪs; ,metempsi'kousis] *n., pl.* **-ses** [-siz; -siːz]. (靈魂之)轉生;輪廻。

***me·te·or** ['mitɪɚ; 'miːtjə, -tiə] *n.* ①〖天文〗流星;隕星;隕石。②〖氣象〗大氣現象(如雹、虹等)。③〖俗〗移動快速的人或事物;一夜之間成名的人。

me·te·or·ic [,mitɪ'ɔrɪk; ,miːti'ɔrik] *adj.* ①隕星的;流星的。②亮如流星的;瞬息的;疾速的。a man's *meteoric* rise to fame. 一個人的迅速成名。③大氣的。—**al·ly,** *adv*

me·te·or·ite ['mitɪər,aɪt; 'miːtjərait] *n.* ①隕石。②流星;流星體。

me·te·or·o·graph ['mitɪərə,græf; 'miːtjərəgrɑːf] *n.* 氣象記錄器。

me·te·or·oid ['mitɪər,ɔɪd; 'miːtjərɔid] *n.* 〖天文〗流星體;隕星體。

me·te·or·o·lite ['mitɪərə,laɪt; 'miːtjərəlait] *n.* =**meteorite.**

me·te·or·o·log·ic [,mitɪərə'lɑdʒɪk; ,miːtjərə'lɔdʒik] *adj.* =**meteorological.**

me·te·or·o·log·i·cal [,mitɪərə'lɑdʒɪkl̩; ,miːtjərə'lɔdʒikəl] *adj.* 氣象的;氣象學的。—**ly,** *adv.*

me·te·or·ol·o·gy [,mitɪə'rɑlədʒɪ; ,miːtjə'rɔlədʒi] *n.* 氣象學。—**me·te·or·ol·o·gist,** *n.*

***me·ter**¹ ['mitɚ; 'miːtə] *n.* ①公尺;米(39.37英寸)。②詩與音樂的韻律。

me·ter² *n.* 計量器。a water *meter.* 水表。—*v.t.* 以計量器計量。

-meter 〖字尾〗①表"測量(某物)之儀器;…計"之義,如: barometer. ②表"有…音步的"之義,如:pentameter. ③表"…公尺的"之義,如:kilometer.

me·ter·age ['mitərɪdʒ; 'miːtəridʒ] *n.* ①度量;測量;計量。②計量費;測度費。

me·tered mail ['mitəd~; 'miːtəd~] 收費郵件(以現金代郵票之郵件,郵資數目用戳子印在郵件上)。

mete·wand ['mit,wɑnd; 'miːt,wɔnd] *n.* =**meteyard.**

mete·yard ['mit,jɑrd; 'miːt,jɑːd] *n.* 〖英〗計量基準。

Meth. Methodist.

meth- 〖字首〗①**meta-** 之異體。②〖化〗=**metho-.**

meth·a·cryl·ic acid [,mɛθə'krɪlɪk~; ,meθə'krilik~] 〖化〗甲基丙烯酸($C_4H_6O_2$)。

meth·a·don(e) ['mɛθə,don; 'meθədoun] *n.* 〖藥〗鹽酸抹殺酮(一種鎮痛劑)。

meth·ane ['mɛθen; 'meθein] *n.* 〖化〗沼氣;甲烷(CH_4)。

meth·a·nol ['mɛθə,nol; 'meθənoul] *n.* 〖化〗甲醇。(亦作 **methyl alcohol** 或 **wood alcohol**)

me·theg·lin [mə'θɛglɪn; mə'θeglin] *n.* 蜂蜜酒。

me·thinks [mɪ'θɪŋks; mi'θiŋks] *v., pt.* **methought.** 〖古〗(=it seems to me) 據我看來;我以爲。

metho- 〖字首〗表 "methyl" 之義。(母音前作 **meth-**)

‡**meth·od** ['mɛθəd; 'meθəd] *n.* ①方法。direct *method* of language teaching. 語言教學之直接法。②做事的條理;計畫。He is a man of *method.* 他是個有條理的人。③順序;有條不紊。④(the M-) 表演逼眞法。—*adj.* (常 M-) 運用表演逼眞法表演的。*Method* actor. 以表演逼眞法表演的演員。

me·thod·ic [mə'θɑdɪk; mi'θɔdik] *adj.* =**methodical.**

me·thod·i·cal [mə'θɑdɪkl̩; mi'θɔdikəl] *adj.* ①有方法的;有順序的。②做事有條不紊的。③緩慢而艱難的。—**ly,** *adv.* —**ness,** *n.*

Meth·od·ism ['mɛθəd,ɪzəm; 'meθədizəm] *n.* ①(基督教)美以美教派。②(m-) 根

據方法之行事。③(m-)對方法之過分强調。

*__Meth·od·ist__ ['mɛθədɪst; 'meθədist] *n.* ①〖基督教〗美以美會教徒。②(m-)過分强調方法的人。—*adj.* =**Methodistic.**

Meth·od·is·tic [ˌmɛθəd'ɪstɪk; ˌmeθə'distik] *adj.* 美以美教派的。

meth·od·ize ['mɛθəˌdaɪz; 'meθədaiz] *v.t.*, **-ized, -iz·ing.** ①使方式化。②依方式加以整理;使有組織、秩序、順序等。

meth·od·ol·o·gy [ˌmɛθəd'ɑlədʒɪ; ˌmeθə'dɔlədʒi] *n., pl.* **-gies.** ①方法論。②〖教育〗課程論。—**meth·od·o·log·i·cal,** *adj.*

me·thought [mɪ'θɔt; mi'θɔːt] *v.* pt. of **methinks.**

Me·thu·se·lah [mə'θjuzələ; mi'θjuːzələ] *n.* ①〖聖經〗麥修撒拉(據傳享年969歲,創世紀五章二十七節)。②年齡極高之人。

meth·yl ['mɛθəl; 'miːθail] *n., adj.* 〖化〗甲基 (CH_3) (的)。*methyl* blue. 甲基藍。

methyl alcohol 〖化〗木精;甲醇。

meth·yl·ate ['mɛθəˌlet; 'meθileit] *n., v.*, **-at·ed, -at·ing.** —*n.* (亦作 **methoxide**)〖化〗甲醇化物。—*v.t.* ①混以甲醇。②〖化〗使與甲基化合。

meth·yl·at·ed spirit ['mɛθəˌletɪd ~; 'meθileitid~] 變質酒精。

meth·yl·ene ['mɛθəˌlin; 'meθiliːn] *n.* 〖化〗次甲基。

me·thyl·ic [mɪ'θɪlɪk; mi'θilik] *adj.* 〖化〗甲荼的;得自甲基的;含甲基的。

me·tic·u·lous [mə'tɪkjələs; mi'tikjuləs] *adj.* 極端注意瑣事的; 拘泥於細節的。—**ly,** *adv.* —**ness, me·tic·u·los·i·ty,** *n.*

mé·tier [me'tje; mei'tjei] *n.* 行業;職業;擅長;專長。

mé·tis [me'tiːs; mei'tiːs] *n.* ①混血兒。②〖加〗白人與北美印第安人之混血兒。

me·tol ['mitol; 'miːtoul] *n.* ①〖化〗甲氨基酚;麥托爾顯像藥。②(M-)其商標名。

me·ton·y·my [mə'tɑnəmɪ; mi'tɔnimi] *n.* 〖修辭〗換喻(如 the crown =king; fur and feather=beasts and birds).

me-too ['mi'tu; 'miː'tuː] *v.t.* 模倣。—*adj.* 模倣的;倣效對方的;值得採用的。

me-too·ism ['mi'tuɪzəm; 'miː'tuːizəm] *n.* 〖俗〗採用反對黨的政綱、政見等。

met·o·pe ['mɛtəˌpi; 'metoup] *n.* 〖建築〗(Doris 式建築中 frieze 上) 兩個 triglyph 之間的方形墻面。

met·ra·zol ['mɛtrəˌzol; 'metrəzoul] *n.* ①美德萊左;四氮五甲烷($C_6H_{10}N_4$,强心劑及精神病之痙攣療法用劑)。②(M-)其商標名。

me·tre ['mitɚ; 'miːtə] *n.* 〖主英〗= **meter.**

met·ric ['mɛtrɪk; 'metrik] *adj.* ①米突的;米突制的;公制的。②測量的。③詩體的。

met·ri·cal ['mɛtrɪkl; 'metrikəl] *adj.* ①用詩體寫的。②測量的。—**ly,** *adv.*

met·ri·cate ['mɛtrɪˌket; 'metrikeit] *v.t. & v.i.*, **-cat·ed, -cat·ing.** 採用米突制;變成米突制。—**met·ri·ca·tion,** *n.*

me·tri·cian [mɛ'trɪʃən; me'triʃən] *n.* 精於韻律的人;韻律學專家;精於作詩法者。

met·rics ['mɛtrɪks; 'metriks] *n.* (作 *sing.* 解) 韻律學;作詩法。

metric system 米突制(以公尺、公升、及克爲單位的十進位度量衡制度);公制。

metric ton 公噸 (=1,000kg).

met·rist ['mɛtrɪst; 'metrist] *n.* ①作詩家;韻律學者。②寫韻文者; 作詩者; 詩人。

Mét·ro, met·ro ['mitro; 'miːtrou] *n., pl.* **-ros.** (歐洲都市之)地下鐵道。

met·ro·log·i·cal [ˌmɛtrə'lɑdʒɪkl; ˌmetrə'lɔdʒikəl] *adj.* 度量衡學的。

me·trol·o·gy [mɪ'trɑlədʒɪ; mi'trɔlədʒi] *n.* 度量衡學;度量衡制。

met·ro·nome ['mɛtrəˌnom; 'metrənoum] *n.* 〖音樂〗節拍器。—**met·ro·nom·ic,** *adj.*

me·tro·nym·ic [ˌmitrə'nɪmɪk; ˌmiːtrə'nimik] *adj.* 出自母親或女性祖先之名的;母姓的。—*n.* 出自母親或女性祖先的名。(亦作 **matronymic**)

*__me·trop·o·lis__ [mə'trɑplɪs; mi'trɔpəlis, me't-, mə't-, -plis] *n., pl.* **-lis·es.** ①首府;主要城市。a cosmopolitan *metropolis.* 世界性的大都市。②大城市;重要中心。Chicago is a busy *metropolis.* 芝加哥是個繁盛的大都市。③〖宗教〗大主教教區。④古希臘之母城(對殖民地而言)。

*__met·ro·pol·i·tan__ [ˌmɛtrə'pɑlətn; ˌmetrə'pɔlitən] *adj.* ①大都市的。*metropolitan* life. 大都市的生活。②母國的。③大主教區的。—*n.* ①大都市之居民。②大主教。③母國的居民。

met·ro·pol·i·tan·ism [ˌmɛtrə'pɑlətəˌnɪzəm; ˌmetrə'pɔlitənizəm] *n.* ①大都市生活之特點。②大都市對其居民之影響。

-metry 〖字尾〗表"測定法; 度量學; 度量術"之義,如: geometry.

Met·ter·nich ['mɛtɚnɪk; 'metənik] *n.* 梅特涅 (Prince Klemens Wenzel Nepomuk Lothar von, 1773–1859, 奧國政治家及外交家)。

met·tle ['mɛtl; 'metl] *n.* ①勇氣;精神。②性格。***be on*** (or ***upon***) ***one's mettle*** 準備奮力而爲;奮發。***put one on one's mettle*** 激勵某人。

met·tled ['mɛtld; 'metld] *adj.* =**mettlesome.**

met·tle·some ['mɛtlsəm; 'metlsəm] *adj.* 有精神的;勇敢的;熱心的。

mew[1] [mju; mjuː] *n.* 咪咪 (貓叫聲)。—*v.i.* 作貓叫聲。

mew[2] *n.* 海鷗。(亦作 **sea mew**)

mew[3] *n.* ①鷹籠(尤指換毛時所用者)。②羽毛的脫換。③(*pl.*)馬廐;倫敦的皇家馬廐。④隱藏處。—*v.t.* ①關(鷹)入籠。②關起來〖up〗.

mew[4] *v.t. & v.i.* (使)脫羽毛。

mewl [mjul; mjuːl] *v.i.* ①(嬰兒)低聲啜泣。②(貓) 低叫。—*v.t.* (嬰兒的) 低聲哭訴〖out〗. —*n.* (嬰兒的)啼哭聲。

Mex [mɛks; meks] *n.* 〖美俗〗墨西哥人。

Mex. ①Mexican. ②Mexico.

*__Mex·i·can__ ['mɛksɪkən; 'meksikən] *adj.* 墨西哥的。—*n.* 墨西哥人; 墨西哥語。

*__Mex·i·co__ ['mɛksɪˌko; 'meksikou] *n.* 墨西哥 (中美洲國家, 首都爲 Mexico City). ***Gulf of Mexico*** 墨西哥灣(美國南部與墨西哥東部間大西洋海灣)。

Mexico City 墨西哥城(Mexico 共和國之首都)。

Mey·er·hof ['maɪɚˌhof; 'maiəhouf] *n.* 梅爾霍夫 (Otto, 1884–1951, 德國生理學家,1922年獲諾貝爾醫學獎)。

mez·za·nine ['mɛzəˌnin; 'mezəniːn] *n.* ①中層樓。②(戲院中之)包廂。

mez·zo ['mɛtso; 'medzou] *adj.* 〖音樂〗中的;適度的。—*adv.* 〖音樂〗中;半。

mezzo forte 〖音樂〗中强。

mezzo piano 〖音樂〗中弱。

mez·zo-re·lie·vo [ˌmɛtsorɪ'livo;

ˌmetsouri'liːvou] *n., pl.* -vos. 半浮雕(品)。
mez·zo-so·pra·no ['mɛtsosə'præno; 'medzousə'prɑːnou] *n., pl.* **-nos, -ni** [-ni; -niː], *adj.* —*n.*【音樂】①次女高音。②其歌者。—*adj.* ①次女高音(部)的。②其歌者的。
mez·zo·tint ['mɛtsəˌtɪnt; 'medzoutint] *n.* ①一種銅板雕刻法(將粗糙之版面磨光一部分，以分出明暗者)。②此種銅板；此種銅板印製之物。—*v.t.* 以此法雕刻。
MF, MF., M.F. ①Middle French. ②medium frequency. **mf.** ①【音樂】mezzo forte. ②【電】millifarad. ③microfarad. **mfd.** ①manufactured. ②microfarad. **mfg.** manufacturing. **M.F.N.** Most Favored Nation. 最惠國。 **mfr.** ①manufacture. ②manufacturer. **mfrs.** manufacturers. **Mg** 化學元素 magnesium 之符號。**mg.** ①milligram. ②milligrams. **M.G.M.** Metro-Goldwin-Mayer. (美國之)米高梅影片公司。**Mgr., mgr.** ①Manager. ②Monseigneur. ③Monsignor. **mgt.** management. **MHG, M.H.G.** Middle High German.
mho [mo; mou] *n., pl.* **mhos.**【電】姆「(歐)(電傳導率的單位)。」
M.H.R. Member of the House of Representatives.
mi [mi; miː] *n.*【音樂】全音階之長音階之「第三音。」
mi. ①mile; miles. ②mill; mills. **M.I., MI** ①Military Intelligence. ②Mounted Infantry. **MIA** missing in action. **M.I.5** 英國情報處負責反間諜及保防工作之部門。
Mi·am·i [maɪ'æmə; mai'æmi] *n.* 邁阿密(美國 Florida 州東南部之一城市)。—**an,** *n.*
Miami Beach 邁阿密海灘(美國 Florida 州東南部 Miami 對岸之一島市)。
mi·aow, mi·aou [mɪ'au; mi(ː)'au] *n., v.* =**mew**[1]. (亦作 **miaul**)
mi·as·ma [maɪ'æzmə; mi'æzmə] *n., pl.* **-mas, -ma·ta** [-mətə; -mətə]. 瘴氣。
mi·as·mal [maɪ'æzml; mi'æzməl] *adj.* 瘴氣的；毒氣的；毒害的。
mi·as·mat·ic [ˌmaɪəz'mætɪk; miəz'mætik] *adj.* =**miasmal.**
mi·aul [mɪ'aul; mi'aul] *n., v.* =**mew**[1].
Mic. Micah. 「—**like,** *adj.*」
mi·ca ['maɪkə; 'maikə] *n.*【礦】雲母。
mi·ca·ceous [maɪ'keʃəs; mai'keiʃəs] *adj.* 雲母的；含雲母的；似雲母的；薄板狀的。
Mi·cah ['maɪkə; 'maikə] *n.* ①彌迦(紀元前八世紀之一希伯來先知)。②【聖經】彌迦書(舊約中之一書)。
Mi·caw·ber·ism [me'kɔbərɪzm; mi'kɔːbərizm] *n.* 幻想的樂天主義(典出自 Dickens 所著 *David Copperfield* 小說中人物 Micawber)。—**Mi·caw·ber·ish,** *adj.*
mice [maɪs; mais] *n.* pl. of **mouse.**
Mich. ①Michael. ②Michaelmas. ③Michigan.
Mi·chael[1] ['maɪkl; 'maikl] *n.* 男子名。
Mi·chael[2] *n.*【聖經】大天使米迦勒(見啓示錄12章7節)。
Mich·ael·mas ['mɪklməs; 'miklməs] *n.* ①米迦勒節(九月二十九日)。②英國四結帳日(quarter day)之一。
Mi·chel·an·ge·lo Buo·nar·ro·ti [ˌmaɪkl'ændʒəˌlo ˌbwɔnar'rɔtɪ; ˌmaikəl 'ændʒilou ˌbwɔːnɑː'rɔːti] 米開蘭基羅(1475-1564, 義大利雕刻家、畫家及建築家)。
Mich·i·gan ['mɪʃəgən; 'miʃigən] *n.* 密西根(美國中西部的一州, 首府 Lansing).
Mich·i·gan·der [ˌmɪʃɪ'gændə; ˌmiʃi'gændə] *n.* =**Michiganite.**
Mich·i·gan·ite ['mɪʃɪgənˌaɪt; 'miʃigənait] *n.* (美國) Michigan 州人。
Mick, mick [mɪk; mik] *n.*【俚】愛爾蘭人(輕蔑語)。
mick·ey finn, Mick·ey Finn ['mɪkɪ~; 'miki~]【美俚】加麻醉藥之酒(飲料)。(亦作**mickey, Mickey**)
mickey mouse, Mickey Mouse 【俚】陳腔濫調的。
mick·le ['mɪkl; 'mikl] *adj., adv., n.*【古、蘇】多；大。 ***Many a little makes a mickle.*** =Every little makes a mickle. 積少成多；集腋成裘。(亦作 **muckle**)
mic·k(e)y ['mɪkɪ; 'miki] *n.* ①馬鈴薯(尤指用野火烤熟者)。②(M-) 加麻醉藥之一杯酒 (=Mickey Finn)。③(M-) 愛爾蘭人(無禮稱呼)。 ***take the mickey out of*** 【英俚】嘲弄；諷刺。
micr-【字首】=**micro-** (用於母音之前)。
mi·cra ['maɪkrə; 'maikrə] *n.* pl. of **micron.**
micro-【字首】①表"極微小"之義。②表"儀器或工具用以擴大者"之義。③表"公制中某單位百萬分之一"之義(在母音前作 **micr-**)。④表"需要顯微鏡"之義。
mi·cro·a·nal·y·sis [ˌmaɪkroə'næləsɪs; ˌmaikrouə'nælisis] *n.*【化】微量分析。
mi·cro·an·a·lyze [ˌmaɪkro'ænḷˌaɪz; ˌmaikrou'ænəlaiz] *v.t.,* **-lyzed, -lyz·ing.** 對(某物)作微量分析。
mi·crobe ['maɪkrob; 'maikroub] *n.* ①微生物。②病菌。*microbe* warfare. 細菌戰。—**mi·cro·bic,** *adj.* —**less,** *adj.*
mi·cro·bi·al [maɪ'krobɪəl; mai'kroubiəl] *adj.* 微生物的；細菌的。(亦作 **microbal, microbian**)
mi·cro·bi·ol·o·gy [ˌmaɪkrobaɪ'ɑlədʒɪ; ˌmaikroubai'ɔlədʒi] *n.* 微生物學。
mi·cro·cam·er·a ['maɪkroˌkæmərə; 'maikrouˌkæmərə] *n.* 顯微鏡照相機。
mi·cro·card ['maɪkroˌkɑrd; 'maikrouˌkɑːd] *n.* (書籍、文件等的)縮影膠片卡。
mi·cro·ceph·a·lous [ˌmaɪkro'sɛfələs; 'maikrou'kefələs] *adj.*【人類、醫】小頭的。
mi·cro·chem·is·try [ˌmaɪkro'kɛmɪstrɪ; 'maikrou'kemistri] *n.* 微量化學。
mi·cro·cli·mate [ˌmaɪkro'klaɪmɪt; 'maikrou-klaimit] *n.*【氣象】小氣候。
mi·cro·cli·ma·tol·o·gy [ˌmaɪkroˌklaɪmə'tɑlədʒɪ; ˌmaikrouˌklaimə'tɔlədʒi] *n.* 小氣候學(研究局部區域內之氣候及其特性)。
mi·cro·coc·cus [ˌmaɪkrə'kɑkəs; ˌmaikrə'kɔkəs] *n., pl.* **-coc·ci** [-'kɑksaɪ; -'kɔksai].【細菌】球狀菌；細球菌。
mi·cro·cop·y ['maɪkrəˌkɑpɪ; 'maikrouˌkɔpi] *n., pl.* **-cop·ies,** *v.,* **-cop·ied, -cop·y·ing.** —*n.* 縮影膠片版。—*v.t.* & *v.i.* 攝製縮影膠片版。
mi·cro·cosm ['maɪkrəˌkɑzəm; 'maikroukɔzəm] *n.* ①小天地；小宇宙(爲macrocosm 之對)。②人(作爲宇宙之縮影)。③縮圖。
mi·cro·cos·mic [ˌmaɪkrə'kɑzmɪk; ˌmaikrou'kɔzmik] *adj.* ①microcosm 的；似 microcosm 的。②【化】磷鹽的。(亦作 **microcosmical**)

mi·cro·cul·ture [ˌmaɪkrəˈkʌltʃɚ; ˌmaikrəˈkʌltʃə] *n.* 一國或一個地區內的小區域(其居民具有特別的生活方式)。
mi·cro·cu·rie [ˈmaɪkroˌkjʊri; ˈmaikrouˌkjuəri] *n.* 〖物理〗微居里(一居里的百萬分之一)。
mi·cro·el·e·ment [ˈmaɪkroˌɛləmənt; ˈmaikrouˌeləmənt] *n.* 〖化〗微量元素。
mi·cro·far·ad [ˌmaɪkroˈfærəd; ˌmaikrouˈfærəd] *n.* 〖電〗微法拉(100萬分之一法拉,電容量單位)。(略作 **mf.**)
mi·cro·fiche [ˈmaɪkrəˌfiʃ; ˈmaikrəfiːʃ] *n., pl.* **-fiche(s).** 單捲的顯微膠片。
mi·cro·film [ˈmaɪkrəˌfɪlm; ˈmaikroufilm] *n.* ①顯微膠片。②顯微鏡照相。—*v.t. & v.i.* 用顯微膠片攝影。
mi·cro·form [ˈmaɪkrəˌfɔrm; ˈmaikrəfɔːm] *n.* 顯微複製材料。
mi·cro·gram(me) [ˈmaɪkroˌgræm; ˈmaikrougræm] *n.* 100萬分之一公分。
mi·cro·graph [ˈmaɪkrəˌgræf; ˈmaikrougrɑːf] *n.* ①作極細之書寫、圖畫或雕刻之用器。②顯微鏡相片或圖片。③微動擴大測定器。—*v.t.* 作…之顯微鏡相片或圖片。
mi·cro·groove [ˈmaɪkrəˌgruv; ˈmaikrougruːv] *n.* ①留聲機唱片上之細溝。②具此種細溝之唱片。
mi·cro·ma·nip·u·la·tion [ˌmaɪkroməˌnɪpjəˈleʃən; ˌmaikrouməˌnipjuˈleiʃən] *n.* 在微小物質上加工之技術。
mi·crom·e·ter [maɪˈkrɑmətɚ; maiˈkrɔmitə] *n.* 測微計(量極微小之距離、角度)。
micrometer caliper 測微鏡。
mi·cron [ˈmaɪkrɑn; ˈmaikrɔn] *n., pl.* **-cra, -crons.** 一百萬分之一公尺。
Mi·cro·ne·sia [ˌmaɪkroˈniʒə; ˌmaikrəˈniːʒə] *n.* 密克羅尼西亞(西太平洋菲律賓以東諸島之集合稱)。
mi·cron·i·za·tion [ˌmaɪkrənaɪˈzeʃən; ˌmaikrənaiˈzeiʃən] *n.* 研磨成微粉;粉化。
mi·cron·ize [ˈmaɪkroˌnaɪz; ˈmaikrənaiz] *v.t.,* **-ized, -iz·ing.** 研磨至極細微狀態。
mi·cro·nu·tri·ent [ˌmaɪkroˈnutrɪənt; ˌmaikrouˈnjuːtriənt] *n.* 微養分(動植物對之只需微量,如維他命或礦物質等)。—*adj.* 微養分的。
mi·cro·or·gan·ism [ˌmaɪkroˈɔrgənˌɪzəm; ˈmaikrouˈɔːgənizəm] *n.* 微生物。
***mi·cro·phone** [ˈmaɪkrəˌfon; ˈmaikrəfoun] *n.* 擴音器。 —**mi·cro·phon·ic,** *adj.*
mi·cro·pho·to·graph [ˌmaɪkrəˈfotəˌgræf; ˌmaikrəˈfoutəgrɑːf] *n.* ①微小照片。②顯微鏡照片。—*v.t.* 拍攝…之顯微鏡照片。
mi·cro·phys·ics [ˌmaɪkroˈfɪzɪks; ˌmaikrouˈfiziks] *n.* 粒子物理學。
mi·cro·phyte [ˈmaɪkrəˌfaɪt; ˈmaikrəfait] *n.* 〖植物〗微小植物。
mi·cro·print [ˈmaɪkrəˌprɪnt; ˈmaikrəprint] *n.* 縮小複印圖片。—*v.t.* 縮小複印。
mi·cro·scope** [ˈmaɪkrəˌskop; ˈmaikrə-skoup] *n.* 顯微鏡。a powerful *microscope.* 高度顯微鏡。 ***focus the microscope upon... 將顯微鏡焦點置於…之上。—*v.t.* ①仔細檢查。to *microscope* a new program. 仔細檢查一個新計畫。②放大;誇大。
mi·cro·scop·ic [ˌmaɪkrəˈskɑpɪk; ˌmaikrəˈskɔpik] *adj.* ①微小的;僅用顯微鏡可見的。②精微的。③顯微鏡的;用顯微鏡的。
mi·cro·scop·i·cal [ˌmaɪkrəˈskɑpɪkḷ; ˌmaikrəˈskɔpikəl] *adj.* =**microscopic.**
mi·cro·scop·i·cal·ly [ˌmaɪkrəˈskɑpɪklɪ; ˌmaikrəˈskɔpikli] *adv.* ①以顯微鏡;用顯微鏡。②精確地。③仔細地。
mi·cros·co·pist [maɪˈkrɑskəpɪst; maiˈkrɔskəpist] *n.* 用或善用顯微鏡者。
mi·cros·co·py [maɪˈkrɑskəpɪ; maiˈkrɔskəpi] *n.* 顯微鏡使用(法);顯微鏡檢查。
mi·cro·seism [ˈmaɪkrəsaɪzṃ; ˈmaikrousaizəm] *n.* 微震(需利用特別測震儀方能探測出之地殼輕微震動)。
mi·cro·skirt [ˈmaɪkrəˌskɝt; ˈmaikrəskəːt] *n.* 超短迷你裙。
mi·cro·some [ˈmaɪkrəˌsom; ˈmaikrəsoum] *n.* 〖生物〗(細胞內之)微粒體。
mi·cro·spore [ˈmaɪkrəˌspor; ˈmaikrəspɔː] *n.* 〖植物〗小胞子;花粉粒。
mi·cro·sur·ger·y [ˌmaɪkroˈsɝdʒərɪ; ˌmaikrouˈsəːdʒəri] *n.* =**micromanipulation.**
mi·cro·tome [ˈmaɪkrəˌtom; ˈmaikrətoum] *n.* 顯微鏡檢查用的薄片切片機。—*v.t.* 以此種切片機切成薄片。
mi·cro·tron [ˈmaɪkrətrən; ˈmaikrətrən] *n.* 〖物理〗電子加速器。
mi·cro·wave [ˈmaɪkrəˌwev; ˈmaikrəweiv] *n.* 〖電信〗微波(波長在10公尺以下之電磁波,尤指在1公尺以下者)。—*v.t.* 以微波傳播。
mic·tu·ri·tion [ˌmɪktʃəˈrɪʃən; ˌmiktjuˈriʃən] *n.* ①排尿;小便。②〖醫〗頻尿(症)。
***mid**[1] [mɪd; mid] *adj.* 中部的;中間的;中央的。in *mid* ocean. 在海洋中。
mid[2]**, 'mid** *prep.* 〖詩〗在…之中(=amid).
mid. ①middle. ②midshipman. ③midland. ④midnight.
mid- 〖字首〗表"中;中部"之義,如:from *mid*-June to *mid*-August. 自六月中至八月中。
mid·af·ter·noon [ˈmɪdˌæftɚˈnun; ˈmidˈɑːftəˈnuːn] *n.* 下午三時(左右)。
mid·air [ˌmɪdˈɛr; ˈmidˈɛə] *n.* ①半空中。②有問題;不確定(前面用in)。
Mi·das [ˈmaɪdəs; ˈmaidæs] *n.* ①麥得斯(希臘傳說中 Phrygia 之王,能點物成金)。②大富翁;善理財者。 ***have the Midas touch*** 知道如何賺大錢。
mid·brain [ˈmɪdˌbren; ˈmidbrein] *n.* 〖解剖〗中腦。
***mid·day** [ˈmɪdˌde; ˈmiddei] *n.* 正午;中午。 They will be back by *midday.* 他們中午就回來。—*adj.* 正午的。 the *midday* meal. 午餐。
mid·den [ˈmɪdṇ; ˈmidn] *n.* ①厨房內堆積之殘餘物。②〖方〗糞堆;垃圾堆。③(亦作 **kitchen midden**)〖考古〗貝殼丘(有可食介類之貝殼及他物,證實爲史前人類居住處)。
‡mid·dle [ˈmɪdḷ; ˈmidl] *adj., n., v.,* **-dled, -dling.** —*adj.* ①中間的;中央的;正中的。He lives in the *middle* house. 他住在中間那所房子裏。②居中的;中等的。③中庸的;不極端的。④(M-) 不古亦非現代的;中世紀的。—*n.* ①(the-) 中央;中間;中部;中心。He is standing in the *middle* of the road. 他正站在路中央。②腰部。 a belt round one's *middle.* 束於腰部的帶子。 ***in the middle*** 進退維谷。You're sure to be caught *in the middle.* 你一定會搞得進退兩難。—*v.t.* 〖航海〗摺疊爲二。
middle age 中年(通常指40-60歲)。
***mid·dle-aged** [ˈmɪdḷˈedʒd; ˈmidlˈeidʒd] *adj.* 中年的。 *middle-aged* love. 中年之戀。

Middle Ages 中古時代(歐洲史上約自5世紀末至15世紀中葉之時期)。

mid·dle-ag·ing [ˈmɪdlˈedʒɪŋ; ˈmidlˈeidʒiŋ] *adj.* 正要進入中年的。

Middle America ①中美洲(卽美國南部及南美北部之拉丁美洲之地域)。②美中階層(指主居美國中西部,政治上走中間路線而收入中等者)。

Middle Americanist 中美洲專家。

mid·dle·brow [ˈmɪdl͵brau; ˈmidlbrau] *adj., n.* 知能、學識等平凡的(人)。

middle class ①中流社會;中產階級。②〖英〗介於貴族及勞工間的中產階級。③中等;中層。

mid·dle-class [ˈmɪdlˈklæs; ˈmidlˈklɑːs] *adj.* ①中流社會的;中產階級的。②中層的;中等貨色的。***a middle-class school*** 中產階級子弟學校。

middle distance ①〖繪畫〗中景。②〖徑賽〗中距離。

middle ear 〖解剖〗中耳。

mid·dle-earth [ˈmɪdl͵ɝθ; ˈmidl̩əːθ] *n.* 〖詩〗地球。

Middle East 中東。

Middle Eastern 中東的。

Middle English 中古英語(1100–1500年間之英語)。

middle finger 中指。

middle ground ①中景(=middle distance). ②(兩極端間之)中間立場。

Middle Kingdom ①〖古〗中國。②紀元前2000至1785年間之埃及。

middle life ①中年。②〖英〗中產階級所過的生活;中等生活。

mid·dle·man [ˈmɪdl͵mæn; ˈmidlmæn] *n., pl.* **-men.** ①經紀人。②居間人。③傳播者。

mid·dle·most [ˈmɪdl͵most; ˈmidlmoust] *adj.* 正中的;近中點的(=midmost).

mid·dle-of-the-road [ˈmɪdləvðəˈrod; ˈmidləvðəˈroud] *adj.* 〖美〗中庸的;不走極端的。

middle passage (非洲與西印度羣島間之)大西洋中央航線。(亦作 **Middle Passage**)

middle school 中學。

mid·dle-sized [ˈmɪdlˈsaɪzd; ˈmidlˈsaizd] *adj.* 中等大小的。

Middle States (美國)中部諸州。

middle term ①〖邏輯〗中名辭。②〖數學〗內項;中項。

middle wall 隔牆。

middle watch 〖航海〗子夜至晨間四時之守望。

middle way 中庸之道;中間路線。

mid·dle·weight [ˈmɪdl͵wet; ˈmidlweit] *n.* ①體重中等之人。②(拳擊、摔角等之)中量級(148–160磅)。—*adj.* ①體重中等的。②(拳擊、摔角等之)中量級的。

Middle West 美國中西部。(亦作 **Midwest**)

Middle Western 美國中西部的。(亦作 **Midwestern**)

Middle Westerner 美國中西部的人。(亦作 **Midwesterner**)

Middle White 〖英〗一種中型的約克賽豬。

mid·dling [ˈmɪdlɪŋ; ˈmidliŋ] *adj.* (大小、品質、等級等)中等的。—*adv.* 〖俗〗略爲;頗爲。—*n.* (*pl.*) ①中等大小、品質或價格之貨物。②帶麩之粗麥粉。—**ly,** *adv.*

mid·dy [ˈmɪdɪ; ˈmidi] *n., pl.* **-dies.** ①〖俗〗=**midshipman.** ②=**middy blouse.**

middy blouse 一種兒童穿着的水手式寬外衣。

midge [mɪdʒ; midʒ] *n.* ①蚊、蚋等類的小蟲。②侏儒;矮人。

midg·et [ˈmɪdʒɪt; ˈmidʒit] *n.* ①侏儒;矮人。②同類中之小者。—*adj.* 同類中之小的。

mid·i [ˈmɪdi; ˈmidiː] *n., pl.* **mid·is.** 迷地裝。(亦作 **longuette**)

mid·i·nette [͵mɪdɪˈnɛt; ͵miːdiːˈnet] 〖法〗*n.* 〖俗〗(巴黎之)女店員。

mid·i·ron [ˈmɪd͵aɪən; ˈmid͵aiən] *n* 〖高爾夫〗一種鐵頭的球棒(通稱 Iron No. 2)。

mid·land [ˈmɪdlənd; ˈmidlənd] *n.* 內陸;(一國)中部。—*adj.* 在內陸的;內陸的。***the Midlands*** 英格蘭中部諸郡。***the midland sea*** 地中海。

mid·leg [ˈmɪd͵lɛg; ˈmidleg] *n.* ①腿之中部。②(昆蟲之)中足。—*adv.* 在(至)腿之中部。

mid-life [ˈmɪd͵laɪf; ˈmidlaif] *n.* 中年(=middle age).

mid mashie 〖高爾夫〗一種鐵頭球棒(現在通稱 Iron No. 3)。

mid·morn·ing [ˈmɪd͵mɔrnɪŋ; ˈmid͵mɔːniŋ] *n.* 上午十時左右。

mid·most [ˈmɪd͵most; ˈmidmoust] *adj.* 正中的;在中點的;近中點的。—*adv.* 在正中地;在中間部分地。—*prep.* 在…之正中;在…之中間部分。

mid·night** [ˈmɪd͵naɪt; ˈmidnait] *n.* 夜半;子夜;午夜。He worked until *midnight.* 他工作至夜半。—*adj.* 夜半的;似夜半的。burn the midnight oil*** 讀書或工作至深夜;焚膏繼晷。

mid·night·ly [ˈmɪd͵naɪtlɪ; ˈmid͵naitli] *adj.* 午夜發生的;每個午夜發生的。—*adv.* 發生於午夜;發生於每個午夜。

midnight sun 夜半太陽(夏季的夜晚在北極和南極所看見的太陽)。

mid·noon [ˈmɪdˈnun; ˈmidˈnuːn] *n.* 正午。

mid-o·cean [ˈmɪdˈoʃən; ˈmidˈouʃən] *n.* 海中央。

mid off 〖板球〗在投手左側位置的野手;其位置。

mid on 〖板球〗在投手右側位置的野手;其位置。

mid·point [ˈmɪd͵pɔɪnt; ˈmidpɔint] *n.* 中點。

mid·rib [ˈmɪd͵rɪb; ˈmidrib] *n.* 〖植物〗(葉之)主脈。

mid·riff [ˈmɪdrɪf; ˈmidrif] *n.* ①〖解剖〗膈。②女服身體中部;使身體中部裸露之女服。—*adj.* 身體中部裸露的(女服)。

mid·se·mes·ter [ˈmɪdsɪˈmɛstɚ; ˈmidsəˈmestə] *n.* ①學期期中。②期中考試。

mid·ship [ˈmɪd͵ʃɪp; ˈmidʃip] *adj.* 〖航海〗船之中部的。

mid·ship·man [ˈmɪd͵ʃɪpmən; ˈmidʃipmən] *n., pl.* **-men.** ①美國海軍學校學生。②英國海軍學校畢業生;與此等畢業生階級相等之軍官。③昔在艦上受訓以備甄選爲軍官之青年。—**ship,** *n.*

mid·ships [ˈmɪd͵ʃɪps; ˈmidʃips] *adv.* =**amidships.**

midst** [mɪdst; midst] *n.* 中間;中央。in the midst of*** 在其中。They departed *in the midst of* a heavy rain. 他們於大雨中離去。—*prep.* 在…中間。—*adv.* 在中間。***first, midst, and last*** 始終一貫;徹頭徹尾。

'midst [mɪdst; midst] *prep.* =**amid.**

mid·stream [ˈmɪd͵strim; ˈmidstriːm] *n.* 中流。

***mid·sum·mer** [ˈmɪdˈsʌmɚ; ˈmid͵sʌmə] *n.* ①仲夏。②夏至期(六月二十一日左右)。—*adj.* 仲夏的。

Midsummer Day 施洗約翰節(六月二十四日,英國四結帳日之一)。

midsummer madness 愚蠢之至;瘋狂之至。

mid·term [ˈmɪdˈtɝm; ˈmidˈtəːm] *adj.*

(學期、總統任期等之)期中的。—*n.* ①(常*pl.*)〖俗〗(大學等之)期中考試。②學期期中。③任期期中。

mid·town [ˈmɪdˌtaun; ˈmidtaun] *n.* 市中心區。—*adj.* (位於) 市中心區的。

mid-Vic·to·ri·an [ˌmɪdvɪkˈtorɪən; ˈmidvikˈtɔːriən] *adj.* ①維多利亞王朝中期的(約 1850–90 年)。②舊式的;操守嚴謹的。③守舊的;落後的。—*n.* ①該時期之人、作家等。②有該時期之思想、習尚、嗜好等之人。

***mid·way** [ˈmɪdˈwe; ˈmidˈwei] *adj.* 中途的;中間的。—*adv.* 在中途地。We stopped *midway* for a light meal. 我們在中途停下來簡單用餐。—*n.* ①中途;中間。②(博覽會中的)遊藝場;娛樂場。

Mid·way Islands [ˈmɪdˌwe～; ˈmidwei～] 中途島(為夏威夷羣島之一部分)。

mid·week [ˈmɪdˈwik; ˈmidˈwiːk] *n.* ①一星期之中間。②(M-)(教友派教徒間之)星期三。—*adj.* 一星期之中間的。

Mid·west [ˈmɪdˈwɛst; ˈmidˈwest] *n.* 美國中西部 (=Middle West). —*adj.* 美國中西部的 (=Midwestern).

Mid·west·ern [mɪdˈwɛstən; ˈmidˈwestən] *adj.* 美國中西部的;有其特性的。

Mid·west·ern·er [mɪdˈwɛstənɚ; ˈmidˈwestənə] *n.* 美國中西部人或居民 (=Middle Westerner).

mid·wife [ˈmɪdˌwaɪf; ˈmidwaif] *n., pl.* **-wives,** *v.t.,* **-wifed** or **-wived, -wif·ing** or **-wiv·ing.** —*n.* 助產士;接生婆。—*v.t.* 為…接生;助…之產生。

mid·wife·ry [ˈmɪdˌwaɪfərɪ; ˈmidwifəri] *n.* ①助產(術);接生(術)。②產科學。

mid·win·ter [ˈmɪdˈwɪntɚ; ˈmidˈwintə] *n.* ①仲冬。②冬至期(十二月二十一日左右)。—*adj.* 仲冬的。

mid·year [ˈmɪdˌjɪr; ˈmidjəː] *adj.* ①年中的。②學年中的。③於(學)年中舉行的。—*n.* ①年中。②學年中。③(常 *pl.*)〖俗〗年中考試。

mien [min; miːn] *n.* 風采;態度;樣子。

miff [mɪf; mif] *n.* 〖俗〗無謂的爭執;發脾氣。—*v.t.*〖俗〗使發脾氣;使生氣。—*v.i.*〖俗〗發脾氣;生氣;作無謂的爭執。

MIG, Mig [mɪg; mig] *n.* 米格機(蘇聯製噴射戰鬥機,為 *Mi*koyan 與 *G*urevich 所設計,故名)。

mig [mɪg; mig] *n.* 遊戲用的指彈石子或珠。(亦作 **migg**)

mig·gle [ˈmɪgl̩; ˈmigl] *n.* =**mig.**

‡**might**[1] [maɪt; mait] *aux., v.* pt. of **may.** ①表過去之"許可","可能"等。The king *might* do nothing without Parliament's consent. 國王沒有國會的同意,甚麼事也不能做。②表"與現狀相反"之事。If he were older he *might* understand. 假如他年紀大些他便能了解。③表比 may 可能性較小之事。It *might* be a good idea to wait and see. 且等着瞧可能是個好辦法。④用於客氣措辭中。You *might* at least apologize. 你至少應該道歉吧。

might**[2] *n.* 强權;權力;能力;勢力。It is beyond your *might.* 此事超出你的力量範圍。with might and main*** 傾全力(=with all one's might). The sailors hauled in the rope *with might and main.* 水手們使盡力氣拉進那條繩子。—**less,** *adj.*

might-have-been [ˈmaɪtəvˌbɪn; ˈmaitəvˈbiːn] *n.* 本可實現或發生(而未實現或發生)之事。

might·i·ly [ˈmaɪtl̩ɪ; ˈmaitili] *adv.* ①强烈地;猛烈地;有力地。②〖俗〗非常;極。

might·i·ness [ˈmaɪtɪnɪs; ˈmaitinis] *n.* ①强大;有力;偉大。②高位;高官。③(M-)閣下(作尊稱用,如:His Mightiness; Their High Mightinesses). his high *mightiness.* (反語)閣下(指高傲的人)。

might·n't [ˈmaɪtn̩t; ˈmaitnt] =**might not.**

‡**might·y** [ˈmaɪtɪ; ˈmaiti] *adj.,* **might·i·er, might·i·est,** *adv., n., pl.* **might·ies.** —*adj.* ①有力的;强大的;有勢力的。*mighty* force. 强大的力量。②巨大的。a *mighty* building. 大廈。***high and mighty*** 〖俗〗很驕傲。—*adv.*〖俗〗很;極。He was *mighty* pleased. 他很高興。—*n.* 有勢力的人。

mi·gnon [ˈmɪnjɑn; ˈminjɔn] *adj.* 小巧玲瓏的;纖美的;可愛的。

mi·gnon·ette [ˌmɪnjənˈɛt; ˌminjəˈnet] *n.* ①〖植物〗木犀草。②灰綠色。

mi·graine [ˈmaɪgren; ˈmaigrein] *n.* ①偏頭痛。②偏頭痛之一次發作。

mi·grant [ˈmaɪgrənt; ˈmaigrənt] *n.* 移居之人或鳥獸等;候鳥。—*adj.* 移居的。

***mi·grate** [ˈmaɪgret; maiˈgreit, ˈmaigreit] *v.i.,* **-grat·ed, -grat·ing.** ①移動;移往。The laboring classes *migrated* to town from rural districts. 勞動階級自鄉村移往城市。②隨季節變化而移居。Some birds *migrate.* 有些鳥類隨季節移居。

***mi·gra·tion** [maɪˈgreʃən; maiˈgreiʃən] *n.* ①移動;移住。*migration* to the suburbs. 向郊區的移居。②(鳥、魚等)成羣移動。③成羣遷徙的人或物;移棲羣;移住者羣。④〖化〗分子中的原子移動。—**al,** *adj.*

mi·gra·to·ry [ˈmaɪgrəˌtorɪ; ˈmaigrətəri] *adj.* 流動的;移動的。—*n.* 移民。

Mi·ka·do, mi·ka·do [məˈkado; miˈkɑːdou] *n., pl.* **-dos.** (日本之)天皇。

mike[1] [maɪk; maik] *n.* 〖俚〗=**microphone.**

mike[2] *v.,* **miked, mik·ing.** —*v.i.* 被用測微計測出某數值。—*v.t.* 以測微計測量。

Mike *n.* 通訊電碼,代表字母 M.

mike fright 站在麥克風前的怯場。

mik·vah [mɪkˈvɛ; mikˈve] *n.* 猶太教中的一種洗禮設施。

mil [mɪl; mil] *n.* ①〖電〗密爾(千分之一英寸,計算電線直徑之單位)。② =**milliliter.** ③以色列之青銅幣。

mil. ①mileage. ②military. ③militia. ④million.

mi·la·dy, mi·la·di [mɪˈledɪ; miˈleidi] *n., pl.* **-dies.** ①夫人(歐洲大陸人對英國貴婦之稱呼);英國貴婦。②貴婦;時髦婦女。

mil·age [ˈmaɪlɪdʒ; ˈmailidʒ] *n.* =**mileage.**

Mi·lan [mɪˈlæn; miˈlæn] *n.* ①米蘭(義大利北部之一城市)。②(亦作 **milan**)編女人草帽用的草。

Mil·an·ese [ˌmɪlənˈiz; ˌmiləˈniːz] *n. sing.* or *pl.* 米蘭人。—*adj.* 米蘭(人)的。

milch [mɪltʃ; miltʃ] *adj.* 生乳的(牛、羊等);為擠乳而飼養的。***treat a person as a milch cow*** 將某人當作搖錢樹。

mild** [maɪld; maild] *adj.* ①溫柔的;和善的。②溫暖的;和暖的。③軟甜的;淡味的。④寬大的;寬容的。a *mild* ruler. 寬大的統治者。⑤輕的;不嚴重的。Draw it mild.*** **a.** 不要誇大。**b.** 行動合理。

mild·en [ˈmaɪldn̩; ˈmaildən] *v.t.* 使變和善、和暖等。—*v.i.* 變和善、和暖等。

mil·dew [ˈmɪlˌdju; ˈmildjuː] *n.* 霉;黴。—*v.t.* & *v.i.* 使生霉;生霉。
mil·dew·y [ˈmɪlˌdjuɪ; ˈmildjuːi] *adj.* 長霉的;像霉的。
mild·ish [ˈmaɪldɪʃ; ˈmaildiʃ] *adj.* 略為和暖的;略為和善的。
mild·ly** [ˈmaɪldlɪ; ˈmaildli] *adv.* ①溫柔地;和善地。②有幾分;略;稍(=somewhat). ***put it mildly 有所忌憚地說;謹愼地說。
mild·ness [ˈmaɪldnɪs; ˈmaildnis] *n.* 溫柔;和善;和暖。
‡**mile** [maɪl; mail] *n.* ①哩;英里 (5,280英尺)。Our school is two *miles* from the sea. 我們的學校離海有二英里。②一英里賽跑。
mile·age [ˈmaɪlɪdʒ; ˈmailidʒ] *n.* ①哩數;哩程。②(以英里計算之)旅費。③以英里計的收費(如出租汽車)。④效益;用途。(亦作 **milage**)
mile·post [ˈmaɪlˌpost; ˈmailpoust] *n.* 哩程標。
mil·er [ˈmaɪlɚ; ˈmailə] *n.* 〖俚〗一英里賽跑之選手或馬。
Mi·le·sian¹ [məˈliʒən; maiˈliːzjən] *adj.* Miletus(希臘之一古城)的。—*n.* Miletus 人。
Mi·le·sian² *adj.* 愛爾蘭(人)的(=Irish). —*n.* ①傳說中之一愛爾蘭祖先。②愛爾蘭人。
mile·stone [ˈmaɪlˌston; ˈmail-stoun] *n.* ①哩程標;哩程碑。②表示進步之重大事件。—*v.t.* 立以哩程碑;以…作特別標誌。
mil·foil [ˈmɪlˌfɔɪl; ˈmilfɔil] *n.* 〖植物〗蓍草。
mil·i·ar·y [ˈmɪlɪˌɛrɪ; ˈmiliəri] *adj.* ①粟粒狀的。②〖醫〗粟粒疹的;粟粒形的。
mi·lieu [miˈljø; ˈmiːljəː, miljø] *n., pl.* **milieus, mi·leux** [miˈljøz; ˈmiːljəːz]. 〖法〗環境。
mil·i·tan·cy [ˈmɪlətənsɪ; ˈmilitənsi] *n.* ①好戰;尙武精神;强硬態度。②交戰狀態。③黷武政策。(亦作 **militance**)
mil·i·tant [ˈmɪlətənt; ˈmilitənt] *adj.* 態度强硬的;從事戰鬥的;好戰的。—*n.* 好戰者;態度强硬者。
mil·i·tant·ly [ˈmɪlətəntlɪ; ˈmilitəntli] *adv.* 好戰地;好鬥地;强硬地。
mil·i·tar·i·a [ˌmɪlɪˈtɛrɪə; ˌmiliˈtɛəriə] *n. pl.* 軍用品。
mil·i·tar·i·ly [ˈmɪləˌtɛrɪlɪ; ˈmilitərili] *adv.* ①以武力;以軍事行動。②在軍事上;從軍事的觀點。
mil·i·ta·rism [ˈmɪlətəˌrɪzəm; ˈmilitərizəm] *n.* ①軍國主義;黷武主義或政策。②尙武精神。③軍人之理想與氣質。
mil·i·ta·rist [ˈmɪlətərɪst; ˈmilitərist] *n.* ①軍國主義者;擁護黷武政策者。②軍事家。—*adj.* 黷武主義的;軍國主義的。—**ic,** *adj.* —**i·cal·ly,** *adv.*
mil·i·ta·ri·za·tion [ˌmɪlətərəˈzeʃən; ˌmilitəraiˈzeiʃən] *n.* 軍隊化。
mil·i·ta·rize [ˈmɪlətəˌraɪz; ˈmilitəraiz] *v.t.*, **-rized, -riz·ing.** ①使軍國主義化;使軍隊化;爲戰爭而裝備。②灌輸尙武精神;使好戰。
‡**mil·i·tar·y** [ˈmɪləˌtɛrɪ; ˈmilitəri] *adj.* ①軍人的;軍事的;戰爭的。*military* academy. 軍校。②軍人所做的。③適於軍人的。④好戰的;尙武的。—*n.* (the-)軍隊;軍人(集合稱)。—**mil·i·tar·i·ness,** *n.*
Military Assistance Advisory Group (美國)軍事援助顧問團。(略作 **MAAG**)
military attaché (大使館的)陸軍武官。
military band 軍樂隊。
military governor 軍政府之首長。
military law 軍法。
military police 憲兵隊。
military review 閱兵式。
military service 兵役。
mil·i·tate [ˈmɪləˌtet; ˈmiliteit] *v.i.*, **-tat·ed, -tat·ing.** 發生作用;影響〖against, for〗. —**mil·i·ta·tion,** *n.*
mi·li·tia [məˈlɪʃə; miˈliʃə] *n.* 人民自衞隊;民團。
mi·li·tia·man [məˈlɪʃəmən; miˈliʃəmən] *n., pl.* **-men.** 人民自衞隊員。
‡**milk** [mɪlk; milk] *n.* ①乳。The babe is sucking *milk.* 嬰兒在吮乳。②乳狀物。the *milk* of a coconut. 椰子汁。***cry over spilt milk*** 對無法挽回的事感到悲傷。***the milk of human kindness*** 慈悲的心腸。—*v.t.* ①擠(牛、羊等之)乳。②擠出…的汁或毒液。③榨取;勒索。to *milk* one's money. 勒索某人的錢。④加牛奶於。—*v.i.* ①產乳。The cows are *milking* well now. 牛現產乳甚佳。②變陰〖常up〗. The weather began to *milk* up. 天氣開始轉陰。—**like,** *adj.*
milk-and-wa·ter [ˈmɪlkənˈwɔtɚ; ˈmilkənˈwɔːtə] *adj.* 無力的;缺少魄力的;索然無味的。
milk chocolate 牛奶巧克力。
milk·er [ˈmɪlkɚ; ˈmilkə] *n.* ①擠牛羊乳的人。②榨乳器。③產乳的牛羊等。
milk fever 〖醫〗授乳熱;生乳熱(產婦最初授乳時之微熱)。②〖獸醫〗乳牛產後之熱病。
milk·fish [ˈmɪlkˌfɪʃ; ˈmilkfiʃ] *n., pl.* **-fish, -fish·es.** 虱目魚。
milk float 〖英〗送牛奶用之馬車。
milk glass 乳色玻璃。
milk house 牛奶處理工廠。
milk·ing [ˈmɪlkɪŋ; ˈmilkiŋ] *n.* 一次所得的乳量。
milking machine 擠乳機。
milk leg 腿白腫病。(亦作 **milk-leg, white leg**)
milk·less [ˈmɪlklɪs; ˈmilklis] *adj.* ①無奶的。②無乳狀液的。
milk-liv·ered [ˈmɪlkˌlɪvɚd; ˈmilkˌlivəd] *adj.* 膽小的;怯懦的。
milk·maid [ˈmɪlkˌmed; ˈmilkmeid] *n.* 擠乳婦;牛奶廠女工。
milk·man [ˈmɪlkˌmæn, -mən; ˈmilkmən] *n., pl.* **-men.** 賣牛奶者;送牛奶者。
milk of magnesia 〖化〗鎂乳 ($Mg(OH)_2$, 用於製酸劑或緩瀉劑)。
milk powder 奶粉。
milk punch 加牛奶、糖、香味等的酒類。
milk run 〖俚〗戰時沒有危險性的飛行任務。
milk shake 加香味冰淇淋等而後搖成泡沫狀的牛奶飲料。
milk snake 一種無毒的灰色小蛇。
milk·sop [ˈmɪlkˌsɑp; ˈmilksɔp] *n.* 儒夫;脂粉氣的男人。
milk sugar 乳糖。
milk toast 和牛奶一道吃的麪包。
milk-toast [ˈmɪlkˌtost; ˈmilktoust] *adj.* 軟弱的;無力的;不堅決的。—*n.* = **milquetoast.**
milk tooth 乳齒。
milk train 〖美〗①運奶火車(將牛奶由產地運至市場者)。②〖俚〗清晨開的火車。
milk walk 牛奶配送區域。
milk·weed [ˈmɪlkˌwid; ˈmilk-wiːd] *n.* 〖植物〗馬利筋屬植物;任何能產生乳狀汁的植物。
milk-white [ˈmɪlkˌhwaɪt; ˈmilk-wait] *adj.* 乳白色的。
***milk·y** [ˈmɪlkɪ; ˈmilki] *adj.*, **milk·i·er, milk·i·est.** ①乳狀的;乳白色的;帶白色的。②乳的。③出乳的;出乳狀液的;含乳的。④柔

和的;軟弱的;怯懦的。—**milk·i·ness,** *n.*

Milky Way 天河;銀河。

Mill [mɪl; mil] *n.* 米爾 (John Stuart, 1806–1873, 英國哲學家及經濟學家)。

‡mill[1] [mɪl; mil] *n.* ①磨粉機; 壓榨機。a cider *mill.* 蘋果榨汁機。②製粉廠; 磨坊。The *mill* cannot grind with water that is past. 水已過去不能推磨(凡事必趁早)。③工廠; 製造廠。④〖俗〗拳戰。⑤緩慢或吃力的過程。***go through the mill*** **a.** 得到徹底的訓練或經驗。 **b.** 由痛苦經驗中學習。***put through the mill*** **a.** 試煉;考驗。**b.** 以痛苦經驗教訓。—*v.t.* ①磨細;磨成粉碎;碾。②磨成漿。③製造。④使(牛羣等)亂轉。⑤〖俗〗以拳打;打。⑥軋齒邊於(錢幣)上。—*v.i.* ①亂轉。The frightened cattle began to *mill.* 受驚的牛羣開始亂轉。②亂鬨鬨地推擠。③被磨。The seed was too wet to *mill* properly. 那些種子太濕而無法磨好。④〖俚〗拳鬥。

mill[2] *n.* 釐 ($ .001)。

mill·board [ˈmɪlˌbord; ˈmilbɔːd] *n.* 厚紙;紙板。

mill·dam [ˈmɪlˌdæm; ˈmildæm] *n.* (供運轉水車用的)水壩或水池。

mil·le·nar·i·an [ˌmɪləˈnɛrɪən; ˌmiliˈnɛəriən] *adj.* 千年的;千福年的。—*n.* 相信千福年說的人。

mil·le·nar·y [ˈmɪləˌnɛrɪ; ˈmilənəri] *adj., n., pl.* **-nar·ies.** —*adj.* ①千的; 成千的; 千年(間)的。②千福年的。③信千福年之人的。—*n.* ①千。②千年(間);千福年。③千周年;千年祭。④相信千福年說的人。

mil·len·ni·al [məˈlɛnɪəl; miˈleniəl] *adj.* 千年(間)的; 千福年的。—*n.* 千周年;千周年紀念。

mil·len·ni·um [məˈlɛnɪəm; miˈleniəm] *n., pl.* **-ni·ums, -ni·a** [-nɪə; -niə]. ①一千年; 一千年之期間。②千年紀念; 千年祭。③〖神學〗千福年(基督將再臨統治人間的神聖的一千年,見聖經啓示錄20章1–5節)。④(理想中將來之)太平盛世;黃金時代。

mil·le·pede [ˈmɪləˌpid; ˈmilipiːd] *n.* 〖動物〗馬陸。(亦作 **millipede**)

mil·le·pore [ˈmɪlɪˌpor, ˈmilipɔː] *n.* 〖動物〗千窩珊瑚;千孔蟲(一種有許多小孔之珊瑚)。

***mill·er** [ˈmɪlə; ˈmilə] *n.* ①廠主 (特指麪粉廠主);磨坊主。②粉蛾。

mill·er·ite [ˈmɪləˌraɪt; ˈmilərait] *n.* 〖礦〗針硫鎳礦 (NiS).

mill·er's-thumb [ˈmɪləzˈθʌm; ˈmiləzˈθʌm] *n.* 杜父魚(一種淡水魚)。

mil·les·i·mal [mɪˈlɛsəməl; miˈlesiməl] *adj.* ①千分之一的。②千分的。—*n.* 千分之一。

mil·let [ˈmɪlɪt; ˈmilit] *n.* 粟。

mill hand 製粉場工人;磨坊工人;水車廠工人。

milli- 〖字首〗①表"千分之一;毫"之義, 如: millimeter. ②表"千"之義, 如: millifold.

mil·li·am·pere [ˌmɪlɪˈæmpɪr; ˌmiliˈæmpɛə] *n.* 〖電〗毫安培。

mil·liard [ˈmɪljəd; ˈmiljɑːd] *n.* 〖英〗十億(美國十億作 **billion**).

mil·li·bar [ˈmɪlɪˌbɑr; ˈmilibɑː] *n.* 〖氣象〗毫巴(氣壓單位)。

mil·li·cu·rie [ˈmɪləˌkjʊri; ˈmiliˌkjuəri] *n.* 毫居里。

mil·li·cy·cle [ˈmɪlɪˌsaɪkl; ˈmiliˌsaikl] *n.* 〖電〗毫週波(一週波的千分之一)。

***mil·li·gram(me)** [ˈmɪləˌgræm; ˈmiligræm] *n.* 千分之一公分;毫克。

***mil·li·li·ter, mil·li·li·tre** [ˈmɪləˌlitə; ˈmiliˌliːtə] *n.* 千分之一公升;公撮;竓。

***mil·li·me·ter, mil·li·me·tre** [ˈmɪləˌmitə; ˈmiliˌmiːtə] *n.* 粍;毫米; 公釐(千分之一米, 卽 0.03937英寸)。

mil·li·mi·cron [ˈmɪlɪˌmaɪkrɑn; ˈmiliˌmaikrɔn] *n.* 微微公尺 (一微公尺的千分之一)。

mil·li·ner [ˈmɪlənə; ˈmilinə] *n.* 製造、裝飾或販賣女帽及帽上飾物者。

mil·li·ner·y [ˈmɪləˌnɛrɪ; ˈmilinəri] *n.* ①女帽(集合稱)。②製造、裝飾或販賣女帽業。③milliner 所製造或出售的貨物。

mill·ing [ˈmɪlɪŋ; ˈmiliŋ] *n.* ①磨粉業。②製造。③幣邊上的齒溝。④鑄幣邊之齒溝。⑤〖俚〗鞭打。

milling machine 銑床。

‡mil·lion [ˈmɪljən; ˈmiljən] *n., adj.* ①百萬(的)。②很多; 很多的。*millions* of reasons. 許多理由。③大衆。education for the *million.* 大衆教育。

***mil·lion·(n)aire** [ˌmɪljənˈɛr; ˌmiljəˈnɛə] *n.* ①百萬富翁。He is a *millionaire* several times over. 他是幾百萬的大富翁。②大富豪。He was born a *millionaire.* 他生來卽爲大富翁。

mil·lion·fold [ˈmɪljənˌfold; ˈmiljənfould] *adj. & adv.* 百萬倍的(地)。

mil·lion·oc·ra·cy [ˌmɪljənˈɑkrəsɪ; ˈmiljənˈɔkrəsi] *n.* 財閥政治。

mil·lionth [ˈmɪljənθ; ˈmiljənθ] *adj.* ①第一百萬的。②百萬分之一的。—*n.* ①第一百萬。②百萬分之一。

mil·li·pede [ˈmɪləˌpid; ˈmilipiːd] *n.* = **millepede.**

mill·man [ˈmɪlˌmæn; ˈmilmən] *n., pl.* **-men.** ①工廠老板。②工廠工頭。③工廠工人。

mill outlet 廠家自營的門市部。

mill·pond [ˈmɪlˌpɑnd; ˈmilpɔnd] *n.* 供推動水車用的水池。

mill·race [ˈmɪlˌres; ˈmilreis] *n.* ①運轉水車之水流。②引水至水車之水溝。

mill run ①= **millrace.** ②〖礦冶〗選礦。

mill-run [ˈmɪlˈrʌn; ˈmilˈrʌn] *adj.* 由工廠大量生產而來 (未經特別檢查或分等級) 的;普通的。(亦作 **run-of-the-mill**)

Mills bomb 一種卵形手榴彈。

mill·stone [ˈmɪlˌston; ˈmil-stoun] *n.* ①石磨; 磨石。②任何能研磨之物。③重擔。

mill·stream [ˈmɪlˌstrim; ˈmil-striːm] *n.* 用以推動水車的溪流。

mill wheel 水車; 水車之輪。

mill·work [ˈmɪlˌwɝk; ˈmilwəːk] *n.* ①水車(工廠)機械; 水車(工廠)機械工作。②工廠之(木工)製品(門、窗等)。

mill·wright [ˈmɪlˌraɪt; ˈmilrait] *n.* ①設計與建築磨坊或磨粉機的人。②工廠之技師。

mi·lor [mɪˈlɔr; miˈlɔː] *n.* = **milord.**

mi·lord [mɪˈlɔrd; miˈlɔː] *n.* ①閣下(歐洲大陸人對英國紳士之尊稱)。②英國紳士。

milque·toast [ˈmɪlkˌtost; ˈmilktoust] *n.* 意志薄弱者;沒勇氣者;膽小者;畏首畏尾者。

mil·reis [ˈmɪlˌres; ˈmilreis] *n. sing.* or *pl.* ①昔葡萄牙之金幣。②昔巴西之銀幣。

milt[1] [mɪlt; milt] *n.* 〖解剖〗脾臟。

milt[2] *n.* ①魚之精液。②雄魚之生殖腺。—*adj.* 生殖期的 (雄魚)。—*v.t.* 使 (魚卵) 受精。

milt·er [ˈmɪltə; ˈmiltə] *n.* ①繁殖期之雄魚。②其精液。

Mil·ton [ˈmɪltn̩; ˈmiltən] *n.* 密爾頓 (John, 1608–1674, 英國詩人)。

Mil·ton·ic [mɪlˈtɑnɪk; milˈtɔnik] *adj.* ① John Milton 的;其作品的。② 似 John Milton 之作品的;有 John Milton 作品之特

微的;莊嚴的;高尙的;雄偉的。

mime [maɪm; maim] *n., v.,* **mimed, mim·ing.** —*n.* ①丑角。②(古希臘及羅馬之)一種笑劇。③此種笑劇之演員。④模仿。⑤啞劇動作。—*v.t.* ①模仿。②以啞劇動作表演。—*v.i.* 扮演笑劇;扮演啞劇。—**mim·er,** *n.*

Mim·e·o·graph [ˈmɪmɪəˌgræf; ˈmimiəgrɑːf] *n.* ①油印機之商標。②(m-)油印機。—*v.t.* (m-)用油印機油印。

mi·me·sis [mɪˈmisɪs; miˈmiːsis] *n.* ①〖修辭〗模寫;模仿。②〖生物〗擬態。③〖醫〗變裝病(某一疾病之呈現另一疾病的徵候)。

mi·met·ic [mɪˈmɛtɪk; miˈmetik] *adj.* ①模仿的。②〖生物〗擬態的。③擬似的;類似的。

mim·ic [ˈmɪmɪk; ˈmimik] *v.,* **-icked, -ick·ing,** *n., adj.* —*v.t.* ①模仿以取笑;戲擬。②仿效;擬態。③與…極相似。④使重現。—*n.* 善於模仿之人或物。 —*adj.* ①假裝的;模擬的。②模仿別人的。

mim·ick·er [ˈmɪmɪkə; ˈmimikə] *n.* 學人樣的人;模仿者。

mim·ic·ry [ˈmɪmɪkrɪ; ˈmimikri] *n., pl.* **-ries.** ①戲擬;模仿。②〖生物〗擬態。protective *mimicry.* 保護性的擬態。

mim-mem [ˈmɪmˈmɛm; ˈmimˈmem] *n.* 模仿記憶法(爲 *mim*icry-*mem*orization 之略).

mi·mo·sa [mɪˈmosə; miˈmouzə] *n.* 〖植物〗含羞草。

Min. Minister; Ministry. **min.** ①minim(s). ②minimum. ③mineral. ④mineralogical; mineralogy. ⑤mining. ⑥minister. ⑦minor. ⑧minute(s).

min·a [ˈmaɪnə; ˈmainə] *n., pl.* **-nae** [-ni; -niː], **-nas.** 古希臘、埃及等之重量及貨幣單位。

mi·na·cious [mɪˈneʃəs; miˈneiʃəs] *adj.* 威脅的;恫嚇的。—**ly,** *adv.* —**ness,** *n.*

min·a·ret [ˌmɪnəˈrɛt; ˈminəret] *n.* 叫拜樓(回教寺院之尖塔)。

min·a·to·ry [ˈmɪnəˌtorɪ; ˈminətəri] *adj.* 威脅的;恫嚇的。

mince** [mɪns; mins] *v.,* **minced, minc·ing,** *n.* —*v.t.* ①切碎;剁碎。②細分(土地等)。③矯飾地說或做。not to mince matters*** (or ***one's words***) 直說;坦白地說。—*v.i.* ①言行矯飾。②婀娜而行。—*n.* ①切碎物。②＝**mincemeat.** —**minc·er,** *n.*

mince·meat [ˈmɪnsˌmit; ˈmins-miːt] *n.* 餅餡(通常用碎肉、蘋果、葡萄乾等調合而成)。***make mincemeat of*** 徹底擊敗;徹底駁倒。

mince pie 碎肉餅(以 mincemeat 爲餡的餅)。

minc·ing [ˈmɪnsɪŋ; ˈminsiŋ] *adj.* ①矯飾的。②用矯飾之談吐、舉止的。③走碎步的。④用以切碎的。—**ness,** *n.*

minc·ing·ly [ˈmɪnsɪŋlɪ; ˈminsiŋli] *adv.* 故作斯文地;矯飾地。

:mind [maɪnd; maind] *n.* ①(思想、感覺、行使意志的)心;意志;理性;精神。②智力;理解力;悟性。An idea has just come into my *mind.* 我剛剛想到一個主意。③心意;意向;欲望;希望;目的;意志。I don't know what is in his *mind.* 我不知道他的心意。④注意力;思想。Keep your *mind* on your work. 專心於你的工作。⑤記憶;記性。⑥智者。He is one of the great *minds* of the age. 他是這個時代的智者之一。⑦追悼會。***absence of mind*** 心不在焉。***a frame*** (or ***state***) ***of mind*** 心境;想法。***bear*** (or ***keep***) ***in mind*** 記住;切記。***be in two minds*** 猶疑不決。***be of*** (***a person's***) ***mind*** 與(某人)意見相同。If you *are* all *of my mind....* 如果你們意見都和我相同…。***be of one*** (or ***a***) ***mind*** 一心。We *are* all *of one mind.* 我們意見相同;我們一條心。***be of the same mind*** **a.** (許多人)同意。*Are* you all *of the same mind?* 你們全體都同意嗎? **b.** 未改變意見、決心等。*Is* he still *of the same mind?* 他還沒有改變主意吧? ***be on one's mind*** 關心;時時放在心上。The approaching trial *was on his mind.* 他關心迫近的審判。***be*** (or ***go***) ***out of one's mind*** 發狂;心神錯亂。***call*** (or ***bring***) ***to mind*** 憶起;回憶。***change one's mind*** 改變主意;變卦。***cross one's mind*** 突然想起。A disturbing thought *crossed my mind.* 我突然想起一件令人心煩的事。***give*** (***a person***) ***a piece*** (or ***bit***) ***of one's mind*** **a.** 把自己對某人之意見坦白告訴他。**b.** 責罵。I'll *give him a piece of my mind* for telling such a lie. 我要責罵他撒這種謊。***give one's mind to*** 注意。***have a good*** (or ***great***) ***mind to*** 幾欲。I *have a good* (or *great*) *mind to* tell him the truth. 我幾乎想把眞情告訴他。***have a mind of one's own*** 有主見。***have half a mind to...*** 有幾分想要…。I *have half a mind to* go. 我有點想走。***have in mind*** 欲;計劃。I don't know whom he *has in mind* for the job. 我不知道他想讓誰做此工作。***have*** (***something***) ***on one's mind*** 關心…;爲…而焦慮。***keep an open mind*** 不作決定。***keep one's mind on*** 集中注意力於…;注意;留意;專心。***know one's own mind*** 不糊塗;有一己之見。***lose one's mind*** 發狂。***make up one's mind*** 決心。He would never *make up his mind.* 他永遠沒有決心。***meeting of minds*** 意見之完全一致。***not to know one's own mind*** 充滿疑慮;猶疑不決。***Out of sight, out of mind.*** 不見則被忘。***pass*** (or ***go***) ***out of*** (***one's***) ***mind*** 被遺忘。***pay no mind*** 〖方〗不要理睬;不理會。*Pay* his insults *no mind!* 不要理會他的侮辱。***presence of mind*** 急智;鎭定。***put in mind*** 使憶起;提醒。You *put* me *in mind* of my cousin. 你使我想起了我的表弟。***set one's mind on*** 決心;急欲。***speak one's mind*** 坦率說出心底的話。***take one's mind off*** 把注意力由…移開;轉移注意力。***tell*** (***a person***) ***one's mind*** 把自己的所思所想告訴某人。***time out of mind*** 遠古。***to one's mind*** **a.** 依(某人)之意;(某人)以爲。**b.** 爲(某人)所喜歡。—*v.t.* ①記住;注意;留心。*Mind* the step! 請留心臺階!②照顧;看管。There was nobody left to *mind* the shop. 沒人留下看管店鋪。③服從。*Mind* your father and mother. 服從你的父母。④介意;反對;關心(多用於疑問句、否定句及條件句中)。Would you *mind* shutting the door (coming here, etc.)? 請你關上門(到這裏來等)可以嗎?⑤〖古〗提醒;使想起。—*v.i.* ①注意;留意;當心。If you don't *mind,* you'll be hurt. 如果不當心,你會受傷的。②服從。③關心;介意。I don't *mind* at all. 我一點也不介意。***mind one's own business*** 管自己的事(毋管閒事)。***mind one's p's and q's*** 謹愼行事;小心翼翼。***never mind*** 毋介意;無疑。*Never mind,* I can do this by myself. 沒有關係,我能自己來做。

mind-blow·ing [ˈmaɪndˌbloɪŋ;

ˈmaindˌblouiŋ] *adj.* 〖俚〗動人心弦(或引起幻覺)的。

mind cure 精神療法;心理療法。

mind doctor 精神科醫師。

***mind·ed** [ˈmaɪndɪd; ˈmaindid] *adj.* ①有某種心向的。②有意的;有心的。He was *minded* to argue. 他有意爭辯。③具有意志的。—**ness,** *n.*

mind·er [ˈmaɪndɚ; ˈmaində] *n.* ①(小孩、機器、家畜等之)照料者;看護人;看守人。②〖英〗被照料者;(特指)託付私人敎養的貧兒。

mind·ful [ˈmaɪndfəl; ˈmaindful] *adj.* ①思索的;自覺的。*Mindful* of your advice, I went slowly. 想到你的勸告,我走得很慢。②留神的;注意的。***be mindful of*** 注意。He *is mindful of* his duties. 他忠於他的職務。—**ly,** *adv.* —**ness,** *n.*

mind·less [ˈmaɪndlɪs; ˈmaindlis] *adj.* ①不聰慧的;愚鈍的。②不留心的;不注意的〖of〗.—**ness,** *n.*

mind reader 測心術者;能測人心思者。

mind reading 測心術。

mind's eye 心眼;想像(力)。

‡mine¹ [maɪn; main] *pron.* ①我的。This book is *mine*. 這書是我的。②我的東西。Your shoes are black; *mine* are brown.你的鞋是黑色的,我的鞋是棕色的。③我的親屬。***of mine*** 屬於我的。He's an old friend *of mine*. 他是我的老朋友。—*adj.* 〖詩,古〗我的(祇用於母音或 h 前,或用於名詞後,如 mine eyes, mine heart, sister mine).

mine²** *n., v.,* **mined, min·ing.** —*n.* ①礦坑。②富源。This book is a *mine* of information. 這一本書是知識的寶庫。③地雷。④水雷。A *mine* is used to blow up enemy ships. 水雷用以炸敵船。salt a mine*** 在空礦坑中放置礦物或金屑等以騙人。—*v.t.* ①開礦。②採礦;尋礦苗。③掘(地道);挖坑。A mole *mines* its way. 鼹鼠挖坑道。④敷設地雷或水雷於。⑤以(水雷)炸毀。The cruiser was *mined* and sank in five minutes. 那驅逐艦被水雷所炸,五分鐘後卽沉。⑥祕密摧毀;慢慢毀掉。⑦爲覓取某產物而加以處理。—*v.i.* ①掘礦。②挖掘。They began to *mine* under the castle. 他們開始在城堡下面挖掘。—**min·a·ble,** *adj.*

mine-cap·tain [ˈmaɪnˌkæptɪn; ˈmainˌkæptin] *n.* 礦山工頭。

mine detector 地(水)雷探測器;偵雷器。

mine field 布地(水)雷區。

mine layer 布雷艇。(亦作 **minelayer**)

***min·er** [ˈmaɪnɚ; ˈmainə] *n.* ①礦工。②地雷工兵。③開礦機。④幼蟲期寄居葉內的昆蟲。

***min·er·al** [ˈmɪnərəl; ˈminərəl] *n.* ①礦物。Coal is a *mineral*. 煤是礦物。China is rich in *minerals*. 中國的礦產豐富。②無機物。③(*pl.*)〖英〗礦泉水;蘇打水;汽水。*Minerals* were served. 有蘇打水供應。—*adj.* ①礦物的。②似礦物的。③含礦物的。

mineral acid 無機酸。

min·er·al·i·za·tion [ˌmɪnərələˈzeʃən; ˌminərəlaiˈzeiʃən] *n.* ①礦石化;礦物化。②礦石化之產物。

min·er·al·ize [ˈmɪnərəlˌaɪz; ˈminərəlaiz] *v.,* **-ized, -iz·ing.** —*v.t.* ①使成礦物;使(金屬)礦石化。Coal is *mineralized* vegetation. 煤是化成礦物的植物。②使含礦物。③使成化石。—*v.i.* ①採礦;探礦。②礦物化。

mineral kingdom 礦物界。

min·er·a·log·i·cal [ˌmɪnərəˈlɑdʒɪkl̩; ˌminərəˈlɔdʒikəl] *adj.* 礦物學的。

min·er·al·o·gy [ˌmɪnəˈælədʒɪ; ˌminəˈrælədʒi] *n.* ①礦物學。②(一地區之)礦物學特徵。—**min·er·a·log·i·cal·ly,** *adv.* —**min·er·al·o·gist,** *n.*

mineral oil 礦油。

mineral spring 礦泉。

mineral water 礦泉水;蘇打水;汽水。

mineral wool 礦綿(作絕緣體用)。

Mi·ner·va [məˈnɝvə; miˈnəːvə] *n.* 〖羅馬神話〗司智慧、工藝及戰爭之女神(卽希臘神話所指之 Athena).

min·e·stro·ne [ˌmɪnəˈstronɪ; ˌminiˈstrouni] *n.* 加蔬菜、大麥、通心粉等煮成之肉羹。

mine sweeper 掃雷艇。(亦作 **mine-sweeper**)

mine sweeping 掃雷;水雷之移除。(亦作 **minesweeping**)

mine thrower 迫擊砲。

min·e·ver [ˈmɪnəvɚ; ˈminivə] *n.* =**miniver.**

Ming [mɪŋ; miŋ] *n.* ①中國之明朝(1368–1644)。②明朝製之瓷器。

***min·gle** [ˈmɪŋgl; ˈmiŋgl] *v.,* **-gled, -gling.** —*v.t.* ①混合。The two rivers *mingle* their waters when they join. 兩河相會時匯流一起。②結合;聯合。Their families are *mingled* by marriage. 他們兩家因婚姻而結合在一起。—*v.i.* ①相混。②相交;交往。They *mingle* very little in society. 他們很少與人交際。—**min·gler,** *n.*

min·gle-man·gle [ˈmɪŋglˈmæŋgl̩; ˈmiŋglˈmæŋgl] *n.* 雜亂之混合物。

min·gy [ˈmɪndʒɪ; ˈmindʒi] *adj.,* **-gi·er, -gi·est.** 〖俗〗鄙吝的。

min·i [ˈmɪni; ˈminiː] *n., pl.* **min·is.** 迷你裝。

mini- 〖字首〗①表"體積或規模極小"之義,如: minibike. ②表"短至膝蓋之上"之義,如: miniskirt.

min·i·a·scape [ˈmɪnɪəˌskep; ˈminiəskeip] *n.* (日本的)盆景。

***min·i·a·ture** [ˈmɪnɪətʃɚ; ˈminjətʃə] *n.* ①縮小之物;縮圖。Paris is France in *miniature*. 巴黎是法國的縮影。②(象牙或精美牛皮紙上的)小畫像。—*adj.* 小規模的;纖小的。—*v.t.* 爲…之縮影。This round orb *miniatures* the world. 這圓球爲世界之縮影。

miniature camera (通常用35mm.以下的窄小軟片的)小型照像機。

min·i·a·tur·ist [ˈmɪnɪətʃərɪst; ˈminjətjuərist] *n.* 微細畫家;製縮最近圖者。

min·i·a·tur·i·za·tion [ˌmɪnɪətʃərəˈzeʃən; ˌminiətʃəraiˈzeiʃən] *n.* 小型化。

min·i·a·tur·ize [ˈmɪnɪətʃəˌraɪz; ˈminiətʃəraiz] *v.t.,* **-ized, -iz·ing.** 使小型化。

min·i·bike [ˈmɪnɪˌbaɪk; ˈminibaik] *n.* 〖美〗迷你摩托車。

min·i·bus [ˈmɪnɪbʌs; ˈminibʌs] *n., pl.* **-bus·es, -bus·ses.** 小型公車。

min·i·car [ˈmɪnɪˌkɑr; ˈminikɑː] *n.* 小型汽車;迷你汽車。

min·i·com·put·er [ˈmɪnɪkəmˈpjutɚ; ˈminikəmˈpjuːtə] *n.* 小型電子計算機。

min·i·fy [ˈmɪnəˌfaɪ; ˈminifai] *v.t.,* **-fied, -fy·ing.** 使縮小;使減少;削減。

min·i·kin [ˈmɪnɪkɪn; ˈminikin] *n.* ①微小之物;侏儒。②〖印刷〗最小活字。③〖廢〗美女。—*adj.* ①微小的。②矯飾的。③雅緻的;考究的。

min·im [ˈmɪnɪm; ˈminim] *n.* ①〖音樂〗二分音符。②米尼姆(液量之最小單位, $=\frac{1}{60}$ dram, 約等於一滴)。③極小之物;微不足道之人或物。④向下垂直書寫之一個筆畫。—*adj.*

最小的;微小的。「少的;最小的;最低的。」

min·i·mal ['mɪnɪml;'miniməl] *adj.* 最

Min·i·mal·ist ['mɪnɪməlɪst; 'miniməlist] *n.* (昔蘇聯社會革命黨之)右派黨員。

min·i·mal·ly ['mɪnɪmlɪ; 'miniməli] *adv.* 最低限度地;最少程度地。

min·i·mi·za·tion [ˌmɪnəmə'zeʃən; ˌminimai'zeiʃən] *n.* ①減到最小量或最少程度。②最低之估計;貶低;輕視。

min·i·mize ['mɪnəˌmaɪz; 'minimaiz] *v.t.*, **-mized, -miz·ing.** ①減…至最小量或最少程度。②作最低之估計;貶低;輕視。

*__min·i·mum__ ['mɪnəməm; 'miniməm] *n., pl.* **-mums, -ma** [-mə; -mə], *adj.* —*n.* 最小量;最低額;最低限度;最低點。—*adj.* ①最小的。②最低的。「之)最低工資。」

minimum wage (維持生活所必需

min·i·mus ['mɪnɪməs; 'miniməs] *adj.* ①(英國公學中)指若干同姓學生中之最年幼者或班次最低的。②〖解剖〗最小的。

*__min·ing__ ['maɪnɪŋ; 'mainiŋ] *n.* ①採礦;採礦業。②敷設水雷或地雷。

mining engineer 採礦工程師。

mining engineering 採礦工程。

min·ion ['mɪnjən; 'minjən] *n.* ①寵僕;嬖倖。②寵愛之人(輕蔑語)。③〖印刷〗七磅因大小之活字。④被敬愛者。

min·ish ['mɪnɪʃ; 'miniʃ] *v.t. & v.i.* 〖古〗(使)變小;(使)減低;(使)減少;(使)縮小。

min·i·skirt ['mɪnɪˌskɝt; 'miniskə:t] *n.* 迷你裙。

:__min·is·ter__ ['mɪnɪstɚ; 'ministə] *n.* ①牧師。②部長。the prime *minister.* 首相;行政院長。③公使。He was appointed Chinese *minister* to Mexico. 他被派任中國駐墨西哥公使。④執行他人之目的與意志者。—*v.i.* ①服事;看護。I *ministered* to him in his last hours. 在他臨終時我在旁侍候。②救助;捐助。It will *minister* to our needs. 此將有助我們的需要。③主持聖事。**—ship,** *n.*

min·is·te·ri·al [ˌmɪnəs'tɪrɪəl; ˌminis'tiəriəl] *adj.* ①牧師、內閣或部長的;部長級的。②行政上的。③附屬的;有助力的。***the ministerial benches*** (英國議會下院之)政府黨議席;與黨議席。

min·is·te·ri·al·ist [ˌmɪnəs'tɪrɪəlɪst; ˌminis'tiəriəlist] *n.*〖英〗政府黨人;與黨黨人。

min·is·te·ri·al·ly [ˌmɪnəs'tɪrɪəlɪ; ˌminis'tiəriəli] *adv.* 以政府首長的身分。

minister plenipotentiary *pl.* **ministers plenipotentiary.** 全權公使。

min·is·trant ['mɪnɪstrənt;'ministrənt] *adj.* 服侍者的;輔佐的。—*n.* 服侍者;輔佐者。

min·is·tra·tion [ˌmɪnə'streʃən;ˌmini'streiʃən] *n.* ①牧師之職務或工作。②服務;輔佐;幫助;給予。**—min·is·tra·tive,** *adj.*

*__min·is·try__ ['mɪnɪstrɪ; 'ministri] *n., pl.* **-tries.** ①部;部長之職務;部長之任期。②教堂衆牧師。③政府諸部長;內閣。④服務;救助;捐助。The *ministry* of books is manifold. 書籍的用處很多。⑤工具;手段。***enter the ministry*** a. 入閣爲閣員。b. 爲牧師。

Ministry of Audit〖中〗審計部。

Ministry of Communications〖中〗交通部。

Ministry of Economic Affairs〖中〗經濟部。「育部。」

Ministry of Education〖中〗教

Ministry of Examination〖中〗考選部。

Ministry of Finance〖中〗財政部。

Ministry of Foreign Affairs〖中〗外交部。

Ministry of Interior〖中〗內政部。

Ministry of Justice〖中〗司法行政部。

Ministry of National Defense〖中〗國防部。「敍部。」

Ministry of Personnel〖中〗銓

min·i·sub ['mɪnɪsʌb; 'minisʌb] *n.* (作研究海底用之)迷你潛艇。

Min·i·track ['mɪnɪˌtræk; 'minitræk] *n.* ①〖商標名〗一種追踪火箭或人造衞星之系統。②(m-)追踪人造衞星之軌道及記載其訊號之程序。

min·i·um ['mɪnɪəm; 'miniəm] *n.* ①〖化〗鉛丹;赤鉛(塗料,製造玻璃用)。②朱砂色。

min·i·ver ['mɪnəvɚ; 'minivə] *n.* ①中古時裝飾女服用之一種白毛皮或灰色毛皮。②任何白色之毛皮;(尤指)白貂皮。

*__mink__ [mɪŋk; miŋk] *n.* ①〖動物〗貂。②貂皮。a *mink* coat. 貂皮大衣。③貂皮衣。The girl was wearing a *mink.* 那女郎穿了貂皮衣。

Minn. Minnesota.

min·ne·sing·er ['mɪnɪˌsɪŋɚ; 'miniˌsiŋə] *n.* (中古德國之)抒情詩人;吟遊詩人。

Min·ne·so·ta [ˌmɪnɪ'sotə; ˌmini'soutə] *n.* 明尼蘇達(美國中北部之一州,首府聖保羅 St. Paul). **—Min·ne·so·tan,** *adj., n.*

Min·nie ['mɪnɪ; 'mini] *n.* 女子名。

min·now ['mɪno; 'minou] *n., pl.* **-nows, -now.** ①鰷魚。②小魚。③較小或不重要之人或物。***a Triton among minnows*** 鶴立鷄羣。***throw out a minnow to catch a whale*** 拋磚引玉。

Mi·no·an [mɪ'noən; mi'nouən] *adj.* 邁諾斯(Minos)文明的;克利特(Crete)文明的。—*n.* 邁諾斯人(太古之 Crete 島人)。

*__mi·nor__ ['maɪnɚ; 'mainə] *adj.* ①較小的;較次要的。It is a *minor* fault. 這是小錯。②〖音樂〗短音階的;小調的。③兩同姓孩子中之年幼者的。④未成年的。*Minor* children follow the nationality of the parents. 未成年的小孩子跟隨其父母的國籍。⑤副修的(課程)。—*n.* ①未成年者。You cannot vote while you are still a *minor.* 你還是未成年的孩子時,不能投票。②〖美〗〖教育〗副科(主科以外的課程)。③〖音〗短音階;小調。We listened to the sweet *minors* of the hymns. 我們傾聽聖歌甜美的短調。—*v.i.* 副修某科〖in〗。

Mi·nor·ca[1] [mɪ'nɔrkə;mi'nɔ:kə] *n.* 米諾卡島(屬西班牙)。**—Mi·nor·can,** *adj., n.*,

Mi·nor·ca[2] *n.* 米諾卡鷄。

Mi·nor·ite ['maɪnəˌraɪt; 'mainərait] *n.* = **Franciscan.**

*__mi·nor·i·ty__ [mə'nɔrətɪ, maɪ-; mai'nɔriti, mi-] *n., pl.* **-ties.** ①少數。The *minority* must often do what the majority decides to do. 少數人必須常常做多數人決定要做的事。②未成年;未屆法定年齡的狀態。He is in his *minority.* 他尚未成年。③(亦作 **minority group**)少數民族;少數黨(派)。—*adj.* ①少數的;構成少數的。a *minority* vote. 居於少數的投票。②屬於少數派的。a *minority* opinion. 少數派的意見。

minority problem 少數民族問題。

minor key ①〖音樂〗小調。②較小規模。

mi·nor-league ['maɪnɚ'lig; 'mainə'li:g] *adj.* 〖美〗①小職業球隊聯盟的;適於

該聯盟的。②二流的;非一流的。
minor piece〖西洋棋〗主教或騎士。
minor premise〖邏輯〗小前題。
Minor Prophets〖聖經〗小預言書。
minor sentence〖文法〗小句(由單獨的單字、片語或子句所成的不完整句子,如:"Yes." "Indeed.")。
Min·o·taur [ˈmɪnəˌtɔr; ˈmainətɔ:] *n.*〖希臘神話〗人身牛頭怪物。
min·ster [ˈmɪnstɚ; ˈminstə] *n.*〖英〗①寺院的教堂。②大教堂。
min·strel [ˈmɪnstrəl; ˈminstrəl] *n.* ①吟遊詩人。②〖詩〗音樂家、歌唱者或詩人。③白人扮演黑人之滑稽歌唱團演員。④白人扮演黑人之滑稽歌唱表演(=minstrel show).
min·strel·sy [ˈmɪnstrəlsɪ; ˈminstrəlsi] *n., pl.* **-sies.** ①吟遊詩人之藝(吟唱、彈奏)。②吟遊詩人(集合稱)。③吟遊詩人所吟唱之歌、民謠等;吟遊詩人之歌集。
***mint**[1] [mɪnt; mint] *n.* ①薄荷。②薄荷糖。 —*v.t.* 以薄荷調味。
mint[2] *n.* ①造幣廠。②巨額;大量。③製造所;僞造所。—*v.t.* ①鑄造(錢幣)。②製造;僞造;創造。③將(金屬)鑄成錢幣。—*v.i.* 造幣;鑄幣。—*adj.* ①造幣廠的。②出廠後未用過的。
mint·age [ˈmɪntɪdʒ; ˈmintidʒ] *n.* ①貨幣鑄造;鑄幣;造幣。②造幣費。③鑄幣上的印記。④製造;製作。⑤(一次發行之)鑄造貨幣。
mint julep 用白蘭地或威士忌酒加冰塊、砂糖及薄荷所調成之飲料。
mint mark (貨幣面上)表示鑄造廠之「刻印。」
mint master 造幣廠廠長。
min·u·end [ˈmɪnjuˌɛnd; ˈminjuend] *n.*〖算術〗被減數。
min·u·et [ˌmɪnjuˈɛt; ˌminjuˈet] *n.* ①小步舞(十七世紀中葉的一種緩慢而莊嚴的舞步)。②小步舞曲。
***mi·nus** [ˈmaɪnəs; ˈmainəs] *prep.* ①減。5 *minus* 3 leaves 2. 5減3剩2。②缺少;無。He came back from the war *minus* a leg. 他戰罷歸來,少了一條腿。—*adj.* ①減的。A mark of B *minus* is not so high as B. B− 沒有B的分數高。②負的。 ③陰性的。plus or *minus* reactions. 陽性或陰性反應。—*n.* ①負號(−)。②負量。
mi·nus·cule [mɪˈnʌskjul; miˈnʌskju:l] *n.* ①(中古抄本之)小寫字體;小寫字。②〖印刷〗小字。 —*adj.* ①小字的;以小字寫的。②微小的。
‡**min·ute**[1] [ˈmɪnɪt; ˈminit] *n.* ①分;六十秒。 The train was ten *minutes* late. 火車誤點十分鐘。②片刻;瞬息。I'll join you in a *minute*. 我立刻就來與你們相會。③分;一度之六十分之一。10°10′ means ten degrees and ten *minutes*. 10°10′ 就是十度十分。④(*pl.*) 會議紀錄。It is on the *minutes*. 這事載於會議紀錄中。***the minute*** (or ***moment***) 一當…卽(=as soon as). I'll tell him *the minute* (that) he gets here. 等他一來到,我便告訴他。 ***to the minute*** 一分不差;準時。He came at five o'clock *to the minute*. 他來時正好五點鐘。 ***up to the minute*** 最近地。 ***wait a minute*** 稍待。 —*v.t.* ①量(時間或速度)。②作…之紀錄。 He *minutes* the proceedings of the meeting. 他作會議紀錄。
***mi·nute**[2] [məˈnjut, maɪ-; maiˈnju:t, mi-] *adj.* ①微小的。*minute* differences. 微小的差別。②詳細的。a *minute* observer. 細心的觀察家。
min·ute book [ˈmɪnɪt~; ˈminit~] 紀錄簿;會議錄。
min·ute gun [ˈmɪnɪt~; ˈminit~] 每隔一分鐘放一響的葬禮砲或遇難信號砲。
min·ute hand [ˈmɪnɪt~; ˈminit~] (鐘之)分針。
min·ute·ly[1] [ˈmɪnɪtlɪ; ˈminitli] *adj.* ①每分鐘一次的。②常常發生的;不斷的。—*adv.* ①每分鐘地。②常常;不斷地。
mi·nute·ly[2] [məˈnjutlɪ; maiˈnju:tli] *adv.* 微小地;詳細地。
min·ute·man [ˈmɪnɪtˌmæn; ˈminitmæn] *n., pl.* **-men.** ①〖美史〗獨立戰爭期間準備立卽應召之民兵。②極警覺的人。③(M-) 美國之義勇兵飛彈。
mi·nute·ness [məˈnjutnɪs; maiˈnju:tnis] *n.* ①詳細。②微小;細微。
mi·nu·ti·a [mɪˈnjuʃɪə; maiˈnju:ʃiə] *n., pl.* **-ti·ae** [-ʃɪˌi; -ʃii:]. (常 *pl.*) 細目;詳細;瑣事;小節。
minx [mɪŋks; miŋks] *n.* 孟浪或輕浮的「少女。」
Mi·o·cene [ˈmaɪəˌsin; ˈmaiəsi:n] *adj.*〖地質〗中新世的。—*n.* (the-)中新世(第三紀之中期)。
mi·o·sis [maɪˈosɪs; maiˈousis] *n.* ①〖生物〗減數分裂(=meiosis)。②〖醫〗瞳孔縮小(=myosis)。
mir [mir; mi:r] *n.* 蘇聯實施集體農場制「度以前之村落共產組織。」
mir·a·cle** [ˈmɪrəkl; ˈmirəkl] *n.* ①奇蹟。Such a *miracle* has never occurred before. 這樣的奇蹟過去從未發生過。②奇事。The doctors said that his recovery was a *miracle*. 醫生們說他的痊癒是件奇事。③驚人的例子。④神蹟劇。to a miracle*** …得若有神助;…到驚人的程度。I understand my part *to a miracle*. 我對自己所扮演的角色有驚人的了解。
miracle man ①演出奇蹟的人。②〖俗〗「做衆信爲不可能之事者。」
miracle play 神蹟劇(中世紀的一種戲劇,係根據聖經故事或聖徒事蹟所寫者)。
mi·rac·u·lous [məˈrækjələs; miˈrækjuləs] *adj.* ①神奇的;不可思議的。②奇異的;非常的。③能創奇蹟的;似乎能創奇蹟的。—**ly,** *adv.* —**ness,** *n.*
mi·rage [məˈrɑʒ; ˈmirɑ:ʒ, miˈrɑ:ʒ] *n.* ①海市蜃樓。②幻想;妄想。—*v.t.* 使如海市蜃樓一般地顯現。
mire [maɪr; ˈmaiə] *n., v.,* **mired, mir·ing.** —*n.* ①泥濘;泥沼;沼池。②泥漿。③困境。 —*v.t.* ①使陷入泥濘;使濺滿泥濘。②使陷於困境中。—*v.i.* 陷入泥濘。
mir·i·ness [ˈmaɪrɪnɪs; ˈmaiərinis] *n.* 「泥濘。」
mirk [mɝk; mə:k] *adj., n.* =**murk.**
mir·ror** [ˈmɪrɚ; ˈmirə] *n.* ①鏡子。②寫眞;眞實之反映。 This book is a *mirror* of the early English life. 此書是英國人早期生活的寫眞。③模範;典型。That knight was a *mirror* of chivalry. 那武士是俠義精神的典範。 ***with mirrors 用法術;用魔術。—*v.t.* 反映。The still water *mirrored* the trees along the bank. 河中靜水反映出沿岸的樹。—**y,** *adj.*
mirror image 反像;翻版。
mirror-image relationship 對「稱關係。」
***mirth** [mɝθ; mə:θ] *n.* 歡樂;歡笑。 uncontrolled outbursts of *mirth*. 忍不住的大笑。
mirth·ful [ˈmɝθfəl; ˈmə:θfəl] *adj.* 歡樂的;喜氣洋洋的;快活的;熱鬧的;歡笑的。—**ly,** *adv.* —**ness,** *n.*
mirth·less [ˈmɝθlɪs; ˈmə:θlis] *adj.* 不快

樂的;悲哀的;憂鬱的。**—ly,** *adv.* **—ness,** *n.*

MIRV Multiple Independent Reëntry Vehicle (一種新式的多彈頭飛彈,每一彈頭可以單獨瞄準某一目標襲擊)。

mir·y [ˈmaɪrɪ; ˈmaiəri] *adj.*, **mir·i·er, mir·i·est.** ①泥濘的;如沼澤的。②骯髒的;污穢的。

Mis. Missouri.

mis- 〖字首〗表"壞、錯誤、否定"之義。

mis·ad·just·ment [ˌmɪsəˈdʒʌstmənt; ˌmisəˈdʒʌstmənt] *n.* 不妥之調整;不協調。

mis·ad·ven·ture [ˌmɪsədˈvɛntʃɚ; ˈmisədˈventʃə] *n.* 不幸; 災難。 **—mis·ad·ven·tur·ous,** *adj.*

mis·ad·vice [ˌmɪsədˈvaɪs; ˌmisədˈvais] *n.*錯的建議。

mis·ad·vise [ˌmɪsədˈvaɪz; ˌmisədˈvaiz] *v.t.*, **-vised, -vis·ing.** 給以謬誤之勸告。

mis·al·li·ance [ˌmɪsəˈlaɪəns; ˈmisəˈlaiəns] *n.* ①身分不相稱的通婚。②不相稱的結合。(亦作 **mésalliance**)

mis·an·thrope [ˈmɪsənˌθrop; ˈmizənθroup] *n.* 恨人類之人;厭世者;厭惡或不信任人類之人。(亦作 **misanthropist**)

mis·an·throp·ic [ˌmɪsənˈθrɑpɪk; ˌmizənˈθrɔpik] *adj.* 厭惡人類的;似厭惡人類的人的。(亦作 **misanthropical**) **—al·ly,** *adv.*

mis·an·thro·pist [mɪsˈænθrəpɪst; miˈzænθrəpist] *n.* =**misanthrope.** **—mis·an·thro·pism,** *n.*

mis·an·thro·py [mɪsˈænθrəpɪ; miˈzænθrəpi] *n.* 對人類之厭惡; 不信任所有的人。

mis·ap·pli·ca·tion [ˌmɪsæpləˈkeʃən; ˈmisˌæpliˈkeiʃən] *n.* 誤用; 錯用;濫用。

mis·ap·ply [ˌmɪsəˈplaɪ; ˈmisəˈplai] *v.t.*, **-plied, -ply·ing.** 誤用。

mis·ap·pre·hend [ˌmɪsæprɪˈhɛnd; ˈmisˌæpriˈhend] *v.t.* 誤解。**—ing·ly,** *adv.*

mis·ap·pre·hen·sion [ˌmɪsæprɪˈhɛnʃən; ˈmisˌæpriˈhenʃən] *n.* 誤解。

mis·ap·pro·pri·ate [ˌmɪsəˈproprɪˌet; ˈmisəˈprouprieit] *v.t.*, **-at·ed, -at·ing.** ①誤用。②侵占; 盜用。**—mis·ap·pro·pri·a·tion,** *n.*

mis·be·come [ˌmɪsbɪˈkʌm; ˈmisbiˈkʌm] *v.t.*, **-came, -come.** 與…不相稱; 與…不適合。

mis·be·got·ten [ˌmɪsbɪˈgɑtn; ˈmisbiˌgɔtn] *adj.* ①私生的。②未好好作成的。③可鄙的;下賤的。

mis·be·have [ˌmɪsbɪˈhev; ˈmisbiˈheiv] *v.t.* & *v.i.*, **-haved, -hav·ing.** 行爲不端。

mis·be·hav·io(u)r [ˌmɪsbɪˈhevjɚ; ˈmisbiˈheivjə] *n.* 不端行爲;品行不良。

mis·be·lief [ˌmɪsbəˈlif; ˈmisbiˈliːf] *n.* ①錯誤的信仰(見解)。②邪教信仰。

mis·be·liev·er [ˌmɪsbəˈlivɚ; ˈmisbiˈliːvə] *n.* ①信仰錯誤者;信仰異端邪說者。②信仰不合正統教義者;信仰異教者。

mis·be·liev·ing [ˌmɪsbɪˈlivɪŋ; ˌmisbiˈliːviŋ] *adj.* 信仰異端邪說的;信仰錯誤的。

mis·brand [mɪsˈbrænd; misˈbrænd] *v.t.* ①打上錯誤的烙印或商標於…。②加上假的商標於…。

misc. ①miscellaneous. ②miscellany.

mis·cal·cu·late [mɪsˈkælkjəˌlet; ˈmisˈkælkjuleit] *v.t.* & *v.i.*, **-lat·ed, -lat·ing.** 誤算;誤估;判斷錯誤。**—mis·cal·cu·la·tor,** *n.*

mis·cal·cu·la·tion [ˌmɪskælkjəˈleʃən; ˈmisˌkælkjuˈleiʃən] *n.* 誤算;判斷錯誤。

mis·call [mɪsˈkɔl; misˈkɔːl] *v.t.* ①誤稱;誤呼。②〖方、俗〗譏罵。**—er,** *n.*

mis·car·riage [mɪsˈkærɪdʒ; misˈkæridʒ] *n.* ①失敗; 未達成公正或預期的結果。②(信件、貨物之) 誤送;未達。③流產;小產。④〖主英〗不按契約規定運送貨物。

mis·car·ry [mɪsˈkærɪ; misˈkæri] *v.i.*, **-ried, -ry·ing.** ①不順遂;失敗。②(信件、貨物等之)誤投;誤送。③流產;小產。

mis·cast [mɪsˈkæst; misˈkɑːst] *v.t.* ①(角色)與演員配合不當。②使擔任不適合之角色。③選派不適合之演員拍電影或演舞臺劇。

mis·ce·ge·na·tion [ˌmɪsɪdʒəˈneʃən; ˌmisidʒiˈneiʃən] *n.* (異種間之)種族混淆;異族通婚;(尤指美國白人與黑人之)雜婚。

mis·cel·la·ne·a [ˌmɪsəˈlenɪə; ˌmisiˈleinjə] *n. pl.* 雜集;雜錄。

***mis·cel·la·ne·ous** [ˌmɪslˈenɪəs; ˌmisiˈleinjəs] *adj.* ①各種的;不同性質的。②多才多藝的;多方面的。a *miscellaneous* artist. 一位多才多藝的藝術家。**—ly,** *adv.*

mis·cel·la·ny [ˈmɪslˌenɪ; miˈseləni] *n.*, *pl.* **-nies.** ①混合。②(*pl.*)雜集;雜錄。

mis·chance [mɪsˈtʃæns; misˈtʃɑːns] *n.* 不幸;壞運;乖舛。**—ful,** *adj.*

mis·chief** [ˈmɪstʃɪf; ˈmis-tʃif] *n.* ①傷害;危害;災禍。Negligence will cause great *mischief.* 疏忽將造成大禍。②導致困難或災害之行爲。The *mischief* is that he did it without permission. 錯處是他做此事未經許可。③惡作劇者。That boy is a regular *mischief!* 那孩子眞是個淘氣鬼! ④戲謔;惡作劇。Boys are fond of *mischief.* 男孩子們歡喜惡作劇。⑤愉快; 嬉戲。Her eyes were full of *mischief.* 她的眼睛裏充滿嬉戲的表情。⑥不和;爭執。⑦〖俗〗魔鬼。play the mischief with*** 傷害;弄壞;弄糟。The wind has *played the mischief with* my papers. 風把我的文件吹得亂七八糟。

mis·chief-mak·er [ˈmɪstʃɪfˌmekɚ; ˈmis-tʃifˌmeikə] *n.* 惡作劇者; 挑撥離間者。

mis·chief-mak·ing [ˈmɪstʃɪfˌmekɪŋ; ˈmis-tʃifˌmeikiŋ] *n.*, *adj.* 惡作劇 (的); 挑撥離間(的)。

***mis·chie·vous** [ˈmɪstʃɪvəs; ˈmistʃivəs] *adj.* ①有害的。②惡作劇的; 淘氣的。a *mischievous* boy. 頑皮的孩子。**—ly,** *adv.* **—ness,** *n.*

mis·ci·bil·i·ty [ˌmɪsəˈbɪlətɪ; ˌmisiˈbiliti] *n.* 可混和(性); 易混合性。

mis·ci·ble [ˈmɪsəbl; ˈmisibl] *adj.* 可混和的; 易混合的。

mis·cite [mɪsˈsaɪt; misˈsait] *v.t.*, **-cit·ed, -cit·ing.** 引用錯誤;誤舉(例證)。

mis·col·or [mɪsˈkʌlɚ; misˈkʌlə] *v.t.* ①作不正確的陳述。②錯用顏色。

mis·con·ceive [ˌmɪskənˈsiv; ˌmiskənˈsiːv] *v.t.* & *v.i.*, **-ceived, -ceiv·ing.** 誤解;誤認。**—mis·con·ceiv·er,** *n.*

mis·con·cep·tion [ˌmɪskənˈsɛpʃən; ˈmiskənˈsepʃən] *n.* 誤解; 錯誤的觀念。

mis·con·duct [*n.* mɪsˈkɑndʌkt; misˈkɔndəkt *v.* ˌmɪskənˈdʌkt; ˈmiskənˈdʌkt] *n.* ①行爲不檢;持身不正。②處置不善;失策。③不貞;通姦。—*v.t.* ①行爲不正。②經營不善;處置不當。—*v.i.* 行爲不端。

mis·con·struc·tion [ˌmɪskənˈstrʌkʃən; ˈmiskənˈstrʌkʃən] *n.* ①曲解; 誤解。②結構不對;錯誤句法。

mis·con·strue [ˌmɪskənˈstru, mɪsˈkɑnstru; ˈmiskənˈstruː] *v.t.*, **-strued,**

-**stru·ing.** 誤解;誤會。
mis·count [mɪsˈkaunt; ˈmisˈkaunt] *v.t., v.i., n.* 誤算;算錯;數錯。
mis·cre·ant [ˈmɪskrɪənt; ˈmiskriənt] *adj.* ①極不道德的; 卑鄙的。②〖古〗信異教的; 信邪教的; 無信仰的。—*n.* ①惡棍。②〖古〗異教徒。
mis·cre·at·ed [ˌmɪskrɪˈetɪd; ˈmiskriˈeitid] *adj.* 殘廢的;奇形怪狀的;醜的。
mis·cue [mɪsˈkju; ˈmisˈkjuː] *n.* ①〖撞球〗撞歪; 球桿滑脫。②失誤。—*v.i.* ①撞歪; (球桿撞球) 滑脫。②(演戲時) 未能接上暗示尾語。③失誤。
mis·date [mɪsˈdet; ˈmisˈdeit] *v.,* **-dat·ed, -dat·ing,** *n.* —*v.t.* 誤塡…之日期;誤記日期(或年代)。—*n.* 錯誤的日期(年代)。
mis·deal [mɪsˈdil; ˈmisˈdiːl] *v.,* **-dealt, -deal·ing,** *n.* —*v.t. & v.i.* 發錯 (紙牌)。—*n.* 分牌錯誤。
mis·deed [mɪsˈdid; ˈmisˈdiːd] *n.* 惡行;罪行。
mis·de·mean·ant [ˌmɪsdɪˈminənt; ˌmisdiˈmiːnənt] *n.* ①品行不端的人。②〖法律〗輕罪犯人。
mis·de·mean·o(u)r [ˌmɪsdɪˈminɚ; ˌmisdiˈmiːnə] *n.* ①〖法律〗輕罪。②卑劣的行爲;不軌的行爲;行爲失檢。
mis·di·rect [ˌmɪsdəˈrɛkt; ˈmisdiˈrekt] *v.t.* ①指錯(方向、地址等)。②寫錯(信封上的地址)。③錯用; 用…在錯的方面。④指示錯誤。⑤瞄準不確;打歪。
mis·di·rec·tion [ˌmɪsdəˈrɛkʃən; ˈmisdiˈrekʃən] *n.* ①錯引。②錯用。③錯誤的指示。
mis·do [mɪsˈdu; ˈmisˈduː] *v.t. & v.i.,* **mis·did, mis·done, mis·do·ing.** ①做錯;失敗。②做壞事。
mis·do·er [mɪsˈduɚ; ˈmisˈduːə] *n.* 做壞事者;行爲不良者。
mis·do·ing [mɪsˈduɪŋ; ˈmisˈduːiŋ] *n.* 惡行;犯罪。
mis·doubt [mɪsˈdaut; misˈdaut] *v.t. & v.i.* 〖古〗①懷疑;疑惑;掛慮;不信任。②恐懼。—*n.* 〖古〗懷疑;疑慮。
mi·se en scène [ˌmizɑ̃ˈsɛn; ˈmiːzɑ̃ːnˈsein] 〖法〗舞臺裝置;舞臺面。
mis·em·ploy [ˌmɪsɪmˈplɔɪ; ˈmisimˈplɔi] *v.t.* 錯用;應用不當。—**ment,** *n.*
***mi·ser** [ˈmaɪzɚ; ˈmaizə] *n.* 守財奴;吝嗇者。
***mis·er·a·ble** [ˈmɪzərəbl, ˈmɪzrə-; ˈmizərəbl] *adj.* ①悲慘的; 可憐的。A sick child is often *miserable*. 一個生病的孩子常常是很可憐的。②帶來苦痛與不幸的。③窮困的;卑賤的。They live in *miserable* surroundings. 他們住在窮苦的環境裏。④可恥的。—*n.* 窮光蛋。—**ness,** *n.*
***mis·er·a·bly** [ˈmɪzərəblɪ; ˈmizərəbli] *adv.* 可憐地;悲慘地。
Mis·e·re·re [ˌmɪzəˈrɛrɪ; ˌmizəˈrɛəri] 〖拉〗 *n.* ①詩篇第五十一篇 ("Have mercy upon me, O God." 爲首句);其樂曲。②(m-) 哀求(乞憐)之聲。③(m-) = **misericord** ③.
mis·er·i·cord(e) [ˌmɪzərɪˈkɔrd; miˈzerikɔːd] *n.* ①(對於修道士之)特免(特別給予戒律所禁之食物、衣服等)。②(修道院中之)免戒室。③教堂中唱詩班可摺合之坐椅下凸出之板 (摺合時供支持站立者用)。④一種短刀 (中古時戰場中用以結束將死之人之生命者)。
mi·ser·ly [ˈmaɪzəlɪ; ˈmaizəli] *adj.* 吝嗇的。—**mi·ser·li·ness,** *n.*
***mis·er·y** [ˈmɪzərɪ; ˈmizəri] *n., pl.* **-er·ies.** ①痛苦;悲慘;不幸。*Misery* loves company. 禍不單行。②窮困; 悲慘的環境。He lives in *misery*. 他生活在窮困中。③〖方〗疼;痛(指肉體上的)。
mis·fea·sance [mɪsˈfizn̩s; misˈfiːzəns] *n.* 〖法律〗不法行爲; 不當行爲; 職權之濫用(特指以不法手段做合法之事);過失。
mis·file [mɪsˈfaɪl; misˈfail] *v.t.,* **-filed, -fil·ing.** 將…歸檔錯誤。
mis·fire [mɪsˈfaɪr; ˈmisˈfaiə] *v.,* **-fired, -fir·ing,** *n.* —*v.i.* ①(槍砲、內燃機等) 不發火;不着火。②失敗。—*n.* ①不發火;不着火。②失敗。
mis·fit [*v.* mɪsˈfɪt; ˈmisˈfit *n.* ˈmɪsˌfɪt; ˈmisfit] *v.,* **-fit·ted, -fit·ting,** *n.* —*v.t. & v.i.* 不適於;不適合。—*n.* ①不適合的東西。②不能適應環境之人;不適合其職位之人。
***mis·for·tune** [mɪsˈfɔrtʃən; misˈfɔːtʃən] *n.* 不幸; 災禍。He had the *misfortune* to break his leg. 他不幸折斷了腿。*Misfortunes* never come single (singly). 禍不單行。One *misfortune* rides upon another's back. 禍不單行。
mis·gave [mɪsˈgev; misˈgeiv] *v.* pt. of **misgive.**
mis·give [mɪsˈgɪv; misˈgiv] *v.,* **-gave, -giv·en, -giv·ing.** —*v.t.* 使懷疑;使焦慮(主詞常爲 mind 或 heart). His mind *misgave* him. 他覺得疑慮不安。—*v.i.* 懷疑;焦慮。
***mis·giv·ing** [mɪsˈgɪvɪŋ; misˈgiviŋ] *n.* 疑懼;焦慮。We started off through the storm with *misgivings*. 我們滿懷焦慮地在風暴中出發。
mis·got·ten [mɪsˈgɑtn̩; misˈgɔtən] *adj.* 用不正當手段得來的。
mis·gov·ern [mɪsˈgʌvən; ˈmisˈgʌvən] *v.t.* 治理不善;行惡政。
mis·gov·ern·ment [mɪsˈgʌvənmənt; ˈmisˈgʌvənmənt] *n.* 惡政;失政。
mis·gov·er·nor [mɪsˈgʌvənɚ; misˈgʌvənə] *n.* 行虐政者;治國不善者。
mis·guid·ance [mɪsˈgaɪdn̩s; ˈmisˈgaidəns] *n.* 指導錯誤;領導錯誤。
mis·guide [mɪsˈgaɪd; ˈmisˈgaid] *v.t.,* **-guid·ed, -guid·ing.** ①予以錯誤之指導;使誤入歧途。②使做錯事;使生荒謬思想。〖注意〗主用於被動式。—**mis·guid·er,** *n.*
mis·guid·ed [mɪsˈgaɪdɪd; ˈmisˈgaidid] *adj.* 被錯誤引導的; 誤入歧途的。—**ly,** *adv.* —**ness,** *n.*
mis·han·dle [mɪsˈhændl̩; ˈmisˈhændl] *v.t.,* **-dled, -dling.** ①不當地使用; 處理不當。②苛待;虐待。
***mis·hap** [ˈmɪsˌhæp, mɪsˈhæp; ˈmishæp, misˈh-] *n.* ①不幸之事;(不太嚴重的)災禍。②惡運;不幸。
mis·hear [mɪsˈhɪr; ˈmisˈhiə] *v.t. & v.i.,* **mis·heard, mis·hear·ing.** 誤聽;聽錯。
mish·mash [ˈmɪʃˌmæʃ; ˈmiʃmæʃ] *n.* 混雜之物;雜集;混雜。
mis·im·prove [ˌmɪsɪmˈpruv; ˌmisimˈpruːv] *v.t.* 誤用;濫用。
mis·in·form [ˌmɪsɪnˈfɔrm; ˈmisinˈfɔːm] *v.t.* 誤報;誤傳。—**a·tion,** *n.*
mis·in·tel·li·gence [ˌmɪsɪnˈtɛlədʒəns; ˌmisinˈtelidʒəns] *n.* 誤解。
mis·in·ter·pret [ˌmɪsɪnˈtɝprɪt; ˈmisinˈtəːprit] *v.t.* 誤譯; 誤解。—**er,** *n.* —**able,** *adj.*
mis·in·ter·pre·ta·tion [ˌmɪsɪnˌtɝprɪˈteʃən; ˈmisinˌtəːpriˈteiʃən] *n.* 誤譯;誤解。
mis·join [mɪsˈdʒɔɪn; misˈdʒɔin] *v.t.* 作錯誤或不合適的接合。
mis·judge [mɪsˈdʒʌdʒ; ˈmisˈdʒʌdʒ] *v.t.*

& *v.i.*, **-judged, -judg·ing.** 判斷不公;判斷錯誤。—**mis·judg·ing·ly,** *adv.*

mis·judg(e)·ment [mɪsˈdʒʌdʒmənt; misˈdʒʌdʒmənt] *n.* 判斷錯誤。

mis·la·bel [mɪsˈlebl̩; misˈleibl] *v.t.* **-bel(l)ed, -bel·(l)ing.** 對…誤加標籤。

mis·lay [mɪsˈle; misˈlei] *v.t.*, **-laid, -lay·ing.** ①誤置;處置不當。②將…置於不能記起之處;暫時遺失。—**er,** *n.*

mis·lead [mɪsˈlid; misˈliːd] *v.t.*, **-led, -lead·ing.** ①領錯路;導入歧途。②使做錯事;使誤作。③使生錯誤思想;欺騙。

mis·lead·er [mɪsˈlidɚ; misˈliːdə] *n.* 誤人者。

mis·lead·ing [mɪsˈlidɪŋ; misˈliːdiŋ] *adj.* 導致錯誤的;使人易生錯覺的;易引起誤解的。—**ly,** *adv.* —**ness,** *n.*

mis·like [mɪsˈlaɪk; misˈlaik] *v.*, **-liked, -lik·ing,** *n.* —*v.t.* ①使不高興;惹怒。②對…不高興;嫌;厭;不贊成。—*n.* 不喜歡;厭煩;不贊成。—**mis·lik·er, mis·lik·ing,** *n.*

mis·make [mɪsˈmek; misˈmeik] *v.t.*, **-made, -mak·ing.** 製造不良;裝配時弄壞。

mis·man·age [mɪsˈmænɪdʒ; ˈmisˈmænidʒ] *v.t.* & *v.i.*, **-aged, -ag·ing.** 管理不善;處置失當。—**mis·man·ag·er,** *n.*

mis·man·age·ment [mɪsˈmænɪdʒmənt; ˈmisˈmænidʒmənt] *n.* 管理不善;處置失當。

mis·match [mɪsˈmætʃ; ˈmisˈmætʃ] *v.t.* ①誤將…配合;使做不適當的結合(尤指婚姻)。—*n.* ①不適當的配合;不適當的婚姻。②實力懸殊的比賽。

mis·mate [mɪsˈmet; ˈmisˈmeit] *v.t.* & *v.i.*, **-mat·ed, -mat·ing.** 誤配;不當結合。

mis·name [mɪsˈnem; ˈmisˈneim] *v.t.*, **-named, -nam·ing.** 誤稱;取名不當。

mis·no·mer [mɪsˈnomɚ; ˈmisˈnoumə] *n.* ①錯誤的名詞。②名詞或名字之誤用。③〖法律〗文件中指定人名的錯誤。

miso- 〖字首〗表"嫌惡"之義。

mi·sog·a·mist [mɪˈsɑgəmɪst; miˈsɔgəmist] *n.* 厭惡結婚的人。

mi·sog·a·my [mɪˈsɑgəmɪ; miˈsɔgəmi] *n.* 厭惡結婚。

mi·sog·y·nist [mɪˈsɑdʒənɪst; maiˈsɔdʒinist] *n.* 厭惡女人的人。—**mi·sog·y·nism,** *n.* —**ic,** *adj.*

mi·sog·y·nous [mɪˈsɑdʒənəs; miˈsɔdʒənəs] *adj.* 痛恨女人的。

mi·sog·y·ny [mɪˈsɑdʒənɪ; maiˈsɔdʒini] *n.* 厭惡女人;對女人之憎恨。

mi·sol·o·gy [mɪˈsɑlədʒɪ; maiˈsɔlədʒi] *n.* 厭惡辯論;討厭推理;厭恨學習。

mis·o·ne·ism [ˌmɪsəˈniɪzm̩, ˌmaɪsə-; ˌmisouˈniːizəm] *n.* 厭新;厭變;保守主義。—**mis·o·ne·ist,** *n.* —**mis·o·ne·is·tic,** *adj.*

mis·o·ri·ent [mɪsˈorɪˌɛnt; misˈɔːrient] *v.t.* 誤置;放錯方向。(亦作 **misorientate**)

mis·per·form [ˌmɪspɚˈfɔrm; ˌmispəˈfɔːm] *v.t.* 執行不當;執行不妥。

mis·place [mɪsˈples; ˈmisˈpleis] *v.t.*, **-placed, -plac·ing.** ①誤置;誤放。②誤給(愛情、信任等)。③〖俗〗忘記將…放在何處。—**ment,** *n.*

misplaced modifier 〖文法〗形容語之誤用。

mis·play [mɪsˈple; ˈmisˈplei] *n.*, *v.t.*, *v.i.* 誤演;誤奏;錯誤的做法(指遊戲等而言);(運動中的)誤傳;誤打。

mis·print [*n.* mɪsˈprɪnt; ˈmisˈprint *v.* mɪsˈprɪnt; misˈprint] *n.* 印刷錯誤;排版錯誤。—*v.t.* 印錯。

mis·pri·sion [mɪsˈprɪʒən; misˈpriʒən] *n.* ①(公務員之)不法行爲;瀆職;怠職。②錯誤;誤會。③〖古〗輕視;鄙視。

misprision of felony 〖法律〗隱匿重罪犯之罪;知情不報之罪。

mis·prize, mis·prise [mɪsˈpraɪz; misˈpraiz] *v.t.*, **-prized, -priz·ing.** 輕視;低估;蔑視。

mis·pro·nounce [ˌmɪsprəˈnaʊns; ˈmisprəˈnauns] *v.t.* & *v.i.*, **-nounced, -nounc·ing.** 發音錯誤。

mis·pro·nun·ci·a·tion [ˌmɪsprəˌnʌnsɪˈeʃən; ˈmisprəˌnʌnsiˈeiʃən] *n.* 發音錯誤。

mis·quo·ta·tion [ˌmɪskwoˈteʃən; ˈmiskwouˈteiʃən] *n.* 錯誤的引用(句)。

mis·quote [mɪsˈkwot; ˈmisˈkwout] *v.t.* & *v.i.*, **-quot·ed, -quot·ing.** 誤引用。

mis·read [mɪsˈrid; ˈmisˈriːd] *v.t.*, **-read** [-ˈrɛd; -ˈred], **-read·ing.** 誤讀;誤解。—**er,** *n.*

mis·reck·on [mɪsˈrɛkən; misˈrekən] *v.i.* 算錯;誤算。

mis·rep·re·sent [ˌmɪsrɛprɪˈzɛnt; ˈmisˌrepriˈzent] *v.t.* 誤傳;誤示;誤言。—*v.i.* 誤言;說與事實不符的話。—**er,** *n.*

mis·rep·re·sen·ta·tion [ˌmɪsrɛprɪzɛnˈteʃən; ˈmisˌreprizenˈteiʃən] *n.* ①訛傳;誤示;誤言。②虛僞的陳述;詐稱。

mis·rule [mɪsˈrul; ˈmisˈruːl] *n*, *v.*, **-ruled, -rul·ing.** —*n.* ①失政;苛政;暴政。②混亂;紊亂。***Lord of Misrule*** 英國宮廷飲宴娛樂事務總管。—*v.t.* 治理不善;施以苛政。—**mis·rul·er,** *n.*

‡**miss**¹ [mɪs; mis] *v.t.* ①未擊中。Both shots *missed* the target. 兩發均未中靶。②未抓住;未捉住。He tried to catch the ball but *missed* it. 他想抓住球,但失手未接住。③未見;未遇;未得到。I *missed* the first part of the speech. 我沒有聽到那演說的前一部分。④失却。He *missed* his chance (*or* opportunity). 他失去了機會。⑤未趕上。You have *missed* (=lost) your train. 你已趕脫了這班火車。⑥懷念。I'm sure that everybody will *miss* him very much. 我相信每個人都會很懷念他。⑦發現遺失。When did you *miss* your purse? 你甚麼時候發現你遺失了錢包? ⑧逃過;避免。He barely *missed* being killed. 他倖免於被殺。⑨省掉;漏去〖out〗. Don't *miss* my name out of your list. 不要在你的表上漏掉了我的名字。⑩忽略。He hasn't *missed* a day's work in years. 多年來他一天也沒有忽略過工作。—*v.i.* ①不中。②失敗。I'm afraid that he may *miss*. 我恐怕他可能失敗。③未獲得〖of, in〗. ***miss fire*** **a.** 未擊中。**b.** 失敗。His speech was carefully planned, but it *missed fire*. 他的演講是經過悉心策劃的,然而失敗了。***miss the boat*** 失去機會。—*n.* ①不中;不得。A *miss* is as good as a mile. 失之毫厘差之千里。②省略。③故意躲避。to give a person a *miss*. 故意躲避某人。④逃脫。a lucky *miss*. 僥倖逃脫。⑤〖俗〗思念。⑥流產。⑦(引擎等之)失火。It will pick up to a fast acceleration without a *miss*. 它能迅速加速而不失火。

‡**miss**² *n.*, *pl.* **miss·es,** *v.* —*n.* ①女郎;少女。She is a saucy *miss*. 她是個孟浪的女郎。②(M-) 小姐 (冠於未婚女子姓名前)。*Miss* McLay. 麥克勒小姐。③小姐 (用以稱呼陌生

的年輕女性)。May I have the menu, *miss?* 給我菜單好嗎?小姐。—*v.t.* 以 miss 稱呼。Don't *miss* her. She is a married woman. 不要以小姐稱呼她, 她是個已婚婦人。〖注意〗指一家的幾個女孩時, 正式用語應爲 Misses, 如 the *Misses* Smith. 史密斯家的小姐們。

Miss. Mississippi.

mis·sal [ˈmɪsl; ˈmisəl] *n.* 〖羅馬天主教〗彌撒書。

mis·say [mɪsˈse; ˈmisˈsei] *v.t. & v.i.*, **mis·said, mis·say·ing.** 〖古〗①說錯; 說不正確的話。②說(…的)壞話; 誹謗。

mis·sel [ˈmɪsl; ˈmizəl] *n.* (歐洲產之)大鶫。(亦作 **missel thrush**)

mis·shape [mɪsˈʃep; ˈmisˈʃeip] *v.t.*, **-shaped, -shaped** or **-shap·en, -shap·ing.** 造形不正; 毀…之形體; 造成畸形。

mis·shap·en [mɪsˈʃepən; ˈmisˈʃeipən] *adj.* 畸形的; 殘缺的。—*v.* pp. of **misshape.** —**ness,** *n.* —**ly,** *adv.*

***mis·sile** [ˈmɪsl; ˈmisail] *n.* ①投射出的武器(箭、石、標槍、矛、子彈等)。②飛彈; 火箭; 導航飛彈。—*adj.* 可發射的。

mis·sile·man [ˈmɪslˌmæn; ˈmisail-mæn] *n., pl.* **-men.** 飛彈製造、發射或保養者。

missile range 飛彈試射場。

mis·sil(e)·ry [ˈmɪslrɪ; ˈmislri] *n.* ①火箭、飛彈科學。②飛彈之集合稱。

miss·ing** [ˈmɪsɪŋ; ˈmisiŋ] *adj.* 缺少的; 不在的; 失蹤的; 行蹤不明的。One book is *missing.* 有一本書不見了。the missing link*** a. 假定在類人猿和人類當中之動物的集合稱。b. 短少之物。

missing in action (美軍)作戰中失蹤者。

***mis·sion** [ˈmɪʃən; ˈmiʃən] *n.* ①使命; 任務。He will take up this *mission.* 他將擔當此任務。②使節團; 負有特殊任務之團體。③傳教的機關、團體、工作、地區等。④人生之目的; 天職。⑤〖軍事〗任務。He flew nineteen *missions* during the war. 大戰期間他完成了十九次飛行任務。—*v.t.* ①對…傳道。②派(人)擔任某項任務。—**al,** *adj.*

***mis·sion·ar·y** [ˈmɪʃənˌɛrɪ; ˈmiʃənəri] *n., pl.* **-ar·ies,** *v.,* **-ar·ied, -ar·y·ing,** *adj.* —*n.* ①傳教士。②工作人員; 負有任務者。He is the Administration's most traveled diplomatic *missionary.* 他是政府旅行最多的外交工作人員。③(某計畫、主義等之)說服或宣傳者。—*v.i.* 作布道工作; 參加布道。—*adj.* ①傳教(士)的。②負有使命的。

mis·sion·er [ˈmɪʃənɚ; ˈmiʃənə] *n.* 傳教士; 教區傳教士。

mis·sion·ize [ˈmɪʃənˌaɪz; ˈmiʃənaiz] *v.,* **-ized, -iz·ing.** —*v.i.* 作傳道工作; 布道。He was then *missionizing* in distant China. 當時他在遙遠的中國布道。—*v.t.* 對…布道。

mission school 〖美〗①傳道學校。②教會學校。③傳教士學校。

mis·sis [ˈmɪsɪz; ˈmisiz] *n.* 〖方、俗〗①妻子。②主婦; 太太(僕人對主婦稱呼)。Yes, *missis.* 是, 太太。(亦作 **missus**)

miss·ish [ˈmɪsɪʃ; ˈmisiʃ] *adj.* 小姐脾氣的; 矜持的; 過分嚴謹的; 做作的。—**ness,** *n.*

Mis·sis·sip·pi [ˌmɪsəˈsɪpɪ; ˌmisiˈsipi] *n.* ①密西西比河。②密西西比州(位於美國南部, 首府傑克遜 Jackson, 略作 **Miss.**).

Mis·sis·sip·pi·an [ˌmɪsəˈsɪpɪən; ˌmisiˈsipiən] *adj.* ①美國密西西比河的。②美國密西西比州的。—*n.* 美國密西西比州人。

mis·sive [ˈmɪsɪv; ˈmisiv] *n.* 公文; 書信。

Mis·sou·ri [məˈzurɪ; miˈzuəri] *n.* ①米蘇里河(美國境內僅次於密西西比河之大河)。②米蘇里州(位於美國中西部, 首府傑佛遜城 Jefferson City, 略作 **Mo.**). ***from Missouri*** 〖俗〗無證據即不信服的; 存疑的; 難以欺詐的。—**an,** *adj., n.*

mis·speak [mɪsˈspik; ˈmisˈspiːk] *v.t. & v.i.*, **-spoke, -spo·ken, -speak·ing.** 誤說; 說錯; 發音錯誤。

mis·spell [mɪsˈspɛl; ˈmisˈspel] *v.t.*, **-spelled** or **-spelt, -spell·ing.** 誤拼。

mis·spell·ing [mɪsˈspɛlɪŋ; ˈmisˈspeliŋ] *n.* ①錯誤的拼法。②拼錯的字。

mis·spelt [mɪsˈspɛlt; ˈmisˈspelt] *adj.* 拼錯了的。—*v.* pt. & pp. of **misspell.**

mis·spend [mɪsˈspɛnd; ˈmisˈspend] *v.t.*, **-spent, -spend·ing.** 浪費; 徒費; 虛度。

mis·spent [mɪsˈspɛnt; ˈmisˈspent] *adj.* 浪費了的。—*v.* pt. & pp. of **misspend.**

mis·state [mɪsˈstet; ˈmisˈsteit] *v.t.*, **-stat·ed, -stat·ing.** 誤說; 僞述。

mis·state·ment [mɪsˈstetmənt; ˈmis-ˈsteitmənt] *n.* 誤說; 僞述。

mis·step [mɪsˈstɛp; ˈmisˈstep] *v.,* **mis-stepped, mis·step·ping,** *n.* —*v.i.* ①踏錯; 失足。②做錯。—*n.* ①失足。②過失; 失策。③(少女之)失身。

mis·strike [mɪsˈstraɪk; misˈstraik] *n.* 圖案鑄偏的硬幣。

mis·sus [ˈmɪsəz; ˈmisəz] *n.* 〖俗, 方〗= **missis.**

miss·y [ˈmɪsɪ; ˈmisi] *n., pl.* **miss·ies,** *adj.* —*n.* 〖俗〗小姑娘; 少女。—*adj.* 少女特有的。

mist** [mɪst; mist] *n.* ①霧。②任何使朦朧不清的東西。A *mist* of prejudice spoiled his judgment. 使他迷惑不清的偏見減損了他的判斷力。③(因病或睡眠使眼睛)朦朧不清。④一種加於碎冰塊上, 並飾以檸檬皮之酒精飲料。be in a mist*** 在迷惑中。***cast*** (or ***throw***) ***a mist before one's eyes*** 蒙蔽某人。—*v.t.* 罩以霧; 使模糊不清。Tears *misted* her eyes. 淚水迷濛了她的眼睛。—*v.i.* ①下霧。It isn't raining; it's only *misting.* 不是下雨, 祇是有霧。②變模糊。—**less,** *adj.*

mis·tak·a·ble [məˈstekəbl; misˈtei-kəbl] *adj.* 易被誤會的; 易被誤解的; 易錯誤的。—**ness,** *n.* —**mis·tak·a·bly,** *adv.*

‡mis·take [məˈstek; misˈteik] *n., v.,* **-took, -tak·en, -tak·ing.** —*n.* 錯誤; 誤會; 誤解。There's no *mistake* about it. 絕對不錯。***and no mistake*** 確實無疑地。It's hot today *and no mistake!* 今天的確很熱啊! ***by mistake*** 誤。I used your towel *by mistake.* 我誤用了你的毛巾。***make a mistake*** 犯錯。You *made a mistake* about the time. 你記錯了時間。—*v.t.* ①誤認; 誤會。He *mistook* you for your brother. 他誤將你當做你的哥哥。②誤選; 選錯。—*v.i.* 犯錯。—**mis·tak·er,** *n.* —**mis·tak·ing·ly,** *adv.*

***mis·tak·en** [məˈstekən; misˈteikən] *v.* pp. of **mistake.** She was *mistaken* for the queen. 她被誤認爲女王。—*adj.* ①犯錯的; 意見錯誤的。A *mistaken* person should admit his error. 一個犯了錯的人應當承認自己的錯誤。②錯誤的; 判斷錯誤的; 誤置的。—**ly,** *adv.* —**ness,** *n.*

***mis·ter** [ˈmɪstɚ; ˈmistə] *n.* ①(M-) 先生(冠於人名或其職務名前, 略作 **Mr.**). *Mr.* Smith. 史密斯先生。*Mr.* Secretary. 部長先生。*Mr.* President. 總統先生。②〖俗〗= **sir.** ③無特別頭銜者; 無博士學位者。—*v.t.* 呼…爲先生。Don't *mister* me. 別叫我先生。

mist·i·ly 〔ˈmɪstəlɪ; ˈmistili〕 *adv.* ①朦朧地。②含糊地。
mis·time 〔mɪsˈtaɪm; ˈmisˈtaim〕 *v.t.*, **-timed, -tim·ing.** ①弄錯…之時間。②作不合時機之（言語、行動）。③打錯拍子。
mist·i·ness 〔ˈmɪstɪnɪs; ˈmistinis〕 *n.* 模糊不清；含糊；不清晰。
mis·tle·toe 〔ˈmɪslˌto; ˈmisltou〕 *n.* ①〖植物〗槲寄生。②槲寄生的小枝（常用做聖誕樹的裝飾）。
mis·took 〔mɪsˈtʊk; misˈtuk〕 *v.* pt. of **mistake.**
mis·tral 〔ˈmɪstrəl; ˈmistrəl〕 *n.* （法國地中海沿岸地方之）乾燥而寒冷的西北風。
mis·trans·late 〔ˌmɪstrænsˈlet; ˈmistrænsˈleit〕 *v.t.*, **-lat·ed, -lat·ing.** 誤譯。—**mis·trans·la·tion,** *n.*
mis·treat 〔mɪsˈtrit; ˈmisˈtri:t〕 *v.t.* 虐待；苛待。—**ment,** *n.*
***mis·tress** 〔ˈmɪstrɪs; ˈmistris〕 *n.* ①主婦；女主人（爲 master 之對）。Is your *mistress* at home? 你的女主人在家嗎？②（被視爲女性的）統治者；支配者。Spain was once the *mistress* of the world. 西班牙一度爲世界之霸。③精通一學科之婦女。④女教師。Miss Chang is our history *mistress.* 張小姐是我們的歷史教師。⑤（M-）夫人（現已以 Mrs. 或 Miss 代之）。⑥妾；情婦。Leaving his wife behind, he travels with his *mistress.* 他遺棄了太太，帶着情婦旅行。⑦使男人爲之顚倒的女人。—**hood,** *n.*
mis·tress-ship 〔ˈmɪstrɪsʃɪp; ˈmistrisʃip〕 *n.* 女主人、女支配者、女教師等之身分。
mis·tri·al 〔mɪsˈtraɪəl; ˈmisˈtraiəl〕 *n.* 〖法律〗①因違反程序而無效之審判。②（因陪審員意見不一致而）未決之審判。
mis·trust 〔mɪsˈtrʌst; ˈmisˈtrʌst〕 *v.t.* & *v.i.* 不信；懷疑。—*n.* 缺乏信心；疑惑。Hate and *mistrust* are the children of blindness. 恨與懷疑爲愚昧之產物。—**er,** *n.* —**ing·ly,** *adv.*
mis·trust·ful 〔mɪsˈtrʌstfəl; ˈmisˈtrʌstfl〕 *adj.* 缺乏信心的；不信任的；懷疑的；狐疑的；猜疑的。—**ly,** *adv.* —**ness,** *n.*
***mist·y** 〔ˈmɪstɪ; ˈmisti〕 *adj.*, **mist·i·er, mist·i·est.** ①霧的。②有霧的；籠罩着霧的。③不清楚的；模糊的。④濛濛的。
***mis·un·der·stand** 〔ˌmɪsʌndəˈstænd; ˈmisʌndəˈstænd〕 *v.t.*, **-stood, -stand·ing.** 誤會；誤解。His intentions were *misunderstood.* 他的意向被誤解了。—**er,** *n.* —**ing·ly,** *adv.*
mis·un·der·stand·ing 〔ˌmɪsʌndəˈstændɪŋ; ˈmisʌndəˈstændiŋ〕 *n.* ①誤解；誤會。②不和；爭執。
mis·un·der·stood 〔ˌmɪsʌndəˈstud; ˈmisʌndəˈstud〕 *v.* pt. & pp. of **misunderstand.** —*adj.* ①被誤解的。②未受到適當重視的。
mis·us·age 〔mɪsˈjusɪdʒ; ˈmisˈju:zidʒ〕 *n.* ①誤用。②濫用；虐待。
***mis·use** 〔*v.* mɪsˈjuz; ˈmisˈju:z *n.* mɪsˈjus; ˈmisˈju:s〕 *v.*, **-used, -us·ing,** *n.* —*v.t.* ①誤用。He *misuses* his knife at the table by lifting food with it. 吃飯時他誤用刀子拿食物。②濫用；虐待。—*n.* 誤用。
M.I.T. Massachusetts Institute of Technology.
mite[1] 〔maɪt; mait〕 *n.* ①（不再適用的）小銅幣；小銅錢。②數量很小的捐助。③幼兒；極小的東西。④少許；一點點（須與冠詞 a 連用）。
mite[2] *n.* 小蜘蛛；小蟲；小蝨等。
mi·ter, mi·tre 〔ˈmaɪtə; ˈmaitə〕 *n.* ①主教參加典禮時所帶之冠。②古代猶太教高僧的法冠。③主教的職位、職務。④〖土木〗斜接；斜接面；斜接規。—*v.t.* ①賜予主教法冠；升爲主教。②斜接。
mi·tered 〔ˈmaɪtəd; ˈmaitəd〕 *adj.* 帶着主教法冠的。
Mith·ra 〔ˈmɪθrə; ˈmiθrə〕 *n.* 〖波斯神話〗密斯拉（光與眞理之神，後成爲太陽神）。（亦作 **Mithras**）
Mith·ras 〔ˈmɪθræs; ˈmiθræs〕 *n.* = **Mithra.**
mith·ri·dat·ize 〔ˈmɪθrəˌdetaɪz; ˈmiθrideitaiz〕 *v.t.*, **-ized, -iz·ing.** 在…之中產生毒物免疫。
mit·i·ga·ble 〔ˈmɪtəgəbl; ˈmitigəbl〕 *adj.* 可緩和的；可減輕的。
mit·i·gate 〔ˈmɪtəˌget; ˈmitigeit〕 *v.*, **-gat·ed, -gat·ing.** —*v.t.* 使緩和；使減輕。—*v.i.* 緩和；減緩。—**mit·i·ga·tor,** *n.*
mit·i·ga·tion 〔ˌmɪtəˈgeʃən; ˌmitiˈgeiʃən〕 *n.* ①緩和；減輕。②緩和或減輕之事物。
mit·i·ga·tive 〔ˈmɪtəˌgetɪv; ˈmitigətiv〕 *adj.* 緩和的；減輕的；緩和性的。—*n.* 緩和劑；減痛劑。
mit·i·ga·to·ry 〔ˈmɪtəgəˌtorɪ; ˈmitigətəri〕 *adj.*, *n.* = **mitigative.**
mi·to·sis 〔mɪˈtosɪs; miˈtousis〕 *n.*, *pl.* **-ses** 〔-ˌsiz; -si:z〕. 〖生物〗（細胞核之）有絲分裂；間接核分裂。
mi·tot·ic 〔mɪˈtɑtɪk; miˈtɔtik〕 *adj.* 〖生物〗有絲分裂的；間接核分裂的。—**al·ly,** *adv.*
mi·trail·leuse 〔ˌmitreˈjɜz; ˌmitraiˈjə:z〕 〖法〗 *n.* 機鎗。
mi·tral 〔ˈmaɪtrəl; ˈmaitrəl〕 *adj.* ①僧帽（狀）的；主教冠的。②〖解剖〗僧帽瓣的。
mitral valve 〖解剖〗僧帽瓣（在心臟左心房與左心室之間防止血液逆流者）；二尖瓣。（亦作 **bicuspid valve**）
***mitt** 〔mɪt; mit〕 *n.* ①一種無指或只帶一部分指頭的長手套（只能保護手背、手掌、腕部者）。②棒球手套；〖俗〗拳擊手套。③ = **mitten.** ④〖俚〗手。
mit·ten** 〔ˈmɪtn̩; ˈmitn〕 *n.* ①拇指除外其他四指連在一起的手套。②一種將手指留在外邊的毛手套。③（*pl.*）〖俗〗拳擊手套。 ***get (or ***give***) ***the mitten*** 〖俗〗 **a.** （男子）求婚被拒。**b.** 被開除。—**like,** *adj.*
mit·ti·mus 〔ˈmɪtəməs; ˈmitiməs〕 *n.* ①〖法律〗徒刑之執行書；下獄狀。②〖法律〗訴訟案卷之移送命令。③〖英〗解雇通知；解聘；免職。④〖英諧〗 = **magistrate.**
mitz·vah 〔ˈmɪtsvɑ; ˈmitsvɑ:〕 *n.*, *pl.* **-voth** 〔-voθ; -vouθ〕, **-vahs.** 〖猶太教〗①戒律。②德行。（亦作 **mitsvah**）
‡**mix** 〔mɪks; miks〕 *v.*, **mixed** or **mixt, mix·ing,** *n.* —*v.t.* ①混合；混和。You can't *mix* oil with water. 你不能使油與水相溶和。②使聯合一起。③加添；混於一起。④配製。Ask the doctor to *mix* some medicine for you. 請醫生配些藥給你。⑤弄錯；搞錯。He *mixed* his dates and arrived a week late. 他弄錯了日期而晚到了一星期。⑥〖動物〗將…作異種交配。—*v.i.* ①相溶。Oil and water will not *mix.* 油和水不相溶和。②相處；交遊。He doesn't *mix* well. 他不善與人相處。③參與〖in〗. It is not in keeping with his position as a judge to *mix* in politics. 他參與政治與他法官的身分不合。④調合。The two colors don't *mix* well. 這兩種顏色不能調和。⑤〖動物〗異種交配。⑥〖拳擊俚〗激烈地互相出拳攻擊。 ***be mixed up in*** 參與其事（多指不

愉快或厭煩的事)。I don't like to *be mixed up in* such a matter. 我不喜歡參與這種事。 ***mix it (up)*** 【俚】互毆;交戰。 ***mix up*** 相混;混亂。We got *mixed up* in our direction. 我們走失了方向。—*n.* ①混合(物)。②【俗】混亂;頭腦混亂的狀態。He was so tired he was in a *mix*. 他疲倦得頭腦混亂。③(材料已配好的)速烹食品;一種不含酒精的速成飲料混合物。**—a·ble, —i·ble,** *adj.* **—a·ble·ness, —i·ble·ness, —a·bil·i·ty, —i·bil·i·ty,** *n.*

***mixed** [mɪkst; mikst] *adj.* ①混合的;由不同成分組成的;由不同種類合成的。②不同種類的;各形各色的;包括一切的。③男女兩性均有的。*mixed* doubles. (球類中的)男女混合雙打。④【俗】糊塗不清的;頭腦混亂的。You are getting *mixed*. 你糊塗了。⑤不同階級或種類的。⑥【股票】榮枯不一的;升降相混的。⑦【語音】中部的;不前不後的。**—ness,** *n.*

mixed-blood [ˈmɪkstˈblʌd; ˈmikstˈblʌd] *n.* 混血兒。(亦作 **mixblood**) **—ed,** *adj.*

mixed farming 農場之多角經營或多目標經營。

mixed feed 混合飼料。

mixed-manned [ˈmɪkstmænd; ˈmikstmænd] *adj.* (部隊)由會員國組成的;聯軍的;包括各國部隊的。

mixed marriage (種族不同或宗教不同的男女之)混合婚姻。

mixed media =**multimedia.**

mixed-me·di·a [ˈmɪkstˈmidɪə; ˈmikstˈmiːdjə] *adj.* =**multimedia.**

mixed number 【數學】帶分數。

mixed train (含客貨車的)混合火車。

mix·er [ˈmɪksɚ; ˈmiksə] *n.* ①混合者;混合器。②【俗】交際家。③調酒用的飲料。

mixing faucet 冷熱水合一而開關分開的自來水龍頭。

mix·ol·o·gist [mɪkˈsɑlədʒɪst; mikˈsɔlədʒist] *n.* 【俚】善於調酒者;酒吧酒師。

mixt [mɪkst; mikst] *v.* pt. & pp. of **mix.**

***mix·ture** [ˈmɪkstʃɚ; ˈmikstʃə] *n.* ①混合;混淆。②混合劑;混合物。Air is a *mixture* of gases. 空氣是氣體的混合物。

mix-up [ˈmɪksˌʌp; ˈmiksˈʌp] *n.* ①混亂;雜亂。②【俗】混戰。③混合的結果;混合物。

miz·(z)en [ˈmɪzn̩; ˈmizn] *n.* ①兩桅或三桅船上最近船尾部之桅。②裝於該桅上的最低之方形帆。—*adj.* 裝於該桅上的。

miz·(z)en·mast [ˈmɪzn̩məst; ˈmiznmɑːst] *n.* 【航海】①(三桅船之)後桅;尾桅。②(四、五桅船之)第三桅。

miz·(z)en·yard [ˈmɪzn̩ˌjɑrd; ˈmiznjɑːd] *n.* 【航海】後桅之帆桁。

miz·zle¹ [ˈmɪzl̩; ˈmizl] *v.*, **-zled, -zl·ing,** *n.* —*v.t.* & *v.i.* 【廢,方】下濛濛雨。—*n.* 細雨;濛濛雨。

miz·zle² *v.i.*, **-zled, -zl·ing.** 【俚】逃走;逃亡。

mk. (*pl.* **mks.**) mark². **MKS, M.K.S.** meter-kilogram-second. **MKS system** MKS 制 (以公尺、公斤及秒爲長度重量及時間的基本單位之制度)。 **mkt.** market. **ML.** ①Mail. ②Medieval Latin. ③Middle Latin. **ml.** ①mail. ②milliliter(s). **M.L.A.** ①Modern Language Association. ②Member of Legislative Assembly. **M.L.F.** Multilateral (nuclear) force. **MLG, M.L.G.** Middle Low German. **Mlle.** (*pl.* **Mlles.**) Mademoiselle. **MLS** 【空】microwave landing system. **MM.** ①(Their) Majesties. ②Messieurs. **mm.** ①millimeter. ②millimeters. **mm², mm.²** square millimeter. **mm³, mm.³** cubic millimeter. **M.M.** ①Master Mason. ②Master Mechanic. **Mme.** (*pl.* **Mmes.**) Madame. **Mn** 【化】manganese. **M.N.E.** Master of Nuclear Engineering.

mne·mon·ic [niˈmɑnɪk; ni(ː)ˈmɔnik] *adj.* ①幫助記憶的;增進記憶的。②記憶的;記憶術的。

mne·mon·ics [niˈmɑnɪks; niːˈmɔniks] *n. pl.* ①(作 *sing.* 解)記憶術;記憶法。②(作 *pl.* 解)幫助記憶的公式;幫助記憶的東西。

Mo 【化】molybdenum.

mo [mo; mou] *n.* 【俚,謔】=**moment.** Wait half a *mo*. 等一會兒。

Mo. ①Missouri. ②Monday. **mo.** ①month. ②months. ③monthly. **M.O., m.o.** ①money order. ②mail order. ③mass observation. ④manually operated. ⑤method of working.

-mo 【字尾】表"(紙張之)…開"之義之名詞字尾。16 mo (=sixteenmo). 16開。

mo·a [ˈmoə; ˈmouə] *n.* 恐鳥(原產 New Zealand, 現已絕種)。

Mo·ab·ite [ˈmoəbˌaɪt; ˈmouəbait] *n.* 【聖經】默阿布人。—*adj.* 默阿布(人)的。**—Mo·a·bit·ic, Mo·a·bit·ish,** *adj.*

***moan** [mon; moun] *n.* ①呻吟。He sank back with a *moan* of pain. 一聲痛苦的呻吟他倒了下去。②似呻吟之聲。—*v.t.* & *v.i.* ①呻吟。The wounded man *moaned* ceaselessly. 這受傷的人不斷地呻吟。②抱怨;悲傷。He *moans* his fate. 他抱怨他的命運。③發似呻吟之聲。The wind *moaned* through the trees. 風發呼嘯聲吹過樹林。**—ing,** *adj.* **—ing·ly,** *adv.*

moan·ful [ˈmonfəl; ˈmounfəl] *adj.* 悲歎的;呻吟的。**—ly,** *adv.*

***moat** [mot; mout] *n.* 壕溝。—*v.t.* 圍以壕溝。

***mob** [mɑb; mɔb] *n., v.*, **mobbed, mobbing.**—*n.* ①羣聚之民衆。②民衆。The *mob* is easily agitated by wild speeches. 民衆易爲激烈的演講所煽動。③暴民;暴徒。*Mobs* collected round the court. 暴民圍聚法庭。—*v.t.* ①(因好奇或憤怒等而)包圍。②行暴;圍攻。The police station was terribly *mobbed*. 警察局慘遭圍攻。—*v.i.* 亂擠。The waiting newsmen *mobbed* forward. 等待中的記者們向前亂擠。**—ber,** *n.*

mob·bish [ˈmɑbɪʃ; ˈmɔbiʃ] *adj.* 如暴徒的;無紀律的;騷擾的。**—ly,** *adv.* **—ness,** *n.*

mob·cap [ˈmɑbˌkæp; ˈmɔbkæp] *n.* (流行於18–19世紀之)袋型的室內用女帽。

mo·bile [ˈmobl̩; ˈmoubail] *adj.* ①動的;自由流動、運動、移動或變動的。②易變的;迅速改變的。③【軍】機動的。

mo·bil·i·ty [moˈbɪlətɪ; mouˈbiliti] *n.* ①易變性;可動性;(人口)流動性。②【物理】遷移率。③【軍】機動性。

mo·bi·li·za·tion [ˌmoblə̩ˈzeʃən; ˌmoubilaiˈzeiʃən] *n.* ①【軍事】動員。②流通。

mo·bi·lize [ˈmobl̩ˌaɪz; ˈmoubilaiz] *v.t.* & *v.i.*, **-lized, -liz·ing.** ①動員。②使流通。③(使)運動。**—mo·bi·liz·a·ble,** *adj.* **—mo·bi·liz·er,** *n.*

mob·oc·ra·cy [mɑbˈɑkrəsɪ; mɔˈbɔkrəsi] *n.* ①暴民政治;暴民統治。②統治階級之暴民(集合稱)。**—mob·o·crat·ic, mob·o-**

crat·i·cal, *adj.*

mob psychology 〖心理〗羣衆心理。

mob rule 暴民統治;暴民政治。

MOBS 〔mɑbz; mɔbz〕 *n.* 多彈頭軌道轟炸系統（由衞星携載彈頭轟炸地球目標以逃過傳統雷達偵測。爲 *M*ultiple *O*rbit *B*ombardment *S*ystem 之略)。

mob·ster 〔ˈmɑbstɚ; ˈmɔbstə〕 *n.* 〖美俚〗「暴徒;盜匪。」

moc·ca·sin 〔ˈmɑkəsn̩; ˈmɔkəsin〕 *n.* ①軟鹿皮。②(*pl.*)(北美印第安人所穿的)鹿皮鞋。③產於美國南部的一種毒蛇。

moccasin flower 〖植物〗鬼督郵。

Mo·cha 〔ˈmokə; ˈmoukə〕 *n.* ①摩加(阿拉伯西南端之一海港)。②(m–)來自摩加的一種咖啡。③(m–) 一種製手套用的軟山羊皮。—*adj.* 加有咖啡的;加有巧克力與咖啡的。

mock** 〔mɑk; mɔk〕 *v.t.* ①嘲弄;愚弄。The naughty boys *mocked* the blind beggar. 淘氣的孩子們愚弄那瞎乞丐。②模仿以嘲弄。③模仿。④抵抗;抗拒。⑤欺騙。⑥輕視;忽視。—*v.i.* 嘲弄;愚弄〖at〗. They *mocked* at my timidity. 他們嘲弄我的膽小。mock up*** 作…之實物大模型。—*adj.* 假的。*mock* modesty. 假謙遜。—*n.* ①嘲笑;戲弄。Don't take to heart what was said in *mock*. 別把人們的嘲笑放在心中。②模仿;模仿的行爲或言語。③被藐視或應受藐視的人或物。—**a·ble,** *adj.*

mock·er 〔ˈmɑkɚ; ˈmɔkə〕 *n.* ①嘲弄者;嘲笑者;作嘲弄性的模仿者。②欺騙者;騙子。③ =**mockingbird.**

mock·er·y** 〔ˈmɑkərɪ; ˈmɔkəri〕 *n., pl.* **-er·ies.** ①嘲弄;愚弄;挖苦。②被嘲弄者;笑柄。Through his foolishness, he became a *mockery* in the village. 因其愚鈍，他成爲全村之笑柄。③嘲弄性的模仿。④蔑視;虛有其表之事。The unfair trial was a *mockery* of justice. 那不公的審判是對公正的一種蔑視。⑤徒勞無功。make a mockery of somebody*** 嘲弄某人。

mock-he·ro·ic 〔ˈmɑkhɪˈro·ɪk; ˈmɔkhiˈrouik〕 *adj.* 模仿英雄氣概的;模擬英雄詩的。—*n.* 模仿英雄氣概的行動;模擬英雄詩。

mock·ing·bird 〔ˈmɑkɪŋˌbɝd; ˈmɔkiŋbəːd〕 *n.* 反舌鳥(產於北美南部及墨西哥)。

mock·ing·ly 〔ˈmɑkɪŋlɪ; ˈmɔkiŋli〕 *adv.* 嘲弄地;愚弄地。

mock moon =**paraselene.**

mock orange 〖植物〗山梅花(=syringa).

mock sun =**parhelion.**

mock turtle soup 假鮮鼈湯(用牛頭肉等製成)。

mock-up 〔ˈmɑkˌʌp; ˈmɔkʌp〕 *n.* (飛機、器具、機械等之)實物大模型。

mod. ①moderate; moderator. ②moderato. ③modern. ④model. ⑤modification; modified; modify. ⑥modulator.

mod·al 〔ˈmod!; ˈmoudl〕 *adj.* ①方式的;樣式的;外形的;形態上的。②〖哲學〗形式(上)的(爲本質、內容之對)。③〖文法〗語態的。④〖音樂〗中古教會調式的。⑤〖邏輯〗表示程式的。⑥典型的;一般的。—**ly,** *adv.*

modal auxiliary (verb) 〖文法〗表動詞語態之助動詞(may, might, must, can, would, should 等均是, 如: Go lest he should be angry. 中之 should).

mo·dal·i·ty 〔moˈdælətɪ; mouˈdæliti〕 *n., pl.* **-ties.** ①形態;樣式;形式。②〖邏輯〗程式。

***mode** 〔mod; moud〕 *n.* ①作法;樣式;方式。②時式;風尙。It is a *mode*. 此爲風尙。③〖音樂〗音階。④〖文法〗=**mood.**

‡mod·el 〔ˈmɑd!; ˈmɔdl〕 *n., v.,* **-el(l)ed, -el·(l)ing,** *adj.* —*n.* ①模型。②(蠟或泥製的)人體模型。a nude *model* in wax. 蠟質裸體模型。③模範;典型。Make him your *model*. 以他做你的模範。④模特兒。His wife served as the *model* for many of his early paintings. 他太太充當了他早期許多繪畫的模特兒。⑤時裝模特兒(穿衣以示顧客,以供彼等挑選)。She left school to go to work as a dress *model* in the garment district. 她離開學校到服裝區當時裝模特兒。⑥時裝模特兒穿的衣帽等。the latest Paris *models*. 最新的巴黎時裝。⑦任何設計之型式。the latest *models* of Ford cars. 福特牌汽車的最新型。a sports *model*. 跑車型汽車。⑧極相似的人。She's a perfect *model* of her mother. 她非常像她母親。—*v.t.* ①塑造;作…的模型。②模倣;倣製。The Constitution of Canada is *modeled* on that of the mother country. 加拿大的憲法是倣效母國(英國)的憲法制定的。③爲(服裝)做模特兒。—*v.i.* ①做模型。She *models* in clay. 她用泥做模型。②做模特兒。③做模範。—*adj.* ①模範的。He is a *model* child. 他是模範兒童。②作模型用的。a *model* apartment. 公寓模型。

mod·el·(l)ing 〔ˈmɑdlɪŋ; ˈmɔdliŋ〕 *n.* ①製作模型;製作模型術。②以可塑物製型(以備用堅牢之材料複製)。③〖繪畫〗使圖面呈立體的輪廓。

Model T ①〖商標名〗美國福特公司第一次大量生產的老型汽車。②初期的;初步的。③老式的;落伍的。

***mod·er·ate** 〔*adj., n.* ˈmɑdərɪt; ˈmɔdərit *v.* ˈmɑdəˌret; ˈmɔdəreit〕 *adj., n., v.,* **-at·ed, -at·ing.** —*adj.* ①適度的;有節制的;不奢的。He is *moderate* in drinking. 他飲酒有節制。②溫和的;不激烈的;穩健的。The party is *moderate* in views. 這政黨的政見穩健。③公平的;中等的;不過分的。Be *moderate* in all things. 萬事守中庸。④有限的。—*n.* 言行中庸之人;穩健之人;溫和主義者。—*v.t.* & *v.i.* ①(使)減輕;(使)緩和。to *moderate* one's enthusiasm. 節制一個人的熱誠。②作主席;主持(會議);作仲裁者。

***mod·er·ate·ly** 〔ˈmɑdərɪtlɪ; ˈmɔdəritli〕 *adv.* ①適度地;不奢地。They lived *moderately*. 他們生活不奢侈。②不過分地。

mod·er·a·tion** 〔ˌmɑdəˈreʃən; ˌmɔdəˈreiʃən〕 *n.* ①緩和;減輕。②適度;節制。③溫和。*moderation* of speech. 言論的溫和。④(*pl.*)牛津大學 B. A. 學位初試(常略作 Mods). ***in moderation 適度。

mod·e·ra·to 〔ˌmɑdəˈrɑto; ˌmɔdəˈrɑːtou〕 〖義〗 *adv.* & *adj.* 〖音樂〗中板。

mod·er·a·tor 〔ˈmɑdəˌretɚ; ˈmɔdəreitə〕 *n.* ①主席;議長。the *moderator* of a town meeting. 鎭民大會主席。②仲裁者;調停者。③〖原子能〗減速劑;緩和劑。④調節器。—**ship,** *n.*

‡mod·ern 〔ˈmɑdɚn; ˈmɔdən〕 *adj.* ①現代的;近世的。*modern* English. 近代英語(十六世紀以後之英語)。*modern* history. 近代史。②新式的;時髦的。*modern* fashions. 時尙。*modern* ideas. 新思想。—*n.* ①現代人;近代人。②有新思想或鑑賞力的人。furniture designed for young *moderns*. 爲新思想的年輕人設計的傢具。③現代派畫家。

mod·ern·ism [ˈmɑdənˌɪzəm; ˈmɔdənizəm] *n.* ①現代作風; 現代語法; 現代思想; 現代方法; 現代主義。②(M-)現代主義(依照科學原理解釋教義之謂)。③現代派美術。

mod·ern·ist [ˈmɑdənɪst; ˈmɔdənist] *n.* ①持有現代見解、思想或應用現代方法者。②以現代科學原理解釋教義者; 現代主義者。

mod·ern·is·tic [ˌmɑdəˈnɪstɪk; ˌmɔdəˈnistik] *adj.* ①現代的; 新式的(指音樂、藝術之當代趨勢或派別)。②現代見解和方法的; 持有現代見解或應用現代方法之人的。

mo·der·ni·ty [mɑˈdɝnətɪ; mɔˈdəːniti] *n., pl.* **-ties.** ①現代性; 現代。②現代之事物。

mod·ern·i·za·tion [ˌmɑdənəˈzeʃən; ˌmɔdənaiˈzeiʃən] *n.* ①現代化。②現代化之版本。

mod·ern·ize [ˈmɑdənˌaɪz; ˈmɔdə(ː)naiz] *v.t.* & *v.i.*, **-ized, -iz·ing.** (使)現代化。—**mod·ern·iz·er,** *n.*

modern pentathlon 新五項運動(包括騎馬、擊劍、手鎗射擊、游泳及賽跑)。

***mod·est** [ˈmɑdɪst; ˈmɔdist] *adj.* ①謙遜的; 有禮貌的。He is *modest* in his behavior. 他的態度謙遜。②羞怯的。a *modest* and meek man. 羞怯而謙和的人。③莊重的; 淑靜的。④不多要的; 適度的。My demands are quite *modest*. 我的要求不大。⑤質樸的。—**ly,** *adv.*

***mod·es·ty** [ˈmɑdəstɪ; ˈmɔdisti] *n., pl.* **-ties.** ①質樸。②羞怯。virgin *modesty*. 嬌羞。③謙遜; 有禮。

mod·i·cum [ˈmɑdɪkəm; ˈmɔdikəm] *n.* 少量。

mod·i·fi·a·bil·i·ty [ˌmɑdəˌfaɪəˈbɪlətɪ; ˌmɔdiˌfaiəˈbiliti] *n.* 可變性。

mod·i·fi·a·ble [ˈmɑdəˌfaɪəbl; ˈmɔdifaiəbl] *adj.* ①可變更的; 可修改的。②可修飾的; 可限制的。③可緩和的。

***mod·i·fi·ca·tion** [ˌmɑdəfəˈkeʃən; ˌmɔdifiˈkeiʃən] *n.* ①修改; 修飾。②減少; 緩和。The *modification* of his anger made him able to think clearly again. 他的怒氣消減使他能再清楚地想一想。③意義的限制。④修改過的形式; 變形。

mod·i·fi·ca·to·ry [ˈmɑdəfəˌketərɪ; ˈmɔdifiˌkeitəri] *adj.* 修改的; 變更的; 修飾的; 限定的; 緩和的。

mod·i·fi·er [ˈmɑdəˌfaɪɚ; ˈmɔdifaiə] *n.* ①〖文法〗修飾語; 形容語。②修改之人或物。

***mod·i·fy** [ˈmɑdəˌfaɪ; ˈmɔdifai] *v.*, **-fied, -fy·ing.** —*v.t.* ①變更; 修改。to *modify* the terms of a lease. 修改租賃條款。②修飾; 限制(意義)。③使減輕; 使緩和。You'd better *modify* your tone. 你最好說得婉轉一點。—*v.i.* 修改; 限制; 修飾。

mo·dil·lion [məˈdɪljən; mouˈdiljən] *n.* 〖建築〗(哥林多式建築等之)飛簷托。

mod·ish [ˈmodɪʃ; ˈmoudiʃ] *adj.* 流行的; 時髦的。—**ly,** *adv.* —**ness,** *n.*

mo·diste [moˈdist; mouˈdiːst] *n.* 裁製或經營時髦之女裝、女帽的婦女; 女裁縫。

Mods [mɑdz; mɔdz] *n. pl.* 〖英俗〗 =**moderation**④.

mod·u·lar [ˈmɑdʒulɚ; ˈmɔdjulə] *adj.* ①(傢具、建材等)組合單元可按需要情形隨意更換或安排的。②module 或 modulus 的。

mod·u·late [ˈmɑdʒəˌlet; ˈmɔdjuleit] *v.*, **-lat·ed, -lat·ing.** —*v.t.* ①調節; 調整。②使柔; 使緩。③改變聲調。④變更(電波)之周波數; 調節頻率。⑤吟唱。 —*v.i.* ①〖音樂〗轉調; 變調。②〖無線電〗產生調幅。

mod·u·la·tion [ˌmɑdʒəˈleʃən; ˌmɔdjuˈleiʃən] *n.* ①調節; 使柔; 變柔; 緩和。②〖音樂〗轉調; 變調。③〖無線電〗電波頻率之轉變; 調幅。④(聲音之)抑揚。

mod·u·la·tor [ˈmɑdʒəˌletɚ; ˈmɔdjuleitə] *n.* ①調節者; 調節物。②〖電信〗(轉變電波周率之)調幅器。③〖音樂〗音階圖。

mod·ule [ˈmɑdʒul; ˈmɔdjuːl] *n.* ①(流水測定之)單位。②(建材等之)標準尺寸; 基本單位; 組合單元。③〖建築〗度(柱式之比例測定單位)。④(易於分離或接合的)組成單位或部分。⑤(電腦或機器內有一定規格而可互換的)組件。

mod·u·lus [ˈmɑdʒələs; ˈmɔdjuləs] *n., pl.* **-li** [-ˌlaɪ; -lai]. 〖物理, 數學〗率; 模數; 係數。—**mod·u·lar,** *adj.*

mo·dus [ˈmodəs; ˈmoudəs] *n., pl.* **mo·di** [ˈmodaɪ; ˈmoudai]. 〖拉〗方法; 樣式 (= measure, manner).

mo·dus o·per·an·di [ˈmodəsˌɑpəˈrændaɪ; ˈmoudəsˌɔpəˈrændai] 〖拉〗做法; 運用法; 處事之方法 (=way of doing or making).

mo·dus vi·ven·di [ˈmodəsvɪˈvɛndaɪ; ˈmoudəsviˈvendai] 〖拉〗①生活方式(=manner of living). ②暫時協定。

mog·gie, mog·gy [ˈmɑgɪ; ˈmɔgi] *n., pl.* **-gies.** 〖英俚〗①貓。②不整潔之婦女。③小牛; 母牛。

Mo·gul [ˈmogʌl; mouˈgʌl] *n.* ①蒙古人。②蒙兀兒人(十六世紀征服並統治印度者或其後裔)。③(m-)顯要人物。movie *moguls*. 電影鉅子。literary *moguls*. 文壇大家。④(m-)一種機車。⑤(m-)極精緻的一種紙牌。

mo·hair [ˈmoˌhɛr; ˈmouhɛə] *n.* ①安哥拉(Angora)山羊毛; 該種羊毛所製之毛布。②上述毛布之仿造品。③上述羊毛所製之衣。

Mo·ham·med [moˈhæmɪd; mouˈhæmed] *n.* 穆罕默德 (570?–632 A.D.). (亦作 **Mahomet, Muhammad**)

Mo·ham·med·an [moˈhæmədən; mouˈhæmidən] *adj.* 穆罕默德的; 伊斯蘭教的; 回教的。—*n.* 回教徒; 伊斯蘭教徒。(亦作 **Mahometan**)

Mo·ham·med·an·ism [moˈhæmədənɪzəm; mouˈhæmidənizəm] *n.* 回教; 伊斯蘭教。(亦作 **Mahometanism**)

Mo·ha·ve [moˈhɑvɪ; mouˈhɑːvi] *n.* 摩哈比族(北美沿 Colorado 河居住之印第安人)之人。—*adj.* 摩哈比族的。

Mo·hawk [ˈmohɔk; ˈmouhɔːk] *n., pl.* **Mo·hawk, Mo·hawks.** ①(*pl.*)摩和克族(北美印第安族之一支, 早先沿 Mohawk 河而居)。②美國 New York 州中部之一河(流入 Hudson 灣)。③摩和克族之一員。

Mo·hi·can [moˈhikən; ˈmouikən] *n.* 摩希根族(北美印第安之一族, 昔居 Hudson 河上游); 摩希根族人。—*adj.* 摩希根族的。(亦作 **Mahican**)

Moh·ism [ˈmoɪzəm; ˈmouizəm] *n.* 墨子哲學; 墨家思想。

Moh·ist [ˈmoɪst; ˈmouist] *n.* 墨家。

Mo·hock [ˈmohɑk; ˈmouhɔk] *n.* 〖史〗魔福克隊員(十八世紀初夜間騷擾倫敦市街之盜匪黨員, 多係貴族子弟)。

M.O.I. ①Ministry of Information. ②Ministry of the Interior.

moi·dore [ˈmɔɪdor; ˈmɔidɔː] *n.* 葡萄牙及西班牙之古金幣。

moi·e·ty [ˈmɔɪətɪ; ˈmɔiəti] *n., pl.* **-ties.** ①〖法律〗(財產等之)一半; 二分之一。②約一

牛。③部分。

moil [mɔɪl; mɔil] *v.i.* 勞苦；辛勞；勞碌。to toil and *moil.* 辛苦做工。—*n.* ①勞苦；辛勞。②混亂；苦惱；麻煩。

moire [mwɑr; mwɑ:] *n.* 波紋花式絲綢。

moi·ré [mwɑ're; 'mwɑ:rei]〖法〗*adj.* 有波紋的。—*n.* ①波紋。②=**moire.**

***moist** [mɔɪst; mɔist] *adj.* ①潮濕的。Grasses were *moist* with dew. 草因露水而沾濕了。②多雨的。a *moist* season. 雨季。③感傷的。—**ly,** *adv.*

moist·en** ['mɔɪsn̩; 'mɔisn] *v.t.* 使濕潤。to be *moistened* by rain. 被雨淋濕。—*v.i.* 變濕。moisten one's clay*** (***lips,*** or ***throat***) 喝酒。—**er,** *n.*

***mois·ture** ['mɔɪstʃɚ; 'mɔistʃə] *n.* ①潮濕；水分；濕氣；水蒸氣。②降雨。About 69 percent of the annual *moisture* occurred during the growing season. 每年約有百分之六十九的雨量是在農作物生長的季節降下的。—**less,** *adj.*

mois·tur·ize ['mɔɪstʃə,raɪz; 'mɔis-tʃəraiz] *v.,* **-ized, -iz·ing.** —*v.t.* 以某種藥物使潮濕。—*v.i.* 使潮濕。

Mo·ja·ve [mo'hɑvɪ; mou'hɑ:vi] *n., adj.* =**Mohave.**

moke [mok; mouk] *n.* ①〖俚〗驢；傻瓜。②〖美俚〗黑人。

mol [mol; moul] *n.* 〖化〗克分子；摩爾。

mol. ①molecular. ②molecule.

mo·lar¹ ['molɚ; 'moulə] *n.* 臼齒。—*adj.* ①臼齒的。②宜於研磨的。

mo·lar² *adj.* ①〖物理〗質量(上)的；物體全體的(爲 molecular, atomic 之對)。②〖化〗克分子的。

***mo·las·ses** [mə'læsɪz; mə'læsiz] *n.* 糖蜜。

mold**¹ [mold; mould] *n.* ①模子；鑄模；字模；鑄型。②模中凝鑄成之形狀；在模中形成的東西。a *mold* of pudding. 在模中做成的布丁。③模型。④性質；氣概。a man of gentle *mold.* 脾氣溫和的人。—*v.t.* ①造型；塑造；鑄。We *mold* statues out of clay. 我們用黏土塑造成塑像。②磨練；鍛鍊。His cold character was *molded* by hardships. 困苦艱難鍛鍊成他那冷酷性格。③給以影響。④造成。The wind *molds* the waves. 風造成浪。—*v.i.* ①形成；變成。②造型；塑造。mold one's own destiny*** 決定自己的命運。

mold² *n.* 黴。—*v.i.* 發黴。—*v.t.* 覆以黴。(亦作 **mould**)

mold³ *n.* ①沃土；糞土(富有有機物之沃土)。②〖古〗土地。—*v.i.* 以糞土覆蓋。

mold·a·ble ['moldəbl̩; 'mouldəbl] *adj.* 可塑造的。—**mold·a·bil·i·ty,** *n.*

mold·board ['mold,bord; 'mould-bɔ:d] *n.* 犁頭後部翻起泥土之曲面鐵板。

mold·er¹ ['moldɚ; 'mouldə] *v.t.* 使腐朽；使崩壞。—*v.i.* 腐朽；敗壞〖常 away〗。(亦作 **moulder**)

mold·er² *n.* 塑造者；造模者。(亦作 **moulder**)

mold·ing ['moldɪŋ; 'mouldiŋ] *n.* ①塑造；鑄造；造型。②塑造物；鑄造物。③〖建築〗裝飾用的嵌線；壁帶(用以掛圖畫或覆蓋電線)。(亦作 **moulding**)

molding board 揉麪板。

mold loft 可在地板上描繪船或飛機之實物設計圖的大建築。

mold·proof ['mold,pruf; 'mould-pru:f] *adj.* 防黴的。

mold·y ['moldɪ; 'mouldi] *adj.,* **mold·i·er, mold·i·est.** ①發黴的。②舊式的；老朽的；陳腐的。(亦作 **mouldy**) —**mold·i·ness,** *n.*

***mole**¹ [mol; moul] *n.* 痣。

***mole**² *n.* 〖動物〗鼹鼠；地鼠子。(as) blind as a *mole.* 完全盲目的；全盲的。

mole³ *n.* ①防波堤；海堤。②防波堤所圍繞的海港。

mole⁴ *n.* 〖化〗=**mol.**

mole cricket 螻蛄。

mo·lec·u·lar [mə'lɛkjəlɚ; mou'lekju-lə] *adj.* 分子的；由分子組成的。—**ly,** *adv.*

molecular formula 〖化〗分子式。

mo·lec·u·lar·i·ty [mə,lɛkjə'lærətɪ; mou,lekju'læriti] *n.* 〖化〗分子狀；分子性。

molecular weight 〖化〗分子量。

***mol·e·cule** ['mɑlə,kjul; 'mɔlikju:l] *n.* ①〖理化〗分子。②微點；些微。a *molecule* of political honesty. 一點點政治上的誠實。

mole·hill ['mol,hɪl; 'moulhil] *n.* ①鼹鼠丘。②不重要的東西。***make a mountain out of a molehill*** 言過其實；誇大困難。

mole·skin ['mol,skɪn; 'moulskin] *n.* ①鼹鼠毛皮。②一種厚棉布。③(*pl.*)此棉布製成之衣服(特指長褲)。

mo·lest [mə'lɛst; mou'lest] *v.t.* ①妨害；干擾；騷擾。②調戲。—*n.* ①妨害；干擾；騷擾(=molestation). He was within his walls, secure from all *molest.* 他在自己屋內，不受任何干擾。②調戲。—**er,** *n.*

mo·les·ta·tion [,moləs'teʃən; ,mou-les'teiʃən] *n.* ①妨害；干擾；騷擾。②調戲。

Mo·lière [,molɪ'ɛr, mɔ̈'ljɛ:r; 'mɔliɛə] *n.* 莫里哀 (1622–1673, 眞名爲 Jean Baptiste Poquelin, 法國喜劇作家)。

Moll [mɑl; mɔl] *n.* 女子名(Mary 之暱稱)。

moll [mɑl; mɔl] *n.* 〖俚〗①盜匪或流氓之姘婦。②妓女。

mol·li·fi·ca·tion [,mɑləfə'keʃən; ,mɔlifi'keiʃən] *n.* ①撫慰；緩和。②撫慰之事物；緩和之事物。

mol·li·fy ['mɑlə,faɪ; 'mɔlifai] *v.t.,* **-fied, -fy·ing.** ①安慰；撫慰。②緩和；減緩。③使柔軟。—**ing·ly,** *adv.*

mol·lusc ['mɑləsk; 'mɔləsk] *n.* 〖英〗=**mollusk.**

Mol·lus·ca [mə'lʌskə; mɔ'lʌskə] *n. pl.* 〖動物〗軟體動物類。

mol·lus·can [mə'lʌskən; mɔ'lʌskən] *adj.* 軟體動物類的；似軟體動物的。—*n.* 軟體動物。

mol·lus·coid [mə'lʌskɔɪd; mɔ'lʌs-kɔid] *adj.* (似)軟體動物的；擬軟體動物的。—*n.* 擬軟體動物。

mol·lus·cous [mə'lʌskəs; mɔ'lʌskəs] *adj.* ①軟體動物的；似軟體動物的。②無脊椎的；無力氣的；柔軟的；衰弱的。

mol·lusk ['mɑləsk; 'mɔləsk] *n.* 軟體動物。

Mol·ly ['mɑlɪ; 'mɔli] *n.* 女子名(Mary 之暱稱)。

mol·ly ['mɑlɪ; 'mɔli] *n.* ①〖俚〗娘娘腔的男人(青年、男孩)；懦夫。②〖俚、方〗=**moll.**

mol·ly·cod·dle ['mɑlɪ,kɑdl̩; 'mɔli-,kɔdl] *n., v.,* **-dled, -dling.** —*n.* ①柔弱的男孩或男人。②歡喜被縱容的人。—*v.t.* 溺愛；嬌慣。—**mol·ly·cod·dler,** *n.*

Mo·loch ['molɑk; 'moulɔk] *n.* ①古代的火神(以人爲祭品)。②任何需要犧牲人命的恐怖事物。(亦作 **Molech**)

mo·loch ['molɑk; 'moulɔk] *n.* (澳洲產之)一種蜥蜴。

Mo·lo·tov cocktail ['mɑlətɔf~; 'mɔlətɔf~] 〖俚〗汽油手榴彈(攻擊戰車用)。

molt [molt; moult] *v.i.* ①換毛；蛻皮。Birds *molt.* 鳥脫毛。—*v.t.* ①換(毛)；蛻

(皮)。②丟棄。—*n.* ①換毛;蛻皮。②脫落之毛或皮。③換毛或蛻皮的時期。(亦作 **moult**)

mol·ten ['moltn̩; 'moultən] *v.* pp. of **melt.** —*adj.* ①鎔化的。②鑄造的。③熱的;熾烈的。the *molten* sunlight. 熾烈的陽光。

mol·to ['molto; 'mɔltou]【義】*adv.*【音樂】極;甚;非常。*molto* adagio. 極慢板。

mol. wt. molecular weight (分子量)。

mo·ly ['molɪ; 'mouli] *n.* ①【希臘神話】有白花和黑根的魔草。②【植物】(歐洲產之)野生蒜。

mo·lyb·de·nite [mə'lɪbdɪ,naɪt; mə'libdənait] *n.*【礦】輝鉬礦。

mo·lyb·de·num [mə'lɪbdənəm; mɔ'libdinəm] *n.*【化】鉬(化學元素,符號Mo).

mom [mɑm; mɔm] *n.*【俗】母;媽媽。

mo·ment ['momənt; 'moumənt] *n.* ①瞬間;片刻。He won't be a *moment.* 他卽刻就來。A busy man will study at odd *moments.* 忙的人抽暇讀書。②重要。It's a matter of *moment.* 這是件重大的事。men of the *moment.* 此時的重要人物。③【物理】矩;力率;能率。④ (the-) 現時。At the *moment* she is at work on her fourth novel. 目前她正執筆寫她的第四本小說。⑤階段;時期。⑥組成分子;要素。***the moment*=as soon as; the minute.** ***to the moment*** 非常準時的。The striking up of the band is timed *to the moment.* 樂隊準時開始奏樂。

mo·men·tar·i·ly ['momən,tɛrəlɪ; 'moumǝntərili] *adv.* ①暫時地;片刻地。②時時刻刻地。③隨時地。④立刻;馬上。

mo·men·tar·y ['momən,tɛrɪ; 'mouməntəri] *adj.* ①刹那的;轉瞬間的。a *momentary* glimpse. 刹那的一瞥。*momentary* joy. 瞬息的喜悅。②時時刻刻的;每刻的。

mo·ment·ly ['momǝntlɪ; 'moumǝntli] *adv.* ①時時刻刻地;每刻地;隨時地。②片刻地;暫時。③立刻。

moment of truth ①鬥牛士卽將刺牛之刹那。②(對人格、才幹、技術等之)極大的考驗;緊要關頭。

mo·men·tous [mo'mɛntəs; mou'mentəs] *adj.* 極重要的。—**ly,** *adv.*

mo·men·tous·ness [mo'mɛntəsnɪs; mou'mentəsnis] *n.* 重要性。

mo·men·tum [mo'mɛntəm; mou'mentəm] *n., pl.* **-tums, -ta** [-tə; -tə]. ①運動量。②動力。③(事件)增加力量與速度的趨勢。④要素。

mom·ism ['mɑmɪzəm; 'mɔmizəm] *n.*【俗】母親對兒子的感情控制;對母親之過分依賴。

mom·my ['mɑmɪ; 'mɔmi] *n.*【俗】媽;媽咪。(亦作 **mummy**)

Mo·mus ['moməs; 'mouməs] *n.* ①【希臘神話】嘲弄之神。②愛挑剔的人;吹毛求疵者。

Mon. ①Monday. ②Monsignor. ③Monaco. **mon.** ①monastery. ②monetary.

mon-【字首】=**mono-** (於母音前用之)。

Mon·a·can ['mɑnəkən; 'mɔnəkən] *adj.* 摩納哥的。—*n.* 摩納哥人。

mon·a·chal ['mɑnək!; 'mɔnəkəl] *adj.* =**monastic.**

mon·a·chism ['mɑnə,kɪzəm; 'mɔnəkizəm] *n.* =**monasticism.**

Mon·a·co ['mɑnə,ko; 'mɔnəkou] *n.* 摩納哥 (法國東南海岸之一小國, 首都摩納哥 Monaco).

mon·ad ['mɑnæd; 'mɔnæd] *n.* ①【生物】單細胞生物;(尤指)鞭毛蟲類之原生動物。②【化】一價原子;一價根;一價元素。③(不可分開之)單體;個體。④【哲學】單子;單元。—**ic, —i·cal,** *adj.* —**i·cal·ly,** *adv.*

mon·a·del·phous [,mɑnə'dɛlfəs; ,mɔnə'delfəs] *adj.*【植物】①有單體雄蕊的。②單體的(雄蕊)。

mon·ad·ism ['mɑnədɪzəm; 'mɔnədizəm] *n.*【哲學】單子論;單元論。

Mo·na Li·za [,monə('mɑnə)'lizə; 'mounə'li:zə] 蒙娜麗莎(Leonardo da Vinci 作之著名人像畫)。

mo·nan·drous [mə'nændrəs; mə'nændrəs] *adj.* ①【植物】單雄蕊(花)的。②一夫制的。③一夫的(不得同時有二夫的)。

mo·nan·dry [mə'nændrɪ; mə'nændri] *n.* ①一夫制。②【植物】單雄蕊。

***mon·arch** ['mɑnək; 'mɔnək] *n.* ①帝王;統治者。an uncrowned *monarch.* 無冕王。②如帝王般的人或物。The lion is called the *monarch* of all beasts. 獅子被稱爲獸中之王。③一種有橘黃色與黑色的大蝴蝶。

mo·nar·chal [mə'nɑrk!; mɔ'nɑ:kəl] *adj.* 王的;君主的;適合於君主的。*monarchal* government. 君主政體。—**ly,** *adv.*

mo·nar·chi·al [mə'nɑrkɪəl; mə'nɑ:kiəl] *adj.* =**monarchal.**

mo·nar·chic [mə'nɑrkɪk; mɔ'nɑ:kik] *adj.* =**monarchical.**

mo·nar·chi·cal [mə'nɑrkɪk!; mɔ'nɑ:kikəl] *n.* ①君主的;帝王的。②君主政治的;君主政體的;似君主政治的。③主張或支持君主政治的。—**ly,** *adv.*

mon·ar·chism ['mɑnə,kɪzəm; 'mɔnəkizəm] *n.* ①君主制。②君主主義(論)。—**mon·arch·ist,** *n., adj.* —**mon·arch·is·tic,** *adj.*

***mon·ar·chy** ['mɑnəkɪ; 'mɔnəki] *n., pl.* **-chies.** ①君主政體。constitutional *monarchy.* 君主立憲政體。②君主國。

mon·as·te·ri·al [,mɑnə'stɪrɪəl; ,mɔnə'stiəriəl] *adj.* 修道院的;僧院的;修道生活的。

***mon·as·ter·y** ['mɑnəs,tɛrɪ; 'mɔnəstəri] *n., pl.* **-ter·ies.** ①修道院;(尤指)僧院;(罕指)女修道院。②修道院中的修道士;僧侶;修女(集合稱)。

mo·nas·tic [mə'næstɪk; mə'næstik] *adj.* ①僧侶的;修女的;修道生活的。②僧院的;修道院的。③隱居的;禁慾的。—*n.* 僧侶;修道士。—**al·ly,** *adv.*

mo·nas·ti·cal [mə'næstɪk!; mə'næstikəl] *adj.* =**monastic.**

mo·nas·ti·cism [mə'næstə,sɪzəm; mə'næstisizəm] *n.* 修道院(僧院)制度;修道生活。

mon·au·ral [mɑn'ɔrəl; 'mɔn'ɔ:rəl] *adj.* ①單耳的。②非立體音響的;單頻道的。

‡Mon·day ['mʌndɪ; 'mʌndi] *n.* 星期一。

Mon·day·ish ['mʌndɪɪʃ; 'mʌndiiʃ] *adj.*【俗】疲勞的;困倦的;不想工作的。

Monday morning quarterback ①足球比賽後批評比賽中所犯錯誤者。②放馬後砲者。

monde [mɔ̃d, mɑnd; mɔ̃d, mɔnd]【法】*n.* 世界;世人;社會(尤指上流社會)。

mon Dieu [mɔ̃'djɜ; mɔ̃'djœ]【法】我的天!(=my God!)

Mo·nel metal [mo'nɛl~; mou'nel~] 蒙銅;銅鎳齊(鎳、銅、鐵、錳、矽及碳之合金,抗酸性甚强)。

mon·e·tar·y ['mʌnə,tɛrɪ; 'mʌnitəri] *adj.* ①貨幣的;幣制的。②金融的;財政的。

monetary unit 貨幣單位。
mon·e·ti·za·tion 〔ˌmʌnətɪˈzeʃən; ˌmʌnitaiˈzeiʃən〕 *n.* 定爲貨幣; 鑄成貨幣。
mon·e·tize 〔ˈmʌnəˌtaɪz; ˈmʌnitaiz〕 *v.t.*, **-tized, -tiz·ing.** ①鑄成貨幣。②定爲貨幣。③使成合法貨幣。
‡mon·ey 〔ˈmʌnɪ; ˈmʌni〕 *n.*, *pl.* **-eys, mon·ies,** *adj.* —*n.* ①金錢;貨幣;財富。They say he is made of *money*. 據說他很有錢。Time is *money*. 時間卽是金錢。He is not everybody's *money*. 他並不受人人歡迎。②一筆款(爲可數名詞)。to appropriate *moneys* for space exploration. 爲太空探險撥款。③獎金(與 first, second 及 third 連用)。His horse took third *money*. 他的馬贏了第三獎。④＝**money of account.** ***coin money*** 很快致富;暴富。***for one's money*** 據某人的看法、選擇或意願。***in the money*** 〖俚〗**a.** 很富有;很有錢。**b.** 賽馬或賽狗之前三名。***make money*** 賺錢。***(pay) money down*** 現金交易。***Money talks.*** 錢能通神。—*adj.* ①管錢的; 處理金錢的。the Wall Street *money* men. 華爾街管錢的人們。②需要大筆錢的。I wanted to invest in the scheme but it was a *money* proposition. 我想投資那計畫, 但這是需要大筆錢的事業。③用以裝錢的。Have you seen my little *money* purse? 你看到我的小錢袋嗎? 〖注意〗**money** 是不可數名詞,形容其多用 much, 不用many.
mon·ey·bag 〔ˈmʌnɪˌbæg; ˈmʌnibæg〕 *n.* ①錢袋。②(*pl.*)〖俗〗財富。③(*pl.*)〖俗〗富人。〖注意〗**moneybags** 作"財富"解時,形式及用法上均爲複數。但作"富人"解時,形式上雖爲複數,用法上卻爲單數。Old *moneybags* is finally giving a little money to charity. 老富翁終於捐出一點錢給救濟事業。
mon·ey-box 〔ˈmʌnɪˌbaks; ˈmʌnibɔks〕 *n.* 貯金箱;捐款箱。
mon·ey·chang·er 〔ˈmʌnɪˌtʃendʒɚ; ˈmʌniˌtʃeindʒə〕 *n.* 以兌換貨幣爲業的人。
money crop 獲利的農產物。
mon·eyed 〔ˈmʌnɪd; ˈmʌnid〕 *adj.* ①有錢的; 富有的。②金錢上的。③錢所造成的。
mon·ey·grub·ber 〔ˈmʌnɪˌgrʌbɚ; ˈmʌniˌgrʌbə〕 *n.* 守財奴。
mon·ey·grub·bing 〔ˈmʌnɪˌgrʌbɪŋ; ˈmʌniˌgrʌbiŋ〕 *adj.* 積蓄錢財的。—*n.* 蓄財; 金錢之爭取。
mon·ey·lend·er 〔ˈmʌnɪˌlɛndɚ; ˈmʌniˌlendə〕*n.* 放利者。
mon·ey·less 〔ˈmʌnɪlɪs; ˈmʌnilis〕 *adj.* 無錢的; 貧窮的。
mon·ey-mak·er 〔ˈmʌnɪˌmekɚ; ˈmʌniˌmeikə〕 *n.* ①賺錢積蓄者; 蓄財家; 會賺錢的人。②有利的工作;獲利豐的事業。
mon·ey·mak·ing 〔ˈmʌnɪˌmekɪŋ; ˈmʌniˌmeikiŋ〕 *n.* ①賺錢; 蓄財。②貨幣的鑄造。—*adj.* ①孜孜求利的;熱心賺錢的。②有利的;獲益的(事業等)。
mon·ey·man 〔ˈmʌnɪmən; ˈmʌnimən〕 *n., pl.* **-men.** 金融家;財政家(＝financier).
money market 金融市場。
money of account ①計算上的貨幣。②虛位通貨(如英國之 guinea, 美國之 mill, 及中國之銀元)。
money of necessity 臨時性錢幣。
money order 匯票。
money player 〖俚〗①在比賽緊要關頭表演最佳者。②擅於賭大筆金錢者。
money spinner ①〖動物〗一種蜘蛛(據傳爬在身上便可發財)。②靠投機或放高利貸發財者。③賺錢的東西。
money's worth 有相當金錢價值之物;值錢之物。
mon·ey·wort 〔ˈmʌnɪˌwɜt; ˈmʌniwəːt〕 *n.* 〖植物〗櫻草科之一種蔓草。
Mong. ①Mongolia. ②Mongolian.
mon·ger 〔ˈmʌŋgɚ; ˈmʌŋgə〕 *n.* 〖英〗販子(多用於複合字中, 如 ironmonger).
Mon·gol 〔ˈmaŋgəl; ˈmɔŋgɔl〕 *n.* ①蒙古人。②蒙古語。—*adj.* ①蒙古人的;蒙古語的。②(常 m-)有先天性愚型徵象的。
Mon·go·li·a 〔maŋˈgoljə; mɔŋˈgouljə〕 *n.* 蒙古(中國北部之一地方,首府庫倫,Kulun 或 Ulan Bator).
Mon·go·li·an 〔maŋˈgolɪən; mɔŋˈgouljən〕 *n.* ①蒙古人。②蒙古語。③黃種人。—*adj.* ①蒙古族的; 蒙古語的。②黃種人的。③(常m-)有先天性愚型徵象的;蒙古種型的。
Mongolian and Tibetan Affairs Commission 蒙藏委員會。
Mongolian race 黃色人種。
Mon·gol·ism 〔ˈmaŋgəlɪzəm; ˈmɔŋgəlizəm〕 *n.* 〖醫〗先天性愚型;伸舌樣愚鈍;蒙古種型。(亦作 **Mongolian idiocy**)
Mon·gol·oid 〔ˈmaŋgəlˌɔɪd; ˈmɔŋgəlɔid〕 *adj.* 似黃色人種的; 黃色人種的。—*n.* ①黃種人。②(常 m-) 患先天性愚型者。
mon·goos(e) 〔ˈmaŋgus; ˈmɔŋguːs〕 *n., pl.* **-goos·es.** 〖動物〗獴(產於印度,形似鼬,善捕殺鼠與蛇)。
mon·grel 〔ˈmʌŋgrəl; ˈmʌŋgrəl〕 *n.* ①雜種狗。②〖蔑〗混血兒。—*adj.* 雜種的。—**ism,** —**ness,** *n.*
mon·ick·er 〔ˈmanɪkɚ; ˈmɔnikə〕 *n.* ＝**moniker.**
mon·ies 〔ˈmʌnɪz; ˈmʌniz〕 *n.* pl. of **money.**
mon·i·ker 〔ˈmanɪkɚ; ˈmɔnikə〕 *n.* ①(流浪者用以代替本人姓名之)符號; 標識; 花押。②〖俚〗姓名; 綽號。(亦作 **monniker, monicker**)
mon·ism 〔ˈmanɪzəm; ˈmɔnizəm〕 *n.* 〖哲學〗一元論。—**mon·ist,** *n.*
mo·nis·tic 〔moˈnɪstɪk; mɔˈnistik〕 *adj.* ＝**monistical.**
mo·nis·ti·cal 〔moˈnɪstɪkl; mɔˈnistikəl〕 *adj.* 一元論的。—**ly,** *adv.*
mo·ni·tion 〔moˈnɪʃən; mouˈniʃən〕 *n.* ①勸告;注意;警告;警戒;通告。②〖法律〗(法庭之)傳喚。③〖宗教〗(主教所發之)訓戒信。
***mon·i·tor** 〔ˈmanətɚ; ˈmɔnitə〕 *n.* ①級長。②勸誡者。③有旋轉砲塔的低舷鐵甲軍艦。④大蜥蜴。⑤〖無線電〗檢音器; 校音器; 鑑聽器。—*v.t.* & *v.i.* ①檢音;校音。②監聽(尤指對外國的廣播)。③監督。to *monitor* an examination. 監考。
mon·i·to·ri·al 〔ˌmanəˈtorɪəl; ˌmɔniˈtɔːriəl〕 *adj.* ①級長的。②〖無線電〗使用檢音器的。③＝**monitory.** —**ly,** *adv.*
mon·i·tor·ship 〔ˈmanətɚˌʃɪp; ˈmɔnitəʃip〕 *n.* ①級長的職位或任期。②監督。
mon·i·to·ry 〔ˈmanəˌtorɪ; ˈmɔnitəri〕 *adj., n., pl.* **-ries.** —*adj.* 勸告的;訓戒的;警告的。—*n.* 訓戒信。
mon·i·tress 〔ˈmanətrɪs; ˈmɔnitris〕 *n.* ＝**monitrix.**
mon·i·trix 〔ˈmanətrɪks; ˈmɔnitriks〕 *n.* monitor 之女性。
***monk** 〔mʌŋk; mʌŋk〕 *n.* 僧侶;修道士。a Buddhist *monk*. 和尚。
monk·er·y 〔ˈmʌŋkərɪ; ˈmʌŋkəri〕 *n., pl.* **-er·ies.** ①僧侶之生活、行爲等。②(*pl.*)修道院之習慣、戒律或信仰。③修道院。④僧侶

之集合稱。

*mon·key [ˈmʌŋkɪ; ˈmʌŋki] n., pl. -keys, v., -keyed, -key·ing. —n. ①猴;猿。②頑皮的孩子。③猴皮裘。④煤礦中之小通道。⑤〖美俚〗吸毒癮。⑥〖英俚〗五百鎊。⑦〖英〗忿怒。⑧〖英〗建築物抵押。*get* (*have*, or *put*) *one's monkey up* 〖英俗〗(使)發怒;(使)生氣。*have a monkey on one's back* 〖俚〗a. 有吸毒癮。b. 沈重的負累。*make a monkey of a person* 戲弄某人。*monkey on one's* (or *the*) *house* 抵押房屋。—*v.i.* 〖美俗〗嘲弄;玩弄〖常 around, with〗. Stop *monkeying* with those tools! 不要亂動那些器具! —*v.t.* ①模仿;學樣。②戲弄;諷嘲。

monkey bread ①一種木棉(baobab)之果實(非洲產)。②此種木棉樹。

monkey business 〖俚〗①不正當的行爲。②輕佻的行爲;惡作劇的行爲。

monkey cup 豬籠草。

mon·key·ish [ˈmʌŋkɪɪʃ; ˈmʌŋkiiʃ] *adj.* 似猿猴的;頑皮的。

monkey jacket (昔時水手的)緊身短外套。

monkey nut 〖英俚〗落花生。

monkey puzzle 〖植物〗智利松(樹枝叢生並有堅銳之葉,故連猴子也爬不上)。

mon·key·shine [ˈmʌŋkɪˌʃaɪn; ˈmʌŋkiʃain] *n.* (常 *pl.*) 〖美俚〗①(猴子似的)頑皮行爲;惡作劇;下流的玩笑。②舞弊。

monkey suit 〖俚〗①制服。②(男用)禮服;晚禮服。

monkey wrench 活動板鉗;活口板頭。

monk·hood [ˈmʌŋkhud; ˈmʌŋkhud] *n.* ①修道僧之身分。②修道僧(集合稱)。

monk·ish [ˈmʌŋkɪʃ; ˈmʌŋkiʃ] *adj.* 修道僧的;修道生活的;修道院的;似修道僧的;和尚似的(常用作輕蔑語)。—**ly,** *adv.*

monks·hood [ˈmʌŋksˌhud; ˈmʌŋkshud] *n.* 〖植物〗附子(一種有毒植物)。

mono- 〖字首〗表"單一"之義(如: monoplane. 在母音前作 mon-, 如: monarch).

mon·o·ba·sic [ˌmɑnəˈbesɪk; ˌmɔnouˈbeisik] *adj.* ①〖化〗一鹽基度的(酸)。②〖生物〗單型的。—**i·ty,** *n.*

mon·o·chord [ˈmɑnəˌkɔrd; ˈmɔnoukɔːd] *n.* ①單弦音響測定器。②〖古〗單弦琴。

mon·o·chro·mat·ic [ˌmɑnəkrəˈmætɪk; ˌmɔnəkrəˈmætik] *adj.* ①單色的;單彩的。②(光線)包括一個波長的。③產生單一波長之光線的。

mon·o·chrome [ˈmɑnəˌkrom; ˈmɔnəkroum] *n.* 單色畫;單色畫法。—*adj.* ①單色的。②黑白的。

mon·o·cle [ˈmɑnəkḷ; ˈmɔnɔkl] *n.* 單眼鏡。

mon·o·cli·nal [ˌmɑnəˈklaɪnḷ; ˌmɔnəˈklainəl] *adj.* 〖地質〗單斜的(地層);單斜地層的。—*n.* =**monocline.** —**ly,** *adv.*

mon·o·cline [ˈmɑnəˌklaɪn; ˈmɔnəklain] *n.* 〖地質〗單斜層。

mon·o·clin·ic [ˌmɑnəˈklɪnɪk; ˌmɔnəˈklinik] *adj.* 〖礦〗單斜(晶系)的。

mon·o·cot·y·le·don [ˌmɑnəˌkɑtḷˈidṇ; ˈmɔnouˌkɔtiˈliːdən] *n.* 〖植物〗單子葉植物。—**ous,** *adj.*

mo·noc·ra·cy [moˈnɑkrəsɪ; mɔˈnɔkrəsi] *n.* 獨裁政治。

mon·o·crat [ˈmɑnəˌkræt; ˈmɔnəkræt] *n.* ①獨裁者。②君主制度主義者。—**ic,** *adj.*

mo·noc·u·lar [məˈnɑkjələ; mɔˈnɔkjulə] *adj.* ①單眼的。②僅有一眼的。③單眼用的。—*n.* 單眼鏡。—**ly,** *adv.*

mon·o·cul·ture [ˈmɑnəˌkʌltʃə; ˈmɔnəˌkʌltʃə] *n.* 〖農〗(田地)單一耕作。

mon·o·dist [ˈmɑnədɪst; ˈmɔnədist] *n.* monody 之作者;唱 monody 者。

mon·o·dra·ma [ˈmɑnəˌdrɑmə; ˈmɔnəˌdrɑːmə] *n.* 一人劇;獨腳戲。—**t·ic,** *adj.* —**tist,** *n.*

mon·o·dy [ˈmɑnədɪ; ˈmɔnədi] *n.* ①(希臘悲劇之)獨唱歌;哀歌;悲歌。②輓歌;追悼詩。③〖音樂〗單音樂曲(=homophony).

mo·noe·cious [məˈniʃəs; mɔˈniːʃəs] *adj.* 〖植物〗雌雄同株的;一家花的。

mo·nog·a·mist [məˈnɑgəmɪst; mɔˈnɔgəmist] *n.* 守一夫一妻制者;一夫一妻論者。—**ic,** *adj.*

mo·nog·a·mous [məˈnɑgəməs; mɔˈnɔgəməs] *adj.* 一夫一妻制的;行一夫一妻制的;主張一夫一妻制的。

mo·nog·a·my [məˈnɑgəmɪ; mɔˈnɔgəmi] *n.* ①一夫一妻;一夫一妻制。②〖動物〗一雄配一雌之習性。

mon·o·gen·e·sis [ˌmɑnəˈdʒɛnəsɪs; ˌmɔnəˈdʒenisis] *n.* ①一元。②〖生物〗一元發生說(主張生物均由單一細胞發達者)。③〖生物〗單性生殖;無性生殖。④人類同源論。

mo·nog·e·nism [məˈnɑdʒənɪzəm; məˈnɔdʒinizm] *n.* 人類同源說。

mon·o·gram [ˈmɑnəˌgræm; ˈmɔnəgræm] *n.* 由姓與名的第一個字母編製而成的圖案。—**mat·ic,** —**mat·i·cal,** —**mic,** *adj.*

mon·o·graph [ˈmɑnəˌgræf; ˈmɔnəgrɑːf] *n.* 專論;專文。(亦作 **monography**)

mo·nog·ra·pher [məˈnɑgrəfə; mɔˈnɔgrəfə] *n.* 小册子的作者;專論作者。

mon·o·graph·ic [ˌmɑnəˈgræfɪk; ˌmɔnəˈgræfik] *adj.* 專論的;專論性質的;專論性的。—**al·ly,** *adv.*

mo·nog·ra·phist [məˈnɑgrəfɪst; mɔˈnɔgrəfist] *n.* =**monographer.**

mo·nog·y·ny [məˈnɑdʒənɪ; məˈnɔdʒini] *n.* ①一妻(主義);一妻制。②一妻多夫制。

mon·o·hull [ˈmɑnəˌhʌl; ˈmɔnəhʌl] *n.* 單身帆船。

mo·nol·a·try [məˈnɑlətrɪ; mɔˈnɔlətri] *n.* 一神崇拜。—**mo·nol·a·trous,** *adj.*

mon·o·lith [ˈmɑnḷˌɪθ; ˈmɔnoliθ] *n.* ①(一塊)巨石;獨石。②由一塊巨石製成的碑、柱、像等。③巨大的結構或組織。

mon·o·lith·ic [ˌmɑnḷˈɪθɪk; ˌmɔnoˈliθik] *adj.* ①由一塊巨石所形成的。②不分派別的;統一的。

monolithic circuit =**integrated circuit.**

mon·o·log [ˈmɑnḷˌɔg; ˈmɔnəlɔg] *n.* =**monologue.**

mon·o·log·ist [ˈmɑnəˌlɔgɪst; mɔˈnɔlədʒist] *n.* ①獨白者;自言自語者。②演獨腳戲者。③獨霸談話(不讓他人有談話機會)者。

mo·nol·o·gize [məˈnɑləˌdʒaɪz; mɔˈnɔlədʒaiz] *v.i.,* **-gized, -giz·ing.** ①獨白;自言自語。②霸占談話。(亦作**monologuize**) —**mo·nol·o·giz·er,** *n.*

mon·o·logue [ˈmɑnḷˌɔg; ˈmɔnəlɔg] *n.* (亦作 **monolog**)①一羣人中一個人的長篇獨語。②(戲劇中一演員的)獨白。③獨腳戲。—*v.i.* 發長篇獨語。

mon·o·logu·ist [ˈmɑnḷˌɔgɪst; ˈmɔnəˌlɔgist] *n.* =**monologist.**

mon·o·ma·ni·a [ˌmɑnəˈmenɪə; ˌmɔnouˈmeinjə] *n.* 〖醫〗偏執狂;專對一事的狂熱。—**cal,** *adj.*

mon·o·ma·ni·ac [ˌmɑnəˈmenɪˌæk; ˈmɔnouˈmeiniæk] *n.* ①偏執狂者。②專對一事的狂熱者。—*adj.* 偏執狂的;狂熱於一事的。

mon·o·me·tal·lic [ˌmɑnəməˈtælɪk; ˌmɔnoumiˈtælik] *adj.* ①一金屬的;使用一金屬的。②單幣制的;單一金屬本位制。③〖化〗每一分子中含有一個金屬原素的。

mon·o·met·al·lism [ˌmɑnəˈmɛtlˌɪzəm; ˌmɔnouˈmetəlizəm] *n.* ①單幣制;單一金屬本位制。②單幣制論;單幣制政策。

mon·o·met·al·list [ˌmɑnəˈmɛtlɪst; ˌmɔnouˈmetəlist] *n.* 主張單幣制政策者。

mo·no·mi·al [moˈnomɪəl; mɔˈnoumiəl] *adj.* ①〖代數〗單項的。②〖生物〗名稱由一字構成的;單名的。—*n.* ①〖代數〗單項式。②〖生物〗一字名稱;單名。

mon·o·mo·lec·u·lar [ˌmɑnəməˈlɛkjələ˞; ˌmɔnəˌmouˈlekjulə] *adj.* ①單分子的。②僅有單分子之厚度的。

mon·o·pho·bi·a [ˌmɑnəˈfobɪə; ˌmɔnəˈfoubjə] *n.* 〖醫〗孤獨恐怖症;獨居恐怖。

mon·o·phon·ic [ˌmɑnəˈfɑnɪk; ˌmɔnəˈfɔnik] *adj.* ①〖音樂〗彈奏或歌唱時無伴奏的。②＝**homophonic.** ③無立體音響效果的;單頻道的。

mon·oph·thong [ˈmɑnəfˌθɔŋ; ˈmɔnəfθɔŋ] *n.* 〖語音〗單母音。

mon·o·plane [ˈmɑnəˌplen; ˈmɔnəplein] *n.* 單翼飛機。

mo·nop·o·list [məˈnɑplɪst; məˈnɔpəlist] *n.* ①專賣者;壟斷者。②主張或贊成專賣者。

mo·nop·o·lis·tic [məˌnɑpəˈlɪstɪk; məˌnɔpəˈlistik] *adj.* 獨占的;專賣的;獨占主義(者)的。—**al·ly,** *adv.*

mo·nop·o·li·za·tion [məˌnɑpləˈzeʃən; məˌnɔpəlaiˈzeiʃən] *n.* 獨占;專賣。

mo·nop·o·lize [məˈnɑplˌaɪz; məˈnɔpəlaiz] *v.t.,* **-lized, -liz·ing.** ①壟斷;專賣。②獨占;據為己有。—**mo·nop·o·liz·er,** *n.*

***mo·nop·o·ly** [məˈnɑplɪ; məˈnɔpəli] *n., pl.* **-lies.** ①壟斷;獨占。the *monopoly* of the trade. 貿易之壟斷。②專賣權;專賣品;專利權。③獨占事業;專賣事業。④享有專賣權之公司。

mon·o·rail [ˈmɑnəˌrel; ˈmɔnoureil] *n.* ①單軌。②單軌鐵路。

mon·o·syl·lab·ic [ˌmɑnəsɪˈlæbɪk; ˈmɔnəsiˈlæbik] *adj.* ①單音節的。②由單音節之字組成的。

mon·o·syl·la·ble [ˈmɑnəˌsɪləbl; ˈmɔnəˌsiləbl] *n.* 單音節字(如 yes, no 等)。

mon·o·the·ism [ˈmɑnəθiˌɪzəm; ˈmɔnouθiːˌizəm] *n.* 一神論;一神教。—**mon·o·the·ist,** *n.* —**mon·o·the·is·tic,** *adj.*

mon·o·tone [ˈmɑnəˌton; ˈmɔnətoun] *n., adj., v.,* **-toned, -ton·ing.** —*n.* ①(聲調、文體、顏色等之)單調;無變化。②單調的演奏或歌唱;作此種表演之人。—*adj.* 單調的。—*v.i.* 單調地歌唱、吟唱、或朗誦。

***mo·not·o·nous** [məˈnɑtṇəs; məˈnɔtənəs] *adj.* ①單調的;無變化的。②因單調而使人厭倦的。*monotonous* life. 單調的生活。

mo·not·o·nous·ly [məˈnɑtənəslɪ; məˈnɔtənəsli] *adv.* 單調地。

mo·not·o·ny [məˈnɑtṇɪ; məˈnɔtəni] *n.* ①單調;單音;無變化。②令人厭倦之單調。

mon·o·trem·a·tous [ˈmɑnəˈtrɛmətəs, -ˈtrimətəs; ˌmɔnəˈtremətəs] *adj.* 〖動物〗單孔類的;一穴類的。

mon·o·treme [ˈmɑnəˌtrim; ˈmɔnətriːm] *n.* 單孔類動物;一穴類動物。—*adj.* ＝**monotrematous.**

mon·o·type [ˈmɑnəˌtaɪp; ˈmɔnətaip] *n., v.,* **-typed, -typ·ing.** —*n.*①〖生物〗單型(構成一屬之唯一的一種)。②〖印刷〗自動鑄字機;用自動鑄字機逐字鑄出之活字。③單刷版畫。—*v.t.* 用自動鑄字機排(字)。

mon·o·va·lent [ˌmɑnəˈvelənt; ˌmɔnəˈveilənt] *adj.* ①〖化〗一價的。②〖細菌〗能抵抗某種病菌的。

mon·ox·ide [mɑnˈɑksaɪd; mɔˈnɔksaid] *n.* 〖化〗一氧化物。

mon·o·zy·got·ic [ˌmɑnəzaɪˈgɑtɪk; ˌmɔnəzaiˈgɔtik] *adj.* 由一個受精的卵細胞分裂而成的;一接合子性的。(亦作 **monovular**)

Mon·roe [mənˈro; mənˈrou] *n.* 門羅 (James, 1758–1831, 於 1817–25 任美國第五任總統)。

Monroe Doctrine ①門羅主義 (James Monroe 任美國總統時,所創歐洲國家不得干涉南北美洲事務的主義)。② 類似門羅主義之政策。

Mon·roe·ism [mʌnˈroɪzṃ; mənˈrouizəm] *n.* ＝**Monroe Doctrine.**

Mons. Monsieur.

Mon·sei·gneur, mon·sei·gneur [ˌmansenˈjɝ; ˌmɔnsenˈjəː] *n., pl.* **Mes·sei·gneurs.** 〖法〗①殿下;閣下(對王族、貴族、主教等之尊稱,通常加在頭銜之前)。②有此稱號之人。(略作 **Mgr., Monsig.**)

mon·sieur [məˈsjɝ; məˈsjəː] *n., pl.* **mes·sieurs.** 〖法〗先生(＝Mr., sir)。

Monsig. ①Monsignor. ②Monseigneur.

Mon·si·gnor, mon·si·gnor [mɑnˈsinjə˞; mɔnˈsiːnjə] *n., pl.* **-gnors.** ①閣下(天主教要人之稱號,＝my lord)。②有此稱號之人。(略作 **Mngr., Mon., Monsig., Msgr.**)

mon·soon [mɑnˈsun; mɔnˈsuːn] *n.* ①季風(印度洋與亞洲南部之季風,夏季從西南吹來,多季自東北吹來)。②西南風帶來之雨季。—**al,** *adj.*

***mon·ster** [ˈmɑnstə˞; ˈmɔnstə] *n.* ①怪物。②巨物;巨獸。The apples were regular *monsters*. 那些蘋果巨大非常。③惡人;殘酷之人。a *monster* of cruelty. 極殘酷的人。④任何醜惡或違反自然之物。⑤畸形之動植物。—*adj.* 巨大的。a *monster* ship. 大船。—**like,** *adj.*

mon·strance [ˈmɑnstrəns; ˈmɔnstrəns] *n.* 〖天主教〗聖體匣。

mon·stros·i·ty [mɑnˈstrɑsətɪ; mɔnˈstrɔsiti] *n., pl.* **-ties.** ①怪物。②畸形;怪異。③巨形;巨大之物。④惡行;窮兇極惡。

***mon·strous** [ˈmɑnstrəs; ˈmɔnstrəs] *adj.* ①巨大的。a *monstrous* sum. 巨大的金額。②異形的;畸形的。③怪異的;荒誕的。④令人吃驚的;恐怖的。a *monstrous* crime. 恐怖的罪行。—*adv.* 〖俗〗非常地;極端地。a *monstrous* fine woman. 非常美麗的女人。—**ly,** *adv.* —**ness,** *n.*

Mont. Montana.

mon·tage [mɑnˈtɑʒ; mɔnˈtɑːʒ] *n., v.,* **-taged, -tag·ing.** —*n.* ①混合畫;混合畫之構成。②〖電影〗蒙太奇(為表示一連串之思想或時間之經過而迅速閃過一連串片段的鏡頭)。③〖廣播〗表示各種意境的多種混雜聲音。④任何不同因素之混合或聯合。—*v.t.* 製成混合畫;拍攝蒙太奇鏡頭。

Mon·taigne [mɑnˈten; mɔnˈtein] *n.* 蒙田 (Michel Eyquem de, 1533–1592, 法國散文家)。—**sque,** *adj.*

Mon·tan·a [mɑn'tænə; mɔn'tænə] *n.* 蒙大拿(美國西北部之一州, 首府爲赫勒拿 Helena).

Mon·tan·an [mɑn'tænən; mɔn'tænən] *adj.* 蒙大拿州的。—*n.* 蒙大拿人。

mon·tane ['mɑnten; 'mɔntein] *adj.* 山的;山地的;居於高山的;山丘的;(尤指)山區的(動、植物)。

mon·tan·ic [mɑn'tænɪk; mɔn'tænik] *adj.* ①山的;多山的。②居山地的。

Mont Blanc [mɑnt'blæŋk; mɔm'blɔŋ] 白朗山(法、義邊境阿爾卑斯山最高峯)。

mont·bre·ti·a [mɑnt'briʃɪə; mɔnt'briːʃjə] *n.* 〖植物〗一種鳶尾科植物。

mon·te ['mɑnte; 'mɔnti] *n.* 發源於西班牙之一種賭博性質的紙牌遊戲。

Mon·te Car·lo [ˌmɑntɪ'kɑrlo; ˌmɔnti'kɑːlou] 蒙地卡羅(摩納哥, Monaco, 之一城市, 俗稱賭城)。

Mon·te·ne·grin [ˌmɑntə'nigrɪn; ˌmɔnti'niːgrin] *adj.* 蒙特尼哥羅 (Montenegro) 的;蒙特尼哥羅人的。—*n.* 蒙特尼哥羅人或居民。

Mon·te·ne·gro [ˌmɑntə'nigro; ˌmɔnti'niːgrou] *n.* 蒙特尼哥羅(第一次大戰前爲一小王國, 現爲南斯拉夫西南部之一省)。

Mon·tes·quieu [ˌmɑntə'skju; ˌmɔntes'kjuː] *n.* 孟德斯鳩 (Charles Louis de Secondat, 1689–1755, 男爵, 法國律師及政治哲學與歷史哲學方面之作家)。

Mon·te·vi·de·o [ˌmɑntəvɪ'deo; ˌmɔntivi'deiou] *n.* 蒙特維多(烏拉圭之首都)。

‡**month** [mʌnθ; mʌnθ] *n.* ①月。this (last, next) *month.* 本(上, 下)月。the *month* after next. 下月後的一個月。the *month* before last. 上月前的一個月。②一個月的期間(三十天)。this day *month.* 下月今日; 一個月後。③懷孕期中之一個月。She was in her eighth *month.* 她懷孕第八個月。***month of Sundays*** 一段無限長的時期。〖注意〗在非正式文體中, 書寫日期時, 如月分名稱的字母在四個以上則縮寫: Jan. 21, 1978. 如祇寫月分或月分及年分, 則很少縮寫。在正式文體中, 所有月分都不縮寫。

***month·ly** ['mʌnθlɪ; 'mʌnθli] *adj., adv., n., pl.* **-lies.** —*adj.* ①每月的; (付款等)按月的;每月一次的。a *monthly* paper (magazine, etc.). 月報(月刊等)。②供一個月用的。③月經的。—*adv.* 每月一次地。He comes here *monthly.* 他每月來一次。—*n.* ①月刊。②(*pl.*)月經。

mon·ti·cule ['mɑntɪˌkjul; 'mɔntikjuːl] *n.* ①小山;小崗;小丘。②火山丘。

***mon·u·ment** ['mɑnjəmənt; 'mɔnjumənt] *n.* ①紀念碑;石碑。This *monument* is in memory of the seventy-two martyrs. 這石碑是紀念七十二烈士的。②紀念物;永垂不朽之事。The professor's researches were *monuments* of learning. 這位教授的研究是學問上不朽的功業。③界碑;界石。④紀念文。

***mon·u·men·tal** [ˌmɑnjə'mɛntl; ˌmɔnju'mentl] *adj.* ①紀念碑的。*monumental* inscription. 碑銘。②做爲紀念的。③似紀念碑的。④不朽的。a *monumental* work. 不朽的作品。⑤巨大的。

mon·u·men·tal·ize [ˌmɑnju'mɛntlˌaɪz; ˌmɔnju'mentəlaiz] *v.t.,* **-ized, -iz·ing.** (以紀念碑等)紀念;傳諸後代;使不朽。

mon·u·men·tal·ly [ˌmɑnjə'mɛntlɪ; ˌmɔnju'mentəli] *adv.* ①龐然地。②非常地。

moo [mu; muː] *n., pl.* **moos,** *v.,* **mooed, moo·ing.** —*n.* 牛鳴聲。—*v.i.* 作牛鳴聲。—*v.t.* 以牛鳴一般的聲音說或唱。

mooch [mutʃ; muːtʃ] *v.i.* 〖俚〗①潛行。②流浪;漂泊。③揩油。—*v.t.* 〖俚〗①偸。②乞求;討。(亦作 **mouch**)

mooch·er ['mutʃɚ; 'muːtʃə] *n.* 〖俚〗潛行者;流浪人;叫化子;小偸;招搖撞騙的人。

***mood**[1] [mud; muːd] *n.* ①心情; 心境。I am in no *mood* for joking. 我無心嬉笑。②(*pl.*)一陣陣的憂鬱心境或壞脾氣。He is a man of *moods.* 他是個喜怒無常的人。③一般態度。

mood[2] *n.* 語氣; 方式; 法。(亦作 **mode**) 〖注意〗在文法中 mood 是動詞敍述的方式, 共分三種, 即: (1)**Indicative Mood** (直述語氣)。(2)**Subjunctive Mood** (假設語氣)。(3) **Imperative Mood** (祈使語氣)。

Moo·dy ['mudɪ; 'muːdi] *n.* 穆地 (William Vaughan, 1869–1910, 美國詩人、劇作家及教育家)。

mood·y ['mudɪ; 'muːdi] *adj.,* **mood·i·er, mood·i·est.** ①心情變幻不定的。②常憂鬱的。③憂鬱的; 不快的。—**mood·i·ly,** *adv.* —**mood·i·ness,** *n.*

moo·la ['mulə; 'muːlə] *n.* 〖美俚〗錢。(亦作 **moolah**)

‡**moon** [mun; muːn] *n.* ①月亮;月球。the crescent *moon.* 新月。the full *moon.* 滿月。the half *moon.* 半月。②月光。He took a walk with her under the *moon.* 他和她在月下散步。③行星的衞星。The planet Jupiter has nine *moons.* 木星有九個衞星。④一個月的時間。Summer is but three *moons* long. 夏季祇有三個月。⑤月形物; 新月形物。⑥〖俚〗私酒 (=moonshine)。⑦人造衞星。***cry for the moon*** 想做不能做到的事; 想要得不到的東西。***once in a blue moon*** 〖俗〗罕有地;永無地。***shoot the moon*** 夜逃; 夜奔。***the man in the moon*** 月中人(指月面的黑斑); 想像的人。—*v.t.* 閒度(時光)〖away〗。to *moon* away one's time. 閒度時光。—*v.i.* ①閒蕩〖about, around〗。He *mooned* around the house all day. 他整日在那房子四周閒蕩。②如癡如醉地想。③如癡如醉地看。

moon·beam ['munˌbim; 'muːnbiːm] *n.* 月光。

moon-blind ['munˌblaɪnd; 'muːnblaind] *adj.* 患夜盲症(月盲症)的。

moon blindness ①〖醫〗夜盲症;雀矇眼。②〖獸醫〗月盲症。

moon cake 〖中〗中秋月餅。

moon·calf ['munˌkæf; 'muːnkɑːf] *n.* ①白癡;天生的低能者。②漫遊者。

moon·craft ['munˌkræft; 'muːnkrɑːft] *n.* 登陸月球之太空船。

moon·eye ['munˌaɪ; 'muːn-ai] *n.* ①〖獸醫〗患月盲病之馬眼。②=**moon blindness.**

moon·faced ['munˌfest; 'muːnfeist] *adj.* 圓臉的。

moon·fish ['munˌfɪʃ; 'muːnfiʃ] *n., pl.* **-fish, -fish·es.** 翻車魚(產於美洲沿岸)。

moon·ish ['munɪʃ; 'muːniʃ] *adj.* ①似月的; 變幻莫測的; 三心兩意的;善變的。②月亮引起的。

***moon·light** ['munˌlaɪt; 'muːnlait] *n.* 月光。They sat in the bright *moonlight.* 他們坐在皎潔的月光下。—*adj.* 有月光的; 月夜的。a *moonlight* night. 月夜。—*v.i.* 兼差。—**er,** *n.*

moon·lit 〔ˈmunˌlɪt; ˈmu:nlit〕 *adj.* 被月光照亮的。
moon probe 月球探測。
moon·rise 〔ˈmunˌraɪz; ˈmu:nraiz〕 *n.* 月出;月出時刻。 「*n.* 月球岩石標本。」
moon·rock 〔ˈmunˌrɑk; ˈmu:nrɔk〕
moon rocket 探月火箭。
moon·scape 〔ˈmunˌskep; ˈmu:n-skeip〕 *n.* 月球上之景色。
moon·shine 〔ˈmunˌʃaɪn; ˈmu:n-ʃain〕 *n.* ①月光。②胡言;妄想。③〖美俗〗私酒。
moon·shin·er 〔ˈmunˌʃaɪnə; ˈmu:n-ˌʃainə〕 *n.* 〖俚〗①偷運私酒者;釀造私酒者。②夜間做非法生意者。
moon·shin·y 〔ˈmunˌʃaɪnɪ; ˈmu:n-ˌʃaini〕 *adj.* ①似月光的;月光皎潔的。②空想的;無意義的;愚蠢的。 「=**mooncraft.**」
moon·ship 〔ˈmunˌʃɪp; ˈmu:nʃip〕 *n.*
moon shoot 向月球發射(火箭等)的試驗。 「月球火箭之發射。」
moon·shot 〔ˈmunˌʃɑt; ˈmu:n-ʃɔt〕 *n.*
moon·stone 〔ˈmunˌston; ˈmu:n-stoun〕 *n.* 〖礦〗月長石。
moon·struck 〔ˈmunˌstrʌk; ˈmu:n-strʌk〕*adj.* 昏迷的;發狂的。「*n.* 月球漫步。」
moon·walk 〔ˈmunˌwɔk; ˈmu:nwɔ:k〕
moon·watch·er 〔ˈmunˌwɑtʃə; ˈmu:nˌwɔtʃə〕 *n.* 月球觀察家。
moon·y 〔ˈmunɪ; ˈmu:ni〕 *adj.*, **moon·i·er, moon·i·est.** ①月亮的。②像月亮的;新月形的。③夢幻的;恍惚的。④瘋狂的。⑤有月光的。⑥似月光的。
Moor 〔mur; muə〕 *n.* 摩爾人(Berber 與阿拉伯人所生之回教人種,居於非洲西北部)。
***moor**[1] 〔mur; muə〕 *n.* 〖英〗①(長有石南屬植物 heather 的)曠野。②狩獵之地。
moor[2] *v.t.* ①使(船)碇泊。②使固定。—*v.i.* ①碇泊;下錨。②繫牢。
moor·age 〔ˈmurɪdʒ; ˈmuəridʒ〕 *n.* ①碇泊。②碇泊處。③碇泊費。
moor cock 雄紅松鷄。
moor·fowl 〔ˈmurˌfaul; ˈmuəfaul〕 *n.* 〖英〗紅松鷄。 「鷸。(亦作 **moorhen**)」
moor hen ①雌紅松鷄。②(歐洲產的)
moor·ing 〔ˈmurɪŋ; ˈmuəriŋ〕 *n.* 碇泊;繫船。
mooring mast 〖航空〗飛艇之繫塔。
Moor·ish 〔ˈmurɪʃ; ˈmuəriʃ〕 *adj.* ①摩爾人的。②摩爾人式的(建築、裝飾等)。
moor·land 〔ˈmurˌlænd; ˈmuələnd〕 *n.* 荒地;沼地。 「〖動物〗麋。」
moose 〔mus; mu:s〕 *n. sing.* or *pl.*
moot 〔mut; mu:t〕 *adj.* ①有討論或辯論餘地的;未決定的。②懷疑的。③假設的。—*v.t.* ①提出討論;辯論。②使失去意義或實質。—*n.* ①(英國早期之)自由市民公會。②(尤指法科學生之)辯論會。*moot* court. 模擬審判。
mop**[1] 〔mɑp; mɔp〕 *n.*, *v.*, **mopped, mop·ping.** —*n.* ①拖把。②亂如拖把的頭髮。a *mop* of hair. 亂蓬蓬的頭髮。—*v.t.* ①洗擦;以拖把擦。to *mop* the floor. 以拖把擦地板。②擦;揩。to *mop* up a mess. 掃清一堆髒亂的東西。—*v.i.* 用拖把洗擦。First she dusted, then she *mopped.* 她首先拂去灰塵,然後用拖把洗擦。 ***mop the floor with (a person) 把(某人)徹底擊敗。 ***mop up*** **a.** 狼吞虎嚥地吃或喝。**b.** 完成;做好。**c.** 掃蕩(殘敵);肅清。**d.** 榨取(利益)。—**per,** *n.*
mop[2] *v.*, **mopped, mop·ping,** *n.* —*v.i.* 作鬼臉;作怪相。***mop and mow*** 作怪相;作鬼臉。—*n.* 怪相;鬼臉。*mops* and mows. 怪相;鬼臉。
mop·board 〔ˈmɑpˌbord; ˈmɔpbɔ:d〕 *n.* 〖建築〗(沿室壁下部之)踢脚板;護壁板。
mope 〔mop; moup〕 *v.*, **moped, mop·ing,** *n.* —*v.t.* & *v.i.* 抑鬱不樂。—*n.* ①抑鬱不樂的人。②(*pl.*)憂鬱。
mop·ish 〔ˈmopɪʃ; ˈmoupiʃ〕 *adj.* 鬱鬱不樂的;茫然若失的。 —**ly,** *adv.* —**ness,** *n.*
mop·pet 〔ˈmɑpɪt; ˈmɔpit〕 *n.* ①〖俗〗布偶。②〖古、謔〗小孩;小姑娘。 「掃蕩戰。」
mop-up 〔ˈmɑpˌʌp; ˈmɔpˈʌp〕 *n.* 掃蕩;
mo·quette 〔məˈkɛt; mouˈket〕 *n.* 一種天鵝絨(做椅面或地毯用)。 「拳遊戲。」
mo·ra 〔ˈmɔrə; ˈmɔ:rə〕 *n.* 一種義大利猜
mo·raine 〔moˈren; mɔˈrein〕 *n.* 〖地質〗(由冰河積成的)石堆。
‡**mor·al** 〔ˈmɔrəl; ˈmɔrəl〕 *adj.* ①品行端正的;公正的。a *moral* man. 品行端正之人。②能辨是非的。Man is a *moral* being. 人是能辨是非的動物。③道德的;道德上的。④教訓的。⑤精神上的;道義上的。to give a person *moral* support. 予某人精神支持。⑥基於良心的。—*n.* ①教訓;寓意。②(*pl.*)品行;風化。He is a man of strict *morals.* 他爲嚴守道德之人。③(*pl.*)倫理學;道德律。④民心;士氣(=morale). The *moral* of the nation is an important factor in war. 在戰爭中民心是個重要因素。
mo·rale 〔moˈræl; mɔˈrɑ:l〕 *n.* 民心;士氣。to bring up the *morale.* 振作士氣。
mor·al·ism 〔ˈmɑrəlɪzm; ˈmɔrəlizəm〕 *n.* ①道德的教論;講道;教訓。②格言。③(別於宗教之)倫理主義;道德上的實踐。 「德家。」
mor·al·ist 〔ˈmɔrəlɪst; ˈmɔrəlist〕 *n.* 道
mor·al·is·tic 〔ˌmɔrəˈlɪstɪk; ˌmɔrəˈlistik〕 *adj.* ①教訓的。②道德主義的。③有道德觀念的。—**al·ly,** *adv.*
***mo·ral·i·ty** 〔moˈrælətɪ; məˈræliti〕 *n.*, *pl.* **-ties.** ①道德;道義。public *morality.* 公共道德。②美德;德行;德性。③教訓;寓意。He ended his lecture with a trite *morality.* 他以陳腐的教訓結束了演講。④(*pl.*)倫理;道德律。the fundamental *moralities* of life. 基本的生活規範。⑤=**morality play.** ⑥道德性。
morality play 十五、六世紀流行的勸善懲惡劇(其中人物如"善"與"惡"等均人格化)。
mor·al·i·za·tion 〔ˌmɔrəlɪˈzeʃən; ˌmɔrəlaiˈzeiʃən〕 *n.* ①講道;教訓。②教化。③道德上的反省。④道德上的解釋。⑤道德化;公正化。
mor·al·ize 〔ˈmɔrəlˌaɪz; ˈmɔrəlaiz〕 *v.*, **-ized, -iz·ing.** —*v.t.* ①以道德意義解說;指出其中的教訓。②教以道德;賦以道德。③使道德化;使公正化。—*v.i.* ①說教;作有關善惡問題的思索、言談、寫作。②教訓;以道德感化。
mor·al·ly 〔ˈmɔrəlɪ; ˈmɔrəli〕 *adv.* ①道德上地。②品行上地。③道義上地;精神上地。④實際地。 「泥沼;濕地。②困境。—**y,** *adj.*」
mo·rass 〔moˈræs; məˈræs〕 *n.*①沼地;
mor·a·to·ri·um 〔ˌmɔrəˈtorɪəm; ˌmɔ:rəˈtɔ:riəm〕 *n.*, *pl.* **-ri·ums, -ri·a** 〔-rɪə; -riə〕. ①〖法律〗延期償付。②延期償付之有效期。③(使用或製造之)禁止或暫停;(某種行爲)暫停。
Mo·ra·vi·an 〔məˈrevɪən; məˈreivjən〕 *adj.* ①摩拉維亞(人)的。②摩拉維亞教徒的;基督教聯合兄弟派的。—*n.* ①摩拉維亞人;摩

拉維亞語(捷克語之一方言)。②基督教聯合兄弟派之教徒。 「(熱帶產之)海鰻。」
mo·ray ['more, mo're; 'mɔːrei] *n.*
mor·bid ['mɔrbɪd; 'mɔːbid] *adj.* ①病態的;不健康的。②由病引起的;病的;關於病的。③病理的;病理學的。*morbid* anatomy. 病理解剖學。④可怕的;恐怖的。—**ness,** *n.*
mor·bi·dez·za [ˌmɔrbɪ'detsɑ; ˌmɔːbi'detsɑː] *n.* 溫柔;細膩。
mor·bid·i·ty [mɔr'bɪdətɪ; mɔː'biditi] *n.* ①病態;不健康狀態。②一地方的疾病率。
mor·bid·ly ['mɔrbɪdlɪ; 'mɔːbidli] *adv.* 不健康地。 「=**morbifical.**」
mor·bif·ic [mɔr'bɪfɪk; mɔː'bifik] *adj.*
mor·bif·i·cal [mɔr'bɪfɪkl; mɔː'bifikəl] *adj.* 引起疾病的。—**ly,** *adv.* 「〖醫〗痲疹。」
mor·bil·li [mɔr'bɪlaɪ; mɔː'bilai] *n. pl.*
mor·da·cious [mɔr'deʃəs; mɔː'deiʃəs] *adj.* ①有腐蝕力的。②銳利的;刻毒的;峻烈的;尖酸刻薄的;譏刺的。—**ly,** *adv.*
mor·dac·i·ty [mɔr'dæsətɪ; mɔː'dæsiti] *n.* 尖酸的諷刺;挖苦;(脾氣的)峻烈。
mor·dan·cy ['mɔrdn̩sɪ; 'mɔːdənsi] *n.* =**mordacity.**
mor·dant ['mɔrdn̩t; 'mɔːdənt] *adj.* ①諷刺的;譏諷的;尖酸的。②有腐蝕性的(酸類)。③媒染的。④激烈的。⑤會咬人的。—*n.* ①媒染劑。②(金屬)腐蝕劑。—*v.t.* 加以媒染。
mor·dent ['mɔrdn̩t; 'mɔːdənt] *n.* 〖音樂〗漣音。
More [mor, mɔr; mɔː] *n.* 摩爾 (Sir Thomas, 1478–1535, 英國政治家及作家)。
more [mor; mɔː] *adj.* comp. of **much, many,** superl., **most,** *n., adv.* —*adj.* ①數目更多的;數量更大的;程度更大的;更重要的。Ten is two *more* than eight. 十比八多兩個。②另外的;外添的;多餘的。One word *more.* 再跟你說一句話。—*n.* ①更大的數量;更多的數量。Give me some *more.* 再多給我一些。I hope to see *more* of you. 我希望能多和你見面。②另外之數量;加添的數量;多餘的數量。*More* is meant than meets the ear. 尙有言外之意。*More* can not be said. 沒有其他可說了。③更重要之人或物。the *more* and the less. 高位的人與低卑的人(高卑上下)。***the more…the more…*** 愈…愈…。*The more* they have, *the more* they want. 他們有的愈多,則需要愈多。—*adv.* ①更(形容形容詞和副詞以造成比較級,相當於字尾 -er 之用途)。*more* beautiful than... 較…更美麗。②(形容動詞)更多;更大。You should sleep *more* than you do. 你應有更多的睡眠。③再。once *more.* 再一次。never *more.* 不再。④(=rather)寧;更甚。He was *more* frightened than hurt. 他受驚較受傷更甚。***all the more*** 格外;越發。***any more*** 再。***more and more*** 越來越多。***more or less*** **a.** 多少;有些。**b.** 大約;大概;左右。**c.** 一點也。***more than*** 多過;大過;比…更。He was *more than* pleased. 他十二分的高興。***more than all*** 尤其 (=above all). ***more than enough*** 很多;較所需者爲多。***more than ever*** 越發;更加。***neither more nor less than*** 恰;正;不多不少;純然。***no more*** **a.** 不再。**b.** 死。***no more than*** **a.** 不過;祇;僅 (=only). **b.** 與…同樣不…;跟…一樣不… (=as little as). ***none the more*** 仍舊;還是 (=not the more). ***not any more than*** =**no more than.** ***not more than*** **a.** 至多 (=at most). **b.** 不致;沒有…的程度 (=not so...as). ***or more*** 至少;或較多。I have walked a mile *or more.* 我至少已經走了一英里路。...***(and) what's more*** 再者;更有甚者;而且。 「比較級, 如: furthermore.」
-more 〖字尾〗附於形容詞及副詞以表示其
mo·reen [mə'rin; mɔː'riːn] *n.* 一種堅牢的羊毛或棉毛交織物(用作窗帘、襯裙等)。
mo·rel [mə'rɛl; mɔ'rel] *n.* 一種小蘑菇。
*__more·o·ver__ [mor'ovɚ, mɔr-; mɔː'rouvə] *adv.* 而且;此外。I did not like the house; *moreover,* it was too high-priced. 我不喜歡這房子,而且它的價錢也太高。
mo·res ['moriz; 'mɔːriːz] *n. pl.* 〖社會〗社會的傳統習慣;習俗。
Mo·resque [mə'rɛsk; mə'resk] *adj.* 摩爾式的(裝飾、建築等)。
Mor·gan[1] ['mɔrgən; 'mɔːgən] *n.* 摩爾根 (Thomas Hunt, 1866–1945, 美國動物學家,曾獲1933年諾貝爾醫學獎)。
Mor·gan[2] *n.* 摩爾根種之馬。
mor·ga·nat·ic [ˌmɔrgə'nætɪk; ˌmɔːgə'nætik] *adj.* 貴族子弟娶平民女爲妻之婚姻的(婚後其妻與子女不得繼承其夫或父之爵位或財產)。—**al·ly,** *adv.*
morgue[1] [mɔrg; mɔːg] *n.* ①(待人認領屍體的)陳屍所。②報館之資料室。
morgue[2] *n.* 驕傲的樣子。
mor·i·bund ['mɔrəˌbʌnd; 'mɔːribʌnd] *adj.* ①將死的。②即將消滅的。③不進步的;呆滯的。—**i·ty,** *n.*
mo·ri·on ['morɪˌɑn; 'mɔriən] *n.* (16–17世紀流行於西班牙之帽型)高頂盔。
Mo·ris·co [mə'rɪsko; mə'riskou] *adj., n., pl.* **-cos, -coes.** —*adj.* 摩爾式的 (=Moorish). —*n.* (特指在西班牙之)摩爾人。
Mor·mon ['mɔrmən; 'mɔːmən] *n.* 摩門教教友 (1830年由 Joseph Smith 所創)。—**ism,** *n.*
*__morn__ [mɔrn; mɔːn] *n.* 〖詩〗=**morning.**
‡**morn·ing** ['mɔrnɪŋ; 'mɔːniŋ] *n.* ①早晨;上午。on Sunday *morning.* 星期日早晨。Good *morning!* 早安! ②早期;初期。the *morning* of life. 生命之初期;幼兒期。***in the morning*** 在早晨;在上午。***top of the morning*** 一個美好的早晨(=a very good *morning*). —*adj.* ①早晨的;上午的;在早晨的;在上午的。②(社交用語)午後的。*morning* call. 午後的正式訪問。
morning after *pl.* **mornings after.** ①宿醉。②任何放縱產生不良後果之時。
morning-after pill (房事後服用的)口服避孕丸。
morn·ing-glo·ry ['mɔrnɪŋˌglorɪ; 'mɔːniŋˌglɔːri] *n., pl.* **-ries.** ①〖植物〗牽牛花。②後勁不足者;虎頭蛇尾者。
morning gown 晨衣。
morning room (日間家屬用之)起居室(別於 drawing room).
morn·ing·tide ['mɔrnɪŋˌtaɪd; 'mɔːniŋtaid] *n.* 〖詩〗晨間;早晨。
Mo·ro ['moro; 'mɔːrou] *n., pl.* **-ros.** ①摩洛族土人(菲律賓羣島南部,屬回敎徒馬來族)。②摩洛語。
Mo·roc·can [mə'rɑkən; mə'rɔkən] *adj.* 摩洛哥的;摩洛哥人的。—*n.* 摩洛哥人。
Mo·roc·co [mə'rɑko; mə'rɔkou] *n.* 摩洛哥(西北非洲一國家,首都爲拉巴特 Rabat). 「摩洛哥山羊皮(釘書用者)。」
mo·roc·co [mə'rɑko; mə'rɔkou] *n.*
morocco leather =**morocco.**

mo·ron ['morɑn; 'mɔːrɔn] *n.* ①智力相等於8-12歲正常兒童的成年人。②低能者。
mo·ron·ic [mo'rɑnɪk; mɔː'rɔnik] *adj.* 低能(者)的;癡笨(人)的。—**al·ly,** *adv.*
mo·ron·ism ['morɑnɪzm̩; 'mɔːrɔnizəm] *n.* 低能。「*n.* 低能。」
mo·ron·i·ty [mə'rɑnətɪ; mɔː'rɔniti]
mo·rose [mo'ros; mə'rous] *adj.* 憂鬱的;陰沉的;壞脾氣的。—**ly,** *adv.* —**ness,** *n.*
morph(ol). morphology. 「之)。」
morph- 〖字首〗=**morpho-**(於母音前用
-morph 〖字尾〗表"…形之物"之義。
mor·pheme ['mɔrfim; 'mɔːfiːm] *n.* 〖語言〗詞素(語言中最小的意義單位);形態素。
mor·phe·mics [mɔr'fimɪks; mɔː'fiːmiks] *n.* 〖語言〗詞素學;形態素學。
Mor·phe·us ['mɔrfɪəs; 'mɔːfjuːs] *n.* 〖希臘神話〗夢之神;睡之神。
mor·phi·a ['mɔrfɪə; 'mɔːfjə] *n.* 嗎啡。(亦作 **morphine**)
mor·phine ['mɔrfin; 'mɔːfiːn] *n.* 嗎啡。
mor·phin·ism ['mɔrfɪnɪzm̩; 'mɔːfinizəm] *n.* ①〖醫〗慢性嗎啡中毒。②嗎啡癮。
mor·phi·no·ma·ni·a [ˌmɔrfɪnə'menɪə; ˌmɔːfinou'meinjə] *n.* 〖醫〗嗜嗎啡狂;嗎啡癮。
mor·phi·no·ma·ni·ac [ˌmɔrfɪnə'menɪˌæk; ˌmɔːfinə'meiniæk] *n.* 嗎啡中毒者。
morpho- 〖字首〗表"形;形態"之義。
mor·pho·log·i·cal [ˌmɔrfə'lɑdʒəkl̩; ˌmɔːfə'lɔdʒikəl] *adj.* ①〖生物〗形態學的。②〖語言〗語形學的;語形論的。(亦作 **morphologic**) —**ly,** *adv.*
mor·phol·o·gist [mɔr'fɑlədʒɪst; mɔː'fɔlədʒist] *n.* 形態學家。
mor·phol·o·gy [mɔr'fɑlədʒɪ; mɔː'fɔlədʒi] *n.* ①〖生物〗形態學。②〖語言〗形態論;語形論。③〖地理〗地形學。④〖生物、語言〗語形;形態(集合稱)。⑤(任何事物之)結構。
mor·ra ['mɔrə; 'mɔːrə] *n.* =**mora.**
mor·ris ['mɔrɪs; 'mɔris] *n.* =**morris dance.** 「可自由調節,坐墊可移去)。」
Morris chair 毛禮斯安樂椅(其靠背
morris dance 英國的一種化裝舞蹈。
mor·row ['mɔro; 'mɔrou] *n.* ①翌日;次日。They reached there on the *morrow.* 他們次日到達該地。②〖古〗=**morning.** ***on the morrow of...*** 緊接…之後。
Morse [mɔrs; mɔːs] *n.* ①摩爾斯 (Samuel Finley Breese, 1791-1872, 美國電報發明者)。②摩爾斯電碼。—*adj.* ①有關摩爾斯電碼的。②有關類似摩爾斯電碼的(如國際電碼等)。「②一種鑲有珠寶的衣夾;別針。」
morse [mɔrs; mɔːs] *n.* ①〖動物〗海象。
Morse code (alphabet or **signals)** 〖電信〗摩爾斯電碼(即用長短線表示字母的電碼)。
mor·sel ['mɔrsəl, -sl̩; 'mɔːsəl] *n.* ①一口。②一小片;少量。a *morsel* of time. 一點點時間。③美肴。④優美小品。
mort[1] [mɔrt; mɔːt] *n.* ①報告獵物已死之號角聲。②屍體。「**much.**」
mort[2] *n.* 〖英方〗多數;多量。—*adv.* =
***mor·tal** ['mɔrtl̩; 'mɔːtl] *adj.* ①不免一死的。Man is *mortal.* 人皆有一死。②人的;人類的。this *mortal* life. 浮生。③致命的。a *mortal* wound. 致命傷。④瀕死的;臨終的。the *mortal* hour. 臨終之時。⑤拚命的;不共戴天的。*mortal* enemy. 不共戴天的仇敵;死敵。⑥很大的;非常的。in a *morta* hurry. 非常匆促。⑦使靈魂死亡的。⑧漫 的。Here they lay for four *morta* hours.他們在這兒躺了漫長的四個小時。—*n.* ①必死的東西。All living creatures ar *mortals.* 一切生物都是必死的東西。②人;人類。—*adv.* 極度地。She was *mortal* angry 她極為憤怒。
***mor·tal·i·ty** [mɔr'tælətɪ; mɔː'tælit *n., pl.* **-ties.** ①不免一死。②大規模死亡。The *mortality* from automobile accident is very serious. 車禍引起的死亡十分嚴重。③死亡率。the *mortality* from disease. 病死亡率。④人類。suffering *mortality.* 苦的人類。⑤失敗率;淘汰率。the *mortalit* among college students. 大學生的被淘汰率。⑥人性。
mor·tal·ly ['mɔrtl̩ɪ; 'mɔːtəli] *adv.* ①致命地。②嚴重地。③觸怒上天地。④非常地
mortal sin 能使靈魂死亡之大罪。
mor·tar[1] ['mɔrtɚ; 'mɔːtə] *n.* 灰泥。—*v.t.* 塗以灰泥;以灰泥黏住(如磚)。
mor·tar[2] *n.* ①臼;乳鉢。②臼砲;迫擊砲 —*v.t. & v.i.* 以迫擊砲攻擊。
mor·tar·board ['mɔrtɚˌbord; 'mɔː təbɔːd] *n.* ①灰泥板;鏝板。②(大學畢業典禮等儀式學生們所戴之)方頂帽。
***mort·gage** ['mɔrgɪdʒ; 'mɔːgidʒ] *n., v.,* **-gaged, -gag·ing.** —*n.* ①抵押。②抵押單據。③義務;精神負擔。—*v.t.* ①抵押。② 誓約;獻身於。Faust *mortgaged* his soul to the devil. 浮士德將其靈魂獻給魔鬼。③使有義務。a view of life in which the individual is *mortgaged* to society. 認為個人對社會負有義務的人生觀。
mort·ga·gee [ˌmɔrgɪ'dʒi; ˌmɔːgə'dʒiː] *n.* 承受抵押者。
mortgage loan 有抵押之貸款。
mort·gag·er, mort·ga·gor ['mɔrgɪdʒɚ; 'mɔːgədʒə] *n.* 抵押者。
mor·tice ['mɔrtɪs; 'mɔːtis] *n., v.t.* = **mortise.** 「*n.* 〖美〗承攬殯葬者;殯儀業者。」
mor·ti·cian [mɔr'tɪʃən; mɔː'tiʃən]
mor·ti·fi·ca·tion [ˌmɔrtəfə'keʃən; ˌmɔːtifi'keiʃən] *n.* ①羞辱;羞恥;懊喪。②制慾;禁慾;苦修。③〖醫〗壞疽。
mor·ti·fy ['mɔrtəˌfaɪ; 'mɔːtifai] *v.,* **-fied, -fy·ing.** —*v.t.* ①使感到羞辱;使蒙屈辱。②抑制(肉慾及情慾)。The saint *mortified* his body. 聖者禁慾苦修。—*v.i.* ①生成壞疽;成為死肉。②禁慾。
mor·ti·fy·ing ['mɔrtəˌfaɪɪŋ; 'mɔːtifaiiŋ] *adj.* ①令人感到羞辱的;叫人嘔氣的;氣死人的;痛心的。②禁慾修行的。—**ly,** *adv.*
mor·tise ['mɔrtɪs; 'mɔːtis] *n., v.,* **-tised, -tis·ing.** —*n.* 枘穴;榫眼。***mortise (and tenon) joint*** 雌雄榫接合。—*v.t.* ①以枘穴接牢;上榫。②接牢;接合。
mort·main ['mɔrtmen; 'mɔːtmein] *n.* 〖法律〗①永代讓渡。②永代管業。
mor·tu·ar·y ['mɔrtʃuˌɛrɪ; 'mɔːtjuəri] *n., pl.* **-ar·ies,** *adj.* —*n.* 停屍處;陳屍處。—*adj.* ①死的;死者的;紀念死者的。②埋葬的。
mos. months.
Mo·sa·ic [mo'ze·ɪk; mə'zeiik] *adj.* 摩西(Moses)的;摩西律的;摩西書的。
mo·sa·ic [mo'ze·ɪk; mə'zeiik] *n., adj., v.,* **mo·sa·ic(k)ed, mo·sa·ic·(k)ing.** —*n.* ①鑲嵌細工;鑲嵌細工所做之物(俗稱瑪賽克)。②任何似鑲嵌細工之物。—*adj.* ①鑲嵌細工

的；鑲嵌細工做成的。②似鑲嵌細工的。③由各種不同物質湊成的。—v.t. 飾以鑲嵌細工。

Mos·cow ['mɑsko; 'mɔskou] *n.* 莫斯科(蘇聯首都,位於蘇聯歐洲部分之中部)。

Mo·selle [mo'zɛl; mə'zel] *n.* ①莫色耳河(源於法國 Vosges 山脈,流入萊因河)。②莫色耳葡萄酒。

Mo·ses ['mozɪz; 'mouziz] *n.* ①〖聖經〗摩西(先知及立法者，率以色列人逃出埃及)。②偉大領袖。

mo·sey ['mozɪ; 'mouzi] *v.i.* 〖美俚〗①躑躅而行。②漫步;徘徊。③走開;離去。

Mos·lem ['mɑzləm; 'mɔzlem] *n., pl.* **-lems, -lem,** *adj.* —*n.*回教徒。—*adj.* 回教徒的;回教的。—**ic,** *adj.* —**ize,** *v.*

mosque [mɑsk; mɔsk] *n.* 回教寺院;清眞寺。(亦作 **mosk**)

***mos·qui·to** [mə'skito; məs'ki:tou] *n., pl.* **-toes, -tos.** ①蚊。*Mosquitoes* buzz. 蚊子嗡嗡叫。②英國的蚊式輕轟炸機。

mosquito boat 魚雷快艇 (=PT boat).

mosquito craft 小型艦艇；小砲艇(集合稱)。

mos·qui·to-cur·tain [mə'skito-ˌkɝtɪn; məs'ki:tou'kə:tn] *n.* 蚊帳。(亦作 **mosquito bar; mosquito net**)

moss** [mɔs, mɒs; mɔs] *n.* 〖植物〗苔。The stones are covered with *moss*. 石頭生滿了青苔。A rolling stone gathers no moss.*** 轉石不生苔,轉業不聚財。—*v.t. & v.i.* (使)生滿青苔。

moss agate 〖礦〗苔紋瑪瑙。

moss·back ['mɔsˌbæk; 'mɔsbæk] *n.* ①〖美俚〗思想落伍之人；極端守舊的人。②(M-)〖美〗(南北戰爭時)藏於沼澤地以逃徵兵的南方人。③背上有苔狀的魚或龜。④鄉下人。

moss-grown ['mɔsˌgron; 'mɔsgroun] *adj.* ①生滿苔的。②落伍的;守舊的。

moss rose 一種西洋薔薇。

moss·troop·er ['mɔsˌtrupɚ; 'mɔs-ˌtru:pə] *n.* ①(17 世紀出沒於英格蘭、蘇格蘭邊境之)匪徒。②流寇;剽匪。

moss·y ['mɔsɪ, 'mɑsɪ; 'mɔsi] *adj.,* **moss·i·er, moss·i·est.** ①生滿苔的;多苔的。②似苔的。③落伍的。*mossy* ideas. 陳腐的思想。

:most [most; moust] *adj.* superl. of **much, many,** comp. **more,** *n., adv.* —*adj.* ①最多的;最大的。The first-prize winner gets the *most* money. 獲頭獎者得最多的錢。②大多數的；幾乎全部的。*Most* children like candy. 大多數的兒童喜愛糖果。***for the most part*** 一般地;主要地。They are good students, *for the most part*. 他們大部分都是好學生。—*n.* ①最多；最大。②大部分。He did *most* of the work. 他做了工作的大部分。***at (the) most*** 至多。I can pay only fifty dollars *at (the) most*. 我最多祇能付五十元。***make the most of*** 善爲利用；獲益。***the most*** 〖俚〗極至;觀止。That movie was *the most*. 那部電影好得不能再好。—*adv.* ①最。**a.** 形容形容詞和副詞以造成最高級,相當於語尾 -est 之用途。**b.** 形容動詞。The thing that troubles me (the) *most* is.... 最使我感到困難的事是…。②極；非常。I shall *most* certainly go there. 我絕對會到那裏去。③〖俗〗幾乎;近乎 (=almost, nearly). You feel the way *most* everybody else has felt. 你的感覺幾乎與其他每個人的感覺是一樣的。

-most 〖字尾〗表"最"之義。

most-fa·vored-na·tion ['most-'fevəd'neʃən; 'moust'feivəd'neiʃən] *adj.* 最惠國的。

***most·ly** ['mostlɪ; 'moustli] *adv.* ①主要地；多半地。The medicine was *mostly* sugar and water. 這藥主要是糖和水。②通常。

mot [mo; mou] *n.* 警句;妙語。

mote[1] [mot; mout] *n.* ①微塵。②小毛病。

mote[2] *v.* 〖古〗=**may, might**[1].

mo·tel [mo'tɛl; mou'tel] *n.* 〖美〗汽車旅館。(亦作 **tourist court**)

mo·tet [mo'tɛt; mou'tet] *n.* 〖音樂〗經文歌(用聖經詩句譜曲)。

***moth** [mɔθ, mɑθ; mɔθ] *n., pl.* **moths.** ①蠹。②蛾。

moth·ball ['mɔθˌbɔl; 'mɔθbɔ:l] *n.* ①(=moth ball) 樟腦丸。②(*pl.*) (由現役)改編爲後備的狀態;被收藏未用的狀態。***in*** (or ***into***) ***mothballs*** **a.** 收藏(舊的武器裝備等)。**b.** 未能積極參加某項工作。**c.** (思想、觀念等)被認爲無價值而遭擱置。—*v.t.* (由現役)改編爲後備；停用並收藏。—*adj.* (由現役)改編爲後備的；被停用並收藏的。

mothball fleet 〖美俗〗海軍中之後備艦隊。

moth-eat·en ['mɔθˌitən; 'mɔθˌi:tn] *adj.* ①蠹蛀的。②破舊的。

:moth·er[1] ['mʌðɚ; 'mʌðə] *n.* ①母親。②根本;源泉。Necessity is the *mother* of invention. 需要是發明之根源。③婦女宗教社會首長；修女院長。④對老年婦女之稱呼。***Mother Carey's chicken*** 海燕類。—*v.t.* ①對…盡母職。Ruth *mothers* her baby sister. Ruth 對她的襁褓妹妹盡母職。②收…爲義子；承認爲…的母親。③生。④照顧。All his life he had to be *mothered* by somebody. 他終生需人照顧。⑤產生。This country has *mothered* many legends. 該國創出了許多傳奇。—*adj.* ①母親的；像母親的。②本國的。one's *mother* tongue. 本國語言;家鄉語。③來源的;根源的。

moth·er[2] *n.* (亦作 **mother of vinegar**) 醋糜。—*v.i.* 變爲醋糜;生醋糜。

mother country 母國;祖國。

Mother Goose 傳說中的英國童謠集之作者。

moth·er·hood ['mʌðɚhud; 'mʌðə-hud] *n.* ①母親之地位;母道。②母性;母權。③母親(集合稱)。

moth·er-in-law ['mʌðərɪnˌlɔ; 'mʌ-ðərinlɔ:] *n., pl.* **moth·ers-in-law.** 婆婆(丈夫之母)；岳母。

moth·er·land ['mʌðɚˌlænd; 'mʌðə-lænd] *n.* ①祖國；故鄉。②祖先所居之地。

moth·er·less ['mʌðəlɪs; 'mʌðəlis] *adj.* 無母的;母親已死的。—**ness,** *n.*

moth·er·like ['mʌðɚˌlaɪk; 'mʌðəlaik] *adj.* 像母親的。

moth·er·li·ness ['mʌðəlɪnɪs; 'mʌ-ðəlinis] *n.* 慈母心；慈愛；慈祥。

moth·er·ly ['mʌðəlɪ; 'mʌðəli] *adj.* 母親的;像母親的。—*adv.* 母親一般地。

Mother of God 聖母瑪利亞。

moth·er-of-pearl ['mʌðəəv'pɝl; 'mʌðərəv'pə:l] *n.* (貝殼等之)珠母層;眞珠母；青貝。—*adj.* 眞珠母的；似眞珠母一般閃亮的。

mother's boy 過分依戀母親的男孩。(亦作 **mama's boy, mamma's boy**)

Mother's Day 〖美,加〗母親節。

mother ship ①將小飛機、火箭等載上天空發射的大飛機。②母船;補給船;護航船。

mother superior *pl.* **mother superiors** or **mothers superior.** 女修道院等之院長。

moth-proof ['mɔθˏpruf; 'mɔθpru:f] *adj.* ①防蟲的。②不怕蟲的。 —*v.t.* ①加以防蟲處理。

moth·y ['mɔθɪ; 'mɔθi] *adj.*, **moth·i·er, moth·i·est.** ①多蠹的; 蠹蛀的。②多蛾的。

mo·tif [mo'tif; mou'ti:f] *n.* ①(文學、藝術作品之)主題;主旨。②圖形;圖式。

mo·tile ['motḷ; 'moutil] *adj.* 〖生物〗能動的; 有自動力的。

mo·til·i·ty [mo'tɪlətɪ; mou'tiliti] *n.* 運動性;自動力。

‡mo·tion ['moʃən; 'mouʃən] *n.* ①運動;移動;動作。 The ship was in *motion.* 船在航行中。②姿態;位置的變動;手的特別動作。All her *motions* were graceful. 她的姿態很優美。 ③動議; 提議。 a *motion* to adjourn. 休會提議。④動機;意向。He refused her offer of his own *motion.* 他拒絕她的贈予係出於己意。⑤(*pl.*) 大便。 ***in motion*** 在運行中;在移動中。—*v.t.* & *v.i.* 以手或頭示意。He *motioned* me to go out. 他示意叫我出去。***motion to somebody*** 向某人點頭或搖手示意。—**er,** *n.*

***mo·tion·less** ['moʃənlɪs; 'mouʃənlis] *adj.* 不動的; 靜止的。 He stood there *motionless.* 他一動不動地站在那兒。 —**ly,** *adv.* —**ness,** *n.*

motion picture 電影。

mo·tion-pic·ture ['moʃən'pɪktʃɚ; 'mouʃən'piktʃə] *adj.* 電影的。

mo·ti·vate ['motəˏvet; 'moutiveit] *v.t.*, **-vat·ed, -vat·ing.** 引起動機; 促起;激發。

mo·ti·va·tion [ˏmotə'veʃən; ˌmouti'veiʃən] *n.* 引起動機;刺激;誘導。—**al,** *adj.*

mo·tive** ['motɪv; 'moutiv] *n.* ①動機;目的。 He did it from selfish *motives.* 他做此事出於自私的動機。②=**motif.** —*adj.* 發動的。 ***motive power **a.** 發動力。**b.** (火車的)機車(集合稱)。**c.** 推力。 —*v.t.* ①賦予動機。②促起;激發。

mo·tive·less ['motɪvlɪs; 'moutivlis] *adj.* 無動機的; 無目的的; 無理由的。—**ly,** *adv.* —**ness,** *n.*

mo·tiv·i·ty [mo'tɪvətɪ; mou'tiviti] *n.* 發動力;原動力;動力。

mot·ley ['mɑtlɪ; 'mɔtli] *n.*, *pl.* **-leys,** *adj.* —*n.* ①雜色花衣(小丑所穿者)。②雜色。③混雜。—*adj.* ①雜色的。②混雜的。③穿雜色花衣的。

‡mo·tor ['motɚ; 'moutə] *n.* ①發動機;馬達。 an electric *motor*. 電動機。②發電機。③內燃機。④汽車。 He bought the fastest *motor* on the market. 他買了市面上最快的汽車。⑤使動的東西。⑥〖解剖〗運動肌; 運動神經。 —*adj.* ①由發動機推動的。 a *motor* bicycle. 機器脚踏車。②運動肌或運動神經的。③推動的。 *motor* power. 動力。④汽車的。*motor* industry. 汽車工業。⑤用於汽車的; 供汽車使用的。—*v.i.* 乘汽車旅行。—*v.t.* ①以汽車載運。 Let me *motor* you to town. 讓我用汽車載你進城。②發動;推動;使運。—**less,** *adj.*

mo·tor·bike ['motɚˏbaɪk; 'moutəbaik] *n.* 〖主英〗 =**motorcycle.**

mo·tor·boat ['motɚˏbot; 'moutəbout] *n.* 汽艇。

mo·tor·bus ['motɚˏbʌs; 'moutə'bʌs] *n.* 公共汽車。

mo·tor·cade ['motɚˏked; 'moutəkeid] *n.*, *v.*, **-cad·ed, -cad·ing.** —*n.*〖美〗汽車行列。 —*v.i.* 〖俗〗參加汽車隊行動。

***mo·tor·car** ['motɚˏkɑr; 'moutəkɑ:] *n.* =**automobile.**

mo·tor·cy·cle ['motɚˏsaɪkḷ; 'moutəˌsaikl] *n.*, *v.*, **-cled, -cling.** —*n.* 機器脚踏車;機車。—*v.i.* 乘機車旅行。

mo·tor·cy·clist ['motɚˏsaɪklɪst; 'moutəˌsaiklist] *n.* 乘機車者。

mo·tor·drome ['motɚˏdrom; 'moutədroum] *n.* 汽車 (摩托車) 賽車或試車場。

mo·to·ri·al [mo'torɪəl; mou'tɔ:riəl] *adj.* ①運動的。②運動神經的。

***mo·tor·ist** ['motərɪst; 'moutərist] *n.* 駕汽車者;乘汽車旅行者。

mo·tor·ize ['motəˏraɪz; 'moutəraiz] *v.t.*, **-ized, -iz·ing.** ①裝發動機於(車)。②使摩托化;使機械化。—**mo·tor·i·za·tion,** *n.*

motor lorry 〖英〗卡車。

mo·tor·man ['motɚmən; 'moutəmən] *n.* ①電車或電動火車司機。②管理發動機者。

motor nerve 〖解剖〗運動神經。

motor scooter 速克達(機車)。

motor ship 摩托船;機船。

motor torpedo boat 魚雷快艇。

mo·tor·way ['motɚˏwe; 'moutəwei] *n.* 〖英〗高速公路。

mo·to·ry ['motərɪ; 'moutəri] *adj.* =**motorial.**

Mo-tse ['mo'dzʌ; 'mɔ:'dzʌ] *n.* 墨子(紀元前五世紀中國哲學家)。(亦作 **Mo Tze, Mo-tze**)

mott(e) [mɑt; mɔt] *n.* 〖美方〗(大草原中之)叢林。

mot·tle ['mɑtḷ; 'mɔtl] *v.*, **-tled, -tling,** *n.* —*v.t.* 使成雜色;弄斑駁。—*n.* 有雜色斑點之色彩或花式。—**ment, mot·tler,** *n.*

mot·tled ['mɑtḷd; 'mɔtld] *adj.* 有斑點的;有雜色斑點的;斑駁的。

***mot·to** ['mɑto; 'mɔtou] *n.*, *pl.* **-toes, -tos.** ①箴言;座右銘。"Think before you speak" is a good *motto.* "考慮後再說話"是個良好的座右銘。②刻於某物上之銘辭;題辭;引用句;題句。

mouch [mutʃ; mu:tʃ] *v.i.* & *v.t.* =**mooch.**

moue [mu; mu:] 〖法〗 *n.* 顰蹙。

mouf·(f)lon ['muflɑn; 'mu:flɔn] *n.*, *pl.* **-lons, -lon.** ①(南歐產之)一種野羊。②其羊毛。

mou·jik ['muʒɪk; 'mu:ʒik] 〖俄〗 *n.* 俄國之農夫。(亦作 **muzhik, muzjik**)

mou·lage [mu'lɑʒ; mu:'lɑ:ʒ] *n.* 供鑑別用的石膏模子。

mould [mold; mould] *v.*, *n.* 〖英〗 = **mold.** —**a·bil·i·ty,** —**i·ness,** *n.* —**a·ble,** *adj.*

mou·lin [ˏmu'læ̃; mu:'læ̃ŋ] *n.* 冰河中近垂直之穴。

moult [molt; moult] *v.*, *n.* 〖英〗=**molt.**

***mound¹** [maʊnd; maund] *n.* ①堤; 土墩;沙堆;石堆。②小山;丘陵;岡;假山。③〖棒球〗投手之踏板。 to take the *mound*. 做投手。④一堆。 —*v.t.* ①圍以堤;圍以土堆等。②堆積。—*v.i.* 逐漸成堆;隆起。

mound² *n.* (王冠上代表權威的)金球。

Mound Builders 於美國 Mississippi 河流域及東南岸諸州築造 Indian mounds 之原始印第安種族。

mounds·man ['maʊndzmən; 'maundzmæn] *n.*, *pl.* **-men.** 〖美俚〗棒球投手。

‡mount¹ [maʊnt; maunt] *v.t.* ①爬上;走上; 登上。 to *mount* stairs. 上樓。 to *mount* a hill. 爬上一小山。 to *mount* a ladder. 爬上一梯。②使…騎乘; 乘於馬上;

備以馬。③裝備；裝設。The fort *mounts* twenty guns. 這砲臺設有二十門砲。④裝以框；裱裝。to *mount* jewels in gold. 鑲寶石於金飾上。⑤供以服裝與道具。⑥演出(戲劇)。⑦擔任（守衛或警備)。to *mount* guard over the person of the emperor. 擔任皇帝的警衛。⑧派(警衛人員)。⑨舉起。Clouds were *mounting* thunderheads in the north. 雲層在北邊正在隆起成爲圓塊積雲。⑩發動(攻擊或攻勢)。to *mount* a successful trade offensive. 發動一次成功的商業攻勢。⑪(雄獸)爬上(雌獸)後背交配。—*v.i.* ①上升；增加。The cost of living is steadily *mounting.* 生活費用不斷上漲。②乘馬。They *mounted* and rode away. 他們騎上馬走了。③被裝置。The transmission *mounts* crosswise in the vehicle. 差速輪横裝於車上。***mount the high horse*** 趾高氣揚。—*n.* ①乘用馬。②框。a picture *mount.* 畫框。③襯布；襯紙。*mount* for a book cover. 書皮的襯紙。④架。⑤騎馬。—**a·ble,** *adj.*

***mount²** *n.* ①山。*Mount* Everest. 埃弗勒斯峯。②(M-)(手相)宮(掌肉隆起處)。

‡**moun·tain**〔'mauntn̩,-tən,-tɪn;'mauntin〕*n.* ①山；高山。Everest is the highest *mountain* in the world. 埃弗勒斯山是世界最高之山。②(*pl.*) 山脈。the Himalayan *mountains.* 喜馬拉雅山脈。③高如山之物。The waves were like *mountains.* 波浪似羣山。④大量之物。⑤巨大的障礙。***the Mountain*** 法國大革命時代國會中的一個急進黨，其領導人爲 Danton 和 Robespierre. —*adj.* ①山的。②生(活)於山上的；在山上發現的。③像山的。

mountain ash 山梨。

mountain chain 山脈。(亦作 **mountain range**)

mountain dew 〖俚〗私釀之威士忌。

***moun·tain·eer**〔,mauntn̩'ɪr; ,maunti'niə〕*n.* ①山居者。②善於登山者。—*v.i.* 爬山。

moun·tain·eer·ing〔,mauntn̩'ɪrɪŋ; ,maunti'niəriŋ〕*n.* 登山。

***moun·tain·ous**〔'mauntn̩əs;'mauntinəs〕*adj.* ①多山的。②巨大的；如山的。a *mountainous* wave. 巨浪。

mountain sickness 〖醫〗高山病。

moun·tain·side〔'mauntn̩,saɪd; 'mauntinsaid〕*n.* 山腹；山坡。

moun·tain·top〔'mauntn̩,tɑp;'mauntintɔp〕*n.* 山頂。

moun·tain·y〔'mauntn̩ɪ; 'mauntini〕*adj.* ①=**mountainous.** ②〖方〗(住在）山地的。

moun·te·bank〔'mauntə,bæŋk; 'mauntibæŋk〕*n.* ①江湖醫生；走方郎中。②騙子；炫言惑衆者。—*v.i.* ①作庸醫；爲江湖醫生。②行騙。—**er·y,** *n.*

mount·ed〔'mauntɪd; 'mauntid〕*adj.* ①騎馬的。*mounted* police. 騎警隊。②〖軍〗機動的(有卡車、戰車、裝甲車或馬等配備的)。③裝架的；裱裝的；鑲嵌的。

Mount·ie〔'mauntɪ; 'maunti〕*n.* 加拿大騎馬警察。(亦作 **Mounty**)

mount·ing〔'mauntɪŋ; 'mauntiŋ〕*n.* ①騎；乘；攀登。②框架。③砲架。④裱裝。

Mount Morrison 玉山(在臺灣，高達3,997公尺，東南亞第一高峯)。(亦作**Yu Shan**)

***mourn**〔morn, mɔrn; mɔːn〕*v.t. & v.i.* ①哀悼；悲悼；憂傷。He *mourned* over his loss. 他爲損失而憂傷。②惋惜。③悲哀地唱。Let the whirlwind *mourn* its requiem. 任由旋風哀唱其輓歌。

mourn·er〔'mɔrnə; 'mɔːnə〕*n.* ①哀悼者；送喪者。②懺悔者；悔罪者。***mourner's bench*** 懺悔者席。

***mourn·ful**〔'mɔrnfl̩; 'mɔːnfəl〕*adj.* ①悲哀的；悽慘的。②悲觀的。He took a *mournful* view of human affairs. 他對人間世事持有悲觀的看法。③令人惋惜的；令人悲傷的。—**ly,** *adv.* —**ness,** *n.*

mourn·ing〔'mɔrnɪŋ; 'mɔːniŋ〕*n.* ①悲哀；哀悼。②穿孝；戴孝；着喪服。③下半旗誌哀。④喪服。⑤服喪期間。***put on mourning*** 着喪服。***wear mourning for somebody*** 爲某人戴孝。—*adj.* 致哀的；戴孝的。

***mouse**〔*n.* maus; maus *v.* mauz; mauz〕*n., pl.* **mice**〔maɪs; mais〕, *v.,* **moused, mous·ing.** —*n.* ①鼠。A *mouse* squeaks. 老鼠吱吱叫。②膽小或羞怯的人。In public affairs he remained a *mouse.* 在公事上，他依然膽小如鼠。③女人。④淤血；青腫。⑤防繩子滑動而打的結。—*v.i.* ①捕鼠。Our cat *mouses* well. 我們的貓善捕鼠。②窺伺(如貓尋鼠狀)。—*v.t.* 尋出；找出。to *mouse* out a neighborhood scandal. 窺探出鄰居的醜行。〖注意〗**mouse** 是小鼠；另一類身體較大的叫 rat.

mouse colo(u)r 鼠色；深灰色。

mouse-ear〔'maus,ɪr; 'maus-iə〕*n.* 〖植物〗鼠耳草。

mous·er〔'mauzə; 'mauzə〕*n.* ①捕鼠動物(貓、狗等)。②窺探的人；四下搜尋東西的人。③〖俚〗偵探。

mouse·trap〔'maus,træp; 'maus-træp〕*n., v.,* **-trapped, -trap·ping.** —*n.* ①捕鼠器。②〖美式足球〗一種引誘戰術。③小地方。—*v.t.* 引誘；引入陷阱。

mousse〔mus; muːs〕*n.* 泡沫冰淇淋。

***mous·tache**〔'mʌstæʃ, mə'stæʃ; məs-'tɑːʃ, mus-〕*n.* =**mustache.**

mous·y〔'mausɪ; 'mausi〕*adj.,* **mous·i·er, mous·i·est.** ①(顏色、氣味、行動等)似鼠的；膽小的；靜如鼠的。②多鼠的；爲鼠所擾的。

‡**mouth**〔*n.* mauθ; mauθ *v.* mauð; mauð〕*n., pl.* **mouths,** *v.* —*n.* ①嘴；口。Tom was born with a silver(*or* golden) spoon in his *mouth.* 湯姆生於富貴之家。②如口之物。③河口。The city is at the *mouth* of the river. 此城位於此河口。④鬼臉；苦相。I don't like her making *mouths* too often. 我不喜她常常做鬼臉。⑤發言人。He is the *mouth* of the House in its relations with the Crown. 他是議會對皇室的發言人。⑥多言。He is not all *mouth,* he gets results. 他並不是祇說不做的人，他也能做事。***down in the mouth*** 悲哀的；沮喪的。***from mouth to mouth*** 一個傳一個地。The news spread like wildfire *from mouth to mouth.* 那消息野火般一個傳一個地迅速傳開。***from the horse's mouth*** 由最原始的來源；由最有權威的來源。***give mouth to one's sentiments*** 吐露感情。***laugh on the wrong side of one's mouth*** 失望；悲傷。***put words into a person's mouth*** **a.** 告訴某人說些甚麼。**b.** 暗示或聲稱某人曾說這些話。***shoot one's mouth off*** 高聲喊叫；信口開河。***take the bread out of a person's mouth*** 剝奪某人的生計；搶去某人的飯碗。***take the words out of a person's mouth*** 搶先說某人所說的話。***word of mouth*** 口傳。

The information got around by *word of mouth*. 那消息由口傳出去。—*v.t.* ①將…置於口中;以口銜…;咬。②裝腔作勢地大聲說出…。③以口或唇舐、磨…。The dog *mouthed* the child's rubber toys. 狗舐小孩的橡膠玩具。④以嘴唇的動作不作聲地說出。⑤使(馬)習慣於轡頭。A horse must be carefully *mouthed* before he is taught to jump. 教一匹馬跳躍之前必需小心使牠習慣於轡頭。⑥檢查…之口部。—*v.i.* ①裝腔作勢地說話。Stop *mouthing* and listen to what I have to say. 別再裝腔作勢, 悉心聽我說的。②扮鬼臉。③流出;放出。

mouth·breed·er 〔ˈmauθˌbridɚ; ˈmauθˌbriːdə〕 *n.* 吳郭魚(在口中孵化魚卵並將幼魚置於口中)。

mouth·er 〔ˈmauðɚ; ˈmauðə〕 *n.* 吹牛「者;說大話者;豪語者。」

mouth-fill·ing 〔ˈmauθˌfɪlɪŋ; ˈmauθˌfiliŋ〕 *adj.* (誓言、讚詞等)誇大的。

***mouth·ful** 〔ˈmauθˌful; ˈmauθful〕 *n.*, *pl.* **-fuls.** ①一口;滿口。He wants to eat it up at a *mouthful*. 他要一口將它吃掉。②少許; 少量。③誇大的措辭。④〖俚〗意味深長的話;中肯的話。You said a *mouthful*. 你的話意味深長。

mouth·ing 〔ˈmauðɪŋ; ˈmauðiŋ〕 *n.* ①誇大的演說、措辭等。②為馬加轡頭。

mouth organ 口琴 (=harmonica).

mouth·piece 〔ˈmauθˌpis; ˈmauθpiːs〕 *n.* ①樂器之吹口。②馬銜;嚼。③(容器、管等之)口;口承。④代言者; 發言人; 機關報。⑤〖俗〗刑事辯護人;律師。

mouth-to-mouth 〔ˈmauθtəˈmauθ; ˈmauθtəˈmauθ〕 *adj.* (人工呼吸)嘴對嘴的。

mouth-to-mouth method 嘴對嘴人工呼吸法。

mouth-wa·ter·ing〔ˈmauθˈwɔtərɪŋ; ˈmauθˈwɔːtəriŋ〕 *adj.* 令人垂涎的;誘人的。

mouth·y 〔ˈmauðɪ; ˈmauði〕 *adj.*, **mouth·i·er, mouth·i·est.** ①說大話的。②愛說話的;多話的。③說話時喜作鬼臉的。—**mouth·i·ly**, *adv.* —**mouth·i·ness**, *n.*

mov(e)·a·bil·i·ty 〔ˌmuvəˈbɪlətɪ; ˌmuːvəˈbiliti〕 *n.* 可動;易動;可動性。

***mov(e)·a·ble** 〔ˈmuvəbl; ˈmuːvəbl〕 *adj.* ①可動的; 活動的。②〖法律〗動產的(為 real 之對)。*movable* property. 動產。③日期隨年而變的;不定的。Easter is a *movable* feast. 復活節是隨年而變日期的節日。④可移動的。—*n.* ①(可移動之) 家具。②(*pl.*) 〖法律〗動產。—**ness**, *n.*

movable type (印刷用之)活字。

mov(e)·a·bly 〔ˈmuvəblɪ; ˈmuːvəbli〕 *adv.* 可動地;易動地。

‡**move** 〔muv; muːv〕 *v.*, **moved, mov·ing,** *n.* —*v.t.*①移動…的位置;搬動。Don't *move* the things on my table. 不要移動我桌上的東西。②使動。The wind was *moving* the branches. 風吹動着樹枝。③使行動;迫使。What *moved* you to do this? 甚麼事情迫使你這樣做呢? ④感動;激動;煽動。Her sad story *moved* me deeply. 她悲楚的身世深深感動了我。⑤(會議中正式)提議。Mr. Chairman, I *move* (that) the meeting be adjourned. 主席, 我提議休會。⑥賣出;出售。That store can *move* these dresses. 那家商店可出售這些衣服。—*v.i.* ①移動; 轉動;改變位置或地方。Keep still—don't *move*. 保持安靜, 不要動。②轉動;進行。The earth *moves* round the sun. 地球繞日運行。③走動。*Move* out of my way. 別擋我的路。④採取行動。God *moves* in a mysterious way. 上帝以神祕不可解方式行事。⑤移居。They *moved* to the country. 他們移居鄉下。⑥移動棋子。It's your turn to *move*. 該你走(棋)了。⑦賣;售。⑧請求;懇求〖for〗。⑨活動; 生活。⑩出發; 走。It's time to be *moving*. 該出發的時候了。***Let's be moving on.*** 〖俗〗我們該走了。***move heaven and earth*** 盡最大努力。 ***move house*** 搬家。***move in*** (***out***) 遷入(出)。***move in on*** **a.** 向…進攻。 **b.** 推翻; 使失去控制或所有權。***move the bowels*** 通便;大便。 ***move up*** (使)晉升。 —*n.* ①一着棋; (棋等)輪到走。Whose *move* is it? 該誰走(棋)啦? ②處置;步驟。What's the next *move*? 下一步驟是甚麼? ③行動;移動。④遷居;移居。***get a move on*** 〖俗〗趕快。We'd better *get a move on* before it rains. 我們最好在下雨之前趕快做。***make a move*** **a.** 採取行動。 **b.** 自(席間等)起立。It's getting late; we ought to *make a move*. 天漸晚, 我們該走了。***on the move*** **a.** 在移動中;遷移。 **b.** 在行動。He wanted to be *on the move*. 他希望行動。 **c.** 在進步中。It is said that civilization is always *on the move*. 有人說文化經常在進步。 **d.** 忙碌的;活動的。—**less,** *adj.*

‡**move·ment** 〔ˈmuvmənt; ˈmuːvmənt〕 *n.* ①動作;移動;運動。He lay there without *movement*. 他安靜地躺在那裏。②(常 *pl.*) 姿態;姿勢。Her *movements* were easy and dignified. 她的姿態安閑而且高貴。③(軍隊、艦隊之) 調動。Not much *movement* could be seen in the enemy's lines. 敵線上看不到甚麼動靜。④(機器等)運轉。⑤活動;行動。Let me know all your *movements* when you are there. 讓我知道你在那裏時的一切活動情形。⑥擺動;振動。⑦移動;遷徙。⑧〖音樂〗 **a.** 節奏; 韻律; 拍子。 **b.** 樂章。the second *movement* of a symphony. 一首交響曲的第二樂章。 ⑨ 社會運動。 the New Life *Movement*. 新生活運動。⑩物價波動。⑪通便;大便。⑫趨向;傾向。⑬事態或形勢之迅速發展。⑭思想、觀念等之發展趨向。

mov·er 〔ˈmuvɚ; ˈmuːvə〕 *n.* ①發動者;原動力。②鼓動者。③提議人。④以為人搬家為業者;搬家公司。⑤行動者。

***mov·ie** 〔ˈmuvɪ; ˈmuːvi〕 *n.* 〖美俗〗①影片。②電影院。a neighborhood *movie*. 鄰近的電影院。 ③(*pl.*)(the-) 電影(指娛樂)。④(*pl.*)(the-)電影事業。

movie fan 影迷。

mo·vie·go·er 〔ˈmuvɪˌgoɚ; ˈmuːviˌgouə〕 *n.* 看電影的人;(尤指)常看電影之人。

movie house 〖俗〗電影院。

mov·ing 〔ˈmuvɪŋ; ˈmuːviŋ〕 *adj.* ①動的。②使發生動作的。③令人感動的;使人悲傷的。④令人感興趣的;令人興奮的。—**ly,** *adv.*

moving picture 電影。(亦作**motion picture**)

moving staircase (or **stairway**) 自動電梯。(亦作 **escalator**)

***mow¹** 〔mo; mou〕 *v.*, **mowed, mowed** or **mown, mow·ing.** —*v.t.* ①(用機器或鐮刀)割;刈。②自…割除草或禾。③掃射;射倒。Our machine guns *mowed* them down like grass. 我們的機鎗如割草般將他們射倒。—*v.i.* ①割草;刈禾。②掃射;射倒。

mow² 〔mau; mau〕 *n.* (亦作**haymow, hayloft**) ①(穀倉內之)草堆; 禾堆。②穀倉內之

禾草貯堆處;乾草棚。—*v.t.* 收入乾草棚〖常away〗. They pitched the hay off the wagon and *mowed* it away. 他們用草叉將乾草拋下車,然後收進乾草棚。

mow³ 〔mau; mau〕 *n.* 鬼臉;揶揄之面容。—*v.i.* 皺眉頭;做鬼臉。(亦作 **mowe**)

mow·er 〔ˈmoɚ; ˈmouə〕 *n.* 刈草者;除草機。

mow·ing 〔ˈmoɪŋ; ˈmouiŋ〕 *n.* ①刈草。②一次所割之草。

mowing machine 刈草機。

mown 〔mon; moun〕 *v.* pp. of **mow¹**. —*adj.* 刈的;割的。

mox·a 〔ˈmɑksə; ˈmɔksə〕 *n.* 〖植物〗艾(針灸用);艾灸。

mox·ie 〔ˈmɑksɪ; ˈmɔksi〕 *n.* 〖俚〗①力氣;精力;勇氣。②技能;經驗。

Mo·zam·bique 〔ˌmozəmˈbik; ˌmouzəmˈbiːk〕 *n.* 莫三鼻克(南非一國,首都馬希多 Maputo).

Mo·zart 〔ˈmozɑrt; ˈmoutsɑːt〕 *n.* 莫扎特 (Wolfgang Amadeus, 1756–1791, 奧國作曲家)。

mo(z)·zet·ta 〔moˈzɛtə; mouˈzetə〕 *n.*, *pl.* **-tas.** 教皇、樞機主教等着的短斗蓬。

MP ①Military Police. ②Mounted Police. **M.P.** ①Member of Parliament. ② Metropolitan Police. ③ Military Police. ④Mounted Police. **M.P.A.** Master of Public Administration.

mpg, m.p.g. miles per gallon. 每加侖汽油所駛英里數。 **mph, m.p.h.** miles per hour. 時速。 **mps, m.p.s.** meters per second. **mR, mr** milliroentgen.

‡**Mr., Mr** 〔ˈmɪstɚ; ˈmistə〕 *n.*, *pl.* **Messrs** 〔ˈmɛsɚz; ˈmesəz〕. 先生 (Mister 之縮寫)。*Mr.* Smith. 史密斯先生。

MRA Moral Re-Armament.

M.R.C.P. Member of the Royal College of Physicians. **M.R.C.S.** Member of the Royal College of Surgeons.

‡**Mrs.** 〔ˈmɪsɪz, ˈmɪsɪs, -əz, -əs; ˈmisiz〕 *n.* 太太;夫人 (Mistress 之縮寫)。*Mrs.* Smith. 史密斯太太。

MRV multiple reentry vehicle. 多彈頭飛彈。 **MS., Ms., ms.** manuscript.

Ms. 〔mɪz; miz〕 *n.* Miss 或 Mrs. 的代用符號(如稱呼一位不知是否已婚的婦女時用)。

M/S ① months after sight. ② motor ship. **M.S.** ①mail steamer. ② Master of Science. ③ Master in Surgery. ④ motor ship. ⑤ multiple sclerosis.

MSA Mutual Security Art (Agency).

M.Sc. Master of Science. **msec** millisecond. **MSG** monosodium glutamate. **Msgr.** Monsignor. **M.Sgt.** master sergeant.

m'sieur 〔məˈsjœ; məˈsjœ〕 *n.* =**monsieur.**

m.s.l. mean sea level. **MSR** missile site radar. 反飛彈飛彈發射雷達。

MSS., Mss., mss. manuscripts.

MST Mountain Standard Time.

MSTS 〖美海軍〗Military Sea Transportation Service.

‡**Mt.** Mount. **mt.** mountain. **M.T.** ①metric ton. ②mean time. ③mechanical (*or* motor) transport. ④Mountain time.

MTB motor torpedo boat. **mtg.** ①mortgage. ②meeting. ③mounting.

mtge. mortgage. **mth.** month.

mtn. mountain. **MTR** material testing reactor. **Mt. Rev.** Most Reverend (archbishop 之尊稱)。

mu 〔mju; mjuː〕 *n.* 希臘字母之第十二字母 (M, μ). 相當於英文之 M, m.

‡**much** 〔mʌtʃ; mʌtʃ〕 *adj.*, **more, most,** *adv.*, **more, most,** *n.* —*adj.* ①多的;大量的。He hasn't *much* money left. 他賸下的錢已不多。②很好的。He's not so *much* on looks, but he really is charming. 他並不很好看,但實在迷人。—*adv.* ①多;甚;極。He doesn't swim *much* (=often). 他不常游泳。That's *much* better. 那樣好多了。②幾乎;差不多。The two boys are *much* the same in arithmetic. 這兩個孩子在算術方面的成績幾乎一樣。—*n.* ①多;許多。*Much* of this is not true. 此事多不眞確。②值得多注意的分量或程度。The evidence did not amount to *much*. 那證據並無多大分量。***as much (...as)*** **a.** (與…) 同量。**b.** (與…) 同限度。You don't come *as much* (often) *as* you used to. 你不像過去那樣常來了。***as much again*** 倍於。***be too much for*** 非力所能抵敵者;(技術等)勝過。***how much*** **a.** 多少(量)。*How much* is there? 有多少? **b.** 多少錢;價值若干。**c.** 如何(程度)。*How much* do you want to go? (=How great is your desire to go?) 你想去的 (欲望) 程度如何? ***make much of*** **a.** 認爲極重要;重視。**b.** 奉承。***much as*** 儘管。***much of a size*** (or ***height***) 約同大(高)。***not much of*** 不算很好的。He is *not much of* a linguist. 他不是個很好的語言學家。***so much (...as)*** **a.** 如此之多。**b.** 如此程度。Don't worry *so much*. 不要如此煩惱。***that*** (or ***this***) ***much*** 那樣(這樣)多。I have only done *that much* so far. 到現在我就只做了那樣多。***too much*** 過多; 過度。***very much*** 很多;很。Thank you *very much*. 多謝。〖注意〗⑴對可數事物用 many, 不可數者用much. ⑵形容動詞的pp. 用 much 或 very much, 而不用very. 但pp. 變成 *adj.* 如: pleased, tired, etc. 時,在習語中亦可用 very.

much·ness 〔ˈmʌtʃnɪs; ˈmʌtʃnis〕 *n.* 大;大量。***much of a muchness*** 大同小異。

mu·cic acid 〔ˈmjusɪk~; ˈmjuːsik~〕 黏液酸。

mu·cif·er·ous 〔mjuˈsɪfərəs; mjuːˈsifərəs〕 *adj.* 含有黏液的;產生黏液的。(亦作 **mucigenous, muciparous**)

mu·ci·lage 〔ˈmjuslɪdʒ; ˈmjuːsilidʒ〕 *n.* ①膠;膠水。②(植物分泌之)膠質。

mu·ci·lag·i·nous 〔ˌmjuslˈædʒənəs; ˌmjuːsiˈlædʒinəs〕 *adj.* ①黏的。②黏液的;分泌黏液的。—**ly,** *adv.*

mu·cin 〔ˈmjusɪn; ˈmjuːsin〕 *n.* 〖生化〗黏液素。

muck** 〔mʌk; mʌk〕 *n.* ①糞;糞肥;肥料。②汚物;垃圾;討厭之物。③〖俗〗雜亂;不潔;汚穢。④拙劣作品;胡說;廢話。The last book he wrote was sheer *muck*. 他寫的最後一本書是毫無價值的東西。⑤〖礦〗廢石。make a muck of*** 弄髒;弄壞。He has *made* such *a muck of* things. 他把東西搞壞成這個樣子。—*v.t.* ①弄髒。They *mucked* up the floor. 他們弄髒了地板。②施肥於。③自…除去髒物。—*v.i.* 〖英〗怠惰;虛擲光陰;混日子〖about〗. ***muck in*** 〖英俚〗磨肩擦背;來往;相交。***muck out*** 清除。***muck up*** 〖俗〗弄壞;弄亂。

muck·er 〔ˈmʌkɚ; ˈmʌkə〕 *n.* ①〖英俚〗粗鄙之人。②笨手笨脚的人。③〖採礦〗清除廢

石的人。④〖俚〗墜落;災難。*come a mucker* 〖俚〗重重跌倒; 失敗。*go a mucker* 〖俚〗遇到災難;破財;亂花錢。

muck·rake 〔'mʌkˌrek; 'mʌk-reik〕 *v.*, **-raked, -rak·ing,** *n.* —*v.t. & v.i.*, 揭發(某人的)貪汚腐敗等。—*n.* 揭發貪汚腐敗等之行爲、文章等。

muck·rak·er 〔'mʌkˌrekɚ; 'mʌkˌreikə〕 *n.* 揭發貪汚腐敗者(尤指新聞記者)。

muck·worm 〔'mʌkˌwɝm; 'mʌkwəːm〕 *n.* ①糞蛆。②守財奴;吝嗇者。③流浪兒童。

muck·y 〔'mʌkɪ; 'mʌki〕 *adj.*, **muck·i·er, muck·i·est.** ①(似)糞的。②汚穢的。③卑鄙的。④汚濁的。⑤泥濘的。

mu·cos·i·ty 〔mju'kɑsətɪ; mjuː'kɔsiti〕 *n.* 黏性。

mu·cous 〔'mjukəs; 'mjuːkəs〕 *adj.* ①黏液的;似黏液的。②分泌黏液的。③有黏液的。

mu·cus 〔'mjukəs; 'mjuːkəs〕 *n.* 〖生物〗黏液。

mud** 〔mʌd; mʌd〕 *n.*, *v.*, **mud·ded, mud·ding.** —*n.* ①泥。Rain turns dust into *mud*. 雨使塵土變成泥。②誹謗。They were using not criticism but *mud*. 他們並不是在批評而是在誹謗。throw*** (***fling***, or ***sling***) ***mud at*** 講…的壞話; 企圖破壞…的名譽。—*v.t.* ①以泥塗。to *mud* pedestrians with careless driving. 駕車不愼使行人身上濺泥。②激起沉澱之泥濘。ducks *mudding* the clear water. 激起清水中沉澱之泥(將清水攪混)的鴨子。—*v.i.* 藏入汚泥;鑽入泥中。a fish that will *mud* when attacked. 遇攻擊時便鑽進汚泥的魚。

mud·di·ness 〔'mʌdɪnɪs; 'mʌdinis〕 *n.* 汚濁不清。

mud·dle 〔'mʌdl̩; 'mʌdl〕 *n.*, *v.*, **-dled, -dling.** —*n.* 一團糟;混亂;紊亂。—*v.t.* ①將…弄成一團糟。②使糊塗。③浪費。④使微醉。⑤使汚濁。—*v.i.* ①微醉。②漫無計畫而糊裏糊塗地混;愚蠢地想。***muddle through*** 混過去。

mud·dled 〔'mʌdl̩d; 'mʌdld〕 *adj.* 混亂的;亂七八糟的。

mud·dle·head 〔'mʌdl̩ˌhɛd; 'mʌdlhed〕 *n.* 頭腦不清者;糊塗蟲。

mud·dle-head·ed 〔'mʌdl'hɛdɪd; 'mʌdl'hedid〕 *adj.* 昏庸的;迷亂的。

mud·dler 〔'mʌdlɚ; 'mʌdlə〕 *n.* ①攪酒棒。②把事情弄糟者; 糊裏糊塗地混下去者。

***mud·dy** 〔'mʌdɪ; 'mʌdi〕 *adj.*, **-di·er, -di·est,** *v.*, **-died, -dy·ing.** —*adj.* ①泥的; 似泥的。②多泥的; 覆有泥的; 泥濘的。a *muddy* road. 泥濘的路。③泥汚的。*muddy* water. 泥水。④混亂的; 不清楚的。*muddy* thinking. 糊塗的想法。⑤貪汚的;腐敗的。⑥棲息於多泥環境的。—*v.t.* ①使泥汚;使汚濁。*muddied* and weary horsemen. 滿身泥汚而疲憊的騎士們。②使不清楚;使混亂。—*v.i.* 變爲泥汚;成爲汚濁。—**mud·di·ly,** *adv.*

mud·fish 〔'mʌdˌfɪʃ; 'mʌdfiʃ〕 *n.*, *pl.* **-fish·es, -fish.** 泥中之魚(如泥鰍等)。

mud·guard 〔'mʌdˌgɑrd; 'mʌdgɑːd〕 *n.* (脚踏車、汽車等之)擋泥板。

mud·hole 〔'mʌdˌhol; 'mʌdhoul〕 *n.* ①汚水坑;汚水洞。②小鎭。

mud lark ①〖俚〗退潮時於河中爛泥上揀拾爛鐵、煤屑等者。②街頭流浪兒。③〖俚〗善於在泥濘跑道上賽跑的馬。

mud·sill 〔'mʌdˌsɪl; 'mʌdsil〕 *n.* ①〖建築〗屋基(置於地中或地上之橫木)。②賤民。

mud·sling·er 〔'mʌdˌslɪŋɚ; 'mʌdˌsliŋə〕 *n.* 愛毀謗他人者。

mud·sling·ing 〔'mʌdˌslɪŋɪŋ; 'mʌdˌsliŋiŋ〕 *n.* (於政治運動中之)毀謗;中傷。

mu·ez·zin 〔mju'ɛzɪn; muː'ezin〕 *n.* (在回教寺院叫拜樓上面的) 報呼禱告時刻的人。

***muff** 〔mʌf; mʌf〕 *n.* ①暖手筒;皮手筒。②笨人。to make a *muff* of oneself. 自討譏笑。③〖球戲〗接球失誤。④笨拙的處理或工作。⑤鳥頭兩側的柔毛。⑥〖機械〗筒;保溫套。*muff* joint. 筒接。⑦不善於運動者。a complete *muff* at cricket. 完全不會玩板球的人。—*v.t.* ①〖球戲〗失(球);沒有接住(球)。to *muff* a ball. 沒有接住球。②〖俗〗拙劣地去作;做錯。He *muffed* a good opportunity for a big contract. 他將一個獲得大合同的好機會弄糟。—*v.i.*〖俗〗笨拙地處理;拙劣地作。

muffed 〔mʌft; mʌft〕 *adj.* 失誤的。

muf·fe·tee 〔ˌmʌfə'ti; ˌmʌfi'tiː〕 *n.* 〖蘇, 英方〗①=**wristlet.** ②=**muffler.**

muf·fin 〔'mʌfɪn; 'mʌfin〕 *n.* 鬆餅。*muffin* man. 賣鬆餅者。

muf·fin·eer 〔ˌmʌfɪ'nɪr; ˌmʌfi'niə〕 *n.* ①(爲保熱附有蓋子的)鬆餅碟子。②用以裝撒在鬆餅上用的糖、鹽及香料之容器。

***muf·fle**[1] 〔'mʌfl̩; 'mʌfl〕 *n.*, *v.*, **-fled, -fling.** —*n.* ①沉悶而低的聲音。②消音器。③窖中之焙室 (裝於此室中之物不直接與火接觸)。—*v.t.* ①圍裹。She *muffled* her throat in a warm scarf. 她用一溫暖的圍巾圍起脖子。②將…蒙起或裹起以使聲音低沉。*muffled* voices. (因蒙住嘴而) 低沉的話聲。③抑制;壓抑。He made an admirable effort to *muffle* his feelings. 他以令人敬佩的努力壓抑感情。

muf·fle[2] *n.* (哺乳動物之)上唇及鼻端部分。

muf·fler 〔'mʌflɚ; 'mʌflə〕 *n.* ①圍巾;頭巾;面紗。②消音裝置;消音器。③拳擊手套。④使沉默或安靜之物。

muf·ti 〔'mʌftɪ; 'mʌfti〕 *n.* ①便服 (爲軍服或制服之對)。②回教法典解說者;法律顧問。

***mug**[1] 〔mʌg; mʌg〕 *n.*, *v.*, **mugged, mug·ging.** —*n.* ①杯 (通指圓筒狀有柄之大杯)。②(該種杯的) 一杯之容量。a *mug* of soup. 一杯湯。③〖俚〗面孔。④〖俚〗嘴。⑤〖俚〗鬼臉;皺眉之臉。to make a *mug*. 作鬼臉。⑥愚人;傻瓜;易受騙者。—*v.t.* ①〖俚〗拍…之照(尤指依公務需要者)。He *mugs* criminals. 他專拍罪犯的照片。②(刺客等之)自背後以前臂扼頸襲擊 (被害者等); 勒死。③皺眉表示。—*v.i.* 扮鬼臉。

mug[2] *v.t.* 學習; 苦讀。—*n.* 苦讀者。

mug·ger[1] 〔'mʌgɚ; 'mʌgə〕 *n.* (印度及東印度羣島產之)一種食人鱷魚。(亦作 **muggar, muggur**)

mug·ger[2] *n.* 〖美俚〗①從背後扼人頸部的强盜。②過分誇張表情(尤指面部表情)的演員。

mug·gins 〔'mʌgɪnz; 'mʌginz〕 *n.* ①〖英〗愚人; 蠢伯; 易受騙的人。②〖牌戲〗一種 dominoes 牌戲。

mug·gle 〔'mʌgl̩; 'mʌgl〕 *n.* 〖美俚〗大麻煙。

mug·gy 〔'mʌgɪ; 'mʌgi〕 *adj.*, **-gi·er, -gi·est.** (空氣、氣候等之) 濕而熱的; 悶人的; 悶熱的。—**mug·gi·ness,** *n.*

mug-up 〔'mʌgˌʌp; 'mʌgʌp〕 *n.* 〖美俗〗兩餐之間的咖啡或點心。

mug·wort 〔'mʌgˌwɝt; 'mʌgwəːt〕 *n.* 〖植物〗艾蒿。

mug·wump 〔'mʌgˌwʌmp; 'mʌgwʌmp〕 *n.* 〖美〗①1884年美國共和黨中不擁護本黨提名之總統候選人 J. G. Blaine 之黨員。②(尤指政治上之)獨立分子。③因猶豫不決而保持中立者;騎牆者。

Mu·ham·mad 〔mu'hæməd; mu'hæməd〕*n.* =**Mohammed.**

mu·jik〔mu'ʒɪk; muː'ʒik〕*n.* =**muzhik.**

Muk·den〔muk'dɛn; 'mukdən〕*n.* 瀋陽(中國遼寧省省會,今譯 Shenyang)。

mu·lat·to〔mə'læto; mjuː'lætou〕*n.*, *pl.* **-toes,** *adj.* —*n.* 白人與黑人所生的第一代混血兒; 一般的黑白混血兒。—*adj.* ①黑白混血的。②有淡褐色的。

***mul·ber·ry**〔'mʌl,bɛrɪ; 'mʌlbəri〕*n.*, *pl.* **-ries.** ①桑樹。②桑椹。③深紫紅色。

mulch〔mʌltʃ; mʌlʃ〕*n.*〖園藝〗爲保護樹根而鋪於地面之一層稻草、樹葉和鬆土等;護根。—*v.t.* 覆以護根。

mulct〔mʌlkt; mʌlkt〕*v.t.* ①詐取;搶奪。②處以罰金。—*n.* 罰金;罰鍰。

***mule**〔mjul; mjuːl〕*n.* ①騾。②〖俗〗倔强之人。③一種紡織機。④一種無後跟的拖鞋。—*adj.* 雜種的;混種的。*mule* lamb. 雜種羔羊。

mu·le·teer〔,mjulə'tɪr; ,mjuːli'tiə〕*n.* 趕騾者。

mu·li·eb·ri·ty〔,mjulɪ'ɛbrətɪ; ,mjuːli'ebriti〕*n.* ①女人之特性;婦人之性格。②=**womanhood.**

mul·ish〔'mjulɪʃ; 'mjuːliʃ〕*adj.* 似騾的;執拗的;倔强的。

mull[1]〔mʌl; mʌl〕*v.t.* (加糖、香料等)溫熱(酒、啤酒等)。

mull[2] *n.* 一種細而軟的棉布。

mull[3] *v.t. & v.i.* (尤指無效果之)研究;思索〖常 over〗。

mull[4] *n.*〖英俗〗失敗;混亂。***make a mull of...*** 把…弄糟。—*v.t.*〖英方〗弄糟;使紛亂;笨拙地操持。

mul·lah, mul·la〔'mʌlə; 'mʌlə〕*n.* 師;先生(回教徒對回教高僧、學者等之尊稱)。(亦作 **mollah**)

mul·lein, mul·len〔'mʌlɪn; 'mʌlin〕*n.*〖植物〗元參科毛蕊花屬之植物。

Mul·ler〔'mʌlɚ; 'mʌlə〕*n.* 墨勒 (Hermann Joseph, 1890-1967, 美國遺傳學家,於1946年獲諾貝爾醫學獎)。

mull·er〔'mʌlɚ; 'mʌlə〕*n.* ①(搗研顏料、藥材等用的)杵。②溫酒容器。

mul·let〔'mʌlɪt; 'mʌlit〕*n.*, *pl.* **-lets, -let.** 鯡鯢鰹。

mul·li·gan〔'mʌlɪgən; 'mʌligən〕*n.*〖美俚〗肉、菜等之雜羹(原爲流浪人之食物)。(亦作 **mulligan stew**)

mul·li·ga·taw·ny〔,mʌlɪgə'tɔnɪ; ,mʌligə'tɔːni〕*n.* 一種咖喱湯(通常加米合食)。

mul·li·grubs〔'mʌlɪ,grʌbz; 'mʌligrʌbz〕*n. sing.* or *pl.*〖俚〗①疝氣痛;腹痛。②意志消沉;憂鬱。

mul·lion〔'mʌljən; 'mʌliən〕*n.*〖建築〗(窗等之)豎框;直櫺。—*v.t.* 造直櫺;以直櫺將(窗)分爲若干部分。

mul·lioned〔'mʌljənd; 'mʌljənd〕*adj.* 有豎框的;有直櫺的。

mul·lock〔'mʌlək; 'mʌlək〕*n.*〖澳〗〖採礦〗(金)礦中之廢土或廢石;廢物;屑。

mul·tan·gu·lar〔mʌl'tæŋgjəlɚ; mʌl'tæŋgjulə〕*adj.* 多角的。

multi-〖字首〗表"多"之義。

mul·ti·cel·lu·lar〔,mʌltɪ'sɛljəlɚ; ,mʌlti'seljulə〕*adj.* 多細胞的。

mul·ti·chan·nel〔,mʌltɪ'tʃænl; ,mʌlti'tʃænl〕*adj.*〖無線電〗多波段的;多頻道的。

mul·ti·col·o(u)r〔,mʌltɪ'kʌlɚ; ,mʌlti'kʌlə〕*adj.* ①多色的(=multicolored)。②能印出多色的。—*n.* 多色。

mul·ti·col·o(u)red〔,mʌltɪ'kʌləd; ,mʌlti'kʌləd〕*adj.* 多色的。

mul·ti·far·i·ous〔,mʌltə'fɛrɪəs; ,mʌlti'fɛəriəs〕*adj.* 種種的;各式各樣的;多方面的;五花八門的。

mul·ti·fid〔'mʌltəfɪd; 'mʌltifid〕*adj.* 分成多部分的;分成許多小塊的。

mul·ti·foil〔'mʌltɪ,fɔɪl; 'mʌltifɔil〕*n.*〖建築〗繁葉飾(窗之葉形飾在五瓣以上者)。

mul·ti·fold〔'mʌltə,fold; 'mʌltifould〕*adj.* ①多種的;繁雜的(=manifold)。②雙摺的;多摺的;摺疊多次的。

mul·ti·form〔'mʌltə,fɔrm; 'mʌltifɔːm〕*adj.* 多形的;多種的;各式各樣的。—*n.* 多形的事物。

mul·ti·for·mi·ty〔,mʌltɪ'fɔrmətɪ; ,mʌlti'fɔːmiti〕*n.* 多樣性;多形性。

mul·ti·graph〔'mʌltə,græf; 'mʌltigrɑːf〕*n.* ①旋轉式零件印刷機。②(M-)其商標名。—*v.t.* 以旋轉式零件印刷機印刷。

mul·ti-in·dus·try〔,mʌltɪ'ɪndəstrɪ; ,mʌlti'indəstri〕*adj.* 涉及多種工業的。(亦作 **multimarket**)

mul·ti·lat·er·al〔,mʌltɪ'lætərəl; 'mʌlti'lætərəl〕*adj.* ①多邊的。②〖政治〗多數國參加的。a *multilateral* treaty. 多邊條約。

mul·ti·lin·gual〔,mʌltɪ'lɪŋgwəl; ,mʌlti'liŋgwəl〕*adj.* ①用多種語言寫成的。②通曉多種語言的。—*n.* 通曉多種語言者。

mul·ti·lith〔'mʌltɪlɪθ; 'mʌltiliθ〕*n.* ①複印文件之凸版印刷機。②(M-)其商標名。

mul·ti·me·di·a〔,mʌltɪ'midɪə; ,mʌlti'miːdjə〕*adj.* (亦作 **mixed-media**)運用多元媒體(使用影片、音響、幻燈片等多種媒體作娛樂、傳播及教學之用)的。—*n. pl.*(作 *sing.* or *pl.* 解)(亦作 **mixed media**)同時對數種傳播或娛樂媒體之運用。

mul·ti·meg·a·ton〔,mʌltɪ'mɛgətʌn; ,mʌlti'megətʌn〕*adj.* (核子武器)威力等於幾百萬噸黃色炸藥的。

mul·ti·mil·lion·aire〔,mʌltə,mɪljən'ɛr; ,mʌltimiljə'nɛə〕*n.* (擁有數百萬的)大富翁;大富豪。

mul·ti·na·tion·al〔,mʌltɪ'næʃənl; ,mʌlti'næʃənl〕*adj.* ①多民族的;多國家的;多國籍的。a *multinational* company. 多國籍公司。②多國籍公司的。—*n.* 多國籍公司。

mul·ti·no·mi·al〔,mʌltɪ'nomɪəl; ,mʌlti'noumiəl〕*adj.*〖數學〗多項的。—*n.* 多項式。

mul·tip·a·rous〔mʌl'tɪpərəs; mʌl'tipərəs〕*adj.* ①〖動物〗一胎多子的。②(女人)產二子以上的;多產的。

mul·ti·par·tite〔,mʌltɪ'pɑrtaɪt; ,mʌlti'pɑːtait〕*adj.* ①分爲多部的。②(協定等)多數國參加的。

mul·ti·ped〔'mʌltə,pɛd; 'mʌltiped〕*adj.*〖罕〗多足的。—*n.* 多足動物。(亦作 **multipede**)

mul·ti·plane〔'mʌltə,plen; 'mʌltiplein〕*n.* 複翼式飛機。

mul·ti·ple〔'mʌltəpl; 'mʌltipl〕*adj.* ①複合的;複式的;多重的;多樣的。a man of *multiple* interests. 有多種興趣的人。②〖電〗二或二以上之平行線路的。③〖數學〗倍數的。④(植物)聚果的。—*n.* ①〖數學〗倍數;倍量。②大量生產之繪畫、雕刻等藝術品。***least common multiple*** (=L.C.M.)最小公倍數。

mul·ti·ple-choice〔'mʌltɪpl'tʃɔɪs; 'mʌltipl'tʃɔis〕*adj.* 有多項選擇的。

multiple-choice test〖教育〗選擇測驗(應試者須在數條答案中擇一正確者)。

mul·ti·plex〔'mʌltə,plɛks; 'mʌltiplexs) *adj.* ①多種的；多樣的；複合的。②〖電信〗多重的；多工的。—*n.* 複合式電子產品(爲收音錄音機合一之一種音響設備)。

mul·ti·pli·a·ble [ˈmʌltəˌplaɪəbl̩; ˈmʌltiˌplaiəbl] *adj.* 可增加的；可乘的。

mul·ti·pli·ca·ble [ˈmʌltəplɪkəbl̩; ˈmʌltiplikəbl] *adj.* =**multipliable.**

mul·ti·pli·cand [ˌmʌltəplɪˈkænd; ˌmʌltipliˈkænd] *n.* 〖算術〗被乘數。

mul·ti·pli·cate [ˈmʌltəpləˌket; ˈmʌltiplikit] *adj.* ①多種的；多樣的。②多重的；多層的。—*n.* 每件相同。

mul·ti·pli·ca·tion [ˌmʌltəpləˈkeʃən; ˌmʌltipliˈkeiʃən] *n.* ①增多；增殖；倍加。to combat the weevil and prevent its *multiplication.* 撲滅穀象蟲並防止其增殖。②〖算術〗乘法。***multiplication table*** 乘法表。

mul·ti·pli·ca·tive [ˈmʌltəplɪˌketɪv; ˌmʌltiˈplikətiv, ˈmʌltiplikeitiv] *adj.* ①增加的；有增殖力的。②乘法的。③〖文法〗倍數詞的。—*n.* 倍數形容詞。

mul·ti·pli·ca·tor [ˈmʌltəplɪˌketɚ; ˈmʌltiplikeitə] *n.* ①〖算術〗乘數。②〖物理〗放大器；倍率器。

mul·ti·plic·i·ty [ˌmʌltəˈplɪsətɪ; ˌmʌltiˈplisiti] *n., pl.* **-ties.** 多；衆多；多樣；重複。

mul·ti·pli·er [ˈmʌltəˌplaɪɚ; ˈmʌltiplaiə] *n.* ①使增加(繁殖)者。②〖算術〗乘數。③〖物理〗(熱、電流、振動等之)放大器。

mul·ti·ply¹** [ˈmʌltəˌplaɪ; ˈmʌltiplai] *v.t. & v.i.,* **-plied, -ply·ing.** ①繁殖；增加；增多。Flies *multiply* enormously. 蒼蠅巨量繁殖。②乘。7 *multiplied* by 9 is (*or* equals) 63. 9 乘 7 得 63。multiply the earth*** 增加世界人口。

mul·ti·ply² [ˈmʌltəplɪ; ˈmʌltipli] *adv.* 「多重地；複式地。」

mul·ti·po·lar [ˌmʌltəˈpolɚ; ˌmʌltiˈpoulə] *adj.* ①〖物理〗多極的。②〖解剖〗有若干樹狀突的。

mul·ti·pur·pose [ˌmʌltɪˈpɝpəs; ˌmʌltiˈpəːpəs] *adj.* 多目標的。

mul·ti·ra·cial [ˌmʌltɪˈreʃəl; ˌmʌltiˈreiʃəl] *adj.* 多種人種的。

mul·ti·ra·cial·ism [ˌmʌltɪˈreʃəlˌɪzəm; ˌmʌltiˈreiʃəlizəm] *n.* 不分種族一律平等之政治或社會制度。

mul·ti·re·sist·ant [ˌmʌltɪrɪˈzɪstənt; ˌmʌltiriˈzistənt] *adj.* 抗拒各種抗生素的。

mul·ti·stage [ˈmʌltɪˌstedʒ; ˈmʌltisteidʒ] *adj.* ①分爲幾個階段的；由若干步驟而成的。②(火箭等)分爲幾節的；多節的。

***mul·ti·tude** [ˈmʌltəˌtjud; ˈmʌltitjuːd] *n.* ①衆多。He has a *multitude* of friends. 他有很多朋友。②羣衆。A great *multitude* gathered in the streets. 一大羣人聚集街上。

mul·ti·tu·di·nous [ˌmʌltəˈtjudn̩əs; ˌmʌltiˈtjuːdinəs] *adj.* ①衆多的。②有許多部分、成分、項目、特色等的。③人數衆多的。

mul·ti·va·lence [ˌmʌltəˈveləns; ˌmʌltiˈveiləns] *n.* ①〖化〗多原子價；多價。②(事物之)多價性。

mul·ti·va·lent [ˌmʌltəˈvelənt; ˌmʌltiˈveilənt] *adj.* 〖化〗①多價(二價或二價以上)的。②多原子價(二種以上之原子價)的。③有多種價值或意義的。

mul·ti·ver·si·ty [ˌmʌltɪˈvɝsətɪ; ˌmʌltiˈvəːsiti] *n., pl.* **-ties.** 多元大學(規模龐大，通常有數個校區，除教學及行政外，尚有多種目標之活動)。

mul·tiv·o·cal [mʌlˈtɪvəkl̩; mʌlˈtivəkəl] *adj.* 表多種意義的；意義曖昧的。

mum¹ [mʌm; mʌm] *adj.* 沉默的；無言的；不說話的。—*interj.* 禁聲；別響！

mum² *n.* ①=**mother.** ②=**madam, ma'am.** ③=**chrysanthemum.**

mum³ *n.* 一種强烈的啤酒。

mum⁴ *v.i.,* **mummed, mum·ming.** ①演啞劇或假面劇。②〖英〗(耶誕節)化裝出遊狂歡。

***mum·ble** [ˈmʌmbl̩; ˈmʌmbl] *v.,* **-bled, -bling,** *n.* —*v.i.* ①喃喃而言；囁嚅；咕噥。The old man was *mumbling* (away) to himself. 那老人喃喃自語。②無齒咀嚼；癟嘴嚼。—*v.t.* ①喃喃說出。②無齒咀嚼；癟嘴嚼。The old woman *mumbled* soft sandwiches. 那老婦人癟嘴嚼柔軟的三明治。③吻。She *mumbled* his cheek and called him "lovely". 她在他臉頰上吻了一下，並叫他一聲"可愛的"。—*n.* 囁嚅；咕噥。His only answer was a *mumble.* 他唯一的回答是一陣喃喃的低語。—**mum·bling·ly,** *adv.*

Mum·bo Jum·bo [ˈmʌmboˈdʒʌmbo; ˈmʌmbouˈdʒʌmbou] ①非洲 Sudan 西部黑人部落之術士(以帶假面具之男人表示之，土人信其能驅邪除祟)。②(m- j-) 迷信的崇拜物；偶像。③(m- j-) 恐怖的東西；可怕的東西。④(m- j-) 無意義的唸咒；胡言亂語。

mum·mer [ˈmʌmɚ; ˈmʌmə] *n.* ①戴假面具、着戲裝作滑稽表演者；啞劇演員。②優伶；伶人(幽默用語)。

mum·mer·y [ˈmʌmərɪ; ˈmʌməri] *n., pl.* **-mer·ies.** ①化裝滑稽表演；啞劇表演。②虛僞的炫耀或儀式。

mum·mi·fy [ˈmʌmɪˌfaɪ; ˈmʌmifai] *v.,* **-fied, -fy·ing.** —*v.t.* ①使爲木乃伊；使不腐爛。②保存。③使乾枯。—*v.i.* 變成木乃伊；乾枯。—**mum·mi·fi·ca·tion,** *n.*

mum·my¹** [ˈmʌmɪ; ˈmʌmi] *n., pl.* **-mies,** *v.,* **-mied, -my·ing.** —*n.* ①(古埃及之)木乃伊；乾屍。②瘦而乾癟之人。beat to a mummy*** 打癟；打個半死。—*v.t.* 製成木乃伊；使像木乃伊。*mummied* cats. 製成木乃伊的貓。

mum·my² *n.* 母親；媽咪(兒語)。

mump [mʌmp; mʌmp] *v.t. & v.i.* 〖方〗①喃喃低語。②行乞；欺騙。③微笑。

mumps [mʌmps; mʌmps] *n. pl.* (作 *sing.* 解)耳下腺炎(俗稱痄腮)；腮腺炎。

mun. ①municipal. ②municipality. ③munitions.

munch [mʌntʃ; mʌntʃ] *v.t. & v.i.* ①用力咀嚼；大聲咀嚼。②用力咬動(下顎)。—*n.* 用力的一嚼。

mun·dane [ˈmʌnden; ˈmʌndein] *adj.* ①世俗的；現世的；塵世的(爲 spiritual 或 heavenly 之對)。②宇宙的；世界的。

mun·go [ˈmʌŋgo; ˈmʌŋgou] *n.* 毛織廠之呢絨碎料(用以與棉混製成一種較廉的毛布)。(亦作 **mongo, mongoe**)

Mu·nich [ˈmjunɪk; ˈmjuːnik] *n.* ①慕尼黑(德國南部之一城市，爲巴伐利亞地區之首府)。②不光榮的妥協；姑息。

***mu·nic·i·pal** [mjuˈnɪsəpl̩; mjuːˈnisipəl] *adj.* ①市的；市政的。a *municipal* council. 市議會。②自治區的。③內政的(以別於外交的)。—*n.* (*pl.*) 市政府或鎮公所發行的公債。

mu·nic·i·pal·ism [mjuˈnɪsəpl̩ˌɪzəm; mjuːˈnisipəlizəm] *n.* 地方自治(論)。

mu·nic·i·pal·ist [mjuˈnɪsəpl̩ɪst; mjuː-

ˈnisipəlist] *n.* ①地方自治主義者。②〖英〗市政專家。

mu·nic·i·pal·i·ty [ˌmjunɪsəˈpælətɪ; mjuːˌnisiˈpæliti] *n., pl.* **-ties.** 自治市(區)。

mu·nic·i·pal·i·za·tion [mjuˌnɪsəpələˈzeʃən; mjuːˌnisiˌpælaiˈzeiʃən] *n.* 歸市有或市營。

mu·nic·i·pal·ize [mjuˈnɪsəpl̩ˌaɪz; mjuːˈnisipəlaiz] *v.t.,* **-ized, -iz·ing.** ①使成爲市。②使歸市有或市營。

mu·nic·i·pal·ly [mjuˈnɪsəplɪ; mju(ː)ˈnisipəli] *adv.* 由市政當局。

mu·nif·i·cence [mjuˈnɪfəsn̩s; mjuːˈnifisns] *n.* 寬厚;慷慨;大度。

mu·nif·i·cent [mjuˈnɪfəsn̩t; mjuːˈnifisnt] *adj.* 寬厚的;慷慨的;毫不吝惜的。

mu·ni·ment [ˈmjunəmənt; ˈmjuːnimənt] *n.* ①防衞;保護;防護之方法或手段。②(*pl.*)〖法律〗(證明權利或特權之)證書;單據; 不動產權利證書。

mu·ni·tion [mjuˈnɪʃən; mjuːˈniʃən] *n.* (常*pl.*) 軍火;軍需品。—*adj.* 軍需品的。—*v.t.* 供以軍火。

M.U.P. Master of Urban Planning.

mu·ral [ˈmjurəl; ˈmjuərəl] *adj.* ①壁上的。a *mural* painting. 一幅壁畫(=a fresco). ②壁的;與壁有關的;似壁的。—*n.* 壁畫。

mu·ral·ist [ˈmjurəlɪst; ˈmjuərəlist] *n.* 壁畫家。

*__mur·der__ [ˈmɝdɚ; ˈməːdə] *n.* 謀殺。an attempted *murder*. 殺人未遂。***get away with murder*** 〖俚〗做壞事而不受處罰。***murder will out*** a. 如要人不知,除非己莫爲。b. 謀殺案是藏不住的。—*v.t.* ①謀殺。He *murdered* her with a knife. 他用刀將她謀殺。②(因缺乏技術或知識而)損毀; 破壞。③浪費時間。—*v.i.* 犯謀殺罪。

*__mur·der·er__ [ˈmɝdərɚ; ˈməːdərə] *n.* 謀殺犯;兇手。

mur·der·ess [ˈmɝdərɪs; ˈməːdəris] *n.* 女謀殺犯; 女兇手。

*__mur·der·ous__ [ˈmɝdərəs; ˈməːdərəs] *adj.* ①能殺害的; 殘酷的; 凶狠的。a *murderous* blow. 凶狠的打擊。②準備謀殺的。a *murderous* villain. 想殺人的惡棍。③殺人的。④很難的;極其危險的;非常費力的。The exams are *murderous*. 考試難得要命。

mu·ri·at·ic acid [ˌmjurɪˈætɪk～; ˌmjuəriˈætik～] 鹽酸(商業用語)。

mu·rine [ˈmjuraɪn; ˈmjuərain] *adj.* ①鼠科的。②老鼠的。 —*n.* 鼠科動物。

murk [mɝk; məːk] *n.* 〖方,詩〗黑暗;陰暗。—*adj.*〖詩〗黑暗的;陰暗的。(亦作 **mirk**)

murk·y [ˈmɝkɪ; ˈməːki] *adj.,* **murk·i·er, murk·i·est.** ①黑暗的;陰暗的;模糊的。②不易懂的;含糊的。—**murk·i·ly,** *adv.* —**murk·i·ness,** *n.*

‡**mur·mur** [ˈmɝmɚ; ˈməːmə] *n.* ①連續之模糊聲。the *murmur* of a stream. 溪水潺潺聲。②微語; 低語。 a *murmur* of thanks. 道謝的低語。③低聲的怨言。He went without a *murmur*. 他毫無怨言地去了。④〖醫〗心臟跳動的雜音;診音。—*v.t.* 低聲而言。 to *murmur* a prayer. 低聲作祈禱。—*v.i.* ①作低而輕的模糊聲。a *murmuring* brook. 流水潺潺的小溪。②低語。We heard the voices *murmuring*. 我們聽到低語聲。③抱怨。

mur·mur·ing [ˈmɝmərɪŋ; ˈməːməriŋ] *n.* 潺潺的聲音;沙沙的聲音;喃喃的聲音;抱怨的聲音。—*adj.* ①抱怨的。②喃喃之聲的; 不斷而模糊之聲的。

mur·mur·ous [ˈmɝmərəs; ˈməːmərəs] *adj.* ①沙沙響的; 作模糊聲的。②細語的;低聲的。③喃喃而語的;低聲怨語的。

mur·phy [ˈmɝfɪ; ˈməːfi] *n., pl.* **-phies.** 〖俚〗馬鈴薯。

mur·rain [ˈmɝɪn; ˈmʌrin] *n.* ①一種牛疫。②瘟疫。 A *murrain* on (*or* to) you! 該死的!天咒你!(=*Murrain* take you!)

mus. ①museum. ②music. ③musical. ④musician.

mus·ca·del [ˌmʌskəˈdɛl; ˌmʌskəˈdel] *n.* =**muscatel.**

mus·ca·dine [ˈmʌskədɪn; ˈmʌskədin] *n.* (美國南部產之) 一種葡萄。

mus·cat [ˈmʌskət; ˈmʌskət] *n.* ①(歐洲產之)一種香葡萄 (muscatel 之原料)。②(=muscatel) 酒。

mus·ca·tel [ˌmʌskəˈtɛl; ˌmʌskəˈtel] *n.* ①(產於法、義等國之)一種芳香、有甜味的白葡萄酒。② (=muscat) 葡萄。

*__mus·cle__[1] [ˈmʌsl; ˈmʌsl] *n., v.,* **-cled, -cling.** —*n.* ①肌肉。Don't move a *muscle!* 不要動! ②膂力。 He is a man of *muscle*. 他是有膂力之人。③力量。***not move a muscle*** 一動不動;保持靜止。—*v.i.* ①干涉; 侵入; 强入〖in〗. to *muscle* in on a territory. 侵入領土。② 純靠膂力或體力行進。—*v.t.* ①使…之肌肉發達。The dancing lessons *muscled* her legs. 跳舞課使她腿部的肌肉發達。②加强。 to *muscle* up our diplomatic approach. 加强我們的外交手腕。③迫使他人讓步。

mus·cle[2] *n.* =**mussel.**

mus·cle-bound [ˈmʌslˌbaund; ˈmʌslbaund] *adj.* ① (因過度運動等而) 肌肉肥大、失去彈性的。②不靈活的;死板的。

mus·cle·man [ˈmʌslˌmæn; ˈmʌslmæn] *n., pl.* **-men.** ①肌肉發達的人。②受雇之惡棍;打手。

mus·co·va·do [ˌmʌskəˈvedo; ˌmʌskəˈveidou] *n.* 粗糖;黑砂糖。

Mus·co·vite [ˈmʌskəˌvaɪt; ˈmʌskəvait] *n.* ①莫斯科人。②Muscovy 人;俄國人。 —*adj.* 莫斯科 (人) 的; Muscovy 的; 俄國的。

Mus·co·vy [ˈmʌskəvɪ; ˈmʌskəvi] *n.* 「莫斯科維(古俄羅斯之名)。

*__mus·cu·lar__ [ˈmʌskjəlɚ; ˈmʌskjulə] *adj.* ①肌的;肌肉的。*muscular* fatigue. 肌肉疲勞。②肌肉發達的; 强壯的。a *muscular* young man. 一個肌肉發達的青年。③含有肌肉的。

mus·cu·lar·i·ty [ˌmʌskjəˈlærətɪ; ˌmʌskjuˈlæriti] *n.* 肌肉發達;强壯。

mus·cu·la·ture [ˈmʌskjələtʃɚ; ˈmʌskjulətʃə] *n.* ①〖解剖〗肌肉組織;肌肉系統。②(組織良好的)結構。

Mus. D., Mus. Doc., Mus. Dr. Musicae Doctor(拉=Doctor of Music).

Muse [mjuz; mjuːz] *n.* ①〖希臘神話〗司文學、藝術、科學等的九位女神之一。the *Muses*. 司文學、藝術、科學等的九女神 (卽 Calliope, Clio, Erato, Euterpe, Melpomene, Polyhymnia, Terpsichore, Thalia, Urania); 詩神; 詩歌; 藝術; 美文學。②(常 m-)詩才;靈感。His *muse* became dumb. 他已江郎才盡。③(m-) 詩。④(m-) 詩人。

*__muse__ [mjuz; mjuːz] *v.i. & v.t.,* **mused, mus·ing.** ①沉思; 冥想。 to *muse* over memories of the past. 緬懷往事。②沉思地凝視;仔細端詳。to *muse* upon a distant scene. 對着遙遠的景象沉思。③沉思地說。—*n.* 沉思。

muse·ful ['mjuzfəl; 'mju:zfəl] *adj.* 沉思的;默想的。

mu·sette [mju'zεt; mju:'zet] *n.* ①一種風笛。②用風笛吹奏的牧歌。③=**musette bag**.

musette bag 士兵或登山者放零星物件之帆布袋。

***mu·se·um** [mju'ziəm, -'zɪəm; mju(:)'ziəm] *n.* 博物院;博物館。

mush[1] [mʌʃ; mʌʃ] *n.* ①〖美〗玉蜀黍粥。②柔軟而濃厚之塊物;軟塊。③〖俗〗脆弱的感情;愚昧的談吐。④〖俚〗嘴巴;臉。***make a mush of*** 〖俗〗弄糟。***mush and molasses*** 〖美〗廢話;糊塗話。

mush[2] *n., v.i.* 〖美西北部,加〗徒步旅行(尤指携犬與橇踏雪之旅行)。

mush[3] *n.* 〖英俚〗①傘。②擁有一部(二部或三部)馬車的車主(自己充馬車夫者)。

***mush·room** ['mʌʃrum, -rʊm; 'mʌʃrum] *n.* ①蕈;菌;蘑菇。②形狀似蕈之物;生長迅速似蕈之物。③〖俗〗暴發戶。④形似蘑菇的雲煙。—*adj.* ①蕈的;似蕈的。②生長極速的(常含滅亡亦速之意)。a *mushroom* millionaire. 暴發富戶。—*v.i.* ①迅速生長或增加。The little town *mushroomed* into a city. 那小鎮迅速發展成一城市。②一端變扁呈菌形;擴張成菌形。③採集蘑菇。④〖軍〗火力加大。—*v.t.* ①使扁。②迅速增加。He *mushroomed* his interests over three quarters of the U. S. 他把自己的事業迅速推廣及美國四分之三的地區。

mush·y ['mʌʃɪ; 'mʌʃi] *adj.*, **mush·i·er, mush·i·est.** ①(似玉蜀黍粥般)柔軟的。②心腸軟的;不堅毅的。

‡**mu·sic** ['mjuzɪk; 'mju:zik] *n.* ①音樂。He loves (*or* is a lover of) *music*. 他愛音樂。②樂曲。to compose *music*. 作曲。③悅耳之聲音。the *music* of the stream. 優美的溪流聲。④譜。He leafed through the *music*. 他一張一張地翻樂譜。⑤對音樂的欣賞力。the man that has no *music* in himself. 一點沒有音樂欣賞力的人。***face the music*** 〖俗〗勇敢地面對麻煩或困難。***set to music*** 配曲。

***mu·si·cal** ['mjuzɪkḷ; 'mju:zikəl] *adj.* ①音樂的。②聲音美妙的。a *musical* voice. 美妙的聲音。③配以音樂的;由音樂組成的。a *musical* entertainment. 配以音樂的娛樂節目。④喜愛音樂的。She comes from a *musical* family. 她來自喜愛音樂的家庭。⑤精於音樂的。—*n.* ①以音樂爲主的電影片或舞臺劇。②=**musicale.** —**ly,** *adv.*

musical comedy 歌舞喜劇。

mu·si·cale [ˌmjuzɪ'kæl; ˌmju:zi'kæl] 〖法〗*n.* (社交上非正式的)音樂會;非公開的演奏會。

mu·si·cal·i·ty [ˌmjuzɪ'kælətɪ; ˌmju:zi'kæliti] *n.* ①聲音美妙。②音樂欣賞力。③音樂才能。

mu·si·cal·ize ['mjuzɪkḷaɪz; 'mju:zikəlaiz] *v.t.*, **-ized, -iz·ing.** 音樂化;歌劇化。

mu·si·cas·sette ['mjuzəkæˌsεt; 'mju:zəkæˌset] *n.* 卡式音樂帶。

music hall ①音樂廳。②〖英〗雜耍戲院。

***mu·si·cian** [mju'zɪʃən; mju(:)'ziʃən] *n.* ①音樂家。②樂師。An orchestra is composed of many *musicians*. 交響樂團由許多樂師組成。③作曲家。④善於音樂者。

mu·si·col·o·gy [ˌmjuzə'kɑlədʒɪ; ˌmju:zi'kɔlədʒi] *n.* 音樂學。

mu·si·co·ther·a·py [ˌmjuzəkə'θεrəpɪ; ˌmju:zikə'θerəpi] *n.* 以音樂治療精神病的方法。

music stand 樂譜架。

music stool 鋼琴演奏時所用之無靠背凳子(可自由升降調節高度者)。

musk [mʌsk; mʌsk] *n.* ①麝香。②麝香之香氣。③麝;有麝香味之動物。④有麝香味之植物。

musk deer 〖動物〗麝;麝香鹿。

musk duck ①(南美產之)莫斯科維鴨。②麝香鴨(澳洲產,交尾期發麝香味)。

mus·kel·lunge ['mʌskəˌlʌndʒ; 'mʌskəlʌndʒ] *n. sing.* or *pl.* (北美東部及中西部產之)一種大梭魚。

mus·ket ['mʌskɪt; 'mʌskit] *n.* 毛瑟槍;滑膛槍。

mus·ket·eer [ˌmʌskə'tɪr; ˌmʌski'tiə] *n.* 配備毛瑟槍之兵;步兵。

mus·ket·ry ['mʌskətrɪ; 'mʌskətri] *n.* ①毛瑟槍(集合稱)。②毛瑟槍射擊(術)。③毛瑟槍兵(集合稱)。

musk·mel·on ['mʌskˌmεlən; 'mʌskˌmelən] *n.* 甜瓜。

musk ox 〖動物〗麝牛。

musk·rat ['mʌskˌræt; 'mʌsk-ræt] *n., pl.* **-rats, -rat.** ①〖動物〗麝鼠。②麝鼠皮。

musk rose 〖植物〗麝香玫瑰。

musk tree 〖植物〗(澳洲產)麝香樹。(亦作 **musk wood**)

musk·y[1] ['mʌskɪ; 'mʌski] *adj.*, **musk·i·er, musk·i·est.** 似麝香的;有麝香氣味的。

musk·y[2] *n.* =**muskellunge.**

Mus·lem, Mus·lim ['mʌzləm; 'muslim] *n., adj.* =**Moslem.**

mus·lin ['mʌzlɪn; 'mʌzlin] *n.* ①(做衣服、窗帷等用之)一種細薄棉布。②(做床單、內衣等用之)一種較厚之棉布。③〖航海俚〗帆(集合稱)。④〖英俗〗女性。a bit of *muslin*. 婦人;少女。—*adj.* 薄棉布製的;棉布製的。

muss [mʌs; mʌs] *v.t.* 〖美俗〗使混亂;使雜亂。—*n.* 〖美俗〗①混亂;雜亂。②吵架;鬧轟轟的局面。

mus·sel ['mʌsḷ; 'mʌsl] *n.* 蠔;貽貝。

Mus·so·li·ni [ˌmuslˈinɪ; ˌmusə'li:ni(:)] *n.* 墨索里尼(Benito, 1883–1945, 義大利法西斯首相及獨裁者,當權時期 1922–43)。

Mus·sul·man ['mʌslmən; 'mʌslmən] *n., pl.* **-mans,** *adj.* —*n.* 回教徒。—*adj.* 回教徒的。

muss·y ['mʌsɪ; 'mʌsi] *adj.*, **muss·i·er, muss·i·est.** 〖美俗〗混亂的;雜亂的;凌亂的。

‡**must**[1] [mʌst; mʌst] *aux. v.* ①不得不;必須;務必。Man *must* eat to live. 人必須吃東西才能活。②應該。You *mustn't* come here. 你不可來此。③必定;必將。You *must* be very tired. 你一定很倦了。④偏巧。Just when we were ready to go away for the holidays, the baby *must* catch measles! 正當我們準備動身出去度假時,偏巧嬰兒出疹子! ⑤必然。Man *must* die. 人必有死。—*n.* 必需做、看、聽的事。This book is a *must*. 此乃必讀之書。—*adj.* 〖俗〗必需的。a *must* item. 必需的條款。This is a *must* book for your reading. 這是一本你們必須讀的書。

must[2] *n.* (發酵前之)葡萄汁;新葡萄酒。

must[3] *n.* 霉臭;霉;黴。—*v.i.* 發霉。

must[4] *adj.* 狂暴的;(尤指雄象、雄駱駝等)發情而狂暴的。—*n.* ①(雄象的)發情期狂暴。②發情期的雄象。

***mus·tache** ['mʌstæʃ, mə'stæʃ; məs'tɑ:ʃ, mus-] *n.* 髭。a pair of *mustaches*.

八字鬍。(亦作 **moustache**)
mus·ta·chio [mə'staʃo; mə'sta:ʃou] *n., pl.* **-chios.** =**mustache.**
mus·tang ['mʌstæŋ; 'mʌstæŋ] *n.* ①(美國平原之)野馬;半野馬。②〖美俚〗由士兵晉升的海軍軍官。
***mus·tard** ['mʌstəd; 'mʌstəd] *n.* ①芥末;芥子粉;芥子泥。②〖植物〗芥菜。③深黃色。④熱烈的興趣。a lot of muscle and *mustard.* 力量强而興趣濃。
mustard oil 芥子油(食用或用於製造肥皂等)。
mustard pot 芥末瓶(餐桌用)。
mus·ter ['mʌstə; 'mʌstə] *v.t.* ①集合;召集;集中。to *muster* soldiers. 召集士兵。②鼓起;振作。③(在數量上)達。—*v.i.* 聚集;集合。***muster in*** (使)入伍。***muster out*** (使)退伍。—*n.* ①集合;召集;集中。②校閱;點兵。an inspection *muster.* 檢閱點名。③召集人員名册。to call the *muster.* 爲召集人員點名。④集合之人數。⑤羣。⑥〖商〗樣品。***pass muster*** **a.** 通過馬虎的檢驗;經得起不嚴格的審閱。**b.** 符合某種標準。
must·n't ['mʌsn̩t; 'mʌsnt]=**must not.**
mus·ty ['mʌstɪ; 'mʌsti] *adj.,* **-ti·er, -ti·est.** ①發霉的;有霉味的;有腐濕氣的。②陳腐的;過時的。③沒有精神的;沒有活力的。—**mus·ti·ness,** *n.*
mut. ①mutilated. ②mutual.
mu·ta·bil·i·ty [ˌmjutə'bɪlətɪ; ˌmju:tə'biliti] *n.* 不定性;易變性;無常。
mu·ta·ble ['mjutəbl̩; 'mju:təbl] *adj.* ①不定的;易變的;無常的。②可變化的。
mu·tant ['mjutənt; 'mju:tənt] *adj.* 變化的;〖生物〗突變的。—*n.* 〖生物〗由突變而產生之新種或新個體;變種。
mu·tate ['mjutet; mju:'teit] *v.t.* & *v.i.,* **-tat·ed, -tat·ing.** ①變化。②〖生物〗突變。③〖語音〗變化(母音)。
mu·ta·tion [mju'teʃən; mju:'teiʃən] *n.* ①變化;變形;變質。②〖生物〗突變;由突變而產生之新種或新個體。③〖語音〗母音變化。④人世之浮沉盛衰。
mu·ta·tive ['mjutətɪv; 'mju:tətiv] *adj.* ①變化的。②〖文法〗表示變化的(動詞)。*mutative* verbs like "fall", "rise". 表示變化的動詞,如:"fall", "rise".
mutch [mʌtʃ; mʌtʃ] *n.* 〖蘇,英方〗(亞麻布製之)女人或小孩用之帽。
***mute** [mjut; mju:t] *adj., n., v.,* **mut·ed, mut·ing.** —*adj.* ①沉默的;無言的。He kept *mute.* 他保持沉默。②啞的;不能說話的。③不讀音的(字母)。The *e* in mute is *mute.* mute 中的 e 是不讀音的。—*n.* ①啞子。②置於樂器上以使音變柔之夾子或墊子;弱音器。③不讀音之字母。—*v.t.* 以夾子或墊子置於(樂器)上使其音變柔。He played the violin with *muted* strings. 他用加了弱音器的小提琴演奏。—**ly,** *adv.* —**ness,** *n.*
mu·ti·late ['mjutl̩ˌet; 'mju:tileit] *v.,* **-lat·ed, -lat·ing,** *adj.* —*v.t.* ①切斷(手足等);使殘廢;毀傷;殘害。②剪掉(樹枝)。③刪改(故事、歌曲等)之主要部分而使不完整;使殘缺不全。—*adj.* ①〖生物〗器官殘缺或發育畸形的。②〖詩〗殘缺不全的。—**mu·ti·la·tor,** *n.*
mu·ti·la·tion [ˌmjutl̩'eʃən; ˌmju:ti'leiʃən] *n.* 切斷;毀傷;殘害。
mu·ti·neer [ˌmjutn̩'ɪr; ˌmju:ti'niə] *n.* 反叛者;背叛者。—*v.i.* 叛變。
mu·ti·nous ['mjutn̩əs; 'mju:tinəs] *adj.* 反叛的;背叛的。—**ly,** *adv.*
***mu·ti·ny** ['mjutn̩ɪ; 'mju:tini] *n., pl.* **-nies,** *v.,* **-nied, -ny·ing.** —*n.* 叛變;兵變。a colonial *mutiny.* 殖民地的叛變。—*v.i.* 叛變;反抗。The extreme left wing *mutinied* just before the election. 極左派在大選前夕叛變。
mut·ism ['mjutɪzm̩; 'mju:tizəm] *n.* ①啞吧(之狀態);無言;沉默。②〖精神病學〗緘默症;不言症。
mutt [mʌt; mʌt] *n.* 〖俚〗①笨人;愚蠢者。②雜種犬。(亦作 **mut**)
***mut·ter** ['mʌtə; 'mʌtə] *v.t.* & *v.i.* ①喃喃而言。He *muttered* to himself. 他自言自語。②作低沉聲響。We heard thunder *muttering* among the hills. 我們聽見山間雷聲隆隆。③出怨言;鳴不平。a *muttering* group of workers. 一羣發牢騷的工人。—*n.* 喃喃低語;呢喃低語聲。the *mutter* of an audience. 聽衆之喃喃低語。
mut·ton** ['mʌtn̩; 'mʌtn] *n.* ①羊肉。We had roast *mutton* for dinner. 我們晚餐吃烤羊肉。②(常 *pl.*)當前要事。Now I must get to my *muttons.* 現在我必須開始做我的當前要事。be as dead as mutton*** 死定了。***eat one's mutton with someone*** 同某人共餐。***return to our mutton*** 話歸本題;言歸正傳。
mutton chop ①羊(肉)排(尤指肋骨或腰部之肉所切成之肉塊,供煮烤食之用)。②臉兩旁所留的上窄下寬的絡腮鬍。
mut·ton·chops ['mʌtn̩ˌtʃaps; 'mʌtntʃɔps] *n., pl.* =**mutton chop②.** (亦作 **muttonchop whiskers**)
mut·ton-head ['mʌtn̩ˌhɛd; 'mʌtnhed] *n.* 〖俚〗愚蠢的人。
mut·ton·y ['mʌtn̩ɪ; 'mʌtəni] *adj.* 似羊肉(味)的。
***mu·tu·al** ['mjutʃuəl; 'mju:tjuəl] *adj.* ①相互的。*mutual* aid. 互助。②〖俗〗共同的。our *mutual* friend. 我們共同的友人。—**ly,** *adv.*
mutual fund 信託基金。
mu·tu·al·ism ['mjutʃuəlɪzəm; 'mju:tjuəlizəm] *n.* ①〖倫理〗互助論。②〖生物〗(有關連之二有機物之)相利共生。
mu·tu·al·i·ty [ˌmjutʃu'ælətɪ; ˌmju:tju'æliti] *n., pl.* **-ties.** 相互關係;相關;相互依存。
mu·tu·al·ly ['mjutʃuəlɪ; 'mju:tjuəli, [-tʃuə-] *adv.* 彼此地;相互地。
Mutual Security Agency 美國共同安全總署。(略作 **MSA**)
mu·tule ['mjutʃul; 'mju:tju:l] *n.* 〖建築〗(Doric 式簷板下之)平面凸塊。
mu·u·mu·u ['muˌmu; 'mu:mu:] *n.* 夏威夷婦女之寬大棉布衣。
mu·zhik, mu·zjik [mu'ʒik; 'mu:ʒik] 〖俄〗 *n.* (俄國帝政時代之)農民;農夫。
muzz [mʌz; mʌz] 〖英俚〗 *v.t.* 使大醉;使昏迷。—*v.i.* ①孜孜苦讀〖over〗。②遊手好閒;閒混。—*n.* ①孜孜苦讀者。②醉;糊塗;混亂。
***muz·zle** ['mʌzl̩; 'mʌzl] *n., v.,* **-zled, -zling.** —*n.* ①(狗、狐、馬等動物之)鼻、口和顎之部分。②(動物之)口絡;鼻籠。③槍口;砲口。*muzzle* cover. 槍口罩。—*v.t.* ①戴口絡於(動物之口部)。to *muzzle* a dog. 使狗戴上口絡。②迫使緘默。The government *muzzled* the press. 政府箝制新聞自由。
muz·zle·load·er ['mʌzl̩ˌlodə; 'mʌzlˌloudə] *n.* 前膛鎗;前膛砲。
muz·zle·load·ing ['mʌzl̩ˌlodɪŋ; 'mʌzlˌloudiŋ] *adj.* 前裝式的;前膛裝填的。
muz·zy ['mʌzɪ; 'mʌzi] *adj.,* **-zi·er, -zi·est.** ①〖俗〗昏迷的;醉得發呆的;酩酊的。②

〖俗〗沒有精神的;呆癡的。

MVD, M.V.D. Ministerstvo Vnutrennikh Del (俄 =Ministry of Internal Affairs). 蘇聯之祕密警察組織。**M.V.Ed.** Master of Vocational Education. **M.V.P.** Most Valuable Player. **MW** 〖英〗megawatt. **M.W.** ①Military Works. ②Most Worshipful. ③Most Worthy.

‡my 〔maɪ; mai〕 *pron.* 我的。This is *my* book (house, dog, etc.). 這是我的書(房子、狗等)。—*interj.* 表示驚訝之詞。*My* goodness! 啊呀! Oh, *my!* 啊呀!

my·al·gi·a 〔maɪˈældʒɪə; maiˈældʒiə〕 *n.* 〖醫〗肌痛。

my·all 〔ˈmaɪɔl; ˈmaiɔːl〕 *n.* ①澳洲土人。②〖植物〗(澳洲產之)阿拉伯護謨樹; 其木材。

my·ce·li·um 〔maɪˈsilɪəm; maiˈsiːliəm〕 *n., pl.* **-li·a** 〔-lɪəl; -liəl〕. 〖植物〗菌絲(體)。

My·ce·nae·an 〔ˌmaɪsɪˈniən; ˌmaisiˈniːən〕 *adj.* ①Mycenae(希臘東南部一古都)的。②(紀元前1500–1100年地中海沿岸諸國之)Mycenae 文明的。

my·col·o·gist 〔maɪˈkɑlədʒɪst; maiˈkɔlədʒist〕 *n.* 黴菌學者。

my·col·o·gy 〔maɪˈkɑlədʒɪ; maiˈkɔlədʒi〕 *n.* ①黴菌學。②(一地域之)黴菌羣。③黴菌之特徵及生活現象。

my·dri·a·sis 〔mɪˈdraɪəsɪs; miˈdraiəsis〕 *n.* 〖醫〗瞳孔散大;瞳孔放大。

my·dri·at·ic 〔ˌmɪdrɪˈætɪk; ˌmidriˈætik〕 *adj.* 瞳孔放大的;促成瞳孔放大的。—*n.* 瞳孔放大劑;散瞳劑。

my·e·li·tis 〔ˌmaɪəˈlaɪtɪs; ˌmaiəˈlaitis〕 *n.* 〖醫〗脊髓炎。

my·na(h) 〔ˈmaɪnə; ˈmainə〕 *n.* (亞洲產之)八哥(能仿人語之鳥)。(亦作 **mina, minah**)

Myn·heer 〔maɪnˈhɛr, -ˈhɪr; mainˈhiə, -ˈhɛə〕 *n.* ①先生(等於Mr. 或 Sir, 爲荷蘭人對男子之尊稱)。②(m-)〖俗〗荷蘭人。

M.Y.O.B. Mind your own business.

my·o·car·di·al in·farc·tion 〔ˌmaɪəˈkɑrdɪəlɪnˈfɑrkʃən; ˌmaiəˈkɑːdiəlinˈfɑːkʃən〕 〖醫〗冠狀動脈栓塞。

my·o·car·di·o·graph 〔ˌmaɪoˈkɑrdɪəˌgræf; ˌmaiəˈkɑːdiəgrɑːf〕 *n.* 心肌搏動描記器。

my·oid 〔ˈmaɪɔɪd; ˈmaiɔid〕 *adj.* 肌肉的;似肌肉的。

my·ol·o·gist 〔maɪˈɑlədʒɪst; maiˈɔlədʒist〕 *n.* 肌肉學家。

my·ol·o·gy 〔maɪˈɑlədʒɪ; maiˈɔlədʒi〕 *n.* ①肌肉學。②肌肉系統。

my·ope 〔ˈmaɪop; ˈmaioup〕 *n.* 近視者。

my·o·pi·a 〔maɪˈopɪə; maiˈoupjə〕 *n.* ①〖醫〗近視。②缺乏遠見。

my·op·ic 〔maɪˈɑpɪk; maiˈɔpik〕 *adj.* ①近視的;近視眼的。②缺乏遠見的。

my·o·py 〔ˈmaɪəpɪ; ˈmaiəpi〕 *n.* = **myopia.**

my·o·sis 〔maɪˈosɪs; maiˈousis〕 *n.* 〖醫〗瞳孔縮小。(亦作 **miosis**)

my·o·so·tis 〔ˌmaɪəˈsotɪs; ˌmaiəˈsoutis〕 *n.* 〖植物〗毋忘我草(屬之植物)。

my·ot·ic 〔maɪˈɑtɪk; maiˈɔtik〕 *adj.* 導致瞳孔縮小的。—*n.* 瞳孔收縮劑。(亦作 **miotic**)

myr·i·ad 〔ˈmɪrɪəd; ˈmiriəd〕 *n.* ①一萬。②巨數; 無數的人或物。There are *myriads* of stars. 有無數的星。—*adj.* ①無數的; 巨數的。②形形色色的。

myr·i·a·pod 〔ˈmɪrɪəˌpɑd; ˈmiriəpɔd〕 *n.* 多足類動物。—*adj.* 多足類的。

Myr·mi·don 〔ˈmɝməˌdɑn, -dən; ˈməːmidən, -dɔn〕 *n.* ①〖希臘神話〗隨 Achilles 出征 Troy 之好戰的 Thessaly 人。②(m-)奉行雇主之命毫不遲疑的人。

myrrh 〔mɝ; məː〕 *n.* 沒藥(一種有香氣、帶苦味之樹脂,用於藥劑及香料等)。

myr·tle 〔ˈmɝtl; ˈməːtl〕 *n.* ①〖植物〗桃金孃。②〖美〗蔓生的長春花屬植物。

‡my·self 〔məˈsɛlf, maɪˈsɛlf; maiˈself, miˈs-, məˈs-〕 *pron., pl.* **our·selves.** ①(我)親自 (me 或 I 的加重語勢)。I *myself* will go. 我要親自去。②我自己 (me 的反身代名詞)。I hurt *myself*. 我傷了自己。③自身;自我。I am not *myself* today. 我今天心神不定;我今天失常。**(all) by myself** 無人幫助;獨自。I don't like going there *all by myself*. 我不喜歡獨自去那裏。

mys·ta·gog·ic 〔ˌmɪstəˈgɑdʒɪk; ˌmistəˈgɔdʒik〕 *adj.* 解釋神祕的;說明(宗教)奧祕的;啓蒙宗教奧祕者的。(亦作 **mystagogical**)

mys·ta·gogue 〔ˈmɪstəˌgɑg; ˈmistəgɔg〕 *n.* 解釋或啓蒙宗教奧祕者。

mys·ta·go·gy 〔ˈmɪstəˌgodʒɪ; ˈmistəgoudʒi〕 *n.* 宗教奧祕之啓示或解釋。

***mys·te·ri·ous** 〔mɪsˈtɪrɪəs; misˈtiəriəs〕 *adj.* ①神祕的;難解的。a *mysterious* stranger. 一個神祕的陌生人。②含有神祕的。a *mysterious* smile. 神祕的一笑。**—ly,** *adv.* **—ness,** *n.*

***mys·ter·y¹** 〔ˈmɪstrɪ, ˈmɪstərɪ; ˈmistəri, ˈmistri〕 *n., pl.* **-ter·ies.** ①神祕; 祕密。He wants to probe the *mystery* to its bottom. 他要探求這祕密之究竟。②不可思議之事務; 祕密的事物; 神祕的事物。How he solved the problem still remains a *mystery*. 他如何解決了那問題仍然是件不可思議的事。③奧理;玄義。④(一種祇准其信徒參加的)祕密宗教儀式。⑤= **mystery play.**

mys·ter·y² *n., pl.* **-ter·ies.** ①職業;行業;手工藝。②同業公會。

mystery play 神蹟劇(中古時代根據聖經事蹟編寫的戲劇)。

mystery ship (or **boat**) = **Q-boat.**

mys·tic 〔ˈmɪstɪk; ˈmistik〕 *adj.* = **mystical.** —*n.* 相信由心靈洞察力能了解眞理或上帝之人;神祕主義者;神祕家。

mys·ti·cal 〔ˈmɪstɪkl; ˈmistikəl〕 *adj.* ①不可思議的; 神祕的。②作爲精神上之象徵的。③神祕家的;神祕主義的。④祕密之宗教儀式的。**—ly,** *adv.*

mys·ti·cism 〔ˈmɪstəˌsɪzəm; ˈmistisizəm〕 *n.* ①神祕主義。②相信眞理或上帝可由心靈洞察力了解之學說。③模糊之思想或空論。

mys·ti·fi·ca·tion 〔ˌmɪstəfəˈkeʃən; ˌmistifiˈkeiʃən〕 *n.* ①迷惑; 困惑; 神祕; 難解。②神祕難解之事;騙局。

mys·ti·fy 〔ˈmɪstəˌfaɪ; ˈmistifai〕 *v.t.,* **-fied, -fy·ing.** ①故意使迷惑;使困惑。②使神祕;使難解。

mys·tique 〔mɪsˈtik; misˈtiːk〕 *n.* ①神祕性; 神祕的氣息; 神祕的氣氛。②神祕的技巧。③神祕之儀式。

***myth** 〔mɪθ; miθ〕 *n.* ①神話。the realm of *myth*. 神話的世界。②任何虛構之故事。③虛構的人或物。

myth. ①mythological. ②mythology.

myth·ic 〔ˈmɪθɪk; ˈmiθik〕 *adj.* = **mythical.**

myth·i·cal 〔ˈmɪθɪkl; ˈmiθikl〕 *adj.* ①神話的;神話中的。②假的; 虛構的; 想像的。

—ly, *adv.*

myth·i·cism 〔'mɪθəsɪzəm; 'miθisizəm〕 *n.* 神話之解釋。

myth·i·cize 〔'mɪθə,saɪz; 'miθisaiz〕 *v.t.*, **-cized, -ciz·ing.** 視爲神話;解釋爲神話。

myth·o·log·i·cal 〔,mɪθə'lɑdʒɪkḷ; ,miθə'lɔdʒikəl〕 *adj.* 神話(學)的。—**ly,** *adv.*

my·tho·lo·gist 〔mɪ'θɑlədʒɪst; mi'θɔlədʒist〕 *n.* 神話學家;神話作者。

my·thol·o·gize 〔mɪ'θɑlə,dʒaɪz; mi'θɔlədʒaiz〕 *v.*, **-gized, -giz·ing.** —*v.t.* = **mythicize.** —*v.i.* ①作神話;說神話。②對神話加以分類或解釋。

***my·thol·o·gy** 〔mɪ'θɑlədʒɪ; mi'θɔlədʒi〕 *n., pl.* **-gies.** ①神話之集合稱。Greek *mythology.* 希臘神話。②神話學。③虛假宣傳。the *mythology* of Fascism. 法西斯主義的虛假宣傳。

myth·o·ma·ni·a 〔,mɪθə'menɪə; ,miθə'meiniə〕 *n.* 誇大狂;渲染狂。

myth·o·ma·ni·ac 〔,mɪθə'menɪæk; ,miθə'meiniæk〕 *n.* 有誇大狂者; 有渲染狂者。—*adj.* 有誇大癖的。

myth·o·p(o)e·ic 〔,mɪθə'piɪk; ,miθə'pi:ik〕 *adj.* ①創作神話的;神話時代的。②產生神話的。

myx·(o)e·de·ma 〔,mɪksɪ'dimə; ,miksi'di:mə〕 *n.* 〖醫〗黏液水腫;黏液腺瘤。

N

N or **n** 〔ɛn; en〕 *n., pl.* **N's** or **n's.** ①英文字母之第十四個字母。 ②〖數學〗不定數。

N ①nitrogen. ②North; Northern.

N. ①North; Northern. ②November. ③Navy. ④New. ⑤Noon. ⑥Nationalist. ⑦Norse. **n.** ①north; northern. ②noun. ③neuter. ④noon. ⑤nominative. ⑥new. ⑦number.

'n 〔ən, ṇ; ən, ṇ〕 *conj.* ①=**and.** sugar *'n* spice. 糖和香料。② =**than.** hotter *'n* blazes. 熱於火。

-n 〖字尾〗① **-en** 在 -er 後之變體。②**-an** 在母音後之變體。 **Na** 化學元素 natrium (拉=sodium)之符號。 **N.A.** ①National Academy. ②National Army. ③North America. **NAA, N.A.A.** National Aeronautic Association. **NAACP, N.A.A.C.P.** National Association for the Advancement of Colored People. **N.A.A.U.** National Amateur Athletic Union.

nab 〔næb; næb〕 *v.t.*, **nabbed, nab·bing.** 〖俗〗①猛然抓住;突攫;偸。②逮捕;捉住。

NAB, N.A.B. National Association of Broadcasters.

na·bob 〔'nebɑb; 'neibɔb〕 *n.* ①(蒙兀兒帝國時代印度之) 土著總督。②在印度發財後歸國之歐洲人。③富豪;大富翁。

Na·both 〔'nebɑθ; 'neibɔθ〕 *n.* 〖聖經〗拿伯(耶斯列人, Ahab 王所羡慕之葡萄園主人,因不應所求而被殺,見列王紀上21章)。

na·celle 〔nə'sɛl; nə'sel〕 *n.* ①(汽球之)吊籃。②〖航空〗(飛機、飛船等之)艙。

na·cre 〔'nekɚ; 'neikə〕 *n.* 珍珠母;青貝;雲母殼;生珍珠母的貝。

na·cred 〔'nekɚd; 'neikəd〕 *adj.* ①(貝殼內側) 有珍珠母的; 被雲母殼包着的。②=**nacreous.**

na·cre·ous 〔'nekrɪəs; 'neikriəs〕 *adj.* ①〖動物〗珍珠母的; 似珍珠母的。②珍珠光澤的;燦爛的。③生珍珠母的。

NAD ①no appreciable disease. ②nothing abnormal discovered.

na·dir 〔'nedɚ; 'neidiə〕 *n.* ①天底 (爲 zenith 之對)。②最低點;最壞之地步。to be at the *nadir* of one's hope. 希望極爲渺茫。

nae 〔ne; nei〕 *adj.* & *adv.* 〖蘇〗=**no, not.**

nae·vus 〔'nivəs; 'ni:vəs〕 *n., pl.* **-vi** 〔-vaɪ; -vai〕. 〖醫〗痣;斑痣。

nag¹ 〔næg; næg〕 *v.*, **nagged, nag·ging,** *n.* —*v.t.* 對…絮聒不休地責罵或抱怨。—*v.i.* ①絮聒不休地責罵或抱怨〖常at〗。②造成痛苦、不適、精神萎靡等〖常 at〗。—*n.* ①絮聒不休。②絮聒不休地責罵或抱怨之人。

nag² *n.* ①供騎用的小馬。②〖俗〗馬。③駑馬;老馬。

Na·ga·sa·ki 〔,nægə'sɑkɪ; ,nægə'sɑ:ki〕 *n.* 長崎 (日本九州西部之一海港)。

nag·ger 〔'nægɚ; 'nægə〕 *n.* 絮聒不休者;好嘮叨的人;愛咒罵的女人;潑婦。

nag·ging 〔'nægɪŋ; 'nægiŋ〕 *adj.* 嘮叨罵人的; 挑剔的。(亦作 **naggish, naggy**)

Na·go·ya 〔nɑ'gojɑ; nɑ:'goujɑ:〕 *n.* 名古屋(日本本州南部之一城市)。

Nah. Nahum.

Na·ha 〔'nɑhɑ; 'nɑ:hɑ:〕 *n.* 那霸 (琉球之首府)。

Na·hum 〔'neəm, 'nehʌm; 'neihəm〕 *n.* 〖聖經〗① 那鴻 (紀元前七世紀之希伯來預言家)。②(舊約中之)那鴻書。

nai·ad 〔'neæd; 'naiæd〕 *n., pl.* **-ads, -a·des.** ①(亦作 **Naiad**)〖希臘、羅馬神話〗保護河泉的女神;水精。②年輕的女游泳者。

na·ïf, na·if 〔nɑ'if; nɑ:'i:f〕 *adj.* =**naive.**

‡nail 〔nel; neil〕 *n.* ①釘子。to pull out a *nail.* 將釘拔出。②手或足指甲;鳥獸之爪。***a nail in one's coffin*** 減壽的東西;催命的東西。Every glass of spirits you take is *a nail in your coffin.* 你所喝的每一杯烈酒都在縮短你的壽命。***as hard as nails*** (身體)結實的;壯碩的;冷酷的(心)。***fight tooth and nail*** 盡全力以攻擊。***hit the nail on the head*** 中的;得其要領;一針見血。***on the nail*** **a.** 立卽;立刻。**b.** 在討論中。***to the nail*** 完全地;徹底地。—*v.t.* ①用釘釘牢。to *nail* the cover on a box. 把箱蓋釘牢。②使固定;使不動。Surprise *nailed* him to the spot. 驚愕使他呆立不動。③〖俗〗抓住;捕獲。The police *nailed* him with the goods. 警察將他人贓俱獲。④〖俗〗覺察或揭發(謊言、虛僞等)。⑤〖俚〗偸。to *nail* an apple. 偸蘋果。⑥〖俚〗打;擊中。***nail a lie to the counter*** 揭露謊言; 拆穿西洋鏡。***nail (a person) down*** 使(某人)履行諾言;使某人負責任。***nail down*** 〖俗〗使成定案;斷然取得或贏得。***nail one's colors to the mast*** 表示決不讓步、投降或承認錯誤等。***nail up*** **a.** 釘牢。**b.** 關緊。

nail-bit·ing 〔'nel,baɪtɪŋ; 'neil,baitiŋ〕 *n.* ①因焦慮而咬指甲的行爲。②焦慮;焦躁。—*adj.* 引起焦慮的。

nail·brush 〔'nel,brʌʃ; 'neilbrʌʃ〕 *n.* 指甲刷。

nail·er 〔'nelɚ; 'neilə〕 *n.* ①製釘者; 釘匠。②敲釘子的人。③〖俚〗非常優秀的東西(人或動物);熱心工作的人〖on, to〗;(競賽等之)能手;好手〖at〗. ***as busy as a nailer*** 忙得很。***work like a nailer*** 〖俗〗工作快而有

勁。

nail·er·y ['nelərɪ; 'neiləri] *n., pl.* **-er·ies.** 製釘所。

nail file 指甲銼刀。

nail·head ['nel,hɛd; 'neilhed] *n.* ①釘頭。②釘頭裝飾。

nail·ing ['nelɪŋ; 'neiliŋ] *adj.* ①敲釘用的。②【俚】極好的;出色的。

nail puller 拔釘器。

nail scissors (or **nippers**) 指甲刀。

nail set 壓釘桿(將釘頭壓至低於平面的短鋼桿)。(亦作 **nailset**)

nail-sick ['nel,sɪk; 'neilsik] *adj.* ①因釘孔過多而失去强度的。②由釘孔漏水的。

nain·sook ['nensuk; 'neinsuk] *n.* (原產印度之)一種薄棉布。

na·ïve, na·ive [nɑ'iv; nɑː'iːv] *adj.* ①像孩子的; 天眞的; 質樸的。 a *naive* girl. 天眞的姑娘。②輕信的;缺乏經驗或判斷力的。③沒有受過科班訓練的; 缺乏高度藝術的。 ④自然的。—**ly,** *adv.*

na·ïve·té, na·ive·te [nɑ,iv'te; nɑː'iːvtei] *n.* ①天眞;質樸。②天眞的話或行爲。

na·ïve·ty, na·ive·ty [nɑ'ivtɪ; nɑː'iːvti] *n., pl.* **-ties.** =**naïveté.**

na·ked** ['nekɪd; 'neikid] *adj.* ①裸體的。*naked* savages. 裸體的野蠻人。②未遮蓋的。*naked* trees. 禿樹。③顯然的;明白的。 the *naked* truth. 顯然的事實。④貧乏的。*naked* belief. 貧乏的信仰。 ⑤缺少的 【of】. hands *naked* of rings. 沒帶戒指的手。⑥【法律】未經證實的。a *naked* confession. 未經證實的供詞。⑦【植物】(種子)無包皮的;(莖、葉等)無細毛的;光滑的。⑧【動物】無羽毛的;無毛裘的。see*** (***something***) ***with the naked eye*** 以肉眼看物。***stark naked*** 全裸;一絲不掛。

na·ked·ly ['nekɪdlɪ; 'neikidli] *adv.* ①無遮蓋地; 顯然地; 明白地; 坦率地。②就…本身。③赤裸地; 暴露地; 無防禦地。④不足地;不完全地。

na·ked·ness ['nekɪdnɪs; 'neikidnis] *n.* ①赤裸; 裸出; 露出。②顯明;明白;坦率。③【聖經】陰部 (=privates).

NAM, N.A.M. National Association of Manufacturers.

nam·a·ble ['neməbḷ; 'neiməbl] *adj.* ①可指名的;可命名的。②値得提及的;値得紀念的。(亦作 **nameable**)

nam·by-pam·by ['næmbɪ'pæmbɪ; 'næmbi'pæmbi] *adj., n., pl.* **-bies.** —*adj.* ①靡弱傷感的。②柔弱的;娘娘腔的。③不徹底的; 不果斷的。—*n.* ①娘娘腔的男人; 傷感的人。②靡弱的傷感;傷感的詩文;傷感的談話。

‡**name** [nem; neim] *n., v.,* **named, nam·ing,** *adj.* —*n.* ①名字; 名稱。first (Christian, *or* given) *name.* 名。last(*or* family) *name.* 姓。What is your (his, etc.) *name?* 你的(他的等)名字叫甚麼? ②辱罵之字;辱罵之話。③名譽; 聲望。 We want men with *names* rather than men with money. 我們要有聲望的人,不要有錢的人。④名人。the great *names* in history. 歷史上的名人。⑤一族;一家;一門。***by name*** **a.** 叫做; 就名字上。I probably know him by sight but not *by name.* 我或許認識他的面貌, 但不知道他的名字。**b.** 以指名的方式。***call*** (***a person***) ***names*** 辱罵。He *called you names.* 他辱罵你。***Give a dog a bad name and hang him.*** 給某人以惡名,那惡名卽永難洗淸。***in name*** 就名義上說。***in the name of*** **a.** 爲…之緣故。**b.** 爲; 替。I speak *in the name of* others. 我爲別人發言。***name names*** 指名。***to one's name*** 屬於某人名下。—*v.t.* ①命名。 The place was *named* after him. 這地方以他爲名。②稱;呼(名字)。③說出某物之名稱。Can you *name* these flowers? 你能說出這些花的名稱嗎? ④提及。He *named* several reasons. 他提出數種原因。⑤訂。to *name* the day. 訂定日期(擇定婚事吉辰等)。 ⑥提名。 They *named* Smith for president. 他們提名史密斯做主席。⑦指控。He was *named* as the thief. 他被控爲賊。⑧(英國下議院議長)指控(某議員)行爲越規。—*adj.* ①用以標示名字的。a leather *name* tag. (繫於行李箱匣等物上的)皮製名牌。②用做標題的。③有名的;著名的。

name·a·ble ['neməbḷ; 'neiməbl] *adj.* =**namable.**

name·board ['nem,bord, –,bɔrd; 'neimbɔːd, –bɔəd] *n.* ①物名牌;地名牌。②用油漆等塗在某物上的名字(如船側之船名)。

name-call·ing ['nem,kɔlɪŋ; 'neim,kɔːliŋ] *n.* 誹謗;中傷。—**name-call·er,** *n.*

name·child ['nem,tʃaɪld; 'neimtʃaild] *n.* 用某人名字命名的小孩。

named [nemd; neimd] *adj.* 有名的;著名的。

name day ①和本人同名的聖徒紀念日。②命名日;受洗日。

name-drop ['nem,drɑp; 'neimdrɔp] *v.i.,* **-dropped, -drop·ping.** (在談話或書信中)高攀名人顯要以擡高身價。—**per,** *n.*

name-drop·ping ['nem,drɑpɪŋ; 'neimdrɔpiŋ] *n.* name-drop 之作風。

***name·less** ['nemlɪs; 'neimlis] *adj.* ①無名的。 *nameless* heroes. 無名英雄。②不可名狀的; 沒有名稱的。I was seized by a *nameless* horror. 我爲莫可名狀的恐懼所控制。③匿名的;隱名的。④不宜說明的;不齒的。*nameless* vices. 爲人所不齒的惡行。⑤不著名的;默默無聞的。⑥私生的。

***name·ly** ['nemlɪ; 'neimli] *adv.* 卽; 就是。The railroad connects two cities, *namely,* New York and Chicago. 這鐵路聯結兩個城市,卽紐約和芝加哥。—*adj.* 【蘇】有名的;著名的。

name of the game (問題的)核心;重點。

name plate ①(門上之)名牌。②報刊等之刊頭。(亦作 **nameplate**)

nam·er ['nemə; 'neimə] *n.* 命名者;呼名者。

name·sake ['nem,sek; 'neimseik] *n.* ①同名的人或物。②從他人之名而取名者。

Nan·cy ['nænsɪ; 'nænsi] *n.* 女子名。

nan·keen, nan·kin [næn'kin; næŋ'kiːn] *n.* ①南京棉花; 紫花布。②(*pl.*) 紫花布製之長褲。③紫花布色;淡黃色。④(N-) 白底藍花之中國細磁。

Nan·king [næn'kɪŋ; næn'kiŋ] *n.* 南京市(中華民國首都)。

nan·ny ['nænɪ; 'næni] *n., pl.* **-nies.** ①【英】(亦作 **nannie**)奶媽。②(亦作 **nanny goat**) 母山羊。

nano- 【字首】表"矮小","十億分之一"之義(在母音前用 **nan-**).

na·no·me·ter ['nenə,mitə; 'neinə,miːtə] *n.* 十億分之一公尺。

na·no·sec·ond ['nenə,sɛkənd; 'neinə,sekənd] *n.* 一秒的十億分之一。

na·no·watt ['nenə,wɑt; 'neinəwɔt] *n.* 十億分之一瓦特。

***nap¹** [næp; næp] *n., v.,* **napped, nap·ping.** —*n.* 小睡;微睡。to take (have, *or* get) a *nap.* 稍睡片刻。—*v.i.* ①小睡;稍睡。②不注意; 無準備。 —*v.t.* 將…在小睡中度過

〖常 away〗. I *napped* the afternoon away. 我睡了一整個下午。

nap² *n.* (絨布等上的)細毛。—*v.t.* 植毛於「(織物等)上。」

nap³ *n.* =**napoleon** ①及②。

nap⁴ *v.t.*, **napped, nap·ping.** 〖俚〗攫取；握住；抓住；偸竊。

na·palm ['nepɑm; 'neipɑ:m] *n.* 燃燒彈、火焰噴射器等所用之膠態汽油；汽油彈。

nape [nep, næp; neip] *n.* 頸背。

na·per·y ['nepərɪ; 'neipəri] *n.* 桌布；餐巾；餐桌用之小布巾。

naph·tha ['næpθə, 'næfθə; 'næfθə, 'næpθə] *n.* ①石油精。②=**petroleum.**

naph·tha·lene ['næfθə,lin; 'næfθəli:n] *n.* =**naphthalin(e).**

naph·tha·lin(e) ['næfθəlɪn; 'næfθəlin] *n.* 〖化〗萘；石腦油精 ($C_{10}H_8$)。

naph·thol ['næfθol; 'næfθoul] *n.* 〖化〗萘酚 ($C_{10}H_7OH$, 用作防腐劑及染料之原料)。

***nap·kin** ['næpkɪn; 'næpkin] *n.* ①餐巾(用餐時蓋於膝上之布)。②似餐巾之物(如小毛巾、尿布等)。

Na·ples ['neplz; 'neiplz] *n.* 那不勒斯(義大利西南部海岸之一海港，以其美麗的海灣著名)。(義亦作 **Napoli**)

na·po·le·on [nə'poljən, -lɪən; nə'pouljən, -liən] *n.* ①昔法國之一種金幣(=20 francs)。②一種紙牌遊戲。③一種多層而夾奶油的法國點心。

Na·po·le·on Bo·na·parte [~ 'bonə,pɑrt; ~'bounəpɑ:t] =**Napoleon I.**

Na·po·le·on I 拿破崙一世 (1769–1821, 法國皇帝，在位期間 1804–15)。

Na·po·le·on·ic [nə,polɪ'ɑnɪk; nə,pouli'ɔnik] *adj.* 法帝拿破崙一世 (Napoleon Bonaparte)的；似拿破崙(一世)的；其時期的。

nap·per¹ ['næpɚ; 'næpə] *n.* 打瞌睡「者；習慣睡午覺的人。」

nap·per² *n.* ①(織物之)植毛機。②使織物起毛之工人。

nap·per³ *n.* 〖俚，英方〗頭。

nap·py ['næpɪ; 'næpi] *n.*, *pl.* **-pies.** 〖英〗「〖俗〗尿布。」

narc, nark [nɑk; nɑ:k] *n.* 〖美俚〗專門執行違反麻醉毒品法之刑警(爲 narcotic agent, narcotic detective 之略)。

nar·ce·ine ['nɑrsɪ,in; 'nɑ:sii:n] *n.* 〖化〗二十三炭罌粟鹼；那碎因 ($C_{23}H_{27}NO_8$)。

nar·cism ['nɑr,sɪzəm; 'nɑ:sizəm] *n.* =**narcissism.** —**nar·cist,** *n.*

nar·cis·sism [nɑr'sɪs,ɪzəm; nɑ:'sisizəm] *n.* ①自我陶醉；自我崇拜。②〖精神分析〗自體觀窺慾；自愛慾。—**nar·cis·sist,** *n.*

Nar·cis·sus [nɑr'sɪsəs; nɑ:'sisəs] *n.*, *pl.* **-sus·es, -cis·si** [-'sɪsaɪ; -'sisai]. ①男子名。②〖希臘神話〗那西塞斯(一美少年，因自戀其水中之影，卒致憔悴而化爲水仙花)。③〖植物〗水仙屬。④(n-)〖植物〗水仙屬之植物；水仙。

nar·co·a·nal·y·sis [,nɑrkoə'nælɪsɪs; ,nɑ:kouə'nælisis] *n.* 麻醉分析法(於輕麻醉之下進行精神分析)。

nar·co·lep·sy ['nɑrkə,lɛpsɪ; 'nɑ:kə,lepsi] *n.* 〖醫〗頻睡病；發作性睡病；麻醉樣昏睡。

nar·co·sis [nɑr'kosɪs; nɑ:'kousis] *n.* 〖醫〗麻醉法；麻醉狀態。

nar·co·syn·the·sis [,nɑrko'sɪnθɪsɪs; ,nɑ:kou'sinθisis] *n.* 麻醉綜合法(利用麻醉劑治療精神錯亂)。

***nar·cot·ic** [nɑr'kɑtɪk; nɑ:'kɔtik] *n.* ①麻醉劑；催眠藥。to sleep with the aid of *narcotic.* 藉安眠藥之助而眠。②吸毒者；有毒癮者。—*adj.* ①麻醉的；催眠的。a *narcotic* lecture. 乏味而使人欲睡的演講。②麻醉劑的。③治吸毒者用的。

nar·co·tine ['nɑrkə,tin; 'nɑ:kəti:n] *n.* 〖化〗那可汀 ($C_{22}H_{23}NO_7$, 罌粟鹼之一種)。

nar·co·tism ['nɑrkə,tɪzəm; 'nɑ:kətizəm] *n.* ①麻醉狀態；昏睡。②麻醉作用。③使用麻醉劑之癖好。

nar·co·tize ['nɑrkə,taɪz; 'nɑ:kətaiz] *v.*, **-tized, -tiz·ing.** —*v.t.* ①使麻醉；施以麻醉劑。②使麻木。—*v.i.* 產生麻醉作用。

nard [nɑrd; nɑ:d] *n.* ①〖植物〗甘松。②甘松香。

na·res ['nɛriz; 'neiri:z] *n.* pl. of **na·ris.** 「['nerɪs; 'neiris].〖解剖〗鼻孔。」

nar·g(h)i·le ['nɑrgəlɪ; 'nɑ:gili] *n.* (東方之)水煙袋。(亦作 **nargileh**)

nark [nɑrk; nɑ:k] *n.* ①〖英俚〗密探；線民。②〖主澳俚〗掃興之人。—*v.i.* ①〖英俚〗密告；作密探；作線民。②〖主澳俚〗使不樂。***nark it*** 〖英俚〗別作聲；停止。

nar·ra·tage ['nærətɪdʒ; 'nærətidʒ] *n.* 旁白(指電影、電視及戲劇)。

nar·rate [næ'ret; næ'reit] *v.*, **-rat·ed, -rat·ing.** —*v.t.* & *v.i.* 敍述；說明。—**nar·ra·tor, nar·rat·er,** *n.*

***nar·ra·tion** [næ'reʃən; næ'reiʃən] *n.* ①敍述。The bare *narration* of the fact took two hours. 單是這事實的敍述已花了兩小時。②故事。a long *narration.* 一個長故事。③敍述文；敍事文。

***nar·ra·tive** ['nærətɪv; 'nærətiv] *n.* ①故事。②敍述；講述。—*adj.* 敍述的；敍事的。a *narrative* poem. 一首敍事詩。—**ly,** *adv.*

‡**nar·row** ['næro; 'nærou] *adj.* ①窄的。a *narrow* path. 窄路。②有限制的；範圍窄的。the *narrowest* sense of a word. 一個字最狹小的意義。③勉强的；間不容髮的。a *narrow* escape. 驚險的逃脫。④褊狹的。He has a *narrow* mind. 他胸襟褊狹。⑤精密的；仔細的。a *narrow* scrutiny. 細察；詳審。⑥貧乏的。a *narrow* majority. 僅超過極少數之多數。⑦〖語音〗狹窄音的；窄喉而發音的(如 e, i 等)。⑧有限的；少量的。*narrow* resources. 有限的資源。⑨〖英方〗小器的；吝嗇的。—*n.* ①(場所或物品之)狹窄部分。②(常 *pl.*)海峽；山峽；隘路。—*v.t.* & *v.i.* ①使狹窄；變窄；變細。The sea *narrows* into a strait. 海洋變窄而形成一海峽。②使眼光狹窄。Living in the countryside has *narrowed* him. 住在鄉下使他眼光變窄了。—**ly,** *adv.* —**ness,** *n.*

nar·row-gauge ['næro'gedʒ, 'nærə-; 'nærougeidʒ] *adj.* ①〖鐵路〗狹軌的。②〖俗〗心地褊狹的；氣量小的。(亦作 **narrow gage**)

narrow gauge 窄軌(兩軌之間距離不到56½英寸的標準寬度)。

nar·row-mind·ed ['næro'maɪndɪd; 'nærou'maindid] *adj.* 心地褊狹的；氣量小的；有偏見的。

nar·whal ['nɑrhwəl; 'nɑ:wəl] *n.* 〖動物〗一角鯨。(亦作 **narwal, narwhale**)

nar·y ['nɛrɪ, 'nerɪ; 'neri, 'neiri] *adj.* 〖方，俗〗=**not any, no** (與冠詞 a 或 an 連用)。

NAS, N.A.S. National Academy of Sciences. **NASA, N.A.S.A.** National Aeronautics and Space Administration. 美國國家航空及太空總署。

na·sal ['nezl; 'neizəl] *adj.* ①鼻的；鼻中的；自鼻而出的。②〖語音〗鼻音的。—*n.* ①

〖語音〗鼻音;鼻音字。②鼻骨。—**ly,** *adv.*

na·sal·i·ty 〔ne'zælətɪ; nei'zæliti〕 *n.* 鼻音(性)。

na·sal·ize 〔'nezḷ,aɪz; 'neizəlaiz〕 *v.,* **-ized, -iz·ing.** —*v.t.* 發以鼻音; 鼻音化。—*v.i.* 以鼻音發聲。—**na·sal·i·za·tion,** *n.*

nas·cen·cy 〔'næsṇsɪ; 'næsnsi〕 *n.* 發生;初生;起源。

nas·cent 〔'næsṇt; 'næsnt〕 *adj.* ①初生的;初期的; 發生中的。②〖化〗新生態的; 初發機的。

na·stur·tium 〔næ'stɝʃəm; nəs'tə:ʃəm〕 *n.* 〖植物〗蔊菜。

***nas·ty** 〔'næstɪ; 'nɑ:sti〕 *adj.,* **-ti·er, -ti·est,** *n.* —*adj.* ①骯髒的;汚穢的。a *nasty* room. 骯髒的屋子。②淫猥的。 a *nasty* mind. 卑鄙的心思。③極不愉快的;不爽快的。*nasty* weather. 不爽快的天氣。④危險的;帶有威脅的。⑤引起麻煩的;尷尬的。⑥不易對付的;危險的。a *nasty* problem. 一個不易解決的難題。⑦討人厭的。a *nasty* child. 一個討厭的孩子。—*n.* 危險的人或物。—**nas·ti·ly,** *adv.* —**nas·ti·ness,** *n.*

nat. ①national. ②native. ③natural. ④naturalist. ⑤naturalized. ⑥natus (拉=born).

na·tal 〔'netḷ; 'neitl〕 *adj.* ①誕生的;出生的。②〖詩〗故土的;故鄉的。

na·tal·i·ty 〔ne'tælətɪ; nei'tæliti〕 *n.* ①出生率(=birth rate). ②出生。

na·tant 〔'netṇt; 'neitənt〕 *adj.* 游泳的;漂浮於水上的。

na·ta·tion 〔ne'teʃən; nei'teiʃən〕 *n.* 游泳;游泳術。

na·ta·to·ri·al 〔,netə'torɪəl; ,neitə'tɔ:riəl〕 *adj.* 游泳的; 適於游泳的。*natatorial* birds. 水鳥。(亦作 **natatory**)

na·ta·to·ri·um 〔,netə'torɪəm; ,neitə'tɔ:riəm〕 *n., pl.* **-ri·ums, -ri·a** 〔-rɪə, -riə〕. (室內之)游泳池。

na·tes 〔'netiz; 'neiti:z〕 *n.pl.* 〖解剖〗臀;臀部。

‡**na·tion** 〔'neʃən; 'neiʃən〕 *n.* ①國家。The United States of America is a *nation.* 美利堅合衆國是一個國家。②民族。the Chinese *nation.* 中華民族。

‡**na·tion·al** 〔'næʃənḷ; 'næʃənl〕 *adj.* ①國家的; 國民的。②全國性的。 a *national* drive. 一個全國性運動。③國立的。 a *national* school. 一所國立學校。④限於一國的。—*n.* 國民。American *nationals* in China. 居留中國的美國人。

National Aeronautics and Space Administration 美國國家航空及太空總署。

national anthem 國歌。

National Assembly ①(中國之)國民大會。②(若干國家中之)下議院。

national debt 國債。

national forest 國有林。

National Guard 美國各州的國民兵。

national holiday 國定假日。

national income 〖經濟〗國民所得。

na·tion·al·ism 〔'næʃənḷ,ɪzəm; 'næʃənəlizəm〕 *n.* ①國家主義; 民族主義; 愛國心。②國有主義(一種社會主義,主張所有工業歸政府所有及控制)。③民族之特性。

na·tion·al·ist 〔'næʃənḷɪst; 'næʃənəlist〕 *n.* 國家主義者; 民族主義者。—*adj.* ①國家主義(者)的; 民族主義(者)的。②(N-)中華民國的。

na·tion·al·is·tic 〔,næʃənḷ'ɪstɪk; ,næʃənə'listik〕 *adj.* 國家主義(者)的;民族主義(者)的。—**al·ly,** *adv.*

***na·tion·al·i·ty** 〔,næʃən'ælətɪ; ,næʃə'næliti〕 *n., pl.* **-ties.** ①國家; 國民。men of all *nationalities.* 各國人民。②國籍。a ship of unknown *nationality.* 一艘不明國籍之船。He changed his *nationality.* 他變更了他的國籍。③國風; 國情; 國民性。*Nationalities* tend to submerge and disappear in a metropolis. 在一個大都市中各種民族特性有淹沒而消失的傾向。④國家之地位;獨立。After the American Revolution the colonies attained *nationality.* 在美國革命後,這些殖民地獲得了獨立。

na·tion·al·i·za·tion 〔,næʃənḷɪ'zeʃən; ,næʃənəlai'zeiʃən〕 *n.* ①國家化。②收歸國有。③歸化。

na·tion·al·ize 〔'næʃənḷ,aɪz; 'næʃənəlaiz〕 *v.t.,* **-ized, -iz·ing.** ①使國家化;歸化。②使(土地、工業、鐵路等)歸國有。③使成爲國家。—**na·tion·al·iz·er,** *n.*

na·tion·al·ly 〔'næʃənḷɪ; 'næʃənəli〕 *adv.* ①由全國民;舉國一致; 從國家立場;以國家爲本位。②遍及全國。

national park 國家公園。

National Socialist Party (德國之)國家社會黨(即希特勒創立之納粹黨)。

na·tion-wide 〔'neʃən,waɪd; 'neiʃənwaid〕 *adj.* 普遍全國的;全國性的。

‡**na·tive** 〔'netɪv; 'neitiv〕 *n.* ①本地人。Are you a *native* of this place? 你是此地人嗎?②土著;不甚開化之人。③土產的動物或植物。 The kangaroo is a *native* of Australia. 袋鼠是澳洲的土產動物。—*adj.* ①生於某地或某國的。②本國的;本土的;本民族的。 one's *native* land. 本國。③生來的;自然的;天賦的。*Native* salt is refined for use. 自然鹽精煉以供食用。④土人的;未開化人民的。⑤土產的;土著的。 Banana is *native* to Taiwan. 香蕉是臺灣的土產。⑥未加修飾的;樸實的。⑦純淨的。 *native* copper. 純銅。⑧土著居住或統治的。 **go native** 過土人的生活。—**ly,** *adv.* —**ness,** *n.*

na·tive-born 〔'netɪv'bɔrn; 'neitiv'bɔ:n〕 *adj.* 土著的;本地生的;本國生的。

na·tiv·ism 〔'netɪvɪzṃ; 'neitivizm〕 *n.* ①〖政治〗土著保護政策(主義)。②〖哲學〗先天論;天性論。—**na·tiv·ist,** *n.* —**na·tiv·is·tic,** *adj.*

na·tiv·i·ty 〔ne'tɪvətɪ; nə'tiviti〕 *n., pl.* **-ties.** ①出生;誕生。②(the N-) 基督的誕生;基督誕生圖;耶誕節。③算命;天宮圖。

NATO, N.A.T.O., Nato 〔'neto; 'neitou〕 *North Atlantic Treaty Organization.* 北大西洋公約組織。

na·tri·um 〔'netrɪəm; 'neitriəm〕 *n.* 〖化〗鈉(符號 Na).

na·tron 〔'netrɑn; 'neitrən, -rɔn〕 *n.* 〖礦〗天然炭酸鈉;鈉鹼 ($Na_2CO_3 \cdot 10H_2O$).

nat·ter 〔'nætɚ; 'nætə〕 *v.i.* ①口出怨言;埋怨。②〖主英〗喋喋不休。—*n.* 〖英〗閒談。

nat·ter·jack 〔'nætɚ,dʒæk; 'nætədʒæk〕 *n.* 〖動物〗(西歐產之)一種蟾蜍。

nat·ty 〔'nætɪ; 'næti〕 *adj.,* **-ti·er, -ti·est.** ①整潔的;乾淨的;整飾的。②靈巧的;敏捷的。 —**nat·ti·ly,** *adv.* —**nat·ti·ness,** *n.*

‡**nat·u·ral** 〔'nætʃərəl; 'nætʃrəl, -tʃur-〕 *adj.* ①天然的; 自然的; 非人造的。 *natural* gas. 天然煤氣。Coal and oil are *natural* products. 煤與油是天然產物。②本能的; 天賦的。*natural* ability. 本能。*natural* gifts.

天賦的才能。③正常的;不勉强的。a *natural* death. 壽終正寢(非橫死)。④(因環境、局勢等)必然的;當然的。a *natural* response. 必然的反應。⑤本能地認爲對的或公正的。*natural* law. 自然法則;天理。⑥像自然的。⑦自然的;不矯揉造作的。It was a very *natural* piece of acting. 這次演出很自然。⑧關於自然的。*natural* sciences. 自然科學。⑨與自然科學有關的。⑩根據從自然中所學得者的。*natural* religion. 自然教(崇拜自然界之現象者)。⑪〖音樂〗本位音的。⑫不合法出生的。—*n.* ①自然物。②〖音樂〗**a.** 本位音。**b.** 本位記號(♮)。**c.** (鋼琴、風琴等之)白鍵。③白癡。④〖俗〗天生的專家;天才。⑤〖俗〗必定的成功。—**ness,** *n.*

nat·u·ral-born [ˈnætʃərəlˈbɔrn; ˈnætʃrəlˈbɔːn] *adj.* 當地生的;生來就有…權利的;生來的;天生的。

natural child 非婚生子;私生子。

natural childbirth 不用藥物的生產。

natural history ①博物學。②有關「博物學的書。」

nat·u·ral·ism [ˈnætʃərəl,ɪzəm; ˈnætʃrəlizəm] *n.* 自然主義;本能主義。

***nat·u·ral·ist** [ˈnætʃərəlɪst; ˈnætʃrəlist] *n.* ①博物學者。②自然主義者;極端寫實的作家或藝術家。

nat·u·ral·is·tic [,nætʃərəlˈɪstɪk; ,nætʃrəˈlistik] *adj.* ①順從自然的;自然主義的;寫實的。②〖宗教〗自然論的。③博物學(者)的。—**al·ly,** *adv.*

nat·u·ral·ize [ˈnætʃərəl,aɪz; ˈnætʃrəlaiz] *v.t.,* **-ized, -iz·ing.** ①使歸化;使入籍。He was *naturalized* as a British subject. 他歸化爲英國國民。②採用(外語、異俗)。③移植。④使自然化。⑤認爲係自然的。⑥使習慣於。⑦用自然現象解釋。—*v.i.* ①歸化。②變得像當地人一樣。③從事博物學研究。—**nat·u·ral·i·za·tion,** *n.*

‡**nat·u·ral·ly** [ˈnætʃərəlɪ; ˈnætʃrəli] *adv.* ①自然地。She speaks *naturally*. 她談話自然。②天然地;天生地。He is a *naturally* quiet child. 他天生是個安靜的孩子。③必然地;未出所料地。④不用人工地。Plants grow *naturally* in such a good climate. 在這種氣候良好的地方,植物能自然生長。

natural philosophy ①物理學。「②物質世界之研究。」

natural resources 天然資源。

natural selection 物競天擇;自然淘汰。

natural sign 〖音樂〗本位記號。

natural year 太陽年 (365日 5 時48分 46 秒)。

‡**na·ture** [ˈnetʃɚ; ˈneitʃə] *n.* ①自然。the laws of *nature.* 自然律。②自然之道;人情;常理。You cannot go against *nature.* 你不能違反人情。③自然之生活;無虛飾之生活。④天性;本性;性質;性情。She has a sweet *nature.* 她有溫和的性情。⑤種類;樣子。That is a book of the same *nature.* 那是一本同種類的書。⑥實際;實況。true to *nature.* 符合實際;逼眞。⑦有特性之人。She is a gentle *nature.* 她是一個溫良的人。⑧體軀;精力。⑨率眞之德行。⑩天生的慾望或生理機能。⑪未開化的狀態。***by nature*** 天生地;天性地。He is timid *by nature.* 他天生怯儒。***in a state of nature*** 裸體。***in the course of nature*** 根據事物之常規。***in*** (or ***of***) ***the nature of*** 類似。His request was *in the nature of* a command. 他的請求跡近命令。***pay the debt of nature*** (or ***pay one's debt to nature***) 死。—**like,** *adj.*

-natured 〖字尾〗表"有…性質或性情的"之義,如: good-*natured*.

nature study 自然現象之硏究。

nature worship 自然崇拜;對自然現象之崇拜。

na·tur·op·a·thy [,netʃəˈrɑpəθɪ; ,neitʃəˈrɔpəθi] *n.* 自然療法。

naught** [nɔt; nɔːt] *n.* ①無。All my work came to *naught.* 我所有的工作都無用了。②零;0。bring to naught*** 破壞;擊敗。***care naught for*** 對…毫不關心;認爲…毫無用處或毫無價值。***set at naught*** 藐視。—*adj.* ①失去的;毀壞了的。②〖古〗無用的;無價值的。(亦作 **nought**)

***naugh·ty** [ˈnɔtɪ; ˈnɔːti] *adj.,* **-ti·er, -ti·est.** ①頑皮的;淘氣的。a *naughty* child. 頑皮的孩子。②不妥的;不適當的。—**naugh·ti·ly,** *adv.* —**naugh·ti·ness,** *n.*

Na·u·ru [nɑˈuru; nɑːˈuːruː] *n.* 諾魯(近赤道之太平洋小島國,於1968年獨立)。

nau·se·a [ˈnɔʒə, ˈnɔzɪə, ˈnɔsɪə; ˈnɔːsjə, ˈnɔːʃiə] *n.* ①反嘔;作嘔;惡心。②暈船。③極端的嫌惡;厭惡。

nau·se·ate [ˈnɔʒɪ,et; ˈnɔːsieit] *v.,* **-at·ed, -at·ing.** —*v.t.* ①使作嘔。②厭惡。—*v.i.* 想嘔;感到惡心。—**nau·se·a·tion,** *n.*

nau·se·at·ing [ˈnɔʒɪ,etɪŋ; ˈnɔːsieitiŋ] *adj.* 使人作嘔的;使人厭惡的。—**ly,** *adv.*

nau·seous [ˈnɔʒəs, -zɪəs; ˈnɔːsjəs, -siəs] *adj.* ①令人作嘔的。②令人厭惡的。—**ly,** *adv.* —**ness,** *n.*

naut. nautical(ly).

nautch [nɔtʃ; nɔːtʃ] *n.* (印度舞女之)舞蹈表演。***nautch girl*** (印度的職業性)舞女。

nau·ti·cal [ˈnɔtɪkl̩; ˈnɔːtikəl] *adj.* 船舶的;船員的;航海的。—**ly,** *adv.*

nau·ti·lus [ˈnɔtl̩əs; ˈnɔːtiləs] *n., pl.* **-lus·es, -li** [-,laɪ; -lai]. ①〖動物〗鸚鵡螺。②〖動物〗魟魚。③(N-) 鸚鵡螺號原子潛艇(美國海軍潛艇及世界第一艘核子動力船)。

nav. ①naval. ②navigable. ③navigation. ④navy.

Nav·a·ho, Nav·a·jo [ˈnævə,ho; ˈnævəhou] *n., pl.* **-hos, -hoes.** 拿佛和人(居於美國 Arizona, New Mexico, 及Utah 各州保留地之一支印第安主要種族)。—*adj.* 拿佛和人的;拿佛和風俗或語言的。

***na·val** [ˈnevl̩; ˈneivəl] *adj.* ①海軍的;軍艦的。*naval* supplies. 海軍補給。②有海軍的;有艦隊的。the *naval* powers. 海軍强國。—**ly,** *adv.* —**ist,** *n.*

Na·varre [nəˈvɑr; nəˈvɑː] *n.* 那瓦爾(昔位於法國西南部與西班牙北部之一王國)。

nave [nev; neiv] *n.* ①教堂的中部;本堂。②(車)轂。

na·vel [ˈnevl̩; ˈneivəl] *n.* ①肚臍。②中央;中心。—**like,** *adj.*

nav·i·cert [ˈnævɪ,sɝt; ˈnævisəːt] *n.* 航海證明書(證明該船係友好或中立國之船隻,且未載運違禁品)。

navig. ①navigation. ②navigator.

nav·i·ga·bil·i·ty [,nævəgəˈbɪlətɪ; ,nævigəˈbiliti] *n.* 可航行;(船之)耐航性。

nav·i·ga·ble [ˈnævəgəbl̩; ˈnævigəbl] *adj.* ①(河、海等)可航行的;適於航行的。②(船隻等)可航行的;耐航的。③(船隻)可駕駛的;可操縱的。—**nav·i·ga·bly,** *adv.*

nav·i·gate [ˈnævə,get; ˈnævigeit] *v.,* **-gat·ed, -gat·ing.** —*v.t.* ①駕駛(船隻、飛

機等)。②航行(海、河等)。③以水運運(貨)。④航行(空中)。—*v.i.* ①航行。②駕駛;領航。

***nav·i·ga·tion** 〔ˌnævəˈgeʃən; ˌnæviˈgeiʃən〕 *n.* ①航海;航行。②航海術;航海學;航空術。—**al,** *adj.*

***nav·i·ga·tor** 〔ˈnævəˌgetɚ; ˈnævigeitə〕 *n.* ①航海者。②精於航海術者。③海上探險者。④(飛機)領航員。⑤〖英〗苦力;濬河工人;修築鐵路工人。

nav·vy 〔ˈnævɪ; ˈnævi〕 *n., pl.* **-vies,** *v.,* **-vied, -vy·ing.** —*n.* 〖英〗鑿河或修路的工人;無特殊技術之工人;粗工。—*v.t.* 挖掘。

***na·vy** 〔ˈnevɪ; ˈneivi〕 *n., pl.* **-vies.** ①海軍。He serves in the *navy.* 他服務於海軍。②海軍人員。③〖古,詩〗艦隊。④深藍色。

navy blue 深藍色。

na·vy-blue 〔ˈnevɪˌblu; ˈneivibluː〕 *adj.* 深藍色的。

Navy Cross 〖美海軍〗英勇十字章。

Navy Exchange 海軍基地福利商店。

navy yard 海軍船塢;海軍工廠。

na·wab 〔nəˈwɑb; nəˈwɑːb〕 *n.* ① = **nabob.** ②(N-) 印度回教王子或顯貴之尊稱。

***nay** 〔ne; nei〕 *adv.* ①〖古〗不;否。②不只於此;而且 (=not only that, but also). —*n.* ①不;否;反對;拒絕。②(投)反對票(者)。The tally was three ayes and two *nays.* 投票結果是三票贊成兩票反對。

Naz·a·rene 〔ˌnæzəˈrin; ˌnæzəˈriːn〕 *adj.* 拿撒勒 (Nazareth) 的;拿撒勒人的。—*n.* ①拿撒勒人。②(the -) 基督。③〖廢〗基督教徒。④拿撒勒教徒(早期基督教之一派)。

Naz·a·reth 〔ˈnæzərəθ; ˈnæzəriθ〕 *n.* 拿撒勒(以色列北部之一小城,爲耶穌之故鄉)。

Naz·a·rite 〔ˈnæzəˌraɪt; ˈnæzərait〕 *n.* ①古代希伯來之虔信者。②〖罕〗= **Nazarene.** (亦作 **Nazirite**)

naze 〔nez; neiz〕 *n.* 岬;岬角;海角。(亦作 **nase**)

Na·zi 〔ˈnɑtsɪ; ˈnɑːtsi〕 *n., pl.* **Na·zis,** *adj.* —*n.*納粹黨人;法西斯黨人。—*adj.* 納粹黨人的。

Na·zi·fi·ca·tion 〔ˌnɑtsɪfɪˈkeʃən; ˌnɑːtsifiˈkeiʃən〕*n.*納粹化。(亦作 **nazification**)

Na·zi·fy 〔ˈnɑtsɪˌfaɪ; ˈnɑːtsifai〕 *v.t.,* **-fied, -fy·ing.** 使納粹化。(亦作 **nazify**)

Na·zism 〔ˈnɑtsɪzəm; ˈnɑːtsizəm〕 *n.*德國國家社會主義;納粹主義。(亦作 **Naziism**)

Nb 化學元素 niobium 的符號。

N.B., n.b. nota bene (拉=note well) 注意。

NBC, N.B.C. National Broadcasting Corporation *or* Company. (美國) 國家廣播公司。**NbE** north by east. **NbW** north by west. **N.C.** ①North Carolina. ②New Church. **NCO, N.C.O.** noncommissioned officer. **Nd** 化學元素 neodymium 之符號。**N.D., N. Dak.** North Dakota. **n.d.** ①no date. ②not dated. ③no delivery. **Ne** 化學元素 neon 之符號。 **NE, n.e.** northeast; northeastern. **N.E.** ① New England. ② northeast; northeastern.

né 〔ne; nei〕〖法〗 *adj.* 原名的;舊姓的。

Ne·an·der·thal 〔nɪˈændɚˌtɑl; niˈændətɑːl〕 *adj.* 尼安德塔人的。

Neanderthal man 尼安德塔人 (1857 年於德國 Neanderthal 河流域發現的舊石器時代之猿人)。

neap 〔nip; niːp〕 *n.* ①小潮;最低潮。②〖俗〗貨車之轅桿。—*adj.* 小潮的。

Ne·a·pol·i·tan 〔ˌniəˈpɑlətn̩; niəˈpɔlitən〕 *adj.* ①義大利那不勒斯 (人) 的。②具有數層之不同顏色與香味的。 ***Neapolitan ice cream*** 分色冰淇淋。—*n.* 那不勒斯人。

‡near 〔nɪr; niə, njəː〕 *adv.* ①近 (爲 far 之對); 不遠地。Come *near.* 走近些。②密切地;親近地。*near* allied nations. 密切聯盟的國家。③〖俗〗幾乎;差不多。④(航海) 靠近風向。 ***be near at hand*** **a.** 在近旁;近在咫尺。**b.** 逼近;卽將發生。The New Year's Day *is near at hand.* 新年就要來臨。***come near doing*** (or ***to do***) ***something*** 差不多做了某件事。The army *came near obtaining* a complete victory. 陸軍差不多得到了全盤勝利。—*adj.* ①近的。 The post office is quite *near.* 郵局甚近。②親密的;親近的。He is my *near* friend. 他是我的密友。③近親的。④短的;直接的。We came by the *nearest* route. 我們從最短的路線來的。⑤勉强的;間不容髮的。a *near* escape. 倖免。⑥左方的 (爲 off 與 right 之對)。The *near* horse and the off horse made a team. 左方的馬和右方的馬成爲一組(聯畜)。⑦近似的;極像的。 ⑧慳吝的。 He's very *near* with his money. 他對於金錢很慳吝。⑨有密切關係的。—*prep.* (空間、時間等) 接近;近。—*v.t.* & *v.i.* 走近;行近。The ship *neared* the land. 這船駛近陸地。

***near·by**〔*adv.* ˈnɪrˈbaɪ; ˈniəˈbai *adj.* ˈnɪrˌbaɪ; ˈniəbai〕 *adj.* & *adv.* 近旁的(地);附近的 (地)。They live *nearby.* 他們住在附近。

Ne·arc·tic 〔nɪˈɑrktɪk; niˈɑːktik〕 *adj.* 〖動物、植物、地理〗新北帶的。

Near East 近東。

‡near·ly 〔ˈnɪrlɪ; ˈniəli〕 *adv.* ①幾乎;近乎 (爲quite之對)。I *nearly* missed the train. 我幾乎誤掉那班車。②密切地;親近地。 This matter concerns you very *nearly.* 此事對你的關係很密切。③親密地。 They are *nearly* related. 他們是近親。④精密地;仔細地。⑤吝嗇地;慳吝地。 ***not nearly*** 絕不;相差甚遠。$200 will *not* be *nearly* enough for my journey. 二百元遠不够我旅行之用。

near-miss 〔ˈnɪrˈmɪs; ˈniəˈmis〕 *n.* ①未直接命中目標。②雖不够理想,但還算差强人意之事。③倖免於難。

near·ness 〔ˈnɪrnɪs; ˈniənis〕 *n.* ①(距離或時間之)近;接近。②親密;密切;親近。③吝嗇。④近似。

near-sight 〔ˈnɪrˌsaɪt; ˈniə-sait〕*n.*近視。

near-sight·ed 〔ˈnɪrˈsaɪtɪd; ˈniəˈsaitid〕 *adj.* 近視的。 —**ly,** *adv.* —**ness,** *n.*

***neat**[1] 〔nit; niːt〕 *adj.* ①整潔的;整齊的。She is always *neat* and tidy. 她總是整潔的。②好整潔的;會乾淨的。③優雅的;雅致的。It is a *neat* design. 此爲優雅的設計。④靈巧的;精巧的。⑤〖英〗(酒)純粹的。⑥簡潔的;巧妙的;得要領的。She gave a *neat* answer. 她作了一個簡潔的回答。⑦〖俚〗很棒的;美妙的。Boy, that's a *neat* car! 嗨,那部車眞棒!⑧淨的。*neat* profits. 淨利。—**ly,** *adv.* —**ness,** *n.*

neat[2] *n. sing.* or *pl.* 牛類動物;牛。—*adj.* 牛類的。

neath, 'neath 〔niθ, nið; niːθ, niːð〕 *prep.* 〖詩〗= **beneath.**

neat-hand·ed 〔ˈnitˈhændɪd; ˈniːtˈhændid〕 *adj.* 手頭兒靈活的。

neat·herd 〔ˈnitˌhɝd; ˈniːthəːd〕 *n.* 牧牛者。

neb 〔nɛb; neb〕 *n.* ①(鳥之)嘴;喙。②(動物之)鼻。③尖;尖端;筆尖。④臉;口。

NEbE northeast by east.

Nebr. Nebraska.

Ne·bras·ka [nəˈbræskə; niˈbræskə] *n.* 內布拉斯加(美國中部之一州,首府爲Lincoln).
Ne·bras·kan [nəˈbræskən; niˈbræskən] *adj.* 美國 Nebraska 州的。—*n.* Nebraska 州人或居民。
Neb·u·chad·nez·zar [ˌnɛbjəkədˈnɛzɚ; ˌnebjukədˈnezə] *n.* 〖聖經〗尼布加尼撒(巴比倫 Chaldean 王)。
neb·u·la [ˈnɛbjələ; ˈnebjulə] *n., pl.* **-lae** [-ˌli; -liː], **-las.** ①〖天文〗星雲。②〖醫〗角膜薄翳;雲翳。③〖醫〗尿之渾濁。④〖藥〗噴霧劑。—**neb·u·lar,** *adj.*
nebular hypothesis 〖天文〗星雲假說。
neb·u·lize [ˈnɛbjəˌlaɪz; ˈnebjulaiz] *v.t.,* **-lized, -liz·ing.** ①使成霧狀。②噴藥水在(傷處)。
neb·u·los·i·ty [ˌnɛbjəˈlɑsətɪ; ˌnebjuˈlɔsiti] *n., pl.* **-ties.** ①星雲狀。②星雲狀物;星雲。③(思想等之)漠然;曖昧;模糊;渾濁。
neb·u·lous [ˈnɛbjələs; ˈnebjuləs] *adj.* ①模糊的; 渾濁的。②雲霧狀的。③星雲的;星雲狀的。(亦作 **nebulose**) —**ly,** *adv.* —**ness,** *n.*
nec·es·sar·i·an [ˌnɛsəˈsɛrɪən; ˌnesəˈsɛəriən] *n., adj.* =**necessitarian.**
***nec·es·sar·i·ly** [ˈnɛsəˌsɛrəlɪ, ˌnɛsəˈsɛrəlɪ; ˈnesisərili, ˌnesiˈserili] *adv.* ①必要地;必須地。No, not *necessarily.* 不,不一定如此。②必然地。War *necessarily* causes misery and waste. 戰爭必引起痛苦與毀壞。
‡**nec·es·sar·y** [ˈnɛsəˌsɛrɪ; ˈnesisəri, -səs-] *adj., n., pl.* **-sar·ies.** —*adj.* ①必須的;必要的;必然的。Death is a *necessary* end. 死爲必然的結局。②〖邏輯〗不能否定的。—*n.* ①必需品; 必要之物。daily *necessaries* 日用必需品。②(*pl.*)〖法律〗(眷屬或無行爲能力人所需之)衣食住必需品。 ***the necessary*** 金錢。
necessary evil 不願意見其發生然又不可避免之事。
ne·ces·si·tar·i·an [nɪˌsɛsɪˈtɛrɪən; niˌsesiˈtɛəriən] *n.* 宿命論者; 必然論者。—*adj.* 宿命論(者)的。(亦作 **necessarian**)
ne·ces·si·tar·i·an·ism [nɪˌsɛsɪˈtɛrɪənɪzəm; niˌsesiˈtɛəriənizm] *n.* 宿命論;必然論;決定論。
***ne·ces·si·tate** [nəˈsɛsəˌtet; niˈsesiteit, neˈs-, nəˈs-] *v.t.,* **-tat·ed, -tat·ing.** ①使成爲必需; 需要。②迫使(主要用於被動式)。No man is *necessitated* to do wrong. 沒有人是被迫去作錯事的。 —**ne·ces·si·ta·tion,** *n.* —**ne·ces·si·ta·tive,** *adj.*
ne·ces·si·tous [nəˈsɛsətəs; niˈsesitəs] *adj.* 窮的;貧困的。—**ly,** *adv.*
‡**ne·ces·si·ty** [nəˈsɛsətɪ; niˈsesiti, neˈs-, nəˈs-] *n., pl.* **-ties.** ①需要; 必要。I am under the *necessity* of doing it. 我必須做此事。②必需品; 必要物。Air, food and water are *necessities.* 空氣、食物與水乃不可缺少者。③貧困。He is now in *necessity.* 他現在很窮。④不可避免之事;必然的事。Night follows day as a *necessity.* 夜以繼晝乃是必然的現象。⑤〖哲學〗必然性。***bow to necessity*** 做被迫而做的事。 ***make a virtue of necessity*** 爽爽快快地去做非做不可的事。 ***Necessity is the mother of invention.*** 需要乃發明之母; 發明皆因需要而產生。 ***Necessity knows no law.*** 需要之前無法律; 饑寒起盜心。 ***of necessity*** 必然;必定;不得已。
‡**neck** [nɛk; nek] *n.* ①頸。②衣領。③似頸之物。④頸肉。⑤〖建築〗柱身之領卷。⑥牙齒之齒根與齒冠間之部分。⑦(賽馬或賽狗等中)一頸之隔的距離。 ***a stiff neck*** 强項;頑强。 ***break one's neck*** 〖俗〗作極大努力。 ***get it in the neck*** a. 受嚴厲懲處;接受痛苦的經驗。Small businesses are *getting it in the neck.* 小企業正大賠其本。b. 被開除;被丟棄。***neck and crop*** (or ***heels***) 迅速而完全地。***neck and neck*** 賽跑時並肩齊驅。 ***neck or nothing*** a. 冒一切危險。b. 孤注一擲。 ***save one's neck*** 得免絞刑;得免一死。***stick one's neck out*** 〖俚〗冒險; 招惹禍事。 ***win by a neck*** 險勝。—*v.i.* 〖美俚〗擁抱;愛撫。—*v.t.* ①强吻;愛撫。②砍…的頭;絞死。
neck·band [ˈnɛkˌbænd; ˈnekbænd] *n.* 圍頸帶;(襯衣等之)領(裝領之部分)。
neck·cloth [ˈnɛkˌklɔθ; ˈnekklɔθ] *n.* =**cravat.**
neck·er·chief [ˈnɛkɚtʃɪf; ˈnekətʃif] *n.* 圍巾;頸巾。
neck·ing [ˈnɛkɪŋ; ˈnekiŋ] *n.* ①〖建築〗柱頂的小嵌線。②〖美俚〗(男女間之) 親吻撫摸。
***neck·lace** [ˈnɛklɪs; ˈneklis] *n.* 頸飾;項鍊。
neck·let [ˈnɛklɪt; ˈneklit] *n.* ①=**necklace.** ②毛皮的圍巾。
neck·line [ˈnɛkˌlaɪn; ˈneklain] *n.* 領口;領圈。
neck·piece [ˈnɛkˌpis; ˈnekpiːs] *n.* ①(衣服之)領。②(甲胄的)圍脖。③毛皮圍巾。
***neck·tie** [ˈnɛkˌtaɪ; ˈnektai] *n.* 領帶。
neck-verse [ˈnɛkˌvɝs; ˈnekvəːs] *n.* (拉丁文舊約中的)免罪詩。(亦作**neck verse**)
neck·wear [ˈnɛkˌwɛr; ˈnek-wɛə] *n.* 圍頸物。
necro- 〖字首〗表"死;屍體"之義。(在母音前作 **necr-**)
ne·crol·o·gist [nɛˈkrɑlədʒɪst; neˈkrɔlədʒist] *n.* (新聞等之)死亡啓事負責人;登記死亡的人。
ne·crol·o·gy [nɛˈkrɑlədʒɪ; neˈkrɔlədʒi] *n.* ①死亡表;死人姓名錄。②死亡啓事;訃聞。—**nec·ro·log·i·cal,** *adj.*
nec·ro·man·cer [ˈnɛkrəˌmænsɚ; ˈnekroumænsə] *n.* 巫師;降神者;行妖術者。
nec·ro·man·cy [ˈnɛkrəˌmænsɪ; ˈnekroumænsi] *n.* ①巫術; 召亡靈以卜未來之術。②魔術;妖術。
nec·ro·man·tic [ˌnɛkrəˈmæntɪk; ˌnekrəˈmæntik] *adj.* 巫術的; 妖術的; 巫術中所使用的。
nec·ro·pho·bi·a [ˌnɛkrəˈfobɪə; ˌnekrəˈfoubiə] *n.* 對死亡或屍體之反常恐怖。
ne·crop·o·lis [nɛˈkrɑpəlɪs; neˈkrɔpəlis] *n.* ①(古代都市之) 墓地。②公共墓地。③史前墳場。—**nec·ro·pol·i·tan,** *adj.*
nec·rop·sy [ˈnɛkrɑpsɪ; ˈnekrɔpsi] *n., pl.* **-sies.** 驗屍。(亦作 **necroscopy**)
ne·cro·sis [nɛˈkrosɪs; neˈkrousis] *n., pl.* **-ses** [-siz; -siːz]. ①〖醫〗壞死;壞疽。②〖植物〗頹壞;黑斑症。
ne·crot·ic [nɛˈkrɑtɪk; neˈkrɔtik] *adj.* ①〖醫〗壞死的;壞疽的。②〖植物〗頹壞的;黑斑症的。
nec·tar [ˈnɛktɚ; ˈnektə] *n.* ①〖希臘神話〗神祇們的飲料;瓊漿玉液。②任何美味的飲料。③花蜜。
nec·tar·ine [ˈnɛktəˌrin; ˈnektərin] *n.* 〖植物〗油桃。
nec·tar·ous [ˈnɛktərəs; ˈnektərəs] *adj.* ①似神酒的; 甘美的。②〖植物〗花蜜的。(亦作 **nectarean, nectareous**)
nec·ta·ry [ˈnɛktərɪ; ˈnektəri] *n., pl.* **-ries.** ①〖植物〗蜜槽;蜜腺。②(昆蟲的)蜜管。

Ned 〔nɛd; ned〕 *n.* 男子名 (Edward, Edmund, Edgar 之暱稱)。

N.E.D., NED New English Dictionary (現稱 Oxford English Dictionary).

NEDC National Economic Development Council (of England).

ned·dy 〔ˈnɛdɪ; ˈnedi〕 *n., pl.* **-dies.** ①(常 N-) 驢; 愚人; 蠢貨。②〖俚〗=life preserver ②.

nee, née 〔ne; nei〕〖法〗*adj.* 娘家姓…的 (置於已婚女子之姓後, 以示其婚前之姓)。

ː̣need 〔nid; niːd〕 *n.* ①缺乏; 缺少。②缺少之物; 必需之物。③必要; 必須。There is no *need* to hurry. 無匆促之必要。④困難之境; 困難之時。A friend in *need* is a friend indeed. 患難之交始爲眞朋友。⑤極端之窮困。Most people were in great *need*. 大多數人在窮困中。***be in need of*** 需要。He *is in need of* money. 他需要錢。***have need to*** 必須; 務必 (=must). ***if need be*** 如果必須的話 (=if it has to be). —*v.t.*①需要(幾與 want 之義相等)。This is what he *needs* most. 此爲他最需要者。②必要。Does he *need* to know? 他必定要知道嗎? —*v.i.* ①必要。He *needn't* go (or He doesn't *need* to go) now. 他不必現在去。②〖古〗需要(用於無人稱結構中)。There *needs* no apology. 無辯解之必要。③窮困。Give to those that *need*. 賙濟貧窮之人。〖注意〗參看 **dare.**

need·ful** 〔ˈnidfəl; ˈniːdful〕 *adj.* ①必須的; 需要的。to do what is *needful*. 做必須做的事。②〖古〗窮乏的。—*n.* 所需之事物。do the needful*** 做該做的事。***the needful*** **a.** 必需之物。**b.**〖俚〗錢。—**ly,** *adv.* —**ness,** *n.*

need·i·ness 〔ˈnidɪnɪs; ˈniːdinis〕 *n.* 窮困; 貧窮。

ː̣nee·dle 〔ˈnidl̩; ˈniːdl〕 *n., v.,* **-dled, -dling.** —*n.* ①針。to thread a *needle*. 穿線於針。She made her living by her *needle*. 她靠做針線度日。②織針。③磁針。④注射針。⑤(松樹等之)針狀葉。⑥(留聲機)唱針。⑦(雕刻用的)針狀刻刀。⑧尖岩; 尖峯; 方尖塔(=obelisk)。⑨針狀活塞。⑩任何針狀物。⑪〖俗〗注射。***give (one) the needle*** 〖俗〗刺激; 激動。***have the pins and needles*** 發麻。***look for a needle in a bundle of hay*** 大海撈針。***the needle*** 揶揄; 喝倒采。—*v.t.* ①揶揄; 嘲弄; 激勵。We *needled* her into going with us. 我們揶揄她逼得她跟我們一起走。②〖俚〗加酒精於(飲料)。—*v.i.* ①用針縫紉。②結晶成針狀。—**like,** *adj.*

needle bath 噴霧狀淋浴。

nee·dle·book 〔ˈnidl̩ˌbuk; ˈniːdlbuk〕 *n.* 針簿(插針用之布片簿)。

nee·dle·case 〔ˈnidl̩ˌkes; ˈniːdlkeis〕 *n.* 針匣子。

nee·dle·fish 〔ˈnidl̩ˌfɪʃ; ˈniːdlfiʃ〕 *n., pl.* **-fish, -fish·es.** ①一種長嘴硬鱗之海魚。②楊枝魚。

nee·dle·ful 〔ˈnidl̩ˌful; ˈniːdlful〕 *n., pl.* **-fuls.** 一次用針適當長度之線。

needle gun 撞針槍。

needle point ①針尖; 針狀物之尖端。②針織花邊。③以毛線在帆布上刺繡之繡品。

nee·dle-point 〔ˈnidl̩ˌpɔɪnt; ˈniːdlpɔint〕 *adj.* 針織花邊的。

need·less** 〔ˈnidlɪs; ˈniːdlis〕 *adj.* 不需要的; 不必要的。If one is enough, the second although useful is *needless*. 假如一個便够, 第二個縱然有用, 也不需要了。needless to say*** 不待言; 無須乎說。—**ly,** *adv.* —**ness,** *n.*

needle valve 〖機械〗針形閥; 針狀活門。

nee·dle·wom·an 〔ˈnidl̩ˌwumən; ˈniːdlˌwumən〕 *n., pl.* **-wom·en.** 做針線活的女人; (尤指)女裁縫。

nee·dle·work 〔ˈnidl̩ˌwɝk; ˈniːdlwəːk〕 *n.* 縫紉; 刺繡; 女紅。(亦作 **needlecraft**) —**er,** *n.* 「處是針的; 充滿了針的。

nee·dly 〔ˈnidlɪ; ˈniːdli〕 *adj.* 如針的; 到

need·ments 〔ˈnidmənts; ˈniːdmənts〕 *n. pl.* 必需品(特指旅行時所携者)。

need·n't 〔ˈnidn̩t; ˈniːdnt〕 =**need not.**

***needs** 〔nidz; niːdz〕 *adv.* 必要地; 一定地。A soldier *needs* must go where duty calls. 職責所在, 一個軍人是必須要去的。He must *needs* go away when I wanted him. 我需要他的時候, 他却偏偏堅持要走。〖注意〗**needs**與**must**二字連用。但如needs放在 must 之後, 則有諷刺的語氣。

need·y 〔ˈnidɪ; ˈniːdi〕 *adj.,* **need·i·er, need·i·est.** 貧窮的。a *needy* family. 貧窮人家。the poor and *needy*. 貧窮的人。

ne'er 〔nɛr; nɛə〕 *adv.* 〖詩〗never 之縮寫。

ne'er-do-well 〔ˈnɛrduˌwɛl; ˈnɛəduːˌwel〕 *n.* 無用之人; 無益之人。—*adj.* 無益的; 無用的。

ne·far·i·ous 〔nɪˈfɛrɪəs; niˈfɛəriəs〕 *adj.* 兇惡的; 邪惡的。—**ly,** *adv.* —**ness,** *n.*

neg. ①negative. ②negatively.

ne·gate 〔ˈniget; niˈgeit〕 *v.t.,* **-gat·ed, -gat·ing.** 否定; 否認; 取消; 使無效。

ne·ga·tion 〔nɪˈgeʃən; niˈgeiʃən〕 *n.* ①否定; 否認。②反對; 拒絕。③反面。④不存在之物; 虛無。⑤反駁。—**al,** *adj.*

neg·a·tive** 〔ˈnɛgətɪv; ˈnegətiv〕 *adj., n., v.,* **-tived, -tiv·ing.**—*adj.* ①否定的; 拒絕的。②消極的。*negative* attitude. 消極的態度。③減的; 負的。*negative* sign. 負號(—)。a *negative* quantity. 負數。④〖電〗陰性的。*negative* electrode. 陰極。*negative* pole. 陰極。⑤〖照相〗明暗相反的; 底片的。⑥無病菌或徵候的。—*n.* ①否定; 否認。Two *negatives* make an affirmative. 兩個否定成爲一個肯定。②(辯論中)反對之一面。③否定的回答、手勢等。④拒絕。to answer a request with a *negative*. 拒絕請求。⑤陰電; 陰極。⑥底片; 乾片。⑦負數; 負量。⑧否決權。in the negative*** 表示反對。The answer is *in the negative*. 回答是否定。—*v.t.* ①否定; 反對。②反駁。③否認。④抵銷。—**ly,** *adv.* —**ness,** *n.*

neg·a·tiv·ism 〔ˈnɛgətɪvˌɪzəm; ˈnegətivizəm〕 *n.* ①〖哲學〗否定論; 消極主義。②〖心理〗反抗癖; 反對傾向。

neg·a·tiv·ist 〔ˈnɛgətɪvɪst; ˈnegətivist〕 *n.* 否定論者; 消極主義者。—*adj.* 否定論(者)的; 消極主義(者)的。

neg·a·tiv·i·ty 〔ˌnɛgəˈtɪvətɪ; ˌnegəˈtiviti〕 *n.* 否定性; 消極性; 陰性。

neg·a·to·ry 〔ˈnɛgəˌtorɪ; ˈnegətəri〕 *adj.* 否定的; 消極的。

neg·a·tron 〔ˈnɛgəˌtrɑn; ˈnegətrɔn〕 *n.* 〖理化〗陰電子(爲 positron 之對)。

***neg·lect** 〔nɪˈglɛkt; niˈglekt〕 *v.t.* ①疏忽; 忽略。He *neglected* his health. 他疏忽了他的健康。②棄置; 不顧; 置而不爲。③遺漏。Don't *neglect* to water the plants. 不要忘了澆花木。—*n.* 疏忽; 忽略; 不留心。He lost his position owing to *neglect* of duty. 他因疏於職守而被撤職。—**er,** *n.*

neg·lect·ful 〔nɪˈglɛktfəl; niˈglektful〕 *adj.* 不留心的; 疏忽的。—**ly,** *adv.* —**ness,** *n.*

né·gli·gé [negliˈʒe; ˈnegliːʒei] 〖法〗 *n., adj.* =**negligee.**
neg·li·gee [ˌnɛglɪˈʒe; ˈnegliːʒei] *n.* ①寬大的女用便服。②便服;長衣。—*adj.* ①服飾不整的。②隨便的;輕率的。
***neg·li·gence** [ˈnɛglədʒəns; ˈneglidʒəns] *n.* ①疏忽;過失。The accident was due to *negligence*. 這次意外乃由於疏忽。②粗心;大意。③疏忽的結果;混亂。—*adj.* 因疏忽造成他人損害,依民法負賠償責任的。
***neg·li·gent** [ˈnɛglədʒənt; ˈneglidʒənt] *adj.* ①疏忽的。He is *negligent* in his business. 他疏忽他的事務。②粗心的; 大意的。③不在意的;瀟灑的。—**ly,** *adv.*
neg·li·gi·ble [ˈnɛglədʒəbl; ˈneglidʒibl] *adj.* 可忽略的; 不足取的; 不關重要的; 很小的。—**neg·li·gi·bil·i·ty, —ness,** *n.*
ne·go·ti·a·bil·i·ty [nɪˌgoʃɪəˈbɪlətɪ; niˌgouʃjəˈbiliti] *n.* ①可磋商性。②可轉讓性;可流通性。③可通行性。
ne·go·ti·a·ble [nɪˈgoʃɪəbl; niˈgouʃiəbl] *adj.* ①可磋商或談判的。②可轉讓的(尤指票據而言)。③可通行的(指道路、河流)。
ne·go·ti·ant [nɪˈgoʃɪənt; niˈgouʃiənt] *n.* =**negotiator.**
***ne·go·ti·ate** [nɪˈgoʃɪˌet; niˈgouʃieit] *v.,* **-at·ed, -at·ing.** —*v.t.* ①商議;商訂(條件等)。②出售;讓渡。③〖俗〗通過;經過。—*v.i.* 磋商;談判。to *negotiate* with someone for something. 與某人協商某事。
***ne·go·ti·a·tion** [nɪˌgoʃɪˈeʃən; niˌgouʃiˈeiʃən] *n.* ①談判;磋商。to enter into *negotiations* with the enemy for a treaty of peace. 與敵人開始作和約之談判。②準備;安排。
ne·go·ti·a·tor [nɪˈgoʃɪˌetɚ; niˈgouʃieitə] *n.* ①商議者; 磋商者; 談判者。②出售者;讓渡者。③〖廢〗交易者;商人。
Ne·gress [ˈnigrɪs; ˈniːgris] *n.* Negro 之女性。
Ne·gril·lo [nɪˈgrɪlo; neˈgrilou] *n., pl.* **-los.** 非洲中南部之小黑人。
Ne·gri·to [nɪˈgrito; neˈgriːtou] *n., pl.* **-tos, -toes.** (特指南洋地方或非洲中南部之)小黑人。—*adj.* 小黑人的。
***Ne·gro** [ˈnigro; ˈniːgrou] *n., pl.* **-groes,** *adj.* —*n.* ①黑人。②有黑人血統之有色人種。—*adj.*黑人的。the *Negro* race. 黑種人。〖注意〗**Negro** 及其衍生字昔均爲小寫, 今常作大寫。
ne·gro·head [ˈnigrəˌhɛd; ˈniːgrəhed] *n.* ①黑色烟草餅。②一種粗樹膠。
Ne·groid [ˈnigrɔɪd; ˈniːgrɔid] *adj.* (亦作 **Negroidal**)(有時 n-) 黑人的;似黑人的;有黑人之特性的。—*n.* (有時 n-)準黑人。
Ne·gro·phile [ˈnigrəˌfaɪl; ˈniːgrəfail] *n.* (有時 n-) 親近或左祖黑人者;主張黑人應獲得平等權利者。(亦作 **Negrophil**)
Ne·groph·i·lism [nɪˈgrɑfəlɪzm; niˈgrɔfilizm] *n.* (有時 n-) 親近或左祖黑人。
Ne·gro·pho·bi·a [ˌnigrəˈfobɪə; ˌniːgrəˈfoubiə] *n.*(有時n-)恐懼黑人;憎惡黑人。
Ne·gus [ˈnigəs; ˈniːgəs] *n.* ①Ethiopia 皇帝之尊稱。②(n-) Ethiopia 王族之尊稱。
ne·gus [ˈnigəs; ˈniːgəs] *n.* 尼加斯酒(以葡萄酒、開水、糖、豆蔻及檸檬汁等製成)。
Neh. Nehemiah.
Ne·he·mi·ah [ˌniəˈmaɪə; ˌniːiˈmaiə] *n.* 〖聖經〗①尼希米(紀元前五世紀之希伯來領導者)。②尼希米記(舊約聖經之一書)。
Neh·ru [ˈneru; ˈnɛəruː] *n.* 尼赫魯 (Jawaharlal, 1889–1964, 於 1947–1964 任印度總理)。
***neigh** [ne; nei] *n.* 馬嘶聲。—*v.i.* (馬)嘶。
‡neigh·bo(u)r [ˈnebɚ; ˈneibə] *n.* ①鄰人;鄰居。next-door *neighbors*. 隔壁鄰居。②相近之人; 鄰近之物。③同胞。The Bible says, "Love thy *neighbor* as thyself." 聖經上說, "愛你的同胞, 像愛你自己一樣。" ④心地仁慈樂於助人者。⑤對陌生人之招呼。—*v.t.* ①鄰接;相鄰。The wood *neighbors* the lake. 樹林鄰近這湖。②使接近;使靠近。—*v.i.* ①鄰接;相鄰。The wood *neighbors* upon the lake. 樹林鄰近這湖。②友好;友善〖常 with〗.—*adj.* 鄰近的;相鄰的。one of our *neighbor* nations. 鄰國之一。
neigh·bo(u)r·hood** [ˈnebɚˌhud; ˈneibəhud] *n.* ①鄰近之地區; 附近之地方。I am a stranger in (*or* to) this *neighborhood*. 我對這附近很陌生。②區域; 地方。③鄰人; 四鄰。The whole *neighborhood* was there. 四鄰都在那裏。④鄰居之情誼;善鄰的行爲。⑤近;接近。in the neighborhood of*** 在…之附近; 近於。She looks to be *in the neighborhood of* 40. 她看上去年約40左右。—*adj.* 鄰近的;鄰區的。
***neigh·bo(u)r·ing** [ˈnebərɪŋ; ˈneibəriŋ] *adj.* 鄰近的;附近的;鄰界的。France and Germany are *neighboring* countries. 法、德爲鄰國。
neigh·bor·less [ˈnebɚlɪs; ˈneibəlis] *adj.* 無鄰人的;孤獨的。
neigh·bor·li·ness [ˈnebɚlɪnɪs; ˈneibəlinis] *n.* 親善;和睦。
neigh·bo(u)r·ly [ˈnebɚlɪ; ˈneibəli] *adj.* 親善的;和睦的。
neigh·bor·ship [ˈnebɚˌʃɪp; ˈneibəʃip] *n.* 鄰人關係。
‡nei·ther [ˈniðɚ, ˈnaɪðɚ; ˈnaiðə, ˈniːðə] *conj.* 既非;既不;亦非。You shall not eat of it, *neither* shall you touch it. 你不許吃它, 也不許你動它。***neither...nor...*** 既非…亦非…。—*adj.* 兩不的;皆不。*Neither* book is satisfactory. 兩本書都不令人滿意。—*pron.* 二者都不。I liked *neither*. 我兩個都不喜歡。〖注意〗以 **neither...nor** 爲連接詞句中之動詞, 須與 nor 後之主詞一致, 例如: *Neither* you *nor* I am wrong. 你和我均未錯。
nek [nɛk; nek] *n.*〖南非〗(山之)鞍部;山峽。
nek·ton [ˈnɛktɑn; ˈnektɔn] *n.* 〖動物〗(成羣而不受潮流影響的)游行動物(如魚羣)。
Nell [nɛl; nel] *n.* 女子名 (Helen 之暱稱)。
Nel·lie, Nel·ly [ˈnɛlɪ; ˈneli] *n.* ①男子名 (Nelson 之暱稱)。②=**Nell.**
Nel·son [ˈnɛlsn̩; ˈnelsn] *n.* ①納爾遜 (Viscount Horatio, 1758–1805, 英國海軍上將, Trafalgar 海戰中以戰勝拿破崙而享盛譽, 並在該戰中殉職)。②納爾遜河(加拿大中部之一河流)。
nel·son *n.* 〖摔角〗在對方頭頸後部及臂部加壓力的一種架式。
nem·a·tode [ˈnɛməˌtod; ˈnemətoud] *adj.* 〖動物〗線蟲類的。—*n.* 〖動物〗線蟲類動物;線蟲。
nem. con. nemine contradicente.
nem. diss. nemine dissentiente.
Ne·me·a [ˈnimɪə; ˈniːmiə] *n.* 尼米亞(古希臘東南方 Argolis 區域之一山谷名)。
Ne·me·an games [nɪˈmiən～; niˈmiən～] 每兩年一次在 Nemea 舉行之古希臘祭典(主要節目爲體育及音樂競賽)。
Nem·e·sis [ˈnɛməsɪs; ˈnemisis] *n., pl.* **-ses** [-ˌsiz; -siːz]. ①〖希臘神話〗司復讎的女神。②(n-) 天罰;公正之懲罰;報應;司報應者。

③(n–) 人力所不能克服或達成之事。④强敵。

ne·mi·ne con·tra·di·cen·te ['nɛmənɪˌkɑntrədɪ'sɛntɪ; 'nemini:ˌkɔntrədi'senti:] 〖拉〗無人反對地；全場一致地(= no one contradicting, unanimously).

ne·mi·ne dis·sen·ti·en·te ['nɛmənɪdɪˌsɛnʃɪ'ɛntɪ; 'nemini:diˌsenʃi'enti:] 〖拉〗= **nemine contradicente** (= no one dissenting).

neo- 〖字首〗表"新；新近；新創"之義。

Ne·o·cene ['niəˌsin; 'ni(:)əsi:n] *adj.* 〖地質〗新第三紀的。—*n.* ①新第三紀。②新第三紀形成之岩石。

ne·o·clas·sic [ˌnio'klæsɪk; ˌni(:)ou'klæsik] *adj.* 新古典主義的。(亦作 **neoclassical**)

Ne·o-Dar·win·ism [ˌnio'dɑrwɪnɪzm; ˌni(:)ou'dɑ:winizm] *n.* 新達爾文主義(否定遺傳而主張 Darwin 之天然淘汰說為進化主因，以 Weismann 為代表)。

ne·o·dym·i·um [ˌnio'dɪmɪəm; ˌni(:)ou'dimiəm] *n.* 〖化〗釹(稀土屬金屬元素之一，符號為 Nd)。

ne·o·im·pres·sion·ism [ˌnio·ɪm'prɛʃənˌɪzəm; ˌni(:)ouim'preʃənizm] *n.* 〖美術〗新印象派。(亦作 **Neo-Impressionism**)

Ne·o-Kant·i·an [ˌnio'kæntɪən; ˌni(:)ou'kæntiən] *adj., n.* 〖哲學〗新康德學派的(學者)。

Ne·o-Lat·in [ˌnio'lætn; ˌni(:)ou'lætin] *n.* 新拉丁語。

ne·o·lith ['niəˌlɪθ; 'ni(:)əliθ] *n.* (新石器時代之)新石器。

ne·o·lith·ic [ˌniə'lɪθɪk; ˌni(:)ou'liθik] *adj.* 新石器時代的。(亦作 **Neolithic**)

ne·o·lo·gi·an [ˌnio'lodʒɪən; ˌni(:)ou'loudʒiən] *n.* 〖神學〗= **neologist.**

ne·ol·o·gism [ni'ɑləˌdʒɪzəm; ni(:)'ɔlədʒizəm] *n.* ①使用新語；創造新義。②新語；新字；新義；有新義之詞句。③新說；新主義。④〖神學〗新教義。

ne·ol·o·gist [ni'ɑlədʒɪst; ni(:)'ɔlədʒist] *n.* ①(亦作 **neoterist**) 造新語者；使用新語(義)者。②〖神學〗主張新教義者。

ne·ol·o·gize [ni'ɑləˌdʒaɪz; ni(:)'ɔlədʒaiz] *v.i.*, **-gized, -giz·ing.** ①造新語；用新義。②〖神學〗用新教義。

ne·ol·o·gy [ni'ɑlədʒɪ; ni(:)'ɔlədʒi] *n.* = **neologism.** —**ne·o·log·i·cal,** *adj.*

Ne·o-Mal·thu·si·an·ism [ˌniomæl'θjuzɪənˌɪzəm; ˌni(:)oumæl'θju:zjənizəm] *n.* 新馬爾薩斯主義(主張以節育控制人口，減少罪惡，提高生活水準)。

ne·o·my·cin [ˌniə'maɪsɪn; ˌni:ou'maisin] *n.* 〖藥〗新鏈絲菌素。

ne·on ['niɑn; 'ni:ən] *n.* 〖化〗氖(氣體元素，符號為 Ne)。

ne·o·phyte ['niəˌfaɪt; 'ni(:)oufait] *n.* ①新信徒；新入教者。②初學者；開始者；生手。③〖天主教〗新聖司鐸。④新入修道院者。

ne·o·plasm ['nioplæzm; 'ni(:)ouplæzm] *n.* 〖醫〗新體素之病態生長物；腫瘍；贅瘤；贅疣。

Ne·o·pla·to·nism [ˌnio'pletnˌɪzəm; ˌni(:)ou'pleitənizm] *n.* 〖哲學〗新柏拉圖學派(綜合 Plato 之思想與東方神祕主義，三世紀時興起於 Alexandria)。

ne·o·prene ['niəˌprin; 'ni:əpri:n] *n.* 尼奧普林(一種合成樹膠)。

Ne·o-Ro·man·ti·cism [ˌnioro'mæntəˌsɪzəm; ˌni:ourə'mæntisizəm] *n.* (有時 n–) 新傳奇主義；新浪漫主義。

Ne·o·sal·var·san [ˌnio'sælvəsæn; ˌni(:)ou'sælvəsæn] *n.* 〖藥〗新六〇六(一種梅毒注射劑之商標名，即九一四)。

ne·o·ter·ic [ˌnio'tɛrɪk; ˌni(:)ou'terik] *adj.* 晚近的；新的。—*n.* 現代人；現代作家或思想家。

Ne·o·trop·i·cal [ˌnio'trɑpɪkl; ˌni(:)ou'trɔpikəl] *adj.* 〖地理〗新熱帶地區的。(亦作 **Neotropic**)

Ne·o·zo·ic [ˌniə'zoɪk; ˌni:ə'zouik] *n., adj.* 〖地質〗新生代(的)。

NEP, N.E.P., Nep, nep [nɛp; nep] *n.* = **New Economic Policy.**

Ne·pal [nɪ'pɔl; ni:'pɔ:l] *n.* 尼泊爾(印度與西藏之間的一小國，首都為 Katmandu)。

Ne·pa·li [nɛ'pɑli; ne'pɑ:li:] *n., pl.* **-lis.** ①尼泊爾語。②尼泊爾人。—*adj.* 尼泊爾(人)的。

ne·pen·the [nɪ'pɛnθɪ; ni'penθi] *n.* ①忘憂藥。②使人忘憂之物。—**an,** *adj.*

ne·pen·thes [nɪ'pɛnθiz; ni'penθi:z] *n., pl.* **-thes.** ① = **nepenthe.** ②(N–) 〖植物〗猪籠草屬。

neph·a·nal·y·sis [ˌnɛfə'næləsɪs; ˌnefə'næləsis] *n., pl.* **-ses** [-ˌsiz; -si:z]. 雲分析。

neph·e·line ['nɛfəlɪn; 'nefəlin] *n.* 霞石。

***neph·ew** ['nɛfju, 'nɛvju; 'nevju(:), 'nefju:] *n.* 姪兒；外甥。

ne·phol·o·gy [nɪ'fɑlədʒɪ; ni'fɔlədʒi] *n.* 雲學。

neph·o·scope ['nɛfəˌskop; 'nefəskoup] *n.* 〖氣象〗測雲器。

neph·rite ['nɛfraɪt; 'nefrait] *n.* 軟玉。

ne·phrit·ic [nɛ'frɪtɪk; ne'fritik] *adj.* ①(亦作 **nephric**)腎臟的。②(患)腎臟炎的。

ne·phri·tis [nɛ'fraɪtɪs; ne'fraitis] *n.* 〖醫〗腎炎；腎臟炎。

nephro- 〖字首〗表"腎臟"之義。

neph·ro·lith ['nɛfrəlɪθ; 'nefrəliθ] *n.* 腎結石。

ne·phrop·a·thy [nə'frɑpəθɪ; nə'frɔpəθi] *n.* 腎病。

ne·phro·sis [nɪ'frosɪs; ni'frousis] *n.* 〖醫〗腎病。

ne plus ul·tra ['niplʌs'ʌltrə; 'neiplus'ultrɑ:] 〖拉〗最高點；極點；極致。

ne·pot·ic [nɪ'pɑtɪk; ni'pɔtik] *adj.* 偏袒親戚的；引用親戚的。

nep·o·tism ['nɛpəˌtɪzəm; 'nepətizəm] *n.* 偏袒親戚；引用親戚；族閥主義。

nep·o·tist ['nɛpətɪst; 'nepətist] *n.* 偏袒親戚者；引用親戚者；族閥主義者。

Nep·tune ['nɛptʃun, -tjun; 'neptju:n, -tʃu:n] *n.* ①〖羅馬神話〗海神(希臘神話之 Poseidon)。②海洋(人格化)。③〖天文〗海王星。

Nep·tu·ni·an [nɛp'tjunɪən; nep'tju:njən] *adj.* ①海神 Neptune 的。②海洋的。③海王星的。④(常 n–)〖地質〗水成的。

Nep·tun·ist ['nɛptjunɪst; 'neptjunist] *n.* 〖地質〗水成論者。

nep·tu·ni·um [nɛp'tunɪəm; nep'tju:njəm] *n.* 〖化〗錼(放射性元素，符號 Np)。

Ne·re·id ['nɪrɪɪd; 'niəriid] *n.* ①〖希臘神話〗海的女神；海神 Nereus 的五十個女兒之一。②(n–) 〖動物〗沙蠋；沙蠶。

Ne·re·us ['nɪrus; 'niərju:s] *n.* 〖希臘神話〗海神(Nereids 之父)。

Nernst [nɛrnst; neənst] *n.* 納爾斯特(Walther Hermann, 1864–1941, 德國物理學家及化學家，曾獲1920年諾貝爾化學獎)。

Ne·ro ['niro, 'nɪro; 'niərou] *n.* 尼祿(A.D. 37–68, 羅馬暴君，在位期間54–68)。

ner·o·li ['nɛrəlɪ; 'nɛərəli] *n.* 橙花油(香水原料)。(亦作 **neroli oil**)
Ne·ro·ni·an [nɪ'ronɪən; niə'rouniən] *adj.* ①羅馬帝國暴君 Nero 的。②似 Nero 般暴虐的;殘暴的;專制的。
nerv·ate ['nɝvet; 'nə:veit] *adj.* 【植物】有葉脈的。
ner·va·tion [nɝ'veʃən; nə:'veiʃən] *n.* 【動、植物】(葉或蟲翼之)脈狀;脈序。(亦作 **nervature, neuration**)
nerve** [nɝv; nə:v] *n., v.,* **nerved, nerv·ing.** —*n.* ①神經。②(*pl.*)神經過敏。He suffered from *nerves* in his late years. 他在晚年患神經質。③勇氣;精力;膽力。He is a man of *nerve.* 他是一個有膽力的人。④【俚】冒失;魯莽;厚顏。He had the *nerve* to say that? 他竟厚顏說那種話嗎? ⑤葉脈;翅脈。⑥中樞;主要部分。Banks are the *nerve* of commerce. 銀行是商業的中樞。⑦筋。get on one's nerves*** 刺激人;攪得人不安。Turn off that radio; it's *getting on my nerves!* 把收音機關上,它攪得我心煩! ***lose one's nerve*** 失去勇氣;氣餒。***strain every nerve*** 盡最大努力。—*v.t.* 使有勇氣;與以力量;激勵。She *nerved* herself for the struggle. 她鼓起勇氣準備奮鬥。
nerve block 【醫】神經阻滯法;神經興奮阻滯。
nerve cell 【解剖,生理】神經細胞。
nerve center ①【解剖,生理】神經中樞。②活動中心;指揮中樞;首腦人物。
(-)nerved [nɝvd; nə:vd] *adj.* ①神經…的。②【植物】有…葉脈的;(蟲)有翅脈的。
nerve fiber 【解剖,生理】神經纖維。
nerve gas 神經瓦斯;神經毒氣。
nerve·less ['nɝvlɪs; 'nə:vlis] *adj.* ①沒有神經的。②沒有力量或勇氣的。③萎弱的;萎頓的。**—ly,** *adv.* **—ness,** *n.*
nerve-(w)rack·ing ['nɝvˌrækɪŋ; 'nə:vˌrækiŋ] *adj.* 極令人頭痛的;極傷腦筋的。
***nerv·ous** ['nɝvəs; 'nə:vəs] *adj.* ①神經的。*nervous* system. 神經系統。②不安的;神經質的;神經過分緊張的。Some are *nervous* in the dark. 有些人在黑暗處就神經緊張。③剛健的;有力的。He is full of *nervous* energy. 他精力充沛。④惴惴不安的;膽怯的。⑤有神經病的;患神經過敏的。⑥有神經的。**—ner·vos·i·ty, —ness,** *n.* **—ly,** *adv.*
nervous breakdown (or **prostration**) 精神崩潰。
ner·vure ['nɝvjur; 'nə:vjuə] *n.* ①【植物】葉脈。②翅脈。
nerv·y ['nɝvɪ; 'nə:vi] *adj.,* **nerv·i·er, nerv·i·est.** ①强壯的;有力的。②需膽力和剛毅的。③【美俚】不害羞的;厚顏的。④【英】神經質的。⑤有勇氣的。
nes·ci·ence ['nɛʃəns; 'nesiəns] *n.* ①無知;不知。②【哲學】不可知論。
nes·ci·ent ['nɛʃənt; 'nesiənt] *adj.* ①無知的;不知的【of】。②【哲學】不可知的。—*n.* 不可知論者。
ness [nɛs; nes] *n.* 【古,方】岬;崎。
-ness 【字尾】附於形容詞或分詞之後造成名詞而表"性質;狀態;程度"之義,如: bitterness, tiredness.
Nes·sel·rode ['nɛsəlrod; 'nesəlroud] *n.* (加於布丁、冰淇淋等中的)果實蜜餞。
‡nest [nɛst; nest] *n.* ①巢;鳥窠。to build a *nest.* 築巢。②(昆蟲、龜、兎等)產卵育幼處。③溫暖安適之處。④(罪惡之)窠;巢窟。a robber's *nest.* 盜匪的窠。⑤一窠(鳥、獸等)。⑥一套(一個比一個小,可重疊放置者)。⑦【俗】飛彈基地。—*v.i.* ①築巢。②獵尋鳥巢。③重疊。—*v.t.* ①爲…築巢;爲…設窩。②安頓;放置。to *nest* dishes in the cabinet. 將碟子放在櫥裏。
nest egg ①放在鷄窠中的眞或假蛋,目的在誘導母鷄在一定的地方生蛋。②爲養老、應變等用的儲蓄。
***nes·tle** ['nɛsl; 'nesl] *v.,* **-tled, -tling.** —*v.i.* ①舒適地坐定;偎依。The child *nestled* close to its mother. 小孩安適地偎依在母親身邊。②位於環境優雅或蔭蔽之處。③築巢;定巢而居。—*v.t.* ①擁抱;緊抱。②置於巢中;安頓;掩蔽。③舒適地安頓下來。He *nestled* himself in the hay for a short nap. 他安適地躺在乾草中小睡片刻。
nest·ling ['nɛslɪŋ; 'nesliŋ] *n.* ①雛鳥。②幼兒;幼嬰。
Nes·tor ['nɛstɚ; 'nestɔ:, 'nestə] *n.* ①【希臘神話】木馬屠城戰爭時希臘軍中最年長而賢明的老人。②賢明的長者;長老。
Nes·to·ri·an [nɛs'torɪən; nes'tɔ:riən] *adj.* Nestorius 的;景教的。—*n.* Nestorius 之信徒;景教徒。
Nes·to·ri·an·ism [nɛs'torɪənɪzəm; nes'tɔ:riənizm] *n.* Nestorius 之教義;Nestorius 教派;景教。
Nes·to·ri·us [nɛs'torɪəs; nes'tɔ:riəs] *n.* 聶思托里(?-?451, Constantinople 教長,任期428-431)。
‡net¹ [nɛt; net] *n., v.,* **net·ted, net·ting.** —*n.* ①網。fish *net.* 魚網。②網狀物。mosquito *net.* 蚊帳。③陷穽;羅網。the *net* of justice. 法網。④網狀之布。⑤(網球等)觸網球。⑥【俗】無線電或電視廣播網。—*v.t.* ①用網捕。to *net* a rich husband. 獵取一有錢的丈夫。②覆以網。③織成網。④以網做。⑤打(球)觸網。—*v.i.* 織網。**—like,** *adj.*
net² *adj., n., v.,* **net·ted, net·ting.** —*adj.* ①淨餘的。*net* earnings. 實得報酬。*net* weight. 淨重。②最後的;結束的。—*n.* 實價,淨利,實重等。—*v.t.* 淨賺。(亦作 **nett**)
Neth. Netherlands.
neth·er ['nɛðɚ; 'neðə] *adj.* ①下界的;冥府的。②【古,詩】下面的(=lower, under). **—ward,** *adj.*
Neth·er·land·er ['nɛðələndɚ; 'neðələndə] *n.* 荷蘭人。
Neth·er·land·ish ['nɛðɚˌlændɪʃ; 'neðəlændiʃ] *adj.* 荷蘭的。
Neth·er·lands ['nɛðələndz; 'neðələndz] *n.* (The -)尼德蘭(西歐一國,卽荷蘭,行政首都,海牙 The Hague, 名義首都,阿母斯特丹 Amsterdam).
Netherlands East Indies 荷屬東印度羣島(卽今之印尼)。
neth·er·most ['nɛðɚˌmost; 'neðəmoust] *adj.* 最下方的。
net national product 國民生產淨額(略作NNP).
net profit 淨利。
NETRC National Educational Television and Radio Center. 【美】全國教育電視廣播中心。
net·ted ['nɛtɪd; 'netid] *adj.* ①用網捕到的。②用網包的;張着網的。③網狀的;網細工的。
net·ting ['nɛtɪŋ; 'netiŋ] *n.* ①結網。②撒網;以網捕魚。③網狀編結物。
net·tle** ['nɛtl; 'netl] *n., v.,* **-tled, -tling.** —*n.* 【植物】蕁蔴;蕁蔴科植物。grasp the nettle*** 堅毅迅速地解決困難。—*v.t.* ①以蕁蔴刺或打。②刺激;激惱;惹怒。**—like,** *adj.*
nettle rash 【醫】蕁蔴疹;風疹塊。

*net·work [ˈnɛtˌwɜk; ˈnet-wəːk] *n.* ①網。②網狀組織。a *network* of railroads. 鐵路網。③無線電或電視廣播網。 —*v.i.* & *v.t.*〖英〗設立廣播網。

Neuf·châ·tel [ˌnjuʃəˈtɛl; ˌnəːʃæˈtel] *n.* 一種軟白乾酪。(亦作 **Neufchâtel cheese**)

neur-〖字首〗=**neuro-** (於母音前用之)。

neu·ral [ˈnjurəl; ˈnjuərəl] *adj.* 神經(系統)的;神經中樞的。

neu·ral·gia [njuˈrældʒə; njuəˈrældʒə] *n.*〖醫〗神經痛(尤指面部和頭部)。

neu·ral·gic [njuˈrældʒɪk; njuəˈrældʒik] *adj.* (患)神經痛的。

neu·ras·the·ni·a [ˌnjurəsˈθinɪə; ˌnjuərəsˈθiːnjə] *n.*〖醫〗神經衰弱。

neu·ras·then·ic [ˌnjurəsˈθɛnɪk; ˌnjuərəsˈθenik] *n., adj.* 神經衰弱者(的)。

neu·ri·tis [njuˈraɪtɪs; njuəˈraitis] *n.*〖醫〗神經炎。—**neu·rit·ic,** *adj.*

neu·ro·bi·ol·o·gy [ˌnjurəbaɪˈɑlədʒɪ; ˌnjuərəbaiˈɔlədʒi] *n.* 神經生理學。

neu·ro·fi·bril [ˌnjurəˈfaɪbrɪl; ˌnjuərəˈfaibril] *n.*〖解剖〗神經原纖維。 —**ar,** *adj.*

neu·ro·gen·ic [ˌnjurəˈdʒɛnɪk; ˌnjuərəˈdʒenik] *adj.*〖醫〗發生神經的;神經發生的。

neu·ro·log·i·cal [ˌnjurəˈlɑdʒɪk]; ˌnjuərəˈlɔdʒikəl] *adj.* 神經學的。

neu·rol·o·gist [njuˈrɑlədʒɪst; njuəˈrɔlədʒist] *n.* 神經學者;神經科專門醫師。

neu·rol·o·gy [njuˈrɑlədʒɪ; njuəˈrɔlədʒi] *n.* 神經(病)學。

neu·ro·ma [njuˈromə; njuəˈroumə] *n., pl.* **-mas, -ma·ta** [-mətə; -mətə].〖醫〗神經瘤。—**tous,** *adj.*

neu·ron [ˈnjurɑn; ˈnjuərɔn] *n.*〖解剖〗神經原;神經細胞。—**ic,** *adj.*

neu·rone [ˈnjuron; ˈnjuəroun] *n.* =neuron.

neu·ro·path [ˈnjurəˌpæθ; ˈnjuərəpæθ] *n.*〖醫〗有神經病體質者;神經病患者。

neu·ro·path·ic [ˌnjurəˈpæθɪk; ˌnjuərəˈpæθik] *adj.*神經病的;患神經病的。—**al·ly,** *adv.*

neu·rop·a·thy [njuˈrɑpəθɪ; njuəˈrɔpəθi] *n.* 神經系病。

neu·ro·sis [njuˈrosɪs; njuəˈrousis] *n., pl.* **-ses** [-siz; -siːz].〖醫〗神經病;神經官能病;精神神經病。

neu·rot·ic [njuˈrɑtɪk; njuəˈrɔtik] *adj.* ①患神經病的。②過於神經質的。 —*n.* 神經病患者。—**ism,** *n.*

neut. ①neuter. ②neutral.

neu·ter [ˈnjutɚ; ˈnjuːtə] *adj.* ①〖文法〗中性的。②〖動、植物〗不雌不雄的;無性的。③中間的;中立的。—*n.* ①中性字。②中性。③中性動物; 中性植物。—*v.t.* ①去勢; 閹割。②使中和; 抵銷。

*neu·tral [ˈnjutrəl; ˈnjuːtrəl] *adj.* ①(戰爭或爭論中)中立的。*neutral* zone. 中立地帶。②中立國的;中立地區的。③(非酸非鹼的)中性的。 *neutral* salts. 中性鹽。④無性的;中性的。⑤無色的;微灰色的。⑥(電流)非陰非陽的;中性的。⑦不確定的。—*n.* ①中立者;中立國。②戰時中立國國民。③〖機械〗齒輪的空檔。—**ly,** *adv.*

neu·tral·ism [ˈnjutrəlɪzəm; ˈnjuːtrəlizm] *n.* ①中立主義;中立政策。②中立。

neu·tral·ist [ˈnjutrəlɪst; ˈnjuːtrəlist] *n.* 中立主義者;採取中立主義之政府。 —*adj.* 遵奉或主張中立主義的。

neu·tral·i·ty [njuˈtrælətɪ; nju(ː)ˈtræliti] *n.* ①中立。②〖化〗中性。

neu·tral·i·za·tion [ˌnjutrələˈzeʃən; ˌnjutrəlaiˈzeiʃən] *n.* ①中立。 ②變無效;消滅。③〖化〗中和。

neu·tral·ize [ˈnjutrəlˌaɪz; ˈnjuːtrəlaiz] *v.t.,* **-ized, -iz·ing.** ①使中立。②使無效;中和。—**neu·tral·iz·er,** *n.*

neutral vowel〖語音〗中性母音(不重讀之母音)。

neu·tret·to [njuˈtrɛto; njuːˈtretou] *n., pl.* **-tos.**〖物理〗中介子。

neu·tri·no [njuˈtrino; njuˈtriːnou] *n., pl.* **-nos.**〖物理〗微中子。

neu·tron [ˈnjutrɑn; ˈnjuːtrɔn] *n.*〖物理〗中子。

neu·tro·phil [ˈnjutrəfɪl; ˈnjuːtrəfil] *n.* 嗜中性細胞; 嗜中性白血球。 —*adj.* 嗜中性的。(亦作 **neutrophile**)

Nev. Nevada.

Ne·vad·a [nəˈvædə; neˈvɑːdə] *n.* 內華達(美國西部之一州, 首府 Carson City).

Ne·vad·an [nəˈvædən; neˈvɑːdən] *adj., n.* 內華達州的(人)。

né·vé [neˈve; ˈnevei]〖法〗*n.* (冰河上層的)粒狀冰雪;萬年雪;萬年雪之原。

‡**nev·er** [ˈnɛvɚ; ˈnevə] *adv.* ①從未地;未曾地;永不地。 I have *never* been there. 我從未到過那裏。②毫不; 決不。 That will *never* do. 那決不行。***Never mind.*** 無妨;請勿介意。***never so*** **a.** 甚至…也不。He *never so* much as smiled. 他甚至連笑也不笑。**b.** 無論怎樣。***now or never*** 勿失良機。

nev·er-end·ing [ˈnɛvɚˈɛndɪŋ; ˈnevəˈendiŋ] *adj.* 不斷的。

nev·er-fail·ing [ˈnɛvɚˈfelɪŋ; ˈnevəˈfeiliŋ] *adj.* 不絕的;不變的。

nev·er·more [ˌnɛvɚˈmor; ˈnevəˈmɔː] *adv.* 永不再; 決不再。

nev·er-nev·er [ˈnɛvɚˈnɛvɚ; ˈnevəˈnevə] *adj.*〖俗〗①想像中的; 非眞實的。②不易瞭解的;似乎不太可信的。—*n.* ①=**never-never land.** ②〖英俚〗分期付款辦法。

never-never land ①想像中的地方; 不易瞭解的情況。②偏僻或人煙稀少之地。

‡**nev·er·the·less** [ˌnɛvɚðəˈlɛs; ˌnevəðəˈles, ˈnev-] *adv.* 雖然如此; 不過; 依然。 She was very tired; *nevertheless* she kept on working. 她雖很疲倦, 却繼續工作。

ne·vus [ˈnivəs; ˈniːvəs] *n.* =**naevus.**

‡**new** [nju, nu; njuː] *adj.* ①從未有過的; 新的。a *new* invention. 新發明。②新生的; 新來的;新製的。③初次用的;新鮮的。④不同的;改變了的。He is a *new* man now. 他現在是另外一個人了。⑤陌生的。⑥不習慣的;不熟悉的。I am *new* to the work. 我對這工作不習慣。⑦新近的;新式的。⑧剛來的;才到的。⑨更進一層的。He sought *new* information on the subject. 他搜尋有關此事更進一層的情報。⑩較近的;最近的。—*adv.* ①新;新近地。a *new*-found friend. 一個新朋友。②再;重新地。—*n.* 新的事物。I prefer the old to the *new*. 我喜舊捨新。

New Amsterdam 新阿姆斯特丹(昔 Manhattan 島上之荷蘭殖民地,現爲紐約市)。

New·ark [ˈnjuɚk; ˈnju(ː)ək] *n.* ①紐華克(美國 New Jersey 州東北部之一城市)。②紐華克 (美國 Ohio 州中部之一城市)。

new·born [ˈnjuˈbɔrn; ˈnjuːbɔːn] *adj.* ①新降生的。②(生活)新生的; 再生的。—*n.* 新生嬰兒。

new·come [ˈnjuˌkʌm; ˈnjuːkəm] *adj.* 新來的; 新到的。—*n.* =**newcomer.**

*new·com·er [ˈnjuˌkʌmɚ; ˈnjuːˈkʌmə]

n. ①新來者。②新到達之移民。

New Del·hi 〔~ˈdɛlɪ; ~ˈdeli〕 新德里(印度聯邦之首府)。

New Economic Policy 新經濟政策(列寧於1921–27年間推行之政策)。

new·el 〔ˈnjuəl; ˈnjuːəl〕 *n.* ①(旋梯的)中心柱。②(梯頂及梯脚的)欄杆支柱。

New Eng·land 〔njuˈɪŋglənd; njuːˈiŋglənd〕 新英格蘭(美國之東北部,包括 Maine, New Hampshire, Vermont, Massachusetts, Rhode Island, Connecticut 六州)。「或居民。」

New Englander 美國新英格蘭人

new·fan·gled 〔ˌnjuˈfæŋgld; ˈnjuːˌfæŋgld〕 *adj.* ①新近流行的。②喜新奇的。—**ness,** *n.*

new·fash·ioned 〔ˈnjuˈfæʃənd; ˈnjuːˈfæʃənd〕 *adj.* 新式的;新型的;新流行的。

New·found·land 〔ˌnjufəndˈlænd, ˈnjufəndlənd; nju(ː)ˈfaundlənd, ˌnjuːfəndˈlænd〕 *n.* 紐芬蘭(加拿大東岸之島嶼)。

New·found·land·er 〔njuˈfaundləndɚ; njuːˈfaundləndə〕 *n.* 紐芬蘭人;紐芬蘭船。「著名牢獄(1902年廢)。」

New·gate 〔ˈnjugɪt; ˈnjuːgit〕 *n.* 倫敦

New Guin·ea 〔njuˈgɪnɪ; njuːˈgini〕 新幾內亞(澳洲北部一大島,半屬澳,半屬印尼)。

New Hamp·shire 〔~ˈhæmpʃɪɚ; ~ˈhæmpʃiə〕 新罕布夏(美國東北部之一州,首府 Concord)。

new·ish 〔ˈnjuɪʃ; ˈnjuːiʃ〕 *adj.* 頗新的。

New Jer·sey 〔njuˈdʒɜzɪ; njuːˈdʒəːzi〕 新澤西(美國東部州名,首府 Trenton)。

New Jerusalem ①〖聖經〗聖城;新耶路撒冷。②天國;天堂。「生下的(蛋)。」

new-laid 〔ˈnjuˈled; ˈnjuːˈleid〕 *adj.* 剛

new look 〖俗〗新面目;新氣象。

new·ly 〔ˈnjulɪ; ˈnjuːli〕 *adv.* ①新近地;最近地。a *newly* wedded couple. 新婚的一對。②重新地。③用新方法;以新方式。

new·ly·wed 〔ˈnjulɪˌwɛd; ˈnjuːliwed〕 *n.* ①新婚者。②(*pl.*)新婚夫婦。

New M. New Mexico.

new-made 〔ˈnjuˌmed; ˈnjuːmeid〕 *adj.* ①新製的。②重新做過的;改裝過的。

New·man 〔ˈnjumən; ˈnjuːmən〕 *n.* 紐曼(Cardinal John Henry, 1801–1890, 英國神學家及作家)。

New·mar·ket 〔ˈnjuˌmɑrkɪt; ˈnjuːˌmɑːkit〕 *n.* ①英格蘭東南部之一城鎮(以賽馬著名)。②(n-)一種緊身長外衣。③(n-)一種紙牌遊戲。「之一州,首府 Santa Fe)。」

New Mexico 新墨西哥(美國西南部

new-mod·el 〔ˈnjuˌmɑdḷ; ˈnjuːˌmɔdl〕 *v.t.* 重新形成;改編;改組。—*adj.* 新型的。

new moon ①新月。②以陰暗一面對地球的月球。「②未熟;不慣。」

new·ness 〔ˈnjunɪs; ˈnjuːnis〕 *n.* ①新。

New Order (德國納粹時代之)新秩序。

New Or·le·ans 〔~ˈɔrlɪənz, ~ɔrˈlinz; ~ˈɔːliənz, ~ɔːˈliːnz〕 新奧爾良(美國 Louisiana 州東南之海港)。

new-rich 〔ˈnjuˈrɪtʃ; ˈnjuːˈritʃ〕 *adj.* 新富的;暴富的。—*n.* 暴發戶。

:news 〔njuz, nuz; njuːz〕 *n.* ①新聞;消息。No *news* is good *news.* 沒有消息便是好消息。*news* agency. 通訊社。*news* analyst. 新聞評論家。*news* editor. 新聞編輯。②有新聞價值的事物或人。You may not like her, but she is *news.* 你也許不喜歡她,但她是新聞人物。③報紙。***be* (*no*) *news to*** 對…是(不是)新聞。*That's news to* me (=I didn't know that). 我不知那事。***break the news* (*to*)** 傳凶訊(給)。—**less,** *adj.* —**less·ness,** *n.* 〖注意〗**news** 形式上爲複數,用法上作單數。

news agent 〖英〗發賣報紙者。

news·beat 〔ˈnjuzˌbit; ˈnjuːzbiːt〕 *n.* ①新聞之獨家報導。②記者採訪新聞之機構或消息來源。「報童;賣報童。」

news·boy 〔ˈnjuzˌbɔɪ; ˈnjuːzbɔi〕 *n.*

news·break 〔ˈnjuzˌbrek; ˈnjuːzbreik〕 *n.* 有新聞價值之事件;重要新聞。

news·cast 〔ˈnjuzˌkæst; ˈnjuːzkɑːst〕 *n.* 新聞廣播。—*v.t.* & *v.i.* 報告新聞;廣播新聞。—**er,** —**ing,** *n.*

news conference 記者招待會。(亦作 **press conference**)

news·deal·er 〔ˈnjuzˌdilɚ; ˈnjuːzˌdiːlə〕 *n.* 販賣報紙、雜誌等的人。(亦作 **news dealer**) 「*n.* 〖俗〗記者;新聞特派員。」

news·hawk 〔ˈnjuzˌhɔk; ˈnjuːzhɔːk〕

news·hound 〔ˈnjuzˌhaund; ˈnjuːzhaund〕 *n.* =**newshawk.**

news·let·ter 〔ˈnjuzˌlɛtɚ; ˈnjuːzˈletə〕 *n.* ①機關、保險公司等定期發行之簡訊。②書信新聞(17世紀後半期自歐洲傳入英國之一種發布新聞的傳單,爲近代報紙之濫觴)。

news·mak·er 〔ˈnjuzˌmekɚ; ˈnjuːzˌmeikə〕 *n.* 〖美〗有新聞價值的人或事。

news·man 〔ˈnjuzmən; ˈnjuːzmən〕 *n., pl.* **-men.** ①賣報人;送報人。②新聞記者。

news·mon·ger 〔ˈnjuzˌmʌŋgɚ; ˈnjuːzˌmʌŋgə〕 *n.* 愛傳述新聞者;好閒談者。

‡news·pa·per 〔ˈnjuzˌpepɚ, ˈnjus-, ˈnu-; ˈnjuːsˌpeipə, ˈnjuːzˌp-〕 *n.* ①報紙。to read a *newspaper.* 看報。to subscribe for (*or* to) a *newspaper.* 訂閱報紙。He corresponds for a *newspaper.* 他爲一報撰通訊。②新聞用紙;白報紙。

news·pa·per·man 〔ˈnjuzˌpepɚˌmæn; ˈnjuːsˌpeipəmæn〕 *n., pl.* **-men.** ①新聞記者。②經營報業者。

news peg 作爲特寫、政治漫畫或社論等之素材的重要消息或事件。

news·print 〔ˈnjuzˌprɪnt; ˈnjuːzprint〕 *n.* 白報紙。「〖美〗新聞影片。」

news·reel 〔ˈnjuzˌril; ˈnjuːzriːl〕 *n.*

news·room 〔ˈnjuzrum; ˈnjuːzrum〕 *n.* 新聞編輯室。(亦作 **news room**)

news·sheet 〔ˈnjuzˌʃit; ˈnjuːzʃiːt〕 *n.* 〖俗〗=**newspaper.**

news·stand 〔ˈnjuzˌstænd; ˈnjuːzstænd〕 *n.* 報攤;雜誌攤。(亦作 **news stall**)

news·wor·thy 〔ˈnjuzˌwɝðɪ; ˈnjuːzˌwəːði〕 *adj.* 有報導價值的;有新聞價值的。

news·y 〔ˈnjuzɪ; ˈnjuːzi〕 *adj.,* **news·i·er, news·i·est,** *n., pl.* **news·ies.** —*adj.* 〖美〗①多新聞的。②饒舌的。—*n.* 〖俗〗①=**newsboy.** ②=**newsman.** —**news·i·ness,** *n.*

newt 〔njut; njuːt〕 *n.* 〖動物〗水蜥;蠑螈。

New Testament 新約聖經。

New·ton 〔ˈnjutn̩; ˈnjuːtn〕 *n.* 牛頓(Isaac, 1642–1727, 英國科學家)。

New·to·ni·an 〔njuˈtonɪən; nju(ː)ˈtounjən〕 *adj.* 牛頓的;牛頓學說的。—*n.* 牛頓信徒。「陸)。」

New World 新世界;新大陸(美洲大

new-world 〔ˈnjuˈwɝld; ˈnjuːˈwəːld〕 *adj.* 新大陸的;西半球的。

new year ①新年。②元旦。③(N-Y-)新年假日。「②=New Year's Eve.」
New Year's ①=New Year's Day.
New Year's Day 元旦。
New Year's Eve 除夕。
***New York** [nju'jɔrk; 'nju:'jɔ:k, nju:'jɔ:k] ①紐約州(位於美國東部, 首府Albany)。②(亦作 New York City) 紐約市。
New York·er [~'jɔrkɚ; ~'jɔ:kə] 紐約州人或居民;紐約市人或居民。
New Zea·land [nju'zilənd; nju:'zi:lənd] 紐西蘭(大英國協在南太平洋之會員國, 首都威靈頓 Wellington)。
New Zea·land·er [~'ziləndɚ; ~'zi:ləndə] 紐西蘭人。
:next [nɛkst; nekst] *adj.* 最近的;其次的。the *next* train. 下班火車。the *next* room. 隔壁房間。*next* Monday. 下星期一。—*adv.* ①下次。When shall I meet you *next?* 我下次何時與你相會? ②(地點、時間、位置等)最近地;鄰接地。His name comes *next*. 其次是他的名字。***get next to someone*** 〖俚〗得某人之好感;成爲某人之朋友。***next door to*** a. 在…隔壁。b. 近乎;差不多。Cheating is an act *next door to* crime. 欺騙是近乎犯罪的行爲。***next to*** a. 相鄰。b. 次於。*Next to* music, he loves tennis best. 除音樂外, 他最愛網球。c. 幾乎。It is *next to* impossible. 幾乎不可能。—*prep.* 與…鄰接。the house *next* the church. 鄰接教堂的房子。
next-door ['nɛks,dɔr; 'neksdɔ:] *adv.* & *adj.* 鄰家(的);隔鄰(的)。
nex·us ['nɛksəs; 'neksəs] *n., pl.* **-us, -us·es.** ①連結;連繫;聯絡;連鎖;關係。the cash *nexus*. 現鈔交易關係。②〖文法〗敍述關係;表達關係。③相互連鎖的一系列。
N.F. ① Newfoundland. ② Norman French. **NFL, N.F.L.** National Football League. **Nfld.** Newfoundland. **N.F.S.** National Fire Service. **N.G.** ①National Guard. ②New Guinea. ③New Granada. **N.H.** New Hampshire. **N.H.P., n.h.p.** nominal horsepower.
Ni 化學元素 nickel 之符號。
ni·a·cin ['naɪəsn̩; 'naiəsn] *n.* 〖化〗尼亞新;菸鹼酸(=nicotinic acid)。
ni·a·cin·a·mide [,naɪəsɪn'æmaɪd; ,naiəsin'æmaid] *n.* 〖生化〗菸醯胺。
Ni·ag·a·ra [naɪ'ægrə; nai'ægərə] *n.* ①尼加拉河(在美、加交界處)。②=Niagara Falls. ③(n-)滔滔不絕的談話;勢不可當的事物。④一種白葡萄。「瀑布。」
Niagara Falls (美、加交界的)尼加拉
nib [nɪb; nib] *n., v.,* **nibbed, nib·bing.** —*n.* ①筆尖;筆嘴;鵝管筆的筆頭。②尖頭;尖端。③鳥嘴;喙。④蘸水鋼筆。⑤極;頂點。⑥鐮柄尖端。⑦可可豆;咖啡豆。—*v.t.* ①裝以筆尖;修(筆尖)。②使尖。—**like,** *adj.*
***nib·ble** ['nɪbl; 'nibl] *v.,* **-bled, -bling,** *n.* —*v.i.* ①細齧;細咬;細食;一點點兒地吃。②輕咬〖常 at〗. A fish *nibbled* at the bait. 一條魚輕咬魚餌。③(對交易或別人意見)做出有意接受的樣子。④慢慢吃以示對食物無興趣。⑤批評;攻擊。—*v.t.* ①細咬;細食;細嚼。②斷續地輕咬(食物)。—*n.* ①細咬;輕咬。I felt a *nibble* at the bait. 我感到(有魚)輕咬一下餌。②一小口;一小塊。—**nib·bler,** *n.* —**nib·bling·ly,** *adv.*
Ni·be·lung·en·lied ['nibə,lʊŋən,lit; 'ni:bə,luŋənli:t] *n.* 尼白龍根之歌(德國中世紀敍事詩)。
nib·lick ['nɪblɪk; 'niblik] *n.* 一種鐵頭高爾夫球棒(現在通稱 Iron No. 9)。
nibs [nɪbz; nibz] *n.* 〖俚〗當權者;在位者。***his nibs*** 〖蔑〗目空一切者;專橫者。
Ni·cae·a [naɪ'siə; nai'si(:)ə] *n.* 尼西亞(小亞細亞西北部 Bithynia 之古都)。
Nic·a·ra·gua [,nɪkə'rɑgwə; ,nikə'rægjuə] *n.* 尼加拉瓜(中美一國, 首都馬拿瓜 Managua). —**Nic·a·ra·guan,** *adj., n.*
Nice [nis; ni:s] *n.* 尼斯(法國東南部港埠)。
:nice [naɪs; nais] *adj.,* **nic·er, nic·est** ①悅人的;令人愉快的;美麗宜人的。*nice* to the taste. 味道鮮美。②親切的;關心的。He was *nice* to us. 他對我們很親切。③精密的;精確的。a *nice* ear for music. 善識音樂的耳朵。④精細的;細緻的;精美的。a *nice* distinction. 精細的區別。⑤講究的;難以取悅的。He is very *nice* in his eating. 他吃東西非常講究。⑥狡黠的;棘手的。⑦適當的;合適的。That's not a *nice* remark. 那句話不該說。⑧謹愼的;行爲極嚴謹的。He's not too *nice* in his business methods. 他的經營方法不太嚴謹。⑨〖古〗謙虛的;保守的。⑩文雅的。a *nice* accent. 文雅的語音。⑪〖諷〗壞的;難的;糟的。You've got us into a *nice* mess! 你使我們陷入困境了! ⑫美味的。⑬循規蹈矩的;令人起敬的。—**ly,** *adv.* —**ness,** *n.* 「['lukɪŋ] *adj.* 漂亮的。」
nice-look·ing ['naɪs'lʊkɪŋ; 'nais-
Ni·cene [naɪ'sin; nai'si:n] *adj.* Nicaea 的。「Nicaea 會議所定之基督徒信條)。」
Nicene Creed 尼西亞信條 (325 年
ni·ce·ty ['naɪsətɪ; 'naisiti] *n., pl.* **-ties** ①精確。②微細差異。③優雅;佳妙。④(常 *pl.*)精美之物;珍饈。⑤細節。***to a nicety*** 正確地;恰好地;精密地。
niche [nɪtʃ; nitʃ] *n., v.,* **niched, nich·ing.** —*n.* ①(置放雕像、花瓶等的)壁龕。②適當的位置, 恰當的處所。③〖生態〗個別生物在動植物界的功能或地位。—*v.t.* 置於壁龕內;安置於適當地位(通常用被動式)。
Nich·o·las ['nɪkl̩əs; 'nikələs] *n.* 男子名。
Nick [nɪk; nik] *n.* ①男子名(Nicholas 之暱稱)。②(常 Old-)魔鬼;撒旦。
nick [nɪk; nik] *n.* ①刻痕;裂口;微凹。②正確時刻;恰於其時。③鉛字下端所刻之凹溝。④骰子擲出後所要的贏點。⑤以刻痕所做之紀錄。***in the nick of time*** 正是時候;不遲。The fire engines arrived *in the nick of time*. 救火車來得正是時候。—*v.t.* ①刻痕於;弄缺。②以刻痕記錄;記錄。③割入;割(馬尾)根部使尾翹高。I *nicked* my chin while shaving. 我刮鬍子的時候割破了下巴。④擊中;猜中;言中。⑤恰好趕上。⑥〖英俗〗逮捕。⑦欺詐;詐騙。He *nicked* me for a thousand dollars. 他騙了我一千塊錢。
***nick·el** ['nɪkl̩; 'nikl] *n., v.,* **-eled, -el·ing.** —*n.* ①鎳。②〖美〗鎳幣;五分鎳幣。—*v.t.* 鍍鎳於。
nick·el·if·er·ous [,nɪkə'lɪfərəs; ,nikə'lifərəs] *adj.* 含鎳的;產鎳的。
nick·el·o·de·on [,nɪkl̩'odɪən; ,nikə'loudiən] *n.* ①〖美〗入場費五分錢之戲院。②一種舊式的自動點唱機。
nick·er ['nɪkɚ; 'nikə] *n., v.i.* 〖英方〗①(馬)嘶。②笑;暗笑;竊笑。
nick·nack ['nɪk,næk; 'niknæk] *n.* =knickknack.
***nick·name** ['nɪk,nem; 'nikneim] *n.,*

v., **-named, -nam·ing.** —*n.* ①綽號;渾名。②小名;暱稱。"Ed" is a *nickname* for "Edward". "Ed" 是 "Edward" 的暱稱。—*v.t.* ①加綽號於。They *nicknamed* the short boy "Shorty". 他們給那矮孩子起個渾名爲"矮子"。②叫錯名字;命名不正確。

Ni·colle [ˌniˈkɔl; ˌniːˈkɔːl] *n.* 尼考爾(Charles Jean Henri, 1866–1936, 法國醫生及細菌學家,曾獲 1928 年諾貝爾生理學及醫學獎)。

ni·co·tian [nɪˈkoʃən; niˈkouʃən] *adj.* 烟草的;得自烟草的。—*n.* ①(原指)烟草。②吸烟者。

nic·o·tin·a·mide [ˌnɪkəˈtɪnəˌmaɪd; ˌnikəˈtinəmaid] *n.* 〖生化〗烟鹼醯胺。

nic·o·tine [ˈnɪkəˌtin; ˈnikətiːn] *n.* 尼古丁(烟草中之毒素)。(亦作 **nicotin**)

nic·o·tin·ic acid [ˌnɪkəˈtɪnɪk～; ˌnikəˈtinik～] 〖化〗烟鹼酸。

nic·o·tin·ism [ˈnɪkəˌtinɪzəm; ˈnikətiːnizm] *n.* 烟鹼中毒。

nic·tate [ˈnɪktet; ˈnikteit] *v.i.*, **-tat·ed, -tat·ing.** 瞬目;霎眼。(亦作 **nictitate**)

nictating membrane 〖動物〗瞬膜。

nid·der·ing [ˈnɪdərɪŋ; ˈnidəriŋ] *n.* 〖古〗怯懦的人;卑劣的人。—*adj.* 〖古〗怯懦的;卑劣的。

nid·i·fi·cate [ˈnɪdɪfɪˌket; ˈnidifikeit] *v.i.*, **-cat·ed, -cat·ing.** 營巢;作巢。(亦作 **nidify**)

nid·i·fi·ca·tion [ˌnɪdɪfɪˈkeʃən; ˌnidifiˈkeiʃən] *n.* 營巢;作巢。—**al,** *adj.*

nid-nod [ˈnɪdˌnɑd; ˈnidˌnɔd] *v.i.* & *v.t.*, **nid-nod·ded, nid-nod·ding.** (使)頻頻垂首;頻頻點頭。

ni·dus [ˈnaɪdəs; ˈnaidəs] *n.*, *pl.* **-di** [-daɪ; -dai], **-dus·es.** ①(昆蟲或蜘蛛)放卵之巢。②(動植物體內病菌或寄生蟲之)繁殖處。

***niece** [nis; niːs] *n.* 姪女;甥女。

ni·el·lo [nɪˈɛlo; niˈelou] *n.*, *pl.* **-li** [-li; -li], **-los,** *v.* —*n.* ①黑金。②黑金鑲嵌品。—*v.t.* 鑲以黑金。

Nie·tzsche [ˈnitʃə; ˈniːtʃə] *n.* 尼采(Friedrich Wilhelm, 1844–1900, 德國哲學家)。

Nie·tzsche·an [ˈnitʃɪən; ˈniːtʃiən] *adj.* 尼采的;尼采哲學的。—*n.* 尼采哲學家。

nif·ty [ˈnɪftɪ; ˈnifti] *adj.*, **nif·ti·er, nif·ti·est,** *n.* —*adj.* 入時的;俏皮的;極好的。—*n.* ①俏皮話。②漂亮的姑娘。

Ni·ger [ˈnaɪdʒɚ; ˈnaidʒə] *n.* 尼日(西非一共和國,首都尼亞美 Niamey)。

Ni·ger·i·a [naɪˈdʒɪrɪə; naiˈdʒiəriə] *n.* 奈及利亞(西非一國,首都拉哥斯 Lagos)。

nig·gard [ˈnɪgɚd; ˈnigəd] *n.* 吝嗇鬼;小氣鬼。—*adj.* ①吝嗇的;小氣的。②少的;不足的。

nig·gard·ly [ˈnɪgɚdlɪ; ˈnigədli] *adj.* ①吝嗇的。②少的。—*adv.* 吝嗇地。

nig·ger [ˈnɪgɚ; ˈnigə] *n.* ①〖俗〗黑人(=Negro)。②有黑人血統者。③其他黑膚色人種(侮蔑語)。④扮成黑人唱黑人之歌者(=nigger minstrel)。⑤〖動物〗瓢蟲或蕪菁蜂之幼蟲。***nigger in the woodpile*** (or ***fence***) 〖俗〗隱密之動機;祕密。***work like a nigger*** 辛勤工作。—**ish,** —**y,** *adj.*

nig·ger·head [ˈnɪgɚˌhɛd; ˈnigəhed] *n.* ①〖美方〗沼澤地區中的暗色植物叢。②一種呈微黑色的淡水蠔。③一種黑色的烟草餅。

nig·gle [ˈnɪgl; ˈnigl] *v.i.*, **-gled, -gling.** ①工作徒勞。②浪費時間與精力於小節或瑣事。③吹毛求疵。

nig·gling [ˈnɪglɪŋ; ˈnigliŋ] *n.* 過於瑣碎的工作;費心(時)的工作。—*adj.* ①爲瑣事操心的;過分注意細節的。②麻煩的;難辦的(工作)。③過於矯飾的。—**ly,** *adv.*

nigh [naɪ; nai] *adj.*, **nigh·er, nigh·est** or **next,** *adv.*, *prep.*, *v.* —*adj.* ①近的。②關係很近的。③短的;直接的。the *nighest* road. 最近之路。④左側的(車輪或馬)。⑤〖方〗吝嗇的。***nigh upon*** (***on,*** or ***about***) 幾乎。—*adv.* ①近地。*nigh* at hand. 在近旁。②〖古〗幾乎。—*prep.* 〖古〗近;近於。—*v.t.* & *v.i.* 〖古〗接近。

‡**night** [naɪt; nait] *n.* ①夜(爲 day 之對)。During the *night* we sleep; during the day we work and play. 我們在夜間睡眠,在白日工作與玩耍。It isn't a place to visit by *night*. 那不是個夜間可去的地方。②晚;黃昏(=evening). Did anybody come last *night?* 昨晚有人來嗎? ③昏暗;黑暗。under cover of *night*. 在黑暗的掩護下。④愚昧、罪惡、悲傷、老年、死亡等所造成之黑暗。to be wrapped in the *night* of ignorance. 處於愚昧的黑暗中。***all night*** (***long***) 徹夜;終夜。***at night*** 在夜間。***from morning till night*** 從早到晚。***have*** (or ***pass***) ***a good*** (or ***bad***) ***night*** 夜裏睡(不)好。***make a night of it*** 狂歡通宵。***night and day*** 日以繼夜。***o'*** (=***on***) ***nights*** 〖方,俗〗在夜間。***turn night into day*** 以夜作晝;夜晚做白天的事情。—*adj.* ①夜晚的。②夜晚發生或看到的。a *night* raid. 夜襲。③夜晚使用的。the *night* entrance. 夜晚的入口處。④夜晚工作的。*night* shift. 夜班。—**less,** *adj.* —**less·ly,** *adv.* —**like,** *adj.*

night bird ①夜鳥;梟;夜鶯。②夜遊者;「乘夜爲惡之人。」

night-blind [ˈnaɪtˌblaɪnd; ˈnait-blaind] *adj.* 患夜盲症的。

night blindness 〖醫〗夜盲(症)。

night-bloom·ing ce·re·us [ˈnaɪtˌblumɪŋˈsɪrɪəs; ˈnaitˌbluːmiŋˈsiəriəs] 曇花。

night·cap [ˈnaɪtˌkæp; ˈnaitkæp] *n.* ①睡帽。②〖俗〗睡前所飲之酒。③〖俗〗運動節目之最後一項,尤指兩場棒球賽之第二場。

night clothes 睡衣。

night club 夜總會。

night·club [ˈnaɪtˌklʌb; ˈnaitklʌb] *n.*, *v.*, **-clubbed, -club·bing.** —*n.* =**night club.** —*v.i.* (亦作 **night-club**)常去夜總會。—**ber,** *n.*

Night Court 〖美〗夜間法庭。

night·dress [ˈnaɪtˌdrɛs; ˈnaitdres] *n.* =**nightgown.**

***night·fall** [ˈnaɪtˌfɔl; ˈnaitfɔːl] *n.* 日暮;黃昏;傍晚。I shall be back by *nightfall*. 我將在傍晚時歸來。

night·glass [ˈnaɪtˌglæs, -ˌglɑs; ˈnait-glɑːs] *n.* 夜間用之望遠鏡。

night·gown [ˈnaɪtˌgaʊn; ˈnaitgaun] *n.* (長的)睡衣。(亦作 **night robe**)

night hag ①(傳說中)夜間飛行空中之女魔。②=**nightmare.**

night·hawk [ˈnaɪtˌhɔk; ˈnaithɔːk] *n.* ①夜鷹。②〖俗〗夜遊者;夜間幹壞事的人。③〖美俚〗(夜裏營業的)出租汽車(司機)。④深夜不眠的人。—*v.i.* 〖俗〗在夜間徘徊。

Night·in·gale [ˈnaɪtn̩ˌgel, -tɪŋ-; ˈnaitiŋgeil] *n.* 南丁格爾(Florence, 1820–1910, 爲近代護理制度創始人)。

***night·in·gale** [ˈnaɪtn̩ˌgel, ˈnaɪtɪn-,

ˈnaɪtɪŋ–; ˈnaitiŋgeil] *n.* 夜鶯。
night·jar [ˈnaɪtˌdʒɑr; ˈnaitdʒɑː] *n.* 蚊母鳥;歐夜鷹。
night key (開彈簧鎖的)鑰匙。
night latch (or **bolt**) 夜鎖;彈簧鎖。
night letter (or **lettergram**) 夜間書信電報(翌晨送達,收費較低)。
night light ①通夜不熄之燈。②夜間之微光。
night line 投置水中過夜之釣魚絲。
night·long [ˈnaɪtˌlɔŋ; ˈnaitlɔŋ] *adj.* 整夜的。—*adv.* 通宵;徹夜。
***night·ly** [ˈnaɪtlɪ; ˈnaitli] *adj.* ①每夜的。②〖詩〗夜間的。*nightly* dew. 夜露。③如夜晚的。④夜晚活躍的;夜晚發生的。—*adv.* ①每夜地。Performances are given *nightly.* 每夜都有演出。②在夜間。
night·man [ˈnaɪtmən; ˈnaitmən] *n., pl.* **-men.** ①夜裏工作的人;守夜者 (通常作 night man)。②(夜裏工作的) 淘糞工人。
***night·mare** [ˈnaɪtˌmɛr; ˈnaitmɛə] *n.* ①夢魘;惡夢。I had a *nightmare* last night. 我昨夜夢魘。②可怕的經驗。
night·mar·ish [ˈnaɪtˌmɛrɪʃ; ˈnaitmɛəriʃ] *adj.* 如惡夢的;似夢魘的;可怕的。—**ly,** *adv.*
night owl ①熬夜的人;深夜不睡的人。②夜裏活動的貓頭鷹。
night piece 夜景畫;夜景文(詩)。
night·rid·er [ˈnaɪtˌraɪdɚ; ˈnaitˌraidə] *n.* ①美國南部夜間騎馬爲非作歹的人。②三K黨員。—**night·rid·ing,** *n.*
night school 夜校。
night·shade [ˈnaɪtˌʃed; ˈnait–ʃeid] *n.* 〖植物〗①龍葵 (=Black Nightshade). ②顛茄 (=Deadly Nightshade).
night·shirt [ˈnaɪtˌʃɝt; ˈnait–ʃəːt] *n.* 男子之睡衣。
night soil 糞便。
night spot 〖俗〗夜總會。
night stick 警棍。(亦作 **nightstick**)
night·stool [ˈnaɪtˌstul; ˈnaitstuːl] *n.* =**closestool.**
night-suit [ˈnaɪtˌsjut; ˈnaitsjuːt] *n.* 睡衣。
night table 床頭几。(亦作 **nightstand**)
night·time [ˈnaɪtˌtaɪm; ˈnaittaim] *n.* 夜間。
night·walk·er [ˈnaɪtˌwɔkɚ; ˈnaitˌwɔːkə] *n.* ①夜間徘徊於街頭者。②夢遊者。—**night·walk·ing,** *n., adj.*
night watch ①守夜者。②守夜;守夜之時間。
night·work [ˈnaɪtˌwɝk; ˈnait–wəːk] *n.* 夜工。
night·y [ˈnaɪtɪ; ˈnaiti] *n., pl.* **night-ies.** 睡衣 (暱稱)。
ni·gres·cence [naɪˈgrɛsəns; naiˈgresəns] *n.*①漸黑;變黑。②(尤指皮膚、毛髮、眼睛等之)黑。
ni·gres·cent [naɪˈgrɛsənt; naiˈgresənt] *adj.* 漸漸變黑的;帶黑色的;近黑的。
nig·ri·tude [ˈnɪgrəˌtjud; ˈnigrətjuːd] *n.* 黑;黑色之物。—**nig·ri·tu·di·nous,** *adj.*
ni·hil [ˈnaɪhɪl; ˈnaihil] 〖拉〗 *n.* ①無;虛無;空。②無價值之物。
ni·hil ad rem [ˈnaɪhɪl ædˈrɛm; ˈnaihil ædˈrem] 〖拉〗不得要領的;牛頭不對馬嘴的 (=nothing to the point).
ni·hil·ism [ˈnaɪəlˌɪzəm; ˈnaiilizəm] *n.* ①〖哲學〗虛無論;虛無主義;極端懷疑論。②(N–) (俄國十九世紀末葉之)無政府主義。③恐怖主義;無政府主義。④徹底破壞主義。
ni·hil·ist [ˈnaɪəlɪst; ˈnaiilist] *n.* ①虛無論者;懷疑論者。②(N–) (俄國十九世紀末葉之)無政府主義者。③破壞論者;恐怖主義者。
ni·hil·is·tic [ˌnaɪəˈlɪstɪk; ˌnaiiˈlistik] *adj.* 虛無論(者)的;虛無主義(者)的;懷疑論(者)的。
ni·hil·i·ty [naɪˈhɪlətɪ; naiˈhiliti] *n.* 虛「無;無。」
-nik 〖字尾〗〖俚〗源於俄語,形成名詞,如: Sputnik 等。beatnik 乃仿 Sputnik 而成。今所形成之字,義多承 beatnik,且稍含輕蔑之意。表"反傳統及追求新奇事物者;…迷;…狂"之義,如: peacenik.
Ni·ke [ˈnaɪki; ˈnaikiː] *n.* ①〖希臘神話〗勝利女神。②美國地對空飛彈名。
nil [nɪl; nil] *n.* 無;零。
nil ad·mi·ra·ri [nɪlˌædmɪˈrerɪ; nilˌædmiˈreiri] 〖拉〗無動於衷;冷漠 (=to wonder at nothing).
Nile [naɪl; nail] *n.* 尼羅河。
nill [nɪl; nil] *v.t.* & *v.i.* 〖古〗不欲;不願。
Ni·lot·ic [naɪˈlɑtɪk; naiˈlɔtik] *adj.* 尼羅河的;尼羅河流域居民的。
***nim·ble** [ˈnɪmbl; ˈnimbl] *adj.,* **-bler, -blest.** ①敏捷的;迅速的。②聰明的;伶俐的。He has a *nimble* mind. 他十分伶俐。③構思很靈巧的。—**nim·bly,** *adv.*
nim·bo·stra·tus [ˌnɪmboˈstretəs; ˌnimbouˈstreitəs] *n., pl.* **-tus, -ti** [–taɪ; –tai]. =**nimbus** ③.
nim·bus [ˈnɪmbəs; ˈnimbəs] *n., pl.* **-bus·es, -bi** [–baɪ; –bai]. ①聖像頭上之光輪;靈光。②(附於神體的)祥雲。③〖氣象〗雨雲。
nim·i·ny-pim·i·ny [ˈnɪmənɪˈpɪmənɪ; ˈniminiˈpimini] *adj.* 故作優雅的;矯飾的。
Nim·rod [ˈnɪmrɑd; ˈnimrɔd] *n.* ①〖聖經〗寧錄(大狩獵家,Noah 之曾孫,載於創世記十章八節及九節)。②善獵者;愛打獵的人。
nin·com·poop [ˈnɪnkəmˌpup; ˈninkəmpuːp] *n.* 愚人;傻子。—**ish,** *adj.*
‡**nine** [naɪn; nain] *n.* ①九。②九個人或物之一組。③棒球隊。*be dressed* (*up*) *to the nines* 穿着華麗衣服;打扮漂亮;過分裝飾。*nine out of ten* 十有八九。*nine-tenths* 十分之九。*the Nine* 司藝術、文學、科學的九女神 (=the nine Muses). —*adj.* 九個;九。
nine·fold [ˈnaɪnˌfold; ˈnainfould] *adj.* & *adv.* 九倍的(地);九重的(地)。
nine·pin [ˈnaɪnˌpɪn; ˈnain–pin] *n.* (九瓶保齡球戲之任一)瓶。
nine·pins [ˈnaɪnˌpɪnz; ˈnain–pinz] *n. pl.* (作*sing.* 解). 九瓶之保齡球(戲)。
‡**nine·teen** [ˈnaɪnˈtin; ˈnainˈtiːn] *n., adj.* 十九;十九個;19;十九(的);十九個(的)。*talk nineteen to the dozen* 不斷說話;喋喋不休。
***nine·teenth** [ˈnaɪnˈtinθ; ˈnainˈtiːnθ] *n., adj.* 第十九(的);第十九;十九分之一。
nineteenth hole 〖俗〗高爾夫俱樂部或酒吧(球賽後休息聊天之處)。
***nine·ti·eth** [ˈnaɪntɪɪθ; ˈnaintiiθ] *n., adj.* 第九十(的);第九十;九十分之一。
‡**nine·ty** [ˈnaɪntɪ; ˈnainti] *n., pl.* **-ties,** *adj.* —*n.* 九十;九十個;90。*ninety-nine times out of a hundred* 一百次中有九十九次;幾乎永遠。*the nineties* 89 與100之間;九十年代(特指 1889–1900 年間)。—*adj.* 九十的;九十個的。
Ning·sia [ˈnɪŋˈʃjɑ; ˈniŋˈʃjɑː] *n.* 寧夏(中國北部之一省,省會爲銀川市,Yinchwan).
nin·ny [ˈnɪnɪ; ˈnini] *n., pl.* **-nies.** 愚人;傻子。—**nin·nish,** *adj.*
ni·non [niˈnɔ̃; niːˈnɔ̃] *n.* 薄綢。

:ninth [naɪnθ; nainθ] *adj., n.* 第九的; 第九;九分之一。

ninth·ly [ˈnaɪnθlɪ; ˈnainθli] *adv.* 在第九;居第九位。

Ni·o·be [ˈnaɪəbɪ; ˈnaiəbi] *n.* ①〖希臘神話〗尼奧比 (Thebes 王 Amphion 之妻, 有子女十四人,常自誇耀,其子女終為 Apollo 及 Artemis 所戮, Niobe 悲傷無已,後被 Zeus 化為頑石, 仍有淚水從石流出)。②(因喪失親人而)終身哀痛之婦女。—**an,** *adj.*

ni·o·bi·um [naɪˈobɪəm; naiˈoubiəm] *n.*〖化〗鈮(金屬元素之一,符號 Nb).

Nip [nɪp; nip] *n., adj.* 〖俚、蔑〗=**Nipponese; Japanese.**

nip¹** [nɪp; nip] *v.,* **nipped, nip·ping,** *n.* —*v.t.* ①箝; 捏; 挾。The crab *nipped* my toe. 螃蟹箝了我的足趾。②箝去; 捏去; 挾掉〖常 off〗。③傷害(尖端部分)。The plants were *nipped* by frost. 花木被霜摧殘。④刺痛。⑤〖俗〗偷取;奪取。⑥〖俚〗突然箝去。⑦〖航海〗(冰塊)從兩旁向船擠壓。—*v.i.* ①箝;捏;挾。②刺痛。The wind *nips* hard this morning. 今晨風寒刺膚。③〖英俗〗急走;急動〖off, away, along〗. ***nip along〖俗〗趕快; 匆忙。***nip in*** 挿入;挿嘴。***nip in the bud*** 在萌芽時摘取;防患於未然。***nip off*** 急忙跑掉。***nip on ahead*** 趕過頭; 迎頭趕上。—*n.* ①箝;挾;捏。He gave me a *nip* on the arm. 他在我的手臂捏了一下。②霜打的損害。③刺膚之寒冷。④一小塊;一點兒。⑤一句尖刻的話。⑥乾酪中的澀味。***nip and tuck*** (比賽中)旗鼓相當;棋逢敵手。

nip² *n.* 小飲。—*v.t. & v.i.* 喝少量的酒;一點一點地喝。

ni·pa [ˈnipə; ˈniːpə] *n.* ①〖植物〗(東印度、菲律賓羣島產)尼巴棕櫚。②尼巴棕櫚之葉(覆蓋屋頂用)。③尼巴酒(以 nipa 之樹液製成)。

nip·per [ˈnɪpɚ; ˈnipə] *n.* ①挾者; 摘取者。②鑷子;鉗。③馬之前齒;蟹之鉗。④(*pl.*)手銬;脚鐐。⑤〖英俗〗小童。

nip·ping [ˈnɪpɪŋ; ˈnipiŋ] *adj.* ①挾的;捏的。②刺骨的 (寒冷)。③譏刺的。—**ly,** *adv.*

nip·ple [ˈnɪpl̩; ˈnipl] *n.* ①乳頭。②(奶瓶的)橡皮乳頭。③(玻璃面、金屬面上的)乳狀隆起物。④任何類似乳頭之物。

Nip·pon·ese [ˌnɪpənˈiz; ˌnipəˈniːz] *adj.* 日本的;日本人的; 日本語的。—*n.* ①日本人。②日本語。

nip·py [ˈnɪpɪ; ˈnipi] *adj.,* **nip·pi·er, nip·pi·est.** ①捏的; 如咬的;銳利的;辛辣的;刺骨的。②〖英俗〗活潑的; 敏捷的。③喜歡咬人的。

Ni·ra, NIRA [ˈnirə; ˈniːrə] 〖美〗 *N*ational *I*ndustrial *R*ecovery *A*ct.

nir·va·na [nɝˈvænə; niəˈvɑːnə] *n.* ①(N-)〖印度教〗生命之火燄的熄滅; 解脫。②(N-)〖佛教〗涅槃; 極樂世界。③(自痛苦、煩惱、世俗之)超脫。

Ni·sei, ni·sei [ˈniˈse; ˈniːˈsei] *n., pl.* **-sei, -seis.** 二世 (日裔美人或加拿大人)。

ni·si [ˈnaɪsaɪ; ˈnaisai]〖拉〗*conj.* 除非;不然則(=unless). decree (order, rule)*nisi.* 在指定時日前不提出反對理由時卽作確定的判決(命令、規則)。

Nis·sen hut [ˈnɪsn̩~; ˈnisn~] (二次大戰期中首由英軍所用之) 半圓形活動營房。(亦作 **Quonset hut**)

nit [nɪt; nit] *n.* ①虱卵; 類似虱之昆蟲的卵。②(虱等之)幼蟲。

ni·ter [ˈnaɪtɚ; ˈnaitə] *n.* 〖化〗①硝酸鉀; 硝石(KNO_3)。②硝酸鈉;智利硝石($NaNO_3$)。

ni·ton [ˈnaɪtɑn; ˈnaitɔn] *n.* 〖化〗 radon 之舊名(符號 Nt).

ni·trate [ˈnaɪtret; ˈnaitreit] *n., v.,* **-trat·ed, -trat·ing.** —*n.* 硝酸鹽;硝酸鉀; 硝酸鈉。—*v.t.* ①以硝酸處理。②使變成硝酸化物。

ni·tra·tion [naɪˈtreʃən; naiˈtreiʃən] *n.* 〖化〗硝化。

ni·tre [ˈnaɪtɚ; ˈnaitə] *n.* 〖主英〗=**niter.**

ni·tric [ˈnaɪtrɪk; ˈnaitrik] *adj.* 〖化〗①氮的;含氮的。②硝石的。

nitric acid 硝酸。

nitric oxide 〖化〗氧化氮。

ni·tride [ˈnaɪtraɪd; ˈnaitraid] *n.* 〖化〗氮化物。

ni·tri·fy [ˈnaɪtrəˌfaɪ; ˈnaitrifai] *v.t. & v.i.,* **-fied, -fy·ing.** 〖化〗①(使)與氮或氮化合物化合。②將硝酸鉀或硝酸鈉注入 (土壤等)。③硝化。—**ni·tri·fi·ca·tion,** *n.*

ni·trile rubber [ˈnaɪtrəl~; ˈnaitril~] 一種不怕汽油等溶劑的人造橡皮。

ni·trite [ˈnaɪtraɪt; ˈnaitrait] *n.* 〖化〗亞硝酸鹽。

nitro- 〖字首〗〖化〗表 "NO_2 基;硝石;硝"之義(母音前作 **nitr-**).

ni·tro·ben·zene [ˌnaɪtrəˈbɛnzin; ˌnaitrəˈbenziːn] *n.* 〖化〗硝基苯($C_6H_5NO_2$)。

ni·tro·cel·lu·lose [ˌnaɪtroˈsɛljəˌlos; ˌnaitrouˈseljulous] *n.* 〖化〗硝化纖維素。

***ni·tro·gen** [ˈnaɪtrədʒən; ˈnaitridʒən] *n.* 〖化〗氮。

nitrogen fixation 氮之固定。

ni·trog·e·nous [naɪˈtrɑdʒənəs; naiˈtrɔdʒinəs] *adj.* (含)氮的;(含)氮化合物的。

ni·tro·glyc·er·in(e) [ˌnaɪtrəˈglɪsrɪn; ˌnaitrouˈglisərin] *n.* 〖化〗硝化甘油。

ni·trous [ˈnaɪtrəs; ˈnaitrəs] *adj.* ①硝石的;含硝的。②氮的;含氮的。

nitrous acid 〖化〗亞硝酸。

nitrous oxide 〖化〗氧化亞氮 (N_2O); 笑氣 (=laughing gas).

nit·ty-grit·ty [ˈnɪtɪˈgrɪtɪ; ˈnitiˈgriti] *n.* 細節。

nit·wit [ˈnɪtˌwɪt; ˈnitwit] *n.* 〖俚〗蠢人。

nix¹ [nɪks; niks] *n., pl.* **nix·es.** 〖德國神話〗水鬼;水妖。

nix² *n.* ①〖俚〗無;全無;無人。②〖俚〗我不同意、不贊成、不允許等。③〖美〗無法遞送的郵件等)。—*adv.* 不;不可。—*interj.* ①停!②當心! —*v.t.* 拒絕;不贊同。

nix³ *interj.* 〖英俚〗(老師等)來了!(警告同伴)。

Nix·on [ˈnɪksn̩; ˈniksn] *n.* 尼克森 (Richard Milhous, 1913–, 1969–1974 任美國第三十七任總統, 因水門事件辭職, 為美國第一位辭職的總統)。

Ni·zam [naɪˈzæm; naiˈzæm] *n.* ①印度 Hyderabad 之君主之稱號。②(n-) 土耳其常備兵;土耳其正規軍。

N.J. New Jersey. **NL, NL., N.L.** New Latin (*or* Neo-Latin). **N. Lat., N. lat.** north latitude. **NLRB, N.L.R.B.** 〖美〗National Labor Relations Board. **N.M., N.Mex.** New Mexico. **nm** ①nanometer. ②nautical mile. ③nonmetallic. **NNE, N.N.E., n.n.e.** north-northeast. **NNW, N.N.W.** north-northwest. **No** 〖化〗元素 nobelium 之符號。

:no [no; nou] *n., pl.* **noes,** *adj., adv.* —*n.* ①不;否定。Two *noes* make a yes. 兩否定成為肯定。②否認;拒絕。He said *no* to this proposal. 他拒絕這一建議。③否決; 投反對票者。The *noes* have it. 反對者占多數。—*adj.* ①沒有;不。There is *no* water. 沒

有水。*No* smoking! 禁止吸烟! ②一點兒;很少。It's *no* distance to the post-office. 到郵局很近。***by no means*** 決不。John is *by no means* a bad swimmer. 約翰決不是個蹩脚的游泳者(是個善泳者)。***in no time*** 立刻。***no account*** 無價值的;不足取的。His opinion is of *no account*. 他的意見沒有價值。***no doubt*** 無疑地。There is *no doubt* that he will come. 他會來是無疑的。***no end*** 非常地;無限地。***no end of*** 很多;大量。***no go*** 不行;失敗。***no wonder*** 自然地;難怪。*No wonder* he should have done it. 難怪他做了此事。—*adv.* ①不。Won't you come? *No*, I won't. 你不願意來嗎?不,我不願意。②毫不;並不。I could do it *no* better than that. 我不能做得比那更好了。***no longer*** 不再(指現狀)。We shall *no longer* live in this house. 我們不再住這房子了。***no more*** **a.** 不再(指將來)。*No more* tea, thank you. 謝謝你,不再要茶了。**b.** 不再(=no longer). **c.** 不比…更;與…一樣。**d.** 永不再。**e.** 亦不。***no sooner said than done*** 卽說卽做。***no sooner... than*** 剛…卽。*No sooner* had he arrived *than* he went away again. 他剛一到便又離開了。

*__No.__ ①north; northern. ②number.〖注意〗**No.** 作 number 之縮寫時,常作大寫,適用於商業性或技術性之英語中。在美國,門牌號碼僅有數字,其前不寫 No.

No·a·chi·an 〔no'ekɪən; nou'eikiən〕 *adj.* ①Noah (時代)的。the *Noachian* deluge. 諾亞時代的洪水。②太古的。(亦作 **Noachic, Noachical, Noahic**)

No·ah 〔'noə; 'nouə〕 *n.*〖聖經〗諾亞(希伯來之一族長,上帝啓示其製一方舟,以拯救自己、其家人、及各種動物雌雄各一脫離大洪水,見舊約創世記)。

Noah's Ark 諾亞的方舟。

nob 〔nɑb; nɔb〕 *n., v.,* **nobbed, nob·bing.** —*n.* ①〖俚〗頭。②打 cribbage 牌時和所翻牌同花之 Jack. ③〖英俗〗富翁;有社會地位之人。—*v.t. & v.i.*〖拳擊俚〗打頭;打…之頭。

nob·ble 〔'nɑbl̩; 'nɔbl〕 *v.t.,* **-bled, -bling.** 〖英俚〗①(賽馬時用麻醉藥等)使(馬)無力競賽。②收買(騎師)使於賽馬失敗;收買。③偷;詐取。④逮捕(罪犯等)。—**nob·bler,** *n.*

nob·by 〔'nɑbɪ; 'nɔbi〕 *adj.,* **-bi·er, -bi·est.** 〖俚〗①時髦的;華麗的。②頭等的。

No·bel 〔no'bɛl; nou'bel〕 *n.* 諾貝爾(Alfred Bernhard, 1833–1896, 瑞典工業家、慈善家、發明炸藥、創設 Nobel prizes).

No·bel·ist 〔no'bɛlɪst; nou'belist〕 *n.* 諾貝爾獎得獎人。

no·bel·i·um 〔no'bɛlɪəm; nou'beliəm〕 *n.*〖化〗鍩(放射性元素之一,符號 No).

*__No·bel prizes__ 〔'no,bɛl~; 'noubel~〕 諾貝爾獎(係 Alfred Bernhard Nobel 遺贈鉅資,以息金每年分贈前一年在物理、化學、醫藥、文學,及促進和平方面有成就者)。

no·bil·i·ar·y 〔nə'bɪlɪ,ɛrɪ; nə'biljəri〕 *adj.* 貴族的。

*__no·bil·i·ty__ 〔no'bɪlətɪ; nou'biliti〕 *n., pl.* **-ties.** ①貴族。②貴族出身;貴族階級。③高貴;高尚。*nobility* of soul. 靈魂的高尚。④華貴。

‡**no·ble** 〔'nobl̩; 'noubl〕 *adj.,* **-bler, -blest,** *n.* —*adj.* ①貴族的;高貴的。*noble* birth. 高貴的出身。②高尚的;偉大的;崇高的。a *noble* leader. 偉大的領袖。③卓越的;優秀的;輝煌的。Niagara Falls is a *noble* sight. 尼加拉瀑布是一壯觀的景色。④〖化〗不發生作用的。⑤寶貴的;不易腐蝕或生銹的。Gold and silver are *noble* metals. 金銀爲貴金屬。—*n.* ①貴族。②一種英國古貨幣。③〖俚〗破壞罷工者之首領。—**ness,** *n.* —**no·bly,** *adv.*

*__no·ble·man__ 〔'nobl̩mən; 'noublmən〕 *n., pl.* **-men.** 貴族。

noble metal 貴金屬(金、銀、水銀、白金等)。

no·ble-mind·ed 〔'nobl̩'maindɪd; 'noubl'maindid〕 *adj.* 心地高尚的;高潔的;豪爽的。—**ly,** *adv.* —**ness,** *n.*

no·blesse 〔no'blɛs; nou'bles〕 *n.* ①貴族之地位或出身。②(尤指法國之)貴族階級;貴族(集合稱)。

no·blesse o·blige 〔no'blɛso'bliʒ; nou'blesou'bli:ʒ〕〖法〗地位高則責任重。

no·ble·wom·an 〔'nobl̩,wumən; 'noubl̩,wumən〕 *n., pl.* **-wom·en.** 貴婦。

‡**no·bod·y** 〔'no,bɑdɪ, 'nobʌdɪ, -bədɪ; 'noubədi, -bɔdi〕 *pron., n., pl.* **-bod·ies.** —*pron.* 無人;無一人。I saw *nobody* there. 我沒看見有人在那裏。—*n.* 不重要之人;庸碌之人。He is just a *nobody*. 他祇是個不足輕重之人。〖注意〗 **nobody, nothing, nowhere** 均應連寫成一個單字。nobody 與 nothing 均作單數解。

nock 〔nɑk; nɔk〕 *n.* ①箭之上端掛弦之處。②弓兩端掛弦之凹痕。—*v.t.* ①裝以矢筈。②作凹痕於(弓)。③搭(箭)於弦。

noct-〖字首〗=**nocti-** (於母音前用之)。

noc·tam·bu·lant 〔nɑk'tæmbjələnt; nɔk'tæmbjulənt〕 *adj.* 夜間步行的;夢遊的。

noc·tam·bu·lism 〔nɑk'tæmbjə,lɪzəm; nɔk'tæmbjulizəm〕 *n.* 夢中步行;夢遊症。—**noc·tam·bu·list,** *n.*

nocti-〖字首〗表"夜"之義。

noc·tiv·a·gant 〔nɑk'tɪvəgənt; nɔk'tivəgənt〕 *adj.* 夜遊的。

noc·tiv·a·gous 〔nɑk'tɪvəgəs; nɔk'tivəgəs〕 *adj.* =**noctivagant.**

noc·to·vi·sion 〔'nɑktə,vɪʒən; 'nɔktə,viʒən〕 *n.* 暗視(利用紅外線於夜間或霧中顯示影像)。

noc·turn 〔'nɑktɝn; 'nɔktə:n〕 *n.* ①〖天主教〗宵禱。②〖音樂〗夜曲。

noc·tur·nal 〔nɑk'tɝnəl, -nl̩; nɔk'tə:nl〕 *adj.* ①夜的;夜間的。②夜間活動的;夜出的;夜晚發生的。③晝閉夜開的(花)。—**ly,** *adv.*

noc·turne 〔'nɑktɝn; 'nɔktə:n〕 *n.*〖音樂〗夜曲;夢幻曲。

‡**nod** 〔nɑd; nɔd〕 *v.,* **nod·ded, nod·ding,** *n.* —*v.i.* ①點頭。②點首答應。I asked if he could come and he *nodded*. 我問他是否能來,他點頭答應。③打盹;懈怠。He *nodded* over his work. 他工作時打盹。④低垂;擺動。Trees *nod* in the wind. 樹在風中搖擺。⑤點首表示嘉許或同意。—*v.t.* ①點頭以表示。②點頭以召喚。He *nodded* me into the room. 他點頭示意要我走進房間。③使(某物)擺動或低垂。***(Even) Homer sometimes nods.*** 最偉大的人有時也會錯。—*n.* ①點頭。He gave me a *nod* as he passed. 他走過時向我點頭。②打盹時之垂頭。③打盹。④擺動。⑤點首同意或嘉許。***land of nod*** 睡鄉。—**der,** *n.* —**ding·ly,** *adv.*

nod·al 〔'nodl̩; 'noudl〕 *adj.* ①node(結,節,瘤)的;有 node 之性質的。②〖物理〗節的;波節的。—**i·ty,** *n.*

nod·die 〔'nɑdɪ; 'nɔdi〕 *n.* =**noddy** ②.

nod·ding 〔'nɑdɪŋ; 'nɔdiŋ〕 *adj.* 點頭的;低垂的;擺動的。

nod·dle¹ [ˈnadl̩; ˈnɔdl] *n.* 〖俗,諧〗頭;腦袋。

nod·dle² *v.t.* & *v.i.*, **-dled, -dling.** 輕輕地或頻頻地點頭。

nod·dy [ˈnadɪ; ˈnɔdi] *n., pl.* **-dies.** ①燕鷗類之熱帶海鳥。②愚人。

node [nod; noud] *n.* ①結;節;瘤。②〖植物〗莖節(莖上生葉的部分)。③〖醫〗硬結腫。④〖天文〗交點。⑤〖物理〗節;波節(波動介質中比較不受振動之點、線或面)。⑥〖數學〗交點;交軌點。⑦(戲劇或小說中之)中心情節。

no·di [ˈnodaɪ; ˈnoudai] *n.* pl. of **nodus.**

nod·i·cal [ˈnadɪkl̩; ˈnɔdikl] *adj.* 〖天文〗交點的。

no·dose [ˈnodos; ˈnoudous] *adj.* 多結節的。

no·dos·i·ty [nəˈdasətɪ; nəˈdɔsiti] *n., pl.* **-ties.** ①有結節;多結節。②節;結節。

nod·u·lar [ˈnadʒələ˞; ˈnɔdjulə] *adj.* ①結節的;結節狀的。②〖礦〗塊狀的;瘤塊狀的。

nod·u·lat·ed [ˈnadʒəˌletɪd; ˈnɔdjuleitid] *adj.* 節的;小節的;結節狀的。

nod·u·la·tion [ˌnadʒəˈleʃən; ˌnɔdjuˈleiʃən] *n.* ①有節;有瘤塊。②結節;結瘤塊。③節;小塊。

nod·ule [ˈnadʒul; ˈnɔdjuːl] *n.* ①小節;小塊。②〖礦〗瘤狀體。③〖植物〗節; 結節。④〖地質〗岩球。

nod·u·lous [ˈnadʒuləs; ˈnɔdjuləs] *adj.* 有小節的;有小塊的。

no·dus [ˈnodəs; ˈnoudəs] *n., pl.* **-di.** ①結節。②〖醫〗硬結腫(＝node). ③困難;困難之點。

No·el [noˈɛl; nouˈel] *n.* ①聖誕節。②(n-)聖誕詩歌。

no·e·sis [noˈisɪs; nouˈiːsis] *n.* ①〖哲學〗純粹理性之認識作用。②〖心理〗認知;認識;認識力。

no·et·ic [noˈɛtɪk; nouˈetik] *adj.* 心的;智力的; 基於純粹理性的; 純理的。—*n.* 有智力之人;智者。

no-fault [ˈnoˈfɔlt; ˈnouˈfɔːlt] *adj.* 〖美〗非過失的(一種汽車保險,不論是否爲被保人之過失,其損失槪由保險公司賠償)。

nog¹ [nag; nɔg] *n., v.,* **nogged, nog·ging.** —*n.* ①(嵌入牆內以承納釘子的)木釘; 木栓;木磚。②支撐礦坑頂的木塊。—*v.t.* 以木釘支持或固定;裝嵌木磚於…。

nog², nogg [nag; nɔg] *n.* ①〖英〗一種强烈麥酒。②〖美〗＝**egg flip.**

nog·gin [ˈnagɪn; ˈnɔgin] *n.* ①小盃;小量之飲料。②液量單位(＝$^1/_4$ pint)。③〖俗〗頭。

nog·ging [ˈnagɪŋ; ˈnɔgiŋ] *n.* 〖英〗①在木板間加襯磚。②(木架間之)磚壁。

no-hit·ter [ˈnoˈhɪtə˞; ˈnouˈhitə] *n.* 〖棒球〗無安打球賽。

no·how [ˈnoˌhau; ˈnouhau] *adv.* 〖方〗毫不;決不;無論如何不 (＝in no way; not at all). —*adj.* 紛亂的; 不舒服的;氣色不好的。

noise** [nɔɪz; nɔiz] *n., v.,* **noised, nois·ing.**—*n.* ①喧聲;噪音。I don't like *noise*. 我不喜歡喧聲。②聲音;響聲。A *noise* woke him up. 一種聲音將他驚醒。③電訊中之干擾音。④〖廢〗謠言; 中傷之言。⑤在性質上多變的能源。 ***make a noise **a.** 吵鬧。It *made a noise* like a train. 它發出的聲音像火車。**b.** 引起談論;引起注意。The song has *made a noise*. 那首歌已引起注意。 ***make a noise in the world*** 引起極大注意; 成爲聳人聽聞之事。—*v.t.* 謠傳;宣稱。 It was *noised* that he killed her. 傳說他將她殺死了。 —*v.i.* ①發出噪音。②議論;公開談論。〖注意〗**noise** 特指不愉快的嘈雜、叫囂、刺耳、震耳之聲。**sound** 是泛指一般的聲音。

***noise·less** [ˈnɔɪzlɪs; ˈnɔizlis] *adj.* ①無聲的;靜的。a *noiseless* step. 無聲的脚步。②聲音很輕的;不出聲的。—**ness,** *n.*

***noise·less·ly** [ˈnɔɪzlɪslɪ; ˈnɔizlisli] *adv.* 輕輕地;寂然無聲地。

noise·mak·er [ˈnɔɪzˌmekə˞; ˈnɔizˌmeikə] *n.* 發出噪音之人或物,如除夕作樂者、或號角等。

noise pollution 噪音汚染。

noi·sette¹ [nwaˈzɛt; nwaːˈzet] *n.* (常 *pl.*) 小片之精瘦肉。

noi·sette² *n.* 〖植物〗一種薔薇。

noi·some [ˈnɔɪsəm; ˈnɔisəm] *adj.* ①使人不快的; 有惡臭的。 ②有害的;有害於健康的;有毒的。—**ly,** *adv.* —**ness,** *n.*

***nois·y** [ˈnɔɪzɪ; ˈnɔizi] *adj.,* **nois·i·er, nois·i·est.** ①喧鬧的。a *noisy* boy. 喧鬧的孩子。②喧囂的。—**nois·i·ly,** *adv.* —**nois·i·ness,** *n.*

no·lens vo·lens [ˈnolɛnz ˈvolɛnz; ˈnoulenzˈvoulenz] 〖拉〗 無論願否 (＝willy-nilly).

no·li me tan·ge·re [ˈnolaɪmiˈtændʒəri; ˈnoulaimiːˈtændʒəriː] 〖拉〗①禁止接觸或干與之警告。 ②復活後之耶穌與 Mary Magdalen 相會之圖畫。③〖植物〗鳳仙花;水金鳳。④〖醫〗狼瘡。(③, ④亦作 **noli-me-tangere**)

nol·le pros·e·qui [ˈnalɪˈprasɪˌkwaɪ; ˈnɔliˈprɔsikwai] 〖法律〗原告撤回訴訟 (＝to be unwilling to prosecute). (略作 **nol. pros.**)

no·lo e·pis·co·pa·ri [ˈnolo ɪˌpɪskəˈperaɪ; ˈnoulou iˌpiskəˈpeirai] 〖拉〗(＝I do not wish to become a bishop). ①〖宗教〗余不願爲主教(主教任命式中之形式上的謙辭)。②對重任之辭謝。

nol-pros [ˌnalˈpras; ˌnɔlˈprɔs] *v.t.,* **-prossed, -pros·sing.** 〖法律〗原告同意中止(訴訟);撤銷(告訴)。

no·mad [ˈnomæd; ˈnɔməd] *n.* ①遊牧部落的人。②流浪的人。 —*adj.* ①遊牧的。②流浪的。

no·mad·ic [noˈmædɪk; nouˈmædik] *adj.* ①遊牧的。②流浪的。—**al·ly,** *adv.*

no·mad·ism [ˈnomædˌɪzəm; ˈnoumædizəm] *n.* 遊牧生活;流浪。

no-man [ˈnoˌmæn; ˈnoumæn] *n.* 〖美俗〗性情乖僻者;常持相反意見者 (爲 yes-man 之對)。

no man's land ①(國境之)無人區域;荒地;無主之土地(常爲爭執之對象)。②(戰爭中兩方戰壕間之)眞空地帶。③〖俗〗(網球、手球等)球場中央一帶對球員不利之地方。

nom de guerre [ˌnɔ̃dəˈgɛr; ˌnɔ̃dəˈgɛːr] 〖法〗假名;藝名;筆名。

nom de plume [ˈnamdəˌplum; ˈnɔmdəˌpluːm] 〖法〗 筆名。

no·men [ˈnomɛn; ˈnoumen] *n., pl.* **nom·i·na** [ˈnamənə; ˈnɔminə]. 古羅馬公民名字的第二個字 (如 Gaius Julius Caesar 中之 Julius 卽是)。

no·men·cla·tor [ˈnomənˌkletə˞; ˈnoumənˌkleitə] *n.* ①宣呼姓名之人(如宴會中宣呼賓客之姓名者)。②學名之命名者。

no·men·cla·ture [ˈnomənˌkletʃə˞, noˈmɛnklətʃə˞; nouˈmenklətʃə, ˈnoumenkleitʃə] *n.* (專門學科中的)有系統的命名法;專門名辭;術語。

nom·i·nal [ˈnamənl̩; ˈnɔminl] *adj.* ①

名義上的（無實權的)。② 極微薄的（象徵性的)。③名字的。④〖文法〗名詞的。⑤記名的。*nominal* shares of stock. 記名股票。⑥賦與名字的。⑦符合計畫的;滿意的。

nom·i·nal·ism [ˈnɑmənlˌɪzm; ˈnɔminlizm] *n.*〖哲學〗唯名論。

nom·i·nal·ist [ˈnɑmənlɪst; ˈnɔminlist] *n.* 唯名論者。—*adj.* 唯名論(者)的。

nom·i·nal·is·tic [ˌnɑmənlˈɪstɪk; ˌnɔminəˈlistik] *adj.* 唯名論（者）的。

nom·i·nal·ize [ˈnɑmənlˌaɪz; ˈnɔminlaiz] *v.t.*, **-ized, -iz·ing.** 使其他詞類轉變爲名詞。「*adv.* 名義上;有名無實地。

nom·i·nal·ly [ˈnɑmənlɪ; ˈnɔminəli]

nominal value (股票等之)面額。

***nom·i·nate** [ˈnɑməˌnet; ˈnɔmineit] *v.*, **-nat·ed, -nat·ing,** *adj.* —*v.t.* ①提名爲…之候選人。He was *nominated* for election. 他被提名爲候選人。②任命;派定。③〖賽馬〗登記(馬匹)參加競賽。—*adj.* ①具有特定之名字的。②被任命的;被提名的。—**nom·i·na·tor,** *n.*

***nom·i·na·tion** [ˌnɑməˈneʃən; ˌnɔmiˈneiʃən] *n.* ①提名（爲候選人)。②任命。③被提名;被任命。His *nomination* to the chairmanship came as a surprise to many people. 他被提名爲主席使許多人覺得奇怪。「minəˈtaivəl] *adj.*〖文法〗主格的。

nom·i·na·ti·val [ˌnɑmənəˈtaɪvl; ˌnɔ-

***nom·i·na·tive** [ˈnɑmənətɪv; ˈnɔminətiv] *adj.* ①〖文法〗主格的。*nominative* case. 主格（例如 I, he, she, we, they 等)。②被提名的;被任命的。③(股票等）記名的。—*n.* ①主格。②主格語。

nominative absolute〖文法〗絕對分詞子句（分詞子句與主句中任何部分不發生關係之結構。例:The day being warm, we took off our coats. 句中的 The day being warm 即絕對分詞子句)。

nom·i·na·tor [ˈnɑməˌnetɚ; ˈnɔmineitə] *n.* 提名者;推薦者;任命者。

nom·i·nee [ˌnɑməˈni; ˌnɔmiˈniː] *n.* 被提名的候選人;被任命者。

non [nɑn; nɔn]〖拉〗*adv.* 不;非(=not).

non-〖字首〗表"無;不;非"之義。

non·ab·stain·er [ˌnɑnəbˈstenɚ; ˌnɔnəbˈsteinə] *n.* 飲酒者;不節制者。

non·ac·cept·ance [ˌnɑnəkˈsɛptəns; ˈnɔnəkˈseptəns] *n.* ①不接受。②〖商〗不承兌。

non·age [ˈnɑnɪdʒ; ˈnounidʒ] *n.* ①〖法律〗未成年。②早期;未成熟期。

non·a·ge·nar·i·an [ˌnɑnədʒəˈnɛrɪən; ˌnounədʒiˈnɛəriən] *adj.* 九十(多)歲的。—*n.* 九十(多)歲的人。

non·ag·gres·sion [ˌnɑnəˈgrɛʃən; ˌnɔnəˈgreʃən] *n.*（國與國之間的）不侵略。—*adj.* 不侵略的。

non·a·gon [ˈnɑnəˌgɑn; ˈnɔnəgɔn] *n.*〖數學〗九邊形;九角形。(亦作 **enneagon**)

non·ag·ri·cul·tur·al [ˌnɑnˌægrɪˈkʌltʃərəl; ˌnɔnˌægriˈkʌltʃərəl] *adj.* 不務農的。「ˌnɔnˌælkəˈhɔlik] *adj.* 不含酒精的。

non·al·co·hol·ic [ˌnɑnælkəˈhɔlɪk;

non·a·ligned [ˌnɑnəˈlaɪnd; ˌnɔnəˈlaind] *adj.* 不結盟的（尤指不與共產或非共產集團結盟)。

non·a·lign·ment [ˌnɑnəˈlaɪnmənt; ˌnɔnəˈlainmənt] *n.* 不結盟;政治中立。

non·ap·pear·ance [ˌnɑnəˈpɪrəns; ˈnɔnəˈpiərəns] *n.*（特指於法庭之)不出席。

no·na·ry [ˈnonərɪ; ˈnounəri] *adj., n. pl.* **-ries.** —*adj.*〖數學〗九進法的。—*n.*〖罕〗九個的一組。

non·as·sess·a·ble [ˌnɑnəˈsɛsəbl; ˌnɔnəˈsesəbl] *adj.*（股份之）除投資額外無其他費用或責任的。

non·at·tend·ance [ˌnɑnəˈtɛndəns; ˈnɔnəˈtendəns] *n.* 缺席;不到;（特指違反義務教育法令之）不就學。

non·be·liev·er [ˌnɑnbəˈlivɚ; ˌnɔnbiˈliːvə] *n.* 無信仰的人(尤指不信上帝者)。

non·bel·lig·er·ent [ˌnɑnbəˈlɪdʒərənt; ˈnɔnbiˈlidʒərənt] *adj.* 非交戰的;非交戰政策的。—*n.* 非交戰國。

nonce [nɑns; nɔns] *n.* 特殊之時間;特殊之場合;現時;目前。—*adj.* 臨時的。

nonce word 僅爲特殊情況而拼成與使用之字,如: *newspaperialist* =journalist.

non·cha·lance [ˈnɑnʃələns; ˈnɔnʃələns] *n.* 無動於衷的神氣。

non·cha·lant [ˈnɑnʃələnt; ˈnɔnʃələnt] *adj.* 冷漠的;滿不在乎的。

non·claim [ˈnɑnˌklem; ˈnɔnkleim] *n.*〖法律〗(於限期內)未提出要求;要求懈怠。

non·col·le·giate [ˈnɑnkəˈlidʒɪɪt; ˈnɔnkəˈliːdʒiit] *adj.* ①不屬於學院(college)的。②非由學院組成的(大學)。③(學歷)在大學以下的。—*n.* ①無所屬之大學生。②非大學出身的人。

non·com [ˌnɑnˈkɑm; ˌnɔnˈkɔm] *n.*〖俗〗士官。—*adj.* 未授官階的。

non·com·bat·ant [nɑnˈkɑmbətənt; ˈnɔnˈkɔmbətənt] *n.* ①非戰鬥人員（如軍中之醫師、牧師等)。②平民;戰時未參與戰鬥的人。—*adj.* 未參加戰鬥的;非戰鬥人員的。

non·com·bus·ti·ble [ˌnɑnkəmˈbʌstəbl; ˌnɔnkəmˈbʌstəbl] *adj.* 非易燃的。—*n.* 非易燃性物質。

non·com·mer·cial [ˌnɑnkəˈmɝʃəl; ˌnɔnkəˈməːʃəl] *adj.* 非營利性的。

non·com·mis·sioned [ˌnɑnkəˈmɪʃənd; ˈnɔnkəˈmiʃənd] *adj.* 無委任狀的;未受任命的。「官;軍士。(略作 **N.C.O.**)

noncommissioned officer 士

non·com·mit·tal [ˌnɑnkəˈmɪtl; ˈnɔnkəˈmitl] *adj.* 不確示意見的;不作確答的;含糊的;曖昧的。—**ly,** *adv.*

non·com·mu·nist [ˌnɑnˈkɑmjunɪst; ˌnɔnˈkɔmjunist] *n., adj.* 非共產主義者(的);非共(的)。

non·com·pli·ance [ˌnɑnkəmˈplaɪəns; ˈnɔnkəmˈplaiəns] *n.* 不承諾;不順從;不同意;不讓步。—*adj.*〖美〗不遵照政府限制而種植之穀物的。—**non·com·pli·ant,** *n.*

non com·pos men·tis [nɑnˈkɑmpəsˈmɛntɪs; nɔnˈkɔmpəsˈmentis]〖拉〗〖法律〗心神喪失的;精神不正常的。(常略作 **non compos**)

non·con·duct·ing [ˌnɑnkənˈdʌktɪŋ; ˈnɔnkənˈdʌktiŋ] *adj.*〖物理〗不傳導的。

non·con·duc·tor [ˌnɑnkənˈdʌktɚ; ˈnɔnkənˌdʌktə] *n.*〖物理〗不良導體;絕緣體。

non·con·fi·dence [ˈnɑnˈkɑnfədəns; ˈnɔnˈkɔnfidəns] *n.* 不信任。

non·con·form·ance [ˌnɑnkənˈfɔrməns; ˈnɔnkənˈfɔːməns] *n.* 不順從;不奉國教。

non·con·form·ist [ˌnɑnkənˈfɔrmɪst; ˈnɔnkənˈfɔːmist] *n.* ①不遵奉國教之人。②(常 N-) 不遵奉英國國教的基督教新教徒。

Nonconformist Churches（英國的）獨立教會。

non·con·form·i·ty 〔ˌnɑnkənˈfɔrmətɪ; ˈnɔnkənˈfɔːmiti〕 *n.* ①不遵從(規則、習慣等)。②不適合;不一致。③不遵奉國教;非國教主義;非國教教徒。④(常 N-) 不遵奉英國國教之基督教教義。

non·co·op·er·a·tion 〔ˌnɑnkoˌɑpəˈreʃən; ˌnɔnkouˌɔpəˈreiʃən〕 *n.* ①不合作。②(對政府之)反抗性的不合作。③(常N-)(印度甘地一派對英國之)消極抵抗政策;不合作主義。(亦作 **nonco-operation, noncoöperation**) **—ist,** *n.*

non·de·liv·er·y 〔ˌnɑndɪˈlɪvərɪ; ˈnɔndiˈlivəri〕*n.* 不(能)引渡;不(能)送達;不交付。

non·de·script 〔ˈnɑndɪˌskrɪpt; ˈnɔndiskript〕 *adj.* 莫可名狀的;難以分類的;無可命名的。—*n.* 難以分類或名狀的人或物。

non·dur·a·ble〔nɑnˈdjurəbl̩; nɔnˈdjuərəbl〕 *adj.* 不耐久的;不經用的。—*n.* 不耐久之物。

‡none[1] 〔nʌn; nʌn〕 *pron.* ①毫無 (=not any). We have *none* of that paper left. 我們絲毫未剩下那種紙。②無一人;無一物(=no one; not one). *None* of these is for me. 這些中沒有一個是給我的。③無人;無物(=no persons or things, 通常當作複數用, 故亦應用複數的動詞)。*None* have arrived. 無人到來。—*adv.* 毫不。He did it *none* too well. 他做的一點也不好。***none the less*** 依然;然而。—*adj.*〖古〗毫無;無。(通常用於母音或h之前)。Thou shalt have *none* other gods but me. 除了我以外你不可有別的神。〖注意〗**none** 是一個字, 而 **no one** 是分寫的兩個字, 且常代替 none 以加强語氣。none 可作複數, 亦可作單數, 但現在則多作複數。

none[2] *n.* sing. of **nones**②.

non·ef·fec·tive〔ˌnɑnəˈfɛktɪv,–ɪˈfɛk–; ˌnɔniˈfektiv〕 *adj.* ①無效的;無用的。②〖軍〗無戰鬥力的。 —*n.* 無戰鬥力之軍人。

non·e·go 〔nɑnˈigo; nɔnˈegou〕 *n., pl.* **-gos.**〖哲學〗非我;客觀;外物;外界。

non·en·ti·ty 〔nɑnˈɛntətɪ; nɔnˈentiti〕 *n., pl.* **-ties.** ①無足輕重之人;無用之人;無價值之物;無用之物。②不存在之物;想像之物。

nones 〔nonz; nounz〕 *n. pl., sing.* **none.** ①(古羅馬曆中) 自 ides 起算之前第九日(三月、五月、七月、十月之第七日或其他各月之第五日)。②(常 N-)〖宗教〗第九時 (依古羅馬計算法日出後之第九時, 卽等於午後三時);第九時之祈禱。

non·es·sen·tial 〔ˌnɑnəˈsɛnʃəl; ˈnɔniˈsenʃəl〕 *adj.* 非本質上的;非必需的; 非主要的。—*n.*非本質上之事物;不必需之事物或人。

none·such 〔ˈnʌnˌsʌtʃ; ˈnʌnsʌtʃ〕 *n.* (亦作 **nonsuch**) ①無雙之人或物;完美之典範。②〖植物〗紅色剪夏羅。—*adj.* 無雙的;無比的。

no·net 〔nəˈnɛt; nəˈnet〕 *n.* 〖音樂〗九重奏(唱)曲。

none·the·less 〔ˌnʌnðəˈlɛs; ˌnʌnðəˈles〕 *adv.* 仍然 (=none the less).

non·ex·ist·ence 〔ˌnɑnɪgˈzɪstəns; ˈnɔnigˈzistəns〕 *n.* ①不存在;非實在;無。②非實在之物。**—non·ex·ist·ent,** *adj.*

non·fea·sance 〔nɑnˈfizn̩s; ˈnɔnˈfiːzəns〕 *n.*〖法律〗不履行義務。

non·fer·rous 〔nɑnˈfɛrəs; nɔnˈferəs〕 *adj.* ①(金屬之)不含鐵的。②非(鋼) 鐵的。

non·fic·tion 〔nɑnˈfɪkʃən; nɔnˈfikʃən〕 *n.* 非小說性的散文文學 (傳記、歷史、小品文等)。

non·flam·ma·ble 〔nɑnˈflæməbl̩; nɔnˈflæməbl〕 *adj.* 不燃性的。

non·ful·fill·ment 〔ˌnɑnfulˈfɪlmənt; ˌnɔnfulˈfilmənt〕 *n.*不履行;不實踐;不應驗。

non·hu·man 〔nɑnˈhjumən; nɔnˈhjuːmən〕 *adj.* 非人類的。

no·nil·lion 〔noˈnɪljən; nouˈniljən〕 *n., pl.* **-lions, -lion.** ①(在美國、法國) 1,000之10方 (1後加30個零之數)。②(在英國、德國) 100萬之9方(1後加54個零之數)。—*adj.* 上述之數的。 **—no·nil·lionth,** *n., adj.*

non·im·mi·grant 〔nɑnˈɪməgrənt; nɔnˈimigrənt〕 *n.* ①非移民入境之外國人;外國訪客。②出境後又回來之外國僑民。

non·im·por·ta·tion 〔ˌnɑnɪmporˈteʃən; ˌnɔnimpɔːˈteiʃən〕 *n.* 不進口;禁止進口。

non·in·ter·ven·tion〔ˌnɑnɪntɚˈvɛnʃən; ˌnɔnintəˈvenʃən〕 *n.* (對他國或對所轄地區之) 不干涉;不介入;放任。 **—al,** *adj.* **—al·ist, —ist,** *n.*

non·join·der 〔nɑnˈdʒɔɪndɚ; nɔnˈdʒɔində〕 *n.*〖法律〗非共同訴訟。

non·ju·ring 〔nɑnˈdʒurɪŋ; nɔnˈdʒuəriŋ〕 *adj.*〖英史〗不肯宣誓效忠的。

non·ju·ror 〔nɑnˈdʒurɚ; ˈnɔnˈdʒuərə〕 *n.* ①拒絕宣誓者。②(N-)〖英史〗1689年革命後拒絕對 William 三世及 Mary 宣誓效忠之英國國教牧師。

non·lead(·ed) 〔ˌnɑnˈlɛd(ɪd); ˌnɔnˈled(id)〕 *adj.* 無鉛的。*nonlead(ed)* gasolines. 無鉛汽油。

non·le·gal 〔nɑnˈligl̩; nɔnˈliːgəl〕 *adj.* 與法律無關的 (別於 illegal).

non·le·thal 〔ˈnɑnˈliθəl; ˈnɔnˈliːθəl〕 *adj.* 非致命性的。

non·log·i·cal 〔ˌnɑnˈlɑdʒɪkl; ˈnɔnˈlɔdʒikəl〕 *adj.* 由邏輯以外之方法的;非邏輯的。

non·mem·ber 〔nɑnˈmɛmbɚ; ˈnɔnˌmembə〕 *n.* 非會員;非黨員。**—ship,** *n.*

non·met·al 〔nɑnˈmɛtl̩; ˈnɔnˌmetl〕 *n.*〖化〗非金屬 (元素)。

non·me·tal·lic 〔ˌnɑnməˈtælɪk; ˌnɔnməˈtælik〕 *adj.*〖化〗①非金屬的。*nonmetallic* elements. 非金屬元素。②非金屬性的。

non·mor·al 〔nɑnˈmɔrəl,–ˈmɑr–; nɔnˈmɔrəl〕 *adj.* 與道德 (倫理) 無關的。

non·nat·u·ral 〔nɑnˈnætʃərəl; nɔnˈnætʃrəl〕 *adj.* 非自然的;不靠自然的。

non·nu·cle·ar 〔ˌnɑnˈnjuklɪɚ; ˌnɔnˈnjuːkliə〕 *n., adj.* 非(原子)核(的)。

no-no 〔ˈnoˌno; ˈnouˌnou〕 *n., pl.* **no-no's, no-nos.**〖美俚〗不可做或不可使用的東西;禁忌。

non·ob·jec·tive 〔ˌnɑnəbˈdʒɛktɪv; ˌnɔnəbˈdʒektiv〕 *adj.* 缺乏客觀性的;抽象的。

non obst. non obstante(拉=notwithstanding). 雖然;縱使(有法律之規定)。

non·of·fi·cial 〔ˌnɑnəˈfɪʃəl; ˈnɔnəˈfiʃəl〕 *adj.* 非官方的;非正式的。

non·pa·reil 〔ˌnɑnpəˈrɛl; ˌnɔnpəˈrel〕 *adj.* 無上的;無比的。—*n.* ①無比之人或物;舉世無雙之人或物。②一種顏色美麗之鶯 (產於美國南部)。③一種蘋果。④〖印刷〗六鎊因 (point) 大小之鉛字。

non·par·ti·san, non·par·ti·zan 〔nɑnˈpartəzn̩; nɔnˈpaːtizn〕 *adj.* 無黨派的;超黨派的。 **—ship,** *n.*

non·par·ty 〔ˈnɑnˈpartɪ; ˈnɔnˈpaːti〕

adj. 不偏不倚的。
non·pay·ment [nɑn'pemənt; 'nɔn-'peimənt] *n.* 不支付;未繳納。
non·per·form·ance [ˌnɑnpɚ'fɔrməns; 'nɔnpə'fɔːməns] *n.* 不履行;不實行。
non·plus [nɑn'plʌs; 'nɔn'plʌs] *v.,* **-plus(s)ed, -plus·(s)ing,** *n.* —*v.t.* 使困惑;使窘困;使狼狽。—*n.* 困惑;窘困;狼狽。
non·pro·duc·tive [ˌnɑnprə'dʌktɪv; ˌnɔnprə'dʌktiv] *adj.* ①不生產的;無出產的。②與生產無直接關係的。—**ly,** *adv.* —**ness, non·pro·duc·tiv·i·ty,** *n.*
non·pro·fes·sion·al [ˌnɑnprə'fɛʃənl; 'nɔnprə'feʃənəl] *adj.* 非職業性的;非專門的。
non·prof·it [nɑn'prɑfɪt; nɔn'prɔfit] *adj.* 非營利的;無利可圖的。
non·pro·lif·er·a·tion treaty [ˌnɑnproˌlɪfə'reʃən～; ˌnɔnprouˌlifə'reiʃən～] 禁止核子擴散條約。(略作 **NPT**)
non·rep·re·sen·ta·tion·al [ˌnɑnrɛprɪzɛn'teʃənl; ˌnɔnreprizen'teiʃənəl] *adj.* 〖美術〗非描寫的;非模倣的;抽象的。—**ism,** *n.*
non·res·i·dent [nɑn'rɛzədənt; 'nɔn-'rezidənt] *adj.* ①不住在自己之產業上(工作地區、就讀之學校地區、任地或管區)的。②非某地之居民的;不在某地居住的。—*n.* ①住家與工作地(產業、就讀學校、任地、或管區)不在同一地區的人。②非本地居民。
non·re·sist·ant [ˌnɑnrɪ'zɪstənt; ˌnɔnri'zistənt] *adj.* 不反抗的;盲從的。—*n.* 不反抗(主義)者。—**non·re·sist·ance,** *n.*
non·re·stric·tive [ˌnɑnrɪ'strɪktɪv; ˌnɔnris'triktiv] *adj.* ①無限制的。②〖文法〗僅加以形容而不限制其意義的。
non·sched·uled [nɑn'skɛdʒuld; nɔn-'ʃedjuːld] *adj.* ①非定期的。②無定期班機之航空公司的。③不按照日程的;不按時間表的。
nonscheduled airline 專做包機(客運或貨運)業務而無定期班機的航空公司。
non·sec·tar·i·an [ˌnɑnsɛk'tɛrɪən; ˌnɔnsek'tɛəriən] *adj.* 不屬於任何宗派的。
non·sense** ['nɑnsɛns; 'nɔnsəns, 'nɔn-'sens] *n.* 無意義;無意義的話或舉動。Don't talk *nonsense!* 不要胡說八道。take the nonsense out of*** 使(某人)之思想或言行合理。
non·sen·si·cal [nɑn'sɛnsɪkl; nɔn-'sensikəl] *adj.* 愚蠢的;荒謬的。—**ly,** *adv.* —**ness,** —**i·ty,** *n.*
non seq. non sequitur.
non se·qui·tur [nɑn'sɛkwɪtɚ; nɔn-'sekwitə] 〖拉〗〖邏輯〗(與前提不符的)不合理的推論或結論(=it does not follow).
non·sked [nɑn'skɛd; nɔn'sked] *n.* 〖俗〗=**nonscheduled airline.**
non·skid ['nɑn'skɪd; 'nɔn'skid] *adj.* (輪胎等)不滑的。
non·stop ['nɑn'stɑp; 'nɔn'stɔp] *adj.* 中途不停的;中途不着陸的;直達的。—*adv.* 中途不停地;中途不降落地;直達地。—*n.* ①直達飛機。②直達飛行。
non·such ['nʌnˌsʌtʃ; 'nʌn-sʌtʃ] *n.* =**nonesuch.**
non·suit [nɑn'sut; 'nɔn'sjuːt] *n.* 〖法律〗訴訟之駁回。—*v.t.* 駁回…之訴訟。
non·sup·port [ˌnɑnsə'port; ˌnɔnsə-'pɔːt] *n.* ①〖法律〗不盡贍養義務。②缺乏支持;無擁護。
non trop·po [nɑn'trɔppo; nɔn'trɔːp-pou] 〖義〗〖音樂〗不過分地(=not too much).
non·un·ion [nɑn'junjən; nɔn'juː-njən] *adj.* ①不屬於工會的;未加入公會的。②不遵守工會規章的。③不承認工會的;反對工會的。—*n.* ①不連(如骨折)。②未能接合;未能團結。
non·un·ion·ism [nɑn'junjənɪzm; nɔn-'juːnjənizm] *n.* 反工會主義(理論或行動)。
non·un·ion·ist [nɑn'junjənɪst; nɔn-'juːnjənist] *n.* ①反對工會(主義)者。②不屬於工會之工人。
non·us·er [nɑn'juzɚ; 'nɔn'juːzə] *n.* 〖法律〗權利不行使;權利消失。
non·vi·o·lence [nɑn'vaɪələns; nɔn-'vaiələns] *n.* ①不訴諸暴力的主張、政策。②無暴力之存在。
noo·dle[1] ['nudl; 'nuːdl] *n.* (常*pl.*)麪條。
noo·dle[2] *n.* ①笨人。②〖俚〗頭;腦袋。
***nook** [nuk; nuk] *n.* ①角落;屋隅。every *nook* and corner. 到處。②隱匿處;隱蔽處;僻遠處。③三角形小塊土地。④角落上掉下之一小片。—**like,** *adj.*
‡**noon** [nun; nuːn] *n.* ①正午;中午。at high *noon.* 正午時。I shall be back by *noon.* 我將在中午回來。②頂點;巔峯;全盛時代。③〖詩〗午夜。—*adj.* 中午的。—*v.i.* 中午停下來吃飯或休息。
***noon·day** ['nunˌde; 'nuːndei] *n., adj.* 正午;正午的。His guilt is as clear as the sun at *noonday.* 他的罪非常顯明。
no one 沒有人(=nobody).(亦作**no-one**)
noon·ing ['nunɪŋ; 'nuːniŋ] *n.* 〖美方〗①正午。②中午休息。③午餐。
noon·tide ['nunˌtaɪd; 'nuːn-taid] *n.* 中午(=noon). —*adj.* 中午的。
***noon·time** ['nunˌtaɪm; 'nuːn-taim] *n.* =**noontide.**
noose [nus; nuːs] *n., v.,* **noosed, noos·ing.** —*n.* ①活結;繩套。②羅網;圈套。***the noose*** 絞刑。—*v.t.* ①以(繩)結成活套。②以活結繩套捕;加圈套。③以羅網捕;誘入圈套。—**noos·er,** *n.*
no-par ['no'pɑr; 'nou'pɑː] *adj.* 無票面價值的。
nope [nop; noup] *adv.* 〖美俚〗=**no.**
‡**nor** [nɔr, nɚ; nɔː, nə] *conj.* ①亦不(與neither連用)。I have neither time *nor* money. 我既無時間也無錢。②亦不;又不。I didn't see it, and *nor* did you. 我沒有看見它,你也沒有。③〖詩〗=**neither** (與另一nor連用)。*Nor* silver *nor* gold can buy it. 金與銀都無法買它。④〖詩〗既非…亦非(其前之 not 或另一 nor 省略時)。Thou *nor* I have made the world. 這世界並非你我所造。⑤〖方〗=**than.**
Nor. ①North. ②Norway. ③Norman. ④Norwegian. ⑤Northern.
No·ra ['nɔrə; 'nɔːrə] *n.* 女子名。
Nor·dic ['nɔrdɪk; 'nɔːdik] *n.* 北歐人。—*adj.* ①北歐人的。②(包括跳躍與越野競賽)滑雪比賽項目的。—**i·ty,** *n.*
Nor·folk ['nɔrfək, -fɔk; 'nɔːfək] *n.* 諾福克(**a.** 美國 Virginia 州東南部之一港埠; **b.** 英格蘭東部之一郡)。
Norfolk jacket 一種有腰帶的男用寬上衣。(亦作 **Norfolk coat**)
nor·land ['nɔrlənd; 'nɔːlənd] *n.* 〖詩〗=**northland.**
norm [nɔrm; nɔːm] *n.* ①標準;規範;模範。②〖數學〗模方;範數。—**less,** *adj.*
Nor·ma ['nɔrmə; 'nɔːmə] *n.* ①女子名。②〖天文〗矩尺座。
***nor·mal** ['nɔrml; 'nɔːməl] *adj.* ①正常

的;正規的;常態的。②〖幾何〗法線的;垂直的;正交的。③〖化〗中和性的;當量的。④〖醫〗無病的。—*n.* ①常態;標準。②〖幾何〗法線;垂直線;垂直面。③正常的人。④智力及情緒穩定力中等的人。—**ly,** *adv.*

nor·mal·cy [ˈnɔrml̩sɪ; ˈnɔːməlsi] *n.* 「常態。」

nor·mal·i·ty [nɔrˈmælətɪ; nɔːˈmæliti] *n.* 正常的狀態;標準。

nor·mal·i·za·tion [ˌnɔrml̩əˈzeʃən; ˌnɔːməlaiˈzeiʃən] *n.* 常態化;標準化。

nor·mal·ize [ˈnɔrml̩ˌaɪz; ˈnɔːməlaiz] *v.,* **-ized, -iz·ing.** —*v.t.* 使常態化;使標準化。—*v.i.* 正常化。

normal pressure 正壓力;標準壓力。

normal saline solution 〖藥〗生理鹽水。

Nor·man [ˈnɔrmən; ˈnɔːmən] *n.* ①法國諾曼第人。②居住於 Normandy 之斯堪的那維亞人與法國人的混血兒。③此種混血兒之斯堪的那維亞祖先;諾曼人。④1066 年征服英國之諾曼第人或其所用之法語。⑤美國 Oklahoma 州中部之一城市。—*adj.* ①諾曼第的。②諾曼或諾曼第人的;其語言的;其文化的。③諾曼第式建築的。④1066年征服英國之諾曼人所用之法語的。

Norman Conquest 諾曼人之征服英國 (1066年 William the Conqueror 率領之諾曼第軍隊於Hastings登陸征服英國)。

Nor·man·dy [ˈnɔrməndɪ; ˈnɔːməndi] *n.* 諾曼第 (法國西北部之一地區,第二次世界大戰期中盟軍登陸地點)。

Nor·man·esque [ˌnɔrmənˈɛsk; ˌnɔːməˈnesk] *adj.* 〖建築〗Norman 式的。

Nor·man-French [ˈnɔrmənˈfrɛntʃ; ˈnɔːmənˈfrentʃ] *n.* (亦作**Norman French**) 諾曼或諾曼第法語。—*adj.* ①諾曼或諾曼第法語的; 用諾曼或諾曼第法語的。②說諾曼或諾曼第法語之人民的。

Nor·man·ize [ˈnɔrmənˌaɪz; ˈnɔːmənaiz] *v.t. & v.i.,* **-ized, -iz·ing.** (使)諾曼化。

nor·ma·tive [ˈnɔrmətɪv; ˈnɔːmətiv] *adj.* ①合於規範的(行爲、語言等)。②規範的;贊同規範的。

Norn [nɔrn; nɔːn] *n.* 〖北歐神話〗司命運之三女神之一。

Norse [nɔrs; nɔːs] *adj.* ①古代斯堪的那維亞的; 古代斯堪的那維亞人(語)的。②挪威的;挪威人(語)的。—*n.* ①古代斯堪的那維亞人(語)。②挪威人(語)。〖注意〗**Norse** 作古斯堪的那維亞人及挪威人解時, 爲單數形作複數用。但作古斯堪的那維亞語或挪威語解時,爲單數形作單數用。

Norse·land [ˈnɔrslənd; ˈnɔːslənd] *n.* 「挪威;斯堪的那維亞。」

Norse·man [ˈnɔrsmən; ˈnɔːsmən] *n., pl.* **-men.** 古代斯堪的那維亞人。

Norsk [nɔrsk; nɔːsk] *adj., n.* =**Norse.**

‡**north** [nɔrθ; nɔːθ] *n.* ①北;北方(略作**N**). a room facing *north.* 朝北的屋子。②(亦作 **North**) 一國之北部。③(the N–) 美國北部。④(N–) =**North Country.**⑤北風。*to* (*on,* or *in*) *the north of* 在…之北。—*adj.* ①北方的;在北部的。*North* China. 華北。②來自北方的。a *north* wind. 北風。—*adv.* 在北方;向北方。I am going *north.* 我要向北去。

North Atlantic Treaty 北大西洋公約 (1949年由12國所簽, 決定設置 North Atlantic Treaty Organization 者)。

North Atlantic Treaty Organization 北大西洋公約組織。(略作 **NATO**)

North Borneo 北婆羅洲 (Sabah 之舊稱, 屬馬來西亞)。

north·bound [ˈnɔrθˌbaund; ˈnɔːθˌbaund] *adj.* 走向北方的;往北的。

North Country ①英格蘭 Humber 河口以北地區。②阿拉斯加及加拿大 Yukon 地區(爲一地理及經濟單元)。

North Dakota 北達科塔(美國中北部之一州, 首府 Bismarck).

***north·east** [ˌnɔrθˈist; ˈnɔːθˈiːst] *adj.* ① 東北的。②向東北的。③ 來自東北的。a *northeast* wind. 東北風。④在東北的。—*n.* ①東北。②東北的地方;向東北的地方。—*adv.* ①向東北地。②自東北地。③在東北地。

northeast by east 東北偏東。(略作 **NEbE**)

northeast by north 東北偏北。(略作 **NEbN**)

north·east·er [ˌnɔrθˈistɚ; nɔːθˈiːstə] *n.* 東北風。

north·east·er·ly [ˌnɔrθˈistɚlɪ; nɔːθˈiːstəli] *adj. & adv.* ①在東北的(地); 向東北的(地)。②來自東北的(地)。

***north·east·ern** [ˌnɔrθˈistɚn; nɔːθˈiːstən] *adj.* ①東北方的; 在東北的; 向東北的。②來自東北的。a *northeastern* wind. 東北風。③(N–) 美國東北部地方的;美國 New England 的;具有該地區之特徵的。

north·east·ward [ˌnɔrθˈistwɚd; nɔːθˈiːstwəd] *adv. & adj.* 向東北地 (的)。—*n.* 東北方;東北;東北地區。

north·east·ward·ly [ˌnɔrθˈistwɚdlɪ; nɔːθˈiːstwədli] *adv. & adj.* ①向東北地(的)。②來自東北地(的)。

north·east·wards [ˌnɔrθˈistwɚdz; nɔːθˈiːstwədz] *adv.* =**northeastward.**

north·er [ˈnɔrðɚ; ˈnɔːðə] *n.* 〖美〗强烈的北風;(尤指冬季墨西哥灣沿岸的)寒冷北風。

north·er·ly [ˈnɔrðɚlɪ; ˈnɔːðəli] *adj.* ①向北的。②來自北方的。③北方的。—*adv.* ①向北方地。②來自北方地。—*n.* 北風。

‡**north·ern** [ˈnɔrðɚn; ˈnɔːðən] *adj.* ①向北的。②來自北方的。③在北方的。He has travelled in *northern* countries. 他曾遊歷過北方諸國。④(N–)美國北方的。—*n.* 北方人;居住北部的人。

north·ern·er [ˈnɔrðɚnɚ; ˈnɔːðənə] *n.* ①北方人。②(N–)美國北部的人。

Northern Ireland 北愛爾蘭自治區 (拒絕參加 Irish Free State, 在政治上仍與大不列顛聯爲一體)。

northern lights 北極光。

Northern Territory 北領地(澳洲北部之地區, 首府爲 Darwin).

north·ing [ˈnɔrθɪŋ, -ðɪŋ; ˈnɔːθiŋ] *n.* ①〖測量、航海〗北距 (北航行經之緯度差)。②(天體的)北行;北進。③〖天文〗北偏。

north·land [ˈnɔrθlənd; ˈnɔːθlənd] *n.* ①(一國之)北部地方; 北國。②(N–) 〖詩〗 **a.** (世界之)北部地帶。 **b.** Scandinavia 半島。—**er,** *n.*

North·man [ˈnɔrθmən; ˈnɔːθmən] *n., pl.* **-men.** ①古代斯堪的那維亞人 (=Norseman, 於八至十一世紀刼掠英國、愛爾蘭及歐洲其他地區之海盜)。②北歐人。

North Pole 北極。

North·um·ber·land [nɔrˈθʌmbɚlənd; nɔːˈθʌmbələnd] *n.* 諾森伯蘭(英國東北部之一郡, 首府 Newcastle).

North·um·bri·a [nɔrˈθʌmbrɪə; nɔːˈθʌmbriə] *n.* 英國 Anglo-Saxon 時代之古王國, 在 Humber 河之北。

North·um·bri·an [nɔrˈθʌmbrɪən;

nɔːˈθʌmbriən] *adj.* ① Northumbria 王國的;其人民或方言的。②Northumberland的;其人民或方言的。—*n.* ① Northumbria 人(或方言)。②Northumberland 人(或方言)。

***north·ward** [ˈnɔrθwəd; ˈnɔːθwəd] *adv.* 向北方地(=northwards). He walked *northward*. 他向北走。—*adj.* 向北方的。The orchard is on the *northward* slope of the hill. 果園在山的北坡上。—*n.* 北方。to the *northward*. 向北方。

north·ward·ly [ˈnɔrθwədlɪ; ˈnɔːθwədli] *adj. & adv.* ①向北的(地)。②來自北方的(地)。

north·wards [ˈnɔrθwədz; ˈnɔːθwədz] *adv.* =**northward.**

***north·west** [ˌnɔrθˈwest; ˈnɔːθˈwest] *adj.* ①西北的。②向西北的。③來自西北的。a *northwest* wind. 西北風。④在西北的。—*n.* ①西北。②西北的地方;向西北的地方。*the Northwest* **a.** 美國西北部 (Washington, Oregon, Idaho 諸州)。**b.** Mississippi 河以東之美國西北部。**c.** 加拿大西北部。—*adv.* ①向西北地。②自西北地。③在西北地。

north·west·er [ˌnɔrθˈwɛstɚ; ˈnɔːθˈwestə] *n.* 西北風。

north·west·er·ly [ˌnɔrθˈwestəlɪ; ˈnɔːθˈwestəli] *adj. & adv.* ①在西北方的(地);向西北的(地)。②來自西北的(地)。

***north·west·ern** [ˌnɔrθˈwɛstən; ˈnɔːθˈwestən] *adj.* ①在西北部的;西北方的;向西北的。②來自西北的。③(N-)美國西北部的;有美國西北部之特徵的。

north·west·ward [ˌnɔrθˈwɛstwəd; ˈnɔːθˈwestwəd] *adv. & adj.* 向西北地(的)。—*n.* 西北方;西北部;西北地區。

north·west·ward·ly [ˌnɔrθˈwɛstwədlɪ; ˈnɔːθˈwestwədli] *adv. & adj.* ①向西北地(的)。②來自西北地(的)。

north·west·wards [ˌnɔrθˈwɛstwədz; ˈnɔːθˈwestwədz] *adv.* =**northwestward.**

nor·ward [ˈnɔrwəd; ˈnɔːwəd] *adv., adj., n.* =**northward.**

***Nor·way** [ˈnɔrwe; ˈnɔːwei] *n.* 挪威(歐洲西北部一國, 首都奧斯陸 Oslo)。

***Nor·we·gian** [nɔrˈwidʒən; nɔːˈwiːdʒən] *adj.* 挪威的;挪威人的;挪威語的。—*n.* ①挪威人。②挪威語。

nor'west·er [ˌnɔrˈwɛstɚ; ˈnɔːˈwestə] *n.* ①强西北風。②(水手用之) 油布防水衣。

Nos.,nos. numbers.

‡nose [noz; nouz] *n., v.,* **nosed, nos·ing.** —*n.* ①鼻子。②嗅覺。A dog has a good *nose*. 狗有好的嗅覺。③偵察的能力。A reporter must have a *nose* for news. 記者必有探聽消息的能力。④突出部分(如機首、船首等)。⑤干涉。Why can't he keep his *nose* out of my business? 他爲甚麼不能少管我的閒事呢? ***as plain as the nose on one's face*** 極爲清楚; 瞭如指掌。***bite*** (or ***snap***) ***a person's nose off*** 不客氣地對某人說;氣勢洶洶地對某人說。***by a nose*** 〖俚〗極微之差。***count noses*** 清點人數。***cut off one's nose to spite one's face*** 與人賭氣反爲自己招來不利。***follow one's nose*** **a.** 向前進;直走。If you *follow your nose* you can't miss it. 假如你一直向前走, 不會看不到它。**b.** 憑直覺。***keep one's nose to the grindstone*** 勞動不息。***lead*** (***a person***) ***by the nose*** 牽着一個人的鼻子 (令之唯命是從)。He lets his wife *lead him by the nose*. 他對太太唯命是從。***look down one's nose at*** 〖俗〗瞧不起…。He had always *looked down his nose at* foreigners. 他一向瞧不起外國人。***on the nose*** 直接地;十分正確地。His estimate was right *on the nose*. 他的估計十分正確。***pay through the nose*** 付出很高的價錢。***poke one's nose into*** 干涉(他人之事)。***put one's nose out of joint*** **a.** 破壞某人之計畫。**b.** 奪人之寵。***thumb one's nose*** 以大姆指按鼻,其餘四指伸開表示輕視。***turn up one's nose at*** 鄙視。***under one's*** (***very***) ***nose*** 在…之面前(而未被其發現);當着…的面。—*v.t.* ①嗅出;靠嗅覺察出。The dog *nosed* out a rat. 這狗嗅出一鼠。②以鼻嗅。③以尖端推進。The ship *nosed* its way into the harbor. 這船駛進港內。④以鼻磨擦。⑤以少許之差擊敗;險勝〖out〗. —*v.i.* ①嗅〖常at, about〗。②(以鼻部或首部)挺進。The boat *nosed* in toward the shore. 這船駛向岸邊。③找;探究;探聽;干涉。④〖英俚〗作間諜。***nose out*** **a.** 探出(祕密等)。**b.** 險勝;倖勝。

nose·band [ˈnozˌbænd; ˈnouzbænd] *n.* (馬等之)鼻羈。—**ed,** *adj.* 鼻出血。

nose·bleed [ˈnozˌblid; ˈnouzbliːd] *n.* 鼻出血。

nose cone 火箭或飛彈之鼻錐體(卽携帶炸彈、儀器或人員之尖端部分,燃料燒完後卽與火箭或飛彈本身脫離)。

nose count 清點人數。

nose dive ①飛機之垂直俯衝。②突降(如物價等)。

nose-dive [ˈnozˌdaɪv; ˈnouzdaiv] *v.i.,* **-dived,** or **-dove, -dived, -div·ing.** ①俯衝。②突降。

nose drops 點鼻藥。

nose·gay [ˈnozˌge; ˈnouzgei] *n.* 花束;花球。

nose·piece [ˈnozˌpis; ˈnouzpiːs] *n.* ①鼻覆;(盔或胄之)鼻甲; (馬之)鼻羈。②(顯微鏡)接物鏡之旋轉盤; (水管等之)口; 嘴。③眼鏡架之夾鼻梁部分。

nos·er [ˈnozɚ; ˈnouzə] *n.* ①〖俚〗對鼻子之一擊。②〖俚〗逆風。

nose-rag [ˈnozˌræg; ˈnouzræg] *n.* 〖俚〗手巾;手帕。

nose ring ①(牛、豬等之)鼻圈。②(野蠻人之)環形鼻飾;鼻環。

nose-thumb·ing [ˈnozˌθʌmɪŋ; ˈnouzˌθʌmiŋ] *n.* (大拇指放在鼻尖上的)輕蔑動作。

nose-warm·er [ˈnozˌwɔrmɚ; ˈnouzˌwɔːmə] *n.* 〖俚〗短烟斗。

nose·wheel [ˈnozˌhwil; ˈnouzˌwiːl] *n.* (飛機機頭之)降落輪。

nos·ey [ˈnozɪ; ˈnouzi] *adj.,* **nos·i·er, nos·i·est,** *n.* —*adj., n.* =**nosy.**

nosh [nɑʃ; nɔʃ] *v.i.* 吃零食; 小吃。—*n.* (三餐外之)零食;小吃。

nosh·er [ˈnɑʃɚ; ˈnɔʃə] *n.* 好吃零食的人。

no-show [ˈnoˌʃo; ˈnouˈʃou] *n.* 在飛機、輪船、或火車上訂座,但未搭乘的人。

nos·ing [ˈnozɪŋ; ˈnouziŋ] *n.* 〖建築〗梯級踏板突出於豎板之部分; 保護此部分之金屬條。

no·sog·ra·phy [noˈsɑgrəfɪ; nouˈsɔgrəfi] *n.* 罹疾病論;病理學。

no·sol·o·gy [noˈsɑlədʒɪ; nouˈsɔlədʒi] *n.* ①疾病之分類。②疾病分類學。

nos·tal·gia [nɑˈstældʒɪə; nɔsˈtældʒiə] *n.* ①鄉愁;懷鄉病。②懷古之思;懷昔。

nos·tal·gic [nɑˈstældʒɪk; nɔsˈtældʒik] *adj.* 懷鄉病的;引起鄉愁的。—**al·ly,** *adv.*

***nos·tril** [ˈnɑstrəl; ˈnɔstril] *n.* 鼻孔。

no-strings [ˈnoˌstrɪŋz; ˈnou-striŋz] *adj.* 無條件或義務拘束的。

nos·trum [ˈnɑstrəm; ˈnɔstrəm] *n., pl.*

-trums. ①祕藥;江湖郎中所賣的藥。②成藥。③(解決社會、政治等之)得意方案(反對者稱之爲 nostrum, 以示不信任)。

nos·y [ˈnozɪ; ˈnouzi] *adj.*, **nos·i·er, nos·i·est,** *n.* —*adj.* 〖俗〗①好管閒事的;好追問的。②有惡臭的。③香的。④鼻子大的。—*n.* 〖俗〗①大鼻子的人。②好管閒事者;好窺探的人。(亦作 **nosey**)

‡not [nɑt; nɔt] *adv.* 不;未。***as likely as not*** 可能。***not a few*** 不少。***not at all*** 毫不。***not but what*** (or ***that***) 〖古〗雖;但。***not for a moment*** 絕不。***not half*** 非常。***not in the least*** 毫不。***not nearly*** = **by no means; far from.** ***not on one's life*** 決不。***not to be thought of*** 不必考慮。***not to speak of*** (or ***not to mention***) 更不必提;不必說。Travelling will need much time, *not to speak of* the expense. 旅行將費許多時間, 費用更不必提。***so as not to*** 爲了不…。I got up early *so as not to* lose the train. 爲了怕趕不上火車, 我起得很早。〖文法〗⑴與助動詞或不完整動詞連用, 形成否定句 (not 在此用法中須緊隨助動詞或不完整動詞之後。又 not 在口語中常被縮爲 n't). It is *not* (or *isn't*) right. 不對。I have *not* (or *haven't*) seen him. 我未曾看見他。應注意, 在否定問句中, not 之正式用法是置於主格的人稱代名詞之後, 但在會話中則置於其前, 例如:Do you *not* (or *Don't* you) understand? 你不明白嗎? ⑵用以造成字或句的部分之否定。*not* my brother (friend). 不是我兄弟(朋友)。*Not* everybody thinks so. 不是每個人都這樣想。I asked him *not* to go. 我請求他不要去。⑶等於以 that 起首的子句。I believe *not*. = I believe that it is *not* so. 我相信不是這樣。〖注意〗**not** 與助動詞連接成省略字時其發音爲[-nt, -n̩t, -t, -n̩; -nt, -n], 如 isn't 等。

no·ta be·ne [ˈnotəˈbinɪ; ˈnoutəˈbiːni] 〖拉〗注意 (=note well, 略作 **N.B.**).

no·ta·bil·i·ty [ˌnotəˈbɪlətɪ; ˌnoutəˈbiliti] *n.*, *pl.* **-ties.** ①值得注意;顯著;著名。②著名的人;名士。

***no·ta·ble** [ˈnotəbl; ˈnoutəbl] *adj.* ①值得注意的; 顯著的;著名的;重要的。a *notable* success. 大成功。②可覺察的;有相當分量的。a *notable* quantity. 相當多的量。③〖俗〗能幹而又勤儉耐勞的(指婦女管家言)。a *notable* housewife. 能幹而又勤儉耐勞之主婦。—*n.* ①著名人士。Many *notables* came to the President's reception. 許多著名人士來參加總統的招待會。②值得注意之事物。—**ness,** *n.* —**no·ta·bly,** *adv.*

no·tar·i·al [noˈtɛrɪəl; nouˈtɛəriəl] *adj.* 公證人的;公證的。—**ly,** *adv.*

no·ta·rize [ˈnotəˌraɪz; ˈnoutəraiz] *v.t.*, **-rized, -riz·ing.** 公證; 公證人證明 (合同、契約等)。—**no·ta·ri·za·tion,** *n.*

no·ta·ry [ˈnotərɪ; ˈnoutəri] *n.*, *pl.* **-ries.** (法律上之)公證人。—**ship,** *n.*

no·ta·tion [noˈteʃən; nouˈteiʃən] *n.* ①(數學、音樂等所用之)一套符號。②以符號表記;符號法。③作筆記。④備忘錄;筆記;註釋。***broad*** (***narrow***) ***notation*** 〖語音〗簡化 (精密)標音法。***decimal notation*** 十進法。***the common scale of notation*** 〖數學〗十進記數法。—**al,** *adj.*

notch** [nɑtʃ; nɔtʃ] *n.* ①V 字形刻痕。②谷道。③〖俗〗程度;等級。This one is a *notch* better than the other. 這一個要比那一個高一等。④(刻在棍子等上的) 計數刻痕。a notch above others*** 高人一等。***take a person down a notch*** 壓低某人之氣燄。—*v.t.* ①刻V字凹痕於。②刻痕計數。He *notched* each hawk he killed. 他每殺死一隻鷹便刻一痕記載。③計分。④得分。to *notch* a run. (棒球)得一分。

notched [nɑtʃt; nɔtʃt] *adj.* =**notchy.**

notch·y [ˈnɑtʃɪ; ˈnɔtʃi] *adj.* 有V字形凹痕的;有刻痕的。

‡note [not; nout] *n.*, *v.*, **not·ed, not·ing.** —*n.* ①摘記;筆記。I must look at my *notes.* 我必須看我的筆記。②注意。③註解; 註釋。④短箋;便條。⑤一個單音。⑥音符;音鍵。⑦歌曲; 調子; 旋律。⑧名聲; 顯著。a man of *note.* 著名的人。⑨期票;定期付款票。⑩外交函件; 備忘錄; 通牒。⑪鳥鳴聲。⑫特徵;以證明眞實不僞之符號。⑬紙幣。⑭圖書館之圖書卡片上有關書本之資料。⑮重要性。⑯〖俗〗新的或未預料的情況。⑰說法;想法。His critics had begun to change their *note.* 他的批評人開始轉變他們的口氣。⑱標點符號;符號。⑲暗示;信號。There is a *note* of anxiety in her voice. 她的聲調中帶有焦慮。***compare notes*** 交換意見。***make a note of*** 記錄;記下。***of note*** 重要的;引人矚目的。***strike the right note*** 說話或行爲合宜。***take note of*** 留心。Please *take note of* these warning signs. 請留心這些警告的標牌。***take notes*** 做筆記。***worthy of note***值得注意。—*v.t.* ①記錄。The contents of the letter have been carefully *noted.* 該信內容已仔細記錄。②注意;留心。These should be thoughtfully *noted.* 這些應留心注意。③註解。④指示;表示。⑤特別提及。⑥配音樂。—**not·er,** *n.*

***note·book** [ˈnotˌbʊk; ˈnoutbuk] *n.* ①筆記本;記錄簿;練習簿。②期票簿。

note broker 股票等有價證券的經紀人。

note·case [ˈnotˌkes; ˈnoutˌkeis] *n.* 〖英〗皮夾子。(亦作 **note-case**)

***not·ed** [ˈnotɪd; ˈnoutid] *adj.* ①著名的; 顯著的。The room was full of *noted* scholars. 這屋內滿是著名的學者。②有音譜的。—**ly,** *adv.* —**ness,** *n.*

note·head [ˈnotˌhɛd; ˈnouthed] *n.* 小型的信箋上方之印刷文句 (=letterhead).

note·less [ˈnotlɪs; ˈnoutlis] *adj.* ①不引人注目的;平凡的; 無名的。②非樂音的; 無聲(音)的。

note·let [ˈnotlɪt; ˈnoutlit] *n.* 便條;短信。

note paper 信紙;信箋。(亦作 **note-paper**)

notes receivable ①債務人簽署的期票。②這種期票的紀錄。

note·wor·thy [ˈnotˌwɝðɪ; ˈnoutˌwəːði] *adj.* 值得注意的; 顯著的。—**note·wor·thi·ly,** *adv.* —**note·wor·thi·ness,** *n.*

‡noth·ing [ˈnʌθɪŋ; ˈnʌθiŋ] *n.* ①無物;無事;無。I saw *nothing* there. 我在那裏甚麼也沒看見。②不關緊要之事務;無足輕重之人;無能之人。That's *nothing!* 那算不得甚麼! ③零。He's five feet *nothing.* 他身高五英尺整。***be nothing, if not*** 是其最大長處;爲其優點。He's *nothing, if not* careful. 謹愼是他最大長處。***care nothing for*** (or ***about***) 不以…爲意。***come to nothing*** 完全失敗;無結果。***for nothing*** **a.** 無酬勞;無收穫。**b.** 免費。**c.** 無理由;無緣故。**d.** 無用地;白費地。***good for nothing*** 無價值的。***have nothing to do but*** (or ***except***) 除…以外毫無辦法。

You have *nothing to do but* wait. 你祇有等待。**have nothing to do with** 與…無關。I advise you to *have nothing to do with* it. 我勸你不要捲入此事。**hear nothing of** 未聞…之消息。**little or nothing** (**of**) 很少。**make nothing of** **a.** 不了解。I can *make nothing of* the letter. 我不懂這信的意思。**b.** 視爲不重要;輕視。**c.** 不能做;未能利用。He *made nothing of* his opportunities. 他坐失良機。**next to nothing** 差不多沒有。**nothing but** (or **except**) 祇;不過。**nothing doing**〖俗〗**a.** 不行。**b.** 完了;不幹了;算了(失敗或拒絕之詞)。**c.** 眼睛看不到的活動、好處等。**nothing less than** (or **short of**) **a.** 與…完全一樣;等於。He is *nothing less than* a tyrant. 他簡直是個暴君。**b.** 完全地;絕對地。**nothing like** 沒有像…者;莫如。There's *nothing like* leather for shoes. 做鞋,沒有比皮革更好的材料。**nothing much** 不多;很少。**say nothing of** 更不待說;何況。**There is nothing to it.** 沒有困難。**think nothing of** **a.** 認爲容易。**b.** 視爲不重要或無價值。—*adv.* 毫不。He is *nothing* wiser than before. 他一點也不比過去聰明。

noth·ing·ness [ˈnʌθɪŋnɪs; ˈnʌθiŋnis] *n.* ①空;不存在的狀態;消滅。②無價值;無價值之事物。③無知覺的狀態。④死亡。**pass into nothingness** 消滅;寂滅。

:no·tice [ˈnotɪs; ˈnoutis] *n., v.,* **-ticed, -tic·ing.** —*n.* ①注意。It was brought to my *notice*. 有人使我注意到這件事。②警告。The driver sounded his horn to give *notice* that he was going to turn. 司機鳴喇叭警告,以示他要轉彎。③標記;招牌。④告示;公告;啓事;通知。They sent me a *notice*. 他們給我一通知。⑤先期通知;預告。He left without *notice*. 他不辭而別。⑥(對新書等之)短評;評介。The new book got a favorable *notice*. 這新書獲得好評。**serve notice** 警告;通知;公布。to *serve notice* that smoking is not allowed. 警告不許吸煙。**sit up and take notice** 病況轉佳。**take notice** 注意;留意;看;(小孩)開始懂事。**take notice of** **a.** 款待;禮遇。**b.** (印象良好的)注意。—*v.t.* ①注意。I didn't *notice* you. 我未曾留意到你。I *noticed* a big difference. 我注意到一大差別。②通知。③提及;評介。④禮遇;知遇;款待。He was too proud to *notice* me. 他太驕傲,對我不客氣。⑤承認相識。She *noticed* him merely with a nod. 她祇點一點頭表示和他相識。—**no·tic·er,** *n.*

***no·tice·a·ble** [ˈnotɪsəbl̩; ˈnoutisəbl] *adj.* ①顯明的;顯著的。The class has made *noticeable* improvement. 這一班已有顯著進步。②值得注意的。—**no·tice·a·bil·i·ty,** *n.*

no·tice·a·bly [ˈnotɪsəblɪ; ˈnoutisəbli] *adv.* 顯明地;顯著地。

notice board 揭示板;布告板。

no·ti·fi·a·ble [ˈnotəˌfaɪəbl̩; ˈnoutifaiəbl] *adj.* 須報告的(指某些傳染病,於發現時必須向衛生當局報告者)。

no·ti·fi·ca·tion [ˌnotəfəˈkeʃən; ˌnoutifiˈkeiʃən] *n.* ①通知;通報。②通知書。

***no·ti·fy** [ˈnotəˌfaɪ; ˈnoutifai] *v.t.,* **-fied, -fy·ing.** ①通知;使知。Please *notify* us when you leave. 你要走時請告訴我們。②報告;公告。③警告。—**no·ti·fi·er,** *n.*

***no·tion** [ˈnoʃən; ˈnouʃən] *n.* ①觀念;概念。He has no *notion* of what I mean. 他不明白我的意思。②意見;信仰。③意念;意向;企圖。He has no *notion* of resigning. 他無意辭職。④愚笨的見解或意見;怪念頭;奇想。He took a *notion* to go to Europe. 他興起到歐洲去的怪念頭。⑤(*pl.*)〖美〗有用的瑣碎之物;雜物(如別針、針、線、帶子、頂針等)。⑥巧妙的裝置;小傢具。

no·tion·al [ˈnoʃənl̩; ˈnouʃənl] *adj.* ①觀念的;概念的。②抽象的;純理論的。③想像中的;虛幻的。④〖美〗充滿幻想的;好空想的。—**i·ty,** *n.* —**ly,** *adv.*

no·to·chord [ˈnotəˌkɔrd; ˈnoutəˌkɔːd] *n.*〖解剖,動物〗脊索。—**al,** *adj.*

no·to·ri·e·ty [ˌnotəˈraɪətɪ; ˌnoutəˈraiəti] *n., pl.* **-ties.** ①狼藉的聲名。②聞名;顯著;衆人皆知。③知名之士;聞人;惡名昭彰者。

***no·to·ri·ous** [noˈtorɪəs; nouˈtɔːriəs, nəˈt-] *adj.* ①聲名狼藉的;罪惡昭彰的。②著名的;衆人皆知的。*notorious* crimes. 衆人皆知的罪惡。—**ly,** *adv.* —**ness,** *n.*〖注意〗**notorious** 通常指因不名譽之原因而著名。**famous** 指因其成就或優越而著名。

No·tre Dame [ˌnotəˈdem; ˌnoutrəˈdɑːm] ①聖母瑪利亞。②(巴黎之)聖母院。

no-trump [ˈnoˈtrʌmp; ˈnouˈtrʌmp] *adj.*〖橋牌〗①無王牌的。②以無王牌叫牌的;無王牌牌戲的。—*n.* 無王牌的牌戲(叫牌)。

***not·with·stand·ing** [ˈnɑtwɪθˈstændɪŋ, -wɪð-; ˌnɔtwiθˈstændiŋ, -wiðˈs-] *prep.* 縱使。He bought it *notwithstanding* the high price. 縱使價錢高,他依然買了。—*conj.* 雖然。He is honest, *notwithstanding* he is poor. 他雖窮,却誠實。—*adv.* 雖然;然而。

nou·gat [ˈnugət, ˈnugɑ; ˈnuːgɑː] *n.* 一種糖果(用杏仁與蜂蜜製成);牛軋糖。

***nought** [nɔt; nɔːt] *n.* ＝**naught.**

nou·me·non [ˈnumɪˌnɑn; ˈnuːminɔn] *n., pl.* **-na** [-nə; -nə].〖哲學〗①(康德哲學)藉純粹理性之直觀作用所了解之事物。②實體;本體(爲現象之本源及原因)。③物自身(與現象相對)。④不可知之事物(在理論上其存在有問題者,如上帝、靈魂等)。

***noun** [naʊn; naun] *n.* 名詞。〖文法〗**noun** 爲人、動物、事物、地方等之名稱,通常分爲下列五類:**abstract noun.** 抽象名詞。**collective noun.** 集合名詞。**common noun.** 普通名詞。**material noun.** 物質名詞。**proper noun.** 專有名詞。—*adj.* (亦作 **nounal**) 名詞的;似名詞的。

***nour·ish** [ˈnɝɪʃ; ˈnʌriʃ] *v.t.* ①滋養。Milk *nourishes* a baby. 牛奶給嬰兒養料。②懷有;孕育。to *nourish* a hope. 懷有一線希望。③供給;支持;助長。—*v.i.* 滋養。Good food *nourishes.* 有益的食物富滋養。—**a·ble,** *adj.* 「滋養的。—**er,** *n.* —**ly,** *adv.*

nour·ish·ing [ˈnɝɪʃɪŋ; ˈnʌriʃiŋ] *adj.*

***nour·ish·ment** [ˈnɝɪʃmənt; ˈnʌriʃmənt] *n.* ①滋養品;養料。②營養;滋養。

nous [naus; naus] *n.* ①〖哲學〗精神;理性;理智;智慧。②〖諧〗機智。

Nov. November.

no·va [ˈnovə; ˈnouvə] *n., pl.* **-vas, -vae** [-vi; -viː].〖天文〗新星。

no·vate [ˈnovet; ˈnouveit] *v.t.,* **-vat·ed, -vat·ing.** ①以新的代替。②〖法律〗以新債務或其他義務代換舊有之債務等。—**no·va·tion,** *n.*

***nov·el** [ˈnɑvl̩; ˈnɔvəl] *adj.* 新奇的;異常的。It's a *novel* idea. 這是個新奇的想法。—*n.* ①小說。a popular *novel.* 流行的小說。

a serial *novel*. 連載小說。②(昔)短篇故事。
nov·el·ette 〔ˌnɑvḷˈɛt; ˌnɔvəˈlet〕 *n.* 短篇或中篇小說。「*n.* 小說家。」
***nov·el·ist** 〔ˈnɑvḷɪst; ˈnɔvəlist, –vḷist〕
nov·el·is·tic 〔ˌnɑvḷˈɪstɪk; ˌnɔvəˈlistik〕 *adj.* 小說的; 似小說的;小說中常有的。
nov·el·ize 〔ˈnɑvḷˌaɪz; ˈnɔvəlaiz〕 *v.t.*, **-ized, -iz·ing.** ①作成小說;小說化。②虛構。
no·vel·la 〔noˈvɛllɑ; noːˈvellɑː〕 *n.*, *pl.* **-vel·le** 〔–ˈvɛllɛ; –ˈvelle〕, **-vel·las.**【義】短篇故事;短篇小說（如 Boccaccio 的"十日談"之任一篇)。
***nov·el·ty** 〔ˈnɑvḷtɪ; ˈnɔvəlti〕 *n.*, *pl.*-**ties.** ①新奇; 新鮮。②新奇之事或物; 異常之事或物。③(*pl.*) 新奇玲瓏之物;玩具;價廉之首飾等。—*adj.* ①新奇的。*novelty* goods. 新奇商品。②有新奇物的。*novelty* shop. 特產商店。「nouˈv–, nəˈv–〕 *n.* 十一月。」
‡No·vem·ber[1] 〔noˈvɛmbɚ; noˈvembə,
No·vem·ber[2] *n.* 通訊電碼,代表字母N.
no·ve·na 〔noˈvinə; nouˈviːnə〕 *n.*, *pl.* **-nae** 〔–ni; –niː〕, **-nas.**【天主教】連續九日之祈禱。
nov·ice 〔ˈnɑvɪs; ˈnɔvis〕 *n.* ①生手; 新手。②見習修士或修女。③新入教者;新信徒。
no·vi·ci·ate 〔noˈvɪʃɪɪt; nouˈviʃiit〕 *n.* =**novitiate.**
no·vi·ti·ate 〔noˈvɪʃɪɪt; nouˈviʃiit〕 *n.* ①見習修行期間。②見習修行者居住訓練之場所。③見習修行者;新手。④見習。
no·vo·cain(e) 〔ˈnovəˌken; ˈnouvəkein〕 *n.* ①奴佛卡因（一種局部麻醉劑)。②(N–) 其商標名。
‡now 〔nau; nau〕 *adv.* ①卽刻;馬上。Do it *now*. 立刻就做。②於是;其次;然後。*Now* we shall see what happens. 我們以下便知其結果。③現在。He is here *now*. 他此刻在這裏。④置於句首或句尾以示說話者之特殊心情與語氣。*Now* listen to me. 且聽我說。⑤那時候。The clock *now* struck three. 那時候時鐘敲了三下。⑥不久以前;剛才。I just *now* saw him. 我剛才還看見他。⑦在目前情況之下; 依此刻情形; 照現狀。I would believe almost anything *now*. 照目前的情形, 我幾乎相信任何事情了。⑧在此刻以前。She must have reached the city *now*. 她此刻必定已到達城市。***not now*** 不再。***now and again*** 有時;偶然。I see my old neighbor *now and again*. 我偶而遇見我的老鄰居。***now and then*** 有時;偶然。***now...now*** 時而…時而。like a stormy day, *now* wind, *now* rain. 像一個暴風雨的日子,時而颳風,時而下雨。***Now or never!*** 勿失良機(時乎不再來)!—*n.* 現在。***by now*** 此時。He should have arrived *by now*. 此時他該已到了。***from now on*** 自現在起。***up to now***; ***until now***; ***till now*** 到現在爲止。—*conj.* 旣然(與 that 連用)。*Now* that you are here, you'd better stay. 旣然你已來,最好住下。
***now·a·days** 〔ˈnauəˌdez; ˈnauədeiz〕 *adv.* (亦作 **nowaday**) 現今;在這時代。*Nowadays* people travel in automobiles. 現今人們旅行都坐汽車了。—*adj.* (亦作 **nowaday**) 現在的;當今的。—*n.* 現在;現時。
no·way(s) 〔ˈnoˌwe(z); ˈnouwei(z)〕 *adv.* 決不;毫不。「1960 年代後期的青年)。」
Now Generation 這一代（特指
no·where** 〔ˈnoˌhwɛr; ˈnouwɛə, ˈnouhw–〕 *adv.* 無處。I have *nowhere* to go. 我沒有地方去。nowhere near*** 【俗】差得遠;遠非。—*n.* ①不存在; 似不存在之事。A gang of thieves appeared from *nowhere*. 一羣盜賊不知從何處突然冒出來。②默默無聞。
no·wise 〔ˈnoˌwaɪz; ˈnouwaiz〕 *adv.* 決不;毫不。「害的,有毒的。」
nox·ious 〔ˈnɑkʃəs; ˈnɔkʃəs〕 *adj.* 有
no·yau 〔nwɑˈjo; ˈnwaiou〕【法】*n.* 果核酒。
noz·zle 〔ˈnɑzl; ˈnɔzl〕 *n.* ①(水管等的)管嘴。②茶壺嘴。③(風箱等之)噴氣口。④燭臺之插燭管。⑤【俚】鼻。
Np ①【物理】neper. ②【化】neptunium.
N.P. ①Notary Public. ②nisi prius(【拉】=unless before). ③【銀行】no protest. ④new paragraph. ⑤Nobel Prize. **n.p.** ①net proceeds. ②【印刷】new paragraph. ③nisi prius. ④no pagination. ⑤no place of publication. ⑥no protest. ⑦notary public. **N.R.** ①North Riding. ②Northern Rhodesia. **NRA, N.R.A.** ①National Rifle Association. ②National Recovery Administration. **N.S.** ①National Society. ②Naval Service. ③New Series. ④【曆法】New Style. ⑤Nova Scotia. ⑥New School. ⑦not specified. **NSC** ①National Safety Council. ②National Security Council. **N/S/F** not sufficient funds. **N.S.P.C.C.** National Society for the Prevention of Cruelty to Children. **NT, NT.** New Testament. **Nt.** 化學元素 niton 的符號。**N.T.** ①New Testament. ②Northern Territory.
-n't not 之連結型,如 didn't;won't.
nth 〔ɛnθ; enθ〕 *adj.* ①【數學】第 n 項的;n 倍的;n次的。②【俗】(一連串事情中之) 最後的;最近的。***to the nth degree*** (or ***power***) **a.**【數學】至n次。**b.** 至無限;至極點。
nt. wt. net weight.
nu 〔nju; njuː〕 *n.*希臘字母之第十三字(N, ν).
nu·ance 〔njuˈɑns; njuːˈɑːns〕 *n.*, *pl.* **-anc·es.** (色彩、音調、措詞、意味、感情等的)細微差異。「②【俗】核心;要點。」
nub 〔nʌb; nʌb〕 *n.* ①瘤;結(煤等的)小塊。
nub·bin 〔ˈnʌbɪn; ˈnʌbin〕 *n.*【美】①小瘤;小片。②玉蜀黍小（或未成熟的) 穗。③未成熟的果物。「塊;小瘤;小瘤。」
nub·ble 〔ˈnʌbḷ; ˈnʌbl〕 *n.* (煤等的) 小
nub·bly 〔ˈnʌblɪ; ˈnʌbli〕 *adj.*, **-bli·er, -bli·est.** 多瘤的;多結節的;小塊狀的。
Nu·bi·an 〔ˈnubɪən; ˈnjuːbiən〕 *adj.* Nubia（西北非一古王國,努比亞)的; 努比亞人(語)的。—*n.* 努比亞人(語)。
nu·bile 〔ˈnjubḷ; ˈnjuːbail〕 *adj.* 結婚期的;及笄的(女人)。
nu·bil·i·ty 〔njuˈbɪlətɪ; njuˈbiliti〕 *n.* (指女性而言)婚期;達結婚年齡;及笄。
***nu·cle·ar** 〔ˈnjuklɪɚ, ˈnu–; ˈnjuːkliə, –jə〕 *adj.* ①【生物】(細胞)核的; 形成核的。②【物理】(原子)核的。*nuclear* weapons. 核子武器。③核子力推動的。a *nuclear* submarine. 核子潛艇。④(國家) 有核子武器的。—*n.* 核子武器（尤指帶有核子彈頭之飛彈)。
nuclear chemistry 核子化學。
nuclear energy【物理】核子能。
nuclear fission【理化】原子核分裂。
nuclear fuel 原子(核)燃料;核子燃料。
nuclear fusion【理化】原子核融合。
nuclear physics 核子物理學。

nu·cle·ar-pow·ered [ˈnjukliə-ˈpauəd; ˈnjuːkliəˈpauəd] *adj.* 核子動力的；原子能推進的。

nuclear reaction 原子核反應。

nuclear reactor 原子爐；核子反應爐。

nuclear warhead 核子彈頭。

nu·cle·ate [*adj.* ˈnjuklɪɪt; ˈnjuːkliit *v.* ˈnjuklɪˌet; ˈnjuːklieit] *adj., v.,* **-at·ed, -at·ing.** —*adj.* 有核的。—*v.t. & v.i.* (使)成核。 —**nu·cle·a·tion, nu·cle·a·tor,** *n.*

nu·cle·ic acid [njuˈklɪɪk～; njuː-ˈkliik～]〖生化〗核酸。

nu·cle·o·lus [njuˈkliələs; njuːˈkliːələs] *n., pl.* **-li** [-ˌlaɪ; -lai].〖生物〗(細胞核內之)小核；核仁；核小體。(亦作 **nucleole**)

nu·cle·on [ˈnjuklɪɑn; ˈnjuːkliːɔn] *n.*〖物理〗核子。

nu·cle·on·ics [ˌnjuklɪˈɑnɪks; ˌnjuː-kliˈɔniks] *n.* (作 *sing.* 解) 核子學。

***nu·cle·us** [ˈnjuklɪəs; ˈnjuːkliəs] *n., pl.* **-cle·i** [-klɪˌaɪ; -kliai], **-cle·us·es.** ①中心；核心；核心組織。②〖理化〗核子；原子核。③〖生物〗細胞核；胚珠心。④基礎；開端。⑤〖天文〗彗星核。「理」核種。

nu·clide [ˈnjuklaɪd; ˈnjuːklaid] *n.*〖物

nude [njud; njuːd] *adj.* ①裸體的；一絲不掛的。②沒有覆蓋的；空的。③〖法律〗無證據的；無考慮的。④肉色的。 —*n.* ①裸體像；裸體畫。②肉色。 ***the nude*** **a.** 裸體人形。**b.** 裸體。 in the *nude.* 裸體地；赤裸裸地。

nudge [nʌdʒ; nʌdʒ] *v.,* **nudged, nudg-ing,** *n.* —*v.t. & v.i.* 以肘輕觸(以喚起注意或予以暗示)。—*n.* 輕推。

nud·ie [ˈnjudɪ; ˈnjuːdi] *n.*〖俚〗黃色電影或雜誌。—*adj.* 裸體畫的。

nud·ism [ˈnjudɪzəm; ˈnjuːdizəm] *n.* 裸體主義；天體主義；裸體運動；天體運動。

nud·ist [ˈnjudɪst; ˈnjuːdist] *n.* 天體運動者；裸體運動者。 —*adj.* 天體運動的；裸體運動的。

nu·di·ty [ˈnjudətɪ; ˈnjuːditi] *n., pl.* **-ties.** ①赤裸。②赤裸之物；裸體像；裸體畫。

nu·ga·to·ry [ˈnjugəˌtorɪ; ˈnjuːgətəri] *adj.* ①無價值的。②無效的；無力的。③無用的。

nug·get [ˈnʌgɪt; ˈnʌgit] *n.* ①塊。②天然金塊。③有價值之物。④〖澳〗**a.** 强有力的動物。**b.** 彪形大漢。

***nui·sance** [ˈnjusn̩s; ˈnjuːsns] *n.* 討厭之人或物。 Flies and mosquitoes are a *nuisance.* 蒼蠅蚊子是討厭的東西。

nuisance tax 消費者所付之小額稅款。

nuke [njuk; njuːk] *n., v.,* **nuked, nuk·ing.** —*n.*〖美俚〗核武器。—*v.t.* 以核武器攻擊。

null [nʌl; nʌl] *adj.* ①無約束力的；無效的。②無意義的。③空的；無的；不存在的。④零。 ***null and void*** (指法律文件)無效。

nul·lah [ˈnʌlə; ˈnʌlə] *n.*〖英印〗水路；河床；乾涸的河床；峽谷。

nul·li·fi·ca·tion [ˌnʌləfəˈkeʃən; ˌnʌ-lifiˈkeiʃən] *n.* ①無效；廢棄；取消。②(常N-)〖美史〗州的不遵從國會法令。

nul·li·fi·er [ˈnʌləˌfaɪə; ˈnʌliˌfaiə] *n.* ①使無效者；廢棄者。②〖美史〗主張州可以不遵從國會之法令者。

nul·li·fy [ˈnʌləˌfaɪ; ˈnʌlifai] *v.t.,* **-fied, -fy·ing.** ①使無約束力；使無效；廢棄；取消。②使不重要；使無意義；抵消。

nul·li·ty [ˈnʌlətɪ; ˈnʌliti] *n., pl.* **-ties.** ①無效；作廢。②不足道的人(物)。③無效之文件(行爲)。④無；全無。

num. ①number(s). ②numeral(s).

***numb** [nʌm; nʌm] *adj.* 麻木的；失去知覺的。 My fingers are *numb* with cold. 我的手指凍僵了。 —*v.t.* ①使麻木。 ②使昏迷。 He was *numbed* with grief. 他因悲傷而昏迷了。—**ly,** *adv.* —**ness,** *n.*

‡num·ber [ˈnʌmbɚ; ˈnʌmbə] *n.* ①數；數字。②數目；總數。 They were fifteen in *number.* 他們總共是十五個。③若干；一些。 I have a *number* of reasons. 我有些理由。 The enemy won by *numbers.* 敵人以人多獲勝。④(節目等)一節。 The program consisted of four musical *numbers.* 節目裏包括四個音樂項目。⑤(雜誌等)一期。 the current *number.* 最近一期。⑥號數(略作 **No.,** 複數作 **Nos.**). Room *No.* 136. 136 號房間。⑦〖文法〗數；數式。⑧(*pl.*)〖文學、詩〗詩；韻律。⑨(*pl.*) 算術。⑩(*pl.*)〖音樂〗音符；樂譜。⑪(歌唱或跳舞之)樂曲。⑫〖俗〗少女；少婦。 a cute little blonde *number.* 一個可愛的金髮女郎。⑬商品(尤指衣物)。 Put those *numbers* in the display window. 把那些商品放進陳列櫥窗去。⑭＝**numbers pool.** ***a number of*** 一些；若干；許多。 ***back number*** **a.** 舊的(雜誌)。**b.** 落伍之人或物。 ***beyond number*** 無數；多不勝數。 ***get*** (or ***have***) ***someone's number*** 〖俚〗曉得某人之眞正動機，意圖。 ***have one's number on it***〖俚〗被認爲對某人之死亡有命運上的關係。 ***in number*** 總共。 ***look after*** (or ***take care of***) ***number one*** 照顧自己；照顧自己利益。 ***one's number is*** (***was,*** or ***will be***) ***up***〖俚〗**a.** 某人(已將)遇到困難。**b.** 某人面臨死亡。 ***the numbers***＝**numbers pool.** ***times without number*** 無數次。 ***to the number of*** 達到…之總數；總數爲。 ***without number*** 無數。—*v.t.* ①標以號數。 to *number* the pages of a book. 標出書頁之頁碼。②有；含有。 The city *numbers* a million inhabitants. 這城有一百萬居民。③計有；達於…之數。 a crew *numbering* 20 men. 數達二十人之船員(機員)。④算作(某類或某集團)之一。 You are *numbered* among his followers. 你算是他的一個門徒。⑤限數；限制。 His days are *numbered.* 他的壽命將盡。⑥數；計算。—*v.i.* ①數。 ②包括在內。 Several eminent scientists *number* among his friends. 他的朋友中有好幾位傑出的科學家。③數目達到。 Casualties *numbered* in the thousands. 傷亡數以千計。

num·ber·less [ˈnʌmbɚlɪs; ˈnʌmbəlis] *adj.* ①無數的；甚多的。②無數字的。

Num·bers [ˈnʌmbɚz; ˈnʌmbəz] *n.* (作 *sing.* 解)〖聖經〗民數記(舊約第四卷)。

numbers pool 一種非法的賭博，以報刊上之某些數目來賭博。(亦作 **numbers game, numbers racket**)

numb·fish [ˈnʌmˌfɪʃ; ˈnʌmfiʃ] *n., pl.* **-fish, -fish·es.** 電魚。 「*n.* ＝**numskull.**

numb·skull [ˈnʌmˌskʌl; ˈnʌmskʌl]

nu·mer·a·ble [ˈnjumərəbl̩; ˈnjuːmə-rəbl] *adj.* 可數的；可計算的。—**ness,** *n.*

***nu·mer·al** [ˈnjumərəl; ˈnjuːmərəl] *n.* ①數字。1, 2, 3, etc. are Arabic *numerals.* 1, 2, 3 等是阿拉伯數字。②(*pl.*) 布質班級號碼(學校給予運動成績卓越者，其號碼爲該生行將畢業之年分)。 —*adj.* ①數字的。②代表數字的。 「rəri] *adj.* 數的；關於數的。

nu·mer·ar·y [ˈnjuməˌrɛrɪ; ˈnjuːmə-

nu·mer·ate [ˈnjuməˌret; ˈnjuːməreit] *v.t.*, **-at·ed, -at·ing.** ①數;計算。②讀(數)。

nu·mer·a·tion [ˌnjuməˈreʃən; ˌnjuːməˈreiʃən] *n.* ①計算;計算法。②讀數;讀數法;命數法。***the numeration table*** 數字表。

nu·mer·a·tor [ˈnjuməˌretɚ; ˈnjuːməreitə] *n.* ①〖數學〗(分數中之)分子(爲denominator 之對)。②計算者;計算器。

nu·mer·i·cal [njuˈmɛrɪkl; njuːˈmerikəl] *adj.* ①數字的;數字上的。*numerical* symbols. 數字符號(如1, 2, 3及Ⅰ, Ⅱ, Ⅲ等)。②以數字表示的。③〖數學〗絕對值的。④擅長於算數的。(亦作 **numeric**)

nu·mer·ol·o·gy [ˌnjuməˈrɑlədʒɪ; ˌnjuːməˈrɔlədʒi] *n.* 命理學(按出生年月日及其他數字測定命運之學)。**—nu·mer·ol·o·gist,** *n.*

‡nu·mer·ous [ˈnjumərəs; ˈnjuːmərəs] *adj.* ①極多的。too *numerous* to be mentioned. 不勝枚舉。②數目衆多的。a *numerous* class. 人數很多的班級。**—ly,** *adv.* **—ness, nu·mer·os·i·ty,** *n.*

nu·mis·mat·ic [ˌnjumɪzˈmætɪk; ˌnjuːmizˈmætik] *adj.* ①錢幣的;獎章的;錢幣與獎章的。a *numismatic* collection. 錢幣、獎章類之蒐集。②錢幣與獎章學的;錢幣、獎章之專家或收藏家的。

nu·mis·ma·ti·cian [njuˌmɪzməˈtɪʃən; njuːˌmizməˈtiʃən] *n.* 錢幣獎章等之收藏家。

nu·mis·mat·ics [ˌnjumɪzˈmætɪks; ˌnjuːmizˈmætiks] *n.* 錢幣與獎章學;錢幣、獎章之蒐集。

nu·mis·ma·tist [njuˈmɪzmətɪst; njuːˈmizmətist] *n.* 貨幣與獎章學家或收藏家。

nu·mis·ma·tol·o·gy [njuˌmɪzməˈtɑlədʒɪ; njuːˌmizməˈtɔlədʒi] *n.* ＝**numismatics.**

num·ma·ry [ˈnʌmərɪ; ˈnʌməri] *adj.* 「貨幣的;金錢的。」

num·mu·lar·y [ˈnʌmjəˌlɛrɪ; ˈnʌmjuləri] *adj.* ＝**nummary.**

num·mu·lite [ˈnʌmjəˌlaɪt; ˈnʌmjulait] *n.* 〖古生物〗貨幣石(一種有孔蟲類,其殼略似錢幣)。

num·skull [ˈnʌmˌskʌl; ˈnʌmskʌl] *n.* 「〖俗〗傻瓜;笨人。」

***nun** [nʌn; nʌn] *n.* 修女;尼姑。

nun buoy 〖航海〗(金屬製)紡錘形浮標。

Nunc Di·mit·tis [ˈnʌŋkdɪˈmɪtɪs; ˈnʌŋkdiˈmitis] *n.* ① Simeon 之頌(路加福音2章29–32節)。②(n–d–)離去之許可;離別;辭世。

nun·ci·a·ture [ˈnʌnʃɪətʃɚ; ˈnʌnʃiətʃə] 「*n.* 羅馬教廷大使之職或任期。」

nun·ci·o [ˈnʌnʃɪˌo; ˈnʌnʃiou] *n., pl.* **-ci·os.** 羅馬教皇之使節;教廷大使。

nun·cu·pate [ˈnʌŋkjuˌpet; ˈnʌŋkjupeit] *v.t.*, **-pat·ed, -pat·ing.** ①口述(遺囑等);口宣。②題獻;銘刻。

nun·cu·pa·tion [ˌnʌŋkjuˈpeʃən; ˌnʌŋkjuˈpeiʃən] *n.* ①(遺囑等之)口述。②題獻;刻銘。

nun·cu·pa·tive [ˈnʌŋkjuˌpetɪv; ˈnʌŋkjuˌpeitiv] *adj.* 口述的(遺囑等)。

Nun·ki·ang [ˈnunˈkɪɑŋ; ˈnunkiˈɑːŋ] *n.* 嫩江(中國東北之一省,省會齊齊哈爾, Tsitsihar 或龍江, Lungkiang)。

nun·ner·y [ˈnʌnərɪ; ˈnʌnəri] *n., pl.* **-ner·ies.** 女修道院;尼庵。

nun's veiling 一種柔細的薄毛織物(用作婦女面紗及衣料)。

nup·tial [ˈnʌpʃəl; ˈnʌpʃəl] *adj.* 婚姻的;婚禮的。the *nuptial* day. 結婚之日。—*n.* (常 *pl.*) 結婚;婚禮。

‡nurse [nɝs; nəːs] *n., v.,* **nursed, nurs·ing.** —*n.* ①護士;看護。②褓姆;乳母。③養育者;保護者。Difficulty is the *nurse* of greatness. 艱難困苦乃偉大人格之溫床。④撫育幼蟲之工蟻或工蜂。***put out to nurse*** 將(嬰兒)交託褓姆或乳母撫養。—*v.t.* ①哺乳。She *nurses* her baby. 她給她自己的孩子奶吃。②做…之褓姆;看護。She *nursed* the sick. 她看護病人。③養育;保護。to *nurse* a plant. 培養植物。④治療;療養。She *nursed* a bad cold by going to bed. 她以臥床休息治重傷風。⑤小心使用或處置。⑥緊抱;擁抱。⑦蓄;懷。to *nurse* feelings of revenge. 蓄意復仇。⑧〖俗〗慢飲。to *nurse* a cocktail. 慢慢地喝一杯雞尾酒。—*v.i.* ①做褓姆或看護。②(嬰兒)吃奶。The child did not *nurse* after he was three months old. 那小孩三個月(大)以後便不吃奶了。③餵奶。

nurse·ling [ˈnɝslɪŋ; ˈnəːsliŋ] *n.* ＝**nursling.**

nurse·maid [ˈnɝsˌmed; ˈnəːsmeid] 「*n.* 照顧幼兒的女僕。」

***nurs·er·y** [ˈnɝsrɪ; ˈnəːsri] *n., pl.* **-er·ies.** ①育兒室;育嬰堂。day *nursery.* 育兒室(供兒童玩耍及用餐);日間托兒所。night *nursery.* 嬰兒寢室;夜間托兒所。②苗圃;花廠。③溫床;培育某物生長之環境或地區。④＝**nursery school.**

nurs·er·y·maid [ˈnɝsrɪˌmed; ˈnəːsrimeid] *n.* ＝**nursemaid.**

nurs·er·y·man [ˈnɝsrɪmən; ˈnəːsrimən] *n., pl.* **-men.** 園主;園丁;花廠工人。

nursery rhyme 兒歌;童歌。

nursery school 托兒所;育幼院。

nurs·ing [ˈnɝsɪŋ; ˈnəːsiŋ] *adj.* 養育的。the *nursing* father (mother). 養父(母)。—*n.* (職業性的)養育;看護。

nursing bottle (嬰兒的)奶瓶。

nursing home ①〖英〗(小規模的)私立療養院。②具有照顧老人或病人設備的私人療養所。

nurs·ling [ˈnɝslɪŋ; ˈnəːsliŋ] *n.* ①「嬰兒。②被小心照顧的人或物。」

nur·ture [ˈnɝtʃɚ; ˈnəːtʃə] *v.,* **-tured, -tur·ing,** *n.* —*v.t.* ①養育;教養。②滋養。—*n.* ①養育;教養。②滋養;食物。

‡nut [nʌt; nʌt] *n., v.,* **nut·ted, nut·ting.** —*n.* ①果核;栗;胡桃;堅果。to crack a *nut.* 打碎胡桃。②核仁。③螺釘帽。④(小提琴等之)絃枕。⑤〖俚〗頭;腦袋。⑥〖俚〗怪人;瘋子;傻瓜;紈袴子。⑦〖俚〗戲或電視節目之製作費用。⑧〖俚,鄙〗睪丸。⑨〖俚〗對某事極爲起勁的人;迷。⑩核心;基本部分。***a hard*** (or ***tough***) ***nut to crack*** a. 難題;難解之事。b. 不易親近或了解的人;不易說服的人。***off one's nut*** 〖俚〗a. 瘋狂。b. 混亂的;不可理喻的。c. 錯誤的。—*v.i.* 採集堅果。

nu·ta·tion [njuˈteʃən; njuːˈteiʃən] *n.* ①垂頭;點頭。②〖天文〗章動(地軸的輕微振動)。③〖植物〗(成長中之莖的)自動旋轉運動。**—al,** *adj.*

nut-brown [ˈnʌtˌbraun; ˈnʌtbraun] 「*adj.* 栗色的;赤褐色的。」

nut·crack·er [ˈnʌtˌkrækɚ; ˈnʌtˌkrækə] *n.* ①胡桃鉗。②(以堅果爲食之)烏鴉屬鳥類;星鳥;五十雀。

nut·gall [ˈnʌtˌgɔl; ˈnʌtgɔːl] *n.* 〖植物〗沒食子;五倍子。

nut·hatch [ˈnʌtˌhætʃ; ˈnʌthætʃ] *n.* 「十五雀(鳥名)。」

nut·meat [ˈnʌtˌmit; ˈnʌtmiːt] *n.* 堅果的(可食的)核仁。

nut·meg [ˈnʌtmɛg; ˈnʌtmeg] *n.* 〖植物〗荳蔻;荳蔻樹。

nut·pick [ˈnʌtˌpɪk; ˈnʌtpik] *n.* 將胡桃等堅果從殼內取出所用之尖銳挑針。
nu·tri·a [ˈnjutrɪə; ˈnjuːtriə] *n.* ①(南美產之)河鼠。②其毛皮。
nu·tri·ent [ˈnjutrɪənt; ˈnjuːtriənt] *adj.* 滋養的;營養的。—*n.* 滋養物;營養物。
nu·tri·ment [ˈnjutrəmənt; ˈnjuːtrimənt] *n.* ①營養品;食物。②有助成長之物。
***nu·tri·tion** [njuˈtrɪʃən; njuːˈtriʃən] *n.* ①食物;營養。A balanced diet provides *nutrition* for your body. 均衡的食物使你的身體獲得營養。②營養的供給。③營養學。—**al,** *adj.*
nu·tri·tion·ist [njuˈtrɪʃənɪst; njuːˈtriʃənist] *n.* 營養專家;營養學家。
nu·tri·tious [njuˈtrɪʃəs; njuːˈtriʃəs] *adj.* 滋養的;營養的。—**ly,** *adv.* —**ness,** *n.*
nu·tri·tive [ˈnjutrətɪv; ˈnjuːtritiv] *adj.* ①營養的;關於營養的。②有滋養成分的;用以營養的。*nutritive* food. 滋養的食物。
nuts [nʌts; nʌts] *adj.* 〖俚〗狂的;瘋的;笨的;蠢的。to go *nuts.* 熱狂;發狂。to drive a person *nuts.* 將某人弄得瘋瘋癲癲。***be (dead) nuts on*** 〖俚〗a. 對…狂熱。b. …的能手。***be nuts about*** 熱愛…;極喜愛…;熱中於。—*interj.* (亦作 **nerts, nertz**)〖俚〗(表示討厭、失望、不信、拒絕等)哼! 不見得!
nuts and bolts 基本特點或成分。
nut·shell [ˈnʌtˌʃɛl; ˈnʌt-ʃel] *n.* ①堅果之殼。②小容器;小房屋。③無價值之物。***in a nutshell*** 簡述之。***lie in a nutshell*** 容易解決;一言可盡。—*v.t.* 簡述;濃縮。
nut tree 堅果樹;(特指)榛。
nut·ty [ˈnʌtɪ; ˈnʌti] *adj.,* **-ti·er, -ti·est.** ①多堅果的。②似堅果的。③〖俚〗極熱心的。④〖俚〗古怪的;瘋狂的。⑤愚笨的。
nux vom·i·ca [ˈnʌksˈvɑmɪkə; ˈnʌks-ˈvɔmikə] 〖植物〗①番木鼈樹。②番木鼈之種子(有毒,供藥用)。
nuz·zle [ˈnʌzl̩; ˈnʌzl] *v.,* **nuz·zled, nuz·zling,** *n.* —*v.t.* ①〖動物〗以鼻掘;將鼻插入。②以鼻觸或摩擦。③伸出(頭、鼻等)。④撫抱。—*v.i.* ①用鼻掘。②將鼻伸出。③卷臥;挨緊。—*n.* 擁抱;撫抱。
N.V. New Version. **NW** ①northwest. ② northwestern. **N.W.** ① North Wales. ②northwest. ③northwestern. **n.w.** ①net weight. ②northwest. ③ northwestern. **NWA** Northwest Airlines. 西北航空公司。 **N.W.T.** Northwest Territories. **n.wt.** net weight. **N.Y.** ①New York State. ② New York City. **NYA, N.Y.A.** 〖美〗National Youth Administration. **N.Y.C.** New York City.
nyc·ta·lo·pi·a [ˌnɪktəˈlopɪə; ˌniktəˈloupiə] *n.* 〖醫〗夜盲症。
nyc·ti·trop·ic [ˌnɪktɪˈtrɑpɪk; ˌniktiˈtrɔpik] *adj.* 〖植物〗夜間變更方向的(葉等)。
***ny·lon** [ˈnaɪlɑn; ˈnailɔn] *n.* ①尼龍(柔韌堅固之合成物,可製衣服、襪子、刷子等)。②(*pl.*) 尼龍襪子。—*adj.* 尼龍製的。
***nymph** [nɪmf; nimf] *n.* ①居住在海上,河上,山林,泉水一帶的女神。②〖詩〗美貌女郎。③〖動物〗(昆蟲的)蛹;活動蛹(介乎幼蟲,larva, 及成長時期之間)。
nym·pha [ˈnɪmfə; ˈnimfə] *n., pl.* **-phae** [-fi; -fiː]. ①活動蛹;蛹。②〖解剖〗小陰唇。
nymph·al [ˈnɪmfl̩; ˈnimfəl] *adj.* ①山林水澤之女神 (nymph) 的;似 nymph 的。②活動蛹的。
nym·phe·an [nɪmˈfiən; nimˈfiːən] *adj.* (似) nymph 的。
nymph·ish [ˈnɪmfɪʃ; ˈnimfiʃ] *adj.* = **nymphean.**
nymph·like [ˈnɪmfˌlaɪk; ˈnimf-laik] *adj.* 似 nymph 的。
nym·pho·lep·sy [ˈnɪmfəˌlɛpsɪ; ˈnimfəˌlepsi] *n.* ①(因看見 nymph 而發生的)狂亂;狂喜。②(因追求不可得之事物而起的)狂熱;妄想。
nym·pho·lept [ˈnɪmfəˌlɛpt; ˈnimfəlept] *n.* 狂熱(亂)者;患 nympholepsy 者。
nym·pho·ma·ni·a [ˌnɪmfəˈmenɪə; ˌnimfəˈmeiniə] *n.* 〖醫〗(女)色情狂;淫亂症。
nys·tag·mus [nɪsˈtægməs; nisˈtægməs] *n.* 〖醫〗眼球震顫。—**nys·tag·mic,** *adj.*
N.Z., N. Zeal. New Zealand.

O

O or **o** [o; ou] *n., pl.* **O's** or **Os; o's** or **os** or **oes.** ①英文字母之第十五個字母。②O形物。③零。④一序列中之第十五。⑤中世紀羅馬數字之11。⑥血型之一種。
‡O [o; ou] *interj., n., pl.* **O's.** —*interj.* 啊! *O* God, save us! 上帝啊,拯救我們! —*n.* "O" 的感歎。
O ①〖電〗ohm. ②old. ③oxygen. ④zero.
O' [o; ou] 〖字首〗置於愛爾蘭姓氏之前表 "son of" 之義,如: O'Brien.
o' [ə, o; ə, ou] *prep.* ①of 之縮寫(如o'clock; man-o'-war 等)。② on 之縮寫。
oaf [of; ouf] *n., pl.* **oafs, oaves.** ①畸形兒童;白癡兒童。②蠢人;莽漢。
oaf·ish [ˈofɪʃ; ˈoufiʃ] *adj.* 蠢笨的;癡呆的。
‡oak [ok; ouk] *n.* ①橡樹。②橡樹木。***sport one's oak*** 〖英大學俚〗關閉住處之外門以示不在家。—*adj.* 橡樹木製的。an *oak* table. 橡木桌。
oak apple (or **gall**) 五倍子;沒食子。
***oak·en** [ˈokən; ˈoukən] *adj.* ①橡木製的。the old *oaken* bucket. 舊橡木桶。②橡樹的。
oa·kum [ˈokəm; ˈoukəm] *n.* (自舊繩中解得之)麻絮(用以塡塞船縫者)。
‡oar [or, ɔr; ɔː, ɔə] *n.* ①櫓;槳。②槳手;划櫓夫。③似槳之物。***put in one's oar*** (or ***put one's oar in***)干涉;插手。***rest on one's oars*** a. 停工;休息。b. 依靠過去之成就而不以現在之努力來保持聲譽。***take an oar*** a. 開始划。b. 幫助。—*v.t.* & *v.i.* 用槳划;划渡。
oar·lock [ˈorˌlɑk; ˈɔːlɔk] *n.* 槳架。(亦作 **rowlock**)
oars·man [ˈorzmən; ˈɔːzmən] *n., pl.* **-men.** 划槳者;櫓夫。
oars·man·ship [ˈorzmənˌʃɪp; ˈɔːzmənʃip] *n.* 划槳術。
OAS, O.A.S. Organization of American States.
***o·a·sis** [oˈesɪs, ˈoəsɪs; ouˈeisis] *n., pl.* **-ses.** ①沙漠中之綠洲。②(枯燥,困難或厭煩之事中)一個輕鬆的變化。
oast [ost; oust] *n.* (忽布、烟葉、麥芽等之)乾燥窯。
oat** [ot; out] *n.* ①(常 *pl.*) 燕麥。②〖詩〗燕麥草做成之笛子。feel one's oats*** 〖美俚〗a. 活潑;雀躍;跳躍。b. 得意揚揚。***sow one's wild oats*** 在年輕時或婚前行爲放蕩。

oat·cake ['ot,kek; 'out'keik] *n.* 燕麥餅。
oat·en ['otn; 'outn] *adj.* ①燕麥製成的。②燕麥莖製成的。an *oaten* pipe. 麥笛;牧笛。
oat·er ['otə; 'outə] *n.* 〖俚〗西部電影或電視節目。
oat grass 似燕麥的草;(尤指)野生燕麥。
oath** [oθ; ouθ] *n., pl.* **oaths.** ①誓約。②表强調或憤怒之字。③咒詛;誓語。on*** (***one's***) ***oath*** 發誓。***put a person on his oath*** 使某人立誓。***take*** (or ***make***) ***an oath*** 宣誓。
***oat·meal** ['ot,mil, -'mil; 'outmi:l] *n.* ①燕麥片。②燕麥片粥。*oatmeal* porridge. 燕麥片粥。—*adj.* ①含燕麥片的。②灰黃色的。
ob. ①obiit (拉=he, *or* she, *or* it died). ②obiter (拉=incidentally). ③oboe.
ob- 〖字首〗①表 "to; toward; before" 之義,如:object. ②表"相反;反對"之義,如:obnoxious. ③表"up;over"之義,如:obfuscate. ④表 "完全;全部" 之義,如: obsolete. ⑤表"逆;反"之義,如: objurgate. 〖注意〗 **ob-** 在 c 之前作 oc-, 如: occur; 在 f 之前作 of-, 如:offer; 在 p 之前作 op-, 如: oppress, 在 m 之前作o-, 如:omit.
Obad., Ob 〖聖經〗 Obadiah.
O·ba·di·ah [,obə'daiə; ,oubə'daiə] *n.* ①男子名。②〖聖經〗俄巴底亞書(舊約之一卷)。
ob·bli·ga·to [,abli'gato; ,obli'ga:tou] *adj., n., pl.* **-tos, -ti** [-ti; -ti:]. —*adj.* 〖音樂〗必要的;不可少的(伴奏)。—*n.*(不可缺的)助奏;助唱。(亦作 **obligato**)
ob·du·ra·bil·i·ty [,abdjərə'biliti; ,obdjurə'biliti] *n.* 硬度與抗力。
ob·du·ra·cy ['abdjərəsi; 'obdjurəsi] *n.* ①無情;鐵石心腸。②執迷不悟;毫無悔意。③頑固;執拗。
ob·du·rate ['abdjərit; 'obdjurit] *adj.* ①無情的;硬心腸的。②執迷不悟的;毫無悔意的。③倔强的;堅決的;執拗的。—**ly,** *adv.*
O.B.E. Officer (of the Order) of the British Empire.
o·be·ah ['obiə; 'oubiə] *n.* ①(常 O-)(西印度羣島或非洲黑人的)一種巫術。②行此種巫術所用之神物(fetish). —**ism,** *n.*
o·be·di·ence** [ə'bidiəns; ə'bi:djəns, ou'b-, -diən-] *n.* 服從;孝順。I shall expect *obedience* from you. 我希望你能聽從我。in obedience to*** 服從。Soldiers acted *in obedience to* orders. 士兵遵守命令行動。
o·be·di·ent** [ə'bidiənt; ə'bi:djənt, ou'b-, -diən-] *adj.* 服從的;順從的;孝順的。be obedient to*** 服從;順從。***Your*** (***most***) ***obedient servant*** 頓首;謹啓;拜上(正式或公開書信中結尾用語)。—**ly,** *adv.*
o·bei·sance [o'besns; ou'beisəns] *n.* ①對尊長表示非常敬意之動作(如鞠躬、道萬福、屈膝等)。②尊敬;順從。
ob·e·lisk ['abl,isk; 'obilisk] *n.* ①方尖形的碑。②〖印刷〗短劍形的符號(†)。③似方尖形碑之物。④=**obelus.**
ob·e·lize ['abl,aiz; 'obilaiz] *v.t.,* **-lized, -liz·ing.** 以劍號(†)或疑句號(—或÷)標示。
ob·e·lus ['abləs; 'obiləs] *n., pl.* **-li** [-,lai; -lai]. ①(古代手寫本中加在可疑之詞句的)疑句號(—或÷)。②=**obelisk**②.
O·ber·on ['obə,ran; 'oubərən] *n.* ①〖中古傳說〗小神仙 (fairies) 之王, Titania 之夫(爲莎士比亞"仲夏夜之夢"中之一角色)。②〖天文〗天王星之第四衞星。
o·bese [o'bis; ou'bi:s] *adj.* 肥的;胖的。—**ly,** *adv.* —**ness,** *n.*
o·bes·i·ty [o'bisəti; ou'bi:siti] *n.* 肥胖。
‡**o·bey** [ə'be, o'be; ə'bei, ou'b-] *v.t.* & *v.i.* 服從;遵奉;順從。Soldiers have to *obey* orders. 軍人須服從命令。
ob·fus·cate [ab'fʌsket; 'obfʌskeit] *v.t.,* **-cat·ed, -cat·ing.** ①使暗;使模糊。②使迷亂;使困惑;使糊塗。—**ob·fus·ca·tor,** *n.*
ob·fus·ca·tion [,abfʌs'keʃən; ,obfʌs'keiʃən] *n.* ①使暗;使模糊;使迷亂。②困惑;模糊。③使困惑之事物。
o·bi ['obi; 'oubi] *n.* =**obeah.** —**ism,** *n.*
ob·i·it ['abiit; 'obiit] 〖拉〗=**he** (or **she**) **died** (略作 **ob.** 而加於死亡年月之前)。
o·bit ['abit; 'obit] *n.* ①忌日;死亡周年之祭典。②訃聞。③安魂彌撒。
ob·i·ter dic·tum ['abitə'diktəm; 'obitə'diktəm] *pl.* **ob·i·ter dic·ta** [~'diktə; ~'diktə]. 〖拉〗①〖法律〗(法官於判決中表示之)附帶的意見。②順便說的話。
o·bit·u·ar·ist [ə'bitʃu,ɛrist; ə'bitjuərist] *n.* 撰寫訃聞的人。
o·bit·u·ar·y [ə'bitʃu,ɛri; ə'bitjuəri] *n., pl.* **-ar·ies.** 訃聞(常附死者略傳)。—*adj.* 死的;關於死的。*obituary* notices. 訃聞。
obj. ①object. ②objection. ③objective.
‡**ob·ject** [*n.*'abdʒikt; 'obdʒikt, -dʒekt *v.* əb'dʒɛkt; əb'dʒekt, ob-] *n.* ①物體;物件。②(情感、思想或行動之)對象;目標。He has no *object* in life. 他沒有生活的目標。③(可憐、荒誕、滑稽或愚蠢的)人或物。What an *object* you look in that old hat! 你戴着那頂舊的帽子,顯得多麼滑稽啊!④目的。The *object* of our visit is to find out the truth of it. 我們此行之目的是欲探知此事之眞相。***fail*** (or ***succeed***) ***in one's object*** 追求某一目標而失敗(成功)。***no object*** 不計較;不成問題。Money is *no object*. 錢不必計較。***propose an object to oneself*** 立志;立下目標。—*v.i.* ①反對。I *object* to the proposal. 我反對這提議。Do you *object* to smoking? 你反對吸烟嗎? ②拒絕。—*v.t.* ①提出(作爲)反對的理由。②拒絕; 不允許。〖文法〗受詞。**direct object.** 直接受詞。**indirect object.** 間接受詞。
object ball 〖撞球〗目的球。
object glass (or **lens**) (望遠鏡、顯微鏡之)接物透鏡。
ob·jec·ti·fy [əb'dʒɛktə,fai; ob'dʒektifai] *v.t.,* **-fied, -fy·ing.** ①使客觀化;視作對象。②使具體化;使現實化。
***ob·jec·tion** [əb'dʒɛkʃən; əb'dʒekʃən] *n.* ①異議。He offered an *objection*. 他提出異議。He took *objection* to what I said. 他反對我所說的話。②反對;厭惡。I have no *objection* to it. 我不反對此事。③反對或拒絕之原因或理由。
ob·jec·tion·a·ble [əb'dʒɛkʃənəbl; əb'dʒekʃnəbl] *adj.* ①應反對的; 可駁的。②使人不愉快的。—**ob·jec·tion·a·bly,** *adv.*
***ob·jec·tive** [əb'dʒɛktiv; ob'dʒektiv] *n.* ①目的;目標。military *objectives*. 軍事目標。②受格;受格的字(如 whom 與 me). ③實物。④(望遠鏡、顯微鏡等中之)接物透鏡。—*adj.* ①實體的;眞實的。Actions are *objective*. 行動是眞實的。②客觀的。A scientist must be *objective*. 科學家必須是客觀的。③受詞的。④目標的。*objective* point. 目標。⑤〖醫〗(症狀之)客觀的。—**ly,** *adv.* —**ness,** *n.*
objective case 〖文法〗受格。
ob·jec·tiv·ism [əb'dʒɛktivizm; ob-

O

ˈdʒektivizəm] *n.*〖哲學, 藝術, 文學〗客觀主義。
ob·jec·tiv·i·ty [ˌɑbdʒɛkˈtɪvətɪ; ˌɔbdʒekˈtiviti] *n.* 客觀性; 對象性。
ob·ject·less [ˈɑbdʒɛktlɪs; ˈɔbdʒiktlis] *adj.* ①無目的的。②無物象的; (視野中) 空無一物的。③無受詞的。
object lesson ①以實物所做的訓解。②實例教訓。
ob·jec·tor [əbˈdʒɛktɚ; əbˈdʒektə] *n.* 反對者。
object staff 〖測量〗函尺; 準尺。
ob·jet d'art [ɔbˈʒɛˈdar; ɔbˈʒɛˈdar] *pl.* **ob·jets d'art** [ɔbˈʒɛˈdar; ɔbˈʒɛˈdar]. 有藝術價值之物品(如小雕像, 小花瓶等)。
ob·jur·gate [ˈɑbdʒɚˌget; ˈɔbdʒəːgeit] *v.t.*, **-gat·ed, -gat·ing.** 嚴責; 嚴叱; 叱責。
ob·jur·ga·tion [ˌɑbdʒɚˈgeʃən; ˌɔbdʒəːˈgeiʃən] *n.* 嚴責; 叱責; 責難。
ob·jur·ga·to·ry [əbˈdʒɝgəˌtorɪ; ɔbˈdʒəːgətəri] *adj.* 叱責的; 譴責的; 非難的。
ob·late[1] [ˈɑblet; ˈɔbleit] *adj.* 〖幾何〗兩極扁平的; 扁圓的。
ob·late[2] *adj.* 〖宗教〗獻身於宗教或修道生活的。—*n.* 獻身於宗教或修道生活者。
ob·la·tion [ɑbˈleʃən; ouˈbleiʃən] *n.* ①聖體(麪包與酒)之奉獻(式); 聖餐式。②(對神之)奉獻; 捐獻; 祭品。—**ob·la·to·ry,** *adj.*
ob·li·gate [ˈɑbləˌget; ˈɔbligeit] *v.*, **-gat·ed, -gat·ing,** *adj.* —*v.t.* ①使負責; 使負義務。②强迫。 —*adj.* ①道義上或法律上受約束的。②必要的; 主要的。
***ob·li·ga·tion** [ˌɑbləˈgeʃən; ˌɔbliˈgeiʃən] *n.* ①義務; 職責。to fulfill every *obligation.* 履行每一義務。②(法令、允諾、義務等之)束縛。He is under no *obligation* to do that. 他沒有必須要做那事的義務。③恩惠; 人情債。④契約。⑤債務。
ob·li·ga·to [ˌɑblɪˈgato; ˌɔbliˈgaːtou] *adj., n.* =**obbligato.**
ob·lig·a·to·ry [əˈblɪgəˌtorɪ; ɔˈbligətəri] *adj.* ①義務上的; 必須做的。②有拘束力的。③强制的 〖on, upon〗. duties *obligatory* on all. 强制大家共同負擔之責任。④〖生物〗專性的。
o·blige** [əˈblaɪdʒ; əˈblaidʒ] *v.*, **o·bliged, o·blig·ing.** —*v.t.* ①使受(諾言、契約、職責等)束縛; 强制。The law *obliges* parents to send their children to school. 法律強制父母送子女入學。②賜; 施於; 加於。She *obliged* us with a song. 她爲我們唱了一首歌。be obliged to*** 不得不; 必須。***be obliged to somebody*** 感激某人。—*v.i.* 取悅; 巴結; 應命。
ob·li·gee [ˌɑblɪˈdʒi; ˌɔbliˈdʒiː] *n.* ①受人施惠者(爲 obliger 之對)。②〖法律〗債權人; 權利人(爲 obligor 之對)。
o·blig·er [əˈblaɪdʒɚ; əˈblaidʒə] *n.* 施惠者。
o·blig·ing [əˈblaɪdʒɪŋ; əˈblaidʒiŋ] *adj.* ①親切的; 熱心助人的; 謙恭的; 仁慈的。② =**obligatory.** —**ly,** *adv.* —**ness,** *n.*
ob·li·gor [ˈɑblɪˌgɔr; ˌɔbliˈgɔː] *n.*〖法律〗債務人; 義務人。
ob·lique [əˈblik; əˈbliːk] *adj., adv., v.*, **-liqued, -liqu·ing,** *n.* —*adj.* ①歪的; 斜的。an *oblique* angle. 斜角。an *oblique* plane. 斜面。②間接的; 迂曲的。③閃爍其詞的; 不爽直的; 歪邪的; 不正的。④〖解剖〗斜紋肌的。⑤〖植物〗兩側不等的(葉等)。⑥〖文法〗從格的。*oblique* case. 從格(主格、呼格或直接目的格以外之各種格)。⑦〖修辭〗間接(敍述)的。***oblique narration*** 〖修辭〗間接敍述法。—*adv.* 〖軍〗以 45 度之角度。—*v.i.* ①歪偏; 傾斜。②〖軍〗斜行進。—*n.* ①〖文法〗從格。②斜的事物。③〖解剖〗斜紋肌。 —**ly,** *adv.*
ob·liq·ui·ty [əˈblɪkwətɪ; əˈblikwiti] *n., pl.* **-ties.** ①傾斜; 歪斜。②不正; 邪曲。③不正的行爲; 不道德。④〖數學〗傾度; 斜度。⑤模稜兩可的文章。⑥精神變態。
ob·lit·er·ate [əˈblɪtəˌret; əˈblitəreit] *v.t.*, **-at·ed, -at·ing.** ①消滅; 毀跡。②塗抹; 擦掉(文字等)。
ob·lit·er·a·tion [əˌblɪtəˈreʃən; əˌblitəˈreiʃən] *n.* ①消滅; 塗抹。②〖醫, 外科〗閉塞; 閉合。
ob·liv·i·on [əˈblɪvɪən; əˈbliviən] *n.* ①煙滅; 埋沒。②遺忘; 忘却。to be buried in *oblivion.* 湮沒無聞。③寬饒; 特赦。
ob·liv·i·ous [əˈblɪvɪəs; əˈbliviəs] *adj.* ①忘記的; 不注意的 〖of〗. I am *oblivious* of my former failure. 我忘了我先前的失敗。②使忘記的。—**ly,** *adv.*
ob·long [ˈɑblɔŋ; ˈɔblɔŋ] *adj.* 長方形的; 長橢圓形的。 —*n.* 長方形; 長橢圓形。 —**ish,** *adj.*
ob·lo·quy [ˈɑbləkwɪ; ˈɔbləkwi] *n., pl.* **-quies.** ①(公衆的) 譴責; 辱罵。②不名譽; 汚名; 恥辱。③毀謗。
ob·nox·ious [əbˈnɑkʃəs; əbˈnɔkʃəs] *adj.* ①令人不悅的; 使人討厭的。②〖法律〗應負責任的。③〖古〗可能遭受傷害的。④〖古〗應受處罰的; 應責備的。—**ly,** *adv.* —**ness,** *n.*
o·boe [ˈobo, ˈobɔɪ; ˈoubou, ˈoubɔi] *n.* 〖音樂〗①雙簧管 (一種樂器)。②風琴中發出似雙簧管音的音栓。
o·bo·ist [ˈoboɪst; ˈoubouist] *n.* 雙簧管吹奏者。
ob·ol [ˈɑbl̩; ˈɔbɔl] *n.* 古希臘之銀幣 (= 1/6 drachma).
Obs., obs. ①observation. ②observatory. ③obsolete.
ob·scene [əbˈsin; ɔbˈsiːn] *adj.* ①猥褻的; 淫穢的。*obscene* pictures. 春宮圖片 (照片)。②討厭的; 厭惡的。
ob·scen·i·ty [əbˈsɛnətɪ; ɔbˈsiːniti] *n., pl.* **-ties.** ①猥褻; 淫穢。②猥褻的言語或行爲。③猥褻的字眼或動作。
ob·scur·ant [əbˈskjurənt; ɔbˈskjuərənt] *n.* ①反啓蒙主義者; 反開化主義者; 蒙昧主義者。②使朦朧者; 使不分明者。 —*adj.* ①反啓蒙主義 (者)的。②使暗的; 使不明顯的。
ob·scur·ant·ism [əbˈskjurəntˌɪzəm; ɔbˈskjuərəntizəm] *n.* ①反啓蒙主義。②反對開化。
ob·scur·ant·ist [əbˈskjurəntɪst; ɔbˈskjuərəntist] *n.* =**obscurant.**—*adj.* (似)反啓蒙主義(者)的; 蒙昧主義(者)的。
ob·scu·ra·tion [ˌɑbskjuˈreʃən; ˌɔbskjuəˈreiʃən] *n.* ①黑暗化; 暗昧; 朦朧。②(良知等的) 蒙昧化; 蒙蔽; (眞理、語意等之)曖昧化。③〖天文〗掩蔽; 掩星。
***ob·scure** [əbˈskjur; əbˈskjuə] *adj.*, **-scur·er, -scur·est,** *v.*, **-scured, -scur·ing,** *n.* —*adj.* ①不著名的; 無名的; 微賤的。an *obscure* poet. 不著名的詩人。②不易發現的; 隱藏的; 幽僻的。an *obscure* meaning. 隱含的意思。③不清楚的; 不分明的。④暗的; 朦朧的。⑤不確定的; 含糊的。an *obscure* vowel. 含糊的母音 (卽ə)。—*v.t.* ①使暗; 使不分明; 使朦朧。②使成爲含糊之母音(ə)。③使意義含混。—*v.i.* 隱蔽。—*n.* =**obscurity.** —**ly,** *adv.* —**ness,** *n.*
***ob·scu·ri·ty** [əbˈskjurətɪ; əbˈskjuəriti] *n., pl.* **-ties.** ①晦澀; 晦澀之文字; 不明

之事。②卑微;默默無聞。Many great men rose from *obscurity* to fame. 許多偉人都是從卑微變成顯赫。③黑暗處;黑暗。④默默無聞之人或地方。

ob·se·cra·tion [ˌɑbsɪ'kreʃən; ˌɔbsi'kreiʃən] *n.* ①懇求;請願。②〖英國教會〗於連禱(Litany)中以"by"開始之祈禱句。

ob·se·qui·al [əb'sikwɪəl; ɔb'siːkwiəl] *adj.* 葬禮的。

ob·se·quies ['ɑbsɪkwɪz; 'ɔbsikwiz] *n. pl.* 葬禮;葬儀。

ob·se·qui·ous [əb'sikwɪəs; əb'siːkwiəs] *adj.* ①逢迎的;諂媚的;卑躬的。②〖罕〗服從的;負責的。**—ly,** *adv.* **—ness,** *n.*

ob·serv·a·ble [əb'zɝvəbl; əb'zəːvəbl] *adj.* ①可見的;顯而易見的。②顯著的。③可(應)遵行或慶祝的。**—ob·serv·a·bly,** *adv.*

***ob·serv·ance** [əb'zɝvəns; əb'zəːvəns] *n.* ①(對法律或習慣之)遵守;奉行〖of〗. *observance* of laws. 法律之遵守。②慶祝典禮;宗教儀式。③遵守之習慣或規則。④觀察。⑤〖古〗尊敬;敬奉。⑥天主教修會或修道院規律;奉此規律之修會或修道院。

ob·serv·ant [əb'zɝvənt; əb'zəːvənt] *adj.* ①善於觀察的;留心的;機警的。②小心遵守(法律、習慣等)的。 *—n.* ①奉行者;遵守者。②(O-) Franciscan 修會之修士(指嚴守St. Francis 之戒律者)。**—ly,** *adv.*

***ob·ser·va·tion** [ˌɑbzə'veʃən; ˌɔbzə'veiʃən] *n.* ①觀察;觀察力。a man of no *observation.* 無觀察力之人。②覺察;注意。to keep a person under *observation.* 注意某人。③觀察所得。④批評;評論。⑤有目的的觀察;研究。〖注意〗**observation, observance** 因其動詞均爲 observe 故常易混淆。**observation** 意爲細心觀察。**observance** 意爲遵守或慶祝。

ob·ser·va·tion·al [ˌɑbzə'veʃənəl; ˌɔbzəː'veiʃnl] *adj.* ①觀察的;觀測的;視察的;監視的。②基於觀察(觀測)的。**—ly,** *adv.*

observation balloon 觀測汽球。

observation car 〖鐵路〗瞭望車。

observation post 〖軍〗觀測所;監視哨;瞭望哨。

***ob·serv·a·to·ry** [əb'zɝvəˌtorɪ; əb'zəːvətri] *n., pl.* **-ries.** 天文臺;氣象臺;瞭望臺。

‡**ob·serve** [əb'zɝv; əb'zəːv] *v.,* **-served, -serv·ing.** *—v.t.* ①觀看;看到。 I *observed* nothing queer in his behavior. 我發現他的行爲沒有怪僻之處。 ②觀察;研究。 An astronomer *observes* the stars. 天文學家研究星辰。③評論;說。"Bad weather," the captain *observed.* "壞天氣,"船長說。④保持;遵守。to *observe* a rule. 遵守規則。⑤慶祝;紀念。 to *observe* Christmas. 慶祝耶誕。 *—v.i.* 觀察;注意。He *observes* keenly but says very little. 他觀察銳敏,但極少發言。

***ob·serv·er** [əb'zɝvɚ; əb'zəːvə] *n.* ①注意者;觀察者;遵奉者。②評論者。③(出席會議之)觀察員。④〖美陸軍〗擔任搜索任務及指導地面砲火的機上人員。⑤〖空軍〗機上觀察員。

ob·serv·ing [əb'zɝvɪŋ; əb'zəːviŋ] *adj.* 觀察的;注意的;留心的。 **—ly,** *adv.*

ob·sess [əb'sɛs; əb'ses] *v.t.* 使分心;使心神困擾(用於被動式中時,與 by 或 with連用)。 He was *obsessed* with the idea of approaching death. 他爲卽將死亡的念頭所困擾。**—ing·ly,** *adv.* **—or,** *n.*

ob·ses·sion [əb'sɛʃən; əb'seʃən] *n.* ①分心;分神;着魔; 感情或意念之縈擾。 to be under an *obsession* of. 爲…所纏繞。②縈繞於心的感情、意念或慾望。

ob·ses·sive [əb'sɛsɪv; əb'sesiv] *adj.* ①分神的;似着魔的;爲…縈繞的。②促成 obsession 的。③過分的;極度的。**—ly,** *adv.*

ob·sid·i·an [əb'sɪdɪən; ɔb'sidiən] *n.* 〖礦〗黑曜石。

ob·so·lesce [ˌɑbsə'lɛs; ˌɔbsə'les] *v.i.,* **-lesced, -lesc·ing.** 成爲過時;成爲廢物。

ob·so·les·cent [ˌɑbsə'lɛsnt; ˌɔbsə'lesnt] *adj.* ①行將作廢的; 卽將過時的。②〖生物〗廢棄性的。 **—ob·so·les·cence,** *n.* **—ly,** *adv.*

ob·so·lete ['ɑbsəˌlit; 'ɔbsəliːt] *adj., v.,* **-let·ed, -let·ing.** *—adj.* ①作廢的;已廢的。an *obsolete* word. 廢字。②過時的。③〖生物〗發育不完整的。*—v.t.* 以新代舊而使舊的成爲過時。**—ly,** *adv.* **—ness,** *n.*

***ob·sta·cle** ['ɑbstəkl; 'ɔbstəkl] *n.* 障礙;妨害物。 Courage knows no *obstacle.* 有勇氣便無障礙。

obstacle race 障礙賽跑。

ob·stet·ric [əb'stɛtrɪk; ɔb'stetrik] *adj.* =**obstetrical.**

ob·stet·ri·cal [əb'stɛtrɪkl; ɔb'stetrikəl] *adj.*①產科的。an *obstetrical* case. 產科病例。②助產的。an *obstetrical* nurse. 助產護士。(亦作 **obstetric**)

ob·ste·tri·cian [ˌɑbstɛ'trɪʃən; ˌɔbste'triʃən] *n.* 產科醫生。

ob·stet·rics [əb'stɛtrɪks; ɔb'stetriks] *n.* (作*sing.* 解) 產科醫學;接生術。

***ob·sti·na·cy** ['ɑbstənəsɪ; 'ɔbstinəsi] *n., pl.* **-cies** for②. ①倔强;頑固。②頑强的行爲或態度。rebuke for their *obstinacies.* 對他們的頑强行爲之拒斥。

***ob·sti·nate** ['ɑbstənɪt; 'ɔbstinit] *adj.* ①倔強的;頑固的。②難控制的;難醫治的。an *obstinate* cough. 難治的咳嗽。**—ly,** *adv.*

ob·strep·er·ous [əb'strɛpərəs; əb'strepərəs] *adj.* ①喧鬧的;吵鬧的。②暴亂的;無秩序的。**—ly,** *adv.*

***ob·struct** [əb'strʌkt; əb'strʌkt] *v.t.* ①阻隔;遮斷。②妨礙;遮蔽。 **—er, —or,** *n.*

***ob·struc·tion** [əb'strʌkʃən; əb'strʌkʃən] *n.* ①障礙物;障礙。Ignorance is an *obstruction* to progress. 無知爲進步之障礙。②閉塞;封鎖。 The enemy adopted a policy of *obstruction.* 敵人採取封鎖政策。③(議會中的)妨害或拖延手段。

obstruction guard 〖鐵路〗(機車之)障礙排除器。

ob·struc·tion·ism [əb'strʌkʃənɪzm; əb'strʌkʃənizəm] *n.* (議會等中之) 有組織的妨害議事進行(政策)。

ob·struc·tion·ist [əb'strʌkʃənɪst; əb'strʌkʃənist] *n.* 妨害議事進行者。*—adj.* 妨害議事進行政策的;妨害議事進行者的。

ob·struc·tive [əb'strʌktɪv; əb'strʌktiv] *adj.* 妨礙的;成爲障礙的。 *—n.* 成爲障礙之人或事物。**—ly,** *adv.* **—ness,** *n.*

‡**ob·tain** [əb'ten; əb'tein] *v.t.* ①得;獲得。to *obtain* a prize. 得獎。②達到(目的)。*—v.i.* ①應用;流行。These views no longer *obtain.* 這些觀點已不合用。②如願以償。**—a·ble,** *adj.* **—er,** *n.*

ob·tect·ed [ɑb'tɛktɪd; ɔb'tektid] *adj.* 有角質外殼的(蛹)。

ob·test [ɑb'tɛst; ɔb'test] *v.t.* ①懇請。②傳喚作證。*—v.i.* ①懇求。②抗議。

ob·tes·ta·tion [ˌɑbtɛs'teʃən; ˌɔbtes-

ˈteiʃən] *n.* 懇請;請求;抗議。

ob·trude [əbˈtrud; əbˈtruːd] *v.*, **-trud·ed, -trud·ing.** —*v.t.* ①强行提出;强使接受。②伸出。—*v.i.* 闖入。—**ob·trud·er,** *n.*

ob·tru·sion [əbˈtruʒən; əbˈtruːʒən] *n.* ①(意見等之)强迫接受。②强迫接受的意見或事物。—**ist,** *n.*

ob·tru·sive [əbˈtrusɪv; əbˈtruːsiv] *n.* ①强行提出的;强入的;闖入的;無顧忌的。②突出的。—**ly,** *adv.* —**ness,** *n.*

ob·tund [ɑbˈtʌnd; ɔbˈtʌnd] *v.t.* 使(感覺、機能等)鈍;緩和(痛苦等)。—**i·ty,** *n.*

ob·tu·rate [ˈɑbtjʊˌret; ˈɔbtjuəreit] *v.t.*, **-rat·ed, -rat·ing.** ①閉;閉塞。②閉錮(鎗砲之後膛等)。

ob·tu·ra·tion [ˌɑbtjʊˈreʃən; ˌɔbtjuəˈreiʃən] *n.* 閉塞;閉錮。

ob·tu·ra·tor [ˈɑbtjʊˌretɚ; ˈɔbtjuəreitə] *n.* ①閉塞物。②錮鎗器。③〖外科〗人工口蓋;閉孔器;阻塞器。

ob·tuse [əbˈtus; əbˈtjuːs] *adj.* ①不銳利的;鈍的。②大於直角的。③〖植物〗(葉、花瓣等)端部呈圓形的。④(理解或感覺)遲鈍的;愚鈍的。⑤(聲音)不尖銳的;(疼痛)不劇烈的。—**ly,** *adv.* —**ness, ob·tu·si·ty,** *n.*

ob·verse [*adj.* əbˈvɝs, ˈɑbvɝs; ˈɔbvəːs *n.* ˈɑbvɝs; ˈɔbvəːs] *adj.* ①正面的(爲 reverse 之對)。②相對的。③底部窄於頂部的。④〖植物〗鈍頭形的;倒生的(葉)。—*n.* ①(貨幣、獎章等之)正面。②正面;前面。③相對物。④〖邏輯〗反換命題。

ob·ver·sion [ɑbˈvɝʃən; ɔbˈvəːʃən] *n.* ①轉向。②〖邏輯〗(命題之)反換;換質。③轉向之事物。

ob·vert [əbˈvɝt; ɔbˈvəːt] *v.t.* ①將…之正面轉向。②〖邏輯〗反換(命題)。

ob·vi·ate [ˈɑbvɪˌet; ˈɔbvieit] *v.t.*, **-at·ed, -at·ing.** 排除;防止;避免。—**ob·vi·a·tion, ob·vi·a·tor,** *n.*

***ob·vi·ous** [ˈɑbvɪəs; ˈɔbviəs] *adj.* 顯然的;明白的。—**ly,** *adv.* —**ness,** *n.*

Oc., oc. ocean.

oc- 〖字首〗＝**ob-** (用於 c 之前)。

oc·a·ri·na [ˌɑkəˈrinə; ˌɔkəˈriːnə] *n.* 洋壎(一種陶質蛋形吹奏樂器)。

:oc·ca·sion [əˈkeʒən; əˈkeiʒən] *n.* ①特殊的時機。It is a favorable *occasion.* 此爲一有利的時機。②特殊的大事;特殊的場合。This sort of thing is usual on *occasions* like (*or* such as) these. 這種事情在此類場合中是尋常的。③機會;良機。I had no *occasion* to see him. 我沒有機會去看他。④理由;原因。There is no *occasion* to be angry. 沒有生氣的理由。***for one's occasion*** 爲某人。***for the occasion*** 臨時。***give occasion to*** 引起;使發生。***have no occasion for*** 沒有…之原因。***have no occasion to*** 無…之必要。***have occasion for*** 有…之必要;必需。***if the occasion arises*** (or ***should arise***) 在必要的時候(＝should occasion arise). ***improve the occasion*** 利用時機;把握機會。***in honor of the occasion*** 爲表示慶祝;爲道賀。***on occasion*** 有時(＝now and then). ***on one occasion*** 曾經;有一次。***on several occasions*** 屢次;好幾次。***on the first occasion*** 一有機會。***on the occasion of*** 在…的時候。***on the present occasion*** 此時。***on this occasion*** 此時。***rise to the occasion*** 表現出有應付某特別事故之能力;善處難局。***seize the occasion to*** 抓住…的機會;乘機。***take occasion to do*** 利用機會以作(某事)。—*v.t.* 產生出;導使;招惹;惹起。His queer behavior *occasioned* talk. 他的古怪行爲引起談論。

***oc·ca·sion·al** [əˈkeʒənl; əˈkeiʒənl] *adj.* ①時常發生的;偶然的。That sort of thing is quite *occasional* and not the rule. 那種事是十分偶然的,並不是慣例。②應時的。*occasional* poetry. 應景詩。③必要時使用的;備不時之需的。④臨時需要而做的。

oc·ca·sion·al·ism [əˈkeʒənlˌɪzəm; əˈkeiʒn̩əlizəm] *n.* 〖哲學〗機會論;偶因說。

***oc·ca·sion·al·ly** [əˈkeʒənlɪ; əˈkeiʒn̩əli] *adv.* 隨時地;偶然地;有時。He writes *occasionally.* 他有時寫信。

Oc·ci·dent [ˈɑksədənt; ˈɔksidənt] *n.* ①(the–)歐美國家(爲 the Orient 之對);西方國家。②(o–) 西方。

oc·ci·den·tal [ˌɑksəˈdɛntl; ˌɔksiˈdentl] *adj.* ①(O–) 西洋的;歐美國家的。②西方的。—*n.* (常 O–) 西洋人。—**i·ty,** *n.* —**ly,** *adv.*

Oc·ci·den·tal·ism [ˌɑksəˈdɛntl̩ˌɪzəm; ˌɔksiˈdentəlizəm] *n.* 西洋式;西洋文化;西洋氣質;西洋習俗;西洋精神。

Oc·ci·den·tal·ist [ˌɑksəˈdɛntl̩ɪst; ˌɔksiˈdentəlist] *n.* ①景仰西洋文明者。②精通西洋事物之人。

Oc·ci·den·tal·ize [ˌɑksəˈdɛntl̩ˌaɪz; ˌɔksiˈdentəlaiz] *v.t.*, **-ized, -iz·ing.** 西化;西洋化;歐化。

oc·cip·i·tal [ɑkˈsɪpətl̩; ɔkˈsipitl] *adj.* 〖解剖〗後頂的;枕骨的。—*n.* 枕骨。

oc·ci·put [ˈɑksɪˌpʌt; ˈɔksipʌt] *n.*, *pl.* **oc·ci·puts, oc·cip·i·ta** [ɑkˈsɪpətə; ɔkˈsipitə]. 〖解剖〗後頂;枕骨部。

oc·clude [əˈklud; ɔˈkluːd] *v.*, **-clud·ed, -clud·ing.** —*v.t.* ①封閉(通道、毛孔等);關閉。②關入;關出;遮斷。③〖化〗(物質等)吸收(氣體等)。—*v.i.* 〖齒科〗(上下牙齒)咬合。

oc·clu·sion [əˈkluʒən; ɔˈkluːʒən] *n.* ①〖醫〗閉塞;阻塞。②〖化〗吸收。③〖齒科〗咬合。④〖語音〗閉鎖。

oc·clu·sive [əˈklusɪv; ɔˈkluːsiv] *adj.* ①閉塞的。②〖語音〗閉鎖音的。—*n.* ①〖語音〗閉鎖音。②任何閉鎖之音。

oc·cult [əˈkʌlt; ɔˈkʌlt] *adj.* ①玄奧的。②超自然法則的。③祕傳的。④隱藏的。—*n.* ①神祕。②(the–)神祕學(研究);玄學。—*v.t.* & *v.i.* 掩蓋。

oc·cul·ta·tion [ˌɑkʌlˈteʃən; ˌɔkʌlˈteiʃən] *n.* ①隱伏;不見。②〖天文〗掩蔽;掩星。

oc·cult·ism [əˈkʌltɪzm̩; ˈɔkəltizəm] *n.* 神祕學;神祕研究;神祕主義;神祕論。—**oc·cult·ist,** *n.*

oc·cu·pan·cy [ˈɑkjəpənsɪ; ˈɔkjupənsi] *n.*, *pl.* **-cies.** ①(土地、房屋等之)占有;占有期間。②〖法律〗先占;占據。③占領。④財產之運用。

***oc·cu·pant** [ˈɑkjəpənt; ˈɔkjupənt] *n.* ①占有者;占領者。Who is the *occupant* of this cottage? 誰住在這個小屋內? ②〖法律〗**a.** 因占有而取得所有權者。**b.** 實際占有人。

***oc·cu·pa·tion** [ˌɑkjəˈpeʃən; ˌɔkjuˈpeiʃən] *n.* ①職業。He has no fixed *occupation.* 他沒有固定的職業。②占領;占據;占有。military *occupation.* 軍事占領。③居住。the *occupation* of a house by a family. 某屋爲某一家庭所居住。④(房屋、田地等)居住期;占有期。⑤人所從事的活動。to become bored for lack of *occupation.* 因

無所事事而感覺無聊。⑥任期。—**less,** *adj.*

oc·cu·pa·tion·al 〔ˌɑkjəˈpeʃənl̩; ˌɔkjuˈpeiʃənl〕 *adj.* ①職業（上）的；業務（上）的。an *occupational* disease. 〖醫〗職業病。②占領的。

occupational hazard 職業上的危險或困擾。

occupational therapy 〖醫〗職業治療法。

oc·cu·pi·er 〔ˈɑkjəˌpaɪə; ˈɔkjupaiə〕 *n.* 占有者；占領者；居住人。

‡oc·cu·py 〔ˈɑkjəˌpaɪ; ˈɔkjupai〕 *v.*, **-pied, -py·ing.** —*v.t.* ①占；填滿。The building *occupies* an entire block. 這建築物占了整整一方街區。②使忙碌；使從事；牽絆。I am fully *occupied.* 我是很忙碌的。③占據；占領。The enemy *occupied* our fort. 敵人占據了我們的堡壘。④住進；居住於。That room is *occupied* by him. 那間屋子爲他所住。⑤占着；居於；充任。—*v.i.* 取得所有權。

‡oc·cur 〔əˈkɝ; əˈkəː〕 *v.i.*, **-curred, -cur·ring.** ①發生。A leap year *occurs* once every four years. 每四年有一次閏年。②被發見；存在。Several misprints *occurred* on the first page. 在第一頁有幾處印刷的錯誤。③被想起；使想到〖常 to〗. An idea *occurred* to me. 我想起一計。

***oc·cur·rence** 〔əˈkɝəns; əˈkʌrəns〕 *n.* ①發生。of frequent *occurrence.* 經常發生的。②事件。an everyday *occurrence.* 每日發生之事。—**oc·cur·rent,** *adj.*

‡o·cean 〔ˈoʃən; ˈouʃən〕 *n.* ①大海。②五大洋(the Atlantic, Pacific, Indian, Arctic, and Antarctic oceans) 之一。③廣漠；無限。an *ocean* of troubles. 無限的麻煩。*oceans* of time (money). 無限的時間(錢)。—**like,** *adj.*

o·cean·ar·i·um 〔ˌoʃəˈnɛrɪəm; ˌouʃəˈnɛəriəm〕 *n., pl.* **-i·ums, -i·a** 〔-ɪə; -iə〕. 海邊附近的海水水族館。

o·cean·aut 〔ˈoʃəˌnɔt; ˈouʃənɔːt〕 *n.* 海洋探險家。

ocean bed 海底。

o·cean-go·ing 〔ˈoʃənˈgoɪŋ; ˈouʃənˈgouiŋ〕 *adj.* 航行遠洋的。

O·ce·an·i·a 〔ˌoʃɪˈænɪə; ˈouʃiˈeiniə〕 *n.* 大洋洲（中南太平洋諸島之集合稱)。(亦作 **Oceanica**)

O·ce·an·i·an 〔ˌoʃɪˈænɪən; ˌouʃiˈeiniən〕 *adj.* 大洋洲的；其人民的。—*n.* 大洋洲人。

o·ce·an·ic 〔ˌoʃɪˈænɪk; ˌouʃiˈænik〕 *adj.* ①大海的；大洋的。②居於海洋中的；海洋出產的。③似海洋的；廣大的。

o·ce·an·ics 〔ˌoʃɪˈænɪks; ˌouʃiˈæniks〕 *n.* 海洋之開發及研究。

O·ce·a·nid 〔oˈsiənɪd; ouˈsiːənid〕 *n., pl.* **O·ce·an·i·des.** 〖希臘神話〗海洋之女神。

ocean liner 郵輪；遠洋客輪。

o·ce·a·nog·ra·pher 〔ˌoʃɪəˈnɑgrəfə; ˌouʃiəˈnɔgrəfə〕 *n.* 海洋學者。

o·ce·a·nog·ra·phy 〔ˌoʃɪənˈɑgrəfɪ; ˌouʃiəˈnɔgrəfi〕 *n.* 海洋學。

oc·el·lat·ed 〔ˈɑsəˌletɪd; ˈɔsəˌleitid〕 *adj.* ①(斑點等)像眼的。②眼狀斑的。(亦作 **ocellate**)

oc·el·la·tion 〔ˌɑsəˈleʃən; ˌɔsəˈleiʃən〕 *n.* 眼狀斑。

o·cel·lus 〔oˈsɛləs; ouˈseləs〕 *n., pl.* **-li** 〔-laɪ; lai〕. 〖動物〗①(昆蟲之)單眼。②(孔雀尾等之)眼狀斑。

o·ce·lot 〔ˈosəˌlɑt; ˈousilɔt〕 *n.* 〖動物〗(中、南美產之)豹貓。—**o·ce·loid,** *adj.*

och 〔ʌk; ʌk〕 *interj.* 〖愛，蘇〗(表示吃驚、遺憾、悲痛等)啊！呀！喲！唷！

o·cher, o·chre 〔ˈokə; ˈoukə〕 *n., adj., v.,* **o·chered, o·chred, o·cher·ing, o·chring.** —*n.* ①〖礦〗赭土；赭石（可作顏料用)。②赭色。③〖美俚〗金錢(尤指金幣)。—*adj.* 赭色的。—*v.t.* 染以赭色。

o·cher·ous, o·chre·ous 〔ˈokərəs; ˈoukərəs〕 *adj.* 赭色的；赭土的；含赭土的。

och·loc·ra·cy 〔ɑkˈlɑkrəsɪ; ɔkˈlɔkrəsi〕 *n.* 暴民政治。

och·lo·crat·ic 〔ˌɑkləˈkrætɪk; ˌɔkləˈkrætik〕 *adj.* 暴民政治的。

‡o'clock 〔əˈklɑk; əˈklɔk〕 ①(=of the clock)點鐘(應用時此字常被略去)。It's just two (*o'clock*). 現在恰爲兩點鐘。②以鐘面爲據而指出相對的方向的方法，卽以12時爲正前方或正上方，以下類推。Enemy aircraft were approaching at 6 *o'clock.* 敵機正從正後方靠近中。

OCR optical character recognition. 〖電腦〗感光讀字。

Oct. October.

oct- 〖字首〗**octa-** 或 **octo-** 之異形。

octa- 〖字首〗表"八" 之義。(亦作 **oct-**)

oc·ta·chord 〔ˈɑktəˌkɔrd; ˈɔktəkɔːd〕 *n.* ①八弦琴。②〖音樂〗八音音階；八之和音。—*adj.* 八弦的。—**al,** *adj.*

oc·tad 〔ˈɑktæd; ˈɔktæd〕 *n.* ①八個之一組或一列。②〖化〗八價元素；八價之基。—**ic,** *adj.*

oc·ta·gon 〔ˈɑktəˌgɑn; ˈɔktəgən〕 *n.* 八角形；八邊形。(亦作 **octangle**)

oc·tag·o·nal 〔ɑkˈtægənl̩; ɔkˈtægənl〕 *adj.* 有八邊的；有八角的；八角形的。—**ly,** *adv.*

oc·ta·he·dral 〔ˌɑktəˈhidrəl; ˈɔktəˈhedrəl〕 *adj.* 有八面的；八面體的。

oc·ta·he·dron 〔ˌɑktəˈhidrən; ˈɔktəˈhedrən〕 *n., pl.* **-drons, -dra** 〔-drə; -drə〕. 八面體。

oc·tane 〔ˈɑkten; ˈɔktein〕 *n.* 〖化〗辛烷(C_8H_{18})。

octane number (or **rating**) 辛烷值(汽油防震性之指數)。

oc·tan·gle 〔ˈɑktæŋgl̩; ˈɔktæŋgl〕 *adj.* 八角的。—*n.* 八角形。

oc·tan·gu·lar 〔ɑkˈtæŋgjələ; ɔkˈtæŋgjulə〕 *adj.* 八角的。—**ness,** *n.*

oc·tant 〔ˈɑktənt; ˈɔktənt〕 *n.* ①八分圓(45° 之弧)。②八分儀。③〖天文〗在離角45度之位置(一天體對另一天體而言)。④〖數學〗卦限（三平面在一點互成直角相交所分成的八個空間之任一)。

Oc·ta·teuch 〔ˈɑktəˌtjuk; ˈɔktətjuːk〕 *n.* 舊約之最初八卷。

oc·tave 〔ˈɑktev, -tɪv; ˈɔktiv, ˈɔkteiv〕 *n.* ①〖音樂〗第八音；第八度音程；一個音階。②〖宗教〗從節日起之第八天；節日及其後的一週。③十四行詩（sonnet）中的起首的八行；八行一節的詩。④八個的一組；一組中的第八個。—*adj.* ①有八個的；八個一組的。②第八度音的；第八度音程的。

oc·ta·vo 〔ɑkˈtevo; ɔkˈteivou〕 *n., pl.* **-vos,** *adj.* —*n.* 八開本；八開(略作 **8vo,** 8°)。—*adj.* 八開的。

oc·ten·ni·al 〔ɑkˈtɛnɪəl; ɔkˈtenjəl〕 *adj.* ①每八年的。②延續八年的。

oc·tet(te) 〔ɑkˈtɛt; ɔkˈtet〕 *n.* ①〖音樂〗八重唱(奏)(曲)；八重唱(奏)團。②八行之詩；十四行詩(sonnet) 之前八行。③八個的一組。

oc·til·lion 〔ɑkˈtɪljən; ɔkˈtiljən〕 *n., pl.* **-lions, -lion,** *adj.* —*n.* ①〖美、法〗$=10^{27}$。②〖英、德〗$=10^{48}$。—*adj.* 上述之數的。

‡Oc·to·ber 〔ɑkˈtobə; ɔkˈtoubə〕 *n.* ①十月。②〖英〗十月釀的麥酒（=ale).

oc·to·dec·i·mo 〔ˌɑktoˈdɛsəˌmo; ˈɔktouˈdesimou〕 *n., pl.* **-mos.** 十八開；十

O

八開本(略作 **18mo, 18°**)。—*adj.* 十八開的。

oc·to·ge·nar·i·an [ˌɑktədʒəˈnɛrɪən; ˌɔktoudʒiˈnɛəriən] *adj.* 八十歲的;八十餘歲的。—*n.* 八十歲的人;八十餘歲的人。

oc·to·nal [ˈɑktənḷ; ˈɔktənl] *adj.* = **octonary.**

oc·to·nar·i·an [ˌɑktəˈnɛrɪən; ˌɔktəˈnɛəriən] *adj.*〖韻律〗八音步的。—*n.* 八音步的詩行。

oc·to·nar·y [ˈɑktəˌnɛrɪ; ˈɔktənəri] *adj., n., pl.* **-nar·ies.** —*adj.* ①八的; 由八個組成的。②〖數學〗八進法的。—*n.* ①八個的一組。②〖韻律〗八行的詩節。(亦作 **octal**)

oc·to·pus [ˈɑktəpəs; ˈɔktəpəs] *n., pl.* **-pus·es, -pi** [-paɪ; -pai]. ①章魚。②似章魚的東西;勢力遠張,强有力且能爲害的組織。

oc·to·roon [ˌɑktəˈrun; ˌɔktəˈruːn] *n.* 黑人血統八分之一的混血兒。

oc·to·syl·lab·ic [ˌɑktəsɪˈlæbɪk; ˈɔktousiˈlæbik] *adj., n.* 八音節的(詩行)。

oc·to·syl·la·ble [ˈɑktəˌsɪləbḷ; ˈɔktouˌsiləbl] *n.* 八音節的字(詩行)。—*adj.* 八音節的。

oc·troi [ˈɑktrɔɪ; ˈɔktrwɑː] *n., pl.* **-trois.** ①(物品)入市稅。②入市稅征收處。③入市稅征收員。

oc·tu·ple [ˈɑktupḷ; ˈɔktjuːpl] *adj., n., v.,* **-pled, -pling.** —*adj.* ①八倍的;八重的。②由八個要素構成的。—*n.* 八倍。—*v.t.* & *v.i.* (使)變成八倍。

oc·u·lar [ˈɑkjələ˞; ˈɔkjulə] *adj.* ①眼睛的; 視覺的。②像眼睛的。—*n.* 望遠鏡、顯微鏡等上的接目鏡。

oc·u·list [ˈɑkjəlɪst; ˈɔkjulist] *n.* 眼科醫生。

OD ①Officer of the Day. ②Ordnance Department. ③outside diameter.

O.D. ①Officer of the Day. ②Old Dutch. ③olive drab. ④overdraft. ⑤overdrawn. ⑥Doctor of Optometry. ⑦outside diameter.

o·da·lisque, o·da·lisk [ˈodḷˌɪsk; ˈoudəlisk] *n.* ①(土耳其宮廷中之)女奴;(土耳其君主之)妾。②上述女奴或妾之圖畫。

odd** [ɑd; ɔd] *adj.* ①剩餘的。Pay the bill with this money and keep the *odd* change. 用這筆錢去付帳,找回的零錢你留着。②一雙或一組中的單隻的。an *odd* stocking. 單隻的襪子。③額外的;附加的。30 *odd* guests. 三十多位客人。④奇數的(爲even之對)。Seven is an *odd* number. 七是奇數。⑤奇異的;古怪的。an *odd* person. 古怪的人。⑥臨時的;零星的;零碎的。*odd* moments. 零碎的空閑時間。⑦不尋常的;偏僻的。⑧(一雙中)不配的。Do you know you're wearing an *odd* pair of socks? 你曉不曉得你穿着左右不配的襪子? ***odd month (有31天的)大月。—*n.* ①奇怪的事物。②怪異;奇特。③〖高爾夫〗**a.** 讓給對方的一桿。**b.** 贏對方的一桿。—**ness,** *n.*

odd·ball [ˈɑdˌbɔl; ˈɔdbɔːl] *n.*〖美俚〗行爲、穿着等古怪的人。—*adj.* 古怪的;乖僻的。

Odd·fel·low [ˈɑdˌfɛlo; ˈɔdˌfelou] *n.* Independent Order of *Oddfellows* (十八世紀創立於英國之一種祕密共濟協會)之會員。(亦作 **Odd Fellow**)

odd·i·ty [ˈɑdətɪ; ˈɔditi] *n., pl.* **-ties.** ①奇怪;古怪;怪癖。②奇異或古怪之人或物。

***odd·ly** [ˈɑdlɪ; ˈɔdli] *adv.* ①奇妙地; 奇怪地。*oddly* enough. 說來奇怪。②零碎地; 成奇數。*oddly* even. 奇數與偶數之積。*oddly* odd. 奇數與奇數之積。③剩餘地。④額外地。

odd·ment [ˈɑdmənt; ˈɔdmənt] *n.* ①殘餘之物;零頭。②(*pl.*)〖印刷〗書籍本文以外之部分。

odds** [ɑdz; ɔdz] *n. pl.* or *sing.* ①賭注與付款之差額。②遊戲中對較弱一方的讓步。③可能性;可能的機會。The *odds* are against us. 我們沒有成功的機會。The *odds* are in our favor. 我們有成功機會。④分別(=difference). What's the *odds?* 有何區別? ⑤不平等;不平均(之事物)。Death makes the *odds* all even. 死亡使一切不平等都平等了。⑥恩惠。I ask no *odds* of them. 我不求他們給以恩惠。at odds*** 不睦;爭吵。She is now *at odds* with fate. 她現在正同命運掙扎(陷於不幸中)。***by all odds; by long odds; by odds*** 毫無疑問地。***fight against longer odds*** 以寡敵衆。***give (receive) odds*** 賭博時讓與(接受)有利條件。***lay*** (or ***give***) ***odds of*** 讓與…的有利條件。***odds and ends*** 殘餘;零星雜物。***take odds of*** 接受…的有利條件。***the odds are*** 很可能(=the chances are).

odds-on [ˈɑdzˈɑn; ˈɔdzˈɔn] *adj.* 有一半以上的勝算的。—*n.* (一半以上的)勝算。

ode [od; oud] *n.* (一種莊嚴的)抒情詩;頌;歌。***the Book of Odes*** 詩經。

o·de·um [oˈdiəm; ouˈdiːəm] *n., pl.* **o·de·ums, o·de·a** [oˈdiə; ouˈdiːə]. ①(古希臘、羅馬之)奏樂堂。②音樂廳。

O·din [ˈodɪn; ˈoudin] *n.*〖北歐神話〗歐丁(司知識、文化、戰爭等之神)。(亦作 **Othin**)

o·di·ous [ˈodɪəs; ˈoudjəs, -diəs] *adj.* 極使人討厭的; 可憎的; 可厭的。The war is *odious* to all the people. 這戰爭是所有人民所憎惡的。—**ly,** *adv.* —**ness,** *n.*

o·di·um [ˈodɪəm; ˈoudiəm] *n.* ①憎恨;厭惡。②譴責;非難;汚名。to expose (one) to *odium.* 使(某人)招反感。

o·do·graph [ˈodəˌgræf; ˈoudəgrɑːf] *n.* ①=**odometer.** ②=**pedometer.**

o·dom·e·ter [oˈdɑmətə˞; ouˈdɔmitə] *n.* (汽車等之)里程錶。(亦作 **hodometer**)

odont- 〖字首〗=**odonto-** (用於母音前)。

o·don·tal·gi·a [ˌodɑnˈtældʒɪə; ˌoudɔnˈtældʒiə] *n.*〖醫〗齒痛;牙痛。

odonto- 〖字首〗表"齒"之義,如: odontology.

O·don·to·glos·sum [əˌdɑntəˈglɑsəm; əˌdɔntəˈglɔsəm] *n.*〖植物〗①蘭屬。②(o-)蘭屬植物。

o·don·toid [əˈdɑntɔɪd; əˈdɔntoid] *adj.*〖解剖, 動物〗①(第二椎骨之)齒狀突起的。②齒狀的。

o·don·tol·o·gy [ˌodɑnˈtɑlədʒɪ; ˌɔdɔnˈtɔlədʒi] *n.* 牙科學。

o·dor, o·dour** [ˈodə˞; ˈoudə] *n.* ①氣味;臭氣。②香氣。the *odor* of roses. 玫瑰的香味。③名譽;聲望。④特有的風味。There is no *odor* of religion about the book. 此書無宗教氣味。be in bad odor*** 聲名狼藉。

o·dor·if·er·ous [ˌodəˈrɪfərəs; ˌoudəˈrifərəs] *adj.* 芳香的;有香味的;有氣味的。*odoriferous* spices. 芳香的香料。

o·dor·less [ˈodə˞lɪs; ˈoudəlis] *adj.* 無氣味的。

o·dor·ous [ˈodərəs; ˈoudərəs] *adj.* 有氣味的;(尤指)有香味的; 芳香的。—**ly,** *adv.*

O·dys·seus [oˈdɪsjus; əˈdisjuːs] *n.*〖希臘神話〗Ithaca 國王, Troy 戰後回程中發生許多冒險事蹟, 爲荷馬(Homer)史詩"奧德賽" *Odyssey* 之主角。(亦作 **Ulysses**)

Od·ys·sey [ˈɑdəsɪ; ˈɔdisi] *n., pl.*

-seys. ①希臘詩人荷馬的史詩名,描述希臘英雄 Odysseus 十年流浪生活及最後還鄉之事。②(亦作 odyssey) 任何長期的流浪生活、漫遊或冒險。—**Od·ys·se·an**, *adj.*

OE, OE., O.E. Old English.

œ o 與 e 之合字。〖注意〗亦分開寫成 oe, 常簡化成 e, 例如: Œdipus, amoeba.

O.E., o.e., oe〖商〗omissions excepted.

OECD, O.E.C.D. Organization for Economic Cooperation and Development.

oe·col·o·gy [ɪ'kɑlədʒɪ; i'kɔlədʒi] *n.* =**ecology.**

oec·u·men·i·cal [,ɛkju'mɛnɪkl; ,i:kju:'menikəl] *adj.* =**ecumenical.** (亦作 **oecumenic**)

O.E.D., OED Oxford English Dictionary.

oe·de·ma [i'dimə; i:'di:mə] *n., pl.* **-ma·ta** [-mətə; -mətə]. =**edema.**

Oe·di·pus ['ɛdəpəs; 'i:dipəs] *n.* 〖希臘傳說〗埃迪帕斯 (Thebes 王 Laius 與后 Jocasta 之子;爲命運擺弄而弒父妻母)。

Oedipus complex 〖精神分析〗戀母情結;兒子對母親戀慕及對父親敵視之傾向。

o'er [or, ɔr; ouə, ɔə, ɔ:] *prep., adv.* 〖詩〗=**over.**

Oer·li·kon ['ɝləkɑn; 'ə:likɔn] *n.* 對空速射砲之一種。

oer·sted ['ɝsted; 'ə:sted] *n.* 〖電〗奧斯忒(磁力單位)。

oe·soph·a·gus [i'sɑfəgəs; i:'sɔfəgəs] *n.* =**esophagus.**

oes·trum ['ɛstrəm, 'is-; 'estrəm, 'i:s-] *n.* =**oestrus.**

oes·trus ['ɛstrəs; 'i:strəs] *n.* ①激烈的慾望(衝動)。②刺激。③(動物之)發情。—**oes·tru·al**, *adj.*

OF, OF. Old French.

:of [ɑv, əv; ɔv, əv, v, f] *prep.* ①屬於。men *of* that time. 那個時代的人。②由…製成;由…組成;包括 (=made from). a house *of* bricks. 磚房。③表性質或狀態。a man *of* tact. 機敏之人。④表距離、方向或位置。to the south *of* Italy. 在義大利之南。⑤關於。to accuse a person *of* taking bribes. 控訴某人納賄。⑥經;由 (=through). to die *of* grief (hunger). 因悲傷(饑餓)而死。⑦除去;剝奪。to cure a person *of* a disease. 醫好某人之病。⑧從(=out of). She came *of* a noble family. 她出身於貴族門第。⑨在其中 (=among). one *of* the best. 最佳者中之一。⑩表原因或動機等。to be proud *of*. 因…而驕傲。⑪表部分關係。a cup *of* tea. 一杯茶。⑫表時間。*of* late years. 近年來。⑬差…到。ten minutes *of* six. 差十分鐘到六點。⑭表同格關係。the city *of* Rome. 羅馬市。⑮表受格關係。the creation *of* man. 人類的創造。

of- 〖字首〗=**ob-** (用於 f 之前), 如: offer.

O.F. ①Odd Fellows. ②Old French.

:off [ɔf, ɑf; ɔ:f, ɔf] *prep.* ①脫落;離開。to be *off* one's balance. 失去平衡。②自;離 (=from 或 away from). Keep *off* the grass. 勿踐踏草地。③正在…之外。The island is *off* the coast. 該島在海岸外。④從。I bought the watch *off* him. 我從他那裏買的這隻錶。⑤少於;低於。He offered me the goods at 10% *off* the regular price. 他願將貨物以九折賣給我。***off color*** 氣色不佳;身體不好。***off duty*** 不當班;不值勤。***off one's eggs*** 誤解。***off one's feed*** 〖俗〗無食慾。***off one's head*** 〖俗〗有點瘋。***off the hinges*** 失序;錯亂。***off the map*** 〖俗〗消滅;不復存在。***off the mark*** a. 未中的。b. 離題;不中肯。—*adv.* ①脫下;除掉。He took *off* his hat. 他脫帽。②離開 (=away). They went *off* on a journey. 他們出外旅行。③表距離之遠。a mile *off*. 一英里外。④表時間距離。The winter vacation is only six weeks *off*. 到寒假祇有六個星期了。⑤停止。Turn the water *off*. 把水關上。⑥表關係斷絕。to lay *off* workmen. 解雇工人。⑦無工作。We have the afternoon *off* on Saturdays. 我們在星期六下午不工作。⑧漸衰;漸冷;漸減。to cool *off*. 冷靜下來。⑨欺騙。to palm *off* a bad coin on a man. 對某人使用假錢。⑩全;盡。Drink it *off*! 乾杯! ***be off*** a. 離開。b. 變壞;失常。***off and on*** (亦作 **on and off**) 有時;偶然;斷斷續續。—*adj.* ①斷的;停的。The electricity is *off*. 電路斷了。②休閒的;不工作的。an *off* day. 休假日。③(金錢、財產等) 特殊情況的。How well (badly) *off* are the Smiths? 史密斯一家是多麼富有(貧窮)? ④不佳的。It is an *off* season in the woolen trade. 此爲羊毛生意清淡之時期。⑤身體不適的。He is feeling rather *off* today. 他今天感到有些不適。⑥不新鮮的。This meat is a bit *off*. 這肉有些壞了。⑦在右手邊的;右邊的。⑧可能性不大的。There is an *off* chance that you may see him there. 你在那兒能看見他的機會不太大。⑨向海的;朝海的。⑩較遠的。the *off* side of a wall. 牆壁的另一面。⑪錯的。You are *off* on that point. 關於那一點你是錯的。⑫頭腦稍不正常。⑬失常;較平時差。⑭開始;啓程。I am *off* to Europe on Monday. 我在星期一啓程到歐洲去。—*interj.* 走開! 躲開! ***off with*** a. 拿去! *Off with* those wet clothes. 將那些濕衣服拿走。b. 排除。*Off with* the old and on with the new! 去舊迎新!—*n.* ①(板球戲中) 擊球員對面的一邊。②離去。***from the off*** 〖英〗從開始起。

off. ①offered. ②office. ③officer. ④official. ⑤officinal.

of·fal ['ɔfl; 'ɔfəl] *n.* ①動物被屠宰後不可食之部分。②廢棄之物;垃圾。

off-and-on ['ɔfən'ɑn; 'ɔ:fən'ɔn] *adj.* 偶爾的;不規則的;時…時…的。

off-bal·ance ['ɔf'bæləns; 'ɔ:f 'bæləns] *adj. & adv.* ①不穩固的(地)。②出乎意外。

off·beat ['ɔf,bit; 'ɔ:fbi:t] *adj.* 〖俗〗不平常的;奇異的。—*n.* 〖音樂〗弱拍;次強拍。

off Broadway 紐約百老匯以外地區演出之舞臺劇(以注重新手法及低預算爲特色)。

off-cam·er·a ['ɔf'kæmərə; 'ɔ:f'kæmərə] *adv. & adj.* ①在電影或電視鏡頭之外地(的)。②私生活地(的)。

off·cast ['ɔf'kæst; 'ɔ:fkɑ:st] *adj., n.* =**castoff.** (亦作 **off-cast**)

off-cen·ter ['ɔf'sɛntə; 'ɔ:f'sentə] *adj.* (亦作 **off-centered**) ①離中央的。②不均衡的。③不合理的。—*adv.* 不平衡地。

off-chance ['ɔf,tʃæns; 'ɔ:ftʃɑ:ns] *n.* 不容易有的機會;萬一之可能性。

off-col·o(u)r ['ɔf'kʌlə; 'ɔ:f'kʌlə] *adj.* ①(寶石等)顏色不佳(不合標準)的。②臉色不好的;身體不好的。③下流的;近於淫猥的。

off day 不當班之日;休息日。

off-du·ty ['ɔf'djutɪ; 'ɔ:f'dju:ti] *adj.* ①不當班的。②下班者的。

of·fence [ə'fɛns; ə'fens] *n.* 〖主英〗=**offense.**

***of·fend** [ə'fɛnd; ə'fend] *v.t.* ①觸怒;傷

…感情。She was *offended* with (*or* by) her husband. 她生她丈夫的氣。②使不快；使不悅。to *offend* the eye. 刺目。③(聖經用語)使犯罪。 —*v.i.* ①犯法；犯罪。to *offend* against custom. 違犯習俗。②拂意；開罪。In what way have I *offended?* 我又在哪兒得罪人了？

***of·fend·er** [əˈfɛndɚ; əˈfendə] *n.* ①罪犯；犯規者。a first *offender*. 初犯。an old (*or* repeated) *offender*. 累犯。②得罪人的人；惹人生氣的人。「*n.* offender之女性。」

of·fend·ress [əˈfɛndrɪs; əˈfendris]

of·fense** [əˈfɛns; əˈfens] *n.* ①犯法；犯罪。an *offense* against good manners. 沒有規矩。②傷感情；不悅；觸怒。No *offense* was meant. 無意傷人之心。③攻擊。④採取攻勢的人、隊、軍隊等。give offense*** 使(某人)動怒(不悅)。***take offense*** 動怒。He easily *takes offense*. 他易於動怒。—**ful,** *adj.*

of·fense·less [əˈfɛnslɪs; əˈfenslis] *adj.* ①無罪的；無咎的。②無攻擊力的。③不爲害的；不討厭的。(亦作 **offenceless**)

of·fen·sive** [əˈfɛnsɪv; əˈfensiv] *adj.* ①令人不快的；冒犯的；無禮的。He has a very *offensive* manner. 他有惹人不快的態度。②難聞的；難看的。Bad eggs have an *offensive* odor. 壞了的蛋有難聞的氣味。③攻擊的；攻勢的。④用於攻擊的。*offensive* weapons. 攻擊武器。—*n.* 攻擊；攻勢。take*** (or ***act on***) ***the offensive*** 攻擊；採取攻勢。—**ly,** *adv.* —**ness,** *n.*

:of·fer [ˈɔfɚ, ˈɑfɚ; ˈɔfə] *v.t.* ①呈贈；奉呈；獻。He *offered* me his help. 他給我幫助。②提供；提出。She *offered* a few ideas to improve the plan. 她提出數種意見以改進那計畫。③供奉；奉獻。to *offer* prayers to God. 向上帝祈禱。④表現。⑤出價。He *offered* three hundred dollars for a radio set. 他出價三百元購一收音機。⑥表示；施以。—*v.i.* ①發生。I shall come if opportunity *offers*. 如果有機會的話我就來。②企圖；試。③供奉；奉獻。***offer one's hand*** **a.** 伸出手以握手。**b.** 求婚。—*n.* ①給與；提供。Thank you for your kind *offer* of help. 感謝你援助的美意。②出價；作價。an *offer* of $10,000 for a house. 出價一萬元購一房屋。③出售。to be on *offer*. 出售。④提議。to make an *offer*. 提議。⑤求婚。⑥企圖；作…姿勢。

***of·fer·ing** [ˈɔfərɪŋ, ˈɑf-; ˈɔfəriŋ] *n.* ①供奉；奉獻。freewill *offering*. 捐獻。②奉獻之物；祭品。③呈贈；提供。④禮物。⑤上市之股票、公債等。No big *offerings* came into the market last week. 上週內沒有大批股票上市。

of·fer·to·ry [ˈɔfɚ,torɪ; ˈɔfətəri] *n., pl.* **-ries.**〖宗教〗①奉獻詩歌或樂曲；奉獻儀式。②奉獻金；捐款。

off·hand [ˈɔfˈhænd; ˈɔːfˈhænd] *adv.* 即刻地；未經準備地。—*adj.* ①即刻的；未經準備的。②不客氣的；隨便的。

off·hand·ed [ˈɔfˈhændɪd; ˈɔːfˈhændid] *adj.* =**offhand.** —**ly,** *adv.*

off-hour [ˈɔfˈaur; ˈɔːfˈauə] *n.* ①不在值勤的時間或時期。②交通不擁擠或無甚活動的時間。—*adj.* 不值勤時的；閒散時的。

:of·fice [ˈɔfɪs, ˈɑfɪs; ˈɔfis] *n.* ①辦公室；事務所；公司；營業所。He works in a lawyer's *office*. 他在一律師事務所工作。②辦公室、事務所或公司等的一部或全部職員。The whole *office* was at her wedding. 公司的全體員工都參加了她的婚禮。③政府的部、局、處等。the War *Office*. 國防部。the Foreign *Office*. 外交部。④職位。⑤職責；任務。A teacher's *office* is teaching. 教員的任務是教書。⑥善意或惡意的行動；幫忙。Through the good *offices* of a friend, he was able to get a job. 經由友人幫忙他找到了一個工作。⑦〖宗教〗聖事；日課。⑧儀式(尤指葬儀)。⑨(*pl.*)住宅中料理家務的房間(如廚房、食物貯藏室等)。

of·fice-bear·er [ˈɔfɪs,bɛrɚ; ˈɔfis,bɛərə] *n.*〖英〗=**officeholder.**

office boy 辦公室的工友。

office copy〖法律〗(經官廳認可或證明之)文書謄本；正式副本；公文。

office girl 女職員；女辦事員。

of·fice·hold·er [ˈɔfɪs,holdɚ; ˈɔfis,houldə] *n.* 公務員；官吏。

office hours 辦公時間；營業時間。

office hunter 希望就公職者；獵官者。

:of·fi·cer [ˈɔfəsɚ, ˈɑf-; ˈɔfisə, ˈɔfsə] *n.* ①軍官。a commanding *officer*. 指揮官；司令官。②公務員；政府官吏；教堂主管。③(會社等之)正副主席、祕書等。④(商船的)高級船員。⑤社團中的職員。⑥公司中的高級職員。⑦警員；警官。a police *officer*. 警官。***officer of the day*** (略作 **O. D.**) 值日官。***officer of the week*** 值星官。—*v.t.* ①配以軍官；配以高級船員。to *officer* an army. 派一軍官統率軍隊。②指揮；指導。

office seeker =**office hunter.**

:of·fi·cial [əˈfɪʃəl; əˈfiʃəl] *n.* 官吏；公務員；職員。An important *official* called to see us. 一位重要的官員來拜訪我們。public *officials*. 公務員。—*adj.* ①公務上的；職務上的；官方的。an *official* report. 官方報告。*official* residence. 官邸。②有權威的；正式的。Is the news *official?* 這是項正式消息嗎？③〖藥〗法定的(處方)。

of·fi·cial·dom [əˈfɪʃəldəm; əˈfiʃəldəm] *n.* ①公務員界；官場。②公務員；官吏(集合稱)。③官僚習氣。

of·fi·cial·ese [ə,fɪʃəˈliz; ə,fiʃəˈliːz] *n.* 官話；公文用語。

of·fi·cial·ism [əˈfɪʃəlɪzm̩; əˈfiʃəlizəm] *n.* ①官廳制度。②官派；形式主義；官僚主義；官僚習氣。③公務員；官吏(集合稱)。

of·fi·cial·ize [əˈfɪʃə,laɪz; əˈfiʃəlaiz] *v.t.,* **-ized, -iz·ing.** ①使成官派。②使歸官廳管轄。③公告；使公開；使正式。

***of·fi·cial·ly** [əˈfɪʃəlɪ; əˈfiʃəli, -ʃli] *adv.* 正式地；官方地；公開地。

of·fi·ci·ant [əˈfɪʃɪənt; əˈfiʃiənt] *n.*〖宗教〗司會者；司祭者。

of·fi·ci·ar·y [əˈfɪʃɪ,ɛrɪ; əˈfiʃiəri] *adj.* (來自)職位的(如頭銜、階級等)。

of·fi·ci·ate [əˈfɪʃɪ,et; əˈfiʃieit] *v.,* **-at·ed, -at·ing.** —*v.i.* ①執行職務；主持會議等。②執行牧師之職務；司祭。—*v.t.* ①執行(職務或公務)。②在(某種場合)執行牧師之職務。③爲(比賽等)執行裁判的任務。—**of·fi·ci·a·tion,** *n.*

of·fic·i·nal [əˈfɪsɪn̩l; ,ɔfiˈsainl] *adj.* ①藥用的。②〖藥〗成藥的；法定的。—*n.* 成藥(非臨時配製者)；法定藥物。—**ly,** *adv.*

of·fi·cious [əˈfɪʃəs; əˈfiʃəs] *adj.* ①好管閒事的。②(外交上)非官方的。—**ly,** *adv.* —**ness,** *n.*

off·ing [ˈɔfɪŋ; ˈɔfiŋ] *n.* ①(由岸上可以見

到之)海面;洋面。②與岸邊之距離;遠離岸邊之位置。 ***in the offing*** **a.** 從岸上可以望見的。**b.** 在不遠之處。 **c.** 即將發生或出現;在醞釀中。 ***gain an offing*** 駛出海面。 ***keep an offing*** 駛行海面(不靠岸)。

off·ish 〔ˈɔfɪʃ; ˈɔfiʃ〕 *adj.* 〖俗〗不喜歡交際的;不親熱的;冷冰冰的。 「外島;近海島嶼。」

off-is·land 〔ˈɔfˌaɪlənd; ˈɔːfˌailənd〕 *n.*

off-key 〔ˈɔfˈki; ˈɔːfˈkiː〕 *adj.* ①走調的;不和諧的。②不適當的;不一致的。

off-li·cense 〔ˈɔfˌlaɪsəns; ˈɔːfˌlaisəns〕 *n.* 〖英〗①准許出售封蓋的瓶裝酒的執照(但不得在店裏飲用)。②有上述執照的商店。—*adj.* 有上述執照的。(亦作 **off-licence**)

off limits 〖美〗禁入(區域);禁區。

off-lim·its 〔ˈɔfˈlɪmɪts; ˈɔːfˈlimits〕 *adj.* 禁止入內的;閒人莫入的。

off-line 〔ˈɔfˈlaɪn; ˈɔːfˈlain〕 *adj.* 〖電腦〗外線的。 「卸貨。」

off-load 〔ˈɔfˌlod; ˈɔːfloud〕 *v.t. & v.i.*

off-print 〔ˈɔfˌprɪnt; ˈɔːfprint〕 *n.*(出版物中某文之)單獨重刊;選刊;單行本。 —*v.t.* 單獨重刊;選刊。 「迫;使不調協。」

off·put 〔ˈɔfˌput; ˈɔːfput〕 *v.t.* 〖英〗使窘

off-put·ting 〔ˈɔfˈputɪŋ; ˈɔːfˈputiŋ〕 *adj.* 〖英俗〗難爲情的;尷尬的。

off·scour·ing 〔ˈɔfˌskaurɪŋ; ˈɔːfˌskauəriŋ〕 *n.* (常 *pl.*) 屑;廢物;汚物;糟粕。 the *offscourings* of society. 社會的渣滓。

off-sea·son 〔ˈɔfˈsizən; ˈɔːfˈsiːzən〕 *adj.* 淡季的;不是時季的。—*adv.* 淡季地;非旺季地。—*n.* 淡季。 Fares are lower when one travels in the *off-season*. 當你淡季去旅行時,各種費用較低。

***off·set** 〔*v.* ɔfˈsɛt; ˈɔːfset *n., adj.* ˈɔfˌsɛt; ˈɔːfset〕 *v.,* **off·set, off·set·ting,** *n., adj.* —*v.t.* ①抵銷;彌補。 He *offsets* his small salary by living economically. 他以生活節儉來彌補其低微之收入。②〖印刷〗以凸版印刷。—*v.i.* ①用凸版印刷。②凸出;伸出分枝。—*n.* ①補償。②(植物的)分枝;短的匍匐枝。③分枝;支族;支脈。④〖機械〗迂廻管。⑤〖建築〗牆上之凸出部分。⑥〖印刷〗透印版。⑦出發;開始。 at the *offset*. 出發時;開始時。⑧〖採礦〗(主坑道外的)縱坑道。—*adj.* 透印版印刷的。 an *offset* press. 透印版印刷機。

off·shoot 〔ˈɔfˌʃut; ˈɔːfʃuːt〕 *n.* ①樹木等之枝條;旁枝。②分枝;支脈;支派;支流。③衍生物;引生物。

off·shore 〔ˈɔfˈʃor; ˈɔːfˈʃɔː〕 *adj.* 離海岸的;向海面的。 *offshore* fisheries. 近海漁業。—*adv.* ①在近海處。②在離海岸相當遠處。

off·side 〔ˈɔfˈsaɪd; ˈɔːfˈsaid〕 *n., adj.* 〖足球〗越位(的)。 an *offside* play. 越位球。

***off·spring** 〔ˈɔfˌsprɪŋ, ˈɑf–; ˈɔːfspriŋ, ˈɔf–〕 *n., pl.* **-spring, -springs.** ①子孫;後裔。 to limit one's *offspring*. 節育。②結果;後果。 the *offspring* of modern times. 近代的產物。

off-stage 〔ˈɔfˈstedʒ; ˈɔːfˈsteidʒ〕 *n., adj.* 舞臺後面(的); 後臺(的)。 —*adv.* 在舞臺後;在後臺;至後臺。

off-street 〔ˈɔfˈstrit; ˈɔːfˈstriːt〕 *adj.* 離開街道的;不占街道的。

off-the-cuff 〔ˈɔfðəˈkʌf; ˈɔːfðəˈkʌf〕 *adj.* 〖俗〗未預備的;隨時的。

off-the-job 〔ˈɔfðəˈdʒɑb; ˈɔːfðəˈdʒɔb〕 *adj.* 不在職的; 非在工作崗位上發生或做的。

off-the-peg 〔ˈɔfðəˈpɛg; ˈɔːfðəˈpeg〕 *adj.* 〖英〗(衣服之)現成的。

off-the-rec·ord 〔ˈɔfðəˈrɛkəd; ˈɔːfðəˈrekɔːd〕 *adj.* 不留記錄的; 非正式的; 非公開的。—*adv.* 非正式;不公開發表。

off·white 〔ˈɔfˈhwaɪt; ˈɔːfˈwait〕 *adj.* (摻着少量灰、黃色的)白色的。—*n.* 上述顏色。

off year ①(如農業、商業或運動)無特殊成就的年分;荒年。②沒有大選的年分。

***oft** 〔ɔft; ɔːft, ɔft〕 *adv.* 〖古〗 = **often.** many a time and *oft*. 常常;屢屢;再三。

‡**of·ten** 〔ˈɔfən, ˈɔftən; ˈɔːfn, ˈɔːftən〕 *adv.* 時常地。 We *often* go there. 我們常常去那裏。 ***every so often*** 時時。 ***more often than not*** 時常。 ***once too often*** (犯規、冒險等) 次數太多一點。

of·ten·times 〔ˈɔfənˌtaɪmz; ˈɔːfntaimz〕 *adv.* = **often.** 「〖古, 詩〗= **oftentimes.**」

oft·times 〔ˈɔftˌtaɪmz; ˈɔːfttaimz〕 *adv.*

o.g. 〖集郵〗 original gum.

og·(h)am 〔ˈɔgəm; ˈɔgəm〕 *n.* 歐甘文字(古代英國及愛爾蘭之一種文字, 由20個字母構成);歐甘碑銘。 —*adj.* 歐甘文字的。

o·gee 〔oˈdʒi; ˈoudʒiː〕 *n., adj.* 〖建築〗 S 形曲線(的);葱花線(的)。

o·gi·val 〔oˈdʒaɪvəl; ouˈdʒaivəl〕 *adj.* 哥德式穹窿之交錯骨的;呈穹窿弧稜之形狀的;尖形拱的。

o·give 〔ˈodʒaɪv; ˈoudʒaiv〕 *n.* ①〖建築〗(哥德式) 穹窿之弧稜; 圓拱之交錯骨。②尖形拱;尖穹窿。③〖統計〗肩形曲線。

o·gle 〔ˈogl; ˈougl〕 *v.,* **o·gled, o·gling,** *n.* —*v.t.* ①向…送秋波;向…作媚眼; 脈脈含情地看。②看。—*v.i.* 送秋波;作媚眼;脈脈含情地看。—*n.* 秋波;媚眼。

o·gre 〔ˈogə; ˈougə〕 *n.* ①(童話中之)食人巨妖。②醜怪殘暴之人。

o·gre·ish 〔ˈogərɪʃ; ˈougəriʃ〕 *adj.* 可怕的;兇暴的。(亦作 **ogrish**)

o·gress 〔ˈogrɪs; ˈougris〕 *n.* ogre 之女性。

‡**Oh, oh** 〔o; ou〕 *interj., n., pl.* **oh's, ohs,** *v.* —*interj.* ①(冠於人名前之稱呼語) 啊!呀! *Oh* Mary, look! 瑪麗啊, 看呀! ②表驚奇、憂懼、快樂、悲傷等。 *Oh,* what a surprise! 啊!多麼令人驚奇呀!—*n.* "啊!","呀!"之驚嘆語。—*v.i.* 發出"啊!","呀!"之聲。 「German.」

OHG, OHG., O.H.G. Old High

O·hi·o 〔oˈhaɪo; ouˈhaiou〕 *n.* ①俄亥俄(美國中東部州名, 首府 Columbus). ②俄亥俄河。 「*adj., n.* Ohio 州的(人)。」

O·hi·o·an 〔oˈhaɪəwən; ouˈhaiəwən〕

Ohm 〔om; oum〕 *n.* 歐姆(Georg Simon, 1787–1854, 德國物理學家)。

ohm 〔om; oum〕 *n.* 〖電〗 歐姆 (電阻單位, 符號 Ω). 「姆的。」

ohm·ic 〔ˈomɪk; ˈoumik〕 *adj.* 〖電〗 歐

ohm·me·ter 〔ˈomˌmitə; ˈoumˌmiːtə〕 *n.* 歐姆計;電阻計。

O.H.M.S. On His (*or* Her) Majesty's Service. 〖英〗公用(公文免郵費之記號)。

Ohm's law 〖電〗歐姆定律。

o·ho 〔oˈho; ouˈhou〕 *interj.* (用以表驚異、高興、嘲諷等)哦嗬! 噯喲!

-oid 〖字尾〗表"如…的(東西);…質的(東西);…狀的(東西); 類似…的(東西)" 之義之形容詞、名詞字尾, 如: alkaloid, negroid.

‡**oil** 〔ɔɪl; ɔil〕 *n.* ①油。 Mineral *oils* are used for fuel. 礦物油用做燃料。②油製顏料。③油畫。④石油。⑤〖俚〗諂媚; 奉承。 ***burn the midnight oil*** 讀書或工作至深夜。 ***pour oil on troubled waters*** 調解爭端。 ***strike oil*** 掘得油;(喻)成暴富。—*v.t.* ①敷

油於;浸以油。to *oil* a lock or bicycle. 擦油於鎖或自行車。②賄賂。③使圓滑;使油滑。④溶化成油(如奶油等)。***oil a person's palm*** 向某人行賄。***oil the wheels*** (or ***works***) (喻)藉圓滑行賄手段使事物順利發展;疏通。—*v.i.* 化爲油。Butter *oils* when heated. 牛油遇熱化爲稀油。—*adj.* ①像油的。②產油的;油的。③油製的。④使用油爲燃料的。—**like,** *adj.*

oil·berg [ˈɔɪlˌbɝg; ˈɔilbəːg] *n.* 大油輪(裝載量達二十萬噸以上者)。

oil burner 油爐。

oil cake (亞麻仁、棉子等之)油渣餅;豆餅。

oil·can [ˈɔɪlˌkæn; ˈɔil-kæn] *n.* 油罐(尤指用以注滑潤油者)。

oil·cloth [ˈɔɪlˌklɔθ; ˈɔilklɔθ] *n., pl.* **-cloths.** 油布;防雨布。

oil color 油畫顏料。

oil crop 可榨油的農作物。

oil·cup [ˈɔɪlˌkʌp; ˈɔilkʌp] *n.* (輸送滑潤油之)油杯;油壺。

oil derrick 開鑿油井時用的起重機。

oiled [ɔɪld; ɔild] *adj.* ①以油浸漬的;以油塗過的。②油滑的。③〖美〗酒醉的。

oil·er [ˈɔɪlɚ; ˈɔilə] *n.* ①加滑潤油於機械之人或器具。②加油壺。③(常 *pl.*)〖美俗〗油布衣。④油輪;油船。

oil field 油田。

oil-fired [ˈɔɪlˌfaɪrd; ˈɔilˌfaiəd] *adj.* 以石油爲燃料的;以石油爲熱源的。

oil lamp 煤油燈;油燈。

oil·man [ˈɔɪlmən; ˈɔilmən] *n., pl.* **-men.** 油商;製油者;賣油者。

oil meal 油渣粉(牲畜飼料或肥料)。

oil of turpentine 松節油。(亦作 **turpentine, spirits of turpentine**)

oil paint 油畫顏料;油漆;油塗料。

oil painting ①油畫。②油畫術。

oil pan (內燃機引擎之)潤滑油槽。

oil·pa·per [ˈɔɪlˌpepɚ; ˈɔilˌpeipə] *n.* 油紙;桐油紙。

oil press 榨油器。

oil·seed [ˈɔɪlˌsid; ˈɔilsiːd] *n.* 花生、可可亞等可榨油之果實。

oil shale 油頁岩。

oil·skin [ˈɔɪlˌskɪn; ˈɔilskin] *n.* ①油布;防水布。②(常 *pl.*) 油布衣。

oil slick 因油而平滑的水面;水面之油漬。

oil·stone [ˈɔɪlˌston; ˈɔilstoun] *n.* 油砥石。

oil well 〖美〗油井。

***oil·y** [ˈɔɪlɪ; ˈɔili] *adj.,* **oil·i·er, oil·i·est,** *adv.* —*adj.* ①油的;似油的;含油的。an *oily* liquid. 油質液體。②塗或沾有油的;油膩的。*oily* rags (hands). 沾有油的地毯(手)。③圓滑的;油腔滑調的;滑頭的。an *oily* hypocrite. 一個圓滑的僞君子。 —*adv.* 圓滑地。—**oil·i·ly,** *adv.* —**oil·i·ness,** *n.*

***oint·ment** [ˈɔɪntmənt; ˈɔintmənt] *n.* 藥膏;油膏。

O·jib·way [oˈdʒɪbwe; ɔˈdʒibwei] *n., pl.* **-way, -ways,** *adj.* —*n.* ①北美印第安人之一大種族之人(居於 Superior 湖地方)。②其語言。 —*adj.* 此族的。

OK, O.K. [ˈoˈke; ˈouˈkei, ouˈkei] *adj., adv., v.,* **OK'd, OK'ing** or **O.K.'d, O.K.'ing,** *n., pl.* **OK's** or **O.K.'s.** —*adj. & adv.* 好;不錯。It's *OK.* 好吧。 —*v.t.* 批准;認可。They finally *OK'd* our plan. 他們最後贊成了我們的計畫。—*n.* 認可;贊同。

o·ka·pi [oˈkɑpɪ; ouˈkɑːpi] *n., pl.* **-pis, -pi.** (中非產之)一種鹿(似長頸鹿,體較小)。

o·kay [ˈoˈke; ˈouˈkei, ouˈkei] *adj., adv., v., n.* =**OK.** (亦作 **okeh, okey**)

O·khotsk, the Sea of [oˈkɑtsk; ouˈkɔtsk] *n.* 鄂霍次克海(在蘇聯亞洲東北堪察加半島之西)。

O·kie [ˈokɪ; ˈouki] *n.* 〖俗〗①美國 Oklahoma 州人。②因旱災等自該州移出之農民。

O·ki·na·wa [ˌokɪˈnɑwə; ˌoukiˈnɑːwə] *n.* 沖繩(琉球羣島之一)。

Okla. Oklahoma.

O·kla·ho·ma [ˌokləˈhomə; ˌoukləˈhoumə] *n.* 俄克拉荷馬(美國中南部之一州,首府 Oklahoma City)。

O·kla·ho·man [ˌokləˈhomən; ˌoukləˈhoumən] *adj., n.* Oklahoma 州的(人)。

o·kra [ˈokrə; ˈoukrə] *n.* ①秋葵。②秋葵莢(可食)。

OL, OL., O.L. Old Latin.

-ol 〖字尾〗①表 "alcohol, phenol" 之義的名詞字尾, 如: menthol, naphthol, lysol. ②**-ole** 之異形, 如: benzol.

Ol., Olym. Olympiad.

:old [old; ould] *adj.,* **old·er** or **eld·er, old·est** or **eld·est,** *n.* —*adj.* ①老的;年代已久的。an *old* wall. 一座老牆。②年高的;年長的;高齡的。He is beginning to look *old.* 他開始看來蒼老了。③年紀若干的;有多少歲的(=of age; in age). She is ten years *old.* 她十歲了。④舊的;不新鮮的。⑤破舊的。*old* clothes. 破舊的衣服。⑥古老的。The superstition is almost as *old* as the hills. 這迷信由來已久。⑦似老的;看來已老的。She is *old* for her age. 她看起來比她的年齡大。⑧有經驗的;老練的。 an *old* head on young shoulders. 少年老成。⑨從前的;昔時的。 An *old* student came back to visit his teacher. 昔時的學生回來探望老師。⑩熟悉的;親密的。It is an *old* story. 這是無人不知的老故事。 ⑪通常置於形容詞後以加强語氣。 We had a fine *old* time. 我們玩得非常高興。 —*n.* ①往時;昔時。②老人。③…歲的人或動物。 a class for six-year-*olds.* 六歲(兒童)的一班。

old age 老年(通常指65歲以後的時期)。

old bean 〖俚〗老兄(對熟識者之稱呼)。

old bird 謹愼老練的人;老手;老世故。

old boy ①〖英〗畢業生;校友。②(O- B-)〖俚〗魔鬼。③富有朝氣的老年人。④〖英〗=**old chap.** (亦作 **old fellow**)

old chap 〖英〗老兄(對熟識者之暱稱)。

old country (移民之)故鄉;(尤指)歐洲。

old·en¹ [ˈoldn̩; ˈouldən] *adj.* 〖古〗往昔的;古老的。

old·en² *v.i.* 變老;變陳舊。—*v.t.* 使變老;使變陳舊。

***old-fash·ioned** [ˈoldˈfæʃənd; ˈouldˈfæʃənd] *adj.* ①老式的;舊式的。an *old-fashioned* dress. 老式的衣服。②守舊的。*old-fashioned* ideas. 守舊的觀念。③(小孩等)思想、行動等成熟的。

old-fo·g(e)y [ˈoldˈfogɪ; ˈouldˈfougi] *adj., n.* —*adj.* 守舊的;過分保守的;老頑固的。—*n.* 老頑固;守舊的人。—**ish,** *adj.*

old gentleman 魔鬼。

Old Glory 美國國旗。

old gold 淺黃至淺橄欖棕色的各種顏色。

Old Guard ①拿破崙一世之御林軍。②美國共和黨中之守舊派。③(常 o- g-)有勢力之保守分子;守舊者。

old hand 老手;有經驗者。

Old Harry 魔鬼;撒旦。

old·ie [ˈoldɪ; ˈouldi] *n.* 老舊的事物(尤指

早期之流行歌曲)。「徵古舊的。
old·ish ['oldɪʃ; 'ouldiʃ] *adj.* 稍老的;稍
old-line ['old'laɪn; 'ould'lain] *adj.* ①歷史悠久的。an *old-line* company. 歷史悠久的公司。②依從傳統的;保守的;守舊的。③系出名門的;歷史悠久之大家族的。
old maid ①老處女。②矜持、過分守舊、無謂紛擾的人。③一種紙牌戲(俗稱"捉烏龜")。④取最後一分的人(尤指吃最後一塊食物者)。
old-maid·ish ['old'medɪʃ; 'ould'meidiʃ] *adj.* 似老處女的;古板的;吹毛求疵的。
old man 〖俗〗①父親。②丈夫。③老板;老總。④老友的暱稱。⑤老經驗的人。
Old Man of the Sea ①(天方夜譚中)糾纏於 Sinbad 背上的老人。②難纏之人或物。
old moon 下弦月。
Old Nick 魔鬼;撒旦。
old school tie ①英國有傳統之私立中學畢業生所打的領帶。②打此種領帶的畢業生。③保守的作風。④勢利眼;極端的保守。
Old Scratch 撒旦。
old·ster ['oldstɚ; 'ouldstə] *n.* ①〖俗〗老人。②(英海軍)已幹了四年的少尉。
old stuff 〖俗〗習見的;很普通的。
Old Testament 〖聖經〗舊約。
***old-time** ['old,taɪm; 'ouldtaim] *adj.* 往昔的;多年的。an *old-time* friend. 老友。
old-tim·er ['old'taɪmɚ; 'ould'taimə] *n.* 〖俗〗①老前輩。②守舊的人。③老年人。
old-wom·an·ish ['old'wumənɪʃ; 'ould'wumәniʃ] *adj.* 老太婆似的;小題大做的;吹毛求疵的;無謂紛擾的。
Old World ①歐、亞、非三洲。②東半球。
old-world ['old'wɝld; 'ould-wəːld] *adj.* ①太古的。②老式的;古色古香的。③舊世界的;東半球的。
o·le·ag·i·nous [,olɪ'ædʒənəs; ,ouli'ædʒinəs] *adj.* ①油質的;含油的;生油的。②油嘴滑舌的;阿諛的。
o·le·an·der [,olɪ'ændɚ; ,ouli'ændə] *n.* 〖植物〗夾竹桃;夾竹桃屬之植物。
ole·ate ['olɪ,et; 'oulieit] *n.* 〖化〗油酸鹽;油酸酯。
o·le·ic [o'liɪk; ou'liːik] *adj.* 〖化〗油酸的。
oleic acid 〖化〗油酸;十八烯酸 ($C_{17}H_{33}COOH$).
o·le·in ['olɪɪn; 'ouliin] *n.* 〖化〗①甘油三油酸酯。②脂肪之液狀部分。
o·le·o ['olɪ,o; 'ouliou] *n.* 〖美〗①=**oleomargarine.** ②=**oleo oil.**
o·le·o·graph ['olɪo,græf; 'ouliougrɑːf] *n.* ①做油畫之石版畫。②油滴在水面上的形狀。
o·le·o·mar·ga·rin(e) [,olɪə'mardʒə,rin; 'ouliou,mɑːdʒə'riːn] *n.* 人造奶油;人造牛酪;油牛酪。(亦作 **margarine**)
oleo oil 液體牛脂。
o·le·o·res·in [,olɪo'rɛzn̩; ,ouliou'rezin] *n.* ①含油樹脂。②〖藥〗樹脂油。
o·le·o·res·in·ous [,olɪo'rɛzənəs; ,ouliou'rezinəs] *adj.* 含油樹脂的;樹脂油的;像樹脂油的。
ol·fac·tion [al'fækʃən; ɔl'fækʃən] *n.* ①嗅。②嗅覺;嗅感。
ol·fac·to·ry [al'fæktərɪ; ɔl'fæktəri] *adj.*, *n.*, *pl.* **-ries.** —*adj.* 嗅覺的。*olfactory* nerves. 嗅神經。the *olfactory* organ. 嗅器官。—*n.* (常 *pl.*) 嗅器官;嗅覺。
ol·i·garch ['alɪ,gark; 'ɔligɑːk] *n.* 寡頭政治家;寡頭政治執政者。
ol·i·gar·chic [,alɪ'garkɪk; ,ɔli'gɑːkik] *adj.* =**oligarchical.**
ol·i·gar·chi·cal [,alɪ'garkɪkl̩; ,ɔli'gɑːkikəl] *adj.* 寡頭政治的;主張寡頭政治的。
ol·i·gar·chy ['alɪ,garkɪ; 'ɔligɑːki] *n.*, *pl.* **-chies.** ①寡頭政治。②行寡頭政治的國家。③寡頭政治執政者之集合稱。
Ol·i·go·cene ['alɪgo,sin; ɔ'ligousiːn] *adj.* 〖地質〗漸新世的;漸新統的。***the Oligocene*** 漸新世;漸新世之岩石;漸新統。
ol·i·gop·o·ly [,alə'gapəlɪ; ,ɔli'gɔpəli] *n.* 求過於供之市場情況。
ol·i·gop·so·ny [,alə'gapsənɪ; ,ɔli'gɔpsəni] *n.* 供過於求之市場情況。
o·li·o ['olɪ,o; 'ouliou] *n.*, *pl.* **o·li·os.** ①什錦湯。②混雜物。③(詩歌、文章等之)雜集。

ol·i·va·ceous [,alɪ'veʃəs; ,ɔli'veiʃəs] *adj.* 橄欖的;似橄欖的;橄欖色的;深綠色的。
ol·i·var·y ['alə,vɛrɪ; 'ɔli,vɛəri] *adj.* ①橄欖形的;卵形的。②〖解剖〗橄欖體的。
***ol·ive** ['alɪv; 'ɔliv] *n.* ①橄欖樹。②橄欖。③橄欖木。④橄欖葉做的花冠。⑤微帶黃色的綠色或褐色。—*adj.* ①黃綠色的。②黃褐色的。
olive branch ①橄欖枝(作爲和平象徵)。②任何和平的象徵。③孩子。
olive drab ①淡綠褐色。②(美國陸軍軍服之一種)淡綠褐色的毛呢。③(*pl.*)此毛呢製成之美軍軍服。
olive oil 橄欖油。
ol·i·ver ['alәvɚ; 'ɔlivә] *n.* 脚踏鐵鎚。
ol·i·vet ['alə,vɛt; 'ɔlivet] *n.* 仿造珍珠。
ol·i·vine ['alə,vin; ,ɔli'viːn] *n.* 〖礦〗橄欖石。
ol·la ['alə; 'ɔlə] *n.* ①(西班牙及南美洲所用的)土甕;土鍋。②(用土鍋烹製之)什錦菜。
ol·la-po·dri·da ['aləpə'dridə; 'ɔləpo'driːdə] *n.* ①什錦菜(=olla)。②任何雜膾。
ol·o·gy ['alədʒɪ; 'ɔlədʒi] *n.*, *pl.* **-gies.** 〖俗〗科學;學術。
-ology 〖字尾〗表"…學;…論"之義,如:geology.
O·lym·pi·a [o'lɪmpɪə; ou'limpiə] *n.* 奧林匹亞(希臘南部一大平原,古代該地每四年舉行競賽一次,以祭 Zeus 神)。
O·lym·pi·ad [o'lɪmpɪ,æd; ou'limpiæd] *n.* ①四年期間(兩次奧林匹克競技會間的一段時期,古希臘自 776 B.C. 起以之計年代)。②現代之世界運動會(每四年舉行一次)。
O·lym·pi·an [o'lɪmpɪən; ou'limpiən] *adj.* ①奧林帕斯山的。②(似奧林帕斯諸神般)威嚴的;氣派十足的。③奧林匹亞的。—*n.* ①〖希臘神話〗奧林帕斯山十二神之一。②昔希臘奧林匹克運動會或今之奧林匹克世運會選手。③奧林匹亞人。
***O·lym·pic** [o'lɪmpɪk; ou'limpik] *adj.* ①與古希臘 Olympia 平原有關的。②與相傳希臘衆神所居的 Mount Olympus 有關的。—*n.* (*pl.*) =**Olympic Games.** They were practicing for the *Olympics*. 他們正在爲參加世運而練習。
Olympic Games ①古希臘人每四年舉行一次的競賽會。②世界運動會。
O·lym·pus [o'lɪmpəs; ou'limpəs] *n.* ①奧林帕斯山(古代神話中衆神所居之處)。②天堂。
O.M. 〖英〗Order of Merit.
O·man [o'mæn; ou'mæn] *n.* 阿曼(阿拉伯東南部一回教國,首都 Muscat).
o·ma·sum [o'mesəm; ou'meisəm] *n.*, *pl.* **-sa** [-sə; -sə]. 〖動物〗重瓣胃(反芻動物之第三胃)。
om·brom·e·ter [am'bramətɚ; ɔm'brɔmitə] *n.* 雨量計;雨計。
o·me·ga [o'mɛgə; 'oumigə] *n.* ①希臘字母之最後一個字母(Ω, ω)。②最後一個;末尾。
om·e·let, om·e·lette ['amlɪt; 'ɔmlit] *n.* 煎蛋捲。***You cannot make omelets***

without breaking eggs. 不打破蛋那能做煎蛋捲(喻作事不能畏首畏尾)。

o·men** [ˈomɪn, ˈomən; ˈoumen, -mən] *n.* 徵兆;預兆。good *omen.* 吉兆。bad (evil, or ill) *omen.* 凶兆。be of good (bad) omen*** 好(壞)預兆。—*v.t.* 給…之預兆;給與事先之警告。The clouds *omen* rain. 雲預示落雨。

om·i·cron [ˈɑmɪˌkrɑn; ouˈmaikrən] *n.* 希臘字母之第十五個字母 (O, o)。

***om·i·nous** [ˈɑmənəs; ˈɔminəs] *adj.* ①惡兆的;不吉的;不利的。②徵兆的;預兆的。It is *ominous* of death. 它預兆死亡。**—ly,** *adv.*

o·mis·si·ble [oˈmɪsəbḷ; ouˈmisibl] *adj.* 可省略的;可忽視的;無必要的。

o·mis·sion** [oˈmɪʃən; ouˈmiʃən, əˈm-] *n.* ①遺漏;省略;刪除。to state without *omission.* 毫無遺漏地敍述。②遺漏之物;省略之物;刪除之物。sins of omission*** 懈怠;應作之事而未作。

o·mis·sive [oˈmɪsɪv; ouˈmisiv] *adj.* 忽略的;省略的。

***o·mit** [oˈmɪt, əˈmɪt; ouˈmit, əˈm-] *v.t.,* **-mit·ted, -mit·ting.** ①遺漏;略去;省去。This chapter may be *omitted.* 這一章可以略去。②疏忽;忽略。Mary *omitted* making her bed. 瑪麗忘了鋪床。

omni- 〖字首〗表"全;總"之義。

***om·ni·bus** [ˈɑmnəˌbʌs, ˈɑmnəbəs; ˈɔmnibəs] *n., pl.* **-bus·es,** *adj.* —*n.* ①公共汽車;公共馬車 (=bus)。②(某一作家或一科目的)全集;精選集。—*adj.* 包含多項的;總括的。an *omnibus* volume. 包含好幾本書的一巨册。

omnibus train 〖英〗每站皆停的火車;慢車。

om·ni·com·pe·tent [ˌɑmnɪˈkɑmpɪtənt; ˌɔmniˈkɔmpitənt] *adj.* 〖法律〗全權的。

om·ni·di·rec·tion·al [ˌɑmnɪdɪˈrɛkʃənḷ; ˌɔmnidiˈrekʃənḷ] *adj.* 〖電子〗全向的。

om·ni·far·i·ous [ˌɑmnəˈfɛrɪəs; ˌɔmniˈfɛəriəs] *adj.* 種種的;各色各樣的。

om·nip·o·tence [ɑmˈnɪpətəns; ɔmˈnipətəns] *n.* ①全能。②(O-)全能的神;上帝。

om·nip·o·tent [ɑmˈnɪpətənt; ɔmˈnipətənt] *n.* 全能者;有絕大權力者。***the Omnipotent*** 上帝。—*adj.* 全能的。**—ly,** *adv.*

om·ni·pres·ence [ˌɑmnɪˈprɛzṇs; ˈɔmniˈprezəns] *n.* 處處都在;無處不在。

om·ni·pres·ent [ˌɑmnɪˈprɛzṇt; ˈɔmniˈprezənt] *adj.* 無處不在的;處處都在的。

om·nis·cience [ɑmˈnɪʃəns; ɔmˈnisiəns] *n.* ①無所不知;全知。②(O-)上帝。

om·nis·cient [ɑmˈnɪʃənt; ɔmˈnisiənt] *adj.* 無所不知的。***the Omniscient*** 上帝。

om·ni·um-gath·er·um [ˈɑmnɪəmˈgæðərəm; ˈɔmniəmˈgæðərəm] *n.* (人或物之)雜聚;雜湊。

om·niv·o·rous [ɑmˈnɪvərəs; ɔmˈnivərəs] *adj.* ①雜食的;動物及蔬菜均食用的。Man is an *omnivorous* animal. 人是肉類與菜蔬都吃的動物。②無所不吸收的。**—ly,** *adv.* **—ness,** *n.*

om·pha·los [ˈɑmfəˌlɑs; ˈɔmfəlɔs] *n., pl.* **-li** [-ˌlaɪ; -lai]. ①〖解剖〗臍。②中心;中心地。③〖古希臘〗盾等的中心之突起。④〖古希臘〗(Delphi 阿波羅神殿中之)半圓形的石祭壇(被稱爲世界之中心)。

ON, ON., O.N. Old Norse.

‡on [ɑn; ɔn] *prep.* ①在…之上;爲…所支持。*on* the table. 在桌上。to hang *on* a nail. 掛於釘上。*on* foot. 徒步走。②環繞;相接觸;包圍;附着於…之上。He put a ring *on* her finger. 他把戒指戴在她的手指上。③接近;靠近。New York is situated *on* the Hudson River. 紐約瀕哈德遜河邊。④向…方向。The house looks out *on* the sea. 這屋子面向大海。⑤表示動作或影響之直接或間接的接受。to call *on.* 拜訪。⑥藉;由。This news is *on* good authority. 這項消息有正確的根據。⑦在…之時;當…之時。*on* Sunday. 在星期日。They greeted us *on* our arrival. 在我們到達之時,他們歡迎我們。⑧關於;論及。a book *on* animals. 一本關於動物的書。⑨爲…之目的。⑩在其中。Who is *on* the committee? 誰在此委員會中? ⑪在某種狀況中。*on* duty. 值班。*on* leave. 休假中。*on* sale. 出售中。⑫在某基礎上;在某條件上。*on* equal terms. 基於平等條件。⑬一次繼一次。Defeat *on* defeat discouraged them. 一次一次的失敗使他們氣餒。⑭冒…之險。*on* pain of death. 冒死亡之險。***on purpose*** 有意;故意。Do you think he made that mistake *on purpose?* 你以爲他故意犯了那錯嗎? ***on second thought*** 經進一步之考慮後。***on the contrary*** 相反地。He is not stupid; *on the contrary,* he is very intelligent. 他不愚蠢,相反地,他很聰明。***on the face of it*** 表面看來;外觀的。***on the one hand*** 一方面(與 on the other hand 連用)。***on the other hand*** 另一方面。***on the*** (or ***one's***) ***way*** (***to***) 在向…之途中。*On my way* home, I ran across him. 在我回家途中,我不期與他相遇。***on the whole*** 大體;一般。***on time*** 準時。—*adv.* ①在上。The walls are up, and the roof is *on.* 牆壁矗立,屋頂在其上。②相接;附着。to hold *on.* 握住。to cling (*or* hang) *on.* 依附;攀住。③指向(某地、某點或某目標)。to look *on.* 旁觀。④向前。to march *on.* 前進。Time is getting *on.* 時間漸晚。He is getting *on* in years. 他漸漸年老。⑤在某種情況、過程、狀態或行動中。Turn the gas *on.* 打開煤氣。The war still went *on.* 戰爭仍繼續中。⑥以後;自從。later *on.* 後來。***and so on*** 等等。***on and off*** = **off and on.** ***on and on*** 繼續不斷地。He talked *on and on.* 他說個不停。***on to*** 到…之上面。He jumped *on to* the shore. 他跳到岸上。—*adj.* 進行中的。The race is *on.* 競賽正進行中。***on to*** 〖俗〗知曉眞情、動機等。I am *on to* your little game. 我知道你搞的甚麼鬼。

on- 〖字首〗表副詞之"on"之義,如: oncoming, onlooker.

o·nan·ism [ˈonənˌɪzəm; ˈounənizəm] *n.* ①體外射精(目的在避孕)。②手淫。

on·board [ˈɑnˈbɔrd; ˈɔnˈbɔːd] *adj.* 裝置在交通工具(如火箭、人造衛星或太空船)上的。an *onboard* computer. 一具裝置電腦。

‡once [wʌns; wʌns] *adv.* ①一次地;一遍地。I've read it *once.* 我曾讀過一遍。②昔時地;往時地。a *once* powerful nation. 昔日一强國。③無論何時地;一旦地。If the facts *once* become known, he will be punished. 事實一旦公開,他會受到處分。***more than once*** 不只一次地;常常地。***not once*** 永未。*Not once* have you done what I asked! 你從來沒有做過我請求你的事! ***once again*** 再一次。Let me hear you sing *once again.* 讓我再聽你唱一次。***once and again*** 重複地;再三地。***once*** (***and***) ***for all*** 堅決地;最終地。I told him *once* (*and*) *for all* that I wouldn't go. 我斷然告訴了他我不願

意去。*once in a while* 有時。*once more* 再一次。Say it *once more*. 再說一遍。*once or twice* 一兩次;幾次。*once upon a time* 昔時。—*n.* 一度;一回。*Once* is enough. 一回卽够了。*all at once* **a.** 突然。**b.** 同時;一同。The soldiers ran away *all at once*. 兵士們一同跑掉了。*at once* **a.** 立刻。She told him to leave the room *at once*. 她要他卽刻離開那屋子。**b.** 同時。*for once* 至少一次。I'm right *for once*. 我至少有一次是對的。—*adj.* 從前的。—*conj.* 如果一旦;每當。*Once* you cross the river you are safe. 你一旦渡過這河,便安全了。

on-cam·er·a [ˈɑnˈkæmərə; ˈɔnˈkæmərə] *adv.* & *adj.* 在電影或電視鏡頭之內地(的)。

once-o·ver [ˈwʌnsˌovɚ; ˈwʌnsˌouvə] *n.* ①〖俚〗粗略的察看;迅速估量的一瞥。②草率的工作。

on·com·ing [ˈɑnˌkʌmɪŋ; ˈɔnˌkʌmiŋ] *adj.* 卽將來臨的;接近的。—*n.* 來臨。

on dit [ɔ̃ˈdi; ɔ̃ˈdiː] 〖法〗①他們說;據說(=they say; it is said)。②(亦作 **on-dit**) 傳聞;謠傳。

‡**one** [wʌn; wʌn] *n.* ①一;1。②一人;一物;一個。*One* went this way, another went that way. 一個向這面走,另一個向那一面走。*all in one* 合在一起。*at one* 一致。I am *at one* with you on that point. 在那一點上我和你的意見一致。*for one* 算做一個(用以表明語氣)。I, *for one*, cannot agree. 我個人不同意。*make one* **a.** 作爲一員。**b.** 團結一致;結婚。*one and all* 每個。*one another* 互相(三者以上)。*one by one* 逐一;陸續。*one up on* 〖俗〗占上風。—*adj.* ①一個的;單一的。No *one* man can do it. 沒有一個人能做。②或有的(=some)。*One* day he will be sorry. 有一天他會悔恨。③相同的。They held *one* opinion. 他們持有同一意見。④一致的。The class was *one* in its approval. 全班人一致贊同。⑤某一的(=a certain)。*One* John Smith was elected. 一個名叫約翰史密斯的人當選了。⑥唯一無二的。This is the *one* thing needful. 這是唯一需要的東西。*all one* 一樣的;相同的。—*pron.* ①某一人;某一物。*One* of the poems was selected for the book. 這些詩中之一首被選入書中。②任何人;任何物。*One* has to do one's best. 人須盡其力。③同一人;同一物。Dr. Jekyll and Mr. Hyde were *one* and the same. 吉柯博士和海德先生是同一個人。

one-arm bandit [ˈwʌnˌɑrm~; ˈwʌnɑːm~] 〖美俚〗吃角子老虎。(亦作 **one-armed bandit**)

one-bag·ger [ˈwʌnˈbægɚ; ˈwʌnˈbægə] *n.* 〖棒球俚〗=**one-base hit.**

one-base hit [ˈwʌnˈbes~; ˈwʌnˈbeis~] 〖棒球〗一壘安打。(亦作 **single**)

one-celled [ˈwʌnˈsɛld; ˈwʌnˈseld] *adj.* 單細胞的。

one-eyed [ˈwʌnˈaɪd; ˈwʌnˈaid] *adj.* ①一隻眼的;獨眼的。②一目失明的。

one·fold [ˈwʌnˌfold; ˈwʌnfould] *adj.* 祇含一個的;單一的;簡單的。

one-horse [ˈwʌnˈhɔrs; ˈwʌnˈhɔːs] *adj.* ①單馬的;由一匹馬拉的;僅用一匹馬的。②祇有一匹馬的。③〖俗〗不重要的;次要的。

one-i·de·aed [ˈwʌnaɪˈdiəd; ˈwʌnaiˈdiəd] *adj.* 祇有一個意見的;固執於一個觀念的;褊狹的。

O'Neill [oˈnil; ouˈniːl] *n.* 歐尼爾 (Eugene Gladstone, 1888–1953, 美國劇作家,曾獲1936年諾貝爾文學獎)。

o·nei·ro·man·cy [oˈnaɪrəˌmænsɪ; ouˈnaiəroumænsi] *n.* 以夢爲根據的占卜術。—**o·nei·ro·man·cer,** *n.*

one-legged [ˈwʌnˈlɛgɪd; ˈwʌnˈlegd] *adj.* ①獨脚的。②單方面的(如議論、觀點等)。③(因缺少基本因素等而)無效力的。

one-lin·er [ˈwʌnˈlaɪnɚ; ˈwʌnˈlainə] *n.* 〖美〗簡短的笑話或妙語。

one-man [ˈwʌnˈmæn; ˈwʌnˈmæn] *adj.* 個人的;僅一人的。

one·ness [ˈwʌnnɪs; ˈwʌnnis] *n.* ①單一。②相同。③統一。④一致。

one-night stand [ˈwʌnˌnaɪt~; ˈwʌnnait~] ①(劇團等)一處祇演一場(隨後便到別處去)。②作上述演出之地方、戲院等。

one-off [ˈwʌnˈɔf; ˈwʌnˈɔːf] *adj., n.* 〖英〗祇一次的(事物);祇供一人使用的(事物)。

on·er [ˈwʌnɚ; ˈwʌnə] *n.* ①〖俚〗獨特之人(物);名手。②〖俚〗猛烈的一擊。

on·er·ous [ˈɑnərəs; ˈɔnərəs] *adj.* ①繁重的;煩苛的。②〖法律〗附有義務的。

one-seat·er [ˈwʌnˈsitɚ; ˈwʌnˈsiːtə] *n.* 單人座的汽車(飛機)。

***one·self** [wʌnˈsɛlf; wʌnˈself] *pron.* 自己;自身。One should not praise *oneself*. 人不應稱讚自己。*be oneself* **a.** 能充分控制個人之身心。**b.** 行動自然。*by oneself* **a.** 獨自(=alone)。She likes to take a walk *by herself*. 她喜歡獨自散步。**b.** 獨力;無幫助。*come to oneself* **a.** (亦作 **come to**) 恢復知覺;恢復意識。**b.** (亦作 **one's self**) 恢復沉着。*for oneself* 獨力;自立。He is old enough to do it *for himself*. 他的年齡已經大到足以獨自做這件事了。

one shot ①只出一期的雜誌。②電影或戲劇中演員的一次(無第二次)出現。③一個人的近鏡頭。④任何祇做一次的事情。

one-shot [ˈwʌnˌʃɑt; ˈwʌnʃɔt] *adj.* 〖俗〗①祇用一次的;臨時性的。②祇出現一次的。—*n.* =**one shot.**

one-sid·ed [ˈwʌnˈsaɪdɪd; ˈwʌnˈsaidid, wʌnˈs-] *adj.* ①祇見問題之一面的。②偏袒的;不公平的;有偏見的。③不均衡的;倒向一面的。④祇有一面的。⑤〖法律〗片面義務的。

one-step [ˈwʌnˌstɛp; ˈwʌnstep] *n.* 一步舞;一步舞之曲。—*v.i.* 跳一步舞。

one·time [ˈwʌnˌtaɪm; ˈwʌntaim] *adj.* ①過去的;從前的。②祇發生過一次的。

one-to-one [ˈwʌntəˈwʌn; ˈwʌntəˈwʌn] *adj.* ①一比一的;成對比的。②〖數學〗一對一的。

one-track [ˈwʌnˈtræk; ˈwʌnˈtræk] *adj.* ①〖鐵路〗單線的;單軌的。②〖俗〗**a.** 固執於一個想法的;褊狹的。**b.** 一次祇能做一件事或祇能有一個想法的;有限的。

one-up·man·ship [ˌwʌnˈʌpmənˌʃɪp; ˌwʌnˈʌpmənʃip] *n.* (在事業、社會地位、特權等)表現高人一等的作風。

one-way [ˈwʌnˈwe; ˈwʌnˈwei] *adj.* ①單行(道)的。a *one-way* ticket. 單程票。②一個方向的。

on·fall [ˈɑnˌfɔl; ˈɔnfɔːl] *n.* ①〖蘇〗攻擊;突擊。②(雨、雪之)大降。③夜晚之降臨。

on·flow [ˈɑnˌflo; ˈɔnflou] *n.* 奔流。

on·go·ing [ˈɑnˌgoɪŋ; ˈɔnˌgouiŋ] *adj.* 前進的;行進的;進行中的。—*n.* ①進行;前

進。②(*pl.*) 程序;處置;行爲。

***on·ion** [ˈʌnjən; ˈʌnjən] *n.* ①洋葱。②洋葱味。③〖俚〗人;傢伙。—*adj.* ①含洋葱的;以洋葱烹調的。②像洋葱的。**—like,** *adj.*

on·ion·skin [ˈʌnjən,skɪn; ˈʌnjənskin] *n.* ①洋葱皮。②葱皮紙(一種半透明的薄紙)。

on·ion·y [ˈʌnjənɪ; ˈʌnjəni] *adj.* 似洋葱的;以洋葱調味的;有洋葱臭的;有洋葱味的。

on·li·cence [ˈɑn,laɪsəns; ˈɔn,laisəns] *n.* 〖英〗賣酒執照。

on·li·est [ˈonlɪɪst; ˈounliist] *adj.* 最好的;最佳的(爲 only 之 superlative).

on-line [ˈɑn,laɪn; ˈɔnlain] *adj.* 〖電腦〗線上的。

on·look·er [ˈɑn,lukə; ˈɔn,lukə] *n.* 旁觀者。

on·look·ing [ˈɑn,lukɪŋ; ˈɔn,lukiŋ] *n., adj.* 旁觀(的);觀看(中的)。

:on·ly [ˈonlɪ; ˈounli] *adj.* ①獨一的;僅有的。They were the *only* people who were wearing summer dresses. 他們是唯一着夏裝的人。②最優的。He is the *only* writer for my taste. 他是我最欣賞的作家。 —*adv.* ①祇;僅。He sold *only* two. 他祇賣掉了兩個。②唯一;無二。There are white ones *only*. 唯有白的了。③最後難免。You will *only* regret your harsh words to him. 你對他說話這樣不客氣,遲早必後悔。***if only*** 我願 (=I wish). *If only* the weather were finer! 但願天氣能好一些就好了! ***only just*** 剛剛 (=just). They've *only just* got up. 他們剛剛起來。***only too*** 很 (=very). I shall be *only too* pleased to come. 我很樂於來。—*conj.* ①惟;但;不過。I would have gone, *only* you objected. 不是你反對,我就去了。②〖主英〗要不是。*Only* for him, you would not be here. 要不是爲了他,你不會在這裏。

on·o·mat·o·poe·ia [,ɑnə,mætəˈpiə; ,ɔnoumætouˈpi(ː)ə] *n.* ①擬聲;擬聲語(如 buzz, tinkle, cuckoo). ②〖修辭〗聲喩法。

on·o·mat·o·poe·ic [,ɑnə,mætəˈpiɪk; ,ɔnoumætouˈpiːik] *adj.* 擬聲的;聲喩的。

on·o·mat·o·po·et·ic [,ɑnə,mætəpoˈɛtɪk; ,ɔnə,mætəpouˈetik] *adj.* =**onomatopoeic.**

on·rush [ˈɑn,rʌʃ; ˈɔnrʌʃ] *n.* ①猛衝。②(水的)急流;奔流。**—ing,** *adj.*

on·set [ˈɑn,sɛt; ˈɔnset] *n.* ①進攻。②開始。

on·shore [ˈɑn,ʃor; ˈɔnʃɔː] *adv. & adj.* 向陸地(的);在陸上(的)。

on·side [ˈɑnˈsaɪd; ˈɔnˈsaid] *adv. & adj.* 〖足球、曲棍球〗在正規位置(的);在界內(的)。

on·slaught [ˈɑn,slɔt; ˈɔnslɔːt] *n.* 猛攻。

Ont. Ontario.

on-the-job [ɑnðəˈdʒɑb; ɔnðəˈdʒɔb] *adj.* 在職的。*on-the-job* training. 在職訓練。

on-the-spot [ɑnðəˈspɑt; ɔnðəˈspɔt] *adj.* ①當場的。②立刻舉行或發生的。

***on·to** [ˈɑntu, -tə, -tu; ˈɔntuː, ˈɔntə] *prep.* 到…之上;在上。to get *onto* a horse. 騎上馬。〖注意〗 **onto** 與 **on to.** 在 on 做副詞用,而 to 爲介詞時,亦可分寫爲兩字。

on·to·gen·e·sis [,ɑntəˈdʒɛnɪsɪs; ,ɔntəˈdʒenisis] *n.* =**ontogeny.**

on·tog·e·ny [ɑnˈtɑdʒənɪ; ɔnˈtɔdʒəni] *n.* 〖生物〗個體發生史;個體發育史。**—on·to·ge·net·ic,** *adj.*

on·to·log·i·cal [,ɑntəˈlɑdʒɪkl; ,ɔntəˈlɔdʒikəl] *adj.* 〖哲學〗本體論上的;實體論的。(亦作 **ontologic**)

on·tol·o·gist [ɑnˈtɑlədʒɪst; ɔnˈtɔlədʒist] *n.* 〖哲學〗本體論學者;實體論者。

on·tol·o·gy [ɑnˈtɑlədʒɪ; ɔnˈtɔlədʒi] *n.* 〖哲學〗①本體論;實體論。②=**metaphysics. —on·tol·o·gis·tic,** *adj.*

o·nus [ˈonəs; ˈounəs] *n.* 負擔;責任;任務。

***on·ward** [ˈɑnwəd; ˈɔnwəd] *adv.* 向前;前進。—*adj.* 向前的;前進的 (=forward).

on·wards [ˈɑnwədz; ˈɔnwədz] *adv.* = **onward.**

on·yx [ˈɑnɪks; ˈɔniks] *n.* 〖礦〗截子瑪瑙。—*adj.* 黑的;烏黑的。

oo·dles [ˈudlz; ˈuːdlz] *n. pl.* (有時作 *sing.* 解)〖俚〗甚多;大量。

oof [uf; uːf] *n.* 〖英俚〗金錢;現錢。

oof·y [ˈufɪ; ˈuːfi] *adj.,* **oof·i·er, oof·i·est.** 〖英俚〗富有的;有錢的。

o·o·gen·e·sis [,oəˈdʒɛnəsɪs; ,ouəˈdʒenisis] *n.* 〖生物〗卵子發生;成卵法。(亦作 **oögenesis**)

o·ö·go·ni·a [,oəˈgonɪə; ,ouəˈgouniə] *n.* pl. of **oögonium.**

o·ö·go·ni·um [,oəˈgonɪəm; ,ouəˈgouniəm] *n., pl.* **-ni·a, -ni·ums.** ①〖生物〗卵原細胞。②〖植物〗藏卵器。(亦作 **oogonium**)

o·ö·lite [ˈoə,laɪt; ˈouəlait] *n.* ①〖礦〗鮞石;魚卵石;鮞狀石灰石。②(O-)〖地質〗歐洲侏儸系之上層部。(亦作 **oolite**) **—o·ö·lit·ic, o·o·lit·ic,** *adj.*

o·öl·o·gy [oˈɑlədʒɪ; ouˈɔlədʒi] *n.* 鳥卵學。(亦作 **oology**)

oo·long [ˈulɔŋ; ˈuːlɔŋ] *n.* 烏龍茶(產於中國之福建、臺灣,色濃)。

oom [om; oum] *n.* 〖南非〗(對長者之暱稱)叔父;伯父。

oomph [umf; umf] *n.* 〖美俚〗①性感;性的魅力。②吸引力。③活力;熱情。

o·o·pho·ri·tis [,oəfəˈraɪtɪs; ,ouəfəˈraitis] *n.* 〖醫〗卵巢炎。(亦作 **oöphoritis**)

oops [ups; ups] *interj.* 對自己之錯誤、笨拙之行爲等表示輕度之驚訝、不滿、懊惱等。

ooze [uz; uːz] *v.,* **oozed, ooz·ing,** *n.* —*v.i.* ①慢慢地流。Blood still *oozed* from his cut. 他的傷口還在流血。②慢慢地洩露。③慢慢消失。④冒出濕氣。—*v.t.* ①淌(汗)。He was *oozing* sweat. 他在淌汗。②流(血)。③流出。—*n.* ①慢慢的滲流。②滲流的東西。③水底的軟泥。④沼澤地。

oo·zy [ˈuzɪ; ˈuːzi] *adj.,* **-zi·er, -zi·est.** ①慢慢滲流的;滲出濕氣的。②軟泥的;泥濘的;含軟泥的;似泥濘的。

Op. opus. **op.** ①opera. ②opposite. ③operation. ④opus.

op- 〖字首〗=**ob-** (用於p之前), 如:oppose.

O.P., o.p. ①out of print. ②overproof. ③〖集郵〗overprint.

o·pac·i·ty [oˈpæsətɪ; ouˈpæsiti] *n., pl.* **-ties.** ①不透明;昏暗;幽暗。②曖昧;意義模糊。③愚鈍;暗昧。④〖照相〗不透明度。⑤不透明體;昏暗部分;不透明部分。⑥愚鈍的人。⑦不透熱;不透聲。

o·pal [ˈopl; ˈoupəl] *n.* 〖礦〗貓眼石;蛋白石。

o·pal·esce [,opəˈlɛs; ,oupəˈles] *v.i.,* **-esced, -esc·ing.** 發(似蛋白石的)乳白光。

o·pal·es·cent [,oplˈɛsn̩t; ,oupəˈlesnt] *adj.* 發似蛋白色之光的;發乳白光的。 **—o·pal·es·cence,** *n.*

o·pal·esque [,opəˈlɛsk; ,oupəˈlesk] *adj.* 似蛋白石的;發乳白光的。

o·pal·ine [ˈoplɪn; *adj.* ˈoupəlain *n.* ˈoupəliːn] *adj.* ①似蛋白石的。②發乳白光的。—*n.* ①乳白玻璃。②乳白色。

o·paque [oˈpek; ouˈpeik] *adj., n., v.,* **o·paqued, o·paqu·ing.**—*adj.* ①不透明的;

不透光的。②不光亮的;幽暗的;昏暗的。③意義不明的; 難解的。④愚鈍的。⑤不傳導電流的;不傳熱的;隔音的。 —*n.* ①不透明物。②難解之物。—*v.t.* 使變爲不透明, 不傳熱, 不傳晉。—**ly,** *adv.*

op. cit. opere citato(〖拉〗=in the work cited).

ope 〔op; oup〕 *v.t. & v.i.,* **oped, op·ing.** 〖古,詩〗=**open.**

OPEC Organization of Petroleum Exporting Countries. 石油輸出國家組織。

:o·pen 〔ˈopən, ˈopm̩; ˈoupən, ˈoupm〕 *adj.* ①開的。Who has left the door *open?* 誰讓門開着未關? ②空的; 空曠的。③未塡滿的; 空缺的。The position is still *open.* 職位仍虛懸着。④可進入的;可使用的;可分享的;可自由競爭的。The race is *open* to all. 任何人皆可參加競跑。⑤不禁止的;開放的。The river is *open* for navigation. 此河可航行。⑥未遮蓋的。The goods are lying *open.* 貨物未遮起而擺在那裏。⑦公開的;公然的。⑧坦率的;開明的。I will be *open* with you about it. 對於這件事, 我將對你坦白無隱。⑨伸開的;展開的; 開放的。The flowers were all *open.* 花都開放了。⑩(商店、醫院、學校等)開着的;(展覽會等)參觀時間的。At what time is the bank *open?* 銀行何時開門? ⑪未解決的。The match seems to be a very *open* one. 這比賽似乎是勝負完全未卜者。⑫未結凍的;未結冰的。⑬易受…感動的;易接受…的;招致…的。⑭〖印刷〗行距寬的。⑮〖航海〗無霧的。The weather is fair and *open.* 天氣清朗無霧。⑯〖醫〗暢通的;不便祕的。The bowels are *open.* 大便暢通。⑰〖語音〗**a.** 開口發音的。**b.** 以母音結尾的(音節)。⑱〖音樂〗**a.** (風笛)上端開口的。**b.** (絃樂器)不由手指所停止的(弦)。⑲多孔的;有網眼的。⑳不設防的。㉑(水道)無冰塊阻塞的;未結冰的。㉒溫和的;不太寒冷的。—*n.* ①曠野;空曠之地; 無垠大海。②公開。All of his dealings are in the *open.* 他的一切來往都是公開的。③孔穴。④空缺;機會。*in open* 公然無隱。*the open* **a.** 野外;戶外。**b.** 衆所周知。**c.** 曠野。 —*v.t.* ①使開;打開; 展開; 睜開。She *opened* her eyes. 她睜開她的眼睛。②開墾; 開拓;開通。③暴露; 展示。④啓發; 發展。His understanding wants to be *opened.* 他的理解力需予以啓迪。⑤開業;創立。He's going to *open* a small shoe shop. 他將開一小鞋店。⑥開放;開通。A communication will be *opened* between the two places. 兩地間的交通卽將開通。⑦開始。to *open* an account with a bank. 在銀行開一戶頭。⑧使(腸)通。The bowels should be well *opened.* 應使大便暢通。⑨〖醫〗切開。⑩看見。We *opened* a white church to the port. 我們看見左舷邊外有一白色教堂。—*v.i.* ①開;展開。The door *opened* and some men came out. 門開了,有些人走出來。②通向。This door *opens* into the dining-room. 這門通向餐廳。③開始。When does the school *open* again? 學校甚麼時候再開學? ④(商店)開張;營業。This grocery has just *opened.* 這雜貨店剛開張。⑤展示;顯出。A wide prospect *opened* below us. 一片廣大的景色在我們下邊展開。⑥發展。His understanding *opened* with the years. 他的理解力與年齡俱增。⑦說明;說出。He did not *open* on the subject. 他沒有說明這題目。⑧翻開。*Open* at page 12. 翻到第十二頁。***open up*** **a.** 打開;開。**b.** 展開。**c.** 開始; 開始射擊。**d.** 吐露眞情。

o·pen·a·ble 〔ˈopənəbl̩; ˈoupənəbl〕 *adj.* 可開的。

open account ①未淸結的帳目。②雙方正在進行中的交易活動。

open admissions 〖美〗=**open enrollment.**

open air 戶外;露天。

o·pen-air 〔ˈopənˈɛr; ˈoupənˈɛə〕 *adj.* 戶外的;室外的;野外的。

o·pen-and-shut 〔ˈopənənˈʃʌt; ˈoupənənˈʃʌt〕 *adj.* 〖美俗〗一望而知的;淸淸楚楚的;極簡單的;明顯的。

o·pen-armed 〔ˈopənˈɑrmd; ˈoupənˈɑːmd〕 *adj.* 伸開兩臂的;衷心的;歡迎的。

open-book examination 可携帶教科書或參考書的一種考試。

o·pen-cast 〔ˈopənˈkæst; ˈoupənkɑːst〕 *adj.* =**open-pit.**

open city 〖軍〗不設防之城市。

open door ①門戶開放;自由進出。②門戶開放政策。

o·pen-door 〔ˈopənˈdor; ˈoupənˈdɔː〕 *adj.* 門戶開放政策的;門戶開放主義的。

o·pen-doored 〔ˈopənˈdord; ˈoupənˈdɔːd〕 *adj.* 好客的。

o·pen-eared 〔ˈopənˈɪrd; ˈoupənˈiəd〕 *adj.* 注意傾聽的。

o·pen-end 〔ˈopənˈɛnd; ˈoupənˈend〕 *adj.* 無限制的;可廣泛解釋的。

o·pen-end·ed 〔ˈopənˈɛndɪd; ˈoupənˈendid〕 *adj.* ① =**open-end.** ②兩端沒有封閉的。③威力無限制的。④沒有時間限制的。

open enrollment 〖美〗大學入學不加限制的政策。

o·pen·er 〔ˈopənɚ; ˈoupn̩ə〕 *n.* ①開啓者;開始者。②開啓瓶蓋、罐頭等之工具。③一連串比賽之第一局。④事物之開始部分。

o·pen-eyed 〔ˈopənˈaɪd; ˈoupn̩ˈaid〕 *adj.* ①睜開眼睛的; 驚醒的; 小心的;機警的;眼光銳敏的。②驚訝的;瞠目吃驚的;駭然張目的。③公然的;公認的;坦白的。

o·pen-faced 〔ˈopənˈfest; ˈoupənˈfeist〕 *adj.* ①相貌誠實的;老實相的。②面上無遮蓋物的。③(鐘錶)錶面只罩玻璃蓋的。④(餡餅、三明治等)有餡但無上面一層的。

o·pen-hand·ed 〔ˈopənˈhændɪd; ˈoupn̩ˈhændid〕 *adj.* 慷慨好施的。

o·pen-heart·ed 〔ˈopənˈhɑrtɪd; ˈoupənˌhɑːtid〕 *adj.* ①坦白的; 無隱私的; 明言的。②慷慨的。

o·pen-hearth 〔ˈopənˈhɑrθ; ˈoupənˈhɑːθ〕 *adj.* 〖冶金〗(使用)敞爐的。—*n.* 敞爐。

open house ①(歡迎親友到家來的) 家庭派對(爲慶祝某事或會晤貴賓等)。②〖美俗〗(學校、宿舍、俱樂部等准許公衆參觀之) 開放日。***keep open house*** 準備隨時款待來賓。

***o·pen·ing** 〔ˈopənɪŋ, ˈopnɪŋ; ˈoupniŋ〕 *n.* ①口;穴; 孔。②初步; 開始。③空缺的職位。④張開。⑤機會。⑥空地;空場。⑦〖法律〗開始提證據前辯護人之陳述。 ⑧開始遊戲之方法。a manual of chess *openings.* 西洋棋入門(初步指南)。⑨正式的開放。⑩開幕。

open letter 公開信(通常爲攻擊或批評某人,並予公開披露者)。

***o·pen·ly** 〔ˈopənlɪ; ˈoupn̩li, -ənli, -m̩li〕 *adv.* ①無隱地;公然地。②坦白地;率直地。

open market 自由市場。

o·pen-mar·ket 〔ˈopənˈmɑrkɪt; ˈoupənˈmɑːkit〕 *adj.* 自由市場的。

o·pen-mind·ed 〔ˈopənˈmaɪndɪd; ˈoupn̩ˈmaindid〕 *adj.* 虛心的;能接納新思想

的;無偏見的。

o·pen-mouthed ['opən'mauðd, -θt; 'oupn̩'mauðd] *adj.* ①張口的。②(因驚奇而)張大著口的;吃驚的。③垂涎的;思食的;貪慾的。④喧噪的;擾嚷的。⑤寬口的;廣口的(容器)。⑥(獵狗之)看到獵物時張口欲撲的。

o·pen·ness ['opənnɪs; 'oupn̩nis] *n.* 公開;率直;無偏見;虛懷。

o·pen-pit ['opən'pɪt; 'oupən'pit] *adj.* 上面暴露的;稍低於地面的。

open sea 公海。

open secret 公開的祕密。

open sesame ①(天方夜譚之 *Ali Baba and the Forty Thieves* 故事中)開盜穴洞門之咒語。②獲得許可、通過等之穩當方法;口令;開門的暗號。

o·pen-shelf ['opən'ʃɛlf; 'oupən'ʃelf] *adj.* 開架式的(圖書館允許借書人進入書架自選書籍的)。

open shop 〖美〗(用工會會員或非工會會員之)開放工廠或商店(爲closed shop 之對)。

o·pen·work ['opən,wɜk; 'oupn̩wəːk] *n.* ①網狀細工;留空眼之細工。②〖採礦〗露天採掘;露天之礦場。—*adj.* 有網狀小孔的。

***op·er·a**[1] ['ɑpərə; 'ɔpərə] *n.* ①歌劇。②歌劇曲譜或歌詞。③歌劇之演出。④歌劇院。

op·er·a[2] 〖拉〗 *n.* pl. of **opus**.

op·er·a·ble ['ɑpərəbl̩; 'ɔpərəbl] *adj.* ①〖醫〗可動手術的;可以開刀的。②可付諸實施的;可實行的。

opera cloak 觀劇用的女外套。

opera glass(es) (觀劇用之)小型雙眼望遠鏡。

opera hat (可以縮扁之男用)大禮帽。

opera hood 觀劇用的女頭巾。

opera house ①歌劇院。②任何劇院。

***op·er·ate** ['ɑpə,ret; 'ɔpəreit] *v.*, **-at·ed, -at·ing.** —*v.i.* ①動作;轉動。The machinery *operates* night and day. 機器日夜轉動。②致;生。Several causes *operated* to bring on the war. 幾種原因使戰爭發生。③奏效;生效。The medicine *operated* quickly. 藥很快地生效了。④施手術。The doctors decided to *operate* at once. 醫生們決定立刻動手術。⑤作軍事活動。⑥買賣股票或公債。—*v.t.* ①使運轉;管理;操縱。The company *operates* several factories. 這公司擁有數個工廠。②產生;使發生。The books have *operated* changes in our way of thought. 這些書籍已使我們的思想發生了變化。—**op·er·at·a·ble,** *adj.*

op·er·at·ic [,ɑpə'rætɪk; ,ɔpə'rætik] *adj.* 歌劇的;似歌劇的;適於歌劇的。—**al·ly,** *adv.*

operating room 手術室。

operating table 手術臺。

‡**op·er·a·tion** [,ɑpə'reʃən; ,ɔpə'reiʃən] *n.* ①動作;工作。②運用法。③作用。④經營;管理。The *operation* of a railroad requires men. 管理鐵路需要很多人。⑤手術。⑥(常 *pl.*)軍事行動;軍事指揮部。*Operations* reported one plane missing. 作戰指揮部報告一機失踪。⑦〖數學〗運算。⑧交易;買賣。*operations* in cotton. 棉花交易。***in operation*** 實行中;生效中。The new system is now ***in*** full *operation*. 新的制度現已全面實施。***come*** (or ***go***) ***into operation*** 開始動作;開始生效。

op·er·a·tion·al [,ɑpə'reʃənl̩; ,ɔpə'reiʃənl] *adj.* ①可使用的。②〖軍〗 **a.** 作戰的。 **b.** 現役的;服戰鬥任務的。③operation 的。

—**ly,** *adv.*

op·er·a·tive ['ɑpə,retɪv; 'ɔpərətiv] *adj.* ①動作的;生效的。②工作的;生產的。③與施手術有關的。④〖數學〗運算用的。—*n.* ①工人;技工。②偵探。③特務;地下工作人員。

***op·er·a·tor** ['ɑpə,retɚ; 'ɔpəreitə] *n.* ①工作者;運用者。②(電話之)接線生;(電報之)收發報員。③廠主;礦主;鐵路經營者。④行手術者。⑤〖數學〗運算素。⑥作大批證券交易者。⑦〖俚〗 **a.** 以巧妙的手段達成目的者;長袖善舞者。**b.** 善於避免困難,或走法律漏洞者。**c.** 很會做生意賺錢者。**d.** 對異性很有辦法者。**e.** 對很多事都能滔滔不絕發表意見者。

o·per·cu·lum [o'pɝkjuləm; ou'pəː-kjuləm] *n.*, *pl.* **-la** [-lə; -lə], **-lums.** ①〖植物〗蘚蓋;果蓋。②〖動物〗(魚)鰓蓋;(腹足動物)殼蓋。

op·er·et·ta [,ɑpə'rɛtə; ,ɔpə'retə] *n.*, *pl.* **-tas, -ti** [-ti; -tiː]. 輕鬆活潑的小歌劇。

op·er·ose ['ɑpə,ros; 'ɔpə,rous] *adj.* ①刻苦的;辛勤的。②費力的;困難的。

O·phel·ia [ə'filjə; ɔ'fiːljə] *n.* ①女子名。②奧菲莉亞(莎士比亞所作 *Hamlet* 之劇中人, Polonius 之女, 因 Hamlet 待之冷熱不定而瘋狂自殺)。

oph·i·cleide ['ɑfɪ,klaɪd; 'ɔfiklaid] *n.* 一種早期之低音大喇叭。

o·phid·i·an [o'fɪdɪən; ɔ'fidiən] *adj.* 蛇類的;似蛇的。—*n.* 蛇。

oph·i·ol·a·ter [,ɑfɪ'ɑlətɚ; ,ɔfi'ɔlətə] *n.* 拜蛇者。

oph·i·ol·a·try [,ɑfɪ'ɑlətrɪ; ,ɔfi'ɔlətri] *n.* 對蛇之崇拜;拜蛇。

oph·ite ['ɑfaɪt; 'ɔfait] *n.* 〖礦〗輝綠岩之一種。

oph·thal·mi·a ne·o·na·to·rum [ɑf'θælmɪə,nɪənə'torəm; ɔf'θælmiə,niənə-'tourəm] 〖醫〗初生兒眼炎。

oph·thal·mic [ɑf'θælmɪk; ɔf'θælmik, ɔp'θ-] *adj.* ①眼的;眼科的。②患眼炎的。

oph·thal·mol·o·gist [,ɑfθæl'mɑlə-dʒɪst; ,ɔfθæl'mɔlədʒist] *n.* 眼科醫師;眼科專家。

oph·thal·mol·o·gy [,ɑfθæl'mɑlədʒɪ; ,ɔfθæl'mɔlədʒi] *n.* 〖醫〗眼科學。

oph·thal·mo·scope [ɑf'θælmə,skop; ɔf'θælməskoup] *n.* 〖醫〗檢目鏡;檢眼器。

o·pi·ate [*n., adj.* 'opɪɪt, -,et; 'oupiit *v.* 'opɪ,et; 'oupieit] *n., adj., v.,* **-at·ed, -at·ing.** —*n.* ①含有鴉片的痲醉劑或安眠藥。②痲醉劑;安眠藥。③任何有緩和作用之事物。—*adj.*①含有鴉片的。②催眠的;痲醉的。—*v.t.* 〖罕〗①(用鴉片)痲醉。②使鈍;使減弱。

o·pine [o'paɪn; ou'pain] *v.t.* & *v.i.*, **-pined, -pin·ing.** 〖諧〗持有意見;表達意見;以爲;想。

‡**o·pin·ion** [ə'pɪnjən; ə'pinjən] *n.* ①意見;見解;信念。They are divided in *opinion*. 他們的意見分歧。②估價;印象。What is your *opinion* of that man? 你對那個人的印象如何?③判斷;評論;輿論。It is a matter of *opinion* only. 這祇是各人看法不同而已。④〖法律〗法官對案件之決定所依據之理由。***have no opinion of*** (=to think badly of)對…有壞印象。***have the courage of one's opinions*** 敢於依自己的信念行動。

o·pin·ion·at·ed [ə'pɪnjən,etɪd; ə'pi-njəneitid] *adj.* 固執己見的;武斷的;固守成見的。—**ly,** *adv.* —**ness,** *n.*

o·pin·ion·a·tive [ə'pɪnjən,etɪv; ə-'pinjəneitiv] *adj.* ①意見的。②=**opinionated.**

***o·pi·um** ['opɪəm; 'oupjəm, -piəm] *n.* 鴉片。

o·pi·um·ism ['opɪəmɪzəm; 'oupjəmizm] *n.* 〖醫〗鴉片癮;鴉片嗜好。

Opium War 鴉片戰爭 (1839-1842 年中英間之戰爭)。

o·pop·a·nax [o'pɑpə,næks; ou'pɔpənæks] *n.* 一種芳香樹脂(製香料用)。

o·pos·sum ['pɑsəm, ə'pɑsəm; ə'pɔsəm] *n., pl.* **-sums, -sum.** 〖動物〗鼬;負鼠。(亦作 **possum**)

opp. ①oppose(d). ②opposite. ③opposition.

Op·pen·heim·er ['ɑpən,haɪmɚ; 'ɔpənhaimə] *n.* 奧本海默(J. Robert, 1904-1967, 美國物理學家, 1963 年獲諾貝爾物理獎, 原子彈計畫主持人)。

op·pi·dan ['ɑpɪdən; 'ɔpidən] *adj.* 都市的;城鎮的。—*n.* ①居於市鎮的人;市民。②(英國 Eton 學院)食宿於校外市鎮中之學生。

***op·po·nent** [ə'ponənt; ə'pounənt] *n.* 對手;敵手;反對者。He defeated his *opponent* in the election. 他在選舉中擊敗了對手。—*adj.* ①相向的;對面的。②敵對的;反對的。③(肌肉)將各部分連在一起的。

op·por·tune [,ɑpɚ'tjun; 'ɔpətju:n] *adj.* 合時宜的;恰逢其時的;及時的。

op·por·tun·ism [,ɑpɚ'tjunɪzəm; 'ɔpətju:nizəm] *n.* 機會主義。

op·por·tun·ist [,ɑpɚ'tjunɪst; 'ɔpətju:nist] *n.* 機會主義者;投機者。—**ic,** *adj.* —**i·cal·ly,** *adv.*

‡**op·por·tu·ni·ty** [,ɑpɚ'tjunətɪ; ,ɔpə'tju:niti, -'tjun, -nət-, -'tju:n̩ti] *n., pl.* **-ties.** 機會;時機。Such *opportunities* should not be missed. 這種機會不應失去。

op·pos·a·bil·i·ty [ə,pozə'bɪlətɪ; ə,pouzə'biliti] *n.* 可對立;可反對;可反抗。

op·pos·a·ble [ə'pozəbl̩; ə'pouzəbl] *adj.* ①可使對立的; 可使與他物相對向的。②可反對(反抗)的。

‡**op·pose** [ə'poz; ə'pouz, ɔ'p-] *v.,* **-posed, -pos·ing.** —*v.t.* ①反對;反抗。A swamp *opposed* the advance of the army. 一沼澤之地阻止了軍隊之前進。②以…對抗。He *opposed* his arms to the blow. 他以兩臂遮擋打擊。③相對;相反。Love is *opposed* to hate. 愛與恨相對。④向。⑤使相對;使相向。The thumb can be *opposed* to any of the fingers. 大姆指能和任何一個指頭對起來。—*v.i.* 採取反對行爲。—**op·pos·er,** *n.*

op·posed [ə'pozd; ə'pouzd] *adj.* ①相向的;相對的。②對立的;反對的;對抗的;敵對的〖to〗。

op·pose·less [ə'pozlɪs; ə'pouzlis] *adj.* 〖罕〗難抵抗的;不可抵抗的(=irresistible).

‡**op·po·site** ['ɑpəzɪt; 'ɔpəzit, -əsit] *adj.* ①相對的;對立的。His house is *opposite* to mine. 他的房子與我的相對。②相反的; 反對的。They are walking in *opposite* ways. 他們正相背而行。③〖植物〗對生的。④〖數學〗對的。⑤〖廢〗相反的;有害的。***opposite number*** 處於相等或相當職位等之人。—*n.* ①相反的人或物;相對的人或物。"High" is the *opposite* of "low". "高"是 "低" 的相反字。②反意語;對語。③〖古〗敵手;對手。—*prep.* 在…對面。—*adv.* 在對側地。—**ly,** *adv.* —**ness,** *n.*

***op·po·si·tion** [,ɑpə'zɪʃən; ,ɔpə'ziʃən, -pou'z-] *n.* ①反對;抵抗。The mob offered *opposition* to the police. 暴徒反抗警察。②反對黨。The Socialist Party was in *opposition*. 社會黨爲(議會中的)反對黨。③對立;對照。It was made bright by *opposition* to blue. 與藍色相襯, 則更鮮明。④〖邏輯〗反對法; 對當法; 對照法。⑤〖天文〗衝(兩天體經線相距180°之地位)。

***op·press** [ə'prɛs; ə'pres, ɔ'p-] *v.t.* ①壓迫;壓制。A good ruler will not *oppress* the poor. 好的統治者不會壓迫貧民。②壓抑;使如負重荷。③〖古〗鎮壓。④〖廢〗壓破;壓碎。—**i·ble,** *adj.*

***op·pres·sion** [ə'prɛʃən; ə'preʃən, ɔ'p-] *n.* ①抑壓;鬱悶。Tears will relieve the *oppression* of the heart. 流淚能舒心頭之鬱悶。②被壓迫;抑壓之情況。They fought against *oppression*. 他們爲反壓迫而戰。③壓迫;高壓手段。

op·pres·sive [ə'prɛsɪv; ə'presiv] *adj.* ①暴戾的;嚴苛的;壓迫的。②難忍的;抑鬱的。

op·pres·sor [ə'prɛsɚ; ə'presə] *n.* 壓迫者;暴虐者。

op·pro·bri·ous [ə'probrɪəs; ə'proubriəs] *adj.* ①可恥的; 可卑的; 不體面的。②表示侮辱、羞辱或凌辱的。

op·pro·bri·um [ə'probrɪəm; ə'proubriəm] *n.* ①恥辱;羞辱;不名譽。②非難;誹謗。③不名譽的事或人。

op·pugn [ə'pjun; ɔ'pju:n] *v.t.* 非難;根據論據推理以抨擊;駁斥;反駁。

OPS, O.P.S. Office of Price Stabilization.

op·son·ic [ɑp'sɑnɪk; ɔp'sɔnik] *adj.* 〖細菌〗噬菌素的;調理素的。

op·so·nin ['ɑpsənɪn; 'ɔpsənin] *n.* 〖細菌〗噬菌素; 調理素(血液中能減弱細菌力量以使白血球易於吞噬之一種物質)。

opt [ɑpt; ɔpt] *v.i.* 選擇。***opt for*** 選擇;贊成。***opt out*** 撤退;退出;辭職。

opt. ①optative. ②optical. ③optician. ④optics. ⑤optional.

op·ta·tive ['ɑptətɪv; 'ɔptətiv, ɔp'teitiv] *adj.* 表願望的; 表祈願的。—*n.* 祈願語態;祈願語態之動詞。—**ly,** *adv.*

op·tic ['ɑptɪk; 'ɔptik] *adj.* 眼睛的; 視覺的。—*n.* 〖俗〗眼。

op·ti·cal ['ɑptɪkl̩; 'ɔptikəl] *adj.* ①眼的;視覺的。②幫助視力的。③光學的。

op·ti·cian [ɑp'tɪʃən; ɔp'tiʃən] *n.* 眼鏡和光學儀器製造者;眼鏡或光學儀器販賣商。

op·tics ['ɑptɪks; 'ɔptiks] *n.* 〖物理〗(作 *sing.* 解)光學。

op·ti·mal ['ɑptəməl; 'ɔptiməl] *adj.* 最好的;最理想的。

op·ti·me ['ɑptə,mi; 'ɔptimi] *n.* 〖英〗(Cambridge 大學數學優等畢業考試)得第二名或第三名者。

***op·ti·mism** ['ɑptə,mɪzəm; 'ɔptimizəm] *n.* ①樂觀。②樂觀主義。

op·ti·mist ['ɑptəmɪst; 'ɔptimist] *n.* 樂觀者;樂觀主義者。

op·ti·mis·tic [,ɑptə'mɪstɪk; ,ɔpti'mistik] *adj.* ①樂觀的。②樂觀主義的。

op·ti·mis·ti·cal [,ɑptə'mɪstɪkl̩; ,ɔpti'mistikəl] *adj.* =**optimistic.** —**ly,** *adv.*

op·ti·mize ['ɑptə,maɪz; 'ɔptimaiz] *v.,* **-mized, -miz·ing.** —*v.i.* 樂觀;表示樂觀。—*v.t.* 作充分之運用;發展至極限;使發揮最大作用。—**op·ti·mi·za·tion,** *n.*

op·ti·mum ['ɑptəməm; 'ɔptiməm] *n., pl.* **-ma** [-mə; -mə], **-mums,** *adj.* —*n.* 〖生物〗(對於生長、繁殖等之溫度、光、濕氣、食物等之)最宜條件。—*adj.* 最適宜的;最佳條件的。

op·tion ['ɑpʃən; 'ɔpʃən] *n.* ①選擇權;選擇自由。②選擇之事物; 可挑選之事物。③

在某一約定期內按某一價格買賣某物品之權。—*v.t.* 獲得或給予在一定期限內以某價格購買某種物品之權。

op·tion·al [ˈɑpʃənl; ˈɔpʃənl] *adj.* 可選擇的;隨意的。

op·tom·e·ter [ɑpˈtɑmətə; ɔpˈtɔmitə] *n.* 〖醫〗視力檢定器;視力計。

op·tom·e·trist [ɑpˈtɑmətrɪst; ɔpˈtɔmitrist] *n.* 驗光醫師;配鏡師。

op·tom·e·try [ɑpˈtɑmətrɪ; ɔpˈtɔmitri] *n.* 視力檢定;驗光。

op·u·lence [ˈɑpjələns; ˈɔpjuləns] *n.* ①財富。②豐饒;豐富。(亦作 **opulency**)

op·u·lent [ˈɑpjələnt; ˈɔpjulənt] *adj.* ①富有的;富裕的。②華麗的;奢侈的;昂貴的。③豐富的;富饒的。—**ly,** *adv.*

o·pus [ˈopəs; ˈoupəs] *n., pl.* **op·er·a, o·pus·es.** ①藝術作品;著作。②樂曲(常縮寫為 op., 其後注以編號, 以示寫作或出版之先後次序)。③〖俗〗廣播劇;電視劇;電影。***opus magnum*** (or ***magnum opus***) 傑作;鉅著。

o·pus·cu·lum [oˈpʌskjuləm; ouˈpʌskjuləm] *n., pl.* **-la** [-lə; -lə]. 小品;小曲。(亦作 **opuscule**)

‡**or**[1] [ɔr, ɚ; ɔ:, ə] *conj.* ①抑;或。Is it sweet *or* sour? 它是甜的還是酸的? ②否則;不然。Put on your overcoat, *or* you will catch cold. 穿上你的大衣, 否則你會着涼。③卽;就是。This is the end *or* last part. 此卽最後部分。④表不定或含混。I put it in the cupboard *or* somewhere. 我大概是把它放在食櫥裏了。⑤用以修改或改換前述語。His autobiography, *or* rather memoirs, is ready for publication. 他的自傳, 或者說是回憶錄, 卽可出版了。***either...or...*** 或…或…。You must *either* tell the truth *or* say nothing. 你須實言, 不然便勿開口。***or else*** (=if not) 否則。Hurry up *or else* you'll be late. 快些, 否則你會晚了。***or so*** 大約 (=about). I want a hundred *or so.* 我要一百左右。***whether...or...*** 究…抑…;不論…或…。I don't know *whether* he is here *or* not. 我不知道他是否在這裏。

or[2] *n.* 〖紋章〗金黃色;黃色。

-or 〖字尾〗①表"動作、狀態、性質"之義, 如: favor, honor. (英國拼法常作 -our)②表"…者;…的人或物;行爲者"之義, 如: inventor, tractor.

***or·a·cle** [ˈɔrəkḷ; ˈɔrəkl, -rik-] *n.* ①神諭。The ancient *oracles* were often vague and equivocal. 古代的神諭常是意義模糊而模稜兩可的。②發布神諭的地方(Delphi 卽是著名的發布神諭的地方)。③代神發布神諭的祭師。④被認爲是可靠的指導的東西。⑤聰明人;賢人;哲人。⑥極聰明之回答。⑦先知。⑧啓示。⑨(*pl.*) 聖經。⑩內殿。

oracle bone 甲骨。*oracle bone* inscriptions. 甲骨文。

o·rac·u·lar [ɔˈrækjələ; ɔˈrækjulə] *adj.* ①神諭的;似神諭的。②意義含混的;難解的。③聰明的。—**ly,** *adv.* —**i·ty,** —**ness,** *n.*

***o·ral** [ˈorəl, ˈɔrəl; ˈɔ:rəl] *adj.* ①口頭的;口述的。the *oral* method. 口授教學法。②口的。*oral* contraceptives. 口服避孕藥。the *oral* cavity. 口腔。③〖語音〗口音的(非鼻音的)。—*n.* ①(大學的)口試(尤指爲取得學位的)。②(*pl.*) 取得博士學位前之一連串口試。—**ly,** *adv.*

o·rang [oˈræŋ; ˈɔ:rəŋ, ɔ:ˈræŋ] *n.* = **orang-utan.**

‡**or·ange** [ˈɔrɪndʒ; ˈɔrindʒ] *n.* ①橘;柑;橙。②橘、柑或橙樹。③橘色;橙黃色。—*adj.* ①橘、柑或橙的。②橘、柑或橙色的。

or·ange·ade [ˌɔrɪndʒˈed; ˈɔrindʒˈeid] *n.* 橘子水。

orange blossom ①橘花(新娘多佩於頭髮上以爲純潔之象徵)。②加冰的鷄尾酒。

orange fin 〖英〗鱒的幼魚。

Or·ange·ism [ˈɔrɪndʒɪzəm; ˈɔrindʒizm] *n.* (北愛爾蘭之)奧蘭治黨之主義;新教與英國王權擁護主義(運動)。—**Or·ange·ist,** *n.*

Or·ange·man [ˈɔrɪndʒmən; ˈɔrindʒmən] *n., pl.* **-men.** 奧蘭治黨員(1795年成立於北愛爾蘭之祕密社團黨員)。

or·ange·ry [ˈɔrɪndʒrɪ; ˈɔrindʒəri] *n., pl.* **-ries.** 橘園;栽培橘樹之溫室。

orange tip 蝶類的一種。

or·ange·wood [ˈɔrɪndʒˌwud; ˈɔrindʒwud] *n.* 橙木。—*adj.* 橙木的。

o·rang-u·tan [oˈræŋuˌtæn; ˈɔ:rəŋˈu:tæn] *n.* 婆羅洲與蘇門答臘的巨猿, 長肢棕毛, 在林間食果實樹葉。(亦作 **orangutan, orangutang, orang-outang, orang**)

o·rate [ˈoret; ɔ:ˈreit] *v.t. & v.i.,* **o·rat·ed, o·rat·ing.** 演說;演講;用演說腔調說。

o·ra·tion [oˈreʃən; ɔ:ˈreiʃən] *n.* 講演;演說。

***or·a·tor** [ˈɔrətɚ, ˈɑrətɚ; ˈɔrətə, -rit-] *n.* ①演說者;講演者。②演說家。—**like,** *adj.* —**ship,** *n.*

or·a·to·ri·al [ˌɔrəˈtorɪəl; ˌɔrəˈtɔriəl] *adj.* ①演說家的;適合於演說家的。②神劇的。—**ly,** *adv.*

or·a·tor·i·cal [ˌɔrəˈtɔrɪkḷ; ˌɔrəˈtɔrikəl] *adj.* ①演說的;演說家的;演說術的。②好雄辯的。—**ly,** *adv.*

or·a·to·ri·o [ˌɔrəˈtorɪo; ˌɔrəˈtɔ:riou] *n., pl.* **-ri·os.** 神劇。

or·a·to·ry[1] [ˈɔrəˌtorɪ; ˈɔrətəri] *n.* ①演說術。②雄辯術;修辭。

or·a·to·ry[2] *n., pl.* **-ries.** 〖宗教〗禱告所;小禮拜堂。

orb [ɔrb; ɔ:b] *n.* ①球。②日;月;星。③地球;世界。④〖廢〗地球、行星等運行的軌道。⑤〖詩〗眼球;眼睛。⑥(象徵王權的)寶球。—*v.t.* ①使成球形;弄圓。②〖詩〗包圍;圍;捲。—*v.i.* ①依軌道運行。②〖詩〗成球形。—**less,** *adj.* —**like,** *adj.*

or·bic·u·lar [ɔrˈbɪkjələ; ɔ:ˈbikjulə] *adj.* ①球狀的;圓形的。②圓滿的。—**i·ty,** —**ness,** *n.* —**ly,** *adv.*

***or·bit** [ˈɔrbɪt; ˈɔ:bit] *n.* ①天體或人造衞星繞行的軌道。②太陽系行星之軌道。③生活的常軌;活動或經驗的範圍。④〖解剖〗眼窠;眼眶。⑤〖動物〗鳥類的眼瞼。⑥勢力範圍。—*v.t.* ①繞軌道而行。The earth *orbits* the sun once every 365.25 days. 地球每365.25天繞太陽軌道一周。②將人造衞星送入軌道。They *orbited* three satellites in a single month. 他們在一個月之內將三枚人造衞星射入軌道。—*v.i.* ①繞軌道而行。The satellite itself will *orbit* around the earth for a period of days. 衞星本身將繞地球軌道運行數日之久。②(人造衞星等)達到繞軌道運行所需的速度;到達軌道。—**ar·y,** *adj.*

or·bit·al [ˈɔrbɪtḷ; ˈɔ:bitl] *adj.* ①〖解剖〗眼窠的;眼眶的。②〖動物〗眼瞼的。③〖天文〗軌道的。

or·bit·er [ˈɔrbɪtɚ; ˈɔ:bitə] *n.* 繞軌道運行之物。

Or·ca·di·an [ɔrˈkedɪən; ɔ:ˈkeidiən] *adj., n.* Orkney 羣島的(人)。

***or·chard** [ˈɔrtʃɚd; ˈɔ:tʃəd] *n.* ①果園。②果樹。

or·chard·ist [ˈɔrtʃɚdɪst; ˈɔ:tʃədist] *n.* 經營果園者。

***or·ches·tra** [ˈɔrkɪstrə; ˈɔːkistrə, -kes-] *n.* ①管絃樂隊。②管絃樂用的諸樂器。③(劇院中)樂隊演奏處(劇臺正前處)。④劇場之前廳。—*adj.* 管絃樂隊的。—**less,** *adj.*

or·ches·tral [ɔrˈkɛstrəl; ɔːˈkestrəl] *adj.* 管絃樂隊的;爲管絃樂隊而作的;管絃樂隊所演奏的。

or·ches·trate [ˈɔrkɪsˌtret; ˈɔːkistreit] *v.t. & v.i.,* **-trat·ed, -trat·ing.** ①改編爲管絃樂;作管絃樂曲。②作調和的組合或安排;配合。—**or·ches·tra·tion,** *n.*

or·ches·tri·na [ˌɔrkɛsˈtrinə; ˌɔːkesˈtriːnə] *n.* (發音似管絃樂之)一種自動風琴。(亦作 **orchestrion**)

or·chid [ˈɔrkɪd; ˈɔːkid] *n.* ①蘭花。②蘭。③淡紫色。—*adj.* 淡紫色的。

or·chi·da·ceous [ˌɔrkɪˈdeʃəs; ˌɔːkiˈdeiʃəs] *adj.* ①〖植物〗蘭科的。②似蘭花的。

or·chid·ist [ˈɔrkɪdɪst; ˈɔːkidist] *n.* 蘭花栽培者;藝蘭者。

or·chil [ˈɔrkəl, -tʃəl; ˈɔːtʃil] *n.* =**archil.**

Or·chis [ˈɔrkɪs; ˈɔːkis] *n.* 〖植物〗①蘭屬。②(o-)蘭;蘭屬植物。

or·chi·tis [ɔrˈkaɪtɪs; ɔːˈkaitis] *n.* 〖醫〗睪丸炎。(亦作 **orchiditis**) —**or·chit·ic,** *adj.*

ord. ①ordained. ②order. ③ordinal. ④ordinance. ⑤ordinary. ⑥ordnance.

***or·dain** [ɔrˈden; ɔːˈdein] *v.t.* ①註定;規定。The law *ordains* that the murderers shall be hanged. 法律規定殺人者受絞刑。②任命(聖職)。He was *ordained* priest. 他被任命爲牧師。—*v.i.* ①任命;命令。Thus do the gods *ordain*. 如此諸神註定一切。②〖廢〗挑選或指派(某人)就職。

***or·deal** [ɔrˈdil; ɔːˈdiːl] *n.* ①神裁判法(古時的一種判罪法,使被告抱灼燒之物或服毒,以視其結果,而認爲係神之判斷)。②嚴酷之考驗;痛苦的經驗。

:or·der [ˈɔrdɚ; ˈɔːdə] *n.* ①次序;順序。②常態;有次序的狀態。Put a room in *order*. 整理房間。③情況;情形;狀態。④常則;定則。⑤制度;規則;秩序。to keep *order*. 遵守規則。⑥命令。Soldiers must obey *orders*. 軍人須服從命令。⑦匯票。⑧定貨單;定貨。I delivered her grocery *order*. 我把她所定的雜貨送去。⑨種類。He has ability of high *order*. 他有優等的才幹。⑩階級;等級。⑪目的(=purpose or intention). ⑫柱式;建築的柱式。⑬會議程序;規程。⑭訓令;指示。⑮〖生物〗目;族。⑯牧師等的地位或階級;神職;神職的任命。the *order* of bishops. 主教們的職位。⑰分類;整頓;整理。⑱教團;修道會;(中世紀)騎士團。the Franciscan *order*. 聖方濟會。⑲結社;公會。the *Order* of Masons. 共濟會。⑳勳位;勳章。the *Order* of the Garter. 英國最高勳位。㉑儀式;典禮。㉒(餐館中的)一客(飯菜)。***a large*** (or ***tall***) ***order*** 困難之事;棘手之事。***be made to order*** 定做的。*Are* your clothes *made to order* or ready made? 你的衣服是定做的還是買現成的? ***by order*** 奉命令。***call to order*** 要求安靜(開始開會);宣布開會。***in order*** **a.** 整齊的;在良好的狀況中。Everything is *in order* for the departure. 出發準備一切就緒。**b.** 工作正常的。**c.** 遵守會議程序的。Questions from the floor are now *in order*. 議員發問現在可以開始了。**d.** 合適的;適宜的。***in order of*** 按照…排列。***in orders*** 任神職。***in order that*** 俾使;爲了(=so that). ***in order to*** (***do something***) 俾能;欲…。*In order to* catch the train, he hurried through his work. 爲了要趕火車,他匆匆辦完了他的工作。***in short order*** 快地;迅速地。He hurried away and returned *in short order*. 他匆匆離開,又迅速地回來。***on order*** 已定購(貨尚未到)。The book is *on order*. 此書已定購。***on the order of*** 與…相似;與…相同。***out of order*** **a.** 壞了。We could not use the telephone because it was *out of order*. 我們不能用這電話,因爲它壞了。**b.** 不適合;不宜。His remark was certainly *out of order*. 他的話極不得體。**c.** 違反會議規程。The chairman told him that he was *out of order*. 主席告訴他說他已違反了議事規程。***take orders*** 任神職。—*v.t.* ①整頓;整理。②命令;指令。The doctor *ordered* me to stay in bed. 醫生囑我不要起床。③向商店等定(貨)。I have *ordered* some new clothes. 我曾定購一些新衣。We *ordered* two steaks. 我們點了兩道牛排。④決定;評定。God has *ordered* death as our fate. 上帝使我們終有一死。⑤任神職。—*v.i.* ①命令;下令。②定貨。Please *order* for me. 請替我點菜。***order about*** (or ***around***) 驅使。***order from*** 向…定購。

order arms 〖軍〗①持槍立正之姿勢。②持槍(口令)!

order book ①〖商〗定貨簿。②〖軍〗命令簿。

order form (or **blank**) 定貨單。

or·der·ly [ˈɔrdɚlɪ; ˈɔːdəli] *adj., adv., n., pl.* **-lies.** —*adj.* ①有順序的;有秩序的。an *orderly* room. 整齊的屋子。②守秩序的。an *orderly* crowd. 守秩序的羣衆。③傳令的;值班的。—*adv.* ①根據規定地。②有條不紊地。We will do this *orderly*. 我們將有條不紊地做這件事。—*n.* ①傳令兵。②醫院侍者。—**or·der·li·ness,** *n.*

orderly officer 〖軍〗①值日官。②〖英〗傳令兵。

order port 商船停泊以裝卸貨物之港口。

***or·di·nal** [ˈɔrdṇəl; ˈɔːdinl] *adj.* ①次序的;順序的。②〖生物〗目的;族的。—*n.* ①序數(=ordinal number). ②〖宗教〗(天主教之)彌撒書;(基督教之)禮拜儀式書。

or·di·nance [ˈɔrdṇəns; ˈɔːdinəns] *n.* ①法令;條例。a Government *ordinance*. 政府法令。②宗教儀式;聖事;聖餐。③習慣;慣例;習俗。

***or·di·nar·i·ly** [ˈɔrdṇˌɛrɪlɪ; ˈɔːdnrili] *adv.* ①正常地;規律地。②平常地。I breakfast *ordinarily* at half past seven. 我平常七點半吃早餐。

:or·di·nar·y [ˈɔrdṇˌɛrɪ; ˈɔːdnri, -dinər-] *adj., n., pl.* **-nar·ies.** —*adj.* ①通常的;普通的;正常的。in *ordinary* dress. 着平常之衣服。②中下等的;平凡的。an *ordinary* speaker. 一位平凡的演說者。③(官員之)正規的;編制內的。④(司法之)直接的(非授權的)。⑤本身有權的。***in an ordinary way*** 就通常之情形;按常例。—*n.* ①客飯。②飯店;飯店的餐廳。③裁判官;宗教裁判官。④(天主教的)彌撒經典;彌撒規程。⑤前輪大後輪小的舊式脚踏車。***in ordinary*** 正規服務的。a physician *in ordinary* to the king. 御醫。***out of the ordinary*** 例外的;特殊的;罕有的。

or·di·nate [ˈɔrdṇˌet; ˈɔːdṇit] *n.* 〖數學〗縱座標。

or·di·na·tion [ˌɔrdṇˈeʃən; ˌɔːdiˈneiʃən] *n.* ①聖職之任命;任命聖職之儀式。②被任命任聖職。③法令之頒布。④整頓;排列。

or·di·nee [ˌɔrdəˈni; ˌɔːdiˈniː] *n.* 新任之教會執事。

ord·nance [ˈɔrdnəns; ˈɔːdnəns] *n.* ①砲;軍械之集合稱。②兵工。

Or·do·vi·cian [ˌɔrdəˈvɪʃən; ˌɔːdəˈviʃən] *adj.* 〖地質〗(古生代之)奧陶紀的;奧陶系的。the *Ordovician* period (system). 奧陶紀(系)。—*n.* 奧陶紀(系)。

or·dure [ˈɔrdʒə, -djur; ˈɔːdjuə] *n.* ①排泄物;糞;肥料。②猥褻;下流的言語。

ore** [or, ɔr; ɔː, ɔə] *n.* 含有金屬的岩石;礦沙。iron *ore.* 鐵礦。be in ore*** 含有礦物。

Ore(g). Oregon.

o·re·ad [ˈorɪˌæd; ˈɔːriæd] *n.* 〖希臘、羅馬神話〗山之女神(=mountain nymph).

ore carrier 運礦砂之貨船。

o·rec·tic [oˈrɛktɪk; ouˈrektik] *adj.* ①〖哲學〗慾望的;願望的。②食慾的。

Or·e·gon [ˈɑrɪˌgɑn; ˈɔrigən] *n.* 俄勒岡(美國太平洋沿岸之一州, 首府 爲 Salem).

Or·e·go·ni·an [ˌɔrɪˈgonɪən; ˌɔriˈgouniən] *n.* ①美國俄勒岡州之人或居民。②居於美國西北部之一族印第安人。—*adj.* 俄勒岡州的。

ore tanker 爲裝運礦石或石油而設計的貨輪。

org. ①organ. ②organic. ③organism. ④organist. ⑤organized.

***or·gan** [ˈɔrgən; ˈɔːgən] *n.* ①器官。the *organs* of speech. 發音器官(舌、牙、唇等)。②機關;工具。A court is one of the chief *organs* of government. 法院爲政府主要機關之一。③(政黨發表意見之)機關報;機關雜誌。④風琴。to play an *organ.* 彈風琴。⑤手風琴;口琴;電風琴;有笛風琴。

or·gan·dy, or·gan·die [ˈɔrgəndɪ; ˈɔːgəndi] *n., pl.* **-dies.** 細薄而硬之棉織品。

organ grinder 於街頭搖奏手風琴者。

***or·gan·ic** [ɔrˈgænɪk; ɔːˈgænik] *adj.* ①器官的。②有機的;含炭的。③有組織的。④有機體的;有機物的。*organic* life. 有機的生命。⑤生來的;固有的。⑥從有機觀點來看或解釋的。⑦用有機肥料而生長的。⑧組織上的;構造上的;本身的;根本的。The Constitution is the *organic* law. 憲法是根本大法。—*n.* 有機物。**—al·ly,** *adv.*

***or·gan·ism** [ˈɔrgənˌɪzəm; ˈɔːgənizəm] *n.* ①生物;有機體。②社會組織;機關。③細小之動植物。**—ic, —al,** *adj.* **—i·cal·ly,** *adv.*

or·gan·ist [ˈɔrgənɪst; ˈɔːgənist] *n.* 風琴彈奏者。

or·gan·iz·a·ble [ˈɔrgənˌaɪzəbl; ˈɔːgənaizəbl] *adj.* 可組織的;可變爲有機體的。**—or·gan·iz·a·bil·i·ty,** *n.*

‡**or·gan·i·za·tion** [ˌɔrgənəˈzeʃən; ˌɔːgənaiˈzeiʃən] *n.* ①組織;構造。He is engaged in the *organization* of a new club. 他正從事於組織一個新社團的工作。②機構;結構。The human body has a very complex *organization.* 人體有很複雜的結構。③團體;組織體。Churches, clubs, and political parties are *organizations.* 教堂、會社及政黨都是團體組織。④有機體。**—al,** *adj.* **—al·ly,** *adv.*

or·gan·i·za·tion·ist [ˌɔrgənəˈzeʃənɪst; ˌɔːgənaiˈzeiʃənist] *n.* 組織之提倡者;善於組織者。

***or·gan·ize** [ˈɔrgənˌaɪz; ˈɔːgənaiz] *v.,* **-ized, -iz·ing.** —*v.t.* ①組織。to *organize* an army. 組織一軍隊。②組成工會。③給與器官;給與生機。④〖俚〗偷竊;說服(某人)使拿出(物品)。—*v.i.* ①團結;成立組織。②成爲有機體;成爲有生命之組織。

or·gan·iz·er [ˈɔrgənˌaɪzə; ˈɔːgənaizə] *n.* ①組織者(尤指組織工人使加入工會者)。②整理文件、檔案的夾子。③組織導體。

organ loft (教堂中)奏風琴者之席位。

or·ga·non [ˈɔrgəˌnɑn; ˈɔːgənɔn] *n., pl.* **-na** [-nə; -nə], **-nons.** ①求知之工具。②〖哲學〗(科學研究之)原則;研究法;思考法;推理法。③(O-) Aristotle 之理則學。

or·ga·num [ˈɔrgənəm; ˈɔːgənəm] *n., pl.* **-na** [-nə; -nə], **-nums.** ①=**organon.** ②〖音樂〗〖古〗和聲的重唱(原旋律加四度、五度、八度等音程之重唱者);(此種)聲部重唱方法。

or·gan·zine [ˈɔrgənˌzin; ˈɔːgənziːn] *n.* 紗絲(主用於上等織物之經絲)。

or·gasm [ˈɔrgæzəm; ˈɔːgæzəm] *n.* ①〖生理〗(性交時)興奮之頂點;高潮。②(感情之)極度興奮;爆發;激烈。

or·gi·as·tic [ˌɔrdʒɪˈæstɪk; ˌɔːdʒiˈæstik] *adj.* ①(祭酒神 Dionysus 或 Bacchus 之)祕密儀式的;似酒神祭禮的。②狂飲的;縱飲的;鬧酒的。③狂歡的。

or·gy [ˈɔrdʒɪ; ˈɔːdʒi] *n., pl.* **-gies.** ①狂飲;狂飲作樂。②恣縱;恣意。③(*pl.*)古希臘、羅馬祭酒神的祕密儀式。(亦作 **orgie**)

o·ri·el [ˈorɪəl, ˈɔ-; ˈɔːriəl] *n.* 〖建築〗凸出於壁外之窗。

o·ri·ent** [*v.* ˈorɪˌɛnt; ˈɔːrient *n.* ˈorɪˌɛnt, -ənt; ˈɔːriənt *adj.* ˈorɪənt; ˈɔːriənt] *v.t.* ①妥定位置;定方位。②使向東。③使適應(環境)。to *orient* one's ideas to new conditions. 使某人的觀念適應新的狀況。④使熟悉新環境、情勢等。⑤使向確定之方向;朝;向。The building is *oriented* north and south. 這建築物是坐南向北。⑥定向;決定…之方向。—*v.i.* 朝向東(或其他方向)。—*n.* ①東方;東。②〖珠寶〗**a.** 東方眞珠。**b.** 眞珠的光澤。the Orient*** 東方諸國;亞洲(特指遠東)。—*adj.* ①〖詩〗東方的。②上升的。③燦爛的;光耀的。

***O·ri·en·tal** [ˌorɪˈɛntl; ˌɔːriˈentl] *adj.* ①東方諸國的;亞洲的。②(o-)東的;東方的。③〖珠寶〗**a.** 東方出產的(珠寶等)。**b.** (o-)燦爛的。—*n.* ①東方人;亞洲人。Both the Chinese and the Koreans are *Orientals.* 中國人與韓國人都是東方人。②受過東方文化薰陶的人。**—ly,** *adv.*

O·ri·en·tal·ism [ˌorɪˈɛntl̩ˌɪzəm; ˌɔːriˈentəlizəm] *n.* (常 o-)①東方之特性;東方之風俗習慣;東方文化。②東方文化之研究。

O·ri·en·tal·ist, o·ri·en·tal·ist [ˌorɪˈɛntlɪst; ˌɔːriˈentəlist] *n.* 精通東方語言、文學、歷史等的人;東方學者;東方通。

O·ri·en·tal·ize [ˌorɪˈɛntl̩ˌaɪz; ˌɔːriˈentəlaiz] *v.t. & v.i.,* **-ized, -iz·ing.** (常 o-)(使)東方化;(使)習慣於東方的風俗。**—O·ri·en·tal·i·za·tion,** *n.*

o·ri·en·tate [ˈorɪɛnˌtet; ˈɔːrienteit] *v.,* **-tat·ed, -tat·ing.** —*v.t.* ①使向東;使成定向。②定(地圖、磁石等)之方位。③使適應新環境。He *orientated* himself on coming to a new city. 他初到一新城市, 便使自己適應新環境。④建立友誼或關係。—*v.i.* ①向東;朝東;朝某一特定方向。②適應新環境。

o·ri·en·ta·tion [ˌorɪɛnˈteʃən; ˌɔːrienˈteiʃən] *n.* ①東向;使向東;定方位。②方向;定位。③〖心理〗認識環境以確定其與自身關係之能力。④〖化〗配向;定位。⑤(動物如鴿等)歸巢之本能。⑥發展或演變之方向。**—o·ri·en·ta·tive,** *adj.*

o·ri·en·teer·ing [ˌorɪənˈtɪrɪŋ; ˌɔːriənˈtiəriŋ] *n.* 越野識圖比賽(與賽者携帶地圖或羅盤前進)。「洞。—**or·i·fi·cial,** *adj.*

or·i·fice [ˈɔrəfɪs, ˈɑr–; ˈɔrifis] *n.* 口;孔;

or·i·flamme [ˈɔrəˌflæm, ˈɑr–; ˈɔriflæm] *n.* ①古代法國國王之親征旗。②王旗;軍旗。

orig. ①origin. ②original(ly). ③originated.

o·ri·ga·mi [ˌɔrəˈgɑmɪ; ˌɔːrəˈgɑːmi]〖日〗*n.* ①折紙;折紙的藝術。②折紙而成之物。

***or·i·gin** [ˈɔrədʒɪn, ˈɑr–; ˈɔridʒin] *n.* ①起源;開端;原始。②出身。③〖數學〗原點。

‡o·rig·i·nal [əˈrɪdʒənḷ; əˈridʒənl] *adj.* ①最初的; 最早的。The *original* plan was afterwards changed. 最初的計畫後來改變了。②新的;新奇的;新穎的。③有創作性的。④獨創的; 不模仿的; 不剽竊的。⑤原作的;原文的。—*n.* ①原物;原作品。This is not the *original*; it's only a copy. 這不是原作品,祇是仿造品。②原文。③怪人;畸人。④起源;原始。⑤〖古〗作者。

***o·rig·i·nal·i·ty** [əˌrɪdʒəˈnælətɪ; əˌridʒiˈnæliti] *n., pl.* **-ties.** ①創作力;獨創力。His work does not show much *originality*. 他的作品缺少創作力。②新鮮; 新穎。③本原;原始;固有。

***o·rig·i·nal·ly** [əˈrɪdʒənḷɪ; əˈridʒṇəli] *adv.* ①最初;自初。a plant *originally* African. 本來產於非洲的一種植物。②原來;本來。③第一;首要。④獨創地; 奇特地。Gauguin paints *originally*. 法國畫家高更以獨創之風格作畫。⑤〖古〗原始地;生就地。

original sin (天主教之)原罪(因Adam和 Eve 墮落而起的人類固有的罪)。

***o·rig·i·nate** [əˈrɪdʒəˌnet; əˈridʒineit] *v.,* **-nat·ed, -nat·ing.** —*v.t.* 創始;發明;使產生。—*v.i.* ①開始;發起(起始於某地或某事多與 in 或 from 連用, 始於某人則用 with 或 from). The quarrel *originated* in a misunderstanding. 此口角由誤會而起。②起站於。This train *originates* at Taipei. 這部列車自臺北開出。—**o·rig·i·na·tor,** *n.*

o·rig·i·na·tion [əˌrɪdʒəˈneʃən; əˌridʒiˈneiʃən] *n.* ①開始; 開端; 草創; 創作; 發明。②起點;起因。③繁殖或發生之形態。

o·rig·i·na·tive [əˈrɪdʒəˌnetɪv; əˈridʒineitiv] *adj.* ①有創作力的;有發明之才能的;新奇的; 奇特的。②有生產能力的; 多產的。—**ly,** *adv.*

o·ri·ole [ˈorɪˌol; ˈɔːrioul] *n.* 金鶯。

O·ri·on [oˈraɪən; ouˈraiən] *n.*〖天文〗獵戶星座。***Orion's Belt*** 獵戶星座的三顆明星。

or·i·son [ˈɔrɪzṇ; ˈɔrizən] *n.*〖古〗祈禱。

Ork·ney Islands [ˈɔrknɪ~; ˈɔːkni~] 奧克尼羣島(在蘇格蘭之北,爲蘇格蘭之一郡)。

or·lon [ˈɔrlən; ˈɔːlən] *n.* ①奧龍(一種合成纖維)。②(O–)其商標名。

or·lop [ˈɔrlɑp; ˈɔːlɔp] *n.*〖航海〗(尤指軍艦之)最下甲板。(亦作 **orlop deck**)

Or·mazd [ˈɔrməzd; ˈɔːməzd] *n.*〖祆教〗善之神;光之神。

or·mo·lu [ˈɔrməˌlu; ˈɔːməluː] *n.* ①金色黃銅(銅、鋅、錫之合金)。②鍍金用之金箔。③鍍金物;鍍過金的金屬物。

***or·na·ment** [*n.* ˈɔrnəmənt; ˈɔːnəmənt *v.* ˈɔrnəˌmɛnt; ˈɔːnəment] *n.* ①美麗之物品;裝飾品。a room crowded with *ornaments*. 布滿了裝飾品的屋子。②增光彩之人或行動;增優美之性質。③裝飾。④教堂的禮拜用品(聖餐器皿、風琴、鐘等)。⑤〖音樂〗裝飾音。—*v.t.* 裝飾;修飾。to *ornament* a dress with lace. 用花邊裝飾衣服。—**er,** *n.*

***or·na·men·tal** [ˌɔrnəˈmɛntḷ; ˌɔːnəˈmentl] *adj.* ①裝飾品的。②用作裝飾品的。③裝飾的。—*n.* 裝飾物(尤指供裝飾用之植物)。—**i·ty,** *n.* —**ly,** *adv.*

or·na·men·tal·ist [ˌɔrnəˈmɛntḷɪst; ˌɔːnəˈmentlist] *n.* 裝飾家;設計家。

or·na·men·tal·ize [ˌɔrnəˈmɛntḷˌaɪz; ˌɔːnəˈmentəlaiz] *v.t.,* **-ized, -iz·ing.** 裝飾;布置。

or·na·men·ta·tion [ˌɔrnəmɛnˈteʃən; ˌɔːnəmenˈteiʃən] *n.* ①裝飾;修飾。②裝飾品(集合稱)。

or·na·ment·ed [ˈɔrnəˌmɛntɪd; ˈɔːnəmentid] *adj.*〖印刷〗花式字體的。

or·nate [ɔrˈnet; ɔːˈneit] *adj.* ①裝飾華麗的。②華麗不實的(文體);特別講究修辭的。—**ly,** *adv.* —**ness,** *n.*

or·ner·y [ˈɔrnərɪ; ˈɔːnəri] *adj.* ①〖方〗壞脾氣的;左性的。②頑固的。③低劣的;下等的。④平凡的;平常的。—**or·ner·i·ness,** *n.*

or·ni·tho·log·i·cal [ˌɔrnɪθəˈlɑdʒɪkḷ; ˌɔːniθəˈlɔdʒikl] *adj.* 鳥類學的。—**ly,** *adv.*

or·ni·thol·o·gist [ˌɔrnɪˈθɑlədʒɪst; ˌɔːniˈθɔlədʒist] *n.* 鳥類學家;禽學家。

or·ni·thol·o·gy [ˌɔrnəˈθɑlədʒɪ; ˌɔːniˈθɔlədʒi] *n.* ①鳥類學。②鳥類學之書籍。

or·ni·tho·rhyn·chus [ˌɔrnɪθəˈrɪŋkəs; ˌɔːniθəˈriŋkəs] *n.* =**duckbill.**

or·o·graph·ic [ˌɔrəˈgræfɪk; ˌɔrouˈgræfik] *adj.* 山嶽誌的; 山嶽論的。(亦作 **orographical**)

o·rog·ra·phy [əˈrɑgrəfɪ; ɔˈrɔgrəfi] *n.* 山嶽誌;山嶽論。

o·ro·ide [ˈoroˌaɪd, –ɪd; ˈourouaid, –id] *n.* 人造金(銅、鋅、錫之合金,爲金之代用品)。

o·rol·o·gy [oˈrɑlədʒɪ; ɔˈrɔlədʒi] *n.* 山嶽學。

o·rom·e·ter [oˈrɑmətɚ; ɔˈrɔmitə] *n.* 山嶽高度計;山嶽氣壓計。

o·ro·tund [ˈorəˌtʌnd; ˈɔroutʌnd] *adj.* ①響朗的;宏亮的(聲音)。②(文體或語調) 誇張的;誇大的。

***or·phan** [ˈɔrfən; ˈɔːfən] *n.* ①孤兒。a war *orphan*. 戰爭孤兒。②被母親遺棄或失去母親的小動物。③孤苦之人或無人支持之事物。—*adj.* ①孤兒的。an *orphan* asylum. 孤兒院。②無父的;無母的;無雙親的。—*v.t.* 使成孤兒。The war *orphaned* him at an early age. 戰爭使他在早年變成孤兒。

or·phan·age [ˈɔrfənɪdʒ; ˈɔːfənidʒ] *n.* ①孤兒院。②孤兒的身分;孤兒(集合稱)。

or·phan·hood [ˈɔrfənhʊd; ˈɔːfənhud] *n.* 孤兒之身分(狀態)。

Or·phe·an [ɔrˈfiən; ɔːˈfi(ː)ən] *adj.* 似 Orpheus (之音樂) 的;美妙的;好聽的; 令人恍惚的;迷人的。

Or·phe·us [ˈɔrfɪəs, –fjus; ˈɔːfjuːs] *n.*〖希臘神話〗阿波羅 (Apollo) 之子,喜彈琴,琴音美,獸類、木石均隨之,故爲音樂之鼻祖。

Or·phic [ˈɔrfɪk; ˈɔːfik] *adj.* ①Orpheus 的。②似 Orpheus 之音樂的;令人恍惚的。③傳以 Orpheus 爲開祖之 Dionysus 或 Bacchus 之崇拜的;其祕密教義或儀式的。④(o–)神祕的;玄奧的。—**al·ly,** *adv.*

or·pi·ment [ˈɔrpɪmənt; ˈɔːpimənt] *n.*〖礦〗雌黃 (As_2S_3)。

or·pin(e) [ˈɔrpɪn; ˈɔːpin] *n.*〖植物〗紫景天。

Or·ping·ton [ˈɔrpɪŋtən; ˈɔːpiŋtən] *n.*(英格蘭Kent郡西部奧屏頓村產之)一種雞。

or·rer·y [ˈɔrərɪ, ˈɑr–; ˈɔrəri] *n., pl.* **-ies.** 太陽系儀(說明太陽、行星、地球、月球等

之運動或位置用)。 「尾。(亦作 orrice)
or·ris¹ [ˈɔrɪs, ˈɑrɪs; ˈɔris] *n.* 〖植物〗鳶
or·ris² *n.* 金(銀)緞;金(銀)花邊。
or·ris·pow·der [ˈɑrɪsˌpaudə; ˈɔrisˌpaudə] *n.* 鳶尾根粉末(藥用或作香料用)。
or·ris·root [ˈɔrɪsˌrut; ˈɔrisruːt] *n.* 鳶尾根。
ort [ɔrt; ɔːt] *n.* (常 *pl.*)吃賸之食物。
or·thi·con [ˈɔrθɪˌkan; ˈɔːθikɔn] *n.* 〖電視〗①直線性光電發像管。②(O-) 其商標名。(亦作 **orthiconoscope**) 「音前作 **orth-**).
ortho- 〖字首〗表"直;正直;正確"之義(母
or·tho·chro·mat·ic [ˌɔrθəkrəˈmætɪk; ˈɔːθoukrouˈmætik] *adj.* ①〖照相〗現天然色濃淡的。②〖醫〗正常染色的。
or·tho·clase [ˈɔrθəˌkles; ˈɔːθəkleis] *n.* 〖礦〗正長石。
or·tho·don·tia [ˌɔrθəˈdɑnʃə; ˌɔːθəˈdɔnʃə] *n.* 畸齒矯正術;正牙學。 **—or·tho·don·tic,** *adj.* **—or·tho·don·tist,** *n.*
or·tho·don·tics [ˌɔrθəˈdɑntɪks; ˌɔːθəˈdɔntiks] *n.* (作 *sing.* 解) =**orthodontia.**
***or·tho·dox** [ˈɔrθəˌdɑks; ˈɔːθədɔks] *adj.* ①思想正確的;正統的(尤指宗教)。②傳統的;慣常的。**—ly,** *adv.* **—ness,** *n.*
orthodox sleep 無夢的睡眠。
or·tho·dox·y [ˈɔrθəˌdɑksɪ; ˈɔːθədɔksi] *n., pl.* **-dox·ies.** 正統學說之信守;正教;正統派之學說;正統。
or·tho·ep·ic [ˌɔrθəˈɛpɪk; ˌɔːθouˈepik] *adj.* 正音的; 正音法的; 正音學的。(亦作 **orthoëpic**)
or·tho·ep·i·cal [ˌɔrθəˈɛpɪkḷ; ˌɔːθouˈepikəl] *adj.* =**orthoepic.** (亦作 **orthoëpical**)
or·tho·ep·ist [ˈɔrθəˌɛpɪst; ˈɔːθouepist] *n.* 正音學者。(亦作 **orthoëpist**)
or·tho·e·py [ɔrˈθo·ɪpɪ; ˈɔːθouepi] *n.* ①正音法;正音學;發音學。②正音;標準音。
or·tho·gen·e·sis [ˌɔrθəˈdʒɛnəsɪs; ˌɔːθouˈdʒenisis] *n.* ①〖生物〗定向進化。②〖社會〗系統發生說。
or·thog·o·nal [ɔrˈθɑgənḷ; ɔːˈθɔgənḷ] *adj.* 〖幾何〗①直角的;正交的。②矩形的。
or·tho·graph·ic [ˌɔrθəˈgræfɪk; ˌɔːθəˈgræfik] *adj.* ①拼字法的; 拼字正確的。②〖幾何〗垂直線的; 直角的。(亦作 **orthographical**)
or·thog·ra·phist [ɔrˈθɑgrəfɪst; ɔːˈθɔgrəfist] *n.* 拼字學者;拼字正確的人。(亦作 **orthographer**)
or·thog·ra·phy [ɔrˈθɑgrəfɪ; ɔːˈθɔgrəfi] *n., pl.* **-phies.** ①正確拼字。②拼字法;拼字式。③拼字學;拼字說。④〖幾何、建築〗直射影法;正投影法。
or·tho·p(a)e·dic [ˌɔrθəˈpidɪk; ˌɔːθouˈpiːdik] *adj.* 整形外科的;矯形術的。
or·tho·p(a)e·dics [ˌɔrθəˈpidɪks; ˌɔːθouˈpiːdiks] *n.* 整形外科;整形術;矯形術。
or·tho·p(a)e·dist [ˌɔrθəˈpidɪst; ˌɔːθouˈpiːdist] *n.* 整形外科醫師。
or·tho·psy·chi·a·try [ˌɔrθosaɪˈkaɪətrɪ; ˌɔːθousaiˈkaiətri] *n.* 精神衞生學。
Or·thop·ter·a [ɔrˈθɑptərə; ɔːˈθɔptərə] *n. pl.* 〖動物〗直翅類。
or·thop·ter·ous [ɔrˈθɑptərəs; ɔːˈθɔptərəs] *adj.* 〖動物〗直翅類的。
or·thop·tic [ɔrˈθɑptɪk; ɔːˈθɔptik] *adj.* 〖眼科〗正視的。
or·to·lan [ˈɔrtələn; ˈɔːtələn] *n.* ①(歐洲產)鳶雀類之鳥。②〖美〗=**bobolink.**
-ory¹ 〖字尾〗附於名詞、動詞形成"似…的;…性質的;作爲…的"之義之形容詞, 如: declamatory, preparatory.
-ory² 〖字尾〗表"場所;爲某種目的之物"之義的名詞字尾, 如: dormitory, factory.
o·ryx [ˈorɪks; ˈɔriks] *n., pl.* **o·ryx·es, o·ryx.** 〖動物〗(非洲產之)一種大羚羊。
Os 化學元素 osmium 之符號。
os¹ [ɑs; ɔs] 〖拉〗 *n., pl.* **os·sa** [ˈɑsə; ˈɔsə]. 〖解剖,動物〗骨。 「口;孔;穴。
os² 〖拉〗 *n., pl.* **o·ra** [ˈorə; ˈourə]. 〖解剖〗
OS Old Saxon.
O·sage [oˈsedʒ; ouˈseidʒ] *n., pl.* **O·sag·es, O·sage.** ①奧色治族之人(昔居住於 Arkansas 河畔之北美印第安人)。②該族之語言。③=**Osage orange.**
Osage orange (or **apple**) (美國 Arkansas 地方產之)一種桑科植物;其果實(不可食)。 「本州南部之一海港)。
O·sa·ka [oˈsɑkə; ˈɔːsəkə] *n.* 大阪(日本
Os·car¹ [ˈɔskə, ˈɑs-; ˈɔskə] *n.* 男子名。
Os·car² *n.* 奧斯卡金像獎(美國電影藝術科學院頒與最優之影片、演員、攝影、導演等者)。
Os·car³ *n.* 通訊電碼, 代表字母 O.
os·cil·late [ˈɑsḷˌet; ˈɔsileit] *v.,* **-lat·ed, -lat·ing.** —*v.i.* ①擺動;在兩點間來回擺動。②(意見、目的之) 游移不定;躊躇。③〖物理〗振動;振盪。④〖數學〗振動。 —*v.t.* ①使擺動。②使振動。
os·cil·la·tion [ˌɑsḷˈeʃən; ˌɔsiˈleiʃən] *n.* ①擺動;(擺動時之)一擺。②(心的) 動搖;躊躇。③〖物理〗振動;振幅。④〖數學〗振幅;消長度;振盪;振動。
os·cil·la·tor [ˈɑsḷˌetə; ˈɔsileitə] *n.* ①振動者。②〖電〗發振器。③〖物理〗振(動)子;振動器。 「*adj.* 擺動的;振動的;動搖的。
os·cil·la·to·ry [ˈɑsələˌtorɪ; ˈɔsilətəri]
os·cil·lo·gram [əˈsɪləˌgræm; əˈsiləgræm] *n.* 波形圖。
os·cil·lo·graph [əˈsɪləˌgræf; əˈsiləgrɑːf] *n.* 〖電〗示波器。 **—ic,** *adj.* **—y,** *n.*
os·cil·lo·scope [əˈsɪləˌskop; əˈsiləskoup] *n.* 〖電〗示波器。
os·cine [ˈɑsɪn; ˈɔsin] *adj.* 鳴禽類的。 —*n.* 鳴禽類之鳥;鳴禽。
os·cu·lant [ˈɑskjulənt; ˈɔskjulənt] *adj.* ①接吻的;接觸的;連接的; 介於二者之間的。②〖生物〗具有兩類共同之特徵的;界於兩類之間的。③〖動物〗固着的;抱合的。
os·cu·lar [ˈɑskjələ; ˈɔskjulə] *adj.* ①嘴的;接吻的。②〖生物〗osculum的。**—i·ty,** *n.*
os·cu·late [ˈɑskjəˌlet; ˈɔskjuleit] *v.t. & v.i.,* **-lat·ed, -lat·ing.** ①接吻。②(使)密接;(使) 結合。③〖幾何〗密切。④〖生物〗(使)具有(共同特徵)。
os·cu·la·tion [ˌɑskjəˈleʃən; ˌɔskjuˈleiʃən] *n.* ①接吻。②密接。③〖幾何〗密切。
os·cu·la·to·ry [ˈɑskjuləˌtorɪ; ˈɔskjulətəri] *adj.* ①接吻的。②密接的。③〖幾何〗密切的。
os·cu·lum [ˈɑskjuləm; ˈɔskjuləm] *n., pl.* **-la** [-lə; -lə]. 〖動物〗(海綿等之)嘴;出水孔;(條蟲等之)吸附器官;吸盤。
-ose¹ 〖字尾〗表"…多的;有…的;…性的"之義的形容詞字尾, 如: bellicose, morose, verbose. 「如: cellulose, fructose.
-ose² 〖字尾〗〖化〗炭水化合物之名稱字尾,
o·sier [ˈoʒə; ˈouʒə] *n.* ①〖英〗一種柳樹。

②其柳條（可編筐籃）。③〖美〗一種山茱萸。—*adj.* 此種柳條製的。—**ed,** —**like,** *adj.*
O·si·ris [o'saɪrɪs; ou'saiəris] *n.* 古代埃及主神之一（Isis 之夫）。—**O·si·ri·an,** *adj.*
-osis 〖字尾〗①表"情況;狀態; 動作"之義,如: osmosis. ②表"變態;病態"之義,如: neurosis.
-osity 〖字尾〗爲 **-ose**（或 **-ous**）及 **-ity** 結合而成之複合字尾, 用與具有 **-ose**或**-ous** 語幹之字作成名詞。如: jocosity, curiosity.
Os·lo ['ɑzlo; 'ɔzlou] *n.* 奧斯陸(挪威之首都,位於挪威之東南部)。
Os·man·li [ɑz'mænlɪ; ɔz'mænli] *n., pl.* **-lis,** *adj.*—*n.* ①土耳其人。②土耳其語。—*adj.* 土耳其（人、語)的。
os·mic ['ɑzmɪk;'ɔzmik] *adj.* 〖化〗鋨的;「含高價之鋨的。」
os·mi·um ['ɑzmɪəm; 'ɔzmiəm] *n.*〖化〗鋨(金屬元素之一, 符號 Os).
os·mo·sis [ɑz'mosɪs; ɔz'mousis] *n.* ①微妙或緩慢的吸收;混合。②〖化,生理〗滲透;滲透分析;滲透性。
os·mot·ic [ɑz'mɑtɪk; ɔz'mɔtik] *adj.* 〖化,生理〗滲透的;滲透性的。—**al·ly,** *adv.*
os·mund ['ɑzmənd; 'ɔzmənd] *n.* 〖植物〗薇。
os·prey ['ɑsprɪ, 'ɔsprɪ; 'ɔspri] *n., pl.* **-preys.** ①鶚。②一種飾帽用之鳥羽。
Os·sa ['ɑsə; 'ɔsə] *n.* 奧塞山(希臘東北部之一山; 希臘神話中巨人們妄圖升天擊神將 Pelion 山疊於 Ossa 山之上,藉以攀登 Olympus 山)。***heap Pelion upon Ossa*** 難上加難;作辦不到的事。
os·se·ous ['ɑsɪəs, -jəs; 'ɔsiəs] *adj.* 由骨構成的;含骨的;似骨的。—**ly,** *adv.*
os·si·cle ['ɑsɪkl; 'ɔsikl] *n.* 〖解剖〗小骨。
os·si·fi·ca·tion [ˌɑsəfə'keʃən; ˌɔsifi'keiʃən] *n.* ①成骨; 化骨。②硬化;變硬。③化骨部分;硬化部分。④遲鈍化;冷淡化。⑤頑固化。
os·si·frage ['ɑsɪfrɪdʒ; 'ɔsifridʒ] *n.* ①=**osprey.** ②(歐洲產) 髭兀鷹;禿鷹。
os·si·fy ['ɑsəˌfaɪ; 'ɔsifai] *v.,* **-fied, -fy·ing.** —*v.t.* ①〖生理〗使骨化;使成爲骨。②使硬化;使僵化。③使冷酷無情。 —*v.i.* ①〖生理〗骨化;成爲骨。②僵化;硬化;不進步。
os·su·ar·y ['ɑsjuˌɛrɪ, 'ɑʃju-; 'ɔsjuəri] *n., pl.* **-ar·ies.** ①藏骨堂。②骨罐;骨甕。
os·ten·si·ble [ɑs'tɛnsəbl; ɔs'tensəbl] *adj.* ①表面的;假裝的;佯的;僞的。②可公開的;非機密的。③明顯的;顯而易見的。 —**os·ten·si·bi·li·ty,** *n.*
os·ten·si·bly [ɑs'tɛnsəblɪ; ɔs'tensə-bli] *adv.* 表面上。
os·ten·sive [ɑs'tɛnsɪv; ɔs'tensiv] *adj.* ①顯示的;明示的。②表面的。—**ly,** *adv.*
os·ten·so·ry [ɑs'tɛnsərɪ; ɔs'tensəri] *n., pl.* **-ries.** =**monstrance.**
os·ten·ta·tion [ˌɑstən'teʃən; ˌɔsten'teiʃən] *n.* ①誇張;虛飾。②〖古〗展示;顯現。
os·ten·ta·tious [ˌɑstən'teʃəs; ˌɔsten'teiʃəs] *adj.* 誇張的; 虛飾的; 招搖 的。—**ly,** *adv.*
os·te·ol·o·gy [ˌɑstɪ'ɑlədʒɪ; ˌɔsti'ɔlədʒi] *n.* ①〖解剖〗骨學。②骨結構。—**os·te·o·log·i·cal,** *adj.* —**os·te·ol·o·gist,** *n.*
os·te·o·my·e·li·tis [ˌɑstɪəˌmaɪə'laɪtɪs; ˌɔstiouˌmaiə'laitis] *n.* 〖醫〗 骨髓炎。
os·te·o·path ['ɑstɪəˌpæθ; 'ɔstiəpæθ] *n.* 整骨療法家;按骨術士。
os·te·o·path·ic [ˌɑstɪə'pæθɪk; ˌɔstiə'pæθik] *adj.* 整骨療法的。
os·te·op·a·thist [ˌɑstɪ'ɑpəθɪst; ˌɔsti'ɔpəθist] *n.* =**osteopath.**
os·te·op·a·thy [ˌɑstɪ'ɑpəθɪ; ˌɔsti'ɔpəθi] *n.* 〖醫〗整骨療法;按骨術。
ost·ler ['ɑslɚ; 'ɔslə] *n.* =**hostler.**
os·tra·cism ['ɑstrəˌsɪzəm; 'ɔstrəsizəm] *n.* ①古希臘之貝殼放逐(由公民投票決定,票書於貝殼上,故名。被放逐者爲擾亂治安者,放逐期間五至十年)。②放逐;排斥;擯棄。
os·tra·cize ['ɑstrəˌsaɪz; 'ɔstrəsaiz] *v.t.,* **-cized, -ciz·ing.** ①(古希臘的由公民以貝殼投票決定)放逐(擾亂治安者)。②放逐;排斥;擯棄。③擯除;禁止。—**os·tra·ciz·er,** *n.*
***os·trich** ['ɔstrɪtʃ; 'ɔstritʃ] *n.* ①鴕鳥。②藏頭露尾者;自欺者。—*adj.* 藏頭露尾的;自欺的。—*v.i.* 藏頭露尾;採自欺態度。
O.T., OT, OT. Old Testament.
O·thel·lo [o'θɛlo; ou'θelou] *n.* ①奧賽羅（莎士比亞四大悲劇之一）。②奧賽羅（該劇之男主角）。
‡oth·er ['ʌðɚ; 'ʌðə] *adj.* ①賸餘的;其餘的。 John is here, but the *other* boys are at school. 約翰在這裏,但其餘的孩子都在學校裏。②另外的; 此外的。 I have no *other* place to go. 我沒有另外的地方可去。③非此的;不同的。Come some *other* day. 改日再來。④不久以前的。 The *other* day it rained. 前幾天曾下了雨。⑤從前的。 in *other* times. 從前。***every other*** **a.** 每隔一個的。I go there *every other* day. 我每隔一天去那裏一次。Write on *every other* line. 隔行寫。**b.** 所有其餘的。Smith didn't come, but *every other* boy (=all the other boys) did come. 史密斯沒有來,但其餘的孩子都來了。***none other than*** 除…之外無他。It was *none other than* Smith. 一定是史密斯(除史密斯外無別人)。***on the other hand*** 另一方面。It's cheap, but *on the other hand* the quality is poor. 它是便宜的,但在另一方面它的質料壞。 ***other than*** 與…不同。I do not wish him *other than* he is. 我不希望他改變現狀(他現狀很好)。***other things being equal*** 如果其它條件都一樣。 ***some day (time) or other*** 某日 (=one day). I hope to go to France *some day or other.* 我希望有一天能到法國去。 ***some one or other*** 某人。 ***the other day*** 數日前 (=a few days ago). Yes, I saw him *the other day.* 是的, 我在數天前看到他。 ***the other world*** 死後之世界。 —*pron.* 其他的人;其他之物。 Please tell the *others.* 請告訴其他的人。***among others*** 和别人 (=and others). Smith, *among others,* was there. 史密斯和其他一些人在那裏。***each other*** (二者間)彼此。 They are exactly like *each other.* 他倆彼此完全相像。 ***of all others*** 所有的當中。on that day *of all others.* 偏偏在那天。 ***one after the other*** 相繼地。They came running *one after the other.* 他們一個接一個地跑來。***one from the other*** 分別;各別。 It is difficult to tell the twins *one from the other.* 很難辨別這對孿生子。***or other*** 某人;某物。He was talking to some man *or other.* 他正與一人談話。—*adv.* 用其他方法;不如此。I can't do *other* than to go. 我祇有去。 I could not do *other* than I did. 我當時非如此做不可。
oth·er-di·rect·ed ['ʌðədɪ'rɛktɪd; 'ʌðədi'rektid] *adj.* 受外力支配的;不自主的。—*n.* 受外力支配者;無自主能力者。

oth·er·guess [ˈʌðəˌgɛs; ˈʌðəges] *adj.* 別種的;不同的。—*adv.* =**otherwise.**
other half ①其他民衆。②配偶。
oth·er·ness [ˈʌðənɪs; ˈʌðənis] *n.* 〖哲學〗差異性;他性。
oth·er·where(s) [ˈʌðəˌhwɛr(z); ˈʌðəhwɛə(z)] *adv.* 〖古,方〗在(至)他處。
:oth·er·wise [ˈʌðəˌwaɪz; ˈʌðəwaiz] *adv.* ①用不同的方法;不同地。 I could not do *otherwise.* 我祇能這樣做。②在別的方面;在其他方面。 He is noisy, but *otherwise* a nice boy. 他愛吵鬧, 但在其他方面却是個好孩子。 ③在其它狀態; 在其它情況。He reminded me of what I should *otherwise* have forgotten. 他提醒我那些不提起或許會忘記的事。 —*conj.* 否則;不然。Do what you are told; *otherwise* you will be punished. 你須聽話,否則你將受懲罰。—*adj.* ①不同的。 It might have been *otherwise.* 此事可能不是如此。②在其他方面的。 Their political enemies were also their *otherwise* friends. 他們的政敵在其他方面是他們的友人。③在不同情況之下的。
oth·er·world·ly [ˈʌðəˈwɜldlɪ; ˈʌðəˈwəːldli] *adj.* 來世的;超脫塵俗的。—**oth·er·world·li·ness,** *n.*
o·tic [ˈotɪk; ˈoutik] *adj.* 〖解剖〗耳的;耳部的。
o·ti·ose [ˈoʃɪˌos; ˈouʃious] *adj.* ①閒散的;懶惰的。②無益的;無效的;徒勞的。③多餘的;無用的。—**ly,** *adv.* —**ness,** *n.*
o·ti·tis [oˈtaɪtɪs; ouˈtaitis] *n.* 〖醫〗耳炎。
o·ti·um cum dig·ni·ta·te [ˈoʃɪəmkʌm ˌdɪgnɪˈtetɪ; ˈouʃiəm kʌmˌdigniˈteiti] 〖拉〗悠閒自適(=leisure with dignity).
o·to·lar·yn·gol·o·gy [ˌotəˌlærɪŋˈgɑlədʒɪ; ˌoutəˌlæriŋˈgɔlədʒi] *n.* 耳鼻喉科。—**o·to·lar·yn·gol·o·gist,** *n.*
o·tol·o·gy [oˈtɑlədʒɪ; ouˈtɔlədʒi] *n.* 〖醫〗耳科學。
o·to·scope [ˈotəˌskop; ˈoutəskoup] *n.* ①檢耳鏡。②一種中耳之聽診器。
ot·ta·va ri·ma [əˈtɑvəˈrimə; əˈtɑːvəˈriːmə] 〖韻律〗八行詩節(一種義大利之詩體,各行11音節,但於英詩則爲10或11音節,押韻如ab ab ab cc).
Ot·ta·wa [ˈɑtəwə; ˈɔtəwə] *n.* ①渥太華(加拿大首都)。②渥太華河(加拿大東南部一河流, 在 Montreal 注入 St. Lawrance 河)。③Algonquian 印第安族之一員,該族散居於 Lake Superior 附近。
Ot·ta·wan [ˈɑtəwən; ˈɔtəwən] *n.* 渥太華人。
ot·ter** [ˈɑtə; ˈɔtə] *n., pl.* **-ters, -ter.** ①〖動物〗獺。②獺皮。sea otter*** 海獺。
ot·to [ˈɑto; ˈɔtou] *n.* =**attar.**
Ot·to·man [ˈɑtəmən; ˈɔtəmən] *n., pl.* **-mans,** *adj.* —*n.* 土耳其人。 —*adj.* 土耳其的;土耳其民族的;土耳其人的;鄂圖曼帝國的。
O.U. Oxford University.
ou·bli·ette [ˌublɪˈɛt; ˌuːbliˈet] *n.* 暗牢;地牢;密獄(其僅有之出入口在上頭)。
ouch¹ [autʃ; autʃ] *interj.* (表示突然疼痛的聲音)啊唷!
ouch² *n.* 〖古〗①(女人佩於領口、胸前之)別針; 胸飾; 釦子(尤指鑲有珠寶者)。②(指環上之)珠座;寶石座。—*v.t.* 〖古〗飾以別針。
:ought¹ [ɔt; ɔːt] *aux. v.* ①應當(表義務)。 You *ought* to obey your parents. 你應服從你的父母。 ②該(表願望)。 ③大概是(表可能性)。It *ought* to rain soon. 大概就要下雨。—*n.* 義務。obedience to the *ought.* 對義務之服從。
ought² *n., adv.* =**aught; anything.**
ought³ *n.* 〖俗〗零; 全無(=nought).
oui·ja [ˈwidʒə; ˈwiːdʒɑː] *n.* 靈應盤(上有字母及其他符號之板,其上再用一種占板planchette, 用於降神術等)。
***ounce¹** [auns; auns] *n.* ①盎斯;英兩(英國重量單位, 常衡爲 1/16 磅, 金衡爲 1/12 磅)。②盎斯(液量名,十六盎斯爲一品脫)。③少量;些許。He hasn't an *ounce* of common sense. 他一點常識都沒有。
ounce² *n.* 〖動物〗雪豹。
:our [aur; ˈauə] *pron.* the possessive of **we.** 我們的; 屬於我們的。*Our* friends are coming to see us next week. 我們的朋友將在下週來看我們。 ***Our Lady*** 聖母瑪利亞。
:ours [aurz; ˈauəz] *pron.* ①我們的; 屬於我們的。 This garden is *ours.* 這個花園是我們的。 ②我們的東西。 *Ours* is a large house. 我們的房子是一所大的房子。
***our·self** [aurˈsɛlf; ˌauəˈself] *pron.* (作家、國王、法官等用語) 我自己。 "We will *ourself* reward the victor," said the King. 國王說,"朕將親自獎勵得勝者"。
:our·selves [aurˈsɛlvz; ˌauəˈselvz] *pron. pl.* ①我們親自(we 或 us 之加重語勢)。We did it *ourselves.* 我們親自做的。②我們自己(us 的反身代名詞)。We hurt *ourselves.* 我們傷了自己。③我們自己的正常及健康狀態。We had been ill, but today we are again *ourselves.* 我們曾感不適,但是今天我們已重獲健康。 ***(all) by ourselves*** **a.** 獨力無助的。 **b.** 我們單獨。Come in; we're *all by ourselves.* 進來;我們沒有外人。
-ous 〖字尾〗①表"多…的;…性的;似…的;有…特徵的; 有…癖的"之義的形容詞字尾, 如: perilous, pompous, rigorous. ②〖化〗表"亞"之義之形容詞字尾,如: nitrousacid. 亞硝酸。
ou·sel [ˈuzl̩; ˈuːzl] *n.* =**ouzel.**
oust [aust; aust] *v.t.* ①逐出;驅逐。②免職;罷黜。③〖法律〗驅逐;剝奪。
oust·er [ˈaustə; ˈaustə] *n.* ①〖法律〗剝奪。②罷黜;免職。
:out [aut; aut] *adv.* ①外出地; 在外地。②向外地。③(動作)突發地。A fire broke *out.* 起火。 Will war break *out?* 戰爭會爆發嗎? ④消失地; 完結地。 The stains will not wash *out.* 污點洗不掉。⑤顯現地;突出地。A big rock stuck *out* of the water. 一塊大巖石突出於水面。⑥高聲地。Speak *out,* please! 請大聲講! ⑦使在外地。 to lock a person *out.* 將一人鎖在外面。 ⑧使消失地; 被遺漏地。 to cross *out* a word. 劃掉一字。 Put the light *out.* 把燈熄滅。 ⑨在相當距離外地(爲表達距離之語氣)。I'm living *out* in the country. 我住在鄉下。 ⑩在家外。 The servant sleeps *out.* 這僕人睡在外面(意指僕人在主人家吃飯,但夜晚在別處睡覺)。⑪到國外。He was sent *out* as ambassador at a critical time. 他在緊要的時候被派往國外任大使。⑫完全地;徹底地。⑬免職。He was voted *out* at the election. 他在選舉時落選而離職。⑭出現;發生。 Fever broke *out.* 熱病發生了。⑮發出;交出。Give *out* the books. 把這些書分發出去。⑯挑出;選出;掘出。She picked *out* a new coat. 她挑選了一件新大衣。⑰錯誤。⑱不滿;不安;窘;爲難。⑲損失。⑳〖棒球〗出局。 ***all out*** 〖俗〗完全地;徹底地;全心全意地。 ***out and away*** 遠;甚;無比。He's *out and away* the cleverest boy in the

class. 他是全班中最聰明的孩子。***out and home*** 來回。***out from under*** 解除困境;脫離艱局。They tried hard to find a way of getting *out from under*. 他們極力設法想出一個解除困境的辦法。***out of***(做介系詞用)。**a.** 在外面。*out of* the house. 在房子外。**b.** 因;由。to act *out of* fear. 因恐懼而爲之。**c.** 表狀態。*out of* breath. 氣喘。*out of* work. 失業。**d.** 在…的範圍外;向…達不到的地方。The boat has gone *out of* sight. 船走得看不見了。**e.** 失去…;沒有…。We are *out of* coffee. 我們沒有咖啡。***out of it*** 處於局外;不明局內事。***out of pocket*** 沒有錢。He did not order beers, being slightly *out of pocket*. 他並沒有叫啤酒,因爲他經濟稍有困難。—*adj.* ①熄滅的。The fire is *out*. 火熄了。②破的;露出的。*out* at the knees. (褲管)膝部破了。③特大的。an *out* size. 特大的尺寸。④錯誤的。to be *out* in one's calculations. 計算錯誤。⑤外邊的。an *out* island. 外邊的島嶼。We shall soon be *out* at sea. 我們不久便到海上。⑥外出的;借出的;出版的。The manager is *out* for dinner. 經理出外吃飯去了。⑦過時;不流行。Full skirts are *out* this season. 這個季節寬大的長裙已過時了。⑧〖棒球〗出局的。He was *out* trying to steal third. 他試偸三壘時被殺出局。⑨結束;完結。before the week is *out*. 在此週結束之前。⑩失勢;未掌握權力;在野。The Democrats are *out*, the Republicans in. 民主黨下野,共和黨執政。⑪(花)開的。The flowers are *out*. 花開了。⑫損失的。to be *out* ten dollars. 損失十塊錢。⑬不和的。He is *out* with his friend over a girl. 他爲一個女孩子與他朋友不和。⑭要出去的;將出去的。the *out* train. 將開出的火車。⑮罷工中的(=on strike). The workers are *out*. 工人在罷工中。***out for*** 努力想得到;期待;求。***out to*** 努力想;極欲。—*v.i.* ①現出;公布。Truth will *out*. 眞相終必大白。Murder will *out*. 兇殺案終必破獲。②〖網球〗將球打出界外。The Australian *outed* and lost the game. 那澳洲人將球打出界外而輸掉那場比賽。***out with*** 拿出;說出。He *outs with* his money. 他拿出錢來。—*v.t.* ①擊倒;打敗(特指拳賽中)。He was *outed* in the first round. 他在第一回合中被擊敗。②熄滅。Please *out* the fire. 請將火滅掉。③罷免;罷黜。④向外伸出。They *outed* oars and pulled hard. 他們向外伸槳用力划船。—*n.* ①(常 *pl.*) 在野黨;不在職者。②缺點;弱點;錯誤。③〖印刷〗漏排;排脫;省略。④〖棒球〗出局者。He was an easy *out*. 他是個容易出局的球員。⑤〖棒球〗出局。It was the last *out* of the game. 這是那一場比賽之最後一次出局。⑥外緣;外邊。the width of the building from *out* to *out*. 那建築物外緣到外緣的寬度。⑦打開僵局的辦法;退路。⑧出路。***at outs*** (or ***on the outs***) 爭執的;不和的。He was *at outs* with most of the kids on the block. 他與那一段街裏的大部分小孩不和。***make a poor out*** 不成功;搞不好。***the ins and the outs*** **a.** 執政黨與在野黨。**b.** 事情的細節。***to out*** 從一頭到另一頭;全長。—*prep.* ①出自;從…出。He went *out* the door. 他走出門。②〖俗〗沿着…離去。Drive *out* Main Street. 沿着大街駕車離去。—*interj.* 〖古〗表示憤怒、責罵之聲音;滾! *Out* upon you! 滾!給我滾!混蛋!

out- 〖字首〗表:①"外"。如:outpatient (不住院之門診病人)。②"向外"或"出"。如:outcast. ③"完;盡"。④"超過"。如:outsell.

out·age ['autɪdʒ; 'autidʒ] *n.* ①出口。②〖商〗(商品於搬運等中發生的)減量。③(由於修理等之船或機器之)停航;停用。④〖電〗停電(期間)。

out-and-out ['autən'aut; 'autən'aut] *adj.* 完全的;徹底的。—*adv.* 完全地;徹底地。(亦作 **out and out**)

out-and-out·er ['autn̩'autɚ; 'autən'autə] *n.*〖俗〗①行家;精通者。②極端主義者。

out·back ['autbæk; 'autbæk] *n.* 〖澳〗人煙稀少的內陸地區。—*adv.* 〖澳〗向人煙稀少的內陸地區。

out·bal·ance [aut'bæləns; aut'bæləns] *v.t.* (在重量、價值、效果等方面)勝過…。

out·bid [aut'bɪd; aut'bid] *v.t.*, **-bid, -bid** or **-bid·den, -bid·ding.** 出價高於(他人);投標時開價低於(他人)。

out·board ['aut,bord; 'autbɔːd] *adj.* 在船外的;在舷側的。—*adv.* 在船外地;在舷側地。—*n.* ①船尾馬達。②裝有船尾馬達的小船。

out·bound ['aut'baund; 'autbaund] *adj.* 開往國外的;往外地的;離埠(港)的。

out·box [aut'bɑks; aut'bɔks] *v.t.* 在拳賽中勝過。

out·brave [aut'brev; aut'breiv] *v.t.*, **-braved, -brav·ing.** ①以勇氣勝過。②(在美麗方面)勝過。③抵抗;不屈於;向…挑戰。

***out·break** [*n.* 'aut,brek; 'autbreik *v.* aut'brek; aut'breik] *n.*, *v.*, **-broke, -bro·ken, -break·ing.** —*n.* ①爆發;發生。the *outbreak* of war. 戰爭的爆發。②暴亂;騷動。Famine conditions led to *outbreaks* in many cities. 饑荒在許多城市引起了暴動。—*v.i.* 發生;爆發。

out·build·ing ['aut,bɪldɪŋ; 'aut,bildiŋ] *n.*(與正屋分離之)附屬建築物(如穀倉等)。

***out·burst** ['aut,bɝst; 'autbəːst] *n.* ①爆發;突發。an *outburst* of anger. 一陣怒氣。②星際間之爆炸;太陽黑子之爆發。

out·cast ['aut,kæst; 'autkɑːst] *n.* 被逐出者;流浪者。Criminals are *outcasts* of society. 罪犯是被社會遺棄者。—*adj.* ①被(家庭、社會等)逐出的;被棄的;無家可歸的。②已丟棄的。③被社會遺棄者的。

out·caste [*n.* 'aut,kæst; 'autkɑːst *v.* aut'kæst; 'autkɑːst] *n.* ①印度失去階級之人;賤民。②無階級之人。—*adj.* 無階級的。—*v.t.* 逐出階級之外。

out·class [aut'klæs; aut'klɑːs] *v.t.* 遠高於;遠優於;遠勝過。

out-col·lege ['aut,kɑlɪdʒ; 'aut,kɔlidʒ] *adj.* 〖英〗不住在大學宿舍的;通學的。

***out·come** ['aut,kʌm; 'autkʌm] *n.* ①結果。The *outcome* of the election is still unknown. 選擧結果依然未詳。②出口。

out·cor·ner ['aut,kɔrnɚ; 'aut,kɔːnə] *n.* 〖棒球〗外角。

out·crop [*n.* 'aut,krɑp; 'autkrɔp *v.* aut'krɑp; aut'krɔp] *n.*, *v.*, **-cropped, -crop·ping.** —*n.* ①(礦脈等)露出地面。②露出於地面上的部分。—*v.i.* 露出地面;出現。

out·cry ['aut,kraɪ; 'autkrai] *n.*, *pl.* **-cries,** *v.*, **-cried, -cry·ing.** —*n.* ①叫喊;高聲尖叫。②喧囂;怒喊;大聲反對。They raised an *outcry* against the man. 他們大聲叫喊以反對這個人。③拍賣;沿街叫賣。—*v.t.* 叫聲高過…。

out·curve ['aut,kɝv; 'autkəːv] *n.* 〖棒球〗外曲球(爲 in-curve 之對)。

out·dare [aut'dɛr; aut'dɛə] *v.t.* ①不顧(危險等)。②比…大膽。
out·dat·ed [aut'detɪd; aut'deitid] *adj.* 過時的;老式的。
out·dis·tance [aut'dɪstəns; aut'distəns] *v.t.*, **-tanced, -tanc·ing.** (在競賽中)領先;勝過;超越。
out·do [aut'du; aut'du:] *v.t.*, **-did, -done, -do·ing.** 超越;勝過。
out·done [aut'dʌn; aut'dʌn] *v.* pp. of **outdo.**
***out·door** ['aut,dor; 'autdɔ:] *adj.* ①戶外的。*outdoor* games. 戶外遊戲。②救濟院外的;醫院外的。*outdoor* relief. 院外救濟。
***out·doors** ['aut'dorz; 'aut'dɔ:z] *adv.* 戶外。Is it cold *outdoors?* 屋外冷嗎? —*n.* 戶外地方。
out·drop ['aut,drɑp; 'autdrɔp] *n.* 〖棒球〗界外。
out·er** ['autə; 'autə] *adj.* 外部的; 外面的。the *outer* suburbs. 郊外。the outer man*** 外貌;外表。
outer city 〖美〗郊區。
out·er·coat ['autə,kot; 'autəkout] *n.* 大衣;風衣;罩袍。
out·er-di·rect·ed ['autədə'rɛktɪd; 'autədi'rektid] *adj.* 外向的。
Outer Mongolia 外蒙古。
out·er·most ['autə,most; 'autəmoust] *adj.* 最外的;最遠的。
outer space 太空。
out·face [aut'fes; aut'feis] *v.t.*, **-faced, -fac·ing.** ①睥睨;盛氣凌(人);威壓。②儼然抗衡。③使無面目;輕侮;蔑視。
out·fall ['aut,fɔl; 'autfɔ:l] *n.* ①河口;渠口;出口。②爭吵。
out·field ['aut'fild, -,fild; 'autfi:ld] *n.* ①〖棒球〗外野; 外野手(集合稱)。②農家遠處之田地。③邊遠之區。
out·field·er ['aut'fildə; 'autfi:ldə] *n.* 〖棒球〗外野手。
***out·fit** ['aut,fɪt; 'autfit] *n., v.*, **-fit·ted, -fit·ting.** —*n.* ①用具; 所需工具; 裝備。a cooking *outfit.* 烹飪用具。②(一般)團體;一同工作的一羣人。③配備。The *outfit* of the exploring party took several months. 探險隊的配備費了數月的時間。④組織;機構;公司。—*v.t.* ①裝備。②供應。—*v.i.* 配備;準備裝束。They *outfitted* for the long journey. 他們爲遠途旅行準備裝束。
out·fit·ter ['aut,fɪtə; 'aut,fitə] *n.* 備辦全套旅行用品之商人。
out·flank [aut'flæŋk; aut'flæŋk] *v.t.* ①包圍(敵軍等)之側翼;迂廻至側翼而襲擊(敵人)。②以計勝過。
out·flow ['aut,flo; 'autflou] *n.* ①流出;流出物。②流出量。
out·fox [aut'fɑks; aut'fɔks] *v.t.* 以計勝過。Since I couldn't outrun him, I had to *outfox* him. 因爲我跑不過他,所以我得以計勝他。
out·gen·er·al [aut'dʒɛnərəl; aut'dʒenərəl] *v.t.*, **-al(l)ed, -al·(l)ing.** ①以軍略勝過;謀勝。②使墮入術中。
out·go ['aut,go; 'autgou] *n., pl.* **-goes,** *v.*, **-went, -gone, -go·ing.** —*n.* ①支出(爲income之對)。②外出。③出口。—*v.t.* 勝過;優於;超過。
out·go·ing ['aut,goɪŋ; 'autgouiŋ] *adj.* ①外出的; 外駛的; 離去的。②友善的; 好交際的。—*n.* ①外出;出發。②(*pl.*)〖英〗開支; 費用。③流出。
out-group ['aut,grup; 'autgru:p] *n.* 〖社會〗外羣; 他羣 (=they-group, 自己所屬的集團以外的集團, 爲 in-group之對)。
out·grow [aut'gro; aut'grou] *v.*, **-grew, -grown, -grow·ing.** —*v.t.* ①過大而不適於。to *outgrow* one's clothes. 身體長得過大,衣服顯小。②較…長得大或快。③因年長放棄或革除。—*v.i.* 生出;長出;突出。
out·growth ['aut,groθ; 'autgrouθ] *n.* ①自然的發展; 自然的結果。②生出之物;枝條;突出物;瘤。③生出;生長。
out·guess [aut'gɛs; aut'ges] *v.t.* 猜測勝過。
out-Her·od [aut'hɛrəd; aut'herəd] *v.t.* ①狂暴之程度勝過(Herod)。②勝過; 超過。
out·hit [aut'hɪt; aut'hit] *v.t.* 〖棒球〗打擊勝於。
out·house ['aut,haus; 'authaus] *n.* ①附屬的建築物(與正屋分開, 如穀倉等)。②戶外便所。
out·ing ['autɪŋ; 'autiŋ] *n.* ①小遊; 遠足;短途旅行。②比賽。—*adj.* 遠足時適用的。
out·jock·ey [aut'dʒɑkɪ; aut'dʒɔki] *v.t.* 欺;騙;哄人上當;用詭計勝。
out·land ['aut,lænd; 'autlænd] *n.* ①(莊園等之)靠近邊界之土地。②〖古〗外國。—*adj.* ①境外的; 邊遠的。②〖古〗外國的。
out·land·er ['aut,lændə; 'aut,lændə] *n.* ①外國人;外來人。②〖俗〗門外漢;局外人。
out·land·ish [aut'lændɪʃ; aut'lændiʃ] *adj.* ①奇異的;古怪可笑的;野蠻的。②似從外國來的;異國風味的。③偏僻的。
out·last [aut'læst; aut'lɑ:st] *v.t.* ①較…耐久;比…持久。②壽命較…長。
out·laugh [aut'lɑf; aut'lɑ:f] *v.t.* ①譏笑;嘲笑。②較…笑得多。—*v.i.* 哄笑。
out·law ['aut,lɔ; 'aut-lɔ:] *n.* ①被放逐者。②惡徒; 罪犯。—*v.t.* ①將…放逐。②使失去法律之保護。③使失去法律上的效力。④宣布…爲非法;使成爲非法。
out·law·ry ['aut,lɔrɪ; 'aut,lɔ:ri] *n., pl.* **-ries.** ①放逐;法律保護的剝奪;失時效。②被放逐者的身分; 惡徒或罪犯的身分。③宣布爲非法。
out·lay [*n.* 'aut,le; 'aut-lei *v.* aut'le; aut'lei] *n., v.*, **-laid, -lay·ing.** —*n.* ①花費;開銷。②費用;花費數目。—*v.t.* 花費。
***out·let** ['aut,lɛt; 'aut-let] *n.* ①出口;出路;排洩口。②銷路;市場。They must find new *outlets* for their industries. 他們必須爲其工業尋找新市場。③出售某種產品的商店。The shoe manufacturer had several *outlets.* 那家製鞋的廠商有幾家代銷店。④牆上裝電插頭的地方。⑤無線電或電視廣播網的分臺。⑥發源於湖泊的河流。⑦河流注入湖泊或海洋之出口。
out·li·er ['aut,laɪə; 'aut,laiə] *n.* ①不住在營業或工作地點者; 寄居外地者。②局外人; 門外漢。③〖地質〗離層。④離開本體之部分;分離物。
out·line** ['aut,laɪn; 'autlain] *n., v.*, **-lined, -lin·ing.** —*n.* ①外形; 輪廓。②略圖。③要點; 大綱。*An Outline of European History.* "歐洲史大綱"。④(*pl.*) 要旨;概要。in outline*** **a.** 梗概的;大概的。**b.** 畫出輪廓。—*v.t.* ①述要點。②畫…之外形或輪廓。③顯示…之輪廓。
out·live [aut'lɪv; aut'liv] *v.t.*, **-lived, -liv·ing.** ①生存得比…更久;比…更經久。②活久而忘掉;久活而失去。
***out·look** [*n.* 'aut,luk; 'aut-luk; *v.* aut'luk; 'aut-luk] *n.* ①景色。②景況。There is a bad *outlook* for trade. 商業的景況欠佳。③對事之展望或看法。④看守; 瞭望。⑤

瞭望處;望樓。—*v.t.* 樣子比…好看。—**er,** *n.*

out·ly·ing ['aut,laiɪŋ; 'aut,laiiŋ] *adj.* ①偏僻的;邊遠的。②邊界以外的;範圍以外的。

out·ma·neu·ver, out·ma·noeu·vre [,autmə'nuvə; ,autmə'nu:və] *v.t.* ①以謀略勝;挫敗(敵人)的計謀。②機動性勝過。

out·march [aut'mɑrtʃ; aut'mɑ:tʃ] 「*v.t.* 進行較速於…;追過;超過。」

out·match [aut'mætʃ; aut'mætʃ] *v.t.* 勝過;凌駕。

out·mod·ed [aut'modɪd; aut'moudid] *adj.* 舊式的;過時的。

out·most ['aut,most; 'autmoust] *adj.* 「最外方的;最遠的。」

out·num·ber [aut'nʌmbə; aut'nʌmbə] *v.t.* 比…多;數目勝過…。

out-of-bounds ['autəv'baundz; 'autəv'baundz] *adv.* 到界外。—*adj.* ①禁止入內的;不得超越的;不許可的。②超出預料之外的。③〖運動〗界外的。

out-of-court settlement ['autəv'kort～; 'autəv'kɔ:t～] 法庭外和解。

out-of-date ['autəv'det; 'autəv'deit] *adj.* 落伍的;老式的;過時的。—**ness,** *n.*

out-of-doors ['autəv'dorz; 'autəv'dɔ:z] *adj.* (亦作 **out-of-door**)=**outdoor.** —*n., adv.* =**outdoors.**

out-of-pock·et ['autəv'pɑkɪt; 'autəv'pɔkit] *adj.* ①現款支付的。②無錢的;無產業的。

out-of-print ['autəv'prɪnt; 'autəv'print] *adj.* 絕版的。—*n.* 絕版書刊。

out-of-the-way ['autəðə'we, 'autəvðə'we; 'autəvðə'wei] *adj.* ①荒僻的;人跡罕至的;不易找到的。②不尋常的;難遇到的;奇怪的。③得罪人的;不得體的。

out-of-work ['autəv'wɝk; 'autəv'wə:k] *n.* 失業者。

out·pace [aut'pes; aut'peis] *v.t.,* **-paced, -pac·ing.** 較…跑得快;追過。

out·par·ty ['aut,pɑrtɪ; 'aut,pɑ:ti] *n.* 在野的政黨。

out·pa·tient ['aut,peʃənt; 'aut,peiʃənt] *n.* 門診之病人(非住院病人)。

out·place [aut'ples; aut'pleis] *v.t.,* **-placed, -plac·ing.** ①取代;擠出。②〖美〗離職前預先安排新的職位;協助覓得新職。

out·play [aut'ple; aut'plei] *v.t.* 打敗;(遊戲之)技術優於…。

out·point [aut'pɔɪnt; aut'pɔint] *v.t.* ①得分較多於。②〖航海〗較(他船)近風航行。

out·port ['aut,port; 'autpɔ:t] *n.* 位於大港口附近而在行政上獨立的小港。

out·post ['aut,post; 'autpoust] *n.* ①哨兵;前哨。②前哨站。③前鋒;前驅;先驅。—*v.t.* 用哨兵防守。

out·pour [*n.* 'aut,por; 'autpɔ: *v.* aut'por; aut'pɔ:] *n.* 瀉出;流出;瀉出之物。—*v.t.* & *v.i.* 瀉出;流出。

out·pour·ing ['aut,porɪŋ; 'aut,pɔ:riŋ] *n.*①流出;傾出。②流出之物。③感情流露。

***out·put** ['aut,put; 'autput] *n.* ①生產額;產量。the *output* of a factory. 工廠之生產量。②發揮;發出(力量)。③(機械動力之)出量。④〖電腦〗輸出。

***out·rage** ['aut,redʒ; 'aut-reidʒ] *n., v.,* **-raged, -rag·ing.** —*n.* ①暴行;迫害。an act of *outrage.* 暴行。②忽視或傷害人格的行爲;要不得的行爲。His request is an *outrage.* 他的請求眞是要不得。—*v.t.* ①觸犯;傷害。②公開違犯(法律等);蔑視。③對…行非禮。—**out·rag·er,** *n.*

***out·ra·geous** [aut'redʒəs; aut'reidʒəs] *adj.* ①暴亂的;侵害的。②極無禮的。*outrageous* language. 極其無禮的措辭。③憤怒的。—**ly,** *adv.* —**ness,** *n.*

out·range [aut'rendʒ; aut'reindʒ] *v.t.,* **-ranged, -rang·ing.** 射程遠於。

out·rank [aut'ræŋk; aut'ræŋk] *v.t.* 階級高於;地位高於。

ou·tré [u'tre; 'u:trei] 〖法〗 *adj.* 逸出常軌的;過激的;奇怪的;奇妙的。—**ness,** *n.*

out·reach [*v.* aut'ritʃ; aut'ri:tʃ *n.* 'aut,ritʃ; aut'ri:tʃ] *v.t.* & *v.i.* ①超越;超過。②伸出;延展(手、腕等)。—*n.* ①範圍。②伸出;延展。

out·re·lief ['autrɪ,lif; 'aut-ri,li:f] *n.* 對於非住救濟院者所施之救濟;院外救濟。

out·ride [aut'raɪd; aut'raid] *v.,* **-rode, -rid·den, -rid·ing,** *n.* —*v.t.* ①騎乘比…更速;騎乘優於。②由騎乘而逃開…。③(船)安全渡過(暴風雨)。a ship strong enough to *outride* any storm. 堅固得能安然渡過任何暴風雨的船。④先…而抵達;越過。to *outride* one's pursuers. 比追蹤者先到。—*v.i.* 騎馬外出。—*n.* ①〖詩〗附加於一音步內之輕音節。②騎馬出遊;遠足。③騎馬場地。

out·rid·er ['aut,raɪdə; 'aut,raidə] *n.* ①(在馬車旁或前面的)騎從;侍衞。②騎馬外出的人。③先驅。

out·rigged ['aut,rɪgd; 'out-rigd] *adj.* 「=**outriggered.**」

out·rig·ger ['aut,rɪgə; 'aut,rigə] *n.* ①任何自主體伸出之暫時支持物。②〖航海〗(伸出船兩邊支槳用的)舷外鐵架;裝有舷外鐵架的小艇;(拴繩子用的)舷外斜木;(防止顚覆用的)舷外浮材。③〖航空〗(支持飛機用的)外架。

out·rig·gered ['aut,rɪgəd; 'aut,rigəd] *adj.* 裝有 outrigger 的。

out·right [*adj.* 'aut,raɪt; 'aut-rait *adv.* 'aut'raɪt; aut'rait] *adv.* ①率直地;坦白地。②立刻地;登時地。③全然地;總共地。④一直向前。—*adj.* ①完全的;徹底的。②率直的;坦白的。③全然的;總共的。④一直向前的。—**ly,** *adv.* —**ness,** *n.*

out·ri·val [aut'raɪvl; aut'raivəl] *v.t.* 勝過(競爭者);擊敗(競爭者)。

out·root [aut'rut; aut'ru:t] *v.t.* 根除;「根絕。」

out·run [aut'rʌn; aut'rʌn] *v.t.,* **-ran, -run, -run·ning.** ①跑得較快。②勝過;追過;超過…的範圍。

out·run·ner [aut'rʌnə, 'aut,rʌnə; 'aut,rʌnə] *n.* ①奔走出來的人。②奔走於馬車前或車旁之侍從。③雪車前一羣曳犬中之最前者。④先驅者。

out·sell [aut'sɛl; aut'sel] *v.t.,* **-sold, -sell·ing.** ①銷數勝過。②較…銷售得快。③賣價較高於。

out·set ['aut,sɛt; 'aut-set] *n.* 開始;起初。

out·shine [aut'ʃaɪn; aut'ʃain] *v.,* **-shone, -shin·ing.** —*v.t.* ①照得比…更亮。②比…更好;勝過。—*v.i.* 放光;照耀。

out·shoot [*n.* 'aut,ʃut; 'aut-ʃu:t *v.* aut'ʃut; aut'ʃu:t] *v.,* **-shot, -shoot·ing,** *n.* —*v.t.* ①比…射得好;比…射得遠。②射越。③射出。—*v.i.* 射出;突出。—*n.* ①射出;突出。②突出物。③〖棒球〗投手所投之球至擊球手附近突向外側曲進之球。

‡**out·side** ['aut'saɪd, aut'saɪd; 'aut'said] *n.* ①外部;外面。The *outside* of it looks all right. 它的外表還可以。②外面的地方或位置;外界。Dreams come from within,

not from the *outside*. 夢由內心產生，非來自外界。③(人之)外觀;外表。Don't judge a man from his *outside*. 不要以貌取人。④極端。**at the (very) outside** 至多;充其量。*At the very outside* there were only fifty people there. 那裏至多有五十個人。**outside in** 外面向裏翻。—*adj.* ①在外面的;外部的。②〖俗〗最高的;最大的。an *outside* estimate. 最高的估計。③局外的;門外的;沒有加入的。*Outside* people tried to get control of the business. 局外之人想控制這項事業。④可能性極小的。—*adv.* ①外面地;外部地。The house was painted green *outside*. 這房子的外部漆成綠色。②在外邊;在戶外。Let's go *outside*. 讓我們到外面去。—*prep.* ①在外;超過…範圍。He was standing just *outside* the door. 他正站在門口外面。②〖俗〗除外。*Outside* of John, none of us liked the play. 除約翰外我們沒一個人喜愛這種遊戲。③超越界限。**be (or get) outside of**〖俚〗吞;吃;喝。to *get outside of* a good dinner. 猛吃一頓盛餐。**outside of**〖俚〗 a. =**outside.** b. 除…之外。*Outside of* her, no one came to the party. 除她之外,沒有人前來赴會。

out·sid·er 〔aut'saɪdɚ; 'aut'saidə〕 *n.* ①在外之人。②圈外之人。③局外人。④〖俗〗不能參加上流社會的粗俗之人。⑤(競賽中)無獲勝機會之馬或選手。

out·sit 〔aut'sɪt; aut'sit〕 *v.t.*, **-sat, -sit·ting.** ①較(他人)久坐。②久坐超過…時間。

out·size 〔'aut,saɪz; 'aut-saiz〕 *n.* ①異常之型;特大號。②特大號之衣服(等)。—*adj.* 特大的(=outsized).

***out·skirt** 〔'aut,skɝt; 'aut-skə:t〕 *v.t.* 沿…之邊界而行。They *outskirted* the lawn. 他們沿草地邊緣走。

out·skirts 〔'aut,skɝts; 'aut-skə:ts〕 *n. pl.* 城鎮之外區;市郊;邊界;邊緣。

out·smart 〔aut'smɑrt; aut'smɑ:t〕 *v.t.*〖美俗〗以機智勝過。***outsmart oneself*** 弄巧成拙。

out·soar 〔aut'sor; aut'sɔ:〕 *v.t.* 飛出。

out·span 〔aut'spæn; aut'spæn〕 *v.*, **-spanned, -span·ning,** *n.* —*v.t.* & *v.i.*〖南非〗去軛;脫卸馬具。—*n.*〖南非〗去軛;脫卸馬具;牲口去軛或休息之地。

out·speak 〔aut'spik; aut'spi:k〕 *v.*, **-spoke, -spo·ken, -speak·ing.** —*v.t.* ①講話勝過。②說出。—*v.i.* 把話說出;發言。

out·spo·ken 〔'aut'spokən; aut'spoukən, 'aut's-〕 *adj.* ①直言無隱的;坦白的。②明顯的(疾病)。—**ly,** *adv.*

out·spread 〔*n., adj.* 'aut,sprɛd; 'aut'spred *v.* aut'sprɛd; aut'spred〕 *adj., v.*, **-spread, -spread·ing,** *n.*—*adj.* 伸開的;張開的。—*v.t.* & *v.i.* 伸開;張開。—*n.* 張開;伸開。

***out·stand·ing** 〔aut'stændɪŋ; aut'stændiŋ〕 *adj.* ①傑出的;顯著的。an *outstanding* person. 傑出的人。②未付的。*outstanding* debts. 未付之債務。*outstanding* account. 未進帳。③突出的。*outstanding* ears. 突出的耳朵。④未完成的;未解決的。—*n. pl.* 未償還的貸款。—**ly,** *adv.*

out·sta·tion 〔'aut,steʃən; 'aut,steiʃən〕 *n.* (遠離大都市、本部、本隊等之)分駐所;支部;市郊的車站。—*adj.* 分駐所的;支部的;偏僻地區的。

out·stay 〔aut'ste; aut'stei〕 *v.t.* ①較…久留。②居留過長。

out·step 〔aut'stɛp; aut'step〕 *v.t.*, **-stepped, -step·ping.** 踏過;越過;犯。

out·stretch 〔aut'strɛtʃ; aut'stretʃ〕 *v.t.* ①伸出;擴張。②伸張超過(某一限制)。

***out·stretched** 〔aut'strɛtʃt; 'aut-stretʃt〕 *adj.* 伸開的;張開的。He welcomed his old friend with *outstretched* arms. 他伸開兩臂歡迎他的老朋友。

out·strip 〔aut'strɪp; aut'strip〕 *v.t.*, **-stripped, -strip·ping.** ①超越;比…更速。②勝過。

out·talk 〔aut'tɔk; aut'tɔ:k〕 *v.t.* 舌戰勝過;講贏。

out·turn 〔'aut,tɝn; 'auttə:n〕 *n.* ①產量。②〖商〗出品;出產(指其品質、數量等而言)。

out·val·ue 〔aut'vælju; aut'vælju:〕 *v.t.* 較…有價值。

out·vie 〔aut'vaɪ; aut'vai〕 *v.t.*, **-vied, -vy·ing.** 賽過;勝過;打敗。

out·voice 〔aut'vɔɪs; aut'vɔis〕 *v.t.* 以大聲壓倒;比…出更大的聲音。

out·vote 〔aut'vot; aut'vout〕 *v.t.*, **-vot·ed, -vot·ing.** 投票之數勝過。

out·walk 〔aut'wɔk; aut'wɔ:k〕 *v.t.* ①比…走得更快(遠、久);走贏。②步行通過或超過(界線)。

***out·ward** 〔'autwɚd; 'aut-wəd〕 *adj.* ①向外的。an *outward* motion. 向外的動作。②外面的;外部的。③外表上的;顯而易見的。④表面的;肉體的。⑤〖藥〗外服的。—*adv.* (亦作 **outwards**) ①向外。The two ends bent *outward*. 兩端向外彎。②在外。—*n.* ①外部;外面。②外界。③外表;外貌。④(*pl.*)外面之物。—**ness,** *n.*

out·ward-bound 〔'autwɚd'baund; 'autwəd'baund〕 *adj.* 開往外國的(機、船等)。

out·ward·ly 〔'autwɚdlɪ; 'aut-wədli〕 *adv.* ①表面地;外觀上地。②向外地。③從外面看來;表面看來。

***out·wards** 〔'autwɚdz; 'aut-wədz〕 *adv.* =**outward.**

out·watch 〔aut'wɑtʃ; aut'wɔtʃ〕 *v.t.* ①比…看(守)得久。②看到看不見爲止;看到最後。

out·wear 〔aut'wɛr; aut'wɛə〕 *v.t.*, **-wore, -worn, -wear·ing.** ①比…更經久;比…生存更久。②穿舊;穿破;用舊;用破;用完。③使筋疲力竭。④消磨(時間);忍耐地度過。

out·weigh 〔aut'we; aut'wei〕 *v.t.* ①重過;比…更重。②優於;勝過;强過;比…更重要。③對…過於沉重;太重使…不勝負擔。

out·wit 〔aut'wɪt; aut'wit〕 *v.t.*, **-wit·ted, -wit·ting.** 以機智勝過;以智敗之;哄騙。

out·work 〔*n.* 'aut,wɝk; 'aut-wə:k *v.* aut'wɝk; aut'wə:k〕 *n., v.*, **-worked** or **-wrought, -work·ing.** —*n.*〖築城〗外堡;外壘。—*v.t.* ①在工作上勝過;比…做得更努力或更快。②做出;完成。

out·work·er 〔'aut,wɝkɚ; 'aut,wə:kə〕 *n.* 在所屬機關外工作的人;屋外工作者。

out·worn 〔'aut'worn; 'aut'wɔ:n〕 *adj.* ①疲倦的。②陳腐的;過時的;已廢的。③穿壞的;穿破的。

ou·zel 〔'uzl; 'u:zl〕 *n.*〖英〗黑鳥。(亦作 **ousel**)

o·va 〔'ovə; 'ouvə〕 *n.* pl. of **ovum.**

***o·val** 〔'ovl; 'ouvəl〕 *adj.* ①卵形的。②橢圓形的。—*n.* ①卵形或橢圓形之物。②卵形或橢圓形。③橢圓形之場地(如徑賽場)。④〖俗〗足球;橄欖球。—**ly,** *adv.* —**ness,** *n.*

o·var·i·an 〔o'vɛrɪən; ou'vɛəriən〕 *adj.* ①〖植物〗子房的。②〖解剖,動物〗卵巢的。

o·var·i·ot·o·my 〔o,vɛrɪ'ɑtəmɪ; ou-

ˌvɛəriˈɔtəmi] *n., pl.* **-mies.** 〖外科〗卵巢切除(術)。

o·va·ri·tis [ˌovəˈraɪtɪs; ˌouvəˈraitis] *n.* 「〖醫〗卵巢炎。」

o·va·ry [ˈovərɪ, ˈovrɪ; ˈouvəri] *n., pl.* **-ries.** ①〖動物〗卵巢。②〖植物〗子房。(亦作 **ovarium**) 「〖植物〗卵形的(葉)。」

o·vate [ˈovet; ˈouveit] *adj.* ①卵形的。②

o·va·tion [oˈveʃən; ouˈveiʃən] *n.* ①熱烈的歡迎;熱烈的鼓掌;大喝采。②(古羅馬之)小凱旋式。—*v.t.* 對…熱烈鼓掌;熱烈歡迎。

ov·en** [ˈʌvən; ˈʌvn] *n.* 烤爐;烤箱。in the same oven*** 〖俗〗處境相同。

ov·en·bird [ˈʌvənˌbɜd; ˈʌvnbəːd] *n.* ①(美國產) 竈巢鳥。②(南美產) 一種鳴禽。

‡o·ver [ˈovɚ; ˈouvə] *prep.* ①在上空(未接觸的, =above). The sky is *over* our heads. 天空在我們的頭上。②在…之上;覆於…之上(相接觸的,=on 或 upon). ③遍於…之上。A blush came *over* her face. 她滿面通紅。④橫過;越過。There is a bridge *over* the river. 河上橫有一橋。⑤在彼面;在彼方。⑥自…落下。He fell *over* the edge of the cliff. 他自山崖上跌下。⑦超過於;高於 (=more than). It costs *over* ten dollars. 它值十元以上。⑧遍經 (=all through). ⑨在…的時間內(=during). ⑩關於。⑪支配;統治;管制;在…之上位。We have a captain *over* us. 我們有一個首領管轄我們。⑫從頭到尾。⑬正從事…的時候;中途。⑭不同於。⑮透過;經過。He spoke to me *over* the telephone. 他用電話跟我說話。⑯直到…之後。She invited us to stay *over* Sunday. 她邀我們逗留至星期日以後。***over a barrel*** 任他人處置;在他人掌握中。They had him *over a barrel.* 他們可以把他任意處置。—*adv.* ①在上空 (=above). ②遍及全面地。③橫過。④越過。Come *over* and see me. 請過來見我。⑤在彼方。*over* in Europe. 遠在歐洲。⑥落下。She went too near the edge and fell *over*. 她走得太靠邊緣而跌了下來。⑦顚倒;反轉。⑧再;又反覆。⑨穿過;經過。⑩自始至終。I have read it *over*. 我曾讀過它一遍。⑪交付。Hand the money *over*. 付錢。⑫太;過度 (=too, 主要用於複合字中)。⑬一直;過(某時)。Please stay *over* till Monday. 請一直逗留到星期一。⑭加之;另外。⑮自一邊到另一邊;自一端到另一端。The mouth of the cave was about 12 feet *over*. 那洞口從一邊到另一邊約有十二英尺。⑯倒下。They knocked the boy *over*. 他們擊倒了那男孩。⑰到家裏。⑱在(某距離)以外。***all over*** **a.** 遍布;到處。**b.** 完全地;徹底地。**c.** 完結。The war was *all over*. 戰爭結束了。***all over with*** 完畢;結束。***be all over with (a person)*** (某人)失敗、將死、或死了。It's *all over with* poor Tom. 可憐的湯姆已完了。***over again*** 再一次。I had to do it *over again*. 我須再做它一次。***over against*** **a.** 對着;面對着。**b.** 對照著。***over and above*** 而且;加之。***over and over (again)*** 再三。I have told you *over and over (again)*. 我曾再三告訴過你。***over here*** 在這邊;在這裏。***over there*** **a.** 在那邊;在那裏。**b.** 〖俗〗(第一次大戰時)在歐洲;往歐洲。—*adj.* ①在上的;表層的。②結束的;完了的。The play is *over*. 戲散了。③賸餘的。④有餘的。The cash is said to be *over*. 據說現款有餘。⑤兩面都煎的(蛋)。He ordered two eggs *over*. 他叫了兩個兩面都煎的蛋。—*n.* 過度之數量。—*v.t.* ①〖方〗自…痊癒。②跳過。

over- 〖字首〗①表"在上;外;優越;傑出"之義。②表"過度;太多"之義。③表"使低於;降服"之義。④表"橫過;越過"之義。〖注意〗①形容詞前加 over, over=too, 例如: overbusy. ②名詞前加 over, over=too much, excessive, 例如: overactivity, overwork. ③動詞前加 over, over=too much, 例如: overburden.

o·ver·a·bun·dance [ˌovərəˈbʌndəns; ˈouvərəˈbʌndəns] *n.* 過多;過豐富。

o·ver·a·chieve [ˈovərəˈtʃiv; ˈouvərəˈtʃiːv] *v.t. & v.i.,* **-chieved, -chiev·ing.** 超過預期標準。

o·ver·act [ˈovɚˈækt; ˈouvərˈækt] *v.t. & v.i.* 爲之過甚;動作過度;表演(角色)過火。

o·ver·age[1] [ˈovərɪdʒ, ˈovrɪdʒ; ˈouvəridʒ] *n.* (商品等的)過賸。「超齡的。」

o·ver·age[2] [ˈovɚˈedʒ; ˈouvərˈeidʒ] *adj.*

***o·ver·all** [*adj.* ˈovɚˌɔl; ˈouvərɔːl *adv.* ˌovɚˈɔl; ˈouvərˈɔːl] *adj.* ①自一端至另一端的。②全面的;全盤的;所有的。—*adv.* ①大體上;就整個來說。*Overall* the film has remarkable power. 就大體而言那電影具有不容忽視的力量。②從頭到尾;從一端到另一端。—*n.* ①(*pl.*)工裝褲。②(*pl.*)防水長綁腿。③〖英〗罩衫;罩衣。

o·ver·arch [ˌovɚˈartʃ; ˈouvərˈaːtʃ] *v.t.* 覆以拱;掩以弓形物;在…上形成穹窿。—*v.i.* 似拱形地彎曲;形成拱形。

o·ver·arm [ˈovɚˌarm; ˈouvəraːm] *adj.* 舉手過肩的;由上向下的。

o·ver·awe [ˌovɚˈɔ; ˌouvərˈɔː] *v.t.,* **-awed, -aw·ing.** 使畏縮;威壓;懾服。

o·ver·bal·ance [ˌovɚˈbæləns; ˌouvəˈbæləns] *v.,* **-anced, -anc·ing,** *n.* —*v.t.* ①重過;重要過;勝過。②使失平衡。—*n.* ①超過量。②使失平衡之物。

o·ver·bear [ˌovɚˈbɛr; ˌouvəˈbɛə] *v.,* **-bore, -borne, -bear·ing.** —*v.t.* ①壓倒;否決;威壓;克服;鎮懾。②重過;勝過。—*v.i.* 結實或產子過多。**—er,** *n.*

o·ver·bear·ing [ˌovɚˈbɛrɪŋ; ˌouvəˈbɛəriŋ] *adj.* ①自大的;專制的;傲慢的;壓倒的;作威作福的。②極重要的。—*n.* 專制;作威作福。**—ly,** *adv.* **—ness,** *n.*

o·ver·bid [*v.* ˌovɚˈbɪd; ˈouvəˈbid *n.* ˈovɚˌbɪd; ˈouvəbid] *v.,* **-bid, -bid·den** or **-bid, -bid·ding,** *n.* —*v.t. & v.i.* ①出價較(他人)爲高。②出價較(物)之價值爲高。③〖牌戲〗(於橋牌戲中)叫牌較(同伴、對方、或自己實力)爲高。—*n.* 所出之高價。

o·ver·blown [ˌovɚˈblon; ˈouvəˈbloun] *adj.* ①盛開期已過的(花);已萎的。②吹過的;被颺去的;過去的;已停歇的。

o·ver·board** [ˈovɚˌbord, -ˌbɔrd; ˈouvəbɔːd] *adv.* 於船外;在船外;落水。go overboard*** 做得太過火。They tend to *go overboard* on this subject. 對這問題他們的言論有過火的傾向。***throw overboard*** **a.** 丟在水中。**b.** 〖俗〗排斥;放棄;除去;棄置。

o·ver·book [ˌovɚˈbʊk; ˈouvəˈbuk] *v.t. & v.i.* 接受超過實有數之訂位(指飛機、船等)。

o·ver·bridge [ˈovɚˌbrɪdʒ; ˈouvəbridʒ] *n., v.,* **-bridged, -bridg·ing.** —*n.* 〖土木〗天橋;陸橋。—*v.t.* 架天橋於…之上。

o·ver·brim [ˌovɚˈbrɪm; ˈouvəˈbrim] *v.,* **-brimmed, -brim·ming.** —*v.t.* 使溢出邊緣;溢出…之邊緣。—*v.i.* 溢出邊緣;滿溢。

o·ver·build [ˈovɚˈbɪld; ˈouvəˈbild] *v.,* **-built, -build·ing.** —*v.t.* ①建於…之

上。②於(某區域)建屋過多。③建造過大、過分精緻或過多。—v.i. 建屋超過需求量。

o·ver·bur·den 〔*v.* ˌovɚˈbɝdn̩; ˌouvəˈbəːdn *n.* ˈovɚˌbɝdn̩; ˌouvəˈbəːdn〕 *v.t.* 使載重過多;使負擔過重。—*n.* ①過重的負擔;重荷。②岩石上的砂土層。

o·ver·buy 〔ˈovɚˈbaɪ; ˈouvəˈbai〕 *v.t.* & *v.i.*, **-bought, -buy·ing.** 購買過多。

o·ver·came 〔ˌovɚˈkem; ˌouvəˈkeim〕 *v.* pt. of **overcome.**

o·ver·can·o·py 〔ˌovɚˈkænəpɪ; ˌouvəˈkænəpi〕 *v.t.*, **-pied, -py·ing.** 以天幕覆蓋;加罩蓋於…之上;如天幕覆蓋。

o·ver·ca·pac·i·ty 〔ˌovɚkəˈpæsɪtɪ; ˈouvəkəˈpæsiti〕 *n.* 生產力過賸。

o·ver·cap·i·tal·i·za·tion 〔ˈovɚˌkæpətl̩ɪˈzeʃən; ˈouvəˌkæpitəlaiˈzeiʃən〕 *n.* ①資本過高估價。②投資過多;過分擴大資本。

o·ver·cap·i·tal·ize 〔ˈovɚˈkæpətl̩ˌaɪz; ˈouvəˈkæpitəlaiz〕 *v.t.*, **-ized, -iz·ing.** ①對…之資本估價過高。②過分擴大(事業)之資本;過多投資於…。

o·ver·care 〔ˌovɚˈkɛr; ˈouvəˈkɛə〕 *n.* 「過慮;杞憂。」

o·ver·care·ful 〔ˈovɚˈkɛrfəl; ˈouvəˈkɛəfəl〕 *adj.* 過分憂慮的;杞憂的;過於謹慎的。—**ly,** *adv.* —**ness,** *n.*

o·ver·cast 〔ˈovɚˌkæst, ˌovɚˈkæst; ˈouvə-kɑːst, ˌouvəˈkɑːst〕 *adj., n., v.,* **-cast, -cast·ing.** —*adj.* ①多雲的;陰暗的;昏黑的。②憂鬱的;愁悶的。③用長針脚縫合的。—*n.* ①一層陰雲。②陰雲密布的天空。—*v.t.* ①使陰暗;使昏黑。②以長針脚縫合(邊)。—*v.i.* 變成陰暗。

o·ver·cer·ti·fy 〔ˌovɚˈsɝtɪfaɪ; ˌouvəˈsəːtifai〕 *v.t.*, **-fied, -fy·ing.** 證明(支票)所支款額超出存款額。

o·ver·charge 〔*v.* ˈovɚˈtʃɑrdʒ; ˈouvəˈtʃɑːdʒ *n.* ˈovɚˌtʃɑrdʒ; ˈouvəˈtʃɑːdʒ〕 *v.,* **-charged, -charg·ing,** *n.* —*v.t.* & *v.i.* ①索價過高。②裝載過多。③誇張;誇大。—*n.* 過高的索價。—**o·ver·charg·er,** *n.*

o·ver·choice 〔ˈovɚˈtʃɔɪs; ˈouvəˈtʃɔis〕 *n.* 過分的挑選;過多的選擇機會。

o·ver·cloud 〔ˌovɚˈklaud; ˌouvəˈklaud〕 *v.t.* ①以雲掩蔽;使似被雲所遮。②使昏暗;使陰沉。—*v.i.* ①變昏暗。②變陰沉。

***o·ver·coat** 〔ˈovɚˌkot; ˈouvəkout〕 *n.* ①大衣;外套。②＝**overcoating**②. —*v.t.* 多塗一層漆於。〖注意〗在美國厚大衣叫 **overcoat,** 輕的稱做 **topcoat.** 在英國 overcoat 或 topcoat 均指輕外套, 厚的叫做 **greatcoat.**

o·ver·coat·ing 〔ˈovɚˌkotɪŋ; ˈouvəˌkoutiŋ〕 *n.* ①縫製外衣或大衣的布料。②爲保護而塗的一層(如油漆)。

o·ver·col·o(u)r 〔ˌovɚˈkʌlɚ; ˈouvəˈkʌlə〕 *v.t.* ①着色過多於…;過分潤飾。②誇張(描寫等)。

***o·ver·come** 〔ˌovɚˈkʌm; ˌouvəˈkʌm〕 *v.,* **-came, -come, -com·ing.** —*v.t.* ①壓倒;克服;擊敗。to *overcome* an enemy. 擊敗一敵人。②(常用被動式)使軟弱;使無能爲力〖with, by〗. to be *overcome* by weariness. 筋疲力盡。—*v.i.* 得勝。

o·ver·com·pen·sate 〔ˈovɚˈkɑmpənset; ˈouvəˈkɔmpenseit〕 *v.t.* 對…作過大的補償。

o·ver·com·pen·sa·tion 〔ˈovɚˌkɑmpənˈseʃən; ˈouvəˌkɔmpenˈseiʃən〕 *n.* 〖精神分析〗過償(作用);代償過度(由自卑感、罪惡感或不成熟感而導致之過分掩飾的極端反應)。

o·ver·con·fi·dence 〔ˈovɚˈkɑnfədəns; ˈouvəˈkɔnfidəns〕 *n.* 過度自信;過分自恃。

o·ver·con·fi·dent 〔ˈovɚˈkɑnfədənt; ˈouvəˈkɔnfidənt〕 *adj.* 過於自信的;過於自恃的。—**ly,** *adv.*

o·ver·count 〔ˌovɚˈkaunt; ˌouvəˈkaunt〕 *v.t.* ①對…作過高之估計。②在數目上超過。

o·ver·cred·u·lous 〔ˈovɚˈkrɛdʒuləs; ˈouvəˈkredjuləs〕 *adj.* 過度輕信的。—**o·ver·cre·du·li·ty,** *n.*

o·ver·crit·i·cal 〔ˈovɚˈkrɪtɪkl̩; ˈouvəˈkritikəl〕 *adj.* 批評過於嚴格的;吹毛求疵的。

o·ver·crop 〔ˌovɚˈkrɑp; ˈouvəˈkrɔp〕 *v.t.,* **-cropped, -crop·ping.** 把(田地)耕種過度;過度耕種而使地力貧瘠。

o·ver·crowd 〔ˌovɚˈkraud; ˌouvəˈkraud〕 *v.t.* & *v.i.* (使)過度擁擠;(使)雜沓。

o·ver·cul·ture 〔ˈovɚˈkʌltʃɚ; ˈouvəˈkʌltʃə〕 *n.* 主要文化。

o·ver·date 〔*n.* ˈovɚˌdet; ˈouvədeit *v.* ˌovɚˈdet; ˌouvəˈdeit〕 *n., v.,* **-dat·ed, -dat·ing.** —*n.* 硬幣上加蓋的新日期。—*v.t.* 加蓋新日期於。

o·ver·de·vel·op 〔ˈovɚdɪˈvɛləp; ˈouvədiˈveləp〕 *v.t.* ①使過度發展。②〖照相〗使(底片)顯影過度。—**ment,** *n.*

o·ver·do 〔ˈovɚˈdu; ˈouvəˈduː〕 *v.,* **-did, -done, -do·ing.** —*v.t.* ①過分;過火;過於鋪張。②過度烹煮;燒得過久。③使疲倦;竭盡。—*v.i.* 過分;過火;過用體力等。***overdo it*** **a.** 竭盡其力;使疲乏。**b.** 過火;過於誇張。

o·ver·dog 〔ˈovɚˌdɑg; ˈouvədɔg〕 *n.* 屬於統治階級或特權階級者;占上風者。

o·ver·done 〔ˈovɚˈdʌn; ˈouvəˈdʌn〕 *adj.* ①做得過分的。②煮得太久的。

o·ver·dose 〔*n.* ˈovɚˌdos; ˈouvədous *v.* ˌovɚˈdos; ˈouvəˈdous〕 *n., v.,* **-dosed, -dos·ing.** —*n.* 藥量過多;過量的一劑藥。—*v.t.* ①配(藥)過量。②使服藥過量。

o·ver·draft 〔ˈovɚˌdræft; ˈouvədrɑːft〕 *n.* ①透支;透支之款。②從火上通過之一股風;向下通過窰或爐之一股風。

o·ver·draught 〔ˈovɚˌdræft; ˈouvəˈdrɑːft〕 *n.* ＝**overdraft.**

o·ver·draw 〔ˈovɚˈdrɔ; ˈouvəˈdrɔː〕 *v.,* **-drew, -drawn, -draw·ing.** —*v.t.* ①透支(銀行存款等);過開(支票等)。②過拉(弓等)。③(描述方面等)誇張;誇大。—*v.i.* ①透支。②誇張。—**er,** *n.*

o·ver·dress 〔ˈovɚˈdrɛs; ˈouvəˈdres〕 *v.t.* & *v.i.* 過度裝飾;穿得太考究。—*n.* 外衣。

o·ver·drink 〔ˌovɚˈdrɪŋk; ˈouvəˈdriŋk〕 *v.,* **-drank, -drunk** or **-drunk·en, -drink·ing.** —*v.t.* 使飲(酒)過量。—*v.i.* 飲(酒)過量。

o·ver·drive 〔ˈovɚˈdraɪv; ˈouvəˈdraiv〕 *v.,* **-drove, -driv·en, -driv·ing,** *n.* —*v.t.* 令過度工作;過度驅使。—*n.* 〖機械〗向推進軸傳達比引擎速度較大速度之一種傳動裝置。

o·ver·due 〔ˈovɚˈdju; ˈouvəˈdjuː〕 *adj.* ①過期的;遲到的。②早已完成準備的。③過大的;過量的;過分的。

***o·ver·eat** 〔ˈovɚˈit; ˈouvərˈiːt〕 *v.t.* & *v.i.,* **-ate, -eat·en, -eat·ing.** 吃得過量。

o·ver·em·pha·sis 〔ˌovɚˈɛmfəsɪs; ˈouvərˈemfəsis〕 *n.* ①過分强調。②(對某一字或音節)過分重讀。

o·ver·em·ploy·ment 〔ˈovɚɪmˈplɔɪmənt; ˈouvərimˈplɔimənt〕 *n.* ①人力之供不應求。②使用過多。

o·ver·es·ti·mate 〔*v.* ˈovɚˈɛstəˌmet; ˈouvərˈestimeit *n.* ˈovɚˈɛstəmɪt; ˈouvərˈestimit〕 *v.*, **-mat·ed, -mat·ing,** *n.* —*v.t.* 對…估計過高。—*n.* 過高的估計。 **—o·ver·es·ti·ma·tion,** *n.*

o·ver·ex·ert 〔ˌovərɪgˈzɝt; ˈouvərigˈzəːt〕 *v.t.* & *v.i.* 過分操勞。

o·ver·ex·pose 〔ˈovərɪkˈspoz; ˈouvəriksˈpouz〕 *v.t.*, **-posed, -pos·ing.** ①過度暴露。②〖照相〗使感光過久。

o·ver·ex·po·sure 〔ˈovərɪkˈspoʒɚ; ˈouvəriksˈpouʒə〕 *n.* ①過度暴露。②〖照相〗使感光過久。

o·ver·ex·tend 〔ˈovərɪkˈstɛnd; ˈouvəriksˈtend〕 *v.t.* ①過分擴張。②使部署於過長的防線或過大區域。***overextend oneself*** 作超出能力之投資或企畫;不自量力。

o·ver·fa·tigue 〔ˌovɚfəˈtig; ˈouvəfəˈtiːg〕 *v.t.* 使過勞;使筋疲力盡。—*n.* 過勞。

o·ver·feed 〔ˈovɚˈfid; ˈouvəˈfiːd〕 *v.*, **-fed, -feed·ing,** *adj.* —*v.t.* & *v.i.* 過度餵飼;(使)吃得太多。—*adj.* 材料或燃料入口在上端的(爲 underfeed 之對)。

o·ver·fill 〔ˈovɚˈfɪl; ˈouvəˈfil〕 *v.t.* 使滿溢;過度塡充。—*v.i.* 漲滿;充滿。

***o·ver·flow** 〔*v.* ˌovɚˈflo; ˌouvəˈflou *n.*, *adj.* ˈovɚˌflo; ˈouvə-flou〕 *v.*, **-flowed, -flown, -flow·ing,** *n.*, *adj.* —*v.t.* ①(液體)流出;溢;氾濫。The river *overflowed* my garden. 河水氾濫淹沒了我的花園。②(人等)擠出。—*v.i.*①(液體)流出;溢;氾濫。②充溢。③充滿;擠出。Banks are *overflowing* with deposits. 銀行充斥着存款。—*n.* ①氾濫;洪水。②充溢;過多。—*adj.* ①溢出的;容納不下的;過剩的。②爆滿的。She sang before *overflow* crowds. 她在爆滿的羣衆前獻唱。 **—a·ble,** *adj.* **—ing·ness,** *n.* **—ing·ly,** *adv.*

o·ver·ful·fil(l) 〔ˌovɚfulˈfɪl; ˌouvəfulˈfil〕 *v.t.* 達成或實現(計畫或目標)而有餘。 **—ment,** *n.*

o·ver·gild 〔ˌovɚˈgɪld; ˈouvəˈgild〕 *v.t.*, **-gild·ed** or **-gilt, -gild·ing.** ①鍍金於。②文飾;掩飾。

o·ver·ground 〔ˈovɚˌgraund; ˈouvəgraund〕 *adj.* 在地上的;地上的(爲 underground 之對)。

o·ver·grow 〔ˈovɚˈgro; ˈouvəˈgrou〕 *v.*, **-grew, -grown, -grow·ing.** —*v.t.* & *v.i.* ①蔓延;生滿。②生長過度;生長過速。③長得大過…。

o·ver·grown 〔ˈovɚˈgron, ˌovɚ-; ˈouvəˈgroun〕 *adj.* ①長滿(草木等)的。②太繁茂的;未修剪的。③發育過速的;長得太高的(人)。④異常發達的。

o·ver·growth 〔ˈovɚˌgroθ; ˈouvəgrouθ〕 *n.* ①繁茂;蔓延;滋蔓。②過度生長。

o·ver·hand 〔ˈovɚˌhænd; ˈouvəhænd〕 *adj.* ①(打球等)舉手過肩的;朝下打的;兩手交拍水面的(游泳)。②重複地穿縫的。—*adv.* ①舉手過肩地;朝下打地。②重複穿縫地。③指關節朝上地。—*n.* 舉手過肩的(發球,游泳等)姿勢。—*v.t.* 重複穿縫。

***o·ver·hang** 〔*v.* ˌovɚˈhæŋ; ˈouvəˈhæŋ *n.* ˈovɚˌhæŋ; ˈouvəhæŋ〕 *v.*, **-hung, -hang·ing,** *n.* —*v.t.* ①懸於…之上;突出於…之上。②懸垂;伸出;突出。A dark sky *overhangs* the earth. 昏暗的天空籠罩大地。③威脅;逼近。A pestilence *overhangs* the country. 瘟疫威脅着那國家。④裝飾以懸掛物。—*v.i.* ①突出;伸出。②威脅;逼近。—*n.* ①突出;突出之物。②〖建築〗懸垂;懸垂之部分(如陽臺等)。③〖航空〗突出翼。

o·ver·hap·py 〔ˈovɚˈhæpɪ; ˈouvəˈhæpi〕 *adj.* 極其快樂的;非常高興的。

o·ver·haul 〔*v.* ˌovɚˈhɔl; ˌouvəˈhɔːl *n.* ˈovɚˌhɔl; ˈouvəhɔːl〕 *v.t.* ①(爲修理)徹底檢查;仔細檢驗。②(爲檢查)拆開;翻過來。③修理;翻修。④追及;趕上。⑤〖航海〗解鬆(船的繩索)。—*n.* 徹底檢查;檢驗;翻修。

***o·ver·head** 〔*adv.* ˈovɚˈhɛd; ˈouvəˈhed *adj.*, *n.* ˈovɚˌhɛd; ˈouvəhed〕 *adv.* ①在空中;在樓上;在高處;在上。②從頭上到脚底;全身地。—*adj.* ①在上面的;經過頭上的。②普通的;經常的。③〖主英〗一般性的。—*n.* ①(稅、租金、保險費、電費等)經常開支;普通用費。There were too many *overheads.* 經常開支太大。②天花板。

overhead railway 〖英〗高架鐵路。

***o·ver·hear** 〔ˌovɚˈhɪr; ˌouvəˈhiə〕 *v.t.*, **-heard, -hear·ing.** 無意聽到;從旁聽到。

o·ver·heat 〔ˌovɚˈhit; ˌouvəˈhiːt〕 *v.t.* ①加熱過大;加熱過度。②使過度興奮或激動。—*n.* 熱度過高。

o·ver·hit 〔ˌovɚˈhɪt; ˌouvəˈhit〕 *v.i.* 打擊過重或過遠。

o·ver·hung 〔ˌovɚˈhʌŋ; ˈouvəˈhʌŋ〕 *v.* pt. & pp. of **overhang.** —*adj.* ①從上面懸下的。②(上頦)突出於下頦之外的。

o·ver·in·dul·gence 〔ˈovərɪnˈdʌldʒəns; ˈouvərinˈdʌldʒəns〕 *n.* 放縱;過度放任;過度耽溺。**—o·ver·in·dul·gent,** *adj.*

o·ver·in·sure 〔ˌovərɪnˈʃur; ˈouvərinˈʃuə〕 *v.t.*, **-sured, -sur·ing.** 作保額過高之投保。

o·ver·is·sue 〔ˈovɚˈɪʃu,-ˈɪʃju; ˈouvərˈisjuː〕 *n.*, *v.*, **-is·sued, -is·su·ing.** —*n.* ①(紙幣、股票、債券等之)濫發;限外發行。②過剩印刷物。—*v.t.* 濫發;限外發行。

o·ver·joy 〔ˈovɚˈdʒɔɪ; ˌouvəˈdʒɔi〕 *v.t.* 使極端欣喜;使大喜;使狂喜。

o·ver·kill 〔*v.* ˌovɚˈkɪl; ˌouvəˈkil *n.* ˈovɚˌkɪl; ˈouvəkil〕 *v.*, *n.* 以超過需要(或數倍)的威力破壞或殺傷。

o·ver·lad·en 〔ˌovɚˈlednˌ; ˈouvəˈleidn〕 *adj.* ①裝貨過多的;(工作等之)負擔過多的。②裝飾過多的。

o·ver·land 〔*adj.* ˈovɚˌlænd; ˈouvəlænd *adv.* ˈovɚˌlænd; ˌouvəˈlænd〕 *adj.* 陸上的;陸路的;經過陸地的。the *overland* route. 陸路;(尤指)從英國經地中海(不繞好望角)到印度的道路;〖美〗橫貫大陸到太平洋岸的道路。—*adv.* 由陸路地;經陸路地。

o·ver·lap 〔*v.* ˌovɚˈlæp; ˌouvəˈlæp *n.* ˈovɚˌlæp; ˈouvəlæp〕 *v.*, **-lapped, -lap·ping,** *n.* —*v.t.* ①重疊。②與…一部分相一致;與…部分時間相同。—*v.i.* ①重複。②(時間上)相同。—*n.* ①重疊;重複。②重疊或重複之部分。③重複之數目。④重複或重疊之處。

o·ver·lay¹ 〔*v.* ˌovɚˈle; ˌouvəˈlei *n.* ˈovɚˌle; ˈouvəlei〕 *v.*, **-laid, -lay·ing,** *n.* —*v.t.* ①置於他物之上;覆蓋;蓋暗;弄陰。②(爲裝飾等)塗上;覆;蓋;鋪;包;鍍。③壓倒;壓制。④〖印刷〗把作輪廓的紙貼在…之上。—*n.* ①蓋於上面之物;外罩;小檯布。②(裝飾用)覆蓋之層;鍍金。③〖印刷〗輪廓紙。④〖軍〗用以蓋在地圖上之透明紙(上載有各地點之軍事上重要資料)。

o·ver·lay² 〔ˌovɚˈle; ˌouvəˈlei〕 *v.* pt. of **overlie.**

o·ver·leaf 〔ˈovɚˈlif, ˈovɚˌlif; ˈouvə-

ˈli:f〕 *adv.* & *adj.* 在(紙之)背面;在(書之)次頁。—*n.* (書頁、信箋等之)次面;次頁。

o·ver·leap 〔ˌovəˈlip; ˌouvəˈli:p〕 *v.t.*, **-leaped** or **-leapt, -leap·ing.** ①跳得較…爲遠。②做得過分而使(自己)失敗。③忽略;省去;不管。④跳過;越過。

o·ver·lie 〔ˌovəˈlaɪ; ˌouvəˈlai〕 *v.t.*, **-lay, -lain, -ly·ing.** ①臥於…之上;覆於…之上。②臥於其上使悶死;壓死。

o·ver·load 〔*v.* ˌovəˈlod; ˈouvəˈloud *n.* ˈovəˌlod; ˈouvəloud〕 *v.t.* ①使裝載過重;充塡過度。②〖電〗過量充電。—*v.i.* 裝載過重。—*n.* 過重負擔。

***o·ver·look** 〔*v.* ˌovəˈlʊk; ˌouvəˈluk *n.* ˈovɜˌlʊk; ˌouvəˈluk〕 *v.t.* ①俯視;俯瞰。②看漏;未注意;忽略。③寬恕。④監督;管理。⑤監視;看守。⑥閱覽。He took down a map and *overlooked* it. 他取下一張地圖把它瀏覽一下。⑦注視而施以魔術。—*n.* ①疏忽;忽略。②可俯視之處。**—er,** *n.*

o·ver·lord 〔ˈovəˌlɔrd; ˈouvəlɔ:d〕 *n.* 大封主;君主;霸王;大地主。**—ship,** *n.*

o·ver·ly 〔ˈovəlɪ; ˈouvəli〕 *adv.* 非常;過度。

o·ver·man 〔*n. for* ① & ②ˈovəmən; ˈouvəmən *for*③ ˈovəˌmæn; ˈouvəmæn *v.* ˌovəˈmæn; ˈouvəˈmæn〕 *n.*, *pl.* **-men** 〔*for* ① & ② -mən; -mən *for* ③ -ˌmɛn; -men〕, *v.*, **-manned, -man·ning.** —*n.* ①監督者;工頭;〖礦場〗坑內監工員。②調停人;仲裁人。③〖哲學〗超人。—*v.t.* 運用過多的人員於…;供以過多的人員。

o·ver·man·tel 〔ˈovəˌmæntl̩; ˈouvəˌmæntl〕 *n.* 壁爐上的飾架。

o·ver·mark 〔ˌovəˈmark; ˌouvəˈmɑ:k〕 *v.t.* 過鬆地給予分數。

o·ver·mas·ter 〔ˌovəˈmæstə; ˈouvəˈmɑ:stə〕 *v.t.* 征服;壓服。**—ing·ly,** *adv.*

o·ver·match 〔ˌovəˈmætʃ; ˌouvəˈmætʃ〕 *v.t.* ①優於…;勝過;壓倒。②使對抗更強之對手。—*n.* 更強之對手。

o·ver·mat·ter 〔ˈovəˌmætə; ˈouvəˌmætə〕 *n.* 留供下期刊載之過賸稿件。

o·ver·meas·ure 〔ˈovəˌmɛʒə; ˈouvəˈmeʒə〕 *n.* 過大之估量;賸餘。—*v.t.* 計量過多;估量過高。

o·ver·much 〔ˈovəˈmʌtʃ; ˈouvəˈmʌtʃ〕 *adj.* 過多的。—*n.* 過賸;過多。—*adv.* 過度地;極端地。**—ness,** *n.*

o·ver·nice 〔ˈovəˈnaɪs; ˈouvəˈnais〕 *adj.* 過於講究的;吹毛求疵的。**—ty, —ness,** *n.*

***o·ver·night** 〔*adv., adj.* ˈovəˈnaɪt; ˈouvəˈnait *n.* ˈovəˌnaɪt; ˈouvəˈnait *v.* ˌovəˈnaɪt; ˌouvəˈnait〕 *adv.* ①在晚上;在夜裏;終夜。②在前一夜;在昨夜。③於短時內。No such perfected technique is born *overnight.* 這樣完善的技術不會在短時內產生。—*adj.* ①晚上的;夜裏的;夜間用的。②前一夜的;昨夜的。—*n.* 前一夜。—*v.i.* 過夜。He *overnighted* at the official presidential residence. 他在總統官邸過夜。

o·ver·oc·cu·pied 〔ˌovəˈɑkjəˌpaɪd; ˌouvəˈɔkjupaid〕 *adj.* 過擠的;空間不寬裕的。

o·ver·pass 〔*n.* ˈovəˌpæs; ˈouvəpɑ:s *v.* ˌovəˈpæs; ˌouvəˈpɑ:s〕 *n., v.*, **-passed** or **-past, -pass·ing.** —*n.* (架於道路、鐵路等上之)天橋;陸橋。—*v.t.* ①越過(一地區、境界、河等)。②超越;勝過。③忽略;置之不顧。④違犯(法律等)。

o·ver·passed 〔ˌovəˈpæst; ˌouvəˈpɑ:st〕 *adj.* 已過去的;已廢除的。(亦作 **overpast**)

o·ver·pay 〔ˈovəˈpe; ˈouvəˈpei〕 *v.*, **-paid, -pay·ing,** *n.* —*v.t.* 過多償付;給錢過多。—*n.* 多付;多給錢。

o·ver·peo·pled 〔ˌovəˈpipl̩d; ˈouvəˈpi:pld〕 *adj.* 人口過多的。

o·ver·per·suade 〔ˈovəpəˈswed; ˈouvəpəˈsweid〕 *v.t.*, **-suad·ed, -suad·ing.** 說服(不贊成者)。

o·ver·play 〔ˌovəˈple; ˈouvəˈplei〕 *v.t.* ①表演過火。②過分强調。③〖高爾夫〗擊(球)超越洞周二十碼以外。④(競賽中)擊敗(對手)。***overplay one's hand*** 〖牌戲〗過分自恃而遭敗績。—*n.* 過分的强調。

o·ver·plus 〔ˈovəˌplʌs; ˈouvə-plʌs〕 *n.* 餘賸;過賸;過多。

o·ver·pop·u·la·tion 〔ˈovəˌpɑpjəˈleʃən; ˈouvəˌpɔpjuˈleiʃən〕 *n.* 人口過多;人口過賸。

***o·ver·pow·er** 〔ˌovəˈpauə; ˌouvəˈpauə〕 *v.t.* ①擊敗;克服。②壓服;壓倒。The heat *overpowered* me. 我熱得受不了。③給以過大動力。Never *overpower* your boat. 不要爲你的船裝過大動力(的馬達)。

o·ver·pow·er·ing 〔ˌovəˈpauərɪŋ; ˌouvəˈpauəriŋ〕 *adj.* 强烈的;難抗拒的;制止不了的。**—ly,** *adv.*

o·ver·praise 〔ˌovəˈprez; ˈouvəˈpreiz〕 *v.*, **-praised, -prais·ing,** *n.* —*v.t.* 過度讚賞;誇獎。—*n.* 過度之讚賞;誇獎。

o·ver·print 〔*v.* ˌovəˈprɪnt; ˈouvəˈprint *n., adj.* ˈovəˌprɪnt; ˈouvə-print〕 *v.t.* ①〖印刷〗加印於(已印之物)上;套印;覆印;添印。②印刷…之册數過多。③〖照相〗曬印過度。④重疊地打(打字機上之字)。—*n.* ①〖印刷〗加印;套印。②(必要册數以上之)多印。③〖集郵〗郵票上特別加印之文字;有加印文字之郵票。—*adj.* 用於套印的。

o·ver·pro·duce 〔ˈovəprəˈdjus; ˈouvə-prəˈdju:s〕 *v.t.* & *v.i.*, **-duced, -duc·ing.** 生產過賸。

o·ver·pro·duc·tion 〔ˈovəprəˈdʌkʃən; ˈouvə-prəˈdʌkʃən〕 *n.* 生產過賸。

o·ver·proof 〔ˈovəˈpruf; ˈouvəˈpru:f〕 *adj.* 所含酒精超過標準的(酒)。

o·ver·pro·tect 〔ˌovəprəˈtɛkt; ˈouvəprəˈtekt〕 *v.t.* 過分保護。

o·ver·proud 〔ˈovəˈpraud; ˈouvəˈpraud〕 *adj.* 太驕傲的;過分自得的。

o·ver·qual·i·fied 〔ˌovəˈkwɑləˌfaɪd; ˌouvəˈkwɔlifaid〕 *adj.* 資格綽綽有餘的。

o·ver·ran 〔ˌovəˈræn; ˌouvəˈræn〕 *v.* pt. of **overrun.**

o·ver·rate 〔ˈovəˈret; ˈouvəˈreit〕 *v.t.*, **-rat·ed, -rat·ing.** 估計過高。

o·ver·reach 〔ˌovəˈritʃ; ˌouvəˈri:tʃ〕 *v.t.* ①過度伸展;伸得過長。②越過(目標);走過頭。③(以奸詐)勝過;越出。④欺騙;哄。⑤普及;廣被。—*v.i.* ①伸展過遠。②行騙。③(馬等)以後脚踢(傷)前脚。④做得過火。***overreach oneself*** **a.** 因不自量力而失敗。**b.** 因操之過急或過於狡詐而失敗。**—er,** *n.*

o·ver·re·fine 〔ˌovərɪˈfaɪn; ˈouvəriˈfain〕 *v.t.*, **-fined, -fin·ing.** ①使過於精緻(精練、文雅、精確)。②將…作太精細的區分。

o·ver·ride 〔ˌovəˈraɪd; ˌouvəˈraid〕 *v.t.*, **-rode, -rid·den, -rid·ing.** ①不顧;不管;藐視;拒絕。②凌駕;勝過。③蹂躪;踐踏。④騎馬橫越(一地區等)。⑤過度乘騎;把(馬)騎累。⑥駕疊;重疊(如斷骨之一端疊於他骨之上)。

o·ver·ripe 〔ˈovəˈraɪp; ˈouvəˈraip〕

adj. ①過熟的。②頹廢的。

o·ver·rule 〔ˌovəˈrul; ˌouvəˈruːl〕 *v.,* **-ruled, -rul·ing.** —*v.t.* ①批駁;不准;廢棄;宣布無效。②克服;支配;壓制。—*v.i.* 作最具權威的決定。

o·ver·run 〔ˌovəˈrʌn; ˌouvəˈrʌn〕 *v.,* **-ran, -run, -run·ning,** *n.* —*v.t.* ①覆蓋;蔓延(含有傷害之意)。②侵占;占領。③超過;逾出。—*v.i.* ①氾濫;溢出。②超過;逾出。***overrun oneself*** 硬跑;跑累。 —*n.* ①超出。②過量;過剩。

o·ver·sea 〔*adv.* ˌovəˈsi; ˈouvəˈsiː *adj.* ˈovəˈsi; ˈouvəˈsiː〕 *adv. & adj.* =**overseas.**

***o·ver·seas** 〔*adv., n.* ˌovəˈsiz; ˈouvəˈsiːz *adj.* ˈovəˈsiz; ˈouvəˈsiːz〕 *adv.* 在海外; 在外國。—*adj.* ①海外的; 國外的。the *overseas* Chinese. 海外華僑。②外國的;來自海外的; 往海外的。*overseas* trade. 海外貿易。—*n.* 國外。

o·ver·see 〔ˌovəˈsi; ˈouvəˈsiː〕 *v.t.,* **-saw, -seen, -see·ing.** ①督導; 監督。②俯視。③無意中看到;偷看到。

o·ver·se·er 〔ˈovəˌsiə; ˈouvəsiə〕 *n.* 監督者。

o·ver·sell 〔ˈovəˈsɛl; ˈouvəˈsel〕 *v.,* **-sold, -sell·ing.** —*v.t.* ①銷售過多而無法交貨。②爲(某物)作過分的宣傳。③對(某人)作過分的宣傳。—*v.i.* 對商品等作過分的宣傳。

o·ver·set 〔ˌovəˈsɛt; ˈouvəˈset〕 *v.,* **-set, -set·ting,** *n.* —*v.t.* ①翻轉; 翻倒; 傾覆。②使精神混亂。③爲…排字過擠。—*v.i.* ①翻倒; 傾覆。②精神混亂。③〖印刷〗排字太擠。—*n.* ①翻倒;傾覆;昏亂。②〖印刷〗排字過擠。

o·ver·sew 〔ˈovəˌso; ˈouvəsou〕 *v.t.,* **-sewed, -sewed** or **-sewn, -sew·ing.** 對縫;縫合。

o·ver·shad·ow 〔ˌovəˈʃædo; ˌouvəˈʃædou〕 *v.t.* ①較…更重要。②使暗;遮蔽。③庇護;保護。—**ing·ly,** *adv.*

o·ver·shoe 〔ˈovəˌʃu; ˈouvəʃuː〕 *n.*(橡皮)套鞋。

o·ver·shoot 〔ˌovəˈʃut; ˈouvəˈʃuːt〕 *v.,* **-shot, -shoot·ing,** *n.* —*v.t.* ①射過;使超過適當限度。②超過;越過。***overshoot the mark*** (or ***oneself***) 做得太過分。—*v.i.* 射越;超過。—*n.* 因目標過高或過多而失敗。

o·ver·shot 〔ˌovəˈʃat; ˈouvəˈʃɔt〕 *v.* pt. & pp. of **overshoot.** —*adj.* ①上顎突出的。②上射式的(水車)(爲 undershot 之對)。③誇張的。④〖俚〗醉了的。

o·ver·side 〔*adv.* ˌovəˈsaɪd; ˌouvəˈsaid *adj., n.* ˈovəˌsaɪd; ˈouvəsaid〕 *adj.* 越舷的;從船邊的。 —*adv.* 越舷地; 從船邊地。—*n.* (唱片等之)反面。

o·ver·sight 〔ˈovəˌsaɪt; ˈouvəsait〕 *n.* ①失察;疏忽;看漏。②監督;監視;照顧。

o·ver·size 〔ˈovəˈsaɪz; ˈouvəsaiz〕 *adj.* 過大的;特大的。—*n.* 特大型;特大之物。

o·ver·sized 〔ˈovəˈsaɪzd; ˈouvəsaizd〕 *adj.* 過大的;特大的。

o·ver·skirt 〔ˈovəˌskɝt; ˈouvəskəːt〕 *n.* 外裙。

o·ver·slaugh 〔ˈovəˌslɔ; ˈouvə-slɔː〕 *n.* ①〖英陸軍〗(爲被派任更重要職務之)免除任務。②〖美方〗(河川中阻礙航行的)洲;沙灘。—*v.t.* ①〖英陸軍〗(爲使就重要任務而)免除任務。②〖美〗(於任職、升官等時)略過(某人)而給予另一人;忽視。③阻礙(議案等)之通過。

o·ver·sleep 〔ˈovəˈslip; ˈouvəˈsliːp〕 *v.,* **-slept, -sleep·ing.** —*v.i.* 睡眠過久。—*v.t.* 睡過(某一時刻)。***oversleep oneself*** 睡眠過久;睡過了頭。

o·ver·sold 〔ˌovəˈsold; ˌouvəˈsould〕 *v.* pt. & pp. of **oversell.** —*adj.* 因出售太多而價錢低落的。

o·ver·soul 〔ˈovəˌsol; ˈouvəsoul〕 *n.* 〖哲學〗超靈;大靈(予宇宙以生命並爲人類靈魂之根源者, 係 Emerson 等唯心論者所倡)。

o·ver·spend 〔ˈovəˈspɛnd,ˌovə-; ˈouvəˈspend〕 *v.,* **-spent, -spend·ing.** —*v.t.* ①花費多於(收入等)。②用錢過多以致(自己)貧窮。③過度使用; 耗盡。—*v.i.* 過度花費; 浪費;揮霍無度。

o·ver·spill 〔*n., adj.* ˈovəˌspɪl; ˈouvə-spil *v.* ˌovəˈspɪl; ˌouvəˈspil〕 *n.* ①溢出之物。②過剩。③都市過剩人口向鄰近地區的分散。—*adj.* 溢出的;過剩的。—*v.i.* 溢出。

o·ver·spray 〔*n.* ˈovəˌspre; ˈouvə-sprei *v.* ˌovəˈspre; ˌouvəˈsprei〕 *n.* ①不黏附於表面之噴霧劑。②超越範圍之噴霧。—*v.t.* 在…之上噴一層。

o·ver·spread 〔ˌovəˈsprɛd; ˌouvə-ˈspred〕 *v.t. & v.i.,* **-spread, -spread·ing.** 滿布;鋪開;撒;覆蓋;蔓延。

o·ver·state 〔ˈovəˈstet; ˈouvəˈsteit〕 *v.t.,* **-stat·ed, -stat·ing.** 誇大敍述;誇張。

o·ver·state·ment 〔ˈovəˈstetmənt; ˈouvəˈsteitmənt〕 *n.* 誇大的敍述; 誇張。

o·ver·stay 〔ˈovəˈste; ˈouvəˈstei〕 *v.t.* ①逗留過久;停留超過(某一時間)。②〖俗〗將(股票、貨物等)保留錯過了最賺錢的時機。

o·ver·step 〔ˌovəˈstɛp; ˈouvəˈstep〕 *v.t.,* **-stepped, -step·ping.** 行過;超越;犯。

o·ver·stock 〔*v.* ˌovəˈstak; ˈouvəˈstɔk *n.* ˈovəˌstak; ˈouvəstɔk〕 *v.t.* 充斥;存貨過多;供給過多。—*n.* 備貨過多;供給過多。

o·ver·strain 〔*v.* ˌovəˈstren; ˈouvə-ˈstrein *n.* ˈovəˌstren; ˈouvə-strein〕 *v.t.* 伸張過度; 用過度; 使過度緊張; 使工作過度。—*v.i.* 過度緊張; 過度努力。—*n.* 緊張過度;努力過度;過勞。

o·ver·strung 〔ˈovəˈstrʌŋ; ˈouvə-ˈstrʌŋ〕 *adj.* 緊張過度的;神經過敏的。

o·ver·stud·y 〔*n.* ˈovəˈstʌdɪ; ˈouvə-ˈstʌdi *v.* ˌovəˈstʌdɪ; ˌouvəˈstʌdi〕 *v.t. & v.i.* 用功過度。—*n.* 過度的用功。

o·ver·stuff 〔ˈovəˈstʌf; ˈouvəˈstʌf〕 *v.t.* ①過度塡塞。②以軟墊完全鋪蓋(傢具)。

o·ver·sub·scribe 〔ˈovəsəbˈskraɪb, ˌovə-; ˈouvəsəbˈskraib〕 *v.t.* 認購(債券等)逾額。—**o·ver·sub·scrib·er,** *n.*

o·ver·sub·scrip·tion 〔ˌovəsəb-ˈskrɪpʃən; ˈouvəsəbˈskripʃən〕 *n.* ①認購逾額。②額外認購之數量。

o·ver·sup·ply 〔*v.* ˌovəsəˈplaɪ; ˈou-vəsəˈplai *n.* ˈovəsəˌplaɪ; ˈouvəsəˌplai〕 *v.,* **-plied, -ply·ing,** *n.* —*v.t.* 過量供應;供給…過多。—*n.* 供給過剩;過量供應。

o·vert 〔ˈovɝt; ˈouvəːt〕 *adj.* 公然的;顯然的;公開的。—**ness,** *n.*

***o·ver·take** 〔ˌovəˈtek; ˌouvəˈteik〕 *v.,* **-took, -tak·en, -tak·ing.** —*v.t.*①追及;趕上。②使突然遭遇。③壓倒;克服。—*v.i.* 〖主英〗超車。Never attempt to *overtake* on the crest of a hill. 在坡頂絕不要企圖超車。

o·ver·tak·ing 〔ˌovəˈtekɪŋ; ˌouvə-ˈteikiŋ〕 *n.* 〖主英〗超車(行爲)。No *overtaking.* 禁止超車。

o·ver·talk 〔ˈovəˈtɔk; ˈouvəˈtɔːk〕 *v.i.* 講話過多。

o·ver·task 〔ˌovəˈtæsk; ˈouvəˈtɑːsk〕 *v.t.* 使負擔過重之工作。

o·ver·tax 〔ˈovəˈtæks, ˌovə-; ˈouvə-ˈtæks〕 *v.t.* ①課以重稅;過度征收。②加以過

重的負擔;使過度勞動。—**a·tion,** *n.*

o·ver-the-count·er [ˈovəðəˈkaʊntə; ˈouvəðəˈkauntə] *adj.* ①不在交換所交易的。②店面交易的。③不需醫生處方的(藥品)。*over-the-counter* drugs. 成藥。

***o·ver·throw** [*v.* ˌovəˈθro; ˌouvəˈθrou *n.* ˈovəˌθro; ˈouvəθrou] *v.*, **-threw, -thrown, -throw·ing,** *n.* —*v.t.* ①打倒;推翻。②使瓦解;使毀滅。③顚倒;顚覆。A dozen trees were *overthrown* by the storm. 成打的樹被暴風推倒。④投球過遠以致超過。The passer *overthrew* the receiver. 傳球者投球過遠而超過了接球者。—*n.* ①推翻;覆沒;瓦解。②投球過遠。—**er,** *n.*

o·ver·time [*n., adv., adj.* ˈovəˌtaɪm; ˈouvətaim *v.* ˌovəˈtaɪm; ˌouvəˈtaim] *n., adv., adj., v.,* **-timed, -tim·ing.** —*n.* ①額外的時間;加班的時間;超出定時的時間。②額外時間的薪給;加班費。—*adv.* 超出時間地。—*adj.* 超出時間的。—*v.t.* 使歷時過久。

o·ver·tire [ˈovəˈtaɪr; ˈouvəˈtaiə] *v.t. & v.i.* (使)過度疲勞。

o·vert·ly [ˈovɜtlɪ, oˈvɜtlɪ; ˈouvəːtli] *adv.* 公然地;公開地。

o·ver·toil [ˌovəˈtɔɪl; ˌouvəˈtɔil] *v.t. & v.i.* = **overwork.**

o·ver·tone [ˈovəˌton; ˈouvətoun] *n.* ①〖音樂〗泛音(一發聲體所發出之音中頻率較高於基音者)。②寓意;絃外之音。

o·ver·top [ˌovəˈtɑp; ˈouvəˈtɔp] *v.t.,* **-topped, -top·ping.** ①聳立於…之上。②比…更高。③超出;勝過。

o·ver·train [ˌovəˈtren; ˈouvəˈtrein] *v.t. & v.i.* (運動員)過度訓練;訓練過度。

o·ver·trick [ˈovəˌtrɪk; ˈouvətrik] *n.* 〖橋牌〗超點。

o·ver·trump [ˌovəˈtrʌmp; ˈouvəˈtrʌmp] *v.t. & v.i.* 〖橋牌〗以較大王牌勝之。

o·ver·ture [ˈovətʃə; ˈouvətjuə] *n., v.,* **-tured, -tur·ing.** —*n.* ①提議;建議;提案。②〖音樂〗序樂;序曲。—*v.t.* ①提議;建議。②向…作提議。③〖音樂〗以序曲開始。

***o·ver·turn** [*v.* ˌovəˈtɜn; ˌouvəˈtəːn *n.* ˈovəˌtɜn; ˈouvətəːn] *v.t.* ①使傾覆。②推翻;使瓦解。③顚倒。—*v.i.* 傾覆。The boat *overturned*. 船翻了。—*n.* 顚覆;滅亡;推翻。

o·ver·use [*v.* ˌovəˈjuz; ˌouvəˈjuːz *n.* ˈovəˈjus; ˈouvəˈjuːs] *v.*, **-used, -us·ing,** *n.* —*v.i.,* *n.* 過度使用;濫用。

o·ver·val·ue [ˈovəˈvælju; ˈouvəˈvæljuː] *v.t.,* **-val·ued, -val·u·ing.** 對…估價過高;估高;過於重視。—**o·ver·val·u·a·tion,** *n.*

o·ver·walk [ˌovəˈwɔk; ˌouvəˈwɔːk] *v.t.* ①步行經過。②步行過多而致疲倦;使走累。—*v.i.* 行走過度;步行太遠。

o·ver·watch [ˈovəˈwɑtʃ; ˈouvəˈwɔtʃ] *v.t.* ①看守;監視。②看守過久(熬夜)而使疲倦。③〖軍〗以砲火掩護。—**er,** *n.*

o·ver·ween·ing [ˈovəˈwinɪŋ; ˈouvəˈwiːniŋ] *adj.* ①自負的;過於自信的;傲慢的。②過火的;過分的。—**ly,** *adv.* —**ness,** *n.*

o·ver·weigh [ˈovəˈwe; ˈouvəˈwei] *v.t.* ①較…爲重;勝過;優於。②使負擔過重;壓迫。

o·ver·weight [*adj., v.* ˈovəˈwet; ˈouvəˈweit *n.* ˈovəˌwet; ˈouvəweit] *adj.* 過重的;超過規定重量的。—*n.* ①過重;超過的重量。②偏重;優勢。—*v.t.* ①使負擔過重。②偏重;過分重視。—**ed,** *adj.*

***o·ver·whelm** [ˌovəˈhwɛlm; ˌouvəˈwelm, -ˈhwelm] *v.t.* ①淹沒;傾覆。②擊潰;使粉碎。The enemy were *overwhelmed* by superior forces. 敵人被優越之兵力擊潰。③控制;壓倒。④使窘。Your kindness *overwhelms* me. 你的好意使我不安。

***o·ver·whelm·ing** [ˌovəˈhwɛlmɪŋ; ˌouvəˈwelmiŋ, -ˈhwelm-] *adj.* 壓倒的;勢不可當的。—**ly,** *adv.* —**ness,** *n.*

o·ver·wind [ˈovəˈwaɪnd; ˈouvəˈwaind] *v.t.,* **-wound, -wind·ing.** 將(發條等)捲得太緊;捲過頭。

***o·ver·work** [*n. for* ① ˈovəˈwɜk; ˈouvəˈwəːk *for* ② ˈovəˌwɜk; ˈouvəwəːk *v.* ˈovəˈwɜk; ˈouvəˈwəːk] *n., v.,* **-worked** or **-wrought, -work·ing.** —*n.* ①過多或過勞之工作。②額外的工作;規定時間外的工作。—*v.t.* ①使工作過度;使過勞;使用過度(常與反身代名詞連用)。②做得過於講究;矯揉做作。③過分刺激。④裝飾…之表面。—*v.i.* 工作過度;過勞。You look as though you've been *overworking*. 你好像工作過度。

o·ver·world [ˈovəˈwɜld; ˈouvəˈwəːld] *n.* ①上流社會。②(有財勢的)特權階級。③精神界。

o·ver·write [ˌovəˈraɪt; ˌouvəˈrait] *v.,* **-wrote, -writ·ten, -writ·ing.** —*v.t.* ①寫在(其他文字或紙)之上;將…寫在其他文字上。②對…寫得過多;將…寫得過分誇張。—*v.i.* (作家等)亂寫;過度多寫。

o·ver·wrought [ˈovəˈrɔt; ˈouvəˈrɔːt] *adj.* ①疲倦的;過勞的。②過度緊張的;過度興奮或激動的。③全面裝飾的。④過於精巧的。

Ov·id [ˈɑvɪd; ˈɔvid] *n.* 奧維德(Publius Ovidius Naso, 43 B.C.–?A. D.17, 羅馬詩人)。

O·vid·i·an [oˈvɪdɪən; ɔˈvidiən] *adj.* Ovid 的; Ovid 之風格的。

o·vi·duct [ˈovɪˌdʌkt; ˈouvidʌkt] *n.* 〖解剖, 動物〗輸卵管。—**al,** *adj.*

o·vi·form [ˈovɪˌfɔrm; ˈouvifɔːm] *adj.* 卵形的。

o·vine [ˈovaɪn, -vɪn; ˈouvain] *adj.* 綿羊的;似綿羊的。

o·vip·a·rous [oˈvɪpərəs; ouˈvipərəs] *adj.* 〖動物〗卵生的;產卵的。

o·vi·pos·it [ˌovɪˈpɑzɪt; ˌouviˈpɔzit] *v.i.* 〖動物〗(昆蟲等以產卵管)產卵。

o·vi·pos·i·tor [ˌovɪˈpɑzɪtə; ˌouviˈpɔzitə] *n.* 〖動物〗(昆蟲之)產卵管;產卵器。

o·void [ˈovɔɪd; ˈouvɔid] *adj.* 卵形的。—*n.* 卵形物。

o·vu·lar [ˈovjulə; ˈouvjulə] *adj.* ①〖植物〗胚珠的。②〖動物〗小卵的。

o·vule [ˈovjul; ˈouvjuːl] *n.* ①〖生物〗小卵。②〖植物〗胚珠。

o·vum [ˈovəm; ˈouvəm] *n., pl.* **o·va** [ˈovə; ˈouvə]. ①〖生物〗卵;卵細胞。②〖建築〗卵形裝飾。

***owe** [o; ou] *v.,* **owed, ow·ing.** —*v.t.* ①欠(某人)債;負有(若干)債。②感恩;感激。I *owe* it to you that I am still alive. 我受你再生之恩。③負有(義務)。We *owe* our duty to our country. 我們對國家應盡義務。④歸功於;由於。—*v.i.* 欠。

ow·ing** [ˈoɪŋ; ˈouiŋ] *adj.* ①負債的。②應付的;到期的。He paid what was *owing*. 他付清了所應付的。owing to*** 因爲;由於。

owl** [aʊl; aul] *n.* ①貓頭鷹;梟。②(面貌)嚴肅的人。as blind*** (or ***stupid***) ***as an owl*** 全瞎(笨透)。***fly with the owls*** 夜遊。***grave*** (or ***wise***) ***as an owl*** 非常嚴肅(聰明)。—*adj.* 活動於夜間的;夜行的。—**like,**

adj. 「梟。②(歐洲產之)一種小梟。
owl·et ['aulɪt; 'aulit] *n.* ①幼貓頭鷹;幼
owl·ish ['aulɪʃ; 'auliʃ] *adj.* ①像貓頭鷹的。②面孔嚴肅的。③似乎聰明而實際上笨的。④夜遊的。 「薄暮。
owl·light ['aul,laɪt; 'aullait] *n.* 微光;
owl train 深夜行駛的火車。
‡**own** [on; oun] *adj.* ①自己的。 I cook my *own* breakfast. 我自己做早飯吃。②親的;同胞的。*Own* brothers have the same parents. 同胞兄弟父母相同。***be one's own man*** 自己作主;不受他人之支配。—*v.t.* ①擁有。 Who *owns* this house? 這所房子爲誰所有? ②自認;承認。I *own* that you are right. 我承認你是對的。—*v.i.* 供認; 自認〖to〗. ***own up***〖俗〗爽爽快快承認。If your ball broke the window, you should *own up.* 如果是你的球擊破那窗戶,你應該爽爽快快地承認。—*n.* 自己的所有物。***come into one's own*** **a.** 得到自己應得之物。**b.** 得到應得的名譽、信用、成功等。Nationalism has rightly *come into its own* in Asia. 民族主義在亞洲已得到應得的成功。***get*** (***a bit of***) ***one's own back***〖俗〗雪恥; 報仇。They're out to *get their own back*. 他們極圖報仇。***hold one's own*** **a.** 堅持不敗;固守。**b.** 維持自己的立場;固守立場。**c.** 支撐。The patient is *holding his own*. 病人還在支撐呢。***of one's own*** 自己的;自己所有的。I have nothing *of my own*. 我自己一無所有。***on one's own***〖俗〗獨力;憑自己。Can you do the work *on your own?* 你能自己單獨做這項工作嗎?
‡**own·er** ['onɚ; 'ounə] *n.* 物主;所有者。the *owner* of a house. 房主。
own·er-oc·cu·pi·er ['onɚ'ɑkjə,paɪɚ; 'ounə'ɔkjupaiə] *n.*〖英〗自己房子自己住的人。 「所有權;主權。
***own·er·ship** ['onɚ,ʃɪp; 'ounəʃip] *n.*
***ox** [ɑks; ɔks] *n., pl.* **ox·en.** 公牛;閹牛(去勢之公牛)。—**like,** *adj.* 「草酸鹽。
ox·a·late ['ɑksə,let;'ɔksəleit] *n.*〖化〗
ox·al·ic [ɑks'ælɪk; ɔk'sælik] *adj.* 酢漿草的;得自酢漿草的。 「等)。
oxalic acid〖化〗草酸(用於漂白、去汚
Ox·a·lis ['ɑksəlɪs; 'ɔksəlis] *n.*〖植物〗①酢漿草屬。②(o-)酢漿草屬之植物;酢漿草。
ox·bow ['ɑks,bo; 'ɔksbou] *n.* ①(牛頸下之)U形牛軛。②(河流之)U形彎曲部分;前述彎曲部分圍繞之土地。—*adj.* U形彎曲的。
Ox·bridge ['ɑks,brɪdʒ; 'ɔksbridʒ] *n.* ①牛津大學或劍橋大學。 He is eager to have his son educated at *Oxbridge*. 他渴望使自己的兒子於牛津大學或劍橋大學受教育。②牛津或劍橋大學之學生或畢業生。③英國之上流知識界。—*adj.* 牛津大學或劍橋大學的;牛津大學或劍橋大學所特有的。
ox·cart ['ɑks,kart; 'ɔkskɑːt] *n.* 牛車。
ox·en ['ɑksn̩; 'ɔksən] *n.* pl. of **ox.**
ox·eye ['ɑks,aɪ; 'ɔksai] *n.*〖植物〗牛眼菊。 「如牛眼的。
ox-eyed ['ɑks,aɪd; 'ɔksaid] *adj.* 眼大
Oxf., Ox. ①Oxford. ②Oxfordshire.
***Ox·ford** ['ɑksfɚd; 'ɔksfəd] *n.* ①牛津(英國一城)。②牛津大學。③(亦作 **oxford**) **a.** 淺口鞋。**b.** 深灰色。
Oxford accent 裝腔作勢的語調。
Oxford bags〖俚〗褲口寬大之長褲。
Oxford blue 深藍色。
Oxford gray 中度灰色至深灰色。
Oxford movement 牛津運動(將天主教之教義及儀式納入英國國教之宗教運動,約於1833年起於牛津大學)。(亦作 **Tractarianism**)
Ox·ford·shire ['ɑksfɚd,ʃɪr; 'ɔksfədʃiə] *n.* 牛津郡 (英格蘭中南部之一郡,首府 Oxford)。(亦作 **Oxford, Oxon**)
Oxford shoe 淺口便鞋。
ox·heart ['ɑks,hart; 'ɔkshɑːt] *n.*〖園藝〗①一種心形的大甜櫻桃。②一種甘藍。
ox·herd ['ɑkshɚd; 'ɔkshəːd] *n.*〖英〗牧牛者。
ox·hide ['ɑks,haɪd; 'ɔkshaid] *n.* 牛皮。
ox·id ['ɑksɪd; 'ɔksid] *n.* =**oxide.**
ox·i·date ['ɑksə,det; 'ɔksideit] *v.t.* & *v.i.,* **-dat·ed, -dat·ing.** =**oxidize.**
ox·i·da·tion [,ɑksə'deʃən; ,ɔksi'deiʃən] *n.* =**oxidization.**
ox·ide ['ɑksaɪd;'ɔksaid] *n.*〖化〗氧化物。
ox·i·di·za·tion [,ɑksədaɪ'zeʃən; ,ɔksidai'zeiʃən] *n.*〖化〗氧化(作用)。
ox·i·dize ['ɑksə,daɪz; 'ɔksidaiz] *v.,* **-dized, -diz·ing.**—*v.t.* 使氧化;使銹。—*v.i.* 氧化;生銹。(亦作 **oxidise**)—**ox·i·diz·er,** *n.*
ox·lip ['ɑks,lɪp; 'ɔkslip] *n.* 黃花九輪草。
Ox·on ['ɑksɑn; 'ɔksɔn] *n.* =**Oxfordshire.**
Oxon. ①Oxonia (拉=Oxford). ②Oxoniensis (拉=of Oxford). ③Oxfordshire. ④Oxford University.
Ox·o·ni·an [ɑks'onɪən; ɔk'sounjən] *adj.* 牛津城的;牛津大學的。—*n.* 牛津城之人;牛津大學之學生(畢業生)。 「用以製湯)。
ox·tail ['ɑks,tel;'ɔksteil] *n.* 牛尾(剝皮
ox·ter['ɑkstɚ;'ɔkstə] *n.*〖蘇〗腋下。—*v.t.* 用手撐住腋下舉起。 「牛舌。②牛舌草。
ox·tongue ['ɑks,tʌŋ;'ɔkstʌŋ] *n.* ①
ox·y·a·cet·y·lene [,ɑksɪə'sɛtl̩,in; 'ɔksiə'setiliːn] *adj.*〖化〗氧炔的。
oxyacetylene torch (or **blowpipe**) 氧乙炔發焰器 (用以鎔接金屬)。
ox·y·ac·id [,ɑksɪ'æsɪd; ,ɔksi'æsid] *n.*〖化〗含氧之酸類;含氧酸。 「〖化〗氧。
***ox·y·gen** ['ɑksədʒən; 'ɔksidʒən] *n.*
oxygen acid〖化〗含氧酸。
ox·y·gen·ate ['ɑksədʒən,et; 'ɔksidʒineit] *v.t.,* **-at·ed, -at·ing.**〖化〗以氧處理;加氧於…;氧化。
ox·y·gen·a·tion [,ɑksədʒən'eʃən; ,ɔksidʒi'neiʃən] *n.*〖化〗加氧;氧化。
ox·y·gen·ic [,ɑksɪ'dʒɛnɪk; ,ɔksi'dʒenik] *adj.*〖化〗氧的;含氧的;似氧的;生氧的。
ox·y·gen·ize ['ɑksədʒən,aɪz; 'ɔksidʒinaiz] *v.t.,* **-ized, -iz·ing.** =**oxygenate.**
oxygen mask〖航空〗氧氣面罩。
ox·yg·e·nous [ɑks'ɪdʒɪnəs; ɔk'sidʒənəs] *adj.* =**oxygenic.**
oxygen tent 氧幕;氧氣篷帳(急救用)。
ox·y·hy·dro·gen[,ɑksɪ'haɪdrədʒən; ,ɔksi'haidrədʒən] *adj.* 氫氧混合的。—*n.* 氫氧混合氣(割切或鎔接金屬用)。
oxyhydrogen torch (or **blowpipe**) 氫氧發焰器(用以割切或鎔接金屬)。
ox·y·mo·ron[,ɑksɪ'morɑn; ,ɔksi'mɔːrɔn] *n., pl.* **-ra** [-rə; -rə], **-rons.**〖修辭〗矛盾修飾法(例如: a wise fool)。
ox·y·salt ['ɑksɪ,sɔlt; 'ɔksisɔːlt] *n.*〖化〗含氧酸鹽。 「*n.* 催產素。
ox·y·to·cin [,ɑksɪ'tosɪn; ,ɔksi'tousin]
ox·y·tone ['ɑksɪ,ton; 'ɔksitoun] *adj., n.*〖希臘文法〗最後音節有重音 (acute ac-

cent）的(字)。

o·yer〔'ojə, 'ɔɪə; 'ɔiə〕*n.*〖法律〗①(刑事案件之)審理。② =**oyer and terminer.**

oyer and terminer〖法律〗①〖美〗(某些州之)高等刑事法院。②〖英〗聽訟裁判庭(爲審理刑事案件之巡廻裁判)。

o·yes, o·yez〔'ojɛs, 'ojɛz; ou'jes, ou'jez〕*interj.* 聽；靜聽；請靜聽(城鎭宣告員或法警促人注意之呼聲，通常喊三次)。—*n.* oyes 之呼聲。

***oys·ter**〔'ɔɪstə; 'ɔistə〕*n.* ①蠔；牡蠣。②(雞背上的)蠔狀暗色肉片。③所有物。④所愛好的事。Mathematics is his *oyster*. 數學是他之所好。⑤守口如瓶者。—**y,** *adj.*

oyster bed 蠔塘；養蠔場。

oyster catcher 蠣鷸；都鳥。

oyster crab 蠔中的寄生蟹。

oyster cracker 與蠔肉同進食的圓形或六角形小鹹餅乾。

oyster culture 牡蠣之養殖。

oyster farm 牡蠣場。

oys·ter·man〔'ɔɪstəmən; 'ɔistəmən〕*n., pl.* **-men.** ①採牡蠣者。②採牡蠣船。

oyster plant〖植物〗婆羅門參(=salsify).

oz. *pl.* **ozs.** ounce.

o·zo·ce·rite〔o'zokə,raɪt, -sə,raɪt; ou'zoukərait〕*n.*〖礦〗地蠟；石蠟。

o·zo·ke·rite〔o'zokə,raɪt; ou'zoukərait〕*n.* =**ozocerite.**

o·zone〔'ozon, o'zon; 'ouzoun〕*n.* ①〖化〗臭氧。②〖俗〗新鮮空氣。

o·zon·er〔'ozonə; 'ouzounə〕*n.*〖美俗〗可駕車進入的劇場(=drive-in-theater).

o·zon·ic〔o'zɑnɪk; ou'zɔnik〕*adj.* 臭氧(ozone)的；似臭氧的；含臭氧的。

o·zo·nif·er·ous〔,ozə'nɪfərəs; ,ouzou'nifərəs〕*adj.* 含臭氧的；生臭氧的。

o·zo·nize〔'ozə,naɪz; 'ouzənaiz〕*v.t.,* **-nized, -niz·ing.** ①以臭氧處理；使含臭氧。②使(氧)變成臭氧。—**o·zo·ni·za·tion,** *n.*

o·zo·niz·er〔'ozə,naɪzə; 'ouzənaizə〕*n.*〖化〗臭氧發生器。

ozs, ozs. ounces.

P

P or p〔pi; piː〕*n., pl.* **P's** or **p's.** 英文字母之第十六個字母。***mind one's P's and Q's*** (or ***p's and q's***)言行謹慎；小心翼翼。

P ①化學元素 phosphorus 之符號。②〖物理〗**a.** parity. **b.** pressure. **P.** ① Pater (拉 =Father). ②President. ③Prince. ④Progressive. **p.** ①page. ②part. ③participle. ④past. ⑤pawn. ⑥penny. ⑦piano (義 =softly). ⑧pint. ⑨pipe. ⑩pitcher. ⑪pole. ⑫population. ⑬professional. **Pa** 化學元素 protactinium之符號。

pa〔pɑ; pɑː〕*n.*〖俗〗爸；父親。

Pa. Pennsylvania. **p.a.** ①participial adjective. ②per an num (拉 =by the year). **PAA** Pan American (World) Airways. 泛美航空公司。

pab·u·lum〔'pæbjələm; 'pæbjuləm〕*n.* ①食物；滋養品。②(精神上之)食糧。

Pac., Pacif. Pacific.

‡**pace**[1]〔pes; peis〕*n., v.,* **paced, pac·ing.** —*n.* ①速度。②一步。to make three *paces.* 走三步。③一步之長度(約爲 $2^1/_2$ 英尺)。six *paces* from the tree. 離樹六步之距。④步態；步法。The trot is a *pace* of the horse. "快步"是馬行的一種步態。⑤馬之蹓行步法(卽將同側兩足同時舉起並落下之步態)；溜蹄。⑥性能之表演。Test pilots put the new planes through their *paces.* 試驗飛行員表演新型飛機的性能。***go at a good pace*** 走(進行)得很快。***go the pace*** 進行極速；花費許多錢。***keep pace with*** 與…並進；與…相匹敵。***put a person through his paces*** 試驗某人的能力。***set the pace*** **a.** 定步調；定速度；調整步子；調整速度(以便他人跟隨)。**b.** 立下榜樣。—*v.t.* ①(以普通之步伐)走過。②以步測量。③使(馬)走慣某種步子。④爲…定步調；爲…調整步調。⑤引導；爲…做前導。Food prices were *pacing* the upsurge. 食物的價格在引導物價上升。⑥配合。⑦指揮(演奏等)。He *paced* the music with sure and tasteful touch. 他以穩而雅的風度指揮那樂曲。—*v.i.* ①(以普通步伐)走。The tiger *paced* up and down his cage. 老虎在籠中走來走去。②(馬)蹓行；溜蹄。

pa·ce[2]〔'pesɪ; 'peisi〕〖拉〗*prep., adv.* 對不起；請…原諒(=by the leave of)(陳述反對意見時用語)。

paced〔pest; peist〕*adj.* ①…步的；步伐…的。②以步測量的；步測的。③〖賽馬〗按照定步調者所定之步調奔馳的。

pace·mak·er〔'pes,mekə; 'peis,meikə〕*n.* ①(競走中)定步調者。②引導者；前導者。③〖解剖〗節律點。

pace·mak·ing〔'pes,mekɪŋ; 'peis,meikiŋ〕*n., adj.* 定步調(的)；整速(的)。

pac·er〔'pesə; 'peisə〕*n.* ①徐行者；步測者。② =**pacemaker.** ③溜蹄的馬。

pa·chi·si〔pə'tʃizɪ, pɑ-; pə'tʃiːzi〕*n.* ①(流行於印度之)一種用貝殼爲骰子之四人遊戲。②(在英國與美國以骰子代替貝殼之)類似上述之一種遊戲。(亦作 **parcheesi, parchesi, parchisi**)

pach·y·derm〔'pækə,dɝm; 'pækidəːm〕*n.* ①〖動物〗厚皮動物(象、河馬、犀牛等)。②厚臉皮的人；神經麻木的人。

pach·y·der·ma·tous〔,pækɪ'dɝmətəs; ,pæki'dəːmətəs〕*adj.* ①厚皮動物的；厚皮的。②厚臉皮的；對批評等無動於衷的；神經麻木的。—**ly,** *adv.*

pach·y·san·dra〔,pækə'sændrə; ,pæki'sændrə〕*n.* 富貴草(作草皮用)。

pac·i·fi·a·ble〔'pæsə,faɪəbl; 'pæsifaiəbl〕*adj.* 可安撫的；可鎭壓的。

***Pa·cif·ic**〔pə'sɪfɪk; pə'sifik〕*n.* 太平洋。—*adj.* ①太平洋的。②太平洋沿岸的；近太平洋的。the *Pacific* States. (美國)太平洋沿岸諸州。

***pa·cif·ic**〔pə'sɪfɪk; pə'sifik〕*adj.* 愛好和平的；求和的；和平的；安靜的。the *pacific* relation of the two countries. 兩國和平的關係。(亦作 **pacifical**) —**al·ly,** *adv.*

pa·cif·i·cate〔pə'sɪfə,ket; pə'sifikeit〕*v.t.,* **-cat·ed, -cat·ing.** =**pacify.**

pac·i·fi·ca·tion〔,pæsəfə'keʃən; ,pæsifi'keiʃən〕*n.* ①講和；和解；鎭定。②和約。③綏靖行動(以堅壁淸野的策略消滅游擊隊或恐怖分子的活動)。

pa·cif·i·ca·tor 〔ˈpæsəfəˌketɚ; pəˈsifikeitə〕 *n.* 調解人;和事人;仲裁者。

pa·cif·i·ca·to·ry 〔pəˈsɪfəkəˌtorɪ; pəˈsifikətəri〕 *adj.* 和解的;安撫的;綏靖的。

pa·cif·i·cism 〔pəˈsɪfəˌsɪzəm; pəˈsifisizm〕 *n.* ＝**pacifism.** —**pa·cif·i·cist,** *n.*

Pacific Ocean 太平洋。

Pacific (**Standard**) **Time** 美國西部標準時間(比臺北標準時間晚16小時,略作 **PT** 或 **PST**)。

pac·i·fi·er 〔ˈpæsəˌfaɪɚ; ˈpæsifaiə〕 *n.* ①安慰者;和解者;調停者;鎮靖者;平定者。②(哄嬰兒用的)奶嘴。

pac·i·fism 〔ˈpæsəˌfɪzəm; ˈpæsifizm〕 *n.* 和平主義; 綏靖主義; 反戰主義。(亦作 **pacificism**)

pac·i·fist 〔ˈpæsəfɪst; ˈpæsifist〕 *n.* ①贊成和平解決一切國際糾紛者。②非戰主義者。③不抵抗主義者。—*adj.* ＝**pacifistic.**

pac·i·fis·tic 〔ˌpæsəˈfɪstɪk; ˌpæsiˈfistik〕 *adj.* 和平主義(者)的。

pac·i·fy 〔ˈpæsəˌfaɪ; ˈpæsifai〕 *v.t.,* **-fied, -fy·ing.** ①鎮定; 平靖。②安慰; 撫慰; 使平靜。③姑息。

:pack¹ 〔pæk; pæk〕 *n.* ①包裹; 包。②一羣; 一組。③(行獵動物之)一羣; 一隊。The *pack* of jets passed overhead on their way to the targets. 一隊噴射機淩空而過飛向目標。④一副紙牌(通常爲52張)。⑤大塊浮冰。⑥馱子; 背包。⑦裝箱、裝罐等之總量; 包裝之數量。⑧乾布塊; 濕布塊(治療用)。⑨包裝; 包裝法。—*v.t.* ①包裝; 綑紮。Have you *packed* (up) your things? 你的東西裝好沒有?②裝塡;塞滿。*Pack* your trunk. 裝好你的箱子。③擠緊;擁擠。A hundred men were *packed* into a small room. 一百個人擠在一間小屋內。④將(水果、肉類等)裝於罐內(使不透空氣)。Meat, fish, and vegetables are often *packed* in cans. 肉類、魚和蔬菜常裝於罐內。⑤打發走;送走。⑥壓緊(使不漏水或漏氣)。⑦把包裹馱在(牲口)身上;負載。⑧〖俗〗搬運;攜帶。—*v.i.* ①包裝; 綑紮。These books *pack* easily. 這些書容易包裝。②緊擠在一起。Excursionists *packed* into a bus. 遠足的旅客擠在一部大客車中。③將物緊密堆放。④搬運貨物。⑤携帶行裝騎馬旅行。***pack in*** 停止。to *pack in* football. 停止玩足球。***pack off*** (or ***away***) **a.** 打發走。**b.** 突然離開。***pack up*** (or ***in***) 〖俗〗**a.** 停止;結束。The motors coughed and *packed up.* 馬達發出空爆聲, 接着停下來。**b.** 死。***send*** (***a person***) ***packing*** 打發人匆匆離去。 —*adj.* 用以搬運貨物的。—**a·ble,** *adj.* —**a·bil·i·ty,** *n.*

:pack² *v.t.* 收買;籠絡;操縱;糾集(以作弊)。***pack cards with*** 共謀; 圖謀。She has *packed cards with* the rebels. 她私通叛徒。—*v.i.* 陰結同謀;通同作弊。

***pack·age** 〔ˈpækɪdʒ; ˈpækidʒ〕 *n., v.,* **-aged, -ag·ing,** *adj.* —*n.* ①包裹。He had a heavy *package* on his back. 他背着一個重包。②包裝。③整批。④〖俚〗(罪犯的)警察紀錄; 前科。⑤(電視等可售與廠商的)完整節目。—*v.t.* 包裝; 裝箱。—*adj.* 整批的。—**a·ble,** *adj.*

package deal 不能分割的整批交易或計畫;躉賣。

pack·ag·er 〔ˈpækɪdʒɚ; ˈpækidʒə〕 *n.* ①包裝者。②(電視等之)節目製作人。

package store 不得在店內喝而僅售瓶裝酒的酒店。

package tour 包辦旅行(由主辦者供應交通工具、食宿及其他一切服務的旅行)。(亦作 **packaged tour**)

pack animal 馱獸(用以搬運貨物之牛、馬等)。

pack drill 〖軍〗①馱運裝卸操練。②全副武裝往復齊步行走的一種處罰。

pack·er 〔ˈpækɚ; ˈpækə〕 *n.* ①包裝者; 包裝機。②罐頭公司;罐頭業者。③挑夫。

***pack·et** 〔ˈpækɪt; ˈpækit〕 *n.* ①包裹;小包;(郵件等的)一捆。②郵船(＝packet boat)。③羣; 組。They watched little *packets* of tanks approach their positions. 他們看着一小隊戰車向他們的陣地迫近。④大量。⑤薪俸袋。⑥〖英俚〗大筆錢。It cost him a *packet* but it cured his indigestion. 這花了他一大筆錢但也治癒了他的消化不良症。—*v.t.* 將…裝進小包裹;將…包成小包裹。

packet boat (埠港間有班期的) 客貨船;郵船;定期客船。

pack horse ①馱馬。②(似馱馬般)做苦工的人;服賤役者。

pack ice 海中被擠而互相重疊的大冰塊。

pack·ing 〔ˈpækɪŋ; ˈpækiŋ〕 *n.* ①包裝; 捆裝。②罐頭之製備。③包裝材料;包裹用品; 塡料。④靠獸力或人力的搬運。⑤集合。

packing case 裝運貨物之箱。

packing house 〖美〗食品包裝工場。(亦作 **packing plant**)

packing needle 打包針。

packing sheet ①包裝布。②〖醫〗(水療法用之)濕布。

pack·man 〔ˈpækmən; ˈpækmən〕 *n., pl.* **-men.** 負販;擔賣者。

pack mule 馱騾。

pack rat ①〖動物〗(北美產之)一種鼠(有搬運及儲藏小物件之習性)。②喜儲藏小物件者。

pack·sack 〔ˈpækˌsæk; ˈpæksæk〕 *n.* 粗厚布料做的行李囊。

pack·sad·dle 〔ˈpækˌsædl; ˈpækˌsædl〕 *n.* 馱鞍;荷鞍。—*v.t.* 用馱獸運送。

pack·thread 〔ˈpækˌθrɛd; ˈpækθred〕 *n.* 捆包或縫包用之粗麻線或繩索。

pack train 馱獸隊。

pact 〔pækt; pækt〕 *n.* 協定;公約。

pac·tion 〔ˈpækʃən; ˈpækʃən〕 *n.* ①同意。②協議書;公約。—**al,** *adj.*

pad¹** 〔pæd; pæd〕 *n., v.,* **pad·ded, pad·ding.** —*n.* ①墊狀物;墊子。②(動物足底之)肉趾。③荷葉。④拍紙簿。⑤橡皮圖章用之印色盒;打印臺。⑥鞍褥。⑦(狗、狐等之)足。⑧(火箭之)發射臺。⑨小片;小塊。hit the pad*** 〖美軍俚〗上床睡覺。—*v.t.* ①(以棉絮等軟物)裝入;塡塞。We *padded* the box with soft cloth. 我們用軟布塡塞那箱子。②塡湊(文章等)篇幅〖常out〗。③對…加不實內容。④誇大。She *padded* her age to work in a cabaret. 她多報自己年齡以便在酒店工作。⑤以不純物增加…之大小。⑥報假帳。

pad² *v.,* **pad·ded, pad·ding,** *n.* —*v.t.* 走路; 徒步; 踏平。*Pad* it. 〖俚〗走着去。—*v.i.* 慢慢地走。***pad the hoof*** 〖俚〗步行。—*n.* ①〖英方,俚〗道路;小徑。②〖罕〗剪徑强盜。③緩行之馬。④笨重的聲音(如脚步聲)。

pad³ *n.* (用以衡量魚、水果等的)籃子。

pad·ded cell (or **room**) 〔ˈpædɪd～; ˈpædid～〕 軟墊病室(壁上有褥的房間,爲防止精神病患者自殺用)。

pad·ding 〔ˈpædɪŋ; ˈpædiŋ〕 *n.* ①塡塞物;塡料。②添湊語;補白。③塡塞;裝塡。

***pad·dle¹** 〔ˈpædl; ˈpædl〕 *n., v.,* **-dled, -dling.** —*n.* ①槳(特指拿在手上之短槳)。②划槳。③(輪船等的)明輪翼。④槳狀物(作攪

拌、擣衣等用者)。—*v.i.* ①盪槳;用槳划。They *paddled* down the stream in a canoe. 他們坐獨木舟划向下游。②用蹼輪或明輪前進。—*v.t.* ①用槳划(小船)。We *paddled* the little boat closer to shore. 我們用槳划那小船靠近岸邊一點。②(船等)用明輪翼划動。③〖俗〗(用槳等)拍打;笞責。④划船帶運。***paddle one's own canoe*** 依賴自己;自立;獨自爲之。

***pad·dle²** *v.i.*, **-dled, -dling.** ①涉水。②輕摩;玩弄。She sat on the edge of the boat and *paddled* in the water with her feet. 她坐在船舷用脚嬉水。③用手划水。④以短而不穩定的脚步行走。His little daughter *paddled* up to him and kissed him. 他的小女兒搖搖晃晃地走過來吻他。

P

pad·dle·board 〔ˈpædḷˌbord, –ˌbord; ˈpædlbɔːd〕 *n.* 一端圓另一端尖的沖浪板。

paddle boat 明輪艇;明輪船;用外輪航行之船。(亦作 **paddleboat**)

paddle box 明輪殼。

pad·dle·fish 〔ˈpædḷˌfɪʃ; ˈpædlfiʃ〕 *n.*, *pl.* **-fish, -fish·es.** 大硬鱗魚。

pad·dler 〔ˈpædlɚ; ˈpædlə〕 *n.* ①划獨木舟者;划船者。②涉水者;涉泥漿者。

pad·dle·steam·er 〔ˈpædḷˌstimɚ; ˈpædlˌstiːmə〕 *n.* =**paddle boat.**

paddle wheel (明輪船的)蹼輪。

pad·dock¹ 〔ˈpædək; ˈpædək〕 *n.* ①小塊空地或圍場(尤指靠近廐或宅的牧地)。②賽馬場之圍場。③〖澳〗有圍欄之一片土地。—*v.t.* ①將…關在小圍場中。②〖澳〗將(地)圍起來。

pad·dock² *n.* 〖蘇、北英, 方〗①蟾蜍。②蛙。

Pad·dy 〔ˈpædɪ; ˈpædi〕 *n.*, *pl.* **-dies.** 〖俚〗愛爾蘭人(綽號)。

pad·dy 〔ˈpædɪ; ˈpædi〕 *n.*, *pl.* **-dies.** ①米(集合稱)。②穀;稻。③稻田。(亦作 **padi**)

pad·dy·field 〔ˈpædɪˌfild; ˈpædifiːld〕 *n.* 稻田。

paddy wagon 〖美俗〗囚車。

pad·dy·whack 〔ˈpædɪˌhwæk; ˈpædihwæk〕 *n.* ①〖美俗〗責打;鞭打。②〖英俗〗暴怒;震怒。

pa·di·shah 〔ˈpadɪˌʃa; ˈpɑːdiʃɑː〕 *n.* ①皇帝;大王。②(P-)(伊朗之)大王。③(P-)(昔之)土耳其皇帝;英王兼任之印度皇帝。④顯要;大牌人物。

pad·lock 〔ˈpædˌlak; ˈpædlɔk〕 *n.* 掛鎖;扣鎖。—*v.t.* ①鎖以掛鎖。②下令關閉。

pa·dre 〔ˈpadrɪ; ˈpɑːdri〕 *n.* ①神父;教士。②〖軍〗隨軍牧師。

pa·dro·ne¹ 〔paˈdrone; pɑːˈdrounei〕 *n.*, *pl.* **-dro·ni** 〔–ˈdroni; –ˈdrouniː〕. ①保護人;主人。②(地中海中之)小船長。③(義大利之)乞丐頭。④(義大利之)客棧主人。

pa·dro·ne² 〔pəˈdronɪ; pəˈdrouni〕 *n.*, *pl.* **-dro·nes.** (在美國等處)控制並供應義大利工人的工頭。

pae·an 〔ˈpiən; ˈpiːən〕 *n.* (亦作 **pean**) 讚美歌;歡樂歌;凱歌。—*v.t.* 歌頌;讚美。

pae·di·at·rics 〔ˌpidɪˈætrɪks; ˌpiːdiˈætriks〕 *n.* 〖主英〗=**pediatrics.**

pae·do·bap·tism 〔ˌpidoˈbæptɪzṃ; ˌpiːdouˈbæptizm〕 *n.* 幼兒洗禮。(亦作 **pedobaptism**)

pae·do·bap·tist 〔ˌpidoˈbæptɪst; ˌpiːdouˈbæptist〕 *n.* 主張幼兒洗禮者。(亦作 **pedobaptist**)

pa·gan 〔ˈpegən; ˈpeigən〕 *n.* ①異教徒(指非基督教徒)。②沒有宗教信仰的人。—*adj.* 異教的;異端的;不信宗教的。—**ly,** *adv.*

pa·gan·dom 〔ˈpegəndəm; ˈpeigəndəm〕 *n.* ①異教徒(集合稱)。②異教國;異教世界。

pa·gan·ish 〔ˈpegənɪʃ; ˈpeigəniʃ〕 *adj.* 異教的;信奉異教的。—**ly,** *adv.*

pa·gan·ism 〔ˈpegənˌɪzəm; ˈpeigənizm〕 *n.* ①異教;邪教;偶像崇拜。②異教精神。

pa·gan·ize 〔ˈpegənˌaɪz; ˈpeigənaiz〕 *v.t.* & *v.i.*, **-ized, -iz·ing.** (使)成異教;(使)異教化。

‡**page¹** 〔pedʒ; peidʒ〕 *n.*, *v.*, **paged, pag·ing.** —*n.* ①頁;(書籍之)一張。Turn the *page* over. 翻轉一頁。②紀錄。the *pages* of history. 歷史的記載。③(歷史等中的)事件;一頁。—*v.t.* ①標明…之頁數。②翻…之頁。He *paged* the book without interest. 他了無興趣地翻書。—*v.i.* 翻頁。He *paged* through the magazine impatiently. 他不耐煩地翻那雜誌。

page² *n.*, *v.*, **paged, pag·ing.** —*n.* ①僮僕。②貴族之隨侍。③(中古)學習騎士。—*v.t.* ①(在旅館、俱樂部等中)喊出其名字以尋找(某人)。②爲…之僮僕。He chose a new boy to *page* him. 他選了一個新男孩爲他的僮僕。—*v.i.* 作僮僕。

***pag·eant** 〔ˈpædʒənt; ˈpædʒənt〕 *n.* ①壯觀;華飾;化裝遊行。The coronation of the new king was a splendid *pageant*. 新王加冕典禮非常壯觀。②歷史遺跡之展覽;露天歷史劇。③虛飾。④連續的變化或發展。⑤華麗;壯麗。For *pageant* of language he has had no equal. 在措辭的華麗方面,他一直是獨一無二的。—*v.t.* 以大遊行慶祝。

pag·eant·ry 〔ˈpædʒəntrɪ; ˈpædʒəntri〕 *n.*, *pl.* **-ries.** ①壯觀;盛觀;華麗。②虛飾;虛華。③(集合稱)=**pageants.**

page boy ①僮僕。②女人的一種髮型(髮長及肩,後端向內捲曲)。(亦作 **pageboy**)

pag·i·nal 〔ˈpædʒənḷ; ˈpædʒinḷ〕 *adj.* ①頁的。②每頁的;一頁對一頁的;對頁的。

pag·i·nate 〔ˈpædʒəˌnet; ˈpædʒineit〕 *v.t.*, **-nat·ed, -nat·ing.** 標記…之頁數。

pag·i·na·tion 〔ˌpædʒəˈneʃən; ˌpædʒiˈneiʃən〕 *n.* ①標記頁數。②表示頁數之文字、數字。③(目錄等中所記之)頁數。

pa·go·da 〔pəˈgodə; pəˈgoudə〕 *n.* (中國、日本、印度等地之)寶塔;浮屠。

pagoda tree ①〖植物〗長成塔狀之東方樹木(如槐樹等)。②〖諧〗搖錢樹。***shake the pagoda tree*** (到印度等地)發橫財。

pah 〔pa; pɑː〕 *interj.* (表憎惡或輕蔑之發聲)呸!哼!

paid 〔ped; peid〕 *v.* pt. & pp. of **pay.** —*adj.* ①有薪金的;僱用的。②已付清的;已還帳的。③已兌現的;已付現款的。***put paid to*** 〖英俗〗處理;結清。

paid-in 〔ˈpedˌɪn; ˈpeidin〕 *adj.* 已經繳納規定之費用的。

paid-in surplus 超出票面額出售股票所得之資本盈餘;繳入盈餘。

paid-up 〔ˈpedˈʌp; ˈpeidˈʌp〕 *adj.* ①已全部償付的。②已繳清全部費用的。

***pail** 〔pel; peil〕 *n.* ①桶。②一桶之量。

pail·ful 〔ˈpelˌfʊl; ˈpeilful〕 *n.* 一滿桶之量。

pail·lasse 〔pælˈjæs; pælˈjæs〕 *n.* 草薦;藁褥。(亦作 **palliasse**)

pail·lette 〔pælˈjɛt; pælˈjet〕 *n.* ①(釉畫用之)金銀箔或有光澤之金屬薄片。②(裝飾衣服用之)閃爍之金屬片。

‡**pain** 〔pen; pein〕 *n.* ①疼痛;苦痛。A

toothache is a *pain*. 牙痛是一痛苦。②(*pl.*) **a.** 勞苦；辛苦。For his *pains* he incurred the enmity of the people. 他的勞苦換來了人們的仇恨。**b.** 產痛。Her *pains* had begun. 她的產痛已經開始。***be at the pains of*** 苦心…。***be in pain*** 苦惱着。***for one's pains*** 作爲勞力的報酬。***No pains, no gains*** (or ***profit***). 不勞則無獲。***on*** (***upon***, or ***under***) ***pain of*** (***death***) 違者處(死)。***pain in the neck*** 〖俚〗極其棘手的事；非常難對付的人。***pains and penalties*** 刑罰。***spare no pains*** 不辭勞苦。*No pains* were *spared* in the workmanship. 不辭勞苦以求做工精巧。***take pains*** 辛苦工作。***with great pains*** 煞費苦心。—*v.t.* 使痛苦。Your laziness *pains* your parents. 你的懶惰使你的父母痛苦。—*v.i.* ①疼痛。②引起苦痛。It *pained* when he moved his arm. 他移動手臂便覺痛苦。

pained 〔pend; peind〕 *adj.* ①痛的；痛苦的。②自尊心受到傷害的；內心感到痛苦的。

***pain·ful** 〔ˈpenfəl; ˈpeinfəl〕 *adj.* ①疼痛的；痛苦的。②困難的；勞苦的。③令人煩惱的；令人厭煩的。—**ly**, *adv.* —**ness**, *n.*

pain·kill·er 〔ˈpenˌkɪlɚ; ˈpeinˌkilə〕 *n.* 〖俗〗止痛藥。

pain·less 〔ˈpenlɪs; ˈpeinlis〕 *adj.* ①無痛苦的。②不感痛苦的；不知痛苦的；無痛覺的。—**ly**, *adv.*

pains·tak·ing 〔ˈpenzˌtekɪŋ; ˈpeinzˌteikiŋ〕 *adj.* 辛苦的；勞苦的；極小心的；下工夫的。—*n.* 勞苦；辛苦；工夫。—**ly**, *adv.*

pains·worth·y 〔ˈpenzˌwɝðɪ; ˈpeinzˌwəːði〕 *adj.* 值得費苦心的；值得下工夫的。

‡**paint** 〔pent; peint〕 *n.* ①油漆；顏料。Fresh *paint!* 油漆未乾！②香粉；臙脂。③繪畫作品。These portraits are great pieces of *paint*. 這一些畫像都是偉大的繪畫作品。—*v.t.* ①油漆；塗色於。He has *painted* the gate. 他已把門漆過。②繪畫。③形容；描寫。He is not so black as he is *painted*. 他不像被人所形容的那樣壞。④塗敷。The doctor *painted* iodine on the cut. 醫生塗碘酒於傷口。⑤掩飾。—*v.i.* ①油漆；着色。②繪畫。The Queen *paints* well. 女王精於繪畫。③塗脂粉。She is aging rapidly and now *paints* heavily. 她老得很快，所以現在她儘量濃妝豔抹。***as painted as a picture*** 搽着很厚的粉。***paint a black*** (or ***rosy***) ***picture of*** 非常悲觀(樂觀)地敍述…。***paint*** (***something***) ***in*** 畫出。to *paint in* the foreground. 畫出前景。***paint*** (***something***) ***out*** 用油漆或顏料塗去。***paint the lily*** 作多餘的事。***paint the town*** (***red***) 〖俚〗狂歡。

paint·box 〔ˈpentˌbɑks; ˈpeintbɔks〕 *n.* 繪具匣(箱)。

paint·brush 〔ˈpentˌbrʌʃ; ˈpeintbrʌʃ〕 *n.* ①畫筆；畫刷。②〖植物〗＝**painted cup.**

paint·ed 〔ˈpentɪd; ˈpeintid〕 *adj.* ①着了色的。②油漆了的。He carelessly scratched the *painted* woodwork. 他不小心擦傷塗有油漆的木器。③搽了脂粉的。④假的；虛飾的。⑤畫(中)的。She treasured the *painted* likeness of her son. 她珍藏她兒子的畫像。⑥如在畫中的。the sunlit *painted* meadow. 陽光照耀下如畫一般的草地。

painted bunting (美國南部產之)羽色鮮明之雀科鳴禽。

painted cup 〖植物〗(北美產)花苞鮮艷之元參屬植物。

painted lady 苧胥(一種蝴蝶，其幼蟲食薊草，故亦作 **thistle butterfly**).

***paint·er**[1] 〔ˈpentɚ; ˈpeintə〕 *n.* ①畫家。②油漆匠。He is a house *painter*. 他是個房屋油漆匠。

paint·er[2] *n.* 舫索；纜索。***cut the painter*** **a.** 使(船)隨波逐流地漂去。**b.** 分開；斷絕關係。

paint·er[3] *n.* 〖動物〗美洲豹；美洲山貓。

paint·er·ly 〔ˈpentəlɪ; ˈpeintəli〕 *adj.* ①畫家的；畫家特有的。②適於繪畫藝術的。—**paint·er·li·ness**, *n.*

paint·er's col·ic 〔ˈpentəzˈkɑlɪk; ˈpeintəzˈkɔlik〕 〖醫〗鉛毒症。

***paint·ing** 〔ˈpentɪŋ; ˈpeintiŋ〕 *n.* ①畫。I've bought several old *paintings*. 我買了幾幅古畫。②繪畫學；繪畫術。She has a talent for *painting*. 她有繪畫的天才。③着色；油漆。

paint·less 〔ˈpentlɪs; ˈpeintlis〕 *adj.* 未油漆的。

paint pot ①油漆罐(或桶)。②〖地質〗有彩色泥漿沸騰之坑穴。

paint·ress 〔ˈpentrɪs; ˈpeintris〕 *n.* ①女畫家。②畫彩陶之女畫師。

paint·y 〔ˈpentɪ; ˈpeinti〕 *adj.*, **paint·i·er, paint·i·est.** ①顏料的。②以顏料(油漆)弄髒的。③漆上了油漆的。④着色過度的(畫等)。

‡**pair** 〔pɛr, pær; pɛə〕 *n.*, *pl.* **pairs** or **pair**, *v.* —*n.* ①一雙；一副。a *pair* of gloves. 一副手套。②(剪刀等)一把；(褲子)一條。a *pair* of scissors (pliers). 一把剪刀(鉗子)。③夫婦；配偶。the happy *pair*. 幸福的一對。④(動物的)偶；一對。⑤(會議中)分屬兩方而約好互相放棄投票權之兩個會員。⑥此種約定。(***quite***) ***another*** (or ***a different***) ***pair of shoes*** (or ***boots***) (完全是)另外一個問題。—*v.t.* & *v.i.* ①使成對；使成配偶；成對；配合。They *paired* him up with an opponent about his equal. 他們使他與實力相當的對手對陣。②(會議中)與對方一個會員約好互相放棄投票權。***pair off*** 配成一對對。***pair off with*** 〖俗〗和…結婚。〖注意〗在商業上或非正式的用語中 **pair** 的複數仍是 pair, 例如：six *pair* of socks. 六雙襪子。其他情形下則用 pairs.

pair-horse 〔ˈpɛrˌhɔrs; ˈpɛəhɔːs〕 *adj.* 雙馬的(車)。

pair-oar 〔ˈpɛrˌor; ˈpɛərɔː〕 *n.* 雙槳艇。—*adj.* 雙槳(艇)的。

pair of stairs 一列階梯。

pais·ley 〔ˈpezlɪ; ˈpeizli〕 *n.* ①伯斯力布(蘇格蘭一城市 Paisley 伯斯力產的毛織品，上有精巧的彩色圖案)。②伯斯力披肩。—*adj.* ①伯斯力布製的。②伯斯力披肩的。

***pa·ja·mas, py·ja·mas** 〔pəˈdʒæməz, pəˈdʒɑməz; pəˈdʒɑːməz〕 *n. pl.* ①睡衣。②(回教徒等所穿之)寬長袴。

Pak·i·stan 〔ˌpɑkɪˈstɑn; ˌpɑːkisˈtɑːn〕 *n.* 巴基斯坦(亞洲一共和國，首都爲伊士蘭馬巴德 Islamabad).

Pak·i·stan·i 〔ˌpɑkəˈstɑnɪ; ˌpɑːkisˈtɑːni〕 *n.*, *pl.* **-stan·is, -stan·i,** *adj.* —*n.* 巴基斯坦人。—*adj.* 巴基斯坦的。

***pal** 〔pæl; pæl〕 *n.*, *v.*, **palled, pal·ling.** —*n.* 〖俗〗朋友；同志；夥伴。—*v.i.* 結爲友。to *pal* up with a person. 同某人結交爲友。

Pal. Palestine.

‡**pal·ace** 〔ˈpælɪs, -əs; ˈpælis〕 *n.* ①宮殿。②華麗之大厦。the *palace* of justice. 司法大厦。③供娛樂用的大厦。movie *palaces*. 電影院。

palace car 〖鐵路〗①〖英〗豪華的特別車廂。②高級的家畜載運車。

pal·a·din [ˈpælədɪn; ˈpælədin] *n.* ①查理曼（Charlemagne）大帝的十二勇士之一。②騎士；武士；遊俠。

palaeo- 〖字首〗＝**paleo-**.

pa·laes·tra [pəˈlɛstrə; pəˈlestrə] *n.*, *pl.* **-tras, -trae** [-tri; -triː]. ①(古希臘之)練習角力及各種競技的公共場所；角力場。②角力學校。③健身房。(亦作 **palestra**)

pal·an·keen [ˌpælənˈkin; ˌpælənˈkiːn] *n.* 轎；肩輿。(亦作 **palanquin**)

pal·at·a·ble [ˈpælətəbl̩; ˈpælətəbl] *adj.* 味美的；怡人的。a *palatable* dish. 美味的菜。②聽得進的。—**pal·at·a·bly,** *adv.*

pal·a·tal [ˈpælətl̩; ˈpælətl] *adj.* ①〖解剖〗口蓋的；上顎的。②〖語音〗上顎音的。—*n.* 〖語音〗上顎音(如 [j], [x], [i] 等)。—**ly,** *adv.*

pal·a·tal·i·za·tion [ˌpælətl̩əˈzeʃən; ˌpælətəlaiˈzeiʃən] *n.* 〖語音〗上顎(音)化。

pal·a·tal·ize [ˈpælətl̩ˌaɪz; ˈpælətəlaiz] *v.t.*, **-ized, -iz·ing.** 〖語音〗發爲上顎音；使上顎音化。

pal·ate [ˈpælɪt; ˈpælit] *n.* ①口蓋；上顎。②味覺；味官。③嗜好；喜愛。

pa·la·tial [pəˈleʃəl; pəˈleiʃəl] *adj.* ①宮殿的；似宮殿的。②宏大的；壯麗的。

Pa·lat·i·nate [pəˈlætn̩ˌet, -ɪt; pəˈlætinit] *n.* ①(the-) 巴列丁奈特(德國萊因河西岸之一地區，昔爲神聖羅馬帝國的選帝侯領地)。②巴列丁奈特之居民。③(p-) palatine 之領地或職位。

pal·a·tine[1] [ˈpæləˌtaɪn; ˈpælətain] *adj.* ①宮殿的。②(在其領地內)有王權的。③(P-) the Palatinate 的。④伯爵的。—*n.* ①(昔於德國或英國)有王權之伯爵。②女用皮圍巾。③(P-) the Palatinate 之居民。④(P-)＝**Palatine Hill.**

pal·a·tine[2] *adj.* 口蓋的；上顎的。—*n.* 〖解剖〗口蓋骨。

Palatine Hill, the 古羅馬七丘之一(羅馬城卽建於其上)。

pal·a·to·gram [ˈpælətəˌgræm; ˈpælətəgræm] *n.* 〖語音〗口蓋圖。

pa·lav·er [pəˈlævɚ; pəˈlɑːvə] *n.* ①商談；談判；交涉(尤指商旅與未開化土人之間的)。②談話；閒談。③阿諛；奉承。—*v.i.* ①空談；閒談。②談判。—*v.t.* 阿諛；甘言誘騙。

***pale**[1] [pel; peil] *adj.*, **pal·er, pal·est,** *v.*, **paled, pal·ing.** —*adj.* ①蒼白的。She turned *pale*. 她的面孔失色。②暗淡的。a *pale* light. 暗淡的光。③無力的；微弱的。*pale* prose. 無力的散文。—*v.i.* 變蒼白；變暗。Her face *paled* with fear. 她嚇得面色灰白。—*v.t.* 使變蒼白。—**ly,** *adv.* —**ness,** *n.*

pale[2] *n.*, *v.*, **paled, pal·ing.** —*n.* ①柵；欄杆；樁。②界限；境界；範圍。③適當範圍。④紋章中部的垂直紋線。—*v.t.* 圍以柵。

pale- 〖字首〗＝**paleo-** (於母音前用之)。

pale·face [ˈpelˌfes; ˈpeilfeis] *n.* (北美印第安人所稱之)白種人。

paleo- 〖字首〗表"古；舊"之義。

pa·le·og·ra·pher [ˌpelɪˈɑgrəfɚ; ˌpeiliˈɔgrəfə] *n.* 古字學家；古文書學家。

pa·le·o·graph·ic [ˌpelɪəˈgræfɪk; ˌpeiliəˈgræfik] *adj.* 古字學的；古文書學的。

pa·le·og·ra·phy [ˌpelɪˈɑgrəfɪ; ˌpeiliˈɔgrəfi] *n.* ①古文書；古字體。②古文書學；古字學。

pa·le·o·lith·ic [ˌpelɪəˈlɪθɪk; ˌpeiliəˈliθik] *adj.* 舊石器時代的。

pa·le·ol·o·gy [ˌpelɪˈɑlədʒɪ; ˌpeiliˈɔlədʒi] *n.* 考古學；古董學。

pa·le·on·tol·o·gist [ˌpelɪɑnˈtɑlədʒɪst; ˌpeiliɔnˈtɔlədʒist] *n.* 古生物學家；化石學家。

pa·le·on·tol·o·gy [ˌpelɪɑnˈtɑlədʒɪ; ˌpeiliɔnˈtɔlədʒi] *n.* 古生物學；化石學。

Pa·le·o·zo·ic [ˌpelɪəˈzo·ɪk; ˌpeiliəˈzouik] *adj.* 〖地質〗①古生代的。②古生代之岩石的；古生統的。***the Paleozoic*** 〖地質〗古生代；古生代之岩石；古生統。

Pal·es·tine [ˈpæləsˌtaɪn; ˈpælistain] *n.* 巴勒斯坦(西南亞瀕地中海東岸古國名，現分屬以色列及約旦)。

Palestine Liberation Organization 巴勒斯坦解放組織。(略作 P.L.O.)

pal·e·tot [ˈpæləˌto; ˈpæltou] *n.* 一種寬外套。

pal·ette [ˈpælɪt; ˈpælit] *n.* ①調色盤；調色板。②(調色盤上之)一套顏料。③某一特定畫家所使用之各種顏料。

Pa·li [ˈpɑlɪ; ˈpɑːli] *n.* 巴利語(印度之古代通俗語之一，爲印度佛典所用者)。

pal·imp·sest [ˈpælɪmpˌsɛst; ˈpælimpsest] *n.* 將原有之文字刮去後用以重寫之羊皮紙等。—*adj.* palimpsest 的；將原有之文字刮去後重寫的。

pal·in·drome [ˈpælɪnˌdrom; ˈpælindroum] *n.* 迴文；迴語(前後讀起均同之語句，如：eye 及 madam，再如：Able was I ere I saw Elba)。

pal·ing [ˈpelɪŋ; ˈpeiliŋ] *n.* ①柵；垣；圍籬。②樁；杙樁。③樁之集合稱。④打樁；築垣。

pal·in·gen·e·sis [ˌpælɪnˈdʒɛnəsɪs; ˌpælinˈdʒenisis] *n.* ①新生；再生。②(靈魂)輪迴說。③〖生物〗動植物個體發育中祖先進化過程之重演。④變態。—**pal·in·ge·net·ic,** *adj.*

pal·i·node [ˈpælɪˌnod; ˈpælinoud] *n.* ①取消前言之詩；改詠詩。②打消前言。

pal·i·sade [ˌpæləˈsed; ˌpæliˈseid] *n.*, *v.*, **-sad·ed, -sad·ing.** —*n.* ①木樁；杙；樁。②柵欄；垣。③(*pl.*) 一列斷崖。—*v.t.* 圍以木柵；用柵圍繞。(亦作 **palisado**)

pal·ish [ˈpelɪʃ; ˈpeiliʃ] *adj.* 稍蒼白的。

pall[1] [pɔl; pɔːl] *n.* ①棺幃；柩衣。②陰暗的幕罩。a *pall* of smoke. 一片濃煙。—*v.t.* 以柩衣覆蓋；以陰暗之幕罩住。

pall[2] *v.i.* (因過分而) 生厭；乏味。—*v.t.* 使饜足(於美味等)；使生厭。

Pal·la·di·an [pəˈledɪən; pəˈleidjən] *adj.* ①智慧女神 Pallas 的。②智慧的；學問的。

Pal·la·di·um [pəˈledɪəm; pəˈleidjəm] *n.*, *pl.* **-di·a** [-dɪə; -diə]. ①智慧女神 Pallas 之像(特指 Troy 城安危所繫之像)。②(p-) (國家、城市等的)守護神。③(常 p-)保障物。

pal·la·di·um [pəˈledɪəm; pəˈleidjəm] *n.* 〖化〗鈀(稀金屬元素之一，符號 Pd)。

Pal·las [ˈpæləs; ˈpælæs] *n.* 〖希臘神話〗智慧女神。(亦作 **Pallas Athena**)

pall·bear·er [ˈpɔlˌbɛrɚ; ˈpɔːlˌbɛərə] *n.* (行葬禮時)扈棺之人。

pal·let[1] [ˈpælɪt; ˈpælit] *n.* 草床；小床。

pal·let[2] *n.* ①(陶工用的)抹子。②(畫家用的)調色板。③(用以搬運或貯放貨物的)金屬或木材之低臺。④(裝訂書籍時)用以印刷文字之器具。⑤〖機械〗棘齒輪之掣子；螯尖。⑥(風琴的)調節瓣。

pal·liasse [pælˈjæs; pælˈjæs] *n.* ＝**paillasse.**

pal·li·ate [ˈpælɪˌet; ˈpælieit] *v.t.*, **-at·ed, -at·ing.** ①減輕(病、痛等)；緩和。②掩飾；辯解；減(罪)。

pal·li·a·tion [ˌpælɪˈeʃən; ˌpæliˈeiʃən] *n.* ①減輕；緩和。②使減輕或緩和之物；辯解；掩飾。

pal·li·a·tive ['pælɪ͵etɪv; 'pæliətiv] *adj.* ①減輕的; 緩和的。②辯解的; 掩飾的。—*n.* 減輕之物; 緩和之物。
pal·lid ['pælɪd; 'pælid] *adj.* ①無色澤的; 蒼白的。②暗淡的。a *pallid* sky. 暗淡的天空。③呆板的。—**ly,** *adv.* —**ness,** *n.*
pal·li·um ['pælɪəm; 'pæliəm] *n., pl.* **-ums, -li·a** [-lɪə;-liə]. ①(古羅馬男人之)大披肩。②〖天主教〗(樞機主教或總主教的)白羊毛袈裟。③〖動物〗(軟體動物的)外膜; 覆膜。④〖解剖〗(腦的灰白質的)外表。
pall-mall ['pɛl'mɛl; 'pel'mel] *n.* ①鐵圈球(在細長的球場上, 一頭用棒吊着鐵圈, 由另一頭用槌打球穿過鐵圈)。②鐵圈球場。
pal·lor ['pælɚ; 'pælə] *n.* (因恐懼、疾病、死亡等所致之)蒼白; 青白; 灰白。***jail pallor*** 監獄的犯人所特有的蒼白色。
palm¹** [pɑm; pɑːm] *n.* ①掌; 手掌。the *palm* of the hand. 手掌。②手掌之寬度(約爲 3 至 4 英寸)。③(手套之)掌部。a fabric glove with soft suede *palm.* 有軟羔皮掌部的布手套。④(於紙牌遊戲或賭博中)藏牌於掌中。grease*** (or ***cross***) ***a person's palm*** 向某人行賄。***have an itching palm*** 貪財。—*v.t.* ①藏匿於掌中。to *palm* a card. 將一張牌藏於掌中。②給出或使接受(不良之物)。***palm off*** 以假物欺騙或騙賣。
palm²** *n.* ①棕櫚。②棕櫚的枝或葉(用作勝利之象徵)。③勝利。bear*** (or ***carry***) ***off the palm*** 獲勝。He *bore off the palm* in both tennis and swimming. 他在網球和游泳兩項運動中均獲勝。***yield the palm to*** 承認爲…所敗。
pal·ma·ceous [pæl'meʃəs; pæl'meiʃəs] *adj.*〖植物〗棕櫚科的。「的; 掌中的。」
pal·mar ['pælmɚ; 'pælmə] *adj.* 手掌
pal·ma·ry ['pælmərɪ; 'pælməri] *adj.* 最優秀的; 勝利者的; 主要的。
pal·mate ['pælmet; 'pælmit] *adj.* ①掌狀的。②〖植物〗(葉等)掌狀的。③〖動物〗蹼足的。「*adj.* =**palmate.**」
pal·mat·ed ['pælmetɪd; 'pælmitid]
pal·ma·tion [pæl'meʃən; pæl'meiʃən] *n.* 掌狀分裂; 掌狀之部分。
Palm Beach 棕櫚灘(美國 Florida 州東南部之一市鎮, 爲一避寒勝地)。
palm·er¹ ['pɑmɚ; 'pɑːmə] *n.* ①(自聖地歸來手持棕葉之)參拜聖地者; 朝聖者。②行脚僧; 遊方僧。—*v.i.*〖蘇〗作行脚僧; 作流浪漢。
palm·er² *n.* (賭牌或骰子的)作弊的人; 行騙者; 郎中。「(亦作 **palmerworm**)」
palmer worm 一種危害果樹的毛蟲。
pal·met·to [pæl'mɛto; pæl'metou] *n., pl.* **-tos, -toes.**〖植物〗有扇形葉之棕櫚。
palm-greas·ing ['pɑm͵grisɪŋ; 'pɑːm-griːsiŋ]〖俚〗*n.* 行賄。—*adj.* 行賄的。
pal·mi·ped ['pælmɪ͵pɛd; 'pælmiped] *adj.* 蹼足的。—*n.* 蹼足鳥; 水禽。
palm·ist ['pɑmɪst; 'pɑːmist] *n.* 手相家。(亦作 **palmister**)
palm·is·try ['pɑmɪstrɪ; 'pɑːmistri] *n.* ①手相術。②(扒手等之)妙手; 手上戲法。
pal·mit·ic [pæl'mɪtɪk; pæl'mitik] *adj.* 棕櫚油的; 得自棕櫚油的。***palmitic acid*** 〖化〗十六酸; 軟脂酸; 棕櫚酸。
pal·mi·tin ['pælmətɪn; 'pælmitin] *n.* 〖化〗棕櫚油; 甘油三軟脂酸酯。
palm leaf 棕櫚葉 (用以製扇、帽等)。
palm oil 棕櫚油 (用以製肥皂、蠟燭等)。
Palm Sunday 聖枝主日; 聖棕樹節(復活節前的禮拜日; 基督入耶路撒冷的紀念日)。
palm·y ['pɑmɪ; 'pɑːmi] *adj.,* **palm·i·er, palm·i·est.** ①(似)棕櫚的; 多棕櫚的; 棕櫚成蔭的。②繁榮的; 興盛的; 得勝的; 得意洋洋的。one's *palmy* days. (某人之)全盛時代。
pal·o·mi·no [͵pælə'mino; ͵pælə'miː-nou] *n., pl.* **-nos.** ①巴洛米諾馬(美國西南部產, 脚細長, 毛呈奶油色)。②奶油色。
pa·loo·ka [pə'lukə; pə'luːkə] *n.*〖美俚〗①無能或無經驗的競賽者。②笨手笨脚者。
palp [pælp; pælp] *n.* =**palpus.**
pal·pa·bil·i·ty [͵pælpə'bɪlətɪ; ͵pælpə-'biliti] *n.* 可觸知性; 明顯; 明白。
pal·pa·ble ['pælpəbl; 'pælpəbl] *adj.* ①可觸知的; 摸得出的。②明顯的; 易覺察的; 明白的。③〖醫〗可觸診的。
pal·pate ['pælpet; 'pælpeit] *v.t.,* **-pat·ed, -pat·ing.** ①(以手)探觸。②〖醫〗觸診。「*adj.* 眼瞼的。」
pal·pe·bral ['pælpɪbrəl; 'pælpibrəl]
pal·pi·tate ['pælpə͵tet; 'pælpiteit] *v.i.,* **-tat·ed, -tat·ing.** ①急速地跳動; 忐忑。②顫動; 抖動。
pal·pi·ta·tion [͵pælpə'teʃən; ͵pælpi-'teiʃən] *n.* ①心臟之急速跳動; 悸動; 忐忑。②顫動; 抖動。
pal·pus ['pælpəs; 'pælpəs] *n., pl.* **-pi** [-paɪ;-pai]. (節足動物等之)觸鬚。
pals·grave ['pɔlz͵grev; 'pɔːlzgreiv] *n.*〖德史〗於其領地內有王權之伯爵。
pal·sied ['pɔlzɪd; 'pɔːlzid] *adj.* ①患中風症的; 麻痺的; 癱瘓的; 半身不遂的。②搖動的; 顫抖的。
pal·sy ['pɔlzɪ; 'pɔːlzi] *n., pl.* **-sies,** *v.,* **-sied, -sy·ing.** —*n.* ①麻痺; 癱瘓; 中風。②震動。—*v.t.* 使麻痺。
pal·sy-wal·sy ['pɔlzɪ'wɔlzɪ; 'pɔːlzi-'wɔːlzi] *adj.*〖俚〗顯得很親熱的。
pal·ter ['pɔltɚ; 'pɔːltə] *v.i.* ①不誠懇地說或作; 騙; 支吾其詞。②兒戲; 戲弄; 含糊處理〖常 with〗。③論價; 討價還價; 斤斤計較。
pal·try ['pɔltrɪ; 'pɔːltri] *adj.,* **-tri·er, -tri·est.** ①無價值的; 微不足道的。②卑鄙的。—**pal·tri·ly,** *adv.* —**pal·tri·ness,** *n.*
pa·lu·dal [pə'ljudl; pə'ljuːdl] *adj.* ①沼澤地的; 多沼澤的。②起於沼澤的; 生瘴氣的。(亦作 **paludic, paludine**)
pal·y ['pelɪ; 'peili] *adj.,* **pal·i·er, pal·i·est.**〖詩〗蒼白的。
Pa·mirs, the [pə'mɪrz; pə'miəz] *n.* 帕米爾(中國新疆西方邊境之一高原)。
pam·pas ['pæmpəz; 'pæmpəz] *n. pl.* 南美(尤指阿根廷)之大草原。
pampas grass〖植物〗pampas 草(產於南美, 有絲光, 可用於裝飾)。
pam·per ['pæmpɚ; 'pæmpə] *v.t.* ①縱容; 姑息; 嬌養。②飽以甘旨; 使飲食過量。
pam·pe·ro [pɑm'pero; pɑːm'pɛərou] *n., pl.* **-ros.** 自南美 Andes 山脈向東北吹過 pampas 的强烈寒風。
***pam·phlet** ['pæmflɪt; 'pæmflit] *n.* 小冊子。scholarly monographs published as articles or *pamphlets.* 以期刊文章或小冊子形式出版的學術性專論。
pam·phlet·eer [͵pæmflɪ'tɪr; ͵pæm-fli'tiə] *n.* 小冊子的作者。—*v.i.* 寫作或發行小冊子。「羊的牧神; 牧羊神。」
Pan [pæn; pæn] *n.*〖希臘神話〗半人半
***pan¹** [pæn; pæn] *n., v.,* **panned, pan-ning.** —*n.* ①平鍋(無蓋之淺鍋); 盤。baking

pan. 烘焙用平鍋。②任何似淺鍋之物;天平盤;淘金盤。a salt-*pan.* 鹽池。③(舊式槍砲的)火藥池。④硬土層。***on the pan*** 受批評;受攻擊。They had him *on the pan* for coddling subversives. 他們攻擊他袒護顚覆分子。—*v.t.* ①淘洗(礦砂);淘(金)。to *pan* gold. 淘金。②捕獲。③在平鍋中燒(菜)。④〖俗〗嚴厲批評;吹毛求疵。The critic *panned* the play. 這批評家對這齣戲作苛刻的批評。—*v.i.* 出金;產金。The gravel *panned* well. 這碎石產金甚豐。***pan out*** **a.** 結果;結局。**b.** 成功。

pan² *v.t. & v.i.,* **panned, pan•ning.** 〖電影〗(爲攝取全景或跟着移動物而)上下、左右移動(鏡頭、攝影機)。

pan³ *adj.* 全色的(=panchromatic).

pan- 〖字首〗表"全;總;汎"之義。

pan·a·ce·a 〔ˌpænəˈsiə; ˌpænəˈsiːə〕 *n.* 萬靈藥。

pa·nache 〔pəˈnæʃ; pəˈnæʃ〕 *n.* ①(盔「等之)羽飾。②燦爛;艷麗;華麗。」

pa·na·da 〔pəˈnɑdə; pəˈnɑːdə〕 *n.* 麪包粥(以麪包加糖、牛奶、調味料等煮成)。

Pan·a·ma 〔ˌpænəˈmɑ; ˌpænəˈmɑː〕 *n.* ①巴拿馬(國名,位於中美洲,首都爲 Panama). ②(亦作 **Panama City**)巴拿馬城(卽巴拿馬首都)。③巴拿馬地峽(介於南美洲及北美洲之間的狹窄地帶)。④巴拿馬灣(太平洋中一海灣,在巴拿馬地峽之南岸)。⑤(p-) 巴拿馬帽(用一種棕櫚狀嫩葉編成,亦作 panama hat).

Panama Canal 巴拿馬運河。

Pan-A·mer·i·can 〔ˈpænəˈmɛrəkən; ˈpænəˈmerikən〕 *adj.* 全美洲的;汎美洲的。*Pan-American* affairs. 全美洲的事務。

Pan-A·mer·i·can·ism 〔ˈpænəˈmɛrəkənɪzəm; ˈpænəˈmerikənizəm〕 *n.* 汎美主義。

Pan-An·gli·can 〔ˌpænˈæŋglɪkən; ˈpænˈæŋglikən〕 *adj.* 全英國國教的。

pan·a·tel·(l)a 〔ˌpænəˈtɛlə; ˌpænəˈtelə〕 *n.* 一端尖削的細長雪茄。

pan·cake 〔ˈpænˌkek, ˈpæŋ-; ˈpænkeik〕 *n., v.,* **-caked, -cak·ing.** —*n.* ①薄煎餅。②(飛機於離地數尺時所作的)平降;垂直降落。③水粉餅(婦女用的一種化粧品)。***flat as a pancake*** 扁平的。—*v.i.* 平降;(飛機離地數尺時)突然着陸。—*v.t.* ①使(飛機)突然着陸;使平降。②壓扁。

pan·chro·mat·ic 〔ˌpænkroˈmætɪk; ˈpænkrouˈmætik〕 *adj.* 〖照相〗易於感受各色之光的;全色的。

pan·cra·ti·um 〔pænˈkreʃɪəm; pænˈkreiʃiəm〕 *n., pl.* **-ti·a** 〔-ʃɪə; -ʃiə〕.(古希臘之)角鬥(拳擊與摔角之混合者)。

pan·cre·as 〔ˈpænkrɪəs, ˈpæŋ-; ˈpæŋkriəs〕 *n.* 胰臟。

pan·cre·at·ic 〔ˌpænkrɪˈætɪk, pæŋ-; ˌpæŋkriˈætik〕 *adj.* 胰的。

pan·cre·a·tin 〔ˈpænkrɪətɪn; ˈpæŋkriətin〕 *n.* 〖生化〗胰酵素(一種消化劑)。

pan·da 〔ˈpændə; ˈpændə〕 *n.* 〖動物〗(中國西南及喜馬拉雅山中產之)熊貓。

panda car 〖英〗警察巡邏車。

Pan·de·an 〔pænˈdiən; pænˈdiːən〕 *adj.* (似)牧神 Pan 的。*Pandean* pipes. 牧神笙。

pan·dect 〔ˈpændɛkt; ˈpændekt〕 *n.* ①(*pl.*) 羅馬法典(六世紀時 Justinian 一世勅編者,共50卷)。②(*pl.*)法律大全;法典。③(某學科的)總論;全論。

pan·dem·ic 〔pænˈdɛmɪk; pænˈdemik〕 *adj.* ①(疾病)流行全國(全世界)的。②(疾病)流行性的。③普遍的;一般性的;通俗的。—*n.* 全國(世界)性的流行病;大疫。

pan·de·mo·ni·um 〔ˌpændɪˈmonɪəm; ˌpændiˈmounjəm〕 *n.* ①(P-) 羣鬼之宮殿;地獄之都城(見 Milton 所著之 *Paradise Lost*)。②魔鬼之居所。③喧囂;騷亂。④大混亂之場所。

pan·der 〔ˈpændə; ˈpændə〕 *n.* ①誘人爲惡之徒;幫人做壞事的人。②淫媒;龜鴇;妓館主人。—*v.t.* 〖古〗爲…作淫媒;幫助(壞事)。—*v.i.* ①爲淫媒。②迎合。

Pan·do·ra 〔pænˈdorə; pænˈdɔːrə〕 *n.* 〖希臘神話〗潘朶娜(Zeus 爲懲罰 Prometheus 偸取天上之火種而命其下凡,是爲世界上第一個女人)。***Pandora's box*** **a.** Pandora 下凡時 Zeus 賜給她的盒子(當 Pandora 開啓之時,所盛之一切災害罪惡全部從裏面跑出來,散布於人間,祇有希望還留在裏面)。**b.** 未意料到的災禍之源。

pan·dore 〔pænˈdor; pænˈdɔː〕 *n.* 三(四)絃琵琶(古代樂器)。(亦作 **pandora**)

pan·dow·dy 〔pænˈdaudɪ; pænˈdaudi〕 *n., pl.* **-dies.** 〖美〗一種加糖蜜的蘋果糕餅或布丁。

***pane** 〔pen; pein〕 *n.* ①門窗上之單塊的玻璃。Hailstones as big as eggs broke several *panes* of glass. 大如鷄卵的雹子打破了好幾塊門窗玻璃。②天花板上之方格。③成一單元而相連接的幾張郵票。④鑽石上部之一面。

paned 〔pend; peind〕 *adj.* 鑲嵌玻璃的;「用雜色小布片拼做的。」

pan·e·gyr·ic 〔ˌpænəˈdʒɪrɪk; ˌpæniˈdʒirik〕 *n.* ①頌詞。②過分的誇獎。—**al,** *adj.*

pan·e·gyr·ist 〔ˌpænəˈdʒɪrɪst; ˌpæniˈdʒirist〕 *n.* 致頌詞者;頌揚者。

pan·e·gy·rize 〔ˈpænədʒəˌraɪz; ˈpænidʒiraiz〕 *v.t. & v.i.,* **-rized, -riz·ing.** 讚頌;寫稱讚的文章;致頌詞。

pan·el** 〔ˈpænḷ; ˈpænl〕 *n., v.,* **-el(l)ed, -el·(l)ing.** —*n.* ①門窗上之方格。②畫板。③鑲板。a wall of prefabricated plywood *panels.* 預製三合板拼成的牆壁。④陪審官名單;全體陪審官。⑤長方形之畫或照片(濶大於長者)。⑥小組討論會。⑦小組。an advisory *panel* of experts. 由專家所構成的顧問小組。⑧對一般民衆之抽樣訪查。⑨一種密封式小貨車。⑩替投過醫藥保險者看病的醫生名單。⑪馬鞍上之墊子或襯裏。on the panel*** 名字列於名單中的。—*v.t.* 裝格子於;鑲板於。

panel board ①有壓紙框架之畫板。②(用廢紙壓製之)硬紙板。③〖電〗配電盤。(亦作 **panelboard**)

panel discussion (題目及討論者預先選定的)討論會;座談會。

panel house (or **den**) 〖美〗(有祕密拉門房間的)娼館;暗窰子。

pan·el·(l)ist 〔ˈpænlɪst; ˈpænəlist〕 *n.* ①panel discussion 之參與者。②〖無線電、電視〗(問答節目等的)回答者;出場者。

panel show 有一組知名人士參加的電視猜謎、討論會或遊戲節目。

panel truck 密封式運貨小卡車。

pan-fry 〔ˈpænˌfraɪ; ˈpænfrai〕 *v.t.,* **-fried, -fry·ing.** 在淺鍋中煎。

***pang** 〔pæŋ; pæŋ〕 *n.* 一陣突然的痛苦;劇痛;悲痛;苦悶。the *pangs* of hunger. 肚子餓得發痛。—*v.t.* 使發生劇痛。

Pan-Ger·man 〔ˌpænˈdʒɝmən; ˈpænˈdʒəːmən〕 *adj.* 全德國人的;汎日耳曼主義的。—*n.* 汎日耳曼主義者。

Pan·Ger·man·ic [ˌpændʒɝˈmænɪk; ˈpændʒəːˈmænik] *adj.* ＝**Pan-German.**
Pan·Ger·man·ism [ˌpænˈdʒɝmənɪzəm; ˈpænˈdʒəːmənizm] *n.* 汎日耳曼主義。
pan·go·lin [pæŋˈgolɪn; pænˈgoulin] *n.* 〖動物〗穿山甲。
pan·han·dle[1] [ˈpænˌhændḷ; ˈpænˌhændl] *n.* ①鍋柄。②（有時 P-）似鍋柄之突出地帶（如: the *Panhandle* of West Virginia, Texas, Oklahoma 等)。
pan·han·dle[2] *v.t.* & *v.i.*, **-dled, -dling.** 〖俚〗在公路上(向人搭訕而)行乞。
pan·han·dler [ˈpænˌhændlɚ; ˈpænˌhændlə] *n.* 〖俚〗在街道上行乞的人;乞丐。
Pan·hel·len·ic [ˈpænhəˈlɛnɪk; ˌpænheˈliːnik] *adj.* ①全希臘人的。②汎希臘主義的。③〖美〗希臘文字俱樂部的。
Pan·hel·len·ism [pænˈhɛlənɪzəm; ˈpænˈhelinizəm] *n.* 汎希臘主義; 希臘統一運動。
***pan·ic**[1] [ˈpænɪk; ˈpænik] *n., pl.* **panics,** *adj., v.,* **pan·icked, pan·ick·ing.** —*n.* ①恐慌;驚惶。When the theater caught fire, there was a *panic.* 戲院着火時, 有一陣驚惶。②經濟上之恐慌。When four banks failed in one day, there was a *panic* among businessmen.當四家銀行在同一天倒閉時, 商人間起了一陣恐慌。—*adj.* ①恐慌的;驚惶的。*panic* fear. 驚惶。②可從裏面推開的(門閂等)。*panic* bars for school doors. 用於校門的可從裏面推開的門閂。—*v.t.* 使恐慌; 使驚惶。A brutal murder *panics* the town. 一件殘忍的兇殺案使全鎮驚惶。—*v.i.* 起恐慌;驚惶。
pan·ic[2] *n.* 〖植物〗稷;稗。(亦作 **panic grass**)
pan·ick·y [ˈpænɪkɪ; ˈpæniki] *adj.* ①恐慌的;驚慌的。②引起恐慌的。③似恐慌的。④起於恐慌的。⑤易起恐慌的。
pan·i·cle [ˈpænɪkḷ; ˈpænikl] *n.*〖植物〗圓錐花(序)。
pan·ic-mon·ger [ˈpænɪkˌmʌŋgɚ; ˈpænikˌmʌŋgə] *n.* 製造恐慌的人。
pan·ic-strick·en [ˈpænɪkˌstrɪkən; ˈpænikˌstrikən] *adj.* 恐慌的;驚慌的。
pa·nic·u·lat·ed [pəˈnɪkjəˌletɪd; pəˈnikjulitid] *adj.* 〖植物〗圓錐花(序)的。(亦作 **paniculate**)
Pan-Is·lam·ic [ˌpænɪzˈlæmɪk; ˌpænizˈlæmik] *adj.* 汎回教主義的。
pan·jan·drum [pænˈdʒændrəm; pænˈdʒændrəm] *n.* 〖蔑〗擺架子的官吏;架子十足的人。
pan·nage [ˈpænɪdʒ; ˈpænidʒ] *n.* 〖英法律〗①在森林中之猪隻之放牧; 其權利或權利金。②林中之猪飼料。
panne [pæn; pæn] *n.* 一種似天鵝絨之織物。
pan·ni·er [ˈpænjɚ; ˈpæniə] *n.* ①(掛於馱獸兩側的) 馱籃。②背籃;肩筐。③(從前用以撐開婦女臀部衣裙之) 鯨骨架。
pan·ni·kin [ˈpænəkɪn; ˈpænikin] *n.* ①一種小鍋。②一種金屬製的小杯子;酒杯。
pa·no·cha [pəˈnotʃə; pəˈnoutʃə] *n.* ＝**panoche.**
pa·no·che [pəˈnotʃɪ; pəˈnoutʃi] *n.* ①(墨西哥產之)粗糖。②赤糖糖果(以赤糖、奶油、牛奶及果仁製成)。
pan·o·plied [ˈpænəplɪd; ˈpænəplid] *adj.* ①披全副盔甲的。②全副穿飾的。
pan·o·ply [ˈpænəplɪ; ˈpænəpli] *n., pl.* **-plies.** ①全副盔甲。②全副穿戴或服裝。③富麗堂皇。④成套或成組的盔甲之圖樣。
pan·op·ti·con [pænˈaptɪˌkan; pæˈnɔptikɔn] *n.* ①圓形監獄。②望遠顯微鏡。
pan·o·ram·a [ˌpænəˈræmə; ˌpænəˈrɑːmə] *n.* ①全景;全圖。②活動畫景; 繼續轉換之景。③範圍。
pan·o·ram·ic [ˌpænəˈræmɪk; ˌpænəˈræmik] *adj.* ①全景的。②似活動畫景的。—**al·ly,** *adv.*
panoramic camera 寬視野照相機。
Pan·pipe [ˈpænˌpaɪp; ˈpænpaip] *n.* 牧神笙(一種原始樂器)。
Pan-Slav·ism [ˌpænˈslɑvɪzəm; ˈpænˈslɑːvizm] *n.* 汎斯拉夫主義;斯拉夫民族統一運動。
***pan·sy** [ˈpænzɪ; ˈpænzi] *n.* ①〖植物〗三色紫羅蘭 (＝heartsease). ②〖俚〗同性戀的男子 (輕蔑語)。③〖俚〗脂粉氣的男子 (輕蔑語)。—*adj.* 〖俚〗①同性戀的。②娘娘腔的。
***pant**[1] [pænt; pænt] *n.* 喘息;心悸。—*v.i.* ①喘息; 氣喘。②渴望 〖for, after〗. The people *panted* after liberty. 人民渴望自由。—*v.t.* ①喘息而言〖out, forth〗. to *pant* out one's last words. 氣喘吁吁地說出遺言。②(心) 猛烈跳動。
pant[2] *n.* 褲子。—*adj.* 褲子的;與褲子有關的。
Pan·ta·gru·el·ism [pænˈtægruˌɛlɪzəm; ˌpæntəˈgruːəlizm] *n.* Pantagruel (法國作家 Rabelais 小說中人物)式幽默; 善意而粗率的諷諷。
pan·ta·let(te)s [ˌpæntḷˈɛts; ˌpæntəˈlets] *n. pl.* ①(19 世紀婦女用的) 寬鬆長內褲。②寬鬆長內褲之飾邊。
pan·ta·loon [ˌpæntḷˈun; ˌpæntəˈluːn] *n.* ①(啞劇中) 爲丑角取笑對象之角色; 老丑角。②(*pl.*) 馬褲;褲子。
pan·tech·ni·con [pænˈtɛknɪˌkan; pænˈteknikən] *n.* 〖英〗①(原指)販賣各種各色東西的市場。②貨棧。③傢具搬運車。
pan·the·ism [ˈpænθiˌɪzəm; ˈpænθiːizəm] *n.* ①宇宙卽神論。②汎神主義;多神崇拜。—**pan·the·ist,** *n.* —**pan·the·is·tic, pan·the·is·ti·cal,** *adj.*
Pan·the·on [ˈpænθɪən; pænˈθiːən] *n.* ①萬神殿 (羅馬之一圓頂廟宇, 建於公元 120–124年)。②(p-) 偉人祠。③(p-)衆神之廟。④(p-) 神話中衆神之集合稱;一國的衆神。
***pan·ther** [ˈpænθɚ; ˈpænθə] *n., pl.* **-thers, -ther,** *adj.* —*n.* ①豹。②美洲豹。③美洲虎。④〖俗〗兇惡之人。—*adj.* 兇猛的。
pan·ther·ess [ˈpænθərɛs; ˈpænθəris] *n.* ①panther 之雌性。②兇狠之婦女。
pant·ies [ˈpæntɪz; ˈpæntiz] *n. pl.* 婦女、兒童之短襯褲。
pan·tile [ˈpænˌtaɪl; ˈpæntail] *n.* 波形瓦。
pan·ti·soc·ra·cy [ˌpæntaɪˈsakrəsɪ; ˌpæntiˈsɔkrəsi] *n.* 理想的平等社會。
panto- 〖字首〗表"全; 每"之義。(母音前作 **pant-**)
pan·to·graph [ˈpæntəˌgræf; ˈpæntəgrɑːf] *n.* ①伸縮繪圖器; 縮圖器。②〖電〗(電車頂上的) 電桿架;檐狀聚電器。
pan·to·mime [ˈpæntəˌmaɪm; ˈpæntəmaim] *n., v.,* **-mimed, -mim·ing.** —*n.* ①啞劇。②手勢。—*v.i.* ①打手勢。②演啞劇。—*v.t.* ①以手勢表示。②演 (啞劇)。—**pan·to·mim·ist,** *n.*
pan·to·mim·ic [ˌpæntəˈmɪmɪk; ˌpæntəˈmimik] *adj.* 啞劇的;似啞劇的。
pan·to·scop·ic [ˌpæntəˈskapɪk; ˌpæntəˈskɔpik] *adj.* ①視野廣闊的。②(透鏡等)

大角度的。

pan·to·then·ic acid 〔ˌpæntəˈθɛnɪk～; ˌpæntəˈθenik～〕【生化】平頭酸；泛酸($C_9H_{17}NO_5$, 維他命B複合體之一種)。

***pan·try** 〔ˈpæntrɪ; ˈpæntri〕 *n., pl.* **-tries.** 餐具室；食品室。

pan·try·man 〔ˈpæntrɪmən; ˈpæntrimən〕 *n., pl.* **-men.** (受雇於旅館等中之)食品或食器貯藏室之管理人。

pants** 〔pænts; pænts〕 *n. pl.* 【美俗】褲子。a pair of *pants.* 一條褲子。wear the pants*** 掌大權；當家。***with one's pants down*** 困窘。【注意】在美國褲子的正式用語是 **trousers.**

pant·skirt 〔ˈpæntˌskɜt; ˈpænt-skəːt〕 *n.* 褲裙。

pant·suit 〔ˈpæntˌsut; ˈpænt-sjuːt〕 *n.* (女用之)套裝。(亦作 **pants suit**)

pan·ty hose 〔ˈpæntɪ～; ˈpænti～〕褲襪。(亦作 **pantyhose, pantihose**)

pan·ty·waist 〔ˈpæntɪˌwest; ˈpænti-weist〕 *n.* ①(原指)幼兒用內衣褲。②【美俚】(幼兒般)柔弱的人；娘娘腔的人。—*adj.* 膽小的；如小孩的；娘娘腔的。

pan·zer 〔ˈpænzə, ˈpɑntsə; ˈpænzə〕 *adj.* 德國裝甲部隊的。a *panzer* division. 德國裝甲師。—*n.* 德國裝甲部隊。(亦作 **Panzer**)

pap 〔pæp; pæp〕 *n., v.,* **papped, pap·ping.** —*n.* ①(嬰兒或病患者食用之)柔軟食物(如麪包粥等)。②【俚】俸給；薪津；津貼。③【俚】政治上的包庇。④純娛樂性讀物。***as soft*** (or ***easy***) ***as pap*** 似同兒戲。***give pap with a hatchet*** 假裝不仁慈，實際上做好事。—*v.t.* 用柔軟食物餵。

***pa·pa** 〔ˈpɑpə, pəˈpɑ; pəˈpɑː〕 *n.* ①爸爸。a promise from *papa* to supply more money. 爸爸給更多錢的允諾。②【俚】丈夫；男友。

Pa·pa *n.* 通訊電碼，代表字母 P.

pa·pa·cy 〔ˈpepəsɪ; ˈpeipəsi〕 *n., pl.* **-cies.** ①羅馬教皇之職位；教皇權。②教皇制度；教皇政治。③教皇之在位期間。④代代相承之全體羅馬教皇。

pa·pal 〔ˈpepl̩; ˈpeipəl〕 *adj.* ①羅馬教皇的。a *papal* delegate. 教皇使節。②羅馬教皇制度的。③天主教的。

pa·pal·ism 〔ˈpepl̩ɪzəm; ˈpeipəlizm〕 *n.* ①教皇制度。②教皇地位、權威之過度推崇。

pa·pal·ist 〔ˈpepl̩ɪst; ˈpeipəlist〕 *n.* 教皇制擁護者；天主教徒。

pa·pal·ize 〔ˈpepl̩ˌaɪz; ˈpeipəlaiz〕 *v.t. & v.i.,* **-ized, -iz·ing.** (使)教皇制度化；(使)奉天主教。

pa·pav·er·a·ceous 〔pəˌpævəˈreʃəs; pəˌpeivəˈreiʃəs〕 *adj.* 【植物】罌粟科的。

pa·pav·er·ous 〔pəˈpævərəs; pəˈpeivərəs〕 *adj.* ①(似)罌粟的。②催眠的。

pa·paw 〔ˈpɔpɔ, pəˈpɔ; pəˈpɔː〕 *n.* 【植物】①生長於美國中部及南部的一種植物；其所生之果。②萬壽果。③木瓜。(亦作 **pawpaw**)

pa·pa·ya 〔pəˈpaɪə, pəˈpɑjə; pəˈpaiə〕 *n.* ①木瓜；蕃瓜。②木瓜樹；蕃瓜樹。

‡**pa·per** 〔ˈpepə; ˈpeipə〕 *n.* ①紙。a sheet of *paper.* 一張紙。②壁紙。③報紙。Have you seen today's *paper?* 你看見今天的報沒有? ④文件；證件。Important *papers* were stolen. 重要文件被竊了。⑤(*pl.*)身分證。⑥(*pl.*)船證；船照。⑦論文。a *paper* on the teaching of English. 一篇關於英語教學之論文。⑧考卷。⑨(學生之)作業。⑩紙袋；紙包。a *paper* of peppermints. 一紙包的薄荷糖。⑪票據。long-term *paper.* 遠期支票。⑫鈔票。⑬票。The *paper* at the box office is all sold. 售票室的票都賣光了。⑭【俚】免費招待的觀衆或聽衆。Most of the first-night audience was *paper.* 第一晚的大部分觀衆都是免費招待的。***on paper*** **a.** 抄寫的；印的。We must get the agreement down *on paper.* 我們必須將那合約寫下來。**b.** 理論上的。The plan looks good *on paper.* 那計畫在理論上看來很好。**c.** 在籌備階段。The project is still *on paper.* 那計畫仍在籌備階段。**d.** 名義上；表面上。*On paper* he was worth nearly $1,000,000. 在表面上他的財產將近 $1,000,000。***send in one's papers*** 辭職。—*adj.* ①紙做的；紙的。a *paper* box. 紙盒子。②薄的。almonds with *paper* shells. 薄皮的杏仁。③理論上的；空泛的。④文字上的；紙上的。⑤文書的。*paper* procedures. 公文程序。⑥大部分由免費招待者所構成的。*paper* audience. 以免費招待爲大多數的觀衆。⑦紙幣的。⑧紙裝的；平裝的。*paper* books. 平裝書。—*v.t.* ①糊紙；包以紙。to *paper* a room. 用紙裱糊房間。②貼於紙上。③【俚】以免費招待的觀衆爲…湊熱鬧(撐場面)。to *paper* a theater for an opening night. 在開演之夜免費招待觀衆爲戲院湊熱鬧。④騙。***paper over*** 粉飾；掩蓋。—*v.i.* 貼壁紙。

pa·per·back 〔ˈpepəˌbæk; ˈpeipəbæk〕 *n.* 用普通紙裝訂作封面的書；廉價的書籍；平裝書。—*adj.* 平裝的。

paper blockade 紙上封鎖(不嚴格「執行之封鎖)。

pa·per·board 〔ˈpepəˌbɔrd; ˈpeipə-bɔːd〕 *n.* 厚紙板；硬紙板。—*adj.* 硬紙板做的。

paper boy 賣報童。(亦作 **paperboy**)

paper chase 一種撒紙追蹤遊戲。

paper clip 紙夾。

paper currency 紙幣。

paper cutter ①裁紙器。②裁紙刀。

paper hanger 裱糊壁紙的工人。(亦作 **paperhanger**)

paper hanging ①裱貼牆紙。②(*pl.*)糊壁用的紙。(亦作 **paperhanging**)

paper knife 裁紙刀。

paper mill 造紙廠。

paper money ①紙幣；鈔票。②票據；支票。

paper profits 帳面盈餘；虛盈。

paper stainer 壁紙製造人(着色人)。

paper tiger 紙老虎；外强中乾者。

paper war(fare) 筆戰；論戰。

pa·per·weight 〔ˈpepəˌwet; ˈpeipə-weit〕 *n.* 書鎮；紙壓。

pa·per·work 〔ˈpepəˌwɜk; ˈpeipəwəːk〕 *n.* 文書業務；書寫工作。

pa·per·y 〔ˈpepərɪ; ˈpeipəri〕 *adj.* ①似紙的；紙狀的；紙質的。②薄的；薄弱的。

pap·e·terie 〔ˈpæpətrɪ; ˈpæpətri〕 *n.* 盒裝的精緻信紙等。

pa·pier-mâ·ché 〔ˈpepəməˈʃe; ˈpæpjeiˈmɑːʃei〕 *n.* 混凝紙。—*adj.* ①混凝紙做成的。②不眞實的；不實在的。

pa·pil·i·o·na·ceous 〔pəˌpɪlɪəˈneʃəs; pəˌpiliəˈneiʃəs〕 *adj.* 【植物】蝶形的(花冠)。

pa·pil·la 〔pəˈpɪlə; pəˈpilə〕 *n., pl.* **-lae** 〔-li; -liː〕. ①【解剖】乳頭。②乳頭狀小突起。

pap·il·lar·y 〔pəˈpɪlərɪ; pəˈpiləri〕 *adj.* =**papillate.**

pap·il·late 〔ˈpæpəˌlet; ˈpæpileit〕 *adj.* 乳頭的；乳頭狀的；有乳頭狀小突起的。

pap·il·lo·ma 〔ˌpæpəˈlomə; ˌpæpiˈloumə〕 *n., pl.* **-ma·ta** 〔-mətə; -mətə〕, **-mas.**

〖醫〗(皮膚或黏膜之)乳頭淋瘤;刺瘤。

pap·il·lon ['pæpə,lɑn; 'pæpilɔn] *n.* 一種小型玩賞狗(毛長光澤如絲, 雙耳豎立如蝴蝶之翅, 爲 spaniel 之一種)。

pap·il·lose ['pæpə,los; 'pæpilous] *adj.* 有乳頭的;多小突起的;多疣的。

pa·pist ['pepɪst; 'peipist] *n.* ①天主教徒;羅馬教徒。②相信羅馬教皇有無上威權者。—*adj.* 羅馬天主教的(惡意之語)。

pa·pis·ti·cal [pe'pɪstɪkl, pə–; pə'pistikəl] *adj.* (羅馬)天主教的。(亦作**papistic**)

pa·pist·ry ['pepɪstrɪ; 'peipistri] *n.* 教皇制度;天主教教義、儀式等(輕蔑語)。

pa(p)·poose [pæ'pus; pə'pu:s] *n.* 北美印第安人之幼嬰。

pap·pus ['pæpəs; 'pæpəs] *n., pl.* **pap·pi** ['pæpaɪ;'pæpai].〖植物〗冠毛。

pap·py ['pæpɪ; 'pæpi] *adj.,* **-pi·er, -pi·est,** *n.* —*adj.* 麪包粥似的;漿糊狀的;半液狀的。—*n., pl.* **-pies.**〖方〗爸爸。

pap·ri·ka [pæ'prikə; pæ'pri:kə] *n.* 乾紅椒;乾紅椒粉。

Pap·u·a ['pæpjʊə; 'pæpjuə] *n.* ①巴布亞(即新幾內亞)。②巴布亞人。

Pap·u·an ['pæpjʊən; 'pæpjuən] *adj.* ①巴布亞的。②新幾內亞土人的。—*n.* ①新幾內亞之土人; 巴布亞人。②西南太平洋諸羣島之語言。③巴布亞語。

pap·u·la ['pæpjʊlə; 'pæpjulə] *n., pl.* **-lae** [–,li; –li:]. =**papule.**

pap·ule ['pæpjul; 'pæpju:l] *n.*〖醫〗「丘疹。」

pa·py·rus [pə'paɪrəs; pə'paiərəs] *n., pl.* **-py·ri** [–'paɪraɪ; –'paiərai]. ①紙草。②由紙草製成之紙。③寫於紙草紙上之古代紀錄;紙草紙之古文書。

*__par__[1] [pɑr; pɑ:] *n.* ①同等;同等地位;同程度。②定額;標準;(健康或精神的)常態。His work is above *par.* 他的工作在水準之上。③(公債、票據、股票等之)票面價值。above *par.* 用票面以上的價格。below *par.* 用票面以下的價格。 at *par.* 照票面價格。④〖高爾夫〗標準桿數。***at par*** (股票)可以票面價購進的。***issue par*** 發行價格。***nominal*** (or ***face***) ***par*** 面額價。***on a par*** 和…同等; 和…同價。The gains and losses are about *on a par.* 得失幾乎相等。***par of exchange*** 匯兌平價。***up to par*** 合乎平均或正常數量。—*adj.* ①平均的;正常的。The acting is only *par.* 演出並無特出之處。②票面價額的。***par value*** 面值。***par value stock*** 面值股票。

par[2] *n.*〖俗〗(報紙之)短篇記事;短評。

par. ①paragraph. ②parallel. ③parenthesis ④parish.

para-[1]〖字首〗①表"側面;並行;超越;錯誤"之義, 如: parallel. ②〖化〗表"同質異構物"之義, 如: paracymene.

para-[2]〖字首〗①表"防護;保安;避難"之義, 如: parachute, parapet. ②表"使用降落傘的"之義, 如: paratroop, paraoperation.

par·a·ble ['pærəbl; 'pærəbl] *n.* ①寓言;比喻; 譬語。②〖古〗隱晦或謎般的格言。***take up one's parable*** 開始講道。

pa·rab·o·la [pə'ræbələ; pə'ræbələ] *n., pl.* **-las.** 拋物線。

par·a·bol·ic[1] [,pærə'bɑlɪk; ,pærə'bɔlik] *adj.*〖幾何〗拋物線(狀)的。

par·a·bol·ic[2] *adj.* 譬喻的;寓言的。

pa·rab·o·loid [pə'ræbə,lɔɪd; pə'ræbəlɔid] *n.*〖幾何〗拋物面;拋物線體。

par·a·brake ['pærə,brek; 'pærəbreik] *n.* 減速降落傘。

pa·rach·ro·nism [pær'ækrənɪzəm; pə'rækrənizəm] *n.* 記時錯誤(尤指將年代或月日誤記較實際爲遲)。

*__par·a·chute__ ['pærə,ʃut; 'pærəʃu:t] *n., v.,* **-chut·ed, -chut·ing.** —*n.* ①降落傘。②飛鼠等可伸張之皮膚皺摺。③=**parabrake.** —*v.t. & v.i.* ①跳傘。The men in the burning plane *parachuted* safely to the ground. 着火飛機中的人員均跳傘安全落地。②由降落傘運送。

par·a·chut·ist ['pærə,ʃutɪst; 'pærə,ʃu:tist] *n.* 使用降落傘降落者;傘兵。

par·a·clete ['pærə,klit; 'pærəkli:t] *n.* ①辯護者; 安慰者。②(P–)〖基督教〗聖靈。

par·a·cy·e·sis [,pærəsaɪ'isɪs; ,pærəsai'i:sis] *n.*〖醫〗子宮外孕。(亦作 **extra-uterine pregnancy**)

P

*__pa·rade__ [pə'red; pə'reid] *n., v.,* **-rad·ed, -rad·ing.** —*n.* ①行列;整隊遊行。funeral *parade.* 出殯的行列。②炫示;誇耀。to make a *parade* of one's virtues. 炫示自己的優點。③公共散步場所。④閱兵;校閱。⑤遊行。a circus *parade.* 馬戲團的遊行。⑥校場; 遊行場所。⑦演奏會;演唱會。—*v.t.* ①遊行過(某處)。②炫示;誇耀。to *parade* one's skill. 炫示個人之技術。③檢閱(軍隊)。—*v.i.* ①列隊行進。②集合軍隊(以備檢閱或操演)。—**pa·rad·er,** *n.*

pa·rade-ground [pə'red,graʊnd; pə'reid'graund] *n.* ①校閱場。②表演場。

par·a·digm ['pærə,dɪm, –,daɪm; 'pærədaim] *n.* ①模範。②〖文法〗(名詞、代名詞及動詞之)變化例或變化表。

par·a·dig·mat·ic [,pærədɪg'mætɪk; ,pærədig'mætik] *adj.* ①典型的; 可爲模範的;例證的。②〖文法〗變化例的; 變化表的。(亦作 **paradigmatical**)

par·a·di·sal [,pærə'daɪsəl; ,pærə'daisəl] *adj.* 天堂的;似天堂的; 樂園的(=paradisiac).

*__par·a·dise__ ['pærə,daɪs; 'pærədais] *n.* ①天堂;天國。②樂園;樂境。a *paradise* for children. 兒童樂園。③伊甸樂園(=Garden of Eden). ④極美的地方。

par·a·dis·i·ac [,pærə'dɪsɪ,æk; ,pærə'disiæk] *adj.* =**paradisiacal.**

par·a·di·si·a·cal [,pærədɪ'saɪəkl; ,pærədi'saiəkəl] *adj.* 天國的;樂園的;至福的。

par·a·dis·i·al [,pærə'dɪsɪəl; ,pærə'disiəl] *adj.* 天堂的; 至福的。(亦作 **paradisian, paradisic, paradisical, paradisiac, paradisiacal, paradisal**)

par·a·dos ['pærə,dɑs; 'pærədɔs] *n.*〖軍〗背牆(砲臺、戰壕等背面之堤,用以防禦敵人自後方來之砲火)。

*__par·a·dox__ ['pærə,dɑks; 'pærədɔks] *n., pl.* **-dox·es.** ①似非而是的雋語。"More haste, less speed," and "The child is father to the man" are *paradoxes.* "越急越慢"與"兒童乃成年人之父" 都是似非而是的雋語。②自相矛盾的話。③充滿矛盾的人或事物。

par·a·dox·i·cal [,pærə'dɑksɪkl; ,pærə'dɔksikəl] *adj.* ①似非而是之論的。②好作奇論的;喜用似非而是之雋語的。③矛盾的。(亦作 **paradoxal, paradoxial**) **—ly,** *adv.*

par·af·fin ['pærəfɪn; 'pærəfin] *n.* ①石蠟。②石蠟油(=paraffin oil). —*v.t.* 塗以石蠟;注以石蠟。

par·af·fine ['pærəfɪn; 'pærəfi:n] *n., v.t.,* **-fined, -fin·ing.** ＝**paraffin.**

par·a·go·ge [ˌpærə'godʒɪ; ˌpærə'goudʒi:] *n.*【文法】語尾音之添加。

par·a·gon ['pærəˌgɑn; 'pærəgən] *n.* ①模範;典型;優秀之人;完美之物;尤物;殊品。②【印刷】二十磅因(20 points) 大小之活字。③罕見之大珍珠。④一百克拉以上之完美大鑽石。—*v.t.* ①比較。②視爲模範。—*adj.* (寶石等)品質極高的;極佳的。

***par·a·graph** ['pærəˌgræf; 'pærəgrɑ:f] *n.* ①(文章等)段;節。Translate the following *paragraphs* into Chinese. 將下列各段譯成中文。②新聞的一節; 短評。③分段符號 (卽¶)。—*v.t.* ①分段。The new version is much better *paragraphed* than the old. 新版比舊版分段分得更好。②寫有關…的短新聞。

par·a·graph·er ['pærəˌgræfɚ; 'pærəgrɑ:fə] *n.* (報章上的)短評作者。

Par·a·guay ['pærəˌgwe, -ˌgwaɪ, ˌpara'gwai; 'pærəgwai, ˌpara'gwai] *n.* ①巴拉圭 (國名, 在南美洲中部, 首都爲亞松森, Asunción)。②巴拉圭河。

par·a·keet ['pærəˌkit; 'pærəki:t] *n.* 長尾鸚鵡。(亦作 **parrakeet, paroquet**)

par·a·leip·sis [ˌpærə'laɪpsɪs; ˌpærə'laipsis] *n.* ＝**paralipsis.**

par·a·lep·sis [ˌpærə'lɛpsɪs; ˌpærə'lepsis] *n., pl.* **-ses** [-siz; -si:z]. ＝**paralipsis.**

par·a·lip·sis [ˌpærə'lɪpsɪs; ˌpærə'lipsis] *n., pl.* **-ses** [-siz; -si:z].【修辭】假省筆法(假裝省略重要部分反而促人注意的表現法, 多以 I say nothing of.... 或 not to mention.... 等筆調開始)。

par·al·lax ['pærəˌlæks; 'pærəlæks] *n.* ①【天文】視差。②【照相】(鏡頭與窺鏡之)視差。

***par·al·lel** ['pærəˌlɛl; 'pærəlel] *adj., n., v.,* **-lel·(l)ed, -lel·(l)ing.** —*adj.* ①平行的。This street is *parallel* to that. 這條街同那條平行。②相同的;相似的。*parallel* points in the characters of different men. 不同人物間個性上之相同點。—*n.* ①平行線; 平行面。②緯線; 緯度圈。③相似之物;相同之物。a brilliant career without (a) *parallel* in modern times. 近世無與倫比之輝煌事蹟。④對比;比較。to draw a *parallel* between this winter and last one. 將今年冬天與去年冬天作一比較。⑤平行的狀態;平行。⑥【電】並聯。—*v.t.* ①(使)與…平行。The street *parallels* the railroad. 這街道與鐵路平行。②找相同的例。③對比;比較。They *paralleled* his life with those of the saints. 他們將他的生活與聖者的生活相比。④與…相同或相似。⑤平行放置。

parallel bars 雙槓。

par·al·lel·e·pi·ped [ˌpærəˌlɛlə'paɪpɪd; ˌpærəle'lepiped] *n.*【幾何】平行六面體。

par·al·lel·ism ['pærəlɛlˌɪzəm; 'pærəlelizm] *n.* ①平行。②相似;類似;對應。③比較。④【哲學】心物平行論; 並行論。⑤【修辭】對句法;對聯。

par·al·lel·o·gram [ˌpærə'lɛləˌgræm; ˌpærə'leləgræm] *n.* 平行四邊形。

pa·ral·o·gism [pə'rælədʒɪzəm; pə'rælədʒizm] *n.*【邏輯】謬誤推理。

pa·ral·y·sis [pə'ræləsɪs; pə'rælisis] *n., pl.* **-ses** [-ˌsiz; -si:z]. ①癱瘓。②(動作、權力等之)終止或破壞等。

par·a·lyt·ic [ˌpærə'lɪtɪk; ˌpærə'litik] *adj.* 麻痺的;無力的。—*n.* 患麻痺者;無力者。

***par·a·lyze, par·a·lyse** ['pærəˌlaɪz; 'pærəlaiz] *v.t.,* **-lyzed, -lyz·ing** or **-lysed, -lys·ing.** ①使麻痺。His left arm was *paralyzed*. 他的左臂癱瘓了。②使無能力; 使不活動。*paralyzed* with fear. 嚇得發呆。—**par·a·ly·za·tion, par·a·ly·sa·tion,** *n.*

par·a·mag·net·ic [ˌpærəmæg'nɛtɪk; ˌpærəmæg'netik] *adj.* 順磁性的;常磁性的。

par·a·mag·net·ism [ˌpærə'mægnətɪzm; ˌpærə'mægnetizm] *n.*【物理】順磁性;常磁性。

par·a·mat·ta [ˌpærə'mætə; ˌpærə'mætə] *n.* 絲與毛或棉與毛交織之一種輕布。

par·a·me·ci·um [ˌpærə'miʃɪəm; ˌpærə'mi:siəm] *n., pl.* **-ci·a** [-ʃɪə; -siə].【動物】草履蟲(原生動物之一種)。

pa·ram·e·ter [pə'ræmətɚ; pə'ræmitə] *n.* ①【數學】通徑;補徑;參數; 變數。②【結晶】半晶軸。

par·a·mount ['pærəˌmaunt; 'pærəmaunt] *adj.* 最重要的; 最高的; 至上的。This duty is *paramount* to all others. 這責任高於其他一切責任。—*n.* 最高統治者;首長。lord *paramount*. 國王;君主。—**ly,** *adv.*

par·a·mount·cy ['pærəˌmauntsɪ; 'pærəˌmauntsi] *n.* 最高; 至要;至上;最上;優越;卓越。

par·a·mour ['pærəˌmur; 'pærəmuə] *n.* ①姦夫;淫婦。②情夫;情婦(＝lover)。

par·a·noe·a [ˌpærə'niə; ˌpærə'ni:ə] *n.* ＝**paranoia.**

par·a·noi·a [ˌpærə'nɔɪə; ˌpærə'nɔiə] *n.*【精神科】偏執狂;妄想狂。

par·a·noi·ac [ˌpærə'nɔɪæk; ˌpærə'nɔiæk] *adj.* 偏執狂的; 患偏執狂的。—*n.* 患偏執狂者。

par·a·noid ['pærəˌnɔɪd; 'pærənɔid] *adj.* 類似偏執狂的。—*n.* 類似偏執狂患者。

par·a·pet ['pærəpɪt; 'pærəpit] *n.* ①【築城】胸牆;胸壁。②(平臺、屋頂、橋樑等邊緣之) 矮垣;欄杆。

par·a·pet·ed ['pærəpɪtɪd; 'pærəpitid] *adj.* ①有胸牆的;有胸壁的。②邊緣有短垣或欄杆的。

par·aph ['pærəf; 'pærəf] *n.* (用防假冒的) 花押; 簽名後之花筆。

par·a·pher·nal·ia [ˌpærəfə'nelɪə; ˌpærəfə'neiliə] *n. pl.* ①隨身用品;行頭;行裝。②【法律】妻的服飾(主要爲衣物、珠寶等)。③裝備。④私人財產。⑤附屬物。

***par·a·phrase** ['pærəˌfrez; 'pærəfreiz] *v.,* **-phrased, -phras·ing,** *n.* —*v.t.* & *v.i.* 意譯;解述意義。—*n.* 意譯;解義。

par·a·phras·tic [ˌpærə'fræstɪk; ˌpærə'fræstik] *adj.* 意譯的; 釋義的。

par·a·ple·gi·a [ˌpærə'plidʒɪə; ˌpærə'pli:dʒiə] *n.*【醫】半身麻痺;半身不遂;截癱。

par·a·ple·gic [ˌpærə'plɛdʒɪk; ˌpærə'pli:dʒik] *adj.* (患)半身麻痺的;(患)截癱的。—*n.* 半身麻痺者;患截癱者。

par·a·pro·fes·sion·al [ˌpærəprə'fɛʃənḷ; ˌpærəprə'feʃənəl] *n.* 受過訓練的職業助手 (尤指教師的助手)。

par·a·psy·chol·o·gy [ˌpærəsaɪ'kɑlədʒɪ; ˌpærəsai'kɔlədʒi] *n.* 靈學 (以傳心術、千里眼等超自然現象爲研究對象)。

par·a·sang ['pærəˌsæŋ; 'pærəsæŋ] *n.* 古波斯之距離單位 (約等於 5km)。

par·a·se·le·ne [ˌpærəsɪ'lini; ˌpærəsi-

ˈliːniː] *n., pl.* **-nae** [-ni;-niː]. 〖氣象〗幻月(現於月暈上之光輪)。

par·a·site [ˈpærəˌsaɪt; ˈpærəsait] *n.* ①寄生蟲或寄生植物。②依人爲生者。Beggars are *parasites.* 乞丐是依人爲生的人。

par·a·sit·ic [ˌpærəˈsɪtɪk; ˌpærəˈsitik] *adj.* ①寄生的; 依人爲生的。②由寄生物引起的(疾病)。

par·a·sit·i·cal [ˌpærəˈsɪtɪkl̩; ˌpærəˈsitikəl] *adj.* = **parasitic.**

par·a·sit·i·cide [ˌpærəˈsɪtɪˌsaɪd; ˌpærəˈsitisaid] *adj.* 消滅寄生蟲的。—*n.* 寄生蟲驅除劑。

par·a·sit·ism [ˈpærəsaɪtˌɪzəm; ˈpærəsaitizəm] *n.* ①寄食; 寄生狀態; 依附; 阿諛; 奉承。②〖生物〗寄生。③〖醫〗(寄生蟲引起的)皮膚病。

par·a·si·tol·o·gy [ˌpærəsaɪˈtɑlədʒɪ; ˈpærəsaiˈtɔlədʒi] *n.* 寄生物學; 寄生蟲學。

***par·a·sol** [ˈpærəˌsɔl; ˌpærəˈsɔl, ˈpærəsɔl] *n.* 陽傘。

par·a·syn·the·sis [ˌpærəˈsɪnθəsɪs; ˌpærəˈsinθisis] *n.* 〖文法〗同時用衍生及複合兩法之字的構成; 雙重造字(如: at-homish, black-eyed)。

par·a·tac·tic [ˌpærəˈtæktɪk; ˌpærəˈtæktik] *adj.* 〖文法〗並列(不用連接詞)的。

par·a·tax·is [ˌpærəˈtæksɪs; ˌpærəˈtæksis] *n.* 〖文法〗並列(不用連接詞而將句、子句、或片語並列, 例如 I came, I saw, I conquered)。

par·a·thy·roid [ˌpærəˈθaɪrɔɪd; ˌpærəˈθairɔid] *adj.* 〖解剖〗①副甲狀腺的; 甲狀旁腺的。②近甲狀腺的。—*n.* 〖解剖〗副甲狀腺; 甲狀旁腺。

parathyroid glands 副甲狀腺; 甲狀旁腺。

par·a·troop [ˈpærəˌtrup; ˈpærətruːp] *adj.* 傘兵的; 空降部隊的。

par·a·troop·er [ˈpærəˌtrupɚ; ˈpærətruːpə] *n.* 傘兵。

par·a·troops [ˈpærəˌtrups; ˈpærətruːps] *n. pl.* 傘兵部隊; 空降部隊。

par·a·ty·phoid [ˌpærəˈtaɪfɔɪd; ˌpærəˈtaifɔid] *adj.* 〖醫〗副腸熱病的; (引起)副傷寒的。—*n.* 副傷寒; 副腸熱病。

paratyphoid fever 副傷寒; 副腸熱病。

par·a·vane [ˈpærəˌven; ˈpærəvein] *n.* ①破雷衞(以鋼索裝於船首兩側沉於水中之鳶形體, 可切斷水雷之繫索)。②一種深水炸彈(裝置似破雷衞, 安置有炸藥, 用以炸毀海底潛艇)。

par a·vi·on [paraˈvjɔ̃; paraˈvjɔ̃] 〖法〗航空郵遞。

par·boil [ˈparˌbɔɪl; ˈpɑːbɔil] *v.t.* ①煮成半熟。②使過熱。—*v.i.* 受過高熱度。

par·buck·le [ˈparˌbʌkl̩; ˈpɑːbʌkl] *n., v.,* **-led, -ling.** —*n.* (拉上或放下大桶等用的)套拉繩; 上下索。 —*v.t.* 以套拉繩拉上或放下〖up, down〗。

par·cel** [ˈparsl̩; ˈpɑːsl] *n., v.,* **-cel(l)ed, -cel·(l)ing,** *adj., adv.* —*n.* ①包裹。②一片; 一塊。 a *parcel* of land. 一片土地。③一羣。④部分。Nature in all her *parcels* fell apart. 自然界整個的瓦解了。part and parcel*** 主要部分。—*v.t.* ①分成數分; 分配〖常 out〗。②〖航海〗以帆布條包裹(纜纜等)。③包裝成包裹。—*adj. & adv.* 部分的(地)。

parcel blind 半盲的。

par·cel·(l)ing [ˈparsəlɪŋ; ˈpɑːsəliŋ] *n.* ①包; 裹。②分配; 區分。③〖航海〗以帆布條包裹; 包裹用之帆布條。

parcel post ①郵政包裹業務。②包裹郵件。③郵寄包裹。

par·ce·nar·y [ˈparsn̩ˌɛrɪ; ˈpɑːsinəri] *n.* 〖法律〗共同繼承。

par·ce·ner [ˈparsn̩ɚ; ˈpɑːsinə] *n.* 〖法律〗共同繼承人。

***parch** [partʃ; pɑːtʃ] *v.t.* ①炒; 烘。*parched* peas. 炒豆。②使(某人)唇舌枯焦; 使極渴。to be *parched* with thirst. 極渴。③使乾透; 使焦乾。—*v.i.* 極爲乾燥; 焦乾。He *parched* with thirst. 他渴死了。—*n.* 烤烘。

parched [partʃt; pɑːtʃt] *adj.* ①枯乾的; 乾透的。*parched* soil. 乾透了的土地。②燒焦的; 焦乾的; 燋的。*parched* peas. 炒豆。

parch·ing [ˈpartʃɪŋ; ˈpɑːtʃiŋ] *adj.* 焦乾的; 灼熱的。 *parching* heat. 炎暑。

parch·ment [ˈpartʃmənt; ˈpɑːtʃmənt] *n.* ①羊皮紙。②寫於羊皮紙上之文件。③假羊皮紙(用以製燈罩等物)。④一種似羊皮紙之上等紙。

pard[1] [pard; pɑːd] *n.* 〖古, 詩〗= **leopard.**

pard[2] *n.* 〖美俚〗夥伴 (= partner)。

***par·don** [ˈpardn̩; ˈpɑːdn] *n.* ①赦宥; 寬恕。 to ask for *pardon.* 請求寬恕。②原諒。 I beg your *pardon.* 請原諒我; 請再說一遍。③赦免; 免罪。 general *pardon.* 大赦。④赦免特狀。—*v.t.* ①寬恕。②原諒。*Pardon* me, madam. 對不起, 夫人。*Pardon* me for interrupting you. 對不起來打攪你。③赦免(罪犯)。The governor *pardoned* the criminal. 州長赦免了那個罪犯。

par·don·a·ble [ˈpardn̩əbl̩; ˈpɑːdnəbl] *adj.* 可寬恕的; 可原諒的; 可赦免的。

par·don·er [ˈpardn̩ɚ; ˈpɑːdnə] *n.* ①寬恕者; 赦罪者。②〖宗教〗賣赦罪符者。

pare** [pɛr, pær; pɛə] *v.t.,* **pared, par·ing.** ①剝; 削。②削去; 剝去(外皮)。③逐漸減少; 削減。pare off*** (***down,*** or ***away***) 削去(角、邊等); 減少(開支等)。 to *pare down* expenses. 節省開支。

par·e·gor·ic [ˌpærəˈgɔrɪk; ˌpærəˈgɔrik] *adj.* 止痛的; 緩和的。—*n.* 止痛藥; 緩和劑; (尤指)複方樟腦浸酒(用以治療咳嗽、腹瀉等)。

pa·rei·ra [pəˈrɛrə; pəˈrɛərə] *n.* 南美產防已科植物之根(用作利尿劑)。(亦作 **pareira brava**)

paren. parenthesis.

pa·ren·chy·ma [pəˈrɛŋkɪmə; pəˈreŋkimə] *n.* ①〖解剖〗(器官之)實質體素; 主質。②〖植物〗柔軟細胞體素; 柔膜組織。

‡**par·ent** [ˈpɛrənt, ˈpærənt, ˈperənt; ˈpɛərənt] *n.* ①父; 母。 He was born of rich *parents.* 他出身富家。②(動植物的)父或母; 母體; 親。③根源; 根本。 Intemperance is the *parent* of many evils. 縱飲爲萬惡之根源。

par·ent·age [ˈpɛrəntɪdʒ; ˈpɛərəntidʒ] *n.* ①出身; 家系。He comes of good *parentage.* 他出身清白。②父或母的地位或狀態。

pa·ren·tal [pəˈrɛntl̩; pəˈrentl] *adj.* 父親的; 母親的; 雙親的; 父母的; 似父母的; 爲父母的。*parental* love. 父母之愛。—**ly,** *adv.*

parental home 問題兒童感化院。(亦作 **parental school**)

parent company (有幾個附屬公司的)母公司。

par·en·ter·al [pəˈrɛntərəl; pəˈrentərəl] *adj.* 腸胃外的。

pa·ren·the·ses [pəˈrɛnθəˌsiz; pəˈrenθisiːz] *n.* pl. of **parenthesis.**

***pa·ren·the·sis** [pəˈrɛnθəsɪs; pəˈrenθisis] *n., pl.* **-ses.** ①挿句; 挿入句間的字或片語。②括弧( )。Some words are enclosed in *parentheses.* 有些字是放在括弧裏。

P

pa·ren·the·size 〔pə'rɛnθə͵saɪz; pə'renθisaiz〕 *v.t.*, **-sized, -siz·ing.** ①插入(字、片語等)作爲插句。②置…於括弧內。③置插句於…中。

par·en·thet·i·cal 〔͵pærən'θɛtɪkḷ; ͵pærən'θetikəl〕 *adj.* ①插句的;似插句的;有插句之性質的;插曲的。②弧形的;弓形的。③標以括號的;置於括號內的。④附加說明的。⑤使用或含有許多括號的。

par·ent·hood 〔'pɛrənt͵hud; 'pɛərənthud〕 *n.* 父母之身分、地位或權力。

pa·ren·ti·cide 〔pə'rɛntə͵saɪd; pə'rentisaid〕 *n.* ①弑父母;弑親。②弑親者。

par·ent-teach·er association 〔'pɛrənt'titʃə~; 'pɛərənt'ti:tʃə~〕〖教育〗教師家長會(相當於中國之家長會或母姊會,略作 P.T.A.)。

pa·re·sis 〔pə'risɪs, 'pærəsɪs; 'pærisis, pə'ri:-〕 *n.* 〖醫〗①局部麻痺;不全麻痺;輕癱。②(起於梅毒之)麻痺性痴呆;腦梅毒(=general paresis)。

pa·ret·ic 〔pə'rɛtɪk, pə'ritɪk; pə'retik, -'ri:-〕 *adj.* (患)局部麻痺的;(患)輕癱的;起於輕癱的。—*n.* 患局部麻痺者;患腦梅毒者。

par ex·cel·lence 〔par'ɛksə͵lans; pa:r'eksəlɑ̃:ns〕〖法〗最卓越;超羣;出類拔萃。

par·fait 〔par'fe, 'parfe; pa:'fei, 'pa:fei〕 *n.* 凍糕(冰淇淋加乳酪、蛋類、水果、糖蜜等製成之一種冰凍甜點心)。

par·get 〔'pardʒɪt; 'pa:dʒit〕 *n., v.,* **-get·(t)ed, -get·(t)ing.** —*n.* ①石膏。②灰泥;牆粉。—*v.t.* 塗以灰泥;粉飾。

par·he·lic 〔par'hilɪk; pa:'hi:lik〕 *adj.* 〖氣象〗幻日的。

par·he·li·on 〔par'hilɪən; pa:'hi:ljən〕 *n., pl.* **-li·a** 〔-lɪə; -liə〕.〖氣象〗幻日(現於日暈上之光點)。

pa·ri·ah 〔pə'raɪə; 'pæriə〕 *n.* ①(P-)印度南部低階級之人民。②被社會遺棄者。

Par·i·an 〔'pɛrɪən; 'pɛəriən〕 *adj.* ①Paros 島的。②(似) Paros 島產之白色大理石的。③Paros 陶器的。—*n.* ①Paros 島人。②Paros 陶器(一種白色陶器)。

pa·ri·e·tal 〔pə'raɪətḷ; pə'raiitl〕 *adj.* ①〖解剖〗腔壁的。②〖解剖、動物〗顱頂部的。③〖植物〗子房壁的。④〖美〗居住大學內的;關於大學內之生活的。⑤在壁上的。—*n.* 〖解剖、動物〗顱頂骨。

par·i-mu·tu·el 〔'pærɪ'mjutʃuəl; 'pæri'mju:tjuəl〕 *n.* ①賽馬賭博之派彩(買中贏馬者,除支付一小部分作爲捐稅手續費外,其餘全部照股平分)。②賽馬賭金計算器。

par·ing 〔'pɛrɪŋ; 'pɛəriŋ〕 *n.* ①剝;削;去皮。②削去物;剝去物;剝去之皮。

***Par·is**[1] 〔'pærɪs; 'pæris〕 *n.* 巴黎(法國的首都)。—*adj.* ①巴黎的。the *Paris* scene. 巴黎的景色。②巴黎式的。

***Par·is**[2] *n.* 〖希臘神話〗Troy 王 Priam 之子,因奪斯巴達王 Menelaus 之妻 Helen 而引起 Trojan War.

Paris blue 〖化〗巴黎藍;紺青(一種天藍色顏料)。

Paris doll (婦女服裝店的)人體模型。

Paris green 〖化〗巴黎綠;乙醯亞砷酸銅(有毒的鮮綠色顏料及殺蟲劑)。

par·ish** 〔'pærɪʃ; 'pæriʃ〕 *n.* ①教區。②居於一教區之住民。the *parish* poor. 賴教區救濟而生活之窮人。③〖英〗地方自治區。④〖美〗Louisiana 州之縣。go to the parish*** 接受教區救濟。

parish clerk 教區書記。

pa·rish·ion·er 〔pə'rɪʃənɚ; pə'riʃənə〕 *n.* 一教區中之居民。

parish lantern 〖英方〗月亮。

parish register 教堂中的紀事錄。

***Pa·ri·sian** 〔pə'rɪʒən, pə'rɪzɪən; pə'rizjən〕 *adj.* 巴黎的;似巴黎的;(似)巴黎人的;(似)巴黎文化的。—*n.* 巴黎人或居民。

Paris white 〖化〗巴黎白;炭酸鈣(精製白堊之一種,作爲顏料)。

par·i·syl·lab·ic 〔͵pærɪsɪ'læbɪk; 'pærisi'læbik〕 *adj.* 有同數之音節的。

par·i·ty 〔'pærətɪ; 'pæriti〕 *n.* ①同等;對等;同價;階級相等。to be on a *parity* with. 和…平等。②類似;相同。③〖商〗平價。④(本國貨幣折合外國貨幣之)折合數目。⑤(各種不同幣制、貨品等之)比率;比值。⑥(農人出售農產物的收入與其生活支出之)平衡。

‡**park** 〔park; pa:k〕 *n.* ①公園。a national *park*. 國立公園。②獵苑。③邸園。④停車處。⑤〖軍〗軍需品營地或停車場。a *park* of artillery. 砲兵營地。⑥〖美〗山區中廣闊的谷地;森林中的空地。—*v.t.* ①停車於。You may *park* your car here.你可把車停在此處。②〖俗〗置於;放於;藏於。He *parked* himself in an easy chair. 他坐在安樂椅中。③將(軍車、砲等)安放於營地。④將…圍起。⑤留置。—*v.i.* ①停車。②〖俗〗停車調情。

par·ka 〔'parkə; 'pa:kə〕 *n.* ①(愛斯基摩人的)皮製外衣。②〖美〗附頭巾之長羊毛衫。

park·ing 〔'parkɪŋ; 'pa:kiŋ〕 *n.* ①(公園、公路中或公路側之)草坪。②(汽車等之)停車。No *parking*. 不准停車! ③停車場所。

parking lot 停車場。

parking meter (停車處所的)停車「計費器。」

parking ramp 停機坪。

parking ticket 給與違反停車規則者的警局報到通知單。

park·way 〔'park͵we; 'pa:k-wei〕 *n.* 有茵草及樹木點綴之大道。

park·y 〔'parkɪ; 'pa:ki〕 *adj.*, **park·i·er, park·i·est.** 〖英俚〗寒冷的。

Parl. ①Parliament. ②Parliamentary.

par·lance 〔'parləns; 'pa:ləns〕 *n.* ①說法;語調;語法;用語;筆調。in legal *parlance*. 用法律上的術語來說。②談話;會談;談判;(尤指)辯論。

par·lay 〔'parlɪ; 'pa:li〕〖美〗*v.t.* & *v.i.* ①將(原本及賭贏的財物)再作另一次的賭注。②成功地利用。③使變爲更有價值之物;成功地將小企業擴展。—*n.* ①將原本及賭贏的財物合在一起下注的賭法。②上述的賭注。

par·ley 〔'parlɪ; 'pa:li〕 *n., pl.* **-leys,** *v.,* **-leyed, -ley·ing.** —*n.* ①談判;商議;非正式商談。②與敵人就停戰、換俘等所作之非正式談判。***beat*** (or ***sound***) ***a parley*** (打鼓或吹號)向敵人表示願開談判。—*v.i.* ①與敵人作非正式談判。②商談;討論。

par·ley·voo 〔͵parlɪ'vu; ͵pa:li'vu:〕 *n.* 〖諧〗法國語;法國人。—*v.i.* 說法語。

***par·lia·ment** 〔'parləmənt; 'pa:ləmənt, -lim-〕 *n.* ①國會;議院。②(P-)英國國會。③(P-)英國自治領、殖民地等之議會。

par·lia·men·tal 〔͵parlə'mɛntḷ; ͵pa:lə'mentəl〕 *adj.* 國會的;議院的(=parliamentary).

par·lia·men·tar·i·an 〔͵parləmɛn'tɛrɪən, -'ter-; ͵pa:ləmen'tɛəriən, -lim-, -mən-〕 *n.* ①精於議會中議事程序與辯論者。②(P-)〖英史〗支持議會反對查理一世者。③國會議員。—*adj.* 議會的;國會的。

par·lia·men·tar·i·an·ism [ˌparləmɛnˈtɛrɪəˌnɪzm̩; ˌpɑːləmenˈtɛəriənizəm] *n.* 代議制政體;議會制政府。

*__par·lia·men·ta·ry__ [ˌparləˈmɛntərɪ; ˌpɑːləˈmentəri] *adj.* ①國會的;議院的。②議院制定的。③遵照議院法的。*parliamentary* procedure. 遵照議院法的程序。④有國會或議院的。⑤國會或議院特有的。*parliamentary* language. 議會特有的措辭。⑥專門負責有關國會事務的。⑦(P-)〖英史〗支持國會反對查理一世的。—*n.* 英國國會議員。

parliamentary agent ①受託在議會中爲某黨派效力的議員。②政黨顧問律師。

parliamentary government 議會政治;議會政體。(亦作 **parliamentary system**)

parliament house 議會大厦;國會大厦。

parliament man (尤指英國)國會議員。

*__par·lo(u)r__ [ˈparlɚ; ˈpɑːlə] *n.* ①客廳;會客室。The *parlors* of the hotels were lavishly furnished. 旅館客廳布置得很豪華。②〖美〗(室內有特殊裝飾的)店鋪。a hairdresser's *parlor*. 美容院。③旅舍中的私室。—*adj.* ①適於會客室的。*parlor* furniture. 適於客廳的傢具。②缺少實際行動的。

parlor boarder ①校長家中之寄宿生;特別寄宿生。②〖俚〗受特別優待的人。

parlor car (火車之)客廳車。

parlor game 室內遊戲。

par·lo(u)r·maid [ˈparlɚˌmed; ˈpɑːləmeid] *n.* 照應客廳、侍候客人之使女。

par·lous [ˈparləs; ˈpɑːləs] *adj.* ①危險的。②可怕的;極大的。③精明的;慧黠的。—*adv.* 非常;極。

Par·me·san [ˌparməˈzæn; ˌpɑːmiˈzæn] *adj.* (來自)義大利巴馬(Parma)城的。—*n.* (亦作 **Parmesan cheese**)巴馬乾酪。

Par·nas·si·an [parˈnæsɪən; pɑːˈnæsiən] *adj.* ①Parnassus 山的。②詩神 Muses 的;詩歌的。③高蹈派(19世紀後半期之法國詩派, 以技巧爲主, 中有 Mendès, Gautier, Beaudelaire 諸人)的。—*n.* 法國高蹈派詩人。

Par·nas·sus [parˈnæsəs; pɑːˈnæsəs] *n.* ①希臘南部山名, 爲古希臘祭 Apollo 及 Muses 之靈地。②希臘傳說中的詩人之山。③詩歌或詩人之集合稱。④文學界;詩壇;學術中心。***try to climb Parnassus*** 學作詩。

pa·ro·chi·al [pəˈrokɪəl; pəˈroukjəl] *adj.* ①教區的;鄉鎮的;地方性的。②狹小的。

pa·ro·chi·al·ism [pəˈrokɪəˌlɪzm̩; pəˈroukjəlizəm] *n.* ①教區制度。②地方觀念;鄉愿;氣量褊狹。

par·o·dy [ˈpærədɪ; ˈpærədi] *n., pl.* **-dies,** *v.,* **-died, -dy·ing.** —*n.* ①(模仿他人之詩文而改作的)遊戲詩文;諷刺詩文。②拙劣的模仿。—*v.t.* ①歪改(他人之詩文);模仿藉以嘲弄。②拙劣地模仿。—**par·o·dist,** *n.*

pa·role [pəˈrol; pəˈroul] *n., v.,* **-roled, -rol·ing.** —*n.* ①假釋。②准許在獄中之有條件的自由。③諾言;誓言(尤指戰俘所作之宣誓)。④口令(=password). —*v.t.* 使(俘虜)宣誓後釋放;假釋。

pa·rol·ee [pəˌroˈli; pəˌrouˈliː] *n.* 〖美〗獲假釋者。

par·o·no·ma·sia [ˌpærənoˈmeʒə; ˌpærənouˈmeiʒə] *n.* 〖修辭〗雙關語。

par·o·nym [ˈpærənɪm; ˈpærənim] *n.* 〖文法〗①同源語(含有相同之字根者, 如 wise, wisdom). ②發音相同之字(如: pair, pare).

par·o·quet [ˈpærəˌkɛt; ˈpærəket] *n.* 長尾鸚鵡。(亦作 **parakeet**)

Par·os [ˈpɛras; ˈpɛərɔs] *n.* 派洛斯島(在希臘東南部,白色大理石之名產地)。

pa·rot·id [pəˈratɪd; pəˈrɔtid] *n.* 〖解剖〗耳下腺;腮腺。—*adj.* 耳邊的;耳下的;耳下腺的。

par·o·ti·tis [ˌpærəˈtaɪtɪs; ˌpærəˈtaitis] *n.* 〖醫〗耳下腺炎;腮腺炎。

par·ox·ysm [ˈpærəksˌɪzəm; ˈpærəksizəm] *n.* ①疾病發作。②(感情)突然激發。

par·ox·ys·mal [ˌpærəkˈsɪzml̩; ˌpærəkˈsizməl] *adj.* 陣發的;突發的。

par·ox·y·tone [pæˈraksəˌton; pæˈrɔksitoun] *adj., n.* 〖希臘文法〗倒數第二音節有重音的(字)。

par·quet [parˈke; ˈpɑːkei] *n., v.,* **-quet·(t)ed, -quet·(t)ing.** —*n.* ①拼花地板。②劇院之優等正廳;正廳之前排。—*v.t.* ①細工鑲嵌。②鋪以鑲花地板。

parquet circle (劇院的)正廳後排;後廳;正廳之圍座。

par·quet·ry [ˈparkɪtrɪ; ˈpɑːkitri] *n.* 鑲木細工。

par·ri·cid·al [ˌpærəˈsaɪdl; ˌpæriˈsaidl] *adj.* (犯)弒父母(罪)的;(犯)殺尊長(罪)的。

par·ri·cide [ˈpærəˌsaɪd; ˈpærisaid] *n.* ①弒父母;殺長上。②弒親罪;殺父母罪;忤逆罪。③殺父母者;弒尊長者。

*__par·rot__ [ˈpærət; ˈpærət] *n.* ①鸚鵡。②重覆別人之話或模仿他人行動。—*v.t.* ①像鸚鵡般重覆或模仿。②教(別人)重覆或模仿。—*v.i.* 重覆或模仿而不解其意義;死背。

par·rot·ry [ˈpærətrɪ; ˈpærətri] *n.* 卑屈的模仿或重覆。

par·ry [ˈpærɪ; ˈpæri] *v.,* **-ried, -ry·ing,** *n., pl.* **-ries.** —*v.t.* ①(格鬥時)擋開;躲開(武器、襲擊等)。②避開;回避。—*v.i.* 避開;擋開;避不作答。—*n.* ①擋開;閃避。②遁辭。

parse [pars; pɑːz] *v.,* **parsed, pars·ing.** —*v.t.* ①對(句子等)作文法上的分析。②分析;剖析。—*v.i.* ①作文法分析。②(句子等)可照文法分析。

par·sec [ˈparˌsɛk; ˈpɑːsek] *n.* 〖天文〗視差距(測天體距離之單位,相當於 3.259 光年)。

Par·see, Par·si [ˈparsi, parˈsi; pɑːˈsiː, ˈpɑːˈsiː] *n.* 印度之拜火教徒;祆教徒(七、八世紀間,由波斯人傳入)。

Par·see·ism [ˈparsiɪzəm; pɑːˈsiːizəm] *n.* 祆教;拜火教。

par·si·mo·ni·ous [ˌparsəˈmonɪəs; ˌpɑːsiˈmounjəs] *adj.* 吝嗇的;小氣的;極度儉省的。—**ness,** *n.* —**ly,** *adv.*

par·si·mo·ny [ˈparsəˌmonɪ; ˈpɑːsiməni] *n.* 吝嗇;小氣;極度節省。

*__pars·ley__ [ˈparslɪ; ˈpɑːsli] *n., pl.* **-leys,** *adj.* —*n.* 〖植物〗芫荽;香菜。—*adj.* ①芫荽的;香菜的。②以芫荽調味的;配以香菜的。

pars·nip [ˈparsnəp; ˈpɑːsnip] *n.* 〖植物〗①防風草(其根可做蔬菜食用)。②防風草根。

*__par·son__ [ˈparsn̩; ˈpɑːsn] *n.* ①教區牧師。②牧師。

par·son·age [ˈparsn̩ɪdʒ; ˈpɑːsnidʒ] *n.* 牧師或教區長之住宅;牧師公館。

par·son·ic [parˈsanɪk; pɑːˈsɔnik] *adj.* 牧師的;教區長的。

‡**part** [part; pɑːt] *n.* ①部分;片段。Only *part* of his story is true. 他的故事(經歷)祇有一部分是眞實的。②(構成整體之)一分。A dime is a tenth *part* of a dollar. 一角是一元的十分之一。③本分;職分。Everyone must do his *part*. 每個人須盡他的本分。④(辯論、競爭或爭吵中之)一面。He always

takes his brother's *part*. 他總是站在他哥哥那一面。⑤劇中人物；脚色；一脚色的臺詞。Mr. A played a very important *part* in the negotiations. 那些談判中，A 先生擔任很重要的脚色。⑥(梳頭髮後之)分界線。⑦(*pl.*)才能。a man of *parts*. 有才能之人。⑧音部；樂曲之一部。⑨區域；地方。I am a stranger in these *parts*. 我在這一帶是個陌生人。**for my part** 就我而論。**for the most part** 一般的；大抵。**in good part** 以友善或欣然的態度。**in ill part** 不愉快。**in part** 一部分；有幾分。**on the part of** a. 在某方面。b. 代表某方。**part and parcel** 主要的部分。**play a part in** 與…有關。**take part in** 參加。**take someone's part** 站在某人一方；爲某人辯護；偏袒某人。—*v.t.* ①分開；使分裂。to *part* gold from silver. 分開金與銀。②迫使分開；排開。The policeman *parted* the crowd. 警察排開衆人。③離開。④將(頭髮)分梳。⑤分成數分；分配。—*v.i.* ①分開。②分離；離別。We'll *part* no more. 我們再也不分離了。**part company** a. 拆夥；散夥；斷絕關係。b. 分離；各自東西。c. 意見不合。**part from** 離開。**part with** 放棄；讓渡；割愛。—*adj.* 部分的。*part*-time. 非整天的。—*adv.* 一部分地；有幾分地。He was at least *part* right. 他至少有幾分道理。

part. ①participle. ②particular. ③participating. ④partner.

***par·take** [pɚ'tek, pɑr-; pɑː'teik] *v.t.* & *v.i.*, **-took, -tak·en, -tak·ing.** ①分擔；分享；參與。They *partook* our triumph. 他們與我們共享勝利。②有幾分。feelings *partaking* of both joy and regret. 又喜又悔之感情。

par·tak·er [pɑr'tekɚ; pɑː'teikə] *n.* 參與者；分享者。

part·ed ['pɑrtɪd; 'pɑːtid] *adj.* ①分成各部分的。②分開的(如頭髮)。③分離的。

par·terre [pɑr'tɛr; pɑː'tɛə] *n.* ①(庭院之)花壇。②(美國)劇場的池子；劇院樓下正廳之後排。

par·the·no·gen·e·sis [ˌpɑrθəno'dʒɛnəsɪs; 'pɑːθinou'dʒenisis] *n.* 〖生物〗單性生殖。

par·the·no·ge·net·ic [ˌpɑrθənodʒɪ'nɛtɪk; 'pɑːθinoudʒi'netik] *adj.* 單性生殖的。

Par·the·non ['pɑrθəˌnɑn; 'pɑːθinən] 巴特農神殿(爲希臘雅典女神 Athena 之神殿，約在紀元前 438 年築成)。

Par·thi·a ['pɑrθɪə; 'pɑːθiə] *n.* 伊朗東北部之古國(位於裏海之東南)。

Par·thi·an ['pɑrθɪən; 'pɑːθjən] *n.* Parthia 人。—*adj.* (關於) Parthia 的。

Parthian glance 臨別的一瞥。

Parthian shot (or **shaft**) 臨退所發之一矢；回馬槍；臨別所作之刻薄言語(因古 Parthia 騎兵臨退之時總向敵射箭，故稱)。

par·ti [pɑr'ti; pɑː'tiː] 〖法〗*n.* 參與者；人；(尤指)(結婚的)理想對象；佳偶。

***par·tial** ['pɑrʃəl; 'pɑːʃəl] *adj.* ①一部分的。②偏向一方的；偏袒的。A parent should not be *partial* to any of his children. 做父母的不應偏袒任何一個孩子。③偏愛的；喜愛的。to be *partial* to sports. 喜愛運動。④偏的。

par·ti·al·i·ty [pɑr'ʃælətɪ; ˌpɑːʃi'æliti] *n., pl.* **-ties.** ①偏袒；偏見。②偏愛。

***par·tial·ly** ['pɑrʃəlɪ; 'pɑːʃəli] *adv.* ①部分地。a determined but only *partially* successful attempt. 堅決但未完全成功的嘗試。②偏袒地；偏愛地。

par·tic·i·pant [pɚ'tɪsəpənt; pɑː'tisipənt] *n.* 參與者；共享者。—*adj.* 參與的；共享的。

***par·tic·i·pate** [pɚ'tɪsəˌpet, pɑr-; pɑː'tisipeit] *v.*, **-pat·ed, -pat·ing.** —*v.i.* 分享；參與。The teacher *participated* in the students' games. 老師參加學生們的遊戲。—*v.t.* 分享；參與。

***par·tic·i·pa·tion** [pɑrˌtɪsə'peʃən, pɚ-; pɑːˌtisi'peiʃən] *n.* 參與；共享。full *participation* in the benefit. 充分共享利益。

par·tic·i·pa·tor [pɑr'tɪsəˌpetɚ; pɑː'tisipeitə] *n.* 分享者；參與者；參加者。

par·ti·cip·i·al [ˌpɑrtə'sɪpɪəl; ˌpɑːti'sipiəl] *adj.* 〖文法〗分詞的。—**ly,** *adv.*

participial adjective 〖文法〗分詞形容詞(本爲動詞分詞的形容詞，如："rolling stone" 中的 "rolling"等)。

***par·ti·ci·ple** ['pɑrtəsəpḷ, 'pɑrtsəpḷ, 'pɑrtəˌsɪpḷ; 'pɑːtsipl, -tis-] *n.* 〖文法〗分詞。

par·ti·ci·pled ['pɑrtəsəpḷd; 'pɑːtisipld] *adv.* 〖俚〗眞；極；怪(分詞形容詞中用以加强語氣的 damned, confounded 等之委婉代用語)。

***par·ti·cle** ['pɑrtɪkḷ; 'pɑːtikl] *n.* ①極小量；分子；微粒。He has not a *particle* of sense. 他沒有一點兒腦筋。②〖物理〗質點。③〖文法〗質詞(包括 preposition, conjunction, article, 或 interjection)。④字首或字尾(如 in-, -ness, -ly 等)。

par·ti-col·o(u)red ['pɑrtɪˌkʌlɚd; 'pɑːtiˌkʌləd] *adj.* ①雜色的；斑駁的。②變化多的；各色各樣的。(亦作**party-colo(u)red**)

‡par·tic·u·lar [pɚ'tɪkjəlɚ; pə'tikjulə] *adj.* ①單個的；單獨的。That *particular* chair is already sold. 那一把椅子已經賣掉了。②個別的；各個的；獨有的。one's *particular* interests. 個人特有之興趣。③特殊的；特別的。a *particular* friend. 一特殊的朋友。④難以取悅的；考究的。He is *particular* about his food. 他對食物很講究。⑤詳盡的。⑥要好的；知己的。my very *particular* friend. 我的知己。—*n.* ①個別部分；單獨事項。to go into *particulars*. 詳細列出；詳述。②詳細說明。I sent you the descriptive *particular*. 我已將詳細說明寄給你。**in particular** 特別地。

par·tic·u·lar·ism [pɚ'tɪkjələˌrɪzəm; pə'tikjulərizm] *n.* ①排他主義；自黨主義。②(聯邦之)各邦自主獨立主義。③〖神學〗特殊神寵論(謂神之恩典祇及於神所揀選之人)。

par·tic·u·lar·ist [pɚ'tɪkjələrɪst; pə'tikjulərist] *n.* ①排他主義者；自黨主義者。②各邦獨立主義者。③〖神學〗特殊神寵論者。—*adj.* ①排他主義的；自黨主義的。②各邦獨立主義的。③〖神學〗特殊神寵論的。

par·tic·u·lar·i·ty [pɚˌtɪkjə'lærətɪ; pəˌtikju'læriti] *n., pl.* **-ties.** ①特別；特殊。②單個；各個。③特質；癖。④詳細；仔細。⑤苛求。⑥特點；特徵。

par·tic·u·lar·ize [pɚ'tɪkjələˌraɪz; pə'tikjuləraiz] *v.*, **-ized, -iz·ing.** —*v.t.* ①使成特殊。②列舉；縷述；逐一敍述。—*v.i.* 縷述；詳說；列舉。—**par·tic·u·lar·i·za·tion,** *n.*

‡par·tic·u·lar·ly [pɚ'tɪkjələlɪ, pɑr-; pə'tikjuləli] *adv.* ①特別地；特殊地。I saw him very often, *particularly* at the club. 我時常看到他，特別是在俱樂部裏。②異常地；顯著地。③詳細地。

***part·ing** 〔'pɑrtɪŋ; 'pɑːtiŋ〕 *n.* ①離別;分別。She cried at *parting*. 她在臨別時哭了。②分歧; 分開。③分歧處。the *parting* of the ways. 道路之分歧處。 —*adj.* ①離別的;臨別的。*parting* words. 離別的話。②離去的;消逝的。a *parting* day. 即將逝去的一天。③分開的;分隔的。

***par·ti·san**[1] 〔'pɑrtəzn̩; ˌpɑːti'zæn, 'pɑː-ti'zæn〕 *n.* ①幫夥;同黨者;(基於感情而非基於理智的)某黨派之支持者。②游擊隊。—*adj.* ①幫夥的;黨派的。*partisan* spirit. 黨派心。②游擊隊的。*partisan* warfare. 游擊戰。(亦作 **partizan**)

par·ti·san[2] *n.* ①(十六、十七世紀所用「的)戟。②棍;棒;杖。

par·ti·san·ship 〔'pɑrtəzn̩ˌʃɪp; ˌpɑː-ti'zænʃip〕 *n.* 黨派心;黨派行爲; 偏頗; 盲從附和。

par·ti·ta 〔pɑr'titə; pɑː'tiːtə〕〖義〗*n.*「變奏曲或組曲的一種。

par·tite 〔'pɑrtaɪt; 'pɑːtait〕 *adj.* ①〖植物〗(葉)深裂的。②分裂的;分成部分的(通常用於複合字,如:tri-*partite* 分成三分的)。

par·ti·tion** 〔pɑr'tɪʃən, pɚ-; pɑː'tiʃən, pə't-〕 *n.* ①分割; 瓜分;分配。the *partition* of a man's wealth when he dies. 人死後其財產之瓜分。②分隔;分畫;區分。③分隔物;房屋之隔牆。④〖植物〗隔膜;隔片。⑤分裂或分割而成的部分。 —*v.t.* ①分割; 瓜分; 分配。to *partition* an empire among three brothers. 三兄弟瓜分一個王國。 ②隔開。partition off*** 隔開。

par·ti·tive 〔'pɑrtətɪv; 'pɑːtitiv〕 *n.*〖文法〗表分之詞(如 some of them 的 some)。 —*adj.* ①〖文法〗 表分的; 表全體中之一部分的。 ②區分的; 用以分爲部分的。 *partitive* tendencies in education. 教育之區分傾向。***partitive adjective*** 表分形容詞。***partitive article*** 表分冠詞。***partitive genitive*** 表分所有格。

***part·ly** 〔'pɑrtlɪ; 'pɑːtli〕 *adv.* 部分地;有幾分地。 It was *partly* my fault. 這有一部分是我的過失。

part·ner** 〔'pɑrtnɚ; 'pɑːtnə〕 *n.* ①分享者;分擔者。to be a *partner* in other's joys and sorrows. 與他人共享憂樂。②股東;合作社社員。③妻或夫。④舞伴。⑤(遊戲中之)同邊者;夥伴。⑥共同協力者。silent partner*** 匿名股東;外股。***special partner; limited partner*** 特別合夥人;有限合夥人。—*v.t.* ①做爲(他人)的夥伴。②使(人們)成爲夥伴。—*v.i.* 合夥;合股。We *partnered* once. 我們一度合夥。

***part·ner·ship** 〔'pɑrtnɚˌʃɪp; 'pɑːtnə-ʃip〕 *n.* ①合股;合夥。a business *partnership*. 商業合股。②合股經營的公司商號。③合作;協力。

part of speech 〖文法〗(字之)詞性。

par·took 〔pɚ'tʊk; pɑː'tuk〕 *v.* pt. of **partake.**

part owner 〖法律〗(船舶之)共有人。

***par·tridge** 〔'pɑrtrɪdʒ; 'pɑːtridʒ〕 *n.*, *pl.* **-tridg·es** or **-tridge.** 鷓鴣;松雞。

par·tridge·ber·ry 〔'pɑrtrɪdʒˌberɪ; 'pɑːtridʒberi〕 *n.*, *pl.* **-ries.** 〖植物〗蔓虎刺。

part song 合唱的歌曲(通常爲男低音,男高音,女低音及女高音四部合成)。

part-time 〔'pɑrt'taɪm; 'pɑːt'taim〕 *adj.* 部分時間的;兼任的。*part-time* student. 半工半讀的學生。—*adv.* 部分時間地;兼任地。

part-tim·er〔'pɑrt'taɪmɚ; 'pɑːt'taimə〕 *n.* 非全日工作(出席)者;兼任者。

par·tu·ri·ent 〔pɑr'tjʊrɪənt; pɑː'tjuə-riənt〕 *adj.* ①將生產的;臨盆的。②關於生產的;分娩的。③將產生某一思想、發現等的。

par·tu·ri·tion 〔ˌpɑrtjʊ'rɪʃən; ˌpɑː-tjuə'riʃən〕 *n.* 生產;分娩。

‡par·ty 〔'pɑrtɪ; 'pɑːti〕 *n.*, *pl.* **-ties**, *adj.*, *v.*, **par·tied**, **par·ty·ing.** —*n.* ①團體;一夥。②(社交、遊戲等之)集會;會。a dinner (dancing) *party*. 宴會(舞會)。to give a *party*. 舉行酒會、宴會等。③政黨。the Democratic *Party*. (美國)民主黨。④參與者;關係人。He was a *party* to our plot. 他是參加我們之計謀的一個。⑤(合同、訴訟等中的)一方。the two *parties* to a marriage contract. 婚約的雙方當事人。⑥〖諧〗人。a rich old *party*. 一個富有老人。—*adj.* ①政黨的;朋黨的。*party* issues. 政黨的問題。②參與的;有關係的。③共有的。④宴會的;晚會的。*party* dress. 晚禮服。—*v.t.* 以晚會款待。to be cocktailed, *partied*, and dined. 被款待以鷄尾酒會、晚會和晚宴。 —*v.i.* 參加或舉行晚會。

par·ty-col·o(u)red 〔'pɑrtɪˌkʌlɚd; 'pɑːtiˌkʌləd〕 *adj.* 雜色的;斑駁的;變化多的。

party girl ①妓女。②被僱參加派對陪伴男人的美女。③〖俚〗特別喜歡參加派對的女人。

party government 政黨政治。

par·ty·ism 〔'pɑrtɪɪzm̩; 'pɑːtiizəm〕 *n.* ①黨派心;黨派(根)性。②黨派制。

party line ①電話合用線。②連接宅邸的分界線。③一政黨採取的政策;黨的路線。④共產黨的路線;共黨產的政策。

party liner 忠於黨之政策者(尤指忠於「共黨者)。

party man 政黨黨員;黨員;忠誠黨員。

party politics 黨派政治。

par·ty-spir·it·ed 〔'pɑrtɪ'spɪrɪtɪd; 'pɑːti'spiritid〕 *adj.* 黨派性强的;有黨派性的。

par value (證券等的)票面價值; 票面額。(略作 **p.v.**)

par·ve·nu 〔'pɑrvəˌnju; 'pɑːvənjuː〕 *n.* ①崛起者。②暴發戶;暴富者。 —*adj.* 暴發戶的;如暴發戶的。

par·vis 〔'pɑrvɪs; 'pɑːvis〕 *n.* ①(建築物,尤指教堂的)前庭。②(教堂前面的)柱廊。

pas 〔pɑ; pɑː〕 *n.*, *pl.* **pas** 〔pɑz; pɑːz〕. 〖法〗①先行權; 優先權;上席。to give the *pas* to…. 讓上席給…;使…坐上席;讓先給…。②舞步。③跳舞; 舞蹈。*pas* de deux. (芭蕾舞之)雙人舞。

PAS para-aminosalicylic acid 對胺水「楊酸(肺病特效藥)。

Pas·cal 〔'pæskl̩, pɑs'kal; 'pæskəl, pɑːs'kal〕 *n.* 巴斯噶 (Blaise, 1623–1662, 法國哲學家、數學家及物理學家)。

Pascal's law 〖物理〗巴斯噶定律。

pas·chal 〔'pæskl̩; 'pɑːskəl〕 *adj.* ①踰越節的。②復活節的。

pash 〔pæʃ; pæʃ〕 *n.* 〖英俚〗= **passion.**

pa·sha 〔'pæʃə; 'pɑːʃə〕 *n.* 巴夏(往時土耳其高級文武官員之尊稱,通常加在姓名之後)。(亦作 **pacha**)

pa·sha·lic, pa·sha·lik 〔pə'ʃɑlɪk; pə'ʃɑːlik〕 *n.* pasha 之管轄權(區域)。(亦作 **pachalic**)

pasque·flow·er 〔'pæskˌflauɚ; 'pæskˌflauə〕 *n.* 〖植物〗白頭翁花的一種。

pas·quin·ade 〔ˌpæskwɪ'ned; ˌpæs-kwi'neid〕 *n.*, *v.*, **-ad·ed, -ad·ing.** —*n.* (揭於公共場所之)諷刺詩文。 —*v.t.* 以此種詩文諷刺或攻擊。

‡pass 〔pæs, pɑs; pɑːs〕 *v.*, **passed, passed**

or **past, pass·ing,** *n.* —*v.t.* ①經過。You will *pass* the post office. 你將經過郵局。②穿過；通過。The ship *passed* the channel. 船駛過了海峽。③傳遞。*Pass* (me) the butter, please. 請把牛油遞給我。④圍；纏。⑤於…成功；使及格。He *passed* the entrance examination. 他的入學考試及格。⑥通過；被批准。to *pass* a bill or law. 通過一議案或法令。⑦度過；消磨。Where will he *pass* the summer holidays? 他將在何處度暑假？⑧使動；使進行；使前進。to *pass* troops in review. 閱兵。⑨超過。His strange story *passes* belief. 他那奇怪的故事令人無法相信。⑩評判；宣告。A judge *passes* sentence on guilty persons. 法官判決犯罪的人。⑪使流通；使用(僞幣)。He was arrested for *passing* forged notes. 他因使用僞幣而被捕。⑫約定；保證。to *pass* one's word. 立誓；發誓；許下諾言。⑬使被接受。⑭力衝；衝刺。⑮排泄。to *pass* water. 小便。—*v.i.* ①走過。Please let me *pass.* 請讓我過去。②度過；過去。The week has *passed* very quickly. 這週很快地過去了。③傳遞；傳。The old man died and his estate *passed* to his heirs. 這老人死了，他的財產傳給了繼承人。④結束；消失。The pain soon *passed.* 疼痛很快便止了。⑤死。King Arthur *passed* in peace. 亞瑟王在平靜中死去。⑥通過；及格。He *passed* (in the examination). 他(考試)及格了。⑦變化。Water *passes* from liquid to a soild state when it freezes. 水冷到冰點時由液體變成固體。⑧發生。Tell me all that *passed.* 把所有經過的情形告訴我。⑨被接受爲；被認爲；冒充〖for, as〗. He *passes* for a great scholar. 他被認爲是個大學者。⑩評判；品評。The judges *passed* on each contestant. 裁判對每位競賽者加以品評。⑪被忽略；不予注意地放過。He was rude, but let that *pass.* 他很粗野，不過算了吧。⑫流通；通用。⑬〖美俗〗暈厥；昏倒。⑭〖劍術〗突然出劍。⑮通便；大便。⑯(玩牌時)放棄叫牌機會。***bring to pass*** 引起；促起。***come to pass*** 發生。***pass away*** **a.** 死去；消滅。**b.** 結束；終止。***pass by*** **a.** 經過。**b.** 疏忽；置之不理。I cannot *pass* the matter *by.* 我不能置此事於不問。**c.** 時間消失。***pass current*** 被普遍接受或相信。***pass for*** 被認爲；被當做。***pass in one's checks*** 〖俗〗死去。***pass muster*** 通過檢查；被認合理。***pass off*** **a.** 以贋品充騙；騙賣。**b.** 消滅；減退。**c.** 進行到底。The meeting *passed off* without incident. 會議順利地進行到底。***pass on*** 死去；去世。***pass out*** 〖俚〗**a.** 昏厥；失知覺。**b.** 死去。***pass over*** **a.** 置之不理；忽視。**b.** 死亡。**c.** (對某人之權益等)置之不理。**d.** 〖俗〗(黑人)被當白人看待。***pass the buck*** 推卸責任。***pass the hat*** 募捐。***pass the time of day*** ***(with...)*** (與…)互相寒喧、問候(早安等)。***pass through*** 經驗。***pass up*** 放棄；拋棄；拒絕。—*n.* ①走過；經過。②考試及格。to get a *pass.* 及格。③免費票；招待券。He has a season *pass* to the ball park. 他有一張棒球賽免費月季票。④執照；通行證。No one can get in the fort without a *pass.* 沒有通行證，任何人均不能進入要塞。⑤情況；境遇。⑥(魔術家或催眠者等)手之動作。⑦狹路；隘口。⑧傳球。He threw a long *pass* into the corner. 他投了一個遠球到那角落。⑨〖劍術〗突然出劍。⑩嘗試；努力。⑪秋波；媚眼。⑫鬥牛士揮動紅布的動作 (=pase). ⑬〖棒球〗保送上壘 (=base on balls). ***hold the pass*** 支持或捍衛到底。***sell the pass*** 放棄基本的安全保障。〖注意〗pass 的過去式或過去分詞多用 passed.

pass. ①passenger. ②passage. ③passive. ④sim.

pass·a·ble [ˈpæsəbl̩; ˈpɑːsəbl] *adj.* ①還好的；尙可的；可及格的。②可通行的。③可通用的；通用的；可通過的。

pass·a·bly [ˈpæsəblɪ; ˈpɑːsəbli] *adv.* 尙可地；也還過得去地。

‡**pas·sage** [ˈpæsɪdʒ; ˈpæsidʒ] *n., v.,* **-saged, -sag·ing.** —*n.* ①通道；走廊。②通行之方法或工具。to take *passage* in a ship. 乘船航行。③通過的權利或自由。The guard refused us *passage.* 守衛不許我們通過。④經過；變遷。a bird of *passage.* 候鳥(隨季節移棲之鳥)；(轉爲)喜流徙之人。⑤(文章或講演等)一節；一段。a *passage* from the Bible. 聖經中的一節。⑥橫過；航行。a stormy *passage.* 有風浪之航行。⑦(議會等)核准；通過。the *passage* of a bill. 法案的通過。⑧(人與人的)招呼；交往。⑨互毆；交戰。a *passage* of arms. 互毆；比武；爭論。⑩〖音樂〗樂節。—*v.i.* ①(馬)斜行；(人)騎馬斜行。②航行。

passage boat 定期客輪。

pas·sage·way [ˈpæsɪdʒˌwe; ˈpæsidʒwei] *n.* ①(人或物經過之)通路；出入口；航路；水路。②走廊。

pas·sant [ˈpæsənt; ˈpæsənt] *adj.* 〖紋章〗(動物)舉右前足向右方前行之步態的。

pass·book [ˈpæsˌbuk; ˈpɑːsbuk] *n.* ①存款簿；(銀行)存摺。②顧客賒購貨物之摺子。③南非共和國有色人種之身分證。

pas·sé [pæˈse; pæˈsei] *adj.* ①已過盛年的；凋殘的；褪色的。②陳舊的；過時的。

passed [pæst; pɑːst] *adj.* ①已經過的；已被傳遞的。②考試已經及格的。③考試及格候缺遞補的。④(紅利)未及時發放的。

passed ball 〖棒球〗捕手漏接。

passe·men·terie [pæsˈmɛntrɪ; pɑːsˈmentəri] *n.* (衣服之)金(銀)飾帶；飾珠。

‡**pas·sen·ger** [ˈpæsn̩dʒɚ; ˈpæsindʒə] *n.* ①旅客；乘客。I was the only *passenger* on the bus. 我是這公共汽車上的唯一乘客。②〖俗〗不生產分子。

passenger list 旅客名單。

passenger pigeon (北美產之)候鴿(善於長距離飛行，今已絕跡)。

passe par·tout [ˌpæspɚˈtu; ˈpæspɑːtuː] ①(原指)護照；通行證。②一種畫框。③能開諸鎖之鑰；總鑰。

pass·er [ˈpæsɚ; ˈpɑːsə] *n.* ①過路人。②考試合格者。③(製品之)合格檢查員。④手錐。⑤傳球者。

pass·er-by [ˈpæsɚˈbaɪ; ˈpɑːsəˈbai] *n., pl.* **pass·ers-by.** 過路客；行人。

pas·ser·ine [ˈpæsərɪn, -ˌraɪn; ˈpæsərain] *adj.* 燕雀類的。—*n.* 燕雀類之鳥。

pas·si·ble [ˈpæsəbl̩; ˈpæsibl] *adj.* 易感動的；感受性强的。

pas·sim [ˈpæsɪm; ˈpæsim] 〖拉〗 *adv.* 各處；到處(用於書籍中以指引喩、成語等)。

pass·ing [ˈpæsɪŋ, ˈpɑs-; ˈpɑːsiŋ] *adj.* ①經過的；路過的。②迅速的；短暫的。③目前的。④及格的。60 will be a *passing* mark. 60是及格的分數。⑤非常的。⑥偶然的。—*adv.* 〖古〗甚；極。—*n.* ①經過。②通過。③議案之通過。④考試及格。⑤消滅。⑥死亡。***in***

passing 順便(提起)。

passing bell 喪鐘;葬鐘。(亦作 **death bell**)

pass·ing·ly [ˈpæsɪŋlɪ; ˈpɑːsiŋli] *adv.* ①走馬看花地;倉卒地。②暫時地。

‡**pas·sion** [ˈpæʃən; ˈpæʃən] *n.* ①熱情;强烈的情感。Hate and fear are *passions.* 恨與懼是强烈的情感。②激怒;忿怒。He flew into a *passion.* 他突然發怒。③愛情。burning *passions.* 燃燒着的情焰。④愛好;嗜癖。She has a *passion* for painting. 她愛好繪畫。⑤熱望之目的物;酷愛之物。Music is her *passion.* 音樂是她所酷愛的。⑥(常 P-) 耶穌在十字架上的受苦難; 聖經中耶穌受難故事。—*v.t.* & *v.i.* (使) 充滿或表露感情或熱情。

pas·sion·al [ˈpæʃənḷ; ˈpæʃənəl] *adj.* ①熱情的;由於熱情的。②情慾的;戀愛的。③激怒的;忿怒的。—*n.* 聖徒或殉教者受難記。

***pas·sion·ate** [ˈpæʃənɪt; ˈpæʃənit] *adj.* ①熱情的; 情深的。②易動感情的; 易怒的。 a *passionate* nature. 熱情的天性。③出自熱情的; 熱烈的。④多情的。 —**ly,** *adv.*

pas·sion·flow·er [ˈpæʃənˌflauɚ; ˈpæʃənˌflauə] *n.* 〖植物〗西番蓮。

pas·sion·less [ˈpæʃənlɪs; ˈpæʃənlis] *adj.* 無熱情的;不爲感情所動的;冷靜的。

passion play or **Passion Play** 描寫耶穌受苦與死的戲劇。

Passion Sunday 復活節前第二個星期日, 即封齋期 (Lent) 中的第五個星期日。

Passion Week 復活節前第二週。

***pas·sive** [ˈpæsɪv; ˈpæsiv] *adj.* ①消極的;被動的。to remain *passive.* 保持被動。a *passive* resister. 消極抵抗者。②不抵抗的。③〖化學〗鈍態的;不易起化學變化的。—*n.* ①被動語態。② 被動語態的動詞。—**ly,** *adv.* —**ness,** *n.*

passive noun 〖文法〗 被動名詞 (如 employee等)。

passive resistance 消極抵抗(不用武力的不合作方式的抵抗)。

passive voice 〖文法〗被動語態。

pas·siv·i·ty [pæˈsɪvətɪ; pæˈsiviti] *n.* 被動;消極;不抵抗。

pass·key [ˈpæsˌki; ˈpɑːs-kiː] *n., pl.* **-keys.**①(能開各種鎖的)總鑰匙;萬能鑰;盜賊用的鑰匙。②門閂鑰匙。 ***passkey man*** 賊。

pass·man [ˈpæsmæn; ˈpɑːsmæn] *n., pl.* **-men.** (英國大學非優等之)普通畢業生。

Pass·o·ver [ˈpæsˌovɚ; ˈpɑːsˌouvə] *n.* ①〖聖經〗踰越節 (猶太人之節日)。②(p-) 踰越節獻祭之羊。③(p-)基督。

***pass·port** [ˈpæsˌport; ˈpɑːs-pɔːt] *n.* ①護照。②達到某種目的之手段。 a *passport* to his favor. 邀寵的手段。③戰時中立國船隻之通行許可證。

pass·word [ˈpæsˌwɝd, ˈpɑs-; ˈpɑːs-wəːd] *n.*〖軍〗口令。

‡**past** [pæst, pɑst; pɑːst] *adj.* ①過去的;結束的。 Our troubles are *past.* 我們的困難過去了。in times *past* (=long ago). 好久以前。②剛過去的。 for the *past* few days (weeks, months, etc.). 過去數日(週、月等)。③卸任的。a *past* president. 一位卸任的總統。④練達的; 老練的。⑤〖文法〗過去的。—*n.* ①過去;往時。She was thinking of the *past.* 她在想念着過去。②過去的生活;往事。We know nothing of his *past.* 我們一點也不知道他的過去歷史。③〖文法〗過去式。—*prep.* ①越過;走過;超越。 It is *past* my power. 非我力所能及。②較…爲遲; 晚於。It is *past* noon. 現已過午。 half *past* two. 兩點半。—*adv.* 過;越過。The cars go *past* once an hour. 汽車一個鐘頭經過一次。

***paste** [pest; peist] *n., v.,* **past·ed, past·ing.** —*n.* ①漿糊。②(用以做餅之) 麪團。③柔軟混合物。 a toothpaste. 牙膏。④假寶石的製造原料。 ⑤原料;材料。 ⑥〖俚〗重擊;猛擊。—*v.t.* ①黏貼。 to *paste* up a notice. 把告示貼在牆上。②〖俚〗重擊;猛擊。③弄成漿;弄成麪團狀。

paste·board [ˈpestˌbord; ˈpeistbɔːd] *n.* ①紙板。②〖俚〗 紙板製品 (如紙牌、名片、車票等)。③擀麪板。④ (*pl.*) 一付撲克牌。—*adj.* ①(似)紙板的。②假的;人造的。***pasteboard peddler*** 〖美俚〗賣假票子的人。

pas·tel [pæsˈtɛl, ˈpæsˌtɛl; pæsˈtel, ˈpæstel] *n.* ①着色粉筆;蠟筆。②蠟筆畫法。③蠟筆畫;着色粉筆畫。④〖植物〗大青;青色染料。⑤輕淡色彩。—*adj.* (色彩)輕淡的;蠟筆畫的。

pas·tel·(l)ist [ˈpæstɛlɪst; ˈpæstelist] *n.* 着色粉筆畫家。

past·er [ˈpestɚ; ˈpeistə] *n.* ①貼箋紙 (一面塗膠的紙片或紙條)。②黏貼人(物)。

pas·tern [ˈpæstɚn; ˈpæstəːn] *n.* (馬等足部之) 骹。 ***great pastern bone*** 大骹骨 (即上趾骨)。 ***small pastern bone*** 小骹骨 (即下趾骨)。

Pas·teur [pæsˈtɝ; pæsˈtəː] *n.* 巴斯德 (Louis, 1822–1895, 法國化學家及細菌學家)。

pas·teur·ism [ˈpæstərɪzṃ; ˈpæstərizm] *n.* ①巴斯德氏病菌接種法;狂犬病菌接種法。②巴斯德氏殺菌法。

pas·teur·i·za·tion [ˌpæstərəˈzeʃən; ˌpæstəraiˈzeiʃən] *n.* ①巴斯德氏殺菌法。②以巴斯德氏殺菌法殺菌。

pas·teur·ize [ˈpæstəˌraɪz; ˈpæstəraiz] *v.t.,* **-ized, -iz·ing.** 以高熱殺菌。

pas·tiche [pæsˈtiʃ; pæsˈtiːʃ, ˈpæstiːʃ] 〖法〗 *n.* 模仿文章;模造畫。

pas·tille [pæsˈtil; pæsˈtiːl] *n.* ①(病室等燻蒸消毒用之)香錠。②菱形物;菱形藥片。③着色粉筆或其原料。(亦作 **pastil**)

***pas·time** [ˈpæsˌtaɪm; ˈpɑːs-taim] *n.* 娛樂;消遣。

past·i·ness [ˈpestɪnɪs; ˈpeistinis] *n.* ①漿糊狀;麪團狀。②(臉色)灰白;發青。③鬆懈。

past master ①曾任某一社團或組織之首領者。②對某種行業或技藝有豐富經驗者。

***pas·tor** [ˈpæstɚ; ˈpɑːstə] *n.* 本堂牧師。

pas·to·ral [ˈpæstərəl; ˈpɑːstərəl] *adj.* ①牧人的;牧人生活的。②用作牧場的;適於牧畜的(土地等)。③田舍風光的; 田舍生活的。 *pastoral* poetry (*or* poem). 牧詩;田園詩。④牧師的。 *pastoral* staff. 〖宗教〗牧杖(主教和修道院長的權標)。 —*n.* ①田園詩; 牧歌; 田園畫; 田園劇。②牧師或主教寫給教區人民的公開信。 —**ly,** *adv.* —**ness,** *n.*

pas·to·ra·le [ˌpæstəˈrɑlɪ; ˌpæstəˈrɑːli] *n., pl.* **-les, -li** [-lɪ; -liː]. ①〖音樂〗田園曲;富田園情調的歌劇或芭蕾舞曲。②田園詩。

pas·to·ral·ism [ˈpæstərəlɪzəm; ˈpɑːstərəlizm] *n.* 田園風味;牧歌體。

pas·to·ral·ize [ˈpæstərəˌlaɪz; ˈpæstərəlaiz] *v.t.,* **-ized, -iz·ing.** 使田園化。

pas·tor·ate [ˈpæstərɪt; ˈpɑːstərit] *n.* ①牧師職(或任期)。②牧師管區。③牧師團。

pas·to·ri·um [pæsˈtorɪəm; pɑːsˈtɔːriəm] *n.* 〖美南部〗牧師或教區牧師公館。

pas·tor·ship [ˈpæstɚˌʃɪp; ˈpɑːstəʃip] *n.* 牧師之職位、任期或管區。

past participle 〖文法〗過去分詞。

past perfect 〖文法〗過去完成式。

past progressive〖文法〗過去進行式。
pas·tra·mi 〔pəˈstrɑmɪ; pəˈstrɑːmi〕 *n.* 五香燻牛肉（常爲肩部肉）。
***pas·try** 〔ˈpestrɪ; ˈpeistri〕 *n., pl.* **-tries.** ①用油和麪烤成的點心。②有餡糕餅（如 pie 等）。
past tense〖文法〗過去式。
pas·tur·a·ble 〔ˈpæstʃərəbl̩; ˈpɑːstjurəbl〕 *adj.* 可作牧場的。
pas·tur·age 〔ˈpæstʃərɪdʒ; ˈpɑːstjuridʒ〕 *n.* ①牧畜；牧養；放牧。②牧草。③牧場；牧畜地。
pas·tur·al 〔ˈpæstʃərəl; ˈpɑːstʃərəl〕 *adj.* 牧場的；草地的。
pas·ture** 〔ˈpæstʃɚ; ˈpɑːstʃə〕 *n., v.,* **-tured, -tur·ing.** —*n.* ①草地；山坡；牧場。②牧草。These lands afford good *pasture.* 這些地方有好的牧草。③放牧。④退休處所。common of pasture***〖法律〗將牲口在他人土地上放牧之權利。—*v.t.* ①放（牛、羊等）於草地。to *pasture* cattle. 牧牛在草地上。②食（青草）。③將（地）用作牧場。—*v.i.*（牛、羊等）在牧場吃草。
past·y[1] 〔ˈpestɪ; ˈpeisti〕 *adj.,* **past·i·er, past·i·est.** ①如糊的；漿糊似的。②（面色）發青的；灰白的。③軟弱的；鬆懈的。
past·y[2] 〔ˈpæstɪ, ˈpɑstɪ; ˈpæsti〕 *n., pl.* **pas·ties.**〖主英〗肉餡烤製之餅；肉包子。
Pat 〔pæt; pæt〕 *n.*〖俗〗愛爾蘭人。
pat**[1] 〔pæt; pæt〕 *v.,* **pat·ted, pat·ting,** *n.* —*v.t.* ①（以掌等扁平物）輕拍。②（以手）撫拍（表示同情、贊同或愛情）。to *pat* a dog. 撫拍一狗。—*v.i.* ①脚步拍搭地走路或跑路。②作出拍搭聲。pat oneself*** (or ***a person***) ***on the back*** 輕拍（某人之）背；（轉爲）恭維；讚美。—*n.* ①輕擊；輕拍。②輕拍聲。③小團（特指牛油）。***a pat on the back***〖俗〗鼓勵之詞；稱讚之詞。
pat[2] *adj.* 合適的；中肯的。a *pat* reply. 中肯的回答。—*adv.* 合適地；確實地。The story came *pat* to the occasion. 那故事正適合那個場合。***have pat*** 完全有。***know pat*** 徹底了解。***stand pat*** **a.** 堅守自己的計畫或政策。**b.**〖撲克〗就發到的一手牌（不再另要）來玩。
pat. ①patent. ②patented. ③patrol. ④pattern.
pa·ta·gi·um 〔pəˈtedʒɪəm; pəˈteidʒiəm〕 *n., pl.* **-gi·a** 〔-dʒɪə; -dʒiə〕.〖動物〗（蝙蝠等之）翼膜。
Pat·a·go·ni·an 〔ˌpætəˈgonjən; ˌpætəˈgounjən〕 *adj.* Patagonia（南美南端一地區）的；Patagonia 人或其文化的。—*n.* Patagonia 人。
patch** 〔pætʃ; pætʃ〕 *n.* ①（衣服等的）補綻。②包傷口之布片。③護眼片；眼罩。④美人斑（昔女人貼在臉上之小黑綢布）。⑤與周圍環境不同的一小塊地。⑥斑點；斑紋。⑦一小塊土地。a garden *patch.* 一塊園地。⑧剩餘之小布片。⑨〖英〗時期；一段時間。not a patch on*** 遠不及…；比…差得遠。***strike a bad patch*** 倒楣。—*v.t.* ①補綴；彌縫。②用作補片。③用布片拼成。④匆促修理；草率作成〖up, together〗. ⑤用美人斑裝飾。***patch up*** **a.** 結束；解決；制止。**b.** 匆匆整理或臨時修整。**c.** 臨時拼湊。
patch·ou·li, patch·ou·ly 〔ˈpætʃulɪ; ˈpætʃuli(ː)〕 *n.* ①〖植物〗（印度產的）一種薄荷。②其所製的香水。
patch test 過敏性測驗。
patch·work 〔ˈpætʃˌwɝk; ˈpætʃwəːk〕 *n.* ①雜色布片之補綴物。②雜湊之物。③草率完成之事。
patch·y 〔ˈpætʃɪ; ˈpætʃi〕 *adj.,* **patch·i·er, patch·i·est.** ①盡是補綻的；由補綴湊成的。a *patchy* excuse. 破綻百出的藉口。②似補綴的；有斑紋的。③不調和的；脾氣彆扭的。
pate 〔pet; peit〕 *n.*〖俗〗①頭；頭頂。bald *pate.* 禿頭。②腦。③有頭腦的人。***empty pate*** 獃子。***shallow pate*** 淺薄的傢伙。
pâ·té 〔pɑˈte; pɑːˈtei〕〖法〗*n.* ①加調味品的肉泥（醬）。②（內塡雞肉、魚、肝、蛤仁等肉醬之）小麪餅。
pâ·té de foie gras 〔pɑˈtedəfwɑˈgrɑ; pɑːˈteidəfwɑːˈgrɑː〕〖法〗肥鵝肝餅。
pa·tel·la 〔pəˈtɛlə; pəˈtelə〕 *n., pl.* **-las, -lae** 〔-li; -liː〕. ①〖解剖〗臏；膝蓋骨。②小淺盤；小皿。③〖動、植物〗盤狀部。④（蟲）基關部。
pa·tel·lar 〔pəˈtɛlɚ; pəˈtelə〕 *adj.*〖解剖〗膝蓋骨的。
pat·en 〔ˈpætn̩; ˈpætn〕 *n.* ①（金銀製之）聖餅碟；祭碟。②（金屬製的）平碟。（亦作 **patin, patina, patine**）
pa·ten·cy 〔ˈpetn̩sɪ; ˈpeitənsi〕 *n.* ①顯著；明顯；公開。②〖醫〗開放性。
***pat·ent** 〔ˈpetn̩t, ˈpætn̩t; ˈpeitənt, ˈpæt-〕 *adj.* ①專利的；專賣的。a *patent* device. 專利發明。②顯著的；明顯的。③開放的；公開的。—*n.* ①執照；特許狀。②專賣；專賣權。③獲專利之發明物。—*v.t.* 特許專賣；特許專利。—**a·ble,** *adj.*
pat·ent·ee 〔ˌpætn̩ˈti; ˌpeitənˈtiː〕 *n.* 獲有專利權的人。
patent leather 黑漆皮。
pa·tent·ly 〔ˈpetn̩tlɪ; ˈpeitəntli〕 *adv.* ①明顯地；顯然地。②公開地。
patent medicine ①成藥。②專利藥品。
Patent Office 專利局。
pat·en·tor 〔ˈpætn̩tɚ; ˈpeitəntə〕 *n.* ①專利許可者。②（誤用）＝**patentee.**
patent right 專利權。
patent roll〖英〗特許專利登記簿。
pa·ter 〔ˈpetɚ; ˈpeitə〕 *n.* ①〖英俗〗父親。②〖宗教〗主禱文。
pa·ter·fa·mil·i·as 〔ˈpetɚfəˈmɪlɪˌæs; ˈpeitəfəˈmiliæs〕 *n., pl.* **pa·tres·fa·mil·i·as** 〔ˌpetrizfəˈmɪlɪæs; ˌpeitriːzfəˈmiliæs〕. 家主；家長；父。
pa·ter·nal 〔pəˈtɝnl̩; pəˈtəːnl〕 *adj.* ①（像）父親的；仁慈的。*paternal* love. 父愛。②父系的。a *paternal* aunt. 姑母。③由父親遺傳的。—**ly,** *adv.*
pa·ter·nal·ism 〔pəˈtɝnl̩ˌɪzəm; pəˈtəːnəlizm〕 *n.* 感情主義；家長政治。—**pa·ter·nal·is·tic,** *adj.*
pa·ter·ni·ty 〔pəˈtɝnətɪ; pəˈtəːniti〕 *n.* ①父道；父權；父職。②父系。③（事物之）起源；根源；（書及文章等之）著者。
pat·er·nos·ter 〔ˈpetɚˈnɑstɚ; ˈpætəˈnɔstə〕 *n.*〖宗教〗①主禱文（尤指拉丁語者）。②念珠串上每隔十粒（第十一粒），顏色及大小與其他不同之念珠。③禱告文。***black paternoster*** 咀咒。***say devil's paternoster*** 咕噥地罵人；發牢騷。
‡**path** 〔pæθ, pɑθ; pɑːθ〕 *n., pl.* **paths.** ①小徑；花園中的小徑。a *path* through the woods. 一條穿過林中之小徑。②道路。③途徑；軌道。④行爲或動作的方式；行徑。the *path* of duty (loyalty). 責任（忠義）之道。⑤〖機械〗路線；動路；路程。***cross one's path*** 不期而遇。
path. ①pathological. ②pathology.
Pa·than 〔pəˈtɑn; pəˈtɑːn〕 *n.* 印度西北境之阿富汗人。

pa·thet·ic** [pəˈθɛtɪk; pəˈθetik] *adj.* ①哀憐的; 悲慘的; 引起憐憫的。 a *pathetic* sight. 悲慘的景象。②感情上的。③引起強烈感情的。 ***the pathetic fallacy (詩人的)將人類的感情賦予自然界的東西,如樹木、太陽等(如 angry wind. 憤怒的風)。

pa·thet·i·cal [pəˈθɛtɪkḷ; pəˈθetikl] *adj.* 〖罕〗 =**pathetic.** —**ly,** *adv.*

path·find·er [ˈpæθˌfaɪndɚ; ˈpɑːθˌfaində] *n.* ①拓荒者;探險者;先導者;先覺者。②〖美俚〗(警察的) 密探。

path·less [ˈpæθlɪs, ˈpɑθ–; ˈpɑːθlis] *adj.* 無路的;人跡未到的。—**ness,** *n.*

path·o·gen·e·sis [ˌpæθəˈdʒɛnəsɪs; ˌpæθəˈdʒenisis] *n.* 〖醫〗疾病之發生或成長;病原。

path·o·gen·ic [ˌpæθəˈdʒɛnɪk; ˌpæθəˈdʒenik] *adj.* 病原的;致病的。

pa·thog·e·ny [pəˈθɑdʒɪnɪ; pəˈθɔdʒini] *n.* =**pathogenesis.**

path·o·log·ic [ˌpæθəˈlɑdʒɪk; ˌpæθəˈlɔdʒik] *adj.* =**pathological.**

path·o·log·i·cal [ˌpæθəˈlɑdʒɪkḷ; ˌpæθəˈlɔdʒikəl] *adj.* ①病理學的;病理上的。②由於疾病的;伴雜疾病的。—**ly,** *adv.*

pa·thol·o·gist [pæˈθɑlədʒɪst; pəˈθɔlədʒist] *n.* 病理學者。

pa·thol·o·gy [pæˈθɑlədʒɪ; pəˈθɔlədʒi] *n., pl.* **-gies.** ①病理學。②病理。③病狀。

pa·thos [ˈpeθɑs; ˈpeiθɔs] *n.* ①(講演、文學作品、音樂等)動人哀感之性質; 使人悽惻之力量。②動人哀感之辭句。

path·way [ˈpæθˌwe; ˈpɑːθ–wei] *n.* ①路;徑;小路。②事物發展的方向。

-pathy 〖字尾〗表下列諸義的名詞字尾:①"痛苦;感情",如: antipathy, sympathy. ②"疾病;療法",如:neuropathy, psychopathy.

pa·tience** [ˈpeʃəns; ˈpeiʃəns] *n.* ①容忍; 忍耐; 耐性。 I've lost *patience* with him. 我已對他無法容忍。②堅忍;耐苦。 ***be out of patience with 對…不能再忍耐; 對…發怒。 ***have no patience with*** 對…無法容忍。 ***the patience of Job*** 無止境的忍耐。

‡pa·tient [ˈpeʃənt; ˈpeiʃənt] *adj.* 忍耐的;容忍的;堅忍的。*patient* with a child. 對小孩忍耐。Please be *patient*. 請忍耐些。 ***patient of*** **a.** 容忍;忍耐。a man *patient of* criticisms. 一個能容忍批評的人。 **b.** 易於招致。 This statement is *patient of* criticism. 這個聲明易招致批評。—*n.* ①病人。The hospital is equipped to handle 500 *patients.* 那醫院有可住500個病人的設備。②(美容院等之)顧客。—**ly,** *adv.*

pat·i·na [ˈpætɪnə; ˈpætinə] *n.* ①古銅上所生的綠銹; 銅綠。②木器等表面因年久所生的顏色變化或苔。③任何外面之物。

pa·ti·o [ˈpatɪˌo, ˈpatjo; ˈpætiou] *n., pl.* **-ti·os.** 西班牙或中南美洲某些國家的房子中的內院。

pat·ois [ˈpætwa; ˈpætwɑː] *n., pl.* **pat·ois.** 〖法〗方言;土語。

pa·tri·arch [ˈpetrɪˌark; ˈpeitriɑːk] *n.* ①家長; 族長。②早期基督教中之主教。③創始者;創辦人。④年高德劭的老人;元老。

pa·tri·ar·chal [ˌpetrɪˈarkḷ; ˌpeitriˈɑːkl] *adj.* ①家長的; 族長的; 教長的。②家長、族長或教長治下的。③可尊敬的。

pa·tri·ar·chate [ˈpetrɪˌarkɪt; ˈpeitriɑːkit] *n.* ①patriarch 之職位、任期、管區等。②族長政治。

pa·tri·ar·chy [ˈpetrɪˌarkɪ; ˈpeitriɑːki] *n., pl.* **-chies.** ①族長(家長)政治。②父系社會(為 matriarchy 之對)。

pa·tri·cian [pəˈtrɪʃən; pəˈtriʃən] *n.* ①古羅馬之貴族。②貴族。—*adj.* ①出身高貴的。②貴族的; 適於貴族的。

pa·tri·ci·ate [pəˈtrɪʃɪɪt; pəˈtriʃiit] *n.* ①貴族身分或地位。②貴族階級。

pat·ri·cid·al [ˌpætrɪˈsaɪdḷ; ˌpætriˈsaidl] *adj.* 弒父罪的;弒父者的;似弒父(者)的。

pat·ri·cide [ˈpætrɪˌsaɪd; ˈpætrisaid] *n.* ①弒父罪。②弒父者。

Pat·rick [ˈpætrɪk; ˈpætrik] *n.* ①男子名。②巴特瑞克(Saint, 約 389-461,愛爾蘭之守護聖徒)。

pat·ri·mo·ni·al [ˌpætrəˈmonɪəl; ˌpætriˈmounjəl] *adj.* 祖傳的;父子相傳的。

pat·ri·mo·ny [ˈpætrəˌmonɪ; ˈpætriməni] *n., pl.* **-nies.** ①世襲之財產;繼承之財產。②教會之財產;贈與教會之錢財等。③任何繼承之事物(如特徵、性格等)。

***pa·tri·ot** [ˈpetrɪət; ˈpeitriət] *n.* 愛國者。

pa·tri·ot·eer [ˌpetrɪəˈtɪr; ˌpætriəˈtiə] *n.* 口是心非的愛國者。—*v.i.* 做口是心非的愛國者。

***pa·tri·ot·ic** [ˌpetrɪˈɑtɪk; ˌpætriˈɔtik, ˌpeit–] *adj.* 愛國的;有愛國心的。a *patriotic* statesman. 愛國的政治家。—**al·ly,** *adv.*

pa·tri·ot·ics [ˌpetrɪˈɑtɪks; ˌpætriˈɔtiks] *n. pl.* 表露愛國精神的言論或行為。

***pa·tri·ot·ism** [ˈpetrɪətɪzəm; ˈpætriətizəm, ˈpeit–] *n.* 愛國心;愛國的精神。the passionate language of *patriotism.* 熱情洋溢流露着愛國精神的話。

pa·tris·tic [pəˈtrɪstɪk; pəˈtristik] *adj.* ①(初期基督教)領袖的; 教父的。②教父之遺著(研究)的。③任何思想或主義創始人遺著的。

***pa·trol** [pəˈtrol; pəˈtroul] *n., v.,* **-trolled, -trol·ling.** —*n.* ①巡邏;巡查。The policemen are now on *patrol.* 警察正在巡邏。②巡邏者。③巡邏隊;斥候兵。④童子軍八人小隊。—*v.i.* 巡查; 巡邏。—*v.t.* ①巡查;巡視;巡邏。to *patrol* the streets. 巡邏街上。②巡遊。

patrol boat 哨艇;巡邏船。

pa·trol·man [pəˈtrolmən; pəˈtroulmæn] *n., pl.* **-men.** ①巡邏人; 巡查者。②〖美〗巡邏警察。

patrol wagon (警察)囚車。

***pa·tron** [ˈpetrən; ˈpeitrən] *n.* ①保護人;資助人;贊助人。②顧客。This little store has many *patrons.* 這小商店主顧甚多。③守護神。—*adj.* 守護的。

***pa·tron·age** [ˈpetrənɪdʒ, ˈpæt–; ˈpætrənidʒ, ˈpet–] *n.* ①鼓勵; 支持; 資助; 庇護;保護。 under the *patronage* of 在…的庇護下。②顧客的惠顧。③恩惠。an air of *patronage.* 施恩於人的那副神情。④委派牧師之權; 施恩惠或派給職位的權力。⑤政治上的職位或恩惠。

pa·tron·ess [ˈpetrənɪs; ˈpeitrənis] *n.* patron 之女性。

pa·tron·ize [ˈpetrənˌaɪz; ˈpætrənaiz] *v.t.,* **-ized, -iz·ing.** ①照顧;光顧。②以施恩的態度對待。③保護;支援;支持。

pa·tron·iz·ing [ˈpetrənˌaɪzɪŋ; ˈpætrənaiziŋ] *adj.* ①照顧的;光顧的。②一面孔恩人氣派的; 神氣十足的; 傲慢的。—**ly,** *adv.*

patron saint ①守護神。②保護者。

pat·ro·nym·ic [ˌpætrəˈnɪmɪk; ˌpætrəˈnimik] *adj.* ①取自父(祖)名的。②表示父(祖)名的(字首或字尾)。—*n.* ①取自父(祖)名的名字(例如 MacArthur, son of Arthur,

Stevenson, son of Steven, O'Brien, son of Brien 等)。②姓。

pa·troon 〔pə'trun; pə'truːn〕 *n.* 〖美史〗(昔 New York 州及 New Jersey 州屬荷蘭政府管轄時)享有采地特權之地主。

pat·ten 〔'pætn̩; 'pætn〕 *n.* ①一種木質套鞋。②一種雨天穿之木套鞋或木屐。

***pat·ter¹** 〔'pætɚ; 'pætə〕 *v.i.* ①發急速輕拍聲。The rain was *pattering* on the roof. 雨正淅瀝落在屋頂上。②發輕拍聲行走。—*v.t.* 使發拍達聲。—*n.* 急速之輕拍聲。

pat·ter² *n.* ①急促的談話;喋喋之語。②行話。***patter song*** 快調滑稽歌。 —*v.t.* & *v.i.* 喋喋而言;喋喋說出。

‡**pat·tern** 〔'pætɚn; 'pætən〕 *n.* ①圖案;花樣;樣式;方式。the *patterns* of wallpaper. 壁紙之花樣。a bicycle of an old *pattern.* 一輛舊式的脚踏車。②模範;模型。*patterns* in English. 英語類型。③〖機械〗模型。*pattern* maker. 製模工人。—*v.t.* 仿作;摹製。to *pattern* a dress on (*or* after) a Parisian model. 模仿巴黎流行樣式裁製衣服。***pattern oneself after*** 模仿。—*v.i.* 形成花樣;創造樣式。

pattern bombing 地毯式轟炸;飽和轟炸。(亦作 **carpet bombing, saturation bombing**)

Pat·ty 〔'pætɪ; 'pæti〕 *n.* 女子名(Martha, Mathilda, Patricia 等之暱稱)。

pat·ty 〔'pætɪ; 'pæti〕 *n., pl.* **-ties.** 小麪餅;小扁圓形的食物。

patty pan 烘焙小麪餅之淺鍋。

pat·u·lin 〔'pætjulɪn; 'pætjulin〕 *n.* 一種抗生素。

pat·u·lous 〔'pætjuləs; 'pætjuləs〕 *adj.* ①張開的。②〖植物〗(樹枝等)張開的;擴展的。

pau·ci·ty 〔'pɔsətɪ; 'pɔːsiti〕 *n.* 少數;少量;稀少;缺乏。

Paul 〔pɔl; pɔːl〕 *n.* ①男子名。②保羅(Saint, ? –A.D.? 67, 原稱 Saul, 耶穌門徒之一, 新約中之書信部分大多出於彼手)。***rob Peter to pay Paul*** 借債還債;挖肉補瘡。

Pau·line¹ 〔pɔ'lin; pɔː'liːn〕 *n.* 女子名。

Paul·ine² 〔'pɔlaɪn; 'pɔːlain〕 *adj.* 使徒聖保羅的;其著作的;其教訓的。

Pau·low·ni·a 〔pɔ'lonɪə; pɔː'louniə〕 *n.* 〖植物〗桐屬。

Paul Pry 過分好奇者。

paunch 〔pɔntʃ; pɔːntʃ〕 *n.* ①胃;腹。②胖子的大肚子。③反芻動物之第一胃。 —*v.t.* ①剩…之肚。②開…之肚;取…肚雜。

paunch·y 〔'pɔntʃɪ; 'pɔːntʃi〕 *adj.*, **paunch·i·er, paunch·i·est.** 有大腹的;大肚子的。—**paunch·i·ness,** *n.*

pau·per 〔'pɔpɚ; 'pɔːpə〕 *n.* 窮人;貧民。—*adj.* 貧民的;窮困的。

pau·per·ism 〔'pɔpə,rɪzəm; 'pɔːpərizəm〕 *n.* ①貧窮;貧困。②貧民(集合稱)。

pau·per·i·za·tion 〔,pɔpərə'zeʃən; ,pɔːpərai'zeiʃən〕 *n.* 貧窮化;貧困化。

pau·per·ize 〔'pɔpə,raɪz; 'pɔːpəraiz〕 *v.t.*, **-ized, -iz·ing.** 使貧窮;使成窮人。

‡**pause** 〔pɔz; pɔːz〕 *v.*, **paused, paus·ing,** *n.* —*v.i.* 中止;躊躇。to *pause* upon a word. 沉思一個字。—*n.* ①中止;躊躇。without a single *pause.* 毫無停止地。②停讀;斷句;停頓。He made a short *pause* and then went on reading. 他停頓一下,隨後就讀下去。③停讀符號;頓號。④〖音樂〗休止;休止符;延長符號(即⌒或⌣)。***give pause*** 使(某人)躊躇。The hazards of the move *gave* them *pause.* 那行動之危險使他們躊躇。

pav·an(e) 〔'pævən; 'pævən〕 *n.* (流行於16世紀之)孔雀舞;其舞曲。(亦作 **pavin**)

pave** 〔pev; peiv〕 *v.t.*, **paved, pav·ing.** 鋪(街道等)。 to *pave* a street. 鋪一條街道。pave the way for*** (or ***to***) 爲…鋪路(預作安排)。

***pave·ment** 〔'pevmənt;'peivmənt〕 *n.* ①(鋪成的)路;公路。He stopped his car just off the *pavement.* 他在路邊停車。②鋪道材料。③〖主英〗人行道。

pavement artist 馬路畫家(用有色粉筆在人行道上作畫討錢的人)。

***pa·vil·ion** 〔pə'vɪljən; pə'viljən〕 *n.* ①亭;閣。②天幕;(運動會的)休息處。③一建築中較高和裝飾較好的部分。④醫院中的一座建築物。⑤〖解剖〗外耳。⑥展覽會等各參加單位之展示館。—*v.t.* 建帳篷;以帳篷蔭蔽。

pav·ing 〔'pevɪŋ; 'peiviŋ〕 *n.* ①鋪路之材料。②=**pavement.**

pav·io(u)r 〔'pevjɚ; 'peivjə〕 *n.* ①鋪石者;砌磚者。②一種用以撞倒砌石的工具。③鋪砌用的石板;鋪磚。④一種堅固的建築用磚。

paw** 〔pɔ; pɔː〕 *n.* ①(貓、狗等有爪之)足掌。②〖俗〗手。make somebody a cat's paw*** 利用某人。He *made me a cat's paw.* 他利用我。—*v.t.* & *v.i.* ①(動物等)用足搔爬;用足觸。②〖俗〗拙笨地處理;盤弄。③艱苦地行走。

pawk·y 〔'pɔkɪ; 'pɔːki〕 *adj.*, **-i·er, -i·est.** 〖蘇,英方〗狡猾的。

pawl 〔pɔl; pɔːl〕 *n.* 〖機械〗(防止齒輪逆轉之)止輪具;(掣動齒輪兼防逆轉之)掣子。

pawn¹ 〔pɔn; pɔːn〕 *v.t.* ①典當;抵押。②以…保證。 —*n.* ①抵押品;典當的狀態。My watch is in *pawn.* 我的錶當了。②人質。

pawn² *n.* ①(象棋的)卒。②可輕易犧牲的不足輕重之人或物。

pawn·bro·ker 〔'pɔn,brokɚ; 'pɔːn,broukə〕 *n.* 典當商;開當鋪者。

pawn·bro·king 〔'pɔn,brokɪŋ; 'pɔːn,broukiŋ〕 *n.* 典當業。—*adj.* 經營典當業的。

pawn·ee 〔pɔn'i; pɔː'niː〕 *n.* 〖法律〗收當人;質權人。

pawn·er, pawn·or 〔'pɔnɚ; 'pɔːnə〕 *n.* 〖法律〗交當人;抵押人。

pawn·shop 〔'pɔn,ʃɑp; 'pɔːnʃɔp〕 *n.* 當鋪。

pawn ticket 當票。

paw·paw 〔'pɔ,pɔ; 'pɔːpɔː〕 *n.* =**papaw.**

pax 〔pæks; pæks〕 *n.* ①天主教之聖像牌。②(P-)〖羅馬神話〗和平女神。③〖英〗(學童語)友誼;朋友。④和平。

Pax Ro·ma·na 〔,pæksro'mɑnə; ,pæksrou'mɑːnə〕 ①古羅馬統治下爲時約200年之和平(自紀元前27年至紀元180年)。②征服者强加諸戰敗國的和平。

‡**pay¹** 〔pe; pei〕 *v.*, **paid,** or **payed** (*v.t.* ⑧), **pay·ing,** *n., adj.* —*v.t.* ①付款(與人);報酬。How much do you *pay* your cook? 你給你的廚子多少工資? ②付(款)。 I *paid* the money yesterday. 我於昨日付掉此款。③對…有價值;有利於。It wouldn't *pay* me to take that job. 做那個工作對我沒有好處。④給;與;致。 to *pay* a lady a compliment. 恭維一位女士。⑤報償;懲罰。⑥生利;獲利。 That stock *pays* me four per cent. 那股票給我賺了百分之四的利錢。⑦遭受;忍受。The one who does wrong must *pay* the penalty. 做惡者必受罰。⑧放出(繩子等)。⑨補償。—*v.i.* ①支付;付款。I have already *paid* for the book. 我已付清此書

價款。②值得;有利。It *pays* to be polite. 客氣不吃虧。③報償;懲罰。You will have to *pay* for this foolish behavior. 你將因此愚蠢之行動而得報應。***pay a call on someone***; ***pay someone a visit*** =visit him. ***pay as you go***〖美〗 a. 付現款(不賒帳)。 b. 量入爲出。c. 從薪金中按期扣繳所得稅。 ***pay attention to*** 注意;留心。 ***pay back*** a. 歸還(欠債)。 b. 報答。c. 報復。 ***pay down*** (分期付款之)即時支付。 ***pay off*** a. 給薪解雇;全部清還。b. 報仇。c. 有了補償;有了收穫。d.〖俗〗付"保護費"。 ***pay one back in his own coin*** 報復;以牙還牙。***pay one's attentions to*** 追求;向…求婚。 ***pay one's own way*** 付自己的帳。***pay one's respects to*** 向…致敬。 ***pay one's*** (or ***its***) ***way*** a. 付分內應付之款。b. 投資產生足够盈利。***pay*** (***a person***) ***out*** 報復某人;懲罰某人。***pay*** (***money***) ***out*** 花費;付出。***pay out*** a. 放(繩子、鍊條等)。 b. 報復;懲罰。***pay through the nose*** 付出高代價。 ***pay up*** a. 全部清還;付清。b. 被迫付錢。 —*n.* ①報酬;薪俸;工資。On what day does he receive his *pay?* 他何日領薪? ②報償。③如期付款的人。***in the pay of*** 受…雇用;受…買通。—*adj.* ①有價值的;可獲利的。②自動收款的。*pay* telephone. 自動收款的電話。③管理付款的。*pay* office. 付款處。

pay² *v.t.*〖航海〗以柏油等塗敷(船底等)以防水。

pay·a·ble [ˈpeəbl; ˈpeiəbl] *adj.* ①到期的;應付的。②可付的。This check is *payable* at the bank. 這張支票在銀行可以支付。③可獲利的(工商業、礦山等)。

pay·box [ˈpeˌbɑks; ˈpeibɔks] *n.*〖英〗①出納處。②售票亭。

pay·check [ˈpeˈtʃɛk; ˈpeiˈtʃek] *n.* 薪水支票。

pay·day [ˈpeˌde; ˈpeidei] *n.* 發薪日。

pay dirt ①值得開採之礦脈等。②有益收穫。

PAYE, P.A.Y.E. ①pay-as-you-earn. ②pay as you enter.

pay·ee [peˈi; peiˈiː] *n.* 受款人;收款人。

pay envelope ①薪水袋。②薪水。

pay·er [ˈpeɚ; ˈpeiə] *n.* 交付人;付款人。

pay·ing [ˈpe·ɪŋ; ˈpeiiŋ] *adj.* ①支付的;付款的。a *paying* guest. 在私人家中寄膳宿的人。②有利的;合算的。—*n.* 支付;付款。

pay load ①(公司等的)經常薪俸負擔。②〖航空〗可以獲得收入之載重(包括乘客、貨物、郵件等)。③火箭所載之人造衞星、原子彈頭、科學儀器或太空船等。

pay·mas·ter [ˈpeˌmæstɚ; ˈpeiˌmɑːstə] *n.* (負責發薪餉之)發款員;軍需官。

paymaster general *pl.* **paymasters general.** ①〖英〗財政部之主計長官。②〖美〗海軍主計總監。

***pay·ment** [ˈpemənt; ˈpeimənt] *n.* ①支付。to demand prompt *payment.* 請即付款。②付出之款。monthly *payments* of $200. 月付兩百元。③報償;懲罰。

pay·off [ˈpeˌɔf; ˈpeiɔːf] *n.* ①發薪餉。②發薪餉的時間。③企業等的收益。④〖俚〗(故事、局勢等的)高潮。Now listen to the *payoff*. 現在仔細聽高潮。⑤分紅;分肥。⑥獎懲之物。

pay·o·la [peˈolə; peiˈoulə] *n.*〖俚〗紅包;賄賂。

pay·out [ˈpeˌaut; ˈpeiaut] *n.* 支出。

pay·roll [ˈpeˌrol; ˈpeiroul] *n.* ①薪水冊。②薪水冊上應付之薪水總數。(亦作 **pay roll**)

pay scale 薪資標準。

pay station 公用電話亭。

pc. ①piece. ②prices. **P/C, p/c** ①petty cash. ②price(s) current. **P.C.** ①Past Commander. ②Police Constable. ③Post Commander. ④Privy Council. ⑤Privy Councilor. **p.c.** ①per cent. ②post card. ③petty cash. ④〖處方〗飯後(=after meals). ⑤price current. **pcs.** pieces. **pct.** per cent. **Pd** 化學元素palladium 之符號。**pd.** paid.已付的;支出。**P.D.** ①Police Department. ②每日(=per diem). ③Postal District. **P.D.Q.**〖美俚〗pretty damn quick(趕緊、馬上)。**P.E.** ①Presiding Elder. ②〖統計〗probable error. ③Protestant Episcopal. ④Petroleum Engineer.

pea** [pi; piː] *n., pl.* **peas,** *adj.* —*n.* ①豌豆。green *peas.* 青豌豆;帶荚之豌豆。split *peas*. 去皮乾豌豆(做湯用者)。②生豌豆的植物。③似豌豆的豆或植物。as like as two peas*** 酷似。—*adj.* 大小如豌豆的。

‡**peace** [pis; piːs] *n.* ①和平。world *peace.* 世界和平。②安寧;平安。③停戰條約或協定;和約。(A) *Peace* was signed between the two countries. 兩國簽訂了和約。④安靜;鎮靜。*peace* of mind. 心地之恬靜。⑤安寧之源。God is our only *peace.* 上帝是我們的唯一安寧之源。***be at peace with*** 與…和平相處。***hold*** (or ***keep***) ***one's peace*** 保持緘默。***keep the peace*** 維持社會安寧;維持治安。***make one's peace with*** 同…解決紛爭。***make peace*** 講和;談和。—*interj.* 靜!別高聲說話!

***peace·a·ble** [ˈpisəbl; ˈpiːsəbl] *adj.* ①和平的;平穩的;安靜的。They settled the dispute in the most *peaceable* and orderly manner. 他們在最和平而秩序井然的情形之下解決了那糾紛。②愛好和平的;溫和的。

peace·a·bly [ˈpisəblɪ; ˈpiːsəbli] *adv.* 和平地;安靜地;安祥地。

Peace Corps 和平工作團(美國政府爲開發中國家提供技術服務)。

Peace Corpsman 和平工作團團員。

***peace·ful** [ˈpisfəl; ˈpiːsful] *adj.* ①和平的;安靜的;寧靜的。a *peaceful* death. 安祥的死。②愛好和平的;喜安靜的。a *peaceful* man. 喜愛安靜的人。

peaceful coexistence 和平共存。

peace·ful·ly [ˈpisfəlɪ; ˈpiːsfuli] *adv.* ①和平地;寧靜地。②愛好和平地。

peace·keep·ing [ˈpisˌkipɪŋ; ˈpiːsˌkiːpiŋ] *adj.* 維護和平的;執行停火協定的。

peace·less [ˈpislɪs; ˈpiːslis] *adj.* 無和平的;不安祥的;不寧靜的。

peace·mak·er [ˈpisˌmekɚ; ˈpiːsˌmeikə] *n.* 調停人;仲裁人;和事佬。

peace marcher 參加反戰示威者。

peace·nik [ˈpisnɪk; ˈpiːsnik] *n.*〖俚〗公開爲反戰而示威者。

peace offensive 和平攻勢。

peace offering ①爲表示願謀取和平而付出之代價;謝罪之禮物。②(古猶太人之)謝恩祭。

peace officer 治安官;警官。

peace pipe 北美土人用以表親睦之烟管(亦用作徵詢和戰之具,受之爲和,拒之爲戰)。

peace sign 和平符號(以手指形成V字母所作之和平表示)。

peace talks 和談。

peace·time [ˈpisˌtaɪm; ˈpiːs-taim] *n.*

和平時期;平時。—*adj.* 和平時期的;平時的。

***peach¹** 〔pitʃ; piːtʃ〕 *n.* ①桃子。②桃樹。③略帶黃色的粉紅色;桃色。④〖俚〗美人。⑤〖俚〗極好的東西或人。He is a *peach* to work with. 他是易於共事的人。—*adj.* 粉紅色的;桃色的。

peach² *v.i. & v.t.* 〖俚〗告密;賣友。to *peach* against (on, *or* upon) one's accomplice. 告發同謀者。

peach·blow 〔ˈpitʃˌblo; ˈpiːtʃblou〕 *n.* ①紫紅色釉藥。②紫紅色。

pea·chick 〔ˈpiˌtʃik; ˈpiːtʃik〕 *n.* ①小孔雀。②好自炫之青年。

peach·y 〔ˈpitʃɪ; ˈpiːtʃi〕 *adj.*, **peach·i·er, peach·i·est.** ①似桃的;桃色的。②〖俚〗愉快的;頂好的;美好的。

pea·cock** 〔ˈpiˌkɑk; ˈpiːkɔk〕 *n., pl.* **-cocks** or **-cock,** *v.* —*n.* ①孔雀。②好自炫的人。a peacock in pride*** 開了屏的孔雀。***be as proud as a peacock*** 非常驕傲。***play the peacock*** 誇耀。—*v.i. & v.t.* 炫耀。

peacock blue 孔雀藍。

pea·cock·er·y 〔ˈpiˌkɑkərɪ; ˈpiːkɔkəri〕 *n.* 虛榮;虛飾;炫耀。

pea·cock·ish 〔ˈpiˌkɑkɪʃ; ˈpiːkɔkiʃ〕 *adj.* 似孔雀的;好虛榮的;虛飾的。

peacock ore 斑銅礦。(亦作 **bornite**)

pea·fowl 〔ˈpiˌfaul; ˈpiːfaul〕 *n.* 孔雀(雌雄通用)。

pea green 淡綠色。

pea·hen 〔ˈpiˌhɛn; ˈpiːˈhen〕 *n.* 雌孔雀。

pea jacket (水手穿) 厚呢短大衣。

***peak¹** 〔pik; piːk〕 *n.* ①山尖;山峯;山頂。The fog hung heavily on the *peak* of the hill. 霧深深地罩住山頂。②孤山。③頂點。at the *peak* of his career. 在他的事業之頂點。④尖頭;尖端。⑤帽舌。⑥船頭與船尾的尖狹部分。⑦斜桁的尖頭。—*v.t. & v.i.* ①豎起。②到達高峯;達於頂點。—*adj.* 巔峯的;最高的。The street at *peak* hours is congested with traffic. 那條街在尖峯時刻交通擁塞。

peak² *v.i.* ①憔悴;衰弱。②漸小或漸弱而終於消失〖常 out〗. ***peak and pine*** 憔悴。

peaked¹ 〔ˈpikɪd, pikt; piːkt〕 *adj.* 尖的;尖頂的。

peak·ed² 〔ˈpikɪd; ˈpiːkid〕 *adj.* 瘦削的;憔悴的。

peak-fresh 〔ˈpikˈfrɛʃ; ˈpiːkˈfreʃ〕 *adj.* (水果、蔬菜等) 新鮮應時的。

peak-hour 〔ˈpikˌaur; ˈpiːkˌauə〕 *adj.* 最高峯時刻的;鼎盛期的。

peak load ①〖電、機械〗(發電所的)最高載荷。②(一定期間內的) 最大運輸量 (荷重、負擔)。

peak·y¹ 〔ˈpikɪ; ˈpiːki〕 *adj.*, **peak·i·er, peak·i·est.** 多峯的;成峯的;似峯的;尖的。

peak·y² *adj.*, **peak·i·er, peak·i·est.** ①〖方〗瘦削的;虛弱的;憔悴的。②〖美俚〗快要爛掉的。

***peal** 〔pil; piːl〕 *n.* ①很響的鈴聲。The bells rang a merry *peal.* 鈴響出悅耳的聲音。②一組鐘之交互鳴響。③〖音樂〗一組鐘;鐘樂。④任何宏亮而延長的響聲。a *peal* of thunder. 雷聲隆隆。—*v.t.* 使響;使鳴。to *peal* a bell. 搖鈴。—*v.i.* 響;鳴。

pe·an 〔ˈpiən; ˈpiːən〕 *n.* =**paean.**

***pea·nut** 〔ˈpiˌnʌt; ˈpiːnʌt〕 *n.* ①花生。②花生米。③花生莢。④微小的人。⑤ (*pl.*) 極小之物;不重要之事;極小數額。Compared to present prices I was getting *peanuts.* 與目前的物價相較,我的收入很少。—*adj.* ①不足爲取的;不重要的。*peanut* politicians. 不足爲取的政客。I haven't got all day for this *peanut* case. 我不能整天爲這芝麻蒜皮的事煩心。②花生的;用花生做的。

peanut gallery 〖俚〗①戲院或公共建築中最後與最高之看臺。②無足輕重的批評者。

***pear** 〔pɛr; pɛə〕 *n.* ①梨。②梨樹。③似梨之果實;似梨樹之植物。

pearl¹** 〔pɜl; pəːl〕 *n.* ①珍珠。a culture(d) *pearl.* 養珠。②似珍珠狀物 (如露珠、淚珠)。*Pearls* of dew glistened on the grass. 露珠在草上閃爍。③(同類中)傑出者;珍貴之物。She is a *pearl* among women. 她是女子中的傑出者。④淡藍灰色;珍珠色。⑤珍珠母。⑥珍珠型鉛字(等於5磅因)。⑦皓齒。cast*** (or ***throw***) ***pearls before swine*** 對牛彈琴。—*adj.* ① 淡藍灰色的;珍珠色的。②結成小圓片的;珍珠狀的。—*v.i.* ①採集珍珠。②珍珠一般地滾動。Rain *pearled* down the window. 雨水珍珠一般滾下了玻璃窗。—*v.t.* 在…成珠。Sweat *pearled* his forehead. 汗水在他額頭上成珠。

pearl² *v.t., n.* =**purl².**

pearl·ash 〔ˈpɜlˌæʃ; ˈpəːlæʃ〕 *n.* 〖化〗珠灰(粗製碳酸鉀)。

pearl barley 眞珠麥;揉搓成圓粒之大麥。

pearl fisher 採珠人;採珠業者。

pearl-fish·er·y 〔ˈpɜlˌfɪʃərɪ; ˈpəːlˌfiʃəri〕 *n.* 採珠業;採珠場。

pearl gray (or **grey**) 珍珠色;稍帶藍色的淡灰色。

Pearl Harbor ①珍珠港(夏威夷Oahu島南部之一海灣)。②毀滅性偷襲。the possibility of atomic *Pearl Harbors.* 原子彈毀滅性偷襲之可能。③對…作毀滅性偷襲。the danger of being *Pearl Harbored.* 受毀滅性偷襲之危險。

pearl·ies 〔ˈpɜlɪz; ˈpəːliz〕 *n.* 〖俚〗有珍珠鈕扣之衣服。

pearl oyster 〖動物〗珍珠貝。

pearl powder 鉛白 (化妝用的白粉)。

pearl shell 〖動物〗珍珠貝;夜光貝。

pearl white ①氯化氧鉍 (白色粉末,用製化妝香粉)。②硝酸氧鉍 (製化妝品、瓷釉等)。③魚鱗粉(人造珠的原料)。④珍珠白(帶微藍色的白色)。—*adj.* 似珍珠一般白的。

pearl-white 〔ˈpɜlˈhwaɪt; ˈpəːlˈwait〕

pearl·y 〔ˈpɜlɪ; ˈpəːli〕 *adj.*, **pearl·i·er, pearl·i·est.** ①似珍珠的。②有珍珠的;飾以珍珠的。

pearly nautilus 〖動物〗鸚鵡螺 (一種海產軟體動物)。

pear·main 〔ˈpɛrmen; ˈpɛəmein〕 *n.* 一種蘋果。

pear-shaped 〔ˈpɛrˌʃept; ˈpɛəʃeipt〕 *adj.* ①梨狀的。②(嗓音) 清脆宏亮的。

Pear·son 〔ˈpɪrsn̩; ˈpiəsn〕 *n.* 皮爾遜 (Lester Bowles, 1897-1972, 加拿大政治家, 1957年獲諾貝爾和平獎)。

peart 〔pɜt, pɪrt; piət〕 *adj.* 〖方〗①活潑的;精神蓬勃的。②聰明的;機智的。

pear tree 梨樹。

***peas·ant** 〔ˈpɛznt; ˈpezənt〕 *n.* ①(歐洲的)農夫。②土包子。—*adj.* 農夫的。*peasant* labor. 農工。

peas·ant·ry 〔ˈpɛzn̩trɪ; ˈpezəntri〕 *n.* ①農夫(集合稱)。②農夫之性格或地位。

pease·cod 〔ˈpizˌkɑd; ˈpiːzkɔd〕 *n.* 豆莢。

pease-pud·ding 〔ˈpizˌpudɪŋ; ˈpiːzˌpudiŋ〕 *n.* 豆粉布丁。

pea·shoot·er 〔ˈpiˌʃutə; ˈpiːˌʃuːtə〕 *n.* 豆槍 (一種玩具)。

pea soup ①豌豆湯。②淡黃色濃霧。

pea-soup·er [ˈpiˌsupɚ; ˈpiːˌsuːpə] *n.* ①〖俗〗濃霧。②〖加俚〗法裔加拿大人。
peat [pit; piːt] *n.* 泥炭;土煤。
peat bog 泥煤田;泥煤沼。
peat moss ①泥煤苔。② =**peat bog.**
peat-reek [ˈpitˌrik; ˈpiːt-riːk] *n.* ①燒泥炭的煙。②燃燒泥炭以蒸餾威士忌的特殊香味。
peat·y [ˈpitɪ; ˈpiːti] *adj.* 似泥炭的;多泥炭的。
pea·vey [ˈpivɪ; ˈpiːvi] *n.* 伐木用皮維桿。
pea·vy [ˈpivɪ; ˈpiːvi] *n., pl.* **-vies.** =**peavey.**
*__peb·ble__ [ˈpɛbl̩; ˈpebl] *n., v.,* **-bled, -bling.** —*n.* ①小圓石。②(皮革、紙等上的)粗表面;粗紋。*pebble* leather. 粗鞣皮。—*v.t.* ①以小圓石投擊。②覆以小圓石或圓石狀物。③用小圓石鋪砌。④製(革)使具粗雜表面。
peb·bly [ˈpɛblɪ, ˈpɛbl̩ɪ; ˈpebli] *adj.,* **-bli·er, -bli·est.** ①多石子的; 多礫的。②粗紋的; 粗面的。
pe·can [pɪˈkɑn; piˈkæn] *n.* ①一種大胡桃(產於美國南部)。②胡桃樹。
pec·ca·bil·i·ty [ˌpɛkəˈbɪlətɪ; ˌpekəˈbiliti] *n.* 易犯罪;易犯過失。
pec·ca·ble [ˈpɛkəbl̩; ˈpekəbl] *adj.* 易犯罪的;易有過失的。
pec·ca·dil·lo [ˌpɛkəˈdɪlo; ˌpekəˈdilou] *n., pl.* **-los, -loes.** 輕罪;小過失。
pec·can·cy [ˈpɛkənsɪ; ˈpekənsi] *n., pl.* **-cies.** 犯罪; 罪過。
pec·cant [ˈpɛkənt; ˈpekənt] *adj.* ①有罪的;犯罪的。②有過錯的;失誤的。③不健康的;有病的;致病的。
pec·ca·ry [ˈpɛkərɪ; ˈpekəri] *n., pl.* **-ries, -ry.** 〖動物〗西貒(美洲產形似豬)。
peck[1] [pɛk; pek] *n.* ①配克(乾量單位,等於二加侖)。②大量;許多。
*__peck__[2] *v.t.* ①以喙啄;以喙啄食。②啄穿。③挖出;掘出。—*v.i.* ①啄。②一點點地慢慢吃。③(以喙)對準而啄。***peck at*** **a.** 〖俗〗不斷地批評或吹毛求疵。My wife keeps *pecking at* me. 我的太太不斷地挑我的毛病。**b.** 〖俗〗祇吃一點兒;慢慢地吃。**c.** 啄。**d.** 〖俗〗扔(石頭)。***peck out*** **a.** 啄出。**b.** 用食指按鍵打字(按美國記者多用這種打字方式)。—*n.* ①啄擊。②被啄之痕跡或傷。③〖俗〗匆匆一吻。④〖英俚〗食物。
peck·er [ˈpɛkɚ; ˈpekə] *n.* ①能啄之鳥(主要用於複合字,如 woodpecker)。②尖頭器具。③〖英俚〗精神;勇氣。 to keep one's *pecker* up. 打起精神來。④〖俚、鄙〗男性生殖器。
peck·ing order [ˈpɛkɪŋ~; ˈpekiŋ~] 任何團體中之長幼尊卑次序。
peck·ish [ˈpɛkɪʃ; ˈpekiʃ] *adj.* ①〖俗〗饑餓的。②好嘮叨的。
peck order =**pecking order.**
Peck·sniff [ˈpɛkˌsnɪf; ˈpek-snif] *n.* 僞君子 (Charles Dickens 小說 *Martin Chuzzlewit* 中之人物)。—**i·an,** *adj.*
pec·ten [ˈpɛktən; ˈpektən] *n., pl.* **-ti·nes** [-tɪˌniz; -tiniːz]. ① 〖解剖〗恥骨。②〖動物〗櫛膜;櫛狀部;櫛狀突起;櫛狀器官。
pec·tin [ˈpɛktɪn; ˈpektin] *n.* 〖化〗果膠;黏膠質。
pec·ti·nate [ˈpɛktɪnˌet; ˈpektineit] *adj.* 櫛狀的;櫛齒狀的。
pec·ti·na·tion [ˌpɛktəˈneʃən; ˌpektiˈneiʃən] *n.* ①櫛狀部分。②犬牙相錯。
pec·to·ral [ˈpɛktərəl; ˈpektərəl] *adj.* ①胸的; 胸腔中的。②佩於胸前的。③發自內心的; 主觀的。④(言語)深沉的。⑤治療胸或肺的。—*n.* ①佩於胸部之飾物或保護物。②治療胸或肺之藥物。③〖動物〗胸鰭;胸肌。
pec·u·late [ˈpɛkjəˌlet; ˈpekjuleit] *v.,* **-lat·ed, -lat·ing.** —*v.t.* 侵吞(公款、公物);盜用(公款、公物)。—*v.i.* 盜用公款。
pec·u·la·tion [ˌpɛkjəˈleʃən; ˌpekjuˈleiʃən] *n.* 盜用公款或公物。
pec·u·la·tor [ˈpɛkjəˌletɚ; ˈpekjuleitə] *n.* 挪用公款者;盜用公物者。
*__pe·cul·iar__ [pɪˈkjuljɚ; piˈkjuːljə] *adj.* ①奇異的; 罕有的; 怪僻的。 a *peculiar* old man. 一怪僻的老人。②特有的; 特殊的。—*n.* 專有之特權或私產。
peculiar institution 南北戰爭前美國南部各州之黑奴制度。
*__pe·cu·li·ar·i·ty__ [pɪˌkjulɪˈærətɪ; piˌkjuːliˈæriti] *n., pl.* **-ties.** ①奇異;怪僻;不平常。*peculiarities* of speech. 言談之怪異。②奇異之事物; 怪僻之事物。③特質; 特色;特性。④特徵;特點;迥異之處。
*__pe·cu·liar·ly__ [pɪˈkjuljəlɪ; piˈkjuːljəli] *adv.* ①特有地。a *peculiarly* French phenomenon. 法國特有的現象。②特別地。③奇異地;不平常地。
pe·cu·ni·ar·i·ly [pɪˈkjunɪˌɛrɪlɪ; piˈkjuːnjərili] *adv.* 在金錢上;在金錢方面。
pe·cu·ni·ar·y [pɪˈkjunɪˌɛrɪ; piˈkjuːnjəri] *adj.* ①金錢的; 金錢上的。*pecuniary* penalties. 罰金。②罰金的。
-ped 〖字尾〗表"足"之義。
ped. ①pedal. ②pedestal.
ped·a·gog [ˈpɛdəˌgɑg; ˈpedəgɔg] *n.* = **pedagogue.**
ped·a·gog·ic [ˌpɛdəˈgɑdʒɪk; ˌpedəˈgɔdʒik] *adj.* ①教師的;小學教師的。②教學的;教學法的;教育學的。
ped·a·gog·i·cal [ˌpɛdəˈgɑdʒɪkl̩; ˌpedəˈgɔdʒikl] *adj.* =**pedagogic.** —**ly,** *adv.*
ped·a·gog·ics [ˌpɛdəˈgɑdʒɪks; ˌpedəˈgɔdʒiks] *n.* =**pedagogy.**
ped·a·gog(u)·ism [ˈpɛdəˌgɑgɪzəm; ˈpedəgɔgizm] *n.* ①兒童教授法。②教師架子;學究氣。
ped·a·gogue [ˈpɛdəˌgɑg; ˈpedəgɔg] *n.* ①教師;小學教師(常蔑)。②好爲人師的腐儒。
ped·a·go·gy [ˈpɛdəˌgodʒɪ; ˈpedəgɔgi] *n.* ①教授;教學。②教育學;教授法;教學技術。
*__ped·al__ [ˈpɛdl̩; ˈpedl] *n., v.,* **-al(l)ed, -al(l)ing,** *adj.* —*n.* 踏板(例如脚踏車或風琴上的踏板)。—*v.t.* 用脚踏動。—*v.i.* ①踏動踏板。②騎脚踏車。—*adj.* ①脚的;與脚有關的。②踏板的;由踏板構成的。
pedal point 〖音樂〗持續音(部); 持續低音(部)。
pedal pusher 〖美〗①騎脚踏車的人;自行車賽跑選手。②(*pl.*)(體育用)女用短外褲(原爲騎脚踏車用)。
ped·ant [ˈpɛdn̩t; ˈpedənt] *n.* ①腐儒;迂闊之人。②愛炫耀學問之人。
pe·dan·tic [pɪˈdæntɪk; piˈdæntik] *adj.* ①好賣弄學問的。②迂腐的。—**al·ly,** *adv.*
ped·ant·ry [ˈpɛdn̩trɪ; ˈpedəntri] *n., pl.* **-ries.** ①自炫博學; 賣弄學問。②迂闊。
ped·ate [ˈpɛdet; ˈpedeit] *adj.* ①〖動物〗有足的。②足狀的。③〖植物〗鳥足狀的(葉)。
ped·dle [ˈpɛdl̩; ˈpedl] *v.,* **-dled, -dling.** —*v.i.* ①沿街叫賣。②作小販。③做無聊事。—*v.t.* ①叫賣; 販賣。②播弄(謠言等)。to *peddle* gossip. 閒談撥弄是非。
*__ped·dler__ [ˈpɛdlɚ; ˈpedlə] *n.* 小販。(亦作 **pedlar, pedler**)

ped·dler·y [ˈpɛdlərɪ; ˈpedləri] *n.* ①擔賣;小販業。②小販所賣的東西。

ped·dling [ˈpɛdlɪŋ; ˈpedliŋ] *adj.* ①不重要的;瑣碎的;小心眼的。②做小販生意的。

ped·es·tal** [ˈpɛdɪstl; ˈpedistl] *n., v.,* **-taled** or **-talled, -tal·ing** or **-tal·ling.** —*n.* ①半身塑像的座。②瓶或燈的座。③根基;基礎。place on a pedestal*** 置於崇高地位;崇拜。***set a person on a pedestal*** 把某人當做十全十美;把某人理想化。—*v.t.* ①置於臺座上。②置於崇高地位。

***pe·des·tri·an** [pəˈdɛstrɪən; piˈdestriən] *n.* 步行者。—*adj.* ①徒步的。②平凡的;缺乏想像的。a *pedestrian* style in writing. 呆板的文體。

pe·des·tri·an·ism [pəˈdɛstrɪənˌɪzəm; piˈdestriənizm] *n.* ①步行;步行主義。②(文體等的)平凡;單調。

pe·di·at·ric [ˌpidɪˈætrɪk, ˌpɛdɪ-; ˌpiːdiˈætrik] *adj.* 〖醫〗小兒科的。

pe·di·a·tri·cian [ˌpidɪəˈtrɪʃən; ˌpiːdiəˈtriʃən] *n.* 小兒科醫師。(亦作 **pediatrist**)

pe·di·at·rics [ˌpidɪ ˈætrɪks; ˌpiːdiˈætriks] *n.* 〖醫〗小兒科。

ped·i·cab [ˈpɛdɪkæb; ˈpedikæb] *n.* (載客之脚踏)三輪車。

ped·i·cel [ˈpɛdəsl; ˈpedisl] *n.* =**pedicle. —lar,** *adj.*

ped·i·cel·late [ˈpɛdəsəlɪt; ˈpedisəlit] *adj.* ①〖植物〗有小花梗的。②〖動物〗有肉莖的。

ped·i·cle [ˈpɛdɪkl; ˈpedikl] *n.* ①〖植物〗小花梗。②〖動物〗肉莖;梗節。

pe·dic·u·lar [pɪˈdɪkjələ˞; piˈdikjulə] *adj.* =**pediculous.**

pe·dic·u·late [pɪˈdɪkjəlɪt; piˈdikjulit] *adj.*〖動物〗柄鰭目的。—*n.* 柄鰭目之魚。

pe·dic·u·lous [pɪˈdɪkjələs; piˈdikjuləs] *adj.* 虱的;多虱的。

ped·i·cure [ˈpɛdɪˌkjʊr; ˈpedikjuə] *n.* ①脚病治療。②脚病醫生。③修脚指甲。

ped·i·gree [ˈpɛdəˌgri; ˈpedigriː] *n.* ①家系;系譜。②血統;門閥。③純種家畜血統表。④語源。⑤根源。—*adj.* 純種的;血統可考的。

ped·i·greed [ˈpɛdəˌgrid; ˈpedigriːd] *adj.* ①(純種家畜)血統可考的。②望族的。

ped·i·ment [ˈpɛdəmənt; ˈpedimənt] *n.* 〖建築〗(古代建築之)山形牆;三角牆。②(門戶、壁爐等上之)三角楣飾。

ped·lar [ˈpɛdlə˞; ˈpedlə] *n.* =**peddler.**

ped·lar·y, ped·ler·y [ˈpɛdlərɪ; ˈpedləri] *n.* =**peddlery.**

pe·do·bap·tism [ˌpidoˈbæptɪzm; ˌpiːdouˈbæptizm] *n.* 幼兒洗禮(論)。—**pe·do·bap·tist,** *n.*

pe·dol·o·gy [pɪˈdɑlədʒɪ; piˈdɔlədʒi] *n.* 土壤之原始與分類學。

pe·dom·e·ter [pɪˈdɑmətə˞; piˈdɔmitə] *n.* 記步器;步程計。

ped·rail [ˈpɛdrel; ˈpedreil] *n.* ①無限軌道式車輪;履帶。②此種車輛。

pe·dun·cle [pɪˈdʌŋkl; piˈdʌŋkl] *n.*〖植物〗花梗;花序柄。②〖動物〗肉莖。③〖解剖〗橋臂。—**pe·dun·cu·lar,** *adj.*

pe·dun·cu·late [pɪˈdʌŋkjʊˌlɪt; piˈdʌŋkjulit] *adj.* ①〖植物〗有花梗的;生於花梗上的。②〖動物〗有肉莖的。

peek [pik; piːk] *v.i.* 偷看;窺見。—*n.* 偷看;瞥望。

peek·a·boo, peek-a-boo [ˈpikəˌbu; ˈpiːkəbuː] *n.* =**bopeep.** —*adj.* 部分顯露的;驚人暴露的。

peel** [pil; piːl] *n.* 果皮。candied *peel.* 蜜餞的果皮。—*v.t.* ①剝…之皮;去…之皮。to *peel* an apple. 削蘋果皮。②剝(皮)。—*v.i.* ①脫皮。The bark *peels* off. 樹皮脫落。②〖俗〗脫去衣服(以作運動等)。③脫離一個團體。peel off* a.** (飛機)突然成陡角度轉彎飛離機羣。**b.** 脫離一個團體。

peeled [pild; piːld] *adj.* 剝去皮的。***keep one's eyes peeled*** 〖美俗〗留意。

peel·er¹ [ˈpilə˞; ˈpiːlə] *n.* ①剝皮者(器)。②脫殼時期的蟹。③脫衣舞孃。④充滿幹勁者。⑤一種棉花。

peel·er² *n.* ①(原指)愛爾蘭的警官。②〖英俚〗警察;警員。

peel·ing [ˈpilɪŋ; ˈpiːliŋ] *n.* 果皮;剝下的(尤指馬鈴薯的)皮;剝皮。

peen [pin; piːn] *n.* 錘之尖頭。—*v.t.* 以錘之尖頭錘。

***peep¹** [pip; piːp] *v.i.* ①(自洞隙中)觀望。②竊視;窺視。to *peep* over a wall. 自牆頭窺視。③微現;現出。Stars are beginning to *peep.* 星星開始出現。—*v.t.* 使微現;使微突。—*n.* ①有限制的瞭望;窺視。②窺視之孔或縫。③一瞥。④初現。*peep* of day. 白晝之初現。

peep² *n.* (小鳥)啾啾的叫聲;唧唧。—*v.i.* ①(小鳥)啾啾叫;唧唧叫。②悄聲地說。

peep·er¹ [ˈpipə˞; ˈpiːpə] *n.* ①偷看者;愛刨根問底的人。②〖俚〗眼睛。③〖俗〗窺視所藉經之物(如鏡子、窗子、眼鏡等)。

peep·er² *n.* ①作啾啾聲之人或物;唧唧叫的鳥;小鳥;小鷄。②蛙的一種。

peep·hole [ˈpipˌhol; ˈpiːphoul] *n.* 窺看之孔隙。

Peeping Tom ①英國傳說中的人物,傳因偷看 Lady Godiva 裸體騎馬而瞎了眼。②(有時作 p- t-)愛偷看(裸體女人等)的人。

peep show 西洋鏡(置各種畫片於箱中,用放大鏡窺視之裝置);洋片。

peep sight (鎗砲等之)覘孔。

***peer¹** [pɪr; piə] *n.* ①同輩;同儕。②匹敵。without *peer.* 無匹敵。③貴族。the king and his *peers.* 國王和他的貴族們。

***peer²** *v.i.* ①細看;凝視。She *peered* at the tag to read the price. 她細看標籤以辨認價格。②窺視。to *peer* into a dark cave. 窺視一黑洞。③出現。The sun was *peering* from behind a cloud. 太陽自雲後出現。

peer·age [ˈpɪrɪdʒ; ˈpiəridʒ] *n.* ①貴族的地位或身分。②貴族(集合稱)。③貴族名鑑。

peer·ess [ˈpɪrɪs; ˈpiəris] *n.* ①貴族夫人。②女貴族;貴婦。

peer·less [ˈpɪrlɪs; ˈpiəlis] *adj.* 無匹敵的;無比的;無雙的;絕世的。**—ly,** *adv.* **—ness,** *n.*

peeve [piv; piːv] *v.,* **peeved, peev·ing,** *n.* —*v.t.* & *v.i.* 〖俗〗(使)惱怒;(使)氣惱;(使)變乖戾。—*n.* 〖俗〗①令人氣惱之事物;討厭的東西。②惱怒;氣惱。

pee·vish [ˈpivɪʃ; ˈpiːviʃ] *adj.* 脾氣乖張的;易怒的;好抱怨的。

pee·wee [ˈpiwi; ˈpiːwiː] *n.* ①=**pewee.** ②〖美俗,方〗矮子;小動物;小東西。—*adj.* 矮小的。

pee·wit [ˈpiwɪt; ˈpiːwit] *n.* =**pewit.**

peg** [pɛg; peg] *n., v.,* **pegged, peg·ging,** *adj.* —*n.* ①木栓;木釘。②釘子;掛釘。hat *pegs.* 掛帽釘。③塞桶洞用的木塞。④衣服夾。⑤軫(調絃鬆緊者)。⑥原因;藉口;遁詞。⑦〖俗〗等級;程度。to come down a *peg.* 稍降一級。⑧〖英〗蘇打水與白蘭地混合之飲料。⑨〖俗〗腿(有時指木質之腿)。⑩〖棒球〗投球(尤指外野手投向守壘者之球)。⑪=**news peg.** ***a peg

to hang* (*something*) *on 作(某事)之藉口。 ***a square peg in a round hole*** 方枘圓鑿;不適任的人。 ***take a person down a peg*** (***or two***) 挫某人之銳氣;使受辱。—*v.t.* ①以木釘釘牢。 to *peg* something down. 用木釘釘於地上。②以木標定界。 to *peg* out a mining claim. 劃定採鑛權地界。③以固定價格抛售或收買(股票等)以穩定其價格。④〖俗〗抛;扔;擲。⑤〖英〗晾(衣服)。⑥認定;斷定。 They *pegged* it as the cause of unemployment. 他們認定這就是失業的原因。⑦投球給守壘者以封殺(跑壘者)。⑧〖新聞〗以…爲題而寫(一則報導或特寫)〖常on〗。—*v.i.* ①孜孜操作。②(槌球戲中)以球擊中標樁。③急行。 She *pegged* down the stairs. 她急步下樓。 ***peg at*** 以木樁打。 ***peg away*** (***at...***) 辛勤地做…。 ***peg down*** 約束某人。 ***peg out*** 失敗;死;力竭。 He may *peg out* at any moment. 他隨時可能死去。—*adj.* (褲管)越往下端越細的。

Peg·a·sus [ˈpɛgəsəs; ˈpegəsəs] *n.* ①〖希臘神話〗Muses 神所騎之飛馬。②詩的靈感。③〖天文〗飛馬座。

Peg·gy [ˈpɛgɪ; ˈpegi] *n.* 女子名。

peg leg 〖俗〗①木製假腿。②裝有木製假腿的人。

peg-legged [ˈpɛgˌlɛgd; ˈpeglegd] *adj.* 裝有木製假腿的。

peg top ①(梨形)木陀螺。②(*pl.*)陀螺形的褲子。③陀螺形的裙子。

peg-top [ˈpɛgˌtɑp; ˈpegtɔp] *adj.* 陀螺形的。

peign·oir [ˈpenwɑr; ˈpeinwɑː] 〖法〗 *n.* 婦女之睡衣;婦女之浴衣。

Pei·ping [ˈpeˈpɪŋ, ˈbeˈpɪŋ; peiˈpiŋ, ˈpeiˈpiŋ] *n.* 北平。

pe·jo·rate [ˈpidʒəˌret; ˈpiːdʒəreit] *v.,* **-rat·ed, -rat·ing.** —*v.t.* 使惡化;使變壞。—*v.i.* 變壞;惡化。

pe·jo·ra·tion [ˌpidʒəˈreʃən; ˌpiːdʒəˈreiʃən] *n.* ①變壞;惡化。②〖語言〗(字義)變壞。

pe·jo·ra·tive [ˈpidʒəˌretɪv; ˈpiːdʒərətiv] *adj.* ①貶損的;變壞的;(使)惡化的(爲 meliorative 之對)。②輕侮的;侮蔑的。—*n.* 蔑稱;輕蔑語,如 poetaster 等。

Pe·kin [ˈpikɪn, ˈpiˈkɪn; piːˈkin, ˈpiːˈk-] *n.* ①=**Peking.** ②北平鴨。③(p-)一種絲織物。

Pe·king [ˈpiˈkɪŋ; piːˈkiŋ] *n.* 北京(北平之舊稱)。

Pe·king·ese [ˌpikɪŋˈiz; ˌpiːkiŋˈiːz] *n., pl.* **-ese,** *adj.* —*n.* ①北平人。②北京官話。③哈巴狗。—*adj.* 北平的;北平人的。

Peking man 北京人。

Pe·king·ol·o·gy [ˌpikɪŋˈɑlədʒɪ; ˌpiːkiŋˈɔlədʒi] *n.* 北京學(特指對中共之研究)。(亦作 **Pekinology**)

pe·koe [ˈpiko; ˈpiːkou] *n.* 由嫩葉製成的上等紅茶。

pel·age [ˈpɛlɪdʒ; ˈpelidʒ] *n.* (哺乳動物的)毛皮;毛。

pe·lag·ic [pəˈlædʒɪk; peˈlædʒik] *adj.* ①遠洋的;大洋的。 *pelagic* fishery. 遠洋漁業。②捕海豹者的。

Pel·ar·go·ni·um [ˌpɛlɑrˈgonɪəm; ˌpeləˈgounjəm] *n.* 〖植物〗①天竺葵屬。②(p-)天竺葵屬之植物;天竺葵。

pel·er·ine [ˌpɛləˈrin; ˈpeləriːn] *n.* (女用)毛皮的細長披肩。

pelf [pɛlf; pelf] *n.* ①金錢;財物;阿堵物(輕蔑語)。②〖英方〗廢物;垃圾。

pel·i·can [ˈpɛlɪkən; ˈpelikən] *n.* 塘鵝;鵜鶘(一種食魚鳥)。

pe·lisse [pəˈlis; peˈliːs] *n.* ①婦女之長外衣。②皮裏的上衣;皮上衣。

pel·la·gra [pəˈlegrə; pəˈleigrə] *n.* 〖醫〗玉蜀黍疹;義大利癩病(一種皮膚病)。

pel·la·grin [pəˈlegrɪn; pəˈleigrin] *n.* 玉蜀黍疹患者。

pel·la·grous [pəˈlegrəs; pəˈleigrəs] *adj.* 〖醫〗玉蜀黍疹的;患玉蜀黍疹的。

pel·let [ˈpɛlɪt; ˈpelit] *n.* ①小球;小丸。②小彈丸。③藥丸。—*v.t.* ①作成小球或小丸。②射擊(小彈丸)。

pel·li·cle [ˈpɛlɪkl; ˈpelikl] *n.* 薄膜;薄皮;表皮。

pell-mell, pell·mell [ˈpɛlˈmɛl; ˈpelˈmel] *adv.* ①雜亂地;混亂地。②紛忙地。—*adj.* ①紛亂的;混亂的。②倉促的。—*v.t.* 使混雜。—*v.i.* 倉促行走。—*n.* 極度混亂。

pel·lu·cid [pəˈlusɪd; peˈljuːsid] *adj.* ①清澈的;透明的。②易解的;明晰的。③帶有光澤的。—**ly,** *adv.*

pe·lo·ta [peˈlotə; peˈloutə] *n.* 回力球(在中南美稱 **jai-alai**).

pelt[1] [pɛlt; pelt] *n.* ①(獸類之)生皮;毛皮。②〖諧〗(人類之)皮膚。

*__pelt__[2] *v.t.* ①投擲;投擊。 The boys were *pelting* the dog with stones. 孩子們以石頭擲向那狗。②抛出;使(雨等)急降。③(以惡言等)質問。—*v.i.* ①投擲。②(雨)急降。 The rain is *pelting* down. 大雨驟降。③惡言相責;惡言相罵。④急急前行。⑤連打。—*n.* ①投擲;投擊。②速力;急速。③連打聲。 ***at full pelt*** 全速地。—**er,** *n.*

pel·tate [ˈpɛltet; ˈpelteit] *adj.* 〖植物〗(葉)楯狀的。

pelt·ry [ˈpɛltrɪ; ˈpeltri] *n., pl.* **-ries.** ①生皮;毛皮(集合稱)。②(一張)毛皮。

pel·vic [ˈpɛlvɪk; ˈpelvik] *adj.* 〖解剖〗骨盤的;骨盆的。

pel·vis [ˈpɛlvɪs; ˈpelvis] *n., pl.* **-ves** [-viz; -viːz]. 〖解剖〗①骨盤;骨盆。②骨盆骨。

pem·mi·can [ˈpɛmɪkən; ˈpemikən] *n.* (北美印第安人所製之)乾肉餅;探險家預備的乾肉餅。(亦作 **pemican**)

‡**pen**[1] [pɛn; pen] *n., v.,* **penned, pen·ning.** —*n.* ①筆;鋼筆。 a fountain *pen.* 自來水筆。 to write in *pen* and ink. 用筆墨寫。②文體;文章;文筆。 to live by one's *pen.* 藉寫作過活。 to draw one's *pen* against... 寫文章攻擊…。 to drive a *pen.* 書寫。 a fluent *pen.* 流利之文體。③作家。—*v.t.* ①寫。 I *penned* a few words to father today. 我今天給父親寫了一封短信。②起草(文件)。

*__pen__[2] *n., v.,* **penned** or **pent, pen·ning.** —*n.* ①(家畜的)圍欄;圈;檻。 a *pen* for pigs. 豬欄。②圍在欄或檻中的家畜。③任何小圍場。 a play *pen* for babies. 供小兒遊玩的小圍場。④〖俚〗感化院;監獄。—*v.t.* ①關入欄中。 Shepherds *pen* their flocks. 牧羊人把他們的羊羣關入欄中。②監禁;關閉。

pen[3] *n.* 雌天鵝。

Pen., pen. peninsula.

P.E.N. International Association of Poets, Playwrights, Editors, Essayists and Novelists. 國際筆會。

pe·nal [ˈpinl; ˈpiːnl] *adj.* ①刑事的;刑罰的。②應受處罰的。③用作處罰之地的。 a *penal* colony. 囚犯隔離區。④作罰金的。—**ly,** *adv.*

penal code 刑事法之集合稱。

pe·nal·ize [ˈpinlˌaɪz; ˈpiːnəlaiz] *v.t.,* **-ized, -iz·ing.** ①宣告有罪。②規定應罰;科罰。 Speeding on city streets is *penalized.* 在市內街道上開快車要受罰。③宣布犯規;處罰。—**pe·nal·i·za·tion,** *n.*

penal servitude〖英〗監禁與苦役之合併處分。

penal sum 罰金。

*__pen·al·ty__ [ˈpɛnltɪ; ˈpenlti] *n.*, *pl.* **-ties.** ①懲罰；刑罰。the *penalty* for speeding. (駛車)逾速之處罰。②罰金；違約金。③(遊戲、運動等中之)罰。*penalty* area. (足球)罰球區。④不利；障礙；困難。***under*** (or ***on***) ***penalty of*** 違法處以…之罰。forbidden *under penalty of* death. 違者處以死刑。

*__pen·ance__ [ˈpɛnəns; ˈpenəns] *n.*, *v.*, **-anced, -anc·ing.** —*n.* ①(贖罪的)懲罰；苦行。②告解(天主教七聖事之一)。***do penance*** 苦修。—*v.t.* 令作苦修；加以懲罰(以贖罪)。

pen-and-ink [ˈpɛnəndˈɪŋk; ˈpenəndˈiŋk] *adj.* 用筆墨書寫或描畫的。

Pe·nang [pɪˈnæŋ; piˈnæŋ] *n.* ①檳榔嶼(在馬來亞聯邦西北部)。②檳榔(馬來亞聯邦之一州，首府 George Town)。

pen·an·nu·lar [pɛˈnænjulɚ; peˈnænjulə] *adj.* 幾乎成環狀的；不完全之圓圈的。

pe·na·tes [pəˈnetiz; pəˈneitiːz] *n. pl.* 〖羅馬神話〗家庭之守護神。

pence [pɛns; pens]〖英〗*n.* pl. of **penny.**

pen·chant [ˈpɛntʃənt; ˈpɑːŋʃɑːŋ] *n.* 傾向；嗜好；愛好。

‡**pen·cil** [ˈpɛnsl; ˈpensl] *n.*, *v.*, **-cil(l)ed, -cil·(l)ing.** —*n.* ①鉛筆。a *pencil* case. 鉛筆盒。②色筆。③似鉛筆之物。④着色之枝形物(如畫眉筆等)。⑤畫筆。⑥光線錐(由一點發出或輻集於一點之一束線條或光線)。⑦畫法；畫風；繪畫術。—*v.t.* 用鉛筆寫；用鉛筆等畫或標出。to *pencil* the eyebrows. 畫眉毛。

pencil compass 圓規。

pen·cil(l)ed [ˈpɛnsld; ˈpensld] *adj.* ①用鉛筆寫或畫的；用眉筆畫的。*penciled* eyebrows. 畫過的眉。②〖動、植物〗有明顯細線的。③〖光學〗光線錐的。

pen·cil·(l)er [ˈpɛnslɚ; ˈpenslə] *n.* ①用鉛筆寫的人。②〖賽馬〗賭帳簿記員。

pencil pusher〖俚〗辦公室工作者；坐辦公桌者；管帳先生。

pencil sharpener 鉛筆鉋。

pen·craft [ˈpɛnˌkræft; ˈpen-krɑːft] *n.* ①筆法；書法；文筆。②書寫。③著作業。

pend [pɛnd; pend] *v.i.* ①下垂；懸垂。②未決；未定。—*v.t.* 使未決；使未定。

pend·ant [ˈpɛndənt; ˈpendənt] *n.* ①(項鍊、耳環、手鐲上的)垂飾。②天花板或屋頂之垂下飾物。③懷錶之有環錶柄。④一雙中之一個。—*adj.* =**pendent.**

pend·en·cy [ˈpɛndənsɪ; ˈpendənsi] *n.* 懸垂；未決；未定。

pend·ent [ˈpɛndənt; ˈpendənt] *adj.* ①下垂的；懸垂的。②伸出的；凸出的。③懸而未決的。④即將發生的；即將來臨的。—*n.* =**pendant.**

pen·den·te li·te [pɛnˈdɛntiˈlaɪti; penˈdentiːˈlaitiː]〖拉〗在訴訟中(=pending the suit)。

pend·ing [ˈpɛndɪŋ; ˈpendiŋ] *adj.* ①未決定的；待解決的。a *pending* question. 懸案。②懸垂的。③即將發生的；即將來臨的。—*prep.* ①在…之中。*pending* these discussions. 在討論中。②在…前；直到。*pending* his return. 在他回來之前。

pen·drag·on [pɛnˈdrægən; penˈdrægən] *n.* (古代 Britain 之)霸主；首領。

pen·du·lous [ˈpɛndʒələs; ˈpendjuləs] *adj.* ①下垂的；懸垂的。②擺動的；振動的。③猶豫不決的；忽高忽低的。

*__pen·du·lum__ [ˈpɛndʒələm; ˈpendjuləm] *n.* 擺；鐘擺。simple (compound) *pendulum.* 單(複)擺。***the swing of the pendulum*** 任何事物(如輿論等)自一極端至另一極端的變化。

pe·ne·plain [ˈpinəˌplen; ˈpiːnəplein] *n.* 〖地質〗準平原。(亦作 **peneplane**)

pen·e·tra·bil·i·ty [ˌpɛnətrəˈbɪlətɪ; ˌpenitrəˈbiliti] *n.* 可入(性)；貫穿性。

pen·e·tra·ble [ˈpɛnətrəbl; ˈpenitrəbl] *adj.* ①可透入的；可貫穿的；可滲透的。*penetrable* to ideas. 能吸收新觀念。②可看破的；可洞察的。

pen·e·tra·li·a [ˌpɛnɪˈtrelɪə; ˌpeniˈtreiliə] *n. pl.* ①內部；內殿；內院。②奧義；祕密。

*__pen·e·trate__ [ˈpɛnəˌtret; ˈpenitreit] *v.*, **-trat·ed, -trat·ing.** —*v.t.* ①穿入；透過。A bullet can *penetrate* a wall. 子彈能穿過牆壁。②刺入；刺破。③滲透；浸透。④洞察；了解。I could not *penetrate* the mystery. 我無法洞察這祕密。⑤侵入(市場)。⑥深深地感動；予…深切之印象。—*v.i.* ①透入；侵入；透徹〖to, through, into〗. Western ideas *penetrate* slowly through the East. 西方觀念逐漸傳入東方。②洞察。③留下深刻印象。

pen·e·trat·ing [ˈpɛnəˌtretɪŋ; ˈpenitreitiŋ] *adj.* ①銳利的；尖銳的；貫穿的。②聰明的；有見識的；有眼光的。

pen·e·tra·tion [ˌpɛnəˈtreʃən; ˌpeniˈtreiʃən] *n.* ①浸入；潰入；穿入。②(對一國家之)滲透行動。③敏銳之智力；洞察力。④天文望遠鏡或顯微鏡等的顯像力。

pen·e·tra·tive [ˈpɛnəˌtretɪv; ˈpenitrətiv] *adj.* ①能浸入的；能貫入的。②聰穎的；敏銳的。—**ly,** *adv.*

pen·friend, pen-friend [ˈpɛnˌfrɛnd; ˈpenfrend] *n.* 〖英〗筆友。

pen·guin [ˈpɛngwɪn; ˈpeŋgwin] *n.* ①企鵝。②〖航空〗不能起飛只供地面教練之教練機。

penguin suit〖俚〗太空衣。

pen·hold·er [ˈpɛnˌholdɚ; ˈpenˌhouldə] *n.* ①鋼筆桿。②筆插；筆架。

pen·i·cil·lin [ˌpɛnɪˈsɪlɪn; ˌpeniˈsilin] *n.* 〖藥〗盤尼西林；青黴素。

pen·i·cil·li·um [ˌpɛnɪˈsɪlɪəm; ˌpeniˈsiliəm] *n.*, *pl.* **-ums, -li·a** [-lɪə; -liə]. 〖植物〗青黴菌。

*__pen·in·su·la__ [pəˈnɪnsələ, -sjulə, -ʃulə; piˈninsjulə, pəˈn-] *n.* 半島。

pen·in·su·lar [pəˈnɪnsəlɚ; piˈninsjulə] *adj.* ①半島的；形成半島的。②似半島的。—*n.* 半島之居民。

pen·in·su·late [pəˈnɪnsəˌlet; pəˈninsjuleit] *v.t.*, **-lat·ed, -lat·ing.** 形成半島。

pe·nis [ˈpinɪs; ˈpiːnis] *n.*, *pl.* **-nes** [-niz; -niːz], **-nis·es.** 〖解剖〗陽物；陰莖。

pen·i·tence [ˈpɛnətəns; ˈpenitəns] *n.* 懺悔；悔悟；悔罪。

pen·i·tent [ˈpɛnətənt; ˈpenitənt] *adj.* ①悔罪的；後悔的。②表示後悔的。—*n.* ①悔罪者；悔悟前非者。②〖天主教〗悔罪苦修者。—**ly,** *adv.*

pen·i·ten·tial [ˌpɛnəˈtɛnʃəl; ˌpeniˈtenʃəl] *adj.* ①悔悟的；悔罪的。②因懺悔而苦修的。—**ly,** *adv.*

pen·i·ten·tia·ry [ˌpɛnəˈtɛnʃərɪ; ˌpeniˈtenʃəri] *n.*, *pl.* **-ries,** *adj.* —*n.* ①感化院。②〖美〗監獄。③悔罪所。④〖天主教〗宗教裁判所；宗教裁判員。—*adj.* ①悔罪的；懺悔

的。②感化的。③應予懲罰的。

pen·knife ['pɛn,naɪf; 'pennaif] *n., pl.* **-knives.** 小刀;削鉛筆刀。

pen·light ['pɛn,laɪt; 'penlait] *n.* 小型電筒。—*adj.* 小型電筒的。

pen·man ['pɛnmən; 'penmən] *n., pl.* **-men.** ①書法家。②文人;作家。③〖英〗謄寫員。

pen·man·ship ['pɛnmən,ʃɪp; 'penmənʃip] *n.* ①書法。②寫作。

Penn., Penna. Pennsylvania.

pen name (著作者之)筆名。

pen·nant ['pɛnənt; 'penənt] *n.* (軍艦等之)旒旗;小旗。

pen·nate ['pɛnet; 'peneit] *adj.* ①有羽毛的;羽狀的。②有翼的;翼狀的。

pen·ni·form ['pɛnɪ,fɔrm; 'penifɔːm] *adj.* 羽狀的。

pen·ni·less ['pɛnlɪs; 'penilis] *adj.* 身無分文的;貧困的。

pen·non ['pɛnən; 'penən] *n.* ①從前騎士矛上之燕尾旗。②槍騎兵團士兵所用之小旗。③(美國)長三角形之校旗。④船上之長旒旗。⑤任何旗幟。

penn'orth ['pɛnəθ; 'penəθ] *n.* 〖俗〗=**pennyworth.**

Penn·syl·va·ni·a [,pɛnsḷ'venjə; ,pensil'veinjə] *n.* 賓夕凡尼亞(美國東部一州,首府 Harrisburg).

Pennsylvania Dutch (or **German**) ①十七、八世紀由德國南部及瑞士遷至 Pennsylvania 州之居民的後裔。②彼等所講混有英語之德國方言。

Penn·syl·va·ni·an [,pɛnsɪl'venɪən; ,pensil'veiniən] *n., adj.* ①Pennsylvania 州(人)(的)。②〖地質〗Pennsylvania紀(的)。

‡pen·ny ['pɛnɪ; 'peni] *n., pl.* **pen·nies,** 〖英〗 **pence.** ①分(美國與加拿大之銅幣);一仙。②辨士(英國幣名,舊制等於1/240鎊,1971年改制後等於1/100鎊)。It isn't worth a *penny*. 它一文錢也不值。③錢量;金額。***a bad penny*** 不受歡迎之人或物;討厭之人或物。***a penny for your thoughts*** 默想。***a pretty penny*** 巨額的金錢。***In for a penny, in for a pound.*** 一不做,二不休;一旦開始,必須完成。***turn an honest penny*** 正當地掙錢。

pen·ny-a-line ['pɛnɪə'laɪn; 'peniə'lain] *adj.* ①每行一辨士的。②(原稿、著作等)便宜的;拙劣的。

pen·ny-a-lin·er [,pɛnɪə'laɪnə; 'peniə'lainə] *n.* (論行計資的)窮文人;下等文人。

pen·ny-in-the-slot ['pɛnɪɪnðə'slɑt; 'peniinðə'slɔt] *n.* 自動販賣機。

pen·ny·roy·al [,pɛnə'rɔɪəl; 'peni'rɔiəl] *n.* ①〖植物〗胡薄荷。②薄荷油。

pen·ny·weight ['pɛnɪ,wet; 'peniweit] *n.* 英國金衡名,等於24克或1/20盎斯。

pen·ny-wise ['pɛnɪ'waɪz; 'peni'waiz] *adj.* 省小錢的;惜分文的。***penny-wise and pound-foolish*** 貪小失大。

pen·ny·worth ['pɛnɪ,wɜθ; 'penəθ, 'peniwə(ː)θ] *n.* ①一辨士之值;一辨士的東西。②少量。③上算的交易。***a good*** (***bad***) ***pennyworth*** 有利(不利)的交易。

pe·no·log·i·cal [,pinə'lɑdʒɪkḷ; ,piːnə'lɔdʒikəl] *adj.* 刑罰學的;典獄學的。

pe·nol·o·gist [pi'nɑlədʒɪst; piː'nɔlədʒist] *n.* 刑罰學者;典獄學者。

pe·nol·o·gy [pi'nɑlədʒɪ; piː'nɔlədʒi] *n.* 刑罰學;典獄學。

pen pal 筆友。(英亦作 **pen-friend**)

pen·sée [pɑ̃'se; pɑ̃'sei] 〖法〗 *n.* ①思想;沉思;回想。②感想錄;箴言;警句。

pen·sile ['pɛnsḷ; 'pensl] *adj.* ①懸的;掛的。②築懸巢的。

pen·sion¹** ['pɛnʃən; 'penʃən] *n.* ①養老金;恩俸。②津貼。③兒童之膳宿及教育費。—*v.t.* 給以養老金(恩俸等)。pension off*** 予以年金而令退休。—*adj.* 養老金的;恩俸的。

pen·sion² ['pɑnsɪ,ɑn, pɑ̃'sjɔ̃; 'pɑ̃ːŋsiɔ̃ːŋ] 〖法〗*n.* (歐洲大陸之)公寓;寄宿學校。

pen·sion·ar·y ['pɛnʃən,ɛrɪ; 'penʃənəri] *adj., n., pl.* **-ies.** —*adj.* ①受年金的;受恩俸的。②養老金的;年金的;恩俸的。③依靠人的;被雇用的。—*n.* ①受年金(恩俸等)者。②雇傭;扈從;傀儡。③昔荷蘭之市長。

pen·sion·er ['pɛnʃənɚ; 'penʃənə] *n.* ①受年金(恩俸等)者。②〖英〗(劍橋大學的)自費生。③受雇者;扈從。

pension fund 養老基金;互助福利金。

pen·sive ['pɛnsɪv; 'pensiv] *adj.* ①沉思的;默想的。②憂鬱的;哀思的。a *pensive* lay. 哀歌。—**ly,** *adv.* —**ness,** *n.*

pen·stock ['pɛn,stɑk; 'penstɔk] *n.* ①水門。②(水力發電所的)水壓管。③(導向水輪之)水道;水渠。

pent [pɛnt; pent] *adj.* 被關閉的;被幽禁的。—*v.* pt. & pp. of **pen.**

pent- 〖字首〗**penta-** 之異體,用在母音之前。

penta- 〖字首〗表"五"之義,如: pentagon. 在母音前作 pent-.

pen·ta·chord ['pɛntə,kɔrd; 'pentəkɔːd] *n.* 五弦琴。

pen·ta·cle ['pɛntəkḷ; 'pentəkl] *n.* (昔時魔術中所用的)五角星形。

pen·tad ['pɛntæd; 'pentæd] *n.* ①五;五個之一組。②五年之期間。③〖化〗五價元素;五價基。

pen·ta·dac·tyl [,pɛntə'dæktɪl; ,pentə'dæktil] *adj.* 有五指的;有五趾的。

pen·ta·gon ['pɛntə,gɑn; 'pentəgən] *n.* ①五角形。②(the P-) 美國國防部五角大廈。

pen·tag·o·nal [pɛn'tægənḷ; pen'tægənl] *adj.* 五角形的。

pen·ta·gram ['pɛntə,græm; 'pentəgræm] *n.* ①五角星形。②〖數學〗五線形。

pen·ta·he·dral [,pɛntə'hidrəl; ,pentə'hiːdrəl] *adj.* 五面體的。

pen·ta·he·dron [,pɛntə'hidrən; ,pentə'hiːdrən] *n., pl.* **-drons, -dra** [-drə; -drə]. 五面體。

pen·tam·e·ter [pɛn'tæmətɚ; pen'tæmitə] *n.* 五音步 (foot) 的詩行。—*adj.* 有五音步的。

pen·tane ['pɛnten; 'pentein] *n.* 〖化〗戊烷 (C_5H_{12})。

pen·tar·chy ['pɛntɑrkɪ; 'pentɑːki] *n.* ①五頭政治。②五國聯盟。

pen·ta·syl·la·ble ['pɛntə,sɪləbḷ; 'pentə,siləbl] *n.* 五音節(字)。

Pen·ta·teuch ['pɛntə,tjuk; 'pentətjuːk] *n.* 舊約聖經開首之五卷書;摩西五書。

pen·tath·lon [pɛn'tæθlən; pen'tæθlən] *n.* 五項運動(跳遠、標槍、二百公尺、鐵餅、及一千五百公尺)。

Pen·te·cost ['pɛntɪ,kɔst; 'pentikɔst] *n.* ①(基督教之)聖靈降臨節(亦作 **Whitsunday**). ②(猶太教之)五旬節。—**al,** *adj.*

pent·house ['pɛnt,haus; 'penthaus] *n.* ①傾斜屋檐;遮檐。②附於大建築物之棚舍(尤指上有傾斜之屋頂者)。③建築於高樓大廈屋頂之小屋。④任何似遮檐之物。***make a penthouse of the eyebrows*** 皺眉頭。

pen·tode ['pɛntod; 'pentoud] *n.* 〖電〗

五極眞空管。

pent roof 單斜屋頂;單斜簷。

pent·ste·mon 〔pɛnt'stimən; pent'stiːmən〕 *n.* 〖植物〗①元參屬。②元參屬之植物。

pent-up 〔'pɛnt'ʌp; 'pent'ʌp〕 *adj.* 被關閉的;被幽禁的;被抑制的。

pe·nult 〔'pinʌlt, pɪ'nʌlt; pi'nʌlt〕 *n.* 倒數第二個;(尤指)一字之倒數第二音節。—*adj.* =**penultimate.**

pe·nul·ti·mate 〔pɪ'nʌltəmɪt; pi'nʌltimit〕 *adj.* ①倒數第二的。②一字中之倒數第二音節的。—*n.* (一字中之)倒數第二音節。

pe·nul·ti·ma·tum 〔pɪˌnʌltə'metəm; piˌnʌltə'meitəm〕 *n.* 最後通牒發出前之宣言、要求等;半最後通牒。

pe·num·bra 〔pɪ'nʌmbrə; pi'nʌmbrə〕 *n., pl.* **-brae** 〔-bri; -briː〕, **-bras.** ①〖天文〗(太陽黑子邊緣之)半暗部;半影。②〖天文〗半陰影(於日蝕、月蝕等時部分入影的區域)。③〖繪畫〗濃淡相交之處。—**pe·num·bral,** *adj.*

pe·nu·ri·ous 〔pə'nurɪəs; pi'njuəriəs〕 *adj.* ①貧窮的;貧困的;赤貧的。②吝嗇的;鄙吝的。③稀少的;不肥沃的;貧瘠的。—**ly,** *adv.*

pen·u·ry 〔'pɛnjərɪ; 'penjuri〕 *n.* 貧窮;窮困;缺乏。

pen·wip·er 〔'pɛnˌwaipɚ; 'penˌwaipə〕 *n.* 拭筆具。

pe·on 〔'piən; 'piːən, *for* ③ pjuːn〕 *n.* ①(南美洲之)工人。②(南美洲之)被迫工作以還債之人;被強制執行勞役以抵償罰金的人。③(印度之)步兵;警察;僕從;侍者。④(西洋象棋中的)卒。

pe·on·age 〔'piənɪdʒ; 'piːənidʒ〕 *n.* ①被迫勞役以抵債者 (peon) 之狀態或工作。②勞役償債制度。

pe·o·ny 〔'piənɪ; 'piəni〕 *n., pl.* **-nies.** ①牡丹;芍藥。②牡丹花。***herbaceous peony*** 芍藥。***tree peony*** 牡丹。

:peo·ple 〔'pipḷ; 'piːpl〕 *n., pl.* **-ple** or (for ②) **-ples,** *v.,* **-pled, -pling.** —*n.* ①人。The streets were crowded with *people.* 街上擠滿了人。②民族。the Chinese *people.* 中華民族。the *peoples* of Asia. 亞洲諸民族。③民衆;人民。"of the *people,* by the *people,* for the *people.*" 民有,民治,民享。④某一地點、階級或團體之人民。Southern *people.* 南方人。⑤低層社會之民衆;平民。The nobles oppressed the *people.* 貴族壓迫平民。⑥庶民;臣民。the king and his *people.* 國王和他的庶民。⑦〖俗〗家族;親戚。to visit one's *people.* 探望家裏人。⑧人類。⑨某一種動物。the monkey *people* of the forest. 森林中的猴羣。—*v.t.* ①供以人民;居於。a thickly *peopled* country. 人口稠密之國家。②飼養;生長。a meadow *peopled* with wild flowers. 長滿野花的草地。

pep 〔pɛp; pep〕 *n.* 〖俚〗精力;元氣。—*v.t.* 〖俚〗予以精神及氣力;激勵士氣〖up〗。

pep·lum 〔'pɛpləm; 'pepləm〕 *n., pl.* **-lums, -la** 〔-lə; -lə〕. ①(婦女裙子的) 荷葉邊裝飾。②附屬於上衣的短裙。

***pep·per** 〔'pɛpɚ; 'pepə〕 *n.* ①胡椒;辣椒;椒。②產椒之植物。③胡椒皿;胡椒瓶。silver salts and *peppers.* 銀質鹽瓶和胡椒瓶。—*v.t.* ①灑以胡椒末調味。②以子彈密擊。③密布。His face is *peppered* with freckles. 他的臉上滿是密密的雀斑。④接二連三的發問。⑤猛烈地打擊。⑥使有生氣。

pep·per-and-salt 〔'pɛpən'sɔlt; 'pepərən'sɔːlt〕 *adj.* 黑白相間精細地交織成的;椒鹽色的(布等)。

pep·per·box 〔'pɛpɚˌbɑks; 'pepəbɔks〕 *n.* ①胡椒盒;胡椒瓶。②〖俚〗脾氣暴燥的人。

pepper caster (or **castor**) = **pepperbox.**

pep·per·corn 〔'pɛpɚˌkɔrn; 'pepəkɔːn〕 *n.* ①乾胡椒;胡椒子。②以胡椒子交付房東的象徵性租金。

pep·per·grass 〔'pɛpɚˌgræs; 'pepəgrɑːs〕 *n.* 〖植物〗胡椒草。

pep·per·mint 〔'pɛpɚˌmɪnt; 'pepəmint〕 *n.* ①薄荷。②薄荷油。③薄荷糖。

peppermint camphor 薄荷腦。

pepper pot ①=**pepperbox.** ②(西印度羣島的)辣椒燉肉。③辣椒肉菜湯。④〖俚〗急性的人。

pepper shaker 頂端有小篩孔的胡椒瓶。

pep·per·y 〔'pɛpərɪ; 'pepəri〕 *adj.* ①胡椒的。②似胡椒的;充滿胡椒的;辛辣的。③(言詞等)尖刻的;譏刺的。④易怒的;暴躁的。

pep·py 〔'pɛpɪ; 'pepi〕 *adj.,* **pep·pi·er, pep·pi·est.** 〖美俚〗精神飽滿的;生氣勃勃的;精力充沛的;活潑的。

pep rally 爲競選活動或球隊等召開的打氣大會。

pep·sin(e) 〔'pɛpsɪn; 'pepsin〕 *n.* ①胃液素;胃蛋白酶。②助消化藥。

pep talk 鼓勵士氣的談話;加油打氣的談話。

pep-talk 〔'pɛpˌtɔk; 'peptɔːk〕 *v.t.* & *v.i.* 〖俗〗作精神講話;鼓勵;爲(人)打氣。

pep·tic 〔'pɛptɪk; 'peptik〕 *adj.* ①消化的;助消化的。②有消化力的。③胃液素 (pepsin) 的;胃蛋白酶的。—*n.* ①助消化藥;健胃劑。②(*pl.*)〖諧〗消化器官。

peptic glands 胃液腺;胃酶腺。

peptic ulcer 〖醫〗消化性潰瘍;胃、十二指腸潰瘍。

pep·tide 〔'pɛptaɪd; 'peptaid〕 *n.* 〖化〗縮氨酸;胜。

pep·tone 〔'pɛpton; 'peptoun〕 *n.* 〖生化〗消化蛋白質;蛋白腖。

pep·to·nize 〔'pɛptəˌnaɪz; 'peptənaiz〕 *v.t.,* **-nized, -niz·ing.** 使化成消化蛋白質;腖化。

per** 〔pɚ; pəː, pə〕 *prep.* ①每。ten cents *per* pound. 每磅一毛錢。②由;經。*Per* Air Mail. 航空郵寄。per usual*** 〖俚〗照常;一如往常 (=as usual).

per- 〖字首〗①表"通;總"之義,如:perceive. ②表"完全;非常"之義,如:persuade. ③〖化〗表"過…"之義,如:peroxide.

per·ad·ven·ture 〔ˌpɜəd'vɛntʃɚ; ˌpərəd'ventʃə〕 *adv.* 〖古〗①或者;也許。②偶然。***if peradventure*** 萬一。***lest peradventure*** 惟恐萬一;以防萬一。—*n.* 〖古〗①偶然之事;不確實之事。②疑惑;疑問。

per·am·bu·late 〔pɚ'æmbjəˌlet; pə'ræmbjuleit〕 *v.,* **-lat·ed, -lat·ing.** —*v.t.* ①巡廻;巡視;巡行;巡查。②巡行以定(森林等)之邊界;勘定…之疆界。—*v.i.* 閒蕩;閒逛;漫步;徘徊;逍遙。

per·am·bu·la·tion 〔pɚˌæmbjə'leʃən; pəˌræmbju'leiʃən〕 *n.* ①巡廻;巡視;巡查;徘徊。②巡行(勘查、測量)區。③勘查報告;巡查紀錄。

per·am·bu·la·tor 〔pɚ'æmbjəˌletɚ; 'præmbjuleitə〕 *n.* ①小兒搖籃車(略作**pram**)。②巡視者;勘查者。③計程器;里程表。

per·am·bu·la·to·ry 〔pɚ'æmbjələˌtorɪ; 'præmbjuˌleitəri〕 *adj.* ①巡廻的;巡視的;勘查的。②喜歡巡遊的。③旅行的。—*n.* 散步的地方。

per annum 每年;每年的;按年計算的(略作 **per an., per ann., p.a.**). Her sal-

ary was $2500 *per annum*. 她的薪水每年二千五百元。「滑細密的棉布。」
per·cale 〔pə'kel; pə'keil〕 *n.* 一種光
per cap·i·ta 〔pə'kæpitə; pə'kæpitə〕 ①〖拉〗每人。②〖法律〗平均分配的。
per capita income 〖經濟〗個人平均所得。
per·ceiv·a·ble 〔pə'sivəbl; pə'si:vəbl〕 *adj.* 可知覺的；可覺察的；可領悟的；可理解的。
***per·ceive** 〔pə'siv; pə'si:v〕 *v.t.*, **-ceived, -ceiv·ing.** ①感覺；知覺。②覺察；理解。I *perceived* that I could not make her change her mind. 我發覺我不能使她改變主意。
‡per cent, per·cent 〔pə'sɛnt; pə'sent〕 *n.* ①每百(%)。6 *per cent* (6%). 百分之六。to get 3 *per cent* interest. 獲利息三分。②(*pl.*)有固定利率之公債。to invest money in the three *per cents.* 投資於三分利公債。③ (*pl.*)＝**percentages.**〖注意〗口語中可以 per cent 代替 percentage.
***per·cent·age** 〔pə'sɛntɪdʒ; pə'sentidʒ〕 *n.* ①百分比；百分率。What *percentage* of children were absent? 未到的兒童占百分之幾? ②部分。③(依百分率計算之) 利息、佣金；折扣。④〖俚〗利益；獲益。
per centum 〖拉〗＝**per cent** ①.
per·cept 〔'pɝsɛpt; 'pə:sept〕 *n.* 〖哲學〗①由知覺或認識得來的印象；知覺表象。②知覺或認識的對象。
***per·cep·ti·ble** 〔pə'sɛptəbl; pə'septəbl〕 *adj.* 易見的；可認知的；可知覺的。The difference is *perceptible.* 其差別顯而易見。—**per·cep·ti·bil·i·ty,** *n.* —**per·cep·ti·bly,** *adv.*
***per·cep·tion** 〔pə'sɛpʃən; pə'sepʃən〕 *n.* ①感覺；知覺。His *perception* of the change came in a flash. 他突然感到有了變化。②感覺力；理解力。③(覺察後之) 了解；悟。
per·cep·tion·al 〔pə'sɛpʃənl; pə'sepʃənl〕 *adj.* 感覺的；知覺的；理解的；知覺力的；理解力的。
per·cep·tive 〔pə'sɛptɪv; pə'septiv〕 *adj.* ①知覺的。②有知覺力的；知覺銳敏的。③觀察入微的。
per·cep·tiv·i·ty 〔ˌpɝsɛp'tɪvətɪ; ˌpə:sep'tiviti〕 *n.* 可知覺；知覺；知覺力。
per·cep·tu·al 〔pə'sɛptʃuəl; pə'septʃuəl〕 *adj.* 知覺(力)的；有知覺的。
perch**[1] 〔pɝtʃ; pə:tʃ〕 *n.* ①(鳥類之)棲木；棲枝。The bird took its *perch.* 鳥棲息。②高的地位；安全的位置或地位。to come off one's *perch.* 沒落。③車輛上御者之高座位。④(亦作 **pole, rod**)英國長度名(＝5½碼)。⑤英國面積單位 (30¼ 平方碼)。⑥石之體積單位 (＝24¾ 立方英尺)。⑦(馬車的)轅桿。hop*** (or ***tip over***) ***the perch*** 敗落；死。***knock one off one's perch*** 打敗；殺死。—*v.i.* ①棲息；棲止〖on, upon〗。The bird *perched* on his finger. 鳥停在他的手指上。②站立；蹲；坐 (於狹小地方上)。—*v.t.* ①放置；擱置；安放 (多用過去分詞)。a castle *perched* on a rock. 築於岩石上之堡壘。②對(剛從紡織機上取下的紡織品)作品質檢查。
perch[2] *n., pl.* **perch·es, perch.** 鱸；鱸類。
per·chance 〔pə'tʃæns; pə'tʃɑ:ns, pə:'tʃ-〕 *adv.* ①或者；或許。②偶然；萬一。
perch·er 〔'pɝtʃə; 'pə:tʃə〕 *n.* ①高坐者；立踞者。②爪適於棲息的鳥。
per·cip·i·ence 〔pə'sɪpɪəns; pə'sipiəns〕 *n.* 知覺；認知；知覺力。
per·cip·i·ent 〔pə'sɪpɪənt; pə'sipiənt〕 *adj.* ①有知覺力的；知覺的；(尤指) 知覺敏銳的。②有辨別力的；有鑑賞力的。—*n.* ①知覺者；感覺者；有知覺力的人。②有超覺力的人。
per·co·late 〔'pɝkəˌlet; 'pə:kəleit〕 *v.,* **-lat·ed, -lat·ing,** *n.* —*v.i.* 濾；濾過；滲透；滴出。—*v.t.* 濾；滲；滴出。—*n.* 濾過之液體；濾液。—**per·co·la·tion,** *n.*
per·co·la·tor 〔'pɝkəˌletə; 'pə:kəleitə〕 *n.* ①(附過濾器的)咖啡壺。②過濾器。
per con·tra 〔pə'kɑntrə; pə'kɔntrə〕 〖拉〗①相反地；反之。②在另一方面。③〖簿記〗在另一方的(一筆記載)。
per·cuss 〔pə'kʌs; pə:'kʌs〕 *v.t.* ①叩；敲。②〖醫〗敲診；叩診。
per·cus·sion 〔pə'kʌʃən; pə:'kʌʃən〕 *n.* ①撞擊；衝擊；衝突。②〖音樂〗敲打；敲擊。③〖軍〗着發；擊發。④(由撞擊而生的)振動；激動；撞擊聲；音響。⑤〖醫〗叩診法；敲診法。
percussion cap (子彈的)雷管；銅帽子。
percussion instrument 打樂器。
per·cus·sion·ist 〔pə'kʌʃənɪst; pə:'kʌʃənist〕 *n.* 打樂器樂手。
per·cus·sive 〔pə'kʌsɪv; pə:'kʌsiv〕 *adj.* ①撞擊的；衝擊的；敲擊的；衝突的。②叩診的；敲診的。
per di·em 〔pə'daɪəm; pə:'daiem〕 〖拉〗①每日。②〖美〗每日津貼；每日出差費。
per·di·tion 〔pə'dɪʃən; pə:'diʃən〕 *n.* ①全滅；全敗；滅亡。②(靈魂之) 沒亡；沉淪；墮地獄。③地獄。
per·du(e) 〔pə'dju; pə:'dju:〕 *adj.* 看不見的；隱藏的；潛伏的。to lie *perdu.* 隱藏；潛伏。
per·dur·a·ble 〔pə'djurəbl; pə(:)'djuərəbl〕 *adj.* 持續的；持久的；不朽的；永久的。
per·dure 〔pə'djur; pə'djuə〕 *v.i.*, **-dured, -dur·ing.** 持久；繼續。
père 〔pɛr; pɛə〕〖法〗 *n.* ①父親 (父子同名時，置於父姓之後以資區別，相當於英文之 Senior)。Dumas *père.* 大仲馬。②(P-) 某些僧侶之頭銜。「*n.* ＝**peregrine.**」
per·e·grin 〔'pɛrəgrɪn; 'perigrin〕 *adj.,*
per·e·gri·nate 〔'pɛrəgrɪˌnet; 'perigrineit〕 *v.t.* & *v.i.*, **-nat·ed, -nat·ing.** 遊歷；遍歷；旅行。—**per·e·gri·na·tion, per·e·gri·na·tor,** *n.*
per·e·grine 〔'pɛrəgrɪn; 'perigrin〕 *adj.* ①外國的；舶來的。②移住的(鳥)。
per·emp·to·ry 〔pə'rɛmptərɪ, 'pɛrəmpˌtorɪ; pə'remptəri, 'perəm-〕 *adj.* ①〖法律〗終局的；決定性的；絕對的。②絕對的；斷然的；不許反抗的 (言詞或命令)。*peremptory* mandamus (*or* edict). 强制執行令。③專橫的；武斷的。—**per·emp·to·ri·ly,** *adv.* —**per·emp·to·ri·ness,** *n.*
per·en·ni·al 〔pə'rɛnɪəl; pə'reniəl〕 *adj.* ①四季不斷的；終年無間斷的。②永久的；不斷的；長久的。③〖植物〗多年生的。—*n.* 多年生植物。—**ly,** *adv.*
perf. ① perfect. ② perforated (of stamps). ③performance. ④performed.
‡per·fect 〔*adj., n.* 'pɝfɪkt; 'pə:fikt *v.* pə'fɛkt, 'pɝfɪkt; pə'fekt, pə:'f-, 'pə:fikt〕 *adj.* ①無瑕的；無缺的；美好的。His behavior was *perfect.* 他的行爲無瑕。②完整的。a *perfect* set of dishes. 一整套盤碟。③全然的。He is a *perfect* stranger to us. 他對我們完全是個陌生人。④熟練的；技術精湛的。⑤理想的 (人選等)。He is a *perfect*

actor to play the role. 他是扮演這個角色的理想演員。⑥純粹的;無雜質的。⑦絕對的。⑧徹頭徹尾的;不折不扣的。⑨絲毫無謬誤的。⑩〖文法〗完成的。*perfect* tense. 完成式。⑪〖植物〗雌雄兩全的。—*v.t.* ①使完美無疵。The artist was *perfecting* his picture. 那畫家在修改他的畫。②改進;改良。③完成。④〖印刷〗印(反面)(指正面已印就)。—*n.* 〖文法〗完成式。**future perfect.** 將來完成式。**past perfect.** 過去完成式。**present perfect.** 現在完成式。—**ness,** *n.*

perfect game 〖棒球〗完美賽局(全場不換投手而使對方無安打、無四壞球上壘及無得分之球賽)。

per·fect·i·ble [pəˈfɛktəbl; pəˈfektəbl] *adj.* 可(使)變成完美的;可完成的。

***per·fec·tion** [pəˈfɛkʃən; pəˈfekʃən] *n.* ①完全;完美;圓滿;精美;完備。He imitates people to *perfection.* 他模仿別人,維妙維肖。②完美之人或物;典型;代表。His work is always *perfection.* 他的作品都是極完美的。③極;極度。*perfection* of rudeness. 粗魯之極。④完成。*perfection* of a poem, picture. 一首詩、一幅畫的完成。⑤(*pl.*)才藝;美德;優點。Beauty is the least of her *perfections.* 美貌是她優點中之最微不足道者。⑥(花果之)盛開;正熟。to come to *perfection.* 成熟。to be at *perfection.* (果之)正熟;(菜之)烹調恰好。*to perfection* 盡善盡美地。

per·fec·tion·ism [pəˈfɛkʃənɪzəm; pəˈfekʃənizm] *n.* ①至善論;圓滿論(謂人在現世可在道德、宗教、社會或政治上達到圓滿的境地)。②至善主義(不達至善境地不肯罷休)。

per·fec·tion·ist [pəˈfɛkʃənɪst; pəˈfekʃənist] *n.* ①至善論者。②力求至善者。—*adj.* 至善至美的;至善主義的。

‡per·fect·ly [ˈpɝfɪktlɪ; ˈpəːfiktli] *adv.* 圓滿地;全然地;正確地。The work was done *perfectly.* 這工作很圓滿。You are *perfectly* right. 你一點也不錯。

per·fec·to [pəˈfɛkto; pəˈfektou] *n., pl.* **-tos.** 一種兩端尖細的中號雪茄。

perfect participle 〖文法〗=**past participle.**

per·fer·vid [pɝˈfɝvɪd; pəːˈfəːvid] *adj.* 極熱的;灼熱的;非常熱心的;熱烈的。

per·fid·i·ous [pəˈfɪdɪəs; pəˈfidiəs] *adj.* 不忠的;不義的;奸詐的。—**ly,** *adv.*

per·fi·dy [ˈpɝfədɪ; ˈpəːfidi] *n., pl.* **-dies.** 背信;不誠實。

per·fo·li·ate [pəˈfolɪˌet; pəˈfoulieit] *adj.* 〖植物〗抱莖的(莖穿過葉子生長的)。

per·fo·rate [*v.*ˈpɝfəˌret; ˈpəːfəreit *adj.* ˈpɝfərɪt, -ˌret; ˈpəːfərit] *v.,* **-rat·ed, -rat·ing,** *adj.* —*v.t.* ①穿孔;打洞;貫穿。②(郵票接縫)打排孔。—*v.i.* 刺穿;貫穿〖into, through〗。—*adj.* 有孔的;打了洞的;鑿穿的;(尤指)刺有排孔的。

per·fo·ra·tion [ˌpɝfəˈreʃən; ˌpəːfəˈreiʃən] *n.* ①穿孔;鑿洞;貫穿;打洞。②洞;孔;眼;接縫孔。

per·fo·ra·tive [ˈpɝfəˌretɪv; ˈpəːfəreitiv] *adj.* 穿孔的;貫穿的;有穿孔力的;穿得過的;穿孔性的。

per·fo·ra·tor [ˈpɝfəˌretɚ; ˈpəːfəreitə] *n.* 穿孔器;穿孔機;穿孔者。

per·force [pəˈfors; pəˈfɔːs] *adv.* 必需地;強迫地;不得已地。—*n.* 必需;強迫;不得已。*by perforce* 強迫地。*of perforce* 不得已地;迫於勢力地。*perforce of* 靠…的力量。

‡per·form [pəˈfɔrm; pəˈfɔːm] *v.t. & v.i.* ①做;行。to *perform* one's duties. 盡責任。②執行;履行。You should always *perform* what you promise. 你應永遠履行你所允諾的事。③表演;演(劇);奏(樂);唱。

***per·form·ance** [pəˈfɔrməns; pəˈfɔːməns] *n.* ①履行;實行;執行。He is faithful in the *performance* of his duties. 他忠於職守。②動作;行爲。③扮演;演奏;奏樂;表演。The evening *performance* is at 8 o'clock. 晚場在八點鐘開演。

per·form·er [pəˈfɔrmɚ; pəˈfɔːmə] *n.* 演奏者;表演者;執行者;動作者。

per·form·ing [pəˈfɔrmɪŋ; pəˈfɔːmiŋ] *adj.* ①行爲的;履行的;執行的。②演藝的。

***per·fume** [*n.* ˈpɝfjum; ˈpəːfjuːm *v.* pəˈfjum; pəˈfjuːm] *n., v.,* **-fumed, -fum·ing.** —*n.* ①香味;芳香。②香水。a bottle of *perfume.* 一瓶香水。—*v.t.* ①使香;薰香。Flowers *perfumed* the air. 空氣中瀰漫着花香。②灑香水於。

per·fum·er [pəˈfjumɚ; pəˈfjuːmə] *n.* ①香料商;香料製造人。②使香的人(物);灑香水的人。

per·fum·er·y [pəˈfjumərɪ; pəˈfjuːməri] *n.* ①一種香水。②香水(集合稱)。③香水業;香水廠。

per·func·to·ry [pəˈfʌŋktərɪ; pəˈfʌŋktəri] *adj.* ①敷衍的;循例的;表面的;草率的。②行爲草率的;不關心的;敷衍塞責的(指人)。—**per·func·to·ri·ly,** *adv.*

per·fuse [pəˈfjuz; pəˈfjuːz] *v.t.,* **-fused, -fus·ing.** 灌;使充滿;鋪滿;灑遍;撒滿。to *perfuse* a room with light. 使房間充滿光線。

per·fu·sive [pəˈfjusɪv; pəˈfjuːsiv] *adj.* (可)撒的;灑水用的。

per·go·la [ˈpɝgələ; ˈpəːgələ] *n.* ①涼亭;陽臺;廊。②(籐蔓棚下之)蔭徑;籐蔓棚。

‡per·haps [pəˈhæps; pəˈhæps, præps] *adv.* 或許;可能。*Perhaps* it will rain. 天可能下雨。

per·hy·drol [pəˈhaɪdrɔl; pəːˈhaidrɔːl] *n.* 〖化〗過氧化氫。(亦作 **hydrogen peroxide**)

pe·ri [ˈpɪrɪ; ˈpiəri] *n.* ①〖波斯神話〗妖精;仙女。②美人。

peri- 〖字首〗表"周圍;近;超;上"之義。

per·i·anth [ˈpɛrɪˌænθ; ˈperiænθ] *n.* 〖植物〗花被;花蓋。

per·i·apt [ˈpɛrɪˌæpt; ˈperiæpt] *n.* 護符。

per·i·blast [ˈpɛrɪˌblæst; ˈperiblæst] *n.* 〖生化〗細胞質;細胞漿。

per·i·carp [ˈpɛrɪˌkɑrp; ˈperikɑːp] *n.* 〖植物〗果皮。

Per·i·cles [ˈpɛrəˌkliz; ˈperikliːz] *n.* 培里克里斯(古時雅典最偉大政治家、大將軍及演說家)。

per·i·cra·ni·um [ˌpɛrɪˈkrenɪəm; ˌperiˈkreiniəm] *n., pl.* **-ni·a** [-nɪə; -niə]. ①〖解剖〗頭骨膜;顱骨外衣。②頭;腦子(諧語)。

per·i·den·tal [ˌpɛrəˈdɛntl; ˌperiˈdentl] *adj.* 牙周的。

per·i·dot [ˈpɛrɪˌdɑt; ˈperidɔt] *n.* 〖礦〗(透明濃綠色的)橄欖石。

per·i·do·tite [ˌpɛrɪˈdotaɪt; ˌperiˈdoutait] *n.* 橄欖岩。

per·i·gee [ˈpɛrəˌdʒi; ˈperidʒiː] *n.* 〖天文〗近地點(天體,尤指月球,在其軌道上最接近地球之點)。

per·i·he·li·on [ˌpɛrɪˈhilɪən; ˌperiˈhiːliən] *n., pl.* **-li·a** [-lɪə; -liə]. 〖天文〗近日

點(天體在其軌道上最接近太陽之點)。

***per·il** [ˈpɛrəl; ˈperil, –rl] *n., v.,* **-il(l)ed, -il·(l)ing.** —*n.*危險。This bridge is not safe; cross it at your *peril.* 此橋不完全,通過時有危險。—*v.t.* 冒於險境。

***per·il·ous** [ˈpɛrələs; ˈperiləs, –rl̩əs] *adj.* 危險的;冒險的。

peril point 進口稅之最低點(如低於此點,該項進口貨將危及本國生產同樣貨物之工業)。

pe·rim·e·ter [pəˈrɪmətɚ; pəˈrimitə] *n.* ①周;周圍;周界;周邊。②周長。③〖光學〗視野計;視野測定器。

per·i·ne·al [ˌpɛrɪˈniəl; ˌperiˈni:əl] *adj.* 〖解剖〗會陰的。

per·i·ne·um [ˌpɛrəˈniəm; ˌperiˈni:əm] *n., pl.* **-ne·a** [–ˈniə; –ˈni:ə].〖解剖〗會陰(肛門與陰部間之部分)。

‡**pe·ri·od** [ˈpɪrɪəd, ˈpir–, –rɪɪd; ˈpiəriəd, ˈpjə:r–] *n.* ①一段時間。He visited us for a short *period.* 他對我們做了一次短短的訪問。②時期;時代。the *period* of the French Revolution. 法國大革命時期。③自然運行中一段固定的時間;周期。④〖地質〗紀。⑤(運動比賽中的)一節。a rest between *periods*. 上下半場比賽間之休息。⑥上課之一節;一堂。⑦病的周期。⑧月經期。⑨句點(.)。⑩〖文法〗完全句。⑪結束;最後階段。The decisive victory put a *period* to the war. 那場決定性的勝利結束了戰爭。—*adj.* 有某一時代之特徵的。—*interj.*〖俗〗就是如此(=That's it!);沒有甚麼可說的了(=That's final!)。

pe·ri·od·ic [ˌpɪrɪˈɑdɪk; ˌpiəriˈɔdik] *adj.* ①周期的;定時的。②不時發生的。③某一時期的。④〖文法〗完全句的。⑤〖修辭〗= **periodic sentence.**

***pe·ri·od·i·cal** [ˌpɪrɪˈɑdɪkl; ˌpiəriˈɔdikəl] *n.* 定期刊物;雜誌。—*adj.* ①刊物的。②定期出版的。③周期的;定時的。

pe·ri·od·i·cal·ism [ˌpɪrɪˈɑdəkl̩ˌɪzm̩; ˌpiəriˈɔdikəlizəm] *n.* 爲雜誌寫稿之工作;發行定期刊物之工作。

pe·ri·od·i·cal·ist [ˌpɪrɪˈɑdəklɪst; ˌpiəriˈɔdikəlist] *n.* 向雜誌投稿者;雜誌發行人。

pe·ri·od·i·cal·ly [ˌpɪrɪˈɑdəklɪ; ˌpiəriˈɔdikəli] *adv.* ①定期地。②偶爾地;不時地。

pe·ri·o·dic·i·ty [ˌpɪrɪəˈdɪsətɪ; ˌpiəriəˈdisiti] *n., pl.* **-ties.** ①定期;周期性;周期數;周律。②〖電〗周率;頻率(=frequency)。

periodic law 〖化〗周期律。

periodic sentence 〖修辭〗掉尾句(整句之主要意義至句尾始完成的句子)。

periodic table 〖化〗元素周期表。

per·i·os·te·um [ˌpɛrɪˈɑstɪəm; ˌperiˈɔstiəm] *n., pl.* **-te·a** [–tɪə; –tiə].〖解剖〗骨膜;骨衣。

per·i·os·ti·tis [ˌpɛrɪɑsˈtaɪtɪs; ˌperiɔsˈtaitis] *n.* 〖醫〗骨膜炎。

per·i·pa·tet·ic [ˌpɛrəpəˈtɛtɪk; ˌperipəˈtetik] *adj.* ①巡行的;巡廻的;遊歷的;徘徊的;逍遙的。②(P–)(亞里斯多德主張之)逍遙學派的。—*n.* ①〖主諧〗巡行者;巡遊者;行商。②(P–)(亞里斯多德主張之)逍遙學派學者。

Per·i·pa·tet·i·cism [ˌpɛrɪpəˈtɛtɪsɪzm̩; ˌperipəˈtetisizm] *n.* ①逍遙學派(亞里斯多德學派)的哲學。②(p–)逍遙(之嗜好);巡遊。

pe·riph·er·al [pəˈrɪfərəl; pəˈrifərəl] *adj.* ①周圍的;外圍的。②非本質的;膚淺的。③補助的。④〖電腦〗外圍器具的。⑤〖解剖〗(神經)末梢的。—*n.*〖電腦〗外圍器具。—**ly,** *adv.*

pe·riph·er·y [pəˈrɪfərɪ; pəˈrifəri] *n., pl.* **-er·ies.** ①周圍;四周;周界。②(球形體之)表面;外圍。③〖解剖〗神經末梢之周圍。

per·i·phrase [ˈpɛrəˌfrez; ˈperifreiz] *v.,* **-phrased, -phras·ing,** *n.* —*v.t. & v.i.* 轉彎抹角地說;用紆說法。—*n.* =**periphrasis.**

pe·riph·ra·sis [pəˈrɪfrəsɪs; pəˈrifrəsis] *n., pl.* **-ses** [–ˌsiz; –si:z]. ①〖修辭〗紆說法。②轉彎抹角的說法。

per·i·phras·tic [ˌpɛrəˈfræstɪk; ˌperiˈfræstik] *adj.* ①〖文法、修辭〗紆說的。②紆遠的;冗贅的。

pe·rique [pəˈrik; pəˈri:k] *n.* (美國 Louisiana 州產的)一種香味濃厚的烟草。

per·i·scope [ˈpɛrəˌskop; ˈperiskoup] *n.* (潛水艇之)潛望鏡。

per·i·scop·ic [ˌpɛrəˈskɑpɪk; ˌperiˈskɔpik] *adj.* ①概見的;概略的。②周視的;可望四面的。③潛望鏡的;潛望鏡式的。(亦作 **periscopical**)

***per·ish** [ˈpɛrɪʃ; ˈperiʃ] *v.i.* 死;毁滅。The city *perished* in an earthquake. 這城於一次地震中毁滅。

per·ish·a·ble [ˈpɛrɪʃəbl; ˈperiʃəbl] *adj.* 易壞的;易滅的;易死的。—*n.* (常*pl.*)易壞之物。

per·ish·er [ˈpɛrɪʃɚ; ˈperiʃə] *n.* ①(使)毁滅之人(物)。②〖英俚〗討厭的人;笨瓜。

per·ish·ing [ˈpɛrɪʃɪŋ; ˈperiʃiŋ] *adj.* 〖俚〗凍死人的;引起毁滅的;極不舒適的;致命的。—*adv.* 非常地;極端地。—**ly,** *adv.*

pe·ris·so·dac·ty·la [pəˌrɪsoˈdæktlə; pəˌrisouˈdæktlə] *n.* 〖動物〗奇蹄類。

per·i·stal·sis [ˌpɛrəˈstælsɪs; ˌperiˈstælsis] *n., pl.* **-ses** [–siz; –si:z].〖生理〗蠕動。

per·i·stal·tic [ˌpɛrəˈstæltɪk; ˌperiˈstæltik] *adj.* 〖生理〗蠕動的。

per·i·stome [ˈpɛrɪˌstom; ˈperistoum] *n.* ①〖植物〗(蘚類的)齒毛;齒環。②〖動物〗口緣;口邊;脣。

per·i·style [ˈpɛrəˌstaɪl; ˈperistail] *n.* 〖建築〗①周圍列柱。②有圓柱列包圍之中庭。

per·i·to·nae·um [ˌpɛrətəˈniəm; ˌperitəˈni:əm] *n., pl.* **-nae·a** [–ˈniə; –ˈni:ə].〖解剖〗腹膜。(亦作 **peritoneum**) —**per·i·to·nae·al,** *adj.*

per·i·to·ni·tis [ˌpɛrətəˈnaɪtɪs; ˌperitəˈnaitis] *n.* 〖醫〗腹膜炎。

per·i·wig [ˈpɛrəˌwɪg; ˈperiwig] *n.* 假髮。

per·i·wigged [ˈpɛrəˌwɪgd; ˈperiwigd] *adj.* 戴假髮的。

per·i·win·kle [ˈpɛrəˌwɪŋkl; ˈperiˌwiŋkl] *n.* ①〖植物〗長春花屬之植物。②〖動物〗玉黍螺。

per·jure [ˈpɝdʒɚ; ˈpə:dʒə] *v.t.,* **-jured, -jur·ing.** 僞證。The witness *perjured* himself. 該證人作僞證。—**per·jur·er,** *n.*

per·jured [ˈpɝdʒɚd; ˈpə:dʒəd] *adj.* 發了假誓的;作了僞證的;犯了僞證罪的。

per·ju·ry [ˈpɝdʒərɪ; ˈpə:dʒəri] *n., pl.* **-ries.** 僞證;僞誓;僞證罪。

perk[1] [pɝk; pə:k] *v.i.* ①行動敏捷。②趾高氣揚。—*v.t.* ①豎起〖up〗。②修飾;修理。*perk up* 快活起來;振作起來。—*adj.* 興高采烈的;趾高氣揚的。

perk[2] *n.* 〖英俗〗=**perquisite.**

perk[3] *v.t. & v.i.* 〖俗〗=**percolate.**

perk·y [ˈpɝkɪ; ˈpə:ki] *adj.,* **perk·i·er, perk·i·est.** ①活潑的;意氣揚揚的。②裝腔作勢的;傲慢的;孟浪的。

per·lite [ˈpɝlaɪt; ˈpə:lait] *n.* 珍珠岩。

perm [pɝm; pə:m] *n.* 〖俗〗=**permanent**

wave. —*v.t.* & *v.i.* 電燙髮;用電將(髮)燙成波浪形。
perm. permanent.
per·ma·frost [ˈpɝməˌfrɔst; ˈpəːməfrɔːst] *n.* 永凍層(北極或寒帶地區之永遠冰凍的下層土)。
per·ma·nence [ˈpɝmənəns; ˈpəːmənəns] *n.* 恆久;永久;不變;不易。
per·ma·nen·cy [ˈpɝmənənsɪ; ˈpəːmənənsi] *n.* ①=**permanence.** ②長久不變之人、物或地位。
***per·ma·nent** [ˈpɝmənənt; ˈpəːmənənt] *adj.* 永久的;不變的;耐久的。a *permanent* job. 固定職業。—*n.* 〖俗〗電燙髮(=permanent wave). —**ly,** *adv.*
permanent address 永久地址;本籍。
Permanent Court of Arbitration 常設國際仲裁法庭(設於 The Hague, 俗稱 The Hague Tribunal).
Permanent Court of International Justice 常設國際法庭(俗稱 World Court).
permanent press 免燙(指衣服類)。
permanent tooth 恆齒;永久齒。
permanent wave 電燙髮;電燙造成的波浪式髮型。
permanent way 永久性公路或鐵路。
per·me·a·bil·i·ty [ˌpɝmɪəˈbɪlətɪ; ˌpəːmiəˈbiliti] *n.* ①可透性;滲透性。②〖物理〗導磁性(率或係數)。③〖航空〗(氣體對完好之氣球、布料之)透氣率;(氣球氣體之)透出量。
per·me·a·ble [ˈpɝmɪəbl̩; ˈpəːmiəbl] *adj.* 可滲入的;可透過的。—**per·me·a·bly,** *adv.*
per·me·ance [ˈpɝmɪəns; ˈpəːmiəns] *n.* ①滲入;透過;可透性。②〖物理〗磁導。
per·me·ant [ˈpɝmɪənt; ˈpəːmiənt] *adj.* 滲透的;透過的。
per·me·ate [ˈpɝmɪˌet; ˈpəːmieit] *v.,* **-at·ed, -at·ing.** —*v.t.* ①瀰漫;擴散;充滿。②滲透;滲入;透過。—*v.i.* 瀰漫;擴散;充滿;滲透〖into, through, among〗.
per·me·a·tion [ˌpɝmɪˈeʃən; ˌpəːmiˈeiʃən] *n.* 瀰漫;充滿;滲入;透過;普及;流布。
Per·mi·an [ˈpɝmɪən; ˈpəːmiən] *adj.* 〖地質〗二疊紀的;二疊系的。*Permian* system. 二疊系。*the Permian* 二疊紀;二疊系。
per·mil·lage [pəˈmɪlɪdʒ; pəˈmilidʒ] *n.* 千分率。
per·mis·si·ble [pəˈmɪsəbl̩; pəˈmisibl] *adj.* 可容許的;可承認的。—**per·mis·si·bil·i·ty,** *n.* —**per·mis·si·bly,** *adv.*
***per·mis·sion** [pəˈmɪʃən; pəˈmiʃən] *n.* 許可;允許;准許。He did it without *permission.* 他做此事未經許可。
per·mis·sive [pəˈmɪsɪv; pəˈmisiv] *adj.* ①表示准許的。②縱容的。—**ly,** *adv.*
‡**per·mit** [*v.* pəˈmɪt; pəˈmit *n.* ˈpɝmɪt, pəˈmɪt; ˈpəːmit] *v.,* **-mit·ted, -mit·ting,** *n.* —*v.t.* ①允許;容許(某人)。*Permit* me to explain. 請讓我解釋。②准許;許可(事物)。Smoking is not *permitted* here. 此處不准吸烟。—*v.i.* 容許;准許。Write me when time *permits.* 有時間請寫信給我。*permit of* 容許。The situation does not *permit of* any delay. 這情況不容有任何耽擱。—*n.* ①許可證。an entry *permit.* 入境證。②許可;准許。
per·mut·a·ble [pəˈmjutəbl̩; pəˈmjuːtəbl] *adj.* ①可變換的;可互換的。②易變的。③〖數學〗可排列的。
per·mu·ta·tion [ˌpɝmjəˈteʃən; ˌpəːmjuː(ː)ˈteiʃən] *n.* ①交換;互換;變換;變化。②〖數學〗順列;排列。③排列中之任一組數字或文字。
permutation and combination 〖數學〗排列組合。
per·mute [pəˈmjut; pəˈmjuːt] *v.t.,* **-mut·ed, -mut·ing.** ①交換;變換;變更…之次序。②〖數學〗排列。
per·ni·cious [pəˈnɪʃəs; pəːˈniʃəs] *adj.* ①有害的;有毒的。②惡性的;致命的。*pernicious* anemia. 惡性貧血。③惡毒的;邪惡的。—**ly,** *adv.*
per·nick·et·y [pəˈnɪkɪtɪ; pəˈnikiti] *adj.* ①吹毛求疵的;好挑剔的。②難對付的;不好惹的;須小心從事的。
per·o·rate [ˈpɛrəˌret; ˈperəreit] *v.i.,* **-rat·ed, -rat·ing.** ①演說;評論;作冗長的(激昂的)演說。②(於演說末了)作結論。
per·o·ra·tion [ˌpɛroˈreʃən; ˌperəˈreiʃən] *n.* ①(演說等之)結論;總結。②慷慨陳辭。
per·o·ra·tor [ˈpɛrəˌretɚ; ˈperəreitə] *n.* 作冗長的(激昂的)演說者。
per·ox·id [pəˈrɑksɪd; pəˈrɔksid] *n.* 〖化〗=**peroxide.**
per·ox·ide [pəˈrɑksaɪd; pəˈrɔksaid] *n.* 〖化〗①過氧化物。②過氧化氫。—*v.t.* 以過氧化氫漂白(頭髮等)。
per·pend [pəˈpɛnd; pəːˈpend] *v.t.* & *v.i.* 仔細考慮;注意。
***per·pen·dic·u·lar** [ˌpɝpənˈdɪkjəlɚ; ˌpəːpənˈdikjulə] *adj.* ①垂直的。a *perpendicular* cliff. 絕壁。②垂直線的;成直角的。—*n.* ①垂直;直立姿勢。②垂直線;垂直面。*be out of (the) perpendicular* 傾斜。—**ly,** *adv.*
per·pen·dic·u·lar·i·ty [ˌpɝpənˌdɪkjəˈlærətɪ; ˈpəːpənˌdikjuˈlæriti] *n.* 垂直;直立。
per·pe·trate [ˈpɝpəˌtret; ˈpəːpitreit] *v.t.,* **-trat·ed, -trat·ing.** ①犯(罪);作(惡)。②開(玩笑);行(詐)。③笨拙地實施或表演。—**per·pe·tra·tion, per·pe·tra·tor,** *n.*
***per·pet·u·al** [pəˈpɛtʃuəl; pəˈpetʃuəl] *adj.* ①永久的;永續的。②終生的;終身的。③不斷的。a *perpetual* stream of visitors. 賓客絡繹不絕。④(花卉)整年開花的。—*n.* 整年開花的雜交種玫瑰。—**ness,** *n.* —**ly,** *adv.*
perpetual calendar 萬年曆。
perpetual motion 〖物理〗永恆運動。
per·pet·u·ate [pəˈpɛtʃuˌet; pəˈpetʃueit] *v.,* **-at·ed, -at·ing,** *adj.* —*v.t.* 使永存;使永恆;使不朽。—*adj.* 已成爲永恆不朽的。—**per·pet·u·a·tion, per·pet·u·a·tor,** *n.*
per·pe·tu·i·ty [ˌpɝpəˈtjuətɪ; ˌpəːpiˈtju(ː)iti] *n.* ①永存;永久。②永存之物;永遠之財產。③終身年金。*in perpetuity* 永遠地。
***per·plex** [pəˈplɛks; pəˈpleks] *v.t.* ①使困窘;使迷惑。to *perplex* a man with questions. 以問題使人困窘。②使難解;使混亂。to *perplex* an issue. 使一問題難解。
per·plexed [pəˈplɛkst; pəˈplekst] *adj.* ①爲難的;困惑的;不知所措的。②混雜的;混亂的。—**ly,** *adv.*
per·plex·ing [pəˈplɛksɪŋ; pəˈpleksiŋ] *adj.* ①使人困窘(困惑)的。②複雜的;麻煩的。—**ly,** *adv.*
***per·plex·i·ty** [pəˈplɛksətɪ; pəˈpleksiti] *n., pl.* **-ties.** 困惑;混亂;困惑、混亂之事物。*in perplexity* 困惑地。He looked at us *in perplexity.* 他困惑地看着我們。
per pro·cu·ra·ti·o·nem [~ˌprɑ-

kjuˌrɛʃɪ'onɛm; ～ˌprɔkjuˌreiʃi'ounem] 〖拉〗〖法律〗經由代理(＝by proxy).

per·qui·site ['pɝkwəzɪt; 'pəːkwizit] *n.* ①正式薪餉以外之任何收入; 額外補貼; 小費; 獎金。②因爲身分、地位等而享有的特權。③〖法律〗自得物(世襲物之相對)。

Per·rin [pɛ'rɛ̃; 'perin] *n.* 伯蘭 (Jean Baptiste, 1870-1942, 法國物理學家, 獲 1926 年諾貝爾物理獎)。

per·ron ['pɛrən; 'perən] *n.* ①〖建築〗石階(大建築物門口等的)。②作講臺用的大石塊。

per·ry ['pɛrɪ; 'peri] *n.* 梨酒。

Pers. Persia(n).

***per·se·cute** ['pɝsɪˌkjut; 'pəːsikjuːt] *v.t.*, **-cut·ed, -cut·ing.** ①迫害; 宗教迫害。Christians were terribly *persecuted*. 基督徒受到嚴重迫害。②困惑; 煩擾。

per·se·cut·ee [ˌpɝsəkju'ti; ˌpəːsəkjuː'tiː] *n.* 受迫害者(尤指曾受迫害的難民)。

***per·se·cu·tion** [ˌpɝsɪ'kjuʃən; ˌpəːsi'kjuːʃən] *n.* ①(宗教上的)迫害。②迫害; 虐待; 煩擾。

persecution mania 〖精神病〗被迫害妄想症。

per·se·cu·tor ['pɝsɪˌkjutɚ; 'pəːsikjuːtə] *n.* 迫害者; 虐待者; 煩擾者。

Per·seph·o·ne [pɚ'sɛfənɪ; pəː'sefəni] *n.* 〖希臘神話〗①冥王之妻。②春之女神; 春之象徵。

Per·se·us ['pɝsjus; 'pəːsjuːs] *n.* ①〖希臘神話〗Zeus 之子, 殺死女怪 Medusa 之英雄。②〖天文〗英仙座。

***per·se·ver·ance** [ˌpɝsə'vɪrəns; ˌpəːsi'viərəns] *n.* 毅力; 堅忍; 堅持。

***per·se·vere** [ˌpɝsə'vɪr; ˌpəːsi'viə] *v.i.*, **-vered, -ver·ing.** 堅忍; 堅持。to *persevere* in one's studies. 孜孜不倦。

per·se·ver·ing [ˌpɝsə'vɪrɪŋ; ˌpəːsi'viəriŋ] *adj.* 堅持的; 不屈不撓的。—**ly,** *adv.*

Per·sia ['pɝʒə, 'pɝʃə; 'pəːʃə, 'pəːʒə] *n.* 波斯(西南亞國名, 1935 年更名爲 Iran).

Per·sian ['pɝʒən, -ʃən; 'pəːʃən, -ʒən] *adj.* 波斯的; 波斯人(語)的。—*n.* ①波斯人(語)。②＝**Persian blinds.** ③〖建築〗人形柱。

Persian blinds 〖建築〗百葉窗。

Persian carpet (or **rug**) 波斯地毯。

Persian cat 波斯貓。

Persian Gulf 波斯灣(伊朗與阿拉伯間之海灣)。

Persian lamb 波斯羔; 波斯羔之毛皮。

per·si·ennes [ˌpɝzɪ'ɛnz; ˌpəːzi'enz] *n. pl.* ＝**Persian blinds.**

per·si·flage ['pɝsɪˌflɑʒ; ˌpɛəsi'flɑːʒ] *n.* 戲謔; 嘲弄; 挖苦。

***per·sim·mon** [pɚ'sɪmən; pəː'simən] *n.* 柿子樹; 柿子。

***per·sist** [pɚ'zɪst; pə'sist] *v.i.* ①堅持; 固執。He *persists* in doing it. 他堅持要做此事。②持久; 耐久。③重複申說; 主張。

per·sist·ence [pɚ'sɪstəns, -'zɪst-; pə'sistəns] *n.* ①堅持; 堅忍; 固執。②繼續存在; 持久; 持續。(亦作 **persistency**)

persistence of vision 視覺暫留。

***per·sist·ent** [pɚ'zɪstənt, -'sɪst-; pə'sistənt] *adj.* ①固執的; 堅持的。②繼續的; 永續的。③一再出現的; 經常重複的。④〖植物〗永久的; 不凋謝的。⑤〖動物〗發展過程中不改變或失掉的。⑥(尤指殺蟲劑)不易分解的。—**ly,** *adv.*

per·snick·e·ty [pɚ'snɪkɪtɪ; pəː'snikəti] *adj.* 〖俗〗＝**pernickety.**

‡per·son ['pɝsn̩; 'pəːsn] *n.* ①人。the average *person*. 常人。②身體; 外貌。He has a fine *person*. 他有優美的容貌。③〖文法〗人稱; 身。**first person.** 第一人稱。**second person.** 第二人稱。**third person.** 第三人稱。④〖神學〗(聖父、聖子、及聖靈之三位一體的)位。the three *persons* of the Godhead. 上帝一體中的三位。⑤小說或戲劇中之角色。*in person* **a.** 親身(出現)。Come *in person*; do not write or phone. 親自來, 不要寫信或打電話。**b.** 在舞臺上出現(非在電影或電視中出現)。

per·so·na [pɚ'sonə; pəː'sounə] 〖拉〗 *n.*, *pl.* **-nae** [-ni; -niː]. ①人。②(*pl.*)(一齣戲劇、一本小說等中之)角色; 人物。

per·son·a·ble ['pɝsn̩əbl̩, 'pɝsnə-; 'pəːsn̩əbl] *adj.* 貌美的; 動人的; 風度好的。

***per·son·age** ['pɝsn̩ɪdʒ, 'pɝsnɪdʒ; 'pəːsn̩idʒ, 'pəːsnidʒ] *n.* ①顯赫之人; 名人。②人; 個人。③(小說、戲劇等中之)人物; 角色。④容貌; 風采。She is stately in *personage*. 她儀容莊麗。

per·so·na (non) gra·ta [pɚ'sonə(ˌnɑn)'gretə; pəː'sounə(ˌnɔn)'greitə] *pl.* **per·so·nae (non) gra·tae** [pɚ'soni(nɑn)-'grɑti; pəː'souniː(nɔn)'grɑːti]. 〖拉〗(不)討人歡喜的人; (不)受(駐在地政府)歡迎的外交官。The ambassador left the country within 24 hours after he was declared *persona non grata*. 該大使在被宣布爲不受歡迎者後二十四小時之內離開了那個國家。

‡per·son·al ['pɝsn̩l; 'pəːsnl] *adj.* ①個人的; 私人的。a *personal* letter. 私人信件。②本人的; 親自的。a *personal* call (*or* visit). 親身拜訪。③身體的; 外貌的。④關於或針對個人的; 攻擊人的。*personal* abuse. 人身攻擊。⑤說話或問題涉及私事的。Don't be too *personal*. 談話不要過於涉及私事。⑥〖文法〗人稱的。⑦〖法律〗動產的。—*n.* 〖美〗①有關個人之短聞。②有關私事的廣告; 人事廣告。

personal effects 〖法律〗個人的財產; 所有物。

***per·son·al·i·ty** [ˌpɝsn̩'ælətɪ; ˌpəːsə'næliti] *n.*, *pl.* **-ties.** ①個性。②人格。The boy is developing a fine *personality*. 這孩子正在發展一個完美的人格。③對人之攻擊; 誹謗。④名人; 人物。⑤人之特性。

personality cult 對個人之偶像式崇拜。

per·son·al·ize ['pɝsn̩l̩ˌaɪz; 'pəːsn̩əlaiz] *v.t.*, **-ized, -iz·ing.** ①使成爲私人的; 使個人化; 使成個人(私人)之物。*personalized* stationery. 私人信紙信封。②賦以個性; 使人格化。③印個人姓名於(支票等)。

***per·son·al·ly** ['pɝsn̩lɪ; 'pəːsnəli] *adv.* ①親自地。②就本人而論。*Personally*, I don't think so. 我個人不這樣想。③就人而論。

personal pronoun 〖文法〗人稱代名詞。

personal property 動產。

personal shopper 百貨公司中協助顧客挑選貨物或辦理挑選郵購物品的雇員。

personal staff 〖軍〗將級軍官的侍從官。

per·son·al·ty ['pɝsn̩ltɪ; 'pəːsnlti] *n.*, *pl.* **-ties.** 〖法律〗動產(爲 realty 之對)。

per·son·ate ['pɝsn̩ˌet; 'pəːsəneit] *v.*, **-at·ed, -at·ing,** *adj.* —*v.t.* ①扮演; 飾演。②假扮; 僞裝。③冒充。④象徵; 代表。—*v.i.* 扮演; 僞裝。—*adj.* 〖植物〗面具狀的。

per·son·a·tion [ˌpɝsn̩'eʃən; ˌpəːsə'neiʃən] *n.* ①扮演; 假裝; 冒充。②身分之假冒; 冒名; 化身。

per·son·a·tor ['pɝsn̩ˌetɚ; 'pəːsəneitə] *n.* 扮演者;演員;假冒者。

per·son·i·fi·ca·tion [pə͵sɑnəfə'keʃən; pəː͵sɔnifi'keiʃən] *n.* ①擬人。②化身。③例子;典型。

per·son·i·fy [pə'sɑnə͵faɪ; pəː'sɔnifai] *v.t.*, **-fied, -fy·ing.** ①擬爲人;視爲人。②爲…之化身。

***per·son·nel** [͵pɝsn̩'ɛl; ͵pəːsə'nel] *n.* 人員(集合稱)。the bureau of *personnel.* 人事室(局)。—*adj.* ①人事的; 人員的。②負責人事的。a *personnel* officer. 人事官。

personnel agency 職業介紹所。

personnel director 人事主任。

per·son-to-per·son ['pɝsəntə'pɝsən; 'pəːsəntə'pəːsən] *adj.* 私人間的;個人的。a *person-to-person* phone call. 叫人電話。—*adv.* ①(打長途電話)給某人。②親自。

***per·spec·tive** [pə'spɛktɪv; pə'spektiv] *n.* ①透視法; 遠近的配合。 in *perspective.* 合於透視法的。 ②透視畫。③正確的眼光。to see things in *perspective.* 正確地觀察事物。④距離對物品外表的效果。⑤事過境遷後對心靈的效果;回顧的見解。⑥前景;遠景;眼界。⑦前途; 希望。—*adj.* 透視的;配景的。*perspective* glass. 望遠鏡。—**ly,** *adv.*

per·spi·ca·cious [͵pɝspɪ'keʃəs; ͵pəːspi'keiʃəs] *adj.* 聰慧的; 明察的。—**ly,** *adv.*

per·spi·cac·i·ty [͵pɝspɪ'kæsətɪ; ͵pəːspi'kæsiti] *n.* 穎悟;敏銳;聰慧;明察。

per·spi·cu·i·ty [͵pɝspɪ'kjuətɪ; ͵pəːspi'kju(ː)iti] *n.* (文體等之)明白; 明晰。

per·spic·u·ous [pə'spɪkjuəs; pə'spikjuəs] *adj.* ①顯明的;明白的;明晰的(文體)。②說話明白的(人)。③=**perspicacious.** —**ly,** *adv.* —**ness,** *n.*

per·spir·a·ble [pə'spaɪrəbl̩; pəː'spaiərəbl] *adj.* ①可出汗的。②可使汗排出的。

per·spi·ra·tion [͵pɝspə'reʃən; ͵pəːspə'reiʃən] *n.* ①汗。②流汗。Genius is one percent inspiration and ninety-nine percent *perspiration.* 天才是百分之一的靈感加上百分之九十九的流汗(努力)。

per·spir·a·to·ry [pə'spaɪrə͵torɪ; pəː'spaiərətəri] *adj.* ①汗的。②引起流汗的。

per·spire [pə'spaɪr; pəs'paiə] *v.*, **-spired, -spir·ing.** —*v.i.* 流汗。—*v.t.* 自毛孔排出;滲出;流(汗)。

per·suad·a·ble [pə'swedəbl̩; pə'sweidəbl] *adj.* 可說服的;可勸說的。

***per·suade** [pə'swed; pə'sweid] *v.t.*, **-suad·ed, -suad·ing.** 說服; 勸誘; 使信。He *persuaded* me to go. 他勸我去。

per·suad·er [pə'swedɚ; pə'sweidə] *n.* ①勸說者; 說客。②〖諧,俚〗用以迫使動物或人服從的東西(如刺馬釘、鎗等)。

per·sua·si·ble [pə'swesəbl̩; pə'sweisibl] *adj.* 可說服的。

***per·sua·sion** [pə'sweʒən; pə'sweiʒən] *n.* ①說服; 勸誘。 All our *persuasion* was of no use; she would not come. 我們所有的勸誘都無效,她不願意來。②說服力。③堅定的信念。④信條;宗派;宗教信仰。⑤〖諧〗種類;性別;階級。

per·sua·sive [pə'swesɪv; pə'sweisiv] *adj.* 能說服的; 能勸誘的; 善於遊說的。—*n.* 勸誘之手段。—**ly,** *adv.* —**ness,** *n.*

PERT [pɝt; pəːt] *n.* 〖電腦〗程式評核術(爲 *P*rogram *E*valuation and *R*eview *T*echnique 之略)。

pert [pɝt; pəːt] *adj.* ①無禮的;粗魯的;孟浪的;魯莽的。②〖方〗活潑的;精神抖擻的;健康的。 ③ 絢爛的; 美麗的; 華麗的; 茂盛的。—*n.* 無禮的人; 淘氣的小孩。 —**ness,** *n.* —**ly,** *adv.*

pert. pertaining.

per·tain [pə'ten; pəː'tein] *v.i.* ①屬於。②有關;關於。The letter does not *pertain* to politics. 這封信與政治無關。③合宜;適於。

per·ti·na·cious [͵pɝtn̩'eʃəs; ͵pəːti'neiʃəs] *adj.* ①頑固的;頑強的;糾纏不放的。②堅持的; 持久的; 繼續不斷的; 不屈不撓的。—**ly,** *adv.* —**ness,** *n.*

per·ti·nac·i·ty [͵pɝtn̩'æsətɪ; ͵pəːti'næsiti] *n.* 頑固;固執;執拗;堅持;糾纏不休。

per·ti·nence ['pɝtn̩əns; 'pəːtinəns] *n.* 適當;恰當;中肯;切題。(亦作 **pertinency**)

per·ti·nent ['pɝtn̩ənt; 'pəːtinənt] *adj.* 有關係的;適當的;中肯的;切題的。Your remark is not *pertinent* to the subject. 你的話不切題。—**ly,** *adv.*

per·turb [pə'tɝb; pə'təːb] *v.t.* ①使心煩意亂。②擾亂;攪亂。—**a·ble,** *adj.*

per·tur·ba·tion [͵pɝtə'beʃən; ͵pəːtəː'beiʃən] *n.* 擾亂;混亂;倉皇;煩亂。

per·tus·sis [pə'tʌsɪs; pə'tʌsis] *n.* 〖醫〗百日咳。

Pe·ru [pə'ru; pə'ruː, pi'ruː] *n.* 秘魯(南美國名,首都利瑪 Lima)。

pe·ruke [pə'ruk; pə'ruːk] *n.* (十七、八世紀男人戴之)假髮。

pe·ru·sal [pə'ruzl̩; pə'ruːzəl] *n.* ①細讀;閱讀。②細察;詳審。

pe·ruse [pə'ruz; pə'ruːz] *v.t.* ①細讀;精讀。②讀;閱讀。③〖古〗詳細考查;觀察。

Pe·ru·vi·an [pə'ruvɪən; pə'ruːvjən] *adj.* 秘魯的;秘魯人的。—*n.* 秘魯人。

***per·vade** [pə'ved; pəː'veid] *v.t.*, **-vad·ed, -vad·ing.** ①遍布;瀰漫;遍及。The air is *pervaded* by a smell. 空氣中瀰漫着一種氣味。②走遍。

per·va·sion [pə'veʒən; pəː'veiʒən] *n.* 遍布;瀰漫。

per·va·sive [pə'vesɪv; pəː'veisiv] *adj.* ①遍布的;瀰漫的;普遍的。②有滲透力的。

per·verse [pə'vɝs; pə'vəːs] *adj.* ①邪惡的。②剛愎的; 固執的; 倔強的。③錯誤的; 荒謬的。④與所希望者相反的。⑤放縱的;任性的。—**ly,** *adv.* —**ness,** *n.*

per·ver·sion [pə'vɝʒən; pə'vəːʃən] *n.* ①顚倒;倒置。②曲解;歪曲;誤用。③反常;變態。④〖心理〗性慾倒錯;性變態。⑤惡化;敗壞。⑥顚倒的形式。

per·ver·si·ty [pə'vɝsətɪ; pə'vəːsiti] *n.*, *pl.* **-ties.** ①邪惡;剛愎;固執;倔強;荒謬。②邪惡的行爲或性格。

per·ver·sive [pə'vɝsɪv; pə'vəːsiv] *adj.* ①偏頗的;枉曲的;曲解的。②敗壞的;導入邪惡的。

per·vert [*v.* pə'vɝt; pə'vəːt *n.* 'pɝvɝt; 'pəːvəːt] *v.t.* ①誘惑;引入邪路;敗壞。②曲解;誤解。③誤用。④使反常;使變惡劣。⑤使降低價值。—*n.* ①墮落的人。②性變態者。—**er,** *n.*

per·vert·ed [pə'vɝtɪd; pə'vəːtid] *adj.* ①誤入歧途的;錯誤的;濫用的。②〖醫〗異常的;變態的。③被曲解的;歪曲的。④惡毒的;邪惡的。⑤性變態的;性變態者的。

perverted image 反像。(亦作 **mirror image**)

per·vert·i·ble [pə'vɝtəbl̩; pə'vəːtibl] *adj.* ①可被曲解的;易被誤解的。②可濫用的。③可導入邪惡的。

per·vi·ca·cious [͵pɝvə'keʃəs; ͵pəː-

vəˈkeiʃəs] *adj.* 任性的;剛愎的。
per·vi·ous [ˈpɝvɪəs; ˈpəːviəs] *adj.* ①(水等)可浸透的。②(光線、空氣)可透過的。Glass is *pervious* to light. 玻璃是透光的。③對理智或情感有感受力的。④可通行的。⑤〖動物〗有孔的。⑥可滲透的。**—ness,** *n.*
Pes·ca·do·res [ˌpɛskɑˈdorɪz; ˌpeskəˈdɔːriz] *n. pl.* 澎湖羣島(中譯爲 Penghu)。
pe·se·ta [pəˈsɛtə; pəˈseitə] *n.* 西班牙銀幣名(與法郎價值同)。
pes·ky [ˈpɛskɪ; ˈpeski] *adj.,* **-ki·er, -ki·est.** 〖俗〗煩惱的;厭煩的;討厭的。
pe·so [ˈpeso; ˈpeisou] *n.* ①披索(中南美、墨西哥及菲律賓之貨幣單位)。②〖美俚〗美元。
pes·sa·ry [ˈpɛsərɪ; ˈpesəri] *n., pl.* **-ries.** 〖醫〗①子宮壓定器。②(避姙用)子宮套。
***pes·si·mism** [ˈpɛsəˌmɪzəm; ˈpesimizəm] *n.* 悲觀;悲觀主義。
pes·si·mist [ˈpɛsəmɪst; ˈpesimist] *n.* ①悲觀者。②悲觀主義者。
pes·si·mis·tic [ˌpɛsəˈmɪstɪk; ˌpesiˈmistik] *adj.* ①悲觀的。②悲觀主義的。**—al·ly,** *adv.*
***pest** [pɛst; pest] *n.* ①令人討厭的人或物;有害的人或物。②疫病。
pes·ter [ˈpɛstɚ; ˈpestə] *v.t.* 使困惱;使厭煩;使苦惱。—*n.* 使人困惱或厭煩的人或物;苦惱之事。
pest·hole [ˈpɛstˌhol; ˈpesthoul] *n.* 疾病瘟疫等容易滋生之處(如貧民窟)。
pest·house [ˈpɛstˌhaus; ˈpesthaus] *n.* 傳染病醫院;隔離病院。
pest·i·cide [ˈpɛstɪsaɪd; ˈpestisaid] *n.* 殺蟲劑。**—pes·ti·cid·al,** *adj.*
pes·tif·er·ous [pɛsˈtɪfərəs; pesˈtifərəs] *adj.* ①傳播疾病的。②有毒害的;敗壞風俗的;有害社會的。③〖俗〗厭煩的;討厭的。
***pes·ti·lence** [ˈpɛstləns; ˈpestiləns] *n.* ①傳染病;流行病;瘟疫;(特指)黑死病;鼠疫。A *pestilence* broke out. 瘟疫發生。②任何有毒害之物;傳布疫病之物。③傷風敗德之事。
pes·ti·lent [ˈpɛstl̩ənt; ˈpestilənt] *adj.* ①瘟疫的;傳染病的;導致死亡的。②敗壞風俗的;破壞治安的。③討厭的;厭煩的(常用作幽默語)。**—ly,** *adv.*
pes·ti·len·tial [ˌpɛstl̩ˈɛnʃəl; ˌpestiˈlenʃəl] *adj.* ①瘟疫的;傳染病的。②產生或可能釀成傳染病的。③惡毒的;毒害的。④極討厭的;極厭煩的。
pes·tle [ˈpɛsl̩; ˈpesl] *n., v.,* **-tled, -tling.** —*n.* 杵。—*v.t. & v.i.* 以杵搗;以杵研。
pet¹** [pɛt; pet] *n., adj., v.,* **pet·ted, pet·ting.** —*n.* ①受寵愛的動物。Do you keep *pets?* 你養小動物嗎? ②愛物;寵物;受寵愛的人。pet aversion*** 最討厭的東西。—*adj.* ①寵愛的;得意的。a *pet* theory. 得意的論調。②〖俗〗特殊的;特別的。—*v.t.* 寵愛;愛撫。She is *petting* her cat. 她在撫摸她的貓。
pet² *n., v.,* **pet·ted, pet·ting.** —*n.* 慍怒;不悅。to be in a *pet*. 在發怒中;生氣。—*v.i.* 不悅;生氣。
***pet·al** [ˈpɛtl̩; ˈpetl] *n.* 花瓣。
pet·al(l)ed [ˈpɛtl̩d; ˈpetld] *adj.* 有花瓣的。
pe·tard [pɪˈtɑrd; piˈtɑːd] *n.* ①古時攻城堡時炸開城門的一種爆炸裝置。②〖英〗一種爆竹。***hoist with*** (or ***by, on***) ***one's own petard*** 害人反害己。
pet·a·sos, pet·a·sus [ˈpɛtəsəs; ˈpetəsəs] *n., pl.* **-si** [-ˌsaɪ; -sai]. ①(古希臘人的)闊邊低頂帽。②〖希臘神話〗Hermes 之有翼帽。
pet·cock [ˈpɛtˌkɑk; ˈpetkɔk] *n.* (蒸汽引擎等之)小活栓;小龍頭;扭塞。(亦作 **pet cock**)
pe·tech·i·a [pəˈtɛkɪə; pəˈtekiə] *n.* 〖醫〗瘀點;瘀斑。
pete·man [ˈpitmən; ˈpiːtmən] *n., pl.* **-men.** 〖俚〗精於開保險箱之竊賊。
Pe·ter [ˈpitɚ; ˈpiːtə] *n.* ①男子名。②彼得(耶穌十二門徒之一)。③彼得書(新約聖經卷名,分前書、後書,相傳爲彼得所作)。***rob Peter to pay Paul*** 借債來還債;東借西還。
pe·ter¹ [ˈpitɚ; ˈpiːtə] *v.i.* 漸小、漸弱而終於消失〖out〗.
pe·ter² *n.* 用作起船信號的旗。
Peter Pan ① J. M. Barrie 作之童話劇。②該劇之主角(一個不願長大而勇敢的少年)。
Peter Principle 彼得原理(主張將員工提升至不能勝任的地步爲止)。
pe·ter·sham [ˈpitɚʃəm; ˈpiːtəʃəm] *n.* ①有棱條的粗呢;用此種呢製成的外套。②有棱條的絲帶。
pet·i·o·lar [ˈpɛtɪəlɚ; ˈpetiələ] *adj.* 〖植物〗葉柄的;生在葉柄上的。
pet·i·o·late [ˈpɛtɪəˌlet; ˈpetiəleit] *adj.* ①〖植物〗有葉柄的。②〖動物〗有肉莖(肉柄)的。
pet·i·ole [ˈpɛtɪˌol; ˈpetioul] *n.* ①〖植物〗葉柄。②〖動物〗肉柄;肉莖。
pet·it [ˈpɛtɪ; ˈpeti] *adj.* 小的;瑣屑的;微不足道的。
pe·tite [pəˈtit; pəˈtiːt] 〖法〗 *adj.* 小的;細的;嬌小的(常用以形容婦女)。
pet·it four [ˈpɛtɪˈfor; ˈpetiˈfouə] *pl.* **pet·its fours** [ˈpɛtɪˈforz; ˈpetiˈfouəz]. 精美的小餅。
***pe·ti·tion** [pəˈtɪʃən; piˈtiʃən, pəˈt-] *n.* ①呈請;請願。②〖法律〗請願書;陳情書;訴狀。*petition* for appeal. 起訴狀。③祈禱;懇求。④所呈請或懇求的東西。—*v.t.* ①請求;呈請。to *petition* the government to do a thing. 呈請政府做某事。②祈求;懇求。—*v.i.* 呈請;祈求。to *petition* for a thing. 請求一事。**—er,** *n.*
pe·ti·tion·ar·y [pəˈtɪʃəˌnɛrɪ; piˈtiʃənəri] *adj.* 請求的;請願的;祈禱的;懇求的。
Petition of Right 〖英史〗權利請願書(1628年由議會向 Charles 一世提出並得承認的人權宣言)。
petit jury =**petty jury.**
pe·tit mal [pətiˈmal; pətiːˈmal] 〖法〗〖醫〗輕癲癇。
pet·it point [ˈpɛtɪ～; ˈpetiː～] ①刺繡時之一個針脚。②一種以帆布作襯布的刺繡。
pet name 暱稱。
pet·nap·per [ˈpɛtˌnæpɚ; ˈpetˌnæpə] *n.* 〖美〗偷竊寵物(pet)的人。
pet·nap·ping [ˈpɛtˌnæpɪŋ; ˈpetˌnæpiŋ] *n.* 〖美〗偷竊寵物。
Pe·trarch [ˈpitrɑrk; ˈpetrɑːk] *n.* 佩脫拉克(1304–1374, 義大利文藝復興時代之詩人與學者)。
pet·rel [ˈpɛtrəl; ˈpetrəl] *n.* 海燕。***stormy petrel*** 不祥之人(其來臨預兆麻煩或爭鬥)。
Pe·tri (or **pe·tri**) **dish** [ˈpetri～; ˈpetriː～] 做細菌培養時用的有蓋玻璃碟子。
pet·ri·fac·tion [ˌpɛtrəˈfækʃən; ˌpetriˈfækʃən] *n.* ①化石。②成爲化石;石化。③嚇呆。(亦作 **petrification**)
pet·ri·fac·tive [ˌpɛtrəˈfæktɪv; ˌpetriˈfæktiv] *adj.* 石化的;有石化力的。
pet·ri·fy [ˈpɛtrəˌfaɪ; ˈpetrifai] *v.,* **-fied, -fy·ing.** —*v.t.* ①使堅硬;使僵硬;使麻木。②使石化;使化爲石。③使發呆;嚇呆。—*v.i.* ①發呆;變僵硬。②成爲石;變成石。

petro- 〖字首〗①表 "石; 岩" 之義。②表 "(含)石油的"之義。(母音前作 **petr-**)

pet·ro·chem·i·cal [ˌpɛtroˈkɛməkl; ˌpetrouˈkemikəl] *n.* 石油化學品。—*adj.* 石油化學品的;石油化學的。

pet·ro·chem·is·try [ˌpɛtroˈkɛmɪstrɪ; ˌpetrouˈkemistri] *n.* ①石油化學。②石油化學品之製造;石油化學工業。③岩石化學。

pet·ro·glyph [ˈpɛtrəglɪf; ˈpetrouglif] *n.* (尤指史前的)岩石雕刻。—**ic,** *adj.*

pe·trog·ly·phy [pɪˈtrɑglɪfɪ; piˈtrɔglifi] *n.* 岩石雕刻術。

pet·ro·graph [ˈpɛtrəˌgræf; ˈpetrəgrɑːf] *n.* =**petroglyph.**

pe·trog·ra·phy [pɪˈtrɑgrəfɪ; piːˈtrɔgrəfi] *n.* 岩石記載(分類)學。

pet·rol [ˈpɛtrəl; ˈpetrəl] *n., v.,* **-rolled, -rol·ling.** —*n.* 〖英〗汽油 (=gasoline). —*v.t.* ①以汽油洗淨。②供以汽油。

pet·ro·la·tum [ˌpɛtrəˈletəm; ˌpetrəˈleitəm] *n.* 〖化〗①得自石油的一種半固體的油性物質(如凡士林等)。②礦油。

petrol bomb 〖英〗汽油彈。

petrol engine 〖英〗汽油發動機。

***pe·tro·le·um** [pəˈtrolɪəm; piˈtrouliəm, pəˈt-] *n.* 石油。

pe·trol·ic [pɪˈtrɑlɪk; piˈtrɔlik] *adj.* 石油的;似石油的;產自石油的。

pe·trol·o·gy [pɪˈtrɑlədʒɪ; piːˈtrɔlədʒi] *n.* 岩石學。—**pet·ro·log·ic,** *adj.*

pet·rous [ˈpɛtrəs; ˈpetrəs] *adj.* ①岩石的;堅硬的。②〖解剖〗岩狀(部)的;顳顬骨的。

pet·ti·coat** [ˈpɛtɪˌkot; ˈpetikout] *n.* ①(婦孺所穿的)裙子(尤指襯裙)。②如裙狀的遮蓋物。③〖俗〗女人;女孩。wear*** (or ***be in***) ***petticoats*** **a.** 幼小;幼稚。The boy *is* still *in petticoats.* 那小孩年紀尚幼。**b.** 行為似婦女。—*adj.* ①女人的。*petticoat* government. 裙帶政治;牝雞司晨。②娘娘腔的。

pet·ti·fog [ˈpɛtɪˌfɑg; ˈpetifɔg] *v.i.,* **-fogged, -fog·ging.** ①作瑣碎的法律事務;以詭詐手段作法律事務;作訟棍。②吹毛求疵。

pet·ti·fog·ger [ˈpɛtɪˌfɑgə; ˈpetifɔgə] *n.* ①非正式之律師; 卑劣之律師; 訟棍。②運用卑劣、欺詐手段的人。

pet·ti·fog·ger·y [ˈpɛtɪˌfɑgərɪ; ˈpetifɔgəri] *n.* =**pettifogging.**

pet·ti·fog·ging [ˈpɛtɪˌfɑgɪŋ; ˈpetifɔgiŋ] *adj.* ①訟棍式的;狡猾的;欺詐的;卑劣的。②瑣碎的。—*n.* 訟棍技倆;歪曲的辯護;詭計。

petting party 〖美〗(可隨便接吻、摟抱的)青年男女的愛撫會。

pet·tish [ˈpɛtɪʃ; ˈpetiʃ] *adj.* 易怒的;壞脾氣的。

pet·ti·toes [ˈpɛtɪˌtoz; ˈpetitouz] *n. pl.* ①(食用之)豬蹄。②人足;(特指)幼兒之足。

***pet·ty** [ˈpɛtɪ; ˈpeti] *adj.,* **-ti·er, -ti·est.** ①細小的; 瑣屑的。②卑賤的;小器的;心胸狹窄的。③低下的;下級的。④表示小器的。⑤次要的;小規模的。—**pet·ti·ly,** *adv.* —**pet·ti·ness,** *n.*

petty cash 少數的現金收支; 零用錢。

petty farmer 小農。

petty jury 小陪審團 (由12人組成)。

petty larceny 小竊盜。

petty officer (海軍的)士官。

pet·u·lance [ˈpɛtʃələns; ˈpetjuləns] *n.* ①性急;暴躁。②性急或暴躁的舉動、脾氣。③暴躁的行動或言語。(亦作 **petulancy**)

pet·u·lant [ˈpɛtʃələnt; ˈpetjulənt] *adj.* 性急的;暴躁的。

pe·tu·ni·a [pəˈtjunjə; piˈtjuːnjə] *n.* ①〖植物〗美洲熱帶土生的一種草本植物, 開各色漏斗形之花(喇叭花)。②深紫紅色。

pe·tun·(t)se [pɛˈtun(t)sɛ; peˈtun(t)se] *n.* 白墩子(精製的白瓷土)。(亦作**petuntze**)

pew [pju; pjuː] *n.* ①教堂中之一排座位。②(=family pew) 教堂內某一家族專用之廂席。*pew* rent. 教堂內家族專用座席之租金。③教堂中教友之集合稱。④〖俗〗任何座位。

pew·age [ˈpjuɪdʒ; ˈpjuːidʒ] *n.* ①教堂座位之集合稱。②教堂內家族專用座席之租金。

pe·wee [ˈpiwi; ˈpiːwiː] *n.* 京燕。

pe·wit [ˈpiwɪt; ˈpiːwit] *n.* ①京燕。②田鳧。③(歐洲之)黑頭鷗。

pew·ter [ˈpjutə; ˈpjuːtə] *n.* ①錫與鉛或其他金屬之合金; 白鑞。②此種合金製成之器皿; 白鑞器。—*adj.* 錫鉛合金製成的; 白鑞製的。

pew·ter·er [ˈpjutərə; ˈpjuːtərə] *n.* 白鑞器工匠。

pf, p.f. 〖音樂〗piu forte (義 = a little louder). **pf.** ①perfect. ②pfennig. ③(of stock) preferred. ④pianoforte (義 =soft, then loud). ⑤proof. **PFC, Pfc.** Private First Class. 一等兵。

pfen·nig [ˈpfɛnɪg; ˈpfenig] *n., pl.* **pfen·nigs, pfen·ni·ge** [ˈpfɛnɪgə; ˈpfenigə]. 德國之小銅幣 (值 1/100 馬克, 略作 **pfg., pf.**).

Pg. ①Portugal. ②Portuguese. **pg.** page. **Ph** 〖化〗phenyl. **pH** 表示酸鹹度的符號 (與數字連用, 如 pH7)。

pha·e·ton [ˈfeətn̩; ˈfeitn] *n.* ①一種輕快的四輪馬車。②一種旅行式的敞篷汽車。

phag·o·cyte [ˈfægəˌsaɪt; ˈfægəsait] *n.* 〖生理〗食菌細胞(如白血球等);吞噬細胞。

phag·o·cyt·ic [ˌfægəˈsɪtɪk; ˌfægəˈsitik] *adj.* 吞噬細胞的;噬菌作用的。

phag·o·cy·to·sis [ˌfægəsaɪˈtosɪs; ˌfægəsaiˈtousis] *n.* (食菌細胞的) 食菌作用;噬菌作用。

phal·ange [ˈfælændʒ; ˈfælændʒ] *n.* 〖解剖〗指骨;趾骨。

pha·lan·ger [feˈlændʒə; feiˈlændʒə] *n.* 〖動物〗(澳洲產的)一種有捲尾的袋鼠。

phal·an·ster·y [ˈfælənˌstɛrɪ; ˈfælənstəri] *n., pl.* **-ster·ies.** ①法國社會主義者 Fourier 之共產同居團體; 其共居之房屋。②共同居住之團體;其房舍。

pha·lanx [ˈfelæŋks; ˈfælæŋks] *n., pl.* **pha·lanx·es,** (for⑤) **pha·lan·ges** [fəˈlændʒiz; fæˈlændʒiːz]. ①古希臘重武裝步兵列成密集的方陣。②列成密集陣形的任何部隊。③大羣集結之人、動物、或物。④為一共同目標而結合的一羣人。⑤〖解剖〗指骨; 趾骨。⑥〖植物〗雄蕊束。

phal·a·rope [ˈfælərop; ˈfæləroup] *n.* (鳥)磯鷸類。

phal·lic [ˈfælɪk; ˈfælik] *adj.* 陰莖的;陰莖像的;陽物崇拜的。

phal·lism [ˈfælɪzəm; ˈfælizəm] *n.* 陽物崇拜;生殖器崇拜。(亦作 **phallicism**)

phal·lus [ˈfæləs; ˈfæləs] *n., pl.* **phal·li** [ˈfælaɪ; ˈfælai]. ①陰莖之圖像。②〖解剖〗陰莖;陰蒂。

phan·er·o·gam [ˈfænərəˌgæm; ˈfænərougæm] *n.* 〖植物〗顯花植物。—**ic,** *adj.*

phan·er·og·a·mous [ˌfænəˈrɑgəməs; ˌfænəˈrɔgəməs] *adj.* 有雄蕊與雌蕊的;有花的;顯花的。

phan·tasm [ˈfæntæzəm; ˈfæntæzəm] *n.* ①幻象; 幻景; 夢景。②幻想;空想。③鬼

魂;幽靈。④〖哲學〗實物之心象。⑤對某種事物之描述。(亦作 **fantasm**)

phan·tas·ma·go·ri·a 〔ˌfæntæzmə'gorɪə; ˌfæntæzmə'gɔriə〕 *n.* ①魔術幻燈。②變幻不定的光景。③連續雜亂的幻象;(夢中的)幻影。—**phan·tas·ma·gor·ic,** *adj.*

phan·tas·mic 〔fæn'tæzmɪk; fæn'tæzmik〕 *adj.* ①幻想的;幻象的。②幻覺的;非眞實的。③幽靈的。(亦作 **phantasmal**)

phan·ta·sy 〔'fæntəsɪ; 'fæntəsi〕 *n., pl.* **-sies.** ①＝**fantasy.** ②〖音樂〗＝**fantasia.**

***phan·tom** 〔'fæntəm; 'fæntəm〕 *n.* ①幻影;幻象。*phantoms* of a dream. 夢中的幻象。②幽靈;鬼怪。③空想;幻想。④外表;有名無實。He is only a *phantom* of a king. 他只是有名無實的國王。—*adj.* 虛幻的;若鬼的。 a *phantom* ship. 鬼船。

phantom order 〖美〗俟官方指示後始有實效的(飛機、武器等)訂購契約。

Phar., phar. ①pharmaceutical. ②pharmacology. ③pharmacopoeia. ④pharmacy.

Phar·aoh 〔'fɛro; 'fɛərou〕 *n.* 法老(古埃及王的尊稱)。

Phar. B. Bachelor of Pharmacy.

Phar. D. Doctor of Pharmacy.

Phar·i·sa·i·cal 〔ˌfærə'se·ɪkl; ˌfæri'seiikəl〕 *adj.* ①古猶太之法利賽教派的。②(p-) 假裝虔誠的;拘泥形式的;僞善的。(亦作 **Pharisaic**)

Phar·i·sa·ism 〔'færəseˌɪzəm; 'færiseiizəm〕 *n.* ①法利賽教派之教義或習俗。②(p-)(宗教上的)形式主義;僞善。

Phar·i·see 〔'færəˌsi; 'færisiː〕 *n.* ①古猶太法利賽教派之教徒。②(p-) 處守宗教儀式而自認聖潔者。③僞善者。

Pharm., pharm. ①pharmaceutic. ②pharmacology. ③pharmacopoeia. ④pharmacy.

phar·ma·ceu·tic 〔ˌfɑrmə'sjutɪk; ˌfɑːmə'sjuːtik〕 *adj.* ＝**pharmaceutical.** —*n.* 藥劑。

phar·ma·ceu·ti·cal 〔ˌfɑrmə'sjutɪkl; ˌfɑːmə'sjuːtikəl〕 *adj.* 製藥的;調藥的。

phar·ma·ceu·tics 〔ˌfɑrmə'sjutɪks; ˌfɑːmə'sjuːtiks〕 *n.* 調劑學;製藥學。

phar·ma·cist 〔'fɑrməsɪst; 'fɑːməsist〕 *n.* 藥劑師;製藥者。(亦作 **pharmaceutist**)

pharmaco- 〖字首〗表"藥"之義。

pharmacol. pharmacology.

phar·ma·col·o·gist 〔ˌfɑrmə'kɑlədʒɪst; ˌfɑːmə'kɔlədʒist〕 *n.* 藥物學者。

phar·ma·col·o·gy 〔ˌfɑrmə'kɑlədʒɪ; ˌfɑːmə'kɔlədʒi〕 *n.* 藥物學;藥理學。

phar·ma·co·p(o)e·ia 〔ˌfɑrməkə'piə; ˌfɑːməkə'piːə〕 *n.* ①處方書;藥劑書;藥典(尤指官方所刊印者)。②藥品;藥類。

phar·ma·cy 〔'fɑrməsɪ; 'fɑːməsi〕 *n., pl.* **-cies.** ①調藥;配藥;製藥學。②藥房。

pha·ros 〔'fɛrɑs; 'fɛərɔs〕 *n.* ①燈塔。②(P-)埃及北部亞歷山大之一半島(古代爲一小島,其上設有一大燈塔)。③(P-)該燈塔(爲古代七大奇觀之一)。

pha·ryn·gal 〔fə'rɪŋgl; fə'riŋgəl〕 *adj.* ①〖語音〗在咽頭發音的;喉音的。②＝**pharyngeal.**

pha·ryn·ge·al 〔fə'rɪndʒɪəl; ˌfærin'dʒiːəl〕 *adj.* 〖解剖〗咽的。

phar·yn·gi·tis 〔ˌfærɪn'dʒaɪtɪs; ˌfærin'dʒaitis〕 *n.* 〖醫〗咽炎。

pha·ryn·go·scope 〔fə'rɪŋgəˌskop; fə'riŋgə-skoup〕 *n.* 〖醫〗咽頭檢診器;檢咽鏡。

phar·ynx 〔'færɪŋks; 'færiŋks〕 *n., pl.* **phar·ynx·es, pha·ryn·ges** 〔fə'rɪndʒiz; fə'rindʒiːz〕. 〖解剖〗咽。

***phase** 〔fez; feiz〕 *n., v.,* **phased, phas·ing.** —*n.* ①局面;狀態;時期;階段。②(對事物觀察研究之)一面。③〖天文〗(月等之)變象;盈虧。④〖物理〗相;周相;金相;震相。*in phase* 〖物理〗同(周)相。*out of phase* 〖物理〗異(周)相。—*v.t.* ①預先安排或定購。②使在時間上一致;使配合。*phase in* 逐漸採用。*phase out* 逐漸淘汰;逐漸撤退。

phase·down 〔'fezˌdaun; 'feizdaun〕 *n.* 一項計畫或作業之漸次縮減。

phase-out 〔'fezˌaut; 'feizaut〕 *n.* 逐步淘汰。

phas·ic 〔'fezɪk; 'feizik〕 *adj.* ①局面的;形勢的。②〖天文〗象的。③〖物理〗相的;相位的。

Ph.D. Doctor of Philosophy.

***pheas·ant** 〔'fɛzn̩t; 'feznt〕 *n., pl.* **-ants, -ant.** ①雉。②美國南部之一種松雞。

pheasant's eye 福壽草屬的植物。

phel·lo·gen 〔'fɛlədʒən; 'felədʒən〕 *n.* 〖植物〗栓質形成組織。—**ic,** *adj.*

phe·nac·e·tin(e) 〔fə'næsətɪn; fi'næsitin〕 *n.* 〖藥〗非那西汀(一種解熱鎭痛藥)。

Phe·ni·cia 〔fə'nɪʃɪə; fi'niʃiə〕 *n.* ＝**Phoenicia.**

phe·nix 〔'finɪks; 'fiːniks〕 *n.* ＝**phoenix.**

pheno- 〖字首〗〖化〗表"苯的;由苯衍生的"之義。(母音前作 **phen-**)

phe·no·bar·bi·tal 〔ˌfinə'bɑrbɪˌtæl; ˌfiːnə'bɑːbitæl〕 *n.* 〖化〗乙苯基丙二醯脲($C_{12}H_{12}O_3N_2$, 用作鎭靜劑及催眠藥)。(亦作 **luminal**)

phe·nol 〔'finol; 'fiːnɔl〕 *n.* 〖化〗酚;石炭酸(C_6H_5OH)。

phe·no·lic 〔fɪ'nɑlɪk; fi'nɔlik〕 *adj.* 〖化〗(含有)石炭酸的。—*n.* (亦作 **phenolic resin**) 一種合成樹脂。

phe·no·lize 〔'finəlaɪz; 'fiːnəlaiz〕 *v.t.,* **-lized, -liz·ing.** 以石炭酸處理。

phe·nol·o·gy 〔fɪ'nɑlədʒɪ; fi'nɔlədʒi〕 *n.* 生物氣候學。 —**phe·nol·o·gist,** *n.*

phe·nol·phthal·ein 〔ˌfinol'θælin; ˌfiːnɔl'fθæliin〕 *n.* 〖化〗酚酞;二羥二苯基苯二甲內酯(用爲鹹性試劑、瀉藥等)。

phe·nom 〔fɪ'nɑm; fi'nɔm〕 *n.* 〖美俚〗優異的人或物。

phe·nom·e·na 〔fə'nɑmənə; fi'nɔminə〕 *n.* pl. of **phenomenon.**

phe·nom·e·nal 〔fə'nɑmənl; fi'nɔminl〕 *adj.* ①現象的。②有現象之性質的;可由感官感知的。③非凡的。—*n.* 可由感官得知之事物。—**ly,** *adv.* —**i·ty,** *n.*

phe·nom·e·nal·ism 〔fə'nɑmənl̩ɪzəm; fi'nɔminlizm〕 *n.* 〖哲〗現象論;唯象論(認爲知識之對象僅爲現象而不及於物本體者)。

phe·nom·e·nol·o·gy 〔fəˌnɑmɪ'nɑlədʒɪ; fiˌnɔmi'nɔlədʒi〕 *n.* 〖哲〗現象學(爲 ontology 之對)。

***phe·nom·e·non** 〔fə'nɑməˌnɑn; fi'nɔminən〕 *n., pl.* **-na** 〔-nə; -nə〕 or (*for* ②) **-nons.** ①現象。 the *phenomena* of nature. 自然界的現象。②特殊的人;特殊的事物。 an infant *phenomenon.* 神童。

phe·no·type 〔'finəˌtaɪp; 'fiːnətaip〕 *n.* 〖生物〗①顯型;表型(非憑遺傳特性,而憑肉眼所能見之特徵爲區別而形成之一型)。②顯型類之所有生物。

phew 〔fju; fjuː〕 *interj.* 呸!啐!(表示憎厭、不耐、驚訝等之聲)。

phi 〔faɪ; fai〕 *n.* 希臘字母之第21個(Φ, φ)。

phi·al 〔'faɪəl; 'faiəl〕 *n.* 小瓶;小藥瓶。

Phi Be·ta Kap·pa [ˈfaɪˌbetəˈkæpə, ~ˌbitə~; ˈfaiˌbeitəˈkæpə, ~ˌbiːtə~] 成績優秀之美國大學生及畢業生所組成之榮譽學會。

Phid·i·as [ˈfɪdɪəs; ˈfidiæs] *n.* 菲狄亞斯（紀元前第五世紀之希臘雕刻家)。

Phil. 〖聖經〗①Philemon. ②Philip. ③Philippians. ④Philippine.

Phil·a·del·phi·a [ˌfɪləˈdɛlfjə, -fɪə; ˌfiləˈdelfjə, -fiə] *n.* 費城（美國賓夕凡尼亞州東南部城名)。

Philadelphia lawyer 〖美俚〗機敏或精明的律師(尤指手段狡猾者)。

phi·lan·der [fəˈlændɚ; fiˈlændə] *v.i.* (指男子)不貞誠地戀愛;調戲女子。 **—er,** *n.*

phil·an·throp·ic [ˌfɪlənˈθrɑpɪk; ˌfilənˈθrɔpik] *adj.* ①慈善心的;慈善事業的。②慈善的; 博愛的; 仁愛的; 仁慈的。(亦作 **philanthropical**)

phi·lan·thro·pism [fɪˈlænθrəpɪzm̩; fiˈlænθrəpizm] *n.* 博愛;慈善;博愛主義。

phi·lan·thro·pist [fəˈlænθrəpɪst; fiˈlænθrəpist] *n.* 博愛主義者; 慈善家。

phi·lan·thro·py [fəˈlænθrəpɪ; fiˈlænθrəpi] *n., pl.* **-pies.** 慈善心。②慈善事業。

phil·a·tel·ic [ˌfɪləˈtɛlɪk; ˌfiləˈtelik] *adj.* 集郵的。

phi·lat·e·list [fəˈlætlɪst; fiˈlætəlist] *n.* 集郵者;集郵家。

phi·lat·e·ly [fəˈlætlɪ; fiˈlætəli] *n.* 集郵。

-phile 〖字尾〗表"愛; 愛人; 愛好者"之義, 如: Anglophile. (亦作 **-phil**)

Phi·le·mon [fəˈlimən; fiˈliːmɔn] *n.*①男子名。②〖聖經〗(新約聖經之）腓利門書。

phil·har·mon·ic [ˌfɪlɚˈmɑnɪk; ˌfilɑːˈmɔnik] *adj.* 愛好音樂的。—*n.* ①愛好音樂者。②(P-) 愛樂協會。③(P-)〖俗〗愛樂協會所資助的樂隊或音樂會。④(P-) 交響樂團。

phil·hel·lene [fɪlˈhɛlin; ˈfilˌheliːn] *n.* ①希臘（人）之愛好者;對希臘友善者。②〖史〗擁護希臘獨立革命運動者。（亦作 **philhellenist**)

phil·hel·len·ic [ˌfɪlhəˈlɛnɪk; ˌfilheˈliːnik] *adj.* 對希臘友善的;支援希臘的。

phil·hel·len·ism [fɪlˈhɛlənɪzm̩; filˈhelinizəm] *n.* 愛好希臘;對希臘的友善;支援希臘。

Phil·ip [ˈfɪləp; ˈfilip] *n.* ①男子名。②〖聖經〗腓力(十二使徒之一)。

Phi·lip·pi [fəˈlɪpaɪ; fiˈlipai] *n.* 菲利比(馬其頓之古都)。***Thou shalt see me at Philippi.*** 後會有期, 咱們等着瞧吧。

Phi·lip·pi·ans [fəˈlɪpɪənz; fiˈlipiənz] *n.* (新約聖經之) 腓立比書。

Phi·lip·pic [fəˈlɪpɪk; fiˈlipik] *n.* ①雅典 Demosthenes 之攻擊馬其頓王的演說。②(p-) 猛烈的抨擊;漫罵演說。

Phil·ip·pine [ˈfɪləˌpin; ˈfilipiːn] *adj.* 菲律賓羣島的;菲律賓人的。(亦作 **Filipine, Filipino**)

Philippine Islands 菲律賓羣島 (位於東南亞, 略作 **P.I.**, 正式名稱爲 Republic of the Philippines, 首都馬尼拉 Manila).

Phil·ip·pines [ˈfɪləˌpinz; ˈfilipiːnz] *n.* (作 *pl.* 解) =**Philippine Islands.**

Phi·lis·tine [fəˈlɪstɪn; ˈfilistain] *n.* ①〖聖經〗非利士人(居於巴勒斯坦西南部)。②思想與風趣庸俗之人。③殘忍的敵人(諧語)。—*adj.* ①非利士人的。②庸俗的;缺乏教養的。

Phi·lis·tin·ism [fəˈlɪstɪnˌɪzəm; ˈfilistinizəm] *n.*鄙俗;庸俗。(亦作 **philistinism**)

phil·lu·men·ist [fɪˈlumənɪst; fiˈljuːminist] *n.* 火柴盒(標籤)收藏家。

philo- 〖字首〗表"愛好;偏好"之義。(母音前作 **phil-**)

phi·log·y·ny [fɪˈlɑdʒənɪ; fiˈlɔdʒəni] *n.* 愛女人(爲 misogyny 之對)。

philol. ①philological. ②philology.

phil·o·log·i·cal [ˌfɪləˈlɑdʒɪkl̩; ˌfiləˈlɔdʒikəl] *adj.* 語言學的。 **—ly,** *adv.*

phi·lol·o·gist [fɪˈlɑlədʒɪst; fiˈlɔlədʒist] *n.* 語言學家。

phi·lol·o·gize [fɪˈlɑləˌdʒaɪz; fiˈlɔlədʒaiz] *v.i.,* **-gized, -giz·ing.** 研究語言學。

phi·lol·o·gy [fɪˈlɑlədʒɪ; fiˈlɔlədʒi] *n.* 語言學 (現在較通用之名詞爲 linguistics).

phil·o·mel [ˈfɪləˌmɛl; ˈfiləmel] *n.*〖詩〗=**nightingale.** (亦作 **Philomel**)

Phil·o·me·la [ˌfɪləˈmilə; ˌfilouˈmiːlə] *n.* ①〖希臘神話〗雅典王 Pandion 之女, 後化身爲夜鶯。②〖詩〗=**nightingale.**

phil·o·p(o)e·na [ˌfɪləˈpinə; ˌfiləˈpiːnə] *n.* ①有雙核的堅果 (胡桃等)。②一種遊戲(將此雙核二人分吃, 其中一人如不能履行某種條件, 則付罰品給對方)。③此種遊戲中的罰品(通常爲一禮物)。(亦作 **philippine**)

phil·o·pro·gen·i·tive [ˌfɪləproˈdʒɛnətɪv; ˌfiləprəˈdʒenətiv] *adj.* ①多產的;多子女的。②愛子女的。 **—ness,** *n.*

philos. ①philosopher. ②philosophical. ③philosophy.

***phi·los·o·pher** [fəˈlɑsəfɚ; fiˈlɔsəfə] *n.* ①研究哲學者。②哲學家。③曠達之人;冷靜達觀者;哲人。

philosophers' stone 點金石;仙石。

phil·o·soph·i·c(al) [ˌfɪləˈsɑfɪk(l̩); ˌfiləˈsɔfik(əl)] *adj.* ①哲學上的。②精於哲學的。③專心於哲學的。④賢明的;冷靜的;明達的。**—phil·o·soph·i·cal·ly,** *adv.*

phi·los·o·phism [fəˈlɑsəfɪzm̩; fiˈlɔsəfizəm] *n.* 虛僞的哲學;詭辯。

phi·los·o·phist [fɪˈlɑsəfɪst; fiˈlɔsəfist] *n.* 虛僞的哲學家;詭辯家。

phi·los·o·phize [fəˈlɑsəˌfaɪz; fiˈlɔsəfaiz] *v.,* **-phized, -phiz·ing.** —*v.t.* 使哲學化; 從哲學的立場解釋。—*v.i.* 作哲理的探究;如哲學家般地思維或推理。

***phi·los·o·phy** [fəˈlɑsəfɪ; fiˈlɔsəfi] *n., pl.* **-phies.** ①哲學。natural *philosophy.* 物理學。moral *philosophy.* 倫理學。②宇宙觀。③人生觀。④哲理;原理。the *philosophy* of science. 科學原理。⑤明達;冷靜;徹悟。

phil·ter, phil·tre [ˈfɪltɚ; ˈfiltə] *n.* ①春藥。②誘淫巫術。③魔藥。—*v.t.* 用春藥或誘淫巫術蠱惑。

phiz [fɪz; fiz] *n., pl.* **phiz·es.** 〖俚〗容貌;顏面; 表情。(爲 physiognomy 之縮寫)。

phle·bi·tis [flɪˈbaɪtɪs; fliˈbaitis] *n.* 〖醫〗靜脈炎。 **—phle·bit·ic,** *adj.*

phle·bot·o·mist [flɪˈbɑtəmɪst; fliˈbɔtəmist] *n.* 刺絡醫;放血者。

phle·bot·o·mize [flɪˈbɑtəˌmaɪz; fliˈbɔtəmaiz] *v.t.* & *v.i.,* **-mized, -miz·ing.** 刺絡;放血。

phle·bot·o·my [flɪˈbɑtəmɪ; fliˈbɔtəmi] *n.*〖醫〗刺絡;放血。

phlegm [flɛm; flem] *n.* ①痰。②黏液。③遲鈍;冷漠。④冷靜;鎮定。

phleg·mat·ic [flɛgˈmætɪk; flegˈmætik] *adj.* =**phlegmatical.**

phleg·mat·i·cal [flɛgˈmætɪkl̩; flegˈmætikəl] *adj.* ①遲鈍的;冷漠的。②冷靜的;鎮定的。③痰的;多痰的。④黏液質的。(亦作

phlegmatic) —ly, *adv.*

phleg·mon ['flɛgmɑn; 'flegmɔn] *n.* 【醫】膿性蜂窩織炎。

phlegm·y ['flɛmɪ; 'flemi] *adj.* ①痰的;似痰的;有痰的;生痰的。②【罕】=**phlegmatic.**

phlo·em, phlo·ëm ['floɛm; 'flouem] *n.*【植物】韌皮部。

phlo·gis·tic [flo'dʒɪstɪk; flɔ'dʒistik] *adj.*①【古化學】燃素的。②【醫】炎症的;炎性的。

phlo·gis·ton [flo'dʒɪstən; flɔ'dʒistən] *n.*【古化學】燃素(未發現氧前被認爲可燃物之主要成分)。

phlor·i·zin ['flɑrɪzɪn; 'flɔrizin] *n.*【化】果樹根皮精(由果樹根皮採取之白色苦味物質)。

phlox [flɑks; flɔks] *n.*【植物】①草夾竹桃。②草夾竹桃之花。

Phnom Penh ['nɑm'pɛn; 'nɔm'pen] *n.* 金邊(高棉之首都)。

-phobe【字尾】表"懼怕者"之義,但亦常含"厭惡;憎恨"之意,如: Anglophobe 恐英病。

pho·bi·a ['fobɪə; 'foubiə] *n.* 恐懼症;異常的恐怖;畏懼。—**pho·bic,** *adj.*

-phobia【字尾】表"恐懼"或"恐…症"之義(如 hydrophobia 恐水病; 狂犬病)。

pho·co·me·li·a [ˌfokə'milɪə; ˌfoukə'mi:liə] *n.*【醫】短肢畸形。(亦作 **phokomelia, phocomely**)

pho·com·e·lus [fo'kɑmɪləs; fou'kɔmiləs] *n., pl.* **-es.**【醫】短肢畸形患者。

Phoe·be ['fibɪ; 'fi:bi] *n.* ①女子名(=Phebe)。②【希臘神話】月之女神。③【詩】月。

phoe·be ['fibɪ; 'fi:bi] *n.* (美國產的)一種京燕(=pewit, pewee)。

Phoe·bus ['fibəs; 'fi:bəs] *n.* ①【希臘神話】太陽神(卽 Apollo)。②【詩】太陽。

Phoe·ni·cia [fə'nɪʃɪə; fi'niʃiə] *n.* 腓尼基(敍利亞西海岸之古國)。(亦作 **Phenicia**)

Phoe·ni·cian [fə'nɪʃən; fi'niʃiən] *adj.* 腓尼基的;腓尼基人的;腓尼基語的。—*n.* ①腓尼基人。②腓尼基語。

phoe·nix ['finɪks; 'fi:niks] *n.* ①長生鳥(相傳此鳥於活五、六百年後,自焚爲灰,然後由灰中復生);鳳凰。②卓越超羣者;絕色佳人;絕世珍品。

phon [fɑn; fɔn] *n.*【物理】聲響的强度單位。

phon. ①phonetic(s). ②phonology.

pho·nate ['fonet; fou'neit] *v.i.,* **-nat·ed, -nat·ing.** 發聲音;發人語;發音。—**pho·na·tion,** *n.*

*__phone__[1] [fon; foun] *n., v.,* **phoned, phon·ing.** —*n., v.* 【美俗】=**telephone.** Some one wants you on the *phone.* 有人打電話給你。My friend *phoned* me at 10 a.m. 上午十時我的朋友打電話給我。

phone[2] *n.* (任何母音或子音之)音;單音。

-phone【字尾】表"聲音"之義的名詞字尾,如: gramophone, microphone.

pho·neme ['fonim; 'founi:m] *n.*【語音】音素;音位(一語言中視爲屬於同一單音的諸語音)。

pho·ne·mic [fo'nimɪk; fou'ni:mik] *adj.*【語音】① 音素的;音位的。②牽涉到意義上之區別的;不同的。(亦作 **phonematic**)

pho·ne·mics [fo'nimɪks; fou'ni:miks] *n.* 音素學;音位學。(亦作 **phonematics**)

pho·net·ic [fo'nɛtɪk, fə–; fou'netik] *adj.* ①語音的; 語音學的。②表示發音的。*phonetic* symbols. 音標。—**al·ly,** *adv.*

pho·ne·ti·cian [ˌfonə'tɪʃən; ˌfouni'tiʃən] *n.* 語音學家。

pho·net·i·cism [fə'nɛtəsɪzṃ; fə'netəsizm] *n.* 表音拼字法(主義);標示語音。

pho·net·i·cize [fo'nɛtɪˌsaɪz; fou'netisaiz] *v.t.,* **-cized, -ciz·ing.** 按照發音拼寫。

pho·net·ics [fo'nɛtɪks; fou'netiks] *n.* 語音學。

pho·ne·tist ['fonətɪst; 'founitist] *n.* ①=**phonetician.** ②主張表音拼字法者。

Phone·vi·sion ['fonˌvɪʒən; 'founˌviʒən] *n.*【商標名】顯像電話。

pho·ney ['fonɪ; 'founi] *adj., n.*【美俚】=**phony.**

phon·ic ['fɑnɪk, 'fonɪk; 'founik, 'fɔn–] *adj.* ①音的;語音的;發音上的。②【罕】有聲的。

phon·ics ['fonɪks; 'founiks] *n.* ①聲學。②【罕】=**phonetics.** ③以基本語音學教初學者朗誦、發音、及拼字的教學法。

phono-【字首】表"聲;音"之義。

pho·no·gen·ic [ˌfonə'dʒɛnɪk; ˌfounə'dʒenik] *adj.* 音響效果好的。

pho·no·gram ['fonəˌgræm; 'founəgræm] *n.* ①音標;(速記等的)表音字。②【罕】留聲機唱片。—(**m**)**ic,** *adj.*

*__pho·no·graph__ ['fonəˌgræf; 'founəgrɑ:f] *n.*【美】留聲機。(英亦作**gramophone**) —**ic,** *adj.* —**i·cal·ly,** *adv.*

pho·nog·ra·pher [fo'nɑgrəfɚ; fou'nɔgrəfə] *n.* 速記者;留聲機錄音技師。

phonograph needle 唱針。

phonograph record 唱片。

pho·nog·ra·phy [fo'nɑgrəfɪ; fou'nɔgrəfi] *n.* ①表音拼(寫)字法。②表音速記法; Pitman 式速記法(1837年 Sir Issac Pitman 所創)。③留聲機製造法。

pho·no·lite ['fonəˌlaɪt; 'founəlait] *n.*【礦】響石;響岩。—**pho·no·lit·ic,** *adj.*

pho·nol·o·gy [fo'nɑlədʒɪ; fou'nɔlədʒi] *n.* ①音韻學。②語音學(指語音的歷史研究)。—**pho·no·log·i·cal,** *adj.* —**pho·nol·o·gist,** *n.*

pho·nom·e·ter [fo'nɑmətɚ; fou'nɔmitə] *n.*【物理】測音器;音波測定器。

pho·no·phore ['fonəˌfor; 'founəfɔ:] *n.*【電】電信電話兩用裝置。(亦作**phonopore**)

pho·no·scope ['fonəˌskop; 'founəskoup] *n.* ①(樂器之)檢弦器。②【物理】檢音器;表音器;樂音自記器。

pho·no·type ['fonəˌtaɪp; 'founoutaip, –nət–] *n.* 音標活字;音標。

pho·no·typ·y ['fonəˌtaɪpɪ; 'founoutaipi] *n.* (特指 Sir Issac Pitman 所創的)表音式速記法(印刷法)。

pho·ny ['fonɪ; 'founi] *adj.,* **-ni·er, -ni·est,** *n., pl.* **-nies.** —*adj.*【美俚】假的;僞造的。—*n.* ①假冒(僞造)之物;假的寶石。②騙徒。

phos·gene ['fɑsdʒin; 'fɔzdʒi:n] *n.*【化】氯化碳醯;光氣。

phos·ge·nite ['fɑzdʒɪˌnaɪt; 'fɔzdʒinait] *n.*【礦】角鉛礦($Pb_2Cl_2CO_3$)。

phosph-【字首】=**phospho-**(於母音前用)。

phos·phate ['fɑsfet; 'fɔsfeit] *n.* ①【化】磷酸鹽。②含磷酸鹽之肥料。③加果汁及磷酸的汽水。*calcium phosphate* 磷酸鈣。

phos·phat·ic [fɑs'fætɪk; fɔs'fætik] *adj.* 磷酸鹽的; 含磷酸鹽的。*phosphatic* manure. 磷肥。

phos·phide ['fɑsfaɪd; 'fɔsfaid] *n.*【化】磷化物。

phos·phine ['fɑsfin; 'fɔsfi:n] *n.*【化】①磷化氫(PH_3, 一種毒氣)。②一種黃色合成染料。

phos·phite ['fɑsfaɪt; 'fɔsfait] *n.*【化】亞磷酸鹽。

phospho- 〖字首〗表"磷的;含磷的"之義。

phos·phor ['fɑsfə; 'fɔsfə] *n.* ①磷。②(P-)〖希臘神話〗啓明星之擬人名(相當於羅馬神話之 Lucifer). ③(P-)〖詩〗啓明星(尤指 Venus). ④〖物理〗發光性合成物質。

phos·pho·rate ['fɑsfə,ret; 'fɔsfəreit] *v.t.*, **-rat·ed, -rat·ing.** 〖化〗使與磷化合;加磷於…。

phosphor bronze 磷青銅。

phos·pho·resce [,fɑsfə'rɛs; ,fɔsfə'res] *v.i.*, **-resced, -resc·ing.** 發磷光。

phos·pho·res·cence [,fɑsfə'rɛsn̩s; ,fɔsfə'resns] *n.* ①發磷光。②磷光;磷火。

phos·pho·res·cent [,fɑsfə'rɛsn̩t; ,fɔsfə'resnt] *adj.* 發磷光的;磷光性的。

phos·phor·ic [fɑs'fɔrɪk; fɔs'fɔrik] *adj.* 磷的;含磷的;(尤指)含五價磷的。***phosphoric acid*** 磷酸。

phos·pho·rism ['fɑsfərɪzm̩; 'fɔsfərizm] *n.* 〖醫〗磷中毒。

phos·pho·rite ['fɑsfə,raɪt; 'fɔsfərait] *n.* 〖礦〗纖核磷灰石。

phos·pho·rous ['fɑsfərəs; 'fɔsfərəs] *adj.* 磷的;含磷的;(尤指)含三價磷的;亞磷的。 ***phosphorous acid*** 亞磷酸。

phos·pho·rus ['fɑsfərəs; 'fɔsfərəs] *n.* 〖化〗磷。red *phosphorus.* 紅磷。

phosphorus necrosis 〖醫〗磷毒性壞死;磷毒性顎骨疽。(俗稱 **phossy jaw**)

phos·phu·ret·(t)ed ['fɑsfjə,rɛtɪd; 'fɔsfjuretid] *adj.* 〖化〗與磷化合的。(亦作 **phosphoreted, phosphoretted**)

phot [fɑt, fot; fɔt, fout] *n.* 〖物理〗輻透(照度之單位:每平方公分一流明的照度)。

pho·tic ['fotɪk; 'foutik] *adj.* ①光的。②〖生物〗生物所發之光的;生物對光之反應的。

***pho·to** ['foto; 'foutou] *n., pl.* **-tos,** *v.,* **pho·toed, pho·to·ing.** 〖俗〗=**photograph.**

photo- 〖字首〗表"光;照相"之義。

pho·to·bi·ot·ic [,fotobaɪ'ɑtɪk; ,foutoubai'ɔtik] *adj.* 〖動、植物〗需靠光線生存的。

pho·to·chem·i·cal [,fotə'kɛmɪkl̩; ,foutə'kemikl] *adj.* 光化學的。—**ly,** *adv.*

pho·to·chem·is·try [,fotə'kɛmɪstrɪ; ,foutə'kemistri] *n.* 光化學。

pho·to·chrome ['fotəkrom; 'foutəkroum] *n.* 彩色照片。

pho·to·chro·my ['fotə,kromɪ; 'foutəkroumi] *n.* 天然色照相術。

pho·to·chron·o·graph [,fotə'krɑnə,græf; ,foutə'krɔnəgrɑːf] *n.* ①動體照相機。②動體相片。③〖物理〗(動體)照相錄秒器。—**y,** *n.*

pho·to·com·pose [,fotokəm'poz; ,foutoukəm'pouz] *v.t.,* **-posed, -pos·ing.** 將(稿件)用照相排版。

pho·to·com·pos·er ['fotokəm,pozə; 'foutoukəm,pouzə] *n.* 照相排版機。

pho·to·cop·i·er [,foto'kɑpɪə; ,fou-tou'kɔpiə] *n.* 影印機。

pho·to·cop·y ['fotə,kɑpɪ; 'foutə,kɔpi] *n., pl.* **-cop·ies,** *v.,* **-cop·ied, -cop·y·ing.** —*n.* 影印(文件等)。—*v.t.* 影印。

pho·to·cube ['fotə,kjub; 'foutəkjuːb] *n.* 透明照片陳列方柱(透明塑膠製,可框照片者)。

pho·to·dra·ma ['fotə,drɑmə; 'foutə,drɑːmə] *n.* =**photoplay.**

pho·to·e·lec·tric [,foto·ɪ'lɛktrɪk; ,foutoui'lektrik] *adj.* 〖物理〗因光而生的電效應的;光電(子)的。*photoelectric* effect. 光電效應。(亦作 **photoelectrical**)

photoelectric cell 〖電子〗光電管。

pho·to·e·lec·tron [,foto·ɪ'lɛktrɑn; ,foutoui'lektrɔn] *n.* 〖物理〗光電子。

pho·to·en·grav·ing [,foto·ɪn'grevɪŋ; ,foutouin'greiviŋ] *n.* 照相雕刻(術);照相雕刻版;照相雕刻版之印刷品。

photo finish ①攝影的終局(競賽者的勝負以攝影判定)。②任何相差極微的競賽。

pho·to·flash lamp ['fotə,flæʃ~; 'foutəflæʃ~] (照相用)閃光燈。

pho·to·flood lamp ['fotə,flʌd~; 'foutəflʌd~] (照相用)强烈溢光燈。

pho·to·gene ['fotə,dʒin; 'foutədʒiːn] *n.* =**afterimage.**

pho·to·gen·ic [,fotə'dʒɛnɪk; ,foutə'dʒenik] *adj.* ①宜於藝術攝影的(人);上鏡頭的。②〖生物〗發磷光的;發光(性)的。③〖醫〗因光而發生的(如皮膚病等)。

pho·to·gram·me·try [,fotə'græmətrɪ; ,foutə'græmitri] *n.* 照相測量術。

pho·to·graph** ['fotə,græf; 'foutəgrɑːf, -græf] *n.* 像片;照片。take a photograph*** (or ***take photographs***) 照一張相(照相)。—*v.t.* 攝影。Let's *photograph* it. 我們把它照下來。 —*v.i.* 攝影; 拍照。 You always *photograph* badly.你拍照總不見佳。

pho·tog·ra·pher [fə'tɑgrəfə; fə'tɔgrəfə] *n.* ①攝影者。②以攝影爲業者。

pho·to·graph·ic [,fotə'græfɪk; ,foutə'græfik] *adj.* ①攝影的; 攝影術的;像相片的。②用於攝影的;攝製的。*photographic* studio. 攝影室。(亦作 **photographical**) —**al·ly,** *adv.*

***pho·tog·ra·phy** [fə'tɑgrəfɪ; fə'tɔgrəfi] *n.* 攝影;攝影術。

pho·to·gra·vure [,fotəgrə'vjur, -'grevjə; ,foutəgrə'vjuə] *n.* ①照相製版法。②照相版;影印版。—*v.t.* 以照相版印;影印。

pho·to·lith·o·graph [,fotə'lɪθə,græf, -,grɑf; ,foutə'liθəgrɑːf, -græf] *n.* 照相石版;影印石版。—*v.t.* 石版影印。

pho·to·li·thog·ra·phy [,fotəlɪ'θɑgrəfɪ; ,foutəli'θɔgrəfi] *n.* 照相(影印)石版術。

pho·to·map ['fotə,mæp; 'foutəmæp] *n., v.,* **-mapped, -map·ping.** —*n.* (由航空照相的)照相地圖。—*v.t.* & *v.i.* 製(…的)照相地圖。

pho·to·me·chan·i·cal [,fotomə'kænɪkl̩; ,foutoumi'kænikəl] *adj.* 印相操作的。

pho·tom·e·ter [fo'tɑmətə; fou'tɔmitə] *n.* 光度計;感光計。

pho·to·met·ric [,fotə'mɛtrɪk; ,foutə'metrik] *adj.* 光度計的; 測定光度的。(亦作 **photometrical**)

pho·tom·e·try [fo'tɑmətrɪ; fou'tɔmitri] *n.* 光度測定(法); 光度學。

pho·to·mi·cro·graph [,fotə'maɪkrə,græf; ,foutə'maikrəgrɑːf] *n.* ①顯微鏡照相的照片。②微小照片。

pho·to·mi·cro·scope [,fotə'maɪkrə,skop; ,foutə'maikrəskoup] *n.* 顯微照相機。

pho·to·mon·tage [,fotəmɑn'tɑʒ; ,foutəmɔn'tɑːʒ] *n.* 集錦照相(術)(爲求美術效果將數幀照片拼合爲一幀者)。

pho·to·mu·ral [,fotə'mjurəl; ,foutə'mjuərəl] *n.* 裝飾牆壁用的大照片。

pho·ton ['fotɑn; 'foutɔn] *n.* 〖物理〗光子;光量子。

pho·to·neu·tron [,fotə'njutrɑn;

ˌfoutəˈnjuːtrɔn] *n.* 〖物理〗光激中子。
pho·to-off·set [ˌfotəˈɔfsɛt; ˌfoutəˈɔːfset] *n.* 照相石版印刷。
pho·to·pho·bi·a [ˌfotəˈfobɪə; ˌfoutəˈfoubiə] *n.* 〖醫〗畏光;羞明;晝盲。
pho·to·play [ˈfotəˌple; ˈfoutəplei] *n.* 電影劇;電影劇脚本。
pho·to·re·con·nais·sance [ˌfotorɪˈkɑnəsəns; ˌfoutouriˈkɔnisəns] *n.* 空中照相偵察。
pho·to·re·cord·er [ˌfotorɪˈkɔrdɚ; ˌfoutouriˈkɔːdə] *n.* 照相記錄器。
pho·to·sen·si·tive [ˌfotəˈsɛnsətɪv; ˌfoutəˈsensitiv] *adj.* 感光的。
pho·to·sphere [ˈfotəˌsfɪr; ˈfoutəsfiə] *n.* 〖天文〗光球(包被太陽周圍的白熱氣體)。
pho·to·stat [ˈfotəˌstæt; ˈfoutəstæt] *n., v.,* **-stat·(t)ed, -stat·(t)ing.** —*n.* ①直接影印機; 複寫照相機。②直接影印照片。③(P–) 其商標名。—*v.t.* 用直接影印機拍攝。
pho·to·syn·the·sis [ˌfotəˈsɪnθəsɪs; ˌfoutəˈsinθisis] *n.* 〖化, 植物〗光合作用。
pho·to·tax·is [ˌfotəˈtæksɪs; ˌfoutəˈtæksis] *n.* 〖生物〗趨光性。(亦作 **phototaxy**)
pho·to·tel·e·graph [ˌfotəˈtɛlɪˌgræf; ˌfoutəˈteligrɑːf] *v.t. & v.i.* 以電報傳眞發送。—*n.* 傳眞電報;電報傳眞像。
pho·to·te·leg·ra·phy [ˌfotətɪˈlɛgrəfɪ; ˌfoutətiˈlegrəfi] *n.* ①閃光通信(如利用日光反射等)。②電報傳眞術。
pho·to·tel·e·scope [ˌfotəˈtɛləˌskop; ˌfoutəˈteliskoup] *n.* 照相望遠鏡。
pho·to·ther·a·py [ˌfotəˈθɛrəpɪ; ˌfoutəˈθerəpi] *n.* 〖醫〗光線療法。
pho·to·tim·er [ˈfotəˌtaɪmɚ; ˈfoutouˌtaimə] *n.* (照相機的)自動曝光調整裝置;賽跑裁判用自動攝影裝置。
pho·tot·ro·pism [foˈtɑtrəˌpɪzəm; fouˈtɔtrəpizəm] *n.* 〖生物〗感光轉動性。
pho·to·tube [ˈfotəˌtjub; ˈfoutətjuːb] *n.* 光電管。
pho·to·type [ˈfotəˌtaɪp; ˈfoutətaip] *n.* 照相凸版(術);照相凸版之印刷物。
pho·to·typ·y [ˈfotəˌtaɪpɪ; ˈfoutəˌtaipi] *n.* 照相凸版術。
pho·to·zin·cog·ra·phy [ˌfotəzɪŋˈkɑgrəfɪ; ˌfoutəziŋˈkɔgrəfi] *n.* 照相鋅版術。
phr. phrase.
phras·al [ˈfrezl; ˈfreizl] *adj.* 詞句的;片語的;組成片語的;使用片語的;成語的。
phrase** [frez; freiz] *n., v.,* **phrased, phras·ing.** —*n.* ①字之組合; 語法。He speaks in simple *phrases* so that the children can understand him. 他用簡單語法講話,所以孩子們能懂他的話。②成語;慣用語。③簡短之警句。④〖文法〗片語。⑤〖音樂〗樂句;樂節。 ***Adjective phrase 形容詞片語。 ***Adverbial phrase*** 副詞片語。 ***Conjunctive phrase*** 連接詞片語。***Noun phrase*** 名詞片語。***Preposition phrase*** 介系詞片語。 ***Verb phrase*** 動詞片語。—*v.t.* ①措辭。She *phrased* her excuse politely. 她很客氣地說出她的藉口。②分(音符)爲節。
phrase book 成語集。(亦作 **phrasebook**)
phrase·mon·ger [ˈfrezˌmʌŋgɚ; ˈfreizˌmʌŋgə] *n.* 愛雕琢詞句者。
phra·se·o·gram [ˈfrezɪəˌgræm; ˈfreiziəgræm] *n.* 代表句子的符號(如速記所使用者)。
phra·se·o·log·i·cal [ˌfrezɪəˈlɑdʒɪkl; ˌfreiziəˈlɔdʒikəl] *adj.* 措辭上的;語法的;句法的。—**ly,** *adv.*
phra·se·ol·o·gy [ˌfrezɪˈɑlədʒɪ; ˌfreiziˈɔlədʒi] *n., pl.* **-gies.** ①措辭;特殊的用語。②語詞;語詞表現法。
phras·ing [ˈfrezɪŋ; ˈfreiziŋ] *n.* ①措辭;語法。②〖音樂〗分節法。
phra·try [ˈfretrɪ; ˈfreitri] *n., pl.* **-tries.** ①〖古希臘〗氏族(部族的分支)。②(原始部族之)氏族;門(如 clans, families 等)。
phre·net·ic [frɪˈnɛtɪk; friˈnetik] *adj.* ①狂亂的。②狂熱的。—*n.* 狂亂者;熱狂者。—**ness,** *n.*
phren·ic [ˈfrɛnɪk; ˈfrenik] *adj.* ①〖解剖〗橫膈膜的。②精神上的。
phre·ni·tis [frɪˈnaɪtɪs; friˈnaitis] *n.* 〖醫〗①膈膜炎。②腦炎。③譫妄;精神錯亂。
phren·o·log·i·cal [ˌfrɛnəˈlɑdʒɪkl; ˌfrenəˈlɔdʒikəl] *adj.* 骨相學的。—**ly,** *adv.*
phre·nol·o·gist [frɛˈnɑlədʒɪst, frɪ–; friˈnɔlədʒist, freˈn–] *n.* 骨相學者;骨相學家。
phre·nol·o·gy [frɛˈnɑlədʒɪ; friˈnɔlədʒi] *n.* 骨相學。
Phryg·i·a [ˈfrɪdʒɪə; ˈfridʒiə] *n.* 佛里幾亞(小亞細亞中部之一古國)。
Phryg·i·an [ˈfrɪdʒɪən; ˈfridʒiən] *adj.* Phrygia 的; 其人民的; 其語言的。—*n.* Phrygia 人; Phrygia 語。
PHS, P.H.S. Public Health Service.
phthis·ic [ˈtɪzɪk; ˈθaisik] *n.* 〖醫〗癆;癆瘵。—*adj.* 癆的;患癆瘵的。
phthis·i·cal [ˈtɪzɪkl; ˈθaisikəl] *adj.* 癆的;患癆瘵的。(亦作 **phthisicky**)
phthi·sis [ˈθaɪsɪs; ˈθaisis] *n.* 癆;癆瘵;肺結核。
phut [fʌt; fʌt] *n., adv.* 啪(模擬汽球、水泡等破裂之聲)。It's gone *phut.*〖俗〗(喻)垮了。
phy·col·o·gy [faɪˈkɑlədʒɪ; faiˈkɔlədʒi] *n.* 海藻學。
phy·lac·ter·y [fəˈlæktərɪ, -trɪ; fiˈlæktəri] *n., pl.* **-ter·ies.** ①經匣(內裝有記載經句的羊皮紙, 猶太人晨禱時佩於頭上及左臂)。②提醒的人或物。③護符。***make broad the phylactery*** 表示理直氣壯。
phy·le [ˈfaɪli; ˈfailiː] *n., pl.* **-lae** [-li; -liː]. (古代希臘之) 種族 (根據血緣的)。
Phyl·lis [ˈfɪlɪs; ˈfilis] *n.* 女子名。
phyl·lox·e·ra [fɪˈlɑksərə; ˌfilɔkˈsiərə] *n., pl.* **-rae** [-ˌri; -riː]. 木虱; 葡萄蟲。
phylo- 〖字首〗表"種族"之義(在母音前作 **phyl-**).
phy·lo·gen·e·sis [ˌfaɪləˈdʒɛnəsɪs; ˌfailəˈdʒenəsis] *n.* 〖生物〗動植物種類史;動植物種類之進化史;種系發生史;種族系統史。(亦作 **phylogeny**)—**phy·lo·ge·net·ic, phy·lo·gen·ic,** *adj.*
phy·lum [ˈfaɪləm; ˈfailəm] *n., pl.* **-la** [-lə; -lə]. ①〖生物〗門;類。②〖語言〗語系。
phys. ①physical. ②physician. ③physics. ④physiological. ⑤physiology.
phys. ed. physical education.
phys·i·at·rics [ˌfɪzɪˈætrɪks; ˌfiziˈætriks] *n.* (作 *sing.* 解) 物理療法。
phys·i·at·rist [ˌfɪzɪˈætrɪst; ˌfiziˈætrist] *n.* 物理醫療家。
phys·ic [ˈfɪzɪk; ˈfizik] *n., v.,* **-icked, -ick·ing.** —*n.* ①藥 (特指瀉藥)。②〖古〗醫術;醫學。—*v.t.* ①使瀉。②以藥物治療;療治。
***phys·i·cal** [ˈfɪzɪkl; ˈfizikəl] *adj.* ①身體的;肉體的。*physical* exercise. 運動;體操。②物質的。*physical* universe. 物質世界。③根據自然法規的;自然的。*physical* laws. 自然

之法則。④物理學的。 *physical beauty* 肉體美。 *physical check-up* 健康檢查；體格檢查。 *physical chemistry* 物理化學。 *physical constitution* 體格。 *physical culture* (or *training*) 體育。 *physical education* 體育。 *physical examination* 身體（體格）檢查。 *physical force* (or *strength*) 體力。 *physical geography* 地文學；自然地理。 *physical jerks*〖俚〗體操。 *physical science* 物理學；自然科學。 *physical therapy* 物理療法。

***phys·i·cal·ly** ['fɪzɪklɪ; 'fizikəli] *adv.* ①依自然的(物理上的)法則；在自然科學(物理學)上。②在物質上（爲 spiritually 之對)。③身體上；體格上；肉體上(爲mentally之對)。

***phy·si·cian** [fə'zɪʃən; fi'ziʃən] *n.* ①醫生。②內科醫生。

phys·i·cist ['fɪzəsɪst; 'fizisist] *n.* ①物理學家。②機械論者；唯物論者。

***phys·ics** ['fɪzɪks; 'fiziks] *n.* 物理學。

physio-〖字首〗表"自然；物理"之義。

phys·i·oc·ra·cy [ˌfɪzɪ'ɑkrəsɪ; ˌfizi'ɔkrəsi] *n.* ①重農主義。②自然政治。

phys·i·o·crat ['fɪzɪəˌkræt; 'fiziəkræt] *n.* 重農主義者。—**ic,** *adj.*

phys·i·og·nom·ic [ˌfɪzɪɑg'nɑmɪk; ˌfiziə'nɔmik] *adj.* 相術的；人相的；相貌的。(亦作 **physiognomical**) —**al·ly,** *adv.*

phys·i·og·no·mist [ˌfɪzɪ'ɑgnəmɪst; ˌfizi'ɔnəmist] *n.* 相面術學者；相士。

phys·i·og·no·my [ˌfɪzɪ'ɑgnəmɪ; ˌfizi'ɔnəmi] *n., pl.* **-mies.** ①相貌。②相法；相面術。③事物之外貌。④地勢。

phys·i·og·ra·pher [ˌfɪzɪ'ɑgrəfɚ; ˌfizi'ɔgrəfə] *n.* ①地文學專家。②地形學家。

phys·i·o·graph·i·c(al) [ˌfɪzɪə'græfɪk(l̩); ˌfiziə'græfik(əl)] *adj.* ①地文學的。②地形學的。

phys·i·og·ra·phy [ˌfɪzɪ'ɑgrəfɪ; ˌfizi'ɔgrəfi] *n.* ①地文學；自然地理。②地形學。

phys·i·o·log·i·cal [ˌfɪzɪə'lɑdʒɪkl; ˌfiziə'lɔdʒikəl] *adj.* 生理學的；生理的。—**ly,** *adv.*

phys·i·ol·o·gist [ˌfɪzɪ'ɑlədʒɪst; ˌfizi'ɔlədʒist] *n.* 生理學家。

phys·i·ol·o·gy [ˌfɪzɪ'ɑlədʒɪ; ˌfizi'ɔlədʒi] *n.* 生理學。

phys·i·o·ther·a·py [ˌfɪzɪo'θɛrəpɪ; ˌfiziou'θerəpi] *n.*〖醫〗物理療法。

phy·sique [fɪ'zik; fi'ziːk] *n.* 體格；身體之構造、形態或發育。

phy·to·ge·og·ra·phy [ˌfaɪtodʒɪ'ɑgrəfɪ; ˌfaitoudʒi'ɔgrəfi] *n.* 植物地理學。

phy·to·hor·mone [ˌfaɪtə'hɔrmon; ˌfaitə'hɔːmoun] *n.* 植物激素。

phy·to·pa·thol·o·gy [ˌfaɪtopə'θɑlədʒɪ; ˌfaitoupə'θɔlədʒi] *n.* 植物病理學。

pi¹ [paɪ; pai] *n., pl.* **pis.** ①希臘字母之第十六個字母 (Π, π)。②〖數學〗圓周率 (以 π 代表, 其值爲 3.14159…)。

pi² *n., v.,* **pied, pie·ing.**〖美〗—*n.* ①混雜的活字堆。②混亂；混雜。—*v.t.* 使(活字等)混雜。(亦作 **pie**)

pi³ *adj.*〖英學生俚〗虔誠的；宗教的(爲 pious 之略)。 a *pi* jaw. 說教；訓話。—*n.* 說教。

P. I. Philippine Islands.

pi·ac·u·lar [paɪ'ækjəlɚ; pai'ækjulə] *adj.* ①贖罪的。②須贖罪的；有罪的；邪惡的。

piaffe [pjæf; pjæf] *v.i.,* **piaffed, piaff·ing.**〖馬術〗用比快步(trot)稍慢的步伐前進。

pi·a ma·ter ['paɪə'metɚ; 'paiə'meitə] ①〖解剖〗軟腦脊膜(爲dura mater之對)。②智慧。

pi·a·nis·si·mo [ˌpiə'nɪsəˌmo; ˌpiːə'nisimou] *adv., adj., n., pl.* **-mos, -mi** [-ˌmi; -miː]. —*adv.* & *adj.*〖音樂〗極弱地(的)。—*n.* 樂曲中以最弱音演奏之一節或一個樂章。

***pi·an·ist** [pɪ'ænɪst, 'piənɪst; 'pjænist, 'piənist, pi'æn-] *n.* 彈鋼琴者；鋼琴師。

‡pi·an·o¹ [pɪ'æno; pi'ænou] *n., pl.* **-an·os.** 鋼琴。 to play (on) the *piano.* 彈鋼琴。 *baby grand piano* 小型平台鋼琴。 *concert grand piano* 大型平台鋼琴。 *cottage piano* 小豎鋼琴。 *grand piano* 平台鋼琴。 *piano player* 鋼琴家；自動鋼琴。 *upright piano* 直立鋼琴。

pi·an·o² [pɪ'ɑno; pi'ɑːnou] *adj.* & *adv.*〖音樂〗柔軟的(地)。

piano duet 鋼琴二重奏曲。

pi·an·o·for·te [pɪ'ænəˌfort; ˌpjænou'fɔːti] *n.* =**piano¹.**

pi·a·no·la [ˌpiə'nolə; pjæ'noulə] *n.* 自動鋼琴之一種。

piano organ 廻轉式自鳴鋼琴。

pi·as·ter, pi·as·tre [pɪ'æstɚ; pi'æstə, pi'ɑːs-] *n.* ①埃及、土耳其的銀幣。②(西班牙、墨西哥之)披索(=peso)。③越南之紙幣。

***pi·az·za** [pɪ'æzə; pi'ætsə, -'ɑːtsə] *n., pl.* **pi·az·zas, piaz·ze** [pɪ'ætse; pi'ætsei]. ①〖美〗走廊。②(義大利城市之)廣場。③〖英〗有頂廻廊。

pi·broch ['pibrɑk; 'piːbrɔk, 'pib-, -ɔx] *n.* (蘇格蘭高地的)風笛曲。

pic [pɪk; pik] *n., pl.* **pix** [pɪks; piks], **pics.** ①〖美俚〗電影。②〖新聞〗照片。(亦作 **pix**)

pi·ca¹ ['paɪkə; 'paikə] *n.*〖印刷〗①12 point 大之活字。②此種活字之縱長。

pi·ca² *n.*〖醫〗異食(症)(如食泥土等)。

pic·a·dor ['pɪkəˌdɔr; 'pikədɔː] *n., pl.* **-dors, -do·res.**〖西〗①(以槍刺牛使牛發怒致鬥牛開始的)騎馬鬥牛士。②機敏的辯論者；機智者。

pic·a·resque [ˌpɪkə'rɛsk; ˌpikə'resk] *adj.* ①惡漢的。②以惡漢及其冒險爲題材的(小說等)。

pic·a·ro ['pɪkəro; 'pikərou] *n., pl.* **-ros.** 壞蛋；流浪漢。

pic·a·roon [ˌpɪkə'run; ˌpikə'ruːn] *n.* ①惡漢；匪徒。②海盜。③海盜船。—*v.i.* 作海盜。—*v.t.* 掠奪；刼奪。

Pi·cas·so [pɪ'kɑso; pi'kæsou] *n.* 畢加索(Pablo, 1881–1973, 西班牙畫家及雕刻家)。

pic·a·yune [ˌpɪkɪ'jun; ˌpiki'juːn] *n.*〖美〗①小錢幣。②瑣屑的東西；不足輕重的人。—*adj.*(亦作 **picayunish**) 瑣屑的；無價值的。

pic·ca·lil·li [ˌpɪkə'lɪlɪ; 'pikəlili] *n.* (東印度之)辛辣醃菜；泡菜。

pic·ca·nin·ny, pick·a·nin·ny ['pɪkəˌnɪnɪ; 'pikənini] *n., pl.* **-nies.**〖美〗①很小的小孩。②黑人的小孩。—*adj.* 非常小的。

pic·co·lo ['pɪkəˌlo; 'pikəlou] *n., pl.* **-los.** 短笛。—**ist,** *n.*

pice [paɪs; pais] *n. sing.* or *pl.* 印度的銅幣(=¼ anna)。

‡pick¹ [pɪk; pik] *v.t.* ①挑選；選擇。*Pick* the best one. 挑最好的一個。②採；摘。 to *pick* flowers. 採花。③鑿；撬開。to *pick* a lock. 撬開鎖。④剔；挖。 to *pick* one's teeth. 剔牙。⑤扯去；拔去(雞、鴨等)的毛以備烹製。⑥撕開；扯開。⑦找；尋求。to *pick* a quarrel. 挑釁；挑戰。⑧掏；竊取。 to *pick* a pocket. 偷口袋內之東西；扒竊。⑨啄食；啃食；〖俗〗細食。 to *pick* a bone. 啃骨頭。⑩〖音樂〗以指

撥奏。—*v.i.* ①鑿;刺;挖。②撥食; 細食。③偷。to *pick* and steal. 偷竊;扒竊。④精選。***pick and choose*** 詳加選擇;挑三揀四。***pick at*** a. 以指彈;以指拖拉。b. 細食;一點一點地吃。to *pick at* one's supper. 慢慢地吃晚飯。c.〖俗〗挑毛病;挑剔。***pick holes in*** 找漏洞;挑毛病。***pick off*** a. 一個個地射 (=shoot one by one). b.〖棒球〗觸殺跑壘者。c. 拔去;摘去。***pick on*** a.〖俗〗揶揄;絮聒不休地抱怨;批評;使煩惱。b. 選擇。***pick one's way*** (or ***steps***) 愼擇道路。***pick one's words*** 愼選最恰當的話。***pick out*** a. 選擇。b. 分別出; 區別。c. 辨出(意義或含義)。***pick over*** 仔細檢查而挑選。***pick someone's brains*** 向別人打聽而不自己研究;抄襲或利用別人的成果。***pick to pieces*** 批評得體無完膚。***pick up*** a. 拾起;舉起。b. 偶獲;偶得;求得。c. (無人教而)學得。d. 攜帶;搭載。The train stopped to *pick up* passengers. 火車停下來搭載乘客。e. 鼓起(勇氣)。f. 改進。g. 再得到;又得到;再開始。h. 增加速度。i. 認識;未與介紹而相識。j. 整理。k.〖俚〗逮捕。l. 偷竊。m. 重獲;恢復(健康、勇氣等)。***pick up with*** 同…交朋友。—*n.* ①選擇;挑揀; 選擇權; 選擇出來的東西或人。to have one's *pick* of.... 選擇…。②最優部分;精華。the *pick* of the bunch. 最優者;出類拔萃者。③穀物一次的收穫量。④指上所戴的彈樂器絃的用具。⑤尖物之一擊。

‡pick² *n.* ①鑿子(尖頭鋤)。②任何尖的工具(常與他字組合)。a toothpick. 牙籤。

pick·a·back [ˈpɪkəˏbæk; ˈpikəbæk] *adv.* 在背上;在肩上。—*adj.* 騎在背上或肩上的。

pick·ax(e) [ˈpɪkˏæks; ˈpikæks] *n.* 尖鋤;鶴嘴鋤。—*v.t.* & *v.i.* 以鶴嘴鋤鑿掘。

picked [pɪkt; pikt] *adj.* ①摘取的。②用尖鋤挖鑿的。③精選的。④廢物已經除盡的。

pick·er [ˈpɪkɚ; ˈpikə] *n.* ①啄者;啄鳥。②摘者;採集者。fruit-*picker*. 摘果者。③用牙籤之人。④扒手。⑤尖鋤;鶴嘴鋤(=pickax). ⑥拆散纖維之器具。⑦織布機上投擲織梭穿過經線之器具。⑧使用⑥及⑦器具的人。

pick·er·el [ˈpɪkərəl; ˈpikərəl] *n., pl.* **-el, -els.** 梭魚。

pick·er·el·weed [ˈpɪkərəlˏwid; ˈpikərəlwiːd] *n.*〖植物〗(美國沼地產的)一種多年生植物。

pick·et [ˈpɪkɪt; ˈpikit] *n.* ①尖樁;籬笆之樁。②〖軍〗哨兵;步哨。③(罷工時阻止工人上工及顧客前往購物之)糾察員。④執行警戒任務的飛機或船隻。⑤站立於公共建築物前的示威羣衆。—*v.t.* ①以柵圍護。②繫(牲口)於樁上。③〖軍〗放步哨以警戒。④派遣糾察員於…。—*v.i.* 充任(名詞③義之)糾察員。

picket fence 柵欄。

picket line ①警戒線。②示威或罷工羣衆排成之線。

pick·ing [ˈpɪkɪŋ; ˈpikiŋ] *n.* ①選擇;採摘; 鑿掘; 扒竊。②採集之量。③(*pl.*) 剩餘之物;殘物。④(*pl.*) 竊得之物;贓物。

pick·le** [ˈpɪkl; ˈpikl] *n., v.,* **-led, -ling.** —*n.* ①(醃肉菜等之) 醃汁; (泡菜等之)酸水。②醃成之黃瓜。③(常*pl.*)任何醃菜。④〖俗〗困難。⑤洗金屬的稀酸。⑥喜歡惡作劇的小孩;頑童。in a pickle*** 處於困難境地中。***in pickle*** 備用。—*v.t.* ①醃。②以稀酸洗(金屬)。

pick·led [ˈpɪkld; ˈpikld] *adj.* ①鹽醃的;醋泡的。②〖美俚〗醉的;酩酊的。

pick·lock [ˈpɪkˏlɑk; ˈpiklɔk] *n.* ①撬鎖具。②撬鎖人; 竊賊。③(術語)高級羊毛。

pick-me-up [ˈpɪkmiˏʌp; ˈpikmiːʌp] *n.*〖俗〗興奮飲料;興奮劑。

pick·pock·et [ˈpɪkˏpɑkɪt; ˈpikˌpɔkit] *n.* 扒手。Beware of *pickpockets*. 當心扒手。

pick·thank [ˈpɪkˏθæŋk; ˈpikˌθæŋk] *n.*〖古,方〗阿諛之人。

pick·up [ˈpɪkˏʌp; ˈpikʌp] *n.* ①拾起。②〖俗〗偶而認識;邂逅。③〖汽車〗a. 加速;加快。b. 小型輕便貨車。c. 中途搭車者。④〖俗〗進步; 改良。⑤〖俗〗刺激物。⑥〖棒球〗球着地後將其捕起擲還。⑦〖無線電〗a. 在發射過程中之接收聲波而轉變爲電波。b. 接收聲波轉變爲電波之裝置。c. 無線電廣播發射之處。d. 干擾。⑧〖電視〗a. 在發射過程中接收影像而轉變爲電波。b. 此種裝置。⑨電唱機之唱頭。⑩〖俗〗消息; 情報。⑪偶然得到的東西。⑫遺失的物件。⑬臨時做的飯。—*adj.* ①卽席的:臨時的。②偶然認識的。

Pick·wick·i·an [pɪkˈwɪkɪən; pikˈwikiən] *adj.* ①匹克尉克 (Pickwick 爲 Charles Dickens 所作 *Pickwick Papers* 中之主角, 以善心樸實著稱)的; 有匹克尉克特性的。②(字或觀念等)意義與通常不同的; 不拘泥於字義的。***in a Pickwickian sense*** 用特殊(滑稽)的意義。—**ly,** *adv.*

***pic·nic** [ˈpɪknɪk; ˈpiknik] *n., v.,* **-nicked, -nick·ing.** —*n.* ①野餐。to go on a *picnic*. 前往郊外擧行野餐。②〖俚〗歡樂的時光; 愉快的經驗; 輕而易擧的工作。It's no *picnic*. 不是容易的事。—*v.i.* ①野餐。②以野餐方式吃。—*adj.* 作爲野餐用的。

pic·nick·er [ˈpɪknɪkɚ; ˈpiknikə] *n.* 參加野餐者。

pic·nick·y [ˈpɪknɪkɪ; ˈpikniki] *adj.* 野餐的;野餐式的;遊樂的。

pico- 〖字首〗米突制表"兆分之一"之義。

pi·cot [ˈpiko; ˈpiːkou] *n.* 花邊上飾邊之小環。

pic·o·tee [ˌpɪkəˈti; ˌpikəˈtiː] *n.*〖植物〗花瓣有紅邊的一種荷蘭石竹。

pic·ric [ˈpɪkrɪk; ˈpikrik] *adj.*〖化〗苦味酸的。*picric* acid. 苦味酸。

Pict [pɪkt; pikt] *n.* 匹克特人(昔住於蘇格蘭東部及北部之民族)。

Pict·ish [ˈpɪktɪʃ; ˈpiktiʃ] *adj.* 匹克特族(文化)的;匹克特語的。—*n.* 匹克特語。

pic·to·graph [ˈpɪktəˏgræf; ˈpiktəgrɑːf] *n.* 繪畫文字;象形文字;用繪畫(象形)文字寫的文獻。—**ic,** *adj.*

pic·tog·ra·phy [pɪkˈtɑgrəfɪ; pikˈtɔgrəfi] *n.* 繪畫文字的使用;繪畫文字。

pic·to·ri·al [pɪkˈtorɪəl; pikˈtɔːriəl] *adj.* ①圖畫的; 以圖畫表示的。②用圖畫說明的;附有插圖的。③生動的。④繪畫的。—*n.* 畫報;畫刊。—**ly,** *adv.*

‡pic·ture [ˈpɪktʃɚ; ˈpiktʃə] *n., v.,* **-tured, -tur·ing.** —*n.* ①畫; 照片。May I take your *picture?* 我給你照張相好嗎? ②景色。③美麗之物。Her hat is a *picture*. 她的帽子很美麗。④肖像; 化身。He is the *picture* of his father. 他極像他的父親。⑤(*pl.*) 電影; 電影院。He goes to the (moving) *pictures* once a week. 他每星期去看一次電影。⑥生動的描寫。⑦印象;記憶。***be out of the picture*** 被拒絕; 不再有可能的。—*v.t.* ①畫。The artists *pictured* the saints. 畫家們畫聖徒的像。②想像。③生動地描述。

picture book 圖畫書(全部或主要爲圖畫者)。

picture card ①花牌(撲克牌中的 king, queen, jack). ②有圖畫的明信片(=picture post card).

picture gallery 畫廊;美術館;美術陳列館。

picture hat (飾以鮀鳥羽毛的)女用闊邊帽。
picture house 電影院。
picture palace 〖英〗電影院。
Pic·ture·phone ('pɪktʃəˌfon; 'pik-tʃəfoun) *n.* 〖商標名〗顯像電話。
picture post card 有圖畫的明信片。
picture show ①畫展。②電影(院)。
*__pic·tur·esque__ (ˌpɪktʃə'rɛsk; ˌpik-tʃə'resk) *adj.* ①如畫的。②栩栩如生的;生動的。③獨特而有趣的(性格)。—**ly,** *adv.* —**ness,** *n.*
picture tube 電視機之映像管。
picture window 大型窗。
picture writing ①畫圖記事法;畫圖通信法。②用圖畫表示的記載或消息。
pic·tur·ize ('pɪktʃəˌraɪz; 'piktʃəraiz) *v.t.,* **-ized, -iz·ing.** 使成圖畫;使成爲電影;電影化。
pic·ul ('pɪkʌl; 'pikʌl) *n., pl.* **pic·ul, pic·uls.** (中國及東方各地之)擔(即一百斤)。
pid·dle ('pɪdl; 'pidl) *v.i. & v.t.,* **-dled, -dling.** ①作無聊事情;虛度(時光)。②〖兒語〗小便;撒尿。
pid·dling ('pɪdlɪŋ; 'pidliŋ) *adj.* 瑣屑的;無用的;不足道的。
pidg·in ('pɪdʒɪn; 'pidʒin) *n.* 不純粹之語言(原爲"business"一字中國讀音之訛)。(亦作 **pigeon**) ***That's not my pidgin.*** 〖俗〗不干我的事;我不管。
pidgin English 洋涇浜英語。(亦作 **pigeon English**)
*__pie__[1] (paɪ; pai) *n.* 派;餡餅(以水果、肉類、蔬菜等包在麪粉內烤成)。an apple *pie.* 蘋果派。***a pie in the sky*** a. 虛幻的承諾。b. 烏托邦;極樂之境。***have a finger in the pie*** 以好管閒事的態度參與某事。***put one's finger into another's pie*** 干涉他人之事。
pie[2] *n., v.,* **pied, pie·ing.** =**pi**[2].
pie[3] *n.* =**magpie.**
pie[4] *n.* (英國宗教改革前的)日課規則書;日課表。(亦作 **pye**)
pie[5] *n.* 印度的小銅幣(=1/12 anna)。
pie·bald ('paɪˌbɔld; 'paibɔːld) *adj.* ①兩色混雜的(尤指黑白或棕白兩色,特指馬言)。②混雜的;雜種的。—*n.* 毛呈兩色混雜的馬;雜種動物。
‡__piece__ (pis; piːs) *n., v.,* **pieced, piec·ing.** —*n.* ①片、塊、段、枝等;斷片。a *piece* of chalk. 一枝粉筆。a *piece* of paper. 一張紙。The cup broke in *pieces.* 那杯子破碎了。②部分。a *piece* of bread. 一片麪包。③(一套中之)一個;一件。a *piece* of furniture. 一件傢具。④幣。a five-cent *piece.* 五分幣。⑤樣本;例子。a *piece* of news. 一項消息。⑥(文學、藝術作品之)一首;一支;一幅;一篇。a *piece* of painting. 一幅畫。a *piece* of music. 一支樂曲。⑦鎗;砲。a fowling *piece.* 鳥鎗。⑧物品之定量;一件。to sell goods by the *piece.* 成件賣貨(非零售者)。⑨工作量。The workmen are paid by the *piece.* 這些工人是按件計酬的。⑩碁子。⑪〖西洋棋〗重要碁子。⑫〖方〗a. 短時間;瞬間。b. 短距離。***be of a piece*** 與…一致;與…有關。***go to pieces*** a. 裂爲碎片。b. 身心崩潰。***piece of one's mind*** 〖俗〗a. 坦率的意見。b. 責備。***speak one's piece*** 表示意見。—*v.t.* ①修補;補綴。②結合;聯結。
pièce de ré·sis·tance (ˌpjɛsdəˌrezis'tɑ̃ːs; ˌpjɛsdəˌreiziːs'tɑ̃s) 〖法〗①(饌肴中的)主菜。②主要物;主要事件;主要作品。
piece goods 疋頭;布疋。(亦作 **yard goods**)
piece·meal ('pisˌmil; 'piːs-miːl) *adv.* ①一件件地;零碎地;逐漸地。②破碎地;粉碎地。—*adj.* 一件件的;一個個的;逐漸的。
piece·work ('pisˌwɜk; 'piːs-wəːk) *n.* 件工(以工作量付錢之工作)。—**er,** *n.*
pie chart 圓形分格統計圖表(狀似切成塊之圓餅,故名)。
pie·crust ('paɪˌkrʌst; 'pai-krʌst) *n.* 派皮;餡餅皮。Promises are, like *piecrust,* made to be broken. 諾言如派皮,容易毀壞。—*adj.* 如餡餅皮般易於毀壞的。
pied (paɪd; paid) *adj.* ①雜色的。②有斑點的;斑駁的。③着雜色服裝的。
pied-à-terre (ˌpjeda'tɛr; ˌpjeita'tɛr) *n., pl.* **pied-à-terre.** 〖法〗臨時住宿處。
Pied·mont ('pidmɑnt; 'piːdmənt) *n.* ①皮得蒙高原(位於美國大西洋岸與 Appalachian 山脈之間)。②皮得蒙(義大利西北部之一省,首府 Turin)。
pied·mont ('pidmɑnt; 'piːdmənt) *adj.* 在山麓的。—*n.* 山麓地帶。
Pied Piper ①穿花衣的吹笛手(德國傳說人物,在 Browning 著 *The Pied Piper of Hamelin* 中,爲 Hamelin 鎮驅鼠,以不獲報酬,而吹笛帶走鎮上小孩)。②(常 p-p-)常以空言而使他人學其榜樣的人;善開空頭支票的領導者。
pie·man ('paɪmən; 'paimən) *n., pl.* **-men.** 賣餡餅的人。
pie·plant ('paɪˌplænt; 'pai-plɑːnt) *n.* 〖美〗〖植物〗大黃(葉莖可製 pie)。
*__pier__ (pɪr; piə) *n.* ①突堤碼頭。②防波堤。③橋脚;橋柱。④窗間壁;戶間壁。⑤方柱。***floating pier*** 浮碼頭。***landing pier*** 碼頭。
*__pierce__ (pɪrs; piəs) *v.,* **pierced, pierc·ing.** —*v.t.* ①戳入;刺透。A tunnel *pierces* the mountain. 一隧道通過此山。②穿洞於。③衝過;響徹。④識破;洞悉。⑤銳厲地影響到。a heart *pierced* with grief. 極度悲痛的心。—*v.i.* 穿過;穿入。
pierced earring 〖美〗穿孔耳環。
pierc·er ('pɪrsɚ; 'piəsə) *n.* ①刺穿之人(物)。②鑽孔器;錐。③〖俚〗銳敏的眼睛。④(昆蟲的)放卵管或針。
pierc·ing ('pɪrsɪŋ; 'piəsiŋ) *adj.* ①刺穿的;刺透的。②響徹的;尖銳的。③銳利的;銳敏的。a *piercing* eye. 銳利的眼光;慧眼。④諷刺的。—**ly,** *adv.*
pier glass 大穿衣鏡。
Pi·e·ri·an (paɪ'ɪrɪən; pai'eriən) *adj.* 派利亞的;繆司(Muses)女神的。
Pierian spring 詩泉(Olympus 山麓的 Muses 之泉);詩才的泉源。
Pi·er·rot (ˌpiə'ro; 'piərou) *n.* ①(法國啞劇中)着白袴及大鈕白色短衣而面塗白色之角色。②(p-)如此裝束之戴假面具者或丑角。
Pie·tà (pje'tɑ; ˌpie'tɑː) 〖義〗 *n.* 聖母抱基督屍體之哀戚畫像或雕像。
Pi·e·tism ('paɪəˌtɪzəm; 'paiətizəm) *n.* ①虔信派(17世紀末德國路德派教會之一宗派);虔信主義。②(p-)虔敬;篤信。③(p-)假虔誠。
Pi·e·tist ('paɪətɪst; 'paiətist) *n.* ①虔信派的信徒。②(p-)虔敬的人。
pi·e·tis·ti·c(al) (ˌpaɪə'tɪstɪk(l̩); ˌpaiə'tistik(l)) *adj.* ①虔敬的。②佯裝或過度虔誠的。
*__pi·e·ty__ ('paɪətɪ; 'paiəti, 'paiiti) *n., pl.* **-ties.** ①虔敬。②孝順;恭敬。filial *piety.* 孝道。③虔敬的行爲、言詞或信仰;孝順的言行。
pi·e·zo·e·lec·tric·i·ty (paɪˌizo·ɪˌlɛk'trɪsətɪ; paiˌiːzouiˌlek'trisiti) *n.* 〖電〗壓電

(於晶體上加壓力時產生之電)。

pi·e·zom·e·ter [ˌpaɪəˈzɑmətɚ; ˌpaiə-ˈzɔmitə] *n.* 壓力計;流壓計;水壓計。

pif·fle [ˈpɪfl; ˈpifl] *v.*, **-fled, -fling,** *n.*, *adj.* —*v.i.* 〖俗〗胡說。—*n.* 〖俗〗胡言亂語;廢話。—*adj.* 無聊的;沒有意義的。

pif·fler [ˈpɪflɚ; ˈpiflə] *n.* 〖俗〗輕浮者;胡言亂語者。

‡pig [pɪg; pig] *n.*, *v.*, **pigged, pig·ging.** —*n.* ①豬。②小豬。③豬肉。roast *pig.* 烤豬肉。④〖俗〗(行動、外表)似豬之人;貪婪、骯髒、愚蠢、遲緩等的人。⑤〖俚〗警察。⑥(鑄成之長方形的)金屬塊。⑦銑鐵。***make a pig of oneself*** 吃得過多。—*v.i.* ①住在骯髒而不舒服的環境中。②產(一胎小豬)。***pig it*** (or ***pig together***) 過豬般的生活。—*v.t.* 將金屬鑄成塊。

pig·boat [ˈpɪgˌbot; ˈpigˌbout] *n.* 〖美海軍俚〗潛水艇。

***pi·geon¹** [ˈpɪdʒən, ˈpɪdʒɪn; ˈpidʒin, -dʒən] *n.* ①鴿子。a carrier (*or* homing) *pigeon.* 傳信鴿。a wood *pigeon.* 野鴿子。②〖俗〗易受騙的人;愚人。③拋於空中做爲射擊目標的泥餅;飛靶。④年輕貌美的女子。⑤〖撲克俚〗從牌堆上拿到的一張好牌。—*v.t.* 欺騙;詐取。

pi·geon² [ˈpɪdʒɪn; ˈpidʒin] *n.* =**pidgin.**

pigeon blood ①深紅色。②〖俗〗醬油。(亦作 **pigeon's blood**)

pigeon breast 〖醫〗鴿胸;鷄胸。

pi·geon-breast·ed [ˈpɪdʒənˈbrɛstɪd; ˈpidʒinˈbrestid] *adj.* 患鴿胸症或鷄胸症的。

pigeon express 通信鴿的通信。

pi·geon-heart·ed [ˈpɪdʒənˈhɑrtɪd; ˈpidʒinˈhɑːtid] *adj.* 怯懦的;膽小的;害羞的。

pi·geon·hole [ˈpɪdʒənˌhol; ˈpidʒin-houl] *n.*, *v.*, **-holed, -hol·ing.** —*n.* ①鴿籠中之隔室。②(寫字台及櫥等中之)裝文件等之架格。—*v.t.* ①置於架格中;貯存。②分類記存。③擱置;置之不理。④在…上裝置架格。

pi·geon·ry [ˈpɪdʒənrɪ; ˈpidʒinri] *n.*, *pl.* **-ries.** 鴿舍;鴿籠。

pi·geon-toed [ˈpɪdʒənˌtod; ˈpidʒin-ˌtoud] *adj.* 趾或脚向內彎的。

pi·geon·wing [ˈpɪdʒənˌwɪŋ; ˈpidʒin-ˌwiŋ] *n.* ①鴿子的翅膀;鴿翼。②〖美〗跳起使兩腿互擊之奇妙跳舞步法。③〖美〗一種滑冰姿勢(狀如展開之鴿翅)。

pig·ger·y [ˈpɪgərɪ; ˈpigəri] *n.*, *pl.* **-ger·ies.** 〖英〗豚舍;豬欄。

pig·gin [ˈpɪgɪn; ˈpigin] *n.* 汲水桶;小手桶;長柄杓。

pig·gish [ˈpɪgɪʃ; ˈpigiʃ] *adj.* 如豬的;貪食的;不潔的。

pig·gy [ˈpɪgɪ; ˈpigi] *n.*, *pl.* **-gies,** *adj.*, **-gi·er, -gi·est.** —*n.* ①小豬。②〖兒語〗嬰兒之手指或脚趾。—*adj.* ①=**piggish.** ②母豬之即將產小豬的。

pig·gy·back [ˈpɪgɪˌbæk; ˈpigibæk] *adj.* & *adv.* =**pickaback.** —*v.t.* & *v.i.* 用火車平板車裝運(卡車拖車)。—*n.* 用火車平板車裝運卡車拖車。

piggy bank 撲滿。

pig·gy·wig(·gy) [ˈpɪgɪˌwɪg(ɪ); ˈpigi-wig(i)] *n.* 〖兒語〗小豬;髒孩子。

pig·head·ed [ˈpɪgˈhɛdɪd; ˈpigˈhedid] *adj.* 頑梗的;愚頑的。

pigiron 銑鐵。

pig·let [ˈpɪglɪt; ˈpiglit] *n.* 小豬。

pig·ling [ˈpɪglɪŋ; ˈpigliŋ] *n.* 小豬。

pig·ment [ˈpɪgmənt; ˈpigmənt] *n.* ①顏料。②〖生物〗色素。—*v.t.* 加顏色。—*v.i.* 變色;成爲有色。

pig·men·tal [pɪgˈmɛntl; pigˈmentl] *adj.* =**pigmentary.**

pig·men·tar·y [ˈpɪgmənˌtɛrɪ; ˈpig-məntəri] *adj.* 顏料的;顏色的;色素的。

pig·men·ta·tion [ˌpɪgmənˈteʃən; ˌpigmənˈteiʃən] *n.* ①〖生物〗染色;色素形成。②皮膚顏色。

pig·my [ˈpɪgmɪ; ˈpigmi] *adj.*, *n.*, *pl.* **-mies.** =**pygmy.**

pig·nut [ˈpɪgˌnʌt; ˈpignʌt] *n.* 〖植物〗①(北美產的)褐色山胡桃(餵豬用)。②(歐洲產的)落花生。

pig·pen [ˈpɪgˌpɛn; ˈpigpen] *n.* ①豬欄;豬圈。②骯髒的地方。

pig·skin [ˈpɪgˌskɪn; ˈpigskin] *n.* ①豬皮。②豬皮製成的革。③〖俗〗足球;橄欖球。④〖俗〗馬鞍。

pig·stick [ˈpɪgˌstɪk; ˈpigstik] *v.i.* 以長矛獵野豬。

pig·stick·er [ˈpɪgˌstɪkɚ; ˈpigˌstikə] *n.* ①獵野豬的人;受過獵野豬訓練的馬。②大號小刀;刺刀。③〖俚〗屠豬者;屠戶。

pig·stick·ing [ˈpɪgˌstɪkɪŋ; ˈpigˌstikiŋ] *n.* (用長矛)獵野豬。

pig·sty [ˈpɪgˌstaɪ; ˈpigstai] *n.*, *pl.* **-sties.** =**pigpen.**

pig·tail [ˈpɪgˌtel; ˈpigteil] *n.* ①辮子。②一種捲煙;撚草煙。

pig·tailed [ˈpɪgˌteld; ˈpigteild] *adj.* ①尾巴如豬尾的。②蓄辮的。

pig·wash [ˈpɪgˌwɑʃ; ˈpigwɔʃ] *n.* ①泔水;豬食(用來飼豬的廚房剩料)。②稀薄的劣等酒(咖啡、湯等)。

pig·weed [ˈpɪgˌwid; ˈpigˌwiːd] *n.* 〖植物〗藜。

pi·ka [ˈpaɪkə; ˈpaikə] *n.* 一種短耳野兎,產於北半球之岩質山中。

pike¹ [paɪk; paik] *n.*, *v.*, **piked, pik·ing.** —*n.* 矛;槍。—*v.t.* 以矛刺傷或刺殺。

pike² *n.* 梭子魚;狀似梭子魚之其他魚類。

pike³ *n.* ①收通行稅之道路;鄉間公路。②收通行稅之關卡。③通行稅。

pike⁴ *n.* ①尖端(如鏃尖、矛尖等)。②〖英方〗有尖峯之山;山峯(多用於專有名詞中,如 Langdale Pikes).

pike⁵ *v.i.*, **piked, pik·ing.** 〖俚〗快走〖常along〗.

pike⁶ *v.i.*, **piked, pik·ing.** 〖俚〗①離開。②死亡。

pike⁷ *v.i.*, **piked, pik·ing.** 極小心謹愼地做事;畏首畏尾。

pike⁸ *n.* 花式跳水姿勢(彎腰、手觸及足趾、膝部保持筆直)。

pike·man¹ [ˈpaɪkmən; ˈpaikmən] *n.*, *pl.* **-men.** 矛兵。

pike·man² *n.*, *pl.* **-men.** 收取通行稅者。

pik·er [ˈpaɪkɚ; ˈpaikə] *n.* ①〖美俚〗小心而客嗇的賭徒;小投機者。②〖俚〗小氣鬼;嗇刻子;膽小鬼;臨陣脫逃的人。

pike·staff [ˈpaɪkˌstæf; ˈpaikstɑːf] *n.*, *pl.* **-staves** [-ˌstevz; -steivz]. ①矛桿;矛柄。②徒步旅行者的手杖(下端尖者)。***as plain as a pikestaff*** 極爲明顯的。

pi·laf(f) [pəˈlɑf; ˈpilæf] *n.* =**pilau.**

pi·las·ter [pəˈlæstɚ; piˈlæstə] *n.* 〖建築〗半露方柱;挨壁柱(一半嵌在牆中之方柱)。

Pi·late [ˈpaɪlət; ˈpailət] *n.* 〖聖經〗比拉多(Pontius, 審判耶穌之 Judea 總督)。

pi·lau [pəˈlo; piˈlau] *n.* 肉飯(米中加肉、魚及香料等)。

pi·law [pɪˈlɔ; piˈlɔː] *n.* =**pilau.**

pilch [pɪltʃ; piltʃ] *n.* (三角形的)尿布兜。

pil·chard [ˈpɪltʃɚd; ˈpiltʃəd] *n.* 鯡科之一種小海魚。

‡pile¹ [paɪl; pail] *n.*, *v.*, **piled, pil·ing.** —*n.* ①一堆;一批;一排。a *pile* of wood. 一堆木頭。②(似丘般的)大堆;大團。a *pile* of dirt. 一大堆垃圾。③〖俗〗大量金錢。He has made his *pile*. 他已發財。④(火葬等時用的)柴堆。⑤大建築物; 一堆建築物。⑥電池。a dry *pile*. 乾電池。⑦電堆。⑧可鑄成鐵條的一堆鐵塊。⑨核子反應爐。—*v.t.* ①堆起;堆疊。②積聚;積蓄〖up〗。③裝載;裝貨於(車)。—*v.i.* ①堆起;堆疊。The snow is *piling* up. 雪正在越堆越高。②蜂湧而行。③積聚;積蓄〖up〗。④成羣結隊攻擊某人。***pile arms*** 架槍。***pile it on***〖俗〗誇耀;誇張。***pile on the agony***〖俗〗把一件事情寫得慘過其實。

pile² *n., v.,* **piled, pil·ing.** —*n.* 木樁。to drive (raise, draw) *piles*. 打(拔)樁。—*v.t.* 固以樁;打樁於。

pile³ *n.* ①軟毛;細毛。②絨毯上的絨毛。

piled 〔paɪld; paild〕 *adj.* 有絨毛的(如絨布等)。

pile driver 打樁機。

pile engine =**pile driver.**

pi·le·ous 〔ˈpaɪlɪəs; ˈpailiəs〕 *adj.* 毛的;有毛的;多毛的。

piles 〔paɪlz; pailz〕 *n. pl.* 痔瘡。

pile-up 〔ˈpaɪlˌʌp; ˈpailˌʌp〕 *n.* ①(工作, 帳單等)堆積。②多數車輛之相撞; 連環車禍。③〖橄欖球〗守護球員疊成堆以阻止進攻。

pil·fer 〔ˈpɪlfɚ; ˈpilfə〕 *v.t. & v.i.* 小量地盜竊;偷竊。—**er,** *n.*

pil·fer·age 〔ˈpɪlfərɪdʒ; ˈpilfəridʒ〕 *n.* ①小竊行爲;小竊盜。②失竊之物。

***pil·grim** 〔ˈpɪlgrɪm; ˈpilgrim〕 *n.* ①參詣聖地者;朝山進香者。②旅客。③(P-)〖美〗1620年創立普里茅斯殖民地(Plymouth Colony)之清教徒。④一地區之原始定居者。

***pil·grim·age** 〔ˈpɪlgrəmɪdʒ; ˈpilgrimidʒ〕 *n., v.,* **-aged, -ag·ing.** —*n.* ①朝聖者之旅途; 朝聖之途程。②漫長之旅途。③人生;生命的途程。—*v.i.* 朝聖。

Pilgrim Fathers 〖美〗1620年建立普里茅斯 (Plymouth Colony) 的清教徒。

Pilgrim's Progress, The 天路歷程(John Bunyan 所著的宗教寓言小說)。

pil·ing 〔ˈpaɪlɪŋ; ˈpailiŋ〕 *n.* ①樁(集合稱)。②打樁。

pill¹** 〔pɪl; pil〕 *n.* ①丸藥。②(the-)口服避孕丸。③小彈丸。④〖俚〗球(尤指棒球和高爾夫球)。⑤〖俚〗惹人厭的人。⑥不愉快但得忍受的事。⑦(*pl.*)〖英俚〗(撞球的) 彈子。gild the pill*** 把討厭的東西弄得好看; 粉飾表面。—*v.t.* ①投丸藥。②將…作成丸藥。③〖俚〗抑貶。—*v.i.* 形成小圓球(如毛線衣上之毛等)。

pill² *v.t.* ①〖古〗掠奪。②〖古,方〗剝(=peel)。③〖廢〗變禿頂;使禿頂。

pil·lage 〔ˈpɪlɪdʒ; ˈpilidʒ〕 *v.,* **-laged, -lag·ing,** *n.* —*v.t. & v.i.* 强刼;掠奪。—*n.* ①强刼;掠奪。②掠奪物。

pil·lar** 〔ˈpɪlɚ; ˈpilə〕 *n.* ①柱子。②柱狀物。③重要的支持者; 棟樑。a *pillar* of the state. 國家的棟樑。from pillar to post*** **a.** 無目標地飄蕩。**b.** 茫然不知下一步做甚麼;遭受一連串的不如意之事。—*v.t.* 以柱子支撐。

pillar box (or **post**) 〖英〗郵筒。

pil·lared 〔ˈpɪlɚd; ˈpiləd〕 *adj.* 有柱的; 以柱支撐的;柱形的。

pill·box 〔ˈpɪlˌbɑks; ˈpilbɔks〕 *n.* ①藥丸盒。②碉堡。③一種無邊的女帽。

pil·lion 〔ˈpɪljən; ˈpiljən〕 *n.* ①鞍褥(供婦女乘騎之用)。②〖英國〗馬鞍後加附之座位。③二輪摩托車之後座。

pil·lo·ry 〔ˈpɪlərɪ; ˈpiləri〕 *n., pl.* **-ries,** *v.,* **-ried, -ry·ing.** —*n.* ①枷(古時刑具)。②受衆辱。—*v.t.* ①施以枷刑。②使受衆辱。

***pil·low** 〔ˈpɪlo; ˈpilou〕 *n.* ①枕頭。②〖機械〗軸襯。③枕頭樣的事物。—*v.t.* ①枕於。②作爲…的枕頭。The earth shall *pillow* my head tonight. 今夜我將露宿(我將以大地作枕頭)。—*v.i.* (像是)枕於枕頭上。

pil·low·case 〔ˈpɪloˌkes; ˈpiloukeis〕 *n.* 枕套。

pillow fight (兒童就寢前做的)枕頭戰。

pillow sham 裝飾用枕頭蓋。

pil·low·slip 〔ˈpɪloˌslɪp; ˈpilouslip〕 *n.* 枕套。

pillow talk 枕邊細語。

pil·low·y 〔ˈpɪləwɪ, ˈpɪləɪ; ˈpiloui〕 *adj.* 枕頭似的;柔軟的;一壓就凹的。

pi·lose 〔ˈpaɪlos; ˈpailous〕 *adj.* 多軟毛的; 覆有柔毛的。(亦作 **pilous**)

pi·los·i·ty 〔paɪˈlɑsətɪ; paiˈlɔsiti〕 *n.* 〖動、植物〗多毛性;有毛。

pi·lot** 〔ˈpaɪlət; ˈpailət〕 *n.* ①航船者; 駕駛船者。②領港者。③飛機駕駛員;飛行員。④嚮導; 領導者。⑤(火車頭、電車等之)排障器。⑥(機械、機器中某一部分的)操縱器; 控制器。⑦(亦作 **coast pilot**) 政府所發有關沿海海洋,港口設施等供航海人員參考的手册。⑧〖電視〗=**pilot film.** ***drop the pilot **a.** 領港員完成任務時令其離船。**b.** 開革可靠的顧問。—*v.t.* ①駕駛 (飛機、船等); 領港。He *pilots* his airplane. 他駕他的飛機。②嚮導;領導。—*adj.* ①示範的; 實驗的。a *pilot* project. 示範計畫。②領港的;導航的。a *pilot* launch. 領港快艇。③總的。—**less,** *adj.*

pi·lot·age 〔ˈpaɪlətɪdʒ; ˈpailətidʒ〕 *n.* ①領港;飛機駕駛(術)。②領導;嚮導。③領港費。

pilot balloon 測風氣球。

pilot biscuit (or **bread**) (船上用)硬餅乾。

pilot cloth (水手外套用的)藍色粗呢。

pilot engine (鐵道上用的)清路車。

pilot film 〖電視〗電視影集之樣片。

pilot fish 鯖類的海魚。

pilot house (船上的)駕駛室。

pilot lamp (or **light**) 〖電〗引示燈(用以指示開關的位置或表示某電路在通電中)。

pilotless aircraft 無人駕駛飛機。

pilot officer 〖英〗空軍少尉。

pilot plant (新生產技術的)試驗工場。

pilot study 初步研究。

Pilt·down man 〔ˈpɪltˌdaun～; ˈpiltdaun～〕 〖人類學〗皮爾丹人 (1912年在英格蘭 Sussex 郡的 Piltdown 發現的頭蓋骨, 曾被認爲洪積世最古的人類, 1953年被證實爲僞物)。

pil·u·lar 〔ˈpɪljəlɚ; ˈpiljulə〕 *adj.* 丸藥的;丸藥狀的。

pil·ule 〔ˈpɪljul; ˈpiljuːl〕 *n.* 小丸藥。

pi·men·to 〔pɪˈmɛnto; piˈmentou〕 *n., pl.* **-tos.** 〖植物〗①西班牙甘椒。②甘椒樹。③美洲熱帶產之一種香料。④鮮紅色。

pi·mien·to 〔pɪmˈjɛnto; pimˈjentou〕 *n., pl.* **-tos.** 西班牙甘椒(作爲菜蔬或香料)。

pim·o·la 〔pɪˈmolə; piˈmoulə〕 *n.* 塡以 pimiento 的橄欖。

pimp 〔pɪmp; pimp〕 *n.* ①淫媒;拉皮條的人;鴇兒;妓院老板。②卑鄙的人。③〖澳〗告密的人;線民。—*v.i.* 拉皮條;寫娼。

pim·per·nel 〔ˈpɪmpɚˌnɛl, -nl; ˈpimpənel, -nl〕 *n.* 〖植物〗紫蘩蔞。

pimp·ing 〔ˈpɪmpɪŋ; ˈpimpiŋ〕 *adj.* 〖俗〗很小的;卑小的;無價值的。②虛弱的。

pim·ple 〔ˈpɪmpl; ˈpimpl〕 *n.* 丘疹;粉刺;面皰。

pim·pled 〔ˈpɪmpld; ˈpimpld〕 *adj.* =**pimply.**

pim·ply 〔ˈpɪmplɪ; ˈpimpli〕 *adj.,* **-pli·er,**

-pli·est. 有丘疹的;多粉刺的。

pin** 〔pɪn; pin〕 *n.* ①大頭針。②飾針;別針;胸針。③有別針的徽章。④釘;栓。⑤支槳的木栓。⑥樂器上調絃的木栓。⑦保齡球戲中的木瓶。⑧〖俗〗腿。⑨小而無價值的東西。⑩(高爾夫球場中用以指示洞口之)旗杆。⑪髮針。⑫指示標的中心之釘等。⑬擀麪棒。neat as a new pin*** 非常整齊。***not to care a pin*** 一點也不在乎。***on pins and needles*** 如坐針氈;焦慮不安。—*v.t.* ①(用針等)釘住。to *pin* papers together. 將紙用針釘在一起。②使不能動。③使固守。to *pin* a person down to a promise. 使某人固守其諾言。④將兄弟會別針贈女孩爲記(通常用被動式)。⑤〖俚〗抓;逮捕。***pin down*** **a.** 約束而採取某行動。**b.** 迫使(某人)採取行動或做決定。**c.** 正確地決定;確立無疑。**d.** 使不能動。***pin in*** 用碎石等塡滿石牆之破洞。***pin one's faith on*** 堅決相信;絕對信賴;堅信。***pin something on someone*** 〖俚〗歸咎於某人;根據證據指控。

pin·a·fore 〔ˈpɪnəˌfor; ˈpinəfɔː〕 *n.* ①(小孩)涎布;胸巾;圍兜。②〖英〗大人用之胸巾或圍裙。

pin·ball 〔ˈpɪnˌbɔl; ˈpinbɔːl〕 *n.* 釘球戲;彈球戲(一種賭博遊戲)。

pin boy 保齡球館內將被打倒的瓶扶起並把球送回打球人的男工。

pince-nez 〔ˈpænsˌne; ˈpɛ̃ːnsnei〕 *n.* 夾鼻眼鏡。

pin·cers 〔ˈpɪnsɚz; ˈpinsəz〕 *n. pl.* or *sing.* ①鉗子;鑷子。a pair of *pincers.* 一把鉗子。②鉗狀物。③〖軍〗鉗形攻勢。(亦作 **pinchers**)

pincers movement 〖軍〗鉗形攻勢(=pincers).

pin·cette 〔ˌpɛ̃ˈsɛt; ˌpɛ̃ˈset〕 *n., pl.* **-cettes.** 〖法〗小鑷子。

pinch** 〔pɪntʃ; pintʃ〕 *v.t.* ①挾;捏;擠。②使皺縮;使困苦。to be *pinched* for money. 細於金錢;在經濟困難中。③〖俚〗逮捕。④〖俚〗偸竊。—*v.i.* ①壓;緊。When hunger *pinches* .... 饑餓逼人的時候…。②用錢吝嗇。to *pinch* and save. 辛苦積蓄。pinch pennies*** 吝嗇;節儉。***That's where the shoe pinches.*** 那就是鞋子挾脚的地方(困難卽在此)。—*n.* ①挾;捏;擠。②撮;捻。a *pinch* of salt. 一撮鹽。③困苦。the *pinch* of poverty. 窮困。④緊急。when it comes to the *pinch.* 到緊急關頭。⑤〖俚〗逮捕。⑥〖俚〗偸。

pinch·beck 〔ˈpɪntʃbɛk; ˈpintʃbek〕 *n.* ①金色黃銅(銅與鋅的合金,用作贋金)。②假東西;冒牌貨;僞造品;廉價寶石類。—*adj.* ①金色黃銅的。②冒牌的。

pinch hit 〖棒球〗代打者擊出的安打。

pinch-hit 〔ˈpɪntʃˈhɪt; ˈpintʃˈhit〕 *v.,* **-hit, -hit·ting.** —*v.i.* ①〖棒球〗(吃緊時)代打。②〖俗〗代替〖for〗。—*v.t.* 代打時擊出安打。

pinch hitter ①〖棒球〗代打者。②代替者;替身。

pinch·pen·ny 〔ˈpɪntʃˌpɛnɪ; ˈpintʃˌpeni〕 *n., pl.* **-nies.** 吝嗇鬼。—*adj.* 吝嗇的。

pinch runner 〖棒球〗代跑者。

pin curl 用髮針挾住的潮濕的髮捲。

pin·cush·ion 〔ˈpɪnˌkuʃən; ˈpinˌkuʃin〕 *n.* 針墊。

Pin·dar 〔ˈpɪndɚ; ˈpində〕 *n.* 平德爾(522?–?443 B.C., 希臘詩人)。

Pin·dar·ic 〔pɪnˈdærɪk; pinˈdærik〕 *adj.* 有 Pindar 風格的。—*n.* 有 Pindar 風格之詩歌(一種流行於十八世紀押韻不規則之詩歌)。

pin·dling 〔ˈpɪndlɪŋ; ˈpindliŋ〕 *adj.* ①〖美俗〗纖弱的;羸弱的;多病的。②〖英方〗脾氣暴躁的;乖張的。

‡**pine**[1] 〔paɪn; pain〕 *n.* ①松樹。②松木。③〖俗〗鳳梨。

***pine**[2] *v.i.,* **pined, pin·ing.** ①渴望;苦思〖常 for〗。He is *pining* for a holiday. 他渴望假日。②消瘦;憔悴。They are *pining* with hunger. 他們因饑餓而消瘦。to *pine* away. 憔悴。

pin·e·al 〔ˈpɪnɪəl, ˈpaɪnɪəl; ˈpiniəl, ˈpainiəl〕 *adj.* ①松毬狀的。②〖解剖〗松果腺的;松果體的。*pineal* gland. 松果腺。

***pine·ap·ple** 〔ˈpaɪnˌæpl; ˈpainˌæpl〕 *n.* ①鳳梨;波羅。②鳳梨叢。③〖俚〗手榴彈。

pine cone 松毬;松果。

pine marten 〖動物〗(歐洲產的)褐貂。

pine needle 松針。

pine nut ①松仁;松子。②松果;松球。

pin·er·y 〔ˈpaɪnərɪ; ˈpainəri〕 *n., pl.* **-er·ies.** ①松林。②鳳梨暖室;波羅園。

pine·y 〔ˈpaɪnɪ; ˈpaini〕 *adj.,* **pin·i·er, pin·i·est.** =**piny.**

pin·feath·er 〔ˈpɪnˌfɛðɚ; ˈpinˌfeðə〕 *n.* 針羽(幼鳥的細線狀的羽毛)。

pin·fold 〔ˈpɪnˌfold; ˈpinfould〕 *n.* ①畜欄。②關閉或約束的地方。—*v.t.* 關入畜欄;關入關閉處所。

ping 〔pɪŋ; piŋ〕 *n.* 乒聲;子彈擊中某物之聲。—*v.i.* 發出乒聲。

***ping-pong** 〔ˈpɪŋˌpɑŋ, –ˌpɔŋ; ˈpiŋpɔŋ〕 *n.* 乒乓球(戲);桌球(戲)。(亦作 **Ping-Pong, Ping-pong, table tennis**)

pin·guid 〔ˈpɪŋgwɪd; ˈpiŋgwid〕 *adj.* ①似油的;含油的;油膩的。②(土地)肥沃的。

pin·head 〔ˈpɪnˌhɛd; ˈpinhed〕 *n.* ①針頭。②細小之物。③〖俚〗愚蠢之人。

pin·head·ed 〔ˈpɪnˌhɛdɪd; ˈpinˌhedid〕 *adj.* ①如針頭的。②〖俚〗愚笨的。

pin·hole 〔ˈpɪnˌhol; ˈpinhoul〕 *n.* 針孔;小孔。

pin·ion 〔ˈpɪnjən; ˈpinjən〕 *n.* ①鳥翼之尖端部分;翮。②〖詩〗翼;翅。③鳥翅上的羽毛。④〖機械〗小齒輪。—*v.t.* ①剪掉或縛住(鳥翼)使不能飛。②束縛。

***pink**[1] 〔pɪŋk; piŋk〕 *n.* ①淡紅色。②最高度;頂點。in the *pink* of health. 非常健康。③石竹。④石竹花。⑤〖美俚〗(常 P–)傾向共產主義的人。—*adj.* ①淡紅色的。②〖美俚〗思想相當左傾的。

pink[2] *v.t.* ①以刀、劍、矛等刺。②將(布邊)剪成鋸齒形。③裝飾。④以小圓孔做裝飾。

pink[3] *n.* 〖英〗幼鮭。

pink[4] *n.* 〖航海〗一種窄尾的小帆船。

pink·eye 〔ˈpɪŋkˌaɪ; ˈpiŋkˌai〕 *n.* ①〖醫〗火眼;傳染性結膜炎。②(馬的)流行性感冒。(亦作 **pink eye**)

pink·ie 〔ˈpɪŋkɪ; ˈpiŋki〕 *n.* 〖俗〗小指。(亦作 **pinky**)

pink·ish 〔ˈpɪŋkɪʃ; ˈpiŋkiʃ〕 *adj.* 略帶淡紅色的。

pink slip 〖俚〗解僱的通知。

Pink·ster 〔ˈpɪŋkstɚ; ˈpiŋkstə〕 *n.* 〖美方〗=**Whitsuntide.**

pinkster flower 產於美國的一種淡紅色杜鵑花。

pink tea 〖俗〗正式茶會。

pink·y 〔ˈpɪŋkɪ; ˈpiŋki〕 *adj.,* **pink·i·er, pink·i·est.** 淡紅色的;帶淡紅色的。

pin money ①男人給他妻子或女兒的零用錢。②零用錢。

pin·na 〔ˈpɪnə; ˈpinə〕 *n., pl.* **-nas, -nae** 〔-ni; -niː〕. ①〖解剖〗耳郭;耳翼。②〖植物〗羽狀複葉的一片;羽片。③〖動物〗羽;翼;鰭。

pin·nace 〔ˈpɪnɪs, –əs; ˈpinis, –nəs〕 *n.* ①附屬於大船的小艇;駁艇。②輕快的小帆船。

pin·na·cle 〔ˈpɪnəkl; ˈpinəkl〕 *n., v.,* **-cled, -cling.** —*n.* ①岩石的尖頂;尖峯。②

極高之名望或地位。③頂點;最高點。④尖塔;尖頂;尖閣。—v.t. ①置於尖頂上;置於極高處。②築(或飾)尖塔、尖頂、尖閣於。
—pin·na·cled, adj.

pin·nate ['pɪnet; 'pinit] adj. ①羽狀的。②〖植物〗有羽狀葉的。(亦作 **pinnated**) —ly, adv.

pin·ner ['pɪnɚ; 'pinə] n. ①以針固定者;揷釘者。②(18世紀初的)一種有長擺下垂的女用頭巾。③=**pinafore.**

pin·ni·ped ['pɪnəpɛd; 'piniped] adj. ①鰭脚類的。②有鰭脚的。—n. 鰭脚類動物。

pin·ny ['pɪnɪ; 'pini] n. 涎圍;涎布(小兒語)。

pi·noc(h)·le ['pi,nʌkl; 'piː,nʌkl] n. 「〖美〗一種紙牌戲。」

pi·no·le [pɪ'nole; pi'noulei] n. (墨西哥及美國西南部的)甜炒玉米粉。

pi·ñon ['pɪnjən; 'pinjən] n.〖美〗(Rocky山脈南部地方產的)矮松樹;其可食之果實。

pin·point ['pɪn,pɔɪnt; 'pin-pɔint] n. ①針尖。②瑣屑之物;一點點。③細小的標的;正確位置或目標。—v.t. ①(插針於地圖上)指示正確的位置;確定(位置)。②正確地瞄準。③精確顯示。—adj. 準確的。

pinpoint bombing 精確轟炸。

pin·prick ['pɪn,prɪk; 'pin-prik] n. ①針刺;針孔。②小刺激;小煩惱。

*__pint__ [paɪnt; paint] n. ①品脫(容量名,等於八分之一加侖)。②一品脫的容器。

pin·ta ['paɪntə; 'paintə] n.〖英〗一品脫的飲料(尤指牛奶)。

pin·tail ['pɪn,tel; 'pin-teil] n., pl. **-tails, -tail.** 長尾鳧。

pin·tle ['pɪntl; 'pintl] n. ①樞軸;(鉸鏈、鎗等的)針栓。②〖造船〗舵針。

pin·to ['pɪnto; 'pintou] adj., n., pl. **-tos.** —adj. 黑白斑紋的;斑駁的。—n.〖美西部〗①(黑白)斑馬。②(亦作 **pinto bean**) 斑豆。

pin-up ['pɪn,ʌp; 'pinʌp] n. ①〖俗〗掛在牆上的漂亮女人照片。②漂亮女人。③掛在牆上的裝置,如壁燈等。—adj. ①漂亮的。②可掛在牆上的。(亦作 **pinup**)

pin·wheel ['pɪn,hwil; 'pinwiːl] n. ①紙風車(一種玩具)。②一種輪狀焰火。③〖機械〗串齒輪。—v.i. 如紙風車似的迅速旋轉。

pin·worm ['pɪn,wɝm; 'pinwəːm] n. 「蟯蟲。」

pinx. pinxit.

pinx·it ['pɪŋksɪt; 'piŋksit]〖拉〗v. …繪(書於繪畫落款之後=he *or* she painted it).

pin·y ['paɪnɪ; 'paini] adj., **pin·i·er, pin·i·est.** 松的;似松的;多松的;松林茂盛的。(亦作 **piney**)

*__pi·o·neer__ [,paɪə'nɪr; ,paiə'niə] n. ①拓荒者;開墾者。②先鋒;首倡者。③〖軍〗工兵。④〖生態〗第一個進入不毛之地而生根或繁殖的動植物。⑤(P-)〖美〗探測月球之無人太空船。⑥(P-)蘇聯共產主義少年團之團員。—v.t. 開拓(道路);爲…開路。to *pioneer* an enterprise. 爲某一事業作先鋒。—v.i. 作先鋒、先驅者。—adj. ①開拓的;先驅的。a *pioneer* method of adult education. 成人教育最早的方法。②開拓者的。

*__pi·ous__ ['paɪəs; 'paiəs] adj. ①虔誠的;虔敬的。②以宗教爲名的(好意或壞意);出自宗教熱誠的;假裝虔誠的。*pious* frauds. 藉宗教之名而行之詐欺。③〖古〗孝順的。

pip[1] [pɪp; pip] n. ①(橘子、梨等的)小粒種子。②〖俚〗很好的事或人。

pip[2] n. ①家禽的一種舌病。②〖諧〗人的任何小病。③〖英俚〗(the-)精神萎靡;感到厭煩。

pip[3] n. ①骰子或紙牌上之點。②鳳梨表面之格子小塊。③〖英俚〗(軍官制服上所佩帶的表示階級之)金屬肩章中之星。④〖植物〗塊根中之一塊。

pip[4] v.t., **pipped, pip·ping.**〖英俗〗①以「彈丸擊。②結束。③排斥。」

pip[5] v., **pipped, pip·ping.** —v.i. 啁啾而鳴。—v.t.(雛鳥)啄破(卵殼);啄破(卵殼)而出。

pip[6] n.〖電子〗雷達幕上的點。

pip·age ['paɪpɪdʒ; 'paipidʒ] n. ①水、瓦斯、油等之以管輸送。②此項輸送管。③用此種方式之輸送費。

pi·pal ['pipəl; 'piːpəl] n. (印度產之)菩提樹。(亦作 **pipal tree, peepul**)

‡**pipe** [paɪp; paip] n., v., **piped, pip·ing.** —n. ①管;導管;筒。②烟斗。He was smoking a *pipe*. 他在以烟斗吸烟。③烟斗一次所裝之烟。④笛;簫。⑤(pl.)風笛。⑥尖銳的聲音;呼嘯聲。⑦水手長的號笛。⑧大酒桶。⑨管狀物。***Put that in your pipe and smoke it.***〖俗〗那是值得你想想的事。—v.t. & v.i. ①以管輸送。②供以管。to *pipe* a house. 給一棟房子裝水管。③吹笛;吹(笛)。④發尖銳聲;以尖聲唱。⑤唱;發呼聲。⑥以水手長之笛聲命令。⑦以笛聲召集。All hands were *piped* on deck. 所有的水手均被召集在甲板上。***pipe down***〖俚〗禁聲;住嘴。***pipe one's*** (or ***the***) ***eye*** 哭泣。***pipe up*** a. 開始吹笛。b.〖俚〗說出。c. 裝飾衣邊。d. 增加速度。

pipe clay 烟斗泥(一種白黏土)。

pipe-clay ['paɪp,kle; 'paipklei] v.t. 以白黏土使變白。

pipe dream〖俗〗妄想。

pipe·fish ['paɪp,fɪʃ; 'paipfiʃ] n., pl. **-fish, -fish·es.** 尖嘴魚;楊枝魚。

pipe·ful ['paɪp,ful; 'paipful] n., pl. **-fuls.** (烟絲等)一管之量;一烟斗之量。

pipe·line ['paɪp,laɪn; 'paiplain] n., v., **-lined, -lin·ing.** —n. ①輸油(天然氣、水等之)管;導管。②祕密消息來源。***in*** (or ***into***) ***the pipeline*** 在進行中。—v.t. 用導管輸送;裝設導管。(亦作 **pipe line**)

pipe of peace 北美印第安人使用之長而有裝飾的烟斗,做爲和平的象徵。

pipe organ 管風琴。

pip·er ['paɪpɚ; 'paipə] n. 吹笛人。***pay the piper*** 承擔後果;負擔玩樂之費用。

pipe rack 烟斗架。

pipe smoker〖美〗鴉片烟鬼;瘾君子。

pipe·stem ['paɪp,stɛm; 'paipstem] n. ①烟管;烟桿。②似烟管軸般細長的東西。

pi·pette, pi·pet [pɪ'pɛt; pi'pet] n., v., **-pet·ted, -pet·ting.** —n. 移液管;吸量管;球管。—v.t. 使用移液管將液體吸移。

pip·ing ['paɪpɪŋ; 'paipiŋ] n. ①管(集合稱)。②管狀或用以製管之材料。③笛聲;尖聲。④笛奏出的音樂。⑤(糕餅等)糖與蛋白等製成的條狀花色。⑥用以裝飾衣物邊縫之管狀窄條。—adj. ①吹笛的;發尖聲的。②太平的;平靜的。the *piping* times of peace. 承平時代。***piping hot*** 極熱的;熱得嘶嘶作響的;滾熱的。

pip·it ['pɪpɪt; 'pipit] n. 天鷚之類;田雲雀。

pip·kin ['pɪpkɪn; 'pipkin] n. ①小瓦壺。②小汲桶。

pip·pin ['pɪpɪn; 'pipin] n. ①一種蘋果。②〖植物〗種子。③〖俗〗受尊崇的人或物。

pip·sis·se·wa [pɪp'sɪsəwə; pip'sisəwə] n.〖植物〗梅笠草;愛多葉。

pip·y ['paɪpɪ; 'paipi] adj., **pip·i·er, pip·i·est.** ①管狀的。②高音調的;發尖聲的。

pi·quan·cy ['pikənsɪ; 'piːkənsi] n.

辛辣;刺激。

pi·quant ['pikənt; 'pi:kənt] *adj.* ①够刺激的;令人痛快淋漓的; 有趣的。②開胃的;辛辣的。③帶有尖刻意味的。—**ly**, *adv.*

pique [pik; pi:k] *n., v.*, **piqued, pi·quing.** —*n.*惱怒;不平之氣。In a *pique*, she left the room. 她生氣地離開房間而去。He took a *pique* against me. 他生我的氣。—*v.t.* ①激怒;激起。②傷 (自尊心等)。③引起感情或使採某行動。④〖航空, 廢〗俯衝。***pique oneself on*** (or ***upon***) 對…感到驕傲。—*v.i.* 使生氣。

pi·qué [pɪ'ke; pi'kei] *n.* 一種凸花棉布;起楞布。—*adj.* 有鑲嵌裝飾的。

pi·quet [pɪ'kɛt; pi'ket] *n.* 一種二人玩之紙牌戲(祇用7及7以上之牌共32張)。

pi·ra·cy ['paɪrəsɪ; 'paiərəsi] *n., pl.* **-cies.** ①海上搶刼。 ②剽竊或盗印著作物。***literary piracy*** 著作權之剽竊。

pi·ra·gua [pɪ'rɑgwə; pi'rɑ:gwə] *n.* ① =**pirogue.** ②一種二桅平底的小帆船。

Pi·ran·del·lo [ˌpɪrən'dɛlo; ˌpirən'delou] *n.* 皮蘭代羅 (Luigi, 1867–1936, 義大利小說家、劇作家及詩人, 1934年獲諾貝爾獎)。

pi·ra·nha [pɪ'rɑnjə; pi'rɑ:njə] *n.* 南美產小魚(在水中會襲擊人畜)。

***pi·rate** ['paɪrət, -rɪt; 'paiərit, -rət] *n., v.*, **-rat·ed, -rat·ing.** —*n.* ①海盜。②海盜船。③違反版權法者;剽竊者;盜印者。literary *pirate*. 侵害著作權者。 ④掠略者; 掠奪者。—*v.t. & v.i.* ①掠奪;做海盜。②盜印;翻印。a *pirated* edition. 非法翻印本。

pi·rat·i·cal [paɪ'rætɪkl; pai'rætikəl] *adj.* ①海盜的;似海盜的;海盜行爲的。②剽竊的; 侵害著作權的; 盜印的。 a *piratical* edition. 盜印版。(亦作 **piratic**) —**ly**, *adv.*

pi·rogue [pə'rog; pi'roug] *n.* ①獨木舟(亦作 **piragua**). ②獨木舟形的船。

pir·ou·ette [ˌpɪru'ɛt; ˌpiru'et] *n., v.*, **-et·ted, -et·ting.** —*n.* ①跳舞時以一足或趾尖所作之急速旋轉。②〖馬術〗馬之以後脚爲軸而做的完全旋轉。 —*v.i.* (跳舞時) 以趾尖旋轉。

Pi·sa ['pizə; 'pi:zə] *n.* 比薩(義大利西北部城名, 以其斜塔著名於世)。

pis al·ler [piza'le; 'pi:z'ælei] 〖法〗 最後之手段; 唯一可能的辦法。

pis·ca·ry ['pɪskərɪ; 'piskəri] *n., pl.* **-ries.** ①〖法律〗(在他人所有之河川之)捕魚權 (現僅用於 common of piscary. 共漁權。一語中)。②漁場。

pis·ca·to·ry ['pɪskəˌtorɪ; 'piskətəri] *adj.* 魚的; 漁夫的; 釣魚的; 漁業的。(亦作 **piscatorial**)

Pis·ces ['pɪsiz; 'pisi:z] *n.* ①〖動物〗 魚類。②〖天文〗 雙魚座。 ③〖天文〗 雙魚宮 (黃道之第十二宮)。

pis·ci·cide ['pɪsəˌsaɪd; 'pisəsaid] *n.* 消滅一個地區的魚類。

pis·ci·cul·tur·al [ˌpɪsɪ'kʌltʃərəl; ˌpisi'kʌltʃərəl] *adj.* 養魚的;養魚法的。

pis·ci·cul·ture ['pɪsɪˌkʌltʃə; 'pisikʌltʃə] *n.* 養魚(法)。

pis·ci·cul·tur·ist [ˌpɪsɪ'kʌltʃərɪst; ˌpisi'kʌltʃərist] *n.* 養魚者;養魚家。

pis·ci·na [pɪ'saɪnə; pi'sainə] *n., pl.* **-nae** [-ni; -ni:], **-nas.** ①〖宗教〗聖杯洗盤;洗手盤。②〖古羅馬〗魚池;浴池。

pis·cine ['pɪsaɪn; 'pisain] *adj.* 魚(類)的;似魚的。

pis·civ·o·rous [pɪ'sɪvərəs; pi'sivərəs] *adj.* (鳥等)食魚的。

pi·sé [ˌpi'ze, 'pize; ˌpi:'zei, 'pi:zei] 〖法〗 *n.* 〖建築〗 墳泥; 砌牆泥。

Pis·gah, Mount ['pɪzgə; 'pizgə] *n.* 〖聖經〗 毗斯迦山 (於此摩西目睹迦南而死)。

pish [pʃ, pɪʃ; piʃ, pʃ] *interj.* 呸! (表示輕視或不耐煩)。 —*n.* 呸聲。 —*v.t.* 向…作呸聲。 —*v.i.* 作呸聲。

pi·si·form ['paɪsɪˌfɔrm; 'paisifɔ:m] *adj.* ①豌豆形的; 豌豆大的。②〖解剖, 動物〗豌豆狀的。

pis·mire ['pɪsˌmaɪr; 'pismaiə] *n.* 〖古〗螞蟻。

piss [pɪs; pis] *v.i.* 〖鄙〗撒尿。—*v.t.* ①和小便同時排出(血等)。②以小便弄濕。—*n.* 小便。

pissed off 〖俚, 鄙〗生氣的。

piss·pot ['pɪsˌpɑt; 'pis-pɔt] *n.* 尿壺。

pis·ta·chi·o [pɪs'tɑʃɪˌo; pis'tɑ:ʃiou] *n., pl.* **-chi·os.** ①〖植物〗阿月渾子樹。②阿月渾子樹的子。③阿月渾子的香味。④淡黃綠色。

***pis·til** ['pɪstḷ; 'pistil] *n.* 〖植物〗 雌蕊。

pis·til·late ['pɪstḷˌet; 'pistileit] *adj.* 〖植物〗 有雌蕊的;僅有雌蕊(而無雄蕊)的。

***pis·tol** ['pɪstḷ; 'pistl] *n., v.*, **-tol(l)ed, -tol·(l)ing.**—*n.* 手鎗。 —*v.t.* 以手鎗射擊。He threatened to *pistol* me. 他威脅着要用手鎗射擊我。

pis·tole [pɪs'tol; pis'toul] *n.* 西班牙的古金幣;其他國家的類似古金幣。

pistol grip 手鎗形鎗把。

pis·tol-whip ['pɪstḷˌhwɪp; 'pistlwip] *v.t.*, **-whipped, -whip·ping.** 以手鎗連續毆打。

***pis·ton** ['pɪstṇ; 'pistən] *n.* 〖機械〗活塞。

***pit**[1] [pɪt; pit] *n., v.*, **pit·ted, pit·ting.** —*n.* ①坑。 a coal *pit*. 煤坑。② (the–)地獄。③〖英〗劇院正廳後面之部分; 坐於正廳後面部分的觀衆。 ④任何低窪之處。 the *pit* of the stomach. 心窩。⑤痘痕; 傷痕。 ⑥陷穽。⑦暗伏的危險。⑧〖美〗交易所中專門從事交易的部分。the corn *pit*. 玉蜀黍交易處。⑨鬥鷄場;鬥犬場。⑩萬人坑;萬人塚。⑪(*pl.*) 賽車場中設置在跑道旁邊的汽車加油、修護及檢查處。 —*v.t.* ①使有痘痕或傷痕。a face *pitted* with smallpox. 麻臉。②使相鬥;使抗衡。to *pit* one person against another. 使一人與另一人相鬥。③置放於坑內。

pit[2] *n., v.*, **pit·ted, pit·ting.** —*n.* 〖美〗 (櫻桃、桃、梅、棗等之) 核。—*v.t.* 去…之核。

pit·a·pat ['pɪtəˌpæt; 'pitə'pæt] *adv., adj., n., v.*, **-pat·ted, -pat·ting.** —*adv.* 有輕快噼啪聲地。 Her heart went *pitapat*. 她的心噗噗地跳。—*adj.* 噗噗跳的。 —*n.* 輕快之噼啪聲。 —*v.i.* 快步而行。(亦作 **pit-a-pat, pitpat, pittypat**)

***pitch**[1] [pɪtʃ; pitʃ] *n.* 瀝青;松脂。He who touches *pitch* shall be defiled therewith. 近朱者赤, 近墨者黑。—*v.t.* 塗以瀝青。

pitch**[2] *v.t.* ①擲; 拋; 投。②〖美〗〖棒球〗投 (球)。③紮;釘牢。 to *pitch* a tent. 張帳幕。④置於固定地位。 ⑤〖音樂〗定(一曲調之)基音。⑥〖俚〗 努力推銷。—*v.i.* ①向前傾跌;向前跳。The man lost his balance and *pitched* down the cliff. 那人失掉平衡, 從懸崖上跌下來。②(船首)上下顚簸。 The ship *pitched* about in the storm. 這船在風暴中上下顚簸。③紮營;張幕。 ***pitch in **a.** 〖俗〗努力工作。 **b.** 參加;貢獻。 ***pitch into*** 〖俗〗攻擊; 大吃。 ***pitch on*** (or ***upon***) 隨意挑選。 —*n.* ①擲;投。a good *pitch*. 好球(擲得好)。 ②高度; 程度; 位置。 ③聲音之高低度。④傾斜;傾斜度;傾坡。⑤〖機械〗 齒節;螺距; 間距。⑥鷹在攫捉獵物猝然下降前先高飛

到的最高點。 to fly a high *pitch*. 飛到高空。⑦推銷商品的宣傳。⑧做事的方法。***make a pitch for***〖俗〗作說服性的請求;爭取。

pitch-and-toss [ˈpɪtʃənˈtɔs; ˈpitʃənˈtɔs] *n.* 一種擲錢遊戲。

pitch-black [ˈpɪtʃˈblæk; ˈpitʃˈblæk] *adj.* 極黑的;漆黑的。

pitch·blende [ˈpɪtʃˌblɛnd; ˈpitʃblend] *n.* 瀝青鈾礦。

pitch-dark [ˈpɪtʃˈdɑrk; ˈpitʃˈdɑːk] *adj.* 極黑的;漆黑的。—**ness,** *n.*

pitched battle [pɪtʃt～; pitʃt～] ①布好陣式的正式會戰。②雙方全力以赴的爭執。

*__pitch·er__[1] [ˈpɪtʃɚ; ˈpitʃə] *n.* ①水罐。②一水罐的容量。***Little pitchers have long*** (or ***wide***) ***ears.***〖諺〗小孩子耳朵快(當着孩子講話時之警告語)。***Pitchers have ears.***〖諺〗隔牆有耳。

*__pitch·er__[2] *n.* ①〖棒球〗投手。②投擲的人。③高爾夫球棒之一種。

pitch·er·ful [ˈpɪtʃɚˌful; ˈpitʃəful] *n., pl.* **-fuls.** 一水罐之量。

pitcher plant〖植物〗猪籠草(科的植物)。

pitch·fork [ˈpɪtʃˌfɔrk; ˈpitʃfɔːk] *n.* 長柄叉(用以叉乾草等者)。—*v.t.* ①以長柄叉舉起並擲出。②强使…進入;投進。

pitch·ing [ˈpɪtʃɪŋ; ˈpitʃiŋ] *n.* ①鋪地石;護堤石。②扔出。③〖棒球〗投球(法)。④(船、飛機的)縱搖;前後簸動。

pitch·man [ˈpɪtʃmən; ˈpitʃmən] *n., pl.* **-men.** ①〖美〗(賣雜貨等的)攤販。②市集或廟會中的攤販。

pitch·out [ˈpɪtʃˌaut; ˈpitʃaut] *n.*〖棒球〗故意投遠離球壘的球(通常爲防盜壘)。

pitch pine〖植物〗脂松。

pitch pipe〖音樂〗(定絃樂器等之音高的)律管;音笛。

pitch·stone [ˈpɪtʃˌston; ˈpitʃstoun] *n.* 瀝青岩;松香岩。

pitch·y [ˈpɪtʃɪ; ˈpitʃi] *adj.,* **-i·er, -i·est.** ①像瀝青的;塗有瀝青的;多瀝青的。②漆黑的。

pit·e·ous [ˈpɪtɪəs; ˈpitiəs] *adj.* 使人同情的;令人憐憫的;可憐的。—**ly,** *adv.*

pit·fall [ˈpɪtˌfɔl; ˈpitfɔːl] *n.* ①捕捉動物之陷穽。②任何不明顯之危險。

pith [pɪθ; piθ] *n.* ①(雙子葉植物之)木髓。②似木髓之柔軟組織。③〖動物〗脊髓;髓。④精華部分。⑤精力。 men of *pith*. 精力飽滿的人。⑥重要性。—*v.t.* ①除去木髓。②割斷(牛等)之脊髓以殺之。③毁脊髓。

pit·head [ˈpɪtˌhɛd; ˈpithed] *n.* 礦坑入口及其附近。

pith·e·can·thrope [ˌpɪθɪˈkænθrop; ˌpiθiˈkænθroup] *n.* 猿人。

Pith·e·can·thro·pus [ˌpɪθɪkænˈθropəs; ˌpiθikænˈθroupəs] *n., pl.* **-pi** [-paɪ; -pai].〖人類學〗猿人屬;猿人屬之動物。

pith·i·ly [ˈpɪθɪlɪ; ˈpiθili] *adv.* ①有力地;精力充沛地。②簡潔地;扼要地。

pith·i·ness [ˈpɪθɪnɪs; ˈpiθinis] *n.* ①有力;精力充沛。②扼要;簡潔。

pith·less [ˈpɪθlɪs; ˈpiθlis] *adj.* ①無髓的。②無氣力的。

pith·y [ˈpɪθɪ; ˈpiθi] *adj.,* **-i·er, -i·est.** ①有力的;精力充沛的。②簡扼的;含蓄的。③多木髓的;像木髓的。

pit·i·a·ble [ˈpɪtɪəbl; ˈpitiəbl] *adj.* ①令人同情與憐憫的。②可憐復可鄙的。—**pit·i·a·bly,** *adv.*

*__pit·i·ful__ [ˈpɪtɪfəl; ˈpitiful] *adj.* ①使人同情的;令人憐憫的;可憐的。②感覺哀憐的。She is *pitiful* to the poor. 她對窮人有憐憫心。③可鄙的。—**ly,** *adv.*

*__pit·i·less__ [ˈpɪtɪlɪs; ˈpitilis] *adj.* 無憐憫心的;無情的。Ambition is *pitiless*. 野心是無情的。—**ly,** *adv.* —**ness,** *n.*

pit·man [ˈpɪtmən; ˈpitmən] *n., pl.* for ① **-men.** for ② **-mans.** ①礦夫;礦工。②〖機械〗連桿;搖桿。

pi·ton [ˈpitɑn; ˈpiːtɔn] *n.* ①爬山者用以攀登懸崖用的鐵栓。②陡立之尖峯或巨岩。

pit·saw [ˈpɪtˌsɔ; ˈpit-sɔː] *n.* (兩人用的)大鋸。(亦作 **pit saw**)

pit·tance [ˈpɪtn̩s; ˈpitəns] *n.* ①微薄的薪俸或津貼。②少量;小分。

pit·ted [ˈpɪtɪd; ˈpitid] *adj.* 有凹痕的;有麻點的。

pit·ter-pat·ter [ˈpɪtɚˌpætɚ; ˈpitəˌpætə] *n.* (下雨等的)拍撻拍撻聲;連續急速的輕擊聲。—*adv.* (雨等) 拍撻拍撻地;劈劈拍拍地。—*v.i.* 發出拍撻拍撻之聲。

pit·tite [ˈpɪtaɪt; ˈpitait] *n.*〖英〗劇院正廳後排的觀衆。

Pitts·burgh [ˈpɪtsbɝg; ˈpitsbəːg] *n.* 匹玆堡(美國 Pennsylvania 州西南部之一城市,爲鋼鐵業之中心)。

pi·tu·i·tar·y [pɪˈtjuəˌtɛrɪ; piˈtjuːitəri] *adj., n., pl.* **-tar·ies.** —*adj.* ①〖解剖〗黏液的;分泌黏液的。②〖解剖〗腦下垂體的。③因腦下垂體分泌過多而致異常碩大的(身材)。—*n.* ①＝**pituitary gland.** ②〖藥〗腦下垂體粉。

pituitary gland (or **body**)〖解剖〗腦下垂體。

‡**pit·y** [ˈpɪtɪ; ˈpiti] *n., pl.* **pit·ies,** *v.,* **pit·ied, pit·y·ing.** —*n.* ①同情;憐憫。②憾事;可惜的原因;可惜之事;可悲之事。It is a *pity* that you can't come. 你不能來很是遺憾。***feel pity for something*** (or ***have a feeling of pity for***) 憐憫某事物。***have*** (or ***take***) ***pity on*** 表示憐憫。—*v.t.* & *v.i.* 同情;憐憫。I *pity* you. 我可憐你。

pit·y·ing [ˈpɪtɪɪŋ; ˈpitiiŋ] *adj.* 憐憫的;同情的。—**ly,** *adv.*

più [pju; pjuː]〖義〗*adv.*〖音樂〗更(＝more);稍(＝somewhat). *più* allegro. 速度轉快。*più* lento. 速度轉慢。

piv·ot [ˈpɪvət; ˈpivət] *n.* ①旋軸;尖軸;樞軸。②〖軍〗基準兵。③中心點;基準點;要點。④〖體育〗轉身。—*v.t.* 裝以旋軸;置於旋軸上。—*v.i.* 於旋軸上旋轉。—*adj.* ＝**pivotal.**

piv·ot·al [ˈpɪvətl̩; ˈpivətl] *adj.* ①旋軸的;作爲旋軸的。②重要的;爲樞紐的。—**ly,** *adv.*

pix[1] [pɪks; piks] *n. pl.*〖俚〗(公開用的)照片;新聞照片;電影(pictures 之縮寫)。

pix[2] *n.* ＝**pyx.**

pix·i·lat·ed [ˈpɪksl̩ˌetɪd; ˈpiksileitid] *adj.* ①有點神經病的;怪模怪樣的。②〖俚〗醉的。③愚蠢而令人發笑的。

pix·y, pix·ie [ˈpɪksɪ; ˈpiksi] *n., pl.* **pix·ies,** *adj.* —*n.* 小仙子;小精靈;小妖精。—*adj.* 頑皮的;戲謔的。

pi(z)·zazz [pəˈzæz; pəˈzæz] *n.*〖美俚〗①精力;精神。②漂亮;時髦派頭。—**y,** *adj.*

piz·za [ˈpitsə; ˈpiːtsə] *n.* 一種義大利肉餅(pie).

piz·ze·ri·a [ˌpitsəˈriə; ˌpiːtsəˈriːə] *n.*〖美〗出售或製 pizza 的餐廳,或麪包店。

piz·zi·ca·to [ˌpɪtsɪˈkɑto; ˌpitsiˈkɑːtou] *adj., adv., n., pl.* **-ti** [-ti; -tiː]. —*adj.* & *adv.*〖音樂〗用指彈(的);撥絃奏(的)。—*n.*〖音樂〗撥絃奏;用指彈的樂曲(樂節、樂句、樂章)。

pj's [ˈpiˈdʒez; ˈpiːˈdʒeiz] *n. pl.*〖俚〗＝**pajamas.**

pk. *pl.* **pks.** ①pack. ②park. ③peak. ④peck.

pkg. *pl.* **pkgs.** package.

pkt. packet.
pl. ①place. ②plate. ③plural.
P.L. ①Paradise Lost.②Poet Laureate.
pla·ca·bil·i·ty [ˌplekəˈbɪlətɪ; ˌpleikəˈbiliti] *n.* 可撫慰;易和解;溫和;寬容。
pla·ca·ble [ˈplekəbl̩; ˈpleikəbl] *adj.* 可撫慰的;易和解的;溫和的;寬容的。
***plac·ard** [*n.* ˈplækard; ˈplækɑːd *v.* plæˈkard, ˈplækard; ˈplækɑːd] *n.* 公告;布告;告示; 招貼。—*v.t.* ①張貼布告於。 to *placard* walls. 在牆上張貼布告。②以公告或招貼公布。to *placard* a meeting. 公告開會。
pla·cate [ˈpleket; pləˈkeit] *v.t.,* **-cat·ed, -cat·ing.** 安慰;撫慰;和解。
pla·ca·to·ry [ˈplekəˌtorɪ; ˈpleikətəri] *adj.* 撫慰的;和解的;懷柔的。
‡**place** [ples; pleis] *n., v.,* **placed, plac·ing.** —*n.* ①地方;所在。I can't be in two *places* at once. 我不能同時在兩個地方。②城; 鎮; 村; 地點。 What's the name of this *place?* 此地叫甚麼名字? ③(有特殊功用之)建築物;場所。a *place* of amusement. 娛樂場所。④住宅; 住處。 Come round to my *place* this evening. 今晚請到我家來。⑤部分;點。Show me the *place* where it hurts. 把痛處指給我看。⑥正當的位置;自然的地位。⑦身分;職位;生活方式。The servant filled his *place* well. 這僕人很稱職。⑧位子;座位。Go back to your *place.* 回到你的位子上去。⑨職分; 職務。It is not my *place* to interfere in such affairs. 干涉此類事情非我之職。⑩情形;環境。If I were in your *place....* 假如我處在你的境地…。⑪步驟。⑫(戲劇等動作)進行的時間; 進展的情形。The play went too slow in several *places.* 這劇有幾處進展太慢。⑬〖數學〗位。in the third decimal *place.* 在第三位的小數。⑭比賽之前三名(尤指第二名)。 John won first *place.* 約翰得第一名。 ***a place in the sun*** 有利之地位。 ***give*** (or ***make***) ***place to*** 讓位於;屈服。***go places***〖俚〗事業一帆風順;有發展。***in place*** 在正當的位置;適當。***in place of*** 代替。***know*** (or ***keep***) ***one's place*** 明瞭自己的地位而不越分。 ***out of place*** **a.** 未在正當位置內。 **b.** 不適當。***put someone in his place*** 挫某人之銳氣;給某人下馬威。***take place*** 發生。***take the place of*** 代替。—*v.t.* ①放;安置。*Place* the books on the table. 把這些書放在桌上。②任命。He was *placed* in command of the regiment. 他被任命爲團長。③認出。④投(資)。to *place* one's money to the best advantage. 將自己的資金作最有利的投資。⑤定(貨);發出(訂單);委託。to *place* an order for coal with one's coal merchant. 向煤商定購煤。⑥(比賽中)位列(前三名,尤指第二)。The duke's horse wasn't *placed.* 公爵的馬在賽馬中未得前三名。—*v.i.* (比賽中)名列前三名而結束。
pla·ce·bo [pləˈsibo; pləˈsiːbou] *n., pl.* **-bos, -boes.** ①〖天主教〗爲死者唱的晚禱歌。②〖醫〗寬心藥;安慰劑。③安慰(物);寬心話。
place card (宴會等之)席次牌。
place kick ①〖足球〗定位踢(將球置於地面然後踢出之踢法)。②〖橄欖球〗定位踢(在持球觸地得分, try, 以後所踢之球)。
place-kick [ˈplesˌkɪk; ˈpleis-kik] *v.t. & v.i.*〖橄欖球,足球〗定位踢出;以定位踢得分。
place·man [ˈplesmən; ˈpleismən] *n., pl.* **-men.** 〖英〗〖常蔑〗官吏。
place mat 置於飯桌上放刀、叉等餐具的墊布。
place·ment [ˈplesmənt; ˈpleismənt] *n.* ①安置;布置;配置。②工作介紹。③〖橄欖球〗置球於地以備射入球門。
place name 地名。(亦作 **place-name**)
pla·cen·ta [pləˈsɛntə; pləˈsentə] *n., pl.* **-tas, -tae** [-ti;-tiː]. ①〖動物,解剖〗胎盤。②〖植物〗胎座。—**r·y, pla·cen·tal,** *adj.*
place of arms ①要塞或設防城市中供兵士集結的地方。②有蓋交通壕中較廣闊之處。
plac·er [ˈplæsɚ; ˈplæsə] *n.* 砂礦床;冲積礦床;含礦之礫;沙金採取場。
place setting ①放於進食人面前的一套碟子、刀叉等餐具。②成套出售之上項餐具。
pla·cet [ˈplesɛt; ˈpleiset]〖拉〗*n.* ①(以placet一語表明的)贊成;贊成票。non *placet.* 不贊成;反對票。②正式之請求書。
***plac·id** [ˈplæsɪd; ˈplæsid] *adj.* 安靜的;平靜的;寧靜的。a *placid* stream. 平靜的溪流。—**ly,** *adv.* —**i·ty,** *n.*
plac·ing-out [ˈplesɪŋˈaut; ˈpleisiŋ-ˈaut] *n.* 寄養制度。
plack·et [ˈplækɪt; ˈplækit] *n.* ①(女裙的)開口(亦作 **placket hole**). ②(尤指女裙的)口袋。③襯裙。④婦女。
plac·oid [ˈplækɔɪd;ˈplækɔid] *adj.* 〖動物〗楯形的(鱗);有楯形鱗的。—*n.* 楯形鱗的魚。
pla·fond [plaˈfɔ̃;plaˈfɔ̃] *n., pl.* **-fonds.** 〖法〗〖建築〗(有雕刻裝飾的)天花板;天花板畫。
pla·gi·a·rism [ˈpledʒəˌrɪzəm; ˈpleidʒjərizəm] *n.* ①剽竊;抄襲。②剽竊之思想、辭句、情節等。
pla·gi·a·rist [ˈpledʒərɪst; ˈpleidʒjərist] *n.* 剽竊者;抄襲者;文抄公。
pla·gi·a·rize [ˈpledʒəˌraɪz; ˈpleidʒjəraiz] *v.t. & v.i.,* **-rized, -riz·ing.**剽竊;抄襲。
pla·gi·a·ry [ˈpledʒɪˌɛrɪ; ˈpleidʒjəri] *n., pl.* **-ries,** *adj.* —*n.* ①剽竊者;抄襲者。②剽竊;抄襲。③剽竊之思想、辭句、情節等。—*adj.* 剽竊的;抄襲的。
pla·gi·o·clase [ˈpledʒɪəˌkles; ˈpleidʒiəkleis] *n.* 〖礦〗斜長石。
***plague** [pleg; pleig] *n., v.,* **plagued, pla·guing.** —*n.* ①瘟疫;疫病。 the black *plague.* 黑死病。②惹人煩惱之人或物。 a *plague* of flies. 蠅患。③上帝的責罰;天譴。—*v.t.* ①折磨;使苦惱。He was *plagued* to death. 他被折磨得要死。②使患瘟疫。
plague spot ①(罹瘟疫時皮膚上的)斑狀出血。②疾病、過失、或罪惡的表記。③惡疫流行地。④罪惡之中心。
pla·gui·ly [ˈplegəlɪ; ˈpleigili] *adv.* 〖俗〗煩累地; 討厭地。
pla·guy [ˈplegɪ; ˈpleigi] *adj.,* **pla·gui·er, pla·gui·est,** *adv.* —*adj.* 〖俗〗煩累的;討厭的。—*adv.* 〖俗〗煩累地;討厭地;非常。(亦作 **plaguey**)
plaice [ples; pleis] *n., pl.* **plaice.** 鰈。
plaid [plæd; plæd] *n.* ①格子布。②蘇格蘭高地人所披之肩巾; 做該肩巾的方格呢。—*adj.* 有格子花紋的。 a *plaid* shawl. 帶方格子的披肩。
plaid·ed [ˈplædɪd; ˈplædid] *adj.* ①穿格子呢肩巾的。②格子呢製成的。③格子花紋的。
‡**plain¹** [plen; plein] *adj.* ①明白的;清楚的;易解的。The meaning is quite *plain.* 這意義十分明顯。②無裝飾的;樸素的。a *plain* dress. 一件樸素的衣服。③一色的。 a *plain* blue dress. 一件純藍的衣服。④平淡的; 淡

泊的。*plain* food. 便飯。⑤一般的;平常的。in *plain* clothes. 着便服(爲uniform 之對)。⑥不美的。a *plain* girl. 不漂亮的女郎。⑦坦白的;誠實的。in *plain* words(=frankly). 坦白地說。⑧容易的;簡單的。*plain* sewing. 簡單的縫法。⑨平的;平坦的。⑩完全的;全然的。*plain* folly. 徹底的愚蠢。—*adv.* ①清晰地。to speak *plain*. 說得很明白。②簡直。He's just *plain* stupid. 他簡直愚不可及。—*n.* ①平原;平地。a vast *plain*. 遼濶的平原。②(*pl.*) 草原。—**ly,** *adv.* —**ness,** *n.*

plain² *v.i.*〖古,詩,方〗歎;悲傷;發牢騷;訴怨。

plain bond〖商〗無擔保債券。

plain-clothes man [ˈplenˈkloz~; ˈpleinˈklouz~] 便衣警察(偵探);便衣隊員。

plain dealing 率直;坦白;光明正大。

plain sailing ①順利而無困難之航行。②輕而易舉之行動; 毫無困難之道路。

plains·man [ˈplenzmən;ˈpleinzmən] *n., pl.* **-men.** 平原的住民;平地居民。

plain song ①(教會中齊唱而無伴奏的)單旋律聖歌。②定旋律。③簡樸的歌調;素歌。

plain·spo·ken [ˈplenˈspokən;ˈplein-ˈspoukən]*adj.*老實說的;率直的;直言無隱的。

plaint [plent; pleint] *n.* ①不平;怨訴。②〖法律〗告訴;控訴。③〖古、詩〗怨訴;悲歎。

plain text (電文等之)明碼;明文。

plain·tiff [ˈplentɪf; ˈpleintif] *n.*〖法律〗原告。

plain·tive [ˈplentɪv; ˈpleintiv] *adj.* 憂愁的;哀傷的;哀愁的。*plaintive* music. 哀怨的音樂。—**ly,** *adv.*

plait [plet; plæt] *n.* ①髮辮;編繩。②褶。—*v.t.* ①編成辮。②褶疊;使生褶。

‡plan [plæn;plæn] *n., v.,* **planned, plan-ning.** —*n.* ①計畫;策略;方法。Everything went according to *plan*. 一切皆照計畫進行。②(房屋等)圖案;設計圖。a floor *plan*. 平面圖。a raised *plan*. 正面圖。③一城鎮或地區的比例尺很大的地圖。—*v.t.* ①計劃。to *plan* a trip. 作旅行之計劃。②設計;作…之圖樣。③籌劃〖out〗. to *plan* out a military campaign. 籌謀一戰役。④意欲;希望;預期。—*v.i.* 計劃。to *plan* ahead. 預爲計劃。

planch·et [ˈplæntʃɪt; ˈplæntʃit] *n.*(未壓成貨幣前的)貨幣形金屬薄片。

plan·chette [plænˈʃɛt; plɑːnˈʃet] *n.* 一種占板(爲一心臟形之木板,支持於兩小輪及一垂直之鉛筆上,以指輕觸可自動寫字)。

‡plane¹ [plen; plein] *n., adj., v.,* **planed, plan·ing.** —*n.* ①平面;水平面。②水準;程度。Keep your work on a high *plane*. 使你的工作保持高的水準。③(飛機)翼面。④飛機。Are you going by *plane?* 你要坐飛機去嗎? —*adj.* ①平的;平面的。a *plane* surface. 平面。②有關平面的。—*v.i.*①乘飛機旅行。②滑行。③(快艇等)微離水面行駛。

‡plane² *n., v.,* **planed, plan·ing.** —*n.* 鉋子。—*v.t.* 用鉋子將…鉋平。to *plane* something smooth. 將某物鉋得光滑。—*v.i.* 鉋平。This tool *planes* well. 這工具很能鉋平(東西)。

plane³ *n.*〖英〗〖植物〗篠懸木。

plane geometry〖數學〗平面幾何學。

plane·load [ˈplenˌlod; ˈpleinloud] *n.* 一飛機所載之乘客或貨物量。

plan·er [ˈplenɚ; ˈpleinə] *n.* ①用鉋的人;鉋匠。②〖機械〗龍門鉋床。③〖木工〗鉋盤;鉋床。

plane·side [ˈplenˌsaɪd; ˈpleinsaid] *n.* 飛機旁邊的區域。

***plan·et** [ˈplænɪt; ˈplænit] *n.* ①行星。②〖星相〗能影響人生與世界大事的天體。③任何能影響人生與世界大事之物。

plane table〖測量〗平板儀。

plan·e·tar·i·um[ˌplænəˈtɛrɪəm;ˌplæniˈtɛəriəm] *n., pl.* **-tar·i·ums, -tar·i·a** [-ˈtɛrɪə; -ˈtɛəriə]. ①行星儀。②天文館。

plan·e·tar·y [ˈplænəˌtɛrɪ;ˈplænitəri] *adj.* ①行星的;有關行星的。*planetary* motions. 行星的運動。the *planetary* system. 太陽系。②繞軌道移動的。③影響人事之天體的。④流浪的;不定的。⑤俗世的;人間的。

plan·e·tes·i·mal [ˌplænəˈtɛsəml; ˌplænəˈtesiməl] *n.* 微星(極小之行星)。—*adj.* 微星的。

plan·et·oid [ˈplænəˌtɔɪd; ˈplænitɔid] *n.* (火星與木星軌道間之)小行星。

plan·e·tol·o·gy[ˌplænɪˈtɑlədʒɪ;ˌplæniˈtɔlədʒi] *n.* 行星學(天文學之一部門)。

plane tree〖植物〗篠懸木。

plane trigonometry〖數學〗平面三角學。

plan·et-strick·en [ˈplænɪtˌstrɪkən; ˈplænitˌstrikən] *adj.* ①受行星影響的;突然受災的。②驚惶的。(亦作 **planet-struck**)

plan·form [ˈplænˌfɔrm; ˈplænfɔːm] *n.* (從上向下看物體如飛機等所呈現之)輪廓。

plan·gent [ˈplændʒənt; ˈplændʒənt] *adj.* ①回響的(聲音); 震顫的;喧鬧的。②衝激的(浪)。

pla·nim·e·ter [pləˈnɪmətɚ; plæˈnimitə] *n.* 測面器; 求積計。

pla·nim·e·try [pləˈnɪmətrɪ; plæˈnimitri] *n.* 測面法;面積測定。

plan·ish [ˈplænɪʃ; ˈplæniʃ] *v.t.* 打(輾)平(金屬板等);磨(砑)光(金屬板、紙等)。

plan·i·sphere [ˈplænɪˌsfɪr; ˈplænisfiə] *n.* ①平面球形圖。②平面天體圖; 星座一覽圖。

plank** [plæŋk;plæŋk] *n.* ①厚板。②(政黨之)政綱條款。③支撐物。walk the plank*** **a.** 在甲板上伸向舷外的木板上向前走而落海中(昔時海盜處死俘虜的一種方法)。 **b.** 被迫放棄某物(如職務);被開除。—*v.t.* ①鋪以厚板。②〖美〗在板上烹煎。③〖俗〗用力放。He *planked* down the package. 他用力放下包裹。④〖俗〗立刻付款。She *planked* out her money. 她立刻付款。

plank·ing [ˈplæŋkɪŋ; ˈplæŋkiŋ] *n.* ①蓋板;鋪板。②板類;板的集合稱。

plank·ton [ˈplæŋktən; ˈplæŋktən] *n.*〖生物〗浮游生物。

plan·less [ˈplænlɪs; ˈplænlis] *adj.* ①無圖面的。②無計畫或方案的;未計畫的。

planned economy 計畫經濟(由政府計畫,控制產、銷、價格等)。

planned parenthood 計畫生育。

plan·ner [ˈplænɚ; ˈplænə] *n.* 計畫者。

pla·no-con·cave [ˌplenəˈkɑnkev; ˌpleinəˈkɔnkeiv] *adj.* (透鏡)平凹的。

pla·no-con·vex [ˌplenəˈkɑnvɛks; ˌpleinəˈkɔnveks] *adj.* (透鏡)平凸的。

plan·og·ra·phy [plæˈnɑgrəfɪ; plæˈnɔgrəfi] *n.* 平版印刷。

pla·nom·e·ter [pləˈnɑmɪtɚ; pləˈnɔmitə] *n.* 測平器;平規。

‡plant [plænt; plɑːnt] *n.* ①植物。②花草;苗木。a house *plant*. 一株室內陳設用的小樹。③工廠。a power *plant*. 電力廠。④(醫院、學校等之)房舍及設備。⑤〖俗〗騙局;欺詐。⑥安置在觀衆裏在適當時機鼓掌,或做其他反應的人。⑦〖戲劇〗伏線。⑧滲透在歹徒中

的線民；引誘歹徒上當的計畫等。—*v.t.* ①栽培；種植；養殖(魚苗、卵、蠔等)。②安置；置放。*Plant* your feet firmly on the ground. 把你的脚穩踏在地上。③建立；建設。They *planted* a colony there. 他們在那裏建立了殖民地。④灌輸；注入(主義、教義等)。⑤〖俗〗藏起(贓物)。⑥〖俗〗打出(一擊)；施出(一拳)。⑦〖戲劇〗加(思想、人、或事)於戲曲中。⑧安放(人)於殖民地。⑨放置(某事)以取得所期望的效果。⑩〖俚〗將金砂、金礦石等置於礦內以矇騙。⑪設置；派遣。to *plant* guards at the cntrance. 在入口處派守衛者。⑫安置線民、反間諜等。to *plant* spies. 派奸細。

Plan·tag·e·net 〔plæn'tædʒənɪt; plæn'tædʒinit〕 *n.*〖英史〗金雀花王朝(1154–1399之英國王朝)。

plan·tain[1] 〔'plæntɪn; 'plæntin〕 *n.*〖植物〗車前屬之植物；車前草。

plan·tain[2] *n.*〖植物〗芭蕉。

plan·tar 〔'plæntə; 'plæntə〕 *adj.*〖解剖，動物〗蹠的；足底的。

*__plan·ta·tion__ 〔plæn'teʃən; plæn'teiʃən, plɑːn-〕 *n.* ①(大規模的)農場；種植地。a cotton *plantation.* 棉花地。②(大的)植林；森林。③殖民。—**like,** *adj.*

plant·er 〔'plæntə, 'plɑntə; 'plɑːntə〕 *n.* ①種植者；耕作者；栽培者。②農場主人。a cotton *planter.* 棉場主。③播種機。④〖歷史〗早期殖民者。⑤花盆。

plan·ti·grade 〔'plæntəˌgred; 'plæntigreid〕 *adj.*〖動物〗蹠行的。—*n.* 蹠行動物(人、猿、熊等)。

plant·ing 〔'plæntɪŋ; 'plɑːntiŋ〕 *n.* ①種植；栽培；植林；播種。②〖方〗種植之植物；森林；樹林。③〖英〗〖建築〗基底。

plant kingdom 植物界(集合稱)。

plant·let 〔'plæntlɪt; 'plɑːntlit〕 *n.* 小植物；幼樹；幼草。

plant louse 蚜蟲 (=aphid).

plant pathology 植物病蟲害學。

plaque 〔plæk; plɑːk〕 *n.* ①(牆壁或傢具上)裝飾用薄金屬板或瓷片等。②板狀針扣飾物或徽章。③〖解剖，動物〗斑。④〖牙科〗牙斑。

plash[1] 〔plæʃ; plæʃ〕 *n.* ①輕輕之拍水聲。②水潭。—*v.i.* ①輕拍水面。②作濺潑聲。—*v.t.* 激濺(水)。

plash[2] *v.t.* ①編結(樹枝)以作籬笆等。②編結樹枝以作或修理(籬笆等)。

plash·y 〔'plæʃɪ; 'plæʃi〕 *adj.,* **-i·er, -i·est.** ①多積水潭的；濕的。②潰潰如濺水之聲的。

plasm 〔'plæzəm; 'plæzəm〕 *n.* =**plasma.**

plas·ma 〔'plæzmə; 'plæzmə〕 *n.* ①原形質。②血漿。③乳漿。④綠玉髓。

plas·mo·di·um 〔plæz'modɪəm; plæz'moudiəm〕 *n., pl.* **-di·a** 〔-dɪə; -diə〕. ①〖生物〗原形體；漿細胞。②〖動物〗瘧原蟲。

*__plas·ter__ 〔'plæstə; 'plɑːstə〕 *n.* ①灰泥。②石膏。③膏藥。④=**plaster of Paris.** —*v.t.* ①塗以灰泥。to *plaster* a wall. 塗灰泥於壁上。②敷以膏藥。to *plaster* a wound. 敷膏藥於傷口。③塗上一層厚的東西。④使平。He *plastered* his hair down. 他將他的頭髮梳平。⑤〖俚〗猛烈攻打；懲罰；徹底破壞。

plas·ter·board 〔'plæstəˌbord; 'plɑːstəbɔːd〕 *n.* 由多層灰泥及紙作成之薄板(用作牆壁)。

plaster cast ①石膏模型；石膏像。②〖外科〗石膏紗布。

plas·ter·er 〔'plæstərə; 'plɑːstərə〕 *n.* 泥水匠；塗石膏者。

plas·ter·ing 〔'plæstərɪŋ; 'plɑːstəriŋ〕 *n.* ①塗灰泥；泥水工；石膏細工；貼膏藥。②(葡萄酒的)加石膏除酸。

plaster of Paris (or **paris**) 燒石膏；石膏粉。

*__plas·tic__ 〔'plæstɪk; 'plæstik〕 *adj.* ①塑造的。Sculpture is a *plastic* art. 雕刻是塑造藝術。②塑膠的。a *plastic* cup. 塑膠杯。③易受影響的；易塑的；有可塑性的。④〖外科〗整形的。⑤有創造性的；富於藝術表現的。⑥〖生物，醫〗成形性的。⑦非自然的；人造的。⑧不眞實的；虛假的。—*n.* (常*pl.*)可塑體；塑膠(如尼龍、玻璃、假象牙等)。

plastic arts 造形美術(雕刻、製陶術等)。

plastic bomb 塑膠炸彈(以有黏着性和可塑性的炸藥造成，多爲恐怖分子使用)。

plas·ti·cine 〔'plæstəˌsin; 'plæstisiːn〕 *n.* 塑像用黏土。

plas·tic·i·ty 〔plæs'tɪsətɪ; plæs'tisiti〕 *n.* 可塑性；柔軟性；適應性。

plas·ti·ciz·er 〔'plæstəˌsaɪzə; 'plæstisaizə〕 *n.* 可塑劑(增加可塑性等之物質)。

plastic operation 整形手術。

plas·tics 〔'plæstɪks; 'plæstiks〕 *n.* ①整形外科。②塑膠。—*adj.* 塑膠的；可塑體的。

plastic surgery 整形外科。

plas·tron 〔'plæstrən; 'plæstrən〕 *n.* ①(中古的)鋼製胸甲。②(劈劍用的)護胸革。③(女衣的)胸飾。④(漿硬的男襯衣的)胸部。⑤〖動物〗(龜等的)腹甲。

plat[1] 〔plæt; plæt〕 *n., v.,* **plat·ted, plat·ting.** —*n.* ①(小塊的)地皮；(作花圃等用的)一塊地。a garden-*plat.* 小花園。②〖美〗(土地的)圖面；地圖。—*v.t.* 〖美〗繪製…的圖面。

plat[2] *n., v.,* **plat·ted, plat·ting.** —*n.* 辮帶；辮條。—*v.t.* 辮；編；編織。

plat[3] 〔plɑ; plɑː〕〖法〗 *n.* 一道菜。

plat·an(e) 〔'plætən; 'plætən〕 *n.* =**plane tree.**

‡**plate** 〔plet; pleit〕 *n., v.,* **plat·ed, plat·ing.** —*n.* ①盤；碟。②盤狀物。③教會中的捐款盤。④一盤所盛之量。⑤(一餐中)一人所食之物。⑥金銀器皿。⑦鍍金或鍍銀器皿。⑧(照相之)感光版。⑨薄金屬板。The warship was covered with steel *plates.* 戰艦外覆有鋼板。⑩金屬片製的甲冑。⑪若板狀的器官、組織等(如動物身上之鱗片)。⑫刻板；電鑄版。⑬以刻板或電鑄版印的印刷品。⑭〖棒球〗本壘。⑮鑲假牙於其上的牙座；假牙床。⑯〖電〗陽極。⑰盛在一盤的全餐。⑱可刻字畫的薄金屬片。⑲書本整頁的挿圖。⑳(賽馬或其他競賽中之)獎杯。㉑(*pl.*)〖英俚〗脚。㉒=**plate glass.** —*v.t.* ①覆以金屬板。②鍍(金、銀等)。gold-*plated* dishes. 鍍金的盤碟。③製成刻板；製電鑄版。

plate armor 薄的裝甲。

*__pla·teau__ 〔plæ'to; 'plætou, plæ'tou〕 *n., pl.* **-teaus, -teaux** 〔-'toz; -'touz〕. ①高地；高原。②〖心理〗學習過程中之停滯狀態。

plate-bas·ket 〔'pletˌbæskɪt; 'pleitˌbɑːskit〕 *n.* 〖英〗餐具籃。

plate·ful 〔'pletˌful; 'pleitful〕 *n., pl.* **-fuls.** 一碟；一盤。

plate glass 厚玻璃板(厚度 5~8mm)。

plate·lay·er 〔'pletˌleə; 'pleitˌleiə〕 *n.* 〖英〗(鐵路)路工。

plate·let 〔'pletlɪt; 'pleitlit〕 *n.* ①血小板。②小盤；小板。

plat·en 〔'plætn; 'plætn〕 *n.* ①(印刷機的)壓印板；壓印滾筒。②(打字機的)滾筒。

plate-pow·der 〔'pletˌpaudə; 'pleitˌpaudə〕 *n.* (金屬餐具器物等之)擦亮粉。

plat·er ['pletɚ; 'pleitə] *n.* ①鍍金（銀）匠;金屬版工;鐵甲工。②〖賽馬〗劣等馬。

plate rail 狹窄的置放裝飾性器皿的壁架。

***plat·form** ['plæt,fɔrm; 'plætfɔːm] *n.* ①月台;講台。A hall usually has a *platform* for speakers. 禮堂裏通常有一個演講台。②(政黨之) 政綱;黨綱。③樓梯中間的駐脚台。④〖軍〗安置大砲的堅固地基。⑤高出之地。

platform car =**flatcar.**

platform ticket 〖英〗月台票。

plat·i·na ['plætɪnə, plə'tinə; 'plætinə, plə'tiːnə] *n.* 〖化〗白金;鉑(=platinum).

plat·ing ['pletɪŋ; 'pleitiŋ] *n.* ①一層極薄之金屬。②包以或鍍以金屬。③電鍍術;包金術。④貼標籤於藏書以標明其所有權。

plating bath 電鍍槽。

pla·tin·ic [plə'tɪnɪk; plə'tinik] *adj.* 〖化〗白金的;含(四價)白金的。

platinic chloride 〖化〗氯化鉑;四氯化鉑。

plat·in·i·rid·i·um [,plætɪnaɪ'rɪdɪəm; ,plætinai'ridiəm] *n.* 鉑銥合金。

plat·i·nize ['plætn̩,aɪz; 'plætinaiz] *v.t.,* **-nized, -niz·ing.** 包以白金;鍍鉑。

plat·i·noid ['plætɪ,nɔɪd; 'plætinɔid] *adj.* 白金狀的; 似白金的。—*n.* ①假鉑;假白金(銅、鎳、鋅及鎢之合金)。②鉑屬之金屬。

plat·i·no·type ['plætɪnə,taɪp; 'plætinoutaip] *n.* 〖照相〗白金照相板; 白金照相(法)。

plat·i·nous ['plætn̩əs; 'plætn̩əs] *adj.* 〖化〗鉑的;似白金的;含(二價)白金的;亞鉑的。

platinous chloride 氯化亞鉑。

***plat·i·num** ['plætn̩əm; 'plætinəm] *n.* ①〖化〗鉑;白金。②白金色。

platinum black 〖化〗鉑黑粉。

platinum blonde 淡金黃頭髮的女人。

plat·i·tude ['plætə,tjud; 'plætitjuːd] *n.* ①陳腔濫調。②陳腐無味。

plat·i·tu·di·nize [,plætə'tjudə,naɪz; ,plæti'tjuːdinaiz] *v.i.,* **-nized, -niz·ing.** 講濫調;寫或說陳腐的話。

plat·i·tu·di·nous [,plætə'tjudn̩əs; ,plæti'tjuːdinəs] *adj.* ①好講濫調的。②平凡的;陳腐的。—**ly,** *adv.*

Pla·to ['pleto; 'pleitou] *n.* 柏拉圖(427?–347 B.C., 希臘哲學家)。

Pla·ton·ic [ple'tɑnɪk; plə'tɔnik] *adj.* ①柏拉圖的。②(亦作 **platonic**) 友誼的;精神的。*Platonic* love. 柏拉圖式戀愛;精神戀愛。③理想的;不切實際的。—**al·ly,** *adv.*

Platonic year 〖天文〗柏拉圖年（約26,000年之周期,經此時期各星辰又歸復原位)。

Pla·to·nism ['pletn̩,ɪzəm; 'pleitənizəm] *n.* ①柏拉圖(派)哲學。②精神戀愛;精神戀愛主義。③柏拉圖主義;柏拉圖格言。

Pla·to·nist ['pletn̩ɪst; 'pleitənist] *adj.* 柏拉圖(學派)的。—*n.* 柏拉圖學派的人。

Pla·to·nize ['pletə,naɪz; 'pleitənaiz] *v.,* **-nized, -niz·ing.** —*v.i.* 信奉柏拉圖哲學;從柏拉圖之說。—*v.t.* 依據柏拉圖哲學解釋;賦以柏拉圖哲學的性質。

pla·toon [plæ'tun; plə'tuːn] *n.* ①〖軍〗排。②一小羣人。③善攻或善守的橄欖球隊。

***plat·ter** ['plætɚ; 'plætə] *n.* ①〖古〗(盛魚、肉等用之)大淺盤。②〖俚〗(棒球之)本壘。③〖俚〗留聲機唱片。

plat·y·pus ['plætəpəs; 'plætipəs] *n., pl.* **-pus·es, -pi** [-,paɪ; -pai]. 〖動物〗鴨嘴獸。

plau·dit ['plɔdɪt; 'plɔːdit] *n.* ①(常 *pl.*) 鼓掌喝采;喝采。②讚揚;嘉許。

plau·si·bil·i·ty [,plɔzə'bɪlətɪ; ,plɔːzə'biliti] *n.* 似眞;似合理;似可取。

***plau·si·ble** ['plɔzəbl; 'plɔːzəbl] *adj.* ①似眞實的;似合理的;似公平的。a *plausible* excuse. 似乎有理的藉口。②似可靠的;似可信的。—**plau·si·bly,** *adv.*

‡play [ple; plei] *n.* ①遊戲; 遊玩; 娛樂。The children are at *play*. 孩子們在遊玩。②(遊戲或競賽中之) 一次;輪值。It's your *play*. 輪到你了。③遊戲或競賽的方法。④劇本;戲劇。Let's go to the *play*. 讓我們去看戲。⑤動作;行動。⑥輕快的動作或變化;變幻。⑦活動之自由;動作之範圍。He gives free *play* to his thoughts. 他自由自在地思想。⑧賭博。***a play on words*** 用雙關語。***as good as a play*** 十分有趣。***bring into play*** 利用。***come into play*** 開始行動。***fair play*** 公正;誠實;公平處置。***foul play*** 犯規;不忠實;不正之行爲。***in play*** **a.** 用於比賽中。**b.** 嬉戲;開玩笑。He didn't want to hurt you; it was only done *in play*. 他並非故意傷害你,祇不過是在開玩笑。***make a play for*** 〖俚〗**a.** 以色情引誘。**b.** 給好印象而得好處。This ad will *make a play for* new consumer markets. 這個廣告將能獲取新的消費市場。***out of play*** 不能用於比賽中。—*v.t.* ①參加 (遊戲等); 玩 (球等)。They are *playing* football. 他們在踢足球。②與…比賽 (遊戲等)。Will you *play* me at chess? 你願意和我下盤棋嗎?③扮演(角色等)。to *play* Hamlet. 扮演哈姆雷特。④彈(琴等); 奏(曲); 吹 (笛等)。to *play* the piano. 彈鋼琴。(注意:在所有樂器前均有固定冠詞 the, 而各種遊戲或運動前則應省去。) ⑤使行動; 使發生作用;做;實行;操作。to *play* a joke on someone. 開某人的玩笑。⑥打賭或下注。⑦利用。He *played* his brothers against each other. 他用計使兄弟們彼此傾軋。⑧拉釣魚線使(上鉤之魚)筋疲力竭。—*v.i.* ①遊玩; 玩耍。Children like to *play*. 孩子們喜歡玩。②參加遊戲。They were *playing* at hockey. 他們在打曲棍球。③扮演;假裝。Let's *play* at being pirates. 讓我們來扮演海盜。④(輕快地) 動(如閃耀、噴水等);活動。A smile *plays* on her lips. 她的唇上泛出微笑。⑤(機器、車輪等) 自由運轉;自在運動。⑥賭博。to *play* for money. 賭錢。⑦玩弄。Don't *play* with matches. 不要玩弄火柴。***play along with*** 與…合作。***play a part*** 扮演一角色。***play a person false*** 出賣某人。***play around with*** **a.** 繼續想(一個思想)。**b.** 同異性鬼混以消磨時間。***play at*** **a.** 假裝。**b.** 做事不認眞。***play both ends against the middle*** 坐收漁利。***play by ear*** 靠記憶彈奏樂器(不使用樂譜)。***play down*** 減低…的重要性;不重視。***play fair*** (***foul***) (不) 公平處置。***play fast and loose with*** 玩弄。***play for time*** 拖延時間。***play into the hands of*** 中計;上當。***play it by ear*** 臨機應變。***play off*** 加賽一場以決勝負。***play off one against the other*** (or ***another***) 使雙方互鬥以坐收漁利。***play on*** (or ***upon***) 利用。***play one's cards*** 執行計畫。***play out*** **a.** 演完一劇。**b.** 結束。**c.** 筋疲力竭。**d.** 陳舊;過時。***play the fool*** 行動愚蠢。***play the game*** 遵照規則;公平誠實。***play the man*** 行動如大丈夫。***play truant*** 逃學。***play up*** 大事宣傳。***play up to*** 〖俗〗諂媚;求寵。***play with*** **a.** 以…自娛。**b.** 玩弄。***play with***

fire 玩火;做危險之事。
play·a·ble ('pleəbl; 'pleiəbl) *adj.* 可遊戲的;可演奏的;適於演出的。 **—play·a·bil·i·ty,** *n.*
play actor 〖蔑〗伶人; 演員。(亦作 **playactor**)
play agent 與戲院經理、製作人等辦交涉的劇作家之經紀人。(亦作 **play broker**)
play·back ('ple,bæk; 'pleibæk) *n.* ①放唱片或錄音帶聽所錄之內容。②playback 的裝置。③錄音的內容(尤指第一次放時)。
play·bill ('ple,bɪl; 'pleibil) *n.* 戲單(碼)。
play·boy ('ple,bɔɪ; 'pleibɔi) *n.* 〖美俗〗耽於遊樂無所事事之富家子;花花公子。
play-by-play ('plebaɪ'ple; 'pleibai-'plei) *adj.* 一件事(尤指運動競賽)之詳細描述的。
play·day ('ple,de; 'pleidei) *n.* (學校的)假日;(礦工等的)休業日。
***play·er** ('pleɚ; 'pleiə) *n.* ①遊戲者; 運動者。He is a good tennis *player*. 他是一個好的網球手。②演員。③音樂師。④自動演奏器。⑤職業運動員。⑥賭徒。
player piano 自動鋼琴。
play·fel·low ('ple,fɛlo; 'plei,felou) *n.* 遊伴。
play field =**playing field.**
***play·ful** ('plefəl; 'pleiful) *adj.* ①嬉戲的; 喜遊玩的。②戲謔的;遊戲的。a *playful* remark. 一句戲言。 **—ly,** *adv.*
play·game ('plegem; 'pleigeim) *n.* 遊戲;兒戲。
play·girl ('ple,gɜl; 'pleigə:l) *n.* 好交際應酬和尋樂的女子。
play·go·er ('ple,goɚ; 'plei,gouə) *n.* 常去看戲的人。
play·go·ing ('ple,goɪŋ; 'plei,gouiŋ) *n.* 看戲;觀劇。 **—*adj.*** 看戲的。
***play·ground** ('ple,graund; 'plei-graund) *n.* ①運動場。②遊樂場。
play·house ('ple,haus; 'pleihaus) *n., pl.* **-hous·es.** ①劇院。②兒童遊戲室。③玩具小屋。
playing card 撲克牌;紙牌。
playing field 〖英〗遊戲場;操場;球場。
play·land ('ple,lænd; 'pleilænd) *n.* ①兒童遊園地。②依靠觀光客的城鎮。
play·let ('plelɪt; 'pleilit) *n.* 短劇。
***play·mate** ('ple,met; 'pleimeit) *n.* 遊伴。
play-off ('ple,ɔf; 'pleiɔ:f) *n.* ①(雙方得分相等時的) 最後決賽。②兩隊間之一連串冠軍賽。
play·pen ('ple,pɛn; 'pleipen) *n.* 可讓小孩獨自在其中遊玩的小圍欄。
play·room ('ple,rum; 'plei,ru:m) *n.* 娛樂室。
play school =**kindergarten.**
play·suit ('ple,sut; 'pleisju:t) *n.* 婦女或小孩的運動裝;海灘裝。
***play·thing** ('ple,θɪŋ; 'plei-θiŋ) *n.* ①玩物;玩具。②被玩弄取樂的人。
play·time ('ple,taɪm; 'plei-taim) *n.* 休息時間;遊戲時間。
play·wright ('ple,raɪt; 'pleirait) *n.* 劇作家。
pla·za ('plæzə; 'plɑ:zə) *n.* 〖西〗城市內之廣場。
***plea** (pli; pli:) *n.* ①懇求; 祈求。a *plea* for pity. 懇求憐憫。②辯解;答辯。③〖法律〗(被告在庭上所作的)抗辯。*cop a plea* 〖俚〗認罪(以逃避較重的處罰)。
pleach (plitʃ; pli:tʃ) *v.t.* 編結(樹枝等)。
***plead** (plid; pli:d) *v.,* **plead·ed** or **pled, plead·ing.** —*v.i.* ①辯護;抗辯。②懇求; 祈求。 —*v.t.* ①爲…辯護。 He had a good lawyer to *plead* his case. 他有一個很好的律師爲他的案子辯護。②以…爲口實; 託稱。The woman who stole *pleaded* poverty. 偷東西的婦人以貧窮爲託詞。
plead·a·ble ('plidəbəl; 'pli:dəbəl) *adj.* 可辯護的;可抗辯的。
plead·er ('plidɚ; 'pli:də) *n.* ①〖法律〗抗辯者;答辯者;辯護士;律師。②懇求者。
plead·ing ('plidɪŋ; 'pli:diŋ) *n.* ①(*pl.*) 原告的訴狀;被告的答辯狀。②辯護。③懇求。 —*adj.* 訴願的;懇求的。 **—ly,** *adv.*
pleas·ance ('plɛzns; 'plezəns) *n.* ①〖古,詩〗愉快;快樂;高興。②(幽靜的)庭園。
‡pleas·ant ('plɛznt; 'pleznt) *adj.* ①愉快的; 可喜的; 可愛的。 She has quite a *pleasant* face. 她有一副十分可愛的面孔。②容易相處的;友愛的。③(天氣)晴朗的。 **—ly,** *adv.* **—ness,** *n.*
pleas·ant·ry ('plɛzntrɪ; 'plezntri) *n., pl.* **-ries.** ①詼諧的笑話; 幽默話。②幽默;詼諧。
‡please (pliz; pli:z) *v.,* **pleased, pleas·ing.** —*v.t. & v.i.* ①願意; 期望; 不反對。Take as many as you *please*. 請你儘量拿(愛拿多少,就拿多少)。Come in, *please*. 請進來。②使快樂;取悅。It's difficult to *please* everybody. 取悅於每一個人是很難的。 ***be pleased*** **a.** 高興;開心。**b.** 選擇;願意;喜歡。 ***if you please.*** **a.** 如君願意;請(常作**please**). **b.**(表示驚訝、憤慨的感嘆句)。The missing letter was in his pocket, *if you please!* 遺失的信就在他的口袋裏,眞是! ***please God*** 如果上帝願意; 如果可能。 ***please oneself*** 隨自己之意。Well, *please yourself*. I don't mind what you do. 好吧!隨你,你做甚麼我都不反對。 **—pleas·a·ble,** *adj.* **—pleas·er,** *n.*
***pleased** (plizd; pli:zd) *adj.* 欣喜的;滿足的;感愉快的。I'm very (much) *pleased* with what he has done. 我對他所做的一切非常滿意。
***pleas·ing** ('plizɪŋ; 'pli:ziŋ) *adj.* 愉快的;嫵媚的;令人喜愛的。 a *pleasing* smile. 嫵媚的一笑。 **—ly,** *adv.*
pleas of the Crown ①〖英〗一切刑事訴訟及程序。②〖蘇〗指搶劫、强姦、凶殺、及縱火等行爲。
pleas·ur·a·ble ('plɛʒrəbl; 'pleʒərəbl) *adj.* 愉快的;悅人的。 **—pleas·ur·a·bly,** *adv.*
‡pleas·ure ('plɛʒɚ; 'pleʒə) *n., v.,* **-ured, -ur·ing.** —*n.* ①快樂;享樂。It gave me much *pleasure* to hear of your success. 聽到你的成功使我很快樂。②愉快之事物;樂趣。It's a *pleasure* to meet with you. 和你相見是件愉快的事。③俗世的享樂。④願望;選擇;意志。 ***at one's pleasure*** 隨意;聽便。 ***take pleasure in*** 以…爲樂。 ***with pleasure*** 願意(=willingly). —*v.t.* 給與快樂。It *pleasures* me to know you. 認識你給我樂趣。 —*v.i.* ①覺得快樂。 I *pleasure* in your company. 跟你一起我很快樂。②〖俗〗享樂(如度假等)。
pleasure boat 遊艇。
pleasure ground 遊樂場。
pleat (plit; pli:t) *n.* 衣服上的褶。 —*v.t.* 摺成褶;將…打褶。
pleb (plɛb; pleb) *n.* 〖俚〗①平民; 庶民(plebeian 之略)。②=**plebe.**
plebe (plib; pli:b) *n.* (尤指陸軍或海軍官校之)最低年級的學生。
ple·be·ian (plɪ'biən; pli'bi(:)ən) *n.* ①古羅馬之平民。②平民。③鄙俗之人。 —*adj.*

①平民的；屬於平民的。②庸俗的。*plebeian* tastes. 庸俗的趣味。—**ly,** *adv.*

ple·be·ian·ism 〔plɪˈbiənˌɪzəm; pliˈbiːənizəm〕 *n.* 平民身分；平民氣質；鄙俗。

ple·bes 〔ˈplibiz; ˈpliːbiːz〕 *n.* pl. of **plebs.**

ple·bis·ci·tar·y 〔plɪˈbɪsɪˌtɛrɪ; pliˈbisitəri〕 *adj.* 公民投票的。

pleb·i·scite 〔ˈplɛbəˌsaɪt; ˈplebisit〕 *n.* 公民投票。

plebs 〔plɛbz; plebz〕 *n., pl.* **ple·bes** 〔ˈplibiz; ˈpliːbiːz〕. ①古羅馬之平民。②平民；平民階級。

plec·tra 〔ˈplɛktrə; ˈplektrə〕 *n.* pl. of **plectrum.**

plec·trum 〔ˈplɛktrəm; ˈplektrəm〕 *n., pl.* **-tra, -trums.** (彈弦樂器時戴於指上的金屬或骨製之)撥子；琴撥；義甲。

pled 〔plɛd; pled〕 *v.* 〖美方，俗〗 pt. & pp. of **plead.**

pledge** 〔plɛdʒ; pledʒ〕 *n., v.,* **pledged, pledg·ing.** —*n.* ①誓言；誓約。②保證；保證物。He left a jewel as *pledge* for the borrowed horse. 他留下一塊寶石當作借馬的保證物。③抵押；被質之狀態。④祝酒。⑤預備會員(經准入會，然尚需一段時間考核方能成爲正式會員者)。 ***hold something in pledge 以某物爲質。 ***take*** (***sign***) ***the pledge*** 發誓(簽誓)戒酒。—*v.t.* ①誓言；保證。to *pledge* one's support. 宣誓支持。②以…作擔保。③飲酒祝…健康。④使發誓；以誓言約束。—*v.i.* ①保證。②喝祝酒。

pledg·ee 〔plɛdʒˈi; pledʒˈiː〕 *n.* 質權人。

pledg·er 〔ˈplɛdʒɚ; ˈpledʒə〕 *n.* ①典質者；當主；〖法律〗設定質權者。②(戒酒等的)發誓人。③舉祝杯之人。

pledg·et 〔ˈplɛdʒɪt; ˈpledʒit〕 *n.* 〖醫〗小拭子(置於傷口上之紗布、脫脂棉花等)。

pledg(e)·or 〔ˌplɛdʒˈɔr; ˌpledʒˈɔː〕 *n.* 〖法律〗設定質權者。

Ple·iad 〔ˈpliəd; ˈplaiəd〕 *n.* Pleiades 之任一個。

Ple·ia·des 〔ˈpliəˌdiz; ˈplaiədiːz〕 *n. pl.* ①〖希臘神話〗 Atlas 與一仙女所生之七個女兒(轉化爲七星)。②〖天文〗金牛宮之七星；昴星團。

Plei·o·cene 〔ˈplaɪəˌsin; ˈplaiəsiːn〕 *adj.* =**Pliocene.**

Pleis·to·cene 〔ˈplaɪstəˌsin; ˈplaistousiːn〕 *adj.* 〖地質〗更新世的；洪積世的。—*n.* 更新世；洪積世。

ple·na·ry 〔ˈplinərɪ; ˈpliːnəri〕 *adj.* ①充分的；完全的。②無限制的；全權的；絕對的。③(會議時)全體出席的。—**ple·na·ri·ly,** *adv.*

plen·i·po·ten·ti·ar·y 〔ˌplɛnəpəˈtɛnʃərɪ; ˌplenipəˈtenʃəri〕 *n., pl.* **-ar·ies,** *adj.* —*n.* 全權大使。—*adj.* ①有全權的。②絕對的；完全的。

plen·i·tude 〔ˈplɛnəˌtjud; ˈplenitjuːd〕 *n.* ①充足；豐饒。②〖醫〗(胃等的)脹。

plen·te·ous 〔ˈplɛntɪəs; ˈplentjəs, -tiəs〕 *adj.* 豐足的；充足的(多用於詩中)。—**ly,** *adv.* —**ness,** *n.*

***plen·ti·ful** 〔ˈplɛntɪfəl; ˈplentiful〕 *adj.* 很多的；豐富的。Ten gallons of gasoline is a *plentiful* supply for a short trip. 十加侖汽油很够一次短程旅行了。—**ly,** *adv.* —**ness,** *n.*

‡**plen·ty** 〔ˈplɛntɪ; ˈplenti〕 *n., pl.* **-ties,** *adj., adv.* —*n.* ①豐富；多；充分。Don't hurry; there's *plenty* of time. 不要忙；我們有充分的時間。②富足；富裕之狀態。 ***in plenty*** 豐富。 ***plenty more*** 尚有許多。 ***years of peace and plenty*** 太平豐收之年。—*adj.* 很多的；豐富的；很够的。Six potatoes will be *plenty*. 六個馬鈴薯很够了。—*adv.* 十分。〖注意〗 there is plenty of 後跟不可數名詞，如 time 等。there are plenty of 後跟可數名詞，如 men 等。

ple·num 〔ˈplinəm; ˈpliːnəm〕 *n., pl.* **-nums, -na** 〔-nə; -nə〕, *adj.* —*n.* ①充滿物質之空間(爲 vacuum 之對)。②充滿；充實。③全體出席之會議；總會；(立法機構之)全院會議。④高壓(封閉空間內的氣壓大於外面大氣壓之狀態)；(在上述高壓狀態中之)封閉的空間。—*adj.* 全體會議的；全會的。

ple·o·nasm 〔ˈpliəˌnæzəm; ˈpli(ː)ənæzəm〕 *n.* 〖修辭〗冗言(法)；贅言(如：a false lie)。

ple·o·nas·tic 〔ˌpliəˈnæstɪk; ˌpliəˈnæstik〕 *adj.* 冗贅的。

ple·si·o·saur 〔ˈplisɪəˌsɔr; ˈpliːsiəsɔː〕 *n.* =**plesiosaurus.**

ple·si·o·sau·rus 〔ˌplisɪəˈsɔrəs; ˈpliːsiəˈsɔːrəs〕 *n., pl.* **-ri** 〔-raɪ; -rai〕. 〖古生物〗蛇頸龍。

ples·sor, ples·ser 〔ˈplɛsɚ; ˈplesə〕 *n.* 〖醫〗 =**plexor.**

pleth·o·ra 〔ˈplɛθərə; ˈpleθərə〕 *n.* ①過多；過賸。②〖醫〗多血症；體液過多。

ple·thor·ic 〔ˈplɛθərɪk; pleˈθɔrik〕 *adj.* ①過多的；過賸的。②多血的；多血症的。

pleu·ra 〔ˈplurə; ˈpluərə〕 *n., pl.* **-rae** 〔-ri; -riː〕. 〖解剖，動物〗肋膜；胸膜。

pleu·ral 〔ˈplurəl; ˈpluərəl〕 *adj.* 肋膜的；胸膜的。

pleu·ri·sy 〔ˈplurəsɪ; ˈpluərisi〕 *n.* 〖醫〗肋膜炎；胸膜炎。

pleu·rit·ic 〔pluˈrɪtɪk; pluəˈritik〕 *adj.* 肋膜炎的；胸膜炎的；患胸膜炎的。

pleu·ro·pneu·mo·ni·a 〔ˌplurənjəˈmonɪə; ˈpluərounju(ː)ˈmounjə〕 *n.* 〖醫〗胸膜肺炎。

plex·i·glass 〔ˈplɛksɪˌglæs; ˈpleksiglɑːs〕 *n.* 樹脂玻璃(作飛機的窗子等用)。

plex·im·e·ter 〔plɛkˈsɪmətɚ; plekˈsimitə〕 *n.* 〖醫〗敲診板；叩診板。

plex·or 〔ˈplɛksɚ; ˈpleksə〕 *n.* 〖醫〗敲診槌；叩診槌。(亦作 **plessor**)

plex·us 〔ˈplɛksəs; ˈpleksəs〕 *n., pl.* **-us·es, -us.** ①〖解剖〗(神經、血管之)叢。②一堆錯綜複雜的事、思想等。

pli·a·ble 〔ˈplaɪəbḷ; ˈplaiəbl〕 *adj.* ①易曲的；柔軟的。②柔順的；易駕馭的。—**pli·a·bil·i·ty,** *n.* —**pli·a·bly,** *adv.*

pli·an·cy 〔ˈplaɪənsɪ; ˈplaiənsi〕 *n.* 易曲(性)；柔軟；柔順。

pli·ant 〔ˈplaɪənt; ˈplaiənt〕 *adj.* ①易曲的；柔軟的。②柔順的；易變的。—**ly,** *adv.*

pli·ca 〔ˈplaɪkə; ˈplaikə〕 *n., pl.* **pli·cae** 〔ˈplaɪsi; ˈplaisiː〕. ①〖解剖〗皺襞。②〖醫〗糾髮病。

pli·cate 〔ˈplaɪket; ˈplaikeit〕 *adj.* =**plicated.** —**ly,** *adv.* —**ness,** *n.*

pli·cat·ed 〔ˈplaɪketɪd; ˈplaikeitid〕 *adj.* 〖動、植物〗有皺襞的；有褶的。

pli·ers 〔ˈplaɪɚz; ˈplaiəz〕 *n. pl.* or *sing.* 鉗子。(英作 **plyers**)

***plight¹** 〔plaɪt; plait〕 *n.* 情勢；情形；情況(通常指惡劣的)。He is in a sad *plight*. 彼陷入悲慘之境。

plight² *v.t.* ①宣誓；誓約。②以誓約束(尤指婚姻)。—*n.* ①誓言；保證。②訂婚。—**er,** *n.*

Plim·soll line (or **mark**) 〔ˈplɪmsḷ ~; ˈplimsəl ~〕 〖航海〗載貨(常備)吃水線。(亦作 **Plimsoll's line, Plimsoll's mark**)

plim·sol(l)s 〔ˈplɪmsəlz; ˈplimsəlz〕 *n. pl.* 〖英〗膠底帆布鞋。(亦作 **plimsoles**)

plink 〔plɪŋk; pliŋk〕 *v.i.* ①以步槍等射擊

隨便選擇的目標。②發出一連串短、輕而響亮的聲音。—*v.t.* ①爲練習或取樂而射擊。②使發出輕、短、響亮聲音。—*n.* 輕、短、響亮聲音。

plinth [plɪnθ; plinθ] *n.* 〖建築〗①(柱等之)基脚;柱脚。②(瓶、像等之)底座。

Pli·o·cene [ˈplaɪəˌsin; ˈplai-əsiːn] *adj.* 〖地質〗鮮新世的。—*n.* 鮮新世;鮮新世之岩層;鮮新統。(亦作 **Pleiocene**)

plod [plɑd; plɔd] *v.,* **plod·ded, plod·ding,** *n.* —*v.t.* 緩步或重步在…走。We *plod* the path of toil. 我們在艱苦的路上慢慢前行。—*v.i.* ①重步或吃力地行走。②孜孜從事;辛苦工作。—*n.* 艱步而行;沉重之脚步聲。

plod·der [ˈplɑdɚ; ˈplɔdə] *n.* ①步履艱難者;重步而行者。②勤學者;勤勞者。

plod·ding [ˈplɑdɪŋ; ˈplɔdiŋ] *adj.* 勤勞而有耐心的。 —**ly,** *adv.*

plop [plɑp; plɔp] *n., v.,* **plopped, plop·ping,** *adv.* —*n.* ①(物件落水之)撲通聲。②撲通落下。—*v.t.* 使撲通一聲落下。—*v.i.* 撲通墜落。—*adv.* 撲通一聲地。

plo·sive [ˈplosɪv; ˈplousiv] *n., adj.* 〖語音〗破裂音(的)。

***plot** [plɑt; plɔt] *n., v.,* **plot·ted, plot·ting.** —*n.* ①陰謀。Two men formed a *plot* to rob the bank. 二人合謀搶劫那銀行。②(戲劇、小說等之)情節。③一小塊土地。④地圖;圖表。⑤〖砲兵〗地圖上之地點。target *plot*. 目標地區。⑥電影或戲劇製作詳細計畫。⑦圖表上表示飛機、船隻等之航線或位置。—*v.t.* ①密謀(壞事);圖謀。②分(地)成小塊。③製…之圖。④標出在圖上之位置。⑤在方格紙上標出位置。⑥描上述位置;(在方格紙上)畫出曲線。⑦詳細計劃電影或戲劇之製作。⑧以圖表做計算。 —*v.i.* 密謀;圖謀。—**ful,** *adj.* —**less,** *adj.* —**less·ness,** *n.*

plot·ter [ˈplɑtɚ; ˈplɔtə] *n.* ①圖謀者;陰謀者。②繪跡器。③〖電腦〗電腦系統中輔助性的輸出部分。

plough [plau; plau] *n., v.t., v.i.* =**plow.**

plov·er [ˈplʌvɚ; ˈplʌvə] *n.* 千鳥之類。

plow** [plau; plau] *n.* ①犂。②犂形器具(如除雪機)。③耕地;田。fifty acres of *plow.* 五十英畝耕地。④(P-)〖天文〗北斗七星。follow*** (or ***hold***) ***the plow*** 以耕田爲業。***look back from the plow*** 中止工作。***put one's hand to the plow*** 開始工作;着手工作。***take a plow*** 〖英俗〗不及格。***under the plow***(田地)耕種中。—*v.t.* ①用犂耕(田);耕(田)。②使生皺紋。a face *plowed* with wrinkles. 長滿皺紋的臉。③乘風破浪前進。④使考試不及格。⑤投資〖常 into〗. ⑥再投資〖常 back〗. —*v.i.* ①耕犂。The land *plows* hard after the drought. 大旱之後土地難耕。②(分開積雪等)前進;刻苦而進。The ship *plowed* through waves. 那船破浪前進。③〖英俗〗考試落第。***plow a lonely furrow*** 孤獨地工作。***plow around*** 〖美俗〗偵探;打聽。***plow one's way*** 費力地前進;推進。***plow the sands*** 做無用之事;徒勞無功。***plow the waves*** 在海上航行。***plow under*** **a.** 用犂耕翻埋入土壤中作綠肥。**b.** 將作物耕起以減少產量。**c.** 〖俗〗擊敗;毀滅;征服。***plow up*** 掘起;鋤起。***plow with one's heifer*** 欲有所求於夫而利用其妻;利用他人財產。(英亦作 **plough**)

plow·back [ˈplauˌbæk; ˈplaubæk] *n.* ①盈餘之用於再投資。②再投資之款額。

plow·boy [ˈplauˌbɔɪ; ˈplaubɔi] *n.* ①莊稼漢;鄉下青年。②村童。(亦作 **ploughboy**)

plow·land [ˈplauˌlænd; ˈplaulænd] *n.* ①耕地;田地。②昔英國之一種地積單位(約等於一年中八頭牛所能耕之地積)。

plow·man [ˈplaumən; ˈplaumən] *n., pl.* **-men.** ①用犂者。②農夫。—**ship,** *n.*

Plow (or **Plough**) **Monday** 主顯節(Epiphany, 1月6日)後之第一個星期一(昔英國於此日開始耕田)。

plow·share [ˈplauˌʃɛr; ˈplauʃɛə] *n.* 「犂刄;犂頭。」

plow·tail [ˈplauˌtel; ˈplauteil] *n.* 犂尾;犂柄。***at the plowtail*** 在種田;從事農業。

ploy [plɔɪ; plɔi] *n.* ①〖俗〗策略(圖占優勢的說話或行動)。②〖蘇〗工作;職業;事業;遠征;消遣;嬉戲。

pluck** [plʌk; plʌk] *v.t.* ①摘;採。to *pluck* flowers. 摘花。②拔;拉。to *pluck* up courage. 振起勇氣。③〖俗〗搶劫;詐欺。④〖英俗〗使…落第;使…不及格。⑤以指撥(樂器之絃)。—*v.i.* 拉;抓。The child *plucked* at its mother's skirt. 孩子拉母親的裙子(引她注意)。pluck up*** **a.** 連根拔起。**b.** 鼓起勇氣。*Pluck up!* You aren't hurt badly. 鼓起勇氣來!你的傷勢不重。—*n.* ①採;摘。②拉;拽。③勇氣;膽量。④供食用之動物的心、肝與肺。—**er,** *n.*

pluck·y [ˈplʌkɪ; ˈplʌki] *adj.,* **pluck·i·er, pluck·i·est.** 有膽量的;有勇氣的。—**pluck·i·ly,** *adv.* —**pluck·i·ness,** *n.*

plug** [plʌg; plʌg] *n., v.,* **plugged, plug·ging.** —*n.* ①塞子;栓。②消防栓;給水栓。③電插頭。Put the *plug* in the socket. 把插頭插在插座內。④火花栓;點火栓。⑤板煙。⑥廣播節目中的廣告。⑦老而無用的馬。⑧〖俗〗賣不出的貨品;劣等陳貨。⑨〖俚〗打擊;拳毆。⑩〖俚〗人造魚餌。⑪小塊草皮。⑫=**plug hat.** —*v.t.* ①以塞子塞住。②射擊;拳擊。③以廣告大事宣傳。to *plug* a new product. 廣爲宣傳一種新產品。④從(西瓜上)削下一片以確定瓜是否已熟。—*v.i.* ①孜孜從事。②打擊。③接插頭。plug away at*** 孜孜工作。***plug in*** 接上插頭通電。

plug·board [ˈplʌgˌbɔrd; ˈplʌgbɔːd] *n.* 電話總機。

plug·ger [ˈplʌgɚ; ˈplʌgə] *n.* ①〖齒〗塡塞器。②〖美俗〗用功學生;孜孜不倦的人。③〖美俚〗廣告播音員;宣傳員。

plug hat 〖美俚〗=**top hat.**

plug-in [ˈplʌgˌɪn; ˈplʌg-in] *adj.* 插進電插座就可用的。—*n.* 可用插座接電的地方。

plug-ug·ly [ˈplʌgˌʌglɪ; ˈplʌgˌʌgli] *n., pl.* **-ug·lies.** 〖美俚〗流氓;暴徒。

***plum** [plʌm; plʌm] *n.* ①李樹;梅樹。②李子;梅子。③(果餅中之)葡萄乾。④陳皮梅。⑤精品;美好之物;精華。His new job is a fine *plum.* 他的新工作是件稱心合意的好差事。⑥深紫色。⑦〖英俚〗**a.** 十萬磅。**b.** 擁資十萬磅者。⑧〖英俚〗額外之紅利。—*adj.* 深紫色的。

plum·age [ˈplumɪdʒ; ˈpluːmidʒ] *n.* 「鳥類之羽毛。」

plumb [plʌm; plʌm] *n.* ①鉛錘;測水錘。②垂直。***in plumb*** 垂直的;成直角的。***out of plumb*** (=off plumb) 不垂直。—*adj.* ①垂直的。②〖俗〗完全的;全然的。—*adv.* ①垂直地。②精確地。③全然地。—*v.t.* ①以鉛錘測定(是否垂直);以鉛錘測深度。②了解;探測。③以鉛緘封。④修理(煤氣、水管等)。—*v.i.* ①成垂直。②當煤氣、水管等之修理工人。

plum·bag·i·nous [plʌmˈbædʒɪnəs; plʌmˈbædʒinəs] *adj.* 〖罕〗黑鉛的;似黑鉛的;含黑鉛的。

plum·ba·go 〔plʌmˈbego; plʌmˈbeigou〕 *n., pl.* **-gos.** ①黑鉛；石墨。②以鉛頭工具繪成之畫。

plumb bob 鉛錘；線鉈。

plum·be·ous 〔ˈplʌmbɪəs; ˈplʌmbiəs〕 *adj.* ①鉛的；似鉛的。②鉛色的。③覆以鉛的。

plumb·er 〔ˈplʌmɚ; ˈplʌmə〕 *n.* ①鉛管工人(修理水管、煤氣管等)。②〖廢〗用鉛的工人。

plumb·er·y 〔ˈplʌmərɪ; ˈplʌməri〕 *n., pl.* **-er·ies.** ①鉛工(業)；鉛管工。②鉛管工場。

plum·bic 〔ˈplʌmbɪk; ˈplʌmbik〕 *adj.* ①〖化〗鉛的；含鉛的。②〖醫〗由於鉛(毒)的。

plum·bif·er·ous 〔plʌmˈbɪfərəs; plʌmˈbifərəs〕 *adj.* 產鉛的；含鉛的。

plumb·ing 〔ˈplʌmɪŋ; ˈplʌmiŋ〕 *n.* ①修理水管等工作；修理水管業。②建築物之水管裝置。

plum·bism 〔ˈplʌmbɪzm̩; ˈplʌmbizəm〕 *n.* 〖醫〗(慢性)鉛中毒；鉛毒症。

plumb·less 〔ˈplʌmlɪs; ˈplʌmlis〕 *adj.* 深不可測的；淵深的。

plumb line ①錘線；鉛垂線；測鉛；測深線。②＝**plumb rule.**

plumb rule 錘規；垂直準測規；懸墨。

plum cake 葡萄乾糕餅。

plum duff 葡萄乾布丁。

plume** 〔plum; pluːm〕 *n., v.,* **plumed, plum·ing.** —*n.* ①羽毛。②裝飾用之羽毛。③羽毛狀的東西。④水底原子爆炸時揚起的中空水柱。⑤帽子上的裝飾羽毛。borrowed plumes*** 借來的衣物而誇爲己有。—*v.t.* ①飾以羽毛。②整刷…之羽毛。The eagle *plumed* its wing. 這鷹整理它的翅膀。***plume oneself on*** 以…爲榮。

plume·let 〔ˈplumlɪt; ˈpluːmlit〕 *n.* ①小羽毛。②〖植物〗幼芽。

plum·met 〔ˈplʌmɪt; ˈplʌmit〕 *n.* ①鉛錘；測水深度之錘。②(釣絲上的)墜子。③＝**plumb rule.** ④抑壓的事物。—*v.t.* 垂直下落。

plum·my 〔ˈplʌmɪ; ˈplʌmi〕 *adj.,* **plum·mi·er, plum·mi·est.** ①似梅子的；多梅子的。②〖俗〗好的；上等的；頂好的；富裕的。

plu·mose 〔ˈplumos; ˈpluːmous〕 *adj.* 有羽毛的；羽毛狀的。

***plump**[1] 〔plʌmp; plʌmp〕 *adj.* 圓胖的；豐滿的。*plump* cheeks. 豐滿的雙頰。—*v.t.* 使成圓胖的〖常up, out〗。—*v.i.* 變爲圓胖的〖常up, out〗。—**ly,** *adv.* —**ness,** *n.*

plump**[2] *v.i.* ①忽然落下。The ducklings *plumped* into the water. 小鴨們突然跳入水中。②〖英〗將選票投給一人。—*v.t.* ①使突然而沉重地落下〖常 down〗。He *plumped* himself down and fell asleep. 他撲通倒下來睡着了。②無保留地說出〖常 out〗。③稱讚。plump for*** **a.** 投票選出(一人)。**b.** 絕對贊成。—*n.* 重落；突落。—*adv.* 直接地；忽然地。He sat down *plump.* 他突然坐下。—*adj.* 直接的；率直的。

plump[3] *n.* 〖古,英方〗羣；隊；族；叢。a *plump* of spears. 槍矛部隊。

plump·er[1] 〔ˈplʌmpɚ; ˈplʌmpə〕 *n.* ①(使)脹起(發胖)之物。②(使腮鼓起的)鼓腮物。

plump·er[2] *n.* ①沉重的墜落。②(雖一次可選數候選人但)將全票僅投給一個候選人的選票；投此等選票者。③〖俚〗大謊。

plum pudding 葡萄乾布丁。

plu·mule 〔ˈplumjul; ˈpluːmjuːl〕 *n.* ①〖鳥〗柔毛。②〖植物〗幼芽。—**plu·mu·lar,** *adj.*

plum·y 〔ˈplumɪ; ˈpluːmi〕 *adj.,* **plum·i·er, plum·i·est.** ①有羽毛的；如羽毛的。②飾以羽毛的。

***plun·der** 〔ˈplʌndɚ; ˈplʌndə〕 *v.t. & v.i.* 搶劫；搶奪。The enemy *plundered* all the goods they found. 敵人把所發現之財物均掠奪而去。—*n.* ①劫奪品。②劫奪；搶劫。③〖美方〗**a.** 行李。**b.** 隨身物件；家庭用具。

plun·der·age 〔ˈplʌndərɪdʒ; ˈplʌndəridʒ〕 *n.* ①掠奪。②〖法律〗**a.** 盜用船貨；盜用的船貨。**b.** 贓物。

plun·der·er 〔ˈplʌndərɚ; ˈplʌndərə〕 *n.* 掠奪者；盜賊。

plunge** 〔plʌndʒ; plʌndʒ〕 *v.,* **plunged, plung·ing,** *n.* —*v.t.* 使投入(水中、洞中等)；使陷入(某種狀態)。to *plunge* a country into war. 使一國家陷入戰爭。—*v.i.* ①投入；跳入；陷入；突入。to *plunge* into the sea. 跳入海中。②衝進；突進。③猛顛；(船首、馬首等)突降。④狂賭；冒險；投機。—*n.* ①跳水。②突進。③跳水的地方；游泳池。take the plunge*** 決意冒險。

plunge bath ①全身浸浴。②可以跳進去的大浴盆。

plung·er 〔ˈplʌndʒɚ; ˈplʌndʒə〕 *n.* ①投入之人或物；跳入者；潛水者。②機器之突動部分(如活塞等)。③冒險的賭博者或投機者。

plunk 〔plʌŋk; plʌŋk〕 *v.t.* ①撥(弦等)；彈(絃樂器等)。②〖俗〗砰地拋出；砰地放下；驟推；猛擲〖常 down〗。—*v.i.* ①發出砰的聲音。②〖俗〗砰地墜落；重跌；重落〖常down〗。***plunk down*** 付款。***plunk for*** 投票贊成。—*n.* ①〖俗〗砰地墜落(擲出)；砰的墜落聲音；重落聲。②〖俗〗撥弦；弦聲。③〖俗〗劈啪的打聲或打擊。④〖美俚〗一元。—*adv.* ①砰地；撲通地。②正着地。

plu·per·fect 〔pluˈpɝfɪkt; ˈpluːˈpəːfikt〕 *n.* 〖文法〗過去完成式。—*adj.* 過去完成式的。***pluperfect tense*** 過去完成式。

plupf. pluperfect.

plur. ①plural. ②plurality.

***plu·ral** 〔ˈplurəl; ˈpluərəl〕 *adj.* 複數的。a *plural* noun. 一複數名詞。—*n.* 〖文法〗複數形。"Books" is the *plural* of "book." "books" 是 "book" 的複數形。—**ly,** *adv.*

plu·ral·ism 〔ˈplurəlɪzm̩; ˈpluərəlizm〕 *n.* ①〖哲學〗多元論。②〖宗教〗兼職。

plu·ral·ist 〔ˈplurəlɪst; ˈpluərəlist〕 *n.* ①〖哲學〗多元論者。②〖宗教〗兼職者。

plu·ral·is·tic 〔ˌplurəlˈɪstɪk; ˌpluərəˈlistik〕 *adj.* ①〖哲學〗多元論(者)的。②〖宗教〗兼職(者)的。—**al·ly,** *adv.*

plu·ral·i·ty 〔pluˈrælətɪ; pluəˈræliti〕 *n., pl.* **-ties.** ①得票最多數與次多數之差。②較多數；大多數。③多數；衆多。④衆多之狀態。⑤〖宗教〗兼職；兼差。

plu·ral·ize 〔ˈplurəlˌaɪz; ˈpluərəlaiz〕 *v.,* **-ized, -iz·ing.** —*v.t.* 使成複數(形)；以複數(形)表示。—*v.i.* ①成爲複數。②〖宗教〗兼職。—**plu·ral·i·za·tion, plu·ral·iz·er,** *n.*

plural marriage 一夫多妻制(尤指摩門教徒)。

plural offices 兼職；兼任。

plural wife 一夫多妻制下之任何一妻。

plus** 〔plʌs; plʌs〕 *prep.* ①加。3 *plus* 2 equals 5. 3加2等於5。②和(＝and also)。—*adj.* ①多的；加的。His mark was B *plus.* 他的分數是B⁺。②表示多的。③正的；正電的。be plus*** 〖俗〗另有。—*n.* ①加號；正號(＋)。②盈餘；餘額。③正數。—*adv.* 以外另加；强。He has personality *plus.* 他有極强的個性。

plus fours (打高爾夫球等時用的)一種寬鬆的半長褲(原爲長及膝下四英寸之義)。

plush 〔plʌʃ; plʌʃ〕 *n.* 厚絨布(一種厚而軟的絲或棉織品)。—*adj.* 〖俚〗豪華的；奢侈的。

Plu·tarch ['plutark; 'plu:ta:k] *n.* 蒲魯塔克 (46?-?120, 希臘傳記作家)。
plute [plut; plu:t] *n.* 〖美〗富豪階級。
Plu·to ['pluto; 'plu:tou] *n.* ①〖希臘、羅馬神話〗冥府之王;閻羅王。②〖天文〗冥王星。
plu·toc·ra·cy [plu'takrəsɪ; plu:'tɔkrəsi] *n., pl.* **-cies.** ①富豪政治;財閥政治。②富豪;財閥。
plu·to·crat ['plutə,kræt; 'plu:təkræt] *n.* ①因財富而有勢力之人;財閥。②〖俗〗富人。
plu·to·crat·ic [,plutə'krætɪk; ,plu:tə'krætik] *adj.* ①富豪政治的; 財閥政治的。②富豪的;財閥的。
plu·to·de·moc·ra·cy ['plutodə'makrəsɪ; 'plu:toudi'mɔkrəsi] *n.* 財閥民主主義。
Plu·to·ni·an [plu'tonɪən; plu:'tounjən] *adj.* ①Pluto 的; 似閻羅王的。②地獄的;冥府的;陰間的。
Plu·ton·ic [plu'tanɪk; plu:'tɔnik] *adj.* ① =**Plutonian.** ②(p-) 〖地質〗火成(岩)的。
plu·to·ni·um [plu'tonɪəm; plu:'touniəm] *n.* 〖化〗鈽(一種放射性元素, 符號 Pu).
Plu·tus ['plutəs; 'plu:təs] *n.* 〖希臘神話〗財富之神。
plu·vi·al ['pluvɪəl; 'plu:vjəl] *adj.* ①雨的;多雨的。②〖地質〗雨成的;由於雨之作用的。
plu·vi·om·e·ter [,pluvɪ'amətə; ,plu:vi'ɔmitə] *n.* 雨量計。—**plu·vi·om·e·try,** *n.* —**plu·vi·o·met·ric,** *adj.*
plu·vi·ous ['pluvɪəs; 'plu:viəs] *adj.* 雨的;多雨的。
***ply**[1] [plaɪ; plai] *v.,* **plied, ply·ing.** —*v.t.* ①使用。The dressmaker *plies* her needle. 這裁縫使用她的針。②經常從事於。③堅持供給。They *plied* him with food and drink. 他們堅持供給他食物和飲料。④追問;盤問。⑤經常在…上來往。Boats *ply* the river. 船隻經常行駛河上。⑥(船夫、汽車司機、脚夫等)經常(在某地方)等候顧客。⑦不斷地攻打。—*v.i.* ①固定地往來。②忙於做事;孜孜工作。
ply[2] *n., pl.* **plies,** *v.,* **plied, ply·ing.** —*n.* ①層;摺;疊。②(紗、繩索等之);絢股。③傾向;癖性。—*v.t.* 使彎曲;扭;摺。
Plym·outh ['plɪməθ; 'pliməθ] *n.* 普里茅斯 (**a.** 英格蘭西南部之一城市。**b.** 美國 Massachusetts 州東南部之一市鎮, 1620 年 Pilgrim Fathers 最初定居之地)。
Plymouth Brethren 普里茅斯教友會(1830年代英人 John Darby 創始於英國 Plymouth, 無正式組織, 惟以聖經爲信仰)。
Plymouth Rock ①在美國 Massachusetts 州 Plymouth 港的岩石(據傳 Pilgrim Fathers 於 1620 年由此登陸)。②美國原產的一種雞。
ply·wood ['plaɪ,wud; 'plaiwud] *n.* 三夾板;合板(用爲建築、細工、飛機等之材料)。
Pm 化學元素 promethium 之符號。
pm. premium.
P.M. ①Past Master. ②Paymaster. ③Police Magistrate. ④Postmaster. ⑤Provost Marshal. ⑥Prime Minister. ⑦post-mortem.
***p.m., P.M.** ['pi'ɛm; 'pi:'em] ①爲 post meridiem (拉=after noon)之縮寫,下午。6 *p.m.* 下午六點。②由中午至午夜。
P.M.G. ①Paymaster General. ②Postmaster General.
PMLA, P.M.L.A. Publications of the Modern Language Association.
P/N, p.n. promissory note.
pneum. ①pneumatic. ②pneumatics.
pneu·mat·ic [nju'mætɪk; nju:'mætik] *adj.* ①空氣的;氣體的;氣體學的。②含有空氣的。③由壓縮空氣推動或操作的。④裝有氣胎的。⑤氣體學的。⑥〖神學〗屬靈的; 精神的。—*n.* ①氣胎。②有氣胎的車輛。—**al·ly,** *adv.*
pneu·mat·ics [nju'mætɪks; nju:'mætiks] *n.* (作 *sing.* 解)氣體學;氣力學。
pneumatic trough 〖化〗集氣槽。
pneumato- 〖字首〗表"空氣;呼吸;靈魂"等義。
pneu·ma·tol·o·gy [,numə'talədʒɪ; ,nju:mə'tɔlədʒi] *n.* ①靈物學。②〖神學〗聖靈論。③〖古〗=**psychology.**
pneu·ma·tom·e·ter [,numə'tamətə; ,nju:mə'tɔmitə] *n.* 〖生理〗肺量器;肺壓計。
pneu·ma·to·phore ['njumətəfɔr; 'nju:mətəfɔ:] *n.* 昆蟲的氣腔。
pneu·mo·co·ni·o·sis [,njumə,konɪ'osɪs; 'nju:mə,kouni'ousis] *n.* 〖醫〗肺塵埃沉着病;塵埃入肺病。
pneu·mo·gas·tric [,njumə'gæstrɪk; ,nju:mə'gæstrik] *adj.* 〖解剖〗肺與胃的; 迷走神經的。—*n.* 迷走神經。
pneumogastric nerve 〖解剖〗迷走神經。
pneu·mo·nia [nju'monjə, -nɪə; nju:'mounjə, -niə] *n.* 〖醫〗肺炎。
pneu·mon·ic [nju'manɪk; nju:'mɔnik] *adj.* ①〖罕〗肺的。②肺炎的;似肺炎的。
Pnom Penh ['nam'pɛn; 'nɔm'pen] *n.* 金邊(高棉之首都)。(亦作 **Phnom Penh, Pnom-penh, Pnompenh**)
Po 化學元素 polonium 之符號。
Po [po; pou] *n.* 波河(在義大利北部)。
po [po; pou] *n., pl.* **pos.** 〖兒語〗=**chamber pot.**
P.O., p.o. ①petty officer. ②postal order. ③post office. ④putout(s).
poach[1] [potʃ; poutʃ] *v.i.* ①侵入他人的土地中獵取獵物。②侵犯他人權利等。③(土地之)因踐踏而多孔穴或成爛泥。④〖俗〗(遊戲或運動中)欺騙。—*v.t.* ①祕密獵取;侵入他人土地中獵取。②侵犯他人權利等。③以不正當手段獲取。④踐踏(土地)使成泥。⑤加水調勻。
poach[2] *v.t.* 煮荷包蛋。—**a·ble,** *adj.*
poach·er ['potʃə; 'poutʃə] *n.* ①偷獵者;偷捕魚類者;擅自進入他人產業者。②侵犯他人領域或搶奪他人主顧的商人。③煮鍋。
P.O.B., POB Post Office Box.
po·chard ['potʃəd; 'poutʃəd] *n., pl.* **-chards, -chard.** (鳥)磯鳬。
pock [pak; pɔk] *n.* ①痘疱;痘瘡;痘痕;痲窩。②〖蘇〗袋子。—*v.t.* 使成痲窩狀。
‡**pock·et** ['pakɪt; 'pɔkit] *n.* ①衣袋。②凹地。③小口袋;囊。④礦穴。The miner struck a *pocket* of silver. 礦工發見一個銀礦穴。⑤(空氣中)部分眞空之處(氣壓過低等處,致使機身突降)。⑥撞球桌之裝球小袋。⑦錢。He will suffer in his *pocket.* 他將要損失錢。⑧封袋(放照片、郵票、唱片等)。⑨牆上等收置拉門之地方。⑩小礦脈。⑪競賽者被對方困住而不得進展的地方。⑫〖解剖〗袋狀物。 ***be in pocket*** 有(或掙)錢。***be out of pocket*** **a.** 損失錢;花錢。**b.** 失敗。***have a person in one's pocket*** 置某人於掌中。He has the audience *in his pocket.* 他完全左右着觀衆。***line one's pocket*** 獲取不法利益。***pick a pocket*** 偷竊袋中之物。***put one's hand in one's pocket*** 花錢。***put one's pride in one's pocket*** 做寡廉鮮恥的事。—*v.t.* ①

關入;封入。②納入袋中。③遏止;壓抑。④忍受。He *pocketed* the insult. 他忍受這侮辱。⑤竊取。 He *pocketed* all the profits. 他竊取了所有的利潤。⑥圍住。The town was *pocketed* in a small valley.那鎮在一小峽谷中。⑦將球撞入撞球桌小袋內。⑧〖美〗(總統等)擱置法案使其無法成爲法律。⑨(競賽中)困住對方。—*adj.* ①可携帶於衣袋中的。②小型的;袖珍的。「水量 10,000噸)。}

pocket battleship 袖珍主力艦(排}

pocket book 小筆記簿;袖珍本。

pock·et·book ['pakɪt,bʊk; 'pɔkit-buk] *n.* ①〖美〗女用錢袋; 女用手提包。②皮夾;皮包。③=**pocket book.**

pocket borough 〖英史〗(1832 年以前) 國會議員選舉被一人或一家族操縱之選舉區。「*n.*, *pl.* **-fuls.** 滿袋;一袋。}

pock·et·ful ['pakɪt,fʊl; 'pɔkitful]}

pock·et-hand·ker·chief ['pakɪt-'hæŋkətʃɪf; 'pɔkit'hæŋkətʃif] *n.* 手帕。

pock·et·knife ['pakɪt,naɪf; 'pɔkit-naif] *n.*, *pl.* **-knives.** (可摺合的)小刀。

pocket money 零用錢。

pocket piece (擱在衣袋裏的)吉利錢。

pocket pistol ①(可放衣袋中的)小手槍。②〖謔〗可裝於口袋中的小瓶;懷中之酒瓶。

pocket veto 〖美〗總統否決議案的一種手段 (總統對於議會提請簽署之議案在議會休會後十天內不予簽署,該議案卽不能成爲法律)。

pock·et·y ['pakətɪ; 'pɔkiti] *adj.* ①〖採礦〗(礦苗)分布不勻的;礦脈呈瘤狀的。②似衣袋的;閉塞的;鬱悶的。

pock·mark ['pak,mark; 'pɔkmaːk] *n.* (常*pl.*) 痘痕;麻點。—*v.t.* 使有痘痕;使千瘡百孔。

pock-marked ['pak,markt; 'pɔk-maːkt] *adj.* 有痘痕的;有麻皮的;千瘡百孔的。

pock·y ['pakɪ; 'pɔki] *adj.*, **pock·i·er, pock·i·est.** ①(有)痘痕的;多麻點的。②(出)水痘的。「少;稍。*poco a poco* 漸漸;徐徐。}

po·co ['poko; 'poukou] 〖義〗*adv.* 〖音樂〗}

po·co·cu·ran·te [,pokokʊ'rræntɪ; 'poukoukjuə'ræntɪ] *adj.*, *n.*, *pl.* **-ti** [-ti; -tiː]. —*adj.* 漫不經心的;冷淡的;不關心的。—*n.* 冷淡的人;不關心的人。

po·co·cu·ran·tism [,pokokʊ'ræn-tɪzm; 'poukoukjuə'ræntizm] *n.* 不在意;冷淡。(亦作 **pococuranteism**)

pod[1] [pad; pɔd] *n.*, *v.*, **pod·ded, pod·ding.** —*n.* ①豆莢;蒴。②機翼或機身外部掩蓋引擎、貨物、武器等的流線型覆蓋。—*v.i.* ①結莢;成莢;生蒴。②豐滿如莢。—*v.t.* 剝掉(豆等)之莢。

pod[2] *n.*, *v.*, **pod·ded, pod·ding.** —*n.* (海豹、鯨、鳥等的)小羣。—*v.t.* 將(海豹等)趕在一塊兒;使(動物)聚集成羣。

P.O.D. ①pay on delivery. ② Pocket Oxford Dictionary. ③Post Office Department. 「〖醫〗足(指)痛風;痛風。}

po·dag·ra [po'dægrə; pə'dægrə] *n.*}

po·dag·ric [pə'dægrɪk; pə'dægrik] *adj.* 足痛風的;患(足)痛風的。

pod·ded ['padɪd; 'pɔdid] *adj.* ①有莢的;生莢的;生於莢中的。②富裕的;小康的;溫飽的;安樂的。「**podg·i·est.** 矮胖的。}

podg·y ['padʒɪ; 'pɔdʒi] *adj.*, **podg·i·er,**}

po·di·a·try [po'daɪətrɪ; pou'daiətri] *n.* 〖醫〗脚病學;脚病治療。

po·di·um ['podɪəm; 'poudjəm] *n.*, *pl.* **-di·ums, -di·a** [-dɪə; -diə]. ①〖建築〗 **a.** 作基礎用的矮牆。**b.** (古代圓形劇場中之) 鬥技場 (arena) 周圍之矮牆。**c.** (管弦樂隊的) 指揮臺;講臺。②〖解剖,動物〗足。③〖植物〗葉柄。④室內綿延不斷之長凳。*take the podium* 開始對羣衆講演或指揮樂隊演奏。

pod·o·phyl·lin [,padə'fɪlɪn; ,pɔdə-'filin] *n.* 足葉草脂 (一種黃色樹脂, 作瀉劑用)。(亦作 **podophyllin resin**)

Po·dunk ['podʌŋk; 'poudʌŋk] *n.* 〖美謔〗(想像中典型之寧靜、單調的) 小城鎮。

Poe [po; pou] *n.* 愛倫坡 (Edgar Allan, 1809–1849, 美國詩人、小說家及批評家)。

‡**po·em** ['po·ɪm; 'pouim] *n.* ①詩篇。This is a lyric *poem.* 這是一首抒情詩。②思想高貴文字優美的作品。③美麗的東西。

po·e·sy ['po·ɪsɪ; 'pouizi] *n.*, *pl.* **-sies.** 〖古〗=**poetry.**

‡**po·et** ['po·ɪt; 'pouit] *n.* 詩人 (女詩人稱 poetess). ***poet laureate*** **a.** 桂冠詩人(英國國王指派的官方詩人, 職務爲作詩祝賀大典)。**b.** 優異之詩人。

po·et·as·ter ['po·ɪt,æstɚ; ,poui'tæs-tə] *n.* 打油詩人;劣等詩人。

***po·et·ic** [po'ɛtɪk; pou'etik] *adj.* (亦作 **poetical**) 詩的;詩人的;適合於詩或詩人的。*poetic* diction. 詩的辭藻。*poetic* licence. 寫詩爲音韻而違反文法規則之特權。 —*n.* = **poetics.**

***po·et·i·cal** [po'ɛtɪk]; pou'etikəl] *adj.* =**poetic.** 〖注意〗平常 poetic 多指詩之內容或本質, poetical 多指詩之形式。—**ly,** *adv.*

po·et·i·cize [po'ɛtə,saɪz; pou'etisaiz] *v.*, **-cized, -ciz·ing.** —*v.i.* 寫或吟詩。—*v.t.* ①使詩化。②爲某事、某場合寫詩。

po·et·ics [po'ɛtɪks; pou'etiks] *n.* (作 *sing.* 解) ①詩學;詩論。②關於詩之論文。③(P-) Aristotle之詩論。

po·et·ize ['po·ɪt,aɪz; 'pouitaiz] *v.*, **-ized, -iz·ing.** —*v.t.* ①詩化。②以詩表達。—*v.i.* 作詩。

***po·et·ry** ['po·ɪtrɪ; 'pouitri] *n.* ①詩(集合稱)。②寫詩的藝術。Have you read the great masters of English *poetry?* 你讀過英國大詩人之作品沒有? ③詩的質地與精神。There is *poetry* in his paintings. 他的畫中有詩。「彈簧單高蹺。}

po·go ['pogo; 'pougou] *n.*, *pl.* **-gos.**}

po·grom ['pogrəm; 'pɔgrəm] *n.* ①有組織的屠殺;集體屠殺 (尤指屠殺猶太人)。②對少數民族之迫害。「種芋製食品。}

po·i [pɔɪ, 'po·ɪ; pɔi, 'poui] *n.* 夏威夷的一}

poign·an·cy ['pɔɪnənsɪ; 'pɔinənsi] *n.* ①銳利;尖刻;深刻。②强烈;嚴酷。③辛辣。

poign·ant ['pɔɪnənt; 'pɔinənt] *adj.* ①痛切的; 傷心刺骨的; 尖刻的;深刻的。②銳利的;强烈的; 痛快的; 生動的。③刺激味覺或嗅覺的;辛辣的。—**ly,** *adv.*

poin·set·ti·a [pɔɪn'sɛtɪə; pɔin'setiə] *n.* 〖植物〗猩猩木(俗稱聖誕紅)。

‡**point** [pɔɪnt; pɔint] *n.* ①尖。②點。Read 4.7 as "four *point* seven."4.7讀爲"四點七." ③地點;場所。Stop at this *point.* 停在此地。④任何確定或特殊的地位; 情況或時間;程度;階段;點。⑤項目; 細節。⑥特點;特質。⑦要點;目的;寓意。I don't see your *point.* 我不懂你的意思。⑧效果;尖刻的力量。⑨方位。⑩時刻; (假想中之) 點。It was a turning *point* in his career. 這是他事業上的轉捩點。⑪突出水中之尖地;岬。⑫分數。We won by five *points.* 我們贏了五分。

⑬〖印刷〗磅因(活字大小單位約合1/72英寸)。⑭〖俗〗暗示。⑮用針刺繡的花邊。⑯〖鐵路〗轉轍器。⑰板球戲等中一球員所占之地位；站於該地位之球員。⑱〖教育〗學分。⑲〖商〗點(美國商業報價之單位，如股票以一元，棉花及咖啡以1/100分，油、穀、肉以一分為一點)。Prices on the stock exchange advanced two *points.* 股票市場的價格漲了兩點。⑳珠寶之單位，等於 1/100 carat. ㉑〖美〗貸款預扣費用(通常為貸款額百分之一)。㉒〖軍〗尖兵。***at all points*** 完全地。 ***at the point of*** 卽將；瀕於。 ***be at the point of the sword*** 在暴力的威脅下；在刀尖的威迫下。***be beside the point*** 不相干；無關重要。***be off*** (***away from,*** or ***beside***) ***the point*** 說題外閒話；離題的。***be on*** (or ***upon***) ***the point of*** 將要。 ***carry*** (or ***gain***) ***one's point*** 達到目的。 ***catch the point of*** 了解…之要點。 ***come to the point*** a. 至緊要關頭。b. 到達要點。 ***in point*** 合適的；與本題有關的；切題的。 ***in point of*** 論及；以…而論。***in point of fact*** 事實上； 就事實而論。***make*** (or ***score***) ***a point*** 證明一主張甚為正確。 ***make a point of*** 堅持；强調；認為必要或重要。 ***not to put too fine a point on it*** 坦白說出；不必加枝添葉地說。 ***point of view*** 見解；論點。 ***strain*** (or ***stretch***) ***a point*** a. (因特殊情形而)通融。b. 超過合理的限度。 ***to the point*** 中肯。—*v.t.* ①使尖；使銳利。②劃上小點；標點。③增加(言語、行動等之) 力量。④指向。⑤瞄準。⑥(獵犬)指示獵物所在處。—*v.i.* ①指；指示。What's he *pointing* at? 他在指甚麼? ②表明；表示；指明。 ***point off*** 用句點或逗點分開。***point out that*** 警告；提醒。***point up*** 强調。

point-blank [ˈpɔɪntˈblæŋk; ˈpointˈblæŋk] *adj.* ①直接瞄準的；直射的；平射的。②坦白的；率直的。—*adv.* ①直接瞄準地；直射地；平射地。②坦白地；率直地。

point-by-point [ˈpɔɪntbaɪˈpɔɪnt; ˈpointbaiˈpoint] *adj.* 逐點詳述的。

point constable 〖英〗交通警察。

point d'ap·pui [ˌpwædaˈpwi; ˈpwɛ̃dæˈpwiː] 〖法〗① 支點；據點。②作戰基地。

point-de·vice, point-de·vise [ˌpɔɪntdɪˈvaɪs; ˌpointdiˈvais] *adj.* & *adv.* 〖古〗完全的(地)；精確的 (地)。

point duty 〖英〗(交通警察等之)站崗；值勤。

***point·ed** [ˈpɔɪntɪd; ˈpointid] *adj.* ①有尖頭的；尖的。②銳敏的；銳利的。③率直的。④顯著的；加重的。He showed her *pointed* attention. 他特別注意她。⑤瞄準的。⑥針對著(某人)的。 —**ly,** *adv.* —**ness,** *n.*

point·er [ˈpɔɪntɚ; ˈpointə] *n.* ①指示者；指示物。②教鞭。③鐘針；(儀器等的) 指針。④〖軍〗瞄準手。⑤一種短毛之獵犬。⑥〖美俗〗暗示；提示。⑦〖海軍〗司調整砲位的射擊手。⑧(P-)(*pl.*)〖天文〗指極星。

Point Four 美國總統杜魯門1949年發表之政策的第四項(對未開發地區的援助計畫)。

poin·til·lism [ˈpwæntəlɪzəm; ˈpwæntilizm] *n.* 〖美術〗(法國印象派的)點描畫法。—**poin·til·list,** *n., adj.*

point·ing [ˈpɔɪntɪŋ; ˈpointiŋ] *n.* ①弄尖；指示。②標點(法)。③〖建築〗(磚縫的)嵌塡。

point lace 針織花邊；手工花邊。

point·less [ˈpɔɪntlɪs; ˈpointlis] *adj.* ①無尖的；鈍的。②無力量的；無意義的；無目標的。③無分數的。—**ly,** *adv.* —**ness,** *n.*

point of departure ①〖航海〗開航點。②出發點。

point of honor 有關一己的名譽之事；面子問題。

point of no return 極限點(超過此點卽不能安全回程)。

point of order 關於議事程序的問題。

point of view ①觀點。②意見。

points·man [ˈpɔɪntsmən; ˈpointsmən] *n., pl.* **-men.** 〖英〗①〖鐵路〗轉轍手；搬閘夫。②值崗的交通警察。

points of the compass 羅盤的32 個方位。

point system ①〖印刷〗磅因制 (以一point, 約合1/72英寸，為單位區分鉛字大小)。②(盲人的)點字法。③〖教育〗評分升級制。

point-to-point [ˈpɔɪnttəˈpɔɪnt; ˈpointtəˈpoint] *adj.* ①從一點直接至他點的；越野的(賽跑等)。②直接的。

***poise** [pɔɪz; poiz] *n., v.,* **poised, pois·ing.** —*n.* ① 精神均衡；寧靜； 泰然自若。②姿態。She has a fine *poise.* 她有優美的姿態。③平衡；均衡。④暫停。⑤猶豫。—*v.t.* ①使均衡。*Poise* yourself on your toes. 用脚尖站立使你保持平衡。②考慮。—*v.i.* 均衡；保持平衡。

poised [pɔɪzd; poizd] *adj.* ①泰然自若的。②平衡的。③搖擺不定的。④懸在半空的。

***poi·son** [ˈpɔɪzn̩; ˈpoizn] *n.* ①毒藥；毒物。rat *poison.* 毒老鼠藥。②敗壞道德之事。③〖俚〗酒類。—*v.t.* ①毒殺；毒害。②置毒於。③敗壞。Slander *poisoned* his mind. 誹謗毀了他的意志。④摧毀；毀掉。—*adj.* 有毒的。—**less,** *adj.* —**less·ness,** *n.*

poi·son·er [ˈpɔɪzn̩ɚ; ˈpoiznə] *n.* ①毒殺者；放毒者。②毒物。

poison gas 毒氣。

poi·son·ing [ˈpɔɪznɪŋ; ˈpoizn̩iŋ] *n.* ①置毒；毒害。②中毒。

poison ivy 〖植物〗野葛。

poison oak 〖植物〗①=**poison ivy.** ②=**poison sumac.**

***poi·son·ous** [ˈpɔɪzn̩əs; ˈpoiznəs] *adj.* ①有毒的。 The snake's bite is sometimes *poisonous.* 蛇咬有時是有毒的。②可厭的；令人不能忍受的。③敗德的；有壞影響的。—**ly,** *adv.* —**ness,** *n.*

poi·son-pen [ˈpɔɪzn̩ˈpɛn; ˈpoiznˈpen] *adj.* ①(信函等)匿名而有惡意的。②匿名而有惡意的信的；毀謗作品的。

poison sumac 〖植物〗生於濕地而有毒的鹽膚木。

poke**¹ [pok; pouk] *v.,* **poked, pok·ing,** *n.* —*v.t.* ①(以尖物)刺；撥；碰；衝。②干預；管閒事。③指。The prosecutor kept *poking* his finger at the defendant. 檢察官老指着被告。—*v.i.* ①游蕩〖常along〗。②尋求〖常around, about〗。③刺；衝。④突出〖常out〗。⑤管閒事。 ***poke fun at (參看 **make fun of**) 嘲弄。 ***poke one's nose into other people's business*** 管閒事；干預他人之事。—*n.* ①刺；碰；衝；戳。②懶惰的人。

poke² *n.* ①〖方〗袋；囊。②〖古〗小口袋；皮夾子。***buy a pig in a poke*** 瞎買東西。

poke³ *n.* =**pokeweed.**

poke⁴ *n.* ①女帽之前緣， 圍着臉龐者。②=**poke bonnet.**

poke·ber·ry [ˈpokˌbɛrɪ; ˈpoukˌberi] *n., pl.* **-ries.** ①〖植物〗 一種商陸 (=pokeweed)。②其果實。

poke bonnet 帽緣向前伸出之女帽；有撐邊的女帽。

pok·er¹ [ˈpokɚ; ˈpoukə] *n.* 撲克牌戲。

pok·er² *n.* ①撥火鐵棒。②刺、衝、碰的人或事物。

poker face〖美俗〗(如撲克牌的能手之對於手中牌不動聲色的)無表情的面孔。
poker work (在白木上做的)烙畫;焦筆畫。(亦作 **pokerwork**)
poke·sy ['poksɪ; 'pouksi] *adj.* 遲緩的;「隨和的。
poke·weed ['pok,wid; 'pouk-wi:d] *n.* 〖植物〗(北美產的)一種商陸。(亦作 **pokeroot, scoke**)
pok·(e)y ['pokɪ; 'pouki] *adj.*, **pok·i·er, pok·i·est,** *n., pl.* **pok·eys, pok·ies.** —*adj.* ①無精打采的;遲鈍的;緩慢的。②狹小擁擠的。③襤褸的;破舊的。—*n.* 〖俚〗監獄。
Pol. ①Poland. ②(亦作 **Pol**) Polish.
pol. ①political. ②politics.
Po·lack ['polæk; 'poulæk] *n.* ①〖廢〗波蘭人。②有波蘭血統的人(輕蔑語)。
Po·land ['polənd; 'poulənd] *n.* 波蘭(歐洲中部國名,首都爲華沙 Warsaw).
Poland China (hog) (美國產的)一種有白花的黑豬。
***po·lar** ['polɚ; 'poulə] *adj.* ①近北極或南極的;屬於北極或南極的。②(電池之)正負極的。③磁極的。④極端相反的;南轅北轍的。⑤中心的。⑥嚮導的;引導的。
polar bear 北極熊。
polar cap 火星兩極處之白色區域。
polar circles 極圈。
polar coordinates〖數學〗極座標。
po·lar·im·e·ter [,polə'rɪmətɚ; ,pou-lə'rimitə] *n.* 〖光學〗偏極計。
Po·lar·is [po'lɛrɪs; pou'lɛəris] *n.* ①北極星飛彈。②〖天文〗北極星。
po·lar·i·scope [po'lærə,skop; pou-'læriskoup] *n.* 〖光學〗偏極光鏡。
po·lar·i·ty [po'lærətɪ; pou'læriti] *n.* ①〖物理〗兩極性;(陰、陽)極性;磁性引力。②〖生物〗(植物之莖與根或動物之頭與尾之)反向性;極性。③(主義、性格等的)正相反。
po·lar·i·za·tion [,polərə'zeʃən; ,pou-lərai'zeiʃən] *n.* ①生極性;得極性。②〖電〗成極作用;極化。③〖光學〗偏極;偏極化。④(集團、思想、勢力等的)分裂爲二;分裂。
po·lar·ize ['polə,raɪz; 'pouləraiz] *v.t.,* **-ized, -iz·ing.** ①〖電〗賦與極性;使極化。*polarizing* action. 極化作用。②〖光學〗使偏光。*polarized* light. 偏光。③使(思想等)偏向。
po·lar·iz·er ['polə,raɪzɚ; 'pouləraizə] *n.* 〖光學〗偏光器;起偏鏡。
polar lights (南、北)極光。
po·lar·oid ['polə,rɔɪd; 'poulərɔid] *n.* ①人造偏光板。②(P-) 其商標名。
pol·der ['poldɚ; 'pouldə] *n.* (荷蘭沿海的)新填築之低地。
Pole [pol; poul] *n.* 波蘭人。
‡**pole**[1] [pol; poul] *n., v.,* **poled, pol·ing.** —*n.* ①竿;柱;桿。②馬車的轅桿。③長度單位名(合5½碼)。④面積單位名(30¼平方碼)。***under bare poles***(船)不張帆航行。***up the pole*** a. 在困難中。b. 瘋狂;發瘋。—*v.t.*〖美〗①以竿撐(船)。②〖棒球,俚〗擊出(二、三壘安打或全壘打)。③供以竿。—*v.i.* 撐船。
***pole**[2] *n.* ①(南、北)極。North *Pole.* 北極。South *Pole.* 南極。②南北兩極附近地帶。③磁極;電極。④任何球軸的兩端。⑤相對;相反。He and his brother are *poles* apart (*or* asunder). 他和他的弟弟完全相反。⑥注意或興趣集中點。⑦〖解剖〗極。⑧〖數學〗極;極點。
pole·ax(e) ['pol,æks; 'poulæks] *n., pl.* **-ax·es** [-,æksɪz; -æksiz], *v.,* **-axed, -ax·ing.** —*n.* ①戰斧;鉞。②殺家畜用之屠斧。—*v.t.* 以斧砍倒或攻打。
pole·cat ['pol,kæt; 'poulkæt] *n.* ①臭貓。②北美產之臭鼬類。
Pol. Econ., pol. econ. political「economy.
pole jump =**pole vault.**
po·lem·ic [po'lɛmɪk; pɔ'lemik] *n.* ①爭論;辯論;論戰。②爭論者;辯論者。—*adj.* (亦作 **polemical**) 爭論的;辯論的。—**al·ly,** *adv.*
po·len·ta [po'lɛntə; pou'lentə] *n.* (義大利人吃的)大麥粥;玉蜀黍粉粥;粟粉粥。
pole position 有利位置。
pole·star ['pol,stɑr; 'poul-stɑ:] *n.* ①北極星。②指標;目標;指導原則。
pole vault 撐竿跳高。
pole-vault ['pol,vɔlt; 'poulvɔ:lt] *v.i.* 作撐竿跳高。—**er,** *n.*
‡**po·lice** [pə'lis; pə'li:s, pou'l-] *n., v.,* **-liced, -lic·ing.** —*n.* ①警察局。②警察。③公安;治安。④〖美陸軍〗營房、營區之整理;營房、營區之整潔狀況。—*v.t.* ①使有秩序;整頓。②以警察管治(一地區)。③管理;管治。〖注意〗**police**一字爲警察及警察局之集合稱,作主詞用時後跟複數動詞。
police action 未經正式宣戰,對游擊隊或叛亂等破壞國際和平者之鎮壓行動。
police box (or **stand**) 警察崗亭。
police constable 警察;警員。
police court 違警罪法庭。
police dog ①警犬。②狼犬。
police inspector 巡官。
police magistrate 違警罪法庭推事。
***po·lice·man** [pə'lismən; pə'li:smən, pou'li:s-] *n., pl.* **-men.** 警察。—**like,** *adj.*
police offense 違警(罪)。
police office〖英〗(市、鎮的)警察局。
police officer ①警官。②警員。
police reporter 採訪警方消息之記者。
police sergeant 警佐。
police state 警察國家(政府有極端統治權之國家)。「(亦作 **station house**)
police station 警察分局;警察派出所。
po·lice·wom·an [pə'lis,wumən; pə-'li:s,wumən] *n., pl.* **-wom·en.** 女警察。
pol·i·clin·ic [,pɑlɪ'klɪnɪk; ,pɔli'klinik] *n.* (病院的)門診部。
***pol·i·cy**[1] ['pɑləsɪ; 'pɔlisi, -ləs-] *n., pl.* **-cies.** ①政策;方針。the foreign *policy* of a country. 一國之外交政策。②治術;權謀。③智慧;深慮。*Policy* demands occasional compromise. 偶而妥協爲深謀遠慮所必需。
pol·i·cy[2] *n., pl.* **-cies.** ①保險單。②搖彩賭博。
pol·i·cy·hold·er ['pɑləsɪ,holdɚ; 'pɔ-lisi,houldə] *n.* 保險客戶;被保人。
pol·i·cy·mak·er ['pɑləsɪ,mekɚ; 'pɔ-lisi,meikə] *n.* 決策者;重要官員。
policy racket〖美〗一種非法搖彩賭博。
po·li·me·tri·cian [,polɪmɛ'trɪʃən; ,poulime'triʃən] *n.* 精於數學及統計學的政治學家。
pol·i·o·my·e·li·tis [,pɑlɪo,maɪə'laɪ-tɪs; ,pɔliou,maiə'laitis] *n.* 〖醫〗小兒麻痺症;脊髓灰白質炎。(亦作 **polio**)
Pol·ish ['polɪʃ; 'pouliʃ] *adj.* 波蘭的;波蘭人的;波蘭語的。—*n.* 波蘭語。
pol·ish** ['pɑlɪʃ; 'pɔliʃ] *v.t.* ①磨光;擦亮。②使優雅;潤飾;洗鍊。His speech needs *polishing.* 他的言語需要潤飾。—*v.i.* 發光澤;變爲光滑。This wood won't *polish.* 這木頭漆不光。polish off*** a.〖俗〗很快地用完;吃

完;做完。b.〖俚〗打倒(某人);擺脫(某人)。*polish up* 使較美觀;改良。—*n.* ①生光澤之物;油漆等物。shoe *polish.* 鞋油。②光澤;光滑。③優雅;精良。

pol·ished [ˈpɑlɪʃt; ˈpɔliʃt] *adj.* ①磨光的;擦亮的;有光澤的。②優美的;文雅的;洗鍊的。③無錯誤的。

pol·ish·er [ˈpɑlɪʃɚ; ˈpɔliʃə] *n.* 磨光之人或物;磨匠。

Po·lit·bu·ro [pəˈlɪtbjuro; pɔˈlitbjuərou] *n.* (蘇聯的)共產黨中央執行委員會政治局(1952 年為 Presidium 所取代)。(亦作 **Politbureau**)

***po·lite** [pəˈlaɪt; pəˈlait, poˈl–] *adj.* ①有禮貌的;客氣的。②文雅的;上流的。 —**ly,** *adv.* —**ness,** *n.*

polite letters 純文學。

pol·i·tic [ˈpɑlə,tɪk; ˈpɔlitik, –lət–] *adj.* ①有智慮的;明達的;精明的。②狡詐的。③有策略的;權宜的。④政治上的。—**ly,** *adv.*

‡po·lit·i·cal [pəˈlɪtɪkl; pəˈlitikəl, poˈl–] *adj.* ①政治學的。*political* economy. 經濟學。②政治上的;政治的。*political* liberties. 政治自由。a *political* prisoner. 政治犯。③政客的;政黨的。a *political* campaign. 政黨選擧。—**ly,** *adv.*

political animal 政治動物(有政治天賦或學問而幹勁十足的政壇人物)。

political asylum 政治庇護。

po·lit·i·cal·ize [pəˈlɪtɪkl,aɪz; pəˈlitikəlaiz] *v.t.,* **-ized, -iz·ing.** 使政治化;使帶政治色彩。—**po·lit·i·cal·i·za·tion,** *n.*

political science 政治學。

political scientist 政治學家。

***pol·i·ti·cian** [,pɑləˈtɪʃən; ,pɔliˈtiʃən, –ləˈt–] *n.* 政治家; 政客; 從政者。〖注意〗politician 略帶輕蔑, statesman 則强調好的一面。

po·lit·i·cize [pəˈlɪtə,saɪz; pəˈlitisaiz] *v.,* **-cized, -ciz·ing.** —*v.t.* ①使政治化;使政黨化。②從政治上討論。—*v.i.* 從政; 參與政事;談論政治。

po·lit·i·co [pəˈlɪtɪ,ko; pəˈlitikou] *n., pl.* **-cos.** =**politician.**

politico- 〖字首〗表"政治與…上的"之義, 如: politicomoral. 政治道德上的。

pol·i·tics [ˈpɑlə,tɪks; ˈpɔlitiks, –lət–] *n.* (作 *sing.* or *pl.* 解) ①政治學。②政論;政治活動。He was engaged in *politics* for many years. 他從事政治活動多年。③政治策略;政治手腕。④(P–) Aristotle 之政治論。*play politics* 玩政治手段(祇圖利益不論是非之手段)。〖注意〗politics可作單數或複數解,但在同段文字中應該統一,不要兩者互用。

pol·i·ty [ˈpɑlətɪ; ˈpɔliti] *n., pl.* **-ties.** ①政府;政治制度。②特殊的政體;國體。③有政府之地區;國家。

pol·ka [ˈpolkə; ˈpɔlkə] *n., pl.* **-kas,** *v.,* **-kaed, -ka·ing.** —*n.* ①波加舞(一種輕快雙人圓舞)。②波加圓舞曲。—*v.i.* 跳波加舞。

polka dot (衣料花樣的)圓點; (衣料的)圓點花樣。

Poll [pɑl; pɔl] *n.* 鸚鵡的俗稱。(亦作 **poll**)

***poll¹** [pol; poul] *n.* ①選擧之投票;所投之票(集合稱)。②投票數目; 投票結果。③投票者人名簿。④ (*pl.*) 〖美〗投票及點票處。⑤〖古〗人頭。⑥一個人; 個人。⑦民意測驗。—*v.t.* ①獲 (選擧票)。He *polled* 25,000 votes. 他獲得兩萬五千張選票。②投(票)。A large vote was *polled.* 投票極為踴躍。③登記…之選票。④(民意測驗中)訪問。⑤剪短…之髮、毛、角、枝等。 —*v.i.* 投票。—*adj.* 〖主英〗無角的。—**a·ble,** *adj.*

poll² [pɑl; pɔl] *n.* 〖英〗(劍橋大學的)普通畢業生(對優等畢業生, honoursman, 而言)。

pol·lack [ˈpɑlək; ˈpɔlək] *n., pl.* **-lack, -lacks.** 鱈屬之魚;狹鱈。

pol·lard [ˈpɑlɚd; ˈpɔləd] *n.* ①頂部枝條被剪削之樹木(以便新生枝葉更密);截頭樹。②解角鹿; 無角之牛、羊等; 無角獸。—*v.t.* 使成截頭樹。

poll-beast [ˈpolbist; ˈpoulbiːst] *n.* 無角牛的一種。

poll·book [ˈpol,buk; ˈpoulbuk] *n.* 選擧人名册。

pol·len [ˈpɑlən; ˈpɔlin, –lən] *n.* 花粉。—*v.t.* 授以花粉。

pol·li·nate [ˈpɑlə,net; ˈpɔlineit] *v.t.,* **-nat·ed, -nat·ing.** 〖植物〗授以花粉。

pol·li·na·tion [,pɑləˈneʃən; ,pɔliˈneiʃən] *n.* 授粉;授粉作用。

poll·ist [ˈpolɪst; ˈpoulist] *n.* =**pollster.**

pol·li·wog, pol·ly·wog [ˈpɑlɪ,wɑg; ˈpɔliwɔg] *n.* 蝌蚪。

pol·lock [ˈpɑlək; ˈpɔlək] *n.* =**pollack.**

poll-ox [ˈpol,ɑks; ˈpoulɔks] *n.* = **poll-beast.**

poll parrot 〖俗〗(受人飼養的)鸚鵡。(亦作 **Poll, Polly**)

poll·ster [ˈpolstɚ; ˈpoulstə] *n.* 民意測驗家。

poll tax 人頭稅。

poll-tax·er [ˈpol,tæksɚ; ˈpoul,tæksə] *n.* (美國) 自有人頭稅之州選出的國會議員。

pol·lu·tant [pəˈlutnt; pəˈluːtnt] *n.* 引起汚染之物。

pol·lute [pəˈlut; pəˈluːt] *v.t.,* **-lut·ed, -lut·ing.** 玷汚;褻瀆;汚染。—**pol·lut·er,** *n.*

pol·lut·ed [pəˈlutɪd; pəˈluːtid] *adj.* ①汚染的。②〖俚〗喝醉的。 —**ness,** *n.*

pol·lu·tion [pəˈluʃən; pəˈluːʃən] *n.* 玷汚;褻瀆;汚染。air *pollution.* 空氣汚染。

poll watcher (投票所之)監票人;監察人(看是否有違法競選者)。(亦作 **watcher**)

Pol·ly·an·na [,pɑlɪˈænə; ,pɔliˈænə] *n.* (有時 p–) 極端樂觀的人(美國 Eleanor Porter 所著小說中的女主角)。—**ish,** *adj.*

Po·lo [ˈpolo; ˈpoulou] *n.* 馬可波羅(Marco, 1254?–?1324, 義大利旅行家)。

po·lo [ˈpolo; ˈpoulou] *n.* ①馬球(類似曲棍球之一種馬上遊戲)。 ②與馬球相類之各種遊戲;水球。*water polo* 水球。—**ist,** *n.*

pol·o·naise [,pɑləˈnez; ,pɔləˈneiz] *n.* ①一種起源於波蘭之慢步舞; 波蘭舞; 波蘭舞曲。②(源自波蘭女人穿著之) 一種女衣。

po·lo·ni·um [pəˈlonɪəm; pəˈlouniəm] *n.* 〖化〗釙(一種放射性元素,符號 Po)。

Po·lo·nize [ˈpolə,naɪz; ˈpoulənaiz] *v.t.,* **-nized, -niz·ing.** ①使(風俗等)波蘭化。②使波蘭語化。 —**Po·lo·ni·za·tion,** *n.*

po·lo·ny [pəˈlonɪ; pəˈlouni] *n.* 一種豬肉香腸;臘腸。

polo shirt 一種短袖、套頭、圓領的棉衫。

pol·ter·geist [ˈpoltɚ,gaɪst; ˈpoultəgaist] 〖德〗 *n.* 吵鬧的鬼。

pol·troon [pɑlˈtrun; pɔlˈtruːn] *n.* 膽怯者;懦夫。

pol·troon·er·y [pɑlˈtrunərɪ; pɔlˈtruːnəri] *n.* 膽怯;怯懦。

poly- 〖字首〗表"多於一的; 多的; 廣濶的"之義, 如 polyangular 多角的。

pol·y·an·drous [,pɑlɪˈændrəs; ,pɔliˈændrəs] *adj.* ①一妻多夫的。②〖動物〗一雌多雄的。③〖植物〗多雄蕊的。

pol·y·an·dry [ˈpɑlɪ,ændrɪ; ˈpɔliændri] *n.* ①一妻多夫; 一妻多夫制。②〖動物〗一雌多雄。③〖植物〗多雄蕊。

pol·y·an·thus 〔,palɪ'ænθəs; ,pɔli'ænθəs〕 *n., pl.* **-thus·es.** 〖植物〗①黃花九輪草。②一種水仙。

pol·y·bas·ic 〔,palɪ'besɪk; ,pɔli'beisik〕 *adj.* 〖化〗多鹽基的。**—i·ty,** *n.*

pol·y·car·pic 〔,palɪ'karpɪk; ,pɔli'ka:pik〕 *adj.* 〖植物〗①結實多次的。②有多子房之雌蕊的。

pol·y·car·pous 〔,palɪ'karpəs; ,pɔli'ka:pəs〕 *adj.* 〖植物〗①多心皮的。②＝**polycarpic.**

pol·y·cen·trism 〔,palɪ'sɛntrɪzəm; ,pɔli'sentrizəm〕 *n.* (共產黨)多元論(主張各共產國家可准予作有限度的獨立，並對共產主義教條作不同的解釋)。

pol·y·chro·mat·ic 〔,palɪkro'mætɪk; ,pɔlikrou'mætik〕 *adj.* 多色的。

pol·y·chrome 〔'palɪ,krom; 'pɔlikroum〕 *adj., n., v.,* **-chromed, -chrom·ing.** —*adj.* ①＝**polychromatic.** ②多色彩飾的；多色印刷的。—*n.* 多色畫；彩像；色彩配合。—*v.t.* 以多色畫。**—pol·y·chro·my,** *n.*

pol·y·clin·ic 〔,palɪ'klɪnɪk; ,pɔli'klinik〕 *n.* 聯合診所；全科臨床講習(所)；綜合醫院。

pol·y·es·ter 〔,palɪ'ɛstɚ; ,pɔli'estə〕 *n.* 〖化〗多元酯。

pol·y·eth·yl·ene 〔,palɪ'ɛθɪlin; ,pɔli'eθili:n〕 *n.* 〖化〗聚乙烯。

po·lyg·a·mist 〔pə'lɪgəmɪst; pɔ'ligəmist〕 *n.* ①實行或贊成一夫多妻者。②贊成或實行一妻多夫者。**—ic,** *adj.*

po·lyg·a·mous 〔pə'lɪgəməs; pɔ'ligəməs〕 *adj.* ①一夫多妻的；一妻多夫的；多婚性的。②〖植物〗同株或異株上有兩性及單性花的。**—ly,** *adv.*

po·lyg·a·my 〔pə'lɪgəmɪ; pɔ'ligəmi〕 *n.* ①一夫多妻；一妻多夫。②〖動物〗多婚性(同時與兩個以上異性同住之習慣)。

pol·y·glot 〔'palɪ,glat; 'pɔliglɔt〕 *adj.* ①通曉數種語言的。②用數種語言寫成的。—*n.* ①通曉數種語言的人。②用數種語言寫成的書(如聖經)。③數種語言之混雜。

pol·y·gon 〔'palɪ,gan; 'pɔligən〕 *n.* (通常指四角以上的)多角形；多邊形。

po·lyg·o·nal 〔pə'lɪgənl; pə'ligənəl〕 *adj.* 四邊或四邊以上的；多邊的。

pol·y·graph 〔'palɪ,græf; 'pɔligra:f〕 *n.* ①複寫器；謄寫版。②多產作家。③多種描記器(同時記錄血壓、呼吸、脈搏等之變化的一種記錄器)。④測謊器。**—ic,** *adj.*

po·lyg·y·nist 〔pə'lɪdʒənɪst; pə'lidʒənist〕 *n.* 一夫多妻主義者；多妻的人。

po·lyg·y·nous 〔pə'lɪdʒənəs; pə'lidʒənəs〕 *adj.* ①一夫多妻的。②〖植物〗多雌蕊的。

po·lyg·y·ny 〔pə'lɪdʒənɪ; pə'lidʒəni〕 *n.* ①一夫多妻。②〖植物〗多雌蕊。

pol·y·he·dron 〔,palɪ'hidrən; ,pɔli'hedrən〕 *n., pl.* **-dra** 〔-drə; -drə〕, **-drons.** 〖數學〗多面體；多面形。**—pol·y·he·dral,** *adj.*

Pol·y·hym·ni·a 〔,palɪ'hɪmnɪə; ,pɔli'himniə〕 *n.* 〖希臘神話〗司聖歌之女神(Nine Muses 中之一)。(亦作 **Polymnia**)

pol·y·mer 〔'palɪmɚ; 'pɔlimə〕 *n.* 〖化〗聚合體；異量體。

pol·y·mer·ic 〔,palɪ'mɛrɪk; ,pɔli'mεərik〕 *adj.* 〖化〗異量的；聚合的；聚合體的。

po·lym·er·i·za·tion 〔,palɪmərɪ'zeʃən; ,pɔliməraі'zeiʃən〕 *n.* 〖化〗聚合(作用)。

pol·y·mer·ize 〔'palɪmə,raɪz; 'pɔliməraiz〕 *v.t. & v.i.,* **-ized, -iz·ing.** 〖化〗(使)聚合。

pol·y·mor·phic 〔,palɪ'mɔrfɪk; ,pɔli'mɔ:fik〕 *adj.* ＝**polymorphous.**

pol·y·mor·phism 〔,palɪ'mɔrfɪzm; ,pɔli'mɔ:fizm〕 *n.* ①〖結晶〗同質異像。②〖化〗多形。③〖生物〗多形(現象)。

pol·y·mor·phous 〔,palɪ'mɔrfəs; ,pɔli'mɔ:fəs〕 *adj.* 多形的；多形態的。

Pol·y·ne·sia 〔,palə'niʒə; ,pɔli'ni:ziə〕 *n.* 玻里尼西亞(中太平洋之一羣島，位於北緯30°與南緯47°間)。

Pol·y·ne·sian 〔,palə'niʒən; ,pɔli'ni:ziən〕 *n.* ①玻里尼西亞人。②玻里尼西亞語言。—*adj.* 玻里尼西亞的；玻里尼西亞人的；玻里尼西亞語的。

pol·y·no·mi·al 〔,palɪ'nomɪəl; ,pɔli'noumiəl〕 *adj.* ①〖數學〗多項的。②〖生物〗多名式的。—*n.* ①多名。②〖數學〗多項式。③〖生物〗多名式學名。

pol·yp 〔'palɪp; 'pɔlip〕 *n.* ①〖動物〗水螅。②〖醫〗息肉(鼻道等黏液面的突起生長物，或爲瘤腫，或爲黏膜的肥大)。

pol·y·pha·gi·a 〔,palɪ'fedʒɪə; ,pɔli'feidʒiə〕 *n.* ①〖醫〗多食症；貪食症。②〖動物〗雜食性。

pol·y·phase 〔'palɪ,fez; 'pɔlifeiz〕 *adj.* 〖電〗多相的。

pol·y·phone 〔'palɪ,fon; 'pɔlifoun〕 *n.* 〖語音〗多音字母(如 read 中之 ea，可讀作〔i; i:〕及〔ε; e〕)；多音符號。

pol·y·phon·ic 〔,palɪ'fanɪk; ,pɔli'fɔnik〕 *adj.* ①多音的。②〖音樂〗**a.** 複調的；對位法上的。**b.** 可同時奏出兩個以上之聲部的(如風琴等)。③〖語音〗(字母等)多音的。

po·lyph·o·ny 〔pə'lɪfənɪ; pə'lifəni〕 *n.* ①多音；多響。②〖音樂〗多聲部樂曲；複調音樂；對位法。③〖語音〗用同一字母或符號代表數音。

pol·y·po·dy 〔'palɪ,podɪ; 'pɔlipədi〕 *n., pl.* **-dies.** 〖植物〗瓦葦屬之植物。

pol·yp·oid 〔'palɪp,ɔɪd; 'pɔlipɔid〕 *adj.* ①〖動物〗似水螅的。②〖醫〗似息肉的。

pol·y·pous 〔'palɪpəs; 'pɔlipəs〕 *adj.* 〖動物〗似水螅的；水螅狀的。

pol·y·pro·py·lene 〔,palɪ'propɪlin; ,pɔli'proupili:n〕 *n.* 〖化〗聚丙烯。

pol·y·pus 〔'paləpəs; 'pɔlipəs〕 *n., pl.* **-pi** 〔-,paɪ; -pai〕, **-pus·es.** ＝**polyp.**

pol·y·sac·cha·ride, pol·y·sac·cha·rid 〔,palɪ'sækə,raɪd; ,pɔli'sækəraid〕 *n.* 〖化〗多醣類。(亦作 **polysaccharose**)

pol·y·sty·rene 〔,palɪ'staɪrin; ,pɔli'stairi:n〕 *n.* 〖化〗多苯乙烯。

pol·y·syl·lab·ic 〔,paləsɪ'læbɪk; 'pɔlisi'læbik〕 *adj.* 多音節的；多於三個音節的。(亦作 **polysyllabical**)

pol·y·syl·la·ble 〔'palə,sɪləbl; 'pɔli,siləbl〕 *n.* 多音節的字；多於三個音節的字。

pol·y·tech·nic 〔,palə'tɛknɪk; ,pɔli'teknik〕 *adj.* 多藝的；各種工藝的；多種學藝的。—*n.* 工藝學校；工業學校。

pol·y·the·ism 〔'paləθi,ɪzəm; 'pɔliθi:izəm〕 *n.* 多神論；多神教。

pol·y·the·ist 〔'palə,θiɪst; 'pɔliθi:ist〕 *n.* 多神論者；信仰多神論者；多神教徒。—*adj.* ＝**polytheistic.**

pol·y·the·is·tic 〔,paləθi'ɪstɪk; ,pɔliθi:'istik〕 *adj.* 多神論的；多神教的；信多神教的。

pol·y·vi·nyl 〔,palɪ'vaɪnɪl; ,pɔli'vainil〕 *adj.* 〖化〗聚合乙烯基的；多乙烯的。

polyvinyl acetate 多乙酸乙烯酯。

pom·ace ['pʌmɪs; 'pʌmis] *n.* ①(爲製蘋果酒等而) 壓碎的蘋果漿或其他水果漿。②任何東西經壓榨後之渣粕;魚渣;蓖麻油渣。

po·ma·ceous [po'meʃəs; pou'meiʃəs] *adj.* ①【植物】梨果的; 梨果狀的。②【詩】有關蘋果的。

po·made [po'med; pə'mɑːd] *n., v.,* **-mad·ed, -mad·ing.** —*n.* 髮油;頭油。—*v.t.* 塗髮油。(亦作 **pomatum**)

po·man·der ['pomændɚ, pə'mæn-; pou'mændə] *n.* 【史】(昔日佩於身上以防疫病的)香盒;香袋。

pome [pom; poum] *n.* 【植物】梨果(卽蘋果、梨、榲桲等)。

pome·gran·ate ['pʌm,grænɪt; 'pɔmgrænit] *n.* ①石榴。②石榴樹。

pom·e·lo ['pɑmə,lo; 'pɔmilou] *n., pl.* **-los.** 【植物】柚子。

pom·fret ['pɑmfrɪt; 'pɔmfrit] *n.* (太平洋、印度洋產的)一種鯧魚。

po·mi·cul·ture ['pomɪ,kʌltʃɚ; 'poumi,kʌltʃə] *n.* 果樹栽培。

pom·mel ['pʌml̩; 'pʌml̩] *n., v.,* **-mel(l)ed, -mel·(l)ing.** —*n.* ①鞍頭(鞍最前端向上突起之部分)。②劍等柄端之圓球;橘頭。—*v.t.* 以橘頭或拳打擊;毆打。(亦作 **pummel**)

pom·my ['pɑmɪ; 'pɔmi] *n., pl.* **-mies.** 【澳俚】①新到之英國移民。②英國人。

po·mol·o·gy [po'mɑlədʒɪ; pou'mɔlədʒi] *n.* 果樹栽培學。

Po·mo·na [pə'monə; pə'mounə, pou'm-] *n.* 【羅馬神話】果樹之女神。

***pomp** [pɑmp; pɔmp] *n.* ①盛觀; 壯麗。The king was crowned with great *pomp.* 國王加冕典禮極爲隆重。②(*pl.*)誇耀;誇示。—**less,** *adj.*

pom·pa·dour ['pɑmpə,dor; 'pɔmpəduə] *n.* ①前髮梳高的女子髮型; 一種向後梳起的男子髮式。②一種胸部開低而成方型的女用胸衣。③一種帶綠的藍色。

pom·pa·no ['pɑmpə,no; 'pɔmpənou] *n., pl.* **-nos.** ①(北美產的)一種鰹(食用)。②(西印度產之)一種鰺(食用)。

Pom·pe·ii [pɑm'pe·i; pɔm'piːai] *n.* 龐貝(義大利西南部 Vesuvius 火山山麓之一古城, 於西元79年因火山爆發而埋入地下)。

Pom·pey the Great ['pɑmpɪ~~; 'pɔmpi~~] 龐培大將 (106–48 B. C., 羅馬大將及政治家)。

pom·pom ['pɑm,pɑm; 'pɔmpɔm] *n.* ①小口徑速射砲。②高射機關砲。(亦作 **pom-pom**)

pom·pon ['pɑmpɑn; 'pɔːmpɔːŋ, 'pɔmpɔn] *n., pl.* **-pons.** ①(軍帽的)毛章。②絨球;絲球(婦女、孩童鞋帽上的裝飾)。③一種開小球形之花的菊花。

pom·pos·i·ty [pɑm'pɑsətɪ; pɔm'pɔsiti] *n., pl.* **-ties.** ①豪華; 華麗; 誇耀。②誇大;傲慢;自大;誇大的行爲、言詞或動作。

pom·pous ['pɑmpəs; 'pɔmpəs] *adj.* ①誇大的;傲慢的;自大的。②華而不實的。③莊嚴炫赫的;鋪張的。—**ly,** *adv.* —**ness,** *n.*

pon·ceau [pɑn'so, 'pɑnso; pɔn'sou, 'pɔnsou] *n.* ①【植物】麗春花。②鮮紅色(染料)。

pon·cho ['pɑntʃo; 'pɔntʃou] *n., pl.* **-chos.** 一種氈狀的寬大防水衣(中開一洞, 供頭部伸出)。—**ed,** *adj.*

‡**pond** [pɑnd; pɔnd] *n.* 池塘。

pond·age ['pɑndɪdʒ; 'pɔndidʒ] *n.* (池的)貯水量。

pon·der ['pɑndɚ; 'pɔndə] *v.t. & v.i.* 考慮;沉思。to *ponder* a question. 考慮一問題。—**er,** *n.*

pon·der·a·ble ['pɑndərəbl; 'pɔndərəbl] *adj.* ①有重量可量的;可估計的。②可深慮的。—*n.* 可予考慮的事物;值得一想的事物。—**pon·der·a·bil·i·ty,** —**ness,** *n.*

pon·der·os·i·ty [,pɑndə'rɑsətɪ; ,pɔndə'rɔsiti] *n.* 重;沉重;笨重;呆鈍;沉悶;呆板。

pon·der·ous ['pɑndərəs; 'pɔndərəs] *adj.* ①沉重的。②笨重的。③令人厭倦的。—**ly,** *adv.* —**ness,** *n.*

pond life 在池塘中生活的小動物。

pond lily 【植物】睡蓮(＝water lily).

pond scum ①死水上面浮的綠藻。②由此等綠藻所形成之一層。

pond·weed ['pɑnd,wid; 'pɔndwiːd] *n.* 【植物】眼子菜(一種水草)。

pone[1] [pon; poun] *n.* 【美國南部】(一塊)玉米麪包。

pone[2] ['ponɪ; 'pouniː] *n.* 【牌戲】切牌的人;莊家(通常爲在分牌人右邊的人)。

pone[3] [pon; poun] *n.* 【美國南部】疙疸;瘤;腫塊。

pon·gee [pɑn'dʒi; pɔn'dʒiː] *n.* 繭綢;府綢。

pon·iard ['pɑnjɚd; 'pɔnjəd] *n.* 匕首;短劍。—*v.t.* 刺以匕首;用短劍戳。

pons [pɑnz; pɔnz] *n., pl.* **pon·tes** ['pɑntiz; 'pɔntiːz]. 【解剖】連接部分;橋。

pon·ti·fex ['pɑntə,fɛks; 'pɔntifeks] *n., pl.* **pon·tif·i·ces** [pɑn'tɪfə,siz; pɔn'tifisiːz] ①.【古羅馬】高僧團之一員。②＝**pontiff.**

pon·tiff ['pɑntɪf; 'pɔntif] *n.* ①教皇;教宗。②主教。③(古羅馬之)高僧;教長;(古猶太之)大祭司。*the Supreme* (or *Sovereign*) *Pontiff* 羅馬教皇;羅馬教宗。

pon·tif·i·cal [pɑn'tɪfɪkl; pɔn'tifikəl] *adj.* ①教皇的;教宗的。②主教的。③高僧的;教長的;大祭司的。—*n.* ①主教儀典。②(*pl.*)主教的法服及徽章;祭服。—**ly,** *adv.*

Pontifical College ①古羅馬之高僧團。②羅馬天主教的主教團。

pon·tif·i·ca·li·a [pɑn,tɪfɪ'kelɪə; pɔn,tifi'keiliə] *n. pl.* 主教之法衣。

pon·tif·i·cate [pɑn'tɪfɪkɪt, -,ket; pɔn'tifikit] *n., v.,* **-cat·ed, -cat·ing.** —*n.* 教皇、主教、高僧之職位或任期。—*v.i.* ①執行教宗之職務。②擔任主教。③倨傲而言; 作訓話式的談話。

pont·lev·is [pɑnt'lɛvɪs; pɔnt'levis] *n.* 吊橋(可開合的)。

pon·ton ['pɑntn̩; 'pɔntn̩] *n.* 【美陸軍】＝**pontoon**[1].

pon·toon[1] [pɑn'tun; pɔn'tuːn] *n.* ①平底船。②【軍】用以支架浮橋的平底船或浮舟。③水上飛機之浮舟或浮橋。④浮揚筒;浮筒。

pon·toon[2] *n.* 【英】二十一點牌戲。

pontoon bridge 浮橋。

Pon·top·pi·dan [pɑn'tɑpɪ,dɑn; pɔn'tɔpidɑːn] *n.* 龐陶普丹 (Henrik, 1857–1943, 丹麥小說家, 1917年獲諾貝爾獎)。

***po·ny** ['ponɪ; 'pouni] *n., pl.* **-nies,** *v.,* **-nied, -ny·ing.** —*n.* ①小馬;駒。②【俗】學生所用的教科書之譯本或註釋本。③【俗】一小杯酒。④某種事物中之小者。⑤【英俚】25鎊。—*v.t. & v.i.* ①用教科書譯本或註釋本準備功課。②付錢(以了帳)【常up】. They made him *pony* up the money he owed. 他們逼他還債。

pony edition 報紙之航空版。

pony express 【美】乘快馬送信的制度。

Pony League 青少年棒球隊。

po·ny·tail ['ponɪ,tel; 'pouniteil] *n.* 馬尾巴(一種髮型)。—**ed,** *adj.*

pooch 〔putʃ; puːtʃ〕 *n.*【俚】犬。

pood 〔pud; puːd〕 *n.* 蘇聯的一種重量單位(＝36.113 磅或 16.38 公斤)。

poo·dle 〔ˈpudl; ˈpuːdl〕 *n.* 一種智力甚高之獅子狗。—**like,** *adj.*

pooh 〔pu; puː〕 *interj.* (表厭惡或輕蔑之聲,通常重複使用)呸！啐！—*n.* 呸；啐。

Pooh-Bah 〔ˌpuˈbɑ; ˈpuːˈbɑː〕 *n.* ①大官；(似)顯要的人物(出自 Gilbert & Sullivan 作喜歌劇 *The Mikado* 中之人物名)。②(p-b-)身兼數職者。

pooh-pooh 〔ˈpuˈpu; puːˈpuː〕 *v.t.* & *v.i.* 輕蔑；藐視；嘲弄；一笑置之。—*interj.* ＝**pooh.**

*__pool__[1] 〔pul; puːl〕 *n.* ①小池；水塘。Our school has a swimming *pool*. 我們的學校有一游泳池。②潭；淵。③水坑。④液體成堆者。⑤在地下之石油或瓦斯。—*v.i.* ①形成爲小池塘等。②(血之)集中於身體之某部。—*v.t.* ①使形成小池塘。②使血集中於身體某部。

pool[2] *n.* ①放在一起供共同使用之錢或物。②公司行號間爲防止競爭而控制價格之措施；聯營。③形成此共同措施之人。④落袋撞球戲。⑤賭金。—*v.t.* 將(錢或物)放在一起供共同使用；聯營。—*v.i.* 加入聯營；共用某物或金錢。

pool·room 〔ˈpulˌrum; ˈpuːlruːm〕 *n.*【美】①撞球場。②公開賭場(對在遠處舉行的賽馬或拳擊下賭注之場所)。

pool·side 〔ˈpulˌsaɪd; ˈpuːlsaid〕 *n.* 游泳池旁邊之區域。—*adj.* 游泳池旁邊的。

poon 〔pun; puːn〕 *n.*【植物】(東印度產之)胡桐；胡桐木(爲製桅、桁、傢具等之良材)。

poop[1] 〔pup; puːp〕 *n.* ①船尾高甲板；舵樓甲板。②船尾。—*v.t.* ①(浪)打擊(船)之尾部。②以船尾受(浪)。

poop[2] *v.t.*【美俚】使筋疲力盡；使上氣不接下氣(通常用被動式)。***poop out***【俚】(因恐懼或疲倦)未能完成某事；筋疲力竭。

poop[3] *n.*【俚】消息；眞實的消息。

poop[4] *n., v.t.* ＝**pope**[2].

poop[5] *n.*【英俚】笨瓜；蠢貨；無用的人。

‡**poor** 〔pur; puə, pɔə, pɔː〕 *adj.* ①貧窮的。He is very *poor*. 他很窮。②壞的；拙劣的；質劣的。a *poor* crop. 歉收。③少量的；薄弱的。④可憐的；不幸的。The *poor* fellow lost both his legs in the war. 這不幸的人在戰爭中失掉了雙腿。⑤瘦弱的；精神萎靡的。What a *poor* creature he is! 他是個多麼沒有精神的人啊！⑥【法律】需要救濟的。***poor as a church mouse*** 窮無立錐之地。***poor as Job's turkey*** 很窮。—*n.* (the-) 窮人(集合稱)。The rich ought to help the *poor*. 富人應幫助窮人。—**ness,** *n.*

poor box (教堂門前之)濟貧箱；慈善箱。

poor farm (政府經營的)濟貧農場。

poor·house 〔ˈpurˌhaus; ˈpuəhaus〕 *n.* 貧民院；救濟院。

poor·ish 〔ˈpurɪʃ; ˈpuəriʃ〕 *adj.* 有些窮的；欠佳的。

poor law 濟貧法。

*__poor·ly__ 〔ˈpurlɪ; ˈpuəli, ˈpɔə-, ˈpɔː-〕 *adv.* ①不足地；貧乏地。He is *poorly* off. 他很窮。②壞地；拙劣地。—*adj.*【俗】不適的；不健康的。

poor-mouth 〔ˈpurˌmauð; ˈpuəmauð〕 *v.i.* & *v.t.*【美】嘆窮；哭窮。

poor·ness 〔ˈpurnɪs; ˈpuənis〕 *n.* ①貧窮；貧乏；不足。②拙劣；劣質；壞。③卑劣；卑鄙。④虛弱；瘦弱。⑤磽瘠。⑥不幸；可憐。

poor rate 濟貧稅。

poor-spir·it·ed 〔ˈpurˈspɪrɪtɪd; ˈpuəˈspiritid〕 *adj.* 無氣力的；懦弱的；怯懦的。

poor white 美國南部之貧苦的白種人。

*__pop__[1] 〔pɑp; pɔp〕 *v.,* **popped, pop·ping,** *n., adv.* —*v.i.* ①發短促爆裂聲。The firecrackers *popped*. 爆竹拍拍響。②突然走動；突然走去或走來；突然動作。*Pop* in and see me some evening. 找一天晚上來看我。③砰然裂開。④(眼睛)睜大或突出(表示驚訝等)。The surprise made her eyes *pop* out. 驚訝使她睜大了眼睛。⑤用火器射擊。⑥【棒球】**a.** 打出高飛球 (pop fly)【常up】。**b.** 高飛球被接住而出局。—*v.t.* ①突然伸出；突然放入。He *popped* his head in at the door. 他突然將頭伸進門內。②【俗】用鎗射擊。③使發出短促的爆裂聲。④開(鎗)。⑤突然發出(問題)。They *popped* a question at him. 他們突然問他一個問題。⑥爆炒(玉蜀黍)。⑦【英俚】將…送進當舖。***pop off*** **a.** 急速離去。**b.**【俚】死。**c.** 衝動地講；不經考慮地說出。**d.** 睡着。***pop out***【棒球】打出之高飛球 (pop fly) 被接住而被判出局。***pop the question***【俗】求婚。***pop up*** 突然出現；突然來臨。—*n.* ①短促爆裂聲。We heard the *pop* of a cork. 我們聽見打開瓶塞的聲音。②汽水類的飲料。③【棒球】＝**pop fly.** —*adv.* 突然地；砰然地。

pop[2]【俚】父親；老伯。

*__pop__[3] *adj.*【俗】通俗的；大衆的。*pop* art. 大衆藝術。—*n.* 通俗音樂會。

pop. ①popular. ②popularly. ③population.

pop·corn 〔ˈpɑpˌkɔrn; ˈpɔpkɔːn〕 *n.* ①玉米花(將玉蜀黍炒裂而成)。②炸玉米花用的玉米。

Pope 〔pop; poup〕 *n.* 波普(Alexander, 1688–1744, 英國詩人)。

*__Pope, pope__[1] 〔pop; poup〕 *n.* ①羅馬教皇。②有如羅馬教皇之權威的人。③主教。

pope[2] 〔pup; puːp〕 *n.* 腿的要害。—*v.t.* (通常用 pp.)打…之腿的要害。

pope·dom 〔ˈpopdəm; ˈpoupdəm〕 *n.* ①(羅馬)教皇之職位、管區或任期。②教皇政治(制度)。③【蔑】＝**popery.**

Pope Joan 〔~dʒon; ~dʒoun〕 (除去方塊 8 點之牌的)一種紙牌戲。

pop·er·y 〔ˈpopərɪ; ˈpoupəri〕 *n.*【蔑】羅馬天主教之教義、儀式等。

pope's-eye 〔ˈpopsˌaɪ; ˈpoups-ai〕 *n.* (牛、羊等之)腿部淋巴腺。

pope's nose【俗】雞、火雞、鴨等之臀部。

pop·eyed 〔ˈpɑpˌaɪd; ˈpɔpaid〕 *adj.* 突眼的；(因驚慌而)睜大眼睛的。

pop fly【棒球】高飛球。

pop·gun 〔ˈpɑpˌgʌn; ˈpɔpgʌn〕 *n.* 玩具氣鎗。

pop·in·jay 〔ˈpɑpɪnˌdʒe; ˈpɔpindʒei〕 *n.* ①紈袴子；花花公子。②(昔時)鸚鵡形之射擊靶。③一種啄木鳥。④【古】鸚鵡。

pop·ish 〔ˈpopɪʃ; ˈpoupiʃ〕 *adj.*【蔑】天主教的。—**ly,** *adv.* —**ness,** *n.*

*__pop·lar__ 〔ˈpɑplɚ; ˈpɔplə〕 *n.* ①【植物】白楊。②白楊木。trembling *poplar*. (普通)白楊。

pop·lin 〔ˈpɑplɪn; ˈpɔplin〕 *n.* 毛葛(一種棉、毛或絲織品)。

pop·lit·e·al 〔pɑpˈlɪtɪəl; pɔpˈlitiəl〕 *adj.*【解剖】腿彎部的；膝膕部的。

pop·o·ver 〔ˈpɑpˌovɚ; ˈpɔpˌouvə〕 *n.* 一種酥餅。

pop·pa 〔ˈpɑpə; ˈpɔpə〕 *n.*【美】爸爸(暱稱)。

pop·per 〔ˈpɑpɚ; ˈpɔpə〕 *n.* ①(使)發短促爆裂聲的人或物；爆竹；鎗；手鎗。②射手；砲手。③爆炒玉米之鍋。

pop·pet 〔ˈpɑpɪt; ˈpɔpit〕 *n.* ①【英方】小乖乖(對小孩的暱稱)。②【機械】**a.** 揚瓣；菌狀氣門(亦作 **poppet valve**)。**b.** 鏃床頭(亦作 **poppethead**)。③(船入水時支持船身的) 枕

木。④〖古〗=**puppet.**

pop·pet·head ['pɑpɪtˌhɛd; 'pɔpithed] *n.* 鏇床頭。(亦作 **poppet, puppet**)

pop·pied ['pɑpɪd; 'pɔpid] *adj.* ①多罌粟的。②受麻醉的;想睡的;沒精打采的。

pop·ping crease ['pɑpɪŋ~;'pɔpiŋ~] 〖板球〗打手線。

pop·ple ['pɑpl̩;'pɔpl] *v.,* **-pled, -pling,** *n.* —*v.i.,* *n.* (水之)滾動;波動;翻動。

***pop·py**[1] ['pɑpɪ; 'pɔpi] *n., pl.* **-pies.** ①罌粟。②罌粟花。③深紅色。④〖建築〗=**poppyhead.** —**like,** *adj.*

pop·py[2] *n.* 〖美俚〗父親(暱稱)。

pop·py·cock ['pɑpɪˌkɑk; 'pɔpikɔk] *n., interj.* 〖俗〗胡說;廢話。

pop·py·head ['pɑpɪˌhɛd; 'pɔpihed] *n.* 〖建築〗(教堂座席一端等之)罌粟狀裝飾;頂花。(亦作 **poppy**)

pop-shop ['pɑpˌʃɑp; 'pɔpʃɔp] *n.* 〖英俚〗當鋪。

Pop·si·cle ['pɑpsəkəl; 'pɔpsikəl] *n.* 〖商標名〗棒棒冰淇淋;冰棒。

pop·u·lace ['pɑpjəlɪs, -ləs; 'pɔpjuləs, -lis] *n.* ①平民;民衆;老百姓。②住民;居民。

‡**pop·u·lar** ['pɑpjələ˞; 'pɔpjulə, -pjələ] *adj.* ①孚衆望的;受人歡迎的。②普遍的;流行的。a *popular* song. 一支流行歌曲。③民衆的;民有的;民治的。④一般的;適合一般人的。*popular* prices. 廉價。

***pop·u·lar·i·ty** [ˌpɑpjə'lærətɪ; ˌpɔpju'læriti] *n.* 流行;普遍;聲望。the *popularity* of baseball. 棒球的普遍。

pop·u·lar·ize ['pɑpjələˌraɪz; 'pɔpjuləraiz] *v.t.,* **-ized, -iz·ing.** 使普遍;使流行;使得人心。—**pop·u·lar·i·za·tion, pop·u·lar·iz·er,** *n.*

pop·u·lar·ly ['pɑpjələlɪ; 'pɔpjuləli] *adv.* ①一般地;由人民投票。②適合大衆地;通俗地;平易地。

popular vote 〖美〗選民投票。

pop·u·late ['pɑpjəˌlet;'pɔpjuleit] *v.t.,* **-lat·ed, -lat·ing.** ①居住於。②殖民於。—**pop·u·la·tor,** *n.*

‡**pop·u·la·tion** [ˌpɑpjə'leʃən; ˌpɔpju'leiʃən] *n.* ①人口。New York City contains 7,876,760 *population.* 紐約市的人口爲7,876,760人。②人口數。The *population* of the city is less than 200,000. 此城的人口不及二十萬。③殖民。—**al,** *adj.*

population explosion 人口之急速膨脹。

population pressure 〖生態〗人口壓力。

Pop·u·lism ['pɑpjəlɪzm; 'pɔpjulizəm] *n.* ①〖美史〗人民黨 (People's Party) 之主義、政策。②俄國1917年革命前的共產主義。

Pop·u·list ['pɑpjəlɪst; 'pɔpjulist] *n.* 〖美史〗人民黨黨員。—*adj.* =**Populistic.**

Pop·u·list·ic [ˌpɑpjə'lɪstɪk; ˌpɔpju'listik] *adj.* 人民黨之政策或主義的;人民黨黨員的。

***pop·u·lous** ['pɑpjələs; 'pɔpjuləs, -pjəl-] *adj.* ①人口稠密的。②多數的。—**ly,** *adv.* —**ness,** *n.*

pop-up ['pɑpˌʌp; 'pɔpˌʌp] *n.* 〖棒球〗=**pop fly.** —*adj.* 彈起的。

por·bea·gle ['pɔrˌbigl; 'pɔːˌbiːgl] *n.* (北大西洋、北太平洋產的)青鮫。

***por·ce·lain** ['porslɪn, 'pɔr-, -slɪn, -ən, -sl̩en; 'pɔːslin] *n.* 瓷;瓷器。Cups and plates are often made of *porcelain.* 杯子和盤碟常是瓷製的。

porcelain clay 瓷土;陶土。

por·ce(l)·la·ne·ous [ˌporsə'lenɪəs; ˌpɔːsə'leiniəs] *adj.* 瓷器的;似瓷器的。

‡**porch** [portʃ, pɔrtʃ; pɔːtʃ] *n.* ①門廊。②走廊(=veranda). —**less,** *adj.* —**like,** *adj.*

porch climber 〖美俚〗竊賊。

por·cine ['pɔrsaɪn; 'pɔːsain] *adj.* ①猪的。②似猪的;髒的;卑劣的。

por·cu·pine ['pɔrkjəˌpaɪn; 'pɔːkjupain] *n.* 豪猪。

porcupine anteater 〖動物〗針鼹;食蟻蝟(=echidna).

***pore**[1] [por, pɔr; pɔː, pɔə] *v.i.,* **pored, por·ing.** ①熟讀;熟視。②沉思;默想〖常over, on, upon〗. to *pore* upon a problem. 熟思一問題。—**por·er,** *n.*

pore[2] *n.* 毛孔;孔。—**like,** *adj.*

por·gy ['pɔrgɪ; 'pɔːgi] *n., pl.* **-gies, -gy.** (地中海及大西洋產之)棘鬣魚。

po·rism ['porɪzm;'pourizm] *n.* 〖幾何〗不定設題;(希臘幾何學的)系;系論。

***pork** [pork, pɔrk; pɔːk] *n.* ①猪肉。②〖美俚〗得自聯邦或州政府的金錢或位置。

pork barrel 〖美政治俚〗議員爲取悅選民而使政府撥出的地方建設經費。

pork·chop ['pɔrkˌtʃɑp; 'pɔːktʃɔp] *n.* 猪排。

pork·er ['porkə˞; 'pɔːkə] *n.* 食用猪;肥胖之小猪。

pork·ling ['porklɪŋ; 'pɔːkliŋ] *n.* 小猪。

pork pie ①猪肉餅。② =**porkpie.**

pork·pie ['porkˌpaɪ; 'pɔːkpai] *n.* 〖美〗一種平頂捲邊圓帽。(亦作 **porkpie hat**)

pork·y ['porkɪ; 'pɔːki] *adj.,* **pork·i·er, pork·i·est.** ①(似)猪肉的。②肥胖的;多脂的。

porn [pɔrn; pɔːn] *n.* 〖俚〗 =**pornography.** (亦作 **porno**)

por·no·graph·ic [ˌpɔrnə'græfɪk; ˌpɔːnə'græfik] *adj.* 色情畫的;色情文學的;淫穢的。—**al·ly,** *adv.*

por·nog·ra·phy [pɔr'nɑgrəfɪ; pɔː'nɔgrəfi] *n.* 春宮;色情畫;色情文學。

po·ros·i·ty [po'rɑsətɪ; pɔː'rɔsiti] *n., pl.* **-ties.** 孔;多孔;多孔性。

po·rous ['porəs; 'pɔːrəs] *adj.* ①多孔的。②能浸漬的;可浸透的。 —**ness,** *n.*

por·phy·ry ['pɔrfərɪ; 'pɔːfiri] *n., pl.* **-ries.** 〖地質〗斑岩。—**por·phy·rit·ic,** *adj.*

por·poise ['pɔrpəs; 'pɔːpəs] *n., pl.* **-pois·es** or **-poise,** *v.,* **-poised, -pois·ing.** —*n.* 海豚。—*v.i.* (快艇或魚雷等)躍上水面。—**like,** *adj.*

por·ridge ['pɔrɪdʒ; 'pɔridʒ] *n.* (和水或牛乳煮成之)麥片粥;粥。 —**like,** *adj.*

por·rin·ger ['pɔrɪndʒə˞; 'pɔrindʒə] *n.* (盛粥或湯之)深碟;小碗。

***port**[1] [port, pɔrt; pɔːt] *n.* ①港;港口。a naval *port.* 軍港。②港市。③〖法律〗進口港(貨物或人員可入境的海關所在地)。④〖俗〗機場 (=airport). —**less,** *adj.*

port[2] *n.* 紫色濃甜的葡萄酒 (由葡萄牙Oporto 城得名)。

port[3] *n.* ①(船上的)艙門;上貨口。②(軍艦的) 砲門。③艙口蓋;砲口的門。④〖機械〗汽口;汽門。⑤〖蘇〗門;城門。

port[4] *n.* (船或飛機的) 左舷。—*adj.* 左舷的。—*v.t.* & *v.i.* (把舵、船等)轉向左邊。

port[5] *n.* ①舉止;態度;姿勢。②舉鎗的姿勢。—*v.t.* 舉鎗;托鎗。

Port. ①Portugal. ②Portuguese.

port·a·bil·i·ty [ˌportə'bɪlətɪ; ˌpɔːtə'biliti] *n.* 可携帶;可移動;輕便。

***port·a·ble** ['portəbḷ, 'pɔr–; 'pɔːtəbl] *adj.* 可攜帶的;可移動的。a *portable* typewriter. 手提打字機。—*n.* 可手提的東西。—**port·a·bly,** *adv.*

port admiral 〖英海軍〗要塞司令官。

por·tage ['portɪdʒ; 'pɔːtidʒ] *n., v.,* **-taged, -tag·ing.** —*n.* ①兩水路間之陸上運送。②兩水路間之陸上運送地點;連水陸路。③搬運;運輸。④搬運費;運費。—*v.t. & v.i.* 於兩水路間運送(船、貨物等)。

***por·tal** ['portḷ, 'pɔr–; 'pɔːtl] *n.* ①大門;入口;正門(常指堂皇者)。②〖解剖〗門脈;脈。③隧道或礦坑的入口。—*adj.* 〖解剖〗門的;門脈的;肝門的。*portal* vein. 門靜脈。—**ed,** *adj.*

portal-to-portal pay 根據自進入工廠或礦場至離開爲止之時間而給付之工資。

por·ta·men·to [ˌportə'mɛnto; ˌpɔːtə'mentou] *n., pl.* **-ti** [–ti; –tiː], **-tos.** 〖義〗〖音樂〗滑音。

port arms ①〖口令〗舉鎗。②舉鎗之姿勢。

Port Ar·thur [~'ɑrθɚ; ~'ɑːθə] 旅順(中譯 Lüshun, 在中國遼東半島)。

por·ta·tive ['portətɪv; 'pɔːtətiv] *adj.* ①可攜帶的;可搬運的。②有搬運能力的;搬運的。—*n.* (亦作 **portative organ**) 歐洲中世紀及文藝復興期中使用的可搬運之風琴。

port authority 港務局。

port charges 港稅;入口稅;噸稅。

port·cray·on [ˌport'kreən; ˌpɔːt'kreiən] *n.* 臘筆夾。

port·cul·lis [port'kʌlɪs; pɔːt'kʌlis] *n.* 古代城堡可升降的鐵閘門;格子吊閘。—**ed,** *adj.*

Porte [port; pɔːt] *n.* 鄂圖曼土耳其帝國政府或宮庭。

porte-co·chere, porte-co·chère ['portkə'ʃɛr; 'pɔːtkə'ʃɛə] *n.* ①〖建築〗車輛可駛入庭院的通道。②〖美〗上下馬車之門廊。

porte-mon·naie [ˌpɔrtˌmɔ'nɛ; pɔrtmɔ'nɛ] *n., pl.* **-mon·naies.** 〖法〗小皮夾;小錢袋。

por·tend [por'tɛnd; pɔː'tend] *v.t.* ①預兆;成爲…的前兆。②表示。

port engineer 船公司負責檢修該公司船隻及監管工程人員的總工程師。(亦作 **superintendent engineer**)

por·tent ['portɛnt; 'pɔːtent] *n.* ①預兆;徵兆。②惡兆;凶兆。③驚異之事; 異常之人或物。

por·ten·tous [por'tɛntəs; pɔː'tentəs] *adj.* ①預示凶事的; 不祥的。②可驚的; 非常的。③自負的;傲慢的。—**ly,** *adv.* —**ness,** *n.*

***por·ter**[1] ['portɚ, 'pɔr–; 'pɔːtə] *n.* ①脚夫;挑夫;火車站之紅帽子。②〖美〗(火車中之) 侍者。

***por·ter**[2] *n.* ①守門者。The *porter* let them in. 守門者放他們進來了。②工友。

***por·ter**[3] *n.* 一種黑啤酒。

por·ter·age ['portərɪdʒ; 'pɔːtəridʒ] *n.* ①搬運;搬運業。②運費。

por·ter·house ['portɚˌhaus; 'pɔːtəhaus] *n., pl.* **-hous·es.** ① (供應 porter, beer 等的) 酒店。② 〖俗〗=**porterhouse steak.**

porterhouse steak 上等腰肉牛排。

port·fire ['portˌfaɪr; 'pɔːtˌfaiə] *n.* 導火筒;引火具(煙火、烽火、礦坑用炸藥等的點火裝置)。

port·fo·li·o [port'folɪˌo; pɔːt'fouljou] *n., pl.* **-li·os.** ①紙夾;公事包。②閣員之職。③銀行或其他投資人的有價證券的財產目錄。

port·hole ['portˌhol; 'pɔːthoul] *n.* ①船側供發砲、採光、通氣等之窗孔;舷窗;艙口;砲門。②牆壁或門上之射擊孔;砲口。③〖機械〗蒸汽口。

por·ti·co ['portɪˌko; 'pɔːtikou] *n., pl.* **-coes, -cos.** 門廊;柱廊;(接於正門之)廻廊。

por·tiere, por·tière [ˌportɪ'ɛr; ˌpɔr'tje] *n., pl.* **-tieres.** 〖法〗門帷;門帘。

‡por·tion ['porʃən, 'pɔr–; 'pɔːʃən] *n.* ①部分;一分。A *portion* of the manuscript is illegible. 這草稿的一部分不易辨讀。②一分(飯菜)。③分得之遺產。④嫁資; 嫁奩。⑤命運。—*v.t.* ①分配;將…分成分。②給與遺產;給嫁奩、嫁資。—**less,** *adj.*

Port·land cement ['portlənd~; 'pɔːtlənd~]波特蘭水泥(石灰石與黏土燒成)。

port·ly ['portlɪ; 'pɔːtli] *adj.,* **-li·er, -li·est,** *n.* —*adj.* ①肥胖的;身體碩大的。②莊嚴的。—*n.* ①肥胖之人。②肥胖者之衣服。—**port·li·ness,** *n.*

port·man·teau [port'mænto; pɔːt'mæntou] *n., pl.* **-teaus, -teaux** [–toz; –touz].〖主英〗一種旅行用的皮箱或皮包。

portmanteau word 結合兩字所造成的字。

port of call 船隻沿途停靠之港口。

port of discharge (or **unloading**) 卸貨港。

port of distress 避難港。

port of entry 進口港。

port of registry 船籍港。

port of sailing 啓航港。

***por·trait** ['portret, 'pɔr–, –trɪt; 'pɔːtrit] *n.* ①人像;肖像。②描寫;描述。a biography that provides a fascinating *portrait* of an 18th-century rogue. 一本描述一個十八世紀歹徒的引人入勝的傳記。③影像;模型;類型。—**like,** *adj.*

por·trait·ist ['portretɪst;'pɔːtritist] *n.* 肖像畫家。

por·trai·ture ['portrɪtʃɚ;'pɔːtritʃə] *n.* ①人像的繪畫。②人像;肖像。③生動的人物描寫。

por·tray [por'tre; pɔː'trei] *v.t.* ①畫像;描繪;寫眞。②扮演;飾演。—**a·ble,** *adj.* —**er,** *n.*

por·tray·al [por'treəl; pɔː'treiəl] *n.* ①描畫;描寫;寫眞。②描畫 (描寫)物;肖像。③扮演;飾演。

port·reeve ['portˌriv; 'pɔːt–riːv] *n.* 〖英史〗市長;(區、鎭的)地方長官。

por·tress ['portrɛs; 'pɔːtris] *n.* 女門房;女搬運工。(亦作 **porteress**)

Port Sa·id [port'sed; pɔːt'said] 塞得港(阿拉伯聯合共和國在地中海之一港口,位於蘇彝士運河之北端)。(亦作 **Port Saïd**)

port·side[1] ['portˌsaɪd; 'pɔːt–said] *n.* 左舷。—*adj.* 左邊的。—*adv.*朝左邊;向左邊。

port·side[2] *n.* 海港之港口附近地區;碼頭區。 —*adj.* 碼頭區的。

Ports·mouth ['portsməθ;'pɔːtsməθ] *n.* 樸次茅斯 (英格蘭南部之一海軍基地,俗名 Pompe)。

***Por·tu·gal** ['portʃəgḷ, 'pɔr–; 'pɔːtjugəl, –tʃu–] *n.* 葡萄牙 (歐洲西南部國家,在西班牙之西,首都爲里斯本 Lisbon)。

***Por·tu·guese** ['portʃəˌgiz, 'pɔr–; ˌpɔːtju'giːz, –tʃu–] *n., pl.* **-guese,** *adj.* —*n.* ①葡萄牙人。②葡萄牙語。—*adj.* 葡萄牙的;

葡萄牙人的;葡萄牙語的。

por·tu·lac·a 〔ˌportʃəˈlækə; ˌpɔːtʃəˈlækə〕 *n.* 〖植物〗馬齒莧屬之植物。

pos. ①position. ②positive. ③possessive.

***pose**[1] 〔poz; pouz〕 *n., v.,* **posed, pos·ing.** —*n.* ①姿勢。②假裝之模樣;僞裝。③心理上的姿態;態度。—*v.i.* ①作姿態。He *posed* an hour for his portrait. 他正襟危坐了一小時讓人替他畫肖像。②假裝; 僞裝。③自任;自命。He likes to *pose* as a judge of literature. 他喜歡自命爲文學批評家。—*v.t.* ①使成某種姿態。②說;陳述。

pose[2] *v.t.,* **posed, pos·ing.** 以困難的問題質問;問難;窘困。

Po·sei·don 〔poˈsaɪdn̩; pɔˈsaidən〕 *n.* ①〖希臘神話〗海神。②美國核子潛艇發射的海神飛彈。

pos·er[1] 〔ˈpozɚ; ˈpouzə〕 *n.* 非常困難的問題;使人困窘的問題。

pos·er[2] *n.* ① =**poseur.** ②擺姿勢的人;提出問題的人。

po·seur 〔poˈzɝ; pouˈzəː〕 *n.* 裝模作樣的人。

posh 〔pɑʃ; pɔʃ〕 *adj.* 舒適的;高雅的;豪華的。

pos·it 〔ˈpɑzɪt; ˈpɔzit〕 *v.t.* ①放置;安置;布置。②〖哲學〗斷定;假定。

‡**po·si·tion** 〔pəˈzɪʃən; pəˈziʃən, puˈz-〕 *n.* ①位置。②被安放的方法;姿勢。③適當位置。④工作;職位。 He got a *position* in the bank. 他在銀行裏找到一分工作。⑤階級;地位(特指高級的)。He was raised to the *position* of captain. 他被擢升爲艦長。⑥見解;立場;態度。⑦〖軍〗陣地; 陣勢。***in position*** 在適當位置的。 ***out of position*** 不在適當位置的。 —*v.t.* ①安放;放置。The nails are *positioned* as desired. 釘被釘在適當的位置。②決定…之位置。 —**er,** *n.* —**less,** *adj.*

po·si·tion·al 〔pəˈzɪʃənl̩; pəˈziʃənl̩〕 *adj.* 位置(上)的;地位(上)的; 職位(上)的。

position paper 意見書(對某一問題所持意見之書面陳述)。

***pos·i·tive** 〔ˈpɑzətɪv; ˈpɔzətiv, -zit-〕 *adj.* ①無問題的; 確實的。②過分相信的; 斷然的。③堅決的;積極的;絕對的。Don't just make criticism; give us some *positive* help. 不要衹是批評, 給我們些積極的援助。④實在的; 存在的。⑤實際的。 a *positive* mind. 實事求是者。⑥陽性的。⑦〖數學〗正的。⑧依前進方向的;往好的方向走的。⑨〖攝影〗正片的。⑩〖文法〗簡單形式的。⑪有病的;有病徵的;有病菌的。⑫〖俗〗徹底的。—*n.* ①形容詞或副詞之簡單形式。②〖電〗(電池之)陽極。③〖攝影〗正片。④〖數學〗正量;正數。—**ness,** *n.*

positive charge 陽電荷。

positive degree 〖文法〗原級。

positive electricity 〖電〗陽電。

positive law 〖法律〗制定法; 實定法; 成文法。

***pos·i·tive·ly** 〔ˈpɑzətɪvlɪ; ˈpɔzitivli〕 *adv.* ①積極地; 確實地。② 毫無疑問地。—*interj.* 表示强烈的肯定。Do you plan to go to the party? *Positively!* 你準備參加派對嗎? 當然!

positive number 〖數學〗正數。

positive philosophy 〖哲學〗實證哲學;實證論。

positive pole 〖電,磁〗正極;陽極。

positive sign 〖數學,物理〗正號(卽+)。

pos·i·tiv·ism 〔ˈpɑzətɪvˌɪzəm; ˈpɔzitivizəm〕 *n.* ①〖哲學〗(亦作P-)實證哲學;實證論;實證主義(爲法人 Auguste Comte 所倡, 故亦稱 Comtism)。②積極性;明確性;積極主義;確信。③獨斷主義;武斷主義。—**pos·i·tiv·is·tic,** *adj.*

pos·i·tiv·ist 〔ˈpɑzətɪvɪst; ˈpɔzitivist〕 *n.* 實證哲學家;實證主義者。

pos·i·tiv·i·ty 〔ˌpɑzəˈtɪvətɪ; ˌpɔziˈtiviti〕 *n.* 確實性;堅決;積極(性)。

pos·i·tron 〔ˈpɑzɪˌtrɑn; ˈpɔzitrɔn〕 *n.* 〖物理〗陽電子;正電子。

poss. ①possession. ②possessive. ③possible. ④possibly.

pos·se 〔ˈpɑsɪ; ˈpɔsi〕 *n.* ①郡執行官(sheriff)爲維持治安所召集之民團。②(警察等之)一隊;一團。

‡**pos·sess** 〔pəˈzɛs; pəˈzes〕 *v.t.* ①有;具有。He *possessed* courage. 他有勇氣。②持有;占有。③支配;控制。 She was *possessed* by the desire to be rich. 她被致富的慾望所支配。④(爲惡魔等) 祟迷; 附體。 What *possesses* you to do such a thing? 甚麼鬼怪在作祟叫你幹出這種事情來? ⑤保持; 維持。⑥通知;使熟悉〖常 of, with〗。⑦使某人獲取(財產、消息等)。⑧使受(感情、觀念等之)支配。⑨(男人之)與(女人)發生性關係;占有(女人)。⑩〖古〗攫取。⑪〖古〗贏。 ***possess oneself of*** 持有。***possess one's soul in patience*** 有耐心。—**or,** *n.*

pos·sessed 〔pəˈzɛst; pəˈzest〕 *adj.* ①被(鬼怪等)纏住的;着了魔的;瘋狂的。②鎮定的。③〖文法〗所有格形的。 ***be possessed of*** 擁有。 —**ly,** *adv.* —**ness,** *n.*

‡**pos·ses·sion** 〔pəˈzɛʃən; pəˈzeʃən〕 *n.* ①持有;握有;所有權。 to come into *possession* of a fortune. 獲得一筆財產。②(*pl.*)所有物;財產;財富。my personal *possessions.* 我的私人財產。③自制。④陰魂附體;着魔。⑤領地;屬國。⑥使人着魔的觀念、感情等。⑦對球的控制。⑧一球隊得分後另一球隊控制球而開始球賽之權。

***pos·ses·sive** 〔pəˈzɛsɪv; pəˈzesiv〕 *adj.* ①所有的。②表示所有的。③有占有慾的;欲據爲己有的。④認爲己所有的。⑤不許自己的小孩或配偶有獨立思想或行動的。⑥〖文法〗所有格的。—*n.* ①所有格。②所有格的字。—**ly,** *adv.* —**ness,** *n.*

possessive adjective 〖文法〗所有格形容詞(如: my, your, his 等)。

possessive case 〖文法〗所有格。

possessive pronoun 〖文法〗所有格代名詞(如:mine, yours, hers, theirs 等)。

pos·ses·so·ry 〔pəˈzɛsərɪ; pəˈzesəri〕 *adj.* ①所有的; 占有的;占有(所有)者的。②由占有(所有)而生的。

pos·set 〔ˈpɑsɪt; ˈpɔsit〕 *n.* 牛奶酒(熱牛奶攙入葡萄酒而成,有時加以香料、糖等)。

***pos·si·bil·i·ty** 〔ˌpɑsəˈbɪlətɪ; ˌpɔsəˈbiliti, -siˈb-〕 *n., pl.* **-ties.** ①可能;可能性。There is a *possibility* that the train may be late. 火車可能誤點。②可能發生之事;可能之人;可能的結果。I see great *possibilities* in this scheme. 我看這方法很可能成功。

‡**pos·si·ble** 〔ˈpɑsəbl̩; ˈpɔsəbl, -sib-〕 *adj.* ①可能的。 Come if *possible.* 如果可能, 就來罷。②可能是眞的;或有的。It is *possible* that he went. 他可能是去了。③可能適當完成或獲選等的。 the only *possible* candidate. 唯一適當的候選人。 —*n.* 可能的候選人;可能的獲勝者。

‡pos·si·bly [ˈpɑsəblɪ; ˈpɔsəbli, –sib–] *adv.* ①可能地。I cannot *possibly* go. 我不可能去。②或許; 或者。*Possibly* you are right. 或許你是對的。

pos·sum [ˈpɑsəm; ˈpɔsəm] *n.* ①〖美俗〗鼴。②〖澳〗(有捲尾之) 袋鼠。***play possum*** 〖美俗〗僞裝; 佯爲; 裝病; 裝死; 裝睡。

post¹** [post; poust] *n.* ①柱; 支柱。the *posts* of a bed. 床柱。②(賽跑用之) 起點標; 終點標。beat a person on the post*** (賽跑) 以一胸之差勝過某人; 險勝某人。***be in the wrong (right) side of the post*** 做得不對 (對)。—*v.t.* ①貼 (布告等)。*Post* no bills! (此處) 不准張貼! ②公布; 揭示。③在公告中譴責。④使(人名)列入公布之名單內。⑤將(船名)列入爲沉沒或失蹤。⑥公告不得侵入。—**less,** *adj.* —**like,** *adj.*

post²** *n.* ①哨站; 崗位。The soldiers stood at their *posts*. 兵士各守崗位。②堡壘; 軍隊駐紮地。③哨兵; 屯兵。④職位; 工作。⑤退伍軍人協會分會。⑥(非文明國度中之) 貿易場。⑦證券交易所內交易某種股票的地方。⑧(英軍中) 熄燈號。take post*** a. 〖昔〗英海軍被任命爲有二十門大砲以上之軍艦的艦長。b. 〖軍〗占領陣地。—*v.t.* ①安置(哨兵); 駐紮。We *posted* guards at the door. 我們在門口設有崗。②任命…擔任軍職或統率之職。

‡post³ *n.* ①書信; 郵件。Has the *post* come yet? 信來過沒有? ②郵政。③〖古〗郵差。④〖古〗郵車; 郵船。⑤郵筒; 郵箱; 郵局。⑥驛館; 驛站。⑦紙張之一種尺寸(約爲20×16英寸)。***by post*** 郵寄。—*v.t.* ①郵寄。I've just come out to *post* some letters. 我剛出來要寄幾封信。②告知; 使知曉。③謄帳; 過帳 (從流水帳記入總帳)。—*v.i.* ①迅速旅行; 匆匆忙忙。②騎驛馬旅行。③隨着馬的跳躍而上下。—*adv.* ①迅速地。②以郵遞地。③以驛馬地。

post⁴ *adv., prep.* 在後; 在…後。

post- 〖字首〗表"在後"之義, 如 postwar.

P.O.S.T. Pacific Ocean Security Treaty.

***post·age** [ˈpostɪdʒ; ˈpoustidʒ] *n.* 郵費。*postage* stamp. 郵票。*postage* due. 信件欠資。

post·age-due stamp [ˈpostɪdʒ-ˈdju~; ˈpoustidʒˈdjuː~] 欠資郵票。

***post·al** [ˈpostl; ˈpoustəl] *adj.* 郵政的; 郵局的。—*n.* (亦作 **postal card, post card**) 明信片。—**ly,** *adv.*

postal card 明信片。

postal delivery zone 郵遞區。

postal order 郵政匯票。

postal savings 郵政儲金。

postal savings bank (美國) 郵政儲蓄銀行。

post·a·tom·ic [ˌpostəˈtɑmɪk; ˌpoustəˈtɔmik] *adj.* 原子彈轟炸(使用)以後的。

post·bag [ˈpostˌbæg; ˈpoustbæg] *n.* ①〖英〗郵件包; 郵袋。②郵件; 信件。

post bel·lum [postˈbɛləm; poustˈbeləm] 〖拉〗戰後。

post-boat [ˈpostˌbot; ˈpoustbout] *n.* 郵船; 短程班輪。

post·box [ˈpostˌbɑks; ˈpoustbɔks] *n.* [=mailbox.]

post·boy [ˈpostˌbɔɪ; ˈpoustbɔi] *n.* ①郵差。②第一列左馬之騎手; 左馬御者。

post captain 〖英海軍〗(從前備砲20門以上之大艦的) 上校艦長。

***post card** ①明信片。②私人製售之明信片(通常有圖畫, 須貼足郵票方可投寄)。(亦作 postcard)

post chaise [~ʃez; ~ʃeiz] (昔之) 驛車; 驛遞馬車。

post·clas·si·cal [postˈklæsɪkl; poustˈklæsikəl] *adj.* (希臘、羅馬文學之) 古典時期之後的。(亦作 **postclassic**)

post·date [ˌpostˈdet; ˈpoustˈdeit] *v.t.,* **-dat·ed, -dat·ing.** ①把日期填遲。②預塡(支票等)之日期。*postdated* bill. 遠期支票。③時間上後於; 繼…之後。

post·di·lu·vi·an [ˌpostdɪˈljuvɪən; ˌpoustdaiˈluːviən] *adj.* 諾亞大洪水 (Deluge) 以後的。—*n.* 諾亞大洪水以後的人。

post·doc·tor·al [postˈdɑktərəl; poustˈdɔktərəl] *adj.* 取得博士學位後的研究或工作的。

post·ed [ˈpostɪd; ˈpoustid] *adj.* ①有地位的。②消息靈通的; 精通的。③有不得侵入之告示的。

***post·er¹** [ˈpostɚ; ˈpoustə] *n.* ①海報; 張貼的大幅廣告。②貼海報或廣告的人。

post·er² *n.* ①=**post horse.** ②脚伕; 遞送快信者。

poste res·tante [ˌpostrɛsˈtɑnt; ˈpoustˈrestɑ̃ːnt] ①郵件上之"存局待取"字樣。②〖主英〗郵局主管此種郵件之部門。

pos·te·ri·or [pɑsˈtɪrɪɚ; pɔsˈtiəriə] *adj.* ①位於後部的(爲 anterior 之對)。②順序上在後的。③時間上在後的; 較遲的〖to〗。④〖動物〗尾部的。⑤〖解剖〗背面的; 背側的。⑥〖植物〗(腋生花之) 位於主莖軸之側的。—*n.* (常 *pl.*) 身體之後部; 臀部。—**ly,** *adv.*

pos·te·ri·or·i·ty [pɑsˌtɪrɪˈɑrətɪ; pɔsˌtiəriˈɔriti] *n.* (時間上或位置上) 在後。

***pos·ter·i·ty** [pɑsˈtɛrətɪ; pɔsˈteriti] *n.* ①後裔; 子孫。②後代。He left behind an immortal example to all *posterity*. 他給後世留下不朽的典範。

pos·tern [ˈpostɚn; ˈpoustəːn] *n.* ①(昔之) 後門; 便門; 旁門。②〖築城〗暗道。③逃遁之道路; 暗門。—*adj.* ①後門或暗道的。②後面的; 在後的。③較小的; 較劣的。④祕密的。

Post Exchange 〖美陸軍〗販賣部; 福利社 (略作 **PX**)。(亦作 **post exchange**)

post·free [ˈpostˈfri; ˈpoustˈfriː] *adj.* ①免付郵費的。②〖英〗郵資已預付的。—*adv.* 〖英〗郵資已付。

post·grad·u·ate [postˈgrædʒuɪt; ˈpoustˈgrædjuit] *n.* (大學畢業後之) 研究生。—*adj.* 畢業後繼續研究的; (大學畢業後之) 研究學程的。*postgraduate* course. 研究科目。

post·haste [ˈpostˈhest; ˈpoustˈheist] *adv.* 急速地; 迅速地。—*n.* 〖古〗火速; 急速。

post·hole [ˈpostˌhol; ˈpousthoul] *n.* 掘在地上插旗桿或電線竿等之洞。

post horn (馬車) 喇叭。

post horse 驛馬。(亦作 **poster**)

post house 驛舍。(亦作 **posthouse**)

post·hu·mous [ˈpɑstʃuməs; ˈpɔstjuməs] *adj.* ①遺著的; 死後出版的。②死後的; 身後的。③父死後生的; 遺腹的。a *posthumous* son. 遺腹子。—**ly,** *adv.* —**ness,** *n.*

post·hyp·not·ic [ˌposthɪpˈnɑtɪk; ˌpousthipˈnɔtik] *adj.* ①催眠後的。②(暗示等) 催眠時所做但醒後亦有效的。

pos·tiche [pɔsˈtiʃ; pɔsˈtiːʃ] *adj.* ①(裝飾等) 多餘的。②人工的; 假的。—*n.* ①仿造品; 代用品。②僞裝。③假髮。

pos·til·(l)ion [poˈstɪljən; pəsˈtiliən] *n.* 第一列(前排)左馬之騎手; 左馬御者。

post·im·pres·sion·ism [ˌpostɪm-

ˈprɛʃənɪzm̩; ˈpoustimˈpreʃn̩izəm] *n.* 〖美術〗後期印象派。(亦作 **post-impressionism, Post-Impressionism**)

post·im·pres·sion·ist [ˌpostɪmˈprɛʃənɪst; ˈpoustimˈpreʃnist] *n.* 後期印象派畫家。—*adj.* 後期印象派的。(亦作 **post-impressionist, Post-Impressionist**)

post·li·min·i·um [ˌpostlɪˈmɪnɪəm; ˌpoustliˈminiəm] *n.* =**postliminy.**

post·lim·i·ny [ˌpostˈlɪmɪnɪ; ˌpoustˈlimini] *n.* 〖國際法〗戰後原狀回復權。

post·lude [ˈpostˌlud; ˈpoustljuːd] *n.* 〖音樂〗(爲prelude 之對) ①(於教會)禮拜完畢後的風琴獨奏。②後奏曲;(樂曲的)尾部。

***post·man** [ˈpostmən; ˈpoustmən] *n., pl.* **-men.** ①郵差。②〖廢〗信使。

post·mark [ˈpostˌmɑrk; ˈpoustmɑːk] *n.* 郵戳。—*v.t.* 蓋以郵戳。

post·mas·ter [ˈpostˌmæstɚ; ˈpoustˌmɑːstə] *n.* ①郵政局長。②驛站站長。

postmaster general 郵政總局長。

post·mas·ter·ship [ˈpostˌmæstɚʃɪp; ˈpoustˌmɑːstəʃip] *n.* ①郵政局長之職位或任期。②驛站站長之職位或任期。

post·me·rid·i·an [ˌpostməˈrɪdɪən; ˈpoustməˈridiən] *adj.* 午後的;午後發生的。

post me·rid·i·em [~mɪˈrɪdɪˌɛm; ~miˈridiem] 〖拉〗午後(略作**P.M.**或**p.m.**).

post·mis·tress [ˈpostˌmɪstrɪs; ˈpoustˌmistris] *n.* 女郵政局長。

post-mor·tem [ˌpostˈmɔrtəm; ˈpoustˈmɔːtem] *adj.* ①死後的。a *post-mortem* examination. 驗屍;屍體解剖。②事後的。—*n.* ①驗屍;屍體解剖。②事後評價或檢討。—*v.t.* & *v.i.* 驗屍;作屍體解剖。

post·na·sal [ˈpostˌnezl̩; ˈpoustˈneizəl] *adj.* 鼻後的。

post·na·tal [postˈnetl̩; ˈpoustˈneitl] *adj.* 出生後的;產後的 (爲 prenatal 之對)。

post·nup·tial [postˈnʌpʃəl; poustˈnʌpʃəl] *adj.* 結婚後的。—**ly,** *adv.*

post-o·bit [postˈobɪt; poustˈoubit] *adj.* 〖法律〗死後生效的。—*n.* 死後償還借據(某人以其將來應得之遺產爲抵押的借據)。

post-of·fice [ˈpostˌɔfɪs; ˈpoustˌɔfis] *adj.* 郵政局的。*post-office* order. 郵政匯票(略作 **P.O.O.**).

***post office** ①郵政局。②(常 P- O-)郵務部。

post-office box 郵政信箱。(略作 **POB, P.O.B.**)

Post Office Department (美國政府)郵政部。

post·paid [ˈpostˈped; ˈpoustˈpeid] *adj.* 郵資已付的。

***post·pone** [postˈpon; poustˈpoun] *v.,* **-poned, -pon·ing.** —*v.t.* & *v.i.* 展緩;延擱。The ball game was *postponed* because of rain. 球賽因雨延期。—**ment,** *n.*

post·po·si·tion [ˌpostpəˈzɪʃən; ˈpoustpəˈziʃən] *n.* ①後置;被後置。②〖文法〗後置詞 (如: all the world over 中之 over). —**al,** *adj.*

post·pran·di·al [postˈprændɪəl; poustˈprændiəl] *adj.* 食後的;正餐後的;宴後的。—**ly,** *adv.*

post road 郵路;驛路。

***post·script** [ˈposˌskrɪpt, ˈpost-; ˈpousskript, ˈpous-kript] *n.* ①(信中)附筆;再啓(略作 **P.S.**). ②(書等之)附加資料。—**al,** *adj.*

post town ①(備有驛馬的)驛站。②有郵局的市鎭。

pos·tu·lant [ˈpɑstʃələnt; ˈpɔstjulənt] *n.* ①請願者;申請者;志願者。②申請加入某修道會者;聖職(牧師)志願者。—**ship,** *n.*

pos·tu·late [ˈpɑstʃəˌlet; ˈpɔstjulit] *n., v.,* **-lat·ed, -lat·ing.** —*n.* ①假定;假說。②條件。③基本原則。—*v.t.* ①主張;要求;需要。②假定。③認爲當然;認爲公理。

pos·tu·la·tion [ˌpɑstʃəˈleʃən; ˌpɔstjuˈleiʃən] *n.* ①假定。②要求;請願。③(須俟上級機關認可的)聖職任命。—**al,** *adj.*

pos·tu·la·tor [ˈpɑstʃəˌletɚ; ˈpɔstjuleitə] *n.* 請求者;要求者;假定人。

pos·ture [ˈpɑstʃɚ; ˈpɔstʃə] *n., v.,* **-tured, -tur·ing.** —*n.* ①姿勢。②條件;情況;位置。③心境。—*v.t.* 令取某種姿勢或態度。—*v.i.* ①取某種姿勢。②裝作…的樣子。—**pos·tur·al,** *adj.* —**pos·tur·er,** *n.*

posture maker 雜技表演者。

posture master 美容體操教師。

post·war [ˈpostˈwɔr; ˈpoustˈwɔː] *adj.* 戰後的。

po·sy [ˈpozɪ; ˈpouzi] *n., pl.* **-sies.** ①花。②花束。③(戒指上之)詩銘。

pot** [pɑt; pɔt] *n., v.,* **pot·ted, pot·ting.** —*n.* ①罐、壺、瓶、盆、鍋等容器或烹飪器(常與他字連用, 例如 teapot, jam-pot 等)。②一鍋(罐…)之物;一鍋(罐…)之量。③酒。④捕魚簍子。⑤〖俗〗一筆巨款。⑥〖俗〗一次所賭之總額;賭注。⑦〖英〗a. =**chimney pot.** b. 〖方〗裝食物之大籃。⑧=**pot shot.** ⑨液體容量單位 (相當於 pint 或 quart). ⑩〖俚〗大麻 (=marijuana). ⑪〖俚〗大腹 (=pot-belly). ⑫(*pl.*)酒。go to pot*** 變弱;變壞;毀滅。***keep the pot boiling*** a. 糊口;謀生。b. 使事情保有生氣。***put a quart into a pint pot*** 不自量力;做不能做之事;知其不可而爲之。***The pot calls the kettle black.*** 五十步笑百步。—*v.t.* ①裝入鍋(罐、盆…)中。②貯於罐中。③在鍋中煮。④射擊。⑤〖俗〗抓;捕;贏。—*v.i.* 射擊。—**like,** *adj.*

po·ta·ble [ˈpotəbl̩; ˈpoutəbl] *adj.* 適於飲用的。—*n.* (常*pl.*) 飲料;酒。

po·tage [pɔˈtaʒ; pɔˈtɑːʒ] 〖法〗 *n.* 湯。minced chicken and corn *potage.* 鷄蓉粟米湯。

pot·ash [ˈpɑtˌæʃ; ˈpɔtæʃ] *n.* 〖化〗①炭酸鉀。②苛性鉀(=caustic potash). ③氧化鉀。④鉀。*potash* water. 人造炭酸水。

po·tas·sic [pəˈtæsɪk; pəˈtæsik] *adj.* 鉀的;含鉀的。

po·tas·si·um [pəˈtæsɪəm; pəˈtæsjəm] *n.* 〖化〗鉀。

potassium bromide 〖化〗溴化鉀(KBr, 供作照相材料、鎭靜劑等)。

potassium carbonate 〖化〗炭酸鉀 (K_2CO_3)。

potassium chlorate 〖化〗氯酸鉀($KClO_3$)。

potassium cyanide 〖化〗氰化鉀(KCN).

potassium hydroxide 〖化〗氫氧化鉀;苛性鉀(KOH).

potassium nitrate 〖化〗硝酸鉀;鉀硝;火硝(KNO_3)。

potassium permanganate 〖化〗高錳酸鉀;灰錳氧($KMnO_4$)。

po·ta·tion [poˈteʃən; pouˈteiʃən] *n.* ①飲;一飲。②(常 *pl.*)飲酒;酒宴。③飲料;酒類。

‡po·ta·to [pəˈteto; pəˈteitou] *n., pl.* **-toes.** 馬鈴薯。***hot potato*** 極難處理的問題。***sweet potato*** 紅薯。

potato beetle (or **bug**) 薯蟲(一種有黑色條紋的黃色甲蟲)。

potato box 〖俚〗口;嘴。

potato chip 油煎馬鈴薯片。(亦作 **Saratoga chip**)
po·ta·to·ry ['potə,torɪ; 'poutətɔri] *adj.* ①飲酒的;有飲酒癖的;耽於飲酒的。②適於飲用的。
pot·bel·lied ['pɑt,bɛlɪd; 'pɔt,belid] *adj.* 腹大的;大腹便便的。
pot·bel·ly ['pɑt,bɛlɪ; 'pɔt,beli] *n., pl.* **-lies.** 大腹;大腹之人。
pot·boil·er ['pɑt,bɔɪlɚ; 'pɔt,bɔilə] *n.* 〖俗〗爲賺稿費而粗製濫造的文學或藝術作品。
pot-bound ['pɑt,baund; 'pɔtbaund] *adj.* ①〖園藝〗根生滿花盆的。②無發展餘地的。
pot·boy ['pɑt,bɔɪ; 'pɔtbɔi] *n.* 〖英〗酒館侍役;酒館助手。(亦作 **potman**)
pot culture 吸毒文化(生活方式以使用大麻煙爲中心)。
po·teen [po'tin; pɔ'ti:n] *n.* (在愛爾蘭)私釀的威士忌。
po·tence ['potṇs; 'poutəns] *n.* =**potency.**
po·ten·cy ['potṇsɪ; 'poutənsi] *n., pl.* **-cies.** ①力量;權勢。②功效;效能。③潛力。④有影響力之人或事物。⑤〖數學〗(集的)勢。
***po·tent** ['potṇt; 'poutənt] *adj.* ①强有力的;有效的。②發生道德影響力的。③(男人或雄性動物之)具有性交能力的。 **—ly,** *adv.*
po·ten·tate ['potṇ,tet; 'poutənteit] *n.* ①有權勢者。②統治者;君主;女王。③强國。
***po·ten·tial** [pə'tɛnʃəl; pə'tenʃəl] *adj.* ①可能的;潛在的。②〖文法〗可能法的(凡用 may, might, can, could 等之語法)。 the *potential* mood of a verb. 某動詞之可能語態。③〖古〗=**potent.** —*n.* ①可能性。②電位;電勢。③〖文法〗可能語態。④〖數學〗位;勢。
potential difference 〖物理〗位差;勢差。
potential energy 〖物理〗位能;勢能。
po·ten·ti·al·i·ty [pə,tɛnʃɪ'ælətɪ; pə,tenʃi'æliti] *n., pl.* **-ties.** ①可能;可能性;潛在性;潛力。②可能之事物;有潛力之事物。
po·ten·tial·ly [pə'tɛnʃəlɪ; pə'tenʃəli] *adv.* 可能地。
po·ten·ti·ate [pə'tɛnʃɪ,et; pə'tenʃieit] *v.t.,* **-at·ed, -at·ing.** 賦與力量;使成爲可能;加强。
po·ten·ti·om·e·ter [pə,tɛnʃɪ'ɑmətɚ; pə,tenʃi'ɔmitə] *n.* 〖電〗①電位計;電勢計。②分壓器。
pot hat =**derby.**
pot·head ['pɑt,hɛd; 'pɔthed] *n.* 〖美俚〗吸大麻煙成癮的人。
po·theen [po'θin; pou'θi:n] *n.* =**poteen.**
poth·er ['pɑðɚ; 'pɔðə] *n.* ①騷動。②烟霧;塵霧。—*v.t.* 騷擾;使困惱。—*v.i.* 無謂紛擾。
pot·herb ['pɑt,ɝb; 'pɔthə:b] *n.* ①葉莖可煮食之植物(如菠菜等);蔬菜。②烹調時用以調味之植物(如麝香草等);香料。
pot·hole ['pɑt,hol; 'pɔthoul] *n.* ①深穴;坑。②河床岩石上之壺狀洞穴。③路上的坑洞。
pot·hook ['pɑt,huk; 'pɔthuk] *n.* ①掛鉤(火爐上支鍋、壺用)。②鐵鉤(鉤舉熱鍋或爐蓋用)。③S形筆畫(尤指兒童所作者)。
pot·house ['pɑt,haus; 'pɔthaus] *n., pl.* **-hous·es.** 〖英〗啤酒店;麥酒店;低級酒店。
pot·hunt·er ['pɑt,hʌntɚ; 'pɔt,hʌntə] *n.* ①(不顧季節及狩獵法的)亂獵者。②以獎品爲唯一目的的運動員。
po·tion ['poʃən; 'pouʃən] *n.* ①(藥等之)一服;一劑。②一種飲料。
pot liquor 鹹肉蔬菜湯。(亦作 **pot-liquor**)
pot·luck ['pɑt,lʌk; 'pɔt'lʌk] *n.* 便飯;便餐;現成菜飯。 ***take potluck*** **a.** 接受便餐招待。Come and *take potluck* with us. 請來和我們便餐。**b.** 接受現有的東西。
Po·to·mac [pə'tomək; pə'toumək] *n.* 波多馬克河(自美國 West Virginia 州流入 Chesapeake 灣)。
pot·pie ['pɑt,paɪ; 'pɔtpai] *n.* ①一種肉餡餅。②鷄或犢肉燉麪糰。
pot·pour·ri [pɑt'purɪ; pou'puri:] *n., pl.* **-ris.** ①乾玫瑰葉或花瓣與香料等之混合物。②〖音樂〗混成曲;接續曲。③文學作品之雜集。④任何不協調事物之混合物。
pot roast 燜燒牛肉。
Pots·dam ['pɑts,dæm; 'pɔtsdæm] *n.* 波茨坦(柏林西南,東德之一城市)。
Potsdam Declaration (or **Surrender Ultimatum**) 波茨坦宣言(或勸告投降最後通牒)(1945年7月26日經中、英、美三國領袖簽署,於 Potsdam 發表要求日本無條件投降的聯合宣言)。
pot·sherd ['pɑt,ʃɝd; 'pɔt-ʃə:d] *n.* 陶器碎片。
pot shot ①僅爲獲取食物而不顧狩獵法的對獵物之射擊。②對人或動物於易命中之近距離的射擊;近距離狙擊或攻擊。
pot still 罐式蒸餾器。
pot·tage ['pɑtɪdʒ; 'pɔtidʒ] *n.* 濃湯。 ***a mess of pottage*** (導致將來吃大虧的)暫時小利。
pot·ted ['pɑtɪd; 'pɔtid] *adj.* ①盆栽的。②裝入壺(或瓶)內的。③〖俚〗喝醉的。④〖英俚〗膚淺的。⑤〖英俚〗錄音的;灌製的。⑥〖英俚〗縮短的;濃縮的。
***pot·ter¹** ['pɑtɚ; 'pɔtə] *n.* 陶工。
pot·ter² *v.i.* & *v.t.* ①懶散而無目的地工作;無效能地忙碌;無事忙。②慢慢地走。③虛度光陰。—*n.* ①懶散而無目的的工作;無事忙。②漫步。③虛度光陰。**—er,** *n.* **—ing·ly,** *adv.*
potter's field 葬貧民或無名屍的公墓。
potter's wheel 製陶器用之轉盤。
***pot·ter·y** ['pɑtərɪ; 'pɔtəri] *n., pl.* **-ter·ies.** ①陶器。②陶器製造術。③陶器場。
pot·tle ['pɑtḷ; 'pɔtl] *n.* ①昔時的一種液量單位(=2 quarts 或 ½ gallon)。②能盛1 pottle 的壺或瓶;盛於此種壺或瓶中之物。③酒。④盛水果的小籃。
pot·ty ['pɑtɪ; 'pɔti] *adj.,* **-ti·er, -ti·est.** 〖英俗〗①瑣屑的;不重要的。②容易的;不予審慎考慮的。③略呈瘋狂的;怪異的。
pot-val·iant ['pɑt,væljənt; 'pɔt,væljənt] *adj.* 酒後膽壯的。
pot-val·o(u)r ['pɑt,vælɚ; 'pɔt,vælə] *n.* 酒後的勇氣。
***pouch** [pautʃ; pautʃ] *n.* ①小袋;小包;囊。②彈藥袋。③裝煙斗及煙葉的小袋(以便携帶於口袋中者);烟具袋。④郵袋。⑤任何袋狀物。⑥〖蘇〗衣服上之口袋。⑦〖古〗銀包;荷包。⑧(袋鼠等之)肚袋。⑨(塘鵝)喙上之袋狀物;(小栗鼠之)頰袋。 —*v.t.* ①裝入袋中。②使成袋狀。③(魚或鳥)吞食。④使乖乖地馴服。⑤〖俗〗給予錢。—*v.i.* 成袋狀。**—y,** *adj.*
pouched [pautʃt; pautʃt] *adj.* ①有袋的。②袋狀的。
poult [polt; poult] *n.* (鷄、火鷄等的)雛。
poult-de-soie [,pudə'swɑ; ,pu:də'swɑ:] 〖法〗 *n.* 波紋綢;縐綢。
poul·ter·er ['poltərɚ; 'poultərə] *n.* 〖英〗家禽販(尤指賣已殺好之鷄鴨等家禽者)。
poul·tice ['poltɪs; 'poultis] *n., v.,* **-ticed, -tic·ing.** —*n.* 敷於傷處以緩痛之麪糊、芥子糊等;膏藥。—*v.t.* 敷藥於;貼膏藥於。
***poul·try** ['poltrɪ; 'poultri] *n.* 家禽

(鷄、鴨、鵝等之集合稱)。—less, *adj.*

poul·try·man ['poltrɪmən; 'poultrimən] *n., pl.* -men. ①飼家禽者。②家禽商。

pounce[1] [pauns; pauns] *v.,* pounced, pounc·ing, *n.* —*v.i.* ①突然跳躍。②突然跳捕〖on, upon, at〗.—*v.t.* (禽獸)突然以利爪抓住。—*n.* 突然之跳躍;突然之跳捕。

pounce[2] *n., v.,* pounced, pounc·ing. —*n.* ①吸墨粉(防止墨水散開用)。②印花粉。—*v.t.* ①撒吸墨粉。②用印花粉印(花樣)。③用金剛砂紙磨光(帽)之表面。—pounc·er, *n.*

‡**pound**[1] [paund; paund] *n., pl.* pounds, pound. ①磅(重量單位,常衡時等於16盎斯,金衡時等於12盎斯)。②鎊(英國貨幣單位)。③埃及、秘魯、土耳其的一種金幣及貨幣單位(與英鎊價值相等)。④蘇格蘭已往計算上之幣制。⑤聖經新約中的一種閃族貨幣單位。

pound[2] *v.t. & v.i.* ①連擊;重擊。②擊碎;搗成粉。③沉重地跑;沉重地走。④重敲發(聲);鼕鼕地打。—*n.* ①沉重的敲擊;用力打;接連的打擊。②用力的一擊。③敲打聲。—er, *n.*

pound[3] *n.* ①(收留迷失牲畜的)獸欄。②(囚野獸的)圍柵。③監牢。—*v.t.* 囚於獸欄。

pound·age[1] ['paundɪdʒ; 'paundidʒ] *n.* ①按磅(重量)或鎊(貨幣)所抽的稅捐或佣金。②磅重;所携帶磅量總數。

pound·age[2] *n.* ①(保管在官設獸欄中的)牲畜釋放費。②監禁。

pound·al ['paundəl; 'paundəl] *n.*〖物理〗磅達(力之單位,作用於質量1磅之物體,使發生每秒1英尺秒之加速度之力)。

pound cake 磅餅(用麪粉、糖、牛油各1磅配製者)。

pound·er[1] ['paundɚ; 'paundə] *n.* ①重量(或價值)與磅(或鎊)有關之人或物。②發射以磅爲單位之砲彈的砲。③〖英〗收入(財產)以鎊爲計算單位的人。

pound·er[2] *n.* 搗者;打者;杵。

pound-fool·ish ['paund'fulɪʃ; 'paund'fu:liʃ] *adj.* 省小錢吃大虧的;因小失大的。

‡**pour** [por, pɔr; pɔ:, pɔə] *v.t.* ①使流;灌;倒;澆。*Pour* the wine into the bottle. 把酒倒在瓶內。②繼續不斷地發出、推出。The hunter *poured* bullets into the moving object. 獵人向在移動的目標不斷地射出子彈。③傾瀉;傾訴〖常out〗. to *pour* out one's troubles to a friend. 向一位朋友傾訴自己的苦惱。—*v.i.* 流;流出;瀉。Tears *poured* from her eyes. 淚水自她眼中流出。***pour cold water on*** 使沮喪;向…澆冷水。***pour it on***〖俗〗a. 努力說服;用力做或表示。b. 勝負雖已成定局,但仍繼續爭取分數。***pour oil on troubled waters*** 調解爭端。—*n.* ①流;注;瀉。②傾盆大雨。—a·bil·i·ty, —er, *n.* —a·ble, *adj.* —ing·ly, *adv.*

pour·boire ['pur,bwɑr; 'puəbwɑ:] *n., pl.* -boires [–,bwɑr; –bwɑ:].〖法〗賞錢;小費;酒錢。

pour·par·ler [pur'pɑrlɪ; puə'pɑ:lei] *n., pl.* -lers [–lez; –leiz].〖法〗(外交上的)非正式會談;預備會議。

pour·point ['pur,pɔint; 'puə,pɔint] *n.* (流行於14–15世紀的)男用緊身棉上衣。

pous·sette [pu'sɛt; pu:'set] *n., v.,* -set·ted, -set·ting.—*n.* 圓舞(一對或數對人携手環繞着跳的鄉間舞蹈)。—*v.i.* 跳圓舞。

pou sto ['pu'sto; 'pu:'stou]〖希〗①立足地。②根據地;基地。

pout**[1] [paut; paut] *v.t. & v.i.* ①撅嘴(小孩生氣或不樂之表示)。②撅嘴發出聲音。—*n.* (生氣或不悅時之)撅嘴。in the pouts*** 不悅;不歡。—ful, *adj.* —ing·ly, *adv.*

pout[2] *n., pl.* pout, pouts. 一種淡水鱈魚。

pout·er ['pautɚ; 'pautə] *n.* ①撅嘴的人;綳臉的人;發脾氣的人。②(亦作 **pouter pigeon**)球胸鴿。

***pov·er·ty** ['pɑvətɪ; 'pɔvəti] *n.* ①貧窮。②缺乏;不足。

poverty line 貧窮線(收入之最低標準,在此以下卽爲貧窮)。

pov·er·ty-strick·en ['pɑvətɪ,strɪkən; 'pɔvəti,strikn] *adj.* 極度貧困的。

POW, P.O.W. prisoner of war. 戰俘(複數爲 POWs 或 POW's).

‡**pow·der**[1] ['paudɚ; 'paudə] *n.* ①粉;細粉。②塗面粉、牙粉、鞋粉等。③火藥。***keep your powder dry*** 準備萬一。***not worth powder and shot*** 不值得費力。—*v.t.* ①使成粉。②塗以粉;搽粉。She *powdered* her nose. 她在鼻子上搽粉。③撒。—*v.i.* ①成爲粉。The soil *powdered* in the heat. 土壤在高溫中成爲粉狀。②搽粉。—er, *n.*

pow·der[2] *v.i.*〖英方〗衝出。—*n.*〖英方〗衝;亂衝。***take a (runout) powder***〖俚〗(爲避不愉快事)匆匆離開;不辭而別。

powder blue ①淺灰藍色。②紫藤顏料粉(淺灰藍色)。

powder box 化妝盒;粉盒。

powdered milk 奶粉。

powdered sugar 粉糖。

powder flask 火藥筒;火藥囊。

powder horn 角製火藥筒。

powder magazine 火藥庫。

powder monkey ①〖史〗(軍艦上)搬火藥的少年。②〖謔〗炸藥保管者;裝炸藥的人。

powder puff 粉撲。

powder room 化妝室;女用盥洗室。

pow·der·y ['paudərɪ; 'paudəri] *adj.* ①粉的;似粉的;粉狀的。②易粉碎的。③塗粉的。

‡**pow·er** ['pauɚ; 'pauə] *n.* ①力;動力。the *power* of a blow. 一擊之力。②能力。③權力;勢力。Knowledge is *power*. 知識卽力量。④有勢力者;强國。⑤職權;權限。⑥乘方;乘冪。27 is the third *power* of 3. 27是3的立方。⑦〖機械〗動力;機力;功率。Running water produces *power* to run mills. 流水可產生動力以推磨。⑧(透鏡之)擴大力。⑨天使之一級。⑩(*pl.*)神祇。***a power of*** 許多的;大量的。***in power*** (政黨等)在朝的。***power politics*** 强權外交。***the powers above*** 天上諸神。***the powers that be*** 當局者。The decision is in the hands of *the powers that be*. 決定權在當局者手裏。—*v.t.* ①供以動力。Atomic energy *powers* the submarine. 原子能供給該潛艇以動力。②使有力量。③鼓勵;激勵;支持。

power amplifier〖電訊〗功率放大器;擴音機。

pow·er·boat ['pauɚ,bot; 'pauəbout] *n.* 快速的汽艇。

power broker〖美〗權力掮客(影響權勢人物而左右權力者)。

power cable〖電〗電纜。

pow·er-dive ['pauɚ,daɪv; 'pauədaiv] *v.,* -dived, -dove, -div·ing. —*v.i.* (飛機)全力俯衝。—*v.t.* 使(飛機)全力俯衝。

power dive (飛機)全力俯衝。

power drill 動力鑽孔機。

(-)pow·ered ['pauɚd; 'pauəd] *adj.* 備有…動力(或發動機)的。a high-*powered* engine. 高馬力引擎。

ːpow·er·ful 〔ˈpauɚfəl; ˈpauəful〕 *adj.* ①有力的;强的。a *powerful* nation. 强大的國家。②(藥物等)强力的;有特效的。a *powerful* drug. 特效藥。③〖主方〗很多的。—**ly,** *adv.* —**ness,** *n.*

pow·er·house 〔ˈpauɚˌhaus; ˈpauəhaus〕 *n., pl.* **-hous·es.** ①〖電〗發電廠。②〖俚〗精力充沛的人。

***pow·er·less** 〔ˈpauəlɪs; ˈpauəlis〕 *adj.* 無力的;無權的;無效能的。I am quite *powerless* in the matter. 我對此事無能爲力。—**ly,** *adv.*

power loom 動力織布機。

power of attorney 〖法律〗委任書。

power plant ①發電廠。②發動機。

power play ①〖運動〗(球賽)集中攻勢(以使帶球人可得分)。②(政治、外交、軍事等)集中壓力。

power politics 强權外交。

power reactor 原子能發電機。

power series 〖數學〗冪級數。

power station 發電廠。

power structure ①(政治、政府、教育等)權力機構。②構成權力機構的人們。

power transmission ①動力傳達;能之傳遞。②電力輸送。

pow·wow 〔ˈpauˌwau; ˈpauwau〕 *n.* ①(北美印第安人之)巫醫;巫祝。②祝禱。③(北美印第安人爲醫病、狩獵等而舉行之)儀式。④(北美印第安人之)會議。⑤〖俗〗任何一種的會議或集會。—*v.i.* ①舉行會議;商議。②行巫術;祝禱。

pox 〔paks; pɔks〕 *n.* 〖醫〗①水痘;天花。②梅毒。 ***A pox on*** (or ***of***) ***you!*** 畜生! 該死的東西! ***What a pox!*** 噯呀!

poz·zo·la·na 〔ˌpatsəˈlanɑ; ˌpɔtsəˈlɑːnɑː〕 *n.* 火山石(作水泥原料)。

poz·zuo·la·na 〔ˌpatswəˈlanɑ; ˌpɔtswəˈlɑːnɑː〕 *n.* =**pozzolana.**

pp, pp. 〖音樂〗pianissimo. **pp.** ①pages. ②past participle. ③pianissimo. ④privately printed. **P.P., p.p.** ①parcel post. ②parish priest. ③past participle. ④postpaid. ⑤prepaid. **P.P.C., p.p.c.** pour prendre congé (法 =to take leave). **PPI** plan position indicator. 平面位置指示器。 **ppr., p.pr.** present participle. **P.P.S., p.p.s.** post-post-scriptum (拉 =an additional postscript). **P.Q.** ①Province of Quebec. ②personality quotient. **Pr** 化學元素 praseodymium 之符號。 **Pr.** ①preferred (stock). ②Priest. ③Prince. ④Provençal. **pr.** ①pair(s). ②paper. ③power. ④preference. ⑤preferred. ⑥present. ⑦price. ⑧priest. ⑨prince. ⑩printing. ⑪pronoun. **P.R.** ①parliamentary report. ②Roman people (拉= populus Romanus). ③press release. ④prize ring. ⑤proportional representation. ⑥public relations. ⑦Puerto Rico.

prac·ti·ca·bil·i·ty 〔ˌpræktɪkəˈbɪlətɪ; ˌpræktikəˈbiliti〕 *n.* 可實行性;實用性。

prac·ti·ca·ble 〔ˈpræktɪkəbl; ˈpræktikəbl〕 *adj.* ①可實行的。a *practicable* idea. 可實行的意見。②能用的。③〖戲院〗(道具等)實用的。—**ness,** *n.* —**prac·ti·ca·bly,** *adv.*

ːprac·ti·cal 〔ˈpræktɪkl; ˈpræktikəl〕 *adj.* ①實際的。Earning a living is a *practical* matter. 謀生是一實際問題。②合乎實際的;實用的;有用的。a *practical* method. 實用的方法。③實際從事的;有實地經驗的。a *practical* politician. 一個有經驗的政壇人物。④實質上的。⑤現實的。

prac·ti·cal·i·ty 〔ˌpræktɪˈkælətɪ; ˌpræktiˈkæliti〕 *n., pl.* **-ties.** ①實際性;實際的可能性。②實際之物;實用之物。

practical joke 惡作劇。

ːprac·ti·cal·ly 〔ˈpræktɪklɪ; ˈpræktikəli〕 *adv.* ①實際地。②〖俗〗幾乎地。Their provisions were *practically* gone. 他們的糧食幾乎沒有了。③實用地。④實驗地。

practical nurse 有實際經驗而未經正式訓練亦無執照的護士。

ːprac·tice 〔ˈpræktɪs; ˈpræktis〕 *n., v.,* **-ticed, -tic·ing.** —*n.* ①實用;實行;應用。to put into *practice.* 實踐;實行(計畫等)。②練習;實習。③習慣;常例。It is our *practice* to get up early in the morning. 早起是我們的習慣。④(醫生或律師之)業務;生意。Dr. Adams has a large *practice.* 亞當斯醫生的業務廣泛。⑤實施;實際應用。⑥(*pl.*)〖古〗策略;詭計。⑦〖法律〗訴訟手續;訴訟程序。 ***in practice*** **a.** 實際上;事實上。**b.** (因練習而)純熟。 ***make a practice of*** 養成…之習慣。 ***out of practice*** (因練習不足而)生疏。—*v.t.* & *v.i.* ①練習;實習。to *practice* playing the piano. 練習彈鋼琴。②慣做;常爲。to *practice* early rising. 養成早起的習慣。③以(醫生、律師等)爲業;營業;操業。He is just beginning to *practice* as a lawyer. 他剛開始操律師業。④實行;爲。to *practice* moderation. 行中庸之道。⑤訓練;教練;使練習。⑥〖古〗圖謀;計畫。⑦利用。—**prac·tic·er,** *n.* 〖注意〗 **practice, practise.** 作名詞時,應該用 practice, 動詞則 practise 或 practice 均可。

prac·ticed 〔ˈpræktɪst; ˈpræktist〕 *adj.* ①熟練的;經驗豐富的;老練的。②由練習而得來的。(亦作 **practised**)

practice teacher 實習教員。

practice teaching 教學實習;試教。

prac·ti·cian 〔prækˈtɪʃən; prækˈtiʃən〕 *n.* ①有經驗的人;熟練的人。②開業者。

***prac·tise** 〔ˈpræktɪs; ˈpræktis〕 *v.,* **-tised, -tis·ing.** =**practice.**

prac·ti·tion·er 〔prækˈtɪʃənɚ; prækˈtiʃn̩ə〕 *n.* ①從業者;開業者。②實行者;實施者。

prae·di·al 〔ˈpridɪəl; ˈpriːdiəl〕 *adj.* ①土地的;長於地上的。②土地占有的。③屬於土地的。(亦作 **predial**)

prae·fect 〔ˈprifɛkt; ˈpriːfekt〕 *n.* =**prefect.**

prae·mu·ni·re 〔ˌprimjəˈnaɪrɪ; ˌpriːmjəˈnairiː〕 *n.* 〖英法律〗王權侵害罪;教皇尊信罪(不服從國王而服從教皇等其他威權之罪);控訴該罪之令狀;對該罪之刑罰。

prae·no·men 〔prɪˈnomɛn; priːˈnoumen〕 *n., pl.* **-no·mi·na** 〔-ˈnɑmɪnə; -ˈnɔminə〕, **-no·mens.** (古羅馬人的)第一個名字(如: Gaius Julius Caesar 之 Gaius). (亦作 **prenomen**)

prae·tor 〔ˈpritɚ; ˈpriːtə〕 *n.* ①(古羅馬)兼負軍事責任之執政官。②(古羅馬之)民選長官(主要掌理司法事務)。

prae·to·ri·an 〔prɪˈtorɪən; priːˈtɔːriən〕 *adj.* ①(古羅馬)兼理軍事之執政官的。②(常 P-)羅馬御衞隊的。—*n.* ①(古羅馬)有執政官階級的人。②(常 P-)羅馬皇帝衞隊中之一員。

prag·mat·ic 〔præg'mætɪk; præg'mætik〕 *adj.* ①(哲學上的)實用主義的。②忙碌的;好事的。③自負的;獨斷的。④實際的。—*n.* ①=**pragmatic sanction.** ②好管閑事的人。
prag·mat·i·cal 〔præg'mætɪkl;præg'mætikəl〕 *adj.* =**pragmatic.** —**ly,** *adv.*
pragmatic sanction 國事詔令(具有基本法效力)。
prag·ma·tism 〔'prægmə,tɪzəm; 'prægmətizəm〕 *n.* ①(哲學上的)實用主義。②忙碌;好事。③自負;獨斷。④實際觀察。—**prag·ma·tist,** *n., adj.*
prag·ma·tis·tic 〔,prægmə'tɪstɪk; ,prægmə'tistik〕 *adj.* 〖哲學〗實用主義的。
prag·ma·tize 〔'prægmə,taɪz; 'prægmətaiz〕 *v.t.,* **-tized, -tiz·ing.** (將想像上的事)實際化;現實化;合理地解釋(神話等)。
Prague 〔preg; prɑːg〕 *n.* 布拉格(捷克斯拉夫首都)。
***prai·rie** 〔'prɛrɪ;'prɛəri〕 *n.* ①大草原。②〖美方〗森林中的一小片空地。③牧場;草地。
prairie chicken 松鷄。
prairie dog 塲撥鼠。
prairie schooner 長形布篷馬車;草原車。
prairie wolf 郊狼;山犬(=coyote).
‡**praise** 〔prez; preiz〕 *n., v.,* **praised, prais·ing.** —*n.* ①讚美;稱讚。Your *praise* pleased her very much. 你的讚譽很使她高興。②讚頌;崇拜。to sing *praises* to God. 唱讚美詩。③〖古〗可受稱讚的理由。④〖廢〗稱讚的對象。***damn with faint praise*** 捧場而不熱心,以致實際上等於貶抑。***sing someone's praise*** 公開讚揚。***sing the praise (of)*** 頌揚;歌頌。—*v.t.* ①稱讚;誇獎;讚譽。Did he *praise* your work? 他稱讚你的工作嗎?②讚頌;頌揚。
praise·wor·thy 〔'prez,wɝðɪ;'preiz,wəːði〕 *adj.* 值得讚美的;應加頌揚的。—**praise·wor·thi·ly,** *adv.* —**praise·wor·thi·ness,** *n.*
pra·line 〔'prɑlin; 'prɑːliːn〕 *n.* 杏仁糖;胡桃糖;乾果糖。
pram[1] 〔præm; præm〕 *n.* 〖英俗〗①搖籃車。②送牛奶之手推車。
pram[2] 〔prɑm;prɑːm〕 *n.* ①(亦作 **praam, prahm**)(荷蘭、德國)一種較輕的平底船。②(挪威)一種小型漁船。
prance 〔præns; prɑːns〕 *v.,* **pranced, pranc·ing,** *n.* —*v.i.*①(馬之)後足立地騰躍。②(騎馬)奮然躍進。③乘馬傲然前進。④高視闊步;意氣揚揚而行。⑤歡躍。—*v.t.* 使(馬)騰躍。—*n.* ①跳躍;歡躍。②昂然而行。
pran·di·al 〔'prændɪəl; 'prændiəl〕 *adj.* 餐膳的;正餐的。
prang 〔præŋ; præŋ〕 *v.t.* 〖英俚〗①與…相撞。②轟炸;炸毀。③打下(敵人飛機)。
prank[1] 〔præŋk; præŋk〕 *n.* ①戲謔。On April Fool's Day people play *pranks* on each other. 在愚人節人們彼此戲謔。②惡作劇。—**ster,** *n.*
prank[2] *v.t. & v.i.* 盛裝;裝飾。
prank·ish 〔'præŋkɪʃ; 'præŋkiʃ〕 *adj.* 戲謔的;頑皮的;愛開玩笑的。—**ly,** *adv.*
prase 〔prez; preiz〕 *n.* 〖礦〗綠石英。
pra·se·o·dym·i·um 〔,prezɪə'dɪmɪəm; ,preiziə'dimiəm〕 *n.* 〖化〗鐠(一種稀土金屬元素,符號 Pr)。
prat 〔præt; præt〕 *n.* 〖美俚〗①(常 *pl.*)臀;屁股。②臀部的褲袋。
prate 〔pret; preit〕 *v.,* **prat·ed, prat·ing,** *n.* —*v.t. & v.i.* 喋喋不休;空談。—*n.* 空談。—**prat·er,** *n.*
prat·fall 〔'prætfɔl; 'prætfɔːl〕 *n.* 〖俚〗①臀部著地的摔交。②可恥的失敗或錯誤。
pra·ties 〔'pretɪz; 'preitiz〕 *n. pl.* 〖方〗洋山芋;馬鈴薯。
pra·tique 〔præ'tik, 'prætɪk; præ'tiːk, 'prætik〕 *n.*(檢疫後發給船隻的)入港許可證。
prat·tle 〔'prætl; 'prætl〕 *v.,* **-tled, -tling,** *n.* —*v.i. & v.t.* ①閑談。②若小孩之談話。—*n.* 閑談;小兒之話。—**prat·tler,** *n.*
Prav·da 〔'prɑvdə; 'prɑːvdə〕 *n.* 眞理報(蘇聯共產黨機關報)。
prawn 〔prɔn; prɔːn〕 *n.* 對蝦(3-4 英寸長)。—*v.t.* 捕(對蝦)。—**er,** *n.*
prax·is 〔'præksɪs; 'præksis〕 *n., pl.* **prax·es** 〔'præksiz; 'præksiːz〕. ①實用;實際。②習慣;慣例。③(文法等的)例題;習題。
‡**pray** 〔pre; prei〕 *v.t. & v.i.* ①祈禱。He *prayed* to God for help. 他祈求上帝幫助。②向…乞求;懇求。I *pray* you to think again. 我請求你再想一想。③請。*Pray* come with me. 請和我一道去。④經禱告與上帝能有精神上的溝通。***pray in aid*** 懇求協助。
‡**prayer** 〔prɛr, for ⑥ 'pre·ɚ; prɛə, for ⑥'preiə *or* 'preə〕 *n.* ①祈禱;禱告。He knelt down in *prayer.* 他跪下祈禱。②所祈禱之事物。③祈禱文。to say one's *prayers.* 讀祈禱文。the Lord's *prayer.* 主禱文。④祈禱式。family *prayers.* 家庭禱告。⑤懇求。⑥祈禱者。
prayer beads 一串念珠。
prayer bones 〖美俚〗膝蓋。
prayer book ①祈禱書。②(the P- B-)英國教會的禮拜儀式及祈禱書。
prayer·ful 〔'prɛrfəl;'prɛəful〕 *adj.* ①常禱告的;虔誠的。②似禱告的;表示禱告的。—**ly,** *adv.*
prayer meeting 祈禱會。
prayer paper 符;咒符。
prayer rug 回教徒禱告跪拜時所用小地毯。
prayer wheel 〖喇嘛教〗地藏車;祈禱輪(祈禱時所用者,轉一周相當於一次祈禱)。
praying mantis 螳螂。(亦作 **praying mantid, praying insect**)
P.R.B. Pre-Raphaelite Brotherhood.
pre- 〖字首〗表"在…先;前;預先"之義。如:prewar. 戰前。(亦作 **prae-**)
preach** 〔pritʃ; priːtʃ〕 *v.t. & v.i.* ①傳教;說教。②宣講(教義等)。to *preach* the Gospel. 宣講福音。③講勸;倡導。④嘮叨。preach down*** **a.** 用宣講斥責。**b.** 用宣講壓制。***preach up*** 公開推介;頌揚。
***preach·er** 〔'pritʃɚ; 'priːtʃə〕 *n.* 傳道者;宣教師;牧師。
preach·i·fy 〔'pritʃə,faɪ;'priːtʃifai〕 *v.i.,* **-fied, -fy·ing.** 〖俗〗說教;勸告;嘮叨地說。
preach·ing 〔'pritʃɪŋ; 'priːtʃiŋ〕 *n.* 傳教;講道;講道法。—*adj.* 傳教的;講道的。
preach·ment 〔'pritʃmənt; 'priːtʃmənt〕 *n.* ①講道;傳教。②冗長的講道。
preach·y 〔'pritʃɪ;'priːtʃi〕 *adj.,* **preach·i·er, preach·i·est.** 〖俗〗似說教的;好講道的;教誨的;冗長的。
pre·ad·am·ite 〔pri'ædəm,aɪt; 'priː'ædəmait〕 *n.* ①亞當(Adam)以前的人。②信亞當以前有人類存在的人。—*adj.* 亞當以前(之人)的。
pre·ad·o·les·cence 〔,priædə'lɛsn̩s; ,priːædou'lesns〕 *n.* 前青年時期(通常指 9歲至12歲之期間)。—**pre·ad·o·les·cent,** *adj., n.*

pre·am·ble [ˈpriæmbḷ; priːˈæmbl] *n.* ①(條約、憲法等之)前文;導言。②緒言;序文。③初步事實;先兆。④(P-)美憲法序文。
pre·ar·range [ˌpriəˈrendʒ; ˈpriːəˈreindʒ] *v.t.*, **-ranged, -rang·ing.** 預先安排;預定。—**ment,** *n.*
pre·a·tom·ic [ˌpriəˈtɑmɪk; ˌpriːəˈtɔmik] *adj.* 原子彈轟炸(使用)以前的。
pre·au·di·ence [priˈɔdiəns; priːˈɔːdiəns] *n.* 〖英法律〗(辯護律師的)優先發言權。
preb·end [ˈprɛbənd; ˈprebənd] *n.* ①牧師(僧侶)的薪俸。②牧師薪俸來源的田產或什一稅。③〖罕〗=**prebendary.**
pre·ben·dal [prɪˈbɛndḷ; priˈbendl] *adj.* 牧師俸祿的;受俸祿之牧師的。
prebendal stall 受祿牧師之座席。
preb·en·dar·y [ˈprɛbəndˌɛrɪ; ˈprebəndəri] *n., pl.* **-dar·ies.** 受祿之牧師。—*adj.* =**prebendal.**
prec. ①preceded. ②preceding.
Pre-Cam·bri·an [priˈkæmbrɪən; priːˈkæmbriən] *adj.* 〖地質〗前寒武紀的;前寒武系的。—*n.* 前寒武紀;前寒武系。
pre·can·cel [priˈkænsḷ; priːˈkænsəl] *v.*, **-celed, -cel·ing,** *n.* —*v.t.* 郵票發行前在(郵票)上蓋作廢的戳子。—*n.* 在發行前蓋過作廢戳子的郵票。
pre·car·i·ous [prɪˈkɛrɪəs; priˈkɛəriəs] *adj.* ①視他人之好惡或環境而定的。②危險的;不安定的;不確定的。A soldier leads a *precarious* life. 軍人度着危險的生活。③無根據的;臆斷的;靠不住的。—**ly,** *adv.* —**ness,** *n.*
prec·a·to·ry [ˈprɛkəˌtorɪ; ˈprekətəri] *adj.* 懇求的;表示懇求的。
***pre·cau·tion** [prɪˈkɔʃən; priˈkɔːʃən] *n.* ①預防;防備。to take *precautions* against fire. 預防火災。②事先之準備;預防法。—*v.t.* 預先警告;使有備。
pre·cau·tion·ar·y [prɪˈkɔʃənˌɛrɪ; priˈkɔːʃṇəri] *adj.* 預防的。
***pre·cede** [priˈsid; pri(ː)ˈsiːd] *v.*, **-ced·ed, -ced·ing.** —*v.t.* ①在前;在先;先行。Truman *preceded* Eisenhower as President. 杜魯門任總統在艾森豪之先。②(地位等)高於;優於。—*v.i.* 在前;在先;在…之上。
prec·e·dence [prɪˈsidṇs; pri(ː)ˈsiːdəns] *n.* ①超出;在先。②更重要。③較高之位置。④遊行或儀式中走於前面的權利;較高之社會聲望。(亦作 **precedency**)
***prec·e·dent** [*n.* ˈprɛsədənt; ˈpresidənt *adj.* prɪˈsidṇt; priˈsiːdənt] *n.* 先例;前例。It is against all *precedents.* 此事違反所有前例。—*adj.* 在先的;在前的。
***pre·ced·ing** [prɪˈsidɪŋ; priˈsiːdiŋ] *adj.* 在前的;在先的。the *preceding* day. 前一日。
pre·cen·sor·ship [priˈsɛnsəʃɪp; priːˈsensəʃip] *n.* 保密文件發表前之預先檢查。
pre·cen·tor [prɪˈsɛntɚ; priːˈsentə] *n.* (唱詩班的)領唱者。
pre·cept [ˈprisɛpt; ˈpriːsept] *n.* ①箴言;教訓。Example is better than *precept.* 身教勝於言教。②(機械等之)操作方法。③〖法律〗命令書;令狀。
pre·cep·tive [prɪˈsɛptɪv; priˈseptiv] *adj.* 箴言的;箴誡的;教訓的。—**ly,** *adv.*
pre·cep·tor [prɪˈsɛptɚ; priˈseptə] *n.* ①教訓者;教師。②聖殿騎士團分團團長。—**i·al,** *adj.*
pre·cep·to·ry [prɪˈsɛptərɪ; priˈseptəri] *n., pl.* **-ries.** 〖史〗①聖殿騎士團的分團或教堂。②其領地。
pre·cep·tress [prɪˈsɛptrɪs; priˈseptris] *n.* preceptor 之女性。
pre·ces·sion [prɪˈsɛʃən; priˈseʃən] *n.* ①=**precedence.** ②前進(運動)。③〖天文〗歲差(=procession of the equinoxes)
pre·ces·sion·al [prɪˈsɛʃənḷ; priːˈseʃənl] *adj.* 〖天文〗歲差的;因歲差而致的。
pre-Chris·tian [ˈpriˈkrɪstʃən; ˈpriːˈkristʃən] *adj.* 基督教以前的。
pre·cinct [ˈprisɪŋkt; ˈpriːsiŋkt] *n.* ①(城市之)區域;區。an election *precinct.* 選舉區。②限定之區域;範圍內之區域。③(常 *pl.*)界限;範圍;環境。within the city *precincts.* 在市區範圍內。④〖主英〗教會、寺廟四周之地。⑤以圍牆等圍住的地方。
pre·ci·os·i·ty [ˌprɛʃɪˈɑsətɪ; ˌpreʃiˈɔsiti] *n., pl.* **-ties.** ①(言語、筆調、趣味等的)過於講究;過於細心;矯揉造作。②有上述習慣之人。③(*pl.*)貴重物件。
‡**pre·cious** [ˈprɛʃəs; ˈpreʃəs] *adj.* ①寶貴的;貴重的。*precious* stones. 寶石。②可愛的;珍愛的。③(言語、行為等)過於考究的;過於精緻的;矯揉造作的。④〖俗〗極大的。⑤好的;很大的(諷刺語)。⑥〖俗〗漂亮的。Her little house is just *precious.* 她的小房子眞是漂亮。—*adv.* 〖俗〗非常地。*precious* little money. 極少的錢。—*n.* 寶貝;被寵愛的人。—**ly,** *adv.* —**ness,** *n.*
***prec·i·pice** [ˈprɛsəpɪs; ˈpresipis] *n.* ①懸崖。②極為危急之情勢;生死存亡關頭。
pre·cip·i·tance [prɪˈsɪpətəns; priˈsipitəns] *n.* ①火急;魯莽。②(*pl.*)魯莽躁急的行為;輕率的舉動。
pre·cip·i·tan·cy [prɪˈsɪpətənsɪ; priˈsipitənsi] *n., pl.* **-cies.** =**precipitance.**
pre·cip·i·tant [prɪˈsɪpətənt; priˈsipitənt] *adj.* ①突然的;急遽的。②下墜的;直竄的。③沉澱的。—*n.* 〖化〗沉澱劑。—**ly,** *adv.*
pre·cip·i·tate [*v.* prɪˈsɪpəˌtet; priˈsipiteit *adj., n.* prɪˈsɪpətɪt; priˈsipitit] *v.*, **-tat·ed, -tat·ing,** *adj., n.* —*v.t.* ①突然引起。②擲下;墜下;猛投。③使(空中水氣)凝為雨露而落下。④使(溶解物)沉澱。—*v.i.* ①倒落;墜落;倉皇。②(溶解物)沉澱。③(空中水氣)凝結為雨露落下。—*adj.* ①急促的;突然的。②匆忙的;鹵莽的。—*n.* 凝結或沉澱而下降之物;沉澱物。—**ly,** *adv.* —**ness,** **pre·cip·i·ta·tor,** *n.*
pre·cip·i·ta·tion [prɪˌsɪpəˈteʃən; priˌsipiˈteiʃən] *n.* ①投下;驀進;猛衝。②匆促;慌張;鹵莽。③催促;促迫。④沉澱(物)。⑤〖氣象〗a. 大氣中水氣凝結之產物(如雨等)。b. 大氣中水氣凝結之量(即雨等之量)。⑥(降神術之)靈魂現形。
pre·cip·i·tous [prɪˈsɪpətəs; priˈsipitəs] *adj.* ①陡峭的。*precipitous* cliffs. 峭壁;危崖。②急轉直下的;突然落下的。③〖罕〗急速的;輕率的。—**ly,** *adv.* —**ness,** *n.*
pré·cis [preˈsi; ˈpreisiː] *n., pl.* **-cis** [-siz; -siːz], *v.*—*n.* 大綱;摘要。—*v.t.* 作大綱;摘要。
***pre·cise** [prɪˈsaɪs; priˈsais] *adj.* ①精確的;正確的。*precise* measurements. 精確的尺寸(或數量)。②考究的;注意的。She is *precise* in her manners. 她在禮貌上是很注意的。③嚴格的。—**ly,** *adv.* —**ness,** *n.*
pre·ci·sian [prɪˈsɪʒən; priˈsiʒən] *n.* ①墨守成規的人;拘泥形式的人(尤指關於宗教事務者)。②十六或十七世紀英國之清教徒。—*adj.* 墨守成規者的。

***pre·ci·sion** 〔prɪˈsɪʒən; priˈsiʒən〕 *n.* ①精確;正確。*precision* in calculation. 計算之精確。②拘泥細節。③〖數學〗精確;精度;精密度。—*adj.* 精確的;精密的。

precision bombing 精密轟炸。(亦作 **pinpoint bombing**)

pre·clear 〔priˈklɪr; priːˈkliə〕 *v.t.* 事先批准;事前證明爲安全。

pre·clin·i·cal 〔priˈklɪnɪkl; priˈklinikəl〕 *adj.* 〖醫〗臨床前的;臨床前期的。

pre·clude 〔prɪˈklud; priˈkluːd〕 *v.t.*, **-clud·ed, -clud·ing.** ①排除。②妨礙;阻止;使不可能。

pre·clu·sion 〔prɪˈkluʒən; priˈkluːʒən〕 *n.* 排除;阻止;預防。

pre·clu·sive 〔prɪˈklusɪv; priˈkluːsiv〕 *adj.* 排除的;除外的;預防的。—**ly,** *adv.*

pre·co·cious 〔prɪˈkoʃəs; priˈkouʃəs〕 *adj.* ①早熟的。②〖植物〗開花結實早的;生葉之前開花的。③過早的。—**ly,** *adv.* —**ness,** *n.*

pre·coc·i·ty 〔prɪˈkɑsətɪ; priˈkɔsiti〕 *n.* ①早熟。②〖植物〗(花等)早開。③過早。

pre·con·ceive 〔ˌprikənˈsiv; ˈpriːkənˈsiːv〕 *v.t.*, **-ceived, -ceiv·ing.** ①預思;預想。②使成先入之見。*preconceived* ideas. 先入之見;成見。

pre·con·cep·tion 〔ˌprikənˈsɛpʃən; ˈpriːkənˈsepʃən〕 *n.* ①預想。②先入之見。③偏見;偏好。

pre·con·cert 〔ˌprikənˈsɝt; ˈpriːkənˈsəːt〕 *v.t.* 預先安排;預先安置。

pre·co·nize 〔ˈprikəˌnaɪz; ˈpriːkənaiz〕 *v.t.*, **-nized, -niz·ing.** ①公開宣布;當衆頌揚。②公開召喚;指名召喚。③〖天主教〗(教宗)公開承認並宣布(新主教)之姓名。

pre-Con·quest 〔priˈkɑnkwɛst, –ˈkɑŋ–; priːˈkɔŋkwest〕 *adj.* 〖英史〗諾曼第人征服(Norman Conquest, 1066年)以前的。

pre·cook 〔priˈkʊk; priːˈkuk〕 *v.t.* 將(食物)預先烹調(以便以後熱一下即可吃)。

pre·cur·sor 〔prɪˈkɝsɚ; pri(ː)ˈkəːsə〕 *n.* ①先驅;先兆。②前輩;先進。

pre·cur·so·ry 〔prɪˈkɝsərɪ; pri(ː)ˈkəːsəri〕 *adj.* ①前驅的;先進的。②預兆的;預先警告的。

pred. ①predicate. ②predicative(ly).

pre·da·cious, pre·da·ceous 〔prɪˈdeʃəs; priˈdeiʃəs〕 *adj.* ①搶掠的;掠奪的。②耽於掠奪或以掠奪爲生的。③〖動物〗捕食其他動物的;肉食的。

pre·date 〔priˈdet; priːˈdeit〕 *v.t.*, **-dat·ed, -dat·ing.** ①塡比實際日期較早之日期。②比…較早到來或發生。

pred·a·tor 〔ˈprɛdətɚ; ˈpredətə〕 *n.* ①掠奪者。②捕食其他動物之動物。

pred·a·to·ry 〔ˈprɛdəˌtorɪ; ˈpredətəri〕 *adj.* ①掠奪的;有掠奪性的;以掠奪爲生的。②〖動物〗食肉的。

pre·de·cease 〔ˌpridɪˈsis; ˈpriːdiˈsiːs〕 *v.*, **-ceased, -ceas·ing,** *n.* —*v.t.* 死於(某人或某事件)之先。—*n.* 早死;先死。

***pred·e·ces·sor** 〔ˌprɛdɪˈsɛsɚ; ˈpriːdisesə〕 *n.* ①(某職位的)前任。②被取代之物。③祖先;前輩。④以前所有的東西。

pre·del·la 〔prɪˈdɛlə; priˈdelə〕 *n.*, *pl.* **-le** 〔–li; –liː〕. ①祭壇之臺;祭壇臺直立面上之繪畫或雕刻。②祭壇後部之高架;此高架上之繪畫或雕刻。

pre·des·ti·nar·i·an 〔prɪˌdɛstəˈnɛrɪən; priˌdestiˈnɛəriən〕 *adj.* 宿命論的;信仰宿命論的。—*n.* 信仰宿命論的人。

pre·des·ti·nate 〔*v.* prɪˈdɛstəˌnet; priːˈdestineit *adj.* prɪˈdɛstənɪt; priːˈdestinit〕 *v.*, **-nat·ed, -nat·ing,** *adj.* —*v.t.* ①命中註定;預定。②〖神學〗(神)預先安排。—*adj.* ①命中註定的;宿命的。②預定的。

pre·des·ti·na·tion 〔prɪˌdɛstəˈneʃən; pri(ː)ˌdestiˈneiʃən〕 *n.* ①預定;前定。②命運;宿命;命定。③〖神學〗a. 世間一切事物均由神預定說。b. 人得救與否由神預定說。

pre·des·tine 〔prɪˈdɛstɪn; priːˈdestin〕 *v.t.*, **-tined, -tin·ing.** 預定;注定。

pre·de·ter·mi·nate 〔ˌpridɪˈtɝmənɪt; ˌpriːdiˈtəːminit〕 *adj.* ①預先決定的。②注定的;預定的。

pre·de·ter·mi·na·tion 〔ˌpridɪˌtɝməˈneʃən; ˈpriːdiˌtəːmiˈneiʃən〕 *n.* ①預先之決定。②先存某種傾向;偏見。

pre·de·ter·mine 〔ˌpridɪˈtɝmɪn; ˈpriːdiˈtəːmin〕 *v.t.*, **-mined, -min·ing.** ①預先決定;註定。②使先有某種傾向;使存偏見。

pred·i·ca·bil·i·ty 〔ˌprɛdɪkəˈbɪlətɪ; ˌpredikəˈbiliti〕 *n.* 可被斷定之情況或性質。

pred·i·ca·ble 〔ˈprɛdɪkəbl; ˈpredikəbl〕 *adj.* ①可斷定的;可肯定的。②可斷定爲…屬性的。—*n.* ①可被斷定者;屬性。②〖邏輯〗賓位語。③範疇。—**pred·i·ca·bly,** *adv.*

pre·dic·a·ment 〔prɪˈdɪkəmənt; priˈdikəmənt〕 *n.* ①處境;苦境;窮境;險境。②〖邏輯〗範疇;賓位語。

pred·i·cant 〔ˈprɛdɪkənt; ˈpredikənt〕 *adj.* 傳道的;說教的。—*n.* 布道者;說教者;牧師。

***pred·i·cate** 〔*n.*, *adj.* ˈprɛdɪkɪt; ˈpredikit *v.* ˈprɛdɪˌket; ˈpredikeit〕 *n.*, *adj.*, *v.*, **-cat·ed, -cat·ing.** —*n.* ①〖文法〗述詞;述語。②〖邏輯〗賓辭;屬性。—*adj.* 〖文法〗屬於述詞的;屬於述語的。—*v.t.* ①宣稱(某事屬實);斷言。Most religions *predicate* life after death. 大多數的宗教宣稱死後仍有生命。②意含;意指。③使(陳述或行動)有根據。④聲稱…爲某人或某物之屬性。

predicate adjective 〖文法〗述詞形容詞。

pred·i·ca·tion 〔ˌprɛdɪˈkeʃən; ˌprediˈkeiʃən〕 *n.* ①斷定;認定。②〖文法〗述語。

pred·i·ca·tive 〔ˈprɛdɪˌketɪv; priˈdikətiv〕 *adj.* ①肯定的;斷定的。②〖文法〗敍述的;述語的。—**ly,** *adv.*

pred·i·ca·to·ry 〔ˈprɛdəkəˌtorɪ; ˈpredikətəri〕 *adj.* ①布道的;說教的;與布道有關的。②〖文法〗述語的。

***pre·dict** 〔prɪˈdɪkt; priˈdikt〕 *v.t.* 預知;預言。The weather bureau *predicts* rain for tomorrow. 氣象局預測明天下雨。—*v.i.* 作預言;預言未來。

pre·dict·a·ble 〔prɪˈdɪktəbl; priˈdiktəbl〕 *adj.* 可預知的。—**pre·dict·a·bil·i·ty,** *n.*

***pre·dic·tion** 〔prɪˈdɪkʃən; priˈdikʃən〕 *n.* 預知;預言;預告;預測;預報。The official *predictions* about the weather often come true. 官方的天氣預報往往是正確的。

pre·dic·tive 〔prɪˈdɪktɪv; priˈdiktiv〕 *adj.* 預言的;預兆的。—**ly,** *adv.*

pre·dic·tor 〔prɪˈdɪktɚ; priˈdiktə〕 *n.* ①預言者。②高射瞄準器(可測定來犯飛機的速度、航路、高度等)。

pre·di·gest 〔ˌpridəˈdʒɛst; ˌpriːdiˈdʒest〕 *v.t.* ①以人工過程處理(食物)使易於消化;預先消化。②使簡化而更易了解。—**pre·di·ges·tion,** *n.*

pre·di·kant 〔ˌpredɪˈkɑnt; ˌpredi–

ˈkɑːnt) n. 荷蘭新教教會之牧師(特指南非者)。
pre·di·lec·tion [ˌpridḷˈɛkʃən; ˌpriːdiˈlekʃən] n. 偏愛;偏好。
pre·dis·pose [ˌpridɪsˈpoz; ˌpriːdisˈpouz] v.t., **-posed, -pos·ing.** ①使傾向於;使偏向於。②使易罹(某種病);使易染(某種病)。Fatigue *predisposes* one to cold. 疲勞使人容易傷風。—*v.i.* 使人易罹(某種病)。
pre·dis·po·si·tion [ˌpridɪspəˈzɪʃən; ˈpriːˌdispəˈziʃən] n. ①性向;傾向;癖性;素質。②〖醫〗易罹病的素質;易致素因。
pre·dom·i·nance [prɪˈdɑmənəns; priˈdɔminəns] n. ①優越;卓越;支配。②多數。(亦作 **predominancy**)
***pre·dom·i·nant** [prɪˈdɑmənənt; priˈdɔminənt] adj. ①主要的;有勢力的;傑出的。②最足注意的;流行的。**—ly,** *adv.*
pre·dom·i·nate [prɪˈdɑməˌnet; priˈdɔmineit] v., **-nat·ed, -nat·ing.** —*v.i.* 占勢力;握主權。—*v.t.* 爲…之主要特色;爲…之主要勢力。
pre·dom·i·na·tion [prɪˌdɑməˈneʃən; priˌdɔmiˈneiʃən] n. =**predominance.**
pre-e·lec·tion [ˌpriɪˈlɛkʃən; ˌpriːiˈlekʃən] adj. 發生在選舉前的;選舉前所說的。—*n.* 預選。
preem [prim; priːm] n. 〖美俗〗=**pre-mière.**
pre·em·i·nence [prɪˈɛmənəns; priːˈeminəns] n. 卓越;傑出。
pre·em·i·nent [prɪˈɛmənənt; priˈeminənt] adj. 優越的;卓越的。**—ly,** *adv.*
pre·empt [prɪˈɛmpt; priˈempt] v.t. ①搶先取得或占用。②預先占有(公地)而取得先買權。(亦作 **pre-empt, preëmpt**) **—or,** *n.*
pre·emp·tion [prɪˈɛmpʃən; priˈempʃən] n. ①搶先購買;優先購買。②優先購買權。③搶先取得。(亦作 **pre-emption, preëmption**)
pre·emp·tive [prɪˈɛmptɪv; priˈemptiv] adj. ①優先購買的;優先購買權的。*preemptive* right. 優先購買權。②先發制人的。(亦作 **pre-emptive, preëmptive**)
preen [prin; priːn] v.t. ①(鳥)以喙整理(羽毛)。②(人)修飾打扮。③覺得驕傲;感到光榮(與反身代名詞連用)。
pre·en·gage [ˌprinˈgedʒ; ˈpriːinˈgeidʒ] v., **-gaged, -gag·ing.** —*v.t.* ①預約;先約。②使先入爲主。③使偏向。—*v.i.* 預約;先約。**—ment,** *n.*
pre·es·tab·lish [ˌpriəsˈtæblɪʃ; ˈpriːisˈtæbliʃ] v.t. 預先設立或制定;預定。
pre·ex·il·i·an [ˌpriɛgˈzɪlɪən; ˈpriːegˈziliən] adj. =**preexilic.**
pre·ex·il·ic [ˌpriɛgˈzɪlɪk; ˈpriːegˈzilik] adj. ①放逐前的。②〖猶太史〗猶太人被放逐到巴比倫以前的。
pre·ex·ist [ˌpriɪgˈzɪst; ˈpriːigˈzist] v.i. 先存;先存在。
pre·ex·ist·ence [ˌpriɪgˈzɪstəns; ˈpriːigˈzistəns] n. 先存;靈魂之先存;前世。
pref. ①preface. ②preference. ③preferred. ④prefix. ⑤prefixed.
pre·fab [ˈpriˈfæb; ˈpriːˈfæb] adj., n., v., **-fabbed, -fab·bing.** —*adj.* 預先建造的。—*n.* 活動房屋。—*v.t.* =**prefabricate.**
pre·fab·ri·cate [priˈfæbrəˌket; ˈpriːˈfæbrikeit] v.t., **-cat·ed, -cat·ing.** ①製造(房屋等之)標準化部分。②預造;預備。**—pre·fab·ri·ca·tion,** *n.*
***pref·ace** [ˈprɛfɪs; ˈprefis] n., v., **-aced, -ac·ing.** —*n.* (書籍、演講之)序言;序文;開端。This book has a *preface* written by the author. 這本書有作者自己寫的序言。—*v.t.* ①作爲…的序文;開始。He *prefaced* his words with a smile. 他先微笑而後開始發言。②以序文介紹;爲…作序文。
pref·a·to·ry [ˈprɛfəˌtorɪ; ˈprefətəri] adj. 序文的;弁言的;開場的。
pre·fect [ˈprifɛkt; ˈpriːfekt] n. ①(古羅馬之)地方行政長官;司令官。②(法國或義大利的)地方行政長官。③〖英〗(學生之)級長;班長。(亦作 **praefect**) **—o·ri·al,** *adj.*
prefect of police 法國之警務總監。
pre·fec·tur·al [prɪˈfɛktʃərəl; priˈfektjurəl] adj. 地方的;地方官署的;地方長官的。
***pre·fec·ture** [ˈprifɛktʃɚ; ˈpriːfektjuə] n. ①地方官之職位、任期、轄區、或官邸。②(羅馬帝國、法國、日本等之)縣。
‡pre·fer [prɪˈfɝ; priˈfəː] v.t., **-ferred, -fer·ring.** ①較喜;寧愛(習慣上多與 to, rather than 連用)。I *prefer* coffee to tea. 我喜咖啡而不喜茶。I *prefer* to read rather than sit idle. 我寧願讀書而不願閒坐着。②提出;呈出。They *preferred* charges against him. 他們對他提出控告。③提升;擢升。
pref·er·a·ble [ˈprɛfrəbḷ; ˈprefərəbl] adj. 寧可取的;較合人意的。Death is *preferable* to dishonor. 死猶勝於受辱。
pref·er·a·bly [ˈprɛfərəblɪ; ˈprefərəbli] adv. 更合人意地;較可取地。
***pref·er·ence** [ˈprɛfərəns; ˈprefərəns] n. ①較愛;寧好;選擇。She has a *preference* for French novels. 她喜讀法國小說。②嗜好物。Her *preference* in reading is a novel. 在讀書方面她喜歡小說。
preference bond 優先公債券。
preference stock 〖英〗優先股。
pref·er·en·tial [ˌprɛfəˈrɛnʃəl; ˌprefəˈrenʃəl] adj. ①優先的。*preferential* right. 優先權。②優惠的;特惠的。
preferential duties 特惠關稅。
preferential shop 工會會員得享特惠待遇之商店、公司或工廠。
pre·fer·ment [prɪˈfɝmənt; priˈfəːmənt] n. ①擢升;晉升。②(僧人等的)高職;高位。③提出。
preferred stock 〖美〗優先股。
pre·fig·u·ra·tion [ˌprifɪgjəˈreʃən; ˈpriːfigjuˈreiʃən] n. ①預示;預表;預兆。②預想;預測。③原型樣本。
pre·fig·ure [priˈfɪgjɚ; ˈpriːˈfigə] v.t., **-ured, -ur·ing.** ①預示;預表。②預想;揣測。
***pre·fix** [n. ˈpriˌfɪks; ˈpriːfiks v. priˈfɪks; priːˈfiks] n. 字首(例如 unkind 中之 un)。—*v.t.* ①加字首。②置於前。We *prefix* "Mr." to a man's name. 我們將"Mr."置於男性姓(名)前。
pre·fix·ion [prɪˈfɪkʃən; priːˈfikʃən] *n.* 加字首。
pre·form [priˈfɔrm; priːˈfɔːm] v.t. 預先決定…之形式;預先形成。
pre·for·ma·tion [ˌprifɔrˈmeʃən; ˌpriːfɔːˈmeiʃən] n. 〖進化論〗預成論。
pre·gla·cial [priˈgleʃəl; ˈpriːˈgleiʃəl] adj. 〖地質〗冰河期前的。
preg·na·ble [ˈprɛgnəbḷ; ˈpregnəbl] adj. ①可用武力奪取的;易受攻擊的。②弱的;有弱點的。
preg·nan·cy [ˈprɛgnənsɪ; ˈpregnənsi] n., pl. **-cies.** ①懷孕;妊娠。②肥沃。
***preg·nant** [ˈprɛgnənt; ˈpregnənt]

adj. ①懷孕的。②充滿的；富饒的〖with〗. words *pregnant* with meaning. 富有意義之言辭。③肥沃的〖in〗. ④有意義的；重要的。⑤極可能的。⑥富概念或想像力的。—**ly,** *adv.*

pregnant construction〖修辭〗含蓄法。

pre·heat [pri'hit; pri:'hi:t] *v.t.* 預先加熱。

pre·hen·sile [prɪ'hɛnsl; pri'hensail] *adj.* ①(動物的尾、手、足等之)能握住或盤住的。②善於領悟的；善於洞察的。

pre·hen·sion [prɪ'hɛnʃən; pri'henʃən] *n.* ①捕捉；抓取。②領會；理解。

pre·his·tor·ic [ˌpriɪs'tɔrɪk, ˌprihɪs-; 'pri:his'tɔrik] *adj.* 史前的。(亦作 **prehistorical**) —**al·ly,** *adv.*

pre·his·to·ry [pri'hɪstərɪ, -trɪ; 'pri:'histəri, -tri] *n.* 史前史；史前背景。

pre·hu·man [pri'hjumən; 'pri:'hju:mən] *adj.* 人類存在以前的。

pre·ig·ni·tion [ˌpriɪg'nɪʃən; ˌpri:ig'niʃən] *n.* (內燃機的)先期點火。

pre·in·duc·tion [ˌpriɪn'dʌkʃən; ˌpri:in'dʌkʃən] *adj.* 入伍以前的。

pre·judge [pri'dʒʌdʒ; 'pri:'dʒʌdʒ] *v.t.,* **-judged, -judg·ing.** ①預斷；預決。②未經詳察事實而做判斷；未獲充分證據而作判斷。

pre·judg(e)·ment [pri'dʒʌdʒmənt; 'pri:'dʒʌdʒmənt] *n.* 審理前之判決；預斷；臆斷。

prej·u·dice** ['prɛdʒədɪs; 'predʒudis] *n., v.,* **-diced, -dic·ing.** —*n.* ①偏見；成見。He has a *prejudice* against all foreigners. 他對所有的外國人存有偏見。②傷害；損害。without prejudice***〖法律〗對法定利益或要求無影響或無損。—*v.t.* ①使存偏見；使有成見。②傷害；損害。

prej·u·diced ['prɛdʒədɪst; 'predʒudist] *adj.* 懷有偏見的；偏頗的。

prej·u·di·cial [ˌprɛdʒə'dɪʃəl; ˌpredʒu'diʃəl] *adj.* ①使生偏見的。②有害的。—**ly,** *adv.*

prel·a·cy ['prɛləsɪ; 'preləsi] *n., pl.* **-cies.** ①大主教、主教等之職位。②大主教、主教等之集合稱。③(教會之)教長政治。

prel·ate ['prɛlɪt; 'prelit] *n.* ①職位甚高的教士(如主教、大主教)。②修道院院長。

pre·lat·i·cal [prɪ'lætɪkl; pri'lætikl] *adj.* ①居高位之聖職者的。②教長政治的。(亦作 **prelatic**)

pre·lect [prɪ'lɛkt; pri'lekt] *v.i. & v.t.* 講演；講課(尤指大學中者)。—**pre·lec·tion,** *n.*

pre·lec·tor [prɪ'lɛktə; pri'lektə] *n.*〖英〗大學講師；講演者。

pre·li·ba·tion [ˌprilaɪ'beʃən; 'pri:lai'beiʃən] *n.* 預嘗；試嘗。

pre·lim [prɪ'lɪm; pri'lim] *n.*〖俗〗初試 (=preliminary examination).

***pre·lim·i·nar·y** [prɪ'lɪməˌnɛrɪ; pri'liminəri] *adj., n., pl.* **-nar·ies.** —*adj.* ①初步的；開始的。a *preliminary* examination. 初試。②在前的。—*n.* ①初步；開端。A physical examination is a *preliminary* to joining the army. 體格檢查是從軍的初步。②(常*pl.*)初步之行動、措施等。—**pre·lim·i·nar·i·ly,** *adv.*

preliminary hearing〖法律〗調查庭。

preliminary remarks 序言。

prel·ude ['prɛljud; 'prelju:d] *n., v.,* **-ud·ed, -ud·ing.** —*n.* ①序言；序幕；前奏；先驅。②〖音樂〗序曲；前奏曲。—*v.t.* ①爲…之前奏；爲…序幕。②以前奏曲開始。—*v.i.* ①爲前奏；爲序幕。②奏序曲。

pre·lu·sive [prɪ'ljusɪv; pri'lju:siv] *adj.* ①序言的。②序曲的；序樂的；前奏曲的。③前驅的。④前兆的；預示的。

prem. premium.

pre·mar·i·tal [pri'mærətl; pri:'mæritəl] *adj.* 婚前的。

pre·ma·ture [ˌprimə'tjur; ˌpremə'tjuə] *adj.* ①未成熟的；太早的。②草率的；匆促的。—*n.* 早熟；早開花；時期過早；時機未熟。—**ly,** *adv.*

premature delivery (or **labor**) 早產。

pre·ma·tu·ri·ty [ˌprimə'tjurətɪ; ˌpremə'tjuəriti] *n.* 未成熟；過早；草率。

pre·med ['primɛd; 'pri:med] *adj.* 醫預科的。—*n.* 醫預科學生。

pre·med·i·cal [pri'mɛdɪkl; 'pri:'medikəl] *adj.* 醫預科的。

pre·med·i·tate [prɪ'mɛdəˌtet; pri'mediteit] *v.t.,* **-tat·ed, -tat·ing.** 預謀。

pre·med·i·tat·ed [prɪ'mɛdəˌtetɪd; pri'mediteitid] *adj.* 預謀的；事先計劃的。

pre·med·i·ta·tion [ˌprimɛdə'teʃən; priˌmedi'teiʃən] *n.* ①預謀；熟慮；預計。②〖法律〗預謀犯罪。

***pre·mier** [*n.* 'primɪə, prɪ'mɪr; 'premjə *adj.* 'primɪə; 'premjə] *n.* 首相；國務總理；(中國之)行政院長。—*adj.* 首要的；第一的。

pre·mière [prɪ'mɪr; 'premiɛə]〖法〗*n.* ①(影劇、歌舞等之)首次公演。②(影劇等中之)首席女主角。—*adj.* 首位的；第一的。

pre·mier·ship ['primɪəˌʃɪp; 'premjəʃip] *n.* 首相、總理等之職位與任期。

prem·ise** [*n.* 'prɛmɪs; 'premis *v.* prɪ'maɪz, 'prɛmɪs; pri'maiz, 'premis] *n.* ①〖邏輯〗前提。②(*pl.*)房屋連地基。③(*pl.*)〖法律〗前述物件。the major premise*** 大前提。***the minor premise*** 小前提。—*v.t. & v.i.* 提論；立前題。Let me *premise* my argument with a bit of history. 讓我引述一些史實作爲我立論的前提。

prem·iss ['prɛmɪs; 'premis] *n.*〖邏輯〗前提 (=premise).

pre·mi·um** ['primɪəm; 'pri:mjəm] *n.* ①報酬；獎品。a *premium* for good conduct. 對於優良品行之獎品。②獎金；賞金。③保險費。④額外費用或價格。⑤(股票等之)超過票面之價格。The shares are selling at a *premium*. 那些股票賣價高於面額。⑥學費(學生付予私人教師者)。⑦不公平的價值；不當的鼓勵。at a premium*** **a.** 估價甚高的(地)；甚受尊敬的(地)。**b.** 非常寶貴的；爲人所冀求的。—*adj.* ①特佳的。②特級的。

premium loan 人壽保險公司借給投保人付保險金的貸款。

premium pay 加班工資；假日工資。

pre·mo·lar [pri'molə; 'pri:'moulə] *adj.*〖解剖〗①臼齒的。②位於臼齒前的。—*n.*〖解剖〗前臼齒；前磨牙。

pre·mo·ni·tion [ˌprimə'nɪʃən; ˌpri:mə'niʃən] *n.* ①預先告誡；預告。②前兆；預感。

pre·mon·i·to·ry [prɪ'mɑnəˌtorɪ; pri'mɔnitəri] *adj.* 預先告誡的；預告的；前兆的。

pre·na·tal [pri'netl; 'pri:'neitl] *adj.* 出生前的；胎兒期的。

pren·tice ['prɛntɪs; 'prentis] *n.* 學徒。—*adj.*〖古〗①學徒的。②無經驗的；未成熟的。

pre·nu·cle·ar [pri'njuklɪə; pri:'nju:kliə] *adj.* 核子武器時代以前的。

pre·oc·cu·pan·cy 〔prɪˈɑkjəpənsɪ; priːˈɔkjupənsi〕 *n., pl.* **-cies.** ①先占；先占權；先取；先得。②心神恍惚之狀態。

pre·oc·cu·pa·tion 〔priˌɑkjəˈpeʃən; pri(ː)ˌɔkjuˈpeiʃən〕 *n.* ①先得；先占；先居住。②先入爲主的偏見。③全神貫注；出神。④令人全神貫注的事物。

pre·oc·cu·pied 〔priˈɑkjəˌpaɪd; pri(ː)ˈɔkjupaid〕 *adj.* ①心不在焉的；心神不定的。②已被先占的。③〖生物〗已被用爲其他種、屬之名稱而不能再用的。

pre·oc·cu·py 〔priˈɑkjəˌpaɪ; pri(ː)ˈɔkjupai〕 *v.t.,* **-pied, -py·ing.** ①盤據（心頭）；使凝神於。②預占；先占。

pre·or·dain 〔ˌpriɔrˈden; ˈpriːɔːˈdein〕 *v.t.* 預定；預先註定。—**pre·or·di·na·tion,** *n.*

prep 〔prɛp; prep〕 *n., adj., v.,* **prepped, prep·ping.** —*n.* ①〖學生俗〗先修班；補習學校。②〖英〗功課。③手術準備。—*adj.* 〖俗〗預備的。—*v.i.* ①上補習學校。②作預習。—*v.t.* ①替…作預習。②替（患者）作手術準備。

prep. ①preparatory. ②preposition.

pre·paid 〔priˈped; ˈpriːˈpeid〕 *v.* pt. & pp. of **prepay.** —*adj.* 先付的；付訖的。

***prep·a·ra·tion** 〔ˌprɛpəˈreʃən; ˌprepəˈreiʃən〕 *n.* ①準備；預備。The car was in excellent *preparation* for the trip. 車子的旅行準備優良。②（常 *pl.*）準備之事物。to make *preparations* for a voyage. 做航行之準備。③（調製成之）藥劑；食物；配製品。pharmaceutical *preparations.* 藥劑。

pre·par·a·tive 〔prɪˈpærətɪv; priˈpærətiv〕 *adj.* ＝**preparatory.** —*n.* ①準備之行爲；準備之事物。②準備。—**ly,** *adv.*

***pre·par·a·to·ry** 〔prɪˈpærəˌtorɪ; priˈpærətəri〕 *adj.* ①預備的；準備的。②初步的。*preparatory* measures. 初步措施。*preparatory to* 先於；作爲…之準備。—**pre·par·a·to·ri·ly,** *adv.*

preparatory school 準備進大學「的私立預備學校。」

‡**pre·pare** 〔prɪˈpɛr; priˈpɛə〕 *v.,* **-pared, -par·ing.** —*v.t.* ①預備；準備。to *prepare* a meal. 預備菜飯。②配製（藥品等）；調製。to *prepare* a drug. 配藥。③爲…之先導；爲…鋪路。—*v.i.* 預備；準備。to *prepare* for an examination. 準備考試。*prepare the way*（爲某事）開路〖for〗。—**pre·par·er,** *n.*

pre·pared 〔prɪˈpɛrd; priˈpɛəd〕 *adj.* ①有準備的。②（食物）經過廠家或零售店預製的。

pre·par·ed·ness 〔prɪˈpɛrɪdnɪs; priˈpɛədnis〕 *n.* ①準備；預備。②戰備。

pre·pay 〔priˈpe; ˈpriːˈpei〕 *v.t.,* **-paid, -pay·ing.** 預付；先付。—**a·ble,** *adj.* —**ment,** *n.*

pre·pense 〔prɪˈpɛns; priˈpens〕 *adj.* 預先計謀的；預謀的；蓄意的；故意的。—**ly,** *adv.*

pre·pon·der·ance 〔prɪˈpɑndrəns; priˈpɔndərəns〕 *n.* ①（數目、重量、力量上之）優勢。②優勢；優越。③主要；首要。

pre·pon·der·ant 〔prɪˈpɑndərənt; priˈpɔndərənt〕 *adj.* ①（在重量、數量、力量、重要性上）占優勢的。②主要的；重要的。

pre·pon·der·ate 〔prɪˈpɑndəˌret; priˈpɔndəreit〕 *v.i.,* **-at·ed, -at·ing.** ①數目超過；重量勝過；力量大過；影響力勝過。②向下垂。③（天平之）往一邊傾斜。④占優勢；爲主要。

***prep·o·si·tion** 〔ˌprɛpəˈzɪʃən; ˌprepəˈziʃən〕 *n.* 介系詞；前置詞。

prep·o·si·tion·al 〔ˌprɛpəˈzɪʃənl; ˌprepəˈziʃənl〕 *adj.* 介系詞的；前置詞的。—**ly,** *adv.*

prepositional phrase 介系詞片「語。」

pre·pos·i·tive 〔prɪˈpɑzətɪv; priˈpɔzitiv〕 *adj.* 〖文法〗置於前的；前置的。—*n.* 〖文法〗前置語。

pre·pos·i·tor 〔prɪˈpɑzətɚ; priːˈpɔzitə〕 *n.*（英國公立學校之）級長；學生自治會主席。（亦作 **praepostor, preposter**）

pre·pos·sess 〔ˌpripəˈzɛs; ˌpriːpəˈzes〕 *v.t.* ①使存有主見；使懷偏見。②使有好感；給予好印象（通常用被動式）。We were *prepossessed* by the boy's modest behavior. 我們因這個孩子的謙遜行爲而對他頗有好感。③（感情、思想之）注入；影響；灌輸（通常用被動式）。He is *prepossessed* with a queer idea. 他有一種奇特的思想。

pre·pos·sess·ing 〔ˌpripəˈzɛsɪŋ; ˌpriːpəˈzesiŋ〕 *adj.* 給人良好印象的；令人愛慕的；吸引人的。

pre·pos·ses·sion 〔ˌpripəˈzɛʃən; ˌpriːpəˈzeʃən〕 *n.* ①先入之見；偏愛；先具的好印象。②先得；先占。③專心貫注。

pre·pos·ter·ous 〔prɪˈpɑstərəs; priˈpɔstərəs〕 *adj.* 反常的；荒謬的。—**ly,** *adv.* —**ness,** *n.*

pre·po·ten·cy 〔prɪˈpotn̩sɪ; priˈpoutnsi〕 *n.* ①〖生物〗遺傳優勢。②優勢；極有權力。

pre·po·tent 〔prɪˈpotn̩t; priˈpoutnt〕 *adj.* ①（權力、力量、影響上）占優勢的；權勢赫赫的。②〖生物〗（具有）遺傳優勢的。

pre·puce 〔ˈpripjus; ˈpriːpjuːs〕 *n.* 〖解剖〗包皮。—**pre·pu·tial,** *adj.*

Pre-Raph·a·el·ite 〔priˈræfɪəˌlaɪt; ˈpriːˈræfəlait〕 *n.* ①前拉斐爾派（the Pre-Raphaelite Brotherhood）的一分子。②有相同目的之現代藝術家。③任何拉斐爾前的義大利畫家。—*adj.* ①前拉斐爾派的；有前拉斐爾派特色的。②拉斐爾前之任何義大利畫家或繪畫的。

pre·re·cord 〔ˌpriːrɪˈkɔrd; ˌpriːriˈkɔːd〕 *v.t.* 將…預先錄音。

pre·req·ui·site 〔priˈrɛkwəzɪt; ˈpriːˈrekwizit〕 *n.* 首要之事物；必備之事物。—*adj.* 必須於預先具備的。

pre·rog·a·tive 〔prɪˈrɑgətɪv; priˈrɔgətiv〕 *n.* 特權；帝王之特權。the royal *prerogative.* 帝王之特權。—*adj.* 特權的；有特權的。a *prerogative* right. 特權。

prerogative court 〖法律〗遺囑事件裁判所。

prerogative of mercy 赦免權。

Pres. ①Presbyterian. ②President.

pres. ①present. ②presidency. ③pressure. ④presumptive.

pres·age 〔*n.* ˈprɛsɪdʒ; ˈpresidʒ *v.* prɪˈsedʒ; ˈpresidʒ〕 *n., v.,* **pre·saged, pre·sag·ing.** —*n.* ①預示；預兆；前兆。a *presage* of a storm. 暴風雨的前兆。②預知；預感。③〖罕〗預測；預言。④意義；含義。—*v.t.* ①預示；預兆。②預感；先覺。③預言；預測。—*v.i.* ①預感；預知。②預言；預測。—**pre·sag·er,** *n.*

pres·by·o·pi·a 〔ˌprɛzbɪˈopɪə; ˌprezbiˈoupiə〕 *n.* 〖醫〗遠視眼。

pres·by·op·ic 〔ˌprɛzbɪˈɑpɪk; ˌprezbiˈɔpik〕 *adj.* 遠視眼的；老花眼的。—*n.* 遠視眼者。

pres·by·ter 〔ˈprɛzbɪtɚ; ˈprezbitə〕 *n.* ①（教會中的）長老；祭司。②（聖公會的）牧師。

pres·by·te·ri·al 〔ˌprɛzbəˈtɪrɪəl; ˌprezbiˈtiəriəl〕 *adj.* 長老的；長老會的；長老會制的；長老政治的。—**ly,** *adv.*

Pres·by·te·ri·an 〔ˌprɛzbəˈtɪrɪən; ˌprezbiˈtiəriən〕 *adj.* ①長老會的。②長老會制的。—*n.* 長老會教友。

Presbyterian Church (基督教)「長老會。」

Pres·by·te·ri·an·ism 〔ˌprɛzbəˈtɪrɪənˌɪzəm; ˌprezbiˈtiəriənizm〕 *n.* ①長老會制。②長老會之教義。

pres·by·ter·y 〔ˈprɛzbəˌtɛrɪ; ˈprezbitəri〕 *n., pl.* **-ter·ies.** ①長老之團體。②(長老會中)由某一地區內全部牧師長老組成之評議會。③上述評議會之轄區; 此轄區內所有之教堂。④〖天主教〗神父居住之房屋。⑤教堂內牧師、教士等之席位。

pre·school 〔ˈpriˈskul; ˈpriːˈskuːl〕 *adj.* 未屆學齡的;學前的。—**er,** *n.*

pre·sci·ence 〔ˈprɛʃɪəns; ˈpresiəns〕 *n.* 預知;先見。

pre·sci·ent 〔ˈprɛʃɪənt; ˈpresiənt〕 *adj.* 「有先見的;預知的。」

pre·sci·en·tif·ic 〔ˌprisaɪənˈtɪfɪk; ˌpriːsaiənˈtifik〕 *adj.* 科學發展以前的。

pre·scind 〔prɪˈsɪnd; priˈsind〕 *v.t.* 分開;使分離;分別思考。—*v.i.* 將思考或注意力從…分開〖from〗。

*__pre·scribe__ 〔prɪˈskraɪb; prisˈkraib〕 *v.t. & v.i.,* **-scribed, -scrib·ing.** ①命令;規定;指定。The law *prescribes* the penalty for this action. 法律規定對這種行爲的懲罰。②開(方); 開藥方。to *prescribe* for a patient. 爲病人開藥方。—**pre·scrib·er,** *n.*

pre·script 〔*adj.* prɪˈskrɪpt; ˈpriːskript *n.* ˈpriskrɪpt; ˈpriːskript〕 *adj.* 命令的;規定的。—*n.* 命令;規則;法律。

*__pre·scrip·tion__ 〔prɪˈskrɪpʃən; prisˈkripʃən〕 *n.* ①命令;指定;規定。②藥方。to fill a *prescription*. 照藥方配藥。③方子; 藥方上所開的藥。a *prescription* for a cough. 治咳嗽的方子。④〖法律〗時間長至足以獲得一物的所有權益之使用或保有; 時效。⑤〖法律〗如此獲得之權益。—**pre·scrip·ti·ble,** *adj.*

prescription drug 非經醫師處方不得買賣的藥品。

pre·scrip·tive 〔prɪˈskrɪptɪv; prisˈkriptiv〕 *adj.* ①規定的。②〖法律〗根據或起於時效的。a *prescriptive* right. 依時效而得之權利。③慣例的。—**ly,** *adv.*

pre·sell 〔ˈpriˈsɛl; ˈpriːˈsel〕 *v.t.,* **-sold, -sell·ing.** 宣傳(將上市的貨品)以引起購買欲。

‡**pres·ence** 〔ˈprɛzn̩s; ˈprezns〕 *n.* ①在場; 出席。Your *presence* is requested. 敬請光臨。②所在地;面前。③態度;儀容。a man of dignified *presence*. 有威嚴的人。④謁見;覲見。⑤(出現之)鬼怪、精靈等。⑥存在率。⑦經雙方協議駐在另一國之外國軍隊。***in the presence of*** 在…面前。***presence of mind*** 鎮定。***saving your presence*** 當面冒瀆, 敬請恕罪。

presence chamber (or **room**) 〖英〗君王或大人物的接見室。

‡**pre·sent**[1] 〔*v.* prɪˈzɛnt; priˈzent *n.* ˈprɛzn̩t; ˈpreznt〕 *v.t.* ①給;贈。He *presented* a gold watch to his girl friend. 他送個金錶給他的女朋友。② 提出。He *presented* reasons for his action. 他提出他的行動的理由。③呈遞; 送呈; 呈獻。The grocer *presented* his bill. 這雜貨商遞上他的帳單。④介紹。May I *present* Mrs. Brown? 請讓我介紹布朗夫人給你好嗎? ⑤演出 (戲劇等)。Our class *presented* a play. 我們班裏演出一劇。⑥呈現出。⑦指向;轉向。⑧出席。to *present* oneself for examination (trial). 參加考試(出席受審)。***present with*** 贈以…作爲禮物。Our class *presented* the school *with* a clock. 我們班上同學送給學校一個鐘作爲禮物。—*n.* 禮物; 贈品。a birthday *present*. 生日禮物。

‡**pres·ent**[2] 〔ˈprɛzn̩t; ˈpreznt〕 *adj.* ①在場的; 出席的。Everybody was *present*. 每個人都到了。②現在的; 此刻的。at the *present* time. 現在。③〖文法〗指現在發生或存在的。④我們正在面對的。the *present* case. 本案。—*n.* ①現在;目前。He is at *present* away on his holidays. 他現在到外地度假去了。②〖文法〗現在時態; 現在時態的動詞。***by these presents*** 據此言;根據此文件。***for the present*** 眼前;目前;現在。—**ness,** *n.*

pre·sent·a·bil·i·ty 〔prɪˌzɛntəˈbɪlətɪ; priˌzentəˈbiliti〕 *n.* 可拿出;可提出;可見人;可介紹於衆人。

pre·sent·a·ble 〔prɪˈzɛntəbl̩; priˈzentəbl〕 *adj.* ①適於贈與的; 可呈贈的。②可上演的。③可見人的; 可介紹於衆人的; 漂亮的。④〖宗教〗可舉薦爲牧師的。⑤可陳述的; 可表現的。

pre·sent arms 〔prɪˈzɛnt~; priˈzent~〕①舉槍致敬。②(徒手隊伍)舉行敬禮。

*__pres·en·ta·tion__ 〔ˌprɛzn̩ˈteʃən, ˌprizɛnˈteʃən; ˌprezenˈteiʃən〕 *n.* ①贈送;進呈。the *presentation* of a gift. 禮物之贈送。②禮物。The ring was a *presentation* to me. 這戒指是給我的一個禮物。③提出。the *presentation* of a plan. 一計畫之提出。④演出。⑤介紹;引見。⑥〖醫〗(胎)產式。face *presentation*. 面產式(面先露之生產)。

pres·en·ta·tion·al 〔ˌprɛzn̩ˈteʃənəl; ˌprezenˈteiʃənl〕 *adj.* ①〖心理〗直覺的; 表象的;觀念的。②贈送的;進呈的。③禮物的;禮品的。④提出的;演出的。⑤介紹的;引見的。

presentation copy 贈送本;獻本。

pres·en·ta·tion·ism 〔ˌprɛzn̩ˈteʃənɪzəm; ˌprezenˈteiʃənizm〕 *n.* 〖心理、哲學〗直覺說。

pre·sent·a·tive 〔prɪˈzɛntətɪv; priˈzentətiv〕 *adj.* ①〖心理、哲學〗直覺的; 表象的。②〖宗教〗有牧師推薦權的。

present company 出席者。

pres·ent-day 〔ˈprɛzn̩tˈde; ˈprezntˈdei〕 *adj.* 今日的;現今的。

pres·en·tee 〔ˌprɛzənˈti; ˌprezənˈtiː〕 *n.* ①被推薦者(尤指爲牧師者)。②受餽贈者。

pre·sent·er 〔prɪˈzɛntɚ; priˈzentə〕 *n.* 贈與者; 申述者; 具呈者; 提出者; 獻與者; 推薦者。

pre·sen·ti·ment 〔prɪˈzɛntəmənt; priˈzentimənt〕 *n.* 預感;預覺。

‡**pres·ent·ly** 〔ˈprɛzn̩tlɪ; ˈprezntli〕 *adv.* ①不久地;卽刻地。The clock will strike *presently*. 鐘卽刻就要響了。②〖古、方〗立刻。③目前;現在。

pre·sent·ment 〔prɪˈzɛntmənt; priˈzentmənt〕 *n.* ①表現;表示;敍述;陳述。②描寫;描繪;畫像。③戲劇之演出。④〖法律〗陪審官之控訴;公訴。⑤〖心理〗表象;心象;概念。⑥暗示。⑦贈予;呈贈。⑧〖商〗依規定時間地點呈出收據、匯票等。

present participle 〖文法〗現在分詞。

present perfect 〖文法〗現在完成式。

present tense 〖文法〗現在式。

present wit 機智。

pre·serv·a·ble 〔prɪˈzɝvəbl̩; priˈzəːvəbl〕 *adj.* 能保存的;能貯藏的。

***pres·er·va·tion** [ˌprɛzəˈveʃən; ˌprezəˈveiʃən] *n.* 保護;保存;保藏。in a good state of *preservation*. 保存良好。

pre·serv·a·tive [prɪˈzɜvətɪv; priˈzəːvətiv] *n.* ①防腐劑;保護物。②預防疾病之藥物。—*adj.* ①保存的;有保存力量的。②防腐的。③預防的。

‡pre·serve [prɪˈzɜv; priˈzəːv] *v.*, **-served, -serv·ing,** *n.* —*v.t.* ①保護;保佑。God *preserve* us! 願上帝保佑我們! ②保持;支持。You look well-*preserved*. 你看起來保養得很好。③保藏;保存。Ice helps to *preserve* food. 冰能幫助保藏食物。④蜜餞(水果等);醃(蔬菜等)。to *preserve* fruit. 蜜餞水果。⑤不准外人(狩獵或釣魚)。The fishing is strictly *preserved*. 嚴禁閒人捕魚。—*v.i.* 被保藏;被保存。—*n.* ①(常 *pl.*)蜜餞水果。strawberry *preserves*. 蜜餞草莓。②(魚或獸之)畜養所。a state game *preserve*. 州立獵物保護區。

pre·serv·er [prɪˈzɜvə; priˈzəːvə] *n.* 保護者;保管者;保存者。

pre-shrunk [priˈʃrʌŋk; priːˈʃrʌŋk] *adj.* (布料)預先縮水過的。(亦作 **preshrunk**)

***pre·side** [prɪˈzaɪd; priˈzaid] *v.*, **-sid·ed, -sid·ing.** —*v.i.* ①開會時做主席。to *preside* over a meeting. 主持一會議。②管理。—*v.t.* 管理;控制;督導。—**pre·sid·er,** *n.*

***pres·i·den·cy** [ˈprɛzədənsɪ, ˈprɛzdən-; ˈprezidənsi] *n.*, *pl.* **-cies.** ①總統、董事長、總經理、社長、會長、大學校長等之職位,職權或任期。He was elected to the *presidency* of the hotel corporation. 他當選爲那旅館之董事長。②管理;督導;監護。

‡pres·i·dent [ˈprɛzədənt; ˈprezidənt] *n.* ①董事長;總經理;社長;會長;大學校長等。*president* of the nation's largest steel company. 全國最大鋼鐵公司之董事長。②(常 P-)總統。the *President* of the Republic of China. 中華民國總統。

pres·i·dent-e·lect [ˈprɛzɪdəntɪˈlɛkt; ˈprezidəntiˈlekt] *n.* 已當選而尚未就職之總統;總統當選人。

***pres·i·den·tial** [ˌprɛzəˈdɛnʃəl; ˌpreziˈdenʃəl] *adj.* ①總統的;議長的;社長的;總經理的;大學校長的。the *presidential* term. 總統(議長、社長、總經理等)之任期。②統轄的;監督的;指揮的。

presidential year (美國)總統選舉年。

pre·sid·i·al [prɪˈsɪdɪəl; priˈsidiəl] *adj.* ①會長的;社長的;議長的。②督導的;主宰的。(亦作 **presidiary**)

pre·sid·ing [prɪˈzaɪdɪŋ; priˈzaidiŋ] *adj.* ①主持者的;主席的;首席的。②主宰的;統轄的。

pre·sid·i·o [prɪˈsɪdɪˌo; priˈsidiou] 〖西〗 *n.* ①衛戍地;要塞;城砦。②(西班牙的)流刑地;充軍地。

pre·sid·i·um [prɪˈsɪdɪəm; priˈsidiəm] *n.* (蘇聯政府的)常務委員會;主席團。

‡press¹ [prɛs; pres] *v.t.* ①壓;按;擠;榨。*Press* the button to ring the bell. 按鈕使鈴響。②擁抱;緊抱。③使平;壓平。to *press* clothes. 熨衣服。④力勸;敦促。We *pressed* our guest to stay all night. 我們力勸我們的客人過夜。⑤迫;逼。to be *pressed* by hunger and cold. 饑寒交迫。⑥催促。⑦堅持。⑧緊壓在(心頭等)。⑨努力進行;極力施行。***be pressed for time (money)*** 時間緊迫(金錢拮据)。***press home*** 堅持到底。—*v.i.* ①壓;壓迫。②擁擠;推進。The boy *pressed* on in spite of the wind. 那孩子不顧風而努力前進。③緊迫;急迫。Time *presses*, make up your mind. 時急矣,速下決心。④作極力的請求。⑤(衣服)被燙。—*n.* ①壓;擠;擁擠。The *press* of many duties keeps her busy. 許多事物纏身使她忙碌不停。②壓力機;壓榨機。a wine *press*. 榨酒機。③印刷機。④印刷;印刷所;印刷事業。The book is now in the *press*.此書正在印刷中。⑤新聞界。The book had a good *press*. 此書頗獲新聞界之好評。⑥羣衆。The little boy was lost in the *press*. 小孩在人羣中走失。⑦緊急。⑧(衣服、書籍等之)櫥。⑨(衣服)燙後的線條。***go to press*** 付印;開始印刷。

press² *v.t.* ①强迫服兵役。to *press* men for naval service. 强迫男子在海軍服役。②徵用(車、馬、船等)。—*n.* 强迫服兵役;强迫服役令。

press agent ①(劇院等的)司廣告與宣傳業務者。②宣傳員;司公共關係者。

press-a·gent [ˈprɛsˌedʒənt; ˈpresˌeidʒənt] *v.t.* 爲…作宣傳。—*v.i.* 擔任宣傳員。

press baron 報業大亨。

press·board [ˈprɛsˌbord; ˈpresbɔːd] *n.* ①一種厚而光的紙。②一種平、硬而光滑的紙板或木板(用以壓紙者)。

press box 新聞記者席。

press conference 記者招待會。

press corrector 校對人員。

press correspondent 新聞通訊員;報社特派員。

press cutting 報紙、雜誌等之剪存;剪報。

press·er [ˈprɛsə; ˈpresə] *n.* ①壓榨者;壓緊者。②燙衣人(尤指燙平新衣或新洗之衣服)。

press gallery ①新聞記者席(尤指英國下院中者)。②採訪議會新聞的新聞記者團。

press-gang [ˈprɛsˌgæŋ; ˈpresgæŋ] *v.t.* ①强迫…服兵役。②强迫…參加活動。

***press·ing** [ˈprɛsɪŋ; ˈpresiŋ] *adj.* ①迫急的;近在眉睫的。a *pressing* need. 迫切的需要。②强求的;執拗的;絮瀆的。—*n.* ①壓;按。②壓製的金屬板。③從模子中壓出來的唱片。④唱片之一次發行數。—**ly,** *adv.*

press law 出版法;新聞法規。

press·man [ˈprɛsmən; ˈpresmən] *n.*, *pl.* **-men.** ①管理印刷機者;印刷工人。②〖英〗新聞記者;新聞採訪員。

press·mark [ˈprɛsˌmark; ˈpresmɑːk] *n.* (圖書館書上的)號碼。

pres·sor [ˈprɛsə; ˈpresə] *adj.* 增高血壓的;刺激的。

press proof 稿件付印前之最後一次校閱。

press·room [ˈprɛsˌrum; ˈpresrum] *n.* 印刷機房。

press·run [ˈprɛsrʌn; ˈpresrʌn] *n.* ①印刷機之印刷。②一次印刷之量。

press-show [ˈprɛsˌʃo; ˈpresʃou] *v.t.* 對新聞界預先公開;預展;試映。

***pres·sure** [ˈprɛʃə; ˈpreʃə] *n.* ①壓。②壓力。the blood *pressure*. 血壓。③困窮;困厄。④壓迫;急迫。the *pressure* of business. 公事之急迫待理。—*v.t.* ①施以壓力。②加高壓烹煮。

pressure cabin 加氣壓的機艙。(亦作 **pressurized cabin**)

pres·sure-cook [ˈprɛʃəˌkuk; ˈpreʃəˈkuk] *v.t.* 以高壓烹煮。

pressure cooker 高壓鍋。

pressure gauge 壓力計。

pressure group 壓力集團(對議員施以壓力,以左右立法或政策以維護自身利益)。

pressure suit 飛行員的壓力服(在高空飛行時,保護飛行員不受氣壓變化之影響)。

pres·sur·ize [ˈprɛʃəˌraɪz; ˈpreʃəraiz] *v.t.*, **-ized, -iz·ing.** 在(飛機)中保持近於正常氣壓(如在高飛或升降時)。

press·work [ˈprɛsˌwɝk; ˈpreswəːk] *n.* 印刷;印刷作業。

Pres·ter John [ˈprɛstɚ~; ˈprestə~] 普勒斯特•約翰(傳說中的一位中世紀基督徒國王及教士,據云曾統治遠東或非洲之某一王國)。

pres·ti·dig·i·ta·tion [ˌprɛstɪˌdɪdʒɪˈteʃən; ˈprestiˌdidʒiˈteiʃən] *n.* (用手的)變戲法;手法;幻術。

pres·ti·dig·i·ta·tor [ˌprɛstɪˈdɪdʒɪˌtetɚ; ˌprestiˈdidʒiteitə] *n.* 變戲法者;演幻術者。

***pres·tige** [ˈprɛstɪdʒ, prɛsˈtiʒ; presˈtiːʒ] *n.* 威望;聲望。His *prestige* rose. 他的威望增高了。

pres·tig·i·ous [prɛsˈtɪdʒɪəs; presˈtidʒiəs] *adj.* 享有聲望的;聲望很高的。**—ly,** *adv.* **—ness,** *n.*

pres·tis·si·mo [prɛsˈtɪsəˌmo; presˈtisimou] *adv.* 〖音樂〗最速地;最快地;非常快。

pres·to [ˈprɛsto; ˈprestou] *adv., adj., n., pl.* **-tos.** *—adv.* ①〖音樂〗急速地;快。②立刻地。*—adj.* ①〖音樂〗快拍子的。②急速的;立刻的。*—n.* 〖音樂〗急速之樂曲或樂章。

pre·sum·a·ble [prɪˈzuməbl; priˈzjuːməbl] *adj.* 可假定的;可能的。

***pre·sum·a·bly** [prɪˈzuməblɪ, -ˈzjum-; priˈzjuːməbli] *adv.* 假定地;推測地;也許;大抵。He knows, *presumably*, what is best for him. 他也許知道甚麼對他是最好的。

***pre·sume** [prɪˈzum; priˈzjuːm] *v.*, **-sumed, -sum·ing.** *—v.t.* ①假定;推測。I *presume* you're tired. 我想你是倦了。②敢於。I won't *presume* to disturb you. 我不敢打攪你。*—v.i.* 占便宜。**—pre·sum·er,** *n.* **—pre·sum·ing,** *adj.* **—ly, pre·sum·ing·ly,** *adv.*

pre·sump·tion [prɪˈzʌmpʃən; priˈzʌmpʃən] *n.* ①僭越;冒昧;無禮;傲慢。②臆測;推定;設定。③推測或假定所依據之理由和根據;可能性。There is a strong *presumption* that he will succeed. 他有很大的成功希望。④〖法律〗事實的推定。⑤假定爲當然如是的事;臆測中之事。

presumption of fact 〖法律〗事實之推定。

pre·sump·tive [prɪˈzʌmptɪv; priˈzʌmptiv] *adj.* 假定的;沒有直接證據的;推定的。***the heir presumptive*** 假定繼承人。

pre·sump·tu·ous [prɪˈzʌmptʃuəs; priˈzʌmptjuəs] *adj.* 僭越的;膽大妄爲的;無顧忌的。**—ly,** *adv.*

pre·sup·pose [ˌprisəˈpoz; ˌpriːsəˈpouz] *v.t.*, **-posed, -pos·ing.** ①預想;假定;推測。②必須先有;以…爲先決條件。

pre·sup·po·si·tion [ˌprisʌpəˈzɪʃən; ˌpriːsʌpəˈziʃən] *n.* ①預想;假定;臆測。②先決條件。

pret. preterit(e).

pre·tax [ˈpritæks; ˈpriːtæks] *adj.* =**before-tax.**

pre·teen [priˈtin; priːˈtiːn] *n.* 〖主美〗快到十三歲(十歲至十二歲)的少年男女。

***pre·tence** [prɪˈtɛns; priˈtens] *n.* 〖主英〗=**pretense.**

***pre·tend** [prɪˈtɛnd; priˈtend] *v.t.* ①佯裝;僞裝。to *pretend* illness. 裝病。②僞稱;佯稱。③聲稱;自命。I don't *pretend* to be a musician. 我不敢自命爲音樂家。④嘗試;企圖。*—v.i.* ①覬覦;主張;爭。to *pretend* to a throne. 僭取王位。②假裝。

pre·tend·ed [prɪˈtɛndɪd; priˈtendid] *adj.* ①假的;虛僞的。②聲稱的;託言的。

pre·tend·er [prɪˈtɛndɚ; priˈtendə] *n.* ①佯爲者;假作者;僞託者。②假裝博學者;冒牌學者。③詐稱者;聲稱者;自命者。④請求者;要求者。⑤王位覬覦者。⑥有大志者;求高位者。***Old Pretender*** 〖英史〗詹姆斯二世(James II) 之子 James Edward. ***Young Pretender*** 〖英史〗詹姆斯二世之孫 Charles Edward.

***pre·tense** [prɪˈtɛns; priˈtens] *n.* ①虛假。That's all *pretense*. 那完全是虛假。②僞裝;掩飾。③藉口;託辭;口實;僞稱。Her illness is only a *pretense*. 她的病祇是一個託辭。④要求。⑤虛飾;矯飾。a man without *pretense*. 實是求是之人。⑥用以炫耀之事物。⑦自命;自負。

pre·ten·sion [prɪˈtɛnʃən; priˈtenʃən] *n.* ①權利;要求。②自命;自負。She makes no *pretensions* to beauty. 她並不自命是美人。③矯飾;虛飾。④口實;託詞。

pre·ten·tious [prɪˈtɛnʃəs; priˈtenʃəs] *adj.* ①虛飾的;矯飾的。②自負的;驕傲的。**—ly,** *adv.* **—ness,** *n.*

preter- 〖字首〗表"超過"之義。

pre·ter·hu·man [ˌpritɚˈhjumən; ˌpriːtəˈhjuːmən] *adj.* 超常人的;超人的。

pret·er·it(e) [ˈprɛtərɪt; ˈpretərit] *n.* 〖文法〗①過去式;過去時態。②過去式動詞。*—adj.* ①〖文法〗過去時態的。②〖罕〗過去的。

pret·er·i·tion [ˌprɛtəˈrɪʃən; ˌpretəˈriʃən] *n.* ①省略;遺漏。②〖法律〗遺囑中對有繼承權者之遺漏。③〖神學〗上帝對非選民之忽略。④〖修辭〗陰述法;暗示省略法。

pre·ter·mis·sion [ˌpritɚˈmɪʃən; ˌpriːtəˈmiʃən] *n.* ①遺漏;略過。②怠慢;忽略。

pre·ter·mit [ˌpritɚˈmɪt; ˌpriːtəˈmit] *v.t.*, **-mit·ted, -mit·ting.** ①忽略;怠忽。②省略。

pre·ter·nat·u·ral [ˌpritɚˈnætʃərəl; ˌpriːtəˈnætʃərəl] *adj.* ①超自然的;不可思議的。②異常的;奇特的。

pre·ter·sen·su·al [ˌpritɚˈsɛnʃuəl; ˌpriːtəˈsensjuəl] *adj.* 超感覺的;超知覺的。

pre·test [*n.* ˈpriˌtɛst; ˈpriːtest *v.* priˈtɛst; priːˈtest] *n.* ①事先之試驗;(產品等的)預行試驗。②測驗學生程度(以決定是否授以新課程)之考試。*—v.t. & v.i.* ①爲測驗學生程度而舉行考試。②預行試驗。

pre·text [*n.* ˈpritɛkst; ˈpriːtekst *v.* prɪˈtɛkst; priːˈtekst] *n.* 藉口。*—v.t.* 以…爲藉口。

pret·ti·fy [ˈprɪtɪˌfaɪ; ˈpritifai] *v.t.*, **-fied, -fy·ing.** 使美;美化;修飾。

pret·ti·ly [ˈprɪtɪlɪ; ˈpritili] *adv.* ①悅人地;精緻地。②有禮貌地;恭敬地。

pret·ti·ness [ˈprɪtɪnɪs; ˈpritinis] *n.* 悅人;精緻;可愛。

‡pret·ty [ˈprɪtɪ; ˈpriti] *adj.*, **-ti·er, -ti·est,** *adv., n., pl.* **-ties,** *v.*, **-tied, -ty·ing.** *—adj.* ①悅人的;漂亮的;精緻的。What a *pretty* house! 一所多麼精緻的房子啊!②很不好的。a *pretty* mess. 一團糟。③太嬌嫩的。④〖古〗勇敢的;好的。⑤〖俗〗大的;廣的。It cost a *pretty* penny. 那花了不少錢。***sitting pretty*** 〖俚〗**a.** 享受幸運;處境優裕。**b.** 占有利地位。*—adv.* 十分;頗。It's *pretty* good. 頗佳。—*n.* 漂亮的人或東西。—*v.t.* 予以美化〖常 up〗. They have curtains to *pretty* up the room. 他們以窗帘美化房間。

pret·ty·ish [ˈprɪtɪɪʃ; ˈpritiiʃ] *adj.* 相當美的;頗美的;有點美的。

pretty penny 〖俗〗大量之金錢。

pret·ty-pret·ty [ˈprɪtɪˌprɪtɪ; ˈpritiˌpriti] *adj., n., pl.* **-pret·ties.** —*adj.* 矯飾的;感傷的。—*n.* (*pl.*) 〖俗〗裝飾品;飾物;浮華而不值錢的玩意兒。

pret·zel [ˈprɛtsl̩; ˈpretsəl] *n.* 一種脆餅乾(作棒狀或紐結狀而外撒以鹽者)。

*__pre·vail__ [prɪˈvel; priˈveil] *v.i.* ①盛行;流行。②占優勢。Truth will *prevail.* 眞理將獲勝。③戰勝。We *prevailed* over our enemies. 我們勝過敵人。④生效;有效。***prevail on*** (***upon*** or ***with***) 勸導;引誘。

*__pre·vail·ing__ [prɪˈvelɪŋ; priˈveiliŋ] *adj.* ①占優勢的。②盛行的;流行的。a *prevailing* style. 流行的式樣。—**ly,** *adv.*

prev·a·lence [ˈprɛvələns; ˈprevələns] *n.* 普遍。

*__prev·a·lent__ [ˈprɛvələnt; ˈprevələnt] *adj.* 普遍的;流行的。Colds are *prevalent* in the winter. 傷風在冬季很普遍。—**ly,** *adv.*

pre·var·i·cate [prɪˈværəˌket; priˈværikeit] *v.i.*, **-cat·ed, -cat·ing.** 支吾其詞;搪塞。—**pre·var·i·ca·tion, pre·var·i·ca·tor,** *n.*

pre·ven·ient [prɪˈvinjənt; priˈviːnjənt] *adj.* ①在前的。②以前的。③預期的。④預防的。⑤在人類行動以前的。

‡**pre·vent** [prɪˈvɛnt; priˈvent] *v.t.* ①阻礙;妨礙。What *prevented* you from coming? 何事使你不能來?②防止;預防。to *prevent* an accident. 預防一意外。The rain *prevented* his coming. 雨使他不能來。③〖古〗前行引導。—*v.i.* 阻礙;妨礙。We shall come tomorrow if nothing *prevents.* 如果沒有甚麼妨礙我們明天會來。

pre·vent·a·ble [prɪˈvɛntəbl̩; priˈventəbl] *adj.* 可防止的;可阻止的。(亦作 **preventible**)

pre·vent·er [prɪˈvɛntɚ; priˈventə] *n.* ①預防者;預防法;預防藥。②妨礙者;障礙物。③〖航海〗副張索。④〖修辭〗預辯法。

*__pre·ven·tion__ [prɪˈvɛnʃən; priˈvenʃən] *n.* ①防止;預防。*Prevention* is better than cure. 預防勝於治療。②阻礙物;防止物。

pre·ven·tive [prɪˈvɛntɪv; priˈventiv] *adj.* ①預防的;妨礙的。*preventive* measures against disease. 預防疾病之方法。②〖醫〗預防疾病的。a *preventive* medicine. 預防藥物。—*n.* ①預防疾病之藥物。②預防之物;預防之策。(亦作 **preventative**)

preventive service 英國海關之緝私機構。

preventive war 先發制人的侵略戰爭。

pre·view [*n.* ˈpriˌvju; ˈpriːˈvjuː *v.* priˈvju; ˈpriːˈvjuː] *n.* ①預先的察看或勘察。②〖電影〗**a.** (公映前之)試映。**b.** 預告片。—*v.t.* ①預先察看或勘察。②試映。(美亦作 **prevue**)

*__pre·vi·ous__ [ˈprivɪəs; ˈpriːvjəs] *adj.* ①在前的;先前的。The *previous* lesson was hard. 前面一課很難。②〖俗〗過快的;過急的。***previous to*** 在以前。*previous to* his marriage. 在他結婚以前。—*adv.* 在前。

previous examination 劍橋大學文學士學位考試之初試。

*__pre·vi·ous·ly__ [ˈprivɪəslɪ; ˈpriːvjəsli] *adv.* 以前;先前。He had served *previously* in the army. 他先前在陸軍服役過。

previous question 先決問題(即議會中正討論之案件應否立即投票表決之動議)。

pre·vise [prɪˈvaɪz; priˈvaiz] *v.t.*, **-vised, -vis·ing.** 〖罕〗①預言;預見。②警告。

pre·vi·sion [prɪˈvɪʒən; priˈviʒən] *n.* ①先見;預知。②預感。—**al,** *adj.*

pre·war [priˈwɔr; ˈpriːˈwɔː] *adj.* 戰前的。—*adv.* 在戰前。

prex·y [ˈprɛksɪ; ˈpreksi] *n., pl.* **-ies.** 〖美俚〗大學校長。

*__prey__ [pre; prei] *n.* ①被捕食之動物。Mice and birds are the *prey* of cats. 鼠和鳥為貓所捕食之動物。②捕食之習慣;掠食。bird of *prey.* 食肉鳥(鷹等);猛禽。③被傷害之人或物;犧牲者。to be a *prey* to fear or disease. 為恐懼或疾病所傷害之人。—*v.i.* 〖on, upon〗. ①捕食;攫食。Cats *prey* upon mice. 貓捕鼠。②使苦惱。③搶奪;掠奪。④使某一階層的人受害。—**er,** *n.*

Pri·am [ˈpraɪəm; ˈpraiəm] *n.* Troy之最後一個國王,為希臘人所殺。

‡**price** [praɪs; prais] *n., v.,* **priced, pric·ing.** —*n.* ①價格;價錢。What's the *price* of this hat? 這帽子值多少錢? ②代價。to pay a heavy *price* for victory. 以重大的代價換取勝利。③價值。a pearl of great *price.* 一顆價值昂貴的珍珠。④捕或殺人之賞格。***at any price*** 不惜任何代價。***at a price*** 以極高代價。***beyond*** (or ***without***) ***price*** 非任何價錢所能購得者。Virtue is *beyond price.* 美德乃無價之寶。***Every man has his price.*** 每個人都可受利誘。***of price*** 極寶貴的;極貴重的。***put a price on the head of...*** 懸賞捕捉或殺死(罪犯、敵人等)。***what price...*** 何價?…何用? *What price* isolation now?當今孤立有何價值? —*v.t.* ①定以價格。All our goods are clearly *priced.* 我們所有的貨物都明定有價格。②問…之價。③估…之價。***price out of the market*** 價格過高致使被擠出市場。

price current 時價表。

price-cut·ter [ˈpraɪsˌkʌtɚ; ˈpraisˌkʌtə] *n.* 減價者(尤指減至造成惡性競爭者)。

price cutting 大減價。

priced [praɪst; praist] *adj.* 附有定價的。a *priced* catalogue. 定價貨目表。

price index 物價指數。

price·less [ˈpraɪslɪs; ˈpraislis] *adj.* ①極貴重的;無價的。*priceless* jewels. 極貴重的寶石。②〖俚〗極有趣的;非常可笑的。

price list 價目表。

pric·er [ˈpraɪsɚ; ˈpraisə] *n.* ①零售商店中決定售價或標價之雇員。②打聽價格者。

price tag ①(商品之)標價籤。②價錢。

price war (同業間之)削價競爭。

*__prick__ [prɪk; prik] *n.* ①尖銳物(如植物之刺,驅牛之刺棒等);刺。②(針尖等所穿刺之)小洞。③戳刺。④刺痛;劇痛。to feel the *prick.* 感到刺痛。***kick against the pricks*** 作無謂之抵抗而徒使自己受到損害;螳臂擋車。***the prick of conscience*** (***remorse,*** etc.) 良心不安;悔恨。—*v.t.* ①以尖銳之物穿刺。②以針孔標示或描畫。③刺痛。④使良心不安;使悔恨。His conscience *pricked* him suddenly. 他的良心突然使他悔恨。⑤驅策。My duty *pricked* me on. 我的責任驅策着我。⑥以尖物挖掘。⑦豎起(耳朵);注意傾聽。The lawyer *pricked* up his ears. 律師豎

耳傾聽。⑧以圓規測量(距離)。⑨選擇。⑩順跡追蹤。to *prick* a hare. 追蹤一野兔。⑪a. 釘馬蹄不當而使跛。b. 切短。—*v.i.* ①刺;刺痛。②感覺刺痛。③豎起〖up〗. The church spire *pricks* up into the air. 教堂尖塔直聳雲霄。④(酒)變酸。⑤策馬前進。***prick up*** 豎立;向上指。 ***prick up the ears*** a. 突然注意。b. 仔細聽。—*adj.* 豎起的(耳朵)。

prick-eared ['prɪk,ɪrd; 'prik-iəd] *adj.* 豎耳的。

prick·er ['prɪkɚ; 'prikə] *n.* ①刺者(人或物);針;小錐。②姥鮫。③穿孔齒輪。

prick·et ['prɪkɪt; 'prikit] *n.* ①蠟燭臺;插燭籤。②兩歲之雄鹿(其角直而不分叉)。③〖植物〗佛甲草。

pricket's sister 兩歲之雌鹿。

prick·le ['prɪkl̩; 'prikl] *n., v.,* **-led, -ling.** —*n.* ①尖刺;刺。②〖俗〗刺痛感覺。—*v.i.* 感覺刺痛。—*v.t.* ①使感覺刺痛。②刺。

prick·ly ['prɪklɪ; 'prikli] *adj.,* **-li·er, -li·est.** ①多刺的。②如針刺的;刺痛的。—**prick·li·ness,** *n.*

prickly heat 痱子。

prickly pear 〖植物〗霸王樹(仙人掌之一種)。

‡**pride** [praɪd; praid] *n., v.,* **prid·ed, prid·ing.** —*n.* ①自負;自尊心。A man without *pride* deserves contempt. 沒有自尊的人應爲人所蔑視。②誇耀之物;引以自豪之人。He is his father's *pride.* 他是他父親引以自豪的人。③驕傲;傲慢。*Pride* goes before a fall. 驕者必敗。④全盛;强盛。a nation in her *pride* of power. 全盛時代的國家。⑤榮耀;自豪。to take (a) *pride* in one's work. 對自己的工作感到自豪。⑥(某些鳥獸之)羣;引人注目的一羣。a *pride* of lions. 一羣獅子。—*v.t.* 自負;驕傲。***pride oneself on*** 以…自傲。We *prided ourselves on* our clean streets. 我們以我們清潔的街道爲榮。—**ful,** *adj.*

pride of the morning 海上所見的晨霧(爲晴天之預兆)。

prie-dieu [pri'djø; 'priːdjəː] 〖法〗 *n.* 祈禱臺。

***priest** [prist; priːst] *n.* 教士;牧師;神父;祭司;僧侶。a *priest* of Apollo. 奉祀太陽神阿波羅的祭師。

priest·craft ['prist,kræft; 'priːst-krɑːft] *n.* 牧師(僧侶、祭司等計劃獲得權力或財富)之方術、策略等。

priest·ess ['pristɪs; 'priːstis] *n.* 女教士;女祭司;尼姑。

priest·hood ['prist·hud; 'priːsthud] *n.* ①僧侶、教士、神父、牧師之職位、階級、或特徵。②僧侶、教士、神父、牧師之集合稱。

priest·ling ['pristlɪŋ; 'priːstliŋ] *n.* 小牧師;小祭司。

priest·ly ['pristlɪ; 'priːstli] *adj.* ①僧侶的;祭司的;教士的;牧師的。②適於僧侶、祭司、教士、神父或牧師的。—**priest·li·ness,** *n.*

priest-rid·den ['prist,rɪdn; 'priːst-,ridn] *adj.* 祭師統治的;受僧侶控制或影響的。

prig¹ [prɪg; prig] *n.* ①一本正經的人。②沾沾自喜者;自命不凡者。

prig² *n., v.,* **prigged, prig·ging.** —*n.* 〖英俚〗賊;小偷;扒手。—*v.t.* 〖英俚〗偷竊。—*v.i.* 〖蘇〗①討價還價。②懇求。***prig down*** 〖俚〗殺價。

prig·ger·y ['prɪgərɪ; 'prigəri] *n., pl.* **-ger·ies.** 沾沾自喜的性格或行爲;自命不凡。

prig·gish ['prɪgɪʃ; 'prigiʃ] *adj.* 自命不凡的;自矜的。—**ly,** *adv.* —**ness,** *n.*

prig·gism ['prɪgɪzm̩; 'prigizm] *n.* 自矜;沾沾自喜;自負。

prim [prɪm; prim] *adj.,* **prim·mer, prim·mest,** *v.,* **primmed, prim·ming.** —*adj.* 拘泥形式的;端端正正的。—*v.t.* 使(面部或口、唇)作一本正經的表情。—*v.i.* 作一本正經的表情。—**ly,** *adv.* —**ness,** *n.*

prim. ①primary. ②primate. ③primitive.

pri·ma bal·le·ri·na [,primə,bælə'rɪnə; 'priːmə,bælə'rinə] *pl.* **pri·ma bal·le·ri·nas.** 芭蕾舞團之首席女星。

pri·ma·cy ['praɪməsɪ; 'praiməsi] *n., pl.* **-cies.** ①首位;首要。②〖宗教〗primate 之職責及權力。③〖天主教〗教皇之最高權力。

pri·ma don·na ['primə'dɑnə; 'priː-mə'dɔnə] *pl.* **pri·ma don·nas.** ①歌劇中的第一女主角;首席女歌星。②〖俗〗喜怒無常或自命不凡的人(尤指女人);(不易合羣的)個性特强者;個人英雄主義者。

pri·ma fa·ci·e ['praɪmə'feʃɪ,i; 'prai-mə'feiʃi(ː)] 〖拉〗①初見的(地);據初步印象的(地)。②自明的;無爭論之餘地的。

prima facie case 〖法律〗表面上證據確鑿的案件。

pri·mage ['praɪmɪdʒ; 'praimidʒ] *n.* ①(昔日)貨主付予船長和水手的禮金(以酬其照料貨物之勞者)。②(今日)運費外另付之酬金(歸船主所得)。

pri·mal ['praɪml̩; 'praiməl] *adj.* ①最初的;第一的;原始的。②主要的;基本的。

***pri·ma·ri·ly** ['praɪ,mɛrəlɪ, praɪ'mɛrə-lɪ; 'praimərili] *adv.* ①主要地;首要地。Napoleon was *primarily* a soldier. 拿破崙主要的是個軍人。②最初地;首先地。

***pri·ma·ry** ['praɪ,mɛrɪ, -mərɪ; 'praimə-ri] *adj., n., pl.* **-ries.** —*adj.* ①第一的;初步的;初級的。*primary* tuberculosis. 初期肺結核。②基本的。③原來的;根本的。④首要的;主要的。⑤〖電機〗主的;原的;第一的。—*n.* ①最主要者。②原色。③〖美〗(政黨之)預選;初選。④〖電機〗主線圈。⑤有另一天體圍繞運行之天體。

primary accent ①主重音。②其符號('或'等)。

primary colors 指紅、黃、藍三原色。

primary election =**primary** *n.* ③.

primary products 農產品。

primary school 小學。

primary stress 主重音。

primary tenses 〖文法〗指現在時態、未來時態與過去時態。

pri·mate ['praɪmɪt, -met; *for* ① & ③ 'praimit, -meit, *for* ② praimeit, ② *pl.* prai'meitiːz *or* 'praimeits] *n.* ①一國或一教區中最高之主教或總主教。②(P-)(*pl.*)〖動物〗靈長類。③領袖;階級或地位最高者。—*adj.* 首要的;第一的。

pri·mate·ship ['praɪmɪt,ʃɪp; 'prai-mit-ʃip] *n.* 主教或總主教之職位或職責。

***prime¹** [praɪm; praim] *adj.* ①首要的;第一的;主要的。of *prime* importance. 最關緊要。②最上等的;最佳的。③基本的;最初的;最早的。④〖數學〗素數的。⑤互爲質數的。2 is *prime* to 9. 二與九互爲質數。—*n.* ①全盛時期;最佳之情況。the *prime* of life. 壯年。②最佳部分。③最初部分;開始。④春天。the *prime* of the year. 春天。⑤青年;壯年。⑥質數。⑦一分(一度的六十分之一)。⑧分號(')。⑨〖宗教〗早課;晨禱。⑩〖擊劍〗第一防守姿勢。—**ness,** *n.*

***prime²** *v.,* **primed, prim·ing.** —*v.t.* ①準備。②上火藥;裝雷管。③倒水於抽水機中(使

能發生吸力)。④〖俗〗塞飽;塞滿。⑤供以消息、細節等。⑥塗頭道油漆。⑦加滿。*prime the pump* 促起作用;使起活動。—*v.i.* ①裝彈藥;上子彈。②倒水於抽水機中使發生吸力。

prime cost 原價;主要成本(商品所需的原料及勞力之成本)。

prime·ly [ˈpraɪmlɪ; ˈpraimli] *adv.* 〖俗〗最好地。

prime meridian 本初子午線。

prime minister 首相;內閣總理。

prime mover ①原動力; 發動者;發起人。②〖電〗原動機。③〖美軍俗〗强力曳引車。

prime number 〖數學〗質數;素數。

prim·er¹ [ˈprɪmɚ; ˈpraimə, ˈprimə] *n.* ①初學用書;初階。a *primer* of phonetics. 語音學入門。②小禱告書。③一種鉛字字體名。

prim·er² [ˈpraɪmɚ; ˈpraimə] *n.* ①裝火藥者。②雷管;引火線。

pri·me·val [praɪˈmivl; praiˈmiːvl] *adj.* 原始時代的;太古的;初期的。*primeval* forest. 原始林。—**ly,** *adv.*

prim·ing [ˈpraɪmɪŋ; ˈpraimiŋ] *n.* ①點火藥;起爆劑。②點火;起爆。③油漆底子;初層之着色。

pri·mip·a·rous [praɪˈmɪpərəs; praiˈmipərəs] *adj.* 初次分娩的;初產的。

***prim·i·tive** [ˈprɪmətɪv; ˈprimitiv] *adj.* ①原始的;上古的。*primitive* culture. 原始文化。②最早的;最初的。③簡單的;幼稚的;古老的。④始創的;基本的。⑤未受正式訓練的;未經陶冶的。—*n.* ①早期的藝術家(尤指文藝復興以前者)。②其作品。③原始人。④原始觀念。⑤〖數學〗本原;原始。

primitive colors 原色。

prim·i·tive·ly [ˈprɪmətɪvlɪ; ˈprimitivli] *adv.* 原始地;以原始的方式。

pri·mo [ˈprimo; ˈpriːmou] *n.* 〖音樂〗第一部;主部。—*adj.* 〖音樂〗第一部的;主部的。—*adv.* 第一;最初。

pri·mo·gen·i·tor [ˌpraɪməˈdʒɛnətɚ; ˌpraiməˈdʒenitə] *n.* 祖先;始祖。

pri·mo·gen·i·ture [ˌpraɪməˈdʒɛnətʃɚ; ˌpraiməˈdʒenitʃə] *n.* ①長子之身分。②〖法律〗長子繼承制。

pri·mor·di·al [praɪˈmɔrdɪəl; praiˈmɔːdjəl] *adj.* ①原始的;原生的;最初的。②根本的。—*n.* 原始物;根本。—**ly,** *adv.*

primp [prɪmp; primp] *v.t.* & *v.i.* 裝飾;打扮。

***prim·rose** [ˈprɪmˌroz; ˈprimrouz] *n.* ①〖植物〗櫻草;櫻草花。②〖植物〗待宵草。③淡黃色。④最盛期;最佳部分。He is in the *primrose* of his life. 他正在他一生之最盛期。—*adj.* ①(多)櫻草的。②歡樂的。③淡黃色的。

Primrose League 櫻草會(英國保守黨的選舉團體)。

primrose path ①歡樂生涯。②容易或有誘惑性但有危險性之行動途徑。

primrose yellow 淡黃色。

prim·u·la [ˈprɪmjulə; ˈprimjulə] *n.* 〖植物〗櫻草科。—**ceous,** *adj.*

pri·mus [ˈpraɪməs; ˈpraiməs] *n.* 蘇格蘭監督教派之監督長。—*adj.* ①第一的; 首位的。②最年長的(小學中,將此字與同姓兒童之姓氏連用,以示區別,如 Jones *Primus*).

pri·mus in·ter pa·res [ˈpraɪməsˈɪntɚˈpɛriz; ˈpraiməsˈintəˈpɛəriːz] 〖拉〗(男性)同輩中第一的。

prin. ①principal. ②principally. ③principle.

‡prince [prɪns; prins] *n.* ①王子;太子。②(小國之)君主;諸侯。the *Prince* of Monaco. 摩納哥王。③巨子;巨頭。a merchant *prince*. 商業巨擘。④極易相處的人。*crown prince* 皇太子;皇儲。

Prince Albert 雙排扣長禮服。

prince consort 女王夫;女皇夫。

prince·dom [ˈprɪnsdəm; ˈprinsdəm] *n.* prince 之權、位或領地。

prince imperial 皇太子。

prince·li·ness [ˈprɪnslɪnɪs; ˈprinslinis] *n.* ①高貴;崇高。②豪華。

prince·ling [ˈprɪnslɪŋ; ˈprinsliŋ] *n.* 幼君;小王子。(亦作 **princekin, princelet**)

prince·ly [ˈprɪnslɪ; ˈprinsli] *adj.,* **-li·er, -li·est.** ①君王的; 王子的; 王侯的; 皇家的。*princely* power. 君王的權力。②似王子的;慷慨的;豐厚的。*princely* gifts. 豐厚的禮物。③與君王(或王侯)相稱的;尊貴的;莊嚴的。

Prince of Darkness 撒旦;魔鬼。

Prince of Peace 耶穌基督。

prince of the blood 皇族。

Prince of the Power of the Air 魔王;撒旦;魔鬼。

Prince of the World 〖聖經〗魔鬼;撒旦。

Prince of Wales 英國皇太子的封號。

prince regent 攝政王。

prince royal 大太子。

prince's-feath·er [ˈprɪnsɪzˈfɛðɚ; ˈprinsizˈfeðə] *n.* 〖植物〗莧屬植物;雞冠花。

***prin·cess** [ˈprɪnsɪs; prinˈses, ˈprinses] *n.* ①公主。②公爵夫人。③女公爵。④(商業廣告的選美會所選出的)公主。the new potato *princess.* 新選出的馬鈴薯公主。〖注意〗英音, princess 冠於人名前時讀爲[ˈprinses], 其他場合時讀爲 [prinˈses]; 美音, 則一律讀爲 [ˈprɪnsɪs].

prin·cesse dress [prɪnˈsɛs(ˈprɪnsɪs)～; prinˈses(ˈprinses)～] 衣裙用一塊布料裁製的女裝。(亦作 **princess dress**)

princess regent ①女攝政王。②攝政王之妻。

princess royal 長公主。

Prince·ton [ˈprɪnstən; ˈprinstən] *n.* 普林斯頓(美 New Jersey 州中部自治城市)。

‡prin·ci·pal [ˈprɪnsəpḷ; ˈprinsəpl] *adj.* 重要的; 首要的; 主要的。 Taipei is the *principal* city of Taiwan. 臺北是臺灣首要的城市。*principal parts* 英文中動詞的三個主要形式, 卽不定詞, 過去式, 過去分詞, 如 do, did, done. —*n.* ①首長。②〖美〗中小學校長(英國多稱 head master 或 head). ③主犯。④(放利息時之)本金。*principal* and interest. 本利。⑤資本;基本財產(可以生息者)。⑥本人(委任代理人之人)。⑦被保應付錢之本人。⑧決鬥者。⑨正樑;主椽。

principal axis 〖物理〗主軸。

principal clause 〖文法〗主要子句。

principal focus 〖光學〗主焦點。

prin·ci·pal·i·ty [ˌprɪnsəˈpælətɪ; ˌprinsiˈpæliti] *n., pl.* **-ties.** ①公國;侯國。②君位;君權; 主權。③(*pl.*) 〖神學〗天使九級之一。*the Principality* (英)威爾斯之別名。

***prin·ci·pal·ly** [ˈprɪnsəpḷɪ; ˈprinsəpəli] *adv.* 大抵;重要地;首要地;主要地。

prin·ci·pal·ship [ˈprɪnsəpḷˌʃɪp; ˈprinsəplʃip] *n.* principal 的任期或職位。

principal tone 〖音樂〗主音。

prin·ci·pate [ˈprɪnsɪˌpet; ˈprinsipit] *n.* ①〖羅馬史〗元首政治。②侯國;侯領。③首要之地位或權威。

prin·cip·i·um [prɪnˈsɪpɪəm; prinˈsipjəm] *n., pl.* **-cip·i·a** [-ˈsɪpɪə; -ˈsipiə]. ①原理；原則。②(*pl.*)基本原理；基本原則。Newton's *Principia*. 牛頓所著之"(數學)原理"。

‡**prin·ci·ple** [ˈprɪnsəpl; ˈprinsəpl] *n.* ①本義；本質；眞諦。the *principles* of democratic government. 民主政體之眞諦。②基本信條；主義。the Three People's *Principles.* 三民主義。③(行動之)規則；常例；戒條。Make it a *principle* to save some money each week. 養成每週儲蓄些錢的習慣。④正直；節操。a man of *principle*. 守節操之人。⑤原理；原則。⑥素；精；主要之質地。⑦操作之方法。⑧來源；根源。***in principle*** 原則上；理論上。***on principle*** **a.** 按固定的方法或規則。**b.** 根據個人之原則或道德觀念。

prin·ci·pled [ˈprɪnsəpld; ˈprinsəpld] *adj.* ①有主義的；有原則的；有節操的(常用於複合字)。high-*principled*. 主義高潔的。loose-*principled*. 無節操的。②合理的。

principle of relativity 〖物理〗(愛因斯坦之)相對論。

prink [prɪŋk; priŋk] *v.t.* 華飾；盛裝。—*v.i.* 打扮；裝飾；對鏡顧盼。

‡**print** [prɪnt; print] *v.t.* ①印刷。The book is well *printed*. 這書印得很好。②出版；刊行。③照印刷體寫。*Print* your name, please. 請將你的名字以印刷體寫下(便於辨認)。④印於；印花樣於。*printed* patterns. 印花圖案。⑤使成爲深刻印象。The scene is *printed* in my memory. 那景象深印在我記憶中。⑥晒印(相片等)。—*v.i.* ①印刷。②印(相片)。③寫印刷體字。—*n.* ①版。in large (small) *print*. 以大(小)字體印刷。②印成之畫片或花樣。③印花布。④印跡。finger *prints*. 指印。⑤印刷物。⑥一版書；一次所出版之書。⑦用以印刷之物。⑧印出之相片。⑨印象。***in print*** 印好的；印刷中；出售中。***out of print*** 絕版。

print·a·ble [ˈprɪntəbl; ˈprintəbl] *adj.* ①可印刷的。②適合於印行的。

print·back [ˈprɪntˌbæk; ˈprintbæk] *n.* 縮影版之放大照片。

print·cloth [ˈprɪntˌklɔθ; ˈprintklɔθ] *n.* 印花用棉布。

printed matter 印刷品。

printed page (the-) 出版物。

***print·er** [ˈprɪntɚ; ˈprintə] *n.* 印刷者；印刷業者；排版工人。

printer's devil 印刷所之學徒。

printer's error 排版錯誤；誤植。

printer's pie ①各種活字的混合堆。②混亂。***make printer's pie of*** 將…搞亂。

print·er·y [ˈprɪntərɪ; ˈprintəri] *n., pl.* **-er·ies.** ①印刷廠。②(布匹)印花工廠。

***print·ing** [ˈprɪntɪŋ; ˈprintiŋ] *n.* ①印刷；印刷術；印刷業。②印刷物；印刷品。③印刷體之字。④一次所印刷之成品。

printing ink 印刷用油墨。

printing machine 〖主英〗印刷機。

printing paper (洗照片用的)感光紙。

printing press 印刷機。

print·out [ˈprɪntˌaut; ˈprintaut] *n.* 〖電腦〗印刷輸出。

print paper 印刷用紙。

print·sell·er [ˈprɪntˌsɛlɚ; ˈprintˌselə] *n.* 版畫店；版畫售賣者。

print shop ①印刷所。②版畫店。

print·works [ˈprɪntˌwɝks; ˈprint-wəːks] *n.* 布匹印花工廠。

pri·or**[1] [ˈpraɪɚ; ˈpraiə] *adj.* ①在前的；較早的。a *prior* engagement. 預先的約會。②較重要的。prior to*** 在…之前。—**ly,** *adv.*

pri·or[2] *n.* 修道院副院長。—**ship,** *n.*

pri·or·ate [ˈpraɪərɪt; ˈpraiərit] *n.* ①修道院副院長之職位或任期。②=**priory.**

pri·or·ess [ˈpraɪərɪs; ˈpraiəris] *n.* 女修道院之副住持；小修道院之院長。

pri·or·i·ty [praɪˈɔrətɪ; praiˈɔriti] *n., pl.* **-ties.** ①(時間上的)在前；在先。②(次序或地位上的)居先；優先。first *priority*. 第一優先。according to *priority*. 按順序。③優先權。to take *priority* of. 得…之優先權。

pri·o·ry [ˈpraɪərɪ; ˈpraiəri] *n., pl.* **-ries.** (通常附屬於 abbey 中之)小修道院。

prise [praɪz; praiz] *v.t.* =**prize**[3].

***prism** [ˈprɪzəm; ˈprizm] *n.* ①稜柱。②稜鏡；三稜鏡。

pris·mat·ic [prɪzˈmætɪk; prizˈmætik] *adj.* ①角柱的；角柱形的。②以三稜鏡分解的。the *prismatic* colors. 光譜的七色。③有三稜解的。④〖礦〗斜方晶系的。⑤彩色繽紛的；光彩奪目的。—**al·ly,** *adv.*

‡**pris·on** [ˈprɪzṇ; ˈprizn] *n.* ①監獄；牢。Put him in *prison*. 將他監禁於獄中。②監禁；禁錮；限制。—*v.t.* 囚禁。

prison breach 越獄。(亦作 **prison break, prison breaking**)

prison breaker 越獄者。

prison camp ①囚犯集中營。②戰俘集中營。

‡**pris·on·er** [ˈprɪznɚ, ˈprɪzṇɚ; ˈpriznə] *n.* ①囚犯；犯人。*prisoner* of war. 戰俘(略作 POW)。②俘虜。He was taken *prisoner* by the enemy. 他被敵人俘虜。

prisoner at the bar 刑事被告。

prisoner of conscience 政治犯。

prisoner of State 國事犯。

prisoner's base 捕人戲。

prison house 監獄。

pris·sy [ˈprɪsɪ; ˈprisi] *adj.,* **-si·er, -si·est.** 〖俗〗①拘謹的；矜持的；過分守禮的。②過分文雅的；過於謙遜的。

pris·tine [ˈprɪstin; ˈpristain] *adj.* ①原始的；原有的。②純正的；純淨的。

prith·ee [ˈprɪðɪ; ˈpriði(ː)] *interj.* 〖古〗請；請你(=I pray thee).

***pri·va·cy** [ˈpraɪvəsɪ; ˈpraivəsi] *n., pl.* **-cies.** ①隱居；獨處；個人的小天地。to live in *privacy*. 隱居。②祕密。in *privacy*. 祕密地。③私事；隱私權。We must respect other's *privacies*. 我們不該打聽他人的私事。④(*pl.*)〖罕〗退隱處。

‡**pri·vate** [ˈpraɪvɪt; ˈpraivit] *adj.* ①私人的；私有的。a *private* letter. 私人信件。②個人的。my *private* opinion. 我個人的意見。③私設的。④祕密的。⑤無官職的；平民的。a *private* citizen. 平民。⑥僻遠的；隔離的。⑦不受他人干擾的。⑧軍階最低的。—*n.* ①列兵。②(*pl.*) 私處；陰部。***in private*** 祕密地(=secretly).

private bed 醫院裏的私人病牀。

private bill 國會中涉及私益的法案。

private car (火車之)私人專用車廂。

private detective 私家偵探。

private enterprise ①私人企業；民營企業。②以民營企業爲基礎的經濟制度。

pri·va·teer [ˌpraɪvəˈtɪr; ˌpraivəˈtiə] *n.* ①私掠船(戰時受命攻擊敵船之民船)。②私掠船之指揮官或船員。—*v.i.* (私掠船)巡弋。

pri·va·teer·ing [ˌpraɪvəˈtɪrɪŋ; ˌpraivəˈtiəriŋ] *n.* 私掠船巡弋；商船私掠。

pri·va·teers·man [ˌpraɪvəˈtɪrzmən;

ˌpraivəˈtiəzmən〕 *n., pl.* **-men.** 私掠船之船長或船員。

private eye 〖俚〗私家偵探。

private first class 〖美軍〗一等兵。

***pri·vate·ly** 〔ˈpraɪvɪtlɪ; ˈpraivitli〕 *adv.* 私下地;不公開地。 「非內閣閣員者。

private member 〖英〗國會議員而

private parts 私處;陰部。

private school 私立學校。

private secretary 私人祕書。

private soldier 列兵。 「展覽。

private view (公開展覽前之)非公開

pri·va·tion 〔praɪˈveʃən; praiˈveiʃən〕 *n.* ①(生活必需品之)匱乏;窮困。to die of *privation.* 死於窮困。②窮困、匱乏境況。to suffer many *privations.* 備嘗艱辛。③剝奪;喪失;欠缺。**—al,** *adj.*

pri·vat·ism 〔ˈpraɪvətɪzəm; ˈpraivətizəm〕 *n.* 不管閒事;退隱。

priv·a·tive 〔ˈprɪvətɪv; ˈprivətiv〕 *adj.* ①缺乏的;欠缺的。②剝奪的;褫奪的。③〖文法〗使肯定詞變成否定意義的;否定的。④消極的;表示性質缺如的。**—***n.* ①缺乏的事物;不存在的事務。②表示否定的字首和字尾(如:a-, un- 等)。**—ly,** *adv.* 「蠟樹。

priv·et 〔ˈprɪvɪt; ˈprivit〕 *n.* 〖植物〗水

priv·i·lege** 〔ˈprɪvlɪdʒ; ˈprivilidʒ〕 *n., v.,* **-leged, -leg·ing.** **—n.* 特權;恩典;特殊利益。the *privilege* of paying half fare. 繳半費之特權。**—***v.t.* 與以特權;特許。

priv·i·leged 〔ˈprɪvḷɪdʒd; ˈprivilidʒd〕 *adj.* 特權的。

privileged communication 〖法律〗證人不得洩漏的消息。(亦作**confidential communication**) 「地;祕密地。

priv·i·ly 〔ˈprɪvəlɪ; ˈprivəli〕 *adv.* 私下

priv·i·ty 〔ˈprɪvətɪ; ˈpriviti〕 *n., pl.* **-ties.** ①共同與聞的祕密;與知。②暗中參與。③祕密。④私事。⑤〖法律〗由法律或契約規定的對同一權利的相互關係。⑥(*pl.*)〖罕〗外陰部。***with his privity and consent*** 得到他的同意。***without the privity of*** 不使…知情;不讓(某人)知道;不與聞。

priv·y 〔ˈprɪvɪ; ˈprivi〕 *adj., n., pl.* **privies.** **—***adj.* ①與聞某事(之祕密)的〖to〗。②私有的;私用的。③君主私有或私用的。④〖古〗祕密的;隱藏的。***Lord Privy Seal*** 掌璽大臣。**—***n.* ①廁所。②〖法律〗當事人;利害關係人。

privy council ①〖英〗(P- C-) 樞密院。②智囊團;顧問團。

privy council(l)or 智囊團之一員。

privy parts 陰部。

privy purse 〖英〗①國王之私人用度(爲皇室費用之一部分)。②(P- P-) 皇室出納官。

privy seal 御璽。

prix fixe 〔ˈpriˈfiks; ˈpriːˈfiːks〕 〖法〗①客飯;和菜;快餐。②客飯或和菜的定價。

prize**[1] 〔praɪz; praiz〕 *n., adj., v.,* **prized, priz·ing.** **—n.* ①獎品。to award a *prize.* 給獎。②值得競爭之目的物。the *prizes* of life. 人生之目的。 **—***adj.* ①做爲獎品的。a *prize* scholarship. 獎學金。②值得給獎的。③獲得獎品的。a *prize* novel. 得獎小說。④突出的。**—***v.t.* ①珍視。②估價。

prize[2] *n.* 戰利品;俘虜。**—***v.t.* 鹵獲。The ship was *prized* for violating neutrality. 那艘船因違犯中立而被鹵獲。

prize[3] *v.t. & v.i.* 撬。to *prize* open a box. 撬開一個箱子。(亦作 **prise**) 「法庭。

prize court 決定戰時鹵獲船貨主權之

prize fight 有獎金的職業拳賽。

prize fighter 職業拳手。

prize fighting 以營利爲目的之職業性拳賽。 「*n., pl.* **-men.** 受賞者;得獎者。

prize·man 〔ˈpraɪzmən; ˈpraizmən〕

prize money ①往時發給虜獲或擊毀敵船有功之船上官兵的獎金。②獎金。

prize ring ①職業性鬥拳之鬥拳臺。②(the-)職業性拳賽。

prize winner 得獎者。

prk. park. **prm.** premium. **prntr.** printer. **PRO** ①Public Relations Office. ②Public Relations Officer.

pro[1] 〔pro; prou〕 *adv., adj., n., pl.* **pros,** *prep.* **—***adv.* 贊成地。**—***adj.* 贊成的;正面的。**—***n.* ①贊成者。②贊成之議論或理由。③贊成票。**—***prep.* 贊成。

pro[2] *n., pl.* **pros,** *adj.* 〖俗〗 = **professional.** a *pro* baseball player. 職業棒球球員。

pro- 〖字首〗①表"在前;居先"之義,如:provision 預備。②表"贊成;親善"之義,如:pro-German親德。③表"代替"之義,如:pronoun 代名詞。④表"向前"之義,如:progress 前進;進步。 「ost.

pro. ①progressive. ②pronoun. ③prov-

pro·a 〔ˈproə; ˈprouə〕 *n.* 馬來亞的快速小帆船。 「業性及業餘性選手混合比賽的。

pro-am 〔ˈproˈæm; ˈprouˈæm〕 *adj.* 職

pro and con 贊成與反對。***pros and cons*** 贊成論與反對論;贊成與反對的理由。

pro-and-con 〔ˈproənˈkɑn; ˈprouənˈkɔn〕 *v.t.,* **pro-and-conned, pro-and-conning.** 辯論。 「lem.

prob. ①probable. ②probably. ③prob-

prob·a·bil·ism 〔ˈprɑbəbəlɪzəm; ˈprɔbəbilizm〕 *n.* ①〖天主教〗對某事有兩種均非決定性意見時,應由判斷者隨意決定之教義。②〖哲學〗或然論。

prob·a·bil·i·ty** 〔ˌprɑbəˈbɪlətɪ; ˌprɔbəˈbiliti〕 *n., pl.* **-ties.** ①可能性;機會。②可能發生之事。A storm is one of the *probabilities* for tomorrow. 明天可能有暴風雨。③〖數學〗可能率;或然率。in all probability*** 很可能;大概(=probably)。

prob·a·ble** 〔ˈprɑbəbḷ; ˈprɔbəbl〕 *adj.* ①或有的;或是的;大概的。It is *probable* that it will rain. 天大概要下雨。②可能的。a *probable* candidate. 可能的候選人。**—n.* ①或有可能之事;可能性相當大之事。②可能之候選人。 「罪的合理基礎。

probable cause 〖法律〗相信被告有

‡prob·a·bly 〔ˈprɑbəblɪ; ˈprɔbəbli〕 *adv.* 或許;大概。*Probably* I can do it. 或許我能做此事。

pro·bang 〔ˈprobæŋ; ˈproubæŋ〕 *n.* 〖外科〗(用以納入咽喉或食道之)除鯁器。

pro·bate 〔ˈprobet; ˈproubit〕 *n., adj., v.,* **-bat·ed, -bat·ing.** **—***n.* ①遺囑之認證。②經認證之遺囑。**—***adj.* 遺囑認證的。**—***v.t.* ①認證(遺囑)之眞實性或效力。②予以緩刑。

probate court 有權認證遺囑與管理死者遺產等的特種法庭。

probate duty 遺囑認證稅。

pro·ba·tion 〔proˈbeʃən; prəˈbeiʃən〕 *n.* ①試驗;試用。②緩刑;監護。three years' *probation.* 三年的緩刑。**—al,** *adj.*

pro·ba·tion·ar·y 〔proˈbeʃənˌɛrɪ; prəˈbeiʃnəri〕 *adj.* ①試用的;試驗的。②試用期間的。

pro·ba·tion·er 〔proˈbeʃənɚ; prə-

ˈbeiʃənə] *n.* ①練習生;試讀生;被試用者;見習者。②緩刑中之犯人。③〖蘇〗見習布道的神學院學生;候補牧師。

pro·ba·tion·er·ship [proˈbeʃənə-ˌʃɪp; prəˈbeiʃənəʃip] *n.* ①試用期間;見習期間。②緩刑期間。

probation officer 觀護員。

pro·ba·tive [ˈprobətɪv; ˈproubətiv] *adj.* ①試驗的;嘗試用的。②提供證明或證據的;立據的。(亦作 **probatory**)

probe [prob; proub] *v.*, **probed, prob·ing,** *n.* —*v.t.* & *v.i.* ①探求;細察。to *probe* deeply into human nature. 探索人性之深處。②〖醫〗以探針探查。—*n.* ①細察;偵察。②調查。③探針(一種外科器械);類似探針之物。④裝有科學儀器以探測太空奧祕的火箭或人造衛星等。⑤空中加油時從加油機上吸取油料用的管子。

pro·bi·ty [ˈprobətɪ; ˈproubiti] *n.* 剛直;廉潔;正直。

‡**prob·lem** [ˈprɑbləm; ˈprɔbləm] *n.* ①問題;難解之問題。The *problem* is to find a suitable man. 問題在於尋找一合適的人。②難解之事物。the *problems* of youth. 青年的問題。③待解之題。a mathematical *problem*. 數學問題。—*adj.* 發生困難的。a *problem* child. 問題兒童。

prob·lem·at·ic [ˌprɑbləˈmætɪk; ˌprɔbliˈmætik] *adj.* 問題的;有疑問的;未決的;成問題的。

prob·lem·at·i·cal [ˌprɑbləˈmætɪkl̩; ˌprɔbliˈmætikl] *adj.* =**problematic.** —**ly,** *adv.*

pro·bos·cis [proˈbɑsɪs; prouˈbɔsis] *n., pl.* **-bos·cis·es, -bos·ci·des** [-ˈbɑsɪˌdiz; -ˈbɔsidiːz]. ①(象等之)長鼻。②(昆蟲等之)針狀吻。③〖諧〗(人之)鼻。

proc. ①proceedings. ②procedure. ③process. ④proctor.

pro·caine [proˈken; prouˈkein] *n.* 〖化〗普魯卡因($C_{13}H_{20}O_2N_2$•HCl, 用作局部麻醉藥)。(亦作 **procaine hydrochloride**)

pro·ca·the·dral [ˌprokəˈθidrəl; ˌprou-kəˈθiːdrəl] *n.* 臨時作主教座堂用的教堂。

pro·ce·dur·al [proˈsidʒərəl; prəˈsiː-dʒərəl] *adj.* 程序的;程序上的;有關程序的。*procedural* details. 程序上的細節。—**ly,** *adv.*

***pro·ce·dure** [prəˈsidʒɚ; prəˈsiːdʒə] *n.* 手續;程序;訴訟程序;議事程序。legal *procedure*. 訴訟程序。code of civil (criminal) *procedure*. 民事(刑事)訴訟法。

‡**pro·ceed** [*v.* prəˈsid; prəˈsiːd *n.* ˈpro-sid; ˈprousiːd] *v.i.* ①(停止後)繼續進行。*Proceed* with your story. 繼續說你的故事。②(動作)開始進行。③進行;進展。④發出;生出。Heat *proceeds* from fire. 熱由火中發出。⑤獲取學位。to *proceed* to the degree of M.A. 獲取文學碩士學位。⑥〖法律〗起訴;進行訴訟程序。to proceed against (a person).控訴(某人)。—*n.*(常 *pl.*)賣得之錢;所得。

***pro·ceed·ing** [prəˈsidɪŋ; prəˈsiːdiŋ] *n.* ①行動;處置。an illegal *proceeding*. 不合法的手段。②(*pl.*)會社等每年發表之記錄;年報。③(*pl.*)訴訟程序。to take legal *proceedings* against a person. 控訴某人。④(*pl.*)經過。

‡**proc·ess**[1] [ˈprɑsɛs, ˈprosɛs; ˈprouses] *n.* ①進行;過程。The tank is in *process* of construction. 水池在建造中。②手續;程序。By what *process* is cloth made from wool? 羊毛織成呢絨經過甚麼手續? ③隆起;突起。④方法。new *process* yielding good result. 產生良好效果之新方法。⑤訴訟程序;傳票。to serve a *process* on. 對…發出傳票。—*v.t.* ①以特種方法處置或調製;對…加工。to *process* leather. 製造皮革。to *process* an application. 處理一件申請案。②起訴;控訴。③對…發出傳票。—*adj.* 以特種方法處置或調製的。*process* sugar. 特製的糖。

proc·ess[2] [proˈsɛs; prəˈses] *v.i.* 〖主英〗列隊前進。

process heat 供工商業用而生產之熱能。

processing tax 農產品之加工稅。

***pro·ces·sion** [prəˈsɛʃən, pro-; prəˈseʃən] *n.* ①行列;前進之物。a funeral *procession*. 送葬行列。to march in *procession*. 列隊進行。②順序前進。

pro·ces·sion·al [prəˈsɛʃənl̩; prəˈseʃənəl] *adj.* (亦作 **processionary**) 遊行的;用於遊行時的;在遊行時唱的。—*n.* ①〖宗教〗遊行聖歌或其歌集。②列隊前進。—**ly,** *adv.*

pro·ces·sive [prəˈsɛsɪv; prəˈsesiv] *adj.* 進步的。

proc·es·sor [ˈprɑsɛsɚ; ˈprousesə] *n.* 製造者;加工者;(尤指)農產品加工者。

process printing 彩色印刷術。

process server 〖法律〗傳票送達員。

pro·cès-ver·bal [proˌsɛvɚˈbɑl; prouˌseivəˈbɑːl] *n., pl.* **-ver·baux** [-vɚˈbo; -vəˈbou]. 〖法〗①報告書;紀錄;筆錄。②〖法國法律〗刑事案之紀錄。

***pro·claim** [proˈklem; prəˈkleim, prou-] *v.t.* ①正式宣布;宣言。War was *proclaimed*. 宣戰了。The people *proclaimed* him king. 人民擁他爲王。②顯示;顯露。③加以法律限制;禁止。④公開讚揚;頌揚。—**er,** *n.*

***proc·la·ma·tion** [ˌprɑkləˈmeʃən; ˌprɔkləˈmeiʃən] *n.* ①文告。The governor issued a *proclamation* declaring martial law. 省長發表戒嚴令文告。②正式宣布;宣言。It becomes legal upon *proclamation*. 它將於正式宣布時成爲合法。

pro·clit·ic [proˈklɪtɪk; prouˈklitik] 〖文法〗*adj.* 後接的。—*n.* 後接語(在日常語言中, 連同其後一字發音, 故而其自身無重音, 如 to be or not to be 中的 to)。

pro·cliv·i·ty [proˈklɪvətɪ; prəˈkliviti] *n., pl.* **-ties.** 癖性;傾向;脾氣〖to, towards〗.

pro·con·sul [proˈkɑnsl̩; prouˈkɔnsl] *n.*(古羅馬之)地方長官;(近代之)殖民地總督。

pro·con·su·lar [proˈkɑnslɚ; prou-ˈkɔnsjulə] *adj.* ①(古羅馬的)地方長官的。②(近代之)英國殖民地總督的。

pro·con·su·late [proˈkɑnslɪt; prou-ˈkɔnsjulit] *n.* proconsul 之職位或任期。

pro·con·sul·ship [proˈkɑnsl̩ˌʃɪp; prouˈkɔnslʃip] *n.* =**proconsulate.**

pro·cras·ti·nate [proˈkræstəˌnet; prouˈkræstineit] *v.t.* & *v.i.,* **-nat·ed, -nat·ing.** 拖延;延宕;遲滯。—**pro·cras·ti·na·tor,** *n.*

pro·cras·ti·na·tion [proˌkræstə-ˈneʃən; prouˌkræstiˈneiʃən] *n.* 拖延;延宕。

pro·cre·ate [ˈprokrɪˌet; ˈproukrieit] *v.t.* & *v.i.,* **-at·ed, -at·ing.** 生育;生殖;產生;產(子)。

pro·cre·a·tion [ˌprokrɪˈeʃən; ˌprou-kriˈeiʃən] *n.* 生產;生殖。

pro·cre·a·tive [ˈprokrɪˌetɪv; ˈprou-krieitiv] *adj.* ①生產的;生殖的。②有生產力的;有生殖力的。

pro·cre·a·tor [ˈprokrɪˌetɚ; ˈprou-krieitə] *n.* 生產者。

Pro·crus·te·an 〔pro'krʌstiən; prou'krʌstiən〕 *adj.* ①Procrustes 的。②硬使與預定之理想、制度等相合的; 激烈的; 施暴力以令服從的。 ***Procrustean bed*** 强使與事實、本性等相配合的觀念、理論或制度。

Pro·crus·tes 〔pro'krʌstiz; prou'krʌsti:z〕 *n.* 〖希臘神話〗古希臘一强盜, 捕得旅客後將之縛於床上, 然後或砍其腿, 或拉之使長, 以適合其床。

pro·cryp·tic 〔pro'krɪptɪk; prou'kriptik〕 *adj.* (昆蟲之)保護色的; 有保護色的(昆蟲)。

proc·tol·o·gy 〔prɑk'tɑlədʒɪ; prɔk'tɔlədʒi〕 *n.* 直腸病學。—**proc·tol·o·gist,** *n.*

proc·tor 〔'prɑktɚ; 'prɔktə〕 *n.* ①訓導長; 訓育主任。②〖法律〗代訴人。

proc·to·ri·al 〔prɑk'torɪəl; prɔk'tɔ:riəl〕 *adj.* 大學之訓導長的; 代理人的。

proc·tor·ize 〔'prɑktəˌraɪz; 'prɔktəraiz〕 *v.,* **-ized, -iz·ing.** —*v.t.* 譴責或處罰(學生)。—*v.i.* 執行其訓導長之職務。

proc·tor·ship 〔'prɑktɚˌʃɪp; 'prɔktəʃip〕 *n.* 訓導長之職位或任期; 代理人之職位。

pro·cum·bent 〔pro'kʌmbənt; prou'kʌmbənt〕 *adj.* ①俯伏的; 平臥的。②〖植物〗匍匐地上生長的。

pro·cur·a·ble 〔pro'kjʊrəbl̩; prə'kjuərəbl〕 *adj.* 可獲得的。

proc·u·ra·tion 〔ˌprɑkjə'reʃən; ˌprɔkjuə'reiʃən〕 *n.* ①獲得; 取得。②代理。③代理人之委任。④賦予之權力。⑤委任狀。⑥(借貸中抽的)佣金。⑦〖宗教〗(教會獻給主教等之)巡視費。⑧淫媒; 替妓女拉皮條。

proc·u·ra·tor 〔'prɑkjəˌretɚ; 'prɔkjuəreitə〕 *n.* ①代理人; 訴訟代理人。②(古羅馬之)太守; 地方稅吏。③檢察官。 ***public procurator*** 檢察官。 ***public procurator general*** 首席檢察官。—**i·al,** *adj.*

proc·u·ra·tor·ship 〔'prɑkjəˌretɚˌʃɪp; 'prɔkjuəreitəʃip〕 *n.* procurator 之職位或任期。

***pro·cure** 〔pro'kjʊr; prə'kjuə〕 *v.,* **-cured, -cur·ing.** —*v.t.* ①取得。A friend *procured* a position in the bank for my big brother. 一個朋友在銀行中爲我哥哥謀得一個職位。②促成。③引誘; 說服。—*v.i.* 蓄娼; 拉皮條。

pro·cure·ment 〔pro'kjʊrmənt; prə'kjuəmənt〕 *n.* ①獲得; 取得。②促成; 成就。

pro·cur·er 〔pro'kjʊrɚ; prə'kjuərə〕 *n.* ①取得者; 獲得者。②蓄娼者; 淫媒。

prod 〔prɑd; prɔd〕 *v.,* **prod·ded, prod·ding,** *n.* —*v.t.* ①(以尖物)刺。②督促; 激勵。—*n.* ①刺; 戳。②有尖鋒之物(如驅家畜之刺棒等)。③鼓勵作用之言語、行動等。 ***on the prod*** 激怒; 暴怒; 狂怒。—**der,** *n.*

prod. ①produce. ②producer. ③produced. ④product. ⑤production.

pro·de·li·sion 〔ˌprodɪ'lɪʒən; ˌproudi'liʒən〕 *n.* 字頭母音之省略(如 I am 之省略爲 I'm)。

prod·i·gal** 〔'prɑdɪgl̩; 'prɔdigəl〕 *adj.* ①浪費的; 揮霍的; 奢侈的。the *prodigal* son. 浪子; 紈袴子。He is *prodigal* of money. 他揮霍無度。②過度慷慨的; 濫用的; 亂給的〖常 of〗. She was *prodigal* of praise. 她亂加稱讚。③極度豐富的; 豐饒的。—*n.* 浪子; 浪費者。the return of the *prodigal.* 浪子回頭。 ***play the prodigal 過放蕩生活; 遊蕩。

prod·i·gal·i·ty 〔ˌprɑdɪ'gælətɪ; ˌprɔdi'gæliti〕 *n.* ①浪費; 揮霍; 奢侈。②豐饒。

prod·i·gal·ly 〔'prɑdɪglɪ; 'prɔdigəli〕 *adv.* ①揮霍地; 奢侈地。②豐饒地; 豐富地。

pro·di·gious 〔prə'dɪdʒəs; prə'didʒəs〕 *adj.* ①很大的。②奇異的; 驚人的。a *prodigious* blunder. 荒謬的錯誤。—**ness,** *n.*

pro·di·gious·ly 〔prə'dɪdʒəslɪ; prə'didʒəsli〕 *adv.* 非常地。

prod·i·gy 〔'prɑdədʒɪ; 'prɔdidʒi〕 *n., pl.* **-gies.** ①可驚之事物; 不凡之人。an infant *prodigy.* 神童。②可驚之例證。③奇特之象徵或朕兆。④反常之事。

‡**pro·duce** 〔*v.* prə'djus; prə'dju:s *n.* 'prɑdjus; 'prɔdju:s〕 *v.,* **-duced, -duc·ing,** *n.* —*v.t.* ①製造; 出產。This factory *produces* cars. 這工廠製造汽車。②引起; 導致。Hard work *produces* success. 努力工作會導致成功。③產; 生產。Hens *produce* eggs. 母鷄會生蛋。④生(子、息、作物等)。⑤產生。⑥呈出; 提出。*Produce* your proof. 拿出你的證明來。⑦演出(戲劇等)。Five new plays were *produced.* 有五部新戲上演了。⑧〖數學〗引長(線段)。—*v.i.* 創作(藝術品等); 寫出作品; 出產。The salvation of trade is to *produce.* 商業的救星即是生產。—*n.* ①出產品。②農產品(集合稱)。Vegetables are a garden's *produce.* 蔬菜是菜園中的農產品。③子嗣。

***pro·duc·er** 〔prə'djusɚ; prə'dju:sə〕 *n.* ①生產者; 製作者。②電影製片人; 戲劇之演出者。③〖化〗瓦斯發生器。④產地。⑤產油之油井。

producers' goods 生產設備及原料。

pro·duc·i·ble 〔prə'djusəbl̩; prə'dju:səbl〕 *adj.* 可生產的; 可製作的; 可提出的; 可延長的。—**pro·duc·i·bil·i·ty,** *n.*

‡**prod·uct** 〔'prɑdəkt, -dʌkt; 'prɔdəkt, -dʌkt〕 *n.* ①產物; 生產品。agricultural *products.* 農產物。②(數字之)乘積; 積。40 is the *product* of 8 by 5. 40 是 8 乘 5 的積。③結果。④〖化〗生成物。

‡**pro·duc·tion** 〔prə'dʌkʃən; prə'dʌkʃən〕 *n.* ①製造; 生產。the *production* of crops. 農作物之生產。②產物; 生產品。③繳驗; 出示。—**al,** *adj.*

production line (工廠之)生產線; 「裝配線。」

***pro·duc·tive** 〔prə'dʌktɪv; prə'dʌktiv〕 *adj.* ①生產的; 能生產的。hasty words that are *productive* of quarrels. 導致口角的躁急的話。②有生產價值的。Farming is *productive* labor. 耕作是有生產價值的勞動。③肥沃的; 豐饒的。a *productive* farm. 肥沃的農場。④多產的。a *productive* writer. 多產作家。⑤可用來造新字或新辭的(字首、字尾等)。

pro·duc·tive·ly 〔prə'dʌktɪvlɪ; prə'dʌktivli〕 *adv.* 有結果地; 有成果地; 有生產地。

pro·duc·tive·ness 〔prə'dʌktɪvnɪs; prə'dʌktivnis〕 *n.* 生產力。

pro·duc·tiv·i·ty 〔ˌprodʌk'tɪvətɪ; ˌproudʌk'tiviti〕 *n.* 生產力。

pro·em 〔'proɛm; 'prouem〕 *n.* 序言; 緒「言。」

pro·ette 〔pro'ɛt; prou'et〕 *n.* 女性職業運動員(尤指高爾夫球)。

prof 〔prɑf; prɔf〕 *n.* 〖俗〗教授。

Prof., prof. professor.

prof·a·na·tion 〔ˌprɑfə'neʃən; ˌprɔfə'neiʃən〕 *n.* ①褻瀆神聖。②濫用。

pro·fan·a·to·ry 〔prə'fænəˌtorɪ; prə'fænətəri〕 *adj.* 褻瀆神靈的。

***pro·fane** 〔prə'fen; prə'fein〕 *adj., v.,* **-faned, -fan·ing.** —*adj.* ①非神聖的; 凡俗

的。②汚穢的；汚神的。*profane* language. 褻瀆神聖的話。③異教的；邪教的。—*v.t.* ①褻瀆；玷汚。②誤用。—**ly,** *adv.*

pro·fane·ness 〔prəˈfennɪs; prəˈfeinnis〕 *n.* 非神聖；瀆神；不敬。

profane history 俗史（以別於宗教史）。

pro·fan·i·ty 〔prəˈfænətɪ; prəˈfæniti〕 *n., pl.* **-ties.** ①不敬；瀆神。②褻瀆的言語或行爲。

***pro·fess** 〔prəˈfɛs; prəˈfes〕 *v.t.* ①聲稱。He *professed* extreme regret. 他表示非常遺憾。②公言；明言。③聲稱信仰。④以…爲業；執業。to *profess* law. 做律師。⑤教授。to *profess* history. 教授歷史。⑥僞稱；佯稱。⑦正式准予歸依；正式准予加入教團。

pro·fessed 〔prəˈfɛst; prəˈfest〕 *adj.* ①公然宣稱的；公然的。a *professed* liar. 一個公然的說謊者。②宣誓加入某教團的。③本行的；專門的。④自稱的；詐稱的。

pro·fess·ed·ly 〔prəˈfɛsɪdlɪ; prəˈfesidli〕 *adv.* ①公言地；公然地。②詐稱地；表面地。

***pro·fes·sion** 〔prəˈfɛʃən; prəˈfeʃən〕 *n.* ①職業（特指須受過特殊教育及訓練者，如教師、律師、醫生等）。the *profession* of an architect. 建築師之職業。②(the~)某種專門職業之團體。to be respected by the *profession.* 爲同行所尊敬。③宣布；表白；表示。*profession* of faith. 信仰的表白。④公開宣布信仰的宗教或信仰。⑤修道誓約。

***pro·fes·sion·al** 〔prəˈfɛʃənḷ; prəˈfeʃənəl〕 *adj.* ①專門職業上的。*professional* skill. 職業上的技術。②從事於專門職業的。A lawyer or a doctor is a *professional* man. 律師或醫生是有專門職業的人。③以(運動、遊藝等)爲專業的。*professional* tennis player. 職業網球家。—*n.* ①以運動、遊藝等爲職業的人。These ballplayers are all *professionals.* 這些球員全是職業球員。②醫生、律師等從事自由職業的人。

pro·fes·sion·al·ism 〔prəˈfɛʃənḷɪzm; prəˈfeʃənəlizm〕 *n.* ①從事於專門職業者的特性、地位或方法。②專業主義。

pro·fes·sion·al·ize 〔prəˈfɛʃənḷˌaɪz; prəˈfeʃənəlaiz〕 *v.t.* & *v.i.,* **-ized, -iz·ing.** (使)職業化。

pro·fes·sion·al·ly 〔prəˈfɛʃənḷɪ; prəˈfeʃənəli〕 *adv.* 在職業上；在專業上。

‡**pro·fes·sor** 〔prəˈfɛsɚ; prəˈfesə〕 *n.* ①教授。a *professor* of French. 法文教授。②〖俗〗= **teacher.** ③公開宣布其信仰的人。④〖美俚〗在下等場所彈奏鋼琴者。

pro·fes·sor·ate 〔prəˈfɛsərɪt; prəˈfesərit〕 *n.* ①教授之職位或聘期。②教授會。③教授之集合稱。(亦作 **professoriate**)

pro·fes·so·ri·al 〔ˌprofəˈsorɪəl; ˌprɔfeˈsɔːriəl〕 *adj.* 教授的；有教授特性的。—**ly,** *adv.*

pro·fes·sor·ship 〔prəˈfɛsɚˌʃɪp; prəˈfesəʃip〕 *n.* 教授之職位。

prof·fer 〔ˈprɑfɚ; ˈprɔfə〕 *v.t.* ①提供；提出。②表示樂意；表示願意。—*n.* 提供；提出；貢獻(意見)。His *proffer* of advice was accepted. 他所提供之意見已被接納。

pro·fi·cien·cy 〔prəˈfɪʃənsɪ; prəˈfiʃənsi〕 *n., pl.* **-cies.** ①熟練；精通。②進步。

***pro·fi·cient** 〔prəˈfɪʃənt; prəˈfiʃənt〕 *adj.* 精通的；熟諳的。She was *proficient* in music. 她精通音樂。—*n.* 專家。

pro·fi·cient·ly 〔prəˈfɪʃəntlɪ; prəˈfiʃəntli〕 *adv.* 熟練地。

***pro·file** 〔ˈprofaɪl; ˈproufail〕 *n., v.,* **-filed, -fil·ing.** —*n.* ①側面像；側面半身像。his handsome *profile.* 他英俊的側面像。②輪廓；外形。③對一個人的能力、人格、事業的簡要描述；寫照。④建築物、橋樑等的橫斷面圖；翼剖面。—*v.t.* ①畫…的側面像；鈎…的輪廓。②對…做扼要描寫。③畫…的側面畫；畫…的橫斷面圖。—*v.i.* (鬥牛士)將左肩轉向牛。

‡**prof·it** 〔ˈprɑfɪt; ˈprɔfit〕 *n.* ①(常 *pl.*)利潤；贏利。The *profits* in this business are not large. 這一行生意利潤不大。②利益。What *profit* is there in worrying? 發愁有甚麼用？—*v.t.* ①有利；有益。It *profited* him nothing. 此事對他毫無利益。②贏利。—*v.i.* ①有益。A wise person *profits* by his mistakes. 聰明的人從過失中獲益。②獲利。③有進步；有改善。—**er,** *n.*

***prof·it·a·ble** 〔ˈprɑfɪtəbḷ; ˈprɔfitəbl〕 *adj.* ①有利潤可圖的。a *profitable* undertaking. 有利可圖的事業。②有利益的；有用的。—**ness,** *n.*

prof·it·a·bly 〔ˈprɑfɪtəblɪ; ˈprɔfitəbli〕 *adv.* 有益地。

profit and loss 盈虧帳目。

prof·it·eer 〔ˌprɑfəˈtɪr; ˌprɔfiˈtiə〕 *n.* 乘機獲暴利者(尤指發國難財者)；奸商。a war *profiteer.* 發戰爭財者。—*v.t.* 獲暴利。

prof·it·eer·ing 〔ˌprɑfəˈtɪrɪŋ; ˌprɔfiˈtiəriŋ〕 *n.* 暴利之獲得。—*adj.* 獲暴利的。

prof·it·less 〔ˈprɑfɪtlɪs; ˈprɔfitlis〕 *adj.* ①無利可得的。②無益的；無用的。—**ly,** *adv.*

profit sharing 勞資雙方分享利潤。

prof·li·ga·cy 〔ˈprɑfləgəsɪ; ˈprɔfligəsi〕 *n.* ①放蕩；淫佚；行爲不檢。②恣意浪費。

prof·li·gate 〔ˈprɑfləgɪt; ˈprɔfligit〕 *adj.* ①放蕩的；行爲不檢的。②浪費的；揮金如土的。—*n.* 放蕩之徒；浪子。—**ly,** *adv.*

prof·lu·ent 〔ˈprɑfluənt; ˈprɔfluənt〕 *adj.* 順利而大量流動的。

pro for·ma 〔proˈformə; prouˈfɔːmə〕〖拉〗僅爲形式之故；僅爲官樣文章；形式上(=for the sake of form).

pro forma invoice 〖商〗估價單。

***pro·found** 〔prəˈfaund; prəˈfaund〕 *adj.* ①極深的；淵深的。a *profound* sleep. 酣睡。②深深感覺的。*profound* despair. 極深的絕望。③深奧的；奧妙的。④低的。—*n.* ①深處。②〖詩〗海洋。

***pro·found·ly** 〔prəˈfaundlɪ; prəˈfaundli〕 *adv.* ①深刻地。②深深地。I was *profoundly* glad to see it. 我非常高興看到它。③完全地(指耳聾之程度而言)。

pro·fun·di·ty 〔prəˈfʌndətɪ; prəˈfʌnditi〕 *n., pl.* **-ties.** ①深奧；深刻；奧妙；淵深。②深處。③(*pl.*)深邃之事物。

pro·fuse 〔prəˈfjus; prəˈfjuːs〕 *adj.* ①很多的。②浪費的。—**ness,** *n.*

pro·fuse·ly 〔prəˈfjuslɪ; prəˈfjuːsli〕 *adv.* 豐富地；豐盛地。

pro·fu·sion 〔prəˈfjuʒən; prəˈfjuːʒən〕 *n.* ①極豐；豐富；大量。②揮霍；浪費。

prog 〔prɑg; prɔg〕 *v.,* **progged, progging,** *n.* —*v.i.* 搜括食物。—*v.t.* (學監)訓誡或處罰(學生)。—*n.* ①〖俚〗食物。②〖英俚〗大學學監。

prog. ①program. ②progress. ③progressive.

pro·gen·i·tive 〔proˈdʒɛnətɪv; prouˈdʒenitiv〕 *adj.* 有生殖力的；能生子的；生殖的。

pro·gen·i·tor 〔proˈdʒɛnətɚ; prouˈdʒenitə〕 *n.* ①祖先；前輩。②起源；前身。

pro·gen·i·tress 〔proˈdʒɛnɪtrɪs; prou-

ˈdʒenitris] *n.* progenitor 之女性。
pro·gen·i·ture [proˈdʒɛnətʃɚ; prouˈdʒenitʃə] *n.* ①出產;生產;生育。②子孫;後裔。
prog·e·ny [ˈprɑdʒənɪ; ˈprɔdʒini] *n., pl.* **-nies.** ①子孫;後裔。②產物;所產;成果。
pro·ges·ter·one [proˈdʒɛstəˌron; prouˈdʒestəroun] *n.* 〖化〗助孕酮;妊娠素;黃體激素(一種荷爾蒙,其分子式爲 $C_{21}H_{30}O_2$)。
pro·ges·tin [proˈdʒɛstɪn; prouˈdʒestin] *n.* ①=**progesterone** (爲較老之名)。②與 progesterone 之作用類似之藥物;子宮內膜刺激素;助孕素;孕激素。
pro·glot·tis [proˈglɑtɪs; prouˈglɔtis] *n., pl.* **-ti·des** [-tɪˌdiz; -tidiːz]. 〖動物〗條蟲之節片;體節。
prog·na·thous [ˈprɑgnəθəs; prɔgˈneiθəs] *adj.* ①頷凸畸形的;突顎的;有突顎的(頭蓋骨或人)。②畸形凸出的(顎、頷)。
prog·no·sis [prɑgˈnosɪs; prɔgˈnousis] *n., pl.* **-ses** [-siz; -siːz]. ①〖醫〗病狀之預斷;豫後;判病結局。②預知;預測。
prog·nos·tic [prɑgˈnɑstɪk; prəgˈnɔstik] *adj.* ①預兆的。②〖醫〗病狀預斷的;豫後的;關於豫後的。—*n.* ①預兆;預知。②病狀預斷。
prog·nos·ti·cate [prɑgˈnɑstɪˌket; prəgˈnɔstikeit] *v.*, **-cat·ed, -cat·ing.** —*v.t.* (由目前之徵兆)預測(將來);預言;預示。—*v.i.* 預言;預卜。
prog·nos·ti·ca·tion [prɑgˌnɑstɪˈkeʃən; prəgˌnɔstiˈkeiʃən] *n.* ①預知;預測;預言。②前兆;徵候。
prog·nos·ti·ca·tor [prɑgˈnɑstɪˌketɚ; prəgˈnɔstikeitə] *n.* 預言者;占卜者。
***pro·gram** [ˈprogræm; ˈprougræm] *n., v.,* **-grammed, -gram·ming.** —*n.* ①節目單;節目。The entire *program* was delightful. 全部節目都很令人愉快。②計畫。What is the *program* for tomorrow? 我們明天做甚麼? ③〖電腦〗程式。—*v.t.* ①排…之節目單。②擬…之計畫。③〖電腦〗爲…規劃程式。 —*v.i.* 使電腦解答一個問題。(亦作 **programme**)
program director (電臺等之)節目部主任。
pro·gram·mat·ic [ˌprogrəˈmætɪk; ˌprougrəˈmætik] *adj.* 計畫的;計畫性的。—**al·ly,** *adv.*
pro·gram·mer [ˈprogræmɚ; ˈprougræmə] *n.* ①編節目單者;安排節目的人;計畫者。②爲電腦規劃程式者。
programming language =**computer language.**
program music 標題音樂;描寫音樂。
program picture 加映影片。
‡**prog·ress** [*n.* ˈprɑgrɛs, ˈpro-; ˈprougres *v.* prəˈgrɛs; prəˈgres] *n.* ①進步;進展;改進;發展。the *progress* of science. 科學的進步。to make *progress.* 有進步。②前進。to make rapid *progress* on a journey. 旅程中進行極速。③(君主之)巡遊。***in progress*** 進展中;進行中。 —*v.i.* ①進步。②前進;進行。—*v.t.* 促進。
pro·gres·sion [prəˈgrɛʃən; prəˈgreʃən] *n.* ①前進;進行。②〖數學〗級數。arithmetic *progression.* 等差(算術)級數。geometric *progression.* 等比(幾何)級數。harmonic *progression.* 調和級數。③進步。
pro·gres·sion·al [prəˈgrɛʃənl̩; prəˈgreʃənl̩] *adj.* ①進步的。②〖數學〗級數的。
pro·gres·sion·ist [prəˈgrɛʃənɪst; prəˈgreʃənist] *n.* 進步論者;改革論者。
***pro·gres·sive** [prəˈgrɛsɪv; prəˈgresiv] *adj.* ①前進的;進步的;進行的。a *progressive* policy. 進步的政策。②提倡進步的;提倡改革的。③日益增長的。④向前流動的;向前移動的。⑤〖稅率〗累進的。⑥〖文法〗(動詞)進行式的。—*n.* 提倡進步論者;前進分子。—**ness,** *n.* 〖文法〗 **progressive form.** 進行式(即 be 的各種變化加上動詞之現在分詞的形式)。
pro·gres·sive·ly [prəˈgrɛsɪvlɪ; prəˈgresivli] *adv.* 日益增多地。
Progressive Party 進步黨(**a.**美國一政黨,成立於1912年,其黨員多爲 Theodore Roosevelt 的追隨者。**b.** 1924 年 Robert M. La Follete 或 1948 年 Henry A. Wallace 領導下組織的美國政黨)。
progressive taxation 累進稅。
pro·gres·siv·ism [prəˈgrɛsɪvɪzm̩; prəˈgresivizm] *n.* 進步主義;改革主義。
***pro·hib·it** [proˈhɪbɪt; prəˈhibit, prou-] *v.t.* ①禁止。We are *prohibited* from smoking on school grounds. 我們不准在校園內吸烟。②阻止;妨礙。Family finances *prohibited* his going to college. 家庭的經濟狀況使他不能上大學。〖注意〗**prohibited** 後面用 from; **prohibition** 後面用 against.
pro·hib·it·er [prəˈhɪbɪtɚ; prəˈhibitə] *n.* 禁止者;阻止者;障礙物。
***pro·hi·bi·tion** [ˌproəˈbɪʃən; ˌprouiˈbiʃən, ˌprouhi-] *n.* ①禁止。The *prohibition* against smoking on school grounds is strictly enforced. 校園內嚴禁吸烟。②禁令;禁律。③〖美〗禁酒令。
pro·hi·bi·tion·ism [ˌproəˈbɪʃənɪzəm; ˌprouiˈbiʃn̩izəm] *n.* 禁酒論者之原則與作風。
pro·hi·bi·tion·ist [ˌproəˈbɪʃənɪst; ˌprouiˈbiʃn̩ist] *n.* ①禁酒論者。②(P-)〖美〗禁酒黨黨員。
pro·hib·i·tive [proˈhɪbɪtɪv; prəˈhibitiv] *adj.* ①禁止的;阻礙的。a *prohibitive* tax. 寓禁稅。②高至令人不敢問津的(價格)。*prohibitive* prices. 嚇人的價格。
pro·hib·i·tor [prəˈhɪbɪtɚ; prəˈhibitə] *n.* 禁止者;阻止者。
pro·hib·i·to·ry [proˈhɪbəˌtorɪ; prəˈhibitəri] *adj.* ①=**prohibitive.** ②有禁止之意的。*prohibitory* laws. 查禁的法令。
***proj·ect** [*n.* ˈprɑdʒɛkt; ˈprɔdʒekt *v.* prəˈdʒɛkt; prəˈdʒekt] *n.* ①計畫;設計。to carry out a new *project.* 實行一新計畫。②事業;企業;工程。—*v.t.* ①計劃;設計。to *project* a new machine. 設計一新機器。②投出;射出。③使落於平面;投影於…上。④畫投影線;畫投影圖。⑤想出;使…在心中形成。⑥表達;表現。⑦使突出。—*v.i.* ①突出。The rocky point *projects* far into the water. 那多石的岬伸入水面很遠。②閒蕩;虛度光陰。
pro·jec·tile [prəˈdʒɛktl̩; ˈprɔdʒiktail] *n.* 拋射物;拋射體;發射體;彈丸。—*adj.* ①投射的;推進的;發射的。*projectile* force. 投射力。②能發射的;適於發射的。a *projectile* missile. 發射飛彈。
pro·ject·ing [prəˈdʒɛktɪŋ; prəˈdʒektiŋ] *adj.* 突出的;凸出的。*projecting* eye. 暴眼。*projecting* teeth. 暴牙。
***pro·jec·tion** [prəˈdʒɛkʃən; prəˈdʒekʃən] *n.* ①投出;發射。②突出;突出部分。a *projection* on a bone. 一骨上之突出物。③投影。④投影法;投影圖。⑤計畫。the *pro-*

jection of a new railroad. 建新鐵路之計畫。⑥推算。⑦表情達意;(心象)描述。
projection booth 電影院中放置放映機的隔音小間。
pro·jec·tion·ist 〔prəˈdʒɛkʃənɪst; prəˈdʒekʃənist〕 *n.* ①電影放映機操作者。②電視攝影員。③作投影畫者。
projection machine 放映機。
projection room (電影)放映室。
pro·jec·tive 〔prəˈdʒɛktɪv; prəˈdʒektiv〕 *adj.* ①投影的;投射的。②〖心理〗心象描述的;投射的。—**ly,** *adv.*
pro·jec·tor 〔prəˈdʒɛktɚ; prəˈdʒektə〕 *n.* ①(電影之)放映機。a slide *projector.* 幻燈片放映機。②計畫者;設計者。
pro·lac·tin 〔proˈlæktɪn; prouˈlæktin〕 *n.* 〖生理〗乳汁刺激素;催乳激素(腦下垂體前葉荷爾蒙,刺激哺乳動物之乳汁分泌)。
pro·lan 〔ˈprolæn; ˈproulæn〕 *n.* 〖生化〗普育蘭;促卵泡激素(在妊娠期中之尿中之一種性激素,藉以診斷早期的懷孕)。***prolan A*** 普育蘭甲;促卵泡成熟激素。***prolan B*** 普育蘭乙;促黃體發生激素。
pro·lapse 〔prəˈlæps; prəˈlæps〕 *n., v.,* **-lapsed, -laps·ing.** —*n.* 〖醫〗(身體內部器官之)脫出;脫垂。—*v.i.* 脫垂;脫出。
pro·lap·sus 〔prəˈlæpsəs; prəˈlæpsəs〕 *n.* 〖醫〗(直腸、子宮之)脫出;脫垂。
pro·late 〔ˈprolet; ˈprouleit〕 *adj.* 〖數學〗偏長的(球體)。
prolate spheroid 〖幾何〗偏長之球體。
pro·la·tive 〔proˈletɪv; prouˈleitiv〕 *adj.* 〖文法〗擴張或補足敍述的(如 must go 中之 go 稱爲 prolative infinitive)。
pro·le·gom·e·na 〔ˌprolɪˈgɑmɪnə; ˌprouləˈgɔminə〕 *n. pl.* 序言;序文;緒論。
pro·lep·sis 〔prəˈlɛpsɪs; prouˈlepsis〕 *n., pl.* **-ses** 〔-siz; -siːz〕. ①預期;預料。②〖修辭〗預辯法。③〖文法〗預期的賓詞法(如 He struck her dead 中之 dead)。④〖哲學〗感覺(知覺)概念。⑤早填日時(即比實際發生之日期較早)。
pro·lep·tic 〔prəˈlɛptɪk; prouˈleptik〕 *adj.* ①預期的;預料的。②前的。③〖修辭〗預辯法的。④〖醫〗早發的;急發的。
pro·le·tar·i·an 〔ˌproləˈtɛrɪən; ˌprouleˈtɛəriən〕 *adj.* 無產階級的。 ***proletarian*** dictatorship. 無產階級獨裁(專政)。 —*n.* 無產階級者。
pro·le·tar·i·at 〔ˌproləˈtɛrɪət; ˌprouleˈtɛəriət〕 *n.* ①(古羅馬之)最下層社會。②無產階級;勞動階級。(亦作 **proletariate**)
pro·lif·er·ate 〔proˈlɪfəˌret; prouˈlifəreit〕 *v.,* **-at·ed, -at·ing.** —*v.i.* ①(細胞等)增生。②增加。—*v.t.* 大量產生。
pro·lif·er·a·tion 〔proˌlɪfəˈreʃən; prouˌlifəˈreiʃən〕 *n.* ①〖生理〗細胞之增生;繁殖。②〖植物〗分芽繁殖。③增加;增多。
pro·lif·ic 〔prəˈlɪfɪk; prəˈlifik〕 *adj.* ①產子的;結實的;有生產力的;肥沃的。②多產的;大量生產的。③豐富的;衆多的。—**al·ly,** *adv.*
pro·lif·i·ca·cy 〔prəˈlɪfɪkəsɪ; prouˈlifikəsi〕 *n.* 多產;豐富;豐饒。
pro·lix 〔proˈlɪks; ˈprouliks〕 *adj.* 冗長的;嚕囌的。—**ly,** *adv.*
pro·lix·i·ty 〔proˈlɪksətɪ; prouˈliksiti〕 *n.* 冗長;嚕囌。
pro·loc·u·tor 〔proˈlɑkjətɚ; prouˈlɔkjutə〕 *n.* ①會議之主席。②代辯者;發言人。
***pro·log** 〔ˈprolɔg, -lɑg; ˈproulɔg〕 *n., v.t.* =**prologue.**
***pro·logue** 〔ˈprolɔg, -lɑg; ˈproulɔg〕 *n., v.,* **-logued, -logu·ing.** —*n.* ①序言;序詞;開場白。②道開場白之演員。③序幕。④作爲序幕之事件〖to〗. —*v.t.* 爲…之序言或序幕。
***pro·long** 〔prəˈlɔŋ; prəˈlɔŋ〕 *v.t.* 延長。to *prolong* one's life. 延長壽命。—**er,** *n.*
pro·lon·gate 〔prəˈlɔŋget; prəˈlɔŋgeit〕 *v.t.,* **-gat·ed, -gat·ing.** 延長;使長。
pro·lon·ga·tion 〔ˌprolɔŋˈgeʃən; ˌproulɔŋˈgeiʃən〕 *n.* ①伸展;延展;延期。②延長或附加之部分。
pro·lu·sion 〔proˈluʒən; prouˈluːʒən〕 *n.* 序文;緒言;序樂;序幕。
prom 〔prɑm; prɔm〕 *n.* 〖俗〗(大學或中學學生舉行之)舞會。 ***prom trotter*** 常常參加舞會的學生。
prom. ①promontory. ②prominent. ③promoted.
***prom·e·nade** 〔ˌprɑməˈned; ˌprɔmiˈnɑːd〕 *n., v.,* **-nad·ed, -nad·ing.** —*n.* ①(散心或炫耀服飾等之)散步;遊行。The Easter *promenade* is well known as a fashion show. 復活節遊行是衆所周知的一種時裝展覽。②公衆散步之場所。③舞會。④舞會開始時全體進入舞廳之行進。—*v.i.* 散步;漫步。He *promenaded* back and forth on the ship's deck. 他在甲板上來回地踱着。—*v.t.* ①散步或遊行通過(某處);徘徊於(某處)。②率領(人羣)遊行。—**prom·e·nad·er,** *n.*
promenade concert 逍遙音樂會(一種聽衆可任意散步或跳舞之音樂會)。
promenade deck 客輪上供乘客散步之上層甲板。
Pro·me·the·an 〔prəˈmiθɪən, -θjən; prəˈmiːθjən〕 *adj.* ①Prometheus 的;賦予生命的。②創造的。
Pro·me·theus 〔prəˈmiθjəs, -jus; prəˈmiːθjuːs〕 *n.* 〖希臘神話〗普洛米休士(一巨人,爲人類自天上竊來火種,因而受懲被縛於 Caucasus 山之岩石上,其肝臟受鷲啄食)。
pro·me·thi·um 〔prəˈmiθɪəm; prəˈmiːθiəm〕 *n.* 〖化〗稀土金屬鉯(illinium)之新名(其符號爲 pm)。
prom·i·nence 〔ˈprɑmənəns; ˈprɔminəns〕 *n.* ①著名;傑出;卓越。②突出物;突起。③太陽的紅焰。(亦作 **prominency**)
***prom·i·nent** 〔ˈprɑmənənt; ˈprɔminənt〕 *adj.* ①著名的;主要的。*prominent* persons. 著名的人物。②顯著的。A single tree in a field is *prominent.* 在田地裏一棵孤樹是顯著的。③突出的;突起的。Some insects have *prominent* eyes. 有些昆蟲有突出的眼睛。
prom·i·nent·ly 〔ˈprɑmənəntlɪ; ˈprɔminəntli〕 *adv.* 顯著地。
prom·is·cu·i·ty 〔ˌprɑmɪsˈkjuətɪ; ˌprɔmisˈkjuːiti〕 *n., pl.* **-ties.** ①雜亂無章;雜亂。②(男女之)雜交。③混雜。
pro·mis·cu·ous 〔prəˈmɪskjuəs; prəˈmiskjuəs〕 *adj.* ①雜亂的;一團糟的。②不加選擇的;男女混雜的;(性交)隨便的;一杯水主義的。*promiscuous* bathing. 男女混浴。*promiscuous* marriage. 亂婚。③〖俗〗偶然的;漫無目的的。—**ness,** *n.*
pro·mis·cu·ous·ly 〔prəˈmɪskjuəslɪ; prəˈmiskjuəsli〕 *adv.* 雜亂地;漫無目的地。
‡**prom·ise** 〔ˈprɑmɪs; ˈprɔmis〕 *n., v.,* **-ised, -is·ing.** —*n.* ①諾言;約定。to make a *promise.* 定約允諾。He never keeps his *promises.* 他從來不守諾言。 to break a *promise.* 失約;食言;失信。②預示;預兆。Clouds give *promise* of rain. 陰雲預示

有雨。③有成功希望之預示。a writer of *promise*. 有希望的作家。—*v.t.* ①允諾；約定。He *promised* (me) to be here at six o'clock. 他和我約好六點鐘到此。②有…希望；有望；預示。—*v.i.* ①約定；應允。②有希望；有前途；樂觀。His plan *promises* well (*or* fair). 他的計畫很可樂觀。

Promised Land ①〖聖經〗上帝答應給亞伯拉罕及其後裔之土地，即迦南(Canaan)。②天堂。③(p- l-)想像的幸福之地。

prom·is·ee 〔ˌprɑmɪsˈi; ˌprɔmiˈsiː〕 *n.* 〖法律〗受約者。

prom·is·er 〔ˈprɑmɪsɚ; ˈprɔmisə〕 *n.* 「約束者；允諾者。」

***prom·is·ing** 〔ˈprɑmɪsɪŋ; ˈprɔmisiŋ〕 *adj.* 有希望的；有前途的。a *promising* young man. 有希望的青年。—**ly,** *adv.*

prom·i·sor 〔ˈprɑmɪsˌɔr; ˈprɔmisɔː〕 *n.* 〖法律〗作許諾者；立約者。

prom·is·so·ry 〔ˈprɑməˌsorɪ; ˈprɔmisəri〕 *adj.* ①允諾的。②訂約的；約定的。***promissory note*** 期票；本票。

pro·mo 〔ˈpromo; ˈproumou〕 *n.* 〖俗〗電視節目預告。

prom·on·to·ry 〔ˈprɑmənˌtorɪ; ˈprɔməntəri〕 *n., pl.* **-ries.** ①海角；岬。②〖解剖〗隆起；岬。—**prom·on·to·ried,** *adj.*

***pro·mote** 〔prəˈmot; prəˈmout〕 *v.t.,* **-mot·ed, -mot·ing.** ①升遷；擢升。He was *promoted* major. 他被升做少校。②提倡；促進；增進；支援；鼓勵。to *promote* a scheme. 提倡一計畫。③〖美〗靠廣告推銷(貨物)。④創辦。Several bankers *promoted* the new company. 幾個銀行家創辦那個新公司。⑤〖俚〗靠技巧或不正當手段獲得。

pro·mot·er 〔prəˈmotɚ; prəˈmoutə〕 *n.* ①擢升者。②支持者；贊助者；提倡者。③鼓舞者；後援者。④(新會社的)發起人；創辦人。⑤(惡意的)帶頭者；發起者。⑥(宗教裁判的)起訴人。

***pro·mo·tion** 〔prəˈmoʃən; prəˈmouʃən〕 *n.* ①晉陞；升遷。The clerk was given a *promotion*. 那書記獲得升級。②促進；提倡；獎勵。③協助組織；創設。

pro·mo·tion·al 〔prəˈmoʃənl̩; prəˈmouʃənl̩〕 *adj.* ①升等的；晉升的。②推廣(銷路)的。③提倡的；促進的；宣傳的。

pro·mo·tive 〔prəˈmotɪv; prəˈmoutiv〕 *adj.* 增進的；獎勵的；提倡的。

prompt** 〔prɑmpt; prɔmpt〕 *adj.* ①迅速的；敏捷的。to be *prompt* to obey. 立刻服從。②即時的；立刻的。a *prompt* reply. 迅速的答覆。—*v.t.* ①使做；激勵；鼓動。Conscience *prompts* us to do right. 良心使我們爲善。②喚起；激起。③提示(演員等)；提醒。—*n.* ①(對演員等之)提示。②提示(之動作)。③〖商〗欠帳償付期限。take a prompt*** (演員)按提示而行動或念臺詞。—*v.i.* 對演員等提示。—**ly,** *adv.* —**ness,** *n.*

prompt·book 〔ˈprɑmptˌbuk; ˈprɔmptbuk〕 *n.* 提示者所用的劇本。

prompt box 後臺提示者之隱席。

prompt day 〖商〗延期交易之收付日。

prompt delivery 限時專送。

prompt·er 〔ˈprɑmptɚ; ˈprɔmptə〕 *n.* ①激勵者；鼓舞者；喚起者。②提示者。

promp·ti·tude 〔ˈprɑmptəˌtjud; ˈprɔmptitjuːd〕 *n.* 機敏；敏捷。

prompt note 〖商〗提示應付款額及日期之通知。

prompt side 〖主英〗面對觀衆時舞臺「之左側(就觀衆論則爲右側)。」

pro·mul·gate 〔prəˈmʌlget; ˈprɔməlgeit〕 *v.t.,* **-gat·ed, -gat·ing.** ①宣布；公布；頒布。②傳播；散播。

pro·mul·ga·tion 〔ˌpromʌlˈgeʃən; ˌprɔməlˈgeiʃən〕 *n.* ①宣布；公布。②傳播。

pro·mul·ga·tor 〔prəˈmʌlgetɚ; ˈprɔməlgeitə〕 *n.* 發布者；公布者；布告者；傳播者。

pron. ①pronoun. ②pronunciation. ③pronounced.

pro·na·tion 〔proˈneʃən; prouˈneiʃən〕 *n.* 〖生理〗反掌；旋前；內轉。

prone 〔pron; proun〕 *adj.* ①有…之傾向的；易於…的。to be *prone* to anger. 易於發怒的。②俯臥的；面向下的。to lie *prone*. 俯臥。to fall *prone*. 面向下跌下去。③手心向下平放的。④傾斜的；斜倚的。a *prone* bombing. 俯衝轟炸。—**ly,** *adv.*

prone·ness 〔ˈpronnɪs; ˈprounnis〕 *n.* 傾向；趣向。

prong 〔prɔŋ; prɔŋ〕 *n.* ①(割乾草等用之)叉子；叉尖。②(吃西餐時用的)叉子。③(鹿角等之)尖部。—*v.t.* ①以叉尖刺。②裝叉尖於。

pronged 〔prɔŋd; prɔŋd〕 *adj.* 有尖頭「(尤指叉形之尖頭)的。」

prong·horn 〔ˈprɔŋˌhɔrn; ˈprɔŋhɔːn〕 *n.* (墨西哥與美國西部產的)麋鹿。

pro·nom·i·nal 〔prəˈnɑmənl̩, pro-; prəˈnɔminl̩〕 *adj.* ①代名詞的。*pronominal* adjective. 〖文法〗代名形容詞(指一個由代名詞變成之形容詞，或有時用作代名詞有時用作形容詞者。前者如：my, his, her, our 等；後者如：all, each, either, both, this 等)。②有代名詞性質的。—**ly,** *adv.*

***pro·noun** 〔ˈpronaun; ˈprounaun〕 *n.* 〖文法〗代名詞(如：he, it 等)。**1. personal pronoun** 人稱代名詞。**2. possessive pronoun** 所有代名詞。**3. reflexive pronoun** 反身代名詞。**4. demonstrative pronoun** 指示代名詞。**5. interrogative pronoun** 疑問代名詞。**6. relative pronoun** 關係代名詞。**7. indefinite pronoun** 不固定代名詞。

***pro·nounce** 〔prəˈnauns; prəˈnauns〕 *v.,* **-nounced, -nounc·ing.** —*v.t.* ①發出…之音。*Pronounce* your words clearly. 把你的字音讀清楚。②宣稱；斷言。③宣判；宣告。to *pronounce* sentence on the criminal. 對罪犯宣告判決。—*v.i.* ①發音；讀音。a difficult word to *pronounce*. 難讀音之字。②聲言。to *pronounce* against (in favor of, for) a proposal. 聲言反對(贊成)一意見。③表示意見；作決定；斷定；判決。—**pro·nounc·er,** *n.*

pro·nounce·a·ble 〔prəˈnaunsəbl̩; prəˈnaunsəbl〕 *adj.* 可發音的。—**ness,** *n.*

***pro·nounced** 〔prəˈnaunst; prəˈnaunst〕 *adj.* 顯著的；明白的；確切的。a *pronounced* tendency. 顯著的傾向。—**ly,** *adv.*

pro·nounce·ment 〔prəˈnaunsmənt; prəˈnaunsmənt〕 *n.* ①發布；發表；公告；文告；聲明。②意見；決定。

pro·nounc·ing 〔prəˈnaunsɪŋ; prəˈnaunsiŋ〕 *adj.* 發音的。a *pronouncing* dictionary. 一本發音的字典。

pron·to 〔ˈprɑnto; ˈprɔntou〕 *adv.* 〖俚〗立即地；即刻地；疾速地。

pro·nun·ci·a·men·to 〔prəˌnʌnsɪəˈmɛnto; prəˌnʌnsiəˈmentou〕 *n., pl.* **-tos.** 正式宣言(尤指革命宣言)；檄文。

***pro·nun·ci·a·tion** 〔prəˌnʌnsɪˈeʃən; prəˌnʌnsiˈeiʃən〕 *n.* 發音；發音方法。She speaks English with a good *pronunciation*. 她說的英語發音很正確。—al, *adj.*

*__proof__ 〔pruf; pruːf〕 *n.* ①證明;證據。It is not capable of *proof*. 那是不能證明的。②證明文件;物證;證言。We shall require *proof(s)* of that statement. 我們將要那項聲明之證據。③考驗。④校樣。to read the *proof*. 看校樣。⑤(酒的) 標準酒精度。⑥耐力。⑦測定原料品質、耐久性等之試驗。—*adj.* ①堅固的; 有耐力的; 不能透入的。to be *proof* against bullets. 不爲子彈所穿入。②够標準的。*proof* gold. 純金。③經證明有效的。—*v.t.* ①校對;校正。books which I edited and *proofed*. 我所編和校對的書。②使對…有抵抗作用;使能防…。

-proof 〖字尾〗表下列諸義:①保護; 防禦。如: weatherproof. ②不能透過。如: waterproof. ③同…一樣堅牢。如: armorproof. ④對…有抗力; 不受…之影響。如: womanproof.

proof·less 〔ˈpruflɪs; ˈpruːflis〕 *adj.* 缺乏證據的;未予證明的。

proof·read 〔ˈpruf,rid; ˈpruːf,riːd〕 *v.t.* & *v.i.*, **-read, -read·ing.** 校正;校對。

proof·read·er 〔ˈpruf,ridɚ; ˈpruːf,riːdə〕 *n.* 校正校樣者;校對員。

proof·read·ing 〔ˈpruf,ridɪŋ; ˈpruːf,riːdiŋ〕 *n.* 校對。

proof·room 〔ˈpruf,rum; ˈpruːf,ruːm〕 *n.* 校對室。

proof sheet 校樣。

proof spirit 含標準量酒精的酒或水與酒精的混合(其酒精含量在美國爲50%, 在英國爲 49.3%)。

proof stress 〖建築〗保證應力;安全限應力。

*__prop__[1] 〔prɑp; prɔp〕 *v.*, **propped, propping,** *n.* —*v.t.* ①支撐。to *prop* the clothesline with a stick. 以一根棒將晒衣繩撐起。②支持; 維持。to *prop* a proof. 支持一個例證。—*n.*①支柱;撐材。a clothes-*prop*. 晒衣柱。②支持者;支持物。the main *prop* of a state. 國之棟樑。—**less,** *adj.*

prop[2] *n.* 〖戲劇、電影俚〗舞台道具。

prop[3] *n.* 〖航空俚〗=**propeller.**

prop. ①proper. ②properly. ③proposition. ④proposed. ⑤propeller. ⑥property. ⑦proprietary. ⑧proprietor.

pro·pae·deu·tic 〔,propɪˈdjutɪk; ,proupiˈdjuːtik〕 *adj.* 初步的; 初階的; 準備的。—*n.* 基本科目;初步研究。

prop·a·ga·ble 〔ˈprɑpəgəbl; ˈprɔpəgəbl〕 *adj.* 可繁殖的;可傳導的;可傳播的。

*__prop·a·gan·da__ 〔,prɑpəˈgændə; ,prɔpəˈgændə〕 *n.* ①宣傳;傳道。to carry out *propaganda* on a large scale. 大事宣傳。②宣傳之言論或信仰; 宣傳資料。③宣傳機構; 宣傳組織。to set up a *propaganda* for.... 設立…之宣傳機構。④〖宗教〗天主教中負責國外傳教的委員會;傳道總會。 —**prop·a·gan·dism,** *n.*

prop·a·gan·dist 〔,prɑpəˈgændɪst; ,prɔpəˈgændist〕 *n.* 宣傳者。—*adj.* 宣傳(性)的。

prop·a·gan·dist·ic 〔,prɑpəgænˈdɪstɪk; ,prɔpəgænˈdistik〕 *adj.* 宣傳的;宣傳家的。—**al·ly,** *adv.*

prop·a·gan·dize 〔,prɑpəˈgændaɪz; ,prɔpəˈgændaiz〕 *v.*, **-dized, -diz·ing.** —*v.t.* ①宣傳。②對…作宣傳。 —*v.i.* 作宣傳。

*__prop·a·gate__ 〔ˈprɑpə,get; ˈprɔpəgeit〕 *v.*, **-gat·ed, -gat·ing.** —*v.t.* ①繁殖;增殖。Trees *propagate* themselves by seeds. 樹木藉種子繁殖。②傳導; 傳送。Sound is *propagated* by vibrations. 聲音係藉震動來傳送。③傳播。 —*v.i.* ①繁殖; 增殖;傳播。②擴展。

prop·a·ga·tion 〔,prɑpəˈgeʃən; ,prɔpəˈgeiʃən〕 *n.* ①繁殖; 增殖。②傳播。③傳導;散發;伸延。 —**al,** *adj.*

prop·a·ga·tive 〔ˈprɑpə,getɪv; ˈprɔpəgeitiv〕 *adj.* 繁殖的;傳播的;傳導的。

prop·a·ga·tor 〔ˈprɑpə,getɚ; ˈprɔpəgeitə〕 *n.* ①繁殖者。②傳播者;散播者;宣傳者。

pro·pane 〔ˈpropen; ˈproupein〕 *n.* 〖化〗丙烷 (C_3H_8)。

pro·par·ox·y·tone 〔,propærˈɑksɪ,ton; ,proupəˈrɔksitoun〕 *adj.*, *n.* 〖希臘文法〗在倒數第三音節有重音的(字)。

pro pa·tri·a 〔proˈpetrɪə; prouˈpeitriə〕 〖拉〗爲國家;爲祖國(=for〔one's〕country).

pro·pel 〔prəˈpɛl; prəˈpel〕 *v.t.*, **-pelled, -pel·ling.** ①推動;推進。②鼓勵; 驅策。 —**ment,** *n.* —**la·ble,** *adj.*

pro·pel·lant 〔prəˈpɛlənt; prəˈpelənt〕 *n.* 推動者;推進者;(尤指)發射火藥。

pro·pel·lent 〔prəˈpɛlənt; prəˈpelənt〕 *adj.* 推進的。—*n.* =**propellant.**

*__pro·pel·ler__ 〔prəˈpɛlɚ; prəˈpelə〕 *n.* ①推動者。②推進器;螺旋槳。*propeller* blade. 螺旋槳葉。

pro·pen·si·ty 〔prəˈpɛnsətɪ; prəˈpensiti〕 *n.*, *pl.* **-ties.** 傾向;嗜好;習性。

‡__prop·er__ 〔ˈprɑpɚ; ˈprɔpə〕 *adj.* ①正確的;正當的。Night is the *proper* time to sleep. 夜晚是睡眠的適當時間。②可敬的;高尚的。*proper* conduct. 高尚的行爲。③獨特的。④就一字句之嚴格意義的 (通常用於名詞後)。Alaska was not part of the United States *proper*. 阿拉斯加原非美國本土的一部分。⑤〖俗〗完全的; 徹底的。a *proper* licking. 一陣痛毆。⑥自己的。with my own *proper* hands. 用我自己的手。⑦只與…有關的。⑧〖文法〗專有的 (名詞、形容詞)。John Adams is a *proper* name. 約翰亞當斯是一專有名字。⑨漂亮的。—*adv.*〖主方〗完全地;徹底地。—**ness,** *n.*

proper fraction 〖數學〗眞分數。

*__prop·er·ly__ 〔ˈprɑpəlɪ; ˈprɔpəli〕 *adv.*①正當地;適當地。Behave *properly*. 行爲要正當。②嚴格地;精確地。*Properly* speaking, a whale is not a fish. 正確地說, 鯨不是魚。③有理由地。④〖俗〗徹底地;完全地。

proper motion 〖天文〗天體之固有運動。

proper noun 專有名詞。

prop·er·tied 〔ˈprɑpɚtɪd; ˈprɔpətid〕 *adj.* 有財產的。 the *propertied* classes. 有產階級。

‡__prop·er·ty__ 〔ˈprɑpətɪ; ˈprɔpəti〕 *n.*, *pl.*-**ties.** ①財產; 所有物。 This stick is my *property*. 這根手杖是我的。②所有;所有權。③性質;屬性;特性。the chemical *properties* of iron. 鐵的化學性質。④(*pl.*) 舞臺道具。—**less,** *adj.*

property man 〖戲劇〗道具管理人。

property master 〖戲劇〗道具主要管理員。

*__proph·e·cy__ 〔ˈprɑfəsɪ; ˈprɔfisi〕 *n.*, *pl.* **-cies.** ①預言。②預言之事物。

proph·e·si·er 〔ˈprɑfə,saɪɚ; ˈprɔfisaiə〕 *n.* 預言者。

*__proph·e·sy__ 〔ˈprɑfə,saɪ; ˈprɔfisai〕 *v.t.* & *v.i.*, **-sied, -sy·ing.** ①預言; 預告。to *prophesy* war. 預言戰爭發生。②(代神)發言。

proph·et** [ˈprɑfɪt; ˈprɔfit] *n.* ①預言者。②先知。③有力的發言人。the Prophet*** **a.** 穆罕默德。**b.** 約瑟夫·史密斯 (Joseph Smith), 摩門 (Mormon) 教的創始者。***the Prophets*** 舊約中先知所寫的預言書。

proph·et·ess [ˈprɑfɪtɪs; ˈprɔfitis] *n.* 女預言家;女先知。

pro·phet·ic [prəˈfɛtɪk; prəˈfetik] *adj.* ①預言的;預示的;預言性的。His words were *prophetic* of his future greatness. 他之所言預示他來日的偉大。②預言者的。③惡兆的。(亦作 **prophetical**) **—al·ly,** *adv.*

pro·phy·lac·tic [ˌprofəˈlæktɪk; ˌprɔfiˈlæktik] *adj.* 預防疾病的。**—***n.* 預防藥;預防法。**—al·ly,** *adv.*

pro·phy·lax·is [ˌprofəˈlæksɪs; ˌprɔfiˈlæksis] *n., pl.* **-lax·es** [-ˈlæksiz; -ˈlæksiz]. 疾病之預防;預防法。

pro·pin·qui·ty [proˈpɪnkwətɪ; prəˈpiŋkwiti] *n.* ①近處。②(時間之)迫切;接近。③(血統之)近親。④(性質之)相近;類似。

pro·pi·ti·ate [prəˈpɪʃɪˌet; prəˈpiʃieit] *v.t.,* **-at·ed, -at·ing.** 懇解;與…和解;邀寵於。**—pro·pi·ti·a·tor,** *n.*

pro·pi·ti·a·tion [prəˌpɪʃɪˈeʃən; prəˌpiʃiˈeiʃən] *n.* ①懇解、和解或邀寵(之事物)。②抵償;贖罪。

pro·pi·ti·a·to·ry [prəˈpɪʃɪəˌtorɪ; prəˈpiʃiətəri] *adj., n., pl.* **-to·ries.** **—***adj.* (作)懇解、和解或邀寵的。**—***n.* **=mercy seat.**

pro·pi·tious [prəˈpɪʃəs; prəˈpiʃəs] *adj.* ①順遂的;順利的。②吉祥的;吉利的。③慈悲的;慈祥的(神等)。**—ly,** *adv.* **—ness,** *n.*

prop·jet [ˈprɑpˌdʒɛt; ˈprɔpdʒet] *n.* **=turboprop.**

pro·po·nent [prəˈponənt; prəˈpounənt] *n.* ①提議者;建議者。②擁護者;支持者。③〖法律〗提出某物(尤指要認證之遺囑)者。

‡pro·por·tion [prəˈporʃən, -ˈpɔr-; prəˈpɔːʃən] *n.* ①比率;比例。The house is tall in *proportion* to its width. 這房子就其寬度的比例而言是很高的。②均衡;相稱。③(*pl.*)大小;容積。④部分。A large (small) *proportion* of the people were not in favor of him. 大(少)部分的人不贊成他。⑤〖數學〗比例。simple *proportion*. 單比例。⑥一個事件的眞正意義。***in proportion*** **a.** 相稱的;均衡的。**b.** 至…同等程度。***out of proportion*** 不相稱;不均衡;不成適當比例。**—***v.t.* 使均衡;使相稱。to *proportion* one's expense to one's income. 量入爲出。**—less,** *adj.*

pro·por·tion·a·ble [prəˈporʃənəbḷ; prəˈpɔːʃənəbl] *adj.* ①相稱的;成相當比例的。②可分配的。**—pro·por·tion·a·bly,** *adv.*

pro·por·tion·al [prəˈporʃənḷ; prəˈpɔːʃənḷ] *adj.* ①成比例的;相稱的。②以比例爲標準的。**—***n.* 〖數學〗比例數。

pro·por·tion·al·ly [prəˈporʃənḷɪ; prəˈpɔːʃṇəli] *adv.* 按比例。

proportional representation 比例代表制(一種選舉制度)。

pro·por·tion·ate [*adj.* prəˈporʃənɪt; prəˈpɔːʃənit *v.* prəˈporʃənˌet; prəˈpɔːʃəneit] *adj.* 成比例的。**—***v.t.* 使成比例;使相稱。**—ness,** *n.*

pro·por·tion·ate·ly [prəˈporʃənɪtlɪ; prəˈpɔːʃənitli] *adv.* 成比例地;相稱地。

pro·por·tioned [prəˈporʃənd; prəˈpɔːʃənd] *adj.* 成比例的;相稱的。well-*proportioned*. 相稱的。

pro·por·tion·ment [prəˈporʃənmənt; prəˈpɔːʃənmənt] *n.* 勻稱之安排;相稱;調和。

***pro·pos·al** [prəˈpozḷ; prəˈpouzəl] *n.* ①建議;提議。to make *proposals* for peace. 做和平之建議。②求婚。to offer (*or* make) a *proposal*. 求婚。

‡pro·pose [prəˈpoz; prəˈpouz] *v.t.* & *v.i.,* **-posed, -pos·ing.** ①提議;建議;推薦。I *propose* Mr. Smith for chairman. 我推薦史密斯先生任主席。Man *proposes,* God disposes. (諺)謀事在人,成事在天。②欲;計劃。We *propose* leaving (*or* to leave) at noon. 我們想在正午離去。③求婚。He *proposed* to her. 他向她求婚。④定爲目標(與反身代名詞連用)。***propose a toast*** (or ***a person's health***) 舉杯祝某人健康。

pro·pos·er [prəˈpozə; prəˈpouzə] *n.* 提議者;提出者。

prop·o·si·tion** [ˌprɑpəˈzɪʃən; ˌprɔpəˈziʃən] *n.* ①提議。②主張;意見。This is a *proposition* that needs no discussion. 這是個不需要討論的意見。③待決的問題;待證明的定理。④〖美〗企業;事業。⑤〖美〗必須處理的事情;必須相與的人。That's a tough *proposition*. 那是件難辦的事。⑥〖邏輯〗命題。**—v.t.* ①向…做提議。②向…調情。

prop·o·si·tion·al [ˌprɑpəˈzɪʃənḷ; ˌprɔpəˈziʃənḷ] *adj.* ①提議的;提案的。②命題的。**—ly,** *adv.*

pro·pound [prəˈpaund; prəˈpaund] *v.t.* 提出(學說、問題、質問、謎語等)。

propr. proprietor.

pro·pr(a)e·tor [proˈpritə; prouˈpriːtə] *n.* 〖羅馬史〗在羅馬任執政官後,派駐外省而仍有執政官權力者。

pro·pri·e·tar·y [prəˈpraɪəˌtɛrɪ; prəˈpraiətəri] *adj., n., pl.* **-tar·ies.** **—***adj.* ①有財產的;所有權的。*proprietary* rights. 所有權。②獨占的;專賣的;專利的。*proprietary* articles. 專利品。③私有的。**—***n.* ①所有者;所有人之集合稱。②所有;所有權。③所有物。④專賣藥品。

proprietary colony 〖美史〗英皇特許之私人殖民地。

***pro·pri·e·tor** [prəˈpraɪətə; prəˈpraiətə] *n.* ①所有者。②有專利權者。

pro·pri·e·to·ri·al [prəˌpraɪəˈtorɪəl; prəˌpraiəˈtɔːriəl] *adj.* ①所有的;所有權的。②因所有權而產生的。

pro·pri·e·tor·ship [prəˈpraɪətəˌʃɪp; prəˈpraiətəʃip] *n.* 所有權。

pro·pri·e·tress [prəˈpraɪətrɪs; prəˈpraiətris] *n.* 女所有者。

***pro·pri·e·ty** [prəˈpraɪətɪ; prəˈpraiəti] *n., pl.* **-ties.** ①適當;適宜。②正當之行爲;禮節。The *proprieties* must be observed. 禮節必須遵守。③(*pl.*)行爲規範。

pro·pri·o·cep·tive [ˌproprɪəˈsɛptɪv; ˌproupriəˈseptiv] *adj.* 〖生理〗本體感受的。

pro·pri·o·cep·tor [ˌproprɪəˈsɛptə; ˌproupriəˈseptə] *n.* 〖解剖〗本體感受器。

prop root (禾本科植物等的)不定根。

props [prɑps; prɔps] *n.* 〖英俚〗道具。

prop·to·sis [prɑpˈtosɪs; prɔpˈtousis] *n.* 〖醫〗前垂(尤指眼球之突出)。

pro·pul·sion [prəˈpʌlʃən; prəˈpʌlʃən] *n.* ①(船、飛機等的)推進。②推進力。

pro·pul·sive [prəˈpʌlsɪv; prəˈpʌlsiv] *adj.* 推進的;(有)推進力的。(亦作 **propulso-**

ry) —ness, *n.*

prop·y·lae·um 〔ˌprɑpəˈliəm; ˌprɔpiˈliːəm〕 *n., pl.* **-laea** 〔-ˈliə; -ˈliːə〕.【希臘、羅馬】神殿或重要建築物之入口。

pro ra·ta 〔proˈretə; prouˈrɑːtə〕【拉】按比例;成比例。

pro·rate 〔proˈret; prouˈreit〕 *v.t. & v.i.*, **-rat·ed, -rat·ing.** 按比例分配。—**pro·ra·tion,** *n.*

pro re na·ta 〔proriˈnetə; prouriːˈneitə〕【拉】臨機應變;爲意外事件 (= for an unexpected contingency).

pro·ro·ga·tion 〔ˌprorəˈgeʃən; ˌprourəˈgeiʃən〕 *n.* (英國議會之) 休會;閉會。

pro·rogue 〔proˈrog; prəˈroug〕 *v.*, **-rogued, -rogu·ing.** —*v.t.* 休會; 閉會 (英國議會)。—*v.i.* 休會;閉會。

pros. ①prosody. ②prosecuting. ③prosecutor.

pro·sa·ic 〔proˈze·ɪk; prouˈzeiik〕 *adj.* ①散文的。②像散文一般的; 平淡無奇的。—**al·ly,** *adv.* —**ness,** *n.*

pro·sa·ism 〔ˈproze·ɪzəm; ˈprouzeiizm〕 *n.* ①散文體。②平凡;無趣。③乏味的話。④散文體的辭句。

pro·sa·ist 〔ˈproze·ɪst; ˈprouzeiist〕 *n.* ①散文家。②無詩意的人;無趣、平凡的人。

pro·sa·teur 〔ˌprozəˈtɝ; ˌprouzəˈtəː〕 *n.* 散文作家。

pro·sce·ni·um 〔proˈsiniəm; prouˈsiːnjəm〕 *n., pl.* **-ni·a** 〔-nɪə; -njə〕. ①舞臺前部(幕與樂隊席之間者)。②舞臺之幕及其拱架。③(古代希臘、羅馬之) 舞臺。④前部。 *proscenium box* 靠近舞臺之包廂。

pro·sciut·to 〔proˈʃuto; prouˈʃuːtou〕 *n.* 烟薰五香火腿。

pro·scribe 〔proˈskraɪb; prousˈkraib〕 *v.t.*, **-scribed, -scrib·ing.** ①摒棄於法律保護之外。②禁止。③排斥。④放逐; 充軍。—**pro·scrib·er,** *n.*

pro·scrip·tion 〔proˈskrɪpʃən; prousˈkripʃən〕 *n.* ①人權剝奪;放逐;禁止;排斥。②【古羅馬】判刑公告。

pro·scrip·tive 〔proˈskrɪptɪv; prousˈkriptiv〕 *adj.* 禁止的。—**ly,** *adv.*

***prose** 〔proz; prouz〕 *n., adj., v.*, **prosed, pros·ing.** —*n.* ①散文。The story is in *prose.* 這故事是用散文寫的。②平凡無奇的性質; 普通的事。③無趣而平凡的談話。—*adj.* ①用散文寫的。②缺乏想像力的; 平凡的。—*v.t. & v.i.* 以散文說或寫;平凡無趣地寫作或談話。

pro·sec·tor 〔proˈsɛktɚ; prouˈsektə〕 *n.* 將屍體解剖示範者。

***pros·e·cute** 〔ˈprɑsɪˌkjut; ˈprɔsikjuːt〕 *v.*, **-cut·ed, -cut·ing.** —*v.t.* ①告發; 檢擧; 對…提起公訴。Trespassers will be *prosecuted.* 請勿擅入;閒人免進。②實行;進行。to *prosecute* a trade. 進行貿易。—*v.i.* 告發; 檢擧。

prosecuting attorney 檢察官。

pros·e·cu·tion 〔ˌprɑsɪˈkjuʃən; ˌprɔsiˈkjuːʃən〕 *n.* ①起訴;訴訟。②原告。③進行;施行。④調查;研究。—**pros·e·cu·tive,** *adj.*

pros·e·cu·tor 〔ˈprɑsɪˌkjutɚ; ˈprɔsikjuːtə〕 *n.* ①檢察官。②原告。***Public Prosecutor*** 檢察官。

pros·e·lyte 〔ˈprɑslˌaɪt; ˈprɔsilait〕 *n., v.*, **-lyt·ed, -lyt·ing.** —*n.* 改變意見或信仰者;改宗者; 改入他黨者。—*v.t.* 使改宗; 使改變思想或意見。—*v.i.* ①改宗; 改變思想或意見。②徵求優秀選手或人員。

pros·e·lyt·ism 〔ˈprɑslaɪtˌɪzəm; ˈprɔsilitizm〕 *n.* 改宗;改黨;變節。

pros·e·lyt·ize 〔ˈprɑsəlaɪtˌaɪz; ˈprɔsilitaiz〕 *v.*, **-ized, -iz·ing.** —*v.t.* 使改宗;使改黨籍。—*v.i.* 改宗; 變節; 改黨。(英亦作 **proselytise**)

pro·sem·i·nar 〔ˈproˈsɛməˌnɑr; ˈprouˈseminɑː〕 *n.* (大學爲研究生或大三、大四學生所開設的)研討會。

pros·en·ceph·a·lon 〔ˌprɑsɛnˈsɛfəlɑn; ˌprɔsenˈsefəlɔn〕 *n.*【解剖】前腦。

pros·er 〔ˈprozɚ; ˈprouzə〕 *n.* ①寫散文者。②寫作或談話平凡乏味者。

Pro·ser·pi·na 〔proˈsɝpɪnə; prəˈsəːpinə〕 *n.*【羅馬神話】地獄之后 (卽希臘之 Persephone). (亦作 **Proserpine**)

pros·i·ly 〔ˈprozɪlɪ; ˈprouzili〕 *adv.* 散文體地;無趣味地;冗長而單調地。

pros·i·ness 〔ˈprozɪnɪs; ˈprouzinis〕 *n.* ①散文體。②乏味;平凡;單調。

pro·sit 〔ˈprosɪt; ˈprousit〕【拉】*interj.* 爲閣下健康乾杯!

pro·slav·er·y 〔proˈslevrɪ; prouˈsleivəri〕 *adj.* 贊成奴隸制度的;(尤指)【美史】贊成黑奴制度的。—*n.* 贊成 (擁護) 奴隸制度。

pro·sod·ic 〔prəˈsɑdɪk; prəˈsɔdik〕 *adj.* 作詩法的;韻律學的。(亦作 **prosodiac, prosodical**) —**al·ly,** *adv.*

pros·o·dy 〔ˈprɑsədɪ; ˈprɔsədi〕 *n.* ①詩體論;韻律學;作詩法。②某種特殊之詩體或韻律。③詩體論著作;韻律學著作。④韻律性;韻律。—**pros·o·dist,** *n.*

pro·so·po·poe·ia 〔proˌsopəˈpiə; prouˌsoupəˈpiːə〕 *n.*【修辭】擬聲法;擬人法。

pros·pect** 〔ˈprɑspɛkt; ˈprɔspekt〕 *n.* ①期望之事物。I see no *prospect* of his recovery. 我看他沒有痊癒的希望。 good *prospects* in business. 事業前途樂觀。②期望;希望。③景色;景象。④【美】可能的顧客、候選人等。⑤眺望處。⑥(*pl.*) 將來可得之財產。⑦(*pl.*)成功、賺錢等之可能性。a young man's *prospects* in life. 一個青年一生中成功之可能性。in prospect*** **a.** 有實現之希望。**b.**在考慮中;預期的。—*v.t. & v.i.* 探勘;尋找。to *prospect* a region for silver. 在一地區探勘銀礦。—**less,** *adj.*

pro·spec·tive 〔prəˈspɛktɪv; prəsˈpektiv〕 *adj.* ①預期的; 有望的; 未來的。*prospective* bride. 未來的新娘。②瞻望未來的。—**ly,** *adv.*

pros·pec·tor 〔ˈprɑspɛktɚ, prəˈspɛk-; prəsˈpektə, prɔs-〕 *n.* 探礦者;礦藏探勘員。

pro·spec·tus 〔prəˈspɛktəs; prəsˈpektəs〕 *n., pl.* **-tus·es.** (卽將出版之新作品等之)內容說明書;(創辦學校、醫院、企業等之)計畫書;發起書。

***pros·per** 〔ˈprɑspɚ; ˈprɔspə〕 *v.t.* 使昌盛;使成功。—*v.i.* 旺盛;成功。Nothing will *prosper* in his hands. 在他手中,一事無成。

***pros·per·i·ty** 〔prɑsˈpɛrətɪ; prɔsˈperiti〕 *n., pl.* **-ties.** 成功; 幸運; 繁榮。Peace brings *prosperity.* 和平帶來繁榮。

***pros·per·ous** 〔ˈprɑspərəs; ˈprɔspərəs〕 *adj.* ①成功的;繁盛的;興隆的。a *prosperous* business. 興旺的事業。②茂盛的。③順利的。—**ly,** *adv.* —**ness,** *n.*

pros·tate 〔ˈprɑstet; ˈprɔsteit〕 *adj.*【解剖】攝護腺的。—*n.*【解剖】攝護腺。

pros·ta·tec·to·my 〔ˌprɑstəˈtɛktəmɪ; ˌprɔstəˈtektəmi〕 *n.*【醫】攝護腺切除術。

prostate gland〖解剖〗攝護腺。

pros·ta·ti·tis [ˌprɑstəˈtaɪtɪs; ˌprɔstəˈtaitis] *n.* 〖醫〗攝護腺炎。

pros·the·sis [ˈprɑsθɪsɪs; ˈprɔsθisis] *n.* ①〖文法〗添頭音或字(如: beloved 中所加之 be)。②〖醫〗彌補術。③彌補物;其製造。

pros·thet·ic [prɑsˈθɛtɪk; prɔsˈθetik] *adj.* ①字頭音或音節之加添的。②彌補的;補形的。

pros·thet·ics [prɑsˈθɛtɪks; prɔsˈθetiks] *n.* 〖醫〗補缺學;贋復學。

pros·tho·don·ti·a [ˌprɑsθəˈdɑnʃɪə; ˌprɔsθəˈdɔnʃiə] *n.* 牙科贋復學;補齒術;鑲牙術。(亦作**prosthodontics**)

pros·tho·don·tist [ˌprɑsθəˈdɑntɪst; ˌprɔsθəˈdɔntist] *n.* 牙科贋復學專家;補齒專家。

pros·ti·tute [ˈprɑstəˌtjut; ˈprɔstitjuːt] *n., v.,* **-tut·ed, -tut·ing.** —*n.* ①娼妓。②爲賺錢而做壞事的人。—*v.t.* ①使賣淫;使賣身。②濫用。—*v.i.* 賣淫;賣身。

pros·ti·tu·tion [ˌprɑstəˈtjuʃən; ˌprɔstiˈtjuːʃən] *n.* ①賣淫;操淫業。②汚辱;沾辱;濫用。

***pros·trate** [ˈprɑstret; ˈprɔstreit] *v.,* **-trat·ed, -trat·ing,** *adj.* —*v.t.* ①平臥;臥倒。The captives *prostrated* themselves before the conqueror. 俘虜們俯伏在征服者面前。②使衰弱;使疲倦。③使沮喪;使憂鬱。—*adj.* ①俯臥的;平臥的。②無力抵抗的;被征服的。③衰弱的;疲倦的。④匍匐生長的。

pros·tra·tion [prɑˈstreʃən; prɔsˈtreiʃən] *n.* ①拜倒;俯身致敬。②倒下。③疲勞;沮喪;憂鬱。④〖醫〗虛脫;虛弱。nervous *prostration.* 神經衰弱。⑤頹唐;蕭條。

pro·style [ˈprostaɪl; ˈproustail] *adj.* 〖建築〗前柱式的。—*n.* ①前柱式廻廊。②前柱式建築。

pros·y [ˈprozɪ; ˈprouzi] *adj.,* **pros·i·er, pros·i·est.** ①散文的;散文體的。②沒趣味的;平凡的;單調的;囉嗦的;缺乏想像的。

Prot. Protestant.

pro·tag·o·nist [proˈtægənɪst; prouˈtægənist] *n.* ①(戲劇、小說中之)主角。②主要人物。

pro·ta·mine [ˈprotəmin; ˈproutəmiːn] *n.* 〖生化〗精蛋白質;卵鹼。

pro tan·to [proˈtænto; prouˈtæntou] 〖拉〗至此爲止;至某一程度。

prot·a·sis [ˈprɑtəsɪs; ˈprɔtəsis] *n., pl.* **-ses** [-siz; -siːz]. ①〖文法〗條件子句。②〖古典戲劇〗開始部分。

Pro·te·an [ˈprotɪən; prouˈtiːən] *adj.* ①(似) Proteus 的。②(p-)變化自如的;變幻無常的;多變化的。③(p-)一人演數角色的。

‡**pro·tect** [prəˈtɛkt; prəˈtekt] *v.t.* 保護;防護。to *protect* the children from catching cold. 防備孩子們受涼。—*v.i.* 有保護作用。—**ing·ly,** *adv.*

pro·tect·ant [prəˈtɛktənt; prəˈtektənt] *n.* 用來殺蟲的撒布劑。

***pro·tec·tion** [prəˈtɛkʃən; prəˈtekʃən] *n.* ①保護;防護。Little children live under the *protection* of their parents. 小孩在父母保護下生活。②保護者;保護物。An apron is a *protection* when doing dirty work. 圍裙是做骯髒工作時之保護物。③保護貿易制度或政策。④通行證;護照。

pro·tec·tion·ism [prəˈtɛkʃənɪzm; prəˈtekʃənizm] *n.* 〖經濟〗保護貿易主義;保護政策。

pro·tec·tion·ist [prəˈtɛkʃənɪst; prəˈtekʃənist] *n.* 保護貿易主義者。—*adj.* 保護貿易主義的。

***pro·tec·tive** [prəˈtɛktɪv; prəˈtektiv] *adj.* 保護的;防護的。a *protective* tariff. 保護關稅。*protective* mimicry. 擬態。—*n.* 保護物。—**ly,** *adv.*

protective coloration 保護色。(亦作 **protective coloring**)

pro·tec·tor [prəˈtɛktə; prəˈtektə] *n.* ①保護者;擁護者;防禦者;支援者。②〖英史〗攝政。③(P-)(=Lord Protector) 護民官(英國共和政治時 Oliver Cromwell 及其子 Richard Cromwell 的稱號)。④保護物;保護裝置。a chest *protector.* 護胸。—**al,** *adj.*

pro·tec·tor·ate [prəˈtɛktərɪt; prəˈtektərit] *n.* ①保護國;保護地。②保護制度;保護關係。③攝政職位;攝政期間。④攝政政治。⑤(P-)〖英史〗攝政之職位;攝政之任期(1653–59)。

pro·tec·tor·ship [prəˈtɛktəˌʃɪp; prəˈtektəʃip] *n.* 攝政的職位及任期。

pro·tec·to·ry [prəˈtɛktərɪ; prəˈtektəri] *n., pl.* **-ries.** ①慈幼院。②少年感化院。

pro·tec·tress [prəˈtɛktrɪs; prəˈtektris] *n.* 女保護者;女攝政。

pro·té·gé [ˈprotəˌʒe; ˈprouteʒei] *n., pl.* **-gés.** 被保護者(指男性)。

pro·té·gée [ˈprotəˌʒe; ˈprouteʒei] *n.* 被保護者(指女性)。

pro·te·ide [ˈprotiˌaɪd; ˈproutiaid] *n.* (亦作 **proteid**)蛋白質。—*adj.* 含蛋白質的。

pro·tein [ˈprotiɪn; ˈproutiːn] *n.* 蛋白質。

pro·te·in·a·ceous [ˌprotɪəˈneʃəs; ˌproutiəˈneiʃəs] *adj.* 蛋白質的。

pro tem [proˈtɛm; prouˈtem] 〖拉〗= **pro tempore.**

pro tem·po·re [proˈtɛmpəˌri; prouˈtempəriː] 〖拉〗(常略作 **pro tem.**) 目前;暫時。

pro·tend [proˈtɛnd; prouˈtend] *v.t.* & *v.i.* ①伸出;突出。②(時間)延長。

pro·ten·sive [proˈtɛnsɪv; prouˈtensiv] *adj.* ①向一方延長的。②時間延長的。

Prot·er·o·zo·ic [ˌprɑtərəˈzoɪk; ˌprɔtərəˈzouik] *n.* 〖地質〗原生代;原生代岩石。—*adj.* 原生代的;原生代之岩石的。

‡**pro·test** [*n.* ˈprotɛst; ˈproutest *v.* prəˈtɛst; prəˈtest] *n.* ①抗議;反對。to make a *protest.* 提出抗議。②鄭重聲明。③〖商〗(票據等之)拒付證書。*under protest* 不願意;不服。—*v.t.* ①反對;抗議。②力言;斷言。③〖商〗拒絕(票據等)之支付。—*v.i.* ①反對〖常 against〗. The boys *protested* against having girls in the game. 男孩子們反對女孩子參加這比賽。②明言;斷言。

***Prot·es·tant** [ˈprɑtɪstənt; ˈprɔtistənt] *n.* ①基督徒;新教徒。②(十七世紀時)路德信徒或英國國教徒。—*adj.* 基督徒,新教徒等的。*Protestant* Reformation. 宗教改革。

***prot·es·tant** [ˈprɑtɪstənt; ˈprɔtistənt] *n.* 抗議者。the *protestants* against war. 對戰爭表抗議者。—*adj.* 抗議的。a *protestant* movement. 抗議運動。

Protestant Episcopal Church 〖宗教〗聖公會。

Prot·es·tant·ism [ˈprɑtɪstəntˌɪzəm; ˈprɔtistəntizm] *n.* ①基督新教;新教。②新教教義。③新教(徒)團體。

Prot·es·tant·ize [ˈprɑtəstənˌtaɪz; ˈprɔtistəntaiz] *v.t.* & *v.i.* (使)奉新教。

prot·es·ta·tion [ˌprɑtəsˈteʃən; ˌprou-

tes'teiʃən] *n.* ①抗議;異議。②明言;斷言。
Pro·te·us ['protjus; 'proutju:s] *n.* ①〖希臘神話〗海神(據傳能隨意變爲各種形狀)。②多變之人; 反覆無常的人或物。③有多種興趣或能力者。
pro·tha·la·mi·on [ˌproθə'lemɪˌɑn; ˌprouθə'leimiɔn] *n.*, *pl.* **-mi·a** [-mɪə; -miə]. 祝婚詩或歌。(亦作 **prothalamium**)
pro·thal·li·um [prə'θælɪəm; prə'θæliəm] *n.*, *pl.* **-li·a** [-lɪə;-liə].〖植物〗原葉體。(亦作 **prothallus**)—**pro·thal·li·al,** *adj.*
proth·e·sis ['prɑθəsɪs; 'prɔθisis] *n.* ①〖文法〗=**prosthesis.** ②〖希臘敎會〗聖餐臺。—**pro·thet·ic,** *adj.*
pro·throm·bin [prə'θrɑmbɪn; pro'θrɔmbin] *n.* 〖生化〗凝血素。
pro·tist ['protɪst; 'proutist] *n.*, *pl.* **-tis·ta** [-'tɪstə; -'tistə]. 單細胞生物。
pro·ti·um ['protɪəm; 'proutiəm] *n.* 〖化〗氕(氫的同位素, H^1)。
proto- 〖字首〗表"第一;主要;最初;原始;最低"之義。(亦作 **prot-**)
pro·to·ac·tin·i·um [ˌprotəæk'tɪnɪəm; ˌproutouæk'tiniəm] *n.* 〖化〗鏷(一種放射性元素)。(亦作 **protactinium**)
pro·to·col ['protəˌkɑl; 'proutəkɔl] *n.* ①議定書;條約草案; 草約。②外交禮節。—*v.i.* 擬作(條約)草案。
pro·to·his·to·ry [ˌproto'hɪstərɪ; ˌproutou'histəri] *n.* 初期歷史;早期歷史。
pro·to·hu·man [ˌproto'hjumən; ˌproutou'hju:mən] *adj.* 似初期人類的; 最初人類之前的。
pro·to·lan·guage ['proto'læŋgwɪdʒ; 'proutə'læŋgwidʒ] *n.* 母語。
pro·to·mar·tyr [ˌproto'mɑrtɚ; ˌproutou'mɑ:tə] *n.* 第一個殉道者(尤指基督敎的 Saint Stephen).
pro·ton ['protɑn;'proutɔn] *n.*〖物理〗質子。
pro·to·plasm ['protəˌplæzəm; 'proutəplæzm] *n.* 〖生物〗原形質。
pro·to·plas·mic [ˌprotə'plæzmɪk; ˌproutə'plæzmik] *adj.* 〖生物〗原形質的。
pro·to·plast ['protəˌplæst; 'proutəplæst] *n.* ①〖生物〗原生質體;原形體。②初成物;原物。③原人。—**ic,** *adj.*
pro·to·type ['protəˌtaɪp; 'proutətaip] *n.* ①原型。②典型;模範。③〖生物〗原形。 —**pro·to·typ·ic, pro·to·typ·i·cal,** *adj.* —**pro·to·typ·i·cal·ly,** *adv.*
Pro·to·zo·a [ˌprotə'zoə; ˌproutə'zouə] *n. pl.* 〖動物〗原生動物;原形動物。
pro·to·zo·an [ˌprotə'zoən; ˌproutə'zouən] *adj.* (=protozoal, protozoic)原生動物的。—*n.* (=protozoon)原生動物。
pro·to·zo·ol·o·gy [ˌprotəzo'ɑlədʒɪ; ˌproutəzou'ɔlədʒi] *n.* 原生動物學。
pro·tract [pro'trækt; prə'trækt] *v.t.* ①延長; 伸張。②伸出。③以量角器或比例尺繪(圖)。 —**ive,** *adj.*
pro·tract·ed [pro'træktɪd;prə'træktid] *adj.* 延長的;引長的。—**ly,** *adv.*
pro·trac·tile [pro'træktɪl;prə'træktail] *adj.* 〖動物〗(動物器官等的) 能伸出的;能引長的。
pro·trac·tion [pro'trækʃən; prə'trækʃən] *n.* ①延長;伸長;擴張。②製圖;所製之圖。
pro·trac·tor [pro'træktɚ;prə'træktə] *n.* ①量角器;分度規。②使(時間、行動等)延長之人(物)。③〖解剖〗伸肌。
pro·trude [pro'trud; prə'tru:d] *v.*, **-trud·ed, -trud·ing.** —*v.t.* 伸出; 吐出。—*v.i.* 凸出;突出。 —**pro·trud·a·ble,** *adj.*
pro·trud·ent [pro'trudənt;prə'tru:dənt] *adj.* 突出的;凸出的;伸出的。
pro·tru·sion [pro'truʒən; prə'tru:ʒən] *n.* ①伸出;突出。②突起 (部分);隆起。
pro·tru·sive [pro'trusɪv;prə'tru:siv] *adj.* 伸出的;突出的。—**ly,** *adv.* —**ness,** *n.*
pro·tu·ber·ance [pro'tjubərəns; prə'tju:bərəns] *n.* ①突出;凸出。②突出物;凸出部分; 結節; 瘤。 ***solar protuberance*** 〖天文〗日珥。
pro·tu·ber·ant [pro'tjubərənt;prə'tju:bərənt] *adj.* ①凸出的; 突出的; 隆起的。②顯著的。 —**ly,** *adv.*
‡**proud** [praud; praud] *adj.* ①自尊的;自重的。He is too *proud* to complain. 他甚自重而不抱怨。②驕傲的;高傲的。She is as *proud* as a peacock. 她十分驕傲。③極愉快的;感到光榮的。 a *proud* moment. 極愉快的時刻。④堂皇的;壯麗的。⑤有精神的(牲口等)。⑥漲水的(河)。***be proud of*** 以…爲榮;爲…沾沾自喜。He *is proud of* his family. 他以自已的家族爲榮。***do one proud*** 〖俗〗 a. 值得驕傲。 b. 優待;使滿意。 —**ly,** *adv.* —**ness,** *n.*
proud flesh (傷口愈後所結的) 贅肉;浮肉。
proud·ful ['praudfəl; 'praudful] *adj.* 〖主方〗自尊的;驕傲的。
proud·heart·ed ['praudˌhɑrtɪd; 'praudˌhɑ:tid] *adj.* 驕傲的。
Prov. ①Provençal. ②Provence. ③Proverbs. ④Province. ⑤Provost.
prov. ①provident. ②province. ③provincial. ④provincialism. ⑤provisional.
prov·a·ble ['pruvəbl; 'pru:vəbl] *adj.* 可證明的; 可證實的。(亦作 **proveable**) —**ness,** *n.* —**prov·a·bly,** *adv.*
‡**prove** [pruv;pru:v] *v.*, **proved, proved** or **prov·en, prov·ing.** —*v.t.* ①證明。His guilt was clearly *proved.* 他的罪明白地證實了。②試驗。 to *prove* a new tool. 試驗一新工具。③表現。 He *proved* himself (to be) a coward. 他表現出是一個懦夫。④〖數學〗驗算;核算。⑤〖法律〗查驗(遺囑)。—*v.i.* 顯示;表明。This book *proved* interesting. 這本書很有趣味。***prove out*** a. 被證明有預期之結果;被知有預期之效果。b. 證明可安全使用。 ***prove up*** 具備 (某某要求的)條件。 —**prov·er,** *n.*
prov·en ['pruvən; 'pru:vən] *v.* pp. of **prove.** —*adj.* 已證明的。 ***not proven*** 〖蘇〗證據不足的(卽宣告無罪)。
prov·e·nance ['prɑvənəns; 'prɔvinəns] *n.* (藝術等的)出處;起源。
Pro·ven·çal [ˌprovən'sɑl; ˌprɔvɑ̃:n'sɑ:l] *n.* ①Provence 的居民。②Provence 的語言; 中世紀法國南部之語言。 —*adj.* ①Provence 的。②Provence 人的。③Provence 語的。
Pro·vence ['prɑvəns;prɔ'vɑ̃:ns] *n.* 法國東南之一地區, 中世紀時以詩歌及武俠著稱。
prov·en·der ['prɑvəndɚ; 'prɔvində] *n.* ①(飼家畜之)芻草;秣料。②〖俗、諧〗食料;食物。
pro·ve·ni·ence [pro'vinɪəns;prou'vi:niəns] *n.* 來源。
prov·en·ly ['pruvənlɪ; 'pru:vnli] *adv.* 已得證明地。

prov·erb** [ˈprɑvɝb; ˈprɔvəːb] *n.* ①諺語;格言。I referred him to the *proverb.* 我以格言規勸他。② 人盡皆知之人或事物;話柄。His ignorance is a *proverb.* 他的無知已成笑柄。the Book of Proverbs***(舊約中的)箴言篇。***to a proverb*** …到無人不知的程度。ridiculous even *to a proverb.* 荒謬絕倫。

pro-verb [ˈprovɝb; ˈprouvəːb] *n.* 〔【文法】代動詞。〕

pro·ver·bi·al [prəˈvɝbɪəl; prəˈvəːbjəl] *adj.* ①諺語的;格言的。②格言或諺語中所表示的。③有名的;天下周知的。

pro·ver·bi·al·ly [prəˈvɝbɪəlɪ; prəˈvəːbjəli] *adv.* 無人不知地。

‡**pro·vide** [prəˈvaɪd; prəˈvaid] *v.*, **-vid·ed, -vid·ing.** —*v.t.* ①供給;供應。Sheep *provide* us with wool. 羊供給我們羊毛。②預先約定;規定。The rules *provide* that dues must be paid monthly. 條文上規定款須按月付。③準備;預備。—*v.i.* ①防備;預備。to *provide* for old age. 預先準備老年之所需。②供應必需品;贍養。③規定。***provide against*** 預先準備。

***pro·vid·ed** [prəˈvaɪdɪd; prəˈvaidid] *conj.* 假若;倘使。She will go *provided* her friends can go also. 假如她的朋友也去,她就去。—*adj.* 享有必需品之供應的。

prov·i·dence** [ˈprɑvədəns; ˈprɔvidəns] *n.* ①上帝之保佑;天佑。to trust in *providence.* 信賴天佑。②準備;預備。③(P-)上帝。a special providence*** 天意;天佑。***make providence*** 預作準備;未雨綢繆。

prov·i·dent [ˈprɑvədənt; ˈprɔvidənt] *adj.* ①預知的;預示的。②深謀遠慮的;有先見之明的。③愼重的;節約的。—**ly,** *adv.*

prov·i·den·tial [ˌprɑvəˈdɛnʃəl; ˌprɔviˈdenʃəl] *adj.* ①幸運的。②天佑的;神意的。

prov·i·den·tial·ly [ˌprɑvəˈdɛnʃəlɪ; ˌprɔviˈdenʃəli] *adv.* ①由神意;按天意。②愼重地;謹愼地。③幸運地。

pro·vid·er [prəˈvaɪdɚ; prəˈvaidə] *n.* 供給者;供應者;準備者;備辦者。***lion's provider*** a.【動物】胡狼(=jackal). b. 爲虎作倀者;爪牙。***universal provider*** 百貨商。

pro·vid·ing [prəˈvaɪdɪŋ; prəˈvaidiŋ] *conj.* =**provided.**

***prov·ince** [ˈprɑvɪns; ˈprɔvins] *n.* ①省。②(*pl.*) 首都以外各地。③適當的工作或活動的範圍。It is not within my *province* to interfere. 此非我所當干涉者。④部門;範圍。⑤古羅馬的義大利以外之領地。⑥大主教之轄區;總主教區。

***pro·vin·cial** [prəˈvɪnʃəl; prəˈvinʃəl] *adj.* ①省的。Taiwan *Provincial* Government. 臺灣省政府。②地方的。③一省居民所特有的(態度、語言、衣着、觀點等)。④狹窄的。a *provincial* point of view. 一種狹窄的意見。⑤粗俗的。—*n.* ①生於一省的人;省中居民。delegations of *provincials.* 省民代表團。②鄉下人。③粗俗的人。—**ly,** *adv.*

pro·vin·cial·ism [prəˈvɪnʃəlˌɪzəm; prəˈvinʃəlizm] *n.* ①粗鄙;粗野。②偏狹;狹窄。③方言;方音。④地方之特性;地方特色。⑤濃厚之地方情感;鄉土觀念。

pro·vin·cial·ist [prəˈvɪnʃəlɪst; prəˈvinʃəlist] *n.* ①省中居民;地方居民。②地方至上主義者。

pro·vin·ci·al·i·ty [prəˌvɪnʃɪˈælətɪ; prəˌvinʃiˈæliti] *n.*, *pl.* **-ties.** =**provincialism.**

pro·vin·cial·ize [prəˈvɪnʃəlˌaɪz; prəˈvinʃəlaiz] *v.t.* & *v.i.*, **-ized, -iz·ing.** ①(使)地方化。②(使)變粗鄙。③(使)變褊狹。④(使)歸於省轄治。

proving ground 試驗場。

pro·vi·sion** [prəˈvɪʒən; prəˈviʒən] *n.* ①條款;規定。one of the *provisions* in a will. 遺囑中之一條。②準備;預備。to make *provision* for the future. 爲將來做準備。③(*pl.*) 供應品(特指食物或飲料的)。a basket of *provisions.* 一籃食物。④供應;提供。the *provision* of a play area for the children. 孩子們遊戲場所之提供。⑤(教會祿位之)敍任。make provision*** 爲未來作打算;預作安排。—*v.t.* 供以食物。

pro·vi·sion·al [prəˈvɪʒənḷ; prəˈviʒənl] *adj.* 臨時的。a *provisional* agreement. 臨時協定。—**ly,** *adv.*

pro·vi·sion·al·i·ty [prəˌvɪʒənˈælətɪ; prəˌviʒənˈæliti] *n.* 臨時性;暫時性。

pro·vi·sion·ar·y [prəˈvɪʒənˌɛrɪ; prəˈviʒənəri] *adj.* =**provisional.**

pro·vi·sion·er [prəˈvɪʒənɚ; prəˈviʒənə] *n.* 糧食供應者。

pro·vi·sion·ment [prəˈvɪʒənmənt; prəˈviʒənmənt] *n.* ①糧食供應。②糧食。

pro·vi·so [prəˈvaɪzo; prəˈvaizou] *n.*, *pl.* **-sos, -soes.** (契約等之)附文;(法律之)但書;條件。***with (a) proviso*** 附有條件。

pro·vi·so·ry [prəˈvaɪzərɪ; prəˈvaizəri] *adj.* ①有條件的。②臨時的;暫時的。

provisory clause 但書;除外條款。

pro·vi·ta·min [proˈvaɪtəmɪn; prouˈvaitəmin] *n.* 維他命元。

prov·o·ca·tion [ˌprɑvəˈkeʃən; ˌprɔvəˈkeiʃən] *n.* ①引起;激怒。②激怒之原因。

pro·voc·a·tive [prəˈvɑkətɪv; prəˈvɔkətiv] *adj.* (亦作 **provocatory**) ①激起的;挑撥的;煽動的。②刺激的。—*n.* ①刺激物;挑撥物。②興奮劑。—**ly,** *adv.* —**ness,** *n.*

***pro·voke** [prəˈvok; prəˈvouk] *v.t.*, **-voked, -vok·ing.** ①引起。②激起。③激怒;刺激。An insult *provokes* a person to anger. 侮辱激怒一個人。—**pro·vok·er,** *n.*

pro·vok·ing [prəˈvokɪŋ; prəˈvoukiŋ] *adj.* ①刺激的;煽動的。②使人惱怒的;惱人的。—**ly,** *adv.*

prov·ost [ˈprɑvəst; ˈprɔvəst. *for* ⑤ ˈprovo; prəˈvou] *n.* ①【英】學院院長(尤用於牛津、劍橋二校)。②(美國若干大學之)負責教務之行政人員。③(蘇格蘭之)市長。④【宗教】大教堂或大學附屬教堂之首長;修道院長。⑤【軍】憲兵軍官。—**ship,** *n.*

provost court 在敵國占領區設立而審理非重大案件的軍事法庭。

provost marshal 憲兵司令。

Provost Marshal Department 憲兵司令部。

prow[1] [praʊ; prau] *n.* ①船首。②類似船首之物。③【詩】船。

prow[2] *adj.* 【古】勇敢的。

prow·ess [ˈpraʊɪs; ˈprauis, -es] *n.* ①勇敢;勇武。②勇敢的行爲。③不凡的技能;好本領;卓越。

prowl [praʊl; praul] *v.t.* & *v.i.* ①潛行以尋覓或偸竊。Wolves *prowl* the forest. 狼在森林裏巡覓食物。②徘徊。—*n.* 潛巡;徘徊。to go on the *prowl.* 潛巡。—**ing·ly,** *adv.*

prowl car 警察乘用之巡邏車。

prowl·er [ˈpraʊlɚ; ˈpraulə] *n.* ①暗巡

者;酒巡者。②徘徊者。③小偸。

prox. proximo.

prox·i·mal ['prɑksəml; 'prɔksiməl] *adj.* ①(時間、空間、次序中)次一個的;最近的。②〖解剖〗近側(近身體中心)的。—**ly,** *adv.*

prox·i·mate ['prɑksəˌmet; 'prɔksimit] *adj.* ①最近的;接近的。②即將來臨的。③近似的;大致準確的。—**ly,** *adv.* —**ness,** *n.*

prox·i·me ac·ces·sit ['prɑksɪmɪæk'sɛsɪt; 'prɔksimiæk'sesit]〖拉〗(賽跑的)第二名;(考試的)第二名;(領獎者的)次席。

prox·im·i·ty [prɑk'sɪmətɪ; prɔk'simiti] *n.* 接近;近似。

proximity fuse 使砲彈等能在目標附近爆炸的一種無線電裝置。「之親。」

proximity of blood 近親;骨肉

prox·i·mo ['prɑksɪmo; 'prɔksimou] *adv.* 下月地;次月地。(略作 **prox.**)

prox·y ['prɑksɪ; 'prɔksi] *n., pl.* **prox·ies,** *adj.* —*n.* ①代理。②代理人;代表。③代理權。④委託書;委託投票書。⑤代替物。 ***stand*** (or ***be***) ***proxy for ...*** 做…的代理;代表…。 —*adj.* 代理的;代替的。

prs. ①pairs. ②present.

prude [prud; pru:d] *n.* 過分(故作)守禮或謙遜的人。「①智慮;謹愼。②節儉。」

***pru·dence** ['prudn̩s; 'pru:dəns] *n.*

***pru·dent** ['prudn̩t; 'pru:dənt] *adj.* ①智慮的;謹愼的。②節儉的。

pru·den·tial [pru'dɛnʃəl; pru:'denʃəl] *adj.* ①有智慮的;有頭腦的。②審愼的;小心的。 —*n.* (常 *pl.*)需就行政或財務研究處理之事。—**ly,** *adv.*

pru·dent·ly ['prudəntlɪ; 'pru:dəntli] *adv.* 謹愼地;愼重地。

prud·er·y ['prudərɪ; 'pru:dəri] *n., pl.* **-er·ies.** ①過分守禮或謙遜;假正經;裝規矩。②(*pl.*)過分守禮或謙遜的行爲或言詞。

prud·ish ['prudɪʃ; 'pru:diʃ] *adj.* 過分守禮或謙遜的;裝得規規矩矩的;過分守禮或謙遜之人的。—**ly,** *adv.* —**ness,** *n.*

pru·i·nose ['pruəˌnos; 'pru:ənous] *adj.* 〖生物〗被一層霜狀排洩物覆蓋的。

***prune**[1] [prun; pru:n] *v.t.* & *v.i.,* **pruned, prun·ing.** ①修剪。to *prune* the twigs off. 剪掉小枝。②刪改;刪掉。

prune**[2] *n.* 乾梅子。 ***prunes and prism (or ***prisms***) 談話或行動時的裝腔作勢。

pru·nel·la [pru'nɛlə; pru:'nelə] *n.* 一種堅牢的斜紋布。

prun·ing ['prunɪŋ; 'pru:niŋ] *n.* ①修剪;修枝;剪枝。②被剪下的殘枝。 —*adj.* 修剪用的;剪枝用的。

pruning hook 修剪用的鐮刀。

pru·ri·ence ['prurɪəns; 'pruəriəns] *n.* ①好色;色慾。②熱望;渴慕。(亦作 **pru·riency**)

pru·ri·ent ['prurɪənt; 'pruəriənt] *adj.* ①好色的;淫亂的。②熱望的;渴想的。③發育過速的;過分茂盛的。 —**ly,** *adv.*

pru·rig·i·nous [pru'rɪdʒənəs; pru'ridʒənəs] *adj.* ①似濕疹的;引起濕疹的;濕疹引起的。②不安的;發癢的。

pru·ri·go [pru'raɪgo; pru'raigou] *n.* 〖醫〗濕疹;癢疹。「*n.* 癬癢症;搔癢。」

pru·ri·tus [pru'raɪtəs; pru'raitəs]

***Prus·sia** ['prʌʃə; 'prʌʃə] *n.* 普魯士。

Prus·sian ['prʌʃən; 'prʌʃən] *adj.* ①普魯士的;普魯士人的;普魯士語的。②普魯士式的;訓練嚴格的。—*n.* 普魯士人;普魯士語。

Prussian blue 普魯士藍(即深藍色)。

Prus·sian·ism ['prʌʃənɪzəm; 'prʌʃənizm] *n.* 普魯士精神;軍國主義。

Prus·sian·ize ['prʌʃənˌaɪz; 'prʌʃənaiz] *v.t.,* **-ized, -iz·ing.** 使普魯士化;使軍國主義化。「〖化〗氫氰酸鹽。」

prus·si·ate ['prʌʃɪɪt; 'prʌʃiit] *n.*

prus·sic acid ['prʌsɪk~; 'prʌsik~] 〖化〗氰酸;氫氰酸。

pry[1] [praɪ; prai] *v.,* **pried, pry·ing,** *n., pl.* **pries.** —*v.i.* 細查;偵查;探問。Don't *pry* into the affairs of others. 莫探問他人之私事;莫管閒事。—*n.* 愛探問閒事的人。 ***Paul Pry*** 愛問閒事的人。

pry[2] *v.,* **pried, pry·ing,** *n., pl.* **pries.** —*v.t.* ①(以槓桿)抬起;舉起;移動。②費力得到。—*n.* 槓桿。

pry·ing ['praɪɪŋ; 'praiiŋ] *adj.* 窺伺的;窺探的;好奇的。—**ly,** *adv.* 「**prithee.**」

pryth·ee ['prɪðɪ; 'pri(:)ði] *interj.* =

Ps. ①Psalm. ②Psalms. **P.S.** ①postscript. ②Public School. ③Privy Seal. ④passenger steamer. ⑤permanent secretary. ⑥private secretary. ⑦prompt side.

***psalm** [sɑm; sɑ:m] *n.* ①讚美歌;讚美詩。②(P-) 舊約中之讚美詩。—*v.i.* 唱讚美歌。—**ic,** *adj.* —**less,** *adj.* 「*n.* 讚美詩集。」

psalm·book ['sɑmˌbuk; 'sɑ:mbuk]

psalm·ist ['sɑmɪst; 'sɑ:mist] *n.* 讚美詩作者。***the Psalmist*** 大衞王(耶教聖經詩篇之作者)。

psal·mod·ic [sæl'mɑdɪk; sæl'mɔdik] *adj.* 唱讚美詩的;朗誦詩篇的;聖詩的。

psal·mo·dist ['sɑmədɪst; 'sælmədist] *n.* ①讚美詩作者;唱讚美詩者。②(the P-) 大衞(聖經詩篇之作者)。

psal·mo·dy ['sɑmədɪ; 'sælmədi] *n., pl.* **-dies.** ①唱讚美詩。②讚美詩;讚美詩集。

psal·ter ['sɔltɚ; 'sɔltə] *n.* ①(P-) 耶教舊約聖經之詩篇。②(祈禱用之)禱告韻文;詩篇集(尤指經翻譯者)。—**i·an,** *adj.*

psal·ter·y ['sɔltrɪ; 'sɔ:ltəri] *n., pl.* **-ter·ies.** ①古代的一種絃樂器。②(P-) 詩篇。

p's and q's 自己應小心之事(常與 mind 或 watch 連用)。He had better watch his *p's and q's*. 他最好注意自己應小心之事。

pseud. pseudonym. 「前)。」

pseud- 〖字首〗**pseudo-** 之異體(用於母音

pseu·do ['sjudo; '(p)sju:dou] *adj.* 假的;僞的。

pseu·do·clas·si·cism [ˌsjudə'klæsəsɪzm̩; '(p)sju:dou'klæsisizm] *n.* 僞古典主義;擬古體。

pseu·do-e·vent [ˌsjudoɪ'vɛnt; '(p)sju:doui'vent] *n.* 爲便於新聞報導或發表而製造的事件。

pseu·do·graph ['sjudoˌgræf; '(p)sju:dougrɑ:f] *n.* 僞書;僞作。

pseu·do·nym ['sjudn̩ˌɪm; '(p)sju:dənim] *n.* 假名;(作家的)筆名。

pseu·do·nym·i·ty [ˌsjudə 'nɪmətɪ; ˌ(p)sju:də'nimiti] *n.* ①筆名;假名。②筆名之使用。

pseu·don·y·mous [sju'dɑnəməs; (p)sju:'dɔniməs] *adj.* ①用假名的;筆名的。②用筆名寫作的。

pseu·do·scope ['sjudəˌskop; '(p)sju:dəskoup] *n.* 反影鏡(映像之凹凸與實物相反)。

pshaw [ʃɔ; pʃɔ:] *interj.* 咄!啐!(表示不

耐煩、輕蔑及討厭等之感嘆聲)。—*v.i.* 發出此種感嘆; 咋。 —*v.t.* 對…發出此種感嘆聲。—*n.* 咄;咋。 「母(Ψ, ψ).
psi [saɪ; sai] *n.* 希臘字母的第二十三個字
psi·lo·sis [saɪ'losɪs; sai'lousis] *n.* ①脫髮症;禿頭病。②口炎性腹瀉。
psit·ta·co·sis [ˌsɪtə'kosɪs; ˌpsitə'kousis] *n.* 〖醫〗鸚鵡病;鸚鵡熱。(亦作 **parrot fever**)
pso·ri·a·sis [sə'raɪəsɪs; (p)sɔː'rai-əsis] *n.* 〖醫〗乾癬;鱗癬;牛皮癬。 「ard Time.
P.S.T., p.s.t., PST Pacific Stand-
psych(e) [saɪk; saik] *v.t.*, **psyched, psych·ing.** ①心理分析。②恐嚇; 用心戰擊敗〖常 out〗。③使爲做某事作心理準備〖up〗。
Psy·che ['saɪkɪ; 'saiki] *n.* ①〖希臘神話〗賽克 (Eros 或 Cupid 所愛之美女, 被視爲靈魂之化身, 昔在藝術中常畫爲蝴蝶或有翼之人)。②(p-)靈魂;精神。
psych·e·del·ic [ˌsaɪkɪ'dɛlɪk; ˌsaiki'delik] *adj., n.* =**psychodelic.**
psy·chi·a·ter [saɪ'kaɪətɚ; sai'kaiətə] *n.* =**psychiatrist.**
psy·chi·at·ric [ˌsaɪkɪ'ætrɪk; ˌsaiki'ætrik] *adj.* 精神病的;精神病治療的。(亦作 **psychiatrical**)
psy·chi·a·trist [saɪ'kaɪətrɪst; sai'kaiətrist] *n.* 精神病醫師;研究精神病之學者。
psy·chi·a·try [saɪ'kaɪətrɪ; sai'kaiətri] *n.* ①精神病之治療與研究;精神病學。②(醫院裏之)精神科。
psy·chic ['saɪkɪk; 'saikik] *adj.* ①靈魂的;精神上的 (爲 physical 之對)。②心靈的;超自然的。 ③對心靈上的影響力特別敏感的;通靈的。—*n.* 特別能感受心靈上影響的人;通靈之人。 「=**psychic.** —**ly,** *adv.*
psy·chi·cal ['saɪkɪkl; 'saikikəl] *adj.*
psy·cho ['saɪko; 'saikou] *adj.* ①〖俚〗精神病治療的。②〖俚〗精神病的。
psy·cho·ac·tive [ˌsaɪko'æktɪv; ˌsaikou'æktiv] *adj.* 對心理有影響的。
psy·cho·a·nal·y·sis [ˌsaɪkoə'næləsɪs; ˌsaikouə'nælisis] *n.* 心理分析;精神分析。
psy·cho·an·a·lyst [ˌsaɪko'ænlɪst; ˌsaikou'ænəlist] *n.* 精神分析學家; 精於心理分析者。
psy·cho·an·a·lyt·ic [ˌsaɪkoˌænl'ɪtɪk; ˌsaikouˌænə'litik] *adj.* 精神分析的。
psy·cho·an·a·lyze [ˌsaɪko'ænlˌaɪz; ˌsaikou'ænəlaiz] *v.t.*, **-lyzed, -lyz·ing.** 以心理分析法診斷與治療。
psy·cho·del·ic [ˌsaɪko'dɛlɪk; ˌsaikou'delik] *adj.* 產生幻覺的; 能使精神恍惚的。—*n.* 能使人產生幻覺之藥劑。
psy·cho·dra·ma [ˌsaɪkə'drɑmə; ˌsaiko'drɑːmə] *n.* 心理戲劇(一種心理療法)。
psy·cho·gen·e·sis [ˌsaɪko'dʒɛnəsɪs; ˌsaikou'dʒenisis] *n.* 精神之起源與發展;心理發生。
psy·cho·gen·ic [ˌsaɪko'dʒɛnɪk; ˌsaikou'dʒenik] *adj.* 精神性的;心理性的。
psy·cho·graph ['saɪkəˌgræf; 'saikəgrɑːf] *n.* ①無意識手動描記器。②分析性格的傳記。
psy·cho·ki·ne·sis [ˌsaɪkokɪ'nisɪs; ˌsaikouki'niːsis] *n.* 個人對無生命物體之影響能力。 「chology.
psychol. ①psychological. ②psy-
***psy·cho·log·i·cal** [ˌsaɪkə'lɑdʒɪkl; ˌsaikə'lɔdʒikəl] *adj.* ①心理上的。②心理學的。 *psychological* tests. 心理測驗。(亦作 **psychologic**)
psy·cho·log·i·cal·ly [ˌsaɪkə'lɑdʒɪklɪ; ˌsaikə'lɔdʒikəli] *adv.* ①心理上。②從心理學的觀點。
psychological moment ①使在心理上發生效果的最恰當的時刻。②緊要關頭。
psychological warfare 心理戰。
psy·chol·o·gist [saɪ'kɑlədʒɪst; sai'kɔlədʒist] *n.* 心理學家。
psy·chol·o·gize [saɪ'kɑləˌdʒaɪz; sai'kɔlədʒaiz] *v.*, **-gized, -giz·ing.** —*v.i.* 研究心理學; 作心理學上之調查或思索。—*v.t.* 從心理學上分析。
***psy·chol·o·gy** [saɪ'kɑlədʒɪ; sai'kɔlədʒi] *n., pl.* **-gies.** ①心理學。 social *psychology.* 社會心理學。②心理學論著。③心理性質;心理狀態。
psy·chom·e·try [saɪ'kɑmətrɪ; sai'kɔmitri] *n.* ①(亦作 **psychometrics**)精神測定學。②(接觸一人或一物即知其一切之)神祕能力。—**psy·chom·e·trist,** *n.*
psy·cho·neu·ro·sis [ˌsaɪkonjʊ'rosɪs; ˌsaikounju'rousis] *n., pl.* **-ses** [-siz; -siːz]. 輕性精神病;心理性神經病。
psy·cho·path ['saɪkəˌpæθ; 'saikəpæθ] *n.* 精神病患者。
psy·cho·path·ic [ˌsaɪkə'pæθɪk; ˌsaikou'pæθik] *adj.* ①精神病的; 精神錯亂的。②治療精神變態症的。③有變爲瘋狂傾向的。
psy·cho·pa·thol·o·gy [ˌsaɪkopə'θɑlədʒɪ; ˌsaikoupə'θɔlədʒi] *n.* 精神病理學;變態心理學。
psy·chop·a·thy [saɪ'kɑpəθɪ; sai'kɔpəθi] *n.* ①精神病。②精神治療法。
psy·cho·phys·ics [ˌsaɪko'fɪzɪks; 'saikou'fiziks] *n.* 精神物理學。
psy·cho·sis [saɪ'kosɪs; sai'kousis] *n., pl.* **-ses** [-siz; -siːz]. ①精神病;精神異狀;精神變態; 變態心理。②特定時間內的意識狀態; 精神狀態。
psy·cho·so·ci·ol·o·gy [ˌsaɪkəˌsoʃɪ'ɑlədʒɪ; ˌsaikəˌsousi'ɔlədʒi] *n.* 社會心理學。
psy·cho·so·ma·tic [ˌsaɪkəso'mætɪk; ˌsaikousou'mætik] *adj.* 精神與身體的; 身心關係的。
psychosomatic medicine 身心醫學(以心理學的方法或原理治療生理疾病)。
psy·cho·ther·a·peu·tics [ˌsaɪkoˌθɛrə'pjutɪks; ˌsaikouˌθerə'pjuːtiks] *n.* =**psychotherapy.**
psy·cho·ther·a·py [ˌsaɪko'θɛrəpɪ; 'saikou'θerəpi] *n.* (精神失常或精神病之)心理療法。 「*adj.* 瘋的;嚴重精神病的。
psy·chot·ic [saɪ'kɑtɪk; sai'kɔtik]
psy·war ['saɪwɔr; 'saiwɔː] *n.* 心戰。
Pt platinum. **pt.** ①part. ②past tense. ③pint. ④point. ⑤payment. ⑥port. ⑦preterit. **P.T.A., PTA** Parent-Teacher Association.
ptar·mi·gan ['tɑrməgən; 'tɑːmigən] *n., pl.* **-gans, -gan.** 松雞類。 「boat).
PT boat 魚雷快艇 (=patrol torpedo
Pte. 〖英陸軍〗Private.
pter·i·do·phyte ['tɛrədoˌfaɪt; 'teridoufait] *n.* 〖植物〗高等隱花植物。
pter·o·dac·tyl [ˌtɛrə'dæktɪl; ˌteərə'dæktil] *n.* 〖古生物〗翼手龍。
Ptg. ①Portugal. ②Portuguese.
P.T.O., p.t.o. please turn over.

Ptol·e·ma·ic 〔,tɑlə'me·ɪk; ,tɔli'meiik〕 *adj.* ①埃及 Ptolemy 王朝之諸王的。②天文學家 Ptolemy 的;天動說的。
Ptolemaic system 天動說。
Ptol·e·my 〔'tɑləmɪ; 'tɔlimi〕 *n.* ①埃及托勒密王 (323–30 B.C. 統治埃及的希臘馬其頓王朝之諸王)。②托勒密 (Claudius Ptolemaeus, 紀元二世紀之希臘天文學家、數學家及地理學家, 以天動說聞名於世)。
pto·main(e) 〔'tomen; 'toumein〕 *n.* 屍毒鹼; 腐敗鹼(腐敗物所產生的一種毒素)。
pts. ①parts. ②payments. ③pints. ④points. ⑤ports.
pty·a·lin 〔'taɪəlɪn; 'taiəlin〕 *n.* 〖生化〗唾液素;唾液澱粉酶;涎酵素。
Pu 〖化〗化學元素 plutonium 之符號。
pub 〔pʌb; pʌb〕 *n.* 〖英俚〗①酒店 (public house 之略)。②旅館;小店。
pub. ①public. ②publication. ③published. ④publisher. ⑤publishing.
pu·ber·ty 〔'pjubətɪ; 'pju:bəti〕 *n.* ①青春發動期(一般之年齡, 男子爲十四歲, 女子爲十二歲)。②〖植物〗開花期。***age of puberty*** 發情期。***arrive at puberty*** 情竇初開。
pu·bes 〔'pjubiz; 'pju:bi:z〕 *n.* ①〖解剖〗陰部。②〖解剖〗陰毛。③〖動、植物〗軟毛。
pu·bes·cence 〔pju'bɛsn̩s; pju'besns〕 *n.* ①屆青春發動期。②〖動、植物〗軟毛覆蓋;軟毛。③長軟毛。
pu·bes·cent 〔pju'bɛsn̩t; pju'besnt〕 *adj.* ①已屆青春發動期的。②〖動、植物〗覆有軟毛的。—*n.* 青春發動期之少年。
pu·bic 〔'pjubɪk; 'pju:bik〕 *adj.* 陰部的; 陰毛的。
pu·bis 〔'pjubɪs; 'pju:bis〕 *n., pl.* **-bes.** 〖解剖〗恥骨。
‡**pub·lic** 〔'pʌblɪk; 'pʌblik〕 *adj.* ①公衆的;公共的。*public* utility. 公用事業。②人民所爲的。③爲人民的。a *public* man. 政府官員。④公立的。⑤公開的。The fact became *public*. 這事實公開了。⑥國家的。—*n.* ①大衆;民衆。the reading *public*. 讀者大衆。②(有共同興趣、目標的) 一群人。③〖英俗〗= **public house.** ***go public*** (公司) 將股票出售給大衆。***in public*** 公然; 公開地。***the public*** 公衆。—**ness,** *n.*
public administration 公共行政(政治學之一部門)。
public administrator 公定遺產之管理人。
pub·li·can 〔'pʌblɪkən; 'pʌblikən〕 *n.* ①〖英〗酒吧老板。②(古羅馬之)收稅官。③被逐出教會者。
*__pub·li·ca·tion__ 〔,pʌblɪ'keʃən; ,pʌbli'keiʃən〕 *n.* ①出版物;發行物。②出版;發行。The firm is engaged in the *publication* of text books. 那公司從事教科書的發行。③發表;公布。
public bill 國會中有關公共利益的法案。
public charge 藉政府救濟以維持生活的窮人。
public debt 國家債務。
public defender 〖美〗刑事案件中之公設辯護律師。
public domain (美國的) 國有土地。***in the public domain*** (著作、發明物等因無版權或專利權保護)爲公衆所共有。
public enemy 公敵。
public health 公共衞生。
public house ①〖英〗酒店。②客棧。
public housing 〖美〗市政府等爲低收入者所建造之房屋。
public indecency 公然猥褻罪。
public international law 國際公法。
pub·li·cist 〔'pʌblɪsɪst; 'pʌblisist〕 *n.* ①公法學家;國際法學家。②政論家;時事評論家;政論作家。③宣傳人員;公共關係人員。
*__pub·lic·i·ty__ 〔pʌb'lɪsətɪ; pʌb'lisiti〕 *n.* ①招引大家注意;出風頭。an actress who seeks (avoids) *publicity*. 一位想要 (避免) 出風頭的女演員。②引大家注意之手段;廣告;宣傳。to give a new car wide *publicity*. 對新車廣事宣傳。③當衆公開的場面。
pub·li·cize 〔'pʌblɪ,saɪz; 'pʌblisaiz〕 *v.t.,* **-cized, -ciz·ing.** 宣揚;引人注意;廣爲宣傳。
public land 公有土地。
public law 公法;國際公法。
*__pub·lic·ly__ 〔'pʌblɪklɪ; 'pʌblikli〕 *adv.* ①公開地;公然地。They cannot support him *publicly*. 他們不能公開支持他。②由公家。③以社團或公衆名義。
public nuisance 〖法律〗妨害公益之人或物。
public opinion 輿論。
pub·lic-o·pin·ion poll 〔'pʌblɪkə'pɪnjən~; 'pʌblikə'pinjən~〕 民意測驗;民意調查。
public prints 報章雜誌。
public prosecutor 檢察官。
public relations 公共關係; 公司、機關等利用報章、雜誌、廣播或電影等宣揚其目的、政策以獲得有利的輿論之活動。
public school ①〖美〗公立學校 (包括小學、中學)。②〖英〗有基金的私立寄宿中學。
public servant 公務員;公僕。
public service ①公用設施。②公共服務。③公職。
public speaker 演說家。
pub·lic-spir·it·ed 〔'pʌblɪk'spɪrɪtɪd; 'pʌblik'spiritid〕 *adj.* 對公衆利益熱心的;熱心公務的。—**ness,** *n.*
public television (不播廣告專播文化、知識和教育性節目的) 大衆電視; 非商業性電視。
public works 公共建設;公共工程。
‡**pub·lish** 〔'pʌblɪʃ; 'pʌbliʃ〕 *v.t.* ①出版;發行。The book was *published* in 1953. 這本書是一九五三年出版的。②發表; 公開。—*v.i.* ①出報; 出書。②出版作品。Several firms offered to *publish* for him. 好幾家公司向他建議要出版他的作品。③發表文章;發表著作。—**a·ble,** *adj.*
*__pub·lish·er__ 〔'pʌblɪʃə; 'pʌbliʃə〕 *n.* 出版者;出版公司;發行人。Editorials tend to reflect the views of the *publisher*. 社論有反映發行人意見的傾向。
pub·lish·ing 〔'pʌblɪʃɪŋ; 'pʌbliʃiŋ〕 *adj.* 出版的;出版業的。*publishing* business. 出版業。—*n.* 出版書籍。
pub·lish·ment 〔'pʌblɪʃmənt; 'pʌbliʃmənt〕 *n.* =**publication.**
puce 〔pjus; pju:s〕 *adj.* 深褐色的。—*n.* 深褐色。
puck 〔pʌk; pʌk〕 *n.* ①(P-) 莎士比亞戲劇"仲夏夜夢"中之小精靈。②喜惡作劇之小精靈;惡鬼。③(冰上曲棍球用的)橡膠製圓盤。
puck·a 〔'pʌkə; 'pʌkə〕 *adj.* 〖英印〗①可靠的;純良的。②上等的。③堅牢的。④永久的。
puck·er 〔'pʌkə; 'pʌkə〕 *v.t.* 皺起;折成褶子。—*v.i.* 皺起來; 成褶子; 縮攏。—*n.* ①皺;褶。②〖俗〗困惑;激動。
puck·er·y 〔'pʌkərɪ; 'pʌkəri〕 *adj.* ①易皺的。②皺起的;皺的。
puck·ish 〔'pʌkɪʃ; 'pʌkiʃ〕 *adj.* 喜惡作劇的;頑皮的;淘氣的。—**ly,** *adv.*

puck-like [ˈpʌkˌlaɪk; ˈpʌk-laik] *adj.* =puckish.

pud. puddling.

*__pud·ding__ [ˈpudɪŋ; ˈpudiŋ] *n.* ①布丁(一種甜食)。②一種臘腸。③似布丁之物。④價值;優點。⑤〖航海〗**a.** 使船隻與他物相碰時能減少損傷或震動用的軟墊等物。**b.** 作此等軟墊用的材料(如舊繩、破布等)。

pudding cloth 紮煮布丁之布。

pud·ding-head [ˈpudɪŋˌhɛd; ˈpudiŋ-hed] *n.* 〖俚〗愚鈍者;傻瓜。

pudding stone 〖礦〗礫岩。

pud·ding·y [ˈpudɪŋɪ; ˈpudiŋi] *adj.* 像布丁的。

pud·dle [ˈpʌdl̩; ˈpʌdl] *n., v.,* **-dled, -dling.** —*n.* ①泥坑。②泥漿。③任何液體之小池。—*v.t.* ①攪濁;混凝。②以黏土與沙混凝的泥漿塡補。③精煉(鐵)。④留泥坑於。—*v.i.* ①在泥或汚水中打滾或移動。②排尿;小便。

pud·dler [ˈpʌdl̩ɚ; ˈpʌdl̩ə] *n.* 攪混者;混凝者;煉鐵者;鎔解金屬之攪拌器;煉鐵鎔爐。

pud·dling [ˈpʌdlɪŋ; ˈpʌdl̩iŋ] *n.* 精煉鐵之過程和方法。

pud·dly [ˈpʌdlɪ; ˈpʌdl̩i] *adj.,* **-dli·er, -dli·est.** ①多泥水坑的(道路)。②汚濁的;泥汚的。

pu·den·cy [ˈpjudn̩sɪ; ˈpjuːdənsi] *n.* 害羞;謙遜;羞怯。

pu·den·dum [pjuˈdɛndəm; pjuː-ˈdendəm] *n., pl.* **-da** [-də; -də]. ①女性生殖器官之外部;陰門;女陰。②(*pl.*)(男性或女性之)生殖器。

pudge [pʌdʒ; pʌdʒ] *n.* 〖俗〗矮胖的人或物。

pudg·y [ˈpʌdʒɪ; ˈpʌdʒi] *adj.,* **pudg·i·er, pudg·i·est.** 矮胖的;短而肥厚的。

pueb·lo [ˈpwɛblo; puˈeblou] *n., pl.* **-los.** ①〖美〗美國西南部印第安人之村落;此等村落以石塊或乾磚所建之居室。②(P-)史前即住於美國 New Mexico 及 Arizona 州之此等村落中的印第安人。③任何印第安人村落。④(西班牙美洲之)市鎭或村落。⑤(菲律賓之)市鎭或自治鎭。

pu·er·ile [ˈpjuəˌrɪl; ˈpjuərail] *adj.* 兒童的;稚氣的;不成熟的;膚淺的。 —**ly,** *adv.*

pu·er·il·i·ty [ˌpjuəˈrɪlətɪ; ˌpjuəˈriliti] *n., pl.* **-ties.** ①幼稚;稚氣。②幼稚之言行或思想;孩子之言行等。

pu·er·per·al [pjuˈɝpərəl; pjuˈəːpərəl] *adj.* 分娩的;生產的;因生產而致的。

Puer·to Ri·can [ˌpwɛrtəˈrikən; ˈpwəːtouˈriːkən] ①波多黎各人。②波多黎各(人)的。

Puer·to Ri·co [ˌpwɛrtəˈriko; ˈpwəː-touˈriːkou] 波多黎各(西印度東部一島,屬美國,首府爲 San Juan)。(亦作 **Porto Rico**)

*__puff__ [pʌf; pʌf] *v.i.* ①吹氣;噴出。Smoke *puffed* up out of the locomotive. 烟自火車頭噴出。②噴着烟移動。③喘息。④輕視;蔑視。⑤膨脹;爆開;張開。The chute *puffed* out behind the plane. 降落傘在飛機後面張開。⑥誇張;吹牛。—*v.t.* ①吹噴;噴出。A brisk breeze *puffs* the clouds away. 輕快的微風吹開雲朵。②(頭髮等)成鬆軟的圓團。③過獎;虛獎。④撲(粉)。⑤氣喘吁吁地說。*puff out* 吹熄;使脹。*puff up* 使充滿傲氣。Be not *puffed up*. 不要得意。—*n.* ①吹;噴。②喘息。③(頭髮、羊毛等)鬆軟的圓團。④粉撲。⑤塡塞以棉絮等的墊褥。⑥誇獎;吹噓。⑦(裝有果醬、攪過的奶油等之)點心(俗名"氣鼓")。⑧(鬆脆的)食品;點心。corn *puff*. 玉米花。 ⑨向女性獻慇懃者。—*adj.* ①膨脹的;張開的。②虛獎的;吹噓的。

puff adder 非洲產的一種毒蛇。

puff·ball [ˈpʌfˌbɔl; ˈpʌfbɔːl] *n.* 〖植物〗蘑菌;馬勃菌。

puff box 粉盒。

puff·er [ˈpʌfɚ; ˈpʌfə] *n.* ①吹氣的人或物。②能使身體因呑氣而膨大的魚類。③(拍賣時)抬高價錢者。④吹噓者;誇獎者。

puff·er·y [ˈpʌfərɪ; ˈpʌfəri] *n., pl.* **-er·ies.**①過度的誇張;虛誇。②虛誇的宣傳或廣告。

puf·fin [ˈpʌfɪn; ˈpʌfin] *n.* 海鴨(盛產於北大西洋之寒帶海鳥)。

puff·i·ness [ˈpʌfɪnɪs; ˈpʌfinis] *n.* ①膨脹。②誇張;誇大。③驕慢;自負。④〖醫〗腫脹。

puff-puff [ˈpʌfˌpʌf; ˈpʌfpʌf] *n.* ①抽煙發出的噗噗聲。②〖兒語〗火車。

puff·y [ˈpʌfɪ; ˈpʌfi] *adj.,* **puff·i·er, puff·i·est.** ①膨脹的。②自負的;自大的。③喘息的。④一陣陣吹來的。⑤肥滿的;肥大的。

pug [pʌg; pʌg] *n., v.,* **pugged, pug·ging.** —*n.* ①哈巴狗。②獅子鼻。③狐。④〖英印〗野獸的足跡。⑤〖俚〗拳師;拳擊家(爲 pugilist 之略)。⑥黏土(製陶器材料)。⑦〖英〗小火車頭。—*v.t.* ①搗(黏土);以水合(泥)。②塗(泥);塞(泥);捏(泥土)。③塗灰泥阻止傳音。④追蹤(獵物等)。

pug·ga·ree [ˈpʌgərɪ; ˈpʌgəri] *n.* =**puggree.**

pug·gree [ˈpʌgri; ˈpʌgri] *n.* 印度人遮太陽的頭布。

pugh [pju; pjuː] *interj.* 呸!(表示輕視、憎惡等之聲音)。

pu·gi·lism [ˈpjudʒəˌlɪzəm; ˈpjuːdʒi-lizm] *n.* 拳擊;拳術。

pu·gi·list [ˈpjudʒəlɪst; ˈpjuːdʒilist] *n.* 拳擊家;職業拳師。

pu·gil·is·tic [ˌpjudʒəˈlɪstɪk; ˌpjuːdʒi-ˈlistik] *adj.* 拳擊的;拳擊家的。

pug·na·cious [pʌgˈneʃəs; pʌgˈneiʃəs] *adj.* 好鬥的;喜戰的。—**ness,** *n.* —**ly,** *adv.*

pug·nac·i·ty [pʌgˈnæsətɪ; pʌgˈnæ-siti] *n.* 好鬥;喜爭。

pug nose 獅子鼻;寬而扁的鼻子。

pug-nosed [ˈpʌgˈnozd; ˈpʌgnouzd] *adj.* (有)獅子鼻的。

puis·ne [ˈpjunɪ; ˈpjuːni] *adj.* ①〖法律〗年紀較輕的;職位較低的。②小的。③晚的。—*n.* ①職位較低的人或年紀較輕的人。②〖英〗(資歷較淺的)推事。

pu·is·sance [ˈpjuɪsn̩s; ˈpju(ː)isns] *n.* 〖古、詩〗力量;權力;威勢。

pu·is·sant [ˈpjuɪsn̩t; ˈpjuisnt] *adj.* 〖古、詩〗强有力的;有勢的;有權的;强大的。

puke [pjuk; pjuːk] *v.i. & v.t.,* **puked, puk·ing.** (使)嘔吐;吐出。

puk·ka(h) [ˈpʌkə; ˈpʌkə] *adj.* =**pucka.**

pul·chri·tude [ˈpʌlkrɪˌtjud; ˈpʌl-kritjuːd] *n.* 美麗;悅目。

pul·chri·tu·di·nous [ˌpʌlkrɪˈtju-dn̩əs; ˌpʌlkriˈtjuːdinəs] *adj.* 美麗的;悅目的;漂亮的。

pule [pjul; pjuːl] *v.i.,* **puled, pul·ing.** (嬰兒)低聲哭泣;啜泣;嗚咽。

Pul·itz·er [ˈpjulɪtsɚ; ˈpulitsə] *n.* 普立玆(Joseph, 1847-1911, 美國新聞記者及慈善家,出生於匈牙利)。

Pulitzer Prize 普立玆獎(由普立玆所設,每年一度頒獎給美國新聞、文學、或音樂等方面傑出之作品)。

‡**pull** [pul; pul] *v.t.* ①拉;拖;扯。She *pulled* him by the ear. 她拉着他的耳朵。②拉住。③拔。④扭傷。The runner *pulled* a ligament in his leg. 這賽跑者扭傷了腿筋。⑤划(船)。⑥採;摘。⑦撕碎。⑧裝備…支槳;以…支槳划。The boat *pulls* eight oars.

這船有八支槳。⑨〖俗〗實行;做。Don't *pull* any tricks. 不要耍詐。⑩擊(高爾夫球)使彎向左邊。⑪打出(校樣)。⑫〖俚〗捉;逮捕(人)。⑬故意減低…之力量;抑制。⑭現出;呈現。⑮吸收;吸引。⑯得到;拿到。—*v.i.* ①拉;拖;拉出;拖出。The drawer won't *pull* out. 這抽屜拉不開。②進行(通常指費力者);拖曳而行。③划行。The boat *pulled* for shore. 船划向岸邊。④飲;喝。⑤吸。⑥被拔。⑦吸引人。This ad *pulled* better than any other we have run. 這廣告比我們用過的其他任何一個都吸引人。***pull (a person* or *thing) about*** **a.** 拖拉(一人或一物)。**b.** 虐待;粗魯地對待。***pull a face*** 蹙眉。***pull a fast one*** 欺騙;欺詐;搶先以做利己之事。***pull a horse*** 拉住馬勒,使之在賽馬中不能獲勝。***pull a lone oar*** 獨立進行。***pull a long face*** 拉長臉;表示不高興。***pull apart*** 嚴厲批評;指出錯誤。***Pull devel, pull baker!*** 拔河比賽等鼓勵雙方加油之詞。***pull down*** **a.**〖俚〗賺錢;掙錢。**b.** 拆除;破壞。**c.** 使降低。**d.** 向下拉;拉下。***pull (a person) down*** 使(人)弱。***pull for***〖俗〗協助;幫助。***pull in*** **a.** 勒緊;拉緊。**b.** 抵達。**c.** 逮捕。***pull off*** **a.** 脫掉。**b.**〖俚〗成功地完成一件需要勇氣、大膽或機智的工作。***pull (a thing) off*** 獲得成功。***pull oneself together*** 恢復正常能力、精力等。***pull one's weight*** **a.** 盡應盡之力。**b.** 划船時有效利用自己的重量。***pull out*** **a.** 離開;撤離。**b.** 突然放棄。***pull over*** 停車在路邊。***pull punches*** (參看 **punch**[1])。***pull round*** 復元;康復。***pull (a person) round*** 使痊癒;使康復。***pull someone's leg*** 取笑某人。***pull (up) stakes*** 離開。***pull the wool over someone's eyes*** 欺騙。***pull through*** 度過難關。***pull (a person* or *thing) through*** 使度過難關。***pull together*** 合作;和諧地一起工作。***pull (something) to pieces*** **a.** 扯碎。**b.** 嚴酷批評。***pull (a person* or *thing) up*** 使停止;阻止。***pull up to*** (or ***with***) 追過;越過。***pull wires*** 在幕後影響某人。—*n.* ①拉;拖;扯。He gave a *pull* at the rope. 他將繩一拉。②吃力的動作。③拉手;把手。④一飲。He took a *pull* at the bottle. 他從瓶口飲一口。⑤一吸。⑥〖高爾夫〗向左彎的擊球。⑦〖美俚〗勢力。⑧划船。He went for a short *pull* on the lake. 他到湖上划一會兒船。⑨引力;吸力。⑩有利條件。—**a·ble,** *adj.*

pull·back [ˈpulˌbæk; ˈpulbæk] *n.* ①反動分子。②撤退;撤離。③裁減;緊縮。

pull·down [ˈpulˌdaun; ˈpuldaun] *adj.* 可拆掉或向下拉的。

pull·er [ˈpulɚ; ˈpulə] *n.* ①拉者;拔者。②拉具;拔具。③吸引人之物。

pull·er-in [ˈpulɚˈɪn; ˈpuləˈrin] *n.*〖俗〗(站在小商店、遊戲場等前面)拉客的人。

pul·let [ˈpulɪt; ˈpulit] *n.* 未滿一歲的小母雞。

pul·ley [ˈpulɪ; ˈpuli] *n., pl.* **-leys.** 滑輪;滑車。

pulley block 絞轆。

pul·li·cate [ˈpʌlɪˌket; ˈpʌlikit] *n.* 彩色手巾;做彩色手巾之材料。

pull-in [ˈpulˌɪn; ˈpulin] *n.*〖英〗路邊小飯館;可開車進入購物、用餐、看電影等的地方。(亦作 **pull-up, drive-in**)

Pull·man [ˈpulmən; ˈpulmən] *n.*〖美〗①(火車之)臥車(=Pullman car)。②(有特別舒適的位置之)火車(由發明者 G. M. Pullman, 1831–97, 而得名)。③大型手提箱。

pull·out [ˈpulˌaut; ˈpulaut] *n.* ①書中之特大折頁。②(軍隊等之)撤離。③(飛機)由俯衝後拉成水平的飛行。—*adj.* 可拉出的。

pull·o·ver [ˈpulˌovɚ; ˈpulˌouvə] *n.* 套頭毛衣。—*adj.* 由頭上套下的。

pull-through [ˈpulˌθru; ˈpulθruː] *n.* 鎗筒清掃繩。

pul·lu·late [ˈpʌljəˌlet; ˈpʌljuleit] *v.i.,* **-lat·ed, -lat·ing.** ①發芽;萌芽。②繁殖;增殖。③(教義等)發展。—**pul·lu·la·tion,** *n.*

pull-up [ˈpulˌʌp; ˈpulʌp] *n.* ①拉單槓使下頦與槓平之動作。②=**pull-in.**

pul·mo·nar·y [ˈpʌlməˌnɛrɪ; ˈpʌlmənəri] *adj.* ①肺的;肺部的。②肺狀的。③〖動物〗有肺的;有肺狀器官的。④影響肺的;對肺有害的。⑤患肺病的。***pulmonary artery (vein)*** 肺動(靜)脈。***pulmonary disease*** 肺病。***pulmonary tuberculosis*** 肺結核。

pul·mo·nate [ˈpʌlməˌnet; ˈpʌlmənit] *adj.*〖動物〗①有肺或似肺之器官的。②有肺類的。—*n.* 有肺類動物。

pul·mon·ic [pʌlˈmɑnɪk; pʌlˈmɔnik] *adj.* ①肺的;肺部的。②肺病的。—*n.* ①肺病藥。②肺病患者。

pul·mo·tor [ˈpʌlˌmotɚ; ˈpʌlmoutə] *n.* ①人工呼吸器。②(P-)此種人工呼吸器之商標名。

***pulp** [pʌlp; pʌlp] *n.* ①水果或蔬菜之可食部分;果肉;果漿。the *pulp* of a grape. 葡萄果肉。②〖解剖〗牙髓。③漿。Paper is made from wood *pulp*. 紙是由木漿做成的。④〖俗〗印刷很壞的低級趣味雜誌。⑤柔軟之物。—*v.t.* ①使成漿狀。②取出果肉。③取出齒髓。—*v.i.* 成爲漿狀。

pulp·i·fy [ˈpʌlpəˌfaɪ; ˈpʌlpifai] *v.t.,* **-fied, -fy·ing.** 使成漿狀;使成果肉狀。

pulp·i·ness [ˈpʌlpɪnɪs; ˈpʌlpinis] *n.* 漿狀;果肉狀;柔軟。

***pul·pit** [ˈpulpɪt; ˈpulpit] *n.* ①(教堂之)講壇;說教壇。to occupy the *pulpit*. 講道;布道。②(the-)教士之集合稱;教士職;聖職。③傳教。—**al,** *adj.* —**less,** *adj.*

pul·pit·eer [ˌpulpɪtˈɪr; ˌpulpiˈtiə] *n.*〖蔑〗傳教士;牧師。

pulp·wood [ˈpʌlpˌwud; ˈpʌlpwud] *n.* ①適於做紙漿的材料。②木質紙漿。

pulp·y [ˈpʌlpɪ; ˈpʌlpi] *adj.,* **-i·er, -i·est.** ①果漿的;似果漿的。②果肉的;多肉的。③柔軟的。—**pulp·i·ly,** *adv.*

pul·que [ˈpulkɪ; ˈpulki] *n.* 墨西哥的「龍舌蘭酒。」

pul·sate [ˈpʌlset; pʌlˈseit] *v.i.,* **-sat·ed, -sat·ing.** ①(脈)有規律地跳動;(心臟)跳動;悸動。②〖物理〗脈動。③震動;搖動。

pul·sa·tile [ˈpʌlsətl; ˈpʌlsətail] *adj.* ①悸動的。②敲擊作響的(樂器)。—*n.* 敲擊作響的樂器;打樂器。

pul·sa·tion [pʌlˈseʃən; pʌlˈseiʃən] *n.* ①有規律的跳動;悸動。②〖物理〗脈動。③震動;搖動。—**al,** *adj.*

pul·sa·tor [ˈpʌlsetɚ; ˈpʌlseitə] *n.* ①跳動或悸動之物。②脈搏跳動計。

pulse**[1] [pʌls; pʌls] *n., v.,* **pulsed, puls·ing.** —*n.* ①脈搏。to feel the *pulse*. 診脈。②(有規律之)鼓動;跳動。③情緒;傾向;意向。④生命力。⑤電流之突然增强或減弱。⑥〖電〗脈波;脈衝。stir one's pulses*** 激起某人之感情。—*v.i.* (脈)搏動;鼓動。My heart *pulsed* with excitement. 我的心因興奮而跳動。—*v.t.* 使鼓動;使跳動。

pulse² *n.* 豆類;豆。
pulse-jet engine 〔ˈpʌlsˌdʒɛt～; ˈpʌlsdʒet～〕 間歇燃燒噴射引擎。
pulse·less 〔ˈpʌlslɪs; ˈpʌlslis〕 *adj.* 無脈搏的;無生氣的;不活潑的。
pulse rate 脈搏率。
pulse-tak·ing 〔ˈpʌlsˌtekɪŋ; ˈpʌlsˌteikiŋ〕 *n.* 〖俗〗民意調查。
pul·sim·e·ter 〔pʌlˈsɪmətɚ; pʌlˈsimitə〕 *n.* 〖醫〗脈搏跳動計。
pul·som·e·ter 〔pʌlˈsɑmətɚ; pʌlˈsɔmitə〕 *n.* ①眞空喞筒。②脈搏跳動計。
pul·ver·ize 〔ˈpʌlvəˌraɪz; ˈpʌlvəraiz〕 *v.*, **-ized, -iz·ing.** —*v.t.* ①磨成粉;搗碎;研碎。②粉碎;毀壞。—*v.i.* 成爲粉末;粉碎。(亦作 **pulverise**) —**pul·ver·i·za·tion,** *n.*
pul·ver·iz·er 〔ˈpʌlvəˌraɪzɚ; ˈpʌlvəraizə〕 *n.* ①研碎機;磨碎者。②研磨機。③經常在沙土中打滾的鳥。
pu·ma 〔ˈpjumə; ˈpjuːmə〕 *n., pl.* **-mas, -ma.** ①〖動物〗美洲山豹(產於南美)。②美洲豹之毛皮。
pum·ice 〔ˈpʌmɪs; ˈpʌmis〕 *n., v.,* **-iced, -ic·ing.** —*n.* (亦作 **pumice stone**) (火山熔岩形成之) 輕石;浮石(磨碎後可作擦粉)。—*v.t.* 用輕石磨擦;用輕石清潔之。—**pu·mi·ceous,** *adj.*
pum·mel 〔ˈpʌml; ˈpʌməl〕 *v.t.,* **-mel(l)ed, -mel·(l)ing.** 打;用拳頭連續打。
***pump¹** 〔pʌmp; pʌmp〕 *n.* ①抽水機;喞筒;打氣機;打氣筒。②心臟。The doctor said I had a good *pump.* 醫生說我的心臟情況甚佳。*prime the pump* a. 增加政府開支以刺激經濟。b. 支持或促進某事之推行或改善。—*v.t.* ①用抽水機等汲(水);用打氣筒等打(氣)。to *pump* up a tire (*or* to *pump* air into a tire). 打氣於輪胎。②(如抽水機柄般)上下動。He *pumped* my hand. 他和我握手。③灌入或抽出。④盤詰(消息);追問。⑤使上氣不接下氣;使不能繼續跑。After the race he was all *pumped* out. 賽跑過後他氣喘如牛。—*v.i.* ①使用喞筒;用喞筒抽水。②如喞筒柄般上下移動。③盤問。④跳動。His heart *pumped* hard. 他的心臟跳得很厲害。⑤間歇地噴出。*pump up* a. 極力造出;努力完成。b. 打氣;充氣。
pump² *n.* 一種低跟輕便舞鞋。
pump·a·ble 〔ˈpʌmpəbl; ˈpʌmpəbl〕 *adj.* 可抽汲的;可灌注的。
pum·per·nick·el 〔ˈpʌmpɚˌnɪkl; ˈpumpənikl〕 *n.* 用未篩過之裸麥製的粗麪包。
pump handle ①喞筒柄。②喞筒式握手(手臂動作如喞筒柄者)。
pump house 抽水站。
pump·ing station 〔ˈpʌmpɪŋ～; ˈpʌmpiŋ～〕 抽水站;抽油站。
***pump·kin** 〔ˈpʌmpkɪn, ˈpʌŋkɪn; ˈpʌmpkin, ˈpʌmkin〕 *n.* ①南瓜。②南瓜藤。*some pumpkins* 重要人物或場所。
pumpkin head ①像南瓜的頭(特指剪平頭者)。②清教徒。③愚蠢的人;傻瓜頭。
pump-ox·y·gen·a·tor 〔ˈpʌmpˈɑksədʒəˌnetɚ; ˈpʌmpˈɔksidʒəneitə〕 *n.* 做大手術時用的人工心臟。
pump rod 喞筒桿。
pump room ①(有礦泉處爲公共便利而設之)飲水廳。②(給水處的)喞筒室。
pump·ship 〔ˈpʌmpˌʃɪp; ˈpʌmpʃip〕 *n., v.i.* 〖鄙〗小便。
pump well ①有喞筒之井。②船上之抽水機室。(亦作 **pumpwell**)
pun 〔pʌn; pʌn〕 *n., v.,* **punned, pun·ning.** —*n.* 雙關語;雙關俏皮話;雙關語之戲用。—*v.i. & v.t.* 諧用雙關語;說雙關俏皮話〖on, upon〗. —**ner,** *n.* —**less,** *adj.*
Punch 〔pʌntʃ; pʌntʃ〕 *n.* ①(在傀儡戲 *Punch and Judy* 中)彎鼻駝背之木偶(與其妻Judy專事爭吵)。②英國一種幽默刊物的名字。
***punch¹** 〔pʌntʃ; pʌntʃ〕 *v.t.* ①以拳擊。②趕(牛、羊羣)。③刺;撥。④打;敲。⑤發出;說出。—*v.i.* ①拳擊。②打;敲。When I entered, he was *punching* away at a typewriter. 當我走進時,他正在打字。③拚命苦幹。—*n.* ①擊;打。②〖俗〗有效的力量。This book has a *punch.* 這本書有力量。*pull punches* a. 拳擊時故意不用力。b.〖俗〗有意約束;自加限制;減少某事之力量。
punch² *v.t.* 打洞;鑽孔。*punch in* 用打卡鐘打卡上班。*punch out* 用打卡鐘打卡下班。—*n.* 打洞器;鑽孔器。
punch³ *n.* 酒、水、牛奶等調以砂糖、檸檬、香料等而成之混合飲料。
punch⁴ *n.* (英國 Suffolk地方產的)短小肥胖的馱馬。
punch·board 〔ˈpʌntʃˌbord; ˈpʌntʃbɔːd〕 *n.* 〖美〗一種賭博機器。
punch bowl ①盛混合飲料 punch 的大碗。②山間或山側之窪地;鉢狀盆地。
punch-drunk 〔ˈpʌntʃˌdrʌŋk; ˈpʌntʃˌdrʌŋk〕 *adj.* 因拳擊而腦部受震盪的。
pun·cheon 〔ˈpʌntʃən; ˈpʌntʃən〕 *n.* ①一種容量爲72至 120 加侖之大桶。②此種大桶之容量。③短柱;架柱;支柱。④(用作支撐地板等表面之)短木料。⑤打印器;有尖端之工具。
punch·er 〔ˈpʌntʃɚ; ˈpʌntʃə〕 *n.* ①穿孔者。②穿孔機;打印機。③〖美俗〗＝**cowboy.**
pun·chi·nel·lo 〔ˌpʌntʃəˈnɛlo; ˌpʌntʃiˈnelou〕 *n., pl.* **-los, -loes.** ①義大利傀儡喜劇之主角。②怪誕之人或物;滑稽角色。
punch·ing bag 〔ˈpʌntʃɪŋ～; ˈpʌntʃiŋ～〕 ①(英亦作 **punching ball**) (練習拳擊用的) 內有氣體或塞有軟物的皮袋。②出氣筒;代罪羔羊。
punch-up 〔ˈpʌntʃˌʌp; ˈpʌntʃʌp〕 *n.* 〖英〗〖俗〗大吵大鬧的打羣架。
punch·y 〔ˈpʌntʃɪ; ˈpʌntʃi〕 *adj.* ①有力的。②＝**punch-drunk.**
punc·tate 〔ˈpʌŋktet; ˈpʌŋkteit〕 *adj.* ＝**punctated.**
punc·tat·ed 〔ˈpʌŋktetɪd; ˈpʌŋkteitid〕 *adj.* ①有斑點的。②施於一點的;加在一點的。
punc·til·i·o 〔pʌŋkˈtɪlɪˌo; pʌŋkˈtiliou〕 *n., pl.* **-i·os.** ①(行爲、儀式、手續等之)細節。②拘謹;拘泥形式。
punc·til·i·ous 〔pʌŋkˈtɪlɪəs; pʌŋkˈtiliəs〕 *adj.* ①留心細節的。②拘泥形式的;拘謹的。—**ly,** *adv.* —**ness,** *n.*
***punc·tu·al** 〔ˈpʌŋktʃuəl; ˈpʌŋktjuəl〕 *adj.* ①敏捷的;守時的。Be *punctual.* 要守時間。②點的;具有點的性質的;限於一點的。③仔細的。—**ly,** *adv.* —**ness,** *n.*
punc·tu·al·i·ty 〔ˌpʌŋktʃuˈælətɪ; ˌpʌŋktjuˈæliti〕 *n.* 準時;守時;迅速;敏捷。
punc·tu·ate 〔ˈpʌŋktʃuˌet; ˈpʌŋktjueit〕 *v.t.,* **-at·ed, -at·ing.** ①加標點於;以標點分開。②(以呼喊等)打斷(他人的話)。③加重。
***punc·tu·a·tion** 〔ˌpʌŋktʃuˈeʃən; ˌpʌŋktjuˈeiʃən〕 *n.* ①標點。②標點法。③(以歡呼聲)打斷別人的話。*punctuation marks* 標點符號。—**al,** *adj.*
punc·tu·a·tor 〔ˈpʌŋktʃuˌetɚ; ˈpʌŋktjueitə〕 *n.* 加標點者;用標點者。
punc·ture 〔ˈpʌŋktʃɚ; ˈpʌŋktʃə〕 *n., v.,*

-tured, -tur·ing. —*n.* ①孔;洞。②穿孔的舉動或過程。—*v.t.* ①穿孔;刺穿。②減低;毀掉;毀壞。—*v.i.* 有破孔。

pun·dit ['pʌndɪt; 'pʌndit] *n.* ①印度的學者;梵文學家;精通印度敎哲學及法律之婆羅門人。②〖諧〗博學之人;權威;學者;空談家。

pun·gen·cy ['pʌndʒənsɪ; 'pʌndʒənsi] *n.*①刺激;辛辣。②尖刻。③劇烈;敏銳。④痛切。

pun·gent ['pʌndʒənt; 'pʌndʒənt] *adj.* ①刺激性的;辛辣的。②嚴厲的;酷苛的。③痛切的。④刺激精神的。⑤〖植物〗堅硬而尖銳的。—*n.* 刺激性物質;有辣味的調味品。

pun·gent·ly ['pʌndʒəntlɪ;'pʌndʒəntli] *adv.* 辛辣地;痛切地。

Pu·nic ['pjunɪk; 'pju:nik] *adj.* ①古迦太基 (Carthage) 的;古迦太基人的。②叛逆的;不信實的。—*n.* 古迦太基語。***Punic faith*** 反叛;背信。***Punic Wars*** 羅馬與迦太基間之三次戰役(西元前 264–146 年間,導致迦太基的傾覆)。

pu·ni·ness ['pjunɪnɪs; 'pju:ninis] *n.* 「弱小;微小;不重要。」

***pun·ish** ['pʌnɪʃ; 'pʌniʃ] *v.t.* ①處罰;懲罰。He was *punished* for his crime. 他因犯罪而受懲罰。to *punish* a man with (by) a fine. 處某人以罰金。②嚴厲對付;使痛苦。③鞭策。④〖俗〗消耗;使告罄。—*v.i.* 懲罰。

pun·ish·a·ble ['pʌnɪʃəbl̩; 'pʌniʃəbl] *adj.* 可處罰的;該處罰的。

pun·ish·er ['pʌnɪʃɚ;'pʌniʃə] *n.* 處罰「者;懲罰者。」

***pun·ish·ment** ['pʌnɪʃmənt; 'pʌniʃmənt] *n.* ①懲罰;處罰;刑罰。The *punishment* for murder is death. 殺人者處死刑。②痛苦;損失。③嚴厲的對待。

pu·ni·tive ['pjunətɪv; 'pju:nitiv] *adj.* ①處罰的;懲罰的;刑罰的。*punitive* justice. 因果報應。②討伐的。*punitive* force. 征討軍;討伐軍。—**ly,** *adv.* —**ness,** *n.*

pu·ni·to·ry ['pjunəˌtorɪ; 'pju:nitəri] *adj.* =**punitive.**

punk [pʌŋk; pʌŋk] *n.* ①(用以燃發煙火等之)引火物。②(用爲引火物之)腐木。③〖俚〗無用廢物;無聊之話。④〖俚〗**a.** 流氓地痞。**b.** 無用之人。**c.** 無經驗之男孩。**d.** 孌童(男子同性戀者之對象)。—*adj.* 〖美俚〗無用的;壞的;沒價值的。

pun·ka(h) ['pʌŋkə; 'pʌŋkə] *n.* 〖英印〗布風扇(尤指懸於天花板上形似布幕用繩拉動者)。

punk·ie ['pʌŋkɪ; 'pʌŋki] *n.* (美國山「區的)一種小蚋。」

pun·net ['pʌnɪt; 'pʌnit] *n.* 淵淺的平籃(盛水果用者)。

pun·ster ['pʌnstɚ; 'pʌnstə] *n.* 好作「雙關諧語者。」

punt[1] [pʌnt; pʌnt] *n.* ①〖英〗方頭平底小船(以篙撐者)。②〖足球〗手中落下球之一踢。—*v.t.* & *v.i.* ①以篙撐(船)。②踢(手中落下球)。—**er,** *n.*

punt[2] *v.i.* ①(在賭博中)對莊家下賭注。②(在賽馬中)對一馬下重賭注。③賭博。—*n.* 賭注;賭博。—**er,** *n.*

pun·ty ['pʌntɪ; 'pʌnti] *n., pl.* **-ties.** 處理熔解玻璃時用的金屬棒。

pu·ny ['pjunɪ; 'pju:ni] *adj.,* **-ni·er, -ni·est.** ①形狀小的;軟弱的。②細微的;不重要的。

pup** [pʌp;pʌp] *n., v.,* **pupped, pup·ping.** —*n.* ①小狗;幼犬。②幼狐、小狼、小海豹等。③傲慢自負的年輕人。④〖俗〗學生 (pupil 之略語)。⑤好看而不中用之物。sell a man a pup*** 在交易中欺騙某人。—*v.i.* 生幼犬等。

pu·pa ['pjupə; 'pju:pə] *n., pl.* **-pae** [-pi;-pi:], **-pas.** 蛹。

pu·pal ['pjupl̩; 'pju:pəl] *adj.* 蛹的。

‡**pu·pil** ['pjupl̩;'pju:pl] *n.* ①學生。②〖法律〗被監護人。③瞳孔;瞳仁。—**less,** *adj.*

pu·pil·(l)age ['pjuplɪdʒ; 'pju:pilidʒ] *n.* ①學生的身分;學生的時期。②幼者身分;幼時。③未成熟或未開化之狀態;學習階段。

pu·pil·lar·y ['pjupəˌlɛrɪ; 'pju:piləri] *adj.* ①學生的;生徒的。②被監護人的。③〖解剖〗瞳孔的。

pupil teacher 小先生(小學中敎低年「級學生的高年級學生)。」

***pup·pet** ['pʌpɪt; 'pʌpit] *n.* ①木偶。*puppet* show. 木偶戲。②傀儡。a *puppet* government. 傀儡政權。

pup·pet·eer [ˌpʌpɪ'tɪr; ˌpʌpi'tiə] *n.* 操縱傀儡的人;設計傀儡的人;給傀儡製或穿衣服的人;演傀儡戲的人。—*v.i.* 演傀儡戲。

puppet play 傀儡戲;木偶戲。

pup·pet·ry ['pʌpɪtrɪ; 'pʌpitri] *n., pl.* **-ries.** ①傀儡;木偶(集合稱)。②木偶之動作。③化裝滑稽表演。④耍傀儡戲之技術。

***pup·py** ['pʌpɪ; 'pʌpi] *n., pl.* **-pies.** ①小狗。②小狐、小狼等。③沒有敎養而自大的青年。—**ish,** *adj.*

pup·py·dom ['pʌpɪdəm; 'pʌpidəm] 「*n.* =**puppyhood.**」

pup·py·hood ['pʌpɪhud; 'pʌpihud] *n.* ①幼犬之狀態;幼犬之時期。②青年的自大時期。

pup·py·ism ['pʌpɪɪzm̩; 'pʌpiizəm] 「*n.* 小犬之性格與行爲。」

puppy love 青春期男女間之短暫的愛。

pup tent 露營用三角小帳蓬。

pur [pɝ; pə:] *v., n.* =**purr.**

Pur·beck ['pɝbɛk; 'pə:bek] *n.* 波白克半島(在英格蘭南部,以產大理石著名)。***Purbeck marble*** 波白克半島產之石灰石(似大理石的建築材料)。***Purbeck stone*** 波白克半島產之硬石灰石。

pur·blind ['pɝˌblaɪnd;'pə:blaind] *adj.* ①半盲的;近視的。②遲鈍的;愚笨的。③〖古〗全盲的。—**ly,** *adv.* —**ness,** *n.*

pur·chas·a·ble ['pɝtʃəsəbl̩; 'pə:tʃəsəbl] *adj.* ①可購買的;可買到的。②可賄買的。

‡**pur·chase** ['pɝtʃəs, -ɪs; 'pə:tʃəs, -is] *v.,* **-chased, -chas·ing,** *n.* —*v.t.* ①購買。②換得;獲得。③〖航海〗藉機械舉起(錨等)。—*n.* ①購買。He has made a good *purchase*. 他以公道的價格買得。②購得之物。③緊束;緊纏。④(每年的)收益;價值。⑤〖機械〗擴力裝置。⑥利益;獲利的手段。⑦土地年租;土地每年收益。⑧纏力;固着力。—**pur·chas·er,** *n.*

pur·chase·less ['pɝtʃəslɪs; 'pə:tʃəslis] *adj.* 無束力的;無纏力的。

purchase tax 〖英〗消費品零售稅。

purchasing power 購買力。

pur·dah ['pɝdə; 'pə:dɑ:] *n.* 〖英印〗①帳;簾(特指在印度爲使婦女避人注視而設者)。②深閨制度(印度上流婦女蟄居內室之制度)。

‡**pure** [pjur; pjuə] *adj.,* **pur·er, pur·est,** *n.* —*adj.* ①純粹的。*pure* gold. 純金。②清潔的。③完美的;正確的。She speaks *pure* French. 她操正確的法語。④僅僅的;全然的。It is a *pure* accident. 這完全是一個意外。⑤純潔的;貞潔的。⑥抽象的;理論的。*pure* mathematics. 理論數學。⑦血統純粹的。***pure and simple*** 完全的;絕對的。—*n.* 純潔的東西。—**ness,** *n.*

pure·bred ['pjurˌbrɛd;'pjuəbred] *adj.* 純種的。—*n.* 純種家畜或家禽。

pu·rée [pju're; 'pjuərei] *n., v.,* **-réed, -ré·ing.** —*n.* 濃湯;將果、菜等搗碎過濾煮成之濃湯。—*v.t.* 將(菜、果)煮成濃湯。

Pure Land 〖佛教〗淨土;西方極樂世界。
***pure·ly** [ˈpjurlɪ; ˈpjuəli] *adv.* ①純粹地。②天眞地;純潔地。③全然地。It was *purely* accidental. 這完全是偶然的。④僅僅地。⑤〖主方〗非常。
pur·fle [ˈpɝfḷ; ˈpəːfl] *v.*, **-fled, -fling,** *n.* —*v.t.* 加邊飾於;鑲邊於。—*n.* 邊飾;緣飾;毛皮之緣。
pur·ga·tion [pɝˈgeʃən; pəːˈgeiʃən] *n.* ①洗罪。②洗滌;清除;整肅。③(吃瀉藥)淨腸。④洗寃;證明無罪。
pur·ga·tive [ˈpɝgətɪv; ˈpəːgətiv] *n.* 〖醫〗瀉藥。—*adj.* ①能通便的;致瀉的。②能清除的。③洗罪的;滌罪的。
pur·ga·to·ri·al [ˌpɝgəˈtorɪəl; ˌpəːgəˈtɔːriəl] *adj.* ①煉獄的。②贖罪的。
pur·ga·to·ry [ˈpɝgəˌtorɪ; ˈpəːgətəri] *n.*, *pl.* **-ries.** ①(天主教)滌罪所;煉獄。②暫時受難或受懲的處所或狀態。③受罪;活受罪。
***purge** [pɝdʒ; pəːdʒ] *v.*, **purged, purg·ing,** *n.* —*v.i.* & *v.t.* ①清除;洗滌。to *purge* the mind from false notions. 清除心中之謬見。②洗罪;滌罪。his attempt to *purge* himself of a charge of heresy. 他之欲洗脫自己被控異端的企圖。③整肅;排除國內或黨內的異己分子。④使瀉;通大便。—*n.* ①洗滌;洗罪。②整肅。③瀉劑;瀉藥。—**a·ble,** *adj.*
purg·ee [pɝˈdʒi; pəːˈdʒiː] *n.* 被整肅者。
purg·er [ˈpɝdʒɚ; ˈpəːdʒə] *n.* ①清除者;洗滌者。②整肅者。③瀉劑。
pu·ri·fi·ca·tion [ˌpjurəfəˈkeʃən; ˌpjuərifiˈkeiʃən] *n.* ①洗滌;洗淨。②齋戒;洗罪。③純化;精鍊。
pu·ri·fi·ca·tor [ˈpjurəfɪˌketɚ; ˈpjuərifikeitə] *n.* 〖宗教〗擦洗聖杯之布巾。
pu·ri·fi·ca·to·ry [pjəˈrɪfɪkəˌtorɪ; ˈpjuərifikeitəri] *adj.* ①淨化的;清滌的。②精製的;精煉的。
pu·ri·fi·er [ˈpjurəˌfaɪɚ; ˈpjuərifaiə] *n.* ①淨化者;清滌者;清潔器。②精煉者;精製者。③精煉裝置。
***pu·ri·fy** [ˈpjurəˌfaɪ; ˈpjuərifai] *v.t.*, **-fied, -fy·ing.** ①使清淨。②洗除罪惡;滌除罪過。to *purify* the heart. 滌除心中之罪念。③純化;精煉;除去雜質。
Pu·rim [ˈpjurɪm; ˈpjuərim] *n.* 普珥節(猶太人爲紀念其種族免受 Haman 計畫之屠殺的節日,於每年二月或三月舉行)。
pu·rine [ˈpjurin; ˈpjuriːn] *n.* 〖化〗嘌呤;普林(尿酸化合物之基元)。
pur·ism [ˈpjurɪzəm; ˈpjuərizm] *n.* (語言、風格等)嚴格的或過度的純正或簡練;修辭癖;練語癖;純正的修辭。
pur·ist [ˈpjurɪst; ˈpjuərist] *n.* 力求語文純正之人。
pu·ris·tic [pjuˈrɪstɪk; pjuəˈristik] *adj.* 力求語言或風格嚴正的;好修辭的;有練語癖之人的。
pu·ris·ti·cal [pjuˈrɪstɪkl; pjuəˈristikəl] *adj.* =**puristic.** —**ly,** *adv.*
***Pu·ri·tan** [ˈpjurətn̩; ˈpjuəritən] *n.* ①清教徒(英國十六、七世紀國家教會的一員,主張嚴肅的生活與簡單的宗教儀式)。②(p-)在道德與宗教方面主張嚴肅者。—*adj.* ①清教徒的。②(p-)生活嚴肅的。—**ly,** *adv.*
pu·ri·tan·ic [ˌpjurəˈtænɪk; ˌpjuəriˈtænik] *adj.* =**puritanical.**
pu·ri·tan·i·cal [ˌpjurəˈtænɪkl; ˌpjuəriˈtænikəl] *adj.* ①(P-)清教徒的。②像清教徒的。③嚴謹的;嚴格的。④反對享樂的。
Pu·ri·tan·ism [ˈpjurətn̩ˌɪzəm; ˈpjuəritənizm] *n.* ①清教;清教教義。②(p-)(道德與宗教上的)謹嚴;嚴正。
pu·ri·tan·ize [ˈpjurətn̩ˌaɪz; ˈpjuəritənaiz] *v.t.* & *v.i.*, **-ized, -iz·ing.** (使)清教徒化;(使)改奉清教教義。
***pu·ri·ty** [ˈpjurətɪ; ˈpjuəriti] *n.* ①純潔。②天眞無邪。③純粹。*purity* of style. 風格之純粹。④貞潔;童貞。
purl¹ [pɝl; pəːl] *n.* ①潺潺流水聲。②小渦流。—*v.i.* ①潺潺而流。②起漩渦。
purl² *v.t.* ①以反針法編織。②以鏈狀小環結(花邊)之緣。—*n.* ①編織之反針法;倒織。②花邊之環緣。③刺綉用之金銀面線。④編織之反針。
purl·er [ˈpɝlɚ; ˈpəːlə] *n.* 〖主英〗墜落。
pur·lieu [ˈpɝlu; ˈpəːljuː] *n.* ①森林邊緣外之空地。②外緣部分。③(*pl.*)近郊。④常往之地。⑤(*pl.*)範圍。⑥〖英史〗劃入皇家林地後復歸還私有之土地。
pur·lin(e) [ˈpɝlɪn; ˈpəːlin] *n.* 〖建築〗平行桁條。
pur·loin [pɝˈlɔɪn; pəːˈlɔin] *v.t.* & *v.i.* 偷竊。—**er,** *n.*
pur·ple** [ˈpɝpḷ; ˈpəːpl] *n., adj., v.*, **-pled, -pling.** —*n.* ①紫色。②深紅色。③紫布;紫衣;紫袍(特指帝王等所穿的)。④皇族;貴族。be born in*** (or ***to***) ***the purple*** 生於皇室(或貴族)。***the purple*** 帝王或樞機主教所穿之紫袍;帝王或樞機主教階級。—*adj.* ①紫色的。to become *purple* with rage. 面孔氣得發紫。②深紅色的。③帝王的;皇家的。④華麗的。*purple* prose. 風格華麗的散文。⑤刺激的。—*v.t.* 使呈紫色。—*v.i.* 變成紫色。—**ness,** *n.*
pur·plish [ˈpɝplɪʃ; ˈpəːpliʃ] *adj.* 略帶紫色的。
pur·ply [ˈpɝplɪ; ˈpəːpli] *adj.* =**purplish.**
pur·port [*n.* ˈpɝport; ˈpəːpət *v.* pɚˈport; ˈpəːpət] *n.* ①意義;主旨。②目的;企圖;目標。—*v.t.* ①聲稱。②〖罕〗意指;意謂。
‡pur·pose [ˈpɝpəs; ˈpəːpəs] *n., v.*, **-posed, -pos·ing.** —*n.* ①目的;意向;宗旨。What was your *purpose* in coming here? 你來此的用意何在? ②決心;果斷力。***of set purpose*** 蓄意地。***on purpose*** 故意地。***to little*** (***no***) ***purpose*** 幾乎(毫)無結果;幾乎(毫)無收穫。***to some purpose*** 有點結果;有些收穫。***to the purpose*** 得要領;切題;合乎目的。—*v.t.* 計劃;意欲;企圖。They *purpose* a further attempt. 他們欲做進一步的嘗試。
pur·posed·ly [ˈpɝpəstlɪ; ˈpəːpəstli] *adv.* 蓄意地;故意地 (=purposely).
pur·pose·ful [ˈpɝpəsfəl; ˈpəːpəsfəl] *adj.* ①有目的的;故意的;蓄意的。②有意義的;意味深長的;重要的。③果斷的。—**ly,** *adv.* —**ness,** *n.*
pur·pose·less [ˈpɝpəslɪs; ˈpəːpəslis] *adj.* ①沒有確定目標的;沒有決斷力的(人)。②沒有目的的(行動);沒有意義的。③無益的;無用的。—**ly,** *adv.* —**ness,** *n.*
pur·pose·ly [ˈpɝpəslɪ; ˈpəːpəsli] *adv.* ①蓄意地;故意地。②專爲;爲某種目的。
pur·pos·ive [ˈpɝpəsɪv; ˈpəːpəsiv] *adj.* ①有目的的;合於目的的。②決斷的;果斷的(人)。
pur·pu·ric [pɝˈpjurɪk; pəːˈpjuərik] *adj.* ①〖醫〗紫斑的;紫斑狀的;有紫斑的。②紫的;紫色的。
***purr** [pɝ; pəː] *v.i.* ①(貓等)作嗚嗚叫的聲音。②發出低而愉快的聲音。—*v.t.* 高興而低聲地說出。She *purred* her approval. 她高興地道出她的贊同。—*n.* 嗚嗚叫的聲音。(亦作 **pur**) —**er,** *n.* —**ing·ly,** *adv.*
pur sang [pyrˈsɑ̃; pyrˈsɑ̃ː] 〖法〗①純血

的；純種的。②純然的；眞正的。He is a militarist *pur sang*. 他是個地道的軍國主義者。

purse** 〔pɝs; pəːs〕 *n.*, *v.*, **pursed, purs·ing.** —*n.* ①錢袋。You cannot make a silk *purse* out of a sow's ears. (諺)母猪耳朵做不出絲質錢袋；瓜藤上長不出茄子。②金錢。Who holds the *purse* rules the house. (諺)有錢就有勢。③一筆錢。a common purse*** 共同基金。***a light purse*** 貧窮。***a long purse*** 財富。***make up a purse*** 爲慈善事業募捐。***open one's purse*** 解囊。***put up a purse*** 捐獎金(給比賽等)。—*v.t.* ①使皺縮；抽緊。She *pursed* up her lips. 她撅着她的嘴唇。②放進錢袋。

purse bearer ①會計員。②〖英〗儀式中的捧璽官。

purse·ful 〔ˈpɝsful; ˈpəːsful〕 *n.* 滿袋；一袋。

purse-proud 〔ˈpɝsˌpraud; ˈpəːspraud〕 *adj.* 以富驕人的。

purs·er 〔ˈpɝsɚ; ˈpəːsə〕 *n.* (商船上之)事務長；(軍艦上之)軍需官。—**ship,** *n.*

purse seine 捕魚用袋網。(亦作 **purse net**)

purse strings ①抽合錢袋口的繩索。②支配金錢的權力。③財政。***control*** (or ***hold***) ***the purse strings*** 控制金錢開支。***loosen the purse strings*** 亂花錢。***tighten the purse strings*** 節省用錢。

pur·si·ness 〔ˈpɝsɪnɪs; ˈpəːsinis〕 *n.* ①喘息。②肥胖。

purs·lane 〔ˈpɝslɪn; ˈpəːslin〕 *n.* 〖植物〗馬齒莧。

pur·su·ance 〔pɚˈsuəns; pəˈsjuːəns〕 *n.* ①(目的之)追求；追踪。②(計畫之)實施；從事。in *pursuance* of one's duties. 履行某人之任務。

pur·su·ant 〔pɚˈsuənt; pəˈsjuːənt〕 *adj.* ①依照的；依循的；遵從的〖to〗。②隨後的。*Pursuant* to his studies he took a job in an office. 他學業完成後在一個機關中找到了一分工作。—*adv.* 依照；符合〖to〗。I have acted *pursuant* to our agreement. 我是按照我們的協定行事。—**ly,** *adv.*

***pur·sue** 〔pɚˈsu, -ˈsɪu; pəˈsjuː, -ˈsuː〕 *v.t.*, **-sued, -su·ing.** ①追捕；追擊。②追逐；追求。to *pursue* pleasure. 尋樂。③繼續。to *pursue* the study of English. 繼續學習英語。④糾纏。⑤永不離開；緊緊追隨。⑥照…而行；沿…而進。

pur·su·er 〔pɚˈsuɚ; pəˈsjuːə〕 *n.* ①追捕者；追逐者。②追求者。

***pur·suit** 〔pɚˈsut, -ˈsjut; pəˈsjuːt, -ˈsuːt〕 *n.* ①追捕；追逐；追求。a dog in *pursuit* of rabbits. 追兔子的狗。②職業；消遣；娛樂。literary *pursuits*. 從事文學著作的生涯。

pursuit plane 〖軍〗驅逐機。

pur·sui·vant 〔ˈpɝswɪvənt; ˈpəːsivənt〕 *n.* ①〖英〗紋章院之屬官。②侍從；從者。③探究者；追究者。

pur·sy[1] 〔ˈpɝsɪ; ˈpəːsi〕 *adj.*, **-si·er, -si·est.** ①因肥胖而喘息的。②肥胖的。

pur·sy[2] *adj.* ①皺起的；有褶子的。②富有的；因富有而驕傲的。

pur·te·nance 〔ˈpɝtɪnəns; ˈpəːtinəns〕 *n.* 〖古〗動物之內臟。

pu·ru·lence 〔ˈpjurələns; ˈpjuərulәns〕 *n.* 化膿；膿汁。

pu·ru·len·cy 〔ˈpjurələnsɪ; ˈpjuərulənsi〕 *n.* =**purulence.**

pu·ru·lent 〔ˈpjurələnt; ˈpjuərulənt〕 *adj.* 化膿性的；充滿膿的；有膿的；流膿的；像膿的。—**ly,** *adv.*

pur·vey 〔pɚˈve; pəˈvei〕 *v.t.* 供給；供應。—*v.i.* 供應；供給〖for〗。

pur·vey·ance 〔pɚˈveəns; pəˈveiəns〕 *n.* ①供應；供給。②供應的糧食。③〖英史〗帝王對平民之糧食或勞役之征購權。

pur·vey·or 〔pɚˈveɚ; pəˈveiə〕 *n.* ①供應糧食者；承辦伙食者。②〖英史〗糧食徵購商。

pur·view 〔ˈpɝvju; ˈpəːvjuː〕 *n.* ①法令之條款；本文(對序文而言)；要項。②(法令、文書、題目等之)範圍；(活動的)範圍。③視界；識界。

pus 〔pʌs; pʌs〕 *n.* 膿。

Pu·sey 〔ˈpjuzɪ; ˈpjuːzi〕 *n.* 蒲賽(Edward Bouverie, 1800–1882, 英國神學家)。

Pu·sey·ism 〔ˈpjuzɪˌɪzəm; ˈpjuːziizm〕 *n.* 〖宗教〗蒲賽主義；牛津運動。

Pu·sey·ite 〔ˈpjuzɪˌaɪt; ˈpjuːziait〕 *n.* 信仰蒲賽主義者；參與牛津運動者。

‡push 〔puʃ; puʃ〕 *v.t.* ①推；衝。*Push* the door; don't pull. 請推門，不要拉。②用力前進；擠。to *push* one's way through a crowd. 自人羣中擠出。③使進行；推進。He *pushed* his plan cleverly. 他巧妙地進行他的計畫。④用力插入。⑤驅策；催迫；力求。to *push* one's claims. 強行要求。⑥擴展。⑦(數目等)將達。—*v.i.* ①用力前進；擠進。What a crowd! Can you *push* by? 好多人呀！你能擠過去嗎？②推；衝。③推行運動；極力活動。④被推。The door *pushed* open. 門被推開。⑤突出；伸出。***be pushed for*** 困於…。***push along*** (or ***forward***) 繼續前進；急進。***push around*** 向…作威作福。***push*** (***up***) ***daisies*** 〖俚〗死而被埋；完蛋。***push off*** 〖俗〗出發；離開。***push on*** **a.** 費力地前進。**b.** 趕快完成。***push one's luck*** 做輕率的冒險。***push one's way*** **a.** 排路前進。**b.** 奮力成功。—*n.* ①推。Give the door a *push*. 推一下門。②堅決的前進。to make a *push*. 奮發；猛攻。③〖俗〗力量；能力。He hasn't enough *push* to succeed as a salesman. 他沒有做推銷員的能力。④危急。at a *push*. 在危急之秋。⑤攻勢。⑥羣。⑦〖澳俚〗一羣流氓。***get the push*** 〖俚〗被解雇。

push·ball 〔ˈpuʃˌbɔl; ˈpuʃbɔːl〕 *n.* ①推球戲(將直徑六英尺之大球推入對方球門的遊戲)。②推球戲中所用之球。

push bike 〖俗〗自行車。(亦作 **push-bike**)

push button 開閉電流之按鈕。

push-but·ton 〔ˈpuʃˌbʌtn̩; ˈpuʃˌbʌtn〕 *adj.* 按鈕操作的。*push-button* war. 按鈕操作的戰爭。

push·cart 〔ˈpuʃˌkart; ˈpuʃkaːt〕 *n.* 手推車。a self-service *pushcart* in the supermarket. 超級市場中之自助手推車。

push·er 〔ˈpuʃɚ; ˈpuʃə〕 *n.* ①推擠之人或物。②推進式飛機(推進器裝於引擎之後者)。③行動積極者。④〖俗〗販賣毒品者。

push·ful 〔ˈpuʃfəl; ˈpuʃful〕 *adj.* 〖俗〗①奮發的；有進取心的；有精力的。②强求的。

push·ing 〔ˈpuʃɪŋ; ˈpuʃiŋ〕 *adj.* ①推的；推進的。②進取的；有精神的；活潑的。③闖入的；好事的。—**ly,** *adv.* —**ness,** *n.*

Push·kin 〔ˈpuʃkɪn; ˈpuʃkin〕 *n.* 普希金(Aleksander Sergeevich, 1799–1837, 俄國詩人)。

push-o·ver 〔ˈpuʃˌovɚ; ˈpuʃˌouvə〕 *n.* 〖俚〗①易完成的事物；閒差事。②易被擊敗、說服、勸誘的(一羣)人；弱敵。③飛機俯衝之開始。

push·pin 〔ˈpuʃˌpɪn; ˈpuʃpin〕 *n.* 圖釘。

push-pull 〔ˈpuʃˈpul; ˈpuʃˈpul〕 〖電〗 *adj.* 推挽式的。—*n.* 推挽式連接。

Push·to, Push·tu 〔ˈpʌʃtu; ˈpʌʃtuː〕

n. 帕圖語(阿富汗之主要語言)。

push-up, push·up [ˈpuʃˌʌp; ˈpuʃʌp] *n.* 伏地挺身。

pu·sil·la·nim·i·ty [ˌpjusl̩əˈnɪmətɪ; ˌpjuːsiləˈnimiti] *n.* 膽怯;懦弱。

pu·sil·lan·i·mous [ˌpjusl̩ˈænəməs; ˌpjuːsiˈlænimәs] *adj.* 懦弱的;膽怯的;無勇氣的。

puss[1] [pus; pus] *n.* ①貓(暱稱或兒語)。②「淘氣的小女孩。③〖英〗野兔。」

puss[2] *n.* 〖俚〗①臉。②嘴。

***puss·y**[1] [ˈpusɪ; ˈpusi] *n., pl.* **puss·ies.** ①小孩對貓之暱稱 (=pussycat). ②〖俗〗毛茸茸而柔軟之物(如柳絮等)。③兒童棒擊小木橛之遊戲。④用於此種遊戲中之小木橛。

pus·sy[2] [ˈpʌsɪ; ˈpʌsi] *adj.* 有膿的;似膿的;多膿的。

puss·y·cat [ˈpusɪˌkæt; ˈpusikæt] *n.* 「貓(= pussy).」

puss·y·foot [ˈpusɪˌfut; ˈpusifut] *v.i.* 〖俚〗①如貓般悄悄而行;潛行。②謹愼行事;模稜兩可地不表示明確態度。 —*n.* 〖俚〗①潛行者。②行事審愼者。③禁酒者。—*adj.* ①行事審愼的。②主張禁酒的;禁酒主義的。—**er,** *n.*

pus·tu·lant [ˈpʌstʃələnt; ˈpʌstʃələnt] *adj.* 使長膿皰的。—*n.* 刺激膿皰生長之物。

pus·tu·lar [ˈpʌstʃələ˞; ˈpʌstjulə] *adj.* (多)膿皰的;有膿皰性質的。

pus·tu·late [ˈpʌstʃəˌlet; ˈpʌstjuleit] *v.,* **-lat·ed, -lat·ing,** *adj.* —*v.t.* & *v.i.* 生膿皰;形成膿皰。—*adj.* ①膿皰的;生膿皰的。②〖植物〗有小隆起物的。

pus·tu·la·tion [ˌpʌstʃəˈleʃən; ˌpʌstjuˈleiʃən] *n.* ①起膿皰;生膿皰。② =**pustule.**

pus·tule [ˈpʌstʃul; ˈpʌstjuːl] *n.* ①〖生理〗膿皰。②任何似膿皰之隆起。

pus·tu·lous [ˈpʌstʃuləs; ˈpʌstjuləs] *adj.* =**pustular.**

‡put[1] [put; put] *v.,* **put, put·ting.** —*v.t.* ①放;安置。Where did you *put* my hat? 你把我的帽子放在何處? ②使成某種狀態或關係。*Put* the children to bed. 使孩子們去睡。③說明;表白;簽署。A teacher should *put* things clearly. 一個教員應當講解清楚。④安裝;供應。to *put* a new handle to a knife. 給一把刀子裝一新柄。⑤提出。He *put* several questions before me. 他向我提出幾個問題。⑥課稅。⑦擲;投(十六磅鉛球等)。⑧估計;估量。He *puts* the distance at five miles. 他估計那距離有五英里。⑨應用。A doctor *puts* his skill to good use. 醫生善用其技術。⑩使向某特定方向進行。⑪使從事某種職業。to *put* a boy to shoemaking. 讓一個男孩去學做鞋。⑫翻譯。Can you *put* this poem into English? 你能將這首詩翻成英文嗎? ⑬賭。—*v.i.* ①(船)駛向;前進。The ship *put* out to sea. 船向大海駛去。②〖植物〗發芽。***put about*** a. 改變…之航路;改變方向。b. 傳說。c. 使不便;帶給…麻煩。d. 使悲痛;使張惶失措。 ***put across*** 〖俗〗a. 完成。b. 使被接受;使被了解。***put all one's eggs in one basket*** 孤注一擲。***put an end to*** 結束。 ***put aside*** a. 放在一旁。b. 儲蓄。c. 擱置;留待以後做。***put a stop to*** 停止;使不能繼續進行。 ***put away*** a. 貯存;儲蓄。b. 收拾整齊。c. 〖俗〗送入瘋人院;送入監獄;擺脫開;抵押。d. 〖俚〗吃;飲。e. 置諸腦後。f. 駛去。 ***put back*** a. 放回原處。b. 撥回。c. 阻礙;阻止。***put by*** a. 儲蓄。b. 躲避;廻避;忽視。 ***put down*** a. 放下。b. 平靖;鎮壓。c. 寫。d. 減縮。e. 表示決心。f. 買;儲藏。g. 制止;遏止。h. 降低地位。i. 認爲;估計。j. 歸於;諉於。***put forth*** a. 長出;發出。b. 使用;盡力。c. 使流行;發行。d. 發表。e. 出發;啓程。***put forward*** a. 提示;提出;建議。b. 推舉。c. 撥快(鐘針)。***put heads together*** 商談;會商。***put in*** a. 任命;使任職;使就職。b. 提出要求;提出證件。c. 做;實行。d. 度過(時間)。e. 進入;駛入;停泊。f. 申請。***put in an appearance*** 露面;出席。 ***put in a word for*** 爲…說句好話。 ***put in black and white*** 記下來;寫下來。***put in for*** a. 請求;申請。b. 做…候選人。***put in motion*** 使動。***put in order*** 按…次序排列;排列整齊。***put in shape*** 使康復;使健康。 ***put into practice*** 實行;實施。***put into words*** 以語言文字表示。***put in*** (or ***into***) ***use*** 應用。***put off*** a. 延期。b. 推脫;推諉;推辭。c. 妨礙;說服使放棄;挫折。 d. 除掉;剷除;消除。e. 出發。***put on*** a. 穿;戴(帽等)(爲 take off 之對)。b. 假裝;僞裝;裝出。c. 增加。***put one in mind of*** 使想起;使憶起。***put one on his feet*** 使站穩;使站住。***put one on to*** 使某人注意;對…引起某人之注意。***put oneself out*** 努力;費神。***put one's finger on*** 找到;判定。***put one's hand to*** 表現技術;能動手做。***put one through one's pace*** 試驗某人的能力。***put one wise*** 使某人知道最近的消息;使知悉。***put out*** a. 熄。b. 逐出。c. 使迷惑;使憂傷。d. 脫臼。e. 給予在家中做的工作。f. 放利息。g. 伸出。h. 生產;製造。i. 航行。j. 〖棒球等〗刺殺;使出局。k. 發行;發表。***put out of action*** 使無用;毀壞。***put out of one's head*** 忘記;忘掉。***put*** (***one***) ***out of the way*** 謀殺。***put over*** a. 成功地完成。b. 欺騙;矇蔽。c. 使了解。***put paid to*** 〖英〗抹殺;使化爲烏有。***put something over on*** 〖俗〗占便宜;欺騙。***put the arm on*** 〖俚〗a. 向…要錢。b. 搶奪。***put the bee*** (or ***bite***) ***on*** 〖俚〗向…借錢或拿錢。 ***put the finger on*** 指控。 ***put through*** a. 順利完成。b. 接通(電話)。***put together*** 建立;創造。 ***put to it*** 使遭遇困難;使遇難題。***put to rights*** 加以整頓。***put two and two together*** 作合理推論。***put up*** a. 舉起。b. 呈獻(祈禱等);出賣(貨品)。c. 提高(價格)。d. 建築。e. 供膳宿。f. 擱置(工作)。g. 蜜餞(水果等);醃。h. 收起;藏起。i. 關(店)。j. 包裝。k. 提名…候選人。l. 使(野獸、鳥等)離窩。m. 密謀;陰謀。n. 公布;張貼。o. 得到。p. 自願做。q. 供給;捐獻。***put upon*** 占…之便宜。***put*** (***a person***) ***up to*** a. 通知;警告。b. 鼓動;激動;唆使。***put up with*** 忍耐。***stay put*** 〖俗〗保持原位。

put[2] [pʌt; pʌt] *v., n.* =**putt.**

pu·ta·men [pjəˈtemən; pjuːˈteimən] *n., pl.* **-tam·i·na** [–ˈtæmənə; –ˈtæminə]. 〖植物〗硬核。

pu·ta·tive [ˈpjutətɪv; ˈpjuːtətiv] *adj.* 推定的;假定的;想像的。—**ly,** *adv.*

put-down [ˈputˌdaun; ˈputdaun] *n.* ①飛機之降落。②〖俚〗反駁;無禮的回答;有意使人丟臉或難爲情的動作。

put-off [ˈputˌɔf; ˈputɔf] *n.* 延宕;推諉;「託辭;拖延。」

put-on [ˈputˌɔn; ˈputɔn] *adj.* 做作的;假裝的;虛飾的。—*n.* 假裝;虛飾。

put-out [ˈputˌaut; ˈputaut] *n.* 〖棒球〗刺殺(即使對方球員出局)。

pu·tre·fac·tion [ˌpjutrəˈfækʃən; ˌpjuːtriˈfækʃən] *n.* ①腐敗。②腐敗物。

pu·tre·fac·tive [ˌpjutrəˈfæktɪv;

ˌpjuːtriˈfæktiv〕*adj.* ①腐敗的。②使腐敗的。
pu·tre·fy 〔ˈpjutrəˌfaɪ; ˈpjuːtrifai〕 *v.t. & v.i.*, **-fied, -fy·ing.** 致腐;使腐;腐朽。
pu·tres·cence 〔pjuˈtrɛsn̩s; pjuːˈtresns〕 *n.* ①腐爛;腐爛物。②腐敗;墮落。
pu·tres·cent 〔pjuˈtrɛsn̩t; pjuːˈtresnt〕 *adj.* 腐爛的;將腐爛的;腐臭的。
pu·trid 〔ˈpjutrɪd; ˈpjuːtrid〕 *adj.* ①腐朽的;腐爛的。②〖俗〗非常壞的;極令人不快的。
putrid fever 〖醫〗斑疹傷寒。
pu·trid·i·ty 〔pjuˈtrɪdətɪ; pjuːˈtriditi〕 *n.* ①腐爛;腐敗。②腐物。
putrid sore throat 〖醫〗壞疽性喉頭炎。
Putsch, putsch 〔pʊtʃ; putʃ〕〖德〗 *n.* 背叛;反抗;暴動(尤指未成功及小規模的)。
putsch·ist 〔ˈpʊtʃɪst; ˈputʃist〕 *n.* 反抗者;暴動者。
putt 〔pʌt; pʌt〕 *v.t. & v.i.* 〖高爾夫〗小心輕擊(球)入洞中。—*n.* 〖高爾夫〗輕擊之動作。
put·tee 〔ˈpʌtɪ; ˈpʌti〕 *n.* 裹腿;綁腿。
put·ter¹ 〔ˈputɚ; ˈputə〕 *n.* ①置放者。②擲鉛球者。
putt·er² 〔ˈpʌtɚ; ˈpʌtə〕 *n.* 〖高爾夫〗①小心輕擊高爾夫球使它入洞的專用擊球棒。②使用此種球棒的擊球者。
put·ter³ *v.i.* ①無精打采或無目的地工作〖常over, along, around〗。②緩緩而行。③漫無目的地散步。—*v.t.* 虛度〖away〗。—*n.* 無精打采的行動;虛度光陰;緩行。 **—er,** *n.*
put·ter⁴ *v.i.* 砰砰作響;發着砰砰聲前進。
putt·ing green 〔ˈpʌtɪŋ~; ˈpʌtiŋ~〕〖高爾夫〗①穴周二十碼以內之場地(有障礙之處除外)。②穴周之輕擊區域。
put·ty¹ 〔ˈpʌtɪ; ˈpʌti〕 *n., pl.* **-ties,** *v.,* **-tied, -ty·ing.** —*n.* ①(磨光玻璃和金屬用的)錫粉;鉛粉。②灰泥(水與石灰塊所混成,但不加沙者)。③油灰(以亞麻仁油、白堊粉所調製者,用以塡孔或粘着玻璃於窗框)。④鐵油灰(用以接合鐵管者)。⑤易受影響之人;易塑之物。⑥淺褐灰色。—*v.t.* 敷以油灰;以油灰接合。
put·ty² *n., pl.* **-ties.** 裹腿;綁腿。
put·ty-col·ored 〔ˈpʌtɪˌkʌlɚd; ˈpʌtiˌkʌləd〕 *adj.* 淺灰色的。
put-up 〔ˈpʊtˌʌp; ˈputˈʌp〕 *adj.* 〖俗〗事先祕密計劃的;與內部人員勾結預謀的。a *put-up* job. 一件預謀的行爲。
put-up·on 〔ˈpʊtəˌpɔn; ˈputəˌpɔn〕 *adj.* 被利用的;被占便宜的。
puz·zle** 〔ˈpʌzl̩; ˈpʌzl〕 *n., v.,* **-zled, -zling.** —*n.* ①難題;難解之事。②(測驗智力之)玩具或問題;謎。a cross-word *puzzle.* 縱橫塡字遊戲。③迷惑;困惑。to be in a *puzzle* about something. 對某事感到迷惑不解。—*v.t.* ①使迷惑;使困惑;使難解。He was *puzzled* how to act. 他不知如何才好。②使苦思。He *puzzled* his brains to find the answer. 他絞盡腦汁以求答案。—*v.i.* ①困惑;不解。②思索。③胡亂尋找。 ***puzzle out 苦思而找出解答;研究出來。
puz·zle·head·ed 〔ˈpʌzl̩ˈhɛdɪd; ˈpʌzlˈhedid〕 *adj.* 頭腦不清的;思想混亂的。
puz·zle·ment 〔ˈpʌzl̩mənt; ˈpʌzlmənt〕 *n.* ①困惑;迷惘。②令人困惑之事;令人迷惘之事。
puz·zle·pat·ed 〔ˈpʌzl̩ˈpetɪd; ˈpʌzlˈpeitid〕 *adj.* =**puzzleheaded.**
puz·zler 〔ˈpʌzlɚ; ˈpʌzlə〕 *n.* 令人困惑的人或物;難題。
puz·zling 〔ˈpʌzlɪŋ; ˈpʌzliŋ〕 *adj.* 困惑的;難解的;令人迷惘的。
puz·zling·ly 〔ˈpʌzlɪŋlɪ; ˈpʌzliŋli〕 *adv.* 令人費解地;莫明其妙地。
puz·zlist 〔ˈpʌzlɪst; ˈpʌzlist〕 *n.* 製作謎語者。
PVC 聚氯乙烯 (=polyvinyl chloride).
Pvt. Private. **PW** Prisoner of War.
PWA Public Works Administration.
P.W.B. Psychological War Bureau.
PWD¹, P.W.D. Public Works Department. **PWD²** Psychological Warfare Division. **pwd.** powder.
pwr power. **PX, P.X.** post exchange. 〖美〗軍中販賣部。 **p.x.** please exchange. **pxt.** pinxit (拉=he *or* she painted it).
py·e·li·tis 〔ˌpaɪəˈlaɪtɪs; ˌpaiiˈlaitis〕 *n.* 〖醫〗腎盂炎。—**py·e·lit·ic,** *adj.*
py·e·mi·a 〔paɪˈimɪə; paiˈiːmjə〕 *n.* 〖醫〗膿(毒)血症。
py·e·mic 〔paɪˈimɪk; paiˈiːmik〕 *adj.* 〖醫〗膿(毒)血症的。
pyg·m(a)e·an 〔pɪgˈmiən; pigˈmiːən〕 *adj.* 侏儒的;矮小的。
pyg·my 〔ˈpɪgmɪ; ˈpigmi〕 *n., pl.* **-mies,** *adj.* —*n.* ①(P-)中非洲的小黑人。②矮小的人;侏儒。③任何東西之細小者。④不甚重要的人。—*adj.* ①侏儒的。②很小的;無意義的。
pyg·my·ish 〔ˈpɪgmɪɪʃ; ˈpigmiiʃ〕 *adj.* 矮小的;很小的。
***py·ja·mas** 〔pəˈdʒæməz; pəˈdʒɑːməz〕 *n. pl.* 〖英〗睡衣褲 (=pajamas).
py·lon 〔ˈpaɪlɑn; ˈpailən〕 *n.* ①飛行指標或目標塔。②(古埃及寺院之)塔門。③架高壓電線之鐵塔。④橋樑、馬路等入口處兩側之塔形建築物。⑤機身或機翼上固定引擎、輔油箱、炸彈等之裝置。
py·lo·ri 〔pəˈloraɪ; paiˈlɔːrai〕 *n.* pl. of **pylorus.**
py·lor·ic 〔pəˈlɔrɪk; paiˈlɔːrik〕 *adj.* 幽門(部)的。
py·lo·rus 〔pəˈlorəs; paiˈlɔːrəs〕 *n., pl.* **-ri.** 〖解剖〗幽門;幽門部。
py·o·der·ma 〔ˌpaɪoˈdɝmə; ˌpaiouˈdəːmə〕 *n.* 〖醫〗任何長膿之皮膚病。
py·o·gen·e·sis 〔ˌpaɪəˈdʒɛnəsɪs; ˌpaiəˈdʒenəsis〕 *n.* 生膿;化膿。
py·oid 〔ˈpaɪɔɪd; ˈpaiɔid〕 *adj.* 膿的;似膿的。
Pyong·yang 〔pjʌŋjɑŋ; pjʌŋjɑːŋ〕 *n.* 平壤。
py·or·rh(o)e·a 〔ˌpaɪəˈriə; ˌpaiəˈriə〕 *n.* 〖醫〗膿溢;膿漏;齒槽膿溢。
pyr·a·mid** 〔ˈpɪrəmɪd; ˈpirəmid〕 *n.* ①角錐。②角錐形之物。③〖數學〗錐體;角錐;稜錐。triangular *pyramid.* 三角錐。④結構。the Pyramids*** 埃及金字塔。—*v.i.* 增大;增廣。—*v.t.* 建立。
py·ram·i·dal 〔pɪˈræmədl̩; piˈræmidl〕 *adj.* ①金字塔的;金字塔形的;尖塔的。②角錐形的;角錐的;稜錐的。③〖結晶〗三角錐狀的。④有角錐狀傾斜面的。—*n.* 〖解剖〗稜錐骨。—**ly,** *adv.*
pyramidal bone 〖解剖〗稜錐骨。
pyramidal tent 露營用錐形帳篷。
pyr·a·mid·i·cal 〔ˌpɪrəˈmɪdɪkl̩; ˌpirəˈmidikəl〕 *adj.* 尖塔狀的;角錐狀的;錐形的。(亦作 **pyramidic**)
pyr·a·mid·i·on 〔ˌpɪrəˈmɪdɪɑn; ˌpirəˈmidiɔn〕 *n.* 小金字塔。
pyr·a·mid·wise 〔ˈpɪrəmɪdˌwaɪz; ˈpirəmidwaiz〕 *adv.* 成尖塔狀地;成角錐狀地。
pyre 〔paɪr; paiə〕 *n.* ①一堆木料或其他易燃物。②火葬時用的柴堆。
Pyr·e·nees 〔ˈpɪrəˌniz; ˌpirəˈniːz〕 *n.* 庇里牛斯山(在法國、西班牙兩國邊境)。
py·ret·ic 〔paɪˈrɛtɪk; paiˈretik〕 *adj.* ①熱病的;引起熱病的;發熱性的。②熱病治療的。

—*n.* 〖罕〗熱病藥;退熱藥。
pyr·e·tol·o·gy 〔ˌpɪrəˈtɑlədʒɪ; ˌpirəˈtɔlədʒi〕 *n.* 熱病學。
pyr·e·to·ther·a·py 〔ˌpɪrətəˈθɛrəpɪ; ˌpirətəˈθerəpi〕 *n.* 發熱療法。
Py·rex 〔ˈpaɪrɛks; ˈpaiəreks〕 *n.* ①一種耐熱玻璃用具的商標名。②(p-)一種耐熱玻璃用具。
py·rex·i·a 〔paɪˈrɛksɪə; paiˈreksiə〕 *n.* 〖醫〗高熱;發熱;熱病。
py·rex·ic 〔paɪˈrɛksɪk; paiˈreksik〕 *adj.* 熱病的;發熱性的。
pyr·he·li·om·e·ter 〔paɪrˌhilɪˈɑmətɚ; paiəˌhiːliˈɔmitə〕 *n.* 太陽熱力計;日溫計。
py·ric 〔ˈpaɪrɪk; ˈpairik〕 *adj.* 燃燒的;與燃燒有關的;由燃燒所引起的。
pyr·i·din 〔ˈpɪrɪdɪn; ˈpiridin〕 *n.* =**pyridine.**
pyr·i·dine 〔ˈpɪrɪˌdin; ˈpiridiːn〕 *n.* 〖化〗吡啶(C_5H_5N,一種無色或淺黃色液體,有刺臭氣味,係蒸餾煤焦油、骨油而得,用做溶媒、酒精變性劑和防腐劑)。
pyr·i·dox·in 〔ˌpɪrɪˈdɑksɪn; ˌpiriˈdɔksin〕 *n.* =**pyridoxine.**
pyr·i·dox·ine 〔ˌpɪrɪˈdɑksin; ˌpiriˈdɔksiːn〕 *n.* 〖生化〗維他命B_6。
pyr·i·form 〔ˈpɪrəˌfɔrm; ˈpirifɔːm〕 *adj.* 梨形的。
py·rite 〔ˈpaɪraɪt; ˈpairait〕 *n.* =**pyrites.**
py·ri·tes 〔pəˈraɪtiz; paiˈraitiːz〕 *n.* ①黃鐵礦(=iron pyrites; fool's gold). ②白鐵礦(=white iron pyrites). ③黃銅礦(=copper pyrites). ④錫鐵礦(=tin pyrites).—**py·rit·ic, py·rit·i·cal, py·ri·tous,** *adj.*
py·ro 〔ˈpaɪro; ˈpaiərou〕 *n.* 〖化〗焦性沒食子酸。
pyro- 〖字首〗①表"火;熱"之義。②〖化〗表"由加熱而得"之義。③〖地質〗表"由熱而形成"之義。
py·ro·e·lec·tric 〔ˌpaɪro·ɪˈlɛktrɪk; ˌpairouiˈlektrik〕 *adj.* (顯示)焦熱電現象的。—*n.* 顯示焦熱電現象之物質。
py·ro·e·lec·tric·i·ty 〔ˌpaɪro·ɪˌlɛkˈtrɪsətɪ; ˌpairouilekˈtrisiti〕 *n.* 焦熱電現象(某些結晶體因溫度變化而生之電極性發展)。
py·ro·graph 〔ˈpaɪrəˌgræf; ˈpairəgrɑːf〕 *n.* 烙畫(以很熱之器具在木、皮等上烙出之圖案)。—*v.t. & v.i.* 畫烙畫;以烙畫術畫。
py·rog·ra·phy 〔paɪˈrɑgrəfɪ; paiˈrɔgrəfi〕 *n.* ①烙畫術。②烙出之畫。
py·ro·gra·vure 〔ˌpaɪrograˈvjur; ˌpairəgrəˈvjuə〕 *n.* =**pyrography.**
py·rol·a·try 〔paɪˈrɑlətrɪ; paiˈrɔlətri〕 *n.* 拜火教;拜火。
py·rol·y·sis 〔paɪˈrɑləsɪs; paiˈrɔlisis〕 *n.* 〖化〗熱解(由熱所引起的分解或化學變化)。
py·ro·man·cy 〔ˈpaɪrəˌmænsɪ; ˈpairomænsi〕 *n.* 火占卜。
py·ro·ma·ni·a 〔ˌpaɪrəˈmenɪə; ˌpaiərouˈmeinjə〕 *n.* 〖醫〗縱火狂;放火癖。
py·ro·ma·ni·ac 〔ˌpaɪrəˈmenɪˌæk; ˌpaiərouˈmeiniæk〕 *n.* 有縱火狂者。—*adj.* 縱火狂的;患有縱火狂的。—**al,** *adj.*
py·rom·e·ter 〔paɪˈrɑmɪtɚ; paiˈrɔmitə〕 *n.* 高溫計;高熱計。
py·ro·pho·bi·a 〔ˌpaɪrəˈfobɪə; ˌpairoˈfoubjə〕 *n.* 恐火症。
py·ro·phor·ic 〔ˌpaɪrəˈfɔrɪk; ˌpaiərəˈfɔrik〕 *adj.* 發火的;自燃的。
py·ro·sis 〔paɪˈrosɪs; paiˈrousis〕 *n.* 〖醫〗胃灼熱。
py·ro·tech·nic 〔ˌpaɪrəˈtɛknɪk; ˌpairouˈteknik〕 *adj.* ①煙火的;如煙火的。②煙火製造術的。③(才智等)炫耀的;動人的;煽動感情的。(亦作 **pyrotechnical**)
py·ro·tech·nics 〔ˌpaɪrəˈtɛknɪks; ˌpairouˈtekniks〕 *n.* ①煙火製造術;煙火使用法。②(用辭等之)炫耀;煽動。
py·ro·tech·nist 〔ˌpaɪrəˈtɛknɪst; ˌpairouˈteknist〕 *n.* 煙火製造者。
py·ro·tech·ny 〔ˈpaɪrəˌtɛknɪ, ˈpɪrə-; ˈpaiəroutekni〕 *n.* ①煙火製造術。②放煙火。
py·ro·tox·in 〔ˌpaɪrəˈtɑksɪn; ˌpairouˈtɔksin〕 *n.* 〖細菌〗熱毒素(一種能使動物發熱之菌毒)。
py·rox·ene 〔ˈpaɪrɑkˌsin; ˈpairɔksiːn〕 *n.* 〖礦〗輝石。
py·rox·y·lin(e) 〔paɪˈrɑksəlɪn; paiˈrɔksilin〕 *n.* 可溶硝棉;綿火藥。
Pyr·rhic 〔ˈpɪrɪk; ˈpirik〕 *adj.* 古代希臘 Epirus 王 Pyrrhus 的。***Pyrrhic victory*** 以重大的犧牲而獲得的勝利。
pyr·rhic 〔ˈpɪrɪk; ˈpirik〕 *n.* ①古希臘之戰舞。②含有兩個短音節或輕讀音節之音步。—*adj.* ①戰舞的。②二短音節之音步的;由二短音節之音步所組成的。
pyrrhic dance 古希臘之戰舞。
Pyr·rho 〔ˈpɪro; ˈpirou〕 *n.* 庇羅(約於紀元前 365–275,希臘懷疑派哲學創始者)。
Pyr·rho·nism 〔ˈpɪrənɪzm; ˈpirənizm〕 *n.* ①Pyrrho 之懷疑學說。②絕對之懷疑論。—**Pyr·rho·nist,** *n.*
Pyr·rhus 〔ˈpɪrəs; ˈpirəs〕 *n.* ①皮拉斯(318–272 B.C.,古希臘 Epirus 國王,295–272 B.C. 在位)。②〖希臘傳說〗Achilles 之子。
Py·thag·o·ras 〔pɪˈθægərəs; paiˈθægəræs〕 *n.* 畢達哥拉斯(約死於 497B.C.,希臘哲學家及數學家)。
Py·thag·o·re·an 〔pɪˌθægəˈriən; paiˌθægəˈri(ː)ən〕 *adj.* 畢達哥拉斯的。—*n.* 信奉畢氏學說者。
Pythagorean proposition (or **theorem**) 〖數學〗畢達哥拉斯定理。
Pyth·i·an 〔ˈpɪθɪən; ˈpiθiən〕 *adj.* 古希臘 Delphi 地方的; Delphi 之 Apollo 神殿的; Apollo 神之女祭司的; Apollo 神的。(亦作 **Pythic**) ***the Pythian*** Delphi 之 Apollo 或其女祭司。
py·tho·gen·ic 〔ˌpaɪθəˈdʒɛnɪk; ˌpaiθəˈdʒenik〕 *adj.* (疾病)由骯髒引起的。(亦作 **pythogenous**)
py·thon 〔ˈpaɪθɑn; ˈpaiθən〕 *n.* ①(P-)〖希臘神話〗Apollo 在 Delphi 附近殺死的巨蛇。②無毒之大蟒。③附體之鬼魂;藉鬼魂附體而作預言之人。
py·tho·ness 〔ˈpaɪθənɪs; ˈpaiθənes〕 *n.* 古希臘 Delphi 地方 Apollo 神之女祭司;女巫。
py·thon·ic[1] 〔paɪˈθɑnɪk; paiˈθɔnik〕 *adj.* 神諭的;預言的。
py·thon·ic[2] *adj.* ①蟒蛇的。②如蟒蛇的。③龐然大物的;巨怪的。
pyx, pix 〔pɪks; piks〕 *n.* ①〖天主教〗聖體容器;聖餅盒。②〖英〗貨幣樣品檢驗箱。***trial of the pyx*** 英國每年舉行一次的硬幣純度及重量檢定。
pyx·id·i·um 〔pɪksˈɪdɪəm; pikˈsidiəm〕 *n., pl.* **-i·a** 〔-ɪə; -iə〕. 〖植物〗蓋果。
pyx·is 〔ˈpɪksɪs; ˈpiksis〕 *n., pl.* **pyx·i·des** 〔ˈpɪksɪˌdiz; ˈpiksidiːz〕. ①小盒或盒狀瓶。②藏珠寶之小箱。③〖植物〗蓋果。

Q

Q or **q** 〔kju; kjuː〕 *n., pl.* **Q's** or **q's.** 英文字母之第十七個字母。「羅馬數字 500。」
Q 〔kju; kjuː〕 *n.* ①Q形之物。②中古時期
Q. ①Queen. ②question. ③quarto. ④quire. **q.** ①quart. ②quarter. ③quarto. ④queen. ⑤query. ⑥quintal. ⑦quire. ⑧quotient. **q. 2h.** 〖處方〗每隔二小時。
Q. and A. question and answer.
Qa·tar 〔'kɑtɑr; 'kɑːtɑː〕 *n.* 卡達（波斯灣之一國, 其首都爲 Doha）。（亦作 **Katar**）
Q.B. Queen's Bench. **Q.B., q.b., qb** 〖足球〗quarterback.
Q-boat 〔'kjuˌbot; 'kjuːbout〕 *n.* 神祕船（第一次大戰末期英國用以誘擊潛艇之僞裝商船）。（亦作 **mystery ship**）
QC, Q.C. ①Quartermaster Corps. ②Queen's Counsel. **Q.E.D.** 〖數學〗quod erat demonstrandum(拉＝which was to be demonstrated). 「冷等)。」
Q fever Q熱（一種熱病, 症狀爲發燒、發
q.h. 〖處方〗每小時。 **q.i.d.** 〖處方〗每天四次。 **QM, Q.M.** Quartermaster.
QMC, Q.M.C. Quartermaster Corps. **QMG, Q.M.G.** Quartermaster-General. **Q.M.S., Q.M. Sgt.** Quartermaster Sergeant.
Qo·mul 〔ko'mul; kou'muːl〕 *n.* 哈密（中國新疆東部一大城）。（亦作 **Hami**）
qr. ①quarter. ②quire. **Q.T.** 〖俚〗quiet. ***on the Q.T.*** 祕密地。 **qt.** ①quantity. ②quart; quarts. **qts.** quarts.
qu. ①quart. ②quarter. ③quarterly. ④quasi（拉 ＝as it were）. ⑤queen. ⑥query. ⑦question.
qua 〔kwe, kwɑ; kwei〕 *adv.* 作爲；以…的資格。 「鳥；未成熟之物。」
quab 〔kwɑb; kwɔb〕 *n.* 尙未生毛的雛
***quack**[1] 〔kwæk; kwæk〕 *n.* 鴨叫聲。—*v.i.* ①作鴨叫；模仿鴨叫。②高聲閒談。
quack[2] *n.* ①庸醫。②任何冒充內行之人；大言不慚之人。—*adj.* ①庸醫的。*quack* doctor. 庸醫。②作僞欺人的。*quack* medicine. 假藥。—*v.i.* 當庸醫。—*v.t.* ①用庸醫之方法或藥物治療。②爲…作誇大宣傳；藉誇大之宣傳出售。
quack·er·y 〔'kwækərɪ; 'kwækəri〕 *n., pl.* **-er·ies.** ①庸醫的醫術；庸醫的治療。②欺騙行爲。
quack-quack 〔'kwæk'kwæk; 'kwæk-'kwæk〕 *n.* ①嘎嘎（鴨叫聲）。②鴨（兒語）。
quack·sal·ver 〔'kwækˌsælvɚ; 'kwæksælvə〕 *n.* 庸醫；江湖郎中。
quack·y 〔'kwækɪ; 'kwæki〕 *adj.*（說話聲）嘎嘎然如鴨叫的。
quad 〔kwɑd; kwɔd〕 *n., v.,* **quad·ded, quad·ding,** *adj.* —*n.* ①〖俗〗方庭；方院。②〖英俚〗牢獄。③〖印刷〗低於活字之鉛塊；空鉛。④〖俗〗四胞胎之一。⑤同類四個之一套或一組。 —*v.t.* 〖印刷〗以空鉛填滿（字行）。—*v.i.* 〖印刷〗被空鉛填滿。 —*adj.*（紙張大小）四倍的。
quad. ①quadrangle. ②quadrant.
quad·ra·ble 〔'kwɑdrəbḷ; 'kwɔdrəbl〕 *adj.*〖數學〗可爲平方的；可爲方形的；可自乘的。
quad·ra·ge·nar·i·an 〔ˌkwɑdrədʒɪ'nɛrɪən; ˌkwɔdrədʒi'nɛəriən〕 *adj.* 四十歲的；四十歲與五十歲間的。—*n.* 四十歲的人；四十歲與五十歲間的人。
Quad·ra·ges·i·ma 〔ˌkwɑdrə'dʒɛsəmə; ˌkwɔdrə'dʒesimə〕 *n.* 四旬節（四旬齋的第一個星期日, 亦稱 Quadragesima Sunday）.
Quad·ra·ges·i·mal 〔ˌkwɑdrə'dʒɛsəmḷ; ˌkwɔdrə'dʒesiməl〕 *adj.* ①四旬節的。②(q-) 連續四十日的（指四旬齋期而言）。
quad·ran·gle 〔'kwɑdræŋgḷ; 'kwɔˌdræŋgl〕 *n.* ①四邊形。②方庭；方院。③方院四邊的建築物。
quad·ran·gu·lar 〔kwɑd'ræŋgjulɚ; kwɔ'dræŋgjulə〕 *adj.* 四邊形的；有四角或四邊的。 —**ly,** *adv.*
quad·rant 〔'kwɑdrənt; 'kwɔdrənt〕 *n.* ①〖幾何〗象限。②象限儀；四分儀。③任何以直交的二直線劃出的一區或一部分。
quad·ran·tal 〔kwɑd'ræntḷ; kwɔ'dræntl〕 *adj.* ①象限的；四分圓的。②象限儀的；四分儀的。

quad·rat 〔'kwɑdrət; 'kwɔdrət〕 *n.* ①〖印刷〗空鉛；嵌塊（塡空白的鉛塊）。②爲研究動植物而劃線標明的長方形或正方形土地。
quad·rate 〔*adj., n.* 'kwɑdrɪt; 'kwɔdrit *v.* 'kwɑdret; kwɔ'dreit〕 *adj., n., v.,* **-rat·ed, -rat·ing.** —*adj.* ①方形的；長方形的。②〖動物〗方骨的。—*n.* ①方形；方形狀；長方形物。②〖動物〗方骨。—*v.t.* ①使一致；使相合。②使成方形。—*v.i.* 適合；一致〖with〗.
quad·rat·ic 〔kwɑd'rætɪk; kwə'drætik〕 *adj.* 〖代數〗二次的。—*n.* 二次方程式。
quadratic equation 二次方程式。
quad·rat·ics 〔kwɑd'rætɪks; kwə'drætiks〕 *n.* 〖數學〗二次方程式論。
quad·ra·ture 〔'kwɑdrətʃɚ; 'kwɔdrətʃə〕 *n.* ①〖數學〗求積。②〖天文〗弦；方照。
quad·rel 〔'kwɑdrəl; 'kwɔdril〕 *n.* ①方形石；方磚；方瓦。②方形草皮。
quad·ren·ni·al 〔kwɑd'rɛnɪəl; kwɔ'dreniəl〕 *adj.* ①每四年一次的。②四年的；四年間的。—*n.* ①一個四年的期間；四年。②每四年發生一次的事。—**ly,** *adv.*
quad·ren·ni·um 〔kwɑd'rɛnɪəm; kwɔ'dreniəm〕 *n., pl.* **-ni·ums, -ni·a** 〔-nɪə; -niə〕. 四年。
quad·ric 〔'kwɑdrɪk; 'kwɔdrik〕 *adj.* 〖數學〗二次的。 —*n.* 〖數學〗二次曲面。
quad·ri·cen·ten·ni·al 〔ˌkwɑdrɪsɛn'tɛnɪəl; ˌkwɔdrisən'teniəl〕 *n.* 四百周年紀念。—*adj.* 四百年的；四百周年的。
quad·ri·cy·cle 〔'kwɑdrəˌsaɪkḷ; 'kwɔdrisaikl〕 *n.* 四輪車。—*adj.* 四輪的。
quad·ri·fid 〔'kwɑdrɪfɪd; 'kwɔdrifid〕 *adj.* 〖植物〗四裂的；四分裂的（葉或瓣）。
quad·ri·ga 〔kwɑd'raɪgə; kwə'driːgə〕 *n., pl.* **-gae** 〔-dʒi; -dʒiː〕. 古羅馬的四馬二輪戰車。
quad·ri·lat·er·al 〔ˌkwɑdrə'lætərəl; ˌkwɔdri'lætərəl〕 *n.* ①〖數學〗四邊形；四角形。②四邊形之地。 —*adj.* ①四邊形的。②有四個關係人的；四方面的；四角的。
quad·ri·lin·gual 〔ˌkwɑdrɪ'lɪŋgwəl; 'kwɔdri'liŋgwəl〕 *adj.* ①用四種語言寫成的。②運用四種語言的；說四種語言的。
qua·dril·lage 〔kwɑ'drɪlɪdʒ; kwə'dri-

lidʒ] *n.* (地圖上的)經緯線。

qua·drille [kwəˈdrɪl; kwəˈdril] *n.* ①由四對組成的方舞。②四對方舞之舞曲。③流行於十八世紀由四人參加之紙牌戲。④大小相同的方格圖樣。—*adj.* 形成許多大小相同之方格的;方眼的。

quad·rilled [kwəˈdrɪld; kwəˈdrild] *adj.* 形成許多大小相同之方格的;方眼的。

quadrille paper 方格紙。

quad·ril·lion [kwadˈrɪljən; kwɔˈdriljən] *n.* ①(美、法為)千萬億(1 後加 15 個零)。②(英、德為) 1 後加24個零。 —*adj.* 達上述數目的。

quad·ril·lionth [kwadˈrɪljənθ; kwɔˈdriljənθ] *adj.* ①第千萬億的。②千萬億分之一的。—*n.* 千萬億分之一。

quad·ri·no·mi·al [ˌkwadrɪˈnomɪəl; ˌkwɔdriˈnoumiəl] *adj.* 【代數】四項的。—*n.* 【代數】四項式。

quad·ri·par·tite [ˌkwadrɪˈpartaɪt; ˌkwɔdriˈpa:tait] *adj.* ①由四部分組成的;可分為四部分的。②由四人或四國形成的。

Q

quad·ri·ple·gi·a [ˌkwadrəˈplidʒɪə; ˌkwɔdrəˈpli:dʒiə] *n.* 【醫】四肢癱瘓。

quad·ri·syl·la·ble [ˈkwadrəˌsɪləbl̩; ˈkwɔdriˌsiləbl] *n.* 四個音節的字。

quad·ri·va·lent [ˌkwadrəˈvelənt; ˌkwɔdriˈveilənt] *adj.* 【化】①四價的。②有四種不同之價的(如錦有 5, 4, 3 及 −3 價是)。

quad·riv·i·al [kwadˈrɪvɪəl; kwɔˈdriviəl] *adj.* ①四條路交會於一點的。②(道路)朝四個方向的。③四科 (quadrivium) 的。—*n.* 四科(算術、幾何、天文、音樂)之任一。

quad·riv·i·um [kwadˈrɪvɪəm; kwɔˈdriviəm] *n., pl.* **-i·ums, -i·a** [-ɪə; -iə]. (中世紀的)四科 (卽算術、幾何、天文、音樂)。

quad·roon [kwadˈrun; kwɔˈdru:n] *n.* 黑人血統占四分之一的人;一白人與黑白混血兒所生的孩子。

quad·ru·ma·nous [kwadˈrumənəs; kwɔˈdru:mənəs] *adj.* 【動物】①四足均可當手用的。②四足皆可當手用之動物 (如猿、猴、狒狒等)的。

quad·ru·ped [ˈkwadrəˌpɛd; ˈkwɔdruped] *n.* 四足獸。—*adj.* 有四足的。

quad·ru·pe·dal [kwadˈrupɪdl̩; kwɔˈdru:pidəl] *adj.* 有四足的;四足獸的。

quad·ru·ple [ˈkwadrupl̩; ˈkwɔdrupl] *adj., adv., n., v.,* **-pled, -pling.** —*adj.* ①四部的。②四倍的;四重的。③【音樂】每小節四拍的。—*adv.* 四拍地。—*n.* 四倍。—*v.t.* 使成四倍;四倍之。—*v.i.* 變成四倍。

quad·ru·plet [ˈkwadrʊˌplɪt; ˈkwɔdruplit] *n.* ①同樣的四個東西組成之一組。②四胞胎中之一個。

quadruple time 四拍子;以每小節四拍為基礎的拍子。

quad·ru·pli·cate [*adj., n.* kwadˈruplɪkɪt; kwɔˈdru:plikit *v.* kwadˈruplɪˌket; kwɔˈdru:plikeit] *adj., v.,* **-cat·ed, -cat·ing,** *n.* —*adj.* ①四倍的;四重的。②四分的(文件)。③相同物中第四的。—*v.t.* 四倍之;四次反覆。—*n.* ①相同四分(文件)中之一。②相同的四分。 —**quad·ru·pli·ca·tion,** *n.*

quad·ru·ply [ˈkwadrʊplɪ; ˈkwɔdrupli] *adv.* 四倍地;四重地。

quae·re [ˈkwɪrɪ; ˈkwiəri] 【拉】 *v.* (祈使語)詢問;查問;疑問;請問。He says he is going to retire, *quaere?* 他說他將退休, 果眞嗎? —*n.* 疑問;問題。

quaes·tor [ˈkwɛstɚ; ˈkwi:stə, -tɔ:] *n.* ①古羅馬的檢察員。②財務官。(亦作 **quaestor**) —**ship,** *n.*

quaff [kwæf; kwa:f, kwɔf] *v.t. & v.i.* 痛飲;暢飲;一飲而盡。—*n.* 痛飲;暢飲。

quag [kwæg; kwæg] *n.* 泥沼。

quag·ga [ˈkwægə; ˈkwægə] *n., pl.* **-ga, -gas.** 【動物】(南非產)斑驢。

quag·gy [ˈkwægɪ; ˈkwægi] *adj.,* **-gi·er, -gi·est.** 多泥沼的;似沼地的;泥濘的。

quag·mire [ˈkwægˌmaɪr; ˈkwægmaiə] *n., v.,* **-mired, -mir·ing.** —*n.* ①沼地;泥沼。②絕境;無法脫身之困境。—*v.t.* 使陷入泥沼;使陷入絕境。

quag·mir·y [ˈkwægˌmaɪərɪ; ˈkwægmaiəri] *adj.* 多泥沼的;多泥濘的。

qua·haug [ˈkwɔhɔg; ˈkwɔhɔg] *n.* =**quahog.**

qua·hog [ˈkwɔhɔg; ˈkwɔhɔg] *n.* 【動物】北美產的一種圓蛤。

Quai d'Or·say [ˌkedɔrˈse; ˌkei dɔ:ˈsei] ①巴黎市沿塞納 (Seine) 河岸之一地名(法國外交部所在地)。②法國外交部。

quail¹ [kwel; kweil] *n., pl.* **quails** or **quail.** ①(集合稱)鵪鶉。②【美俚】妙齡女郎。*quail call* 誘鶉入網之哨笛聲。*quail pipe* 誘鶉入網所用之哨笛。

quail² *v.i.* 畏縮;畏懼;沮喪。

***quaint** [kwent; kweint] *adj.* ①古怪而有趣的。②奇怪的。*quaint* methods. 奇怪的方法。③做得很精巧的;製作得很聰明的。—**ly,** *adv.* —**ness,** *n.*

quake [kwek; kweik] *v.,* **quaked, quaking,** *n.* —*v.i.* 震動;戰慄。He was *quaking* with fear (cold). 他因恐懼(寒冷)而發抖。—*n.* ①震動;戰慄。②地震。

quake·proof [ˈkwekˌpruf; ˈkweikpru:f] *adj.* 防震的 (建築物等)。

***Quak·er** [ˈkwekɚ; ˈkweikə] *n.* 教友派 (Society of Friends) 的信徒。

quak·er·bird [ˈkwekɚˌbɝd; ˈkweikəbə:d] *n.* (鳥名)信天翁。

Quaker City 美國 Philadelphia 之別稱。

Quak·er·ess [ˈkwekərɪs; ˈkweikəris] *n.* 教友派之女教徒。

Quaker gun 騙敵用的假砲 (常爲木所製成, 因 Quakers 反對任何戰爭, 故名)。

Quak·er·ish [ˈkwekərɪʃ; ˈkweikəriʃ] *adj.* ①教友派(教徒)的。②謹嚴的;樸素的。

Quak·er·ism [ˈkwekɚˌɪzəm; ˈkweikərizm] *n.* 教友派之主義與習慣。

Quak·er-la·dies [ˈkwekɚˌledɪz; ˈkweikəˌleidiz] *n. pl.* 【植物】矢車菊等之藍色小花。

Quak·er·ly [ˈkwekəlɪ; ˈkweikəli] *adj. & adv.* ①似教友派教徒的(地)。②謹嚴的(地);樸素的(地)。

Quaker meeting ①教友派的集會(非因感召不得講話)。②較為沉默的任何集會。(亦作 **Quakers' meeting**)

quaker moth 一種夜蛾。

Quaker's bargain 不二價之交易。

quak·y [ˈkwekɪ; ˈkweiki] *adj.,* **quak·i·er, quak·i·est.** 戰慄的;震顫的。

qual·i·fi·a·ble [ˈkwaləˌfaɪəbl̩; ˈkwɔlifaiəbl] *adj.* 可修飾的;可改變的;可限制的。

***qual·i·fi·ca·tion** [ˌkwaləfəˈkeʃən; ˌkwɔlifiˈkeiʃən] *n.* ①資格。 a doctor's *qualifications.* 醫生的資格。②限制; 限定。③賦予資格。

qual·i·fi·ca·to·ry [ˈkwaləfɪˌketərɪ; ˈkwɔlifikətəri] *adj.* 資格的;資格上的;限定

的;附有條件的。
qual·i·fied [ˈkwɑləˌfaɪd; ˈkwɔlifaid] *adj.* ①合格的;合式的;可採用的。②受限制的。*qualified* acceptance. 有限度的接受。
qual·i·fi·er [ˈkwɑləˌfaɪɚ; ˈkwɔlifaiə] *n.* ①賦予資格或權限之人或物;限定物。②〖文法〗修飾詞。③合格者。
***qual·i·fy** [ˈkwɑləˌfaɪ; ˈkwɔlifai] *v.*, **-fied, -fy·ing.** —*v.t.* ①使合格;使勝任。You must *qualify* yourself for the post. 你必須使自己有充任這職位的資格。②限制。③形容;修飾。Adjectives *qualify* nouns. 形容詞形容名詞。④描寫;敍述。⑤緩和;減輕…之激烈程度。⑥改變香味等。—*v.i.* 合格;適合。Can you *qualify* for the Boy Scouts? 你做童子軍能合格嗎?
qual·i·ta·tive [ˈkwɑləˌtetɪv; ˈkwɔlitətiv] *adj.* ①與性質有關的;性質上的;品質上的;質地上的。②〖化〗定性的。*qualitative* analysis. 定性分析。—**ly,** *adv.*
qual·i·tied [ˈkwɑlətɪd; ˈkwɔlitid] *adj.* 被賦以某種性質的。
‡qual·i·ty [ˈkwɑlətɪ; ˈkwɔliti] *n., pl.* **-ties,** *adj.*—*n.* ①特質;性質。One *quality* of iron is hardness. 堅硬是鐵的特質之一。②種類;等第。cloth of a poor (excellent) *quality.* 壞(好)布。③品質。We aim at *quality* rather than quantity. 我們重質不重量。④本性;脾氣。⑤品德;德性。She has many fine *qualities.* 她有很多優良的品德。⑥關係;地位。⑦上流社會;上流社會之人。a man of good *quality.* 世家出身之人。⑧〖物理〗音質;音色。—*adj.* ①上流社會的。to bring *quality* people to the wedding. 請上流社會的人們參加婚禮。②上等品質的。*quality* leather. 上等皮革。
quality control 品質管制。
quality of life 生活要素。
qualm [kwɑm; kwɔːm] *n.* ①暫時之昏暈或惡心之感覺。②不安;疑懼。③良心之譴責。
qualm·ish [ˈkwɑmɪʃ; ˈkwɔːmiʃ] *adj.* ①似要作嘔的。②於心不安的。
quan·da·ry [ˈkwɑndrɪ; ˈkwɔndəri] *n., pl.* **-ries.** 困惑;窘境;進退兩難之境。
quant [kwænt; kwænt] *n.* =**quant pole.** —*v.t.* & *v.i.* 用桿撐船。
quan·ti·fi·er [ˈkwɑntəˌfaɪɚ; ˈkwɔntifaiə] *n.* ①定量辭。②精於計量或計數者。
quan·ti·fy [ˈkwɑntəˌfaɪ; ˈkwɔntifai] *v.t.*, **-fied, -fy·ing.** ①定…之量。②〖邏輯〗使…之量更明確(如用 all, none 或 some);限定(賓辭等)之量。
quan·ti·ta·tive [ˈkwɑntəˌtetɪv; ˈkwɔntitətiv] *adj.* ①與量有關的。②〖化〗定量的。*quantitative* analysis. 定量分析。③能量的。—**ly,** *adv.*
‡quan·ti·ty [ˈkwɑntətɪ; ˈkwɔntiti] *n., pl.* **-ties.** ①量;數量。I prefer quality to *quantity.* 我重質不重量。②特定的量。a small *quantity* of water. 少量的水。③大量;大宗。The baker bought flour in *quantity.* 這麪包商買下大量的麪粉。④可量的東西。⑤〖音樂〗音符長度;音量。⑥一母音或一音節的長度;音量。⑦〖數學〗量;數。an unknown *quantity.* 未知數;(喻)不可測的人。
quantity theory of money 〖經濟〗物價隨貨幣流通量多寡而升降之理論。
quan·ti·va·lence [ˌkwɑntɪˈveləns; ˌkwɔntiˈveiləns] *n.* 〖化〗原子價。
quant pole 撐船用的竿。
quan·tum [ˈkwɑntəm; ˈkwɔntəm] *n., pl.* **-ta** [-tə; -tə]. ①量;額。②某定量;部分。③〖物理〗能獨立存在的最小能量;量子。
quantum mechanics 〖物理〗量子力學。
quantum theory 〖物理〗量子論。
quar·an·tine [ˈkwɔrənˌtin; ˈkwɔrəntiːn] *v.*, **-tined, -tin·ing,** *n.*—*v.t.* ①使受檢疫停船;使受檢疫拘留。②使(在政治上或商業上)孤立。—*n.* ①在港口或邊境爲避免疾病傳染而行之拘留、隔離等措施。②停船檢疫期間;檢疫拘留期間(通常爲四十日)。③檢疫所。④四十日之期間。⑤(在政治或商業上之)隔絕。
quarantine flag 表示船上未發生疾病的黃旗,挿在船上作爲請求入港許可的信號。(亦作 **yellow flag**)
quarantine period 檢疫期間。
‡quar·rel[1] [ˈkwɔrəl, ˈkwɑr-; ˈkwɔrəl] *n., v.,* 〖美〗**-reled, -rel·ing,** 〖英〗**-rel·led, -rel·ling.** —*n.* ①爭論;爭吵;口角。*Quarrels* are often followed by fights. 爭吵後往往是打鬥。②爭論之原因;爭吵之原故。I have no *quarrel* against (with) him. 我沒有與他爭論的理由。***fight another person's quarrels for him*** 幫着別人吵鬧。***make up a quarrel*** 和解;言歸於好。***pick (seek) a quarrel with*** 向…挑釁。***take up another's quarrel*** 支持某人。—*v.i.* ①爭論;爭吵。Children sometimes *quarrel.* 孩子們有時愛爭吵。②怨;挑剔。***quarrel with one's bread and butter*** 挑剔自己的行業;違背自己的利益。
quar·rel[2] *n.* ①方鏃箭。②菱形玻璃板。
quar·rel·(l)er [ˈkwɔrəlɚ; ˈkwɔrələ] *n.* 爭吵者;吵鬧者;好爭論者。
***quar·rel·some** [ˈkwɔrəlsəm, ˈkwɑr-; ˈkwɔrəlsəm] *adj.* 愛爭吵的;好口角的。—**ly,** *adv.* —**ness,** *n.*
quar·ri·er [ˈkwɑrɪɚ; ˈkwɔriə] *n.* =**quarryman.**
quar·ry[1] [ˈkwɔrɪ, ˈkwɑrɪ; ˈkwɔri] *n., pl.* **-ries,** *v.*, **-ried, -ry·ing.** —*n.* ①採石場。②(知識、事實、消息等之)源泉。a *quarry* of knowledge. 知識之源泉。—*v.t.* ①自採石場挖出。②闢爲採石場;闢採石場於…。③(自書中等)探索(資料)。—*v.i.* ①採石。②探索資料。
quar·ry[2] *n., pl.* **-ries.** ①(常 *sing.*)獵物。②急急追求之事物或目標。
quar·ry[3] *n.* ①菱形玻璃板。②機製地磚。
quar·ry·ing [ˈkwɔrɪɪŋ; ˈkwɔriiŋ] *n.* 採石;採石業。
quar·ry·man [ˈkwɑrɪmən; ˈkwɔrimən] *n., pl.* **-men.** 採石工人。
quart**[1] [kwɔrt; kwɔːt] *n.* ①夸;夸脫(容量名,等於四分之一加侖或二品脫)。a *quart* of beer. 一夸脫啤酒。②裝一夸脫的容器。try to put a quart into a pint pot*** 欲使小的裝大的;徒勞。
quart[2] [kɑrt; kɑːt] *n.* ①〖牌戲〗同花連續之四張牌。②〖劍術〗=**quarte.** ***quart major*** 點數最大的四張同花牌(即 ace, king, queen, jack). ***quart minor*** 點數次大的四張同花牌(即 king, queen, jack, ten).
quart. ①quarter. ②quarterly.
quar·tan [ˈkwɔrtn; ˈkwɔːtən] *adj.* 每四天發一次的(熱病)。—*n.* 〖醫〗四日熱。
quar·ta·tion [kwɔrˈteʃən; kwɔːˈteiʃən] *n.* 金銀的硝酸分解法。
quarte [kɑrt; kɑːt] 〖法〗 *n.* 〖劍術〗八種防禦姿勢中的第四種。
‡quar·ter [ˈkwɔrtɚ; ˈkwɔːtə] *n.* ①四

分之一。a *quarter* of an hour. 一刻鐘;十五分鐘。②一刻鐘;十五分鐘。 a *quarter* to two. 差一刻到兩點。a *quarter* past six. 六點一刻。③〖美〗一元錢的四分之一;二角五分。④二角五分之銀幣。⑤季;一年的四分之一;三個月。He pays his rent at the end of each *quarter*. 他每三個月付一次租金。⑥一碼的四分之一;九英寸。⑦一hundredweight的四分之一;二十五磅或二十八磅。⑧區域;地方。the Chinese *quarter* in San Francisco. 舊金山的華人區。⑨社區或一羣體的某一部分。⑩(*pl.*)住處;寓所。⑪方位;方角;方向。from all *quarters*. 來自四方。⑫(對敵人等之)饒命;寬恕。⑬鳥獸屍體被四分後之一肢。⑭腿及其附近的部分。⑮船尾附近部分。⑯〖紋章〗盾的四分之一;盾形右上角四分之一部分的表徵。⑰〖音樂〗四分音符。⑱〖軍〗營盤;軍營。⑲(消息、錢等的)來源。⑳就位備戰。Officers and men at once took up their *quarters*. 官兵均就位備戰。***at close quarters*** 極爲接近;幾乎相接觸。***cry (for) quarters*** 求饒。—*v.t.* ①四等分。②駐紮。③將…切成四塊;肢解。④將紋章安於(盾的右上角四分之一處)。⑤來回地橫越;在…上來回。—*v.i.* ①駐紮;居住。②(風)吹向船尾。③在一地區上來回移動(以尋找)。—*adj.* 四分之一的。

quar·ter·age 〔ˈkwɔrtərɪdʒ; ˈkwɔːtəridʒ〕 *n.* ①每季的付款、收入或津貼。②軍隊食宿之供給。③兵營。

quar·ter·back 〔ˈkwɔrtəˌbæk; ˈkwɔːtəbæk〕 *n.* 〖橄欖球〗①前鋒與中衛間之位置;踢此位置之球員。②進攻時指揮本隊之球員。—*v.i.* (橄欖球隊中) 擔任前鋒與中衛間之位置。—*v.t.* 指揮;領導。

quarter-bell (時鐘的) 每一刻鐘鳴一次的鈴。

quar·ter-bound 〔ˈkwɔrtəˈbaund; ˈkwɔːtəˈbaund〕 *adj.* (書本的)背皮裝訂的。

quar·ter-breed 〔ˈkwɔrtəˌbrid; ˈkwɔːtəbriːd〕 *n.* 有四分之一白人血統(祖父或祖母爲白人)的印第安人。

quarter butt 〖撞球〗短球桿。

quarter day 四季之結帳日期或付款日期(英國爲三月二十五日,六月二十四日,九月二十九日與十二月二十五日;美國爲一,四,七,十各月之一日)。

quar·ter-deck, quar·ter·deck 〔ˈkwɔrtəˌdɛk; ˈkwɔːtədek〕 *n.* 〖航海〗①後甲板。②(the –)高級船員或軍官之集合稱。—*v.i.* 來回徘徊;散步。

quar·tered 〔ˈkwɔrtəd; ˈkwɔːtəd〕 *adj.* ①四等分的。②設有房間的。③(木料)縱鋸成四等分,然後鋸成木板的。

quar·ter·fi·nal 〔ˌkwɔrtəˈfaɪnl; ˈkwɔːtəˈfainl〕 *adj.* 〖運動〗準決賽前之比賽的。

quar·ter-hour 〔ˈkwɔrtəˈaur; ˈkwɔːtərˈauə〕 *n.* ①一刻鐘。②鐘面上標明第一刻鐘或第三刻鐘之點。(亦作 **quarter hour**)

quar·ter·ing 〔ˈkwɔrtərɪŋ; ˈkwɔːtəriŋ〕 *adj.* ①〖航海〗吹在船舷尾部的(風)。②直交的。—*n.* ①四等分;分爲四等分。②軍營或其他住所之分配。③〖紋章〗盾形之四等分;盾的四分之一。

quar·ter·ly 〔ˈkwɔrtəlɪ; ˈkwɔːtəli〕 *adj., adv., n., pl.* **-lies.** —*adj.* 一年四次的;每季的。—*adv.* 每季地。—*n.* 季刊。

quar·ter·mas·ter 〔ˈkwɔrtəˌmæstə; ˈkwɔːtəˌmɑːstə〕 *n.* ①〖軍〗經理官;後勤部隊軍官。②海軍掌信號、舵、羅盤等之士官。

Quartermaster Corps 〖美陸軍〗經理部隊。

quartermaster general 經理署署長。

quartermaster sergeant 補給士官。

quar·tern 〔ˈkwɔrtən; ˈkwɔːtən〕 *n.* ①(液量)四分之一品脫。②重四磅之圓形麪包。

quarter ripsaw =**handsaw.**

quar·ter·saw 〔ˈkwɔrtəˌsɔ; ˈkwɔːtəsɔː〕 *v.t.*, **-sawed, -sawed** or **-sawn, -saw·ing.** 將(木材)直鋸成四等塊,然後鋸成木板。

quar·ter·stretch 〔ˈkwɔrtəˌstrɛtʃ; ˈkwɔːtəstretʃ〕 *n.* (賽馬等之)最後直線賽程。

quar·ter-turn stair 〔ˈkwɔrtəˌtɜn～; ˈkwɔːtətəːn～〕 每上下一層即須作90度轉彎的樓梯。

quarter wind 〖航海〗向船後稍斜而吹的風;船尾風。

quar·ter-year·ly 〔ˈkwɔrtəˈjɪrlɪ; ˈkwɔːtəˈjəːli〕 *adv. & adj.* 每季一次(的)。

quar·tet(te) 〔kwɔrˈtɛt; kwɔːˈtet〕 *n.* ①四個(人或物)組成的一組。②四部合唱;四重奏。③四部合唱曲;四部合奏曲。

quar·to 〔ˈkwɔrto; ˈkwɔːtou〕 *n., pl.* **-tos.** ①四開(通常爲9×12英寸)。②四開本。③四開樂譜。—*adj.* 四開的;四開本的。

quar·tus 〔ˈkwɔrtəs; ˈkwɔːtəs〕 *adj.* 〖處方〗第四。

***quartz** 〔kwɔrts; kwɔːts〕 *n.* 石英石。

quartz·ite 〔ˈkwɔrtsaɪt; ˈkwɔːtsait〕 *n.* 石英岩;硅岩。

quash 〔kwɑʃ; kwɔʃ〕 *v.t.* ①取消;作廢。②壓碎;擠碎;鎮壓。

qua·si 〔ˈkwesaɪ; ˈkwɑːzi(ː)〕 *adj.* 類似的;準的。*quasi* cholera. 假性霍亂。—*adv.* 類似地;準地。

quasi- 〖字首〗表"類似;準;半"之義。

qua·si-ju·di·cial 〔ˌkwesaɪdʒuˈdɪʃəl; ˈkwɑːzidʒuːˈdiʃəl〕 *adj.* 準司法的。

qua·si-pub·lic 〔ˌkwesaɪˈpʌblɪk; ˌkwɑːziˈpʌblik〕 *adj.* 私有但屬公共性質的。

quas·si·a 〔ˈkwɑʃɪə; ˈkwɔʃə〕 *n.* 〖植物〗①(南美所產的)苦木科植物。②苦木科植物之木材。③由苦木科植物中提煉的苦味液(用做強壯劑及驅蟲劑)。

qua·ter·cen·te·nar·y 〔ˌkwetəˈsɛntəˌnɛrɪ; ˌkwætəsenˈtiːnəri〕 *n.* 四百年紀念。

qua·ter·na·ry 〔kwəˈtɜnərɪ; kwəˈtəːnəri〕 *adj., n., pl.* **-ries.** —*adj.* ①四要素組成的。②〖化〗四元素組成的。③四個一組的;有四部分的。④(Q-)〖地質〗第四紀的。—*n.* ①四;四個。②四個一組。③(Q-)〖地質〗第四紀。***the Quaternary*** 第四紀及其岩石。

qua·ter·ni·on 〔kwəˈtɜnɪən; kwəˈtəːnjən〕 *n.* ①四個一組。②(*pl.*)〖數學〗四元法。

qua·ter·ni·ty 〔kwəˈtɜnətɪ; kwəˈtəːniti〕 *n., pl.* **-ties.** ①四個一組;四人一組。②〖神學〗四位一體。

quat·rain 〔ˈkwɑtren; ˈkwɔtrein〕 *n.* 四行詩(通常隔句押韻)。

qua·tre 〔ˈkatə; ˈkɑːtə〕 *n.* ①四。②紙牌、骰子等之四點。

quat·re·foil 〔ˈkætəˌfɔɪl; ˈkætəfɔil〕 *n.* ①〖建築〗四葉飾。②有四瓣之花。③有四葉片之葉。④〖紋章〗楯形上之四葉飾。

quat·tro·cen·to 〔ˌkwɑttroˈtʃɛnto; ˌkwɑːtrouˈtʃentou〕 *n.* 第十五世紀(指義大利該時期之文學藝術)。—*adj.* (文藝、建築等)屬於此一時期的。

qua·ver 〔ˈkwevə; ˈkweivə〕 *v.i.* 震顫。—*v.t.* 以震顫聲說出或唱出。—*n.* ①抖顫;顫音。②〖音樂〗八分音符。

qua·ver·ing·ly 〔ˈkwevərɪŋlɪ; ˈkweivəriŋli〕 *adv.* 震顫地;顫音地;抖顫地。

qua·ver·y 〔ˈkwevərɪ; ˈkweivəri〕 *adj.* 震顫的;多顫音的;顫音的。

quay 〔ki; kiː〕 *n.* 碼頭。

quay·age 〔ˈkiɪdʒ; ˈkiːidʒ〕 *n.* ①碼頭使用稅;泊船費。②碼頭用地。③碼頭(集合稱)。④碼頭設備。

quay·side 〔ˈkiˌsaɪd; ˈkiːsaid〕 *n.* 碼頭邊土地。

Que. Quebec.

quean 〔kwin; kwiːn〕 *n.* ①輕佻的婦女。②妓女;淫蕩的婦女。③〖蘇〗(未婚)女子。

quea·sy 〔ˈkwizɪ; ˈkwiːzi〕 *adj.*, **-si·er, -si·est.** ①令人作嘔的(食物)。②易嘔的;不易消化食物的(胃)。③不安的;不舒服的。④脾氣古怪的;過分講究細節的;難於取悅的。⑤需要小心處理的。—**quea·si·ly,** *adv.* —**quea·si·ness,** *n.*

Que·bec¹ 〔kwɪˈbɛk; kwiˈbek〕 *n.* 魁北克(加拿大之一省;其首府)。

Que·bec² *n.* 通訊電碼,代表字母 Q.

‡queen 〔kwin; kwiːn〕 *n.* ①皇后。②女王。③最有權力之女子;最有吸引力之女子。movie *queen.* 影后。④最佳者;最美者。⑤雌蜂;雌蟻。⑥(撲克牌及棋中之)女王。***to the queen's taste*** 足以使最有辨別力的人感到滿意的。—*v.t.* 立爲女王(或后)。—*v.i.* 統治;作女王。***queen it*** 做女王統治;行動像女王一般。

queen ant 蟻王;雌蟻。

queen bee ①蜂王;雌蜂。②〖俚〗統治一羣人的女人;領導社交活動的婦女。

queen·dom 〔ˈkwindəm; ˈkwiːndəm〕 *n.* ①女王之地位或尊嚴。②女王統治(之國家)。

queen dowager 孀居之王后。

queen·hood 〔ˈkwinhʊd; ˈkwiːnhud〕 *n.* ①女王之地位、階級或尊嚴。②女王統治時期。

queen·ing 〔ˈkwinɪŋ; ˈkwiːniŋ〕 *n.* 一種蘋果。

queen·like 〔ˈkwinˌlaɪk; ˈkwiːnlaik〕 *adj.* =**queenly.**

queen·ly 〔ˈkwinlɪ; ˈkwiːnli〕 *adj.*, **-li·er, -li·est,** *adv.* —*adj.* ①皇后的;女王的;適於皇后或女王的。②似皇后或女王的。—*adv.* 似皇后地;似女王地。—**queen·li·ness,** *n.*

queen mother 母后;皇太后。

queen post 〖建築〗直立橫梁上支撐屋頂的兩內柱之一;雌柱。

Queen's Bench 英國高等法院。

queen's counsel 英國王室法律顧問。

queer** 〔kwɪr; kwiə〕 *adj.* ①奇怪的;古怪的。There is something *queer* about him. 他有些古怪。②〖俗〗可疑的;費解的。③(身體)覺得不舒服的;暈眩的;眼花的。④〖俚〗假的;僞造的。*queer* money. 僞幣。⑤心智失去平衡的。⑥同性戀的。—*v.t.* 〖俚〗糟蹋;破壞。queer a person's pitch*** 暗中破壞某人計畫;顛覆某人。—*n.* 〖俚〗①僞鈔。②同性戀者。—**ly,** *adv.* —**ness,** *n.*

Queer Street 經濟上的拮据。

quell 〔kwɛl; kwel〕 *v.t.* ①撲滅;壓服。②緩和;使鎮靜。

***quench** 〔kwɛntʃ; kwentʃ〕 *v.t.* ①結束;停止。to *quench* hope. 絕望。②熄滅;消滅。③(鍛鐵時之)淬火;驟冷。—*v.i.* 熄滅。—*n.* 終止;熄滅;淬火。—**a·ble,** *adj.*

quench·er 〔ˈkwɛntʃɚ; ˈkwentʃə〕 *n.* ①熄滅者;熄滅器。②抑制者(人或物)。③冷却器。④〖俚〗飲料;解渴之物。

quench·less 〔ˈkwɛntʃlɪs; ˈkwentʃlis〕 *adj.* 不可消滅的;不能鎭壓的。

que·nelle 〔kəˈnɛl; kəˈnel〕 *n.* 〖烹飪〗油炸雞肉或牛肉丸。

que·rist 〔ˈkwɪrɪst; ˈkwiərist〕 *n.* 質問者;詢問者。

quer·u·lous 〔ˈkwɛrələs; ˈkwerulәs〕 *adj.* ①愛抱怨的;好發牢騷的;吹毛求疵的。②易怒的;暴躁的。—**ly,** *adv.*

que·ry 〔ˈkwɪrɪ; ˈkwiəri〕 *n., pl.* **-ries,** *v.,* **-ried, -ry·ing.** —*n.* ①問題;質問;詢問;疑問。to raise a *query.* 發問。②問號。③用以介紹一問句。*Query,* where are we to find the funds? 請問我們到那裏去找這筆經費呢? —*v.t. & v.i.* ①質問;詢問。②表示懷疑。③加問號。

***quest** 〔kwɛst; kwest〕 *n.* ①探詢;搜尋。They went to Australia in *quest* of gold. 他們到澳洲去找金子。②探求;(尤指中世紀騎士之)遠征。③中古遠征之騎士。④探求物。⑤〖古〗驗屍。crowner's *quest* (=coroner's inquest). 驗屍。—*v.t. & v.i.* 搜尋;找。

‡ques·tion 〔ˈkwɛstʃən; ˈkwestʃən〕 *n.* ①訊問;疑問。②問題;討論(爭執)之事物;論點。He asked me a lot of *questions.* 他問我許多問題。③(待表決之)提議;提案。④疑問句。⑤疑義;論點。⑥表決。***beside the question*** 離題;在問題外。***beyond*** (or ***without***) ***question*** 無疑問。This story is true *beyond* all *question.* 這話眞實無疑。***call in*** (or ***into***) ***question*** 表示異議;表示不服;表示懷疑。He *called* my statement *in question.* 他懷疑我的話。***come into question*** 成問題;有實際重要性。***in question*** **a.** 正被談論的(人或物)。**b.** 在爭議中。***out of question*** 無疑問。***out of the question*** 不可能。***put the question*** 表決。***Question!*** (公開集會中之喊聲) **a.** 離題了(促言歸本題)。**b.** 有疑問;有異議! —*v.t.* ①詢問;質問;審問。②懷疑。I *question* the truth of his story. 我懷疑他的故事是否眞實。③提出異議,認爲有待商榷。—*v.i.* 詢問;質問;審問。

ques·tion·a·ble 〔ˈkwɛstʃənəbl; ˈkwestʃənəbl〕 *adj.* ①引起爭論的;有問題的;可疑的。②(道德上、行爲上等)有問題的。

ques·tion·a·bly 〔ˈkwɛstʃənəblɪ; ˈkwestʃənəbli〕 *adv.* 有問題地;可疑地。

ques·tion·ar·y 〔ˈkwɛstʃənˌɛrɪ; ˈkwestʃənəri〕 *adj., n., pl.* **-ar·ies.** —*adj.* 質問的;疑問的。—*n.* =**questionnaire.**

ques·tion·er 〔ˈkwɛstʃənɚ; ˈkwestʃənə〕 *n.* 質問者;詢問者。

ques·tion·ing·ly 〔ˈkwɛstʃənɪŋlɪ; ˈkwestʃəniŋli〕 *adv.* 質問地;訊問地;疑惑地。

ques·tion·less 〔ˈkwɛstʃənlɪs; ˈkwestʃənlis〕 *adj. & adv.* 無疑的(地);確然的(地)。

question mark ①問號(?)。②〖俗〗困難的問題;爭議中的問題。③疑問。His identity is still a *question mark* to most of us. 他究竟是誰我們大多數人依舊不知道。④一種蝴蝶(後翅底面有問號狀之銀色花紋)。

ques·tion·mas·ter 〔ˈkwɛstʃənˌmæstɚ; ˈkwestʃənˌmɑːstə〕 *n.* 〖英〗〖廣播、電視〗猜謎節目主持人。(亦作 **question-master**)

ques·tion·naire 〔ˌkwɛstʃənˈɛr; ˌkwestʃəˈnɛə〕 *n.* 一組問題(通常印好並留空白,以資調查或測驗用)。—*v.t.* 向…提出一組問題。

question time 議會之質詢時間。

quet·zal 〔kɛtˈsal; ketˈsɑːl〕 *n.* ①〖動物〗中美洲產的一種鳥(爲瓜地馬拉之國鳥)。②瓜地馬拉的貨幣單位。(亦作 **quezal**)

queue 〔kju; kjuː〕 *n., v.,* **queued, queu·ing.** —*n.* ①辮子。②一行人或汽車等。to form a *queue.* 排成一行。③一種盛酒之容器。—*v.i. & v.t.* 〖英〗排成一行(=line up).

queu·er 〔ˈkjuə; ˈkjuːə〕 *n.* 排隊者。
Que·zon City 〔ˈkesɔn～; ˈkeisɔːn～〕 奎松城(菲律賓之正式首都,在馬尼拉近郊)。
quib·ble 〔ˈkwɪbl; ˈkwibl〕 *n., v.,* **-bled, -bling.** —*n.* ①雙關語。②遁辭;模稜兩可的話。—*v.i.* 以雙關語說出;模稜兩可地說。
quib·bling 〔ˈkwɪblɪŋ; ˈkwibliŋ〕 *adj.* 雙關語的;遁辭的。—*n.* 用雙關語;作遁辭。
:quick 〔kwɪk; kwik〕 *adj.* ①迅速的;迅急的;敏捷的。②即刻的;立即的。a *quick* reply. 即時答覆。③急躁的;性急的。④機伶的;活潑的。a *quick* wit (*or* mind). 機智。⑤短時間的。⑥旺盛的;熊熊的(火)。a *quick* fire. 熊熊的火。⑦即可兌現的(支票)。⑧銳角的;尖銳的。⑨顯示有生命的。⑩可以很快變賣的。—*n.*①(皮肉)細嫩敏感的部分;(感覺的)要害。②活人;生物。the *quick* and the dead. 生者及死者。③最重要之部分。***cut to the quick*** 深深地傷害;損傷(某人之)感情。—*adv.* = quickly (常位於動詞之後)。Run as *quick* as you can. 儘量快跑。Come *quick!* 快來!
quick-change 〔ˈkwɪkˌtʃendʒ; ˈkwik-tʃeindʒ〕 *adj.* ①換裝迅速的。②容易改變主意的。
quick-eared 〔ˈkwɪkˈɪrd; ˈkwikˈiəd〕 *adj.* 耳敏於聽的。
·quick·en 〔ˈkwɪkən; ˈkwikən〕 *v.t.* ①使加速;催促。*Quicken* your pace. 加速你的脚步。②鼓舞;使復甦。—*v.i.* ①加速。The pace *quickened*. 脚步加快了。②鼓舞;復甦。③(孕婦)感覺胎動。④(胎兒)蠕動。
quick·en·ing 〔ˈkwɪkənɪŋ; ˈkwikniŋ〕 *n.* ①復生;活潑;興奮。②胎動期(懷孕後十八週左右)。
quick-eyed 〔ˈkwɪkˈaɪd; ˈkwikˈaid〕 *adj.* 眼力銳敏的;慧眼的。
quick-fir·er 〔ˈkwɪkˌfaɪrə; ˈkwikˌfaiə-rə〕 *n.* 速射砲。
quick-fir·ing 〔ˈkwɪkˈfaɪrɪŋ; ˈkwik-ˈfaiəriŋ〕 *adj.* 速射的。*quick-firing* gun. 速射砲。(亦作 **quick-fire**)
quick-freeze 〔ˈkwɪkˈfriz; ˈkwikfriːz〕 *v.t.,* **-froze, -fro·zen, -freez·ing.** 急凍。
quick goods 家畜;畜生。
quick·ie 〔ˈkwɪkɪ; ˈkwiki〕 *n.* 〖俚〗①匆匆製成的劣品;(尤指)粗製濫造的電影。②任何需時甚短暫之事物。—*adj.* ①迅速的;速成的。a *quickie* training course. 速成訓練班。②未作事先警告的;突然發生的。
quickie strike 未經工會許可的罷工。(亦作 **wildcat strike**)
quick·ish 〔ˈkwɪkɪʃ; ˈkwikiʃ〕 *adj.* 相當快的。
quick·lime 〔ˈkwɪkˌlaɪm; ˈkwik-laim〕 *n.* 生石灰。
quick-lunch 〔ˈkwɪkˈlʌntʃ; ˈkwik-ˈlʌntʃ〕 *n.* 簡速餐廳。
:quick·ly 〔ˈkwɪklɪ; ˈkwikli〕 *adv.* 快地;迅速地。He did it *quickly*. 他做得很快。
quick-mix 〔ˈkwɪkˈmɪks; ˈkwikˈmiks〕 *n.* 市場上質料已經調配現成的食物。
quick·ness 〔ˈkwɪknɪs; ˈkwiknis〕 *n.* ①迅速。②活潑;敏捷;機敏。③急速;急;急躁。④尖銳化。
quick parts 才智;穎悟。
quick·sand 〔ˈkwɪkˌsænd; ˈkwiksænd〕 *n.* ①流沙。②危險而不可信賴的事。
quick-scent·ed 〔ˈkwɪkˌsɛntɪd; ˈkwikˌsentid〕 *adj.* 嗅覺敏銳的。
quick·set 〔ˈkwɪkˌsɛt; ˈkwikset〕 *n.* ①以山楂樹等植物做的樹籬。②做樹籬而種的植物。—*adj.* 以山楂樹等植物做成的(籬)。
quick-set·ting 〔ˈkwɪkˈsɛtɪŋ; ˈkwik-ˌsetiŋ〕 *adj.* (水泥、油漆等)很快凝結的。
quick-sight·ed 〔ˈkwɪkˈsaɪtɪd; ˈkwikˈsaitid〕 *adj.* 目力敏銳的;眼快的。
·quick·sil·ver 〔ˈkwɪkˌsɪlvə; ˈkwik-ˌsilvə〕 *n.* ①水銀;汞。②像水銀一般敏捷、閃爍、不可捉摸之人或物。—*v.t.* 塗以水銀。
quick·step 〔ˈkwɪkˌstɛp; ˈkwikstep〕 *n.* ①快步走。②活潑的舞步。③〖音樂〗快速之進行曲。④〖美俗〗痢疾。—*v.i.* ①以輕快的步伐前進。②以活潑的舞步跳舞。
quick study 記憶力强的人。
quick-tem·pered 〔ˈkwɪkˈtɛmpəd; ˈkwikˈtempəd〕 *adj.* 性情急躁的;易怒的。
quick time 〖美軍〗齊步(每分鐘120步,每步步幅30英寸)。
quick-trig·gered 〔ˈkwɪk ˈtrɪgəd; ˈkwikˈtrigəd〕 *adj.* 射擊迅速的;動作敏捷的。
quick·wa·ter 〔ˈkwɪkˌwɔtə; ˈkwik-ˌwɔːtə〕 *n.* 水流湍急之處。
quick-wit·ted 〔ˈkwɪkˈwɪtɪd; ˈkwik-ˈwitid〕 *adj.* 才思敏捷的。
quid¹ 〔kwɪd; kwid〕 *n.* 咀嚼物;咀嚼用的烟草塊。
quid² *n., pl.* **quid.** 〖英俚〗一鎊;二十先令。
quid·di·ty 〔ˈkwɪdətɪ; ˈkwiditi〕 *n., pl.* **-ties.** ①實質;本質。②無關緊要的區分。③詭辯。④遁詞。
quid·nunc 〔ˈkwɪdˌnʌŋk; ˈkwidnʌŋk〕 *n.* 有好奇心的人;好管閑事者;搬弄是非者。
qui·es·cence 〔kwaɪˈɛsṇs; kwaiˈesns〕 *n.* 靜;靜寂;安靜;靜止。(亦作 **quiescency**)
qui·es·cent 〔kwaɪˈɛsṇt; kwaiˈesnt〕 *adj.* ①安靜的。②靜止的;不活動的。
:qui·et¹ 〔ˈkwaɪət; ˈkwaiət〕 *adj.* ①平穩的;靜止的。a *quiet* sea. 風平浪靜的海。②安閒的;安靜的。Be *quiet!* I want to listen to the music. 安靜些!我要聽音樂。③恬靜的;鎮靜的。④靜寂的;靜謐的。⑤溫和的;文雅的。*quiet* manners. 文雅的舉止。⑥樸素的;暗淡的。⑦祕密的;內心的。⑧平靜的;不積極的。a *quiet* country life. 平靜的鄉村生活。—*v.t.* ①使靜。②使鎮定。③使不作聲。④使減少(恐懼、疑慮等)。—*v.i.* 靜止。The wind *quieted* down. 風停了。—*adv.* =**quietly.**
qui·et² *n.* ①閒適;安靜。②平安;寧靜。
qui·et·en 〔ˈkwaɪətṇ; ˈkwaiətn〕 *v.t.* & *v.i.* 使靜;靜。
qui·et·ism 〔ˈkwaɪətɪzṃ; ˈkwaiitizəm〕 *n.* ①〖宗教〗寂靜主義(十七世紀末期西班牙教士 Molinos 倡導的一種宗教神祕主義,主張排除人類的意志、俗世慾望與事物,而對上帝及神聖事物做完全的沉思冥想)。②平靜;寂靜。
qui·et·ist 〔ˈkwaɪətɪst; ˈkwaiətist〕 *n.* 信奉寂靜主義者。—*adj.* 寂靜主義的;信奉寂靜主義者的。
:qui·et·ly 〔ˈkwaɪətlɪ; ˈkwaiətli〕 *adv.* ①和平地;平靜地。②無動靜地;無行動地。③靜寂地。
qui·et·ness 〔ˈkwaɪətnɪs; ˈkwaiətnis〕 *n.* 靜寂;鎮定。
qui·e·tude 〔ˈkwaɪəˌtjud; ˈkwaiitjuːd〕 *n.* 安靜;靜止;鎮靜。
qui·e·tus 〔kwaɪˈitəs; kwaiˈiːtəs〕 *n.* ①(債務的)償清;(義務的)解除;清除。②根絕之物。③死。④最後之一擊;終止。⑤使安靜之物。⑥退隱期;靜止期。⑦收據。
quiff 〔kwɪf; kwif〕 *n.* ①一陣風;一口煙。②〖英俚〗掛在額角上的一束頭髮。③〖俚〗賤女人;妓女。
quill 〔kwɪl; kwil〕 *n.* ①翎管。②翎做的筆等;翎管所製之物。③剛毛;硬毛。④(翼或尾部硬直的)羽毛。⑤牙籤。⑥彈奏曼陀林、豎琴等用的撥子。⑦捲成圓筒形之桂皮。***drive the quill*** 揮毫;寫字。—*v.t.* 將(衣服、布料等)摺成翎管形之褶紋。—*v.i.* 將紗、線等繞在翎管上。

quill driver 〖蔑〗①著作家;著述家。②抄寫員;小書記;錄事。

quill·ing 〔ˈkwɪlɪŋ; ˈkwiliŋ〕 *n.* 表面似一排羽莖之帶飾;襞褶。

quilt 〔kwɪlt; kwilt〕 *n.* 棉被;與棉被相似之物。—*v.t.* ①(加軟墊於內)縫合。②縫成線條或花樣。The bedcover was *quilted* in a flower design. 床單縫成花形圖案。—*v.i.* 製棉被。

qui·na 〔ˈkinə; ˈkwainə〕 *n.* ①金雞納樹皮。②奎寧。

qui·na·ry 〔ˈkwaɪnərɪ; ˈkwainəri〕 *adj.* 由五個構成的;五個的;五的。

quince 〔kwɪns; kwins〕 *n.* 〖植物〗①榲桲(一種薔薇科植物的果實)。②榲桲樹。

quin·cen·te·nar·y 〔kwɪnˈsɛntɪˌnɛrɪ; ˌkwinsenˈtiːnəri〕 *adj.* ①五百年的。②五百的;第五百的。—*n.* ①五百年紀念。②由五百所成之物;含有五百之物。(亦作 **quincentennial**)

quin·cun·cial 〔kwɪnˈkʌnʃəl; kwinˈkʌnʃəl〕 *adj.* ①五點形排列的。②〖植物〗五葉或五瓣成疊覆排列的。

quin·cunx 〔ˈkwɪnkʌŋks; ˈkwinkʌŋks〕 *n.* ①五點形排列(在一正方形或長方形上,四角中每角置一個,中間置一個,如 ⁙ 之排列形式)。②〖植物〗五葉或五瓣的一種疊覆排列(即兩個在外,兩個在內,一個一半在外一半在內)。

quin·gen·te·na·ry 〔kwɪnˈdʒɛntɪˌnɛrɪ; ˈkwindʒenˈtiːnəri〕 *adj.* =**quincentenary.**

qui·nine 〔ˈkwaɪnaɪn; kwiˈniːn〕 *n.* 〖藥〗金雞納霜;奎寧。(亦作 **quinin, quinina**)

quin·qua·ge·nar·i·an 〔ˌkwɪnkwədʒɪˈnɛrɪən; ˌkwiŋkwədʒiˈnɛəriən〕 *adj.* 五十多歲的。—*n.* 五十歲的人;五十多歲的人。

quin·quag·e·nar·y 〔kwɪnˈkwædʒɪˌnɛrɪ; kwinˈkwædʒinəri〕 *n.* 五十年紀念。

Quin·qua·ges·i·ma 〔ˌkwɪnkwəˈdʒɛsəmə; ˌkwiŋkwəˈdʒesimə〕 *n.* 四旬齋前的星期日。(亦作 **Quinquagesima Sunday**)

quin·quan·gu·lar 〔kwɪnˈkwæŋgjʊlə; kwinˈkwæŋgjulə〕 *adj.* 有五角的。

quinque- 〖字首〗表"五"之義。(在母音前作 **quinqu-**)

quin·quen·ni·al 〔kwɪnˈkwɛnɪəl; kwiŋˈkweniəl〕 *adj.* ①延續五年的。②每隔五年發生一次的。—*n.* ①每五年發生的事件。②持續五年的事件。

quin·quen·ni·um 〔kwɪnˈkwɛnɪəm; kwiŋˈkweniəm〕 *n., pl.* **-ni·ums, -ni·a** 〔-nɪə; -niə〕. 五年期間。(亦作 **quinquenniad**)

quin·que·par·tite 〔ˌkwɪnkwɪˈpɑrtaɪt; ˌkwiŋkwiˈpɑːtait〕 *adj.* 由五部分構成的。

quin·que·reme 〔ˈkwɪnkwɪˌrim; ˈkwiŋkwiriːm〕 *n.* 有五行槳的大划船。

quin·que·va·lent 〔ˌkwɪnkwɪˈvelənt; ˌkwiŋkwiˈveilənt〕 *adj.* 〖化〗五價的;有五種不同價的(如磷有5, 4, 3, 1, 及−3五種價)。

quin·qui·na 〔kwɪnˈkwaɪnə; kwinˈkwainə〕 *n.* 金雞納樹(=cinchona);金雞納皮。

quins 〔kwɪnz; kwinz〕 *n. pl.* 〖俗〗=**quintuplets.**

quin·sy 〔ˈkwɪnzɪ; ˈkwinzi〕 *n.* 〖醫〗扁桃腺發炎;咽門炎。

quint 〔kwɪnt; kwint〕 *n.* ①〖音樂〗第五度音程。②〖音樂〗風琴高 1/5 音的音栓。③〖音樂〗小提琴的E絃。④同花相連的五張牌。⑤〖俗〗=**quintuplet.** ⑥〖美〗籃球隊。

quin·tain 〔ˈkwɪntɪn; ˈkwintin〕 *n.* ①刺槍靶子。②在此等靶子上刺槍之遊戲。

quin·tal 〔ˈkwɪntl; ˈkwintl〕 *n.* ①百千克;百公斤。②=**hundredweight.**

quin·tan 〔ˈkwɪntən; ˈkwintən〕 *adj.* 隔五天一發作的。—*n.* 〖醫〗五日熱。

quinte 〔kɛ̃t; kɛ̃t〕 *n.* 〖劍術〗八種防禦姿勢中的第五種。

quin·tes·sence 〔kwɪnˈtɛsn̩s; kwinˈtesns〕 *n.* ①精髓;精華;實體;本質。②最完美之榜樣。③第五元素(土、水、氣、火以外者)。—**quin·tes·sen·tial,** *adj.*

quin·tet(te) 〔kwɪnˈtɛt; kwinˈtet〕 *n.* ①五人(或物)之一組。②合唱或合奏之五人。③〖音樂〗五部曲;五重奏。④〖俗〗男子籃球隊。

quin·til·lion 〔kwɪnˈtɪljən; kwinˈtiljən〕 *n.* ①(在美、法兩國爲)1後附 18 個零所代表的數目。②(在英、德兩國爲)1後附30個零所代表的數目。—*adj.* 達於此等數目的。

quin·tu·ple 〔ˈkwɪntjupl̩; ˈkwintjupl〕 *adj., n., v.,* **-pled, -pling.** —*adj.* 五倍的;五重的;五部分組成的。—*n.* 五倍。—*v.t.* 使成五倍。—*v.i.* 成爲五倍。

quin·tu·plet 〔ˈkwɪntəplɪt; ˈkwintjuplit〕 *n.* ①(*pl.*) 一胎所產的五子;五胞胎。②五胞胎之一。③任何五個所成的一組。

quin·tu·pli·cate 〔*adj., n.* kwɪnˈtjuplɪkɪt; kwinˈtjuːplikit *v.* kwɪnˈtjupləˌket; kwinˈtjuːplikeit〕 *adj., v.,* **-cat·ed, -cat·ing,** *n.* —*adj.* 五倍的。—*v.t.* 使成五倍。—*n.* 一組五個中之一。***in quintuplicate*** 一式五分。

quip 〔kwɪp; kwip〕 *n., v.,* **quipped, quip·ping.** —*n.* ①譏諷語。②妙語;警語。③雙關語;遁詞。④奇異之舉動或事物。—*v.t.* 向…作譏諷語、妙語、雙關語等。—*v.i.* 譏諷;作妙語;作雙關語。

quip·ster 〔ˈkwɪpstɚ; ˈkwipstə〕 *n.* 作警語者;說諷刺話者;用雙關語或遁詞者。

quire 〔kwaɪr; kwaiə〕 *n.* ①二十四或二十五張同質同大小的一刀紙。②已摺疊並排好順序而未裝訂的一部分書葉。***in quires*** (書之)散頁;印好疊就而未加裝訂。—*v.t.* 將(未裝訂之書葉)摺疊並按順序放好。

Quir·i·nal 〔ˈkwɪrənl; ˈkwirənl〕 *n.* ①羅馬七丘之一(羅馬即建於此七丘之上)。②(建於此丘上之)義大利皇宮。③義大利政府或王朝(以別於梵蒂岡教廷)。—*adj.* 羅馬七丘之一的;義大利皇宮的;義大利政府或王朝的。

quirk 〔kwɝk; kwəːk〕 *n.* ①奇行;怪癖。②雙關語;遁辭;詭辯。③急扭;急轉。④(書寫等之)花體;花體字。⑤〖建築〗銳角;缺口;槽。—*adj.* 有缺口的。

quir·l(e)y 〔ˈkwɝlɪ; ˈkwəːli〕 *n., pl.* **-leys, -lies.** 〖美俚〗用手捲的香烟。

quirt 〔kwɝt; kwəːt〕 *n.* 一種短柄皮梢馬鞭。—*v.t.* 以短柄馬鞭擊。

quis·le 〔ˈkwɪzl; ˈkwizl〕 *v.i.,* **-led, -ling.** 〖俚〗當賣國賊;當敵人之傀儡。

quis·ling 〔ˈkwɪzlɪŋ; ˈkwizliŋ〕 *n.* 賣國賊;內奸;第五縱隊(典出挪威政客 Vidkun Quisling, 1887–1945, 因賣國投向納粹德國,被立爲挪威傀儡政府之首領)。

***quit** 〔kwɪt; kwit〕 *v.,* **quit** or **quit·ted, quit·ting,** *adj.* —*v.t.* ①停止;棄。The men *quit* work. 工人們停工。②離去。③根絕;脫去。He has *quit* drinking. 他已戒酒。④還淸;償還(債務等)。⑤除去;清除。to *quit* oneself a nuisance. 爲自己除去一件討厭之

事。⑥放手。***quit hold of*** 放開。***quit the scores*** 湔雪遺恨。—*v.i.* ①停工。When do you *quit?* 你何時停工？②離去。③辭職。④罷手；認輸。—*adj.* 清除的；了結的〖常 of〗.

quitch 〔kwɪtʃ; kwitʃ〕 *n.* 〖植物〗茅草之類。(亦作 **quitch grass**)

quit·claim 〔ˈkwɪtˌklem; ˈkwitkleim〕 *n.* 〖法律〗①放棄要求；放棄權利。②放棄權利(或要求)之證書。—*v.t.* 放棄對(財產、權利等)之要求。

‡quite 〔kwaɪt; kwait〕 *adv.* ①完全地。It's not *quite* finished. 尙未全部結束。②(表贊成、同感等之應答)眞實的；的確的。Oh, *quite.* (Yes, *quite.* or *Quite* so.)的確。③〖俗〗頗；有幾分。***quite a few*** 相當的；相當多的。***quite other*** (or ***another***) 完全不同的。***quite some*** 非常多。***quite the thing*** 時髦；時興。

quits 〔kwɪts; kwits〕 *adj.* 兩相抵銷的；無勝負的。***be quits with*** 向…報復或復讎。I will *be quits with* him. 我要向他報復。***call it quits*** a. 暫時或永久停止。b. 罷手；放棄。***cry quits*** 承認沒有勝負。***double or quits*** (連賭兩次時的)加倍(輸贏)或(輸贏)相銷。

quit·tance 〔ˈkwɪtn̩s; ˈkwitəns〕 *n.* ①免除；赦免；解除。②領取；領收證；收據。③償還；報答。

quit·ter 〔ˈkwɪtɚ; ˈkwitə〕 *n.* 〖俗〗怕事者；懦夫；遇困難即罷手者。

***quiv·er**[1] 〔ˈkwɪvɚ; ˈkwivə〕 *v.t. & v.i.* 使振動；振動；戰慄。to *quiver* with cold. 冷得發抖。—*n.* 振動；戰慄。

quiv·er[2] *n.* 箭囊；箭筒。***have an arrow left in one's quiver*** 還有本錢；尙未用盡。

quiv·er·ful 〔ˈkwɪvɚˌful; ˈkwivəful〕 *n.* ①滿箭筒的箭。②〖謔〗大家庭；大家族。

qui vive 〔kiˈviv; kiːˈviːv〕 〖法〗誰在那兒走？誰？(哨兵之口令)。***on the qui vive*** 警覺；警戒着。

Quix·ote 〔kɪˈhotɪ; ˈkwiksət〕 *n.* ①吉訶德(Don, 西班牙 Cervantes 小說中主角)。②如吉訶德之人物；俠義的空想家。

quix·ot·ic 〔kwɪksˈɑtɪk; kwikˈsɔtik〕 *adj.* ①如吉訶德的；愚俠的；傳奇的。②幻想的；不切實際的。

quix·ot·ism 〔ˈkwɪksətɪzəm; ˈkwiksətizəm〕 *n.* 不切實際之思想或行動。(亦作 **quixotry**)

quiz 〔kwɪz; kwiz〕 *v.*, **quizzed, quiz·zing,** *n., pl.* **quiz·zes.** —*v.t.* ①(非正式地)測驗(學生等)。②戲弄；嘲弄。—*n.* ①〖美〗非正式的考試。②戲弄別人的人；嘲弄別人的人。③戲弄；嘲弄；惡作劇。④怪人；乖僻之人。

quiz·mas·ter 〔ˈkwɪzˌmæstɚ; ˈkwizˌmɑːstə〕 *n.* 猜謎節目之主持人。(亦作 **questionmaster**)

quiz program 〖電視、廣播〗猜謎節目。(亦作 **quiz show**)

quiz·zee 〔kwɪˈzi; kwiˈziː〕 *n.* ①被詢問或質問的人。②參加測驗者。

quiz·zer 〔ˈkwɪzɚ; ˈkwizə〕 *n.* ①詢問者；考問者。②嘲弄者；惡作劇者。

quiz·zi·cal 〔ˈkwɪzɪkl̩; ˈkwizikəl〕 *adj.* ①古怪的；奇異的；滑稽的。②戲弄的；揶揄的。③疑問的；迷惑的。

quod 〔kwɑd; kwɔd〕 *n.* 〖英俚〗監獄。(亦作 **quad**)

quoin 〔kɔɪn; kɔin〕 *n.* ①〖建築〗突角；外角；外角石；隅石。②楔形之石塊、木塊等；楔形支持物。③〖印刷〗穩定活字於框架內之楔子。—*v.t.* ①置以隅石。②加楔使緊牢或高起。

quoit 〔kwɔɪt; kwɔit〕 *n.* ①鐵圈；繩圈；橡皮圈；金屬環(用於擲環套樁遊戲者)。②(*pl.*)擲環套樁遊戲。—*v.t.* 擲圈環於〖away, down, off, out〗.

quon·dam 〔ˈkwɑndəm; ˈkwɔndəm〕 *adj.* 過去的；以前的。

Quon·set hut 〔ˈkwɑnsɪt～; ˈkwɔnsit～〕 活動房屋(以鋼質桁爲基，以金屬浪板爲頂，頂成半圓拱狀，第二次世界大戰時美軍首先使用)。

quo·rum 〔ˈkworəm; ˈkwɔːrəm〕 *n.* ①法定人數。②特選的一羣人。

quot. quotation.

quo·ta 〔ˈkwotə; ˈkwoutə〕 *n.* ①分；配分；承擔或得到的部分。②(外國輸入品、移民等的)限額；配額；定額。

quot·a·ble 〔ˈkwotəbl̩; ˈkwoutəbl〕 *adj.* ①值得引用的。②適於引用的。—**quot·a·bil·i·ty,** *n.*

***quo·ta·tion** 〔kwoˈteʃən; kwouˈteiʃən〕 *n.* ①引用；引用文；引用句。*quotations* from Shakespeare. 自莎士比亞作品中引來之文句。②價格。today's *quotation* on wheat. 今日小麥之價格。③〖商〗估價；報價。④報價單；估價單。

quotation mark 引號之任一邊("" 或' ')。(亦作 **quote mark**)

quo·ta·tive 〔ˈkwotətɪv; ˈkwoutətiv〕 *adj.* 好引用的。

***quote** 〔kwot; kwout〕 *v.*, **quot·ed, quot·ing,** *n.* —*v.t.* ①引用。②定價；喊價。It is *quoted* at $10. 定價十元。③引證；舉例證明。④納入引號中。—*v.i.* 引用他人之文句。The minister *quoted* from the Bible. 傳教士引用聖經。—*n.* ①引用文(句)。②引號。

quoth 〔kwoθ; kwouθ〕 *v.t.* 〖古〗說。

quo·tid·i·an 〔kwoˈtɪdɪən; kwouˈtidiən〕 *adj.* 每日的；每日發生的。—*n.* 每日發生之事；(尤指)每日發作之熱病。

quo·tient 〔ˈkwoʃənt; ˈkwouʃənt〕 *n.* 〖數學〗商數。

quo·ti·e·ty 〔kwoˈtaɪətɪ; kwouˈtaiəti〕 *n., pl.* **-ties.** 〖數學〗率；係數。

qy. query.

R

R or **r** 〔ɑr; ɑː〕 *n., pl.* **R's** or **r's.** 英文之第十八個字母。***the three R's*** 讀，寫，算。

R. ①River. ②Republican. ③railroad. ④railway. ⑤Royal. ⑥King (拉=rex). ⑦Queen (拉=regina). ⑧rector. ⑨right. ⑩road. ⑪rupee(s). **r.** ①rod. ②road. ③ruble(s). ④rupee(s). ⑤king (拉=rex). ⑥queen (拉=regina). ⑦rabbi. ⑧radius. ⑨railroad. ⑩railway. ⑪rain. ⑫rare. ⑬〖商〗received. ⑭rector. ⑮residence. ⑯resides. ⑰retired. ⑱right. ⑲rises. ⑳river. ㉑royal. ㉒rubber. ㉓〖棒球〗run(s).

Ⓡ 〖商〗registered trademark. 註册商標。

Ra 〔rɑ; rɑː〕 *n.* 〖埃及神話〗太陽神。

Ra radium. **R.A.** ①Rear Admiral. ②Royal Academy. ③Royal Academician. ④Royal Artillery. ⑤Regular Army.

rab·bet 〔ˈræbɪt; ˈræbit〕 *n.* ①(木板上的)一種槽口。②相嵌接合。—*v.t.* ①在(木板等)上挖槽口。②以相嵌槽口連接。—*v.i.* 以相嵌槽口連接〖on, over〗.

rab·bi 〔ˈræbaɪ; ˈræbai〕 *n., pl.* **-bis,**

-bies. ①猶太教之法律專家;法師;教師;先生。②猶太教牧師。*the Chief Rabbi* 猶太教會之領袖。(亦作 **rabbin**)

rab·bin·ic [ræˈbɪnɪk; ræˈbinik] *n.* ①(R-)中世紀猶太法師寫作所用的希伯來語文。②(R-)後期希伯來語。—*adj.* (亦作 **rabbinical**) 猶太法師的;猶太法師之理論的;猶太法師之學問及所用語言的。***Rabbinic Hebrew*** 後期希伯來語。***rabbinic(al) literature*** 希伯來之神學與哲學。

rab·bin·ism [ˈræbɪnˌɪzəm; ˈræbinizəm] *n.* 猶太法師之教義或學說。

rab·bin·ist [ˈræbɪnɪst; ˈræbinist] *n.* 信奉猶太經典 (Talmud) 及法師之不成文宗教法典與教條者。

:rab·bit [ˈræbɪt; ˈræbit] *n.* ①兔子。②兔毛;兔皮。③〖俗〗不良之運動員(尤指不佳之網球員)。—*v.i.* 打兔子; 獵兔。to go *rabbiting.* 去獵兔子。

rabbit fever 〖醫〗兔熱;土拉倫斯菌病。

rabbit hutch 兔檻;兔籠。

rabbit punch 對頸後之一記有力的打擊。

rab·bit·ry [ˈræbɪtrɪ; ˈræbitri] *n., pl.* -ries. ①養兔場;兔棚。②一羣兔。

rabbit's foot ①作爲幸運象徵而保存的兔之後腿。②一種苜蓿。

rabbit warren ①養兔場。②飼兔圈地。③過度擁擠之共同住宅。

rab·bit·y [ˈræbɪtɪ; ˈræbiti] *adj.,* -bit·i·er, -bit·i·est. ①如兔的。②多兔的。

rab·ble¹ [ˈræbḷ; ˈræbl] *n., v.,* -bled, -bling, *adj.* —*n.* 暴民。*the rabble* 賤民。—*v.t.* 如暴民似地攻擊(人身)或破壞(財產)。—*adj.* 混亂的;粗魯的;卑鄙的。

rab·ble² *n., v.,* -bled, -bling. —*n.* 〖冶金〗熔鐵時用以攪拌或撇掉浮渣的鐵棒。—*v.t.* 以此等鐵棒攪拌。

rabble rouser 煽動暴民者。(亦作 **rabble-rouser**)

Rab·e·lai·si·an [ˌræbḷˈezɪən; ˌræbˈleiziən] *adj.* ①法國諷刺家拉伯雷(François Rabelais 1494?—1533)的。②粗俗之幽默的。—*n.* 崇拜拉伯雷者;研究拉伯雷之作品者。

Rab·e·lai·si·an·ism [ˌræbḷˈezɪənɪzəm; ˌræbˈleiziənizəm] *n.* 粗俗的幽默。

rab·id [ˈræbɪd; ˈræbid] *adj.* ①狂暴的;激烈的; 狂熱的; 猛烈的。②狂怒的;發狂的。③有恐水症的; 恐水症的; 狂犬症的;瘋的。—ness, *n.*

ra·bid·i·ty [ræˈbɪdətɪ; ræˈbiditi] *n.* 不講理;瘋狂。

ra·bies [ˈrebiz; ˈreibiːz] *n.* 〖醫〗恐水症(狂犬病)。

R.A.C. Royal Automobile Club (of Great Britain).

rac·coon [ræˈkun; rəˈkuːn] *n.* ①浣熊。②浣熊之皮毛。(亦作 **racoon**)

:race¹ [res; reis] *n., v.,* raced, rac·ing. —*n.* ①競賽;賽跑。②人生之旅程。His *race* is nearly run. 他的壽命將盡。③(*pl.*)固定時期內之一組賽馬。④競爭。⑤急流;急潮。⑥小海峽。⑦溝;水道。⑧(機器中滑動部分之)溝;槽。⑨前進之行動或路線。⑩爲飛機螺旋槳迫向後方之氣流。***with a strong race*** 凶猛地;猛烈地。—*v.t.* ①與…賽跑。②使(人或馬等)跑;使競走。③使疾進。to *race* a motor. 加速開動馬達。—*v.i.* ①疾行; 跑。Hearing the bell, we *raced* to the class. 聽見鐘響,我們趕快跑到課堂。②加疾;加速。

:race² *n.* ①(生物的)族類;種屬。the human *race.* 人類。②種族;人種。the white *race.* 白種人。③血統;家系;門第。of noble *race.* 貴族出身的。④優秀的血統。⑤生動或刺激性的品質。

race³ *n.* (生薑等之)根。

race·a·bout [ˈresəˌbaut; ˈreisəbaut] *n.* ①一種競賽用的遊艇。②競賽用的汽車。

race·ball [ˈresˌbɔl; ˈreisbɔːl] *n.* 賽馬時舉行的舞會。

race card 賽馬之順序單。

race·course [ˈresˌkors; ˈreis-kɔːs] *n.* ①=**race track.** ②用以推磨的流水。(亦作 **race course**)

race·go·er [ˈresˌgoɚ; ˈreisˌgouə] *n.* 經常去看賽馬、賽牛等各種比賽的人。

ra·ceme [reˈsim; reiˈsiːm] *n.* 〖植物〗串狀花;總狀花序。

race meet (or **meeting**) 賽馬會;「(腳踏車等)競賽會。」

ra·ce·mic [rəˈsimɪk; rəˈsiːmik] *adj.* ①葡萄的;葡萄中含有的。②串狀花狀的;葡萄狀的。③〖化〗葡萄酸化合物的。

rac·e·mose [ˈræsəˌmos; ˈræsəmous] *adj.* 〖植物〗①串狀花序的。②串狀排列的。③開串狀花的。

rac·er [ˈresɚ; ˈreisə] *n.* ①參加賽跑之人、動物或機械等。②美洲產之黑蛇。③重砲之旋轉盤。

race track ①賽馬場。②競賽場。

race·way [ˈresˌwe; ˈreiswei] *n.* ①導水溝;水路。②電線保護管。

ra·chis [ˈrekɪs; ˈreikis] *n., pl.* -chis·es, rach·i·des [ˈrækəˌdiz; ˈrækidiːz]. ①〖植物〗花軸;葉軸。②〖解剖〗脊椎;脊柱。③〖動物〗羽軸。

ra·chit·ic [rəˈkɪtɪk; rəˈkitik] *adj.* 〖醫〗佝僂病的;患佝僂病的。

ra·chi·tis [rəˈkaɪtɪs; rəˈkaitis] *n.* 〖醫〗佝僂病。

***ra·cial** [ˈreʃəl; ˈreiʃəl] *adj.* 人種的; 種族的。*racial* prejudice. 種族偏見。—**ly,** *adv.*

ra·cial·ism [ˈreʃəlˌɪzəm; ˈreiʃəlizəm] *n.* ①民族性; 民族精神; 民族主義。②種族偏見;種族優劣論。

rac·i·ly [ˈresəlɪ; ˈreisili] *adv.* ①有力地;爽利地;活潑地。②味美地;芬芳地;新鮮地。③刺激地;辛辣地;有趣地。④略涉淫猥地。

rac·i·ness [ˈresɪnɪs; ˈreisinis] *n.* ①有力;爽利;活潑。②味美; 芬芳; 新鮮。③刺激;辛辣;有趣。④略涉淫猥。

rac·ing [ˈresɪŋ; ˈreisiŋ] *n.* ①競走; 賽跑。②賽馬;賽船。—*adj.* ①賽馬的;適於賽馬的;賽馬用的。②比賽用的。

racing form ①有關賽馬資料之出版品。②任何比賽中有關參加者之詳細記錄。(亦作 **form sheet**)

rac·ism [ˈresɪzəm; ˈreisizəm] *n.* ①種族差別論;種族優越感。②種族差別政策。③以種族差別論爲基礎的政治或社會制度。

rac·ist [ˈresɪst; ˈreisist] *adj.* 種族差別論的;懷種族偏見的。 —*n.* 種族差別論者;懷種族偏見者。

rack¹** [ræk; ræk] *n.* ①掛物或裝物之架。a hat *rack.* 帽架。②裝草架;馬槽。③配裝齒輪之齒棒。④拷問臺(古時之一種刑具,扯人之四肢而拷問者)。⑤(身體上或精神上的)巨大痛苦。⑥拉緊;繃緊。be on the rack*** **a.** 受拷刑;十分苦痛。**b.** 受到壓力。***in a high rack*** 在高位。***live at rack and manger*** 過豪華奢侈的生活。***put to*** (or ***on***) ***the rack*** 加以拷問。—*v.t.* ①使痛苦; 拉; 絞。to be *racked* with a cough. 爲咳嗽所苦。②以拷問臺行刑。***rack one's brains*** 苦苦思索;絞腦汁。***rack up*** 〖美俗〗累積。

rack² *n.* (馬的) 輕跑; 小跑之步法。—*v.i.* (馬)輕跑;溜蹄。

rack³ *n.* ①飛雲。②記號; 痕跡。 —*v.i.* 順風駕駛或移動。
rack⁴ *n.* 毀滅。***go to rack and ruin*** 破壞;毀滅。
rack⁵ *v.t.* 從葡萄渣榨取(酒等)。
rack·a·bones [ˈrækəˌbonz; ˈrækəbounz] *n.* 〖謔〗瘦弱的人或獸。
***rack·et¹** [ˈrækɪt; ˈrækit] *n.* ①網球拍。②(*pl.*)一種拍球戲。
rack·et² *n.* ①喧嘩; 吵嚷。②〖俗〗以威脅手段騙錢之計策。③〖俗〗職業。④〖俗〗有組織之非法行動(如勒索、欺詐等)。⑤闊宴;歡樂之聚會。⑥不利的結果。***give away the racket*** 無心地把祕密洩漏出去。***go on a racket*** 遊蕩;縱情歡鬧。***make a racket*** 惹起大亂子。***stand the racket*** **a.** 付帳。**b.** 長久保持;負責任。***What is the racket?*** 甚麼事? 怎麼啦? —*v.i.* ①喧鬧。②過放蕩生活。
racket ball 網球。
racket court 網球場。
rack·et·eer [ˌrækɪtˈɪr; ˌrækiˈtiə] *n.* 〖美俚〗以威脅手段詐財者;勒索者;歹徒。—*v.i.* 以威脅手段詐財。
racket press 網球拍夾(夾網球拍以保持其平整之框架)。
rack·et·y [ˈrækɪtɪ; ˈrækiti] *adj.* ①喧鬧的。②放蕩的。
rack railway (or **railroad**) 齒狀鐵道。
rack-rent [ˈrækˌrɛnt; ˈræk-rent] *n.* (亦作 **rack rent**) 極高的地租。—*v.t.* ①向…索極高地租。②强索(農田等)之盡可能最高之租金。
rack wheel 大齒輪。
ra·con [ˈrekɑn; ˈreikɔn] *n.* 雷達信標(爲 *ra*dar bea*con* 之略)。
rac·on·teur [ˌrækɑnˈtɝ; ˌrækɔnˈtəː] 〖法〗 *n.* 健談者;善講故事者;說書人。
ra·coon [ræˈkun; rəˈkuːn] *n.* =**raccoon.**
rac·quet [ˈrækɪt; ˈrækit] *n.* =**racket¹.**
rac·y [ˈresɪ; ˈreisi] *adj.*, **rac·i·er, rac·i·est.** ①有力的;爽利的;活潑的。②味美的;芬芳的;新鮮的。③辛辣的;有趣的。④猥褻的;挑逗性的。
rad. ①radial. ②radical. ③radius. ④radix.
***ra·dar** [ˈredɑr; ˈreidə, -dɑː] *n.* ①〖電〗雷達。(爲*ra*dio *d*etecting *a*nd *r*anging 之略) ②由雷達原理裝配之機械。
ra·dar·scope [ˈredɑrˌskop; ˈreidɑːskoup] *n.* 雷達指示器。
rad·dle [ˈrædl; ˈrædl] *n.*, *v.*, **-dled, -dling.** —*n.* 〖礦〗赭色赤鐵礦;代赭石;赭土。—*v.t.* 塗赭土於;用赭土着色。(亦作 **ruddle, reddle**)
ra·di·al [ˈredɪəl; ˈreidjəl] *adj.* ①光線的;光線狀的。②〖數學〗半徑的。③〖物理〗沿徑的。④成輻射狀的;放射狀的;櫛形的。⑤〖植物〗射出花的。⑥〖動物〗射出狀的。⑦〖解剖〗橈骨的;靠近橈骨的。*radial* artery. 橈骨動脈。—*n.* ①放射部分。②橈骨神經;橈骨動脈。—**ly,** *adv.*
radial engine 輻射引擎。
ra·di·an [ˈredɪən; ˈreidjən] *n.* 〖數學〗弳;度弧(角度的單位, 約等於 57.295°)。
***ra·di·ance** [ˈredɪəns, -djəns; ˈreidjəns, -diəns] *n.* ①燦爛; 閃爍。 the *radiance* of the sun. 太陽的燦爛。②發光;射光。③輻射。
***ra·di·an·cy** [ˈredɪənsɪ; ˈreidjənsi, -diən-] *n.* =**radiance.**
***ra·di·ant** [ˈredɪənt; ˈreidjənt, -diənt] *adj.* ①閃鑠的;明亮的。②滿面春風的。a *radiant* smile. 嫣然微笑。③放射光線的;輻射的。We get *radiant* energy from the sun. 我們自陽光中得到輻射能。④發光的;放熱的。—*n.* 〖物理〗輻射點;輻射體。—**ly,** *adv.*
radiant energy 輻射能。
radiant heating 在建築物內裝設電熱器、熱水管或蒸汽管於牆壁中或地板下以取暖的方法。
***ra·di·ate** [ˈredɪˌet; ˈreidieit] *v.*, **-at·ed, -at·ing,** *adj.*, *n.* —*v.t.* ①發射(光線等)。②放出; 射出。Her face *radiates* joy. 她的面孔洋溢着喜悅。—*v.i.* ①射出; 放出。②輻射出;向四周伸張。—*adj.* ①發光的;光輝的。②輻射狀的。③有輻射結構之動物的。 —*n.* 有輻射結構之任何無脊椎動物。
ra·di·a·tion [ˌredɪˈeʃən; ˌreidiˈeiʃən] *n.* ①輻射; 放射之過程。②輻射線; 輻射能。③〖醫〗放射線治療。④輻射狀排列。⑤〖測量〗射出測量法。***direct radiation*** 直接輻射。
radiation sickness 輻射病(因接受過多之輻射能而引起之病症)。
ra·di·a·tive [ˈredɪˌetɪv; ˈreidieitiv] *adj.* ①放熱的;放射光的。②放射的;輻射的。***radiative capture*** 輻射捕獲。
***ra·di·a·tor** [ˈredɪˌetɚ; ˈreidieitə] *n.* ①暖氣爐;放熱器。②(汽車引擎的)冷却器。③發光或發熱的人或物。 Stars are *radiators* of vast power. 恒星是强力的發光體。
***rad·i·cal** [ˈrædɪkl; ˈrædikl] *adj.* ①根本的; 基本的。②急進的; 極端的; 急烈的。 the *Radical* Party. 急進黨。③〖植物〗根的;根生的。④〖數學〗根的。 the *radical* sign. 根號(如 $\sqrt{\ }$)。—*n.* ①急進分子。②〖化〗根;基(如 NH_4 是 NH_4OH 及 NH_4Cl 之根)。③〖數學〗根號($\sqrt{\ }$)。④〖語音〗語根。⑤〖文法〗字根;(中國字的)偏旁;部首。⑥基本;基礎。
rad·i·cal·ism [ˈrædɪklˌɪzəm; ˈrædiklizəm] *n.* 急進;急進主義。
radical left 極左派分子(亦稱新左派分子)。
rad·i·cal·ly [ˈrædɪklɪ; ˈrædikli] *adv.* ①根本上。②徹底;完全。
rad·i·cle [ˈrædɪkl; ˈrædikl] *n.* ①〖解剖〗小根(神經、血管等的根狀部)。②〖植物〗幼根;胚根。③〖化〗=**radical.**
rad·ic-lib [ˈrædɪkˈlɪb; ˈrædikˈlib] *n.* 〖美〗左傾自由分子。
‡**ra·di·o** [ˈredɪˌo; ˈreidiou] *n.*, *pl.* **-di·os,** *adj.*, *v.*, **-di·oed, -di·o·ing.** —*n.* ①無線電報;無線電話;無線電播音。②收音機。I heard it on the *radio*. 我在收音機中聽到的。③〖俗〗無線電通訊;由無線電所發之消息。—*adj.* ①無線電報的; 收音機的。②每秒超過 15,000 週率以上的; 中波週率以上的。—*v.t.* 以無線電廣播。They *radioed* a call for help. 他們發出無線電報求救。②以無線電通信。 —*v.i.* 以無線電傳送消息、音樂等。
radio- 〖字首〗表下列諸義: ①光射的;似光射的, 如: radiolarian. ②由無線電的, 如: radiotelegraphy.③〖解剖〗橈骨及…。④〖醫〗用輻射能治療的, 如: radiotherapy. ⑤〖理化〗放射性的;有輻射能的。
ra·di·o·ac·tive [ˌredɪoˈæktɪv; ˌreidiouˈæktiv] *adj.* 有輻射能的;放射性的。—*v.t.* 使有放射性;使有輻射能。
radioactive fallout 放射塵。
radioactive isotope 放射同位素。
ra·di·o·ac·tiv·i·ty [ˌredɪˌoækˈtɪvətɪ; ˈreidiouækˈtiviti] *n.* 放射性;放射現象。
ra·di·o·am·pli·fi·er [ˌredɪoˈæmpləˌfaɪɚ; ˌreidiouˈæmplifaiə] *n.* 〖無線電〗高周波增幅機;高頻放大器。

ra·di·o·au·to·graph [ˌredɪoˈɔtəˌgræf; ˌreidiouˈɔːtəgrɑːf] *n.* 自動放射照相。(亦作 **autoradiograph**)

ra·di·o·bi·ol·o·gy [ˌredɪobaɪˈɑlədʒɪ; ˌreidioubaiˈɔlədʒi] *n.* 放射生物學。

ra·di·o·broad·cast [ˈredɪoˈbrɔdˌkæst; ˈreidiouˈbrɔːdkɑːst] *n., v.,* **-cast** or **-cast·ed, -cast·ing.** —*n.* 無線電廣播。—*v.t.* 用無線電廣播。—**er,** *n.*

radiobroadcasting station 無線電臺。

radio car 有無線電話收發機設備的警車。

ra·di·o·cast [ˈredɪoˌkæst; ˈreidioukɑːst] *v.,* **-cast** or **-cast·ed, -cast·ing,** *n.* —*v.t. & v.i.* (用)無線電廣播。—*n.* 無線電廣播。

ra·di·o·chem·is·try [ˌredɪoˈkɛmɪstrɪ; ˌreidiouˈkemistri] *n.* 放射化學。

ra·di·o·co·balt [ˌredɪoˈkobɔlt; ˌreidiouˈkoubɔːlt] *n.* 放射性鈷同位素。

ra·di·o·de·tec·tor [ˌredɪodɪˈtɛktɚ; ˌreidioudiˈtektə] *n.* 【無線電】檢波器。 ***crystal radiodetector*** 晶體檢波器。

ra·di·o·e·col·o·gy [ˌredɪoɪˈkɑlədʒɪ; ˌreidiouiˈkɔlədʒi] *n.* 環境輻射學。

ra·di·o·gen·ic [ˌredɪoˈdʒɛnɪk; ˈreidiouˈdʒenik] *adj.* ①由於放射現象而產生的。②適於電臺廣播的。

ra·di·o·go·ni·om·e·ter [ˌredɪoˌgonɪˈɑmɪtɚ; ˌreidiouˌgouniˈɔmitə] *n.* 無線電方位計。

ra·di·o·gram [ˈredɪəˌgræm; ˈreidiəgræm] *n.* ①無線電報。②【英】收音電唱機。③【英】放射線;放射線照片。

ra·di·o·gram·o·phone [ˈredɪoˈgræməfon; ˈreidiouˈgræməfoun] *n.* 收音電唱機。

ra·di·o·graph [ˈredɪəˌgræf; ˈreidiougrɑːf] *n.* ①放射線照相;放射線攝照之相片。②陽光强度與期間之測量儀或記錄器。—*v.t.* 作…之放射線照相。

ra·di·o·graph·ic [ˌredɪoˈgræfɪk; ˌreidiouˈgræfik] *adj.* 放射照相的;放射照相術的。

ra·di·og·ra·phy [ˌredɪˈɑgrəfɪ; ˌreidiˈɔgrəfi] *n.* 放射線照相術。

ra·di·o·i·so·tope [ˌredɪoˈaɪsətop; ˌreidiouˈaisətoup] *n.* 放射性同位素。

ra·di·o·lo·cate [ˌredɪoloˈket; ˈreidioulouˈkeit] *n.* 雷達測向;雷達定位(探測敵機等之方位及方向)。—**ra·di·o·lo·ca·tion,** *n.*

ra·di·o·lo·ca·tor [ˌredɪoloˈketɚ; ˈreidioulouˈkeitə] *n.* 【英】=**radar** (舊名)。

ra·di·ol·o·gist [ˌredɪˈɑlədʒɪst; ˌreidiˈɔlədʒist] *n.* 放射線研究者。

ra·di·ol·o·gy [ˌredɪˈɑlədʒɪ; ˌreidiˈɔlədʒi] *n.* ①放射學;應用輻射學。②【醫】放射線科。—**ra·di·o·log·i·cal,** *adj.*

ra·di·o·me·te·or·o·graph [ˌredɪoˈmitɪərəˌgræf; ˌreidiouˈmiːtiərəgrɑːf] *n.* 電波氣象記錄器。

ra·di·om·e·ter [ˌredɪˈɑmətɚ; ˌreidiˈɔmitə] *n.* 輻射計。

ra·di·om·e·try [ˌredɪˈɑmətrɪ; ˌreidiˈɔmitri] *n.* 輻射能測量。

ra·di·o·news [ˈredɪoˌnjuz; ˈreidiounjuːz] *n.* 無線電臺廣播之消息。

ra·di·o·nu·clide [ˌredɪoˈnjuklaɪd; ˌreidiouˈnjuːklaid] *n.* 【物理】放射性核種。

ra·di·o·phone [ˈredɪəˌfon; ˈreidioufoun] *n., v.,* **-phoned, -phon·ing.** —*n.* ①無線電話(機)。②【物理】任何使放射能變成聲音的儀器。—*v.t. & v.i.* 用無線電話發送(信息);打無線電話。

ra·di·o·pho·to [ˌredɪoˈfoto; ˈreidiouˈfoutou] *n., pl.* **-tos.** =**radiophotograph.**

ra·di·o·pho·to·graph [ˌredɪoˈfotəˌgræf; ˈreidiouˈfoutəgrɑːf] *n.* 無線電傳眞照片。

ra·di·o·pho·tog·ra·phy [ˌredɪəfəˈtɑgrəfɪ; ˈreidioufəˈtɔgrəfi] *n.* 無線電傳眞。

ra·di·o·press [ˈredɪoˌprɛs; ˈreidioupres] *n.* 無線電新聞。

ra·di·o·pro·tec·tion [ˌredɪoprəˈtɛkʃən; ˌreidiouprəˈtekʃən] *n.* 輻射防護。

ra·di·o·scope [ˈredɪoˌskop; ˈreidiouskoup] *n.* 放射鏡。

ra·di·o·scop·ic [ˌredɪoˈskɑpɪk; ˌreidiouˈskɔpik] *adj.* ①放射鏡的。②放射觀察法的。

ra·di·os·co·py [ˌredɪˈɑskəpɪ; ˌreidiˈɔskəpi] *n.* 射線檢查法;放射觀察法。

ra·di·o·sonde [ˈredɪoˌsɑnd; ˈreidiousɔnd] *n.* 無線電探空儀;無線電測候器。

ra·di·o·tel·e·gram [ˈredɪoˈtɛləˌgræm; ˈreidiouˈteligræm] *n.* 無線電報。

ra·di·o·tel·e·graph [ˌredɪoˈtɛləˌgræf; ˈreidiouˈteləgrɑːf] *n.* 無線電報機。—*v.t. & v.i.* 以無線電報機發送。

ra·di·o·tel·e·graph·ic [ˈredɪoˌtɛləˈgræfɪk; ˈreidiouˌteləˈgræfik] *adj.* 無線電報的。

ra·di·o·te·leg·ra·phy [ˈredɪˌotəˈlɛgrəfɪ; ˈreidioutəˈlegrəfi] *n.* 無線電報(術)。

ra·di·o·tel·e·phone [ˌredɪoˈtɛləfon; ˈreidiouˈtelifoun] *n., v.,* **-phoned, -phon·ing.** —*n.* 無線電話(機)。—*v.i. & v.t.* 以無線電話發送(信息);打無線電話。

ra·di·o·te·leph·o·ny [ˈredɪˌotəˈlɛfənɪ; ˈreidioutəˈlefəni] *n.* 無線電通話;無線電話。

radio telescope 無線電天文望遠鏡。

ra·di·o·tel·e·type [ˌredɪoˈtɛlɪtaɪp; ˈreidiouˈtelitaip] *n.* 無線電自動打字機。

ra·di·o·ther·a·pist [ˌredɪoˈθɛrəpɪst; ˈreidiouˈθerəpist] *n.* 放射治療家。

ra·di·o·ther·a·py [ˈredɪoˈθɛrəpɪ; ˈreidiouˈθerəpi] *n.* X光療法;放射線療法。

ra·di·o·ther·my [ˈredɪoˌθɝmɪ; ˈreidiouˌθəːmi] *n.* 放射線療法;X光療法。

radio wave 無線電波。

rad·ish [ˈrædɪʃ; ˈrædiʃ] *n.* 蘿蔔。

***ra·di·um** [ˈredɪəm; ˈreidjəm, -diəm] *n.* 【化】鐳。

ra·di·um·ther·a·py [ˈredɪəmˈθɛrəpɪ; ˈreidjəmˈθerəpi] *n.* 以鐳的放射線治療法。

***ra·di·us** [ˈredɪəs; ˈreidjəs, -diəs] *n., pl.* **-di·i** [-dɪˌaɪ; -diai], **-di·us·es.** ①半徑。②以半徑畫成之圓形面積。He has visited every shop within a *radius* of two miles. 周圍兩英里以內的店鋪他都去過了。③橈骨。④範圍;地區。

radius vector *pl.,* **radii vec·tor·es** [~vɛkˈtoriz; ~vekˈtɔːriz], **radius vec·tors.** ①【數學】輻;矢徑;向徑。②【天文】向徑。

ra·dix [ˈredɪks; ˈreidiks] *n., pl.* **ra·di·ces** [ˈrædəˌsiz; ˈrædisiːz], **ra·dix·es.** ①【數學】根;基數。②【植物】根(尤指藥用植物之根)。③【文法】語根;語幹。

ra·don [ˈredɑn; ˈreidɔn] *n.* 【化】氡(符號 Rn, 係一種放射性元素)。

RAF, R.A.F. Royal Air Force. 英國皇家空軍。

raff [ræf; ræf] *n.* ①大量;多量;衆多。②

R

〖英方〗垃圾；廢物。③賤民；下流社會(輕蔑語)。
raff·ish ['ræfɪʃ; 'ræfiʃ] *adj.* ①放蕩的；聲名狼籍的。②俗氣的；低級的。
raf·fle¹ ['ræfl; 'ræfl] *n., v.,* **-fled, -fling.** —*n.* 抽籤售賣法。—*v.t.* 以抽籤法售賣〖常 off〗. —*v.i.* 加入抽籤銷售。
raf·fle² *n.* ①垃圾；廢物。②〖航海〗繩索，帆等弄成的糾結；紛亂。
***raft¹** [ræft; rɑːft] *n.* 筏；救生艇。—*v.t.* ①以筏運送。②製成筏。—*v.i.* 搭乘筏子；使用筏子。
raft² *n.* 〖俗〗大量；許多。
***raft·er** ['ræftɚ; 'rɑːftə] *n.* 椽。
rafts·man ['ræftsmən; 'rɑːftsmən] *n.* 筏夫；撐木筏的人。(亦作 **rafter**)
rag¹** [ræg; ræg] *n.* ①破布；碎布。②一小塊布。③(*pl.*) 破衣服；襤褸的衣服。He was clad in *rags.* 他穿着破衣。④少量；不足道的一點點。⑤〖蔑〗手帕；旗子；戲臺布幕；鈔票等。⑥爲人輕視的報紙或雜誌。be cooked to rags*** 煮爛。***chew the rags*** 〖俚〗閒談；瞎聊天。***from rags to riches*** 從赤貧而暴富。***like a red rag to a bull*** 使人憤怒的；極端令人煩惱的。***spread every rag of sail*** 掛起所有的風帆。***take the rag off*** 强過；超過。—*adj.* 破布片製的。a *rag* doll. 破布縫的洋囡囡。—*v.t.* 使襤褸；使破爛。—*v.i.* 變得襤褸。

rag² *v.,* **ragged, rag·ging,** *n.* —*v.t.* 〖俚〗①罵。②逗；惹。③開…的玩笑；戲弄。—*n.* 〖英〗嘲笑；逗弄。
rag·a·muf·fin ['rægəˌmʌfɪn; 'rægəˌmʌfin] *n.* ①衣衫襤褸且骯髒之無賴。②衣衫襤褸之流浪兒童。
rag baby=**rag doll.**
rag·bag ['rægˌbæg; 'rægbæg] *n.* ①裝破衣服、破布之布袋。②雜湊。
rag bolt 有倒鈎的棘釘。
rag doll 用碎布做的玩偶。
rage** [redʒ; reidʒ] *n., v.,* **raged, rag·ing.** —*n.* ①憤怒；激怒；盛怒。He flew (*or* fell) into a *rage.* 他勃然大怒。②風行之物；流行之物。③極端的熱情；熱情之激發。④狂暴。have a rage for*** 有…癖；迷於…。***the rage*** 短時的風尚。—*v.i.* ①憤怒；發怒；狂暴。A storm is *raging.* 風雨狂作。②(疾病等) 蔓延；傳布。③激烈地進行。***rage itself out*** (暴風雨)平息；完結。
***rag·ged** ['rægɪd; 'rægid] *adj.* ①破爛的；襤褸的。②着破爛衣服的；衣衫襤褸的。③嶙峋的。*ragged* rocks. 嶙峋之石。④粗啞的 (=harsh). a *ragged* voice. 沙啞的聲音。⑤不整潔的；粗糙的。a *ragged* garden. 不潔的庭園。⑥凹凸不平的；潰爛的；皮肉有破損的。a *ragged* wound. 破爛的傷口。⑦不完全的；不整齊的。*ragged* time. (競舟中)不整齊的划法。—**ly,** *adv.* —**ness,** *n.*
ragged edge 邊緣。***on the ragged edge*** 在危險狀態中。
ragged robin 石竹科之一種野花。
ragged school 貧民學校。
rag·ged·y ['rægədɪ; 'rægədi] *adj.* 襤褸的；破爛的；不整的。
rag·gle-tag·gle ['rægḷˌtægḷ; 'rægəlˌtægəl] *adj.* 〖俗〗①衣衫襤褸的；衣冠不整的。②雜湊的。
rag·ing ['redʒɪŋ; 'reidʒiŋ] *adj.* ①激怒的；憤怒的。a *raging* anger. 狂怒。②猛烈的。③劇痛的。—**ly,** *adv.*
rag·man ['rægˌmæn; 'rægmæn] *n., pl.* **-men.** 收買破爛東西的人。
ra·gout [ræ'gu; ræ'guː] *n., v.,* **-gouted** [-'gud; -'guːd], **-gout·ing** [-'guɪŋ; -'guːiŋ]. —*n.* 一種蔬菜燉肉。—*v.t.* 將…作成此種菜餚。
rag·pick·er ['rægˌpɪkɚ; 'rægˌpikə] *n.* 以撿破爛東西爲生的人。
rag·tag ['rægˌtæg; 'rægtæg] *n.* 衣衫襤褸之羣衆。***ragtag and bobtail*** 下層社會；賤民。—*adj.* 下流社會的；烏合之衆的。
rag·time ['rægˌtaɪm; 'rægtaim] *n.* 〖俗〗①(黑人音樂中)旋律中重音落在非常地方之音律；切分音甚多之音律。②重音落在非常地方之音樂；爵士樂。—*adj.* 不嚴肅的；滑稽的。
rag·weed ['rægˌwid; 'rægwiːd] *n.* 〖植物〗豕草(花粉可致乾草熱病)。
rag wheel 鏈輪。
rah [rɑ; rɑː] *interj., n.* =**hurrah.**
raid** [red; reid] *n.* ①襲擊；突擊。an air-*raid.* 空襲。②搜捕。③搶㓨。④挖角；爭取競爭者之員工。make a raid upon*** (or ***on***) 抄查；襲擊；侵略。—*v.t.* ①襲擊；侵入。The police *raided* the gambling house. 警察搜查賭窟。②搶㓨。③挖角。—*v.i.* 搜捕；襲擊；突擊。
raid·er ['redɚ; 'reidə] *n.* ①襲擊者(尤指偷襲的飛機和軍艦)。②(美國海軍陸戰隊的)突擊大隊的士兵。
‡rail¹ [rel; reil] *n.* ①欄杆。stair *rails.* 樓梯之扶欄。②鐵軌。③鐵路；鐵道。④船舷上之欄杆。***off the rails*** 出軌；擾亂秩序；狂亂；解散。***ride (someone) out on a rail*** 嚴懲(某人)。—*v.t.* ①鋪以鐵軌。②圍以欄杆。***rail in*** 用欄杆或籬笆圍起。
rail² *v.i.* 罵；嘲罵；奚落。—**er,** *n.*
rail³ *n., pl.* **rails, rail.** 秧鷄之類。
rail·bird ['relˌbɝd; 'reilbəːd] *n.* ①〖美俚〗喜在賽馬場欄杆旁邊觀看賽馬或練馬的人。②=**rail³.**
rail fence 柵欄。
rail·head ['relˌhɛd; 'reilhed] *n.* ①〖鐵路〗已鋪鐵軌之最遠點。②〖軍〗鐵運末地；兵站車站；軍需站。③最遠點。
***rail·ing** ['relɪŋ; 'reiliŋ] *n.* ①柵欄；圍欄；欄杆。②欄杆之材料。③欄杆之集合稱。
rail·ler·y ['relərɪ; 'reiləri] *n., pl.* **-ler·ies.** ①善意的嘲笑；玩笑；嘲弄。②玩笑話。
‡rail·road ['relˌrod; 'reilroud] *n.* ①〖美〗鐵路；鐵道。②〖美〗鐵路界。③(*pl.*) 鐵路公司之股票或債劵。—*v.t.* ①〖美〗以鐵路運輸。②供以鐵路。③〖美俗〗以極大速度提出並使之通過。④〖美俗〗輕率審判而定罪。—*v.i.* 〖美〗服務於鐵路界。
rail·road·er ['relˌrodɚ; 'reilˌroudə] *n.* 〖美〗鐵路從業人員。
rail·split·ter ['relˌsplɪtɚ; 'reilˌsplitə] *n.* 將木頭劈成欄杆者。***the Railsplitter*** 林肯的綽號。
‡rail·way ['relˌwe; 'reilwei] *n.* ①〖英〗=**railroad.** ②鐵軌。③電車路軌。
rai·ment ['remənt; 'reimənt] *n.* 〖古、詩〗衣服。
‡rain [ren; rein] *n.* ①雨。We've had too much *rain* this summer. 今年夏天的雨太多了。②雨之降落。Has the *rain* stopped yet? 雨停了沒有？③如雨般之降落。***rain or shine*** 不論晴雨；無論如何；在任何情況之下。***the rains*** **a.** 雨季。**b.** 雨季中所降之雨。—*v.i.* ①降雨；下雨。Is it *raining?* 在下雨嗎？②似雨滴般降下。③(似雨般) 降落。Tears *rain* down his cheeks. 他淚流滿面。—*v.t.* 使傾注；灑落。***It never rains but it pours.*** 不雨則已，一雨傾盆。***It rained cats and dogs.*** 降傾盆大雨。***rain off*** 〖英〗=**rain out.**

rain out 因雨取消。
rain·band 〔ˈrenˌbænd; ˈreinbænd〕 *n.* 〖氣象〗雨線(太陽光譜黃色部分顯出的暗色帶)。
***rain·bow** 〔ˈrenˌbo; ˈreinbou〕 *n.* 虹。
rain check ①雨票(戶外比賽因雨停止舉行時,散發給觀衆留待後用的票)。②被邀赴宴會因故不能到,而希望以後改期再請的要求。
rain·coat 〔ˈrenˌkot; ˈreinkout〕 *n.* 雨衣。
rain dance 美國印第安人之祈雨舞。
rain doctor 祈雨法師。(亦作 **rain maker**)
rain·drop 〔ˈrenˌdrɑp; ˈrein-drɔp〕 *n.* 雨滴;雨點。
***rain·fall** 〔ˈrenˌfɔl; ˈreinfɔːl〕 *n.* ①降雨。②雨量。the annual *rainfall* in Keelung. 基隆每年的雨量。
rain gauge 雨量計。
rain glass 晴雨計。
rain·i·ness 〔ˈrenɪnɪs; ˈreininis〕 *n.* 多雨。
rain·mak·er 〔ˈrenˌmekɚ; ˈreinˌmeikə〕 *n.* 造雨者。
rain·mak·ing 〔ˈrenˌmekɪŋ; ˈreinˌmeikiŋ〕 *n.* 藉人工方法或法術造雨。
rain·proof 〔*adj.* ˈrenˈpruf; ˈreinˈpruːf *v.* ˈrenˌpruf; ˈreinpruːf〕 *adj.* 防雨的。—*v.t.* 使能防雨。
rain·spout 〔ˈrenˌspaut; ˈreinspaut〕 *n.* 屋頂的排水孔。
rain·squall 〔ˈrenˌskwɔl; ˈreinskwɔːl〕 *n.* 一陣風雨。
rain·storm 〔ˈrenˌstɔrm; ˈrein-stɔːm〕 *n.* 暴風雨。
rain water 雨水。
rain·wear 〔ˈrenˌwɛr; ˈreinwɛə〕 *n.* 雨天穿着之物,如雨衣、雨鞋等。
‡rain·y 〔ˈrenɪ; ˈreini〕 *adj.*, **rain·i·er, rain·i·est.** ①下雨的;多雨的。②帶來雨的。*rainy* winds. 帶來雨水的風。③爲雨所淋濕的。***rainy day*** 將來可能有的苦日子。
‡raise 〔rez; reiz〕 *v.*, **raised, rais·ing,** *n.* —*v.t.* ①舉起;扶起。to *raise* one's hand. 舉起手。②使升;揚起。③擢升。④增加;提高。⑤使(聲音)增高。*Raise* your voice. 提高你的聲音。⑥聚集;招募;徵。⑦產生;惹起。A funny remark *raises* a laugh. 滑稽的話惹人發笑。⑧(自口中)發出。to *raise* a shout. 發出呼喊。⑨建立。⑩驚起;激起。⑪飼育;栽培。⑫結束;解除。to *raise* a siege. 解圍。⑬提出。to *raise* a question. 提出一問題。⑭籌募;募集。to *raise* money. 募款。⑮(賭博時)加多賭金。⑯(酵素)使(麪包)膨起。Yeast *raises* bread. 發酵粉使麪包膨起。⑰起死回生。⑱看見(陸地)。After a long voyage the ship *raised* land. 在長時間的航行之後,這船看見了陸地。⑲使出現。⑳塗改(支票等)。㉑以無線電建立通信。㉒從下面向上挖礦坑。***raise a dust*** 激起騷動。***raise Cain; raise hell*** (or ***the devil***)〖俚〗引起大風波;引起擾亂。***raise from the dead*** 起死復生。***raise*** (***a soldier***) ***from the ranks*** 擢升(士兵)爲軍官。***raise his*** (or ***its***) ***head*** 出現;顯現。***raise one's voice against*** 向…抗議。***raise the wind*** 〖俚〗籌款;取得所需之款。—*v.i.* ①升高。②提高賭注或叫價。—*n.* ①(量、價格、待遇等之)增高;提高。They promised him a *raise.* 他們答應給他加薪。②高地;隆起之地。③由下朝上挖掘而成之礦坑。
raised 〔rezd; reizd〕 *adj.* ①浮雕的。②浮起的;凸起的。③(以酵素等)發起的(麪包等)。
rais·er 〔ˈrezɚ; ˈreizə〕 *n.* 〖美〗栽植者;飼養者。a cattle *raiser.* 飼牛者。
***rai·sin** 〔ˈrezn̩; ˈreizn〕 *n.* ①葡萄乾。②葡萄乾色。
raj 〔rɑdʒ; rɑːdʒ〕 *n.* 〖英印〗統治;支配;主權。
ra·ja, ra·jah 〔ˈrɑdʒə; ˈrɑːdʒə〕 *n.* (印度、爪哇、婆羅洲之)統治者;首領;酋長;土王。
***rake¹** 〔rek; reik〕 *n., v.*, **raked, rak·ing.** —*n.* 耙子。—*v.t.* ①耙。②搜尋。③縱射(軍艦或敵軍等);沿…縱線掃射。④大量收集〖常 in〗。⑤揭露〖常 up〗。⑥拂;括;抓。—*v.i.* ①用耙子。②搜求。③用眼睛掃視。④沖刷。The sea *rakes* against the shore. 海浪沖刷海岸。
rake² *n.* 流氓;浪子。
rake³ *n., v.*, **raked, rak·ing.** —*n.* 〖航海〗傾斜。—*v.i.* (船頭、船尾、舵、桅杆、煙囪等)傾斜。—*v.t.* 使(桅杆、煙囪等)向後傾斜。
rake·hell 〔ˈrekˌhɛl; ˈreikhel〕 *n.* 放蕩者;無賴漢。—*adj.* 放蕩的;無賴的。
rake-off 〔ˈrekˌɔf; ˈreikɔf〕 *n.* 〖俚〗①(以正當或不正當的方法獲得的)一分。②盈利之一分。③折扣。
rak·ish¹ 〔ˈrekɪʃ; ˈreikiʃ〕 *adj.* ①漂亮的;俏皮的。②輕快的;速度很快似的。
rak·ish² *adj.* 放蕩的;遊蕩的;淫邪的。
râle 〔rɑl; rɑːl〕 *n.* 〖醫〗囉音;肺鳴(正常呼吸聲中所帶之一種嘎嘎聲或水泡聲,通常爲肺部或支氣管病之徵候)。
rall. rallentando.
ral·len·tan·do 〔ˌrælənˈtændo; ˌrælenˈtændou〕 *adj.* & *adv.* 〖音樂〗漸緩的(地)。—*n.* 演奏漸緩之處。
ral·li·car(t) 〔ˈrælɪˌkɑr(t); ˈrælikɑː(t)〕 *n.* 〖英〗供四人乘坐之兩輪馬車。
***ral·ly¹** 〔ˈrælɪ; ˈræli〕 *v.*, **-lied, -ly·ing,** *n., pl.* **-lies.** —*v.t.* ①收集;重整。②鼓起;重振。—*v.i.* ①集合;集隊。The soldiers *rallied.* 兵士集隊。②前去幫助一人、一黨或一運動〖常 to, around〗。③恢復氣力;(部分)復原。④〖網球〗將球迅速打來打去(至一方不能接住爲止)。⑤(價格)回升。⑥〖棒球〗一局中得分一次或一次以上。⑦振作力氣、精神等。—*n.* ①恢復。②集會。③(網球或其它球賽)連續來回的打。④拳賽中之迅速互相出拳。⑤價格之回升。⑥長途賽車。⑦〖棒球〗一局中得分一次或一次以上。
ral·ly² *v.t.* & *v.i.*, **-lied, -ly·ing.** 嘲笑;挖苦。
***ram** 〔ræm; ræm〕 *n., v.*, **rammed, ram·ming.** —*n.* ①(未去勢之)牡羊;公羊。②撞擊機;機器之撞擊部分。③戰艦前端之撞角。④有撞角之戰艦。⑤抽水機之活塞。⑥抽水機。⑦(R-)〖天文〗白羊宮。
—*v.t.* ①撞;撞倒。②擠入;撞入。③猛力向下打。④用力塞進。⑤堅定地推進。to *ram* a bill through the Senate. 將一個法案在參院中以强力通過。⑥自前膛裝(彈藥)。
R.A.M. Royal Academy of Music. 皇家音樂學院。
Ram·a·dan 〔ˌræməˈdɑn; ˌræməˈdɑːn〕 *n.* ①回教曆之第九月;齋月。②齋月戒齋。
***ram·ble** 〔ˈræmbl̩; ˈræmbl〕 *v.*, **-bled, -bling,** *n.* —*v.i.* ①漫步;漫遊。to *ramble* about the streets. 漫步於街頭。②漫談;隨筆。③蔓延。—*v.t.* 在…漫步。—*n.* 漫步;漫遊。
ram·bler 〔ˈræmblɚ; ˈræmblə〕 *n.* ①漫步者;漫遊者。②漫談者;隨筆者。③〖植物〗攀緣薔薇。④郊區之平房。
ram·bling 〔ˈræmblɪŋ; ˈræmbliŋ〕 *adj.* ①漫步的;漫遊的。②漫談的;閑談的;隨筆的。③排列散漫不整的。④思想散漫的。⑤〖植物〗攀緣的;蔓延的。⑥移動的。
ram·bunc·tious 〔ræmˈbʌŋkʃəs; ræmˈbʌŋkʃəs〕 *adj.* 〖俗〗①騷亂的;喧囂的。

R

②暴亂的;剛愎的;難控制的。
ram·e·kin ['ræməkɪn;'ræməkin] *n.* ①烤蛋(以麪包屑、乾酪、蛋等烤成的一種食品)。②盛此種食品的烤盆。(亦作 **ramequin**)
ram·ie ['ræmɪ; 'ræmi] *n.* ①〖植物〗苧麻。②苧麻纖維。
ram·i·fi·ca·tion [ˌræməfə'keʃən; ˌræmifi'keiʃən] *n.* ①分枝; 分枝狀。②樹枝;枝狀物。③區分; 支流; 枝節。④分枝法。
ram·i·fy ['ræməˌfaɪ;'ræmifai] *v.*, **-fied, -fy·ing.** —*v.t.* 使分枝; 出枝; 分派。—*v.i.* 分派;分歧;分成網狀。
ram·jet ['ræmdʒɛt; 'ræmdʒet] *n.* 衝壓噴射。
ram·mer ['ræmɚ; 'ræmə] *n.* ①撞者。②撞器。③擦槍之通條;前膛槍之裝藥棒。
ram·mish ['ræmɪʃ; 'ræmiʃ] *adj.* ①公羊的;有腥臊味的。②淫亂的。
ra·mose [rə'mos;rə'mous] *adj.* 多分枝的(根或莖);分枝的。
ra·mous ['reməs; 'reiməs] *adj.* ①有分枝的。②枝狀的。
ramp¹ [ræmp; ræmp] *n.* ①(連接高低不平之兩平面之)盤道;上下飛機之活動梯。②(樓梯扶手)盤曲部分。③坡道; 斜路。④停機坪。
ramp² *v.i.* ①(如紋章內之獅等) 舉前足而立;以後脚立起。②作恫嚇之姿態。③猛衝;猛襲;暴跳。—*n.* ①直立躍起。②作恫嚇姿態。③猛衝; 暴跳。④〖俗〗動怒; 發怒。⑤〖俚〗欺騙;欺詐。
ram·page [*n.* 'ræmpedʒ; 'ræmpeidʒ *v.* ræm'pedʒ; ræm'peidʒ] *n., v.,* **-paged, -pag·ing.** —*n.* 一陣狂暴或興奮之行動。—*v.i.* 狂暴地亂衝;暴跳;猛烈地舉動。
ram·pa·geous [ræm'pedʒəs; ræm'peidʒəs] *adj.* 狂暴的;騷鬧的。
ramp·an·cy ['ræmpənsɪ; 'ræmpənsi] *n.* ①繁茂; 蔓延。②猖獗。③暴亂; 激烈。④〖紋章〗(獅子的)舉前脚直立。⑤跳躍。
ramp·ant ['ræmpənt; 'ræmpənt] *adj.* ①蔓延的;繁茂的。②無約束的;猖獗的。③憤怒的;激烈的;狂暴的。④〖紋章〗舉前肢而起立的;用後脚立起的。
ram·part ['ræmpɑrt; 'ræmpɑ:t] *n.* ①圍繞堡壘四周所建之土堤, 頂上與外緣置有石扶牆。②任何防禦物。③〖喻〗防禦; 保護。—*v.t.* 以壁壘防禦;保護。
ramp bus 機坪載客車。
ram·pi·on ['ræmpɪən; 'ræmpiən] *n.* 〖植物〗歐洲產的山小菜(其根可做生菜)。
ram·rod ['ræmˌrɑd; 'ræmrɔd] *n., v.,* **-rod·ded, -rod·ding.** —*n.* ①(前膛槍之)裝藥棒。②(槍之) 通條; 洗桿。***as stiff as a ramrod*** 保持僵直;僵直如通條。—*v.t.* ①〖俗〗用力推進。②約束;管教。
ram·shack·le ['ræmʃækl; 'ræmˌʃækl] *adj.* ①傾頹的;傾斜的;要倒塌的。②衰弱的;無力量的。③腐敗的;頹廢的。
Ran [rɑn; rɑ:n] *n.* 〖北歐神話〗海之女神。
*__ran__ [ræn; ræn] *v.* pt. of **run**.
*__ranch__ [ræntʃ; ræntʃ] *n.* ①大農場(包括房屋在內)。②農場。a chicken *ranch*. 養雞場。③在農場工作或居住的人。—*v.i.* 主持農場;在農場工作。—*v.t.* 使(家畜)在農場吃草;牧(牛、羊等)。
ranch·er ['ræntʃɚ; 'ræntʃə] *n.* ①農場主人或管理人。②牧童;農場工人。
ran·che·ro [ræn'tʃero; ræn'tʃɛərou] *n., pl.* **-ros.** =**rancher.**
ranch·man ['ræntʃmən; 'ræntʃmən] *n., pl.* **-men.** =**rancher.**
ran·cho ['ræntʃo; 'ræntʃou] 〖西〗*n.* ①農場工人所住之小茅屋。②農場。
ran·cid ['rænsɪd; 'rænsid] *adj.* ①陳腐的;敗壞的。②惡臭的。③難以相處的。
ran·cid·i·ty [ræn'sɪdətɪ; ræn'siditi] *n.* 腐敗;惡臭;腐臭氣味。
ran·co(u)r ['ræŋkɚ; 'ræŋkə] *n.* 深仇;怨恨。
ran·cor·ous ['ræŋkərəs; 'ræŋkərəs] *adj.* 深仇的;懷惡意的。
ran·dan¹ [ræn'dæn, 'rændæn; ræn'dæn] *n.* 〖方,俚〗①恣肆的行爲; 縱飲。②行爲狂亂的人。
ran·dan² *n.* 供三人划的小舟。
R & D research and development.
*__ran·dom__ ['rændəm; 'rændəm] *adj.* 隨便的;無目的的。a *random* remark. 一句無意的話。—*n.* 隨便; 無目的的工作。***at random*** 隨便地;無目的地。
random access 〖電腦〗隨機出入;雜亂進出。
ran·dy ['rændɪ; 'rændi] *adj.* 〖蘇〗①粗魯的;粗野的。②喧鬧的;大聲的。③淫蕩的。④難馴的。—*n.* ①强索的乞丐。②粗野的女人。
ra·nee ['rɑnɪ; 'rɑ:ni] *n.* (印度之) 王妃或女王;土王之妻。(亦作 **rani**)
rang [ræŋ; ræŋ] *v.* pt. of **ring**.
‡**range** [rendʒ; reindʒ] *n., v.,* **ranged, rang·ing,** *adj.* —*n.* ①範圍;界限。the *range* of vision. 視力範圍;眼界。②射程。out of (in) *range*. 在射程外(內)的。③射擊場。④放牧區。⑤列; 行。⑥(烹飪用之)爐竈。⑦槍砲至目標間之距離。⑧徘徊。⑨(動、植物的)分布或繁殖的區域。⑩方向; 方向線。The two barns are in direct *range* with the house. 那兩間穀倉與這間房子在同一個方向。⑪階級; 種類; 次序。***in range*** 〖航海〗(從船上看兩個以上物體)位於同一直線上的。—*v.t.* ①漫遊; 漫步。The buffaloes *ranged* the plains. 水牛漫遊於原野。②排列; 使成行。③列於某人一邊。④分門;別類。⑤使成直線;排整齊。⑥將(天文望遠鏡)對準目標; 瞄準。⑦調整槍砲角度。⑧在(某一區域)到處搜尋。⑨將(牛羣等)放在牧場吃草。—*v.i.* ①在某範圍之內變化。Prices *ranged* from $5 to $10. 價格自五元至十元不等。②伸展;延及。③漫遊;徘徊;漫步。The dogs *ranged* through the woods. 獵犬走過森林。④發現;產生;蔓生。⑤找出某物之距離或方向。⑥搜索某一區域。—*adj.* 牧場的;放牧區的。
range finder 測距器。
rang·er ['rendʒɚ; 'reindʒə] *n.* ①守林人。②〖英〗皇家森林或公園看守者。③巡邏人; 巡邏隊員。④(R-)(第二次世界大戰中美國之)突擊隊員;游擊隊員。⑤漫遊者;徘徊者。
Ran·goon [ræŋ'gun; ræŋ'gu:n] *n.* 仰光(緬甸之首都)。
rang·y ['rendʒɪ; 'reindʒi] *adj.,* **rang·i·er, rang·i·est.** ①適於漫遊的。②四肢瘦長的(動物或人)。③寬大的。④〖澳〗似山脈的;有山脈的;多山的。
ra·ni ['rɑnɪ;'rɑ:ni:] *n., pl.* **-nis.** =**ranee.**
‡**rank¹** [ræŋk; ræŋk] *n.* ①一行兵士。②(*pl.*) 軍隊; 兵士。③官階; 職位。④高位; 顯貴。A duke is a man of *rank*. 公爵是一顯貴之人。⑤社會階層。people of all *ranks* and classes. 各階層之人民。⑥等級。a scholar of the first *rank*. 第一流學者。⑦橫隊(別於縱隊)。***close ranks*** 團結。***pull (one's) rank (on)*** 利用職權;以權勢凌人。***take rank with*** 和…並列;和…並肩。—*v.t.* ①使成行列;排列。②分類;按秩序排列。*Rank* the provinces in the order of size. 按

面積大小依次排列各省。③強過；階級高於…之上。A major *ranks* a captain. 少校比上尉階級高。—*v.i.* ①列於。New York City *ranks* first in wealth. 紐約市在財富上居第一位。②居高位。③排成橫隊。

rank² *adj.* ①粗的；繁茂的。②生長茂盛的。③肥沃的。④野樹雜草叢生的。⑤腥臭的。⑥極端的；很厲害的。⑦下賤的；猥褻的；卑鄙的。

rank and file ①士兵（別於軍官）。②任何組織中占多數的普通人；平民（別於領袖）。

rank·er [ˈræŋkɚ; ˈræŋkə] *n.* ①占有某種地位之人。②〖英〗出身行伍之軍官。③士兵。

***rank·ing** [ˈræŋkɪŋ; ˈræŋkiŋ] *adj.* 出類拔萃的；第一流的。—*n.* 等級；順次。

ran·kle [ˈræŋkl̩; ˈræŋkl] *v.*, **-kled, -kling.** —*v.i.* ①使人心痛；痛。②發炎；化膿。—*v.t.* 使酸痛。

ran·sack [ˈrænsæk; ˈrænsæk] *v.t.* ①細細搜索；遍搜。②洗刼；掠奪。

ran·som** [ˈrænsəm; ˈrænsəm] *n.* ①贖金；贖回。to hold persons for *ransom*. 擄人待贖；綁票。②〖俗〗換取特權之錢等。a king's ransom*** 一大筆款子。—*v.t.* ①贖回。②向(爲)…索取贖金。③補贖；以奉獻贖罪。

rant [rænt; rænt] *v.i.* 作狂言；怒吼。—*v.t.* 怒喊。***rant and rave*** (劣等演員)瞎叫；亂喊。—*n.* ①狂言；壯語。②喧嚷；亂吵。③〖英方〗喧鬧作樂。

ran·tan·ker·ous [rænˈtæŋkərəs; rænˈtæŋkərəs] *adj.* 〖俗〗＝**cantankerous.**

rant·er [ˈræntɚ; ˈræntə] *n.* ①喧嚷者。②(R-)〖宗教〗美以美會初期之熱心說教者。

ra·nun·cu·lus [rəˈnʌŋkjələs; rəˈnʌŋkjuləs] *n., pl.* **-lus·es, -li** [-ˌlaɪ; -lai]. 〖植物〗毛茛科植物。

rap¹** [ræp; ræp] *v.*, **rapped, rap·ping,** *n.* —*v.t.* ①敲擊。②銳聲說出。to *rap* out an answer. 厲聲回答。③斥責。—*v.i.* 敲。The chairman *rapped* on the table for order. 主席敲桌維持秩序。—*n.* ①敲擊。a *rap* on the head. 打在頭上的一擊。②敲擊聲。③〖美俚〗斥責。④〖美俚〗判決；判刑。a bum rap*** 〖俚〗冤獄。***beat the rap*** 逃過刑責；獲宣判無罪。***take the rap*** 付罰款；受懲罰；代人受過。

rap² *n.* 〖俗〗些微；毫末。

ra·pa·cious [rəˈpeʃəs; rəˈpeiʃəs] *adj.* ①强取的；搶刼的。②貪婪的；貪得無厭的。③〖動物〗捕食生物的。

ra·pac·i·ty [rəˈpæsətɪ; rəˈpæsiti] *n.* ①强取；强刼性。②貪婪；貪得性。

rape¹ [rep; reip] *n., v.,* **raped, rap·ing.** —*n.* ①刼取。②强姦。③〖美法律〗誘姦。④强占；欺凌。—*v.t.* ①强刼。②强姦。—*v.i.* 犯强姦罪。

rape² *n.* 〖植物〗蕓薹；油菜。

rape³ *n.* 汁液被榨出後之葡萄渣。

rape·seed [ˈrepˌsid; ˈreipsiːd] *n.* ①油菜籽。②油菜。

***rap·id** [ˈræpɪd; ˈræpid] *adj.* ①迅速的；敏捷的；急促的。a *rapid* river. 水流甚急的河。②急陡的。—*n.* (常 *pl.*)急湍；急流。—**ly,** *adv.*

rapid eye movement 眼的迅速跳動(指人夜間作夢時)。(略作 **REM**)

rap·id-fire [ˈræpɪdˈfaɪr; ˈræpidˈfaiə] *adj.* ①速射的(砲)。a *rapid-fire* gun. 速射鎗。②急速做的；急速進行的。a *rapid-fire* talk. 急速的談話。

***ra·pid·i·ty** [rəˈpɪdətɪ; rəˈpiditi] *n.* 迅速；急促。(亦作 **rapidness**)

ra·pi·er [ˈrepɪɚ; ˈreipiə] *n.* ①銳利的短劍。②兩刃劍。③似短劍般銳利的；透過的。

rap·ine [ˈræpɪn; ˈræpin] *n.* 强奪；搶刼。

rap·pee [ræˈpi; ræˈpiː] *n.* 一種强烈的鼻煙。

rap·port [ræˈport; ræˈpɔːt] *n.* ①關係。②一致；和諧；親善。

rap·proche·ment [raprɔ̃ʃˈmɑ̃; ræˈprɔʃmɑ̃ːŋ] 〖法〗 *n.* 建立或恢復友誼或和睦關係。

rap·scal·lion [ræpˈskæljən; ræpˈskæljən] *n.* 惡棍；流氓。

rap session 〖美俚〗專題討論；小組討論。

***rapt** [ræpt; ræpt] *adj.* ①狂喜的。②精神貫注的。*rapt* in thought. 全神集中於思索。③心移神馳的。④狂喜所致的。

rap·to·ri·al [ræpˈtorɪəl; ræpˈtɔːriəl] *adj.* ①適於捕捉小生物的。②〖動物〗猛禽類的。—*n.* 猛禽。

***rap·ture** [ˈræptʃɚ; ˈræptʃə] *n.* ①奪魂；銷魂；精神貫注。He gazed at the picture with *rapture*. 他全神貫注地凝視那圖片。②(常 *pl.*)狂喜；大喜。

rap·tur·ous [ˈræptʃərəs; ˈræptʃərəs] *adj.* 表示或感到狂喜的。

***rare¹** [rɛr; rɛə] *adj.*, **rar·er, rar·est.** ①罕見的；珍奇的；稀罕的。②罕有的；不常發生的。③稀薄的。④極好的；極偉大的。Edison had *rare* powers as an inventor. 愛迪生是一個極有才能的發明家。

rare² *adj.*, **rar·er, rar·est.** 未完全煮熟的。

rare·bit [ˈrɛrˌbɪt; ˈrɛəbit] *n.* 麪包上所塗之已溶的乳酪(＝Welsh rabbit).

rar·ee show [ˈrɛri～; ˈrɛəriː～] 奇觀鏡；西洋鏡。

rar·e·fac·tion [ˌrɛrəˈfækʃən; ˌrɛəriˈfækʃən] *n.* 稀釋。

rar·e·fied [ˈrɛrəˌfaɪd; ˈrɛərifaid] *adj.* ①極高尚的；崇高的。②有選擇性的；精選的。

rar·e·fy [ˈrɛrəˌfaɪ; ˈrɛərifai] *v.*, **-fied, -fy·ing.** —*v.t.* ①(使)稀釋。②(使)變更純；(使)變精良。—*v.i.* 變稀。

***rare·ly** [ˈrɛrlɪ; ˈrɛəli] *adv.* ①罕見地；罕有地。I *rarely* met him. 我很少碰見他。He is *rarely* ill. 他極少生病。②非常地；非常好地。

rare·ness [ˈrɛrnɪs; ˈrɛənis] *n.* 稀少；稀薄；珍貴。

rare·ripe [ˈrɛrˌraɪp; ˈrɛəraip] *adj.* 早熟的。—*n.* 早熟的水果、菜蔬等(尤指桃子)。

rar·i·ty [ˈrɛrətɪ; ˈrɛəriti] *n., pl.* **-ties.** ①珍品；罕見之物。②稀薄。③不常發生。

***ras·cal** [ˈræskl̩; ˈræskl] *n.* ①流氓；惡棍。②〖謔〗傢伙(對頑皮孩子的暱稱)。You little *rascal!* 你這小傢伙！—*adj.* 卑鄙的；下賤的。

ras·cal·i·ty [ræsˈkælətɪ; ræsˈkæliti] *n., pl.* **-ties.** ①卑鄙的根性或行爲。②壞事；惡事；流氓行爲。(亦作 **rascalism**)

ras·cal·ly [ˈræsklɪ; ˈræskəli] *adj. & adv.* 卑鄙的(地)；邪惡的(地)。

rase [rez; reiz] *v.t.*, **rased, ras·ing.** ＝**raze.**

***rash¹** [ræʃ; ræʃ] *adj.* ①輕率的；不留心的。to make *rash* promises. 作輕率的諾言。②行動不加思考的。a *rash* young man. 一個行動不加思考的青年。—**ly,** *adv.* —**ness,** *n.*

rash² *n.* (痧子、猩紅熱等的)發疹；瘍腫。

rash·er [ˈræʃɚ; ˈræʃə] *n.* (供烹飪之)鹹肉薄片。

rasp [ræsp; rɑːsp] *n.* ①銼。②刺耳聲。—*v.i.* ①用銼子銼。②發刺耳聲。—*v.t.* ①用銼子銼。②以刺耳聲說出。③刺激。

rasp·ber·ry [ˈræzˌbɛrɪ; ˈrɑːzbəri] *n., pl.* **-ries,** *adj.* —*n.* ①〖植物〗覆盆子；蔗莓。②覆盆子樹。③〖俚〗咂舌、唇之聲；嘲笑輕蔑之聲；譏一笑。*adj.* 紫紅色的。

***rat** [ræt; ræt] *n., v.,* **rat·ted, rat·ting.**

—*n.* ①鼠。The house swarms with *rats.* 此屋多鼠。②卑鄙之人；下賤之人。③〖美〗髮墊。④叛徒；變節者。⑤告密者。 ***like a drowned rat*** 渾身濕透。***Rat!*** 〖俚〗胡說八道；我不信。 ***smell a rat*** 覺得可疑。—*v.i.* ①捕鼠；獵鼠。②變節；背叛。③告密。***rat on*** a. 食言；背信。b. 告密。

rat·a·bil·i·ty [ˌretəˈbɪlətɪ; ˌreitəˈbiliti] *n.* ①可估價或應課稅之性質或狀態；課稅資格。②〖英〗負擔地方稅之義務。

rat·a·ble [ˈretəbl; ˈreitəbl] *adj.* ①可估價的；應課稅的。②按比例的；比例上的。③〖英〗應負擔地方稅的。(亦作 **rateable**)

rat·a·fee [ˌrætəˈfi; ˌrætəˈfiː] *n.* = **ratafia.**

rat·a·fi·a [ˌrætəˈfiə; ˌrætəˈfiə] *n.* ①果酒；果汁與香劑。②一種甜餅乾。

rat·al [ˈretl; ˈreitl] *n.* 課稅額。—*adj.* 課稅額的；納稅的。

ra·tan [ræˈtæn; ræˈtæn] *n.* ①籐。②籐條。③籐杖。

rat·a·plan [ˌrætəˈplæn; ˌrætəˈplæn] *n., v.,* **-planned, -plan·ning.** —*n.* 擊鼓聲；咚咚如鼓聲。—*v.t.* & *v.i.* (使)作鳴鼓之聲。

rat-a-tat [ˈrætəˈtæt; ˈrætəˈtæt] *n.* 砰砰(連續叩擊聲)。

ratch·et [ˈrætʃɪt; ˈrætʃit] *n.* ①棘齒輪；棘齒棒。②節制棘齒輪(棒)的掣子；制輪機。③棘齒輪(棒)與掣子構成之整套機械；棘輪機。

‡rate¹ [ret; reit] *n., v.,* **rat·ed, rat·ing.** —*n.* ①比率；率。conversion *rate.* 折換率。multiple *rate.* 多元匯率。birth (death) *rate.* 出生(死亡)率。the *rate* of exchange. 兌換率。②價格。buying *rate.* 買價。selling *rate.* 賣價。official *rate.* 官價。③等級。first *rate.* 一等。④(常 *pl.*)〖英〗捐稅；地方稅。water *rates.* 自來水費。*rates* and taxes. 地方稅與全國稅。⑤情況；樣子。***at any rate*** 無論如何。***at that rate*** 如照你所說的；如照那種情形。***at this rate*** 照此情形下去。***by no rate*** 決沒有。—*v.t.* ①估價。②認爲。③定等級(如船或海員)。④征地方稅；定稅率。My property was *rated* at £20 per annum. 我的地產稅率核定爲每年二十鎊。⑤評分。to *rate* a student's class performance. 爲學生的學業成績評分。⑥爲某種速度而設計。⑦決定…之速度。—*v.i.* ①有價值；有等級。②被認爲；被列入。

rate² *v.t.* & *v.i.,* **rat·ed, rat·ing.** 申斥；叱責；罵。

rate·a·ble [ˈretəbl; ˈreitəbl] *adj.* = ratable. —**rate·a·bly,** *adv.*

rate card 廣告費卡(列舉收費標準者)。

ra·tel [ˈretəl; ˈreitəl] *n.* 〖動物〗食蜜獾。

rate·pay·er [ˈretˌpeə; ˈreitˌpeiə] *n.* 〖英〗納(地方)稅者。

rat·er [ˈretə; ˈreitə] *n.* ①評價者。②某一等級之人或物。③〖俚〗小型遊艇。

rat·fink [ˈrætfɪŋk; ˈrætfiŋk] *n.* 〖美俚〗壞蛋；惡棍；告密者。

‡rath·er [ˈræðə, ˈrɑðə; ˈrɑːðə] *adv.* ①寧可；寧願。He said he would *rather* stay at home. 他說他寧願留在家裏。②更合理；更恰當。③更正確地說；更確實。④頗；有幾分。She felt *rather* tired. 她有些倦了。⑤反之；相反地。***had rather*** 寧願(=prefer to). I *had rather* dance than eat. 我寧願跳舞不願吃飯。—*interj.* 〖俗〗當然！一定！怎麼不！Is it worth going to? *Rather!* 值得去嗎？當然(怎麼不)！

rat·hole [ˈrætˌhol; ˈræthoul] *n.* ①被鼠咬成的洞。②鼠窠。③狹小齷齪之地。***down the rathole*** 白費；浪費。

raths·kel·ler [ˈrɑtsˌkɛlə; ˈrɑːtsˌkelə] *n.* ①(德國)會堂地下室(常做酒館、餐館之用)。②地下室內的酒店或餐館；德國式酒館。

rat·i·cide [ˈrætɪˌsaɪd; ˈrætisaid] *n.* 滅鼠藥；殺鼠藥。

rat·i·fi·ca·tion [ˌrætəfəˈkeʃən; ˌrætifiˈkeiʃən] *n.* 批准；承認。

rat·i·fi·er [ˈrætəˌfaɪə; ˈrætifaiə] *n.* 批准者；認可者。

***rat·i·fy** [ˈrætəˌfaɪ; ˈrætifai] *v.t.,* **-fied, -fy·ing.** 批准。The treaty has been *ratified.* 這條約已被批准。

rat·ing¹ [ˈretɪŋ; ˈreitiŋ] *n.* ①估計；評價。a *rating* of 80% in English. 英語八十分。②(船艦或海員等的)等級；地位。the *rating* of a ship according to tonnage. 按照噸位決定船的等級。③(*pl.*) 某一等級之全體船員。④〖英〗地方稅之課賦。⑤廣播或電視節目收聽(視)率。

rat·ing² *n.* 責罵；申斥。to give a sound *rating.* 痛斥一頓。

***ra·ti·o** [ˈreʃo; ˈreiʃiou] *n., pl.* **-ti·os.** 比；比率；比例。direct *ratio.* 正比。inverse *ratio.* 反比。

ra·ti·oc·i·nate [ˌræʃɪˈɑsn̩ˌet; ˌrætiˈɔsineit] *v.i.,* **-nat·ed, -nat·ing.** 推論；推理。

ra·ti·oc·i·na·tion [ˌræʃɪˌɑsn̩ˈeʃən; ˌrætiɔsiˈneiʃən] *n.* ①推理；推論；推斷。②推理後所獲之結論。

ra·ti·oc·i·na·tive [ˌræʃɪˈɑsɪˌnetɪv; ˌrætiˈɔsineitiv] *adj.* 推理的；推論的；好議論的。

ra·tion** [ˈræʃən, ˈreʃən; ˈræʃən] *n.* ①定食；口糧；(軍隊)一日之定量配糧。a daily *ration* of meat and bread. 每日定量的肉類和麪包。②分。a *ration* of coffee. 一分咖啡。③(*pl.*) 糧食。put on rations*** 計口授糧；定額配授。***the iron ration*** (攜帶以備緊急時食用的)隨身口糧。—*v.t.* ①供以口糧。to *ration* an army. 以口糧供應軍隊。②定量配給。

***ra·tion·al** [ˈræʃənl̩; ˈræʃənl̩] *adj.* ①合理的。a *rational* explanation. 合理的解釋。②懂道理的；理智的。③理性的；有辨別力的。Man is a *rational* animal. 人是有理性的動物。④頭腦清楚的；神智清醒的。⑤推理的。*rational* faculty. 推理力。⑥〖數學〗有理的。a *rational* expression. 有理式。—*n.* 〖數學〗有理數；命分數。—**ly,** *adv.*

ra·tion·ale [ˌræʃəˈnæl, -ˈnɑlɪ; ˌræʃiəˈnɑːli] *n.* ①基本理由；理論基礎。②理論或原理的說明或解釋。

ra·tion·al·ism [ˈræʃənl̩ˌɪzəm; ˈræʃn̩əlizəm] *n.* 理性主義；唯理論。

ra·tion·al·ist [ˈræʃənl̩ɪst; ˈræʃn̩əlist] *n.* 唯理主義者；理性論者。—*adj.* =**rationalistic.**

ra·tion·al·is·tic [ˌræʃənl̩ˈɪstɪk; ˌræʃn̩əˈlistik] *adj.* 唯理主義的；理性論者的。

ra·tion·al·i·ty [ˌræʃəˈnælətɪ; ˌræʃəˈnæliti] *n., pl.* **-ties.** ①理性；合理。②有理性的行爲、信仰等。

ra·tion·al·i·za·tion [ˌræʃənəlɪˈzeʃən; ˌræʃn̩əlaiˈzeiʃən] *n.* ①合理化。②合於經濟原則。③〖數學〗化根號式爲有理式。

ra·tion·al·ize [ˈræʃənl̩ˌaɪz; ˈræʃn̩əlaiz] *v.,* **-ized, -iz·ing.** —*v.t.* ①使合於理性。②以科學知識解釋。③尋求(常是意識的)藉口。④使(事業之經營)合於經濟原則。—*v.i.* ①尋藉口。②合理地思索。

rat·lin(e) [ˈrætlɪn; ˈrætlin] *n.* 〖航海〗(常 *pl.*)梯索。

RATO rocket assist for take-off.
rat race〖俗〗勞神而無法逃避的日常工作。
rats·bane [ˈrætsˌben; ˈrætsbein] *n.* ①殺鼠藥。②某些有毒植物之共名。
rat·tail [ˈrætˌtel; ˈrætteil] *adj.* 細而長的;柄或尾巴細長的。
rat·tan [ræˈtæn; rəˈtæn] *n.* =**ratan.**
rat-tat [ˌrætˈtæt; ˌrætˈtæt] *n.* 砰砰(連續之叩擊聲)。
rat·ten [ˈrætn̩; ˈrætn] *v.t. & v.i.*〖英俚〗擾亂(工人),破壞或取走(機器工具等)以迫使(雇主)答應工會的要求。
rat·ter [ˈrætɚ; ˈrætə] *n.* ①捕鼠者;善捕鼠之人、狗、或貓。②〖俚〗變節者;告密者;叛徒。
***rat·tle** [ˈrætl̩; ˈrætl] *v.*, **-tled, -tling,** *n.* —*v.t.* ①使發嘎嘎聲。The wind *rattled* the windows. 風使窗發嘎嘎聲。②喋喋說出。③〖俗〗使紊亂;使緊張。Don't get *rattled*. 勿緊張。④〖俗〗使激動;激起。⑤用力追趕(獵物)。—*v.i.* ①發嘎嘎聲。②喋喋而言。③帶嘎嘎聲而移動。The cart *rattled* down the street. 那二輪馬車沿街發嘎嘎聲駛過。—*n.* ①嘎嘎聲;喋喋聲。the *rattle* of empty bottles. 空瓶的嘎嘎聲。②格咯格咯(肺疾時或臨死前的喉嚨聲)。③吵鬧;喧囂。④嘎嘎作響的玩具或器械。⑤(響尾蛇的)音響器官。
rat·tle·box [ˈrætl̩ˌbɑks; ˈrætlbɔks] *n.* ①轟匣(小兒玩具)。②〖植物〗野百合。
rat·tle·brain [ˈrætl̩ˌbren; ˈrætlbrein] *n.* 浮躁而愚鈍之人;魯鈍而愛說話之人。
rat·tled [ˈrætl̩d; ˈrætld] *adj.*〖俗〗困惑的;狼狽的;慌張的;混亂的。
rat·tler [ˈrætlɚ; ˈrætlə] *n.* ①響尾蛇。②作嘎啦響聲之人或物。③〖俗〗快速之運貨列車。④〖俗〗極好之事物;能幹的人;多才多藝者。
rat·tle·snake [ˈrætl̩ˌsnek; ˈrætlsneik] *n.* 響尾蛇。
rat·tle·trap [ˈrætl̩ˌtræp; ˈrætltræp] *n.* ①因破舊而發嘎聲之物(如車輛)。②〖俚〗饒舌的人。③〖俚〗嘴。④(*pl.*)零星雜物(=odds and ends). —*adj.* 破舊的;發嘎聲的。
rat·tling [ˈrætlɪŋ; ˈrætliŋ] *adj.* ①發嘎嘎之聲的。②〖俗〗快速的;快活的。③〖俗〗良好的;痛快的。—*adv.*〖俗〗很;甚;非常。
rat·trap [ˈrætˌtræp; ˈrættræp] *n.* ①捕鼠機。②絕望之境地。③(脚踏車之)有鋸齒形的防滑的踏脚板。④〖俚〗嘴。—*adj.* 如捕鼠機的。
rat·ty [ˈrætɪ; ˈræti] *adj.*, **-ti·er, -ti·est.** ①多鼠的。②(似)鼠的。③〖俚〗卑賤的;襤褸的。
rau·cous [ˈrɔkəs; ˈrɔːkəs] *adj.* 粗啞的;聲音沙啞的。—**ly,** *adv.* —**ness,** *n.*
raugh·ty [ˈrɔtɪ; ˈrɔːti] *adj.* =**rorty.**
***rav·age** [ˈrævɪdʒ; ˈrævidʒ] *v.*, **-aged, -ag·ing,** *n.* —*v.t. & v.i.* 蹂躪;破壞;毀掉。—*n.* 蹂躪;荼毒;破壞。War causes *ravage*. 戰爭產生大破壞。
***rave** [rev; reiv] *v.*, **raved, rav·ing,** *n.*, *adj.* —*v.i.* ①發譫語;發狂言。The patient began to *rave* again. 病人又發譫語了。②過分而言〖about, of〗. He *raved* about her beauty. 他過分揄揚她的美。③怒吼。—*v.t.* 叫囂地說出。—*n.* ①叫囂;發狂;怒吼。②〖俚〗過分之讚揚。③〖俚〗青春發動期內對某一異性之迷戀。—*adj.* 過分誇獎的。
rav·el [ˈrævl̩; ˈrævl] *v.*, **-el(l)ed, -el(l)ing,** *n.* —*v.t.* ①使糾纏;使混亂。②拆開(繩索);拆散(織物)。③使明白;使一目了然〖out〗. —*v.i.* ①拆開;解決〖常 out〗. ②變爲錯綜複雜。—*n.* ①糾結之物。②拆開的部分(尤指繩索)。③混亂;錯綜;糾纏。
rave·lin [ˈrævlɪn; ˈrævlin] *n.*〖築城〗半月堡。
rav·el·(l)ing [ˈrævlɪŋ; ˈrævliŋ] *n.* 縷析之物;(尤指)散線。
ra·ven¹ [ˈrevən; ˈreivn, -vən] *n.* 烏鴉。—*adj.* 黑若烏鴉的;烏黑的。*raven* hair. 烏黑的頭髮。
rav·en² [ˈrævɪn; ˈrævn] *v.t.* 貪婪地吞食。—*v.i.* ①搜尋;捕食;掠奪。②狼吞虎嚥;急欲。—*n.* 掠奪;掠奪物。
rav·en·ing [ˈrævənɪŋ; ˈrævniŋ] *adj.* 貪婪而饑餓的。—*n.* 掠奪;掠奪物。
rav·en·ous [ˈrævənəs; ˈrævinəs] *adj.* ①極餓的。②貪婪的。③捕他種動物爲食的。④渴望的。(亦作 **ravin**) —**ly,** *adv.*
ra·vine [rəˈvin; rəˈviːn] *n.* 峽谷;深谷;山澗。
rav·ing [ˈrevɪŋ; ˈreiviŋ] *adj.* ①發譫語的;精神錯亂的;狂亂的。②〖俗〗卓越的;非凡的。a *raving* beauty. 絕代佳人。—*n.* 譫語。
ra·vi·o·li [ˌrɑvɪˈolɪ; ˌrɑːviˈouli] *n.* (作 *sing.* or *pl.* 解) 一種包餡的點心。
rav·ish [ˈrævɪʃ; ˈræviʃ] *v.t.* ①攫奪;强搶。to *ravish* a kiss. 强吻。②使狂喜;迷住;使銷魂。③强姦。④搶刼。⑤將(婦女)擄走。
rav·ish·ing [ˈrævɪʃɪŋ; ˈræviʃiŋ] *adj.* 使狂喜的;銷魂的;使人陶醉的。—**ly,** *adv.*
rav·ish·ment [ˈrævɪʃmənt; ˈræviʃmənt] *n.* ①狂喜;銷魂。②掠奪;强奪。③强姦。④擄走(婦女)。
raw** [rɔ; rɔː] *adj.* ①生的;未煮過的。*raw* fish. 生魚。②未精煉過的;粗的。③無經驗的;未訓練的。④陰寒的;濕冷的。*raw* weather. 陰寒的天氣。⑤皮膚綻開的;痛的;刺痛的。⑥〖俚〗嚴苛的;不公平的。⑦未製造過的。*raw* sugar. 粗糖。⑧未開化的;野蠻的。⑨粗糙的;不精細的。⑩未稀釋的。*raw* whiskey. 未加水的威士忌。—*n.* ①生的肉。②身上的痛處。③未經提煉過的糖或油。in the raw*** **a.**〖俚〗裸體的。**b.** 天然的;未經琢磨的。***touch one on the raw*** 觸及某人痛處。—**ly,** *adv.*
Ra·wal·pin·di [ˌrɑvəlˈpɪndɪ; ˌrɑːwəlˈpindi] *n.* 洛瓦平第(巴基斯坦之臨時首都)。
raw·boned [ˈrɔˈbond; ˈrɔːbound] *adj.* 骨瘦如柴的;消瘦的。
raw·hide [ˈrɔˌhaɪd; ˈrɔːhaid] *n.*, *adj.*, *v.*, **-hid·ed, -hid·ing.** —*n.* ①生牛皮。②生牛皮的繩或鞭。—*adj.* 生牛皮做的。—*v.t.* 以生牛皮鞭鞭撻。
raw·ish [ˈrɔɪʃ; ˈrɔiʃ] *adj.* 略帶一些生的(食物);似未精製的。
raw material 原料。duty-free *raw materials*. 免稅的原料。
raw milk 未經殺菌的牛乳。
raw·ness [ˈrɔnɪs; ˈrɔːnis] *n.* ①生;不熟。②未精製狀態;粗糙。③不熟練;無經驗。④皮破露肉;擦傷。⑤陰濕寒冷。⑥傷心。
raw silk 生絲。
‡ray¹ [re; rei] *n.* ①光線。②線;熱線;電流。③射線。X *rays*. X光(射線)。④微光。a *ray* of hope. 一線希望。⑤似射線的部分。a star with six *rays*. 六稜星形。⑥〖植物〗射出花。⑦〖動物〗刺鰭。⑧視線。—*v.t.* ①放射;射出(光線等)。②以射線治療。③照射。④〖俗〗用 X 光拍照。—*v.i.* ①放射光線;閃現。②照射。
ray² *n.* 鰩魚。
Ray·leigh [ˈrelɪ; ˈreili] *n.* 雷利 (John William Strutt, 3rd Baron, 1842–1919, 英國物理學家,1904年獲諾貝爾物理獎)。
Ray·mond, Ray·mund [ˈremənd; ˈreimənd] *n.* 男子名。

ray·on ['reɑn; 'reiɔn] *n.* ①人造絲。②人造絲織物。
raze [rez; reiz] *v.t.*, **razed, raz·ing.** ①(從記憶中)消逝;忘却。②擦傷;微傷。③摧毀;毀滅;夷爲平地。
***ra·zor** ['rezɚ; 'reizə] *n.* 剃刀;刮鬍刀。safety *razor.* 安全剃刀。—*v.t.* 用剃刀刮(鬍子);用剃刀刮去。to *razor* a beard. 刮鬍子。
ra·zor·back ['rezɚ,bæk; 'reizəbæk] *n.* ①野豬;半野豬(產於美國南部,身瘦、脊高、腿長)。②剃刀鯨。
ra·zor·bill ['rezɚ,bɪl; 'reizəbil] *n.* 「一種海鳥。」
ra·zor-edge ['rezɚ,ɛdʒ; 'reizəedʒ] *n.* ①剃刀之刄。②危機。to be on a *razor-edge.* 在千鈞一髮中。②鋒銳之刀刄。④尖銳之山脊。
razor shell 〖動物〗①竹蟶。②細長之蚌殼。
razor strop 磨剃刀的皮革。(亦作「**razorstrop**)」
razz [ræz; ræz] *v.t. & v.i.* 〖美俚〗嘲弄;嘲笑;惡作劇。—*n.* 〖美俚〗①嚴厲的批評;嘲笑。②嘲笑、輕蔑發出之聲。
raz·zi·a ['ræzɪə; 'ræziə] *n.* 侵略;攻擊;掠奪;(非洲回教徒爲掠奪奴隸財物之)侵掠。
raz·zle-daz·zle ['ræzl̩,dæzl; 'ræzl-,dæzl] *n., adj., v.,* **-zled, -zling.** —*n.* 〖俚〗①混亂;惶惑。②酩酊大醉。③波浪式廻轉木馬。④球賽中使敵方迷亂的一種策略。⑤噱頭。—*adj.* 〖俚〗令人目眩的;擺噱頭的。—*v.t.* 〖俚〗使迷惑;使頭暈眼花。

Rb 化學元素rubidium之符號。 **R.B.A.** Royal Society of British Artists. **RBI, rbi** run(s) batted in. 〖棒球〗安打得分。 **RC, R.C.** ①Red Cross. ②Reserve Corps. ③Roman Catholic. **R.C.A.** ①Radio Corporation of America. ②Royal Canadian Academy of Arts. ③Royal Canadian Army. **R.C.Ch.** Roman Catholic Church. **R.C.P.** Royal College of Physicians. **Rd.** Road. **rd.** ①road. ②rod; rods. **R.D.** ①refer to drawer. ②Royal Dragoons. ③Rural Delivery. **R.D.C.** ①Royal Defence Corps. ②Rural District Council. **Re** 化學元素 rhenium 之符號。
re¹ [re; rei] *n.* 〖音樂〗長音階的第二音。
re² [ri; riː] *prep.* 關於。*re* your esteemed favor of lst inst. 〖商,俗〗關於本月一日尊函。*in re* 〖法律〗關於…。*in re* Mr. A vs. Mr. B. 關於 A 先生對 B 先生的訟案。
're are 之縮寫。
re- 〖字首〗表下列諸義:①又;再;屢;重;反覆。如:reappear 再出現, rebuild 重建。②還;返;互。如:repay 還錢, replace 放回原位。③反對;反抗;逆。如:resist 抵抗。
R.E. ①Reformed Episcopal. ②Right Excellent. ③Royal Exchange.
‡reach [ritʃ; riːtʃ] *v.t.* ①到;達;抵。to *reach* the top of a hill. 爬到山頂。②伸出。③觸及;接觸。I can't *reach* the bottom of it. 我摸不到底。④影響;感動。Men are *reached* by flattery. 人受諂媚的影響。⑤(用手)遞;交給。Please *reach* me the newspaper. 請把報紙遞給我。⑥總達;計有;等於。⑦得到或獲得(結論);做(決定)。No conclusion has been *reached* yet. 尙未獲得結論。⑧建立通信。I called but couldn't *reach* you. 我曾經打電話給你可是找不到你(無法和你通話)。—*v.i.* ①伸出;伸出手臂。②伸展;延長。③(伸手)欲得;欲達。④及;達;起作用。The speaker's voice did not *reach* to the back of the hall. 這講演者的聲音達不到後廳(後座)。⑤〖航海〗順風行駛。⑥數達〖to〗. sums *reaching* to a considerable total. 總數加起來達到相當可觀的款項。—*n.* ①伸出;伸展。to make a *reach* for a rope. 伸手抓繩。②範圍;能力所及之範圍。the *reach* of the mind. 智力之範圍;心力之領域。③寬廣的一片。a *reach* of water (woodland). 一大片水(林地)。④河區;江區。⑤運河兩水閘間的部分。⑥一個航向的航程。***as far as the eye can reach*** 至地平線;極目。***out of one's reach*** 手所不能及;力所不能及。***within one's reach*** 手所能及;力所能及。
reach-me-down ['ritʃmɪ,daun; 'riːtʃmidaun] *adj.* 〖俚〗現成的;舊的;便宜的。—*n.* (常 *pl.*) 現成衣服;二手貨;舊衣服;陳舊的意見。
***re·act** [rɪ'ækt; ri'ækt] *v.i.* ①反動;反抗;反作用。to *react* against the opposition. 反抗對方。②反應;受感應。A dog *reacts* to kindness by wagging its tail. 狗搖尾以報答人們之愛護。③起化學反應。Acids *react* on metals. 酸與金屬起化學反應。④復舊;恢復原狀。
re-act [ri'ækt; riː'ækt] *v.t.* 再作;重做;「再演;重演。」
re·act·ance [rɪ'æktəns; ri'æktəns] *n.* 〖電〗電抗。***inductive reactance*** 感電抗。***reactance coupling*** 電抗偶合。
***re·ac·tion** [rɪ'ækʃən; ri(ː)'ækʃən] *n.* ①反作用。②反動;反動力。③(政治趨勢的)復古。④反應。Our *reaction* to a joke is to laugh. 我們對詼諧的反應是笑。⑤化學反應。
***re·ac·tion·ar·y** [rɪ'ækʃən,ɛrɪ; ri(ː)-'ækʃnəri] *adj., n., pl.* **-ar·ies.** —*adj.* 反動的;保守的;復古的。—*n.* 反動分子。
reaction engine 噴射引擎。
re·ac·tion·ist [rɪ'ækʃənɪst; ri'æk-ʃənist] *n.* 反動主義者;復古主義者;保守論者。—*adj.* =**reactionary.**
re·ac·ti·vate [ri'æktɪ,vet; riː'ækti-veit] *v.,* **-vat·ed, -vat·ing.** —*v.t.* 使恢復活動。—*v.i.* 再度活躍。
re·ac·tive [rɪ'æktɪv; ri(ː)'æktiv] *adj.* ①反動的。②〖化〗反應的。③〖物理〗反作用的;無功的。④復古的。—**ly,** *adv.*
re·ac·tor [rɪ'æktɚ; ri'æktə] *n.* ①反動者。②起反應者。③〖物理〗原子爐。④〖化〗反應器。
‡read¹ [rid; riːd] *v.,* **read** [rɛd; red], **read·ing.** —*v.t.* ①閱讀。②誦;朗讀。*Read* it to me. 把它讀給我聽。③(表記、圖形等)指示;表示。The thermometer *reads* 70 degrees. 寒暑表指出70度。④學習;研究。⑤讀作;原文作。⑥解釋;解答;解說;預測。to *read* a dream. 詳夢。⑦觀測;了解。God *reads* men's heart. 上帝知人之心。⑧閱讀至某種狀態。He *reads* himself to sleep. 他讀到入睡。⑨可讀;可解釋。⑩叱責。—*v.i.* ①閱讀;讀書。②朗讀;誦讀。*Read* to me, please. 請讀給我聽。③閱悉;讀知。We *read* of heroes of other days. 我們由讀書知道昔日的英雄豪傑。④讀時產生某印象;讀時有…之效果。⑤有某種含義。⑥有某些字樣。The sentence *reads* as follows. 此句文字如下。⑦研究;學習。to *read* for the Bar. 學習法律預備做律師。***read a subject up*** 對某科目作特殊之研究。***read between the lines*** 尋言外之意;了解絃外之音。***read into***

作某種解釋；加以解釋。*read out of* 自(政黨等)逐出。*read over* (or *through*) 讀一遍。

read² 〔rɛd; red〕 *adj.* 有學識的；熟知的(通常用於複合詞)。a well-*read* man. 博學之人。—*v.* pt. & pp. of **read¹**.

read·a·bil·i·ty 〔͵ridəˈbɪlətɪ; ͵riːdəˈbiliti〕 *n.* 可讀性；易讀；清晰；(字體)秀麗。

read·a·ble 〔ˈridəbl; ˈriːdəbl〕 *adj.* ①可讀的；易讀的；清楚的。②字體秀麗的；易辨識的。

re·ad·dress 〔͵riəˈdrɛs; ˈriːəˈdres〕 *v.t.* ①再致詞；再向之交談。②改寫收信人地址。

‡**read·er** 〔ˈridɚ; ˈriːdə〕 *n.* ①讀者；誦讀者。I hope my *readers* will excuse me. 希望讀者能原諒我。②書店雇請之審閱稿件者。③讀本。The First *Reader*. 第一册讀本。④教堂儀式中朗讀聖經者。⑤(某些英國大學中)講師。He was appointed *reader* in English history. 他被任爲英國歷史講師。⑥批改考卷的教授助理；助教。

read·er·ship 〔ˈridɚʃɪp; ˈriːdəʃip〕 *n.* ①reader 之身分。②(報章等之)讀者。③審閱稿件人的職務、身分。④(英大學中)講師職位。

***read·i·ly** 〔ˈrɛdlɪ, -ɪlɪ; ˈredili〕 *adv.* ①迅速地。②容易地。③願意地。He *readily* agreed to help us. 他欣然同意幫助我們。

***read·i·ness** 〔ˈrɛdɪnɪs; ˈredinis〕 *n.* ①準備好的狀態。②迅速；敏捷。③容易。④願意。

***read·ing** 〔ˈridɪŋ; ˈriːdiŋ〕 *n.* ①閱讀。②誦讀；朗讀。③讀書。④讀物。to get through a good deal of *reading*. 讀完許多讀物。⑤(標記、儀器等)指出之物；指示之數。⑥(在一作品之某一版本中)一字、一句、或一節之變化(變體)。⑦見解；解釋。What is your *reading* of the facts? 你對這些事實作何解釋？⑧個人學識的範圍；文學上的知識。a man of wide *reading*. 博識之士。⑨法案在立法機構中之正式誦讀。The bill has passed the second *reading*. 該法案已經二讀通過。—*adj.* ①讀書的；愛讀書的。②關於讀書的；讀時用的。*reading* glasses. 讀書用的眼鏡。

reading book 讀本。

reading desk ①書桌。②教堂中的讀經臺。

reading room (圖書館等之)閱覽室。

re·ad·just 〔͵riəˈdʒʌst; ˈriːəˈdʒʌst〕 *v.t.* 重新調整；再整理；使適應。—**a·ble,** *adj.* —**er,** *n.*

re·ad·just·ment 〔͵riəˈdʒʌstmənt; ˈriːəˈdʒʌstmənt〕 *n.* 重新調整；重新整理；重新安排；重新適應。

read·out 〔ˈrid͵aut; ˈriːdaut〕 *n.* 〖電腦〗資料輸出；讀出。

‡**read·y** 〔ˈrɛdɪ; ˈredi〕 *adj.*, **read·i·er, read·i·est,** *v.*, **read·ied, read·y·ing,** *n.*, *interj.* —*adj.* ①已預備好的；齊備的。Dinner is *ready*. 飯已好了。②願意的；情願的。③敏捷的；迅速的。*ready* reply. 迅速的答覆。④喜好的；傾向的；易於的。Don't be so *ready* to find fault. 不要過於喜歡吹毛求疵。⑤即時可有的；在手邊的。*ready* money. 現款。⑥隨時可發生的。***Get ready!*** 就位！(賽跑時之口令。整個口令爲 *Get ready!* Get set! Go! 就位！預備！跑！) ***make ready*** 準備。—*v.t.* 準備。***ready up*** 〖英澳俚〗欺騙。—*n.* ①〖俗〗現款。②預備好的狀態。—*interj.* (賽跑時之口令)就位！*Ready!* Set! Go! (參看 **Get ready!**)

***read·y-made** 〔ˈrɛdɪˈmed; ˈrediˈmeid〕 *adj.* ①現成的；做好的。a *ready-made* suit. 一套現成衣服。②陳腐的；無甚新奇的。*ready-made* ideas. 陳腐的觀念。③應急而做的。—*n.* 現成之事物(尤指衣服)。

ready room 飛機工作人員出勤任務講解室。

read·y-to-wear 〔ˈrɛdɪtəˈwɛr; ˈreditəˈwɛə〕 *adj.* 現成的；做成的(衣服)。—*n.* 現成衣服。

read·y-wit·ted 〔ˈrɛdɪˈwɪtɪd; ˈrediˈwitid〕 *adj.* 機敏的；有機智的；有急智的。

re·af·firm 〔͵riəˈfɝm; ˈriːəˈfəːm〕 *v.t.* 再斷定；再肯定；再證實。—**er,** *n.*

re·af·fir·ma·tion 〔͵riæfɚˈmeʃən; ͵riːæfəˈmeiʃən〕 *n.* 再斷言；再肯定；再證實。(亦作 **reaffirmance**)

re·a·gent 〔riˈedʒənt; riːˈeidʒənt〕 *n.* ①〖化〗試藥；試劑。②反應力；呈反應之物；對刺激呈反應之人。

‡**re·al¹** 〔ˈriəl, ril, ˈrɪəl; riəl, ˈriːəl, riːl〕 *adj.* ①實際的；眞實的。This is a story of *real* life. 這是一篇眞實的故事。②純粹的；眞的。a *real* diamond. 眞鑽石。③〖法律〗不動產的。④〖數學〗實數的。the *real*. 實數。⑤〖光學〗實像的。*real* image. 實像。—*adv.* 〖俗〗=really. to have a *real* good time. 玩得眞痛快。—*n.* ①實數。②眞實。***for real*** 〖俚〗眞的。You mean she dyed her hair green *for real?* 你說她把頭髮染成綠色是眞的嗎？***the real*** 眞實存在的事物；眞實。

re·al² *n.*, *pl.* **re·als.** ①昔西班牙之一種銀幣(若干拉丁美洲國家現仍使用)。②昔西班牙之幣制單位。

real estate ①不動產(爲 personal estate 之對)。②房地產。

re·al·gar 〔rɪˈælgɚ; riˈælgə〕 *n.* 〖礦〗雄黃；雄精；鷄冠石(舊名)。

re·a·li·a 〔rɪˈelɪə; riˈeiliə〕 *n. pl.* ①〖教育〗教師用來敍述日常生活的各種實物(如錢幣、工具等)。②〖哲學〗實物。

real income 實所得(以金錢所得所能購到的貨物與勞務之總和)。

re·al·ism 〔ˈriəl͵ɪzəm; ˈriəlizəm〕 *n.* ①現實；現實主義；尙實的傾向。②(文學上之)寫實主義。③〖哲學〗實體論；實在論；實念論。④〖美術〗現實主義。

re·al·ist 〔ˈriəlɪst; ˈriəlist〕 *n.* ①尙實之人。②寫實主義者。③實在論者。

re·al·is·tic 〔͵riəˈlɪstɪk; riəˈlistik〕 *adj.* ①似實物的；逼眞的。②寫實的。③就事實方面觀察的；實際的。④尙實(者)的；寫實主義(者)的；實在論(者)的；實體論(者)的。—**al·ly,** *adv.*

re·al·i·ty** 〔rɪˈælətɪ; ri(ː)ˈæliti〕 *n.*, *pl.* **-ties.** ①實在；眞實。②實體；實物；實事。We are here face to face with *realities*. 我們正面對現實。in reality*** 實際上。

re·al·iz·a·ble 〔ˈriəl͵aɪzəbl; ˈriə͵laizəbl〕 *adj.* ①可實現的；可實行的。②可認識的。③可換現錢的。

***re·al·i·za·tion** 〔͵riələˈzeʃən; ͵riəlaiˈzeiʃən〕 *n.* ①了解；覺察。②實現。③變賣。④(金錢、財產等之)獲得。

‡**re·al·ize** 〔ˈriə͵laɪz, ˈrɪə-; ˈriəlaiz〕 *v.*, **-ized, -iz·ing.** —*v.t.* ①認知；了解。Does he *realize* his error yet? 他認知他的錯誤沒有？②實現。③如實表現；寫實。④變賣。Before going abroad, he *realized* all his property. 在出國以前，他把所有財產都變賣了。⑤賺得(若干利潤)。He *realized* $10,000 from his investment. 他投資賺了一萬元。—*v.i.* ①變賣財產；賣出求現。②賺錢。(亦作 **realise**)

re·al-life 〔ˈriəlˈlaɪf; ˈriːəlˈlaif〕 *adj.* 眞的；眞人眞事的。

real line 〖數學〗實線。

‡**re·al·ly** 〔ˈriəlɪ, ˈrɪəlɪ, ˈrɪlɪ; ˈriəli〕 *adv.* ①實際地；實在地；眞正地。Do you *really* wish to go? 你眞地想去嗎？②果然 (=indeed.

表驚奇、興趣、懷疑等)。"We're going to Mexico this summer." "Oh, *really?*" "今年夏天我們要去墨西哥。" "啊!眞的?"

***realm** [rɛlm; relm] *n.* ①王國。laws of the *realm*. 國法。②地區;地域。③領域。the *realm* of biology. 生物學的範疇(範圍)。

real number 〖數學〗實數。

real property 〖法律〗不動產。

real time 〖電腦〗眞時。

re·al·tor ['riəltɚ; 'ri:əltə] *n.* 不動產經紀人。

re·al·ty ['riəltɪ; 'riəlti] *n., pl.* **-ties.** ①不動產(爲 personalty 之對)。②〖廢〗忠心;誠實。

real wages 實際工資(不以錢之多寡而以購買力爲準的工資)。

ream¹ [rim; ri:m] *n.* ①令; 二十刀(480至516張紙)。long *ream*. 大令(500 張以上)。printer's (*or* perfect) *ream*. 印刷紙的一令(516張)。short *ream*. 小令(480張)。②〖俗〗(常 *pl.*) 很多。I wrote *reams* to you last week. 上星期我寫了很多信給你。

ream² *v.t.* ①以擴孔器擴大(孔)。②擴大(鎗)之口徑〖常 out〗。③擠出(檸檬等)之汁。

ream·er ['rimɚ; 'ri:mə] *n.* ①鑽孔者; 鑽孔器;整孔鑽。②榨檸檬汁、柑汁等用的器具。

re·an·i·mate [ri'ænəˌmet; ri:'ænimeit] *v.t.,* **-mat·ed, -mat·ing.** ①使復有生氣;使復活。②鼓舞。—**re·an·i·ma·tion,** *n.*

reap** [rip; ri:p] *v.t. & v.i.* ①收割;刈。②收穫;獲得。Kind acts *reap* happy smiles. 善意的行動得到幸福的微笑。reap where one has not sown*** 不勞而獲。***sow the wind and reap the whirlwind*** 做蠢事得到報應。

reap·er** ['ripɚ; 'ri:pə] *n.* ①刈者; 收割者。②收割機。③(=Grim Reaper, the Reaper) 手拿大鐮刀的人(死亡之擬人化)。reaper and binder*** 收割捆紮機。

reap·hook ['ripˌhuk; 'ri:phuk] *n.* 鐮刀;彎月刀。(亦作 **reaping hook**)

reaping machine 收割機。

***re·ap·pear** [ˌriə'pɪr; 'ri:ə'piə, 'riə'p-] *v.i.* 再出現。—**ance,** *n.*

re·ap·point [ˌriə'pɔɪnt; 'ri:ə'pɔint] *v.t.* 再任命;再委派;再指定;復職。—**ment,** *n.*

re·ap·prais·al [ˌriə'prezḷ; ˌri:ə'preizəl] *n.* 新估價;再考慮。

re·ap·praise [ˌriə'prez; ˌri:ə'preiz] *v.t.,* **-praised, -prais·ing.** 再考慮;重新估價。

rear¹** [rɪr; riə] *n.* ①後部; 背後。at the *rear* of the buildings. 在這些建築物之後面。②(軍隊、艦隊之) 後陣; 尾部。bring up the rear*** 隨後; 殿後。—*adj.* 後部的; 後面的。the *rear* door. 後門。

***rear²** *v.t.* ①養育;飼養。to *rear* children. 養育兒女。②建立; 豎起。to *rear* a monument. 建立一紀念碑。③抬起; 揚起。—*v.i.* ①(馬等動物)以後腿站立〖常up〗. The horse *reared* at the sight of the fire engine. 看見救火車,馬突然後肢直立(前肢懸空)。②豎立。

rear admiral 海軍少將。

rear·er ['rɪrɚ; 'riərə] *n.* ①養育者; 培養者;飼養者。②有後脚站立癖的馬。

rear guard 〖軍〗後衛。

rear·guard ['rɪrˌgɑrd; 'riəgɑ:d] *adj.* 後衛的;目的在防止、延遲或逃避的。

rear·horse ['rɪrˌhɔrs; 'riəhɔ:s] *n.* 螳螂。

rearing pond 魚池;魚苗養殖池。

re·arm ['ri'ɑrm; 'ri:'ɑ:m] *v.t. & v.i.* ①重整軍備;再武裝。②供給或改良武器裝備。

re·ar·ma·ment [ri'ɑrməmənt; ri:'ɑ:məmənt] *n.* 重新武裝; 重整軍備; 裝備改良之新武器。***Moral Rearmament*** 道德重整運動。

rear·most ['rɪrˌmost; 'riəˌmoust] *adj.* 最後面的;最後的;最末的。

re·ar·range [ˌriə'rendʒ; 'ri:ə'reindʒ] *v.t.,* **-ranged, -rang·ing.** ①重新編排;再排列;再整理。②以新的或不同的方式排列。

rear-view mirror ['rɪrˌvju~; 'riəvju:~] (汽車的)後視鏡。

rear·ward ['rɪrwɚd; 'riəwəd] *adj.* 後面的; 最末的; 靠近末端的。—*adv.* 向後面地(亦作 **rearwards**). —*n.* 最後面的位置。

‡**rea·son** ['rizṇ; 'ri:zn] *n.* ①理由;原因;動機。He refused to explain his *reasons*. 他拒絕解釋他的理由。②理性; 思考力; 理智。Only man has *reason*. 祇有人有理智。***bring (a person) to reason*** 使遵循道理; 說服;使改變主張;使聽話。***by reason of*** 由於。***in reason*** 合理的。I'm willing to do anything *in reason*. 我願意做一切合理的事。***It stands to reason (that...).***大多數認爲; 按照常情;難怪;無怪乎。***listen to*** (or ***hear***) ***reason*** 聽從道理; 合乎人情。***reason of state*** 統治者、政府或高級官員,採取某項行動之動機(尤指不能公開宣布者)。***stand to reason*** 得當;合道理。***within reason*** =in reason. ***with reason*** 有理由。—*v.i.* 思考; 推理。—*v.t.* ①說服; 勸服。to *reason* a person out of his fear. 說服某人使他勿懼。②合理地安排;使合邏輯。a well-*reasoned* statement. 很合邏輯的陳述。③想出; 想到;思索。

***rea·son·a·ble** ['riznəbl; 'ri:znəbl] *adj.* ①知理的;通人情的。②正當的;合理的。③不貴的; 低廉的; 公道的。The price seems *reasonable*. 價錢似乎不貴。④有理性的;能思考的。—**ness,** *n.* —**rea·son·a·bly,** *adv.*

rea·soned ['rizṇd; 'ri:zənd] *adj.* ①據理的;經過考慮的。②含有理由的。

rea·son·ing ['rizṇɪŋ; 'ri:zniŋ] *n.* ①推論之過程(由已知或假定之事實推斷結論或道理)。sound *reasoning*. 正確的推論。②道理;論據;理由。—*adj.* 能推理的。

rea·son·less ['rizṇlɪs; 'ri:znlis] *adj.* ①不明道理的;無理性的。②不合理的。

re·as·sem·ble [ˌriə'sɛmbḷ; 'ri:ə'sembl] *v.t. & v.i.,* **-bled, -bling.** 再集合;再聚集。

re·as·sert [ˌriə'sɝt; 'ri:ə'sə:t] *v.t.* 再主張;再斷言;再言明。

re·as·ser·tion [ˌriə'sɝʃən; ˌri:ə'sə:ʃən] *n.* 再斷言;再主張;再言明。

re·as·sess [ˌriə'sɛs; ˌri:ə'ses] *v.t.* 再評價;再估定;再評定;再課以賦稅。

re·as·sign [ˌriə'saɪn; ˌri:ə'sain] *v.t.* 再分配;再指定;再選派;再讓與。

re·as·sume [ˌriə'sjum; ˌri:ə'sju:m] *v.t.,* **-sumed, -sum·ing.** ①再取; 取回。②再承擔;再擔任。③再假定。④再開始。

re·as·sump·tion [ˌriə'sʌmpʃən; 'ri:ə'sʌmpʃən] *n.* 取回; 再取; 再承擔;再開始;重就(職位);再假定。

re·as·sur·ance [ˌriə'ʃurəns; ˌri:ə'ʃuərəns] *n.* ①再保證;再保險。②勇氣或信心的恢復。

re·as·sure [ˌriə'ʃur; ˌri:ə'ʃuə] *v.t.,* **-sured, -sur·ing.** ①使恢復信心。His remarks *reassured* me. 他的話使我恢復信心。②再保證。③再保險。—**re·as·sur·ing,** *adj.*

Ré·au·mur ['reəˌmjur; 'reiəmjuə] *adj.* 列氏(寒暑表)的(以零度爲冰點, 80° 爲沸

點)。—*n.* 列氏寒暑表。

re·bap·tism [riˈbæptɪzm; riːˈbæptizm] *n.* 再施洗禮; 再命名; 再受洗。

re·bap·tize [ˌribæpˈtaɪz; ˌriːbæpˈtaiz] *v.t.*, **-tized, -tiz·ing.** 爲…再施洗或命名。

re·bate[1] [ˈribet; ˈriːbeit] *n., v.*, **-bat·ed, -bat·ing.** —*n.* ①部分款項之退還; 折扣。②部分減免之款項; 折扣金。—*v.t.* ①將部分款項減免; 予以折扣。②使(尖銳武器)變鈍。③將尖銳武器蓋住使其無法戮或劈。—*v.i.* 允許有回扣。

re·bate[2] [ˈræbɪt; ˈræbit] *n., v.*, **-bat·ed, -bat·ing.** =**rabbet.**

re·bec(k) [ˈribɛk; ˈriːbek] *n.* 雷貝克琴(中世紀的一種三絃樂器, 呈梨形, 以弓拉之)。

Re·bec·ca [rɪˈbɛkə; riˈbekə] *n.* ①〖聖經〗利百加 (Isaac 之妻, Esau 及 Jacob 之母: 創世記24章)。②女子名。(亦作 **Rebekah**)

***reb·el** [*n., adj.* ˈrɛbl̩; ˈrebl *v.* rɪˈbɛl; riˈbel, rəˈb-] *n., adj., v.*, **re·belled, re·bel·ling.** —*n.* ①叛徒; 謀反者。②(有時R-)美國南北戰爭時之南軍士兵。—*adj.* 反叛的; 謀反的。the *rebel* army. 叛軍。—*v.i.* ①反叛; 謀反。②厭惡; 不從; 反對。

***re·bel·lion** [rɪˈbɛljən; riˈbeljən] *n.* ①反叛; 謀反。to rise in *rebellion.* 造反。②反抗; 不從。*rebellion* against fate. 反抗命運。

re·bel·lious [rɪˈbɛljəs; riˈbeljəs, rəˈb-] *adj.* ①謀反的; 反叛的。②難治的; 難處理的。—**ly,** *adv.* —**ness,** *n.*

re·bind [riˈbaɪnd; ˈriːˈbaind] *v.t.*, **-bound, -bind·ing.** 再束; 重縛; 重新裝訂。

re·birth [riˈbɝθ; ˈriːˈbəːθ] *n.* ①(受洗禮後靈魂得以)再生; 復生; 重生。②復興; 新生; 新發展。③轉世; 再生。

re·born [riˈbɔrn; ˈriːˈbɔːn] *adj.* 再生的。

re·bound [*n.* ˈriˌbaund, rɪˈbaund; riˈbaund, ˈriːb- *v.* rɪˈbaund; riˈbaund] *v.i.* 彈回; 跳回。—*v.t.* 使彈回; 使跳回。—*n.* ①彈回; 跳回。②〖籃球〗籃板球。***on the rebound*** **a.** 突然失戀後之惶惑狀態。**b.** 彈回; 跳回。***take*** (or ***catch***) ***a person on*** (or ***at***) ***the rebound*** 利用感情的反激使某人採取相反的行動。

re·broad·cast [riˈbrɔdˌkæst; riːˈbrɔːdkɑːst] *n., v.*, **-cast** or **-cast·ed, -cast·ing.** —*n.* ①〖無線電〗再播; 轉播。②再播之節目。—*v.t.* & *v.i.* 再播; 轉播。

re·buff [rɪˈbʌf; riˈbʌf] *n.* ①(計畫、希望等的)挫折; 阻礙。②(對請求等)斷然的拒絕。—*v.t.* 挫折; 阻擋; 嚴拒; 驅逐。

re·build [riˈbɪld; ˈriːˈbild] *v.*, **-built,** or (古) **-build·ed, -build·ing.** —*v.t.* 再建; 重建; 再造。—*v.i.* 重建; 再建。

***re·buke** [rɪˈbjuk; riˈbjuːk, rəˈb-] *v.*, **-buked, -buk·ing,** *n.* —*v.t.* 指責; 叱責; 非難。He *rebuked* him strongly for his negligence. 他嚴斥他的疏忽。—*n.* 指責; 叱責; 非難。

re·bus [ˈribəs; ˈriːbəs] *n., pl.* **-bus·es.** 謎; 謎畫。

re·but [rɪˈbʌt; riˈbʌt] *v.*, **-but·ted, -but·ting.** —*v.t.* ①舉證據以辯駁; 反駁。②拒絕。—*v.i.* 舉出反證。

re·but·ment [rɪˈbʌtmənt; riˈbʌtmənt] *n.* =**rebuttal.**

re·but·tal [rɪˈbʌtl̩; riˈbʌtl] *n.* 舉證據辯駁; 反駁。

re·but·ter [rɪˈbʌtɚ; riˈbʌtə] *n.* ①〖法律〗被告的第三度答辯。②反駁者。③反駁之辯論。

rec. ①receipt. ②recipe. ③record. ④recorded. ⑤recorder.

re·cal·ci·trance [rɪˈkælsɪtrəns; riˈkælsitrəns] *n.* 不服從; 反抗; 頑强; 固執。

re·cal·ci·tran·cy [rɪˈkælsɪtrənsɪ; riˈkælsitrənsi] *n.* =**recalcitrance.**

re·cal·ci·trant [rɪˈkælsɪtrənt; riˈkælsitrənt] *adj.* 反抗的; 不服從的; 固執的。—*n.* 反抗者; 不服從的人。

re·cal·ci·trate [rɪˈkælsɪˌtret; riˈkælsitreit] *v.i.*, **-trat·ed, -trat·ing.** ①踢回; 用力踢。②不服從; 頑抗。

re·cal·ci·tra·tion [rɪˌkælsɪˈtreʃən; riˌkælsiˈtreiʃən] *n.* ①踢回。②反抗; 頑梗。

re·ca·lesce [ˌrikəˈlɛs; ˌriːkəˈles] *v.i.*, **-lesced, -lesc·ing.** 發生復輝現象。

re·call** [*v.* rɪˈkɔl; riˈkɔːl *n.* ˈriˌkɔl, rɪˈkɔl; riˈkɔːl] *v.t.* ①記起; 憶起。②召回; 挽回。to *recall* an ambassador. 召回一大使。③挽回; 復活。④撤回; 取消。to *recall* a promise. 取消一諾言。—*n.* ①回憶; 回想。②召回; 喚回。③用以召回人、船等的訊號。④撤回; 取消。⑤(由人民投票的) 罷免。beyond*** (or ***past***) ***recall*** **a.** 不能召回或撤回。**b.** 不能記憶; 記不起。

re·cant [rɪˈkænt; riˈkænt] *v.t.* 正式或公然撤回或取消(言論、意見等)。—*v.i.* 正式或公然撤回言論、意見或信仰。

re·can·ta·tion [ˌrikænˈteʃən; ˌriːkænˈteiʃən] *n.* 正式或公然的撤回或取消言論、意見、決心等。

re·cap[1] [*n.* ˈriˌkæp; ˈriːkæp *v.* riˈkæp; riːˈkæp] *n., v.*, **-capped, -cap·ping.** —*n.* 翻新過之輪胎。—*v.t.* 翻新(輪胎)。

re·cap[2] [*v.* rɪˈkæp; riˈkæp *n.* ˈriˌkæp; ˈriːkæp] *n., v.*, **-capped, -cap·ping.** —*n.* =**recapitulation.** —*v.t.* =**recapitulate.**

re·ca·pit·u·late [ˌrikəˈpɪtʃəˌlet; ˌriːkəˈpitjuleit] *v.*, **-lat·ed, -lat·ing.** —*v.t.* ①撮要說明; 簡述要旨。②〖音樂〗反復。③〖生物〗各進化階段重現。—*v.i.* 簡述要旨。

re·ca·pit·u·la·tion [ˌrikəˌpɪtʃəˈleʃən; ˈriːkəˌpitjuˈleiʃən] *n.* ①重述要點; 撮要。②〖音樂〗反復。③〖生物〗個體成長中其所屬種族各進化階段之重現(尤指胎兒期中者)。

re·ca·pit·u·la·to·ry [ˌrikəˈpɪtʃuləˌtorɪ; ˌriːkəˈpitjuleitəri] *adj.* 撮要的; 重述要點的。(亦作 **recapitulative**)

re·cap·ture [riˈkæptʃɚ; ˈriːˈkæptʃə] *v.*, **-tured, -tur·ing,** *n.* —*v.t.* ①再捕獲; 收復; 重新占領。②記憶; 回憶。③歸公。—*n.* ①再捕獲; 收復; 再占領。②再獲得之物。③歸公。④〖國際法〗合法的收回從前之領土等。

re·cast [*v.* riˈkæst; ˈriːˈkɑːst *n.* ˈriˌkæst; ˈriːˈkɑːst] *v.*, **-cast, -cast·ing,** *n.* —*v.t.* ①再鑄; 重鑄。②改正; 改作; 改寫(文章、文件、字句等); 改算(數目)。③改變劇中演員; 換角。—*n.* ①再鑄; 改作; 再計算。②再鑄物; 改正物。

recd., rec'd. received.

re·cede**[1] [rɪˈsid; riˈsiːd] *v.i.*, **-ced·ed, -ced·ing.** ①後退。②向後傾斜。③退出; 撤回; 撤銷。He *receded* from the agreement. 他撤回協定。④變模糊。Memories of childhood *recede.* 童年的記憶漸漸模糊。⑤縮小; 減退; 降低。recede into the background*** **a.** (人的) 勢力消失; 失去重要性。**b.** (問題、權利等)利益減少; 減少趣味; 減少重要性。

re·cede[2] [ˌriˈsid; riːˈsiːd] *v.t.*, **-ced·ed, -ced·ing.** 返還; 歸還。

***re·ceipt** [rɪˈsit; riˈsiːt, rəˈs-] *n.* ①收據; 收條。Please send me a *receipt* for the money. 請給我一張關於此款的收據。②

(*pl.*) 收到之款；進款。③收到；領收。④收到之事物。⑤〖方〗 =**recipe.** ***on*** (or ***upon***) ***receipt of*** 當收到…時。—*v.t.* 〖美〗開收據。

re·ceipt·or [rɪˈsitɚ; riˈsiːtə] *n.* 收受人。

re·ceiv·a·ble [rɪˈsivəbl̩; riˈsiːvəbl] *adj.* ①適於接收的。②待付款的。③可收到的。—*n.* (*pl.*) 可收取之帳目或帳單。

re·ceiv·al [rɪˈsivl̩; riˈsiːvəl] *n.* 接受；收到。

‡**re·ceive** [rɪˈsiv; riˈsiːv, rəˈs-] *v.,* **-ceived, -ceiv·ing.** —*v.t.* ①收到；領收。When did you *receive* the letter? 你何時接到那信？②接受；領受。He *received* a good education. 他受過良好的教育。③裝載；支持；負擔；容納。④聽（告解）；同意聽取。⑤經歷；遭受。⑥款待；歡迎。⑦收容；收留。⑧容許；准予進入。—*v.i.* ①收到；領收；接受。Freely ye have *received*. (聖經)你已爽快地接受了。②接見；會客。She *receives* on Tuesdays. 她星期二在家會客。③〖無線電〗 接收；收受。

re·ceived [rɪˈsivd; riˈsiːvd] *adj.* ①一般承認的。②收訖的；收到的。

Received Standard 英國標準英語。

***re·ceiv·er** [rɪˈsivɚ; riˈsiːvə, rəˈs-] *n.* ①收受者。②收話器；接收機；收信機。③電話的耳機。④〖法律〗(破產財團之) 管理人。⑤〖商〗收款人。⑥收贓物的人；贓物商。⑦容器。⑧〖棒球〗捕手。

re·ceiv·er·ship [rɪˈsivɚˌʃɪp; riˈsiːvəʃip] *n.* ①〖法律〗監管他人財產者的地位或任期。②〖法律〗受監管者代管之狀態。

re·ceiv·ing [rɪˈsivɪŋ; riˈsiːviŋ] *adj.* 收容的；吸收的(用於特別名詞)。

receiving order 〖法律〗宣告破產及指定財產監管人的命令。

receiving set 收音機；收報機；電視機。

receiving station 〖無線電〗接收站。

re·cen·cy [ˈrisn̩sɪ; ˈriːsnsi] *n.* 新近；晚近。***law of recency*** 〖心理〗近因律。

re·cen·sion [rɪˈsɛnʃən; riˈsenʃən] *n.* ①校訂。②校訂本；校訂版。

‡**re·cent** [ˈrisn̩t; ˈriːsnt] *adj.* ①最近的；近來的。*recent* events. 最近的事件。②近代的。③(R-)〖地質〗近世的。—*n.* (R-)〖地質〗近世。

‡**re·cent·ly** [ˈrisn̩tlɪ; ˈriːsntli] *adv.* 最近地；近來地。*Recently* I met him in the street. 我最近在街上碰見了他。

re·cep·ta·cle [rɪˈsɛptəkl̩; riˈseptəkl] *n.* ①容器。②〖植物〗花托；花床。③〖電〗收容器；插座。

***re·cep·tion** [rɪˈsɛpʃən; riˈsepʃən, rəˈs-] *n.* ①接待；歡迎。②容納；收入。③歡迎之態度。The book met with a favorable *reception*. 此書很受歡迎。④歡迎會；酒會；茶會。⑤收受；接受。⑥〖無線電〗接收；收受。*Reception* was poor. (收音機)收聽不清楚。

re·cep·tion·ist [rɪˈsɛpʃənɪst; riˈsepʃənist] *n.* 招待員；(公司等)招呼訪客的人。

reception room 客廳；候診室。

re·cep·tive [rɪˈsɛptɪv; riˈseptiv] *adj.* ①能接受的；能容納的。②易接納要求、建議等的。③易接受新思想的。

re·cep·tiv·i·ty [rɪˌsɛpˈtɪvətɪ; risepˈtiviti] *n.* 感受性；容受性(=receptiveness).

re·cep·tor [rɪˈsɛptɚ; riˈseptə] *n.* ①〖生理〗(感受刺激的) 神經末梢；感受體。②=**receiver.**

***re·cess** [*n.* rɪˈsɛs, ˈrisɛs; riˈses, ˈriːses *v.* rɪˈsɛs; riˈses] *n.* ①休閒時間；休假期；休會期；休業期。②牆壁之凹部；壁凹。③深奧之處；深幽處。—*v.t.* ①置於隱密處；隱藏。②於…形成凹處；作凹處。—*v.i.* 休憩；休假。The convention *recessed* till afternoon. 會議休會至下午。

re·ces·sion¹ [rɪˈsɛʃən; riˈseʃən] *n.* ①退；引退；退却。②(壁等的)凹處。③〖經濟〗商業暫時衰落現象；蕭條。

re·ces·sion² [ˌriˈsɛʃən; ˌriːˈseʃən] 「*n.* 交還原主。」

re·ces·sion·al [rɪˈsɛʃənəl; riˈseʃnl] *adj.* ①退後的；引退的。②禮拜儀式結束後牧師與歌詠團退往聖衣室的。③禮拜結束後所唱之讚美歌或音樂的。④〖英〗議會休會的。—*n.* 禮拜結束時之讚美歌或音樂。

re·ces·sion·ar·y [rɪˈsɛʃənˌɛrɪ; riˈseʃənəri] *adj.* 經濟萎縮的。

re·ces·sive [rɪˈsɛsɪv; riˈsesiv] *adj.* ①退後的；倒退的；有倒退傾向的。②〖生物〗隱性的；潛性的。③〖語音〗逆行的；移向字首的。—*n.* 〖生物〗隱性；潛性；隱性遺傳因子。

Rech·ab·ite [ˈrɛkəˌbaɪt; ˈrekəˌbait] *n.* ①〖聖經〗 Jonadab (Rechab之子)的後裔。②禁酒者。

re·change [riˈtʃendʒ; riːˈtʃeindʒ] *v.,* **-changed, -chang·ing,** *n.* —*v.t.* & *v.i.* 再變更；再變異。—*n.* 進一步之變更。

re·check [riˈtʃɛk; riːˈtʃek] *v.t.* & *v.i.* 再核對。

re·cher·ché [rəˈʃɛrʃe; rəˈʃɛəʃei] *adj.* ①精心求出的。②罕有的；不平常的。③精選的。④優美的。⑤供不應求的；大家爭取的。

re·cid·i·vism [rɪˈsɪdəˌvɪzəm; riˈsidivizəm] *n.* 〖法律〗罪行之累犯習性；累犯；常習犯(指犯罪行爲)。

re·cid·i·vist [rɪˈsɪdəvɪst; riˈsidivist] *n.* 常犯罪的人；慣犯；累犯；常習犯 (指犯罪者)。—*adj.* 累犯的；再犯的。

***rec·i·pe** [ˈrɛsəpɪ, -ˌpi; ˈresipi] *n.* ①烹飪法；食譜。Give me your *recipe* for cookies. 把你的製餅乾法給我。②製法；祕訣；祕法。③祕方。

re·cip·i·ent [rɪˈsɪpɪənt; riˈsipiənt] *n.* 接受者。—*adj.* 容納的；接受的；願領受的。

***re·cip·ro·cal** [rɪˈsɪprəkl̩; riˈsiprəkəl] *adj.* ①交往的；互惠的。*reciprocal* treaties. 互惠條約。②相互的；交互的。③〖文法〗 相互的。*reciprocal* pronoun. 相互代名詞(如each other, one another 等)。—*n.* ①相互事物；對等物。②〖數學〗倒數。3 is the *reciprocal* of ⅓. 3 是 ⅓ 的倒數。—**ly,** *adv.*

reciprocal ohm 〖電〗姆歐(=mho).

reciprocal trade 最優惠國通商協定。

re·cip·ro·cate [rɪˈsɪprəˌket; riˈsiprəkeit] *v.t.* & *v.i.,* **-cat·ed, -cat·ing.** ①回報；報答；回信。②〖機械〗往復；來回。

re·cip·ro·ca·tion [rɪˌsɪprəˈkeʃən; riˌsiprəˈkeiʃən] *n.* ①交換。②圖報；報答。③往復運動。

re·cip·ro·ca·tor [rɪˈsɪprəˌketɚ; riˈsiprəkeitə] *n.* ①報答者；往返者。②往復機。

rec·i·proc·i·tar·i·an [ˌrɛsəprɑsəˈtɛrɪən; ˌresiprɔsiˈtɛəriən] *adj.* 互惠的；通商互惠的。—*n.* 主張通商互惠者。

rec·i·proc·i·ty [ˌrɛsəˈprɑsətɪ; ˌresiˈprɔsiti] *n.* ①相互的動作、依靠等。②互換；交易。③互惠 (特指兩國間商業上的互惠)。a *reciprocity* treaty. 互惠條約。

re·cit·a·ble [rɪˈsaɪtəbl̩; riˈsaitəbl] *adj.* 可詳述的；可吟誦的。

re·cit·al [rɪˈsaɪtl̩; riˈsaitl] *n.* ①述說；

吟誦。②故事。③音樂會（常爲一人獨奏或獨唱）。④表演會。

rec·i·ta·tion〔ˌrɛsəˈteʃən; ˌresiˈteiʃən〕*n.* ①再述；重述。②(功課等之)背誦。③所背誦之篇章。

rec·i·ta·tive¹〔ˌrɛsətəˈtiv; ˌresitəˈtiːv〕*n.*【音樂】敍唱調；敍唱部。—*adj.* 敍唱調的。

rec·i·ta·tive²〔ˈrɛsəˌtetɪv, rɪˈsaɪtətɪv; ˈresiteitiv, riˈsaitətiv〕*adj.* 背誦的；重述的；詳述的。

***re·cite**〔rɪˈsaɪt; riˈsait〕*v.*, **-cit·ed, -cit·ing.** —*v.t.* ①背誦。to *recite* a lesson. 背誦一課。②詳述。③朗讀(詩歌等)。—*v.i.* ①誦(詩或演詞)以娛聽衆。②背誦。

re·cit·er〔rɪˈsaɪtɚ; riˈsaitə〕*n.* ①背誦者；吟調者。②朗誦集。

reciting note 朗吟調；朗吟符。

reck〔rek; rɛk〕*v.i. & v.t.*【古】①干係。②顧慮；注意。The brave soldiers *recked* little of danger. 勇敢的士兵不大顧及危險。【注意】此字經常在問話或否定語中使用。

***reck·less**〔ˈrɛklɪs; ˈreklis〕*adj.* 鹵莽的；不顧一切的。a *reckless* driver. 鹵莽的駕駛者。—**ly,** *adv.* —**ness,** *n.*

reck·on**〔ˈrɛkən; ˈrekən〕*v.t.* ①計算。②斷定；推定；公認。③【俗】認爲。You are the boss here, I *reckon.* 我想你是此地的老板。—*v.i.* ①計算；算帳。②依賴；仗恃【on, upon】. You can *reckon* on our help. 你可依恃我們的幫助。reckon for*** 顧及；體諒；酌量。***reckon in*** 計及。***reckon up*** 計算。***reckon with*** a. 考慮到。b. 處理。***reckon without one's host*** 忽略了困難或他人之反對；作計畫時對有關重要因素未予考慮。

reck·on·er〔ˈrɛkənɚ; ˈreknə〕*n.* ①計算者；清算人。②計算表。

reck·on·ing〔ˈrɛkənɪŋ; ˈrekniŋ〕*n.* ①計算法；計算；數。②算帳；結帳。③(尤指酒館等的)帳單。④船隻位置的推算。⑤所推算出的位置。***be out in one's reckoning*** 計算錯誤；估計不準。***the day of reckoning*** a. 結帳日。b. 贖罪日；報應來到的日子。c. 最後審判日(＝the Day of Judgment).

***re·claim**〔rɪˈklem; riˈkleim〕*v.t.* ①糾正；矯正(某人)的錯誤；拯救(某人)於罪惡；教化(野蠻人)。②使恢復有用、良好之狀態；開拓(沙漠、荒地等)使成爲可耕地或可居住之地；墾殖；塡(海、沼地等)。*reclaimed* land. 新生地；新墾地。③從(廢物中)取得(有用之物)；廢物利用；再製(天然產物)。④馴服(野獸等)。⑤取回；要求(土地)的歸還。—*n.* ①糾正；矯正；挽救。He is past (*or* beyond) *reclaim.* 他是無可救藥。②新的要求。

re·claim·a·ble〔rɪˈkleməbl̩; riˈkleiməbl〕*adj.* ①可取回的；可挽救的。②可改正的；可矯正的。③可開墾的。④可馴服的。⑤可教化的。⑥可再予利用的。

rec·la·ma·tion〔ˌrɛkləˈmeʃən; ˌrekləˈmeiʃən〕*n.* ①改正；矯正；挽救。②取回；收復。③廢物利用。④抗議。

rec·li·nate〔ˈrɛklənet; ˈrekləneit〕*adj.*【植物】內曲的；臥垂的。

***re·cline**〔rɪˈklaɪn; riˈklain, rəˈk-〕*v.*, **-clined, -clin·ing.** —*v.t.* 斜倚；橫臥；憑依。to *recline* one's head on (*or* upon) ... 將頭斜靠於…上。—*v.i.* 斜倚；橫臥【on, upon, against】. The tired girl *reclined* on the couch. 這疲倦的女孩斜臥榻上。

reclining chair 臥椅。

re·clothe〔riˈkloð; riːˈklouð〕*v.t.*, **-clothed** or **-clad, -cloth·ing.** ①再着衣。②換着新衣；更衣。

rec·luse〔*n.* ˈrɛklus, rɪˈklus; riˈkluːs *adj.* rɪˈklus; riˈkluːs〕*n.* 遁世者；隱士。—*adj.* 遁世的；隱居的。

re·clu·sion〔rɪˈkluʒən; riˈkluːʒən〕*n.* ①遁世；隱居；退隱。②幽禁。③隱士之生活。

re·clu·sive〔rɪˈklusɪv; riˈkluːsiv〕*adj.* 蟄居的；隱居的；隱遁的。

re·coal〔ˈriˈkol; ˈriːˈkoul〕*v.t. & v.i.* 重新供以煤；再裝以煤。

***rec·og·ni·tion**〔ˌrɛkəgˈnɪʃən; ˌrekəgˈniʃən, -kig-〕*n.* ①認識；認出；認得。*recognition* of an old friend. 認出舊友。②承認；認可。an official *recognition.* 官方的承認；公認。③察覺；注意。④讚譽。The actor soon won *recognition* from the public. 這演員不久便獲得衆人的讚譽。

recognition signal【軍】識別訊號。

rec·og·niz·a·ble〔ˈrɛkəgˌnaɪzəbl̩; ˈrekəgnaizəbl〕*adj.* 可被認出的；可被承認的。—**rec·og·niz·a·bly,** *adv.*

re·cog·ni·zance〔rɪˈkɑgnɪzəns; riˈkɔgnizəns〕*n.* ①【法律】保證書；具結。②【法律】保證金；抵押金。

re·cog·ni·zant〔rɪˈkɑgnɪzənt; riˈkɔgnizənt〕*adj.* 認識的；認可的。

‡**rec·og·nize**〔ˈrɛkəgˌnaɪz; ˈrekəgnaiz, -kig-〕*v.t.*, **-nized, -niz·ing.** ①認識；認得。②認出；辨認。③承認；認可。They *recognized* him as the lawful heir. 他們承認他是合法的繼承人。④覺察；注意。⑤(在會議中)予以發言權。⑥感激；讚揚；表揚。to *recognize* merit. 表揚功績。⑦承認(私生子)爲己出。(亦作 **recognise**)

re·cog·ni·zee〔rɪˌkɑgnəˈzi; riˌkɔgniˈziː〕*n.*【法律】被具保人。

re·cog·ni·zor〔rɪˌkɑgnəˈzɔr; riˌkɔgniˈzɔː〕*n.*【法律】具保人。

re·coil〔rɪˈkɔɪl; riˈkɔil〕*v.i.* ①退却；退縮。②彈回；跳回。③起反應；呈反作用。④【物理】反衝。—*n.* ①退却；退縮。②彈回；跳回。the *recoil* of a gun. 砲的回彈(後座力)。③反應；反作用。

re·coil·less〔rɪˈkɔɪllɪs; riˈkɔillis〕*adj.* 無座力的。a *recoilless* rifle. 無座力砲。

re·coin〔riˈkɔɪn; riːˈkɔin〕*v.t.* 改鑄；重鑄；再鑄。

re·coin·age〔rɪˈkɔɪnɪdʒ; riˈkɔinidʒ〕*n.* ①改鑄。②改鑄貨幣；經重鑄之物。

***rec·ol·lect**〔ˌrɛkəˈlɛkt; ˌrekəˈlekt〕*v.t. & v.i.* ①記起；憶起。as far as I *recollect.* 就我所記得的；倘若我記得不錯。②(禱告時)沉思。

re-col·lect〔ˌrikəˈlɛkt; ˈriːkəˈlekt〕*v.t.* ①重新收集；再收集。②鼓起(勇氣)；提起(力量)；集中(心思)。③恢復(冷靜)。***re-collect oneself*** 恢復頭腦冷靜。

***rec·ol·lec·tion**〔ˌrɛkəˈlɛkʃən; ˌrekəˈlekʃən〕*n.* ①記起；憶記；記憶力。to the best of my *recollection.* 就我所能記憶；如我記得不錯。②回憶；記憶；記性。③(常 *pl.*)回想的事物。

re·com·mence〔ˌrikəˈmɛns; ˌriːkəˈmens〕*v.t. & v.i.*, **-menced, -menc·ing.** 再開始；重新開始。

***rec·om·mend**〔ˌrɛkəˈmɛnd; ˌrekəˈmend〕*v.t.* ①介紹；推薦。They *recommended* me for the job. 他們介紹我擔任這工作。②勸告。③使得人歡心。④託交；託付。

R

He *recommended* his soul to God. 他將他的心靈交給了上帝。

rec·om·mend·a·ble [ˌrɛkəˈmɛndəbl̩; ˌrekəˈmendəbl] *adj.* 可推薦的;可褒獎的。

***rec·om·men·da·tion** [ˌrɛkəmɛnˈdeʃən; ˌrekəmenˈdeiʃən] *n.* ①推薦;介紹。to buy something on the *recommendation* of a friend. 經朋友之推薦而購買某物。②推薦書;介紹信。③勸告;讚譽之言。④可取之處。⑤被推薦之事物、方法等。

rec·om·mend·a·to·ry [ˌrɛkəˈmɛndəˌtorɪ; ˌrekəˈmendətəri] *adj.* ①推薦的。②勸告的。

re·com·mit [ˌrikəˈmɪt; ˌriːkəˈmit] *v.t.*, **-mit·ted, -mit·ting.** ①再委託。②將(議案等)再交付委員會。③再投獄。④再犯。

re·com·mit·ment [ˌrikəˈmɪtmənt; ˌriːkəˈmitmənt] *n.* ①再委託;再信託。②再交付委員會。③再下獄。④再犯。

re·com·mit·tal [ˌrikəˈmɪtl̩; ˌriːkəˈmitəl] *n.* =**recommitment.**

***rec·om·pense** [ˈrɛkəmˌpɛns; ˈrekəmpens] *v.*, **-pensed, -pens·ing,** *n.* —*v.t.* ①償還;報答;報酬。to *recompense* good with evil. 以怨報德。②補償;賠償。to *recompense* a person for his loss. 賠償某人的損失。—*v.i.* 償還;補償。—*n.* ①酬金;報酬;償還金。to work without *recompense.* 工作而不受報酬;義務工作。②賠償;補償金。

re·com·pose [ˌrikəmˈpoz; ˈriː-kəmˈpouz] *v.t.*, **-posed, -pos·ing.** ①重新組織;改組。②〖印刷〗重排。③改作(樂曲、詩文等)。④恢復鎮靜。

re·com·po·si·tion [ˌrikɑmpəˈzɪʃən; ˌriːkɔmpəˈziʃən] *n.* ①改組;重組。②〖印刷〗重排。③(詩文、樂曲的)改作。④恢復鎮靜。

rec·on·cil·a·ble [ˈrɛkənˌsaɪləbl̩; ˈrekənsailəbl] *adj.* ①可調停的;有和解希望的;可復交的。②調諧一致的。

***rec·on·cile** [ˈrɛkənˌsaɪl; ˈrekənsail] *v.t.*, **-ciled, -cil·ing.** ①復交;和解。②調停(口角等)。③使一致。to *reconcile* one's statements with one's conduct. 使言行一致。④使滿足;使安於。I must *reconcile* myself to a life of poverty. 我須安於貧困。⑤再供獻(教堂、公墓等)。⑥使被逐出教會之人再加入教會。

rec·on·cile·ment [ˈrɛkənˌsaɪlmənt; ˈrekənsailmənt] *n.* =**reconciliation.**

rec·on·cil·i·a·tion [ˌrɛkənˌsɪlɪˈeʃən; ˌrekənsiliˈeiʃən] *n.* ①復交;修好。②調停;調和。

rec·on·cil·i·a·to·ry [ˌrɛkənˈsɪlɪəˌtorɪ; ˌrekənˈsiliətɔːri] *adj.* 和解的;調停的;有和解傾向的。

rec·on·dite [ˈrɛkənˌdaɪt; riˈkɔndait] *adj.* ①爲一般人所不解的;深奧的;奧妙的。②默默無聞的;隱藏的;祕密的。

re·con·di·tion [ˌrikənˈdɪʃən; ˌriːkənˈdiʃən] *v.t.* 使恢復良好或滿意的狀態;修復。

re·con·nais·sance [rɪˈkɑnəsəns; riˈkɔnisəns] *n.* ①〖軍〗偵察;搜索。*reconnaissance* in force. 實力偵察;强行偵察。②(地形或地勢的)勘查。③事先的考查。

reconnaissance car 偵察車。

rec·on·noi·ter [ˌrikəˈnɔɪtɚ, ˌrɛkə-; ˌrekəˈnɔitə] *v.t.* ①〖軍〗偵察(敵情)。②勘測(地形、地勢);勘查(地區)。③觀察;考查;探究。—*v.i.* 偵察;勘測;觀察;考查。

rec·on·noi·tre [ˌrikəˈnɔɪtɚ; ˌrekəˈnɔitə] *v.*, **-tred, -tring.** =**reconnoiter.**

re·con·sid·er [ˌrikənˈsɪdɚ; ˈriː-kənˈsidə] *v.t.* ①再考慮;再斟酌。②(會議中)覆議;重新討論(決議案)。—*v.i.* 再考慮或覆議一事。—**re·con·sid·er·a·tion,** *n.*

re·con·sign·ment [ˌrikənˈsaɪnmənt; ˌriːkənˈsainmənt] *n.* ①再委託。②〖商〗改變原提貨單上之交貨地點、運輸路線、收貨人等。

re·con·sti·tute [riˈkɑnstəˌtjut; ˈriːˈkɔnstitjuːt] *v.t.*, **-tut·ed, -tut·ing.** ①再組成;再構成。②再任命;再選定。③再設立。④重制定。⑤使還原;使成原狀。

***re·con·struct** [ˌrikənˈstrʌkt; ˈriː-kənsˈtrʌkt] *v.t.* ①重建;改造。②〖語言〗自現存語言推測古代語言的字形、發音等。

***re·con·struc·tion** [ˌrikənˈstrʌkʃən; ˈriː-kənsˈtrʌkʃən] *n.* ①再建;重建。②(R-)〖美〗**a.** 美國南方諸州於內戰後重新組織並與聯邦政府重建關係之過程。**b.** 此一時期(1865-1877)。③重建物;改建物。

re·con·struc·tive [ˌrikənˈstrʌktɪv; ˈriː-kənsˈtrʌktiv] *adj.* 再建的;重建的。

re·con·ver·sion [ˌrikənˈvɝʃən; ˈriː-kənˈvəːʃən] *n.* ①再改宗;再改信仰。②再改黨。③復黨;歸隊;再歸依。④(工業的)由戰時狀態重回平時狀態;復原;此種改變的時期。

re·con·vert [ˌrikənˈvɝt; ˈriː-kənˈvəːt] *v.t.* ①使再改宗;使再改黨;使復黨;使再歸依。②使(工業等)恢復平時狀態;使復原。—*v.i.* ①再改宗;再改黨;復黨;再歸依。②故態復萌。③由戰時狀態改爲平時狀態;復原。

‡re·cord [*v.* rɪˈkɔrd; riˈkɔːd *n., adj.* ˈrɛkɚd; ˈrekɔːd] *v.t.* ①記錄。Listen to the speaker and *record* what he says. 靜聽演說者,並把他說的話記錄下來。②記載。We *record* history in books. 我們將歷史記載在書上。③錄於留聲機片;將…錄音。④顯出;表示。The thermometer *recorded* 40°C. 寒暑表上顯出攝氏40度。—*v.i.* 記錄;記載。—*n.* ①記錄;報告。②官方記載;案卷。③唱片。④(人之)履歷;(船隻、動物等之)行動記載。She had a fine *record* at school. 她在學校曾有良好的行爲記載。⑤〖美〗犯罪記錄;前科。⑥最高成績;比賽記錄。***a matter of record*** 有記錄的事實;有案可稽之事件。***bear record to*** 給…作證;證實。***break a record*** 打破記錄。***break*** (or ***beat***) ***the record*** 打破記錄;超過前例。***go on record*** 公開聲明。***have a good*** (***bad***) ***record*** 已知之事實證明具有良好(壞)品格。***off the record*** 不可記錄或引用的;不可以公開的。***of record*** 根據正式記載。***on record*** 被記錄的;有案可稽的。—*adj.* 造成記錄的;最高記錄的。a *record* wheat crop. 最高記錄的小麥收成。

rec·ord-break·er [ˈrɛkɚdˌbrekɚ; ˈrekɔːdˌbreikə] *n.* ①打破記錄者。②打破記錄之表演、事件等。(亦作 **record breaker**)

rec·ord-break·ing [ˈrɛkɚdˌbrekɪŋ; ˈrekɔːdˌbreikiŋ] *n., adj.* 打破記錄(的)。

record changer 自動換唱片器。

re·cord·er [rɪˈkɔrdɚ; riˈkɔːdə] *n.* ①記錄員;書記。②記錄器;錄音機。③(某些城市之)法院推事。④一種簫(古樂器)。

rec·ord-hold·er [ˈrɛkɚdˌholdɚ; ˈrekɔːdˌhouldə] *n.* 保持最高記錄者;記錄保持者。(亦作 **record holder**)

re·cord·ing [rɪˈkɔrdɪŋ; riˈkɔːdiŋ] *n.* ①記錄。②被記錄的東西。③錄音。—*adj.* 記錄的;可記錄的。

recording telegraph 記錄電報機。

re·cord·ist 〔rɪˈkɔrdɪst; riˈkɔːdist〕 *n.* 作記錄的人;錄音員。
re·cord·mak·er 〔ˈrɛkəd͵mekɚ; ˈrekəd͵meikə〕 *n.* 唱片製造商。
record player 電唱機。
re·count 〔rɪˈkaunt; riˈkaunt〕 *v.t.* ①詳述;敍述;描述。②依次數說;列舉。
re-count 〔*v.* ͵rɪˈkaunt; ˈriːˈkaunt *n.* ˈri͵kaunt, riˈkaunt; ˈriːˈkaunt〕 *v.t.* 覆算;再計算;重數。—*n.* 覆算;覆算票數。
re·coup 〔rɪˈkup; riˈkuːp〕 *v.t.* ①取得補償;彌補。②付還。③〖法律〗扣留(應付給之一部分款額)。—*v.i.* 獲得補償。—*n.*〖法律〗補償;付還;扣留應付款項之一部分。
re·coup·ment 〔rɪˈkupmənt; riˈkuːpmənt〕 *n.* ①補償;付還;扣除。②補償物;付還之款。
re·course 〔riˈkɔrs; riˈkɔːs〕 *n.* ①求助;請求保護。②賴以幫助或保護之人或物。③〖法律〗(對商業票據等之)追索權;請求償還。***have recourse to*** 求助於。
re·cov·er 〔͵riˈkʌvɚ; ˈriːˈkʌvə〕 *v.t.* ①再覆蓋。②裝以新面。
***re·cov·er** 〔rɪˈkʌvɚ; riˈkʌvə〕 *v.t.* ①尋回;復得;恢復。to *recover* consciousness. 恢復知覺。②補償;補救。to *recover* one's losses. 補償損失。③使復元;使痊癒;使清醒。④恢復適當的位置或狀況。⑤(因法院判決)獲得;取回。⑥援救;救出。⑦恢復有用;重新利用;再生。—*v.i.* ①痊癒;復元。He has *recovered* from his illness. 他已痊癒。②〖法律〗打勝官司;勝訴。
re·cov·er·a·ble 〔rɪˈkʌvərəbl̩; riˈkʌvərəbl〕 *adj.* 可痊癒的;可收回的。
***re·cov·er·y** 〔rɪˈkʌvərɪ; riˈkʌvəri〕 *n., pl.* **-er·ies.** ①恢復;尋回;復得。②痊癒;復元。*recovery* from influenza. 流行性感冒之痊癒。③恢復適當的位置或狀況。④〖法律〗取得某項權益。
rec·re·an·cy 〔ˈrɛkrɪənsɪ; ˈrekriənsi〕 *n., pl.* **-cies.** ①懦弱;畏縮。②不義;變節。
rec·re·ant 〔ˈrɛkrɪənt; ˈrekriənt〕 *adj.* ①怯懦的;卑劣的。②不忠實的;叛逆的。—*n.* ①懦夫。②叛徒;賣國賊。—**ly,** *adv.*
rec·re·ate 〔ˈrɛkrɪ͵et; ˈrekrieit〕 *v.,* **-at·ed, -at·ing.** —*v.t.* 休養;娛樂。—*v.i.* 消遣。
re-cre·ate 〔͵rikrɪˈet; ˈriː-kriˈeit〕 *v.t.,* **-at·ed, -at·ing.** 重新創造;改造;重做。
***rec·re·a·tion** 〔͵rɛkrɪˈeʃən; ͵rekriˈeiʃən〕 *n.* 娛樂;消遣;休養。*recreation* room. 康樂室。—**rec·re·a·to·ry,** *adj.*
re-cre·a·tion 〔͵rikrɪˈeʃən; ˈriː-kriˈeiʃən〕 *n.* ①再創造;重新創造;改造。②重新創造之物。
rec·re·a·tion·al 〔͵rɛkrɪˈeʃənl̩; ͵rekriˈeiʃənl〕 *adj.* 娛樂的;消遣的。
rec·re·a·tive 〔ˈrɛkrɪ͵etɪv; ˈrekrieitiv〕 *adj.* 供娛樂的;供消遣的;振奮精神的。
re·crim·i·nate 〔rɪˈkrɪmə͵net; riˈkrimineit〕 *v.i.,* **-nat·ed, -nat·ing.** 反控;反責;反唇相譏。
re·crim·i·na·tion 〔rɪ͵krɪməˈneʃən; ri͵krimiˈneiʃən〕 *n.* ①反控告;反責;反唇相譏。②反控的罪狀;反責的話。
re·crim·i·na·tive 〔rɪˈkrɪmə͵netɪv; riˈkrimineitiv〕 *adj.* ①反控訴的。②反責的;反唇相譏的。(亦作 **recriminatory**)
rec room 〔rɛk～; rek～〕〖俗〗康樂室。
re·cru·desce 〔͵rikruˈdɛs; ͵riː-kruːˈdes〕 *v.t.,* **-desced, -desc·ing.** (疼痛、疾病、憤怨等)再發作;復發。
re·cru·des·cence 〔͵rikruˈdɛsn̩s; ˈriː-kruːˈdesns〕 *n.* (病、瘡等)復發;再發;(疾病經過潛伏期後)發作。(亦作 **recrudescency**) —**re·cru·des·cent,** *adj.*
***re·cruit** 〔rɪˈkrut; riˈkruːt〕 *n.* ①新兵。②(任何團體之)新加入者;新會員。Our club needs *recruits*. 我們的俱樂部需要新會員。③〖古〗任何事物之補充。—*v.t.* ①使入伍;招募;增添兵額。②吸收(新分子)。③恢復。④補充。Before sailing, we *recruited* our provisions. 在開船前,我們補充了給養。—*v.i.* ①招募新兵。②養病。③靜養。He has gone to the country to *recruit*. 他已去鄉下靜養。
re·cruit·ment 〔rɪˈkrutmənt; riˈkruːtmənt〕 *n.* 補充;招募。
rect- 〖字首〗 **recti-** 之異體,用於母音前。
rect. ①receipt. ②rectified. ③rector. ④rectory.
rec·tal 〔ˈrɛktl̩; ˈrektəl〕 *adj.* 直腸的;近直腸的。—**ly,** *adv.*
***rec·tan·gle** 〔ˈrɛktæŋgl̩; ˈrektæŋgl〕 *n.* 長方形;矩形。
rec·tan·gu·lar 〔rɛkˈtæŋgjəlɚ; rekˈtæŋgjulə〕 *adj.* 長方形的;直角的。
recti- 〖字首〗表"直;正直;正確"之義(在母音前作 **rect-**)。
rec·ti·fi·a·ble 〔ˈrɛktə͵faɪəbl̩; ˈrektifaiəbl〕 *adj.* ①可修正的。②可精鍊的。③可調整的。④〖數學〗(曲線之)可求長的。
rec·ti·fi·ca·tion 〔͵rɛktəfəˈkeʃən; ͵rektifiˈkeiʃən〕 *n.* ①改正;訂正;矯正。②〖化〗蒸餾。③〖電學〗整流。④〖數學〗求(曲線之)長。
rec·ti·fi·er 〔ˈrɛktə͵faɪɚ; ˈrektifaiə〕 *n.* ①修正者;矯正者;改正者。②〖電〗整流器。③〖化〗蒸餾器。
rec·ti·fy 〔ˈrɛktə͵faɪ; ˈrektifai〕 *v.t.,* **-fied, -fy·ing.** ①修正;改正;矯正。②精鍊。③〖電〗整流。
rectifying tube (or **valve**) 整流管。
rec·ti·lin·e·al 〔͵rɛktəˈlɪnɪəl; ͵rektiˈliniəl〕 *adj.* =**rectilinear.**
rec·ti·lin·e·ar 〔͵rɛktəˈlɪnɪɚ; ͵rektiˈliniə〕 *adj.* ①成直線進行的。②成直線的。③由直線構成的。
rec·ti·tude 〔ˈrɛktə͵tjud; ˈrektitjuːd〕 *n.* ①正直的行爲或品行。②誠實;正直。③正確的判斷或方法。
rec·to 〔ˈrɛkto; ˈrektou〕 *n., pl.* **-tos.** ①書的右頁。②紙張的正面。
rec·to·cele 〔ˈrɛktə͵sil; ˈrektəsiːl〕 *n.* 〖醫〗脫肛;直腸脫出。
rec·tor** 〔ˈrɛktɚ; ˈrektə〕 *n.* ①教區長;牧師。②(某些學校之)校長。Lord Rectro*** 蘇格蘭各大學的校長。
rec·tor·ate 〔ˈrɛktərɪt; ˈrektərit〕 *n.* 教區長、牧師、(某些學校)校長之職位及任期。
rec·to·ri·al 〔rɛkˈtorɪəl; rekˈtɔːriəl〕 *adj.* ①牧師的;教區長的。②校長的。
rec·tor·ship 〔ˈrɛktɚʃɪp; ˈrektəʃip〕 *n.* =**rectorate.**
rec·to·ry 〔ˈrɛktərɪ; ˈrektəri〕 *n., pl.* **-ries.** ①聖公會牧師之住宅。②〖英〗主管一教區之牧師的俸祿或住宅。
rec·tum 〔ˈrɛktəm; ˈrektəm〕 *n., pl.* **-tums, -ta** 〔-tə; -tə〕. 〖解剖〗直腸。
re·cum·bent 〔rɪˈkʌmbənt; riˈkʌmbənt〕 *adj.* ①橫臥的;斜靠的。②休息着的;不活潑的。—*n.* 斜靠的人、動物或植物。—**re·cum·bence, re·cum·ben·cy,** *n.* —**ly,** *adv.*

re·cu·per·ate [rɪˈkjupəˌret; riˈkjuːpəreit] *v.i.* & *v.t.*, **-at·ed, -at·ing.** ①恢復（健康）; 休養。②恢復（損失）。—**re·cu·per·a·tion,** *n.*

re·cu·per·a·tive [rɪˈkjupəˌretɪv; riˈkjuːpəreitiv] *adj.* ①恢復中的。②有恢復能力的。

*__re·cur__ [rɪˈkɝ; riˈkəː] *v.i.*, **-curred, -cur·ring.** ①重現; 再發生。Leap year *recurs* every four years. 每四年閏年一次。②再回到。Old memories constantly *recurred* to him. 舊事經常浮現在他的腦海裏。③訴諸。

re·cur·rence [rɪˈkɝəns; riˈkʌrəns] *n.* ①再發生;重覆;復現。②求助;保護。

re·cur·rent [rɪˈkɝənt; riˈkʌrənt] *adj.* ①再現的; 再發的; 回歸性的。②周期性的;反覆的。③〖解剖〗回歸性的。—*n.* 回歸動脈;回歸神經。

recurring decimal 〖數學〗循環小數。

re·cur·vate [rɪˈkɝvet; riˈkəːveit] *adj.* 反曲的;曲回的。

re·curve [rɪˈkɝv; riːˈkəːv] *v.t.* & *v.i.*, **-curved, -curv·ing.** 曲回;折回;反彎。

rec·u·san·cy [ˈrɛkjuzn̩sɪ; ˈrekjuzənsi] *n.* ①拒絕服從。②不從國教;悖逆。

rec·u·sant [ˈrɛkjuzn̩t; ˈrekjuzənt] *n.* ①拒不服從者。②〖英史〗拒不參加英國國教且否認其權威者(尤指天主教徒)。—*adj.* ①不服從的;不屈從的。②不從英國國教的。

re·cy·cle [riˈsaɪkl̩; riːˈsaikl] *v.t.*, **-cled, -cling.** 將…再經過製造俾能再使用。—**re·cy·cla·ble,** *adj.*

‡**red** [rɛd; red] *n.*, *adj.*, **red·der, red·dest.** —*n.* ①紅色。②紅色顏料。Put a little more *red* in the picture. 再稍加些紅顏色在這畫片上。③紅布;紅衣。a girl in *red*. 紅衣女郎。④帶紅色之人、動物或物品。⑤(R-) 激進分子; 赤色分子; 共產黨員。⑥(the-) 赤字; 虧空; 負債。to be in (out of) the *red*. 虧欠(贏利)。***in the red*** 〖俗〗賠本; 欠債。***out of the red*** 〖俗〗有盈餘。***see red*** 〖俗〗極爲震怒;憤怒欲狂。—*adj.* ①紅的。He painted the gate *red*. 他將大門漆成紅色。②紅腫的;發炎的。③羞紅的;紅臉的。④(R-)極端急進的; 共產黨的。the *Red* Army. 紅軍。***a red rag*** 任何用以激使人發怒、動情、仇恨等的東西。***have red hands*** 犯殺人罪。***paint the town red*** 狂歡作樂。

re·dact [rɪˈdækt; riˈdækt] *v.t.* ①編纂;編輯;修訂。②草擬(政府命令、布告等)。

re·dac·tion [rɪˈdækʃən; riˈdækʃən] *n.* ①編輯;編纂;編修。②校訂;修訂。③修正版;改編本。

re·dac·tor [rɪˈdæktɚ; riˈdæktə] *n.* 編輯者;修訂者。

red alert 〖防空〗緊急警報。

re·dan [rɪˈdæn; riˈdæn] *n.* 〖築城〗凸角堡;矢堡。

red arsenic 雄黃 (=realgar).

red-bait [ˈrɛdˌbet; ˈredbeit] *v.t.* & *v.i.* 抨擊(某人或某團體)爲共產黨分子。

red-bait·er [ˈrɛdˌbetɚ; ˈredˌbeitə] *n.* 指斥他人爲共產黨的人。

red-bait·ing [ˈrɛdˌbetɪŋ; ˈredˌbeitiŋ] *n.* 指斥他人爲共產黨。

red·bird [ˈrɛdˌbɝd; ˈredbəːd] *n.* 紅雀。

red-blind [ˈrɛdˌblaɪnd; ˈredblaind] *adj.* 紅色色盲的。

red blood cell 紅血球。

red-blood·ed [ˈrɛdˈblʌdɪd; ˈredˈblʌdid] *adj.* ①意志堅强的;活潑有力的(人)。②充滿動作的;令人興奮的(小說等)。

*__red·breast__ [ˈrɛdˌbrɛst; ˈredbrest] *n.* 知更鳥(亦作 **robin redbreast**).

red·bud [ˈrɛdˌbʌd; ˈredbʌd] *n.* 〖植物〗紫荊(其葉爲心形, 開淺紅色如蕾般的小花)。

red·cap [ˈrɛdˌkæp; ˈredkæp] *n.* ①戴紅帽的人(如火車站上搬行李之脚伕)。②〖動物〗歐洲產之金翅雀。③〖英俗〗憲兵。

red carpet ①迎接貴賓用的紅地毯。②隆重的接待。

red-car·pet [ˈrɛdˈkɑrpɪt; ˈredˈkɑːpit] *adj.* 隆重的;殷勤的。

red cell 紅血球。

red cent 〖俗〗一分錢;一辨士。

Red Chamber 〖加俗〗加拿大國會之上院。

red clover 紅苜蓿。

red·coat [ˈrɛdˌkot; ˈredkout] *n.* 昔之英國兵。

red corpuscle 紅血球。

Red Cross 紅十字會。

red cross 紅十字(紅十字會之會徽)。

*__red·den__ [ˈrɛdn̩; ˈredn] *v.t.* & *v.i.* ①使紅; 變紅。②使面紅; 赧顏。He *reddened* with anger. 他因憤怒而臉紅。

*__red·dish__ [ˈrɛdɪʃ; ˈrediʃ] *adj.* 微紅色的;帶紅色的。

red·dle [ˈrɛdl̩; ˈredl] *n.*, *v.*, **-dled, -dling.** =**raddle.**

*__re·deem__ [rɪˈdim; riˈdiːm] *v.t.* ①買回(已賣之物);收回。②贖回。to *redeem* a mortgage. 贖回抵押品。③實踐;履行。④贖出;救贖。⑤補償;補救。⑥換(紙幣)成硬幣。

re·deem·a·ble [rɪˈdiməbl̩; riˈdiːməbl] *adj.* 可買回的;可贖回的;可拯救的。

re·deem·er [rɪˈdimɚ; riˈdiːmə] *n.* ①買回者;贖回者。②拯救者; 贖罪者; 超度者。③(the R-) 救世主;耶穌。

re·demp·tion [rɪˈdɛmpʃən; riˈdempʃən] *n.* ①買回;收回。②贖出;贖回。③換(紙幣)爲硬幣。④贖罪;拯救;濟度。⑤補救;改正。⑥買回物; 贖回物。⑦(諾言等的) 履行;實踐。⑧補償。

re·demp·tive [rɪˈdɛmptɪv; riˈdemptiv] *adj.* 用以買回的;用以贖出的;用以拯救的。

re·demp·to·ry [rɪˈdɛmptərɪ; riˈdemptəri] *adj.* =**redemptive.**

re·de·ploy [ˌridɪˈplɔɪ; ˈriː-diˈplɔi] *v.t.* 將(軍隊)自一戰區調至另一戰區; 將(部隊)調防。—*v.i.* 調防;重作布署。—**ment,** *n.*

re·de·vel·op [ˌridɪˈvɛləp; ˈriːdiˈveləp] *v.t.* ①再開發。②〖照相〗再沖洗。—*v.i.* 再發現。

redevelopment company 土地開發公司。

red-eyed [ˈrɛdˈaɪd; ˈredˈaid] *adj.* 紅眼圈的;哭至眼圈紅的。

red-hand·ed [ˈrɛdˈhændɪd; ˈredˈhændid] *adj.* & *adv.* ①有血染之手的;殘忍的。②在犯罪現場的;當場的。

red·head [ˈrɛdˌhɛd; ˈredhed] *n.* ①紅髮的人。②北美產的一種紅頭鴨。③紅頭啄木鳥。

red·head·ed [ˈrɛdˌhɛdɪd; ˈredˌhedid] *adj.* 有紅頭髮的(人); 紅頭的(鳥)。(亦作 **red-headed**)

red-hot [ˈrɛdˈhɑt; ˈredˈhɔt] *adj.* ①紅熱的;極熱的。②十分熱心的;激昂的;激烈的。③嶄新的; 最新近的(新聞等)。—*n.* (亦作 **red hot**) =**frankfurter.**

red·in·gote [ˈrɛdɪŋˌgot; ˈrediŋgout] *n.* ①昔日男人所着的一種胸前有雙層之外衣。②一種女人所着的無襯裏的輕長外衣。

red·in·te·grate [rɪˈdɪntəˌgret, rɛd-ˈɪn-; reˈdintigreit] *v.t.*, **-grat·ed, -grat·ing.** 使再完整;使再完善;重建;更新。

red·in·te·gra·tion [rɪˌdɪntəˈgreʃən; reˌdintiˈgreiʃən] *n.* ①更新;重建。②〖心理〗

重整作用。

re·di·rect [ˌridəˈrɛkt; ˈriːdiˈrekt] *v.t.* 重新繕寄(信件)。—*adj.*〖法律〗對方對己方證人詰問(cross-examination)後之詰問的。

re·di·rec·tion [ˌridəˈrɛkʃən; ˈriːdiˈrekʃən] *n.* ①重新繕寄(指信件)。②〖法律〗對方對己方證人詰問後之詰問。

re·dis·count [riˈdɪskaunt; riːˈdiskaunt] *v.t.* 再折扣;重貼現。—*n.* ①再折扣。②(常*pl.*)重貼現之票據。

re·dis·trib·ute [ˌridɪˈstrɪbjut; ˈriː-disˈtribjuːt] *v.t.*, **-trib·ut·ed, -trib·ut·ing.** 再分配; 再分發; 再分送。—**re·dis·tri·bu·tion,** *n.*

re·dis·trict [riˈdɪstrɪkt; riːˈdistrikt] *v.t.* 將…再分區(尤指選擧區)。

red-let·ter [ˈrɛdˈlɛtɚ; ˈredˈletə] *adj.* ①標有紅字的。②値得紀念的; 特別快樂的。***a red-letter day*** a. 聖徒之節日。b. 有喜事或慶典的日子。

red light ①危險信號。②使車輛停止行駛的紅燈。③停止某行爲的命令。

red-light district [ˈrɛdˈlaɪt～; ˈredˈlait～]〖美〗紅燈區;風化區;花街柳巷。

red·line [ˈrɛdˌlaɪn; ˈredlain] *v.t.*, **-lined, -lin·ing.** ①確定(飛機之)安全速度。②劃紅線以註銷。③使(飛機)停飛。

red·ness [ˈrɛdnɪs; ˈrednis] *n.* 紅;紅色。

re·do [riˈdu; ˈriːˈduː] *v.t.*, **re·did, re·done.** 再作;重作。

red·o·lent [ˈrɛdl̩ənt; ˈredoulənt] *adj.* ①香的;芬芳的。②有强烈氣味的〖常of〗。③有某種意味的;使人回憶或連想到某事的〖常of〗。—**red·o·lence, red·o·len·cy,** *n.*

re·dou·ble [riˈdʌbl̩; riˈdʌbl] *v.*, **-bled, -bling,** *n.* —*v.t.* ①加倍; 增添; 激增。②重述或重作。③發回聲。④再加倍(通常用於橋牌中再加倍對方)。—*v.i.* ①加倍;激增。②發回聲。③循原路折回。④〖橋牌〗再加倍。—*n.*〖橋牌〗再加倍。

re·doubt [rɪˈdaut; riˈdaut] *n.*〖兵學〗內堡;臨時堡;堡壘。

re·doubt·a·ble [rɪˈdautəbl̩; riˈdautəbl] *adj.* ①可畏的;勇敢的。②令人起敬的。

re·dound [rɪˈdaund; riˈdaund] *v.i.* ①有助於; 增加; 提高;有損於;及於。②歸之於;歸返於。③(波等)返流;返捲。

red-pen·cil [ˈrɛdˈpɛnsl̩; ˈredˈpensl] *v.t.*, **-cil(l)ed, -cil·(l)ing.** 用紅筆删改。

red pepper ①辣椒。②辣椒粉。

re-dress [riˈdrɛs; ˈriːˈdres] *v.t.* ①再爲…穿衣; 再供以衣服。②再裝飾; 再處理;再調製;再整理。

re·dress [*v.* rɪˈdrɛs; riˈdres *n.* ˈridrɛs, rɪˈdrɛs; ˈriːdres, riˈdres] *v.t.* ①修正;改正;重新修理。②矯正;匡正;補救。③補償。④調整。—*n.* ①補償。②修正;改正。

Red Sea 紅海(阿拉伯與非洲間之狹海,爲印度洋之一部分, 由蘇彝士運河而與地中海相連,長1,450英里,面積178,000平方英里)。

red·shank [ˈrɛdˌʃæŋk; ˈredʃæŋk] *n.* 赤足鷸。***run like a redshank*** 走得很快。

red-short [ˈrɛdˈʃɔrt; ˈredˈʃɔːt] *adj.*〖冶金〗紅熱時即脆的(指含硫過多的鐵和鋼)。

red·skin [ˈrɛdˌskɪn; ˈred-skin] *n.* 北美洲印第安人(常含蔑視之意)。

red·start [ˈrɛdˌstɑrt; ˈred-stɑːt] *n.* ①歐洲產的一種尾部呈紅褐色的小鳥。②一種捕蠅爲食的鶯科鳥。

red tape ①(繫公文等的)紅帶。②官樣文章;繁文縟節。

red-tape [ˈrɛdˌtep; ˈredteip] *adj.* 官樣文章的;繁文縟節的;官僚作風的。

red-tap·ism [ˌrɛdˈtepɪzəm; ˈredˈteipizəm] *n.* 官樣文章; 繁瑣手續; 官僚作風。(亦作 **red-tapery**)

red-tap·ist [ˌrɛdˈtepɪst; ˌredˈteipist] *n.* 好官樣文章者。

red·top [ˈrɛdˌtɑp; ˈredtɔp] *n.*〖植物〗小糠草。

‡re·duce [rɪˈdjus; riˈdjuːs, rəˈd-] *v.*, **-duced, -duc·ing.** —*v.t.* ①減少;減縮;減低。to *reduce* speed. 減低速度。②將…貶爲;使賤; 使陷於。③使變形; 分解; 使簡化。The chalk was *reduced* to powder. 粉筆變成了粉末。④征服。⑤〖醫〗使(折骨)復位。⑥〖化〗使還原。⑦減價。⑧沖淡。⑨以水將酒中之酒精沖淡。—*v.i.* ①節食以減肥。His doctor advised him to *reduce*. 他的醫生勸他節食減肥。②減少。—**re·duc·er,** *n.*

re·duc·i·ble [rɪˈdjusəbl̩; riˈdjuːsəbl] *adj.* ①可減縮的; 可減少的。②可降的; 可貶的。③〖數學〗可約的; 可化簡的。④〖化〗可分解的;可還原的。⑤(折骨)可復位的。

***re·duc·tion** [rɪˈdʌkʃən; riˈdʌkʃən, rəˈd-] *n.* ①減少;減縮;減低。②減少或減低之數量。The *reduction* in cost was $5. 成本減低了五元。③地圖照相等之縮版。④變形;變。⑤〖化〗還原。⑥(爲傳教及教育印第安人在南美洲建立的)小村莊。

reduction division〖生物〗減數分裂(=meiosis).

re·duc·tive [rɪˈdʌktɪv; riˈdʌktiv] *adj.* ①減縮的。②還原的。—*n.* 還原劑。—**ly,** *adv.*

re·dun·dan·cy [rɪˈdʌndənsɪ; riˈdʌndənsi] *n.* ①過多;累贅。②冗長;重複。③累贅之部分; 重複之部分; 過多之量。(亦作 **redundance**)

re·dun·dant [rɪˈdʌndənt; riˈdʌndənt] *adj.* ①過多的。②冗贅的。③多餘的。④豐裕的。—**ly,** *adv.*

re·du·pli·cate [*v.* rɪˈdjupləˌket; riˈdjuːplikeit *adj.* rɪˈdjupləkɪt; riˈdjuːplikit] *v.*, **-cat·ed, -cat·ing,** *adj.* —*v.t. & v.i.* 加倍;重複。—*adj.* 加倍的;雙重的。—**re·du·pli·ca·tion,** *n.*

re·du·pli·ca·tive [rɪˈdjupləˌketɪv; riˈdjuːplikeitiv] *adj.* 加倍的; 重複的; 重疊的。(亦作 **reduplicatory**) —**ly,** *adv.*

red wine 紅葡萄酒。

red·wing [ˈrɛdwɪŋ; ˈredwiŋ] *n.* 紅翼鶇。

red·wood [ˈrɛdˌwud; ˈredwud] *n.* ①美國加州產之杉樹。②此種杉木。③木質紅色之樹或木材。

re·ech·o, re-ech·o [riˈɛko; riːˈekou] *v.*, *n.*, *pl.* **-oes.** —*v.t.* 回響…之聲音。—*v.i.* 回響。—*n.* 回響之回聲。(亦作 **reëcho**)

reed** [rid; riːd] *n.* ①蘆葦; 蘆葦桿。②蘆桿製成之物; 似蘆桿之物。③(樂器之)簧; 蘆笛。④做屋頂用之茅草。⑤〖詩〗矢; 箭。a broken reed*** 懦弱得不能依賴的人或物。***the reeds*** 管絃樂隊中的簧樂器。—*v.t.* ①以茅草做屋頂。②以蘆葦裝飾。—**like,** *adj.*

reed·bird [ˈridˌbɝd; ˈriːdbəːd] *n.* 食米鳥。

reed·ed [ˈridɪd; ˈriːdid] *adj.* ①長滿蘆葦的。②覆以蘆葦的。③有蘆飾的。

re·ed·i·fy, re-ed·i·fy [riˈɛdəˌfaɪ; riːˈedifai] *v.t.*, **-fied, -fy·ing.** 重建;恢復。(亦作 **reëdify**)

reed instrument 簧樂器。

re·ed·it, re-ed·it [riˈɛdɪt; riːˈedit] *v.t.* 重編(輯)。(亦作**reëdit**)

reed mace〖植物〗香蒲。

reed organ 簧風琴。

reed pipe 簧管。

reed stop 簧管音栓。

re·ed·u·cate 〔riˈɛdʒəˌket; riːˈedju-keit〕 *v.t.*, **-cat·ed, -cat·ing.** 再教育;重新教育。—**re·ed·u·ca·tion,** *n.*

reed·y 〔ˈridɪ; ˈriːdi〕 *adj.*, **reed·i·er, reed·i·est.** ①多蘆葦的。②蘆葦做的。③長而細的;像蘆葦的。④像簧樂器發出的(聲音);尖的。—**reed·i·ness,** *n.*

***reef**[1] 〔rif; riːf〕 *n.* ①礁;灘;暗礁;暗灘。The ship was wrecked on the hidden *reef.* 那艘船撞到暗礁沉沒。②礦脈。—**y,** *adj.*

reef[2] *n.* ①帆之可捲疊或收縮部分。②此部分之捲疊。***take in a reef*** 捲疊一部分帆;小心前進;緊縮費用。—*v.t.* ①縮帆;收帆。②降低(中檣、斜檣等)。—**a·ble,** *adj.*

reef·er[1] 〔ˈrifɚ; ˈriːfə〕 *n.* ①縮帆者。②(亦作 **reefing jacket**) 一種結實的短衣。③(亦作 **reef knot**) 方結。

reef·er[2] *n.* ①〖美〗冷藏車;冷藏船。②〖俚〗含 marijuana 的香煙。

reef knot 方結。

reek 〔rik; riːk〕 *n.* ①水汽;濕氣;煙。②強烈的氣味;臭味。—*v.i.* ①發出水汽或煙。②發出強烈臭氣。③瀰漫臭氣。④爲汗、血等濕透。⑤充滿(某種意味)。—*v.t.* ①燻。②發出(蒸氣、臭氣、煙霧等)。③表現…態度。

reek·y 〔ˈrikɪ; ˈriːki〕 *adj.*, **reek·i·er, reek·i·est.** ①冒蒸氣的;冒臭氣的。②冒煙的;多煙的。③被煙燻汚的。

reel**[1] 〔ril; riːl〕 *n.* ①紡車;繞線機。②線軸;捲線筒。③捲在軸上的東西(如一軸線)。a *reel* of cotton. 一軸棉線。④一捲電影片。(right***) ***off the reel*** a. 迅速不停地。b. 立刻。—*v.t.* ①繞(線軸)〖in〗。②抽(線軸)〖out〗。③捲收〖in〗。He *reels* in a fish. 他收釣線把魚拖近。***reel off*** 迅速而容易地說出或寫出。—**a·ble,** *adj.*

***reel**[2] *v.i.* ①站立不穩;搖幌。to *reel* under a heavy blow. 受重擊而搖幌。②撤退。③蹣跚而行;搖搖欲墜。④暈眩。⑤搖擺;擺盪;旋轉。—*v.t.* ①使眩暈;使動搖。②蹣跚而行。—*n.* 退縮;動搖;蹣跚;旋轉;搖幌;暈眩。

reel[3] *n.* ①一種活潑的蘇格蘭舞蹈。②此種舞曲。

re-e·lect 〔ˌriəˈlɛkt; ˈriːiˈlekt〕 *v.t.* 重選;再選。

re-e·lec·tion 〔ˌriəˈlɛkʃən; ˈriːiˈlekʃən〕 *n.* 再選;重選;再度當選。

re-em·pha·size 〔riˈɛmfəˌsaɪz; riː-ˈemfəsaiz〕 *v.t.* & *v.i.*, **-sized, -siz·ing.** 再度強調。

re-em·ploy 〔ˌriɛmˈplɔɪ; ˈriːemˈplɔi〕 *v.t.* 再度雇用。

re-en·act, re·en·act 〔ˌriɪnˈækt; ˈriːiˈnækt〕 *v.t.* 再制定(法律)。

re-en·force, re·en·force 〔ˌriɪn-ˈfors; ˈriːinˈfɔːs〕 *v.t.*, **-forced, -forc·ing,** *n.* =reinforce. (亦作 **reënforce**)—**ment,** *n.*

re-en·grave 〔ˌriɪnˈgrev; ˈriːinˈgrev〕 *v.t.* **-graved, -grav·ing.** 再雕上。

re-en·list 〔ˌriɛnˈlɪst; ˈriːinˈlist〕 *v.i.* & *v.t.* ①再從軍。②延長服役。(亦作 **re-enlist, reënlist**)

re·en·ter 〔riˈɛntɚ; ˈriːˈentə〕 *v.t.* ①再使進入;再入。②再加入。③再記入;再登記。—*v.i.* ①又進去;再入。②再加入。③再登記。(亦作 **re-enter, reënter**) —**re·en·trance,** *n.*

re·en·trant, re·en·trant 〔riˈɛn-trənt; riːˈentrənt〕 *adj.* ①再進入的。②再登記的。③凹角的。—*n.* 凹角。(亦作 **reëntrant**)

re·en·try, re·en·try 〔riˈɛntrɪ; riː-ˈentri〕 *n., pl.* **-tries.** ①再進入。②〖法律〗回復土地所有權。③〖橋牌〗奪得一磴並奪回出牌權之牌。④(火箭、太空船等)重返大氣層。(亦作 **reëntry**)

re·es·tab·lish, re·es·tab·lish 〔ˌriəˈstæblɪʃ; ˈriːisˈtæbliʃ〕 *v.t.* ①使復位;使復職;恢復。②再建;使重新定居。(亦作 **reëstablish**) —**ment,** *n.*

re·es·ti·mate 〔ˌriˈɛstəˌmet; ˈriːˈesti-meit〕 *v.t.* & *v.i.* 重新估計;再估計。

reeve[1] 〔riv; riːv〕 *n.* ①〖英史〗鄉、鎮、區長。②家宰;執事。③(加拿大)鄉鎮議會議長。④雌千鳥。⑤〖英〗昔時代表英皇家的高級官員。

reeve[2] *v.t.*, **reeved** or **rove, reev·ing.** ①〖航海〗貫穿(繩等)。②綑縛。③將繩穿過(滑車等)。④(船)穿過(暗礁、浮冰等之間隙)航進。

re·ex·am·i·na·tion, re·ex·am·i·na·tion 〔ˌriɪgˌzæməˈneʃən; ˈriːig-ˌzæmiˈneiʃən〕 *n.* 再試驗;再調查;覆問。(亦作 **reëxamination**)

re·ex·am·ine, re·ex·am·ine 〔ˌriɪgˈzæmɪn; ˈriːigˈzæmin〕 *v.t.*, **-ined, -in·ing.** 再試驗;再調查;覆問(證人)。(亦作 **reëxamine**)

re·ex·change, re·ex·change 〔ˌriɛksˈtʃendʒ; ˈriːeksˈtʃeindʒ〕 *n.* ①再交換;再交易。②〖商〗回匯;回兌。(亦作 **reëxchange**) ***re-exchange bill*** 退回之匯票。

re·ex·port, re·ex·port 〔*v.* ˌriɪks-ˈport; ˈriːeksˈpɔːt *n.* riˈɛksˌport; ˈriː-ˈekspɔːt〕 *v.t.* 再輸出。—*n.* 再輸出;再輸出之貨物。(亦作 **reëxport**) —**er,** *n.*

re·ex·por·ta·tion, re·ex·por·ta·tion 〔ˌriɪksporˈteʃən; ˈriːikspɔːˈteiʃən〕 *n.* 再輸出。(亦作 **reëxportation**)

ref 〔rɛf; ref〕 *n., v.t.* & *v.i.*, **reffed, ref-fing.** 〖體育俚〗裁判(referee 之略)。

ref. ①referee. ②reference. ③referred. ④reformation. ⑤reformed. ⑥reformer. ⑦refund.

re·face 〔riˈfes; ˈriːˈfeis〕 *v.t.*, **-faced, -fac·ing.** 重裝表面。

re·fash·ion 〔riˈfæʃən; ˈriːˈfæʃən〕 *v.t.* 再作成某種模樣;重作。—**er,** *n.*

re·fec·tion 〔rɪˈfɛkʃən; riˈfekʃən〕 *n.* ①點心。②便餐。

re·fec·to·ry 〔rɪˈfɛktərɪ; riˈfektəri〕 *n., pl.* **-ries.** (寺院及學校的)餐廳;膳廳。

***re·fer** 〔rɪˈfɝ; riˈfəː, rəˈf-〕 *v.*, **-ferred, -fer·ring.** —*v.t.* ①指示。The asterisk *refers* the reader to a footnote. 星標指示讀者參閱註解。②使諮詢。③歸之於;諉於。④交給;提交。⑤將…列某一類或認爲…屬於某一時代等。—*v.i.* 〖to〗 ①指示;言及。②參考;諮詢。Writers often *refer* to a dictionary. 著作家時常參考字典。③應用。

re·fer·(r)a·ble 〔ˈrɛfərəbl; riˈfəːrəbl〕 *adj.* ①可歸因於…的;起因於…的。②可參考的;可參看的。③可交付的。(亦作 **referrible**)

ref·er·ee 〔ˌrɛfəˈri; ˌrefəˈriː〕 *n., v.*, **-eed, -ee·ing.** —*n.* ①裁判員。②仲裁者;公斷人。—*v.t.* & *v.i.* 裁判。

ref·er·ence** 〔ˈrɛfərəns; ˈrefrəns, -fər-〕 *n., v.*, **-enced, -enc·ing.** —*n.* ①指示;查照。mark of *reference.* 參照符號(如*, +等)。②附註;旁註。③參考;諮詢。④(品性、能力等之)證明人;保證人。⑤(對品性、能力等之)證明書;介紹書。⑥言及;提及。⑦計較。cross reference*** 一書之內前後參照。***in*** (or ***with***) *reference to* 關於。*make reference to* 參考;提及;提到。*without reference to* 不顧;不管。—*v.t.* ①(書、論文等)加附註。Each new volume is thoroughly *referenced.* 每一本新書都有詳細的附註。②編排附註,以便易於參閱。「書、地圖、年鑑等)。

reference book 參考書(如百科全

reference frame 〖物理〗參考坐標。

ref·er·en·dum [ˌrɛfəˈrɛndəm; ˌrefəˈrendəm] *n., pl.* **-dums, -da** [-də;-də]. ①人民複決;人民複決權。②複決投票。③外交官向本國政府請示特別訓令之文書。

ref·er·en·tial [ˌrɛfəˈrɛnʃəl; ˌrefəˈrenʃəl] *adj.* ①提及…的〖to〗。②參考的;指示的。

re·fill [*v.* riˈfɪl; ˈriːˈfil *n.* ˈriˌfɪl; ˈriːˈfil] *v.t.* 再注滿;再填滿。—*n.* ①再注滿;再填滿。②(再填滿之)附加物。

***re·fine** [rɪˈfaɪn; riˈfain] *v.*, **-fined, -fin·ing.** —*v.t.* ①使純;精煉;精製。②使精美;使文雅。Reading good books helped to *refine* her speech. 讀好的書有助於使她的言談文雅。③使精確。—*v.i.* ①變純。②變精美。③改善;改進〖on, upon〗. *refine on* (or *upon*) **a.** 精於;擅長於。**b.** 改進。

***re·fined** [rɪˈfaɪnd; riˈfaind] *adj.* ①精煉的;精製的。*refined* sugar. 精製糖。②文雅的;高尚的。③精確的。*refined* measurements. 精確的測量。④精微的。—**ness,** *n.*

***re·fine·ment** [rɪˈfaɪnmənt; riˈfainmənt] *n.* ①文雅;高尚;精美。②文雅之行爲;高尚之舉動。③精煉;精製;改良。④精密;巧妙;精微的區別。⑤精製之物;改良之物;巧妙之物。*refinements* of cruelty. 極端之殘酷。

re·fin·er [rɪˈfaɪnɚ; riˈfainə] *n.* 精製者;精製機。

re·fin·er·y [rɪˈfaɪnərɪ; riˈfainəri] *n., pl.* **-er·ies.** 精製廠;煉製廠;精煉設施。

re·fit [riˈfɪt; ˈriːˈfit] *v.*, **-fit·ted, -fit·ting,** *n.* —*v.t.* ①修裝;修繕。②改裝;重新裝配。—*v.i.* ①修理。②改裝。—*n.* ①修理;修復。②船隻的改裝。

re·fit·ment [riˈfɪtmənt; riːˈfitmənt] *n.* (船等的)修理;改裝;修復。

refl. ①reflection. ②reflective. ③reflex. ④reflexive. ⑤reflexively.

re·flate [rɪˈflet; riˈfleit] *v.t. & v.i.*, **-flat·ed, -flat·ing.** (使)通貨再膨脹。—**re·fla·tion,** *n.*

***re·flect** [rɪˈflɛkt; riˈflekt] *v.t.* ①反射(光、熱、聲音等)。A mirror *reflects* light. 鏡子反光。②反映(形像)。③反映(意見、思想等);表達。④帶給。—*v.i.* ①反映。②考慮。③歸咎〖on〗. Bad behavior *reflects* on home training. 壞的品行歸咎於家庭教育。

re·flect·ing [rɪˈflɛktɪŋ; riˈflektiŋ] *adj.* ①反射的;反映的。*reflecting* telescope. 反射望遠鏡。②內省的;沉思的。③咎責的。—**ly,** *adv.*

***re·flec·tion** [rɪˈflɛkʃən; riˈflekʃən] *n.* ①反射;反射作用。②反射光;反射熱;反射色。③映像;影像。④內省;考慮。⑤意見;感想;評論。I have a few *reflections* to offer on what you have said. 對於你所說的話我有幾點意見貢獻給你。⑥損及名譽的言行;非難。⑦咎責;不名譽。⑧〖解剖〗反折;回反。—**al,** *adj.*

re·flec·tive [rɪˈflɛktɪv; riˈflektiv] *adj.* ①反射的;反映的。②沉思的。—**ly,** *adv.*

re·flec·tor [rɪˈflɛktɚ; riˈflektə] *n.* ①反射者;表達意見者。②反射望遠鏡。③反射器。*parabolic reflector* 拋物柱面反射鏡。

re·flex [*adj., n.* ˈriflɛks; ˈriː-fleks *v.* rɪˈflɛks; riˈfleks] *adj.* ①不自主的。②反射(作用)的。③反省的。④回復的。⑤彎曲的。⑥(角度)180度以上 360 度以下的。—*n.* ①反射作用。②反映;反照。③改編之物;副本。④反射之事物,如光線等。—*v.t.* ①使經過反射作用。②使折回;使摺回。—**ness,** *n.*

reflex arc 〖心理〗反射弧。

reflex camera 反射照相機。

re·flex·i·ble [rɪˈflɛksɪbl; riˈfleksibl] *adj.* 可反射的;反射性的。—**re·flex·i·bil·i·ty,** *n.* 「*n.* =reflection. —**al,** *adj.*

re·flex·ion [rɪˈflɛkʃən; riˈflekʃən]

re·flex·ive [rɪˈflɛksɪv; riˈfleksiv] *adj.* ①〖文法〗反身的。②反射的。③反應的。④〖數學〗自反的。—*n.* 反身動詞;反身代名詞。*reflexive pronoun* 反身代名詞。*reflexive verb* 反身動詞。

re·flex·ol·o·gy [ˌriflɛkˈsɑlədʒɪ; ˌriːflekˈsɔlədʒi] *n.* 反射論。

re·flo·res·cent [ˌrifloˈrɛsn̩t; ˌriːflɔːˈresənt] *adj.* 再開花的。

ref·lu·ent [ˈrɛfluənt; ˈreflu(ː)ənt] *adj.* 逆流的;倒流的(潮水、血液等)。

re·flux [ˈriˌflʌks; ˈriː-flʌks] *n.* 逆流;退潮。(亦作 **refluence**)

re·fo·cus [riˈfokəs; ˈriːˈfoukəs] *v.t. & v.i.*, **-cused, -cus·ing, -cussed, -cus·sing.** 再集中;再定焦點。「再造林;再植樹。

re·for·est [riˈfɔrɪst; ˈriːˈfɔrist] *v.t.*

re·for·est·a·tion [ˌrifɔrɪsˈteʃən; ˈriːfɔrisˈteiʃən] *n.* 再造林。

re-form [ˌriˈfɔrm; ˈriːˈfɔːm] *v.t.* ①再形成;再組成;再作。②改編(軍隊)。—*v.i.* ①變成一新形。②改編。—**er,** —**a·tion,** *n.*

***re·form** [rɪˈfɔrm; riˈfɔːm, rəˈf-] *v.t. & v.i.* 改造;改進;改革;改過自新。—*n.* ①改善;改進;改革。social *reform.* 社會改革。②思想、行爲等之改進。—**a·ble,** *adj.* —**ing·ly,** *adv.*

***ref·or·ma·tion** [ˌrɛfɚˈmeʃən; ˌrefəˈmeiʃən, -fɔːˈm-] *n.* ①改革;改善;改良。②(R-)宗教改革(歐洲十六世紀之宗教改革)。

ref·or·ma·tion·al [ˌrɛfɚˈmeʃənl̩; ˌrefəˈmeiʃənl] *adj.* ①改革的;改良的。②宗教改革的。

re·form·a·to·ry [rɪˈfɔrməˌtorɪ; riˈfɔːmətəri] *adj., n.*, **-ries.** —*adj.* (亦作 **reformative**) ①改革的;改善的。②感化的。—*n.* (亦作 **reform school**) 少年感化院。

re·formed [rɪˈfɔrmd; riˈfɔːmd] *adj.* ①革新的;改革的。②改過自新的。③(R-)宗教改革派的。*the Reformed Faith* 新教。*the Reformed Church* **a.** 基督教派。**b.** 基督教新教(喀爾文派)。

reformed spelling 改革拼法(簡化拼法,如以 thru 代替 through, tho 代替 though, slo 代替 slow 等)。

***re·form·er** [rɪˈfɔrmɚ; riˈfɔːmə, rəˈf-] *n.* ①改革者。②(R-)宗教改革家。

reform school 少年感化院。

re·fract [rɪˈfrækt; riˈfrækt] *v.t.* 使(光)屈折;使折射。—**ed·ly,** *adv.* —**ed·ness,** *n.*

re·frac·tile [rɪˈfræktəl; riˈfræktail] *adj.* 折射(光線)的。

re·frac·tion [rɪˈfrækʃən; riˈfrækʃən] *n.* ①〖物理〗折光;折射。②〖光學〗眼之折光能力;折光度之測量(指眼)。—**al,** *adj.*

re·frac·tive [rɪˈfræktɪv; riˈfræktiv]

adj. ①折射(光線等)的;有折光力的。②屈折的;因折射而引起的。(亦作**refractile**)

refractive index 折射率。

re·frac·tom·e·ter [ˌrifræk'tɑmətɚ; ˌriːfræk'tɔmitə] *n.* 折射計;折光計。

re·frac·tor [rɪ'fræktɚ; ri'fræktə] *n.* ①任何能折光之物。②折射望遠鏡。

re·frac·to·ry [rɪ'fræktərɪ; ri'fræktəri] *adj., n., pl.* **-ries.** —*adj.* ①難駕御的;倔强的;固執的。②難治療的。③難鎔化的;難處理的;耐高溫的。—*n.* ①耐火物。②(*pl.*)火爐內用的耐火磚。③〖生理〗不應期;反拗期。

***re·frain**[1] [rɪ'fren; ri'frein] *v.i. & v.t.* 抑制;制止;禁止。to *refrain* from smoking. 節制吸煙。—**er,** —**ment,** *n.*

***re·frain**[2] *n.* ①詩歌中之重疊句。②重複唱詞的樂曲。

re·fran·gi·bil·i·ty [rɪˌfrændʒə'bɪlətɪ; riˌfrændʒi'biliti] *n.* (可)折射性;折射。

re·fran·gi·ble [rɪ'frændʒəbḷ; ri'frændʒibl] *adj.* 可折射的;折射性的。—**ness,** *n.*

re·freeze [ri'friz; riː'friːz] *v.t.,* **-froze, -fro·zen, -freez·ing.** 再冰凍;使再結冰。

***re·fresh** [rɪ'frɛʃ; ri'freʃ, rə'f-] *v.t.* ①使爽快;使消除疲勞。to *refresh* oneself with a cup of tea. 喝一杯茶提神。②恢復(記憶);補充;補足。③使再新鮮。④使恢復原狀。—*v.i.* ①提起精神;恢復精神。②飲用飲料提神;吃點心提神。③補充。—**ful,** *adj.* —**ful·ly,** *adv.*

re·fresh·er [rɪ'frɛʃɚ; ri'freʃə] *adj.* 複習的;溫習的。—*n.* ①清涼劑;酒。②〖英〗(訴訟進行中)暫付律師之額外費。

re·fresh·ing [rɪ'frɛʃɪŋ; ri'freʃiŋ] *adj.* ①令人精神爽快的;提神的;給人以力量的。②清鮮而悅人的。—**ly,** *adv.* —**ness,** *n.*

***re·fresh·ment** [rɪ'frɛʃmənt; ri'freʃmənt, rə'f-] *n.* ①爽快;心曠神怡。②提神之事物。③(*pl.*)點心。

refreshment room (鐵路車站等中的)飲食店;餐室。

re·frig·er·ant [rɪ'frɪdʒərənt; ri'fridʒərənt] *n.* ①冷凍劑。②退熱劑;清涼劑。—*adj.* ①冷却的。②降低體溫或高熱的。

re·frig·er·ate [rɪ'frɪdʒəˌret; ri'fridʒəreit] *v.t.,* **-at·ed, -at·ing.** 使冷却;使清涼。

re·frig·er·a·tion [rɪˌfrɪdʒə'reʃən; riˌfridʒə'reiʃən] *n.* ①冷却;冷凍。②〖地質〗地球之冷却。③冷藏。④〖醫〗消熱;解熱。

re·frig·er·a·tive [rɪ'frɪdʒəˌretɪv; ri'fridʒəreitiv] *adj.* 冷却的;冷凍的;清涼的。—*n.* 冷凍劑;清涼劑。

***re·frig·er·a·tor** [rɪ'frɪdʒəˌretɚ; ri'fridʒəreitə, rə'f-] *n.* 電冰箱。

refrigerator car 〖鐵路〗冷藏貨車。

re·frig·er·a·to·ry [rɪ'frɪdʒərəˌtorɪ; ri'fridʒərətəri] *adj., n., pl.* **-ries.** —*adj.* 冷却的;清涼的。—*n.* ①冷却裝置;冷凍裝置;冷却器;結冰槽。②(蒸餾器的)蒸汽凝結機。

reft [rɛft; reft] *v.* pt. & pp. of **reave.**

re·fu·el [ri'fjuəl; 'riː'fjuːəl] *v.,* **-el(l)ed, -el·(l)ing.** —*v.t.* 再供以燃料。—*v.i.* 取得新燃料。

***ref·uge** ['rɛfjudʒ; 'refjuːdʒ] *n., v.,* **-uged, -ug·ing.** —*n.* ①安全;保護。②避難所;避難處。③慰藉物。He found a *refuge* in books. 他以讀書自娛。④〖英〗(馬路上的)安全島。—*v.t.*〖古〗予以保護。—*v.i.*〖古〗避難。

ref·u·gee [ˌrɛfju'dʒi; ˌrefju'dʒiː] *n.* 避難者;難民。—**ism,** *n.*

re·ful·gence [rɪ'fʌldʒəns; ri'fʌldʒəns] *n.* 光輝;燦爛。(亦作 **refulgency**)

re·ful·gent [rɪ'fʌldʒənt; ri'fʌldʒənt] *adj.* 光輝的;燦爛的。—**ly,** *adv.* —**ness,** *n.*

re·fund[1] [*v.* rɪ'fʌnd; riː'fʌnd *n.* 'riˌfʌnd; 'riːfʌnd] *v., n.* —*v.t.* 償付;償還;退還。—*v.i.* 償付;退錢。—*n.* 退款;退還之款。—**a·ble,** *adj.* —**er,** *n.*

re·fund[2] [ˌri'fʌnd; ˌriː'fʌnd] *v.t.* 〖財政〗①發行公債以償付(借款)。②以新公債換回(舊公債)。

re·fund·ment [rɪ'fʌndmənt; ri'fʌndmənt] *n.* 退款;退還;所退還之金額或物。

re·fur·bish [ri'fɝbɪʃ; 'riː'fəːbiʃ] *v.t.* 整修;刷新。—**ment,** *n.*

re·fur·nish [ri'fɝnɪʃ; 'riː'fəːniʃ] *v.t.* ①再供給。②重新陳設或布置。—**ment,** *n.*

re·fus·a·ble [rɪ'fjuzəbḷ; ri'fjuːzəbl] *adj.* 可拒絕的;可謝絕的。

re·fus·al** [rɪ'fjuzḷ; ri'fjuːzəl] *n.* ①拒絕;謝絕。②取捨權;選擇的自由;先買權。take no refusal*** 堅持。

‡**re·fuse**[1] [rɪ'fjuz; ri'fjuːz] *v.,* **-fused, -fus·ing.** —*v.t. & v.i.* ①拒絕;謝絕。He *refused* my offer of help. 他拒絕我的幫助。②不願;不肯。He *refused* to obey. 他不肯服從。

ref·use[2] ['rɛfjus; 'refjuːs] *n.* 垃圾;棄物。—*adj.* 被棄的。*refuse* matter. 垃圾。

ref·u·ta·ble ['rɛfjutəbḷ; 'refjutəbl] *adj.* 可駁斥的。—**ref·u·ta·bly,** *adv.*

ref·u·ta·tion [ˌrɛfju'teʃən; ˌrefju(ː)'teiʃən] *n.* 反駁;辯駁。(亦作 **refutal**)

re·fute [rɪ'fjut; ri'fjuːt] *v.t.,* **-fut·ed, -fut·ing.** 反駁;駁斥。—**re·fut·er,** *n.*

Reg. ①Regent. ②Regiment. ③Regina (拉=Queen). **reg.** ①regent. ②regiment. ③region. ④register. ⑤registered. ⑥registrar. ⑦registry. ⑧regular. ⑨regularly. ⑩regulation. ⑪regulator.

***re·gain** [rɪ'gen; ri'gein] *v.t.* ①復得;恢復。to *regain* health. 恢復健康。②重回;復至。—**ment,** *n.* —**a·ble,** *adj.*

***re·gal** ['rigḷ; 'riːgəl] *adj.* ①帝王的;王室的。②似帝王的;華麗的;莊嚴的。It was a *regal* banquet. 那是豪華的酒宴。—**ly,** *adv.*

re·gale[1] [rɪ'gel; ri'geil] *v.,* **-galed, -gal·ing,** *n.* —*v.t.* ①款以盛饌;款讌;款待。②使喜悅;使享受。—*v.i.* 享用盛餐〖on〗。—*n.* ①盛宴。②佳餚美酒。③點心。—**ment,** *n.* —**re·gal·er,** *n.*

re·gale[2] *n.* sing. of **regalia.**

re·ga·li·a [rɪ'gelɪə; ri'geiliə] *n. pl.* ①王權的標識。②〖古〗王權;特權。③任何團體之任何標識。④華麗的衣服。

re·gal·ism ['rigəlɪzṃ; 'riːgəlizm] *n.* 帝王教權論。

re·gal·ist ['rigəlɪst; 'riːgəlist] *n.* 君主主義者。

re·gal·i·ty [rɪ'gælətɪ; riː'gæliti] *n., pl.* **-ties.** ①王位;王權。②君主國;王國。③(國王賜予的)地方管轄權;管轄區。***the lord of regality***〖蘇史〗國王委派的地方管轄者。

‡**re·gard** [rɪ'gɑrd; ri'gɑːd] *v.t.* ①視爲;當作。②尊敬;敬重。③注視;熟視。④關係;關於。⑤注意。None *regarded* her screams. 沒有人注意她的尖叫。⑥考慮。***as regards*** 至於。—*v.i.* ①注意。②注視。—*n.* ①考慮;關心。②注視;熟視。③尊敬;敬重;好感。④(*pl.*)問候。Please give my kind *regards* to your brother. 請代向令兄問候。With

kind *regards*. 謹致問候之意(用於信尾)。⑤關係。⑥方面;特點。*in* (or *with*) *regard to* 關於。*in this regard* 關於此事。*without regard to* 不顧;不管。

re·gard·ant [rɪˈgardənt; riˈgɑːdənt] *adj.* ①〖紋章〗側面向後視的。②〖古,詩〗回顧的;熟視的。(亦作 **reguardant**)

re·gard·ful [rɪˈgardful; riˈgɑːdful] *adj.* ①注意的;小心的〖常 of〗。②恭敬的;表示敬意的。—**ly,** *adv.* —**ness,** *n.*

***re·gard·ing** [rɪˈgardɪŋ; riˈgɑːdiŋ] *prep.* 關於。

***re·gard·less** [rɪˈgardlɪs; riˈgɑːdlis] *adj.* 不顧;不拘〖of〗. *regardless* of consequence. 不顧後果。*regardless* of sex. 不拘性別。—*adv.* ①不顧地。②不管;雖然。—**ly,** *adv.* —**ness,** *n.*

re·gat·ta [rɪˈgætə; riˈgætə] *n.* ①賽船。②賽船會。③一種條紋厚棉布。

re·ge·late [ˈridʒəˌlet; ˈriːdʒəleit] *v.i.,* **-lat·ed, -lat·ing.** (冰雪等溶化後)再凍結一起;復冰。

re·ge·la·tion [ˌridʒəˈleʃən; ˌriːdʒəˈleiʃən] *n.* 〖物理〗復冰現象。

re·gen·cy [ˈridʒənsɪ; ˈriːdʒənsi] *n., pl.* **-cies,** *adj.* —*n.* ①攝政政治;攝政職位;攝政期限;攝政執政團。②(R-)英史 1811 至 1820 年之時期。③(R-) 法史 1715 至 1723 年之時期。④攝政統治的地域。—*adj.* 攝政(時代)的。

re·gen·er·a·cy [rɪˈdʒɛnərəsɪ; riˈdʒenərəsi] *n.* 新生;革新;復生。

re·gen·er·ate [*v.* rɪˈdʒɛnəˌret; riˈdʒenəreit *adj.* rɪˈdʒɛnərɪt; riˈdʒenərit] *v.t.,* **-at·ed, -at·ing,** *adj.* —*v.t.* ①使重獲新生;使改過自新。②重生。③〖物理〗產生再生現象。—*v.i.* ①精神更生。②重生;再生。—*adj.* ①精神重生的。②改造過的。

re·gen·er·a·tion [rɪˌdʒɛnəˈreʃən; riˌdʒenəˈreiʃən] *n.* ①改造;改革;重建。②復活;復興。③〖宗教〗更生;新生;再生。④〖生理〗細胞組織之再生。⑤〖物理〗再生現象。

re·gen·er·a·tive [rɪˈdʒɛnəˌretɪv; riˈdʒenəreitiv] *adj.* ①再生的;重獲新生的。②〖機械〗回熱式的。③〖無線電〗再生式的。

re·gen·er·a·tor [rɪˈdʒɛnəˌretə; riˈdʒenəreitə] *n.* ①再生者;更生者;改革者;刷新者。②〖機械〗蓄熱器;復熱爐。③〖無線電〗再生器。

re·gen·e·sis [rɪˈdʒɛnəsɪs; riˈdʒenəsis] *n.* 再生;更新。

***re·gent** [ˈridʒənt; ˈriːdʒənt] *n.* ①攝政。②(大學之)董事。③統治者。—*adj.* ①攝政的。②〖古〗校董的。③〖古〗統治的。—**ship,** *n.*

re·ges, Re·ges [ˈridʒiz; ˈriːdʒiːz] *n.* pl. of **rex, Rex.**

reg·i·cid·al [ˌrɛdʒəˈsaɪdl̩; ˌredʒiˈsaidl] *adj.* 弒君的;弒君者的。

reg·i·cide [ˈrɛdʒəˌsaɪd; ˈredʒisaid] *n.* ①弒君。②弒君者。

ré·gie [ˌreˈʒi; reiˈʒiː] 〖法〗*n.* (法、義、西等國的菸、鹽等之)專賣;專賣局;(公共事業之)官營;公營。

***re·gime, ré·gime** [rɪˈʒim; reiˈʒiːm, reˈʒ-] *n.* ①政權;政治系統。②某一政府當政之期間;某一政制當權之期間。③生活規律;紀律。

reg·i·men [ˈrɛdʒəˌmɛn; ˈredʒimen] *n.* ①攝生法。②統治;控制。③政體;制度。

***reg·i·ment** [*n.* ˈrɛdʒəmənt; ˈredʒimənt *v.* ˈrɛdʒəˌmɛnt; ˈredʒiment] *n.* ①〖軍〗團。②多數;簇;團。③〖廢〗政府;統治。—*v.t.* ①編成團。②嚴格而統一地管理;統制。③整理;納入同一制度或體系。

reg·i·men·tal [ˌrɛdʒəˈmɛntl̩; ˌredʒiˈmentl] *adj.* 團的。—*n.*(*pl.*)軍服。—**ly,** *adv.*

reg·i·men·ta·tion [ˌrɛdʒəmɛnˈteʃən; ˌredʒimenˈteiʃən] *n.* ①編成團。②組織;編組。③統制。

Re·gi·na, re·gi·na [rɪˈdʒaɪnə; riˈdʒainə] 〖拉〗*n.* 女王(=Queen).

‡**re·gion** [ˈridʒən; ˈriːdʒən] *n.* ①地方;區域。the *region* of the equator. 赤道區域。②(身體之)一部;部位。③領域;境界。the *region* of art. 藝術的領域。

re·gion·al [ˈridʒənl̩; ˈriːdʒənl] *adj.* 某一地方的;某一地區內的;區域性的。—**ly,** *adv.*

re·gion·al·ism [ˈridʒənl̩ˌɪzəm; ˈriːdʒənlˌizəm] *n.* ①行政區域之劃分或其原則。②地域性。③鄉土主義。④〖文學〗鄉土色彩。

ré·gis·seur [reʒiˈsœr; reʒiˈsœːr] *n., pl.* **-seurs** [-ˈsœr; -ˈsœːr]. 〖法〗舞臺劇或電影導演。

***reg·is·ter** [ˈrɛdʒɪstə; ˈredʒistə] *n.* ①名單;名簿。a *register* of attendance. 出席人名單。②登記簿;註冊簿。③記錄器。④登記;註冊。⑤登記者;註冊主任。⑥屋頂或地板上調節氣流或溫度的裝置。⑦〖音樂〗音域。⑧(表示國籍之)商船登記證。⑨書籤(尤指附在書背的小絲帶)。⑩商店中附有計算機之收銀櫃。—*v.t.* ①登記;註冊。②指示。③掛號。*Register* this letter. 把此信掛號。④以表情或行爲表示(驚訝、快樂、憂傷等)。⑤〖印刷〗排整齊(行、欄、色版等)以能印刷。⑥登記商船之國籍。—*v.i.* ①登記;註冊。to *register* at a hotel. 到旅館登記(投宿)。②〖印刷〗排整齊。③發生效力。

reg·is·tered [ˈrɛdʒɪstəd; ˈredʒistəd] *adj.* ①登記過的。②註過册的。③掛號的。④記名的。⑤(家畜等)有血統證明書的。

registered bond 記名公債。

registered nurse 考試合格而有執照之護士。

reg·is·tra·ble [ˈrɛdʒɪstrəbl̩; ˈredʒistrəbl] *adj.* 可登記的;可註册的;可掛號的。

reg·is·trant [ˈrɛdʒɪstrənt; ˈredʒistrənt] *n.* 登記者。

reg·is·trar [ˈrɛdʒɪˌstrar; ˌredʒisˈtrɑː] *n.* ①登記員;(學校裏的)註册主任。②(銀行、信託公司等)負責登記、證明股票的人。

***reg·is·tra·tion** [ˌrɛdʒɪˈstreʃən; ˌredʒisˈtreiʃən] *n.* ①登記;註册。②登記之一項。③登記或註册人員之數目。④登記證。

reg·is·try [ˈrɛdʒɪstrɪ; ˈredʒistri] *n., pl.* **-tries.** ①登記;註册。②登記處;註册處。③登記簿;記錄簿。④商船之登記國籍。

re·gi·us [ˈridʒɪəs; ˈriːdʒiəs] *adj.* 國王的(指英國或蘇格蘭大學中由國王指定所設之講座而言,如 a *regius* professor, 擔任此種講座之教授)。

reg·nal [ˈrɛgnəl; ˈregnəl] *adj.* ①國的;朝的。②國王的;君主的。

reg·nant [ˈrɛgnənt; ˈregnənt] *adj.* ①統治的(用於名詞後)。②占優勢的;流行的。

re·gorge [rɪˈgɔrdʒ; riˈgɔːdʒ] *v.,* **-gorged, -gorg·ing.** —*v.t.* ①擲回;拋回;吐出;嘔出。②〖罕〗再吞下。—*v.i.* 倒流。

re·gress [*n.* ˈrigrɛs; ˈriːgres *v.* rɪˈgrɛs; riˈgres] *n.* ①回歸;後退。②復歸權。③退步。—*v.i.* ①後退;復舊。②〖天文〗逆行。—**or,** *n.*

re·gres·sion [rɪˈgrɛʃən; riˈgreʃən] *n.* ①回歸;復歸。②退步。③〖心理〗退轉。④〖統計〗迴歸。⑤〖天文〗逆行。⑥〖生物〗退化。⑦(疾病之)消退。

re·gres·sive [rɪˈgrɛsɪv; riˈgresiv]

adj. ①回歸的; 逆行的。②退步的; 退化的。③(稅率之)累減的。—**ly,** *adv.* —**ness,** *n.*

re·gret** [rɪˈɡrɛt; riˈɡret] *n.*, *v.*, **-gret·ted, -gret·ting.** —*n.* ①悔恨; 懊悔; 悼惜。②抱歉; 遺憾。He refused with many *regrets* (*or* much *regret*). 他非常抱歉地謝絕。③(*pl.*) 表示客氣的婉言謝絕。Please accept my *regrets.* (不能奉陪)謹致歉意。④敬謝之回帖。express regret at*** 對…表示惋惜。***express regret for*** 對…表示遺憾之意。***have no regrets*** 不後悔。***to my regret*** 抱歉。—*v.t.* 悔恨;惋惜;抱歉。I *regret* being unable to come (*or* that I cannot come). 我不能來甚爲抱歉。

re·gret·(t)a·ble [rɪˈɡrɛtəbl; riˈɡretəbl] *adj.* ①可後悔的; 可抱歉的。②不幸的。—**ness,** *n.* —**re·gret·a·bly,** *adv.*

re·gret·ful [rɪˈɡrɛtfl; riˈɡretful] *adj.* ①後悔的; 懊悔的。②抱歉的; 遺憾的。—**ly,** *adv.* —**ness,** *n.*

re·group [riˈɡrup; ˈriːˈɡruːp] *v.t.* & *v.i.* ①再集合;再集成羣。②〖軍〗整編。—**ment,** *n.*

Regt. ①regent. ②regiment.

regt. regiment.

‡**reg·u·lar** [ˈrɛɡjələ; ˈreɡjulə, -ɡjəl-] *adj.* ①通常的; 正常的。②依法的; 循規的。③常例的;定期的。Sunday is a *regular* holiday. 星期日是例假。④習慣性的; 不變的; 經常的。⑤齊整的;端正的。⑥對稱的。⑦〖幾何〗角與邊均相等的;等邊等角的。⑧〖植物〗整齊的(花)。⑨有規律的;有秩序的。to lead a *regular* life. 過着有規律的生活。⑩〖文法〗變化規則的。⑪合格的;有訓練的。⑫永久組織的;常備的;常備軍的。the *regular* army. 常備軍。⑬〖宗教〗屬於教團的;受教規束縛的。⑭〖俗〗完全的;徹底的。a *regular* rascal. 一個十足的流氓。⑮〖俗〗良好的;討人喜歡的。⑯〖運動〗最好的;第一流的。a *regular* team. 第一流的球隊。—*n.* ①常備兵;正規兵。②修士;和尚。③(政黨中的)忠貞不貳分子。④老顧客。⑤普通尺寸的現成衣服。⑥參加幾乎全部競賽的運動員。—**ness,** *n.*

reg·u·lar·i·ty [ˌrɛɡjəˈlærətɪ; ˌreɡjuˈlæriti] *n.* 規律;秩序;慣常;整齊;定期。

reg·u·lar·ize [ˈrɛɡjələˌraɪz; ˈreɡjuləraiz] *v.t.*, **-ized, -iz·ing.** ①使規律化。②使組織化;使合法化。—**reg·u·lar·i·za·tion,** *n.*

***reg·u·lar·ly** [ˈrɛɡjələlɪ; ˈreɡjuləli] *adv.* ①有規則地。②定期地。

***reg·u·late** [ˈrɛɡjəˌlet; ˈreɡjuleit, -ɡjəl-] *v.t.*, **-lat·ed, -lat·ing.** ①管理;節制;規定。to *regulate* one's conduct. 管理自己的行爲。②調節; 調整。—**reg·u·lat·a·ble, reg·u·la·tive, reg·u·la·to·ry,** *adj.*

***reg·u·la·tion** [ˌrɛɡjəˈleʃən; ˌreɡjuˈleiʃən] *n.* ①管理; 節制; 規定。②規則; 條例; 法令。traffic *regulations.* 交通規則。—*adj.* ①標準的; 正規的; 合乎規定的。the *regulation* speed. 規定速度。②正常的; 通常的; 習慣上的。—**ist,** *n.*

reg·u·la·tor [ˈrɛɡjəˌletə; ˈreɡjuleitə] *n.* ①調整者; 規定者。②調整器; 調節器。③標準時計。

reg·u·lus [ˈrɛɡjuləs; ˈreɡjuləs] *n.*, *pl.* **-lus·es, -li** [-laɪ; -lai]. ①(R-)〖天文〗獅子星座(Leo)之第一星。②〖冶金〗礦石熔化時在底層沉澱之金屬塊。

re·gur·gi·tate [riˈɡɝdʒəˌtet; riːˈɡəːdʒiteit] *v.*, **-tat·ed, -tat·ing.** —*v.t.* 使湧回;使流回;反芻。—*v.i.* 流回;湧回;反芻;反胃。

re·gur·gi·ta·tion [rɪˌɡɝdʒəˈteʃən; riˌɡəːdʒiˈteiʃən] *n.* ①湧回; 流回。②(反芻動物之)反芻。③(血液)反流。

re·ha·bil·i·tant [ˌrihəˈbɪlətənt; ˌriːhəˈbilitənt] *n.* (健康、心理等)恢復康健者。

re·ha·bil·i·tate [ˌriəˈbɪləˌtet; ˌriːəˈbiliteit] *v.t.*, **-tat·ed, -tat·ing.** ①恢復; 修復。②恢復原有的職位、地位、權利、名譽等。③使恢復心理健康;精神重建。—**re·ha·bil·i·ta·tive,** *adj.*

re·ha·bil·i·ta·tion [ˌriəˌbɪləˈteʃən; ˈriːəˌbiliˈteiʃən] *n.* ①恢復; 修復。②復權; 復職;復位;恢復名譽。③身心之重建。

re·hash [*v.* riˈhæʃ; ˈriːˈhæʃ *n.* ˈriˌhæʃ; ˈriːˈhæʃ] *v.t.* 再處理; 改造(舊材料)成新形式。—*n.* ①再處理;改成新形式。②改成新形式之舊材料;舊調新唱。

re·hear [rɪˈhɪr; ˈriːˈhiə] *v.t.*, **-heard, -hear·ing.** 再聽;(尤指)再審;覆審。

re·hear·ing [riˈhɪrɪŋ; ˈriːˈhiəriŋ] *n.* 〖法律〗覆審;再審。

re·hears·al [rɪˈhɝsl; riˈhəːsəl] *n.* ①預演;預習;再三訓練。②詳述;復述。

***re·hearse** [rɪˈhɝs; riˈhəːs, rəˈh-] *v.*, **-hearsed, -hears·ing.** —*v.t.* ①預演;演習。②詳述;複述。to *rehearse* all the happenings of the day. 詳述當日所發生的一切事件。—*v.i.* 預演;演習。

Reich [raɪk; raik] *n.* ①自九世紀至十九世紀初之神聖羅馬帝國。②德國或德國政府(尤指納粹時期的)。

Reichs·bank [ˈraɪksˌbæŋk; ˈraiksbæŋk] 〖德〗*n.* 德國國家銀行。

reichs·mark [ˈraɪksˌmɑrk; ˈraiksmɑːk] *n.*, *pl.* **-marks, -mark.** 德國馬克(德國之錢幣單位)。

Reichs·tag [ˈraɪksˌtɑɡ; ˈraikstɑːɡ] *n.* 德國之議會。

reign** [ren; rein] *n.* ①(一帝王之)統治時代; 朝代; 王朝。②王權; 君權; 統治。the Reign of Terror*** (法國大革命期間, 許多人被處決的)恐怖時代。—*v.i.* ①爲王; 爲君;統治。A king *reigns* over his kingdom. 一國王統治其王國。②占優勢;盛行。

re·im·burse [ˌriɪmˈbɝs; ˌriːimˈbəːs] *v.t.*, **-bursed, -burs·ing.** 補償;退款。—**re·im·burs·a·ble,** *adj.* —**ment,** *n.*

re·im·port [ˌriɪmˈport; ˈriːimˈpɔːt] *v.t.* 再輸入;逆輸入。—*n.* ①再輸入;逆輸入。②再輸入的東西;再進口貨。

re·im·por·ta·tion [ˌriɪmporˈteʃən; ˌriːimpɔːˈteiʃən] *n.* ①再輸入; 逆輸入。②再輸入的東西。

re·im·pres·sion [ˌriɪmˈprɛʃən; ˈriːimˈpreʃən] *n.* (原版未予變動的)再版;重版。

re·im·print [ˌriɪmˈprɪnt; ˌriːimˈprint] *v.t.* 再版。

rein** [ren; rein] *n.* ①韁繩。a pair of *reins.* 一副韁繩。②(*pl.*) 駕馭; 箝制; 權勢。assume*** (***drop***) ***the reins of government*** 握(失)政權。***draw rein*** a. 勒韁。b. 慢下來;緩行;停止。***give*** (***the***) ***rein***(***s***) ***to one's imagination*** 任想像縱情奔放。***hold the reins*** 統馭; 支配。***keep a tight rein on*** 抑制。***take the reins*** 控制。—*v.t.* 駕馭; 統制。*Rein* your tongue. 住嘴罷;不要講了。***rein in*** a. 勒住馬。b. 控制;抑制。***rein up*** (or ***back***) 止馬。—*v.i.* ①服從駕馭。②駕馭馬或其他動物。—**less,** *adj.*

re·in·car·nate [*v.* ˌriɪnˈkɑrnet; riːˈinkɑːneit *adj.* ˌriɪnˈkɑrnɪt; ˈriːinˈkɑːnit] *v.t.*, **-nat·ed, -nat·ing.** 賦予(靈魂)一新肉體；使再化身。 —*adj.* 再化身的。 —**re·in·car·na·tion,** *n.*

***rein·deer** ['rendɪr; 'reindiə] *n., pl.* **-deer, -deers.** 馴鹿。

re·in·fec·tion [ˌriɪn'fɛkʃən; ˌri:in-'fekʃən] *n.* 再感染。

re·in·force [ˌriɪn'fors; ˌri:in'fɔ:s] *v.,* **-forced, -forc·ing,** *n.* —*v.t.* ①增援。②增强。—*n.* 增强物。(亦作 **re-enforce, reënforce, reenforce**) —**re·in·forc·er,** *n.*

reinforced concrete 鋼筋混凝土。

re·in·force·ment [ˌriɪn'forsmənt; ˌri:in'fɔ:smənt] *n.* ①增援；加强。②增援或加强之物。③(*pl.*) 援兵；援艦。(亦作 **reënforcement**)

rein·less ['renlɪs; 'reinlis] *adj.* ①無韁繩的。②不受拘束的；自由的；放縱的。

reins [renz; reinz] *n. pl.* 〖古〗①腎臟。②腰；腰部。③情感；情緒。

re·in·sert [ˌriɪn'sɝt; ˌri:in'sə:t] *v.t.* 重新插入；再插入。—**re·in·ser·tion,** *n.*

re·in·state [ˌriɪn'stet; 'ri:in'steit] *v.t.,* **-stat·ed, -stat·ing.** ①使復原位；恢復原職；恢復。②使復原；重建。 —**re·in·sta·tion, —ment, re·in·sta·tor,** *n.*

re·in·sur·ance [ˌriɪn'ʃurəns; 'ri:in-'ʃuərəns] *n.* 再保險；再保險金額。

re·in·sure [ˌriɪn'ʃur; 'ri:in'ʃuə] *v.t.,* **-sured, -sur·ing.** 再保險。—**re·in·sur·er,** *n.*

re·in·te·grate [rɪ'ɪntɪˌgret; ri'intigreit] *v.t.,* **-grat·ed, -grat·ing.** ①使再完整；恢復；再建；復興。②使再統一。 —**re·in·te·gra·tion,** *n.*

re·in·ter [ˌriɪn'tɝ; ˌri:in'tə:] *v.t.,* **-terred, -ter·ring.** 再埋葬；改葬。—**ment,** *n.*

re·in·tro·duce [ˌriɪntrə'djus; 'ri:ˌintrə'dju:s] *v.t.,* **-duced, -duc·ing.** 再介紹；再導入；再引入；再提出；再採用。

re·in·vest [ˌriɪn'vɛst; 'ri:in'vest] *v.t. & v.i.* 再投(資)；重新投(資)。—**ment,** *n.*

re·in·vig·or·ate [ˌriɪn'vɪgəˌret; ˌri:in'vigəreit] *v.t.,* **-at·ed, -at·ing.** 使恢復生命；使恢復活力；使有新的勇氣。

re·is·sue [ri'ɪʃu; ri:'isju:] *v.,* **-sued, -su·ing,** *n.* —*v.t.* 再發行(證券、書籍等)。—*n.* 再發行；再版。 —**re·is·su·ance,** *n.*

re·it·er·ate [ri'ɪtəˌret; ri:'itəreit] *v.t.,* **-at·ed, -at·ing.** ①重述；反覆地說。②反覆地做。③反覆。—**re·it·er·a·tion,** *n.*

re·it·er·a·tive [rɪ'ɪtəˌretɪv; ri:'itəreitiv] *n.* ①重疊語；疊成語(如 dillydally)。②〖文法〗表反覆動作之字；反覆語。—*adj.* 反覆的。—**ly,** *adv.*

reive [riv; ri:v] *v.t. & v.i.,* **reived, reiv·ing.** 〖蘇〗搶；掠。—**reiv·er,** *n.*

***re·ject** [*v.* rɪ'dʒɛkt; ri'dʒekt *n.* 'ri-dʒɛkt; 'ri:dʒekt] *v.t.* ①拒絕；不受。 He tried to join the army but was *rejected.* 他想從軍但被拒絕了。②丟；丟棄。③嘔吐。④駁斥；不理會。 —*n.* 被拒之人；被棄之物。 —**a·ble, —ive,** *adj.* —**er,** *n.*

re·ject·ee [rɪˌdʒɛk'ti; ridʒek'ti:] *n.* 被(軍中)拒絕者。

re·jec·tion [rɪ'dʒɛkʃən; ri'dʒekʃən] *n.* ①拒絕。②被拒。③被棄之物。

rejection slip 出版商附在退稿上之拒絕通知。

re·joice** [rɪ'dʒɔɪs; ri'dʒɔis] *v.,* **-joiced, -joic·ing.** —*v.t.* 使喜；使樂。—*v.i.* 喜歡；高興。I *rejoice* to hear your success. 聽到你的成功我很高興。rejoice at*** (or ***in***) 爲…而快樂。—**ful,** *adj.* —**re·joic·er,** *n.*

***re·joic·ing** [rɪ'dʒɔɪsɪŋ; ri'dʒɔisiŋ] *n.* ①欣喜；喜悅；狂喜；高興。②歡樂；歡宴。Widespread *rejoicings* celebrated the victory. 普天同歡共慶勝利。③使歡欣之事；喜慶之事。 —**ly,** *adv.*

re·join[1] [ˌri'dʒɔɪn; 'ri:'dʒɔin] *v.t. & v.i.* ①再參加；再加入。②再接；再接合。

re·join[2] [rɪ'dʒɔɪn; ri'dʒɔin] *v.t. & v.i.* 應答；回答。

re·join·der [rɪ'dʒɔɪndə; ri'dʒɔində] *n.* 回答。

re·ju·ve·nate [rɪ'dʒuvəˌnet; ri'dʒu:vineit] *v.,* **-nat·ed, -nat·ing.** —*v.t.* ①使返老還童；使充滿活力。②〖地質〗使(河流)恢復其浸蝕力。—*v.i.* 恢復青春；恢復活力。 —**re·ju·ve·na·tion, re·ju·ve·na·tor,** *n.*

re·ju·ve·nesce [rɪˌdʒuvə'nɛs; ˌri:dʒu:vi'nes] *v.t. & v.i.,* **-nesced, -nesc·ing.** ①(使)返老還童；(使)更新。②〖生物〗(使)細胞再生。

re·ju·ve·nes·cence [rɪˌdʒuvə'nɛsn̩s; ˌri:dʒu:vi'nesns] *n.* ①返老還童；新生；復壯。②〖生物〗(細胞的)再生；更新。

re·ju·ve·nes·cent [rɪˌdʒuvə'nɛsn̩t; ˌri:dʒu:vi'nesnt] *adj.* 返老還童的；新生的；復壯的。

re·ju·ve·nize [rɪ'dʒuvəˌnaɪz; ri'dʒu:vinaiz] *v.t.* =**rejuvenate.**

re·kin·dle [ri'kɪndl̩; 'ri:'kindl] *v.,* **-dled, -dling.** —*v.t.* ①再點火；再燃。②再使精神振奮。—*v.i.* 再振作；再燃起。—**ment,** *n.*

rel. ①relating. ②relative(ly). ③religion. ④religious.

re·laid [ˌri'led; 'ri:'leid] *v.* pt. & pp. of **re-lay.**

re·lapse [rɪ'læps; ri'læps] *v.,* **-lapsed, -laps·ing,** *n.* —*v.i.* ①回復。②復發。③又陷入不良嗜好、壞行爲。—*n.* 復發。

re·laps·ing fever [rɪ'læpsɪŋ~; ri-'læpsiŋ~] 〖醫〗回歸熱。

***re·late** [rɪ'let; ri'leit] *v.,* **-lat·ed, -lat·ing.** —*v.t.* ①敍述；說。②使有關係；使關聯。③有親戚關係。I am not *related* to him in any way. 我與他絲毫沒有親戚關係。—*v.i.* ①有關係；關於〖常 to〗. This letter *relates* to the sale of the house. 這封信與賣屋有關係。②與人或事物協調或建立某種關係。

re·lat·ed [rɪ'letɪd; ri'leitid] *adj.* ①所敍述的；所陳述的。②有相互關係的；有關連的。③親戚的；同源的。④〖音樂〗(在樂音、和音上)有密切連繫的。—**ly,** *adv.* —**ness,** *n.*

‡**re·la·tion** [rɪ'leʃən; ri'leiʃən] *n.* ①敍述；述說。②(思想與意義上之)關係。the *relation* between cause and effect. 因果關係。③(常 *pl.*) **a.** (特殊之)關係。the *relations* between husband and wife. 夫妻間之關係。 **b.** 性行爲。④親戚。Is he any *relation* to you? 他是你的親戚嗎? ***bear no*** (***not much,*** etc.) ***relation to*** 與…無關係 (=be out of relation to). ***in*** (or ***with***) ***relation to*** 關於。—**less,** *adj.*

re·la·tion·al [rɪ'leʃən!; ri'leiʃənl] *adj.* ①關係的；表關係的。②親戚的。③〖文法〗表關係的。—**ly,** *adv.*

***re·la·tion·ship** [rɪ'leʃənˌʃɪp; ri'leiʃənʃip] *n.* ①親戚關係。What is the *relationship* between you and George? 你和喬治有甚麼親戚關係? ②關聯；關係。

rel·a·ti·val [ˌrɛlə'taɪvəl; ˌrelə'taivəl] *adj.* ①親戚的；親族的。②〖文法〗關係詞的。

***rel·a·tive** [ˈrɛlətɪv; ˈrelətiv] *n.* ①親戚;親族。②關係詞(尤指關係代名詞)。—*adj.* ①有關係的; 表關係的。②比較的。③相對的(爲 absolute 之對);相互的。East and west are *relative* terms. 東和西是相對的名詞。*relative to* a.關於;和…有關。b.和…成比例。

relative adverb 關係副詞。

relative clause 關係子句。

relative humidity 相對濕度。

***rel·a·tive·ly** [ˈrɛlətɪvlɪ; ˈrelətivli] *adv.* ①相對地;比較上。②相關地;關係上。③成比例地。*relatively speaking* 比較地說。

relative major 〖音樂〗關係大調。

relative minor 〖音樂〗關係小調。

relative pronoun 關係代名詞。

rel·a·tiv·ism [ˈrɛlətɪvɪzem; ˈrelətivizəm] *n.* 〖倫理〗相對說;相對主義。

rel·a·tiv·ist [ˈrɛlətɪvɪst; ˈrelətivist] *n.* ①〖倫理〗相對論者;相對主義者。②〖物理〗相對論者。—**ic,** *adj.*

rel·a·tiv·i·ty [ˌrɛləˈtɪvətɪ; ˌreləˈtiviti] *n.* ①相關;相對。②相對論。Einstein's theory of *relativity*. 愛因斯坦的相對論。

re·la·tor [rɪˈletə; riˈleitə] *n.* ①敍述者;陳述者。②〖法律〗告發人;原告。

***re·lax** [rɪˈlæks; riˈlæks] *v.t.* ①放鬆; 鬆弛。②放寬;鬆懈。③使(心神)輕鬆。—*v.i.* ①放鬆。②鬆懈。You must not *relax* in your efforts. 你不能鬆懈,要繼續努力。—**ed,** *adj.* —**er,** —**ed·ness,** *n.* —**ed·ly,** *adv.*

re·lax·ant [rɪˈlæksənt; riˈlæksənt] *adj.* 〖醫〗有緩和力的。—*n.* 〖醫〗緩和劑。

re·lax·a·tion [ˌrilæksˈeʃən; ˌri:lækˈseiʃən] *n.* ①鬆弛。②減輕; 緩和。③娛樂。④〖數學〗放鬆;張弛。

re·lay [rɪˈle; ri:ˈlei] *v.,* **-layed, -lay·ing,** *n.* —*v.t.* 接轉。—*v.i.* 〖電〗轉送。—*n.* ①新補充之人或物。②接力。to work in (*or* by) *relays.* 接力工作。③備替換之馬、犬等。④〖電〗繼電器。⑤(R-)〖美〗一系列的高度較低的通信衞星。⑥接力賽跑;接力賽跑中之一段的距離。

re-lay [ˌriˈle; ˈri:ˈlei] *v.t.,* **-laid, -lay·ing.** 再鋪設;再安置。

relay race 接力賽跑。

relay station 轉播電臺。

***re·lease** [rɪˈlis; riˈli:s] *v.,* **-leased, -leas·ing,** *n.* —*v.t.* ①解放; 解開; 釋放。to *release* a prisoner. 釋放囚犯。②解除;免除。③准予發表。④讓與(財產等); 放棄(權利等)。—*n.* ①解放;釋放。②解除;免除。③棄權;讓渡;讓渡證書。④准許發表、展覽或售賣等。⑤准許電影片上演;准予上演的影片。⑥使動的機械裝置;彈簧;鈎子。⑦擬在報章或電台發表的文章或聲明。a news *release.* 送給新聞機構發表的消息。—**ment, re·leas·er,** *n.*

re-lease [riˈlis; ri:ˈli:s] *v.t.,* **-leased, -leas·ing.** 訂新契約再租貸(土地、房屋等)。

re·leas·ee [rɪˌlisˈi; riˌli:ˈsi:] *n.* ①被免除債務者。②〖法律〗(權利、財產等之)受讓人。

re·lea·sor [rɪˈlisə; riˈli:sə] *n.* 〖法律〗棄權者;(權利、財產等之)讓渡者。

rel·e·gate [ˈrɛləˌget; ˈreligeit] *v.t.,* **-gat·ed, -gat·ing.** ①貶謫;貶黜。②放逐;驅逐。③丟棄; 拋棄。④置於不重要之地位〖to, into, out of〗。⑤使歸於(某屬、某類)。⑥移轉;委託。—**rel·e·ga·tion,** *n.*

re·lent [rɪˈlɛnt; riˈlent] *v.i.* ①變溫和。②變寬容;動憐憫〖toward〗。

re·lent·ing·ly [rɪˈlɛntɪŋlɪ; riˈlentiŋli] *adv.* 寬和地;緩和地;憐憫地。

re·lent·less [rɪˈlɛntlɪs; riˈlentlis] *adj.* 無慈悲心的;殘酷的;不放鬆的。—**ly,** *adv.*

rel·e·van·cy [ˈrɛləvənsɪ; ˈrelivənsi] *n.* 切題;中肯。(亦作 **relevance**)

rel·e·vant [ˈrɛləvənt; ˈrelivənt] *adj.* 有關的;切題的;中肯的。matters *relevant* to the subject. 與該問題有關的各節。—**ly,** *adv.*

re·li·a·bil·i·ty [rɪˌlaɪəˈbɪlətɪ; riˌlaiəˈbiliti] *n.* 可靠性;可信賴性。

***re·li·a·ble** [rɪˈlaɪəbl; riˈlaiəbl] *adj.* 可靠的;可信賴的。*reliable* sources of information. 消息之可靠的來源。—**ness,** *n.* —**re·li·a·bly,** *adv.*

re·li·ance [rɪˈlaɪəns; riˈlaiəns] *n.* ①信賴;信任;依賴。②信心。③所依賴的東西。

re·li·ant [rɪˈlaɪənt; riˈlaiənt] *adj.* ①有依賴的。②有信心的。③靠自己的。—**ly,** *adv.*

***rel·ic** [ˈrɛlɪk; ˈrelik] *n.* ①遺跡; 遺物; 遺俗。precious *relics* of ancient day. 古代的寶貴遺物。②聖徒遺物;聖徒遺骸。③紀念物。④(*pl.*) 遺骸; 廢墟。(亦作 **relique**) —**like,** *adj.*

rel·ict [ˈrɛlɪkt; ˈrelikt] *n.* ①殘存的動植物。②〖罕〗未亡人;寡婦。③生存者;殘存者。

‡re·lief [rɪˈlif; riˈli:f, rəˈl-] *n.* ①(痛苦、負擔等之)減輕;解除;解救。②慰藉。To his great *relief,* the difficulties were overcome. 使他大爲欣慰,困難都克服了。③調劑。④賑濟;救濟。to provide *relief* for refugees. 賑濟難民。⑤換班;接替。⑥輪班者;接替者。⑦浮雕。*relief* printing. 凸版印刷術。⑧顯著;明顯。⑨地面的凹凸起伏。⑩鮮明;顯著; 輪廓鮮明。*in relief* a. 從表面突出的。b. 鮮明的; 明顯的。*on relief* 接受救濟的。—**less,** *adj.*

relief map 立體圖;模型地圖;有等高線的地圖。

relief pitcher 〖棒球〗候補投手; 臨時換上的投手。

relief tube 太空人使用之導尿管。

re·li·er [rɪˈlaɪə; riˈlaiə] *n.* 信賴者;依賴者。

re·liev·a·ble [rɪˈlivəbl; riˈli:vəbl] *adj.* ①可救濟的; 可援助的。②可安慰的; 可減輕的。③可使浮凸的;可使明顯的;可襯托的。④可換班的;可被接替的。

***re·lieve** [rɪˈliv; riˈli:v] *v.t.,* **-lieved, -liev·ing.** ①減輕;使較少; 使輕易。②解除;免除。Your coming *relieves* me of the trouble of writing a letter. 你的來臨使我免了寫信的麻煩。③解救;援助。④襯托;使明顯; 使免除單調。⑤換班; 接替。to *relieve* a sentry. 換哨。⑥〖棒球〗更換投手。—*v.i.* 〖棒球〗充任更換的投手。*relieve nature* (or *oneself*) 大便;小便。

re·lie·vo [rɪˈlivo; riˈli:vou] *n., pl.* **-vos.** 浮雕; 凸形。*alto* (*basso, mezzo*) *relievo* 高(低、中)浮雕。*in relievo* 顯著;明顯。

‡re·li·gion [rɪˈlɪdʒən; riˈlidʒən] *n.* ①宗教。②宗教信仰。What is your *religion?* 你信奉何教? ③神聖之物; 必爲之事。④宗教生活;修道生活。⑤(*pl.*)〖古〗宗教儀式。⑥〖古〗嚴格的信仰。—**less,** *adj.*

re·li·gion·ism [rɪˈlɪdʒənɪzəm; riˈlidʒənizəm] *n.* ①過度的宗教熱忱。②僞裝的宗教熱忱;虛僞的信仰。

re·li·gion·ist [rɪˈlɪdʒənɪst; riˈlidʒənist] *n.* 有宗教狂熱的人;宗教心極强的人;宗教狂。

re·lig·i·ose [rɪˌlɪdʒɪˈos; riˌlidʒiˈous] *adj.* 狂熱信仰的;有狂熱信仰的。

re·lig·i·os·i·ty [rɪˌlɪdʒɪˈɑsətɪ; riˌlidʒiˈɔsiti] *n.* ①宗教心;宗教情感;信心。②狂熱

的信仰。

ː**re·li·gious** [rɪˈlɪdʒəs; riˈlidʒəs] *adj., n., pl.* **-gious.** —*adj.* ①宗教的;宗教上的。a *religious* house. 修道院;僧院。②信奉宗教的; 虔誠的。③嚴密的; 謹愼的。*religious* care. 嚴謹。—*n.* ①僧侶;尼姑;修士;修女。②僧尼的集合稱。***the religious*** 虔誠的信徒。—**ly,** *adv.* —**ness,** *n.*

re·lin·quish [rɪˈlɪŋkwɪʃ; riˈliŋkwiʃ] *v.t.* ①放棄。②放手;放鬆。③讓出。—**ment,** *n.*

rel·i·quar·y [ˈrɛləˌkwɛrɪ; ˈrelikwəri] *n., pl.* **-quar·ies.** 聖骨箱;聖物箱; 遺物盒。

re·liq·ui·ae [rɪˈlɪkwɪˌi; riˈlikwii:] *n. pl.* ①遺物。②遺作。③〖地質〗動植物之化石。④〖植物〗枯葉(仍留枝上者)。

rel·ish** [ˈrɛlɪʃ; ˈreliʃ] *n.* ①美味; 滋味。②調味品;香料。Hunger is the best *relish* for food. 饑不擇食。③喜好; 胃口; 享受。He eats with great *relish.* 他吃得津津有味。④少量; 些許。have no relish for*** 不喜;不好。—*v.i.* ①有…的味道;有…的氣味。②愉快; 快活。—*v.t.* 愛好; 喜好。A cat *relishes* cream. 貓喜歡乳酪。—**a·ble,** *adj.*

re·live [riˈlɪv; ˈri:ˈliv] *v.,* **-lived, -liv·ing.** —*v.t.* 再生;再體驗。—*v.i.* 再生;復甦。

re·load [riˈlod; ˈri:ˈloud] *v.t.* 再裝;再裝(砲彈等)。

re·load·er [riˈlodɚ; ri:ˈloudə] *n.* (火車、輪船等之)自動輸煤機。

re·lo·cate [riˈloket; ˈri:louˈkeit] *v.t.,* **-cat·ed, -cat·ing.** ①再定…之位置。②徙置於另一新地方。—**re·lo·ca·tion,** *n.*

rel. pron. relative pronoun.

***re·luc·tance** [rɪˈlʌktəns; riˈlʌktəns] *n.* ①不願;勉强。to show *reluctance* to do something. 表示不願作某事。②因勉强而行動遲緩。③〖電〗磁阻。(亦作 **reluctancy**)

***re·luc·tant** [rɪˈlʌktənt; riˈlʌktənt] *adj.* ①不願的; 勉强的。He is *reluctant* to accept. 他不願接受。②因不願而遲緩的。③難以處理的;難駕馭的;頑抗的。—**ly,** *adv.*

rel·uc·tiv·i·ty [ˌrɛləkˈtɪvətɪ; ˌreləkˈtiviti] *n.* 〖物理〗磁阻率。

re·lume [riˈlum, -ˈljum; ri:ˈlju:m] *v.t.,* **-lumed, -lum·ing.** 〖古,詩〗再點燃;再照明;再照耀。(亦作 **relumine**)

***re·ly** [rɪˈlaɪ; riˈlai] *v.i.,* **-lied, -ly·ing.** 依賴; 信賴 〖on, upon〗. Never *rely* on a broken reed. 永勿信賴不可靠之人。

REM rapid eye movement.

ː**re·main** [rɪˈmen; riˈmein] *v.i.* ①停留;居住。②繼續;依然。He *remained* poor all his life. 他依然貧窮。③剩下;剩餘。If you take (away) 7 from 10, 3 *remains.* 10 減 7 餘 3。④保留。

***re·main·der** [rɪˈmendɚ; riˈmeində] *n.* ①餘物;餘數;殘餘。②(*pl.*)〖集郵〗被廢用後尙剩餘的郵票。③出版商所留下的不再出售的書的一册。—*adj.* 餘下的; 剩下的。—*v.t.* 當殘餘物出售或處理。

re·main·der·ship [rɪˈmendɚˌʃɪp; riˈmeindəʃip] *n.* 〖法律〗殘留權;繼承權。

re·mains [rɪˈmenz; riˈmeinz] *n. pl.* ①殘物;殘餘。②遺跡;遺物。③殘存者;遺族;生還者。④遺體; 遺骸; 屍體。⑤遺稿。⑥遺風。⑦(古生物之)化石。

re·make [rɪˈmek; ˈri:ˈmeik] *v.,* **-made, -mak·ing,** *n.* —*v.t.* ①再做;重做;改做。②〖電影〗重拍。—*n.* 重拍的電影或劇本。

re·man [riˈmæn; ri:ˈmæn] *v.t.,* **-manned, -man·ning.** ①再供以人員;再派人給…。②使恢復剛勇;使恢復男子氣概。

re·mand [rɪˈmænd; riˈmɑ:nd] *v.t.* ①送回。②命令回返。③將(犯人或被告)再送回牢獄;還押。④將(案件)發回下級法院重審。—*n.* (亦作 **remandment**)①送回。②還押。③發回一案件複審。④召還。

remand home 〖英〗少年拘留所。

ː**re·mark** [rɪˈmɑrk; riˈmɑ:k, rəˈm-] *v.t.* ①談起;述及;評論。②注意;留意。—*v.i.* 評論;談論〖常 on, upon〗. This point has often been *remarked* upon. 此點常被談論。—*n.* ①短語;短評;註;摘要。 to make a few *remarks.* 說幾句話。②注意;留意。We saw nothing worthy of *remark.* 我們看不到値得注意之物。

re-mark [ˈriˈmɑrk; ˈri:ˈmɑ:k] *v.t.* ①重作標記。②〖商〗改標價。

***re·mark·a·ble** [rɪˈmɑrkəbl; riˈmɑ:kəbl] *adj.* 値得注意的;不平常的。a *remarkable* change. 顯著的變化。—**ness,** *n.* —**re·mark·a·bly,** *adv.*

re·mar·riage [riˈmærɪdʒ; ˈri:ˈmæridʒ] *n.* 再婚。

re·mar·ry [riˈmærɪ; ˈri:ˈmæri] *v.t. & v.i.,* **-ried, -ry·ing.** 再婚;再娶;再嫁。

re·me·di·a·ble [rɪˈmidɪəbl; riˈmi:diəbl] *adj.* 可補救的;可治療的;可修補的;可矯正的。—**ness,** *n.* —**re·me·di·a·bly,** *adv.*

re·me·di·al [rɪˈmidɪəl; riˈmi:diəl] *adj.* ①治療(上)的。②補救的。③修補的;矯正的。—**ly,** *adv.*

re·me·di·a·tion [rɪˌmidɪˈeʃən; riˌmi:diˈeiʃən] *n.* 矯正;補救。

rem·e·di·less [ˈrɛmɪdɪlɪs; ˈremidilis] *adj.* 無法補救的; 無法醫治的; 無法修補的。

***rem·e·dy** [ˈrɛmədɪ; ˈremidi] *n., pl.* **-dies,** *v.,* **-died, -dy·ing.** —*n.* ①藥物;治療法。②補救方法。This is the only *remedy* for the situation. 此爲解救這局面之唯一方法。—*v.t.* ①治療。②修理;補救。③抵銷。

ː**re·mem·ber** [rɪˈmɛmbɚ; riˈmembə] *v.t.* ①追憶;憶及。②記得;記着。I *remember* having met her. 我記得曾經見過她。③牢記;不忘。*Remember* what I told you. 記住我告訴你的話。④問候;致意。Please *remember* me to your brother. 請代向令兄問候。⑤給與餽贈;報酬;給小費。Grandfather *remembered* us all in his will. 祖父在他的遺囑中給我們大家遺贈物。—*v.i.* ①記憶。②有記憶力。Dogs *remember.* 狗有記憶力。—**a·ble,** *adj.* —**er,** *n.*

re·mem·brance** [rɪˈmɛmbrəns; riˈmembrəns] *n.* ①記憶。②紀念物;紀念。③記憶力。It has escaped my *remembrance.* 我已把它忘記。④(*pl.*)問候;致意。Give my *remembrances* to your sister. 請代向令姊致候。in remembrance of*** 紀念。

re·mem·branc·er [rɪˈmɛmbrənsɚ; riˈmembrənsə] *n.* ①記憶喚起者; 提醒者。②紀念物。③(R-)〖英〗爲王室收債之官吏(= King's *or* Queen's Remembrancer). ④(R-)〖英〗高等法院之官員。

re·mil·i·ta·rize [riˈmɪlətəˌraɪz; ri:ˈmilitəraiz] *v.t.,* **-rized, -riz·ing.** 重整軍備;再武裝。—**re·mil·i·ta·ri·za·tion,** *n.*

***re·mind** [rɪˈmaɪnd; riˈmaind] *v.t.* 使憶起;提醒。This *reminds* me of a story. 這使我想起一個故事。

re·mind·er [rɪˈmaɪndɚ; riˈmaində] *n.* 提醒者;助人記憶之事物。

re·mind·ful [rɪˈmaɪndful; riˈmaindful] *adj.* ①使憶起的;提醒的〖of〗. ②想到的。

rem·i·nisce [ˌrɛməˈnɪs; ˌremiˈnis] *v.i.*, **-nisced, -nisc·ing.** 說往事;回憶;話舊。
rem·i·nis·cence [ˌrɛməˈnɪsn̩s; ˌremiˈnisns] *n.* ①回憶;回想;追懷。②記憶中之事物。③喚起記憶之事物。④(常*pl.*) 回憶(錄)。
rem·i·nis·cent [ˌrɛməˈnɪsn̩t; ˌremiˈnisnt] *adj.* ①回憶的;喜回憶的;喜談論往事的。②引起回憶的;引起聯想的〖常 of〗。—**ly,** *adv.*
re·mint [riˈmɪnt; riːˈmint] *v.t.* 再鑄;改鑄(貨幣)。
re·mise [rɪˈmaɪz; riˈmaiz] *v.t.*, **-mised, -mis·ing.** 〖法律〗放棄對…之權利要求;讓渡。
re·miss [rɪˈmɪs; riˈmis] *adj.* ①疏忽的;不小心的。②無氣力的。—**ly,** *adv.* —**ness,** *n.*
re·mis·si·ble [rɪˈmɪsəbl̩; riˈmisibl] *adj.* 可寬恕的;可赦免的。—**ness,** *n.*
re·mis·sion [rɪˈmɪʃən; riˈmiʃən] *n.* ①免除;釋免。②赦免;容恕。③和緩;減輕。
re·mis·sive [rɪˈmɪsɪv; riˈmisiv] *adj.* ①減輕的。②赦免的。—**ly,** *adv.* —**ness,** *n.*
*__re·mit__ [rɪˈmɪt; riˈmit] *v.*, **-mit·ted, -mit·ting,** *n.* —*v.t.* ①匯寄。to *remit* money to a person. 匯款給某人。②緩和;減輕。③赦免;豁免。to *remit* a sin. 赦罪。④將(案件)發回下級法院重審。⑤送回(監獄);放回原處。⑥將…送呈某人請求裁決。⑦延期。—*v.i.* ①匯款。Enclosed is our bill; please *remit*. 奉上帳單,敬請匯款。②變少;和緩;鬆懈。—*n.* (案件)轉移(原審法院)。—**ta·ble,** *adj.*
re·mit·tal [rɪˈmɪtl̩; riˈmitl] *n.* = **remission.**
re·mit·tance [rɪˈmɪtn̩s; riˈmitəns] *n.* ①匯寄之款。②匯款。(亦作**remitment**)
remittance man 寄居外國而靠國內匯款生活的人。
re·mit·tee [rɪmɪˈti; rimiˈtiː] *n.* 受款人。
re·mit·tent [rɪˈmɪtn̩t; riˈmitn̩t] *adj.* 忽輕忽重的;間歇性的;弛張的(病、高熱等)。—*n.* 弛張熱。—**re·mit·tence,** *n.* —**ly,** *adv.*
re·mit·ter [rɪˈmɪtɚ; riˈmitə] *n.* ①匯款人。②赦免者。③〖法律〗(以前情況或權力之)恢復;復權。④〖法律〗將案件移送(低級法院)審理。
re·mit·tor [rɪˈmɪtɚ; riˈmitə] *n.* 〖法律〗匯款人。
*__rem·nant__ [ˈrɛmnənt; ˈremnənt] *n.* ①殘餘;遺物。a *remnant* sale. 出清底貨之減價出賣。②剩餘的布料。③痕跡;遺跡。—*adj.* 殘餘的;遺留的。—**al,** *adj.*
re·mod·el [riˈmɑdl̩; ˈriːˈmɔdl] *v.t.*, **-el(l)ed, -el·(l)ing.** ①再塑。②修改;改作。
re·mold [riˈmold; ˈriːˈmould] *v.t.* 再造形;再塑。(亦作 **remould**)
re·mon·e·tize [riˈmɑnɪˌtaɪz; riːˈmʌnitaiz] *v.t.*, **-tized, -tiz·ing.** 使(金屬)再做貨幣使用;使(貨幣)再通用。
re·mon·strance [rɪˈmɑnstrəns; riˈmɔnstrəns] *n.* ①抗議。②忠告;告誡;諫疏。
re·mon·strant [rɪˈmɑnstrənt; riˈmɔnstrənt] *adj.* ①忠告的;諫言的;告誡的。②抗議的。—*n.* ①忠告者;諫言者;告誡者。②抗議者。③(R-)荷蘭神學家 Arminius 派的信仰者。—**ly,** *adv.*
re·mon·strate [rɪˈmɑnstret; riˈmɔnstreit] *v.*, **-strat·ed, -strat·ing.** —*v.i.* ①抗議;抗辯。②忠告;規勸〖with〗. —*v.t.* 抗議;抗辯。—**re·mon·stra·tor,** *n.*
re·mon·stra·tion [ˌrimɑnˈstreʃən; ˌriːmɔnˈstreiʃən] *n.* ①抗議。②規諫;勸告。
re·mon·stra·tive [rɪˈmɑnstrətɪv; riˈmɔnstrətiv] *adj.* ①忠告的。②抗議的。
rem·o·ra [ˈrɛmərə; ˈremərə] *n.* ①印魚。②〖古〗妨礙;障礙物。
*__re·morse__ [rɪˈmɔrs; riˈmɔːs] *n.* 懊悔;悔恨。without *remorse.* 無悔意。
re·morse·ful [rɪˈmɔrsfəl; riˈmɔːsful] *adj.* 懊悔的;悔恨的。—**ly,** *adv.* —**ness,** *n.*
re·morse·less [rɪˈmɔrslɪs; riˈmɔːslis] *adj.* 不知懊悔的;無惻隱心的。—**ly,** *adv.*
*__re·mote__ [rɪˈmot; riˈmout] *adj.*, **-mot·er, -mot·est,** *n.* —*adj.* ①遠的。②古的。③遠親的。a *remote* relative. 遠親。④輕微的。a *remote* possibility. 極少的可能性。⑤隱祕的。⑥遠隔的;抽象的。⑦非直接的。⑧冷淡的。—*n.* (亦作 **nemo**)〖電視、廣播〗現場轉播節目。—**ly,** *adv.* —**ness,** *n.*
remote control (以無線電等所作之)遙控。
re·mote-con·trol [riˈmotkənˈtrol; riːˈmoutkənˈtroul] *adj.* 藉遙控的。(亦作 **remote-controlled**)
re·mount [riˈmaʊnt; riːˈmaunt] *v.t.* & *v.i.* ①再上(馬等)。②再爬上(山等)。③供給新馬。④重安裝(砲等)。⑤回溯。—*n.* 新馬;預備作爲補充之馬;新馬之補充。
re·mov·a·ble [rɪˈmuvəbl̩; riˈmuːvəbl] *adj.* ①可移動的;可除去的。②可免職的。③〖數學〗可去的。—**re·mov·a·bil·i·ty,** *n.*
*__re·mov·al__ [rɪˈmuvl̩; riˈmuːvəl] *n.* ①撤除;排除。②遷移;移動。③免職;解職。the *removal* of an official. 一官員的解職。
‡**re·move** [rɪˈmuv; riˈmuːv] *v.*, **-moved, -mov·ing,** *n.* —*v.t.* ①(自某處)移動;取去。*Remove* your hat. 脫去你的帽子。②除去;排除。③離去;遷移。④免職;開除。to *remove* a boy from school. 開除一學生。⑤殺死。***remove oneself*** 離開。—*v.i.* ①遷移;移居。They have *removed* from this town. 他們已遷離此城。②離開;消失。—*n.* ①移動;遷移。Three *removes* are as bad as a fire. 遷居三次不啻遭火一場;家搬三次窮。②等級;程度;距離。③親戚等次;關係程度。④〖英〗(學童之)跳級。⑤〖英〗一道菜。
*__re·moved__ [rɪˈmuvd; riˈmuːvd] *adj.* ①遠離的。②親屬關係相隔一等或多等的。
re·mov·er [rɪˈmuvɚ; riˈmuːvə] *n.* ①移運者。②除去物。③(法院之)移轉管轄。
re·mu·ner·ate [rɪˈmjunəˌret; riˈmjuːnəreit] *v.t.*, **-at·ed, -at·ing.** 報酬;酬勞。
re·mu·ner·a·tion [rɪˌmjunəˈreʃən; riˌmjuːnəˈreiʃən] *n.* 報酬;薪水。
re·mu·ner·a·tive [rɪˈmjunəˌretɪv; riˈmjuːnərətiv] *adj.* 有報酬的;有利益的。
re·mu·ner·a·tor [rɪˈmjunəˌretɚ; riˈmjuːnəˌreitə] *n.* 報償者;酬勞者。
Re·mus [ˈriməs; ˈriːməs] *n.* 〖羅馬神話〗雷摩斯(與其孿生兄弟 Romulus 同受狼哺乳,後爲 Romulus 所殺)。
*__ren·ais·sance__ [ˌrɛnəˈzɑns, rɪˈnesn̩s; rəˈneisəns, riˈn-, -sɑːns, -sɔːns] *n.* 再生;新生;復興。***the Renaissance*** **a.** 文藝復興(歐洲的藝術、文學之復興運動)。**b.** 文藝復興時期。**c.** 文藝復興時期的藝術、建築等之形式。—*adj.* 文藝復興的;其藝術、建築等的。
re·nal [ˈrinl̩; ˈriːnl] *adj.* 腎臟的;關於腎臟的。
re·name [riˈnem; ˈriːˈneim] *v.t.*, **-named, -nam·ing.** 予以新名;再命名。
Ren·ard [ˈrɛnəd; ˈrenəd] *n.* = **Reynard.**
re·nas·cence [rɪˈnæsn̩s; riˈnæsns] *n.* ①新生;再生;復活;復興。②(R-) = **Renaissance.**

re·nas·cent [rɪˈnæsn̩t; riˈnæsnt] *adj.* 再生的;復活的;復興的。

Re·nault [rəˈno; rəˈnou] *n.* 雷諾(Louis, 1843–1918, 法國法學家, 1907 年得諾貝爾和平獎)。

ren·con·tre [rɛnˈkɑntɚ; renˈkɔntə] *n.* =**rencounter.**

ren·coun·ter, ren·coun·tre [rɛnˈkauntɚ; renˈkauntə] *n.* ①衝突;決鬥。②偶遇。—*v.t.* & *v.i.* ①衝突;爭鬥。②邂逅。

***rend** [rɛnd; rend] *v.*, **rent, rend·ing.** —*v.t.* ①撕;扯破。*rent* to pieces. 撕成碎片。②割裂;使分裂。③干擾;震動。④強使分離〖常 away, off, up〗。⑤(因憤怒或悲傷)撕破衣裳或拉頭髮。—*v.i.* ①散開;揭開。The mist *rends.* 霧散開。②分裂。—**er,** *n.* —**i·ble,** *adj.*

‡ren·der [ˈrɛndɚ; ˈrendə] *v.t.* ①使成;致使。An accident has *rendered* him helpless. 一件意外使得他束手無策。②給與。③報答;報復。to *render* thanks. 答謝。④納付;納貢。⑤扮演;演唱;演奏。⑥報告;呈遞。The treasurer *rendered* an account of all the money spent. 財務員呈遞了一個所有費用的報告。⑦翻譯。to *render* a passage into English. 將一段文字翻譯成爲英文。⑧放棄;投降。⑨煎熬(脂肪)。⑩表示(服從,關心等)。⑪〖法律〗給付。⑫正式宣布;傳遞。⑬表現;描繪。⑭還給;恢復〖常 back〗。***render good for evil*** (***blow for blow***) 以德報怨(以牙還牙)。***render one a service*** (or ***render a service to one***) 爲某人服務;幫忙某人。—*v.i.* ①報酬。②煎熬。—**a·ble,** *adj.* —**er,** *n.*

ren·der·ing [ˈrɛndərɪŋ; ˈrendəriŋ] *n.* ①翻譯;譯文。②表現;表演;演奏。③精煉油脂。④牆壁之初次塗泥。

rendering works (作 *sing.* 解) 處理家畜屍體爲脂肪、皮革、肥料的工廠。(亦作 **rendering plant**)

ren·dez·vous [ˈrɑndəˌvu; ˈrɔndivuː] *n., pl.* **-vous** [-ˌvuz; -vuːz], *v.,* **-voused** [-vud; -vuːd], **-vous·ing** [-ˌvuɪŋ; -vuːiŋ]. —*n.* ①約會;集會;集合。②約會地;集會地。—*v.t.* & *v.i.* 集合;集會;約見。

ren·di·tion [rɛnˈdɪʃən; renˈdiʃən] *n.* ①翻譯。②對音樂或劇本之解釋;表演;演奏。

ren·e·gade [ˈrɛnɪˌged; ˈrenigeid] *n., adj., v.,* **-gad·ed, -gad·ing.** —*n.* ①叛教者。②叛黨者。—*adj.* 叛教的;變節的。—*v.i.* ①成爲叛教者;成爲變節者。②叛教;變節。

re·nege [rɪˈnɪg; riˈniːg] *v.,* **-neged, -neg·ing,** *n.* —*v.i.* ①〖牌戲〗手中有可跟之牌而違例不跟。②〖俗〗違背諾言;背信;毀約。—*v.t.*〖古〗否認;放棄。—*n.*〖牌戲〗有牌而不跟。

re·ne·go·ti·ate [ˌrinɪˈgoʃɪˌet; ˌriːniˈgouʃiːeit] *v.t.* & *v.i.,* **-at·ed, -at·ing.** ①再協商。②〖政府〗再審查。—**re·ne·go·ti·a·ble,** *adj.* —**re·ne·go·ti·a·tion,** *n.*

***re·new** [rɪˈnju; riˈnjuː] *v.t.* ①更新;恢復。to *renew* one's youth. 恢復青春。②再始;復始。③重訂。to *renew* a contract. 重訂契約。④換新;補充;補足。—*v.i.* ①再始。②更新;重訂。③恢復。—**er,** *n.*

re·new·a·ble [rɪˈnjuəbl̩; riˈnjuːəbl] *adj.* 可更新的;可繼續有效的(契約);可修整的。

re·new·al [rɪˈnjuəl; riˈnjuːəl] *n.* ①更新;復始;恢復。②更換。③繼續。

re·new·ed·ly [rɪˈnjuɪdlɪ; riˈnjuːidli] *adv.* 重新地;再度。

ren·i·form [ˈrɛnəˌfɔrm; ˈrenifɔːm] *adj.* 腎臟形的。

ren·net¹ [ˈrɛnɪt; ˈrenit] *n.* ①牛犢第四胃之內膜。②該胃膜的凝乳。③用於凝乳之物。

ren·net² *n.* 法國產的一種蘋果。

ren·nin [ˈrɛnɪn; ˈrenin] *n.*〖生化〗凝乳酶。

re·nom·i·nate [riˈnɑməˌnet; riːˈnɔmineit] *v.t.,* **-nat·ed, -nat·ing.** 再提名。—**re·nom·i·na·tion,** *n.*

***re·nounce** [rɪˈnauns; riˈnauns] *v.,* **-nounced, -nounc·ing.** —*v.t.* ①放棄。He *renounces* his claim to the money. 他放棄對這筆錢的要求。②否認;與…斷絕關係。—*v.i.* 正式投降。—**a·ble, re·nun·ci·a·ble,** *adj.* —**ment, re·nounc·er,** *n.*

ren·o·vate [ˈrɛnəˌvet; ˈrenouveit] *v.t.,* **-vat·ed, -vat·ing.** ①革新;使變新。②修理。—**ren·o·va·tion, ren·o·va·tor, ren·o·va·ter,** *n.*

***re·nown** [rɪˈnaun; riˈnaun] *n.* 名望;聲譽。a man of great *renown.* 極有聲望之人。—**less,** *adj.*

re·nowned [rɪˈnaund; riˈnaund] *adj.* 著名的。—**ly,** *adv.* —**ness,** *n.*

rent¹** [rɛnt; rent] *n.* ①租金。land *rent.* 地租。②〖經濟〗耕地或地產之純利。③生產事業之純利。for rent*** 出租的。house *for rent.* 吉屋召租。—*v.t.* ①租用。②出租。

rent² *v.* pt. & pp. of **rend.** —*n.* ①破裂處;裂口。②破裂;不和。—*adj.* 破裂的;破碎的。

rent·a·ble [ˈrɛntəbl̩; ˈrentəbl] *adj.* 可租的;可出租的。

rent·al [ˈrɛntl̩; ˈrentl] *n.* ①租金總額。②租金收入。③出租的公寓(房子)。④=**rent roll.** —*adj.* 租賃的。

rental library 出租圖書館。

rent charge (依遺囑或契約,土地所有權的繼承人應向第三人繳納之)定期地租。

rent control 政府對租金之控制。

rente [rɑ̃t; rɑ̃t] *n., pl.* **rentes** [rɑ̃t; rɑ̃t].〖法〗①歲收;年金。②(*pl.*)法國政府發行之長期公債;其利息。

rent·er [ˈrɛntɚ; ˈrentə] *n.* 租用者。

rent-free [ˈrɛntˈfri; ˈrentˈfriː] *adj.* & *adv.* 不收租金的(地)。

ren·tier [ˌrɑ̃ˈtje; ˈrɔntiei, rɑ̃tje] *n., pl.* **-tiers** [-tɪe; -tiei].〖法〗靠地租、利息等固定收入度日之人。

rent roll 租摺;地租帳。(亦作**rent-roll**)

rent service 代地租之勞役。

rent strike 〖美〗房租罷繳(以抗議增加租金及服務不佳等)。

re·nun·ci·ate [rɪˈnʌnsɪˌet; riˈnʌnsieit] *v.t.,* **-at·ed, -at·ing.** 棄絕;拒絕。

re·nun·ci·a·tion [rɪˌnʌnsɪˈeʃən; riˌnʌnsiˈeiʃən] *n.* ①放棄;棄絕。②否認;拒絕。③自制;克己。—**re·nun·ci·a·tive, re·nun·ci·a·to·ry,** *adj.*

ren·voi [rɛnˈvɔɪ; renˈvɔi] *n.* ①驅逐外人(尤指外交官)出境。②將國際法中管轄權發生疑義案件,向當地以外有管轄權法院之移轉。

re·o·pen [riˈopən; ˈriːˈoupən] *v.t.* ①再打開。②再討論。③繼續。—*v.i.* 再開始。

re·or·der [riˈɔrdɚ; riːˈɔːdə] *v.t.* ①再命令。②再整理。③重訂(貨物)。—*v.i.*〖商〗重訂(貨物)。—*n.*〖商〗重訂貨物。

re·or·gan·i·za·tion [ˌriɔrgənəˈzeʃən; ˈriːˌɔːgənaiˈzeiʃən] *n.* ①重新組織;改組。②再編制。③整理。

re·or·gan·ize [riˈɔrgəˌnaɪz; ˈriːˈɔːgənaiz] *v.t.* & *v.i.,* **-ized, -iz·ing.** 重新組織;改組。

re·or·i·ent [*v.* riˈɔrɪɛnt; riːˈɔːrient

adj. ri'ɔrɪənt; ri:'ɔ:riənt) *v.t.* & *v.i.* 再改方向;再適應(環境);再定方位。—*adj.* 再改方向的。—**a·tion,** *n.*

rep¹ 〔rɛp; rep〕 *n.* 有稜線或稜條的編製物。(亦作 **repp, reps**) —**ped,** *adj.*

rep² *n.* 放蕩者。

rep³ *n.* 〖俚〗爲 repertory, repetition, representative, reputation 諸字之略寫形。

Rep. ①Representative. ②Republic. ③Republican. **rep.** ①repeat. ②report. ③reported. ④reporter. ⑤representative. ⑥republic.

re·pack·age 〔ri'pækədʒ; ri:'pækidʒ〕 *v.t.,* **-aged, -ag·ing.** 重新包裝。

re·paint 〔ri'pent; ri:'peint〕 *v.t.* 再油漆;再着色;再繪畫。—*n.* 重漆或畫過的部分。

***re·pair¹** 〔rɪ'pɛr; ri'pɛə〕 *v.t.* ①修補;修理。②補救;補償。How can I *repair* the harm done? 我怎能賠償這損害呢? —*n.* ①(常 *pl.*)修補;修理。This house needs a lot of *repairs.* 此屋需大加修理。②可應用之狀態。Keep the roads in *repair.* 保持道路之完好。③修理狀況。The house was in bad *repair.* 這屋子失修(破損不堪)。④(*pl.*)(會計)維護保養費用。—**er,** *n.*

re·pair² *v.i.* 往(某地);赴。—*n.* 常往的地方;巢窟。

re·pair·a·ble 〔rɪ'pɛrəbl; ri'pɛərəbl〕 *adj.* 可修補的;可修理的;可補救的;可補償的。

re·pair·man 〔rɪ'pɛr,mæn; ri'pɛəmæn〕 *n., pl.* **-men.** 修補工人。

repair shop 修理廠。

rep·a·ra·ble 〔'rɛpərəbl; 'repərəbl〕 *adj.* ①可修繕的。②能補救的;可補償的。

rep·a·ra·tion 〔,rɛpə'reʃən; ,repə'reiʃən〕 *n.* ①補償。②(*pl.*)賠款;賠償。③修復;修理。④=**repair**④.

re·par·a·tive 〔rɪ'pærətɪv; ri'pærətiv〕 *adj.* ①修繕的。②賠償的。③恢復的。(亦作 **reparatory**)

rep·ar·tee 〔,rɛpə'ti; ,repɑ:'ti:〕 *n.* ①捷巧應答(之才能)。②有捷巧應答之談話。

re·par·ti·tion 〔,ripɑr'tɪʃən; ,ri:pɑ:'tiʃən〕 *n.* ①區分;分配。②再區分;再分配。—*v.t.* 再區分;再分配。

re·pass 〔ri'pæs; 'ri:'pɑ:s〕 *v.i.* 再通過;回頭通過。—*v.t.* ①再渡過(河、海等)。②再通過(門、通路等)。③再通過(議案)。

re·past 〔rɪ'pæst; ri'pɑ:st〕 *n.* 餐;食事;食物。a light *repast.* 點心。—*v.i.* 進餐〖常 on, upon〗。

re·pa·tri·ate 〔ri'petrɪ,et; ri:'pætrieit〕 *v.t.* 遣返。—*v.i.* 歸國。—*n.* 被遣返之人。—**re·pa·tri·a·tion,** *n.*

***re·pay** 〔rɪ'pe; 'ri:'pei〕 *v.,* **-paid, -pay·ing.** —*v.t.* ①付還。②報答;回報。—*v.i.* 報答;償還;酬答。God will *repay.* 上天會有報應的。

re·pay·a·ble 〔rɪ'peəbl; ri:'peiəbl〕 *adj.* ①可付還的;可回報的。②必須付還(回報)的。

re·pay·ment 〔rɪ'pemənt; ri:'peimənt〕 *n.* ①償還;賠償。②報答;報酬。③付還之款。

***re·peal** 〔rɪ'pil; ri'pi:l〕 *v.t.* ①撤銷;撤回。②廢止;廢棄。—*n.* ①撤銷。②廢止。He voted for the *repeal* of that law. 他投票贊成廢止那一法律。

re·peal·er 〔rɪ'pilə; ri'pi:lə〕 *n.* ①撤銷者;廢止者。②〖英史〗主張廢止英國與愛爾蘭合併者。③〖美〗廢止某一條早期法律的議案。

‡re·peat 〔rɪ'pit; ri'pi:t〕 *v.t.* ①重做;重複。to *repeat* a mistake. 重犯一錯誤。②重說;再述。③誦讀;背誦。④跟着說;照樣講。*Repeat* the oath after me. 跟我宣讀誓言。⑤向他人轉述。—*v.i.* ①重做;覆述。②重發生。③(在一次選舉中)投票多於一次。④(小數等)循環。***repeat itself*** 以後再發生。History *repeats itself.* 歷史會重演。***repeat oneself*** 覆述。—*n.* ①重複;重述。②重複之物;重複之處。③〖音樂〗重覆句;反覆符號。④(電視、廣播之)重播節目。—**a·bil·i·ty,** *n.* —**a·ble,** *adj.*

***re·peat·ed** 〔rɪ'pitɪd; ri'pi:tid〕 *adj.* 再三的;反覆的。I've given him *repeated* warnings. 我曾再三地警告他。—**ly,** *adv.*

re·peat·er 〔rɪ'pitə; ri'pi:tə〕 *n.* ①反覆動作之人或物。②(亦作 **repeating watch**)可鳴打兩次時刻的鐘或錶。③連發槍。④曾多次入一監獄者。⑤在一次選舉中用詐術投票多次者。⑥重修某課程者。⑦〖數學〗循環小數。⑧〖電訊〗重發器;替續增音器。

re·peat·ing 〔rɪ'pitɪŋ; ri'pi:tiŋ〕 *adj.* 反覆的;循環的;連發的。

repeating decimal 循環小數。

repeating rifle 連發鎗。(亦作**repeating firearm**)

re·pe·chage 〔rəpɛ'ʃɑʒ; rəpe'ʃɑ:ʒ〕 〖法〗 *n.* (爲參加準決賽的)敗部的複賽。

***re·pel** 〔rɪ'pɛl; ri'pel〕 *v.,* **-pelled, -pel·ling.** —*v.t.* ①逐退;驅逐;拒絕。to *repel* a temptation. 拒絕一誘惑。②使不愉快;使憎惡。③排斥。④不透水。—*v.i.* ①排斥;驅逐。②使人不愉快。—**lence,** —**len·cy,** *n.*

re·pel·lent, re·pel·lant 〔rɪ'pɛlənt; ri'pelənt〕 *adj.* ①逐回的。②不透水的。③拒人於千里之外的;不討人喜歡的。—*n.* ①驅除劑。②防水劑;防蟲(防腐)劑。—**ly,** *adv.*

***re·pent¹** 〔rɪ'pɛnt; ri'pent〕 *v.i.* 悔悟;懊悔;悔恨。He *repented* of his sin. 他悔悟他的罪過。—*v.t.* 懊悔;後悔。She *repented* her choice. 她懊悔選擇錯了。〖注意〗**repent** 及物動詞之古用法,反身式與 me, him 連用,如: I *repent* me full sore. 余痛悔萬分。以 it 爲主詞,用作非人稱動詞,如:It *repents* me that I did it. 余作此事甚感遺憾。

re·pent² 〔'ripənt; 'ri:pənt〕 *adj.* ①〖動物〗匍匐的;爬行的。②〖植物〗蔓延的。

***re·pent·ance** 〔rɪ'pɛntəns; ri'pentəns〕 *n.* ①悔恨;懊悔。②悛改。

re·pent·ant 〔rɪ'pɛntənt; ri'pentənt〕 *adj.* 悔恨的;悛改的。—**ly,** *adv.*

re·peo·ple 〔ri'pipl; 'ri:'pi:pl〕 *v.t.,* **-pled, -pling.** ①再殖民。②再供以牲畜。

re·per·cus·sion 〔,ripə'kʌʃən; ,ri:pə:'kʌʃən〕 *n.* ①反應;影響。②回聲;回響。③(光之)反射。④彈回;撞回;躍回。⑤〖醫〗消腫作用。⑥〖醫〗觸子宮檢胎法;反擊觸診。

rep·er·toire 〔'rɛpə,twɑr; 'repətwɑ:〕 *n.* ①戲目;演唱目錄。②某一藝術領域內之全部作品。(亦作 **répertoire**)

rep·er·to·ry 〔'rɛpə,torɪ; 'repətəri〕 *n., pl.* **-ries.** ①倉庫;寶庫。②貯藏;蒐集。③目錄;目錄表。④=**repertoire.**

repertory theater 由固定劇團演出各種選定之劇目的戲院。

rep·e·tend 〔'rɛpə,tɛnd; 'repətend〕 *n.* ①〖數學〗循環節。②反覆語句。③〖音樂〗重複唱的詞句。

***rep·e·ti·tion** 〔,rɛpɪ'tɪʃən; ,repi'tiʃən〕 *n.* ①重複;重說;重做。②重複之事物。③摹仿;仿效;副本;複製品。—**al,** —**ar·y,** *adj.*

rep·e·ti·tious [ˌrɛpɪˈtɪʃəs; ˌrepiˈtiʃəs] *adj.* 重複的;令人厭倦地反覆的。—**ness,** *n.*
re·pet·i·tive [rɪˈpɛtɪtɪv; riˈpetitiv] *adj.* =**repetitious.**
re·phrase [riˈfrez; riːˈfreiz] *v.t.*, **-phrased, -phras·ing.** 再措辭; 改變措辭。
re·pine [rɪˈpaɪn; riˈpain] *v.i.*, **-pined, -pin·ing.** 不滿;抱怨;自嘆。
***re·place** [rɪˈples; riˈpleis] *v.t.*, **-placed, -plac·ing.** ①代替。to be *replaced* by (*or* with). 爲…所代替。②替換; 更換。③放回; 置於原處。*Replace* the books on the shelves. 把書放還架上。
re·place·a·ble [rɪˈplesəbl̩; riˈpleisəbl] *adj.* 可歸原處的; 可替換的。—**re·place·a·bil·i·ty,** *n.*
re·place·ment [rɪˈplesmənt; riˈpleismənt] *n.* ①代替;接替。②代替之人或物。③〖化〗取代。④〖軍〗補充兵員。
re·plac·er [rɪˈplesɚ; riˈpleisə] *n.* ①代替者;復原者。②代用品;取代者。
re·plan [riˈplæn; riːˈplæn] *v.t. & v.i.*, **-planned, -plan·ning.** 再計劃;重新計劃。
re·plant [riˈplænt; ˈriːˈplɑːnt] *v.t.* ①移植。②移植樹木於。③新殖民於。—*v.i.* 移植樹木。—*n.* 經過再移植之物。
re·play [*v.* riˈple; ˈriːˈplei *n.* ˈriˌple; ˈriː-plei] *v.t., n.* 再比賽;再演奏。
re·plead [riˈplid; riːˈpliːd] *v.t. & v.i.*, **-plead·ed** or **-pled, -plead·ing.** 再申訴; 再懇求。
re·plead·er [riˈplidɚ; riːˈpliːdə] *n.* 〖法律〗再申辯;再申辯權。
re·plen·ish [rɪˈplɛnɪʃ; riˈpleniʃ] *v.t.* ①再裝滿;補充。②再添以燃料等。③再殖民於…;再居住於…。—**ed,** *adj.*
re·plen·ish·ment [rɪˈplɛnɪʃmənt; riˈpleniʃmənt] *n.* ①再裝滿; 再被裝滿。②補充。
re·plete [rɪˈplit; riˈpliːt] *adj.* ①充滿的;飽足的。②充分供應的。
re·ple·tion [rɪˈpliʃən; riˈpliːʃən] *n.* ①充滿;飽滿;盈滿;充足。He ate to *repletion.* 他吃得很飽。②〖醫〗多血;充血。
re·plev·in [rɪˈplɛvɪn; riˈplevin] *n.* 〖法律〗①具保結取回扣押物;被扣押物的發還。②取回扣押物之令狀或訴訟。—*v.t.* ①以訴訟取回(被扣押之物)。②保釋。
re·plev·i·sa·ble [rɪˈplɛvəsəbl̩; riˈplevisəbl] *adj.* 可具結取回的。(亦作 **repleviable**)
re·plev·y [rɪˈplɛvɪ; riˈplevi] *v.*, **-plev·ied, -plev·y·ing,** *n.*, *pl.* **-plev·ies.** —*v.t.* ①以訴訟收回 (被扣押物)。②憑令狀取回(被扣押物)。—*v.i.* 憑令狀取回被扣押物。—*n.* 取回被扣押物。
rep·li·ca [ˈrɛplɪkə; ˈreplikə] *n.* ①(原作者自己的)複製品;摹寫品。②複製。
rep·li·cate [*n., adj.* ˈrɛplɪkɪt; ˈreplikit *v.* ˈrɛplɪˌket; ˈreplikeit] *adj., v.*, **-cat·ed, -cat·ing,** *n.* —*adj.* 〖植物〗折轉的;折返的。—*v.t.* 折返;折轉。—*n.* 〖音樂〗高(或低)八度之反覆音。
rep·li·ca·tion [ˌrɛpləˈkeʃən; ˌrepliˈkeiʃən] *n.* ①折轉;折疊。②回答;答覆。③回聲。④模寫;複製品。⑤〖法律〗原告的答辯。⑥重作實驗。
re·pli·er [rɪˈplaɪɚ; riˈplaiə] *n.* 答覆者。
‡re·ply [rɪˈplaɪ; riˈplai] *v.*, **-plied, -ply·ing,** *n.*, *pl.* **-plies.** —*v.t. & v.i.* ①答覆;回答。to *reply* to a question. 答覆一問題。②採取報復行動;反應。—*n.* 答覆;回答。in *reply* to your letter. 爲答覆你的信。
ré·pon·dez s'il vous plaît [re-pɔ̃ˈdesilvuˈplɛ; reipɔ̃ːˈdeisiːlvuːˈple] 〖法〗敬請賜覆 (=reply, if you please. 請帖中用語, 簡寫爲 R.S.V.P. 或 rsvp)。
‡re·port [rɪˈport; riˈpɔːt] *n.* ①報導;紀事;紀錄。②報告;通知。a schoolboy's *report.* 學生成績報告單。③(鎗彈等)爆聲。④傳聞; 謠言。The *report* goes that the Smiths are leaving town. 據說史密斯一家人將離開本鎮。⑤名譽;聲譽。a man of good *report.* 有好名譽的人。⑥(法庭的)宣判;裁決。⑦(*pl.*) 判例大全。—*v.t.* ①宣告。②正式報導;報告。③敍述;描述。④報到;復命。*Report* yourself to the manager. 向經理報到。⑤寫報告。⑥報導(新聞事件);寫採訪稿。⑦告發;控告。to *report* one to the police. 向警局告發某人。—*v.i.* ①作報告。I'll *report* to the police. 我要報告警察。②報到。*Report* for duty at the office. 至辦公處報到。③採訪新聞。***It is reported that....*** 據報導…;據說…。***report out*** (專門委員會)將法案提交大會並附審查報告。
re·port·a·ble [rɪˈportəbl̩; riˈpɔːtəbl] *adj.* 可報告的;可報導的; 有報導價值的。
re·port·age [rɪˈportɪdʒ; ˌrepɔːˈtɑːʒ] *n.* ①報導。②報導之消息。③報導之文章。
report card 學生的成績報告單。
re·port·ed·ly [rɪˈportɪdlɪ; riˈpɔːtidli] *adv.* 據說;據傳。
***re·port·er** [rɪˈportɚ; riˈpɔːtə] *n.* ①報告者。②通訊員;採訪員;記者。
rep·or·to·ri·al [ˌrɛpɚˈtorɪəl; ˌrepəˈtɔːriəl] *adj.* ①屬於或有關 reporter 的。②報導的。
re·pos·al [rɪˈpozəl; riˈpouzəl] *n.* ①安臥;休息。②信賴;信託;信靠。
***re·pose**[1] [rɪˈpoz; riˈpouz] *n., v.*, **-posed, -pos·ing.** —*n.* ①休息;睡眠。②安靜。—*v.t.* 使休息;使安眠。—*v.i.* ①休息;安眠。to *repose* on a couch. 躺在長椅上。②長眠。③依賴。④信賴。His faith *reposed* in God. 他信靠上帝。⑤安靜地處於…。
re·pose[2] *v.t.*, **-posed, -pos·ing.** 置;放。
re·pose·ful [rɪˈpozfəl; riˈpouzful] *adj.* 鎮靜的;沉着的;從容不迫的。—**ly,** *adv.*
re·pos·it [rɪˈpɑzɪt; riˈpɔzit] *v.t.* ①放回。②儲藏。—**re·po·si·tion,** *n.*
re·pos·i·to·ry [rɪˈpɑzəˌtorɪ; riˈpɔzitəri] *n.*, *pl.* **-to·ries.** ①貯藏器;收藏用之容器。②貯藏所;倉庫;棧房。③墓。④被信賴的人;被告訴心腹之話的人。
re·pos·sess [ˌripəˈzɛs; ˌriːpəˈzes] *v.t.* 再取得; 再取回; 再具有; 復有。to *repossess* oneself of... 取回…; 恢復…所有權。—**re·pos·ses·sion,** *n.*
re·pous·sage [rəpuˈsɑʒ; rəpuːˈsɑːʒ] *n.* 敲花(藝)術。
re·pous·sé [rəpuˈse; rəˈpuːsei] 〖法〗*adj.* (從反面)敲出花樣的。—*n.* 敲花細工。
repp [rɛp; rep] *n.* =**rep**[1].
rep·re·hend [ˌrɛprɪˈhɛnd; ˌrepriˈhend] *v.t.* 責難;譴責;申斥。
rep·re·hen·si·ble [ˌrɛprɪˈhɛnsəbl̩; ˌrepriˈhensəbl] *adj.* 應受譴責的; 應受責難的。—**rep·re·hen·si·bly,** *adv.*
rep·re·hen·sion [ˌrɛprɪˈhɛnʃən; ˌrepriˈhenʃən] *n.* 叱責;譴責;非難。
rep·re·hen·sive [ˌrɛprɪˈhɛnsɪv; ˌrepriˈhensiv] *adj.* 譴責的;非難的;叱責的。
‡rep·re·sent [ˌrɛprɪˈzɛnt; ˌrepriˈzent] *v.t.* ①表示;象徵。Phonetic signs *represent*

sounds. 音標表示聲音。②代表。③扮演(角色)。④描寫;描繪。This painting *represents* a hunting scene. 這幅畫描繪一個獵場。⑤陳述;描述〖常 as〗. He *represented* the plan as safe, but it was not. 他說這計畫是安全的,但並非如是。⑥使人想起;使人認爲。⑦作爲例子。⑧相當於。

re·pre·sent [ˌripri'zɛnt; ˌri:pri'zent] *v.t.* 再贈予;再提出;再上演(劇本)。

***rep·re·sen·ta·tion** [ˌrɛprizɛn'teʃən; ˌreprizen'teiʃən] *n.* ①代表;象徵。②選舉代表的權利與制度。Taxation without *representation* is tyranny. 徵稅而不准選舉代表是虐政。③代表之集合稱。④畫像;模型。⑤戲劇的表演。⑥形成想像或觀念之過程。⑦抗議;陳情。to make *representations* to somebody. 向某人抗議。⑧(常 *pl.*) 陳述;申述;描述。⑨〖外交〗**a.** 外交交涉。**b.** 代表國家所作之發言。

rep·re·sen·ta·tion·al [ˌrɛprizɛn'teʃənḷ; ˌreprizen'teiʃənḷ] *adj.* ①代表的。②(藝術)具象派的(與抽象派的相反)。

‡rep·re·sent·a·tive [ˌrɛprɪ'zɛntətɪv; ˌrepri'zentətiv] *n.* ①代表。We sent a *representative.* 我們派了一個代表。②(R-)〖美〗衆議員。③樣本;典型。***the House of Representatives*** (美國)衆議院。—*adj.* ①代議制的。②表明的;象徵的。③代表性的;典型的。④相當於某種類的。

re·press [rɪ'prɛs; ri'pres] *v.t.* ①阻止;抑制。②鎮壓;壓服。

re·press·i·ble [rɪ'prɛsəbḷ; ri'presəbl] *adj.* 可鎮壓的;可抑制的;可阻止的。

re·pres·sion [rɪ'prɛʃən; ri'preʃən] *n.* ①鎮壓;制止。②抑制。

re·pres·sive [rɪ'prɛsɪv; ri'presiv] *adj.* 抑制的;鎮壓的。

re·prieve [rɪ'priv; ri'pri:v] *v.*, **-prieved, -priev·ing,** *n.* —*v.t.* ①緩刑。②暫救;暫減。—*n.* ①緩刑。②暫緩;暫時解脫。

rep·ri·mand [*n.* 'rɛprəˌmænd; 'reprimɑ:nd *v.* 'rɛprəˌmænd, ˌrɛprə'mænd; 'reprimɑ:nd, ˌrepri'm-] *n.* 申斥;申戒;懲戒。—*v.t.* 嚴斥;申戒。

re·print [*v.* ri'prɪnt; 'ri:'print *n.* 'riˌprɪnt; 'ri:'print] *v.t.* 再印;再版;翻印。—*n.* ①再版;再版本。②郵票之再版。

re·pris·al [rɪ'praɪzḷ; ri'praizəl] *n.* ①(對敵國人民、財產等)報復性的侵占或掠奪;報復。②報復之行爲。③(常 *pl.*) 賠償;補償。

re·prise [rɪ'praɪz; ri'praiz] *n.*, *v.*, **-prised, -pris·ing.** —*n.* ①(常 *pl.*) 每年由貴族采邑或財產中扣除之養老金等。②〖音樂〗再現部;挿入部。—*v.t.* 再現;挿入。

re·pro ['ripro; 'ri:prou] *n.*, *pl.* **-pros.** 〖俗〗複製品(爲 reproduction 之略)。

***re·proach** [rɪ'protʃ; ri'proutʃ] *n.* ①譴責;責備。②恥辱;不名譽。to bring *reproach* on one's family. 玷辱門庭。③譴責之原因;不名譽之原因。—*v.t.* ①譴責;叱斥〖常 with〗. He *reproached* me with extravagance. 他責罵我浪費。②汚辱。

re·proach·a·ble [rɪ'protʃəbḷ; ri'proutʃəbl] *adj.* 可譴責的;可責備的。

re·proach·ful [rɪ'protʃfəl; ri'proutʃful] *adj.* 責備的;表示譴責的。—**ly,** *adv.*

re·proach·ing·ly [rɪ'protʃɪŋlɪ; ri'proutʃiŋli] *adv.* 非難地;譴責地。

re·proach·less [rɪ'protʃlɪs; ri'proutʃlis] *adj.* 無可非難的;無可譴責的。

rep·ro·bate ['rɛprəˌbet; 'reproubeit] *n.*, *adj.*, *v.*, **-bat·ed, -bat·ing.** —*n.* 墮落的人;無賴漢。—*adj.* ①墮落的;放蕩的。②被神所棄的(人)。③無價值的;下等的。—*v.t.* ①非難;斥責。②拒絕。

rep·ro·ba·tion [ˌrɛprə'beʃən; ˌreprou'beiʃən] *n.* ①非難;指責。②拒斥;拒絕。③〖神學〗定罪(認爲永不能得救)。—**rep·ro·ba·tive,** *adj.*

re·proc·ess [ri'prɑsɛs; ri:'prɔses] 「*v.t.* 將…再加工。」

re·proc·essed [ri'prɑsɛst; ri:'prɔsest] *adj.* 經過再加工的。

***re·pro·duce** [ˌriprə'djus; ˌri:prə'dju:s] *v.*, **-duced, -duc·ing.** —*v.t.* ①再生。②複製。③生殖;產。—*v.i.* 生殖;繁殖。Most plants *reproduce* by seeds. 大多數植物靠種子繁殖。

re·pro·duc·er [ˌriprə'djusɚ; ˌri:prə'dju:sə] *n.* 複製者;再生者。

re·pro·duc·i·ble [ˌriprə'djusəbḷ; ˌri:prə'dju:səbl] *adj.* 可再生的;可複製的。

***re·pro·duc·tion** [ˌriprə'dʌkʃən; ˌri:prə'dʌkʃən] *n.* ①再生;複製。②拷貝;複製品。③生殖;繁殖。

re·pro·duc·tive [ˌriprə'dʌktɪv; ˌri:prə'dʌktiv] *adj.* ①再生的;複製的。②再生、複製或繁殖用的;與再生、複製或繁殖有關的。

***re·proof** [rɪ'pruf; ri'pru:f] *n.* 譴責;斥責;斥責的話。a word of *reproof.* 譴責之言。

re·prov·a·ble [rɪ'pruvəbḷ; ri'pru:vəbl] *adj.* 應受譴責的。

re·prov·al [rɪ'pruvḷ; ri'pru:vəl] *n.* 「譴責;責難。」

re·prove [ri'pruv; ri:'pru:v] *v.t.* & *v.i.*, **-proved, -proved** or **-prov·en, -prov·ing.** 再證明。

***re·prove** [rɪ'pruv; ri'pru:v] *v.*, **-proved, -prov·ing.** —*v.t.* 譴責;責罵。to *reprove* a boy for being rude. 責罵孩子,因其無禮。—*v.i.* 責罵。

re·prov·ing·ly [rɪ'pruvɪŋlɪ; ri'pru:viŋli] *adv.* 譴責地。

reps [rɛps; reps] *n.* =**rep**[1].

rep·tant ['rɛptənt; 'reptənt] *adj.* 〖動、植物〗匍匐的;爬行的;蔓延的。

***rep·tile** ['rɛptḷ, -tɪl; 'reptail] *adj.* ①卑鄙的;卑劣的。②匍匐的;爬行的。—*n.* ①卑鄙的人。②爬蟲。

Rep·til·i·a [rɛp'tɪlɪə; rep'tiliə] *n. pl.* 「〖動物〗爬蟲類。」

rep·til·i·an [rɛp'tɪlɪən; rep'tiliən] *adj.* ①爬蟲類的;似爬蟲類的。②卑鄙的;惡意的。***the reptilian age*** 〖地質〗爬蟲時代;中生代。—*n.* 爬蟲類動物。

Repub. ①Republic. ②Republican.

re·pub·lic** [rɪ'pʌblɪk; ri'pʌblik] *n.* 共和國。the Republic of China*** 中華民國。

‡re·pub·li·can [rɪ'pʌblɪkən; ri'pʌblikən] *adj.* ①共和國的;共和政體的。②(R-)〖美〗共和黨的。③贊成共和的。***the Republican Party*** 〖美〗共和黨。—*n.* ①擁護共和政體者。②(R-)〖美〗共和黨員。

re·pub·li·can·ism [rɪ'pʌblɪkənˌɪzəm; ri'pʌblikənizəm] *n.* ①共和政體。②共和主義。③對共和主義的擁護。④(R-)美國共和黨的政策。

re·pub·li·can·ize [rɪ'pʌblɪkənˌaɪz; ri'pʌblikənaiz] *v.t.*, **-ized, -iz·ing.** 使成共和政體;使成共和國。

re·pub·li·ca·tion [ˌripʌblɪ'keʃən; 'ri:ˌpʌbli'keiʃən] *n.* ①再發行;再版;再發表。②再發行之書刊;再版之書刊。

republic of letters ①文學界;文壇。②文學。

re·pub·lish [riˈpʌblɪʃ; ˈriːˈpʌbliʃ] *v.t.* ①再公布;再頒布。②再版;再印行。
re·pu·di·ate [rɪˈpjudɪˌet; riˈpjuːdieit] *v.t.*, **-at·ed, -at·ing.** ①拒絕;駁斥。②否認;棄絕。③用離婚手段丟棄。
re·pu·di·a·tion [rɪˌpjudɪˈeʃən; riˌpjuːdiˈeiʃən] *n.* ①拒絕。②否認。③棄絕。④拒絕支付。
re·pu·di·a·tor [rɪˈpjudɪˌetɚ; riˈpjuːdieitə] *n.* ①離婚者;休妻者。②拋棄者;否認者;拒絕者。③賴債者;國債廢棄論者。
re·pugn [rɪˈpjun; riˈpjuːn] *v.t.* ①使不愉快;使憎恨;使厭惡。②反對;抵抗。—*v.i.* 〖古〗①反抗;反對;抵抗〖against〗. ②矛盾;衝突〖to, against〗.
re·pug·nance [rɪˈpʌgnəns; riˈpʌgnəns] *n.* ①嫌惡;厭棄。②矛盾。(亦作 **repugnancy**)
re·pug·nant [rɪˈpʌgnənt; riˈpʌgnənt] *adj.* ①令人厭棄的;使人討厭的。②不調和的;相違反的。③反對的。④相反的;敵對的。
***re·pulse** [rɪˈpʌls; riˈpʌls] *v.*, **-pulsed, -puls·ing,** *n.* —*v.t.* ①驅逐;擊退。②拒絕;不受。—*n.* ①擊退。②拒絕。Her *repulse* was to be expected. 她的拒絕乃意料中事。
re·pul·sion [rɪˈpʌlʃən; riˈpʌlʃən] *n.* ①厭惡。②驅逐;拒絕。③〖物理〗斥力;拒力。
re·pul·sive [rɪˈpʌlsɪv; riˈpʌlsiv] *adj.* ①使人厭惡的;討厭的。②排斥的;冷淡的。③〖物理〗拒斥的;排斥的。—**ly,** *adv.*
re·pur·chase [riˈpɝtʃəs; riːˈpəːtʃəs] *v.*, **-chased, -chas·ing,** *n.* —*v.t.* 再買;買回。—*n.* 再買;買回。
rep·u·ta·ble [ˈrɛpjətəbl̩; ˈrepjutəbl] *adj.* 名譽好的;有聲望的;可尊敬的;高尚的。—**rep·u·ta·bly,** *adv.*
***rep·u·ta·tion** [ˌrɛpjəˈteʃən; ˌrepju(ː)ˈteiʃən] *n.* ①名譽;名聲。He is a man of good (*or* high) *reputation.* (*or* He has a good *reputation.*) 他是個名譽很好的人。②美名;聲望。
***re·pute** [rɪˈpjut; riˈpjuːt] *n., v.*, **-put·ed, -put·ing.** —*n.* ①名譽;名聲。to know a man by *repute.* 僅聞某人之名(未見過面)。②美名;聲望。—*v.t.* 被認為;被稱為(祇用於被動式)。He was *reputed* to be a millionaire. 他被認為是一個百萬富翁。
re·put·ed [rɪˈpjutɪd; riˈpjuːtid] *adj.* ①有好名聲的;出名的。②一般認為的;號稱的。the *reputed* author of a book. 一般所認為的某書的作者。—**ly,** *adv.*
‡re·quest [rɪˈkwɛst; riˈkwest] *v.t.* ①請求;要求。to *request* a loan. 請求一項借款。②邀請;請。He *requested* her to go with him. 他邀她一同去。—*n.* ①請求。We did it at his *request.* 我們應他的請求而做此事。②請求之事物。③需要。These imported materials are in great *request*. 這些進口物資極為需要。④請求書。***at*** (or ***by***) ***request*** 應允請求。Miss Day will sing *at request.* 戴小姐將應大衆要求而唱歌。
re·quick·en [riˈkwɪkən; ˈriːˈkwikən] *v.t. & v.i.* (使)甦醒;(使)重振。
Re·qui·em, re·qui·em [ˈrikwɪəm; ˈrekwiem, -iəm] *n.* ①〖羅馬天主教〗**a.** 為死者舉行的安靈彌撒。 **b.** 安靈彌撒的儀式。 **c.** 安靈彌撒曲;奠祭曲。②為安慰死者而作之任何音樂追悼儀式、讚美歌或輓歌。
re·qui·es·cat [ˌrɛkwɪˈɛskæt; ˌrekwiˈeskæt] 〖拉〗 *n.* 願死者靈魂安息之祈禱。
requiescat in pa·ce [~~ˈpesɪ; ~~ˈpeisi] 〖拉〗願彼安息(=may he *or* she rest in peace. 常刻於墓碑上, 簡寫為 R.I.P.).
‡re·quire [rɪˈkwaɪr; riˈkwaiə] *v.*, **-quired, -quir·ing.** —*v.t.* ①需要。We did all that was *required* of us. 我們做了所需要我們做的一切。②命令;要求。They *required* me to keep silent. 他們命令我不要作聲。—*v.i.* 命令;要求。
required course 必修課程。
required reading 必讀書籍。
***re·quire·ment** [rɪˈkwaɪrmənt; riˈkwaiəmənt] *n.* ①需要;需要之事物。②要求;要求之事物。③命令;規定。to fulfil the *requirements* of the law. 履行法律之規定。
req·ui·site [ˈrɛkwəzɪt; ˈrekwizit] *adj.* 需要的;必要的。—*n.* 必需品;需要物。
req·ui·si·tion [ˌrɛkwəˈzɪʃən; ˌrekwiˈziʃən] *n.* ①需要。②要求;請求(特指書面之正式要求或請求)。③需用或徵用。④必備條件。***be called into requisition*** 被徵用。—*v.t.* ①徵用;徵發。②向…徵用。
re·quit·al [rɪˈkwaɪtl̩; riˈkwaitl] *n.* ①報答;酬答;酬勞;回報。②報仇;處罰。***in requital for*** (or ***of***) 作為…的報酬;報恩;報答。
re·quite [rɪˈkwaɪt; riˈkwait] *v.t.*, **-quit·ed, -quit·ing.** ①回報;報還。②報酬;酬謝。③報復;報仇。④補償;報償。***requite like for like*** 以恩(怨)報恩(怨)。
re·ra·di·ate [riˈredɪˌet; riːˈreidieit] *v.t. & v.i.*, **-at·ed, -at·ing.** 〖物理〗再輻射。—**re·ra·di·a·tion,** *n.*
re·read [riˈrid; ˈriːˈriːd] *v.t. & v.i.*, **-read** [-ˈrɛd; -ˈred], **-read·ing.** 再讀;再念;重讀。
re-re·cord [ˌririˈkɔrd; ˌriːriˈkɔːd] *v.t.* ①再錄音;重錄音。②改灌(如將轉速78轉唱片改灌成$33^1/_3$者)。
rere·dos [ˈrɪrdɑs; ˈriədɔs] *n.* 祭壇背後牆壁上的雕刻裝飾或屏風。
re·route [riˈrut; ˈriːˈruːt] *v.t.*, **-rout·ed, -rout·ing.** 以新(不同)路線遞送。
re·run [*v.* riˈrʌn; ˈriːˈrʌn *n.* ˈriˌrʌn, ˈriːrʌn] *v.*, **-ran, -run, -run·ning,** *n.* —*v.t. & v.i.* ①再上演(電影)。②再跑。—*n.* ①電影之再上演。②(比賽之)再跑。
res [riz; riːz] *n., pl.* **res.** 〖拉〗①物;物件。②事件。③財產。
res. ①research. ②reserve. ③residence. ④resides. ⑤residue. ⑥resigned. ⑦resistance. ⑧resolution.
res ad·ju·di·ca·ta [rizəˌdʒudəˈketə; riːzəˌdʒuːdiˈkeitə] 〖拉〗最高法院已作最後判決之案件。(亦作 **res judicata**)
re·sail [riˈsel; riːˈseil] *v.i.* 再航行;重航海。
re·sal·a·ble [riˈseləbl̩; riːˈseiləbl] *adj.* 可轉售的;可再賣的。
re·sale [riˈsel; riːˈseil] *n.* ①再賣;轉賣。②出售舊物。
re·scind [rɪˈsɪnd; riˈsind] *v.t.* 廢止;撤銷;取消;宣告無效。
re·scis·si·ble [rɪˈsɪsəbl̩; riˈsisibl] *adj.* 可廢止的;可取消的。
re·scis·sion [rɪˈsɪʒən; riˈsiʒən] *n.* ①削除;除掉。②使失效;廢止;取消。③撤銷;撤回。
re·scis·so·ry [rɪˈsɪsərɪ; riˈsisəri] *adj.* 廢止的;撤銷的。
re·script [ˈriskrɪpt; ˈriːskript] *n.* ①(羅馬皇帝或教皇之)敕令;敕答;詔書。②命令;法令。③抄本;副本。④重寫;重寫之物。
***res·cue** [ˈrɛskju; ˈreskjuː] *v.*, **-cued,**

-cu·ing, *n.* —*v.t.* ①解救；救出。to *rescue* a man from bandits. 從盜匪手裏救出一人。②〖法律〗以暴力奪回(扣押之人或物)。—*n.* ①解救；援助。②〖法律〗暴力奪回。***come*** (or ***go***) ***to the rescue*** 援救。

res·cu·er ('rɛskjuɚ; 'reskjuə) *n.* 救助者。

re·search (ri'sɝtʃ; 'riː'səːtʃ) *v.t.* & *v.i.* 再尋找。

***re·search** (*n.* 'risɝtʃ, rɪ'sɝtʃ; ri'səːtʃ, rə's–, 'riːsəːtʃ *v.* rɪ'sɝtʃ, 'risɝtʃ; ri'səːtʃ, rə's–) *n.* ①研究；探索。②研究工作(常作複數或以不定冠詞 a 置於前，但不可冠以數字)。to carry out a *research* into (*or* for) the causes of cancer. 進行探究癌症原因之研究工作。—*v.i.* & *v.t.* 研究；探索。**—er, —ist,** *n.*

re·search·ful (rɪ'sɝtʃfəl; ri'səːtʃful) *adj.* 研究的；好探討的；好問的。

research library 一種專供學者與專家獲得某方面資料的圖書館。

research reactor 供研究用的核子反應爐。

re·seat (ri'sit; 'riː'siːt) *v.t.* ①使再就坐；再坐。②供以新座位。③換(椅子座或褲襠等)。④使復王位。

re·seau, ré·seau (re'zo; rei'zou) *n.*, *pl.* **-seaux** (–zoz, –zo; –zouz, –zou). ①網；網狀物。②〖氣象〗受一機構控制的一系列氣象臺。

re·sect (rɪ'sɛkt; ri'sekt) *v.t.* 〖外科〗切除；部分切除。

re·sec·tion (rɪ'sɛkʃən; ri'sekʃən) *n.* 〖古〗削除；割去。②〖外科〗切除術。

Re·se·da (rɪ'sidə; ri'siːdə) *n.* ①〖植物〗木犀草屬。②(r–) 木犀草。③(r–) 灰綠色。—*adj.* (r–) 灰綠色的。

re·seize (ri'siz; riː'siːz) *v.t.*, **-seized, -seiz·ing.** ①再賦與；使再具有；使恢復(原來地位或尊嚴)。②奪回；取回。

re·sei·zure (ri'siʒɚ; riː'siːʒə) *n.* 再占有；奪回；回復；復位。

re·sell (ri'sɛl; 'riː'sel) *v.t.*, **-sold, -sell·ing.** 再賣；轉售。

re·sem·blance** (rɪ'zɛmbləns; ri'zembləns) *n.* ①相似(之處)。Twins often show great *resemblance*. 雙生子常極相似。②外表；表面。③副本；形像。bear resemblance to*** 與…相像。

re·sem·blant (rɪ'zɛmblənt; ri'zemblənt) *adj.* ①相似的〖有時 to〗。②像眞的。

***re·sem·ble** (rɪ'zɛmbl; ri'zembl) *v.t.*, **-bled, -bling.** ①相似。She strongly *resembles* her mother. 她酷似她的母親。②〖古〗比較；比擬。

re·send (ri'sɛnd; riː'send) *v.t.*, **-sent, -send·ing.** 再送。

***re·sent** (rɪ'zɛnt; ri'zent) *v.t.* 憤恨；憎惡。She *resented* being called a baby. 她厭惡被稱爲小孩子。

re·sent·ful (rɪ'zɛntfəl; ri'zentful) *adj.* 憤恨的；憤慨的。

re·sent·ment (rɪ'zɛntmənt; ri'zentmənt) *n.* 憤恨。

res·er·pine ('rɛsəpɪn; 'resəpin) *n.* 〖藥〗蛇根鹼(高血壓治療劑)。

***res·er·va·tion** (ˌrɛzɚ'veʃən; ˌrezə'veiʃən) *n.* ①隱藏；隱諱。②限制條件；保留條件。to accept without *reservation*. 無條件地接受。③〖美〗留作專用之土地。④〖美〗(常 *pl.*)(車座、旅館房間、戲座等)預定。Have you made your *reservations?* 你已定好(房間等)沒有？⑤保留的事物。

‡**re·serve** (rɪ'zɝv; ri'zəːv) *v.*, **-served, -serv·ing,** *n.*, *adj.* —*v.t.* ①隱藏；保留。to *reserve* criticism. 不予置評。②延遲；改期。③貯備；貯藏。④預定(車座、戲座等)。to *reserve* rooms at a hotel. 預定旅館房間。⑤留作專用。time *reserved* for recreation. 專供娛樂的時間。—*n.* ①留作專用之公地。a forest *reserve*. 留作造林之地。②貯以待用之人或物；貯藏物。the bank's *reserves*. 銀行之準備金。③〖軍〗**a.** 預備部隊(非現役部隊)。**b.** 後備部隊。**c.** (*pl.*)〖美〗美陸軍中無正式編制之部隊。④隱藏；保留。We accept your conditions without *reserve*. 我們無保留地接受你的條件。⑤謹愼；節制。⑥冷漠；隔閡。***in reserve*** 保留的。money *in reserve*. 準備金。***without reserve*** 毫無保留的(地)。—*adj.* 預備的；後備的；限制的。a *reserve* fund. 準備金。

reserve bank 〖美〗聯邦準備銀行。

reserve book (圖書館中)不外借的書。

re·served (rɪ'zɝvd; ri'zəːvd) *adj.* ①預定的；儲備的。a *reserved* seat. 預定的座位。②自制的；有所保留的；緘默的；性格孤獨的。③分開的；保留的。

re·serv·ed·ly (rɪ'zɝvɪdlɪ; ri'zəːvidli) *adv.* ①保留地；預備地；預定地。②自制地；緘默地。

reserved powers 〖美〗非憲法賦與但爲國家或人民保留之權力。

reserve officer 預備軍官。

re·serv·ist (rɪ'zɝvɪst; ri'zəːvist) *n.* 後備兵；預備兵。

***res·er·voir** ('rɛzɚˌvɔr; 'rezəvwaː) *n.* ①貯水池；水庫。This *reservoir* supplies the entire city. 這水庫供給全城用水。②任何儲藏液體之部分。③儲藏庫；儲藏處。④大量的供應。

re·set (*v.* ri'sɛt; 'riː'set *n.* 'riˌsɛt; 'riːˌset) *v.*, **-set, -set·ting,** *n.* —*v.t.* ①再設；重組；重新放置；再磨快。②重排(活字)。③重鑲；重嵌。④〖外科〗接骨。—*n.* ①重組；重排；重鑲。②重組、重排或重鑲之物。

re·set·tle (ri'sɛtl; riː'setl) *v.t.* & *v.i.*, **-tled, -tling.** 再安頓；再建立；再安置。**—ment,** *n.*

re·shape (ri'ʃep; 'riː'ʃeip) *v.*, **-shaped, -shap·ing.** —*v.t.* 再賦以形；使再形成；採行新方針。—*v.i.* 形成新形態。

re·ship (ri'ʃɪp; 'riː'ʃip) *v.*, **-shipped, -ship·ping.** —*v.t.* ①再裝船運送。②改裝他船。③使再乘船。—*v.i.* ①再乘船。②(船員)簽約參加另一次航行。**—ment,** *n.*

re·shuf·fle (ri'ʃʌfl; 'riː'ʃʌfl) *v.*, **-fled, -fling,** *n.* —*v.t.* ①再洗(紙牌)。②改革；轉變。—*n.* ①再洗牌。②轉變；改革；改組。

***re·side** (rɪ'zaɪd; ri'zaid) *v.i.*, **-sid·ed, -sid·ing.** ①居住。②存在。Her charm *resides* in her happy smile. 她的魅力在於她快樂的微笑中。

res·i·dence** ('rɛzədəns; 'rezidəns) *n.* ①居住。②住宅；住處。official *residence*. 官邸。③居留之時間。④總公司所在地。in residence*** **a.** 住公家宿舍的；住校的。**b.** 駐於任所的。a doctor *in residence*. 住院醫師。

res·i·den·cy ('rɛzədənsɪ; 'rezidənsi) *n.*, *pl.* **-cies.** ①=**residence.** ②舊印度總督代表在土邦的官邸。③舊荷屬東印度羣島之行政區。④住院醫師之職務或任期。

***res·i·dent** ('rɛzədənt; 'rezidənt) *n.* ①居住者；居民。the *residents* of the suburbs. 市郊的居民。②駐外國宮廷之代表(通常爲低於大使者)。③派駐印度土邦宮廷之英總督代表。④舊荷屬東印度羣島之行政官。⑤住院醫師。—*adj.* ①居住的；居留的。the *resident* population. 居民人口。②駐在任所的。a *resident* physician. 住院醫師。③不

遷居的;定居的。

resident commissioner〖美〗派駐國會（衆議院）的屬地代表（可發言但無投票權)。

res·i·den·tial [ˌrɛzəˈdɛnʃəl; ˌreziˈdenʃəl] *adj.* ①適於居住的;居所的。②居住的;與居住有關的。the *residential* qualification for voters. 選擧者之居住資格。

res·i·den·ti·ar·y [ˌrɛzəˈdɛnʃɪˌɛrɪ; ˌreziˈdenʃiˌɛəri] *adj., n., pl.* **-ar·ies.** —*adj.* ①住於官舍的;應住官邸的。②居住的;住在的。—*n.* ①居住者;居民。②駐在牧師。

re·sid·u·al [rɪˈzɪdʒʊəl; riˈzidjuəl] *adj.* ①殘餘的; 剩餘的。*residual* property.〖法律〗剩餘財產;餘產。②〖數學〗差的;剩餘的。*residual* error. 剩餘誤差。③〖醫〗殘留的。④附加酬報的。—*n.* ①殘餘; 殘渣。②〖數學〗差;剩餘。③〖地質〗殘丘。④(常 *pl.*)(病癒後)後遺症狀。⑤(常 *pl.*) 電視節目提供人付與演員的附加酬報。—**ly,** *adv.*

re·sid·u·ar·y [rɪˈzɪdʒʊˌɛrɪ; riˈzidjuəri] *adj.* ①殘餘的; 剩餘的。some *residuary* odds and ends. 一些剩下的零碎東西;零頭。②〖法律〗剩餘財產的。*residuary* bequest. 餘產的遺贈。*residuary* legatee. 餘產承受者。

res·i·due [ˈrɛzəˌdju; ˈrezidjuː] *n.* ①殘餘;剩餘。②〖法律〗剩餘財產。③〖化學〗殘渣;剩餘物。④〖數學〗殘數;留數;剩餘。

re·sid·u·um [rɪˈzɪdʒʊəm; riˈzidjuəm] *n., pl.* **-u·a** [-ʊə; -juə]. ①殘餘;殘餘物。②〖化〗殘渣;副產物。③〖數學〗剩餘;剩餘誤差。④〖喩〗最下層的人;賤民。⑤〖法律〗剩餘財產;餘產。

re-sign [ˌriˈsaɪn; ˈriːˈsain] *v.t.* 再簽署;再署名。

***re·sign** [rɪˈzaɪn; riˈzain] *v.t.* & *v.i.* ①辭職;辭退。to *resign* office. 辭職。②順從;聽從。to *resign* to one's fate. 聽天由命。③放棄;捨棄。④委託。*resign oneself* 順從。to *resign oneself* to one's fate. 聽天由命。

***res·ig·na·tion** [ˌrɛzɪgˈneʃən; ˌrezigˈneiʃən] *n.* ①辭職。②辭呈。to hand in one's *resignation.* 提出辭呈。③忍受;順從。She bore the pain with *resignation.* 她默默地忍受着痛苦。

re·signed [rɪˈzaɪnd; riˈzaind] *adj.* 順從的;聽天由命的;逆來順受的。—**ly,** *adv.*

re·sile [rɪˈzaɪl; riˈzail] *v.i.,* **-siled, -sil·ing.** ①跳回;彈回;(有彈性物體被壓扁後) 恢復原狀。②縮回;退縮。③(契約等)撤銷。

re·sil·i·ence [rɪˈzɪlɪəns; riˈziliəns] *n.* ①彈力; 彈性。②精神恢復力; 輕快; 愉快。(亦作 **resiliency**)

re·sil·i·ent [rɪˈzɪlɪənt; riˈziliənt] *adj.* ①彈回的; 有彈性的。②活潑的; 愉快的。

re·sil·i·om·e·ter [rɪˌzɪlɪˈɑmətɚ; riˌziliˈɔmitə] *n.* 彈力計。

res·in [ˈrɛzn̩; ˈrezin] *n.* 樹脂（尤指松脂與樅脂);樹脂狀沉澱物。synthetic *resin.* 合成樹脂。—*v.t.* 用樹脂處理或摩擦。

res·in·ate [ˈrɛzɪˌnet; ˈrezineit] *v.,* **-at·ed, -at·ing,** *n.* —*v.t.* 以樹脂注入;用樹脂使香。—*n.*〖化〗樹脂酸鹽。

res·in·i·fy [rɛˈzɪnəˌfaɪ; reˈzinifai] *v.,* **-fied, -fy·ing.**〖化〗—*v.t.* ①使成爲樹脂狀。②以樹脂處理。—*v.i.* 變爲樹脂。

res·in·oid [ˈrɛzɪˌnɔɪd; ˈrezinɔid] *adj.* 似樹脂的;樹脂狀的。—*n.* 樹脂性物質; 合成樹脂;松香脂。

res·in·ous [ˈrɛzn̩əs; ˈrezinəs] *adj.* ①樹脂的。②係樹脂的。③含樹脂的;多樹脂的。(亦作 **resiny**)

res·i·pis·cent [ˌrɛsəˈpɪsənt; ˌresiˈpisənt] *adj.* 改變心意的;悛悔的。

***re·sist** [rɪˈzɪst; riˈzist] *v.t.* ①抵抗; 對抗。to *resist* temptation. 抵抗誘惑。②抵住;忍住。I was unable to *resist* laughing. 我忍不住笑了。③防止。—*v.i.* 抵抗; 對抗。—*n.* 有防止(如防銹)作用的物質。

***re·sist·ance** [rɪˈzɪstəns; riˈzistəns] *n.* ①抵抗。 The bank clerk made no *resistance* to the robber. 那銀行職員沒有向强盜作抵抗。②抵抗力。③抵抗之物或行動;阻力。④〖電〗電阻。⑤具有電阻性能之導體。⑥反抗之意志;反對。⑦(常R-) 在被占領地區從事破壞運動或游擊戰的地下組織。

resistance coil〖電〗電阻線圈。

resistance thermometer〖物理〗電阻溫度計。

re·sist·ant [rɪˈzɪstənt; riˈzistənt] *adj.* 抵抗的。—*n.* ①抵抗者。②=**resistor.**

re·sist·er [rɪˈzɪstɚ; riˈzistə] *n.* ①抵抗者;反對者。② =**resistor.**

re·sist·i·bil·i·ty [rɪˌzɪstəˈbɪlətɪ; riˌzistiˈbiliti] *n.* 可抵抗性;可抗拒性;抵抗力。

re·sist·i·ble [rɪˈzɪstəbl̩; riˈzistibl] *adj.* 可被抵抗的;可反抗的。

re·sis·tive [rɪˈzɪstɪv; riˈzistiv] *adj.* =**resistant.**

re·sis·tiv·i·ty [ˌrizɪsˈtɪvətɪ; ˌriːzisˈtiviti] *n.* ①〖物理〗電組係數。②抵抗力。

re·sist·less [rɪˈzɪstlɪs; riˈzistlis] *adj.* ①不可抵抗的。②無抵抗力的。③無法抵抗的。

re·sis·tor [rɪˈzɪstɚ; riˈzistə] *n.*〖電〗電阻器;電阻。

re·site [ˈriˈsaɪt; ˈriːˈsait] *v.t.,* **-sit·ed, -sit·ing.** 放於一新地方。

re·soil [riˈsɔɪl; riːˈsɔil] *v.t.* 補充（浸蝕掉的)上層土壤。

re·sole [riˈsol; ˈriːˈsoul] *v.t.,* **-soled, -sol·ing.** 換鞋底。

res·ol·u·ble [rɪˈzɑljəbl̩; riˈzɔljubl] *adj.* ①可分解的;可溶解的。②可解決的。

***res·o·lute** [ˈrɛzəˌlut; ˈrezəluːt] *adj.* 堅決的;斷然的;勇敢的。a *resolute* attitude. 果決的態度。—**ly,** *adv.*

***res·o·lu·tion** [ˌrɛzəˈljuʃən; ˌrezəˈluːʃən] *n.* ①已決定之事物;決心;決意;堅決;決定。to make good *resolutions.* 定良好的決策。②果斷力;決斷力。③決議;決議案。④分解;分析。⑤〖光學〗分辨。⑥(對某問題、爭執的)解決;解釋。⑦變換;由繁變簡。⑧〖醫〗(發炎等之)消散。

res·o·lu·tion·er [ˌrɛzəˈljuʃənɚ; ˌrezəˈluːʃənə] *n.* 附議人;支持決議案的人。(亦作 **resolutionist**)

res·o·lu·tive [ˈrɛzəˌljutɪv; ˈrezəluːtiv] *adj.* ①可溶解的;有溶解力的。②可消散的;能消腫的。③解除的。—*n.* 消腫藥。

re·solv·a·bil·i·ty [rɪˌzɑlvəˈbɪlətɪ; riˌzɔlvəˈbiliti] *n.* ①可決定; 可表決; 可議決。②可分解(性); 可溶解(性)。③可解決。④可改變。

re·solv·a·ble [rɪˈzɑlvəbl̩; riˈzɔlvəbl] *adj.* ①可決定的; 可表決的; 可議決的。②可分解的;可溶解的。③可解決的。④可改變的。

***re·solve** [rɪˈzɑlv; riˈzɔlv] *v.,* **-solved, -solv·ing,** *n.* —*v.t.* ①決定; 下決心。He *resolved* to do better work in the future. 他決定以後要更努力工作。②分解。③解決;解答。④議決;投票表決。It was *resolved* that our school have a lunchroom. 我們學校決定闢一間午餐廳。⑤改變。The assembly *resolved* itself into a committee.

大會改組成委員會。⑥〖光學〗分辨。⑦〖醫〗(發炎等)消散。—*v.i.* ①決定;決心。He *resolved* on (*or* upon) making an early start. 他決定即早着手。②分解。—*n.* ①決定之事物。He kept his *resolve* to do better. 他堅決地要做得再好一些。②決心。He is a man of great *resolve*. 他是有大決心的人。

***re·solved** [rɪˈzɑlvd; riˈzɔlvd] *adj.* 有決心的;意志堅決的;不屈不撓的;審愼的。—**ly**, *adv.*

re·sol·vent [rɪˈzɑlvənt; riˈzɔlvənt] *adj.* ①〖化〗分解的;溶解的;有分解力的;有溶解力的。②〖醫〗能消腫的。—*n.* ①分解物;溶劑。②消腫劑。③〖數學〗分解式。④(問題等之)解決方法。

resolvent equation 〖數學〗豫解方程式。

resolving power 〖光學〗分辨能力;分辨率。

res·o·nance [ˈrɛzn̩əns; ˈreznəns] *n.* ①回響;反響。②共鳴。*resonance* box. 共鳴箱。③〖電〗諧振;共振。④〖醫〗叩響(敲診時所生之響聲)。

resonance pendulum 〖物理〗共振擺。

resonance radiation 〖物理〗共振輻射。

res·o·nant [ˈrɛzn̩ənt; ˈreznənt] *adj.* ①(聲音)反響的;回響的;繼續增加音量的;繼續延長的。②共鳴的。③〖電〗諧振的;共振的。—*n.* 母音;有聲子音或半母音如: m, ŋ, n, l, r, j, w 等。—**ly**, *adv.*

res·o·nate [ˈrɛzəˌnet; ˈrezəneit] *v.*, **-nat·ed, -nat·ing.** —*v.i.* ①共鳴;反響。②產生共振。—*v.t.* 使共鳴或共振。

res·o·na·tor [ˈrɛzəˌnetɚ; ˈrezəneitə] *n.* 共鳴器;共振器。

res·o·na·to·ry [ˈrɛzənəˌtorɪ; ˈrezənətəri] *adj.* 產生共鳴的。

re·sorb [rɪˈsɔrb; riˈsɔːb] *v.i.* 再吸收;再吞。

re·sorb·ent [rɪˈsɔrbənt; riˈsɔːbənt] *adj.* 再吸收的。

res·or·cin·ol [rɛzˈɔrsɪˌnol, -nɑl; rezˈɔːsinoul, -nɔl] *n.* 樹脂酚(用於染料、醫術、攝影等方面)。(亦作 **resorcin**)

re·sorp·tion [rɪˈsɔrpʃən; riˈsɔːpʃən] *n.* 再吸收;再吞。

re-sort [ˌriˈsɔrt; ˈriːˈsɔːt] *v.t.* 再分類。

re·sort** [rɪˈzɔrt; riˈzɔːt] *v.i.* ①去;常去。to *resort* to the seaside. 常去海濱。②求助;依賴;訴諸。If other means fail, we shall *resort* to force. 如果其他手段均失敗,我們將訴諸武力。—*n.* ①常去之處;常往;聚集。a summer *resort*. 避暑地。②憑藉;手段。It must be done without *resort* to violence. 此事不可用暴力爲之。③最後所憑藉者。Good friends are the best *resort* in trouble. 好友是困難時最佳的憑藉。in the last resort*** 作爲最後之手段。

re-sound [ˌriˈsaund; ˈriːˈsaund] *v.t.* & *v.i.* (使)再響。

***re·sound** [rɪˈzaund; riˈzaund] *v.i.* ①回響;發回聲。②高聲響。③充滿響聲。The room *resounded* with the children's shouts. 屋裏充滿孩子們的鬧聲。④轟傳;被稱頌;揚名;馳名。His name *resounds* throughout the land. 他的名聲滿天下。—*v.t.* ①使成回聲;使共鳴。②高聲說或讀出。③使揚名於天下。

re·sound·ing [riˈzaundɪŋ; riːˈzaundiŋ] *adj.* ①發出回聲的;很響的。②宏亮的。

re·source** [rɪˈsors; riˈsɔːs] *n.* ①(供應、幫助、救濟等之)來源。②(*pl.*)資源。natural *resources*. 天然資源。③(常 *pl.*)策略;機智。a man of great *resources*. 多計謀之人。④解決困難或獲得成功之方法。be at the end of one's resources*** 至山窮水盡之地步;智窮力竭。

re·source·ful [rɪˈsorsfəl; riˈsɔːsful] *adj.* ①有機智的;多策略的。②多資源的。—**ly**, *adv.* —**ness**, *n.*

re·source·less [rɪˈsorslɪs; riˈsɔːslis] *adj.* ①缺乏資源的;無資源的。②無謀略的(人);無隨機應變之才的(人)。

‡**re·spect** [rɪˈspɛkt; risˈpekt] *n.* ①尊敬;敬重;尊重。Show *respect* to those who are older. 尊敬長者。②顧慮;關心。We must have (*or* pay) *respect* to the needs of the general reader. 我們須顧慮一般讀者之需要。③(*pl.*)敬意。Please give my *respects* to your brother. 請向令兄致候。④細事;點;方面。I think you are wrong in every *respect*. 我覺得你全部都錯了。⑤差別待遇;歧視。***in respect of*** (or ***to***) =**with regard to.** ***in respect that*** 〖古〗由於;因爲。***in some*** (***all***) ***respects*** 在某些(各)方面。***pay one's respects to*** 拜謁以示敬意。***with respect to*** 關於;顧慮到。—*v.t.* ①尊敬;敬重。to *respect* oneself. 尊重自己;自重。②顧慮;考慮。③重視;遵奉。to *respect* the law. 遵守法律。④關於;與…有關。***as respects*** 關於;說到。

re·spect·a·bil·i·ty [rɪˌspɛktəˈbɪlətɪ; risˌpektəˈbiliti] *n.*, *pl.* **-ties.** ①值得尊敬之性質或狀態。②受人尊敬之品格、名譽及社會地位等。③(常 *pl.*)受尊敬之人或物。

***re·spect·a·ble** [rɪˈspɛktəbl̩; risˈpektəbl] *adj.* ①有好名譽的;有聲望的;應受尊敬的。Such behavior is hardly *respectable*. 此種行爲不值得尊敬。②相當好的;大小(數量)適度的。a *respectable* amount. 適度的量。③(事物、行爲)文雅的;高尙的。④可以讓人看的;尙可的。—**re·spect·a·bly**, *adv.*

re·spect·er [rɪˈspɛktɚ; risˈpektə] *n.* 尊重者。(***no***) ***respecter of persons*** (不)視人之地位與重要性而以不同之態度相待者。

***re·spect·ful** [rɪˈspɛktfəl; risˈpektful] *adj.* 表示尊敬的;有禮貌的。He is always *respectful* to older people. 他對年齡較大的人總是彬彬有禮。—**ly**, *adv.*

***re·spect·ing** [rɪˈspɛktɪŋ; risˈpektiŋ] *prep.* 關於(=with regard to).

***re·spec·tive** [rɪˈspɛktɪv; risˈpektiv] *adj.* 個別的;各個的。The classes went to their *respective* rooms. 各班學生走進他們各自的教室。

***re·spec·tive·ly** [rɪˈspɛktɪvlɪ; risˈpektivli] *adv.* 個別地;各自地。Tom, Dick, and Harry are 16, 18, 20 *respectively*. 湯姆,狄克和哈利各爲 16, 18及 20歲。

re·spell [riˈspɛl; ˈriːˈspel] *v.t.* 再拼字;重拼字。

Res. Phys. Resident Physician. 住院醫師。

re·spir·a·ble [rɪˈspaɪrəbl̩; ˈrespirəbl] *adj.* ①能被呼吸的。②能呼吸的。

res·pi·ra·tion [ˌrɛspəˈreʃən; ˌrespəˈreiʃən] *n.* 呼吸。

res·pi·ra·tor [ˈrɛspəˌretɚ; ˈrespəreitə] *n.* ①口罩。②〖英〗防毒面具。③人工呼吸器。

re·spir·a·to·ry [rɪˈspaɪrəˌtorɪ; risˈpaiərətəri] *adj.* 關於呼吸的;呼吸用的。the *respiratory* organs. 呼吸器官。

re·spire [rɪˈspaɪr; risˈpaiə] *v.t.* & *v.i.*, **-spired, -spir·ing.** 呼吸。

res·pi·rom·e·ter [ˌrɛspəˈrɑmətɚ; ˌrespiˈrɔmitə] *n.* 呼吸運動計;呼吸計。

res·pite [ˈrɛspɪt; ˈrespait] *n.*, *v.*, **-pit·ed, -pit·ing.** —*n.* ①休息; 中止。②緩刑; 死刑之暫緩執行。—*v.t.* ①使有喘息機會。②緩期執行。

re·splend·ence [rɪˈsplɛndəns; risˈplendəns] *n.* 輝耀; 燦爛;華麗。(亦作 **resplendency**)

***re·splend·ent** [rɪˈsplɛndənt; risˈplendənt] *adj.* 燦爛的;華麗的;輝耀的;赫赫的。—**ly,** *adv.*

***re·spond** [rɪˈspɑnd; risˈpɔnd] *v.i.* ①回答。to *respond* briefly to a question. 簡短地回答一問題。②回應; 反應。Nerves *respond* to a stimulus. 神經對刺激起反應。③負責。to *respond* in damage. 對損失負責。

re·spond·ence [rɪˈspɑndəns; risˈpɔndəns] *n.* ①相應;一致。②反應;感應;答應。(亦作 **respondency**)

re·spond·ent [rɪˈspɑndənt; risˈpɔndənt] *adj.* ①回答的; 應答的; 感應的。②被告立場的。—*n.* ①回答者; 答辯者。②被告(尤指上訴及離婚案件)。

re·spon·den·ti·a [ˌrispɑnˈdɛnʃɪə; ˈriːspɔnˈdenʃiə] *n.* 〖法律〗船貨押借(俟貨安抵目的地後始付還者);冒險借款。

re·spond·er [rɪˈspɑndɚ; risˈpɔndə] *n.* ①回答者。②對刺激起反應之機械裝置。

***re·sponse** [rɪˈspɑns; risˈpɔns] *n.* ①回答; 回應。 in *response* to your inquiry. 為回答你的詢問。②會衆或唱詩班應答牧師之祈禱文或歌唱。③〖生理〗反應。—**less,** *adj.*

***re·spon·si·bil·i·ty** [rɪˌspɑnsəˈbɪlətɪ; risˌpɔnsəˈbiliti] *n.*, *pl.* **-ties.** ①責任。You should take up your *responsibility.* 你應負起你的責任。②負擔。*on one's own responsibility* 主動地;自己負責地。

***re·spon·si·ble** [rɪˈspɑnsəbl; risˈpɔnsəbl] *adj.* ①負責任的; 應負責任的〖for〗。I am not *responsible* for it. 我不負此事之責任。②可信賴的; 可靠的。③有責任的。④明白是非的;能負責任的。⑤對…負責的〖常for, to〗。⑥能履行責任的(如還債等)。 —*n.* ①負責任的人。②(*pl.*)〖戲劇〗**a.** (作*pl.*解) 小但重要的角色。**b.** (作*sing.*解)演此角色的演員。

re·spon·sion [rɪˈspɑnʃən; risˈpɔnʃən] *n.* ①應答;答覆。②(*pl.*)牛津大學 B.A. 學位三次考試中之初試。

re·spon·sive [rɪˈspɑnsɪv; risˈpɔnsiv] *adj.* ①回答的;應答的。②易感動的;易感應的;敏感的。③(做禮拜時)應用或含有應答歌的。④〖生理〗反應的。

re·spon·so·ry [rɪˈspɑnsərɪ; risˈpɔnsəri] *n.*, *pl.* **-ries.** 〖宗教〗日課完畢後獨唱者和唱詩班的對答歌唱。

‡**rest**[1] [rɛst; rest] *n.* ①睡眠。 I had a good night's *rest.* 我有一夜的安睡。②休息;休憩。③靜止; 安靜。The lake was at *rest.* 湖水平靜。④支持物(托、架、臺等)。 a back *rest.* 後架。⑤休息處。⑥〖音樂〗休止;休止符。⑦(讀書中之) 頓挫。⑧死。 The poor man is now at *rest.* 這可憐的人死去了。⑨旅客休息處; 旅館。 ***at rest*** **a.** 休息;睡覺。**b.** 死亡。**c.** 休止; 不動。**d.** 安靜;無憂。 Nothing could put his mind *at rest.* 甚麼事都無法使他的心安下來。***go*** (or ***retire***) ***to rest*** 就寢。***lay...to rest*** 安葬。***set a person's mind at rest*** 使安心。***take a rest*** 休息。—*v.i.* ①睡眠;休息;停止。Lie down and *rest.* 躺下休息。②被支持;倚靠。③倚賴〖常 on〗。Our hope *rests* on you. 我們的希望寄託在你的身上。④繫於; 以…為基礎; 在於。⑤信賴; 信任。 We *rest* in your promise. 我們信任你的諾言。⑥停留於;徘徊於。⑦盯住;注視(如視線等)。⑧〖法律〗自動停止向庭上提供證據。⑨死後永遠安息。 He *rests* in the churchyard. 他長眠在墓地裏。—*v.t.* ①使休息。②倚靠。We *rest* our hope(s) on (*or* in) you. 我們將希望寄托在你身上。③(法律案件中)自動停止提出證據。④指向(如目光)。⑤以…為根據;使依賴。⑥使停止。***rest on*** (or ***upon***) **a.** 為…所支持。**b.** 散布於…之上。**c.** (眼睛)凝視。***rest on one's oars*** **a.** 停止划船。**b.** 努力工作之後得到一段時間休息。***rest with*** 全在於。It *rests with* you to decide. 這全要看你決定的。

‡**rest**[2] *n.* ①其餘之物;其餘之人;餘者。The *rest* of the money is his. 其餘的錢是他的。②〖英,銀行〗剩餘。***and*** (***all***) ***the rest*** (***of it***) 其他等等。***for the rest*** 至於其他。—*v.i.* 依然;繼續。

rest[3] *n.*中古騎士甲冑胸板上支撐矛柄之處。

re·start [riˈstart; riːˈstaːt] *v.t.* & *v.i.* 重新開始;再發動。—*n.* 新的開始。

re·state [riˈstet; ˈriːˈsteit] *v.t.*, **-stat·ed, -stat·ing.** 重新陳述;重講;再聲明。

re·state·ment [riˈstetmənt; ˈriːˈsteitmənt] *n.* ①重述;再聲明。②重述的話;重作的聲明。

***res·tau·rant** [ˈrɛstərənt; ˈrestərɔ̃ːŋ, -rɔnt] *n.* 飯店;餐館。

restaurant car 〖英〗餐車。

res·tau·ra·teur [ˌrɛstərəˈtɝ; ˌrestɔ(ː)rəˈtəː] *n.*, *pl.* **-teurs.** 〖法〗飯店主人。

rest cure 〖醫〗(精神病等之)靜養療法。

rest day 休息日;安息日。

rest energy 〖物理〗靜能。

re·ster·i·lize [riˈstɛrəlˌaɪz; riːˈsterilaiz] *v.t.*, **-lized, -liz·ing.** 再消毒。

rest·ful [ˈrɛstfəl; ˈrestful] *adj.* ①平靜的;休止的;不受打擾的。②休息充足的;給人休息的。—**ly,** *adv.*

rest·har·row [ˈrɛstˌhæro; ˈrestˌhærou] *n.* 〖植物〗歐洲產的一種豆科植物。

rest home 為照顧恢復康健中的病人、老人、或殘廢者並有特別設備的住家。

rest house (印度的) 旅客休息的場所。(亦作 **resthouse**)

rest·ing [ˈrɛstɪŋ; ˈrestiŋ] *adj.* ①〖植物〗休眠的。②休息的。

resting place 休息處; 休息所。***the final*** (or ***last***) ***resting place*** 墳墓。

res·ti·tute [ˈrɛstəˌtjut; ˈrestitjuːt] *v.t.*, **-tut·ed, -tut·ing.** ①歸還。②補償。

res·ti·tu·tion [ˌrɛstəˈtjuʃən; ˌrestiˈtjuːʃən] *n.* ①歸還;償還。②賠償。③復位;復職;(夫婦)恢復同居關係。④〖物理〗(彈力體的)恢復。

res·tive [ˈrɛstɪv; ˈrestiv] *adj.* ①不安寧的;動亂的; 不穩的。②難駕馭的; 倔強的。③(馬等)不肯前進的。—**ly,** *adv.* —**ness,** *n.*

***rest·less** [ˈrɛstlɪs; ˈrestlis] *adj.* ①不安靜的;好動的;紛擾的。②無睡眠的。③無休止的。—**ly,** *adv.* —**ness,** *n.*

rest mass 〖物理〗靜質量。

re·stock [riˈstɑk; ˈriːˈstɔk] *v.t.* & *v.i.* 再供以物品;重新進貨(於);再補充。

re·stor·a·ble [rɪˈstorəbl; risˈtɔːrəbl]

adj. 可挽回的;可復職的;可復舊的。

***res·to·ra·tion** [ˌrɛstəˈreʃən; ˌrestəˈreiʃən, -tɔːˈr-] *n.* ①恢復; 復原。Closed during *restorations.* 內部裝修暫停營業。②修復之物。③復職。**the Restoration**〖英史〗**a.** 王權復興 (1660年 Charles II 之復辟)。**b.** 王權復興時代(1660-1688)。

re·stor·a·tive [rɪˈstorətɪv; risˈtɔrətiv] *adj.* ①交還的; 回復的。②可恢復的; 能恢復健康或體力的。—*n.* ①恢復健康或體力之物(如補劑、新鮮空氣等)。②興奮劑。

***re·store** [rɪˈstor, -ˈstɔr; risˈtɔː, rəs-, -ˈtɔə] *v.t.*, **-stored, -stor·ing.** ①恢復;重建。②修補;修復。③使痊癒;使復原。to feel completely *restored.* 健康完全復原。④歸還;交還。to *restore* money to its owner. 將錢交還遺失者。⑤使再出現;重新使用。

rest period ①(工場、學校、或軍中之)休息時間。②〖植物〗生長暫停期。

restr. restaurant.

***re·strain** [rɪˈstren; risˈtrein] *v.t.* ①克制; 抑制; 約束; 阻止。to *restrain* a child from doing mischief. 阻止孩子惡作劇。You must not *restrain* them of their liberty. 你不可約束他們的自由。②監禁。

re·strain·ed·ly [rɪˈstrenɪdlɪ; risˈtreinidli] *adv.* 受約束地;克制地;謹愼地。

***re·straint** [rɪˈstrent; risˈtreint] *n.* ①抑制;遏制。He gave himself up to evil without *restraint.* 他縱情作惡。②限制; 約束。③監禁。to be held in *restraint.* 受監禁。④(情感等之)抑制。

restraint of trade 貿易管制。

***re·strict** [rɪˈstrɪkt;risˈtrikt] *v.t.* 限制; 約束。Our club membership is *restricted* to twelve. 我們的社員以十二位爲限。

re·strict·ed [rɪˈstrɪktɪd; risˈtriktid] *adj.* ①限制的; 受約束的; 拘束的。②僅限於某一團體或人羣的。*restricted* hotel. 僅限白人居住的旅館。③〖美政府,軍〗密(機密分類之最低級。其餘爲 confidential 機密, secret 極機密, top secret 絕對機密)。—**ly,** *adv.*

***re·stric·tion** [rɪˈstrɪkʃən; risˈtrikʃən] *n.* ①限制。to place *restrictions* on foreign trade. 管制對外貿易。②帶有限制性之條件或規則。

re·stric·tion·ism [rɪˈstrɪkʃənˌɪzm̩; risˈtrikʃənizəm] *n.* 商業(尤指進口)限制政策。—**re·stric·tion·ist,** *n., adj.*

re·stric·tive [rɪˈstrɪktɪv; risˈtriktiv] *adj.* ①帶有限制性的; 限制的。②〖文法〗限制的。—**ly,** *adv.*

restrictive clause 〖文法〗限制子句。

rest room (商店等之)厠所;洗手間。

‡re·sult [rɪˈzʌlt; riˈzʌlt, rəˈz-] *n.* ①結果;效果。We worked without *result.* 我們的工作無效果。②成績; 成效。③計算所得之答案;答數。—*v.i.* ①產生;起於〖常from〗. Sickness often *results* from eating too much. 疾病常起於過度飲食。②終歸; 致成〖常 in〗. The accident *resulted* in his death. 這意外事件使他身死。

re·sult·ant [rɪˈzʌltn̩t; riˈzʌltənt] *adj.* ①結果的;產生結果的。②合成的。*resultant* force. 〖機械〗合力。—*n.* ①結果。②〖物理〗合力;合成運動。③〖數學〗結式。

re·sult·ful [rɪˈzʌltfəl; riˈzʌltful] *adj.* 有結果的;有成果的;有成績的;有效果的。

re·sult·less [rɪˈzʌltlɪs; riˈzʌltlis] *adj.* 無結果的;無成果的;無效果的;無益的。

re·sum·a·ble [rɪˈzjuməbl̩; riˈzjuːməbl] *adj.* 可重獲的;可恢復的;再開始的;可繼續的。

***re·sume** [rɪˈzum, -ˈzɪum; riˈzjuːm, rəˈz-, -ˈzuːm] *v.*, **-sumed, -sum·ing.** —*v.t.* ①重新開始;繼續。to *resume* work. 恢復工作; 復業。②重獲; 再取。He *resumed* his seat. 他重回原座。—*v.i.* 更始;復始。

ré·su·mé [ˌrɛzuˈme; ˈrezju(ː)mei] *n.* ①摘要;概略。②(人之)簡歷。(亦作**resume**)

re·sump·tion [rɪˈzʌmpʃən; riˈzʌmpʃən] *n.* 重新開始;重獲。

re·sump·tive [rɪˈzʌmptɪv; riˈzʌmptiv] *adj.* ①取回的;收回的;恢復的;再開始的。②摘要的;概要的。

re·su·pi·nate [rɪˈsupəˌnet; riˈsjuːpineit] *adj.* ①〖植物〗倒生的(蘭花等)。②仰臥的;仰翻的。

re·sur·face [riˈsɝfɪs; ˈriːˈsəːfis] *v.t.*, **-faced, -fac·ing.** 賦與一新表面; 爲…再鋪一層不同的表面。

re·surge [rɪˈsɝdʒ;riˈsəːdʒ] *v.i.*, **-surged, -surg·ing.** ①再起; 復活。②(波浪)再起伏; 再澎湃。

re·sur·gent [rɪˈsɝdʒənt; riˈsəːdʒənt] *adj.* 再起的; 復活的。—*n.* 再起者;復活者。—**re·sur·gence,** *n.*

res·ur·rect [ˌrɛzəˈrɛkt; ˌrezəˈrekt] *v.t.* ①使蘇醒;使復活。②恢復;復興。③〖俗〗掘起;挖出。—*v.i.* 蘇醒;復活。

res·ur·rec·tion [ˌrɛzəˈrɛkʃən; ˌrezəˈrekʃən] *n.* ①復活。②恢復;修復;恢復使用。③發掘屍體。④(R-)基督教義中最後審判日之死者復活。**the Resurrection** 耶穌的復活。

res·ur·rec·tion·ist [ˌrɛzəˈrɛkʃənɪst; ˌrezəˈrekʃənist] *n.* ①掘屍的人;盜屍賊。②相信死者復活的人。③闡釋者;(祕密的)暴露者。

resurrection man 盜屍者。

re·sus·ci·tate [rɪˈsʌsəˌtet; riˈsʌsiteit] *v.*, **-tat·ed, -tat·ing.**—*v.t.*使蘇醒;使復活;恢復。—*v.i.* 復活;復蘇。—**re·sus·ci·ta·tion,** *n.*

re·sus·ci·ta·tive [rɪˈsʌsəˌtetɪv; riˈsʌsiteitiv] *adj.* 復蘇的;復活的;復興的。

re·sus·ci·ta·tor [rɪˈsʌsəˌtetə; riˈsʌsiteitə] *n.* ①人工呼吸器。②救生者; 作人工呼吸者。

ret [rɛt; ret] *v.t.*, **ret·ted, ret·ting.** 以水浸漬(蔴、木材等)。

ret. ①retard. ②retired. ③returned.

***re·tail** [*n., adj.* ˈritel; ˈriːteil, riːˈt- *v.* ˈritel, for *v.t.* ②also rɪˈtel; riːˈteil, riˈt-, ˈriː-] *n.* 零售。to sell by (*or* at) *retail.* 零售。—*adj.* ①零碎的;少量的。②零售的。the *retail* price. 零售價格。—*v.i.* 零售。These shoes *retail* at (*or* for) $10 a pair. 這些鞋子零賣十元一雙。—*v.t.* ①零售。②轉述;再說。—**er,** *n.*

retail store 〖美〗零售店。

***re·tain** [rɪˈten; riˈtein, rəˈt-] *v.t.* ①保留;保持。to *retain* an old custom. 保留舊的習俗。②不忘;記憶。③僱;聘請。to *retain* a lawyer. 聘請一律師。④留住。

re·tain·er[1] [rɪˈtenə; riˈteinə] *n.* ①保留者;保持者;保留物。②侍從;家臣;門客。③〖機械〗承盤;制動。

re·tain·er[2] *n.* ①保留職務。②〖法律〗**a.** 聘請律師、顧問等。**b.** 律師、顧問等之聘請費。

retaining wall 護堤壁。

re·take [*v.* riˈtek; ˈriːˈteik, riːˈt- *n.* ˈriˌtek; ˈriːˈteik] *v.*, **-took, -tak·en, -tak·ing,** *n.* —*v.t.* ①再取;取回。②奪回。③〖電影,攝影〗重攝。—*n.* 重攝;重攝之景、像。

re·tal·i·ate [rɪˈtælɪˌet; riˈtælieit] *v.i. & v.t.*, **-at·ed, -at·ing.** 報復;復讎;回敬。to *retaliate* upon one's enemy. 向敵人報復。—**re·tal·i·a·tive, re·tal·i·a·to·ry,** *adj.* —**re·tal·i·a·tor, re·tal·i·a·tion,** *n.*

re·tard [rɪˈtɑrd; riˈtɑːd] *v.t.* ①阻礙;妨礙。②延遲。—*n.* 阻礙;延緩。***in retard*** 阻礙的;遲緩的。—**er,** *n.*

re·tard·ate [rɪˈtɑrdet; riˈtɑːdeit] *n.* 白痴。

re·tar·da·tion [ˌritɑrˈdeʃən; ˌriːtɑːˈdeiʃən] *n.* ①阻礙。②躭延;遲滯。③導致阻礙或遲滯之事物。④〖心理〗落退。(亦作 **retardment**) —**re·tard·a·tive, re·tard·a·to·ry,** *adj.*

re·tard·ed [rɪˈtɑrdɪd; riˈtɑːdid] *adj.* 智力遲鈍的。

re·tard·ee [rɪˌtɑrˈdi; riˌtɑːˈdiː] *n.* 智力遲鈍的人;白痴。

retch [rɛtʃ; riːtʃ] *v.i.* 嘔;作嘔;乾嘔。

retd. ①retained. ②retired. ③returned.

re·tell [riˈtɛl; ˈriːˈtel] *v.t.*, **-told, -tell·ing.** 再講述;再告知;再說。

re·ten·tion [rɪˈtɛnʃən; riˈtenʃən] *n.* ①保留;保持。②保持力。③記憶;記憶力。④拘留;扣押。⑤〖醫〗留滯;存留;閉止。

re·ten·tive [rɪˈtɛntɪv; riˈtentiv] *adj.* ①保留的;有保持力的。②有記憶力的;記性好的。—**ly,** *adv.* —**ness,** *n.*

re·ten·tiv·i·ty [ˌritɛnˈtɪvətɪ; ˌriːtenˈtiviti] *n.* ①保持力;記憶力。②〖物理〗頑磁(感應强度)。

re·think [riˈθɪŋk; riːˈθiŋk] *v.t.*, **-thought, -think·ing.** 再想;再考慮。

re·ti·ar·y [ˈrɪʃɪˌɛrɪ; ˈriːʃiəri] *adj.* ①網(狀)的。②結網的。③有網的。④巧於糾纏的。—*n.* ①古羅馬帶網之角鬥士。②結網蜘蛛。

ret·i·cence [ˈrɛtəsn̩s; ˈretisəns] *n.* 沉默;緘口;無言。(亦作 **reticency**)

ret·i·cent [ˈrɛtəsn̩t; ˈretisənt] *adj.* 沉默的;寡言的。—**ly,** *adv.*

ret·i·cle [ˈrɛtək!; ˈretikəl] *n.* 〖光學〗(望遠鏡等之)線網。

re·tic·u·lar [rɪˈtɪkjələ; riˈtikjulə] *adj.* ①網狀(組織)的。②多孔的;蜂窩狀的。③錯綜複雜的。④〖解剖〗(反芻動物之)蜂巢胃的。

re·tic·u·late [*adj.* rɪˈtɪkjəlɪt; riˈtikjulit *v.* rɪˈtɪkjəˌlet; riˈtikjuleit] *adj., v.,* **-lat·ed, -lat·ing.** —*adj.* (亦作 **reticulated**) ①網狀(組織)的。②〖植物〗有網狀脈的(葉)。—*v.t. & v.i.* (使)呈網狀。

re·tic·u·la·tion [rɪˌtɪkjəˈleʃən; riˌtikjuˈleiʃən] *n.* 網目;網狀物;網狀細工;(繪畫等之)方眼複寫法。

ret·i·cule [ˈrɛtɪˌkjul; ˈretikjuːl] *n.* ①女用手提網袋。②〖光學〗(望遠鏡等之)線網。

re·tic·u·lum [rɪˈtɪkjələm; riˈtikjuləm] *n., pl.* **-la** [-lə; -lə]. *gen.* **-li** [-laɪ; -lai] *for* ②. ①網狀物;網狀組織;網狀花紋;網狀結構。②(R-)〖天文〗網罟座(南天之一星座)。③〖生物〗細胞原生質中發現的一種網狀組織;網狀膜。④〖動物〗(反芻動物之)第二胃;蜂巢胃。⑤〖植物〗(葉上的)網脈。

re·ti·form [ˈritɪˌfɔrm; ˈriːtifɔːm] *adj.* 網狀(組織)的。a *retiform* tissue. 網狀組織。

ret·i·na [ˈrɛtn̩ə; ˈretinə] *n., pl.* **-nas, -nae** [-ni; -niː]. 〖解剖〗視網膜。

ret·i·nal [ˈrɛtɪnəl; ˈretinəl] *adj.* 視網膜的;視網膜上的。

ret·in·ene [ˈrɛtɪˌnin; ˈretiniːn] *n.* 〖生物〗視黃質(眼球網膜桿狀細胞之視紫經光線作用所變成之黃色素, =visual yellow).

ret·i·ni·tis [ˌrɛtəˈnaɪtɪs; ˌretiˈnaitis] *n.* 〖醫〗視網膜炎。

ret·i·nue [ˈrɛtn̩ˌju; ˈretinjuː] *n.* 侍從;隨員;家僕。

***re·tire** [rɪˈtaɪr; riˈtaiə, rəˈt-] *v.*, **-tired, -tir·ing,** *n.* —*v.i.* ①隱居;隱退。to *retire* from the world. 遁世。②就寢。We *retire* early. 我們很早就寢。③退休;退職。He *retired* at the age of sixty. 他於六十歲時退休。④(軍隊)撤退。⑤離去;退去。—*v.t.* ①使解職。②收回(債券、股票等);撤回。③〖棒球〗使(打擊手)出局。—*n.* 退却號。to sound *retire*. 吹退却號。—**re·tir·er,** *n.*

re·tired [rɪˈtaɪrd; riˈtaiəd] *adj.* ①退職的;已退休的。*retired* pay. 退休金。②隱退的。to lead a *retired* life. 度隱居生活。③隱蔽的。—**ly,** *adv.* —**ness,** *n.*

retired list (軍中)退役軍人名册。

re·tir·ee [rɪˈtaɪri; riˈtaiəriː] *n.* 退休者。

***re·tire·ment** [rɪˈtaɪrmənt; riˈtaiəmənt] *n.* ①退休。②退隱之生活方式;退隱之所。She lives in *retirement*. 她過着退隱的生活。③收回(股票等)。④〖軍〗有計畫的撤退。—*adj.* 退休的。*retirement* pay. 退休金。

re·tir·ing [rɪˈtaɪrɪŋ; riˈtaiəriŋ] *adj.* ①隱退的。②退職的;退休的。③羞怯的。

re·tir·ing-room [rɪˈtaɪrɪŋˌrum; riˈtaiəriŋ-ruːm] *n.* 休息室。

re·tool [riˈtul; ˈriːˈtuːl] *v.t.* ①換或更改(工廠之)機器、工具。②改組。—*v.i.* 替換或更改機器、工具。

re·tort**¹ [rɪˈtɔrt; riˈtɔːt, rəˈt-] *v.t.* 回嘴。"It's none of your business," he *retorted*. "你管不着,"他回嘴道。—*v.i.* 反擊。retort insult for insult*** (or ***blow for blow***) 以牙還牙。—*n.* 回嘴。a sharp *retort*. 銳利刺人的回嘴。

re·tort² *n.* ①〖化〗蒸餾皿;蒸餾器。②罐頭食物消毒器。—*v.t.* 以蒸氣或高溫消毒已密封之罐頭。

re·tor·tion [rɪˈtɔrʃən; riˈtɔːʃən] *n.* ①返回;折回;曲回。②〖國際法〗報復行爲。

re·touch [riˈtʌtʃ; ˈriːˈtʌtʃ] *v.t.* ①〖照相〗修描(底片或照片)。②修飾;潤色;修改(繪畫等)。—*n.* 修改;潤色。

re·trace [rɪˈtres; riˈtreis] *v.t.*, **-traced, -trac·ing.** ①折回;退回;引還。②回顧;退想。③追溯;探源。

re-trace [riˈtres; riːˈtreis] *v.t. & v.i.*, **-traced, -trac·ing.** 再模寫;再描模。

re·tract [rɪˈtrækt; riˈtrækt] *v.t.* ①縮回。②收回。—*v.i.* ①縮回。②收回聲明、承諾等。

re·tract·a·ble [rɪˈtræktəb!; riˈtræktəbl] *adj.* ①可撤回的;可翻悔的。②可收縮的;伸縮自如的。

re·trac·ta·tion [ˌritrækˈteʃən; ˌriːtrækˈteiʃən] *n.* ①(約束、意見、陳述等之)取消;翻悔。②撤回;撤銷。

re·trac·tile [rɪˈtrækt!; riˈtræktl] *adj.* ①〖動物〗有收縮能力的。②取消的;收回的。

re·trac·til·i·ty [ˌritrækˈtɪlətɪ; ˌriːtrækˈtiliti] *n.* 伸縮性;伸縮能力。

re·trac·tion [rɪˈtrækʃən; riˈtrækʃən] *n.* 縮回;收回。

re·trac·tive [rɪˈtræktɪv; riˈtræktiv] *adj.* 可收縮的;能收縮的;有收縮傾向的。

re·trac·tor [rɪˈtræktə; riˈtræktə] *n.* ①〖外科〗牽引器;牽引繃帶。②〖解剖〗縮肌。③抓子鈎。④翻悔者。

re·train [riˈtren; ˈriːˈtrein] *v.t.* 再訓練;授以新技術。—*v.i.* 接受再訓練。

***re·treat** [rɪˈtrit; riˈtriːt, rəˈt-] *v.i.* ①撤

退;退却。②向後傾斜。—*v.t.* ①撤退;拿走。②〖西洋棋〗將(棋子)後移。—*n.* ①撤退;退却。The whole army was in full *retreat.* 全軍總退却。②撤退號;退軍號。③安靜的地方;安全的地方。④(酗酒者或瘋子的)收容所或療養院。⑤暫時退隱;〖天主教〗避靜。⑥〖軍〗a. 降旗典禮。b. 降旗時之號音或鼓號。***beat a retreat*** a. 撤退;逃走。b. 放棄某項工作。

re·tree [rɪ'tri; ri'triː] *n.* 微有破損的紙。

re·trench [rɪ'trɛntʃ; ri'trentʃ] *v.t.* ①減少(支出);節省。②刪除;省略。③〖軍〗以複廓或堡壘防護。—*v.i.* 減少支出;節省。

re·trench·ment [rɪ'trɛntʃmənt; ri'trentʃmənt] *n.* ①減少支出;節省。②刪除;省略。③〖軍〗a. 複廓。b. 壕溝;堡壘。

re·tri·al [ri'traɪəl; 'riː'traiəl] *n.* ①〖法律〗再審;覆審。②再試驗。

ret·ri·bu·tion [ˌrɛtrə'bjuʃən; ˌretri'bjuːʃən] *n.* ①報應;果報;罰。②報償;復讎。

re·trib·u·tive [rɪ'trɪbjətɪv; ri'tribjutiv] *adj.* 報應的;報償的。

re·triev·a·ble [rɪ'trivəbl̩; ri'triːvəbl] *adj.* 可取回的;可恢復的;可補償的;可挽回的。

re·triev·al [rɪ'trivl̩; ri'triːvəl] *n.* ①取回;恢復;補償;挽回。②恢復或挽回之可能性。***beyond*** (or ***past***) ***retrieval*** 不能恢復的;不能挽回的。

re·trieve [rɪ'triv; ri'triːv] *v.,* **-trieved, -triev·ing,** *n.* —*v.t.* ①尋回。②恢復。③補救。④替人尋得並帶回。⑤拉回(釣魚線)。⑥援救。—*v.i.* ①尋回獵獲物。②拉回釣魚線。—*n.* ①尋回;恢復。②尋回的可能性。

re·triev·er [rɪ'trivɚ; ri'triːvə] *n.* ①(能尋回獵物之)獵犬。②尋回東西者。③恢復者。

retro- 〖字首〗表"向後;回復;回溯;歸還;後方"之義(如 retrogress 倒退)。

ret·ro·act [ˌrɛtro'ækt; ˌretrou'ækt] *v.i.* ①逆溯;反動。②〖法律〗追溯既往。

ret·ro·ac·tion [ˌrɛtro'ækʃən; ˌretrou'ækʃən] *n.* ①反應力。②反動;反應。③相反之行動。

ret·ro·ac·tive [ˌrɛtro'æktɪv; ˌretrou'æktiv] *adj.* ①追溯既往的。②加薪之追溯既往生效的。—**ly,** *adv.* —**ret·ro·ac·tiv·i·ty,** *n.*

ret·ro·cede¹ [ˌrɛtro'sid; ˌretrou'siːd] *v.t.,* **-ced·ed, -ced·ing.** 歸還;返還(占領的領土)。—**ret·ro·ces·sion,** *n.*

ret·ro·cede² *v.i.,* **-ced·ed, -ced·ing.** ①後退;退回。②〖醫〗(病症之)內攻。—**ret·ro·ces·sion,** *n.*

ret·ro·fire ['rɛtroˌfaɪr; 'retroufaiə] *n., v.,* **-fired, -fir·ing.** —*n.* 減速火箭之發動。—*v.i.* 發動減速火箭。

ret·ro·flex ['rɛtrəˌflɛks; 'retroufleks] *adj.* ①反曲的;折返的;翻轉的。②〖語音〗a. 尖端上升並向後捲的(舌)。b. 捲舌的(音)。(亦作 **retroflexed**)

ret·ro·flex·ion [ˌrɛtrə'flɛkʃən; ˌretrou'flekʃən] *n.* ①反曲;翻轉。②〖醫〗器官(如子宮)之後屈。③〖語音〗捲舌音。(亦作 **retroflection**)

ret·ro·gra·da·tion [ˌrɛtrəgre'deʃən; ˌretrəgrei'deiʃən] *n.* ①後退;退去。②退步;衰退;退化。③〖天文〗逆行。

ret·ro·grade ['rɛtrəˌgred; 'retrougreid] *adj., adv., n., v.,* **-grad·ed, -grad·ing.** —*adj.* ①後退的;倒退的。②退化的;退步的。③〖天文〗逆行的。④相反的;顛倒的。—*adv.* 逆行地;倒流地。—*n.* =**retrogression.** —*v.i.* ①退後;倒退。②退化;退步。③衰落;墮落。④〖天文〗逆行。—*v.t.* 使後退;使退步。

ret·ro·gress ['rɛtrəˌgrɛs; ˌretrə'gres] *v.i.* 後退;倒退;衰退;墮落;衰微。

ret·ro·gres·sion [ˌrɛtrə'grɛʃən; ˌretrou'greʃən] *n.* ①後退;退步;衰退。②〖生物〗退化。③〖天文〗逆行運動。

ret·ro·gres·sive [ˌrɛtrə'grɛsɪv; ˌretrou'gresiv] *adj.* 退步的;退化的;衰退的;墮落的。

ret·ro·rock·et ['rɛtroˌrɑkɪt; 'retrouˌrɔkit] *n.* (太空船或飛彈之)減速火箭。

ret·ro·spect ['rɛtrəˌspɛkt; 'retrouspekt] *n.* 反顧;回溯。***in*** (***the***) ***retrospect*** 回顧。—*v.t.* & *v.i.* 回想。

ret·ro·spec·tion [ˌrɛtrə'spɛkʃən; ˌretrou'spekʃən] *n.* 回顧。

ret·ro·spec·tive [ˌrɛtrə'spɛktɪv; ˌretrou'spektiv] *adj.* ①回顧的;追想的。②溯及既往的。—*n.* 回顧展。—**ly,** *adv.*

retrospective show 回顧展。

ret·rous·sé [ˌrɛtru'se, rə'truse; rə'truːsei] *adj.* 向上翻的(尤指鼻子)。

ret·ro·ver·sion [ˌrɛtrə'vɝʃən; ˌretrou'vəːʃən] *n.* ①回顧;退轉。②〖醫〗(器官的)後傾;後轉;後向。

ret·ro·vert [ˌrɛtrə'vɝt; ˌretrou'vəːt] *v.t.* 使向後彎曲;使反轉;使後屈;使後傾。

re·try [ri'traɪ; 'riː'trai] *v.t.,* **-tried, -try·ing.** 再試驗;再審;重審。

ret·ting ['rɛtɪŋ; 'retiŋ] *n.* (麻等之)浸漬。

‡**re·turn** [rɪ'tɝn; ri'təːn] *v.i.* ①回;歸。to *return* home. 回家。②回復。③回答。④回想。—*v.t.* ①歸還。②回答。③獲利。④宣告。⑤選出(議員等)。⑥(牌戲中)回打。⑦報答。to *return* evil for good. 以怨報德。⑧反射(聲、光等)。—*n.* ①回來;歸。②歸還;報答。a poor *return* for kindness. 以怨報德。③(常*pl.*) 贏利。*returns* from a sale. 一次販賣所得之利潤。④(常*pl.*)報告;陳述。election *returns.* 選舉報告。⑤回答;報答;反擊;送回。⑥〖英〗來回票。⑦(*pl.*) 退貨。***in return*** 以為報答。***Many happy returns of the day!*** (賀生日用語)祝你長壽! —*adj.* ①回來的;歸來的。a *return* ticket. 回程票。②送回的;回報的。

re·turn·a·ble [rɪ'tɝnəbl̩; ri'təːnəbl] *adj.* ①可以退還的。②必須返還的;目的在使之返回的。—*n.* 〖美〗可退回的空瓶或空罐。

return address 退信地址。

re·turned [rɪ'tɝnd; ri'təːnd] *adj.* 已歸的;已回來的。***returned students*** 回國之留學生。

re·turn·ee [rɪˌtɝ'ni; ritəː'niː] *n.* ①(自海外或囚禁等)回來者。②自海外服役回來者。

return receipt (雙掛號郵件之)回執。

re·tuse [rɪ'tjus; ri'tjuːs] *adj.* 〖植物〗前端微凹形的。

re·un·ion [ri'junjən; 'riː'juːnjən] *n.* ①重行結合;重修舊好;融合。②重聚。③團圓。

re·un·ion·ist [ri'junjənɪst; 'riː'juːnjənist] *n.* 主張重行結合者;(尤指)擁護英國國教同天主教重行聯合者。

re·u·nite [ˌriju'naɪt; 'riːjuː'nait] *v.t.* & *v.i.,* **-u·nit·ed, -u·nit·ing.** (使)再結合;(使)重聚;(使)團聚。

re·use [*v.* ri'juz; 'riː'juːz *n.* ri'jus; 'riː'juːs] *v.,* **-used, -us·ing,** *n.* —*v.t.* 再使用。—*n.* 再使用。—**re·us·a·ble,** *adj.*

Reu·ters ['rɔɪtɚz; 'rɔitəz] *n.* 路透通訊社。

rev 〔rɛv; rev〕 *n., v.,* **revved, rev·ving.** —*n.* 〖俗〗發動機之旋轉。 —*v.t.* 〖俗〗改變(引擎、馬達等)之速度；加速〖常 up〗. —*v.i.* 〖俗〗加速旋轉。

Rev. ①Reverend. ②Revelation. ③Revelations. **rev.** ①revenue. ②reverse. ③review. ④revise. ⑤revised. ⑥revision. ⑦revolution. ⑧revolving.

re·val·or·i·za·tion 〔ˌrivælərɪˈzeʃən; ˌri:vælәriˈzeiʃәn〕 *n.* 貨幣價值之恢復。

re·val·u·a·tion 〔ˌriväljuˈeʃən; ˌri:væljuˈeiʃən〕 *n.* ①重新估價；再評價。②幣值之重新調整(貶值或升值)。

re·val·ue 〔riˈvælju; ri:ˈvælju:〕 *v.t.,* **-ued, -u·ing.** 重新評價；再估價。

re·vamp 〔riˈvæmp; ri:ˈvæmp〕 *v.t.* ①修訂；修改。②修補；換新鞋面。

‡re·veal 〔rɪˈvil; riˈvi:l, rәˈv-〕 *v.t.* ①洩露；透露。 Never *reveal* my secret. 絕不要洩露我的祕密。②顯示；顯出。 ***reveal oneself*** 出現；顯示身分。—*n.* 洩露；透露。

revealed religion 天啓教（根據天啓的宗教,特指猶太教、基督教)。

re·veal·ment 〔rɪˈvilmənt; riˈvi:lmәnt〕 *n.* 洩露；透露。

rev·eil·le 〔ˈrɛvl̩ˌi, ˌrɛvl̩ˈi; riˈvæli〕 *n.* 〖軍〗起床號；晨間第一次集合(號)。

rev·el 〔ˈrɛvl̩; ˈrevl〕 *v.,* **-el(l)ed, -el(l)ing,** *n.* —*v.i.* ①大悅；狂喜；沉迷〖in〗. to *revel* in a book. 沉迷於書。②狂歡；縱酒；鬧飲。—*n.* (常 *pl.*) 狂歡；宴樂；鬧飲。

***rev·e·la·tion** 〔ˌrɛvl̩ˈeʃən; ˌreviˈleiʃən, -vl̩ˈei-〕 *n.* ①洩露；顯示。②顯示之事物；啓示。 Her true nature was a *revelation* to me. 她的眞性格對我是個新發現。③天啓。④(R-)(常 *pl.*)〖新約〗啓示錄。

rev·e·la·tion·al 〔ˌrɛvl̩ˈeʃənl̩; ˌreviˈleiʃənl〕 *adj.* ①天啓的；默示的；啓示的。②顯示的；暴露的；洩露的。③意外發現的。

rev·e·la·tion·ist 〔ˌrɛvl̩ˈeʃənɪst; ˌreviˈleiʃәnist〕 *n.* ①信仰啓示錄者。②(the R-)啓示錄作者。

rev·e·la·tor 〔ˈrɛvəˌletə; ˈrevəˌleitə〕 *n.* 洩露者；透露者。

rev·el·(l)er 〔ˈrɛvələ, ˈrɛvl̩ə; ˈrevl̩ə〕 *n.* 狂歡者；鬧酒者；宴樂者。

rev·el·ry 〔ˈrɛvəlrɪ, ˈrɛvl̩rɪ; ˈrevlri〕 *n., pl.* **-ries.** 狂歡；飲宴作樂。

re·venge** 〔rɪˈvɛndʒ; riˈvendʒ, rəˈv-〕 *n., v.,* **-venged, -veng·ing.** —*n.* ①報仇；復仇。a blow struck in *revenge.* 洩忿的一擊。②報仇心；復仇心。 ***take (or ***have***) ***one's revenge*** 報仇。 ***take revenge on somebody*** 向某人報仇。—*v.t.* 報仇；報復。 I'll *revenge* that insult. 我將報復那次侮辱。—*v.i.* 報仇。 ***revenge oneself on*** (or ***upon***) ***a person*** 向某人報仇。

re·venge·ful 〔rɪˈvɛndʒfl; riˈvendʒful, rəˈv-〕 *adj.* 懷深仇的；報復的。—**ly,** *adv.*

***rev·e·nue** 〔ˈrɛvəˌnju; ˈrevinju:, riˈvenju:, rəˈvenju:〕 *n.* ①收入總額；國家之歲入。②(*pl.*) 收入項目；收入數目。③稅務局；稅捐處。

revenue agent 稅務員。

revenue cutter 緝私船。

revenue stamp 印花。

re·ver·ber·ant 〔rɪˈvɝbərənt; riˈvə:bərənt〕 *adj.* =**reverberative.**

re·ver·ber·ate 〔rɪˈvɝbəˌret; riˈvə:bəreit〕 *v.,* **-at·ed, -at·ing,** *adj.* —*v.i.* ①起回聲；回響；反響。②彈回；跳回。③(光、熱)反射；屈折。—*v.t.* ①使起回聲；使有回響。②使(光、熱等)反射；使屈折。③置入反射爐等以處理。***reverberating furnace*** 反射爐；反焰爐。—*adj.* =**reverberant.**

re·ver·ber·a·tion 〔rɪˌvɝbəˈreʃən; riˌvə:bəˈreiʃən〕 *n.* ①回聲；回響。②反響；響應。③(熱、光的) 反射；反射熱；(反射爐的)反射焰。④反射爐處理法。

re·ver·ber·a·tive 〔rɪˈvɝbəˌretɪv; riˈvə:bəˌreitiv〕 *adj.* ①起回聲的；回響的；反響的。②彈回的；跳回的。③反射的。

re·ver·ber·a·tor 〔rɪˈvɝbəˌretə; riˈvə:bəˌreitə〕 *n.* 反射器；反射燈；反射鏡；反射爐。

re·ver·ber·a·to·ry 〔rɪˈvɝbərəˌtorɪ; riˈvə:bəreitəri〕 *adj., n., pl.* **-ries.** —*adj.* ①反射的；反響的；回響的。②反射爐的。—*n.* 反射爐；反射器。

***re·vere** 〔rɪˈvɪr; riˈviə, rəˈv-〕 *v.t.,* **-vered, -ver·ing.** 尊敬；尊崇。 We *revere* sacred things. 我們尊敬神聖事物。

rev·er·ence** 〔ˈrɛvərəns; ˈrevərəns〕 *n., v.,* **-enced, -enc·ing.** —*n.* ①崇敬；尊敬。②(R-)對教士之尊稱。③深度鞠躬。 ***hold a thing (or ***person***) ***in reverence*** 尊敬一物(人)。 ***pay reverence to*** 向…致敬。—*v.t.* 尊敬；尊崇。

***rev·er·end** 〔ˈrɛvərənd; ˈrevərənd〕 *adj.* 應受尊敬的。—*n.* (R-) 牧師之尊稱（略作 **Rev.**). 〖注意〗 **Reverend** 之正式用法,其前加 the, 不單獨與姓 (last name) 連用,且不用縮寫式,如: the *Reverend* James Shaw, the *Reverend* J. T. Shaw. 縮寫式 (Rev.) 係報章雜誌及其他非正式用法,如: *Rev.* James Shaw, *Rev.* J. T. Shaw. 縮寫式於書寫信封時亦用之,如: "The *Rev.* Allen Price".

rev·er·ent 〔ˈrɛvrənt; ˈrevərənt〕 *adj.* 恭敬的；虔誠的。—**ly,** *adv.*

rev·er·en·tial 〔ˌrɛvəˈrɛnʃəl; ˌrevəˈrenʃəl〕 *adj.* 恭敬的；表示虔誠的。

rev·er·ie 〔ˈrɛvərɪ; ˈrevəri〕 *n.* ①幻想；深想。②〖音樂〗幻想曲。(亦作 **revery**)

re·vers 〔rəˈvɪr, rəˈvɛr; riˈviə, -ˈvɛə〕 *n., pl.* **-vers** 〔rəˈvɪrz, -ˈvɛrz; riˈviəz, -ˈvɛəz〕. 衣裏翻在外面的部分。(亦作 **revere**)

re·ver·sal 〔rɪˈvɝsəl; riˈvə:səl〕 *n.* ①反轉；倒轉；逆轉；顚倒。②〖法律〗(下級法院裁判之)廢棄；撤銷。

re·verse** 〔rɪˈvɝs; riˈvə:s, rəˈv-〕 *n., adj., v.,* **-versed, -vers·ing.** —*n.* ①顚倒；反轉。 Your remarks were the *reverse* of polite. 你說的話很粗魯。 Is she pretty? No, quite the *reverse.* 她漂亮嗎?不,正相反。②不幸；逆運。③背面；反面。④使機械倒退的裝置。⑤反向；相背之方向。 ***put in reverse (駕駛汽車用語)倒開。—*adj.* 向後的；顚倒的；相反的。 in *reverse* order. 次序顚倒的。—*v.t.* ①逆行；反轉；顚倒。②取消；廢棄。 to *reverse* a decision. 取消一項決定。③轉過來；翻過來；顚倒過來。④作相反之決定。—*v.i.* ①逆行；反行；倒開。②用倒退排擋。—**ly,** *adv.*

re·vers·i·bil·i·ty 〔rɪˌvɝsəˈbɪlətɪ; riˌvə:səˈbiliti〕 *n.* ①可翻轉；可倒轉。②轉換可能性。③(衣服之) 正反面均可用。④(命令等之)撤銷可能。⑤可逆性；可廻溯性。

re·vers·i·ble 〔rɪˈvɝsəbl̩; riˈvə:səbl〕 *adj.* ①可反轉的。②〖化〗可逆的。③可廢棄的。④（衣料之）兩面都可用的。⑤兩面可穿的。—*n.* 正反兩面均可穿着之上衣或短外衣。

re·ver·sion 〔rɪˈvɝʒən, -ˈvɝʃ-; riˈvə:ʃən〕 *n.* ①歸屬。②承繼權。③隔代遺傳。④反回。

re·ver·sion·al 〔rɪˈvɝʒənḷ, -ˈvɝʃ-; riˈvəːʃənḷ〕 *adj.* ①反轉的;倒轉的。②復歸的;歸屬的。③〖法律〗應繼承的; 將來可繼承的。④隔代遺傳的。(亦作 **reversionary**)

re·ver·sion·er 〔rɪˈvɝʃənɚ; riˈvəːʃənə〕 *n.* 〖法律〗將來享有繼承權者。

re·vert 〔rɪˈvɝt; riˈvəːt, rəˈv-〕 *v.i.* ①回到(原來之話題)。②恢復原狀; 重返舊觀。③(耕地)重成荒地。④〖生物〗返回祖先狀態。⑤回想;重思。⑥復歸;歸屬。 —*n.* ①反回者。②〖法律〗歸屬;繼承。

re·vert·i·ble 〔rɪˈvɝtəbḷ; riˈvəːtibl〕 *adj.* 可恢復原狀的;可復歸的;可歸屬的。

re·vet 〔rɪˈvɛt; riˈvet〕 *v.t.*, **-vet·ted, -vet·ting.** (以磚、石等)被覆(堡壁等)。

re·vet·ment 〔rɪˈvɛtmənt; riˈvetmənt〕 *n.* ①〖築城〗被覆。②〖土木〗擁壁; 護岸。③(飛機場之)機堡。

re·vict·ual 〔riˈvɪtḷ; ˈriːˈvitl〕 *v.*, **-ual(l)ed, -ual·(l)ing.** —*v.t.* 再供糧食;再補給。 —*v.i.* 補充糧食。

***re·view** 〔rɪˈvju; riˈvjuː, rəˈv-〕 *v.t.* ①覆閱;溫習。to *review* a lesson. 溫習功課。②回顧。③細察; 觀察。④檢閱;檢查。⑤評論;批評。⑥覆審或再審(案件)。 —*v.i.* 評論;批評。He *reviewed* for a small-town paper. 他替一家小城的報紙寫評論。—*n.* ①復習;溫習。②回顧;檢討。to pass one's life in *review*. 回顧過去。③檢查; 檢閱。a *review* copy. (送交編輯審查的)原稿。 ④(對著作之)評論。⑤評論雜誌。 a motion-picture *review*. 電影評論。⑥ =**revue.** ⑦(上級法院等之) 覆審(一案件); 再審。 *come under review* 接受檢查;被考慮。—**er,** *n.*

re·view·al 〔rɪˈvjuəl; riˈvjuːəl〕 *n.* ①再調查。②校閱; 校訂。③批評; 評論。④檢閱;閱兵。⑤復習;溫習。⑥回顧。

re·vile 〔rɪˈvaɪl; riˈvail〕 *v.t.* & *v.i.*, **re·viled, re·vil·ing.** 辱罵;誹謗。—**ment,** *n.*

re·vis·al 〔rɪˈvaɪzḷ; riˈvaizḷ〕 *n.* 校正;訂正;修正。

***re·vise** 〔rɪˈvaɪz; riˈvaiz, rəˈv-〕 *v.*, **-vised, -vis·ing,** *n.* —*v.t.* ①校訂;校對;改訂。the *revised* edition. 修訂版。②更改;改變。③〖英〗溫習。—*n.*①校訂。②校訂後之形式或版本。③改正之校樣。—**re·vis·a·ble, re·vis·i·ble,** *adj.*

re·vis·er, re·vi·sor 〔rɪˈvaɪzɚ; riˈvaizə〕 *n.* 校訂者;修正者;校對。

***re·vi·sion** 〔rɪˈvɪʒən; riˈviʒən, rəˈv-〕 *n.* ①校訂;校對; 校正; 改變。②校訂後之形式。 —**al,** —**ar·y,** *adj.*

re·vi·sion·ism 〔rɪˈvɪʒənɪzəm; riˈviʒənizm〕 *n.* 修正主義;修正的社會主義。

re·vi·sion·ist 〔rɪˈvɪʒənɪst; riˈviʒənist〕 *n.* ①修正主義者;修正的社會主義者。②訂正者。—*adj.* 修正主義(者)的;修正的社會主義(者)的;訂正者的。

re·vis·it 〔riˈvɪzɪt; ˈriːˈvizit〕 *v.t.*, *n.* 再訪;重遊。

re·vi·so·ry 〔rɪˈvaɪzərɪ; riˈvaizəri〕 *adj.* ①修正的;訂正的。②有修正權的。

re·vi·tal·ize 〔riˈvaɪtḷˌaɪz; ˈriːˈvaitəlaiz〕 *v.t.*, **-ized, -iz·ing.** 使復蘇;使復活;使復興。 *adj.* 可復活的;可復興的。

re·viv·a·ble 〔rɪˈvaɪvəbḷ; riˈvaivəbḷ〕 *adj.* 可復活的;可復興的。

***re·viv·al** 〔rɪˈvaɪvḷ; riˈvaivəl, rəˈv-〕 *n.* ①復活;蘇醒。②(精力、健康等之)恢復。③再興;復用;重演。the *revival* of an old custom. 舊習俗之再興。④(對宗教之)信仰復興;信仰復興運動。

re·viv·al·ism 〔rɪˈvaɪvḷˌɪzəm; riˈvaivəlizəm〕 *n.* ①宗教信仰復興運動。②復古傾向;復古論。

re·viv·al·ist 〔rɪˈvaɪvḷɪst; riˈvaivəlist〕 *n.* ①信仰復興論者。②領導宗教復興運動者。

Revival of Learning (Letters or **Literature)** 文藝復興。

***re·vive** 〔rɪˈvaɪv; riˈvaiv, rəˈv-〕 *v.*, **-vived, -viv·ing.** —*v.i.* ①復活; 蘇醒。②重振;振興。 Our hopes *revived*. 我們的希望重振起來。③再興;復用;重新流行。④〖化〗還原。—*v.t.* ①使復甦;使振作。②使重現;重演;使重變爲時髦。③〖化〗使還原。

re·viv·er 〔rɪˈvaɪvɚ; riˈvaivə〕 *n.* ①復活者; 蘇醒者。②使復活或振作的人(或物)。③〖俚〗刺激劑;興奮劑。④恢復光澤的藥劑;生色素;擦銅油。⑤恢復使用某件東西的人;重建者。⑥修補舊衣的人。

re·viv·i·fi·ca·tion 〔rɪˌvɪvəfəˈkeʃən; riːˌvivifiˈkeiʃən〕 *n.* ①蘇醒; 復活; 恢復氣力。②〖化〗還原。

re·viv·i·fy 〔rɪˈvɪvəˌfaɪ; riːˈvivifai〕 *v.*, **-fied, -fy·ing.** —*v.t.* ①使蘇醒; 使復活; 使恢復氣力。②〖化〗還原。 —*v.i.* ①〖化〗還原。②復活;蘇醒。

rev·i·vis·cence 〔ˌrɛvɪˈvɪsn̩s; ˌreviˈvisns〕 *n.* 蘇醒;復活;恢復氣力。

rev·i·vis·cent 〔ˌrɛvɪˈvɪsn̩t; ˌreviˈvisnt〕 *adj.* 復活的;蘇醒的;氣力恢復的。

rev·o·ca·ble 〔ˈrɛvəkəbḷ; ˈrevəkəbl〕 *adj.* 可廢止的;可撤銷的;可解除的。

rev·o·ca·tion 〔ˌrɛvəˈkeʃən; ˌrevəˈkeiʃən〕 *n.* ①廢棄;取消。②〖法律〗 取消或撤銷(要約)。

rev·o·ca·to·ry 〔ˈrɛvəkəˌtorɪ; ˈrevəkətəri〕 *adj.* 廢止的;取消的;解除的。

re·voke 〔rɪˈvok; riˈvouk〕 *v.*, **-voked, -vok·ing,** *n.* —*v.t.*廢棄;廢除;廢止;宣告…無效;取消。—*v.i.* ①(命令、權利、契約等)取消;廢止; 宣告無效。②〖牌戲〗 有牌不跟。 —*n.* 〖牌戲〗有牌不跟。

***re·volt** 〔rɪˈvolt; riˈvoult, rəˈv-〕 *n.* 叛亂; 背叛。 The fleet was already in *revolt*. 這艦隊已叛變。—*v.i.* ①叛亂; 背叛。The people *revolted* against their rulers. 人民反叛他們的統治者。②嫌惡; 起惡感。—*v.t.* 使嫌惡;使起惡感。

re·volt·ing 〔rɪˈvoltɪŋ; riˈvoultiŋ〕 *adj.* ①背叛的;叛亂的;造反的。②違反的。③令人震驚的;使生反感的;討厭的。—**ly,** *adv.*

rev·o·lute[1] 〔ˈrɛvəˌlut; ˈrevəljuːt〕 *adj.* 〖植物〗背捲的;下捲的(葉)。

rev·o·lute[2] *v.i.*, **-lut·ed, -lut·ing.** 〖俚〗革命;從事革命工作。

‡rev·o·lu·tion 〔ˌrɛvəˈluʃən; ˌrevəˈluːʃən〕 *n.* ①革命。 the French *Revolution*. 法國大革命。②改革;大改變。③周轉。④旋轉。⑤一轉之時間或距離。⑥循環一周。 The *revolution* of the four seasons fills a year. 四季循環而成一年。

***rev·o·lu·tion·ar·y** 〔ˌrɛvəˈluʃənˌɛrɪ; ˌrevəˈluːʃn̩əri〕 *adj.* ①革命(性)的。②廻旋的。③(R-)美國革命戰爭的。—*n.* 革命者;改革者。

Revolutionary War 美國革命戰爭(指 1775–1783 年獨立戰爭)。

rev·o·lu·tion·ist 〔ˌrɛvəˈluʃənɪst; ˌrevəˈluːʃn̩ist〕 *n.* 革命者;革命家。

rev·o·lu·tion·ize 〔ˌrɛvəˈluʃənˌaɪz; ˌrevəˈluːʃn̩aiz〕 *v.t.*, **-ized, -iz·ing.** ①鼓吹革命思想;引起革命。②大舉革新; 大事改革;推翻。(亦作 **revolutionise**)

***re·volve** [rɪˈvɑlv; riˈvɔlv, rəˈv-] *v.i.* ①周轉。The earth *revolves* round the sun. 地球繞太陽運轉。②旋轉。③周而復始; 循環。④熟思;考慮。—*v.t.* ①使旋轉。②考慮; 熟思。

***re·volv·er** [rɪˈvɑlvə; riˈvɔlvə, rəˈv-] *n.* ①連發手鎗;左輪。②周轉者。

re·volv·ing [rɪˈvɑlvɪŋ; riˈvɔlviŋ] *adj.* 廻旋的;廻轉的。

revolving door 旋轉門。

revolving fund ①周轉金。②〖美〗周轉基金。

re·vue [rɪˈvju; riˈvjuː] *n.* 時事諷刺劇(常含輕鬆歌舞之幽默喜劇)。(亦作 **review**)

re·vul·sion [rɪˈvʌlʃən; riˈvʌlʃən] *n.* ①(心情之)突變;劇變。②〖醫〗誘導法。③拉回;牽回。④厭惡;討厭。

re·vul·sive [rɪˈvʌlsɪv; riˈvʌlsiv] *adj.* ①心情突變的;致使心情突變的。②〖醫〗誘導的。—*n.* 〖醫〗誘導藥;誘導器。

Rev. Ver. Revised Version.

***re·ward** [rɪˈwɔrd; riˈwɔːd] *n.* ①報答; 報酬。The *rewards* of study cannot always be measured in money. 讀書所得的報酬不能以金錢衡量。②酬勞金; 賞金。—*v.t.* ①酬報;酬謝(人)。②酬報;酬謝(事蹟)。

re·ward·ing [rɪˈwɔrdɪŋ; riˈwɔːdiŋ] *adj.* 有報酬的;有用的;有益的。

re·ward·less [rɪˈwɔrdlɪs; riˈwɔːdlis] *adj.* 無報酬的;徒勞無功的。

re·wire [riˈwaɪr; ˈriːˈwaiə] *v.t.* & *v.i.*, **-wired, -wir·ing.** ①裝以新電線。②再打電報。

re·word [riˈwɜd; ˈriːˈwəːd] *v.t.* ①重說;改寫。②重複。

re·work [riˈwɜk; ˈriːˈwəːk] *v.t.* 修改; 修正。

re·write [*v.* riˈraɪt; ˈriːˈrait *n.* ˈriˌraɪt; ˈriːrait] *v.*, **-wrote, -writ·ten, -writ·ing,** *n.* —*v.t.* ①重寫;改寫。②〖美〗改寫新聞稿。—*n.* ①改寫之作品。②〖美〗經改寫之新聞稿。

rewrite man 〖美〗做報紙改寫工作的編輯或記者。

Rex [rɛks; reks] *n.*, *pl.* **re·ges.** 王;君。George *Rex.* 喬治王。(亦作 **rex**; 略作 **R.**)

Rex·ine [ˈrɛksin; ˈreksiːn] *n.*〖商標名〗做沙發套或書封面用的一種人造皮。

Rey·mont [ˈremɔnt; ˈreimɔːnt] *n.* 雷蒙特(Wladyslaw Stanislaw, 1868–1925, 波蘭小說家, 1924 年得諾貝爾獎)。

Reyn·ard [ˈrɛnəd; ˈrenəd] *n.* ①寓言或民間故事中狐之專名。②(r-) 狐。(亦作 **Renard**)

rf. 〖棒球〗①right field. ②right fielder.

R.F. ①Royal Fusiliers. ②radio frequency. ③Reserve Force. **r.f.** ①radio frequency. ②range finder. ③rapid-fire. ④reducing flame. ⑤〖棒球〗right field.

RFC Reconstruction Finance Corporation. **R.F.C.** Royal Flying Corps.

RFD, R.F.D. Rural Free Delivery.

R.G.S. Royal Geographical Society.

Rh 化學元素 rhodium 之符號。**Rh, Rh.**〖生化〗=**Rh factor. R.H.** ①Royal Highness. ②Royal Highlanders. **r.h.** ①relative humidity. ②〖音樂〗right hand.

Rhad·a·man·thine [ˌrædəˈmænθɪn; ˌrædəˈmænθin] *adj.* (像)Rhadamanthys 的;嚴峻的;剛直的。

Rhad·a·man·thys [ˌrædəˈmænθɪs; ˌrædəˈmænθis] *n.* ①〖希臘神話〗主神 Zeus 與 Europa 之子(死後爲冥府三判官之一)。②嚴正之審判官。(亦作 **Rhadamanthus**)

rhap·sod·ic [ræpˈsɑdɪk; ræpˈsɔdik] *adj.* ①史詩的; 吟誦詩的; 狂文狂詩的。②狂熱的;狂想的。(亦作 **rhapsodical**)

rhap·so·dist [ˈræpsədɪst; ˈræpsədist] *n.* ①吟誦史詩者; 遊唱詩人。②狂文、狂詩或狂想曲作者。③發狂熱言論者。

rhap·so·dize [ˈræpsəˌdaɪz; ˈræpsədaiz] *v.*, **-dized, -diz·ing.** —*v.t.* 將…作爲史詩般吟誦; 朗誦; 熱狂地講。—*v.i.* ①作狂文、狂詩或狂想曲;吟誦史詩。②熱狂地說。

rhap·so·dy [ˈræpsədɪ; ˈræpsədi] *n.*, *pl.* **-dies.** ①狂熱的言論或詩文。②〖音樂〗狂想曲。③史詩; 敍事詩; 史詩之一節。***go into rhapsodies over*** 顯現對…之强烈之喜悅。

rhat·a·ny [ˈrætənɪ; ˈrætəni] *n.*, *pl.* **-nies.** ①南美所產的一種多年生灌木。②此種植物之根(可做藥用)。③此種根製之藥劑。

Rhe·a [ˈriə; ˈriːə] *n.*①〖希臘神話〗Zeus, Poseidon, Hades, Demeter, Hera 與 Hestia 之母, 被稱爲"諸神之母"。②(r-)〖動物〗三趾鴕鳥(南美產)。③〖天文〗土星之第五衞星。

Rhen·ish [ˈrɛnɪʃ; ˈriːniʃ, ˈren-] *adj.* 萊茵河的;萊茵河流域的。—*n.* 萊茵酒(現在通常稱爲 Rhine wine).

rhe·ni·um [ˈrinɪəm; ˈriːniəm] *n.* 〖化〗錸(一種稀有金屬元素, 化學符號爲 Re).

rhe·ol·o·gy [rɪˈɑlədʒɪ; riˈɔlədʒi] *n.* 〖物理〗流變學。

rhe·om·e·ter [rɪˈɑmətə; riˈɔmitə] *n.* ①電流計。②〖醫〗血流速度計。

rhe·om·e·try [riˈɑmətrɪ; riːˈɔmətri] *n.* ①電流測定。②〖醫〗血流測定。

rhe·o·scope [ˈriəˌskop; ˈriːəskoup] *n.* 〖物理〗檢電器。

rhe·o·stat [ˈriəˌstæt; ˈriːəstæt] *n.* 〖電〗變阻器。

rhe·sus [ˈrisəs; ˈriːsəs] *n.* (印度產的)恆河猴。

Rhe·sus factor [ˈrisəs~; ˈriːsəs~] =**Rh factor.**

rhet. ①rhetoric. ②rhetorical.

rhe·tor [ˈritə; ˈriːtə] *n.* ①修辭學家;修辭學教師。②演說家。

***rhet·o·ric** [ˈrɛtərɪk; ˈretərik] *n.* ①修辭學; 修辭學書籍。②浮誇之言語。

rhe·tor·i·cal [rɪˈtɔrɪkl; riˈtɔrikəl] *adj.* ①修辭的;用修辭法的。②矯飾的;誇張的。③詞藻華美的。④演說的。***a rhetorical question*** 反語(用以加重語氣而非眞正之問句, 如: Why not? 行呀! 好呀!)。—**ly,** *adv.*

rhet·o·ri·cian [ˌrɛtəˈrɪʃən; ˌretəˈriʃən] *n.* ①修辭學者;修辭學教師。②雄辯家。

rheum [rum; ruːm] *n.* 〖醫〗①炎性分泌物 (如淚液、唾液等)。②鼻黏膜炎; 感冒。

rheu·mat·ic [ruˈmætɪk; ruːˈmætik] *adj.* 風濕症的;患風濕症的;引起風濕症的;風濕症致起的。—*n.* ①風濕症患者。②(*pl.*) 風濕症。—**al·ly,** *adv.*

rheumatic fever 風濕性熱。

rheu·mat·ick·y [ruˈmætəkɪ; ruːˈmætiki] *adj.* 〖俗〗患風濕症的。

***rheu·ma·tism** [ˈruməˌtɪzəm; ˈruːmətizəm] *n.* ①風濕症。②風濕性熱。

rheum·y [ˈrumɪ; ˈruːmi] *adj.*, **rheum·i·er, rheum·i·est.** ①炎性分泌物的;粘膜分泌液的。②鼻炎的。③引起鼻炎的。④(空氣中)水氣過多的;粘濕的。

Rh factor 〖生化〗獮因子(人類血液中的一種凝血素)。

rhi·nal [ˈraɪnl; ˈrainəl] *adj.* 鼻的; 鼻腔的。the *rhinal* cavities. 鼻腔。

Rhine [raɪn; rain] *n.* 萊茵河 (自瑞士中

部經德國流入北海)。

rhine·stone [ˈraɪnˌston; ˈrainstoun] *n.* ①萊因石(水晶之一種)。②假金鋼鑽。

Rhine wine ①萊茵河流域產之色白帶香味之酒。②他處類似之酒。

rhi·ni·tis [raɪˈnaɪtɪs; raiˈnaitis] *n.* 〖醫〗鼻炎。

rhi·no [ˈraɪno; ˈrainou] *n., pl.* **-nos, -no.** ①〖俗〗犀牛。②〖英俚〗金錢。ready *rhino.* 現金。③〖美俗〗鐵舟(架浮橋所用者)。

rhi·noc·er·os [raɪˈnɑsərəs; raiˈnɔsərəs] *n., pl.* **-os·es, -os.** 犀牛。

rhi·nol·o·gy [raɪˈnɑlədʒɪ; raiˈnɔlədʒi] *n.* 鼻科學。

rhi·no·plas·ty [ˈraɪnəˌplæstɪ; ˈrainouplæsti] *n.* 〖醫〗造鼻術;鼻成形術;鼻修補術。—**rhi·no·plas·tic,** *adj.*

rhi·no·scope [ˈraɪnəˌskop; ˈrainəskoup] *n.* 檢查鼻腔用的小鏡;鼻鏡;鼻窺器。

rhi·nos·co·py [raɪˈnɑskəpɪ; raiˈnɔskəpi] *n.* 利用鼻鏡的鼻腔檢查;檢鼻術;鼻窺器檢查法。

rhi·zoid [ˈraɪzɔɪd; ˈraizɔid] *adj.* 根狀的。—*n.* 假根。

rhi·zo·ma [raɪˈzomə; raiˈzoumə] *n.* 〖植物〗根莖;地下莖。(亦作 **rhizome**)

rhi·zo·pod [ˈraɪzəˌpɑd; ˈraizəpɔd] *n.* 〖動物〗根足類動物。

rho [ro; rou] *n.* 希臘字母之第十七個字母 (Ρ, ρ, 相當於英文字母之 R, r)。

Rho., Rhod. Rhodesia.

Rhode Is·land [rodˈaɪlənd; roudˈailənd] 羅德島 (美國東部之一州, 首府為 Providence).

Rhode Island Red 羅島紅(一種美國鷄)。

Rho·de·sia [roˈdiʒɪə; rouˈdiːzjə] *n.* 羅德西亞(南非一國, 首都 Salisbury).

Rho·de·si·an [roˈdiʒɪən; rouˈdiːzjən] *adj.* 羅德西亞的。—*n.* 羅德西亞人。

Rhodes scholar 領羅氏(羅德玆Cecil John Rhodes, 1853–1902, 英殖民地資本家及南非行政長官)獎學金的研究生。

Rho·di·an [ˈrodɪən; ˈroudjən] *adj.* 羅德斯島的;羅德斯島人民的;羅德斯島文化的。—*n.* 羅德斯島人;羅德斯島居民。

Rhodian law 羅德斯海商法(制定於紀元前九世紀, 為世界最古之海商法)。

rho·di·um [ˈrodɪəm; ˈroudjəm] *n.* 〖化〗銠(一種化學元素, 化學符號為 Rh)。

rho·do·den·dron [ˌrodəˈdɛndrən; ˌroudəˈdendrən] *n., pl.* **-drons, -dra** [-drə; -drə]. 〖植物〗石楠;石楠屬植物。

rho·do·ra [roˈdorə; rouˈdɔːrə] *n.* 〖植物〗石楠屬植物。

rhomb [rɑmb, rɑm; rɔm] *n.* 菱形。(亦作 **rhombus**)

rhom·bic [ˈrɑmbɪk; ˈrɔmbik] *adj.* ①菱形的;斜方形的。②底面或橫切面為菱形的。③〖結晶〗斜方晶系的。

rhom·bo·he·dron [ˌrɑmbəˈhidrən; ˌrɔmbəˈhiːdrən] *n., pl.* **-drons, -dra** [-drə; -drə]. 〖結晶〗菱面體;斜方六面體。

rhom·boid [ˈrɑmbɔɪd; ˈrɔmbɔid] *adj.* ①長斜方形的; 長菱形的。②〖解剖〗菱形的。—*n.* ①長斜方形;長菱形。②〖解剖〗菱形肌。

rhom·boi·dal [rɑmˈbɔɪdəl; rɔmˈbɔidəl] *adj.* 長斜方形的;長菱形的。

rhom·bus [ˈrɑmbəs; ˈrɔmbəs] *n., pl.* **-bi** [-baɪ; -bai], **-bus·es.** ①〖數學〗菱形;斜方形。②〖結晶〗菱面體;斜方六面體。

rhon·chus [ˈrɑŋkəs; ˈrɔŋkəs] *n., pl.* **-chi** [-kaɪ; -kai]. 〖醫〗(氣管之)水泡音;乾囉音;鼾音。

R.H.S. ①Royal Historical Society. ②Royal Horticultural Society. ③Royal Humane Society.

rhu·barb [ˈrubɑrb; ˈruːbɑːb] *n.* ①〖植物〗大黃。②大黃根 (藥用)。③大黃葉柄 (食用)。④〖美俚〗吵架;爭吵。

rhumb [rʌm, rʌmb; rʌm] *n.* ①羅盤方位線。②海員所用羅盤的三十二點的任何一點。

rhum·ba [ˈrʌmbə; ˈrʌmbə] *n., v.i.,* **-baed, -ba·ing.** =**rumba.**

rhumb line 羅盤方位線。

rhyme** [raɪm; raim] *v.,* **rhymed, rhym·ing,** *n.* —*v.t. & v.i.* 使押韻; 押韻。"Long" and "song" *rhyme.* long 和 song 押韻。—*n.* ①韻。②押韻的字或行。"Cat" is a *rhyme* for "mat". "Cat" 是 "mat" 的押韻字。③押韻詩。nursery *rhymes.* 兒歌;童謠。④節奏。without rhyme or reason*** 不可解;雜亂無章。(亦作 **rime**)〖注意〗**rime** 較簡單, 且為英文之原始拼法, 正逐漸普遍被使用。

rhyme·less [ˈraɪmlɪs; ˈraimlis] *adj.* 無韻的;不押韻的。

rhym·er [ˈraɪmɚ; ˈraimə] *n.* =**rhymist.** ***the Rhymer*** 十三世紀末葉蘇格蘭最古的詩人 Thomas the Rhymer.

rhyme royal 英國詩人 Chaucer 首用的一種詩的格式, 每節七行, 每行五步, 為抑揚格, 其韻脚為 ababbcc.

rhyme·ster [ˈraɪmstɚ; ˈraimstə] *n.* 作詩者;詩人(指缺乏詩才的二流小詩人)。(亦作 **rimester**)

rhyming dictionary 韻書(如我國之"廣韻"等是)。

rhym·ist [ˈraɪmɪst; ˈraimist] *n.* 詩人;作詩者。

rhy·o·lite [ˈraɪəˌlaɪt; ˈraiəlait] *n.* 火山岩之一種。

***rhythm** [ˈrɪðəm; ˈriðəm] *n.* ①節奏;韻律。the *rhythm* of music. 音樂的節奏。②按重音或拍子的劃分。triple *rhythm.* 三拍的韻律。

rhyth·mic [ˈrɪðmɪk; ˈriðmik] *adj.* 韻律的;有韻律的;依節奏的。—*n.* (*pl.*)韻律學。

rhyth·mi·cal [ˈrɪðmɪkl; ˈriðmikl] *adj.* ①韻律的;有節奏的。②依節奏的。—**ly,** *adv.*

rhythm·less [ˈrɪðəmlɪs; ˈriðəmlis] *adj.* 無韻律的;無節奏的。

rhythm method 周期避孕法。

R.I. ①Regina et Imperatrix (拉=Queen and Empress). ②Rex et Imperator(拉=King and Emperor). ③Rhode Island. ④Royal Institute.

ri·al [rɪˈɔl; riˈɔːl] *n.* 伊朗之貨幣單位。

ri·al·to [rɪˈælto; riˈæltou] *n., pl.* **-tos.** 市場;交易場。

ri·ant [ˈraɪənt; ˈraiənt] *adj.* 大笑的;微笑的;愉快的;歡樂的。

rib** [rɪb; rib] *n., v.,* **ribbed, rib·bing.** —*n.* ①肋骨。to dig (*or* poke) a person in the *ribs.* 觸一人之肋骨(使其注意)。②肋骨狀物。③樹葉之粗大葉脈。④(布或針織物上之) 稜線。⑤〖俚〗取笑。tickle the ribs*** 使人大笑。—*v.t.* ①供以肋狀物; 以肋狀物支持或加强。②綴以稜線。③〖俚〗取笑。

rib·ald [ˈrɪbld; ˈribld] *adj.* 下流的;猥褻的;不敬的。—*n.* 卑賤的人; 下流人; 無賴漢; 說話粗鄙的人。

rib·ald·ry [ˈrɪbldrɪ; ˈribldri] *n.* ①下流;猥褻。②下流話;猥褻語。

rib·band [ˈrɪbˌbænd, ˈrɪbənd; ˈribənd] *n.* 〖造船〗支材(造船時用以支撐船身使不移動之狹長木板)。(亦作 **riband**)

ribbed [rɪbd; ribd] *adj.* (織物)有稜線的。

rib·bing [ˈrɪbɪŋ; ˈribiŋ] *n.* ①肋骨;肋狀組織(集合稱)。②肋材之安裝;橫木之安裝。

***rib·bon** [ˈrɪbən; ˈribən] *n.* ①絲帶;緞帶;絨帶。②帶;條。a typewriter *ribbon*. 打字機色帶。③(勳章之)綬帶。④(*pl.*)碎片;斷片。torn to *ribbons*. 撕成碎片。⑤(*pl.*)韁繩。—*v.t.* ①飾以緞帶。②撕成帶;撕成碎片。

ribbon park 道路兩側之林園。

ri·bo·fla·vin [ˌraɪbəˈflevɪn; ˈraibouˌfleivin] *n.* 維他命 B_2;核黃素。

ri·bo·nu·cle·ic acid [ˌraɪboˈnjuklɪɪk ～; ˌraibouˈnjuːkliːik～] 核糖核酸。(略作 RNA)

***rice** [raɪs; rais] *n., v.,* **riced, ric·ing.** —*n.* ①米;飯。②稻。—*v.t.* 使變成米狀。

rice·bird [ˈraɪsˌbɝd; ˈraisbəːd] *n.* ①爪哇麻雀。②美國南部產的一種鳥。

rice bowl ①飯碗。②產米區。

rice paddy 稻田。

rice paper ①宣紙。②通草紙。

ric·er [ˈraɪsɚ; ˈraisə] *n.* 〖美〗一種炊具(用時將煮熟之山芋等壓過小孔,使成細條)。

‡**rich** [rɪtʃ; ritʃ] *adj.* ①有錢的;富的。a *rich* man. 富人。②富饒的;豐富的。a land *rich* in minerals. 礦產富饒的土地。③肥沃的。*rich* soil. 肥沃的土壤。④貴重的。*rich* jewels. 貴重的珠寶。⑤昂貴的;華貴的。*rich* dress. 華貴的服裝。⑥甘美的;油膩的。a *rich* fruitcake. 甘美的水果餅。⑦(顏色)濃的;(聲音)宏亮圓潤的;(氣味)馥郁的;醇厚的。a *rich* tone. 宏亮圓潤的音調。⑧〖俗〗好玩的;可笑的。⑨隆重的;盛大的。a *rich* funeral. 隆重的葬禮。***the rich*** 富人。—**ness,** *n.*

Rich·ard [ˈrɪtʃɚd; ˈritʃəd] *n.* 男子名。

Richard Roe 某甲(公文契約中用以代表不知姓名者的用語)。

Rich·ards [ˈrɪtʃɚdz; ˈritʃədz] *n.* 理查玆(Theodore William, 1868–1928, 美國化學家,曾獲1914年諾貝爾化學獎)。

Rich·ard·son [ˈrɪtʃɚdsn̩; ˈritʃədsn] *n.* 理查生(Owen Williams, 1879–1959, 英國物理學家,曾獲1928年諾貝爾物理獎)。

rich·es** [ˈrɪtʃɪz; ˈritʃiz] *n. pl.* 財富;財寶。from rags to riches*** 從赤貧變爲鉅富。

Ri·chet [riˈʃɛ; riˈʃei] *n.* 黎歇(Charles Robert, 1850–1935, 法國生理學家,曾獲 1913 年諾貝爾生理及醫學獎)。

***rich·ly** [ˈrɪtʃlɪ; ˈritʃli] *adv.* ①富麗地。*richly* dressed. 服裝富麗。②充分地。He *richly* deserved it. 他有充分資格去獲得它。

rick [rɪk; rik] *n.* 禾堆;乾草堆。—*v.t.* 堆成禾堆。

rick·ets [ˈrɪkɪts; ˈrikits] *n.* 軟骨病;佝僂病;佝僂病。

rick·ett·si·a [rɪkˈɛtsɪə; rikˈetsiə] *n., pl.* **-si·as, -si·ae** [-sɪˌi; -siiː]. 發疹及傷寒等的病原體。

rick·et·y [ˈrɪkɪtɪ; ˈrikiti] *adj.* ①患佝僂病的。②佝僂病的;似佝僂病的。③蹣跚的;虛弱的。④搖搖晃晃的;東倒西歪的。

rick·ey [ˈrɪkɪ; ˈriki] *n.* 〖美〗一種檸檬汁、酒、汽水等混合之飲料。

rick·shaw [ˈrɪkʃɔ; ˈrikʃɔː] *n.* 人力車;黃包車。(亦作 **ricksha**)

rick·y-tick [ˈrɪkiˌtɪk; ˈrikiːˌtik] *adj.* 〖美俚〗=**rinky-dink.**

ric·o·chet [ˌrɪkəˈʃe; ˈrikəʃet] *n., v.,* **-cheted** [-ˈʃed; -ʃeid], **-chet·ing** [-ˈʃeɪŋ; -ʃeiiŋ], or **-chet·ted** [-ˈʃɛtɪd; -ʃetid], **-chet·ting** [-ˈʃɛtɪŋ; -ʃetiŋ]. —*n.* ①躍起;回跳;掠平面而飛。②〖軍〗跳彈。—*v.i.* 躍起;回跳;掠平面而飛。—*v.t.* 使躍起;使回跳;使掠平面而飛。

rid** [rɪd; rid] *v.t.,* **rid** or **rid·ded, rid·ding.** 免除;解除。to *rid* oneself of debt. 清除債務。be rid of*** 免除;不受…之擾。***get rid of*** 免除;解除。

rid·a·ble [ˈraɪdəbl̩; ˈraidəbl] *adj.* ①可騎乘的(馬等)。②可騎乘而過的(小路或溪流)。

rid·dance [ˈrɪdn̩s; ˈridns] *n.* 除去;擺脫。***good riddance*** 樂得沒有;樂得除去。

‡**rid·den** [ˈrɪdn̩; ˈridn] *v.* pp. of **ride.** —*adj.* 受折磨的;受支配的。a country *ridden* by soldiers. 軍人跋扈的國家。

***rid·dle**[1] [ˈrɪdl̩; ˈridl] *n., v.,* **-dled, -dling.** —*n.* ①不可解之問題;謎。He speaks in *riddles.* 他說話令人費解。②謎樣的人;費解之人。—*v.i.* 講話含糊;出言若謎。—*v.t.* 解(謎)。*Riddle* me this. 爲我解釋此事。

rid·dle[2] *n., v.,* **-dled, -dling.** —*n.* 粗篩。—*v.t.* ①篩。②穿孔。③挑剔(言論)中的漏洞。—*v.i.* 穿過。

rid·dling·ly [ˈrɪdlɪŋlɪ; ˈridliŋli] *adv.* 謎般地;不可解地。

‡**ride** [raɪd; raid] *v.,* **rode, rid·den, rid·ing,** *n.* —*v.i.* ①乘馬、驢、駱駝、脚踏車等而行。He *rode* over to see me yesterday. 他昨天騎馬(或脚踏車)來看我。②乘坐;跨。to *ride* in a train (bus). 乘火車(公共汽車)。③前進;飄行;浮。④(車、馬等載人而)行。That horse *rides* easily. 那匹馬走起來很輕快。⑤依;靠。⑥(錢)被賭。—*v.t.* ①騎;乘。to *ride* a bicycle. 騎脚踏車。②飄行;御行。The eagle *rides* the winds. 鷹御風飛翔。③控制;駕馭。He was *ridden* by foolish fears. 他爲愚妄的恐懼所控制。④騎(馬等)、乘(車等)經過或通過。⑤(騎乘而)做;作。to *ride* a race. 騎馬比賽。⑥使騎乘。to *ride* a child on one's shoulders. 使小孩騎在肩上。⑦〖俗〗揶揄;嘲弄。⑧克服。***ride at anchor*** 拋錨。***ride down*** **a.** 擊倒。**b.** 克服;征服。**c.** 騎馬追及。**d.** 由騎乘而使力竭。***ride for a fall*** 魯莽行事;自討苦吃;自取滅亡。***ride gain*** 控制聲音之强弱使適於廣播或傳播。***ride herd on*** 監督;監視;管教。***ride high*** 做事成功;百事遂意。***ride out*** **a.** 抵擋(狂風等)而不受損。**b.** 安然度過。***ride roughshod over*** 蹂躪;嚴酷地對待;擊敗。***ride the beam*** 〖航空〗沿無線電波束指示的航線飛行。***ride up*** 滑上去而離了原位;走樣。The coat *rides up* at the back. 這件外衣背後會往上縮。—*n.* ①乘馬(車等);乘在馬(車等)上的短程旅行。to go for a *ride.* 騎馬(或乘車等)出去兜風。②供騎馬之道路。***take for a ride*** 〖俚〗**a.** 帶到他處而加以謀殺。**b.** 欺騙。

***rid·er** [ˈraɪdɚ; ˈraidə] *n.* ①騎馬者;騎車者;乘車者。motorcycle *rider.* 摩托車騎士。②(文件等上之)附加物;附文;附件。③籬笆之支柱。

rid·er·less [ˈraɪdɚlɪs; ˈraidəlis] *adj.* ①無騎(乘)者的。②無附件的;無附文的。

***ridge** [rɪdʒ; ridʒ] *n., v.,* **ridged, ridg·ing.** —*n.* ①脊。②屋脊。③狹長之山脈;山脊。④任何隆起的窄物。the *ridge* of the nose. 鼻梁。—*v.t.* 使成脊。—*v.i.* 成脊形。

ridge beam 房屋之正樑;營帳之中央橫木。

ridge·piece [ˈrɪdʒˌpis; ˈridʒpiːs] *n.* =**ridgepole.**

ridge·pole [ˈrɪdʒˌpol; ˈridʒpoul] *n.* 〖建築〗棟木。

ridg·y [ˈrɪdʒɪ; ˈridʒi] *adj.,* **ridg·i·er,**

ridg·i·est. 有脊的;有壟的;隆起的。

*rid·i·cule 〔'rɪdɪˌkjul; 'ridikjuːl〕 v., -culed, -cul·ing, n. —v.t. 訕笑;譏笑;嘲弄。 —n. 訕笑;譏笑;嘲弄。 to pour *ridicule* on a person or thing. 對人或事物加以譏嘲。

*ri·dic·u·lous 〔rɪ'dɪkjələs; ri'dikjuləs〕 *adj.* 可笑的;荒謬的。 a *ridiculous* suggestion. 可笑的意見。—ness, *n.* —ly, *adv.*

rid·ing¹ 〔'raɪdɪŋ; 'raidiŋ〕 *n.* ①英國 Yorkshire 郡之三個行政區 (the North Riding, the East Riding 及 the West Riding) 之一。②他處類似之區畫。 ***The Three Ridings*** 英國約克郡。

rid·ing² *n.* ①騎馬;乘車。to take a *riding.* 騎馬;乘車。②馬路;跑馬場。—*adj.* ①騎乘的。②騎乘用的。③旅行用的。

riding boot 馬靴;長統靴。

riding breeches 騎馬褲。

riding crop 一端有帶圈可握的短馬鞭。

riding habit 女用騎裝。

riding lamp (or **light**) 〖航海〗停泊燈。

riding master 騎術師。

riding school 騎術學校。

riding suit 騎裝。

rife 〔raɪf; raif〕 *adj.* ①流行的;盛行的;常發生的;無數的。②衆多的;充斥的〖with〗.

riff 〔rɪf; rif〕 *v.i.* & *v.t.* ①迅速輕翻(書頁等)。②迅速過目。

rif·fle 〔'rɪf!; 'rifl〕 *n., v.,* -fled, -fling. —*n.* ①溪流中激起漣漪或激流之淺灘、暗礁或岩石。②溪流中被淺灘、暗礁等激起的漣漪。③〖採礦〗排置於水門或洗礦槽底部之木條或木板。④此種槽溝中的任一木板或木條。⑤此種槽溝。⑥洗牌之動作及方法。 ***make the riffle*** 在淺灘上逆流而上;(喻) 在困苦環境中努力掙扎力求上游。—*v.t.* & *v.i.* ①(使)形成漣漪; 變成漣漪。②用姆指迅速輕翻書頁。③洗牌。④流過暗礁。⑤(使)飄動。

riff·raff 〔'rɪfˌræf; 'rifræf〕 *n.* ①流氓;暴民;賤民。②廢物;碎屑;渣滓。—*adj.* 下等的;破爛的。

*ri·fle¹ 〔'raɪf!; 'raifl〕 *n., v.,* -fled, -fling. —*n.* ①來福槍; 步槍。②來福線。③(*pl.*) 步槍兵。—*v.t.* 加來福線於(槍械)。

ri·fle² *v.,* -fled, -fling. —*v.t.* ①搶刼; 擄取; 偸竊。②搜取一空。—*v.i.* 搜刼;搜索。

ri·fle³ *v.t.* 用力擊出或投出。

ri·fle·man 〔'raɪf!mən; 'raiflmən〕 *n., pl.* -men. ①荷有來福槍之士兵。②精於使用來福槍的人。

rifle pit 〖軍〗散兵坑;散兵壕。

rifle range ①靶場。②來福槍的射程。

ri·fle·scope 〔'raɪf!ˌskop; 'raiflskoup〕 *n.* 步槍望遠瞄準器。

ri·fle·shot 〔'raɪf!ˌʃɑt; 'raiflʃɔt〕 *n.* 步槍彈;步槍射擊。

ri·fling 〔'raɪflɪŋ; 'raifliŋ〕 *n.* ①膛線之鐫刻。②(槍內之)一序列膛線。

rift 〔rɪft; rift〕 *n.* ①裂縫;罅隙; 裂口。②不和;失睦。 ***a rift in the lute*** 不和、失睦的預兆; 破裂的徵兆。—*v.t.* & *v.i.* 劈開; 破開; 裂開。—*adj.* 劈開的;(沿木紋理)鋸開的。

*rig¹ 〔rɪg; rig〕 *n., v.,* rigged, rig·ging. —*n.* ①船具裝置法。②設備; 裝置物。③服裝。④〖美俗〗配有馬之馬車。—*v.t.* ①裝索具於(船)。②將(橫桅索、帆之下桁、支索等)移置其適當位置。③裝置;配備。④〖俗〗裝束。⑤準備。⑥匆促湊成;草草做成。⑦欺詐;作弊。Speculators *rigged* the market. 投機者壟斷市場。***rig down*** 置於靜止狀態。***rig up*** 裝備;配備。

rig² *n.* ①蕩婦;娼妓。②狎戲;詭計。

rig·a·doon 〔ˌrɪgə'dun; ˌrigə'duːn〕 *n.* ①一種用跳躍步調之對舞。②此種舞之音樂。

rig·ger 〔'rɪgɚ; 'rigə〕 *n.* ①索具裝置者。②搖絞轆者。③裝配飛機、飛船者。④建築工程進行中預防工具材料等落下傷人之搭架。

rig·ging 〔'rɪgɪŋ; 'rigiŋ〕 *n.*①船之纜索。②裝備。③〖俗〗服裝。

‡right 〔raɪt; rait〕 *adj.* ①好的;公正的; 合法的。*right* conduct. 正當的行爲。②對的; 眞實的。Your opinions are quite *right.* 你的意見極是。③正當的; 適當的。He's the *right* man for the position. 他是適合這職位的人。④合適的。If the weather is *right,* we'll go. 如果天氣適宜,我們便去。⑤健康的; 正常的。 Do you feel all *right?* 你感到舒適嗎? ⑥右方的;右面的(left 之對)。one's *right* hand. 右手。⑦直的。 a *right* line. 直線。⑧垂直的。 a *right* angle. 直角。 ***All right!*** 好;是;對(表贊同或滿意)。 ***at right angles*** 成直角地。 ***be in one's right mind*** (or ***senses***) 神智健全。 ***get something right*** 徹底了解一事。***not right in the head*** 發狂;瘋。***on the right side of*** 尙未及…歲。 ***put*** (or ***set***) ***something*** (or ***somebody***) ***right*** 整頓; 使恢復健康。***right arm*** 右臂;得力助手。(***as***) ***right as rain*** (or ***a trivet***) 極對; 舒服; 滿意。—*adv.* ①好地; 公正地; 合法地。He acted *right.* 他行動正當。②對地; 正確地。 She guessed *right.* 她猜得對。③好地; 合適地; 適當地。Nothing seems to go *right* with him. 一切對他都不順利。④向右地; 右方地。Turn *right.* 向右轉。⑤恰好地。Put it *right* here. 把它就放在這裏。⑥〖美〗卽刻地; 立時地。Stop playing *right* now. 馬上停止玩耍。⑦很; 極 (=very, 用在尊稱之前, 意爲極受人尊敬的)。 the *Right* Reverend. (對主教之尊稱)。⑧一直地; 照直地。 Go *right* to the end of this road and then turn left. 一直走完這條路後向左轉。 ⑨完全地; 徹底地。 The apple was rotten *right* through. 這蘋果爛透了。⑩〖方,俗〗非常地;極。He knows *right* well. 他知道得非常淸楚。⑪直接地; 直線地。 Look me *right* in the eye. 正視着我。***right along***不停地;不斷地。***right and left*** 向各方面;無拘束地。Look *right and left* before you cross a street. 過街之前要向各方面看看。***right away*** 立刻; 直截了當地。 He said he couldn't do the job *right away.* 他說他不能立刻做那工作。***right down*** 極其地。 *right down* clever. 極其聰明。 ***right off***=**right away**. —*n.* ①正義; 公理; 道理。*right* and wrong. 是非。②權利。the *right* to vote. 表決權; 投票權。③右;右方;右翼。 the school on the *right.* 在右方的學校。④右手所擊之拳。⑤(常 R-)右派(較爲保守者)。⑥購買新股之特權;此種特權證。⑦〖棒球〗右外野。⑧〖方〗義務。You have a *right* to behave better. 你行爲應更檢點一些。 ***by right(s)*** 公正地; 恰當地。***by right of*** 因爲; 由於。***in one's own right*** a. 由於本人之繼承權。b. 因本身之能力、條件等。***in right of*** 根據…所有的權利。***in the right*** 在對的一邊。***Mr. Right*** 〖美俗〗女人之合適的結婚對象。 ***right of way*** 通行權; 優先通行權。 ***stand on*** (or ***assert***) ***one's rights*** 固守其權利。 ***to rights***〖俗〗就緒;有次序。—*v.t.* ①糾正;改正。

to *right* errors. 糾正錯誤。②整頓；整理。③扶正；扶直；扶起。④公正對待。*right about!* 〖軍〗向後轉！—*v.i.* (船從傾斜中)恢復直立。

right·a·bout ['raɪtə,baut; 'raitəbaut] *n.* ①反對之方向。②向後轉。—*adv. & adj.* 反對方向地(的)。(亦作 **right-about**)

right·a·bout-face ['raɪtə,baut'fes; 'raitəˌbaut'feis] *n.* ①〖軍〗向後轉。②(信仰、行爲等之)完全轉變。—*interj.*〖軍〗向後轉！(亦作 **right about-face, right-about-face**)

right-and-left ['raɪtn̩'lɛft; 'raitənd'left] *adj.* ①成雙製造供左右兩邊使用的(如鞋、手套等)。②左右對稱的。③有左右向之線的。

right angle 直角。

right-an·gled ['raɪt'æŋgl̩d; 'rait'æŋgld] *adj.* 直角的；含有直角的；成直角的。

right-cen·ter ['raɪt'sɛntɚ; 'rait'sentə] *adj.* (政治上)中間而偏右的。

right-down ['raɪt'daun; 'rait'daun] *adj.* 完全的；徹底的。

***right·eous** ['raɪtʃəs; 'raitʃəs] *adj.* ①行爲正當的。②正當的；公正的。*righteous* anger (*or* indignation). 義憤。

right·eous·ly ['raɪtʃəslɪ; 'raitʃəsli] *adv.* 正當地；公正地。

***right·eous·ness** ['raɪtʃəsnɪs; 'raitʃəsnis] *n.* 公正；正當。

right face 〖軍〗向右轉。

right field 〖棒球〗右外野。

right fielder 〖棒球〗右外野手。

right·ful ['raɪtfəl; 'raitful] *adj.* ①合法的。②正直的；公正的。

right·ful·ly ['raɪtfəlɪ; 'raitfuli] *adv.* ①合法地；公正地。②合理地。

right hand ①右手。②最得力的助手。

***right-hand** ['raɪt'hænd; 'raithænd] *adj.* ①右方的；向右方的。②右手的；右手用的；用右手的。③最得力的。

right-hand·ed ['raɪt'hændɪd; 'rait'hændid] *adj.* ①習慣於用右手的；右手的。②以右手用的。③順時針方向的；右旋的。④可恕的；可原諒的。—*adv.* 以右手。

right-handed screw 正螺旋；右旋螺釘。

right-hand·er ['raɪt'hændɚ; 'rait'hændə] *n.* ①用右手的人。②右手拳。

right-hand man 得力助手。

right·ism ['raɪtɪzm̩; 'raitizm] *n.* 〖政治〗保守之思想或行動；右派。

right·ist ['raɪtɪst; 'raitist] *n.* 〖政治〗保守主義者；右派分子。—*adj.* 〖政治〗右派的；保守派的。

***right·ly** ['raɪtlɪ; 'raitli] *adv.* ①正直地；正當地；無誤地。②有道理地；合理地。

right-mind·ed ['raɪt'maɪndɪd; 'rait'maindid] *adj.* 公正的；合理的。

right·ness ['raɪtnɪs; 'raitnis] *n.* 正直；公正；適切。

right·o ['raɪto; 'rait'ou] *interj.* 〖主英〗=all right; O. K.(亦作 **right-oh**)

right of asylum ①(國家之)庇護權。②(個人之)要求庇護權。

right of search 〖海上法〗公海搜索權。

right of way ①(車輛或船隻優先通過之)先行權。②可依法使用之道路。③(可在別人土地上通過之)通行權。④用做鐵路路線之土地。⑤公路分布之土地；高壓線通過之地區。(亦作 **right-of-way**)

rights [raɪts; raits] 〖俗〗*n.* (作 *pl.* 解) 民權。—*adj.* 民權的；民權運動的。

right section 橫截面。

right smart ①很大的。②很；非常。③很多。

right triangle 正三角形。

right·ward ['raɪtwɚd; 'rait-wəd] *adj. & adv.* 向右的(地)。

right·wards ['raɪtwɚdz; 'raitwədz] *adv.* 向右地。

right whale 露脊鯨。

right-wing ['raɪt,wɪŋ; 'rait-wiŋ] *adj.* 〖政治〗右派的；右翼的。

right wing 〖政治〗右派；右翼；保守派。(亦作 **Right Wing**)

right·wing·er ['raɪt'wɪŋɚ; 'rait'wiŋə] *n.* 右派的人；右翼主義者；右翼分子。

***rig·id** ['rɪdʒɪd; 'ridʒid] *adj.* ①僵硬的；穩固的。②嚴格的；嚴厲的。*rigid* rules. 嚴格的規則。③精確的。—**ly**, *adv.* —**ness**, *n.*

ri·gid·i·ty [rɪ'dʒɪdətɪ; ri'dʒiditi] *n.* ①堅硬；硬；僵硬。②〖物理〗剛性。③嚴峻；嚴格；嚴厲；嚴正。④剛直；不屈。⑤難以改變之處。

rig·ma·role ['rɪgmə,rol; 'rigməroul] *n.* ①冗長散亂之言語；廢話。②無意義的手續。

rig·or ['rɪgɚ; 'rigə] *n.* ①嚴厲；嚴酷；苛刻。②剛強；不屈。③嚴寒；酷熱。④戰慄；惡寒。⑤精確性；嚴密性。(亦作 **rigour**)

rig·or·ism ['rɪgərɪzəm; 'rigərizm] *n.* ①〖倫理〗嚴肅主義。②嚴格性。—**rig·or·ist**, *n.*

rig·or mor·tis ['raɪgɔr'mɔrtɪs; 'raigɔː'mɔːtis] 〖拉〗屍體之僵硬。

rig·o·ro·so [rɪgə'roso; rigə'rousou] *adj.* 〖音樂〗非常有節奏的；完全合拍子的。

rig·or·ous ['rɪgərəs; 'rigərəs] *adj.* ①堅硬的；嚴厲的。②確實的；合邏輯的；嚴密的。③尖刻的；極冷的。—**ly**, *adv.* —**ness**, *n.*

Rigs·dag ['rɪgz,dɑg; 'rigzdɑːg] *n.* 丹麥國會。

Riks·dag ['rɪks,dɑg; 'riksdɑːg] *n.* 瑞典國會。

rile [raɪl; rail] *v.t.*, **riled, ril·ing.** ①〖俗〗惹怒；激怒；使煩躁。②〖美〗攪渾；攪濁。

ri·lie·vo [rɪ'ljɛvo; ˌrili'eivou] *n.*, *pl.* **-vi** [-vi; -viː]. 〖義〗浮雕。

rill [rɪl; ril] *n.* 小河；小川。

***rim** [rɪm; rim] *n.*, *v.*, **rimmed, rim·ming.** —*n.* 邊緣。—*v.t.* ①加邊於；鑲邊於。red-*rimmed* eyes. 哭紅了眼眶的眼睛。②沿洞之邊緣滾。—*v.i.* 成邊。

rim-brake ['rɪm,brek; 'rimbreik] *n.* 輪緣制動機。

***rime** [raɪm; raim] *n.*, *v.*, **rimed, rim·ing.** =**rhyme.**

rim·less ['rɪmlɪs; 'rimlis] *adj.* 無邊緣的。*rimless* glasses. 無邊之眼鏡。

ri·mose ['raɪmos; 'raimous] *adj.* 有裂隙的；有罅隙的。(亦作**rimous**)

rim·y ['raɪmɪ; 'raimi] *adj.*, **rim·i·er, rim·i·est.** 覆以霜的；霜寒的。

***rind** [raɪnd, raɪn; raind] *n.* ①樹皮；植物皮；果皮；種子外殼；獸皮。*rind* of a tree. 樹皮。②硬殼；外殼。③外觀；外表。

rin·der·pest ['rɪndɚ,pɛst; 'rindəpest] 〖德〗*n.* 〖獸醫〗牛瘟。

‡ring[1] [rɪŋ; riŋ] *n.*, *v.*, **ringed, ring·ing.** —*n.* ①環；圈。The children danced in a *ring.* 孩子們圍成一圈跳舞。②金屬環；指環。③樹木之年輪。④(圓形物之)外沿。⑤圓形競技場。⑥惡黨。a spy *ring.* 一羣間諜。⑦競爭。He threw his hat into the presidential *ring.* 他宣布參加總統競選。⑧馬戲表演場。⑨拳擊賽場。*in the ring for election* 競選。*run rings around* 顯然優於…；超過。—*v.t.*①戴以環；圍繞。They had their palace *ringed* with barbed wire. 他們以鐵絲網將大厦圍住。②擲環以套(短樁等)。③供以環。④套環於(動物之鼻)。⑤環剝樹皮。⑥在…之周圍環行。—**less,** *adj.* —**like,** *adj.*

‡**ring²** *v.,* **rang, rung, ring·ing,** *n.* —*v.i.* ①鳴;響。Begin work when the bell *rings.* 鈴響時開始工作。②回響;發震聲。The room *rang* with shouts of laughter. 這屋裏響起一陣歡笑聲。③鳴鈴呼喚。to *ring* for the maid. 鳴鈴召喚女僕。④有鐘鳴之感。My ears *ring.* 我耳鳴。⑤聽起來;似乎。—*v.t.* ①使鳴;使響。to *ring* the bell. 鳴鈴;搖鈴。②高聲而言;散布;傳播。to *ring* one's praises. 高聲稱頌。③發(鳴聲)。④以鐘聲召集。⑤以鐘聲宣告。*Ring* out the old year; *ring* in the new. 鐘聲宣告舊年已逝,新年來臨。⑥打電話給。***ring a bell*** 引起反應;引起共鳴。***ring down the curtain*** **a.** 鳴鈴拉下戲幕。**b.** 結束。***ring in*** **a.** 以不正當手段引入。**b.** 打卡上班。***ring off*** 掛斷電話。***ring the bell*** 說服;使人相信。***ring the changes on*** **a.** 以同一事物產生新的效果。**b.** 以不同方法或次序一再應用。***ring the knell of*** 宣布…之結束或崩潰;敲…之喪鐘。***ring true*** 似乎是眞的。***ring up*** **a.** 用電話聯絡;打電話。I'll *ring* you *up* tomorrow. 我明天打電話給你。**b.** 用收銀機記載售貨數量。***ring up the curtain*** **a.** 鳴鈴拉開戲幕。**b.** 開始表演;開始行動。—*n.* ①鈴聲;鐘聲。There was a *ring* at the door. 有人按門鈴。②打鐘或搖鈴。③特別的聲音;特性。There was a *ring* of sincerity in his promise. 他的允諾語氣眞誠。④打電話。Give me a *ring* as soon as you're in town. 你一到城裏就給我打個電話。

ring·bolt [ˈrɪŋˌbolt; ˈriŋboult] *n.* 有環螺釘。

ring·dove [ˈrɪŋˌdʌv; ˈriŋdʌv] *n.* 斑鳩。

ringed [rɪŋd; riŋd] *adj.* ①有環狀飾物的。②以環狀飾物裝飾的;爲環所圍繞的。③輪狀的。④戴指環的。⑤正式結了婚的。

ring·er¹ [ˈrɪŋɚ; ˈriŋə] *n.* ①鳴鐘者;鳴鈴者。②〖礦〗鐵梃;起貨鉤。③詐僞出場比賽之人或馬。④極相似之人或物(常與 dead 連用)。⑤〖俚〗非本球隊之正式隊員;臨時隊員。

ring·er² *n.* ①包圍者;包圍物。②擲鐵樁之馬蹄鐵或圓環。③擲環遊戲之一擲。

ring fence 圍垣;圍籬。

ring finger (左手之)無名指。

ring-goal [ˈrɪŋˌgol; ˈriŋgoul] *n.* 一種投環遊戲。

ring·ing¹ [ˈrɪŋɪŋ; ˈriŋiŋ] *n.* ①鐘響;鈴響。②響聲;響的感覺。—*adj.* ①如鐘響的;如鈴響的。②響亮的;有力的(話)。a *ringing* appeal. 有力的訴願。

ring·ing² *adj.* 圍繞的;打圈圈的。

ring·ing·ly [ˈrɪŋɪŋlɪ; ˈriŋiŋli] *adv.* 響亮地;(說話)有力地。

ring·lead [ˈrɪŋˌlid; ˈriŋliːd] *v.t. & v.i.,* **-led** [-lɛd; -led], **-lead·ing.** 當魁首。

ring·lead·er [ˈrɪŋˌlidɚ; ˈriŋˌliːdə] *n.* 叛黨首領;暴動之魁首;倡導作亂的人。

ring·let [ˈrɪŋlɪt; ˈriŋlit] *n.* ①小環;環形物。②鬈髮。

ring·let·ed [ˈrɪŋlɪtɪd; ˈriŋlitid] *adj.* 有小環的;成小環的。

ring·man [ˈrɪŋmən; ˈriŋmən] *n., pl.* **-men.** 拳擊者。

ring·mas·ter [ˈrɪŋˌmæstɚ; ˈriŋˌmɑːstə] *n.* 馬戲場管理人。

ring·side [ˈrɪŋˌsaɪd; ˈriŋsaid] *n.* ①(拳賽場、馬戲場等)場邊。②可供近看的地方。—*adj.* 場邊的;可近看的。—*adv.* 在場邊;在可以近看處。

ring·ster [ˈrɪŋstɚ; ˈriŋstə] *n.* 〖俗〗結黨營私者;黨徒。

ring·worm [ˈrɪŋˌwɝm; ˈriŋwəːm] *n.* 〖醫〗癬;錢癬。

rink [rɪŋk; riŋk] *n.* ①溜冰場。②供滑冰用的光滑地板。③室內溜冰場。④供作冰上遊戲之滑冰場。⑤可做比賽用的滾球戲草坪。⑥滾球戲競技者之一方;冰上遊戲參加比賽之一方。—*v.i.* (在滑冰場中)溜冰。

rin·ky-dink [ˈrɪŋkɪˌdɪŋk; ˈriŋkiˌdiŋk] *adj.* 〖美俚〗過時的;陳腔濫調的。

***rinse** [rɪns; rins] *v.,* **rinsed, rins·ing,** *n.* —*v.t.* ①清洗。②洗濯;漂洗。③漱(口);涮洗。④沖去;洗去。⑤〖俗〗以水沖進(食物)。—*v.i.* 被漂清;被沖掉。This soap *rinses* easily. 這肥皂很容易漂清。—*n.* ①漱洗;漂洗;漂清;洗淨。②(潤髮用)潤絲精。

rins·ing [ˈrɪnsɪŋ; ˈrinsiŋ] *n.* ①沖洗;洗刷;漂洗。②(*pl.*) **a.** 洗刷用之液體。**b.** 渣滓。

Ri·o de Ja·nei·ro [ˈriodədʒəˈnɪro; ˈriːou də dʒəˈniərou] 里約熱內盧(巴西舊都,新都爲 Brasilia)。

ri·ot** [ˈraɪət; ˈraiət] *n.* ①騷擾;紊亂;騷動。②鮮艷之展示。③非常有趣或好玩之事物。④有趣之人或表演。He was a *riot* at the party. 他在派對中談笑風生。⑤喧鬧。to break out in a *riot* of laughter. 縱聲大笑。⑥放縱;恣情逸樂。run riot*** **a.** 行動無約束。His tongue *runs riot.* 他放肆地胡言亂語。**b.** 生長茂盛。—*v.i.* ①喧鬧;歡鬧。②恣情;耽。③騷動;騷擾。—*v.t.* 浪費;亂花。—**er,** *n.*

Riot Act 〖英〗取締暴動法案。***read the riot act*** **a.** 下令取締暴動。**b.** 嚴詞責備。

riot gun 鎭暴鎗。

ri·ot·ous [ˈraɪətəs; ˈraiətəs] *adj.* ①暴亂的;引起暴亂的。②恣情的;放縱的。③滋蔓的;豐盛的。—**ly,** *adv.*

riot squad 鎭暴隊。

rip¹** [rɪp; rip] *v.,* **ripped, rip·ping,** *n.* —*v.t.* ①撕開;扯開;扯掉。*Rip* the cover off this box. 把這個盒子的封套扯掉。②(沿木紋理)直鋸或直劈(木材)。③〖俗〗出言不遜;胡說;亂講。He *ripped* out an angry oath. 他破口大罵。—*v.i.* ①裂開;破開。A seam *rips.* 一條衣縫裂開了。②〖俗〗向前直闖。③〖俗〗出言不遜;胡說〖out〗。He *ripped* out with an oath. 他破口大罵。let her*** (or ***it***) ***rip*** 別管它;讓它去(指船、機器等)。***let rip*** 〖主英〗 **a.** 發出一連串的咒罵。**b.** 滔滔不絕地說或寫。***let things rip*** 擱着不管。***rip into*** 〖俗〗攻擊;批評。***rip off*** 〖美俚〗偸;搶。***rip out*** 〖俗〗怒罵。—*n.* 裂開之處;破痕。***rip cord*** 〖空軍〗開傘索;裂索。

rip² *n.* 〖俗〗①邪惡之人;浪子。②劣馬。③廢物。

rip³ *n.* ①激流。②浪濤。(亦作 **riptide**)

R.I.P., RIP Requiesca(n)t in pace (拉=May he, she *or* they rest in peace!) 願他(她、他們)安息!

ri·par·i·an [rɪˈpɛrɪən, raɪ-; raiˈpɛəriən] *adj.* ①河岸上的;水濱的。②生於水濱的(植物)。③棲居河岸的(動物)。—*n.* 河岸居住者。

ripe** [raɪp; raip] *adj.,* **rip·er, rip·est.** ①成熟的;紅潤飽滿的。a *ripe* apple. 一隻熟蘋果。②發展完成的;十分的。*ripe* scholarship (knowledge). 成熟的學識(知識)。③準備成熟的〖for〗。④已化膿的;可刺破的。a *ripe* boil. 已化膿的疔瘡。⑤足够的。⑥年長的。Soon ripe, soon rotten.*** 〖諺〗早熟早

爛。—ly, *adv.* —ness, *n.*

***rip·en** ['raɪpən; 'raipən] *v.t.* & *v.i.* 使熟；成熟。to *ripen* into maturity. 成熟。

rip·off ['rɪpɑf; 'ripɔf] *n.* 〖美俚〗偸；搶。

ri·post(e) [rɪ'post; ri'poust] *n.*, *v.*, **-post·ed, -post·ing.** —*n.* ①〖劍術〗擋後還刺。②機敏之應對；反駁。③反擊。—*v.i.* ①〖劍術〗擋後還刺。②機敏地回答；反駁。

rip-pan·el ['rɪpˌpænl̩; 'ripˌpænəl] *n.* ①氣球的裂瓣。②〖機械〗裂幅。(亦作 **rip panel**)

rip·per ['rɪpɚ; 'ripə] *n.* ①撕裂者；裂開之工具；裂具。②一種雙撬(=double-ripper)。③〖英俚〗非常好的人或東西。

rip·ping ['rɪpɪŋ; 'ripiŋ] *adj.* 〖英俚〗非凡的；頂好的；絕妙的；愉快的。—*adv.* 〖英俚〗非凡地；非常地；頂好地；愉快地。a *ripping* good time. 非常愉快的時間。—ly, *adv.*

***rip·ple**[1] ['rɪpl̩; 'ripl] *n.*, *v.*, **-pled, -pling.** —*n.* ①微波；漣漪。②微波狀物(如髮浪等)。③聲浪；一陣聲音。a *ripple* of laughter in the crowd. 人羣中一陣笑聲。—*v.t.* & *v.i.* 使起微波；生波紋。

rip·ple[2] *v.*, **-pled, -pling,** *n.* —*v.t.* 以篦梳梳下(亞麻等之)種子。—*n.* 篦梳。

ripple mark 風和浪在沙上造成的波浪。

rip·plet ['rɪplɪt; 'riplit] *n.* 小漣漪。

rip·pling ['rɪplɪŋ; 'ripliŋ] *adj.* 起漣漪的；起皺的。—ly, *adv.*

rip·ply ['rɪplɪ; 'ripli] *adj.*, **rip·pli·er, rip·pli·est.** ①有微波的；起漣漪的。②若漣漪聲的。

rip·rap ['rɪpˌræp; 'ripræp] *n.*, *v.*, **-rapped, -rap·ping.** —*n.* ①亂堆石基。②此種碎石。—*v.t.* 以亂石基鞏固。

rip·roar·ing ['rɪp'rɔrɪŋ; 'rip'rɔːriŋ] *adj.* 〖俚〗喧囂的；騷亂的；吵鬧的。

rip·saw ['rɪpˌsɔ; 'ripsɔː] *n.* 粗齒鋸。

rip·snort·er ['rɪpˌsnɔrtɚ; 'ripsnɔːtə] *n.* ①精力充沛、談吐豪爽者；暴怒者。②達到極點之事物。

rip·tide ['rɪpˌtaɪd; 'riptaid] *n.* ①令人團團轉的情況或力量。②與另一股海流反向的海流。

Rip Van Win·kle [ˌrɪpvæn'wɪŋkl̩; 'ripvæn'wiŋkl] ①美國作家 Washington Irving 所著 Sketch Book 中 "Rip van Winkle" 的主角，Rip 在 Catskill 山中一睡二十年，醒來發現一切全非。②對環境之變化不够警覺的人。

‡rise [raɪz; raiz] *v.*, **rose, ris·en, ris·ing,** *n.* —*v.i.* ①立起；起身；起床(用 get up 較普通)。to *rise* from a chair. 自椅上起立。He *rises* very early. 他起床很早。②升起；上升。③矗立。The tower *rises* to a height of 60 feet. 那塔高矗達六十英尺。④斜升；漸高。⑤(程度、強度、數量等)增高；漲。Prices are *rising*. 物價在上漲。⑥升級；晉升。to *rise* in the world. 成名；功成名就。⑦起源；開始。⑧發生。⑨築；蓋。⑩振作；高興。His spirit *rose*. 他的精神振奮起來。⑪反抗；叛變。⑫變大；變鬆。⑬再生。Christ *rose* from the dead. 耶穌從死中復生。⑭休會；閉會。⑮熱烈歡呼鼓掌。The audience *rose* to his verve and wit. 聽衆對他的精力和機智熱烈歡呼鼓掌。⑯(魚)上升至水面(以吃餌)。—*v.t.* 使升起。***rise to*** **a.** 相等於。**b.** 能應付。They *rose to* the occasion. 他們能應付那情勢。—*n.* ①(向上的)斜坡。②增加；增高。a *rise* in prices. 物價之增高。③起源；開始。④上升。⑤(魚之)上升至水面(以吃餌)。⑥(臺階、斜坡、拱形等之)垂直高度。⑦升至地平線之上。⑧刺人的回答。***get a rise out of*** 〖俚〗激起預期之反應；激怒。***give rise to*** 引起；惹起。

‡ris·en ['rɪzn̩; 'rizn] *v.* pp. of **rise.**

ris·er ['raɪzɚ; 'raizə] *n.* ①起床者。an early (late) *riser*. 早(晚)起的人。②升起之物。③〖建築〗梯級間之豎板。

ris·i·bil·i·ty [ˌrɪzə'bɪlətɪ; ˌrizi'biliti] *n.*, *pl.* **-ties.** ①笑的能力；笑的傾向與性質。②(*pl.*)〖美〗發笑感；笑癖；幽默感。③笑。

ris·i·ble ['rɪzəbl̩; 'rizibl] *adj.* ①能笑的；善笑的；愛笑的。②笑的；與笑有關的。③可笑的。—*n.* (*pl.*)笑感；幽默感。

***ris·ing**[1] ['raɪzɪŋ; 'raiziŋ] *adj.* 上升的；增强的；蒸蒸日上的；隆盛的。—*prep.* ①〖俗〗多於。②〖方〗接近。He was *rising* 45. 他快45歲了。

***ris·ing**[2] *n.* ①上升；起床。my usual hour of *rising*. 我通常起床的時間。②叛亂；暴動。③復活。④瘍腫；瘤。⑤閉會；散會。

risk** [rɪsk; risk] *n.* ①危險。②被保險人；被保險物。③被冒險一試之事物。a poor *risk* for surgery. 手術成功的希望不大的病患。at all risks*** (or ***at any risk***) 不顧一切；無論如何。***run a risk*** 冒險。***run*** (or ***take***) ***the risk of*** 冒…之險。He was ready to *run the risk of* being captured by the enemy. 他準備冒被敵人俘虜的危險。—*v.t.* ①使冒危險；作賭注。to *risk* one's happiness (fortune, etc.). 以幸福(財產等)作賭注。②冒…之險。to *risk* failure. 冒失敗之險。***risk it*** 碰運氣。I dare not *risk it*; it's too dangerous. 我不敢碰運氣，太危險了。

risk·ful ['rɪskfəl; 'riskfəl] *adj.* = **risky.**

risk·i·ly ['rɪskɪlɪ; 'riskili] *adv.* 危險地；冒險地；投機地。

risk·less ['rɪsklɪs; 'risklis] *adj.* 無危險的；安全的。*riskless* investments. 安全的投資。

risk·y ['rɪskɪ; 'riski] *adj.*, **risk·i·er, risk·i·est.** ①危險的。②冒險的；投機的。③好冒險的。④=**risqué.** —**risk·i·ness,** *n.*

ris·qué [rɪs'ke; ris'kei] 〖法〗*adj.* 淫穢的；敗壞風俗的；猥褻的。

rit., ritard. 〖音樂〗ritardando.

ri·tar·dan·do [ˌritɑr'dændo; ˌritɑː'dændou] *adj.* 〖音樂〗漸緩的。—*n.* 漸緩之樂曲。

***rite**[1] [raɪt; rait] *n.* 儀式；典禮；禮儀。funeral *rites*. 殯葬之儀式。

rit·u·al ['rɪtʃuəl; 'ritjuəl] *n.* ①典禮；儀式。②儀式之程序。③儀式之舉行。④儀式典範；儀式書。—*adj.* 儀式的；典禮的。—ly, *adv.*

rit·u·al·ism ['rɪtʃuəlˌɪzəm; 'ritjuəlizm] *n.* 拘泥儀式；儀式主義；教會儀式；儀式研究。

rit·u·al·ist ['rɪtʃuəlɪst; 'ritjuəlist] *n.* ①研習儀式者；精通儀式者。②拘泥儀式者；主持儀式者；墨守教會儀式者。

rit·u·al·is·tic [ˌrɪtʃuəl'ɪstɪk; ˌritjuə'listik] *adj.* 儀式的；固守儀式的；喜歡儀式的。

rit·u·al·i·ty [ˌrɪtʃu'ælətɪ; ˌritju'æliti] *n.* 拘泥儀式；儀式。

rit·u·al·ize ['rɪtʃuəlˌaɪz; 'ritjuəlaiz] *v.t.*, **-ized, -iz·ing.** 使儀式化。—**rit·u·al·i·za·tion,** *n.*

ritz·y ['rɪtsɪ; 'ritsi] *adj.*, **ritz·i·er, ritz·i·est.** 〖俚〗豪華的；奢侈的；流行的；優美的(常用於諷刺意義)。

***ri·val** ['raɪvl̩; 'raivəl] *n.*, *adj.*, *v.*, **-valed, -val·ing.** —*n.* ①競爭者；對手；敵手。*rivals* in love. 情敵。②匹對者；足堪比擬者。—*adj.*

競爭的;敵對的。—*v.t.* ①爭勝;求勝過。②匹敵。The sunset *rivaled* the sunrise in beauty. 日落可與日出媲美。—*v.i.* 競爭。—less, *adj.*

***ri·val·ry** [ˈraɪvlrɪ; ˈraivəlri] *n.* 競爭;敵對。friendly *rivalry.* 友善的競爭。(亦作 **rivality, rivalship**)

rive [raɪv; raiv] *v.*, **rived, rived** or **riv·en, riv·ing.** —*v.t.* ①扯裂;撕開;劈開。②使傷心;使悲痛。—*v.i.* 裂開;撕裂。

‡riv·er [ˈrɪvɚ; ˈrivə] *n.* ①河;江。the Yellow *River.* 黃河。the Yangtze *River.* 長江。②任何湧流之物。*rivers* of blood. 血流成渠。***sell down the river*** **a.**(昔美國)將(黑奴)賣給密西西比河下游的農場以爲懲罰。**b.** 使…之境遇更差;爲害;出賣;背棄。***up the river*** 〖俚〗**a.** 到監獄裏。**b.** 在監獄中。

riv·er·ain [ˈrɪvəˌren; ˈrivərein] *adj.* 河的;河邊的;居於河濱的。—*n.* ①居於河濱的人。②河濱地區。

river basin 江河流域。

riv·er·bed [ˈrɪvɚˌbɛd; ˈrivəˈbed] *n.* 河床。

riv·er·boat [ˈrɪvɚˌbot; ˈrivəbout] *n.* 河船。

riv·er·head [ˈrɪvɚˌhɛd; ˈrivəhed] *n.* 河川發源地。

river horse 河馬(=hippopotamus).

riv·er·ine [ˈrɪvəˌraɪn; ˈrivərain] *adj.* ①河的;似河的。②位於河邊的;居住河邊的。

riv·er·side [ˈrɪvɚˌsaɪd; ˈrivəsaid] *n.* 河岸。—*adj.* 在河岸上的。

riv·et** [ˈrɪvɪt; ˈrivit] *n.* 鉸釘;包頭釘。—*v.t.* ①用鉸釘釘之;用鉸釘固結之。②敲扁(螺釘之一端)使之牢固;使有包頭。③固守;緊牢。to stand *riveted* to the spot. 站在那裏一動也不動。④凝視;盯牢;集中注意。⑤獲得;吸引(注意力)。rivet one's attention*** (or ***eyes***)***upon*** (使)深深注意。—**er,** *n.*

riv·et·ing [ˈrɪvɪtɪŋ; ˈrivitiŋ] *adj.* 令人意醉神迷的;驚人的。

Riv·i·er·a [ˌrɪvɪˈɛrə, riˈvjɛːrɑ; ˌriviˈɛərə] *n.* 里維耶拉(從法國東南之 Nice, 沿地中海至義大利西北之 La Spezia, 爲著名之避寒遊憩勝地)。

riv·u·let [ˈrɪvjəlɪt; ˈrivjulit] *n.* 小河;溪流。

rix-dol·lar [ˈrɪksˌdɑlɚ; ˈriksˈdɔlə] *n.* 荷蘭、德國、丹麥等國之銀幣(現大部已不流通)。

R.L.S. Robert Louis Stevenson. **RM, RM., r.m.** reichsmark(s). **RM.** Remittance. **rm.** *pl.* **rms.** ①room. ②ream (of paper). **R.M.** ①resident magistrate. ②royal mail. ③Royal Marines. **R.M.S.** Royal Mail Steamer. **Rn** 化學元素 radon 之符號。**R.N.** ①registered nurse. ②Royal Navy. **RO.** Remittance Order.

roach[1] [rotʃ; routʃ] *n.*, *pl.* **roach·es, roach.** ①歐洲產之一種鯉科淡水魚。②美洲所產之翻車魚。

roach[2] *n.* 蟑螂。

‡road [rod; roud] *n.* ①公路;道路。Is this the *road* to Taipei? 這是通臺北的路嗎? ②路;道(廣義的)。the *road* to ruin. 趨毀滅(墮落)之路;敗亡之道。③(常 *pl.*)(近岸之)碇泊處;拋錨處。shipping lying in the *roads.* 碇泊的船隻。***be on the road*** **a.** 旅行(特指推銷員)。He *was on the road* for a dress manufacturer. 他替一家服裝工廠當旅行推銷員。**b.** 旅行演出,特指樂團或劇團。***burn up the road*** 〖俗〗開快車;迅速行動。***by road*** 由公路 (by rail 之對)。***for the road*** 以(向某人)餞行。***get in one's road*** 阻礙;妨害。***get out of the road*** 不阻礙;讓路。***hit the road*** 〖俚〗啓程;首途。We *hit the road* before sunrise. 我們在日出前啓程。***hold the road*** 安全而順利地旅行、駕車等。***in the road*** 阻礙。***one for the road*** 餞行的最後一杯。***on the road*** 在途中;旅行中。The team is *on the road.* 該隊現正在外訪問。***take to the road***(由公路)出發。***the road*** **a.** 紐約市區以外供旅行演出的劇團上演之處。**b.** 劇團等之旅行演出。—**less,** *adj.*

road·a·ble [ˈrodəbl; ˈroudəbl] *adj.* 可在公路上駕駛的。—**road·a·bil·i·ty,** *n.*

road agent 〖美〗攔路强盜。

road·bed [ˈrodˌbɛd; ˈroudbed] *n.* 鋪築鐵路、馬路等的路基。

road·block [ˈrodˌblɑk; ˈroudblɔk] *n.* ①道路障礙。②障礙;阻礙。—*v.t.* 以道路障礙阻止。

road book 路程指南。

road·craft [ˈrodˌkræft; ˈroudkrɑːft] *n.* 〖英〗駕車的知識或能力;駕駛技術。

road hog 將車開行於道路中央或接近道路中央致使他人難於或不能通過者。

road·house [ˈrodˌhaus; ˈroudhaus] *n.* 公路旁供旅客休息娛樂的酒店、旅社等。

road·ing [ˈrodɪŋ; ˈroudiŋ] *n.* 道路之建設與保養。

road map 公路線路圖(尤指供汽車駕駛人使用者)。

road metal 築路用的碎石、煤屑等。

road runner 美國西南部沙漠地帶產的一種長尾鳥。

road show 旅行劇團之簡陋的街頭表演。

***road·side** [ˈrodˌsaɪd; ˈroudsaid] *n.* 路邊;路旁。—*adj.* 路旁的。a *roadside* inn. 路旁的旅館。

road sign 公路標誌;道路標誌。

road·stead [ˈrodˌstɛd; ˈroudsted] *n.* 拋錨處;碇泊所。

road·ster [ˈrodstɚ; ˈroudstə] *n.* ①供二人乘坐之單排座位之敞頂汽車。②街頭乘騎或駕車用之馬。③馬車車伕。④從前的一種腳踏車。⑤慣於徒步旅行的人。

road test 車輛實地試驗。

road-test [ˈrodˌtɛst; ˈroudtest] *v.t.* 實地試驗。

***road·way** [ˈrodˌwe; ˈroudwei] *n.* ①馬路。②快車道。

road·work [ˈrodˌwɝk; ˈroudwəːk] *n.* 跑步運動。

***roam** [rom; roum] *v.i.* & *v.t.* 閒逛;漫遊;流浪。to *roam* over the country. 在鄉間流浪。—*n.* 徘徊;閒逛;流浪。—**er,** *n.*

roan [ron; roun] *adj.* ①雜有灰色或白色毛之黃棕色的(馬、牛);雜色的。②飾以雜色皮的。—*n.* ①該種顏色之馬或其他動物。②(做書皮用的)柔軟羊皮(多爲仿製摩洛哥皮)。

‡roar [ror, rɔr; rɔː] *v.i.* ①吼;轟鳴;怒號。to *roar* with laughter. 哄然大笑。②大笑。③大聲吼叫而過。The train *roared* past us. 火車從我們身邊吼叫而過。—*v.t.* ①大聲說出。to *roar* out an order. 大聲發出命令。②因大聲叫吼而使之。The crowd *roared* itself hoarse. 羣衆叫至聲嘶。③使轟鳴。—*n.* 吼;轟鳴;怒號。He set the room in a *roar.* 他使滿屋的人哄笑。

roar·er [ˈrorɚ; ˈrɔːrə] *n.* ①咆哮者;怒吼者。②〖獸醫〗患喘鳴症之馬。③〖美俚〗極受稱讚的人或物。

roar·ing [ˈrorɪŋ; ˈrɔːriŋ] *n.* ①咆哮;怒吼;咆哮聲;喧噪。②〖獸醫〗(馬的)喘鳴症。—*adj.* ①吼叫的;喧噪的;風急雨大的。②〖俗〗興隆的;昌盛的。a *roaring* trade. 非常興隆

的生意。③健康的。

roaring forties ①北緯四十度至五十度間之大西洋風暴地帶。②(R- F-)紐約市第四十街與第五十街間 Broadway 附近之繁華地帶。

Roaring Twenties 爵士樂時代「(1920–1930)。」

roast** [rost; roust] *v.t.* ①烤;炙;焙。to *roast* beef. 烤牛肉。②烤乾;烘乾。③熬;煅燒。④使暖;使熱。to *roast* oneself at the fire. 爐邊取暖。⑤取笑;嚴加批評。—*v.i.* ①變暖。②被烤。—*n.* ①烤肉;待烤之肉。pork *roast*. 豬的裏脊肉。②烤肉野餐會。③烤肉(之動作)。④【俗】嚴厲之批評。rule the roast*** 做主人;當家(=to rule the roost). —*adj.* 烘烤的。*roast* duck. 烤鴨。

roast·er ['rostɚ;'roustə] *n.* ①烤炙者。②烤炙用具。③可供烤炙的幼豚或雞等。

roasting jack 烤肉叉旋轉器。

Rob [rab; rɔb] *n.* 男子名。

rob** [rab; rɔb] *v.*, **robbed, rob·bing.** —*v.t.* ①搶刼;盜取;偷取。to *rob* a man of his money. 搶刼某人之錢。②剝奪。The disease had *robbed* him of his strength. 那一場病剝奪了他的力氣。—*v.i.* 搶刼。rob Peter to pay Paul*** 借東還西;挖肉補瘡。

***rob·ber** ['rabɚ; 'rɔbə] *n.* 強盜;盜賊。The *robbers* have not been caught yet. 強盜尚未被捕。

robber baron ①【英史】搶刼路過其土地之旅客的貴族。②十九世紀後期不擇手段而致富的美國資本家。

robber fly 捕食昆蟲的一種大蒼蠅。

***rob·ber·y** ['rabərɪ; 'rɔbəri] *n.*, *pl.* **-ber·ies.** 搶刼;盜取;盜案。

robe** [rob; roub] *n.*, *v.*, **robed, rob·ing.** —*n.* ①寬鬆的外袍。②禮服;官服。③外套。④覆蓋物。⑤(the-)律師業。to follow the *robe* as a profession. 執律師之業。⑥衣櫥;衣櫃。the long robe*** **a.** 律師業。**b.** 書記業。***the robe*** 【主英】律師業。***the short robe*** 行伍生涯;軍中生涯。—*v.t.* & *v.i.* ①穿;穿衣。*robed* in black. 着黑衣。②覆蓋。He *robes* himself in moonlight. 他浸沈於月光之中。—**less,** *adj.*

robe-de-cham·bre [ˌrɔbdə'ʃɑ̃brə; ˌrɔːbdə'ʃɑ̃ːbrə] 【法】*n.* 一種婦女輕便服。

Rob·ert¹ ['rabɚt; 'rɔbət] *n.* 男子名(暱稱時作 Bob, Rob, Robin).

Rob·ert² *n.* 【英俗】警察。

***rob·in** ['rabɪn; 'rɔbin] *n.* 知更鳥;紅襟鳥。(亦作 **robin redbreast**)

Robin Good·fel·low [~'gudˌfɛlo; ~'gudˌfelou] 英國民間故事中的頑皮鬼怪;小精靈。

Robin Hood 羅賓漢(英國傳說中的一「俠盜)。」

rob·in's-egg blue ['rabɪnzˌɛg~; 'rɔbinzeg~] 綠藍色。

Rob·in·son ['rabɪnsn̩; 'rɔbinsn] *n.* 羅賓孫(Sir Robert, 1886–, 英國化學家, 獲1947年諾貝爾化學獎)。

Rob·in·son Cru·soe ['rabɪnsn̩ 'kruso; 'rɔbinsn'kruːsou] ①魯賓孫漂流記(英國小說家 Defoe 所著之小說, 1719 年出版)。②魯賓孫(前述小說中之主角)。

ro·bomb ['roˌbam; 'roubɔm] *n.* = **robot bomb.**

ro·bot ['robət; 'roubɔt] *n.* ①機器人。「②行動機械的人。」

robot bomb 無人飛機;自動炸彈。

robot pilot 自動駕駛儀。

ro·bust [ro'bʌst; rə'bʌst, rou'b-] *adj.* ①强壯的。②需要體力的。③粗鹵的。④强烈的;濃厚的。—**ly,** *adv.* —**ness,** *n.*

ro·bus·tious [ro'bʌstʃəs; rou'bʌstʃəs] *adj.* ①强壯的;健壯的。②粗暴的;騷亂的。③活潑的;豪爽的。—**ly,** *adv.* —**ness,** *n.*

ROC, R.O.C. the Republic of China.

roc [rak; rɔk] *n.*(阿拉伯及波斯傳奇中的)大怪鳥;大鵬。

roch·et ['ratʃɪt; 'rɔtʃit] *n.* 主教或方丈「等的一種法衣。」

‡rock¹ [rak;rɔk] *n.* ①岩石;礁。The ship was wrecked on the *rocks*. 船觸礁而碎。②石(=stone). ③如岩石般穩固之物;支持物。The Lord is my *rock*. 主是我的庇護者。④礦石。⑤硬糖。⑥(*pl.*)【俚】錢。⑦危險。⑧愚蠢的錯誤。⑨【俚】鑽石;寶石。⑩=**rock candy.** ***on the rocks*** **a.** 觸礁而碎。**b.**【俗】處於災難中。**c.**【俗】破產;窮困。**d.**(飲料等)放有小冰塊的。***the Rock*** 直布羅陀海峽(=Gibraltar). —*adj.* 岩石製的。a *rock* cavern. 一個石洞。—**like,** *adj.*

rock²** *v.t.* & *v.i.* ①搖擺;搖動。to *rock* a baby in its cradle. 搖動搖籃中之嬰兒(使之入睡)。②受極深之感動或震驚。③洗礦。rock along*** 安穩而順利地進行。—*n.* ①搖擺;搖動。the gentle *rock* of the boat. 船之輕微的蕩漾。②英國一種專騎摩托車且打扮怪異之少年。

rock³ *n.* 【古】紡條;捲紗竿。

rock·a·bil·ly ['rakəˌbɪlɪ; 'rɔkəˌbili] *n.* 有搖滾及鄉村音樂特色的熱門音樂。

rock and roll 搖滾樂;搖滾舞。(亦作 **rock-and-roll, rock'n'roll**)

rock bottom 最低層;最低限度。

rock-bot·tom ['rak'batəm; 'rɔk'bɔtəm] *adj.* 最低的;最低限度的。

rock-bound ['rakˌbaund;'rɔkbaund] *adj.* ①被岩石封閉的;多岩石的。②鞏固的;難以改變的。

rock cake 一種表面堅硬的糕餅。

rock candy 冰糖。

rock-climb·ing ['rakˌklaɪmɪŋ;'rɔkˌklaimiŋ] *adj.* 攀登岩壁的;攀登岩壁術的。

rock crystal 無色水晶。

rock drill 鑿石機。

Rock·e·fel·ler ['rakɪˌfɛlɚ, 'rakə-; 'rɔkifelə] *n.* ①洛克斐勒(John Davison, 1839–1937, 美國石油大王及慈善家)。②洛克斐勒(Nelson Aldrich, 1908–, 前者之孫, 1974–1977任美國第四十一任副總統)。

rock·er ['rakɚ; 'rɔkə] *n.* ①(搖椅、搖籃等下面的)彎軸。②搖椅。③搖者;搖動搖籃者。④底部呈弧形的溜冰鞋。⑤洗礦盤。⑥=**rock² ②.** ***off one's rocker*** 神經失常。

rocker arm *n.*【機械】搖臂(桿)。

rock·er·y ['rakərɪ; 'rɔkəri] *n.*, *pl.* **-er·ies.** ①假山庭園(為種植高山植物而造者)。②石園。

***rock·et¹** ['rakɪt;'rɔkit] *n.* 火箭。—*v.i.* ①(如火箭般)向上直衝。②被火箭送入軌道。—*v.t.* ①用火箭攻擊。②用火箭推動。to *rocket* a satellite into orbit. 用火箭推動衛星進入軌道。③使急速上升。

rock·et² *n.*【植物】歐洲產可做生菜的芥「子科植物。」

rocket airplane ①用火箭推動的飛機。②用火箭作武器的飛機。

rocket astronomy 以火箭設備從事天文資料之收集。

rocket bomb 用火箭推進的炸彈。

rock·et·drome ['rakɪtdrom; 'rɔkitdroum] *n.* 火箭發射場。

rock·et·eer 〔ˌrɑkəˈtɪr; ˌrɔkiˈtiə〕 *n.* ①發射火箭者。②火箭專家。(亦作**rocketer**)
rocket engine 火箭引擎。
rocket gun 火箭砲。
rocket launcher (步兵用)火箭砲。(亦作 **bazooka**)
rock·et-pro·pelled 〔ˈrɑkɪtprəˈpɛld; ˈrɔkitprəˈpeld〕 *adj.* 用火箭推動的。
rocket propulsion 火箭推進。
rock·et·ry 〔ˈrɑkətrɪ; ˈrɔkitri〕 *n.* ①火箭學。②火箭(集合稱)。
rock·fish 〔ˈrɑkˌfɪʃ; ˈrɔkfiʃ〕 *n., pl.* **-fish, -fish·es.** 停留在礁石中的魚類;(尤指)有條紋的鱸魚;石魚;黑鰕。
rock garden 岩石庭園。
rock hound 〖俚〗①以收集岩石並研究之作爲嗜好之人;愛石者。②地質學家。
rock·ing 〔ˈrɑkɪŋ; ˈrɔkiŋ〕 *adj.* 搖動的。
rocking chair 搖椅。
rocking horse 兒童玩耍時所騎的搖動木馬。
rock·ing-turn 〔ˈrɑkɪŋˈtɜn; ˈrɔkiŋtəːn〕 *n.* 搖轉(一種溜冰式)。
rock·man 〔ˈrɑkmən; ˈrɔkmən〕 *n., pl.* **-men.** ①採石場劈石板的工人。②操作氣壓鑽孔機的工人。③礦工。
rock'n'roll 〔ˈrɑkənˈrol; ˈrɔkənˈroul〕 *n.* =**rock and roll.** —*adj.* 搖滾樂的。—**er,** *n.*
rock oil 〖英〗石油。
rock·oon 〔rɑˈkun; rɔˈkuːn〕 *n.* 氣球火箭。
rock plant 在岩石間生長的植物。
rock rabbit 家兔。
rock-ribbed 〔ˈrɑkˈrɪbd; ˈrɔkribd〕 *adj.* ①有岩石層的;有岩石突出的。②堅定的;頑强的。③穩妥的;不太可能失敗的。
rock·rose 〔ˈrɑkˌroz; ˈrɔkˈrouz〕 *n.* 〖植物〗岩薔薇。
rock salt 岩鹽。
rock·shaft 〔ˈrɑkˌʃæft; ˈrɔkʃɑːft〕 *n.* 〖機械〗搖軸。
rock·slide 〔ˈrɑkˌslaɪd; ˈrɔk-slaid〕 *n.* ①岩石崩落。②崩落的岩石。
rock tripe *n.* 生長在北方或高山上一種帶狀植物,緊急時可作食物用。
rock wool 岩綿;石毛(用以做絕緣材料)。
rock·work 〔ˈrɑkˌwɝk; ˈrɔkwəːk〕 *n.* ①一大堆天然岩石。②模倣天然岩之刻石或砌石。③=**rockery.**
***rock·y**[1] 〔ˈrɑkɪ; ˈrɔki〕 *adj.,* **rock·i·er, rock·i·est.** ①多岩石的。②岩石製的。③如岩石的;穩固的。*rocky* heart. 鐵石心腸。
rock·y[2] *adj.,* **rock·i·er, rock·i·est.** ①搖動的;搖顫的。②〖俗〗弱的;眩暈的。③不堅決的;動搖的。④困難的。⑤猥褻的。
Rocky Mountains 落磯山脈(爲北美主要山脈)。(亦作 **Rockies**)
ro·co·co 〔rəˈkoko; rəˈkoukou〕 *n.* ①洛可可式(十七、八世紀時歐洲流行的一種纖巧華麗的建築和音樂形式)。②過於華麗的文體。③裝飾得過於華麗之傢具。—*adj.* ①洛可可形式的(建築物或樂曲)。②過分修飾的;華麗而乏味的;俗不可耐的。③陳舊的;過時的。
rod** 〔rɑd; rɔd〕 *n., v.,* **rod·ded, rod·ding.** —*n.* ①桿;棒;竿。②苔鞭;教鞭。③釣竿。④竿(長度名,等於16½英尺或5½碼)。⑤處罰。⑥〖美俚〗手鎗。⑦家族中之一支;家系。⑧象徵官階、階級、權威之杖;權杖。⑨權力;權威。⑩〖解剖〗桿。*rod* cell. 桿細胞。retinal *rod.* 視網膜桿。⑪〖機械〗桿;棒。lightning *rod.* 避雷針。⑫桿菌。⑬避雷針。kiss the rod*** 甘心受罰。***Spare the rod and spoil the child.*** 孩子不打不成材。—*v.t.* ①供以棒;裝避雷針。②用金屬棒加强(模心)。
‡**rode** 〔rod; roud〕 *v.* pt. of **ride.**
ro·dent 〔ˈrodn̩t; ˈroudənt〕 *n.* 〖動物〗囓齒類。—*adj.* ①囓齒類動物的。②嚙的;咬的。③侵蝕性的。
ro·de·o 〔ˈrodɪˌo, roˈdeo; rouˈdeiou, ˈroudiou〕 *n., pl.* **-de·os.** 〖美〗①(美國西部之)將牛馬驅集於一起以備烙印。②圍起驅集一起之牛馬的場地。③牧童用繩索驅集牛馬之絕技;牧童騎術競演會。④任何絕技競演會。
Ro·din 〔roˈdæn; rouˈdæn〕 *n.* 羅丹(Auguste, 1840–1917, 法國雕刻家,現代寫實派代表)。
rod·man 〔ˈrɑdmən; ˈrɔdmən〕 *n., pl.* **-men.** ①〖測量〗標尺手。②垂釣者。③〖美俚〗持手鎗之强盜。
rod·o·mon·tade 〔ˌrɑdəmɑnˈted; ˌrɔdəmɔnˈteid〕 *n., adj., v.,* **-tad·ed, -tad·ing.** —*n.* 大言;狂放荒謬的言論。—*adj.* 大言的;放誕的。—*v.i.* 大言不慚。(亦作 **rhodomontade**)
roe[1] 〔ro; rou〕 *n.* ①魚子;魚卵。②魚白;雄魚精。③有殼水族(如蟹、蚌、蝦等)之卵。
roe[2] *n., pl.* **roes, roe.** ①麅;一種產於歐、亞洲的小雌鹿。②雌鹿。(亦作 **roe deer**)
roe·buck 〔ˈroˌbʌk; ˈroubʌk〕 *n.* 雄roe deer;雄鹿。
roe deer =**roe**[2].
Roent·gen, Rönt·gen 〔ˈrɛntgən; ˈrɔntjən〕 *n.* ①樂琴 (Wilhelm Konrad, 1845–1923, 德國物理學家,X光線的發現者)。②(r-)X 光的光量單位。—*adj.* X光的;有關X光的。*Roentgen* examinations. X光檢查。
roent·gen·ize 〔ˈrɛntgənˌaɪz; ˈrentgənaiz〕 *v.t.,* **-ized, -iz·ing.** 使暴露於X光或珈瑪線之作用。(亦作 **röntgenize**)
roent·gen·o·gram 〔ˈrɛntgənəˌgræm; rɔntˈgenəgræm〕 *n.* X光照片。
roent·gen·og·ra·phy 〔ˌrɛntgənˈɑgrəfɪ; ˌrɔntgeˈnɔgrəfi〕 *n.* X光照相術。
roent·gen·ol·o·gy 〔ˌrɛntgənˈɑlədʒɪ; ˌrɔntgeˈnɔlədʒi〕 *n.* X光射線學。
roent·gen·o·ther·a·py 〔ˌrɛntgənəˈθɛrəpɪ; ˈrentgənəˈθerəpi〕 *n.* X光治療法。
roentgen rays X光線。(亦作**Roentgen rays**)
ROG, R.O.G., r.o.g. receipt of goods.
ro·ga·tion 〔roˈgeʃən; rouˈgeiʃən〕 *n.* ①〖羅馬史〗法案之提出;提出之法案。②(常 *pl.*)〖宗教〗(耶穌升天節前三天所做的)祈禱;懇求;祈禱之儀式。
Rogation Days 祈禱節(耶穌升天節之前三天)。
Rog·er 〔ˈrɑdʒɚ; ˈrɔdʒə〕 *n.* ①男子名。②(亦作 r-) 海盜旗(黑底白骷髏旗 =Jolly Roger).
rog·er 〔ˈrɑdʒɚ; ˈrɔdʒə〕 *interj.* ①〖美俚〗好!是!(=O.K.! right!)②收到了!(=received, 無線電話用語,表示對方所說的都聽到了)。—*v.t. & v.i.* 〖鄙〗(男女間)有曖昧。
***rogue** 〔rog; roug〕 *n., v.,* **rogued, rogu·ing,** *adj.* —*n.* ①惡棍;流氓;無賴漢;流浪者。②欺詐者;騙子。to play the *rogue.* 欺騙。③黠兒;乖兒;小淘氣(親暱語)。④離羣而居脾氣乖張的野象;離羣獸。⑤〖園藝〗生長不良果實之植物。—*v.i.* ①幹壞事;流浪;遊蕩;過流氓般的生活。②除去生長不良之植物。—*v.t.* ①欺騙;欺詐。②除去(生長不良之植物)。—*adj.* ①兇惡的;兇猛的。②離羣的。
ro·guer·y 〔ˈrogərɪ; ˈrougəri〕 *n., pl.* **-guer·ies.** ①詭譎;欺騙;奸詐。②惡作劇;搗

鬼。③歹徒的圈子;黑社會。

rogues' gallery 罪犯照片陳列室。

rogue's march 放逐曲(在某人被逐出隊伍或團體時所奏的嘲笑的音樂)。

ro·guish 〔ˈrogɪʃ; ˈrougiʃ〕 *adj.* ①不誠實的;流氓的。②惡作劇的;淘氣的。

roil 〔rɔil; rɔil〕 *v.t.* 〖美〗①攪渾;攪濁。②激怒;觸怒。③使紊亂。—*v.i.* ①翻騰。②動盪。—*n.* 動盪。

roil·y 〔ˈrɔɪlɪ; ˈrɔili〕 *adj.*, **roil·i·er, roil·i·est.** ①渾濁的;骯髒的。②被激怒的。

roist·er 〔ˈrɔɪstɚ; ˈrɔistə〕 *v.i.* ①作威作福;擺架子;逞威。②鬧飲;喧鬧無度。—**ing,** *adj.*

roist·er·er 〔ˈrɔɪstərɚ; ˈrɔistərə〕 *n.* ①作威作福者。②鬧飲者。

roist·er·ous 〔ˈrɔɪstərəs; ˈrɔistərəs〕 *adj.* ①作威作福的;逞威的。②鬧飲的。

ROK Republic of Korea.

Ro·land 〔ˈrolənd; ˈroulənd〕 *n.* ①男子名。②羅蘭德(傳說中 Charlemagne 大帝手下的一員勇將)。 ***a Roland for an Oliver*** 一報還一報;旗鼓相當;不分勝負(源於傳說中之 Roland 與其友 Oliver 連戰五日而不分勝負)。

role, rôle** 〔rol; roul〕 *n.* ①(戲劇中之)角色。 the leading *role*. 主角。②眞實生活中之角色;職分。 ***play an important role 占重要的位置;起重要的作用。

‡roll 〔rol; roul〕 *v.i.* ①滾;轉。 Round things *roll* easily. 圓物易於滾動。②旋轉而行。The car *rolled* along. 車向前駛進。③(天體)運行;(歲月)推移。The years *roll* on. 歲月推移。④搖擺;顚簸。 The ship *rolls* in the waves. 船在浪中顚簸。⑤起伏。miles of *rolling* country. 綿延起伏的土地。⑥發隆隆聲。Thunder *rolls*. 雷聲隆隆。⑦(眼球)左右轉動。 Her eyes *rolled* with curiosity. 她的眼睛因好奇而左右轉動。⑧滾流。Waves *roll* in on the beach. 波濤滾滾而來湧上海灘。⑨打滾。⑩搖搖幌幌而行。⑪漫步;徘徊。⑫〖俗〗所有較所需爲多;富有。to *roll* in money. 富有。⑬(乘車而)行。⑭被捲(成筒形或球形)。⑮有作爲;有成績。⑯運轉。The cameras were ready to *roll*. 攝影機隨時可運轉。⑰(鳥)啁啾而鳴。⑱(飛機)滾轉飛行。—*v.t.* ①使滾;使轉動。②包捲;纏。to *roll* string (wool, etc.) into a ball. 將繩(毛線等)捲成球。③滾成;揉成;輾平。④以顫聲發(音)。to *roll* one's r's. 以顫聲發 r 音。⑤使(眼球)左右轉動。⑥〖印刷〗以滾筒敷油墨於。⑦連續而快地擊(鼓)。⑧使運轉。⑨翻轉…的身體搜索全身以搶物。***roll back*** a. 使(物價等)全面回降。b. 擊退。***roll in*** a. 滾滾而來;大量湧進。b. 上床;睡覺。c. 大量擁有。***roll out*** a. 起床。b. 展開;壓平。to *roll out* dough. 擀麪。***roll out the red carpet*** 正式歡迎。***roll up*** a. 累積;增加。to *roll up* a huge fortune. 累積很大一筆財產。b. 坐車抵達。c. 捲起。—*n.* ①一捲;捲物。a *roll* of cloth. 一捲布。②捲形物;團。He has *rolls* of fat on him. 他一身是肥油(胖得發圓)。③滾動;搖擺;顚簸。She walks with a slight *roll*. 她走路有點搖擺。④名單;名簿。a *roll* of honor. 陣亡將士名册。⑤一種小的圓形軟麪包;小餅。⑥隆隆聲。⑦鼓的連續疾敲。⑧滾筒機;壓路機;輾壓機。⑨起伏。***call the roll*** 點名。***strike off*** (or ***from***) ***the rolls*** 除名;開除。

Rol·land 〔rɔˈlɑ̃; rɔːˈlɑ̃〕 *n.* 羅蘭 (Romain, 1866–1944, 法國小說家及劇作家, 曾獲1915 年諾貝爾文學獎)。

roll·a·way 〔ˈroləˌwe; ˈrouləwei〕 *n.* (有滑輪可折疊的)活動床。(亦作 **rollaway bed**)

roll·back 〔ˈrolˌbæk; ˈroulbæk〕 *n.* ①全面壓回。 a *rollback* of prices. 物價之全面回跌。②擊退。

roll book 出席登記簿;勤惰登記簿。

roll call ①點名。②點名鼓號;點名時間。

roll-call 〔ˈrolˌkɔl; ˈroul-kɔːl〕 *v.t.* 予以點名。

roll-cu·mu·lus 〔ˈrolˌkjumjələs; ˈroulˈkjumjuləs〕 *n.* 〖氣象〗捲軸積雲。

rolled gold 包金;金箔。

***roll·er** 〔ˈrolɚ; ˈroulə〕 *n.* ①滾動之物;輪。*roller* skate. 輪式溜冰鞋。②滾子;滾轉機;滾軸。③巨浪。④一捲紗布。⑤滾轉某種東西的人。⑥一種鳴聲尖脆的金絲雀。⑦一種翻飛鴿。⑧會搖擺的船。

roller bearing 滾子軸承。

roller coaster 一種敞車(遊樂用)。

roller mill 在滾筒間軋碎物料的磨子。

roll·er-skate 〔ˈrolɚˌsket; ˈrouləˌskeit〕 *v.i.*, **-skat·ed, -skat·ing.** 用輪式溜冰鞋溜冰。

roller towel 掛在滾筒上滾轉的擦手毛巾。

roll film 攝影用的成捲軟片。

rol·lick 〔ˈrɑlɪk; ˈrɔlik〕 *v.i.* 嬉戲;耍鬧;縱情地玩。—*n.* 嬉戲;耍鬧;歡噪。—**er,** *n.*

rol·lick·ing 〔ˈrɑlɪkɪŋ; ˈrɔlikiŋ〕 *adj.* 喧鬧作樂的;歡樂的。(亦作 **rollicksome**)

roll·ing 〔ˈrolɪŋ; ˈrouliŋ〕 *adj.* ①轉動的;滾動的。②起伏的。③作隆隆聲的。④搖擺的。⑤波動的。⑥周而復始的。***A rolling stone gathers no moss.*** 滾石不生苔;(喩)轉業不聚財(見異思遷終無所獲)。—*n.* ①轉動;輾動;滾;輾壓。②隆隆聲。

rolling chair 輪椅。

rolling kitchen 炊事車。

rolling mill ①輾壓機。②輾壓工廠。

rolling pin 擀麪杖。

rolling press 印刷機;壓光機。

rolling stock ①鐵路機車及車輛。②(運輸業者所有之)車輛。

rolling stone 無固定職業者。

roll-neck 〔ˈrolˌnɛk; ˈroulnek〕 *adj.* (衣服)有套頭高翻領的。

roll·top desk 〔ˈrolˌtɑp～; ˈroul-tɔp～〕 有可以捲縮之頂蓋之寫字枱。

ro·ly-po·ly 〔ˈrolɪˌpolɪ; ˈrouliˈpouli〕 *n., pl.* **-lies.** ①矮胖之人(尤指兒童);矮胖之獸。②〖英〗含有果醬、葡萄乾之捲形布丁。—*adj.* 矮胖的。

Rom, rom 〔rɑm; rɔm〕 *n.* 吉卜賽男人;吉卜賽男孩。

Rom. ①Roman. ②Romance. ③Romans. ④Romania. ⑤Romanian. ⑥Romanic.

rom. roman (type).

Ro·ma·ic 〔roˈmeɪk; rouˈmeiik〕 *n.* 現代希臘語。—*adj.* 現代希臘語的;現代希臘的。

ro·maine 〔roˈmen; rouˈmein〕 *n.* 〖植物〗萵苣之一種。

***Ro·man** 〔ˈromən; ˈroumən〕 *adj.* ①羅馬的;羅馬人的。②羅馬天主教的。③(r-)羅馬字體的。④堅忍不拔的。—*n.* ①羅馬人。②羅馬天主教徒。③(r-)羅馬字體。

ro·man 〔ˌroˈmɑ̃; ˌrɔˈmɑ̃〕 〖法〗*n.* ①(特指中古法國的)韻文小說。②小說;傳奇故事。

ro·man à clef 〔rɔˈmɑ̃naˈkle; rɔː-ˈmɑ̃naˈklei〕 〖法〗根據眞人眞事所寫的故事;影射小說。

Roman alphabet 羅馬字母;羅馬字。

Roman arch 半圓形拱門。
Roman candle 羅馬煙火。
Roman Catholic ①天主教的；天主教會的。②天主教徒。
Roman Catholic Church 天主教會。
Roman Catholicism 天主教；天主教的教義、儀式、習慣等。
Ro·mance [rə'mæns; rə'mæns] *adj.* 拉丁語系的；使用拉丁系語言的。—*n.* 拉丁語系。
*__ro·mance__[1] [*n.* ro'mæns, rə-, 'romæns; rə'mæns, rou- *v.* ro'mæns, rə-; rə'mæns, rou-] *n.*, *v.*, **-manced, -manc·ing.** —*n.* ①愛情故事。②描寫英雄故事的小說或詩歌。Have you read the *romances* about King Arthur and his knights? 你讀過有關亞瑟王及其武士的故事嗎？③冒險故事。④艷事；風流事跡；羅曼史。⑤虛構的故事；傳奇。⑥所夢想之事物。—*v.i.* ①編寫 romances. ②作奇想。③誇大；說謊。
ro·mance[2] [ro'mæns; rou'mæns] *n.* ①〖音樂〗浪漫曲（簡短的小調或速度中庸的短樂曲）。②〖西班牙文學〗短敍事詩；短抒情詩。—*v.t.* ①加以誇大。②向…獻媚；求…之歡心。③與…談情說愛。
Romance language 自拉丁文演變出的許多語言之任何一種，包括如法語、西班牙語、葡萄牙語、義大利語及羅馬尼亞語等。
ro·manc·er [rə'mænsɚ; rə'mænsə] *n.* ①傳奇作家。②空想家。
ro·manc·ist [rə'mænsɪst; rə'mænsist] *n.* 傳奇小說家。
Roman Curia 天主教教廷。
Roman Empire 羅馬帝國（紀元前27年 Augustus 建立，紀元395年分裂）。
Ro·man·esque [ˌromən'ɛsk; ˌroumə'nesk] *n.* ①羅馬式建築（圓頂，弧形拱門及厚牆之建築）。②羅馬式之繪畫、藝術。③拉丁系語言。—*adj.* ①羅馬式的（建築、繪畫、雕刻等）。②拉丁語系的。③(r-)傳奇的；荒誕的。
ro·man-fleuve [rɔ'mɑ̃ 'flœv; rɔː'mɑ̃'flœv] 〖法〗 *n.* 以家族世系的生活思想發展爲題材寫成的長篇小說。
Roman holiday 得自他人之痛苦的快樂。
Ro·ma·nia [ro'menjə; rou'meinjə] *n.* =**Rumania.** —**Ro·ma·ni·an,** *n.*, *adj.*
Ro·man·ic [ro'mænɪk; rou'mænik] *adj.* ①古羅馬的；古羅馬人的；羅馬帝國的；羅馬帝國之文化的。②拉丁語系的。③古羅馬人之後裔的。—*n.* 拉丁系語言。
Ro·man·ism ['romənˌɪzəm; 'roumənizm] *n.* ①〖蔑〗羅馬天主教；天主教教義。②古羅馬風；古羅馬影響；古羅馬精神。
Ro·man·ist ['romənɪst; 'roumənist] *n.* ①羅馬天主教徒；天主教徒。②羅馬法學家；羅馬文物制度學者。—**ic,** *adj.*
Ro·man·i·za·tion [ˌromənɪ'zeʃən; ˌroumənai'zeiʃən] *n.* ①古羅馬化。②皈依天主教。③羅馬字之採用；以羅馬字拼寫。
Ro·man·ize ['romənˌaɪz; 'roumənaiz] *v.*, **-ized, -iz·ing.** —*v.t.* ①使有羅馬風；使羅馬化。②使皈依天主教。③以羅馬字書寫；以羅馬字拼音。—*v.i.* ①皈依天主教。②羅馬化。
Roman law 羅馬法。
Roman nose 高鼻梁鼻子；鷹鼻。
Roman numerals 羅馬數字（即 I, V, X, L, C, D, M, 通常 I=1, V=5, X=10, L=50, C=100, D=500, M=1,000)。
Roman peace 以武力維持的和平。
Ro·mans ['romənz; 'roumənz] *n.*（作 *sing.* 解）羅馬書（爲耶教聖經新約之一書）。
*__ro·man·tic__ [ro'mæntɪk; rə'mæntik] *adj.* ①傳奇性的；空想的；想像的。a *romantic* adventure. 傳奇性的冒險故事。②有浪漫思想的；喜幻想的。③浪漫的；合於傳奇故事的。④浪漫主義的。⑤富於感情的；多情的。—*n.* ①浪漫派作家，藝術家；浪漫主義者。②(*pl.*) 富幻想的感情與語言表現；浪漫成分。—**al·ly,** *adv.* —**al·ness,** *n.*
ro·man·ti·cism [ro'mæntəˌsɪzəm; rə'mæntisizm] *n.* ①浪漫的精神或傾向。②〖文學〗浪漫主義。
ro·man·ti·cist [ro'mæntəsɪst; rə'mæntisist] *n.* 浪漫主義者；浪漫派作家。—*adj.* 浪漫主義的；浪漫派的。
ro·man·ti·cize [ro'mæntəˌsaɪz; rə'mæntisaiz] *v.*, **-cized, -ciz·ing.** —*v.t.* 使浪漫化；使傳奇化。—*v.i.* 浪漫化；傳奇化。
Rom·a·ny ['rɑmənɪ; 'rɔməni] *n.*, *pl.* **-nies.** ①吉卜賽人。②吉卜賽語。—*adj.* 吉卜賽人的；吉卜賽語的；吉卜賽人之習俗的。
ro·maunt [ro'mɑnt; rou'mɔːnt] *n.* 〖古〗韻文傳奇小說。
Rom. Cath. Roman Catholic.
*__Rome__ [rom; roum] *n.* ①羅馬（義大利首都）。*Rome* was not built in a day. 羅馬城不是一天造成的；巨大工作不是短時期能做成的。②古羅馬帝國。③羅馬天主教會。
Ro·me·o[1] ['romɪˌo; 'roumiou] *n.* ①羅蜜歐（莎士比亞著的 *Romeo and Juliet* 中之男主角）。②愛人；害相思病的青年。
Ro·me·o[2] *n.* 通訊電碼，代表字母R。
romp [rɑmp; rɔmp] *v.i.* ①頑皮喧鬧地嬉戲；亂跑亂叫地遊戲。②〖俚〗輕快地跑。③(在比賽中) 輕取勝利。The horse *romped* home. 這匹馬輕易地獲勝了。④談情說愛；調情。—*n.* ①頑皮的嬉戲。②頑皮的人（尤指女孩）；頑皮姑娘。③輕取的勝利。
romp·er ['rɑmpɚ; 'rɔmpə] *n.* ①（孩童遊戲時所着之）背心。②(*pl.*) 孩童所着之背心連褲子的衣服。③嬉戲喧鬧者。
romp·ish ['rɑmpɪʃ; 'rɔmpiʃ] *adj.* 嬉戲喧鬧的；頑皮的；亂跑亂叫的。
Rom·u·lus ['rɑmjələs; 'rɔmjuləs] *n.* 〖羅馬傳說〗古羅馬之建國者 (753 B.C.)，亦爲其第一代之國君（是 Mars 與 Rhea Silvia 所生之兒子，和 Remus 爲孿生兄弟，嬰兒時被棄，由一狼哺育長大，羅馬人尊爲守護神)。
ron·deau ['rɑndo; 'rɔndou] *n.*, *pl.* **-deaux** [-doz, -'doz; -douz, -'douz]. ①〖詩〗一種短詩的形式，包括十三(或十)行，用兩個韻，以開始之字或短語在兩處做爲不押韻之重疊。②〖音樂〗=**rondo.**
ron·del ['rɑndl; 'rɔndl] *n.* 十四行短詩（爲 rondeau 之變體）。
ron·do ['rɑndo; 'rɔndou] *n.*, *pl.* **-dos.** 〖義〗〖音樂〗輪旋曲。
ro·ne·o ['ronɪo; 'rouniou] *n.* 〖英〗①(R-) 一種複寫機的商標名。②複寫機；謄寫版。—*v.t.* 以此種複寫機複寫。
rood [rud; ruːd] *n.* ①（亦作**rood tree**)（耶穌受難之）十字架；象徵性之十字架。②十字架之耶穌像；苦像（尤指置於聖壇內者)。③〖英〗路得（長度單位，各地方規定不一，約等於五碼半至八碼)。④路得（面積單位，約等於四分之一英畝)。***by the* (*holy*) *rood*** 對着十字架；的確；必定（誓言）。
rood loft 教堂中之十字架壇。
rood screen 教堂內的聖壇隔板；聖壇屏。
‡**roof** [ruf; ruːf] *n.* ①屋頂。a leaking *roof.* 漏的屋頂。②似屋頂之物。③房屋。***hit***

the roof【俚】勃然大怒。***raise the roof***【俚】a. 發出高聲。b. 高聲抗議或抱怨。***the roof of the world*** 世界的屋頂(即最高處)。***under one's roof*** 在某人之家內。—*v.t.* 蓋以頂;覆遮。

roofed 〔ruft, ruft; ru:ft〕 *adj.* 有屋頂的;…屋頂的。flat-*roofed* house. 平頂的屋。

roof·er 〔'rufɚ; 'ru:fə〕 *n.* ①以蓋或修屋頂爲業者。②做屋頂所用之材料。③【英俚】客人別後之謝函。

roof garden 屋頂花園。

roof·ing 〔'rufɪŋ; 'ru:fiŋ〕 *n.* ①蓋屋頂。②蓋屋頂之材料。③屋頂。—*adj.* 蓋屋頂用的。

roof·less 〔'ruflɪs; 'ru:flis〕 *adj.* ①沒有屋頂的。②沒有家的。

roof·top 〔'ruf,tap; 'ru:ftɔp〕 *n.* 屋頂。

roof·tree 〔'ruf,tri, 'ruf-; 'ru:ftri:〕 *n.* ①屋頂之棟樑。②屋頂。③家;屋。

rook[1] 〔ruk; ruk〕 *n.* ①歐洲的一種烏鴉。②賭博騙子。—*v.t.* ①以賭博騙取。②敲詐。—*v.i.* ①行騙。②敲竹槓。

rook[2] *n.* 城堡形棋子。

rook·er·y 〔'rukərɪ; 'rukəri〕 *n., pl.* **-er·ies.** ①白嘴鴉、企鵝等的巢;海豹等之穴。②白嘴鴉、海豹等之羣。③一叢枝間有白嘴鴉窩巢之樹。④貧民窟。

rook·ie 〔'rukɪ; 'ruki〕 *n.* 【俚】①無經驗的新兵。②生手;新手。

rook·y 〔'rukɪ; 'ruki〕 *adj.* 多白嘴鴉的;「白嘴鴉常至的。」

‡**room** 〔rum, rum; rum, ru:m〕 *n.* ①房間;室。This *room* is a very pleasant one. 這間屋子很悅目。②(*pl.*)一組房間;住所。③屋內的人。The whole *room* laughed. 全屋子裏的人都笑了。④場所;地方;空位。Standing *room* only! 只剩站位了! ⑤機會;餘地。There is no *room* for dispute. 沒有爭論之餘地。⑥地位。He fought for *room* at the top. 他力爭上游。⑦能力。***make room for*** 給…讓地方。***no room to swing a cat*** 狹窄的空間。—*v.i.* 占一房間;居;寓。—*v.t.* 給予…住處;留住(客人)。

room and board 膳宿。

room conditioning 室內空氣調節「裝置。」

roomed 〔rumd; ru:md〕 *adj.* 有…房間的。

room·er 〔'rumɚ; 'ru:mə〕 *n.* 房客;寄宿者。

room·ette 〔rum'ɛt; ru:m'et〕 *n.* 臥車「裏的小房間(內有床鋪及衞生設備)。」

room·ful 〔'rum,ful; 'ru:mful〕 *n., pl.* **-fuls.** ①滿室。②一室內的人或物。—*adj.* ①有許多房間的。②有很多空間的。

rooming house 【美】公寓。

room·ing-in 〔'rumɪŋ'ɪn; 'ru:miŋ'in〕 *n.* ①僕人在主人家中住宿的安排。②醫院中初生嬰兒與產婦住在一起的安排。

room·mate 〔'rum,met; 'ru:mmeit〕 *n.* 【美】同屋者;同室者;室友。

room service ①(旅社之)房內服務。②(旅社之)房內服務部。

room·y 〔'rumɪ; 'ru:mi〕 *adj.,* **room·i·er, room·i·est.** 寬敞的;寬大的。—**room·i·ly,** *adv.* —**room·i·ness,** *n.*

roor·back, roor·bach 〔'rurbæk; 'ruəbæk〕 *n.* 【美】在選舉前爲中傷政敵而作的揑造的誹謗故事。

Roo·se·velt[1] 〔'rozə,vɛlt; 'rouzəvelt〕 *n.* 羅斯福 (Franklin Delano, 1882–1945, 於1933–45 任美國第32任總統)。 —**ian,** *adj.*

Roo·se·velt[2] *n.* 羅斯福 (Theodore, 1858–1919, 於 1901–09 任美國第26任總統)。

*__roost__ 〔rust; ru:st〕 *v.i.* 棲息;夜宿。A bird *roosts* on a rod. 鳥棲於木上。—*v.t.* 使棲息。***come home to roost*** 對行動者本身產生不利;使行動者自食其果。—*n.* ①棲木;鳥巢。②(人的)安歇之處;睡眠之處。to go to *roost*. 上床睡覺。③窩藏處。④一巢或一窩鳥。***rule the roost*** 爲首;爲王;爲領袖。

*__roost·er__ 〔'rustɚ; 'ru:stə〕 *n.* ①雄鷄。②【俚】自負者。

*__root__[1] 〔rut; ru:t〕 *n.* ①植物之根;植物生於地下之任何部分。They pulled up the tree by the *roots*. 他們將那樹連根拔起。②(形狀、位置、用途等)似根之物。③根源;原因。④【文法】字根。⑤【數學】根。2 is the square *root* of 4. 2 是4的平方根。⑥根基;必需的部分。⑦【音樂】和絃的基礎音。⑧基礎;基本。⑨底部。*root* of a hill. 山的底部。⑩祖先。⑪後裔。⑫(*pl.*) a. 人之原籍、環境及文化。b. 人事關係,對當地的各種情況之適應等。***root and branch*** 連根帶枝;徹底地;完全地。***root out*** (or ***up***) 拔去;根絕。***take root*** 開始生長;生根;固定;確立。—*v.i.* ①生根。Some plants *root* more quickly than others. 有一部分植物生根較其他的植物快。②固定不移;固着。I'll *root* forever here. 我要永遠停在這裡不走。③發源。—*v.t.* ①使固定;使根深蒂固。He was *rooted* to the spot by suprise. 他嚇得呆在那裏不能動彈。②拔出;拉出;掘出。③使有基礎。We need a peace *rooted* in justice and law. 我們需要基於公正及法律的和平。

root[2] *v.i.* ①以鼻將土翻起。②搜尋;尋覓。③【俚】以喝采鼓舞或支持。—*v.t.* ①以鼻翻起。②發掘;揭發;尋獲。

root·age 〔'rutɪdʒ; 'ru:tidʒ〕 *n.* ①生根;紮根;固定。②根之集合稱。

root beer 【美】用藥草根製成的一種可「口飲料。」

root crop 食用根之農作物(如馬鈴薯、甜菜等)。

root·ed 〔'rutɪd; 'ru:tid〕 *adj.* ①有根的;生根的;紮於根的。②根深蒂固的;牢不可破的。—**ness,** *n.*

root·er 〔'rutɚ; 'ru:tə〕 *n.* ①拔根的人;以鼻掘土的動物。②連土帶根一併掘起的堆土機。③聲援者;啦啦隊。

root hair 【植物】根鬚。

root·hold 〔'rut,hold; 'ru:thould〕 *n.* ①根之固着力。②使根固着之處。

root·less 〔'rutlɪs; 'ru:tlis〕 *adj.* ①無根據的。②無所寄托的。③無根的。④不穩固的。—**ness,** *n.*

root·let 〔'rutlɪt; 'ru:tlit〕 *n.* 【植物】小「根;支根;幼根。」

root·stalk 〔'rut,stɔk; 'ru:t-stɔ:k〕 *n.* 【植物】根莖;地下根。

root·stock 〔'rut,stak; 'ru:t-stɔk〕 *n.* ①塊根;根莖。②根源;起源。

root·y 〔'rutɪ; 'ru:ti〕 *adj.,* **root·i·er, root·i·est.** 多根的;根狀的;似藥草根的。

‡**rope** 〔rop; roup〕 *n., v.,* **roped, rop·ing.** —*n.* ①粗繩。②串;貫。a *rope* of pearls. 一串眞珠。③【美】一端有活結的繩索。④絞人用的繩索。⑤吊死。⑥賣藝人走的繩索。⑦黏絲;黏線。⑧行動之自由(尤指有害者)。⑨(*pl.*)祕訣。***be at*** (or ***come to***) ***the end of one's rope*** 智窮力盡。***be on the high ropes*** 得意揚揚。***be outside the ropes*** 不懂內情。***Give a fool rope enough, and he'll hang himself.*** 放任愚人,他必自取滅亡。***give a person a rope's end*** 鞭笞某人。***give one enough rope*** 放任某人讓他自取滅亡。***give one rope*** (or ***plenty of rope***)

任其自由行動。*know the ropes* 熟悉內情、規則等。*learn the ropes* 學習規則、內情等。*on the ropes* a. 〖拳擊〗被迫至拳臺繩邊。b. 無力奮戰。*put up to the ropes* 授以祕訣。*rope of sand* 無法使團結之物。*show a person the ropes* 教以方法。*stretch a rope* 被絞死。—*v.t.* ①以繩將…縛、繫、結住。②圍以繩以隔開或圈起。③〖美〗以有活結之繩捉(馬、牛等)。—*v.i.* ①形成黏漿。②彼此以繩繫結而行。*rope (a person) in* 說服(某人)參加一項運動;使(某人)入圈套。*rope in* a. 以繩圍起。b. 〖俚〗用欺騙使人上鈎。*rope off* 用繩隔開。

rope·danc·er [ˈropˌdænsɚ; ˈroupˌdɑːnsə] *n.* 走繩索者。

rope·danc·ing [ˈropˌdænsɪŋ; ˈroupˌdɑːnsiŋ] *n.* 走繩索;繩技。

rope ladder 繩梯。

rop·er·y [ˈropərɪ; ˈroupəri] *n., pl.* **-ies.** 製繩所。(亦作 **ropewalk**)

rope's end 一種笞打罪犯之刑具。

rope·walk·er [ˈropˌwɔkɚ; ˈroupˌwɔːkə] *n.* 走繩索者。

rope·walk·ing [ˈropˌwɔkɪŋ; ˈroupˌwɔːkiŋ] *n.* 走索。

rope·way [ˈropˌwe; ˈroupwei] *n.* 運重物之空中索道。

rope yarn 製繩之紗;瑣屑之物。

rop·i·ness [ˈropɪnɪs; ˈroupinis] *n.* 黏稠;黏着性。

rop·y [ˈropɪ; ˈroupi] *adj.*, **rop·i·er, rop·i·est.** ①像繩的。②成黏線的;黏稠的。③肌肉發達的。④〖俚〗令人不滿的;很糟糕的。

roque [rok; rouk] *n.* 槌球戲之一種。

Roque·fort [ˈrokfɚt, rŏkˈfɔ̄ːr; ˈrɔkfɔː] 〖法〗*n.* 羊乳酪。(亦作 **Roquefort cheese**)

ro·quet [rəˈke, ˈroke; ˈrouki] *v.t. & v.i.* 擊中(他人之球)。—*n.* (Croquet 球戲中) 擊中他人之球。

ror·qual [ˈrɔrkwəl; ˈrɔːkwəl] *n.* 〖動物〗鰮鯨。

Ror·schach test [ˈrɔrʃɑx ~; ˈrɔːʃɑːk ~] 〖心理〗羅沙測驗(視對墨水點及畫之反應而分析性格之測驗)。

ror·ty [ˈrɔrtɪ; ˈrɔːti] *adj.*, **ror·ti·er, ror·ti·est.** 〖俚〗 愉快的; 有趣的。(亦作 **raughty**)

Ro·sa [ˈrozə; ˈrouzə] *n.* 女子名。

ro·sace [ˈrozes; ˈrouzeis] 〖法〗 *n.* 〖建築〗圓花飾;圓花窗。

ro·sa·ceous [roˈzeʃəs; rouˈzeiʃəs] *adj.* ①〖植物〗薔薇科的。②〖植物〗 有五瓣花冠的。③似玫瑰的。④玫瑰色的。

Ros·a·mond [ˈrɑzəmənd; ˈrɔzəmənd] *n.* 女子名。

ros·an·i·line [roˈzænəˌlin, -lɪn; rouˈzænilin, -liːn] *n.* 玫瑰色素。

ro·sar·i·an [rəˈzɛrɪən; rouˈzɛəriən] *n.* 栽植薔薇者;熱愛薔薇者。

ro·sa·ry [ˈrozərɪ; ˈrouzəri] *n., pl.* **-ries.** ① a. (天主教之) 玫瑰經。 b. (念玫瑰經用之) 一串念珠;(普通之) 一串念珠。②玫瑰園;玫瑰花壇。

ros·coe [ˈrɑsko; ˈrɔskou] *n.* 〖俚〗左輪;手槍。

‡**rose**[1] [roz; rouz] *n., adj., v.,* **rosed, ros·ing.** —*n.* ①玫瑰;薔薇。②薔薇科植物。the Chinese *rose.* 月季花。the *rose* of May. 白水仙。③似玫瑰的東西。④美麗之女子。She is the *rose* of Paris. 她是巴黎最美的女子。⑤玫瑰色。the *roses* in her cheeks. 她雙頰上之玫瑰色。⑥玫瑰香水。⑦英國的五瓣玫瑰國徽。⑧〖建築〗圓花飾。⑨令人高興之事。*a bed of roses* 十分安樂之境地。*gather (life's) roses* 享樂。*no rose without a thorn* 沒有無刺之薔薇(有樂必有苦)。*not all roses* 不完美。*under the rose* 祕密的。—*adj.* 玫瑰色的。—*v.t.* 使成玫瑰色;使帶玫瑰花香味。—**like,** *adj.*

rose[2] *v.* pt. of **rise.**

ro·sé, Ro·sé [roˈze; rouˈzei] *n.* 粉紅色的葡萄酒。

rose acacia 〖植物〗產於 Alleghenies 南部之一種灌木(開玫瑰色之大花)。

ro·se·ate [ˈrozɪɪt; ˈrouziit] *adj.* ①玫瑰色的;粉紅色的。②容光煥發的;愉快的。③幸福的;樂觀的。—**ly,** *adv.*

rose·bay [ˈrozˌbe; ˈrouzbei] *n.* 〖植物〗 ①夾竹桃。②石南。

rose beetle 一種爲害玫瑰花之甲蟲。(亦作 **rose bug**)

***rose·bud** [ˈrozˌbʌd; ˈrouzbʌd] *n.* ①玫瑰花蕾;(形狀或美麗)似玫瑰花蕾之物。a *rosebud* mouth. 美如玫瑰之口;櫻桃小口。②妙齡少女。③〖美俚〗初入社交界之少女。

rose·bush [ˈrozˌbuʃ; ˈrouzbuʃ] *n.* 玫瑰樹; 玫瑰花。

rose colo(u)r 玫瑰紅;淡紅色。

rose-col·ored [ˈrozˌkʌlɚd; ˈrouzˌkʌləd] *adj.* ①玫瑰色的。②樂觀的。

rose diamond 二十四面體之金鋼鑽石。

rose hip 玫瑰實。

rose leaf 玫瑰花瓣。

rose·mar·y [ˈrozˌmɛrɪ; ˈrouzməri] *n., pl.* **-mar·ies.** ①〖植物〗迷迭香(用以象徵忠實、貞操、記憶等)。②(*pl.*)迷迭香叢。

rose oil 玫瑰油。

ro·se·o·la [roˈziələ; rouˈziːələ] *n.* 〖醫〗玫瑰疹;紅疹。

rose pink 玫瑰色。

rose red 玫瑰紅;紫紅色。

ro·ser·y [ˈrozərɪ; ˈrouzəri] *n.* 薔薇園。

Ro·set·ta [roˈzɛtə; rouˈzetə] *n.* 羅塞達(埃及尼羅河口一市鎮)。

Rosetta stone 一七九九年在埃及尼羅河口羅塞達發現之一塊石板,上刻有希臘文、埃及象形文及簡體字,使埃及文字得以推考。

ro·sette [roˈzɛt; rouˈzet] *n.* ①薔薇形飾物。②薔薇形緞帶結。③〖建築〗薔薇形之雕飾。

rose water 玫瑰香水。

rose·wa·ter [ˈrozˌwɔtɚ; ˈrouzˌwɔːtə] *adj.* ①撒以玫瑰香水的。②有玫瑰香水味的。③矯飾的;矯揉造作的。

rose window 配有玫瑰式線紋裝飾或窗櫺的圓窗。

rose·wood [ˈrozˌwud; ˈrouzwud] *n.* ①〖植物〗花梨木。②花梨屬之熱帶樹。

Rosh Ha·sha·na(h) [ˌrɑʃhəˈʃɑnə; ˌrɔʃhəˈʃɑːnə] 猶太新年。

Ro·si·cru·cian [ˌrozəˈkruʃən; ˌrouziˈkruːʃiən] *n.* ①十七、十八世紀流行的宣揚神祕教義之祕密結社的會員。②近代承襲上述教義、習慣等各團體之會員。

ros·i·ly [ˈrozlɪ; ˈrouzili] *adv.* ①帶玫瑰色地。②樂觀地;興高采烈地。

ros·in [ˈrɑzn̩, ˈrɑzɪn; ˈrɔzin] *n.* ①松香。②樹脂;松脂。—*v.t.* 用樹脂、松香擦抹。

Ros·i·nan·te, Roz·i·nan·te [ˌrɑzɪˈnæntɪ; ˌrɔziˈnænti] *n.* ①Don Quixote 所乘之老瘦馬。②瘦弱無力之老馬;駑馬。

ros·i·ness [ˈrozɪnɪs; ˈrouzinis] *n.* ①淡紅色;玫瑰紅。②光明;愉快。

ros·ter [ˈrɑstɚ; ˈroustə] *n.* 名單; 名簿。—*v.t.* 列入名單內。

ros·tral [ˈrɑstrəl; ˈrɔstrəl] *adj.* ①喙狀突起的;隆起的。②講壇的。③(船上) 附有喙狀突起之裝飾的。

ros·trat·ed [ˈrɑstretɪd; ˈrɔstreitid] *adj.* ①〖動物〗有喙的;有喙狀突起的。②裝飾有喙狀柱的(船)。

ros·trum [ˈrɑstrəm; ˈrɔstrəm] *n., pl.* **-trums, -tra** [-trə; -trə]. ①嘴;喙。②船首。③古羅馬公所內之演講臺。④演說臺。⑤公開演講;演講者之集合稱。⑥嘴狀突起物。

***ros·y** [ˈrozɪ; ˈrouzi] *adj.*, **ros·i·er, ros·i·est.** ①玫瑰色的;淡紅色的。*rosy* cheeks. 紅潤的雙頰。②玫瑰花做成的。③光明的;愉快的;樂觀的。

***rot** [rɑt; rɔt] *v.*, **rot·ted, rot·ting,** *n.* —*v.i.* ①腐爛;枯朽。The flowers *rotted* off. 花凋謝了。②衰弱;消瘦;成爲無用。The prisoners were left to *rot* in jail. 任令囚徒們在獄中變成無用的人。③胡說;嘲弄。He is only *rotting.* 他祇是在胡說。④(在精神上)腐敗。—*v.t.* ①使腐爛;使枯朽;敗壞;破壞。God *rot* them! 那羣混蛋東西算得了甚麼(詛咒語)! ②挖苦;取笑。—*n.* ①腐蝕;腐爛。*Rot* has set in. 開始腐爛了。②腐爛之物。③囈語;愚事。Don't talk *rot.* 不要胡說。④一種植物及動物的慢性腐蝕爛。⑤(板球比賽中)一連串的失敗。⑥敗壞;腐敗。

rot. ①rotary. ②rotating. ③rotation. ④rotten.

ro·ta [ˈrotə; ˈroutə] *n.* ①〖英〗輪流;輪唱。②輪值表;勤務簿。③(R-)羅馬天主教之教廷法院。

ro·tam·e·ter [roˈtæmətɚ; rouˈtæmitə] *n.* 曲線測量儀;輪距測量儀。

Ro·tar·i·an [roˈtɛrɪən; rouˈtɛəriən] *n.* 扶輪社(Rotary Club)之社員。—*adj.* 扶輪社的;扶輪社活動的。

ro·ta·ry [ˈrotərɪ; ˈroutəri] *adj.* ①旋轉的。a *rotary* engine. 廻轉機。②輪流的。③使用輪轉印刷機的。—*n.* ①(亦作 **rotary press**) 輪轉印刷機。②(亦作 **rotary intersection**)(道路交會的)圓環。

Rotary Club 扶輪社(富有的商人領袖及專門職業者之地方的聯誼性組織,一九〇五年創於美國芝加哥)。

Rotary International 國際扶輪社。

rotary plow (or **tiller**) ①轉動犂。②公路除雪機。

rotary press〖印刷〗輪轉機。

ro·ta·ry-wing aircraft [ˈrotərɪˌwɪŋ~; ˈroutəriwiŋ~] 旋轉翼機。(亦作 **rotating-wing aircraft, rotorcraft**)

***ro·tate** [ˈrotet; rouˈteit] *v.*, **-tat·ed, -tat·ing.** —*v.i.* ①旋轉。②更迭;輪廻。The seasons *rotate.* 季節交替。—*v.t.* ①使旋轉。②輪植。to *rotate* crops. 輪栽農作物。③使替換;使輪值。

ro·ta·tion** [roˈteʃən; rouˈteiʃən] *n.* ①旋轉。②輪流;更迭。③輪栽;輪植。*rotation* of crops. 農作物的輪栽。④按輪流制調回國內休假。 ***in rotation 輪流;交替。

ro·ta·tion·al [roˈteʃənl; rouˈteiʃənəl] *adj.* 旋轉的;輪流的;交替的;循環的;輪植的。***rotational inertia***〖物理〗轉動慣性。

ro·ta·tive [ˈrotətɪv; ˈroutətiv] *adj.* ①旋轉的。②使起旋轉運動的。③循環的。

ro·ta·tor [ˈrotetɚ; rouˈteitə] *n., pl. for* ① **ro·ta·tors,** *for* ② **ro·ta·tor·es** [ˌrotəˈtorɪz; ˌroutəˈtɔːriz]. ①旋轉者;廻轉機;旋轉爐。②〖解剖〗旋轉肌。

ro·ta·to·ry [ˈrotəˌtorɪ; ˈroutətəri] *adj.* ①旋轉的;廻轉的;循環的。②引起旋轉的。③循環的;更迭的。

rotatory power〖物理〗旋光本領;旋光力。

ROTC, R.O.T.C. Reserve Officers' Training Corps.

rote [rot; rout] *n.* ①機械的方法;固定程序。②背誦;强記(僅用於 by rote 中)。

rot·gut [ˈrɑtˌgʌt; ˈrɔtgʌt] *n.*〖俚〗劣等的威士忌酒。—*adj.* 劣等的(酒)。

ro·ti·fer [ˈrotɪfɚ; ˈroutifə] *n.*〖動物〗輪蟲。

ro·tis·se·rie [roˈtɪsərɪ; rouˈtisəri] *n.* ①烤食物用之電動炙叉。②賣烤肉之飯店。

ro·to·graph [ˈrotəˌgræf; ˈroutəgrɑːf] *n.*〖攝影〗①旋印照片;速印相片。②原稿等直接曬印之照片(卽不用底片)。

ro·to·gra·vure [ˌrotəgrəˈvjʊr; ˌroutəgrəˈvjuə] *n.*〖印刷〗①凹版照相印刷術。②用凹版照相法印刷之圖畫等。③報紙上刊登照相版圖片的部分。

ro·tor [ˈrotɚ; ˈroutə] *n.* ①〖電〗廻轉子。②〖航海〗廻旋圓筒。③〖航空〗旋轉翼。④〖機械〗廻轉輪。

***rot·ten** [ˈrɑtn̩; ˈrɔtn] *adj.* ①腐爛的;腐朽的。a *rotten* egg. 腐壞的蛋。②惡臭的;臭的。③不健全的;弱的。*rotten* ice. 薄冰。④腐敗的;不誠實的。⑤〖俗〗壞的。a *rotten* book. 壞書。⑥〖俗〗不舒服。

rotten borough ①〖英史〗某些祇有少數投票人但仍在議會有代表之市鎭。②居民減少而仍保持選擧議員權利之市鎭。

rot·ten·stone [ˈrɑtn̩ˌston; ˈrɔtnstoun] *n.* 擦亮石(用做磨光金屬)。

rot·ter [ˈrɑtɚ; ˈrɔtə] *n.*〖英俚〗無用之人;可厭之人;下流坯。

ro·tund [roˈtʌnd; rouˈtʌnd] *adj.* ①圓胖的。②聲音洪亮的。③文體華麗的。

ro·tun·da [roˈtʌndə; rouˈtʌndə] *n.* ①(有圓頂之)圓形建築物。②圓廳。

ro·tun·di·ty [roˈtʌndətɪ; rouˈtʌnditi] *n., pl.* **-ties.** ①肥胖;脂肪過多。②(聲音)洪亮。③(文體等的)華麗;虛誇。④圓胖之物。

ro·tu·rier [rɔtyˈrje; rotyˈrjei] *n., pl.* **-riers.**〖法〗平民;黔首;庶民。

rou·ble [ˈrubl̩; ˈruːbl] *n.* 盧布(俄國貨幣)。(亦作 **ruble**)

rou·é [ruˈe; ˈruːei]〖法〗*n.* 遊蕩者;浪子;好色者。

***rouge** [ruʒ; ruːʒ] *n., v.,* **rouged, roug·ing.** —*n.* ①胭脂。②過氧化鐵;鐵丹。—*v.t.* & *v.i.* ①搽胭脂。②(使)發紅。

rouge et noir [ˈruʒeˈnwɑr; ˈruːʒeiˈnwɑː]〖法〗一種賭博牌戲。

‡rough [rʌf; rʌf] *adj.* ①不平滑的;粗糙的;崎嶇的。②未琢磨的;未精製的。*rough* rice. 糙米。③艱苦的。④未完成的;概略的。⑤粗而不齊的。⑥粗魯的;不雅的。*rough* manners. 粗魯的態度。⑦狂暴的;激烈的;亂的。⑧有風暴的。*rough* weather. 有風暴的天氣。a *rough* sea. 洶湧的海(風浪甚大)。⑨祇需力不需智慧或技巧的。*rough* work. 粗重工作。⑩性烈的。*rough* wine. 烈酒。⑪笨拙的;粗心的。⑫沙啞的(聲音)。⑬〖語音〗帶 h 音的;氣音的。a *rough* vowel. 帶 h 音的母音。***be rough on*** 有害於;傷害。***rough and ready*** 適合實際需要但不精確的。—*n.* ①粗暴之人;莽漢。A gang of *roughs* broke in. 一羣莽漢闖了進來。②粗糙的東西或情況。③高爾夫球場生有長草的部分。④野草漫生之荒地。⑤未琢磨之寶石。⑥大綱;大意。***in the rough*** **a.** 粗糙。**b.** 隨便地;不特別講究形式地。**c.** 蠻荒。***take the rough with the smooth*** 逆來順受。—*v.t.* ①使粗糙;使不平。②粗製;粗割;略繪。to *rough* out a plan. 草擬一計畫。

③過艱苦生活。to *rough* it. 過艱苦生活。④對…舉止粗魯;毆打〖常up〗. ⑤〖運動〗對對方球員採取粗暴的動作。 —*v.i.* ①(面等) 變粗糙。②舉止粗魯。*rough it* 過不舒適的生活; 過野外生活。—*adv.* ①粗暴地; 粗魯地。Treat him *rough*. 粗暴地對付他。②粗糙地。to live *rough*. 過簡陋生活。

rough·age 〔ˈrʌfɪdʒ; ˈrʌfidʒ〕 *n.* ①粗糙原料。②飼料或食料之粗糙而無營養價值的部分(如果皮、稻草、糠等)。

rough-and-read·y 〔ˈrʌfənˈrɛdɪ; ˈrʌfənˈredi〕 *adj.* ①不精美但足可應用的(東西)。②豪爽能幹的。

rough-and-tum·ble 〔ˈrʌfn̩ˈtʌmbl; ˈrʌfənˈtʌmbl〕 *adj.* ①莽撞的;騷亂的。②草率作成的。 —*n.* 混戰;扭鬥。

rough·cast 〔ˈrʌfˌkæst;ˈrʌfkɑːst〕 *n.*, *v.*, **-cast, -cast·ing.** —*n.* ①塗壁之粗灰泥。②粗的形式;粗形;粗型。—*v.t.* ①塗粗灰泥於(牆壁等)。②粗寫(故事)大綱;草草準備。

rough coat 油漆等用以打底的一層。

rough-dry 〔ˌrʌfˈdraɪ; ˌrʌfˈdrai〕 *v.*, **-dried, -dry·ing,** *adj.* —*v.t.* (洗衣後)晒乾不燙。—*adj.* 晒乾而未燙的。(亦作 **roughdry**)

rough·en 〔ˈrʌfən; ˈrʌfən〕 *v.t.* 弄粗糙;使成崎嶇不平。—*v.i.* 變粗糙;變得崎嶇不平。

rough-foot·ed 〔ˈrʌfˈfutɪd; ˈrʌfˈfutid〕 *adj.* (鳥類之)趾有羽毛的。

rough-heart·ed 〔ˈrʌfˈhɑrtɪd; ˈrʌfˈhɑːtid〕 *adj.* 無同情心的;硬心腸的。

rough-hew 〔ˌrʌfˈhju; ˈrʌfˈhjuː〕 *v.t.*, **-hewed, -hewn** or **-hewed.** 粗砍; 粗削(木材、石等);粗製;粗粗地形成或雕成。

rough-hewn 〔ˌrʌfˈhjun; ˈrʌfˈhjuːn〕 *adj.* ①粗削的; 粗製的。②粗野的;無教養的。

rough·house 〔ˈrʌfˌhaus; ˈrʌfhaus〕 *n.* 〖俚〗室內喧嚣之遊戲或打鬥。—*v.t.* 〖俚〗粗魯而喧鬧地對待(某人);戲弄(某人)。—*v.i.* 〖俚〗參加喧嚣之遊戲或打鬥。—*adj.* 喧嚣打鬥的;粗魯對待的。

rough·ish 〔ˈrʌfɪʃ; ˈrʌfiʃ〕 *adj.* ①稍帶粗魯的;稍粗略的。②稍有風浪的。

rough-legged 〔ˈrʌfˌlɛgd; ˈrʌflegd〕 *adj.* (鳥)脚上生羽毛的。

***rough·ly** 〔ˈrʌflɪ; ˈrʌfli〕 *adv.* ①粗暴地;粗魯地。②大約地;約略地。*roughly* speaking. 大致說來;大體上講。

rough·neck 〔ˈrʌfˌnɛk; ˈrʌfnek〕 *n.* 〖俚〗粗魯的人;惡棍。—*adj.* 粗魯的;野蠻的。

rough·ness 〔ˈrʌfnɪs; ˈrʌfnis〕 *n.* ①不平滑;粗糙。②令人難受;令人不快。③粗暴;粗魯。④不平靜;不暖和。⑤未開化。⑥粗糙之處;不雅之處。

rough·rid·er 〔ˈrʌfˌraɪdə;ˈrʌfˌraidə〕 *n.* ①馴馬師。②慣騎劣馬的人。

rough·shod 〔ˈrʌfˈʃɑd; ˈrʌfʃɔd〕 *adj.* ①釘有防滑鐵蹄的(馬)。②穿釘鞋的。③無情的。*ride roughshod over* 不顧別人意見或情緒而任意行動;殘酷自私地恣意孤行。

rough-spo·ken 〔ˈrʌfˌspokən; ˈrʌfˈspoukən〕 *adj.* 言語粗魯的。

rough·wrought 〔ˈrʌfˌrɔt;ˈrʌf-rɔːt〕 *adj.* 粗製的;草草做成的。

rou·lade 〔ruˈlɑd; ruːˈlɑːd〕 *n.* ①〖音樂〗急奏。②以薄肉片捲包碎肉烹成的菜餚。

rou·leau 〔ruˈlo;ruːˈlou〕 *n., pl.* **-leaus, -leaux** 〔-ˈloz; -ˈlouz〕. 細長的小卷;用紙包的一卷硬幣。

rou·lette 〔ruˈlɛt; ruːˈlet〕 *n., v.,* **-let·ted, -let·ting.** —*n.* ①輪盤賭。②用在版面刻點或線之齒輪。③在郵票等上刻騎縫刻痕之齒輪。④郵票四周爲便於撕開之齒孔刻痕。—*v.t.* 用齒輪鏤刻。

Rou·ma·nia 〔ruˈmenɪə;ru(ː)ˈmeinjə〕 *n.* =**Rumania.** —**Rou·ma·ni·an,** *n., adj.*

‡round¹ 〔raund;raund〕 *adj.* ①圓的;圓形的;球形的;圓筒形的。 It is neither *round* nor square. 它既不圓又不方。②豐滿的;肥胖的。③循圓而動的;圓舞的。The waltz is a *round* dance. 華爾玆是圓舞。④滿的;整數的。a *round* dozen. 一整打。a good *round* sum of money. 一筆巨款。⑤率直的;坦白的。⑥音調圓潤宏亮的。a mellow, *round* voice. 圓潤宏亮的聲音。⑦有力的;輕快的。a *round* trot. 快步。⑧用圓脣發出的(音)。a *round* vowel. 用圓脣發聲的母音。⑨豐盛的; 多的; 大的。⑩彎彎曲曲的 (字體)。 a *round* schoolboy hand. 彎彎曲曲的學童筆跡。⑪猛烈的;痛烈的。I gave him a *round* hiding. 我給他一頓痛打。⑫完全的;完整的。*in round numbers* 以約略數字言之 (卽以幾千幾百等整數而言)。 —*n.* ①圓形物;球狀物。 the *rounds* of a ladder. 梯子上的橫木。②巡行;巡察。 The night watchman makes his *rounds*. 守夜者巡察。③旋轉。the earth's yearly *round*. 地球之公轉。④(職責、事件等) 一連串。 the daily *round*. 例行公事。a *round* of duties. 一連串的職務。⑤(競賽等之)一回合。a fight of ten *rounds*. (拳擊)十回合之交戰。⑥範圍。the *round* of human knowledge. 人類知識的範圍。⑦(彈藥之)一發。⑧一齊射擊。⑨一齊射擊所需之彈藥。⑩(喝采、歡呼等)一次;一起。 a *round* of cheers. 一陣歡呼。⑪輪唱之歌。⑫牛後腿肉。⑬圓舞。a light fantastic *round*. 輕盈而美妙的圓舞。⑭ (*pl.*) 消息等傳播的路線。 ⑮循環。 the annual *rounds*. 一年一年的循環。 *go the rounds* (消息、謠言等)流傳。 *in the round* **a.** (雕刻等)形狀完整的;非浮雕的。**b.** 完全地;完整地。*make the rounds* **a.** 走遍;作例行之巡視等。**b.** (演員、自由作家等) 與製片人、編輯等接頭找差事。*out of round* 扭曲而失去眞圓性的。—*v.t.* ①使圓;使圓滿完成〖off, out〗. to *round* out a career. 完成一事業。②繞行。The car *rounded* the corner. 汽車拐過角隅。 ③使轉向。④以四捨五入簡化 (數字)。—*v.i.* ①轉身。②變圓;成圓形。③成熟;完成。*round in* 〖航海〗收纜。*round off* **a.** 使十全十美。 **b.** 以四捨五入表示。 **c.** =**round out.** *round on* (or *upon*) 突然以言語或行動攻擊。*round out* **a.** 使成圓形;成圓形。**b.** 完成;結束。*round to* 〖航海〗使船首當風。*round up* 聚集;捕捉。to *round up* cattle. 逐牛聚在一起。—*adv.* ①周行地。 A wheel goes *round*. 車輪旋轉。②四處地;遍及地。Shall I show you *round?* 我領你四處看看好嗎? ③圓周地;周圍地。The ball measures 5 inches *round*. 這球周圍有5英寸。④繞道地。⑤傳遞地;流轉地。The news was soon carried *round*. 這消息不久便傳遍各地。 ⑥(時間)循環地。Summer will soon come *round* again. 夏天又快來到了。⑦在附近地;在近處地(=about, around). What are you hanging *round* for? 〖俗〗你逗留在這附近做甚麼? ⑧至或自說話者所在或將去的地方。Come *round* and see me this evening. 今晚請過來看我。⑨爲大家(=for all). There is just enough cake to go *round*. 有恰够的糕分給大家吃。 ⑩向後轉地。 He turned *round* in his chair to look. 他坐在椅子上轉向後面看看。⑪至正常狀態。—*prep.* ①在…之四周。②至…之各處。We took them *round* the town. 我們帶他們到城裏各處遊逛。③繞着。④沿着…之邊緣。⑤沿着(曲線)。⑥約在;在…前後。**get** (or **come**) **round a person** a. 以機智勝過某人。 b. 以甜言蜜語誘勸某人。**round the corner** 在轉角處。He lives *round the corner.* 他住在轉角的地方;他住得很近。〖注意〗**round, around** 在正式用法中,有一種趨勢,卽將 around 祇解釋爲處處、到處, round 祇解釋爲一種旋轉的行動: I have looked all *around.* 我到處都看過了。He is going *round* the world. 他正作環球旅行。

round² *v.t.* & *v.i.* 〖英古,廢〗耳語。

round·a·bout [ˈraundəˌbaut;ˈraund-əbaut] *adj.* ①間接的;繞遠的。②豐滿的。—*n.* ①間接的方式;委婉說法;繞彎的話。②短而緊的男上衣。③〖英〗=**merry-go-round.** ④繞遠路;繞道;繞圈子。—**ness,** *n.*

round dance 圓舞;圓舞曲。

roun·del [ˈraundl; ˈraundl] *n.* ①小圓形物;環;小圓盤。②圓形飾物。③小圓形窗。④圓盾。⑤〖紋章〗圓形紋。⑥圓舞 (=round dance). ⑦〖詩〗rondeau 之變體(三節,每節三行,第一及第三節之後有疊句)。

roun·de·lay [ˈraundəˌle; ˈraundilei] *n.* ①輪旋曲(一種有覆唱詞之短歌)。②配合此種歌曲之音樂。③圓舞;輪舞。

round·er [ˈraundɚ; ˈraundə] *n.* ①巡廻者。②作圓之人; 範圓之具。③行跡放蕩之揮霍者;習常犯罪者;醉鬼。④(*pl.*)(作 *sing.* 解)一種類似棒球之遊戲。⑤(R-)〖英〗基督教美以美會之巡廻牧師。⑥(包括若干回合的)一場拳擊賽。

round-eyed [ˈraundˈaɪd;ˈraundˈaid] *adj.* 因驚訝而睜大眼睛的。

round game 四個或四個人以上參加而無夥伴制的遊戲(如麻將)。

round hand 一種書寫字體(字母圓而豐滿,別於 running hand).

Round·head [ˈraundˌhɛd;ˈraundhed] *n.* 1642–52英國內亂時議會派或清教派分子。

round·house [ˈraundˌhaus; ˈraund-haus] *n.* ①圓形機車庫。②〖航海〗甲板室。③〖古〗監獄。—*adj.* 〖俚〗在空中劃一條大弧線的(如棒球投手之投球或拳擊家之出拳)。

round·ish [ˈraundɪʃ; ˈraundiʃ] *adj.* 略圓的。

round·ly [ˈraundlɪ; ˈraundli] *adv.* ①呈圓形地。②努力地;熱心地;活潑地;神高氣爽地。③率直地;直言無隱地。④徹底地;周到地。⑤嚴苛地;苛刻地。to scold *roundly.* 痛罵。⑥約略地;按整數計地。The number was estimated *roundly* at 500. 其數約略估計爲 500。

round·ness [ˈraundnɪs; ˈraundnis] *n.* 圓(指其性質或狀態)。

round number ①整數。②可用 10, 100, 1,000等整除的偶數。

round of beef 牛股肉。

round robin ①陳情書或抗議書(署名者的簽字列爲圓形,使不能辨認簽名之次序)。②一連串;一系列。③〖運動〗循環賽。④圓桌會議。

round-shoul·dered [ˈraundˈʃol-dɚd; ˈraundˈʃouldəd] *adj.* 圓肩的。

rounds·man [ˈraundzmən; ˈraundz-mən] *n., pl.* **-men.** ①巡邏者;巡查者。②送牛奶、麪包等的人。

round steak 牛後腿上部之肉。

Round Table ①圓桌 (Arthur 王與其武士坐圓桌席位,以免爭論席次尊卑)。②圓桌武士 (Arthur 王與其武士)。③(r- t-)圓桌會議。a *round* table conference. 圓桌會議。

round-the-clock [ˈraundðəˈklɑk; ˈraundðəklɔk] *adj.* 整天的;二十四小時的。—*adv.* 不分晝夜;無休止。(亦作**around-the-clock**)

round·top [ˈraundˌtɑp; ˈraundtɔp] *n.* 〖航海〗檣樓。

round trip 來回旅行;雙程旅行。(亦作 **return trip**)

round-trip [ˈraundˈtrɪp; ˈraundˈtrip] *adj.* 來回的; 往返的; 雙程的。a *round-trip* ticket. 來回票;雙程票。

round-trip·per [ˈraundˈtrɪpɚ; ˈraundˈtripə] *n.* 〖俚〗全壘打。

round·up [ˈraundˌʌp; ˈraundʌp] *n.* ①驅集(牛羊等)。②被驅集於一處之牛羊羣。③負責驅集牛羊於一處之牧童、馬等。④類似的驅集一處之行動。⑤(新聞之)綜合報導。

round·worm [ˈraundˌwɝm; ˈraund-wəːm] *n.* 線蟲(特指寄生人腸內者,如蛔蟲)。

roup¹ [rup; ruːp] 〖蘇〗 *v.t.* 拍賣。—*n.* 拍賣(通常作 public roup).

roup² *n.* ①〖獸醫〗家禽所患的一種眼睛及鼻腔之黏膜炎。②沙啞聲。

*__rouse¹__ [rauz; rauz] *v.,* **roused, rous·ing,** *n.* —*v.t.* ①喚醒;驚醒。I was *roused* by the telephone. 我被電話驚醒。②激勵;激動。to *rouse* a man to action. 激勵一人使之行動。③驚起(鳥、獸)。—*v.i.* ①醒來。②奮起。③驚起。④被激起。—*n.* ①被激起之狀態。②激起或行動之信號。

rouse² *n.* 〖古〗①酒會; 酒宴。to take a *rouse.* 鬧飲。②乾杯。to give a *rouse.* 乾杯。

rous·er [ˈrauzɚ; ˈrauzə] *n.* ①喚起者;激動者。②〖俚〗最大者;最厲害者。

rous·ing [ˈrauzɪŋ; ˈrauziŋ] *adj.* ①鼓舞的;興奮的;動人的。②活潑的;敏捷的。③〖俗〗驚人的; 大的。—*n.* ①喚起; 激動; 激勵。②〖俚〗責罵。—**ly,** *adv.*

Rous·seau [ruˈso; ˈruːsou] *n.* 盧梭 (Jean Jacques, 1712–1778, 生於瑞士之法國哲學家及作家,民約論作者)。—**e·an,** *adj.*

Rous·seau·ism [ruˈsoɪzəm;ˈruːsou-izm] *n.* 盧梭主義;盧梭之思想及作風。

roust·a·bout [ˈraustəˌbaut; ˈraustə-baut] *n.* 〖美〗①碼頭搬運伕。②馬戲場中的雜工。③船上雜工。④油田粗工。⑤短工;雜工。

*__rout¹__ [raut; raut] *v.i.* & *v.t.* ①(獸類)以鼻挖土;挖掘。②尋找;搜尋。③强迫。④打敗;擊敗。to *rout* an enemy. 打敗敵人。⑤排除。—*n.* ①潰敗。②暴動;騷動。③烏合之衆。④一羣。⑤時髦人物的聚會。**put to rout** 擊潰並驅散;使混亂。

rout² *n.* ①咆哮;吼。②嘈雜; 騷亂。—*v.i.* ①咆哮;吼。②發鼾聲。—*v.t.* 咆哮而言。

‡**route** [rut, raut; ruːt, raut] *n., v.,* **rout-ed, rout·ing.** —*n.* ①路;道路。Which *route* did you take? 你走那條路?②〖軍〗前進命令;開拔令。to get the *route.* 奉令開拔。a *route* march. 旅次行軍。③路線。④一英里以上之賽馬。**en route** 在途中。**go the route** a. 貫徹始終。 b. 〖棒球俚〗投手投完整個比賽。—*v.t.* ①安排…之道路;定以路線。②經某路投送。letters *routed* via... 經…寄出之信件。—**rout·man,** *n.*

route·way [ˈrutˌwe; ˈruːt-wei] *n.* 通路;路線。

*__rou·tine__ [ruˈtin; ruːˈtiːn, ruˈt-] *n.* 例

行公事;慣例;常規。the daily *routine*. 日常事務;日課。—*adj.* 慣行的;例行的。*routine* duties. 例行職務。*routine* work. 例行事務。—*v.t.* 使化爲慣例。

rou·ti·neer [ˌrutɪ'nɪr; ˌruːti'niə] *n.* 循常規辦事的人;因循現狀而缺進取心的人。

rou·tin·ism [ru'tinɪzm; ruː'tiːnizm] *n.* 遵行慣例常規。—**rou·tin·ist**, *n.*

rou·tin·ize [ru'tinaɪz; ruː'tiːnaiz] *v.t.*, **-ized, -iz·ing.** 使慣例化。

*__rove__[1] [rov; rouv] *v.*, **roved, rov·ing,** *n.*—*v.i.* ①流浪;漫遊;漂泊。to *rove* over the fields and woods. 在田野和樹林中漫遊。②(眼睛)轉來轉去。③(愛情等)時時改變;飄忽不定。—*v.t.* 徘徊於;漫遊於。—*n.* 徘徊;飄動;轉動。

rove[2] *v.*, **roved, rov·ing,** *n.* —*v.t.* ①引(纖維等)過小孔。②梳(羊毛)。③紡前引捻(纖維)。—*n.* 經引捻的毛、棉纖維;粗紡線。

rove[3] *v.* pt. & pp. of **reeve.**

rove beetle 身細長而行動迅速之甲蟲。

rov·er ['rovə; 'rouvə] *n.* ①漂泊者。vacation *rover*. 渡假中的漂泊者。②海盜。③海盜船。④〖箭術〗任意選擇的標的。⑤〖英〗十八歲以上的男童軍。

roving ambassador 〖美〗巡廻大使;無任所大使。

roving life 放浪生活。

‡**row**[1] [ro; rou] *n.* ①行列;排。The children stood in a *row*. 孩子們站成一排。②(劇院等中)一排座位。a pair of seats in the fifth *row*. 在第五排的兩個座位。③連續;一連串。④連接成排的房屋之任一(=row house). street lined with *rows*. 房屋成排的街道。⑤橫格(別於 column, 縱格)。***a hard*** (or ***long***) ***row to hoe*** 一件困難的工作。***in a row*** **a.** 成排。three houses *in a row*. 三幢成排的房屋。**b.** 接連。for the third day *in a row*. 接連第三天。—*v.t.* 放成一排;列成排。

‡**row**[2] *v.i.* 划船。—*v.t.* ①以槳划(船);以船渡。Let's *row* a race. 讓我們做划船比賽。②用(若干把的槳)划。The boat *rows* two oars. 那小舟用兩把槳划。***row down*** 在划船比賽中越過。***row out*** 使划到筋疲力竭。—*n.* 划船。Let's go for a *row* on the lake. 我們到湖上划船去吧。—**er**, *n.*

*__row__[3] [rau; rau] *n.* ①爭吵;吵鬧。What's the *row?* 發生了甚麼事? ②喧鬧聲。There is too much *row* going on. 吵鬧聲太厲害了。③挑剔受責。***kick up a row*** **a.** 爭吵。**b.** 引起亂子。—*v.t.* 〖俗〗責備;責斥。—*v.i.* 〖俗〗爭吵;吵鬧。

row·an ['roən; 'rau-ən] *n.* 〖植物〗①(亦作 **rowan tree**) 歐洲產之山梨。②(亦作 **rowanberry**) 其所產之果。

row·boat ['roˌbot; 'roubout] *n.* 以槳划行的船;划艇。(亦作**rowing boat**)

row-de-dow ['raudɪ'dau; 'raudi'dau] *n.* 〖俚〗喧鬧;喧囂。

row·dy ['raudɪ; 'raudi] *n.*, *pl.* **-dies,** *adj.*, **-di·er, -di·est,** *v.* —*n.* 粗暴而喧嚷者;流氓;地痞。—*adj.* 粗暴的;喧嚷的。—*v.i.* 喧嚷。—**row·di·ly,** *adv.* —**row·di·ness,** *n.*

row·dy-dow·dy ['raudɪ'daudɪ; 'raudi'daudi] *adj.* 〖俗〗喧囂的;吵鬧的。

row·dy·ish ['raudɪɪʃ; 'raudiiʃ] *adj.* 暴亂的;喧囂的;粗野的;粗暴的。—**ly,** *adv.* —**ness,** *n.*

row·dy·ism ['raudɪɪzəm; 'raudiizm] *n.* 粗暴行爲;粗暴作風。

row·el ['rauəl; 'rauəl] *n.*, *v.*, **-el(l)ed, -el(l)ing.** —*n.* ①馬刺上之小齒輪;距輪。②〖獸醫〗揷環打膿器。—*v.t.* ①揷環打膿。②以小齒輪刺(馬)。③挖掘。④衝破;刺破。⑤擾亂。⑥配以距輪。

row house ①連接成排的房屋之任一。②與鄰屋起碼有一堵共同牆壁之房屋。

row·lock ['roˌlɑk; 'rɔlək] *n.* 〖英〗槳架;槳架(美語中作 oarlock).

‡**roy·al** ['rɔɪəl; 'rɔiəl] *adj.* ①王室的;皇家的。the *royal* family. 皇室;皇族。②屬於皇家的;爲國王或皇后所贊成的;爲王室服務的。*royal* power. 王權。the *Royal* Navy. 〖英〗皇家海軍。③欽定的;勅建的。a *royal* command. 勅令;聖旨。④盛大的;輝煌的。a *royal* feast. 盛宴。⑤威嚴的。⑥深豔的;鮮亮的。*royal* blue. 深藍色。⑦極好的。to have a *royal* time. 過極好的時光。⑧極大的。⑨容易的。⑩不易發生化學變化的。—*n.*①皇族。②一種棕樹(=royal palm). ③紙張的一種尺寸(寫字紙爲19×24英寸,印刷紙爲20×25英寸)。

Royal Academy 〖英〗皇家藝術院。

Royal Air Force 英國(皇家)空軍。

royal bay 月桂樹。

royal flush (撲克牌的)同花大順。

Royal Institution 英國科學研究所(1799年創設,以促進民衆科學知識爲宗旨)。

roy·al·ism ['rɔɪəlɪzəm; 'rɔiəlizm] *n.* 尊王主義;忠君主義。

roy·al·ist ['rɔɪəlɪst; 'rɔiəlist] *n.* 保皇者;保皇黨。—*adj.* 尊王主義的;保皇黨的。

roy·al·is·tic [ˌrɔɪə'lɪstɪk; ˌrɔiə'listik] *adj.* 尊王的;勤王的;保皇黨的。

roy·al·ly ['rɔɪəlɪ; 'rɔiəli] *adv.* ①由國王;以國王之名義。②輝煌地。③大規模地。

royal mast 〖航海〗最上桅。

royal palm 美洲產高大的羽狀葉棕樹。

royal purple 深藍紫色。

royal road 平坦易行之道路;近路;捷徑。

Royal Society 〖英〗皇家學會。

royal standard 英皇家旗。

*__roy·al·ty__ ['rɔɪəltɪ; 'rɔiəlti] *n.*, *pl.* **-ties.** ①皇族;皇室。②王權;王位。③莊嚴;高貴。④王國。⑤皇族之一員。⑥國王所授之土地。⑦使用費;版稅;上演稅。

royal water 王水(=aqua regia).

royal "we" 朕(帝王自稱, 以代替"I").

royal yellow 〖礦〗雌黃。

R.P. ①Reformed Presbyterian. ②Regius Professor. **RPM, rpm, r.p.m.** revolutions per minute. **R.P.O.** Railroad Post Office. **RPQ** request for price quotation. **rps, r.p.s.** revolutions per second. **rpt.** ①report. ②reported. ③reporting. ④repeat. **rptd.** ①repeated. ②reported. ③reprinted. ④ruptured. **R.R.** ①railroad. ②Right Reverend. ③rural route. **RSFSR** (亦作 **R.S.F.S.R.**) Russian Soviet Federated Socialist Republic. **R.S.L.** Royal Society of Literature. **RSPCA, R.S.P.C.A.** 〖英〗 The Royal Society for the Prevention of Cruelty to Animals. **R.S.S.** Regiae Societatis Socius (拉 = Fellow of the Royal Society). **RSV, R.S.V.** Revised Standard Version (of the Bible). **R.S.V.P., r.s.v.p.**(亦作 **RSVP, rsvp**) Répondez s'il vous plaît. (法 = Please answer.)請答覆。**rt.** right. **R/T** radio telegraphy. **'rt**〖俗〗art. **rtd.** ①retired.

②returned. **rte.** route. **R.T.F.** Radio diffusion et Television Françaises. **Rt. Hon.** Right Honorable. **Rt. Rev.** Right Reverend. **Rts.** rights. **Ru** 化學元素 ruthenium 之符號。

rub** [rʌb; rʌb] *v.*, **rubbed, rub·bing,** *n.* —*v.t.* ①磨;擦。He *rubbed* his hands with soap. 他在手上擦肥皂。②揉;按摩。③擦去;磨光;擦亮。—*v.i.* ①摩擦。It won't *rub* out. 擦不掉它。②使人惱火;令人易發脾氣。③勉强維持下去。rub a person the wrong way*** 傷害某人的感情;激怒某人。***rub down*** **a.** 徹底擦乾淨。**b.** 擦平;擦亮。**c.** 按摩。***rub elbows*** 互相接觸。***rub in*** **a.** 擦入。*Rub* the oil *in* well. 將油好好擦入。**b.** 强迫學習;迫使承認或接受不快之事實;强調。***rub off*** 擦掉;擦去。***rub off on*** 附着於…;成爲…之一部分。***rub out*** **a.** 擦去;拭去。**b.**〖俚〗謀殺。***rub shoulders with*** 同(他人)相遇;與(他人)交際。***rub the right way*** 安撫;使平息怒氣。***rub up*** **a.** 擦淨;擦亮。**b.** 重溫。My Latin needs to be *rubbed up*. 我的拉丁文需要重新溫習一下。—*n.* ①摩擦。to give something a good *rub*. 好好擦某物。②刺傷感情之事物(譴責、嘲弄、譏諷等)。③困難;障礙。Aye, there's the *rub*. 是的,難處就在這裏了。

rub. ①rubbed. ②rubber. ③〖處方〗ruddy.

rub-a-dub [ˈrʌbəˌdʌb; ˈrʌbədʌb] *n.*, *v.*, **-dubbed, -dub·bing.** —*n.* (鼓之)咚咚聲;與鼓聲相似之聲音。—*v.i.* 發出咚咚聲。

ru·ba·to [ruˈbato; ru:ˈbɑ:tou] *n.*, *pl.* **-tos.**〖音樂〗彈性速度(唱、奏不受節拍約束)。

***rub·ber**[1] [ˈrʌbɚ; ˈrʌbə] *n.* ①橡皮;橡膠。②橡皮製成物(如膠套鞋)。③摩擦者;摩擦器。④輪胎。⑤橡皮擦。—*adj.* 橡皮製的。*rubber* shoes. 橡膠鞋。—*v.t.* 包以橡皮;覆以橡皮。—*v.i.*〖俚〗引頸而望;回頭而望。

rub·ber[2] *n.* ①(牌戲中)連續的三次比賽。②三次比賽中的兩勝;三次比賽中決定勝負的一次比賽。

rubber band (包裝等所用)橡皮筋。

rubber check 空頭支票。

rub·ber·ize [ˈrʌbəˌraɪz; ˈrʌbəraiz] *v.t.*, **-ized, -iz·ing.** 塗以橡膠;以橡膠塡充。

rub·ber·neck [ˈrʌbɚˌnɛk; ˈrʌbənek] *n.*〖美俚〗引頸而望者;好奇觀覽者;遊客。—*adj.*〖美俚〗供遊覽使用的。—*v.i.* ①〖美俚〗引頸而望;好奇觀看;東張西望。②觀光;遊覽。

rubber plant ①橡膠樹。②一種桑科觀賞植物。

rubber sheet 橡膠布(用於病床或嬰孩尿布者)。

rubber stamp ①橡皮圖章。②〖俗〗不加考慮卽表贊同或予批准之人或機構。③陳腔濫調。

rub·ber-stamp [*v.* ˌrʌbɚˈstæmp; ˌrʌbəˈstæmp *adj.* ˈrʌbɚˈstæmp; ˈrʌbəˈstæmp] *v.t.* ①蓋以橡皮圖章。②〖俗〗不加思考卽贊同或批准。—*adj.* ①用橡皮圖章的。②〖俗〗不加思索而批准的;爲形式而批准的。

rub·ber·y [ˈrʌbərɪ; ˈrʌbəri] *adj.* 像橡皮的;有彈性的;强韌的。

rub·bing [ˈrʌbɪŋ; ˈrʌbiŋ] *n.* ①摩擦;研磨。②搨印。

rub·bish** [ˈrʌbɪʃ; ˈrʌbiʃ] *n.* ①廢物;垃圾。②胡說;毫無價值的話或思想。*Rubbish!* 胡說!③甚少價值的東西。a good riddance of bad rubbish*** 眼中釘可算拔掉了。

rub·bish·y [ˈrʌbɪʃɪ; ˈrʌbiʃi] *adj.* ①無用的;垃圾一般的。②遍地是垃圾的。

rub·ble [ˈrʌbl̩; ˈrʌbl] *n.*, *v.*, **rub·bled, rub·bling.** —*n.* ①粗石;碎石;瓦礫。②碎石建築。—*v.t.* 破壞成爲瓦礫;使化爲瓦礫。

rub·ble·work [ˈrʌbl̩ˌwɝk; ˈrʌblwə:k] *n.* 碎石構造物;表面粗糙之石建築物。

rub·down [ˈrʌbˌdaun; ˈrʌbdaun] *n.* ①摩擦全身。②按摩。

rube [rub; ru:b] *n.*〖美俚〗村夫;鄉下佬。—*adj.* 村夫的;像鄉下佬的。

ru·be·fa·cient [ˌrubəˈfeʃənt; ˌru:biˈfeiʃjənt] *adj.*〖醫〗使皮膚發紅色的。—*n.* 使皮膚發紅色的藥劑;發紅劑;紅皮劑。

ru·bel·la [ruˈbɛlə; ru:ˈbelə] *n.*〖醫〗風疹;德國麻疹。

ru·bel·lite [ruˈbɛlaɪt; ru:ˈbelait] *n.*〖礦〗紅電氣石。

Ru·bens [ˈrubɪnz; ˈru:binz] *n.* 魯賓斯(Peter Paul, 1577–1640, Flanders之畫家)。

ru·be·o·la [rəˈbiələ; ru:ˈbi:ələ] *n.*〖醫〗①紅疹。②德國麻疹;風疹。

Ru·bi·con [ˈrubɪˌkɑn; ˈru:bikən] *n.* 盧比孔河(義大利中部之河名,紀元前49年凱撒領兵過此河與龐培作戰)。***cross*** (or ***pass***) ***the Rubicon*** 破釜沉舟;有去無回。

ru·bi·cund [ˈrubəˌkʌnd; ˈru:bikənd] *adj.* ①帶紅色的。②臉色紅潤的。—**i·ty,** *n.*

ru·bid·i·um [ruˈbɪdɪəm; ru:ˈbidiəm] *n.*〖化〗銣(銀白色金屬元素,化學符號爲Rb)。

ru·big·i·nous [ruˈbɪdʒənəs; ru:ˈbidʒinəs] *adj.* 褐紅色的;銹色的。

ru·ble [ˈrubl̩; ˈru:bl] *n.* 盧布(俄國錢幣單位)。(亦作 **rouble**)

ru·bric [ˈrubrɪk; ˈru:brik] *n.* ①朱字;朱印;紅標題。②標題。③禮拜規程;教儀。④習俗;成例。—*adj.* =**rubrical.** —**ian,** *n.*

ru·bri·cal [ˈrubrɪkl̩; ˈru:brikl] *adj.* ①〖宗教〗禮拜儀式之規程的。②朱色的;朱字的。

ru·bri·cate [ˈrubrɪˌket; ˈru:brikeit] *v.t.*, **-cat·ed, -cat·ing.** ①以紅色標出;塗以紅色。②以紅色印刷或書寫。

ru·bri·ca·tion [ˌrubrɪˈkeʃən; ˌru:briˈkeiʃən] *n.* ①紅色印刷;紅色書寫。②紅色印刷之印刷品;用紅字寫的東西。

rub·stone [ˈrʌbˌston; ˈrʌbstoun] *n.* 磨石;砥石。

***ru·by** [ˈrubɪ; ˈru:bi] *n.*, *pl.* **-bies,** *adj.* —*n.* ①紅寶石。②紅寶石色。③紅酒。④〖英俚〗血。—*adj.* 紅寶石色的。*ruby* lips. 紅嘴唇。*ruby* wine. 紅酒。

ruby wedding 紅寶石婚(結婚四十五周年紀念)。

ruch·ing [ˈruʃɪŋ; ˈru:ʃiŋ] *n.* ①做褶帶或襞布之材料。②褶帶或襞布之集合稱。

ruck[1] [rʌk; rʌk] *n.* ①羣衆。②一大堆東西。③(賽馬)落伍之馬羣。④任何落伍之一羣。⑤(時間)在後之事物。***the ruck*** 大衆。

ruck[2] *v.t.* & *v.i.* 摺;使皺;變皺。—*n.* 摺;皺。

ruck·le[1] [ˈrʌkl̩; ˈrʌkl] *n.*, *v.*, **ruck·led, ruck·ling.** —*n.*〖蘇,英方〗一堆。—*v.t.*〖蘇,英方〗堆起。

ruck·le[2] *v.*, **ruck·led, ruck·ling,** *n.* —*v.i.*〖蘇,英方〗喉中咯咯響。—*n.*〖蘇,英方〗喉鳴聲。

ruck·sack [ˈrʌkˌsæk; ˈruksæk] *n.* 一種軟式背囊。

ruck·us [ˈrʌkəs; ˈrʌkəs] *n.* 爭吵;激辯。

ruc·tion [ˈrʌkʃən; ˈrʌkʃən] *n.*〖俗〗鼓噪;騷擾;吵鬧。—**ruc·tious,** *adj.*

rud·beck·i·a [rʌdˈbɛkɪə; rʌdˈbekiə] *n.*〖植物〗黃雛菊屬植物。

rudd [rʌd; rʌd] *n.* 赤睛魚(鯉科淡水魚)。

***rud·der** [ˈrʌdɚ; ˈrʌdə] *n.* ①船舵;方向舵。②領導者;掌舵者。③〖諧〗魚尾;鳥尾;

獸尾。 ***ease the rudder!***〖航海〗減少方向舵轉動角度! ***full rudder!***〖航海〗急轉彎! ***left rudder!***〖航海〗方向舵靠左(使船首向左轉)! ***right rudder!***〖航海〗方向舵靠右(使船首向右轉)!

rudder angle 舵角(舵面與船身間之銳角)。

rudder fish 追隨船舶之魚。

rud·der·less [ˈrʌdəlɪs; ˈrʌdəlis] *adj.* 無舵的;漂流的;無人指導的。

rud·der·post [ˈrʌdɚˌpost; ˈrʌdəpoust] *n.* ①舵柱。②=**rudderstock**.

rud·der·stock [ˈrʌdɚˌstɑk; ˈrʌdəstɔk] *n.* 舵桿。

rud·de·va·tor [ˈrʌdəˌvetɚ; ˈrʌdəveitə] *n.*〖航空〗方向升降舵。

rud·di·ly [ˈrʌdɪlɪ; ˈrʌdili] *adj.* 現赤紅色。

rud·dle [ˈrʌdl; ˈrʌdl] *n., v.,* **-dled, -dling.** —*n.*〖礦〗紅土;代赭石。—*v.t.*①塗以代赭石;用紅土塗或作記號。②使發紅;使紅。

rud·dock [ˈrʌdək; ˈrʌdək] *n.* (歐洲產之) 知更鳥。

*__rud·dy__ [ˈrʌdɪ; ˈrʌdi] *adj.,* **-di·er, -di·est,** *adv., v.,* **rud·died, rud·dy·ing.** —*adj.* ①(淺)紅色的。a *ruddy* sky. 淡紅色的天空。②紅潤的(表示健康)。a *ruddy* complexion. 紅潤的臉色。③〖英〗極大的; 非常的。—*adv.*〖英〗非常;很。—*v.t.* 使變紅;使帶紅色。—**rud·di·ness,** *n.*

ruddy duck 北美洲產的一種淡水鴨。

*__rude__ [rud; ru:d] *adj.,* **rud·er, rud·est.** ①無禮貌的。 It's *rude* to interrupt. 插嘴搶話是無禮貌的。②粗製的。③粗暴的; 猛烈的。*rude* blast. 狂風。④野蠻的。⑤健壯的。in *rude* health. 粗壯的。⑥刺耳的。⑦窮人的。⑧發展或發育不全的。⑨突然的; 令人不知所措的。⑩無法抗拒的;無法避免的。

*__rude·ly__ [ˈrudlɪ; ˈru:dli] *adv.* ①無禮地。 You spoke *rudely* to him. 你對他說話無禮。②概略地; 大約地。

rude·ness [ˈrudnɪs; ˈru:dnis] *n.* ①無禮; 粗暴。②無禮的行爲; 粗暴的行爲。

ru·di·ment [ˈrudəmənt; ˈru:dimənt] *n.* ①基礎。②(常*pl.*)初階; 初步。③(常*pl.*)初期。④(動植物)發育不完全的部分或器官。

ru·di·men·tal [ˌrudəˈmɛntḷ; ˌru:diˈmentl] *adj.* = **rudimentary.**

ru·di·men·ta·ry [ˌrudəˈmɛntərɪ; ˌru:diˈmentəri] *adj.* ①基本的;初期的。②未發展的;發展不完全的。③〖生物〗發育未全的;衰退的。

rud·ish [ˈrudɪʃ; ˈru:diʃ] *adj.* 稍微粗魯的;稍微無禮的。

rue[1] [ru; ru:] *n.*〖植物〗芸香。

rue[2] *v.,* **rued, ru·ing,** *n.* —*v.t.* ①後悔;悔恨;懺悔。You shall *rue* it. 你要後悔的。②願望(某事未曾發生)。to *rue* a bargain. 後悔不該作一宗交易。—*v.i.* ①感覺悲傷。②抱憾。—*n.*〖古〗①悔恨。②憐憫。—**ru·er,** *n.*

rue·ful [ˈrufəl; ˈru:ful] *adj.*①悲哀的;悲慘的。②悔恨的;悲傷的。—**ness,** *n.* —**ly,** *adv.*

ru·elle [ruˈɛl; ru:ˈel] *n.* 小街;小巷。

ruff[1] [rʌf; rʌf] *n.* ①襞襟。②鳥獸之頸毛。③千鳥之一種。④一種有頸毛之鴿。

ruff[2] *n.* 鱸鮒(歐洲產淡水魚)。(亦作**ruffe**)

ruff[3] *n.*①昔日流行的一種紙牌(略似whist)。②〖牌戲〗出王牌取磴。—*v.t.* & *v.i.*〖牌戲〗出王牌取磴;以王牌取勝(=trump).

ruffed [rʌft; rʌft] *n.* 有皺領的; 有襞狀物的;飾有皺領的。

ruffed grouse 北美洲產的一種松鷄。

*__ruf·fi·an__ [ˈrʌfɪən; ˈrʌfjən] *n.* 兇漢;惡棍; 無賴。—*adj.* 兇惡的;殘暴的。

ruf·fi·an·ism [ˈrʌfɪənˌɪzəm; ˈrʌfjənizm] *n.* 兇惡;兇暴;惡漢行徑。

ruf·fi·an·ly [ˈrʌfɪənlɪ; ˈrʌfjənli] *adj.* 似惡漢的;兇惡的;殘暴的;無法無天的。

*__ruf·fle__[1] [ˈrʌfḷ; ˈrʌfl] *v.,* **-fled, -fling,** *n.* —*v.t.* ①摺皺; 使皺; 振(羽)。 A breeze *ruffled* the lake. 一陣輕風吹皺湖水。②滋擾;打擾。③加以襞飾。④洗牌。⑤急速翻動(書頁)。***ruffle it*** 欺凌弱小;擺臭架子。—*v.i.* ①起皺。②生氣。③飄盪。④欺凌弱小; 擺臭架子。 —*n.* ①皺摺;皺紋。②鑲於衣邊的摺邊。③滋擾;煩亂。④忙亂。without *ruffle.* 不慌不忙。⑤漣漪;微波。⑥振羽。

ruf·fle[2] *n., v.,* **-fled, -fling.** —*n.* 連續的低聲敲鼓(檢閱時或喪葬中用之)。—*v.t.* & *v.i.* 連續地低敲(鼓)。

ruf·fly [ˈrʌflɪ; ˈrʌfli] *adj.* 有皺摺的。

ru·fous [ˈrufəs; ˈru:fəs] *adj.* ①發紅色的;赤褐色的。②面色紅潤的。

Ru·fus [ˈrufəs; ˈru:fəs] *n.* 男子名。

*__rug__ [rʌg; rʌg] *n., v.,* **rugged, rug·ging.** —*n.* ①地毯。②厚毯。 ***cut a rug***〖美俚〗輕快地跳舞;跳搖滾舞。***pull the rug from under*** 破壞…之計畫。—*v.t.* 以厚毯包。

Rug·by [ˈrʌgbɪ; ˈrʌgbi] *n.* ①英國中部 Warwickshire 之一城市。②該地之一著名男校。③(亦作 **Rugby football**) 橄欖球戲(爲美式橄欖球之濫觴)。—**Rug·bei·an,** *adj., n.*〖注意〗橄欖球在美國稱爲 football 或American football, 在英國稱爲 Rugby 或 Rugby football; 足球在美國稱爲 soccer, 在英國稱爲 football 或 association football.

rug-cut·ter [ˈrʌgˌkʌtɚ; ˈrʌgˌkʌtə] *n.* 跳搖滾舞者。

*__rug·ged__ [ˈrʌgɪd; ˈrʌgid] *adj.* ①崎嶇的;不平坦的。*rugged* face. 多皺紋的面孔。②〖美〗強壯的;強健的。③狂暴的;粗野的。*rugged* weather. 狂暴的天氣。④艱苦的。⑤忠誠、坦直而嚴厲的(人)。⑥不雅的;粗陋的。⑦刺耳的。—**ly,** *adv.* —**ness,** *n.*

Rug·ger [ˈrʌgɚ; ˈrʌgə] *n.*〖英俚〗橄欖球戲(=Rugby football). (亦作 **rugger**)

ru·gose [ˈrugos; ˈru:gous] *adj.*①有皺紋的;多皺紋的;脊形的。②〖植物〗支葉脈凹進而其間葉面突起的; 起皺痕的 (葉)。(亦作 **rugous**) —**ly,** *adv.* —**ru·gos·i·ty,** *n.*

Ruhr [rur; ruə] *n.* ①魯爾河 (德國西部一河名)。②魯爾(沿魯爾河之礦業及工業區)。

‡**ru·in** [ˈruɪn, ˈrɪuɪn; ruin, ˈru:in] *n.* ①滅亡; 毀滅; 破壞; 推翻。 the *ruin* of one's hopes. 希望之毀滅。②頹廢;傾覆。 a house gone to *ruin.* 頹塌之房屋。③衰敗的原因。Gambling was his *ruin.* 賭博是使他衰敗之原因。④(*pl.*)廢墟。The building is in *ruins.* 那建築物已成廢墟。⑤破產。⑥(婦女之)失去貞操。⑦害。—*v.t.* ①使滅亡;破壞。You will *ruin* your prospects. 你將毀滅你的前途。②使破產。—*v.i.* 衰敗; 毀滅。 —**a·ble,** *adj.* —**er,** *n.*

ru·in·a·tion [ˌruɪnˈeʃən; ruiˈneiʃən] *n.* ①滅亡;破壞;頹廢。②滅亡之原因。

ru·ined [ˈruɪnd; ruind] *adj.* ①受破壞的; 被毀滅的;荒廢的。②衰退的。

ru·in·ous [ˈruɪnəs; ˈruinəs] *adj.* ①毀壞的; 毀滅的。 ②招致毀滅的。 ③廢墟的。—**ly,** *adv.* —**ness,** *n.*

‡**rule** [rul; ru:l] *n., v.,* **ruled, rul·ing.** —*n.* ①規則; 法規。to break a *rule.* 違犯規則。②法院的命令;法令。③教會中的教規;

教條。④章程。standing *rule*. 章程；規章。⑤統治；管理。⑥慣例；經常發生之事。⑦米突尺；尺。carpenter's *rule*. 曲尺。slide *rule*. 計算尺。***as a rule*** 照例地；通常地。***out of rule*** 與習俗相反。—*v.t.*①規定；裁決。②統治；管理。Don't be *ruled* by your passions. 不要受你情感的控制。③畫線於。④畫界；以線分隔。⑤畫(線)。—*v.i.* ①統治；管理；裁判。The court will *rule* on the matter. 此事將由法庭裁決。②(價格等)保持某種程度或比率。***ruled paper*** 有橫格的紙。***rule off*** **a.** 劃線隔開。**b.** 不准參加比賽。***rule out*** **a.** 以尺劃線。**b.** 拒絕承認；消滅；排除。***rule (something) out*** **a.** 拒絕考慮某事；宣判某事爲違法。**b.** 排除(某物)。**c.** 使爲不可能。***rule the roast*** (or ***roost***) 當領袖。

rule·book 〔ˈrulˌbuk; ˈruːlbuk〕 *n.* 規則手冊。(亦作 **rule book**)

rule joint 肘狀接合裝置(可隨意伸直「折合)。

rule·less 〔ˈrullɪs; ˈruːllis〕 *adj.* 無規則的；不法的。

rule of law 法治。

rule of thumb 根據經驗(而非根據理論)的規則；粗略而實際的處事方法。(亦作 **rule o'thumb**)

***rul·er** 〔ˈrulɚ; ˈruːlə〕 *n.* ①統治者。②尺；米突尺。

rul·er·ship 〔ˈrulɚˌʃɪp; ˈruːləʃip〕 *n.* 「統治者的地位及職權。

rul·ing** 〔ˈrulɪŋ; ˈruːliŋ〕 *n.* ①統治；管理。②法院之裁判。③以尺劃線。④以尺所劃之線。⑤以尺衡量。—*adj.* ①管理的；統治的。the *ruling* race (class). 統治民族(階級)。the *ruling* party. 執政黨。②主要的。the *ruling* passion. 主要的情緒(支配行爲者)。③流行的。the *ruling* price. 時價。④劃線用的。ruling gradient*** 制限傾斜度。

rum¹ 〔rʌm; rʌm〕 *n.* ①蘭酒(由甘蔗或糖蜜製成的甜酒)。②酒。***rum runner*** 非法輸入酒之人或船。—*adj.* 【英俚】可笑的；奇異的。a *rum* customer. 奇怪的人(或動物)。

rum² *n.* 一種紙牌戲(=rummy²)。

Ru·ma·ni·a 〔ruˈmenɪə; ruːˈmeinjə〕 *n.* 羅馬尼亞(南歐國家，首都爲布加勒斯特 Bucharest).

Ru·ma·ni·an 〔ruˈmenɪən; ruːˈmeiniən〕 *adj.* 羅馬尼亞的；羅馬尼亞人的；羅馬尼亞語的。—*n.* ①羅馬尼亞人。②羅馬尼亞語。

rum·ba 〔ˈrʌmbə; ˈrʌmbə〕 *n.* ①侖巴舞。②侖巴舞曲。—*v.i.* 跳侖巴舞。

***rum·ble** 〔ˈrʌmbl̩; ˈrʌmbl〕 *v.*, **-bled, -bling,** *n.* —*v.i.* ①發隆隆聲；發轆轆聲。The thunder *rumbles*. 雷聲隆隆。②隆隆地進行；帶轆轆聲進行。③帶隆隆聲說話。④鬧；爲患。—*v.t.* ①使發隆隆聲；使隆隆地進行。②以隆隆聲說出。—*n.* ①隆隆聲；轆轆聲。②汽車或馬車後部之車座或裝行李處。a *rumble* seat. 汽車或馬車後部之座位。③【俚】街上打鬥。

rum·ble-tum·ble 〔ˈrʌmbl̩ˈtʌmbl̩; ˈrʌmblˈtʌmbl〕 *n.* ①走動時發出轆轆聲的車輛。②轆轆搖動；搖晃。

rum·bly 〔ˈrʌmblɪ; ˈrʌmbli〕 *adj.* ①使發隆隆聲的；崎嶇不平的(道路)。②隆隆作響的(車、輪、雷等)。

rum·bus·tious 〔rʌmˈbʌstʃəs; rʌmˈbʌstʃəs〕 *adj.* 【俗】喧鬧的；難馴的。

ru·men 〔ˈrumɪn; ˈruːmən〕 *n.*, *pl.* **-mi·na** 〔-mɪnə; -minə〕. 瘤胃(反芻動物之第一胃)。

ru·mi·nant 〔ˈrumənənt; ˈruːminənt〕 *n.* 反芻類動物(如牛、羊、鹿等)。—*adj.* ①反芻的；反芻動物的。②沉思的。—**ly,** *adv.*

ru·mi·nate 〔ˈruməˌnet; ˈruːmineit〕 *v.t.* & *v.i.*, **-nat·ed, -nat·ing.** ①反芻。②再嚼。③沉思。—**ru·mi·na·tive,** *adj.*

ru·mi·na·tion 〔ˌruməˈneʃən; ˌruːmiˈneiʃən〕 *n.* ①反芻。②沉思。

rum·ly 〔ˈrʌmlɪ; ˈrʌmli〕 *adv.* = **rummily.**

rum·mage 〔ˈrʌmɪdʒ; ˈrʌmidʒ〕 *v.*, **rum·maged, rum·mag·ing,** *n.* —*v.i.* & *v.t.* ①翻尋。②搜檢。***rummage out*** (or ***up***) 搜尋出。—*n.* ①搜尋。②搜尋出來的東西。③零星雜物。④義賣。

rummage sale ①義賣。②出清存貨的大拍賣；倉庫中無人提取之物品的拍賣。

rum·mer 〔ˈrʌmɚ; ˈrʌmə〕 *n.* ①大酒杯。②一杯酒或其他液體。

rum·mi·ly 〔ˈrʌmɪlɪ; ˈrʌmili〕 *adv.* 【俚】「奇妙地；古怪地。

rum·my¹ 〔ˈrʌmɪ; ˈrʌmi〕 *adj.*, **-mi·er, -mi·est,** *n.*, *pl.* **-mies.** —*adj.* ①像甜酒的；甜的。②因醉而無力的。—*n.* 【俚】醉漢。

rum·my² *adj.*, **-mi·er, -mi·est,** *n.*, *pl.* **-mies.** —*adj.* 【英俚】古怪的；奇異的。—*n.* ①一種紙牌戲。②【英俚】古怪的人(輕蔑語)。

***ru·mo(u)r** 〔ˈrumɚ; ˈruːmə〕 *n.* 謠言；傳說；流言。*Rumors* have it that there will be a change in the Cabinet. 謠傳內閣將改組。—*v.t.* 謠傳；傳聞。It is *rumored* that there will be a holiday tomorrow. 謠傳明天放假。—**er,** *n.* —**ous,** *adj.*

ru·mor·mon·ger 〔ˈrumɚˌmʌŋgɚ; ˈruːməmʌŋgə〕 *n.* 造謠者；傳布謠言者。

rump 〔rʌmp; rʌmp〕 *n.* ①(動物之)臀部。②牛之臀肉。③最後的不重要部分；渣滓；剩餘的一羣。—*adj.* 小的；不重要的；次等的。

rum·ple 〔ˈrʌmpl̩; ˈrʌmpl〕 *v.*, **-pled, -pling,** *n.* —*v.t.* & *v.i.* 使皺；起皺。—*n.*縐紋；縐摺。

rum·pus 〔ˈrʌmpəs; ˈrʌmpəs〕 *n.* 【俗】喧鬧；騷擾。***rumpus room*** 休憩室。

rum·run·ner 〔ˈrʌmˌrʌnɚ; ˈrʌmˌrʌnə〕 *n.* 【美】祕密輸入私酒者；偷運私酒入境的走私船。

‡run 〔rʌn; rʌn〕 *v.*, **ran, run, run·ning,** *n.*, *adj.* —*v.i.* ①跑；奔。She *ran* to meet me. 她跑來迎接我。②逃。He had to *run* for his life. 他不得不逃命。③行；進行；行駛。This train *runs* to Tainan. 這班火車開往臺南。④爬；攀登。Vines *run* along the sides of the road. 葛藤蔓生在道路兩旁。⑤(機器等)轉動。The machine won't *run* properly. 那機器轉動不靈。⑥伸展；伸延。The road *runs* across a plain. 此路穿過一平原。⑦延續；延長；繼續。a lease to *run* two years. 一項兩年有效的租約。⑧流。Blood *ran* in torrents. 血流如泉湧。⑨成爲；變爲。His blood *ran* cold. 他嚇得血都涼了。I have *run* short of money. 我沒有錢了。⑩發散；散播。⑪流逝。Time *runs*. 時間流逝。⑫有某種性質、形式、大小等。These potatoes *ran* large. 這些馬鈴薯很大。⑬發生；感到。A thought *ran* through my mind. 一個意念閃過我的腦際。⑭【美】競選。⑮輕快地移動；撫。⑯脫針；抽絲。Silk stockings often *run*. 絲襪常抽絲。⑰說；敍述。So the story (letter) *runs*. 這故事(信上)這樣說。⑱通用；有效。The law does not *run* here.此項法律在此地無效。⑲(戲劇等)連續上演；(書等)續版；(物價)續漲。The play *ran* for six months. 那個戲劇連演六個月。⑳表現；寫出。How does the first verse *run?* 第一節詩如何寫

的? ㉑融化; 變爲液體。The butter *ran*. 奶油融化了。㉒傳播。The news of his promotion *ran* all over town. 他獲得晉陞的消息傳遍全城。㉓一再出現; 連續重現。㉔延續到某種長度。㉕朝某一個方向延伸。This road *runs* north to Keelung. 這條道路朝北通達基隆。㉖向人求助。㉗作非正式拜訪;在某地作短暫停留。I'll *run* over to see you after dinner. 晚餐後我將來看你。㉘參加比賽;獲得名次。The horse *ran* second. 那匹馬在比賽中獲得第二名。—*v.t.*①使跑;開(車)進。They *ran* the car into the garage. 他們將車駛入汽車間。②使插入;使刺入。③使遭受。to *run* a risk. 冒險。④經營;管理。⑤穿過;衝過。⑥追溯;溯源。⑦傳說。The story *runs* that school will close early today. 傳說今天要提早放學。⑧使流入。⑨追趕。⑩〖美〗登載於報紙。He *ran* an ad in the evening paper. 他在晚報上登了一個廣告。⑪鎔鑄。⑫推舉;舉出。We *run* him for the Senate. 我們推舉他競選參議員。⑬將(馬)報名參加比賽。⑭與…比賽。I will *run* you a mile. 我將和你作一英里賽跑。⑮在表面上畫(線)。⑯走私;偷運。⑰携帶; 運送。⑱流着。The streets *ran* blood. 血流滿街。⑲使迅速經過。She *ran* her eyes over the old notes. 她將舊筆記匆匆閱過。 ***cut and run*** 逃脫。***run about*** 到處亂跑;自由自在地跑着玩。***run across*** 偶遇。***run after*** 追;追逐。The policeman was *running after* the thief. 警察在追賊。***run against*** **a.** 撞及。**b.** 偶遇。**c.** 對…不利。***run along*** 走;出發。***run around*** 在外尋歡;有外遇。***run around with*** 交遊;結交。***run at*** **a.** 向…跑去。**b.** 攻擊。***run a temperature*** 發高燒;發燒。***run away*** 逃走; 離家。***run away with*** **a.** 偸;挾…而逃。**b.** 同…私奔。**c.** 匆匆接受;不加考慮而接受。**d.** 失去控制。**e.** 用盡(錢等)。**f.** 在…方面做得遠較別人爲佳。***run*** (***a person*** or ***thing***) ***close*** (在競跑中)幾乎追上某人;幾乎相等。 ***run down*** **a.** 停止。**b.** 誹謗。**c.** 搜捕。**d.** 撞倒。**e.** 毀壞; 疲倦。**f.** 尋找後而發現。 ***run errands*** 供差遣。***run for it*** 逃走;逃往安全地點。***run foul of*** **a.** 撞及。**b.** 違反。***run in*** **a.** 作非正式訪問。**b.** 投入獄中。 ***run into*** **a.** 陷入。**b.** 偶遇。**c.** 到達。**d.** 會合; 合併。**e.** 撞及;撞到。***run in with*** 接近;靠近。***run off*** **a.** 逃跑。**b.** 使流出。**c.** 出版;印出。**d.** 如流水般寫出或背出。**e.**決定;獲勝。***run on*** **a.**〖印刷〗字與字或行與行接排;連起。**b.** 繼續行動;繼續談論。**c.** 關於;涉及。**d.** 在正文末附加。***run out*** **a.** 用盡;結束。**b.** 伸出;突出。**c.** (繩子) 抽出; 拉出。**c.** 逐出。***run out of*** 耗盡。***run out on*** 背棄;未予支持。***run over*** **a.** 輾過; 壓過。**b.** 複習;覆查。**c.** 超過。**d.** 溢出; 流出(容器)。**e.** 很快地讀一遍。***run ragged*** 折磨;使筋疲力竭。***run short*** (東西)缺乏。***run short of***(人)缺乏(東西)。***run the gauntlet*** 受嚴厲批評。***run the show*** 〖俚〗稱霸; 逞威; 作威作福。 ***run the streets*** 做流浪兒。 ***run through*** **a.** 浪費;濫用。**b.** 複習;預演。**c.** 刺入;貫穿。**d.** 畫線將(字)刪掉。***run to*** **a.** 約有;到達。**b.** 有足够金錢或能力以做。***run to earth*** 歸根究底地找出。***run up*** **a.** 升起(旗)。**b.** 匆匆蓋起。**c.** 加起(許多數字)。**d.** 增加。**e.** 迅速地縫。**f.** (在拍賣時)追使(對方)出高價。***run up against*** 遭遇。***run upon*** **a.** 撞及。**b.** 連續不斷地說。**c.** 偶然發現。 ***run wild*** **a.** 無控制; 亂鬧。**b.** 亂長。**c.** 荒廢。

—*n.* ①跑; 賽跑。a five-mile *run*. 五英里賽跑。②進行;趨向。③旅行;旅程。a *run* to Paris. 去巴黎旅行。④(壘球、板球比賽中之)分數單位。⑤連續。a *run* of bad luck. 一連串惡運。⑥繼續演出;連演。⑦擠兌。There was a *run* on the bank. 銀行發生擠兌。⑧種類;階級;普通人。the common *run*. 老百姓。⑨自由使用。to let a person have his *run*. 讓某人自由去做。⑩獸羣; 魚羣。a *run* of salmon. 一羣鮭魚。⑪(供動物用之)圍場。a cattle *run*. 牧場。⑫絲襪上脫針之處。⑬猛跌。Prices came down with a *run*. 價格猛跌。⑭(工廠中的機器)動作時間;此時間內之出產量。⑮(汁液)流出;流出之量。⑯水流;小溪。⑰私貨之上岸。⑱〖音樂〗急奏。⑲擁擠。⑳力氣。㉑足跡。㉒斜道。㉓野獸常走之小徑。㉔槽;水管。㉕大量而持續的需求、銷售等。a *run* on umbrellas during the rainy season. 雨季中對傘的大量需求。㉖普通或典型的種類。㉗受大衆歡迎的一段時間。***a run for one's money*** **a.** 激烈的競爭。**b.** 付出代價後獲得的滿足或利益。 ***at a run*** 跑。***in the long run*** 終久。***in the short run*** 暫時; 目前。***on the*** (or ***a***) ***dead run*** 全速進行。 ***on the run*** **a.** 逃跑。**b.** 紛忙;忙碌。**c.** 在奔跑中; 匆忙地。**d.** 逃避警察追捕。***the runs***〖俚〗瀉肚。—***adj.*** ①融化的。*run* butter. 融化的奶油。②鑄造的。③走私的。*run* diamonds. 走私的鑽石。

run·a·bout 〔ˈrʌnəˌbaut; ˈrʌnəbaut〕 *n.* ①游蕩者。②小型單座敞篷馬車或汽車。③小型摩托船。④幼童。

run·a·gate 〔ˈrʌnəˌget; ˈrʌnəgeit〕 *n.* ①逃亡者。②流浪者。③變節者;背教者。

run-a·round 〔ˈrʌnəˌraund; ˈrʌnəraund〕 *n.* 〖俚〗一連串的藉口;遁詞。②〖印刷〗在一圖畫周圍用較狹之段欄的排字法。③〖俚〗(圍繞指甲而不傷及骨的)瘭疽。④繞過障礙物之道路、小路等。⑤刨刀所刨旋的一圈。⑥〖採礦〗豎坑柱上挖的通徑。(亦作 **runround**)

run·a·way 〔ˈrʌnəˌwe; ˈrʌnəwei〕 *n.* ①逃亡者; 亡命之徒。②脫韁之馬。③逃亡; 私奔。④美國公司在海外拍攝的電影。—***adj.*** ①逃亡的; 私逃的。②容易獲得的。③由私逃者做的。a *runaway* marriage. 私奔結婚。④輕易獲勝的。⑤迅速升高的; 迅速增加的。*runaway* inflation. 急速增加的通貨膨脹。⑥美國公司在海外拍攝之電影的。

runaway ship 在外國登記或懸掛外國旗幟的美國商船。

run·ci·ble spoon 〔ˈrʌnsəbl̩~;ˈrʌnsəbl~〕一種有三個闊尖頭的叉子。

run·ci·nate 〔ˈrʌnsɪnɪt; ˈrʌnsinit〕 *adj.* 〖植物〗鋸齒狀的; 有下向裂片的。

run-down 〔ˈrʌnˈdaun; ˈrʌndaun〕 *adj.* ①疲憊的;健康不佳的。②敗壞的;破爛的。③(鐘錶等)因未上緊發條而停止的。—*n.* ①〖棒球〗刺殺出局。②口述大要。③逐項核對、檢查或報告。④減少;衰退。 〔=**run-down.**〕

run·down 〔ˈrʌnˈdaun; ˈrʌndaun〕 *n.*

rune 〔run; ruːn〕 *n.* ①古北歐之文字;前種文字之記述。②神祕之文字或記號。③芬蘭詩篇。 ④古斯堪的那維亞 (Scandinavian) 詩。⑤〖詩〗詩歌。

rung¹ 〔rʌŋ; rʌŋ〕 *v.* pp. of **ring.**

rung² *n.* ①椅子的四條腿之間的横撐; 梯級。②車軸。③階級;級位。—**less,** ***adj.***

ru·nic 〔ˈrunɪk; ˈruːnik〕 *adj.* ①古北歐文字的。②有古北歐風的(詩)。③古北歐人之紀念碑、金屬製品等上之交叉花紋的。④用

rune 文字之古北歐人的。—*n.* ①古北歐文字刻的碑文。②〖印刷〗一種用做裝飾的活字。

run-in 〔ˈrʌnˌɪn; ˈrʌnˈin〕 *n.* ①(文稿中)插入部分(尤指不另起一段的)。②爭吵。—*adj.* 〖印刷〗加入正文而不必另起一段的。

run·less 〔ˈrʌnlɪs; ˈrʌnlis〕 *adj.* 〖棒球〗無得分的。

run·let[1] 〔ˈrʌnlɪt; ˈrʌnlit〕 *n.* =**runnel.**

run·let[2] *n.* 〖古〗小罈(酒等的桶)。

run·na·ble 〔ˈrʌnəbḷ; ˈrʌnəbl〕 *adj.* 可追捕的;可獵取的。

run·nel 〔ˈrʌnḷ; ˈrʌnl〕 *n.* 小河;細流;小水路。

***run·ner** 〔ˈrʌnɚ; ˈrʌnə〕 *n.* ①奔跑者。②(橇之)滑行部分;溜冰鞋之滑刀。③信差。④管機器者。⑤走私者。⑥長條布、毯、花邊等。a *runner* of carpet in the hall. 大廳中之長條地毯。⑦〖植物〗纖匐枝;蔓。⑧糾纏處。⑨〖棒球〗跑壘員。⑩(亦作**runner bean**)扁豆類之豆。⑪跑腿者。⑫融解之金屬從鍋爐倒進模型中時所經之槽。⑬兩爿磨石中之轉動的一爿磨石。⑭襪子上脫線之處。⑮裝有滑輪以移液狀物之架。⑯戲院兩翼中減低舞臺以外雜音之地毯。

run·ner-up 〔ˈrʌnɚˈʌp; ˈrʌnərˈʌp〕 *n., pl.* **run·ners-up.** ①競賽中之第二名;亞軍。②(*pl.*)比賽中冠軍以下之優勝者(如前三名,前五名或前十名之內者)。

run·ning** 〔ˈrʌnɪŋ; ˈrʌniŋ〕 *n.* ①跑;流。②液狀物之流出。a *running* of the nose in a cold. 着涼時流鼻涕。③力氣;衝動。④管理;管理的責任。⑤跑道之情況;跑道之好壞。be in* (*out of*) *the running*** 有(無)獲勝機會。***make the running*** 先跑;率先。***out of the running*** **a.** 未參加比賽。**b.** 不在競賽中的前幾名內。***take up the running*** 領導;率先。—*adj.* ①連接的;連續的。I've won three times *running.* 我連勝三次。②草書體的。a *running* hand. 草書體。③流膿的(傷口)。④流動的。⑤液體的;溶解的。⑥重複的。a *running* pattern. 一再重複的花樣。⑦跑的;奔跑的。a *running* race. 賽跑。⑧匍匐的(植物)。⑨流行的;現在的;當時的。a *running* rumor through the town. 傳遍滿城的謠言。the *running* month. 本月;當月。⑩運轉的;開動着的(機器)。⑪以直線量的。⑫跑着做的。a *running* jump. 連跑帶跳。⑬易滑動的;易滑的。—*adv.* 連續地。They won the championship 3 years *running.* 他們連續地保持冠軍有三年之久。

running board (汽車兩旁下部的)踏腳板。

running dog 走狗;跟班。

running expenses 經常開支。

running gear ①任何機器的運動部分。②車輛的輪、軸、附件等(別於車身)。

running head (or **title**) 每頁頁首之標題。

running knot 可以隨繩牽引而收緊的活結。

running light 飛機或船隻夜航時經常開著的燈光。

run·ning·ly 〔ˈrʌnɪŋlɪ; ˈrʌniŋli〕 *adv.* 奔跑地;流動地;迅速地。

running mate ①在賽馬時,屬於同一主人,用以定步調之馬。②競選夥伴(如副總統候選人)。③〖俗〗常被看見同另一人在一起者。

running shed 〖英〗〖鐵路〗圓形機車車房。

running shooting 對急動目標之射擊。

running start ①〖運動〗需要跑步之開始(如跳遠、跳高等)。②任何事業開始時所占之便宜或上風。

running story ①分期刊登的故事。②分段發排的新聞稿。

running water ①流水。②由水管流出的水;自來水。

run·ny 〔ˈrʌnɪ; ˈrʌni〕 *adj.* ①過於鬆軟的;水分過多的。②流鼻涕的。

run-off 〔ˈrʌnˌɔf; ˈrʌnˈɔːf〕 *n.* ①流走之物(如雨水被土地吸收後,其餘流走之量)。②最後的決賽(如分數相同而舉行者)。③(初賽中獲得勝利者參加的)決賽。④在製造過程中排出之廢物。

run-of-mill 〔ˈrʌnəvˈmɪl; ˈrʌnəvˈmil〕 *adj.* 普通的;平庸的。(亦作**run-of-the-mill**)

run-of-mine 〔ˈrʌnəvˈmaɪn; ˈrʌnəvˈmain〕 *adj.* 平庸的(=run-of-mill).(亦作 **run-of-the-mine**)

run-of-pa·per 〔ˈrʌnəvˈpepɚ; ˈrʌnəvˈpeipə〕 *adj.* 可登在版面上任何位置的。

run-of-riv·er 〔ˈrʌnəvˈrɪvɚ; ˈrʌnəvˈrivə〕 *adj.* 利用河川天然動力的。

run-on 〔ˈrʌnˌɑn; ˈrʌnɔn〕 *adj.* ①〖印刷〗連續接排的。②衍生的;加添的。—*n.* 連續接排的印刷物;加添之物。

run·out 〔ˈrʌnˌaut; ˈrʌnaut〕 *n.* ①〖板球〗刺殺。②背棄;遺棄;逃避。

run-o·ver 〔ˈrʌnˈovɚ; ˈrʌnˈouvə〕 *adj.* 超出有限篇幅的。

run·o·ver 〔ˈrʌnˌovɚ; ˈrʌnˌouvə〕 *n.* (報上文章)轉續另一版之部分。

run·proof 〔ˈrʌnˌpruf; ˈrʌnpruːf〕 *adj.* ①不綻線的;不抽紗的(如襪)。②(顏色)下水不會化開的。

runt 〔rʌnt; rʌnt〕 *n.* ①小種的牛。②矮小的人、畜或植物。③動物一胎中之最小者。④〖英俗〗老牛。⑤〖英俗〗老嫗。⑥〖英俗〗老樹殘株。—**ish,** *adj.*

run-through 〔ˈrʌnˌθru; ˈrʌnθruː〕 *n.* ①概要;大綱。②預演。

runt·y 〔ˈrʌntɪ; ˈrʌnti〕 *adj.,* **runt·i·er, runt·i·est.** 矮小的。—**runt·i·ness,** *n.*

run-up 〔ˈrʌnˌʌp; ˈrʌnʌp〕 *n.* ①(價錢之)抬高。②將引擎加速使熱或供檢查。③跳遠者之跑向起跳線。④〖英〗前奏;醞釀時期。

run·way 〔ˈrʌnˌwe; ˈrʌnwei〕 *n.* ①跑道。②鹿或其他動物踏出的小徑。③獸苑;供家禽或家畜活動的場地。④飛機跑道。⑤河牀。⑥將保齡球送回球道頂端之槽。⑦夜總會、戲院等之伸展臺;突出之表演臺。

ru·pee 〔ruˈpi; ruːˈpiː〕 *n.* 盧比(印度及巴基斯坦錢幣單位,縮寫作 R., r., Re.)。

Ru·pert 〔ˈrupɚt; ˈruːpət〕 *n.* 男子名。

ru·pi·ah 〔ruˈpiə; ruːˈpiːə〕 *n.* 印尼之貨幣單位。

rup·ture 〔ˈrʌptʃɚ; ˈrʌptʃə〕 *v.,* **-tured, -tur·ing,** *n.* —*v.i. & v.t.* ①破裂。A blood vessel *ruptured.* 血管破裂。②斷絕;決裂。③〖醫〗脫出。—*n.* ①破裂。②絕交。③〖醫〗(腸)脫出。—**rup·tur·a·ble,** *adj.*

***ru·ral** 〔ˈrurəl; ˈruərəl〕 *adj.* ①鄉村的;農村的。②有關農業的。—*n.* 鄉下人。—**ly,** *adv.*

rural free delivery 鄉村地區郵件的免費遞送。

ru·ral·ism 〔ˈrurəlˌɪzəm; ˈruərəlizm〕 *n.* ①田園風味。②農村習用語。

ru·ral·ist 〔ˈrurəlɪst; ˈruərəlist〕 *n.* ①田園生活者;提倡田園生活者。②精通農事者。

ru·ral·i·ty 〔ruˈrælətɪ; ruəˈræliti〕 *n., pl.* **-ties.** 田園生活;田園風景;田園風味。

ru·ral·ize 〔ˈrurəlˌaɪz; ˈruərəlaiz〕 *v.,* **-ized, -iz·ing.** —*v.t.* 田園化;農村化。—*v.i.* 鄉居;過田園生活。

rural sociology 農村社會學。

rur·ban [ˈrʌrbən; ˈrʌbən] *adj.* 近都市農村的。
Rus. ①Russia. ②Russian.
ruse [ruz; ruːz] *n.* 策略;計謀;詐術。
ru·sé [ˈruze; ˈruːzei] 〖法〗 *adj.* 狡猾的;有計謀的。
:rush¹ [rʌʃ; rʌʃ] *v.i.* ①衝進。They *rushed* out of the room. 他們從屋裏衝出去。②急進;急促行事。Don't *rush* through your work. 不要匆促趕完你的工作。to *rush* into print. 匆匆付印。③急流。Tears *rushed* to her eyes. 淚水湧入她的眼睛。④〖橄欖球〗帶球衝向敵線。—*v.t.* ①使急進;猛攻;猛衝。Fresh troops were *rushed* up to the front. 新軍被急急調赴前線。②急促運送;匆促進行。③向…索高價。How much did they *rush* you for this? 他們對這件東西向你要多少錢? ④撲向;衝入。They *rushed* the enemy. 他們向敵人猛攻。⑤向…求寵;向…獻慇懃。⑥以晚會或同樂會等予以招待以便爭取爲(大學姊妹會或兄弟會之)會員。—*n.* ①衝進;突進;激流。②匆促;匆忙。I don't like the *rush* of modern life. 我不喜歡熙熙攘攘之近代生活。③搶購;追求某目標的熱潮。the Christmas *rush*. 耶誕季的搶購。a gold *rush*. 淘金潮。④〖美〗兩組學生間的競技。⑤〖橄欖球〗企圖帶球衝入敵線內。⑥慇懃;特別的關心。He seems to be giving her quite a *rush*. 他似乎對她予以特別的關心。⑦〖電影〗尚未經過剪輯的鏡頭。***at a rush*** 迅速地;很快地。***with a rush*** 突然地;匆匆地。—*adj.* ①緊急的;急迫的。②熙熙攘攘的;擁擠的。—**er,** *n.*
rush² *n.* ①燈心草。②無價值的東西。not worth a *rush*. 毫無價值。—**like,** *adj.*
rush candle 燈心草蠟燭。
rush·ee [rʌʃˈi; rʌˈʃiː] *n.* 被大學姊妹會或兄弟會爭取爲會員的新生。
rush hour (早晚之)交通擁擠時間。
rush·ing [ˈrʌʃɪŋ; ˈrʌʃiŋ] *adj.* ①急奔的;急流的。②興隆的。—*n.* 大學姊妹會或兄弟會爲爭取會員而舉行的活動。—**ly,** *adv.*
rush·light [ˈrʌʃˌlaɪt; ˈrʌʃlait] *n.* ①燈心草蠟燭。②不受重視的人。(亦作 **rush light**)
rush line 〖橄欖球〗前鋒線。
rush·work [ˈrʌʃˌwɜk; ˈrʌʃwəːk] *n.* 以燈心草爲材料的編織手工。
rush·y [ˈrʌʃɪ; ˈrʌʃi] *adj.,* **rush·i·er, rush·i·est.** ①燈心草製成的。②多燈心草的。③似燈心草的。
rus in ur·be [ˈrʌs ɪnˈɜbi; ˈrʌs in ˈəːbi] 〖拉〗都市中的田園;田園都市。
rusk [rʌsk; rʌsk] *n.* 乾麪包;餅乾。
Rus·kin [ˈrʌskɪn; ˈrʌskin] *n.* 羅斯金 (John, 1819–1900, 英國散文家、批評家及社會改革者)。—**i·an,** *adj.*
Russ [rʌs; rʌs] *n., pl.* **Russ,** or **Russ·es.** 俄國人;俄國語。—*adj.* 俄國的;俄國人的;俄語的。
Russ. ①Russia. ②Russian.
Rus·sell [ˈrʌsl; ˈrʌsl] *n.* 羅素 (Bertrand Arthur William, 1872–1970, 英國數學家及哲學家)。—**i·an,** *adj.*
rus·set [ˈrʌsɪt; ˈrʌsit] *n.* ①赤褐色。②赤褐色粗布。③一種皮色粗而駁雜之多季蘋果。—*adj.* ①赤褐色的。②褐色粗布製的。—*v.t.* & *v.i.* (使)帶赤褐色。—**ish,** *adj.*
rus·set·y [ˈrʌsɪtɪ; ˈrʌsiti] *adj.* 枯葉色的;赤褐色的。
·Rus·sia [ˈrʌʃə; ˈrʌʃə] *n.* 俄羅斯;蘇聯。
·Russia leather 俄國皮革(一種精細光滑的皮革,常染製成深紅色)。(亦作 **russia**)
·Rus·sian [ˈrʌʃən; ˈrʌʃən] *adj.* 俄國的;俄國人的;俄國語的。—*n.* ①俄國人。②俄語。
Russian Church (1918年前的)俄國國教(爲希臘正教之一支)。
Russian dressing 一種濃烈的調味品(用蛋黃醬加切碎之醃菜、辣椒醬及西班牙甘椒調成者)。
Rus·sian·ism [ˈrʌʃənˌɪzəm; ˈrʌʃənizm] *n.* 俄國特色;俄國風格;俄國精神。
Rus·sian·ize [ˈrʌʃənˌaɪz; ˈrʌʃənaiz] *v.t.,* **-ized, -iz·ing.** 俄國化;使有俄國風格。—**Rus·sian·i·za·tion,** *n.*
Russian roulette 一種危險而賭運氣的遊戲(參加者輪流持祇裝一顆子彈的左輪手槍,先將彈膛旋轉,然後以槍口指向自己頭部並扣扳機)。
Russian Soviet Federated Socialist Republic 俄羅斯社會主義聯邦蘇維埃共和國(爲蘇聯中最大之共和國,占全面積四分之三,首都莫斯科 Moscow; 簡稱蘇俄 Soviet Russia)。
Russian wolfhound 一種俄國種「獵犬」。
Rus·sism [ˈrʌsɪzəm; ˈrʌsizm] *n.* 俄語化的辭句。
Russo- 〖字首〗表"俄國"之義 (如: *Russo*-「Japanese 日俄的)。
Rus·so·phile [ˈrʌsəˌfaɪl; ˈrʌsəfail] *adj.* 親俄國的。—*n.* 親俄者。
Rus·so·phobe [ˈrʌsəˌfob; ˈrʌsəfoub] *n.* 懼俄者;恨俄者。
Rus·so·pho·bi·a [ˌrʌsəˈfobɪə; ˌrʌsəˈfoubjə] *n.* 恐俄或恨俄症。
·rust [rʌst; rʌst] *n.* ①銹。to gather *rust*. 生銹。②陳腐;荒廢;不活動;懶惰。a life of *rust*. 懶惰的生活。③〖植物〗銹菌;銹病。④紅褐色。—*v.i.* ①生銹。Don't let your machines *rust*. 不要使你的機器生銹。②陳舊;朽腐。③〖植物〗生銹病。④變成紅褐色。The leaves slowly *rust*. 樹葉慢慢變成紅褐色。—*v.t.* ①使銹;荒廢。②使變成紅褐色。***rust together*** 使兩塊金屬或鐵管之接頭處生銹以連接之。—*adj.* 銹色的;紅褐色的。
rust·a·ble [ˈrʌstəbl; ˈrʌstibl] *adj.* 會生銹的。
·rus·tic [ˈrʌstɪk; ˈrʌstik] *adj.* ①鄉村的;農村的。*rustic* charm. 鄉村的美色。②單純的;質樸的;樸素的。*rustic* simplicity. 質樸。③粗野的;不雅觀的;鄉土氣的。*rustic* dress. 粗俗的衣服。④用帶皮的樹枝做的。⑤表面粗糙的。—*n.* 鄉下人;粗野之人。
rus·ti·cal·ly [ˈrʌstɪklɪ; ˈrʌstikli] *adv.* ①粗野地;鄉土氣地。②質樸地;樸素地。
rus·ti·cate [ˈrʌstɪˌket; ˈrʌstikeit] *v.,* **-cat·ed, -cat·ing.** —*v.i.* ①去鄉村。②暫居鄉村;過鄉間生活。—*v.t.* ①送往鄉村;使定居鄉村。②使田園化;使質樸;使粗俗。③〖英〗勒令停學做爲處罰。④粗略地完成(磚造物等)。—**rus·ti·ca·tion, rus·ti·ca·tor,** *n.*
rus·ti·cism [ˈrʌstəˌsɪzəm; ˈrʌstisizm] *n.* 鄉下人特有的措辭或舉止。
rus·tic·i·ty [rʌsˈtɪsətɪ; rʌsˈtisiti] *n., pl.* **-ties.** ①田園風格;田園風味;田園生活。②粗俗。③質樸;率直。
rus·ti·cize [ˈrʌstəˌsaɪz; ˈrʌstisaiz] *v.t.,* **-cized, -ciz·ing.** 使鄉下化。
rust·i·ly [ˈrʌstɪlɪ; ˈrʌstili] *adv.* ①銹蝕地。②(因久不用而)生疏地。
rust·i·ness [ˈrʌstɪnɪs; ˈrʌstinis] *n.* ①生銹。②荒廢;荒疏。③陳腐;褪色。
·rus·tle [ˈrʌsl; ˈrʌsl] *n., v.,* **-tled, -tling.** —*n.* 風吹樹葉之沙沙聲;沙沙聲。—*v.i.* ①發

沙沙聲。Leaves *rustled* in the breeze. 樹葉在風中發沙沙聲。②穿着發出沙沙聲的衣服。③〖俗〗奮力工作。—*v.t.* ①使發沙沙聲。The wind *rustled* the leaves. 風吹樹葉發出沙沙之聲。②〖俗〗奮力地作；奮力而得到。③〖俗〗偷家畜。**rustle up** 費力尋找、湊集。

rus·tler ['rʌslɚ; 'rʌslə] *n.* 〖美俗〗①偷牛賊。②富有活力而好動的人。③發出沙沙聲之物。

rust·less ['rʌstlɪs; 'rʌstlis] *adj.* ①不生銹的。②無銹的。

rust·proof ['rʌst,pruf; 'rʌstpru:f] *adj.* 防銹的;不銹的。*rustproof* steel. 不銹鋼。—*v.t.* (亦作**rust-proof**)加以防銹處理。

rust·y**[1] ['rʌstɪ; 'rʌsti] *adj.*, **rust·i·er, rust·i·est.** ①生銹的。②陳腐的;(學問、技術等)荒疏的; 荒廢的。He is getting *rusty.* 他漸漸落伍了。③褪色的(指黑色衣服)。④〖植物〗生葉澀病的。⑤紅褐色的。The leaves were turning *rusty.* 樹葉正在變成紅褐色。turn rusty*** 發脾氣。

rust·y[2] *adj.*, **rust·i·er, rust·i·est.** 倔強的; 執拗的。***ride*** (or ***run***) ***rusty*** 行動固執或令人不悅。

rut[1] [rʌt; rʌt] *n., v.,* **rut·ted, rut·ting.** —*n.* ①轍跡。②常規。③凹痕。***get into a rut*** 墨守成規。***go on in the same old rut*** 總是作同一件事。***move in a rut*** 按常規從事; 因襲成規。—*v.t.* ①留轍跡於。②使生凹痕。

rut[2] *n., v.,* **rut·ted, rut·ting.** —*n.* 雄鹿、羊等之周期性的春情發動;春情發動期。—*v.i.* 春情發動。

ru·ta·ba·ga [,rutə'begə; ,ru:tə'beigə] *n.* 〖植物〗蕓薹。

Ruth [ruθ; ru:θ] *n.* ①女子名。②舊約路得記。③舊約路得記中之女子。

ruth [ruθ; ru:θ] *n.* 〖古〗憐憫;慈悲。

ru·the·ni·um [ru'θinɪəm; ru:'θiniəm] *n.* 〖化〗釕(一種金屬元素,符號 Ru)。

Ruth·er·ford ['rʌðɚfɚd; 'rʌðəfəd] *n.* 拉塞福 (Ernest, 1871–1937, 生於 New Zealand 的英國化學家及物理學家,曾獲1908年諾貝爾化學獎)。

Rutherford scattering 〖物理〗拉塞福散射。

ruth·ful ['ruθfʊl; 'ru:θful] *adj.* ①充滿憐憫心的。②哀傷的;悲傷的。—**ly,** *adv.*

***ruth·less** ['ruθlɪs; 'ru:θlis] *adj.* 無情的;殘忍的。—**ly,** *adv.* —**ness,** *n.*

ru·ti·lant ['rutələnt; 'ru:tilənt] *adj.* 發光的;閃爍的。

ru·tile ['rutil, -taɪl; 'ru:ti:l, -tail] *n.* 〖礦〗金紅石。

ru·tin ['rutɪn; 'ru:tin] *n.* 芸香苷; 路丁(一種治出血的藥)。

rut·ted ['rʌtɪd; 'rʌtid] *adj.* 多車轍的。

rut·tish ['rʌtɪʃ; 'rʌtiʃ] *adj.* 淫亂的; 好色的。

rut·ty ['rʌtɪ; 'rʌti] *adj.*, **rut·ti·er, rut·ti·est.** ①多車轍的道路。② =**ruttish.**

RV, R.V. Revised Version of the Bible. **R.V.S.V.P.** (亦作 **rvsvp, r.v.s.v.p.**) Répondez vite s'il vous plait. (法 =Please reply at once.) 請速答覆。 **RW** radiological warfare. **RW., rw.** railway. **R/W** right of way. **R.W.** ①Right Worshipful. ②Right Worthy.

Rwan·da [ru'ɑndə; ru'ɑ:ndə] *n.* 盧安達(中非一共和國,首都吉佳利 Kigali)。

R.W.S. Royal Society of Painters in Watercolours. **Rwy., rwy.** railway.

Rx ['ɑr'eks; 'ɑ:'reks] *n., pl.* **Rx's.** ①處方。②任何補救辦法; 行動; 解決方法。③〖處方〗服用。④幾十個盧比。

Ry. Railway.

-ry 〖字尾〗①表"狀況;執業;行業"等抽象名詞之字尾, 如: husbandry, dentistry. ②表"集合稱"之名詞之字尾, 如: tenantry, jewelry. ③裸麥麪。④裸麥酒。

***rye** [raɪ; rai] *n.* ①裸麥;黑麥。②裸麥粒。

rye grass 一種牧草。

ry·ot ['raɪət; 'raiət] *n.* 〖英印〗農夫;佃農。

R.Y.S. Royal Yacht Squadron.

Ryu·kyu ['rju'kju; 'rju:'kju:] *n.* 琉球。

Ryu·kyu·an ['rju'kjuən; 'rju:'kju:ən] *n.* ①琉球民族。②琉球人。

S

S or s [ɛs; es] *n., pl.* **S's or s's.** ①英文字母之第十九個字母。②S形之物。 —*adj.* S 形的。

S [ɛs; es] *n.* 中世紀羅馬數字中之7 或 70。

S 化學元素 sulfur 之符號。

S. ①south. ②southern. ③Saint. ④School. ⑤Saturday. ⑥Sunday. ⑦September.

s. ①shilling (*or* shillings). ② son. ③ second(*or* seconds). ④singular. ⑤south.

-s 〖字尾〗①加於名詞表示複數。②加於動詞表示第三人稱單數現在式。

-'s ①加於名詞之後表示所有格。②〖俗〗has, is, us 等之縮寫。③us 在 let 後之縮寫。

SA ①storm troops. ②surface-to-air.

Sa 化學元素 samarium 之符號。 **Sa.** Saturday. **S.A.** ①Salvation Army. ②South Africa. ③ South America. ④ South Australia. **s.a.** ①secundum artem(拉=according to art). ②sine anno (拉 =without year or date). ③ subject to approval. ④ semiannual. ⑤ small arms. ⑥sex appeal. **Saam** small arms ammunition. 輕武器彈藥。

Saa·ve·dra La·mas [sɑ'veðrɑ'lɑmɑs; sɑ:'veiðrɑ:'lɑ:mɑ:s] 薩維妓拉(Carlos, 1880–1959, 阿根廷律師及外交家,曾獲1936年諾貝爾和平獎)。

SAB 〖美〗Science Advisory Board. 科學顧問委員會。**Sab.** Sabbath.

Sa·bae·an [sə'biən; sə'bi:ən] *adj., n.* =**Sabean.**

Sa·ba·ism ['sebɪɪzəm; 'seibiizm] *n.* 星辰崇拜;拜星。—**Sa·ba·ist,** *n.*

Sab·a·oth ['sæbɪ,ɑθ; sæ'beiɔθ] *n.* 〖聖經〗軍隊;萬軍。***the Lord of Sabaoth*** 上帝。

Sab·ba·tar·i·an [,sæbə'tɛrɪən; ,sæbə'tɛəriən] *adj.* 安息日的; 守安息日的。—*n.* ①守安息日 (星期六)的人。②嚴守星期日爲安息日的人。—**ism,** *n.*

Sab·bath** ['sæbəθ; 'sæbəθ] *n.* ①安息日(基督徒以星期日爲安息日,猶太人以星期六爲安息日)。②(s-) 休息、寧靜的日子。 the *sabbath* of the tomb. 長眠之安息。 ***a witches' Sabbath 女巫子夜之集會。 ***keep the Sabbath*** 守安息日(在安息日休息)。***the great Sabbath*** 復活節之前一日。—*adj.*安息日的。***Sabbath day*** 安息日。—**less,** *adj.*

Sab·bath-break·er ['sæbəθ,brekɚ;

ˈsæbəθˌbreikə〕*n.* 不守安息日的人。

sab·bat·ic〔səˈbætɪk; səˈbætik〕*adj.*, *n.* =**sabbatical.**

sab·bat·i·cal〔səˈbætɪkl; səˈbætikl〕*adj.* ①(S-) 安息日的。②安息的;休息的;安寧的。—*n.*(大學給予教師每七年一次之)休假年。(亦作 **sabbatic**)　「**year**②.」

sabbatical leave = **sabbatical**

sabbatical year ①安息年(猶太人每七年中停止耕作及釋放債務人之一年)。②(大學教師之)休假年。　「破壞工作者。」

sab-cat〔ˈsæbˌkæt; ˈsæbkæt〕*n.* 從事

Sa·be·an〔səˈbiən; səˈbiːən〕*adj.* 希巴(古義大利山地一民族 Saba) 的; 希巴人的; 希巴語的。—*n.* 希巴人;希巴語。

sa·ber〔ˈsebɚ; ˈseibə〕*n.*(騎兵所用的)軍刀。 ***saber jet*** 軍刀機(F-86型噴射機)。—*v.t.* 以軍刀砍傷或斬殺。　「脅。」

saber rattling 以炫耀軍力而作的威

sa·ber-toothed〔ˈsebɚˌtuθt; ˈseibətuːθt〕*adj.* 有軍刀形(長而銳利)的上犬齒的。

saber-toothed tiger 劍齒虎(一種古生物)。　「nizm〕*n.* 拜星教。」

Sa·bi·an·ism〔ˈsebɪənɪzəm; ˈseibiə-

Sa·bine〔ˈsebaɪn; ˈseibain〕*n.* 古義大利中部 Apennines 山脈中居住的一民族, 紀元前 290 年爲羅馬所征服。—*adj.* 該民族的。

Sa·bin vaccine〔ˈsebɪn~; ˈseibin~〕沙賓疫苗(防治小兒痲痺疫苗, 爲 Albert B. Sabin 所發明, 故名)。

sa·ble〔ˈsebḷ; ˈseibl〕*n.* ①黑貂。②黑貂皮。③黑色。④黑貂皮大衣。⑤(*pl.*)喪服。—*adj.* ①黑貂皮製成的。②黑色的。

S

sa·ble·fish〔ˈsebḷˌfɪʃ; ˈseiblfiʃ〕*n.*, *pl.* **-fish·es, -fish.** 北太平洋產的一種大黑魚。

sab·ot〔ˈsæbo; ˈsæbou〕*n.* ①歐洲農民所穿的一種木鞋。②粗革面之木底鞋。③狀似此種木鞋之小艇。④〖軍〗彈底板。

sab·o·tage〔ˈsæbəˌtɑʒ; ˈsæbətɑːʒ〕*n.*, *v.*, **-taged, -tag·ing.** —*n.* ①破壞行動(工人於勞資糾紛中所從事之毀壞機器、浪費材料及怠工等)。②任何惡意之破壞。—*v.t.* 破壞;故意損壞。

sab·o·teur〔ˌsæbəˈtɝ; ˌsæbəˈtəː〕*n.* 從事破壞工作。　「生的人。」

sa·bra〔ˈsɑbrə; ˈsɑːbrə〕*n.* 在以色列出

sa·bre〔ˈsebɚ; ˈseibə〕*n.*, *v.*, **-bred, -bring.**〖英〗=**saber.**

sa·bre·tache〔ˈsebɚˌtæʃ; ˈsæbətæʃ〕*n.* 騎兵所佩戴之佩囊。

sa·breur〔saˈbrœr; saˈbrœr〕〖法〗*n.* ①佩軍刀者。②以軍刀擊劍者。　「强烈炸藥。」

sab·u·lite〔ˈsæbjuˌlaɪt; ˈsæbjulait〕*n.*

sab·u·lous〔ˈsæbjələs; ˈsæbjuləs〕*adj.* ①多砂的;砂狀的; 像砂的。②〖醫〗多沉渣的(尿)。　「mand.」

SAC, S.A.C. Strategic Air Com-

Sac〔sæk, sɔk; sæk, sɔːk〕*n.*, *pl.* **Sacs, Sac.** 北美印第安人之一族;此族人。(亦作 **Sauk**)

sac〔sæk; sæk〕*n.*(動、植物組織中之)囊;液囊。　「的;有囊的。」

sac·cate〔ˈsæket; ˈsækeit〕*adj.* 囊狀

sac·cha·rate〔ˈsækəˌret; ˈsækəreit〕*n.*〖化〗糖酸鹽。

sac·char·ic〔səˈkærɪk; səˈkærik〕*adj.* 糖的;含有糖的。***saccharic acid*** 糖酸。

sac·cha·ride〔ˈsækəˌraɪd; ˈsækəraid〕*n.*〖化〗糖類。②糖酸鹽。

sac·cha·rif·er·ous〔ˌsækəˈrɪfərəs; ˌsækəˈrifərəs〕*adj.* 含糖的;產糖的。

sac·char·i·fy〔səˈkærəˌfaɪ; səˈkærifai〕*v.t.*, **-fied, -fy·ing.**(以化學方法)糖化;製成糖。

sac·cha·rim·e·ter〔ˌsækəˈrɪmətɚ; ˌsækəˈrimitə〕*n.*〖化〗糖量計。

sac·cha·rin〔ˈsækərɪn; ˈsækərin〕*n.* 糖精;沙卡林。

sac·cha·rin·at·ed〔ˈsækərəˌnetɪd; ˈsækərineitid〕*adj.* 有糖精的;含有糖精的。

sac·cha·rine〔*adj.* ˈsækəˌraɪn; ˈsækərain *n.* ˈsækərɪn; ˈsækərin〕*adj.* ①糖的; 含有糖分的。②十分甜蜜的。③過甜的。④含糖的;可製糖的。—*n.* =**saccharin.**

sac·cha·roid〔ˈsækəˌrɔɪd; ˈsækərɔid〕*adj.*〖地質〗結構似糖狀的(岩石)。(亦作 **saccharoidal**)

sac·cha·rom·e·ter〔ˌsækəˈrɑmətə; ˌsækəˈrɔmitə〕*n.* 糖量計;驗酵管。

sac·cha·rose〔ˈsækəˌros; ˈsækərous〕*n.*〖化〗蔗糖。　「fɔːm〕*adj.* 囊狀的。」

sac·ci·form〔ˈsæksəˌfɔrm; ˈsæksi-

sac·cu·late〔ˈsækjuˌlet; ˈsækjuleit〕*adj.* 小囊形成的;分裂成小囊的。

sac·cu·la·tion〔ˌsækjəˈleʃən; ˌsækjuˈleiʃən〕*n.* ①分裂成小囊。②囊狀組織。

sac·cu·lus〔ˈsækjuləs; ˈsækjuləs〕*n.*, *pl.* **-li**〔-ˌlaɪ; -lai〕. ①小囊。②〖解剖〗(內耳中的)球狀囊。

sac·er·do·tal〔ˌsæsɚˈdotḷ; ˌsæsəˈdoutl〕*adj.* ①僧侶的;祭司的。②尊重僧權的。—**ly,** *adv.*

sac·er·do·tal·ism〔ˌsæsɚˈdotḷɪzəm; ˌsæsəˈdoutəlizm〕*n.* ①祭司制度;僧侶氣質。②僧侶之方術、策略等(通常含敵對之意)。

sac fungus 子囊菌類。

sa·chem〔ˈsetʃəm; ˈseitʃəm〕*n.* ①北美印第安人之酋長; 印第安人聯盟之領袖。②紐約市 Tammany Society 的幹事。③大人物。 —**ic,** *adj.* —**dom,** —**ship,** *n.*

sa·chet〔sæˈʃe; ˈsæʃei〕*n.* ①香囊(置於衣櫃、抽屜等中)。②(裝於上述香囊中之)香粉。③〖英〗(裝細巧物品如手帕等之)小袋。

sack**[1]〔sæk; sæk〕*n.* ①粗布袋; 牛皮紙袋;囊; 包。②一袋(之量); 一包(之量)。two *sacks* of candy. 兩包糖果。③(類似布袋裝之)寬鬆外衣。④〖古〗女人鬆大的袍子。⑤〖英俚〗解雇;革職。get the sack*** 被解雇。***give*** (***one***) ***the sack*** 解雇(某人)。***hit the sack***〖俚〗上牀睡覺。***hold the sack*** **a.** 被迫擔負全責。**b.** 兩手空空; 一無所獲。—*v.t.* ①置於囊中。②〖俚〗解雇。③獲得; 贏得。***sack in*** (or ***out***)〖俚〗上床睡覺。

sack[2] *v.t.* 刼掠;掠奪。—*n.* 刼掠;掠奪。

sack[3] 十六、十七世紀流行於英國的西班牙之一種白葡萄酒。

sack·but〔ˈsækˌbʌt; ˈsækbʌt〕*n.* ①中世紀時之一種管樂器(形似喇叭)。②(聖經但尼爾書 Daniel中)一種形似七弦琴之弦樂器。

sack·cloth〔ˈsækˌklɔθ; ˈsækklɔθ〕*n.* ①麻袋布;粗麻布。②懺悔服。***in sackcloth and ashes*** 懺悔;悲苦。

sack coat 男用之寬短上衣。

sack dress 布袋裝(寬鬆直線條女裝)。

sack·er〔ˈsækɚ; ˈsækə〕*n.* ①掠奪者;刼掠者。②製囊者;製袋者;裝袋者。③〖棒球〗壘手(=baseman).

sack·et〔ˈsækət; ˈsækit〕*n.* 小袋。

sack·ful〔ˈsækˌfʊl; ˈsækful〕*n.* ①一袋之量;一袋。②大量。

sack·ing〔ˈsækɪŋ; ˈsækiŋ〕*n.* 麻袋布。

sack·less ['sæklɪs; 'sæklis] *adj.* 〖蘇〗①沒精打采的。②頭腦衰弱的;愚鈍的。
sack race 把兩腿或頸部以下之身體套入袋內之競走。
sac·like ['sæk,laɪk; 'sæklaik] *adj.* 囊狀的。
sacque [sæk; sæk] *n.* 婦孺等穿的一種寬而短的外衣。
sacr- 〖字首〗表"神聖"之義。
sa·cra ['sekrə; 'seikrə] *n.* pl. of sacrum.
sa·cral[1] ['sekrəl; 'seikrəl] *adj.* 〖解剖〗薦骨的。—*n.* 薦椎骨。
sa·cral[2] *adj.* 聖禮的;聖事的。
sa·cral·ize ['sækrəl,aɪz; 'sækrəlaiz] *v.t.*, **-ized, -iz·ing.** 使神聖。
sac·ra·ment ['sækrəmənt; 'sækrəmənt] *n.* ①(基督教會之)聖禮; 聖事。②(常 S-) 聖體;聖餐;聖餐之麪包或麪包與酒。③神聖之事物。④記號;表徵。⑤誓言;誓約。
sac·ra·men·tal [,sækrə'mɛntl; ,sækrə'mentl] *adj.* ①聖禮的;聖事的;聖餐的。②重視聖禮的。③表徵的。④特殊神聖的。⑤莊重如聖禮的。 —*n.* 天主教會所創類似聖事之禮儀或事物(如十字架、用聖水等)。
sac·ra·men·tal·ism [,sækrə'mɛntl,ɪzəm; ,sækrə'mentəlizm] *n.* 重視聖餐的教義。 —**sac·ra·men·tal·ist,** *n.*
sac·ra·men·tar·i·an [,sækrəmɛn'tɛrɪən; ,sækrəmen'teəriən] *n.* ①(S-)主張聖餐中麪包與酒祇是一種象徵, 而非基督眞正之血肉的新教神學家。②主張重視聖餐論者。—*adj.* ①(S-) 上述之神學家的。 ②聖禮的。
Sac·ra·men·to [,sækrə'mɛnto; ,sækrə'mentou] *n.* ①薩克拉曼多 (美國 California 州之首府)。②薩克拉曼多河(自Califorina 北部流入San Francisco 灣)。
*__sa·cred__ ['sekrɪd; 'seikrid] *adj.* ①神聖的;宗教上的; 屬於或奉獻予上帝的。 *sacred* music. 聖樂。*sacred* number. 宗教上視爲神聖之數(如七)。②受崇敬的; 不可侵犯的。*sacred* oaths. 不可違背之誓言。③奉獻的;獻給…的。
sacred book (任何宗教之)聖經。
Sacred College 羅馬天主教樞機主教之集合稱。(亦作 **College of Cardinals**)
sacred cow 神聖不可侵犯的人或物。
‡**sac·ri·fice** ['sækrə,faɪs, -,faɪz; 'sækrifais] *n., v.,* **-ficed, -fic·ing.** —*n.* ①供奉;獻祭;祭祀。②祭品; 犧牲。③犧牲的行爲; 獻身。 Parents often make *sacrifices* in order to educate their children. 父母常爲教育子女而犧牲自己。④損失; 虧本出售。 to sell a house at a *sacrifice*. 虧本出售房屋。⑤〖棒球〗犧牲打。 ***the great*** (or ***last***) ***sacrifice*** 爲祖國戰死。 —*v.t. & v.i.* ①供奉;獻祭;祭祀。②犧牲。 to *sacrifice* lives for the sake of freedom. 爲自由犧牲生命。 ③賤賣。 The owner *sacrificed* his house. 屋主將其房屋予以賤賣。④〖棒球〗犧牲打以使(跑壘者)進壘。 —**sac·ri·fic·er,** *n.*
sacrifice bunt 〖棒球〗犧牲短打。
sacrifice fly 〖棒球〗犧牲長打(常指使在三壘之跑壘員能得分者)。
sacrifice hit 〖棒球〗犧牲打。
sac·ri·fi·cial [,sækrə'fɪʃəl; ,sækri'fiʃəl] *adj.* 犧牲的;祭祀的;獻祭的;供奉的。 —**ly,** *adv.*
sacrificial lamb 被犧牲之人或物。
sac·ri·lege ['sækrəlɪdʒ; 'sækrilidʒ] *n.* ①褻瀆神聖; 瀆聖之事。②褻瀆聖物;竊取聖物;褻瀆聖地(之罪)。
sac·ri·le·gious [,sækrɪ'lɪdʒəs; ,sækri'lidʒəs] *adj.* 褻瀆聖物的;褻瀆神聖的; 盜竊聖物的。 —**ly,** *adv.* —**ness,** *n.*
sac·ri·le·gist [,sækrə'lidʒɪst; ,sækri'li:dʒist] *n.* 瀆神者;褻瀆聖物者。
sa·cring ['sekrɪŋ; 'seikriŋ] *n.* 〖古〗聖餐用之麪包與酒之被祝聖。
sacring bell 聖餐祝聖時所響之鈴。
sa·crist ['sekrɪst; 'seikrist] *n.* 聖器監護者。
sac·ris·tan ['sækrɪstən; 'sækristən] *n.* =sacrist.
sac·ris·ty ['sækrɪstɪ; 'sækristi] *n., pl.* **-ties.** 聖器收藏室。
sacro- 〖字首〗①表"神聖"之義。②表"薦骨"之義。
sac·ro·sanct ['sækro,sæŋkt; 'sækrousæŋkt] *adj.* 神聖不可侵犯的。—**i·ty,** *n.*
sa·crum ['sekrəm; 'seikrəm] *n., pl.* **sa·cra, sa·crums.** 〖解剖〗薦骨。
‡**sad** [sæd; sæd] *adj.,* **sad·der, sad·dest.** ①悲哀的;憂愁的。a *sad* countenance. 愁容。②使人悲哀的;悽慘的。*sad* news. 噩耗。③暗色的;黑的。④非常壞的。 a *sad* mess. 一團糟。He is a *sad* coward. 他是個無恥的懦夫。 ⑤〖方〗(麪包等) 發酵不充分的。***a sadder and wiser man*** 經歷坎坷而變爲明智之人。***a sad dog*** 一個大流氓。
sad·den ['sædn̩; 'sædn] *v.t.* 使悲哀;使悲傷。②使帶暗色。 —*v.i.* 悲哀; 悲傷。 —**ing·ly,** *adv.*
sad·dish ['sædɪʃ; 'sædiʃ] *adj.* 稍微悲哀的;稍微可悲的。
*__sad·dle__ ['sædl̩; 'sædl] *n., v.,* **-dled, -dling,** *adj.* —*n.* ①鞍;鞍座。 ②(腳踏車等的)車座。③鞍狀物。④兩山峯間的凹下部分; 鞍部。⑤(羊等的) 帶脊骨之腰肉。 ***in the saddle*** **a.** 乘馬的。**b.** 在位的;在職的。***put the saddle on the right*** (or ***wrong***) ***horse*** 責備得(不)當。 —*v.t.* ①套以馬鞍。②使負擔。He was *saddled* with heavy debts. 他負著很重的債。③(爲使參加賽馬而)訓練(馬)。—*v.i.* 套馬鞍。—*adj.* ①在馬上用的。②因騎馬所引起的。③騎馬的。
sad·dle·back ['sædl̩,bæk; 'sædlbæk] *n.* ①鞍狀峯。②背部呈鞍狀之動物。
sad·dle-backed ['sædl̩,bækt; 'sædlbækt] *adj.* ①鞍狀的。②背部如鞍狀的。
sad·dle·bag ['sædl̩,bæg; 'sædlbæg] *n.* 鞍囊;旅囊。
sad·dle·bow ['sædl̩,bo; 'sædlbou] *n.* 鞍之前穹。
sad·dle·cloth ['sædl̩,klɔθ; 'sædlklɔθ] *n.* 鞍褥。
saddle girth 馬之腹帶。
saddle horse 乘用之馬;鞍馬。
saddle iron 馬鐙。
saddle nose 鼻梁下陷之扁塌鼻。
saddle pin 腳踏車車座下之栓。
sad·dler ['sædlɚ; 'sædlə] *n.* 製造、出售或修理馬鞍、馬具的人。
saddle roof 〖建築〗鞍狀屋頂。
sad·dler·y ['sædlərɪ; 'sædləri] *n., pl.* **-ries.** ①馬具。②出售馬具的店。③馬具業;馬具製造術。
saddle shoe 鞋面中部顏色不同之運動鞋或便鞋。
sad·dle·tree ['sædl̩,tri; 'sædltri:] *n.* ①鞍架。②〖美〗〖植物〗百合木。
Sad·du·ce·an [,sædʒʊ'siən; ,sædju'si:ən] *adj.* 撒都該教信徒的;撒都該教教義的。
Sad·du·cee ['sædʒə,si; 'sædjusi:] *n.* 撒都該(Zadok)派信徒(猶太教之一派,不信死後之生命及天使之存在);撒都該人。—**ism,** *n.*
sa·dhu ['sɑdu; 'sɑ:du:] *n.*〖印度教〗聖人。
Sad·ie ['sedɪ; 'seidi] *n.* 女子名, 爲 Sarah

之暱稱。 「熨斗。」
sad·i·ron ['sæd,aɪən; 'sæd,aiən] *n.*
sa·dism ['sædɪzəm, 'sedɪzəm;'sædizm, 'seid-]*n.*〖精神病學〗①性虐待狂。②虐待狂。
sad·ist ['sædɪst; 'sædist] *n.* 性虐待狂者;虐待狂者。 「性虐待狂的;虐待狂的。」
sa·dis·tic [sæ'dɪstɪk; sæ'distik] *adj.*
***sad·ly** ['sædlɪ; 'sædli] *adv.* ①悲慘地;可悲地; 傷心地。 He stood *sadly* beside the grave. 他傷心地站在墓旁。②非常地。③〖古〗堅强地;堅決地。④嚴肅地。⑤安靜地。⑥著黑色地。 *sadly* dressed. 著黑色衣服。 —*adj.* 身體不適的; 健康不佳的。 to feel *sadly.* 感覺不適。
***sad·ness** ['sædnɪs; 'sædnis] *n.* ①悲傷;悲慘。②令人悲傷之事物;悲慘的事物。
sa·do·mas·och·ism [,sædo'mæsəkɪzəm, ,se-; ,sædou'mæsəkizəm, ,sei-] *n.* 施虐受虐狂(虐待狂與被虐待狂混合之心理病態)。 **—sa·do·mas·och·ist,** *n.* **—sa·do·mas·och·is·tic,** *adj.* 「的人。」
sad sack 〖美俚〗不中用的士兵;不中用
SAE, S.A.E. Society of Automotive Engineers.
saf. safety.
sa·fa·ri [sə'farɪ; sə'fa:ri] *n.* ①(在非洲東部之)狩獵旅行;狩獵遠征隊。②任何遠征或探險。③一日的行程。—*v.i.* 參加狩獵遠征。
‡safe [sef; seif] *adj.*, **saf·er, saf·est,** *n.*, *adv.* —*adj.* ①安全的;無危險的。Put them in a *safe* place. 把這些放在一個安全地方。②穩妥的;不致引起危險的。③可靠的;可信賴的。④必定。He is *safe* to win. 他一定獲勝。⑤不能爲害的。He is *safe* in jail. 他在獄中才不能爲害。⑥〖棒球〗安然上壘的;安打的。⑦(選區)不會被敵對黨派候選人贏去的。⑧不會出岔子的;不會錯的。***be on the safe side*** 萬無一失;妥加準備以防萬一。***safe and sound*** 平安無恙。—*n.* ①保險箱(櫃)。②冷藏櫃;冷藏室。a meat *safe.* 肉類冷藏櫃。③〖俚〗保險橡皮套(防花柳病傳染用者)。④接濕水之地。—*adv.*安全地;不冒險地。**—ness,** *n.*
safe·blow·er ['sef,bloə;'seif,blouə] *n.* 以炸藥炸開保險箱而搶扨的人。
safe·blow·ing ['sef,bloɪŋ;'seif,blouiŋ] *n.* 以炸藥炸開保險箱而搶扨。—*adj.* 用炸藥開保險箱的。
safe·break·er ['sef,brekə;'seif,breikə] *n.* 打開保險箱而搶扨之人。
safe-con·duct ['sef'kandʌkt; 'seif'kɔndəkt] *n.* ①安全通行證。②安全通行權。③護衞或護送持有通行證者之衞兵或衞隊。***under*** (***in*** or ***with***) ***safe-conduct*** 持有安全通行證; 享有安全通行權。—*v.t.* ①頒給安全通行證。②護送使通過敵區。
safe·crack·er ['sef,krækə;'seif,krækə] *n.* 打開保險箱而搶扨之人。
safe·crack·ing ['sef,krækɪŋ; 'seif,krækiŋ] *n.* 打開保險箱而搶扨。
safe-de·pos·it ['sefdɪ,pazɪt; 'seifdi,pɔzit] *adj.* 安全保管的。—*n.* 貴重物品保管處。 「(特指銀行地下室者)。」
safe-deposit box 安全庫;保險箱
***safe·guard** ['sef,gard; 'seifga:d] *v.t.* 保護;防護。—*n.* ①保護;防護。Clean food is a *safeguard* against disease. 清潔的食物是防止疾病的保障。②保護者;保鑣;護航。
safe hit 〖棒球〗安打。
safe·keep·ing ['sef'kipɪŋ; 'seif'ki:piŋ] *n.* 保護;保管。 「〖相〗暗室中之燈。」
safe·light ['sef,laɪt; 'seiflait] *n.* 〖照
***safe·ly** ['seflɪ; 'seifli] *adv.* 安全地;確切地。 「加…之安全度;減少…之危險性。」
saf·en ['sefən; 'seifən] *v.t.* 使安全;增
safe period 安全期(婦女受孕可能性極少之期間)。
safe-time ['sef,taɪm; 'seiftaim] *n.* 飛彈或火箭在飛行時彈頭不會引爆之安全時間。
‡safe·ty ['seftɪ; 'seifti] *n.* ①平安;安全;穩妥。*Safety* in aviation is improving. 航空的安全日益進步。a place of *safety.* 安全地點。②安全裝置; 安全瓣; 保險器。③〖棒球〗安打。④〖橄欖球〗球之置於本隊球門線後(如此對方可得兩分)。***in safety*** 安全;無恙。***play for safety*** 不冒險。—*adj.* 保障安全的;保險的。
safety belt ①(繫於飛機或汽車座位的)安全帶。②救生帶;浮袋(使人在水中不下沉)。
safety cage 礦坑中的安全升降機。
safety catch =**safety lock②.**
safety curtain 防火幕。
safe·ty-de·po·sit ['seftɪdɪ,pazɪt; 'seiftidi,pɔzit] *adj.* =**safe-deposit.**
safety factor 安全因素。(亦作 **factor of safety**)
safety film 安全膠片(影片用)。
safety fuse ①安全信管。②〖電〗保險絲。
safety glass安全玻璃。 「安全墨水。」
safe·ty-ink ['seftɪ,ɪŋk;'seiftiiŋk] *n.*
safety island (馬路上之)安全島。
safety lamp (礦坑用之)安全燈。
safety lock ①保險鎖。②(槍砲上之)保險機栓 (=safety catch).
safety match 安全火柴。
safety pin 安全別針。
safety razor 安全剃刀。
safety squeeze 〖棒球〗搶分近擊球(三壘上跑壘員等打擊手將球短打後才跑回本壘得分之打法)。(亦作 **squeeze play**)
safety switch 安全開關。
safety valve ①安全瓣。②使人消除怒氣、緊張等而不生危險之事物。
safety zone 安全地帶(指候車、過街等保護旅客、行人之指定區域)。
saf·flow·er ['sæ,flauə; 'sæflauə] *n.* 〖植物〗紅花;紅花染料。
safflower oil 紅花子油。
saf·fron ['sæfrən; 'sæfrən] *n.* ①〖植物〗番紅花。②(取自番紅花的)一種橘黃色染料(用於糖果、飲料等之着色及添加香味)。③橘黃色。—*adj.* 橘黃色的。—*v.t.* 以番紅花染料着色;以番紅精調味。
saffron yellow 橘黃色。
S. Afr. South Africa(n).
saf·ra·nine ['sæfrə,nin; 'sæfrəni:n] *n.* 番紅精。(亦作 **safranin**)
sag [sæg; sæg] *v.*, **sagged, sag·ging,** *n.* —*v.i.* ①壓陷;中間下墜。The roof is *sagging.* 房頂下陷了。②不整齊地下垂。③消沉。④跌價。⑤〖船〗漂離航線。—*n.* ①下陷處。②跌價。③精神消沉。
sa·ga ['sagə; 'sa:gə] *n.* ①古代北歐之英勇故事。②任何英勇冒險故事。
sa·ga·cious [sə'geʃəs; sə'geiʃəs] *adj.* ①睿智的;明敏的;精明的。②伶俐的(動物)。 —**ly,** *adv.* —**ness,** *n.*
sa·gac·i·ty [sə'gæsətɪ; sə'gæsiti] *n.*, *pl.* **-ties.** 睿智;明敏;精明。
sag·a·more ['sægə,mor; 'sægəmɔ:] *n.* 北美印第安人之酋長。
SAGE Semi-Automatic Ground En-

vironment.〖美〗半自動防空管制組織。

***sage** [sedʒ; seidʒ] *adj.*, **sag·er, sag·est,** *n.* —*adj.* ①賢明的;明智的。②嚴肅的。—*n.* 聖人;哲人。—**ly,** *adv.* —**ness,** *n.*

sage² *n.* ①〖植物〗鼠尾草屬植物(葉可作藥及調味)。②=**sagebrush.**

sage·brush ['sedʒ,brʌʃ; 'seidʒbrʌʃ] *n.* 山艾樹(產於美國西部的一種灰綠色灌木)。

sage cock sage grouse 之雄性。

sage green 灰綠色。

sage grouse 北美西部生長山艾之草原產的松鷄。

sage hen ①大松鷄。②雌性大松鷄。

Sage-King ['sedʒ'kɪŋ; 'seidʒ'kiŋ] *n.* 聖君(中國古代三皇五帝之任一)。

sag·gar ['sægɚ; 'sægə] *n.*, *v.* =**sagger.**

sag·ger ['sægɚ; 'sægə] *n.* ①火泥箱(用耐火泥製的一種容器,陶器入窰時裝入其內,可使質地精良)。②製火泥箱的耐火泥。—*v.t.* 裝入火泥箱烘燒。

Sa·ghal·ien [,sægə'lin; ,sægə'li:n] *n.* 庫頁島(=Sakhalin).

Sa·git·ta [sə'dʒɪtə; sə'dʒitə] *n.* ①〖天文〗矢星座(北天之一小星座)。②(s-)〖數學〗矢。③(s-)〖動物〗箭蟲。

Sag·it·tar·i·us [,sædʒɪ'tɛrɪəs; ,sædʒi'tɛəriəs] *n.* 〖天文〗人馬宮;射手座。

sag·it·tate ['sædʒɪ,tet; 'sædʒiteit] *adj.* 〖植物〗鏃狀的(葉)。

sa·go ['sego; 'seigou] *n.* 由 sago palm (西穀椰子)之莖髓所製成的食物;西米;西穀。

sa·gua·ro [sə'gwɑro; sə'gwɑ:rou] *n.* (美國南部及墨西哥所產之)一種仙人掌。(亦作 **sahuaro**)

Sa·har·a [sə'hɛrə, -'hɑrə; sə'hɑ:rə] *n.* ①撒哈拉(非洲北部的大沙漠)。②(s-)任何不毛之地或冷冷清清的情景。—**Sa·har·an,** *adj.*

sa·hib ['sɑ·ɪb, 'sɑhɪb; 'sɑ:hib] *n.* 先生;閣下;大人(印度人對歐洲人之尊稱)。

***said** [sɛd; sed] *v.* pt.& pp. of **say.**—*adj.* 上述的;該。the *said* witness. 該證人。

Sai·gon [saɪ'gɑn; sai'gɔn] *n.* 西貢(越南南部第一大都市)。

‡sail [sel; seil] *n.* ①帆。to hoist a *sail.* 揚帆。to lower a *sail.* 下帆。②帆狀物;用途如帆之物。③**a.** 帆船;船。**b.** 船隊;船團。a fleet of thirty *sail.* 三十艘船之艦隊。④航行;航程(不專指帆船而言)。It is ten days' *sail* from Shanghai. 此處距上海有十日之航程。***in*** (***under***) ***full sail*** 張滿帆。***in sail*** 在帆船上。***make sail*** **a.** 張帆。**b.** 在海上起程。***set sail*** 起航。***take in sail*** **a.** 減少或放低船帆。**b.** 減少活動;減低雄心。***take the wind out of a person's sails*** 使對方啞然無以對答。***under sail*** 張帆前進中。—*v.i.* ①(帆船)張帆而行;(汽船等)航行;起航。The ship *sails* for New York on Mondy. 該船於星期一駛往紐約。②(鳥、雲等)飛行於空中;平穩地行動。③駕駛船隻。④由海路起程。We *sail* at 2 p.m. 下午二時我們將起航。—*v.t.* ①航行;渡。②駕駛(船舶)。③使輕盈滑行或飛行。***sail in*** 懷有信心地開始做某事。***sail into*** 〖俗〗**a.** 熱心地做;努力做。**b.** 批評;斥責。**c.** 痛擊;攻擊。***sail near*** (or ***close***) ***to the wind*** 幾乎犯規;幾乎違法。

sail·boat ['sel,bot; 'seilbout] *n.* 帆船。

sail·cloth ['sel,klɔθ; 'seilklɔθ] *n.* 帆布。

sail·er ['selɚ; 'seilə] *n.* ①掛帆行駛的船;帆船。②快速之船。

sail·fish ['sel,fɪʃ; 'seilfiʃ] *n.*, *pl.* **-fish, -fish·es.** (有齒及極大脊鰭之)帆魚;旗魚。

sail·fly·ing ['sel,flaɪɪŋ; 'seil,flaiiŋ] *n.* 滑翔術。

sail·ing ['selɪŋ; 'seiliŋ] *n.* ①航海術;航海法。②航行;啓帆;出航;船期。③航行的情況。④船啓航時所載的客、貨。***plain sailing*** 順利。—*adj.* ①使用帆的。②有關船或航運的。

sailing day ①客輪的啓航日;開航日。②貨船收貨的截止日。

sailing directions 〖航海〗水路誌。

sailing master 航海官。

sailing orders (船長所下的)出航命令。

sailing ship 大帆船。

sail·less ['sellɪs; 'seillis] *adj.* 無帆的。

sail lizard 產於麻六甲羣島的一種大蜥蜴。

sail·mak·er ['sel,mekɚ; 'seil,meikə] *n.* ①縫帆工;製帆者。②〖美海軍〗帆纜軍士長。

‡sail·or ['selɚ; 'seilə] *n.* ①水手;船夫;船員;海員。②平頂硬草帽。(亦作 **sailor hat**) ***a bad*** (***good***) ***sailor*** (不)暈船的人。***talk sailor*** 說話時用航海術語。—*adj.*像水手用的。

sailor collar 水手領(領後部寬而方)。

sail·or·ing ['selərɪŋ; 'seiləriŋ] *n.* 水手生涯或職務。

sail·or·ly ['selɚlɪ; 'seiləli] *adj.* 似水手的;適於水手的。

sail·or·man ['selɚ,mæn; 'seiləmæn] *n.*, *pl.* **-men.** 水手。

sailor suit 男童之水手裝。

sail·plane ['sel,plen; 'seilplein] *n.*, *v.*, **-planed, -plan·ing.** —*n.* 輕滑翔機。—*v.i.* 駕輕滑翔機飛行。

sail room 船中的藏帆室。

sail·ship ['sel,ʃɪp; 'seilʃip] *n.* 帆船(=sailing ship).

sail yard 帆桁。

sain·foin ['senfɔɪn; 'sæn-fɔin] *n.* 〖植物〗紅豆草。

Saint [sent; seint] *n.* 聖(放在聖賢的姓名前,縮寫作 St., 複數之縮寫爲 SS. 或 Sts.). *Saint* Matthew. 聖馬太。〖注意〗英語用於姓名前無重音,讀作 [sənt, sɪnt; sənt, sint]; 現代美語, 不因上下文而異, 皆讀作 [sent; seint].

‡saint [sent; seint] *n.* ①聖徒;聖者。②聖人; 道德崇高之人。③已進天國之人; 死者。④天使。⑤聖徒之像。The *saint* was cast eighty-two years ago. 那聖徒像鑄造於82年前。—*v.t.* 列爲聖徒; 使成爲聖徒。—*v.i.* 過聖徒生活;行爲如聖徒。

Saint Agnes's Eve 聖艾格奈節前夕(爲一月二十日之夜,相傳少女於此時擧行某些儀式後,可見其未來丈夫之幻象)。

saint·ed ['sentɪd; 'seintid] *adj.* ①神聖的。②似聖徒的; 似聖者的。③升天國的。④被宣稱爲聖徒的。

saint·hood ['sent,hud; 'seinthud] *n.* ①聖徒的地位;品格。②聖徒(集合稱)。

saint·like ['sent,laɪk; 'seintlaik] *adj.* 爲聖徒的;適宜於聖者的。

saint·ly ['sentlɪ; 'seintli] *adj.*, **-li·er, -li·est.** ①似聖人的; 神聖的。②品德高尙的。—**saint·li·ly,** *adv.* —**saint·li·ness,** *n.*

saint's day 聖徒之紀念日。

saint·ship ['sent·ʃɪp; 'seint-ʃip] *n.* 聖徒之地位及品格。

Saint Valentine's Day 情人節(二月十四日,原爲紀念第三世紀殉敎聖徒 St. Valentine 者,情人多於是日互贈紀念物,但與 St. Valentine 無關)。

‡sake [sek; seik] *n.* 緣故;原因;關係;目的。She did it for her brother's *sake.* 她爲了她兄弟而做這事。***for God's*** (***goodness'***, ***Heaven's***, or ***mercy's***) ***sake*** 看在

上帝面上;千萬;務請。*For God's sake* don't fire that gun. 看在上帝面上,不要放那槍。***for old sake's sake***為了過去(或老朋友)的緣故。***for the sake of*** 為了;因為。We must be patient *for the sake of* peace. 為了和平,我們必須有耐心。

sa·ker 〔'sekə; 'seikə〕 *n.* 南歐產的一種大獵鷹。

Sa·kha·lin 〔ˌsækəˈlin; ˌsækəˈliːn〕 *n.* 庫頁島(在西伯利亞之東,日本之北,原以北緯50°為界,北屬俄國,南屬日本,1945年 Yalta 協定全歸蘇聯所有)。

Sa·kya·mu·ni 〔'sɑkjəˌmʊnɪ; 'sɑːkjəˌmuni〕 *n.* 釋迦牟尼。

Sal 〔sæl; sæl〕 *n.* Sarah 之暱稱。

sal[1] 〔sɑl; sɑːl〕 *n.* 〖植物〗婆羅雙樹。

sal[2] 〔sæl; sæl〕 *n.* 鹽(主要用於藥劑)。

sa·laam 〔səˈlɑm; səˈlɑːm〕 *n.* ①印度之額手鞠躬禮(以右手掌按於額部而行之深鞠躬禮)。—*v.t.* & *v.i.* 行額手鞠躬禮。②回教國家人民見面時歡迎詞,意為"和平"。

sal·a·bil·i·ty 〔ˌseləˈbɪlətɪ; ˌseiləˈbiliti〕 *n., pl.* **-ties.** ①可賣;易賣。②暢銷。(亦作 **saleability**)

sal·a·ble 〔'seləbl̩; 'seiləbl〕 *adj.* 可銷售的;適於銷售的;易賣的。(亦作 **saleable**) **—ness,** *n.* **—sal·a·bly,** *adv.*

sa·la·cious 〔səˈleʃəs; səˈleiʃəs〕 *adj.* ①好色的;淫蕩的。②(書籍、圖片等)猥褻的;淫穢的;黃色的。**—ness,** *n.* **—ly,** *adv.*

***sal·ad** 〔'sæləd; 'sæləd〕 *n.* ①沙拉;生菜食品;涼拌食品。②雜燴;混雜物。

salad bowl 沙拉碗(拌生菜用的碗)。

salad days 少不更事之時期。

salad dressing 生菜食品之調味汁。

salad fork 吃生菜食品或糕餅所用之短叉(有四寬叉齒)。

sal·ad·ing 〔'sælədɪŋ; 'sælədiŋ〕 *n.* 〖主英〗用於生菜食品的蔬菜。

salad oil 沙拉油(調製生菜用的上等橄欖油)。

salad plate ①沙拉盤(生菜盤)。②午餐食用之生菜。

sal·a·man·der 〔'sæləˌmændə; 'sæləˌmændə〕 *n.* ①〖動物〗鯢;蠑螈。②昔時被信為生活於火中之蜥蜴或其他爬蟲。③喜愛或能耐酷熱的人。④能耐火中高熱之器具(如火箸、烤板等)。⑤生活於火中之精靈。

sal·a·man·drine 〔ˌsæləˈmændrɪn; ˌsæləˈmændrin〕 *adj.* ①似蠑螈的;蠑螈的。②耐火的;耐熱的。—*n.* 能耐火耐熱的人或物。

sa·la·mi 〔səˈlɑmɪ; səˈlɑːmi〕 *n.* 義大利臘腸。

sal·an·gane 〔'sælənˌgæn; 'sæləngæn〕 *n.* 海燕(能造燕窩供食用者)。

sa·lar·i·at 〔səˈlɛrɪˌæt; səˈlɛəriæt〕 *n.* 薪水階級。

‡**sal·a·ry** 〔'sælərɪ; 'sæləri〕 *n., pl.* **-ries,** *v.,* **-ried, -ry·ing.** —*n.* 薪水;俸給。What is your *salary?* 你支薪若干? —*v.t.* 付薪水給…。**—sal·a·ried,** *adj.* 〖注意〗**salary, wages** 為同義字,前者常指勞心工作之報酬,其支付期間之間隔較長,後者常指勞力之報酬。

salary savings insurance 雇主從雇員薪水中扣除保險費而直接繳與保險公司之人壽保險制度。

‡**sale** 〔sel; seil〕 *n.* ①售賣。②銷數。Today's *sales* were larger than yesterday's. 今天的銷數較昨天為佳。③銷路。④賤賣。⑤拍賣。***for*** (or ***on***) ***sale*** 出售。Not *for sale*. 非賣品。***on sale*** 廉價出售。—*adj.* 大量製售的。*sale* tools. 大量製售的工具。

sale·a·ble 〔'seləbl̩; 'seiləbl〕 *adj.* = **salable.**

sale and leaseback 業主將產業售給他人之同時向新業主長期租用該產業之安排(卽新業主變為房東而原業主成為租戶之安排)。(亦作 **leaseback**)

sal·ep 〔'sælɛp; 'sælep〕 *n.* 蘭科植物的乾球莖製造之澱粉(供食用及藥用)。

sal·e·ra·tus 〔ˌsæləˈretəs; ˌsæləˈreitəs〕 *n.* 烹飪用的重碳酸鈉;小蘇打;酸粉。

sale-ring 〔'selˌrɪŋ; 'seilriŋ〕 *n.* 圍在拍賣者四周的購買人羣。

sale·room 〔'selˌrum; 'seilruːm〕 *n.* 賣貨場(特指拍賣場)。

sales 〔'selz; 'seilz〕 *adj.* 售貨的;有關售貨的。*sales* agency. 經銷處。*sales* department. 門市部。—*n. pl.* 售貨總量;銷售工作。

sales·clerk 〔'selzˌklɝk; 'seilzklɑːk〕 *n.* 店員;售貨員。

sales·girl 〔'selzˌgɝl; 'seilzgəːl〕 *n.* 女店員;女售貨員。

sales·la·dy 〔'selzˌledɪ; 'seilzˌleidi〕 *n., pl.* **-dies.** 〖美俗〗女店員;女售貨員。

***sales·man** 〔'selzmən; 'seilzmən〕 *n., pl.* **-men.** 店員;售貨員;推銷員(女性稱 saleswoman 或 salesgirl)。

sales·man·ship 〔'selzmənˌʃɪp; 'seilzmənʃip〕 *n.* ①售貨員的工作。②推銷能力;銷貨術;推銷術。③宣傳。

sales·peo·ple 〔'selzˌpipl̩; 'seilzˌpiːpl〕 *n. pl.* 售貨員;店員。

sales·per·son 〔'selzˌpɝsn̩; 'seilzˌpəːsn〕 *n.* 售貨員;店員。

sales promotion 銷路推廣。

sales resistance ①〖商〗推銷阻力(顧客對貨品、高價或商店招徠之反感)。②反感;厭惡。

sales·room 〔'selzˌrum; 'seilzruːm〕 *n.* 售貨場(尤指拍賣場)。

sales talk 推銷或宣傳之文章、演說;說辭。

sales tax 貨物稅;銷售稅。

sales·wom·an 〔'selzˌwʊmən; 'seilzˌwumən〕 *n., pl.* **-wom·en.** 女店員;女售貨員。

sale·work 〔'selˌwɝk; 'seilwəːk〕 *n.* ①供銷售而非自用之貨品。②偷工減料之物;次等貨色。

sale·yard 〔'selˌjɑrd; 'seiljɑːd〕 *n.* 買賣家畜之圍場。

Sal·ic 〔'sælɪk; 'sælik〕 *adj.* ①舍拉族人的。②舍拉法典(Salic law)的。(亦作 **Salique**)

sal·i·cin 〔'sæləsɪn; 'sælisin〕 *n.* 〖化〗柳皮精;水楊糖甙;水楊素(一種無色的結晶糖原質,$C_{13}H_{18}C_7$,由美洲柳樹之皮中取得,可做解熱劑)。

sal·i·cyl 〔'sæləsɪl; 'sælisil〕 *n.* 〖化〗水楊酸基。

sal·i·cyl·ate 〔'sæləˌsɪlet, səˈlɪsəˌlet; sæˈlisileit〕 *n.* 〖化〗水楊酸鹽。

sal·i·cyl·ic 〔ˌsæləˈsɪlɪk; ˌsæliˈsilik〕 *adj.* 〖化〗水楊酸的。

sa·li·ence 〔'selɪəns; 'seiljəns〕 *n.* ①突出;突起。②顯著;特徵。③突出部分;突角。④要點。(亦作 **saliency**)

sa·li·ent 〔'selɪənt; 'seiljənt〕 *adj.* ①顯著的。②突出的;凸出的。③跳躍的。④向上噴出的。—*n.* (陣地等之)凸出部分;凸角。**—ly,** *adv.*

sa·lif·er·ous 〔səˈlɪfərəs; səˈlifərəs〕 *adj.* 含鹽的;產鹽的。

sal·i·fy 〔'sæləˌfaɪ; 'sælifai〕 *v.t.,* **-fied, -fy·ing.** 使成鹽;使同鹽混合。

sa·line 〔'selaɪn; 'seilain〕 *adj.* ①鹽的;似鹽的;有鹽的。②含鹽的。—*n.* ①鹽井;鹽沼;鹽礦。②含鎂、鉀等金屬之鹽類;含鹽劑。③〖醫〗鹽水。**—ness,** *n.*

saline soil 鹽性土壤(含鹽過多以致不適種植)。

saline water 鹽水。

sa·lin·i·ty 〔səˈlɪnətɪ; səˈliniti〕 *n.* 鹽

分;鹽性;鹽度。 「li'nɔmitə] n. 鹽量計。
sal·i·nom·e·ter [ˌsælɪ'nɑmətɚ;ˌsæ-
Salis·bur·y steak ['sɔlzˌbɛrɪ~; 'sɔːlzbəri~] 以碎牛肉、蛋、牛乳、麪包屑及作料等混合煎成或烹成的牛肉餅。
sa·li·va [sə'laɪvə; sə'laivə] n. 唾液。
sal·i·var·y ['sæləˌvɛrɪ; 'sælivəri] adj. 唾液的;分泌唾液的。
sal·i·vate ['sæləˌvet; 'sæliveit] v., **-vat·ed, -vat·ing.** —v.i. 〖生理〗分泌唾液。—v.t. 〖生理〗使分泌過量之唾液。
saliva test 賽馬之賽後唾液試驗(以確定曾否使用興奮劑)。
sal·i·va·tion [ˌsælə'veʃən; ˌsæli'veiʃən] n. ①流涎。②流涎過多。③水銀中毒。
Salk [sɔlk; sɔːlk] n. 沙克 (Jonas Edward, 1914–, 美國細菌學家爲沙克疫苗之發明者)。
Salk vaccine 沙克疫苗(預防小兒痲痺)。
salle [sæl; sɑːl] 〖法〗 n. 室;廳;大廳。
sal·let ['sælɪt; 'sælit] n. 十五世紀時一種輕便的盔。
sal·low[1] ['sælo; 'sælou] adj. 病黃色的(皮膚或面色)。—v.t. 使發病黃色。
sal·low[2] n. ①一種柳樹。②柳枝。
sal·low·ish ['sæloɪʃ; 'sælouiʃ] adj. 微帶病黃色的。
sal·low·y ['sælo·ɪ; 'sæloui] adj. 多柳樹的。
Sal·ly ['sælɪ; 'sæli] n. 女子名 (Sarah 之暱稱)。
***sal·ly** ['sælɪ; 'sæli] v., **sal·lied, sal·ly·ing,** n., pl. **sal·lies.** —v.i. ①突然出擊。②出發。We *sallied* forth at dawn. 我們黎明時出發了。③突然衝出。④出發旅行或遠足。⑤長出;發出。—v.t. 故意使(船)搖擺。—n. ①俏皮的評語。②突擊。The soldiers made a successful *sally*. 士兵們作了一次有效的突擊。③突發。④出發旅行;遠足旅行。
sally port ①〖築城〗暗門;地道。②〖航海〗船上的太平門。
sal·ma·gun·di [ˌsælmə'gʌndɪ; ˌsælmə'gʌndi] n. ①一種義大利雜燴(由碎肉、鹹魚、醋、油、胡椒、葱等製成)。②任何混雜物;雜錄。
sal·mi ['sælmɪ; 'sælmi] n. 以酒烹煮的禽肉。
***salm·on** ['sæmən; 'sæmən] n., pl. **salm·ons** or **salm·on,** adj. —n. ①鮭。②橙紅色。—adj. 橙紅色的。
salmon brick 燒烤不足的紅磚。
salmon colo(u)r 鮭肉色;橙紅色。
salm·on-col·o(u)red ['sæmənˌkʌlɚd; 'sæmənˌkʌləd] adj. 鮭肉色的;橙紅色的。
sal·mo·noid ['sælməˌnɔɪd; 'sælmənɔid] adj. 鮭魚屬的。—n. 鮭魚屬之魚。
salmon oil 鮭魚油(用於皮革、肥皂等之製造)。
salmon pink 橙紅色。
salmon trout 一種似鮭的鱒魚。
salmon wheel 一種捕捉溯水而上的鮭魚之輪狀裝置。
Sa·lo·me [sə'lomɪ; sə'loumi] n. 〖聖經〗莎樂美(希律王之侄女,因其舞使希律王大悅,遂應其請將施洗約翰之頭給她,見馬太福音 14 章 8 節)。
sa·lon** [sa'lõ; 'sælɔ̃ː] n., pl. **-lons.** ①客廳。②在客廳中集會的人。③美術展覽或展覽所。④藝術家、文學家等之聯誼會;文藝沙龍。⑤(營業性的)廳。a beauty *salon*. 美容院。the Salon*** 沙龍畫展(現代藝術家在巴黎每年舉行一次的展覽)。
salon music 一種室內輕音樂(通常由小樂隊演奏)。
sa·loon** [sə'lun; sə'luːn] n. ①公用之大廳或場所。billiard *saloon*. 撞球場。dancing *saloon*. 跳舞廳。hair-dressing *saloon*. (女)理髮店。refreshment *saloon*. 飲食店。②〖美〗酒店。③(輪船等之)大廳。④＝**saloon car.** ***shaving saloon 〖美〗理髮店。
sa·loon·a·tic [sə'lunətɪk;sə'luːnətik] n. 熱烈擁護酒店制度者。
saloon bar 高級酒店。
sa·loon-cab·in [sə'lunˌkæbɪn; sə'luːnˌkæbin] n. 頭等艙。
saloon car (or **carriage**) 〖鐵路〗頭等客車;頭等餐車。
saloon deck 頭等艙乘客之專用甲板。
sa·loon·keep·er [sə'lunˌkipɚ; sə'luːnˌkiːpə] n. 〖美〗酒店主人。
saloon pistol 〖英〗射擊場中用的手鎗。
saloon rifle 〖英〗射擊場中用的步鎗。
sa·loop [sə'lup; sə'luːp] n. 以黃樟皮等加味之熱飲料。
Sa·lo·pi·an [sə'lopɪən; sə'loupjən] adj. Shropshire 地方的; Shropshire人的。—n. Shropshire 人或居民。
sal·pi·glos·sis [ˌsælpɪ'glɑsɪs; ˌsælpi'glɔsis] n. 〖植物〗喇叭舌屬之植物或其花。
sal·pin·gi·tis [ˌsælpɪn'dʒaɪtɪs; ˌsælpin'dʒaitis] n. 〖醫〗輸卵管炎。
sal·pinx ['sælpɪŋks; 'sælpiŋks] n., pl. **sal·pin·ges** [sæl'pɪndʒiz; sæl'pindʒiːz]. 〖解剖〗①輸卵管。②歐氏管(＝Eustachian tube).
sal·si·fy ['sælsəfɪ; 'sælsifi] n. 〖植物〗婆羅門參。
SALT [sɔlt; sɔːlt] n. 戰略武器限制談判 (*S*trategic *A*rms *L*imitation *T*alks 之略)。
‡**salt** [sɔlt; sɔːlt] n. ①鹽;食鹽。②有經驗的水手。③餐桌上的鹽罐(＝saltcellar). ④譏刺;機智。⑤要素;刺激;趣味。Adventure is the *salt* of life to some men. 對某些人說起來,冒險是生活的刺激。⑥〖化〗鹽;酸類和鹽基的化合物。⑦(pl.)瀉鹽。⑧(pl.)嗅鹽(＝smelling salts). ⑨懷疑。***attic salt*** 文雅的機智;雅而不俗的譏刺。***eat one's salt*** 在某人家作客。***not*** (or ***hardly***) ***worth one's salt*** 沒有用;不稱職。He is *not worth his salt*. 他不稱職。***sit above*** (***below***) ***the salt*** 坐在上(末)席。***the salt of the earth*** 社會中堅分子(新約馬太福音 5:13)。***with a grain of salt*** 稍有保留的態度;懷疑地。—adj. ①鹽的;含鹽的。②鹹的。③鹽醃的。④生長於鹹水中的。⑤辛辣的;有力的;中肯的。—v.t. ①加鹽。②用鹽醃以便保藏。③餵以鹽。④作苛刻批評。⑤〖化〗以鹽處理;加鹽於。⑥使變灰白。Experience has *salted* his hair. 經歷使他頭髮灰白。⑦使更有趣。⑧使悲痛。***salt away*** (or ***down***) **a.** 用鹽醃以便保藏。**b.** 積蓄;儲存。***salt out*** 在溶液中加鹽使(溶解之物質)分離。—**ness,** n.
sal·tant ['sæltənt; 'sæltənt] adj. ①跳舞的;跳躍的。②〖紋章〗飛躍姿勢的。
sal·tate ['sæltet;'sælteit] v.i., **-tat·ed, -tat·ing.** 跳躍;跳舞。
sal·ta·tion [sæl'teʃən; sæl'teiʃən] n. ①跳躍。②激變;突變;急動。③〖生物〗突變。④心臟之急速跳動。⑤跳舞。
sal·ta·to·ri·al [ˌsæltə'torɪəl; ˌsæltə'tɔːriəl] adj. ①舞踊的;跳躍的。②〖動物〗適於跳躍的。
sal·ta·to·ry ['sæltəˌtorɪ; 'sæltətəri]

S

adj. ①跳躍的。②躍進的;以疾速動作前進的。③舞蹈的。

saltatory evolution 〖生物〗飛躍的進化。

salt·box ('sɔlt͵bɑks; 'sɔːltbɔks) *n.* ①十八世紀美國康乃狄克州的一種正方形二樓房屋。②鹽匣。

salt·cel·lar ('sɔlt͵sɛlɚ; 'sɔːlt͵selə) *n.* 「餐桌上的鹽罐。

salt·ed ('sɔltɪd; 'sɔːltid) *adj.* ①用鹽醃漬的; 以鹽治療的; 以鹽處理的。②〖俗〗老練的;有經驗的。③〖獸醫〗對傳染病免疫的。④(核子武器)經特別處理使產生大量放射塵的。

salt·er ('sɔltɚ; 'sɔːltə) *n.* ①製鹽者;鹽商。②鹹漬者(鹹肉、魚等者)。③鹹肉的槽等。

salt·ern ('sɔltɚn; 'sɔːltən) *n.* ①鹽場。②鹽田。

salt field 鹽田。

salt flat ①有鹽礦的廣大平地。②淤泥盆地。

salt horse 〖航海俚〗醃牛肉。

sal·tim·ban·co (͵sæltɪm'bæŋko; ͵sæltim'bæŋkou) *n.* ①江湖醫生。②騙子。

salt·ine (sɔl'tin; sɔːl'tiːn) *n.* 撒鹽餅乾。

salt·i·ness ('sɔltɪnɪs; 'sɔːltinis) *n.* ①鹹;含有鹽分。②尖銳;尖刻。

salt·ing ('sɔltɪŋ; 'sɔːltiŋ) *n.* ①醃製;加鹽。②〖英〗時遭海水泛濫之土地。

sal·tire ('sæltɪr; 'sɔːltaiə) *n.* (亦作 **sal·tier**)〖紋章〗X形十字。—*adj.* 成X形的。

salt·ish ('sɔltɪʃ; 'sɔːltiʃ) *adj.* 略帶鹹味的。

salt lake 鹹水湖。

Salt Lake City 鹽湖城(美國 Utah 州首府,靠近 Great Salt Lake)。

salt·less ('sɔltlɪs; 'sɔːltlis) *adj.* ①無鹽的。②無味的。

salt lick 野獸舐食天然岩鹽之鹽地。

salt·like ('sɔlt͵laɪk; 'sɔːltlaik) *adj.* 似鹽的(尤指在離子的特性上)。

S

salt·ly ('sɔltlɪ; 'sɔːltli) *adv.* 辛辣地。

salt marsh 鹽澤;鹽沼。

salt mine 岩鹽坑;岩鹽產地。

salt·pan ('sɔlt͵pæn; 'sɔːltpæn) *n.* ①製鹽用的鹽釜。②海岸的鹽田。③(*pl.*)鹽場。(亦作 **salt pan**)

salt·pe·ter, salt·pe·tre (͵sɔlt'pitɚ; 'sɔːlt͵piːtə) *n.* ①硝石。②硝酸鈉(肥料)。③硝酸鉀(亦稱智利硝石 Chile saltpeter)。

salt pit 鹽坑。

salt pork 醃豬肉。

salt·shak·er ('sɔlt͵ʃekɚ; 'sɔːlt͵ʃeikə) *n.* 餐桌上用的鹽瓶(瓶蓋有細孔可撒鹽者)。

salt spoon 鹽匙。

sal·tus ('sæltəs; 'sæltəs) *n. sing.* or *pl.* ①急變。②〖邏輯〗速斷(證明中必要步驟之遺漏)。

salt-wa·ter ('sɔlt'wɔtɚ; 'sɔːlt'wɔːtə) *adj.* ①鹽水的; 含鹽水的。②棲居鹹水中的。③海的;海洋的。

salt water ①鹽水;海(水)。②淚。③水手。

salt·works ('sɔlt͵wɝks; 'sɔːltwəːks) *n. sing.* or *pl.* 製鹽場; 鹽廠。

salt·wort ('sɔlt͵wɝt; 'sɔːltwəːt) *n.* 〖植物〗藜科鬮羊栖菜屬植物。

salt·y ('sɔltɪ; 'sɔːlti) *adj.*, **salt·i·er**, **salt·i·est.** ①含鹽的; 有鹹味的。②尖銳的; 警闢的;機智的;有趣的。—**salt·i·ly,** *adv.*

sa·lu·bri·ous (sə'lubrɪəs; sə'ljuːbriəs) *adj.* 有益健康的(現特指空氣、氣候等)。—**ly,** *adv.* —**ness,** *n.*

sa·lu·bri·ty (sə'lubrətɪ; sə'ljuːbriti) *n.* 適於衛生;增進健康。

sal·u·tar·y ('sæljə͵tɛrɪ; 'sæljutəri) *adj.* ①有益健康的;合於衛生的。②有益的。

sal·u·ta·tion (͵sæljə'teʃən; ͵sæljuː'teiʃən) *n.* ①致意;敬禮。②(信件開頭的)稱呼。③寒暄。a word of *salutation.* 寒暄語。

sa·lu·ta·to·ri·an (sə͵lutə'torɪən; sə͵ljuːtə'tɔːriən) *n.* 〖美〗畢業典禮上對來賓致歡迎詞的畢業生代表(通常爲成績第二名者)。

sa·lu·ta·to·ry (sə'lutə͵torɪ; sə'luːtətəri) *adj., n., pl.* **-ries.** —*adj.* 致意的;致敬的;祝賀的。—*n.* 歡迎詞(尤指畢業生代表在畢業典禮上之致詞)。

sa·lute** (sə'lut; sə'luːt) *v.,* **-lut·ed, -lut·ing,** *n.* —*v.t.* ①向…敬禮;(以鳴砲、升旗等方式)致敬。②向…致意;歡迎;祝賀。③傳到;傳入。④頌揚;讚頌。—*v.i.* 致意;祝賀;致敬禮。—*n.* ①致意; 致候。He did not return my *salute.* 他並沒有回我的致意。②敬禮;禮砲;擧鎗(等)致敬。③敬禮之姿勢或位置。④鞭砲。fire a salute*** 鳴禮砲。***stand at*** (***the***) ***salute*** 立正致敬;立正敬禮。***take the salute*** 還禮;接受敬禮。—**sa·lut·er,** *n.*

salute to the Union 美國獨立紀念日中午鳴放的禮砲。

sal·va·ble ('sælvəbl; 'sælvəbl) *adj.* ①〖神學〗可獲救的。②(船、貨等)可以打撈(搶救)的。

Sal·va·dor ('sælvə͵dɔr; 'sælvədɔː) *n.* ①薩爾瓦多(巴西東部之一海港)。②= El Salvador. —**an,** *adj., n.*

sal·vage ('sælvɪdʒ; 'sælvidʒ) *n., v.,* **-vaged, -vag·ing.** —*n.* ①對遇險之船舶、船員及貨物之救護。②(船東或保險公司付予援救者之)援救費。③獲救之船舶、貨物或船員。④(潛水伕或打撈器具對沉於海底貨物之)打撈。⑤〖保險〗**a.** 火災中對貨物、財產之搶救。**b.** 火災中搶救出來之財產。**c.** 火災搶救費。**d.** 獲救財產之價值。**e.** 獲救財產變賣所得之款。⑥救助; 救濟。⑦廢物利用。⑧(財產之)搶救。⑨〖醫〗救治。—*v.t.* ①援救…於海難。②打撈(沉船)。③利用廢物。④搶救(財產)。⑤〖醫〗救;治。—**sal·vag·er,** *n.*

sal·vage·a·ble ('sælvədʒəbl; 'sælvidʒəbl) *adj.* 可搶救的;可救的。

salvage boat 海難救助船。

salvage company 海難救援公司;沉船打撈公司。

Sal·var·san ('sælvɚ͵sæn; 'sælvəsən) *n.* 〖商標名〗六〇六;606;洒爾佛散; 阿斯凡納明(=arsphenamine);鹽酸二氨基砷酚(一種治梅毒之特效針藥)。

***sal·va·tion** (sæl'veʃən; sæl'veiʃən) *n.* ①救助;拯救。②救助者。③救世;超度。

sal·va·tion·al (sæl'veʃənḷ; sæl'veiʃənəl) *adj.* 救世的。

Salvation Army 救世軍(1865年由 William Booth 創於英國)。

Sal·va·tion·ism (sæl'veʃənɪzṃ; sæl'veiʃənizm) *n.* 救世軍的教義。

Sal·va·tion·ist (sæl'veʃənɪst; sæl'veiʃənist) *n.* ①救世軍之一員。②(s-) 傳道者。—*adj.* 救世軍的。

salve¹ (sæv; sɑːv, sælv) *n., v.,* **salved, salv·ing.** —*n.* ①藥膏;軟膏。②緩和物;安慰物。—*v.t.* ①敷以藥膏。②安慰;緩和。

salve² (sælv; sælv) *v.t.,* **salved, salv·ing.** 救助;救護。

sal·ve³ ('sælvɪ; 'sælvi) *interj.* 歡呼祝賀之聲;祝人安好之語。

sal·ver ('sælvɚ; 'sælvə) *n.* 盤;盆(用以放置信件、名片等,俾便僕人托送者)。

Sal·vi·a ('sælvɪə; 'sælviə) *n.* 〖植物〗①琴柱草屬。②(s-) 琴柱草;鼠尾草。

sal·vo¹ ('sælvo; 'sælvou) *n., pl.* **-vos,**

-voes, *v.* —*n.* ①排砲;同時發射;齊發。②禮砲。③齊聲歡呼或喝采。**salvo bombing** 齊投轟炸。**salvo fire** 集中發射。**salvo release** 集中投下。—*v.t.* 同時發射;齊發。

sal·vo² *n., pl.* **-vos.** ①保留條款;但書。②遁詞;口實。③挽救名譽、緩和感情的方法。

sal vo·la·ti·le [ˈsælvoˈlætḷ,i; ˌsælvəˈlætəli] 碳酸銨水;揮發鹽(用作提神藥)。

sal·vor [ˈsælvɚ; ˈsælvə] *n.* 救難者;救難船。

salv·y [ˈsælvɪ; ˈsælvi] *adj.* 似軟膏的。

Sal·ween [ˈsælˌwin; ˈsælwiːn] *n.* 薩爾溫江(源於中國之西康省, 流經緬甸入印度洋)。

SAM surface-to-air missile(s). 地對空飛彈。

Sam [sæm; sæm] *n.* 男子名 (Samuel 之暱稱)。**stand Sam** 負擔費用(特指酒帳)。**take one's Sam upon it** 〖俗〗敢於承當。**upon my Sam** 誓必。

Sam. 〖聖經〗 Samuel.

S. Am. ① South America. ②South American.

sam·a·ra [ˈsæmərə; ˈsæmərə] *n.* 〖植物〗翅果;翼果。

Sa·mar·i·a [səˈmɛrɪə; səˈmɛəriə] *n.* 撒馬利亞(巴勒斯坦北部, 約旦河與地中海之間的一古國, 後改為一省;又, 該國之首都)。

Sa·mar·i·tan [səˈmærətṇ; səˈmæritn] *n.* ①撒馬利亞人。②同情並援助貧病者的善人(通常為 good Samaritan). —*adj.* ①撒馬利亞(人)的。②有同情心的;援助貧病者的。

sa·mar·i·um [səˈmɛrɪəm; səˈmɛəriəm] *n.* 〖化〗釤(稀金屬元素, 符號為Sa或Sm)。

sam·ba [ˈsæmbə; ˈsæmbə] *n., pl.* **-bas,** *v.,* **-baed, -ba·ing.** —*n.* 森巴舞。 —*v.i.* 跳森巴舞。

sam·bar [ˈsæmbɚ; ˈsɑːmbə] *n., pl.* **-bars, -bar.** 印度產的一種大鹿。

sam·bo¹ [ˈsæmbo; ˈsæmbou] *n., pl.* **-bos.** 黑人與印第安人或黑白混血所生之混血兒。

sam·bo² *n.* 運用柔道技巧的角力。

sam·bur [ˈsæmbɚ; ˈsæmbə] *n., pl.* **-burs, -bur.** =**sambar.**

‡same [sem; seim] *adj.* ①同一的。They were both born on the *same* day and in the *same* town. 他們在同一天誕生於同一城。②相同的;同樣的。Her name and mine are the *same.* 她的名字和我的相同。He gave me the *same* answer as before. 他給我的答覆和從前一樣。③無變化的。The town was still the *same* after fifty years. 這城市過了五十年仍然沒有改變。④上述的。**at the same time** a. 可是。b. 同時。**come to the same thing** 結果相同。—*pron.* ①同一之人;同樣之事物。We must all say the *same.* 我們大家所說的必須一致。②上述之物;該物。**all** (or **just**) **the same** a. 同樣地;仍然。 b. 無關重要。**be all** (or **just**) **the same to** (**somebody**) 對(某人)是一樣的。**one and the same** =**the very same. same here** 我也一樣。**the same** 同樣地(=in the same manner). **the very same** 就是那個;與那個完全一樣的。 —*n.* 相同或同一之人或物。*sames* and differences. 相同點和相異點。—*adv.* ①相同地。②正;恰。

same·ly [ˈsemlɪ; ˈseimli] *adj.* 單調的;無變化的;千篇一律的。

same·ness [ˈsemnɪs; ˈseimnis] *n.* ①千篇一律;無變化。②共同之處;相同之處。

S. Amer. ① South America. ②South American.

Sa·mi·an [ˈsemɪən; ˈseimiən] *adj.* Samos 島的; Samos 島之居民的。 —*n.* Samos 島上的居民。

sam·ite [ˈsæmaɪt; ˈsæmait] *n.* 中世紀的一種織錦。

sam·let [ˈsæmlɪt; ˈsæmlit] *n.* 〖魚〗幼鮭。

Sam·my [ˈsæmɪ; ˈsæmi] *n., pl.* **-mies.** ①〖俚〗(第一次世界大戰時之) 美國兵。②(常 s-)〖英方〗愚人;蠢貨。**stand Sammy** = **stand Sam.**

Sam·nite [ˈsæmnaɪt; ˈsæmnait] *adj.* 義大利一古國 Samnium 人(或語)的。—*n.* Samnium 人。

Sa·mo·a [səˈmoə; səˈmoə] *n.* 薩摩亞羣島(南太平洋一羣島)。

Sa·mo·an [səˈmoən; səˈmoən] *adj.* Samoa 的; Samoa 人的。—*n.* Samoa人; Samoa 語。

Sa·mos [ˈsemɑs; ˈseimɔs] *n.* 薩摩斯島(愛琴海中一島, 屬希臘)。

SAMOS [ˈsæmos; ˈsæmous] *n.* 美國之偵察衞星(為 *s*atellite *a*nti*m*issile *o*bservation *s*ystem 之略)。

sam·o·var [ˈsæməˌvɑr; ˌsæmouˈvɑː] *n.* 俄國煮茶之銅壺。

Sam·o·yed [ˌsæməˈjɛd; ˌsæmɔiˈed] *n.* ①撒摩耶族人(西伯利亞北極區之黃種人)。②白色厚毛的西伯利亞犬。—*adj.* ①撒摩耶族的 (=Samoyedic). ②撒摩耶族語的。

Sam·o·yed·ic [ˌsæməˈjɛdɪk; ˌsæmɔiˈedik] *adj.* 撒摩耶族的。

samp [sæmp; sæmp] *n.* 〖美〗玉蜀黍䅟;玉蜀黍粥。

sam·pan [ˈsæmpæn; ˈsæmpæn] *n.* (中國的)舢板。

sam·phire [ˈsæmfaɪr; ˈsæmfaiə] *n.* ①歐洲沿岸的一種繖形科多肉之植物(可做沙拉用)。②=**glasswort.**

***sam·ple** [ˈsæmpḷ; ˈsɑːmpl] *n., adj., v.,* **-pled, -pling.** —*n.* ①樣品;樣本。It comes up to *sample.* 它和樣品相符。②例;範例。③抽樣檢查。—*adj.* 樣品的。 —*v.t.* ①取…的貨樣;提出…的貨樣;試驗…的貨樣。②抽樣調查。③將…迅速過目。

sample cards 貨物樣品卡片。

sam·pler [ˈsæmplɚ; ˈsɑːmplə] *n.* ①檢驗貨物樣品者。②抽查者。③樣品;集粹。④刺繡花樣(用以表示女孩子之刺繡技藝者)。

sample room ①樣品陳列室。②〖俗〗酒吧。

sam·pling [ˈsæmplɪŋ; ˈsɑːmpliŋ] *n.* ①提取或試驗貨樣的行動或程序。②提取或試驗之樣品。

sam·sa·ra [səmˈsɑrə; səmˈsɑːrə] *n.* 〖佛教、印度教〗輪廻。

Sam·son [ˈsæmsṇ; ˈsæmsn] *n.* ①〖聖經〗參孫(力大無雙之以色列的士師)。②大力士。

Sam·u·el [ˈsæmjuəl; ˈsæmjuəl] *n.* ①男子名。②〖聖經〗撒母耳(希伯來之士師兼先知)。③舊約聖經中之撒母耳書(分上下兩卷)。

sam·u·rai [ˈsæmuˌraɪ; ˈsæmurai] 〖日〗 *n. pl.* or *sing.* ①封建時代的日本武士;武士階級。②日本之陸軍軍官;日本軍閥。

san·a·tive [ˈsænətɪv; ˈsænətiv] *adj.* 有治療效力的;醫治的。

san·a·to·ri·um [ˌsænəˈtorɪəm; ˌsænəˈtɔːriəm] *n., pl.* **-ri·ums, -ri·a** [-rɪə; -riə]. 療養院;休養地。(亦作 **sanitarium, sanatarium**)

san·a·to·ry [ˈsænəˌtorɪ; ˈsænətəri] *adj.* 有益於健康的;治療的。

san·be·ni·to [ˌsænbəˈnito; ˌsænbəˈniːtou] *n., pl.* **-tos.** ①悔改之異教徒所著之

黃色懺罪服。②受宗教裁判被判死刑者所著之黑色悔罪服。

San·cho Pan·za ['sæŋko 'pænzə; 'sæŋkou'pænzə] *Don Quixote* 中主角 Don Quixote 之侍者，其實際的經驗常識與其主人之幻想的理想主義成對比。

sanc·ti·fi·ca·tion [ˌsæŋktəfə'keʃən; ˌsæŋktifi'keiʃən] *n.* 神聖化；神聖；聖潔。

sanc·ti·fy ['sæŋktəˌfaɪ; 'sæŋktifai] *v.t.*, **-fied, -fy·ing.** ①使神聖。②使聖潔；使純潔。③使成爲正當；認可。④使無罪過。⑤使專供聖用。—**sanc·ti·fi·er,** *n.*

sanc·ti·mo·ni·al [ˌsæŋktə'monɪəl; ˌsæŋktə'mouniəl] *n.* 修女。

sanc·ti·mo·ni·ous [ˌsæŋktə'monɪəs; ˌsæŋkti'mounjəs] *adj.* 僞裝神聖的；僞裝虔誠的。

sanc·ti·mo·ni·ous·ly [ˌsæŋktə'monɪəslɪ; ˌsæŋkti'mouniəsli] *adv.* 僞裝神聖地；僞裝虔誠地。

sanc·ti·mo·ny ['sæŋktəˌmonɪ; 'sæŋktiməni] *n.* 僞裝之神聖氣概；僞裝的虔誠。

***sanc·tion** ['sæŋkʃən; 'sæŋkʃən] *n.* ①批准；認可。②制裁。moral *sanction.* 道德制裁。③處罰。④良心制裁。⑤制裁力；約束力。⑥道德之影響力。—*v.t.* ①批准；認可。②授權；准許。—**er,** *n.*

sanc·tion·a·tive ['sæŋkʃənətɪv; 'sæŋkʃənətiv] *adj.* 認可的；制裁的；約束的。

sanc·tion·ist ['sæŋkʃənɪst; 'sæŋkʃənist] *n.* (對違反國際法國家之)制裁國。

sanc·ti·tude ['sæŋktəˌtjud; 'sæŋktitju:d] *n.* 神聖；純潔。

sanc·ti·ty ['sæŋktətɪ; 'sæŋktiti] *n., pl.* **-ties.** ①神聖。②(*pl.*)神聖的義務或感情。③神聖之物。

sanc·to·ri·um [ˌsæŋk'torɪəm; ˌsæŋk'touriəm] *n.* 廟；祠。

sanc·tu·a·rize ['sæŋktʃʊəˌraɪz; 'sæŋktʃuəraiz] *v.t.*, **-rized, -riz·ing.** 予以庇護；給予避難所。

***sanc·tu·ar·y** ['sæŋktʃʊˌɛrɪ; 'sæŋktjuəri] *n., pl.* **-ar·ies.** ①聖所；聖堂；神殿。②至聖所；內殿。③避難所；隱匿地；庇護所。④庇護。The escaped prisoner found *sanctuary* in the temple. 這個逃犯隱匿在廟裏。⑤耶路撒冷的聖廟。⑥耶路撒冷聖廟中保存約櫃(ark of the covenant)的聖地。

sanc·tum ['sæŋktəm; 'sæŋktəm] *n., pl.* **-tums, -ta** [-tə; -tə]. ①聖所。②私室；書房。

Sanc·tus ['sæŋktəs; 'sæŋktəs] *n.* 彌撒禮中以"Holy, holy, holy Lord God of hosts"開始之讚美歌。

‡**sand** [sænd; sænd] *n.* ①沙。②(*pl.*)沙地；沙岸；沙漠。Children enjoy playing on the *sands.* 孩子們喜歡在沙中玩。③(*pl.*)沙漏中之沙粒；時刻；壽命。The *sands* are running out. 餘時不多了。④〖美俚〗勇氣。⑤眼屎。***be built on sand*** 未打穩固的基礎。***make ropes of sand*** 做徒勞無功的事。***numberless as the sand(s)*** 恒河沙數。***plough the sands*** 徒勞無功。—*v.t.* ①撒以沙；摻以沙；埋於沙。②以沙紙或沙擦淨或磨光。The stain will have to be *sanded* out. 這汚點必須用沙紙磨淨。***sand up*** 被沙阻塞。

***san·dal** ['sændl; 'sændl] *n., v.*, **-dal(l)ed, -dal·(l)ing.** —*n.* ①涼鞋；草鞋。②矮幫的便鞋。③矮幫的膠皮套鞋。④草鞋或矮幫便鞋之繫帶。—*v.t.* 供給(或穿以)草鞋或便鞋。

san·dal·wood ['sændlˌwʊd; 'sændlwud] *n.* 檀香木。

sand·bag ['sændˌbæg; 'sændbæg] *n., v.*, **-bagged, -bag·ging.** —*n.* 沙袋；沙包。—*v.t.* ①供以沙袋；以沙袋圍起。②以沙袋擊。③〖俗〗猛擊；威脅。④〖撲克〗手中有好牌時不下注，誘(對手)不退出，以便在稍後下高注。—*v.i.* 〖撲克俚〗手中有好牌時誘人入彀。

sand·bag·ger ['sændˌbægɚ; 'sændˌbægə] *n.* ①〖美〗以沙袋擊倒人的惡徒。②〖俗〗吃水淺且以沙袋做壓艙物的帆船。③任何以蔽詐爲目的之議案。

sand·bank ['sændˌbæŋk; 'sændbæŋk] *n.* 沙洲。

sand bar (由潮汐或水流所造成的)沙洲。

sand bath ①化學實驗室中用的沙鍋。②沙浴(將身體埋於熱沙中，用以治病)。

sand bed 沙床。

sand belt ①磨物用的沙帶。②狹長之沙丘地帶。

sand binder 使沙不移動的任何植物。

sand·blast ['sændˌblæst; 'sændblɑ:st] *n.* ①噴沙(洗滌或打磨玻璃等的表面)。②噴沙器。—*v.t.* & *v.i.* 以噴沙器清洗或打磨。—**er,** *n.*

sand-blind ['sændˌblaɪnd; 'sændblaind] *adj.* 〖古，方〗半盲的；目力不佳的。—**ness,** *n.*

sand·box ['sændˌbɑks; 'sændbɔks] *n.* ①火車機車或街車上之沙箱。②沙匣(上面有小孔以撒沙於未乾之墨水上)。③沙匣樹(=sandbox tree).

sand·boy ['sændˌbɔɪ; 'sændbɔi] *n.* ①賣沙的孩子。②沙岸上能跳的任何昆蟲(如沙蚤)。***as happy (jolly, merry, etc.) as a sandboy*** 極爲高興；非常開心。

Sand·burg ['sænbɝg, 'sænd-; 'sændbə:g] *n.* 桑德堡(Carl, 1878–1967, 美國詩人、作家及民謠蒐集家)。

sand-cast ['sændˌkæst; 'sændkɑ:st] *v.t.*, **-cast, -cast·ing.** 沙模鑄造。—**ing,** *n.*

sand cat 沙漠的一種野貓。

sand cloth 戲臺上畫成沙或土地狀之地毯。

sand crack 馬之裂蹄症。

sand·cul·ture ['sændˌkʌltʃɚ; 'sændˌkʌltʃə] *n.* 沙床水耕法。

sand dollar 〖動物〗海膽。

sand-drift ['sændˌdrɪft; 'sændrift] *n.* 流沙。

sand dune 沙丘。

sand·ed ['sændɪd; 'sændid] *adj.* ①覆有沙的；撒有沙的；沙的。②沙色的；有小斑點的。③沙質的；沙所形成的。④有沙摻雜的。

sand eel 落潮時鑽進海灘沙中之魚類。

sand·er ['sændɚ; 'sændə] *n.* 磨沙者；磨沙機；以沙紙磨光者。

sand·er·ling ['sændəlɪŋ; 'sændəliŋ] *n.* 三趾鷸。

sand finish (牆面等之)洗石。

sand·glass ['sændˌglæs; 'sændglɑ:s] *n.* (計時用的)沙漏。

S and H 星期例假(=Sundays and holidays).

san·dhi ['sændhi; 'sændhi:] *n.* 〖語言〗變音(如"a cow"中之"a"及"an old cow"中之"an"，或中國語言上聲在另一上聲之前變爲陽平等是)。

sand hill 沙丘。

sand·hill ['sændˌhɪl; 'sændhil] *adj.* 沙丘的；多沙丘的。

sand·hog ['sændˌhɔg, -ˌhɑg; 'sændhɔg] *n.* ①挖沙苦力。②在水底工作之勞工。(亦作 **sand hog**)

Sand·hurst ['sændhɝst; 'sændhə:st] *n.* ①散德赫斯特(英格蘭南部一鄉村)。②英國陸軍軍官學校(其所在地即 Sandhurst).

San Di·e·gan ['sændɪ'egən; 'sændi-

ˈeigən] 美國 California 州聖地牙哥 (San Diego)人。
San Di·e·go [ˌsæn·diˈego; ˌsæn-di:-ˈeigou] 聖地牙哥 (美國 California 州一海港,爲海軍基地)。
sand·lot [ˈsændˌlɑt; ˈsændlɔt] *n.* 〖美〗市郊供運動和遊戲之空曠沙地。—*adj.* 市郊沙地上的。
sand·man [ˈsændˌmæn; ˈsændmæn] *n., pl.* **-men.** 神話中之睡魔(能將沙放入兒童眼內使之昏昏欲睡)。
sand mar·tin [~ˈmɑrtɪn; ~ˈmɑ:tin] 〖英〗燕之一種。
sand·pa·per [ˈsændˌpepɚ; ˈsændˌpei-pə] *n.* 沙紙。—*v.t.* 用沙紙磨光。—**er,** *n.*
sand·pip·er [ˈsændˌpaɪpɚ; ˈsændˌpai-pə] *n.* 磯鷸。
sand pit 採沙場;沙坑。(亦作 **sandpit**)
San·dra [ˈsændrə; ˈsɑ:ndrə] *n.* 女子名。(亦作 **Saundra, Sondra**)
sand·rock [ˈsændˌrɑk; ˈsænd-rɔk] *n.* 沙岩 (=sandstone).
sand shoe 〖英〗一種輕便的網球鞋;運動鞋。
sand star 海盤車;星魚。
***sand·stone** [ˈsændˌston; ˈsændstoun] *n.* 〖地質〗沙岩。
sand·storm [ˈsændˌstɔrm; ˈsænd-stɔ:m] *n.* 大風沙;沙暴。
sand table 沙盤(供軍事演習或兒童遊戲之用)。
sand trap ①分沙器(用以分離沙與水)。②〖高爾夫〗沙坑障礙。
***sand·wich** [ˈsændwɪtʃ; ˈsænwidʒ, -tʃ] *n.* ①夾以肉類或果醬等物之麪包;三明治。②兩面均被夾緊之物。—*v.t.* ①夾在中間;挿入。②將…夾在三明治中。
sandwich board 夾板廣告伕背後及胸前所掛之廣告牌。
sand·wi·che·ri·a [ˌsændwɪˈtʃɪrɪə; ˌsændwiˈtʃiəriə] *n.* 三明治飲食店。(亦作 **sandwich bar**)
sandwich man 夾板廣告伕(背後及胸前均掛有廣告牌者)。
sand·wort [ˈsændˌwɝt; ˈsændwə:t] *n.* 〖植物〗蚤綴。
San·dy [ˈsændɪ; ˈsændi] *n.* ①男子名 (Alexander 之暱稱)。②女子名 (Sandra 之暱稱)。
***sand·y** [ˈsændɪ; ˈsændi] *adj.,* **sand·i·er, sand·i·est,** *n.* —*adj.* ①沙的;沙質的;多沙的。a *sandy* beach. 沙灘。②沙色的;淺茶色的(髮等)。③易滑動如沙的;不安穩的。—*n.* 〖俗〗蘇格蘭人。—**sand·i·ness,** *n.*
sand·y·ish [ˈsændɪɪʃ; ˈsændiiʃ] *adj.* 略帶沙質的。
***sane** [sen; sein] *adj.,* **san·er, san·est.** ①神志清明的;頭腦清楚的。②健全的;穩健的。—**ly,** *adv.* —**ness,** *n.*
***San Fran·cis·co** [ˌsænfrənˈsɪsko; ˌsæn frənˈsiskou] 舊金山;三藩市(美國 California 州太平洋岸之大城)。
San Francisco Bay 舊金山灣 (美國 California 州太平洋岸之一港灣)。
***sang** [sæŋ; sæŋ] *v.* pt. of **sing.**
san·ga·ree [ˌsæŋgəˈri; ˌsæŋgəˈri:] *n.* 一種由水、葡萄酒、糖、香料等調成的清涼飲料。
sang-froid [sɑ̃ˈfrwɑ; sɑ̃:ŋˈfrwɑ:] 〖法〗*n.* 沉着;冷靜;鎮定。
San·graal [sæŋˈgrel; sæŋˈgreil] *n.* =**Sangreal.**
San·gre·al [ˈsæŋgrɪəl; ˈsæŋgriəl] *n.* 聖杯(耶穌於最後晚餐中所用之杯)。(亦作 **the Holy Grail**)
san·guif·er·ous [sæŋˈgwɪfərəs; sæŋ-ˈgwifərəs] *adj.* 載運血液的(如血管)。
san·gui·mo·tor [ˈsæŋgwəˌmotɚ; ˈsæŋgwimoutə] *adj.* 血液循環的。
san·gui·nar·y [ˈsæŋgwɪnˌɛrɪ; ˈsæŋ-gwinəri] *adj.* ①殺傷甚多的;死屍枕藉的。②有血的;血淋淋的;血跡斑斑的。③血的。④嗜殺的;殘暴的。⑤粗暴的(話)。—**san·gui·nar·i·ly,** *adv.* —**san·gui·nar·i·ness,** *n.*
san·guine [ˈsæŋgwɪn; ˈsæŋgwin] *adj.* ①樂天的。②自信的;有望的。③面色紅潤的。④多血的。⑤血紅的。—**ly,** *adv.* —**ness,** *n.*
san·guin·e·ous [sæŋˈgwɪnɪəs; sæŋ-ˈgwiniəs] *adj.* ①血的;含有血的。②血色的;紅色的。③流血的。④有信心的;有希望的。
san·guin·i·ty [sæŋˈgwɪnətɪ; sæŋˈgwi-niti] *n.* 樂天。
San·he·drim [ˈsænɪˌdrɪm; ˈsænidrim] *n.* =**Sanhedrin.**
San·he·drin [ˈsænɪˌdrɪn; ˈsænidrin] *n.* 古猶太國之最高法院及參議院。
san·i·cle [ˈsænɪkl; ˈsænikl] *n.* 〖植物〗繖形科變形菜屬植物。
san·i·fy [ˈsænəˌfaɪ; ˈsænifai] *v.t.,* **-fied, -fy·ing.** 使有益健康。—**san·i·fi·ca·tion,** *n.*
san·i·tar·i·an [ˌsænəˈtɛrɪən; ˌsæni-ˈtɛəriən] *adj.* 衛生的。—*n.* 衛生學家。
san·i·tar·i·ly [ˈsænəˌtɛrəlɪ; ˈsænitə-rili] *adv.* 在衛生上。
san·i·tar·i·um [ˌsænəˈtɛrɪəm; ˌsæni-ˈtɛəriəm] *n., pl.* **-i·ums, -i·a** [-ɪə; -iə]. ①療養院。②療養地。(亦作 **sanatorium**)
***san·i·tar·y** [ˈsænəˌtɛrɪ; ˈsænitəri] *adj.* ①衛生的;衛生方面的。*sanitary* cup. (紙製的)衛生杯。*sanitary* inspection. 衛生檢查。②清潔的。—*n.* 廁所等衛生設備。—**san·i·tar·i·ness,** *n.*
sanitary belt 月經帶。
sanitary cordon 傳染病流行區邊界上爲防止疾病散布而布置的士兵或警衛人員。
sanitary engineer ①衛生工程師。②鉛管匠 (誇大語)。
sanitary engineering 衛生工程。
sanitary napkin (婦女用) 衛生棉。
sanitary sewer 汚水道;汚水下水道。
sanitary towel 月經帶。
sanitary ware 衛生器具。
san·i·tate [ˈsænətet; ˈsæniteit] *v.t.* & *v.i.,* **-tat·ed, -tat·ing.** 使清潔;使合衛生;添置衛生設施。
san·i·ta·tion [ˌsænəˈteʃən; ˌsæniˈtei-ʃən] *n.* 衛生;衛生設施;衛生設備。
san·i·ta·tion·ist [ˌsænəˈteʃənɪst; ˌsæniˈteiʃənist] *n.* 衛生專家;衛生學家。
san·i·tize [ˈsænəˌtaɪz; ˈsænitaiz] *v.t.* (對可能危害健康之物) 採取衛生措施; 消毒。
san·i·tiz·er [ˈsænəˌtaɪzɚ; ˈsænitaizə] *n.* 食物加工設備所用之消毒殺菌劑。
san·i·ty [ˈsænətɪ; ˈsæniti] *n.* ①心智健全;神智清明。②公正;明達。
san·jak [ˈsændʒæk; ˈsændʒæk] 〖土〗*n.* 土耳其之省。
San Jose scale 聖約瑟蟲(果樹的害蟲)。
sank [sæŋk; sæŋk] *v.* pt. of **sink.**
San Ma·ri·no [ˌsæn məˈrino; ˌsæn məˈri:nou] 聖馬利諾 (義大利半島東部一小國,首都 San Marino).
san·nup [ˈsænʌp; ˈsænʌp] *n.* 印第安人之已婚男性。
sann·ya·si [sʌnˈjɑsi; sʌnˈjɑ:si:] 〖印度〗*n.* 印度的托鉢僧。(亦作 **sonnyasin**)
sans [sænz, sɑ̃; sænz, sɑ̃:] *prep.* 〖古,詩〗=**without.**
Sans., Skr., Skt. Sanskrit.

San Sal·va·dor〔sæn'sælvə,dɔr; sæn'sælvədɔː〕聖薩爾瓦多(**a.** 薩爾瓦多之首都。**b.** 巴哈馬羣島之一島,又名 Watlings)。

sans-cu·lotte〔,sænzkju'lɑt, sɑ̃ky'lɔ̃t; ,sænzkju'lɔt〕*n.* ①法國大革命時貴族對過激共和黨人之蔑稱。②過激革命家。

San·sei, san·sei〔'sɑn'se; 'sɑːn'sei〕*n., pl.* **-sei, -seis.** 三世(祖父母爲日本人的美國公民)。

san·ser·if〔sæn'sɛrɪf; sæn'serif〕*n.*〖印刷〗無細線之活字(如 **abc**)。—*adj.* 無細線的(活字)。

San·skrit〔'sænskrɪt; 'sænskrit〕*n.* 「梵文。—*adj.* 梵文的。

San·skrit·ist〔'sænskrɪtɪst; 'sænskritist〕*n.* ①精通梵文的學者。②利用梵文神話支持自己之見解者。

sans-ser·if〔sæn'sɛrɪf; sæn'serif〕*n., adj.*〖印刷〗=**sanserif.**

Sans Sou·ci〔sɑ̃su'si; sɑ̃suː'siː〕〖法〗①無憂宮(在 Prussia 之 Potsdam, 爲 Frederick the Great 所建)。②(s- s-) 無憂無慮;逍遙自在地。

***San·ta Claus**〔'sæntɪ,klɔz; ,sæntə'klɔːz〕聖誕老人。(亦作 **Santa Klaus**)

San·ta Ma·ri·a〔'sæntəmə'riə; 'sɑːntə mə'riːə〕①聖大瑪利亞(哥倫布 1492 年航海發現美洲大陸時之旗艦)。②聖大瑪利亞(Guatemala 西部之一個活火山)。

San·ti·a·go〔,sæntɪ'ɑgo; ,sænti'ɑːgou〕*n.* 聖地牙哥(智利之首都)。

san·to〔'sɑnto; 'sɑːntou〕〖西〗*adj., n., pl.* **-tos.** —*adj.* 神聖的。—*n.* 聖者;聖像。

san·to·nin〔'sæntənɪn; 'sæntənin〕*n.*〖化〗山道年;蛔蒿素;茵陳素(用以驅除蛔蟲)。

São Pau·lo〔,sɑ̃u'paulu; sɑ̃u'paulu〕聖保羅(巴西東南, 南美第二大城)。

Saor·stat〔'sɛrstɑt; 'sɛəstɑːt〕*n.*〖愛〗自由邦。

São To·mé and Prin·ci·pe〔,sɑ̃utə'me～'prɪnsəpə; ,sɑ̃utə'mei～'prinsəpə〕聖多美及普林西比(非洲一共和國, 首都聖多美 São Tomé)。

***sap¹**〔sæp; sæp〕*n.* ①樹液;汁液;(樹皮下的)白木質。②血;元氣;精力。③〖俗〗蠢材。

sap² *v.,* **sapped, sap·ping,** *n.* —*v.t.* ①腐蝕;挖掘使不穩;使逐漸損壞。②挖地道。③由地道中行進而接近(敵陣)。④削弱;耗竭。—*n.* ①地道;對壕。②地道之挖掘。③逐漸損壞;削弱;耗竭。

sap·a·jou〔'sæpədʒu; 'sæpədʒuː〕*n.* 南美產之一種捲尾猿。

sa·pan·wood〔sə'pæn,wud; sə'pænwud〕*n.*〖植物〗蘇方;蘇木。

sap·ful〔'sæpfəl; 'sæpfəl〕*adj.* 多液汁的。

sap green 暗綠色;一種暗綠色之顏料。

sap·head〔'sæp,hɛd; 'sæphed〕*n.*〖美俗〗蠢人;呆子。—**ed,** *adj.* —**ed·ness,** *n.*

sap·id〔'sæpɪd; 'sæpid〕*adj.* ①有味的;有風味的。②有趣味的;適意的。—**i·ty,** *n.*

sa·pi·en·cy〔'sepɪənsɪ; 'seipjənsi〕*n.* 智慧。(亦作 **sapience**)

sa·pi·ent〔'sepɪənt; 'seipjənt〕*adj.* 有智慧的;有知識的(常含諷刺之意)。—**ly,** *adv.*

sa·pi·en·tial〔,sepɪ'ɛnʃəl; ,seipi'enʃəl〕*adj.* 智慧的;表現智慧的;給予智慧的。

sap·less〔'sæplɪs; 'sæplis〕*adj.* ①無樹液的;枯萎的。②無精力的。③無價值的;沒趣味的。

sap·ling〔'sæplɪŋ; 'sæpliŋ〕*n.* ①樹苗。②青年。—**hood,** *n.*

sap·o·dil·la〔,sæpə'dɪlə; ,sæpə'dilə〕*n.* ①(西印度及中美洲所產的一種)大常青樹。②此種樹的果實(可食,叫做sapodilla plum)。

sap·o·na·ceous〔,sæpə'neʃəs; ,sæpou'neiʃəs〕*adj.* 似肥皂的;石鹼質的。

sa·pon·i·fi·ca·tion〔sə,pɑnəfə'keʃən; sə,pɔnifi'keiʃən〕*n.* 石鹼化;鹼化。

sa·pon·i·fy〔sə'pɑnə,faɪ; sə'pɔnifai〕*v.t.* & *v.i.,* **-fied, -fy·ing.** 使石鹼化;使鹼化。

sa·por〔'sepɔr, -pɚ; 'seipɔː〕*n.* ①味;滋味(主要爲科學用語)。②風味。

sap·o·rif·ic〔,sæpə'rɪfɪk; ,sæpə'rifik〕*adj.* 有味的;能刺激味覺的。

sap·o·rous〔'sæpərəs; 'sæpərəs〕*adj.* 有味的;美味的。—**sap·o·ros·i·ty,** *n.*

sap·per〔'sæpɚ; 'sæpə〕*n.* ①〖英〗挖壕之工兵。②炸彈、水雷處理專家。***Royal Sappers and Miners***〖英〗工兵。

Sap·phic〔'sæfɪk; 'sæfik〕*adj.* Sappho 的;有 Sappho 之風格的; Sappho 之詩體的。—*n.* 有 Sappho 風格之詩。

***sap·phire**〔'sæfaɪr; 'sæfaiə〕*n.* ①青玉;藍寶石。②青玉色。③剛石之一種。—*adj.* ①蔚藍色的。②用藍寶石做的。

sap·phir·ic〔sə'fɪrɪk; sə'firik〕*adj.* 有青玉之特色的;像青玉的。

sap·phir·ine〔'sæfərɪn; 'sæfərain〕*adj.* 青玉的;青玉色的;像青玉的。—*n.* 碧石英。

sap·phism〔'sæfɪzm̩; 'sæfizm〕*n.* 女子間的同性戀。—**sap·phist,** *n.*

Sap·pho〔'sæfo; 'sæfou〕*n.* 莎孚(紀元前 600 年左右的希臘女詩人)。

sap·py〔'sæpɪ; 'sæpi〕*adj.,* **-pi·er, -pi·est.** ①多樹汁的;多汁液的。②精力充沛的。③〖俗〗愚蠢的。

sa·pr(a)e·mi·a〔sə'primɪə; sæ'priːmiə〕*n.*〖醫〗敗血症。—**sa·pre·mic,** *adj.*

sap·ro·phyte〔'sæpro,faɪt; 'sæproufait〕*n.*〖植物〗腐生菌(寄居生物屍體內)。

sap·suck·er〔'sæp,sʌkɚ; 'sæp,sʌkə〕*n.* 一種以樹汁爲食物的啄木鳥。

sap·wood〔'sæp,wud; 'sæpwud〕*n.*〖植物〗白木質;液質木質。

SAR Sons of the American Revolution.

sar·a·band〔'særə,bænd; 'særəbænd〕*n.* ①莎拉本舞(緩慢的西班牙舞)。②其舞曲。

Sar·a·cen〔'særəsn̩; 'særəsn〕*n.* ①阿拉伯人之古稱。②十字軍東征時之回教徒。—*adj.* 回教徒的。

Sar·a·cen·ic〔,særə'sɛnɪk; ,særə'senik〕*adj.* 回教徒的。(亦作 **Saracenical**)

Sar·ah〔'sɛrə; 'sɛərə〕*n.* ①女子名。②〖聖經〗Abraham 之妻, Isaac 之母。

sa·ran〔sə'ræn; sə'ræn〕*n.* 耐火塑膠。

Sa·ra·wak〔sə'rɑwɑk, -wɑ; sə'rɑːwək〕*n.* 沙勞越(馬來西亞之一邦, 首府 Kuching)。

sar·casm〔'sɑrkæzəm; 'sɑːkæzm〕*n.* 「譏諷;諷刺。

sar·cas·tic〔sɑr'kæstɪk; sɑː'kæstik〕*adj.* 諷刺的;辛辣的;好諷刺的。—**ness,** *n.*

sar·cas·ti·cal·ly〔sɑr'kæstəkəlɪ; sɑː'kæstikəli〕*adv.* 諷刺地。

sarce·net〔'sɑrsnɪt; 'sɑːsnet〕*n.* =**sarsenet.**

sar·co·carp〔'sɑrko,kɑrp; 'sɑːkoukɑːp〕*n.*〖植物〗①核果之果肉。②肉果皮。

sar·co·ma〔sɑr'komə; sɑː'koumə〕*n., pl.* **-mas, -ma·ta**〔-mətə; -mətə〕.〖醫〗惡性毒瘤;肉瘤。

sar·coph·a·gus〔sɑr'kɑfəgəs; sɑː'kɔfəgəs〕*n., pl.* **-gi**〔-,dʒaɪ; -dʒai〕, **-gus·es.** (古希臘、羅馬、埃及之)雕刻精美之石棺。

sar·co·phile〔'sɑrkə,faɪl; 'sɑːkəfail〕

n. 食肉動物。
sard [sard; sɑːd] *n.* 〖礦〗肉紅石髓。
sar·dine**[1] [sɑr'din; sɑː'diːn] *n., pl.* **-dines, -dine.** 沙丁魚。packed like sardines*** 擠得像沙丁魚一般。
sar·dine[2] ['sardɪn, -daɪn; 'sɑːdain] *n.* =**sard.**
sar·don·ic [sɑr'danɪk; sɑː'dɔnik] *adj.* 諷刺的;譏誚的;嘲笑的。
sar·don·i·cal·ly [sɑr'danɪklɪ; sɑː'dɔnikəli] *adv.* 諷刺地;譏誚地。
sar·don·i·cism [sɑr'danə,sɪzəm; sɑː'dɔnisizm] *n.*諷刺。
sar·do·nyx ['sardənɪks; 'sɑːdəniks] *n.* ①〖礦〗纏絲瑪瑙(帶紅白條紋)。②深紅色。
sar·gas·so [sɑr'gæso; sɑː'gæsou] *n., pl.* **-so(e)s.** 〖植物〗馬尾藻。
Sar·gas·so Sea [sɑr'gæso～; sɑː'gæsou～] 藻海(北大西洋西印度羣島東北之海域)。
sa·ri, sa·ree ['sari; 'sɑːriː] *n.* 紗麗(印度女裝,以長布做成,穿着時半披半裹)。
sark [sark; sɑːk] *n.* 〖蘇, 古〗襯衣;內衣。
sa·rong [sə'rɔŋ, 'sarɔŋ; sə'rɔŋ] *n.* ①(馬來羣島等地男女所着之)布裙。②裙布。
sar·sa·pa·ril·la [,sarspə'rɪlə; ,sɑːsəpə'rilə] *n.* ①撒爾沙(美洲產的熱帶植物)。②由撒爾沙根中提煉的藥(可治梅毒)。③撒爾沙根爲香料所做之冷飲;沙士。
sar·sar ['sarsɚ; 'sɑːsə] *n.* 刺骨寒風。
sarse·net ['sarsnɪt; 'sɑːsnet] *n.* 一種薄絹。
sar·to·ri·al [sɑr'torɪəl; sɑː'tɔːriəl] *adj.* 〖諧〗裁縫的;衣服的。
SAS Scandinavian Airlines System. 斯堪的那維亞航空公司。
sash[1] [sæʃ; sæʃ] *n.* 窗框。—*v.t.* 裝以窗框。
***sash**[2] *n.* 帶;飾帶;肩帶;腰帶。
sa·shay [sæ'ʃe; sæ'ʃei] *v.i.* 行;走;滑。—*n.* ①旅行。②探險。
sash chain (上下拉動窗戶的)曳鍊。
sash cord (上下拉動窗戶之)繩。(亦作 **sash line**)
sash house 小溫室。
sash pulley (上下拉動窗之)窗框滑輪。
sash weights 上下拉動窗之平衡棒。
sash window 可上下拉動之窗。
sass [sæs; sæs] *n.* ①頂嘴。②蔬菜。—*v.t.* 向…出言不遜。—*v.i.* 言行粗魯。
sas·sa·fras ['sæsə,fræs; 'sæsəfræs] *n.* ①〖植物〗北美洲產之一種樟科植物。②該種植物之根皮。
Sas·se·nach ['sæsn̩,æk; 'sæsənæk] *n., adj.* 撒克遜人(的);英格蘭人(的)。
sas·sy ['sæsɪ; 'sæsi] *adj.*, **-si·er, -si·est.** 〖美俗〗①莽撞的;無禮的;唐突的。②很帥的。
sas·tra ['sastrə; 'sɑːstrə] *n.* ①〖印度教〗聖書。②有關科學或藝術之權威著作。
***sat** [sæt; sæt] *v.* pt. & pp. of **sit.**
SAT Scholastic Aptitude Test.
Sat. ①Saturday. ②Saturn.
***Sa·tan** ['setn̩; 'seitən] *n.* 撒旦;惡魔。
sa·tan·ic, Sa·tan·ic [se'tænɪk; sə'tænik] *adj.* ①惡魔的;魔王的。②如惡魔的;極邪惡的。③極難看的;醜惡的。④極惡劣的。
sa·tan·i·cal [se'tænɪkl̩; sə'tænikl] *adj.* =**satanic.**
sa·tan·i·cal·ly [se'tænəklɪ; sə'tænikəli] *adv.* 似魔王地;極邪惡地。
Sa·tan·ism ['setənɪzəm; 'seitənizm] *n.* 魔道;惡魔根性;惡魔崇拜。
Sa·tan·ist ['setənɪst; 'seitənist] *n.* 崇拜惡魔者;本性邪惡者。
sa·tan·ize ['setən,aɪz; 'seitənaiz] *v.t.*, **-ized, -iz·ing.** 使入邪道;使有惡魔特性。
satch·el ['sætʃəl; 'sætʃəl] *n.* 小皮包;小學生用之書包。
sate[1] [set; seit] *v.t.*, **sat·ed, sat·ing.** ①充分滿足(食慾或其他欲望)。②供給過多致使厭棄;使膩。
sate[2] [set, sæt; sæt] *v.* 〖古〗pt. & pp. of **sit.**
sa·teen [sæ'tin; sæ'tiːn] *n.* 假緞(一種棉織物)。
sate·less ['setlɪs; 'seitlis] *adj.* 〖詩〗不知足的。
***sat·el·lite** ['sætl̩,aɪt; 'sætəlait] *n.* ①〖天文〗衛星。The moon is a *satellite* of the earth. 月亮爲地球之衛星。②隨從人員;僕從。③諂媚的追隨者;食客。④附庸國。⑤人造衛星。⑥附屬社區。⑦附屬品。—*adj.* ①衛星的。②附庸的。*satellite* states. 附庸國。
sat·el·lit·ic [,sætə'lɪtɪk; ,sætə'litik] *adj.* ①〖天文〗衛星的;同衛星般運行的。②附屬的。③衛星國的。
sat·el·loid ['sætəlɔɪd; 'sætəlɔid] *n.* ①速度慢不能久作軌道運行的太空船。②一種半飛機,半人造衛星式的有人太空船。
sa·ti·a·ble ['seʃɪəbl̩; 'seiʃjəbl] *adj.* 可使滿足的;可使飽的。
sa·ti·ate [*v.* 'seʃɪ,et; 'seiʃieit *adj.* 'seʃɪɪt; 'seiʃiit] *v.*, **-at·ed, -at·ing,** *adj.* —*v.t.* (通常用於被動式)①使飽;使滿足。②使因供給過度而厭倦;使膩。—*adj.* 滿足的。
sa·ti·a·tion [,seʃɪ'eʃən; ,seiʃi'eiʃən] *n.* ①滿足(的狀態)。②滿足(的行動)。
sa·ti·e·ty [sə'taɪətɪ; sə'taiəti] *n.* 飽足;饜足;滿足。
sat·in ['sætɪn; 'sætin] *n.* 緞。figured *satin.* 花緞。—*adj.* ①緞的。②光澤如緞的。
sat·i·net(te) [,sætɪ'nɛt; ,sæti'net] *n.* 一種含棉的劣質緞。
sat·in·ize ['sætɪn,aɪz; 'sætinaiz] *v.t.*, **-ized, -iz·ing.** 使有如緞光澤;予以光澤加工。
satin stitch 刺繡的一種針法(繡線彼此平行,形成一種似緞之表面)。
sat·in·wood ['sætn̩,wud; 'sætinwud] *n.* 緞木(印度產之一種良質木材)。
sat·in·y ['sætɪnɪ; 'sætini] *adj.* 似緞的;光滑的;有光澤的。
***sat·ire** ['sætaɪr; 'sætaiə] *n.* ①諷刺;譏刺。②諷刺詩;諷刺文;諷刺作品。③諷刺文學。
sa·tir·ic [sə'tɪrɪk; sə'tirik] *adj.* 諷刺的;譏刺的。(亦作 **satirical**)
sat·i·rist ['sætərɪst; 'sætərist] *n.* 諷刺詩(文)作者;諷刺家。
sat·i·rize ['sætə,raɪz; 'sætəraiz] *v.t.* & *v.i.*, **-rized, -riz·ing.** 諷刺;譏刺。—**sat·i·riz·er,** *n.*
sat·is ['sætɪs; 'sætis] 〖拉〗 *n., adv.* 充分(地);考試成績合格(地);及格。
sat·is·fac·tion** [,sætɪs'fækʃən; ,sætis'fækʃən] *n.* ①滿足;滿意。She felt *satisfaction* at winning a prize. 她得了獎,覺得很滿意。②令人滿意之事物(前面須加不定冠詞,且鮮用複數)。The news was a great *satisfaction* to all of us. 此項消息使我們全體都極感滿意。③賠償;補償;償還。I demand some *satisfaction* for that loss. 爲那項損失我要求一些補償。④補贖;償罪;贖罪。⑤報復的機會(如決鬥等)。find satisfaction in*** 由某事感到滿足。***give satisfaction*** a. 使滿意;使滿足。b. 因侮辱而作決鬥。***to one's (own) satisfaction*** 使某人(自感)滿意。***to the satisfaction of*** 使…滿意。

***sat·is·fac·to·ry** [ˌsætɪsˈfæktərɪ; ˌsætisˈfæktəri] *adj.* 滿意的;令人滿意的;適意的;圓滿的。The answer was not quite *satisfactory* to him. 這項答覆未使他完全滿意。—**sat·is·fac·to·ri·ly,** *adv.*

sat·is·fi·a·ble [ˈsætɪsˌfaɪəbl; ˈsætisˌfaiəbl] *adj.* 可使滿足的。

sat·is·fied [ˈsætɪsˌfaɪd; ˈsætisfaid] *adj.* ①滿足的。a *satisfied* look. 滿足的表情。②已付清的。③被說服的。

‡**sat·is·fy** [ˈsætɪsˌfaɪ; ˈsætisfai] *v.,* **-fied, -fy·ing.** —*v.t.* ①使滿意;使滿足。I am *satisfied* with your explanation. 我對於你的解釋是滿意了。to *satisfy* one's thirst. 止渴。②償還;賠償;補償。to *satisfy* a creditor. 清償欠債。③使確信;使消除疑慮。I am *satisfied* that he is guilty. 我確信他有罪。④解決;解答。—*v.i.* ①令人滿意。Riches do not always *satisfy*. 財富並不永遠令人滿足。②補償;贖罪。

sat·is·fy·ing [ˈsætɪsˌfaɪɪŋ; ˈsætisˌfaiiŋ] *adj.* 使滿足的;使滿意的。—**ly,** *adv.*

sa·to·ri [sɑˈtɔrɪ; sɑːˈtɔːri] *n.* 【禪宗】心靈的醒悟;悟道。

sa·trap [ˈsetræp; ˈsætrəp] *n.* ①古波斯之省長。②殖民地的總督。③暴吏。④主管;主持人。

sa·trap·y [ˈsetrəpɪ, ˈsætrə-; ˈsætrəpi] *n., pl.* **-trap·ies.** ①古波斯之省。②長官階級制度。

sat·u·ra·ble [ˈsætʃərəbl; ˈsætʃərəbl] *adj.* 可浸透的;可使飽和的。

sat·u·rant [ˈsætʃərənt; ˈsætʃərənt] *adj.* 【化】飽和的。—*n.* ①【化】飽和劑。②【醫】制酸劑。

sat·u·rate [ˈsætʃəˌret; ˈsætʃəreit] *v.,* **-rat·ed, -rat·ing,** *adj., n.* —*v.t.* ①浸;浸透;滲透。During a fog, the air is *saturated* with moisture. 下霧時空氣被濕氣浸透。②使滿;使達飽和點。③【化】使飽和。a *saturated* compound. 飽和化合物。a *saturated* solution. 飽和溶液。—*adj.* 【化】飽和的。—*n.* 【化】飽和化合物。

sat·u·rat·ed [ˈsætʃəˌretɪd; ˈsætʃəˌreitid] *v.* pt. & pp. of **saturate.** —*adj.* ①飽和的。an already *saturated* market. 已達飽和的市場。②充滿的;塞滿的。③濕透的;浸水的。④未被白色弄淡的(顏色)。⑤完成的;成熟的。

sat·u·ra·tion [ˌsætʃəˈreʃən; ˌsætʃəˈreiʃən] *n.* ①浸透;浸潤。②飽和。falling off of sales due to market *saturation*. 由於市場之飽和而引起的銷路減退。③【化】飽和;飽和狀態。*saturation* point. 飽和點。④普及的程度;普及度。⑤純色性。⑥密集攻擊。

saturation bombing 密集轟炸。

‡**Sat·ur·day** [ˈsætədɪ; ˈsætədi] *n.* 星期六。

Saturday night special 【美】價廉而易購到的手槍。

Sat·ur·days [ˈsætədɪz; ˈsætədiz] *adv.* 每星期六。

Sat·ur·day-to-Mon·day [ˈsætədɪtəˈmʌndɪ; ˈsætəditəˈmʌndi] *n.* 週末休假。—*adj.* 週末的。

***Sat·urn** [ˈsætən; ˈsætən] *n.* ①【羅馬神話】農神。②【天文】土星。③鉛(鍊丹術用語)。④美國之農神火箭。

Sat·ur·na·li·a [ˌsætəˈnelɪə; ˌsætəːˈneiljə] *n. pl.* ①古羅馬之祭農神 Saturn 節。②(s-)狂歡喧鬧;縱情狂歡之時節。

sa·tur·na·li·an [ˌsætəˈnelɪən; ˌsætəːˈneiljən] *adj.* 喧鬧的;放肆的;縱情狂歡的。

Sa·tur·ni·an [sæˈtɜnɪən; sæˈtəːnjən] *adj.* ①【天文】土星的。②【羅馬神話】農神 Saturn 的。③繁榮的;快樂的;安寧的。—*n.* (假想的)土星人。

sa·tur·nic [səˈtɜnɪk; səˈtəːnik] *adj.* 鉛毒的;鉛毒性的。

sat·ur·nine [ˈsætəˌnaɪn; ˈsætəːnain] *adj.* ①憂鬱的;沉默的;嚴肅的。②譏誚的。③鉛中毒的。—**sat·ur·nin·i·ty,** *n.*

sat·ur·nism [ˈsætənɪzəm; ˈsætəːnizm] *n.* 【醫】慢性鉛中毒。

sat·ya·gra·ha [ˈsʌtjəˌgrʌhə; ˈsʌtjəˌgrʌhə] *n.* 【印度】(甘地之)不合作主義。

sat·ya·gra·hi [ˈsʌtjəˌgrʌhi; ˈsʌtjəˌgrʌhiː] *n.* 【印度】實行(甘地)不合作主義者。

sat·yr [ˈsætə, ˈsetə; ˈsætə] *n.* ①【希臘神話】半人半獸的森林之神。②色狼;色情狂者。

sat·y·ri·a·sis [ˌsætɪˈraɪəsɪs; ˌsætiˈraiəsis] *n.* 【醫】男性的情慾亢進;色情狂。

sat·yr·o·ma·ni·ac [ˌsætɪrəˈmenɪˌæk; səˌtirəˈmeiniæk] *n.* 有色情狂之男人。

sauce** [sɔs; sɔːs] *n., v.,* **sauced, saucing.** —*n.* ①調味汁;醬油。②【美】果醬。tomato *sauce.* 番茄醬。③任何增加趣味或刺激的東西。④【俗】無禮之言;冒昧;莽撞。⑤【俚】酒。None of your sauce!*** 別胡說八道!—*v.t.* ①加味道;調味。②使有趣味;使有情趣。③【俗】對…唐突莽撞;對…無規矩。④緩和或減輕…之嚴厲。—**less,** *adj.*

sauce·boat [ˈsɔsˌbot; ˈsɔːsbout] *n.* (餐桌上之)船形醬汁碟器。

sauce·box [ˈsɔsˌbɑks; ˈsɔːsbɔks] *n.* 【俗】魯莽無禮之人;(尤指)頑皮的孩子。

***sauce·pan** [ˈsɔsˌpæn; ˈsɔːspən] *n.* 長柄有蓋的煮鍋。

sauce·pot [ˈsɔsˌpɑt; ˈsɔːspɔt] *n.* (普通)煮鍋。

***sau·cer** [ˈsɔsə; ˈsɔːsə] *n.* ①茶碟。②小碟。③碟狀物。a flying *saucer.* 飛碟。④小盆地。—**like,** *adj.*

saucer eye 大而圓之眼睛。

sau·cer-eyed [ˈsɔsəˌaɪd; ˈsɔːsəraid] *adj.* 眼大而圓的。

sau·cer·ful [ˈsɔsəful; ˈsɔːsəful] *n., pl.* **-fuls.** 一碟之量。

sau·cer·man [ˈsɔsəmən; ˈsɔːsəmən] *n.* 來自外太空的飛碟人。

***sau·cy** [ˈsɔsɪ; ˈsɔːsi] *adj.,* **-ci·er, -ci·est.** ①鹵莽的;無禮的;孟浪的。②俊俏的;慧黠的。—**sau·ci·ly,** *adv.* —**sau·ci·ness,** *n.*

Sa·u·di [sɑˈudɪ, ˈsaudɪ; sɑːˈuːdi, ˈsaudi] *adj.* ①沙烏地阿拉伯(人)的。②(阿拉伯)沙烏地王朝的。—*n.* ①沙烏地阿拉伯人。②(阿拉伯)沙烏地王朝之人。③該王朝之擁護者。

Saudi Arabia 沙烏地阿拉伯(阿拉伯半島中部之一國,首都爲麥加 Mecca與利雅得 Riyadh)。

Saudi Arabian ①沙烏地阿拉伯王國的;沙烏地阿拉伯人的;沙烏地阿拉伯語的。②沙烏地阿拉伯人。

sauer·kraut [ˈsaurˌkraut; ˈsauəkraut] *n.* 一種泡菜(以白菜切細加鹽發酵製成)。

Saul [sɔl; sɔːl] *n.* ①【聖經】掃羅(以色列的第一位君主)。②掃羅(使徒 Paul 的原名)。

saul [sɔl; sɔːl] *n.* 【植物】婆羅雙樹。

Sau·mur [soˈmyr; ˈsoumjuə] *n.* (法國產的一種)白葡萄酒。

sau·na [ˈsaunɑ; ˈsaunə] *n.* 芬蘭蒸汽浴。

saun·ter [ˈsɔntə; ˈsɔːntə] *v.t.* 閒逛;漫步。—*n.* ①漫步;閒遊。②悠閒之步態。

Sau·ri·a [ˈsɔrɪə; ˈsɔːriə] *n. pl.* 【動物】蜥蜴類。

sau·ri·an ['sɔrɪən; 'sɔːriən] *adj.* 蜥蜴類的。—*n.* 蜥蜴類動物。
sau·roid ['sɔrɔɪd; 'sɔːrɔid] *adj.* 似蜥蜴的。—*n.* 似蜥蜴的動物。
sau·ry ['sɔrɪ; 'sɔːri] *n., pl.* **-ries.** 〖魚〗針魚;鱵魚。
***sau·sage** ['sɔsɪdʒ; 'sɔsidʒ] *n.* 臘腸;香腸。
sausage balloon 觀測用的繫留汽球。
sausage curl 如香腸的一束捲髮。
sausage meat 製臘腸用之肉。
sausage roll 臘腸捲。
sau·té [so'te; 'soutei] *adj., n., v.,* **-téed, -té·ing.** —*adj.* 煎的;炸的。*sauté* potatoes. 煎洋芋片。—*n.* 煎或炸的菜肴。—*v.t.* 煎;炸;炒。
sau·terne [so'tɝn; sou'təːn] *n.* (法國產的一種)白葡萄酒。
sauve qui peut [ˌsovki'pœ; ˌsouvkiː'pəː] 〖法〗(自顧自的)潰散;四散逃生 (= save himself who can).
sav·a·ble ['sevəbl̩; 'seivəbl] *adj.* ①可救助的。②可儲蓄的。③可節省的。
***sav·age** ['sævɪdʒ; 'sævidʒ] *adj., n., v.,* **-eagd, -ag·ing.** —*adj.* ①天然的;荒野的。②野蠻的;未開化的。*savage* customs. 野蠻的習俗。③兇暴的;殘酷的。④未經馴服的;野生的。—*n.* ①野人;野蠻人。②殘酷之人。—*v.t.* ①(尤指馬)亂踏;痛打;傷害。②使變爲野蠻、殘暴等。
sav·age·ly ['sævɪdʒlɪ; 'sævidʒli] *adv.* 野蠻地;殘酷地。The gangsters beat him up *savagely.* 歹徒們將他痛毆。
sav·age·ness ['sævɪdʒnɪs; 'sævidʒnis] *n.* ①蠻荒;荒野。②殘酷;野蠻。
sav·age·ry ['sævɪdʒrɪ; 'sævidʒəri] *n., pl.* **-ries.** ①蠻荒狀態;野蠻狀態;未開化。②殘忍;殘暴。③荒涼;凄涼。④野獸或野蠻人(集合稱)。(亦作 **savagism**)
sa·van·na(h) [sə'vænə; sə'vænə] *n.* ①大草原。②(熱帶、亞熱帶的)無樹的大平原。
sa·vant [sə'vɑnt, 'sævənt; 'sævənt] *n., pl.* **-vants** [-vənts, -'vɑn; -vənts, -'vɑːn]. 著名學者;博學之士。
sa·vate [sæ'væt; sæ'væt] 〖法〗 *n.* 法國古代的一種拳擊(脚手均可用)。
‡**save**[1] [sev; seiv] *v.,* **saved, sav·ing.** —*v.t.* ①援救;拯救;保全。He *saved* the boy from drowning. 他救了這個男孩,使他未被溺死。②儲蓄;貯存。to *save* money. 儲蓄金錢。③節省;省去;免去。Large print *saves* one's eyes. 大字可節省目力。④減少。to *save* trouble. 減少麻煩。⑤救(球)(使不入球門)。***save appearances*** (or ***honor***)保全體面。***save one's breath*** 緘默。***save oneself*** 偸懶。***save one's face*** 保全面子。***save one's neck*** 謀自保;明哲保身。***save one's pains*** 不濫費氣力。***save one's skin*** 免受損傷(往往指以卑鄙的手段)。***save the mark*** 〖古〗對不起(說錯話時的道歉)! ***save the situation*** 收拾時局;挽救難關。***save the tide*** 趁水漲時出(入)港;把握機會。***save up*** 貯錢。***Save us!*** 哎呀!嚇了一跳! —*v.i.* ①儲蓄。②節省。She *saves* in every way she can. 她在各方面盡可能的節省。③解脫(罪惡)。④保全;保護。⑤貯藏食物等使不變壞。⑥救球(使不入球門)。
***save**[2] *prep., conj.* 除…外。All is lost *save* honor. 除榮譽外一切都喪失了。
save-all ['sevˌɔl; 'seivɔːl] *n.* ①任何防止浪費或損傷的東西。②燭臺的底盤。③外套;外衣。④〖航海〗脚帆。⑤兒童之撲滿。⑥〖方〗吝嗇鬼。
sav·e·loy ['sævəˌlɔɪ; 'sævilɔi] *n.* 一種乾臘腸。
sav·er ['sevɚ; 'seivə] *n.* ①救助者;援助之人;救星。②儉省之人。③節省的方法或機械;省費器(有時用於複合字中)。
sav·in(e) ['sævɪn; 'sævin] *n.* 杜松屬的一種藥用植物。
sav·ing** ['sevɪŋ; 'seiviŋ] *adj.* ①援救的;救助的。②儉約的;節儉的。③儲蓄的。④保留的。⑤補償的;補不足的。a saving clause*** 保留條款。—*prep.* ①除…外;除非。He is never idle *saving* in sleep. 他除睡覺時外從不閒着。②對…合乎禮貌;敬重。***saving your reverence*** (or ***presence***) 說句失敬的話。—*conj.* 除…之外;除非。—*n.* ①拯救;救助。②節省;節約。From *saving* comes having. 節儉爲致富之本。③節省之錢。The discount gave me a *saving* of $25. 打一個折扣使我省下25元。④儲蓄。⑤(*pl.*)儲金。*savings* of years. 多年的儲金。
saving grace 足以補償其他缺點之特質。
savings account 儲蓄存款戶頭。
savings and loan association 信用合作社。
savings bank 儲蓄銀行。
savings bond 〖美〗儲蓄公債。
sav·io(u)r** ['sevjɚ; 'seivjə] *n.* 救濟者;拯救者。the Savior*** 救世主。
sa·voir-faire ['sævwɑr'fɛr; 'sævwɑː'fɛə] 〖法〗 *n.* 能幹;處世機警;隨機應變之道。
sa·voir-vi·vre [ˌsa'vwar'vivr; ˌsa'vwar'viːvr] 〖法〗 *n.* 對人情世故社交禮儀之知識。
***sa·vo(u)r** ['sevɚ; 'seivə] *n.* ①味;滋味;風味。②特質;意味。—*v.t.* ①欣賞…的味;嘗味。②調味;加以香味。③現出…的影響;具有…之意味。④盡情享受。—*v.i.* 具有某種氣味、意味或性質〖of〗. His speech *savors* of wisdom. 他的言語中顯露着智慧。
sa·vor·i·ness ['sevərɪnɪs; 'seivərinis] *n.* 風味;佳味。
sa·vo(u)r·less ['sevəlɪs; 'seivəlis] *adj.* 無香味的;無風味的;無興味的。
sa·vor·y[1] ['sevərɪ; 'seivəri] *adj.,* **-vor·i·er, -vor·i·est,** *n., pl.* **-vor·ies.** —*adj.* ①味香的;可口的;開胃的。②怡人的。③高尚的;高貴的。—*n.* 開胃的點心。(英作 **savoury**) —**sa·vor·i·ly,** *adv.*
sa·vor·y[2] *n., pl.* **-vor·ies.** 歐洲產的一種香薄荷。
Sa·voy [sə'vɔɪ; sə'vɔi] *n.* 法國東南部地名(昔爲一公國)。
sa·voy [sə'vɔɪ; sə'vɔi] *n.* 〖植物〗皺葉甘藍。
Sa·voy·ard [sə'vɔɪɚd; sə'vɔiɑːd] *n.* Savoy 人。—*adj.* ①Savoy 的; Savoy 人的。②倫敦 Savoy 歌劇院的。
sav·vy ['sævɪ; 'sævi] *v.,* **-vied, -vy·ing,** *n., adj.* —*v.t.* & *v.i.* 知道;了解。—*n.* 理解;見識。—*adj.* 聰明的;知曉的;懂道理的。
***saw**[1] [sɔ; sɔː] *n., v.,* **sawed, sawed** or **sawn, saw·ing.** —*n.* 鋸。—*v.t.* 鋸;鋸開;鋸成。—*v.i.* ①鋸;被鋸開。②用鋸;使鋸。③似鋸一般切開;似鋸地往復而動。—**er,** *n.*
***saw**[2] *v.* pt. of **see.**
saw[3] *n.* 格言;諺語。
saw·bones ['sɔˌbonz; 'sɔːbounz] *n.* 〖俚〗外科醫生。
saw·buck ['sɔˌbʌk; 'sɔːbʌk] *n.* ① = **sawhorse.** ②〖俚〗面額十元或二十元之鈔票。
saw·der ['sɔdɚ; 'sɔːdə] *v.t.* 〖俗〗奉承;諂媚。—*n.* 〖俗〗奉承;諂媚;甘言;諛詞。
saw-doc·tor ['sɔˌdɑktɚ; 'sɔːˌdɔktə]

n. 整鋸齒之工具。
saw·dust [ˈsɔˌdʌst; ˈsɔːdʌst] n. 鋸屑。
sawed-off [ˈsɔdˌɔf; ˈsɔːdˈɔf] adj. ①鋸短了的。②〖俚〗矮小的;小型的。
saw·fish [ˈsɔˌfɪʃ; ˈsɔː-fiʃ] n., pl. **-fish, -fish·es.** 鋸鮫;鋸鱝。
saw·fly [ˈsɔˌflaɪ; ˈsɔːflai] n. 鋸蠅。
saw frame 鋸架。(亦作 **saw gate**)
saw·horse [ˈsɔˌhɔrs; ˈsɔːhɔːs] n. 鋸木架。
saw log 鋸木。
saw·mill [ˈsɔˌmɪl; ˈsɔːmil] n. ①鋸木廠。②鋸木機。
sawn [sɔn; sɔːn] v. pp. of **saw¹**.
saw·ney [ˈsɔnɪ; ˈsɔːni] n. ①小丑;傻瓜。②(S-)〖蔑〗蘇格蘭人。—adj. 愚蠢的。—v.i. 愚蠢地說。
saw pit 鋸木坑。
saw set 整鋸齒之工具。
saw·tooth [ˈsɔˌtuθ; ˈsɔːtuːθ] n., pl. **-teeth** [-ˌtiθ; -tiːθ], adj. —n. 鋸齒。—adj. =**saw-toothed.**
saw-toothed [ˈsɔˌtuθt; ˈsɔːtuːθt] adj. 鋸齒狀的。
saw·yer [ˈsɔjɚ; ˈsɔːjə] n. ①鋸木匠。②被絆羈河中之樹。③幼蟲藏居木頭中之甲蟲。
sax [sæks; sæks] n. 〖俗〗=**saxophone.**
Sax. ①Saxon. ② Saxony.
saxe [sæks; sæks] n. ①薩克森藍(一種染料)。②(德製)蛋白照相紙。
Saxe-Co·burg-Go·tha [ˈsæksˈkobɝgˈgotə; ˈsæksˈkoubəːgˈgouθə] n. 英國王室名(從 1901 至 1917, Edward VII 及 George V 爲國王的一個時期)。
sax·horn [ˈsæksˌhɔrn; ˈsækshɔːn] n. 〖音樂〗薩克號(一種有鍵銅管樂器)。
sax·i·frage [ˈsæksəfrɪdʒ; ˈsæksifridʒ] n. 〖植物〗虎耳草。
Sax·on [ˈsæksn̩; ˈsæksn] n. ①撒克遜人。②撒克遜語。③盎格魯撒克遜人。④現代德國 Saxony 地方之人或其語言。—adj. ①撒克遜人的;撒克遜語的。②盎格魯撒克遜的。③英國的;英語的;英國人的。④Saxony 地方的。
Sax·on·ism [ˈsæksn̩ɪzm̩; ˈsæksnizm] n. 撒克遜語風;撒克遜氣質。
Sax·on·ist [ˈsæksənɪst; ˈsæksənist] n. 精通撒克遜語者;主張用純粹撒克遜語者。
Sax·on·ize [ˈsæksn̩ˌaɪz; ˈsæksənaiz] v.t., **-ized, -iz·ing.** 使撒克遜化;使盎格魯撒克遜化。
Saxon words 原有之英語(對外來語而言)。
Sax·o·ny [ˈsæksn̩ɪ; ˈsæksni] n. ①薩克森(德國地區名)。②(有時作 s-) 一種高級毛料或毛線。
sax·o·phone [ˈsæksəˌfon; sækˈsəfoun] n. 薩克管(一種裝有單簧片的管樂器)。
sax·o·phon·ist [ˈsæksəˌfonɪst; sækˈsɔfounist] n. 薩克管吹奏者。
sax·tu·ba [ˈsæksˌtjubə; ˈsæksˌtjuːbə] n. 低音大薩克號。
:say [se; sei] v., **said** [sɛd; sed], **say·ing**, n. —v.t. ①言;說。What did you *say?* 你說甚麼? ②表達;宣布。*Say* what you think. 把你的意思宣布出來。③背誦;誦讀。to *say* one's lessons. 背誦功課。to *say* one's prayers. 祈禱。④假定 (=if);姑且說(=let us say). *Say* it were true, what then? 假使這是眞的,那麼怎樣呢? ⑤表達意見。It is hard to *say* what is wrong. 甚麼地方出了毛病很難說。—v.i. 言;說。So he says. 他是這樣說。***as much as to say*** 好像是說…一樣;像要說…似的。***Easier said than done.*** 〖諺〗說着容易做着難。***I say!*** 哎呀! 喂喂!我是說…。***It is said*** (or ***They say***) …. 據說…。***No sooner said than done.*** 〖俗〗一說就實行;即說即做。***not to say*** 即使不能說。It is warm, *not to say* hot. 雖不能說熱, 亦很暖和了。***Say away!*** 完全說出來! ***say nothing of*** 更不待言。***say on*** 繼續說下去。***say to*** (***do something***) 〖俗〗叫;命。He *said to tell* you not to come. 他叫(我)告訴你不要來。***say*** (***something***) ***to oneself*** 自言自語;想;以爲。***that is to say*** 即是;換言之。***Who shall I say, sir?*** (傳達者問來客)請問尊姓大名? —n. ①言辭;欲言之事。I have had my *say.* 我已盡所欲言。②發言權。***have a say*** 有發言權;有參加決定權。***have the say*** 居於領導地位;有決定權。Who *has the say* in the matter? 關於這事誰有決定權? —**er,** n.
say·a·ble [ˈseəbl̩; ˈseiəbl] adj. ①可以說的;可表達的。②可有力或流利地說出來的。
Sa·yan Mountains [sɑˈjɑn~; sɑːˈjɑːn~] 薩彥嶺(在外蒙西北部,爲中俄界山)。
say·est [ˈseɪst; ˈseiist] v.t. & v.i. 〖古〗say 之第二人稱、單數、現在式。(亦作 **sayst**)
ˈsay·ing [ˈseɪŋ; ˈseiiŋ] n. ①言語;陳述。*Sayings* and doings are two things. 言和行是兩回事。②格言;諺語;名言。***as the saying goes*** (or ***is***) 常言道;俗語說得好。***go without saying*** 不待言;不消說。
sa·yo·na·ra [ˈsɑjoˈnɑrɑ; ˈsɑːjouˈnɑːrɑː] 〖日〗 n. 再會。
Say's law [sez~; seiz~] 〖經濟〗賽氏定律。
say-so [ˈseˌso; ˈseisou] n. 〖美俗〗①並無證據支持之個人聲明。②最後決定權;權威。
Sb 化學元素 stibium(拉 =antimony) 之符號。 **Sb, s.b.** 〖棒球〗stolen base(s). **sb.** substantive. **S.B.** ①Scientiae Baccalaureus(拉=Bachelor of Science). ②simultaneous broadcasting. ③South Britain. **S.b.E.(W.)** South by East (West).
'sblood [zblʌd; zblʌd] interj. 〖古〗該死的! (God's blood 之略語)。
SbW South by West. **Sc** ①化學元素 scandium 之符號。②〖氣象〗 stratocumulus. **sc** small capitals. **SC.** Service Charge. **Sc.** ①Scotch. ②Scotland. ③Scots. ④Scottish. ⑤science. **sc.** ① scale. ②scene. ③science. ④scientific. ⑤ scilicet. ⑥screw. ⑦scruple(s). **S.C.** ①Sanitary Corps. ②Signal Corps. ③ South Carolina. ④Staff Corps. ⑤Supreme Court. ⑥Staff College. **s.c.** ①〖印刷〗small capitals. ②supercalendered.
scab [skæb; skæb] n., v., **scabbed, scab·bing.** —n. ①創口上結的疤;痂。②癬;(特指羊的)疥癬。③(植物的)斑點病。④〖俚〗不加入工會的工人; 不參加工會或罷工而接受罷工工人位置的工人。⑤〖俚〗鄙夫; 無賴; 流氓。—v.i. ①(創口)結疤;生疙痂;生疥癬。②〖俚〗破壞罷工;不加入工會而工作。
scab·bard [ˈskæbɚd; ˈskæbəd] n. 劍鞘;鞘。***throw*** (or ***fling***) ***away the scabbard*** 丟開劍鞘;採取斷然處置;決心作戰;奮鬥到底。—v.t. 將…插入(劍)鞘中。
scabbard fish 大刀魚。
scab·bed [ˈskæbɪd; ˈskæbid] adj. ①有痂的。②〖廢,方〗卑賤的;無價值的。
scab·by [ˈskæbɪ; ˈskæbi] adj., **-bi·er, -bi·est.** ①結痂的。②由痂組成的。③〖俗〗卑鄙的;卑劣的。④患疥癬病的。
sca·bi·es [ˈskebɪˌiz; ˈskeibiiːz] n. 〖醫〗疥癬。
sca·bi·o·sa [ˌskebɪˈosə; ˌskeibiˈousə]

n. =scabious[2]. 「疥癬的；多痂的。」
sca·bi·ous[1] [ˈskebɪəs; ˈskeibjəs] *adj.*
sca·bi·ous[2] *n.* 〖植物〗山蘿蔔；輪峯菊。
scab·land [ˈskæbˌlænd; ˈskæb-lænd] *n.* 不毛的火山地帶。
sca·brous [ˈskebrəs; ˈskeibrəs] *adj.* ①粗糙的。②多困難的。③稍帶猥褻的。
scad [skæd; skæd] *n.* 鰺魚。
scad(s) [skæd(z); skæd(z)] *n.* 〖俚〗①許多；大量。②錢；硬幣。
scaf·fold [ˈskæfld; ˈskæfəld] *n.* ①足臺；鷹架（建築或修繕房屋時所搭之架）。②斷頭臺；絞臺。③（物品之）陳列臺；看臺。④任何所搭之臺。***go to*** (or ***mount***) ***the scaffold*** 上斷頭臺。***send to the scaffold*** 送上斷頭臺。—*v.t.* 搭臺；設鷹架。
scaf·fold·ing [ˈskæfldɪŋ; ˈskæfəldiŋ] *n.* ①足臺；鷹架；臺架；絞刑臺。②其建築材料。
scag, skag [skæg; skæg] *n.* 〖美俚〗海洛英。 「人造大理石。」
scagl·io·la [skælˈjolə; skælˈjoulə] *n.*
scal·a·ble [ˈskeləbl; ˈskeiləbl] *adj.* ①可攀登的。②可去鱗的。③可秤的。
scal·age [ˈskelɪdʒ; ˈskeilidʒ] *n.* ①木材之概算量。②潮濕物品或易損耗物品在重量或價格方面之折扣。③打這種折扣。
sca·lar [ˈskelɚ; ˈskeilə] *adj.* ①梯狀的。②由一數可表明的。③〖數學〗數量的。—*n.* 數量。
sca·lar·i·form [skəˈlærəˌfɔrm; skəˈlærifɔːm] *adj.* 〖生物〗梯狀的；階狀的。
sca·la·tion [skeˈleʃən; skeiˈleiʃən] *n.* 鱗之性質及形態。
scal·(l)a·wag [ˈskæləˌwæg; ˈskælə-wæg] *n.* =scallywag.
***scald**[1] [skɔld; skɔːld] *v.t.* ①燙。He was *scalded* with hot water. 他被熱水燙傷。②煮熱（牛乳等）。③用沸水或蒸氣澆燙。—*v.i.* ①被煮燙。②被燙傷。—*n.* ①燙傷。②樹葉在酷暑時之變褐色。③植物寄生蟲病。
scald[2] [skɔld; skɔːld] *n.* 〖俚〗頭瘡；白癬。
scald[3] *n.* 古代北歐之遊唱詩人。(亦作**skald**)
scald·er [ˈskɔldɚ; ˈskɔːldə] *n.* 煮沸器；煮沸消毒器。
scald·fish [ˈskɔldˌfɪʃ; ˈskɔːldfiʃ] *n., pl.* **-fish, -fish·es.** 一種比目魚。
scald head (小孩子的)癩痢頭。
scale**[1] [skel; skeil] *n., v.,* **scaled, scal·ing.** —*n.* ①天秤盤。②(常*pl.*)天秤；秤。hang in the scale*** 未有決定。***hold the scales even*** 公平裁判。***tip the scales*** **a.** 稱得體重。He *tips the scales* at 150 pounds. 他體重爲 150 磅。**b.** 因一邊過重而使失去平衡。**c.** 轉變爲有利情勢。***turn the scale(s)*** 改變情勢；決定。***turn the scale at...pounds*** 重(若干)磅。—*v.t.* ①用秤稱。②重(若干)。He *scales* 175 pounds. 他體重一百七十五磅。—*v.i.* ①過磅。②有重量。
scale**[2] *n., v.,* **scaled, scal·ing.** —*n.* ①鱗。②鱗狀物。③鱗片。④鍋垢；銹皮。⑤〖植物〗鱗苞。⑥甲蟲。⑦(*pl.*) **a.** 使聖保羅暫時失明之眼疾(新約使徒行傳9章18節)。**b.** 使人看不清眞相之事物。remove the scales from a person's eyes*** 使某人看清眞相。—*v.t.* ①剝鱗。②使生鱗垢；使在…上生銹皮。—*v.i.* ①剝落；脫落。②生鱗狀物。—**like,** *adj.*
***scale**[3] *n., v.,* **scaled, scal·ing.** —*n.* ①等級；階級。A duke is high in the social *scale*. 公爵的社會地位是崇高的。②尺；尺度；刻度。③比例尺；縮尺；比例。④〖音樂〗音階。⑤記數法；進法。decimal *scale*. 十進位。⑥規模。They are preparing for war on a large *scale*. 他們正在大規模地準備戰爭。—*v.t.* ①攀登；以梯登；爬越。②(按比例)增加〖up〗；(按比例)減低〖down〗。Income tax was *scaled* up 10%. 所得稅增加百分之十。All prices were *scaled* down 15%. 一切物價都減低百分之十五。③按照比例尺而做。—*v.i.* 攀登；逐步增高。
scale armor 鱗甲；甲葉鎧(古代戰袍)。
scale beam 天平桿。
scale·board [ˈskelˌbord; ˈskeilbɔːd] *n.* ①極薄之木板。②〖印刷〗插於活字行間的薄木條。③鑲蓋表面用的薄木片。
scaled [skeld; skeild] *adj.* ①〖動物〗有鱗的；覆有鱗的。②已剝掉鱗的。③鱗狀排列的(羽毛等)。④用雲梯登城而占領的。
scale-down [ˈskelˌdaun; ˈskeildaun] *adj.* 縮小的；減低的。 「蟲。」
scale insect 〖動物〗介殼科昆蟲；介殼
scale leaf 〖植物〗鱗葉。 「鱗的。」
scale·less [ˈskellɪs; ˈskeillis] *adj.* 無
scale model 與原物成比例的模型。
sca·lene [skeˈlin; ˈskeiliːn] *adj.* ①〖解剖〗斜角肌的。②〖數學〗不規則的；不等邊的。③〖數學〗斜的(圓錐體)。
scal·er [ˈskelɚ; ˈskeilə] *n.* ①攀登者。②除鱗器。③牙齒去垢器。④〖電〗定標器。
scale-up [ˈskelˌʌp; ˈskeilˈʌp] *adj.* 增加的；擴大的。 「②魚鱗之排列。」
scal·ing [ˈskelɪŋ; ˈskeiliŋ] *n.* ①鱗。
scaling ladder 雲梯。
scall [skɔl; skɔːl] *n.* 頭皮疥癬。
scal·lion [ˈskæljən; ˈskæljən] *n.* 〖植物〗①青葱。②多葱。③韮菜。
scal·lop [ˈskɑləp; ˈskɔləp] *n.* ①〖動物〗干貝。②海扇殼之一扇。③淺鍋；貝皿。④(衣服邊、袖口等之)扇形皺褶。—*v.t.* ①焙；烤。②弄成扇形皺褶。
scal·lop·er [ˈskɑləpɚ; ˈskɔləpə] *n.* ①焙烤者。②弄成扇形皺褶者。③撈海扇用的船。
scal·lop·ing [ˈskɑləpɪŋ; ˈskɔləpiŋ] *n.* ①捕捉海扇類之漁業。②扇形飾物。③做扇形飾物。 「禮之徽章)。②貝殼皿；淺鍋。」
scallop shell ①海扇殼(昔日聖地巡
scal·ly·wag [ˈskælɪˌwæg; ˈskæliwæg] *n.* ①〖諧〗無賴；流氓；惡棍。②美國內戰後重建時期與北方政府合作之南方白人。
scalp** [skælp; skælp] *n.* ①頭皮。②連髮頭皮之一部分。③勝利紀念品。④〖俗〗買賣轉手所賺的薄利。have the scalp of*** 打敗(某人)。***out for scalps*** 去出征；挑戰似地。***take one's scalp*** 剝掉頭皮；打勝；報讎。—*v.t.* ①剝去…的頭皮。②做(股票)小投機。③賣(黃牛票)。—*v.i.* ①賣黃牛票。②炒股票。—**less,** *adj.*
scal·pel [ˈskælpɛl; ˈskælpəl] *n.* 外科醫生用之小刀。 「戲票等牟利之)黃牛。」
scalp·er[1] [ˈskælpɚ; ˈskælpə] *n.* (轉售
scalp·er[2] *n.* 〖外科〗刮骨刀；解剖刀。
scalp lock 若干印第安部落戰士留在頭皮上的一束頭髮以表示其戰士之身分。
scal·y [ˈskelɪ; ˈskeili] *adj.,* **scal·i·er, scal·i·est.** ①鱗狀的；多鱗的。②有介殼類甲蟲的。③一層層地剝落的。④〖俗〗卑鄙的；可憎的。 「lin)。(亦作**scaly lizard**)」
scaly anteater 穿山甲(=pango-
scam·mo·ny [ˈskæmənɪ; ˈskæməni] *n.* ①〖植物〗一種旋花科植物。②自此種植物根中提煉之樹脂(做瀉藥用)。

scamp [skæmp; skæmp] *n.* 流氓;無賴漢。—*v.t.* 潦草從事。—*v.i.* 吝嗇;小量供給。—**ish,** *adj.*

scam·per ['skæmpɚ; 'skæmpə] *v.i.* ①疾走;急馳;逃走。②跑來跑去;跳來跳去。—*n.* 疾走;急馳;逃走。

scan [skæn; skæn] *v.,* **scanned, scan·ning,** *n.* —*v.t.* ①細察;審視。②〖俗〗匆匆一閱。③按韻律吟誦(詩)。④在(詩句上)作韻律記號。⑤〖電視〗掃描範圍。—*v.i.* ①〖詩〗合於韻律。②〖電視〗掃描。—*n.* ①審視。②押韻。③〖電視〗掃描範圍。

Scan., Scand. ①Scandinavia. ②Scandinavian.

scan·dal** ['skændl; 'skændl] *n.* ①恥辱;汚辱;醜行;醜聞。a railroad *scandal.* 鐵路貪汚案件。②誹謗;詆毀。Don't talk *scandal.* 不要誹謗人。③反感;憤慨。be the scandal of*** 使爲之驚駭;使不悅。***raise a scandal*** 使世人憤慨;引起物議。

scan·dal·ize ['skændlˌaɪz; 'skændəlaiz] *v.t.,* **-ized, -iz·ing.** 使(人)憤慨;使(人)駭異。—**scan·dal·i·za·tion,** *n.*

scan·dal·mon·ger['skændlˌmʌŋgɚ; 'skændlˌmʌŋgə] *n.* 散布惡意中傷之言者。

scan·dal·ous ['skændləs; 'skændələs] *adj.* ①可恥的;令人發生反感的。②誹謗的;惡意中傷的。—**ly,** *adv.*

scandal sheet 揭人陰私的報紙或雜誌。

Scan·di·na·vi·a [ˌskændə'nevɪə; ˌskændi'neivjə] *n.* ①斯堪的那維亞(挪威、瑞典、丹麥、冰島之集合稱)。②斯堪的那維亞半島(由挪威及瑞典構成)。

Scan·di·na·vi·an [ˌskændə'nevɪən; ˌskændi'neivjən] *adj.* 斯堪的那維亞(人、語)的;北歐(人、語)的。—*n.* 斯堪的那維亞語(人);北歐語(人)。

Scandinavian Peninsula 斯堪的那維亞半島。

scan·di·um ['skændɪəm; 'skændiəm] *n.* 〖化〗鈧(稀有金屬元素,化學符號爲 Sc)。

scan·ner ['skænɚ; 'skænə] *n.* ①詳察者。②精於分析詩之韻律者。③〖電視〗掃描機。

scan·ning ['skænɪŋ; 'skæniŋ] *n.* ①詳察;細察;審視。②〖電視〗掃描。

scanning disk 〖電視〗掃描盤。

scanning telescope 掃描望遠鏡。

scan·sion ['skænʃən; 'skænʃən] *n.* 詩之韻律分析;按照輕重節奏而讀詩。—**ist,** *n.*

scan·so·ri·al [skæn'sorɪəl; skæn'sɔːriəl]*adj.* ①(適於)攀登的。②〖動物〗攀禽類的。

***scant** [skænt; skænt] *adj.* ①欠缺的;少量的。②剛剛够用的。③不足的〖of〗。She was *scant* of breath. 她在喘息。④節省的;吝嗇的。—*v.t.* ①減少;限制。②尅扣;不給。—*adv.* 殆不;幾乎不。

scan·ties ['skæntɪz; 'skæntiz] *n. pl.* 極短之短褲。

scant·i·ly ['skæntɪlɪ; 'skæntili] *adv.* 缺乏地;不足地;僅。(亦作 **scantly**)

scant·ling ['skæntlɪŋ; 'skæntliŋ] *n.* ①小木材。②此等小木材之集合稱。③建築材料之尺寸。④小的直立木材。⑤少量。

***scant·y** ['skæntɪ; 'skænti] *adj.,* **scant·i·er, scant·i·est.** 缺乏的;不足的。He is *scanty* of words. 他沈默寡言。—**scant·i·ness,** *n.*

SCAP Supreme Commander for the Allied Powers.

scape[1] [skep; skeip] *n.* ①〖植物〗根生花梗;花莖。②〖動物〗羽軸;觸角根。③〖建築〗柱身。

scape[2] *n., v.,* **scaped, scap·ing.** —*n.* 〖古〗逃脫;逃遁。—*v.t.* & *v.i.* 逃脫。

scape·goat ['skepˌgot; 'skeipgout] *n.* 替罪羊;代人受過者。to be made the *scapegoat* for... 作…之替罪者。

scape·goat·ism ['skepˌgotɪzṃ; 'skeipgoutizəm] *n.* 諉過;卸罪。

scape·grace ['skepˌgres; 'skeipgreis] *n.* 無賴漢;流氓;惡棍。

scaph·oid ['skæfɔɪd; 'skæfɔid] *adj.* ①舟形的。②〖解剖〗舟形的。—*n.* 〖解剖〗舟骨;船形骨。

scap·u·la ['skæpjələ; 'skæpjulə] *n., pl.* **-lae** [-ˌli; -liː], **-las.** 〖解剖〗肩胛骨。

scap·u·lar ['skæpjəlɚ; 'skæpjulə] *adj.* 肩胛骨的。—*n.* ①〖宗教〗肩衣;無袖法衣。②〖動物〗肩翼;肩羽。③〖外科〗肩胛繃帶。

***scar**[1] [skɑr; skɑː] *n., v.,* **scarred, scar·ring.** —*n.* ①傷痕;疤;痕跡。a vaccine *scar.* 痘疤。②心上之創傷。—*v.t.* 使有傷痕。—*v.i.* 結疤;痊癒。

scar[2] *n.* ①巉岩;斷崖;峭壁。②(海中之)孤岩;岩礁。

scar·ab ['skærəb; 'skærəb] *n.* ①蜣螂。②古埃及的蜣螂雕像(用作護身符)。(亦作 **scarabee**)

scar·a·bae·us [ˌskærə'biəs; ˌskærə'bi(ː)əs] *n., pl.* **-bae·i** [-'biaɪ; -'biːai], **-bae·us·es.** =**scarab.**

scar·a·mouch ['skærəˌmautʃ; 'skærəmautʃ] *n.* ①(古代義大利喜劇中的)愛虛張聲勢的懦夫;愛吹嘘者。②無賴漢。

scarce** [skɛrs; skɛəs] *adj.,* **scarc·er, scarc·est,** *adv.* —*adj.* ①缺乏的。②稀罕的;難得的。a *scarce* book. 難得之書;珍本。make oneself scarce*** 〖俗〗**a.** 退避;不出來。**b.** 突然離去。—*adv.* =**scarcely.**

‡**scarce·ly** ['skɛrslɪ; 'skɛəsli] *adv.* ①殆無;殆不(=hardly). I *scarcely* saw him. 我簡直沒有看見他。②一定不(=definitely not). He can *scarcely* have said so. 他一定不會如此說。③將近;不充分;不完全(=not quite). He is *scarcely* eighteen. 他將近十八歲。④甫…卽(與 when 或 before 連用)。*Scarcely* had I seen the lightning, when I heard a clap of thunder. 我剛一看見閃電就聽見雷聲。〖注意〗**scarcely** 本身含有否定的意思,應避免與否定式連用。

scarce·ment ['skɛrsmənt; 'skɛəsmənt] *n.* 〖建築〗壁階。

***scar·ci·ty** ['skɛrsətɪ; 'skɛəsiti] *n., pl.* **-ties.** ①缺乏;不足。②稀罕;難得。

scare** [skɛr; skɛə] *v.,* **scared, scar·ing,** *n.* —*v.t.* 恐嚇;驚嚇。I was *scared* to death. 嚇死我了!—*v.i.* 受驚;驚駭;驚恐。be more scared than hurt*** 無事自擾;有驚無險。***be scared stiff*** (or ***hollow***) 嚇呆了。***scare up*** 〖俗〗**a.** (將財物)嚇出來;蔽詐出來;得到。**b.** 籌措。—*n.* 驚恐;恐慌。a war *scare.* 以爲戰爭將至的恐慌。

scare buying (恐物資缺乏之)搶購。

***scare·crow** ['skɛrˌkro; 'skɛə-krou] *n.* ①稻草人。②衣服襤褸者。③嚇唬人之物。

scared [skɛrd; skɛəd] *adj.* 受驚的;嚇了的;害怕的。Don't be *scared.* 不要怕。***run scared*** **a.** 戰戰兢兢地從事競選活動生怕失敗似的。**b.** 害怕得拚命跑。

scared·y-cat ['skɛrdɪˌkæt; 'skɛədikæt] *n.* 〖俗〗容易受驚的人;膽小鬼。

scare·head ['skɛrˌhɛd; 'skɛəhed] *n.* 〖美俗〗聳人聽聞之報紙大標題。(亦作 **scare-heading**)

scare·mon·ger ['skɛrˌmʌŋgɚ;

ˈskɛəˌmʌŋgə] *n.* 散布駭人聽聞之謠言的人。
scare·mon·ger·ing [ˈskɛrˌmʌŋgərɪŋ; ˈskɛəˌmʌŋgəriŋ] *n.* 散布駭人聽聞謠言。
scar·er [ˈskɛrɚ; ˈskɛərə] *n.* 嚇人者。
***scarf**[1] [skɑrf; skɑːf] *n.*, *pl.* **scarfs** or **scarves** [skɑrvz; skɑːvz], *v.* —*n.* ①圍巾;頸巾;肩巾;腰巾。②領巾。③桌巾;檯巾。—*v.t.* 以圍巾包;以桌布蓋。
scarf[2] *n.*, *pl.* **scarfs**, *v.* —*n.* ①(木材、金屬等之)嵌接。②(嵌接之)割口;切口; 接榫。—*v.t.* 嵌接(木材、金屬等)。
scar-faced [ˈskɑrˌfest; ˈskɑːfeist] *adj.* 滿臉是疤的;臉上有疤的。
scarf joint 〖機械〗嵌接。
scarf·pin [ˈskɑrfˌpɪn; ˈskɑːfpin] *n.* 領帶扣針。
scarf-ring [ˈskɑrfˌrɪŋ; ˈskɑːfriŋ] *n.* 「〖英〗領帶(圍巾)的固定環。」
scarf·skin [ˈskɑrfˌskɪn; ˈskɑːfskin] *n.* 〖解剖〗表皮。
scar·i·fi·ca·tion [ˌskærəfəˈkeʃən; ˌskɛərifiˈkeiʃən] *n.* 〖外科〗劃痕。
scar·i·fi·ca·tor [ˈskærəfɪˌketɚ; ˈskɛərifikeitə] *n.* 〖外科〗劃痕器。
scar·i·fy [ˈskærəˌfaɪ; ˈskɛərifai] *v.t.*, **-fied, -fy·ing.** ①〖外科〗在(皮膚)上劃痕。②嚴厲批評。③鬆(土)。④刻劃細痕於(種子)表皮上, 使其提早萌芽。—**scar·i·fi·er,** *n.*
scar·la·ti·na [ˌskɑrləˈtinə; ˌskɑːləˈtiːnə] *n.* 〖醫〗猩紅熱。
***scar·let** [ˈskɑrlɪt; ˈskɑːlit] *n.* ①深紅;緋紅;猩紅。②深紅色的布或衣着。—*adj.* ①深紅的;緋紅的;猩紅的。②面紅耳赤的。③明顯的;昭彰的。 a *scarlet* crime. 滔天大罪。
scarlet fever 〖醫〗猩紅熱。
scarlet hat 天主教的樞機主教之帽子。
scarlet letter 猩紅A字(昔時被判通姦罪之婦女所佩帶的標記)。
scarlet runner 〖植物〗美洲熱帶之一種食用豆類植物。
Scarlet Woman 緋衣婦(參見新約「聖經啓示錄第十七章)。」
scarlet woman 妓女;淫婦。
scarp [skɑrp; skɑːp] *n.* ①懸崖;陡坡。②〖築城〗內壁。—*v.t.* ①使成陡坡。②備以內壁。
scarp·er [ˈskɑrpɚ; ˈskɑːpə] *v.i.* 〖英〗「突然離去(尤指不付帳而潛走)。」
scar·y [ˈskɛrɪ, ˈskærɪ; ˈskɛəri] *adj.*, **scar·i·er, scar·i·est.** 〖俗〗①使驚恐的;可怕的。②易驚恐的;膽怯的。
scat [skæt; skæt] *v.*, **scat·ted, scat·ting,** *interj.* —*v.t.* & *v.i.* 〖美俗〗叱退;(使)立刻走開(常用於命令語氣)。—*interj.* 趕走動物聲。
scathe [skeð; skeið] *n.*, *v.*, **scathed, scath·ing.** —*n.* 〖古〗損傷;傷害。 —*v.t.* ①酷評;苛責。②〖古〗傷害。③〖古〗使枯萎。
scathe·less [ˈskeðlɪs; ˈskeiðlis] *adj.* 無傷害的;無損害的。 —**ly,** *adv.*
scath·ing [ˈskeðɪŋ; ˈskeiðiŋ] *adj.* ①傷害的。②嚴苛的;苛刻的。—**ly,** *adv.*
sca·tos·co·py [skəˈtɑskəpɪ; skəˈtɔskəpi] *n.* 〖醫〗糞便檢查。(亦作**skatoscopy**)
‡scat·ter [ˈskætɚ; ˈskætə] *v.t.* ①散播;撒播。to *scatter* seed. 撒播種子。②驅散。③〖物理〗散射。—*v.i.* 分散;離散。The mob *scattered*. 暴徒們散去了。***scatter about*** 撒布; 散布。 ***scatter* (*something*) *to the winds*** 浪費。—*n.* ①散布;散播;離散。②散播之物。③〖俚〗房間。
scat·ter·a·tion [ˌskætəˈreʃən; ˌskætəˈreiʃən] *n.* 散播;分散。
scat·ter·brain [ˈskætɚˌbren; ˈskætəbrein] *n.* 注意力不集中的人。(亦作 **scatterbrains**) —**ed,** *adj.*
scat·tered [ˈskætɚd; ˈskætəd] *adj.* 散亂的;分散的。 —**ly,** *adv.* —**ness,** *n.*
scat·ter·good [ˈskætɚˌgʊd; ˈskætəgud] *n.* 揮霍無度的人。
scat·ter·gun [ˈskætɚˌgʌn; ˈskætəːgʌn] *n.* 〖俚〗獵槍。
scat·ter·ing [ˈskætərɪŋ; ˈskætəriŋ] *adj.* ①分散的。②散落的。③不集中的(選票)。
scatter rug 小地毯。
scatter shot ①大型鉛彈。②獵槍散彈「之擴散範圍。」
scat·ter·shot [ˈskætɚˌʃɑt; ˈskætəʃɔt] *adj.* ①擴散很廣的。②廣泛的;一般的。
scat·ty [ˈskætɪ; ˈskæti] *adj.*, **-ti·er, -ti·est.** 〖俗〗浮躁的;思想不集中的。
sca·tu·ri·ent [skəˈtʊrɪənt; skəˈturiənt] *adj.* 湧出的;流出的。
scaup duck [skɔp~; skɔːp~] 〖動物〗鈴鴨。(亦作 **scaup**)
scaur [skɑr; skɑː] *n.* 斷崖;巖礁。
scav·enge [ˈskævɪndʒ; ˈskævindʒ] *v.*, **-enged, -eng·ing.** —*v.t.* ①清掃(街道等)。②排出內燃機氣缸內(廢氣)。③〖冶金〗(加入另一種物質, 同渣滓化合而)清除(鎔化之金屬)。—*v.i.* ①作清掃者;清掃街道等。②覓食。
scav·en·ger [ˈskævɪndʒɚ; ˈskævindʒə] *n.* ①清道夫。②以腐物腐屍爲食之動物。
Sc.B. Bachelor of Science. **Sc.B.C.** Bachelor of Science in Chemistry. **Sc.B.E.** Bachelor of Science in Engineering. **Sc. D.** Doctor of Science. **Sc. D. Hyg.** Doctor of Science in Hygiene. **Sc. D. Med.** Doctor of Medical Science.
sce·nar·i·o [sɪˈnɛrɪˌo; siˈnɑːriou] *n.*, *pl.* **-nar·i·os.** ①劇情說明書。②電影脚本。③行動方案。
sce·na·rist [sɪˈnɛrɪst; ˈsiːnərist] *n.* 「電影脚本作者。」
sce·na·rize [ˈsinəraɪz; ˈsiːnəraiz] *v.t.*, **-rized, -riz·ing.** 將…改寫成電影脚本。
scend [send; send] *n.*, *v.i.* ＝**send**[2].
‡scene [sin; siːn] *n.* ①出事地點。②(常 *pl.*)情景;實況。③(戲劇等的)一場、一幕;景;布景;(小說上所假設之)時間、地點或環境。④風景;景色。The sunrise was a beautiful *scene*. 日出是一美景。 ⑤吵鬧;發脾氣。***appear* (*come* or *enter*) *on the scene*** 出現舞臺上;登場。***behind the scenes*** a. 祕密地;暗中。 b. 後臺;幕後。 ***have a nice scene with*** 和…大鬧。***lay* (or *place*) *the scene in*** 取…做場面;用…做舞臺。***make the scene*** 〖美俚〗在某地出現;參加某項活動。***on the scene*** 在出事地點; 當場。 ***quit the scene*** 退場;死。***scene of battle*** 戰場。
scene·man [ˈsinmən; ˈsiːnmən] *n.*, *pl.* **-men.** 移置與排列舞臺布景者。
scene master 戲院中控制數條燈光電路的開關。
scene painter 舞臺背景畫幕之畫家;「畫布景者。」
***scen·er·y** [ˈsinərɪ; ˈsiːnəri] *n.*, *pl.* **-er·ies.** ①舞臺之布景;道具布置。②風景;景色。I enjoy mountain *scenery* very much. 我很喜歡山景。
scenery wagon 有脚輪之布景臺。
scene·shift·er [ˈsinˌʃɪftɚ; ˈsiːnˌʃiftə] *n.* ＝**sceneman.**
scene-steal·er [ˈsinˌstilɚ; ˈsiːnˌstiːlə] *n.* 在舞臺上出風頭之演員。
sce·nic [ˈsinɪk, ˈsɛn-; ˈsiːnik, ˈsen-] *adj.*

①舞臺的;戲劇的。②風景的;多風景的。*scenic* spots. 風景區。③背景的。

sce·ni·cal ['sinəkl; 'si:nikəl] *adj.* = scenic. —ly, *adv.*

scenic dome 火車客車車廂頂部之玻璃或塑膠拱頂,供旅客欣賞風景之用。

sce·no·graph ['sinə,græf; 'si:nəgra:f] *n.* 配景畫。

sce·nog·ra·phy [si'nɑgrəfɪ; si:'nɔgrəfi] *n.* 配景圖法; 寫景術。 **—sce·nog·raph·er,** *n.* **—sce·no·graph·i·cal,** *adj.*

scent** [sɛnt; sent] *n.* ①香;臭;氣味。②香水。③嗅覺。④蹤跡; 線索。The police are on the *scent* of the thieves. 警方正在追蹤竊賊。⑤臭跡;遺臭。follow up the scent*** (獵犬)聞着臭跡追趕。 ***get scent of*** 聞出…; 發覺…。 ***put one off the scent; put one on a wrong scent*** 使人迷失線索。 ***put one on the scent*** 使人跟着追;使人跟蹤追趕。—*v.t.* ①嗅出;聞出。②使香。③察覺。—*v.i.* ①發出香味;發出氣味。②藉嗅覺行獵。

scent bag (麝鹿等之)香囊。

scent bottle 香水瓶。

scent·ed ['sɛntɪd; 'sentid] *adj.* ①灑有香水的; 加有香料的。②芳香的。③有…嗅覺的。 keen-*scented*. 嗅覺敏銳的。

scent·ful ['sɛntful; 'sentful] *adj.* ①氣味濃厚的。②嗅覺敏銳的; 能靠嗅覺追踪的。

scent·less ['sɛntlɪs; 'sentlis] *adj.* 無氣味的;無香氣的;無嗅覺的。

scep·ter ['sɛptɚ; 'septə] *n.* ①王節;寶杖。②王權; 王位。 —*v.t.* ①授以王節;授以王權。②以王節輕觸表示嘉許。(亦作 **sceptre**) **—less,** *adj.* **—scep·tral,** *adj.*

scep·tered ['sɛptɚd; 'septəd] *adj.* ①有王權的。②持王節的。

scep·tic ['skɛptɪk; 'skeptik] *n.* 懷疑(論)者; 懷疑基督教眞理的人。 —*adj.* 懷疑的。(亦作 **skeptic**) **—al,** *adj.*

scep·ti·cism ['skɛptə,sɪzəm; 'skeptisizəm] *n.* ①懷疑。 ②懷疑說;懷疑主義。③對宗教之懷疑。(亦作 **skepticism**)

scha·den·freu·de ['ʃɑdən,frɔɪdə; 'ʃa:dən,frɔidə]〖德〗*n.* 幸災樂禍。

***sched·ule** ['skɛdʒul; 'ʃedju:l] *n., v.,* **-uled, -ul·ing.** —*n.* 目錄;表; 一覽表;時間表。Trains are sure to arrive on *schedule.* 火車必定按照時間表準時到達。—*v.t.* ①作目錄;列於表中。②列入時間表中; 排定(在某時間作某事)。 The President's speech is *scheduled* for next Tuesday. 總統定於下星期二發表演說。③〖俗〗安排(某事)於將來某特定的日期。**—sched·u·lar,** *adj.*

schee·lite ['ʃilaɪt; 'ʃeilait, 'ʃi:-] *n.* 〖礦〗重石;鎢酸鈣礦。

sche·ma ['skimə; 'ski:mə] *n., pl.* **-ma·ta** [-mətə;-mətə]. ①圖表;圖解;略圖;綱要。②〖修辭〗詞藻;形容;比喻。 ③(康德哲學的)先驗圖式。—**t·ic,** *adj.* **—tism,** *n.*

sche·ma·tize ['skimə,taɪz; 'ski:mətaiz] *v.t. & v.i.,* **-tized, -tiz·ing.** 按計畫行事;照公式安排。**—sche·ma·ti·za·tion,** *n.*

***scheme** [skim; ski:m] *n., v.,* **schemed, schem·ing.** —*n.* ①方案; 計畫; 設計。 He has a *scheme* for increasing his income. 他有一個增加收入的計畫。②圖謀;陰謀;奸策。③圖解;圖表。—*v.t. & v.i.*計劃;設計;圖謀。

schem·er ['skimɚ; 'ski:mə] *n.* 陰謀者;計劃者;設計者。

schem·ing ['skimɪŋ; 'ski:miŋ] *adj.*①計劃的;設計的。②詭詐的。 **—ly,** *adv.*

scher·zan·do [skɛr'tsɑndo; skeət'sændou]〖義〗*adj. & adv.*〖音樂〗遊戲的(地); 諧謔的(地)。

scher·zo ['skɛrtso; 'skeətsou] *n., pl.* **-zos, -zi** [-tsi; -tsi:].〖義〗〖音樂〗諧謔曲。

Schick test [ʃɪk~; ʃik~]〖醫〗希克氏試驗(檢驗是否易染白喉)。

Schie·dam [skɪ'dɑm; ski'dæm] *n.* ①斯奇丹(荷蘭西南部之一城市)。②該地產之杜松子酒。

schiff·li ['ʃɪflɪ; 'ʃifli] *n.* ①刺繡機。②刺繡器所繡之花式。

Schil·ler ['ʃɪlɚ; 'ʃilə] *n.* 席勒(Johann Friedrich von, 1759–1805, 德國詩人及劇作家)。

schil·ling ['ʃɪlɪŋ; 'ʃiliŋ] *n.* ①昔德國錢幣名。②奧國的貨幣單位。

schip·per·ke ['skɪpəkɪ; 'ʃipəki] *n.* (原產於比利時的一種)小犬。

schism ['sɪzəm; 'sizəm] *n.* ①(一個組織之)分裂。②分裂宗教(或教會之)罪。③宗派;派別;派系。 ***the Great Schism*** 公元800 年開始的基督教東西教會之分裂。

schis·mat·ic [sɪz'mætɪk; siz'mætik] *adj.* (亦作 **schismatical**)①分裂的;分離的;派別的;宗派的。②(宗教上)有分離趨向的;犯分離罪的。—*n.* 分裂宗教(或教會)之人。

schist [ʃɪst; ʃist] *n.* 〖地質〗片巖。

schist·ous ['ʃɪstəs; 'ʃistəs] *adj.* 片巖的;片巖質的;片巖狀的。 (亦作 **schistose**)

schiz·o·gen·e·sis [,skɪzə'dʒɛnɪsɪs; ,skizə'dʒenisis] *n.* 〖生物〗分裂生殖。

schiz·oid ['skɪzɔɪd; 'skizɔid] *adj.*〖醫〗精神分裂症的。—*n.* 患精神分裂症的人。

schiz·o·phrene ['skɪzə,frin; 'skitsoufri:n] *n.* 精神分裂症患者。

schiz·o·phre·ni·a [,skɪzə'frinɪə; ,skitsou'fri:njə] *n.* 〖精神病學〗精神分裂症。

schiz·o·phren·ic [,skɪzə'frɛnɪk; ,skitsou'frenik] *adj.* 患精神分裂症的。—*n.* 精神分裂症患者。

schiz·o·phyte ['skɪzə,faɪt; 'skizəfait] *n.* 分裂菌;分裂植物。

schiz·o·thy·mi·a [,skɪzə'θaɪmɪə; ,skizə'θaimiə] *n.* 瀕臨精神分裂之狀態。

schle·miel, schle·mihl [ʃlə'mil; ʃlə'mi:l] *n.* 〖俚〗笨手笨脚的人;笨蛋。

schlepp [ʃlɛp; ʃlep]〖俚〗*v.t.* 携帶。—*n.* 不足輕重之人;無成就之人。

schli·ma·zel [ʃlɪ'mɑzəl; ʃli'ma:zəl] *n.* 〖俚〗無能而經常運氣不佳者。(亦作 **schlimazl, shlimazel, shlimazl**)

schlock [ʃlɑk; ʃlɔk]〖俚〗*adj.* 賤的;不值錢的。—*n.* 不值錢的東西。

schmaltz, schmalz [ʃmɑlts; ʃma:lts] *n.* ①〖俚〗音樂、藝術、文學中之情感的渲染或誇張。②鷄油。**—y,** *adj.*

schmo(e) [ʃmo; ʃmou] *n.* 〖俚〗笨人;愚人。(亦作 **shmo**)

schmoos(e) [ʃmuz; ʃmu:z] *n., v.,* **schmoosed, schmoos·ing.**〖俚〗—*n.* 流言蜚語;閒話。—*v.i.* 搬弄是非。(亦作 **shmooze**)

schmuck [ʃmʌk; ʃmʌk] *n.* 〖俚〗笨瓜。

schnap(p)s [ʃnæps; ʃnæps] *n.* ①荷蘭杜松子酒。②任何烈酒。

schnau·zer ['ʃnauzɚ; 'ʃnauzə] *n.* 德國產的一種小獵犬。

schnook [ʃnuk; ʃnuk] *n.* 〖俚〗笨人。

schnor·kle, schnor·kel ['ʃnɔrkəl; 'ʃnɔ:kəl] *n.* =**snorkel.**

schnoz·zle ['ʃnɑzəl;'ʃnɔzəl] *n.* 〖俚〗鼻子。

***schol·ar** 〔ˈskɑlɚ; ˈskɔlə〕 *n.* ①學者。②學生；學習者。③享有獎學金之學生。④〖鄙〗受過教育的人。

schol·arch 〔ˈskɑlɑrk; ˈskɔlɑːk〕 *n.* 古代雅典哲學學校之校長；任何學校校長。

schol·ar·ly 〔ˈskɑlɚlɪ; ˈskɔləli〕 *adj.* ①有學者之風的；學者派頭的。②博學的。③適於做學者的。④好學的。⑤學習方法透徹而井然有序的。—*adv.* 學者派頭地。

***schol·ar·ship** 〔ˈskɑlɚˌʃɪp; ˈskɔləʃip〕 *n.* ①學識；學問；學業。②獎學金。He applied for a *scholarship* of two hundred dollars. 他申請一個二百元的獎學金。③獎學基金。

scho·las·tic 〔skoˈlæstɪk; skəˈlæstik〕 *adj.* (亦作 **scholastical**) ①學校的；學者的；學術的。a *scholastic* year. 學年。②煩瑣哲學的；煩瑣學派的。③學究的；迂腐的；教條式的；形式的。④中學的。—*n.* ①煩瑣學者。②迂腐之學究。③學生。④耶穌會之學習教士。

Scholastic Aptitude Test 美國大學入學考試中的學力、智力及性向測驗。

scho·las·ti·cate 〔skəˈlæstəkɪt; skəˈlæstikit〕 *n.* 耶穌會教士學校。

scho·las·ti·cism 〔skoˈlæstəˌsɪzəm; skəˈlæstisizəm〕 *n.* ①經院哲學；煩瑣哲學。②墨守傳統教條或方法。

scho·li·ast 〔ˈskolɪˌæst; ˈskouliæst〕 *n.* 評註者；註釋者；訓詁學者。

scho·li·as·tic 〔ˌskolɪˈæstɪk; ˌskouliˈæstik〕 *adj.* 註釋(者)的；訓詁(學者)的。

scho·li·um 〔ˈskolɪəm; ˈskouljəm〕 *n.*, *pl.* **-li·a**〔-lɪə; -liə〕, **-li·ums.** 評註；註釋；旁註。

‡school¹ 〔skul; skuːl〕 *n.* ①學校；校舍。primary (elementary) *school.* 小學；國民學校。②授課時間 (=period of teaching, 不用冠詞)。 *School* begins at eight o'clock. 八點鐘開始上課。③課業；授課(=lesson, teaching 不用冠詞)。He is at *school* now. 他現在在上課。④全體學生(=pupils)；全體師生。⑤學派；派。⑥大學內的院、系。⑦大學院、系之房屋；館；樓。⑧訓練所；養成所。⑨學院。medical *school.* 醫學院。 ***keep a school*** 辦(私立)學校。***tell tales out of school*** 洩漏秘密；搬弄是非。—*v.t.* ①教授；教育。He is well-*schooled.* 他受過良好教育。②訓練；克制。He *schools* himself to patience. 他養成忍耐性。③指導(演員)如何表演。—*adj.* 學校的。

school² *n.* (魚及水族動物之) 羣；隊。a *school* of dolphins. 一羣海豚。—*v.i.* 成羣地游。

school·a·ble 〔ˈskuləbl; ˈskuːləbl〕 *adj.* 適於學校的；適於入學的。

school age ①入學年齡。②應接受義務教育之年齡。

school·bag 〔ˈskulˌbæg; ˈskuːlbæg〕 *n.* 書包。

school board 地方教育委員會。

school·book 〔ˈskulˌbuk; ˈskuːlbuk〕 *n.* 教科書。—*adj.* 〖主美〗過分簡化的；教科書式的。

***school·boy** 〔ˈskulˌbɔɪ; ˈskuːlbɔi〕 *n.* 學童；學生。

school bus 校車。

school·child 〔ˈskulˌtʃaɪld; ˈskuːltʃaild〕 *n.*, *pl.* **-chil·dren.** 學童。

school day ①授課日期。②每日授課時數。③(*pl.*)求學時代。

school district 學區。

school edition 書籍作教科書用之版本。

school·fel·low 〔ˈskulˌfɛlo; ˈskuːlˌfelou〕 *n.* 同學。

***school·girl** 〔ˈskulˌgɝl; ˈskuːlgəːl〕 *n.* 女學生。—*adj.* 少女的。

school house ①〖英〗(public school 的校長之)公館。②(集合稱) 住校長公館與校長一同生活的學生們。

***school·house** 〔ˈskulˌhaus; ˈskuːlhaus〕 *n.* 校舍。

school·ing 〔ˈskulɪŋ; ˈskuːliŋ〕 *n.* ①學校教育。②學費。③授課。④訓練。⑤〖古〗譴責。

school inspector 督學。

school-leav·er 〔ˈskulˌlivɚ; ˈskuːlˌliːvə〕 *n.* 〖英〗中途輟學者。

school-leav·ing 〔ˈskulˌlivɪŋ; ˈskuːlˌliːviŋ〕 *n.* 〖英〗中途輟學。

school·ma'am 〔ˈskulˌmɑm; ˈskuːlmɑːm〕 *n.* 〖美俗〗=**schoolmarm.**

school·man 〔ˈskulmən; ˈskuːlmən〕 *n.*, *pl.* **-men.** ①教師；教育家；學者。②(S-) 中世紀大學的哲學、理則學及神學教授；煩瑣派學者。

school·marm 〔ˈskulˌmɑrm; ˈskuːlmɑːm〕 *n.* 〖俗, 方〗女教師。

***school·mas·ter** 〔ˈskulˌmæstɚ; ˈskuːlˌmɑːstə〕 *n.* ①校長。②教師。—*v.t.* & *v.i.* 擔任校長或教師職務。

school·mate 〔ˈskulˌmet; ˈskuːlmeit〕 *n.* 同學。

school·miss 〔ˈskulˈmɪs; ˈskuːlˈmis〕 *n.* 女學生。

school·mis·tress 〔ˈskulˌmɪstrɪs; ˈskuːlˌmistris〕 *n.* ①女校長。②女教師。

***school·room** 〔ˈskulˌrum, -ˌrum; ˈskuːlrum, -ruːm〕 *n.* 教室。

school·ship 〔ˈskulˌʃɪp; ˈskuːlʃip〕 *n.* 海事學校之訓練船。

school·teach·er 〔ˈskulˌtitʃɚ; ˈskuːlˌtiːtʃə〕 *n.* 教師。

school·teach·ing 〔ˈskulˌtitʃɪŋ; ˈskuːlˌtiːtʃiŋ〕 *n.* 教職。

school·time 〔ˈskulˌtaɪm; ˈskuːltaim〕 *n.* ①授業時間；開課時間。②求學時代。

school·work 〔ˈskulˌwɝk; ˈskuːlwəːk〕 *n.* 學業；學業成績。

school·yard 〔ˈskulˌjɑrd; ˈskuːljɑːd〕 *n.* 校園；運動場。

school year 學年。

schoon·er 〔ˈskunɚ; ˈskuːnə〕 *n.* ①(有兩桅以上之)縱帆式帆船。②(美國拓荒者乘用之)大篷車。③〖俗〗盛啤酒之大玻璃杯。

schooner rig 〖航海〗縱帆裝置。

schoon·er-rigged 〔ˈskunɚˌrɪgd; ˈskuːnərigd〕 *adj.* 有縱帆裝置的；縱帆式的。

Scho·pen·hau·er 〔ˈʃopənˌhauɚ; ˈʃoupənhauə〕 *n.* 叔本華(Arthur, 1788–1860, 德國哲學家)。

schot·tisch(e) 〔ˈʃɑtɪʃ; ʃɔˈtiːʃ〕 *n.* ①類似 polka 的二拍子圓舞。②其舞曲。

Schör·ding·er 〔ˈʃrœdɪŋɚ; ˈʃrœdiŋə〕 *n.* 士洛丁格 (Erwin, 1887–1961, 德國人, 波動力學之確定者, 曾獲1933年諾貝爾物理獎)。

Schu·bert 〔ˈʃubɚt; ˈʃuːbəːt〕 *n.* 舒伯特 (Franz, 1797–1828, 奧國作曲家)。

Schu·mann 〔ˈʃumən; ˈʃuːmən〕 *n.* 舒曼 (Robert, 1810–1856, 德國作曲家)。

schwa 〔ʃwɑ; ʃwɑː〕 *n.* 〖語音〗中性元音；不重讀之母音(如 about 中之 *a* 〔ə;ə〕)。

Schweit·zer 〔ˈʃvaɪtsɚ; ˈʃvaitsə〕 *n.* 史懷哲(Albert, 1875–1965, 牧師、哲學家、醫師, 在非洲行醫, 獲1952年諾貝爾和平獎)。

sci. ①science. ②scientific.

sci·am·a·chy 〔saɪˈæməkɪ; saiˈæməki〕 *n.* 同影子作戰；假想戰。(亦作 **sciomachy, skiamachy, skiomachy**)

sci·at·ic 〔saɪˈætɪk; saiˈætik〕 *adj.* ①坐骨的。②坐骨神經(痛)的。

sci·at·i·ca [saɪˈætɪkə; saiˈætikə] *n.* 〖醫〗坐骨神經痛。

‡**sci·ence** [ˈsaɪəns; ˈsaiəns] *n.* ①科學;學術。natural *science.* 自然科學。He is a man of *science.* 他是科學家。②技術。③知識。④(S-) 基督敎精神療法(= Christian Science).

science fiction 科學小說。(亦作「**sci-fi**」)

sci·en·tial [saɪˈɛnʃəl; saiˈenʃəl] *adj.* ①知識的。②學識豐富的。

*__sci·en·tif·ic__ [ˌsaɪənˈtɪfɪk; ˌsaiənˈtifik] *adj.* 科學(上)的;合乎科學的。*scientific* method. 科學方法。—**al·ly,** *adv.*

*__sci·en·tist__ [ˈsaɪəntɪst; ˈsaiəntist] *n.* ①科學家。②(S-)基督敎精神療法者。

scil. scilicet (拉=namely).

scil·i·cet [ˈsɪlɪˌsɛt; ˈsailiset] 〖拉〗 *adv.* 換言之;卽是;就是。(略作**sc., scil., SS., ss.**)

scim·i·tar, scim·i·ter [ˈsɪmətɚ; ˈsimitə] *n.* (波斯人、阿拉伯人等用之)彎刀;曲劍。

scin·til·la [sɪnˈtɪlə; sinˈtilə] *n.* ①火花。②微粒;痕跡;一點;極少。

scin·til·lant [ˈsɪntələnt; ˈsintələnt] *adj.* 發火花的;閃爍的。

scin·til·late [ˈsɪntlˌet; ˈsintileit] *v.i.,* **-lat·ed, -lat·ing.** ①放火花。②放智慧之光。

scin·til·la·tion [ˌsɪntlˈeʃən; ˌsintiˈleiʃən] *n.* ①放射火花。②火花閃爍。③天才橫溢。④〖天文〗閃動。

scintillation counter 閃爍計數器。(亦作 **scintillation detector**)

scin·til·lom·e·ter [ˌsɪntəˈlɑmətɚ; ˌsintiˈlɔmitə] *n.* 閃爍計數器。

sci·o·lism [ˈsaɪəˌlɪzəm; ˈsai-əlizəm] *n.* 淺學。

sci·o·list [ˈsaɪəlɪst; ˈsaiəlist] *n.* 淺學之人。

sci·o·lis·tic [ˌsaɪəˈlɪstɪk; ˌsaiəˈlistik] *adj.* 一知半解(者)的。

sciol·to [ˈʃɔlto; ˈʃɔːltou] 〖義〗 *adv.* 〖音樂〗自由地;斷音地。

sci·on [ˈsaɪən; ˈsaiən] *n.* ①(爲接枝或栽植而剪下之)芽或小枝。②後裔;子孫。(亦作 **cion**)

scir·rhous [ˈsɪrəs; ˈsirəs] *adj.* 〖醫〗硬性癌的。

scir·rhus [ˈsɪrəs; ˈsirəs] *n., pl.* **-rhi** [-raɪ; -rai], **-rhus·es.** 〖醫〗①硬性癌。②硬瘤。

scis·sile [ˈsɪsɪl; ˈsisil] *adj.* 可以切割的。

scis·sion [ˈsɪʒən; ˈsiʒən] *n.* 切斷;分裂;分割;分離。

scis·sor [ˈsɪzɚ; ˈsizə] *v.t.* 剪斷;剪下〖off, up, out〗.

*__scis·sors__ [ˈsɪzɚz; ˈsizəz] *n. pl.* ①剪刀。a pair of *scissors.* 一把剪刀。②摔角時用雙脚拌或夾。

scissors and paste 剪貼工作;編輯工作。

scissors kick 游泳時的一種剪水姿勢。

scis·sor·tail [ˈsɪzɚˌtel; ˈsizəteil] *n.* 〖動物〗鋏尾鳥。

sclaff [sklæf; sklæf] *n.* ①〖蘇〗輕擊。②〖蘇〗輕擊聲。③〖高爾夫〗以球棒刮地之一擊。—*v.t.* & *v.i.* 在擊着球前以球棒刮地。

Sclav [sklɑv; sklɑːv] *n., adj.* =**Slav.**

scle·ra [ˈsklɪrə; ˈsklirə] *n.* 〖解剖〗(眼球之)鞏膜。—**scler·al,** *adj.*

scle·ren·chy·ma [sklɪˈrɛŋkɪmə; skliˈreŋkimə] *n.* ①〖植物〗厚壁組織。②〖動物〗石核組織。

scle·rite [ˈsklɪraɪt; ˈsklirait] *n.* 〖動物〗(角素的石灰質之)硬甲片;硬針骨。

scle·ri·tis [sklɪˈraɪtɪs; skliˈraitis] *n.* 〖醫〗鞏膜炎。(亦作 **sclerotitis**)

scle·ro·der·ma [ˌsklɪrəˈdɝmə; ˌskliraˈdəːmə] *n.* 〖醫〗皮膚硬化症;皮硬化。(亦作 **sclero dermia**)

scle·rom·e·ter [sklɪˈrɑmətɚ; skliˈrɔmətə] *n.* 〖機械〗硬度計(測礦之硬度者)。

scle·ro·pro·tein [ˌsklɪrəˈprotin; ˌskliraˈproutiːn] *n.* 〖生化〗硬蛋白。

scle·rose [sklɪˈros; skliˈrous] *v.t.* & *v.i.,* **-rosed, -ros·ing.** 硬化;使硬化。

scle·ro·sis [sklɪˈrosɪs; skliˈrousis] *n., pl.* **-ses** [-siz; -siːz]. ①〖醫〗硬化症。②〖植物〗細胞壁硬化。

scle·rot·ic [sklɪˈrɑtɪk; skliˈrɔtik] *adj.* ①〖植物〗硬的;厚的。②〖解剖〗鞏膜的。③〖醫〗硬結的。—*n.* ①〖解剖〗鞏膜。②硬化劑。

scle·ro·ti·um [sklɪˈroʃɪəm; skliˈrouʃiəm] *n., pl.* **-ti·a** [-ʃɪə; -ʃiə]. 〖植物〗菌核。

scle·ro·tize [ˈsklɪrəˌtaɪz; ˈskliratạiz] *v.t.* & *v.i.,* **-tized, -tiz·ing.** 硬化;使硬化。—**scle·ro·ti·za·tion,** *n.*

Sc. M. Master of Science.

Sc. M. Hyg. Master of Science in Hygiene.

*__scoff__ [skɔf; skɔf] *n.* ①嘲笑;嘲弄。②笑柄。—*v.i.* & *v.t.* 嘲笑;嘲弄。to *scoff* at a person. 嘲笑某人。—**er,** *n.* —**ing·ly,** *adv.*

scoff·law [ˈskɔfˌlɔ; ˈskɔflɔː] *n.* 〖美俗〗違反法律者(尤指飲用私酒者)。

*__scold__ [skold; skould] *v.t.* & *v.i.* 叱責;責罵。He was *scolded* for being lazy. 他因懶惰而受叱責。—*n.* 叱責者;高聲罵人之婦女。—**a·ble,** *adj.* —**er,** *n.*

scold·ing [ˈskoldɪŋ; ˈskouldiŋ] *n.* 罵;叱;斥責。—*adj.* 責罵的。—**ly,** *adv.*

sco·lex [ˈskolɛks; ˈskouleks] *n., pl.* **sco·le·ces** [skoˈlisiz; skouˈliːsiːz], **sco·li·ces** [ˈskɑlɪˌsiz; ˈskɔlisiːz]. 〖動物〗頭節(絛蟲頭部之環節)。

scol·lop [ˈskɑləp; ˈskɔləp] *n., v.t.* =**scallop.**

scom·broid [ˈskɑmbrɔɪd; ˈskɔmbrɔid] *adj.* 〖動物〗①青花魚科的。②似青花魚的。—*n.* 青花魚;青花魚科之魚。

sconce¹ [skɑns; skɔns] *n.* 裝於牆上的蠟燭臺。

sconce² *n., v.,* **sconced, sconc·ing.**—*n.* 砲臺;堡砦。—*v.t.* 以砲臺保護。

sconce³ *v.,* **sconced, sconc·ing,** *n.* —*v.t.* 課以罰金(尤指對牛津大學生)。—*n.* 罰金。

sconce⁴ *n.* ①〖俗〗頭;頭蓋。②〖俗〗才智;智慧。③盔。④避難處。

scone [skon; skɔn] *n.* 一種扁平的圓餅。

*__scoop__ [skup; skuːp] *n.* ①杓子;戽斗。②鏟子;煤鏟;沙斗。③舀。④一舀之量;一鏟之量。⑤汲取;舀取。⑥洞;穴。⑦〖俚〗獨家新聞。—*v.t.* ①汲取;舀取。②掘;挖。③〖俚〗比…搶先登出獨家新聞。—*v.i.* 挖;掘。—**er,** *n.*

scoop·ful [ˈskupˌful; ˈskuːpful] *n., pl.* **-fuls.** 一杓之量;一戽斗之量;一鏟之量。

scoop net 抄網;攩網。

scoop wheel 汲水車。

scoot [skut; skuːt] *v.i.* 快走;疾走。—*n.* 疾走。—*interj.* 快走!

scoot·er¹ [ˈskutɚ; ˈskuːtə] *n.* ①滑行車;踏板車。②機車;速克達。③冰上或水上行駛之帆船。—*v.i.* 乘滑行車;坐冰上行駛之帆船。

scoot·er² *n.* =**scoter.**

*__scope¹__ [skop; skoup] *n.* ①範圍;眼界;見識。a mind of wide *scope.* 見識廣博之人。②機會;餘地。***give scope to*** (or ***for***) 給發揮…的機會。***have full*** (***free*** or ***large***) ***scope*** 有充分的餘地;能充分發揮能力。***seek scope for*** 尋求發揮…的機會;找…(活動的)機會。***within the scope of*** 在…的範圍內;

在…及得到的地方。

scope² *n.* 〖俗〗①=**radarscope.** ②步槍之望遠鏡瞄準儀。

-scope 〖字尾〗表"觀察或實驗之用具"之義。

sco·pol·a·mine [sko'pɑləmin; skou'pɔləmi:n] *n.* 〖化〗莨菪鹼 ($C_{17}H_{21}O_4N_4$)。(亦作 **hyoscine**)

scor·bu·tic [skɔr'bjutɪk; skɔ:'bju:tik] *adj.* (亦作**scorbutical**)(患)壞血症的。—*n.* ①患壞血症者。②壞血症特效藥。

***scorch** [skɔrtʃ; skɔ:tʃ] *v.t.* ①烘焦;燒焦。②使萎;使枯。③大罵。—*v.i.* ①焦;萎;枯。②〖俗〗以全速奔馳。—*n.* ①燒焦。②騎馬騎得極快;(汽車等的)飛跑。

scorched earth policy 焦土政策。

scorch·er ['skɔrtʃɚ; 'skɔ:tʃə] *n.* ①燒焦者。②〖俗〗大熱天。③嚴苛之事物。④〖俗〗駕車過速者。⑤〖俗〗嚴厲之斥責或批評。

scorch·ing ['skɔrtʃɪŋ; 'skɔ:tʃiŋ] *adj.* ①灼熱的;燃燒般的。②猛烈的;苛刻的。—*n.* 疾走;疾馳。—**ly,** *adv.*

‡score [skor, skɔr; skɔ:, skɔə] *n., v.,* **scored, scor·ing.**—*n.*①劃痕;截痕;劃線;記號。②(競技之)得分;得點;點數。The *score* is 9 to 2 in our favor. 我隊以九對二的比數領先。③帳;欠款;夙怨。④理由;緣故。⑤總樂譜。⑥二十。two *score* of eggs. 四十個蛋。⑦(*pl.*)許多。*scores* of years. 許多年。***by scores*** 不少;許多;很多。***Death pays all scores.*** 〖諺〗一死百了。***have an old score to settle with*** 跟…有宿怨。***in scores*** 很多;大批;大羣。***make a score off one's own bat*** 獨力做。***on the score of*** 因爲;爲了。***pay off*** (or ***settle***) ***old scores*** 報復舊怨宿仇;還清舊帳。***pay one's score*** 付帳。***run up a score*** 負債。***the score*** 〖俗〗眞情;事實;情形。—*v.t.* ①加截痕;劃線;作記號。②記載;記(點數)。③獲得;成功。to *score* a success. 獲得成功。④〖美俗〗刻薄地批評;罵。⑤爲(電影、戲劇等)作曲;寫樂譜。—*v.i.* ①記點數。He was appointed to *score* for both sides. 他奉派替雙方記分。②得點數。③獲勝;得利益。The new product *scored* with the public. 新產品受到大衆的歡迎。④做記號;刻痕;劃線。⑤負債。

score·board ['skor,bord; 'skɔ:bɔ:d] *n.* ①記分板。②記錄。

score·book ['skor,buk;'skɔ:buk] *n.* 運動會之記分簿。

score card ①高爾夫球等之記分卡片。② 記載運動員姓名、體重等之卡片。(亦作 **scorecard**)

score·keep·er ['skor,kipɚ; 'skɔ:,ki:pə] *n.* 記分員;記錄員。

score·less ['skorlɪs; 'skɔ:lis] *adj.*①無點的;未得分的。②未留記號的。

scor·er ['skorɚ; 'skɔ:rə] *n.* 記分員。

sco·ri·a ['skorɪə; 'skɔ:riə] *n., pl.* **-ri·ae** [-rɪ,i; -rii:]. ①金屬熔渣。②火山之岩燼。—**ceous,** *adj.*

sco·ri·fy ['skorə,faɪ; 'skɔ:rifai] *v.t.,* **-fied, -fy·ing.** 使化爲熔渣;煅成礦渣。

scor·ing ['skorɪŋ, 'skɔr-; 'skɔ:riŋ, 'skɔər-] *n.*①得分。②勝利;成功。③作曲;作譜。④曲譜。—*adj.* 得分的。

scorn** [skɔrn; skɔ:n] *n.* ①輕蔑;蔑視。We feel *scorn* for a draft dodger. 我們輕視開空頭支票的人。②輕蔑的對象。That bully is the *scorn* of the school. 全校都瞧不起那個橫行霸道的傢伙。③諷刺;譏嘲。think*** (or ***hold***) ***it scorn to*** (***do***) 不屑(做)。***think scorn of*** 藐視;蔑視;瞧不起。—*v.t.* & *v.i.*①輕蔑;輕視。②不屑。to *scorn* to tell a lie. 不屑說謊。—**er,** *n.*

***scorn·ful** ['skɔrnfəl; 'skɔ:nful] *adj.* ①輕蔑的。②受輕蔑的。—**ly,** *adv.* —**ness,** *n.*

Scor·pi·o ['skɔrpɪ,o;'skɔ:piou] *n.* ①〖動物〗蠍屬。②〖天文〗天蠍宮。③〖天文〗天蠍座。

scor·pi·on ['skɔrpɪən; 'skɔ:pjən] *n.* ①蠍。②鞭;笞。③(S-) =**Scorpio.** —**ic,** *adj.*

***Scot** [skɑt; skɔt] *n.* 蘇格蘭人。

scot [skɑt; skɔt] *n.* 稅;應分擔的給付。

Scot. ①Scotch. ②Scotland. ③Scottish.

scot and lot 以前之一種市稅。

Scotch** [skɑtʃ; skɔtʃ] *adj.* 蘇格蘭的;蘇格蘭人(語)的。—*n.* ①蘇格蘭人。②〖俗〗(蘇格蘭)威士忌酒。out of all Scotch*** 〖鄙〗過度地;非常地。

scotch¹ [skɑtʃ; skɔtʃ] *v.t.* ①傷害;傷及;使負傷。②鎮壓;撲滅;遏止。③割;抓;刻痕於。

scotch² *n.* 防止車輪、木材等滾動之木塊;軔。—*v.t.* 以木塊制止(車輪等)滾轉。

Scotch and soda 威士忌蘇打。

Scotch broth 以羊肉、大麥、野菜等煮之濃湯。

Scotch cousin 遠親。

Scotch-I·rish ['skɑtʃ'aɪrɪʃ; 'skɔtʃ'aiəriʃ] *n., adj.* 蘇格蘭與愛爾蘭血統均有的人(的)。

Scotch·lite ['skɑtʃ,laɪt; 'skɔtʃlait] *n.* 〖商標名〗反光膠帶。

Scotch·man ['skɑtʃmən; 'skɔtʃmən] *n., pl.* **-men.** 蘇格蘭人。

Scotch mist ①(蘇格蘭山地之)濕氣多的濃霧。②霪雨。

Scotch tape 〖商標名〗透明膠紙帶。

scotch-tape [,skɑtʃ'tep; ,skɔtʃ'teip] *v.t.,* **-taped, -tap·ing.** 用透明膠紙帶封口(補、貼等)。

Scotch terrier 蘇格蘭種狗。(亦作 **Scottish terrier**)

Scotch whisky 蘇格蘭威士忌酒。

Scotch·wom·an ['skɑtʃ,wumən; 'skɔtʃ,wumən] *n., pl.* **-wom·en.** 蘇格蘭女人。

Scotch woodcock 煮蛋加風尾魚漿和麪包一起吃的食物。

sco·ter ['skotɚ; 'skoutə] *n.* 〖動物〗黑鳧。(亦作 **scooter**)

scot-free ['skɑt'fri; 'skɔt'fri:] *adj.* ①免稅的。②安全無恙的。

Sco·tia ['skoʃə; 'skouʃə] *n.* 〖詩〗蘇格夏(蘇格蘭的拉丁名稱)。

sco·tia ['skoʃə;'skouʃə] *n.* 〖建築〗柱基的凹形邊飾。

Scot·ic ['skɑtɪk; 'skɔtik] *adj.* 蘇格蘭人(語)的。

***Scot·land** ['skɑtlənd; 'skɔtlənd] *n.* 蘇格蘭。

Scotland Yard 倫敦警察廳;倫敦警察廳偵緝部(卽蘇格蘭場,以所在地得名)。

scot·o·graph ['skɑtə,græf; 'skɔtəgrɑ:f] *n.* ①黑暗中寫字器;盲人寫字器。②〖物理〗X 光照像機。

sco·to·ma [skə'tomə; skə'toumə] *n., pl.* **-ma·ta** [-mətə;-mətə]. 〖醫〗暗點;盲點。

sco·to·pi·a [sko'topɪə; skou'toupiə] *n.* ①對黑暗之適應。②黑暗中能睹物之能力。

sco·top·ic [sko'tɑpɪk;skou'tɔpik] *adj.* ①對黑暗能適應的。②能在黑暗中睹物的。

Scots [skɑts;skɔts] *adj.* 蘇格蘭的。—*n.*①(作 *sing.*解)蘇格蘭語。②(作 *pl.*解)蘇格蘭人。

Scots·man ['skɑtsmən; 'skɔtsmən] *n., pl.* **-men.** 蘇格蘭人 (=Scotchman).

Scots·wom·an ['skɑts,wumən; 'skɔts,wumən] *n., pl.* **-wom·en.** =**Scotchwoman.**

Scott [skɑt; skɔt] *n.* 司各脫 (Sir Walter, 1771-1832, 蘇格蘭詩人及小說家)。

Scot·ti·cism ['skɑtə,sɪzəm; 'skɔtisizəm〕 *n.* 蘇格蘭語風；蘇格蘭方言（習語、發音）。（亦作 **Scoticism**）

Scot·ti·cize 〔'skɑtə,saɪz; 'skɔtisaiz〕 *v.t.* & *v.i.*, **-cized, -ciz·ing.** （使）具有蘇格蘭風格；（使）蘇格蘭化。

***Scot·tish** 〔'skɑtɪʃ; 'skɔtiʃ〕 *adj.* 蘇格蘭的；蘇格蘭人（語）的（此爲雅語；普通用 Scotch）. —*n.* ①蘇格蘭人（集合稱）。②蘇格蘭語。

***scoun·drel** 〔'skaundrəl; 'skaundrəl〕 *n.* 無賴；惡漢。—*adj.* 無賴的；無惡不作的；卑鄙的。—**ly,** *adj.*

scoun·drel·ism 〔'skaundrəlɪzəm; 'skaundrəlizm〕 *n.* ①卑劣；無賴。②卑劣之行爲。

scour[1] 〔skaur; 'skauə〕 *v.t.* ①磨擦；洗滌。*Scour* the rust off. 將銹跡磨洗掉。②清除；掃淨。to *scour* the shame away. 洗盡恥辱。③沖洗。④懲罰；打。⑤打蟲；清腸。—*v.i.* ①磨亮；擦淨。②除去灰塵、油脂等。③變得乾淨發亮。④容易擦乾淨。⑤（鏟、犁等）因使用而發亮。—*n.* ①磨擦；沖洗；清除。②經洗擦之處。③用以洗擦之物。④流水之磨蝕力。⑤牛馬等之腹瀉。

scour[2] *v.t.* ①搜索。The police *scoured* the city for the thief. 警察巡行全城搜索盜賊。②疾走。—*v.i.* 疾走。

scour·er 〔'skaurə; 'skauərə〕 *n.* ①洗擦者。②用以洗擦之物。household *scourers.* 家庭用之洗擦物。③清腸劑；瀉藥。

***scourge** 〔skɝdʒ; skə:dʒ〕 *n., v.,* **scourged, scourg·ing.** —*n.* ①鞭；笞。②懲罰；災害；禍患。③引起災害之人或物。—*v.t.* ①鞭笞。②懲罰；使受痛苦。—**scourg·er,** *n.* —**scourg·ing·ly,** *adv.*

scour·ing pad 〔'skaurɪŋ~; 'skauəriŋ~〕 洗擦用的鋼絲絨或塑膠絲團。

scouring rush 〖植物〗木賊。

scour·ings 〔'skaurɪŋz; 'skauəriŋz〕 *n. pl.* ①殘屑。②穀皮。

scouse 〔skaus; skaus〕 *n.* 〖航海〗水手吃的一道菜（含有硬餅乾、菜蔬及肉，有時無肉）。

scout**[1] 〔skaut; skaut〕 *n.* ①斥候；偵察；偵察兵。②斥候艦；偵察機。③童子軍。boy *scout.* 男童子軍。girl *scout.* 女童子軍。④〖俚〗人；傢伙。⑤英國牛津大學之校工。on the scout*** 在偵察中。—*v.i.* 斥候；偵察；尋找。—*v.t.* ①觀察；偵察；研究。②尋找〖常 out, up〗。

scout[2] *v.t.* 輕蔑地拒絕。—*v.i.* 嘲笑。

scout car 輕裝甲巡邏車。

scout·craft 〔'skaut,kræft; 'skaut-krɑ:ft〕 *n.* 斥候技術；斥候活動；童子軍之活動。

scout cruiser 偵察巡洋艦。

scout·er 〔'skautə; 'skautə〕 *n.* ①偵察者；尋找者。②18歲以上之男童軍。

scout·ing 〔'skautɪŋ; 'skautiŋ〕 *n.* 童子軍之活動；斥候或偵察活動。

scout·mas·ter 〔'skaut,mæstə; 'skaut,mɑ:stə〕 *n.* ①童子軍教練。②斥候長。

scow 〔skau; skau〕 *n.* 大型平底船。

***scowl** 〔skaul; skaul〕 *v.i.* 蹙額；皺眉；作不豫之色。to *scowl* at a person. 對某人作不豫之色。—*v.t.* 皺眉表示。—*n.* 蹙額；不豫之色。—**er,** *n.*

scrab·ble 〔'skræbl; 'skræbl〕 *v.,* **-bled, -bling,** *n.* —*v.t.* & *v.i.* ①爬尋。②亂塗；亂寫。③掙扎；奮鬥。—*n.* ①亂塗；亂寫（的字）。②爬；抓。③掙扎；奮鬥。—**scrab·bler,** *n.*

scrab·bly 〔'skræblɪ; 'skræbli〕 *adj.* 次要的；不重要的。

scrag 〔skræg; skræg〕 *n., v.,* **scragged, scrag·ging.** —*n.* ①骨瘦如柴的人或動物。②羊頸肉。③〖俚〗頸部。—*v.t.*〖俚〗扭（絞）…之頸。

scrag·gly 〔'skræglɪ; 'skrægli〕 *adj.,* **-gli·er, -gli·est.** 散亂的；不整齊的（毛）。

scrag·gy 〔'skrægɪ; 'skrægi〕 *adj.,* **-gi·er, -gi·est.** ①瘦而多骨的。②＝**scraggly.**（亦作 **scranny**）

scram 〔skræm; skræm〕 *v.i.,* **scrammed, scram·ming.** 〖美俚〗出去；走開（命令語氣）。

scram·ble** 〔'skræmbl; 'skræmbl〕 *v.,* **-bled, -bling,** *n.* —*v.i.* ①爬；攀緣。②爭取；爭奪。③混雜一起。④〖美俚〗（軍機）緊急起飛擔任攔截任務等。 —*v.t.* ①攪炒（蛋）。*scrambled* eggs. 炒蛋。②匆忙湊合；湊攏。③〖美俚〗使緊急起飛。④將無線電或電視訊號分散攪亂，使截聽者無法了解。 ***scramble after 搜求；拚命找。***scramble along*** (or ***on***) 爬向前；勉强對付過去。—*n.* ①爬；攀緣。②爭取；爭奪。 the *scramble* for power. 權力之爭。③任何混亂之動作。④〖美空軍〗緊急起飛。—**scram·bler,** *n.*

scram·jet 〔'skræm,dʒɛt; 'skræmdʒet〕 *n.* 一種衝壓噴射引擎。

scran 〔skræn; skrɑ:n〕 *n.* ①〖俚，方〗食物屑；食物。②〖愛俚〗運氣。***Bad scran to you!*** 〖愛〗你這倒霉鬼！***out on the scran*** 在外討飯。

scran·nel 〔'skrænl; 'skrænəl〕 *adj.* 〖古〗①細小的；微弱的。②刺耳的（聲音）。

***scrap**[1] 〔skræp; skræp〕 *n., v.,* **scrapped, scrap·ping,** *adj.* —*n.* ①小片；碎屑。It's only a *scrap* of paper. 這不過是一張紙而已（指不可靠之字據）。②殘物。*scraps* of food. 剩餘的食物。③斷簡；殘篇。④（*pl.*）油渣。—*v.t.* ①使成碎片。②丟棄；廢棄。 —*adj.* 碎片的；殘剩的；廢棄的。

scrap[2] *v.,* **scrapped, scrap·ping,** *n.* —*v.i.* & *v.t.* 〖俚〗打架；口角；格鬥。—*n.* 〖俚〗打架；口角；格鬥。

scrap·bas·ket 〔'skræp,bæskɪt; 'skræp,bɑ:skit〕 *n.* 廢紙籃；字紙桶。

***scrap·book** 〔'skræp,buk; 'skræpbuk〕 *n.* 雜貼簿；集錦簿。

scrape** 〔skrep; skreip〕 *v.,* **scraped, scrap·ing,** *n.* —*v.t.* ①刮；削；擦；刮落；擦淨；擦傷。②摩擦發聲。③挖掘；穿（孔）。④積攢。⑤用推土機鏟平。—*v.i.* ①刮；削；擦。The branch of the tree *scraped* against the window. 樹枝擦着窗戶。②積攢。③摩擦作聲。④亂彈（絃樂器）；發出怪聲音。⑤勉强維持。⑥打扦；行一脚往後退之鞠躬。bow and scrape*** 打躬屈膝；奉承；巴結。***pinch and scrape*** 省吃省用地貯蓄。***scrape a living*** 收入僅够維生。***scrape (up) an acquaintance with*** 極力與（某人）結交。***scrape through*** 勉强通過。—*n.* ①刮；削；摩擦。②刮削聲；摩擦聲；軋轢聲。③困境；困難。He is always in some kind of a *scrape.* 他老是遭遇困難。④刮痕；擦傷。⑤打扦。⑥意見不合；吵架。***bread and scrape*** 塗了一點點奶油的麪包。

scrap·er 〔'skrepə; 'skreipə〕 *n.* ①刮削者；擦響者。②刮削所用的器具。③儉約之人；吝嗇之人。

scrap heap 塵芥堆；鐵屑堆。「***be fit for the scrap heap*** 無用。」

scrap·ing 〔'skrepɪŋ; 'skreipiŋ〕 *n.* ①刮削的動作。②刮削的聲音。③（常 *pl.*）被刮削下的東西。—**ly,** *adv.*

scrap iron 廢鐵；碎鐵。

scrap·per 〔'skræpə; 'skræpə〕 *n.* 〖俚〗①拳擊家。②好打架者。

scrap·ple ['skræpl̩; 'skræpl] *n.* 〖美〗玉米肉片(以碎肉、玉米粉等烹炸而成)。

scrap·py ['skræpɪ; 'skræpi] *adj.*, **-pi·er, -pi·est.** ①由殘餘東西做成的;殘餘的。②片斷的;散漫的。③〖俗〗好鬥的。

Scratch [skrætʃ; skrætʃ] *n.* 惡魔。

scratch** [skrætʃ; skrætʃ] *v.t.* ①搔;抓。The cat *scratched* me. 貓抓我。②以爪挖掘。③潦草書寫。④勾消;畫線塗掉。⑤搔癢。⑥擦。He *scratched* a match. 他擦了一支火柴。⑦將(馬等)退出比賽。⑧刻劃。⑨〖美〗**a.** 支持本黨候選人,但將票投給黨外人。**b.** 拒絕投本黨候選人。—*v.i.* ①搔;抓。②積錢。③勉强維持。④退出比賽。—*n.* ①抓痕。②微傷。③賽跑之出發線(單數,不加冠詞)。④搔聲;擦聲。⑤潦草之書寫。⑥運氣。⑦(紙牌戲之)零分。⑧=**scratch hit.** ***a scratch of the pen 隨手寫的幾個字;簽字。***come up to scratch*** 準備開始競賽;(喻)準備執行任務;踐約。***from scratch*** **a.** 從開始;從出發點。**b.** 從一無基礎的情況;無辦法或依賴。After the depression he started another business *from scratch.* 不景氣後他在毫無基礎情況下經營另一生意。***up to scratch*** 够上水準;情況良好。—*adj.* ①臨時湊成的。a *scratch* football team. 臨時湊成之足球隊。②起草的。③偶然的;靠機會的。④平等比賽的。**—er,** *n.*

scratch·cat ['skrætʃ,kæt; 'skrætʃkæt] *n.* 懷惡意的女人;狠毒的女人。

scratch hit 〖棒球〗很勉强的安打。

scratch pad 拍紙簿。

scratch paper 便條紙。

scratch sheet 〖美俚〗記錄退出比賽之馬及其他有關賽馬消息的刊物。

scratch test 過敏性測驗。

scratch wig 僅覆蓋頭部之一部分的假髮。

scratch·y ['skrætʃɪ; 'skrætʃi] *adj.*, **scratch·i·er, scratch·i·est.** ①草率的;亂畫的。②有沙沙爬聲的。③雜湊成的。④發癢的。⑤稀少的。⑥不均勻的;時好時壞的。**—scratch·i·ness,** *n.*

scrawl [skrɔl; skrɔ:l] *v.i. & v.t.* 潦草書寫;亂塗。—*n.* 潦草書寫;塗鴉。**—er,** *n.* **—y,** *adj.*

scraw·ny ['skrɔnɪ; 'skrɔ:ni] *adj.*, **-ni-er, -ni·est.** 〖美俗〗細而瘦的。

screak [skrik; skri:k] *v.i.* 尖叫;作軋壓聲。—*n.* 尖叫聲;(磨擦的)刺耳聲。

scream** [skrim; skri:m] *v.i. & v.t.* ①尖聲叫喊;大笑;高聲說話。to *scream* with laughter. 高聲大笑。②產生驚人的效果或予人以新穎的印象。—*n.*①尖叫(聲)。②非常可笑的事物;極爲有趣的人。a* (*perfect*) *scream*** 〖俗〗極其可笑之人或物。

scream·er ['skrimə; 'skri:mə] *n.* ①尖叫者;發急劇尖聲之物。②〖俚〗令人驚奇叫絕之事物;極漂亮的女人;極準確的射擊。③〖新聞俚〗**a.** 駭人聽聞之標題。**b.** 報紙上橫貫全頁的大標題。④〖印刷俚〗驚嘆號。⑤南美洲產的一種鳥。⑥〖運動俚〗**a.** 打得很遠的高爾夫球。**b.** 用力擊中的棒球。

scream·ing ['skrimɪŋ; 'skri:miŋ] *adj.* ①尖叫的;發尖叫聲的。②令人驚愕的。③使發笑的。—*n.* 尖叫;尖叫聲。**—ly,** *adv.*

scream·ing-mee·mies ['skrimɪŋ-'mimiz; 'skri:miŋ'mi:mi:z] *n.*(作 *sing.* or *pl.*解)〖俗〗歇斯底里;神經極度緊張之狀態。

scree [skri; skri:] *n.* 〖英〗①碎石;石子。②碎石堆。

***screech** [skritʃ; skri:tʃ] *v.i.* 尖叫。The brakes *screeched.* 煞車尖響一下。—*v.t.* 以尖銳刺耳聲喊出。—*n.* 尖叫;尖叫聲。The boy let out a *screech.* 這孩子發出一聲尖叫。**—er,** *n.* **—y,** *adj.*

screech owl ①一種叫聲很尖的梟。②預言凶事者。

screed [skrid; skri:d] *n.* ①長篇大論。②勻泥尺。③〖方〗**a.** 一小片;碎片。**b.** 一塊撕下的布。**c.** 邊緣;邊條。④〖蘇〗**a.** 分裂。**b.** 撕布聲。—*v.t. & v.i.* 〖方〗撕破;裂開。

screen** [skrin; skri:n] *n.* ①幕;屛;簾;帳(等遮蔽物)。a folding *screen.* 屛風。②金屬線織成之紗。③銀幕;電影。④篩。⑤似幕之物;矮牆。⑥執行護航任務的驅逐艦。⑦〖軍〗保護主力的前衛部隊。make a screen version of*** 將…改編成電影。***put on a screen of indifference*** 假裝冷淡。***show* (or *throw*) *on the screen*** 放映。***under screen of night*** 在黑夜的掩護之下。—*v.t.* ①(用屛、幕之類)遮蔽;阻隔;掩護。②篩。③放映(電影);改編爲電影;攝成影片。④甄別;審查;調查。***screen off*** 用幕(屛)隔間。—*v.i.* 適於拍成電影。This novel does not *screen* well. 這部小說不適於拍成電影。**—a·ble, —like,** *adj.* **—er,** *n.*

screen·dom ['skrindəm; 'skri:ndəm] *n.* 〖美〗電影界。

screen·ing ['skrinɪŋ; 'skri:niŋ] *n.* ①作紗窗、濾器等用的細鐵紗。②審查;調查。Your application is under *screening.* 你的申請正在審查中。③電影之上映。

screen·ings ['skrinɪŋz; 'skri:niŋz] *n. sing.* or *pl.* 篩屑;篩後殘餘之物。

screen·play ['skrin,ple; 'skri:nplei] *n.* 〖電影〗電影脚本。

screen test (電影演員之)試鏡。

screen-test ['skrin,tɛst; 'skri:ntest] *v.t.* 讓(電影演員)試鏡。

screen-wip·er ['skrin,waɪpə; 'skri:n,waipə] *n.* 〖英〗汽車前擋風玻璃上之刷子。

screen·writ·er ['skrin,raɪtə; 'skri:n,raitə] *n.* 電影劇本作家。

screeve [skriv; skri:v] *n., v.*, **screeved, screev·ing.** —*n.* 〖俚〗在路旁作行乞文字或圖畫。—*v.i.* 〖俚〗作求乞文字或畫於路旁以求布施。**—screev·er,** *n.*

screw** [skru; skru:] *n.* ①螺旋;螺旋釘。a *screw* bolt. 螺釘。②螺旋推進機。③螺旋狀物。④螺旋式之轉動;螺絲之一轉。⑤〖桌球〗捩;轉。⑥捲在紙中之物。⑦吝嗇鬼;守財奴。⑧〖俗〗薪水;工錢。⑨老弱之馬。⑩(常*pl.*)恐嚇。a screw loose*** 毛病;故障。There's *a screw loose* somewhere. 甚麼地方出了故障。***have a screw loose*** 〖俚〗瘋瘋癲癲的;古怪。***put the screw on*** 逼使。—*v.t.* ①用螺旋釘釘住;扭螺旋。②榨取;勒索。③强迫做某事;壓低(價格);壓迫(某人)說或放棄某項事業。④鼓起(勇氣);加强(效率)。⑤壓價;强迫(賣主)殺價〖down〗。⑥〖俚〗欺騙;利用(某人)。⑦〖俚,鄙〗與…性交。—*v.i.* ①旋轉。②用螺絲轉緊,轉鬆或轉開〖常on, together, off〗。③勒索。④〖俚,鄙〗性交。***have one's head screwed on the right way*** 通達事理。***screw around*** 〖俚〗鬼混。***screw off*** 拔螺絲。***screw up*** 〖俚〗搞成一團糟。***screw up one's courage*** 鼓起勇氣。***screw up one's face*** 扭曲面容。

screw·ball ['skru,bɔl; 'skru:bɔ:l] *n.* ①〖美俚〗畸人;奇異之人。②〖棒球〗旋轉球。—*adj.* 〖美俚〗奇特的;異常的;怪僻的。

screw·driv·er ['skru,draɪvə; 'skru:-,draivə] *n.* ①螺絲刀;起子。②一種伏特加酒和桔子汁的混合飲料。

screwed [skrud; skru:d] *adj.* ①以螺

釘固定的。②有螺旋紋的。③(亦作 **screwed up**) 扭曲的; 扭轉的。④〖英俚〗有幾分醉的。

screw eye 頂上有環狀頭的螺旋。

screw gear ①螺旋齒輪。②螺輪聯動裝置。

screw gearing 螺輪聯動。

screw·head [ˈskru,hɛd; ˈskru:hed] *n.* 螺旋頂端。

screw hook 頂端呈鈎形的螺旋。

screw jack =**jackscrew.**

screw·loose [ˈskru,lus; ˈskru:lu:s] *adj.* 〖俚〗脾氣很古怪的。—*n.* 脾氣古怪的人。

screw nut 螺帽。

screw press 螺旋壓榨機。

screw propeller 螺旋槳推進器。

screw steamer 用螺旋槳推進之汽船。

screw thread 螺紋。

screw·y [ˈskruɪ; ˈskru:i] *adj.*, **screw·i·er, screw·i·est.** ①像螺旋的。②〖俚〗微醉的。③嚴苛的; 吝嗇的。④〖俗〗無用的。⑤彎曲的; 扭曲的。⑥特別的; 怪異的。⑦不實際的。⑧易使人誤解的。

scrib·al [ˈskraɪbl̩; ˈskraibl] *adj.* 手寫的; 記錄的。

scrib·ble [ˈskrɪbl̩; ˈskribl] *v.*, **-bled, -bling,** *n.* —*v.t.* & *v.i.* 潦草書寫。—*n.* ①潦草書寫。②潦草或胡亂寫成之文字。

scrib·bler [ˈskrɪblɚ; ˈskriblə] *n.* ①潦草書寫的人。②小文人。

scribe [skraɪb; skraib] *n.* ①書記; 抄寫者。②(猶太法的)學者。③作者; 作家。—*v.t.* 書寫; 銘刻; 刻以標記。

scrib·er [ˈskraɪbɚ; ˈskraibə] *n.* ①畫線器。②書寫者; 刻劃者。

scrim [skrɪm; skrim] *n.* 作窗幕等用的棉或麻織品。

scrim·mage [ˈskrɪmɪdʒ; ˈskrimidʒ] *n.*, *v.*, **-maged, -mag·ing.** —*n.* ①混戰; 扭打。②〖橄欖球〗並列爭球。③〖橄欖球〗分成兩隊練球。—*v.i.* ①參與混戰。②〖橄欖球〗並列爭球。③忙忙碌碌地尋求。—*v.t.* 〖橄欖球〗練球時對抗。—**scrim·mag·er,** *n.*

scrimp [skrɪmp; skrimp] *v.i.* ①節儉。②尅扣。—*v.t.* 節省。—*adj.* 節縮的; 不足的。

scrimp·y [ˈskrɪmpɪ; ˈskrimpi] *adj.*, **scrimp·i·er, scrimp·i·est.** ①缺乏的; 不足的。②吝嗇的。

scrim·shank [ˈskrɪm,ʃæŋk; ˈskrimʃæŋk] *v.i.* 〖英俗〗逃避責任; 推諉責任; 偷懶。

scrim·shaw [ˈskrɪmʃɔ; ˈskrimʃɔ:] *n.* (水手於暇時雕刻之)貝殼、鯨骨、象牙、鋼、木等細工。—*v.i.* & *v.t.* 雕刻此等細工。

scrip¹ [skrɪp; skrip] *n.* 〖古〗旅行者所携帶之小袋。

scrip² *n.* ①證書。②紙片; 紙條。③臨時證券。④〖俗〗(昔美國面值一元以下之)紙幣。

***script** [skrɪpt; skript] *n.* ①書寫之字母、數字、符號(等); 手跡。②戲劇脚本原稿。③廣播原稿。④草體之鉛字字體。⑤〖法律〗正本。—*v.t.* ①為…寫脚本或廣播稿。②將…寫成脚本。—*v.i.* 寫廣播或電視稿; 寫脚本。

Script. ①Scriptural. ②Scripture.

script editor 廣播或電視臺節目稿之編輯。

script girl 〖電影〗場記; 電影導演之女祕書。

scrip·to·ri·um [skrɪpˈtorɪəm; skripˈtɔ:riəm] *n.*, *pl.* **-ri·ums, -ri·a** [-rɪə; -riə]. (寺院內之)繕寫室。

***scrip·ture** [ˈskrɪptʃɚ; ˈskriptʃə] *n.* ①經文; 經典。②(S-)聖經(亦作 **the Scriptures, the Holy Scripture**). —**scrip·tur·al, Scrip·tur·al,** *adj.* —**scrip·tur·al·ly,** *adv.*

scripture reader 對平民家庭或不能讀書家庭讀聖經的信徒; 傳教者。

script·writ·er [ˈskrɪpt,raɪtɚ; ˈskript,raitə] *n.* (廣播、電影、電視)劇作家; 編撰者。(亦作 **scripter**)

scrive·ner [ˈskrɪvnɚ; ˈskrivnə] *n.* 代書人; 公證人。

scrod [skrɑd; skrɔd] *n.* 〖美〗小鱈魚。

scrof·u·la [ˈskrɔfjələ; ˈskrɔfjulə] *n.* 〖醫〗瘰癧; 斯科夫拉。

scrof·u·lous [ˈskrɑfjələs; ˈskrɔfjuləs] *adj.* ①瘰癧的。②似斯科夫拉的。③患斯科夫拉的。④(文學等)腐敗的。

***scroll** [skrol; skroul] *n.* ①紙卷; 卷軸。②渦卷形的裝飾。③簽名時所加之渦卷花紋。—*v.t.* ①將…寫在卷軸上; 題記; 銘刻。②使形成卷軸或渦卷形花紋。③以渦卷形裝飾點綴。

scroll painting 卷軸畫; 橫軸畫。

scroll saw ①一種用以鋸彎曲線條之窄鋸。②此等鋸鋸成的裝飾圖案。

scroll·work [ˈskrol,wɝk; ˈskroulwə:k] *n.* 渦形裝飾。

Scrooge [skrudʒ; skru:dʒ] *n.* ①Dickens 作 *A Christmas Carol* 中的一個吝嗇漢。②(常 s-) 吝嗇的人; 小氣鬼。

scroop [skrup; skru:p] *v.i.* 〖方〗發軋轢聲。—*n.* 〖方〗軋轢聲。

scro·tal [ˈskrotl̩; ˈskroutəl] *adj.* 陰囊的。

scro·tum [ˈskrotəm; ˈskroutəm] *n.*, *pl.* **-ta** [-tə; -tə], **-tums.** 〖解剖〗陰囊。

scrounge [skraundʒ; skraundʒ] *v.*, **scrounged, scroung·ing.** —*v.t.* ①〖俚〗擅取; 擅用; 偷取。②求; 乞討。—*v.i.* ①搜尋。②敲詐。***scrounge around*** 搜尋。

***scrub**¹ [skrʌb; skrʌb] *v.*, **scrubbed, scrub·bing,** *n.* —*v.t.* ①(用力)擦洗。②從(氣體中)除去雜質。③〖俚〗取消。—*v.i.* 洗。—*n.* (用力)擦洗。—**ba·ble,** *adj.* —**ber,** *n.*

scrub² *n.* ①矮樹; 灌木叢。②渺小之物。③(球隊之) 預備隊員。④(*pl.*) 由二流運動員組成的球隊。⑤作賤役者。—*adj.* ①渺小的。②(球隊之)預備隊員的。

scrubbing brush 硬毛刷子。(亦作 **scrub brush**)

scrub·board [ˈskrʌb,bord; ˈskrʌbbɔ:d] *n.* ①洗衣板。②(房間牆壁下方之) 踢脚板。

scrub·by [ˈskrʌbɪ; ˈskrʌbi] *adj.*, **-bi·er, -bi·est.** ①雜木叢生的。②過小的; 卑劣的; 下等的。③破舊的。

scrub·man [ˈskrʌbmən; ˈskrʌbmən] *n.*, *pl.* **-men.** 〖美俗〗做雜役的人。

scrub nurse 手術室遞手術用具之護士。

scrub·wo·man [ˈskrʌb,wumən; ˈskrʌb,wumən] *n.* 打掃清潔之女傭。

scruff [skrʌf; skrʌf] *n.* 頸背之鬆皮; 頸背。

scruf·fy [ˈskrʌfɪ; ˈskrʌfi] *adj.*, **-fi·er, -fi·est.** 〖主英〗①長滿頭屑的; 頭皮滿頂的。②破舊的; 卑鄙的。

scrum [skrʌm; skrʌm] *n.* = **scrummage.**

scrum·mage [ˈskrʌmɪdʒ; ˈskrʌmidʒ] *n.*, *v.i.* 〖英〗=**scrimmage.**

scrump·tious [ˈskrʌmpʃəs; ˈskrʌmpʃəs] *adj.* 〖俚〗①極好的; 卓越的; 優美的; 第一流的。②愉快的。—**ness,** *n.*

scrunch [skrʌntʃ; skrʌntʃ] *v.*, *n.* = **crunch.**

scru·ple** [ˈskrupl̩; ˈskru:pl] *n.*, *v.*, **-pled, -pling.** —*n.* ①躊躇; 猶豫; 顧忌。He did it without *scruple*. 他無所躊躇地做這件事。②衡量名(等於二十喱, 1.296公分)。③微量。make scruple*** 猶豫; 勉强。—*v.i.* 躊躇; 顧慮(常用於否定語)。to *scruple* at nothing. 毫無顧忌。—*v.t.* 對…有顧忌。—**less,** *adj.*

scru·pu·los·i·ty [,skrupjəˈlɑsətɪ;

ˌskru:pju'lɔsiti] *n., pl.* **-ties.** 猶豫；躊躇；深慮；謹嚴；小心。

scru·pu·lous ['skrupjələs; 'skru:pjuləs] *adj.* ①多顧慮的；小心翼翼的；審愼的。②完全的；無疵可指的。—**ly,** *adv.* —**ness,** *n.*

scru·ta·ble ['skrutəbl; 'skru:təbl] *adj.* 可以瞭解的；可以窺測的。

scru·ta·tor [skru'tetɚ; skru:'teitə] *n.* 檢查者；調查者。

scru·ti·neer [ˌskrutə'nɪr; ˌskru:ti'niə] *n.* ①檢查者。②〖英〗選票檢查人；監票者。

scru·ti·nize ['skrutṇˌaɪz; 'skru:tinaiz] *v.t. & v.i.,* **-nized, -niz·ing.** 細察；詳審。

scru·ti·ny ['skrutṇɪ; 'skru:tini] *n., pl.* **-nies.** ①細察；詳審。②投票之再檢查。

scry [skraɪ; skrai] *v.i.,* **scried, scry·ing.** 以水晶體占卜。

scu·ba ['skubə; 'sku:bə] *n.* 水肺。

scud [skʌd; skʌd] *v.,* **scud·ded, scud·ding,** *n.* —*v.i.* ①疾行；飛駛。②乘風前進。—*v.t.* 迅速經過；匆匆跑過。—*n.* ①疾行；飛駛。②飛雲；急雨；風吹起之浪或水花。③掌擊。

scu·do ['skudo; 'sku:dou] *n., pl.* **-di** [-di; -di:]. 〖義〗古銀幣名。

scuff [skʌf; skʌf] *v.i.* 拖足而行；曳足而行。—*v.t.* ①拖（足）；曳（足）而行；以足擦（地）。②磨壞。—*n.* ①拖曳行走；拖步。②磨壞之處。③無後跟之拖鞋。

scuf·fle ['skʌfl; 'skʌfl] *v.,* **-fled, -fling,** *n.* —*v.i.* ①混戰；亂打。②拖足而行。—*n.* ①混戰。②(走路時之)拖足。

scull [skʌl; skʌl] *n.* ①船之尾櫓；舢槅。②一葉槳；雙槳中之一葉。③尾櫓划船；短槳划船。④〖蘇〗淺口大籃。—*v.t. & v.i.* 以尾櫓或短槳划(船)。—**er,** *n.*

scul·ler·y ['skʌlərɪ; 'skʌləri] *n., pl.* **-ler·ies.** 〖英〗廚房旁做粗活的小室。

scullery maid 女幫廚。

scul·lion ['skʌljən; 'skʌljən] *n.* ①在廚房操粗重工作的僕人。②卑賤的人。

sculp. ①sculptor.②sculptural. ③sculpture.

sculp [skʌlp; skʌlp] *v.t. & v.i.* 〖俚〗「=**sculpture.**」

scul·pin ['skʌlpɪn; 'skʌlpin] *n.* ①〖動物〗一種牛尾魚。②〖蔑〗不中用的東西（人）。—*adj.* 〖美〗無價值的；不中用的。

sculp·sit ['skʌlpsɪt; 'skʌlpsit] 〖拉〗 *v.* (他或她)雕刻(此作品)；(某某)謹刻。(略作 **sculp., sculpt.**)

sculpt [skʌlpt; skʌlpt] *v.t. & v.i.* ①雕刻。②做(頭髮)；梳(髮式)。

***sculp·tor** ['skʌlptɚ; 'skʌlptə] *n.* 雕刻師；雕刻家。

sculp·tress ['skʌlptrɪs; 'skʌlptris] 「*n.* 女雕刻家。」

***sculp·ture** ['skʌlptʃɚ; 'skʌlptʃə] *n., v.,* **-tured, -tur·ing.** —*n.* 雕刻術；雕刻；雕塑；雕刻品。—*v.t.* ①雕刻；雕塑。②用雕刻物裝飾。③〖地質〗以侵蝕改變地形。—*v.i.* 從事雕刻。—**sculp·tur·al,** *adj.*

sculp·tur·esque [ˌskʌlptʃə'rɛsk; ˌskʌlptʃə'resk] *adj.* 似雕刻的；精緻的；肅穆的。—**ly,** *adv.*

scum [skʌm; skʌm] *n., v.,* **scummed, scum·ming.** —*n.* ①泡沫；浮渣。②卑賤之人。—*v.i.* ①變成泡沫；浮有浮渣。②生浮皮。—*v.t.* ①自表面上撇取(浮沫等)。②迅速的掠過。③在…上形成泡沫或浮渣。

scum·ble ['skʌmbl; 'skʌmbl] *v.,* **-bled, -bling,** *n.* —*v.t.* ①〖油畫〗(爲修改原有色彩之效果而)薄施彩色於。②〖炭畫、鉛筆畫〗(爲使粗硬輪廓變得柔和)塗擦粉筆於。—*n.* 薄施彩色或粉；所施之彩色或粉。

scum·my ['skʌmɪ; 'skʌmi] *adj.,* **-mi·er, -mi·est.** ①有浮渣的。②無價值的。

scun·ner ['skʌnɚ, 'skunɚ; 'skʌnə] *n.* 〖方〗①憎惡；反感；偏見。②令人討厭之物。—*v.i. & v.t.* 〖蘇，英方〗討厭；憎惡。

scup [skʌp; skʌp] *n.* 一種鯛魚。

scup·per[1] ['skʌpɚ; 'skʌpə] *n.* 船甲板兩側之排水孔。

scup·per[2] *v.t.* 〖英俚〗①毀滅；擊潰；使紊亂；殺。②故意沉(船)。

scup·per·nong ['skʌpɚˌnɔŋ; 'skʌpənɔ:ŋ] *n.* ①美洲南部產的一種葡萄(黃綠色、有梅子味道)。②此種葡萄釀製之酒。

scurf [skɝf; skə:f] *n.* ①頭皮屑；頭垢。②皮屑；任何鱗狀外皮。—**y,** *adj.*

scur·ril(e) ['skɝɪl; 'skʌril] *adj.* 下流的；卑俗的；無禮的。

scur·ril·i·ty [skə'rɪlətɪ; skʌ'riliti] *n., pl.* **-ties.** ①下流。②粗俚之言語或行爲。

scur·ri·lous ['skɝələs; 'skʌriləs] *adj.* ①粗野無禮的。②嘲弄辱罵的。—**ly,** *adv.*

scur·ry ['skɝɪ; 'skʌri] *v.,* **-ried, -ry·ing,** *n., pl.* **-ries.** —*v.i.* 疾走。—*v.t.* 使疾走；使快跑。—*n.* ①疾走；倉皇而跑；疾走聲。②短跑。③一陣風雨；一陣風雪。

scur·vied ['skɝvɪd; 'skə:vid] *adj.* 患壞血症的。

scur·vy[1] ['skɝvɪ; 'skə:vi] *adj.,* **-vi·er, -vi·est.** 卑鄙的；可鄙的。—**scur·vi·ly,** *adv.* —**scur·vi·ness,** *n.*

scur·vy[2] *n.* 〖醫〗壞血症。(亦作 **scorbutus**)

scurvy grass 〖植物〗壞血病草。

scut [skʌt; skʌt] *n.* ①(兔、鹿之)短尾。②〖俚〗卑鄙小人。

scu·tage ['skjutɪdʒ; 'skju:tidʒ] *n.*(古代之)兵役免役稅。

scu·tate ['skjutet; 'skju:teit] *adj.* ①〖植物〗圓楯狀的。②〖動物〗有鱗甲的。

scutch [skʌtʃ; skʌtʃ] *v.t.* ①打（麻、棉等）之纖維使散。②以打麻機打。—*n.* 打麻機；打棉機。

scutch·eon ['skʌtʃən; 'skʌtʃən] *n.* ①盾形標牌；盾飾。②任何盾形金屬板。 ***a blot on the scutcheon*** 玷辱門楣的事。

scutch·er ['skʌtʃɚ; 'skʌtʃə] *n.* ①打麻者；打棉者。②打麻機；打棉機。

scute [skjut; skju:t] *n.* 〖動物〗鱗甲。

scu·tel·late ['skjutḷˌet, 'skju:təleit] *adj.* ①〖動物〗有鱗甲的；生鱗甲的。②盾形的；盤狀的。(亦作 **scutellated**)

scu·tel·lum [skju'tɛləm; skju:'teləm] *n., pl.* **-la** [-lə; -lə]. ①〖動物〗盾狀甲；(鳥足之)角質鱗片。②〖植物〗子葉盤。

scut·ter ['skʌtɚ; 'skʌtə] *v.i., n.* 〖蘇，英方〗急走；疾馳。

scut·tle[1] ['skʌtḷ; 'skʌtl] *n.* 煤斗；煤箱。

scut·tle[2] *n., v.,* **-tled, -tling.** —*n.* ①天窗；小艙口。②天窗蓋；小艙口蓋。—*v.t.* ①鑿沈(船)。②放棄。③破壞；毀壞。

scut·tle[3] *n., v.,* **-tled, -tling.** —*n.* 疾走；急行。—*v.i.* 疾走；快走。

scut·tle·butt ['skʌtḷˌbʌt; 'skʌtlbʌt] *n.*①船上的飲水噴泉。②〖美俚〗謠言；閒話。

scu·tum ['skjutəm; 'skju:təm] *n., pl.* **-ta** [-tə; -tə]. ①〖動物〗鱗甲。②〖解剖〗膝蓋骨。③(古羅馬的)長盾。

Scyl·la ['sɪlə; 'silə] *n.* ①義大利西端一塊危險之大石，隔 the Strait of Messina 與 Charybdis 渦流相對。②神話中六頭十二臂之妖怪，居於 Scylla 石上，專捕船上水手。

between Scylla and Charybdis 腹背受敵;左右爲難。

scythe [saɪð; saið] *n., v.,* **scythed, scyth·ing.** —*n.* 大鐮刀。—*v.t.* & *v.i.* 用大鐮刀割。

Scyth·i·a [ˈsɪθɪə; ˈsiθiə] *n.* 塞西亞(亞洲與歐洲東南部之一古地區)。

Scyth·i·an [ˈsɪθɪən; ˈsiθiən] *adj.* 塞西亞(人、語)的。—*n.* 塞西亞人(語)。

S/D sight draft. 見票卽付之匯票。 **S.D.** ① Scientiae Doctor (拉 = Doctor of Science). ②Senior Deacon. ③(亦作 **S. Dak.**) South Dakota. ④standard deviation. **s.d.** ①sight draft. ②sine die (拉= without a day). 無限期地。③〖數學〗standard deviation. **S. Dak.** South Dakota.

'sdeath [zdɛθ; zdeθ] *interj.*〖古〗該死!畜生! (God's death 之略)。

SE, S.E. ①southeast. ②southeastern.

S/E Stock Exchange. 股票交換所。

Se 化學元素 selenium 之符號。

s.e. ①southeast. ②southeastern.

‡sea [si; si:] *n.* ①(the-)海;洋。Boats sail on the *sea.* 船在海上航行。②海上之情形(可用定冠詞或不定冠詞)。The *sea* was calm. 海上風平浪靜。a rough *sea.* 波濤洶湧的海。③大的淡水湖。④波浪;大浪。A high *sea* swept away the ship's masts. 一個高浪沖去了那艘船的桅桿。⑤很多;大量。⑥寬廣;寬闊。***arm of the sea*** 海灣。***a sea of*** 多量的;無限的。*a sea of* troubles. 無窮的煩擾。***at full sea*** 滿潮;絕頂;極端。***at sea*** a. 在海上。b. 茫然;迷惑。I am quite *at sea* in regard to his explanation.他的解釋使我如墮五里霧中。***between the devil and the deep sea*** 腹背受敵;進退維谷。***beyond the sea(s)*** 在海外。***by sea*** 由海路。***command of the sea*** 制海權。***follow the sea*** 當海員;做水手。***freedom of the seas*** 海上通航權。***go to sea*** a. 航海。b. 當海員。***half seas over*** 喝酒太多;有點醉。***on the sea*** a. 在海上。b. 在船上;乘船。c. 臨海;在海岸。***put (out) to sea*** 出港。***take the sea*** 乘船;下水;開船。***take to sea*** 啓航。***the closed sea*** 領海。—*adj.* 海的;海上用的。*sea* forces. 海軍。

sea anchor (帆布製之)浮錨。

sea anemone 〖動物〗海葵。

sea bag 海員裝隨身行李用的帆布袋。

sea bass 棕黑色大鱗闊嘴之食用魚。

sea-bath·ing [ˈsiˈbeðɪŋ; ˈsi:ˈbeiðiŋ] *n.* 海水浴。

sea·beach [ˈsiˌbitʃ; ˈsi:bi:tʃ] *n.* 海灘。

sea bear 北極熊;白熊。

sea-bea·ver [ˈsiˌbivɚ; ˈsi:ˌbi:və] *n.* 〖動物〗海獺。

sea·bed [ˈsiˌbɛd; ˈsi:bed] *n.* 海底。

Sea·bee [ˈsiˌbi; ˈsi:bi:] *n.*〖美〗①海軍工程營之一員。②(略作 CB)海軍工程營。

sea beef 海豚或鯨之肉。

sea bells 〖植物〗旋花屬植物。

sea bird 海鳥。

sea biscuit 可供久藏的硬餅干。

sea·board [ˈsiˌbord; ˈsi:bɔ:d] *n.* 海岸;海濱。—*adj.* 海岸的;海濱的。

sea boat 海船;海上救急船。

sea boots 海員用的高統防水靴。

Sea·borg [ˈsibɔrg; ˈsi:bɔ:g] *n.* 西堡格 (Glenn Theodore, 1912–, 美國化學家, 1951年獲諾貝爾化學獎)。

sea-born [ˈsiˌbɔrn; ˈsi:bɔ:n] *adj.* ①生於海中的。②海產的。

sea-borne [ˈsiˌborn; ˈsi:bɔ:n] *adj.* ①海上運送的(人員或貨物)。②(船)浮在海上的。

sea bread 船上吃的硬麪包。(亦作 **ship biscuit, hardtack**)

sea breeze 海風。

sea calf 〖動物〗海豹。

sea captain 船長。

sea change ①海水造成之變化(如珍珠之形成)。②重大的轉變。

sea chest 水手之衣箱。

sea chestnut 〖動物〗海膽。

sea coal 〖英史〗煤(英格蘭南方無煤礦,故煤炭需從 Newcastle 海運而來, 以別於木炭 charcoal).

***sea·coast** [ˈsiˌkost; ˈsi:ˈkoust] *n.* 海岸;海濱。

sea cock 船底與海水相通之管口之活瓣。

sea cook 船上之廚師。

sea·cop·ter [ˈsiˌkɑptɚ; ˈsi:kʌptə] *n.* 水陸兩用直升機。

sea cow 〖動物〗海牛。

sea·craft [ˈsikræft; ˈsi:krɑ:ft] *n.* ①航行海上之船隻。②航海術。

sea crow 〖動物〗一種鷗屬之海鳥。

sea cucumber 海參。

sea-cut [ˈsiˌkʌt; ˈsi:kʌt] *adj.* 海浪侵蝕成的。

sea devil 華臍魚。

sea dog ①有經驗的海員或水手。②海豹。③小鯊。

sea·drome [ˈsiˌdrom; ˈsi:droum] *n.* 海上(浮起的)飛機場。

sea eagle 〖動物〗以魚爲食之海鷹。

sea-ear [ˈsiˌɪr; ˈsi:iə] *n.* 〖動物〗石決明;鮑魚。

sea elephant 〖動物〗海象(一種大海豹)。

sea·far·er [ˈsiˌfɛrɚ; ˈsi:ˌfɛərə] *n.* ①海員;水手。②海上旅行者。

sea·far·ing [ˈsiˌfɛrɪŋ; ˈsi:ˌfɛəriŋ] *adj.* ①海上旅行的。②航海的。—*n.*航海業;航海。

sea fight 海戰。

sea fisherman *pl.* **-men.** 在海上以捕魚爲業者。

sea·flow·er [ˈsiˌflauɚ; ˈsi:ˌflauə] *n.* 〖動物〗海葵。

sea foam ①海水之泡沫。②〖礦〗海泡石。

sea fog 海霧。

sea food 海產食物。

sea·fowl [ˈsiˌfaul; ˈsi:faul] *n.* 海鳥。

sea fox 〖動物〗長尾鮫。

sea front ①城市濱海之部分;海邊;海岸區。②房屋建築等對海之一面。

sea gauge ①(船的) 吃水深度。②氣壓測深器。

sea·girt [ˈsiˌgɝt; ˈsi:gə:t] *adj.* 爲海所環繞的。

sea-god [ˈsiˌgɑd; ˈsi:gɔd] *n.* 海神。(亦作 **sea god**)

sea-god·dess [ˈsiˌgɑdɪs; ˈsi:ˌgɔdis] *n.* 海之女神。(亦作 **sea goddess**)

sea·go·ing [ˈsiˌgo·ɪŋ; ˈsi:ˌgouiŋ] *adj.* ①航海的。②適於海上航行的 (以別於河上航行)。③從事航海事業的。—*n.* 航海。

sea grape ①馬尾藻。②(*pl.*) 烏賊之卵。③(美國 Florida 州沿海所產)一種結葡萄狀果實之植物。

sea green 海綠色。

sea gull 海鷗。

sea hedgehog 〖動物〗①海膽。②魚虎;海豚。

sea hog 〖動物〗海豚。

sea horse ①海馬。②〖動物〗海象。③(神話中)半馬半魚之怪獸。

sea kale 〖植物〗歐洲產的一種肥厚蔬菜。

sea king 中古時代北歐的海盜王。

seal[1]** [sil; si:l] *n.* ①捺印;封緘。②印章;圖章。③火漆;封蠟;封條(等)。④保證;表示。⑤圖記;記號。affix one's seal to*** 在…上

蓋印。 ***set one's seal to*** **a.** 在…上蓋印。 **b.** 批准;贊同。 ***speak under the seal of confession*** (天主教徒向神父) 告解。 ***take off the seal*** 拆信;開封。 ***the Great Seal*** 國璽。 ***under my hand and seal*** 經我簽名蓋印。 ***under seal of secrecy*** 保守祕密。—*v.t.* ①蓋印;蓋章。②封緘。③決定。④密封。⑤(用某種記號以)保證。 ***seal off*** = **seal up.** ***seal up*** 封;阻塞。—**a•ble,** *adj.*

***seal²** *n., pl.* **seals** or **seal,** *v.* —*n.* ①海豹。②海豹之皮毛。③海豹皮所製之革。—*v.i.* 獵海豹。

Sea·lab ['si,læb; 'si:læb] *n.* 海底實驗室(供潛水者棲息之美國海軍水下船隻)。

sea lane 海中之航道。

sea lawyer ①〖俗〗好批評詢問的水手。②〖動物〗鮫。

sealed [sild; si:ld] *adj.* ①經蓋印批准或證實的。②經蓋印證明合格或不短少的。③封口的。④謎樣的;不知的。

sealed book 未知之事;無法獲知之事。

sea legs 在動盪之船中仍能行走的能力。 ***get one's sea legs*** 經起初的暈船後對船身顛簸開始習慣。 ***have sea legs on*** 不暈船。

sea leopard 〖動物〗南極產的海豹。

seal·er¹ ['silɚ; 'si:lə] *n.* 檢查度量衡之官吏;蓋印者。

seal·er² *n.* ①捕海豹的人。②獵海豹的船。

seal·er·y ['silərɪ; 'si:ləri] *n., pl.* **-er·ies.** ①捕海豹業。②捕海豹之地方。

sea letter 〖航海〗中立船證(中立國船隻之航行許可證)。(亦作 **sea pass**)

sea level 海面;海拔。

seal fishery 海豹漁業;海豹漁場。

sea lily 〖植物〗海百合。

sea line ①水平線;海岸線。②深水捕魚用之釣線。

seal·ing wax ['silɪŋ~; 'si:liŋ~] 封蠟。

sea lion 〖動物〗一種大海豹。

Sea Lord 〖英〗武官出身之海軍大臣。

seal ring 有印之指環。

seal rookery 海豹繁殖之地。

seal·skin ['sil,skɪn; 'si:l-skin] *n.* ①海豹皮。②海豹革或皮毛。③海豹革或皮毛之製品。—*adj.* 用海豹皮製的。

Sea·ly·ham ['silɪ,hæm; 'si:liəm] *n.* 㹴之一種。

***seam** [sim; si:m] *n.* ①縫; 接縫。②接合線; 綴合處。③似縫之線; 皺紋。④地層; 層。⑤〖方〗針線活。⑥〖方〗油脂; 豬油。—*v.t.* ①縫合; 接合。②使有痕跡; 使有皺紋 (常用 pp.). His face is *seamed* with sorrow. 他的臉因憂愁而生皺紋。—*v.i.* ①生裂痕。②形成一條縫。

sea-maid ['si,med; 'si:meid] *n.* ①美人魚。②海上女神。(亦作 **sea-maiden**)

***sea·man** ['simən; 'si:mən] *n., pl.* **-men.** ①船員。②水兵。—**like,** —**ly,** *adj., adv.*

sea·man·ship ['simən,ʃɪp; 'si:mən-ʃip] *n.* 船藝;船舶操縱術;良好船員之能力。

sea·mark ['si,mark; 'si:ma:k] *n.* ①海岸上標明海潮最高點之線。②航海標幟。

sea mat 〖動物〗(尤指板枝介屬之)苔蘚蟲。

seamed [simd; si:md] *adj.* ①縫合的。②有線條的;有皺紋的。

sea mew 一種海鷗(產於歐洲)。

sea mile 海里; 浬 (英國爲 6,080 英尺; 美國爲 6076.1033 英尺)。

seam·less ['simlɪs; 'si:mlis] *adj.* 無縫的。

sea monster 海怪;海妖。

sea moss ①苔蘚蟲。②(苔狀的) 海草。

seam·stress ['simstrɪs; 'semstris] *n.* 女裁縫。(亦作 **sempstress**)

sea mud (當肥料用的)海泥。

sea mule (箱形)拖船。

sea-mus·sel ['si,mʌsl; 'si:,mʌsl] *n.* 〖動物〗貽貝;淡菜。

seam·y ['simɪ; 'si:mi] *adj.,* **seam·i·er, seam·i·est.** ①露出縫線的。②道德低落的; 卑鄙的。 ***the seamy side*** 黑暗面。

Sean·ad Eir·eann ['sænad'ɛrən; 'sænad'ɛərən] 愛爾蘭國會之上院。

sé·ance ['seɑns; 'seiɑ̃:ns] 〖法〗 *n.* ①會社團體之一次或一屆會議。②巫者之降神會。

sea nettle 〖動物〗刺螫水母。

sea nymph 水神。

sea otter 〖動物〗 海獺。

sea ox 〖動物〗海象 (=walrus).

sea parrot =**puffin.**

sea pen 〖動物〗 一種水螅; 海鰓。(亦作 **sea feather**)

sea pie ①〖英〗捉蠔者。②水手食用的肉拌蔬菜裹以麪糊或以麪糊分層烤成之食品。

sea·piece ['si,pis; 'si:pi:s] *n.* 海景畫。

sea pig 〖動物〗海豚。

sea pink 〖植物〗海石竹。

sea·plane ['si,plen; 'si:-plein] *n.* 水上飛機。

***sea·port** ['si,port; 'si:-pɔ:t] *n.* 海港; 海口;港埠。

sea power ①海軍强國。②海軍力量。③制海權。

sea purse 〖動物〗鮫等之卵囊。

sea·quake ['si,kwek; 'si:kweik] *n.* 海底地震。

sear [sɪr; siə] *v.t.* ①使枯萎;使憔悴。②灼燒; 燒焦。③加烙印於。④使(良心等)麻痺無情;使冷酷。—*v.i.* ①枯萎。②灼傷。③變得無情或麻木不仁。 —*adj.* 枯乾的; 枯萎的(葉、花等)。—*n.* 烙印;燒痕。

‡search [sɝtʃ; sə:tʃ] *v.t.* ①搜尋;搜查;探查。to *search* the dictionary for a word. 查字典。②(寒冷、風、火器等)刺穿。—*v.i.* ①尋覓; 搜索。②探求; 調查; 研究。to *search* for the truth. 探求眞理。 to *search* into a matter. 調查事件。 ***search me*** 〖俚〗不知道 (回答問題時用)。 ***search one's heart*** 仔細檢查自己的信仰與行爲。 ***search out*** 尋找;尋到。—*n.* 搜尋;探求;調查; 研究。I have made a *search* for the missing papers. 我已尋找過遺失的文件。 ***in search of*** 尋找。 I am at present *in search of* a house. 我現在正在找房子。 ***right of search*** 戰時交戰國搜查中立國船隻的權利。—**a•ble,** *adj.* —**er,** *n.*

search·ing ['sɝtʃɪŋ; 'sə:tʃiŋ] *adj.* ①仔細的; 徹底的。②銳利的; 洞察的。③刺骨的。—**ly,** *adv.* —**ness,** *n.*

***search·light** ['sɝtʃ,laɪt; 'sə:tʃ-lait] *n.* ①探照燈;照空燈。②光線;光柱。

search party 搜索隊。

search warrant 〖法律〗住宅搜索狀。

sea robber 海盜;海賊。

sea robin (魚)魴鮄的一種。

sea room ①船隻可以自由航行之無障礙物的海面。②自由行動之機會。

sea route ①航線;航路。②航路圖。

sea rover ①海賊;海盜。②海賊船; 海盜船。

sea salt 海鹽。

sea·scape ['si,skep; 'si:skeip] *n.* ①海景。②海景畫。

sea·scout ['si,skaut; 'si:skaut] *n.* 海洋童子軍。

sea serpent ①海蛇。②任何有毒之大海蛇。

sea shell 海產軟體動物之介殼;海貝。

***sea·shore** [ˈsi,ʃor; ˈsiːˈʃɔː] *n.* 海岸;海濱。—*adj.* 海濱的。a *seashore* resort. 海濱勝地。

***sea·sick** [ˈsi,sɪk; ˈsiː-sik] *adj.* 暈船的。—**ness,** *n.*

***sea·side** [ˈsi,saɪd; ˈsiːˈsaid] *n.* 海邊。—*adj.* 海濱的。a *seaside* inn. 海濱旅館。

sea sleeve 〖動物〗烏賊;墨魚。

sea slug 〖動物〗海參。

sea snake ①傳說中之大海蛇。②海蛇。

sea soldier 海軍陸戰隊隊員。

‡sea·son [ˈsizn̩; ˈsiːzn] *n.* ①季。the four *seasons.* 四季。②時期; 季節; 當令之時。the rainy *season.* 雨季。③短暫的一段時間。④合宜的時間。⑤〖俗〗月季票。⑥〖運動〗**a.** 舉辦某項競賽的期間(指所舉行比賽之次數)。**b.** 某隊輸贏記錄。***for a season*** 一段時間; 一會兒。***in good season*** 有足夠時間的; 儘早的。***in season*** **a.** 當令、合宜的時間。 a word in *season.* 適合時宜的話。**b.** =**in good season.** ***in season and out of season*** 在所有的時候。***out of season*** 不當令。 —*v.t.* ①使適應;使適用。to *season* oneself to cold. 使自己適應寒冷。②調味。③緩和。④使更有趣;使更適宜。⑤使木材變硬(俾不變形)。—*v.i.* 變爲適用。—**less,** *adj.*

sea·son·a·ble [ˈsizn̩əbl̩; ˈsiːzn̩əbl] *adj.* 合時的; 應時的; 適合時機的; 及時的。—**ness,** *n.* —**sea·son·a·bly,** *adv.*

sea·son·al [ˈsizn̩əl; ˈsiːzənl] *adj.* 季節的;季節性的。—**ly,** *adv.*

sea·soned [ˈsizn̩d; ˈsiːznd] *adj.* ①經調味的。highly *seasoned* dishes. 香料很濃的菜肴。②經加工即可使用的; 變乾的; 晒乾的。③習慣於…的; 訓練有素的; 有經驗的。a *seasoned* soldier. 經驗豐富的老兵。

sea·son·er [ˈsizn̩ɚ; ˈsiːznə] *n.* 調味者;調味器;調味料。

sea·son·ing [ˈsizn̩ɪŋ; ˈsiːzn̩iŋ] *n.* ①調味品。②增添興味的東西。—**like,** *adj.*

season ticket 長期票。

sea spider 〖動物〗①蜘蛛蟹。②鱆魚。③海盤車(魚)。

sea squirt 〖動物〗海鞘;石勃卒(海生小軟體動物)。

sea swallow 燕鷗。(亦作 **tern**)

‡seat [sit; siːt] *n.* ①座;坐位。 to take a *seat.* 坐下。to take one's *seat.* 坐在自己的座位上。②席位;席次。to lose one's *seat.* 落選;失去議員席次。③(椅子等的)座部。④臀部(或褲子上之臀部)。⑤所在地;中心; 場所; 位置。a *seat* of commerce. 商業中心。⑥邸宅; 別莊。⑦坐的姿勢; 騎乘的姿勢。That rider has a good *seat.* 那個騎馬者騎乘姿勢很好。⑧基礎。⑨被認爲某情感或機能所在之身體一部分。The heart is the *seat* of passion. 心是熱情所寓之處。⑩國王、主教等之職權、職位。⑪證券交易所中會員之特權。—*v.t.* ①使坐;使就座。We are all *seated.* 我們都就座了。②有(若干)座位;可容納。The hall *seats* 2,000. 這個會場有兩千個座位。③供以座位。④修(椅等)之座部。⑤使得職位,或議會中席次。—**less,** *adj.*

seat belt (飛機或汽車上的) 安全帶。

seat·er [ˈsitɚ; ˈsiːtə] *n.* 可供…人乘坐的汽車、飛機等。a four-*seater.* 可供四人乘坐的飛機或汽車。

sea term 航海用語。

seat·ing [ˈsitɪŋ; ˈsiːtiŋ] *n.* ①座位之備置。②座墊。③(乘馬等之) 坐姿。—*adj.* 座位的。

seat·mate [ˈsit,met; ˈsiːtmeit] *n.* 鄰座的人。

SEATO, S.E.A.T.O. South East Asia Treaty Organization. 東南亞公約組織。

sea·train [ˈsi,tren; ˈsiːtrein] *n.* 運火車車廂之輪船。

sea trout 海鱒(魚)。

Se·at·tle [siˈætl̩, ˈsiætl; siˈætl] *n.* 西雅圖(美國 Washington 州西部一海港)。

sea urchin 〖動物〗海膽。

sea wall 海堤;防波堤。

sea·ward [ˈsiwɚd; ˈsiːwəd] *adv.* 向海地。—*adj.* 向海的。 —*n.* 向海的方向。

sea·wards [ˈsiwɚdz; ˈsiːwədz] *adv.* 向海地。

sea·wa·ter [ˈsi,wɔtɚ, -,wɑt-; ˈsiː,wɔːtə] *n.* 海水。

sea·way [ˈsi,we; ˈsiːwei] *n.* ①航路;航道;海路。②公海;大海。③(船舶之)航行。④波濤洶湧之海。⑤運河或拓寬之河川。

***sea·weed** [ˈsi,wid; ˈsiːwiːd] *n.* 海藻;海菜。

sea·wor·thy [ˈsi,wɝðɪ; ˈsiː,wəːði] *adj.* ①適於航海的(船)。②建造與設備很好的(船);能耐風浪的(船)。—**sea·wor·thi·ness,** *n.*

sea wrack 海藻。

se·ba·ceous [sɪˈbeʃəs; siˈbeiʃəs] *adj.* 脂肪的;似脂肪的;分泌脂肪的。

sebaceous gland 〖解剖〗皮脂腺。

SEbE southeast by east.

SEbS southeast by south.

sec [sɛk; sek] 〖法〗 *adj.* 無甜味的(酒)。

SEC 〖美〗Securities and Exchange Commission. **sec** secant. **Sec.** Secretary.

sec. ①secretary. ②second; seconds. ③section; sections. ④secant. ⑤according to. ⑥secondary. ⑦sector. ⑧secundum.

S.E.C. ①Supreme Economic Council. ②Securities and Exchange Commission.

se·cant [ˈsikənt, ˈsikænt; ˈsiːkənt] *n.* 〖數學〗正割。—*adj.* 分割的;交割的。

sec·a·teur [,sɛkəˈtɝ; ˈsekətəː] *n.* (常 *pl.*) 修剪樹木之大剪刀;截斷鐵絲之大鉗子。

sec·co·tine [ˈsɛkə,tin; ˈsekətiːn] *n., v.,* **-tined, -tin·ing.** —*n.* 一種膠水。—*v.t.* 以此種膠水黏合。

se·cede [sɪˈsid; siˈsiːd] *v.i.,* **-ced·ed, -ced·ing.** 退出一機構、組織等。—**se·ced·er,** *n.*

se·cern [sɪˈsɝn; siˈsəːn] *v.t. & v.i.* ①分別;辨別。②〖生理〗分泌。—**ment,** *n.*

se·cern·ent [sɪˈsɝnənt; siˈsəːnənt] *adj.* 〖生理〗分泌的;分泌性的。—*n.* ①〖生理〗分泌器官;分泌機能。②促進分泌之藥物。

se·ces·sion [siˈsɛʃən; siˈseʃən] *n.* ①脫離;退出。②(常 S-)〖美史〗1860–1861美南方11州之退出聯邦(因而引起美國內戰)。

se·ces·sion·ism [siˈsɛʃən,ɪzəm; siˈseʃn̩izəm] *n.* 脫離論; 分離主義。—**se·ces·sion·ist,** *n., adj.*

***se·clude** [sɪˈklud; siˈkluːd] *v.t.,* **-clud·ed, -clud·ing.** 隔離;隔絕;使隱居。to *seclude* oneself from society. 過隱居生活。

se·clud·ed [sɪˈkludɪd; siˈkluːdid] *adj.* 隔離的;隱退的。—**ly,** *adv.* —**ness,** *n.*

se·clu·sion [sɪˈkluʒən; siˈkluːʒən] *n.* ①蟄居;隱遁。She lives in *seclusion.* 她過隱居生活。②幽僻之地。

se·clu·sive [sɪˈklusɪv; siˈkluːsiv] *adj.* ①喜蟄居的; 隱遁的。②趨於隔離的; 隔離性的。—**ly,** *adv.* —**ness,** *n.*

‡sec·ond[1] [ˈsɛkənd; ˈsekənd] *adj.* ①第二的。February is the *second* month of the year. 二月是一年的第二個月。②次的;

二等的;較劣的。He is *second* to none. 他不亞於任何人。③另一個;又一個。④額外的。⑤〖音樂〗音調較低的;唱奏音調較低之部分的。*second* soprano. 次高音。***in the second place*** 說到第二點。***on second thoughts*** 重加考慮。—*adv.* 第二地;次要地。The English swimmer came *second*. 那個英國游泳選手得第二。—*n.* ①第二人;第二物;第二者。②(月之)初二;二日。③(*pl.*) **a.** 次等品;劣物。**b.** 粗劣的麪粉。**c.** 用次等麪粉做的麪包。④輔助者;助手。⑤〖音樂〗第二度音程;第二音。—*v.t.* ①贊成。to *second* a motion. 附議。②支持;輔助。Deeds must *second* words. 言行必須一致。③〖英〗被暫時調任。④做(拳擊家或決鬥者的)助手。

***sec·ond[2]** *n.* ①秒;(鐘錶之)秒針。②片刻。Please wait a *second*. 請稍待片刻。③秒(角度單位)。

second advent 基督再臨。(亦作「Second Advent」)

Second Adventist, second adventist 基督再臨派信徒。

***sec·ond·ar·y** [ˈsɛkənˌdɛrɪ; ˈsekəndəri] *adj.*, *n.*, *pl.* **-ar·ies.** —*adj.* ①第二的;從屬的。*secondary* product. 副產品。②次要的;較不重要的。③〖物理〗感應電流的;次級電流的。④〖醫〗在一種病症之後繼發的。⑤〖醫〗第二期的。*secondary* eruptions. 第二期的發作。⑥(S-)〖地質〗發生於或屬於 Mesozoic era 的。⑦非原始的;間接的。⑧〖化〗次(的);副的。⑨〖語言〗次重音的。—*n.* ①次要的人;次要的東西。②產生感應電流的線圈。③〖語音〗次重音。—**sec·ond·ar·i·ly,** *adv.* —**sec·ond·ar·i·ness,** *n.*

secondary accent ①次重音。②次重音標號。(亦作 **secondary stress**)

secondary color 等和色(以兩原色等量混合而成的顏色)。

secondary education 中等教育。

secondary planet 衞星。

secondary school 中等學校。

secondary sex characteristic 〖醫〗第二性徵。(亦作 **secondary sex character**)

second ballot ①第二次投票。②第二次投票數。

second base 〖棒球〗第二壘。

second baseman 〖棒球〗二壘手。

sec·ond-best [ˈsɛkəndˈbɛst; ˈsekəndˈbest] *adj.* 第二等的。—*n.* 二等角色;二等貨色。—*adv.* 第二等地。

Second Chamber 荷蘭的衆議院。(參議院稱為 First Chamber).

second childhood 因年老而致的愚蠢或幼稚行為;第二童年。

second class ①(火車等之)二等。②〖美郵政〗新聞紙類。

sec·ond-class [ˈsɛkəndˈklæs; ˈsekəndˈklɑːs] *adj.* 二流的;二等的。—*adv.* 坐二等艙地;坐二等車地。

second-class matter 〖美郵政〗新聞紙類。

Second Coming 基督再臨。

second cousin 從堂、表兄弟姊妹。

se·cond-de·gree burn [ˈsɛkənddɪˈgri～; ˈsekənddiˈgriː～] 二級灼傷(起水疱程度的灼傷)。

se·conde [sɪˈkɑnd, səˈgɔ̃d; siˈkɔnd, səˈgɔ̃d] *n.*, *pl.* **-condes** [-ˈkɑndz, -ˈgɔ̃d; -ˈkɔndz, -gɔ̃d]. 〖劍術〗一種撥擊之姿勢。

sec·ond·er [ˈsɛkəndɚ; ˈsekəndə] *n.* 補助者;贊成者;附議者。

second estate (英、法等國)貴族。

second fiddle ①交響樂隊中第二小提琴部;該部的小提琴手。②第二流的人;次要地位。***play second fiddle*** 扮演次要的角色。

second gear 汽車之第二檔。

sec·ond-gen·er·a·tion missile [ˈsɛkəndˌdʒɛnəˈreʃən～; ˈsekəndˌdʒenəˈreiʃən～] 改良飛彈;新型飛彈。

second growth 原始林破壞後長出之草木。

sec·ond-guess [ˈsɛkəndˈgɛs; ˈsekəndˈges] *v.t.* & *v.i.* ①〖俗〗用事後聰明;放馬後砲。②預言;猜測。—**er,** *n.*

***sec·ond-hand** [ˈsɛkəndˈhænd; ˈsekəndˈhænd] *adj.* ①用過的;舊的。②非原始的;得自他人的。③販賣舊物的。a *second-hand* bookstore. 舊書店。—*adv.* 間接地。He heard the news *second-hand*. 他間接地聽到消息。

second hand ①(鐘、錶之)秒針。②媒介物;中間人。***at second hand*** 間接地。

second lieutenant (陸空軍、海軍陸戰隊)少尉。(略作 **2d Lt.**)

***sec·ond·ly** [ˈsɛkəndlɪ; ˈsekəndli] *adv.* 第二。

second mate 〖航海〗二副。

sec·ond·ment [ˈsɛkəndmənt; ˈsekəndmənt] *n.* 〖英〗暫調;借調。

second mortgage 第二抵押。

second nature 第二天性。

se·con·do [seˈkondo; seˈkɔndou] *n.*, *pl.* **-di** [-di; -diː]. 〖音樂〗二重奏等之附屬部分。

second papers 外國人入美國籍的最後申請;申請歸化。

second person 〖文法〗第二人稱。

second pilot 副駕駛員。

sec·ond-rate [ˈsɛkəndˈret; ˈsekəndˈreit] *adj.* ①二等的;二流的。②平凡的;庸劣的。—**ness, sec·ond-rat·er,** *n.*

second self 第二自我(指知心密友)。

second sight 千里眼;預知力。

sec·ond-strike [ˈsɛkəndˈstraɪk; ˈsekəndˈstraik] *adj.* ①反擊的(指核子武力受到偷襲後仍有能力反擊的)。②報復的。

sec·ond-string [ˈsɛkəndˈstrɪŋ; ˈsekəndˈstriŋ] *adj.* ①第二流的;次要的。②〖體育〗非正選隊的;預備隊的。

second thought(s) 愼思熟慮後做之決定。

second wind ①(激烈運動等後的)呼吸恢復正常狀態。②〖俗〗恢復常態;恢復元氣。

Second World War 第二次世界大戰(1939–45)。

se·cre·cy** [ˈsikrəsɪ; ˈsiːkrisi] *n.*, *pl.* **-cies.** ①祕密。②保密的能力;守祕密。③掩飾;不坦白。in*** (or ***with***) ***secrecy*** 祕密地。

‡se·cret [ˈsikrɪt; ˈsiːkrit] *adj.* ①隱祕的。a *secret* room. 密室。②祕密的。Be as *secret* as the grave. 要極端的保守祕密。③只有少數人知道的。a *secret* society. 祕密會社。④隱退的;隱居的。⑤難解的;不易發現的。⑥守祕密的。⑦〖美政府,軍〗極機密的。***keep something secret*** 保守某事之祕密。—*n.* ①祕密。②祕訣。*secret* of success. 成功的祕訣。③奧妙;玄妙。*secrets* of nature. 自然界的奧祕。④〖美政府,軍〗極機密(機密分類之一種)。***in secret*** 祕密地。***in the secret*** 參與祕密。***keep something a secret*** 保守某事之祕密。***let someone into a*** (or ***the***) ***secret*** 告某人以某項祕密;使某人參與某項祕密工作。—**ly,** *adv.*

secret agent 特務;間諜。

sec·re·taire [səˌkreˈtɛr; səˌkreiˈtɛə] *n.* ①寫字台。②祕書。(亦作 **secrétaire**)

sec·re·tar·i·al [ˌsɛkrəˈtɛrɪəl; ˌsekrəˈtɛəriəl] *adj.* ①祕書的；書記的。②部長的。
sec·re·tar·i·at(e) [ˌsɛkrəˈtɛrɪət; ˌsekrəˈtɛəriət] *n.* ①書記之職；祕書之職；部長之職。②祕書處；文書課。
‡**sec·re·tar·y** [ˈsɛkrəˌtɛrɪ; ˈsekrətri, -krit-] *n., pl.* **-tar·ies.** ①書記；祕書。②大臣；部長。*Secretary* of State.(美國)國務卿；(英國)國務大臣。③寫字台。
secretary bird 〖動物〗鷲鷹；食蛇鳥。
sec·re·tar·y-gen·er·al [ˈsɛkrəˌtɛrɪˈdʒɛnərəl; ˈsekrətriˈdʒenərəl] *n., pl.* **sec·re·tar·ies-gen·er·al.** 祕書長；書記長。
sec·re·tar·y·ship [ˈsɛkrəˌtɛrɪˌʃɪp; ˈsekrətriʃip] *n.* 書記、祕書、部長之職位、任期等。
secret ballot 祕密投票。
se·crete [sɪˈkrit; siˈkriːt] *v.t.,* **-cret·ed, -cret·ing.** ①隱匿；隱藏。②分泌。
se·cre·tion [sɪˈkriʃən; siˈkriːʃən] *n.* ①隱匿；隱藏。②分泌。③分泌物。
se·cre·tive [sɪˈkritɪv; siˈkriːtiv] *adj.* ①隱匿的；祕而不宣的；隱密的。②〖生理〗分泌的；促進分泌的。—**ly,** *adv.* —**ness,** *n.*
se·cre·to·ry [sɪˈkritərɪ; siˈkriːtəri] *adj., n., pl.* **-ries.** —*adj.* 分泌的；使分泌的。—*n.* 分泌器官。
secret police 祕密警察。
secret service ①(S- S-)特務工作局(美國財政部之一部門，專司僞幣偵察及總統保護等)。②特務機構。③特務工作。
***sect** [sɛkt; sekt] *n.* 派；宗派；教派。
sect. section.
sec·tar·i·an [sɛkˈtɛrɪən; sekˈtɛəriən] *adj.* 宗派的；派系的；有門戶之見的。—*n.* 宗派門徒；派系意識濃厚的人。—**ly,** *adv.*
sec·tar·i·an·ism [sɛkˈtɛrɪənˌɪzəm; sekˈtɛəriənizəm] *n.* 門戶之見；宗派意識。
sec·tar·i·an·ize [sɛkˈtɛrɪənˌaɪz; sekˈtɛəriənaiz] *v.t.,* **-ized, -iz·ing.** 使有門戶之見；使有宗派心。
sec·ta·ry [ˈsɛktərɪ; ˈsektəri] *n., pl.* **-ries.** ①(某一特殊宗派之)門徒；信徒；宗教心極强的人。②(常 S-)英國獨立新教派之教徒。
sec·tile [ˈsɛktɪl; ˈsektil] *adj.* (礦物等)可用刀切斷但一經重擊會粉碎的。
‡**sec·tion** [ˈsɛkʃən; ˈsekʃən] *n.* ①切開；切斷。②斷片；部分。③節；項。④區域；地段。a residential *section.* 住宅區。⑤斷面；截面。vertical *section.* 豎斷面；縱斷面。a cross (*or* transverse) *section.* 橫斷面。⑥一平方英里的面積。⑦(鐵路的)一組工人負責保養的一段。⑧臥車中包括上下鋪的一部分。⑨可裝成一整體的各部分；零件。⑩〖數學〗截口；截面。⑪〖外科〗切片。⑫〖軍〗 **a.** 兩班或兩班以上的小部隊。**b.** 參謀下之一部門。**c.** 海、空軍的小戰術部隊。⑬兩部或兩部以上火車、巴士等之任何一部。⑭樂隊中同種樂器之部分。the string *section.* 絃樂器部分。⑮=**section mark.** —*v.t.* ①切成部分；分成章節。②拆散(機器等)。③割切使成斷面。④〖外科〗將…切片。
sec·tion·al [ˈsɛkʃənl̩; ˈsekʃənl] *adj.* ①部分的；分節的。②區域的；地段的。③由數獨立部分組合而成的。—*n.* 可獨立分開來使用，亦可拼成爲一個使用的沙發。—**ly,** *adv.*
sec·tion·al·ism [ˈsɛkʃənl̩ˌɪzəm; ˈsekʃənlizəm] *n.* ①地方主義；地域偏見。②派系主義。
sec·tion·al·ist [ˈsɛkʃənlɪst; ˈsekʃənlist] *n.* 地方主義者；地方利益第一主義者。
sec·tion·al·ize [ˈsɛkʃənl̩ˌaɪz; ˈsekʃənəlaiz] *v.t.,* **-ized, -iz·ing.** ①區分；劃分。②使成派別或地方性；造成黨派之見。—**sec·tion·al·i·za·tion,** *n.*
section mark 節標(卽§)。
section paper 方眼紙。
sec·tor [ˈsɛktɚ; ˈsektə] *n.* ①〖數學〗扇形。②尺規；函數尺。③〖軍〗戰區；陣線。—*v.t.* 分割爲扇形或戰區。—**al,** *adj.*
sec·u·lar [ˈsɛkjəlɚ; ˈsekjulə] *adj.* ①現世的；塵世的；世俗的；非宗教的。*secular* affairs. 俗事。②住於俗世的(爲regular 之對)。③永久的；長期的。④百年一度的；一世紀一次的。—*n.* 居住俗界的牧師。—**ly,** *adv.*
sec·u·lar·ism [ˈsɛkjələˌrɪzəm; ˈsekjulərizəm] *n.* ①現世主義；世俗主義。②G. J. Holyoak (1817-1906) 倡導之世俗主義。—**sec·u·lar·ist,** *n.* —**sec·u·lar·is·tic,** *adj.*
sec·u·lar·i·ty [ˌsɛkjəˈlærətɪ; ˌsekjuˈlæriti] *n., pl.* **-ties.** ①=**secularism.** ②世俗；俗事；俗心。
sec·u·lar·ize [ˈsɛkjələˌraɪz; ˈsekjuləraiz] *v.t.* ①使俗化；使現世化。②使(教育)脫離宗教。③使(教會財產)供俗用。—**sec·u·lar·i·za·tion,** *n.*
se·cund [ˈsikʌnd; ˈsiːkʌnd] *adj.* 〖動植物〗偏向一側的；側向一方的(如鈴蘭)。—**ly,** *adv.*
se·cun·do [sɪˈkʌndo; siˈkʌndou] 〖拉〗 *adv.* 第二(=secondly).
se·cun·dum [sɪˈkʌndəm; siˈkʌndəm] 〖拉〗 *prep.* 依照；按照；由(=according to).
secundum le·gem [~ˈlidʒɛm; ~ˈliːdʒem] 〖拉〗從法律；根據法律。
secundum na·tu·ram [~nəˈtjuræm; ~nəˈtjuːəræm] 〖拉〗天然地；自然地。
se·cur·a·ble [sɪˈkjurəbl̩; siˈkjuərəbl] *adj.* 可獲得的。
‡**se·cure** [sɪˈkjur; siˈkjuə] *adj., v.,* **-cured, -cur·ing.** —*adj.* ①無受損、受害、受攻擊之虞的；安全的。to be *secure* from harm. 無受害之虞。②確定的；無疑的。③安心的；無慮的。He hoped for a *secure* old age. 他希望有一個無憂無慮的晚年。④可靠的；穩固的。⑤不能逃脫的。—*v.t.* ①使安全；保護。②擔保；保證。to *secure* a debt by mortgage. 以抵押擔保債務。③繫緊；緊閉。④得到；獲得。to *secure* one's end. 達到目的。—**ly,** *adv.*
se·cu·ri·form [sɪˈkjurɪˌfɔrm; siˈkjuərifɔːm] *adj.* 〖植物〗斧狀的。
***se·cu·ri·ty** [sɪˈkjurətɪ; siˈkjuəriti] *n., pl.* **-ties,** *adj.* —*n.* ①安全。personal (public) *security.* 身家的(公共的)安全。②安全的保障。③確信；確然。④疏忽；過度的自信。fatal *security.* 致命的忽略。⑤保證；擔保。personal *security.* 人保。in *security* for. 爲…保證。⑥抵押品；擔保品。⑦(*pl.*) 公債；股票。government *securities.* 公債。⑧擔保人；保證人。—*adj.* 保安的；安全的。*security* guard. 警衞。
security analyst 股市分析家。
security clearance ①忠貞調查。②通過上項調查。
Security Council (聯合國)安全理事會。
security police 祕密警察。
security risk 〖美〗①聯邦政府雇用人員中，因各種原因而被認爲不可靠，或不應使其參與國家機密者。②任何可能危害國家安全之事。
security system 國家安全制度；國際安全制度。
secy., sec'y. secretary.

se·dan [sɪˈdæn; siˈdæn] *n.* ①(亦作**sedan chair**) 轎;肩輿。②轎車。
sedan chair 轎;肩輿。
se·date [sɪˈdet; siˈdeit] *adj., v.,* **-dat·ed, -dat·ing.** —*adj.* 安詳的; 靜肅的。—*v.t.* 以鎮靜劑使靜。—**ly,** *adv.* —**ness,** *n.*
se·da·tion [sɪˈdeʃən; siˈdeiʃən] *n.* ①安詳;沉靜(尤指用鎮靜劑後)。②〖醫〗鎮靜作用。
sed·a·tive [ˈsɛdətɪv; ˈsedətiv] *adj.* ①鎮定的; 定神的。②撫慰的; 安靜的。—*n.* 鎮定劑;止痛劑。
sed·en·tar·y [ˈsɛdn̩ˌtɛrɪ; ˈsedntəri] *adj.* ①慣坐的; 久坐的;不活動的。②須坐的。③少動的; 罕動的。④固定於一點的。⑤非候鳥的;定居的。⑥(蜘蛛等)結網等候的。—**sed·en·tar·i·ly,** *adv.* —**sed·en·tar·i·ness,** *n.*
sedge [sɛdʒ; sedʒ] *n.* 〖植物〗蘆葦。
sedg·y [ˈsɛdʒɪ; ˈsedʒi] *adj.,* **sedg·i·er, sedg·i·est.** ①蘆葦的。②似蘆葦的。
se·di·le [sɪˈdaɪli; seˈdaili] *n., pl.* **-dil·i·a** [-ˈdɪlɪə; -ˈdiljə]. 〖宗教〗(內殿聖壇近側的)司祭席。
sed·i·ment [ˈsɛdəmənt; ˈsedimənt] *n.* ①沈澱物;渣。②沖積物。—*v.t.* & *v.i.* 沈澱。—**ous,** *adj.*
sed·i·men·ta·ry [ˌsɛdəˈmɛntərɪ; ˌsediˈmentəri] *adj.* ①沈澱物的; 有沈澱物性質的;含有沈澱物的。②〖地質〗沖積的;水成的。(亦作 **sedimental**)
sed·i·men·ta·tion [ˌsɛdəmənˈteʃən; ˌsedimənˈteiʃən] *n.* 沈澱;沈澱作用;沈降。
sed·i·men·tol·o·gy [ˌsɛdəmənˈtɑlədʒɪ; ˌsedimənˈtɔlədʒi] *n.* 水成岩學。
se·di·tion [sɪˈdɪʃən; siˈdiʃən] *n.* ①煽動叛亂之言行。②暴動;叛亂。
se·di·tion·ar·y [sɪˈdɪʃənˌɛrɪ; siˈdiʃənəri] *adj., n., pl.* **-ar·ies.** —*adj.* 騷動的;暴亂的;煽動暴亂的。—*n.* 倡亂者;煽動暴亂者。
se·di·tious [sɪˈdɪʃəs; siˈdiʃəs] *adj.* ①煽動(性)的;妨害治安的;煽動叛變的。②妨害治安罪的。—**ly,** *adv.* —**ness,** *n.*
se·duce [sɪˈdjus; siˈdjuːs] *v.t.,* **-duced, -duc·ing.** ①誘惑。②使入歧途。③誘姦(婦女)。—**se·duc·ive,** *adj.* —**se·duc·er,** *n.*
se·duce·ment [sɪˈdjusmənt; siˈdjuːsmənt] *n.* 引誘;誘惑;勾引;詭計。
se·duc·i·ble [sɪˈdjusəbl̩; siˈdjuːsibl] *adj.* 可引誘的;可誘姦的。(亦作 **seduceable**)
se·duc·tion [sɪˈdʌkʃən; siˈdʌkʃən] *n.* ①引誘;誘惑。②勾引;誘姦。③誘惑物;魔力。
se·duc·tive [sɪˈdʌktɪv; siˈdʌktiv] *adj.* ①引誘的; 誘惑的。②勾引的; 誘姦的。—**ly,** *adv.* —**ness,** *n.*
se·du·li·ty [sɪˈdjulətɪ; siˈdjuːliti] *n.* 勤勉;恒心。
sed·u·lous [ˈsɛdʒələs; ˈsedjuləs] *adj.* 勤勉的;努力不倦的。—**ly,** *adv.* —**ness,** *n.*
Se·dum [ˈsidəm; ˈsiːdəm] *n.* ①〖植物〗景天屬。②(s-)景天屬植物。
‡**see**[1] [si; siː] *v.,* **saw** [sɔ; sɔː], **seen** [sin; siːn], **see·ing,** *interj.* —*v.t.* ①看;見;視。I *saw* something move (*or* moving). 我看見有甚麼東西在動。②了解;領會(=understand); 察覺(=perceive). I *see* what you mean. 我明白你的意思。③發現; 察知。④經驗; 閱歷。He has *seen* a lot in his life. 他閱歷很多。⑤會面;晤見(=meet);訪晤(=call on);商談(=talk with); 接見(=receive a call from). He is too ill to *see* anyone. 他病得不能接見任何人。⑥護送;照顧。Who's going to *see* Miss Green home? 誰送葛琳小姐回家? ⑦參加; 參觀。We *saw* the World's Fair. 我們參觀了世界博覽會。⑧讓; 允許。⑨注意; 負責。*See* that the defect is made good. 注意要把毛病修好。⑩期待; 等待到最後。⑪〖牌戲〗下(與賭注)同樣多的賭金。—*v.i.* ①看; 見; 視。Can you *see* to write? 你能看得見寫字否? ②具有視力。③察看。④考慮。Now, then, let's *see.* 那麼,讓我們考慮考慮。⑤了解;領會。I *see.* 我明白啦。*See?* 懂不懂? ⑥注意; 留心。***see about*** a. 注意。b. 考察; 查詢。***see after*** 照顧(=look after). ***see into*** 調查。***see one's way*** 明瞭做某事之可能性。***see out*** 完成; 貫徹。***see over*** 檢查; 調查。***see red*** a. 生氣; 發怒。b. 有破壞或攻擊人的欲望。***see service*** a. 因富經驗而成專家。b. 因久用而破舊。***see somebody off*** 送行。***see the back of*** 送去;擺脫。***see the last of*** 和…斷絕關係;趕走(某人)。***see things*** 有幻想;有幻覺。***see through*** a. 看透; 眞正了解。b. 堅持到底; 貫徹始終。***see to*** 注意(=to take care of). ***see visions*** 做先知;做卜者。—*interj.* 瞧! 看啊! *See,* here he comes! 瞧,他來了!
see[2] *n.* 主教的職權;主教的轄區。***the Holy See*** 羅馬教廷;教宗;教宗之職權。
see·a·ble [ˈsiəbl̩; ˈsiːəbl] *adj.* 可看見的。
‡**seed** [sid; siːd] *n., pl.* **seeds, seed,** *v.* —*n.* ①種; 種子。to sow *seed* in the ground. 播種於地。②子孫;後裔。③根源。She planted the *seeds* of virtue in her children. 她在孩子們心田裏播下了道德的種子。④誕生。⑤精子;卵子。⑥=**seed oyster.** ⑦玻璃中的氣泡。***go*** (or ***run***) ***to seed*** a. 結子。b. 衰頹。***in seed*** a. (某些植物)結成熟種子的。b. (田地、草坪等)播着種子的。—*v.i.* ①結實;成熟。②播種。—*v.t.* ①播種於。②去…之種子。③〖運動〗配(種子隊)於比賽之各組。④撒(乾冰等)於雲以造人造雨。—**like,** *adj.*
seed·bed [ˈsidˌbɛd; ˈsiːdbed] *n.* ①苗床。②發源地;醞釀地。
seed·cake [ˈsidˌkek; ˈsiːdkeik] *n.* ①香餅。②油被榨出後的棉子餅。
seed capsule 蒴。
seed·case [ˈsidˌkes; ˈsiːdkeis] *n.* 〖植物〗① =**seed capsule.** ②種子外衣。
seed coat 種子外皮。
seed coral (作裝飾用的)珊瑚粒。
seed corn 穀種。
seed·eat·er [ˈsidˌitɚ; ˈsiːdˌiːtə] *n.* 吃穀物的小鳥。
seed·er [ˈsidɚ; ˈsiːdə] *n.* ①播種機; 播種者。②除果核之裝置; 除種子機。③爲取種子而栽植的植物。④造人造雨之裝置。
seed·ing-ma·chine [ˈsidɪŋməˌʃin; ˈsiːdiŋməˌʃiːn] *n.* 播種機。
seed leaf 子葉。
seed·less [ˈsidlɪs; ˈsiːdlis] *adj.* 無子的; 無核的。
seed·ling [ˈsidlɪŋ; ˈsiːdliŋ] *n.* ①從種子中長出的植物。②不滿三尺之小樹。③苗圃中供移植的任何小樹。—*adj.* ①從種子栽培的。②原始狀態的。③(牡蠣之)從種子繁殖的。
seed oyster 供繁殖用之牡蠣。
seed pearl ($^{1}/_{4}$ grain 以下之) 珍珠; 米珠。
seed plant 種子植物。
seed plot ①苗床。②(罪惡等之)淵藪;策源地。
seed·pod [ˈsidˌpɑd; ˈsiːdpɔd] *n.* =**pod**[1]①.
seeds·man [ˈsidzmən; ˈsiːdzmən] *n., pl.* **-men.** 播種者;賣種子者。
seed·time [ˈsidˌtaɪm; ˈsiːdtaim] *n.*

播種時期。

seed vessel 包種子的莢、外殼等。

seed·y ['sidɪ; 'si:di] *adj.*, **seed·i·er, seed·i·est.** ①多種子的。②結子的。③衣服襤褸的。④〖俗〗精神不佳的;不適的。⑤不很高尚的。—**seed·i·ly,** *adv.* —**seed·i·ness,** *n.*

***see·ing** ['siɪŋ; 'si:iŋ] *conj.* 因為;既然;鑑於 (=since). Your child reads well, *seeing* that he has attended school so short a time. 鑑於你的小孩子上學的時間才這麼短,他的書可以說是讀得很好了。—*n.* ①看。*Seeing* is believing. 眼見是實。②視覺。—*adj.* 看的。—**ly,** *adv.* —**ness,** *n.*

Seeing Eye 導盲犬訓練所。

Seeing Eye dog 導盲犬。

:seek [sik; si:k] *v.*, **sought** [sɔt; sɔ:t], **seek·ing.** —*v.t.* ①尋覓。to *seek* shelter from rain. 尋找避雨之所。②尋求;求得;請求。to *seek* fame. 求名。③企圖獲得;嘗試。He *sought* to make peace. 他企圖講和。④往。⑤〖古〗尋找;探測。—*v.i.* 尋覓。to *seek* for employment. 謀職。***be sought after*** 被爭取;被需要。***to seek*** **a.** 被尋找 (=to be sought). The reason is not far *to seek*. 理由不難找到。**b.** 尚未尋到;缺如。**c.** 〖古〗迷惑;不解。—**er,** *n.*

seel [sil; si:l] *v.t.* ①以線縫閉(鷹等之)眼瞼。②閉(目)。③使盲。

:seem [sim; si:m] *v.i.* 似乎是;看似;似乎;似覺。There *seems* no need to wait longer. 似乎無須再等了。It *seems* to me that it will rain. 我看天要下雨。

***seem·ing** ['simɪŋ; 'si:miŋ] *adj.* 彷彿的;似乎的;表面上的。*seeming* happiness. 表面上的快樂。—*n.* 外貌;外觀。the *seeming* and the real. 表面與實際。—**ly,** *adv.* —**ness,** *n.*

seem·ly ['simlɪ; 'si:mli] *adj.*, **-li·er, -li·est,** *adv.* —*adj.* ①合適的;端莊的。②貌美的。—*adv.* 合適地。—**seem·li·ness,** *n.*

***seen** [sin; si:n] *v.* pp. of **see**[1]. —*adj.* 有技巧的;有經驗的;熟悉的。

seep[1] [sip; si:p] *v.i.* ①滲。②(觀念等)滲入。③混合;滲透。—*n.* ①滲出之濕氣。②地下湧出之水灘;小泉。

seep[2] *n.* 水陸兩用之吉普車。

seep·age ['sipɪdʒ; 'si:pidʒ] *n.* ①滲。②滲出物。

seep·y ['sipɪ; 'si:pi] *adj.*, **seep·i·er, seep·i·est.** ①排水不良的。②濕氣很重的。

seer[1] [sɪr *for* ①, 'siɚ *for* ②; 'si(:)ə] *n.* ①預言家;先知;卜者。②觀看者。

seer[2] [sɪr; siə] *n.* 印度之重量單位(等於2.057 磅)。

seer·ess ['sɪrɪs; 'si:əris] *n.* 女預言者。

seer·suck·er ['sɪr,sʌkɚ; 'siə,sʌkə] *n.* 印度織的一種縐起的條子布(棉或麻)。

***see·saw** ['si,sɔ; 'si:-sɔ:] *n.* ①蹺蹺板;軒輊戲。to play at *seesaw*. 玩蹺蹺板。②上下或前後移動。—*v.i.* 玩蹺蹺板;上下動;前後動。—*adj.* ①上下或前後動的。②拉鋸性的。—*adv.* 上下動地;前後動地。

seesaw game 拉鋸戰。

seethe [sið; si:ð] *v.*, **seethed** or (廢) **sod, seethed** or (廢) **sod·den** or **sod, seeth·ing,** *n.* —*v.i.* ①煮沸;沸騰。②起泡沫。③激昂;騷動。to *seethe* with anger. 大發雷霆。—*v.t.* ①漬;浸。②煮。—*n.* ①煮沸。②激動;激昂。

see-through ['si,θru; 'si:θru:] *adj.* 透明的。—*n.* ①透明的服飾。②穿着此種服飾之時尚。

se·gar [sɪ'gar; si'gɑ:] *n.* cigar 之誤寫。

seg·ment ['sɛgmənt; 'segmənt] *n.* ①片;部分;斷片。②〖數學〗節。—*v.i.* & *v.t.* 分割成(部分)。—**ar·y,** *adj.*

seg·men·tal [sɛg'mɛntl; seg'mentl] *adj.* ①部分的;斷片的。②〖生物〗環節的;分節片的。③弓形的。—**ly,** *adv.* —**ize,** *v.*

seg·men·ta·tion [,sɛgmən'teʃən; ,segmən'teiʃən] *n.* ①分割;切斷。②〖動物〗環節構成。③〖生物〗細胞分裂。

se·go ['sigo; 'si:gou] *n.* 百合之一種。(亦作 **sego lily**)

seg·re·gate [*v.* 'sɛgrɪ,get; 'segrigeit *adj.*, *n.* 'sɛgrəgɪt; 'segrigit] *v.*, **-gat·ed, -gat·ing,** *adj.*, *n.* —*v.t.* ①隔離。②强制隔離(不同種族、宗教信仰等)。—*v.i.* ①分離。②實行種族等之强制隔離。—*adj.* 隔離的;分離的。—*n.* 隔離或分離物。—**seg·re·ga·ble,** *adj.*

seg·re·gat·ed ['sɛgrə,getɪd; 'segrigeitid] *adj.* ①種族隔離的。②只限於一種族的。③在設施上採取種族隔離的。④(因種族而)歧視的。—**ly,** *adv.* —**ness,** *n.*

seg·re·ga·tion [,sɛgrɪ'geʃən; ,segri'geiʃən] *n.* ①隔離;分離。②被隔離之部分。③種族隔離。④〖機械〗離析性。—**al,** *adj.*

seg·re·ga·tion·ist [,sɛgrɪ'geʃənɪst; ,segri'geiʃənist] *n.* 主張種族隔離者。—*adj.* 主張種族隔離(者)的。

seg·re·ga·tive ['sɛgrɪ,getɪv; 'segrigeitiv] *adj.* ①分離的;隔離的;有隔離傾向的。②不合羣的(人)。

seg·re·ga·tor ['sɛgrɪ,getɚ; 'segrigeitə] *n.* ①分離器。②主張隔離主義者。

sei·del ['saɪdl; 'saidəl] *n.* 有蓋的大型啤酒杯。

Seid·litz powder ['sɛdlɪts～; 'sedlits～] 塞德利茨散(緩瀉劑)。

seign·ior ['sinjɚ; 'si:njə] *n.* ①(封建之)君主;領主;諸侯。②君(尊稱,相當於Sir)。(亦作 **seigneur**)

seign·ior·age ['sinjərɪdʒ; 'si:njəridʒ] *n.* ①君主特權;統治權。②以國王特權所要求或拿取的東西。③鑄幣稅。(亦作**seignorage**)

seign·ior·y ['sinjərɪ; 'si:njəri] *n.*, *pl.* **-ior·ies.** ①君權;領主權。②領地。③(尤指中世紀義大利之)領主團體。(亦作 **signory**)

sei·gno·ri·al [sin'jorɪəl; si:n'jouriəl] *adj.* 君主的;領主的。(亦作 **seignioral, seigniorial, seignoral**)

Seine [sen; sein] *n.* 塞納河(在法國北部)。

seine [sen; sein] *n.*, *v.*, **seined, sein·ing.** —*n.* 大捕魚網;拖地大圍網;拉網。—*v.i.* & *v.t.* 以該種網捕魚。

seise [siz; si:z] *v.t.*, **seised, seis·ing.** 〖法律〗扣押;占有 (=seize).

seis·mal ['saɪzml; 'saizml] *adj.* =**seismic.**

seis·mic ['saɪzmɪk; 'saizmik] *adj.* 地震的;與地震有關的;由地震引起的;易生地震的。(亦作 **seismical**) —**al·ly,** *adv.*

seismic vertical 震央。

seismo- 〖字首〗表"地震"之義。

seis·mo·gram ['saɪzmə,græm; 'saizməgræm] *n.* 地震計記錄圖。

seis·mo·graph ['saɪzmə,græf; 'saizməgrɑ:f] *n.* 地震計。

seis·mog·ra·pher [saɪz'mɑgrəfɚ; saiz'mɔgrəfə] *n.* 地震檢測專家;地震學家。

seis·mo·graph·ic [,saɪzmə'græfɪk; ,saizmə'græfik] *adj.* 地震儀的。(亦作 **seismographical**)

seis·mog·ra·phy 〔saɪzˈmɑgrəfɪ; saizˈmɔgrəfi〕 *n.* ①地震檢測法; 地震記錄法。②地震學。
seis·mo·log·i·cal 〔ˌsaɪzməˈlɑdʒɪkl; ˌsaizməˈlɔdʒikəl〕 *adj.* 地震學的。**—ly,** *adv.*
seis·mol·o·gist 〔saɪzˈmɑlədʒɪst; saizˈmɔlədʒist〕 *n.* 地震學家;地震專家。
seis·mol·o·gy 〔saɪzˈmɑlədʒɪ; saizˈmɔlədʒi〕 *n.* 地震學。**—seis·mo·log·ic,** *adj.*
seis·mom·e·ter 〔saɪzˈmɑmətɚ; saizˈmɔmitə〕 *n.* 地震儀。
seis·mo·scope 〔ˈsaɪzməˌskop; ˈsaizməskoup〕 *n.* 簡易地震計。
seiz·a·ble 〔ˈsizəbl; ˈsi:zəbl〕 *adj.* ①可捕捉的。②可扣押的。③可奪取的。
‡**seize** 〔siz; si:z〕 *v.*, **seized, seiz·ing.** —*v.t.* ①捉;握取;把攫。to *seize* an opportunity. 把握機會。②了解。③侵襲。to be *seized* with an illness. 患病。④占有;扣押。⑤結;接。⑥〖法律〗=**seise.** —*v.i.* ①攫取;強取〖on, upon〗. ②(機器)因過熱而停止轉動。③訴諸〖常 on, upon〗.
seiz·er 〔ˈsizɚ; ˈsi:zə〕 *n.* ①捕捉者。②扣押者。③捕捉獵物之獵犬。
sei·zin 〔ˈsizɪn; ˈsi:zin〕 *n.* 〖法律〗土地之占有;占有地;占有物;財產。(亦作 **seisin**)
seiz·ing 〔ˈsizɪŋ; ˈsi:ziŋ〕 *n.* ①捕捉; 強奪;強占;扣押。②〖航海〗用細繩索綑紮; 綑紮用的細繩。(英亦作 **seising**)
sei·zor 〔ˈsizɚ, -zɔr; ˈsi:zə〕 *n.* 〖法律〗扣押者;占有者。
sei·zure 〔ˈsiʒɚ; ˈsi:ʒə〕 *n.* ①捕獲; 奪取。②押收;沒收。③侵襲;(疾病的)發作。④押收品; 捕獲物。(英亦作 **seisure**)
se·jant 〔ˈsidʒənt; ˈsi:dʒənt〕 *adj.* 〖紋章〗前足直立而坐的(獅等)。(亦作 **sejeant**)
se·lah 〔ˈsilə; ˈsi:lə〕 *n.* 〖聖經〗常出現於希伯來文"詩篇"中之字,意義不明。可能是禮拜儀式或音樂方面之一符號。
se·lam·lik 〔sɛˈlɑmlɪk; seˈlɑ:mlik〕 *n.* ①(回教國中)室內男子居住部分。②蘇丹朝拜回教寺院之儀式。
‡**sel·dom** 〔ˈsɛldəm; ˈseldəm〕 *adv.* 很少;不常;罕。He is *seldom* ill. 他很少生病。—*adj.* 稀少的;不常的。
‡**se·lect** 〔səˈlɛkt; siˈlekt〕 *v.t.* 選擇;挑選。—*adj.* ①精選的。②挑剔的;苛擇的。She is very *select* in the people she invites. 她對於所邀請的人選擇得很苛。—*n.* 被挑選之人或物。**—a·ble,** *adj.* **—ly,** *adv.* **—ness,** *n.*
select committee (立法機關等)特別委員會。(亦作 **special committee**)
se·lect·ed 〔sɪˈlɛktɪd; siˈlektid〕 *adj.* 經選擇的;挑選的;精選的。
se·lect·ee 〔səˌlɛkˈti; ˌselekˈti:〕 *n.* 應召兵;選募兵。
***se·lec·tion** 〔səˈlɛkʃən; siˈlekʃən〕 *n.* ①選擇;挑選; 淘汰。 *natural* selection. 自然淘汰。②選擇出之人或物;精選品。 *selections* from Shakespeare. 莎士比亞選集。
se·lec·tive 〔səˈlɛktɪv; siˈlektiv〕 *adj.* ①選擇的;淘汰的。②〖無線電〗有好選擇性的。**—ly,** *adv.*
selective buying =**boycott.**
selective service 義務兵役。
se·lec·tiv·i·ty 〔səˌlɛkˈtɪvətɪ; silekˈtiviti〕 *n.* 〖無線電〗選擇性。
se·lect·man 〔səˈlɛktmən; siˈlektmən〕 *n.*, *pl.* **-men.** (美國新英格蘭各州之)行政委員。
se·lec·tor 〔səˈlɛktɚ; siˈlektə〕 *n.* ①選擇者;選拔者;精選者。②選擇器; 選波器。③(澳洲之)小農。
selector switch ①電話交換機之自動接線機。②電視機之選臺旋鈕。
select society 上流社會。
Se·le·ne, Se·le·na 〔səˈlini, -nə; siˈli:nə〕 *n.* 〖希臘神話〗月之女神(相當於羅馬神話中之 Luna).
se·le·nic acid 〔sɪˈlinɪk～; siˈli:nik～〕 〖化〗硒酸。
sel·e·nite[1] 〔ˈsɛləˌnaɪt, sɪˈlinaɪt; siˈli:nait〕 *n.* 月球上之居民。
sel·e·nite[2] 〔ˈsɛləˌnaɪt; ˈselinait〕 *n.* ①〖化〗亞硒酸鹽。②〖礦〗透明石膏。
se·le·ni·um 〔səˈlinɪəm; siˈli:niəm〕 *n.* 〖化〗 硒(符號為 Se).
selenium cell 〖電〗硒質光電管。
se·le·no·graph 〔sɪˈlinəˌgræf; siˈli:nəgrɑ:f〕 *n.* 月面圖。
sel·e·nog·ra·phist 〔ˌsɛləˈnɑgrəfɪst; ˌseliˈnɔgrəfist〕 *n.* 月理學者。
sel·e·nog·ra·phy 〔ˌsɛləˈnɑgrəfɪ; ˌseliˈnɔgrəfi〕 *n.* 月理學。
sel·e·nol·o·gy 〔ˌsɛləˈnɑlədʒɪ; ˌseliˈnɔlədʒi〕 *n.* 〖天文〗月學;月理學。
‡**self** 〔sɛlf; self〕 *n.*, *pl.* **selves** 〔sɛlvz; selvz〕, *adj.*, *pron.*, *v.* —*n.* ①自身;自己;自我。my own *self*. 我自己。②品質;本質;性質。his better *self*. 他的較高尚的品質。③自私心;私欲。④〖俗〗我;我自己(=me; myself). ⑤顏色一致的花。—*adj.* (品質、顏色等)相同的;一致的。—*pron.* 我自己、他自己等。—*v.t.* & *v.i.* 自花授粉。
self- 〖字首〗表"及於自己的;由自己發出的"之義。
self-a·ban·doned 〔ˌsɛlfəˈbændənd; ˈselfəˈbændənd〕 *adj.* 自暴自棄的; 放肆的。
self-a·ban·don·ment 〔ˌsɛlfəˈbændənmənt; ˈselfəˈbændənmənt〕 *n.* 自暴自棄;放肆。
self-a·base·ment 〔ˌsɛlfəˈbesmənt; ˈselfəˈbeismənt〕 *n.* 自卑;自謙;自貶。
self-ab·hor·rence 〔ˌsɛlfəbˈhɔrəns; ˈselfəbˈhɔ:rəns〕 *n.* 自嫌。
self-ab·ne·ga·tion 〔ˈsɛlfˌæbnəˈgeʃən; ˈselfˌæbniˈgeiʃən〕 *n.* 自我犧牲;克己。
self-ab·sorbed 〔ˌsɛlfəbˈsɔrbd; ˈselfəbˈsɔ:bd〕 *adj.* 專心於自身利益或事務的;不管別人的;自私的。
self-ab·sorp·tion 〔ˌsɛlfəbˈsɔrpʃən; ˈselfəbˈsɔ:pʃən〕 *n.* 專心於一己之利益或事務。
self-a·buse 〔ˌsɛlfəˈbjus; ˈselfəˈbju:s〕 *n.* ①自暴自棄。②手淫。
self-ac·cu·sa·tion 〔ˈsɛlfˌækjəˈzeʃən; ˈselfˌækjuˈzeiʃən〕 *n.* 自責。
self-ac·cus·ing 〔ˌsɛlfəˈkjuzɪŋ; ˈselfəˈkju:ziŋ〕 *adj.* 自責的。
self-act·ing 〔ˈsɛlfˈæktɪŋ; ˈselfˈæktiŋ〕 *adj.* 自動的。
self-ad·dressed 〔ˈsɛlfəˈdrɛst; ˈselfəˈdrest〕 *adj.* 有發信人姓名住址的; 寄給自己的。
self-ad·just·ing 〔ˈsɛlfəˈdʒʌstɪŋ; ˈselfəˈdʒʌstiŋ〕 *adj.* 自動調節的。
self-ad·min·is·tered 〔ˌsɛlfədˈmɪnɪstɚd; ˈselfədˈministəd〕 *adj.* 自治的;自己管理的。
self-ag·gran·dize·ment 〔ˌsɛlfəˈgrændɪzmənt; ˈselfəˈgrændizmənt〕 *n.* ①自己發展(權力、財富等)。②自大;自誇。
self-a·nal·y·sis 〔ˌsɛlfəˈnæləsɪs; ˈselfəˈnælisis〕 *n.* 自我精神分析。
self-ap·point·ed 〔ˈsɛlfəˈpɔɪntɪd; ˈselfəˈpɔintid〕 *adj.* 自己指定的。
self-as·ser·tion 〔ˌsɛlfəˈsɝʃən; ˈself-

əˈsəːʃən] *n.* ①堅持己見。②逞強;逞能。
self-as·ser·tive [ˌsɛlfəˈsɝtɪv; ˈselfəˈsəːtiv] *adj.* ①堅持己見的; 自作主張的。②冒昧的;任性的;逞強的;好出風頭的。
self-as·sumed [ˌsɛlfəˈsumd; ˈselfəˈsjuːmd] *adj.* 武斷的;專斷的;僭越的。
self-as·sur·ance [ˌsɛlfəˈʃurəns; ˈselfəˈʃuərəns] *n.* ①自信。②自足;自滿。
self-as·sured [ˌsɛlfəˈʃurd; ˈselfəˈʃuəd] *adj.* ①自信心强的。②自滿自足的。
self-a·ware·ness [ˈsɛlfəˈwɛrnɪs; ˈselfəˈwɛənis] *n.* 自覺;覺悟。
self-be·tray·al [ˌsɛlfbɪˈtreəl; ˈselfbiˈtreiəl] *n.* 自欺。
self-bind·er [ˈsɛlfˈbaɪndɚ; ˈselfˈbaində] *n.* ①自動裝釘機。②自動束禾(草)機。
self-care [ˈsɛlfˈkɛr; ˈselfˈkɛə] *n.* 自顧。
self-cen·tered [ˈsɛlfˈsɛntɚd; ˈselfˈsentəd] *adj.* ①自我中心的。②自私自利的。
self-charg·ing [ˈsɛlfˈtʃɑrdʒɪŋ; ˈselfˈtʃɑːdʒiŋ] *adj.* 自動充電的。
self-clos·ing [ˈsɛlfˈklozɪŋ; ˈselfˈklouziŋ] *adj.* 自動關閉的。
self-col·lect·ed [ˌsɛlfkəˈlɛktɪd; ˈselfkəˈlektid] *adj.* 沉着的;泰然自若的。
self-col·or [ˈsɛlfˈkʌlɚ; ˈselfˈkʌlə] *n.* ①單色。②天然色(非染之色)。
self-col·o(u)red [ˈsɛlfˈkʌlɚd; ˈselfˈkʌləd] *adj.* ①單色的。②天然色的;本色的。
self-com·mand [ˌsɛlfkəˈmænd; ˈselfkəˈmɑːnd] *n.* 自制;克己。
self-com·mun·ion [ˌsɛlfkəˈmjunjən; ˈselfkəˈmjuːnjən] *n.* 自省;內省。
self-com·pla·cence [ˌsɛlfkəmˈplesṇs; ˈselfkəmˈpleisṇs] *n.* 自我陶醉;自滿。(亦作 **self-complacency**) —**self-com·pla·cent,** *adj.*
self-com·posed [ˌsɛlfkəmˈpozd; ˈselfkəmˈpouzd] *adj.* 自若的;鎮靜的。
self-con·ceit [ˌsɛlfkənˈsit; ˈselfkənˈsiːt] *n.* 自大;自滿;自負。
self-con·demned [ˌsɛlfkənˈdɛmd; ˈselfkənˈdemd] *adj.* 自責的。
self-con·fi·dence [ˈsɛlfˈkɑnfədəns; ˈselfˈkɔnfidəns] *n.* 自信。
self-con·fi·dent [ˈsɛlfˈkɑnfədənt; ˈselfˈkɔnfidənt] *adj.* 自信的;自恃的。
self-con·scious [ˈsɛlfˈkɑnʃəs; ˈselfˈkɔnʃəs] *adj.* 自覺的;自覺意識濃厚的;神經過敏的;不自然的。—**ly,** *adv.* —**ness,** *n.*
self-con·se·quence [ˈsɛlfˈkɑnsəˌkwɛns; ˈselfˈkɔnsikwəns] *n.* 自尊。—**self-con·se·quent,** *adj.*
self-con·sist·ent [ˌsɛlfkənˈsɪstənt; ˈselfkənˈsistənt] *adj.* 前後一致的; 不矛盾的。—**self-con·sist·en·cy,** *n.* —**ly,** *adv.*
self-con·sti·tut·ed [ˌsɛlfˈkɑnstəˌtjutɪd; ˈselfˈkɔnstitjuːtid] *adj.* 自我構成的;自我任命的;自行設立的。
self-con·tained [ˌsɛlfkənˈtend; ˈselfkənˈteind] *adj.* ①能克制自己言行的;寡言的;不衝動的。②包括所有必需物的;完備的。③自足的; 獨立的。④所有各部分在一個盒子或覆蓋之下的。
self-con·tempt [ˌsɛlfkənˈtɛmpt; ˈselfkənˈtempt] *n.* 自卑;自輕。
self-con·tent [ˌsɛlfkənˈtɛnt; ˈselfkənˈtent] *n.* 自滿自足。—**ed,** *adj.*
self-con·tra·dic·tion [ˈsɛlfˌkɑntrəˈdɪkʃən; ˈselfˌkɔntrəˈdikʃən] *n.* ①自相矛盾;前後矛盾。②前後矛盾之聲明。
self-con·tra·dic·to·ry [ˈsɛlfˌkɑntrəˈdɪktərɪ; ˈselfˌkɔntrəˈdiktəri] *adj.* 自相矛盾的;前後矛盾的。
self-con·trol [ˌsɛlfkənˈtrol; ˈselfkənˈtroul] *n.* 克己;自制。
self-crit·i·cal [ˈsɛlfˈkrɪtɪkl; ˈselfˈkritikəl] *adj.* 自我批判的。—**self-crit·ic·ism,** *n.*
self-de·ceived [ˌsɛlfdɪˈsivd; ˈselfdiˈsiːvd] *adj.* ①自負的;自命不凡的。②自欺的。
self-de·cep·tion [ˌsɛlfdɪˈsɛpʃən; ˈselfdiˈsepʃən] *n.* 自欺。(亦作 **self-deceit**) —**self-de·cep·tive,** *adj.*
self-de·feat·ing [ˌsɛlfdɪˈfitɪŋ; ˈselfdiˈfiːtiŋ] *adj.* 不利於自己之企圖的; 弄巧成拙的。
self-de·fense [ˌsɛlfdɪˈfɛns; ˈselfdiˈfens] *n.* 自衛;正當防衞。(亦作 **self-defence**)
self-de·ni·al [ˌsɛlfdɪˈnaɪəl; ˈselfdiˈnaiəl] *n.* 自我犧牲;無私。
self-de·ny·ing [ˌsɛlfdɪˈnaɪɪŋ; ˌselfdiˈnaiiŋ] *adj.* 自我犧牲的;無私的。
self-de·pend·ent [ˌsɛlfdɪˈpɛndənt; ˈselfdiˈpendənt] *adj.* 依靠自己的;獨立的。—**ly,** *adv.* —**self-de·pend·ence,** *n.*
self-dep·re·cat·ing [ˈsɛlfˈdɛprəˌketɪŋ; ˈselfˈdeprikeitiŋ] *adj.* 抑貶自己的;謙虛的。—**ly,** *adv.* —**self-dep·re·ca·tion,** *n.*
self-de·struct [ˈsɛlfdɪsˈtrʌkt; ˈselfdisˈtrʌkt] *v.i.* 自我毀滅;自動毀壞。
self-de·struc·tion [ˌsɛlfdɪˈstrʌkʃən; ˈselfdisˈtrʌkʃən] *n.* 自殺;自毀。
self-de·struc·tive [ˌsɛlfdɪˈstrʌktɪv; ˈselfdisˈtrʌktiv] *adj.* ①自毀的。②有自殺傾向的。
self-de·ter·mi·na·tion [ˈsɛlfdɪˌtɝməˈneʃən; ˈselfdiˌtəːmiˈneiʃən] *n.* ①自決。②民族自決。—**self-de·ter·mined,** *adj.*
self-de·ter·min·ing [ˈsɛlfdɪˈtɝmɪnɪŋ; ˈselfdiˈtəːminiŋ] *n., adj.* ①自決(的)。②有自決能力(的)。
self-de·vo·tion [ˌsɛlfdɪˈvoʃən; ˈselfdiˈvouʃən] *n.* 自我犧牲;獻身。
self-dis·ci·pline [ˈsɛlfˈdɪsəplɪn; ˈselfˈdisiplin] *n.* 自我訓練;自己修養;自律;自制。—**self-dis·ci·plined,** *adj.*
self-dis·trust [ˌsɛlfdɪsˈtrʌst; ˈselfdisˈtrʌst] *n.* 缺乏自信。—**ful,** *adj.*
self-doubt [ˈsɛlfˈdaut; ˈselfˈdaut] *n.* 缺乏對自己之信心。
self-drive car [ˈsɛlfˈdraɪv～; ˈselfˈdraiv～] 〖英〗出租汽車。
self-ed·u·cat·ed [ˈsɛlfˈɛdʒəˌketɪd; ˈselfˈedjuːkeitid] *adj.* 自修的;自習的。
self-ef·face·ment [ˌsɛlfɛˈfesmənt; ˈselfeˈfeismənt] *n.* 謙讓;避免出風頭。
self-em·ployed [ˌsɛlfɛmˈplɔɪd; ˈselfemˈplɔid] *adj.* 自雇的。
self-es·teem [ˌsɛlfəˈstim; ˈselfisˈtiːm] *n.* 自尊;自負;自大;自滿。
self-e·val·u·a·tion [ˌsɛlfɪˌvæljuˈeʃən; ˈselfiˌvæljuˈeiʃən] *n.* 自己的評價。
self-ev·i·dent [ˈsɛlfˈɛvədənt; ˈselfˈevidənt] *adj.* 不證自明的。
self-ex·am·i·na·tion [ˈsɛlfɪgˌzæməˈneʃən; ˈselfigˌzæmiˈneiʃən] *n.* 反省; 自我批判。
self-ex·ist·ent [ˌsɛlfɪgˈzɪstənt; ˈselfigˈzistənt] *adj.* 自存的;自然而然的。
self-ex·plain·ing [ˌsɛlfɪkˈsplenɪŋ;

ˈselfiksˈpleiniŋ] *adj.* 意義自明的。

self-ex·plan·a·to·ry [ˌsɛlfɪkˈsplænəˌtorɪ; ˈselfiksˈplænətəri] *adj.* 意義明顯的；不解自明的。

self-ex·pres·sion [ˌsɛlfɪkˈsprɛʃən; ˈselfiksˈpreʃən] *n.* 自我表現。

self-feed [ˈsɛlfˈfid; ˈselfˈfiːd] *v.t.*, **-fed, -feed·ing.** 〖農〗充分供飼料(給家畜)。

self-feed·er [ˈsɛlfˈfidɚ; ˈselfˈfiːdə] *n.* 自給器。

self-feed·ing [ˈsɛlfˈfidɪŋ; ˈselfˈfiːdiŋ] *adj.* 自給式的。

self-fer·tile [ˌsɛlfˈfɝtl̩; ˌselfˈfəːtail] *adj.* 〖植物〗自花受精的。

self-fer·ti·li·za·tion [ˈsɛlfˌfɝtl̩əˈzeʃən; ˈselfˌfəːtilaiˈzeiʃən] *n.* 〖植物〗自花受精。

self-fill·er [ˈsɛlfˈfɪlɚ; ˈselfˈfilə] *n.* 自動吸墨水之筆。

self-for·get·ful [ˌsɛlffɚˈgɛtfəl; ˈselffəˈgetful] *adj.* 自我犧牲的；不顧自己利害的；無私慾的。(亦作 **self-forgetting**)

self-gen·er·a·tion [ˌsɛlfˌdʒɛnəˈreʃən; ˈselfˌdʒenəˈreiʃən] *n.* 自家產生。

self-glo·ri·fi·ca·tion [ˌsɛlfˌglorɪfəˈkeʃən; ˈselfˌglɔːrifiˈkeiʃən] *n.* 自讚。

self-gov·erned [ˈsɛlfˈgʌvɚnd; ˈselfˈgʌvənd] *adj.* ①自治的；獨立的。②自律的。

self-gov·ern·ing [ˈsɛlfˈgʌvɚnɪŋ; ˈselfˈgʌvəniŋ] *adj.* ①自治的。②克己的。

self-gov·ern·ment [ˈsɛlfˈgʌvɚnmənt; ˈselfˈgʌvənmənt] *n.* ①自制；克己。②自治；自治制。

self-heal [ˈsɛlfˈhil; ˈselfˈhiːl] *n.* 〖植物〗滁州夏枯草。

self-help [ˈsɛlfˈhɛlp; ˈselfˈhelp] *n.* 自助；自立。

self·hood [ˈsɛlfhud; ˈselfhud] *n.* ①自我；個性。②人格。③自私自利心。

self-hyp·no·sis [ˌsɛlfhɪpˈnosɪs; ˈselfhipˈnousis] *n.* 自我催眠；自己催眠。

self-ig·nite [ˌsɛlfɪgˈnaɪt; ˈselfigˈnait] *v.i.*, **-nit·ed, -nit·ing.** 自燃。

self-im·por·tant [ˌsɛlfɪmˈpɔrtn̩t; ˈselfimˈpɔːtənt] *adj.* 自誇的；自大的；自視過高的。—**self-im·por·tance,** *n.* —**ly,** *adv.*

self-im·posed [ˌsɛlfɪmˈpozd; ˈselfimˈpouzd] *adj.* 自己加給自己的。

self-im·prove·ment [ˌsɛlfɪmˈpruvmənt; ˈselfimˈpruːvmənt] *n.* 自我改進；自修。

self incrimination 〖法律〗自認犯罪。

self-in·duced [ˌsɛlfɪnˈdjust; ˈselfinˈdjuːst] *adj.* 〖電〗自誘導的；自感應的。

self-in·duc·tion [ˌsɛlfɪnˈdʌkʃən; ˈselfinˈdʌkʃən] *n.* 〖電〗自感應。

self-in·dul·gence [ˌsɛlfɪnˈdʌldʒəns; ˈselfinˈdʌldʒəns] *n.* 放縱自己。—**self-in·dul·gent,** *adj.*

self-in·flict·ed [ˌsɛlfɪnˈflɪktɪd; ˈselfinˈfliktid] *adj.* 自使蒙受的。

self-in·sur·er [ˌsɛlfɪnˈʃurɚ; ˈselfinˈʃuərə] *n.* 自己保險者。—**self-in·sured,** *adj.*

self-in·ter·est [ˈsɛlfˈɪntərɪst; ˈselfˈintrist] *n.* 私利；利己。—**ed,** *adj.*

self-in·vit·ed [ˌsɛlfɪnˈvaɪtɪd; ˈselfinˈvaitid] *adj.* ①不請自來的；不速之客的。②自己引起的。

***self·ish** [ˈsɛlfɪʃ; ˈselfiʃ] *adj.* 自私的；自利的。 *selfish* behavior. 自私的行爲。—**ly,** *adv.* —**ness,** *n.*

self-jus·ti·fi·ca·tion [ˌsɛlfˌdʒʌstəfəˈkeʃən; ˈselfˌdʒʌstifiˈkeiʃən] *n.* 自己辯白。

self-jus·ti·fy·ing [ˈsɛlfˈdʒʌstəfaɪɪŋ; ˈselfˈdʒʌstifaiiŋ] *adj.* 自己辯白的。

self-knowl·edge [ˈsɛlfˈnɑlɪdʒ; ˈselfˈnɔlidʒ] *n.* 自知；自覺。

self·less [ˈsɛlflɪs; ˈselflis] *adj.* 忘我的；無私的。—**ly,** *adv.* —**ness,** *n.*

self-liq·ui·dat·ing [ˈsɛlfˈlɪkwəˌdetɪŋ; ˈselfˈlikwədeitiŋ] *adj.* 可使貨物迅速變現款的。

self-load·ing [ˈsɛlfˈlodɪŋ; ˈselfˈloudiŋ] *adj.* (火器之)自動上彈藥的；自動的。

self-lock·ing [ˈsɛlfˈlɑkɪŋ; ˈselfˈlɔkiŋ] *adj.* 自動上鎖的。

self-love [ˈsɛlfˈlʌv; ˈselfˈlʌv] *n.* ①利己。②自大；自負。③自愛。④自我陶醉。—**self-lov·ing,** *adj.*

self-made [ˈsɛlfˈmed; ˈselfˈmeid] *adj.* ①自製的；自做的。②白手起家的；自力成功的。

self-mail·er [ˈsɛlfˈmelɚ; ˈselfˈmeilə] *n.* 廣告或小册子等可塡寫姓名,地址,即可寄,而不需另加信封者。

self-mas·ter·y [ˈsɛlfˈmæstərɪ; ˈselfˈmɑːstəri] *n.* 自制 (=self-control).

self-med·i·ca·tion [ˌsɛlfˌmɛdɪˈkeʃən; ˈselfˌmediˈkeiʃən] *n.* ①不經醫師指示而自己醫治或吃藥。②沒有醫師時自己醫療。

self-mo·tion [ˈsɛlfˈmoʃən; ˈselfˈmouʃən] *n.* 自動。

self-mov·ing [ˈsɛlfˈmuvɪŋ; ˈselfˈmuːviŋ] *adj.* 自動的。

self-mur·der [ˈsɛlfˈmɝdɚ; ˈselfˈməːdə] *n.* 自殺。

self·ness [ˈsɛlfnɪs; ˈselfnis] *n.* 自我中心；自私自利；利己主義。

self-op·er·at·ing [ˈsɛlfˈɑpəˌretɪŋ; ˈselfˈɔpəreitiŋ] *adj.* 自動的。(亦作 **self-operative**)

self-o·pin·ion [ˌsɛlfəˈpɪnjən; ˈselfəˈpinjən] *n.* ①自負。②固執己見。③對自身之意見。

self-o·pin·ion·at·ed [ˌsɛlfəˈpɪnjənˌetɪd; ˈselfəˈpinjəneitid] *adj.* 固執己見的；執迷不悟的；頑固的；執拗的。

self-o·pin·ioned [ˌsɛlfəˈpɪnjənd; ˈselfəˈpinjənd] *adj.* 固執己見的；執迷不悟的。

self-or·dained [ˌsɛlfɔrˈdend; ˈselfɔːˈdeind] *adj.* 自己制定的。

self-pit·y [ˈsɛlfˈpɪtɪ; ˈselfˈpiti] *n.* 自憐。

self-poised [ˈsɛlfˈpɔɪzd; ˈselfˈpɔizd] *adj.* ①自己平衡的。②泰然自若的。

self-pol·li·nat·ed [ˈsɛlfˈpɑləˌnetɪd; ˈselfˈpɔlineitid] *adj.* 〖植物〗自花受粉的。—**self-pol·li·na·tion,** *n.*

self-pol·lu·tion [ˌsɛlfpəˈluʃən; ˈselfpəˈluːʃən] *n.* 手淫。

self-por·trait [ˈsɛlfˈportret; ˈselfˈpɔːtrit] *n.* 自畫像。

self-pos·ses·sion [ˌsɛlfpəˈzɛʃən; ˈselfpəˈzeʃən] *n.* 沉着；鎭靜；泰然自若。—**self-pos·sessed,** *adj.* —**self-pos·sess·ed·ly,** *adv.*

self-praise [ˈsɛlfˈprez; ˈselfˈpreiz] *n.* 自讚；自誇。

self-pres·er·va·tion [ˈsɛlfprɛzəˈveʃən; ˈselfˌprezəˈveiʃən] *n.* 自保；自衞。

self-pride [ˈsɛlfˈpraɪd; ˈselfˈpraid] *n.* 自尊；自負。

self-pro·pelled [ˌsɛlfprəˈpɛld; ˈselfprəˈpeld] *adj.* ①自己推動的。②(車輛等)自動的。③(火箭或火砲)自帶推動器的。(亦作 **self-propelling**)

self-pro·tec·tion [ˌsɛlfprəˈtɛkʃən; ˈselfprəˈtekʃən] *n.* 自衞；自保。

self-rais·ing ['sɛlf'rezɪŋ; 'self'reiziŋ] *adj.* 製造時卽攙有發酵物質的。(亦作 **self-rising**)
self-re·al·i·za·tion ['sɛlf,riələ'zeʃən; 'self,riəlai'zeiʃən] *n.* 自我實現;自己能力之發揮。
self-re·cord·ing [,sɛlfrɪ'kɔrdɪŋ; 'selfri'kɔ:diŋ] *adj.* 自動記錄的。
self-re·gard [,sɛlfrɪ'gard; 'selfri'gɑ:d] *n.* ①自利;祇顧自己之利益。②自尊;自重。—**ing**, *adj.*
self-reg·is·ter·ing ['sɛlf'rɛdʒɪstərɪŋ; 'self'redʒistəriŋ] *adj.* 自動記錄的。
self-reg·u·lat·ed ['sɛlf'rɛgjə,letɪd; 'self'regjuleitid] *adj.* 自動調節或調整的。
self-reg·u·lat·ing ['sɛlf'rɛgjə,letɪŋ; 'self'regju,leitiŋ] *adj.* 自動調節的。
self-reg·u·la·tion ['sɛlf,rɛgju'leʃən; 'self,regju'leiʃən] *n.* 自動調節。
self-re·li·ance [,sɛlfrɪ'laɪəns; 'self-ri'laiəns] *n.* 自恃。—**self-re·li·ant**, *adj.*
self-re·nun·ci·a·tion ['sɛlfrɪ,nʌnsɪ'eʃən; 'self-ri,nʌnsi'eiʃən] *n.* 自己放棄權利;自我犧牲;大公無私。
self-re·pres·sion [,sɛlfrɪ'prɛʃən; 'self-ri'preʃən] *n.* 自我抑制。
self-re·proach [,sɛlfrɪ'protʃ; 'self-ri'proutʃ] *n.* 自責;自譴。
self-re·spect [,sɛlfrɪ'spɛkt; 'self-ris'pekt] *n.* 自尊;自重。—**ful**, *adj.*
self-re·spect·ing [,sɛlfrɪ'spɛktɪŋ; 'self-ri'spektiŋ] *adj.* 自重的;有自尊心的。
self-re·straint [,sɛlfrɪ'strent; 'self-ri'streint] *n.* 自制;克己。
self-rev·e·la·tion ['sɛlf,rɛvə'leʃən; 'self,revi'leiʃən] *n.* 無意的表露自己之情感;表露自己之本性。
self-right·eous ['sɛlf'raɪtʃəs; 'self-'raitʃəs] *adj.* 僞善的;自以爲是的。
self-right·ing ['sɛlf'raɪtɪŋ; 'self'raitiŋ] *adj.* 打翻後能自動立起來的;能自動扶正的。a *self-righting* doll. 不倒翁。
self-rule [,sɛlf'rul; 'self'ru:l] *n.* 自治。
self-sac·ri·fice ['sɛlf'sækrə,faɪs; 'self'sækrifais] *n.* 自我犧牲。
***self·same** [,sɛlf'sem; 'selfseim] *adj.* 同一的;同樣的。—**ness**, *n.*
self-sat·is·fac·tion ['sɛlfsætɪs'fækʃən; 'self,sætis'fækʃən] *n.* 自滿;自足。
self-sat·is·fied ['sɛlf'sætɪs,faɪd; 'self-'sætisfaid] *adj.* 自滿的;自足的;自負的。
self-sat·is·fy·ing [,sɛlf'sætɪs,faɪɪŋ; 'self'sætis,faiiŋ] *adj.* 能引起自滿的。
self-seal·ing [,sɛlf'silɪŋ; 'self'si:liŋ] *adj.* 自行封口的;自固的。
self-seek·er ['sɛlf'sikɚ; 'self'si:kə] *n.* 自私自利的人;唯圖自利的人。
self-seek·ing ['sɛlf'sikɪŋ; 'self'si:kiŋ] *adj.* 自私的;祇圖私利的。—*n.* 自利;自私。
self-se·lec·tion [,sɛlfsɪ'lɛkʃən; 'selfsi'lekʃən] *n.* ①自己選擇。②不需商店店員之協助而自己挑選商品。
self-serv·ice ['sɛlf'sɝvɪs; 'self'sə:vis] *n.* 自助;自取食物;自取商品。—*adj.* 自助餐廳的;自助商店的。
self-slaugh·ter [,sɛlf'slɔtɚ; 'self-'slɔ:tə] *n.* 自殺。
self-sown ['sɛlf'son; 'self'soun] *adj.* ①自然播種的。②自行播種的。
self-start·er ['sɛlf'startɚ; 'self'stɑ:tə] *n.* ①自行發動器。②有自發裝置的汽車引擎。③〖俗〗自行發起某項工作或計畫者。
self-styled ['sɛlf'staɪld; 'self'staild] *adj.* 自稱的。
self-suf·fi·cient [,sɛlfsə'fɪʃənt; 'selfsə'fiʃənt] *adj.* ①自給自足的。②傲慢的;自負的。—**ly**, *adv.* —**self-suf·fi·cien·cy**, *n.*
self-suf·fic·ing [,sɛlfsə'faɪsɪŋ; 'self-sə'faisiŋ] *adj.* ①自立的;自足的。②自信的;傲慢的。
self-sug·ges·tion [,sɛlfsəg'dʒɛstʃən, -sə'dʒɛs-; 'selfsə'dʒestʃən] *n.* 自我暗示。
self-sup·port [,sɛlfsə'port; 'selfsə-'pɔ:t] *n.* 自立;自給;自營生計。
self-sup·port·ing [,sɛlfsə'portɪŋ; 'selfsə'pɔ:tiŋ] *adj.* 自給自足的;不依賴他人的。—**ly**, *adv.*
self-sur·ren·der [,sɛlfsə'rɛndɚ; 'selfsə'rendə] *n.* 自讓;自屈;忍從;捨己從人。
self-sus·tain·ing [,sɛlfsə'stenɪŋ; 'selfsə'steiniŋ] *adj.* 自立的;自給的。
self-taught ['sɛlf'tɔt; 'self'tɔ:t] *adj.* 自修的;自學的。
self-tim·er ['sɛlf'taɪmɚ; 'self'taimə] *n.* (照相機上之)快門定時自動關閉裝置。
self-tor·ture ['sɛlf'tɔrtʃɚ; 'self'tɔ:tʃə] *n.* 自我折磨。
self-will ['sɛlf'wɪl; 'self'wil] *n.* 固執己見;執拗。—**self-willed**, *adj.*
self-wind·ing ['sɛlf'waɪndɪŋ; 'self-'waindiŋ] *adj.* 自動上發條的(錶等)。
:**sell** [sɛl; sel] *v.*, **sold** [sold; sould], **sell·ing**, *n.* —*v.t.* ①售賣;販賣;出賣。Do you *sell* wine? 你賣酒嗎? ②背叛;放棄;出賣。③使接受;使贊成。to *sell* an idea to the public. 使民衆接受一種觀念。④使能售出。Advertisements *sold* many new cars. 廣告使許多新車得以售出。⑤使購買。⑥〖俚〗欺騙。⑦迫使付出一代價。—*v.i.* ①售賣。to *sell* at a bargain. 廉價出售。②(商品)銷售(= be sold). On a rainy day, umbrellas really *sell*. 下雨天傘的銷路好。③能被接受。an idea that will *sell*. 一個能被接受的觀念。④當店員;當推銷員。⑤售價爲〖常 at, for〗. Eggs *sell* at 60 cents a dozen. 鷄蛋售價爲每打六毛。***sell off*** 清除存貨的廉價出售。***sell on*** a. 使人有購買或擁有…之欲望。b. 使人相信…之價值、優點等。***sell one's life dear(ly)*** 使敵蒙受重大損失而後死。***sell one up*** 變賣債務人之財產以償還債權人。***sell out*** a. 完全脫售。b. 〖俚〗背棄。***sell up*** 將(某債務人之貨物)拍賣以抵債。—*n.* 〖俚〗①欺騙;欺詐。②〖英俚〗失望。③〖俗〗貨品之能銷售的條件。
sell·a·ble ['sɛləbl; 'seləbl] *adj.* 可以出售的;可以使人接受的。
***sell·er** ['sɛlɚ; 'selə] *n.* ①售賣人。②售賣之物。This book is a best *seller*. 這書是一種暢銷書。
seller's market 貨物稀少價錢較高的市場。
sell·ing ['sɛlɪŋ; 'seliŋ] *n.* 售賣;販賣;出售。—*adj.* ①可售賣的;可出售的。a low *selling* price. 可使貨物易於出售的低價。②售賣的;出售的;關於出售的。a *selling* agent. 代銷店。
sell-off ['sɛl,ɔf; 'selɔ:f] *n.* (股票等之)大量出售。
sell·out ['sɛl,aut; 'selaut] *n.* 〖俚〗①售罄。②賣滿座的演出。③〖美〗密告;出賣。
Selt·zer ['sɛltsɚ; 'seltsə] *n.* 德國 Wiesbaden 地方之礦水。(亦作 **Seltzer water**)
selt·zo·gene ['sɛltsə,dʒin; 'seltsə-dʒi:n] *n.* 製造蘇打水的輕便用具。

sel·vage ['sɛlvɪdʒ; 'selvidʒ] *n.* 布的織邊。(亦作 **selvedge**)
sel·vaged ['sɛlvɪdʒd; 'selvidʒd] *adj.* 有織邊的(織物)。(亦作 **selvedged**)
sel·va·gee [,sɛlvə'dʒi; ,selvə'dʒi:] *n.* 〖航海〗束環索。
selves [sɛlvz; selvz] *n.* pl. of **self.**
Sem, Sem. ①Seminary. ②Semitic.
sem. semicolon.
se·man·tic [sə'mæntɪk; si'mæntik] *adj.* ①與意義有關的。②語意學的。**—al·ly,** *adv.*
se·man·ti·cist [sə'mæntəsɪst; si'mæntisist] *n.* 語意學學者;精通語意學的人。(亦作 **semantician**)
se·man·tics [sə'mæntɪks; si'mæntiks] *n.* (作 *sing.* 解)語意學。(亦作 **semantology**)
sem·a·phore ['sɛmə,for; 'seməfɔ:] *n., v.,* **-phored, -phor·ing.** —*n.* 信號機;信號燈;信號旗;旗語。—*v.t.* 以信號通知。—*v.i.* 以信號通訊。
se·ma·si·ol·o·gy [sɪ,mesɪ'ɑlədʒɪ; si,meisi'ɔlədʒi] *n.* =**semantics.**
se·mat·ic [sɪ'mætɪk; si'mætik] *adj.* 〖生物〗作爲危險警告之表示的。
sem·blance ['sɛmbləns; 'sembləns] *n.* ①肖像。②相似;類似。There is some *semblance* between the two stories. 這兩個故事有些相似之處。③外觀;外貌。
se·mei·ol·o·gy [,simaɪ'ɑlədʒɪ; ,si:mai'ɔlədʒi] *n.* ①〖醫〗徵候學。②記號學。③手語。(亦作 **semiology**)
se·men ['simən; 'si:men] *n., pl.* **sem·i·na** ['sɛmɪnə; 'seminə]. ①〖生理〗精液。②〖植物〗胚種。
se·mes·ter [sə'mɛstɚ; si'mestə] *n.* 半學年;一學期。
semi- 〖字首〗表:①"半"之義(如: semiannual. 半年一次的)。②"不完全地"或"部分地"之義 (如: semicivilized. 部分文明化的)。③"次於"之義(如: semifinal. 準決賽)。
sem·i·an·nu·al [,sɛmɪ'ænjuəl; ,semi'ænjuəl] *adj.* 半年的;每半年的。**—ly,** *adv.*
sem·i·ar·id [,sɛmə'ærɪd; ,semi'ærid] *adj.* 半乾燥的。
sem·i·au·to·mat·ic [,sɛmə,ɔtə'mætɪk; 'semi,ɔ:tə'mætik] *adj.* 半自動的(機器、火器等)。
sem·i·au·ton·o·mous [,sɛmɪɔ'tɑnəməs; 'semiɔ:'tɔnəməs] *adj.* (內政等)半自治的。
sem·i·breve ['sɛmə,briv; 'semibri:v] *n.* 〖音樂〗全音符。
sem·i·cen·ten·ni·al [,sɛməsɛn'tɛnɪəl; 'semisen'teniəl] *adj.* 五十周年的。—*n.* ①五十周年。②五十周年慶典。(亦作 **semicentenary**)
sem·i·cen·tu·ry [,sɛmə'sɛntʃurɪ; 'semi'sentʃuri] *n., pl.* **-ries.** 半世紀;五十年。
sem·i·cho·rus ['sɛmə,korəs; 'semi,kɔ:rəs] *n.* 〖音樂〗①半合唱。②半合唱曲。**—sem·i·cho·ric,** *adj.*
sem·i·cir·cle ['sɛmə,sɝkl̩; 'semi,sə:kl] *n.* 半圓形。(亦作 **semicircumference**)
sem·i·cir·cu·lar [,sɛmɪ'sɝkjələ; ,semi'sə:kjulə] *adj.* 半圓形的。
semicircular canal 〖解剖〗(耳之)半規管。
sem·i·civ·i·lized [,sɛmə'sɪvl̩,aɪzd; 'semi'sivilaizd] *adj.* 半文明的。
sem·i·clas·sic [,sɛmə'klæsɪk; 'semi'klæsik] *adj.* (亦作 **semiclassical**) 半古典的。—*n.* 半古典的作品(音樂、書等)。
***sem·i·co·lon** ['sɛmə,kolən; 'semi'koulən] *n.* 半支點;分號(;)。
sem·i·co·lo·ni·al [,sɛməkə'lonɪəl; 'semikə'louniəl] *adj.* 半殖民的。
sem·i·com·mer·cial [,sɛməkə'mɝʃəl; 'semikə'mə:ʃəl] *adj.* 半商業性的。
sem·i·con·duc·tor [,sɛməkən'dʌktɚ; 'semikən'dʌktə] *n.* 半導體。
sem·i·con·scious [,sɛmə'kɑnʃəs; 'semi'kɔnʃəs] *adj.* 半意識的; 半自覺的。**—ness,** *n.* **—ly,** *adv.*
sem·i·con·so·nant [,sɛmə'kɑnsənənt; 'semi'kɔnsənənt] *n.* 半子音(如 **you** [ju; ju:] 中之j)。
sem·i·dai·ly [,sɛmə'delɪ; 'semi'deili] *adj.* 每半日的;半日一次的;每天兩次的。
sem·i·dem·i·sem·i·qua·ver [,sɛmə'dɛmɪ'sɛmə,kwevɚ; ,semi'demi'semi,kweivə] *n.* 〖音樂〗六十四分音符。
sem·i·de·tached [,sɛmədɪ'tætʃt; 'semidi'tætʃt] *adj.* ①半分離的(指中隔公牆之兩所毗連房屋而言)。②部分分離的。
sem·i·de·vel·oped [,sɛmədɪ'vɛləpt; 'semidi'veləpt] *adj.* ①發育不全的。②半開發的。
sem·i·di·am·e·ter [,sɛmɪdaɪ'æmətɚ; 'semidai'æmitə] *n.* 半徑 (=radius).
sem·i·doc·u·men·ta·ry [,sɛmə,dɑkju'mɛntərɪ; 'semi,dɔkju'mentəri] *adj., n., pl.* **-ries.** —*adj.* 半紀錄的; 半實在的。—*n.* 半紀錄書、影片、電視片。
sem·i·dome ['sɛmə,dom; 'semidoum] *n.* 〖建築〗半穹窿式屋頂。
sem·i·do·mes·ti·cat·ed [,sɛmədə'mɛstə,ketɪd; 'semidə'mestikeitid] *adj.* (動物等)半馴服的。
sem·i·dor·mant [,sɛmə'dɔrmənt; 'semi'dɔ:mənt] *adj.* 半睡眠的。
sem·i·ed·u·cat·ed [,sɛmə'ɛdʒu,ketɪd; 'semi'edjukeitid] *adj.* 半受教育的。
sem·i·em·pir·i·cal [,sɛmɪɛm'pɪrəkl̩; 'semiem'pirikəl] *adj.* 半憑經驗的。
sem·i·feu·dal [,sɛmə'fjudl̩; 'semi'fju:dl] *adj.* 半封建的。
sem·i·fic·tion·al [,sɛmə'fɪkʃənl̩; 'semifikʃənl] *adj.* 半虛構的。
sem·i·fi·nal [,sɛmə'faɪnl̩; 'semi'fainl] *n., adj.* 準決賽(的)。
sem·i·fi·nal·ist [,sɛmə'faɪnl̩ɪst; 'semi'fainlist] *n.* 參加準決賽者。
sem·i·fin·ished [,sɛmə'fɪnɪʃt; 'semi'finiʃt] *adj.* 半完成的;半成品的。
sem·i·flu·id [,sɛmə'fluɪd; 'semi'flu:id] *n.* 半流體。—*adj.* 半流體的。
sem·i·for·mal [,sɛmə'fɔrml̩; 'semi'fɔ:məl] *adj.* 半正式的。
sem·i·gov·ern·men·tal [,sɛmə,gʌvən'mɛntl̩; 'semi,gʌvən'mentəl] *adj.* 半官方的。
sem·i·in·de·pend·ent [,sɛmə,ɪndɪ'pɛndənt; 'semi,indi'pendənt] *adj.* 半獨立的。
sem·i·in·dus·tri·al·ized [,sɛməɪn'dʌstrɪəl,aɪzd; 'semiin'dʌstriəlaizd] *adj.* 半工業化的。
sem·i·liq·uid ['sɛmə'lɪkwɪd; 'semi'likwid] *n., adj.* =**semifluid.**
sem·i·lit·er·ate [,sɛmə'lɪtərɪt; 'semi'litərit] *adj.* ①粗識字的。②識字但不諳書寫的。

sem·i·lu·nar [ˌsɛmə'lunɚ; 'semi'lu:nə] *adj.* 半月形的。—*n.* 半月形之事物。

sem·i·man·u·fac·ture [ˌsɛməˌmænju'fæktʃɚ; 'semiˌmænju'fæktʃə] *n.* 半成品。

sem·i·me·chan·i·cal [ˌsɛmәmә'kænәkḷ; 'semimi'kænikәl] *adj.* 半機械的。

sem·i·month·ly [ˌsɛmə'mʌnθlɪ; 'semi'mʌnθli] *adj., adv., n., pl.* **-lies.** —*adj.* 半月的;半月一次的。 —*adv.* 每半月地;每半月一次地。 —*n.* 半月刊。

sem·i·nal ['sɛmənḷ; 'si:minl] *adj.* ①精液的。*seminal* duct. 輸精管。②〖植物〗胚子的;種子的。③繁殖的。④潛在的;含蓄的。⑤發育不全的;未發達的。⑥根本的;基本的。

sem·i·nar ['sɛməˌnɑr; 'semi'nɑ:] *n.* ①大學學生在指導下進行研究討論之班次或課程。②上述班次之教室。③講習會; 討論會。

sem·i·nar·y ['sɛməˌnɛrɪ; 'seminəri] *n., pl.* **-nar·ies.** ①學校;學院。②神學院。③=**seminar.** ④發源地;溫床。

sem·i·nate ['sɛmənet; 'semineit] *v.t.,* **-nat·ed, -nat·ing.** 播種;傳播;散發。

sem·i·na·tion [ˌsɛmə'neʃən; ˌsemi'neiʃən] *n.* 播種;傳播。

sem·i·nif·er·ous [ˌsɛmə'nɪfərəs; ˌsemi'nifərəs] *adj.* ①〖解剖〗生精液的;輸液的。②〖植物〗結種子的。

Sem·i·nole ['sɛməˌnol; 'seminoul] *n.* 塞米奴人(為北美印第安人 Creek 族之一支,居於 Florida 州)。—*adj.* 塞米奴族人的。

sem·i·no·mad·ic [ˌsɛməno'mædɪk; 'seminou'mædik] *adj.* 半遊牧的。

sem·i·nude [ˌsɛmə'nud; 'semi'nju:d] *adj.* 半裸的。

sem·i·of·fi·cial [ˌsɛmɪə'fɪʃəl; 'semiə'fiʃəl] *adj.* 半官方的。a *semiofficial* gazette. 半官方報紙。—**ly,** *adv.*

se·mi·ol·o·gy [ˌsimɪ'ɑlədʒɪ; ˌsi:mi'ɔlədʒi] *n.* ①〖醫〗徵候學。②記號學。③手勢語言。

se·mi·ot·ics [ˌsimɪ'ɑtɪks; ˌsi:mi'ɔtiks] *n.* 〖醫〗徵候學。(亦作 **semeiotics**)

sem·i·o·val [ˌsɛmə'ovəl; 'semi'ouvəl] *adj.* 半橢圓形的。

sem·i·per·ma·nent [ˌsɛmə'pɝmənənt; 'semi'pə:mənənt] *adj.* 半永久的。

sem·i·per·me·a·ble [ˌsɛmə'pɝmɪəbḷ; 'semi'pə:miəbl] *adj.* 半透性(小粒可透過)的。

sem·i·po·lit·i·cal [ˌsɛmɪpə'lɪtəkḷ; ˌsemipə'litikəl] *adj.* 半政治性的。

sem·i·post·al [ˌsɛmə'postḷ; 'semi'poustəl] *n., adj.* 慈善捐款性的高價郵票(的)。

sem·i·pre·cious [ˌsɛmə'prɛʃəs; 'semiˌpreʃəs] *adj.* 半珍貴的。

sem·i·pri·vate [ˌsɛmə'praɪvɪt; 'semi'praivit] *adj.* 半私用的(如醫院病房,床數較少者)。

sem·i·pro [ˌsɛmə'pro; 'semi'prou] *n., pl.* **-pros,** *adj.* —*n.* 〖俗〗半職業性選手。—*adj.* 半職業性的。

sem·i·pro·fes·sion·al [ˌsɛmәprә'fɛʃәnḷ; 'semiprә'feʃәnḷ] *adj.* 半職業性的。—*n.* 半職業性之選手或其他人。

sem·i·pub·lic [ˌsɛmə'pʌblɪk; 'semi'pʌblik] *adj.* 半公開的。

sem·i·qua·ver ['sɛməˌkwevɚ; 'semiˌkweivə] *n.* 〖音樂〗十六分音符。

sem·i·re·li·gious [ˌsɛmɪrɪ'lɪdʒəs; 'semiri'lidʒəs] *adj.* 半宗教性的。

sem·i·rig·id [ˌsɛmə'rɪdʒɪd; 'semi'ridʒid] *adj.* 半硬式的。

sem·i·sav·age [ˌsɛmə'sævɪdʒ; 'semi'sævidʒ] *adj.* 半野蠻的。 —*n.* 半野蠻人。

sem·i·skilled [ˌsɛmə'skɪld; 'semi'skild] *adj.* 半熟練的(工人)。

sem·i·sol·id [ˌsɛmə'sɑlɪd; 'semi'sɔlid] *adj.* 半固體的。—*n.* 半固體物質。

sem·i·star [ˌsɛmə'stɑr; 'semi'stɑ:] *n.* 〖美俗〗二流電影明星。

sem·i·starved [ˌsɛmə'stɑrvd; 'semi'stɑ:vd] *adj.* 半饑餓的。

sem·i·sweet [ˌsɛmə'swit; 'semi'swi:t] *adj.* 半甜的;不很甜的。

Sem·ite ['sɛmaɪt; 'si:mait] *n.* 閃族;塞姆族(包括希伯來人、阿拉伯人、亞述人、腓尼基、巴比倫人等);(今特指)猶太人。

Se·mit·ic [sə'mɪtɪk; si'mitik] *adj.* 閃族的; 閃族語的。—*n.* ①閃族人。②閃族語(包括 Hebrew, Arabic 等文字的語系)。

Sem·i·tism ['sɛməˌtɪzəm; 'semitizəm] *n.* ①閃族人(尤指猶太人)之性格、氣質。②閃族的語言。

sem·i·tone ['sɛməˌton; 'semitoun] *n.* 〖音樂〗半音。

sem·i·to·tal·i·tar·i·an [ˌsɛmɪtoˌtælə'tɛrɪən; 'semitouˌtæli'tɛəriən] *adj.* 半極權(主義)的。

sem·i·trans·lu·cent [ˌsɛmətrænz'lusənt; 'semitrænz'lu:snt] *adj.* 似半透明的。

sem·i·trans·par·ent ['sɛmətræns'pɛrənt; 'semitræns'pɛərənt] *adj.* 半透明的。

sem·i·trop·i·cal [ˌsɛmə'trɑpɪkḷ; 'semi'trɔpikəl] *adj.* 亞熱帶的。(亦作 **semitropic**)

sem·i·ur·ban [ˌsɛmə'ɝbən; 'semi'ə:bən] *adj.* 半城市的。

sem·i·vi·bra·tion [ˌsɛməvaɪ'breʃən; 'semivai'breiʃən] *n.* 半震動。

sem·i·vo·cal [ˌsɛmə'vokḷ; 'semi'voukəl] *adj.* 〖語音〗半母音的。

sem·i·vol·un·tar·y [ˌsɛmə'vɑlənˌtɛrɪ; 'semi'vɔləntəri] *adj.* 半志願的。

sem·i·vow·el ['sɛməˌvauəl; 'semi'vauəl] *n.* 〖語音〗半母音。

sem·i·week·ly [ˌsɛmə'wiklɪ; 'semi'wi:kli] *adj.* 一週二次的;每半週一次的。—*n.* 半週刊; 三日刊。—*adv.* 一週二次地。

sem·i·year·ly [ˌsɛmə'jɪrlɪ; 'semi'jə:li] *adj.* 每年兩次的; 半年一次的。 —*n.* 半年刊。—*adv.* 每年兩次地;半年一次。

sem·o·li·na [ˌsɛmə'linə; ˌsemə'li:nə] *n.* 粗小麥粉。(亦作 **semola**)

sem·pi·ter·nal [ˌsɛmpɪ'tɝnḷ; ˌsempi'tə:nl] *adj.* 〖古,詩〗永遠的;永久的。

sem·pli·ce ['sɛmplɪtʃe; 'semplitʃi] 〖義〗 *adj.* 〖音樂〗單純的;無裝飾音的。

sem·pre ['sɛmpre; 'sempri] 〖義〗 *adv.* 〖音樂〗自始至終。

semp·stress ['sɛmpstrɪs; 'sempstris] *n.* 縫紉婦。(亦作 **seamstress**)

Sen., sen. ①Senior. ②Senate. ③Senator. **sen., senr.** senior.

sen·a·ry ['sɛnərɪ; 'si:nəri] *adj.* 六的; 六個的。

‡sen·ate ['sɛnɪt; 'senit] *n.* ①(S-) 參議院;上議院。②(古羅馬的)元老院。③(若干大學之) 評議會。

senate house ①參議院議場。②英國劍橋大學評議員辦公處。

‡sen·a·tor ['sɛnətɚ; 'senətə] *n.* ①參議院議員;上議院議員。②(S-)〖美〗對現任或前任參議員的尊稱。

sen·a·to·ri·al [ˌsɛnəˈtorɪəl; ˌsenəˈtɔːriəl] *adj.* ①上議院或參議院的。②參議員的。

sen·a·tor·ship [ˈsɛnətəˌʃɪp; ˈsenətəʃip] *n.* (參院、上院)議員之職位及任期。

ːsend[1] [sɛnd; send] *v.*, **sent, send·ing.** —*v.t.* ①遣; 派; 使往。 to *send* a person for the doctor. 遣人去請醫生。②送;傳遞;傳達。I have *sent* him several letters. 我已寄給他好幾封信。③促使 (=cause to become). The noise will *send* me mad. 這喧囂將使我發狂。④施與;賜給。God *sends* rain. (上帝)降雨。⑤拋;擲。⑥送出;送到。⑦發出〖常 forth, off, out, through〗. ⑧〖電〗發出信號。⑨〖俚〗使興奮。⑩迫使。⑪引起…上升或下降。 The news *sent* the stock market up. 這個消息使股票上揚。 —*v.i.* ①遣使。to *send* for a taxi. 遣人去叫計程車。②〖電〗送出(信號)。 ***send away*** **a.** 解僱(僕人等)。 **b.** 寫信或派人至遠方。 ***send down*** **a.** 使下降; 使減低。 to *send down* prices. 使物價下降。 **b.** (英牛津, 劍橋大學等) 開除 (學生); 勒令退學。 ***send for*** 延請。 ***send forth*** (***out***) **a.** 生出; 發出。**b.** 出口。 ***send in*** **a.** 參加展覽。 **b.** 使宣布; 使爲人知。 to *send in* one's resignation. 呈請辭職。 ***send off*** **a.** 發貨;送貨。Please *send* the goods *off* today. 請於今天把貨物運出。**b.** 送別。 to *send* a person *off*. 送別某人。**c.** 差遣; 辭退。 ***send on*** **a.** 轉送;轉寄。**b.** 先送;先寄。 ***send one's love*** 寄語問候。 ***send out*** **a.** 放射;放出。**b.** 生出; 長出。 **c.** 分發。 ***send packing*** 驅逐;開革。***send up*** **a.** 使上揚;使升高。to *send up* prices. 使物價上揚。**b.** 使高升(職位)。 **c.** 〖俚〗 判刑;送進監獄。***send word*** 通知。

send[2] *n.* 〖航海〗①波浪的推力。②船之縱搖。—*v.i.* (船受波浪推進而)上掀。

send·ee [sɛnˈdi; sendˈiː] *n.* 收貨人。

send·er [ˈsɛndɚ; ˈsendə] *n.* ①送者;發送人;發貨人。②(電話之)送話器;(電報之)發報機。

send-off [ˈsɛndˌɔf; ˈsendˈɔːf] *n.* 〖俗〗①話別會; 送別會。He was given a good *send-off*. 他受到盛大的歡送。②開創(事業等)之衝動;開始。

sen·e·ga [ˈsɛnɪgə; ˈsenigə] *n.* 〖植物〗①茅香;森伊加 (遠志屬之植物)。②此種植物之根 (藥用, 可做化痰劑)。

Sen·e·gal [ˌsɛnɪˈgɔl, seneˈgal; ˌseniˈgɔːl] *n.* ①塞內加爾(非洲西海岸一共和國, 首都達喀爾, Dakar). ②塞內加爾河。

Sen·e·ga·lese [ˌsɛnɪgɔˈliz; ˌsenigɔːˈliːz] *adj.*, *n.*, *pl.* **-lese.** —*adj.* 塞內加爾的;塞內加爾人的。 —*n.* ①塞內加爾人(主要爲 Moors 及黑人)。②塞內加爾語。

se·nes·cence [səˈnɛsn̩s; səˈnesns] *n.* 衰老;老年。

se·nes·cent [səˈnɛsn̩t; səˈnesnt] *adj.* 衰老的;開始有衰老現象的。

sen·es·chal [ˈsɛnəʃəl; ˈseniʃəl] *n.*(中世紀皇宮或貴族莊園中的)管家;執事。

se·nhor [seˈnjor; seiˈnjouə] *n.*, *pl.* **se·nhors,** *Port.* **se·nho·res.**〖葡〗①先生;君(=Mr., Sir). ②上流社會的人;紳士。

se·nho·ra [seˈnjorə; seiˈnjourə] *n.*, *pl.* **se·nho·ras.**〖葡〗夫人(=Mrs., Madam).

se·nho·ri·ta [ˌsenjoˈritə; ˌseinjouˈriːtə] *n.*, *pl.* **-tas.** 〖葡〗小姐 (=Miss).

se·nile [ˈsinaɪl; ˈsiːnail] *adj.* 老年的;衰老的。—*n.* 老年人;衰老者。

se·nil·i·ty [səˈnɪlətɪ; siˈniliti] *n.* ①年老; 老耄。②衰老。

***sen·ior** [ˈsinjɚ; ˈsiːnjə] *adj.* ①年長的;同名的父子或兄弟二人中之長者 (如 John Brown, *Senior* 指老 John Brown, 大 John Brown, 卽 John Brown 之父或兄;常略作 **Sen., Senr.** 或 **Sr.**). ②上級的;高級的;前輩的。a *senior* partner. 社長; 經理。③〖美〗(大學或四年制中學之)四年級的;畢業班的。④資深的(軍官等)。—*n.* ①年長者。He is my *senior* by three years. 他比我大三歲。②上司;長官;前輩;長者。③〖美〗(大學或四年制中學之)四年級學生;畢業班學生。

senior citizen 〖美〗老年人。

se·ni·o·res pri·o·res [ˌsinɪˈoriz praɪˈoriz; ˈsiːniˈouriːz praiˈouriːz] 〖拉〗年長者居先(=elders first).

senior high school〖美〗高級中學。

sen·ior·i·ty [sinˈjɔrətɪ; ˌsiːniˈɔriti] *n.*, *pl.* **-ties.** ①年長。②年資深;年資。

seniority rule 〖美〗資深規則。

sen·na [ˈsɛnə; ˈsenə] *n.* ①〖植物〗旃那。②旃那葉(用作通便劑)。

sen·net [ˈsɛnɪt; ˈsenit] *n.* 大西洋中一種攻擊游泳者的大魚。

sen·nit [ˈsɛnɪt; ˈsenit] *n.* ①〖航海〗編索。②草帽辮。

se·no·pi·a [səˈnopɪə; səˈnoupiə] *n.* 近視眼因年長而目力趨於正常的現象。

se·ñor [senˈjɔr; seˈnjɔː] *n.*, *pl.* **-ñors, -ño·res.** 〖西〗 ①…先生 (=Mr. 略作 Sr.). ②紳士。

se·ño·ra [senˈjorə; seˈnjɔːrə] *n.*, *pl.* **se·ño·ras.**〖西〗①夫人(與姓氏連用)。②女士。

se·ño·ri·ta [ˌsenjəˈritə; ˌsenjəˈriːtə] *n.*, *pl.* **-tas.** 〖西〗 ①小姐(與姓氏連用)。②女士。

senr. senior.

***sen·sa·tion** [sɛnˈseʃən; senˈseiʃən] *n.* ①感覺;感覺力。Fire gives a *sensation* of warmth. 火予人以溫暖的感覺。②感情;感動;感情之激動。③激動感情之事物。—**less,** *adj.*

***sen·sa·tion·al**[sɛnˈseʃənl̩;senˈseiʃənl] *adj.*①聳人聽聞的; 令人激動的。a *sensational* crime. 轟動社會的犯罪。②意圖激動感情的。③感覺的;感情的;感動的。④〖哲學〗感覺論的。—**ly,** *adv.*

sen·sa·tion·al·ism[sɛnˈseʃənl̩ˌɪzəm; senˈseiʃnəlizəm] *n.* ①激情的方法; 聳人聽聞的作品、語言等。②〖哲學〗感覺論。③〖倫理〗快樂主義。④煽情主義;激情主義。—**sen·sa·tion·al·ist,** *n.*

ːsense [sɛns; sens] *n.*, *v.*, **sensed, sens·ing.** —*n.* ①感官;官能; 感覺; 知覺。 the five *senses*. 五官。②意念; 意識; 辨識力。 *sense* of honor (duty, humor). 榮譽 (責任, 幽默)感。③判斷力;見識。He has plenty of *sense*. 他富有見識。④(*pl.*) 理性;本性;健全之神智。 We must bring him to his *senses*. 我們必須使他醒悟。⑤意義; 意味。In what *sense* do you use the word? 你此語用爲何義?⑥一般意見;輿情。⑦〖數學〗指向;向旨。⑧理由。***come to one's senses*** **a.** 醒悟。**b.** 恢復知覺。 ***common sense*** 常識。***in a sense*** 在某一方面來說。***in one's*** (***right***) ***senses*** 神智正常; 感覺清醒。***lose one's senses*** **a.** 變爲愚蠢。**b.** 昏厥。***make sense*** 理解;合理。Can you *make sense* of what he says? 你懂得他所說的話的意義嗎? ***out of one's*** (***right***) ***senses*** 神智失常; 糊塗。 ***talk sense*** 說有意義的話。 —*v.t.* ①覺得;感知。②〖俗〗了解;理解;明白。

sense-cen·ter [ˈsɛnsˌsɛntɚ; ˈsens-

ˌsentə] *n.* 感覺中樞。

***sense·less** [ˈsɛnslɪs; ˈsenslis] *adj.* ①無感覺的;不省人事的。to fall *senseless.* 失去知覺。②無知的;愚蠢的。③(語詞等)無意義的。

sense organ 感覺器官。

***sen·si·bil·i·ty** [ˌsɛnsəˈbɪlətɪ; ˌsensiˈbiliti] *n., pl.* **-ties.** ①感性; 感覺能力。②敏感;敏感性。③(*pl.*)情感。

***sen·si·ble** [ˈsɛnsəbl̩; ˈsensəbl] *adj.* ①可感覺的。②聰明的; 明智的;明達的;有理性的。③感知 (=aware, conscious). I am very *sensible* of your kindness. 我深感你的好意。④敏感的。⑤有知覺的。⑥(數量等)相當大的。a *sensible* reduction in price. 相當大的減價。—**sen·si·bly,** *adv.*

***sen·si·tive** [ˈsɛnsətɪv; ˈsensitiv] *adj.* ①有感覺的。②敏感的;神經過敏的;感覺靈敏的。The eye is *sensitive* to light. 眼睛對光敏感。③敏於理解的; 能辨好壞的。④易受影響的。⑤仁慈的; 易受感動的。⑥易受傷害的。⑦易感光的。*sensitive* paper. 感光紙。⑧(職務等)涉及高度機密而微妙之情報或工作的。⑨(秤或溫度器等)能記錄微小之變化的。—**ly,** *adv.* —**ness,** *n.*

sensitive plant 含羞草。

sen·si·tiv·i·ty [ˌsɛnsəˈtɪvətɪ; ˌsensiˈtiviti] *n., pl.* **-ties.** ①感受性; 敏感性。②感光度。③〖無線電〗對外來電波之感受性。

sen·si·tize [ˈsɛnsəˌtaɪz; ˈsensitaiz] *v.t.,* **-tized, -tiz·ing.** ①使易感; 使敏感。②使 (照像底片) 易於感光。 —**sen·si·ti·za·tion, sen·si·tiz·er,** *n.*

sen·so·ri·al [sɛnˈsorɪəl; senˈsɔːriəl] *adj.* =**sensory.**

sen·so·ri·um [sɛnˈsorɪəm; senˈsɔːriəm] *n., pl.* **-ri·ums, -ri·a** [-rɪə;-riə].〖解剖〗①頭腦;感覺中樞。②感覺機關;感覺所。

sen·so·ry [ˈsɛnsərɪ; ˈsensəri] *adj.* ①感覺的。②〖生理〗知覺器官的;感覺器官的。

sen·su·al [ˈsɛnʃuəl; ˈsensjuəl] *adj.* ①肉體上的;五官的。②(耽於)肉慾的;好色的。③享樂主義的。④顯示淫蕩之本性的。—**ly,** *adv.*

sen·su·al·ism [ˈsɛnʃuəlˌɪzəm; ˈsensjuəlizəm] *n.* ①〖哲學〗感覺論。②〖藝術〗感覺主義。③〖倫理〗快樂主義。④耽於肉慾; 好色。 —**sen·su·al·ist,** *n.*

sen·su·al·i·ty [ˌsɛnʃuˈælətɪ; ˌsensjuˈæliti] *n., pl.* **-ties.** ①淫蕩;好色。②感覺性;感能。(亦作 **sensualness**)

sen·su·al·ize [ˈsɛnʃuəlˌaɪz; ˈsensjuəlaiz] *v.t.,* **-al·ized, -al·iz·ing.** 使縱於肉慾;使墮落。

sen·su·ous [ˈsɛnʃuəs; ˈsensjuəs] *adj.* ①感官的; 感覺的。②訴諸感覺的。③易受感官快樂的。—**ly,** *adv.* —**ness,** *n.*

‡sent [sɛnt; sent] *v.* pt. & pp. of **send.**

sen·tence** [ˈsɛntəns; ˈsentəns] *n., v.,* **-tenced, -tenc·ing.** —*n.* ①句; 文句。②(對某問題的)意見;決策。③宣判;判決。④刑罰。⑤格言。be under sentence of death*** 已被宣判死刑。 ***pass sentence*** 宣判刑罰。***serve a sentence*** 服刑。—*v.t.* 宣判;判決。He was *sentenced* to death. 他被判死刑。〖文法〗句是表現一個完全思想的一組字,必須由主語 (subject) 和述語 (predicate) 兩個部分組合而成。句有下列四類:⑴**declarative sentence.** 敍述句。⑵**interrogative sentence.** 疑問句。⑶**imperative sentence.** 祈使句。⑷**exclamatory sentence.** 感歎句。

sentence stress 句中之重讀。(亦作 **sentence accent**)

sen·ten·tial [sɛnˈtɛnʃəl; senˈtenʃəl] *adj.* ①句子的。②判斷的; 判決的。

sen·ten·tious [sɛnˈtɛnʃəs; senˈtenʃəs] *adj.* ①簡潔精鍊的。②警句的。③好說教的;自以爲正義的。 —**ly,** *adv.* —**ness,** *n.*

sen·tience [ˈsɛnʃəns; ˈsenʃəns] *n.* ①感覺性; 知覺力。②感覺; 知覺。(亦作 **sentiency**)

sen·tient [ˈsɛnʃənt; ˈsenʃənt] *adj.* 知覺的;感覺的; 有知覺力的。—*n.* ①有知覺或感覺力的人或物。②心(=mind).

***sen·ti·ment** [ˈsɛntəmənt; ˈsentimənt] *n.* ①感情;情緒;情操。②傷感;感情的弱點。③(常 *pl.*)意見;觀點。What are your *sentiments* in this matter? 你對此事意見如何?

***sen·ti·men·tal** [ˌsɛntəˈmɛntl̩; ˌsentiˈmentl] *adj.* ①感情的;情緒的。②感情用事的;多愁善感的;感傷的。a *sentimental* girl. 一個多愁善感的女孩子。—**ly,** *adv.*

sen·ti·men·tal·ism [ˌsɛntəˈmɛntl̩ˌɪzəm; ˌsentiˈmentəlizəm] *n.* ①感情主義。②溺於情感。③脆弱的感情之流露。

sen·ti·men·tal·ist [ˌsɛntəˈmɛntl̩ɪst; ˌsentiˈmentlist] *n.* 感情主義者;多愁善感者。

sen·ti·men·tal·i·ty [ˌsɛntəmɛnˈtælətɪ; ˌsentimenˈtæliti] *n., pl.* **-ties.** 溺於感情;多愁善感;傷感。

sen·ti·men·tal·ize [ˌsɛntəˈmɛntl̩ˌaɪz; ˌsentiˈmentlaiz] *v.,* **-ized, -iz·ing.** —*v.i.* 沉溺於情感; 感情用事; 傷感。 —*v.t.* ①使溺於感情;使傷感; 使有感情。②傷感於;對…傷感。

sen·ti·nel** [ˈsɛntənl̩; ˈsentinl] *n., v.,* **-nel(l)ed, -nel·(l)ing.** —*n.* ①哨兵;步哨。②守衛人。 ***stand sentinel over 守衛。—*v.t.* 站崗;看管。

sen·try** [ˈsɛntrɪ; ˈsentri] *n., pl.* **-tries,** *v.,* **-tried, -try·ing.** —*n.* ①哨兵; 步哨。②放哨;守望。 ***come off sentry 落哨;退哨。***go on sentry*** 上哨;當哨。***relieve a sentry*** 換哨。 ***stand sentry*** 站崗; 看顧; 守護。—*v.t.* 上哨; 站崗。

sentry box 哨兵崗位;哨兵之小屋。

sentry go 步哨線; 步哨勤務。(亦作 **sentry-go**)

sen·za tem·po [ˈsɛntsɑˈtɛmpo; ˈsentsɑːˈtempou]〖義〗〖音樂〗不拘泥節拍。

Se·oul [sol, seˈol; soul, seiˈoul] *n.* 漢城 (大韓民國首都)。

Sep., Sept. ①September. ②Septuagint. **sep.** ①sepal. ②separate. ③septic.

se·pal [ˈsipl̩; ˈsiːpəl] *n.*〖植物〗萼片。

sep·a·ra·bil·i·ty [ˌsɛpərəˈbɪlətɪ; ˌsepərəˈbiliti] *n.* 可分離;可分性。

sep·a·ra·ble [ˈsɛpərəbl̩; ˈsepərəbl] *adj.* 能分開的;可區分的。 —**sep·a·ra·bly,** *adv.*

‡sep·a·rate [*v.*ˈsɛpəˌret; ˈsepəreit *adj., n.* ˈsɛpərɪt; ˈseprit] *v.,* **-rat·ed, -rat·ing,** *adj., n.* —*v.t.* ①分離;分開;隔開。The sea *separates* Taiwan from the Chinese mainland. 海隔開了臺灣和中國大陸。②開除;開革;遣散。—*v.i.* 分離;分開;分居。I hear that Mr. and Mrs. White have *separated.* 我聽說懷特夫婦已經分居。—*adj.* 分離的;分開的;各別的; 單獨的。The children all sleep in *separate* beds. 孩子們都各人睡各人的床。—*n.* ①分開的事物。②(*pl.*)可分開穿着的女裝。③抽印本。 —**ly,** *adv.*

separate but equal 黑白種族隔

離,但使黑人在教育,就業,交通等有同等待遇。
separate estate (or **property**) (妻之)獨有財產。「居後妻之」贍養費」
separate maintenance (夫婦分」
sep·a·ra·tion** [ˌsɛpəˈreʃən; ˌsepəˈreiʃən] *n.* ①分離;分開。②分離的期間。③分居。④缺口;孔;裂口。 ***judicial separation 經法庭判定的夫婦分居。
separation allowance 征屬津貼。
separation center 軍隊復員中心。
separation of powers 〖政府〗權能之分立(如行政、立法、司法權之分立)。
separation pay 遣散費。
sep·a·ra·tism [ˈsɛpərəˌtɪzəm; ˈsepərətizəm] *n.* ①(政治、宗教上的)分離主義。②獨立主義。
sep·a·ra·tist [ˈsɛpəˌretɪst; ˈsepəreitist] *n.* ①(宗教與政治上的)分離主義者。②獨立主義者。—*adj.* 獨立主義(者)的;政教分離主義(者)的。
sep·a·ra·tive [ˈsɛpəˌretɪv; ˈsepəreitiv] *adj.* ①傾向分離的;主張分離的;造成分離的。②區別的;分別的。
sep·a·ra·tor [ˈsɛpəˌretɚ; ˈsepəreitə] *n.* ①分離者。②分離器;選礦機;脫脂器。
sep·a·ra·to·ry [ˈsɛpərəˌtorɪ; ˈsepərətəri] *adj.* 分離的;分離用的。
Se·phar·di [sɪˈfɑrdi; seˈfɑːdi] *n.* sing. of **Sephardim.**
Se·phar·dim [sɪˈfɑrdɪm; seˈfɑːdim] *n. pl.* 西班牙及葡萄牙籍之猶太人;其後裔。—**Se·phar·dic,** *adj.*
se·pi·a [ˈsipɪə; ˈsiːpjə] *n., pl.* **-pi·as, -pi·ae** [-pɪi; -piiː], *adj.* —*n.* ①烏賊之黑墨汁。②用烏賊墨汁製成之深褐色顏料或墨水;用此顏料或墨水所繪製之圖。③深褐色。—*adj.* ①暗褐色的。②以上述顏色畫的。
se·pi·o·lite [ˈsipɪəˌlaɪt; ˈsiːpiəlait] *n.* 〖礦〗海泡石。「隊中的印度兵。」
se·poy [ˈsipɔɪ; ˈsiːpɔi] *n.* 〖昔〗英國軍」
sep·sis [ˈsɛpsɪs; ˈsepsis] *n.* 〖醫〗腐敗;腐敗作用;敗血症;敗血作用;膿毒病。
sept [sɛpt; sept] *n.* ①(中古愛爾蘭的)種族;家族。②〖人類學〗源自同一祖先的族人。
Sept. ①September. ②Septuagint.
sept- 〖字首〗表"七"之義。如 septenary, 七年一次的。(亦作 **septem-, septi-**)
sep·ta [ˈsɛptə; ˈseptə] *n.* pl. of **septum.**
sep·tal [ˈsɛptl̩; ˈseptl] *adj.* 〖動、植物〗隔壁的;隔膜的;芽胞壁的;中隔的。
sep·tan [ˈsɛptən; ˈseptən] *adj.* 〖醫〗每隔七日發作的。 a *septan* fever. 七日熱。
sep·tan·gle [ˈsɛpˌtæŋgl̩; ˈsepˌtæŋgl] *n.* 七角形。 —**sep·tan·gu·lar,** *adj.*
septem- 〖字首〗 **sept-** 之異體。
‡Sep·tem·ber [sɛpˈtɛmbɚ; səpˈtembə] *n.* 九月。(略作 **Sept., Sep.**)
sep·te·nar·y [ˈsɛptəˌnɛrɪ; ˈseptənəri] *adj., n., pl.* **-nar·ies.**—*adj.* 七的;七個的;由七個組成的;七年一度的。—*n.* ①七;七個一組;七年間。②〖詩〗七音步的詩行。
sep·ten·ni·al [sɛpˈtɛnɪəl; sepˈtenjəl] *adj.* 七年的;每七年的;七年一次的。
sep·tet, sep·tette [sɛpˈtɛt; sepˈtet] *n.* ①七人或七個一組。②〖音樂〗七重奏;七部合唱;七部合奏曲。「膜;隔片"之義。」
septi- 〖字首〗 ①**sept-** 之異體。②表"隔」
sep·tic [ˈsɛptɪk; ˈseptik] *adj.* 致使腐敗的;致使敗血的。—*n.* 致使腐敗或敗血之物。
sep·ti·cae·mi·a [ˌsɛptəˈsimɪə; ˌseptiˈsiːmiə] *n.* 〖醫〗敗血症。(亦作 **septicemia**) —**sep·ti·cae·mic,** *adj.* 「腐敗;腐敗性。」
sep·tic·i·ty [sɛpˈtɪsətɪ; sepˈtisiti] *n.*」
septic tank 化糞池。
sep·til·lion [sɛpˈtɪljən; sepˈtiljən] *n.* 數字名(法美兩國為 10^{24};英德兩國為 10^{42})。—*adj.* 上述數字的。「*adj.* 七的。」
sep·ti·mal [ˈsɛptɪməl; ˈseptiməl]」
sep·time [ˈsɛptim; ˈseptiːm] *n.* 〖劍術〗八種防禦姿勢中的第七種。
sep·tu·a·ge·nar·i·an [ˌsɛptʃuədʒəˈnɛrɪən; ˌseptjuədʒiˈnɛəriən] *n., adj.* 〖主英〗=**septuagenary.**
sep·tu·ag·e·nar·y [ˌsɛptʃuˈædʒəˌnɛrɪ; ˌseptjuˈædʒinəri] *n., pl.* **-nar·ies,** *adj.* —*n.* 七十歲老者; 七十至八十歲之間的人。—*adj.* 七十歲的;七十至八十歲之間的。
Sep·tu·a·ges·i·ma [ˌsɛptʃuəˈdʒɛsəmə; ˌseptjuəˈdʒesimə] *n.* 四旬節 (Lent) 前之第三個星期日。(亦作 **Septuagesima Sunday**)
Sep·tu·a·gint [ˈsɛptʃuəˌdʒɪnt; ˈseptjuədʒint] *n.* 希臘文舊約聖經(傳稱應埃及王 Ptolemy II 之請, 由七十或七十二位猶太學者在七十或七十二日內譯成)。
sep·tum [ˈsɛptəm; ˈseptəm] *n., pl.* **-ta.** ①〖動、植物〗隔膜;隔壁;芽胞壁;中隔。
sep·tu·ple [ˈsɛptupl̩; ˈseptjupl] *adj., v.,* **-pled, -pling.** —*adj.* 七倍的。—*v.t.* 以七倍之;以七乘之。
sep·tup·let [sɛpˈtʌplɪt; sepˈtʌplit] *n.* ①同樣的七個東西組成之一組。②同胎七子中之一個。③(*pl.*) 七胞胎。
sep·tu·pli·cate [*adj., n.* sɛpˈtjupləkɪt; sepˈtjuːplikit *v.* sɛpˈtjupləˌket; sepˈtjuːplikeit] *adj., n., v.,* **-cat·ed, -cat·ing.** —*adj.* 一式七分的。—*n.* (複寫之) 七分〖常 in〗. Type the letter in *septuplicate.* 這封信打七分複寫。—*v.t.* 乘七。
sep·ul·cher, sep·ul·chre [ˈsɛpl̩kɚ; ˈsepəlkə] *n.* 墳墓; 塚。 ***a whited sepulchre*** 偽君子。***the Holy Sepulchre*** 聖墓(耶穌之墓)。—*v.t.* 埋葬。
se·pul·chral [səˈpʌlkrəl; siˈpʌlkrəl] *adj.* ①墓的。②陰沉的;陰森森的。
sep·ul·ture [ˈsɛpl̩tʃɚ; ˈsepəltʃə] *n.* ①埋葬。②〖古〗墳墓。
seq. ①sequel. ②sequentes *or* sequentia (拉=the following). **seqq.** the following (ones).
se·qua·cious [sɪˈkweʃəs; siˈkweiʃəs] *adj.* ①盲從的;順從的; 附和的。②有條理的;合邏輯的;前後一貫的。
se·quel [ˈsikwəl; ˈsiːkwəl] *n.* ①繼續;後續。②結果;結局。③(小說等的) 續集; 續篇。 ***as a sequel to*** (or ***of***) 由於…的結果。 ***in the sequel*** 結果;到後來。
se·que·la [sɪˈkwilə; siˈkwiːlə] *n., pl.* **-lae** [-li; -liː]. 〖拉〗 ①〖醫〗後發病。②結果。
***se·quence** [ˈsikwəns; ˈsiːkwəns] *n.* ①繼續; 繼起。②次第; 順序; 關聯。 in *sequence.* 順序地。③後果;結局。④〖數學〗序列;數貫。〖文法〗 **the sequence of tenses.** 時態的關聯。
se·quent [ˈsikwənt; ˈsiːkwənt] *adj.* ①繼續的;連續的。②結果的。③繼起的;繼承的。—*n.* 結果;繼起之事物。—**ly,** *adv.*
se·quen·tial [sɪˈkwɛnʃəl; siˈkwenʃəl] *adj.* 隨之而來的;連續的;結果的。—**ly,** *adv.*
se·ques·ter [sɪˈkwɛstɚ; siˈkwestə]

v.t. ①扣押;沒收。②使退隱;隱遁;分離(作反身動詞用,或以過去分詞作形容詞用)。③〖國際法〗扣押(敵產)。

se·ques·tered [sɪˈkwɛstɚd; siˈkwestəd] *adj.* 退隱的;孤立的;幽僻的。

se·ques·trate [sɪˈkwɛstret; siˈkwestreit] *v.t.,* **-trat·ed, -trat·ing.** ①〖法律〗**a.**假扣押。**b.** 查封;沒收。②〖古〗隔離;分離。—**se·ques·tra·tion, se·ques·tra·tor,** *n.*

se·ques·trum [sɪˈkwɛstrəm; siˈkwestrəm] *n., pl.* **-tra** [-trə; -trə]. 〖醫〗(同健全骨頭分開的)腐骨片;死骨片。

se·quin [ˈsikwɪn; ˈsi:kwin] *n.* 衣服上作飾物用之小金屬片。

se·quoi·a [sɪˈkwɔɪə; siˈkwɔiə] *n.* 〖植物〗美洲杉。

ser [sɪr, sɛr; siə, sɛə] *n.* =**seer²**.

se·ra [ˈsɪrə; ˈsiərə] *n.* pl. of **serum.**

sé·rac [seˈrak; ˈseræk] *n., pl.* **-racs.** (常 *pl.*)冰河上的塔狀冰塊。

se·ragl·io [sɪˈræljo; seˈrɑ:liou] *n., pl.* **-ios.** ①土耳其皇宮。②(回教國家之)後宮。(亦作 **serail**)

se·rai [səˈraɪ; seˈrai] *n.,* **-rais.** ①(中東國家的)旅店;客棧。②(回教國家之)後宮;王宮。

se·rang [səˈræŋ; səˈræŋ] *n.* 〖英印〗東印度的水手長;東印度的船長。

se·ra·pe [sɛˈrapɪ; seˈrɑ:pi] *n.* (拉丁美洲人穿的)灰色披肩或披身毛毯。

ser·aph [ˈsɛrəf; ˈserəf] *n., pl.* **-aphs, -a·phim** [-əˌfɪm; -əfim]. ①六翼天使(九級天使中地位最高者)。②撒拉弗(見舊約以賽亞書六章二節)。

se·raph·ic [səˈræfɪk; seˈræfik] *adj.*六翼天使的;適於天使的;崇高的;純潔的;美的。(亦作 **seraphical**)

Serb [sɝb; sə:b] *adj.* 塞爾維亞的;塞爾維亞人的;塞爾維亞語的。 —*n.* 塞爾維亞人;塞爾維亞語。(亦作 **Serbian**)

Ser·bi·a [ˈsɝbɪə; ˈsə:bjə] *n.* 塞爾維亞(昔巴爾幹半島上之一王國,今爲南斯拉夫之一地區)。(舊稱 **Servia**)

Ser·bo·ni·an [sɚˈbonɪən; sə:ˈbounjən] *adj.* 古埃及北部 Serbonis 大沼澤的。

Serbonian bog ①昔日尼羅河三角洲與蘇彝士地峽間的大沼澤。②絕境;困境。

sere [sɪr; siə] *adj.* 〖詩〗乾枯的; 凋萎的。(亦作 **sear**)

se·rein [səˈræ̃; səˈræ̃] 〖法〗 *n.* 〖氣象〗白撞雨(日落後晴空中降下之濛濛細雨)。

***ser·e·nade** [ˌsɛrəˈned; ˌseriˈneid] *n., v.,* **-nad·ed, -nad·ing.** —*n.* 夜曲; 小夜曲(尤指情人在其女友窗外所奏唱者)。—*v.t.* 向…奏或唱小夜曲。—*v.i.* 歌唱或奏小夜曲。The young Spaniards go *serenading* every night. 年輕的西班牙人每天夜晚奏唱小夜曲。

ser·en·dip·i·ty [ˌsɛrənˈdɪpətɪ; ˌserənˈdipəti] *n.* 發掘或發見的才能(此字爲英國文豪 Horace Walpole 所造,因其所著童話 *The Three Princes of Serendip* 的主人翁善於發掘珍寶)。

ser·en·dip·per [ˌsɛrənˈdɪpɚ; ˌserənˈdipə] *n.* 善於發掘或發見的人。

***se·rene** [səˈrin; siˈri:n] *adj.* ①安詳的;平靜的; 寧靜的; 沈着的; 晴朗的。a *serene* look. 沈着的神情。②(常 S-)對皇族的尊稱(常與 his, your 等連用)。his *Serene* Highness. 殿下。—**ly,** *adv.*

se·ren·i·ty [səˈrɛnətɪ; siˈreniti] *n., pl.* **-ties.** ①安靜;平靜;沈着;晴朗。②(常 S-)對皇族的尊稱(常與 his, your 等連用)。

serf [sɝf; sə:f] *n.* ①農奴。②奴隸。③被虐待如農奴的人。

serf·dom [ˈsɝfdəm; ˈsə:fdəm] *n.* ①農奴之身分;農奴之境遇。②蓄奴之風俗;奴隸制。(亦作 **serfage, serfhood**)

serg., sergt. sergeant.

serge [sɝdʒ; sə:dʒ] *n.* ①一種毛嗶嘰。②棉、尼龍或絲織之斜紋布料。

ser·gean·cy [ˈsɑrdʒənsɪ; ˈsɑ:dʒənsi] *n., pl.* **-cies.** 士官之職位或階級。

***ser·geant** [ˈsɑrdʒənt; ˈsɑ:dʒənt] *n.*①(陸軍)中士;(空軍)下士。②(警察)警官。③(S-)〖美〗地對地單節飛彈。

sergeant at arms(議會、法院等的)衛士。

sergeant first class 陸軍上士。

sergeant major 軍士長;士官長。

ser·geant·ship [ˈsɑrdʒəntˌʃɪp; ˈsɑ:dʒənt-ʃip] *n.* 士官之職務、地位或階級。

se·ri·al [ˈsɪrɪəl; ˈsiəriəl] *n.* ①連載小說;連續性的廣播或電視等。②(報紙以外之)定期刊物。—*adj.* ①連載的。②連續刊行物的;連續廣播的。③連續的;排成系列的。

se·ri·al·ize [ˈsɪrɪəlˌaɪz; ˈsiəriəlaiz] *v.t.,* **-ized, -iz·ing.** 連續刊載;連載。

se·ri·al·ly [ˈsɪrɪəlɪ; ˈsiəriəli] *adv.* 逐次地;連續地;連續刊載地。

serial number ①依次編列的號碼。②人員或物品之編號(如軍籍號碼等)。

se·ri·ate [*adj.* ˈsɪrɪɪt; ˈsiəriit *v.* ˈsɪrɪˌet; ˈsiərieit] *adj., v.,* **-at·ed, -at·ing.** —*adj.* 連續的。—*v.t.* 按順序排列。

se·ri·a·tim [ˌsɪrɪˈetɪm; ˌsiəriˈeitim] 〖拉〗 *adv.* 順次地; 連續地;逐一地。

se·ri·ceous [sɪˈrɪʃəs; siəˈriʃəs] *adj.*①絲狀的; 似絲的。②〖植物〗有絲狀柔毛的。

ser·i·cul·tur·al [ˌsɛrɪˈkʌltʃərəl; ˌseriˈkʌltʃurəl] *adj.* 養蠶的。(亦作**sericicultural**)

ser·i·cul·ture [ˈsɛrɪˌkʌltʃɚ; ˈseriˌkʌltʃə] *n.* 養蠶(業)。(亦作 **sericiculture**)

ser·i·cul·tur·ist [ˌsɛrɪˈkʌltʃərɪst; ˌseriˈkʌltʃərist] *n.* 養蠶者。(亦作 **sericiculturist**)

‡**se·ries** [ˈsɪrɪz; ˈsiəri:z] *n., pl.* **-ries,** *adj.* —*n.* ①連續; 系列。a *series* of victories. 一連串的勝利。②級數。arithmetical *series.* 算術級數。③〖電〗串聯。④叢書。⑤一套(如硬幣,郵票等)。⑥由同隊比賽的一連串競賽(常作爲一個單位)。***in series*** 連續地;順序地。—*adj.* 〖電〗串聯的。

se·ries-wound [ˈsɪrɪzˌwaund; ˈsiəri:zwaund] *adj.* 〖電〗串聯的。

ser·if [ˈsɛrɪf; ˈserif] *n.* 〖印刷〗襯線(特指附加字母上做裝飾之細線)。

se·ri·graph [ˈsɛrəˌgræf; ˈserəgrɑ:f] *n.* 綢網彩色印刷。—**y,** *n.*

se·ri·o·com·ic [ˌsɪrɪoˈkɑmɪk; ˈsiəriouˈkɔmik] *adj.* 半嚴肅半詼諧的。

‡**se·ri·ous** [ˈsɪrɪəs; ˈsiəriəs, ˈsjə:r-] *adj.* ①莊重的;嚴肅的。I want to have a *serious* talk with you. 我要同你作一次鄭重的談話。②認眞的;非開玩笑的。Are you really *serious* when you say you'll help me? 你說你要幫助我,這是眞話嗎? ③重要的;需加考慮的。④危險的;嚴重的。a *serious* injury. 重傷。—*n.* 重要,嚴肅,或嚴重的事物。—**ly,** *adv.* —**ness,** *n.*

se·ri·ous-mind·ed[ˈsɪrɪəsˈmaɪndɪd; ˈsiəriəsˈmaindid] *adj.* 熱誠的;認眞的。

ser·jeant [ˈsɑrdʒənt; ˈsɑ:dʒənt] *n.*

〖英〗=**sergeant.**

***ser·mon**〔ˈsɝmən; ˈsəːmən〕*n.* ①說教;講道。Ministers preach *sermons* in church. 牧師們在教堂中布道。②訓誡。③使人厭煩的長篇演講。

ser·mon·ic〔səˈmɑnɪk; səːˈmɔnik〕*adj.* 講道的;訓誡的。(亦作 **sermonical**)

ser·mon·ize〔ˈsɝmən,aɪz; ˈsəːmənaiz〕*v.i.*, **-ized, -iz·ing.** 說教;布道;訓誡。

Sermon on the Mount(耶穌之)登山訓衆(見馬太5–7章;路加6:20–49)。

se·rol·o·gy〔sɪˈrɑlədʒɪ; siəˈrɔlədʒi〕*n.* 血清學。—**se·ro·log·i·cal,** *adj.*

se·ros·i·ty〔sɪˈrɑsətɪ; siəˈrɔsiti〕*n., pl.* **-ties.** ①〖生理〗漿液。②漿液狀;漿液性。

se·rot·i·nous〔sɪˈrɑtɪnəs; siəˈrɔtinəs〕*adj.* 〖植物〗晚生的;晚開花的。

se·rous〔ˈsɪrəs; ˈsiərəs〕*adj.* ①漿液的;漿液性的;漿液狀的;生漿液的。②稀薄的;似水的。

Ser·pens〔ˈsɝpɛnz; ˈsəːpenz〕*n.* 〖天文〗巨蛇座。

***ser·pent**〔ˈsɝpənt; ˈsəːpənt〕*n.* ①蛇。②狡猾的人。③(S–) 巨蛇座。④魔鬼;撒旦。⑤作蛇行的烟火。⑥一種蛇形的舊木管樂器。

ser·pent-charm·er〔ˈsɝpənt,tʃɑrmɚ; ˈsəːpənt,tʃɑːmə〕*n.*(尤指吹笛)弄蛇者。

ser·pen·tine〔ˈsɝpən,tin; ˈsəːpəntain〕*adj.* ①蛇的;似蛇的。②繞曲的;蜿蜒的。③狡猾的。—*n.* 〖礦〗蛇紋石。—*v.i.* & *v.t.* (如蛇)繞曲;蜿蜒。

ser·pent's-tongue〔ˈsɝpənts,tʌŋ; ˈsəːpəntstʌŋ〕*n.* ①〖植物〗瓶兒草。②雙尖短刀。

ser·rate〔ˈsɛrɪt; ˈserit〕*adj., v.,* **-rat·ed, -rat·ing.** —*adj.* 〖生物〗鋸齒狀的;有鋸齒的。—*v.t.* 加鋸齒;使有鋸齒。

ser·rat·ed〔ˈsɛretɪd; seˈreitid〕*adj.* =**serrate.**

ser·ra·tion〔sɛˈreʃən; seˈreiʃən〕*n.* 鋸齒狀;鋸齒狀突起。

ser·ried〔ˈsɛrɪd; ˈserid〕*adj.* 擁擠的;密集的;林立的。

ser·ru·late〔ˈsɛrjʊ,let; ˈseruleit〕*adj.* 小鋸齒狀的。(亦作 **serrulated**)

se·rum〔ˈsɪrəm; ˈsiərəm〕*n., pl.* **-rums, -ra**〔-rə; -rə〕. ①血漿;漿液。②血清。③乳漿。—**al,** *adj.*

ser·val〔ˈsɝvəl; ˈsəːvəl〕*n.* 〖動物〗非洲產的一種野貓。

‡serv·ant〔ˈsɝvənt; ˈsəːvənt〕*n.* ①僕人;服務者。A priest is a *servant* of God. 牧師爲上帝之忠僕。②有用的東西。③公務員。***a civil*** (or ***public***) ***servant*** 文官;公僕。

servant girl (or **maid**) 女僕。

‡serve〔sɝv; səːv〕*v.,* **served, serv·ing,** *n.* —*v.t.* ①服務;服役。She *served* the family faithfully for many years. 她在這家忠實服務多年。②供應;侍候(顧客)。There was no one in the shop to *serve* me. 店鋪裏沒有人來接待我。③備置(餐食);開(飯);上(菜)。The waiter *served* the soup. 侍者上湯。④適合;達。It will *serve* my purpose. 此物適我之用。⑤對待;待遇。He *served* me shamefully.他對待我極壞。⑥度過(=pass, spend);奉(職);服(刑)。to *serve* a term in prison. 服有期徒刑。⑦送達。⑧(網球)發球。to *serve* a ball. 發球。⑨使用(鎗砲等)。⑩貢獻。to *serve* a cause. 獻身於某主義。⑪滿足(慾望,需要等)。⑫(雄性動物)與(雌性動物)交配。—*v.i.* ①服務;服役。He *serves* in the navy. 他在海軍服役。②侍候。③使人滿意;利於;合適。④可作…用〖as, for〗. A worm will *serve* as bait. 蟲可作餌用。⑤發球。to *serve* well. 球發得好。⑥彌撒時充任輔祭。***serve a person a trick*** (or ***serve a trick on someone***) 欺詐某人。***serve one right*** 活該;得到應受之處罰。***serve out*** 處罰。***serve time*** 服刑。—*n.* 發球。Whose *serve* is it? 該誰發球?

serv·er〔ˈsɝvɚ; ˈsəːvə〕*n.* ①服務者;服役者。②盤;盆。③大調羹,叉子等用以將食物分到小盤者。④輔祭(彌撒時神父的助手)。⑤(網球等的)發球人

Ser·vi·a〔ˈsɝvɪə; ˈsəːvjə〕*n.* =**Serbia.**

‡serv·ice〔ˈsɝvɪs; ˈsəːvis〕*n., v.,* **-iced, -ic·ing,** *adj.* —*n.* ①服務。The food was good but the *service* was bad. 食物很好, 但服務不周。②僕人的職業;雇傭。③公職;公職之部門或其全體人員。military *service*. 兵役;軍役。④陸軍或海軍。We entered the *service* together. 我們一起去服役。⑤陸海軍中的任務。⑥助益;貢獻。His *services* to the country were immense. 他對國家的貢獻非常大。⑦幫助;照顧。Do you need the *services* of a doctor? 你需要醫生的照顧嗎?⑧上菜;所上之菜。⑨一套碟子。a silver tea *service*. 一套銀質茶具。⑩(網球中) 發球。His *service* is weak. 他發球無力。⑪(傳票等的)送達。⑫(車,船等之)交通服務。⑬禮拜式;儀式。We attend church *services* twice a week. 我們每星期去教堂做兩次禮拜。⑭公用事業(如水,電,瓦斯等)之供應。⑮服務業;服務公司。a television repair *service*. 電視修理公司。⑯裝彈及發射大砲。⑰禮拜式中歌唱的配樂。⑱雄性動物與雌性動物交配。***at someone's service*** 隨時提供服務。***be of service*** 能幫助的;有用的。***do somebody a service*** 對某人幫忙。—*v.t.* ①使…適於使用;修理。The mechanic *serviced* our automobile. 機械師把我們的汽車修好了。②提供服務或消息等。③(雄性動物)與雌性交配。—*adj.* ①服務的;有用的。②僕傭的。③服務業的。④修理服務的。⑤〖軍〗後勤的。

serv·ice·a·ble〔ˈsɝvɪsəbḷ; ˈsəːvisəbl〕*adj.* ①有用的;適用的。②耐用的。—**serv·ice·a·bly,** *adv.*

service book 祈禱書;禮拜儀式書。

service cap 〖軍〗軍帽。

service charge 服務費。

service club ①以服務公衆及以會員福利爲目的之組織。②軍人俱樂部。

service court (網球場之)發球區。

serv·ice-dress〔ˈsɝvɪs,drɛs; ˈsəːvisdres〕*n.* 軍服。

service elevator 員工或送貨人使用之電梯。

service entrance 傭人或送貨人使用之門。

service line ①〖電機〗用戶進線。②(網球場之)發球線。

serv·ice·man〔ˈsɝvɪs,mæn; ˈsəːvismæn〕*n., pl.* **-men.** ①軍人。②修理員。(亦作 **service-man, service man**)

service pipe (自來水、煤氣等之)輸送管。

service station ①汽油站。②供應或修理電機零件之服務站。

service tree 〖植物〗花楸樹。

ser·vi·ette〔,sɝvɪˈɛt; ,səːviˈet〕〖法〗*n.* 餐桌用之拭巾;餐巾。

ser·vile〔ˈsɝvḷ; ˈsəːvail〕*adj.* ①奴隸的。②奴隸性的;卑屈的〖常 to〗。③(藝術作品等)徹底模倣的;無創作性的。④僕人的。

ser·vil·i·ty〔səˈvɪlətɪ; səːˈviliti〕*n.* 卑躬屈節;奴隸性。

ser·vi·tor〔ˈsɝvətɚ; ˈsəːvitə〕*n.* 〖詩〗從者;僕從。

ser·vi·tude ['sɝvə,tjud; 'sə:vitju:d] *n.* ①奴役;苦役。②〖法律〗可處分另外一人財產之權利。

ser·vo·con·trol ['sɝvəkən'trol; 'sə:voukən'troul] *n.* ①=**servo mechanism.** ②=**servomotor.**

ser·vo mechanism ['sɝvə~; 'sə:və~] ①補助動力裝置;自動控制裝置。②〖航空〗自動駕駛裝置。

ser·vo·mo·tor ['sɝvə,motɚ; 'sə:və,moutə] *n.* 補助發電機。

ses·a·me ['sɛsəmɪ; 'sesəmi] *n.* ①〖植物〗芝蔴。②(通常作 Open sesame! 係"天方夜譚"中叫開盜穴大門的咒語)獲取通過或進入(關口)之口令等。③克服困難之簡易方法。

ses·a·moid ['sɛsə,mɔɪd; 'sesəmɔid] *adj.* 〖解剖〗芝蔴實狀的;種子狀的。—*n.* 〖解剖〗種子骨;種子軟骨;滑骨。

ses·qui·cen·ten·ni·al [,sɛskwɪsɛn'tɛnɪəl; ,seskwisen'teniəl] *adj.* 一百五十年的。—*n.* 一百五十周年紀念。

ses·qui·pe·da·li·an [,sɛskwɪpə'delɪən; 'seskwipi'deiljən] *adj.* ①一英尺半長的。②〖諧〗非常長的(話語)。③長語的;好用長語的。—*n.* ①一英尺半長的人;矮小的人;侏儒。②長單語;長字。

sess [sɛs; ses] *n.* =**cess.**

ses·sile ['sɛsḷ; 'sesail] *adj.* ①〖植物〗無柄的。②〖動物〗固着的;不能自由走動的。

***ses·sion** ['sɛʃən; 'seʃən] *n.* ①(議會等之)開會;(法庭之)開庭。The court is now in *session.* 法庭現正開庭。②開會期;開庭期。③學期。④一日內連續授課的時間。morning (afternoon) *session.* 上(下)午授課時間。⑤(*pl.*)〖英法律〗法官開庭。⑥一羣人為某一目的而約集一處的時間。⑦長老會的地區性管理機構。—**al,** *adj.*

ses·tet [sɛs'tɛt; ses'tet] *n.* ①〖音樂〗六重奏;六部合唱。②〖詩〗任何六行的一節詩(尤指義大利型十四行詩之最後六行)。

ses·ti·na [sɛs'tinə; ses'ti:nə] *n., pl.* **-ti·nas, -ti·ne** [-'tinɪ; -'ti:ni]. 〖詩〗六節詩。(亦作 **sextain**)

:set [sɛt; set] *v.,* **set, set·ting,** *adj., n., interj.* —*v.t.* ①置;放。She *set* food and drink before the travelers. 她把食物飲料放在旅客面前。②調整。The doctor will *set* the broken bone. 醫生將把斷骨接合。③對準。to *set* a clock. 將鐘對準。④致;使。⑤指定;規定。to *set* a limit. 定一限度。⑥使從事。He *set* the men to chop wood. 他讓那些人去伐木。⑦種;植。to *set* a tree. 植樹。⑧使(母鷄)孵蛋。⑨使移動。to *set* a pen to paper. 開始寫字。⑩裝起;裝好。⑪鑲嵌(寶石)於。⑫釋放。He *set* the prisoners free. 他釋放了囚犯。⑬使(植物)結果實。⑭為(詩,詞)做樂譜;改寫(樂曲)。⑮〖印刷〗排(鉛字)。⑯捲(頭髮)。⑰致力於;專心於。to *set* one's mind to a task. 專心於一工作。⑱使坐下。⑲(獵狗)以鼻指着(獵物)以指示其位置。⑳〖戲劇〗安排舞臺道具、布景。㉑蓋(印)。The king *set* his seal to the decree. 國王將璽印在敕令上。㉒磨(刀)。㉓使凝固;使變硬。㉔煽動攻擊;使生敵意。They *set* his friends against him. 他們使他的朋友反對他。㉕使朝某一方向。to *set* one's feet homeward. 朝回家的方向走。㉖使(顏色)固着。㉗使緊〖常up〗。—*v.i.* ①固定;凝固。②沉落;沒入。The sun rises in the east and *sets* in the west. 日出於東而沒於西。③流向;傾向。The current *sets* to the east. 水向東流。④(母鷄)孵卵。⑤適合。That coat *sets* well. 那件外套非常合身。⑥(獵犬以某種姿勢)指示獵物所在。⑦開始活動。to *set* to work. 開始工作。⑧(花)結成實。⑨固定;變爲僵硬;變爲無情。His face *set.* 他面部無情。⑩(頭髮)捲。⑪攻擊。⑫開始工作。⑬(顏色)固着。***set about*** a. 着手。b. 散布。to *set* a rumor *about.* 散布謠言。c. 攻打。***set afloat*** a. 使下水。b. 發動;使動。***set against*** a. 使猜忌;使反對。b. 對比;襯托。***set apart*** a. 撥出;劃歸某種用途。b. 使特殊;使受到注意。***set aside*** a. 提出;保留。b. 忽視;不注意。c. 拒絕。d. 〖法律〗廢止;取消。***set at defiance*** 蔑視;反對。***set a thief to catch a thief*** 以賊捉賊;讓壞人懲治壞人。***set back*** a. 阻礙;妨礙。b. 撥慢。***set by*** 保留。***set down*** a. 放下;卸下。b. 使下車。c. 寫下;填入(表中)。d. 視爲;認爲。e. 歸之於;歸功於。f. 規定;制定。g. 挫銳氣;凌辱;使蒙羞。h. 降落。***set eyes on*** 看;望;注視。***set forth*** a. 宣布。b. 啓程;動身。***set forward*** a. 動身啓程。b. 宣布;事先公布。c. 將(鐘錶時間)撥快。***set free*** 釋放。***set in*** a. 開始。b. 向…前進;流向。c. 置於…中。***set off*** a. 出發。b. 使爆發;燃放。c. 襯托;使更爲美觀。d. 使開始做。e. 分開。***set on*** (or ***upon***) a. 前進。b. 攻擊。c. 煽動;鼓動。***set one's hand*** (***name, signature,*** or ***seal***) ***to a document*** 在一文件上簽名(或蓋印)。***set one's teeth*** 咬緊牙關;決心幹。***set*** (***a person***) ***on his feet*** 使能自立。***set out*** a. 出發。b. 裝飾;點綴。c. 發表。d. 種植。e. 打算;企圖。f. 設計;計劃。g. 解釋;描述。***set right*** a. 修理。b. 糾正。***set*** (or ***lay***) ***store by*** 敬重;珍視。***set the axe to*** a. 開始砍。b. 摧毀。***set the Thames on fire*** 做不平凡的事。***set things to rights*** a. 使一切有條不紊。b. 改革。***set to*** a. 開始積極地做。b. 開始打鬥。***set up*** a. 設立。b. 創立。c. 建立;開始。d. 使獲權;勝過。He was *set up* over his rivals. 他勝過了他的敵對者。e. 提議。f. 喊出。g. 供應;供給(常用被動式)。to be well *set up* with clothes. 被供以很多衣服。h. 訓練或發展身體;恢復健康與力量。Change will *set* her *up* again. 環境改變會使她恢復健康的。i. 排活字。j. 爲(病)的原因。k. 提高;晉陞。l. 宣稱;假裝。m.〖俚〗請客。n. 促成。o.〖俚〗刺激。—*adj.* ①確定的。at a *set* time. 在確定的時間。②固定的;不動的。③固執的;頑固的。a man *set* in his opinions. 固執己見之人。④決心的;決定的。He is *set* on going today. 他決心今天就走。⑤習慣的。***all set*** 〖俗〗準備就緒。***get set*** (對賽跑人之口令)預備! On your mark! *Get set!* Go! 就位!預備!跑!—*n.* ①套;組。a *set* of furniture. 一套傢具。②一班志趣相投的人。the smart *set.* 一羣時髦的人。③收受機。a television *set.* 電視機。④(戲劇中的)布景;大道具。⑤型式;形狀;姿勢;體態。⑥方向;趨向。the *set* of public opinion. 輿論之趨向。⑦轉;彎曲。a *set* to the right. 向右的轉彎。⑧鋪路用花崗石。⑨樹苗。⑩剛結成的小果實。⑪日落。⑫(網球等比賽中)一局。⑬(獵犬的)指示獵物。⑭(著作之)全集。⑮〖籃球〗長射。***make a dead set at*** a. 猛攻。b. 力謀影響;力謀獲得友誼、信仰等。—*interj.* (對賽跑人的口令)預備! Ready! *Set!* Go! 就位! 預備! 跑!

se·ta ['sitə; 'si:tə] *n., pl.* **-tae** [-ti; -ti:].

〔動、植物〕剛毛;棘毛。

se·ta·ceous [sɪˈteʃəs; siˈteiʃəs] *adj.* 似剛(棘)毛的。

set·back [ˈsɛtˌbæk; ˈsetbæk] *n.* ①挫折。②高樓外牆之逐漸縮入。

set·down [ˈsɛtˌdaun; ˈsetdaun] *n.* ①責罵;斥責;反駁。②(搭車的)一段路。

set-in [ˈsɛtˌɪn; ˈsetin] *n.* 開始;(尤指)潮之起漲(時間);雨、雪之開始降落。—*adj.* 附建在建築物上的;附連在某物上的。

set·off [ˈsɛtˌɔf; ˈsetˈɔːf] *n.* ①抵銷。②債務抵銷。③襯托裝飾物。④〔建築〕牆之突出部分。⑤(旅行之)出發。

se·ton [ˈsitn; ˈsiːtn] *n.* 〔醫〕①串線;排液線。②(揷排液線於皮下之)排液。

se·tose [ˈsitos; ˈsiːtous] *adj.* =**setaceous.**

set·out [ˈsɛtˌaut; setˈaut] *n.* 〔俗〕①一套器具。②開始;出發。③陳列。

set piece ①花式煙火。②戲院中可移動之個別立體布景。③有固定形式的文藝、音樂或藝術作品。④根據固定計畫而實施的軍事行動。

set scene 舞臺上之立體布景。

set·screw [ˈsɛtˌskru; ˈset-skruː] *n.* 締合螺釘;固定螺釘。

set-square [ˈsɛtˈskwɛr; ˈsetˈskwɛə] *n.* 三角板。(亦作 **set square**)

set·tee [sɛˈti; seˈtiː] *n.* ①有靠背及扶手之長椅。②中型沙發。③一種三角帆船。

set·ter [ˈsɛtɚ; ˈsetə] *n.* ①安放者;排字者;鑲嵌者。②一種長毛獵狗。

***set·ting** [ˈsɛtɪŋ; ˈsetiŋ] *n.* ①置放;裝置。②環境;背景等。③鑲嵌(寶石等)之框子。④(戲劇的)景;布景。with a sea *setting*. 以海爲背景。⑤〔音樂〕爲歌詞所配之音樂。⑥(母鷄正在孵的)蛋的集合稱。⑦(日、月之)沉落。the *setting* of the sun. 落日。⑧凝固;硬化。⑨安置機器用之架、床等,如鉋床。⑩一套餐具。⑪小說、戲劇等故事之背景。

setting rule 〔印刷〕排字規則。

‡**set·tle**[1] [ˈsɛtl̩; ˈsetl] *v.*, **-tled, -tling.** —*v.t.* ①決定;解決。The affair is now satisfactorily *settled*. 此事現在圓滿解決了。②安排;弄妥當;弄淸楚。③淸算;淸償。The account is not yet *settled*. 此帳尙未付淸。④安頓;使定居。We are *settled* in our new home. 我們住入新居。⑤使沈;使降。The rain *settled* the dust. 雨使灰塵平息。⑥鎭定。A vacation will *settle* your nerves. 休假可以鎭定你的神經。⑦殖民(某地)。⑧使堅固;使堅實。⑨贈予。⑩〔法律〕和解。⑪使緊密。⑫調整。—*v.i.* ①決定;確定。Have you *settled* on a time for leaving? 你已決定離去的時間否?②安居;居住。He *settled* in America. 他定居美國。③僑居;殖民。④安身。He is *settling* down to his new job. 他漸漸安於並且熟習他的新工作。⑤平靜;鎭靜。⑥澄淸;沉澱。⑦下陷;陷落。The road bed *settled*. 路基塌陷。⑧償付;淸算。He won't *settle* without court action. 不經法庭訴訟他不肯償付。⑨棲息。⑩和解。⑪(雌性動物)懷胎。***settle down*** **a.** 定居;定操某業。When I *settle down*, I shall invite you to our house. 等我住定的時候,我將請你到我們家來。**b.** 恢復鎭靜。**c.** 認眞做事。***settle in*** 遷入(新居)。***settle on*** (or ***upon***) 決定。

set·tle[2] *n.* 有背的長櫈。

***set·tled** [ˈsɛtl̩d; ˈsetld] *adj.* ①一定的;固定的;確立的。a *settled* habit. 固定的習慣。②深切的。③決定的;解決的。④(天氣晴朗)不變的。a *settled* weather. 晴朗的天氣。⑤淸償的;付淸的。

‡**set·tle·ment** [ˈsɛtl̩mənt; ˈsetlmənt] *n.* ①解決。to reach a *settlement*. 獲得解決。②和解。*settlement* of a dispute. 紛爭之和解。③整理;淸理;安排。④淸償;淸算。*settlement* of debt. 淸償欠債。⑤決定。*settlement* of a date. 日期之決定。⑥殖民地。⑦殖民。⑧居留地。⑨產業的贈予。⑩產業贈予之數目。⑪社會福利實施區;社會改革示範區。⑫〔英〕**a.** 法定居留。**b.** 貧民對政府機關要求救濟的權利。⑬建築物之下陷。⑭(*pl.*)建築物下陷所造成之裂隙或其他損害。

***set·tler** [ˈsɛtlɚ; ˈsetlə] *n.* ①居留者;定居者。②移住者;殖民者。The first white *settlers* came to New York from Holland in 1626. 第一批來到紐約的白種移民於1626年來自荷蘭。③贈予者。④調停者。

set·tling [ˈsɛtlɪŋ; ˈsetliŋ] *n.* ①固定。②移住;殖民;居留。③決定;解決。④和解。⑤鎭靜。⑥沉澱。⑦(*pl.*)沉澱物;沉渣。

settling day 決算日;結帳日。

set-to [ˈsɛtˌtu; ˈsetˈtuː] *n.*, *pl.* **-tos.** 〔俗〕①爭鬥;爭論。②競爭;比賽。

set·up [ˈsɛtˌʌp; ˈsetʌp] *n.* ①組織;結構;機械裝置。②體格;身體之構造(=physique)。③〔美俗〕身體之姿態;舉止。④冰、蘇打水、酒杯等飲酒所需的東西。⑤〔美俚〕**a.** 故意使雙方實力懸殊之比賽。**b.** 易打敗的對手。⑥容易做的事。⑦爲某事而準備,安排的工具。⑧計畫。

‡**sev·en** [ˈsɛvən; ˈsevn] *adj.* 七;七個。to be frightened out of one's *seven* senses. 嚇得魂不附體。—*n.* 七;七個。in *sevens*. 七個一組的;七人成羣的。***at sixes and sevens*** 亂七八糟。

seven deadly sins 七大罪(卽pride, covetousness, lust, anger, gluttony, envy, sloth, 犯此等罪者卽入地獄)。

sev·en·fold [ˈsɛvənˈfold; ˈsevnfould] *adj.* 七倍的;七重的。—*adv.* 七倍地;七重地。

Seven Hills 羅馬七丘(羅馬城卽建於其上及其周圍)。

seven seas 七大洋(卽北冰洋、南冰洋、北大西洋、南大西洋、北太平洋、南太平洋及印度洋);世界之全部海洋。

‡**sev·en·teen** [ˌsɛvənˈtin; ˈsevnˈtiːn] *n.* 十七;十七個;17。sweet *seventeen*. 妙齡十七。—*adj.* 十七的。

***sev·en·teenth** [ˌsɛvənˈtinθ; ˈsevnˈtiːnθ] *adj.* ①第十七的。②十七分之一的。—*n.* ①第十七個。②十七分之一。

seventeen-year locust 〔動物〕(美國產的)十七年蟬。

‡**sev·enth** [ˈsɛvənθ; ˈsevnθ] *adj.* ①第七的。②七分之一的。—*n.* ①第七。②七分之一。—**ly,** *adv.*

sev·enth-day [ˈsɛvənθˌde; ˈsevnθˈdei] *adj.* 守星期六爲安息日的。(亦作 **Seventh-Day**)

seventh heaven ①七重天(天之最高處)。②極樂;極樂世界。

***sev·en·ti·eth** [ˈsɛvəntɪɪθ; ˈsevntiiθ] *adj.* ①第七十的。②七十分之一的。—*n.* ①第七十。②七十分之一。

‡**sev·en·ty** [ˈsɛvəntɪ; ˈsevnti] *n.*, *pl.* **-ties,** *adj.* —*n.* 七十;七十個;70。***seventies*** 70到79之數;七十年代。—*adj.* 七十的。

sev·en-up [ˈsɛvənˈʌp; ˈsevnˈʌp] *n.* 一種紙牌戲。

Seven Wonders of the World 古代世界七大奇觀,卽:1. 埃及的

金字塔。2. Artemisia 在 Halicarnassus 建的墳墓。3. 在 Ephesus 的 Artemis 廟。4. 巴比倫的空中花園。5. Rhodes 的巨像。6. 奧林匹亞的 Zeus 雕像。7. 亞歷山大港的燈塔。

Seven Years' War 七年戰爭(1756–63, 英國與普魯士聯盟戰勝法、奧、俄等國)。

***sev·er** [ˈsɛvɚ; ˈsevə] *v.t.* ①切斷。 to *sever* a rope with a knife. 用刀割斷繩子。②斷絕; 終止。 to *sever* friendship. (與朋友)絕交。③〖法律〗分割(產業等)。④區別。 —*v.i.* ①分裂。 The church *severed* into two factions. 教會分裂爲二派。②斷。

‡sev·er·al [ˈsɛvərəl; ˈsevrəl] *adj.* ①幾個;數個。 *Several* people went out. 有幾個人出去了。②個別的; 各個的; 單獨的。 on three *several* occasions. 在三個不同的時機。③〖法律〗有連帶責任的。 —*pron.* 數個; 數人。*Several* have given their consent. 有幾個人已經同意。

sev·er·al·fold [ˈsɛvərəlˌfold; ˈsevrəlfould] *adv. & adj.* 好幾倍地(的)。

sev·er·al·ly [ˈsɛvərəlɪ; ˈsevrəli] *adv.* 分別地;個別地;各個地。

sev·er·al·ty [ˈsɛvrəltɪ; ˈsevrəlti] *n., pl.* **-ties.** ①各自;各個。②(土地的) 單獨租用;單獨所有。

sev·er·ance [ˈsɛvərəns; ˈsevərəns] *n.* 隔斷;分離;斷絕。

severance pay 離職金;遣散費。

***se·vere** [səˈvɪr; siˈviə, səˈv-] *adj.*, **-ver·er, -ver·est.** ①嚴厲的; 苛刻的。a *severe* punishment. 嚴厲的懲罰。②嚴重的。 His illness was a *severe* one. 他的病很嚴重。③劇烈的; 酷烈的。 *severe* cold. 嚴寒。④樸素的; 無飾的。⑤困難的; 艱難的; 嚴格的。⑥條理分明的; 精確的。 *severe* reasoning. 精確的推理。—**ness,** *n.*

se·vere·ly** [səˈvɪrlɪ; siˈviəli, səˈv-] *adv.* ①劇烈地; 酷烈地; 嚴重地。 He is *severely* wounded. 他負重傷。②嚴厲地; 嚴格地。 ***leave (or ***let***) (***a person*** or ***a thing***) ***severely alone*** 故意躲避 (某人或某物);對(某人或某物)敬而遠之。

***se·ver·i·ty** [səˈvɛrətɪ; siˈveriti, səˈv-] *n., pl.* **-ties.** ①嚴厲;苛刻。②嚴重。③劇烈;酷烈。 the *severity* of pain. 疼痛的劇烈。④正確; 精確。⑤樸素; 樸實。 the *severity* of a nun's dress. 修女服裝之樸質無華。⑥(*pl.*) 嚴苛的對待。

Sè·vres [ˈsɛvrə; seivr] *n.* ①塞弗爾(法國巴黎附近之一城市)。②該地出產之昂貴瓷器。

sew** [so; sou] *v.t. & v.i.,* **sewed, sewed** or **sewn, sew·ing.** 縫合;縫紉。 You can *sew* by hand or with a machine. 你可以用手縫或用機器縫。 ***sew up **a.** 〖俗〗壟斷;控制。**b.** 縫合。**c.** 〖俚〗成功地完成(協商、合約等)。**d.** 使確定。

sew·age [ˈsjuɪdʒ; ˈsjuːidʒ] *n.* 下水道中之汚物。(亦作 **sewerage**)

sewage farm 汚物處理場。

***sew·er**[1] [ˈsoɚ; ˈsouə] *n.* 從事於縫製的人或工具。

sew·er[2] [ˈsjuɚ; ˈsjuə] *n.* 陰溝;下水道。

sew·er[3] *n.* 昔日負責侍膳之家僕。

sew·er·age [ˈsjuəɪdʒ; ˈsjuːəridʒ] *n.* ①下水道設備; 下水道系統。②下水道排水或汚物。③下水道中的汚物 (=sewage).

***sew·ing** [ˈsoɪŋ; ˈsouiŋ, ˈsoiŋ] *n.* ①縫紉。②縫物。 —*adj.* 縫紉用的。

sewing circle 定期集會爲教會或慈善事業從事縫紉的婦女會。

sewing machine 縫紉機。

sewn [son; soun] *v.* pp. of **sew.**

sex** [sɛks; seks] *n.* ①性;性別。 female *sex.* 女性。 male *sex.* 男性。 both *sexes.* 兩性;男女。②性特徵。③性之吸引力。④性交。 ***have sex 〖俗〗性交。 ***the fair*** (***gentle, softer*** or ***weaker***) ***sex*** 女性。 ***the sex*** 女性。 ***the sterner*** (***stronger***) ***sex*** 男性。 —*v.t.* 判斷 (小鷄等之) 性別。 ***sex it up*** 〖俚〗 兩性間熱情的愛撫。 ***sex up*** 〖俗〗 **a.** 勾引;吸引。**b.** 增加吸引力;使更刺激。—*adj.* 性的;與性有關的。

sex- 〖字首〗表"六"之義。如 sexennial (六年的;六年一次的)。(亦作 **sexi-**)

sex·a·ge·nar·i·an [ˌsɛksədʒəˈnɛrɪən; ˌseksədʒiˈnɛəriən] *n.* 六十歲或六十至七十歲間之人。—*adj.* 六十歲或六十至七十歲間的。

sex·ag·e·nar·y [sɛksˈædʒɪˌnɛrɪ; seksˈædʒinəri] *adj.* ①六十的。 the *sexagenary* cycle. 六十年之周期。②=**sexagenarian.** —*n.* =**sexagenarian.**

Sex·a·ges·i·ma [ˌsɛksəˈdʒɛsəmə; ˌseksəˈdʒesimə] *n.* 四旬節 (Lent) 前之第二個星期日。(亦作 **Sexagesima Sunday**)

sex·a·ges·i·mal [ˌsɛksəˈdʒɛsəml; ˌseksəˈdʒesiml] *adj.* 六十的;六十進位的。 —*n.* 〖數學〗六十分數(卽以60爲分母之分數)。

sex appeal 性感。

sex·cen·te·nar·y [sɛksˈsɛntɪˌnɛrɪ; seksˈsentinəri] *adj., n., pl.* **-nar·ies.** —*adj.* 六百年的。—*n.* 六百周年紀念。

sex chromosome 〖生物〗性染色體。

sex·en·ni·al [sɛksˈɛnɪəl; seksˈeniəl] *adj.* 六年間的; 六年一度的; 連續六年的。 —*n.* 六周年紀念。

sex·foil [ˈsɛksˌfɔɪl; ˈseksfɔil] *n.* 〖建〗「築〗六葉飾。

sex hormone 〖生化〗性激素。

sexi- 〖字首〗表"六"之義 (sex- 之異體)。

sex·il·lion [sɛksˈɪljən; seksˈiljən] *n.* =**sextillion.**

sex·ism [ˈsɛksɪzəm; ˈseksizəm] *n.* 性別歧視 (在商業、政治、藝術等領域對女性之歧視)。

sex·ist [ˈsɛksɪst; ˈseksist] *n.* 歧視女「性的人。

sex·less [ˈsɛkslɪs; ˈsekslis] *adj.* ①無性的;中性的。②性慾冷淡的。③無性感的。

sex·ol·o·gy [sɛksˈɑlədʒɪ; seksˈɔlədʒi] *n.* 性行爲學。

sex·par·tite [sɛksˈpɑrtaɪt; seksˈpɑː-tait] *adj.* 分爲六部分的; 由六部分構成的。

sex pot 富於性感的人;肉彈。

sext [sɛkst; sekst] *n.* ①〖宗教〗第六時禱告 (卽正午的禱告);其儀式。②〖音樂〗第六度音程。

sex·tain [ˈsɛksten; ˈsekstein] *n.* 〖詩〗「六行之詩節。

sex·tan [ˈsɛkstən; ˈsekstən] *adj.* 每六日發生一次的。—*n.* 〖醫〗六日熱 (=sextan fever).

Sex·tans [ˈsɛkstənz; ˈsekstənz] *n., gen.* **Sex·tan·tis** [sɛksˈtæntɪs; seksˈtæntis]. 〖天文〗六分儀座。

Sex·tant [ˈsɛkstənt; ˈsekstənt] *n.* ①〖天文〗六分儀座(=Sextans). ②(s-)六分儀。

sex·tet, sex·tette [sɛksˈtɛt; seksˈtet] *n.* ①六重唱曲;六重奏曲。②合唱或合奏之六人。③六人或六物之一組。(亦作 **sestet**)

sex·til·lion [sɛksˈtɪljən; seksˈtiljən] *n., adj.* (英德兩國) 10^{36} (的); (美法兩國) 10^{24} (的)。

sex·to [ˈsɛksto; ˈsekstou] *n., pl.* **-tos.** 「六折本;六開本。

sex·to·dec·i·mo [ˌsɛkstoˈdɛsɪˌmo; ˈsekstouˈdesimou] *n., pl.* **-mos,** *adj.* —*n.* 十六折本;十六開本。—*adj.* 十六開本的。

sex·ton [ˈsɛkstən; ˈsekstən] *n.* 教堂司事。

sex·tu·ple [ˈsɛkstjupl̩; ˈsekstjupl] *adj., v.,* **-pled, -pling.** —*adj.* ①六重的;六倍的;六部分組成的。②〖音樂〗六拍子的。—*v.t.* & *v.i.* 六倍之;增至六倍。

sex·tu·plet [ˈsɛkstuplɪt; seksˈtjuplit] *n.* ①六胞胎之一個。②以六組成之事物。

sex·u·al [ˈsɛkʃuəl; ˈseksjuəl] *adj.* ①性的;有雌雄分別的。*sexual* desire. 性慾。②兩性之間的。—**ly,** *adv.*

sexual intercourse 性交。

sex·u·al·i·ty [ˌsɛkʃuˈælətɪ; ˌseksjuˈæliti] *n.* ①性之具有;性之性質;有性。②對性方面之興趣或注意;性能力;性感。

sexual organs 性器官。

sexual reproduction 〖生物〗有性生殖。

sexual selection 〖生物〗雌雄淘汰(達爾文學說,兩性彼此吸引特徵的自然選擇)。

sex·y [ˈsɛksɪ; ˈseksi] *adj.,* **sex·i·er, sex·i·est.** 〖俚〗①性感的;涉及性的。②因加裝飾而更爲有趣的。

Sey·chelles [seˈʃɛl(z); seiˈʃel(z)] *n.* 塞席爾(西印度洋一島國,在 Madagascar 東北,首都維多利亞 Victoria).

SF, sf science fiction.

sf., sfz. sforzando.

sfer·ics [ˈsfɛrɪks; ˈsferiks] *n.* 〖氣象〗天電偵測。

sfor·zan·do [sforˈtsɑndo; sfɔːtˈsændou] 〖義〗 *adj.* & *adv.* 〖音樂〗加强的(地)。(亦作 **sforzato**)

s.g. specific gravity. **Sgt., sgt.** Sergeant. **sh.** ①share. ②sheet. ③shilling(s). ④〖裝訂〗 sheep. ⑤shunt.

***shab·by** [ˈʃæbɪ; ˈʃæbi] *adj.,* **-bi·er, -bi·est.** ①破舊的;襤褸的。He looks *shabby*. 他的樣子寒酸。②卑鄙的;卑劣的。a *shabby* trick. 卑鄙的把戲。③簡陋的;低劣的。—**shab·bi·ly,** *adv.* —**shab·bi·ness,** *n.*

shab·by-gen·teel [ˈʃæbɪdʒɛnˈtil; ˈʃæbidʒenˈtiːl] *adj.* 襤褸破敝而仍圖裝着高貴尊嚴的;窮擺架子的。

shack[1] [ʃæk; ʃæk] *n.* ①〖美〗簡陋的房屋;小木屋。②〖鐵路俚〗火車上控制煞車者(=brakeman)。③〖俗〗無線電收發室。—*v.i.* 多眠;蟄居;避寒。**shack up** 〖俚〗 **a.** 過夜。**b.** 同居。**c.** 畸戀。

shack[2] *v.t.* 〖俗〗追趕、撿拾並扔回;取回。

shack·le [ˈʃækl̩; ˈʃækl] *n., v.,* **-led, -ling.** —*n.* ①(*pl.*)桎梏;手銬;足鐐。②(*pl.*)束縛物;羈絆物。—*v.t.* ①加桎梏;加枷鎖。②束縛;羈絆。

shad [ʃæd; ʃæd] *n., pl.* **shad, shads.** 鯡魚。

shad·ber·ry [ˈʃædˌbɛrɪ; ˈʃædbəri] *n., pl.* **-ries.** 〖植物〗扶移屬植物;其果實。

shad·bush [ˈʃædˌbuʃ; ˈʃædbuʃ] *n.* 〖植物〗(美洲產之)扶移。

shad·dock [ˈʃædək; ˈʃædək] *n.* 〖植物〗朱欒;其果實。

‡**shade** [ʃed; ʃeid] *n., v.,* **shad·ed, shad·ing.** —*n.* ①蔭;陰。What a pleasant *shade* these trees give us! 這些樹供給我們多麼好的蔭涼!②蔭涼處。③(*pl.*)薄暗;闇黑。Little children are afraid to walk in the *shades* of night. 小孩怕在夜色闇黑中走路。④遮蔽光熱之物(幔、帷、簾、罩、陽傘等)。Pull down the *shades* of the windows. 把窗簾拉下來。⑤色度;顏色之深淺。all *shades* of blue. 各種色度的藍。⑥微末;少許。Your coat is a *shade* too long. 你的外衣稍微長了一點。⑦鬼魂;幽靈;陰間。⑧相片的陰影。⑨(*pl.*)〖俚〗太陽眼鏡。**cast** (or **put**) **someone in** (or **into**) **the shade** 使某人(物)相形失色。**in** (or **into**) **the shade** **a.** 在蔭暗中。**b.** 沒落;衰微。**the shades** **a.** 夜晚之黑暗。**b.** 地獄。**c.** 地獄居民。—*v.t.* ①遮蔽。②使暗。③微減。Can't you *shade* the price for me? 你不能把價錢減少些嗎? —*v.i.* 漸變;微現不同。This scarf *shades* from deep rose to pink. 這條圍巾漸漸從深玫瑰色變爲淡紅色。

shade·less [ˈʃedlɪs; ˈʃeidlis] *adj.* 無陰影的。

shad·i·ness [ˈʃedɪnɪs; ˈʃeidinis] *n.* 蔭蔽。

shad·ing [ˈʃedɪŋ; ˈʃeidiŋ] *n.* ①遮蔽。②(繪畫之)陰影;描影法;濃淡。③(顏色、種類、性質等之)細微的變化或差別。

‡**shad·ow** [ˈʃædo; ˈʃædou] *n.* ①影。the *shadow* of a man. 人影。②蔭;蔭暗。③黑暗;幽暗。a twilight *shadow*. 暮色蒼茫。④微末;少許。There is not a *shadow* of doubt. 毫無可疑之處。⑤模糊的影像。⑥庇護。under the *shadow* of the Almighty. 在神的庇護下。⑦憂愁;陰鬱。⑧祕密跟蹤他人的人。⑨經常在一起的伴侶。⑩憂愁寡歡之神色。⑪預兆。Coming events cast *shadows* before them. 事情發生,必有預兆。⑫沒落;微賤。to be content to live in the *shadow*. 甘願屈居於微賤之中。⑬幽靈;鬼;幻象。⑭籠罩的陰暗;陰暗的氣氛。⑮暫時的中斷。A *shadow* came over their friendship. 他們的友誼暫時中斷。**the shadows** 日落後之陰暗。—*v.t.* ①遮蔽;隱憂。The grass is *shadowed* by huge oaks. 草被巨大的橡樹所遮蔽。②投影於…上。③使憂鬱。④預示;預兆。⑤祕密尾隨。**shadow forth** 預示;預兆。**under** (or **in**) **the shadow of** 非常近;和…靠得很近。

shadow box 長方形淺玻璃箱(爲展覽及保護圖畫、貨幣、首飾等之用)。(亦作 **shadow box frame**)

shad·ow·box [ˈʃædoˌbɑks; ˈʃædoubɔks] *v.i.* ①與假想對手鬥拳。②避免積極或直接的決定。

shad·ow·box·ing [ˈʃædoˌbɑksɪŋ; ˈʃædouˌbɔksiŋ] *n.* 〖拳擊〗(練習時與假想對手之搏鬥,特指)太極拳。

shadow cabinet ①影子內閣(在野政黨計畫中之預備內閣)。②總統或首相之智囊團。

shadow factory 〖英〗戰時可轉變爲軍火生產之工廠。

shad·ow·graph [ˈʃædoˌɡræf; ˈʃædouɡrɑːf] *n.* ①將陰影投諸亮幕上所製之圖像。②放射線照相(=radiograph)。③=**shadow play.**

shad·ow·less [ˈʃædolɪs; ˈʃædoulis] *adj.* 無陰影的。

shadow play 影子戲。(亦作 **shadowgraph, shadow pantomime, shadow show, shadow theater**)

***shad·ow·y** [ˈʃædəwɪ; ˈʃædoui] *adj.* ①多蔭影的;鬱蒼的。*shadowy* woods. 鬱蒼之樹林。②朦朧的;模糊的。a *shadowy* excuse. 含糊的託辭。③鬼魂般的;非眞實的。—**shad·ow·i·ness,** *n.*

***shad·y** [ˈʃedɪ; ˈʃeidi] *adj.,* **shad·i·er, shad·i·est.** ①多蔭涼的;遮蔭的。a *shady* tree. 一棵遮蔭的樹。②在蔭處的;蔭蔽的。a *shady* path. 樹蔭小道。③陰黑的;不清楚的。④〖俗〗令人懷疑的;成問題的。He has engaged in rather *shady* occupations.

他從事於相當不明不白的職業。***keep shady*** 〖俚〗隱匿;躲藏。***on the shady side of*** 〖俚〗(年齡)大於。

SHAEF 〔ʃef; ʃeif〕 *S*upreme *H*eadquarters *A*llied *E*xpeditionary *F*orces. (二次世界大戰)盟軍最高指揮部。(亦作 **Shaef**)

***shaft** 〔ʃæft, ʃɑft; ʃɑːft〕 *n.* ①箭幹;矛柄。②箭;矛。 *shafts* of satire. 諷刺之箭。③(植物之)幹;莖;柄。④羽軸。⑤車杠;轅。⑥器械之柄。 the *shaft* of an axe. 斧柄。⑦煙突。⑧機械之軸。⑨〖礦〗豎坑。⑩光線。⑪柱;柱身。⑫旗桿。⑬井狀通道。 —*v.t.* 以桿推動。 to *shaft* a boat through a tunnel. 以桿推一小船通過隧道。

shaft horse 轅馬。

shaft·ing 〔'ʃæftɪŋ, 'ʃɑftɪŋ; 'ʃɑːftiŋ〕 *n.* 〖機械〗①軸系。②傳動軸。③做軸之材料。

shag[1] 〔ʃæg; ʃæg〕 *n., v.,* **shagged, shag·ging.** —*n.* ①粗毛;尨毛。②織物上的絨毛;表面有絨毛之織物。③一種切成細片的粗煙草。—*v.t.* ①使粗糙。②〖俚〗追捕犯人;追蹤。③〖棒球俚〗追趕撿拾並扔回。—*v.i.* 〖俚〗①散步。②立刻走開;離開。

shag[2] *n., v.,* **shagged, shag·ging.**—*n.*一種左右脚交互躍起之舞步。 —*v.i.* 跳此種舞。

shag·bark 〔'ʃæg,bɑrk; 'ʃægbaːk〕 *n.* 〖植物〗①一種粗皮胡桃樹。②此種樹所結的胡桃。③此種樹之木。

***shag·gy** 〔'ʃægɪ; 'ʃægi〕 *adj.,* **-gi·er, -gi·est.** ①多粗毛的; 毛髮蓬鬆的。a *shaggy* dog. 長毛狗。②長濃而粗的。*shaggy* eyebrows. 濃眉;粗眉。③表面粗糙的。—**shag·gi·ness,** *n.*

shaggy dog story ①冗長的敍述後有一個預料不到的結局的故事。②以一個會講話的動物,如狗爲主角的故事或笑話。

sha·green 〔ʃə'grin; ʃæ'griːn〕 *n.* ①鯊皮。②一種表面粗糙而有顆粒狀的生皮(通常呈綠色)。—*adj.* (亦作 **shagreened**) 用上述皮做的;蓋着上述之皮的。

shah 〔ʃɑ; ʃɑː〕 *n.*伊朗國王稱號。(亦作**Shah**)

shai·tan, shei·tan 〔ʃaɪ'tɑn; ʃai'tɑːn〕 *n.* ①(常 S-) 惡魔;魔王;撒旦。②〖俗〗惡人;壞人。③〖印度〗塵霾。

Shak., Shaks. Shakespeare.

‡shake 〔ʃek; ʃeik〕 *v.,* **shook** 〔ʃuk; ʃuk〕, **shak·en** 〔'ʃekən; 'ʃeikən〕, **shak·ing,** *n.* —*v.t.* ①搖動;搖撼;揮動;使震動。He *shook* the fruit down. 他將果實搖落。②動搖(信念、決心等)。His lie *shook* my faith in his honesty. 他的謊言動搖了我對於他爲人誠實的信心。③〖俚〗擺脫。Can't you *shake* him? 你不能擺脫開他嗎? ④(在手裏)搖動骰子。—*v.i.* ①抖動;震顫;戰慄。②擺動;搖曳。③動搖。His courage began to *shake*. 他的勇氣開始動搖。④搖動。*Shake* before using. 使用前搖一搖。***shake down*** **a.** 搖落。**b.** 使安居下來。**c.** 整理使有秩序。**d.** 〖俚〗敲詐(金錢)。**e.** 鋪(草等)於地板做床。**f.** 測驗。**g.** 〖俚〗搜査;搜(身)。***shake hands*** 握手。***shake in one's shoes*** 戰慄。***shake off*** **a.** 脫落。**b.** 擺脫。to *shake off* a bad companion. 擺脫一壞伴侶。***shake one's fist*** 揮拳威脅。***shake one's head at something*** (or ***somebody***) 對某事(或某人)搖頭(表示不以爲然,懷疑,躊躇或對某人某事不贊成之意)。***shake one's sides with laughter*** 捧腹大笑。***shake the dust from one's feet*** 憤然離開。***shake up*** **a.** 猛搖。**b.** 激起。**c.** 震動(身體,神經)。—*n.* ①搖動;震動。②(常*pl.*)戰慄。 We knew he'd get the *shakes* when he saw the enemy. 我們知道當他看到敵人時他會戰慄。③震驚。④搖動數種原料混合而成之飲料。 a milk *shake*. 雪果(冰淇淋牛奶攪合飲料)。⑤〖俗〗地震。⑥〖俚〗片刻。⑦樹上裂隙。⑧〖音樂〗顫音。⑨握手的行爲或方式。⑩命運;運氣。⑪地上的龜裂。⑫自扭扭舞變化出來的一種舞步。***a brace of shakes*** 片刻。 ***a fair shake*** 〖俚〗公平的安排;公平的待遇。***in half a shake*** 立刻。***in two shakes***=in half a shake. ***no great shakes*** 並無不平凡處。***two shakes of a lamb's tail***; ***two shakes*** 片刻。

shake·down 〔'ʃek,daun; 'ʃeik'daun〕 *n.* ①臨時的便床。②搖落。③整備。④敲詐;勒索。⑤徹底的尋找; 搜索。⑥新機或新船的試飛或試航;練習。—*adj.* (飛行或航行)爲使機(船)上人員熟悉新機(船)上各種新設備而擧行的。(亦作 **shake-down**)

shak·en 〔'ʃekən; 'ʃeikən〕 *v.* pp. of **shake.**

shake·out 〔'ʃek,aut; 'ʃeikaut〕 *n.* ①**a.** 輕度經濟衰落。**b.** (因競爭激烈或其他優良產品應市所導致的) 公司或產品之淘汰。②股票之暴跌。③=**shake-up**②.

shak·er 〔'ʃekɚ; 'ʃeikə〕 *n.* ①搖動者。②搖盪機; 搖盪器。③(有帶小孔之蓋的) 胡椒粉罐、鹽罐(等)。④(S-)(美國的)震盪教徒。⑤配混合飲料用的搖杯。

***Shake·speare** 〔'ʃek,spɪr; 'ʃeikspiə, -pjəː〕 *n.* 莎士比亞 (William, 1564–1616, 英國詩人, 劇作家)。 (亦作 **Shakspere, Shakespear**)

Shake·spear·i·an 〔ʃek'spɪrɪən; ʃeiks'piəriən〕 *adj.* 莎士比亞的;莎士比亞風格的;莎士比亞之著作的。—*n.* 研究莎士比亞之專家。

shake-up 〔'ʃek,ʌp; 'ʃeik'ʌp〕 *n.* ①〖俗〗攪動; 激動; 動亂; 騷動。②(因人事變動而導致之)重新組織;政策變更;大改革。

shak·ing 〔'ʃekɪŋ; 'ʃeikiŋ〕 *n.* ①振動或搖動之人或事物。②〖醫〗瘧。③(*pl.*) 塞船縫用的帆布碎片、斷繩等。—*adj.* 搖動的; 振動的。

shaking palsy 〖醫〗振顫癱瘓 (一種腦病)。

shak·o 〔'ʃæko; 'ʃækou〕 *n., pl.* **-oes, -os.** 一種軍帽(狀略似圓筒, 頂上有綫)。

Shak·sper·i·an, Shak·sper·e·an 〔ʃek'spɪrɪən; ʃeiks'piəriən〕 *adj., n.* =**Shakespearian.**

shak·y 〔'ʃekɪ; 'ʃeiki〕 *adj.,* **shak·i·er, shak·i·est.** ①搖動的;震撼的;戰慄的。②不可靠的。③不穩固的;不結實的。—**shak·i·ly,** *adv.* —**shak·i·ness,** *n.*

shale 〔ʃel; ʃeil〕 *n.* 〖地質〗頁岩;泥板岩。

shale oil 頁岩油(由油頁岩乾餾而成)。

‡shall 〔ʃæl, ʃəl; ʃæl, ʃəl〕 *aux. v., 2nd sing.* also **shalt**; past **should.** (**shall not** 常略作 **shan't**; **should not** 常略作 **shouldn't**) ①將(限第一人稱)。②須;應;非…不可(如加重 shall 之語勢, 表示義務或强制;如不特別加重 shall 之語勢, 表示諾言或威嚇) (限第二或第三人稱)。He says he won't go, but I say he *shall*. 他說他不去, 但是我說他必須去。③用於疑問句中之第一人稱及第三人稱, 表請示之意。*Shall* I open the window? 我可以把窗子打開嗎? ④shall we 等於或補充 let us 之義。Let's start tomorrow, *shall we?* 我們明天動身吧, 好不好? ⑤在以 if, when 等開始的附屬子句中 shall 之第一人稱表未來, 其第二或第三人稱表不確定。 例: If he *shall* come, we shall be saved. 倘若他來了,我們就會得救了。〖注意〗參看 will.

shal·loon [ʃəˈlun; ʃəˈluːn] *n.* 一種輕軟的毛織斜紋布(主要做襯裏用)。

shal·lop [ˈʃæləp; ˈʃæləp] *n.* ①〖詩〗輕舟;小舟。②一種小型戰船。

shal·lot [ʃəˈlɑt; ʃəˈlɔt] *n.* 〖植物〗多蔥。

***shal·low** [ˈʃælo; ˈʃælou] *adj.* ①淺的。②淺薄的; 膚淺的。③(呼吸之)淺而短的。④〖棒球〗較近本壘的。—*n.* (常*pl.*)淺灘。—*v.t.* & *v.i.* (使)變淺。—*adv.* 較近本壘地。

shal·low-brained [ˈʃæloˌbrend; ˈʃæloubreind] *adj.* 愚蠢的;膚淺的。(亦作 **shallow-headed, shallow-pated**)

sha·lot [ʃəˈlɑt; ʃəˈlɔt] *n.* =**shallot.**

shalt [ʃælt; ʃælt] *v.* 〖古〗=**shall** (用於第二人稱、單數、現在式,與 thou 連用)。

shal·y [ˈʃelɪ; ˈʃeili] *adj.*, **shal·i·er, shal·i·est.** 頁岩的;頁岩狀的;含頁岩的。

sham [ʃæm; ʃæm] *n., adj., v.,* **shammed, sham·ming.** —*n.* ①僞物; 贋品。②欺騙者。③虛僞; 欺詐。④僞裝物。—*adj.* 假的;虛僞的;假裝的;仿製的。—*v.t.* 假裝;佯爲。—*v.i.* 假裝;佯爲。

sha·man [ˈʃɑmən; ˈʃæmən] *n.* 黃教「僧;巫師。」

sha·man·ism [ˈʃɑmənɪzm̩; ˈʃæmənizm] *n.* ①黃教(亞洲北部盛行的原始宗教)。②(如北美印第安人信奉的)類似黃教之宗教。

sham·a·teur [ˈʃæmətɚ, -tʃur; ˈʃæmətəː, -tjuə] *n.* 〖俚〗冒牌業餘選手。

sham·ble [ˈʃæmbl̩; ˈʃæmbl] *v.*, **-bled, -bling,** *n.* —*v.i.* 蹣跚而行; 踉蹌而行。—*n.* 蹣跚之步態;踉蹌之步態。

sham·bles [ˈʃæmbl̩z; ˈʃæmblz] *n. pl.* or *sing.* ①屠宰場;肉鋪。②被轟炸後之廢墟。③任何毀壞之地方。④任何屠殺之場面。⑤紊亂之地方。

‡**shame** [ʃem; ʃeim] *n., v.,* **shamed, sham·ing.** —*n.* ①羞愧;羞恥。He blushed with *shame.* 他羞慚得臉紅。②恥辱。He put her to *shame.* 他使她羞慚。③可恥之事、人或物。What a *shame!* 多麼可恥! ④可惋惜之事。It is a *shame* to be so wasteful. 這樣浪費太可惜了。⑤羞恥心;羞辱感。He has no *shame.* 他毫無羞恥心。***feel shame at something*** 因某事而感羞愧。***For shame!*** 多麼可羞! ***put to shame*** **a.** 使蒙羞。**b.** 勝過;使黯然失色。***Shame on you!*** 好可羞!—*v.t.* ①使羞愧。It *shames* me to hear this. 聽到這話使我羞愧。②使蒙羞。③使相形見絀;使黯然失色。

shame·faced [ˈʃemˌfest; ˈʃeimfeist] *adj.* ①怕羞的; 羞怯的。②表現慚愧和窘迫的。*shamefaced* apologies. 赧顏的道歉。—**ly,** *adv.*

***shame·ful** [ˈʃemful; ˈʃeimful] *adj.* 可恥的。a *shameful* defeat. 慘敗。—**ly,** *adv.* —**ness,** *n.*

shame·less [ˈʃemlɪs; ˈʃeimlis] *adj.* 無恥的;厚顏的。a *shameless* liar. 無恥的說謊者。—**ly,** *adv.*

sham·mer [ˈʃæmɚ; ˈʃæmə] *n.* 虛僞者;說謊者;欺騙者;冒充者。

sham·my [ˈʃæmɪ; ˈʃæmi] *n., pl.* **-mies.** ①〖動物〗(南歐及西南亞山地產之)羚羊。②羚羊、山羊、鹿等之柔皮。(亦作**chamois, shamoy**)

sham·poo [ʃæmˈpu; ʃæmˈpuː] *v.*, **-pooed, -poo·ing,** *n.* —*v.t.* ①洗(頭及髮)。②按摩。③以特別洗滌劑洗(地毯等)。—*n.* ①洗髮;洗頭。②洗髮粉;洗髮劑。

sham·rock [ˈʃæmrɑk; ˈʃæmrɔk] *n.* 〖植物〗酢漿草(愛爾蘭的國花)。

sha·mus [ˈʃeməs; ˈʃɑːməs, ˈʃei-] *n., pl.* **-mus·es.** 〖俚〗①偵探。②警官。

shan·dry·dan [ˈʃændrɪˌdæn; ˈʃændridæn] *n.* 〖方〗①搖幌不穩的舊馬車。②愛爾蘭的二輪輕便馬車。

shan·dy [ˈʃændɪ; ˈʃændi] *n.* 一種啤酒與檸檬水混合成之飲料。

shan·dy·gaff [ˈʃændɪˌgæf; ˈʃændigæf] *n.* 〖英〗一種啤酒與薑汁混合成之飲料。

Shang·hai [ˈʃæŋˈhaɪ; ʃæŋˈhai, ˈʃæŋˈhai] *n.* 上海(中國東海岸之大都市)。

shang·hai [ˈʃæŋhaɪ, ʃæŋˈhaɪ; ˈʃæŋhai, ʃæŋˈhai] *v.t.*, **-haied, -hai·ing.** ①灌以麻醉劑而綁架至船上服勞役; 誘拐。②〖俚〗以武力或卑劣手段强迫他人做事。

Shan·gri·la, Shan·gri-La [ˈʃæŋgrɪˈlɑ; ˈʃæŋgriˈlɑː] *n.* ①香格里拉(人間的理想樂園)。②美國陸軍航空隊之祕密基地。③〖美軍俗〗厠所。

shank [ʃæŋk; ʃæŋk] *n.* ①脛; 脛骨。②腿。③(用具等之)幹; 身; 柄部。④鞋襪之脛部。⑤鉛字之身。⑥任何東西的末端或後部。***go*** (or ***ride***) ***on shank's*** (or ***shanks'***) ***mare*** 步行;走。***shank of the evening*** 晚上最好之時間。—*v.i.* ①(樹葉等)因病掉下。②〖主蘇〗徒步;步行。***shank it*** 步行。***shank off*** (樹莖)腐爛。

Shan·si [ˈʃɑnˈsi; ˈʃɑːnˈsiː] *n.* 山西(中國北部之一省,省會太原 Taiyuan).

shan't, sha'n't [ʃænt, ʃɑnt; ʃɑːnt] =**shall not.**

Shan·tung[1] [ˈʃænˈtʌŋ; ˈʃænˈtʌŋ] *n.* 山東(中國北部之一省,省會濟南 Tsinan).

Shan·tung[2] [ʃænˈtʌŋ; ʃænˈtʌŋ] *n.* (有時 s-) 山東綢。

shan·ty[1] [ˈʃæntɪ; ˈʃænti] *n., pl.* **-ties,** *adj., v.,* **-tied, -ty·ing.** —*n.* 簡陋的小屋。—*adj.* ①簡陋小屋的。②窮困的。—*v.i.* 居住於簡陋小屋。

shan·ty[2] *n., pl.* **-ties.** 船歌; 櫂歌。(亦作**chantey**)

shan·ty·town [ˈʃæntɪˌtaun; ˈʃæntitaun] *n.* ①(城市裏)貧民窟。②以簡陋小屋形成的市鎭。

shap·a·ble [ˈʃepəbl̩; ˈʃeipəbl] *adj.* 可造形的;形狀好的。(亦作 **shapeable**)

SHAPE, Shape Supreme Headquarters, Allied Powers in Europe. 駐歐盟軍最高指揮部。

‡**shape** [ʃep; ʃeip] *n., v.,* **shaped, shap·ing.** —*n.* ①形;形狀;形式。In *shape,* it was like a bell. 其形如鐘。②假裝的形狀。③想像中的或模糊的形影;輪廓。④定形;適當之配置。He could not give *shape* to his ideas. 他不能將他的觀念具體表達出來。⑤種類。⑥模;模型。⑦在模中形成的東西;任何形狀的金屬。⑧狀態; 情形。His affairs are in bad *shape.* 他的事務很糟糕。⑨生活方式。⑩姿態身段等(尤指女人富於性感者)。She's got a great *shape.* 她身材很好。***get something into shape*** 使成適當形式;整理。***take shape*** 成形;實現。—*v.t.* ①造成(某)形。The child *shapes* clay into balls. 小孩將泥土摶成圓球。②定…的方向。③定形;塑造。④使適合。That hat is *shaped* to your head. 那帽子正適合你的頭。⑤以言語表示。⑥把鋸齒銼勻。—*v.i.* ①成形;有某種形式。His plan is *shaping* well. 他的計畫有一點樣子了。***shape up*** **a.** 成形;具體化。**b.** 發展;進展。**c.** (碼頭工人)

排除等候分配工作。**d.** 表現某種趨勢;有…之傾向。 「狀的。

shaped 〔ʃept; ʃeipt〕 *adj.* 形成的;有形

***shape·less** 〔'ʃeplɪs; 'ʃeiplis〕 *adj.* ①無定形的;無樣式的。②形狀醜陋的。—**ly,** *adv.*

shape·ly 〔'ʃeplɪ; 'ʃeipli〕 *adj.,* **-li·er, -li·est.** 形狀美好的;比例勻稱的(尤指女人姿態)。—**shape·li·ness,** *n.*

shap·er 〔'ʃepɚ; 'ʃeipə〕 *n.* ①造形者;塑形者。②〖機械〗成形機;牛頭鉋床。

shape-up 〔'ʃep,ʌp; 'ʃeip-ʌp〕 *n.* 〖美〗從前雇用碼頭工人的方法;工人每天到碼頭去由工會人員挑選雇用。

shard 〔ʃard; ʃɑːd〕 *n.* ①(陶器、瓦等摔破之)碎片;破片。②牛蟲翼翅外的硬殼;蝸牛之殼;蛋殼。③〖英方〗糞便;牛糞。

‡share[1] 〔ʃɛr; ʃɛə〕 *n., v.,* **shared, shar·ing.** —*n.* ①部分;分。Everybody ought to have his proper *share.* 每人均應得其應得之分。②股份。The company was formed with 2,000 *shares.* 該公司由兩千股組成。③參與;貢獻。I had no *share* in the matter. 我未參與其事。***bear*** (or ***take***) ***one's share of*** 負擔…的部分;付…的分。***come in for a share*** 受到分配;分得一分。***deferred*** (***preference,*** or ***preferred***) ***shares*** 紅利扣存股(優先股)。***fall to one's share*** 由某人負擔;歸某人的分。***go shares in something*** 平分;均攤。***have*** (or ***take***) ***a*** (or ***one's***) ***share in*** 分擔;參加。***on*** (or ***upon***) ***shares*** 共同承受風險或利益;利害與共。***the lion's share*** 最大(或最好)部分。—*v.t.* ①分配。They *shared* the profits between them. 他們分利潤。②共有;分享;分擔。They *shared* their joys and sorrows. 他們苦樂與共。—*v.i.* 分受;分享;共同負擔。I will *share* with you in the undertaking. 我將與你共同擔負這項事業。***share and share alike*** **a.** 有相等的分子;平均分配。**b.** 一切與他人分享。***share out*** 分配。—**shar·a·ble, —a·ble,** *adj.*—**shar·er,** *n.*

share[2] *n.* 犂頭。

share·bro·ker 〔'ʃɛr,brokɚ; 'ʃɛə,broukə〕 *n.* 〖英〗股票經紀人。

share certificate 股票。

share·crop·per 〔'ʃɛr,krapɚ; 'ʃɛə,krɔpə〕 *n.* 佃農;佃戶。 「də〕 *n.* 股東。

share·hold·er〔'ʃɛr,holdɚ;'ʃɛə,houl-

share-list 〔'ʃɛr,lɪst; 'ʃɛəlist〕 *n.* 〖英〗股市行情表。 「作社的)配給物。

share-out 〔'ʃɛr,aut; 'ʃɛəraut〕 *n.* (合

***shark** 〔ʃark; ʃɑːk〕 *n.* ①鯊;鮫。②騙子;放高利貸者。③〖俚〗傑出者。—*v.t.* & *v.i.* 欺騙;詐騙。

shark·skin 〔'ʃark,skɪn; 'ʃɑːk-skin〕 *n.* ①鯊皮;鯊革。②一種結實的人造絲。

‡sharp 〔ʃarp; ʃɑːp〕 *adj.* ①銳利的。②尖的。③急轉的;峭急的。④嚴寒的;凜冽的。⑤劇烈的;猛烈的。⑥敏捷的;輕快的。⑦迫切的;强烈的。*Sharp* stomachs make short graces.〖諺〗衣食足然後知禮儀(餓著肚子,飯前感恩祈禱詞也說得短)。⑧敏銳的;聰明的。a *sharp* boy. 聰明的孩子。⑨機警的;注意的。⑩嚴厲的;苛刻的。*sharp* words. 苛刻的話。⑪清楚的;顯明的。⑫聲調高的;尖聲的。⑬〖音樂〗升半音的;高調的;嬰音的。⑭〖語音〗無聲的;氣音的(如 p, t, k 等)。⑮(味道之)辣的。⑯精明的;門檻很精的。He is a *sharp* lawyer. 他是個精幹的律師。⑰(衣服等)過分講究的。—*adv.* ①準;整。one o'clock *sharp.* 一點鐘正。②尖銳地;銳利地。③機警地;注意地。④突然地;急速地。The road turns *sharp(ly)* to the left. 該路向左急轉。***Look sharp!*** 趕快!注意!小心!—*n.* ①〖音樂〗高調;嬰音;嬰記號(即#)。②騙子。③〖俗〗專家。④(*pl.*)小麥的粗粉。—**ly,** *adv.* —**ness,** *n.*

***sharp·en** 〔'ʃarpən; 'ʃɑːpən〕 *v.t.* ①使銳利;使尖銳;磨(刀);削(鉛筆)。He was *sharpening* his knife. 他在磨刀。②加强;使敏銳。—*v.i.* ①變爲銳利;變爲尖銳。②增强;變爲敏銳。—**er,** *n.*

sharp·er 〔'ʃarpɚ; 'ʃɑːpə〕 *n.* ①詐欺者;騙子。②賭博郎中。(亦作 **sharpie**)

sharp-eyed 〔'ʃarp'aɪd;'ʃɑːp'aid〕 *adj.* ①目光敏銳的;有慧眼的。②注意的;警覺的。

sharp-freeze 〔'ʃarp,friz; 'ʃɑːp'friːz〕 *v.t.,* **-froze, -fro·zen, -freez·ing.** 急速冷凍。

sharp·ie 〔'ʃarpɪ; 'ʃɑːpi〕 *n.* ①一種長的平底船(單桅或雙桅)。②〖美俗〗狡猾的人。(亦作 **sharpy**)

sharp-set 〔'ʃarp,sɛt; 'ʃɑːp'set〕 *adj.* ①甚餓的;急欲進食的。②急切的;急迫的。

sharp·shoot·er 〔'ʃarp,ʃutɚ; 'ʃɑːp-,ʃuːtə〕 *n.* ①善射者;神鎗手。②狙擊兵;狙擊手。③〖美軍〗優等射手。

sharp-sight·ed 〔'ʃarp'saɪtɪd; 'ʃɑːp-'saitid〕 *adj.* ①目光敏銳的;有慧眼的。②機警的;機智的。

sharp-tongued 〔'ʃarp'tʌŋd; 'ʃɑːp-'tʌŋd〕 *adj.* (講話之)刻薄的;挖苦的。

sharp-wit·ted 〔'ʃarp'wɪtɪd; 'ʃɑːp-'witid〕 *adj.* 敏悟的;機敏的。

Shas·ta daisy 〔'ʃæstə~; 'ʃæstə~〕〖植物〗沙斯塔雛菊。 「教的)聖典。

shas·tra 〔'ʃastrə; 'ʃɑːstrə〕 *n.* (印度

shat·ter** 〔'ʃætɚ; 'ʃætə〕 *v.t.* 使粉碎;損毀;使破滅。—*v.i.* 粉碎;破碎。—*n.* (常 *pl.*)破片;碎塊。in shatters*** 破碎不堪;七零八落。

shat·ter·proof 〔'ʃætɚ,pruf; 'ʃætə-pruːf〕 *adj.* 防破碎的;不碎的。

***shave** 〔ʃev; ʃeiv〕 *v.,* **shaved, shaved** or **shav·en, shav·ing,** *n.* —*v.t.* ①剃;薙;修面;刮鬍子。②鉋;刮;削;切成薄片。③擦過;掠過。The car *shaved* a wall. 汽車從牆邊擦過。④以低於合法的折扣價購買(有價證券)。⑤減(價);削(價)。⑥〖俚〗減少;減輕。—*v.i.* ①刮鬍子;修面。②斤斤較量。—*n.* ①修面;刮鬍子。②修面刀;刮具;鉋。③削片;薄片。④驚險的脫免。The shot missed him, but it was a close *shave.* 這發子彈沒有打中他,但實在是間不容髮。—**shav·a·ble, —a·ble,** *adj.*

shave·ling 〔'ʃevlɪŋ; 'ʃeivliŋ〕 *n.* ①剃掉鬚髮之人;僧人(輕蔑語)。②青年人。

***shav·en** 〔'ʃevən; 'ʃeivn〕 *v.* pp. of **shave.** —*adj.* ①修過臉的;刮過臉的。②削髮的。

shav·er 〔'ʃevɚ; 'ʃeivə〕 *n.* ①理髮師;剃頭者;刮臉者。②剃頭刀;剃具。③討價還價斤斤計較的人。④〖俗〗年輕人;男孩。⑤傢伙。

shave·tail 〔'ʃev,tel; 'ʃeivteil〕 *n.* ①〖美軍俚〗新授職的少尉。②(軍隊中用的未馴服的)騾子。 「伯納的。—*n.* 蕭伯納的崇拜者。

Sha·vi·an 〔'ʃevɪən; 'ʃeiviən〕 *adj.* 蕭

shav·ing 〔'ʃevɪŋ; 'ʃeiviŋ〕 *n.* ①刮臉;修面。②刨;削。③(常 *pl.*)削片;刨花等之薄片。

shaving brush 修面刷。

shaving cream 刮鬍膏。

shaving horse 削架;刨架。

shaving soap 刮鬍皂。

Shaw [ʃɔ; ʃɔː] *n.* 蕭伯納(George Bernard, 1856–1950, 英國劇作家、批評家、小說家及社會改革者)。

shaw [ʃɔ; ʃɔː] *n.* ①〖古,方〗小林; 林叢。②〖蘇〗馬鈴薯之莖和葉。

***shawl** [ʃɔl; ʃɔːl] *n.* 披肩;圍巾。

shawl pattern 披巾花樣。

shawm [ʃɔm; ʃɔːm] *n.* 從前的一種笛。

shay [ʃe; ʃei] *n.* 〖俗〗輕便馬車。

‡she [ʃi; ʃiː] *pron., sing. nom., poss.* **her** or **hers,** *obj.* **her,** *pl.* **they.** 她(第三人稱, 單數, 主格, 所有格爲 her 及 hers, 受格爲 her. 指女人、女孩或雌性動物, 亦用以指船或其他擬爲女性之物)。—*n.* ①女人; 女孩。Is the baby a "he" or a "*she*"? 這小孩是個男的還是女的? ②雌者;雌性動物。

sheaf [ʃif; ʃiːf] *n., pl.* **sheaves,** *v.* —*n.* 束;捆。—*v.t.* 將…捆成束。

shear** [ʃɪr; ʃiə] *v.,* **sheared, sheared** or **shorn** [ʃorn; ʃɔːn], **shear·ing,** *n.* —*v.i.* & *v.t.* ①修剪;剪羊毛。②刈;割。③剝奪;詐取 〖of〗. The mansion is *shorn* of its splendors. 此邸已失去豪華景象。④飛越。⑤如割開一般地越過。a shorn lamb*** **a.** 被剪去羊毛的羔羊。**b.** 被騙去金錢的愚人。***shear off*** **a.** 折斷。**b.** 挫折。—*n.* ①修剪;刈割。②被剪下的東西。③剪刀的一片。④一把剪刀。⑤剪斷機;剪床。⑥〖物理〗**a.** 切力。**b.** 切變。⑦剪羊毛之次數;羊的一歲。a sheep of one *shear*. 一歲的羊。

shear hulk 備有剪脚起重機的舊船。

shear·ing [ˈʃɪrɪŋ; ˈʃiəriŋ] *n.* ①剪羊毛; 剪毛。②剪下之羊毛。③〖機械〗剪斷;剪割。

shear legs 剪脚起重機; 合掌起重機。(亦作 **shearlegs**)

shearing strength 抗剪強度。

shear·ling [ˈʃɪrlɪŋ; ˈʃiəliŋ] *n.* ①祇剪過一次毛的綿羊。②自上項綿羊身上剪下之短毛。③上項綿羊之皮(帶毛而揉過的)。

shears [ʃɪrz; ʃiəz] *n. pl.* ①大剪刀。②似剪刀之工具。③剪脚起重機。

shear·wa·ter [ˈʃɪrˌwɔtə; ˈʃiəˌwɔːtə] *n.* 海鷗。

sheat·fish [ˈʃitˌfɪʃ; ˈʃiːtfiʃ] *n., pl.* **-fish, -fish·es.** 大鯰魚(一種淡水魚, 產於中、東歐)。

***sheath** [ʃiθ; ʃiːθ] *n., pl.* **sheaths** [ʃiðz; ʃiːðz], *v.* —*n.* ①鞘。②(植物之) 葉鞘。③(昆蟲之)翅鞘。④包皮; 護套。⑤〖解剖〗鞘。—*v.t.* =**sheathe.**

sheathe [ʃið; ʃiːð] *v.t.,* **sheathed, sheath·ing.** ①(將刀、劍)插入鞘。②包;覆。③將(刀、劍、利角等)刺入敵人身體內。

sheath·ing [ˈʃiðɪŋ; ˈʃiːðiŋ] *n.* ①包覆物;包板;包鞘;覆板;覆蓋。②插入鞘中。

sheath knife 鞘刀。

sheave¹ [ʃiv; ʃiːv] *v.t.,* **sheaved, sheav·ing.** 束;捆。

sheave² *n.* 帶槽輪;滑輪;滑車。

sheaves [ʃivz; ʃiːvz] *n.* pl. of **sheaf.**

She·ba [ˈʃibə; ˈʃiːbə] *n.* ①希巴(古國名, 在阿拉伯南部, 因做香料、寶石生意而著名)(亦作 **Saba**)。②〖美俗〗有魔力之美人。

she·bang [ʃəˈbæŋ; ʃəˈbæŋ] *n.* 〖俚〗①事情;事務;事件。②建築物;小屋;住宅;店鋪。

she·been [ʃɪˈbin; ʃiˈbiːn] *n.* 〖愛,蘇〗賣私酒之小酒店。—*v.i.* 〖愛,蘇〗開賣私酒的小酒店;賣私酒。

***shed¹** [ʃɛd; ʃed] *n.* (車)棚;小屋。

shed²** *v.,* **shed, shed·ding,** *n.* —*v.t.* ①流出;落下。②使(他人之血)流出;殺死。③發散;放射。 The sun *sheds* light. 太陽發射光。④脫落;蛻;擺脫。⑤遮蔽。—*v.i.* 脫毛或殼等;脫換。shed blood*** 喪生;殺死。—*n.* ①脫落之物。②分水嶺;高地之脊。

she'd [ʃid; ʃiːd] =**she had; she would.**

shed·der [ˈʃɛdə; ˈʃedə] *n.* ①脫落者;放射者。②開始脫殼之龍蝦或蟹。③剛換過殼的龍蝦或蟹。

she-dev·il [ˈʃiˈdɛvl; ˈʃiːˈdevl] *n.* 女魔鬼;殘暴的女人。

sheen [ʃin; ʃiːn] *n.* 光輝。—*adj.* 〖詩〗光輝的;綺麗的。—*v.i.* 〖詩,方〗發亮;照耀。

sheen·y¹ [ˈʃinɪ; ˈʃiːni] *adj.,* **sheen·i·er, sheen·i·est.** 發亮的;有光澤的;閃爍的。

sheen·y² *n., pl.* **sheen·ies.** 〖蔑〗猶太人。(亦作 **sheeney, sheenie**)

‡sheep [ʃip; ʃiːp] *n., pl.* **sheep.** ①羊; 綿羊。a flock of *sheep*. 一羣羊。②懦怯之人。③羊皮。④信徒; 教友; 教區民。***a black sheep*** 敗類;不肖之徒;害羣之馬。***a wolf in sheep's clothing*** 假裝善良之惡人。***cast*** (or ***make***) ***sheep's eyes at a person*** 向人眉目傳情。***follow like a sheep*** 盲從。***lost sheep*** 迷途之羊; 迷失正途之人。***One may as well be hanged for a sheep as a lamb.*** 如果所得處罰相同, 則寧願犯大罪而捨小惡;一不做二不休。***separate the sheep from the goats*** 分辨好人壞人。***sheep and goats*** 善人與惡人。***sheep that have no shepherd*** 烏合之衆。

sheep·ber·ry [ˈʃipˌbɛrɪ; ˈʃiːpbəri] *n.* 〖植物〗(北美)莢蒾屬落葉灌木;此種灌木之實。

sheep·cot [ˈʃipˌkɑt; ˈʃiːpkɔt] *n.* 羊欄; 羊舍。

sheep·dip [ˈʃipˌdɪp; ˈʃiːpdip] *n.* 羊消毒液。

sheep dog 牧羊犬。(亦作 **sheepdog**)

sheep·fold [ˈʃipˌfold; ˈʃiːpfould] *n.* 羊欄;羊舍。

sheep·herd·er [ˈʃipˌhɝdə; ˈʃiːpˌhəːdə] *n.* 〖美〗牧羊人。

sheep·hook [ˈʃipˌhuk; ˈʃiːphuk] *n.* 牧羊杖。

sheep·ish [ˈʃipɪʃ; ˈʃiːpiʃ] *adj.* ①羞怯的; 靦腆的。②如綿羊的; 怯懦的; 愚鈍的。—**ly,** *adv.*

sheep·man [ˈʃipˌmæn; ˈʃiːpmæn] *n., pl.* **-men.** ①以養羊爲業者。②牧羊人。

sheep range 牧羊場。

sheep run 大牧羊場。

sheep·shank [ˈʃipˌʃæŋk; ˈʃiːpʃæŋk] *n.* ①羊脛。②纖細的東西。③〖航海〗縮短結。

sheeps·head, sheep's-head [ˈʃipsˌhɛd; ˈʃiːpshed] *n.* ①(食用)羊頭。②愚蠢的人。③羊首魚。—*v.i.* 〖美俗〗釣羊首魚。

sheep·skin [ˈʃipˌskɪn; ˈʃiːp-skin] *n.* ①(尤指帶毛之)羊皮。②羊皮衣。③羊革; 羊皮紙。④〖美俗〗文憑;證書。⑤〖俚〗獲得文憑的人。—*adj.* ①羊皮做的。②(衣服之) 以帶毛羊皮鑲邊的。

sheep sorrel 〖植物〗一種開紅花的酸模。

sheep·walk [ˈʃipˌwɔk; ˈʃiːpwɔːk] *n.* 〖英〗牧羊場。

***sheer¹** [ʃɪr; ʃiə, ʃjəː] *adj.* ①純粹的; 全然的;絕對的。*sheer* impossibility. 絕對不可能之事。②極薄的。stockings of *sheer* silk. 薄絲襪。③垂直的; 峻峭的。 a *sheer* cliff. 懸崖;絕壁。—*adv.* ①完全地;全然地。②峻峭地; 垂直地。The rock rises *sheer* from the water. 岩石矗立水面。—*n.* 薄衣服。—**ly,** *adv.*

sheer² *v.i.* 躲開;躲避 〖off, away〗. —*v.t.* 使避開。—*n.* 〖航海〗①逸出路線;轉向。②舷弧。③船舶拋單錨時的位置。

sheer legs =**shear legs.**

sheers [ʃɪrz; ʃiəz] *n. pl.* =**shears.**

‡**sheet** [ʃit;ʃiːt] *n.* ①被單;褥單。②薄片;薄板;(紙之)一張。a *sheet* of paper. 一張紙。③報紙。④廣闊之一片。a *sheet* of water. 一片汪洋。⑤〖航海〗帆脚索。⑥帆。⑦〖地質〗岩床。⑧〖數學〗葉。***a sheet in the wind*** (or ***wind's eye***)〖俗〗微有醉意。***get between the sheets*** 就寢。***stand in a white sheet*** 懺悔;悔改。***three sheets in*** (or ***to***) ***the wind***〖俗〗酒醉。—*v.t.* ①鋪以床單。②包(屍)。③使延展成薄片。The river was *sheeted* with ice. 河上結了一層冰。***sheet home*** 用帆脚索扣住(風帆)。

sheet anchor ①緊急時始使用之大錨。②緊急時可依恃的人或物;最後的依恃。

sheet glass 大片平板玻璃。

sheet·ing [ˈʃitɪŋ; ˈʃiːtiŋ] *n.* ①被單布;床單布。②護板;貼板。③做護板;用被單覆蓋。

sheet iron 薄鐵板;鐵板。

sheet lightning 大片之閃電(由於遠方之閃電反照而成者)。

sheet metal 薄金屬片;金屬板。

sheet music 單張樂譜。

Sheet·rock [ˈʃit,rɑk;ˈʃiːt–rɔk] *n.*〖商標名〗(作室內隔間用的)石膏紙板。

Shef·field [ˈʃɛfild; ˈʃefiːld] *n.* 雪菲耳(英格蘭中北部之一城市,爲鋼鐵工業中心)。

Sheffield plate 銀片銅片合鑄的盤子。

sheik(h) [ʃik; ʃeik] *n.* ①(阿拉伯之)酋長;族長。②回教領袖;教主。③回教徒所用的尊稱。④〖俚〗小白臉;大情人。

sheik(h)·dom [ˈʃikdəm; ˈʃeikdəm] *n.* (阿拉伯)酋長統轄之領土;酋長國。

shek·el [ˈʃɛkl; ˈʃekl] *n.* ①古希伯來人及巴比倫人等所用之衡名。②希伯來之金及銀幣名(重半英兩者)。③(常 *pl.*)〖俚〗錢。

she·ki·nah [ʃɪˈkaɪnə; ʃiˈkainə] *n.*〖猶太教〗神之顯現;神顯現時之光雲。(亦作 **Shekinah, Shechinah, shechinah**)

shel·drake [ˈʃɛl,drek;ˈʃel–dreik] *n.*, *pl.* **-drakes, -drake.** 淚鳧;冠鴨(一種捕食魚類的野鴨)。

shelf** [ʃɛlf; ʃelf] *n.*, *pl.* **shelves.** ①架。②崖路;岩棚。③暗礁。off the shelf*** 現貨供應。***on the shelf*** **a.** 被棄置的;無人問津的。**b.** (女性之)無結婚希望的(如解除婚約等)。

shelf (or **storage**) **life** 儲藏商品之有效或有用期間。

‡**shell** [ʃɛl; ʃel] *n.* ①殼;介殼;甲。to cast the *shell*. 脫殼;脫皮。②貝;有介殼之軟體動物。③競渡用之輕舟。④砲彈。illuminating *shell*. 照明彈。tear *shell*. 催淚彈。⑤房屋的框架;船體;骨架。⑥外表;外觀;外形。⑦無袖無領的女上衣。***come out of one's shell*** 不再羞怯沈默。***go*** (or ***retire***) ***into one's shell*** 與旁人在一起時羞怯沈默。—*v.t.* ①去殼;剝殼。②砲轟。The enemy *shelled* the town. 敵人砲轟該城鎮。③〖棒球俚〗(投手)使對方獲得多次安打或得分。—*v.i.* ①脫殼;(由穗或莢中)脫出。②砲擊。***as easy as shelling peas*** 像剝豌豆一樣的容易;極其容易。***shell out***〖俗〗付款;捐獻。

she'll [ʃil; ʃiːl] =**she shall; she will.**

shel·lac(k) [ʃəˈlæk; ʃəˈlæk] *n.*, *v.*, **-lacked, -lack·ing.** —*n.* ①充漆;假漆。②(造充漆的)蟲膠。③用假漆做的唱片。—*v.t.* ①塗以充漆。②〖俚〗徹底擊敗。

shell·back [ˈʃɛl,bæk; ˈʃelbæk] *n.* ①老水手。②乘船橫過赤道者。

shell·bark [ˈʃɛl,bɑrk; ˈʃelbɑːk] *n.*〖植物〗=**shagbark.**

shell bean 不連豆莢吃的豆類。

shell egg 帶殼的蛋(以別於加工過的蛋)。

shell·er [ˈʃɛlɚ;ˈʃelə] *n.* 去殼者;去殼機。

Shel·ley [ˈʃɛlɪ; ˈʃeli] *n.* 雪萊 (Percy Bysshe, 1792–1822, 英國詩人)。

shell·fire [ˈʃɛl,faɪr; ˈʃel,faiə] *n.*〖軍〗砲火;砲轟。

***shell·fish** [ˈʃɛl,fɪʃ; ˈʃel–fiʃ] *n.*, *pl.* **-fish·es** or **-fish.** 貝;甲殼類。—**er·y,** *n.*

shell game ①類似thimblerig 的一種遊戲。②欺騙。

shell heap 貝塚。

shell jacket 熱帶地方的陸軍軍官便服。

shell·less [ˈʃɛllɪs; ˈʃellis] *adj.* 無殼的。

shell-lime [ˈʃɛllaɪm; ˈʃellaim] *n.* 貝殼灰。

shell mound 貝塚。

shell·proof [ˈʃɛlˈpruf; ˈʃel–pruːf] *adj.* 防彈的。

shell shock 彈震症(由戰爭的緊張而造成的神經病或精神病)。

shell-shocked, shell·shocked [ˈʃɛl,ʃɑkt; ˈʃelʃɔkt] *adj.* 彈震症的。

shell·work [ˈʃɛl,wɝk; ˈʃelwəːk] *n.* 貝殼細工。

shell·y [ˈʃɛlɪ; ˈʃeli] *adj.*, **shell·i·er, shell·i·est.** ①多介殼的。②由介殼做成的。③似介殼的。

‡**shel·ter** [ˈʃɛltɚ; ˈʃeltə] *n.* ①庇護所;避難所;遮蔽物。Trees are a *shelter* from the sun. 樹木可供遮蔭(避免日晒)。②庇護;保護;遮蔽。He took *shelter* in vague excuses. 他用含混的託辭來掩飾。***air-raid shelter*** 空襲避難所;防空洞。—*v.t.* ①庇護;保護;掩護。He *sheltered* an escaping prisoner. 他庇護一名逃犯。②供住宿。③隱匿。—*v.i.* 托庇;隱匿。to *shelter* from the rain. 避雨。—**less,** *adj.* —**y,** *adj.*

shelter belt 防風林;有保持水土作用的森林。(亦作 **shelter wood**)

shelter tent 軍用雙人帳篷。(亦作 **pup tent**)

shelter trench 爲避砲火的臨時戰壕。

shel·ty [ˈʃɛltɪ; ˈʃelti] *n.*, *pl.* **-ties.** ①Shetland 所產之小狗。②Shetland 出產之牧羊狗。(亦作 **sheltie**)

shelve[1] [ʃɛlv; ʃelv] *v.t.*, **shelved, shelv·ing.** ①將…置於架上。②擱置。③解雇;辭退。④裝架子於;做架子。—**shelv·er,** *n.*

shelve[2] *v.i.* 傾斜(通常指海岸)。

***shelves** [ʃɛlvz; ʃelvz] *n.* pl. of **shelf.**

shelv·ing[1] [ˈʃɛlvɪŋ; ˈʃelviŋ] *n.* ①搭架之材料。②棚架之集合稱。③搭棚架。④擱置;延誤。⑤免職;解職。

shelv·ing[2] *n.* (漸成)斜坡。

shelv·y [ˈʃɛlvɪ;ˈʃelvi] *adj.* 逐漸傾斜的。

Shem·ite [ˈʃɛmaɪt;ˈʃemait] *n.* =**Semite.**

She·mit·ic [ʃɛˈmɪtɪk; ʃeˈmitik] *adj.* =**Semitic.**

she·nan·i·gan [ʃəˈnænə,gæn; ʃəˈnænigæn] *n.*〖俗〗(常 *pl.*)無聊的話;胡說;詭計。

Shen·si [ˈʃɛnˈsi; ˈʃenˈsiː] *n.* 陝西(中國西北之一省,省會西安 Sian)。

shent [ʃɛnt; ʃent] *adj.*〖古〗①羞愧的。②被譴責的。③打敗的。④毀壞的。

She·ol [ˈʃiol; ˈʃiːoul] *n.* ①〖舊約聖經〗陰間;冥府。②(s-)〖俗〗地獄。

shep·herd** [ˈʃɛpɚd; ˈʃepəd] *n.* ①牧羊人。②保護者;領導人。③(喩)牧師。④牧羊狗。the*** (***Good***) ***Shepherd*** 基督。—*v.t.* ①牧;放牧。②照看。③指導;引領。

shepherd dog 牧羊犬。

shep·herd·ess [ˈʃɛpɚdɪs;ˈʃepədis] *n.* 牧羊女。

shepherd god 牧羊神（=Pan).
Shepherd Kings = **Hyksos.**
shepherd's pie 上鋪碎馬鈴薯的肉餅。
shep·herd's-purse 〔'ʃɛpədz'pɝs; 'ʃepədz'pə:s〕 *n.* 〖植物〗薺。
Sher·a·ton 〔'ʃɛrətn̩; 'ʃerətn〕 *n.* 雪里頓(Thomas, 1751–1806, 英國傢具設計家)。—*adj.* 雪里頓的;雪里頓式的(傢具)。
sher·bet 〔'ʃɝbɪt; 'ʃə:bət〕 *n.* ①一種由果汁、糖、水、牛奶或蛋白製成之冷凍食品。②一種由果汁、糖及水製成的清涼飲料。
sherd 〔ʃɑrd, ʃɝd; ʃə:d〕 *n.* **=shard.**
she·reef 〔ʃɛ'rif; ʃe'ri:f〕 *n.* ①穆罕默德之後裔。②阿拉伯王公。③麥加 (Mecca) 之地方長官。④摩洛哥之蘇丹。
Sher·i·dan 〔'ʃɛrədn̩; 'ʃeridn〕 *n.* 雪利敦 (Richard Brinsley, 1751–1816, 愛爾蘭劇作家及政治領袖)。
she·rif 〔ʃə'rif; ʃə'ri:f〕 *n.* **=shereef.**
***sher·iff** 〔'ʃɛrɪf; 'ʃerif〕 *n.* 一個 county 裏執行法律的主要官吏;行政司法長官。
sher·lock 〔'ʃɝlɑk; 'ʃə:lɔk〕 *n.* 〖俗〗①私家偵探。②善勘破奧祕者。(亦作**Sherlock**)
Sher·lock Holmes 〔'ʃɝlɑk'homz; 'ʃə:lɔk'houmz〕 ①福爾摩斯 (Conan Doyle 小說中的偵探名)。②名偵探。
Sher·pa 〔'ʃɝpə; 'ʃə:pə〕 *n.* (住在喜馬拉雅山地的) 雪爾帕人。
Sher·ring·ton 〔'ʃɛrɪŋtən; 'ʃeriŋtən〕 *n.* 雪令頓 (Sir Charles Scott, 1861–1952, 英國生理學家, 曾獲 1932 年諾貝爾醫學獎)。
sher·ry 〔'ʃɛrɪ; 'ʃeri〕 *n., pl.* **-ries.** ①雪利酒(西班牙南部所產之白酒)。②任何與此相似之酒。
sherry cobbler 一種由 sherry, 柑橘汁及冰混成之飲料。
sher·ry-glass 〔'ʃɛrɪ͵glæs; 'ʃeriglɑ:s〕 *n.* 雪利酒酒杯。
she's 〔ʃiz; ʃi:z〕 **=she is; she has.**
Shet·land 〔'ʃɛtlənd; 'ʃetlənd〕 *n.* 謝德蘭羣島 (在蘇格蘭 Okney 羣島之東北, 爲蘇格蘭之一郡)。(亦作 **Zetland, Shetland Islands**) ***Shetland pony*** 該地所產之小狗。 ***Shetland sheepdog*** 該地所產之牧羊狗。 ***Shetland wool*** 該地所紡之羊毛。
shew 〔ʃo; ʃou〕 *v.t. & v.i.,* **shewed, shewn, shew·ing.** 〖英, 古〗**=show.**
shew·bread 〔'ʃo͵brɛd; 'ʃoubred〕 *n.* 猶太教用作祭品之無酵餅。(亦作**showbread**)
Shi·ah 〔'ʃiə; 'ʃi:ə〕 *n.* ①回教兩大派之一, 認穆罕默德之婿 Ali 爲正統之繼承者。②此派之信徒。
shib·bo·leth 〔'ʃɪbəlɪθ; 'ʃibəleθ〕 *n.* ①〖聖經〗Gileadite 人用以辨別逃亡之 Ephraimite 人所用語, 蓋彼等不能發 "sh" 音 (見舊約士師記十二章六節)。②暗號語; (一黨一派之)切口。③一國或一階級特有的語言、習慣。
shield** 〔ʃild; ʃi:ld〕 *n.* ①盾。 Return with your *shield* or upon it. 不能戰勝歸來便應馬革裹屍;不成功便成仁。②防禦物;保護物;庇護人。③盾形物。④警察、偵探或保安官的徽章。⑤大砲上保護操作人員的鐵板。⑥〖電〗電屏。⑦〖天文〗盾牌座。look on both sides of the shield*** 察明一件事情(或一個問題) 的兩面。 ***the other*** (or ***reverse***) ***side of the shield*** 事情的另一 (反)面。—*v.t.* 防禦;保護。—*v.i.* 當作盾用;防禦。
shield hand 左手。
shield·ing 〔'ʃildɪŋ; 'ʃi:ldiŋ〕 *n.* 防止輻射線突透之保護物質。
shift** 〔ʃɪft; ʃift〕 *v.t.* ①移動;變換;更易。to *shift* the blame on to someone else. 諉過於他人。to *shift* one's ground. 改變立場。②〖古、方〗換…的衣服。③除去; 解脫。*Shift* this rubbish out of the way. 把這些垃圾從路上清除掉。④變(汽車排擋)的位置。—*v.i.* ①移動;變換;更易。The scene *shifts.* 場面變換。②策劃; 籌劃; 設法過活。 They had to *shift* for themselves. 他們必須自謀生計。③瞞騙; 圖謀; 托辭; 閃避。④〖古〗換衣服。 ***shift and contrive 千方百計。 ***shift off*** 拖延; 逃避。 —*n.* ①變換; 更易; 轉移。②方策;計畫;計謀。③輪值;換班。two *shifts* of work. 兩班工作。④一班之輪值工人。the night *shift.* 夜班(工人)。⑤輪值時間;換班之工作時間。⑥〖古〗女內衫。⑦〖足球〗(開賽前)球員陣勢的變動。⑧汽車排擋。⑨輪作之任一農作物。⑩用以輪作之農地。***make shift*** a. 設法過活或度日。b. 設法繼續或維持。c. 盡力做。***the shifts and changes of life*** 人生之禍福榮枯。—**er,** *n.*
shift key 打字機換大寫字體所按的鍵。
shift·less 〔'ʃɪftlɪs; 'ʃiftlis〕 *adj.* ①懶惰的。②不中用的。—**ly,** *adv.* —**ness,** *n.*
shift·y 〔'ʃɪftɪ; 'ʃifti〕 *adj.,* **shift·i·er, shift·i·est.** ①多策略的; 善於應變的。②不正直的;詭詐的。—**shift·i·ly,** *adv.* —**shift·i·ness,** *n.*
Shi·ite 〔'ʃiaɪt; 'ʃi:ait〕 *n.* Shiah 派之信徒。(亦作 **Shii**)
shi·kar 〔ʃɪ'kɑr; ʃi'kɑ:〕 *n., v.t. & v.i.,* **-karred, -kar·ring.** 〖印度〗狩獵。
shi·ka·ri, shi·ka·ree 〔ʃɪ'kɑri; ʃi'kæri〕 〖印度〗 *n.* 獵人。
shill 〔ʃɪl; ʃil〕 *n.* 〖美俚〗(賭攤等之)假顧客;誘餌;囮子。
shil·la·la(h), shil·le·la(g)h 〔ʃə'lelə; ʃi'leilə〕 *n.* (愛爾蘭的)橡樹棍;棍杖。
shil·ling** 〔'ʃɪlɪŋ; 'ʃiliŋ〕 *n.* 先令(英國幣名)。 ***cut someone off with a shilling 剝奪某人之繼承權。***take the King's*** (or ***Queen's***) ***shilling*** 從軍;當兵。
shil·ling-mark 〔'ʃɪlɪŋ͵mɑrk; 'ʃiliŋmɑ:k〕 *n.* 書寫或印刷的(／)記號。
shilling shocker 〖英〗聳人聽聞的短篇小說(每本賣一先令之故)。
shil·ling's·worth 〔'ʃɪlɪŋz͵wɝθ; 'ʃiliŋzwə:θ〕 *n.* 一先令可購之物量。
shil·ly-shal·ly 〔'ʃɪlɪ͵ʃælɪ; 'ʃili͵ʃæli〕 *n., pl.* **-shal·lies,** *adj., adv., v.,* **-lied, -ly·ing.** —*n.* 優柔寡斷;逡巡不決。—*adj.* 猶豫不決的。 —*adv.* 躊躇不定地。 —*v.i.* 逡巡; 猶豫。
shi·ly 〔'ʃaɪlɪ; 'ʃaili〕 *adv.* 羞怯地; 膽怯地 (=shyly).
shim 〔ʃɪm; ʃim〕 *n., v.,* **shimmed, shim·ming.** —*n.* 填隙用的木片或金屬片。 —*v.t.* 以木片或金屬片填入。
shim·mer 〔'ʃɪmə; 'ʃimə〕 *v.i.* 發閃爍之光;發閃光。—*n.* 微光;閃光。—**y,** *adj.*
shim·my 〔'ʃɪmɪ; 'ʃimi〕 *n., pl.* **-mies,** *v.,* **-mied, -my·ing.** —*n.* ①美國流行的一種搖肩擺臀的爵士舞。②汽車前輪的急劇搖盪。③〖俗, 方〗婦女穿的寬鬆內衣 (=chemise). —*v.i.* ①跳搖肩擺臀的爵士舞。②(汽車)震顫。
***shin** 〔ʃɪn; ʃin〕 *n., v.,* **shinned, shin·ning.** —*n.* ①外脛;脛骨。 ②牛的小腿肉。 —*v.t. & v.i.* 爬(樹)。
shin·bone 〔'ʃɪn͵bon; 'ʃinboun〕 *n.* 〖解剖〗脛骨。
shin·dig 〔'ʃɪndɪg; 'ʃindig〕 *n.* 〖美俚〗舞會;其他作樂的集會。
shin·dy 〔'ʃɪndɪ; 'ʃindi〕 *n., pl.* **-dies.** 〖俚〗①喧囂;喧嘩。②舞會; 其他作樂的集會。
‡shine 〔ʃaɪn; ʃain〕 *v.,* **shone** 〔ʃon; ʃɔn〕

or **shined, shin·ing,** *n.* —*v.i.* ①發光;射光;照耀。The sun was *shining.* 陽光在照耀。The boy's eyes *shone* with excitement. 這小孩子的眼睛因興奮而發出光芒。②卓越;出類拔萃。He *shines* in conversation. 他談吐出衆。③(眼睛、面孔等)發亮。④(情感等)顯出。—*v.t.* ①使發亮;磨光;擦亮。He *shined* my shoes. 他擦亮我的皮鞋。②使照耀;使發光。*Shine* your flashlight over here. 把你的手電筒往這裏照射。***shine up to*** 〖俚〗**a.** 竭力討好以博取…的友誼。**b.** 竭力博取異性之歡心。—*n.* ①光輝;光亮;光采。②日光;晴天。③擦鞋。Have a *shine?* 擦皮鞋嗎? ④〖俚〗愛好;喜愛。⑤〖俚〗惡作劇;詭計。⑥騷擾。⑦〖蔑〗黑人。***kick up*** (or ***make***) ***a shine*** 引起大騷動。***make no end of a shine*** 大鬧。(***come***) ***rain or shine*** **a.** 晴雨無阻。**b.** 不管怎麼樣。***take a shine to*** 〖俚〗變爲喜好;愛上;看中。***take the shine out of*** (***off of,*** or ***off***) **a.** 奪去…的光澤;使黯然無光。**b.** 勝過;使相形見絀。**—less,** *adj.* 〖注意〗*pt.* & *pp.* **shined,** 祇適用於 *v.t.* ①。

shin·er [ˈʃaɪnɚ; ˈʃainə] *n.* ①發光體;有光亮之物(如星星、鑽石等)。②出類拔萃的人;聰明的人;服飾漂亮的人。③擦皮鞋者。④〖俚〗青腫之黑眼圈。⑤銀色小魚。⑥〖英俚〗錢幣(特指金幣)。⑦〖俚〗(賭棍所用的)反射鏡。

shin·gle[1] [ˈʃɪŋgl; ˈʃiŋgl] *n., v.,* **-gled, -gling.** —*n.* ①屋頂板;木瓦。②一種婦人之短髮式。③〖美俗〗小招牌(尤指醫師或律師所用者)。***hang out one's shingle*** 掛牌;開業。—*v.t.* ①蓋屋頂板。②剪短(頭髮)。

shin·gle[2] *n.* 〖主英〗①海濱沙石;砂礫。②覆有砂礫的地方(如海濱等)。

shin·gles [ˈʃɪŋglz; ˈʃiŋglz] *n.* 〖醫〗帶狀匍行疹(herpes zoster 之俗稱)。

shin·gly[1] [ˈʃɪŋglɪ; ˈʃiŋgli] *adj.* 以木瓦或石板覆蓋的。

shin·gly[2] *adj.,* **-gli·er, -gli·est.** 多礫的;多小石子的;似砂礫的;覆有砂礫的。

shin guard (踢足球用的) 護脛。

shin·ing [ˈʃaɪnɪŋ; ˈʃainiŋ] *adj.* ①發光的;光亮的。②顯赫的;傑出的;顯明的。

shin·ny [ˈʃɪnɪ; ˈʃini] *n., pl.* **-nies,** *v.,* **-nied, -ny·ing.** —*n.* ①一種簡易的 hockey 球戲。②此種球戲所用之球棒。—*v.i.* ①玩此種球戲。②擊球。③〖美俗〗攀;爬〖up〗。***shinny on one's own side*** 〖俗〗約束自己的行動使不超越適當的範圍。(亦作 **shinney**)

shin·plas·ter [ˈʃɪnˌplæstɚ; ˈʃinˌplɑːstə] *n.* ①治脛部用之膏藥。②小額紙幣。③濫發之紙幣。

Shin·to [ˈʃɪnto; ˈʃintou] *n.* 日本之神道教。(亦作 **Shintoism**)

Shin·to·ist [ˈʃɪntoɪst; ˈʃintouist] *n.* 神道教徒。

***shin·y** [ˈʃaɪnɪ; ˈʃaini] *adj.,* **shin·i·er, shin·i·est.** ①發光的;輝煌的;晴朗的。What *shiny* shoes you're wearing! 你穿的皮鞋多麼亮啊!②穿至發光的;磨亮的。

:ship [ʃɪp; ʃip] *n., v.,* **shipped, ship·ping.** —*n.* ①船;艦(單數代名詞用she, her)。to go on board a *ship.* 登船。on (*or* in) a *ship.* 在船上(裏)。on board *ship.* 在船上。to go by *ship.* 乘船去。②三桅船;全裝帆船。③船(艦)上之全體人員。④飛艇;飛機。⑤財富。***about ship*** 〖航海〗掉頭;轉向。***burn one's ship*** 破釜沉舟。***clear a ship*** 卸貨。***gauge a ship*** 量船的吃水量。***heave a ship to*** 停船。***jump ship*** **a.** 棄船潛逃。**b.** 潛逃;背棄。***lose*** (or ***spoil***) ***the ship for a ha'p'orth*** (=***halfpennyworth***) ***of tar*** 因小失大。***take ship*** 乘船;搭船。***when one's ship comes in*** (or ***home***) 當某人時來運轉時;當某人有錢時。***wind a ship*** 掉轉船頭。—*v.t.* ①以船運送;運送。The goods were *shipped* (to you) last week. 貨物已於上週運送。②雇用(水手)。③〖航海〗(因浪打入等, 自一側)灌入(海水)。④裝置(船具);安上。⑤〖俗〗送走。—*v.i.* ①乘船;坐船旅行。②在船上服務。He *shipped* as cook. 他在船上作廚子。***ship oars*** 把槳自槳架上取出置於船中。***ship off*** 送往;遣去。***ship out*** **a.** (坐船)離(故)國。**b.** 送(某人上船)到海外去。**c.** 〖俗〗辭職;被開除。***ship water*** (or ***a sea***) 波浪打上甲板;冒着風浪。

-ship 〖字尾〗①表"狀態; 性質"之義。如: friendship. ②表"身分;職位"之義。如:kingship. ③表"技術;能力"之義。如:leadership.

ship biscuit 船上用的一種粗硬餅乾。

ship·board [ˈʃɪpˌbord; ˈʃipbɔːd] *n.* 船。***on shipboard*** 在船上;在船裏。

ship bread=**ship biscuit.**

ship breaker 廢船解體業者。

ship broker 船舶經紀人; 水險掮客。

ship·build·er [ˈʃɪpˌbɪldɚ; ˈʃipˌbildə] *n.* ①造船者;造船匠。②造船公司。

ship·build·ing [ˈʃɪpˌbɪldɪŋ; ˈʃipˌbildiŋ] *n.* 造船學;造船術。—*adj.* 用於或關於造船的。

ship canal (可供大船航行的)運河。

ship carpenter 造船工人;造船木匠。

ship chandler 船具商。

ship chandlery ①船具業。②船具(集合稱)。

ship fever 〖醫〗傷寒。

ship·fit·ter [ˈʃɪpˌfɪtɚ; ˈʃipˌfitə] *n.* 〖造船〗輪船裝配者。

ship letter 郵船外其他船隻運送之信件。

ship·load [ˈʃɪpˌlod; ˈʃiploud] *n.* ①船貨。②船載量。

ship·man [ˈʃɪpmən; ˈʃipmən] *n., pl.* **-men.** ①〖古〗水手。②船長。

ship·mas·ter [ˈʃɪpˌmæstɚ; ˈʃipˌmɑːstə] *n.* (商船的)船長。

ship·mate [ˈʃɪpˌmet; ˈʃipmeit] *n.* 船夥;同事之船員。

***ship·ment** [ˈʃɪpmənt; ˈʃipmənt] *n.* ①裝船。②所載之貨。

ship money 〖英史〗建艦稅。

ship of the desert 駱駝。

ship of the line 帆船時代之戰鬥巨艦。

ship·own·er [ˈʃɪpˌonɚ; ˈʃipˌounə] *n.* 船主。

ship·pa·ble [ˈʃɪpəbl; ˈʃipəbl] *adj.* 適於裝船的;可船運的。

ship·per [ˈʃɪpɚ; ˈʃipə] *n.* ①運貨者。②交運貨物者。

***ship·ping** [ˈʃɪpɪŋ; ˈʃipiŋ] *n.* ①船運;航運; 運輸。the *shipping* business. 運輸業。②船舶的總稱(=ships). ③船舶總噸數。④某一個國家、城市、企業界等的船舶集合稱。

shipping agent 裝船代理處; 運貨代理人;運貨經紀人。

shipping articles 船員雇用合同。

shipping bill (or **note**) 出口貨詳單;請求退還原稅單。

shipping clerk 運務員(負責貨物打包及裝運之人)。

shipping lane 航路。

shipping line 船公司;航業公司。

shipping office 貨運業事務所;海員監督事務所。

shipping room (商號、工廠等之)發貨室。

ship-rigged [ˈʃɪpˌrɪgd; ˈʃiprigd] *adj.*

〖航海〗①有三桅橫帆的。②有方形帆的。

ship's company 一船之全體船員。

ship·shape 〔'ʃɪpˌʃep; 'ʃipʃeip〕 *adj. & adv.* 井然有序的(地);整齊的(地)。

ship's husband 隨船押貨人。

ship's paper 船證;船照。

ship·way 〔'ʃɪpˌwe; 'ʃipwei〕 *n.* ①造船臺。②=ship canal.

ship·worm 〔'ʃɪpˌwɜm; 'ʃipwəːm〕 *n.* 〖動物〗鑿船蟲;攻木蛤。

ship·wreck** 〔'ʃɪpˌrɛk; 'ʃip-rek〕 *n.* ①船舶失事;船之遇難。②破毀的船。③毀滅。make shipwreck of one's life*** 毀滅其生命。***suffer*** (or ***make***) ***shipwreck of one's hopes*** 絕望。—*v.t.* ①使(船隻)遭難。②毀滅。—*v.i.* 船隻遭難或失事。

ship·wright 〔'ʃɪpˌraɪt; 'ʃip-rait〕 *n.* 造船者;修船者。

ship·yard 〔'ʃɪpˌjɑrd; 'ʃipˈjɑːd〕 *n.* 造船所;修船所;船塢。(亦作**shipbuilding yard**)

shire 〔ʃaɪr; 'ʃaiə〕 *n.* (英國之)州;郡。***the Shires*** 英國中部各州(以獵狐出名)。

-shire 〖英〗〖字尾〗郡名之字尾, 如: Lancashire.

shire horse (用於拖車之)大種馬。

shirk 〔ʃɜk; ʃəːk〕 *v.t. & v.i.* 規避;躲避。—*n.* 規避者。—**er,** *n.*

shirr 〔ʃɜ; ʃəː〕 *n.* 鬆緊線。—*v.t.* ①縫鬆緊線於…中。②(以奶油、麪包屑等)烤(蛋)。

shirr·ing 〔'ʃɜɪŋ; 'ʃəːriŋ〕 *n.* =shirr.

‡shirt 〔ʃɜt; ʃəːt〕 *n.* ①襯衣;襯衫。He has not a *shirt* to his back. 他無蔽體之衣;他極窮。②婦女的寬鬆外衣。***a black*** (***green,*** or ***brown***) ***shirt*** 各政治組織會員所著之一種有顏色的襯衫;該特殊組織之會員。***get a person's shirt out*** (or ***off***) 激怒某人。***give away the shirt off one's back*** 送掉身上所有的東西。***give one a wet shirt*** 使某人做到汗流浹背。***have one's shirt out*** 發怒。***in one's shirt sleeves*** (or ***shirt-sleeves***)祇穿襯衣的(地)。***keep one's shirt on*** 〖俚〗保持冷靜;別生氣。***lose one's shirt*** 〖俚〗失去一切;丟得精光。***Near*** (or ***Close***) ***is my shirt, but nearer*** (or ***closer***) ***is my skin.*** 爲人不如爲己。***put one's shirt on*** 以所有的錢打賭。—*v.t.* 供以襯衣。

shirt·band 〔'ʃɜtˌbænd; 'ʃəːtbænd〕 *n.* 襯衫的領口或袖口。

shirt front 襯衣的前胸。

shirt·ing 〔'ʃɜtɪŋ; 'ʃəːtiŋ〕 *n.* 襯衣布;襯衣料。

shirt·mak·er 〔'ʃɜtˌmekɚ; 'ʃəːtˌmeikə〕 *n.* ①做襯衣的人。②一種婦女上衣。

shirt-sleeve 〔'ʃɜtˌsliv; 'ʃəːtsliːv〕 *adj.* ①簡單的;樸素的;非正式的。②祇穿襯衫的。(亦作 **shirtsleeved**)

shirt·tail 〔'ʃɜtˌtel; 'ʃəːtteil〕 *n.* 襯衣之後幅。***hang onto one's shirttails*** 依靠某人。—*adj.* 隨便的;不拘泥的;非正式的。

shirt·waist 〔'ʃɜtˌwest; 'ʃəːt-weist〕 *n.* 一種婦女的寬鬆上衣。

shirt·y 〔'ʃɜtɪ; 'ʃəːti〕 *adj.*, **shirt·i·er, shirt·i·est.**〖俚〗發怒的;被激怒的;脾氣暴的。

shit 〔ʃɪt; ʃit〕 *n., v.*, **shit, shit·ting,** *interj.* 〖俚, 鄙〗—*n.* ①糞。②通便。③假裝;誇大。—*v.i.* 通便。—*interj.* 用以表示厭惡、蔑視、失望等。

Shi·va 〔'ʃivə; 'ʃivə〕 *n.* =Siva.

shiv·a·ree 〔ˌʃɪvə'ri; ˌʃivə'riː〕 *n., v.*, **-reed, -ree·ing.** —*n.* ①朋友或鄰居等敲打鍋、鐵桶等鬧新房。②〖俗〗吵吵鬧鬧的慶祝會。—*v.t.* 做 shivaree 鬧新婚夫婦。

shiv·er¹** 〔'ʃɪvɚ; 'ʃivə〕 *v.i.* 顫抖。—*n.* 顫抖。It gives me the *shivers.* 它使我不寒而慄。the shivers*** **a.** 瘧疾。**b.** 寒顫。

shiv·er² *v.t. & v.i.* (使)破碎;打碎;碎裂。***Shiver my timbers!*** (水手罵人語) 粉身碎骨!他媽的!—*n.* 碎片;破片。

shiv·er·y 〔'ʃɪvərɪ; 'ʃivəri〕 *adj.* ①(冷或怕得)發抖的。②寒冷的。

***shoal¹** 〔ʃol; ʃoul〕 *n.* ①羣;魚羣。②(*pl.*)〖俗〗大量;許多。*shoals* of time. 許多時間。—*v.i.* (魚)羣聚;成羣。

shoal²** *n.* ①水淺處;淺灘。②沙洲;沙灘。③(常*pl.*)隱伏的危機或困難。the shoals*** 海之淺水部分。—*adj.* 淺的。—*v.t.* ①駛入淺水處。②使淺。—*v.i.* 變淺。

shoal·y 〔'ʃolɪ; 'ʃouli〕 *adj.*, **shoal·i·er, shoal·i·est.** 多淺灘的。—**shoal·i·ness,** *n.*

shoat 〔ʃot; ʃout〕 *n.* 不滿一歲之小猪。(亦作 **shote**)

‡shock¹ 〔ʃɑk; ʃɔk〕 *n.* ①震動。②地震。A slight *shock* occurred last night. 昨夜有輕微地震。③衝突;撞擊。④電擊。If you touch a live wire you will get a *shock.* 如果你摸有電流的電線, 你就會遭電擊。⑤震驚;激動。His wife's death was a terrible *shock* to him. 他太太的死對他是個很大的打擊。⑥〖醫〗震擾;休克。⑦〖俗〗暈厥。⑧=**shock absorber.** —*v.t.* ①震動。②使震驚。I was very much *shocked* at the sight. 這情景使我大爲驚駭。③使受電擊。—*v.i.* 衝突;碰撞。

shock² *n.* ①(豎立之)穀捆堆;禾束堆。②一大堆;一大批。—*v.t. & v.i.* 堆成穀捆堆。

shock³ *n.* 蓬亂的一堆(如頭髮)。***a shock of hair*** 一堆蓬亂的頭髮;亂髮。

shock absorber ①吸收或減少震動之物;緩衝器。②(汽車之)減震器。

shock·er 〔'ʃɑkɚ; 'ʃɔkə〕 *n.* ①引起震驚之人或物。②〖英俗〗動人感情而無甚價值之作品。

shock-head·ed 〔'ʃɑk'hɛdɪd; 'ʃɔk-ˌhedid〕 *adj.* 頭髮蓬亂的。

shock·ing 〔'ʃɑkɪŋ; 'ʃɔkiŋ〕 *adj.* ①可驚的;駭人的。②使人厭惡的。③〖俗〗極劣的;極壞的。④震動的;觸電的。—**ly,** *adv.*

shock·proof 〔'ʃɑkˌpruf; 'ʃɔkpruːf〕 *adj.* ①防震的。②可防電擊的。

shock tactics 突襲;奇襲。

shock therapy (對精神病的)震擊療法。

shock treatment ①=**shock therapy.** ②任何類似之行動。

shock troops 突擊隊;奇襲隊。

shock wave 激震波;駭波。

shod 〔ʃɑd; ʃɔd〕 *v.* pt. & pp. of **shoe.**

shod·dy 〔'ʃɑdɪ; 'ʃɔdi〕 *adj.*, **-di·er, -di·est,** *n., pl.* **-dies.** —*adj.* ①舊毛絨等再製的。②冒充好貨的;次品的。—*n.* ①舊毛絨再製品。②虛飾外觀之劣等貨。

‡shoe 〔ʃu; ʃuː〕 *n., pl.* **shoes,** *v.*, **shod** or **shoed, shoe·ing.** —*n.* ①鞋;靴。a pair of *shoes.* 一雙鞋。②鞋形物。③蹄鐵。④(手杖等的)金屬環箍。⑤(輪部的)刹車。⑥(輪胎的)外胎。⑦外套(保護裏面事物者)。***be in another man's shoes*** (or ***in someone's shoes***) 處於他人的位置。***cast aside like an old shoe*** 棄如敝屣。***die in one's shoes*** 橫死;慘死;被絞死。***fill someone's shoes*** 代替別人的義務。***fling an old shoe after*** 向…丟舊鞋(新婚夫婦旅行時的幸運的表示)。***look after*** (or ***wait for***) ***dead***

men's shoes 等候別人死(以奪其地位或財產)。 ***Over shoes, over boots.*** 一不做二不休。 ***put the shoe on the right foot*** 責備得當。***shake in one's shoes*** 顫慄；害怕。***stand in another's shoes*** 代替別人；處於別人位置。***That's another pair of shoes.*** 那又是一回事。***The shoe is on the other foot.*** 情況完全相反。***where the shoe pinches*** 困苦之所在。—*v.t.* ①穿以鞋(祇能用過去分詞)。neatly *shod* feet. 鞋子穿得很好的脚。②爲(馬)釘蹄鐵。 A blacksmith *shoes* horses. 鐵匠釘馬蹄鐵。③裝金屬環箍於…之頂端。a stick *shod* with steel. 裝有鋼箍的手杖。

shoe·black [ˈʃuˌblæk; ˈʃuː-blæk] *n.* 擦鞋匠。(亦作 **bootblack**)

shoe·brush [ˈʃuˌbrʌʃ; ˈʃuː-brʌʃ] *n.* 鞋刷。

shoe buckle 鞋扣。

shoe·horn [ˈʃuˌhɔrn; ˈʃuːhɔːn] *n.* 鞋拔。—*v.t.* 將…擠進或塞進。

shoe·lace [ˈʃuˌles; ˈʃuːleis] *n.* 鞋帶。

shoe leather 製鞋用之皮革；皮鞋之集合稱。

shoe lifter 鞋拔。

***shoe·mak·er** [ˈʃuˌmekɚ; ˈʃuːˌmeikə] *n.* 鞋匠。

shoe·mak·ing [ˈʃuˌmekɪŋ; ˈʃuːˌmei-kiŋ] *n.* 製鞋；補鞋；製鞋業。

shoe·shine [ˈʃuˌʃaɪn; ˈʃuːʃain] *n.* ①擦鞋。②擦鞋者。③經擦亮之鞋面。

shoe·string [ˈʃuˌstrɪŋ; ˈʃuːstriŋ] *n.* ①鞋帶。②〖俗〗開始經營企業或投資等所用之極少數金錢。***on a shoestring*** 以極少之資本。—*adj.* 資金極少的。

shoe tree 鞋楦。

sho·gun [ˈʃoˌgun; ˈʃouˌguːn] *n.* (日本封建時代之)將軍。

sho·gun·ate [ˈʃoˌgʌnɪt; ˈʃouˌgʌnit] *n.* (日本之)幕府。

***shone** [ʃon; ʃɔn] *v.* pt. & pp. of **shine.**

shoo [ʃu; ʃuː] *interj., v.,* **shooed, shoo·ing.** —*interj.* 趕走鳥獸之呼聲。—*v.t.* 以此呼聲趕走(鳥獸)。—*v.i.* 發出此聲音。

shoo-in [ˈʃuˌɪn; ˈʃuːin] *n.* 〖俗〗①被認爲可輕易當選的候選人或獲勝的競賽人。②有把握之事。

shook¹ [ʃuk; ʃuk] *v.* pt. of **shake.** —*adj.* (亦作 **shook up**)〖俚〗受嚴重打擊的。

shook² *n.* ①可造一木桶的一批木板。②可拼成一盒或一件傢具等的部分。③一捆東西。

‡shoot [ʃut; ʃuːt] *v.,* **shot** [ʃɑt; ʃɔt], **shoot·ing,** *n.* —*v.t.* ①射中；射死。The three prisoners were *shot.* 這三個囚犯被槍斃了。I'll be *shot* (= I'll be damned) if I do it. 我決不做這種事。②發射；射擊。He *shot* a pistol at me. 他用手槍向我射擊。③發出；提出。He *shot* question after question at us. 他接二連三向我們提出問題。④投；拋。⑤迅疾通過；穿過。⑥發(芽)；生(枝)。⑦拍(照)；攝影。⑧傾倒；排出。⑨以不同顏色等加變化；加不同顏色之紋理於。⑩測量…的高度。⑪攻(球)入門；送(物)入囊袋等。⑫突然或迅速地指向。⑬突然地移動。⑭伸出。⑮使爆炸。⑯〖航空〗重複練習。—*v.i.* ①射擊；放槍；射箭。to *shoot* at a target. 向目標射擊。He *shoots* well. 他善射擊。②出獵。③突進；疾馳。A car *shot* by us. 一輛車從我們身旁急馳而過。④生長；迅速發育。The boy is *shooting* up. 這孩子長得很快。⑤發芽。⑥急痛；劇痛。Pains *shot* up his arm. 他的手臂陣陣作痛。⑦拍照；攝影。⑧突出；伸入。⑨〖俗〗開始講話。***shoot a bolt*** 關上或打開插梢。***shoot a covert*** (***an estate***)在獵場(莊園)打獵。***shoot ahead*** 迅速地前進；(喻)追過。***shoot away*** a. 繼續射擊。b. 射完(子彈等)。***shoot dice*** 擲骰子。***shoot down*** 打下；擊落。***shoot for*** (or ***at***) 期望；企圖達到(目標)。***shoot off one's mouth*** (or ***face***)〖俚〗 a. 信口雌黃。b. 誇張。***shoot rubbish*** 從車上等處傾倒垃圾。***shoot the breeze*** 〖俚〗聊天；胡扯。***shoot the bull*** 〖俚〗 a. 漫談；閑聊。b. 誇張；渲染。***shoot the works*** 〖俚〗盡力而爲；傾全力而作。***shoot up*** a. 〖美俚〗放槍使(村舍、地區等)驚恐。b. 漲價。c. 迅速成長。d. 射傷。—*n.* ①射擊；狩獵。to make a *shoot.* 發射。②射擊或狩獵之行程、團體、競賽、地區等。③芽；苗；嫩枝。bamboo *shoots.* 筍；筍。bean *shoots.* 豆芽菜。④瀉槽；斜槽。⑤發射。

shoot-'em-up [ˈʃutəmˌʌp; ˈʃuːtəm-ˌʌp] *n.* 〖美俚〗鎗戰影片。

shoot·er [ˈʃutɚ; ˈʃuːtə] *n.* ①射擊者；獵者。②射擊用物, 如槍、砲等(通常用於複合詞, 如 pea-*shooter* 豆子槍)。

shoot·ing [ˈʃutɪŋ; ˈʃuːtiŋ] *n.* ①發射；射擊。②狩獵；遊獵。③(某一地區之)狩獵權。④遊獵地；獵場。

shooting box (or **lodge**) 〖英〗狩獵小屋。

shooting gallery 射擊場；打靶場。

shooting iron 〖美俚〗火器；(尤指)手槍。

shooting script 根據拍攝次序排好的電影劇本。

shooting star 流星；隕星。

shooting war 熱戰(爲cold war 之對)。

‡shop [ʃɑp; ʃɔp] *n., v.,* **shopped, shop·ping,** *interj.* —*n.* ①店鋪；商店。a barber *shop.* 理髮店。②工廠；修理廠。He works in a carpenter's *shop.* 他在一家木工廠裏做工。③大商店中之某一部門。④〖教育〗 a. 手工藝(如木工、印刷等)。 b. 上此課程的教室。⑤職業；業務。***all over the shop*** 〖俚〗在各處；紛亂地散置；零亂；雜亂。***come*** (or ***go***) ***to the wrong shop*** 〖俗〗託錯人幫助、打聽消息等。***set up shop*** 開店；開始營業。***shut up shop*** 歇業；停止營業；停止做某些事。***talk shop*** 談論本行、本業、自己特別有趣的事物等。—*v.i.* 購物。My sister is out *shopping.* 我的妹妹出去買東西去了。***shop around*** 極力尋找(較好職位或便宜貨等)。—*v.t.* ①找或細查(貨物、財物等)準備購買。②〖英俗〗 a. 關進監獄。 b. 出賣(某人)。—*interj.* 商店中, 叫店員服侍顧客的喊聲。

shop·boy [ˈʃɑpˌbɔɪ; ˈʃɔpbɔi] *n.* 店鋪的伙計；小店員。

shop·girl [ˈʃɑpˌgɝl; ˈʃɔpgəːl] *n.* 女店員。

shop hours (商店正式的)營業時間。

***shop·keep·er** [ˈʃɑpˌkipɚ; ˈʃɔpˌkiːpə] *n.* 小商人；零售商人；小店主。

shop·lift·er [ˈʃɑpˌlɪftɚ; ˈʃɔpˌliftə] *n.* 佯爲顧客而偷竊貨品者。—**shop·lift·ing,** *n.*

shop·man [ˈʃɑpmən; ˈʃɔpmən] *n., pl.* **-men.** ①售貨員。②零售商人；小商人；店主。

shop·per [ˈʃɑpɚ; ˈʃɔpə] *n.* ①看貨、購物之人。②替商店購貨的人。③到競爭者商店收集情報、樣式、價錢等的雇員(=comparison shopper)。

shop·ping** [ˈʃɑpɪŋ; ˈʃɔpiŋ] *n.* ①購物。I have some *shopping* to do this afternoon. 今天下午我要出去買些東西。 ②購物者可利用的設施或可買到的商品。go*** (***out***) ***shopping*** 去購物。He *went out shopping* with his wife. 他和他的太太出去購物。—*adj.* 購物的。

shopping center(郊區之)購物中心。

shop·py [ˈʃɑpɪ; ˈʃɔpi] *adj.*, **shop·pi·er, shop·pi·est.** ①小商人(特性)的。②商店林立的。③〖俗〗有關自身職業的;商業上的。
shop steward (工會的)工廠代表。(亦作 **committeeman, shop chairman**)
shop·talk [ˈʃɑpˌtɔk; ˈʃɔptɔːk] *n.* ①有關自己行業之談話。②職業用語。
shop·walk·er [ˈʃɑpˌwɔkɚ; ˈʃɔpˌwɔːkə] *n.* (大商店中的)巡視員;招待員。
shop·win·dow [ˈʃɑpˈwɪndo; ˈʃɔpˈwindou] *n.* 商店的櫥窗。
shop·worn [ˈʃɑpˌworn; ˈʃɔpwɔːn] *adj.* 店中擺舊的; 經久曝露而陳舊的。
sho·ran [ˈʃoræn; ˈʃɔːræn] *n.* 〖航空〗測定自己位置的一種儀器。
‡**shore**[1] [ʃor, ʃɔr; ʃɔː, ʃɔə] *n.* ①岸。to go on *shore*. 上岸。②陸地; 土地; 國土。③〖法律〗滿潮線和退潮線中間的地區。***in shore*** 近岸。***off shore*** 在離岸不遠的海中。***on shore*** 在岸上。***within these shores*** 四海之內;在此國內。—*adj.* 陸地的;海岸的。
shore[2] *n., v.,* **shored, shor·ing.** —*n.* (支撐建造或修理中之船、不穩之建築物等的)支柱;撐柱。—*v.t.* 用支柱支撐〖up〗。
shore leave 〖海軍〗①准許船上人員登岸之休假證。②此項休假之時間。
shore·less [ˈʃorlɪs; ˈʃɔːlis] *adj.* ①無可供登陸之海岸的; 無岸的。②無邊的;無涯的。
shore line 海岸線。(亦作 **shoreline**)
shore patrol 〖美〗海岸巡邏隊。
shore·ward [ˈʃorwɚd; ˈʃɔːwəd] *adj.* 向岸方的。—*adv.* (亦作 **shorewards**) 向岸方地。
shor·ing [ˈʃorɪŋ; ˈʃɔːriŋ] *n.* ①(建築物、船等的)支柱之集合稱。②支柱的支撐。
shorn [ʃorn; ʃɔːn] *v.* pp. of **shear.** —*adj.* ①被剪過的。②被拿去的;被搶奪去的。
‡**short** [ʃort; ʃɔːt] *adj.* ①短的; 短暫的。a *short* time ago. 不久之前。②矮的。③簡短的; 簡潔的。to be *short* and to the point. 短而扼要。④不足的;短少的;缺少的。I am a little *short*. 我的錢不够花。The sum comes *short* by ten dollars. 總額尙差十元。⑤唐突的;無禮的。⑥油和麪的;鬆脆的(餅等)。⑦〖語音〗短音的。⑧〖商〗賣空的;無存貨的。⑨〖商〗靠跌價賺錢的。⑩卽將到期的;卽將兌現的。⑪達不到(目標)的;不够遠的。⑫(金屬等)易斷的。⑬(飲料之)含酒精量少的。⑭〖英〗(威士忌之)純的。⑮(黏土之)可塑度不足的。***be short of*** **a.** 未達到;在…近處。**b.** 缺乏;短少。 We *are short of* money. 我們缺乏金錢。***be*** (or ***become***) ***short of breath*** 易喘。 ***cut something short*** 使短促;使中斷;提早結束。***have a short temper*** 易怒;脾氣急躁。***make a long story short*** 簡而言之。***make short work of*** 迅速處理、毀壞等。***nothing short of*** 除…外, 完全無…的。***short and*** 代表 and 的符號(卽 &)。***short and sweet*** **a.** 短而愉快的。**b.** 扼要的。***short for***…之簡稱。***short of*** **a.** 較差於…。**b.** 除了…以外。***short sight*** 近視; (喩)無眼光。***short time*** 縮短的工作時間。***short waist*** (上衣之) 短身材。—*adv.* ①短地。to cut a thing *short*. 截短某物。②突然。③不足地; 缺乏地。④未達某程度地〖of〗。⑤〖商〗賣空。It is risky to sell *short*. 賣空危險。⑥簡短地。***cut short*** 中斷; 中止。***fall*** (or ***come***) ***short*** **a.** 不達;不及。**b.** 不足;缺乏。***run short*** 不足;不够。***sell short*** **a.** 〖商〗(股票等)賣空。**b.** 小看;低估。—*n.* ①短的東西。②缺乏或不足者。③〖電〗短路。④〖商〗賣空之人; 賣空。⑤〖語音〗短音節。⑥(*pl.*) 短褲。⑦(*pl.*) 短而寬鬆的運動褲。⑧(*pl.*) 嬰兒的短裝。⑨麪糠和粗粉之混合物。***for short*** 簡略之。***in short*** 總而言之。***the long and*** (***the***) ***short of it*** 這事的概略。—*v.t.* & *v.i.* 〖電〗(使)生短路;設短路。—**ness,** *n.*
***short·age** [ˈʃortɪdʒ; ˈʃɔːtidʒ] *n.* ①缺乏;不足。a *shortage* of grain. 穀物缺乏。②不足之額;缺陷。
short-armed [ˈʃortˌɑrmd; ˈʃɔːtɑːmd] *adj.* ①短臂的。②短距離的。
short bill 短期票據。
short·bread [ˈʃortˌbrɛd; ˈʃɔːtbred] *n.* 鬆脆的酥餅。
short·cake [ˈʃortˌkek; ˈʃɔːtkeik] *n.* (一種上面覆有漿果或其他水果之)油酥糕餅。
short·change [ˌʃortˈtʃendʒ; ˌʃɔːtˈtʃeindʒ] *v.t.*, **-changed, -chang·ing.** 〖美俗〗①找錢不足;少找錢給(某人)。②欺騙。
short circuit 〖電〗短路。
short-cir·cuit [ˌʃortˈsɝkɪt; ˈʃɔːtˈsəːkit] *v.t.* & *v.i.* ①〖電〗(使)生短路;設短路。②使(公文)走捷徑。③〖外科〗做捷徑手術。
short clothes (小兒着用之)短褲。
short·com·ing [ˈʃortˌkʌmɪŋ; ʃɔːtˈkʌmiŋ] *n.* 缺點;短處。
short cut ①近路。②省時、省力、省錢的方法;捷徑。
short-cut [ˈʃortˌkʌt; ˈʃɔːtkʌt] *v.t.* & *v.i.*, **-cut, -cut·ting.** (使)走捷徑。
***short·en** [ˈʃortn̩; ˈʃɔːtn] *v.t.* ①使短;縮短。Please have this coat *shortened*. 請把這件上衣改短。②使鬆脆。③〖航海〗收(帆)。④(網球拍、球棒等)抓短(手的位置抓得特別低)。⑤將(母音或音節)讀成短音。—*v.i.* ①縮短。②(價錢等)減少。
short-end·er [ˈʃortˈɛndɚ; ˈʃɔːtˈendə] *n.* 〖俗〗競賽中被認爲沒有希望獲勝者。
short·en·ing [ˈʃortn̩ɪŋ; ˈʃɔːtniŋ] *n.* ①使麪食、糕餅等酥脆之奶油、豬油等; 油酥。②〖語音〗成短音節之步驟。③〖語言〗將長字縮短。
short field 〖棒球〗內野第二壘與第三壘間之地區, 由游擊手 (shortstop) 守衞。
short fuse 〖美〗暴燥脾氣。
***short·hand** [ˈʃortˌhænd; ˈʃɔːthænd] *n.* ①速記法。②用速記記錄的文法。—*adj.* ①用速記的。a *shorthand* writer. 速記員。②以速記寫下的。
short-hand·ed [ˈʃortˈhændɪd; ˈʃɔːtˈhændid] *adj.* 人手不足的。—**ness,** *n.*
short·hand-typ·ist [ˈʃortˌhændˈtaɪpɪst; ˈʃɔːthændˈtaipist] *n.* 〖英〗速記員。
short-haul [ˈʃortˈhɔl; ˈʃɔːtˈhɔːl] *adj.* 短距離的;短程的。
short·horn [ˈʃortˌhɔrn; ˈʃɔːthɔːn] *n.* (原產於英國之)短角牛。
short·ish [ˈʃortɪʃ; ˈʃɔːtiʃ] *adj.* 略短的;稍短的。
short-lived [ˈʃortˈlaɪvd; ˈʃɔːtˈlivd] *adj.* 短命的; 持續不久的; 曇花一現的。
***short·ly** [ˈʃortlɪ; ˈʃɔːtli] *adv.* ①卽刻;不久。Mr. Wang will arrive *shortly*. 王先生不久就會到來。②簡略地。③唐突地;無禮地。
short order 餐廳中可速成的一道菜。
short-or·der [ˈʃortˈɔrdɚ; ˈʃɔːtˈɔːdə] *adj.* ①很快可做好菜的。②立刻供應的。
short-range [ˈʃortˈrendʒ; ˈʃɔːtˈreindʒ] *adj.* 短射程的;短期間的。
short rib ①假肋骨;(牛肉)假肋。②(*pl.*) 假肋骨部分。
short sale 〖商〗賣空 (未買貨卽預作銷售)。

short seller〔商〕賣空者。
short selling〔商〕賣空行爲。
short short story 短短篇小說（比 short story 更短的小說）。
short shrift ①(死刑犯在行刑前之)簡短懺悔。②(無耐心或同情心所致之)不理會。③硬心腸；不予展緩。***give short shrift (to)*** a. 不理會。b. 立刻嚴厲地處理。
***short·sight·ed** 〔ˈʃɔrtˈsaɪtɪd; ˈʃɔːt-ˈsaitid〕*adj.* ①近視的。②目光短淺的；無遠見的。a *shortsighted* policy. 無遠見的政策。
short-spo·ken 〔ˈʃɔrtˈspokən; ˈʃɔːt-ˈspoukən〕*adj.* ①言簡的。②粗魯的；唐突的。
short·stop 〔ˈʃɔrt,stɑp; ˈʃɔːtstɔp〕*n.* ①〔棒球〕(第二壘與第三壘間的)游擊手。②〔照相〕一種能立刻制止顯影作用之溶劑。
short story 短篇小說。
short subject〔電影〕加演之短片。
short-tem·pered 〔ˈʃɔrtˈtɛmpəd; ˈʃɔːtˈtempəd〕*adj.* 易怒的；脾氣暴燥的。
short-term 〔ˈʃɔrtˈtɝm; ˈʃɔːttəːm〕*adj.* 短期的。
short ton 短噸；美噸（常衡2000磅）。
short wave 短波。
short-wave 〔ˈʃɔrt,wev; ˈʃɔːt-weiv〕*v.,* **short-waved, short-wav·ing,** *adj.* —*v.t.* 以短波播送。—*adj.* 短波的；用短波播送的。
short wave radio 短波無線電發「射機。」
short-wind·ed 〔ˈʃɔrtˈwɪndɪd; ˈʃɔːt-ˈwindid〕*adj.* ①氣促的；呼吸困難的。②(文章、講話等)簡短扼要的。
short·y 〔ˈʃɔrtɪ; ˈʃɔːti〕*n., pl.* **short·ies,** *adj.* —*n.*〔俗〕①矮子。②短的衣服。—*adj.* 短衣服的。
shot[1] 〔ʃɑt; ʃɔt〕*v.* pt. and pp. of **shoot.** —*adj.* ①(布等) 彩色閃變的。②有顏色穿透的。③破舊的；損壞的。④〔俚〕酒醉的。
shot**[2] *n., pl.* **shots** or **shot,** *v.,* **shot·ted, shot·ting,** *adj.* —*n.* ①彈丸；砲彈；鐵球。a solid *shot.* 實彈。②射擊；一發；一射。He heard two *shots.* 他聽見兩聲鎗響。③瞄準；襲擊；狙擊。That was a good *shot.* 那一鎗打得很準。④射程。⑤射手；砲手。He is a good *shot.* 他是個優秀的鎗手。⑥似彈丸等之物。⑦尖刻的批評。⑧試圖；試爲；猜測。⑨〔運動〕鉛球。⑩照片；(電影之)單幅。⑪〔俚〕飲。⑫〔俚〕一劑；一服。a *shot* of some drug. 一劑藥。⑬〔採礦〕爆炸。⑭應付之款；賬。⑮散彈。⑯打針；注射。⑰打賭輸贏的機會。⑱照相；攝影。a long shot*** 試爲困難之事；大膽的企圖。***big shot***〔美俗〕重要人物；大人物。***by a long shot*** 不顧一切。***call one's shots*** 事先說出所要做的事及如何做法。***call the shots***〔俚〕控制；指揮。***like a shot*** 立刻。***not by a long shot*** 毫不；毫無；不行。***off like a shot*** 高速地；不稽延地；似彈矢般地。***put the shot*** 擲鉛球。***shot in the arm***〔俚〕鼓勵之事物。***shot in the dark***〔俚〕胡猜。***shot in the locker***〔俗〕(戰艦彈艙僅存之一彈，轉義)金錢。—*v.t.* ①裝以彈丸等。②試圖。—*adj.* ①射出的。②〔俗〕用舊了的。***shot through with*** 充滿著；遍是。
shote 〔ʃot; ʃout〕*n.* ①斷奶的小豬。②〔方〕廢料；一文不值之人。
shot effect〔電子〕散粒效應。
shot·gun 〔ˈʃɑt,gʌn; ˈʃɔtgʌn〕*n.* 散彈槍；獵槍；鳥槍。—*adj.* ①以散彈槍射擊或强迫的。②不分皂白的；漫無選擇的。③包羅萬象的。④强迫的。—*v.t.*①以散彈槍射擊。②强迫。
shotgun wedding (or **marriage**)〔俚〕①因已懷孕而不得不舉行的結婚。②爲需要而作的妥協；勉强的結合或同意。
shot-proof 〔ˈʃɑt,pruf; ˈʃɔtpruːf〕*adj.* 防彈的。
shot-put 〔ˈʃɑt,put; ˈʃɔtput〕*n.*〔運動〕擲鉛球。
shot-put·ter 〔ˈʃɑt,putə; ˈʃɔt,putə〕*n.* 擲鉛球者。
shot tower 彈丸製造塔。
‡should 〔ˈʃud, ,ʃud, ʃəd, ʃd, ʃt; ʃud, ʃəd, ʃd, ʃt〕*aux. v.* pt. of **shall.** ①普通用法：作 shall 的過去式，參看 shall. I said on Thursday that I *should* see my friend the next day. 我在星期四說我將於第二天訪晤我的朋友。②特殊用法：**a.** 表示一種責任或義務之意（=ought to. 應該）。You *should* try to make fewer mistakes. 你應該設法少犯一些錯誤。**b.** 表示一種不確定的狀態。If it *should* rain tomorrow, I *should* not go; 如果明天下雨，我就不去了。**c.** 表示一種可能發生而實際並未發生的情形。I *should* have bought it if I had had enough money. 如果我當時有足够的錢，我就會把它買來了。**d.** 表示預料或可能之意。They *should* arrive by one o'clock, I think. 我想他們在一點鐘以前可以到達。**e.** 表示一種比較委婉的說法。*Should* you like to go? 你願意去嗎？**f.** 表示事物之狀態或理由。He was pardoned on the condition that he *should* leave the country. 他可得到赦免，其條件是必須離開國境。**g.** 表示不合理、難以相信或不應該之事（常用於 why 問句）。Why *should* you think that I did not like the book? 你有甚麼理由認爲我不喜歡這本書呢？
‡shoul·der 〔ˈʃoldə; ˈʃouldə〕*n.* ①肩。to shrug one's *shoulders.* 聳聳肩。②(*pl.*) 雙肩及背的上部。③衣服的肩部；衣肩。④(豬、牛等連前腿的) 肩膀肉。⑤肩狀的部分或突出部。⑥道路的兩側之任一。⑦〔印刷〕鉛字超出筆畫之平面部分；字肩。⑧〔築城〕肩角。⑨(常*pl.*)〔俗〕負責任、願受譴責或表同情的能力。***cry on someone's shoulder*** 向某人傾訴以獲同情。***give*** (or ***turn***) ***a cold shoulder to a person*** 冷淡對待某人。***have broad shoulders*** 肩膀寬；可當重任。***lay the blame on the right shoulders*** 責備得當。***put one's shoulder to the wheel*** 努力工作。***rub shoulders with*** 與…爲伍；和…在一起。***shift the blame on to other shoulders*** 諉過於他人。***shoulder to shoulder*** 並肩；團結一致。***square one's shoulders*** 將兩肩向後收縮俾與身體之垂直軸成直角。***stand head and shoulders above somebody*** 遠勝於某人。***straight from the shoulder*** 公然地；直接地；坦白地。—*v.t. & v.i.* ①肩負；揹於肩上。②負擔；擔任。He *shouldered* his son's debts. 他負擔他兒子的債務。③以肩衝；擠。***Shoulder arms!***〔口令〕槍上肩！
shoulder bag 有肩帶的女用手提包。
shoulder belt〔軍〕從肩上和胸部穿過的斜皮帶。
shoulder blade 肩胛骨。
shoulder brace 拱背矯正器。
shoulder knot 肩飾。
shoulder loop〔美〕軍隊制服兩肩上掛階級或肩章之布條。
shoulder mark〔美〕海軍的肩章。
shoulder strap ①肩帶；負革。②〔軍〕肩章。
should·n't 〔ˈʃudn̩t; ˈʃudnt〕=should not.

shouldst [ˈʃudst;ʃudst] *v.*〖古〗should 之第二人稱, 單數。(亦作 **shouldest**)

‡**shout** [ʃaut; ʃaut] *v.i.* & *v.t.* ①呼;喊;叫;喊出;叫出。They *shouted* as with one voice. 他們異口同聲地呼喊。②高聲談笑。The crowd *shouted* with laughter. 羣衆縱聲大笑。③〖澳〗請(某人)喝酒,吃飯,玩樂。***shout a person down*** 大聲喝倒某人;大聲喝使某人沉默。—*n.* ①叫; 喊。He gave a *shout* of welcome. 他發出歡迎的呼聲。②突發的大笑;陣笑。—**er,** *n.*

shout·ing [ˈʃautɪŋ; ˈʃautiŋ] *n.* 叫;喊;陣笑。***all over but the shouting*** 大致已成定局。***within shouting distance*** 在距離很近(一喊就聽得見)的地方。

shove** [ʃʌv; ʃʌv] *v.,* **shoved, shov·ing,** *n.* —*v.t.* ①推; 推擠; 撞。②置放。*Shove* it in your pocket. 把它放在口袋中。—*v.i.* 推;擠;撞。Don't *shove,* wait your turn. 不要推, 等著依次輪到你。shove off*** a. 推船離岸。b. 動身;出發。—*n.* 推。—**shov·er,** *n.*

shove-half·pen·ny [ˈʃʌvˈhepənɪ; ˈʃʌvˈheipəni] *n.* 一種推移錢幣的遊戲。(亦作 **shove-ha'penny**)

shov·el** [ˈʃʌvl̩; ˈʃʌvl] *n., v.,* **-el(l)ed, -el·(l)ing.** —*n.* ①鏟; 鐵鍬。②一鏟或一鍬之量。③鏟形帽。put to bed with a shovel*** 〖俗〗埋葬。—*v.t.* ① 用鏟子鏟起並投送。②用鏟子挖成。③大量地投送。—*v.i.* 用鏟或鍬工作。***shovel up*** (or ***in***) ***money*** 大量地賺錢。

shov·el·board [ˈʃʌvl̩ˌbord; ˈʃʌvlbɔːd] *n.* =**shuffleboard.**

shov·el·(l)er [ˈʃʌvl̩ɚ; ˈʃʌvlə] *n.* ①用鏟之工人; 鏟東西的工具。②〖動物〗廣味鳧。

shov·el·ful [ˈʃʌvl̩ˌful; ˈʃʌvlful] *n., pl.* **-fuls.** 滿鏟之量。

shovel hat (英國教會牧師戴的)鏟形帽。

shov·el-nosed [ˈʃʌvl̩ˌnozd; ˈʃʌvəl-nouzd] *adj.* (鳥或魚等)嘴濶扁如鏟的。

‡**show** [ʃo;ʃou] *v.,* **showed, shown**[ʃon; ʃoun] or **showed, show·ing,***n., adj.* —*v.t.* ①顯示; 表現; 顯露; 表示。*Show* what you have in your hands. 把你手裏的東西給我看看。②解釋; 說明; 告知; 指示; 引導。Can you *show* me how to do it? 你可以告訴我怎樣做這事嗎? ③證明;表明。He *showed* that it was true. 他證明那是對的。④施與。⑤表演;演出;上映。⑥出示(爲出售等)。—*v.i.* ①顯現; 可見; 出現。②顯得。③展覽;表演。④〖俚〗(賽跑)跑前三名; 跑第三名。⑤〖俗〗赴約。He said he would be there, but he didn't *show.* 他說他會來,但他沒有到。⑥〖俗〗參加演出;上演。***have nothing to show for it*** 無成就可言。***show a person the door*** 叫人走出房子; 逐出。***show fight*** 堅決地抗拒; 願戰; 反抗。***show off*** a. 誇耀;炫示。b. 顯露自己之成就、能力或才華等; 賣弄。***show oneself*** 露臉; 出面; 出現。(***not to***) ***show one's face*** (or ***head***) (不)露臉;(不)出現。***show one's hand*** 表明計畫或意圖。***show one's teeth*** 發怒。***show up*** a. 〖俗〗出現。b. 突出;顯眼。c. 使別人相形見絀。***show*** (***a person*** or ***thing***) ***up*** 暴露;揭發。—*n.* ①顯示;展覽。②展覽會。③虛飾;外觀。She is fond of *show.* 她好虛飾。④表示。⑤徵象;痕跡。⑥〖俗〗演藝; 電影。⑦〖俗〗機會。⑧嘲弄的對象;怪物;異象。Don't make a *show* of yourself. 不要做怪樣子。⑨藉口。⑩電影院。⑪戲劇之演出;劇團。⑫光景。⑬〖醫〗a. 初次月經。b. 臨產現血。⑭〖英俗〗事情;一羣人;事。***be on show*** 展覽中。***by*** (***a***) ***show of hands*** 以舉手表決。***for show*** 爲效果起見; 爲引人注意。***give the*** (***whole***) ***show away*** 露出任何事物之錯誤、缺點等; 露馬脚; 失言。***put up a good show*** 演出精采。***run the show*** 當家;掌權。***stand a show*** 〖俗〗有希望。***steal the show*** a. 搶鏡頭。b. 在一羣人中成爲最受歡迎的;出鋒頭。***stop the show*** 贏得熱烈掌聲而使表演爲之停頓。—*adj.* ①爲表演用的。②戲劇的; 表演的。—**a·ble,** *adj.*

Sho·wa [ˈʃowɑ;ˈʃouwɑː] *n.* 昭和(日本天皇裕仁之年號, 自1926始)。

show bill 招貼;(演出之)廣告;戲單。

show biz 〖俗〗=**show business.**

show·boat [ˈʃoˌbot; ˈʃoubout] *n.* 演藝船。—*v.i.* 〖俗〗炫耀。

show·bread [ˈʃoˌbrɛd; ˈʃoubred] *n.* =**shewbread.**

show business 影劇業。

show card 招貼;貨樣卡片。

show·case [ˈʃoˌkes; ˈʃoukeis] *n., v.,* **-cased, -cas·ing.** —*n.* ①店鋪或博物院等之玻璃櫃櫥。②示範。—*v.t.* 展覽;展示。

show·down [ˈʃoˌdaun; ˈʃoudaun] *n.* 攤牌。***force a showdown*** 迫使攤牌。

***show·er**[1] [ˈʃauɚ; ˈʃau-ə] *n.* ①陣雨。②任何似陣雨之物。③淋浴。to take a *shower.* 作一次淋浴。④送禮物給新娘或待產婦之聚會。⑤大量之事物。—*v.t.* ①淋濕。②大量地給與。③如陣雨般抛擲。They *showered* stones on the enemy. 他們向敵人如雨般投石頭。④爲…淋浴。⑤送禮給(新娘或待產婦)。—*v.i.* ①下驟雨;如陣雨般降下。②淋浴。

show·er[2] [ˈʃoɚ; ˈʃouə] *n.* 顯示者; 表演人。

shower bath 淋浴。

show·er·y [ˈʃauərɪ; ˈʃau-əri] *adj.* 陣雨的;多陣雨的;似陣雨的;大量的。

show girl ①歌舞女郎。②廣告女郎。

show·ing [ˈʃoɪŋ; ˈʃouiŋ] *n.* ①印象;表現。②展示;展覽。③陳述; 指陳。④外觀; 外表。***make a good showing*** 壯觀瞻。

show·man [ˈʃomən; ˈʃoumən] *n., pl.* **-men.** ①主持演藝或展覽的人。②長於引起別人興趣和注意的人。

show·man·ship [ˈʃomənˌʃɪp; ˈʃou-mənʃip] *n.* 引人注意之技術或能力。

‡**shown** [ʃon; ʃoun] *v.* pp. of **show.**

show-off [ˈʃoˌɔf; ˈʃouɔːf] *n.* ①炫耀。②炫耀的人。

show of hands 舉手表示贊成, 反對, 或志願等。

show·piece [ˈʃoˌpis; ˈʃoupiːs] *n.* ①展出之事物。②值得展出之事物。

show·place [ˈʃoˌples; ˈʃoupleis] *n.* ①可遊覽的地方; 名勝。②裝潢美麗典雅的家庭、辦公室或建築物等。

show·room [ˈʃoˌrum; ˈʃourum] *n.* 貨品陳列室。

show-stop·per [ˈʃoˌstɑpɚ; ˈʃouˌstɔ-pə] *n.* 〖戲院〗臺詞或表演等因贏得掌聲而使演劇一時中斷者。(亦作 **showstopper**)

show trial (極權國家舉行的)公審。

show·up [ˈʃoˌʌp; ˈʃouʌp] *n.* 〖俗〗暴露;出現;揭發。

show window 商店之櫥窗。

show·y [ˈʃoɪ; ˈʃoui] *adj.,* **show·i·er, show·i·est.** 華麗的; 炫耀的。—**show·i·ly,** *adv.* —**show·i·ness,** *n.*

shrank [ʃræŋk;ʃræŋk] *v.* pt. of **shrink.**

shrap·nel [ˈʃræpnəl;ˈʃræpnl̩] *n. sing.* or *pl.* 榴霰彈;榴霰彈片。

***shred** [ʃrɛd; ʃred] *n., v.,* **shred·ded** or **shred, shred·ding.** —*n.* ①碎片; 細條。

The wind tore the sail to *shreds.* 風將帆撕成了碎片。②微量；些微；一點。—*v.t.* & *v.i.* 撕成碎片；切成細條。—**der,** *n.*

shrew [ʃru; ʃruː] *n.* ①潑婦；悍婦。②〖動物〗鼩鼱；地鼠。—**like,** *adj.*

*__shrewd__ [ʃrud; ʃruːd] *adj.* ①明敏的；精明的。He is a *shrewd* business man. 他是一個精明的商人。②銳利的；酷烈的。③惡意的；毒惡的。**shrewd turn** 卑鄙的欺詐手段。—**ly,** *adv.* —**ness,** *n.*

shrew·ish [ˈʃruɪʃ; ˈʃruːiʃ] *adj.* 脾氣暴躁的；潑悍的。—**ly,** *adv.* —**ness,** *n.*

shrew·mouse [ˈʃruˌmaus; ˈʃruːmaus] *n., pl.* **-mice.** 〖動物〗鼩鼱；地鼠。

*__shriek__ [ʃrik; ʃriːk] *n.* 尖銳的叫聲、響聲、或笑聲。—*v.i.* ①尖叫。②(樂器、哨子、風等)發出尖銳聲音。—*v.t.* 以尖銳的聲音發出或道出。—**er,** *n.*

shriev·al·ty [ˈʃrivl̩tɪ; ˈʃriːvəlti] *n., pl.* **-ties.** sheriff 之職務，轄區或任期等。

shrift [ʃrɪft; ʃrift] *n.* 〖古〗①懺悔；臨終懺悔。②懺悔後僧侶所定的苦行。

shrike [ʃraɪk; ʃraik] *n.* 百舌鳥；伯勞。

*__shrill__ [ʃrɪl; ʃril] *adj.* ①聲音尖銳的。Crickets and locusts make *shrill* noises. 蟋蟀和蟬發出刺耳尖鳴聲。②多尖銳聲的。③強烈的(情感等)。—*v.i.* 發出尖銳的聲音。—*v.t.* 以尖銳聲音發出或道出。—*n.* 尖銳的聲音。—*adv.* 以尖銳聲地。—**ness,** *n.* —**y,** *adv.*

shrimp [ʃrɪmp; ʃrimp] *n., pl.* **shrimps, shrimp,** *v., adj.* —*n.* ①小蝦。②短小或無足輕重的人。—*v.i.* 捉蝦。—*adj.* ①含小蝦的。②捕蝦的。—**er,** *n.*

*__shrine__ [ʃraɪn; ʃrain] *n., v.,* **shrined, shrin·ing.** —*n.* ①神龕。②廟；祠。③古蹟；聖地；聖物。④聖者之墓。—*v.t.* 將…置於神龕內；奉祀於廟中(=enshrine). —**like,** *adj.*

*__shrink__ [ʃrɪŋk; ʃriŋk] *v.,* **shrank** [ʃræŋk; ʃræŋk], **shrunk** [ʃrʌŋk; ʃrʌŋk] or **shrunk·en** [ˈʃrʌŋkən; ˈʃrʌŋkən], **shrink·ing,** *n.* —*v.i.* ①收縮；縐縮；萎縮。②退縮；畏縮。The dog *shrank* from the whip. 那狗退縮以躲避鞭子。—*v.t.* 使收縮；使縐縮。—*n.* 收縮；萎縮。—**a·ble,** *adj.* —**er,** *n.*

shrink·age [ˈʃrɪŋkɪdʒ; ˈʃriŋkidʒ] *n.* ①縮少；縐縮；收縮。②收縮的量或程度。③家畜原重量與販賣時重量之差額。

shrinking violet 怕羞，謙虛的人。

shrive [ʃraɪv; ʃraiv] *v.,* **shrived** or **shrove, shriv·en** or **shrived, shriv·ing.** —*v.t.* (教士)聽(悔罪者)懺悔；使懺悔而赦罪。—*v.i.* ①聽懺悔。②懺悔。

shriv·el [ˈʃrɪvl̩; ˈʃrivl] *v.,* **-el(l)ed, -el(l)ing.** —*v.t.* ①使枯萎；使縐縮；使捲縮。②使失去效力；使成爲無用。—*v.i.* ①枯萎；縐縮；捲縮。②變爲虛弱無用。

shroff [ʃrɑf; ʃrɔf] *n.* ①(印度)錢幣兌換者。②(中國)錢幣鑑定者。—*v.t.*鑑定(錢幣)。

Shrop·shire [ˈʃrɑpʃɪr; ˈʃrɔpʃiə] *n.* ①什羅浦郡(英格蘭西部之一郡)。②英國種的無角食用羊(面部及腿爲深褐色，毛爲白色)。

*__shroud__ [ʃraud; ʃraud] *n.* ①屍衣；壽衣。②遮蔽物；覆蓋物。③(*pl.*)(船之)橫桅索。—*v.t.* ①包以屍衣。②遮蔽；覆蓋。The earth is *shrouded* in darkness. 黑暗籠罩着大地。③隱察；隱藏。④〖古〗掩蔽(=shelter).

shrove [ʃrov; ʃrouv] *v.* pt. of **shrive.**

Shrove Monday 聖灰瞻禮前之星期一。

Shrove Sunday 懺悔星期日(聖灰瞻禮前之星期日)。

Shrove·tide [ˈʃrovˌtaɪd; ˈʃrouvtaid] *n.* 懺悔節(卽聖灰瞻禮日之前三日)。

Shrove Tuesday 四旬齋開始之前一日。

*__shrub__¹ [ʃrʌb; ʃrʌb] *n.* 灌木。

shrub² *n.* 果汁、糖、酒混成之飲料。

shrub·ber·y [ˈʃrʌbərɪ; ˈʃrʌbəri] *n., pl.* **-ber·ies.** ①灌木(集合稱)。②灌木叢。

shrub·by [ˈʃrʌbɪ; ˈʃrʌbi] *adj.,* **-bi·er, -bi·est.** ①像灌木的。②覆有灌木的。③多灌木的。

*__shrug__ [ʃrʌg; ʃrʌg] *v.,* **shrugged, shrug·ging,** *n.* —*v.t.* 聳(肩)。to *shrug* one's shoulders. 聳肩(表示嫌惡、懷疑、冷淡、不耐煩等意)。—*v.i.* 聳肩。He *shrugged.* 他聳聳肩。**shrug off a.** 不理；一笑置之。**b.** 擺脫。—*n.*①聳肩。With a *shrug,* he left us. 他聳一下肩，走開了。②一種下擺垂至腰部的上衣。

shrunk [ʃrʌŋk; ʃrʌŋk] *v.* pt. & pp. of **shrink.**

shrunk·en [ˈʃrʌŋkən; ˈʃrʌŋkən] *v.* pp. of **shrink.** —*adj.* 縐縮的；萎縮的。

shuck [ʃʌk; ʃʌk] *n.* 殼；筴；外皮。—*v.t.* 剝…之殼，筴或皮。**shuck off** 〖俗〗**a.** 脫衣；除去。**b.** 革除；揚棄。—**er,** *n.*

shucks [ʃʌks; ʃʌks] *interj.* 〖蔑〗呸！—*n.* 無價值之物。

*__shud·der__ [ˈʃʌdɚ; ˈʃʌdə] *v.i.* 戰慄；發抖。He *shuddered* at the sight of blood. 他看見血便戰慄起來。—*n.* 戰慄；發抖。to give a person (the) *shudders.* 使某人戰慄。

*__shuf·fle__ [ˈʃʌfl̩; ˈʃʌfl] *v.,* **-fled, -fling,** *n.* —*v.t.* ①曳(足)；曳(足)而行。②弄混；洗(牌)。to *shuffle* cards. 洗牌。③亂堆；亂塞。④推來推去；推動。⑤曳步而舞。—*v.i.* ①曳足而行。The old man *shuffles* feebly along. 那老人微弱地曳足而行。②洗牌。③支吾；閃避；蒙混；閃爍其辭。④曳步而舞。⑤笨拙地移動〖常 into〗. **shuffle off a.** 除去；排除；推卸。to *shuffle off* responsibilities upon others. 把自己的責任推卸給別人。**b.** 曳足而行。**shuffle on** 匆匆穿上。—*n.* ①曳足而行；曳步。②洗牌。Give the pack a good *shuffle.* 把這副紙牌好好洗一下。③支吾之辭。④詭計。⑤亂堆；混合。⑥曳步而舞。—**shuf·fler,** *n.*

shuf·fle·board [ˈʃʌfl̩ˌbord; ˈʃʌflbɔːd] *n.* 推移板遊戲；推移板。(亦作 **shovelboard**)

*__shun__ [ʃʌn; ʃʌn] *v.t.,* **shunned, shun·ning.** 規避；避免；避開。She was lazy and *shunned* work. 她懶惰，規避工作。—**ner,** *n.*

'**shun** [ʃʌn; ʃʌn] *interj.* 立正！(口令，爲 attention 之縮語。)

shun·pike [ˈʃʌnˌpaɪk; ˈʃʌnpaik] *n., v.,* **-piked, -pik·ing.** —*n.* 〖美俚〗汽車駕駛人爲逃避繳過路費而繞道走的路。—*v.i.* 〖美〗選偏僻小路駕車以欣賞鄉村景色。

shunt [ʃʌnt; ʃʌnt] *v.t.* ①移向一旁；轉避。②使(火車)轉到另一軌道(以讓更重要車輛通過)；使(火車)轉轍。③擱置(一個計畫)；廻避(問題之討論)；丟棄；除去。④分路傳送(電流)。—*v.i.* (火車)開上側路；轉轍。—*n.* ①轉開；側移。②〖鐵路〗轉轍器。③〖電〗分路；分流。—*adj.* 〖電〗分路的。

shunt·er [ˈʃʌntɚ; ˈʃʌntə] *n.* ①〖鐵路〗轉轍手；轉轍器。②有組織能力的人；有手腕的人。③(倫敦股票交易所的)套利者。

shush [ʃʌʃ, ʃuʃ; ʃʌʃ] *interj.* 噓！(命人小聲或安靜的感歎詞)。—*v.t.* 使肅靜。—**er,** *n.*

‡**shut** [ʃʌt; ʃʌt] *v.,* **shut, shut·ting,** *adj., n.* —*v.t.* ①關；閉。*Shut* the door. 關

上門。②摺起；合攏。*Shut* your books, please. 請把書合起來。③關閉(店等)。All the shops were *shut*. 所有店鋪都關門了。④關入；幽禁。⑤拒絕；排出。⑥閂(門)。—*v.i.* 關上；閉起。Suddenly the door *shut*. 門忽然關上了。**shut down** a. 關閉；停工。b. 包圍而使暗。The fog *shut down* rapidly. 霧很快地籠罩下來。**shut down on (upon)**〖俗〗禁止。**shut in** a. 圍繞；圍住。b. 迫近。c. 臥床；臥病。d. 使中止；壓制。**shut off** a. 遮斷；停閉(水,電,煤氣等)。*Shut off* the radio, please. 請把收音機關閉。b. 隔離；隔絕。**shut one's eyes (ears) to** 假裝沒有看見(聽見)；拒絕去看(聽)。**shut one's face (head)**〖俚〗緘默。**shut one's heart to** 對…不動心。**shut one's light (off)** 死。**shut one's mind to** 死不答應。**shut one's mouth** 緘默。**shut one's teeth** 咬緊牙關。**shut out** a. 遮蔽。b. 拒絕。c. 使對方不能得分。**shut the door upon** 不許進入(出去)；不理睬。**shut to** 關閉。*Shut* the door *to*. 請關門。**shut together** 接合；焊接。**shut up** a. 關閉門窗。to *shut up* shop. 關店鋪門。b. 囚禁；妥藏。c.〖俗〗使不開口。Oh, *shut up!* I am tired of your talk. 啊，不要講了！我已經聽厭了你的話。d.〖俗〗緘默。—*adj.* ①關閉的；摺合的；合攏的；圍繞的。The door is *shut*. 這門關着。②〖語音〗閉口音的；閉鎖音的；音節末端有子音的。*shut* consonants. 閉鎖子音(如 p, b, t, d, k 等)。—*n.* ①閉合之動作或時間。②兩塊焊接金屬之接合線。

shut·down [ˈʃʌtˌdaun; ˈʃʌtdaun] *n.* ①(工廠等之)暫時休業。②〖遊戲〗決賽。③〖俗〗最後一幕。④礦坑之停止開採。(亦作 **shut-down**)

shut-eye [ˈʃʌtˌaɪ; ˈʃʌtˌai] *n.*〖俚〗睡覺。

shut-in [ˈʃʌtˌɪn; ˈʃʌtin] *adj.* ①關在家中或醫院的。②有孤獨傾向的。—*n.* (因病不能離家的)病人。

shut·off [ˈʃʌtˌɔf; ˈʃʌtɔːf] *n.* ①栓；關閉裝置。②停閉；阻塞。(亦作 **shut-off**)

shut·out [ˈʃʌtˌaut; ˈʃʌtaut] *n.* ①遮斷；關閉。②被遮斷或關閉之狀態。③〖運動〗迫使對方得零分；一方得零分之比賽。④(雇主抵制工人非法要求之)停工。(亦作**shut-out**)

***shut·ter** [ˈʃʌtɚ; ˈʃʌtə] *n.* ①(*pl.*)百葉窗；窗板；遮門。②(照相機鏡頭之)遮蔽器；光開關；快門。③關閉者；關閉物。**put up the shutters**(商店)上板；關門。—*v.t.* 裝以百葉窗或遮門；以百葉窗或遮門關閉。—**less,** *adj.*

shut·ter·bug [ˈʃʌtɚˌbʌg; ˈʃʌtəbʌg] *n.*〖俚〗業餘的照相迷。

***shut·tle** [ˈʃʌtl̩; ˈʃʌtl] *n., v.,* **-tled, -tling.** —*n.* ①梭。②往返移動之物。③短距離往返的火車(=shuttle train)。④=**shuttlecock.** —*v.t. & v.i.* (使)穿梭般往返移動。

shuttle bus 機坪載客車。

shut·tle·cock [ˈʃʌtl̩ˌkak; ˈʃʌtlkɔk] *n.* ①羽毛球。②羽毛球戲。③在幾個意見之間徘徊的人。—*v.t. & v.i.* 拋來拋去；往復移動；被踢來踢去。—*adj.* 往復移動的。

shuttle train 短程往返開駛之火車。

***shy**[1] [ʃaɪ; ʃai] *adj.,* **shy·er, shy·est** or **shi·er, shi·est,** *v.,* **shied, shy·ing,** *n., pl.* **shies.** —*adj.* ①怕羞的；羞怯的。②膽怯的；易被驚走的。A deer is a *shy* animal. 鹿是膽怯的動物。③畏縮的；審愼的。This made him *shy* of trying it again. 這使他不敢輕於再作嘗試。④懷疑的；不信任的。⑤(動、植物)不易繁殖的。**fight shy of** 設法避開。**shy of** 缺乏；不足。This house is *shy of* a bathroom. 這房子缺少一間浴室。—*v.i.* ①驚跳；驚逸。The horse *shied* at the approaching car. 那匹馬見到駛近的車子就嚇跑了。②(人)拒絕做事。**shy away from** 躲避。—*n.* 驚跳；驚避。—**ness,** *n.* —**er,** *n.*

shy[2] *v.,* **shied, shy·ing,** *n., pl.* **shies.** —*v.t.* 投；擲。—*n.* ①投；擲。②〖俗〗譏笑。**have a shy at something** 嘗試做某事。

Shy·lock [ˈʃaɪlɑk; ˈʃailɔk] *n.* 毒狠無情的放高利貸者(原爲 Shakespeare 所作 *The Merchant of Venice* 中的猶太放高利貸者)。

***shy·ly** [ˈʃaɪlɪ; ˈʃaili] *adv.* 羞怯地；膽小地。(亦作 **shily**)

shy·ster [ˈʃaɪstɚ; ˈʃaistə] *n.*〖俚〗奸猾的人；奸猾的律師。

Si 化學元素 silicon 之符號。

si [si; siː] *n.*〖音樂〗音階的第七音。

Si·am [saɪˈæm, ˈsaɪæm; saiˈæm, ˈsai-æm] *n.* 暹羅(Thailand, 泰國之舊名，首都爲曼谷, Bangkok)。

Siam, Gulf of *n.* 暹羅灣。

Si·a·mese [ˌsaɪəˈmiz; ˌsaiəˈmiːz] *adj., n., pl.* **-mese.** —*adj.* 暹羅的；暹羅人的；暹羅語的。—*n.* ①暹羅人；暹羅語。②暹羅貓。

Siamese cat 暹羅貓。

Siamese twins 暹羅連體雙胞胎；劍突聯胎(1811–74, 二人胸部有一肉條相連一起)；連體雙胞胎。

sib [sɪb; sib] *adj.* 血親的；血族的；近親的。—*n.* 血親；血族；氏族。

Si·be·ri·a [saɪˈbɪrɪə; saiˈbiəriə] *n.* 西伯利亞。—**Si·be·ri·an,** *adj., n.*

sib·i·lant [ˈsɪbl̩ənt; ˈsibilənt] *adj.* 有嘶嘶聲的；發嘶嘶聲的。—*n.* 嘶音(如s, z, ʃ, ʒ)。—**ly,** *adv.* —**sib·i·lance, sib·i·lan·cy,** *n.*

sib·i·late [ˈsɪbl̩ˌet; ˈsibileit] *v.t. & v.i.,* **-lat·ed, -lat·ing.** 發嘶音；發齒擦音；以嘶嘶音發聲。—**sib·i·la·tion,** *n.*

sib·ling [ˈsɪblɪŋ; ˈsibliŋ] *n.* ①(同父母所生的)兄弟或姊妹。②(同父異母或同母異父所生的)兄弟或姊妹。③〖人類學〗一氏族的成員。—*adj.* 兄弟或姊妹的。

sib·yl [ˈsɪbl̩; ˈsibil] *n.* ①古希臘、羅馬之女預言家。②女預言家；女巫；算命者。

sib·yl·line [ˈsɪbl̩ˌin; siˈbilain] *adj.* ①神巫的；神巫所言(作)的。②如神諭的；預言的；神祕的。

sic[1] [sɪk; sik]〖拉〗*adv.* 原文如此(=so; thus. 於引用文句時，如遇原文謬誤或欠妥之處，於其後標 sic 於方括弧〔 〕內)。

sic[2] *adj.*〖方〗如此的；這樣的。

sic[3] *v.t.* =**sick**[2].

sic·ca·tive [ˈsɪkətɪv; ˈsikətiv] *adj.* 使乾燥的。—*n.* 乾燥劑。

sice[1] [saɪs, saɪz; sais] *n.* 骰子之六點。

sice[2] [saɪs; sais] *n.* (印度的)馬夫。(亦作 **syce**)

Si·cil·i·an [sɪˈsɪlɪən; siˈsiljən] *n.* ①西西里島人。②西西里島通行之義大利語。—*adj.* 西西里島的；西西里島人的。

si·cil·i·a·no [sɪˌsɪlɪˈɑno; siˌsiliˈɑːnou] *n., pl.* **-nos.** 西西里島的民族舞；其舞曲。(亦作 **siciliana**)

Sic·i·ly [ˈsɪsl̩ɪ; ˈsisili] *n.* 西西里島。

‡sick[1] [sɪk; sik] *adj.* ①患病的；有病的。He's been *sick* for six weeks. 他已病了六星期。to fall *sick*. 得病。②作嘔的；欲嘔的。to feel *sick*. 欲嘔。The smell made him *sick*. 這氣味使他欲嘔。③厭惡的；厭煩

的。He was *sick* at heart. 他甚爲厭惡。I am *sick* of flattery. 我厭惡諂媚。④渴望的;戀慕的;憔悴的〖for〗. He is *sick* for his home. 他懷念家鄉。⑤蒼白的;有倦容的。⑥壞的;不健全的。⑦月經來潮的。⑧〖農〗a. 不適於栽種某種作物的。b. 含有害微生物的。⑨殘忍的;有虐待狂的。**go** (or **report**) **sick**〖軍〗宣布因病而不能執行任務。**sick of**; **sick and tired of**; **sick to death of** 厭惡;倦於。—*n.* (the-)(作*pl.* 解)病人;病患(集合稱)。The *sick* need special care. 病患需要特別看護。〖注意〗**sick, ill** 兩字略有分別, ill 是較正式的字。在英國 sick 專指"惡心;嘔吐"而言, 在美國則指一切疾病。參看**ill.**

sick² *v.t.* 命令(犬)攻擊;追擊。

sick bay 船上的醫務室。

sick·bed [ˈsɪkˌbɛd; ˈsikbed] *n.* 病床。

sick call ①召喚醫生、牧師等去看病者。②〖軍〗a. 集合病人去醫務室的號音。b. 聽到此等號音而集合的病人。

***sick·en** [ˈsɪkən; ˈsikn] *v.i.* ①患病;生病。②厭惡;厭倦。He soon *sickened* of his new wife. 他不久就對他的新妻生厭了。③作嘔;欲嘔。—*v.t.* ①使厭惡;使厭倦。Cruelty *sickens* me. 殘酷使我厭惡。②使作嘔;使病。

sick·en·er [ˈsɪkənɚ; ˈsiknə] *n.* ①使厭惡或作嘔的東西。②〖學生用語〗討厭的人。

sick·en·ing [ˈsɪkənɪŋ; ˈsikniŋ] *adj.* ①使人生病的;使人作嘔的;使人昏暈的。②使人厭惡的。③生病的。—**ly,** *adv.*

sick flag 檢疫船旗;傳染病船旗。

sick headache 伴有嘔吐的頭痛;偏頭痛。

sick·ish [ˈsɪkɪʃ; ˈsikiʃ] *adj.* ①有病的。②令人作嘔的。

sick·le [ˈsɪkl; ˈsikl] *n.* 鐮刀。

sick leave 病假。

sickle cell anemia〖醫〗鐮狀細胞貧血症。

sick list 病患名簿。

sick·ly [ˈsɪklɪ; ˈsikli] *adj.*, **-li·er, li·est,** *adv.* —*adj.* ①多病的;不健康的;憔悴的;委靡的。②致病的。③令人作嘔的。④微弱的;暗淡的。—*adv.* 有病地;憔悴地。

***sick·ness** [ˈsɪknɪs; ˈsiknis] *n.* ①疾病;患病。He's had a lot of *sickness* during the last five years. 他過去五年中患了很多病。②作嘔;嘔吐。③不健康。

sick·room [ˈsɪkˌrum; ˈsik-ruːm] *n.* 病房;病室。

‡side [saɪd; said] *n., adj., v.,* **sid·ed, sid·ing.** —*n.* ①邊;側;面。He was sitting by the *side* of the road. 他坐在路旁。②脇;身體之兩邊。I have a pain in the left *side.* 我左脇痛。③山或河岸的斜坡。④河岸。⑤方面。all *sides* of a question. 問題的各方面。⑥集團;黨;派系。Which *side* are you on? 你屬於哪一個集團?⑦血統;家系;世系。The man is English on his mother's *side.* 這人的母系是英國血統。⑧(打彈子球時迅速打一面而形成的)旋轉運動。⑨〖英俗〗自負的態度;擺架子。⑩(丘陵等之)斜側。⑪演員臺詞之一頁。**blind** (or **weak**) **side** 弱點;缺點。**by one's side** 與某人並列;在某人附近。**by the side of**＝by one's side. **change sides** 離黨;加入他黨;叛逆。**clear side**〖航海〗露出水面部分。**credit** (**debit**) **side**〖簿記〗貸(借)方。**from side to side** 左右地。**on** (or **from**) **all sides**; **on** (or **from**) **every side** 從各方面;到處;處處。**on one side** 在一邊;在一傍。**on** (**off**) **side**〖橄欖球〗(不)合規則的位置。**on the other side** 在反面;在對面。**on the right** (**wrong**) **side of forty** 不足(已過)四十歲。**on the side**〖俗〗a. 與主題分開的。b. 本行, 或主要工作等之外。She tried selling cosmetics *on the side.* 她要以賣化妝品爲副業。c. 作爲小菜, 添菜。**on the... side** 有幾分…的意味;相當;頗。Prices are *on the* high *side.* 物價相當高。**on this side** (**of**) **the grave** 在現世;在世上;活着。**place on one side** 置於一邊;蔑視。**shake** (or **burst**) **one's sides with laughter** (or **laughing**) 捧腹大笑。**side by side** a. 並肩地;互相支持地。They walked *side by side.* 他們並肩而行。b. 相等地。c. 共存地;相鄰地。**split one's sides** 捧腹大笑。**stand by a person's side** 支持某人。**take sides** 加入;袒護〖常 with〗. —*adj.* ①側的;旁的。②斜的。a *side* glance. 斜視。③不重要的;枝節的。—*v.i.* 援助;參與;袒護〖常 with〗.

side·arm [ˈsaɪdˌɑrm; ˈsaidɑːm] *adj.* 〖棒球〗側投的(手的位置與腰等高的)。

side arms 隨身佩帶的劍、刀、手槍等武器。

side band〖電訊〗旁頻率。

side·board [ˈsaɪdˌbord; ˈsaidbɔːd] *n.* ①餐室中之餐具櫥;餐具架。②(*pl.*)＝**side whiskers.**

side-box [ˈsaɪdˌbɑks; ˈsaidbɔks] *n.* 戲院兩側的廂座。

side·burns [ˈsaɪdˌbɝnz; ˈsaidbəːnz] *n. pl.* 緊接鬢角頭髮下兩頰上之鬍鬚;短腮鬍。

side·car [ˈsaɪdˌkɑr; ˈsaidkɑː] *n.* ①(附於機器脚踏車旁可載一人或行李的)側車。②一種以白蘭地, 橘子酒, 檸檬汁混合的鷄尾酒。

side chain ①〖化學〗側鏈。②摩托車上連接車輪與引擎之鏈條。

side chapel 禮拜堂之側堂。

side dish 正菜外加的菜;小菜。

side door (or **entrance**) 側門。

side effect (藥物之)副作用。

side issue 與正題無關的問題。

side-kick [ˈsaɪdˌkɪk; ˈsaidkik] *n.*〖美俚〗夥伴;密友;合作者;助手。

side light ①從側面射來之光;側光;側燈。②(船上的)舷燈。③(船或建築物側面的)窗。④偶然啓示;間接說明。(亦作**sidelight**)

side line ①界線。②(*pl.*)界線外之地。③副業。④支線。

side·line [ˈsaɪdˌlaɪn; ˈsaidlain] *v.,* **-lined, -lin·ing,** *n.* —*v.t.* (因負傷或病而)迫使或被迫退出。—*n.* ＝**side line.**

side·long [ˈsaɪdˌlɔŋ; ˈsaidlɔŋ] *adj.* ①橫的;斜的。②側面的;非直接的。—*adv.* 橫地;斜地;側面地。

side·piece [ˈsaɪdˌpis; ˈsaidpiːs] *n.* 物之側部。

si·de·re·al [saɪˈdɪrɪəl; saiˈdiəriəl] *adj.* 星的;星座的。—**ly,** *adv.*

sidereal day 恒星日(較標準日約短四分鐘)。

sidereal year 恒星年(等於365天6小時又10分)。

sid·er·ite [ˈsɪdəˌraɪt; ˈsidərait] *n.* ①〖礦〗菱鐵礦。②隕鐵。

side·sad·dle [ˈsaɪdˌsædl; ˈsaidˌsædl] *n.* 橫鞍;偏座鞍;女鞍。—*adv.* 鞍上偏坐着。

side show ①附屬的表演。②附屬事件;枝節問題。

side·slip [ˈsaɪdˌslɪp; ˈsaidslip] *n., v.,* **-slipped, -slip·ping.** —*n.* ①橫滑;滑向一邊。②〖航空〗側滑。—*v.i.* 橫滑;側滑。

sides·man [ˈsaɪdzmən; ˈsaidzmən]

n., pl. **-men.** (英國之)輔助教會委員。
side·split·ting [ˈsaɪdˌsplɪtɪŋ; ˈsaidˌsplitiŋ] *adj.* 令人捧腹大笑的。—**ly,** *adv.*
side step ①側步。②(船、車等之)側梯。
side-step [ˈsaɪdˌstɛp; ˈsaidstep] *v.t. & v.i.,* **-stepped, -step·ping.** ①走側步。②閃開;規避。
side street 小巷。
side stroke 側泳。
side·swipe [ˈsaɪdˌswaɪp; ˈsaidswaip] *v.,* **-swiped, -swip·ing,** *n.* —*v.t.* 自側方橫擊;掠過;擦過。—*n.* 橫擊; 側擊。
side·track [ˈsaɪdˌtræk; ˈsaidtræk] *n.* ①〖鐵路〗側線;旁軌。②規避;擱置;搪塞。—*v.t.* ①將(火車)轉入側線。②轉移(某人)之目標。
side view 側景;側面圖。
***side·walk** [ˈsaɪdˌwɔk; ˈsaid-wɔːk] *n.* 〖美〗人行道(英國用 **pavement**).
sidewalk artist 路邊畫家。
side wall 車胎之外壁。
side·ward [ˈsaɪdwəd; ˈsaidwəd] *adj.* 向側面的。—*adv.* = **sidewards.**
side·wards [ˈsaɪdwədz; ˈsaidwədz] *adv.* 向側方地。
side·way [ˈsaɪdˌwe; ˈsaidwei] *n.* ①小路。②人行道。—*adj. & adv.* =**sideways.**
side·ways [ˈsaɪdˌwez; ˈsaid-weiz] *adv.* ①斜向一邊地。②自一邊地。③一邊向前地。—*adj.* 向一邊的; 橫斜的。(亦作 **sidewise**)
side-wheel [ˈsaɪdˌhwil; ˈsaidhwiːl] *adj.* 每側均有外輪的(汽船)。—**er,** *n.*
side whiskers (蓄於兩頰之) 側鬢。
side·wind·er [ˈsaɪdˌwaɪndə; ˈsaidˌwaində] *n.* ①一種小的響尾蛇。②(S-) 響尾蛇飛彈(美國海軍之空對空導向飛彈)。
side·wise [ˈsaɪdˌwaɪz; ˈsaidwaiz] *adj. & adv.* =**sideways.**
sid·ing [ˈsaɪdɪŋ; ˈsaidiŋ] *n.* ①〖鐵路〗側線;旁軌。②〖美〗外壁板 (集合稱)。
si·dle [ˈsaɪdl; ˈsaidl] *v.,* **-dled, -dling,** *n.* —*v.i.* (羞澀或膽怯地)側身而行。—*n.* 側身前行。—**si·dling·ly,** *adv.*
Sid·ney [ˈsɪdnɪ; ˈsidni] *n.* 西德尼 (Sir Philip, 1554–1586, 英國詩人及政治家)。
Si·do·ni·an [saɪˈdonɪən; saiˈdounjən] *adj.* 西頓的;西頓人的。—*n.* 西頓人。
Sieg·bahn [ˈsigbɑn; ˈsiːgbaːn] *n.* 西格班 (Karl Manne Georg, 1886–, 瑞典物理學家, 曾獲1924年諾貝爾物理獎)。
siege** [sidʒ; siːdʒ] *n., v.,* **sieged, sieg·ing.** —*n.* ①圍困; 圍攻; 圍城。to raise a *siege.* 展開圍攻。to stand a *siege.* 頑強抵抗圍攻。②任何長期的或堅持不斷的征服抵抗之努力;任何長期的攻擊。③長期的困擾。lay siege to*** a. 圍困。b. 以長期持續不斷的努力企圖獲得。—*v.t.* 包圍;圍攻。—**a·ble,** *adj.*
siege train 隨軍攜帶的攻城裝備、武器、彈藥等。
Sieg·fried [ˈsigfrid, ˈziːkfriːt; ˈsiːg-friːd,ˈziːkfriːt] *n.*齊格飛(德國傳說中英雄)。
Siegfried Line 齊格飛防線 (德國於1940年構成之防線, 1944年爲美軍所突破)。
Sien·kie·wicz [ʃɛnˈkjɛvɪtʃ; ʃenˈkje-vitʃ] *n.* 顯克維支 (Henryk, 1846–1916, 波蘭小說家, 獲 1905 年諾貝爾文學獎)。
si·en·na [sɪˈɛnə; siˈenə] *n.* ①濃黃色; 赭色。②濃黃土(一種顏料)。
si·er·ra [sɪˈɛrə, ˈsɪrə; ˈsiərə, siˈerə] *n.* ①有如鋸齒狀峯巒之山脈。②西班牙鯖。
Si·er·ra *n.* 通訊電碼, 代表字母 S。
Sierra Le·o·ne [~lɪˈonɪ; ~liˈoun] 獅子山(西非一國, 首都自由城 Freetown).
Sierra Nevada 內華達山脈 (a. 在美國 California 州東部; b. 在西班牙南部, 最高峯爲 Mulhacén, 高達 11,421 英尺)。
si·es·ta [sɪˈɛstə; siˈestə] *n., v.,* **-taed, -ta·ing.** —*n.* 午睡;午後小睡(尤指氣候炎熱國家中者)。—*v.i.* 午後小睡。
sieve [sɪv; siv] *n., v.,* **sieved, siev·ing.** —*n.*①篩;漏杓。We use a *sieve* to strain soup. 我們用漏杓濾湯。②不能保密的人。***draw water with a sieve; pour water into a sieve*** 白費氣力。***have a memory*** (or ***head***) ***like a sieve*** 善忘;健忘。—*v.t.* 以篩篩。
sif·fleur [sɪˈflɝ; siˈfləː] 〖法〗*n.* 吹口哨的人。
***sift** [sɪft; sift] *v.t.* ①篩;篩撒。*Sift* sugar on the top of the cake. 將糖篩撒在糕餅上。②詳察;細審。③盤問。—*v.i.* 篩下; (雪等)紛落。—**er,** *n.*
sift·ings [ˈsɪftɪŋz; ˈsiftiŋz] *n.* (作 *pl.* 解)①篩過的東西。②篩過後多餘的東西。
Sig., sig. ①signal. ②signature. ③signor. ④signore. ⑤signori.
‡**sigh** [saɪ; sai] *v.i.* ①歎息。②發出類似歎息之聲。③熱望;渴想〖for〗. She *sighed* for home and friends. 她渴念家和朋友。④悲歎。—*v.t.* 歎息說出;以歎息表示〖out〗. to *sigh* out one's grief. 以哀歎表示其憂愁。—*n.* ①歎息。 to heave a *sigh.* 發出一聲歎息。②似歎息之聲。—**er,** *n.* —**less,** *adj.* —**like,** *adj.*
‡**sight** [saɪt; sait] *n.* ①視力; 視覺。 His *sight* is not very good. 他的目力不很好。②觀覽;見。 He fell in love with her at first *sight*. 他對她一見鍾情。③眼界;視界。Land was in *sight*. 陸地已在望。④看見的東西;瞥見。I caught a *sight* of him. 我瞥見了他。⑤情景;景象。⑥ (*pl.*) a. 名勝。to see the *sights*. 遊覽名勝;觀光。b. 目標。⑦奇異的東西。⑧意見;心目;面前。 to lose (find) favor in a person's *sight*. 失(得)寵於某人。 ⑨(槍砲等之) 瞄準;瞄準具。 to take *sight*. 瞄準。⑩很多。It cost a *sight* of money. 它值很多錢。***a*** (***long***) ***sight*** 〖俗〗很多。It is *a long sight* better. 這樣好得多。***a sight for sore eyes*** 願見的人或物。 ***at first sight*** 初見。 ***at*** (or ***on***) ***sight*** 見到立卽。The check is payable *at sight*. 這支票見票卽付。***at the sight of*** 一看見…。***catch sight of*** 看見。***in sight*** 在望;看得見。Peace is now *in sight*. 和平在望(可期)。 ***in sight of*** 在看得見…的地方;在…所看得見的地方。***keep sight of*** 記住;考慮。***know by sight*** 認得某人; 面熟。***lose sight of*** a. 看不見。b. 不得音訊。c. 遺漏; 忽略。***not by a long sight*** 差得遠;遠不如。 ***out of sight*** 看不到; 不被看到。***Out of sight, out of mind.*** 去者日以疏;離久則情疏。—*v.t.* ①看見。We *sighted* land at last. 我們終於看見陸地了。②瞄準。③調整(鎗砲的)瞄準器。④供以瞄準器。—*v.i.* ①瞄準。 The hunter *sighted* carefully before firing his gun. 獵者射擊前小心瞄準。②朝某方向觀看。—**a·ble,** *adj.*
sight bill 卽期票據。
‡**sight draft** 卽期票據 (見票卽付之支票或匯票, 縮寫爲 S/D).
sight·less [ˈsaɪtlɪs; ˈsaitlis] *adj.* ①盲的。②不可見的; 不在目前的。

sight·ly [ˈsaɪtlɪ; ˈsaitli] *adj.*, **-li·er, -li·est.** 悅目的;美麗的。—**sight·li·ness,** *n.*

sight-read [ˈsaɪtˌrid; ˈsaitˌriːd] *v.t.* & *v.i.*, **-read, -read·ing.** 隨看隨讀(外語文章);隨看隨奏(樂譜)。

sight reader ①隨看隨讀者。②隨看隨奏之樂師。

sight reading 不經練習，看着樂譜卽席演奏或演唱。

sight·see [ˈsaɪtˌsi; ˈsait-siː] *v.i.* 遊覽;觀光。

***sight·see·ing** [ˈsaɪtˌsiɪŋ; ˈsaitˌsiːiŋ] *n.* 觀光; 遊覽。—*adj.* 觀光的; 遊覽的。a *sightseeing* car. 遊覽車。

sight-se·er [ˈsaɪtˌsiɚ; ˈsaitˌsiːə] *n.* 觀光者;遊覽者。

sight unseen 未曾看一眼地。

sight·wor·thy [ˈsaɪtˌwɝðɪ; ˈsaitˌwəːði] *adj.* 值得觀賞的。—**sight·wor·thi·ness,** *n.*

sig·il [ˈsɪdʒəl; ˈsidʒil] *n.* ①印章。②符咒。—**lar·y,** *adj.*

sig·ma [ˈsɪgmə; ˈsigmə] *n.* 希臘文之第十八個字母 (Σ, σ).

sig·mate [ˈsɪgmet; ˈsigmeit] *adj., v.*, **-mat·ed, -mat·ing.** —*adj.* S 形的;Σ形的。—*v.t.* 加 s 於…之語尾。

sig·moid [ˈsɪgmɔɪd; ˈsigmɔid] *adj.* ① S 形的。②〖解剖〗乙狀結腸的。③C 形的。(亦作 **sigmoidal**)

sigmoid flexure ①〖動物〗S狀彎曲。②〖解剖〗結腸之最後彎曲部分;乙狀結腸。

‡**sign** [saɪn; sain] *n.* ①記號;符號。Words are the *signs* of ideas. 語言是思想的符號。②手勢;姿勢。We talked to the deaf man by *signs*. 我們用手勢同那聾子談話。③痕跡;跡象; 徵兆。There are no *signs* of life about the house. 這房子沒有生命的跡象(卽無人居住)。The weather shows no *signs* of getting better. 天氣沒有轉佳的徵兆。④足跡。The hunter found *signs* of deer. 獵人發現了鹿的足跡。⑤祕語;暗號。*sign* and countersign. 黑話;行話;隱語。⑥告示;牌示。The *sign* reads: "Keep off the grass." 牌子上寫的是:"勿踐踏草地"。⑦〖天文〗(黃道十二宮之)宮。***at the sign of*** 在有…之牌示的酒店、店號等。—*v.t.* & *v.i.* ①簽字。He's forgotten to *sign* his name. 他忘記簽名。②做信號;做手勢。③以手勢或信號表示。to *sign* someone to enter. 對某人做手勢要他進來。④雇; 聘。⑤供以標誌。⑥以手畫十字記號。⑦顯示;爲…之徵兆。***sign away*** 簽字讓渡。***sign off*** a. 廣播電臺宣布廣播節目結束。b. 不開口; 停止說話。***sign on*** (or ***up***) 簽字於雇用契約。***sign over*** 簽字移交。—**er,** *n.* —**a·ble,** *adj.*

***sig·nal** [ˈsɪgnl; ˈsignl] *n., v.*, **-nal(l)ed, -nal·(l)ing,** *adj.* —*n.* ①信號;暗號。A red light is a *signal* of danger. 紅燈是危險的信號。②導火線; 動機。③〖牌戲〗給同伴某種暗示的叫牌。—*v.t.* ①向…作信號。He *signaled* the car to stop by raising his hand. 他舉手叫車停住。②以信號報知。③表示。—*v.i.* 發信號;作信號。to *signal* for help. 發信號求救。—*adj.* ①信號的; 信號用的。②顯著的;重大的。—**er,** *n.*

sig·nal-book [ˈsɪgnlˌbuk; ˈsignlbuk] *n.* (陸海空軍之)信號書。

signal box 〖鐵路〗信號所。

Signal Corps (美陸軍的)通訊隊。

signal fire 烽火。

signal flag 信號旗。

signal gun 信號槍。

sig·nal·ize [ˈsɪgnəˌlaɪz; ˈsignəlaiz] *v.t.*, **-ized, -iz·ing.** ①使著名;使顯著。②表現; 表露。③以信號通知。④供以交通標誌。—**sig·nal·i·za·tion,** *n.*

sig·nal·ly [ˈsɪgnlɪ; ˈsignəli] *adv.* 顯著地;非常地。

sig·nal·man [ˈsɪgnlˌmæn; ˈsignlmən] *n., pl.* **-men.** 信號手;信號兵。

sig·nal·ment [ˈsɪgnlmənt; ˈsignəlmənt] *n.* ①有關通緝犯特徵之描述。②特殊記號。

signal tower 信號塔。

sig·na·to·ry [ˈsɪgnəˌtorɪ; ˈsignətəri] *adj., n., pl.* **-ries.** —*adj.* ①簽名的;簽署的。—*n.* 簽名者;簽約國。(亦作 **signatary**)

***sig·na·ture** [ˈsɪgnətʃɚ; ˈsignitʃə] *n.* ①簽字。②〖音樂〗調號。③(廣播節目的)信號調;信號曲。④〖印刷〗紙上裝釘用的折疊號碼;印有此號碼之紙張。⑤〖醫〗藥方上註明附於藥瓶上的說明。—**sig·na·tur·al,** *adj.* —**less,** *adj.*

sign·board [ˈsaɪnˌbord; ˈsainbɔːd] *n.* 廣告牌;告示牌。

sig·net [ˈsɪgnɪt; ˈsignit] *n.* 小印章; 圖章。

signet ring 刻有小印章的戒指; 名字戒指。

***sig·nif·i·cance** [sɪgˈnɪfəkəns; sigˈnifikəns] *n.* ①重要; 重大。a matter of *significance*. 重大事情。②意義;意味。③意味深長。(亦作 **significancy**)

***sig·nif·i·cant** [sɪgˈnɪfəkənt; sigˈnifikənt] *adj.* ①有意義的;含有意味的。Smiles are *significant* of pleasure. 笑表示快樂。②意味深長的; 重大的。③表示某種含義的; 暗示的。—*n.* 符號;記號。

sig·nif·i·cant·ly [sɪgˈnɪfəkəntlɪ; sigˈnifikəntli] *adv.* ①另有含意地。②值得注目地;非偶然地。

sig·ni·fi·ca·tion [sɪgˌnɪfəˈkeʃən; ˌsignifiˈkeiʃən] *n.* ①正確之意義; 意味。②表明;表示。

sig·nif·i·ca·tive [sɪgˈnɪfəˌketɪv; sigˈnifikətiv] *adj.* ①指示的; 表示的。②有象徵意義的。—**ly,** *adv.*

***sig·ni·fy** [ˈsɪgnəˌfaɪ; ˈsignifai] *v.*, **-fied, -fy·ing.** —*v.t.* 表示…之義; 表示。What does that *signify*? 那表示甚麼?—*v.i.* 有重要性;有關係。What a fool says does not *signify*. 一個愚人說的話無關重要。—**sig·ni·fi·a·ble,** *adj.*

si·gnior [ˈsinjɔr; ˈsiːnjɔː] *n.* =**signor.**

sign language (聾者等之)手勢語言。

sign manual ①特殊之記號、品質等。②文件上君主或官員之簽字。

sign-off [ˈsaɪnˌɔf; ˈsainˌɔːf] *n.* 廣播結束之宣布。

si·gnor [ˈsinjor; ˈsiːnjɔ, siːˈnjɔː] 〖義〗 *n.* ①君;先生。②紳士;上流人。

si·gno·ra [sinˈjorə; siːˈnjɔːrə] *n., pl.* **si·gnore.** 〖義〗①太太;夫人。②貴婦人。

si·gno·re [sinˈjore; siːˈnjɔːrei] *n., pl.* **-ri** [-rɪ; -ri]. 〖義〗①紳士; 上流人。②君; 先生(用於直接稱呼; 如用於人名前, 須寫做 signor).

si·gno·ri·na [ˌsinjəˈrinə; ˌsiːnjəˈriːnə] *n., pl.* **-ne** [-ne; -nei]. 〖義〗①小姐(=Miss). ②女郎;少女。

si·gno·ry [ˈsinjərɪ; ˈsiːnjəri] *n., pl.* **-ries.** =**seigniory.**

sign painter 畫廣告者;畫招牌者。

sign·post [ˈsaɪnˌpost; ˈsainpoust] *n.* ①廣告柱。②路標 (=guidepost). ③任何明顯的徵兆、線索等。—*v.t.* ①指引。②〖英〗設置路標。

Si·gurd [ˈsɪgɚd; ˈsiguəd] *n.* 齊格(北歐神話中的英雄)。

Si·kang [ˈʃiˈkaŋ; ˈʃiːˈkaːŋ] *n.* 西康(中

國西南之一省, 省會康定, Kangting).
Sikh [sik; siːk] *n.* (印度之)塞克教徒。
Sikh·ism [ˈsikɪzm̩ ;ˈsiːkizm] *n.* 塞克教(十六世紀時起源於印度北部)。
Sik·kim [ˈsɪkɪm; ˈsikim] *n.* 錫金(又名哲孟雄, 位於中國西藏與印度之間, 昔爲印度之保護國, 1974 年 9 月併爲印度一自治省, 首府 Gangtok).
si·lage [ˈsaɪlɪdʒ; ˈsailidʒ] *n.* 保藏於糧秣庫中之草料。
‡si·lence [ˈsaɪləns; ˈsailəns] *n., v.,* **-lenced, -lenc·ing,** *interj.* —*n.* ①寂靜;無聲。A profound *silence* prevailed over all. 萬籟俱寂。②緘默;無言。I can't understand his *silence*. 我不懂他何以不作答覆。—*v.t.* ①使(敵人軍艦砲臺等)停止射擊;制壓。We *silenced* the enemy's batteries. 我們(發出猛烈砲火)使敵方停止發砲。②使閉口無言。③使停止。—*interj.* 肅靜; 不要作聲(=be silent). *Silence*, please! 請不要講話!
si·lenc·er [ˈsaɪlənsɚ; ˈsailənsə] *n.* ①使沉默之人或物。②消音器。
‡si·lent [ˈsaɪlənt; ˈsailənt] *adj.* ①寂靜的;無聲的。All is *silent*. 萬籟俱寂。②緘默的; 無言的。You had better be *silent*. 你最好不開口。③匿名的。④不發音的。The "e" in "time" is a *silent* letter. "time" 中的 "e" 是個不發音的字母。⑤不積極活動的。⑥(敍述中或故事中)沒有提到的。⑦無聲電影的。the *silent* screen. 無聲電影。⑧(頻率過低以致)無法被人的耳朵聽到的。—*n.* (常 *pl.*) 無聲電影片。—**ness,** *n.* —**ly,** *adv.*
silent butler 一種用以收拾飯屑烟灰等之有柄容器。
Silent Majority 〖主美〗沉默的大多數(指在政治上不表示意見的大多數美國人)。
silent partner 不出名股東;匿名股東。
silent picture 無聲電影;默片。
silent spring 寂靜的春天(有毒的化學物品對大自然的任意摧殘而使春天了無生氣)。
Si·le·nus [saɪˈlinəs; saiˈliːnəs] *n.* 〖希臘神話〗①森林神祇之首領(爲酒神 Bacchus 之養父)。②(s-) 森林神祇之一。
Si·le·sia [saɪˈliʃɪə; saiˈliːzjə] *n.* 西里西亞(東歐之一地區, 包括Sudeten 山地及 Oder 河盆地, 煤、鐵、及其他金屬藏量甚豐)。—**Si·le·sian,** *adj., n.*
si·le·sia [səˈliʃə; səˈliːʃə] *n.* 作襯裏用的一種細布。
si·lex [ˈsaɪlɛks; ˈsaileks] *n.* ①矽土。②耐熱性石英玻璃。③此種玻璃製的咖啡壺。④(S-) 此種咖啡壺之商標名。
sil·hou·ette [ˌsɪluˈɛt; ˌsilu(ː)ˈet] *n., v.,* **-et·ted, -et·ting.** —*n.* ①黑色半面畫像; 側面影像; 側面輪廓畫;剪影。②輪廓。*in silhouette* 以輪廓或黑像白底表示的(地)。—*v.t.* 使現出黑色影像。
sil·i·ca [ˈsɪlɪkə; ˈsilikə] *n.* 〖化〗矽土(二氧化矽)。
silica gel 矽膠凝體(作吸收劑用)。
sil·i·cate [ˈsɪlɪkɪt; ˈsilikit] *n.* 〖化〗矽酸鹽。
si·li·ceous [sɪˈlɪʃəs; siˈliʃəs] *adj.* ①含有矽土的;由矽土構成的;像矽土的。②生長在含多量矽土之土壤中的。
si·lic·ic [səˈlɪsɪk; siˈlisik] *adj.* 〖化〗①含矽的;矽土的;似矽土的。②矽的;矽酸的。
silicic acid 〖化〗矽酸。
si·lic·i·fy [sɪˈlɪsəˌfaɪ; siˈlisifai] *v.t. & v.i.,* **-fied, -fy·ing.** (使)化爲矽土。
sil·i·con [ˈsɪlɪkən; ˈsilikən] *n.* 〖化〗矽。
sil·i·cone [ˈsɪləˌkon; ˈsiləkoun] *n.* 〖化〗一種含矽原子與氧原子的聚合體。
sil·i·co·sis [ˌsɪlɪˈkosɪs; ˌsiliˈkousis] *n.* 〖醫〗石末沉着病(因吸入過量矽土而致之肺病)。
‡silk [sɪlk; silk] *n.* ①絲。②綢。③(*pl.*)綢衣。dressed in *silks* and satins. 著錦衣; 穿好衣服。④人造絲。⑤任何似絲之物。corn *silk*. 玉蜀黍鬚。⑥〖英〗皇室律師;高級的律師。to take *silk*. 作皇室的律師。⑦降落傘。***hit the silk*** 〖俚〗從飛機上跳傘降落。—*adj.* 絲的;像絲的;與絲有關的。—*v.t.* 覆以絲; 繫以絲。—*v.i.* (玉蜀黍)生花絲。—**like,** *adj.*
silk cotton 木棉。
silk-cot·ton tree [ˈsɪlk ˈkɑtn̩~; ˈsilkˈkɔtn~] 木棉樹。
***silk·en** [ˈsɪlkən; ˈsilkən] *adj.* ①如絲的; 絲製的。②光滑柔軟的。③溫柔的;嬌滴滴的。④穿綢衣的。⑤奢華的; 優美的。⑥溫和的。—*v.t.* ①使如絲一般地光滑柔軟。②使穿綢衣。
silk hat 帽身呈圓筒形之黑呢帽;大禮帽。
silk·screen [ˈsɪlkˌskrin; ˌsilkˈskriːn] *n.* 以絲幕上模型複製圖案之方法。—*adj.* 此種方法的。
silk stocking ①絲襪。②穿絲襪的人;富人。
silk-stock·ing [ˈsɪlkˈstɑkɪŋ; ˈsilkˈstɔkiŋ] *adj.* ①穿絲襪的。②豪華的; 奢侈的。③貴族的; 富有的。—*n.* ①奢侈階級的人;貴族。②〖美史〗〖俗〗=Whig.
silk·weed [ˈsɪlkˌwid; ˈsilkwiːd] *n.* 〖植物〗絲藻。
***silk·worm** [ˈsɪlkˌwɝm; ˈsilkwəːm] *n.* 蠶。
silk·y [ˈsɪlkɪ; ˈsilki] *adj.,* **silk·i·er, silk·i·est,** *n., pl.* **silk·ies.** —*adj.* ①像絲的; 平滑的;亮的。②絲的。③巴結的;設法討好的。④〖植物〗覆有絲狀細毛的。—*n.* 一種二至三磅重的短尾鷄。—**silk·i·ness,** *n.*
***sill** [sɪl; sil] *n.* 門檻;窗臺。
sil·la·bub [ˈsɪləˌbʌb; ˈsiləbʌb] *n.* 乳酒凍(一種牛乳或奶油同酒、果汁等混合之食物)。
sil·ler [ˈsɪlɚ; ˈsilə] *n.* 〖蘇〗①銀。②金錢。
***sil·ly** [ˈsɪlɪ; ˈsili] *adj.,* **-li·er, -li·est,** *adv., n., pl.* **-lies.** —*adj.* ①愚蠢的;無智慧的。You were very *silly* to trust him. 你信賴他, 眞是愚蠢得很。②可笑的。③〖古〗純樸的;天眞的。④〖俗〗驚呆的;昏了頭的。—*adv.* 愚蠢地。—*n.* 傻瓜;蠢貨。—**sil·li·ly,** *adv.* —**sil·li·ness,** *n.*
silly season 〖英〗七、八月間新聞缺乏期。
si·lo [ˈsaɪlo; ˈsailou] *n., pl.* **-los,** *v.* —*n.* ①圓筒形倉。②貯藏穀物或草料之地下建築物或地窖。③地下飛彈發射室。—*v.t.* 將(草料)藏於 silo 中。
silt [sɪlt; silt] *n.* ①淤泥。②微沙;沙泥(比粘土粗而比沙細)。—*v.t.* 以淤泥充塞。—*v.i.* ①爲淤泥充塞。②淤積。
silt·y [ˈsɪltɪ; ˈsilti] *adj.* 微沙質的;沙泥質的。
Si·lu·ri·an [səˈlurɪən; saiˈljuəriən] *adj.* 〖地質〗志留利亞紀的; 與志留利亞紀有關的。
sil·va [ˈsɪlvə; ˈsilvə] *n., pl.* **-vas, -vae** [-vi; -viː]. ①某一地區內之森林樹木(集合稱)。②林木誌。(亦作 **sylva**)
sil·van [ˈsɪlvən; ˈsilvən] *adj.* ①森林的; 關於森林的。②居住於森林的。③多林木的; 樹木茂盛的。—*n.* ①森林之神。②森林居民。(亦作 **sylvan**)
‡sil·ver [ˈsɪlvɚ; ˈsilvə] *n.* ①銀。②銀幣; 銀錢。③銀器。table *silver*. 銀餐具。④銀色。⑤似銀的東西。—*adj.* ①銀的; 與銀有關的;銀質的。*silver* coin. 銀幣。②製銀的;賣銀的。③銀色的。*silver* hair. 銀髮;白髮。④清越的(聲音);流利的。He has a *silver* tongue. 他能言善辯。Speech is *silver*, but silence is golden. 沈默勝於多言。⑤第二等

的。⑥二十五周年的。*be born with a silver spoon in one's mouth* 生於富貴之家。—*v.t.* ①包以銀;鍍以銀;敷以似銀之物。②使呈銀色。—*v.i.* 變爲銀白色。
Silver Age ①白銀時代(人類神話時代的第二個時代,次於第一個黃金時代,爲奢侈與不敬神之時代)。②文學上之白銀時代(拉丁文學之一個時期,從 Augustus 大帝之死到 Hadrian 大帝之死, 14–138)。③(s- a-) 緊接着全盛時期以後的一個時代。
silver bath 〖攝影〗①硝酸銀液;感光液。②盛感光液之盤或碟。
silver certificate 銀票(美國政府發行的一種紙幣,可隨時兌換與票面等值之銀)。
sil·ver·fish [ˈsɪlvɚ͵fɪʃ; ˈsilvəfiʃ] *n., pl.* **-fish, -fish·es.** ①銀色金魚;銀魚。②蠹蟲。
silver foil 銀箔。
silver fox ①銀狐(毛爲黑色,但在近尖端處則有白條)。②銀狐毛皮。
silver gilt ①鍍金之銀。②塗黃色油漆於銀箔上之仿製品。—**sil·ver-gilt,** *adj.*
sil·ver-gray [ˈsɪlvɚ͵gre; ˈsilvəˈgrei] *adj.* 銀灰色的。
sil·ver-haired [ˈsɪlvɚˈhɛrd; ˈsilvəˈhɛəd] *adj.* 頭髮銀灰色的。
sil·ver·ing [ˈsɪlvərɪŋ; ˈsilvəriŋ] *n.* ①鍍銀;包銀。②所鍍之銀。
silver jubilee 二十五周年紀念。
silver leaf 銀箔。
silver lining ①黑雲之白色邊緣。②光明之前途;漸入佳境之希望。
sil·ver·ly [ˈsɪlvəlɪ; ˈsilvəli] *adj.* 似銀的;聲如銀鈴的。
sil·vern [ˈsɪlvən; ˈsilvən] *adj.* 〖古〗銀的;銀製的;如銀的;銀白色的。
silver paper ①銀紙。②(包銀器用的)一種上等薄紙。③感光紙。
silver plate ①銀器類(集合稱)。②銀製的盤。
sil·ver-plat·ed [ˈsɪlvɚˈpletɪd; ˈsilvəˈpleitid] *adj.* 包銀的;鍍銀的。
silver point 銀之熔解點 (960.8°C).
silver print 〖攝影〗印於銀鹽感光表面之照像。
silver sand 白沙。
silver screen ①銀幕。②電影。
sil·ver·side [ˈsɪlvɚ͵saɪd; ˈsilvəsaid] *n.* ①〖英〗最上部分之牛股肉。②銀魚。
sil·ver·smith [ˈsɪlvɚ͵smɪθ; ˈsilvəsmiθ] *n.* 銀匠。
silver standard 銀本位。
Silver Star 〖美陸軍〗銀星勳章。
silver streak 〖俗〗英吉利海峽。
silver thaw ①結於地上物表面之一層薄冰。②白霜。
sil·ver-tongue [ˈsɪlvɚˈtʌŋ; ˈsilvəˈtʌŋ] *n.* 口才;雄辯。
sil·ver-tongued [ˈsɪlvɚˈtʌŋd; ˈsilvəˈtʌŋd] *adj.* 有口才的;雄辯的。
sil·ver·ware [ˈsɪlvɚ͵wɛr; ˈsilvəwɛə] *n.* 銀器。
silver wedding 銀婚(結婚二十五周年紀念)。
sil·ver·weed [ˈsɪlvɚ͵wid; ˈsilvəwiːd] *n.* 〖植物〗鵝金梅。
sil·ver·work [ˈsɪlvɚ͵wɝk; ˈsilvəwəːk] *n.* 銀飾品。
***sil·ver·y** [ˈsɪlvərɪ; ˈsilvəri] *adj.* ①如銀的;銀色的。②清越的(聲音)。③產銀的;含銀的。—**sil·ver·i·ness,** *n.*
sil·vi·cul·ture [ˈsɪlvɪ͵kʌltʃɚ; ˈsilvi͵kʌltʃə] *n.* 林學;造林術。(亦作**sylviculture**)
Sim [sɪm; sim] *n.* 男子名 (Simeon, Simon 之暱稱)。
Sim·e·on [ˈsɪmɪən; ˈsimiən] *n.* 男子名。
sim·i·an [ˈsɪmɪən; ˈsimiən] *adj.* 似猿的;似猴的;猿的;猴的。—*n.* 猴;猿。—**i·ty,** *n.*
‡**sim·i·lar** [ˈsɪmələ; ˈsimilə] *adj.* 類似的;同樣的。Gold is *similar* in color to brass. 金子的顏色和黃銅相似。—*n.* 類似物;類似者。
sim·i·lar·i·ty [͵sɪməˈlærətɪ; ͵simiˈlæriti] *n., pl.* **-ties.** ①類似;相似。②相似之點。
***sim·i·lar·ly** [ˈsɪmələlɪ; ˈsimiləli] *adv.* 同樣地;相同地。
sim·i·le [ˈsɪmə͵li; ˈsimili] *n.* ①直喻;明喻(如:He is as brave as a lion. 他勇猛如獅)。②相似;類似。
si·mil·i·tude [səˈmɪlə͵tjud; siˈmilitjuːd] *n.* ①相似;類似。②比喻。③相似之人或物。
sim·i·tar [ˈsɪmɪtɚ; ˈsimitə] *n.* 彎刀;偃月刀。(亦作 **scimitar, scimiter**)
Sim·la [ˈsɪmlə; ˈsimlə] *n.* 西姆拉(印度北部之一市鎮,爲避暑勝地)。
sim·mer [ˈsɪmɚ, ˈsimə] *v.t.* 慢慢煮(使溫度在沸點下)。—*v.i.* ①溫火慢煮。②發出將沸時之聲。③將爆發。*simmer down* 平靜下來;冷靜下來。—*n.* ①慢煮使沸的狀態。②文火;溫火。
Si·mon¹ [ˈsaɪmən; ˈsaimən] *n.* 男子名。
Si·mon² *n.* 〖聖經〗耶穌門徒彼得 (Peter) 之原名。
si·mo·ni·ac [səˈmonɪ͵æk; siˈmouniæk] *n.* 買賣聖職者。
si·mo·ni·a·cal [͵saɪməˈnaɪək]; ͵saiməˈnaiəkl] *adj.* 買賣聖職的;犯買賣聖職罪的。
si·mon-pure [ˈsaɪmənˈpjur; ˈsaimənˈpjuə] *adj.* ①眞正的;道地的。②心地純正的。
sim·o·ny [ˈsaɪmənɪ; ˈsaiməni] *n.* ①買賣聖職;買賣聖職罪。②賣聖物牟利。
si·moom [sɪˈmum; siˈmuːm] *n.* (阿拉伯、敍利亞、非洲等地之)熱風(常捲有黃沙,令人窒息)。(亦作 **simoon**)
sim·per [ˈsɪmpɚ; ˈsimpə] *v.i.* 假笑;癡笑。—*v.t.* 假笑着說出;假笑着表示出。—*n.* 癡笑;假笑。—**er,** *n.* —**ing·ly,** *adv.*
‡**sim·ple** [ˈsɪmpl̩; ˈsimpl] *adj.,* **-pler, -plest,** *n.* —*adj.* ①簡單的;簡易的。Such a dress is *simple* to make. 這種衣服做起來很簡單。②樸實的;樸素的。He lives a *simple* life. 他過着樸實的生活。③單純的;天眞爛漫的;無虛飾的。He is *simple* and honest. 他爲人眞誠。④愚蠢的;無知的。⑤完全的;純然的。⑥單一的;非複合的。⑦普通的。⑧微賤的;卑下的。⑨無條件的。—*n.* ①愚蠢的人。②簡單之事物。③草藥;藥用之植物。④祇含一種成分的藥。⑤身分卑微者;平民。*gentle and simple* 上下貴賤;富貴貧賤。
simple conversion 〖邏輯〗簡單變換(主辭與賓辭互調而仍不失爲眞)。
simple equation 〖數學〗一次方程式。
simple fraction 單分數。
simple fracture 單純骨折;無創骨折。
sim·ple-heart·ed [ˈsɪmpl̩ˈhartɪd; ˈsimplˈhaːtid] *adj.* ①天眞的;直率的。②誠實的。
simple interest 單利。
simple leaf 單叉葉。
simple machine 〖物理〗簡單機械(槓桿、輪等)。
sim·ple-mind·ed [ˈsɪmpl̩ˈmaɪndɪd; ˈsimplˈmaindid] *adj.* ①無經驗的;頭腦簡單的。②愚蠢的。③低能的。—**ness,** *n.* —**ly,** *adv.*
simple motion 〖物理〗簡單運動(直線運動、圓弧運動等)。
simple proposition 〖邏輯〗簡單命題。
simple sentence 簡單句。
simple syllogism 〖邏輯〗簡單三段論法。

simple time 〖音樂〗單純拍子（每小節有兩拍或三拍）。

sim·ple·ton 〔ˈsɪmpl̩tən; ˈsimpltən〕*n.* 愚人；蠢貨。

sim·plex 〔ˈsɪmplɛks; ˈsimpleks〕*adj.* ①單純的；單一的。②〖電訊〗單式的(不能同時發報與收報的)。—*n.* 單字(爲複合字之對)。

simplex telegraphy 單工電報。

sim·plic·i·ty** 〔sɪmˈplɪsətɪ; simˈplisiti〕*n., pl.* **-ties.** ①簡單；簡易。②樸素；樸實。③單純；無虛飾。④遲鈍；癡呆；頭腦簡單。⑤忠誠；忠實。⑥單純樸素之事物。be simplicity itself*** 極爲容易；十分簡易。

sim·pli·fi·ca·tion 〔ˌsɪmpləfəˈkeʃən; ˌsimplifiˈkeiʃən〕*n.* 單純化；簡易化；簡化。

***sim·pli·fy** 〔ˈsɪmpləˌfaɪ; ˈsimplifai〕*v.t.*, **-fi·ed, -fy·ing.** ①使單純；使簡化。The story has been *simplified* by Mr. Wang. 這故事已由王先生簡化了。②過分簡化。—**sim·pli·fi·er,** *n.* —**sim·pli·fi·ca·tive,** *adj.*

sim·plis·tic 〔sɪmˈplɪstɪk; simˈplistik〕*adj.* 過分簡化的。—**al·ly,** *adv.*

‡**sim·ply** 〔ˈsɪmplɪ; ˈsimpli〕*adv.* ①實在；簡直。I had *simply* nothing to say. 我簡直無話可說。②簡單地。The questions can be answered quite *simply*. 這些問題可以回答得十分簡單。③樸素地。She dresses *simply*. 她衣着樸素。④僅；祇。He failed *simply* because he was lazy. 他失敗，只因他懶惰。⑤愚蠢地。He acted as *simply* as an idiot. 他的舉動愚蠢如白痴。⑥純然地；絕對地。*simply* perfect. 非常完善的。

sim·u·la·crum 〔ˌsɪmjəˈlekrəm; ˌsimjuˈleikrəm〕*n., pl.* **-cra** 〔-krə; -krə〕, **-crums.** ①影像；像。②僞物；僞裝的東西。

sim·u·lant 〔ˈsɪmjulənt; ˈsimjulənt〕*adj.* 〖生物〗擬態的；擬色的。

sim·u·late 〔ˈsɪmjəˌlet; ˈsimjuleit〕*v.*, **-lat·ed, -lat·ing,** *adj.* —*v.t.* ①假裝；僞裝。②扮演。③〖生物〗擬態；擬色。④類似。—*v.i.* 假裝。—*adj.* ①僞裝的。②擬態的。

sim·u·la·tion 〔ˌsɪmjəˈleʃən; ˌsimjuˈleiʃən〕*n.* ①假裝；佯爲。②擬態；擬色。③外表；外觀。

sim·u·la·tive 〔ˈsɪmjəˌletɪv; ˈsimjuleitiv〕*adj.* 僞裝的；假裝的。

si·mul·cast 〔ˈsaɪmlˌkæst; ˈsiməlkɑːst〕*v.*, **-cast, -cast·ing,** *n.* —*v.t.* 以電視與無線電同時廣播。—*n.* 電視與無線電之同時廣播同一節目。

si·mul·ta·ne·i·ty 〔ˌsaɪml̩təˈniətɪ; ˌsiməltəˈniəti〕*n.* 同時；同時發生；同時存在。

***si·mul·ta·ne·ous** 〔ˌsaɪml̩ˈtenɪəs; ˌsiməlˈteinjəs〕*adj.* 同時的；同時存在的；同時發生的。—**ly,** *adv.*

simultaneous equations 〖數學〗聯立方程式。

‡**sin** 〔sɪn; sin〕*n., v.*, **sinned, sin·ning.** —*n.* ①罪；罪惡。deadly (*or* mortal) *sin.* 大罪。②犯罪；犯法。③不該做的事。It's a *sin* to stay indoors on such a fine day. 這樣好天氣留在屋裏實在不該。—*v.i.* 犯罪；獲罪；違背。to *sin* against propriety. 違背禮儀。—*v.t.* ①犯(罪)。②違反天意而爲。***sin one's mercies*** 忘恩負義。—**less,** *adj.*

sin sine.

Si·nai 〔ˈsaɪnaɪ; ˈsainiai〕*n.* ①西奈半島(埃及東北部，紅海北端，蘇彝士灣與 Aqabá 間一半島)。②〖聖經〗西奈山(上帝授摩西十誡處)。

Si·na·it·ic 〔ˌsaɪnɪˈɪtɪk; ˌsaineiˈitik〕*adj.* ①西奈山的。②西奈半島的。

Sin·an·thro·pus 〔ˌsɪnænˈθropəs; ˌsinænˈθroupəs〕*n.* 〖考古〗北京人（在北平附近周口店發現其骸骨）。

sin·a·pism 〔ˈsɪnəpɪzəm; ˈsinəpizm〕*n.* 〖醫〗芥子泥；芥子糊。

Sin·bad 〔ˈsɪnbæd; ˈsinbæd〕*n.* ①辛巴德(天方夜譚中之水手)。②水手；海員。（亦作 **Sindbad**)

‡**since** 〔sɪns; sins〕*prep.* 自…以後；自…以來。I have eaten nothing *since* yesterday. 我自昨日起卽未吃任何東西。—*conj.* ①自…以後；自…以來。What have you been doing *since* I last saw you? 自我上次和你見面以後，你在做甚麼事情? ②旣然；因爲。*Since* you ask, I will tell you. 你旣然問，我就告訴你。—*adv.* 自彼時至此時；其後。He caught cold last Saturday and has been in bed ever *since*. 他上星期六傷風了，從那時起便一直躺在床上。***long since*** 很久以前。

***sin·cere** 〔sɪnˈsɪr; sinˈsiə〕*adj.*, **-cer·er, -cer·est.** ①眞實的；誠摯的；篤實的。②自信心極强的。—**ness,** *n.*

sin·cere·ly** 〔sɪnˈsɪrlɪ; sinˈsiəli〕*adv.* 眞實地；誠懇地；篤實地。I *sincerely* hope you will soon recover. 我誠懇地盼望你不久卽告康復。Yours sincerely*** 信文後簽名前的問候語。

***sin·cer·i·ty** 〔sɪnˈsɛrətɪ sinˈseriti〕*n., pl.* **-ties.** ①眞實；誠懇；眞摯。in all *sincerity.* 極其誠懇。②眞實的感情。

sin·ci·put 〔ˈsɪnsɪˌpʌt; ˈsinsipʌt〕*n.* 〖解剖〗前頂；前頭部；頭頂部。

sine[1] 〔saɪn; sain〕*n.* 〖三角〗正弦。

si·ne[2] 〔ˈsaɪnɪ; ˈsaini〕〖拉〗*prep.* 無（= without).

si·ne·cure 〔ˈsaɪnɪˌkjur; ˈsainikjuə〕*n.* 閒差；領乾俸的職位。—*adj.* 領乾俸的。

si·ne·cur·ist 〔ˈsaɪnɪˌkjurɪst; ˈsainikjuərist〕*n.* 居閒職者(尤指掛名牧師)。

si·ne di·e 〔ˈsaɪnɪˈdaɪ·i; ˈsainiˈdaii(ː)〕〖拉〗無限期地；無確定日期地。

si·ne qua non 〔ˈsaɪnɪkweˈnɑn; ˈsainikweiˈnɔn〕〖拉〗必要條件；必要之物。

***sin·ew** 〔ˈsɪnju; ˈsinjuː〕*n.* ①腱。②力量；能力。a man of mighty *sinews.* 力大無窮的人。③(*pl.*)力量的來源。Men and money are the *sinews* of war. 人力與財力是戰爭的力量之來源。—*v.t.* 給予力量；加强。

sin·ew·y 〔ˈsɪnjəwɪ; ˈsinju(ː)i〕*adj.* ①多腱的。②强壯的；有力的。③(文體等)有力的。④如腱的；堅韌的。—**sin·ew·i·ness,** *n.*

sin·ful 〔ˈsɪnful; ˈsinfəl〕*adj.* 有罪的；充滿罪惡的。—**ness,** *n.*

sin·ful·ly 〔ˈsɪnfəlɪ; ˈsinfəli〕*adv.* ①充滿罪惡地；不道德地。②荒唐地；無理地。

‡**sing** 〔sɪŋ; siŋ〕*v.*, **sang** 〔sæŋ; sæŋ〕or **sung** 〔sʌŋ; sʌŋ〕, **sung, sing·ing,** *n.* —*v.i.* ①歌唱。The children are learning to *sing.* 孩子們在學唱歌。②囀；啼。③歌頌；吟詠。He *sang* of war. 他吟詠戰爭。④(溪流、水壺、風等)作鳴聲。⑤被唱。⑥作詩。⑦有美妙效果；有節奏。⑧響。⑨叫；喊。⑩密告。—*v.t.* ①歌唱。②唱出；唱歌般說出。The priest *sings* Mass. 牧師吟誦彌撒曲。③歌頌；吟詠。④歌唱以使…。She *sang* the baby to sleep. 她唱歌使小兒入睡。⑤(鳥等)鳴；囀。⑥宣布；聲明。***sing another song*** (or ***tune***) 受屈辱後變沉默；變謙遜。***sing one's praises*** 稱頌某人；歌頌某人。***sing out*** 大聲喊出。They *sang out* for help. 他們大聲呼救。***sing small*** = **sing another**

song. *sing the blues* 發牢騷;打抱不平;說洩氣話。*sing up* 更用力唱。—*n.* ①歌唱聲;鳴聲;玎玲聲。②歌唱;合唱;歌唱會。—**a·ble,** *adj.*
sing. ①single. ②singular.
Sin·ga·pore [ˈsɪŋgəˌpor; ˌsiŋgəˈpɔː] *n.* 新加坡(位於馬來半島南端的國家, 首都新加坡, Singapore).
singe [sɪndʒ; sindʒ] *v.,* **singed, singe·ing,** *n.* —*v.t.* ①微燒; 燙焦。②燙(頭髮)。③傷害;損害。④使(多管閒事而)惹上麻煩。—*v.i.* 燒焦; 燙焦。*singe one's feathers* (or *wings*) **a.** 損壞名譽。**b.** 事業失敗; 鎩羽。—*n.* 輕微的燒灼。
***sing·er** [ˈsɪŋɚ; ˈsiŋə] *n.* ①歌者;歌手。②鳴禽。③詩人。
Sin·gha·lese [ˌsɪŋgəˈliz; ˌsiŋhəˈliːz, ˌsiŋgəˈl-] *adj.* 錫蘭的;錫蘭族的;錫蘭語的。—*n.* 錫蘭人;錫蘭語。
sing·ing [ˈsɪŋɪŋ; ˈsiŋiŋ] *n.* ①歌唱; 唱歌;歌聲。②鳴; 響。③耳鳴。—*adj.* 歌唱的; 鳴囀的。—**ly,** *adv.*
‡**sin·gle** [ˈsɪŋgḷ;ˈsiŋgl] *adj., n., v.,* **-gled, -gling,** *adv.* —*adj.* ①單一的; 單獨的; 單式的。a *single* bed. 單人床。Not a *single* word was said. 一語未發。②〖植物〗單瓣的。③每邊祇有一個的; 一人對一人的。④獨身的; 未婚的。a *single* man. 獨身男子。*single* life. 獨身生活。⑤誠實的;單純的。⑥獨特的。He is *single* among his fellows. 他在他夥伴中顯得很獨特。⑦唯一的。⑧祇關心(某事)的。⑨一致的;無例外的。—*n.* ①一個; 單個。The guests arrive in *singles* and pairs. 客人們有的獨自來,有的成雙地來。②〖棒球〗一壘安打。③兩個人玩的遊戲。④(*pl.*)(作 *sing.* 解)單打比賽。⑤一元美鈔。⑥單人房。The apartment is a *single.* 那寓所是一間單人房。⑦單人表演。⑧一邊祇有一支曲子的唱片。—*v.t.* ①選;挑選〖常 out〗。②〖棒球〗以一壘安打護送(隊友)。③〖棒球〗以一壘安打使(隊友)得分〖常 in〗。—*v.i.* 〖棒球〗擊出一壘安打。—*adv.* 單獨地。
single blessedness 獨身狀態。
sin·gle-breast·ed [ˈsɪŋgḷˈbrɛstɪd; ˈsiŋglˈbrestid] *adj.* 單襟的;單排扣的(上衣)。
single combat 兩人之間的戰鬥;一人對一人的毆鬥。
sin·gle-crop [ˈsɪŋgḷˈkrɑp; ˈsiŋglˈkrɔp] *v.i. & v.t.,* **-cropped, -crop·ping.** 行單一耕種(在同一農地反覆種同一種農作物)。
single entry 〖簿記〗單式記帳。—**sin·gle-en·try,** *adj.*
sin·gle-eyed [ˈsɪŋgḷˈaɪd; ˈsiŋglˈaid] *adj.* ①單眼的; 獨眼的。②純眞的; 誠實的。
single file ①一列縱隊。②成一列縱隊地。
sin·gle-foot [ˈsɪŋgḷˌfut; ˈsiŋglfut] *n.* 單步(馬走的一種步態)。—*v.i.* 以單步行進。
sin·gle-hand·ed [ˈsɪŋgḷ ˈhændɪd; ˈsiŋglˈhændid] *adj.* ①獨力的;無助的。②祇須一人的。③單手使用的; 單手操作的。④僅用一手的;用單手的。—*adv.* 獨力地; 單人地; 單手地。—**ness,** *n.*
sin·gle-heart·ed [ˈsɪŋgḷˈhɑrtɪd;ˈsiŋglˈhɑːtid] *adj.* ①忠誠的; 眞心的。②一心一意的;目的專一的。—**ness,** *n.* —**ly,** *adv.*
sin·gle-mind·ed [ˈsɪŋgḷˈmaɪndɪd; ˈsiŋglˈmaindid] *adj.* ①一心一意的。②專誠的;赤誠的。—**ly,** *adv.*
sin·gle-mind·ed·ness [ˈsɪŋgḷˈmaɪndɪdnɪs; ˈsiŋglˈmaindidnis] *n.* 專誠;專心。
sin·gle-name paper [ˈsɪŋgḷˈnem ~; ˈsiŋglˈneim ~] 祇有開票人背書的期票。
sin·gle·ness [ˈsɪŋgḷnɪs; ˈsiŋglnis] *n.* ①單一; 單一性; 單獨。②獨身狀態; 未婚狀態。③誠實;眞誠。
sin·gle-phase [ˈsɪŋgḷˈfez;ˈsiŋglˈfeiz] *adj.* 〖電〗單相的。
single quotes 單點引號, 即' '。
single rhyme 單音節之押韻。
sin·gle-seat·er [ˈsɪŋgḷˈsitɚ; ˈsiŋglˈsiːtə] *n.* 單人乘坐之汽車、飛機等。
sin·gle-shot [ˈsɪŋgḷˈʃɑt; ˈsiŋglˈʃɔt] *adj.* (手鎗等)單發的; 不用彈夾的。
sin·gle-space [ˈsɪŋgḷˈspes; ˈsiŋglˈspeis] *v.t. & v.i.,* **-spaced, -spac·ing.** (用打字機)不隔行地打;打成單空白。
single standard ①單本位制(或用銀本位、或用金本位)。②全體適用之道德標準。
sin·gle·stick [ˈsɪŋgḷˌstɪk; ˈsiŋgl-stik] *n.* ①用於劍術之劍狀棍棒。②(使用此種棍棒之)劍術。
sin·glet [ˈsɪŋglɪt; ˈsiŋglit] *n.* 〖英方〗襯衣;汗衫。
single tax 單一稅。
single ticket 〖英〗單程票。
sin·gle·ton [ˈsɪŋgḷtən; ˈsiŋgltən] *n.* ①單獨存在之物。②(橋牌等)弔單之牌。
sin·gle-track [ˈsɪŋgḷˈtræk; ˈsiŋglˈtræk] *adj.* ①〖鐵路〗單軌的。②狹窄的;褊狹的。
sin·gle·tree [ˈsɪŋgḷˌtri; ˈsiŋgltriː] *n.* 〖美〗馬車、犂等前頭兩端繫曳繩之橫木。
sin·gly [ˈsɪŋglɪ; ˈsiŋgli] *adv.* ①單獨地; 個別地。②一個一個地。③獨力地;無助地。
Sing Sing [ˈsɪŋˌsɪŋ; ˈsiŋsiŋ] 紐約州 Ossining 附近之州立監獄。
sing·song [ˈsɪŋˌsɔŋ; ˈsiŋsɔŋ] *n.* ①單調的節奏。②單調的聲調。③單調幼稚的劣詩。④即席唱歌會。—*adj.* ①單調的;節奏單調的。②不精采的;平凡的。—*v.t. & v.i.* 以單調的聲調吟唱。
***sin·gu·lar** [ˈsɪŋgjəlɚ;ˈsiŋgjulə] *adj.* ①非凡的;卓異的。a man of *singular* courage. 勇敢非凡的人。②奇特的;奇異的。③單一的;單獨的。④〖文法〗單數的。⑤個別的;各個的;私人的。all and *singular* interests. 各人的利益。—*n.* ①〖文法〗單數式;單數的字。②個人;個體。—**ness,** *n.*
sin·gu·lar·i·ty [ˌsɪŋgjəˈlærətɪ;ˌsiŋgjuˈlæriti] *n., pl.* **-ties.** ①奇異;特異;非凡。②特性。③個體。
sin·gu·lar·ly [ˈsɪŋgjələlɪ;ˈsiŋgjuləli] *adv.* 特異地;奇異地。a *singularly* charming woman. 嫵媚異常的女人。
sin·gul·tus [sɪŋˈgʌltəs; siŋˈgʌltəs] *n., pl.* **-tus·es.** 〖醫〗呃逆;打嗝。—**sin·gul·tous,** *adj.*
Sin·ha·lese [ˌsɪnhəˈliz;ˌsiŋhəˈliːz] *n., adj.* =Singhalese.
Sin·i·co-Jap·a·nese [ˈsɪnəkoˌdʒæpəˈniz;ˈsinikouˌdʒæpəˈniːz] *n.* 日語之漢字。
***sin·is·ter** [ˈsɪnɪstɚ; ˈsinistə] *adj.* ①邪惡的;兇惡的;陰險的。②不吉的;不祥的;凶兆的。③在左方的; 左的。—*adv.* 向左。*bar sinister* 一個人的盾牌或盾形徽章左邊之符號, 表示其爲私生子。—**ness,** *n.*
sin·is·ter·ly [ˈsɪnɪstəlɪ;ˈsinistəli] *adv.* 不祥地;陰險地。
sin·is·tral [ˈsɪnɪstrəl; ˈsinistrəl] *adj.* ①左的;左方的;向左方的。②有左旋紋的 (貝殼等)。—**ly,** *adv.* —**i·ty,** *n.*
Si·nit·ic [sɪˈnɪtɪk; siˈnitik] *adj.* 中國人的;有關中國人、中國語或中國文化的。(亦作 Sinetic)
‡**sink** [sɪŋk; siŋk] *v.,* **sank** [sæŋk; sæŋk]

or **sunk** [sʌŋk; sʌŋk], **sunk** or **sunk·en** [ˈsʌŋkən; ˈsʌŋkən], **sink·ing**, *n.* —*v.i.* ①沉;沉落;沉下;下傾。The sun was *sinking* in the west. 夕陽西下。②沮喪。His spirits *sank*. 他的精神沮喪。③減弱;降低。The wind has *sunk* down. 風勢已弱。④滲入。The rain *sank* into the dry and thirsty ground. 雨水滲入乾旱的地裏。⑤陷於;墮入(某種狀態)。⑥予人以深刻印象。Let the warning *sink* into your mind. 要把這個警告銘記在心。⑦坐;躺〖down in, down on, in, into, on, onto 等〗. He *sank* down on the bench and waited for the next bus.他在長櫈上坐下等下一班公共汽車。—*v.t.* ①使沉。The submarine *sank* two ships. 這隻潛艇擊沉兩隻船。②使低落;使衰落。*Sink* your voice. 放低聲音。③掘。④挿入;埋入;打入。⑤對…作無利的投資。⑥掩飾。⑦忽視;不重視。⑧使凹。He *sank* his chin on his hands. 他的下顎因托在手中而凹進去。⑨壓倒。⑩廢棄不用。⑪使沉淪;使墮落。⑫爲獲暴利而對…投資。***sink in*** 被了解。***sink in one's estimation*** 失去某人的信任。***sink in the world*** 沒落;式微。***sink one's teeth*** 咬。***sink or swim*** 成敗。*Sink or swim*, I will try. 不論成敗,我必一試。—*n.* ①溝渠。②污水槽。③窩;罪惡或腐敗滋生之地;藏垢納污之地。 a *sink* of iniquity. 罪惡的淵藪。④田地中滲水之低地。 —**a·ble**, *adj.*

sink·er [ˈsɪŋkɚ; ˈsiŋkə] *n.* ①沉下之人或物;掘井者。②(釣絲或漁網之)鉛錘。③〖美俚〗炸麪餅。

sink·hole [ˈsɪŋk͵hol; ˈsiŋkhoul] *n.* ①(爲水所穿之)石灰岩豎洞。②陰溝;污水溝。③下流酒館或賭博場所(=dive). ④〖美俗〗不合算之企業。⑤窩;窟;藏垢納污之地。

Sin·kiang [ˈsɪnˈkjæŋ, ˈʃɪnˈdʒɪɑŋ; ˈsinˈkjæŋ, ˈʃinˈdʒiɑːŋ] *n.* 新疆(中國西北之一省,省會廸化 Tihwa 或 Urumchi)。

sink·ing [ˈsɪŋkɪŋ; ˈsiŋkiŋ] *n.* ①沉陷;低陷。②〖建築〗凹處。③沮喪;頹廢。④虛弱。

sinking fund (政府、公司等準備的)償債基金。

sink·less [ˈsɪŋklɪs; ˈsiŋklis] *adj.* 不沉的。

sin·less [ˈsɪnlɪs; ˈsinlis] *adj.* 無罪的;淸白的;無辜的。—**ly**, *adv.* —**ness**, *n.*

sin money 贖罪金。

***sin·ner** [ˈsɪnɚ; ˈsinə] *n.* (宗敎、道德上的)罪人。

Sinn Fein [ˈʃɪnˈfen; ˈʃinˈfein] 愛爾蘭之新芬黨(成立於 1905 年,主張愛爾蘭完全脫離英國而獨立)。

Sino- 〖字首〗表"中國的"之義,如:Sino-Japanese.

sin offering 贖罪之供品。

Si·no-Jap·a·nese [͵saɪno͵dʒæpəˈniz; ˈsinou͵dʒæpəˈniːz] *adj.* 中國及日本的;中日的。—*n.* 漢化日語。

Si·nol·o·gist [saɪˈnɑlədʒɪst; siˈnɔlədʒist] *n.* 漢學家。

Si·no·logue [ˈsaɪnə͵lɔg; ˈsinəlɔg] *n.* 研究中國文化者;漢學家。

Si·nol·o·gy [saɪˈnɑlədʒɪ; siˈnɔlədʒi] *n.* 漢學(研究中國文學、藝術、語言、歷史等)。

Si·no-Ti·bet·an [͵saɪnotɪˈbɛtn; ͵sinoutiˈbetən] *n.*, *adj.* 漢藏語系(的)。

SINS Ship's Inertial Navigation System (用於核子動力潛艇中)。

sin·ter [ˈsɪntɚ; ˈsintə] *n.* ①泉華(礦泉所生石灰質或矽質的多孔性沉澱物)。②(鑄鐵時之)非金屬鎔塊;灰。 —*v.t.* & *v.i.* 〖冶金〗燒結。

sin·u·ate¹ [ˈsɪnjuɪt; ˈsinjuit] *adj.* 彎曲的;波狀的。—**ly**, *adv.*

sin·u·ate² [ˈsɪnju͵et; ˈsinjueit] *v.i.*, **-at·ed, -at·ing.** 蜿蜒;彎曲;曲折。 —**sin·u·a·tion**, *n.*

sin·u·os·i·ty [͵sɪnjuˈɑsətɪ; ͵sinjuˈɔsiti] *n.*, *pl.* **-ties.** ①蜿蜒;彎曲。②波狀物。③(道路等的)彎處。

sin·u·ous [ˈsɪnjuəs; ˈsinjuəs] *adj.* ①彎彎曲曲的;蜿蜒的;迂迴的。②間接的。③邪惡的。④〖植物〗有波狀邊緣的(葉)。 —**ly**, *adv.* —**ness**, *n.*

si·nus [ˈsaɪnəs; ˈsainəs] *n.*, *pl.* **-nus·es, -nus.** ①〖解剖〗竇。②〖醫〗瘻;瘻管。③彎曲。④海彎。

si·nus·i·tis [͵saɪnəˈsaɪtɪs; ͵sainəˈsaitis] *n.* 〖醫〗竇炎。

Si·on [ˈsaɪən; ˈsaiən] *n.* =**Zion.**

-sion 〖字尾〗與 **-tion** 同義。

Siou·an [ˈsuən; ˈsuːən] *n.* 蘇族(北美印第安人之一大語族)。—*adj.* 蘇族的。

Sioux [su, *pl.* su(z); suː, *pl.* suːz] *n. sing.* or *pl.* 蘇族(北美印第安人之一族);蘇族人。—*adj.* Sioux 族的; Sioux 語的。

***sip** [sɪp; sip] *v.*, **sipped, sip·ping,** *n.* —*v.t.* & *v.i.* 啜;啜飮。 She *sipped* her tea. 她啜茶。—*n.* 一啜;啜飮。to take a *sip.* 啜飮。

si·phon [ˈsaɪfən; ˈsaifən] *n.* ①彎管;虹吸管。②〖動物〗某些甲殼類排水及汲水的吸管。 ***siphon barometer*** 虹吸式氣壓計。***siphon bottle*** 彎管瓶。 ***siphon gauge*** 曲管壓力計。 —*v.t.* & *v.i.* ①用虹吸管吸出;通過虹吸管。②外流;消耗。(亦作 **syphon**) —**al**, *adj.*

si·phon·ic [saɪˈfɑnɪk; saiˈfɔnik] *adj.* 虹吸的;虹吸作用的。

sip·per [ˈsɪpɚ; ˈsipə] *n.* ①啜飮者。②從瓶中吸取液體或飲料的吸管、麥管等。

sip·pet [ˈsɪpɪt; ˈsipit] *n.* ①小片;碎片。②浸於牛奶或肉湯中的小麪包片。

SIR Submarine Intermediate Reactor. 核子動力潛艇上使用的一種原子反應爐。

‡sir [sɝ; səː] *n.*, *v.*, **sirred, sir·ring.** —*n.* ①先生;君;閣下。②(S-) 爵士或從男爵的尊稱,置於名前。如: *Sir* Charles Brown. ③先生(=Mr. *or* Master). I'd be very grateful, *sir*, for your advice. 先生,我將非常感激您的忠告。④寫信時開始之稱呼。如 My dear *Sir*; Dear *Sir*; Dear *Sirs*. —*v.t.* 以 sir 稱呼。〖注意〗**Sir** 作爵士或貴族尊號解時通常和名字或連名帶姓一起,但不可與姓單獨使用。例: Sir William Craigie 可稱之爲 Sir William, 但不可稱之爲 Sir Craigie.

sir·dar [sɚˈdɑr; ˈsəːdɑː] *n.* (印度的)酋長;指揮官。—**ship**, *n.*

sire [saɪr; ˈsaiə] *n.*, *v.*, **sired, sir·ing.** —*n.* ①〖詩〗父;祖先。②(四足獸之)雄親;父獸(=male parent). ③閣下;陛下(昔日對貴族,今日對君主之尊稱)。—*v.t.* ①(尤指雄的種馬等)使生。②爲…之父。③創作(作品)。 ***Base things sire base.*** 賤東西生賤東西;有其父必有其子。

si·ren [ˈsaɪrən; ˈsaiərin] *n.* ①〖希臘神話〗海上女妖。②引誘男人的美婦人。③號笛(如警報器等)。—*adj.* 海上女妖的;誘惑人的。 ***siren song*** 誘惑。—*v.i.* 響着號笛行駛。

si·re·ni·an [saɪˈrinɪən; saiəˈriːniən] *n.* 〖動物〗海牛。

siren suit 〖英〗=**coveralls.**

Sir·i·an [ˈsɪrɪən; ˈsiriən] *adj.* 〖天文〗天狼星的。

si·ri·a·sis [sɪˈraɪəsɪs; siˈraiəsis] *n.* 〖醫〗日射病;中暑。

Sir·i·us [ˈsɪrɪəs; ˈsiriəs] *n.* 〖天文〗天狼星。

sir·loin [ˈsɝlɔɪn; ˈsəːlɔin] *n.* 牛腰上部之肉。
si·roc·co [səˈrɑko; siˈrɔkou] *n., pl.* **-cos.** ①由非洲東北部之利比亞沙漠經地中海吹向南歐之熱風。②熱風。
sir·rah [ˈsɪrə; ˈsirə] *n.* 〖古〗對男子輕蔑責罵之稱呼。
sir·up [ˈsɪrəp; ˈsirəp] *n., v.t.* =**syrup.**
sir·up·y [ˈsɪrəpɪ; ˈsirəpi] *adj.* 糖漿的;似糖漿的。
SIS Scientific Intelligence Survey.
Sis [sɪs; sis] *n.* 女子名 (Cecilia, Cecily 等之暱稱)。
sis [sɪs; sis] *n.* ①〖俗〗=**sister.** ②〖俗〗女郎;愛人。③〖俚〗=**sissy.**
si·sal [ˈsaɪsl; ˈsaisəl] *n.* 〖植物〗瓊麻。
sis·kin [ˈsɪskɪn; ˈsiskin] *n.* 金雀;金翅雀。
sis·sy [ˈsɪsɪ; ˈsisi] *n., pl.* **-sies,** *adj.*—*n.* ①〖俗〗=**sister.** ②〖俗〗有女人氣的男人。③小女孩。④膽小者。—*adj.* 女人氣的。
‡**sis·ter** [ˈsɪstɚ; ˈsistə] *n.* ①姊;妹;姊妹。elder *sister*. 姊。younger *sister*. 妹。②女會員;女社友。③修女;女教士;尼。④親切的女人。⑤相似物;可相比之物。⑥〖俚〗女人;小姐(多用於稱呼)。⑦〖英〗護士;護士長。***the Fatal Sisters*** 命運三女神。***weak sister*** 能力不强者。—*adj.* 如姊妹一般的;極相似的。—*v.t.* 可與…比;可爲…之姊妹作。—**less,** *adj.* —**like,** *adj.*
sis·ter-ger·man [ˈsɪstɚˈdʒɝmən; ˈsistəˈdʒəːmən] *n.* 同父同母之姊妹。
sis·ter·hood [ˈsɪstɚhud; ˈsistəhud] *n.* ①姊妹的關係;姊妹之道。②婦女會社。③結社;組織;聯合。
sis·ter-in-law [ˈsɪstərɪn,lɔ; ˈsistərin-lɔː] *n., pl.* **sis·ters-in-law.** ①夫或妻之姊妹;姑;姨。②兄或弟之妻;嫂;弟婦。③姻兄弟之妻。
sis·ter·ly [ˈsɪstɚlɪ; ˈsistəli] *adj.* 似姊妹的。—*adv.* 似姊妹一般地;以姊妹的作法。
sister ship 姊妹艦;同級之船艦。
Sis·tine [ˈsɪstin; ˈsistain] *adj.* 羅馬教皇 Sixtus 的。
Sistine Chapel 羅馬梵諦岡教皇之小禮拜堂(爲 Sixtus 四世所建,有 Michelangelo 之壁畫,因而著名)。
Sistine Madonna 義大利 Piacenza 的 San Sisto 教堂中拉飛爾 (Raphael) 畫的聖母像。
sis·tra [ˈsɪstrə; ˈsistrə] *n. pl.* of **sistrum.**
sis·trum [ˈsɪstrəm; ˈsistrəm] *n., pl.* **-trums, -tra.** 古埃及人祭 Isis 時用的樂器。
Sis·y·phe·an [,sɪsəˈfiən; ,sisiˈfiːən] *adj.* ①Sisyphus 的。②無止境而困難的;操勞的。
Sis·y·phus [ˈsɪsəfəs; ˈsisifəs] *n.* 〖希臘神話〗科林斯王(詭譎而貪婪,被罰在冥府推一巨石上山,該石推上去後必會自動滾下)。
‡**sit** [sɪt; sit] *v.,* **sat** [sæt; sæt], **sit·ting,** *n.* —*v.i.* ①坐。 *Sit* up straight. 坐正。②位於。The city *sits* on a hill. 此城坐落在一山上。③在會議中有一席位;爲會議中之一員。④開會;開庭。The parliament is *sitting.* 國會正在開會。⑤做姿勢。⑥棲。There was a bird *sitting* on the branch. 一鳥棲息在樹枝上面。⑦孵卵。⑧適合;適於。⑨合身。The coat *sits* well. 這件上衣很合身。⑩在休息的狀態中;不活動。⑪重壓。Care *sat* heavy on his brow. 他的眉間顯出憂慮;他愁眉苦臉。⑫(風)來自(某方向)。⑬當臨時褓母〖with〗。—*v.t.* ①使坐;使就座。She *sat* her guests at the table. 她使客人們就座(進餐)。②騎乘。***make a person sit up*** a. 使某人驚起。b. 鼓舞某人從事活動。***sit around*** 無所事事。***sit at home*** 蟄居家中;不活動。***sit down*** a. 坐下;就座。b. 會商;協議。c. (飛機)降落。***sit down under (insults)*** 無怨言地忍受(凌辱)。***sit for an examination*** 參加考試。***sit in*** a. 參加(競賽、會議等)。b. 參加靜坐抗議。c. 不採取行動;不干預。***sit in on*** a. 作旁觀者或訪客。b. 參加。***sit loose*** 不關心;不注意。***sit on (or upon)*** a. (陪審團)調查;審詢。b.〖俗〗壓制;冷待。They *sat upon* the bad news as long as they could. 他們儘可能扣壓這個壞消息。c. 占有一席次。d. 延遲;擱置。***sit on a fence*** 騎牆;持觀望態度。***sit on thorns*** 如坐針氈;侷促不安。***sit out*** a. 貫徹始終。b. 保持坐着而不參加。c. 留得比(別人)更久。***sit pretty***〖俗〗適意;諸事順遂。***sit through*** 從頭到尾不離座地聽或看。***sit tight*** a. 坐穩(馬背)。b. 堅守目標;固執意見。c. 不採取行動;靜觀待變。***sit up*** a. 不睡。b. 坐直。c. 保持直坐姿勢。d. 驚起;發生興趣。—*n.* ①坐。②(衣服)與身材之配合;合身。
sit. situation.
sit-down [ˈsɪt,daun; ˈsitdaun] *n.* ①〖美〗靜坐罷工;在廠罷工。②座位。③〖英俗〗坐下聊天。—*adj.* 坐着享受的;坐而行的。
sit-down strike =**sit-down** ①.
***site** [saɪt; sait] *n., v.,* **sit·ed, sit·ing.** —*n.* 位置;場所。—*v.t.* ①使位於某處。②使(火砲)放列以備發射。
sith [sɪθ; siθ] *adv., conj., prep.* 〖古〗=**since.**
sit-in [ˈsɪt,ɪn; ˈsit-in] *n.* ① =**sit-down strike.** ②〖美〗爲反對種族歧視而集體在餐館等地坐下不離開之抗議方式。
si·tol·o·gy [saɪˈtɑlədʒɪ; saiˈtɔlədʒi] *n.* 營養學。
Si·tsang [ˈʃiˈtsɑŋ; ˈʃiːˈtsaːŋ] *n.* 西藏(中國西部之自治區,亦稱 Tibet, 首府拉薩, Lhasa)。
sit·ter [ˈsɪtɚ; ˈsitə] *n.* ①坐者。②坐供畫像者。③孵卵的禽鳥。④棲息的鳥;坐臥的獸。⑤臨時看護嬰兒者 (=baby sitter)。⑥易擊中的目標。
sit·ter-in [ˈsɪtɚˈɪn; ˈsitərˈin] *n.* 〖主英〗替人看家並照顧小孩者。
sit·ting [ˈsɪtɪŋ; ˈsitiŋ] *n.* ①開會或開庭的期間。②一次坐着不動的期間。He finished reading the book at one *sitting.* 他一口氣把那本書讀完了。③坐。④ a. 孵蛋。b. 一鳥所孵的卵數。⑤教堂中的座位。—*adj.* ①坐着的。②在議會中占有席位的。③容易射中的。④孵卵的。⑤供座次用的。
sitting duck 容易射中的目標;易於欺騙或傷害的對象。
sitting room 起居室;客廳。
sit·u·ate [*v.* ˈsɪtʃu,et; ˈsitjueit *adj.* ˈsɪtʃuɪt; ˈsitjueit] *v.t.* 置於某處;使處於某種境地。—*adj.* 〖古〗=**situated.**
***sit·u·at·ed** [ˈsɪtʃu,etɪd; ˈsitjueitid] *adj.* 坐落(某處)的;處於(某種)境地的。The village is *situated* by a river. 這個村莊坐落河濱。
‡**sit·u·a·tion** [,sɪtʃuˈeʃən; ,sitjuˈeiʃən] *n.* ①位置;場所。Choose an attractive *situation* for our camp. 選一個很好的場地供我們紮營。②情形;情勢;境遇。 The *situation* at the front has not changed recently. 前線的情況最近沒有變化。③職業;工作(現大抵指卑微的職業)。④戲劇、小說等中的緊要情節或場面。
situation comedy 〖美〗〖廣播、電視〗喜劇集(角色及背景相同,而各集內容獨立

者)。(亦作 **sitcom**)
sit-up [ˈsɪtˌʌp; ˈsitʌp] *n.* 從平臥姿勢所作之坐起運動。
si·tus [ˈsaɪtəs; ˈsaitəs]【拉】*n.* 位置;「地位。」
sitz [sɪts; sits]【德】*n.* 坐。*sitz* bath. 坐浴;坐浴室。
sitz·krieg [ˈsɪtsˌkrig; ˈsitskri:g] *n.*一再出現僵持局面而雙方都沒有大進展的戰事。
Si·va [ˈsivə; ˈsi(ː)və] *n.* 濕婆; 大自在天(印度三大神中司破壞之神)。
si·wash [ˈsaɪwɑʃ; ˈsaiwɔʃ] *n., pl.* **-wash·es,** *adj.* —*n.* ①(常作 S-) 位於內陸鄉下的小規模大學。②(S-) 北美太平洋海岸之印第安人。—*adj.* (S-) 北美太平洋海岸之印第安人的。
‡**six** [sɪks; siks] *adj.* 六;六個。*six* years. 六年。 —*pron.* 六個人; 六個。*Six* were found. 找到了六個。 —*n.* ①六; 六個。It is *six* of one and half a dozen of the other. 這是半斤對八兩。②六的號碼。③六點的骰子或紙牌。④(大小號碼之)六號。She wears a *six*. 她穿六號衣(或鞋)。⑤(S-)歐洲共同市場之六個原始會員國(即比、法、荷、義、德及盧森堡)。 ***at six(es) and seven(s)*** a. 亂七八糟。b. 不協調。 ***knock*** (or ***hit***) ***for six*** 【英俚】痛擊;消滅;擊敗。
six·er [ˈsɪksɚ; ˈsiksə] *n.* ①含六之物;一組六件之物。②【俗】板球得六分之一擊。
six·fold [ˈsɪksˌfold; ˈsiksfould] *adj. & adv.* 六倍的(地);六重的(地)。
six-foot·er [ˈsɪksˈfutɚ; ˈsiksˈfutə] *n.* 身高六英尺者。
six-gun [ˈsɪksˌgʌn; ˈsiksgʌn] *n.* =「**six-shooter.**」
six·mo [ˈsɪksmo; ˈsiksmou] *n.* (紙張之)六開。
six-o-six [ˈsɪkˌsoˈsɪks; ˈsikˌsouˈsiks] *n.* 梅毒特效藥六〇六 (=arsphenamine).
six-pack [ˈsɪksˌpæk; ˈsikspæk] *n.* (以六瓶或六罐而裝成之)一箱(飲料等)。
six·pence [ˈsɪkspəns; ˈsikspəns] *n.* ①六辨士。②六辨士之銀幣。
six·pen·ny [ˈsɪksˌpɛnɪ; ˈsikspəni] *adj.* ①值六辨士的。②廉價的; 殊少價值的。③兩英寸的。
six-shoot·er [ˈsɪksˈʃutɚ; ˈsiksˈʃuː-「tə] *n.* (六發)左輪手鎗。」
sixte [sɪkst; sikst] *n.*【劍術】八種防禦姿勢中之第六種。
‡**six·teen** [sɪksˈtin, ˈsɪksˈtin; ˈsiksˈtiːn, ˈsikstiːn, siksˈtiːn] *adj.* 十六的;十六個的。—*pron.* 十六個。*Sixteen* are here. 這裏有十六個。 —*n.* ①十六; 十六個。②十六的號碼。③(大小號碼之) 十六號。She wears a *sixteen*. 她穿十六號。
six·teen·mo [sɪksˈtinmo; siksˈtiːnmou] *n., pl.* **-mos.** 十六開本 (= sextodecimo).
***six·teenth** [sɪksˈtinθ, ˈsɪksˈt-; ˈsiksˈtiːnθ, ˈsikst-, siksˈt-] *adj.* ①第十六的。②十六分之一的。—*n.* ①第十六。②十六分之一。
sixteenth note【音樂】十六分音符。
sixteenth rest【音樂】十六分休止符。
‡**sixth** [sɪksθ; siksθ] *adj.* ①第六的。the *sixth* day. 第六天。②六分之一的。—*n.* ①第六。the *sixth* of the month. 當月六號。②六分之一。—*adv.* 第六地。**—ly,** *adv.*
sixth column ①第六縱隊(間接或直接幫助敵方第五縱隊地下工作者之集合稱)。②反第五縱隊之工作人員。
six-three-three [ˈsɪksˌθriˈθri; ˈsiksˌθriːˈθriː] *adj.*【教育】六三三制的(小學六年,初中三年,高中三年)。
sixth sense 第六感;直覺。
***six·ti·eth** [ˈsɪkstɪɪθ; ˈsikstiiθ] *adj.* ①第六十的。②六十分之一的。—*n.* ①第六十。②六十分之一。
‡**six·ty** [ˈsɪkstɪ; ˈsiksti] *pron., n., pl.* **-ties,** *adj.* —*pron.* 六十個。*Sixty* are here. 有六十個人在這兒。—*n.* ①六十;60。②六十的記號。 ***in one's sixties*** 在六十到六十九歲之間的年齡。***in the sixties*** a. 在六十到六十九之間。b. 六十年代(一世紀中60到69年間)。***like sixty*** a. 拚命地。b. 激烈地。It was raining *like sixty*. 天正下着傾盆大雨。c. 容易地;迅速地。—*adj.* 六十的。
six·ty-first [ˈsɪkstɪˈfɝst; ˈsikstiˈfəːst] *adj.* ①第六十一的。②六十一分之一的。—*n.* ①第六十一。②六十一分之一。
six·ty·fold [ˈsɪkstɪˈfold; ˈsikstiˈfould] *adj.* 六十倍的。—*adv.* 六十倍地;六十重地。
sixty-four-dollar question【俗】基本問題;最後而主要的問題。
six·ty-four·mo [ˌsɪkstɪˈformo; ˌsikstiˈfɔːmou] *n.* 六十四開本。
six·ty-fourth note [ˈsɪkstɪˈforθ～; ˈsikstiˈfɔːθ～]【音樂】六十四分音符。
sixty-fourth rest【音樂】六十四分休止符。
six·ty·ish [ˈsɪkstɪɪʃ; ˈsikstiiʃ] *adj.* 將「近六十歲的;大約六十歲的。」
six·ty-sec·ond [ˈsɪkstɪˈsɛkənd; ˈsikstiˈsekənd] *adj.* ①第六十二的。②六十二分之一的。—*n.* ①第六十二。②六十二分之一。
six·ty-third [ˈsɪkstɪˈθɝd; ˈsikstiˈθəːd] *adj.* ①第六十三的。②六十三分之一的。—*n.* ①第六十三。②六十三分之一。
six-wheel·er [ˈsɪksˈhwilɚ; ˈsiksˈhwiːlə] *n.* 六輪大卡車。
siz·a·ble [ˈsaɪzəbl̩; ˈsaizəbl] *adj.* 頗大的。(亦作 **sizeable**) **—siz·a·bly,** *adv.*
siz·ar [ˈsaɪzɚ; ˈsaizə] *n.*【英】(以前Cambridge 大學、Dublin 大學之 Trinity 學院中的)公費生。(亦作 **sizer**) **—ship,** *n.*
‡**size**[1] [saɪz; saiz] *n., v.,* **sized, siz·ing.** —*n.* ①大小; 容量 ;面積; 尺寸。They're both of a *size*. 他們大小一樣。②實力;範圍。③(鞋、帽等的)號。His shoes are *size* 10. 他的鞋是十號的。④【俗】實況; 眞確的描述。That's about the *size* of it. 其眞相大致如此。⑤聲望; 地位。⑥人口數目; 數量。 ***cut*** (or ***chop***) ***down to size*** 使露眞面目。***for size*** a. 看看大小是否合適。b. 看看是否勝任。***life size*** 實物的大小。***of a size*** 同一大小。***take the size of*** 量…的尺寸。—*v.t.* ①按大小排列。②量(其)大小;估量【up】。③作成某種大小。④按大小分。 ***size up*** a. 估量;打量。b. 到達某種標準。
size[2] *n., v.,* **sized, siz·ing.** —*n.* 膠水; 漿糊。—*v.t.* 上膠於;上漿於。
size·a·ble [ˈsaɪzəbl̩; ˈsaizəbl] *adj.* = **sizable.** **—size·a·bly,** *adv.*
sized [saɪzd; saizd] *adj.* 有…大小的。large-*sized*. 大型(號)的。
siz·er [ˈsaɪzɚ; ˈsaizə] *n.* ①分大小之分類器; 分粒器; 作大小分類的人。②【英俗】(某物之)特大號。③=**sizar.**
size stick 鞋匠用尺。
size-up [ˈsaɪzˌʌp; ˈsaizʌp] *n.* 估量。
siz·ing [ˈsaɪzɪŋ; ˈsaiziŋ] *n.* ①上膠或上漿; 上膠或上漿之過程。②增加紙面光澤所塗之膠。③依大小比例配列;分配。
siz·y [ˈsaɪzɪ; ˈsaizi] *adj.,* **siz·i·er, siz·i-**

est. 黏稠的;有黏性的。—**siz·i·ness,** *n.*

sizz 〔sɪz; siz〕 *n.* 嘶嘶聲。—*v.i.* 發嘶嘶聲。—*v.t.* 使發出嘶嘶聲。

siz·zard 〔ˈsɪzəd; ˈsizəd〕 *n.* 〖美俗〗潮熱天;熱浪。

siz·zle 〔ˈsɪzl̩; ˈsizl〕 *n., v.,* **-zled, -zling.** —*n.* 嘶嘶聲。—*v.i.* ①發出嘶嘶聲;發嘶嘶聲地煎炒着。②表現良好; 進行順利。—*v.t.* ①燒之使焦。②惡言相罵。

siz·zler 〔ˈsɪzlɚ; ˈsizlə〕 *n.* ①〖俚〗特出之事物;令人振奮之事物;危險事物。②〖俗〗熱天。

siz·zling 〔ˈsɪzlɪŋ; ˈsizliŋ〕 *adj.* ①發嘶嘶聲的。②議論紛紛的。③酷暑的; 極熱的。—*adv.* …得發嘶嘶聲。—**ly,** *adv.*

S.J. Society of Jesus.

sjam·bok 〔ˈʃæmbɑk; ˈʃæmbɔk〕 *n.* 〖南非〗皮鞭。—*v.t.* 以皮鞭鞭打。

S.J.D. Doctor of Juridical Science.

sk. ①sack. ②sick. ③sink. ④sinking. ⑤sketch. ⑥skewbald. ⑦skewness. ⑧skip.

skald 〔skɔld; skɔːld〕 *n.* 古代斯堪的那維亞的詩人。(亦作 **scald**) —**ic,** *adj.*

skat 〔skɑt; skɑːt〕 *n.* 一種三人玩共用32張牌的紙牌戲。

*__skate__¹ 〔sket; skeit〕 *n., v.,* **skat·ed, skat·ing.** —*n.* 溜冰鞋。—*v.i.* ①溜冰。②比賽溜冰。③滑行。④輕描淡寫。—*v.t.* 沿…溜冰。 ***skate over thin ice*** 巧妙地論述困難問題。—**skat·a·ble,** *adj.*

skate² *n., pl.* **skates, skate.** 鰩魚;魟魚。

skate³ *n.* ①〖美俚〗老馬; 廢馬。②卑劣的人;吝嗇的人; 小氣鬼; 墮落的人。③傢伙。

skat·er 〔ˈsketɚ; ˈskeitə〕 *n.* 溜冰者。

skat·ing 〔ˈsketɪŋ; ˈskeitiŋ〕 *n.* 溜冰。—*adj.* ①(溜冰時)正在滑動的。②(溜冰時)與滑動的脚同在一邊的。

skating rink 溜冰場。

skean 〔skin; skiːn〕 *n.* (愛爾蘭與蘇格蘭用的)一種銀柄雙刃短劍。(亦作 **skene**)

ske·dad·dle 〔skɪˈdædl̩; skiˈdædl〕 *n., v.i.,* **-dled, -dling.** 〖俚〗逃竄。—**ske·dad·dler,** *n.*

skee 〔ski; skiː〕 *n., pl.* **skee** or **skees,** *v.,* **skeed, skee·ing.** =**ski.**

skee·sicks 〔ˈskizɪks; ˈskiːziks〕 *n.* 〖美俗〗小流氓;無用的人。

skeet¹ 〔skit; skiːt〕 *n.* 〖航海〗長柄水杓。—*v.t.* 以長柄水杓潑水於(帆上)。

skeet² *n.* 一種飛靶射擊。

skeet³ *v.i.* 〖方〗①急行; 奔馳。②噴。—*v.t.* 〖方〗①使急行;使奔馳。②使噴。

skeet·er 〔ˈskitɚ; ˈskiːtə〕 *n.* ①〖美俗〗蚊子。②一種在冰上滑行的小帆船。

skeg 〔skɛg; skeg〕 *n.* 〖航海〗龍骨之後部。

skein 〔sken; skein〕 *n.* ①一束(紗)。②一羣(野禽)。③混亂。

skel·e·tal 〔ˈskɛlətl̩; ˈskelitəl〕 *adj.* ①骨骼的;骸骨的。②輪廓的。③好像骨骼的。

*__skel·e·ton__ 〔ˈskɛlətn̩; ˈskelitn〕 *n.* ①骨骼; 骨架。②鋼骨。③很瘦的人或動物。④輪廓;梗概;綱要。 ***family skeleton; skeleton in the cupboard*** (***closet*** or ***house***) 家醜。—*adj.* ①骨骼的;似骨骼的;似骸骨的。a *skeleton* hand. 瘦骨嶙峋的手。②輪廓的;綱要的。a *skeleton* plan. 概略的計畫。③只有最起碼之人數的。

skeleton at the feast 掃興者。

skeleton construction 鋼骨建築。

skeleton crew 〖航海〗基幹船員。

skel·e·ton·ize 〔ˈskɛlətn̩ˌaɪz; ˈskelitənaiz〕 *v.,* **-ized, -iz·ing.** —*v.t.* ①使成骸骨;使成骨架。②大量裁減(軍隊之)員額。③概略地記述。—*v.i.* 變成骨架。—**skel·e·ton·i·za·tion, skel·e·ton·iz·er,** *n.*

skeleton key 萬能鑰。

skel·ter 〔ˈskɛltɚ; ˈskeltə〕 *v.i.* 急行;匆忙。

skep 〔skɛp; skep〕 *n.* ①蜂窩。②一種大而深的籃子。③一籃之量。

skep·sis 〔ˈskɛpsɪs; ˈskepsis〕 *n.* 懷疑哲學;哲學的懷疑。

skep·tic 〔ˈskɛptɪk; ˈskeptik〕 *n.* ①懷疑者;懷疑論者。②對宗教表示懷疑者。—*adj.* 懷疑的。(亦作 **sceptic**)

skep·ti·cal 〔ˈskɛptɪkl̩; ˈskeptikəl〕 *adj.* ①懷疑論者的; 多疑的。②懷疑的; 不信的。(亦作 **sceptical**) —**ly,** *adv.*

skep·ti·cism 〔ˈskɛptəˌsɪzəm; ˈskeptisizm〕 *n.* ①懷疑。②懷疑說;懷疑論。(亦作 **scepticism**)

skep·ti·cize 〔ˈskɛptəˌsaɪz; ˈskeptisaiz〕 *v.i.,* **-cized, -ciz·ing.** 主張懷疑論; 表示懷疑。

sker·rick 〔ˈskɛrɪk; ˈskerik〕 *n.* 〖澳〗少量;微量。

sker·ry 〔ˈskɛrɪ; ˈskeri〕 *n., pl.* **-ries.** 〖蘇〗①多岩石的小島。②沿岸有許多岩石小島的海岸線。③(海中的)孤石。

*__sketch__ 〔skɛtʃ; sketʃ〕 *n.* ①略圖;草稿;素描。②概略;輪廓。③小品文字;短篇;短劇;短曲。④〖俗〗滑稽可笑的人。—*v.t.* & *v.i.* ①繪略圖;素描;寫生。②記述(其)概略。—**a·ble,** *adj.* —**er,** *n.*

sketch block 寫生簿。(亦作 **sketchblock**)

sketch·book 〔ˈskɛtʃˌbʊk; ˈsketʃbuk〕 *n.* ①素描簿。②見聞錄; 小品文集。(亦作 **sketch book**)

sketch·i·ly 〔ˈskɛtʃəlɪ; ˈsketʃili〕 *adv.* 輕描淡寫地;不完全地;簡略地。

sketch·i·ness 〔ˈskɛtʃɪnɪs; ˈsketʃinis〕 *n.* 不完全;不徹底;不周到;簡略。

sketch map 略圖。

sketch·y 〔ˈskɛtʃɪ; ˈsketʃi〕 *adj.,* **sketch·i·er, sketch·i·est.** ①概略的; 草圖的; 草稿的。②不完全的;不徹底的。③不足的。

skew 〔skju; skjuː〕 *adj.* ①歪的; 斜的;不直的。②不對稱的。—*n.* ①歪斜; 傾斜。②〖建築〗牆帽脚蹬石。***on the*** (or ***a***) ***skew*** 斜的;傾斜地。—*v.i.* ①歪斜。②斜進;斜行。③〖方〗斜視。—*v.t.* ①使歪斜;使偏。②歪曲;曲解。—**ness,** *n.*

skew·back 〔ˈskjuˌbæk; ˈskjuːbæk〕 *n.* 〖建築〗起拱石;拱座。

skew·bald 〔ˈskjuˌbɔld; ˈskjuːbɔːld〕 *adj.* 有斑點的。—*n.* 有斑點的馬。

skew bridge 與河堤斜交的橋。

skew curve 立體弧線。

skew·er 〔ˈskjuɚ; skjuə〕 *n.* ①(烤肉的)串肉針。②形狀或功用類若串肉針之物。—*v.t.* ①以串肉針串起;以似串肉針之物串起。②刺。

skew-eyed 〔ˈskjuˌaɪd; ˈskjuːaid〕 *adj.* 斜視(眼)的。

skew·whiff 〔ˈskjuˌhwɪf; ˈskjuːhwif〕 *adj.* 〖英方〗歪的;歪曲的。

*__ski__ 〔ski; skiː〕 *n., pl.* **skis** or **ski,** *v.,* **skied, ski·ing.** —*n.* 滑雪屐。—*v.i.* 滑雪。to go *skiing* at New Year. 新年去滑雪。—*v.t.* 滑雪行走於…。—**a·ble,** *adj.* —**er,** *n.*

ski·a·gram 〔ˈskaɪəˌgræm; ˈskaiəgræm〕 *n.* ①X光照片。②物體輪廓中塗墨而成的圖。(亦作 **skiogram**)

ski·a·graph 〔ˈskaɪəˌgræf; ˈskaiəgrɑːf〕 *n.* X光照片。—*v.t.* 攝取…之X光照片。(亦作 **skiograph**) —**er,** *n.* —**ic,** *adj.*

ski·ag·ra·phy 〔skaɪˈægrəfɪ; skaiˈægrəfi〕 *n.* X光攝影術。

ski·a·scope 〔ˈskaɪəˌskop; ˈskaiəskoup〕

n.〖醫〗檢眼鏡。—**ski•as•co•py,** *n.*
ski boot 滑雪靴。
skice 〔skaɪs; skais〕 *v.i.* **skiced, skic-ing.** 疾走;快走。
skid¹ 〔skɪd; skid〕 *n., v.,* **skid•ded, skid-ding.** —*n.* ①滑向一邊。②制輪機;制輪器。③滑材。④飛機之滑橇。⑤(常 *pl.*)船之墊木。⑥墊木;臺架。***on the skids*** 走上被解雇、失敗或其他災禍之路。—*v.i.* ①(行進時)滑向一側。②(車輪)不轉動而滑進。③(從滑材上)滾下;滑下。④下降。—*v.t.* ①以制輪機制(輪)。②置於滑材上。③使輪不轉動而滑行。④使滑向一側。⑤墊起來。—**der,** *n.*
skid² *v.i.,* **skid•ded, skid•ding.** 疾行;快走。(亦作 **scud**)
skid•doo 〔skɪˈdu; skiˈduː〕 *v.i.*〖俚〗走開;離開(通常用於命令語)。
skid•dy 〔ˈskɪdɪ; ˈskidi〕 *adj.* 易滑的。
skid fin 〖航空〗早期某些飛機上層主翼的輔助風板。
skid•proof 〔ˈskɪdˌpruf; ˈskidpruːf〕 *adj.* 防滑的。
skid road ①拖木材用的滑行道。②(常 S– R–) =**skid row.**
skid row 貧民區之街道;破舊之街道。
skiff 〔skɪf; skif〕 *n.* 輕舟;小艇。
skif•fle 〔ˈskɪfəl; ˈskifəl〕 *n.* ①一種爵士樂。②英國的一種搖滾樂。
ski•ing 〔ˈskiɪŋ; ˈskiːiŋ〕 *n.* 滑雪;滑雪術。
ski•jor•ing 〔skiˈdʒɔrɪŋ; skiːˈdʒɔːriŋ〕 *n.* (着滑雪鞋,而由馬拉之)滑雪運動。
ski jump ①滑雪跳;穿雪屐所做之跳躍。②供滑雪跳之跑道。
ski lift 載運滑雪遊客之纜車。
***skil(l)•ful** 〔ˈskɪlfəl; ˈskilful〕 *adj.* 熟練的;巧妙的。a *skillful* physician. 良醫;醫道熟練之醫生。—**ly,** *adv.* —**ness,** *n.*
***skill** 〔skɪl; skil〕 *n.* ①技能;技巧;巧妙;熟練。It takes *skill* to repair a clock. 修理鐘錶需要技巧。②有技術的人(集合稱)。Immigration of *skill* is welcomed in all undeveloped areas. 所有未開發地區均歡迎技術人員前往移民。—**skil•less,** *adj.*
skilled** 〔skɪld; skild〕 *adj.* ①巧妙的;熟練的。②需要技能的。skilled labor*** 熟練工人。
skil•let 〔ˈskɪlɪt; ˈskilit〕 *n.* ①有長柄之淺鍋。②長柄煮鍋(通常帶有支脚)。
skil•ly 〔ˈskɪlɪ; ˈskili〕 *adj.*〖英方〗熟練的。
***skim** 〔skɪm; skim〕 *v.,* **skimmed, skim-ming,** *n., adj.* —*v.t.* ①撇去(牛乳等)的浮皮;撇取(浮沫)。to *skim* the cream from the milk. 撇取牛奶之乳酪。②掠過。③拋之使掠過。④草草閱讀。⑤覆以薄薄一層冰等。⑥取…之精華。—*v.i.* ①掠過;飛掠。②草草閱讀。③覆有薄薄一層冰等;被一層薄冰所覆。—*n.* ①撇取。②被撇取之物。③掠過。④薄薄的表層。bread with a *skim* of jam on it. 塗上一層果醬的麪包。—*adj.* ①用以撇取的。②以脫脂牛乳製成的。
skim•ble-skam•ble, skim•ble-scam•ble 〔ˈskɪmblˈskæmbl; ˈskimbl-ˈskæmbl〕 *adj.* 毫無意義的;亂七八糟的。—*n.* 毫無意義的談話;胡說八道。
skim•mer 〔ˈskɪmɚ; ˈskimə〕 *n.* ①撇取者;網杓。②除沫器。③撇水鳥。④略讀者。⑤寬邊平頂草帽。
skim milk 脫脂牛乳。(亦作**skimmed milk**)
skim•ming 〔ˈskɪmɪŋ; ˈskimiŋ〕 *n.* ①撇取浮皮。②(*pl.*)被撇去之糟粕。
ski•mo•bile 〔ˈskiməbil; ˈskiːməbiːl〕 *n.* 運滑雪者上山坡之有軌小汽車。
skimp¹ 〔skɪmp; skimp〕 *v.t.* ①吝於供應;不足量地供給。②草率從事。—*v.i.*節儉;吝嗇。
skimp² *adj.* 很少的;有限的。
skimp•ing•ly 〔ˈskɪmpɪŋlɪ; ˈskimpiŋli〕 *adv.* 吝嗇地。
skimp•y 〔ˈskɪmpɪ; ˈskimpi〕 *adj.,* **skimp-i•er, skimp•i•est.** ①太少的;不足的。②吝嗇的;過於節省的。
‡**skin** 〔skɪn; skin〕 *n., v.,* **skinned, skin-ning.** —*n.* ①皮;皮膚。She is only *skin* and bone. 她瘦成皮包骨了。②鳥皮;獸皮;生皮;毛皮。③革製品。④(果實等之)外皮;殼。⑤皮製之囊袋(裝液體用者)。⑥殼板;殼。⑦〖俚〗騙子。⑧〖俚〗吝嗇之人。⑨(液體表面之)表皮。***by the skin of one's teeth*** 相差極微;僅。***change one's skin*** 改變本性。***get under one's skin***〖俚〗a. 激怒;刺激。His laugh really *gets under my skin.*他的笑聲眞叫我受不了。b. 深深地感動;深深地影響。***have a thick skin*** 麻木不仁。***have a thin skin*** 敏感的;易受傷害的。***in*** (or ***with***) ***a whole skin*** 安全無恙。***in one's skin*** 赤裸地。***no skin off one's back*** (***nose*** or ***teeth***)不相干。***out of one's skin*** (高興、緊張或驚慌得)不能自制。***save one's skin*** 免受損傷;安然逃脫。***skin deep*** 膚淺。***the ass in the lion's skin*** 狐假虎威。***under the skin***在心裏;在肚子裏。—*v.t.* ①剝皮;去皮;去殼。②覆以皮。③〖俗〗欺騙。④〖俚〗責罵。⑤竭盡…之資源。⑥驅逐(牲口)。—*v.i.* ①爲皮所覆蓋;長皮。The wound has *skinned* over. 傷處已長好皮。②爬。③勉強通過。④匆匆通過。***skin alive***〖俗〗a. 刑責。b. 痛斥;嚴厲批評。c. 徹底擊敗。***skin out***〖俚〗溜走;逃走。
skin and bones 骨瘦如柴之人。
skin boat 皮製輕舟。
skinch 〔skɪntʃ; skintʃ〕 *v.i.* 簡省;節約。
skin-deep 〔ˈskɪnˈdip; ˈskinˈdiːp〕 *adj.* ①表面的。②膚淺的。—*adv.* 膚淺地。
skin disease 皮膚病。
skin dive =**skin-dive.**
skin-dive 〔ˈskɪnˌdaɪv; ˈskindaiv〕 *v.i.,* **-dived, -div•ing.** (不穿潛水衣僅戴氧氣面罩等簡單裝備而)潛水;切膚潛水。
skin diver 切膚潛水者。
skin diving 切膚潛水。
skin•flint 〔ˈskɪnˌflɪnt; ˈskin-flint〕 *n.* 吝嗇鬼;卑鄙之人。
skin-food 〔ˈskɪnˌfud; ˈskinfud〕 *n.* (面霜等)皮膚化妝營養品。
skin friction 〖物理〗表面摩擦。
skin•ful 〔ˈskɪnˌful; ˈskinful〕 *n.* ①滿皮袋。②〖俗〗滿腹。to have a *skinful.* 喝得大醉。
skin game 〖美俗〗詐欺。
skin graft 供移植用的皮膚。
skin grafting 〖醫〗皮膚移植;植皮術。
skin•head 〔ˈskɪnˌhɛd; ˈskinhed〕 *n.* 〖俚〗①禿頭者。②頭髮剪得很短的青少年。③海軍陸戰隊新兵。
skink 〔skɪŋk; skiŋk〕 *n.* 〖動物〗石龍子(一種有鱗的小蜥蜴)。
skin•less 〔ˈskɪnlɪs; ˈskinlis〕 *adj.* ①無皮的。②敏感的。
skin•ner 〔ˈskɪnɚ; ˈskinə〕 *n.* ①剝皮者。②皮革商。③騙子;騙取錢財者。④〖美俗〗趕牲口的人。⑤重型土木機械駕駛人。
skin•ner•y 〔ˈskɪnərɪ; ˈskinəri〕 *n., pl.* **-ner•ies.** 獸皮加工場。
skin•ny 〔ˈskɪnɪ; ˈskini〕 *adj.,* **-ni•er, -ni•est.** ①很瘦的。②似皮的;皮狀(質)的。③貧乏的。④吝嗇的。—**skin•ni•ness,** *n.*
skin•ny-dip 〔ˈskɪnɪˌdɪp; ˈskinidip〕

v.i., -dipped, -dipt, -dip·ping. 〖俗〗裸體游泳。—per, *n.*
skin resistance 〖物理〗表面阻力。
skin test 〖醫〗皮膚反應測驗。
skin-tight [ˈskɪnˈtaɪt; ˈskinˈtait] *adj.* 緊身的(衣服)。—*n.* 緊身衣。
***skip**[1] [skɪp; skip] *v.*, skipped, skip·ping, *n.* —*v.i.* ①輕快地跳;跳躍。He *skipped* out of the way. 他很快地跳往一旁。②沿一表面跳進。③遺漏;漏過。④〖俗〗匆匆離去。⑤跳讀。—*v.t.* ①輕輕跳過。The girls *skipped* rope. 女孩子們跳繩。②抛出…使沿一表面跳進。③遺漏; 漏讀; 跳讀。④〖俗〗匆匆離開(某地)。⑤使跳年升級。⑥無故不到。—*n.* ①跳; 跳躍。②遺漏; 漏讀; 跳讀。I read the book without a *skip*. 我一字不漏地讀了那本書。③遺漏的部分;可刪節的部分。—ping·ly, *adv.*
skip[2] *n.* (bowling 及 curling 戲之)主將。
skip[3] *n.* 礦場中運人或物件上下之籃框、桶、箱等。
ski pants 滑雪褲。
ski patrol 滑雪區巡邏救生隊。
skip-bomb [ˈskɪpˌbɑm; ˈskipbɔm] *v.t.* & *v.i.* (水面)低空轟炸。
skip bombing 在水面目標以上之低空轟炸。
skip distance 〖無線電〗越程。
Skip·e·tar [ˈskɪpətɑr; ˈskipətɑː] *n.* ①阿爾巴尼亞人。②阿爾巴尼亞文。
skip·jack [ˈskɪpˌdʒæk; ˈskipdʒæk] *n.* ①〖動物〗飛魚類。②〖動物〗叩頭蟲。③〖航海〗一種小帆船。④一種跳躍之玩具人。⑤小紈袴子。
ski·plane [ˈskiˌplen; ˈskiː-plein] *n.* 裝有雪橇可在雪地升降的飛機。
ski pole 滑雪杖。(亦作 **ski stick**)
skip·pa·ble [ˈskɪpəbl̩; ˈskipəbl] *adj.* ①可跳的。②可跳讀的。
skip·per [ˈskɪpɚ; ˈskipə] *n.* ①跳躍者。②船長;隊長。③飛魚。④叩頭蟲;弄花蝶。⑤跳讀者。
skip·per's daugh·ters [ˈskɪpɚzˈdɔtɚz; ˈskipəzˈdɔːtəz] 〖航海俚〗白浪。
skipping rope 跳繩用的繩子。
skip straight 〖撲克〗五張牌隔號順序(如 7,9, Jack 和 King)。(亦作 **alternate straight, Dutch straight**)
skip tracer 〖俗〗專門尋找逃債者的偵探。
skip vehicle 重入大氣層時在大氣層外圍作打水漂式跳躍若干次始降落的太空船。
skirl[1] [skɝl; skəːl] *n.* 〖蘇方〗風笛之尖銳響聲。—*v.i.* (風笛)響出尖銳聲。
skirl[2] *v.i.* 旋動;廻旋。—*n.* 旋動;廻旋;廻旋物。
skir·mish [ˈskɝmɪʃ; ˈskəːmiʃ] *n.* 小戰;小衝突。—*v.i.* 從事小戰; 從事小爭論。
skir·mish·er [ˈskɝmɪʃɚ; ˈskəːmiʃə] *n.* 〖軍〗斥候;前衞;散兵羣中之一員。
skirmish line 〖軍〗散兵線。
skirr [skɝ; skəː] *v.i.* 急忙離開;逃。—*v.t.* ①找遍。②〖方〗使跳進。—*n.* 轟轟聲。
‡**skirt** [skɝt; skəːt] *n.* ①裾(長外衣腰部以下下垂之部分)。②女裙。③邊緣;邊界。to live on the *skirts* of a town. 住在城郊。④〖俗〗年輕姑娘; 女人。⑤馬鞍兩側的垂下部分。—*v.t.* ①沿(某地)的邊緣而行。②位於…邊緣; 住於…邊緣。The road *skirted* the wood. 這條路位於森林的邊緣。—*v.i.* ①繞行。②位於邊緣;沿邊緣。—er, *n.* —less, *adj.*
skirt dance 大裙舞(一種盛行於十九世紀的芭蕾舞,以着大裙舞姿優美著稱)。
skirt-dance [ˈskɝtˈdæns; ˈskəːtˌdɑːns] *v.i.*, -danced, -danc·ing. 跳大裙舞。—skirt-danc·er, *n.*
skirt·ing [ˈskɝtɪŋ; ˈskəːtiŋ] *n.* ①〖建築〗壁脚板。②女裙之集合稱; 女裙材料。③邊;緣;邊境。
skirt·like [ˈskɝtˌlaɪk; ˈskəːtlaik] *adj.* 裙狀的。
ski run 適於滑雪的山坡。
ski runner 滑雪者。
ski running 滑雪。
ski stick 滑雪杖。(亦作 **ski pole**)
ski suit 滑雪裝。
skit[1] [skɪt; skit] *n.* 幽默而諷刺之短劇或短篇文字;笑罵文章。
skit[2] *v.i.*, skit·ted, skit·ting. 〖蘇〗衝刺;跳躍。
skite[1] [skaɪt; skait] *v.*, skit·ed, skit·ing, *n.* —*v.i.* 〖蘇方〗①匆匆移動; 急跳; 滑動;跌落。②突然地打擊。—*n.* 〖蘇方〗①突然的一擊;一拳;一巴掌。②驟雨。
skite[2] *v.i.* 〖澳方〗自誇;誇張。
ski tow 將滑雪者拉上山坡用的電纜。
ski train 開往滑雪地的火車專車。
ski troops 滑雪部隊。
skit·ter [ˈskɪtɚ; ˈskitə] *v.i.* ①輕快地跑; 滑行。②掠過水面。—*v.t.* 使掠過。
skit·ter·y [ˈskɪtərɪ; ˈskitəri] *adj.* ①滑溜溜的。②害怕的;緊張的。
skit·tish [ˈskɪtɪʃ; ˈskitiʃ] *adj.* ①易驚恐的; 易驚惶的。②輕浮的; 易變的。③怕羞的; 愛羞怯的。④小心翼翼的。—ly, *adv.*
skit·tle [ˈskɪtl̩; ˈskitl] *n.*, *v.*, skit·tled, skit·tling. —*n.* ①(*pl.*) 九柱戲。②九柱戲之小柱。***Life is not all beer and skittles.*** 人生非僅遊樂而已。—*v.i.* 玩九柱戲。
skittle alley 九柱戲場。
skittle ball 九柱戲用球。
skive [skaɪv; skaiv] *v.*, skived, skiv·ing, *n.* —*v.i.* 〖方〗急掠而過。—*v.t.* ①刨或割(皮革)成薄片。②磨光(寶石之表面)。—*n.* (磨寶石用的)鑽石輪。—skiv·er, *n.*
skiv·vies [ˈskɪvɪz; ˈskiviz] *n. pl.* 〖美航俚〗內衣。
skiv·vy [ˈskɪvɪ; ˈskivi] *n.*, *pl.* -vies. 〖俚〗男人(尤指水手)的汗衫。
skiv·y [ˈskɪvɪ; ˈskivi] *n.*, *pl.* skiv·ies. 〖英蔑〗女傭。
ski·wear [ˈskiˌwɛr; ˈskiːwɛə] *n.* 滑雪衣。
skoal [skol; skoul] *interj.* 舉杯祝人健康的歡呼聲。—*n.* 歡呼"skoal!"所表示之敬禮或祝福。
skoo·kum [ˈskukəm; ˈskuːkəm] *adj.* ①强壯的。②品質優良的。
skoo·kum-house [ˈskukəmˈhaus; ˈskuːkəmˈhaus] *n.* 監獄。
Skr., Skrt., Skt. Sanskrit.
sku·a [ˈskjuə; ˈskjuːə] *n.* 〖動物〗一種似鷗的食肉鳥。(亦作 **skua gull**)
skul·dug·ger·y [skʌlˈdʌgərɪ; skʌlˈdʌgəri] *n.*, *pl.* -ger·ies. 〖美俗〗陰謀; 欺騙。(亦作 **sculduggery**)
skulk [skʌlk; skʌlk] *v.i.* 藏匿;潛行。—*v.t.* 偷偷地逃避。—*n.* 潛伏者。—er, *n.*
skull** [skʌl; skʌl] *n.* ①頭蓋骨; 腦殼。②頭;腦子。③頭頂。have a thick skull*** 愚蠢。***skull(s) and crossbones*** a. (海盜用的)骷髏旗;骷髏畫。b. 危險的標誌。—ed, *adj.*
skull·cap [ˈskʌlˌkæp; ˈskʌlkæp] *n.* ①頭巾; (室內所着之)無邊便帽。②古鐵胄。③頭頂部。④〖植物〗並頭草。
skull cracker 用以拆毀建築物之大鐵球。(亦作 **ball breaker, wrecking ball**)
skull·fish [ˈskʌlˌfɪʃ; ˈskʌlfiʃ] *n.*, *pl.* -fish·es, -fish. 鯨魚;兩隻以上之老鯨魚。

skull·guard [ˈskʌlˌgɑrd; ˈskʌlgɑːd] *n.* 土木工人所戴之頭盔。
skull practice (or **session**) ①體育教練之理論講解課；用圖表等解釋運動比賽戰略之課程。②任何會議或商討。
*__skunk__ [skʌŋk; skʌŋk] *n.* ①〖動物〗臭鼬。②臭鼬毛皮。③〖俗〗卑鄙之人；下流胚。***Let every man skin his own skunk.*** 〖諺〗各人自掃門前雪。—*v.t.* 〖俚〗①全然打敗(對手)；使(對手)得零分。②對…不付錢。③剝奪。 —**y,** *adj.*
‡**sky** [skaɪ; skai] *n., pl.* **skies** [skaɪz; skaiz], *v.*, **skied** or **skyed, sky·ing.** —*n.* ①天；天空。If the *sky* fall, we shall catch larks. 如天塌下來，我們可捕捉雲雀（喻，勿作杞人之憂）。②(常 *pl.*) 天氣；氣候。the sunny *skies* of Honolulu. 檀香山的晴朗天氣。③天堂；天國。***out of a clear*** (or ***clear-blue***) ***sky*** 突然地；出其不意地；晴天霹靂地。 ***to the skies*** (or ***sky***) 很高地；非常。 to praise *to the skies.* 大爲稱讚。—*v.t.* ①將(球等)高高擊入空中。②將（照片等）高掛在牆上或靠天花板處。—*v.i.* ①將球等高高擊入空中。The batter *skied* to the center fielder. 打擊手擊出一個高飛球到中外野。②上升。 ***sky up*** (獵物) 向上飛。
sky blue 天藍色。 「天藍色的。
sky-blue [ˈskaɪˈblu; ˈskaiˈbluː] *adj.*
sky-born [ˈskaɪˌbɔrn; ˈskaibɔːn] *adj.* 生於天上的 (=heaven-born).
sky·borne [ˈskaɪˌbɔrn; ˈskaibɔːn] *adj.* =**airborne.** 「飛機場搬運工人。
sky·cap [ˈskaɪˌkæp; ˈskaikæp] *n.* 〖美〗
sky-clad [ˈskaɪˌklæd; ˈskai-klæd] *adj.* 〖俗〗裸體的；赤裸的。
sky·coach [ˈskaɪˌkotʃ; ˈskaikoutʃ] *n.* 經濟飛行之招待(票價廉，但不供應免費餐點)。
sky·dive [ˈskaɪˌdaɪv; ˈskaidaiv] *v.i.*, **-dived** or **-doved, -dived, -div·ing.** 〖俗〗從事於儘量延遲打開降落傘的跳傘運動。
sky diver 作 sky diving 的人。
sky diving 在打開降落傘以前用各種姿勢控制身體降落路線的跳傘運動。
Skye [skaɪ; skai] *n.* ①斯開島(蘇格蘭西北部 Hebrides 羣島中最大之一島)。②=**Skye terrier.** 「高球。
sky·er [ˈskaɪɚ; ˈskaiə] *n.* 〖板球〗飛球；
Skye terrier 蘇格蘭種短腿長毛獵犬。
sky·ey [ˈskaɪɪ; ˈskaii] *adj.* 〖詩〗①天的；天空的；天藍色的。②來自天空的；天降的；在天空的。③高的；高聳的。 「數量。
sky·ful [ˈskaɪˌful; ˈskaiful] *n.* 滿天之
sky-high [ˈskaɪˈhaɪ; ˈskaiˈhai] *adv.* ①極高地；高入雲霄地。②支離破碎地。 —*adj.* ①極高的。②極昂貴的。
sky·hook [ˈskaɪˌhʊk; ˈskaihuk] *n.* 一種空投補給品用的載貨工具。 「氣球。
skyhook balloon 高空宇宙線觀測
sky·jack [ˈskaɪˌdʒæk; ˈskaidʒæk] *v.t.* 空中刼機。—**er,** *n.* 「ˌdʒækiŋ] *n.* 刼機。
sky·jack·ing [ˈskaɪˌdʒækɪŋ; ˈskai-
Sky·lab [ˈskaɪˌlæb; ˈskailæb] *n.* 太空實驗室(美國太空計畫之一，目的在地球上空建立太空科學研究站)。
*__sky·lark__ [ˈskaɪˌlɑrk; ˈskailɑːk] *n.* ①雲雀。②〖俗〗嬉戲。—*v.i.* 〖俗〗嬉戲。—**er,** *n.*
sky·lark·ing [ˈskaɪˌlɑrkɪŋ; ˈskailɑː-kiŋ] *n.* 〖俗〗嬉戲；調笑。 「布不見藍天的。
sky·less [ˈskaɪlɪs; ˈskailis] *adj.* 烏雲密
sky·light [ˈskaɪˌlaɪt; ˈskailait] *n., v.*, **-light·ed** or **-lit, -light·ing.** —*n.* 天窗。—*v.t.* 裝天窗。
sky·line [ˈskaɪˌlaɪn; ˈskailain] *n.* ①地平線。②以天空爲背景而映出的建築物、山、樹等之輪廓；天空線。
sky·lin·er [ˈskaɪˌlaɪnɚ; ˈskailainə] *n.* (定期航線之)客機。 「窗的。
sky·lit [ˈskaɪˌlɪt; ˈskailit] *adj.* 裝有天
sky·man [ˈskaɪˌmæn; ˈskaimæn] *n., pl.* **-men.** 〖俗〗①飛行員。②傘兵。
sky·mark [ˈskaɪˌmɑrk; ˈskaimɑːk] *n.* 以天空爲背景而映出的顯著目標。
sky marshal 〖美〗(預防刼機，着便衣的)空中安全人員。
sky·mo·tel [ˈskaɪmoˌtɛl; ˈskaimou-tel] *n.* 設於機場附近專供空中旅行者住宿的汽車旅館。 「上層之房間。
sky parlor 〖俚〗①閣樓。②(屋裏) 最
sky pilot 〖俗〗①牧師。②飛行員。
sky·port [ˈskaɪˈpɔrt; ˈskaipɔːt] *n.* 屋頂直升機場。 「*n.* 空中飛人。
sky-rid·er [ˈskaɪˌraɪdɚ; ˈskaiˌraidə]
sky·rock·et [ˈskaɪˌrɑkɪt; ˈskaiˌrɔ-kit] *n.* 流星烟火。—*v.i.* ①曇花一現。②(物價等)猛漲。③失去自制。—*v.t.* 使急增；使(物價等)猛漲；使急升。 「第三桅上帆。
sky·sail [ˈskaɪˌsel; ˈskaiseil] *n.* 〖航海〗
sky·scape [ˈskaɪˌskep; ˈskai-skeip] *n.* ①天空景色。②天空景色畫。
*__sky·scrap·er__ [ˈskaɪˌskrepɚ; ˈskai-ˌskreipə] *n.* ①摩天樓。②任何特高之物。
sky·scrap·ing [ˈskaɪˌskrepɪŋ; ˈskai-ˌskreipiŋ] *adj.* ①非常高的；高達天空的。②住在摩天大樓中的；摩天大樓之生活的。
sky show 飛機內放映的電影。
sky sign 〖英〗空中廣告；屋頂廣告。
sky·sweep·er [ˈskaɪˌswipɚ; ˈskai-ˌswiːpə] *n.* 用雷達瞄準的75糎口徑高射砲，每分鐘能發射45發子彈。 「成的航空機羣。
sky train 由一架飛機拖曳若干滑翔機而
sky·troop·er [ˈskaɪˌtrupɚ; ˈskai-ˌtruːpə] *n.* 傘兵 (=paratrooper).
sky·troops [ˈskaɪˌtrups; ˈskaitruːps] *n.* 傘兵部隊 (=paratroops).
sky truck 大型運輸機。
sky·u·gle [skaɪˈjugḷ; skaiˈjuːgl] *v.t.*, **-gled, -gling.** 〖俚〗偷竊。
sky·ward [ˈskaɪwɚd; ˈskaiwəd] *adj.* 向天空的；向上的。—*adv.* =**skywards.**
sky·wards [ˈskaɪwɚdz; ˈskaiwədz] *adv.* 向天空地；向上地。
sky wave 〖無線電〗天空電波。
sky·way [ˈskaɪˌwe; ˈskaiwei] *n.* ①小飛機或私家飛機之航線。②高架公路。
sky·write [ˈskaɪˌraɪt; ˈskairait] *v.*, **-wrote, -writ·ing.** —*v.i.* 以飛機噴出之煙在空中寫字。—*v.t.* ①以飛機噴出之煙在空中寫。②大事宣傳。—**sky·writ·er,** *n.*
sky·writ·ing [ˈskaɪˌraɪtɪŋ; ˈskaiˌrai-tiŋ] *n.* 飛機在空中噴出之煙所形成之文字(係一種廣告)。
*__slab__[1] [slæb; slæb] *n., v.*, **slabbed, slab-bing.** —*n.* ①板；片(如石、木等)。a *slab* of cheese. 一塊乾酪。②製材之木屑。—*v.t.* ①製成厚板。②以厚板鋪、撐等。③大量塗上。to *slab* butter on bread. 在麪包上大量塗上奶油。 「黏稠的；濃的。
slab[2] *adj.*, **slab·ber, slab·best.** 〖古方〗
slab·ber [ˈslæbɚ; ˈslæbə] *v.i.* & *v.t.*, *n.* =**slobber.** —**er,** *n.*

slab·ber·y ['slæbərɪ; 'slæbəri] *adj.* 濕的;泥濘的。

slab·by[1] ['slæbɪ; 'slæbi] *adj.*, **-bi·er, -bi·est.** ①黏的;膠黏的。②泥濘的;濕的。—**slab·bi·ly,** *adv.*

slab·by[2] *adj.* 石板鋪成的;覆有木片的;「似石板的。」

slab·like ['slæb,laɪk; 'slæb-laik] *adj.* 石板狀的;扁平寬厚的。

slab-on-ground ['slæb,ɑn'graʊnd; 'slæb,ɔn'graund] *adj.* 基礎混凝土直接打在地上(無地下室)的。

slab-sid·ed ['slæb'saɪdɪd; 'slæb'sai-did] *adj.* ①側面扁平的。②細長的。

slab·stone ['slæb,ston; 'slæbstoun] *n.* 石板。

slab top 用木板或石板做的頂或桌面等。

slab-top ['slæb,tɑp; 'slæbtɔp] *adj.* 以(木、石或混凝土之)厚板爲頂的。

slack**[1] [slæk; slæk] *adj.* ①鬆弛的;寬的。②懈怠的;疏忽的。③不活潑的;不景氣的。Business is *slack* at this season. 這一季營業蕭條。④緩慢的。at a *slack* pace. 緩步。—*n.* ①鬆弛之部分。②營業蕭條季節。③(*pl.*)寬鬆的褲子。④水流之滯緩。—*v.t.* & *v.i.* (使)鬆弛 (=slacken). ***slack back (千斤頂)因受到繼續不斷之重壓而部分縮回。***slack off*** a. 使鬆。b. 鬆懈力量。***slack up*** 漸緩;慢行。—**ly,** *adv.*

slack[2] *n.* 煤渣;煤屑。

slack·age ['slækɪdʒ; 'slækidʒ] *n.* 鬆弛之程度。

slack-baked ['slæk,bekt; 'slæk-beikt] *adj.* ①烘烤不完全的。②設計不良的;粗製濫造的。

slack·en ['slækən; 'slækən] *v.t.* & *v.i.* ①使緩慢;變爲緩慢。②遲滯;變爲不景氣。③使鬆弛;變爲鬆弛。—**er,** *n.*

slack·er ['slækɚ; 'slækə] *n.* 規避責任者;戰時逃避兵役者。

slack·er·ism ['slækərɪzm; 'slækərizm] *n.* 規避責任的行爲;逃避兵役的行爲。

slack-filled ['slæk'fɪld; 'slæk'fild] *adj.* 裝得過於稀鬆的。

slack ice 流動碎冰。

slack jaw 乏味之言;無禮之言。

slack-jawed ['slæk'dʒɔd; 'slæk-'dʒɔ:d] *adj.* 發呆的。

slack-off ['slæk,ɔf; 'slækɔ:f] *n.* 〖俗〗趨緩;蕭條;鬆弛;減少。

slack-spined ['slæk'spaɪnd; 'slæk-,spaind] *adj.* 無骨氣的;軟骨頭的;無毅力的。

slack suit 便服。

slack-twist·ed ['slæk,twɪstɪd; 'slæk-,twistid] *adj.* ①纖維鬆弛的。②不堅毅的。

slack water 緩慢流動或靜止不動的水;靜水;平潮。(亦作 **slack tide**)

slack-water ['slæk,wɔtɚ; 'slæk-,wɔ:tə] *adj.* 靜水的。—*v.t.* 使形成靜水。

slag [slæg; slæg] *n.*, *v.*, **slagged, slag-ging.** —*n.* ①礦渣;鎔渣。②火山鎔岩;火山岩燼。③廢物;渣滓。—*v.t.* 使化爲鎔渣。—*v.i.* 變爲鎔渣。—**less,** *adj.*

slag·gy ['slægɪ; 'slægi] *adj.*, **-gi·er, -gi·est.** 礦渣的;鎔岩的;似礦渣或鎔岩的。

slain [slen; slein] *v.* pp. of **slay.**

slake [slek; sleik] *v.*, **slaked, slak·ing.** —*v.t.* ①解(渴);息(怒);雪(恨);使得到滿足而減消。②使較不活躍、有力、强烈等;減弱;緩和。③使(火)漸滅或熄滅。④消和或沸化(石灰)。*slaked* lime. 消石灰;熟石灰。⑤使淋濕。—*v.i.* ①(石灰)消和;沸化。②〖罕〗減弱;緩和。***slake one's lust of blood*** 滿足殺伐的慾望。

slake·less ['sleklɪs; 'sleiklis] *adj.* 不能滿足的;貪得無厭的。

slak·y ['slekɪ; 'sleiki] *adj.* 多泥濘的。

sla·lom ['slɑləm; 'sleiləm] 〖挪威〗 *n.* 彎道滑雪比賽。—*v.i.* 做彎道滑雪比賽。

slam** [slæm; slæm] *v.*, **slammed, slam-ming,** *adv.*, *n.* —*v.t.* & *v.i.* ①砰然關閉(門、窗等);(門、窗等)砰然關起。to *slam* the door in one's face. 當某人之面將門砰然關閉。②猛力投擲或放置。③猛擊。④〖美俗〗猛烈而苛刻地抨擊。slam the door*** 拒絕考慮;拒絕商討。—*adv.* 砰然地。—*n.* ①砰然聲。He threw his books down with a *slam.* 他砰然將書擲落。②〖美俗〗苛刻的抨擊。③〖橋牌〗滿貫。

slam-bang ['slæm'bæŋ; 'slæm'bæŋ] *adv.* 〖俗〗①猛烈有聲地;砰噹一聲地。②魯莽地。—*v.i.* 〖俗〗很有力地行動;急而響地移動。

slam·bang ['slæm'bæŋ; 'slæm'bæŋ] *adj.* ①極喧鬧的;極大聲的。②極有力的。③極好的。—*n.* 巨響。

slanch·wise ['slæntʃ,waɪz; 'slæntʃ-waiz] *adv.* 歪斜地。

slan·der ['slændɚ; 'slɑ:ndə] *n.* ①誹謗。②散布謠言;造謠。—*v.t.* & *v.i.* 誹謗;造謠中傷。—**er,** *n.*

slan·der·ous ['slændərəs; 'slɑ:ndə-rəs] *adj.* 誹謗的;惡毒的;造謠中傷的。—**ly,** *adv.*

***slang** [slæŋ; slæŋ] *n.* ①俚語。a piece of *slang.* 一句俚語。②某一階層或行業中所用的特殊習用語。schoolboy *slang.* 學生用語。—*v.t.* & *v.i.* ①辱罵;責罵。②用俚語說。—**ism,** *n.*

slan·guage ['slæŋgwɪdʒ; 'slæŋgwidʒ] *n.* 〖諧〗俚俗之言詞或寫作。

slang·y ['slæŋɪ; 'slæŋi] *adj.*, **slang·i-er, slang·i·est.** ①俚語或特殊習用語的。②用很多俚語或特殊習用語的。

***slant** [slænt; slɑ:nt] *v.i.* & *v.t.* ①(使)傾斜;歪向。②曲解;歪曲。to *slant* the news. 歪曲新聞。—*n.* ①傾斜;斜面。②心向;觀點;意見。③斜看。I took a *slant* at him. 我斜看了他一下。④〖俗〗語調。—*adj.* 傾斜的;歪斜的。—**a·ble,** *adj.* —**er,** *n.*

slant drilling (岩孔、油井等之)斜鑽。

slant·ing ['slæntɪŋ; 'slɑ:ntiŋ] *adj.* 斜的;歪的;傾斜的。—**ly,** *adv.*

slant·ing·ways ['slæntɪŋ,wez; 'slɑ:ntiŋweiz] *adv.* =**slantwise.**

slant·ing·wise ['slæntɪŋ,waɪz; 'slɑ:ntiŋwaiz] *adv.* =**slantwise.**

slant·wise ['slænt,waɪz; 'slɑ:nt-waiz] *adv.* 傾斜地。—*adj.* 傾斜的。

slap** [slæp; slæp] *n.*, *v.*, **slapped, slap-ping,** *adv.* —*n.* ①掌擊;摑。He got a *slap* in the face. 他挨了一個耳光。②拒斥;侮辱。③掌擊聲;似掌擊之聲音。④嘗試。a slap in the eye*** (or ***face***) 公然侮辱。***a slap on the wrist*** 效果不大的溫和懲戒。—*v.t.* ①掌擊;摑;拍擊。I *slapped* him in the face. 我打他一個耳光。②用力放置;擲。③肆意施加。④申斥;申戒。⑤取締;依法對付。—*v.i.* 拍擊。Rain *slapped* at the win-dow. 雨打在窗戶上。***slap around*** 揍一頓;予以痛打。***slap down*** 壓制。***slap in the face*** 侮辱。***slap on the wrist; slap the wrist of; slap one's wrist*** 略予申斥。***slap together*** 草率作成。—*adv.* ①直接地;正面地。The thief ran *slap* into a policeman. 那賊和一個警察迎面相撞。②突然地。—**per,** *n.*

slap-bang ['slæp'bæŋ; 'slæp'bæŋ] *adv.* ①魯莽地;喧鬧地。②立刻;馬上。—*adj.* 魯莽的;喧鬧的;草率的。

slap·dab ['slæp,dæb; 'slæpdæb] *adv.* 正好;恰恰 (=exactly).

slap·dash ['slæp,dæʃ; 'slæpdæʃ] *adv.* ①草率地。②正好地;直接地。—*adj.* 草率的;粗心的。—*n.* 魯莽的行動、方法或工作。

slap·dash·ery ['slæp,dæʃərɪ; 'slæp-dæʃəri] *n.* 草率; 不整齊;髒亂。

slap·hap·py ['slæp,hæpɪ;'slæphæpi] *adj.*, **-pi·er, -pi·est.** 〖俚〗①被打得或好像被打得頭昏眼花的。②愚蠢的; 胡塗的。③興高采烈而無責任心的。—**slap·hap·pi·ness,** *n.*

slap·jack ['slæp,dʒæk; 'slæpdʒæk] *n.* 〖美〗①烤焙之薄餅。②一種簡單之牌戲。

slap·ping ['slæpɪŋ; 'slæpiŋ] *adj.* 〖俗〗①非常快的;甚速的。②大的;高大的。

slap·stick ['slæp,stɪk; 'slæpstik] *n.* ①擊板;敲板(能發響聲,演諧劇等時用之)。②下等滑稽劇;鬧劇。—*adj.* 鬧劇的;胡鬧的。

slap-up ['slæp,ʌp; 'slæpʌp] *adj.* 〖俗〗第一流的;上等的;新式的。

***slash** [slæʃ; slæʃ] *v.t.* ①(以劍、刀等)砍;斬;砍傷;戳傷。②鞭撻;鞭打。③酷評;非難。④削減;大大地減少。Our budget has been *slashed*. 我們的預算已經削減了。⑤在(衣服上)開長縫;開叉。⑥割裂。⑦猛動;猛揮;猛拉。—*v.i.* ①砍;斬;戳。②酷評。③猛進;猛飛;衝。—*n.* ①砍;斬;戳。②砍痕;斬傷;傷痕。③(衣服上的)長縫;叉。④林中空地;(布滿林中空地的)殘葉;斷枝等。⑤(常*pl.*)矮樹叢生的濕地。⑥削減。⑦斜線符號(/)。 —**er,** *n.*

slash-and-burn ['slæʃən'bɝn; 'slæʃən'bə:n] *n.* 砍燒耕種法。

slash·ing ['slæʃɪŋ; 'slæʃiŋ] *adj.* ①亂砍的。②嚴峻的;苛刻的。③雄赳赳的;有精神的。④〖俗〗大的;巨大的; 盛大的。⑤奪目的;生動的。 —*n.* 砍斬;削減;鞭打。—**ly,** *adv.*

slash pine 濕地松;此等松木。

slash pocket 懸掛於衣服反面而開口在外的斜口袋。

slat[1] [slæt; slæt] *n.* ①(木、石、金屬等之)板條。②(*pl.*)〖俚〗肋骨。—*v.t.* ①供以板條;以板條作成。②關起…之板條。—*adj.* 板條作成的。

slat[2] *v.*, **slat·ted, slat·ting,** *n.* —*v.t.* 〖方〗①用力拋。②打; 擊。 —*v.i.* 猛烈地拍擊(如帆索之猛擊船桅)。—*n.* 〖方〗猛烈打擊。

S. Lat., S. lat. south latitude.

slate**[1] [slet; sleit] *n., v.,* **slat·ed, slat·ing,** *adj.* —*n.* ①板石; 粘板岩。②石板。③石板瓦。④深藍灰色。⑤〖美〗備提名或任命的候選人名單。⑥行爲記錄。 ***have a clean slate 有清白的記錄;沒有犯過罪。 ***on the slate*** 記在帳上。 ***slate club*** 〖英〗(每人每週繳出一點錢的)互助會。 ***slate pencil*** 石筆(寫石板用)。 ***start with a clean slate*** 重新開始; 改過自新。—*v.t.* ①以石板瓦蓋於(屋頂)。②列(名) 於候選人名單上。③譴責;斥責。④預定。 Elections are *slated* July 1–2. 選舉預定於七月一號到二號舉行。⑤注定。 —*adj.* ①深藍灰色的。②石板的; 石板瓦的。 a *slate* roof. 石板瓦的屋頂。

slate[2] *v.t.*, **slat·ed, slat·ing.** 〖英〗縱狗咬(人或獸)。

slat·ed ['sletɪd; 'sleitid] *adj.* 狀似石板的 (=slaty).

slat·er ['sletə; 'sleitə] *n.* ①鋪石板瓦之工匠; 製石板瓦的人。②嚴苛的批評者。③鼠婦(=wood louse). ④一種有斜刃的工具(用以刮掉獸皮上的肉)。

slath·er ['slæðə; 'slæðə] *v.,* **slath·ered, slath·er·ing,** *n.* —*v.t.* ①〖方,俗〗大量使用;大量浪費。②〖方〗濺洒;以口涎弄濕。—*v.i.* 滑行;曳足而進。—*n.* (常*pl.*)〖方,俗〗大量。 ***open slather*** 自由執行權。

slat·ing ['sletɪŋ; 'sleitiŋ] *n.* ①石板瓦。②蓋石板瓦;製石板瓦。③斥責。

slat·ish ['sletɪʃ; 'sleitiʃ] *adj.* (顏色)略似石板的。

slat·ted ['slætɪd; 'slætid] *adj.* 木條作成的。

slat·ter ['slætə; 'slætə] *v.t.* 〖英〗溢出;浪費;亂撒。

slat·tern ['slætən; 'slætən] *n.* 懶散的女人;衣着不整潔的女人。—*adj.* 不整潔的 (=slatternly). —*v.t.* 浪費;消磨。

slat·tern·li·ness ['slætənlɪnɪs;'slætənlinis] *n.* 不整潔。

slat·tern·ly ['slætənlɪ; 'slætənli] *adj.* 不整潔的。

slat·y ['sletɪ; 'sleiti] *adj.*, **slat·i·er, slat·i·est.** ①石板的;似石板的;有關石板的。②深藍灰色的。③含板石的。

***slaugh·ter** ['slɔtə; 'slɔ:tə] *n.* 屠殺;殺戮;屠宰。—*v.t.* ①屠殺;殺戮;屠宰。②使遭大敗。—**er,** *n.*

slaugh·ter·house ['slɔtə,haus; 'slɔ:təhaus] *n.* 屠宰場。(亦作 **slaughter house**)

slaugh·ter·man ['slɔtəmən; 'slɔ:təmən] *n., pl.* **-men.** ①屠夫。②劊子手。

slaugh·ter·ous ['slɔtərəs; 'slɔ:tərəs] *adj.* 殘酷的;嗜殺的;破壞的。—**ly,** *adv.*

Slav [slɑv, slæv; slɑ:v, slæv] *n.* 斯拉夫族人。—*adj.* 斯拉夫人的; 斯拉夫語的。

Slav. ①Slavic. ②Slavonian. ③Slavonic.

Slav·dom ['slɑvdəm, 'slæv-; 'slɑ:vdəm, 'slæv-] *n.* 斯拉夫民族(集合稱)。

‡**slave** [slev; sleiv] *n., v.,* **slaved, slav·ing,** *adj.* —*n.* ①奴隸。②被欲望、習慣或影響所控制者。 a *slave* to drink. 沈湎於杯中物之人。③苦工; 奴工。④被俘而被迫做苦工的螞蟻。—*v.i.* ①作苦工。Many mothers *slave* for their children. 許多母親爲她們的兒女辛苦工作。②從事奴隸販賣。—*v.t.* ①〖古〗使淪爲奴隸。②〖機械〗 自動控制。③使作苦工;使役;驅使。—*adj.* ①奴隸的;有關奴隸的。②〖機械〗自動控制的。

slave driver ①監督奴隸工作者。②嚴苛的工頭或監工。

slave·hold·er ['slev,holdə; 'sleiv,houldə] *n.* 奴隸的主人。

slave·hold·ing ['slev,holdɪŋ; 'sleiv,houldiŋ] *adj.* 擁有奴隸的;實行奴隸制度的。—*n.* 奴隸之擁有。

slave hunter 擄賣奴隸者。

slave labor ①苦役;奴役。②作苦役之奴工。

slave market 奴隸市場。

slave·oc·ra·cy [slev'ɑkrəsɪ; slei'vɔkrəsi] *n.* 美國南北戰爭前南方之奴隸主人集團。(亦作 **slavocracy**)

slav·er[1] ['slevə; 'sleivə] *n.* ①販賣奴隸者;奴隸販子。②販賣奴隸所用之船。

slav·er[2] ['slævə; 'slævə] *v.i.* ①流涎;垂涎。②奉承;諂媚。—*v.t.* 以涎弄濕或弄汚。—*n.* ①涎;口水;吐沫。②愚言;妄語。

***slav·er·y** ['slevərɪ; 'sleivəri] *n.* ①奴役;奴隸狀態。②奴隸制度。③苦役。④束縛。

slave ship 販賣奴隸的船。

Slave States 南北戰爭前美國承認奴隸制的各州。

slave station 〖無線電〗遠隔操縱發射臺。

slave trade 販賣奴隸。
slave trader 奴隸販子。
slav·ey ['slevɪ; 'slævi, 'sleivi] *n., pl.* **-eys.** 〖英俗〗女傭;打雜之女僕。
Slav·ic ['slævɪk; 'slævik] *adj.* 斯拉夫人的;斯拉夫語的。—*n.* 斯拉夫語。
Slav·i·cist ['slævəsɪst; 'slævisist] *n.* 斯拉夫語文專家。(亦作 **Slavist**)
slav·ish ['slevɪʃ; 'sleiviʃ] *adj.* ①奴隸的。②卑屈的;卑賤的;奴隸性的。③無創造性的;無獨立性的。—**ness,** *n.*
slav·ish·ly ['slevɪʃlɪ; 'sleiviʃli] *adv.* ①卑屈地。②無獨立性地;不作獨立判斷地。
Slav·ism ['slævɪzm; 'slɑːvizm] *n.* 斯拉夫風格;斯拉夫氣質;斯拉夫語氣;斯拉夫主義。(亦作**Slavicism**)
Sla·von·ic [slə'vɑnɪk; slə'vɔnik] *adj.* 斯拉夫民族的。—*n.* 斯拉夫人;斯拉夫語。
Slav·o·phil ['slɑvəfɪl; 'slɑːvəfil] *n.* (亦作 **Slavophile**) 親斯拉夫人者;崇拜斯拉夫習俗、文化等者。—*adj.* 親斯拉夫人的。
Slav·o·phobe ['slɑvəˌfob, 'slæv–; 'slɑːvəfoub, 'slæv–] *n., adj.* 畏懼或憎恨斯拉夫人、其文化或其影響者(的)。
slaw [slɔ; slɔː] *n.* (生或熟的)甘藍片;白菜片。
***slay** [sle; slei] *v.,* **slew** [slu; sluː], **slain** [slen; slein], **slay·ing.** —*v.t.* ①殺(爲詩中或文雅的用語)。②毀。③〖俗〗深深感動;壓倒;克服。—*v.i.* 造成死亡。—**er,** *n.*
SLBM satellite-launched ballistic missile. 從人造衛星上發射的彈道飛彈。
sld. ①sailed. ②sealed. ③solder.
sleave [sliv; sliːv] *n., v.,* **sleaved, sleav·ing.** —*n.* ①絲線。②散絲;粗絲。③任何糾纏之物。—*v.t.* 解開;析開;理(絲等)。
slea·zy ['slizɪ, 'slezɪ; 'sliːzi, 'slei–] *adj.,* **-zi·er, -zi·est.** ①薄而質料不佳的(織物)。②簡陋的;破爛的。③低級的。—**slea·zi·ly,** *adv.*
***sled** [slɛd; sled] *n., v.,* **sled·ded, sled·ding.** —*n.* 雪車;橇;滑臺。—*v.t.* 以橇載運。—*v.i.* 乘橇。—**like,** *adj.*
sled·der ['slɛdɚ; 'sledə] *n.* ①乘雪車者;駕橇者。②拉雪車或橇之狗或馬等。
sled·ding ['slɛdɪŋ; 'slediŋ] *n.* ①乘橇滑行。②進行的狀況。Business was hard *sledding.* 商業不景氣。
sled dog 拉雪車之狗。(亦作**sledge dog**)
***sledge**[1] [slɛdʒ; sledʒ] *n., v.,* **sledged, sledg·ing.** —*n.* 雪車;橇。—*v.t.* 以橇運送。—*v.i.* 乘橇。—**sledg·er,** *n.*
sledge[2] *n., v.,* **sledged, sledg·ing.** —*n.* 大鍾;任何强而有力之物 (=sledge hammer). —*v.i. & v.t.* 以大鍾鍾擊。
sledge hammer ①長柄大槌。②有壓服力的東西。
sledge-ham·mer ['slɛdʒˌhæmɚ; 'sledʒˌhæmə] *v.t.* 以大鍾鍾打;以任何强而有力之物壓服。—*adj.* 强有力的;壓服的;無情的。—*adv.* 全面地;毫無保留地。
sled-length ['slɛd'lɛŋθ; 'sled'leŋθ]
***sleek** [slik; sliːk] *adj.* ①有光澤的;光滑的。②有光滑皮膚或毛髮的。③圓滑的;花言巧語的;諂諛的。a *sleek* salesman. 花言巧語的售貨員。④很帥的。—*v.t.* ①使光滑;使整齊。②掩飾。—**ly,** *adv.*
sleek·en ['slikən; 'sliːkən] *v.t.* 使光滑;使有光澤。
‡sleep [slip; sliːp] *v.,* **slept** [slɛpt; slept], **sleep·ing,** *n.* —*v.i.* ①睡眠。Did you *sleep* well? 你睡得好嗎? ②靜止;不活動。③死;長眠。—*v.t.* ①睡。②供給住宿。This hotel *sleeps* 300 guests. 這旅館可供 300 人住宿。③藉睡眠驅散或消除。④藉睡眠使達到某狀態(常與反身代名詞連用)。**sleep away** a. 在睡眠中消磨。She *slept away* the whole morning. 她將整個上午在睡眠中度過。b. 藉睡眠驅散或消除。**sleep in** a. 住在雇主家內。Two of the maids *sleep in.* 女傭有兩個住在(主人)家中。b. 睡到很晚才起身。**sleep like a top** (or **log**) 睡得很熟。**sleep off** 用睡眠除去;睡掉。**sleep on** (**upon,** or **over**) **a question** 把一問題留待第二天解決。**sleep out** a. 未住在雇主家內。Our cook *sleeps out.* 我們的厨師住在外面。b. 離家外宿。c. =**sleep away. sleep the clock round** 連續睡十二小時。—*n.* ①睡眠。I can't get to *sleep.* 我睡不着。to send (*or* put) to *sleep.* 使入睡。②睡眠時間。a short *sleep.* 小睡。③靜止;安息。④死;長眠。⑤夜。⑥睡意。eyes heavy with *sleep.* 昏昏欲睡的眼睛。**cry oneself to sleep** 一直哭到睡着。**go to sleep** 睡着。**last sleep** 死。**the sleep that knows no waking** 長眠;長逝。
sleep around 人盡可夫(妻)。
sleep·coat ['slipˌkot; 'sliːpkout] *n.* 男用便袍或睡袍。
***sleep·er** ['slipɚ; 'sliːpə] *n.* ①睡眠者。a light (heavy) *sleeper.* 淺(沉)睡者。②〖美〗臥車。③〖英〗枕木(美亦作 **tie**)。④(*pl.*)幼兒自頸至脚之連身睡衣。
sleeper plane 有睡眠設備之飛機。
sleep·ful ['slipfəl; 'sliːpful] *adj.* 在睡眠中過去的。—**ly,** *adv.* —**ness,** *n.*
sleep-in[1] ['slipˌɪn; 'sliːpin] *adj.* 住在(雇主)家內的。
sleep-in[2] *n.* 睡臥抗議(羣據公共場所睡臥以抗議、示威或表示主權等)。—*v.i.* 參加睡臥抗議。
***sleep·ing** ['slipɪŋ; 'sliːpiŋ] *n.* 睡眠;休息。—*adj.* 睡眠的;供睡眠用的。—**ly,** *adv.*
sleeping bag (露營用的)睡袋。
Sleeping Beauty 睡美人(童話中公主)。
sleeping car (or **carriage**) (鐵路之)臥車。
sleeping draught 安眠藥;催眠劑。
sleeping partner 不參與實際業務的股東;匿名股東;外股。
sleeping pill 安眠藥丸。
sleeping powder 安眠藥粉。
sleeping sickness 〖醫〗①睡眠症;昏睡病。②昏睡性腦炎。
sleep·less ['sliplɪs; 'sliːp-lis] *adj.* ①失眠的;不眠的。②無休息的。③警覺的;戒備的。—**ly,** *adv.* —**ness,** *n.*
sleep-out ['slipˌaut; 'sliːpaut] *adj.* 不住在雇主家內的。
sleep·walk ['slipˌwɔk; 'sliːpwɔːk] *v.i.* 夢遊。—*n.* 夢遊。
sleep·walk·er ['slipˌwɔkɚ; 'sliːpˌwɔːkə] *n.* 夢遊者;患夢遊症者。
sleep·walk·ing ['slipˌwɔkɪŋ; 'sliːpˌwɔːkiŋ] *n.* 夢遊;夢遊症。—*adj.* 夢遊的。
sleep·wear ['slipˌwɛr; 'sliːpwɛə] *n.* 睡衣。
***sleep·y** ['slipɪ; 'sliːpi] *adj.,* **sleep·i·er, sleep·i·est.** ①欲睡的。She felt *sleepy.* 她覺得瞌睡。②不活潑的;懶惰的;靜寂的。a *sleepy* little village. 靜寂無生氣之小村。③催眠的。④開始腐爛的。—**sleep·i·ly,** *adv.* —**sleep·i·ness,** *n.*
sleep·y-eyed ['slipɪˌaɪd; 'sliːpi-aid]

adj. 睡意甚濃的;睡眼惺忪的。
sleep·y·head ['slipɪ,hɛd; 'sli:pihed] *n.* 貪眠者;懶惰者。
sleep·y-voiced ['slipɪ,vɔɪst; 'sli:pivɔist] *adj.* 聲音單調的;說話聲有氣無力的。
***sleet** [slit; sli:t] *n.* 霰; 霙。—*v.i.* ①降霰;下雨雪;雨雹。It *sleets.* 降霰。②如雨雹般下降。—*v.t.* ①使如降霰一般落下。②以霰或雪雹覆蓋。
sleet·y ['slitɪ; 'sli:ti] *adj.*, **sleet·i·er, sleet·i·est.** 霰的;似霰的;覆以霰的。
sleeve** [sliv; sli:v] *n., v.,* **sleeved, sleeving.** —*n.* ①袖。②筒;套管。hang on one's sleeve*** 聽從某人。***have a plan*** (or ***a card***) ***up one's sleeve*** 胸有成竹;胸有定策。***laugh up*** (or ***in***) ***one's sleeve*** 竊笑。***turn*** (or ***roll***) ***up one's sleeves*** 捲起袖子(準備做工等)。***up one's sleeve*** 祕密備用。***wear one's heart on one's sleeve*** 胸懷坦白;開誠布公。***work in one's sleeves*** 祇穿襯衫工作。—*v.t.* ①供以袖子。②以袖子擦。—**like,** *adj.*
sleeve·board ['sliv,bord; 'sli:vbɔ:d] *n.* (熨衣袖用的)熨袖架。
sleeved [slivd; sli:vd] *adj.* 有袖子的。
sleeve dog 小到可以放在衣袖中的狗(如北京狗)。
sleeve·less ['slivlɪs; 'sli:vlis] *adj.* ①無袖子的。②無利益的; 無用的。—**ness,** *n.*
sleeve·let ['slivlɪt; 'sli:vlit] *n.* 袖套。
sleeve link 袖扣。
sleeve nut 套筒螺母;鬆緊螺旋扣。
sleeve target (飛機所拖之)筒靶。
***sleigh** [sle; slei] *n.* 〖美〗橇; 雪車; 馬拉之雪車。—*v.i.* & *v.t.* ①乘雪車旅行。②以雪車運送。—**er,** *n.*
sleigh·ing ['sle·ɪŋ; 'sleiiŋ] *n.* ①乘橇;橇運。②雪路適於行橇之狀況。
sleight [slaɪt; slait] *n.* ①巧妙; 熟練。②〖罕〗狡計; 巧計。***sleight of hand*** **a.** 變戲法。**b.** 手動作之熟練或技巧。
***slen·der** ['slɛndɚ; 'slendə] *adj.* ①細長的;纖細的。*slender* waist. 纖腰。②微少的;微薄的。a *slender* hope. 微渺之希望。
slen·der·ize ['slɛndə,raɪz; 'slendəraiz] *v.,* **-ized, -iz·ing.** —*v.t.* 使細長(微薄)。—*v.i.* 變細長(微薄)。—**slen·der·i·za·tion,** *n.*
slen·der·ly ['slɛndəlɪ; 'slendəli] *adv.* ①微少地;微薄地。②細長地;苗條地。
***slept** [slɛpt; slept] *v.* pt. & pp. of **sleep.**
sleuth [sluθ; slu:θ] *n.* ①一種嗅覺敏銳之警犬。②〖美俗〗偵探。—*v.t.* & *v.i.* 跟蹤。
sleuth·hound ['sluθ,haʊnd; 'slu:θ'haund] *n.* =**sleuth.**
slew¹ [slu; slu:] *v.* pt. of **slay.**
slew² *v.t.* & *v.i.* 使旋轉;廻旋;廻轉。—*n.* 旋轉。(亦作 **slue**)
slew³ *n.* 濕地;沼地。(亦作**slough, slue**)
slew⁴ *n.* 〖俗〗多量; 大量。*slews* (*or* a *slew*) of money (people). 許多錢(人)。
***slice** [slaɪs; slais] *n., v.,* **sliced, slic·ing.** —*n.* ①片;薄片。a *slice* of bread. 一片麪包。②刀刃薄而寬的刀或其他器具。③部分。a *slice* of luck. 好運氣。④〖運動〗斜擊。—*v.t.* ①切成薄片。②切去〖off〗。③分…爲若干分。④〖運動〗擊(球)使斜向右方。—*v.i.* ①切。②〖運動〗**a.** (擊球者)斜出。**b.** (球)斜飛。—**a·ble,** *adj.*
slic·er ['slaɪsɚ; 'slaisə] *n.* ①(切麪包、鹹肉等之)切片機。②切片的人。
slick [slɪk; slik] *adj.* ①有光澤的; 光滑的。②圓滑的;善僞詐的。③精巧的;巧妙的。④〖俗〗(文章等)有技巧而無內容的。⑤〖俚〗良好的;精美的。—*n.* ①光滑之處。②〖美俚〗紙面光滑之雜誌(內容高級者, 爲 pulp 之對)。③有油跡之光滑水面。④狡猾不可靠者。⑤任何使表面光滑之工具。—*adv.* 〖俗〗直接地;正面地。—*v.t.* ①使平滑;使光滑。②加以修飾〖常up〗。③占…之便宜。—*v.i.* 打扮起來〖常up〗.
slicked-up ['slɪkt'ʌp; 'slikt'ʌp] *adj.* 〖俚〗①打掃乾淨的。②流線型的;吸引人的。
slick·en·side ['slɪkən,saɪd; 'slikənsaid] *n.* 岩石之較光滑的表面(因與相鄰之岩石磨擦而造成)。
slick·er ['slɪkɚ; 'slikə] *n.* ①〖美〗寬長的雨衣。②〖美俗〗騙子。③〖俗〗大都市中油腔滑調者。
slick-pa·per ['slɪk'pepɚ; 'slik'peipə] *adj.* 印刷在厚而光滑的紙上的。
slick·rock ['slɪk,rɑk; 'slik-rɔk] *n.* 平滑的岩石。
slide** [slaɪd; slaid] *v.,* **slid** [slɪd; slid], **slid** or **slid·den** ['slɪdn̩; 'slidn], **slid·ing** ['slaɪdɪŋ; 'slaidiŋ], *n.* —*v.i.* ①滑動。②潛行;溜進;溜過。③在不知不覺中逝去。Time *slides* by. 光陰在不知不覺中過去。—*v.t.* ①使滑動;使輕輕溜過。②順溜地放入。let slide*** 忽視;不加努力。He *let slide* his studies. 他任學業荒蕪。***let things slide*** 聽其自然。***slide into bad habits*** 沾染惡習。***slide over*** (***a matter, a delicate subject***) 迅速越過;輕觸(事情、困難問題)。—*n.* ①滑。②滑面。ski *slide.* 滑雪場地。③滑梯。playground *slide.* 兒童遊戲場之滑梯。④滑蓋。⑤玻璃板;幻燈片。⑥伸縮喇叭中可拉出推進的U形管。⑦大量滑落的土塊、雪堆等; 雪崩; 土崩。⑧婦女用的髮針。⑨墮落。—**slid·a·ble,** *adj.* —**slid·a·bly,** *adv.*
slide fastener 拉鍊。
slide projector 幻燈片放映機;幻燈機。
slid·er ['slaɪdɚ; 'slaidə] *n.* ①滑雪者;滑冰者。②(機器之)滑子;滑塊。③拉鍊有齒部分。
slide rule 滑尺;計算尺。
slide valve 〖機械〗滑瓣。
slide·way ['slaɪd,we; 'slaidwei] *n.* 〖機械〗滑槽;導槽;導路。
slid·ing ['slaɪdɪŋ; 'slaidiŋ] *adj.* ①滑的;滑動的。②易變的; 不可靠的。③視情形而升降的;有伸縮性的;富彈性的。—**ly,** *adv.*
sliding axle 滑動軸。
sliding bearing 滑動軸承。
sliding door 滑門。
sliding gear 滑動齒輪。
sliding rule 計算尺。
sliding scale ①按價格、收入等條件而升降之課稅率、工資計算率、收費標準等。②=**slide rule.**
‡slight [slaɪt; slait] *adj.* ①輕微的; 細微的。There won't be the *slightest* difficulty. 毫無困難。②纖細的;苗條的。She is a *slight* girl. 她是個苗條的女孩。③纖弱的。④脆弱的;不穩固的。***make slight of*** 輕視。***not in the slightest*** 完全不 (=not at all).—*v.t.* 輕視;藐視;忽略。—*n.* 輕蔑。***put a slight upon*** 輕視;侮辱。—**er,** *n.*
slight·ing ['slaɪtɪŋ; 'slaitiŋ] *adj.* 輕視的;蔑視的;侮辱的。—**ly,** *adv.*
***slight·ly** ['slaɪtlɪ; 'slaitli] *adv.* ①輕微地。He is *slightly* deaf. 他微聾。②怠慢地。③纖細地;苗條地。She is *slightly* built. 她身材苗條。
slight·ness ['slaɪtnɪs; 'slaitnis] *n.* ①輕微;不足取。②纖細;苗條。

sli·ly 〔ˈslaɪlɪ; ˈslaili〕 *adv.* ＝**slyly.**
slim** 〔slɪm; slim〕 *adj.*, **slim·mer, slim·mest,** *v.*, **slimmed, slim·ming.** —*adj.* ①細長的;纖弱的。②微少的;微弱的;不充實的。Her chances for getting well were very *slim.* 她痊癒的希望甚微。③狡猾的。 —*v.t.* & *v.i.* 使變細。She is trying to *slim* by dieting. 她想以節食減肥。slim down*** 減少;減縮。—**ly,** *adv.* —**ness,** *n.*
slime 〔slaɪm; slaim〕 *n.* ①黏土;黏泥;類似黏泥之物。②(魚、蝸牛等之)黏液。③令人噁心的髒東西。
slime pit 瀝青坑。
slim-jim 〔ˈslɪmˌdʒɪm; ˈslimdʒim〕 *n.* 瘦子。—*adj.* 〖俚〗細長的。
slim·mer 〔ˈslɪmɚ; ˈslimə〕 *n.* 〖英〗減肥者。
slim·ming 〔ˈslɪmɪŋ; ˈslimiŋ〕 *adj.* 使顯苗條的。—*n.* 減肥。
slim·mish 〔ˈslɪmɪʃ; ˈslimiʃ〕 *adj.* 略嫌不足的;略嫌貧乏的。
slim·sy 〔ˈslɪmzɪ; ˈslimzi〕 *adj.*, **-si·er, -si·est.** ①〖美俗〗脆弱的; 纖弱的。②〖英俗〗懶惰的。(亦作 **slimpsy**)
slim·y 〔ˈslaɪmɪ; ˈslaimi〕 *adj.*, **slim·i·er, slim·i·est.** ①覆有黏土的。②黏土的;似黏土的。③汚穢的。④卑俗的。⑤卑劣的。—**slim·i·ly,** *adv.* —**slim·i·ness,** *n.*
sling**[1] 〔slɪŋ; sliŋ〕 *n.*, *v.*, **slung, sling·ing,** *adj.* —*n.* ①吊索。②吊腕帶。③投石器。④投擲。—*v.t.* ①投擲; 抛; 以投石器投擲。②吊; 懸。③以吊索吊起或繫下。④〖俗〗混合。sling hash*** 〖俚〗在低級飯館當侍者或侍女。***sling mud at a person*** 詬罵某人。—*v.i.* 衝。—*adj.* 披在肩上的。—**er,** *n.*
sling[2] *n.* 由酒、水、糖、檸檬汁等合成之冷飲。
sling·back 〔ˈslɪŋˌbæk; ˈsliŋbæk〕 *n.* 後跟敞開祇有一條帶子掛住的女用皮鞋。
sling cart 搬運大砲、機械等重物之大吊車。
sling chair 用布或帆布做椅座與靠背的椅子。
sling dog 索端之掛鈎。
sling·man 〔ˈslɪŋmən; ˈsliŋmən〕 *n.*, *pl.* **-men.** 用投石器作武器的士兵。
sling·shot 〔ˈslɪŋˌʃɑt; ˈsliŋʃɔt〕 *n.* 〖美〗小彈弓。
sling·stone 〔ˈslɪŋˌston; ˈsliŋ-stoun〕 *n.* 供投石器投射之石彈。
slink 〔slɪŋk; sliŋk〕 *v.*, **slunk** or **slank, slunk, slink·ing,** *n.*, *adj.* —*v.i.* 潛行; 溜走;潛逃〖away, off, about〗。—*v.t.* (動物)早產。 —*n.* ①早產之犢或其他動物。②偷偷的一動。—*adj.* 早產的。—**ing·ly,** *adv.*
slink·skin 〔ˈslɪŋkˌskɪn; ˈsliŋk-skin〕 *n.* 早產動物之皮;用此等皮所製的革。
slink·y 〔ˈslɪŋkɪ; ˈsliŋki〕 *adj.* ①偷偷的。②線條優美的。
‡slip[1] 〔slɪp; slip〕 *v.*, **slipped, slip·ping,** *n.*, *adj.* —*v.i.* ①滑; 溜。The newspaper *slipped* off my knees. 報紙從我的膝部滑落下去。②失足; 滑倒。③失去; 逸失。Don't let this opportunity *slip.* 不要錯過這個機會。④滑脫;突然溜往錯誤方向。⑤悄悄溜去。Time *slips* by. 光陰在不知不覺中過去。⑥犯錯誤; 失誤。He often *slips* (up) in his grammar. 他常犯文法上的錯誤。⑦被忘記。⑧迅速穿衣。He *slipped* into his coat. 他迅速地穿上外套。⑨放錯。⑩減退; 減少。⑪衰弱。—*v.t.* ①使滑。②迅速俐落地穿上或脫下。③失去;使逸去;脫漏;自…逸去。④放開;釋放。⑤濳置。⑥無意中提到。⑦(家畜) 早產;流產。⑧使脫關節。⑨使失安定。⑩閃避。***let slip*** 無意說出;洩漏。***let slip the dogs of war*** 開戰。***slip a cog*** 犯錯。***slip into*** 迅速地或輕易地穿(衣)。***slip off*** 脫(衣)。***slip on*** 穿 (衣)。***slip one's attention*** 未被注意。***slip one's memory*** 被遺忘。***slip someone's mind*** 被遺忘。***slip something over on*** 欺騙(某人);占(某人)的便宜。***slip up*** 〖俗〗犯錯誤;失誤。—*n.* ①滑;溜;滑跌。②錯誤;失誤。a *slip* of the tongue. 失言。a *slip* of the pen. 筆誤。③下跌。a *slip* in stock prices. 股票行情之下跌。④枕套; (婦女之)套裙; (小兒之)胸巾等。⑤〖美〗碼頭或船塢中船的停泊處。⑥碼頭上用以修理船隻的人造斜坡。⑦繫犬索。⑧〖板球〗守三柱門球員旁的位置或球員。⑨(家畜)早產或流產。⑩潤滑性。***give someone the slip*** 躲避某人。***There's many a slip ('twixt the cut and the lip).*** 總有事故妨礙計畫實現。—*adj.* 利用滑動作用的。—**less,** *adj.* —**ping·ly,** *adv.*
‡slip[2] *v.*, **slipped** or **slipt, slipped, slip·ping,** *n.* —*v.t.* ①剪(枝)備挿種; 從(植物)剪下挿枝。②記在紙條(單子)上。—*n.* ①狹長的紙片、木片等。a *slip* of paper. 一張細長的紙。②紙條;單子。deposit *slip.* 存款單。③年輕而瘦弱的人。④剪下備挿的枝。⑤任何狹小之物。
slip carriage 〖英〗脫留車廂(在火車駛過不停之車站脫下之一節車廂)。(亦作 **slip coach**)
slip·case 〔ˈslɪpˌkes; ˈslipkeis〕 *n.* 有一邊敞開便書脊外露的書套。
slip cover 椅套;沙發套。
slip·cov·er 〔ˈslɪpˌkʌvɚ; ˈslipkʌvə〕 *v.t.* 蓋以椅套。—*n.* ①＝**slip cover.** ②書皮。
slip knot 活結;滑結。(亦作 **slipknot**)
slip noose 活結繩套。(亦作 **slipnoose**)
slip-on 〔ˈslɪpˌɑn; ˈslipɔn〕 *n.* 自頭部套穿之衣服。—*adj.* ①便於穿脫的。②自頭部套穿的(衣服)。
slip·o·ver 〔ˈslɪpˌovɚ; ˈslipˌouvə〕 *adj.*, *n.* ＝**slip-on.**
slip·page 〔ˈslɪpɪdʒ; ˈslipidʒ〕 *n.* ①滑移。②滑動量。③滑動造成之動 (motion)與功率 (power)之損失。④後退;墮落。
***slip·per**[1] 〔ˈslɪpɚ; ˈslipə〕 *n.* 輕便的淺幫鞋;拖鞋。—*v.t.* 以拖鞋打。—*v.i.* 穿着拖鞋走。
slip·per[2] *adj.* 〖主方〗 ＝**slippery.**
slipper chair 臥室中用的一種矮脚小椅。
slip·pered 〔ˈslɪpɚd; ˈslipəd〕 *adj.* 穿拖鞋的。
***slip·per·y** 〔ˈslɪpərɪ; ˈslipəri〕 *adj.* ①表面光滑的。②不可靠的;狡猾的。③不安定的;不穩固的。④含糊的;難以解釋的。
slippery elm ①〖植物〗赤楡。②赤楡皮(用作緩和劑)。
slip·py 〔ˈslɪpɪ; ˈslipi〕 *adj.* 〖方、俗〗 ①易滑的。②快速的;靈便的;敏捷的。
slip ring 〖機械〗①滑環;集電環。②轂緣。
slip road 〖英〗(通達高速公路之)交流道。
slip·sheet 〔ˈslɪpˌʃit; ˈslipʃiːt〕 *v.t.* & *v.i.* 將空白紙張夾在(印好的紙張)之間以防未乾的油墨玷汚。 —*n.* 作上述用途之空白紙。
slip·shod 〔ˈslɪpˌʃɑd; ˈslipʃɔd〕 *adj.* ①隨便的;不整飾的;懶散的。②曳足而行的; 攪混的。③磨損不堪的。④穿拖鞋的。—**ness,** *n.*
slip·slop 〔ˈslɪpˌslɑp; ˈslip-slɔp〕 *n.* ①淡薄之酒。②隨便寫的文字; 信口之談。③拖鞋拍地聲。 —*adj.* 隨便的; 馬馬虎虎的。
slip-slop 〔ˈslɪpˌslɑp; ˈslip-slɔp〕 *adj.*, *v.*, **-slopped, -slop·ping.** —*adj.* 內容膚淺的。—*v.i.* 穿着拖鞋走。
slip·stick 〔ˈslɪpˌstɪk; ˈslip-stik〕 *n.* 〖俚〗＝**slide rule.**
slip stream 〖機械〗 沖流。(亦作 **slip-stream**)

slipt 〔slɪpt; slipt〕 *v.* 【古】pt. of **slip.**
slip-up 〔ˈslɪpˌʌp; ˈslipʌp〕 *n.* 【美俗】錯誤;疏忽。
slip·ware 〔ˈslɪpˌwɛr; ˈslipwɛə〕 *n.* 用稀黏土塗過而烤成的陶器。
slip·way 〔ˈslɪpˌwe; ˈslipwei〕 *n.* (船塢)船台;滑動式造船架。
slit 〔slɪt; slit〕 *v.,* **slit, slit·ting,** *n., adj.* —*v.t.* ①割裂;劃破。②使變細;使變窄。—*n.* 裂縫;豁口。—*adj.* ①細長的。②有裂縫的;有豁口的。—**less,** *adj.* —**ter,** *n.*
slith·er 〔ˈslɪðɚ; ˈsliðə〕 *v.i.* 滑動;滑行。—*v.t.* 使滑動;使滑行。—*n.* 滑動;滑行。
slith·er·y 〔ˈslɪðərɪ; ˈsliðəri〕 *adj.* 滑溜溜的。
slit trench ①狹窄之防空壕或散兵壕。②散兵坑。
slit·ty 〔ˈslɪtɪ; ˈsliti〕 *adj.,* **-ti·er, -ti·est.** ①有裂縫的;像裂縫的。②細長的。
sliv·er 〔ˈslɪvɚ; ˈslivə〕 *n.* ①長條;裂片;細片。②(毛、棉等待梳整成條之)疏鬆纖維束。—*v.t.* 切成長條;裂成細片。—*v.i.* 裂開。
sliv·o·vitz 〔ˈslɪvəvɪts; ˈslivəvits〕 *n.* 一種用梅子釀成的烈性白蘭地酒。
slob 〔slɑb; slɔb〕 *n.* ①【方】泥;河底的軟泥;(尤指)軟泥的海岸。②【俚】蠢貨;笨蛋。
slob·ber 〔ˈslɑbɚ; ˈslɔbə〕 *v.i.* ①流涎;唾涎;淌口水。②極端感情用事;不自制地發洩感情。—*v.t.* ①以涎等弄濕或弄污。②口齒不清地說或唱。 ***slobber over a person*** 將人弄得滿身是口水;流着口水接吻;拚命寵愛;哭訴。 —*n.* ①涎;口津。②極端感情用事的談話或舉動。③口齒不清的發音。(亦作 **slabber**) —**er,** *n.*
slob·ber·y 〔ˈslɑbərɪ; ˈslɔbəri〕 *adj.* ①流口涎的;爲口涎所濕汚的。②易動感情的;泣涕而言的。③潮濕的。—**slob·ber·i·ness,** *n.*
sloe 〔slo; slou〕 *n.* 【植物】野李(樹);野梅(樹)。 *sloe* gin. 野梅酒。
sloe-eyed 〔ˈsloˌaɪd; ˈslouaid〕 *adj.* ①眼睛烏黑的。②斜眼的。
slog 〔slɑg; slɔg〕 *v.,* **slogged, slog·ging,** *n.* —*v.t. & v.i.* ①猛擊;痛毆。②掙扎行走;辛苦工作。—*n.* ①痛打;猛擊。②艱苦努力。
***slo·gan** 〔ˈslogən; ˈslougən〕 *n.* ①標語;口號。"Safety First" is our *slogan.* 我們的口號是"安全第一"。②戰爭中士兵們的吶喊聲。
slo·gan·eer 〔ˌslogəˈnɪr; ˌslougəˈniə〕 *n.* 創造口號者;口號製造家。
slo·gan·eer·ing 〔ˌslogəˈnɪrɪŋ; ˌslougəˈniəriŋ〕 *n.* 喊口號;呼口號;用口號。
slo·gan·ize 〔ˈslogəˌnaɪz; ˈslougənaiz〕 *v.t.,* **-ized, -iz·ing.** ①化爲口號;以口號表達或宣傳。②用口號影響或說服。
slog·ger 〔ˈslɑgɚ; ˈslɔgə〕 *n.* ①猛擊者;亂打者。②艱苦的工作者。
slog·ging 〔ˈslɑgɪŋ; ˈslɔgiŋ〕 *n.* 苦工;辛勞。 —*adj.* ①艱苦的。②猛擊的;痛打的。
sloid, slojd 〔slɔɪd; slɔid〕 *n.*＝**sloyd.**
sloop 〔slup; sluːp〕 *n.* 一種單桅帆船。
sloop of war ①昔裝十至三十二門砲的軍艦(帆船)。②僅在甲板上裝砲的小軍艦。
slop[1] 〔slɑp; slɔp〕 *v.,* **slopped, slop·ping,** *n.* —*v.t.* ①洒;潑。②洒液體於。③狼吞虎嚥地吃。④以食物殘渣餵。 —*v.i.* ①洒;潑。②在泥濘中走。③閒蕩。 ***slop over*** 【俚】表現過分的熱心。 —*n.* ①洒的水;濺出的水(或其他液體)。②(常 *pl.*) 穢水。③殘湯賸飯。④稀泥;泥水。⑤(*pl.*) 液體食物。⑥(*pl.*) 大小便。⑦食物之殘渣。
slop[2] *n.* 【英俚】警察。
slop[3] *n.* ①廉價之現成衣服。②水手用之被服。③寬大之外衣。
slop basin 餐桌上盛殘渣的淺碟;髒水盆。(亦作 **slop bowl, slop bucket**)
slop chest ①商船上之日用品販賣部。②昔時船上裝日用品之箱。
***slope** 〔slop; sloup〕 *v.,* **sloped, slop·ing,** *n.* —*v.i. & v.t.* ①傾斜;使傾斜;使成斜坡。②走;行。—*n.* ①傾斜;坡度。②斜坡;傾斜面。③經濟衰退。
slop·ing 〔ˈslopɪŋ; ˈsloupiŋ〕 *adj.* 傾斜的;有斜坡的。
slop pail (盛殘湯賸菜供餵家畜之用的)汚水桶。
slopped 〔slɑpt; slɔpt〕 *adj.* ①爲水濺濕或弄髒的。②酒醉的。
slop·py 〔ˈslɑpɪ; ˈslɔpi〕 *adj.,* **-pi·er, -pi·est.** ①濕的;泥濘的。②爲水濺濕或玷汚。③乏味的(食物或飲料)。④【俗】不留心的;不整潔的。⑤【俗】脆弱的;愚痴的;易動感情的。⑥浪濤很大的。⑦酒醉的。—**slop·pi·ly,** *adv.*
slop·sell·er 〔ˈslɑpˌsɛlɚ; ˈslɔpselə〕 *n.* 賣現成衣服的商人。
slop·shop 〔ˈslɑpˌʃɑp; ˈslɔpʃɔp〕 *n.* 賣現成服裝之店鋪。
slop·work 〔ˈslɑpˌwɝk; ˈslɔpwəːk〕 *n.* ①現成衣服或廉價衣服(之縫製)。②廉價衣服。③任何匆匆完成之工作;任何劣質品。
slop·y 〔ˈslopɪ; ˈsloupi〕 *adj.,* **slop·i·er, slop·i·est.** 傾斜的。
slosh 〔slɑʃ; slɔʃ〕 *n.* ①雪泥;稀泥;軟土;(尤指)泥濘的道路。②【俗】味淡的飲料。③水之磅拍聲。④少量的液體。⑤一擊。—*v.i.* ①濺着水而行;在泥水中輾轉而行;在爛泥路上走。②發出濺水的聲音;潑潑地響。③【美俚】遊蕩。—*v.t.* ①在液體中攪動或搖動。②在水中用力地洗。③【方,俚】(尤指用軟的東西或液體)擊;拋擊。④【方】潑水於;濺洒。⑤匆忙地倒(液體)。
slot[1] 〔slɑt; slɔt〕 *n., v.,* **slot·ted, slot·ting.** —*n.* ①口;狹縫。②【機械】槽溝。③(自動售貨機的)放錢口。④位置;空位。—*v.t.* 鑿狹縫;開一狹縫或槽溝於…之中。—**ter,** *n.*
slot[2] *n., v.,* **slot·ted, slot·ting.** —*n.* ①獸類(尤指鹿)的足跡。②任何足跡;蹤跡。—*v.t.* 循…之足跡追蹤。
sloth 〔sloθ; slouθ〕 *n.* ①怠惰。②緩慢。③樹獺(產於中南美洲)。
sloth bear 印度的一種長毛熊。
sloth·ful 〔ˈsloθfəl; ˈslouθful〕 *adj.* 怠惰的;懶惰的;行動遲緩的。 —**ly,** *adv.*
sloth·ful·ness 〔ˈsloθfəlnɪs; ˈslouθfulnis〕 *n.* 怠惰;沉滯。
slot machine 自動售貨機;自動體重計;吃角子老虎(賭具名);(投入硬幣使用的)公共電話。
slot man 【美】報館之編輯主任(＝copy editor). (亦作 **slotman**)
slouch 〔slaʊtʃ; slautʃ〕 *v.i.* ①以呆拙而垂頭彎腰的姿態站立、坐、走路或行動。②低垂。—*v.t.* ①使低垂;下垂。②以垂頭彎腰的姿勢走(路)。—*n.* ①頭及肩部之低垂;(動作)消沉之姿態。②帽沿等的低垂。③笨拙之人;懶人;不中用之人。He's no *slouch* at tennis. 他打網球很行。④懶惰;怠惰。
slouch hat 垂邊軟帽。
slouch·ing 〔ˈslaʊtʃɪŋ; ˈslautʃiŋ〕 *adj.* 垂頭喪氣的;不振作的;有氣無力的。 —**ly,** *adv.*
slouch·y 〔ˈslaʊtʃɪ; ˈslautʃi〕 *adj.,* **slouch·i·er, slouch·i·est.** 不振作的;垂頭的;不修邊幅的。—**slouch·i·ly,** *adv.*
slough[1] 〔for ①③slaʊ; slau, for ②slu; sluː〕 *n.* ①泥沼;泥坑。②【美,加】沼澤。③絕望、無助、沮喪的情況。 ***slough of despond***

沮喪之深淵。—*v.t.* ①使淹沒於泥沼。②〖俚〗逮捕;監禁〖in, up〗。—*v.i.* 行於泥中。

slough² 〔slʌf; slʌf〕 *n.* ①(蛇等之)蛻皮;蛻殼。②〖醫〗腐肉;瘸;死皮膚。③任何脫褪或被捨棄之物。—*v.i.* ①被蛻下;被脫除。②脫皮;長瘸;脫落。—*v.t.* 蛻去;脫除;廢棄。 ***slough over*** 忽略;不予注意。

slough·y¹ 〔ˈslauɪ; ˈslaui〕 *adj.*, **slough·i·er, slough·i·est.** 泥濘的;多泥沼的。

slough·y² 〔ˈslʌfɪ; ˈslʌfi〕 *adj.*, **slough·i·er, slough·i·est.** (像)蛻皮的;(像)死皮的。

Slo·vak 〔ˈslovæk; ˈslouvæk〕 *n.* ①斯洛伐克人(卽居住於捷克 Slovakia 省之斯拉夫人)。②斯洛伐克語。—*adj.* 斯洛伐克人的;斯洛伐克語的。

Slo·vak·i·an 〔sloˈvɑkɪən, -ˈvæk-; slouˈvækiən〕 *n., adj.* =**Slovak.**

slov·en 〔ˈslʌvən; ˈslʌvən〕 *n.* 潦草的人;不整潔的人。—*adj.* 不整潔的;骯髒的。

Slo·vene 〔sloˈvin; ˈslouviːn〕 *n.* 居於 Slovenia (南斯拉夫之西北地區) 的斯拉夫人;其南部斯拉夫語。—*adj.* Slovenia 的;住於 Slovenia 的斯拉夫人的;其語言的。

slov·en·ly 〔ˈslʌvənlɪ; ˈslʌvənli〕 *adj.*, **-li·er, -li·est,** *adv.* —*adj.* 不整潔的;疏忽的;潦草的。—*adv.* 不整潔地;潦草地。

‡slow 〔slo; slou〕 *adj.* ①遲緩的;緩慢的。The clock is *slow*. 這個鐘慢。ten minutes *slow*. 慢十分鐘。②遲鈍的;呆笨的。He's *slow* of hearing. 他聽覺不靈。③無趣味的;不精采的。a very *slow* book. 索然無味的書。④不急速的;不輕易的。He's *slow* to show his anger. 他不輕易怒形於色。⑤遲到的;不準時的。He is *slow* in arriving. 他遲到。⑥燃燒緩慢或溫和的(火)。⑦不景氣的。⑧不陡峭的;不險峻的。⑨使遲緩的。⑩落伍的。a *slow* town. 一個落伍的市鎭。⑪〖照相〗需要曝光很久的。⑫(時間)過得很慢的。It's been a *slow* afternoon. 這一個下午過得眞慢。⑬(跑道)雨後不久因而尙有些黏脚的。—*v.t.* & *v.i.* 使遲緩;緩行;變爲遲緩。to *slow* down (*or* up) a car. 將車開慢。—*adv.* ①緩慢地。②審愼地。I advise you to go *slow* in what you are doing. 我勸你審愼從事。—**ly,** *adv.* —**ness,** *n.*

slow burn 〖俚〗怒氣之逐漸形成(與突然暴怒成對比)。

slow coach 〖俚〗遲鈍的人。

slow·down 〔ˈsloˌdaun; ˈsloudaun〕 *n.* 〖俗〗①減速。②減低生產;怠工。②趨於不活潑;變爲緩慢。

slow-foot·ed 〔ˈsloˌfutɪd; ˈslouˈfutid〕 *adj.* 脚步緩慢的;速度緩慢的。—**ness,** *n.* (亦作 **slow-foot**)

slow·go·ing 〔ˈsloˈgoɪŋ; ˈslouˈgouiŋ〕 *adj.* 徐徐前進的;不慌不忙的;悠閒的。

slow·ish 〔ˈsloɪʃ; ˈslouiʃ〕 *adj.* 速度較慢的;速度稍慢的。

slow match 導火線;引信。

slow motion (影片之)慢動作。

slow-mo·tion 〔ˈsloˈmoʃən; ˈslouˈmouʃən〕 *adj.* ①移動較常速緩慢的;操作較常速緩慢的;慢動作的。②高速攝製之影片的(如以常速放映,則動作顯得緩慢)。

slow-mov·ing 〔ˈsloˈmuvɪŋ; ˈslouˈmuːviŋ〕 *adj.* 慢吞吞的;悠哉遊哉的。

slow-paced, slow·paced 〔ˈsloˈpest; ˈslouˈpeist〕 *adj.* 速度或進行緩慢的。

slow·poke 〔ˈsloˌpok; ˈsloupouk〕 *n.* 〖俚〗動作特別遲鈍的人。

slow-poke 〔ˈsloˌpok; ˈsloupouk〕 *v.i.*, **-poked, -pok·ing.** 慢吞吞地走。

slow-spo·ken 〔ˈsloˌspokən; ˈslouˌspoukən〕 *adj.* 慢慢講話的(人)。

slow time 〖俗〗標準時間(日光節約時間之對)。

slow·up 〔ˈsloˌʌp; ˈslouʌp〕 *n.* 減速;趨緩。

slow-wit·ted 〔ˈsloˈwɪtɪd; ˈslouˈwitid〕 *adj.* 遲鈍的;笨的。

slow·worm 〔ˈsloˌwɝm; ˈslouwəːm〕 *n.* 〖動物〗無足蜥蜴。

sloyd 〔slɔɪd; slɔid〕 *n.* 手工藝訓練法(尤指木工手藝)。(亦作 **sloid, slojd**)

slsmgr. sales manager. **slsmn.** salesman. **slt.** ①searchlight. ②sleet.

slub 〔slʌb; slʌb〕 *n., v.,* **slubbed, slub·bing.** —*n.* 輕搓過的一捲羊毛(或棉、絲)。—*v.t.* 輕搓(毛、絲)以備紡績。

slub·ber 〔ˈslʌbɚ; ˈslʌbə〕 *v.t.* ①弄污;塗髒。②馬馬虎虎地做。—**ing·ly,** *adv.*

sludge 〔slʌdʒ; slʌdʒ〕 *n.* ①泥;軟泥;泥濘。②淤泥。③鍋爐或水箱內壁之沉澱物。④小塊的浮冰。⑤水與粉狀物質之混合物。⑥含有大量微生物之溝中沉澱物。—**sludg·y,** *adj.*

sludg·er 〔ˈslʌdʒɚ; ˈslʌdʒə〕 *n.* 清除污泥等所用之抽水機或其他裝置。

slue¹ 〔slu; sluː〕 *v.,* **slued, slu·ing,** *n.* —*v.t.* & *v.i.* 轉;旋轉。—*n.* 旋轉。

slue² *n.* 沼澤;沼地(=slough¹).

slue³ *n.* 大量。

slug¹ 〔slʌg; slʌg〕 *n.* ①蛞蝓(類似蝸牛而無硬殼之動物)。②似蛞蝓的毛蟲或蠋等。③行動遲緩的人、動物、車輛等。④金屬塊。⑤小彈丸。⑥排版用之鉛條;自動鑄字機鑄出來的一行相連的鉛字。⑦〖俚〗一杯酒。a *slug* of whisky. 一杯威士忌。⑧〖新聞〗稿紙上角顯示稿子內容的簡短說明(通常祇用一兩個字)。

slug² *v.,* **slugged, slug·ging,** *n.* —*v.t.* (以拳)重擊。***slug it out*** 打到勝負決定爲止。—*v.i.* 猛擊;出拳有力。—*n.* 拳擊;重擊。

slug³ *v.,* **slugged, slug·ging.** —*v.i.* ①虛擲時光。②慢行。—*v.t.* 虛擲(時光)。

slug·a·bed 〔ˈslʌgəˌbed; ˈslʌgəbed〕 *n.* 睡懶覺的人;懶人。—*adj.* 晏起的;睡懶覺的。

slug·fest 〔ˈslʌgˌfɛst; ˈslʌgfest〕 *n.* 〖俚〗①激烈的競爭場合;混戰;互毆。②安打次數頻繁的棒球賽。③(雙方祇顧出拳打擊對方而不注意防衞的)拳賽。

slug·gard 〔ˈslʌgɚd; ˈslʌgəd〕 *n.* 怠惰者;懶人。—*adj.* 怠惰的;懶的。—**ly,** *adv.*

slug·ger 〔ˈslʌgɚ; ˈslʌgə〕 *n.* ①猛擊之人。②〖俚〗職業拳擊家。③〖俚〗〖棒球〗強打者。

slug·ging 〔ˈslʌgɪŋ; ˈslʌgiŋ〕 *n.* 〖俗〗重擊。

slugging average 〖棒球〗打擊率。(亦作 **slugging percentage**)

slug·gish 〔ˈslʌgɪʃ; ˈslʌgiʃ〕 *adj.* ①行動遲緩的;緩慢的。②怠惰的;呆滯的。③不景氣的;不振的;不活潑的。—**ly,** *adv.*

slug·gish·ness 〔ˈslʌgɪʃnɪs; ˈslʌgiʃnis〕 *n.* ①遲緩;呆滯。②不振;不活潑;不景氣。

sluice 〔slus; sluːs〕 *n., v.,* **sluiced, sluic·ing.** —*n.* ①堰;堰內之水。②水門;水閘。③排水道(溝)。④〖採礦〗斜水槽;洗礦槽。⑤(運送木材等之)人工水道。—*v.t.* ①開水閘放(水);開水閘灌漑。②沖洗。③放(木材等)入水道。—*v.i.* 流出;奔流;泛濫。—**like,** *adj.*

sluice gate 水門;水閘。

sluice valve 洩水閥;水閘。

sluice·way 〔ˈslusˌwe; ˈsluːs-wei〕 *n.* ①有閘門控制之水道。②任何人工水道。

sluic·y 〔ˈslusɪ; ˈsluːsi〕 *adj.* ①傾瀉的。②潮濕的。

slum¹ [slʌm; slʌm] *n.*, *v.*, **slummed, slum·ming.** —*n.* ①(常*pl.*)貧民窟;貧民區。②(*pl.*)極度的貧窮;赤貧。—*v.i.*(爲慈善目的而)去貧民區視察。
slum² *n.*〖主英〗潤滑油的殘渣。
***slum·ber** ['slʌmbɚ; 'slʌmbə] *v.i.* ①睡眠;安睡。②不活躍。—*v.t.* 以睡眠度過。—*n.* 睡眠;微睡。—*adj.* 睡時用的。—**er,** *n.* —**less,** *adj.*
slum·ber·land ['slʌmbɚ,lænd; 'slʌmbəlænd] *n.* 夢鄉。
slum·ber·ous ['slʌmbərəs; 'slʌmbərəs] *adj.* ①昏昏欲睡的。②催眠的;使人思睡的。③與睡眠有關的;有睡眠特徵的;似睡眠的。④不活潑的。⑤安靜的;寧靜的。—**ly,** *adv.*
slumber party 女孩子在寢室裏穿上睡衣以談話過夜的集會。(亦作 **pajama party**)
slum·ber·y ['slʌmbərɪ; 'slʌmbəri] *adj.* 昏睡的;思睡的。
slum·brous ['slʌmbrəs; 'slʌmbrəs] *adj.* =**slumberous.**
slum clearance 爲建築新住宅區或其他市政建設而拆除違章建築。
slum·dom ['slʌmdəm; 'slʌmdəm] *n.* ①貧民區。②貧民區之居民。③貧民區之地位。
slum·dwell·er ['slʌm,dwɛlɚ; 'slʌm,dwelə] *n.* 貧民區之居民。
slum·gul·lion [slʌm'gʌljən; slʌm'gʌljən] *n.* ①肉與馬鈴薯和洋葱等混合煮的連湯食物。②洗鑛槽中稠而有黏性的渣滓。③〖俚〗卑賤之人;無價值之人。
slum·gum ['slʌm,gʌm; 'slʌmgʌm] *n.* 蜂房取出蠟後所剩之殘渣。
slum·land ['slʌm,lænd; 'slʌmlænd] *n.* 貧民區;貧民地帶(=slumdom).
slum·lord ['slʌm,lɔrd; 'slʌmlɔːd] *n.* 〖美〗貧民區中之房東。
slum·mer ['slʌmɚ; 'slʌmə] *n.* ①赴貧民窟訪問之人。②居住貧民窟的人。
slum·ming ['slʌmɪŋ; 'slʌmiŋ] *n.* 貧民窟之訪問。
slum·my ['slʌmɪ; 'slʌmi] *adj.*, **-mi·er, -mi·est.** 多貧民窟的;有貧民窟性質的。
***slump** [slʌmp; slʌmp] *v.i.* ①陷;猛然落下。②衰落。—*n.* ①猛然落下。②暴跌。a *slump* in prices. 價格的暴跌。③衰落;不景氣。④運動員表現失常的一段時期。⑤傴腰彎背之不振作姿勢。
slung [slʌŋ; slʌŋ] *v.* pt. & pp. of **sling.**
slung shot 附於皮帶上的小塊金屬或石頭,用做武器者。
slunk [slʌŋk; slʌŋk] *v.* pt. & pp. of **slink.**
slup [slʌp; slʌp] *v.t.*, **slupped, slup·ping.** 啜食(=slurp).
slur [slɝ; sləː] *v.*, **slurred, slur·ring,** *n.* —*v.t.* ①忽略;忽視;草率看過〖常over〗。②含糊讀出;不清楚地講。③〖音樂〗標以連音符;輕快地唱(奏);滑唱(奏)。④侮辱;蔑視;中傷。⑤弄汚;致模糊。—*v.i.* 含糊而讀;潦草書寫;馬虎了事。—*n.* ①含糊之發音、聲音等。②〖音樂〗二個或二個以上滑唱(奏)音調之組合。③〖音樂〗連音符;連結線(‿,⁀)。④〖印刷〗模糊不清之點;滑汚;印花。⑤汚點;瑕疵;輕蔑或藐視之言辭。
slurp [slɝp; sləːp] *v.t.* & *v.i.* 啜食。—*n.*①一啜;發出聲音之一飲一啜。②潺潺聲。
slur·ry¹ ['slɝɪ; 'sləːri] *v.t.*〖英方〗弄髒;弄汚。
slur·ry² *n.*, *pl.* **-ries.** 泥;黏土;水泥;灰泥等混合成的稀泥。
slur·ry³ *adj.*〖罕〗不清楚的;模糊的。
slur·vi·an ['slɝvɪən; 'sləːviən]〖蔑〗*adj.* 口齒不清之演說的。—*n.* 口齒不清楚者所作之演說。—**ism,** *n.*
slush [slʌʃ; slʌʃ] *n.* ①半融之雪;雪泥。②稀泥;軟土。③愚痴而感傷之談話、文章等。④脂肪;潤滑油。—*v.t.* ①濺以雪泥、稀泥等。②塗以油脂或潤滑油。③塡以或覆以灰泥或水泥〖up〗。④(以大量之水)沖洗。—*v.i.* ①行於泥中或水中。②發出擊水聲。—**er,** *n.*
slush fund 行賄基金。
slush·i·ness ['slʌʃɪnɪs; 'slʌʃinis] *n.* ①多稀泥。②愚痴而感傷。
slush lamp 洋鐵罐做的粗劣油燈,通常以破布爲芯。
slush·y ['slʌʃɪ; 'slʌʃi] *adj.*, **slush·i·er, slush·i·est.** ①多雪泥的;多稀泥的。②雪泥的;似雪泥的;稀泥的;似稀泥的。③愚痴而感傷的。—**slush·i·ly,** *adv.*
slut [slʌt; slʌt] *n.* ①齷齪而不整潔的女子;懶女人。②放蕩的女子。③頑皮的女孩。④母狗。
slut·ter·y ['slʌtərɪ; 'slʌtəri] *n.* 齷齪或放蕩女人之行爲。
slut·tish ['slʌtɪʃ; 'slʌtiʃ] *adj.* ①齷齪的;不整潔的。②放蕩的。—**ly,** *adv.* —**ness,** *n.*
slv. ①sleeve. ② solvent.
sly** [slaɪ; slai] *adj.*, **sly·er** or **sli·er, sly·est** or **sli·est,** *n.*, *v.*, **slied, sly·ing.** —*adj.* ①能祕密作事而不爲他人所知的;狡猾的。②詭譎的;狡詐的;狡黠的。a *sly* plot. 一個狡詐的陰謀。③淘氣的;幸災樂禍的;若有所悟的。—*n.* 祕密;狡猾。on the sly*** 祕密地;暗暗地。—*v.i.* 偸偸行走;溜。
sly·boots ['slaɪ,buts; 'slaibuːts] *n.* *pl.* (作 *sing.* 解)〖諧〗狡猾的人。
sly·ly ['slaɪlɪ; 'slaili] *adv.* 狡猾地;詭譎地;狡黠地;陰險地;淘氣地。(亦作 **slily**)
sly·ness ['slaɪnɪs; 'slainis] *n.* 狡猾;詭譎;狡黠。
slype [slaɪp; slaip] *n.*〖建築〗(禮拜堂中)有覆蓋之走廊。
SM Service Men. **Sm** 化學元素 samarium 之符號。 **sm.** small. **S.M.** ①Master of Science. ②Sergeant Major. ③〖詩〗short meter. ④Soldier's Medal. ⑤State Militia.
***smack**¹ [smæk; smæk] *n.* ①氣味;滋味。②遺痕;風味。The old sailor still had a *smack* of the sea about him. 這老水手仍然帶有海上的風味。③微量。—*v.i.* 微有(某)味;帶有(某種)風味〖of〗. The medicine *smacks* of sulphur. 這藥有硫磺味。
smack**² *v.t.* ①咂(脣)作響。to *smack* one's lips. 咂脣作響。②拍擊;摑;掌擊。③使(鞭子等)發爆裂聲。④響吻。—*n.* ①咂脣聲;掌摑聲;響吻聲(等)。②掌摑;拍擊。③響吻。a *smack* on the lips. 響吻。a smack in the eye*** 出乎意料的失望。—*adv.*〖俗〗①直接地;平平正正地。②突然地。He hit me *smack* in the face. 他突然打我一耳光。
smack³ *n.* 單桅帆船;單桅漁舟。
smack·er ['smækɚ; 'smækə] *n.* ①有響聲之接吻。②有響聲之打擊。③惹人注意的人。④〖美俚〗一元。
smack·ing ['smækɪŋ; 'smækiŋ] *adj.* ①發輕爆聲的。a *smacking* kiss. 發輕爆聲的一吻。②爽快的;活潑的。③疾吹的。④巨大的;極佳的。
smacks·man ['smæksmən; 'smæksmən] *n.*, *pl.* **-men.** 單桅漁舟上的漁翁;單桅帆船上的水手。
‡**small** [smɔl; smɔːl] *adj.* ①小的;少的;不重要的。a *small* sum of money. 一小筆錢。②鄙劣的;吝嗇的。It is *small* of him

to wish for recompense. 他還希望得到報酬, 眞是卑鄙。③淡薄的;弱的。④資本或資產不大的。a *small* dealer. 小本商人。⑤低的;輕的。a *small* voice. 細小的嗓音。⑥地位低微的; 謙卑的。Both great and *small* people mourned Lincoln's death. 擧國上下均哀悼林肯之死。⑦普通的;本領平常的;不太有名的。a *small* author. 一個名氣不大的作家。⑧(字母) 小寫的。⑨年幼的。a *small* boy. 幼童。***feel small*** 感到慚愧;自慚形穢。***in a small way*** 小規模地; 儉約地。—*adv.* ①成爲碎塊地。②(聲音)低低地; 輕輕地。to speak *small*. 低聲說。***sing small*** 轉成謙遜之音調或態度。—*n.* ①小東西;小用品。He kept a good stock of *smalls*. 他存有一大批的小玩意。②(*pl.*) 短褲;小件包裹。***the small of the back*** 背部最窄之處; 後腰。—**ness,** *n.*

small and early 客人較少而散會較早的小晚會。

small arms 輕武器(如手槍、步槍等)。

small beer ①淡啤酒。②瑣事; 不重要的人物。***think small beer of*** 〖俗〗瞧不起。

small capital 〖印刷〗小號的大寫字母。

small change ①小額錢幣; 零錢。②無足輕重之人或物。

small·clothes [ˈsmɔlˌkloz; ˈsmɔːl-klouðz] *n. pl.* ①〖古〗短褲。②小件衣着(如內衣、手帕等)。

small-fry [ˈsmɔlˌfraɪ; ˈsmɔːlfrai] *adj.* 不重要的;不受重視的。

small game 野兔、鴿等小獵物。

small·hold·er [ˈsmɔlˌholdɚ; ˈsmɔːl-ˌhouldə] *n.* 小自耕農。

small hours 午夜後最初幾小時。

small intestines 小腸。

small·ish [ˈsmɔlɪʃ; ˈsmɔːliʃ] *adj.* 略小的。

small letter 小寫字母。

small-mind·ed [ˈsmɔl ˈmaɪndɪd; ˈsmɔːlˈmaindid] *adj.* 心胸狹窄的; 氣量小的。—**ly,** *adv.* —**ness,** *n.*

small potatoes 〖俗〗小人物;小物件。

***small·pox** [ˈsmɔlˌpɑks; ˈsmɔːl-pɔks] *n.* 〖醫〗痘症;天花。

small-scale [ˈsmɔlˈskel; ˈsmɔːlˈskeil] *adj.* ①小規模的。②按小比例畫或製的。

small·sword [ˈsmɔlˌsord; ˈsmɔːlsɔːd] *n.* 衝刺用的輕劍。

small talk 閑談;聊天。

small-time [ˈsmɔlˈtaɪm; ˈsmɔːlˈtaim] *adj.* 〖俚〗有限的; 次要的;小規模的;平庸的。

small-tim·er [ˈsmɔlˈtaɪmɚ; ˈsmɔːl-ˈtaimə] *n.* ①屬於小劇團者。②從事小規模之事業者。

small·wares [ˈsmɔlˌwɛrz; ˈsmɔːl-wɛəz] *n. pl.* 〖英〗①雜貨。②窄邊布料。③女用化妝品。

smalt [smɔlt; smɔːlt] *n.* 深青色; 深青色顏料。

smarm [smɑrm; smɑːm] *v.i.* 〖英俗〗奉承;獻媚。

smarm·y [ˈsmɑrmɪ; ˈsmɑːmi] *adj.,* **smarm·i·er, smarm·i·est.** 〖俗〗奉承的;討好賣乖的。

‡**smart** [smɑrt; smɑːt] *v.i.* ①感到劇痛。②招致劇痛。③精神上感痛苦。***smart for*** 因…而受罰。***smart under*** 受苦。—*n.* ①劇痛; 痛苦; 傷心。②樣子漂亮或時髦的人。—*adj.* ①刺痛的;劇烈的。②活潑的; 輕快的。③聰敏的; 伶俐的; 機敏的; 精明能幹的。a *smart* boy. 伶俐的孩子。④漂亮的;時髦的。a *smart* motorcar. 漂亮的汽車。⑤整齊的;清新的。*smart* in his uniform. 穿着制服整齊清新。⑥〖俗、方〗相當大的。a *smart* distance (earthquake). 相當大的距離(地震)。⑦俏皮的。—*adv.* 聰明伶俐地; 輕快地; 漂亮地。to talk *smart*. 說話聰明伶俐。

smart al·eck [~ˈælɪk; ~ˈælik] 自負而令人討厭的人。

smart-al·eck·ism [ˈsmɑrtˈæləkɪzm̩; ˈsmɑːtˈæləkizm] *n.* 自負而令人討厭的言行。

smart-al·eck·y [ˈsmɑrt ˌælәkɪ; ˈsmɑːtˌæləki] *adj.* 自負而令人討厭的。

smart bomb 〖美軍俚〗精靈炸彈(以雷射及電視導向特定轟炸目標之炸彈)。

smarted up 打扮起來的。

smart·en [ˈsmɑrtn̩; ˈsmɑːtn] *v.t.* ①裝飾; 修整; 弄漂亮。②使輕快; 使活潑。—*v.i.* 變漂亮; 變輕快; 變活潑。to *smarten* up. 漂亮起來;活潑起來。

smart·ly [ˈsmɑrtlɪ; ˈsmɑːtli] *adv.* ①用力地;劇烈地。②大大地。③乾淨俐落地;熟練地。④機智地;聰明地。⑤漂亮地;時髦地。

smart money ①罰金; 賠償金。②爲逃避某種不愉快之事而付的錢。③有經驗者所下的注或作的投資。④有經驗之下注者或投資者。⑤〖英〗負傷津貼。

smart·ness [ˈsmɑrtnɪs; ˈsmɑːtnis] *n.* ①聰明。*smartness* in business. 商業才幹。②機智。③輕快有力。④漂亮;時髦;帥。

smart set 一羣精通世故講究時髦的人。

smart·weed [ˈsmɑrtˌwid; ˈsmɑːt-wiːd] *n.* 〖植物〗水蓼類植物。

smash** [smæʃ; smæʃ] *v.t.* ①搗碎; 使破碎。②擊敗; 使瓦解。③以快急而擧手過肩之姿勢擊(網球); 殺球。④〖俗〗重擊; 投擲。—*v.i.* ①粉碎;破碎。②破產。③碰撞。smash in*** (or ***down***) 擊破(阻撞物)。—*n.* ①破碎; 粉碎;破碎聲。②碰撞。③破產;慘敗;瓦解;災難。④(網球的)殺球。⑤痛擊。⑥薄荷、水、白蘭地或其他烈性酒所混合成之一種飲料。⑦大成功。a box-office *smash*. 票房之大成功。***go to smash*** 垮臺; 毀滅。***to smash*** **a.** 成爲碎片。**b.** 毀壞。—*adv.* 破碎地。—*adj.* 非常成功的;極好的。the *smash* best seller of the year. 當年之極爲成功的暢銷書。

smashed [smæʃt; smæʃt] *adj.* 〖俚〗酒醉的。

smash·er [ˈsmæʃɚ; ˈsmæʃə] *n.* ①龐然大物。②破壞者。③優異之人或物。④殺球的球員。⑤重擊; 重跌。⑥刻薄的言語; 挖苦的回答。⑦壓書機。⑧使用壓書機者。

smash hit 演出極爲成功之電影或戲劇。

smash·ing [ˈsmæʃɪŋ; ˈsmæʃiŋ] *adj.* ①粉碎的。②猛烈的。③極好的;絕妙的。

smash·up [ˈsmæʃˌʌp; ˈsmæʃʌp] *n.* ①猛撞(尤指火車之撞毁)。②失敗;破產;毁滅。③不幸;災難。④健康衰落;不支。

smat·ter [ˈsmætɚ; ˈsmætə] *n.* 一知半解; 膚淺的知識。—*v.i.* 一知半解地說或寫〖in〗。—*v.t.* 膚淺地學習或研究。

smat·ter·ing [ˈsmætərɪŋ; ˈsmætə-riŋ] *n.* ①淺薄的知識;一知半解(通常用作單數, 前加不定冠詞, 後連 of)。to have a *smattering* of English. 略諳英語。②小量;少數。—*adj.* 一知半解的;淺薄的。

smaze [smez; smeiz] *n.* 煙霧。

***smear** [smɪr; smiə] *v.t.* ①塗;敷;弄髒;弄污。②使污; 玷辱。③以塗抹的動作弄熄。④〖俚〗擊潰;痛擊。⑤〖俚〗賄賂。—*v.i.* 塗污;弄成污濁一片。—*n.* ①污點; 污跡。②(供顯微鏡檢查的)塗抹標本。③中傷。

smear word 有損名譽之字語。

smear·y [ˈsmɪrɪ; ˈsmiəri] *adj.*, **smear·i·er, smear·i·est.** ①被塗汚的；被弄髒的。②造成汚痕的。

‡**smell** [smɛl; smel] *v.*, **smelled** or **smelt** [smɛlt; smelt], **smell·ing,** *n.* —*v.t.* ①嗅；聞；嗅出。I can *smell* the dinner cooking. 我聞到燒飯的氣味。②覺出…的跡象。We *smelled* trouble. 我們覺得會有麻煩。③藉嗅覺而探索或發現〖out〗. The dog will *smell* out a thief. 狗會靠其嗅覺而找到賊。④有…之味。—*v.i.* ①有嗅覺；嗅；聞。Can a fish *smell?* 魚有嗅覺否？②發出氣味。Roses *smell* sweet. 玫瑰發出香氣。The house *smells* of paint. 這房屋有油漆的氣味。③發出臭味；發出壞味。④有…之跡象。The plan *smells* of trickery. 這計畫中似有詭詐。⑤似有不當；似不誠實。***smell a rat*** 懷疑其中有詭詐。***smell of the lamp*** 像是深夜趕製出來的。***smell out*** **a.** 以嗅覺檢查或發現。**b.** 由細心研究而發現。***smell round*** 到處打聽消息。***smell up*** 使充滿難聞的氣味。—*n.* ①嗅覺。*Smell* is keener in dogs than in men. 狗的嗅覺比人靈敏。②嗅；聞。Take a *smell* of this wine. 聞一聞這酒味。③氣味。④跡象。

smell·er [ˈsmɛlɚ; ˈsmelə] *n.* ①嗅者；有嗅覺的動物。②有味道的東西。③受雇用嗅覺檢驗東西的人。④〖俚〗鼻。⑤(動物之)觸角；觸鬚。⑥往鼻子上的重擊；重擊。

smell·ie [ˈsmɛlɪ; ˈsmeli] *n.* 〖俗〗加有氣味的電影。

smelling bottle 嗅鹽瓶。

smelling salts 嗅鹽。

smell-less [ˈsmɛllɪs; ˈsmellis] *adj.* ①無嗅覺的。②無臭味的。

smell·y [ˈsmɛlɪ; ˈsmeli] *adj.*, **smell·i·er, smell·i·est.** 臭的；有臭味的；放臭味的。

smelt[1] [smɛlt; smelt] *v.t.* ①鎔煉；鎔解(礦石)。②精煉；製煉。—*v.i.* ①煉礦。②(礦苗)經過煉礦程序。

smelt[2] *n.*, *pl.* **smelts, smelt.** 香魚；沙鑽魚。

smelt[3] *v.* pt. & pp. of **smell.**

smelt·er [ˈsmɛltɚ; ˈsmeltə] *n.* ①熔煉業者；熔煉工。②熔煉物。③煉鑛所。

smew [smju; smjuː] *n.* 〖動物〗鸍鵰。

smi·lax [ˈsmaɪlæks; ˈsmailæks] *n.* 〖植物〗牛尾菜屬植物。

‡**smile** [smaɪl; smail] *v.*, **smiled, smil·ing,** *n.* —*v.i.* ①微笑；現笑容；現喜色。What were you *smiling* at? 你笑甚麼？②眷顧；示好意。Fortune has always *smiled* at him. 他的命運一向很好。③冷笑；嗤笑。—*v.t.* 發出(一種微笑)；微笑以示。to *smile* away grief. 笑以解愁。***smile at*** **a.** 對…表示欣慰。**b.** 對…覺得好笑。**c.** 耐心忍受。—*n.* ①微笑；喜色。②冷笑。③眷顧。to enjoy the *smiles* of fortune. 時運亨通。***be all smiles*** 面露得色；極爲高興。

smil·ing [ˈsmaɪlɪŋ; ˈsmailiŋ] *adj.* ①含笑的；微笑的。②明媚的(風景)。***come up smiling*** 拳擊時第一回合失敗後鼓起勇氣再競賽；遇困難後再鼓起勇氣做。—**ly,** *adv.*

smirch [smɝtʃ; sməːtʃ] *v.t.* 使汚；玷汚；汚辱。—*n.* 汚點；汚斑；瑕疵。

smirk [smɝk; sməːk] *v.i.* 傻笑；得意地笑〖at, on, upon〗. —*n.* 佯笑；得意之笑。

smite** [smaɪt; smait] *v.*, **smote** [smot; smout], **smit·ten** [ˈsmɪtn̩; ˈsmitn] or **smit** [smɪt; smit], **smit·ing** [ˈsmaɪtɪŋ; ˈsmaitiŋ]. —*v.t.* ①打；擊。②責備。③擊敗。④突然照到。⑤突擊。⑥使在心理上深有感受。—*v.i.* 打；擊；震。be smitten by*** 迷戀(某人)。***smite hip and thigh*** 猛烈攻擊；擊敗。

Smith [smɪθ; smiθ] *n.* ①男子名。②亞當斯密斯(Adam, 1723–1790, 蘇格蘭經濟學家。)

***smith** [smɪθ; smiθ] *n.* ①鍛工；冶工；工匠。②鐵匠。—*v.t.* 鍛鍊。

smith·er·eens [ˌsmɪðəˈrinz; ˈsmiðəˈriːnz] *n. pl.* 〖俗〗碎片；碎屑。to break into *smithereens.* 破爲碎片。

smith·er·y [ˈsmɪθərɪ; ˈsmiθəri] *n.*, *pl.* **-er·ies.** 鍛冶工廠；鍛冶術。

Smith·so·ni·an Institution [smɪθˈsonɪən～; smiθˈsounjən～] 斯密生博物館(在美國首都華盛頓)。

smith·y [ˈsmɪθɪ; ˈsmiði] *n.*, *pl.* **smith·ies,** *v.*, **smith·ied, smith·y·ing.** —*n.* ①鍊冶場；鐵匠店。②鐵匠。—*v.t.* 鍛鍊(金屬)。

smit·ten [ˈsmɪtn̩; ˈsmitn] *v.* pp. of **smite.** —*adj.* ①受到重大打擊的。②深深墜入情網的。

S.M.M. ①〖拉〗Sancta Mater Maria. 聖母瑪麗亞。②Master of Sacred Music.

smock [smɑk; smɔk] *n.* ①罩衫；工作服。②〖古〗女襯衣。—*v.t.* ①着以罩衫。②用針線(在布料上)縫成一叢蜂窩形的皺褶。

smock frock (歐洲農夫等所穿的)一種寬鬆的罩衫。

smock·ing [ˈsmɑkɪŋ; ˈsmɔkiŋ] *n.* 保持布褶平整的裝飾縫線；褶飾。

***smog** [smɑg; smɔg] *n.* 〖美〗煙霧(爲smoke 與 fog 兩字合組而成)。—**gy,** *adj.* —**less,** *adj.*

smog·bound [ˈsmɑgˌbaund; ˈsmɔgbaund] *adj.* 煙霧籠罩的。

smog·out [ˈsmɑgˌaut; ˈsmɔgaut] *n.* 煙霧籠罩的情況。

‡**smoke** [smok; smouk] *n.*, *v.*, **smoked, smok·ing.** —*n.* ①煙；煙霧；蒸發氣。No *smoke* without fire. 有煙必有火(空穴來風，不爲無因)。②一縷煙。③吸煙。Have a *smoke.* 吸一根煙。④似煙之事物；空幻。⑤煙(香煙、雪茄、板煙等)。⑥似煙霧之物。⑦速度。***go up*** (or ***end***) ***in smoke*** 成爲泡影。—*v.i.* ①冒煙；起煙霧；發蒸氣。②吸煙。Do you *smoke?* 你吸煙嗎？③奔馳。—*v.t.* ①燻製。②吸(煙)。He has *smoked* himself ill. 他吸煙致病。③燻黃；燻壞。④以煙燻而驅除。***smoke out*** **a.** 以煙燻逐出。**b.** 發現並宣布。

smoke ball 煙幕彈之一種。

smoke bomb 煙幕彈。

smoke·chas·er [ˈsmokˌtʃesɚ; ˈsmoukˌtʃeisə] *n.* 森林消防隊員。

smoke curtain 煙幕。

smoked [smokt; smoukt] *adj.* ①用煙燻製的。②被煙燻黑的。③灰色的。

smoke-dried [ˈsmokˌdraɪd; ˈsmoukdraid] *adj.* 燻製的。

smoke-eat·er [ˈsmokˌitɚ; ˈsmoukˌiːtə] *n.* 〖美俚〗森林救火隊員。

smoke-filled room [ˈsmokˌfɪld～; ˈsmoukfild～] 政客在旅館裏的會談室。

smoke helmet 消防帽；防毒面具。

smoke·house [ˈsmokˌhaus; ˈsmoukhaus] *n.* 燻製所；燻肉貯藏所。

smoke·jack [ˈsmokˌdʒæk; ˈsmoukdʒæk] *n.* 轉炙叉機。

smoke-jump·er [ˈsmokˌdʒʌmpɚ; ˈsmoukˌdʒʌmpə] *n.* 〖美〗使用降落傘之森林消防隊隊員。(亦作 **smoke jumper**)

smoke·less ['smoklɪs; 'smouk-lis] *adj.* 無煙的。
smokeless powder 無煙火藥。
smoke mask 消防帽;防毒面具。
smoke pipe 連接火爐與煙囱的管子。
smoke·proof ['smok,pruf; 'smouk-pru:f] *adj.* 不透煙的;防煙的。
smok·er ['smokɚ; 'smoukə] *n.* ①吸煙者。②燻製者。③吸煙車(=smoking car);吸煙室。
smok·er·y ['smokərɪ; 'smoukəri] *n., pl.* **-er·ies.** 吸煙室。
smoke screen ①煙幕。②隱瞞眞正目的或企圖等之行動;障眼法。
smoke signal ①狼煙;用煙做的信號。②朕兆;象徵。
smoke·stack ['smok,stæk; 'smouk-stæk] *n.* 煙囱。
smoke tree 〖植物〗黃櫨。
***smok·ing** ['smokɪŋ; 'smoukiŋ] *adj.* ①發煙的;煙燻的。②吸煙的。—*n.* ①吸煙。No *smoking.* 禁止吸煙。②燻製。
smoking car (列車上的)吸煙車廂。
smoking carriage 〖英〗=**smoking car.**
smoking concert 准許吸煙之音樂會。
smoking jacket 吸煙時所穿之衣服。
smoking room =**smokery.**
smok·ing-room ['smokɪŋ,rum; 'smoukiŋ,rum] *adj.* ①吸煙室內用的;吸煙室內的。②猥褻的;下流的。
smoking stand 煙灰臺。
smok·y ['smokɪ; 'smouki] *adj.*, **smok·i·er, smok·i·est.** ①發煙的;多煙的;如煙的。②充滿煙的;煙霧瀰漫的。③燻黑的;燻汚的。④煙色的;煙味的。⑤愛抽煙的;有煙癮的。—**smok·i·ly,** *adv.*
smol·der ['smoldɚ; 'smouldə] *v.i.* ①無火燄而燃燒或冒煙;悶燒。②潛伏;鬱積(在內心)。③現出壓抑的情緒。—*n.* ①悶火;悶燒;濃煙。②壓抑的情緒。(亦作 **smoulder**)
smolt [smolt; smoult] *n.* 兩歲之小鮭。
smooch¹ [smutʃ; smu:tʃ] *v.t.* 〖美〗弄髒;弄汚。—*n.* 〖美〗髒汚;汚點(=smutch).
smooch² *v.i.* 〖俚〗接吻;擁抱;求愛。—*n.* 〖俚〗接吻。
‡**smooth** [smuð; smu:ð] *adj.* ①光滑的;平滑的。a *smooth* surface. 光滑之面。②平穩的;安靜的。The sea was *smooth.* 海上風平浪靜。③流暢的;圓通的。He has a *smooth* tongue. 他口齒伶俐。④無毛的。a *smooth* face. 無鬚的臉。⑤無麻煩或困難的;順利的。The way is now *smooth.* 前途現在毫無阻礙。⑥持重的;安祥的。a *smooth* temper. 持重的性格。⑦溫和的。*smooth* wine. 溫和的酒。⑧匀和的;無結塊的。⑨文雅的;有禮貌的。That salesman is a *smooth* talker. 那位售貨員講話彬彬有禮。⑩悅耳的。—*v.t.* ①使平滑;使光滑;燙平。She *smoothed* her dress. 她弄平她的衣服。②使和順;使平和。to *smooth* away differences. 協調歧見。③洗練;潤飾。***smooth away*** 消除(麻煩、困難等)。***smooth down*** 使平靜;安慰。***smooth over*** 掩飾過去。—*v.i.* 變爲平靜。—*adv.* 平滑地;平穩地;流利地。—*n.* ①光滑平穩之事物。②摩挲平滑。to give a *smooth* to the hair. 將頭髮摩挲平滑。***take the rough with the smooth*** 逆來順受。—**ness,** *n.*
smooth·bore ['smuð,bor; 'smu:ðbɔ:] *adj.* 無膛線的。—*n.* 無膛線的槍砲。
smooth dogfish 大西洋中的一種小鯊。
smooth·en ['smuðən; 'smu:ðən] *v.t. & v.i.* =**smooth.**
smooth-faced ['smuð,fest; 'smu:ð-feist] *adj.* ①表面光滑的;平滑的。②無鬚的;臉刮得乾淨的。③言談舉止均取悅他人的。
smooth·ie ['smuðɪ; 'smu:ði] *n.* =**smoothy.**
smoothing iron 熨斗。
smoothing plane 鉋子。
***smooth·ly** ['smuðlɪ; 'smu:ðli] *adv.* 通順地;順利地;圓滑地。
smooth-shav·en ['smuð'ʃevn̩; 'smu:ð'ʃeivn] *adj.* 臉刮得很乾淨的。
smooth-spo·ken ['smuð 'spokən; 'smu:ð'spoukn] *adj.* 口若懸河的;談吐優雅的。
smooth-talk·ing ['smuð 'tɔkɪŋ; 'smu:ð'tɔ:kiŋ] *adj.* 企圖說服他人的;鼓舌如簧的。
smooth-tongued ['smuð'tʌŋd; 'smu:ð'tʌŋd] *adj.* 甜言蜜語的;慇懃的;口慧舌巧的。
smooth·y ['smuðɪ; 'smu:ði] *n.* ①舉止優雅的人。②善於對女人獻慇懃的男性。(亦作 **smoothie**)
smor·gas·bord ['smɔrgəs ,bɔrd; 'smɔ:gəsbɔ:d] 〖瑞典〗 *n.* ①正餐前的開胃食品(=hors d'oeuvres). ②包括有此等開胃食品之餐。③有此等開胃食品供應之餐館。
smote [smot; smout] *v.* pt. of **smite.**
***smoth·er** ['smʌðɚ; 'smʌðə] *v.t.* ①使窒息。②悶死;悶熄。③遏制。④覆蓋;掩蔽。⑤蒸煑;燉。⑥大敗。—*v.i.* ①窒息。②被抑止。③〖方〗悶燒。—*n.* ①塵、烟、霧汽等。②使窒息之物。③窒息。④混亂。
smoth·er·y ['smʌðərɪ; 'smʌðəri] *adj.* 易使窒息的;充滿灰塵或烟霧的。
smoul·der ['smoldɚ; 'smouldə] *v.i., n.* =**smolder.**
smudge [smʌdʒ; smʌdʒ] *n., v.,* **smudged, smudg·ing.** —*n.* ①汚點;汚斑。②令人窒息的濃烟。③燻蚊火;燻蟲火;燻火;蚊烟。—*v.t.* ①塗汚;弄髒。②以燻火燻。—*v.i.* ①形成汚斑。②被塗汚。
smudg·y ['smʌdʒɪ; 'smʌdʒi] *adj.,* **smudg·i·er, smudg·i·est.** ①髒汚的;塗汚的。②模糊不清的。③有濃烟的;窒息的。④〖英方〗溽暑的。—**smudg·i·ly,** *adv.* —**smudg·i·ness,** *n.*
smug [smʌg; smʌg] *adj.,* **smug·ger, smug·gest.** ①沾沾自喜的;自鳴得意的;自滿的。②整潔的;服飾修整的。—**ness,** *n.*
***smug·gle** ['smʌgl̩; 'smʌgl] *v.t. & v.i.,* **-gled, -gling.** 偸運;私運;走私。
smug·gler ['smʌglɚ; 'smʌglə] *n.* ①走私者;偸運者。②走私船。
smut [smʌt; smʌt] *n., v.,* **smut·ted, smut·ting.** —*n.* ①汚物;積烟;炱煤。②汚處;汚點。③猥褻之談話或文字;淫詞。④(穀類之)黑穗病。—*v.t.* ①(給汚物等)汚染;弄髒。②使患黑穗病。—*v.i.* ①變汚;弄髒。②患黑穗病。
smutch [smʌtʃ; smʌtʃ] *n., v.t., v.i.* =**smudge.**
smut·ty ['smʌtɪ; 'smʌti] *adj.,* **-ti·er, -ti·est.** ①染汚的;多汚物的。②暗黑的;汚髒的。③猥褻的。④患黑穗病的。—**smut·ti·ly,** *adv.* —**smut·ti·ness,** *n.*
Sn 化學元素 stannum 之符號。
S.N. shipping note. 裝貨通知單。
snack [snæk; snæk] *n.* ①小吃;點心。②分;部分。***go snack(s)*** 分享(利潤)。—*v.i.* 吃零食;吃點心。

snack bar 小吃店;賣小吃的櫃臺。
snack table 可摺疊的單人小餐桌。(亦作 TV table)
snaf·fle ['snæfl; 'snæfl] *n.*, *v.*, **-fled, -fling.** —*n.* 一種輕馬銜; 輕勒。***ride* (*one*) *on* (or *with*) *the snaffle*** 輕易地控制;用和平手段控制。—*v.t.* ①用輕馬銜控御; 裝上輕勒。②〖英俗〗偷。
sna·fu [snæ'fu; snæ'fu:] *adj.* 〖軍俚〗混亂的 (*s*ituation *n*ormal, *a*ll *f*ouled *u*p). —*n.* 〖軍俚〗混亂狀態。—*v.t.* ①〖軍俚〗使混亂。②處理不當。
snag [snæg; snæg] *n.*, *v.*, **snagged, snag·ging.**—*n.* ①水中隱樹;沉樹。②任何銳利而突出之尖端(如枝椿等)。③牙根;暴牙;齜牙; 缺牙。④暗礁。⑤斷線部分。⑥裂片; 裂塊。⑦一批; 一筆。⑧斷裂的樹枝。⑨預料之外的阻礙。—*v.t.* ①用沉樹破壞(船)或阻礙。②阻礙;妨害。③清除沉樹; 切枝; 修枝。④使絆住。⑤偷取;攫取;奪取。—*v.i.* ①纏結。②(船)撞上沉樹或暗礁。
snagged [snægd; snægd] *adj.* ①多水中障礙的;多障礙的。②爲障礙所礙的。
snag·gle·tooth ['snægl,tuθ; 'snægl-tu:θ] *n.*, *pl.* **-teeth.** 殘缺不齊的牙齒; 斜出之牙齒。—**ed,** *adj.*
snag·gy ['snægɪ; 'snægi] *adj.*, **-gi·er, -gi·est.** ①水底多沉樹的 (河川)。②〖蘇,方〗暴躁的;易怒的;壞脾氣的。③突出的。
snail** [snel; sneil] *n.* ①蝸牛;蝸牛類之軟體動物。②懶惰而遲緩的人。at a snail's pace*** 緩慢地。***slow as a snail*** 慢如蝸牛。—*v.i.* 蝸牛一般地緩慢進行。—**like,** *adj.*
snail·er·y ['snelərɪ; 'sneiləri] *n.*, *pl.* **-er·ies.** 食用蝸牛飼養場。
snail-paced ['snel,pest; 'sneilpeist] *adj.* 蝸步的;行動遲緩的。
snail-slow ['snel,slo; 'sneilslou] *adj.* 像蝸牛一樣緩慢的。
snake** [snek; sneik] *n.*, *v.*, **snaked, snak·ing.** —*n.* ①蛇。②陰險之人。③通陰溝或水管等之通條。a snake in the grass*** a. 隱敝;潛伏的危機。b. 陰險之人。***raise snakes*** 引起騷亂。***snake charmer*** 弄蛇者。***warm a snake in one's bosom*** 引狼入室。—*v.i.* 蜿蜒轉折而行。—*v.t.* 〖俗〗①(用力地)拖;拉。②突拉; 急抽。③曲折前進。④〖俗〗用通條通(陰溝等)。
snake·bird ['snek,bɝd; 'sneikbə:d] *n.* 蛇鳥。
snake·bite ['snek,baɪt; 'sneikbait] *n.* 蛇咬傷。
snake dance ①蛇舞。②彎曲的遊行行列。
snake doctor ①蜻蜓。②美洲產之翅蟲幼蟲。
snake feeder 〖美〗蜻蜓。
snake fence 〖美〗曲折之圍柵。(亦作 **Virginia fence, Virginia rail fence, worm fence**)
snake·head ['snek,hɛd; 'sneikhed] *n.* 〖植物〗①(歐洲產的) 一種百合科植物。②(美洲產的)玄參科山玄參屬之各種草本植物。
snake·let ['sneklɪt; 'sneiklit] *n.* 小蛇。
snake oil 走方郎中販賣的液質萬靈藥。
snake pit ①瘋人院。②混亂悲慘之處; 混亂悲慘。③蛇坑。
snake·root ['snek,rut; 'sneik-ru:t] *n.* 〖植物〗蛇根草;蛇根草之根。
snake·skin ['snek,skɪn; 'sneik-skin] *n.* 蛇皮;蛇皮製的革。
snake·stone ['snek,ston; 'sneik-stoun] *n.* ①〖古生物〗菊石;蛇石。②被蛇咬後用以從傷口吸取毒汁的一種多孔物質。
snake·wood ['snek,wud; 'sneikwud] *n.* ①〖植物〗蛇木。②蛇紋材。
snak·y ['snekɪ; 'sneiki] *adj.*, **snak·i·er, snak·i·est.** ①蛇的。②似蛇的。③多蛇的。④彎曲的;迂廻的;蜿蜒的。⑤狡詐的;陰險的。
snap** [snæp; snæp] *v.*, **snapped, snap·ping,** *n.*, *adj.* —*v.t.* ①使發脆快之響聲。②折斷。③咬;攫奪。④急促發布。⑤拍…的快照。Tourists were *snapping* the scenery. 旅客們正對着風景拍快照。⑥急速發射。⑦使迅速完成或成立〖常up〗. —*v.i.* ①發爆裂聲;發脆快之響聲。②折斷;突斷。③咬;攫取〖at〗. to *snap* at the chance. 抓住機會。④突然關閉、移動等。⑤急迅移動。⑥發閃光;發火花。⑦聲音尖而快地說。snap back*** 〖俗〗彈回;突然恢復。***Snap into it!*** 〖美〗趕快做;好好趕。***snap one's fingers at*** a. 輕蔑(某人)。b. 對…漠不關心; 將…不當一回事。***snap out of it*** 〖俚〗a. 突然改變態度、習慣等。b. 恢復原狀; 重新振作起來。***snap someone's head off*** 〖俗〗對某人咆哮; 斥責某人。***snap the whip*** (亦作 **crack the whip**) 要求被雇者服從; 督促下屬工作。—*n.* ①爆裂聲。②折斷;突斷。③突然的一咬;攫取。④急促之說話態度。⑤〖俗〗(照相之) 快照; 快攝。⑥〖俗〗急促之情形;俐落。⑦一短時間之寒冷(炎熱)天氣。a cold (hot) *snap*. 一陣短暫的寒冷(炎熱)之天氣。⑧扣;鉤。⑨一種薄的脆餅。a gingersnap. 鬆薑餅。⑩〖美俚〗輕而易舉之事。⑪精力。There is no *snap* left in him. 他已精疲力竭。⑫兒童的一種牌戲。***not a snap*** 一點也不 (=not at all). ***not give*** (or ***care***) ***a snap*** (***of one's finger for***) 不當一回事; 不在乎。—*adj.* ①倉卒的; 突然的; 急就的。a *snap* election. 倉促的選舉。②〖俚〗容易的。③以彈簧作用自動扣緊的。
snap·back ['snæp,bæk; 'snæpbæk] *n.* ①〖橄欖球〗(中鋒之)突然將球踢回。②〖橄欖球〗中鋒。③突然彈回;突然好轉。
snap·bolt ['snæp,bolt; 'snæpboult] *n.* 彈簧鎖。
snap bug 磕頭蟲。
snap cap 雷管;引信管。
snap·drag·on ['snæp,drægən; 'snæp-,drægən] *n.* ①〖植物〗金魚草。②火中取栗(一種從燃燒中的白蘭地中取葡萄乾的遊戲)。
snap lock 有彈簧之自動鎖。
snap·per ['snæpɚ; 'snæpə] *n.* ①攫奪者;折斷者;發出突然的響聲者。②磕頭蟲。③鼈;鰵龜。
snapping beetle 磕頭蟲。
snapping turtle 鼈;鰵龜。
snap·pish ['snæpɪʃ; 'snæpiʃ] *adj.* ①好咬的;有嚙咬之習慣的。②(言語、態度上)不耐煩的;暴躁的;尖刻的。
snap·py ['snæpɪ; 'snæpi] *adj.*, **-pi·er, -pi·est.** ①好咬的;暴躁的。②聲音尖脆的;爆裂聲的。③〖俗〗活潑的; 强壯的;迅速的;銳利的;刺激的;有力的。④〖俗〗時髦的;漂亮的。a *snappy* piece of work. 迷人的姑娘。***make it snappy*** 〖俗〗a. 趕快。b. 直截了當;乾脆。
snap·shoot ['snæp,ʃut; 'snæpʃu:t] *v.t.*, **snap·shot, snap·shoot·ing.** 拍…之快照。
snap shooter 快槍手。
snap shooting 快槍射擊。
snap shot 快槍射出之一發。
snap·shot ['snæp,ʃɑt; 'snæpʃɔt] *n.*, *v.*, **-shot·ted, -shot·ting.** —*n.* ①快照;快相。②簡短的描述。③迅速射擊;倉猝的射擊。—*v.t.* 快攝;攝…之快照。—*v.i.* 拍快照。

***snare** [snɛr; snɛə] *n., v.,* **snared, snar·ing.** —*n.* ①羅網；陷阱。to fall into a *snare.* 陷入羅網。②誘惑物；圈套。③【外科】鉉圈套器。—*v.t.* ①以羅網捕捉。②誘陷；陷害。
snare drum 響弦鼓。「想的動物名)。
snark [snɑrk; snɑ:k] *n.* 蛇鯊(詩人幻
***snarl**[1] [snɑrl; snɑ:l] *v.t. & v.i.* ①咆哮；狺狺。②咆哮而言；怒吼。—*n.* ①咆哮。②怒語；罵詈。「糾纏；纏結。
snarl[2] *n.* 纏結；糾結；混亂。—*v.t. & v.i.*
snarl·y[1] [ˈsnɑrlɪ; ˈsnɑ:li] *adj.,* **snarl·i·er, snarl·i·est.** 好咆哮的；壞脾氣的；乖戾的。
snarl·y[2] *adj.,* **snarl·i·er, snarl·i·est.** 糾結的；糾纏不清的；混亂的；雜亂的。
snatch** [snætʃ; snætʃ] *v.t. & v.i.* ①攫奪；奪取。to *snatch* at a chance. 把握機會。②以迅速之行動拯救。③【俚】綁架。—*n.* ①攫取。②片刻；短時間。He had a *snatch* of sleep sitting in his chair. 他坐在椅子上面小睡片刻。③小量；片段。④【俚】綁架。by*** (or ***in***) ***snatches*** 斷斷續續地；一陣鬆一陣緊地。***put the snatch on*** 向…作强硬要求。
snatch·y [ˈsnætʃɪ; ˈsnætʃi] *adj.,* **snatch·i·er, snatch·i·est.** 斷續的；時作時輟的；不規則的。「柄。(亦作 **snathe**)
snath [snæθ; snæθ] *n.* 【美】大鐮刀之
snaz·zy [ˈsnæzɪ; ˈsnæzi] *adj.* 美麗奪目的；非常時髦的。
sneak** [snik; sni:k] *v.i.* ①潛行。②行爲鬼祟。③(學童用語)向教師密告同學之過失。—*v.t.* ①潛行過。②【俗】偸竊。③悄悄地做。sneak out of*** 偸巧規避。—*n.* ①行爲鬼祟之人。②向教師告密之學生。③小偸。④【俚】潛離。⑤(*pl.*)＝**sneakers.** ⑥＝**sneak preview.** ***on the sneak*** 偸偸地。—*adj.* 偸偸的；鬼祟的。a *sneak* attack. 偸襲。
sneak·er [ˈsnikɚ; ˈsni:kə] *n.* ①(*pl.*)【美】膠底之運動鞋。②潛行者；卑劣之人。
sneak·ing [ˈsnikɪŋ; ˈsni:kiŋ] *adj.* ①卑怯的；詭祕的；隱密的；鬼祟的。②心中感覺到但不明言的。—**ly,** *adv.* 「宣布的預演。
sneak preview 【俗】電影片不公開
sneak thief 小偸。「逃的；卑劣的。
sneak·y [ˈsnikɪ; ˈsni:ki] *adj.* 潛行的；潛
***sneer** [snɪr; sniə] *v.i. & v.t.* ①輕蔑；鄙夷；嘲笑；譏誚。to *sneer* a person out of countenance. 譏誚某人使之惶悚不安。②發噓聲。③以輕蔑的口吻說。—*n.* 嘲弄；鄙夷的態度；譏誚之辭。「的；嘲笑的。—**ly,** *adv.*
sneer·ing [ˈsnɪrɪŋ; ˈsniəriŋ] *adj.* 輕蔑
sneeze** [sniz; sni:z] *v.,* **sneezed, sneez·ing,** *n.* —*v.i.* 打噴嚏。—*v.t.* 打噴嚏而噴出。sneeze at*** 輕視；卑視。—*n.* 噴嚏。—**sneez·y,** *adj.* —**sneez·er,** *n.* 「**ing gas**)
sneeze gas 噴嚏性毒氣。(亦作 **sneez-**
snell [snɛl; snel] *n.* 連接釣鉤釣桿的短線。
snick[1] [snɪk; snik] *n.* ①刻痕；凹痕。②【板球】輕擊。—*v.t.* ①刻淺痕於。②猛擊。③【板球】輕擊(球)。
snick[2] *n.* 滴答聲；卡答聲。—*v.i.* 發出卡答聲。—*v.t.* 使發出卡答聲。
snick·er [ˈsnɪkɚ; ˈsnikə] *v.i.* (不懷敬意地)暗笑；竊笑。—*n.* (不懷敬意的)暗笑；竊笑。(亦作 **snigger**) 「ˈsni:] *n.* 短刀。
snick·er·snee [ˈsnɪkɚˌsni; ˈsnikə-
snide [snaɪd; snaid] *adj.,* **snid·er, snid·est,** *n.* —*adj.* 【俚】①假的；僞造的。②卑劣的；下等的；卑鄙的。—*n.* 【俚】①贋造物；人造寶石。②卑劣的人。③卑鄙之事。
snides·man [ˈsnaɪdzmən; ˈsnaidzmən] *n., pl.* **-men.** 【俗】使用僞幣者。
***sniff** [snɪf; snif] *v.i.* ①以鼻吸氣。②嗤之以鼻【at】。③發出呼呼吸氣之聲而聞。—*v.t.* ①以鼻吸入(空氣等)。②嗅出；發覺；覺察出；懷疑。I can *sniff* something burning. 我嗅到有甚麼東西燃燒的氣味。to *sniff* danger. 覺得有危險。③以輕蔑的口吻說。—*n.* ①以鼻吸氣；以鼻吸氣聲。②吸入的東西。③氣味。
snif·fle [ˈsnɪfl̩; ˈsnifl] *v.,* **-fled, -fling,** *n.* —*v.i.* 頻頻以鼻吸氣作聲；作鼻聲；抽搐。—*n.* 鼻聲；鼻塞聲。***the sniffles*** 【俗】 **a.** 傷風。**b.** (哭泣時的)抽搐聲；鼻聲。
sniff·y [ˈsnɪfɪ; ˈsnifi] *adj.,* **sniff·i·er, sniff·i·est.** 【俗】①有以鼻呼吸之傾向的。②鄙夷的；不友善的。
snif·ter [ˈsnɪftɚ; ˈsniftə] *n.* ①【蘇，方】鼻吸氣；噴鼻息。②【蘇，方】(*pl.*)頭冷痛。③【蘇，方】嚴重的一擊。④【蘇，方】逆運；困難。⑤【俚】一特拉姆(dram)酒；一口酒。⑥【英方】瞬息。⑦(毒品之)微量。—*v.i.* 【蘇，方】以鼻吸氣；噴鼻息；發鼻聲。—*adj.* 【俚】好的；卓
snifting valve 洩汽閥。「越的。
snif·ty [ˈsnɪftɪ; ˈsnifti] *adj.* 【俚】①有香味的。②卑視的；鄙夷的。
snig [snɪg; snig] *n.* 【方】小鱔魚；小鰻魚。
snig·ger [ˈsnɪgɚ; ˈsnigə] *v.i.* 低聲暗笑；竊笑。—*n.* 暗笑；竊笑。
snig·gle [ˈsnɪgl̩; ˈsnigl] *v.,* **snig·gled, snig·gling,** *n.* —*v.i. & v.t.* 將魚餌投入鰻穴中捕(鰻)。—*n.* 捕鰻用的一種鉤。
snip [snɪp; snip] *v.,* **snipped, snip·ping,** *n.* —*v.t. & v.i.* 剪；剪斷；剪去。*Snip* the ends off. 剪去末端。—*n.* ①剪；一剪。②剪下之小片；斷片；碎片。③【俗】渺小之人；不足道的人。④(*pl.*)鐵絲剪；鋏子。⑤鐵定之事。⑥貨眞價實之物。***go snips*** 均分。
snipe [snaɪp; snaip] *n., pl.* **snipes, snipe,** *v.,* **sniped, snip·ing.** —*n.* ①鷸；沙雖鳥。②伏擊；狙擊。③【俚】香煙頭。—*v.i.* ①獵鷸；打沙雖鳥。②伏擊；狙擊。—*v.t.* 狙擊；伏擊。「擊兵；狙擊手。
snip·er [ˈsnaɪpɚ; ˈsnaipə] *n.* 【軍】狙
snip·er·scope [ˈsnaɪpɚˌskop; ˈsnaipəskoup] *n.* 步槍用紅外線夜間瞄準器。
snip·per-snap·per [ˈsnɪpɚˌsnæpɚ; ˈsnipəˌsnæpə] *n.* 無足輕重之人。
snip·pet [ˈsnɪpɪt; ˈsnipit] *n.* ①小片；斷片；碎片。②【美俗】無關重要之人。③(*pl.*)零碎的知識；片段的引敍。
snip·pet·y [ˈsnɪpətɪ; ˈsnipiti] *adj.* ①零碎的；不完整的。②傲慢的。
snip·py [ˈsnɪpɪ; ˈsnipi] *adj.,* **snip·pi·er, snip·pi·est.** ①【俗】傲慢的。②零碎的；片斷的。③【英方】吝嗇的；小氣的。
snip-snap [ˈsnɪpˌsnæp; ˈsnipsnæp] *n.* ①機敏之回答。②剪。③【罕】咔嗒咔嗒的剪刀聲。—*adj.* ①機敏的；針鋒相對的。②暴躁的。
snip·snap·sno·rum [ˈsnɪpsnæpˈsnɔrəm; ˈsnipsnæpˈsnɔ:rəm] *n.* 一種牌戲。
snit [snɪt; snit] *n.* 心情緊張或紊亂。
snitch [snɪtʃ; snitʃ] *v.t.* 【俚】偸竊(價值不大的小物件)。—*v.i.* ①偸竊；做小偸。②告密。—*n.* 【俚】告密者。—**er,** *n.*
sniv·el [ˈsnɪvl̩; ˈsnivl] *v.,* **-el(l)ed, -el(l)ing,** *n.* —*v.i.* ①啜泣；抽抽搭搭。②假泣；假裝悲傷。③流鼻涕。④吸鼻涕作響；響鼻子。—*v.t.* ①以啜泣或響鼻子發出(聲音)。②哭哭啼啼地說。—*n.* ①假哭；假裝悲哀。②啜泣；抽搭。③鼻涕。—**er,** *n.*
snob [snɑb; snɔb] *n.* 勢利小人；諂上傲下

的人;瞧不起窮人者;注重派頭者。
snob appeal (商品之)派頭。
snob·ber·y [ˈsnɑbərɪ; ˈsnɔbəri] *n., pl.* **-ber·ies.** 勢利的行爲。
snob·bish [ˈsnɑbɪʃ; ˈsnɔbiʃ] *adj.* 勢利眼的;諂上凌下的;注重派頭的。 **—ness,** *n.*
snol·ly·gos·ter [ˈsnɑlɪˌgɑstɚ; ˈsnɔligɔstə] *n.* 野心勃勃而愛吹牛的小人。
snood [snud; snuːd] *n.* ①少女所用的束髮帶。②婦女用的髮袋。③類似髮袋之帽子或帽上之一部分。④連結釣鉤與釣絲之線。—*v.t.* 以髮帶束縛。
snook [snuk; snuːk] *n.* 以拇指頂住鼻尖並張搖其他四指以示輕蔑之手勢。***cock*** (***cut***, or ***make***) ***a snook at***;***cock one's snook*** 對…表示鄙視。
snook·er [ˈsnukɚ; ˈsnuːkə] *n.* 撞球遊戲的一種。
snoop [snup; snuːp] *v.i. & v.t.* 〖俗〗窺察;窺探;管閒事〖常 around〗. —*n.* 〖俗〗①窺察;管閒事。②窺探之人;愛管閒事者。
snoop·er [ˈsnupɚ; ˈsnuːpə] *n.* 窺察者;窺探者。
snoop·er·scope [ˈsnupɚˌskop; ˈsnuːpəskoup] *n.* 夜間觀察敵軍動態用的紅外線裝置。
snoop·y [ˈsnupɪ; ˈsnuːpi] *adj.* 〖美俗〗愛窺探或愛管閒事的。
snoot [snut; snuːt] *n.* 〖俗〗①鼻。②臉。③表示輕視之鬼臉。 —*v.t. & v.i.* 〖俗〗(向某人)作輕視的鬼臉;譏笑;瞧不起。
snoot·y [ˈsnutɪ; ˈsnuːti] *adj.*, **snoot·i·er, snoot·i·est.** 〖美俗〗傲慢的;勢利的;侮慢的。
snooze [snuz; snuːz] *v.*, **snoozed, snooz·ing,** *n.* —*v.i.* 〖俗〗小睡;假寐。 —*n.* 〖俗〗小睡;假寐。
***snore** [snor; snɔː] *v.*, **snored, snor·ing,** *n.* —*v.i.* ①發鼾聲。②發轟轟聲。 —*v.t.* ①發鼾聲熟睡度過。②〖方〗斷言。—*n.* ①鼾聲。②轟隆聲。
snor·kel [ˈsnɔrkḷ; ˈsnɔːkl] *n.* 潛水艇吸入及排出空氣之裝置。
***snort**[1] [snɔrt; snɔːt] *v.i. & v.t.* ①自鼻噴氣作聲;噴鼻息。②噴鼻息而言;噴鼻息表示輕蔑或不耐之意。③作噴噴聲。 —*n.* ①噴鼻息;噴鼻聲。②〖俚〗一杯(酒)。
snort[2] *n.* 潛水艇之吸氣排氣之裝置。
snort·er [ˈsnɔrtɚ; ˈsnɔːtə] *n.* ①大聲噴鼻息者;發鼾聲者。②〖俚〗聲音喧鬧的東西;特別重的東西;打架;喧鬧。③打在鼻上的一記重擊。④豐收。⑤大言不慚的人;自負的人。⑥〖英方〗天氣。⑦傑出的人或物。
snot [snɑt; snɔt] *n.* ①鼻涕。②〖俚〗討厭或可鄙之人。
snot-rag [ˈsnɑtˌræg; ˈsnɔt-ræg] *n.* 〖鄙〗手帕。
snot·ty [ˈsnɑtɪ; ˈsnɔti] *adj.* ①流鼻涕的。②討厭的;傲慢的。
snout [snaut; snaut] *n.* ①(尤指豬之)口鼻部。②管嘴;噴口。③〖動物〗吻狀突起;吸盤。④〖諧,蔑〗(人之)鼻;大鼻。—*v.i.*(動物)以鼻挖。
snout beetle 象鼻蟲。
‡snow [sno; snou] *n.* ①雪。as white as *snow.* 潔白如雪。②下雪。③〖詩〗純白色。④似雪之物。⑤〖俚〗海洛英;嗎啡精;古柯鹼(=cocaine)。⑥年。 forty *snows* ago. 四十年以前。 —*v.i.* ①下雪。 It is *snowing* in great flakes. 正在大雪紛飛。②似雪片般飛來。Presents *snowed* in on my birthday. 我生日時,禮物紛紛而來。—*v.t.* ①使似雪般落下。②以雪蓋、阻等。③使變白。 hair *snowed* by age. 年老而變白的頭髮。④〖俚〗對…吹牛。⑤〖俚〗使產生很深的印象。⑥〖俚〗欺騙;說服。 ***snow in*** 以雪包圍或阻塞。***snow under*** a. 以雪掩蓋。b. 〖俗〗以多得無法應付的(信件、工作等)壓倒。 **—less,** *adj.*
snow·ball [ˈsnoˌbɔl; ˈsnoubɔːl] *n.* ①雪球。②山楽樹。—*v.t.* ①向…擲雪球。②使迅速增大或增加。—*v.i.* ①滾雪球般地迅速增大或增加。②作擲雪球遊戲。
snow·bank [ˈsnoˌbæŋk; ˈsnoubæŋk] *n.* 雪堆;雪丘。
snow bear 〖動物〗白熊。
snow·ber·ry [ˈsnoˌbɛrɪ; ˈsnouberi] *n., pl.* **-ries.** ①結白色漿果的灌木。②其所結之漿果。
snow·bird [ˈsnoˌbɝd; ˈsnoubəːd] *n.* ①雪鵐。②〖俚〗有嗎啡癮者。
snow-blind [ˈsnoˌblaɪnd; ˈsnou-blaind] *adj.* 雪盲的。
snow blindness 雪盲。
snow·blow·er [ˈsnoˌbloɚ; ˈsnouˌblouə] *n.* 氣爆式剷雪機。
snow boot 雪靴。
snow-bound [ˈsnoˌbaund; ˈsnou-baund] *adj.* 爲雪所封閉的;爲雪所阻的(旅行)。
snow bunting 〖動物〗雪鵐。
snow-capped [ˈsnoˌkæpt; ˈsnou-kæpt] *adj.* 爲積雪蓋頂的(山)。
snow-clad [ˈsnoˌklæd; ˈsnou-klæd] *adj.* 〖詩〗爲雪所覆蓋的。
snow·drift [ˈsnoˌdrɪft; ˈsnou-drift] *n.* ①爲風吹成之雪堆。②隨風吹飄之雪。
snow·drop [ˈsnoˌdrɑp; ˈsnoudrɔp] *n.* 〖植物〗雪花。
snow·fall [ˈsnoˌfɔl; ˈsnou-fɔːl] *n.* ①降雪。②降雪量。
snow fence 〖鐵路〗避雪垣。
snow field 雪原;雪野。(亦作**snowfield**)
snow·flake [ˈsnoˌflek; ˈsnou-fleik] *n.* ①雪花;雪片。②=**snow bunting.**
snow goose 白雁。
snow job 〖俚〗欺騙或說服他人之企圖。
snow line ①雪線(在高山上,此線以上之積雪終年不融化)。②海平面上之降雪線(即緯度上之降雪極限)。
snow·man [ˈsnomæn; ˈsnoumæn] *n., pl.* **-men.** ①雪人(傳說中居住於喜馬拉雅山上者)。②雪人(用雪堆成的人形)。
snow·mo·bile [ˈsnomoˌbil; ˈsnou-moubiːl] *n.* 摩托雪車。
Snow Mountains 雪山(在西新幾內亞)。
snow-on-the-moun·tain [ˈsno-ɑnðəˈmauntn̩; ˈsnouɔnðəˈmauntin] *n.* 〖植物〗(美國西部產之)甘遂。
snow·plow [ˈsnoˌplau; ˈsnouˈplau] *n.* ①雪鋤(用以清除街道、鐵道上之積雪之機器)。②雪橇制動法。—*v.i.*用雪鋤清除積雪。(英亦作 **snow-plow, snowplough**)
snow pudding 蛋白布丁。
snow·scape [ˈsnoˌskep; ˈsnou-skeip] *n.* 雪景。
snow shed 〖鐵路〗防雪崩之建築。
snow·shoe [ˈsnoˌʃu; ˈsnou-ʃuː] *n., v.*, **-shoed, -shoe·ing.** —*n.* 雪鞋。—*v.i.* 着雪鞋行走或旅行。
snow·slide [ˈsnoˌslaɪd; ˈsnou-slaid] *n.* ①雪崩。②崩落之雪塊。(亦作 **snowslip**)
snow·storm [ˈsnoˌstɔrm; ˈsnou-stɔːm] *n.* 大風雪;暴風雪。
snow·suit [ˈsnoˌsut; ˈsnou-sjuːt] *n.* 兒童禦寒之服裝或斗篷;雪衣;雪裝。
snow sweeper 推雪機。
snow tire 雪上輪胎。
snow white =**zinc white.**
snow-white [ˈsnoˈhwaɪt; ˈsnou-

ˈwait] *adj.* 雪白的;純白的。
*__snow·y__ [ˈsnoɪ; ˈsnoui] *adj.*, **snow·i·er, snow·i·est.** ①似雪的;雪白的。②多雪的;大雪的;雪封的。 *snowy* mountains. 積雪之山。
snub [snʌb; snʌb] *v.*, **snubbed, snubbing,** *n.*, *adj.* —*v.t.* ①輕待;冷落。②斷然拒絕;責罵。③突然使(船、馬等)停住。④制止;喝止。⑤剪斷。⑥栓住。—*n.* ①輕待;冷落。②斥退;責罵。③突然之喝止。—*adj.* 短、扁、而微向上翻的。*snub* nose. 獅子鼻。
snub·ber [ˈsnʌbɚ; ˈsnʌbə] *n.* ①〖航海〗錨鏈制止機。②汽車之減震裝置。③突然使馬停跑之人。
snub·by [ˈsnʌbɪ; ˈsnʌbi] *adj.*, **snub·bi·er, snub·bi·est.** ①短而向上翻的(鼻)。②鼻子短而向上翻的。③好輕視人的。
snub-nosed [ˈsnʌbˈnozd; ˈsnʌbnouzd] *adj.* 獅子鼻的。
*__snuff__[1] [snʌf; snʌf] *v.t.* & *v.i.* ①吸入鼻中。②聞(=sniff)。③吸鼻烟。—*n.* ①鼻烟。②吸鼻烟。③氣味。 ***up to snuff*** a. 〖俗〗很好;够標準。b. 〖俚〗不易受騙;精明;老油條。
*__snuff__[2] *v.t.* ①剪(燭花)。②消滅〖out〗. —*v.i.* 〖俚〗死〖常out〗. ***snuff it*** 〖俚〗死。***snuff out*** a. 熄滅。b. 壓制;擊潰。c. 〖俗〗死。—*n.*①燭花。②任何衰頽或無價值之事物。
snuff·box [ˈsnʌfˌbɑks; ˈsnʌfbɔks] *n.* 鼻煙盒。
snuff color 黃褐色。
snuff-col·o(u)red [ˈsnʌfˌkʌləd; ˈsnʌfˌkʌləd] *adj.* 黃褐色的。
snuff·er [ˈsnʌfɚ; ˈsnʌfə] *n.* ①以鼻吸(尤指表示輕視)者。②吸鼻煙者。③〖動物〗五島鯨。④剪燭花者。
snuff·ers [ˈsnʌfɚz; ˈsnʌfəz] *n. pl.* 剪燭花用的剪刀。
snuf·fle [ˈsnʌfl; ˈsnʌfl] *v.*, **-fled, -fling,** *n.* —*v.i.* ①嗅;聞。②大聲地吸氣或吸鼻涕。③帶鼻音說話;以塞鼻之聲說話。④哭泣。—*v.t.* ①以鼻聲說出。②大聲用鼻子吸。—*n.* ①嗅聞;大聲之吸氣或吸鼻涕等。②鼻塞聲;鼻音。③(*pl.*)鼻塞;鼻傷風。
snuff·y [ˈsnʌfɪ; ˈsnʌfi] *adj.*, **snuff·i·er, snuff·i·est.**①如鼻煙的;爲鼻煙弄污的。②(外表)令人厭惡的;不引人的。③惱怒的;易怒的。
*__snug__ [snʌg; snʌg] *adj.*, **snug·ger, snug·gest,** *v.*, **snugged, snug·ging,** *adv.*, *n.* —*adj.* ①舒適的;溫暖的。②整潔的。③緊貼的(短上衣等)。④少而足够的。⑤隱匿的。⑥建造良好的;適於海上航行的。—*v.t.* ①使舒適、溫暖、整潔等。②使緊貼。③整備(船隻)以度過風暴。—*v.i.* 蜷伏;緊貼。—*adv.* 舒適地;整潔地。—*n.* 客棧中之酒吧間。
snug·ger·y [ˈsnʌgərɪ; ˈsnʌgəri] *n.*, *pl.* **-ger·ies.** 舒適的地方、位置、房間(等)。
snug·gle [ˈsnʌgl; ˈsnʌgl] *v.*, **-gled, -gling.** —*v.i.* 蜷伏;貼近;挨緊。—*v.t.* ①緊抱;擁抱;挨近;(將孩子等)拉抱過來。②安放;安置。
snug·ly [ˈsnʌglɪ; ˈsnʌgli] *adv.* ①舒舒服服地。②緊緊地。
‡__so__[1] [so; sou] *adv.* ①如是;如此;如彼。Hold your pen *so*. 這樣拿筆。②如上所述。Is that really *so?* 那眞是這樣嗎?③至此程度。Do not walk *so* fast. 不要走那麼快。④如…那樣…;如此…乃至於…。It is not *so* good as I thought. 沒有我想的那麼好。It *so* happened that he was not there. 他剛巧不在那裏。⑤很。You are *so* kind. 你眞好。⑥因此。⑦亦;亦復如此。She likes dogs; *so* does he. 她喜歡狗;他亦復如此。***and so*** a. 同樣地;也。b. 因而。***and so forth*** (***so on***) 諸如此類;等等。***or so*** 大約;左右。It cost a dollar *or so*. 它值一元左右。***so as to*** 以便;以求。***so far*** 迄今。*So far* so good. 到現在爲止,一切都很好。***so far as*** 至此程度。*so far as* I know. 就我所知。***so far from*** 毫不…地。***So long!*** 〖俗〗再會! ***so long as*** 只要。***so much as*** 甚至。***so much for...***其他便不必說了。***so much the better*** 那更好。***so so*** 〖俗〗還好;馬馬虎虎。***so that*** 以致;以便。***so to speak*** 可以說;如同;活像。***So what?*** 有甚麼了不起?那又怎麼樣? —*pron.* ①左右;約。a pound or *so*. 一磅左右。②如是;如此。Is that *so?* 是這樣嗎? ③同樣。—*conj.* ①倘若;假使;只要。*So* it be done, I care not who does it. 只要那事做好,我不管是誰做的。②因此;所以。He was sick, *so* they were quiet. 他病了,所以他們很肅靜。③爲了要。Be quiet *so* he can sleep. 肅靜些,好使他能睡覺。***so that's that*** 〖俗〗用於一段陳述之後,表示强調"完了"。—*interj.* ①好啦!就如此罷!②眞的嗎?
so[2] *n.* 〖音樂〗全音階之長音階的第五音。
So. ①South. ②southern.
s.o. ①seller's option. ②shipping order.
*__soak__ [sok; souk] *v.t.* ①浸;濡濕。to *soak* oneself in history. 專心鑽研歷史。②吸收〖in, up〗. A sponge *soaks* up water. 海綿吸水。③狂飲。④〖美俚〗重罰;重擊。⑤〖俚〗使…付過多;徵重稅。—*v.i.* ①浸濕;浸透。②〖俗〗狂飲。③深入腦際。***be soaked to the bone*** 全身濕透。***soak up*** a. 吸收。b. 牢記心頭。—*n.* ①浸;漬。②浸液;漬液。③〖俗〗酒徒;酒鬼。④〖俚〗典當。
soak·age [ˈsokɪdʒ; ˈsoukidʒ] *n.* ①浸漬。②浸漬液。③浸漬時吸收之液量。④滲透。
soak·er [ˈsokɚ; ˈsoukə] *n.* ①浸漬者。②浸漬物。③〖俗〗豪飲者。④〖俗〗大雨。
so-and-so [ˈsoənˌso; ˈsouənsou] *n.*, *pl.* **-sos,** *adj.* —*n.* 〖俗〗①某某;某人;某事物。②討厭的傢伙;可惡的傢伙。—*adj.* 咀咒語。
*__soap__ [sop; soup] *n.* ①肥皂。②〖美俚〗錢(尤指賄款)。***no soap*** a. 毫無用處;毫無結果。b. 建議、計畫等被拒絕;不行。—*v.t.* ①以肥皂擦洗。②諂媚;奉承。
soap·ber·ry [ˈsopˌbɛrɪ; ˈsoupberi] *n.*, *pl.* **-ries.** 〖植物〗①無患子屬之植物;無患子。②無患子之果實。
soap boiler 肥皂製造者。
soap·box [ˈsopˌbɑks; ˈsoupbɔks] *n.*①肥皂箱。②街頭演說臺。—*v.i.* 作街頭演說。—*adj.* ①街頭演說(者)的。②煽動性的。
soapbox oratory 街頭演說;煽動性的演說。
soap bubble ①肥皂泡。②短暫虛幻之物。
soap dish (洗臉臺之)肥皂盤。
soap·er [ˈsopɚ; ˈsoupə] *n.* ①用肥皂的人。②連續廣播劇(=soap opera).
soap·er·y [ˈsopərɪ; ˈsoupəri] *n.*, *pl.* **-er·ies.** 肥皂廠。
soap flakes 雪花狀的肥皂粉。(亦作soap chips)
soap·less [ˈsoplɪs; ˈsouplis] *adj.* ①無肥皂的。②未洗的;骯髒的。
soap opera 逐日連播的廣播劇。
soap plant 有一部分可當肥皂用的植物。
soap powder 清潔粉;肥皂粉。
soap·stone [ˈsopˌston; ˈsoupstoun] *n.* 肥皂石;凍石。
soap·suds [ˈsopˌsʌdz; ˈsoupsʌdz] *n. pl.* 有泡沫的肥皂水。
soap·wort [ˈsopˌwɝt; ˈsoupwəːt] *n.*

【植物】石鹼草屬之植物;石鹼草。
soap·y 〔ˈsopɪ; ˈsoupi〕 *adj.*, **soap·i·er, soap·i·est.** ①爲肥皂或肥皂泡沫所覆蓋的。②含肥皂的。③似肥皂的;圓滑的。④油腔滑調的;甜言蜜語的。⑤有連續廣播劇之味道的。
***soar** 〔sor; sɔː〕 *v.i.* ①翱翔; 高飛。②升騰;升高;高聳。③滑翔。④高唱;高歌。—*v.t.* 飛騰至;經…朝上飛。—*n.* 翱翔;高飛。
sob¹** 〔sɑb; sɔb〕 *v.*, **sobbed, sob·bing,** *n., adj.* —*v.i.* ①嗚咽; 啜泣; 欷歔。She *sobbed* herself to sleep. 她嗚咽而致入睡。②(風等)作類似嗚咽之聲。sob one's heart out*** 哭得死去活來。—*v.t.* ①使啜泣。②以啜泣發洩。 —*n.* 嗚咽;啜泣;欷歔。—*adj.* 〖美俚〗意欲引起憐憫及傷感之情的。
sob² 〔ˈɛˌsoˈbi; ˈeˌsouˈbiː〕 *n.* 狗娘養的;卑鄙傢伙;混蛋(爲 son of a bitch 之略)。(亦作 **s.o.b., S.O.B.**)
so·ber** 〔ˈsobɚ; ˈsoubə〕 *adj.* ①未醉的;清醒的。②適度的; 有節制的。③冷靜的; 審愼的。④端莊的;嚴肅的。⑤樸素的(顏色等)。⑥不誇張的。⑦合理的。⑧能自我控制的。—*v.t. & v.i.* ①(使)清醒。②使沈着;變爲沈着。③使端莊; 變爲端莊; 變爲嚴肅。sober down*** 變冷靜。***sober up*** (or ***off***) 酒醒。—**ly,** *adv.* —**ness,** *n.*
so·ber-mind·ed 〔ˈsobɚˈmaɪndɪd; ˈsoubəˈmaindid〕 *adj.* 頭腦冷靜的。
so·ber·sides 〔ˈsobɚˌsaɪdz; ˈsoubəsaidz〕 *n.* 〖諧〗嚴肅而正經的人。
so·bri·e·ty 〔səˈbraɪətɪ; souˈbraiəti〕 *n., pl.* **-ties.** ①清醒。②節制。③沈着。④端莊; 嚴肅。⑤節酒。
so·bri·quet 〔ˈsobrɪˌke; ˈsoubrikei〕 *n.* 渾名;別名;綽號。(亦作 **soubriquet**)
sob sister 傷感故事作者;傷感消息記者。
sob story 傷感的故事。
Soc. ①Socialist.②Society. **soc.** society.
***so-called** 〔ˈsoˈkɔld; ˈsouˈkɔːld〕 *adj.* 所謂的。We went to see the *so-called* circus. 我們去看所謂的馬戲(意謂不精采)。
***soc·cer** 〔ˈsɑkɚ; ˈsɔkə〕 *n.* 足球。
so·cia·bil·i·ty 〔ˌsoʃəˈbɪlətɪ; ˌsouʃəˈbiliti〕 *n.* ①好交際;友善。②交際行動。
so·cia·ble 〔ˈsoʃəbḷ; ˈsouʃəbl〕 *adj.* ①好交際的; 友善的。②社交的。 —*n.* ①〖美〗非正式的社交集會。②一種S形雙人沙發椅。—**so·cia·bly,** *adv.*
‡so·cial 〔ˈsoʃəl; ˈsouʃəl〕 *adj.* ①社會的。*social* reform. 社會改革。②羣居的。Man is a *social* animal. 人是羣居動物。③社交的;交誼的。He has too little *social* life. 他的社交生活太少。④好交際的;友善的。She has a *social* nature. 她天性好交際。⑤與上流社會有關的。a *social* leader. 社會領袖。⑥社會主義的。⑦性的;性交的。*social* hygiene. 性衞生。⑧有禮貌的。—*n.* 交誼會。
social climber 想盡辦法加入上流社會者;攀高枝者。
Social Credit 〖經濟〗社會債權說。
social dance 社交舞。
social democracy 社會民主主義。
Social Democrat 社會民主黨黨員。
social disease 花柳病(=venereal disease).
social evil ①賣淫(=prostitution). ②對社會有害之事。
social insurance 社會保險。
***so·cial·ism** 〔ˈsoʃəlˌɪzəm; ˈsouʃəlizm〕 *n.* ①社會主義。②社會主義運動。
***so·cial·ist** 〔ˈsoʃəlɪst; ˈsouʃəlist〕 *n.* ①社會主義者。②(S-)社會黨黨員。—*adj.* 社會主義的。a *socialist* state. 社會主義國家。—**ic,** *adj.* —**i·cal·ly,** *adv.*
Socialist Party 社會黨。
so·cial·ite 〔ˈsoʃəˌlaɪt; ˈsouʃəlait〕 *n.* 〖美俗〗社會名流;名士;聞人。
so·ci·al·i·ty 〔ˌsoʃɪˈælətɪ; ˌsouʃiˈæliti〕 *n., pl.* **-ties.** ①社交活動; 社交; 交際。②社交性;羣居性。
so·cial·i·za·tion 〔ˌsoʃələˈzeʃən; ˌsouʃəlaiˈzeiʃən〕 *n.* ①社會化。②社會主義化。
so·cial·ize 〔ˈsoʃəˌlaɪz; ˈsouʃəlaiz〕 *v.*, **-ized, -iz·ing.**—*v.t.* ①使社會化; 使適於社會生活。②使社會主義化; 依照社會主義而設立或管理。③〖教育〗使個人活動成爲羣體活動。—*v.i.* ①參加社會活動。②交際; 來往。
socialized medicine 公醫制度。
so·cial·ly 〔ˈsoʃəlɪ; ˈsouʃəli〕 *adv.* ①在社交上。②社會上。③由社會。
so·cial-mind·ed 〔ˌsoʃəlˈmaɪndɪd; ˌsouʃəlˈmaindid〕 *adj.* 具社會思想的(尤指對社會福利方面);關注社會問題及情況的。
social psychology 社會心理學。
social register 〖美〗社交界名人錄。
social science 社會科學。
social secretary (私人的)社交祕書。
social security ①社會安全制度; 社會生活保障制度。②〖美〗社會生活保障制度下的支給。
social service (or **work**) 社會服務。
social worker 社會服務工作人員。
so·ci·e·tal 〔səˈsaɪətḷ; səˈsaiətəl〕 *adj.* 社會的;與社會有關的。
‡so·ci·e·ty 〔səˈsaɪətɪ; səˈsaiəti〕 *n., pl.* **-ties,** *adj.* —*n.* ①社會。a danger to *society*. 社會之害。②交際; 交往; 社交界。I enjoy your *society*. 我以和你交往爲樂。③會;社; 團體。*Society* of Friends. 教友派。④上流社會。*society* people. 上流社會人士。⑤文明。—*adj.* 社交界的;與社交界有關的。*society* page. 社交版。
society column 社交欄。
so·ci·o·bi·ol·o·gy 〔ˌsosɪobaɪˈɑlədʒɪ; ˌsousiouˌbaiˈɔlədʒi〕 *n.* 社會生物學。
so·ci·o·e·co·nom·ic 〔ˌsosɪəˌikəˈnɑmɪk; ˌsousiəˌiːkəˈnɔmik〕 *adj.* 社會與經濟的。
so·ci·ol·o·gese 〔ˌsosɪˌɑləˈdʒiz; ˌsousiˌɔləˈdʒiːz〕 *n.* 社會學用語。
so·ci·o·log·i·cal 〔ˌsoʃɪəˈlɑdʒɪkḷ; ˌsousjəˈlɔdʒikl〕 *adj.* 社會的;社會學的。—**ly,** *adv.*
so·ci·ol·o·gist 〔ˌsoʃɪˈɑlədʒɪst; ˌsousiˈɔlədʒist〕 *n.* 社會學家。
so·ci·ol·o·gy 〔ˌsoʃɪˈɑlədʒɪ; ˌsousiˈɔlədʒi〕 *n.* ①社會學。②社會學上的分析或敍述。
so·ci·o·po·lit·i·cal 〔ˌsosɪopəˈlɪtɪkḷ; ˌsousioupəˈlitikəl〕 *adj.* 社會與政治的。
so·ci·o·re·li·gious 〔ˌsosɪorɪˈlɪdʒəs; ˌsousiouriˈlidʒəs〕 *adj.* 社會與宗教的。
so·ci·o·tech·no·log·i·cal 〔ˌsosɪoˌtɛknəˈlɑdʒɪkḷ; ˌsousiouˌteknəˈlɔdʒikəl〕 *adj.* 社會與科技的。
***sock¹** 〔sɑk; sɔk〕 *n.* ①短襪。a pair of *socks*. 一雙短襪。②(鞋的)襯底。③古希臘及羅馬喜劇演員所穿之軟鞋。④喜劇。⑤儲金器。
sock² *v.t.* 〖俚〗重擊。***sock away*** 儲蓄;作準備金。***sock in*** 因氣候不佳而停飛。***sock it*** 〖俚〗拚命做; 拚命說。—*n.* 〖俚〗①一擊。②威力。③極爲成功的演出。***give a person socks*** 〖俚〗毆打某人; 在辯論或競爭中擊敗某人。—*adv.* 〖俚〗正着地; 不偏不倚地。—*adj.*

〖俚〗非常成功的。
sock·dol·a·ger [sɑk'dɑlədʒɚ; sɔk-'dɔlədʒə] *n.* 〖俚〗①龐大之物。②決定性的回答或辯論。③致命的一擊。(亦作**sockdologer**)
sock·er ['sɑkɚ;'sɔkə] *n.* 〖英〗=**soccer.**
***sock·et** ['sɑkɪt; 'sɔkit] *n.* ①凹處;承口。②電線之插頭等。—*v.t.* 裝入插頭或承口中。
so·cle ['sɑkl̩; 'sɔkl] *n.* 〖建築〗①承放美術品之方平臺。②承壁之基部。
Soc·ra·tes ['sɑkrə,tiz; 'sɔkrəti:z] *n.* 蘇格拉底 (469–399 B.C., 希臘哲學家)。
So·crat·ic [so'krætɪk; sɔ'krætik] *adj.* 蘇格拉底的;其哲學的。—*n.* 蘇格拉底之門徒。
Socratic method 問答法; 對話法。
sod** [sɑd; sɔd] *n., v.,* **sod·ded, sod·ding.** —*n.* 草地;草皮。be under the sod*** 已被掩埋;在黃泉之下。***the old sod*** 故土;故鄉。—*v.t.* 鋪以草皮。
***so·da** ['sodə; 'soudə] *n.* ①蘇打;碳酸鈉。②蘇打水;汽水。whisky and *soda.* 威士忌蘇打。③發酵粉。④鈉(非正式用法)。
soda ash 蘇打灰。
soda biscuit 蘇打餅乾。(亦作 **soda cracker**)
soda fountain 蘇打水供應器。
soda jerk 〖俚〗在出售飲料與點心之櫃臺後工作者。(亦作 **soda jerker**)
so·dal·i·ty [so'dælətɪ; sou'dæliti] *n., pl.* **-ties.** ①交誼;友誼。②協會;會社;團體。③羅馬天主教之慈善團體。
soda water 蘇打水;汽水。
sod·den ['sɑdn̩; 'sɔdn] *adj.* ①水漬的;浸透的; 漲濕的。②黏而實的 (未烘透的)。③恍惚的;愚蠢的。—*v.t.* ①浸濕。②使變呆;使變愚蠢。—*v.i.* 濕透。
Sod·dy ['sɑdɪ;'sɔdi]*n.* 蘇第(Frederick, 1877–1956, 英國人, 獲1921年諾貝爾化學獎)。
sod·dy ['sɑdɪ;'sɔdi]*adj.,* **sod·di·er, sod·di·est,** *n., pl.* **-dies.** —*adj.* 草皮的;覆有草皮的;草泥的。—*n.* 〖美西部〗草泥小屋。
Sö·der·blom ['sœdɚ,blum; 'sœdə-blum] *n.* 蘇德卜龍 (Nathan, 1866–1931, 瑞典神學家, 獲1930年諾貝爾和平獎)。
so·di·um ['sodɪəm; 'soudjəm] *n.* 〖化〗鈉 (符號爲 Na).
sodium bicarbonate 碳酸氫鈉;重碳酸鈉;小蘇打。
sodium carbonate 碳酸鈉。
sodium chloride 氯化鈉;食鹽。
sodium cyanide 氰化鈉。
sodium hydroxide 氫氧化鈉。
sodium lamp =**sodium-vapor lamp.**
sodium nitrate 硝酸鈉。
sodium silicate 矽酸鈉;偏矽酸鈉。
sodium thiosulfate 硫代硫酸鈉。
sodium-vapor lamp 鈉燈(內充鈉蒸氣之電燈泡, 通以電流則發黃光)。(亦作 **sodium lamp**)
Sod·om ['sɑdəm; 'sɔdəm] *n.* 〖聖經〗所多瑪城(死海邊之城邑名, 上帝以其居民罪惡重大降火盡焚之)。
sod·om·ite ['sɑdəm,aɪt;'sɔdəmait] *n.* ①男色者;雞姦者。②(S-)Sodom 城之居民。
sod·om·y ['sɑdəmɪ; 'sɔdəmi] *n.* 男色;雞姦;獸姦。
so·ev·er [so'ɛvɚ; sou'evə] *adv.* …到任何可想像的程度 (用以加强語氣)。
***so·fa** ['sofə; 'soufə] *n.* 沙發。
sofa bed 可兼用作沙發的兩用牀。
so·far ['sofɑr;'soufɑ:] *n.* 水中測音裝置。
sof·fit ['sɑfɪt; 'sɔfit] *n.* 〖建築〗(樑、拱等之)下邊之一面;下端。

So·fi ['sofɪ; 'soufi] *n.* =**Sufi.**
So·fi·a ['sofɪə, so'fiə; 'soufjə, sou'fi:ə] *n.* 索非亞(保加利亞首都)。(亦作 **Sofiya**)
:soft [sɔft; sɔft] *adj.* ①柔軟的; 軟的。a *soft* bed. 軟床。②軟滑的;細嫩的。*soft* skin. 細嫩的皮膚。③溫和的。a *soft* voice. 溫和的聲音。④不顯的; 柔和的。*soft* light. 柔和的光。⑤弱的; 沒有男人氣概的。⑥愚蠢的。⑦〖語音〗軟音的(如city 中之 c 與 gentle 中之 g 爲軟音, soft sound). ⑧〖俗〗輕鬆的;隨和的。a *soft* job. 一件輕鬆的工作。⑨不險峻的; 徐緩的。⑩透力較低的。*soft* X rays. 軟性 X 射線。⑪紙裝的。***be soft on someone*** 對某人發生愛慕之情。—*adv.* 柔和地; 柔軟地; 安靜地。to speak *softer.* 低聲點說話。—*n.* 柔軟、柔和等之物。—**ly,** *adv.* —**ness,** *n.*
soft·ball ['sɔft,bɔl; 'sɔftbɔ:l] *n.* 壘球。
soft-boiled ['sɔft'bɔɪld; 'sɔft'bɔild] *adj.* 煮得半熟的(蛋)。
soft coal 煙煤;生煤。
soft-cov·er ['sɔft,kʌvɚ; 'sɔft,kʌvə] *adj.* (書)紙裝的;平裝的。
soft currency 準備金不足的貨幣;與其他貨幣兌換時須打折扣的貨幣。
soft drink 不含酒精的飲料。
***soft·en** ['sɔfən; 'sɔfn] *v.t.* ①使變軟;使柔軟。②緩和; 減輕。③使溫柔。④使柔弱。⑤使(價錢)降低。—*v.i.* ①軟化; 變軟。②憐憫;同情;變爲溫柔。③變柔弱。④變不振。
sof·ten·ing ['sɔfənɪŋ; 'sɔfniŋ] *n.* 變軟;軟化。***softening of the brain*** **a.** 〖醫〗腦軟化症。**b.** 呆癡。
soft glances 媚眼;秋波。
soft goods 織物類貨品; 無耐久性之貨品。
soft·head ['sɔft,hɛd; 'sɔfthed] *n.* 愚蠢之人;傻瓜。
soft-head·ed ['sɔft'hɛdɪd; 'sɔft,hedid] *adj.* 愚蠢的。
soft-heart·ed ['sɔft'hɑrtɪd; 'sɔft-'hɑ:tid] *adj.* 心慈的;溫柔的;寬大的。
soft lens 軟性隱形眼鏡。
soft line 溫和路線(尤指政治方面)。
soft loan 利息低而償還期間長的貸款。
soft money 〖美俗〗紙幣。
soft pedal ①柔音踏瓣(使樂器降低音調之踏板)。②〖俗〗抑制之事物。
soft-ped·al [,sɔft'pɛdl̩; 'sɔft'pedl] *v.t. & v.i.,* **-aled, -al·ing.** ①使(樂器)降低音調;使(聲音)降低。②〖俚〗減弱;變低;緩和;減輕。③減少關於…之宣傳或渲染。
soft science 軟性科學(凡社會及行爲科學均屬之, 如政治學、經濟學、社會學及心理學等)。
soft sell 軟式推銷法。
soft sex 女性。
soft-shoe ['sɔft'ʃu; 'sɔft'ʃu:] *adj.* 穿軟底鞋跳踢躂舞的。—*v.i.* 穿軟底鞋跳踢躂舞。
soft soap ①液體或半液體之肥皂。②〖俗〗阿諛之詞;諂媚。
soft-soap ['sɔft'sop; 'sɔft'soup] *v.t. & v.i.* ①用軟肥皂洗。②〖俗〗諂媚。—**er,** *n.*
soft solder (焊接所用之)軟鑞。
soft-spo·ken ['sɔft'spokən; 'sɔft-,spoukn] *adj.* ①說話溫和的。②用溫和聲調說出的。
soft spot (感情上或防衞上之) 弱點。
soft top 可以捲合的帆布汽車頂篷。
soft touch①易利用者。②易擊敗的對手。
soft·ware ['sɔft,wɛr; 'sɔft-wɛə] *n.* ①機械零件等之設計階段。②電腦系統之標準

作業程序。
soft water 軟水。 「*adj.* 愚蠢的。」
soft-wit·ted 〔'sɔft'wɪtɪd; 'sɔft'witid〕」
soft·wood 〔'sɔft,wud; 'sɔft-wud〕 *n.* ①組織鬆軟的木材。②松柏科的林木。—*adj.* 與上述之木材有關的;以上述之木材做成的。
soft·y 〔'sɔftɪ; 'sɔfti〕 *n., pl.* **soft·ies.** 〖俗〗①柔軟之人。②易受騙的人;愚人。
sog·gi·ness 〔'sagɪnɪs; 'sɔginis〕 *n.* ①濕;濡濕。②愚蠢;遲鈍。
sog·gy 〔'sagɪ; 'sɔgi〕 *adj.*, **-gi·er, -gi·est.** ①濕透的;濡濕的。②黏而濕的;未烘透的;生的(麪包等)。③遲鈍的;愚蠢的;沒精打采的。
So·ho 〔so'ho; sou'hou〕 *n.* 倫敦的一區(以多餐館著稱)。 「步的聲音。」
so·ho 〔so'ho; sou'hou〕 *interj.* 喝馬使止」
soi-di·sant 〔swadi'zɑ̃; swadi:'zɑ̃〕〖法〗 *adj.* 自稱的;自命的。
soi·gné 〔swa'nje; swa'njei〕〖法〗 *adj.* 被細心照料的;整齊的;整潔的。
‡**soil**[1] 〔sɔɪl; sɔil〕 *n.* ①土壤;土。poor (rich) *soil.* 貧瘠(肥沃)的土壤。②土地;國。one's native *soil.* 故鄉;祖國。③溫床;生育地。
soil**[2] *v.t.* ①汚損;弄髒。②汚辱;玷汚。—*v.i.* 變汚;變髒。refuse to soil one's hands*** **a.** 不肯弄髒自己的手。**b.** 不肯做卑鄙或不榮譽的事情。—*n.* ①汚穢;汚點。②汚物。③糞便;堆肥。 「馬)瀉糞。」
soil[3] *v.t.* 以青草餵(牛馬);餵以青草使(牛」
soil·less 〔'sɔɪllɪs; 'sɔillis〕 *adj.* ①無土壤的。②無汚垢的。
soil pipe 地下排水管;汚水管。
soil science 土壤學。
soi·rée 〔swɑ're; 'swɑ:rei〕 *n.* 晚會。
so·ja 〔'sodʒə; 'soujə〕 *n.* ①大豆;黃豆。②醬油。***soja bean*** 大豆;黃豆。
***so·journ** 〔*n.* 'sodʒɜn; 'sɔdʒə:n *v.* so'dʒɜn, 'sodʒɜn; 'sɔdʒə:n〕 *n.* 逗留;寄居。—*v.i.* 逗留;寄居。to *sojourn* at an inn. 寄居在旅館。 「逗留者;寄居者。」
so·journ·er 〔'sodʒɜnɚ; 'sɔdʒə:nə〕 *n.*」
soke 〔sok; souk〕 *n.*〖英史〗裁判權;司法權;施行裁判權之區域。 「〖煉金〗黃金。」
Sol 〔sal; sɔl〕 *n.* ①太陽神。②太陽。③」
sol[1] 〔sol; soul〕 *n.*〖音樂〗全音階的長音階之第五音。 「之一種銀幣。」
sol[2] 〔sol; soul〕 *n., pl.* **sols, soles.** 秘魯」
sol[3] 〔sal; sɔl〕 *n.*〖化〗溶膠。
Sol. ①Solicitor. ②Solomon. **sol.** ①solicitor. ②soluble. ③solution. ④soldier. ⑤solenoid. **S.O.L.** strictly out of luck.〖俚〗運氣不佳;倒霉。
so·la[1] 〔'solə; 'soulə〕 *n.* ①〖植物〗(熱帶所產)合萌屬植物(莖中有木髓,可製遮陽盔帽)。②此種植物木髓所做之盔帽。(亦作 **shola**)
so·la[2] 〖拉〗 *adj.* feminine of **solus.**
sol·ace 〔'salɪs, -əs; 'sɔləs, -lis〕 *n., v.,* **-aced, -ac·ing.** —*n.* 安慰;慰藉。—*v.t.* ①安慰;慰藉。to *solace* oneself with a book. 以書籍自遣。②(以安慰)減輕。
sola check 單張匯票。(略作 SOLA)
so·lan 〔'solən; 'soulən〕 *n.*〖動物〗塘鵝。(亦作 **solan goose**)
***so·lar** 〔'solɚ; 'soulə〕 *adj.* ①太陽的。②與太陽有關的。③從太陽來的。④藉太陽的光或熱之作用而工作或運轉的。a *solar* engine. 藉太陽熱作用而運轉的引擎。—*n.* 日光浴室。
solar battery 太陽電池。
solar cell 太陽電池。
solar day 太陽日。
solar eclipse 日蝕。 「設計的房屋。」
solar house 爲吸收並保留日光熱度而」
so·lar·ism 〔'solərɪzm; 'soulərizm〕 *n.* 太陽神話中心說。
so·lar·i·um 〔so'lɛrɪəm; sou'lɛəriəm〕 *n., pl.* **-i·a** 〔-ɪə; -iə〕. 日光浴室。
so·lar·ize 〔'solə,raɪz; 'souləraiz〕 *v.,* **-ized, -iz·ing.** —*v.t.* ①使受日光之作用。②過曝(照相底片)。③根據太陽神話中心說加以解釋。—*v.i.* 過曝而受損傷;曝光過久。—**so·lar·i·za·tion,** *n.*
solar month 一年的十二個月之一。
solar plexus 〖解剖〗胃後方的太陽神」
solar system 太陽系。 「經叢。」
solar year 太陽年(約三百六十五日五時四十八分四十六秒)。
so·la·ti·um 〔so'leʃɪəm; sou'leiʃiəm〕 *n., pl.* **-ti·a** 〔-ʃɪə; -ʃiə〕. 賠償;慰藉物;賠償物;安慰金。
***sold** 〔sold; sould〕 *v.* pt. & pp. of **sell.**
sol·der 〔'sadɚ; 'sɔldə〕 *n.* ①合金;白鑞;焊藥;焊料。②接合物。—*v.t.* ①以白鑞修補或焊接。②結合。—*v.i.* ①焊合;接合。②被」
soldering iron 電焊棒。 「焊。」
soldering paste 焊漿。
‡**sol·dier** 〔'soldʒɚ; 'souldʒə〕 *n.* ①軍人。②士兵。③軍事家。④爲任何目標而奮鬥之人。⑤〖動物〗一種頭及口特大之工蟻;一種大頭白蟻。***an old soldier*** **a.** 老兵。**b.** 以詭計達其目的者。—*v.i.* ①當兵。②〖俗〗逃避職責。
soldier color 〖美〗全部一色。
soldier crab 〖動物〗寄居蟹。
sol·dier·like 〔'soldʒɚ,laɪk; 'souldʒə-laik〕 *adj.* =**soldierly.**
sol·dier·ly 〔'soldʒɚlɪ; 'souldʒəli〕 *adj.* 像軍人的;適於軍人的;勇敢的;英勇的。
soldier of fortune ①以金錢、冒險或享樂爲從軍目的而不論所服役之政府者;軍事冒險者。②追求財富或享樂等的冒險家。
sol·dier·ship 〔'soldʒɚ,ʃɪp; 'souldʒə-ʃip〕 *n.* ①軍人之身分、地位、精神等。②武略;兵學;軍事手腕。 「所;榮民之家。」
soldiers' home 〖美〗退役軍人招待」
soldier's wind 〖航海〗順風;側風。
sol·dier·y 〔'soldʒərɪ; 'souldʒəri〕 *n.* ①軍人(集合稱);軍隊。②軍事訓練;軍事知識。
sol·do 〔'saldo; 'sɔldou〕 *n., pl.* **-di** 〔-di; -di:〕. 義大利之銅幣名(等於1/20里拉)。
sold-out 〔'sold,aut; 'souldaut〕 *adj.* 完全售罄的。 「品供不應求的。」
sold-up 〔'sold,ʌp; 'sould'ʌp〕 *adj.* 產」
***sole**[1] 〔sol; soul〕 *adj.* ①唯一的;獨一的。the *sole* heir. 唯一的繼承人。②僅有的。③專用的。the *sole* right of use. 專用權。④單獨進行的。⑤單獨的;獨自的。—**ness,** *n.*
***sole**[2] *n., v.,* **soled, sol·ing.** —*n.* ①脚掌;蹠。②鞋底;靴底。③底部。④高爾夫球棒之下端。—*v.t.* ①上以鞋底;配以鞋底。②將高爾夫球球棒的下端在球後面觸地。
sole[3] *n., pl.* **soles, sole.** 鰈(魚)。
sol·e·cism 〔'salə,sɪzəm; 'sɔlisizm〕 *n.* ①違反語法;文法錯誤。②舉止失態;失禮;背理。 「反文法的人。②失禮者。」
sol·e·cist 〔'salɪsɪst; 'sɔlisist〕 *n.* ①違」
sol·e·cis·tic 〔,salɪ'sɪstɪk; ,sɔli'sistik〕 *adj.* ①違反文法或語法的。②失禮的。
***sole·ly** 〔'sollɪ; 'soulli〕 *adv.* 唯一地;單獨地;祇。I am *solely* responsible.我獨自負責。
***sol·emn** 〔'saləm; 'sɔləm〕 *adj.* ①嚴肅的;莊重的。a *solemn* warning. 嚴正警告。

②鄭重的;莊嚴的。③合於儀式的;神聖的。④陰沉的;幽暗的。⑤法律上正確的。—**ness,** *n.*

so·lem·ni·ty [sə'lɛmnətɪ; sə'lemniti] *n., pl.* **-ties.** ①莊嚴;嚴肅。②(常*pl.*)莊嚴的儀式。③〖法律〗使契約等生效而須做的手續。

sol·em·ni·za·tion [ˌsɑləmnəˈzeʃən; ˌsɔləmnaiˈzeiʃən] *n.* ①儀式;舉行儀式。②莊嚴化。

sol·em·nize [ˈsɑləmˌnaɪz; ˈsɔləmnaiz] *v.t.,* **-nized, -niz·ing.** ①以莊嚴儀式慶祝。②舉行(儀式)。③使嚴肅;使端莊。

sol·emn·ly [ˈsɑləmlɪ; ˈsɔləmli] *adv.* 莊嚴地;嚴肅地;鄭重地。

solemn mass 〖宗教〗盛式彌撒。

solemn vow 〖宗教〗盛式誓願。

so·len [ˈsolən; ˈsoulən] *n.* ①〖解剖〗管;脊椎管。②〖動物〗馬蛤;竹蟶(貝介類)。

so·le·noid [ˈsoləˌnɔɪd; ˈsoulinɔid] *n.* 〖電〗螺線管;螺形線圈。

sole·plate [ˈsolˌplet; ˈsoulpleit] *n.* 〖機械〗底板。

sol-fa [solˈfɑ; sɔlˈfɑː] *n.* ①全音階唱名(即 do, re, mi, fa, sol, la, ti, do)。②以全音階唱名所作的聲音練習。 —*v.t. & v.i.* 用全音階唱名歌唱。—*adj.* 使用全音階唱名的。

sol·feg·gi·o [sɑlˈfɛdʒo; sɔlˈfedʒiou] *n., pl.* **-gi** [-dʒi; -dʒiː]. 〖音樂〗視唱練習。

so·li [ˈsoli; ˈsouliː] *n.* pl. of **solo.**

***so·lic·it** [səˈlɪsɪt; səˈlisit] *v.t. & v.i.* ①懇求;請求。to *solicit* a person for help. 懇求某人幫助。②教唆;引誘。③促起。④吸引。

so·lic·i·tant [səˈlɪsətənt; səˈlisitənt] *n.* 懇求者;請求者。—*adj.* 懇求的;請求的。

so·lic·i·ta·tion [səˌlɪsəˈteʃən; səˌlisiˈteiʃən] *n.* ①懇求;請求。②教唆;引誘;誘惑。

so·lic·i·tor [səˈlɪsətɚ; səˈlisitə] *n.* ①懇求者。②律師。③城市或州之地方法律官。

solicitor general ①副檢察長。②〖美〗(無檢察長之州之)首席檢察官。

so·lic·it·ous [səˈlɪsɪtəs; səˈlisitəs] *adj.* ①懸慮的;焦慮的;掛念的。②渴望的;熱望的;切望的。③講究的;細心的。 —**ly,** *adv.*

so·lic·i·tude [səˈlɪsəˌtjud; səˈlisitjuːd] *n.* ①懸慮;焦慮;掛念。②(*pl.*)懸慮之原因。

***sol·id** [ˈsɑlɪd; ˈsɔlid] *adj.* ①固體的。*solid* food. 固體食物。②立體的;立方體的。③堅實的;可靠的。a *solid* house. 堅固的房屋。④實心的;充實的。⑤純粹的;齊一的。*solid* silver (gold). 純銀(金)。⑥一致的;團結的。 a *solid* vote. 一致的選擧。⑦完整的;連續的。 He spent two *solid* hours on his arithmetic. 他作算術足足花了兩個鐘頭。⑧實質的;純的。⑨眞正的。⑩內容充實的;明達的。⑪經濟穩固的。a *solid* business. 一個經濟穩固的商號。⑫空間很少的。⑬沒有連字符號(hyphen)的;排字排得很緊的。⑭〖俚〗友善的(前面常用 in)。to get in *solid* with one's employer. 取得老板的歡心。⑮〖俚〗第一流的;很棒的。⑯徹底的;有力的;直截了當的。 —*n.* ①固體。②立體。③(溶液中之)固體物質。—**ly,** *adv.* —**ness,** *n.*

sol·i·da·rist [ˈsɑlədərɪst; ˈsɔlidərist] *n.* 社會連帶主義者。

sol·i·dar·i·ty [ˌsɑləˈdærətɪ; ˌsɔliˈdæriti] *n., pl.* **-ties.** 團結。

sol·i·da·rize [ˈsɑlɪdəˌraɪz; ˈsɔlidəraiz] *v.i.,* **-rized, -riz·ing.** 團結。

solid fuel 固體燃料。

solid geometry 立體幾何。

so·lid·i·fy [səˈlɪdəˌfaɪ; səˈlidifai] *v.,* **-fied, -fy·ing.** —*v.t.* ①使凝固;使堅硬;使成固體。②使一致;使團結。③使成結晶。④予以充實。—*v.i.* ①凝固;變爲堅硬。②成爲晶體。③團結一起。 —**so·lid·i·fi·ca·tion,** *n.*

solidifying point 〖物理〗凝點。

so·lid·i·ty [səˈlɪdətɪ; səˈliditi] *n., pl.* **-ties.** ①堅實性;固體性。②實質。③殷實可靠性。④〖數學〗體積。⑤固體。

solid rocket 用固體燃料推進的火箭。

Solid South (美國民主黨地盤鞏固之)南方諸州。

sol·id-state [ˈsɑlɪdˈstet; ˈsɔlidˈsteit] *adj.* 固態物理的;固態電子學的;電子裝置(如電晶體、礦石等)的;全晶體的。

solid-state electronics 固態電子學。

solid-state physics 固態物理學。

sol·i·dus [ˈsɑlɪdəs; ˈsɔlidəs] *n., pl.* **-di** [-ˌdaɪ; -dai]. ①斜線(即/)。②〖物理〗固態。

sol·i·fid·i·an [ˌsɑlɪˈfɪdɪən; ˌsɔliˈfidiən] *n.* 〖神學〗唯信說者。—*adj.* 唯信說(者)的。

sol·i·fid·i·an·ism [ˌsɑlɪˈfɪdɪənɪzm̩; ˌsɔliˈfidiənizm] *n.* 〖神學〗唯信說。

so·lil·o·quist [səˈlɪləkwɪst; səˈliləkwist] *n.* 獨語者;獨白者。

so·lil·o·quize [səˈlɪləˌkwaɪz; səˈliləkwaiz] *v.,* **-quized, -quiz·ing.** —*v.i.* 自言自語;獨語;獨白。—*v.t.* 自言自語地說。

so·lil·o·quy [səˈlɪləkwɪ; səˈliləkwi] *n., pl.* **-quies.** ①自言自語。②〖戲劇〗獨白。

sol·i·ped [ˈsɑlɪpɛd; ˈsɔliped] *n.* 〖動物〗單蹄獸(如馬等)。—*adj.* 〖動物〗單蹄獸的。

sol·ip·sism [ˈsɑlɪpsɪzm̩; ˈsɔlipsizm] *n.* 〖哲學〗唯我論。 —**sol·ip·sist,** *n.*

sol·i·taire [ˌsɑləˈtɛr; ˌsɔliˈtɛə] *n.* ①獨粒寶石;鑲嵌於戒指等裝飾品的單粒鑽石。②一人獨玩之紙牌戲;單人球戲。③隱居者。

sol·i·tar·y** [ˈsɑləˌtɛrɪ; ˈsɔlitəri] *adj., n., pl.* **-tar·ies.** —*adj.* ①單一的;唯一的。②孤獨的。③幽寂的;人跡罕到的。④〖動物〗單獨生活的。⑤〖植物〗單獨生長的。solitary confinement*** 單獨拘禁。 —*n.* ①孤獨生活的人。②被遺棄的人。 ③單獨拘禁。 The prisoner was put in *solitary.* 那犯人被單獨拘禁。—**sol·i·tar·i·ly,** *adv.*

***sol·i·tude** [ˈsɑləˌtjud; ˈsɔlitjuːd] *n.* ①孤獨;單獨;獨居;孤寂。②荒僻之地;人跡罕到之所。to live in *solitude.* 獨居。

sol·mi·za·tion [ˌsɑlmɪˈzeʃən; ˌsɔlmiˈzeiʃən] *n.* 〖音樂〗階名唱法。

***so·lo** [ˈsolo; ˈsoulou] *n., pl.* **-los, -li** [-li; -liː], *adj., v.,* **-loed, -lo·ing,** *adv.* —*n.* ①獨唱曲;獨奏樂;獨唱;獨奏。②單獨表演;獨作。—*adj.* 單獨的。a *solo* part. 獨奏(唱)部分。—*v.i.* (飛行教練中)放單飛。—*adv.* 單獨地。

so·lo·ist [ˈsoˌloɪst; ˈsoulouist] *n.* 獨唱者;獨奏者。

so·lo·is·tic [ˌsoloˈɪstɪk; ˌsoulouˈistik] *adj.* 獨唱或獨奏的;與獨唱或獨奏有關的。

Sol·o·mon [ˈsɑləmən; ˈsɔləmən] *n.* ①所羅門王(聖經記述之 Israel 的賢明國王)。②大智者;大賢人;聖人。***the Book of the Wisdom of Solomon*** 〖聖經〗所羅門智慧篇。***the Song(s) of Solomon*** 〖聖經〗雅歌。

Solomon's seal 六線形"✡"。

so long 〖俗〗再見 (=good-by).

sol·stice [ˈsɑlstɪs; ˈsɔlstis] *n.* ①〖天文〗至;至日。 summer *solstice.* 夏至。winter *solstice.* 多至。②〖天文〗二至點。③最遠點。

sol·sti·tial [sɑlˈstɪʃəl; sɔlˈstiʃəl] *adj.* ①至的;(尤指)夏至的。②在夏至或多至的。

sol·u·bil·i·ty [ˌsɑljəˈbɪlətɪ; ˌsɔljuˈbiliti〕 *n.*, *pl.* -ties. ①可溶性;溶解性;溶解度。②可解決之性質。

sol·u·ble 〔'saljəbl; 'sɔljubl〕 *adj.* ①可溶解的。②可解決的。③可解釋的。—*n.* 可溶物質。

so·lu·nar 〔sə'lunə; sə'lu:nə〕 *adj.* 日月的共同作用所造成的。

so·lus 〔'soləs; 'souləs〕〖拉〗 *adj.* 單獨的。

sol·ute 〔'saljut; 'sɔlju:t〕 *n.* 〖化〗溶質。—*adj.* ①溶解的; 呈溶液狀態的。②〖植物〗游離的;分離的。

***so·lu·tion** 〔sə'luʃən; sə'lu:ʃən〕 *n.* ①解決;解答。②解釋。③溶解;分解。④溶液。⑤分散。⑥〖醫〗 **a.** 疾病之終止。 **b.** 疾病之危機。

so·lu·tion·ist 〔sə'luʃənɪst; sə'lu:ʃənist〕 *n.* 解答者;解答專家。

sol·u·tiz·er 〔'saljə,taɪzə; 'sɔljutaizə〕 *n.* 助溶劑。

solv·a·bil·i·ty 〔,salvə'bɪlətɪ; ,sɔlvə'biliti〕 *n.* 能解決;能闡明;溶解性。

solv·a·ble 〔'salvəbl; 'sɔlvəbl〕 *adj.* ①可解決的;可解答的;可闡明的。②可溶解的。

***solve** 〔salv; sɔlv〕 *v.t.*, **solved, solv·ing.** ①解釋;解答;解決。to *solve* a problem in mathematics. 解答數學題。②付給;償付。③溶解。

sol·ven·cy 〔'salvənsɪ;'sɔlvənsi〕*n.*, *pl.* **-cies.** ①償清全部債務之能力。②溶解力。

sol·vent 〔'salvənt; 'sɔlvənt〕 *adj.* ①能償債的。②有溶解力的。③有緩和力量的。—*n.* ①溶劑;溶媒。②解釋物; 闡明物。③緩和之物;減弱之物。④解決法。

Sol·zhe·ni·tsyn 〔,solʒə'nitsən; ,soulʒə'ni:tsən〕 *n.* 索忍尼辛 (Aleksandr Isayevich, 1918—, 蘇聯小說家, 曾獲1970年諾貝爾文學獎)。

so·ma 〔'somə; 'soumə〕 *n.*, *pl.* **-ma·ta** 〔-mətə; -mətə〕. 〖生物〗體幹。

So·ma·li 〔so'malɪ; sə'ma:li〕 *n.*, *pl.* **-li, -lis.** ①索馬利人。②索馬利語。

So·ma·li·a 〔sə'malɪə; sə'ma:liə〕 *n.* 索馬利亞(東非一國家, 首都 Mogadiscio)。

So·ma·li·an 〔sə'malɪən; sə'ma:liən〕 *adj.* ①索馬利亞的。②索馬利亞人的。—*n.* 索馬利亞人。

So·ma·li·land 〔sə'malɪ,lænd;sə'ma:lilænd〕 *n.* 索馬利蘭(東非之一地區)。

so·mat·ic 〔so'mætɪk; sou'mætik〕 *adj.* ①身體的;肉體的。②〖解剖〗 體幹的;軀幹的;身體之本體的。

somatic cell 體細胞。

so·ma·tol·o·gy 〔,somə'talədʒɪ;,soumə'tɔlədʒi〕 *n.* ①人體論;體質論。②有機體性質論;生體學。

***som·ber, som·bre** 〔'sambə; 'sɔmbə〕 *adj.* ①陰沈的; 幽暗的。②憂鬱的; 鬱悶的。③暗色的。 **—ly,** *adv.*

som·bre·ro 〔sam'brero; sɔm'brεərou〕 *n.*, *pl.* **-ros.** (西班牙、墨西哥及美國西南部等地人所戴的)一種闊邊帽。

som·brous 〔'sambrəs;'sɔmbrəs〕 *adj.* 〖古,詩〗 =**somber.**

‡**some** 〔'sʌm, ,sʌm, səm, sm̩; sʌm, səm, sm〕 *adj.* ①少許;一些; 少數(用於不可數之名詞、複數名詞或名詞代用語之前,甚少用於疑問句及條件句中,絕對不能用於否定句中,否定句應用 any)。 Give me *some* money, please. 請給我一些錢。Will you buy *some* stamps? 你要買些郵票嗎? ②某些; 有些。*Some* wood is soft. 有些木頭是軟的。③某一;一個;任一;某種的(通常用於單數名詞或名詞代用語之前)。He went to *some* place in Africa. 他到非洲某地去了。④大約的。We waited *some* 20 minutes. 我們等了大約二十分鐘。⑤〖美俗〗好的;大的。 Boy, this is *some* soup! 啊, 這眞是好湯! ***and then some*** 〖俚〗遠不止於此;此外尙有更多。***some day*** 來日;他日;在將來的某時。***some day or other*** 遲早。—*pron.* 若干;一部分;少數;少許。*Some* of the boys were early and *some* of them were late. 有些男孩子早到,有些則晚了。—*adv.* ①〖俗〗稍;略 (=somewhat). He is *some* better today. 他今天稍好些了。②〖美俗〗 極爲。 That's going *some!* 那眞不得了!

-some 〖字尾〗①表"某種傾向"之形容詞字尾(如 awesome)。②與數字相接的集合字尾(如 twosome)。③表"體"之義。

***some·bod·y** 〔'sʌm,badɪ, -,bʌdɪ, 'sʌmbədɪ; 'sʌmbədi, -bɔdi, -bdi〕 *pron.*, *n.*, *pl.* **-bod·ies.** ①有人;某人。 There's *somebody* who wants to speak to you. 有人要同你講話。②重要人物。 He thinks he's *somebody,* but really he's nobody. 他自以爲是個了不起的人, 但是實際上却是個小角色。

some·day 〔'səm,de; 'sʌmdei〕 *adv.* 來日;將來總有一天。

some·how** 〔'sʌm,hau; 'sʌmhau〕 *adv.* 以某種方法;未知如何。 I must get it finished *somehow.* 我必設法將其完成。somehow or other*** 設法;藉某種方法。

‡**some·one** 〔'sʌm,wʌn;'sʌmwʌn〕 *pron.* 有人;某人。*Someone* has to lock up the house. 總得有人把這房屋鎖起來。

some·place 〔'sʌmples; 'sʌmpleis〕 *adv.* 在某處。

som·er·sault 〔'sʌmə,sɔlt; 'sʌməsɔ:lt〕 *n.* ①觔斗。to turn a *somersault.* 翻觔斗。②意見之徹底轉變。 —*v.i.* 翻觔斗。(亦作 **summersault**)

som·er·set 〔'sʌmə,set; 'sʌməset〕 *n.*, *v.i.* =**somersault.**

‡**some·thing** 〔'sʌmpθɪŋ,'sʌmθɪŋ;'sʌmθiŋ, -mpθ-〕 *pron.* ①某事; 某物。 There was *something* (that) I wanted to show you. 我有一樣東西要給你看。②若干;幾分。He is *something* of a scholar. 他略有學問。③重要之事物。 He thinks he's *something.* 他認爲他了不起。④該類事物。 He's a wool merchant or *something.* 他是個羊毛商之類的人。***something for nothing*** 不勞而獲。***something like*** 大約。—*adv.* ①稍;略。*something* like two o'clock. 大約兩點鐘光景。②非常地。He swears *something* awful. 他咒罵得很厲害。—*n.* ①某事;某物。 I felt the presence of an unknown *something.* 我感覺到了不可知的某物之存在。②有價值或重要之人或物。 He is really *something!* 他眞是個了不起的人!

***some·time** 〔'sʌm,taɪm; 'sʌmtaim〕 *adv.* ①來日;改天。Come over and see me *sometime.* 改天有時間, 請過來看我。②某時。 It happened *sometime* last month. 此事發生在上月某一個時候。 —*adj.* ①以前的;昔時的。 Miss Lee was a *sometime* pupil of our school. 李小姐是本校從前的一個學生。②不可靠的。

‡**some·times** 〔'sʌm,taɪmz, sʌm'taɪmz, səm'taɪmz; 'sʌmtaimz, səm'taimz〕 *adv.* 有時; 間或。 *Sometimes* he does it this way and *sometimes* he does it that

way. 他有時這樣做, 有時那樣做。
some·way(s) [ˈsʌmˌwe(z); ˈsʌmwei(z)] *adv.* 以某種方法。(亦作**some way**)
‡some·what [ˈsʌmˌhwɑt, ˈsʌmhwət; ˈsʌmwɔt, -mhw-] *adv.* 有幾分; 略。The earth is *somewhat* round. 地球是略帶圓形的。—*pron.* 幾分。He is *somewhat* of a musician. 他可算是音樂家。—*n.* ①某分量; 某程度; 某東西。②重要或有價值之人或事物。
‡some·where [ˈsʌmˌhwɛr, -ˌhwær; ˈsʌmwɛə, -mhw-] *adv.* ①在某處。He lives *somewhere* in the neighborhood. 他住在附近某處。②在某時。③往某處; 向某地。④到較滿意的境界。⑤大約。*somewhere* about nine o'clock. 大約九點鐘。—*n.* 某地。
som·nam·bu·lant [sɑmˈnæmbjələnt; sɔmˈnæmbjulənt] *adj.* 有夢遊習慣的; 患夢遊症的。
som·nam·bu·lar [sɑmˈnæmbjələ; sɔmˈnæmbjulə] *adj.* 夢遊症的。
som·nam·bu·late [sɑmˈnæmbjəˌlet; sɔmˈnæmbjuleit] *v.*, **-lat·ed, -lat·ing.** —*v.i.* 夢遊。—*v.t.* 夢中走過; 夢遊。
som·nam·bule [sɑmˈnæmbjul; sɔmˈnæmbjuːl] *n.* 夢遊症患者。
som·nam·bu·lism [sɑmˈnæmbjəˌlɪzəm; sɔmˈnæmbjulizm] *n.* 夢遊症。***artificial somnambulism*** 催眠術。
som·nam·bu·list [sɑmˈnæmbjəlɪst; sɔmˈnæmbjulist] *n.* 夢遊者。
somni- 〖字首〗表"睡眠"之義。
som·ni·fa·cient [ˌsɑmnəˈfeʃənt; ˌsɔmniˈfeiʃənt] *n.* 催眠劑。—*adj.* 催眠的。
som·nif·er·ous [sɑmˈnɪfərəs; sɔmˈnifərəs] *adj.* ①致睡的; 催眠的。②昏昏欲睡的; 有睡意的。
som·nil·o·quy [sɑmˈnɪləkwɪ; sɔmˈniləkwi] *n.* ①說夢話。②作囈語之習慣。
som·no·lence [ˈsɑmnələns; ˈsɔmnələns] *n.* 想睡; 瞌睡; 嗜眠狀態; 幻夢。(亦作 **somnolency**)
som·no·lent [ˈsɑmnələnt; ˈsɔmnələnt] *adj.* ①思睡的; 欲眠的。②促睡的; 催眠的。③似在夢鄉中的。
‡son [sʌn; sʌn] *n.* ①兒子。②子孫。③孩子(年長者或牧師對年輕人的稱呼)。④女婿。⑤擁戴者。*sons* of liberty. 自由的擁戴者。⑥(S-)〖天主教〗聖子(三位一體之第二位)。
so·nance [ˈsonəns; ˈsounəns] *n.* ①有聲音之性質或狀態。②〖古〗聲音; 音調。(亦作 **sonancy**)
son and heir 嗣子。
so·nant [ˈsonənt; ˈsounənt] *adj.* ①聲音的; 有聲響的。②〖語音〗有聲的。—*n.* ①〖語音〗音節主音。②有聲之音(voiced sound). ③〖語音〗=**sonorant.**
so·nar [ˈsonɑr; ˈsounɑː] *n.* 聲納(軍艦用以偵測潛艇之儀器, 爲*so*und *na*vigation *r*anging 之略)。
so·na·ta [səˈnɑtə; səˈnɑːtə] *n.* 〖音樂〗奏鳴曲。
so·na·ti·na [ˌsɑnəˈtinə; ˌsɔnəˈtiːnə] *n., pl.* **-nas, -ne** [-ne; -nei]. 〖音樂〗小奏鳴曲。
‡song [sɔŋ; sɔŋ] *n.* ①歌; 詩; 曲。a *song* of praise. 讚美歌。②歌唱; 鳴聲。The bird burst into *song*. 鳥歌唱。③低價。④老花樣; 老調子。***for a song*** 以極低的代價。***nothing to make a song about*** 不值得爲之麻煩的; 不重要的。***not worth an old song*** 沒有價值。***song and dance*** 〖美俚〗花言巧語的解釋。
song·bird [ˈsɔŋˌbɝd; ˈsɔŋbəːd] *n.* ①鳴禽。②女歌手。
song·book [ˈsɔŋˌbuk; ˈsɔŋbuk] *n.* 歌集; 歌謠集。
song·fest [ˈsɔŋfɛst; ˈsɔŋfest] *n.* 非正式之音樂會或歌唱聚會。
song·ful [ˈsɔŋfəl; ˈsɔŋfəl] *adj.* 富於歌曲的; 旋律悅耳的。—**ly,** *adv.* —**ness,** *n.*
song·less [ˈsɔŋlɪs; ˈsɔŋlis] *adj.* 不唱的; 不能唱的。—**ly,** *adv.*
song sparrow 一種雀科鳴禽。
song·ster [ˈsɔŋstə; ˈsɔŋstə] *n.* ①歌者。②詩歌之作者。③鳴禽; 鳴鳥。
song·stress [ˈsɔŋstrɪs; ˈsɔŋstris] *n.* 女歌手; 女作歌者; 女詩人。
song thrush 畫眉鳥。
song·writ·er [ˈsɔŋˌraɪtə; ˈsɔŋˌraitə] *n.* 流行歌曲作家。
son·ic [ˈsɑnɪk; ˈsɔnik] *adj.* 音的; 音波的; 音速的。
sonic barrier 〖物理〗音速障礙。
sonic boom 音爆。
sonic depth finder 一種海洋測深儀。
sonic mine 音感水雷。
son·ics [ˈsɑnɪks; ˈsɔniks] *n.* (作*sing.* 解)實用音響學。
sonic speed 音速。
so·nif·er·ous [soˈnɪfərəs; souˈnifərəs] *adj.* 傳聲的; 發音的。
son-in-law [ˈsʌnɪnˌlɔ; ˈsʌninlɔː] *n., pl.* **sons-in-law.** 婿。
son·less [ˈsʌnlɪs; ˈsʌnlis] *adj.* 無子的。
***son·net** [ˈsɑnɪt; ˈsɔnit] *n.* 十四行詩。
son·net·eer [ˌsɑnəˈtɪr; ˌsɔniˈtiə] *n.* ①十四行詩作者; 短詩作者。②劣等詩人。—*v.t.* & *v.i.* 作十四行詩。
son·net·ist [ˈsɑnətɪst; ˈsɔnitist] *n.* 十四行詩作者。
son·net·ry [ˈsɑnətrɪ; ˈsɔnitri] *n.* 十四行詩(集合稱)。
son·ny [ˈsʌnɪ; ˈsʌni] *n., pl.* **-nies.** 寶寶; 乖兒。
son·o·buoy [ˈsɑnəˌbɔɪ; ˈsɔnəbɔi] *n.* 無線電深水音響偵測浮標(偵察潛艇用)。
son of a bitch *pl.* **sons of bitches.** ①狗娘養的; 王八蛋; 卑鄙的傢伙(略作 **S. O. B.**). ②討厭之事; 苦差。③表示不耐煩、驚異、不高興等之感歎詞。
son of Adam 男人; 男孩。
son of a gun *pl.* **sons of guns.** ①歹徒; 流氓。②討厭之事; 苦差。③表示親暱的招呼。④表示不耐煩、驚奇、不悅等的感歎詞。
Son of God 耶穌基督; 救世主; 聖子。
Son of Heaven (中國往時之)天子。
son of man ①人; 必有一死者。②(有時 S- of M-) 耶穌基督之別稱。
son of toil 勞動者。
so·no·graph [ˈsɑnəˌgræf; ˈsounəgrɑːf] *n.* 錄聲器。
so·nom·e·ter [soˈnɑmətə; souˈnɔmitə] *n.* ①弦音計。②聽力計。
so·no·rant [səˈnorənt; səˈnɔːrənt] *n.* 〖語音〗可作音節主音之子音(如 l, r, m, n, y, w).
son·o·rif·ic [ˌsɑnəˈrɪfɪk; ˌsɔnəˈrifik] *adj.* 發音的; 發音響的。
so·nor·i·ty [səˈnɔrətɪ; səˈnɔriti] *n., pl.* **-ties.** 響亮。
so·no·rous [səˈnorəs; səˈnɔːrəs] *adj.* ①發宏亮聲音的。②響亮的; 宏亮的。③浮誇的; 華麗的。—**ly,** *adv.* —**ness,** *n.*
‡soon [sun; suːn] *adv.* ①即刻; 不久。He will *soon* be back. 他馬上就回來。②早; 快。What makes you come so *soon*? 你怎麼來得這樣早? ③寧願(=rather). He would

sooner die than consent to such a plan. 他寧死也不肯同意這計畫。④較早。Spring came *soon* this year. 今年春天來得較早。***as soon as*** 即刻。Come *as soon as* possible. 儘可能地早來。***had sooner*** 寧可；寧願。***Least said, soonest mended.***〖諺〗話少易了(爭論中少說話，則事情容易解決)。***no sooner ... than*** 剛…就。*No sooner* said *than* done. 說了就做。***sooner or later*** 遲早。***Soon got, soon gone.***〖諺〗得來容易去得快。***The sooner the better.*** 愈早愈好；愈快愈好。

soon·er [ˈsunɚ; ˈsuːnə] *adv.* soon 之比較級。—*n.*〖美俚〗①在法定開放前移居公地之人。②搶先以謀不正利益之人。

***soot** [sut, sʊt; sut, suːt] *n.* 煤煙；煤灰；油煙。—*v.t.* 蓋或燻以煤煙；油煙。

sooth [suθ; suːθ] *n.*〖古〗眞實；事實；實際。***for sooth*** 事實上；的確。***in (good, very) sooth*** 實際。***sooth to say; to tell the sooth*** 老實說；說老實話。—*adj.* ①〖古〗眞實的。②〖詩〗撫慰的；柔和的；爽快的。

***soothe** [suð; suːð] *v.t.*, **soothed, sooth·ing.** ①安慰；撫慰；使安靜。②緩和；使減輕痛苦。—**sooth·er,** *n.*

sooth·ing [ˈsuðɪŋ; ˈsuːðiŋ] *adj.* ①安慰的；撫慰的。②〖藥〗鎮痛的；發生鎮靜作用的；緩和的。—**ly,** *adv.*

sooth·say [ˈsuθˌse; ˈsuːθsei] *v.i.*, **-said, -say·ing.** 預言。

sooth·say·er [ˈsuθˌseɚ; ˈsuːθˌseiə] *n.* 預言者；占卜者。

sooth·say·ing [ˈsuθˌse·ɪŋ; ˈsuːθˌseiiŋ] *n.* ①預言未來之事；占卜。②預言。

soot·y [ˈsutɪ; ˈsuti] *adj.*, **soot·i·er, soot·i·est,** *v.*, **-tied, -ty·ing.** —*adj.* ①爲煤煙燻污的。②黑如煤煙的；黑的；幽暗的。③產生許多煤煙的。—*v.t.* 以煤煙弄髒。—**soot·i·ly,** *adv.* —**soot·i·ness,** *n.*

SOP, S.O.P. standard (*or* standing) operating procedure. 標準作業程序。

sop [sɑp; sɔp] *n., v.*, **sopped, sop·ping.** —*n.* ①(浸於牛奶、羹湯等裏的)食物。②浸透之物；濕透的東西。③安慰物；使安寧之物；賄賂。***give (or throw) a sop to Cerberus*** 以賄賂收買；賄賂貪婪的敵人以求相安無事。—*v.t.* ①用液體浸；浸之於液體中。②吸去(水等)；揩；抹〖常up〗。—*v.i.* ①變濕；漬濕；淋濕。②(水、液體)浸入；滲入〖in〗。

sop. soprano.

soph [sɑf; sɔf] *n.*〖俗〗=**sophomore.**

soph. ①sophister. ②sophomore.

So·phi·a [səˈfaɪə; səˈfaiə] *n.* 女子名。

soph·ism [ˈsɑfɪzəm; ˈsɔfizm] *n.* 詭辯；巧辯；似是而非的理論。

soph·ist [ˈsɑfɪst; ˈsɔfist] *n.* ①詭辯家；巧辯家。②(常 S-) 古希臘之修辭學、哲學、雄辯術、倫理學等教師。③博學之人。

soph·ist·er [ˈsɑfɪstɚ; ˈsɔfistə] *n.* ①詭辯家。②古希臘之修辭學、哲學、倫理學教師。③博學之士。④某些英國大學之二、三年級學生。

so·phis·tic [səˈfɪstɪk; səˈfistik] *adj.* ①巧辯的；詭辯的；强辭奪理的。②(古希臘)詭辯家的；詭辯學派的。(亦作 **sophistical**)

so·phis·ti·cate [səˈfɪstɪˌket; səˈfistikeit] *v.t.* ①使熟悉世故；使失去天眞；使矯飾。②使迷惑；使誤解。③攙雜；攙假。④使複雜。—*v.i.* 詭辯。—*n.* 失去天眞的人；矯飾者；老於世故者。—*adj.* =**sophisticated.**

so·phis·ti·cat·ed [səˈfɪstɪˌketɪd; səˈfistikeitid] *adj.* ①通世故的；老練的；失去了天眞的；矯揉造作的。②複雜的；高級的。③攙雜的；攙假的。

so·phis·ti·ca·tion [səˌfɪstɪˈkeʃən; səˌfistiˈkeiʃən] *n.* ①詭辯。②矯飾而不自然的狀態。③摻雜；不純之混和物。④通世故；富於經驗；老練。

soph·ist·ry [ˈsɑfɪstrɪ; ˈsɔfistri] *n.*, *pl.* **-ries.** 詭辯；詭辯術；詭辯法。

Soph·o·cles [ˈsɑfəˌkliz; ˈsɔfəkliːz] *n.* 沙孚克理斯 (495?–?406 B.C., 古希臘三大悲劇作家之一)。

soph·o·more [ˈsɑfm̩ˌor; ˈsɔfəmɔː] *n.* ①大學或四年制高級中學之二年級學生。②有兩年經驗者。—*adj.* 二年級的。

soph·o·mor·ic [ˌsɑfəˈmɔrɪk; ˌsɔfəˈmɔrik] *adj.* ①大學或四年制中學之二年級的。②〖美〗一知半解的。

So·phy [ˈsofɪ; ˈsoufi] *n.* 女子名 (Sophia之暱稱)。

so·po·rif·er·ous [ˌsopəˈrɪfərəs; ˌsoupəˈrifərəs] *adj.* 致睡的；催眠的。

so·po·rif·ic [ˌsopəˈrɪfɪk; ˌsoupəˈrifik] *adj.* ①致睡的；催眠的。a *soporific* drug. 催眠藥。②困乏的；疲倦的。—*n.* 催眠劑。

sop·ping [ˈsɑpɪŋ; ˈsɔpiŋ] *adj.* 濕透的。*sopping* wet. 很濕的；濕透的。

sop·py [ˈsɑpɪ; ˈsɔpi] *adj.*, **-pi·er, -pi·est.** ①浸透的；甚濕的。②多雨的。③〖英俚〗易傷感的；容易落淚的。

so·pra·no [səˈpræno; səˈprɑːnou] *n.*, *pl.* **-pra·nos,** *adj.* —*n.*〖音樂〗①女高音；最高音。②女高音歌唱者；最高音歌唱者。③最高音部；女高音部。—*adj.* 女高音的；最高音的。*soprano* solo. 女高音獨唱。

Sor·bonne [sɔrˈbɑn; sɔːˈbɔn] *n.* ①巴黎以前之一神學院。②巴黎大學文理學院。

sor·cer·er [ˈsɔrsərɚ; ˈsɔːsərə] *n.* 魔法師；弄妖術者；男巫。

sor·cer·ess [ˈsɔrsərɪs; ˈsɔːsəris] *n.* 女魔法師；女妖術者；女巫。

sor·cer·y [ˈsɔrsərɪ; ˈsɔːsəri] *n.*, *pl.* **-cer·ies.** 魔法；妖術；巫術。

sor·did [ˈsɔrdɪd; ˈsɔːdid] *adj.* ①汚穢的；不潔的。②卑賤的。—**ly,** *adv.* —**ness,** *n.*

sore** [sor, sɔr; sɔː, sɔə] *adj.*, **sor·er, sor·est,** *n.* —*adj.* ①疼痛的。②使人痛苦的；傷心的。a *sore* subject. 使人傷心的話題。③痛心的；憂傷的；惱怒的。④極端的；劇烈的。He is in *sore* need of help. 他極端需要幫助。⑤惱怒的。a sight for sore eyes*** 悅目之情景或人。***like a bear with a sore head*** 脾氣極壞的。—*n.* ①傷處；痛處。an open *sore.* 破開的傷口。②痛苦；不幸；傷心事。old *sores.* 舊創。—**ness,** *n.*

sore·head [ˈsorˌhɛd; ˈsɔːhed] *n.*〖美俗〗生氣者；鳴不平者；(尤指)比賽或競爭失敗後而發怒者。—*adj.*〖美俗〗生氣的；鳴不平的。

***sore·ly** [ˈsorlɪ, ˈsɔr-; ˈsɔːli, ˈsɔə-] *adv.* ①痛苦地；悲傷地；痛心地。②嚴厲地；狂暴地。③極端地；迫切地。Help was *sorely* needed. 援助是迫切地需要的。

sore spot 容易得罪或易於生氣的事。

sore throat 喉嚨痛；喉嚨發炎。

sor·ghum [ˈsɔrgəm; ˈsɔːgəm] *n.* ①〖植物〗高粱；蘆粟；帚蜀黍。②由此種植物液中提煉之糖漿。

sor·go [ˈsɔrgo; ˈsɔːgou] *n.*, *pl.* **-gos.**〖植物〗一種帚蜀黍。

so·ri·tes [səˈraɪtiz; souˈraitiːz] *n.*〖邏輯〗連鎖推理；連鎖詭辯法。

sor·o·ban [ˈsɔrəˌbɑn; ˈsɔrəbɑːn] *n.* 日式算盤。

so·rop·ti·mist [səˈrɑptəmɪst; sɔːˈrɔptimist] *n.* 職業婦女會之會員。

so·ror·i·ty [sə'rɔrətɪ; sə'rɔriti] *n., pl.* **-ties.** ①(尤指大學之)姊妹會。②婦女團體；婦女會。 「**-ized, -iz·ing.** 結爲姊妹。」
sor·o·rize ['sɑrə,raɪz; 'sɔrəraiz] *v.i.,*
so·ro·sis [sə'rosɪs; sə'rousis] *n.* ①〖植物〗桑果。②〖美俗〗婦女俱樂部；婦女會社。
sorp·tion ['sɔrpʃən; 'sɔːpʃən] *n.* 〖理化〗吸收作用。 「化〗吸收作用的。」
sorp·tive ['sɔrptɪv; 'sɔːptiv] *adj.* 〖理
sor·rel¹ ['sɔrəl; 'sɔrəl] *adj.* 紅褐色的；栗色的。—*n.* ①紅褐色；栗色。②紅褐色馬；栗色馬。③三歲之雄鹿。
sor·rel² *n.* 〖植物〗酸模；酸模屬之植物。
‡**sor·row** ['sɑro; 'sɔrou] *n.* ①悲哀；憂愁；悔憾。a life full of *sorrow.* 充滿憂苦的一生。②(常 *pl.*) 可悲之事；憂患。to share one's joys and *sorrows.* 苦樂與共。***the Man of Sorrows*** 耶穌基督。—*v.i.* 悲苦。
***sor·row·ful** ['sɑrofəl; 'sɔrəful] *adj.* ①悲哀的；憂愁的；悔恨的。②可悲的。③顯得悲傷的。a *sorrowful* smile. 慘笑。—**ly,** *adv.*
‡**sor·ry** ['sɔrɪ, 'sɑrɪ; 'sɔri] *adj.,* **-ri·er, -ri·est.** ①悲哀的；憂愁的；遺憾的；難過的。I'm *sorry* to hear that your father is dead. 我聽到令尊去世，甚爲難過。②可惜的。I'm *sorry* for him. 我爲他感到可惜。③可憐的；可鄙的。a *sorry* sight. 可憐的情景。④不好的；沒有價值的。a *sorry* excuse. 理由不充足的藉口。⑤帶感歎意味的道歉用語。Did I bump you? *sorry.* 我撞到了你嗎？對不起。—**sorri·ly,** *adv.* —**sor·ri·ness,** *n.*
‡**sort** [sɔrt; sɔːt] *n.* ①種；類；品等；品質。What *sort* of book do you want? 你要那一類的書？people of every *sort.* 各色人等。②某種人或物；有某特性之人或物。He is a good *sort.* 他是個好人。③一套鉛字。④樣子；態度；方式。***after a sort*** **a.** 幾分；稍爲。**b.** 某種的。***of sorts*** **a.** 某種的。**b.** 品質平常的。***out of sorts*** **a.** 不適；心情不佳；不舒服。I am *out of sorts.* 我有些不舒服。**b.** 缺少某種鉛字。***sort of*** 〖美俗〗稍稍地；有幾分。—*v.t.* ①分類；整理。②揀選；揀別。—**er,** *n.* —**a·ble,** *adj.*
sor·tie ['sɔrti; 'sɔːti(ː)] *n.* ①(自被圍攻之陣地)突擊；出擊；反攻。②出擊之部隊；突圍之部隊。③(單架飛機之)出動或出擊；架次。
sor·ti·lege ['sɔrtḷɪdʒ; 'sɔːtilidʒ] *n.* ①拈鬮；籤卜。②魔法；巫術。
sor·ti·tion [sɔr'tɪʃən; sɔː'tiʃən] *n.* 拈鬮。 「-raɪ]. 〖植物〗胞子囊羣。」
so·rus ['sorəs; 'sɔːrəs] *n., pl.* **-ri** [-raɪ;
***SOS** ['ɛs,o'ɛs; 'es,ou'es] ①(無線電訊之)求救信號；求救電碼(按 Morse 國際符號爲…— — —…)。②任何緊急求救之表示。
so-so ['so,so; 'sousou] *adj.* 〖俗〗平常的；不好不壞的；馬馬虎虎的。—*adv.* 平常地；不好不壞地；過得去地；馬馬虎虎地。(亦作 **so so**)
sos·te·nu·to [,sɑstə'nuto; ,sɔstə'nuːtou] 〖義〗*adj.* 〖音樂〗音延長的；音持續的。—*n.* 以延長或持續之音調演唱的樂章。
sot [sɑt; sɔt] *n., v.,* **sot·ted, sot·ting.** —*n.* 因飲酒過多而愚鈍麻木的人；酒徒；酒鬼。—*v.t.* 喝酒浪費掉。 「星的。」
so·thic ['soθɪk; 'souθik] *adj.* 〖天文〗天狼
sot·tish ['sɑtɪʃ; 'sɔtiʃ] *adj.* ①飲酒過多而癡呆麻木的；醉的。②酒徒的；濫喝的。③遲鈍的；愚蠢的。 「tʃi] 〖義〗音調甚低地；低聲地。」
sot·to vo·ce ['sɑto'votʃɪ; 'sɔtou'vou-
sou [su; suː] *n.* ①蘇(法國錢幣名)。②無甚價值之物。
sou·brette [su'brɛt; suː'bret] 〖法〗*n.* ①紅娘之流；扮演紅娘角色之女演員。②賣俏侍女；輕薄少婦。
sou·bret·tish [su'brɛtɪʃ; suː'bretiʃ] *adj.* 輕薄的；搔首弄姿的。
sou·bri·quet ['subrɪ,ke; 'suːbrikei] *n.* =**sobriquet.**
sou·chong ['su'ʃɔŋ; 'suː'ʃɔŋ] 〖中〗*n.* 小種(一種紅茶名)。(亦作 **Souchong**)
souf·flé [su'fle, 'sufle; 'suːflei] 〖法〗*n.* 蛋白牛奶酥；凡攪拌鷄蛋、牛乳等烘成酥鬆之食品。—*adj.* 攪拌成疏鬆的；起酥的。
sough [sʌf, sau; sau] *n.* 颼颼；颯颯(風聲)。—*v.i.* 作颯颯聲。
sought [sɔt; sɔːt] *v.* pt. & pp. of **seek.**
sought-af·ter ['sɔt,æftɚ; 'sɔːt,ɑːftə] *adj.* 很吃香的；爭相羅致的。a *sought-after* speaker. 一個很吃香的演說者。
‡**soul** [sol; soul] *n.* ①靈魂。He has hardly enough food to keep body and *soul* together. 他沒有足够的食物來維持生命。②熱情；魄力。She put her whole *soul* into her work. 她把全部心力貫注於工作。③主腦；中心人物；精髓。Brevity is the *soul* of wit. 言以簡爲貴。④人。Not a *soul* was to be seen in the street. 街上看不到一個人。⑤推動者；推動力。⑥具體的表現；化身。He is the *soul* of honor. 他乃節義之化身。⑦幽靈。⑧崇高的德性或品格。⑨黑人音樂及藝術中令人感情激動或引起共鳴的成分。***upon my soul*** 眞的；確確實實的。
soul·ful ['solfəl; 'soulfəl] *adj.* ①充滿情感的；深情的；熱情的。②靈的；精神的。
soul kiss 以舌頭伸入對方口中的接吻。(亦作 **deep kiss, French kiss**)
soul-kiss ['sol,kɪs; 'soulkis] *v.t.* & *v.i.* 以舌頭伸入對方口中接吻。
soul·less ['sollɪs; 'soullis] *adj.* ①無精神的；無靈魂的。②卑陋的。—**ly,** *adv.*
soul mate ①情人。②密友。
soul music 靈魂音樂(由黑人歌唱家發展推廣而出，爲哀歌及聖樂的一種混合節奏)。
soul-search·ing ['sol,sɝtʃɪŋ; 'soul-,səːtʃiŋ] *n.* 深思；反省。
soul-sick ['sol,sɪk; 'soulsik] *adj.* 精神頹唐的。 —**ness,** *n.*
soul-stir·ring ['sol'stɝɪŋ; 'soul'stəː-riŋ] *adj.* 使精神奮發的；使興奮的。
‡**sound¹** [saund; saund] *n.* ①聲音。We heard strange *sounds* in the distance. 我們聽到遠處有各種奇怪的聲音。②聲。③聲音所及之距離。within *sound* of his voice. 在可聽到他聲音的距離之內。④語言中之一單音；音。a vowel *sound.* 母音。a consonant *sound.* 子音。—*v.i.* ①發聲；響。The trumpet *sounds* for battle. 作戰號響着。②聽起來；似乎。How sweet the music *sounds!* 這音樂聽起來多悅耳！ That excuse *sounds* queer. 那個藉口似乎有點怪。③發音。④有聲音。⑤基於某物〖in〗。⑥被提到。⑦〖法律〗可以金錢衡量賠償。—*v.t.* ①使發聲；使響。to *sound* the alarm. 發警報。②發表。③發(聲)。④以聽聲試測。⑤以聲音發布。⑥說；講。⑦慶祝。***sound off*** 〖俗〗**a.** 坦白說出；高聲埋怨。**b.**〖軍〗報數；報名。**c.** 吹牛；誇大。
‡**sound²** *adj.* ①健全的；完好的。a *sound* body and mind. 健全之身心。②穩固的；堅實的；殷實的。a *sound* firm. 殷實之公司。③正確的；確實的；穩健的。a *sound* advice. 正確的忠告。④徹底的；痛快的。a *sound* sleep.

酣睡。⑤〖法律〗無問題的;有效的。⑥正統的;傳統的。⑦誠實可靠的。a *sound* friend. 誠實可靠的朋友。⑧頭腦清晰的;判斷正確的。—*adv.* 舒暢地。to be *sound* asleep. 酣睡。

sound³** *v.t.* ①(以測錘)測量(水之深淺)。②試探;打聽。We *sounded* mother on the subject of a picnic. 我們就舉行野餐的問題試探母親的意見。③〖醫〗以探桿探測。—*v.i.* ①(以測錘)測量水之深淺。②下潛。③試探;打聽。sound the well*** 測量船艙積水之深度。—*n.* 〖醫〗(外科醫生用之)探桿;探子。

sound⁴ *n.* ①海峽。②海灣。③氣泡;鰾。

sound arrester 〖機械〗防音裝置。

sound articulation 發音清晰度。

sound barrier 〖物理〗音速障礙。(亦作 **sonic barrier, sound wall**)

sound·board 〔'saund,bord; 'saund-bɔ:d〕 *n.* =**sounding board.**

sound box ①(唱機之)唱頭。②〖音樂〗共鳴箱;反響體。(亦作 **soundbox**)

sound camera 錄音攝影機。

sound effects(電影、收音機等之)音響效果。

sound-ef·fects man 〔'saundə-'fɛkts~; 'saundi'fekts~〕(廣播、電視等之)音響效果技師。

sound·er 〔'saundə; 'saundə〕 *n.* ①音響機;發聲器。②測深機;測深人員。

sound field 〖物理〗聲場。

sound film 有聲電影。

sound·ful 〔'saundfəl; 'saundful〕 *adj.* 充滿聲音的。

sound·ing¹ 〔'saundɪŋ; 'saundiŋ〕 *adj.* ①響的;響亮的。②發聲的。③誇張的;堂皇的。

sound·ing² *n.* ①以測錘測水深度。②(*pl.*) 以測錘測出水之深度。③水深可測之處(不超過600英尺處)。④調查;探測。***get off soundings*** **a.** (船)駛離水深可測之處。**b.** 參預自己不能做的事。***get on soundings*** **a.** (船)駛到水深可測之處。**b.** 參預自己能做的事。***off soundings*** 〖航海〗在深度100尋以上之水域中。***on soundings*** 〖航海〗在深度不到100尋之水域中。***strike soundings*** 測量水深。***take soundings*** 不動聲色地調查事態的發展。

sounding balloon 〖氣象〗探測氣球。

sounding board ①共鳴盤;(講壇上面或背面使聲音響亮的)響板。②樂器內擴大音響之薄板;風琴內風箱頂部之插管處。③地板或隔間中的消音板。④對某一建議、計畫等之意見可視爲對該建議、計畫之一般反應的人。⑤宣揚觀念、意見等的人或團體;宣傳家。

sounding line 測深索。

sound·less¹ 〔'saundlɪs; 'saundlis〕 *adj.* 無聲音的;寂靜的。—**ly,** *adv.*

sound·less² *adj.* 〖罕〗深不可測的。

sound·ly 〔'saundlɪ; 'saundli〕 *adv.* ①健全地;完好地。②穩固地; 殷實地。③正確地;確實地。④完全地;猛烈地。⑤酣暢地。

sound·ness 〔'saundnɪs; 'saundnis〕 *n.* ①健康;健全。②殷實;可靠性。③正確性;合理性。④穩固;安穩。

sound·proof 〔'saund,pruf; 'saund-pru:f〕 *adj.* 防音的;有防音設備的;不致發出音響的。—*v.t.* 加以防音設備或處置。

sound track (電影膠片上之)聲帶。

sound truck 裝有擴音器之卡車。

sound wave 〖物理〗聲波。

soup** 〔sup; su:p〕 *n.* 〖俚〗①湯;羹湯;肉汁。ox-tail *soup.* 牛尾湯。②(使飛行困難的)惡劣天氣;濃霧。③速度能力;馬力。His new car has plenty of *soup.* 他的新車馬力很大。④(相片)顯像劑。The prints were in the *soup.* 印洗的相片在顯像劑中。⑤硝化甘油(=nitroglycerin)。from soup to nuts*** 從頭到尾;無所不包。***in the soup*** 〖俚〗處於困境;陷於困難。—*v.t.* 〖俚〗加速;加強;增加活潑生動;增加馬力〖up〗。

soup·çon 〔sup'sõ; 'su:psɔ̃:ŋ〕〖法〗 *n.* 少量;輕微的形跡或氣味。

soup kitchen 施食處;施粥場。

soup plate 湯碟;湯盆;深盤。

soup·spoon 〔'sup,spun; 'su:p-spu:n〕 *n.* 大湯匙。

soup·y 〔'supɪ; 'su:pi〕 *adj.,* **soup·i·er, soup·i·est.** ①似羹湯的;羹湯的。②傷感的。③有濃霧的;陰沉的。

sour** 〔saur; 'sauə〕 *adj.* ①酸的;有酸味的。②發酵的;酸敗的。 *sour* milk. 發酵的牛奶。③乖戾的;壞脾氣的。④陰濕的。*sour* weather. 陰濕的天氣。⑤令人不快的。sour grapes*** 酸葡萄;因得不到而反說不願得到的東西。—*v.t.* & *v.i.* ①(使)變酸。②(使)變爲乖戾。③失去興趣。④惡化;變壞。—*n.* ①酸的東西。②苦事。The sweet and *sour* go together. 苦樂相伴相生。—*adv.* 酸酸地;乖戾地;不高興地。to look *sour.* 一臉不高興。—**er,** —**ness,** *n.* —**ly,** *adv.*

:source 〔sors, sɔrs; sɔ:s, sɔəs〕 *n.* ①源;泉源。The river takes its *source* from the lake. 這河發源於這湖。②來源;出處。Books are a *source* of knowledge. 書籍是知識的一個來源。③消息來源;供給消息的人。The news comes from a reliable *source.* 這項消息出自一個可靠的來源。

source book 資料書。

source material (調查、研究等之)資料。

sour·dough 〔'saur,do; 'sauədou〕 *n.* ①酵頭(發麫用)。②美國西部、阿拉斯加或加拿大之拓荒者。

sour·puss 〔'saur,pus; 'sauəpus〕 *n.* 〖俚〗陰鬱之人。

sou·sa·phone 〔'suzə,fon; 'su:zəfoun〕 *n.* 蘇沙低音號(低音大喇叭)。 —**sou·sa·phon·ist,** *n.*

souse 〔saus; saus〕 *v.,* **soused, sous·ing,** *n., adv.* —*v.t.* ①投入水中。②浸溼。③澆;潑(水)。④澆水於…;潑水於…。⑤醃漬;泡在鹽水裏。⑥〖俚〗使醉。⑦撲向;向…猛飛下來。***souse it*** 〖美〗不聲不響;不做聲。 ***souse oneself*** 〖美〗洗手臉。—*v.i.* ①跳進水裏;水花四濺地落入水裏。②浸溼;泡。③〖俚〗飲醉。④〖古〗猛飛下來。—*n.* ①投入水中;浸溼;泡在水裏。②醃貨(如醃猪耳、醃蹄膀等)。③鹽汁;醃水。④〖俚〗酒鬼;酒徒。⑤〖俚〗狂飲。⑥〖古〗〖放鷹術〗(使鳥)猛向上飛;(使鷹)猛撲下來(捕捉向上飛之鳥)。—*adv.* 突然地;猛然地;水花四濺地。

sou·tache 〔su'tæʃ; 'su:tæʃ〕〖法〗 *n.* 狹而扁的飾帶。

sou·tane 〔su'tan; su:'ta:n〕 *n.* 天主教神父所着之黑色法衣。

:south 〔sauθ; sauθ〕 *n.* ①南。 Mexico is to the *south* of the U. S. A. 墨西哥在美國之南。②南方;南國。③(S-) 美國南北戰爭時之南方聯邦。 ***south by east*** (***west***) 正南偏東(西)。***the South*** 美國南部。—*adj.* 南方的;來自南方的;向南的。a *south* wind. 南風。—*adv.* 向南;在南地。to go *south.* 向南行。—*v.t.* 朝南移動;轉向南方。

South Africa, Republic of 南非共和國(首都 Pretoria 與 Capetown).

South America 南美洲。

South·amp·ton 〔sauθ'hæmptən;

sauθ'æmptən] *n.* 南安普敦(英南部一港埠)。
south·bound ['sauθ,baund; 'sauθbaund] *adj.* 往南的。
south by east 南偏東。
south by west 南偏西。
South Carolina 南卡羅來納(美國東南部之一州, 其首府爲 Columbia)。
South Dakota 南達科他(美國中北部之一州, 其首府爲 Pierre)。
South·down ['sauθ,daun; 'sauθdaun] *n.* (英格蘭南部產之)無角短毛羊;此種羊肉。
*__south·east__ [,sauθ'ist; 'sauθ'i:st] *adj.* 東南的; 來自東南的; 向東南的; 在東南的。—*adv.* 來自東南;向東南。—*n.* ①東南;東南部。②(S-) 美國東南部。
southeast by east (south) 東南偏東(南)。
south·east·er [,sauθ'istə; sauθ'i:stə] *n.* 東南風;來自東南的暴風。
south·east·er·ly [,sauθ'istəlɪ; sauθ'i:stəli] *adj.* 向東南的;在東南的;自東南的。—*adv.* 向東南;自東南。—*n.* 東南風。
south·east·ern [,sauθ'istən; sauθ'i:stən] *adj.* ①向東南的。②來自東南的。③東南的。④東南部的。⑤(S-) 美國東南部的。
south·east·ward [,sauθ'istwəd; sauθ'i:stwəd] *adj.* & *adv.* 向東南的(地)。—*n.* 東南;東南方。
south·east·wards [,sauθ'istwədz; sauθ'i:stwədz] *adv.* 向東南地。
south·er ['sauðə; 'sauðə] *n.* 南風; 來自南方之强風。
south·er·ly ['sʌðəlɪ; 'sʌðəli] *adj.* (亦作 **southernly**) ①向南的。②從南方吹來的(風)。—*adv.* 向南地;從南地。—*n.* 南風。
‡**south·ern** ['sʌðən; 'sʌðən] *adj.* ①南的;南方的;來自南方的;向南方的。Patients on the *southern* side of a hospital recover faster. 住於醫院南側的病人復元較快。②南部的。③(S-)美國南部的。*Southern* belle. 南部美女。—*n.* ①(S-) 南方人 (= Southerner)。②美國南部方言。
Southern Cross 〖天文〗南十字座。
south·ern·er ['sʌðənə; 'sʌðənə] *n.* ①南方人;南部人。②(S-) 美國南方人。
Southern Hemisphere 南半球。
south·ern·most ['sʌðən,most; 'sʌðənmoust] *adj.* 極南的;最南的;最南端的。
Southern Rhodesia 羅德西亞(南非之一國, 首都 Salisbury)。(亦作 **Rhodesia**)
south·ern·wood ['sʌðən,wud; 'sʌðənwud] *n.* 〖植物〗(南歐產的)青蒿。
south·ing ['sauðɪŋ; 'sauðiŋ] *n.* ①〖航海, 測量〗南距 (航海向南進行之緯度差)。②〖天文〗任何天體在赤道以南的距離。③南行;南進;南航。
South Korea 南韓(正式名稱大韓民國, Republic of Korea, 首都漢城, Seoul)。
south·land ['sauθlənd; 'sauθlənd] *n.* 南國; 南部地方。
south·most ['sauθmost; 'sauθmoust] *adj.* 最南的。
south·paw ['sauθ,pɔ; 'sauθpɔ:] *n.* ①〖俚〗慣用左手的運動員。②〖棒球〗用左手投球之投手。—*adj.* 〖俚〗慣用左手的。
South Pole 南極。
south·ron ['sʌðrən; 'sʌðrən] *n.* ①南方人。②(常 S-)〖蘇方〗英格蘭人(輕蔑語)。
South Sea 南半球之海洋的;南太平洋的。
South Sea Islands 南太平洋諸島。
South Seas ①南半球之海洋;赤道以南之各海洋。②南太平洋。
South Temperate 南溫帶的。
*__south·ward__ ['sauθwəd; 'sauθwəd] *adv.* & *adj.* 向南。—*n.* 南方;南部。
south·ward·ly ['sauθwədlɪ; 'sauθwədli] *adj.* & *adv.* ①向南的 (地)。②來自南方的(地)。
*__south·west__ [,sauθ'west; 'sauθ'west] *adj.* 西南的; 來自西南的; 向西南的; 在西南的。—*adv.* 向西南;來自西南。—*n.* ①西南方;西南部。②(S-) 美國西南部。
southwest by south 西南偏南。
southwest by west 西南偏西。
south·west·er [*for* ①,sauθ'westə; sauθ'westə *for* ②,sau'westə; sau'westə] *n.* ①西南風。②一種後沿較寬可護頸之防水帽。
south·west·er·ly [,sauθ'westəlɪ; sauθ'westəli] *adj.* 向西南的; 來自西南的。—*adv.* 向西南;來自西南。—*n.* 西南風。
*__south·west·ern__ [,sauθ'westən; sauθ'westən] *adj.* ①西南的;來自西南的;向西南的;在西南的。②(S-)美國西南部的。
south·west·ward [,sauθ'westwəd; sauθ'westwəd] *adj.* & *adv.* 向西南的(地)。—*n.* 西南;西南方。
south·west·wards [,sauθ'westwədz; sauθ'westwədz] *adv.* 向西南地。
sou·ve·nir [,suvə'nɪr; 'su:vəniə] *n.* 紀念物;紀念品。—*v.t.* 收爲紀念品。
sou'·west·er, sou·west·er [,sau'westə; sau'westə] *n.* =**southwester.**
SOV., sov. sovereign.
*__sov·er·eign__ ['sɑvrɪn, 'sʌv-; 'sɔvrin] *n.* ①君主; 最高統治者。②金鎊 (英國之金幣)。③獨立國。—*adj.* ①最高的; 無上的。Character is of *sovereign* importance. 人品最爲重要。②至尊的;握至高無上之權的。③有主權的; 獨立的; 自主的。④極好的;極有效的。a *sovereign* cure for colds. 治感冒的妙藥。—**ly,** *adv.*
sovereign state 主權國;獨立國。
*__sov·er·eign·ty__ ['sɑvrɪntɪ, 'sʌv-; 'sɔvrənti, -rin-] *n., pl.* **-ties.** ①主權;君權;統治權。②至高無上之權威。③獨立國。
*__so·vi·et__ ['sovɪɪt, ,sovɪ'ɛt; 'souviet, 'sɔv-] *n.* ①〖蘇聯〗委員會;評議會。②(S-)蘇維埃。③(S-)(*pl.*)蘇聯人民及官吏。—*adj.* ①委員會的; 評議會的。②(S-) 蘇維埃的; 蘇聯的。③共產的。
so·vi·et·ism ['sovɪə,tɪzəm; 'souvietizm] *n.* ①蘇維埃制度。②共產主義。
so·vi·et·ist ['sovɪətɪst; 'souvietist] *n.* 蘇維埃主義者。—*adj.* ①蘇維埃主義的; 蘇維埃主義者的。②蘇維埃統治的。
so·vi·et·ize ['sovɪə,taɪz; 'souvietaiz] *v.t.*, **-ized, -iz·ing.** 蘇維埃化;共產化;赤化。—**so·vi·et·i·za·tion,** *n.*
Soviet Russia ①蘇聯(=Soviet Union)。②蘇俄(蘇聯之最大的一個共和國)。
Soviet Union 蘇聯(正式名稱 Union of Soviet Socialist Republics 蘇維埃社會主義共和國聯邦, 首都莫斯科 Moscow)。
sov·khoz [sɔv'kɔz; sɔ:v'kɔ:z] *n., pl.* **-khoz·es, -khoz·y** [-'kɔzɪ; -'kɔ:zi]. 〖蘇聯〗蘇聯國營農場。
sov·ran ['sɑvrən; 'sɔvrən] *n., adj.* 〖詩〗=**sovereign.**
*__sow¹__ [so; sou] *v.*, **sowed** [sod; soud], **sown** [son; soun] or **sowed, sow·ing.** —*v.t.* ①撒(種子)於田地中; 以種子種於 (田地); 播種。The farmer *sowed* the field with wheat. 農夫在田中種小麥。②散布;傳

播。 to *sow* the seeds of hatred. 散布仇恨的種子。—*v.i.* 播種。***As a man sows, so shall he reap.*** 如何播種,如何收穫(種瓜得瓜,種豆得豆)。***sow one's wild oats*** 在年輕時或婚前行爲放蕩。***sow the wind and reap the whirlwind*** 爲惡者終食更惡之果;惡有惡報。 **—a·ble,** *adj.*

sow² 〔sau; sau〕 *n.* 母豬。

sow·bel·ly 〔ˈsauˌbɛlɪ; ˈsauˌbeli〕 *n.* 〖俗〗醃肥豬肉。

sow·bread 〔ˈsauˌbrɛd; ˈsaubred〕 *n.* 〖植物〗中歐所產櫻草屬之植物;篝火花。

sow bug 〔sau~; sau~〕 蛜蝛。

sow·er 〔ˈsoɚ; ˈsouə〕 *n.* ①播種者; 播種機。②傳播者。③煽動者。

sown 〔son; soun〕 *v.* pp. of **sow¹**.

sow thistle 〔sau~;sau~〕〖植物〗苦菜。

sox 〔sɑks; sɔks〕 *n. pl.* 〖俗〗短襪。

soy 〔sɔɪ; sɔi〕 *n.* ①醬油。②黃豆;大豆。

soy·a 〔ˈsɔɪə; ˈsɔiə〕 *n.* =**soybean.**

soy·bean 〔ˈsɔɪˈbin; ˈsɔiˈbiːn〕 *n.* 大豆;黃豆。(亦作 **soya bean**)

soybean milk 豆漿。(亦作 **soya milk**)

soz·zled 〔ˈsɑzəld; ˈsɔzəld〕 *adj.* 喝醉的。

SP¹ Stand Playing (Record). 標準唱片(每分鐘78轉)。

SP², S.P. ①Shore Patrol. ②Submarine Patrol. **Sp.** ①Spain. ②Spaniard. ③Spanish. **sp.** ①space. ②spare. ③special. ④specialist. ⑤species. ⑥specific. ⑦specimen. ⑧speck. ⑨speech. ⑩speed. ⑪spell. ⑫spelling. ⑬spelled. ⑭spine. ⑮spirit. ⑯sponge. ⑰spoon. ⑱sport.

spa 〔spɑ; spɑː〕 *n.* ①礦泉; 溫泉。②有礦泉、溫泉之處。③溫泉名勝。

‡space 〔spes;speis〕 *n., v.,* **spaced, spac·ing.** —*n.* ①太空;空間。Our earth moves through *space*. 我們的地球在太空中運行。②場所;地位。Is there any *space* left? 還有空地方嗎? ③間隔;距離;空白。This road is bad for a *space* of ten miles. 這條道路上有十英里是壞的。④時間;一段時間。in the *space* of an hour. 一小時之間。⑤〖古〗間歇的一段時間。⑥機會。⑦〖印刷〗空鉛。⑧〖音樂〗間(五線譜上線與線間之空白)。⑨(火車等之)坐位或鋪位。⑩空幻狀態。⑪篇幅。*Space* in the newspapers is always restricted. 報上的篇幅總是受到限制的。⑫無線電、電視等的廣告時間。—*v.t.* ①隔開(字母、字、行等)。*Space* your words evenly when you write. 寫字的時候要把字均勻地隔開。②分隔。***single*** (or ***double***) ***spacing*** (打字時行與行間所留之)單(雙)空白。***space out*** 於字與字或字母與字母間之空白放寬。**—less,** *adj.*

space age, Space Age 太空時代。

space bar 打字機上用以打出空格之橫槓。

space capsule 太空囊;太空船。

space carrier (火箭、飛彈等之)太空發射臺。

space·craft 〔ˈspesˌkræft; ˈspeis-krɑːft〕 *n. sing.* or *pl.* 太空船。

space fiction (想像的)宇宙小說;有關將來太空旅行的小說。

space flight 太空飛行。

space·less 〔ˈspeslɪs; ˈspeislis〕 *adj.* ①不受空間限制的;無窮的。②不占空間的。

space·man 〔ˈspesˌmæn; ˈspeismæn〕 *n., pl.* **-men.** ①太空人。②太空科學家。

space medicine 太空醫學。

space opera 以太空探險爲主題之電影,電視或無線電廣播劇。

space platform 太空站。

space·port 〔ˈspesˌport; ˈspeis-pɔːt〕 *n.* 太空船發射降落場。

space probe 太空探測火箭。

spac·er 〔ˈspesɚ; ˈspeisə〕 *n.* ①隔離物;間隔物。②隔離者。③〖印刷〗空鉛; 倒空。④逆電流器。

space rate 按篇幅計算的稿酬。

space satellite 人造衛星。

space-sav·ing 〔ˈspesˌsevɪŋ; ˈspeis-ˌseiviŋ〕 *adj.* 節省空間的;所占空間不大的。—*n.* 空間之節省。

space·ship 〔ˈspesˌʃɪp; ˈspeisʃip〕 *n.* 太空船。(亦作 **space ship, space rocket**)

space shuttle 太空梭;太空車(用以運輸人員及物資至太空站,略作 **shuttle**).

space·sick 〔ˈspesˌsɪk; ˈspeissik〕 *adj.* 太空暈機症的。

space station 太空站(用作太空旅行中途站之有人的人造衛星)。

space suit 太空衣。(亦作 **spacesuit**)

space time 以時間作爲第四度空間之理論。

space travel 太空旅行。

space·walk 〔ˈspesˌwɔk; ˈspeiswɔːk〕 *n., v.i.* 太空漫步。

space writer (or **man**) 以稿件所占篇幅計酬之作家(尤指新聞記者)。

spa·cial 〔ˈspeʃəl;ˈspeiʃəl〕*adj.*=**spatial.**

spac·ing 〔ˈspesɪŋ; ˈspeisiŋ〕 *n.* ①取間隔。②位置上之安排;位置關係。③間隔;空白。

***spa·cious** 〔ˈspeʃəs; ˈspeiʃəs〕 *adj.* ①廣大的;廣闊的。The rooms of the palace were *spacious*. 這座華廈的房間很寬敞。②令人心曠神怡的。③無拘無束的; 自在的。**—ly,** *adv.* **—ness,** *n.*

spade** 〔sped; speid〕 *n., v.,* **spad·ed, spad·ing.** —*n.* ①鏟;鍬。②紙牌中之有鍬形花樣者(俗稱黑桃)。③鏟頭一掘的深度。call a spade a spade*** 直言無隱。 ***in spades*** **a.** 〖俚〗毫無疑問地。**b.** 毫不留情地。—*v.t.* 鏟;鍬。*Spade* up the garden. 把花園的土掘翻一下。**—spad·er, —ful,** *n.*

spade·work 〔ˈspedˌwɝk;ˈspeid-wəːk〕 *n.* 艱難的基本工作。

spad·ger 〔ˈspædʒɚ;ˈspædʒə〕 *n.* ①〖英〗雀;麻雀。②〖俚〗小男孩。

spa·dix 〔ˈspedɪks; ˈspeidiks〕 *n., pl.* **spa·di·ces** 〔speˈdaɪsiz; speiˈdaisiːz〕. 〖植物〗肉穗花序。

spa·ghet·ti 〔spəˈgɛtɪ;spəˈgeti〕 *n.* ①義大利式麪條。②〖電〗(包纏裸線之)細絕緣管。

spa·hi, spa·hee 〔ˈspɑhi; ˈspɑːhiː〕 *n.* 〖昔〗①土耳其之非正規騎兵。②法國陸軍之阿爾及利亞籍騎兵。

***Spain** 〔spen; spein〕 *n.* 西班牙(歐洲大陸一國家,首都馬德里, Madrid).

spake 〔spek;speik〕 *v.* 〖古〗pt. of **speak.**

spall 〔spɔl; spɔːl〕 *n.* 碎片;碎石塊。—*v.t.* 將(礦石)敲成碎片; 斫碎。—*v.i.* ①〖物理〗原子蛻裂。②碎成片。**—a·tion, —er,** *n.*

spal·peen 〔ˈspælpin;spælˈpiːn〕 *n.*〖愛〗①無用之人;下賤之人;惡棍;無賴。②〖諧〗勇敢之男孩。③少年。

Spam 〔spæm; spæm〕 *n.* 〖商標名〗豬肉罐頭。

***span¹** 〔spæn; spæn〕 *n., v.,* **spanned, span·ning.** —*n.* ①一指距;一指長(拇指尖至小指尖間伸張時之距離,約爲九英寸)。②短時間。How brief is the *span* of life! 人生何其短促! ③(二橋礅間的)礅距; 兩支柱間

的距離。④(橋樑等的)架徑。⑤全長;全幅。⑥〖美,南非〗拉車之一對馬、騾或牛。⑦精神活動之持續時間。—*v.t.* ①以指距量。②跨過;架。A bridge *spanned* the railroad tracks. 一座橋跨在路軌之上。③持續。④越過。⑤拉緊;張緊。

span² *v.* 〖古〗pt. of **spin**.

span·drel ['spændrəl; 'spændrəl] *n.* 〖建築〗三角壁;拱側。

spang [spæŋ; spæŋ] *adv.* 〖俗〗①照直地;「突然地。②完全地。」

span·gle** ['spæŋgḷ; 'spæŋgl] *n.*, *v.*, **-gled, -gling.** —*n.* ①(作裝飾用的)燦爛發光的金屬片;小金箔。②任何閃爍的小片。This rock shows *spangles* of gold. 這石頭中顯出一些小金片。—*v.t.* ①飾以閃爍之小金屬片。②以光耀之小片撒布。The sky is *spangled* with stars. 天空裏散布着光亮之星。—*v.i.* 閃亮;燦爛發光。The Star-Spangled Banner*** a. 美國國旗。b. 美國國歌。—**span·gly,** *adj.*

Span·glish ['spæŋglɪʃ; 'spæŋgliʃ] *n.* 混有西班牙語之英語(流行於美國西部及拉丁美洲)。

***Span·iard** ['spænjəd; 'spænjəd] *n.* 「西班牙人。」

span·iel ['spænjəl; 'spænjəl] *n.* ①一種長毛垂耳之小犬(爲西班牙種)。②佞人;走狗;搖尾乞憐的人。—*v.t.* 向…搖尾乞憐。

***Span·ish** ['spænɪʃ; 'spæniʃ] *adj.* 西班牙的;西班牙人的;西班牙語的。—*n.* ①西班牙人(集合稱)。②西班牙語。

Spanish America 西班牙美洲(包括南美洲之大部〔巴西與圭亞那除外〕、中美洲〔英屬宏都拉斯除外〕、墨西哥、古巴、海地、波多黎各、多明尼加及西印度羣島中之若干島嶼)。

Spanish American ①西班牙美洲居民。②美籍西班牙人。

Span·ish-A·mer·i·can ['spænɪʃə'mɛrəkən; 'spæniʃə'merikən] *adj.* ①西班牙美國的。②(美國國內)美籍西班牙人區的。

Spanish-American War 美西戰爭(發生於1898年)。

Spanish bayonet 〖植物〗(沙漠中「產的)麟鳳蘭。」

Spanish fly 〖蟲〗斑蝥;芫菁。

Spanish mackerel 鰆屬之青花魚。

Spanish Main ①(原指)西班牙大陸美洲(即西班牙美洲之大陸部分)。②加勒比海,或鄰近南美洲北海岸之海面。

spank [spæŋk; spæŋk] *v.t.* ①(用巴掌、拖鞋等)打(尤指打屁股)。②鞭策急趨;使急速前進。③痛斥。—*v.i.* ①疾走(介乎 trot 與 gallop 之間)。②砰然而落。—*n.* 拍打;一巴掌。

spank·er ['spæŋkɚ; 'spæŋkə] *n.* ①〖俗〗拍擊者;疾走者。②〖俗〗駿馬。③〖航海〗後斜桁帆;後檣縱帆。④卓越超羣之人或物。⑤〖古,俚〗錢;黃金。

spank·ing ['spæŋkɪŋ; 'spæŋkiŋ] *adj.* ①疾走的;敏捷活潑的。②迅速有力的。③疾吹的。④〖俗〗非常好的;非常大的。—*adv.* 〖俗〗非常地。—*n.* (用巴掌)拍擊;打巴掌。—**ly,** *adv.*

span·less ['spænlɪs; 'spænlis] *adj.* 不「能以指距測度的。」

span·ner ['spænɚ; 'spænə] *n.* 螺旋鉗;螺旋起子;扳鉗;扳手。

span·worm ['spæn,wɝm; 'spæn-wə:m] *n.* (蟲)尺蠖。

SPAR, Spar [spɑr; spɑ:] *n.* 〖美〗海岸防衞隊婦女預備隊隊員。

spar¹ [spɑr; spɑ:] *n.*, *v.*, **sparred, spar·ring.** —*n.* ①〖航海〗帆桅;檣;桁。②〖航空〗(機翼之)縱骨;翼樑(翼肋附於其上)。—*v.t.* 裝以桅、檣等。

spar² *v.*, **sparred, spar·ring,** *n.* —*v.i.* ①拳擊。②(雄鷄)以足鬥。③爭論;辯論;對罵。④戰鬥。⑤遲遲不行動;拖延行爲。—*n.* ①拳擊;揮拳;拳擊比賽。②爭論;辯論。③鬥鷄。

spar³ *n.* 〖礦〗晶石。

spar·a·ble ['spærəbḷ; 'spærəbl] *n.* (做鞋用的)無頭小釘。

spar buoy 圓柱浮標;桿浮標。

spar deck 從船首至船尾的上層甲板。

‡spare [spɛr; spɛə] *v.*, **spared, spar·ing,** *adj.*, **spar·er, spar·est,** *n.* —*v.t.* ①恕宥;赦免。He *spared* his enemy. 他恕宥了敵人。②節省使用;吝惜。*Spare* the rod and spoil the child. 〖諺〗孩子不打不成器。③不用;省却;捨棄;讓與。I have no time to *spare*. 我沒有餘暇。④使免於苦役、痛苦等。not to *spare* oneself. 不遺餘力地工作。⑤使免於。He did the work to *spare* you the trouble. 他做了那件事以使你免却麻煩。—*v.i.* 節約;節省。***and to spare*** 太多;過多。He has enough *and to spare*. 他很寬裕。—*adj.* ①剩餘的;備用的。*spare* room. 備客人居住之房間。*spare* tire. 備用輪胎。②瘦的;貧乏的。③節儉的;節約的。He is habitually *spare* of speech. 他經常沉默寡言。—*n.* ①備用之物。②〖保齡球〗滾球兩次將所有之木瓶擊倒。—**spar·er,** —**ness,** *n.* —**ly,** *adv.* —**a·ble,** *adj.*

spare hand 備用之人手。

spare part (供更換使用之機器的)零件。

spare·rib ['spɛr,rɪb; 'spɛərib] *n.* 豬肉的帶肉肋骨;排骨肉。

spare·time ['spɛr,taɪm; 'spɛətaim] *n.* 閒暇;閒時。—*adj.* 閒暇的;閒時的。

sparge [spɑrdʒ; spɑ:dʒ] *v.t.* & *v.i.*, **sparged, sparg·ing.** 散播;擴散;撒;潑;灑。

spar·ing ['spɛrɪŋ; 'spɛəriŋ] *adj.* ①謹慎的;小心的。②節省的;儉約的。③缺少的;不足的;貧乏的。④仁慈的;寬容的。⑤愛惜的;吝惜的。—**ness,** *n.* —**ly,** *adv.*

***spark¹** [spɑrk; spɑ:k] *n.* ①火星;火花。②閃光;閃耀。③少量;一點。to have not a *spark* of interest. 絲毫不感興趣。④痕跡;生命活力之標誌。a *spark* of genius. 天才的火花。—*v.i.* ①放散火花;放散火星;(內燃機)發火。②閃爍。Her eyes *sparked* with fury. 她氣得眼睛冒火。③大感興趣;大表熱心。—*v.t.* ①鼓勵(朋友或隊友);爲(朋友或隊友)加油。②給以靈感。—**less,** *adj.*

spark² *n.* ①快樂的青年;紈袴子;翩翩少年。②漂亮的青年;愛人。—*v.i.* & *v.t.* 求婚;調情;追求女性。

spark arrester ①防止火花擴散之裝置。②〖電〗減低或防止電花擴散之裝置。

spark coil 〖電〗電花線圈;感應線圈。

spark·er ['spɑrkɚ; 'spɑ:kə] *n.* ①放火花者;內燃機之點火裝置。②〖電〗= **spark arrester.** ③〖美俚〗戀人;情夫。

sparking plug 〖英〗= **spark plug.**

spark·ish ['spɑrkɪʃ; 'spɑ:kiʃ] *adj.* ①活潑的;快活的。②風流的;艷麗的;服裝優美的。

***spar·kle** ['spɑrkḷ; 'spɑ:kl] *v.*, **-kled, -kling,** *n.* —*v.i.* ①放散火花;放散火星。The fireworks *sparkled*. 烟火冒出火花了。②閃耀;閃爍。Diamonds *sparkle*. 鑽石閃閃發光。③起泡沫。④晶瑩顯露。—*v.t.* ①使閃爍。The sun *sparkled* wet grass. 陽光使濕草閃閃發光。②顯露。—*n.* ①火花;火星。②閃耀。I like the *sparkle* of her eyes. 我喜歡她眼睛的閃耀。③燦爛。④隱約可見的

痕跡。

spar·kler [ˈsparklɚ; ˈspɑːklə] *n.* ①閃爍有光之物。②放異彩的人；才子；佳人。③寶石。④〖俗〗明眸。⑤烟火。

spark·ly [ˈsparklı; ˈspɑːkli] *adj.* 閃爍的。

spark plug ①(內燃機之)火花塞；火星塞。②〖俗〗領導團體活動而保持其高度熱烈情緒之人。

spark·plug [ˈspark͵plʌg; ˈspɑːkplʌg] *v.t.*, **-plugged, -plug·ging.** 給以推力；推動；鼓勵。

spark transmitter 〖電訊〗電花放送機。

spar·ling [ˈsparlıŋ; ˈspɑːliŋ] *n.* ①歐洲產的銀色鱗香魚。②小青魚。

***spar·row** [ˈspæro; ˈspærou] *n.* 雀；麻雀。

sparrow hawk (鳥)鷂。

spar·ry [ˈsparı; ˈspɑːri] *adj.*, **-ri·er, -ri·est.** ①像晶石的。②含晶石的；多晶石的。

sparse [spars; spɑːs] *adj.*, **spars·er, spars·est.** ①稀少的；稀疏的。②不足的；貧瘠的。—**ness,** *n.*

sparse·ly [ˈsparslı; ˈspɑːsli] *adv.* 稀疏地；稀少地。

spar·sim [ˈsparsım; ˈspɑːsim] *adv.* 稀疏地；散見於。

spar·si·ty [ˈsparsətı; ˈspɑːsiti] *n.* 稀少；稀薄；缺少；不足。

Spar·ta [ˈspartə; ˈspɑːtə] *n.* 斯巴達(古希臘的最重要城邦之一，以尙武著稱)。

Spar·ta·cus [ˈspartəkəs; ˈspɑːtəkəs] *n.* 第一次世界大戰末期德國的社會主義過激派組織之一政黨。

Spar·tan [ˈspartn̩; ˈspɑːtn] *adj.* ①斯巴達的；斯巴達式的。②剛勇的。③簡樸的。—*n.* ①斯巴達人。②剛勇之人。—**ly,** *adv.*

Spar·tan·ism [ˈspartənızm̩; ˈspɑːtənizm] *n.* 斯巴達主義；斯巴達精神；尙武精神。

spasm [ˈspæzəm; ˈspæzm] *n.* ①痙攣。②突發的一陣。

spas·mod·ic [spæzˈmadık; spæzˈmɔdik] *adj.* ①〖醫〗痙攣的；痙攣性的；間歇性的。②一陣奮發的；間斷的；時作時停的；勤惰無常的。③狂熱的；興奮的。

spas·mod·i·cal [spæzˈmadıkl̩; spæzˈmɔdikəl] *adj.* =**spasmodic.** —**ly,** *adv.*

spas·tic [ˈspæstık; ˈspæstik] *adj.* 〖醫〗①痙攣性的。②患痙攣性癱瘓的。—*n.* 患痙攣性癱瘓者。—**al·ly,** *adv.*

spat[1] [spæt; spæt] *n., v.*, **spat·ted, spat·ting.** —*n.* ①口角；小爭論；鬥嘴。②輕打；掌擊；拍擊。③一濺；一灑；一潑。④(如雨般的)連擊聲。—*v.i.* ①〖俗〗口角；鬥嘴；作小爭論。②輕打；拍擊。—*v.t.* ①輕打；拍打。②(如雨般)連擊。

spat[2] *v.* pt. & pp. of **spit.**

spat[3] *n.* (常*pl.*)鞋罩；覆於足面之短綁腿。

spat[4] *n., v.*, **spat·ted, spat·ting.** —*n.* ①貝卵；介卵。②蠔卵；牡蠣卵。③幼牡蠣；幼牡蠣羣(集合稱)。—*v.i.* & *v.t.* (蠔等)產卵。

spatch·cock [ˈspætʃ͵kak; ˈspætʃkɔk] *n.* 殺後拔毛剖腹立刻烤食之雞。—*v.t.* ①殺(雞)以烹食。②插入(文句)。

spate [spet; speit] *n.* 〖英〗①洪水泛濫。②暴雨。③突然傾流；迸發。④大量。

spathe [speð; speið] *n.* 〖植物〗大花苞。—**spathed,** *adj.*

spath·ic [ˈspæθık; ˈspæθik] *adj.* 晶石的；似晶石的。

spa·tial [ˈspeʃəl; ˈspeiʃəl] *adj.* ①空間的。②存在於空間的；占有空間的。—**ly,** *adv.*

spa·ti·o·tem·po·ral [͵speʃıoˈtɛmpərəl; ͵speiʃiouˈtempərəl] *adj.* 〖哲學〗空間與時間上的；時空的。

spat·ter [ˈspætɚ; ˈspætə] *v.t.* ①濺。②灑；潑。③濺汚；灑汚。④(如雨般)連擊。⑤誹謗；玷辱；汚蔑。—*v.i.* ①濺出水滴(如沸水)。②灑落；紛紛落下。③(子彈)雨般射來。④誹謗。—*n.* ①濺灑；紛擊。②滴落之聲；淅瀝聲。③汚點；濺汚之處。

spat·ter·dash·es [ˈspætɚ͵dæʃız; ˈspætədæʃiz] *n. pl.* 護腿；綁腿套。—**spat·ter·dashed,** *adj.*

spat·ter·dock [ˈspætɚ͵dak; ˈspætədɔk] *n.* 〖植物〗萍蓬草；黃睡蓮。

spat·u·la [ˈspætʃələ; ˈspætjulə] *n.* ①(用以混合藥物，塗敷油漆等之)濶扁而有彈性的抹刀；調刀；藥刀；小鏟。②〖醫〗壓舌板；壓舌器。—**spat·u·lar,** *adj.*

spat·u·late [ˈspætʃəlıt, -͵let; ˈspætjulit, -leit] *adj.* ①闊扁之薄片的；壓舌片的。②狀如抹刀的。

spav·in [ˈspævın; ˈspævin] *n.* 〖獸醫〗①馬足之跗節內腫。②因止血而引起之腫瘤。

spav·ined [ˈspævınd; ˈspævind] *adj.* 殘廢的。

spawn [spɔn; spɔːn] *n.* ①(魚類、兩棲類、介類及其他水產動物之)卵；子。②由此類卵中孵出之小動物。③〖植物〗菌絲。④子孫；產物(輕蔑語)。⑤凝膠狀之物。—*v.i.* (魚類)產卵；孵卵。—*v.t.* ①(魚類等)產(卵)。②產；生產。③〖植物〗以菌絲種植。

spay [spe; spei] *v.t.* 割去(雌獸)之卵巢。

S.P.C.A. Society for the Prevention of Cruelty to Animals. **S.P.C.C.** Society for the Prevention of Cruelty to Children. **S.P.E.** Society for Pure English.

‡speak [spik; spiːk] *v.*, **spoke, spo·ken, speak·ing.** —*v.i.* ①說話。*Speak* more slowly. 說得再慢些。②表示意思、感情等。Their eyes *spoke.* 他們的眼睛表示出他們的情感。③演說。Mr. Smith will *speak* now. 史密斯先生要演說了。④發響聲。The cannon *spoke.* 大砲發巨響。⑤請求；要求。⑥(狗)受命而吠。⑦表示；代表；象徵。Schools and museums all *speak* of the past. 學校和博物館全象徵着過去。⑧預示。—*v.t.* ①說。to *speak* the truth. 說實話。②操，說，使用(語言)。③〖古〗顯示；表示出。His conduct *speaks* him honorable. 他的行爲顯示他是可敬的。④招呼；聯絡。⑤表明；表達。⑥爲…發言。⑦請求。***nothing to speak of*** 無可稱述；不值一述。***not to speak of*** 且不提。***so to speak*** 可謂；可以說。***speak by the book*** 有權威性地說；精確地說。***speak for*** a. 爲…說情；替…講好話。b. 選擇；已留作自用。***speak one's mind*** 直言無隱。***speak up*** (or ***out***) a. 大聲說。The chairman asked him to *speak out* or sit down. 主席要他大聲說話，要不就坐下來。b. 毫不拘束地說出自己的意見。***speak volumes for*** 極足以證明。(***not***) ***to be on speaking terms with*** a. 與…之交情足可(不足)交談。b. (不)願與…交談；與…和好(不和)。***to speak of*** 值得一提。The islands have no trees *to speak of.* 這些島上毫無樹木可言。—**a·ble,** *adj.*

speak-eas·y [ˈspik͵izı; ˈspiːk͵iːzi] *n., pl.* **-eas·ies.** 〖美俚〗販賣私酒的酒店。

***speak·er** [ˈspikɚ; ˈspiːkə] *n.* ①說話者。②演說者。Mr. Wang is the *speaker* of the evening. 王先生是今晚之演說者。③主席；議長。④揚聲機；擴音喇叭(= loudspeaker). ⑤演講辭選集。

speak·er·phone ['spikɚ,fon; 'spi:kəfoun] *n.* (揚聲器和麥克風合成的)揚聲麥克風。

speak·ing ['spikɪŋ; 'spi:kiŋ] *adj.* ①談話用的;適於談話的。②可談話的;可搭言的。a *speaking* acquaintance. 泛泛之交。③祇到講話程度的。④像要開口似的;逼眞的;生動的;感動的。a *speaking* likeness. 一幅維妙維肖的肖像。⑤演說的。⑥雄辯的; 動人的。—*n.* ①談話; 講話; 演說。②政治集會。

speaking trumpet 船與船間通話用的揚聲筒。

speaking tube ①=**speaking trumpet.** ②通話管;傳聲筒(如兩房之間所用的)。

***spear**¹ [spɪr; spiə] *n.* ①槍;矛。②光線。—*v.t.* 用槍刺。—*v.i.* 衝。—**er,** *n.*

spear² *n.* (植物之)芽; 苗; 小根; 葉片。—*v.i.* (植物)發長莖;發芽。

spear·fish ['spɪr,fɪʃ; 'spiəfiʃ] *n., pl.* **-fish, -fish·es,** *v.* —*n.*①眞旗魚。②=**marlin.** —*v.i.* 以矛射魚;以矛捕魚。

spear·head ['spɪr,hɛd; 'spiəhed] *n.* ①槍尖;矛頭。②先鋒;前鋒;先頭部隊。—*v.t.* 爲…作先鋒。—*v.i.*作爲槍頭;作先鋒。

spear·man ['spɪrmən; 'spiəmən] *n., pl.* **-men.** 持矛者;持槍者。

spear·mint ['spɪr,mɪnt; 'spiəmint] *n.* 〖植物〗薄荷。

spear side 父系的(與 spindle side 或 distaff side 相反)。

spec [spɛk; spek] *n.* ①〖俗〗=**speculation.** ②=**specification.** ③=**spectacle.** ④=**spectacular.** ***on spec*** 投機;冒險。

spec. ①special. ②specialist. ③specially. ④specialty. ⑤species. ⑥specific. ⑦specifical(ly). ⑧specification. ⑨specimen. ⑩spectacle. ⑪spectacular. ⑫spectrum. ⑬speculation. ⑭ spectra.

‡**spe·cial** ['spɛʃəl; 'speʃəl] *adj.* 特別的;特殊的;專門的。Is there anything *special* in the papers today? 今天報上有甚麼特殊消息嗎? —*n.* ①專車。②特殊之人或物。③(報紙的) 專號; 專輯。Newsboys were hawking the afternoon *specials.* 報童們在沿街叫賣晚報專號。④〖美〗(店鋪及飯館等之)特製品、特價品等。The store is featuring *specials* on meats today. 該店今天以肉爲特價品。⑤特殊之事。

special delivery (信件的)限時專送。

special effects 電影中之特殊效果。

spe·cial·ism['spɛʃəl,ɪzəm;'speʃəlizm] *n.* ①專門; 專修; 專科。②專門化; 專科化。

***spe·cial·ist** ['spɛʃəlɪst; 'speʃəlist] *n.* 專家。Dr. white is an eye *specialist.* 懷德醫師是眼科專家。

spe·ci·al·i·ty [,spɛʃɪ'ælətɪ; ,speʃi'æliti] *n., pl.* **-ties.** 〖主英〗=**specialty.**

spe·cial·i·za·tion [,spɛʃəlɪ'zeʃən; ,speʃəlai'zeiʃən] *n.* ①特殊化。②專門化。③局限化;限制。④〖生物〗分化。

***spe·cial·ize, spe·cial·ise** ['spɛʃəl,aɪz; 'speʃəlaiz] *v.,* **-ized, -iz·ing, -ised, -is·ing.** —*v.i.* ①專攻; 專門研究。Many students *specialize* in agriculture. 許多學生專攻農業。②〖生物〗爲適應新環境或新功能而發展。③深入。—*v.t.* ①使專門;限制。②特別指出。③〖生物〗適應新環境或新功能而發展。④在(支票等)上背書指名受款人。

***spe·cial·ly** ['spɛʃəlɪ; 'speʃəli] *adv.* 特別地; 專門地。I came here *specially* to see you. 我專爲看你而來。

spe·cial·ty ['spɛʃəltɪ; 'speʃəlti] *n., pl.* **-ties.** ①特性; 特質。②專門研究;專門職業;專長。③特製品。④特徵。⑤細節;特別項目。⑥特級品。⑦新產品;極爲人歡迎之產品。(亦作 **speciality**)

spe·cie ['spiʃɪ; 'spi:ʃi:] *n.* 錢幣; 硬幣(爲紙幣之對)。***in specie*** **a.** 照原樣。**b.** 用硬幣。**c.** 〖法律〗與指定者同樣。***specie par*** 法定平價。

spe·cies** ['spiʃɪz,-ʃiz; 'spi:ʃi:z,-ʃiz] *n., pl.* **-cies.** ①種;類。②〖生物〗種。Wheat is a *species* of grass. 小麥是禾本植物的一種。③外表; 外形。④彌撒中所用之麪包及聖酒。the four species***〖數學〗四則。***the species*** 人類。

specif. ①specific. ②specifically.

***spe·cif·ic**[spɪ'sɪfɪk;spi'sifik, spə's-]*adj.* ①明確的。There was no *specific* reason for the quarrel. 這場口角並無明確的緣由。②特種的; 特殊的。③有特效的。 *specific* remedy (*or* medicine). 特效藥。④由特殊原因產生的。⑤〖生物〗種 (species) 的。—*n.* ①特別聲明、品質等。②特效藥。 Quinine is a *specific* for malaria. 奎寧是瘧疾的特效藥。—**al·ly,** *adv.* —**ness,** *n.*

spec·i·fi·ca·tion [,spɛsəfə'keʃən; ,spesifi'keiʃən] *n.* ①指明;明確陳述;詳述。②(建築物、道路、船等之)詳細計畫書。③詳細說明書。④所列舉之事項;特殊項目。

specific duty 〖商〗從量稅。

specific gravity 〖物理〗比重。

specific heat 〖物理〗比熱。

specific name 〖生物〗種名。

***spec·i·fy** ['spɛsə,faɪ; 'spesifai] *v.i.* & *v.t.,* **-fied, -fy·ing.** ①指定。He delivered the paper as *specified.* 他把指定的報紙送到了。②載明。—**spec·i·fi·er,** *n.*

***spec·i·men** ['spɛsəmən; 'spesimin, -mən] *n.*①樣品; 標本。zoological *specimens.* 動物標本。②〖俗〗人類; 人。The tramp was a queer *specimen.* 那流浪者是個古怪的人。—*adj.* 作爲樣品的。*specimen* pages. 樣張。

spe·ci·ol·o·gy [,spiʃɪ'ɑlədʒɪ; ,spi:ʃi'ɔlədʒi] *n.* 種族學。

spe·ci·os·i·ty [,spiʃɪ'ɑsətɪ; ,spi:ʃi'ɔsiti] *n., pl.* **-ties.** ①華而不實; 華而不實之物。②似是而非;似是而非之物。

spe·cious ['spiʃəs; 'spi:ʃəs] *adj.* ①似是而非的; 像是眞的。②華而不實的; 金玉其外的;外表美麗的;僞善的。—**ly,** *adv.*

***speck** [spɛk; spek] *n.* ①斑點; 汚點; 瑕疵。②微片;些微;微塵。 I've got a *speck* in my eye. 我的眼裏掉進一點灰塵。 —*v.t.* 沾以或似沾以汚點。

***speck·le** ['spɛkl̩; 'spekl] *n., v.,* **-led, -ling.** —*n.* 小點;斑點。This hen is gray with white *speckles.* 這隻母鷄是灰色上帶白斑點。—*v.t.* 加以斑點。

specs [spɛks; speks] *n. pl.* 〖俗〗眼鏡(spectacles 之略)。

spec·ta·cle** ['spɛktəkl̩; 'spektəkl] *n.* ①景象;奇觀; 壯觀。 A big army parade is a fine *spectacle.* 大規模的陸軍閱兵極爲壯觀。②(*pl.*) 眼鏡。 to wear a pair of *spectacles.* 戴一付眼鏡。③(*pl.*) 見解;看法。look*** (or ***see all things***) ***through rose-colored spectacles*** 持樂觀態度。***make a spectacle of oneself*** 出醜; 丟人。

spec·ta·cled ['spɛktəkl̩d; 'spektəkld]

adj. ①戴眼鏡的。②〖動物〗有眼鏡狀斑點的。a *spectacled* bear.(南美產之)眼鏡斑熊。

spec·tac·u·lar 〔spɛkˈtækjələ; spekˈtækjulə〕 *adj.* 壯觀的；壯麗的；蔚爲巨觀的；奇觀的；戲劇化的。—*n.* ①昂貴豪華的彩色電視片。②奇景；壯觀。 —**i·ty,** *n.* —**ly,** *adv.*

spec·tate 〔ˈspɛktet; ˈspekteit〕 *v.i.,* **-tat·ed, -tat·ing.** 旁觀；作壁上觀。

*__spec·ta·tor__ 〔ˈspɛktetə, spɛkˈtetə; spekˈteitə〕 *n.* 觀者；旁觀者。There were many *spectators* at the football match. 這場足球賽有許多觀衆。

spec·ter, spec·tre 〔ˈspɛktə;ˈspektə〕 *n.* 鬼；幽靈。

spec·tra 〔ˈspɛktrə; ˈspektrə〕 *n.* pl. of **spectrum.**

spec·tral¹ 〔ˈspɛktrəl; ˈspektrəl〕 *adj.* 「妖怪的；幽靈的。—**ly,** *adv.*

spec·tral² *adj.* 分光譜的。

spectral analysis 光譜分析。

spectral colors 譜色。

spec·tro·gram 〔ˈspɛktrəˌgræm; ˈspektrougræm〕 *n.* 〖物理〗光譜圖。

spec·tro·graph 〔ˈspɛktrəˌgræf; ˈspektrougrɑːf〕 *n.*〖物理〗攝譜儀。—**ic,** *adj.*

spec·trol·o·gy 〔spɛkˈtrɑlədʒɪ; spekˈtrɔlədʒi〕 *n.* 光譜分析學。

spec·trom·e·ter 〔spɛkˈtrɑmətə; spekˈtrɔmitə〕 *n.* 分光計。

spec·tro·pho·tom·e·ter 〔ˌspɛktrofoˈtɑmətə; ˌspektroufouˈtɔmitə〕 *n.* 分光光度計。

spec·tro·scope 〔ˈspɛktrəˌskop; ˈspektrəskoup〕 *n.* 分光器。

spec·tro·scop·ic 〔ˌspɛktrəˈskɑpɪk; ˌspektrousˈkɔpik〕 *adj.* ①分光器的。②用分光器完成的。(亦作 **spectroscopical**)

spec·tros·co·py 〔spɛkˈtrɑskəpɪ; spekˈtrɔskəpi〕 *n.* 光譜學；光譜研究。

spec·trum 〔ˈspɛktrəm; ˈspektrəm〕 *n., pl.* **-tra, -trums.** ①〖物理〗光譜。*spectrum* analysis. 光譜分析。solar *spectrum.* 太陽光譜。②〖無線電〗自3公分至 30,000 公尺間之波長。③(有相互關係之不同觀念、物體等的)範圍。

spec·u·lar 〔ˈspɛkjələ; ˈspekjulə〕 *adj.* ①鏡的；如鏡的。②反射的。③〖醫〗用窺器的；用耳鬥鏡的；用子宮鏡的。

spec·u·late 〔ˈspɛkjəˌlet; ˈspekjuleit〕 *v.i.,* **-lat·ed, -lat·ing.** ①沉思；默想；思索。②投機。to *speculate* in stocks. 投機股票買賣。③推測；猜測。—*v.t.* 對(有風險之事業)投資。

*__spec·u·la·tion__ 〔ˌspɛkjəˈleʃən; ˌspekjuˈleiʃən〕 *n.* ①思索；沉思；推想。②臆測。③投機；投機買賣。The government forbids *speculation* in rice. 政府禁止做米的投機生意。

spec·u·la·tive 〔ˈspɛkjəˌletɪv; ˈspekjulətiv〕 *adj.* ①思索的；純理論的。*speculative* philosophy. 思辨哲學。*speculative* geometry. 純正幾何學。②投機的。*speculative* market. 投機市場。③冒險的。④臆測的。

spec·u·la·tor 〔ˈspɛkjəˌletə; ˈspekjuleitə〕 *n.* 投機者。

spec·u·lum 〔ˈspɛkjələm; ˈspekjuləm〕 *n., pl.* **-la** 〔-lə; -lə〕, **-lums.** ①鏡銅(昔作鏡用)。②金屬鏡；反射鏡。③(醫生檢查用之)窺器；耳鬥鏡；子宮鏡。④(蟲翼上的)眼狀斑。

sped 〔spɛd; sped〕 *v.* pt. & pp. of **speed.**

:**speech** 〔spitʃ; spiːtʃ〕 *n.* ①說話；言語；言辭。*Speech* is silver but silence is golden. 言語是銀，但沈默是金(能保持沈默比能說話更好)。②說話能力。Animals lack *speech.* 動物沒有語言能力。③演說。He made a very good *speech.* 他發表一篇很好的演說。④說話的情形、態度。⑤語言。⑥〖文法〗語法。the direct (indirect) *speech.* 直(間)接語法。part of *speech.* 〖文法〗詞性；詞類。

speech clinic 語言矯正醫院。

speech community 使用同一種語言或方言之人民的集合稱。

speech day (英國學校的)給獎日。

speech·i·fy 〔ˈspitʃəˌfaɪ; ˈspiːtʃifai〕 *v.i.,* **-fied, -fy·ing.** 〖諧,蔑〗演說；高聲演說。 —**speech·i·fi·er,** *n.*

speech·less 〔ˈspitʃlɪs; ˈspiːtʃlis〕 *adj.* ①啞的；不能說話的。②暫時失去說話能力的。③緘默的。④不能說出的；未說出的。—**ness,** *n.*

speech organs 發聲器官。

speech reading 唇讀術(聾者視說話人口部動作而理解其意)。(亦作 **lip reading**)

:**speed** 〔spid; spiːd〕 *n., v.,* **sped** or **speed·ed, speed·ing.** —*n.* ①迅速；速率；速度。We are traveling at a *speed* of thirty miles an hour. 我們以每小時三十英里的速率行進。②汽車的排擋。③〖古〗好運道；成功。 ***at full*** (or ***top***) ***speed*** **a.** 全速；最快速度。**b.** 盡力之所能。***More haste, less speed.*** 欲速則不達。 —*v.i.* ①速進；急行。②〖古〗成功。③超速。 The motorist was fined for *speeding.* 駕車者因超速而被罰款。—*v.t.* ①使速進；使急行。*Speed* up the work. 加緊工作。②使趕快離開。③推進；促進。④〖古〗使成功。God *speed* you. 願上帝祝福你。***speed up*** 加速。

speed·boat 〔ˈspidˌbot; ˈspiːdbout〕 *n.* 「快艇。

speed cop 〖美俚〗取締汽車超速之警察。

speed·er 〔ˈspidə; ˈspiːdə〕 *n.* ①急馳之人或物；超速駕車者。②加速器。③速度調節器。

*__speed·i·ly__ 〔ˈspidlɪ; ˈspiːdili〕 *adv.* 迅速地。

speed·i·ness 〔ˈspidɪnɪs; ˈspiːdinis〕 *n.* 迅速；快捷。

speed limit ①速度限制。②受限制的最高速度。

speed·om·e·ter 〔spiˈdɑmətə; spiˈdɔmitə〕 *n.* (汽車等之)速度計。

speed-read 〔ˈspidˌrid; ˈspiːd-riːd〕 *v.t.* 「速讀。

speed·ster 〔ˈspidstə; ˈspiːdstə〕 *n.* ① =**speeder.** ②高速雙人座汽車。

speed trap 汽車超速監視區。

speed-up 〔ˈspidˌʌp; ˈspiːdʌp〕 *n.* ①生產率之提高；生產增高制度。②加速。

speed·way 〔ˈspidˌwe; ˈspiːd-wei〕 *n.* ①高速公路。②賽車跑道。

speed·well 〔ˈspidwɛl; ˈspiːd-wel〕 *n.* 〖植物〗草本威靈仙屬之植物。

*__speed·y__ 〔ˈspidɪ; ˈspiːdi〕 *adj.,* **speed·i·er, speed·i·est.** 迅速的；快的。a *speedy* decision. 一個快速的決定。

spe·l(a)e·ol·o·gy 〔ˌspilɪˈɑlədʒɪ; ˌspiːliˈɔlədʒi〕 *n.* 洞穴學(研究洞穴與穴居人生活之學科)。—**spe·le·ol·o·gist,** *n.*

*__spell¹__ 〔spɛl; spel〕 *v.,* **spelled** or **spelt, spell·ing.** —*v.t.* ①拼(某字)字母。How do you *spell* your name? 你的名字如何拼法？②(字母)拼成(字、音節等)。③意指；招致。 Delay *spells* danger. 遲延招致危險。④艱難地讀。—*v.i.* 拼字；綴字。We learn to *spell* in school. 我們在學校學習拼字。***spell out*** **a.** 詳細說明；詳加解釋。 Must I *spell* it *out* for you? 我非詳加解釋不可

嗎? b. 拼出來。c. 費力地求解。

*spell² n. ①符咒;咒語。②魔力。She cast a *spell* on him. 她把他迷住了。—ful, adj.

*spell³ n., v., spelled, spell·ing. —n. ①工作時間; 輪值時間。②一段時期; 一陣子。a long *spell* of fine weather. 一段長時期的好天氣。③替代他人工作。④〖美俗〗短時;片刻。⑤〖澳〗休息。 —v.t. ①〖俗〗暫代(他人)。②〖澳〗給…以暫時休息。—v.i.〖澳〗休息。

spell·bind (ˈspɛlˌbaɪnd; ˈspelbaind) v.t.,-bound, -bind·ing. ①以符咒迷住。②迷惑。

spell·bind·er (ˈspɛlˌbaɪndɚ; ˈspelˌbaində) n.〖美俗〗①能吸引聽衆的演說家。②能吸引觀衆的演出;能吸引讀者的作品。

spell·bound (ˈspɛlˌbaund; ˈspelbaund) adj. 被迷住的;意亂情迷的。

spell·er (ˈspɛlɚ; ˈspelə) n. ①拼字者;綴字者。②拼字書。

***spell·ing** (ˈspɛlɪŋ; ˈspeliŋ) n. ①拼字;綴字。②拼(綴)字法。"Ax" has two *spellings*. Ax 有兩種拼法。

spelling bee 〖美〗拼字比賽;綴字比賽。

spelling book 綴字書。

spelling match 綴字比賽。

spelt¹ (spɛlt; spelt) v. pt. & pp. of **spell**.

spelt² n.〖植物〗一種小麥。

spel·ter (ˈspɛltɚ; ˈspeltə) n. 鋅(尤指鋅錠);亞鉛。

spe·lunk·er (spɪˈlʌŋkɚ; spiˈlʌŋkə) n. 「洞穴探險者。」

Spe·mann (ˈʃpemɑn; ˈʃpeimɑːn) n. 施培曼(Hans, 1869–1941, 德國動物學家,曾獲1935年諾貝爾醫學獎)。

Spen·cer (ˈspɛnsɚ; ˈspensə) n. 斯賓塞(Herbert, 1820–1903, 英國哲學家)。

spen·cer¹ (ˈspɛnsɚ; ˈspensə) n. 一種短的羊毛外套。

spen·cer² n.〖航海〗前桅之縱帆。

Spen·ce·ri·an (spɛnˈsɪrɪən; spenˈsiəriən) adj. ①英國哲學家 Herbert Spencer 的;其哲學體系的。②美國教師 Platt Rogers Spencer (1800–1864) 所教之書法的(其特徵爲:清晰、圓形、右斜)。—n. Herbert Spencer 學派之信徒。

:spend (spɛnd; spend) v., **spent, spend·ing.** —v.t. ①花用; 耗費。He doesn't like *spending* money. 他不好花錢。②用盡; 使竭盡。The storm has *spent* its force. 暴風雨已經靜息。 —v.i. 花錢; 浪費。He *spends* easily. 他隨便花錢。—er, n.

spend·a·ble (ˈspɛndəbl; ˈspendəbl) adj. 可花費的。

spending money 個人的零用錢。

spend·thrift (ˈspɛndˌθrɪft; ˈspendθrift) n. 揮金如土的人; 浪費者。—adj. 浪費的;揮霍無度的。

Spen·ser (ˈspɛnsɚ; ˈspensə) n. 斯賓塞(Edmund, 1552?–1599, 英國詩人, 1591–99 爲桂冠詩人)。

Spen·se·ri·an (spɛnˈsɪrɪən; spenˈsiəriən) adj. 英國詩人 Edmund Spenser的;其詩的。—n. ①模仿或追隨 Spenser 者。②=**Spenserian stanza.**

Spenserian stanza 〖詩〗斯賓塞體(Spenser 寫 The Faerie Queene 的詩體)。

:spent (spɛnt; spent) v. pt. & pp. of **spend.** —adj. 耗盡的;疲竭的。

sperm¹ (spɝm; spəːm) n. 精液; 精蟲。

sperm² n. ①〖動物〗抹香鯨。②鯨腦;鯨蠟。③鯨腦油。

sper·ma·cet·i (ˌspɝməˈsɛtɪ; ˌspəːməˈseti) n. 鯨腦;鯨蠟。

sper·ma·ry (ˈspɝmərɪ; ˈspəːməri) n., pl. -ries. ①〖解剖〗精囊。②〖植物〗雄器。

sper·mat·ic (spɝˈmætɪk; spəːˈmætik) adj. 精液的;精蟲的;精囊的。(亦作**spermous**)

spermatic fluid 〖生理〗精液。

sper·ma·tid (ˈspɝmətɪd; ˈspəːmətid) n. 〖生物〗精子細胞。

sper·ma·ti·um (spɝˈmeʃɪəm; spəːˈmeiʃiəm) n., pl. -ti·a (-ʃɪə; -ʃiə).〖植物〗雄子;雄性原;雄精體。

sper·ma·to·phore (ˈspɝmətəˌfor; ˈspəːmətəfɔː) n.〖動物〗(無脊椎動物之)精囊。

sper·ma·to·phyte (ˈspɝmətəˌfaɪt; ˈspəːmətəfait) n. 〖植物〗種子植物。

sper·ma·tor·rhoe·a, sper·ma·tor·rhe·a (ˌspɝmətəˈriə; ˌspəːmətəˈriːə) n. 〖醫〗遺精。

sper·ma·to·zo·on (ˌspɝmətəˈzoɑn; ˌspəːmətouˈzouɔn) n., pl. -zo·a (-ˈzoə; -ˈzouə).〖生物〗精蟲;精子。

sperm oil 抹香鯨油。

sper·mo·phile (ˈspɝməˌfaɪl; ˈspəːməfail) n. 〖動物〗美洲西部產的小地鼠。

sperm whale 〖動物〗抹香鯨。

spew (spju; spjuː) v.t. 嘔吐出; 吐出。—v.i. 作嘔;吐出;嘔吐。—n.嘔吐物;吐出物;作嘔。(亦作 **spue**) —er, n.

sp. gr. specific gravity.

sphac·e·late (ˈsfæsəˌlet; ˈsfæsəleit) v.t. & v.i., -lat·ed, -lat·ing. (使)成壞疽性;(使)成死肉;(使)生脫疽;腐爛。

Sphag·num (ˈsfægnəm; ˈsfægnəm) n., pl. -na (-nə; -nə).〖植物〗①水苔屬;水蘚屬。②(s-)水苔屬或水蘚屬之任一種植物。

sphe·noid (ˈsfinɔɪd; ˈsfiːnɔid) adj. ①楔狀的。②〖解剖〗楔狀(骨)的。—n.〖解剖〗楔狀骨。

spher·al (ˈsfɪrəl; ˈsfiərəl) adj. ①球的;球狀的。②對稱的;勻整的。—i·ty, n.

***sphere** (sfɪr; sfiə) n. ①球; 球形; 球體;球面。②天體。 The earth, sun, and moon are *spheres*. 地球、太陽和月亮均爲天體。③地球儀;渾天儀。④範圍;領域; 社會地位。We move in different *spheres*. 我們在不同的社會裏活動。—v.t. ①包圍; 罩住。②將…做成球體。③使升起;使浮起。

spher·i·cal (ˈsfɛrəkl; ˈsferikəl) adj. ①球的;球狀的;球面的。②天體的。③星相的。

spherical aberration 〖光學〗球面像差。

spherical geometry 球面幾何學。

spherical surface 球面。

spherical triangle 球面三角形。

spherical trigonometry 〖數學〗球面三角。

sphe·ric·i·ty (sfɪˈrɪsətɪ; sfiəˈrisiti) n. 球形;圓。

spher·ics (ˈsfɛrɪks; ˈsferiks) n.〖數學〗球面幾何學;球面三角法。

sphe·roid (ˈsfɪrɔɪd; ˈsfiərɔid) n. 橙形體;橢圓體; 類似球狀體。—adj. 橙形的; 橢圓體的。

sphe·roi·dal (sfɪˈrɔɪdl; sfiəˈrɔidl) adj. ①類似球形的。②橢圓體的。(亦作 **spheroidic**) —ly, adv.

sphe·rom·e·ter (sfɪˈrɑmətɚ; sfiəˈrɔmitə) n. 球徑計;球面計。

spher·ule (ˈsfɛrul; ˈsferjuːl) n.小球體。

sphinc·ter (ˈsfɪŋktɚ; ˈsfiŋktə) n. 〖解

部〗括約肌。—al, *adj.*

***sphinx** 〔sfɪŋks; sfiŋks〕 *n., pl.* **sphinxes** 〔'sfɪŋksɪz; 'sfiŋksiz〕. ①獅身人頭(羊頭或鷹頭)之雕像。②(S-) 埃及首都開羅附近的獅身人面大雕像。③〖希臘神話〗獅身人面且有翅膀之怪物。④神祕的人;怪人。⑤天蛾。

sphra·gis·tics 〔sfrə'dʒɪstɪks; sfrə'dʒistiks〕 *n.* 印章學。—**sphra·gis·tic,** *adj.*

sphyg·mo·graph 〔'sfɪgmə,græf; 'sfigməgrɑːf〕 *n.* 〖醫〗脈搏計;脈波計。

sphyg·mo·ma·nom·e·ter 〔,sfɪgmomə'nɑmətɚ; ,sfigmoumə'nɔmitə〕 *n.* 〖醫〗脈搏血壓計;血壓測量計。

sphyg·mus 〔'sfɪgməs; 'sfigməs〕 *n.* 〖醫〗脈搏。

spi·ca 〔'spaɪkə; 'spaikə〕 *n., pl.* **-cae** 〔-si; -siː〕. ①〖植物〗穗狀花。②〖醫〗穗狀繃帶。③(S-)〖天文〗角宿第一星(卽 Virgo 座中之第一星)。

spi·ca·to 〔spɪ'kɑto; spi'kɑːtou〕 *n., pl.* **-tos,** *adj.* 〖音樂〗跳弓(的)(奏小提琴時,左手手腕放鬆,任弓上下跳躍之奏法)。

spi·cate 〔'spaɪket; 'spaikeit〕 *adj.* ①〖植物〗有穗的。②〖動物〗尖的。

***spice** 〔spaɪs; spais〕 *n., v.,* **spiced, spicing.** —*n.* ①香料;調味品。②香味。③氣味;意味;風味;趣味。There is a *spice* of madness in his character. 他的性格帶有狂氣。—*v.t.* ①加以香料。②爲…加添興趣。

spice·ber·ry 〔'spaɪs,bɛrɪ; 'spaisberi〕 *n., pl.* **-ries.** 〖植物〗①(產於西印度羣島及美國 Florida 州之)一種小樹;其果實。②白珠樹。

spice·bush 〔'spaɪs,bʊʃ; 'spaisbuʃ〕 *n.* 〖植物〗北美所產之安息香。

Spice Islands 香料羣島(卽 Molucca 羣島)。

spic·er·y 〔'spaɪsərɪ; 'spaisəri〕 *n., pl.* **-ies.** ①香料(集合稱);香料之氣味。②有香味的東西;作料。③〖古〗香料貯藏所。

spick-and-span 〔'spɪkən'spæn; 'spikən'spæn〕 *adj.* ①嶄新的;新鮮的。②整潔的。

spic·u·late 〔'spɪkjə,let; 'spikjuleit〕 *adj.* ①針骨狀的。②有針骨的。

spic·ule 〔'spɪkjul; 'spaikjuːl〕 *n.* ①針狀體。②〖解剖〗針骨;骨片。③〖植物〗小穗狀花。

spic·y 〔'spaɪsɪ; 'spaisi〕 *adj.,* **spic·i·er, spic·i·est.** ①加有香料的;有香味的。②像香料味的。③火辣的;尖刻的。④下流的。⑤產香料的;多香料的。

***spi·der** 〔'spaɪdɚ; 'spaidə〕 *n.* ①蜘蛛。②像蜘蛛的東西。③一種有柄的淺鍋。④(在火上撐鍋用的)三脚架。

spider crab 〖動物〗蜘蛛蟹。

spider monkey 〖動物〗蜘蛛猿。

spi·der·wort 〔'spaɪdɚ,wɝt; 'spaidəwəːt〕 *n.* 〖植物〗紫鴨跖草。

spi·der·y 〔'spaɪdərɪ; 'spaidəri〕 *adj.* ①細長如蜘蛛足的。②似蜘蛛網的。③多蜘蛛的。

spie·gel·ei·sen 〔'spigəl,aɪzən; 'spiːgəlaizən〕 *n.* 鏡鐵(一種含錳之白色鑄鐵)。

spiel 〔spil; spiːl〕 *n.* 〖俚〗談話;講話;演說。—*v.i.* 〖俚〗談話;演講。—**er,** *n.*

spi·er 〔'spaɪɚ; 'spaiə〕 *n.* 偵探;密探。

spiff·y 〔'spɪfɪ; 'spifi〕 *adj.,* **spiff·i·er, spiff·i·est.** 〖俚〗①服裝漂亮的;整潔的;優秀的。②愜意的;安逸的。—**spiff·i·ness,** *n.*

spig·ot 〔'spɪgət; 'spigət〕 *n.* ①栓;塞子。②活門。③〖美〗(自來水的)龍頭。

spike**¹ 〔spaɪk; spaik〕 *n., v.,* **spiked, spik·ing.** —*n.* ①長釘;大釘。②釘狀物。The ballplayers wear shoes with *spikes.* 打球者穿釘鞋。③(*pl.*)釘鞋。—*v.t.* ①以大釘釘牢。②將釘裝於(鞋上)。③用鞋釘傷(人)。④將釘穿入(鎗的裝藥口)使失效。⑤阻止;使失效;使失敗。⑥加酒於(飲料)。spike one's gun*** 破壞一個人的計畫;使某人計不得逞。

***spike**² *n.* ①穗。②穗狀花。

spiked heel 高跟鞋上之後跟。

spike lavender 歐洲產的一種薄荷(其油可做香料)。

spike·let 〔'spaɪklɪt; 'spaiklit〕 *n.* 〖植物〗小穗狀花;小穗。

spike·nard 〔'spaɪknɚd, 'spaiknɑːd〕 *n.* ①(東印度所產有香味之)一種敗醬科植物。②(古時的)一種香油膏(據測爲上述植物所製成)。③(美洲所產有香根的)一種五加科植物。

spik·y 〔'spaɪkɪ; 'spaiki〕 *adj.* ①如樁的;有尖頭的。②打釘的;多釘的。③如穗的。

spile 〔spaɪl; spail〕 *n., v.,* **spiled, spil·ing.** —*n.* ①栓;塞。②取楓汁之插管。③樁;杙。—*v.t.* ①塞以栓;開小孔於…以插栓。②自插管中抽取(液汁)。③給…打樁;以樁支撐。

spil·i·kin 〔'spɪlɪkɪn; 'spilikin〕 *n.* ①jackstraws 等遊戲用之小木片。②(*pl.*)(作 *sing.* 解) 用此類小木片所做之遊戲。(亦作 **spillikin**)

spil·ing 〔'spaɪlɪŋ; 'spailiŋ〕 *n.* ①打樁。②栓或塞(集合稱)。

spill**¹ 〔spɪl; spil〕 *v.,* **spilled** or **spilt, spilling,** *n.* —*v.t.*①使(水等)流出或落下;灑(水)。②使自馬上、車中、船中等顚落或墮下。③使(帆)露風。④洩露(祕密);道出。—*v.i.* 溢出;灑。It is no use crying over spilt milk.*** 爲灑了的牛奶而哭號是無益的;(喩)往者不諫。***spill blood*** 使流血。***spill the beans*** 〖美俚〗無意中洩漏機密。—*n.* ①流出;溢出。②濺出之量。③〖俗〗跌落。④傾盆大雨。⑤溢洪道。

spill² *n.* ①小栓;小塞。②紙捻。③木片。

spill·age 〔'spɪlɪdʒ; 'spilidʒ〕 *n.* ①溢出。②溢出之物;溢出之量。

spil·li·kin 〔'spɪlɪkɪn; 'spilikin〕 *n.* = **spilikin.**

spill·o·ver 〔'spɪl,ovɚ; 'spil,ouvə〕 *n.* ①溢出;超出範圍。②溢出物;氾濫;充沛。

spill·way 〔'spɪl,we; 'spilwei〕 *n.* (堰、河等之)溢洪道;放水堰。

spilt 〔spɪlt; spilt〕 *v.* pt. & pp. of **spill.**

spilth 〔spɪlθ; spilθ〕 *n.* ①溢出;流出。②溢出之物;流出物。③剩餘物。

spin** 〔spɪn; spin〕 *v.,* **spun, spin·ning,** *n.* —*v.t.* ①紡;紡織。②抽(絲)織網。Spiders *spin* webs. 蜘蛛織網。③將(玻璃、金)抽成線。④編製;講述。⑤使旋轉。⑥拖延;拉長〖常 out〗. He *spun* the project out for three years. 他將該計畫拖延了三年時間。⑦故意使(火箭或飛彈)滾轉。—*v.i.* ①紡織。②旋轉。The wheel *spins* round. 輪子旋轉。③暈眩。④迅速地跑, 開車, 騎馬等。spin a coin*** 擲錢於空中, 待落下後看哪一面朝上。***spin along*** 很快移動;疾馳。***spin a yarn*** (or ***story***)講故事。***spin off*** 創造新事物而不影響原物之大小或穩定性等。***spin out*** 拖長。***spin round*** 旋轉。—*n.* ①旋轉。The pitcher gave a *spin* to the ball. 投手使球旋轉。②疾行;疾馳。③(飛機)螺旋下降。

spin·ach, spin·age 〔'spɪnɪdʒ; 'spinidʒ〕 *n.* 菠菜。

spi·nal 〔'spaɪnl̩; 'spainl̩〕 *adj.* 脊骨的;脊柱的。

spinal column 脊柱;脊;脊椎骨。

spinal cord 脊髓。

***spin·dle** 〔'spɪndl̩; 'spindl〕 *n., adj., v.,* **-dled, -dling.** —*n.* ①紡錘。②紗之長度單位。③細長如紡錘之物。④警告棒(一端有燈,插於石上以警告船隻)。⑤液體比重計。⑥〖生

物〕紡錘狀細胞。⑦軸；轉軸。⑧〖建築〗旋梯中柱。—*adj.* ①紡錘的；紡錘狀的。②母系的；母方的。—*v.i.* ①〖植物〗發長莖。②長成細長。—*v.t.* 使成細長如軸；裝以軸。

spin·dle-leg·ged [ˈspɪndḷˌlɛgɪd; ˈspindllegd] *adj.* 有細長之腿的。

spin·dle·legs [ˈspɪndḷˌlɛgz; ˈspindllegz] *n. pl.* ①細長腿。②〖俗〗(作 *sing.* 解)細長腿者。

spin·dle-shanked [ˈspɪndḷˌʃæŋkt; ˈspindlʃæŋkt] *adj.* 有細長腿的。

spindle side 母方；母系。

spindle tree 〖植物〗桃葉衛矛。

spin·dling [ˈspɪndlɪŋ; ˈspindliŋ] *adj.* 細長的。—*n.* 細長的人或物。

spin·dly [ˈspɪndlɪ; ˈspindli] *adj.*, **-dli·er, -dli·est.** 紡錘形的；細長的。

spin·drift [ˈspɪnˌdrɪft; ˈspin-drift] *n.* (强風吹起的)浪花。(亦作 **spoondrift**)

spin dryer (or **drier**) 旋轉式衣服乾燥機。

***spine** [spaɪn; spain] *n.* ①脊骨。②針；刺；棘狀突起。The cactus has *spines.* 仙人掌有刺。③脊骨狀物。④人面臨危險或逆境時所表現的勇敢剛毅。

spined [spaɪnd; spaind] *adj.* 有脊椎的；有刺的。

spi·nel, spi·nelle [spɪˈnɛl, ˈspɪnəl; spiˈnel] *n.* 〖礦〗尖晶石。

spine·less [ˈspaɪnlɪs ˈspainlis] *adj.* ①無脊椎的。②無刺的；無棘狀突起的。③跛的。④優柔寡斷的；沒骨氣的。—**ly,** *adv.* —**ness,** *n.*

spi·nes·cent [spaɪˈnɛsənt; spaiˈnesənt] *adj.* ①〖植物〗a. 長成刺的。b. 有刺的。②〖動物〗粗糙、尖銳的(如羽毛等)。

spin·et [ˈspɪnɪt; spiˈnet] *n.* 〖音樂〗①小瑟。②早期之小方形鋼琴。

spin·na·ker [ˈspɪnəkɚ; ˈspinəkə] *n.* 〖航海〗遊艇順風時所用之大三角帆。

spin·ner [ˈspɪnɚ; ˈspinə] *n.* ①紡織者；善紡織者。②紡織機。③〖動物〗蜘蛛。④〖動物〗怪鴟。⑤蜘蛛等之絲囊。⑥〖航空〗機頭罩；槳轂整流器。⑦說故事者。

spin·ner·et [ˈspɪnəˌrɛt; ˈspinəret] *n.* (蜘蛛等的)絲囊。

spin·ner·y [ˈspɪnərɪ; ˈspinəri] *n., pl.* **-ries.** 紡織廠；紡紗廠。

spin·ney [ˈspɪnɪ; ˈspini] *n.* 〖英〗雜木林。

***spin·ning** [ˈspɪnɪŋ; ˈspiniŋ] *adj.* ①紡織的。②旋轉的。—*n.* 紡織。—**ly,** *adv.*

spinning jenny 多軸紡織機。

spinning machine 紡織機。

spinning mill 紡織廠。

spinning wheel 紡車。

spin-off [ˈspɪnˌɔf; ˈspinɔf] *n.* ①將新公司或子公司股份分配給母公司股東之措施。②(電視劇之)續集。③副產物。

spi·nose [ˈspaɪnos; ˈspainous] *adj.* 有刺的；多刺的。

spi·nos·i·ty [spaɪˈnɑsətɪ; spaiˈnɔsiti] *n.* ①有刺；多刺。②譏諷；諷刺的話。③有刺之部分；有刺之物。

spi·nous [ˈspaɪnəs; ˈspainəs] *adj.* 有刺的；多刺的；棘狀的。

Spi·no·za [spɪˈnozə; spiˈnouzə] *n.* 斯賓諾莎 (Baruch *or* Benedict, 1632–1677, 荷蘭哲學家)。

spin·ster [ˈspɪnstɚ; ˈspinstə] *n.* ①未婚女性。②老處女。③紡織女。—**hood,** *n.*

spin·thar·i·scope [spɪnˈθærəˌskop; spinˈθæriskoup] *n.* 〖物理〗閃爍鏡。

spi·nule [ˈspaɪnjul; ˈspainju:l] *n.* 小刺。

spin·y [ˈspaɪnɪ; ˈspaini] *adj.* ①多針的；多刺的；覆有針或刺的。②刺狀的；似針的。③困難的；麻煩的。④不易相處的；脾氣古怪的。

spin·y-finned [ˈspaɪnɪˌfɪnd; ˈspaini-find] *adj.* (魚類)鰭上多硬刺的。

spi·ra·cle [ˈspaɪrəkḷ; ˈspaiərəkl] *n.* ①昆蟲的呼吸孔。②鯨類的噴水孔。③通風孔；通氣孔。—**spi·rac·u·lar,** *adj.*

spi·rae·a [spaɪˈriə; spaiˈriə] *n.* 〖植物〗繡線菊。

***spi·ral** [ˈspaɪrəl; ˈspaiərəl] *adj., n., v.,* **-ral(l)ed, -ral·(l)ing.** —*adj.* ①螺旋形的；盤旋的。②〖數學〗螺線的。a *spiral* line. 螺線。—*n.* ①螺旋形之物。②〖數學〗螺線。③〖經濟〗成本、工資、物價等之不斷上升 (inflationary spiral) 或不斷下降 (deflationary spiral). —*v.t.* 使形成螺旋；螺旋狀接近。The plane *spiraled* the airport before landing. 飛機在降落前在機場上空盤旋。—*v.i.* ①成螺旋狀移動或旋轉。②(飛機)成螺旋狀下降。—**ly,** *adv.*

spiral galaxy (or **nebula**) 〖天文〗旋渦星雲。

spi·rant [ˈspaɪrənt; ˈspaiərənt] *n., adj.* 摩擦音(的)。

***spire**[1] [spaɪr; spaiə] *n., v.,* **spired, spir·ing.** —*n.* ①塔尖；尖頂。②最高點；頂點。the *spire* of one's profession. 事業之最高峯。③芽。—*v.i.* ①高聳。②出嫩芽。—*v.t.* 建以尖頂。

spire[2] *n.* 螺線；單廻螺旋線。

spi·re·a [spaɪˈriə; spaiˈriə] *n.* =**spiraea.**

spi·reme [ˈspaɪrim; ˈspaiəri:m] *n.* 〖生物〗染色體之旋絲；染色質細；絲毬。

Spi·ril·lum [spaɪˈrɪləm; spaiəˈriləm] *n., pl.* **-la** [-lə; -lə]. ①螺旋狀菌屬。②(s-) 螺旋狀菌。

‡**spir·it** [ˈspɪrɪt; ˈspirit] *n.* ①精神。He is vexed in *spirit.* 他精神煩惱。②靈魂。③幽靈；鬼。④(*pl.*)心境。He is in good *spirits.* 他很愉快。⑤人；人格。a brave *spirit.* 英勇之士。⑥勇氣；銳氣。⑦眞意；要旨。⑧(常 *pl.*) 火酒；酒精；酒。He drinks beer but no *spirits.* 他飲啤酒而不飲烈性的酒。⑨影響；風氣。⑩熱心與忠實。⑪個性；脾氣。***Holy Spirit*** 聖靈。***in high*** (***low***) ***spirits*** 高興(不高興)。***out of spirits*** 憂傷的；怏怏然。***the departed spirits*** 亡靈。***the Spirit*** a. 上帝。b. 聖靈。—*v.t.* ①誘拐〖away, off〗. The child has been *spirited* away. 這孩子被拐走了。②鼓勵。③以魔法變出。

spir·it·ed [ˈspɪrɪtɪd; ˈspiritid] *adj.* ①精神飽滿的；生氣勃勃的；活潑的；勇猛的。②(用於複合詞中)有…精神的；有…心境的。high-*spirited.* 高興的。—**ly,** *adv.* —**ness,** *n.*

spir·it·ism [ˈspɪrɪtɪzm; ˈspiritizm] *n.* 招魂術；降神術。—**spir·it·is·tic,** *adj.*

spirit lamp 酒精燈。

spir·it·less [ˈspɪrɪtlɪs; ˈspiritlis] *adj.* 無精神的；無生命力的；沒有勇氣的；委靡不振的；垂頭喪氣的。—**ly,** *adv.* —**ness,** *n.*

spirit level 酒精水準器。

spi·ri·to·so [ˌspɪrɪˈtoso; ˌspiriˈtousou] 〖義〗*adj.* 〖音樂〗活潑的。

spirit rapper 招魂者；降神者。

spirit rapping 降神術；招魂術。

spirits of turpentine 松香油。

spirits of wine 酒精。

spir·it·u·al** [ˈspɪrɪtʃuəl; ˈspiritjuəl, -tʃuəl] *adj.* ①精神的；靈魂的；精神上的。②神聖的；宗教上的。*spiritual* songs. 聖歌。③脫俗的；崇高的。a *spiritual* mind. 崇高的精神。Lords Spiritual*** 英國上議院的主教或

大主教。—*n.* ①(美國南方黑人所唱的一種極富感情的)靈歌。②(*pl.*) **a.** 宗教事務。**b.** 精神事務。—ly, *adv.*

spir·it·u·al·ism 〔ˈspɪrɪtʃuəlˌɪzəm; ˈspiritjuəlizəm〕 *n.* ①〖哲〗唯心論;唯靈論。②招魂術; 降神術; 招魂論。—**spir·it·u·al·ist,** *n.* —**spir·it·u·al·is·tic,** *adj.*

spir·it·u·al·i·ty 〔ˌspɪrɪtʃuˈælətɪ; ˌspiritjuˈæliti〕 *n., pl.* **-ties.** ①精神性;心靈性。②專注於精神或靈性之事物。③(常 *pl.*) 敎堂或敎士之財產與收入。

spir·it·u·al·ize 〔ˈspɪrɪtʃuəlˌaɪz;ˈspiritʃuəlaiz〕 *v.t.,* **-ized, -iz·ing.** ①使精神化;使靈化;使淸心; 使脫俗; 使高尚。②予以精神的意義; 釋爲屬靈的意義。③〖罕〗鼓舞。(亦作 **spiritualise**) —**spir·it·u·al·i·za·tion,** *n.*

spi·ri·tu·el 〔ˌspɪrɪtʃuˈel; ˌspiritʃuˈel〕 〖法〗 *adj.* 活潑的;愉快的;嫻雅的。

spi·ri·tu·elle 〔ˌspɪrɪtʃuˈɛl; ˌspiritʃuˈel〕 〖法〗 *adj.* 活潑的;愉快的;嫻雅的(指婦女言)。

spir·it·u·ous 〔ˈspɪrɪtʃuəs;ˈspiritʃuəs〕 *adj.* ①酒精的; 似酒精的。 ②含酒精成分强的。③快樂的;有精神的。

spi·ro·ch(a)ete 〔ˈspaɪrəˌkit; ˈspaiərəkiːt〕 *n.* 螺旋菌。

spi·ro·graph 〔ˈspaɪrəˌgræf; ˈspaiərəgrɑːf〕 *n.* 〖醫〗呼吸記錄器。

Spi·ro·gy·ra〔ˌspaɪrəˈdʒaɪrə;ˌspaiərəˈdʒairə〕 *n.* 〖植物〗①水綿屬。②(s-) 水綿屬之植物;水綿。

spi·rom·e·ter 〔spaɪˈrɑmətɚ; ˌspaiəˈrɔmitə〕 *n.* 〖醫〗肺活量計;呼吸計。

spirt 〔spɝt; spəːt〕 *v., n.* =**spurt.**

spir·y¹ 〔ˈspaɪrɪ;ˈspaiəri〕 *adj.,* **spir·i·er, spir·i·est.** 螺旋狀的;渦卷的。

spir·y² *adj.,* **spir·i·er, spir·i·est.** 尖閣的;尖塔的;多尖塔的;細長的。

spit**¹ 〔spɪt; spit〕 *v.,* **spat** or **spit, spit·ting,** *n.* —*v.i.* ①唾;吐唾液。Don't *spit* in the bus. 不要在公共汽車內吐口水。②落小雨;降小雪。③發如吐之聲音。The cat *spat* at the dog. 貓向狗呼呼叫。—*v.t.* 吐出;放出。The gun *spits* fire. 砲噴吐砲火。spit at*** 向…吐口水; 藐視; 侮辱。***spit in one's face*** (***teeth***) 吐口水於某人面(嘴)上; 侮辱某人。***spit in*** (or ***on***) ***one's hand*** 吐口水於掌上;加緊努力。***spit it out*** 坦白說出。***spit upon*** 輕蔑; 侮辱。—*n.* ①唾液。②唾吐;唾吐聲。③某些昆蟲分泌的唾液狀液體。④小雨;小雪。⑤酷似。***be the*** (***dead***) ***spit of a person*** 〖俗〗酷似某人。

spit² *n., v.,* **spit·ted, spit·ting.** —*n.* ①烤肉叉;炙叉。②突伸海中的狹長陸地;崎;岬。—*v.t.* 刺穿;刺戳。

spit³ *n.* 〖英〗一鋤、一鍬或一鏟之深。

spit·al 〔ˈspɪtl̩; ˈspitl〕 *n.* ①醫院(尤指貧民、患麻瘋病者等之醫院)。②令人厭惡之場所。③大路旁供旅人休息之小棚。

spit·ball 〔ˈspɪtˌbɔl; ˈspitbɔːl〕 *n.* ①小孩投擲作戲的以唾液弄濕之小紙團。②〖棒球〗將球一側唾濕而投之曲球(今已視爲違規)。

spitch·cock 〔ˈspɪtʃˌkɑk; ˈspitʃkɔk〕 *n.* 烤炙之鰻魚片。—*v.t.* ①剖開而炙(鷄、鰻等)。②簡略地處理;粗魯地應付。

spit curl 在額前或兩鬢弄濕並壓平之髮卷。

spit-dev·il 〔ˈspɪtˌdɛvl̩; ˈspitˌdevl〕 *n.* 煙火的一種。

‡spite 〔spaɪt; spait〕 *n., v.,* **spit·ed, spit·ing.** —*n.* 惡意; 怨恨。He has a *spite* against me. 他對我懷有惡意。***in spite of*** 雖然;儘管…仍。We succeeded *in spite of* all difficulties. 我們雖遭遇種種困難,終獲成功。—*v.t.* ①使困惱; 使難堪; 輕蔑。②敵視;仇視。***cut off one's nose to spite one's face*** 洩怒反以自害。

spite·ful 〔ˈspaɪtfəl; ˈspaitful〕 *adj.* 懷恨的;有惡意的。—**ly,** *adv.*

spit·fire 〔ˈspɪtˌfaɪr; ˈspitˌfaiə〕 *n.* ①易怒之人(尤指婦女)。②噴火之物(如大砲等)。

Spit·te·ler 〔ˈʃpɪtəlɚ; ˈʃpitələ〕 *n.* 斯比特勒 (Carl, 1845–1924, 筆名Felix Tandem, 瑞士作家, 曾獲1919年諾貝爾文學獎)。

spit·ter¹ 〔ˈspɪtɚ; ˈspitə〕 *n.* ①吐唾液之人。②〖俗〗〖棒球〗=**spitball.**

spit·ter² *n.* ①以肉叉烤肉者。②開始長角之小鹿。

spit·tle 〔ˈspɪtl; ˈspitl〕 *n.* ①唾液;口水。②泡泡蟲 (spittle insect) 所分泌的泡沫。***lick one's spittle*** 諂媚。

spit·toon 〔spɪˈtun;spiˈtuːn〕 *n.* 痰盂。

spitz 〔spɪts; spits〕 *n.* 狐狸狗。(亦作 **spitz dog**)

spit·zen·burg 〔ˈspɪtsn̩ˌbɝg; ˈspitsnbəːg〕 *n.* 美國產之一種冬季蘋果。

spiv 〔spɪv; spiv〕 *n.* 〖英俚〗作奸犯科者。

spiv·(v)er·y 〔ˈspɪvərɪ; ˈspivəri〕 *n.* 〖英俗〗不務正業的生活;似寄生蟲之生活。

splanch·nic 〔ˈsplæŋknɪk;ˈsplæŋknik〕 *adj.* 內臟的。

splash** 〔splæʃ; splæʃ〕 *v.t.* ①濺 (水、泥等)。Stop *splashing* the water about. 不要亂撩水啦。②濺污; 濺濕。The mud has *splashed* my dress. 泥濺污了我的衣服。③涉水、泥而進。—*v.i.* ①激濺水、泥等。The waves *splashed* on the beach. 波浪激濺在海灘上。②涉水、泥而進。He *splashed* across the brook. 他涉水過溪。—*n.* ①激濺; 激濺聲。②(激起之水、泥等遺留之)污跡;斑痕。③張揚;渲染。④ **a.** 用水沖走木料。**b.** 將木料沖走之水。make a splash*** 引起他人注意。

splash·board 〔ˈsplæʃˌbord; ˈsplæʃbɔːd〕 *n.* ①遮泥板; 擋泥板; 擋水板。②水壩溢洪道之開關。

splash·down 〔ˈsplæʃˌdaun; ˈsplæʃdaun〕 *n.* ①太空船等之在海中降落。②此種降落之地點。③此種降落之時間。

splash·er 〔ˈsplæʃɚ; ˈsplæʃə〕 *n.* ①濺灑者;濺灑器。②防水濺灑之物(如油布等)。

splash guard 車後輪之擋泥橡皮條。

splash·y 〔ˈsplæʃɪ;ˈsplæʃi〕 *adj.,* **splash·i·er, splash·i·est.** ①濺灑的; 飛濺的。②易濺的;濕的; 泥濘的。③有污斑的; 有斑痕的。④炫耀的;鋪張的。

splat 〔splæt;splæt〕 *n.* ①(椅背中間用的)扁平木板。②噼啪聲。

splat·ter 〔ˈsplætɚ; ˈsplætə〕 *v.t. & v.i.* 濺污;發潑濺聲;不淸晰地說。

splay 〔sple; splei〕 *v.t.* ①擴張;延展。②使(窗口、門口之壁) 傾斜。③使 (骨節)脫臼。—*v.i.* ①傾斜。②擴張; 擴大。—*adj.* ①擴張的;延展的。②粗陋的; 笨拙的。③傾斜的; 歪斜的。—*n.* ①擴大;展開。②〖建築〗(門、窗、壁等之)斜面或斜角。

splay·foot 〔ˈspleˌfut; ˈspleifut〕 *n., pl.* **-feet,** *adj.* —*n.* 扁平外撇之脚;八字脚。—*adj.* =**splayfooted.**

splay·foot·ed 〔ˈspleˌfutɪd; ˈspleiˌfutid〕 *adj.* ①有扁平外撇之脚的。②笨拙的。

spleen 〔splin; spliːn〕 *n.* ①脾;脾臟。②發脾氣;憤怒。③抑鬱。

spleen·ful 〔ˈsplinfəl; ˈspliːnful〕 *adj.* 易怒的;有惡意的;乖張的。—**ly,** *adv.*

spleen·wort ['splinˏwɝt; 'spli:nwə:t] *n.* 〖植物〗脾草(用以治脾臟病)。

splen·dent ['splɛndənt; 'splendənt] *adj.* ①光亮的; 發光的。②外觀漂亮的; 鮮明的。③顯赫的; 著名的。—**ly,** *adv.*

:splen·did ['splɛndɪd; 'splendid] *adj.* ①華麗的; 壯麗的; 堂皇的; 輝煌的。a *splendid* victory. 輝煌的勝利。②〖俗〗絕妙的; 極佳的。—**ly,** *adv.* —**ness,** *n.*

splen·dif·er·ous [splɛn'dɪfərəs; splen'difərəs] *adj.* 〖俗, 諧〗華麗的; 燦爛的。

***splen·do(u)r** ['splɛndɚ; 'splendə] *n.* ①光彩; 光輝。②華麗; 壯麗。③顯赫; 卓越。the *splendor* of one's achievements. 一個人的成就之卓越。

sple·nec·to·my [splɪ'nɛktəmɪ; spli'nektəmi] *n.* 〖外科〗脾臟切除術。

sple·net·ic [splɪ'nɛtɪk; spli'netik] *adj.* (亦作 **splenetical**) ①脾的; 脾臟的。②壞脾氣的; 易怒的; 性情乖戾的。—*n.* 壞脾氣的人; 易怒的人。—**sple·net·i·cal·ly,** *adv.*

splen·ic ['splɛnɪk, 'splinɪk; 'splenik, 'spli:nik] *adj.* ①脾臟的; 與脾臟有關的。②在脾中的; 在脾臟附近的。

sple·ni·tis [splɪ'naɪtɪs; spli'naitis] *n.* 〖醫〗脾臟炎。

sple·ni·us ['splinɪəs; 'spli:niəs] *n., pl.* **-ni·i** [-nɪˏaɪ; -niai]. 〖解剖〗頸部之扁肌。

splice [splaɪs; splais] *v.,* **spliced, splic·ing,** *n.* —*v.t.* ①編結而接起 (繩或纜頭); 接合 (斷裂的錄音帶等)。②疊接 (兩塊木材)。③〖俗〗結合; 接結。④〖俗〗結婚。to get *spliced.* 結婚。***splice the main brace*** 〖航海〗**a.** 發酒給所有船員。**b.** 喝酒。—*n.* ①結接; 疊接。②結合; 結婚。—**splic·er,** *n.*

spline [splaɪn; splain] *n., v.,* **splined, splin·ing.** —*n.* 〖機械〗制轉楔; 方栓; 方栓之槽。—*v.t.* 〖機械〗裝以方栓; 備以方栓槽。

splint [splɪnt; splint] *n.* ①(固定斷臂、斷骨等用之)夾板。②〖解剖〗(亦作**splint bone**) 腓骨。③〖獸醫〗管骨瘤。④(編結籃子、做椅面等用之)細軟木條。—*v.t.* 以夾板固定。

splint bone 〖解剖〗腓骨。

***splin·ter** ['splɪntɚ; 'splintə] *n.* 片; 碎片; 裂片。—*adj.*分裂的。—*v.t. & v.i.* 分裂; 碎裂。The Labor Party has *splintered* hopelessly. 工黨已四分五裂無法挽救了。

splinter bar 馬車之橫木。

splinter bone =**splint bone.**

splin·ter·proof ['splɪntɚˏpruf; 'splintəpru:f] *adj.* 防彈片的。

splin·ter·y ['splɪntərɪ; 'splintəri] *adj.* ①易裂的。②碎片的。③多碎片的。④粗糙的。

split** [splɪt; split] *v.,* **split, split·ting,** *n., adj.* —*v.t.* ①割裂; 劈開。②分配; 分派。The two men *split* the cost of the dinner between them. 那兩個人均攤餐費。③分化; 使(團體等)分裂。④將(分子)分裂爲原子。⑤(强加一中子而)使(原子核)分裂爲量相近似的兩部分。⑥分割。The old farm has been *split* up into house lots. 那塊從前的農田被分割成建地。—*v.i.* ①裂開; (團體等之)分裂; 分開。My head is *splitting.* 我的頭疼痛欲裂。②〖俗〗出賣祕密。Please don't *split* on me. 不要出賣我。③分道揚鑣。split hairs*** 作極其細微之區別; 剖析瑣屑之點。***split one's sides*** 捧腹大笑。***split one's vote*** (or ***ticket***) 投票給異黨候選人。***split the difference*** **a.** 妥協; 折中; 互相讓步。**b.** 將剩餘部分均分。—*n.* ①分裂。There was a *split* in the Republican Party. 共和黨曾有分裂。②裂開。③〖俚〗分; 部分。④〖俗〗比平常小一半的一瓶酒等。⑤由水果、冰淇淋等混合的甜飲料。⑥(常 *pl.*) (馬戲團中) 兩腿大劈叉落地表演。—*adj.* 分裂的。—**ter,** *n.*

split decision (如拳賽等中之)不一致的決定。

split-level ['splɪtˏlɛvl; 'splitˏlevl] *n.* 地板水平面有兩種以上高度的平房。

split personality ①精神分裂; 雙重人格。②有雙重人格之人。

split second 一瞬間。

split ticket ①分裂票 (投給不同黨的候選人之選票)。②包括非黨員在內之政黨提名的候選人名單。

split·ting ['splɪtɪŋ; 'splitiŋ] *adj.* ①破裂的; 裂開的。②劇裂的 (頭痛); 極端的; 劇痛的(頭)。③刺耳的。④飛快的; 極快的。⑤〖俗〗令人捧腹的。—*n.* (常 *pl.*)分裂物; 碎片。

split-up ['splɪtˏʌp; 'splitʌp] *n.* ①分裂; 裂開。②決裂; 絕交。

splosh [splɑʃ; splɔʃ] *n.* ①濺水聲。②〖英俗〗金錢。—*adv.* 帶濺水聲地。 —*v.t. & v.i.* =**splash.**

splotch [splɑtʃ; splɔtʃ] *n.* 汚痕; 汚漬。—*v.t.* 玷汚。 —*v.i.* ①易髒。②玷汚。(亦作 **splodge**)

splotch·y ['splɑtʃɪ; 'splɔtʃi] *adj.,* **splotch·i·er, splotch·i·est.** 有汚點的; 有汚痕的。

splurge [splɝdʒ; splə:dʒ] *n., v.,* **splurged, splurg·ing.** —*n.* ①〖俗〗誇示; 炫耀; 賣弄。②突然迸發。—*v.i.* 〖俗〗①誇示; 炫耀; 賣弄。②浪費; 亂花錢。 —*v.t.* 浪費(金錢); 引人注目地花(錢)。

splut·ter ['splʌtɚ; 'splʌtə] *v.i.* ①急促地亂說。②發細急之爆裂聲。③飛濺。—*v.t.* ①急促地亂說出。②激濺; 使飛濺。③濺汚。—*n.* ①雜亂而急促的話; 雜亂的聲音。②(液體的)飛濺。 —**er,** *n.*

:spoil [spɔɪl; spɔil] *v.,* **spoiled** or **spoilt, spoil·ing,** *n.* —*v.t.* ①損傷; 損害; 破壞。Our holidays were *spoiled* by bad weather. 我們假期的樂趣被惡劣天氣所破壞。②姑息; 寵壞。Spare the rod and *spoil* the child. 小孩不打不成器。③搶刧; 掠奪。—*v.i.* ①腐敗; 變壞。The fruit will soon *spoil* if you keep it too long. 水果如放得太久, 便將變壞。②搶刧。***be spoiling for*** 迫切地要做。He *is spoiling for* a fight. 他想打架。***spoil the Egyptians*** 從剝奪者手中搶奪; 從有錢有勢者手中搶刧。—*n.* ①(常 *pl.*)掠奪品; 戰利品。②(常 *pl.*)〖美〗**a.** (執政黨所取得之)肥差事。**b.** 獎品。③開礦、採石等所掘起的無用之物。

spoil·age ['spɔɪlɪdʒ; 'spɔilidʒ] *n.* ①損壞; 損害。②損壞物; 損壞量。③搶刧; 掠奪。④〖印刷〗印壞作廢之紙。

spoil·er ['spɔɪlɚ; 'spɔilə] *n.* ①損壞者; 寵壞者; 搶刧者。②收贓者。③機翼低部之襟翼。④〖俚〗可擊敗强隊之球隊; 可擊敗高手之運動員。⑤〖美〗搗亂性的第三黨候選人 (其所得票數足以破壞另一候選人之得勝機會)。

spoiler party 〖美〗搗亂性第三黨 (美國兩黨中之任何一黨所分裂出之第三黨, 目的在破壞該黨在競選中得勝之機會)。

spoils·man ['spɔɪlzmən; 'spɔilzmən] *n., pl.* **-men.** ①擁護政黨分肥制者。②資助一政黨以期獵官分肥者。

spoil·sport ['spɔɪlˏsport; 'spɔil-spɔ:t] *n.*破壞或妨礙他人之遊戲或娛樂者; 掃興的人。

spoils system 〖美〗政黨之分贓制（將政黨獲勝後有權委派之官職視爲戰利品，以之分與黨的有功幹部）。

spoilt 〔spɔɪlt; spɔilt〕 *v.* pt. & pp. of **spoil.**

‡spoke¹ 〔spok; spouk〕 *v.* pt. of **speak.**

spoke²** *n.* ①輪輻。②船舵輪柄。put a spoke in a person's wheel*** 使某人之計畫挫敗。—*v.t.* 裝以輪輻；裝以船舵輪柄。

‡spo·ken 〔ˈspokən; ˈspoukən〕 *v.* pp. of **speak.** —*adj.* 口頭的；口述的。*spoken* English. 口講之英語。

spoke·shave 〔ˈspokˌʃev; ˈspoukʃeiv〕 *n.* (製車輻之)輻刀(現祇用於修光圓形物表面)。

spokes·man 〔ˈspoksmən; ˈspouksmən〕 *n.*, *pl.* **-men.** 代言人；發言人。

spoke·wise 〔ˈspokˌwaɪz; ˈspoukˌwaiz〕 *adj.* & *adv.* 輻射狀的(地)。

spo·li·a·tion 〔ˌspolɪˈeʃən; ˌspouliˈeiʃən〕 *n.* ①强奪；掠奪。②戰時作戰國對中立國船隻之擄捕。③〖法律〗毀棄或變造文書、票據等。

spon·da·ic 〔spɑnˈde·ɪk; spɔnˈdeiik〕 *adj.* 〖詩〗揚揚格的。

spon·dee 〔ˈspɑndi; ˈspɔndiː〕 *n.* 〖詩〗揚揚格(每一音步包含兩個長或重音節)。

spon·dy·li·tis 〔ˌspɑndɪˈlaɪtɪs; ˌspɔndiˈlaitis〕 *n.* 〖醫〗脊椎炎。

sponge** 〔spʌndʒ; spʌndʒ, spʌnʒ〕 *n.*, *v.*, **sponged, spong·ing.** —*n.* ①〖動物〗海綿。②海綿軟而多空之骨；海綿(沐浴等用以浸水者)。③海綿擦浴。④海綿狀之物。⑤寄食者；食客。⑥開刀時，用以擦血的消毒紗布或藥棉。⑦擦砲管的布拖把。⑧能吸收之物。pass the sponge over*** a. 擦掉。b. 同意重修舊好。***throw in*** (or ***up***) ***the sponge*** 放棄；承認失敗。—*v.t.* ①用海綿揩乾或吸乾。*Sponge* up the spilled water. 吸乾那灑了的水。②依賴；敲取。③做衣服前先將(布料)縮水。—*v.i.* ①用海綿吸取液體。②採海綿。③依賴；敲詐。

sponge bath 用海綿或浴巾擦洗而不進入水中之沐浴。

sponge cake 鬆糕；軟糕；海綿蛋糕。

spong·er 〔ˈspʌndʒɚ; ˈspʌndʒə〕 *n.* ①採集海綿者；海綿採集船。②用海綿洗滌之人。③寄人籬下者；依賴他人爲生的人；食客。

sponge rubber 海綿橡皮(做椅墊等物之材料)。

spon·gi·ness 〔ˈspʌndʒɪnɪs; ˈspʌndʒinis〕 *n.* 海綿狀；海綿質。

spon·gy 〔ˈspʌndʒɪ; ˈspʌndʒi〕 *adj.*, **-gi·er, -gi·est.** ①像海綿的；輕軟而多孔的。②多孔的。（亦作 **spongeous, spongiose, spongious**）

spon·sion 〔ˈspɑnʃən; ˈspɔnʃən〕 *n.* ①保證。②〖國際法〗(權限外之)約定；擔保。

spon·son 〔ˈspɑnsn̩; ˈspɔnsn〕 *n.* ①船舷側之突出處。②水上飛機身側之浮舟（使停泊水面上時保持平衡)。

***spon·sor** 〔ˈspɑnsɚ; ˈspɔnsə〕 *n.* ①保證人；負責人。②教父；教母。③資助者；主持者；贊助者。④電臺或電視臺之節目提供者。—*v.t.* 〖美〗資助；主持；支持。to *sponsor* a program. 資助(或主持)一項計畫。

spon·so·ri·al 〔spɑnˈsɔrɪəl; spɔnˈsɔːriəl〕 *adj.* ①保證人的；負責人的。②教父(母)的。③資助者的；主持者的。

spon·sor·ship 〔ˈspɑnsɚˌʃɪp; ˈspɔnsəʃip〕 *n.* 保證；負責；資助；主持。

spon·ta·ne·i·ty 〔ˌspɑntəˈniətɪ; ˌspɔntəˈniːiti〕 *n.*, *pl.* **-ties.** ①自發的情況；自發性。②自然發生。③自發的行爲、活動等。

***spon·ta·ne·ous** 〔spɑnˈtenɪəs; spɔnˈteiniəs〕 *adj.* ①自然的；自發的。spontaneous combustion. 自燃。②自然生長的；非培育的。—**ly,** *adv.* —**ness,** *n.*

spontaneous generation 自生；自發(有機體之自然創生)。

spoof 〔spuf; spuːf〕 *n.* 〖俚〗諷刺；騙局；笑話。—*v.t.* & *v.i.* 〖俚〗欺騙；欺詐；愚弄；開玩笑。—**er,** *n.*

spook 〔spuk; spuːk〕 *n.* 〖俗〗鬼；幽靈。—*v.t.* ①作祟。②〖俚〗唬。

spook·y 〔ˈspukɪ; ˈspuːki〕 *adj.*, **spook·i·er, spook·i·est.** 〖俗〗①似鬼的；有鬼的；鬼魂出現的。②令人害怕的；毛骨悚然的。③(馬)不安的；神經緊張的。(亦作 **spookish**)

spool 〔spul; spuːl〕 *n.* ①線軸。②形狀和用途與線軸相似之物。—*v.t.* ①纏…於線軸。②將…從線軸上轉下〖off, out〗。

spoon¹** 〔spun; spuːn〕 *n.* ①匙；調羹。②匙狀物。③有木端的高爾夫球棒。be born with a silver spoon in one's mouth*** 生於富貴之家。—*v.t.* ①以匙取〖out, up〗。②〖俗〗愚蠢地向…求愛。③輕擊(高爾夫球)。—*v.i.* 愚蠢地求愛；接吻或撫弄以調情。

spoon² *n.* 〖俚〗愚人；痴戀者。

spoon bait 用作魚餌的微曲之金屬片。

spoon·bill 〔ˈspunˌbɪl; ˈspuːnbil〕 *n.* 篦鷺(鳥名)。

spoon bread 〖美〗一種用牛乳、鷄蛋同玉蜀黍粉混合製成的麪包(焙後仍軟，故食時仍需匙)。

spoon·drift 〔ˈspunˌdrɪft; ˈspuːndrift〕 *n.* 浪花。

spoon·er·ism 〔ˈspunəˌrɪzəm; ˈspuːnərizəm〕 *n.* (講話或讀書時，因不小心而致)二字(或二字以上)的部分聲音之互換(如 It is kistomary to cuss the bride. 爲 It is customary to kiss the bride. 之誤)。

spoon-fed 〔ˈspunˌfɛd; ˈspuːn-fed〕 *adj.* ①以羹匙餵食的(小兒、病人等)。②被縱容的；嬌生慣養的；被溺愛的。③不給予自發練習機會的；不使有獨立行動或思想的(學生等)。

spoon-feed 〔ˈspunˌfid; ˈspuːn-fiːd〕 *v.t.* & *v.i.*, **-fed, -feed·ing.** ①用匙餵。②溺愛；嬌寵。③給予塡鴨式的教育。

***spoon·ful** 〔ˈspunˌful; ˈspuːnful〕 *n.* 一匙；滿匙。two *spoonfuls* of sugar. 兩匙糖。

spoon meat 流質食物；羹湯。

spoon net 手撈網。

spoon·y 〔ˈspunɪ; ˈspuːni〕 *adj.*, **spoon·i·er, spoon·i·est,** *n.*, *pl.* **spoon·ies.** —*adj.* 〖俗〗①〖英〗愚蠢的。②癡愛的；迷戀的。—*n.* 〖俗〗①癡情者。②〖英〗愚人。(亦作 **spooney**)

spoor 〔spur; spuə〕 *n.* (野獸的) 足跡。—*v.t.* & *v.i.* 追蹤。—**er,** *n.*

spo·rad·ic 〔spoˈrædɪk; spəˈrædik〕 *adj.* ①零星的；時有時無的。②散在的；散發性的。③單獨發生的；散見於各地的。(亦作 **sporadical**) —**al·ly,** *adv.* —**i·ty,** *n.*

sporadic cholera 〖醫〗假霍亂；似霍亂病。

spo·ran·gi·um 〔spəˈrændʒɪəm; spɔˈrændʒiəm〕 *n.*, *pl.* **-gi·a** 〔-dʒɪə; -dʒiə〕. 〖植物〗胞子囊。

spore 〔spor; spɔː〕 *n.*, *v.*, **spored, spor·ing.** —*n.* ①〖生物〗芽胞；胞子。②胚種；種子；生殖細胞。—*v.i.* 形成芽胞；發育成芽胞。

spo·ro·phyl(l) 〔ˈsporəfɪl; ˈspɔːrəfil〕 *n.* 〖植物〗胞子葉；芽胞葉。

spo·ro·phyte 〔ˈsporəˌfaɪt; ˈspɔːrəfait〕 *n.* 〖植物〗胞子體。

spor·ran 〔ˈspɑrən; ˈspɔrən〕 *n.* 蘇格蘭高地男子腰帶上所繫之毛皮袋。

:sport [sport, spɔrt; spɔːt] *n.* ①遊戲;戶外運動。He's very fond of *sport*. 他很喜歡戶外運動。②娛樂。③戲謔;玩笑。He said it in *sport*. 他講的是玩笑話。④戲謔的對象。That fat boy is the *sport* of other boys. 那個胖孩子是其他的孩子們戲謔的對象。⑤(*pl.*)運動會。the school *sports*. 學校運動會。⑥〖俗〗有運動道德的人;堂堂正正的人。Be a *sport!* 做一個堂堂正正的人! ⑦賭鬼。⑧〖俗〗愛炫耀的人。⑨變態或畸形的動物或植物。***for*** (or ***in***) ***sport*** 開玩笑的。***make sport of*** 取笑;嘲弄。***turn to sport*** 當作開玩笑。—*v.i.* ①遊戲。Lambs *sport* in the fields. 小羊在田裏遊戲。②戲弄;嘲弄。③變態。—*v.t.* ①炫耀。②浪費(金錢)〖常away〗。③將時間消磨於(娛樂或運動)。***sport one's oak*** 〖英〗(大學生)將門關上以示不在家。—*adj.* ①適於戶外穿戴的;非正式場合穿戴的。②運動的。—**er,** *n.* —**ful,** *adj.*

sport·ing [ˈsportɪŋ; ˈspɔːtiŋ] *adj.* ①遊戲的;運動的。a *sporting* page. 體育版。②遵守運動規則的;堂堂正正的。③愛好運動或含有賭博性質之遊戲的;愛好狩獵的。④〖俗〗帶有冒險性的;有企業心的;賭博性的。a *sporting* chance. 一個成敗不定的機會。—**ly,** *adv.*

sporting goods 運動服裝及器材。

sporting house 妓院;狎遊之所。

spor·tive [ˈsportɪv; ˈspɔːtiv] *adj.* ①(好)嬉戲的。②開玩笑的;不是認眞的。③運動的。④〖古〗淫蕩的。⑤〖生物〗變種的。—**ly,** *adv.*

sports [sports; spɔːts] *adj.* 運動的;適於運動的。a *sports* shirt. 運動衫(=a sport shirt). a *sports* page. 體育版。

sports car 跑車。

sports·cast [ˈsports,kæst; ˈspɔːts-kaːst] *n.* 〖電視,廣播〗運動比賽之實況轉播。—**er,** *n.*

sport shirt 運動衫;香港衫。

***sports·man** [ˈsportsmən; ˈspɔːts-mən] *n., pl.* **-men** [-mən; -mən]. ①作戶外運動者(尤指狩獵、垂釣或賽跑)。②喜歡戶外運動者。③有運動道德之人;堂堂正正之人。④願意冒險者。

sports·man·like [ˈsportsmən,laɪk; ˈspɔːtsmənlaik] *adj.* 似運動家的;堂堂正正的。(亦作 **sportsmanly**)

sports·man·ship [ˈsportsmən,ʃɪp; ˈspɔːtsmənʃip] *n.* 運動道德;運動員精神;堂堂正正的態度。

sports·wear [ˈsports,wɛr; ˈspɔːts-wɛə] *n.* 運動裝;便服。

sports·wom·an [ˈsports,wumən; ˈspɔːts,wumən] *n., pl.* **-wom·en.** 女運動員。

sports·writer [ˈsports,raɪtɚ; ˈspɔːts-,raitə] *n.* 體育記者;體育新聞稿作者。

sport·y [ˈsportɪ; ˈspɔːti] *adj.,* **sport·i·er, sport·i·est.** 〖俗〗①似運動家的;適於運動家的。②庸俗而炫誇的;華麗的(服飾等)。③時髦的。

spor·ule [ˈsparjul; ˈspɔrjuːl] *n.* 〖生物〗小芽胞;小胞子。—**spor·u·lar,** *adj.*

:spot [spat; spɔt] *n., v.,* **spot·ted, spot·ting,** *adj.* —*n.* ①斑點;污點。His tie is blue with white *spots*. 他的領帶是藍底帶白點的。②瑕疵;污點。a *spot* on one's fame. 名譽上的污點。③地點;場所。④〖俗〗一丁點;一些;少許。⑤〖俗〗=**spotlight.** ⑥〖俗〗**a.** 職位。**b.** 節目安排位置。⑦一種鴿子。⑧太陽黑子。⑨葉斑症。⑩〖美俚〗鈔票。⑪骰子或紙牌上之點。⑫ =**spot announcement.** ***hit the high spots*** 〖俗〗僅遊覽主要名勝。***hit the spot*** 〖俗〗滿足;正好。***in a*** (***bad***) ***spot*** 〖美俚〗在困難中;處於窘境。***in spots*** **a.** 在若干點上;在某些方面。**b.** 有時。***on*** (or ***upon***) ***the spot*** **a.** 當地;就地。**b.** 立刻。**c.** 〖美俗〗在困難中。**d.** 〖俚〗成爲暗殺對象。***put on the spot*** **a.** 使處於困惱中。**b.** 謀殺。***touch the tender spot*** 觸及痛處。—*v.t.* ①加以斑點;沾污。②去(衣服上)之污點。③〖俗〗察出;認出。④被置於某一地點。Lookouts were *spotted* all along the coast. 沿海岸均有瞭望臺。⑤用聚光圈照射。⑥將…散置。⑦〖軍〗定…之位置。⑧〖軍〗觀察(彈着點以便矯正射擊)。⑨〖運動〗向(對手)作若干讓步。⑩〖器械操〗協助(表演者)使不致受傷。—*v.i.* 變污;染污。This silk will *spot*. 這綢會變污的。—*adj.* 當場的;當場交付的。*spot* transaction. 現貨買賣;當場交易。

spot announcement 〖電視、廣播〗節目前或節目中插播的短廣告或通告。

spot cash 〖商〗當場交付之現金。

spot check ①抽樣調查。②抽查;突擊檢查。

spot-check [ˈspat,tʃɛk; ˈspɔttʃek] *v.t.* 抽樣調查。

spot·less [ˈspatlɪs; ˈspɔtlis] *adj.* ①無斑點的;純色的。②潔白的;無瑕疵的。③一塵不染的;非常清潔的。

spot·light [ˈspat,laɪt; ˈspɔtlait] *n., v.,* **-light·ed, -lit, -light·ing.** —*n.* ①劇院用之反光燈。②聚光圈。③注意之中心。—*v.t.* ①用聚光燈照射。②引起對…之注意。

spot·ted [ˈspatɪd; ˈspɔtid] *adj.* ①有斑點的。②有污點的。

spotted fever 〖醫〗斑疹熱。

spot·ter [ˈspatɚ; ˈspɔtə] *n.* ①〖美〗(公司、銀行等職員之)監視人。②私人偵探;刑警。③〖美〗〖鐵路〗檢路器。④〖軍〗彈落觀測員。⑤監視敵機動態之民防人員。⑥洗清污點(如衣服上者)的人。⑦觀測用之飛機;觀測員。⑧去污點機。⑨保齡球柱自動排列機。

spot·ty [ˈspatɪ; ˈspɔti] *adj.,* **-ti·er, -ti·est.** ①有斑點的;多斑點的。②不規則的;不一律的;不穩定的;時好時壞的。—**spot·ti·ly,** *adv.* —**spot·ti·ness,** *n.*

spous·al [ˈspauzl; ˈspauzl] *n.* 〖罕〗(常*pl.*)婚禮;結婚儀式。—*adj.* 結婚的。

spouse [spauz; spauz] *n.* 夫;妻;配偶。

spout** [spaut; spaut] *v.t.* ①噴。A whale *spouts* water when it breathes. 鯨魚呼吸時噴水。②裝腔作勢說出。③使大量湧出。④〖俚〗當;典押。—*v.i.* ①噴出;湧流出。Water *spouted* from the break in the pipe. 水從水管破裂處噴出。②裝腔作勢地說。He's too fond of *spouting*. 他太喜歡裝腔作勢地說話。—*n.* ①(管等流水的)嘴;噴口;噴水孔。②承霤(房簷下的水筧)。go up the spout*** 〖俚〗毀滅;化爲烏有。***put up the spout*** 〖俚〗典當。***upon the spout*** 〖俗〗**a.** 典當的。**b.** 毀壞的。—**er,** *n.* —**less,** *adj.*

S.P.Q.R., SPQR ①Senatus Populusque Romanus (拉 =the Senate and the Roman people). ②small profits and quick returns.

sprag [spræg; spræg] *n., v.,* **spragged, sprag·ging.** —*n.* ①制輪木板;制輪木條。②〖採礦〗(煤坑中用之)支柱。—*v.t.* 用制輪木條使(輪)靜止。

sprain [spren; sprein] *v.t.* 扭傷(關節或筋等)。—*n.* 扭傷;扭筋。

***sprang** [spræŋ; spræŋ] *v.* pt. of **spring.**

sprat [spræt; spræt] *n.* ①一種類似鯡

之小海魚。②小人物；無足輕重之人或物。***throw a sprat to catch a herring*** (or ***whale***) 小魚釣大魚；小本賺大錢。

sprawl 〔sprɔl; sprɔːl〕 *v.i.* ①伸手足而臥或坐；仰臥。②展開；蔓延。③匍匐而行；笨拙地行走。④很亂地散開。—*v.t.* ①使(軍隊)散開。②使伸手足而臥或坐。—*n.* ①手足伸開而臥。②雜亂無章的蔓延。

***spray¹** 〔spre; sprei〕 *n.* ①小枝。②小枝狀之裝飾物。

***spray²** *n.* ①水沫；浪花。We were wet with the sea *spray*. 我們被海水的浪花濺濕。②類似浪沫之物。③噴霧器。④用噴霧器噴出之藥物。—*v.t.* ①用噴霧器噴射。②掃射。The soldiers *sprayed* the enemy with bullets. 士兵們用子彈掃射敵人。—*v.i.* 噴霧；噴射。The hose *sprayed* over the flowers. 水管向花上噴水。—**er,** *n.*

spray gun 噴霧器。

‡spread 〔sprɛd; spred〕 *v.,* **spread, spread·ing,** *n., adj.*—*v.t.*①展開；塗敷；羅列。The table was *spread* with good things to eat. 桌子上擺滿了好吃的東西。②伸出；使延展。He was *spreading* his hands to the fire. 他伸手烤火。③傳布；傳播。Flies *spread* disease. 蒼蠅傳播疾病。④遮蓋；覆蓋。*Spread* a cloth on the table. 把桌布鋪在桌子上。⑤撒開。⑥鋪(桌面)；上(菜)。⑦登記；記錄。—*v.i.* ①展開；伸展；擴展。②傳布；流傳；蔓延。The news soon *spread*. 這消息很快傳播開了。③淹沒。④(時間) 延長。***spread oneself*** **a.** 好客。**b.** 自我炫示以討好。**c.** 誇耀地說；華而不實地寫。***spread oneself thin*** 同時從事多項活動以致沒有一樣能做得好或使健康受損。***spread the table*** 將食物等擺在桌上；開飯。—*n.* ①伸展；擴展。②廣袤；範圍。③飛機之翼幅。④傳布；蔓延。⑤〖俗〗酒席；宴會。⑥塗於麪包上的牛油、果醬等。⑦鋪於桌上的桌布；床上的被單。⑧成本與售價間之差。⑨買價與賣價間之差別。⑩廣告新聞等所占之版面(以欄計算)。⑪報章雜誌面對面之兩頁(在編排時視作一個單元)。⑫〖俗〗地產；莊田；牧場。—*adj.* 伸展的；擴延的。

spread eagle ①(美國國徽) 展翼鷹。②像展翼鷹之物。③〖美俗〗自誇之人。④溜冰的一種姿勢。

spread-ea·gle 〔ˈsprɛdˌigl; ˈspredˈiːgl〕 *adj., v.,* **-ea·gled, -ea·gling.** —*adj.* ①有展翼鷹之圖像的；似展翼鷹的。②〖美俗〗誇大的；(尤指)誇張的(愛國主義)。—*v.t.* ①如展翼鷹伸展。②將(人)四肢分綑作為處罰。③徹底擊敗。—*v.i.* 溜冰時作展翼鷹之姿勢。

spread·er 〔ˈsprɛdɚ; ˈspredə〕 *n.* ①推廣者。②延展機。③塗奶油的刀。

spread-o·ver system 〔ˈsprɛdˌovɚ～; ˈspredˌouvə～〕 工作時間依工作需要而伸縮之制度。(亦作 **spread-over**)

spree 〔spri; spriː〕 *n., v.,* **spreed, spree·ing.** —*n.* ①喧樂；遊樂。②縱飲；狂飲。③一段極其放縱或活躍之時間。***go on the spree*** 痛飲。—*v.i.* 狂飲；痛飲。

sprig 〔sprɪg; sprig〕 *n., v.,* **sprigged, sprig·ging.** —*n.* ①嫩枝；小枝。②枝狀裝飾或圖案。③少年；小夥子。④後裔；產物。⑤無頭小釘。—*v.t.* ①以小枝狀裝飾或圖案做在(陶器、織物)上。②從(植物)上折下小枝。③以小釘固定。

sprig·gy 〔ˈsprɪgɪ; ˈsprigi〕 *adj.,* **sprig·gi·er, sprig·gi·est.** 多小枝的；多嫩枝的。

spright·ly 〔ˈspraɪtlɪ; ˈspraitli〕 *adj.,* **-li·er, -li·est,** *adv.* —*adj.* 活潑的；愉快的。—*adv.* 活潑地；愉快地。—**spright·li·ness,** *n.*

sprig-tailed 〔ˈsprɪgˌteld; ˈsprigteild〕 *adj.* 尖尾巴的。

‡spring 〔sprɪŋ; spriŋ〕 *v.,* **sprang** or **sprung, sprung, spring·ing,** *n., adj.* —*v.i.* ①跳；躍起。He *sprang* over the river. 他跳過河去。②彈回。③萌芽；發出；迸發。Sparks *sprang* from the fire. 火花自火中迸出。④開始動；開始行動。⑤彎曲；扭曲；裂開。⑥突然出現。His anger *springs* to the surface easily. 他容易發怒。⑦突然湧出〖常 forth, out, up〗。⑧爆炸。—*v.t.* ①使躍起；使跳躍。②使突然發生；(藉彈簧之力)發動。③使爆發；使破裂；裂開。④〖俚〗使(某人)獲得釋放或免役。⑤炸(礦坑)。***spring a mine*** **a.** 炸礦。**b.** 使驚訝。***spring from obscurity*** 出身微賤。***spring surprises on people*** 驚人；駭世。—*n.* ①跳躍。②彈簧；發條。a watch *spring*. 錶的發條。③彈性；彈力。④春季。in the *spring* of 1950. 在一九五〇年春天。this (next, last) *spring*. 今年(明年，去年) 春天。⑤泉；泉源。hot *spring*. 溫泉。⑥起源；動機。⑦裂縫；破隙。***set all springs going*** 盡全力。—*adj.* ①裝有彈簧的；以彈簧操作的。②掛在彈簧上的。③春天的。*spring* flowers. 春季的花卉。④適於春天的；春天使用的。⑤來自礦泉的。

spring beauty 〖植物〗馬齒莧屬野花。

spring·board 〔ˈsprɪŋˌbord; ˈspriŋbɔːd〕 *n.* ①(跳水用之)跳板。②(跳高、翻觔斗等起跳的)彈性板。③為達成某種目的所必經之途徑；出發點。

spring·bok 〔ˈsprɪŋˌbak; ˈspriŋbɔk〕 *n.* 南非洲產的一種羚羊。

spring chicken ①小雞(尤指未滿十個月之小雞，供烤食用者)。②〖俚〗無經驗而天眞的年輕人(尤指少女)。

spring-clean 〔ˈsprɪŋˈklin; ˈspriŋˈkliːn〕 *v.t.* 春季掃除(房屋等)。—**ing,** *n.*

springe 〔sprɪndʒ; sprindʒ〕 *n., v.,* **springed, spring·ing.** —*n.* (利用彈性物捕捉魚獸之)網羅；陷阱。—*v.t.* 以此等網羅捕捉。—*v.i.* 設置網羅。

spring·er 〔ˈsprɪŋɚ; ˈspriŋə〕 *n.* ①跳躍者；跳躍的東西。②幼草；嫩樹。③青年。④〖建築〗起拱石。⑤一種用以驚起獵物之獵犬。⑥＝**springbok.** ⑦＝**grampus.** ⑧＝**spring chicken.**

spring fever 春天感到的一種睏倦。

spring·halt 〔ˈsprɪŋˈhɔlt; ˈspriŋhɔːlt〕 *n.* 〖獸醫〗馬的跛行症。

spring·head 〔ˈsprɪŋˌhɛd; ˈspriŋhed〕 *n.* ①源泉；源頭。②來源。

spring·house 〔ˈsprɪŋˌhaus; ˈspriŋhaus〕 *n.* 〖美〗室內有泉水或小溪流過的小型建築物(用以冷却牛奶等)。

springing bow (弦樂器的)彈奏法。

spring·let 〔ˈsprɪŋlɪt; ˈspriŋlit〕 *n.* 小溪；小泉。

spring·lock 〔ˈsprɪŋˌlak; ˈspriŋlɔk〕 *n.* 彈簧鎖。

spring·tail 〔ˈsprɪŋˌtel; ˈspriŋteil〕 *n.* 躍尾蟲。

spring tide ①(新月及滿月所引起之)滿潮；潮之最高者。②奔流；充沛。

***spring·time** 〔ˈsprɪŋˌtaɪm; ˈspriŋtaim〕 *n.* ①春天；春季。②早期。

spring·wood 〔ˈsprɪŋwud; ˈspriŋwud〕 *n.* ①每年春季樹木所長的外層。②幼樹叢。

spring·y 〔ˈsprɪŋɪ; ˈspriŋi〕 *adj.,* **spring·i·er, spring·i·est.** ①有彈性的。②多泉的。③潮濕的。—**spring·i·ness,** *n.*

***sprin·kle** 〔ˈsprɪŋkl; ˈspriŋkl〕 *v.,* **-kled,**

-kling, *n.* —*v.t.* ①撒；灑。②散置；漫布。—*v.i.* ①灑；撒落。②下微雨。—*n.* ①少量。The cook put a *sprinkle* of nuts on the cake. 廚師在糕上灑了一點果仁。②微雨；毛毛雨。③(*pl.*) 餅干上面作裝飾用的巧克力糖小圓點。

sprinkler head 灑水裝置之蓮蓬頭。

sprinkler system 田野或草地等之自動灑水裝置(溫度到某一點時卽自動灑水)。

sprin·kling [ˈsprɪŋklɪŋ; ˈspriŋkliŋ] *n.* ①散布之微量；待撒灑之微量。②灑水。

sprint [sprɪnt; sprint] *v.i.* 以全速奔跑(尤指短距離者)。—*n.* ①短距離賽跑。②短時間之劇烈活動。—**er,** *n.*

sprit [sprɪt; sprit] *n.* 〖航海〗張帆用的斜杠。

sprite [spraɪt; sprait] *n.* ①妖精；鬼怪；小精靈。②〖古〗鬼。

sprit·sail [ˈsprɪtˌsel; ˈspritseil] *n.* 〖航海〗斜杠帆。

sprock·et [ˈsprɑkɪt; ˈsprɔkit] *n.* ①〖機械〗鏈輪。②扣鏈齒。

sprocket wheel 鏈輪。

sprout** [spraut; spraut] *v.i.* ①長出；發芽；萌芽。Seeds *sprout*. 種子發芽。②〖俗〗迅速地發展。—*v.t.* ①使長出；使發芽；使萌芽；生長。②去掉…之芽。—*n.* ①芽；苗。②(*pl.*)芽甘藍。a course of sprouts*** 〖俗〗嚴格的訓練。

spruce[1] [sprus; spruːs] *n.* ①〖植物〗針樅。②針樅木。

spruce[2] *adj.,* **spruc·er, spruc·est,** *v.,* **spruced, spruc·ing.** —*adj.* 整潔的；漂亮的；瀟灑的。—*v.t.* & *v.i.* 修飾；打扮得整潔漂亮。—**ly,** *adv.* —**ness,** *n.*

spruce beer 針樅啤酒。

sprue[1] [spru; spruː] *n.* ①鑄型的注入口。②該處之金屬鑄物廢片；渣滓。

sprue[2] *n.* 〖醫〗口炎性腹瀉。

‡**sprung** [sprʌŋ; sprʌŋ] *v.* pt. & pp. of **spring.** —*adj.* ①已被弄鬆的。②裂開的。③彎曲的。④〖俚〗醉醺醺的。

spry [spraɪ; sprai] *adj.,* **spry·er** or **spri·er, spry·est** or **spri·est.** 活潑的；輕快的；敏捷的。—**ly,** *adv.* —**ness,** *n.*

spt. seaport.

spud [spʌd; spʌd] *n., v.,* **spud·ded, spud·ding.** —*n.* ①小鏟。②用以除去樹皮之鑿狀器具。③〖俗〗馬鈴薯。—*v.t.* ①以小鏟挖〖up, out〗。②初步鑽(油井)。***spud in*** 裝置鑽井設備。

spue [spju; spjuː] *v.t.* & *v.i.,* **spued, spu·ing.** =**spew.**

spume [spjum; spjuːm] *n., v.,* **spumed, spum·ing.** —*n.* 泡沫。—*v.i.* & *v.t.* 起泡沫。

spu·mes·cence [spjuˈmɛsəns; spjuˈmesəns] *n.* 發泡沫。

spu·mes·cent [spjuˈmɛsənt; spjuˈmesənt] *adj.* 起泡沫的；似泡沫的；泡沫的。

spu·mo·ne [spuˈmone; spuːˈmounei] 〖義〗*n.* 一種冰淇淋(通常含有蜜餞水果或切碎之栗子)。(亦作 **spumoni**)

***spun** [spʌn; spʌn] *v.* pt. & pp. of **spin.** —*adj.* 撚成絲的。

spun glass 玻璃絲。

spunk [spʌŋk; spʌŋk] *n.* ①〖俗〗勇氣；膽量；毅力。②火花；微火。③引火之木材。***get one's spunk up*** 表現(鼓起)勇氣、膽量等。***spunk of fire*** 小火。—*v.i.* 點燃；燃起。

spunk·y [ˈspʌŋkɪ; ˈspʌŋki] *adj.,* **spunk·i·er, spunk·i·est.** 〖俗〗①有膽量的；有勇氣的；有毅力的；精神蓬勃的。②易怒的；暴躁的。—**spunk·i·ly,** *adv.* —**spunk·i·ness,** *n.*

spun sugar 棉花糖。

spur** [spɝ; spəː] *n., v.,* **spurred, spur·ring.** —*n.* ①刺馬釘。②激勵物；刺激物；驅策力；激勵；刺激。③類似刺馬釘的東西。A cock has *spurs* on his legs. 公鷄腿上有肉距。④山之支脈；横嶺。⑤支線。⑥爬竿用之足蹬。on the spur of the moment*** 憑一時衝動。***set*** (or ***put***) ***spurs to*** 用刺馬釘刺；驅策。***win one's spurs*** 獲得名聲；證明能力。—*v.t.* ①以刺馬釘刺(馬)。②策勵；刺激。③裝以刺馬釘。—*v.i.* ①以刺馬釘刺馬。②疾馳；疾驅。

spurge [spɝdʒ; spəːdʒ] *n.* 〖植物〗甘遂。

spu·ri·ous [ˈspjurɪəs; ˈspjuəriəs] *adj.* ①假的；僞造的。②私生的；庶出的。③〖生物〗假性的；擬似的。—**ly,** *adv.* —**ness,** *n.*

***spurn** [spɝn; spəːn] *v.t.* ①擯斥；趕走。②狂傲地拒絕。The judge *spurned* the bribe. 法官拒絕受賄。③〖古〗踢開。—*v.i.* 藐視；看不起。They *spurned* at restraint. 他們反對節制。—*n.* ①擯斥；藐視。②踢開。—**er,** *n.*

spurred [spɝd; spəːd] *adj.* ①有馬刺的。②(鳥)有距的。

spur·ri·er [ˈspɝɪə; ˈspəːriə] *n.* 製造馬刺者。

spur·ry [ˈspɝɪ; ˈspəːri] *n., pl.* **-ries.** 〖植物〗石竹科的各種小草。

spurt [spɝt; spəːt] *v.i.* ①噴出；湧出；迸出。②作一短時間之奮力活動；衝刺。—*v.t.* 噴出；湧出；迸出。—*n.* ①噴出；湧出；猝發。②(短時間的)奮力活動；衝刺。③物價之暫時上揚；商業之短時興隆。***put a spurt on*** 〖俗〗趕緊；趕快；作最後奮鬥。(亦作 **spirt**)

spur track 〖鐵路〗支線。

sput·nik [ˈspʌtnɪk, ˈsput-; ˈsputnik, ˈspʌt-] *n.* 史潑尼克(蘇聯發射之人造衛星，此字原爲俄語"衛星"之義)。

sput·ter [ˈspʌtə; ˈspʌtə] *v.i.* ①作拍拍聲。②噴出(唾沫、飯屑等)；爆出微粒(木塊燃燒時或油煮沸時等)。③雜亂急話。—*v.t.* ①噴出。②唾沫飛濺地急速說出。③略帶爆炸地少量噴出。—*n.* ①急速雜亂的談話。②爆濺聲。③噴濺出之微粒。

spu·tum [ˈspjutəm; ˈspjuːtəm] *n., pl.* **-ta** [-tə; -tə]. ①唾液；口水。②痰。

spy** [spaɪ; spai] *n., pl.* **spies** [spaɪz; spaiz] *v.,* **spied** [spaɪd; spaid], **spy·ing.** —*n.* 間諜；斥候；偵探；偵察者。—*v.t.* ①偵察；窺探。②發現。③瞥見；看見。—*v.i.* 偵察；探索；窺探。spy out*** a. 祕密地或注意地監視。b. 由祕密或注意地偵查而發現。

spy·glass [ˈspaɪˌglæs; ˈspai-glɑːs] *n.* 小型單管望遠鏡。

spy-hole [ˈspaɪˌhol; ˈspaihoul] *n.* 窺視孔。

Sq. ①Squadron. ②Square (廣場)。

sq. ①sequence. ②square.

squab [skwɑb; skwɔb] *n.* ①(羽毛未豐的)幼鴿；雛鳥。②矮胖的人。③未成熟或無經驗的人。④坐褥；椅墊。⑤沙發；長椅。—*adj.* ①矮胖的。②新孵出的。③怕羞的；嬌羞的。—*adv.* 〖俗〗突然而沉重地。

squab·ble [ˈskwɑbl; ˈskwɔbl] *n., v.,* **-bled, -bling.** —*n.* 小爭吵；小爭論；小口角。—*v.i.* 爭吵；爭論；口角。—*v.t.* 〖印刷〗拆亂(排好的活字)。—**squab·bler,** *n.*

squab·by [ˈskwɑbɪ; ˈskwɔbi] *adj.,* **-bi·er, -bi·est.** 肥胖的；矮胖的。

***squad** [skwɑd; skwɔd] *n., v.,* **squad·ded, squad·ding.** —*n.* ①一小羣人；小隊。②〖軍〗班。—*v.t.* ①使成班或隊。②將…派至班或隊。

squad car 警察巡邏車。

***squad·ron** [ˈskwɑdrən; ˈskwɔdrən]

n. ①海軍戰隊。② **a.** 空軍中隊。**b.** 航空隊。③騎兵中隊。④隊。

squadron leader 〖英〗空軍中隊長。

squail [skwel; skweil] *n.* ①(投擲樹上之小鳥或果實之)小棒。②(*pl.*)一種以小圓木片自桌四周向中央目標投擲之遊戲。③此種遊戲中用的小圓木片。—*v.i.* ①(向樹上棲息之小鳥或果實)投擲。②玩 squails 遊戲。—*v.t.* 〖方〗投擊。

squal·id [ˈskwalɪd; ˈskwɔlid] *adj.* ①污穢的; 不潔的。②卑劣的; 下流的; 不幸的。

squa·lid·i·ty [skwaˈlɪdətɪ; skwɔˈlidəti] *n.* =**squalor.**

squall[1] [skwɔl; skwɔːl] *v.t.* & *v.i.* 大聲叫喊;尖聲叫喊;悲鳴。—*n.* 大聲尖叫。

squall[2] *n.* ①狂風(常夾雨、雪等); 颮。②〖俗〗騷擾;麻煩。—*v.i.* 颳狂風(指短時間的)。

squall·y [ˈskwɔlɪ; ˈskwɔːli] *adj.*, **squall·i·er, squall·i·est.** ①暴風的。②(風)强勁的;强烈的。③〖俗〗威脅的;來勢洶洶的。

squal·or [ˈskwalɚ; ˈskwɔlə] *n.* ①不潔;污穢;窮苦。②卑劣;下流。

squa·ma [ˈskwemə; ˈskweimə] *n., pl.* **-mae** [-mi; -miː]. 〖生物〗鱗片。

squa·mate [ˈskwemet; ˈskweimeit] *adj.* 鱗片的;生鱗片的;覆有鱗片的。

squa·mous [ˈskweməs; ˈskweiməs] *adj.* 〖生物〗有鱗片的;鱗片狀的。(亦作**squamose**)

squan·der [ˈskwandɚ; ˈskwɔndə] *v.t.* ①浪費〖常 away〗。②使散開; 散開。—*v.i.* 被浪費。—*n.* 浪費;虛擲。—**er,** *n.*

squan·der·ma·ni·a [ˌskwandɚˈmenɪə; ˌskwɔndəˈmeiniə] *n.* 浪費狂。

‡**square** [skwɛr; skwɛə] *n., adj.,* **squar·er, squar·est,** *v.,* **squared, squar·ing,** *adv.* —*n.* ①正方形。②方形物。③〖英〗街區;(四面有街道之) 房屋區。④四圍植樹以供休息的方場; 廣場。⑤街區或廣場四圍的建築物。⑥規矩;曲尺。T *square.* 丁字尺。⑦平方;自乘。The *square* of 5 is 25. 五的平方是二十五。⑧〖軍〗方陣。***by the square*** 精確地。***live on the square*** 營正業。***on the square*** **a.** 成直角的。**b.** 〖俗〗爽直;誠實; 公正。***out of square*** **a.** 斜的;不正的;無秩序的。**b.** 不規則的;錯誤的; 不正確的。—*adj.* ①正方形的;四方形的。②四方形每邊有定長的。③成直角的;直角的。④收支相抵的;清算的。⑤直的;平直的。⑥坦率的;率直的。⑦方正的;公正的。⑧平方的。⑨令人滿足的;豐足的。⑩直接的;直截了當的。⑪〖俚〗保守的; 不時髦的。He was real *square.* 他很保守。***a square peg in a round hole*** (or ***a round peg in a square hole***) 方枘圓鑿;不適任者。***get square with a person*** 同某人算清帳目;報仇。***get (things) square*** 整理。—*v.t.* ①使成方形; 使成直角。②使直; 使平。③調整;整理;結算。④自乘。—*v.i.* 一致;符合。Your idea and mine do not *square.* 你的意思同我的不一致。***square accounts with a person*** 向某人復仇。***square away*** **a.** 〖航海〗調正帆桁,以便在風前行駛。**b.** 重新做起;採取或使採取新路線。**c.** 〖俗〗準備。**d.** 採攻勢或守勢。***square off*** 〖俗〗取自衞或攻擊之陣式。***square the circle*** **a.** 作一方形,使其面積與一已知圓相等。**b.** 做不可能之事。***square up*** 清償所欠;還帳;清算。—*adv.* ①〖俗〗公平地;忠實地。②成方形地。③照直地。to hit a man *square* on the jaw. 照直打一個人的下巴。④結實地。—**ness,** *n.*

square bracket 〖印刷〗方括弧〔 〕。

square-built [ˈskwɛrˌbɪlt; ˈskwɛəbilt] *adj.* 堅實的;粗壯的。

square dance 方塊舞。

square deal 〖俗〗公平交易;誠實交易。

square·face [ˈskwɛrˌfes; ˈskwɛəfeis] *n.* 〖英俚〗杜松子酒 (=gin).

square-faced [ˈskwɛrˌfest; ˈskwɛəfeist] *adj.* 方臉的。

square·head [ˈskwɛrˌhɛd; ˈskwɛəhed] *n.* ①〖美俚、蔑〗德國人。②〖俗〗斯堪的那維亞人;北歐人。③笨人。

***square·ly** [ˈskwɛrlɪ; ˈskwɛəli] *adv.* ①方正地。②直接地;不閃避地。He faced the problem *squarely.* 他勇敢地面對該難題。③直截了當地;誠實地;公平地。

square-rigged [ˈskwɛrˈrɪgd; ˈskwɛəˈrigd] *adj.* 〖航海〗有橫帆裝置的;主帆與桅桿成直角的。

square root 平方根。

square shooter 〖俗〗公平正直的人。

square-toed [ˈskwɛrˈtod; ˈskwɛəˈtoud] *adj.* ①方頭的(鞋)。②嚴正的; 拘謹的;保守的。

square-toes [ˈskwɛrˌtoz; ˈskwɛətouz] *n.* 墨守成規之人。

squar·ish [ˈskwɛrɪʃ; ˈskwɛəriʃ] *adj.* 近似方形的。

squar·son [ˈskwarsn̩; ˈskwaːsn] *n.* 〖英,諧〗兼任牧師之地主。

squash[1] [skwaʃ; skwɔʃ] *v.t.* ①壓潰;壓爛;壓扁。②鎮壓;撲滅。③〖俗〗以諷刺的言語使(人)緘默。—*v.i.* ①潰;被壓爛。②擠。③發出擠壓聲;帶着擠壓聲行進。—*n.* ①壓碎之物;壓爛的果物。②壓碎;壓爛;壓碎聲。③以壓出的果汁製成的飲料。④一種類似手球和網球的球戲。

squash[2] *n.* 南瓜。

squash bug 南瓜蟲(有害於南瓜藤等)。

squash·y [ˈskwaʃɪ; ˈskwɔʃi] *adj.,* **squash·i·er, squash·i·est.** ①易爛的。②軟而鬆的;濕而軟的。③表面壓爛的。

***squat** [skwat; skwɔt] *v.,* **squat·ted** or **squat, squat·ting,** *adj., n.* —*v.i.* ①蹲踞。②〖俗〗坐。③擅自居住於他人之土地上。④爲取得所有權而居住於公家之土地上。—*v.t.* 使蹲踞。—*adj.* ①蹲踞的。②矮胖的。—*n.* 蹲踞;蹲踞的姿勢。

squat·ter [ˈskwatɚ; ˈskwɔtə] *n.* ①蹲踞着之人或動物。②無權而定居於公地者。③合法居住於政府公地以期取得所有權者。④〖澳〗牧場借用者;家畜所有者。

squat·ty [ˈskwatɪ; ˈskwɔti] *adj.,* **-ti·er, -ti·est.** 矮胖的;粗短的。

squaw [skwɔ; skwɔː] *n.* ①(印第安人之)女子或妻。②〖諧〗女子;妻子。

squawk [skwɔk; skwɔːk] *v.i.* ①粗厲地叫; 咯咯地叫。②粗聲說出。③〖俗〗高聲抱怨。—*n.* 咯咯的叫聲。—**er,** *n.*

squawk·box [ˈskwɔkˌbaks; ˈskwɔːkbɔks] *n.* 〖美俚〗公衆講話系統中之擴音器。(亦作 **squawk box**)

squaw man 娶北美印第安人爲妻之白人。

squeak** [skwik; skwiːk] *v.i.* ①發尖銳叫聲;吱吱而叫;作輾軋聲。A mouse *squeaks.* 鼠吱吱叫。②〖俚〗 **a.** 作告密者。**b.** 招供。③〖俗〗勉强通過。—*v.t.* ①以尖銳叫聲發出或說出 (言語、呼聲等) 〖out〗。② 使發尖銳聲。squeak by*** (or ***through***) 險勝;勉强合格。—*n.* 尖銳聲; 吱吱叫聲; 輾軋聲。***a narrow squeak*** 幸免於難;險勝。—**y,** *adj.*

squeak·er [ˈskwikɚ; ˈskwiːkə] *n.* ①尖叫者;吱吱叫者; 咕咕叫者。②〖俗〗小鴿;小豬。③〖俚〗告密者; 背叛者。④最後關頭才分出優劣勝敗的比賽。

*squeal [skwil; skwiːl] *v.i.* ①發出長而尖銳的叫聲。②〖俚〗告密。③〖俗〗高聲埋怨;大聲訴苦。—*v.t.* ①以尖而拉長的聲音說出或發出。②〖俚〗揭露;揭發。—*n.* ①長而尖銳的叫聲。②〖俗〗告密。③〖俗〗高聲訴苦。—**er,** *n.*

squeam·ish [ˈskwimɪʃ; ˈskwiːmiʃ] *adj.* ①過於拘謹的;易感驚訝的;神經質的。②過於仔細、審慎的。③有潔癖的;苛求的。④易於嘔吐的。⑤〖方〗謙遜的;害羞的。—**ly,** *adv.*

squee·gee [ˈskwidʒi, skwiˈdʒi; ˈskwiːˈdʒiː, skwiːˈdʒiː] *n., v.,* **-geed, -gee·ing.** —*n.* ①(以熟革或橡皮爲邊之) T 形拖把。②(壓平相片並吸收其上水分的)橡皮滾子。—*v.t.* 以此等工具拖擦或輾。

*squeeze [skwiz; skwiːz] *v.,* **squeezed, squeez·ing,** *n.* —*v.t.* ①壓榨;緊握;緊挾。to *squeeze* a person's hand. 緊握某人之手。②緊抱。③榨取;勒索;逼迫。④擠;塞。to *squeeze* oneself into a room. 擠入一個房間。⑤〖棒球〗用犧牲打得分。—*v.i.* ①擠。He *squeezed* through the crowd. 他從人羣擠過。②壓縮。③用手捏擠。—*n.* ①壓榨;緊挾;緊握。②勒索;榨取。③擁擠;緊塞。④緊抱。⑤榨出之物。⑥鑄型;印模;拓印之物。⑦難逃脫的境遇。

squeeze bottle 用手一捏裏面液質即噴出的塑膠瓶。

squeeze play ①〖棒球〗(第三壘有人,一人出局時之)犧牲打。②〖橋牌〗迫使對方拋出可能贏牌之牌。③對某人或集團從各方面加壓力迫使就範。

squeez·er [ˈskwizɚ; ˈskwiːzə] *n.* ①壓榨之人或物。②果汁機。

squelch [skwɛltʃ; skweltʃ] *v.t.* ①壓制。②使緘默。—*v.i.* ①(踏地時)發格吱聲。②發格吱之激濺聲。—*n.* ①(踏地時所發出之)格吱聲。②被壓碎或壓擠之物。③〖俗〗銳利之反駁。—**er,** *n.*

squib [skwɪb; skwib] *n., v.,* **squibbed, squib·bing.** —*n.* ①諷刺。②起花(一種爆竹)。③〖英〗爆竹。—*v.t. & v.i.* ①作詩文諷刺。②點燃爆炸物。③發尖小聲而爆炸。④作迅速而不規則之移動。

squid [skwɪd; skwid] *n., pl.* **squids, squid,** *v.,* **squid·ded, squid·ding.** —*n.* ①烏賊;魷魚。②烏賊鉤(一種人工魚鉤)。—*v.i.* 用烏賊爲餌釣魚。

squif·fy [ˈskwɪfɪ; ˈskwifi] *adj.,* **-fi·er, -fi·est.** 〖俚〗喝醉的;醉酒的。

squig·gle [ˈskwɪgḷ; ˈskwigl] *n., v.,* **-gled, -gling.** —*n.* 彎彎曲曲的線(如心電圖或地震儀所畫之線)。—*v.i.* 蠕動。—*v.t.* 使成彎彎曲曲之線。

squill [skwɪl; skwil] *n.* ①〖植物〗海葱;海葱根(利尿劑)。②〖動物〗蝦蛄;螳螂。

squinch [skwɪntʃ; skwintʃ] *n.* 〖建築〗內角拱。

squint [skwɪnt; skwint] *v.i.* ①斜視;瞇眼而看。②傾向。③偏斜出;越出原意等。—*v.t.* ①半閉着(眼睛)。②使斜視;使傾向;使斜出或越出。—*n.* ①斜視;瞥視;看。②〖醫〗斜視眼。③傾向;偏向。④間接提及;暗示。—*adj.* ①斜視的。②斜視眼的。—**er,** *n.*

squint-eyed [ˈskwɪntˈaɪd; ˈskwintˈaid] *adj.* ①斜視眼的。②惡意的。

*squire [skwaɪr; ˈskwaiə] *n., v.,* **squired, squir·ing.** —*n.* ①鄉紳(英國的紳士名稱)。②〖美〗地方法官。③隨侍 knight 的青年(以後他亦變爲 knight)。④護衞。⑤婦女的護衞。—*v.t.* 侍從;護衞(婦女)。***squire it*** 作鄉紳;當婦女之護衞。

squire·ar·chy [ˈskwaɪ,rɑrkɪ; ˈskwaiərɑːki] *n.* ①地主階級;鄉紳(集合稱)。②(英國1832年 Reform Bill 制定前之)地主政治;鄉紳政治。

squir·een [skwaɪˈrin; ˌskwaiəˈriːn] *n.* 〖愛〗小鄉紳;小地主。

squirm [skwɝm; skwəːm] *v.i.* ①蠕動;扭曲。②侷促不安。—*n.* 蠕動。—**y,** *adj.*

*squir·rel [ˈskwɝəl, skwɝl; ˈskwirəl] *n.* ①松鼠。②松鼠皮毛。③〖俚〗不顧危險開快車者。—*v.t.* 將…儲備起來〖常 away〗.

squirrel corn 〖植物〗罌粟科野草之一。

squir·rel·(l)y [ˈskwɝrəlɪ; ˈskwəːrili] *adj.* 古怪的;乖癖的。

squirt [skwɝt; skwəːt] *v.t.* ①噴出。②噴濕。—*v.i.* 自狹口中噴出。—*n.* ①液體之噴出。②噴出之液體。③噴出液體之工具;注射器;灌腸器;玩具手槍。④夜郎自大的人。⑤愛管閒事的青年。⑥矮子。—**er,** *n.*

squirt gun ①兒童玩具水槍。②噴霧器。

squish [skwɪʃ; skwiʃ] *v.t. & v.i., n.* 〖方〗=**squash¹**. —**y,** *adj.*

Sr strontium. **Sr.** ①senior. ②〖西〗Señor. ③Sir. **Sra.** 〖西〗Señora.

Sri Lan·ka [ˌsrɪˈlæŋkə; ˌsriˈlæŋkə] 斯里蘭卡(印度洋中一島國,首都可倫坡 Colombo; 昔稱錫蘭 Ceylon).

S.R.O. standing room only. 僅有站位。

Srta. 〖西〗Señorita. **SS, S.S., S/S** steamship. **SS., ss.** ① Sancti (拉=Saints). ②scilicet(拉=namely). ③sections. **ss.** 〖棒球〗shortstop. **SSA** Social Security Administration. **SSDDS** self-service discount department store. **SSDS** self-service discount store. **SSE, S.S.E., s.s.e.** south-southeast. **SSM** surface-to-surface missile. 地對地飛彈。 **SSR, S.S.R.** Soviet Socialist Republic. **SSW, S.S.W., s.s.w.** south-southwest.

*St. ①Saint. ②Strait. ③Street. ④Statute(s).

*st. ①street. ②stone (weight). ③stanza. ④stitch; stitches. ⑤statute(s). **s.t.** short ton.

*stab [stæb; stæb] *v.,* **stabbed, stab·bing,** *n.* —*v.t.* ①刺;刺傷。to *stab* a person to death. 刺死某人。②使貫穿;以(刀等)刺入。③傷害;損傷。④〖俗〗嘗試;企圖。—*v.i.* 刺;刺死。to *stab* at a person. 向某人刺戳。***stab a person in the back*** 背後陷害某人;暗傷某人。—*n.* ①刺;戳。②刺戳的傷;劇痛。③傷心;悲痛。④〖俗〗企圖;嘗試。***a stab in the back*** 暗害。***have*** (or ***make***) ***a stab at*** 嘗試;作…之嘗試。—**ber,** *n.*

Sta·bat Ma·ter [ˈstabatˈmatɚ; ˈstɑːbætˈmɑːtə] 〖拉〗〖宗教〗聖母哀悼基督之聖歌。

*sta·bil·i·ty [stəˈbɪlətɪ; stəˈbiliti, -ləti] *n., pl.* **-ties.** ①穩固;穩定。②堅定;有恆。He is a man of great *stability*. 他是一個很堅定的人。③永恆性;耐久性。

sta·bi·lize [ˈstebḷ,aɪz; ˈsteibilaiz] *v.t.,* **-lized, -liz·ing.** 使穩定。—**sta·bi·li·za·tion,** *n.*

sta·bi·liz·er [ˈstebə,laɪzɚ; ˈsteibilaizə] *n.* ①使平衡者;使穩定者。②〖機械〗穩定器。③〖化工〗安定劑。④〖航空〗使飛機在飛行時保持穩定之裝置;平衡器。

*sta·ble¹ [ˈstebḷ; ˈsteibl] *n., v.,* **-bled, -bling.** —*n.* ①廐;畜舍。②畜舍中的一羣家畜。the whole *stable*. 全廐中的馬羣。③(*pl.*) 訓練賽馬之馬廐。④一個主人的一羣賽

馬。⑤賽馬之馬夫及訓練者等。⑥〖俗〗同僚；同夥；志同道合者。⑦〖俚〗受同一個經紀人控制的拳擊手。—*v.t.* & *v.i.* 納入廐中；居於廐中。

*__sta·ble²__ *adj.* ①堅固的；穩定的。②堅定的；不動搖的。The whole world needs a *stable* peace. 全世界需要穩定的和平。

sta·ble·man 〔ˈstebl͵mæn; ˈsteiblmən〕 *n., pl.* **-men.** 馬夫。

stab·lish 〔ˈstæblɪʃ; ˈstæbliʃ〕 *v.t.* 〖古〗 =**establish.**

sta·bly 〔ˈsteblɪ; ˈsteibli〕 *adv.* 穩固地；「平穩地；固定地。」

stacc. staccato.

stac·ca·to 〔stəˈkɑto; stəˈkɑːtou〕 *adj.* ①〖音樂〗斷音的。②不連接的；突然中斷的。—*adv.* ①斷音地。②不連接地；突然中斷地。—*n.* ①〖音樂〗斷奏；斷唱。②突然中斷之事物。

*__stack__ 〔stæk; stæk〕 *n.* ①堆。a *stack* of hay. 一堆乾草。②烟囪；烟筒。③大量；大宗；多數。a *stack* of people. 一羣人。④書架。⑤英國衡量木及煤之單位。⑥架起之槍；槍架。⑦(亦作 **air stack**) 在機場上空盤旋等待降落之機羣。⑧(*pl.*) **a.** 圖書館中之書箱。**b.** 圖書館中之主要藏書放置處。***blow one's stack*** 〖俚〗發脾氣；光火。—*v.t.* ①堆起；堆積。*Stack* arms! 架槍！(軍隊之口令)。②做(牌)(洗牌時作弊)。③選派(有偏見的陪審團團員以作不公正之判決)。④因特殊情形而使(前來之飛機)在機場上空不同高處盤旋，以便挨次候命降落。***have the cards stacked against one*** 對某人有極大的不利。***stack up*** **a.** 〖航空〗控制候命降落飛機之飛行路線。**b.** 〖俚〗比較。**c.** 〖俚〗似乎有理。**d.** 疊積。

stacked 〔stækt; stækt〕 *adj.* 〖俚〗妖艷的；身材婀娜多姿的。

stac·te 〔ˈstæktɪ; ˈstæktiː〕 *n.* 古猶太人用以製供神香之一種香料。

stac·tom·e·ter 〔stækˈtɑmətɚ; stækˈtɔmitə〕 *n.* 滴量計。

stad(t)·hold·er 〔ˈstæd͵holdɚ; ˈstæd͵houldə〕 *n.* 荷蘭一省之行政長官。

sta·di·a¹ 〔ˈstedɪə; ˈsteidiə〕 *n.* pl. of **stadium.**

sta·di·a² *n.* 〖測量〗①視距儀；視距準尺。「②視距儀測量法。」

*__sta·di·um__ 〔ˈstedɪəm; ˈsteidiəm〕 *n., pl.* **sta·di·ums** or **sta·di·a.** 有多層看臺的露天運動場。

*__staff__ 〔stæf, stɑf; stɑːf〕 *n., pl.* **staffs** or **staves** (定義①-④可用 staffs 或 staves，定義⑤、⑥ 只能用 staffs), *v., adj.* —*n.* ①棒；杖；竿。②旗竿。③依靠。A son should be the *staff* of his father's old age. 兒子應是父親老年時的依靠。④(輔佐的)全體人員。editorial *staff*. 編輯部全體職員。⑤〖軍〗參謀；幕僚；參謀部；(團營等之) 本部。the general *staff*. 參謀本部。⑥音度線；五線譜。***the staff of life*** **a.** 生命的支持物。**b.** 麪包。—*v.t.* 供以職員；供以幕僚。—*adj.* 參謀的；行政業務的。*staff* duties. 參謀作業。

staf·fer 〔ˈstæfɚ; ˈstɑːfə〕 *n.* 〖美〗①職員。②報社之編輯。

staff officer ①〖軍〗參謀。②〖美海軍〗不能當艦長或機長之軍官(如軍醫、軍中牧師等)。

*__stag__ 〔stæg; stæg〕 *n., adj., v.,* **stagged, stag·ging.** —*n.* ①雄鹿。②其他多種動物之雄性。③單獨參加舞會、宴會等的男子。④〖美俗〗限男子參加之聚會等。⑤〖英俚〗購買某公司之股票而立刻出售以賺錢者。—*adj.* 僅男子參加的。—*v.t.* 購買(股票)立刻出售以賺錢。

stag beetle 鹿角蟲；鍬蟲。

‡__stage__ 〔stedʒ; steidʒ〕 *n., v.,* **staged, stag·ing.** —*n.* ①壇；臺。②舞臺；劇場；劇壇；戲劇業。Shakespeare wrote for the *stage*. 莎士比亞寫劇本。③活動的場所。the *stage* of politics. 政治舞臺；政界。④驛；站；驛程。⑤驛馬車。⑥階段；進程；時期。at this *stage* of his life. 在他生命中的這一階段。⑦足臺；鷹架。⑧(火箭或飛彈之)節。⑨〖美〗水位。***by easy stages*** 慢慢地；不慌不忙地。***go on the stage*** 做演員。***hold the stage*** **a.** 繼續上演。**b.** 成爲注目之中心；引人注目。***the stage*** 戲劇生涯。—*v.t.* ①表演；上演。to *stage* a play. 上演一劇。②供給舞臺。③以某時間或地點作編劇之背景。④使每個參加者都有特定任務而準備計畫或展開某項活動。—*v.i.* ①乘驛車旅行。②上演。That scene will not *stage* well. 那一景不會演得好。

stage·coach 〔ˈstedʒ͵kotʃ; ˈsteidʒkoutʃ〕 *n.* 驛馬車。

stage·craft 〔ˈstedʒ͵kræft; ˈsteidʒkrɑːft〕 *n.* 編劇術；上演術。

stage direction ①舞臺指導。②導演。

stage door 後臺門。

stage effect 舞臺效果。

stage fever 演員熱(想做演員之熱望)。

stage fright 怯場。

stage·hand 〔ˈstedʒ͵hænd; ˈsteidʒhænd〕 *n.* 管理舞臺布景、道具及燈光等之人。

stage-man·age 〔ˈstedʒ͵mænɪdʒ; ˈsteidʒ͵mænidʒ〕 *v.t.,* **-aged, -ag·ing.** ①指揮；督導。②暗中安排或指導。③替…作舞臺監督。—*v.i.* 當舞臺監督。

stage manager 舞臺監督。

stag·er 〔ˈstedʒɚ; ˈsteidʒə〕 *n.* ①經驗豐富之人或物；老手 (常與 old連用)。②驛馬車之馬。③〖古〗優伶。

stage-struck 〔ˈstedʒ͵strʌk; ˈsteidʒstrʌk〕 *adj.* ①熱望做演員的。②對演劇界特別景仰的。

stage whisper ①演員意欲使觀衆聽見的大聲自語。②意欲使別人聽見的低語。

stage·wise 〔ˈstedʒ͵waɪz; ˈsteidʒwaiz〕 *adj.* ①熟知演劇的。②善於演出的。—*adv.* ①在舞臺上。②與舞臺有關。

stag·fla·tion 〔ˈstæg͵fleʃən; ˈstæg͵fleiʃən〕 *n.* 〖英〗停滯性的經濟萎縮 (失業人數與通貨膨脹同時猛烈上升的情況)。

*__stag·ger__ 〔ˈstægɚ; ˈstægə〕 *v.i.* ①蹣跚；搖擺。②猶豫；躊躇。③不穩；崩潰。—*v.t.* ①使蹣跚；使搖擺。②使猶豫；使躊躇。③使驚愕。I was *staggered* by the news. 這消息使我驚愕。④間隔(不使集中在一個時間發生)。⑤使無助。—*n.* ①蹣跚；躊躇。②(*pl.*) (作 *sing.* 解)〖獸醫〗牛馬等之暈倒症。—**er,** *n.*

stag·ger·ing 〔ˈstægərɪŋ; ˈstægəriŋ〕 *adj.* ①驚人的；使吃驚的。②巨大的；龐大的。—**ly,** *adv.*

stag·hound 〔ˈstæg͵haund; ˈstæghaund〕 *n.* 獵鹿用之獵犬。

Stag·i·rite 〔ˈstædʒə͵raɪt; ˈstædʒirait〕 *n.* ①古馬其頓 Stagira 城的居民。②(the-) 亞里斯多德(因其出生於 Stagira 之故)。

stag·nant 〔ˈstægnənt; ˈstægnənt〕 *adj.* ①停滯的；不流動的。②不活潑的；不興旺的；不景氣的。—**ly,** *adv.* —**stag·nan·cy,** *n.*

stag·nate 〔ˈstægnet; ˈstægneit〕 *v.i.* & *v.t.,* **-nat·ed, -nat·ing.** ①(使)停滯；(使)不流動；(使)變爲腐濁。②(使)不振；(使)不景氣。—**stag·na·tion,** *n.*

stag·y 〔ˈstedʒɪ; ˈsteidʒi〕 *adj.,* **stag·i·er, stag·i·est.** ①舞臺的；演劇的 (通常含有惡意)。②假的；做作的；誇張的。

staid [sted; steid] *adj.* 穩定的;沉着的;沉靜的。—**ly,** *adv.* —**ness,** *n.*

*__stain__ [sten; stein] *n.* ①汚點;染汚之處。②汚辱;恥辱;瑕疵。③顏料;染料。—*v.t.* ①汚;染汚。②玷汚;汚辱。His character was *stained* by cruelty. 殘酷玷汚了他的品性。③染;着色於。—*v.i.* ①受汚。②染汚他物;造成汚跡。—**er,** *n.* —**a·ble,** *adj.*

*__stain·less__ [ˈstenlɪs; ˈsteinlis] *adj.* 無汚點的;無瑕疵的;不銹的。—*n.* 不銹鋼(餐具)。

stainless steel 不銹鋼。

‡**stair** [stɛr; stɛə] *n.* ①階梯之一級。He was standing on the bottom *stair.* 他在階梯的最下面一級上站着。②階梯之一段;室內或與建築物相連的樓梯。a winding *stair.* 螺旋梯。③(*pl.*) 樓梯;階梯。The *stairs* are steep. 這樓梯很陡。***below stairs*** a. 一幢房屋的地下室,卽僕人所居之處。b. 樓下。

*__stair·case__ [ˈstɛrˌkes; ˈstɛəkeis] *n.* ①樓梯。②樓梯間。

stair rod 樓梯踏板上壓住地毯之條狀物。

*__stair·way__ [ˈstɛrˌwe; ˈstɛəwei] *n.* 樓梯。

*__stake__[1] [stek; steik] *n., v.,* **staked, stak·ing.** —*n.* ①樁;杙。②火刑柱。③在火刑柱上燒死。④小型鐵砧。***drive stakes*** 〖俗〗a. 搭篷帳。b. 用樁標出所要求的地界。c. 定居下來。***go to the stake*** 受火焰之刑。***pull up stakes*** 〖美俗〗a. 搬家;遷居。b. 辭職。—*v.t.* ①以樁支持;繫於樁上。②以樁爲界。③保留或要求(土地、利潤、功勞等)〖常out, off〗. ***stake out*** 〖俚〗a. (警察)釘梢(嫌犯)。b. 派警察看管一嫌犯或一地。

*__stake__[2] *v.,* **staked, stak·ing,** *n.* —*v.t.* ①以…爲賭注;賭。I *stake* my reputation on his honesty. 我把我的名譽賭在他的誠實上面(我保證他很誠實)。②〖俗〗供應。—*n.* ①賭物;賭金。②(*pl.*)(賽馬或競技的)獎金。③利害關係。④〖俗〗=**grubstake.** ***at stake*** 得失攸關;瀕於危險。

stake·hold·er [ˈstekˌholdɚ; ˈsteikˌhouldə] *n.* 賭金保管者。

Sta·kha·nov·ism [stəˈkɑnoˌvɪzəm; stəˈkɑːnouvizm] *n.* 蘇聯之勞動競賽制(工人自動以改良技術而增加生產,可分紅並享受福利以爲酬勞)。—**Sta·kha·no·vite,** *adj., n.*

sta·lac·tite [stəˈlæktaɪt; ˈstæləktait] *n.* ①鐘乳石。②形狀或位置似鐘乳石之物。

stal·ac·tit·ic [ˌstælækˈtɪtɪk; ˌstæləkˈtitik] *adj.* 鐘乳石的;鐘乳石狀的。

sta·lag [ˈstæləg, ˈʃtɑlɑk; ˈstæləg, ˈʃtɑːlɑːk] 〖德〗*n.* 戰俘營(收容士兵者)。

sta·lag·mite [stəˈlægmaɪt; ˈstæləgmait] *n.* ①石筍。②形狀類似石筍之物。

stal·ag·mit·ic [ˌstæləgˈmɪtɪk; ˌstæləgˈmitik] *adj.* 石筍的;石筍狀的。

stal·ag·mom·e·ter [ˌstæləgˈmɑmətɚ; ˌstæləgˈmɔmitə] *n.* 〖理化〗滴數計。(亦作 **stactometer**)

*__stale__[1] [stel; steil] *adj.,* **stal·er, stal·est,** *v.,* **staled, stal·ing.** —*adj.* ①不新鮮的;陳舊的;陳腐的。a *stale* joke. 老笑話。②精力喪失的。③〖法律〗(權利等,因多年未行使而)失效的。—*v.t.* 使陳舊。—*v.i.* 變爲陳舊。—**ly,** *adv.* —**ness,** *n.*

stale[2] *n., v.,* **staled, stal·ing.** —*n.*(牛、馬之)尿。—*v.i.* (牛、馬)放尿。

stale·mate [ˈstelˌmet; ˈsteilˈmeit] *n., v.,* **-mat·ed, -mat·ing.** —*n.* ①(奕棋中之)王棋受困;將死。②停頓。—*v.i.* ①使王棋受困;將死。②使停頓。

Sta·lin [ˈstɑlɪn; ˈstɑːlin] *n.* 史達林(Joseph V., 1879–1953, 蘇聯的獨裁者)。—**ism,** *n.* —**ist,** *adj., n.*

*__stalk__[1] [stɔk; stɔːk] *n.* ①(植物的)莖;柄。②莖狀物;羽莖。③動物的似莖的部分。④任何似柄的支撐物。—**like,** *adj.*

*__stalk__[2] *v.i. & v.t.* ①潛行;潛近(獵物等)。②高視闊步。③(疾病、災害等)蔓延。—*n.* ①潛近;潛蹤。②高視闊步。—**er,** *n.*

stalk·ing-horse [ˈstɔkɪŋˌhɔrs; ˈstɔːkiŋhɔːs] *n.* ①獵人掩於其後以潛近獵物之馬或假馬。②託詞;口實;煙幕。③〖政治〗爲掩護另一更重要候選人的候選人。

*__stall__[1] [stɔl; stɔːl] *n.* ①廐;畜舍;畜舍之一欄。②攤;商場中之貨攤。③(禮拜堂之)教士座位。④(劇院之)正廳前排座位。⑤教堂中合唱團之席次。⑥〖航空〗失速。⑦圖書室中設有座位的小角落。⑧爲某一用途而設的小隔間。a shower *stall.* 淋浴間。⑨停車場劃開的長方形停車位置。⑩護指或護脚趾。—*v.t.* ①納於廐中;在廐中飼肥。②(如陷入泥中等)使進退不得。③阻礙或停止…的前進;使靜。④使(飛機等)失速。—*v.i.* ①(馬、車等因遇爛泥、積雪等而)停止。②(發動機等因缺乏燃料或負荷過度而)停止。③(飛機)失速下降。④〖美俗〗假裝忙碌而磨蹭;拖時間。⑤被納入廐中。

*__stall__[2] *n.* 〖俚〗①口實;託辭;拖延行爲。②扒手黨。—*v.i.* 〖俚〗①推托;躲閃;拖延。②(運動員)故意不做好的表現。—*v.t.* 〖俗〗延宕;妨礙;閃避;推托〖off〗.

stall bar (體操用)肋木。

stall-feed [ˈstɔlˌfid; ˈstɔːlfiːd] *v.t.,* **-fed, -feed·ing.** 在廐中飼肥;用乾芻飼肥。

stal·lion [ˈstæljən; ˈstæljən] *n.* 未閹之雄馬;種馬。

stal·wart [ˈstɔlwɚt; ˈstɔːlwət] *adj.* ①強壯的。a *stalwart* man. 壯健的人。②強壯而勇敢的。③堅定的;堅毅的。—*n.* ①強壯之人;勇敢之人。②政黨之中堅分子。

sta·men [ˈstemən; ˈsteimen] *n., pl.* **sta·mens, stam·i·na** [ˈstæmənə; ˈstæminə]. 〖植物〗雄蕊。

stam·i·na [ˈstæmənə; ˈstæminə] *n.* 體力;精力;(對疾病、疲勞等之)耐力;持續力。

stam·i·nal [ˈstæmɪnəl; ˈstæminəl] *adj.* ①本質的;精力的。②〖植物〗雄蕊的。

stam·i·nate [ˈstæmənɪt; ˈstæminit] *adj.* 〖植物〗有雄蕊的;生雄蕊的;僅有雄蕊的。

*__stam·mer__ [ˈstæmɚ; ˈstæmə] *v.i. & v.t.* 口吃;結巴〖out〗. —*n.* 口吃。He had a nervous *stammer.* 他有緊張的口吃毛病。—**er,** *n.*

‡**stamp** [stæmp; stæmp] *v.t.* ①頓(足);踏。to *stamp* out a fire. 踏滅火。②鎭服;撲滅。③蓋印於;加記號於。④表徵。⑤貼以郵票或印花。⑥銘刻於。His words were *stamped* on my mind. 他的話深深銘刻在我的心上。⑦壓碎(礦石等)。—*v.i.* 踏足;頓足。He *stamped* with rage. 他頓足大怒。***stamp down*** (or ***flat***) 用脚踏碎;踩平。***stamp out*** a. 毀掉;踏滅。b. 鎭服。—*n.* ①踏足;頓足。②印章;圖記。③打印器;壓印器;壓碎機。④痕跡;表徵。⑤郵票;印花。⑥種;類。⑦=**trading stamp.**

stamp album (or **book**) 集郵簿。

stamp collector 集郵人。

stamp duty 印花稅。

stam·pede [stæmˈpid; stæmˈpiːd] *n., v.,* **-ped·ed, -ped·ing.** —*n.* ①(受驚恐之牛、馬羣的)驚逃;逃竄。②任何驚逃;奔竄。

③風起雲湧的行動。④〖美西部,加〗一年一次之慶祝會,包括牧童技術競賽、展覽、舞蹈等。⑤〖美西北部〗牧童技術競演會。—*v.i.* ①驚逃;奔竄。②紛紛行動。—*v.t.* 使驚逃;使奔竄。

stamp·er [ˈstæmpɚ; ˈstæmpə] *n.* ①頓足者。②郵局蓋郵戳的職員。③印記之用具。④碎石機之杵。⑤模子(尤指作唱片用的)。

stamp machine 自動郵票販賣機。

stance [stæns; stæns] *n.* ①(高爾夫球等) 擊球時之脚的位置。②站立時之姿勢。③姿態; 態度。

stanch¹ [stæntʃ, stɑntʃ; stɑːntʃ] *v.t.* ①止住(血等)。②止住(傷口)之流血。—*v.i.* (血等)止流;停止流出。(亦作 **staunch**)

stanch² *adj.* ①堅固的; 堅强的。②忠誠的;堅定的。③不漏水的。(亦作 **staunch**)

stan·chion [ˈstænʃən, -tʃən; ˈstɑːnʃən] *n.* ①(窗戶、廐欄等之) 支柱。②牛欄中夾限牛頸之隔框。—*v.t.* ①支以支柱。②以隔框夾限(牛頸)。

‡stand [stænd; stænd] *v.*, **stood, stand·ing,** *n.* —*v.i.* ①站立; 站住; 立起。*Stand* up, please. 請起立。His hair *stood* on end. 他的毛髮悚然。②位於;處於某種地位或情形。He *stands* first in his class. 他在班中名列第一。The thermometer *stands* at 90°. 寒暑表達九十度。③站立時身高。He *stands* six feet in his socks. 他着襪(脫鞋)時身高六英尺。④停住;勿動。*Stand* and deliver! 站住,把錢交給我! ⑤存在;不變;持久。This color will *stand.* 這顏色會持久。⑥有效。The order will still *stand.* 這命令仍將有效。⑦航行。The ship *stood* out to sea. 那船出航海上。⑧充當;作爲。⑨採取某種政策或行爲。He *stands* for free trade. 他贊成自由貿易。⑩(帳目、分數等)顯示。⑪(水等)停滯不動。⑫〖主英〗候選(公職)〖常 for〗。⑬(指雄性動物,尤指種馬) 待顧客召喚而交配傳種。⑭(獵犬) 指示獵物之方向。—*v.t.* ①豎起;使直立。*Stand* the box here. 把匣子豎放在這兒。②忍耐;忍受。Can you *stand* the pain? 你能受得了這痛苦嗎?③不受…之損傷。④供給;付帳。Who is going to *stand* treat? 誰付帳? ⑤執行(任務);參與(某事)。***stand a chance*** (or ***show***) 有機會;有可能性。***stand alone*** **a.** 沒有支援者。**b.** 沒有敵手。***stand at attention*** (***at ease***) 立正(稍息)。***stand by*** **a.** 旁觀。**b.** 援助。**c.** 遵守;維持。**d.** 保持。**e.** 準備行動。***stand down*** **a.** 離開證人席。**b.** 退休;撤退;退出競爭。***stand firm*** **a.** 固守不變;堅守不移。**b.** 拒絕撤退。***stand for*** **a.** 代替;代表。**b.** 擁護;贊成。**c.** 爲…候選人。**d.**〖俗〗容忍;允許。***stand in*** 參加;分擔一分。***stand in the way*** 妨礙。***stand in with***〖俗〗**a.** 與…爲伍;與…合謀。**b.** 與…友善;獲…之青睞。***stand off*** 避開;不接近。***stand on*** (or ***upon***) **a.** 爲…之基礎;依賴。**b.** 要求;聲言。***stand on ceremony*** 拘禮。***stand one's ground*** **a.** 堅守陣地。**b.** 堅持立場。***stand on one's own legs*** 自助;自立。***stand out*** **a.** 支撐。**b.** 顯著; 傑出。**c.** 突出;伸出。**d.**〖航海〗保持離開海岸的航線。**e.** 不讓步;頑抗。***stand over*** **a.** 延緩;展期(再作考慮、決定等)。**b.** 密切注意;嚴格監督。***stand to*** **a.** 固守。**b.** 繼續做下去。**c.** 準備行動。***stand to reason*** 得當;合道理。***stand up*** **a.** 站着。**b.** 仍强硬;仍可信服;站得住。**c.**〖俚〗使(人)空等;不守約。**d.** 經久。***stand up for*** 堅持;維護;辯護。***stand up to*** 對抗;抵禦。***stand up with*** 作…之儐相、伴娘等。—*n.* ①停止;停頓。②位置。③講臺。④(*pl.*)看臺。⑤置物臺;架。⑥攤。a newspapers *stand.* 報攤。⑦抵抗。⑧旅行劇團爲在某處演出而做之停留。⑨旅行劇團演出之市鎮。⑩一叢正生長之樹或植物。⑪(法院之)證人席。⑫車輛之招呼站。a taxicab *stand.* 計程車招呼站。⑬在招呼站停放的車輛。⑭立場。***take a*** (or ***one's***) ***stand on*** **a.** 依據。**b.** 主張。***take the stand*** 前往證人席作證。

‡stand·ard [ˈstændɚd; ˈstændəd] *n.* ①標準;模範。Your work is not up to the *standard.* 你的工作不够標準。②本位;官定重量。gold *standard.* 金本位。③旗;軍旗;象徵。④支柱。⑤〖園藝〗有樹幹般高而直之莖的園藝植物。⑥(*pl.*) 道德、倫理、習慣等之標準。⑦(英國小學之) 班級。⑧〖美〗小牛肉;嫩牛肉。***raise the standard of revolt*** 揭竿而起。—*adj.* ①標準的; 模範的; 本位的。*standard* weights and measures. 標準度量衡。②品質最差的;最低級的。

standard atmosphere ①標準大氣。②零氣壓高度。

stand·ard-bear·er [ˈstændɚdˌbɛrɚ; ˈstændədˌbɛərə] *n.* ①掌旗官; 掌旗兵。②指導者;領袖。

standard candle 〖光學〗標準燭光。

stand·ard·ize [ˈstændɚdˌaɪz; ˈstændədaiz] *v.t.*, **-ized, -iz·ing.** 使與標準一致; 標準化。 —**stand·ard·iz·a·ble,** *adj.* —**stand·ard·i·za·tion,** *n.*

standard of living 生活水準。

standard time 標準時間。

stand-by [ˈstændˌbaɪ; ˈstændbai] *n.*, *pl.* **-bys,** *adj.* —*n.* ①可靠的人或物;主要的支持。②準備隨時救急的船。③令船待命的信號。④備好隨時可代替的人或事。⑤等待; 待命。***on stand-by*** 等待着;待命。—*adj.* ①待命的;隨時可接替的。②等待期間的。

stand·ee [stænˈdi; stænˈdiː] *n.* 〖俗〗(劇院或交通工具中之)站立者。

stand·er-by [ˈstændɚˈbaɪ; ˈstændəˈbai] *n.*, *pl.* **stand·ers-by.** 旁觀者;在場者。

stand-in [ˈstændˌɪn; ˈstændˈin] *n.* ①〖電影〗替身。②任何代替物。③〖俚〗具有影響力之地位;有利地位。④〖美〗黑人參加排隊以示反對公共場所中種族歧視之抗議。

***stand·ing** [ˈstændɪŋ; ˈstændiŋ] *n.* ①地位;身分;名望。a man of high *standing.* 地位高的人;名望高的人。②持續;期間。③站立;站立處;站立期間。④(*pl.*)〖運動〗顯示得分、比賽結果、名次等的表。—*adj.* ①直立的。②持續的;永存的;固定的。a *standing* army. 常備軍。③靜止的;停滯的。

standing order 〖軍〗標準作業程序。

standing room ①站立的空間。②(劇院、巴士等之)站位。

stand·ish [ˈstændɪʃ; ˈstændiʃ] *n.* 〖古〗「墨水瓶架。」

stand·off [ˈstændˌɔf; ˈstændɔːf] *n.* ①站於一旁。②旁觀;冷漠;孤立。③競賽中打成平手。④任何使均衡之物。⑤支撐之物。—*adj.* 冷眼旁觀的;孤高的;冷漠的;置身事外的。

stand·off·ish [stændˈɔfɪʃ; ˈstændˈɔːfiʃ] *adj.* 旁觀的;保留的;不友誼的。(亦作 **stand-offish**) —**ly,** *adv.* —**ness,** *n.*

stand·out [ˈstændˌaut; ˈstændaut] *n.* ①出類拔萃的人物。②〖俗〗堅持己見者;孤立主義者。—*adj.* 顯著的;傑出的;堅持己見的。

stand·pat [ˈstændˌpæt; ˈstændpæt]

adj. 〖俗〗主張維持現狀的;反對改革的;保守的;頑固的。—n. 〖俗〗保守之人。—tism, n.

stand·pat·ter [ˈstændˌpætɚ; ˈstændˌpætə] n. 〖俗〗頑固的人;保守的人。

stand·pipe [ˈstændˌpaɪp; ˈstændpaip] n. ①儲水塔;蓄水塔。②房屋內之消防用水管。

***stand·point** [ˈstændˌpɔɪnt; ˈstændpɔint] n. 立場;見地;觀點。 from a material *standpoint*. 從物質的觀點來說。

stand·still [ˈstændˌstɪl; ˈstændstil] n. 停頓; 停滯。 ***come to a standstill*** 停頓。—adj. ①停頓的;停滯的。②造成停頓的。

stand-up [ˈstændˌʌp; ˈstændʌp] adj. ①直立的;豎立的。②站立着做的。③堂堂正正的; 結結實實的。④直立或膨大的姿態的。⑤〖戲劇〗(丑角)在舞臺上獨自做詼諧獨白的。

stan·hope [ˈstænhop, ˈstænəp; ˈstænəp] n. 一種單座二輪或四輪之輕便馬車。

Stan·ley[1] [ˈstænlɪ; ˈstænli] n. 斯坦萊 (Sir Henry Morton, 1841–1904, 英國非洲探險家)。

Stan·ley[2] n. 斯坦萊 (Wendell Meredith, 1904–1971, 美國生物化學家,曾獲 1946 年諾貝爾化學獎)。

stan·na·ry [ˈstænərɪ; ˈstænəri] n., pl. -ries, adj. —n. 〖英〗錫礦坑;錫礦區;鎔錫場。—adj. 〖英〗採錫的;錫礦的。

stan·nate [ˈstænet; ˈstæneit] n. 〖化〗錫酸鹽。

stan·nic [ˈstænɪk; ˈstænik] adj. ①錫的;含錫的。②四價錫的。

stan·nite [ˈstænaɪt; ˈstænait] n. 〖礦〗黃錫礦。

stan·nous [ˈstænəs; ˈstænəs] adj. 〖化〗錫的;含二價錫的。

stan·num [ˈstænəm; ˈstænəm] n. 〖化〗錫。

St. Anthony's fire 丹毒。

***stan·za** [ˈstænzə; ˈstænzə] n. (詩之)一節。

sta·pes [ˈstepiz; ˈsteipiːz] n., pl. sta·pes, sta·pe·dez [stəˈpidiz; stəˈpiːdiːz]. 〖解剖〗(中耳之)鐙骨。

staph·y·lo·coc·cus [ˌstæfɪləˈkɑkəs; ˌstæfiləˈkɔkəs] n., pl. -coc·ci [-ˈkɑksaɪ; -ˈkɔksai]. 葡萄狀球菌。

***sta·ple**[1] [ˈstepl̩; ˈsteipl] n., adj., v., -pled, -pling. —n. ①主要物產; 土產; 名產。 Sugar is the *staple* of Taiwan. 糖是臺灣的主要物產。②原料。③纖維。④主要的貿易中心。⑤主要部分。—adj. ①主要的;最重要的。②經常大量生產的。 the *staple* commodities of Taiwan. 臺灣的主要生產品。—v.t. 按纖維之性質將(羊毛、棉等)分類。

sta·ple[2] n., v., -pled, -pling. —n. ①U形大釘。②釘書釘。—v.t. 釘以U形釘。

sta·pler[1] [ˈsteplɚ; ˈsteiplə] n. 釘書機。

sta·pler[2] n. ①將纖維分等的人。②從事主要物產買賣的商人。

‡star [stɑr; stɑː] n., v., starred, starring, adj. —n. ①星; 恒星。 fixed *star*. 恒星。 shooting *star*. 流星。②星宿; 命運。③明星; 主角; 名角; 泰斗; 大家。 a movie (*or* film) *star*. 電影明星。④星標;星符; 星狀物(如☆等)。⑤〖美軍〗 星章 (佩帶於衣袖, 表示參加某戰役)。⑥馬額上之白點。 ***see stars*** (因被打) 眼睛冒金星; 目眩。 ***thank one's (lucky) stars*** 感謝好運氣。 —v.t. ①以星裝飾。②加星標於。③以…爲主角。—v.i. 擔任主要角色;主演。—adj. 主要的;最好的;卓越的。 a *star* performance. 卓越的表演。

star·board [ˈstɑrˌbord; ˈstɑːbəd] n. (船之)右舷。—adj. 在右舷的。 —adv. 向右舷地。—v.t. & v.i. 將(舵)轉向右邊。

starch** [stɑrtʃ; stɑːtʃ] n. ①澱粉。②(漿硬衣服用之)漿糊。 *Starch* is used to stiffen clothes. 漿糊用來漿硬衣服。③態度拘泥;古板。④〖俗〗精力。⑤(pl.) 澱粉成分甚高之食物。 ***take the starch out of 〖俗〗挫…之銳氣;使洩氣。—v.t. 漿硬(衣服等)。

Star Chamber ①星法院(以濫刑專斷著聞於世)。②任何專斷不公之裁判機構。

star-cham·ber [ˈstɑrˌtʃembɚ; ˈstɑːˌtʃeimbə] adj. ①星法院的。②舉行星法院式祕密審訊的。

star chart 〖天文〗星位圖。

starch·y [ˈstɑrtʃɪ; ˈstɑːtʃi] adj., starch·i·er, starch·i·est. ①漿的;漿造成的。②含漿的。③拘泥的。—starch·i·ness, n.

star-crossed [ˈstɑrˌkrɔst; ˈstɑːkrɔst] adj. 〖詩〗命運不佳的。

star·dom [ˈstɑrdəm; ˈstɑː-dəm] n. ①電影明星;舞臺明星(集合稱)。②明星之地位。

star dust ①(肉眼不能分辨之)星團。②流星塵。③〖俗〗魅力;恍惚。

‡stare [stɛr; stɛə] v., stared, star·ing, n. —v.t. ①凝視;睇視;瞪着眼睛看。 to *stare* a person up and down. 上下打量某人。②瞪眼注視而使之。 to *stare* a person into silence. 瞪視某人使之緘默。 —v.i. ①睇視;瞪眼。②顯著;刺目(通常只用現在分詞指色彩而言)。 *staring* colors. 刺目之顏色。③(頭髮、羽毛等)聳起。 ***stare a person down*** (or ***out of countenance***) 把某人盯視得侷促不安。 ***stare one in the face*** 迫在眼前;顯而易見。—n. 睇視;瞪視。 to look at a person with a cold *stare*. 以冷眼瞪視某人。 —star·er, n.

star·fish [ˈstɑrˌfɪʃ; ˈstɑː-fiʃ] n., pl. -fish·es, -fish. 〖動物〗海盤車。

star·gaze [ˈstɑrˌgez; ˈstɑːgeiz] v.t., -gazed, -gaz·ing. ①凝視星辰。②耽於幻想。

star·gaz·er [ˈstɑrˌgezɚ; ˈstɑːˌgeizə] n. ①凝視星辰者(如天文學家等)。②做白日夢的人。③不實際的理想主義者。④頭舉得過高的馬。⑤眼睛長在頭頂上的一種魚。

Stark [ʃtark; ʃtɑːk] n. 施塔克 (Johannes, 1874–1957, 德國物理學家, 曾獲 1919 年諾貝爾物理獎)。

***stark** [stark; stɑːk] adj. ①僵硬的。②完全的;純然的。③嚴厲的。④〖古〗 强壯的。—adv. ①完全;全然。②嚴厲地。

star·less [ˈstarlɪs; ˈstɑːlis] adj. 無星的。

star·let [ˈstarlɪt; ˈstɑːlit] n. ①小星。②〖俗〗〖電影〗正接受訓練的小明星。

star·light [ˈstarˌlaɪt; ˈstɑːlait] n. 星光。—adj. (亦作 **starlighted**) 星光閃閃的。

star·like [ˈstarˌlaɪk; ˈstɑːlaik] adj. ①如星的;星形的。②閃爍的。

star·ling [ˈstarlɪŋ; ˈstɑːliŋ] n. ①(歐洲產之)椋鳥;燕八哥。②橋墩四周之木樁。

star·lit [ˈstarˌlɪt; ˈstɑːlit] adj. 星光照耀的。

Star of Bethlehem 伯利恆之星(引導來自東方的博士至嬰兒耶穌的星)。

star-of-Beth·le·hem [ˈstarəvˈbɛθlɪəm; ˈstɑːrəvˈbeθliəm] n., pl. stars-of-Beth·le·hem. 〖植物〗 星花百合。

starred [stard; stɑːd] adj. ①以星爲飾的; 有星標的。②被認爲受星辰影響的。③被派爲主角的。

***star·ry** [ˈstarɪ; ˈstɑːri] adj., -ri·er, -ri·est. ①多星的。 a *starry* night. 一個繁星之夜。②輝耀如星的。③星狀的。④星的;

與星有關的。—**star·ri·ness,** *n.*

star·ry-eyed ['stɑrɪ,aɪd; 'stɑːri-aid] *adj.* 過於理想的;不實際的;打如意算盤的。

Stars and Stripes 星條旗(美國國旗)。

star shell 〖軍〗照明彈。

star-span·gled ['stɑr,spæŋgḷd; 'stɑː,spæŋgld] *adj.* 星點散布的; 飾以星點的。***the Star-Spangled Banner*** **a.** 美國國旗。**b.** 美國國歌。

:start [stɑrt; stɑːt] *v.i.* ①起身;出發(不能用 begin 代替)。to *start* on a journey. 首途;動身旅行。He *started* for (= left for) London this morning. 他今晨動身前往倫敦。②開始 (大致均可用 begin 代替)。You have *started* well. 你開始得很好。③發生;發起(可用 begin 代替)。How did the war *start?* 戰爭怎樣發生的?④驚起; 突動。⑤突來; 突流出。Tears *started* from her eyes. 眼淚突然從她的眼睛裏流出來。⑥突出;伸出。⑦變鬆;脫節; 脫出。—*v.t.* ①開始(可用 begin 代替); 開始旅程(有時可用 begin 代替)。She *started* singing. 她開始歌唱。②發動;使開動;創始(不能用 begin 代替)。We couldn't *start* the car. 我們不能開動這輛汽車。③驚起。④使鬆; 使脫線。⑤協助…使開始。⑥發信號使開始。***start in*** 〖俗〗開始(做某事)。***start off*** 開始。***start out*** 企圖做…;着手做。***start to one's feet*** 受驚而立起;突然站起。***start up*** **a.** 突然升起;突然起立。**b.** 突然出現。**c.** 發動(引擎)。**d.** 開始做某事。***to start with*** **a.** 首先;第一。*To start with,* we haven't enough money. 首先, 我們沒有足够的錢。**b.** 開始時。We had ten members *to start with.* 開始時我們有十位會員。 —*n.* ①開始; 着手; 動身。You must make a new *start.* 你必須重新開始。②使開始賽跑等的信號;起跑線。③發展之機緣或助力。④驚動。⑤奮發之動作。⑥先發之便利(如在競走中);優先地位。You have got the *start* of me. 你已較我占優勢。

start·er ['stɑrtɚ; 'stɑːtə] *n.* ①起始之人或物; (尤指)一系列中之最先者。②賽跑時的起跑者。③賽跑中之發令員。④發令使汽車開車或飛機起飛之人員。⑤〖機械〗起動裝置;(尤指)自動起動裝置。***as*** (or ***for***) ***a starter*** 〖俗〗起始地(的)。

start·ing ['stɑrtɪŋ; 'stɑːtiŋ] *n.* 出發;開始;出發點;起動; 開動; 開車。***starting place*** 起點。***starting point*** 出發點; 起點。***starting post*** (賽馬的)出發點。

***star·tle** ['stɑrtḷ; 'stɑːtl] *v.*, **-tled, -tling,** *n.* —*v.t.* 使吃驚;使驚愕;驚動。—*v.i.* 吃驚;驚動。He *startled* from sleep. 他從睡中驚起。—*n.* 驚愕;驚恐。—**star·tler,** *n.*

***star·tling** ['stɑrtlɪŋ; 'stɑːtliŋ] *adj.* 使驚駭的;駭人聽聞的。a *startling* discovery. 駭人聽聞之發現。—**ly,** *adv.*

star·va·tion** [stɑr'veʃən; stɑː'veiʃən] *n.* 饑餓; 餓死。starvation wages*** 低於基本生活費的工資。

starve** [stɑrv; stɑːv] *v.i.* & *v.t.*, **starved, starv·ing.** ①(使)饑餓。to *starve* a man to death. 使人餓死。②渴望。to *starve* for news. 渴望消息。③(使)餓死。I am *starving!* 我要餓死了!④〖英方〗(因缺乏某物)(使) 受困苦;挨凍。starve down*** (or ***out***)以饑餓使屈服。***starve for*** 渴望。

starve·ling ['stɑrvlɪŋ; 'stɑːvliŋ] *adj.* ①饑餓的; 營養不良的。②饑饉而窮困的。③品質低劣或數量不足的。—*n.* 饑餓者。

stash [stæʃ; stæʃ] *v.t.* & *v.i.* 〖美俚〗貯藏以備用 〖常 away〗。—*n.* 〖美俚〗貯藏備用之物。

sta·sis ['stesɪs; 'steisis] *n.* 〖醫〗血液停滯;淤血;壅滯。

stat. ①statics. ②station. ③statistical. ④statistics. ⑤statuary. ⑥statue. ⑦statute.

:state [stet; steit] *n.*, *v.*, **stat·ed, stat·ing,** *adj.* —*n.* ①情形; 狀態。He is in a *state* of poor health. 他健康不佳。②國;國家;政府;(美國等之)州。Department of *State* (or *State* Department). 〖美〗國務院。③身分;地位; 威嚴; 榮耀。④隆重儀式。***lie in state*** (屍體)放於無蓋棺材中任人憑弔。***the States*** 〖俗〗美國。—*v.t.* 說;陳述。to *state* one's views. 陳述見解。—*adj.* ①國的;國家的。a *state* criminal. 國事犯。②儀式用的;官方的;正式的。 a *state* call. 正式訪問。

state bank ①國家銀行。②〖美〗州銀行。

state capitalism 國家資本主義。

state·craft ['stet,kræft; 'steitkrɑːft] *n.* ①政策;政略;治國方策。②政客手腕。

stat·ed ['stetɪd; 'steitid] *adj.* ①被陳述的;明白說出的。②確定的; 規定的; 一定的。—**ly,** *adv.*

State flower 〖美〗州花(代表美國各州之花)。

state·hood ['stethud; 'steithud] *n.* 〖美〗州之狀態或地位。

State·house ['stet,haus; 'steithaus] *n.* 〖美〗州議會大廈。(亦作 **State house**)

state·less ['stetlɪs; 'steitlis] *adj.* ①無國籍的。②無國家主權的;無疆界的。

***state·ly** ['stetlɪ; 'steitli] *adj.*, **-li·er, -li·est,** *adv.* —*adj.* 威嚴的;莊嚴的; 堂皇的。—*adv.* 莊嚴地;堂皇地。—**state·li·ness,** *n.*

:state·ment ['stetmənt; 'steitmənt] *n.* ①陳述; 記載; 聲明; 聲明書。a verbal *statement.* 口頭聲明。②(法庭上之)供述。③(商業上之)計算書; 報告書。 a bank *statement.* 銀行存款支付報告書。

State of the Union message 美總統每年一月向國會提出之國情咨文。

sta·ter ['stetɚ; 'steitə] *n.* 古希臘及波斯之各種金幣或銀幣。

state·room ['stet,rum; 'steit-rum] *n.* (船或火車上之)艙房;包房。

State's attorney 〖美〗州檢察官。

state·side ['stet,saɪd; 'steitsaid] *adj.* 〖俗〗美國(本土)的。—*adv.* 〖俗〗在美國本土;向美國本土。

***states·man** ['stetsmən; 'steitsmən] *n.*, *pl.* **-men** [-mən; -mən]. 治政家。—**ly,** *adj.*

states·man·ship ['stetsmən,ʃɪp; 'steitsmənʃip] *n.* 政治才能;治國之才。

state socialism 國家社會主義。

States' righter 〖美〗極力主張 States' rights 的人。

States' rights 〖美〗憲法賦予州的權利。

states·wom·an ['stets,wumən; 'steits,wumən] *n.*, *pl.* **-wom·en.** 女政治家。

State university 〖美〗州立大學。(亦作 **state university**)

state visit 國家元首至他國之正式訪問。

state·wide, state-wide ['stet'waɪd; 'steit'waid] *adj.* 延及(遍及)全州的。—*adv.* (有時 S-)延及(遍及)全州地。

stat·ic ['stætɪk; 'stætik] *adj.* (亦作 **statical**)①靜止的;靜態的。②(社會生活等)受傳統約束的。—*n.* ①(尤指無線電信號之)靜

電干擾。②靜電;天電。—al·ly, *adv.*
static electricity 靜電。
stat·ics ['stætɪks; 'stætiks] *n.* 〖物理〗靜力學。
‡**sta·tion** ['steʃən; 'steiʃən] *n.* ①立脚地;位置;場所;指定的崗位。to take up a convenient *station.* 占一方便位置。②車站。a bus *station.* 公共汽車站。③(軍隊之)營所;根據地。a police *station.* 警察派出所。④地位;身分。⑤(無線電之)電臺。⑥〖澳〗牧場。⑦(侍者或軍人)服勤的地方。⑧站立;立姿。⑨靜立。—*v.t.* 配置;安置。
station agent 〖鐵路〗站長。
sta·tion·ar·y ['steʃən,ɛrɪ; 'steiʃnəri] *adj., n., pl.* -ar·ies. —*adj.* ①固定的;不動的。*stationary* troops.駐屯軍。②無增減的;不變的。—*n.* 固定或不動的人或事物。
stationary engine 〖機械〗固定引擎。
station break 〖廣播,電視〗節目與節目之間播放的呼號、通告等(通常每隔半小時或一小時出現一次)。
sta·tion·er ['steʃənɚ; 'steiʃnə] *n.* 文具商。
sta·tion·er·y ['steʃən,ɛrɪ; 'steiʃṇəri] *n.* 文具;信紙。
station house ①警察派出所;消防隊。②(火)車站。
sta·tion·mas·ter ['steʃən,mæstɚ; 'steiʃən,mɑːstə] *n.* 〖鐵路〗站長。
sta·tion-to-sta·tion ['steʃəntə'steʃən; 'steiʃəntə'steiʃən] *adj.* (長途電話之)叫號的。—*adv.* ①自一站至另一站地。②以電話叫號費率地。
station wagon (有摺疊式後座之)旅行車。(亦作 **beach wagon, ranch wagon.** 英亦作 **estate car, estate wagon**)
stat·ism ['stetɪzṃ; 'steitizm] *n.* ①國家主權說。②中央政府經濟統制說。
stat·ist ['stetɪst; 'steitist] *n.* ①統計學家;統計人員。②主張中央政府統制經濟者。—*adj.* 主張中央統制經濟的。
sta·tis·tic [stə'tɪstɪk; stə'tistik] *adj.* =**statistical.**
sta·tis·ti·cal [stə'tɪstɪkḷ; stə'tistikəl] *adj.* 統計的;統計上的;統計學的。—ly, *adv.*
stat·is·ti·cian [,stætə'stɪʃən; ,stætis'tiʃən] *n.* 統計學家(或專家);統計人員。(亦作 **statist**)
***sta·tis·tics** [stə'tɪstɪks; stə'tistiks, stæ'-t-] *n.* ①(作 *sing.* 解)統計學。②(作 *pl.* 解)統計;統計表。*statistics* of population. 人口統計。
sta·tor ['stetɚ; 'steitə] *n.* ①〖機械〗固定部。②〖電〗固定子;靜定子。
stat·o·scope ['stætə,skop; 'stætəskoup] *n.* ①微動氣壓計。②〖航空〗升降計。
stat·u·ar·y ['stætʃu,ɛrɪ; 'stætjuəri] *n., pl.* -ar·ies, *adj.* —*n.* ①雕像;塑像(集合稱)。②雕塑術。③雕刻家。—*adj.* 雕像的;雕塑的;雕塑用的。
***stat·ue** ['stætʃu; 'stætjuː] *n.* 像;雕鑄;鑄像。The *Statue* of Liberty is in New York Bay. 自由女神像是在紐約港內。
stat·ued ['stætʃud; 'stætjuːd] *adj.* ①以雕像爲裝飾的。②雕像狀的。
stat·u·esque [,stætʃu'ɛsk; ,stætju'esk] *adj.* 莊嚴、優美如雕像的。—ly, *adv.*
stat·u·ette [,stætʃu'ɛt; ,stætju'et] *n.* 小雕像;小塑像。
***stat·ure** ['stætʃɚ; 'stætʃə] *n.* ①身材;身長。②重要性;道德的或智能的價值。③發展;身體、心智或道德之發展。a minister of great *stature.* 一位了不起的大臣。
***sta·tus** ['stetəs; 'steitəs] *n.* ①情形;狀態。②身分;地位。his *status* as a teacher. 他的教師身分。③〖法律〗法律地位。
status symbol ①可藉以判斷社會地位、經濟成就的事物或習慣。②藉以誇耀自己身分的事物。
stat·u·ta·ble ['stætʃutəbḷ; 'stætjutəbl] *adj.* =**statutory.**
***stat·ute** ['stætʃut; 'stætjuːt] *n.* ①成文法;法規。②規章;規程。the *statute* of a university. 大學規程。③〖國際法〗條約之附件。
statute book 法令全書。
statute law 成文法。
statute mile 法定英里。
statute of limitations 〖法律〗時效。
stat·u·to·ry ['stætʃu,torɪ; 'stætjutəri] *adj.* ①法律的;法令的;法規的。②法令所定的;依照法令的。*statutory* tariff. 國定稅率。③依法應處罰的。④合乎法令的。
Stau·ding·er ['ʃtaudɪŋɚ; 'ʃtaudiŋə] *n.* 史陶汀耳(Hermann, 1881–1965, 德國化學家,曾獲1953年諾貝爾化學獎)。
staunch [stɔntʃ; stɔːntʃ] *adj., v.t., v.i.* =**stanch.**
stau·ro·scope ['stɔrə,skop; 'stɔːrəskoup] *n.* 〖結晶〗十字鏡(測偏光面方向用)。
stave [stev; steiv] *n., v.,* **staved** or **stove, stav·ing.** —*n.* ①桶板。②棍;棒。③譜表(=staff)。④詩節;詩句。⑤梯之橫木。—*v.t.* ①鑿孔;擊穿(桶、船等)〖in〗。②防止;避開;延緩〖off〗。③裝以桶板;裝以橫木。—*v.i.* (船等)穿破。
stave rhyme 〖韻律〗古代詩歌的頭韻。
staves [stevz; steivz] *n.* ①pl. of **staff.** ②pl. of **stave.**
‡**stay**[1] [ste; stei] *v.,* **stayed, stay·ing,** *n.* —*v.i.* ①停止;停留;繼續停留於某個地方或某種狀態;繼續不變。Why did you *stay* away from school? 你爲甚麼不來(去)上課? *Stay* where you are. 站在那兒不要動。②暫住;居留。③等待。Time and tide *stay* for no man. 歲月不待人。④能持久;有耐力。*staying* powers. 耐久力。—*v.t.* ①止住。to *stay* one's hand. 住手。②延緩。③等待。④結束;滿足。⑤遏制。***stay out*** 停留的時間到達或超過某種限度。***stay put*** 〖俗〗停留原地不動。—*n.* ①逗留;逗留時期。You're making a very long *stay* here. 你在這裏停留很長時間了。②(法律上的)延緩執行;裁判手續之中止。③妨礙;抑制。④耐久力;持久力。
stay[2] *n., v.,* **stayed, stay·ing.** —*n.* ①支持物;支柱;船桅上的支索。②(*pl.*)婦人的胸衣;緊衣褡。③胸衣上之薄鐵片。—*v.t.* ①以(繩索、支柱等)支持〖有時 up〗。②支撐。
stay-at-home ['steət,hom; 'steiəthoum] *n.* 〖俗〗甚少離家外出的人。—*adj.* 〖俗〗常在家的;不常外出的。
stay·er ['steɚ; 'steiə] *n.* ①停留者。②能耐久之人或動物(尤指賽跑的馬)。③使停止者;壓制者;延緩者。④支撐者。
stay-in ['ste,ɪn; 'stei'in] *n.* 〖英〗靜坐罷工。(亦作 **stay-in strike**)
stay·lace ['ste,les; 'steileis] *n.* 婦人束胸之細帶。
stay·sail ['ste,sel; 'steiseil] *n.* 〖航海〗支索帆。
S.T.D. Sacrae Theologiae Doctor (拉=Doctor of Sacred Theology).
Ste., Ste Sainte (法文 Saint 之女性)。
***stead** [stɛd; sted] *n.* ①(人或物所處的)位置。②利益;好處;用處。③〖廢〗地方。

in one's stead 代替某人。*stand one in good stead* 於某人有好處。

***stead·fast** ['stɛd,fæst; 'stedfəst] *adj.* ①固定的；堅定的。a *steadfast* belief. 堅定的信仰。②不變的；不移的。a *steadfast* gaze. 凝視。(亦作**stedfast**) **—ly,** *adv.* **—ness,** *n.*

***stead·i·ly** ['stɛdəlɪ; 'stedili] *adv.* 有規則地；穩固地；不動搖地。The situation worsened *steadily.* 情勢越來越壞。

stead·i·ness ['stɛdɪnɪs; 'stedinis] *n.* 穩固；堅定不移；鎮靜。to maintain *steadiness* under fire. 在槍林彈雨中保持鎮靜。

stead·ing ['stɛdɪŋ; 'stediŋ] *n.* ①農場；農場內之建築。②建築物之基址。

‡stead·y ['stɛdɪ; 'stedi] *adj.,* **stead·i·er, stead·i·est,** *v.,* **stead·ied, stead·y·ing,** *n., pl.* **stead·ies,** *interj., adv.* **—***adj.* ①穩定的；不動搖的。(as) *steady* as a rock. 穩如磐石。②無變化的；同樣的；有規律的。He is making *steady* progress in his work. 他的工作着着進步。③沉着的；鎮定的。④穩健的；殷實的；可靠的。a *steady* young man. 穩健的青年。⑤(船)在洶湧之海上保持平穩的。*go steady* 〖俗〗祇跟一個固定的異性約會。**—***v.t.* 使堅定；使穩定；使沉着。**—***v.i.* 變爲堅定；變爲穩定；變爲沉着。**—***n.* 男(女)朋友；經常約會的一個固定異性朋友。**—***interj.* 穩住；不要慌。**—***adv.* 穩定地。

stead·y-state ['stɛdɪ,stet; 'stedi-steit] *adj.* 不變的；變動性很少的；靜恆狀態的。

***steak** [stek; steik] *n.* ①牛排。a beefsteak. 炸牛排。Hamburg *steak.* 漢堡牛排。②煎炸用的魚片或肉片。a cod-*steak.* 炸魚片。

steak·house ['stek,haus; 'steikhaus] *n., pl.* **-hous·es.** 牛排餐廳。(亦作 **steak house**)

steak knife 切牛排的小刀(通常有鋸齒)。

steak maul 在牛排未炸前將之敲打使嫩的工具。

‡steal [stil; sti:l] *v.,* **stole** [stol; stoul], **sto·len** ['stolən; 'stoulən], **steal·ing,** *n.* **—***v.t. & v.i.* ①偷；竊取。It's wrong to *steal.* 偷東西是不應該的。②獲得；贏得。to *steal* away one's heart. 博得某人歡心。③潛行；偷偷行走。to *steal* one's way. 潛行。④緩進；緩動。⑤〖棒球〗盜(壘)。⑥偷偷地搬運、移動〖常 away, from, in, into〗。⑦贏得分外的注意，喝采。*steal someone's thunder* **a.** 借用他人的話、觀念、計畫等。**b.** 喧賓奪主；反客爲主。**—***n.*①〖俗〗偷竊。②〖俗〗贓物。③〖俗〗很便宜買到的東西。④買賣中的欺詐行爲。⑤〖棒球〗盜壘。

steal·ing ['stilɪŋ; 'sti:liŋ] *n.* ①偷竊。②(常 *pl.*) 被竊之物。③〖棒球〗盜壘。**—***adj.* 偷竊的。

stealth [stɛlθ; stelθ] *n.* 祕密行動；祕密。*by stealth* 祕密地；偷偷地。

stealth·i·ly ['stɛlθəlɪ; 'stelθili] *adv.* 偷偷地；悄悄地。

stealth·y ['stɛlθɪ; 'stelθi] *adj.,* **stealth·i·er, stealth·i·est.** 祕密而爲的；隱祕的。

‡steam [stim; sti:m] *n.* ①蒸氣；水氣。②〖俗〗氣力；精力。to get up *steam.* 鼓起精神。*let* (or *blow*) *off steam* 〖俗〗 **a.** 發洩過多的精力。**b.** 發洩感情。*run out of steam* 〖俗〗洩氣；失去力氣。**—***v.i.* ①蒸發；發蒸氣。②藉蒸氣力行駛。③(玻璃窗等)凝結蒸氣。④〖俗〗生氣；發脾氣。⑤〖俗〗疾行。**—***v.t.* ①蒸(食物等)。to *steam* the meat. 蒸肉。②發出(蒸氣)。③以蒸氣力運送或推進。**—***adj.* ①蒸氣熱的。②蒸氣機的。③引導蒸氣的。④受蒸氣影響的。⑤蒸氣的。

steam bath 蒸氣浴。

***steam·boat** ['stim,bot; 'sti:mbout] *n.* 輪船；汽船。

steam boiler 汽鍋。

steam box (or **chest**) 蒸氣瓣室。

steam color 利用蒸氣以染着於織物或纖維上之顏色。

***steam engine** 蒸氣機。

steam·er** ['stimɚ; 'sti:mə] *n.* ①汽船。②蒸氣機。③蒸籠；蒸器。**—v.i.* 坐輪船。

steam fitter 裝修汽管、汽鍋之工人。

steam heat 蒸氣熱。

steam-heat·ed ['stim'hitɪd; 'sti:m'hi:tid] *adj.* 用蒸氣熱的。

steam iron 噴霧式電熨斗。

steam jacket 〖機械〗蒸氣套。

steam locomotive 蒸氣火車頭。

steam port 〖機械〗汽門；蒸氣口。

steam power 蒸氣的力量。

steam power plant 火力發電廠。

steam roller ①蒸氣壓路機。②〖俗〗壓制反對的方法。

steam-roll·er ['stɪm,rolɚ; 'sti:m,roulə] *v.t.* ①〖俗〗壓；輾。②壓倒對方或克服障礙以通過。**—***v.i.* 輾壓而前。**—***adj.* ①如壓路機的。②壓倒性的；無情地强壓的。(亦作 **steamroller, steam-roll, steamroll**)

steam room 土耳其浴室中的蒸氣室。

***steam·ship** ['stim,ʃɪp; 'sti:mʃip] *n.* 汽船；輪船。

steam shovel 汽鏟。

steam table 食物之蒸氣保溫箱。

steam·tight ['stim'taɪt; 'sti:m'tait] *adj.* 不漏氣的；氣密的；防止漏氣的。

steam turbine 蒸氣渦輪機。

steam·y ['stimɪ; 'sti:mi] *adj.,* **steam·i·er, steam·i·est.** ①蒸氣的；似蒸氣的。②多蒸氣的；發出蒸氣的。③又熱又潮濕的。

ste·ap·sin [stɪ'æpsɪn; sti'æpsin] *n.* 胰脂酶(胰液中分解脂肪的酵素)。

ste·a·rate ['stiə,ret; 'sti:əreit] *n.* 〖化〗硬酯酸鹽。

ste·ar·ic [stɪ'ærɪk; sti'ærik] *adj.* 〖化〗硬酯的。

ste·a·rin ['stiərɪn; 'stiərin] *n.* 〖化〗①硬酯；三硬酯酸甘油酯。②(商用) 硬酯酸 (=stearic acid). (亦作 **stearine**)

ste·a·tite ['stiə,taɪt; 'stiətait] *n.* 〖礦〗塊滑石。**--ste·a·tit·ic,** *adj.*

***sted·fast** ['stɛd,fæst; 'stedfəst] *adj.* =**steadfast.** **—ly,** *adv.* **—ness,** *n.*

steed [stid; sti:d] *n.* 〖詩〗馬；駿馬。

‡steel [stil; sti:l] *n.* ①鋼。②鋼製品(如刀等)。an enemy worthy of one's *steel.* 强敵；勁敵。③鋼鐵般的堅硬或力量。④胸衣的支撐。⑤(*pl.*)鋼鐵公司的股票。**—***adj.* 鋼的；如鋼的。*steel* weapons. 鋼鐵製的武器。**—***v.t.* ①使堅如鋼。②加以鋼刃等；以鋼包裹。

steel-clad ['stil,klæd; 'sti:l,klæd] *adj.* 穿甲冑的。

steel engraving 鋼版雕刻；鋼版雕刻術；鋼版雕刻品。

steel gray 稍帶藍色的灰色。

steel mill 煉鋼廠。

steel wool 鋼絲絨(磨光、去銹等用)。

steel·work ['stil,wɝk; 'sti:lwə:k] *n.* ①鋼鐵製品。②鋼架。

steel·work·er ['stil'wɝkɚ; 'sti:l'wə:kə] *n.* 鋼鐵工人。

steel·y ['stilɪ; 'sti:li] *adj.,* **steel·i·er, steel·i·est.** ①鋼的；鋼製的。②鋼色的；堅硬如鋼的。③嚴酷的；無情的；頑固的。**—steel·i·ness,** *n.*

steel·yard ['stɪljəd, 'stil,jɑrd; 'stiljɑ:d] *n.* 秤。

steen·bok ['stin,bɑk; 'sti:nbɔk] *n., pl.* **-boks, -bok.**【動物】一種南非產的小羚羊。(亦作 **steinbo(c)k, steinbuck**)

***steep**[1] [stip; sti:p] *adj.,* **steep·er,steep·est,** *n.* —*adj.* ①陡峭的;險峻的。②【俗】過分的;不合理的。a *steep* price. 過昂之價格。③【俗】(敍述等)極端的;無法相信的。④【廢】高的。—*n.* 陡峭的地方。—**ly,** *adv.* —**ness,** *n.*

***steep**[2] *v.t.* 浸; 漬; 濡濕; 沾染。to be *steeped* in liquor. 沉湎於酒。—*v.i.* 浸。—*n.* ①浸;漬。②浸液;漬液。

steep·en ['stipən; 'sti:pən] *v.t.* & *v.i.* (使)變爲峻急;(使)變爲陡峭。

***stee·ple** ['stipl̩;'sti:pl] *n.*(教堂的)尖塔。

stee·ple·bush ['stipl̩,buʃ;'sti:plbuʃ] *n.*【植物】美洲產的一種繡線菊屬之灌木。

stee·ple·chase['stipl̩,tʃes;'sti:pltʃeis] *n., v.,* **-chased, -chas·ing.** —*n.* ①障礙馬賽; 障礙賽跑。②越野賽馬;越野賽跑。—*v.i.* 參加障礙馬賽。

stee·ple-crowned ['stipl̩,kraund; 'sti:pl,kraund] *adj.* (帽子等)尖頂的。

stee·ple·jack ['stipl̩,dʒæk; 'sti:pl-dʒæk] *n.* 爬上塔尖、煙囪等從事修建者。

***steer**[1] [stɪr; stiə] *v.t.* ①駕駛。to *steer* an automobile. 駕駛汽車。②引導。③取(道)。—*v.i.* 駕駛;航行。The pilot *steered* for the harbor. 那駕駛員向港口航去。*steer clear of* 避開。—*n.*【美俚】勸告;消息;念頭。—**a·ble,** *adj.* —**er,** *n.*

steer[2] *n.* ①公犢(常指2–4歲者)。②公牛。

steer·age ['stɪrɪdʒ;'stiəridʒ] *n.* ①(客船之)統艙。②操舵;駕駛(船隻)。③船隻對舵之反應。

steer·age·way ['stɪrɪdʒ,we; 'stiə-ridʒwei] *n.*【航海】能使船應舵而轉動的最低前進速度。

steer·ing ['stɪrɪŋ; 'stiəriŋ] *n.* ①操舵。*steering* compass. 舵用羅盤。*steering* engine. 操舵機。*steering* gear. 操縱船隻、車輛、飛機方向等之裝置。*steering* wheel. 駕駛盤;方向盤;舵輪。②指導。

steering committee 程序委員會。

steers·man ['stɪrzmən; 'stiəzmən] *n., pl.* **-men.** ①舵手。②(汽車等之)司機。③操作機器的人。

steeve[1] [stiv; sti:v] *n., v.,* **steeved, steev·ing.** —*n.* ①【航海】船首斜桅仰角。②杠重桅吊桿。—*v.t.* ①使(船首斜桅)與水平成仰角。②以吊桿裝(貨物)於船內。—*v.i.* (斜桅)與水平成仰角。

steeve[2] *v.,* **steeved, steev·ing,** *n.* —*v.i.*將貨物裝滿船艙。—*n.* 船內裝貨之吊桿。

steg·o·my·ia [,stɛgə'maɪə; ,stegə-'maiə] *n.* 黃熱蚊(傳染黃熱病之蚊子)。

steg·o·sau·rus [,stɛgə'sɔrəs; ,stegə-'sɔ:rəs] *n.*【古生物】劍龍(已絕跡之巨大披甲爬蟲,爲恐龍之一種)。

stein [staɪn; stain] *n.* 一種有柄之陶製啤酒杯;任何類似之玻璃啤酒杯。

Stein·beck ['staɪnbɛk; 'stainbek] *n.* 斯坦培克(John Ernst, 1902–1968, 美國小說家, 1962年獲諾貝爾文學獎)。

ste·le ['stili; 'sti:li:] *n., pl.* **-lae** [-li; -li:], **-les.** ①【考古】石碑;石柱。②建築物或岩石上備刻字之平面。③【植物】(脈管纖維束形成之)中柱。

Stel·la ['stɛlə; 'stelə] *n.* 女子名。

stel·lar ['stɛlɚ; 'stelə] *adj.* ①星的; 似星的;星狀的。②主要的;主角的。

stel·late ['stɛlɪt;'stelit] *adj.* ①星狀的。②星狀排列的。③【植物】放射狀的。

stel·li·form ['stɛlɪ,fɔrm; 'stelifɔ:m] *adj.* 星形的; 放射狀的。

stel·lu·lar ['stɛljulɚ; 'steljulə] *adj.* ①小星狀的。②點綴以星狀點的; 星點花樣的。

stel·lu·late ['stɛljulet; 'steljuleit] *adj.* =**stellular.**

***stem** [stɛm; stem] *n., v.,* **stemmed, stem·ming.** —*n.* ①莖;幹;葉柄; 花梗。②莖狀物;(工具之)柄。the *stem* of a pipe. 煙斗之柄。③家系; 族。④語幹。⑤船首。⑥一束香蕉;一串香蕉。*from stem to stern* **a.** 從船首至船尾。**b.** 任何物體之縱貫全長。—*v.t.*①去(葉、果實等之)梗。②阻止。to *stem* the enemy's attack. 阻止敵人的攻擊。③逆…而上。—*v.i.* ①滋長; 發展。②源自。

stem·ma ['stɛmə; 'stemə] *n., pl.* **-ma·ta** [-mətə; -mətə]. ①家系;血統;家系譜。②【動物】單眼。

stemmed [stɛmd;stemd] *adj.* ①有某「種莖的。②去了莖的。」

stem·mer ['stɛmɚ;'stemə] *n.* ①去煙葉梗之人。②抽葡萄等之蒂的裝置;除梗器。

stem·ware ['stɛm,wɛr; 'stemwɛə] *n.*【美】高脚酒杯。

stem-wind·er ['stɛm'waɪndɚ;'stem-'waində] *n.* ①【俗】用轉柄上發條之錶(即今通常形式之錶)。②【俗】上等之人或物。

stem-wind·ing ['stɛm'waɪndɪŋ; 'stem'waindiŋ] *adj.* 以轉柄上發條的。

stench [stɛntʃ; stentʃ] *n.* 臭氣; 惡臭。

sten·cil ['stɛnsl̩;'stensl] *n., v.,* **-cil(l)ed, -cil·(l)ing.** —*n.* ①有雕空文字或花紋用以印刷之金屬板或紙板。②用此種模板印刷之文字或花紋。—*v.t.* 以上述模板印刷。

sten·cil·(l)er ['stɛnsl̩ɚ; 'stensl̩ə] *n.* 模板工; 模板印刷具。

stencil paper 蠟紙。

stencil pen 鐵筆。

stencil plate 蠟板;模板。

Sten·dhal [stɑ̃'dal; stɑ̃'dal] *n.* 斯當達爾 (1783–1842, 法國小說家及評論家, 本名爲 Marie Henri Beyle).

Sten gun [stɛn~; sten~] 英製輕機鎗。

sten·o ['stɛno; 'stenou] *n., pl.* **sten·os** for ①. ①速記員。②速記術。

sten·o·graph ['stɛnə,græf; 'stenə-grɑ:f] *n.*①速記之文件。②速記符號。③印刷速記符號之機器。 —*v.t.* & *v.i.* 速記。

***ste·nog·ra·pher** [stə'nɑgrəfɚ; ste-'nɔgrəfə] *n.*速記員。(亦作 **stenographist**)

sten·o·graph·ic[,stɛnə'græfɪk;,ste-nə'græfik] *adj.* 速記的; 速記術的。(亦作 **stenographical**) —**al·ly,** *adv.*

ste·nog·ra·phy [stə'nɑgrəfɪ;ste'nɔ-grəfi] *n.* 速記;速記術。

sten·o·type ['stɛnə,taɪp;'stenətaip] *n.* ①用普通字母的速記打字機。②(S-) 其商標名。③此種速記法中代替某音、某字或某詞之字母。

sten·o·typ·ist['stɛnə,taɪpɪst;'stenə-「,taipist] *n.* 速記打字員。」

sten·o·typ·y ['stɛnə,taɪpɪ; 'stenə-,taipi] *n.* ①普通字母之速記法。②用普通字母速記打字機作記錄。

Sten·tor ['stɛntɔr;'stentɔ:] *n.* ①【希臘神話】Troy 戰爭中之希臘傳令官(在 *Iliad* 中敍述其聲音之洪亮相當於五十人同時呼喊)。②(s-)聲音洪亮之人。

sten·to·ri·an [stɛn'torɪən; sten'tɔ:-riən] *adj.* 聲音洪亮的;極響亮的。

:step 〔stɛp; step〕 *n., v.*, **stepped, stepping.** —*n.* ①步; 脚步。He turned his *steps* towards the river. 他轉步向河走去。②一步的距離。She was three *steps* away when he called her back. 他喚回她時, 她才走了三步。③很短的距離。The school is only a *step* away. 學校就在附近。④步態; 步調。⑤脚步聲;足跡。⑥步驟; 手段; 措置。What *steps* are you taking in the matter? 這件事你打算怎麼辦? ⑦階段;踏級。A flight of *steps* leads up to the house. 一段踏級通上這所房屋。⑧官階的一級; 升級。to get one's *step*. 晉級; 升官。⑨坐子。⑩〖音樂〗度;一度。⑪ (*pl.*) = **stepladder.** ***a false step*** 錯誤; 愚蠢之行爲。***break step*** 不以一致的步伐行走。***change step*** 改正步伐俾與他人一致。***in step*** a. 與…同一步伐。b.和諧。***keep step*** 齊步伐; 跟上;配合; 與…一致。 ***out of step*** a. 不合步伐;不合拍子。b. 不和諧。***step by step*** 一步一步地; 慢慢地。 ***take steps*** 採取行動。***watch one's step*** 小心謹愼。—*v.t.* ①踏。②以步測量〖off〗。*Step* off the distance from the door to the window. 用步量一量從門到窗有多遠。③裝梳於…。 ④裝階梯於。—*v.i.* ①踏足;舉步行走。He *stepped* back quickly. 他迅速後退。②踩。***step aside*** a. 走到一旁;避在一邊。b. 讓職位給別人;下臺。***step down*** a. 走下來。b. 辭職; 讓位。c. 減少;減低。 ***step in*** a. 走進。Please *step in*. 請(走) 進來。b. 干涉; 介入。c. 參加。***step into*** 不費力地得到。***step it*** 走;跳舞。***step lively*** 〖俚〗快一點;快走。***step on it*** 〖俗〗快走。 ***step out*** 〖美俗〗 a. 外出尋樂。b. 快走。c. 暫時離開。***step up*** a. 爬上。b. 加速。c. 增加。

step- 〖字首〗表"後、繼"之義 (指因父母再婚而產生之家庭關係, 如 stepfather 繼父)。

step·broth·er 〔ˈstɛpˌbrʌðɚ; ˈstepˌbrʌðə〕 *n.* 繼父或繼母前次婚姻中所生之子。

step·child 〔ˈstɛpˌtʃaɪld; ˈsteptʃaild〕 *n., pl.* **step·chil·dren.** 夫或妻前次婚姻所生之子女。

step·dame 〔ˈstɛpˌdem; ˈstepdeim〕 *n.* 〖古〗=**stepmother.**

step·dance 〔ˈstɛpˌdæns; ˈstepdɑːns〕 *n.* 以舞步爲主的舞 (常指雙手放在口袋中的跳舞)。

step·daugh·ter 〔ˈstɛpˌdɔtɚ; ˈstepˌdɔːtə〕 *n.* 夫或妻前次婚姻所生之女; 繼女。

step-down 〔ˈstɛpˌdaun; ˈstepˌdaun〕 *adj.* ①〖電〗電壓降低的。②使逐漸減少的。

step·fa·ther 〔ˈstɛpˌfɑðɚ; ˈstepˌfɑːðə〕 *n.* 繼父; 後父。

Steph·a·no·tis 〔ˌstɛfəˈnotɪs; ˌstefəˈnoutis〕 *n.* 〖植物〗①白蘭科植物之一屬。②(s-)此屬之植物或花。

Ste·phen 〔ˈstivən; ˈstiːvn〕 *n.* 男子名。

Ste·phen·son 〔ˈstivənsn̩; ˈstiːvnsn〕 *n.* 斯蒂芬生 (George, 1781–1848, 英國工程師, 改進蒸氣機車, 1825年首創客貨火車)。

step-in 〔ˈstɛpˌɪn; ˈstepˌin〕 *adj.* (鞋之) 伸脚卽可穿上的;(服裝之) 伸進卽可穿上的。—*n.* ①此種服裝。②(*pl.*) 三角褲;女子內褲。

step·lad·der 〔ˈstɛpˌlædɚ; ˈstepˌlædə〕 *n.* 四脚梯(踏板扁平, 頂部有鉸鏈連接)。

***step·moth·er** 〔ˈstɛpˌmʌðɚ; ˈstepˌmʌðə〕 *n.* 繼母;後母。

step·ney 〔ˈstɛpnɪ; ˈstepni〕 *n.* 汽車之備用輪胎。

step·par·ent 〔ˈstɛpˌpɛrənt; ˈstepˌpɛərənt〕 *n.* 後父或後母;繼父或繼母。

steppe 〔stɛp; step〕 *n.* 無樹的大平原。***the Steppes*** a. 蘇聯之東南歐及西南亞部分之大草原。b. 吉爾吉斯 (Kirghiz)大草原。

stepped 〔stɛpt; stept〕 *adj.* 有階梯的; 成梯狀的。

stepped-up 〔ˈstɛptˌʌp; ˈsteptˌʌp〕 *adj.* 〖美俗〗①增加速度的。②增强的。

step·per 〔ˈstɛpɚ; ˈstepə〕 *n.* ①以濶步行走之人或動物。②〖俗〗跳舞者。

step·ping-off place 〔ˌstɛpɪŋˈɔf~; ˌstepiŋˈɔːf~〕 國外航線終點。

step·ping-stone 〔ˈstɛpɪŋˌston; ˈstepiŋ-stoun〕 *n.*①踏脚石。②進身之階。

step·sis·ter 〔ˈstɛpˌsɪstɚ; ˈstepˌsistə〕 *n.* 繼父或繼母以前婚姻中所生之女。

step·son 〔ˈstɛpˌsʌn; ˈstepsʌn〕 *n.* 夫或妻以前婚姻中所生之子;繼子。

step stool 梯凳。

step-up 〔ˈstɛpˌʌp; ˈstepʌp〕 *adj.* ①增强的;强化的。②〖電〗電壓增高的。—*n.* 增加; 增强。

step·wise 〔ˈstɛpˌwaɪz; ˈstepwaiz〕 *adv.* 逐步地;按級地;如踏級地。

ster. ①stereotype. ②sterling.

-ster 〖字尾〗表"是何種人;有某種習慣或職業者"之義, 如 oldster. (常帶蔑視之意)。

ster·co·ra·ceous 〔ˌstɝkəˈreʃəs; ˌstəːkəˈreiʃəs〕 *adj.* 〖生理〗糞便的;糞狀的。

stere 〔stɪr; stiə〕 *n.* 一立方公尺。

ster·e·o 〔ˈstɛrɪo; ˈstiəriou〕 *n.* ①〖俗〗=**stereotype.** ②立體鏡照相(術)。③立體音響效果;立體音響設備 (如電唱機等)。—*adj.* 立體鏡照相的; 立體音響的。—*v.t.* 〖印刷〗澆製鉛版。

stereo- 〖字首〗表"實體的; 立體的; 堅固的"之義。(母音前作 **stere-**)

ster·e·o·chem·is·try 〔ˌstɛrɪəˈkɛmɪstrɪ; ˌstiəriəˈkemistri〕 *n.* 立體化學(研究分子內原子或原子羣在空間之關係位置)。

ster·e·o·gram 〔ˈstɛrɪəˌgræm; ˈstiəriəgræm〕 *n.* ①立體照片。②立體畫。

ster·e·o·graph 〔ˈstɛrɪəˌgræf; ˈstiəriəgrɑːf〕*n.* 立體照片(在實體鏡下現立體像)。

ster·e·og·ra·phy 〔ˌstɛrɪˈɑgrəfɪ; ˌstiəriˈɔgrəfi〕*n.* ①立體畫法;實體畫法。②形畫幾何學 (研究規則多面體之構成)。 —**ster·e·o·graph·ic, ster·e·o·graph·i·cal,** *adj.*

ster·e·ol·o·gy 〔ˌstɛrɪˈɑlədʒɪ; ˌstiəriˈɔlədʒi〕 *n.* 立體學。

ster·e·om·e·try 〔ˌstɛrɪˈɑmətrɪ; ˌstiəriˈɔmitri〕 *n.* ①測體(積)術;測體(積)學。②比重測定法。

ster·e·o·mi·cro·scope 〔ˌstɛrɪoˈmaɪkrəˌskop; ˌstiərioulˈmaikrəskoup〕 *n.* 立體顯微鏡。

ster·e·o·phone 〔ˈstɛrɪəˌfon; ˈstiəriəfoun〕 *n.* 立體音響耳機。

ster·e·o·phon·ic 〔ˌstɛrɪəˈfɑnɪk; ˌstiəriəˈfɔnik〕 *adj.* 〖物理〗立體音響(效果)的。

ster·e·op·ti·con 〔ˌstɛrɪˈɑptɪkən; ˌstiəriˈɔptikən〕 *n.* 一種雙燈放映機。

ster·e·o·scope 〔ˈstɛrɪəˌskop; ˈstiəriəskoup〕 *n.* 實體(立體)鏡。

ster·e·o·scop·ic 〔ˌstɛrɪəˈskɑpɪk; ˌstiəriəsˈkɔpik〕 *adj.* 實體(立體)鏡的。(亦作 **stereoscopical**) —**al·ly,** *adv.*

stereoscopic microscope 立體顯微鏡。

ster·e·o·tape 〔ˈstɛrɪəˌtep; ˈstiəriəteip〕 *n.* 立體音響錄音帶。

ster·e·o·type 〔ˈstɛrɪəˌtaɪp; ˈstiəriətaip〕 *n., v.,* **-typed, -typ·ing.** —*n.* ①鉛版印刷術。②用紙型澆製之鉛版。③固定的

形式；老套。—*v.t.* ①澆製鉛版。②用鉛版印刷。③使成定型。

ster·e·o·typed ['stɛrɪə,taɪpt; 'stiəriətaipt] *adj.* ①用鉛版印刷的。②形式固定的；陳舊的。*stereotyped* phrases. 陳腔濫調。

ster·e·o·typ·y ['stɛrɪə,taɪpɪ; 'stiəriətaipi] *n.* ①製鉛版之手續。②鉛版印刷。

ster·ile ['stɛrəl; 'sterail] *adj.* ①不肥沃的；磽薄的(土地)。②不能生育的(婦女或雌性動物)；不結果實的(植物)。③無生氣的；枯燥無味的(演講、文體等)。④無細菌的；消毒的。⑤(工作等)無結果的。—**ste·ril·i·ty,** *n.*

ster·i·lize ['stɛrə,laɪz; 'sterilaiz] *v.t.*, **-lized, -liz·ing.** ①剝奪…之生產能力。②殺…的菌；消…的毒。③使無用；使不結果。—**ster·i·li·za·tion,** *n.*

ster·ling ['stɝlɪŋ; 'stə:liŋ] *n.* ①英國貨幣。②純銀；純銀製品。—*adj.* ①英國貨幣的(通常寫於金額之後，略作**stg.**). five pounds *sterling.* 英幣五鎊。②標準成分的；含92.5%純銀的。③由標準成分純銀製成的(刀、叉等)。④眞正的；極佳的；可靠的。

sterling area (or **bloc**)英鎊地區。

sterling silver 標準純銀(純度92.5%)。

Stern [stɝn; stə:n] *n.* 斯德恩 (Otto, 1888–1969, 生於德國的美國物理學家，曾獲1943年諾貝爾物理獎)。

***stern¹** [stɝn; stə:n] *adj.* ①嚴厲的；嚴格的。a *stern* look. 嚴厲的面容。②堅決的；不讓步的。*stern* measures. 堅決的手段。③可怖的；令人害怕的。—**ly,** *adv.*

***stern²** *n.* ①船尾。②臀部。③野獸之尾(尤指一種獵狐狗之尾)。④任何事物之後部。

ster·nal ['stɝnḷ; 'stə:nəl] *adj.* 〖解剖〗胸骨的；近胸骨的。

stern chase 〖航海〗艦尾追擊。

stern chaser 艦尾砲。

stern·most ['stɝn,most; 'stə:nmoust] *adj.* ①最接近船尾的。②最後的；最末的。

stern·ness ['stɝnnɪs; 'stə:nnis] *n.* ①嚴格；嚴厲。②堅決。③苛刻；嚴酷。

ster·no·cos·tal [,stɝno'kɑstḷ; ,stə:nou'kɔstəl] *adj.* 〖解剖，動物〗胸肋的；胸骨肋骨的。

stern·post ['stɝn,post; 'stə:npoust] *n.* 〖造船〗船尾骨。(亦作 **body post**)

ster·num ['stɝnəm; 'stə:nəm] *n., pl.* **-na** [-nə; -nə], **-nums.** 〖解剖〗胸骨。

ster·nu·ta·tion [,stɝnju'teʃən; ,stə:nju'teiʃən] *n.* ①噴嚏。②打噴嚏。

ster·nu·ta·tive [stə'njutətɪv; stə'nju:tətiv] *adj.* 促打噴嚏的。—*n.* 催嚏劑。

ster·nu·ta·to·ry [stə'njutə,torɪ; stə'nju:tətəri] *adj., n., pl.* **-ries.** —*adj.* 催嚏的；促打噴嚏的。—*n.* 催嚏劑。

stern·ward ['stɝnwəd; 'stə:nwəd] *adj.* 船尾的；後方的。—*adv.* 向船尾地；向後方地。

stern·wards ['stɝnwədz; 'stə:nwədz] *adv.* 向船尾地；向後方地。

stern·way ['stɝn,we; 'stə:nwei] *n.* 船之後退。

stern-wheel ['stɝn,hwil; 'stə:nwi:l] *adj.* 船尾外輪推進的。—**er,** *n.*

ster·tor ['stɝtə; 'stə:tə] *n.* 〖醫〗大鼾聲；鼾息。

ster·to·rous ['stɝtərəs; 'stə:tərəs] *adj.* 發鼾聲的；打呼的。

stet [stɛt; stet] *n., v.,* **stet·ted, stet·ting.** —*n.* "不刪" (〖拉〗=let it stand). —*v.t. & v.i.* 在已刪之稿邊上寫 "不刪"。

steth·o·scope ['stɛθə,skop; 'steθəskoup] *n.* 〖醫〗聽診器。—**steth·o·scop·ic,** *adj.*

ste·thos·co·py [stɛ'θɑskəpɪ; ste'θɔskəpi] *n.* 〖醫〗聽診；聽診法。

stet·son ['stɛtsṇ; 'stetsən] *n.* ①牛仔帽。②(S-) 其商標名。

Steve [stiv; sti:v] *n.* 男子名(Stephen之暱稱)。

ste·ve·dore ['stivə,dor; 'sti:vidɔ:] *n., v.,* **-dored, -dor·ing.** —*n.* 碼頭之裝卸工人。—*v.t. & v.i.* 裝卸(船上貨物)。

Ste·ven·son ['stivənsṇ; 'sti:vnsn] *n.* 斯蒂文生(Robert Louis, 1850–1894, 蘇格蘭詩人及小說家)。

stew¹** [stju; stju:] *v.t. & v.i.* ①燜；燉。to *stew* meat. 燉肉。②〖俗〗憂慮；憤悶。③悶熱而感覺不舒服。stew in one's own juice*** 自作自受。—*n.* ①燜菜；燉菜。beef *stew.* 燉牛肉。②煩惱；憂慮。to be in a *stew.* 煩惱；憂慮。—**a·ble,** *adj.*

stew² *n.* 養魚池；牡蠣繁殖場。

***stew·ard** ['stjuwəd; stjuəd, 'stju:əd] *n.* ①管理人；管家。He is the *steward* of that great estate. 他是那大筆財產的管理人。②(輪船、火車、飛機或俱樂部等之)膳務員。③(客船、客機等之)服務生(員)；空中少爺。④餐會、舞會、其他表演等之籌備人。⑤爲一機構管理某些事項者。⑥〖美海軍〗管理軍官食宿的士官。—*v.t. & v.i.* ①管理。②作管理人。

***stew·ard·ess** ['stjuwədɪs; 'stjuədis] *n.* ①女管理人；女管家。②輪船、客機等之女招待；空中小姐。

stew·ard·ship ['stjuwəd,ʃɪp; 'stjuədʃip] *n.* ①管理人之職位。②管理。

stew·pan ['stju,pæn; 'stju:pæn] *n.* 燉鍋；煮鍋。

stge. storage. **stg.** sterling.

St. Ex. Stock Exchange.

St. He·le·na ['senthə'linə; ,senti'li:nə] 聖赫勒拿(大西洋南部之一英屬小島，拿破崙於1815年被放逐於此)。

sthen·ic ['sθɛnɪk; 'sθenik] *adj.* 〖醫〗精力過盛的；亢進性的；(病態之)活潑性的。

stib·i·um ['stɪbɪəm; 'stibiəm] *n.* 〖化〗銻(符號爲 Sb).

stib·nite ['stɪbnaɪt; 'stibnait] *n.* 〖礦〗輝銻礦。

‡**stick¹** [stɪk; stik] *n., v.,* **sticked, stick·ing.** —*n.* ①杖；棍；棒。a walking *stick.* 手杖。②棒形物；柄；槌。a *stick* of chalk. 一支粉筆。③柴枝。④〖俗〗固執之人；蠢夫。⑤控制飛機的操縱桿。⑥船桅；桅之一部分。⑦加於飲料中之酒。⑧〖印刷〗植字盒。⑨〖俗〗(the-)(*pl.*)偏僻之區。⑩〖俚〗印度大麻菸。⑪從飛機上投下之一串炸彈。⑫賽跑中之高欄或障礙。⑬〖俚〗飛機掠過某區時一次跳出的一羣傘兵。⑭〖俚〗不熱心的人。***give*** (***a boy***) ***the stick*** 棍責(兒童)。***have*** (or ***get***) ***hold of the wrong end of the stick*** 誤解一種情勢。***on the stick*** 〖俚〗警惕；活躍。***shake a stick at*** 〖俗〗注意。—*v.t.* ①以桿撐(植物、藤等)。②在植字盒中排(字)。—**like,** *adj.*

stick²** *v.,* **stuck, stick·ing,** *n.* —*v.t.* ①刺；戳；插；貫穿。②以尖刀殺死。③插於。He *stuck* his hands in his pockets. 他把手插入口袋。④插於針上展覽。⑤伸出；使突出。Don't *stick* your head out of the window. 不要將頭伸出窗外。⑥黏貼。to *stick* a stamp on the envelope. 將郵票黏在信封上。⑦〖俗〗使困惑。This question will *stick* him up. 這個問題將把他難倒。⑧〖俚〗欺騙。⑨阻止；使停止。⑩忍受；容忍。I can't *stick* it (out) any longer. 我不能再忍受了！*Stick* it. 堅持下去。⑪放於指定位置。⑫〖俗〗將不愉快之事加諸(某人)。—*v.i.* ①黏着;附着;不離。Whatever happens, we must *stick* together. 不論甚麼情形發生,我們必須團結。②堅持;固執。to *stick* to one's country. 忠於國家。③陷住。The key *stuck* in the lock. 鑰匙插在鎖中拔不出來。④刺入;梗塞;卡住。⑤突出;豎起〖out, up〗. hair *sticking* up on end. 豎起來的頭髮。⑥躊躇;困惑〖常at〗. ⑦久留不去;縈繞。stick around*** 〖俚〗在附近逗留或等待。***stick at*** **a.** 繼續做某事。**b.** 遲疑。**c.** 顧慮。***stick by*** (or ***to***) 忠貞於。***stick it on*** 〖俚〗 **a.** 誇大。**b.** 索高價。***stick one's neck out*** 冒險;自找麻煩。***stick out*** **a.** 突出;伸出。**b.** 觸目;顯眼。**c.** 〖俗〗忍耐到底。***stick out for*** 堅索。***stick to one's guns*** 不顧反對堅持立場。***stick to the*** (or ***one's***) ***ribs*** 〖俗〗(如一頓飯等)豐盛的;有營養的。***stick up*** 〖俚〗搶刼;持槍搶刼。***stick up for*** 〖俗〗爲…辯護;維護。***stick up to*** 抗拒。—*n.* ①刺。②停止。③阻礙。④黏着之物。**—a·ble,** *adj.*

stick candy 棒棒糖;手杖糖。

stick·er [ˈstɪkɚ; ˈstikə] *n.* ①黏貼之人;黏貼告示或廣告之人。②固執的人。③(反面塗有膠等的)標紙;郵票。④蒺藜;刺鉤;芒刺。⑤殺豬之人。⑥久坐不去之客人。⑦賣不掉之陳貨。⑧〖俗〗難題;謎。⑨〖俚〗(歹徒之)小刀。

stick figure 〖美術〗把人或動物的頭畫成圓形,其他部分畫成直線的畫法。(亦作 **stick drawing**)

stick·ful [ˈstɪkˌful; ˈstikful] *n., pl.* **-fuls.** 〖印刷〗滿植字架;滿字盤。

stick·i·ness [ˈstɪkɪnɪs; ˈstikinis] *n.* 黏;黏稠。

stick·ing [ˈstɪkɪŋ; ˈstikiŋ] *adj.* 黏的;有黏性的。

sticking place ①固定的地方;搭脚處;永不退轉的地步。②(屠刀刺入的)獸頸下部。***screw one's courage to the sticking place*** 鼓起最大勇氣。

sticking plaster 膠布。

sticking point ①阻礙;談判中之絆脚石。②=**sticking place**①.

stick insect 竹節蟲。

stick-in-the-mud [ˈstɪkn̩ðəˌmʌd; ˈstikinðəmʌd] *adj.* 守舊的;頑固的;心胸狹窄的。—*n.* ①守舊的人。②無主動精神的人;想不出主意的人。

stick·jaw [ˈstɪkˌdʒɔ; ˈstikdʒɔː] *n.* 〖俚〗難嚼的糕點等。

stick·le [ˈstɪkl̩; ˈstikl] *v.i.*, **stick·led, stick·ling.** ①爲瑣事爭論。②反對;過慮。

stick·le·back [ˈstɪkl̩ˌbæk; ˈstiklbæk] *n.* 棘魚;絲魚。(亦作 **prickleback**)

stick·ler [ˈstɪklɚ; ˈstiklə] *n.* ①堅持…之人〖常for〗. ②困難的問題。

stick·man [ˈstɪkˌmæn; ˈstikmæn] *n., pl.* **-men.** 〖美俚〗①賭場雇用的人。②〖棒球〗打擊手。

stick·out [ˈstɪkˌaut; ˈstikaut] 〖俗〗 *n.* 傑出的人;能幹的人。—*adj.* 傑出的。

stick·pin [ˈstɪkˌpɪn; ˈstikpin] *n.* 〖美〗領帶上裝飾用的別針。

stick·tight [ˈstɪkˌtaɪt; ˈstiktait] *n.* 〖植物〗牛蒡。

stick-to-it·ive [ˌstɪkˈtuɪtɪv; ˌstikˈtuːitiv] *adj.* 〖美俚〗頑固的;執拗的;堅持的。(亦作 **stick-to-it-ive**) **—ness,** *n.*

stick-up [ˈstɪkˌʌp; ˈstikʌp] *n.* 〖俚〗搶刼;攔路搶奪。—*adj.* 豎直的(硬領)。(亦作 **stickup**)

stickup man 〖俚〗攔路搶奪的歹徒。

***stick·y** [ˈstɪkɪ; ˈstiki] *adj.*, **stick·i·er, stick·i·est.** ①黏的。②濕熱的。③需要細心處理的;困難的。④非常令人討厭的。**—stick·i·ly,** *adv.*

sticky tape 膠帶。

***stiff** [stɪf; stif] *adj.* ①硬的;堅硬的;不易彎曲的。a *stiff* collar. 硬領。②濃黏的。③不易移動的。④倔强的;執拗的。a *stiff* denial. 倔强之否認。⑤不自然的;拘泥虛禮的;呆板的。a *stiff* manner. 不自然的態度。⑥强烈的;過分的。a *stiff* price. 高價。⑦拉緊的;緊張的。⑧費力的;難應付的。⑨嚴厲的。a *stiff* punishment. 嚴罰。⑩不易跌價的(如股票等)。⑪〖蘇,英北部〗强壯的。—*n.* 〖俚〗①屍首。②拘泥形式的人;呆板的人。③小費給得很少的人。④醉漢。⑤〖俚〗 **a.** 傢伙。**b.** 流浪漢。**c.** 工人;勞動者。⑥〖俚〗 **a.** 僞造支票。**b.** 期票。**c.** 密函。⑦〖俚〗穩輸的選手或馬。—*adv.* ①僵硬地。②徹底地。—*v.t.* 〖俚〗不給…小費。**—ly,** *adv.* **—ness,** *n.*

***stiff·en** [ˈstɪfən; ˈstifn] *v.t. & v.i.* ①使硬;使堅挺;變硬;堅挺。The market *stiffens.* 市價堅挺。②使濃黏;使凝固;變爲濃黏;凝固。③使堅强;使猛烈;倔强;變强;變爲猛烈。**—er, —ing,** *n.*

stiff-necked [ˈstɪfˈnɛkt; ˈstifˈnekt] *adj.* ①頸子硬直的。②頑固的。**—ly,** *adv.*

***sti·fle¹** [ˈstaɪfl̩; ˈstaifl] *v.t.*, **-fled, -fling.** ①使窒息。②使窒息而死。③熄滅;抑止。—*v.i.* 窒悶;有窒息之感。**—stifl·er,** *n.*

sti·fle² *n.* (馬、狗等之)後膝關節。(亦作 **stifle joint**)

sti·fling [ˈstaɪflɪŋ; ˈstaifliŋ] *adj.* 窒息的;不透氣的。**—ly,** *adv.*

stig·ma [ˈstɪgmə; ˈstigmə] *n., pl.* **stig·mas** for ①, ④, ⑤&⑥, **stig·ma·ta** [ˈstɪgmətə; ˈstigmətə] for ②, ③&⑦. ①恥辱;瑕疵。②聖傷(似耶穌釘痕之傷)。③皮膚上的紅斑。④〖植物〗柱頭。⑤〖古〗奴隸或罪犯身上之烙印。⑥〖動物〗氣孔;氣門。⑦〖醫〗紅斑(如歇斯的里症之特徵)。**—stig·mal,** *adj.*

stig·mat·ic [stɪgˈmætɪk; stigˈmætik] *adj.* (亦作 **stigmatical**) ①瑕疵的;特徵的。②〖植物〗柱頭的。③〖眼科〗小孔的;眼點的。—*n.* 有聖傷(stigmata)的人。**—al·ly,** *adv.*

stig·ma·tize [ˈstɪgməˌtaɪz; ˈstigmətaiz] *v.t.*, **-tized, -tiz·ing.** ①描繪;敍述。②非難;指責;誣衊。③加烙印於。**—stig·ma·ti·za·tion,** *n.*

stile [staɪl; stail] *n.* ①梯磴;階梯。②十字形旋門。③〖建築〗主框條;豎框條。

sti·let·to [stɪˈlɛto; stiˈletou] *n., pl.* **-tos, -toes,** *v.*, **-toed, -to·ing.** —*n.* ①小劍;短劍。②刺繡用之穿孔錐。—*v.t.* 用小劍刺傷或刺死。**—like,** *adj.*

‡still¹ [stɪl; stil] *adj.* ①靜止的;不動的。Please stand *still.* 請靜立勿動。②靜寂的;無聲的。How *still* everything is! 一切都是多麼的寂靜!③(酒等)不起泡的。④低沉輕柔的(聲音)。⑤拍靜止照片用的。a *still* camera. 拍靜止照片用的攝影機。—*v.t. & v.i.* ①(使)安靜;(使)靜止;(使)寂靜。②解脫。—*n.* ①〖詩〗靜止;寂靜。in the *still* of night. 在寂靜的夜晚。②靜止之人或物之照片。③作爲廣告用之電影的單張照片。—*adv.* ①仍;仍然。The matter is *still* unsettled. 那事情尚未解決。②更;愈。His brother is *still* taller. 他的兄弟還要高些。③然則;可是依然。④靜止地。⑤〖古,詩〗持續地;常常。—*conj.* 但是;然而。He is dull; *still* he tries hard. 他很笨,然而他甚爲努力。***still and all*** 〖美〗雖如此。

still² *n.* 蒸餾器;蒸餾所。
still alarm 以電話等非一般性報火警系統所作的火警報告。
still·birth [ˈstɪlˌbɜθ; ˈstilbəːθ] *n.* ①死於胎中的嬰兒;死胎。②死胎的產下;死產。
still·born [ˈstɪlˌbɔrn; ˈstilbɔːn] *adj.* ①死後生下的; 死產的。②注定不會實現的。③絲毫未能吸引觀(聽)衆的。
still house 蒸餾房。
still hunt ①潛行或僞裝的追捕獵物。②〖俗〗對任何目標的悄悄追求。
still-hunt [ˈstɪlˌhʌnt; ˈstilhʌnt] *v.t.* & *v.i.* 悄悄追捕(獵物); 暗暗追求(目標)。—**er,** *n.*
still life ①靜物。②靜物畫。
***still·ness** [ˈstɪlnɪs; ˈstilnis] *n.* ①靜止。②安靜;肅靜。
still·room [ˈstɪlˌrum; ˈstilrum] *n.* ①(廚房外之)蒸餾室。②(大房舍中之)食物堆儲所。(亦作 **still-room**)
Still·son wrench [ˈstɪlsn̩~; ˈstilsn~] 〖商標名〗斯蒂爾遜鉗(用以夾管子等之鉗)。
still trailer 靜靜地追蹤獵物的獵狗。
still water (河流中之)靜水。
stil·ly [*adj.* ˈstɪlɪ; ˈstili *adv.* ˈstɪllɪ; ˈstilli] *adj.* 〖詩〗寂靜的。—*adv.* 寂靜地。
stilt [stɪlt; stilt] *n.* ①高蹺。②(架於水上等建築物之)支柱。③千鳥類之涉禽。—*v.t.* (如)使踏高蹺而升高。—**like,** *adj.*
stilt·ed [ˈstɪltɪd; ˈstiltid] *adj.* ①矜持的。②虛飾的;浮誇的。③如踏高蹺而升高的。④〖建築〗建於支柱上的。(亦作 **stilty**) —**ly,** *adv.*
stilted arch 〖建築〗有座子的圓拱。
Stil·ton [ˈstɪltn̩; ˈstiltn] *n.* 一種上等乾酪。(亦作 **Stilton cheese**)
stim·u·lant [ˈstɪmjələnt; ˈstimjulənt] *n.* ①〖醫〗興奮劑。②刺激物; 酒。③激勵; 鼓舞。—*adj.* ①刺激(性)的;興奮的。②鼓舞的。
***stim·u·late** [ˈstɪmjəˌlet; ˈstimjuleit] *v.*, **-lat·ed, -lat·ing.** —*v.t.* ①刺激;激勵;鼓舞。②增進(身體某部分等)之暫時活動。③用酒刺激;使醉。—*v.i.* 用作刺激物或興奮劑;起刺激作用。—**stim·u·lat·er, stim·u·la·tor,** *n.*
stim·u·la·tion [ˌstɪmjəˈleʃən; ˌstimjuˈleiʃən] *n.* 刺激;激勵。
stim·u·la·tive [ˈstɪmjəˌletɪv; ˈstimjulətiv] *adj.* 刺激的; 鼓舞的。—*n.* 刺激劑。
***stim·u·lus** [ˈstɪmjələs; ˈstimjuləs] *n.*, *pl.* **-li** [-ˌlaɪ; -lai]. ①刺激物;刺激;激勵。②〖植物〗刺。
sti·my [ˈstaɪmɪ; ˈstaimi] *n.*, *pl.* **-mies,** *v.t.*, **sti·mied, sti·my·ing.** =**stymie.**
***sting** [stɪŋ; stiŋ] *v.*, **stung** [stʌŋ; stʌŋ], **sting·ing,** *n.* —*v.t.* ①刺;螫。A bee *stung* him. 一隻蜜蜂螫了他。②刺痛; 刺傷。to be *stung* with remorse. 痛感悔恨。③激勵;刺激。④〖俚〗欺騙;索求過多。—*v.i.* ①刺人;螫人。Bees and wasps *sting.* 蜜蜂和黃蜂螫人。②感覺劇痛。—*n.* ①刺; 螫。②刺傷; 刺痛。③劇痛;痛苦。④使劇痛之物。⑤刺激物;激勵。⑥能傷人之特質。—**less,** *adj.*
sting·a·ree [ˈstɪŋəˌri; ˈstiŋəriː] *n.* =**sting ray.**
stinged [stɪŋd; stiŋd] *adj.* (昆蟲等)有螫的;有針的。
sting·er [ˈstɪŋə; ˈstiŋə] *n.* ①〖動物〗刺; 螫;針。②刺人之物。③〖俗〗嚴重的打擊;尖刻話。④有刺或針的動、植物。⑤一種鷄尾酒。⑥〖英俗〗威士忌與蘇打的混合酒。
sting·ing [ˈstɪŋɪŋ; ˈstiŋiŋ] *adj.* ①有針刺的;有刺毛的。②刺痛的; 尖銳的; 尖酸刻薄的。—**ly,** *adv.*
stinging hair 〖植物〗刺毛。
stin·go [ˈstɪŋgo; ˈstiŋgou] *n.* 〖俚〗①烈性啤酒或麥酒。②精力;活力。
sting ray 黃貂魚。(亦作 **stingray**)
stin·gy¹ [ˈstɪndʒɪ; ˈstindʒi] *adj.*, **stin·gi·er, stin·gi·est.** ①吝嗇的。②缺乏的;不足的。—**stin·gi·ly,** *adv.* —**stin·gi·ness,** *n.*
sting·y² [ˈstɪŋɪ; ˈstiŋi] *adj.*, **sting·i·er, sting·i·est.** 有刺的;有螫的;刺痛的。
stink [stɪŋk; stiŋk] *n.*, *v.*, **stank** [stæŋk; stæŋk] or **stunk** [stʌŋk; stʌŋk], **stunk, stink·ing.** —*n.* ①臭味; 臭氣。②(*pl.*)(作 *sing.* 解)〖俗〗化學。③〖俚〗醜聞;不愉快的紛擾。***raise a stink*** 〖俚〗激起不滿、批評或混亂。—*v.i.* ①發臭味。②聲名狼藉。③〖俚〗品質極低劣。④〖俚〗有大量的某種東西〖常 of, with〗. They *stink* of money. 他們很有幾個錢。⑤有某種氣味的。—*v.t.* ①使發臭〖常 up〗. ②以臭氣驅逐〖out〗.
stink·ball [ˈstɪŋkˌbɔl; ˈstiŋkbɔːl] *n.* (昔海戰用)臭彈。
stink bomb 臭彈。(亦作**stench bomb**)
stink·bug [ˈstɪŋkˌbʌg; ˈstiŋkbʌg] *n.* 放惡臭的蟲。
stink·er [ˈstɪŋkə; ˈstiŋkə] *n.* ①任何放惡臭之人或物。②臭彈(=stinkpot). ③大海燕。④臭角菌(=stinkhorn). ⑤〖俚〗卑鄙的人;討厭的人。⑥極度困難之事物。
stink·ing [ˈstɪŋkɪŋ; ˈstiŋkiŋ] *adj.* 發惡臭的;臭的。—**ly,** *adv.* —**ness,** *n.*
stinking smut (小麥之)黑穗病。
stink·pot [ˈstɪŋkˌpɑt; ˈstiŋkpɔt] *n.* ①(昔日海戰用之)臭彈。②小氣的人。
stink·stone [ˈstɪŋkˌston; ˈstiŋkstoun] *n.* 〖礦〗臭石。
stink·weed [ˈstɪŋkˌwid; ˈstiŋk-wiːd] *n.* 〖植物〗臭椿。
stint [stɪnt; stint] *v.t.* ①吝惜; 緊縮; 限制;節儉。②〖古〗停止。—*v.i.* ①節用;節儉。②〖古,方〗限制。—*n.* ①限制;吝惜。②定量;定額。③指定必做之工作。④〖古〗停止。
stint·less [ˈstɪntlɪs; ˈstintlis] *adj.* 慷慨的;不吝嗇的。
stipe [staɪp; staip] *n.* ①〖植物〗葉柄; 蕈柄;子房柄。②〖動物〗莖狀部分。
sti·pel [ˈstaɪpl̩; ˈstaipl] *n.* 〖植物〗小托葉。
sti·pend [ˈstaɪpend; ˈstaipend] *n.* ①薪水;薪俸。②定期的付款如獎學金、補助金等。
sti·pen·di·ar·y [staɪˈpendɪˌɛrɪ; staiˈpendjəri] *adj.*, *n.*, *pl.* **-ar·ies.** —*adj.* ①受薪給的; 有薪水的; 爲薪給而服務的。②薪給的;與薪水有關的。③納稅的;服勞役的。—*n.* 受薪給者;有薪俸之牧師、官員等。
sti·pes [ˈstaɪpiz; ˈstaipiːz] *n.*, *pl.* **stip·i·tes** [ˈstɪpɪˌtiz; ˈstipitiːz]. ①〖動物〗甲殼類及昆蟲之第一對足的第二節。②〖植物〗=**stipe.**
stip·ple [ˈstɪpl̩; ˈstipl] *n.*, *v.*, **-pled, -pling.** —*n.* ①點刻法; 點畫法。②點刻; 點畫。—*v.t.* & *v.i.* 點刻;點畫。
stip·pling [ˈstɪplɪŋ; ˈstipliŋ] *n.* ①點刻;點刻法;點刻細工。②點畫;點畫法。
stip·u·lar [ˈstɪpjələ; ˈstipjulə] *adj.* 〖植物〗①(似)托葉的; 有托葉的。②長於托葉上或托葉附近的。
stip·u·late¹ [ˈstɪpjəˌlet; ˈstipjuleit] *v.*, **-lat·ed, -lat·ing.** —*v.t.* ①(條約或契約上)規定; 記明。②堅持要求以…爲協議之條件。—*v.i.* 契約規定;約定〖常 for〗. —**stip·u·la·tor,** *n.*
stip·u·late² [ˈstɪpjəlɪt; ˈstipjulit] *adj.* 有托葉的。
stip·u·la·tion [ˌstɪpjəˈleʃən; ˌstipju-

ˈleiʃən] *n.* ①契約; 約定; 合同。②(契約上之)規定;條文;條件。

stip·ule [ˈstɪpjul; ˈstipjuːl] *n.* 〖植物〗「托葉。」

‡stir¹ [stɝ; stəː] *v.*, **stirred, stir·ring,** *n.* —*v.t.* ①使動;移動。②攪和。to *stir* sugar into one's coffee. 將糖攪和在咖啡裏。③激動;惹起。to *stir* up a quarrel. 惹起爭論。④〖古〗提出討論; 引起注意。—*v.i.* ①動; 活動。No one was *stirring* in the house. 全家都在休息。②攪和; 拌動。③興奮; 奮起; 受感應。***not to stir a finger*** 袖手旁觀。***not to stir an eyelid*** 一動不動。***stir one's stumps*** 〖俗〗疾迅地行動。***stir the blood*** 激使興奮或熱心。***stir up*** 激起;鼓動;煽動。—*n.* ①移動; 撥動; 攪和。Give the soup a *stir*. 把這湯攪和一下。②激動;騷動。③推;衝;刺。④感情;衝動。—**ra·ble,** *adj.* —**rer,** *n.*

‡stir² *n.* 〖俚〗監獄。

stir·a·bout [ˈstɝəˌbaut; ˈstəːrəbaut] *n.* ①燕麥粥。②激動;匆忙;騷動;紛亂。③匆忙的人。—*adj.* 騷動的;忙碌的。

stirps [stɝps; stəːps] *n., pl.* **stir·pes** [ˈstɝpiz; ˈstəːpiːz]. 〖拉〗①種族;家系。②〖法律〗祖先。③〖生物〗受精卵內之遺傳因子。

stir·ring [ˈstɝɪŋ; ˈstəːriŋ] *adj.* ①活動的; 繁忙的。②激動的;鼓舞人心的。—**ly,** *adv.*

stir·rup [ˈstɪrəp, ˈstɝəp; ˈstirəp] *n.* ①馬鐙。②鐙形物。—**less,** *adj.* —**like,** *adj.*

stirrup bone 〖解剖〗鐙骨。

stirrup cup ①餞別酒。②餞別酒的酒杯。

stirrup leather 馬鐙皮帶。

stirrup pump 一種輕便的消防抽水機。

stirrup strap =**stirrup leather.**

stitch** [stɪtʃ; stitʃ] *n.* ①一針;一縫。②針法; 縫法。③縫線; 針脚。to put *stitches* in a wound. 縫合傷口。④布片; 衣片。⑤〖俗〗小片; 一點點。⑥突然疼痛; 劇痛。A stitch in time saves nine.*** 〖諺〗及時縫一針省却將來的九針;及時行事, 事半功倍。***have not a dry stitch on*** 全身淋濕。***have not a stitch on*** 一絲不掛;赤裸。—*v.t.* 縫;綴連。—*v.i.* 縫級。—**er,** *n.* —**like,** *adj.*

stitch·er·y [ˈstɪtʃərɪ; ˈstitʃəri] *n.* 針法;針線工作。(亦作 **stitchwork**)

stith·y [ˈstɪðɪ; ˈstiði] *n., pl.* **stith·ies.** ①鐵砧。②鍛冶場;鐵工廠。

sti·ver [ˈstaɪvɚ; ˈstaivə] *n.* ①一種荷蘭錢幣。②瑣屑之物;微量。

stk. stock.

St. Law·rence [sentˈlɔrəns; sntˈlɔrəns] 聖羅倫斯河(在加拿大東南部)。

St. Lou·is [sentˈluɪs; sntˈluis] 聖路易(美國 Missouri 州東部之一城市)。

St. Luke's summer (10月18日的 St. Luke's Day 前後的)秋日艷陽天。

St. Martin's summer (11月11日的 St. Martin's Day 前後的)小陽春天氣。

sto·a [ˈstoə; ˈstouə] *n., pl.* **sto·ae** [ˈstoi; ˈstouiː], **sto·ai** [ˈstoaɪ; ˈstouai], **sto·as.** ①〖希臘建築〗有頂的柱廊或廻廊。②〖哲學〗斯多亞哲學 (Stoicism) 之任何一方面。

stoat [stot; stout] *n.* 〖動物〗白鼬。

sto·chas·tic [stəˈkæstɪk; stəˈkæstik] *adj.* 猜測的。

‡stock [stɑk; stɔk] *n.* ①貯蓄; 蓄積。a *stock* of knowledge. 積貯之知識。②貯藏品; 存貨; 現貨。The store keeps a large *stock* of toys. 該店有大批的玩具存貨供應。③(通常作 livestock)家畜。④股票。common *stock*. 普通股。⑤公債。⑥先祖;家系; 血統; 種族。He comes of (a) good *stock*. 他出身世家。⑦原料; 材料。⑧作爲支持物或把柄之部分。the *stock* of a rifle. 槍托。⑨(樹木等之)幹;莖;地下莖。⑩無生命之物;愚鈍的人。⑪嘲笑的對象。⑫一種舊式的硬頸帶。⑬湯料; 原湯。⑭某固定劇團在一劇院長期演出的各種戲劇。⑮斷株; 殘立之幹。⑯用作切取接枝的植物。⑰(插入接木的)臺木; 本幹。⑱紫羅蘭花。⑲(*pl.*)造船臺。⑳(*pl.*)足或手枷。A thief was put in the *stocks*. 一個賊被械在枷裏。㉑同一語系之語文。㉒語系之分類。㉓(鞭或釣竿等之)柄。㉔〖古〗木片; 木材。㉕〖古〗襪子。㉖〖鐵路〗機車。***have*** (or ***keep***) ***in stock*** 有現貨。***in stock*** 備有;持有;現貨供應。goods *in stock*. 現貨。***lock, stock, and barrel*** 完全地;全部地;包括每一部分地。***on the stocks*** 在建造中。***out of stock*** 無現貨;售罄; 賣光。***take stock*** **a.** 清點存貨;清點盤存。**b.** 估定;清査。***take***(or ***put***) ***stock in*** **a.** 〖俗〗對…有興趣; 視爲重要;信靠。**b.** 參加(公司)的股份。***take stock of*** **a.** 仔細推想;鑑定。**b.** 計算; 估價。—*v.t.* ①供應;備置。a well-*stocked* library. 收藏豐富的圖書館。②裝托柄; 繫以柄狀物。③以野生物供給。④備以馬、牛等。⑤以草等播種(土地)。⑥〖古〗加以足枷。—*v.i.* ①發芽。②採辦; 貯存〖常 up〗. —*adj.* ①經常備有的。*stock* sizes. 常備的尺碼。②普通的;日常的。③股票的;公債的。*stock* clerk. 股票經理人。④豢養家畜的。⑤存貨的。*stock* clerk. 倉庫管理員。⑥長期演出之戲劇的。

stock account 〖英〗〖簿記〗原賬;股本賬。

stock·ade [stɑkˈed; stɔˈkeid] *n., v.,* **-ad·ed, -ad·ing.** —*n.* ①〖築城〗以直立之木柱等構成之障礙物。②欄;柵欄; 圍欄。③〖美軍〗拘留室。—*v.t.* 以柵欄保護、防衞或圍起。

stock·age [ˈstɑkɪdʒ; ˈstɔkidʒ] *n.* ①貯藏。②存貨。

stock book 〖商〗存貨簿。

stock·breed·er [ˈstɑkˌbridɚ; ˈstɔkˌbriːdə] *n.* 豢養家畜者。

stock·bro·ker [ˈstɑkˌbrokɚ; ˈstɔkˌbroukə] *n.* 證券經紀人。

stock·bro·ker·age [ˈstɑkˌbrokərɪdʒ; ˈstɔkˌbroukəridʒ] *n.* 證券交易; 證券買賣;證券經紀人的業務。

stock·bro·king [ˈstɑkˌbrokɪŋ; ˈstɔkˌbroukiŋ] *n.* 證券交易。

stock car ①〖鐵路〗家畜載運車。②賽車用之跑車。

stock certificate 股票;證券。

stock company ①股份公司。②通常在一個劇院長期演出多個戲劇的固定劇團。

stock dividend 〖金融〗股票股利。

stock dove 歐洲產的一種野鴿。

stock exchange 證券交易所。

stock farm 畜牧場。

stock farmer 牧畜者。

stock farming 畜牧事業。

stock·fish [ˈstɑkˌfɪʃ; ˈstɔkfiʃ] *n., pl.* **-fish, -fish·es.** 風乾之鱈魚;乾魚。

stock·hold·er [ˈstɑkˌholdɚ; ˈstɔkˌhouldə] *n.* ①股東。②〖澳〗牧場主。

stock·hold·ing [ˈstɑkˌholdɪŋ; ˈstɔkˌhouldiŋ] *adj.* 持有股份的。—*n.* 股份之持有。

Stock·holm [ˈstɑkˌhom; ˈstɔkhoum] *n.* 斯德哥爾摩(瑞典首都)。

stock·i·net [ˌstɑkɪnˈɛt; ˌstɔkiˈnet] *n.* 〖英〗一種鬆緊織物。

‡stock·ing [ˈstɑkɪŋ; ˈstɔkiŋ] *n.* ①長襪。a pair of *stockings*. 一雙長襪。②似

長襪之物。***in one's stocking feet*** 祇穿襪子(不穿鞋)的。

stocking cap 圓錐形編織的帽子。

stock·inged ['stakɪŋd; 'stɔkiŋd] *adj.* 穿襪子的。

stock in trade ①店鋪的存貨;現貨。②工具;原料;生財;營業用具。③老手段;慣用手段。(亦作 **stock-in-trade**)

stock·ist ['stakɪst; 'stɔkist] *n.*【英】有存貨的批發商或零售商。

stock·job·ber ['stak,dʒabɚ; 'stɔk,dʒɔbə] *n.* ①【美】證券經紀人。②【英】股票投機者。

stock·job·bing ['stak,dʒabɪŋ; 'stɔk,dʒɔbiŋ] *n.* 證券交易;股票買賣。—*adj.* 從事證券交易的。

stock·man ['stakmən; 'stɔkmən] *n., pl.* **-men.** ①【美】飼養牲畜者;牧人。②管理存貨者;倉庫管理員。

stock market ①證券市場;證券交易所。②證券交易;證券市場;證券行情。

stock option 認股權。

stock ownership 股權。

stock·pile ['stak,paɪl; 'stɔkpail] *n.* ①原料及必需品之儲備。②爲戰爭準備的核子武器。—*v.t. & v.i.* 儲備(原料及必需品)。—**stock·pil·er,** *n.*

stock·pot ['stak,pat; 'stɔkpɔt] *n.* 「湯罐;肉汁罐。」

stock power 股份轉讓授權書。

stock·proof ['stak'pruf; 'stɔk'pruːf] *adj.* 防止家畜穿越的。

stock raiser 畜牧業者。

stock raising 畜牧(業)。

stock record 存貨簿。

stock-rid·er ['stak,raɪdɚ; 'stɔk,raidə] *n.*【澳】騎馬牧人。

stock·room ['stak,rum; 'stɔk-rum] *n.* ①商品儲藏室。②商品陳列室。(亦作 **stock room**)

stock split 股票分股。

stock-still ['stak'stɪl; 'stɔk'stil] *adj.* 靜止的;不動的。

stock·tak·ing ['stak,tekɪŋ; 'stɔk,teikiŋ] *n.* ①清查存貨;盤存。②全盤檢討。

stock ticker (股票)報成交機。

stock·whip ['stak,hwɪp; 'stɔkwip] *n.*【英】牧人使用之鞭,柄短而梢長。

stock·y ['stakɪ; 'stɔki] *adj.,* **stock·i·er, stock·i·est.** 堅實的;矮而壯的;粗短的。—**stock·i·ly,** *adv.*

stock·yard ['stak,jard; 'stɔk-jaːd] 「*n.* 畜牲圍欄。」

stodge [stadʒ; stɔdʒ] *v.,* **stodged, stodg·ing,** *n.* —*v.t.* ①填滿;塞滿。②滿足;充分地滿足。③拌攪。—*v.i.* ①像在泥濘中蹣跚而行。②暴食。—*n.* ①暴食者;貪食者。②硬厚的一塊食物;固體食物。③矮壯的人;畸形的人。④枯燥無味的作品或題目。

stodg·y ['stadʒɪ; 'stɔdʒi] *adj.,* **stodg·i·er, stodg·i·est.** ①缺乏趣味的;令人生厭的。②庸俗的;平凡的(人)。③軀體笨重的(人)。④不容易消化的;味不美的(食物)。⑤塞得滿滿的。—**stodg·i·ly,** *adv.* —**stodg·i·ness,** *n.*

sto·gie, sto·gy ['stogɪ; 'stougi] *n., pl.* **-gies.** ①長而細的劣等雪茄。②粗而堅牢的靴或鞋。

sto·ic ['sto·ɪk; 'stouik] *n.* ①(S-)古希臘 Stoicism 的信奉者;堅忍主義者。②堅忍之人;不介意於苦樂之人;克制感情者。—*adj.* ①(S-)與 Stoic 學派有關的。②=**stoical.**

sto·i·cal ['sto·ɪkl; 'stouikəl] *adj.* 堅忍的;不介意於苦樂的;苦修的。—**ly,** *adv.*

sto·i·cism ['sto·ɪ,sɪzəm; 'stouisizəm] *n.* ①(S-)斯多亞學派(主義)。②堅忍;禁慾。

stoke [stok; stouk] *v.,* **stoked, stok·ing.** —*v.t.* ①撥(火);添加燃料於(火爐中);照管(火爐);司(爐)。②【俗】吃;吞食。—*v.i.* ①撥火。②司爐。***stoke up*** **a.** 加燃料於(火或爐)中。**b.** 供以大量食物;使多吃食物。

stoke·hold ['stok,hold; 'stoukhould] *n.* 汽船上的鍋爐室;鍋爐口。

stoke·hole ['stok,hol; 'stoukhoul] *n.* ①鍋爐室。②鍋爐口。③火伕工作時站立之處。

stok·er ['stokɚ; 'stoukə] *n.* ①司爐。②自動添燃料機器。③【英】火車頭之司爐。

stole¹ [stol; stoul] *v.* pt. of **steal.**

stole² *n.* ①(教士所披之)聖帶;袈裟。②(婦女之)毛皮長圍巾;長圍巾。③【古】長袍。

sto·len ['stolən; 'stoulən] *v.* pp. of **steal.**

stol·id ['stalɪd; 'stɔlid] *adj.* 不易感動的;不易激動的;不動聲色的;遲鈍的。—**ly,** *adv.*

sto·lid·i·ty [stə'lɪdətɪ; stɔ'liditi] *n., pl.* **-ties.** 漠然;冷淡無感覺;遲鈍。

sto·lon ['stolan; 'stoulɔn] *n.*【植物】匍匐枝。—**ate,** *adj.*

sto·ma ['stomə; 'stoumə] *n., pl.* **-ma·ta** [-mətə; -mətə], **-mas.** ①【解剖】小孔;口。②【植物】葉孔;氣孔。—**tal,** *adj.*

***stom·ach** ['stʌmək; 'stʌmək] *n.* ①胃。I have a pain in my *stomach.* 我胃(腹)痛。②腹。③胃口;食慾。④愛好;慾望。A coward has no *stomach* for fighting. 懦夫無鬥志。—*v.t.* ①能吃;能消化。②忍受。

stomach ache 胃痛;腹痛。(亦作 **stomach-ache**)

stom·ach·er ['stʌməkɚ; 'stʌməkə] *n.* 胸衣(15-17 世紀間男女通用,以作裝飾)。

sto·mach·ic [sto'mækɪk; stou'mækik] *adj.* (亦作 **stomachical**) 胃的;健胃的;促進消化的。—*n.* 健胃藥;開胃劑。

stom·ach·less ['stʌməklɪs; 'stʌməklis] *adj.* ①無胃的。②無胃口的;無食慾的。

stomach pump 洗胃器;胃唧筒。

stom·ach·y ['stʌməkɪ; 'stʌməki] *adj.* ①【英方】易怒的。②有大腹的。

sto·ma·ti·tis [,stomə'taɪtɪs; ,stoumə'taitis] *n.*【醫】口炎;口腔發炎。

sto·ma·tol·o·gy [,stomə'talədʒɪ; ,stoumə'tɔlədʒi] *n.*【醫】口腔學;口腔病學。

stomp [stamp; stɔmp] *v.t.*【俗】=**stamp.** —*v.i.*【俗】①=**stamp.** ②跳爵士樂曲。—*n.* ①【俗】=**stamp.** ②早期的爵士樂曲。③合此樂曲的舞。

:stone [ston; stoun] *n., pl.* **stones,** *adj., v.,* **stoned, ston·ing.** —*n.* ①石;石材。a heart of *stone.* 鐵石心腸。②紀念碑;墓石。③某些似小石之物。④【醫】結石。⑤【植物】核。plum *stones.* 李核。⑥寶石;玉。⑦【英】㖊(重量單位,十四磅,不用複數)。***A rolling stone gathers no moss.*** 滾石不生苔(喻常改業則不聚財)。***a stone's throw*** (or ***cast***) 擲石可及之距離。***cast the first stone*** 起頭批評或攻擊;作過於魯莽的批評。***leave no stone unturned*** 不遺餘力。***throw stones at*** (喻)攻擊某人之品格等。—*adj.* ①石(製)的。a *stone* wall. 石牆。②用粗陶器或粗泥製成的。—*v.t.* ①以石砌築。②以石投向。to *stone* a person to death. 用石擊死某人。③投石擊死。④去核。⑤磨之以石。—**like,** *adj.*

Stone Age 石器時代。
stone-blind ['ston'blaɪnd; 'stoun'blaind] *adj.* 全盲的;全瞎的。—**ness,** *n.*
stone-broke ['ston'brok; 'stoun'brouk] *adj.* 〖俚〗一文不名的;手無分文的。(亦作 **stony-broke**)
stone bruise 脚掌傷痛。
stone·cast ['ston,kæst; 'stounkɑ:st] *n.* =**stone's cast.**
stone·chat ['ston,tʃæt; 'stountʃæt] *n.* 野鷄。
stone coal ①無煙煤。②天然煤。
stone-cold ['ston'kold; 'stoun'kould] *adj.* 冰冷如石的;冷透的。—*adv.* 完全地;徹底地。
stone·crop ['ston,krɑp; 'stounkrɔp] *n.* 〖植物〗景天。
stone crusher 築路用的碎石機。
stone·cut·ter ['ston,kʌtɚ; 'stoun,kʌtə] *n.* ①石工;石匠。②琢石機。
stoned [stond; stound] *adj.* ①〖俚〗醉酒的。②多石的。③去核的。
stone-dead ['ston'dɛd; 'stoun'ded] *adj.* 僵死如石的;完全斷了氣的。
stone-deaf ['ston'dɛf; 'stoun'def] *adj.* 全聾的。
stone fruit 核果。
stone·heart·ed ['ston'hɑrtɪd; 'stoun'hɑ:tid] *adj.* 鐵石心腸的;殘酷的。
Stone·henge ['ston'hɛndʒ; 'stoun'hendʒ] *n.* 英格蘭 Salisbury 平原上的史前巨石柱。
stone-horse ['ston,hɔrs; 'stounhɔ:s] *n.* 〖古,方〗種馬;雄馬。
stone·man ['stonmən; 'stounmən] *n.* 石匠。
stone·ma·son ['ston,mesn̩; 'stoun,meisn] *n.* 石匠。(亦作 **stone mason**)
stone·ma·son·ry ['ston,mesn̩rɪ; 'stoun,meisnri] *n.* 琢石藝術;石匠之工作。
stone oil 石油 (=petroleum).
stone pine 〖植物〗(南歐地中海沿岸產之) 石松。
stone pit 石坑;採石場。
ston·er ['stonɚ; 'stounə] *n.* ①琢石者。②去果核之工具。
stone's cast 一(投) 石之遙;短距離。(亦作 **stonecast, stone's throw**)
stone·wall [,ston'wɔl; 'stoun'wɔ:l] *v.i.* ①〖板球〗愼重防守。②〖俚〗在議會作滔滔不絕之演講以阻碍議程之進行。—*v.t.* 〖英〗藉冗長之辯論以阻止(法案之通過)。—**er,** *n.*
stone·wall·ing ['ston,wɔlɪŋ; 'stoun'wɔ:liŋ] *n.* 〖英〗延宕或妨害(議會)議事。
stone·ware ['ston,wɛr; 'stounwɛə] *n.* 粗陶器。
stone·work ['ston,wɝk; 'stounwə:k] *n.* ①石工;石造物。②建築物中石造的部分。③(*pl.*)做石工的地方。
stone·wort ['ston,wɝt; 'stounwə:t] *n.* 〖植物〗一種淡水藻。
stonk [stɑŋk; stɔŋk] *n.* (猛烈集中)砲擊。
***ston·y** ['stonɪ; 'stouni] *adj.,* **ston·i·er, ston·i·est.** ①多石的。The beach is *stony.* 那海濱多石。②如石的;鐵石心腸的;無情的。a *stony* heart. 鐵石心腸。③〖俚〗無錢的;一文不名的。④僵硬的;不動的。⑤使化成石的。⑥(水果等)有核的。(亦作 **stoney**) —**ston·i·ly,** *adv.*
ston·y-broke ['stonɪ'brok; 'stouni'brouk] *adj.* 〖俚〗=**stone-broke.**
ston·y-faced ['stonɪ,fest; 'stouni-feist] *adj.* 繃着臉的;無表情的。
ston·y·heart·ed ['stonɪ'hɑrtɪd; 'stouni,hɑ:tid] *adj.* 無情的;殘酷的。(亦作 stony-hearted) —**ly,** *adv.* —**ness,** *n.*
‡stood [stʊd; stud] *v.* pt. & pp. of **stand.**
stooge [studʒ; stu:dʒ] *n., v.,* **stooged, stoog·ing.** —*n.* 〖俗〗①滑稽演員之副手。②混於觀衆間的此類演員之副手。③(蔑)爲他人作襯托者;他人之跟班。—*v.i.* 充做副手。
stook [stuk; stu:k] *n.* 〖英〗一堆刈下之禾束(通常12束爲一堆)。—*v.t.* & *v.i.* 堆(禾束)。
stool** [stul; stu:l] *n.* ①凳。②便器;大便。to go to *stool.* 大便;如厠。*stool* examination. 糞便檢驗。③厠所。④母樹。⑤一簇新枝。⑥(引誘其他鳥前來之)媒鳥。⑦縛繫媒鳥用的桿。⑧窗臺。⑨主教之座椅。⑩某些非洲國王之寶座。fall between two stools*** 兩頭落空。—*v.i.* ①(老根株) 發出新枝;生新枝。②〖俚〗告密;做線民。③上厠所;大便。—**like,** *adj.*
stool pigeon ①(誘使他鴿入羅網的)媒鴿;囮鴿。②〖美俚〗告密人;線民。③〖俚〗職業賭徒用以引人上鉤之助手。
stoop**[1] [stup; stu:p] *v.i.* ①屈身;彎腰;傴僂。to *stoop* over one's books. 埋首於書本。②屈尊;降格;卑屈。to *stoop* to ask. 不恥下問。③(樹、懸崖等) 前曲;彎下。④(鷹等) 撲下;攫。—*v.t.* ①屈 (身);俯 (首)。②〖古〗使屈從;壓倒。stoop to conquer*** (or ***win***) 含垢忍辱以求雪恥。—*n.* ①屈身;傴僂。Grandfather walks with a *stoop.* 祖父走起路來傴僂着身子。②屈尊;卑屈。③下撲;下攫。—**er,** *n.* —**ing·ly,** *adv.*
stoop[2] *n.* 〖美〗門廊;門階;門口之平臺。
‡stop [stɑp; stɔp] *v.,* **stopped, stop·ping,** *n.* —*v.t.* ①使停止;止住;阻止。*Stop* crying! 不要哭了! We *stopped* thinking. 我們停止再想下去。What *stopped* you from coming? 你爲甚麼不能來? ②塡塞;阻塞;堵塞。to *stop* one's ears. 塞住耳朵。③截斷;扣留。to *stop* supplies. 截斷補給品。④用軟木塞、栓等關閉(容器);密封(物品)於關閉的容器或地方;蓋;藏。⑤妨礙;攔阻。A fallen tree *stopped* traffic. 一棵倒下的樹妨礙交通。⑥止付(支票)。⑦制止(打擊等);擋開。⑧〖競賽〗擊敗。⑨加標點於。⑩〖音樂〗**a.** 按(管樂器之指孔等) 以發某一特定的樂音。**b.** 捺(絃樂器之絃) 以變其音調。—*v.i.* ①停止。We *stopped* to think. 我們停下來想一想。②逗留;住 (=stay). We'll *stop* at a hotel tonight. 我們今夜將住在旅館裏。***stop a gap*** 在需要之際用作代用物。***stop by*** 中途作短暫的訪問。I'll *stop by* on my way home. 回家途中我將前來拜訪。***stop dead*** (or ***short***) 突然停止。***stop down*** 〖攝影〗將鏡頭之鏡徑縮小。***stop in*** 作短暫而未計畫的訪問。If you're in town, be sure to *stop in.* 如果你到城裏一定要來舍下。***stop off*** 〖俗〗作短暫逗留。***stop over*** **a.** 停留片刻。**b.** 中途下車(機、船等);中途停留。***stop up*** **a.** 塞;阻。to *stop up* a hole. 塞住一洞。**b.** 醒着;沒有睡 (=sit up). —*n.* ①中止;停止。②逗留;泊宿。③停留之處;車站。Where is the nearest bus *stop?* 最近的公共汽車站在哪兒? ④阻塞物;塞子。⑤阻塞;妨礙。⑥控制或阻止機械活動之器具;觸止器;制子。⑦句點。a full *stop.* 句點 (=period). ⑧〖音樂〗音栓;音節柱。⑨〖語音〗**a.** 閉鎖。**b.** 閉鎖子音(卽 p, b, t, d, k, g). ⑩〖商業〗**a.** (支票的)止付。**b.** =**stop order.** ***come to a (full) stop*** 停;停止。***pull out all stops*** 盡最大的力量;全力以赴。***put a stop to*** 使終止;制止。—**less,** *adj.* —**less·ness,** *n.* 〖注意〗

stop 作 *v.t.* ①解時, 其受詞用名詞、代名詞、或動名詞, 而不用不定詞。
stop-and-go ['stɑpən'go; 'stɔpən'gou] *adj.* 定期而不斷被迫停止的(如交通等)。
stop·cock ['stɑp,kɑk; 'stɔpkɔk] *n.* (水管、煤氣管上的)開關; 龍頭。
stope [stop; stoup] *n., v.,* **stoped, stop·ing.** —*n.* 〖採礦〗掘礦室。 —*v.t.* & *v.i.* 在掘礦室內採礦 〖out〗.
stop·gap ['stɑp,gæp; 'stɔpgæp] *n.* ①塞孔之物。②應急之策; 權宜之計。③臨時代替之人(物)。—*adj.* 權宜的; 彌縫的。
stop light ①裝於車後之刹車燈。②令停駛之交通信號燈(通常爲紅燈)。
stop-off ['stɑp,ɔf; 'stɔpɔːf] *n.* =stop-over.
stop order 投資人對股票經紀人之指示當股票跌至某一限度時卽售出該股票。
stop·o·ver ['stɑp,ovɚ; 'stɔp,ouvə] *n.* ①(在長途旅程中的)中途下車暫停(原車票以後仍繼續有效)。②可中途下車而後繼續有效的車票。③旅途中暫時停留(爲吃飯等)。
stop·pa·ble ['stɑpəbl̩; 'stɔpəbl] *adj.* 可停止的。
stop·page ['stɑpɪdʒ; 'stɔpidʒ] *n.* ①停止; 中止; 塞住。②阻礙; 阻塞; 障礙。③停工。
stop payment (支票之)止付。
stop·per ['stɑpɚ; 'stɔpə] *n.* ①阻止者; 阻塞物。②(瓶等之)塞子; 栓。③〖俗〗引起注意的人或事。④〖棒球俚〗**a.** 可使本球隊不輸球賽的好投手。**b.** 緊急時接替的投手。—*v.t.* (亦作 **stopper down**)加以塞子; 塞住。
stop·ping ['stɑpɪŋ; 'stɔpiŋ] *n.* 〖礦〗阻止空氣或瓦斯流通的阻塞物。
stopping place 停車場。
stop·ple ['stɑpl̩; 'stɔpl] *n., v.,* **-pled, -pling.** —*n.* (瓶等的)塞子。 —*v.t.* 用塞子塞住; 將…閉塞。
stop press (報紙付印時臨時加的) 最後消息。(亦作 **stop-press**)
stop street 車輛必須停車後再開之街道交叉點。
stop valve 停止閥; 關斷閥。
stop watch (記錄時間用之) 計時錶; 碼錶。
stor·a·ble ['storəbl̩; 'stɔːrəbl] *adj.* 可貯藏的。—*n.* (常 *pl.*) 可貯藏的物品。
***stor·age** ['storɪdʒ; 'stɔːridʒ] *n.* ①貯藏。cold *storage.* 冷藏。②倉庫; 貯藏所。③棧租; 倉庫費。
storage battery 〖電〗蓄電池。
storage cell 〖電〗蓄電池。
storage tank 水槽; 油槽; 瓦斯槽。
storage wall 壁櫥。
‡**store** [stor, stɔr; stɔː, stɔə] *n., v.,* **stored, stor·ing.** —*n.* ①〖美〗商店。He keeps a *store.* 他開一家商店。②貯藏; 積蓄; 大量; 豐富。a *store* of knowledge. 豐富的知識。③(*pl.*) 貯存待用的物品; 貯藏品; 必需品; 原料品。military *stores.* 陸軍軍需品。④倉庫; 棧房。⑤〖英〗(*pl.*) 百貨店。***in store*** **a.** 準備着; 貯藏着。**b.** 必將來到或發生。***set no store by*** 輕視。***set*** (or ***lay***) ***store by*** 重視; 珍視。She *sets* great *store by* good character. 她很重視好的品格。—*v.t.* ①供給; 裝配。②貯藏; 積蓄。to *store* up wealth. 積財。③存入倉庫; 交於棧房。—*v.i.* ①貯藏。②可久放(而不壞)。
store·front ['stor,frʌnt; 'stɔːfrʌnt] *n.* 店面。
***store·house** ['stor,haus, 'stɔr-; 'stɔːhaus, 'stɔə-] *n., pl.* **-hous·es.** ①倉庫; 棧房。②寶庫; 寶藏。
store·keep·er ['stor,kipɚ; 'stɔː,kiːpə] *n.* ①〖美〗店主; 店商。②倉庫管理人。③〖英〗軍需官。—**store·keep·ing,** *n.*
store·man ['stor,mæn; 'stɔːmæn] *n., pl.* **-men.** ①〖美〗店主; 店商。②倉庫管理人。
store·room ['stor,rum; 'stɔːrum] *n.* 儲藏室。
stores ledger 存貨簿。(亦作 **stock book, stock ledger, stock record**)
store·wide ['stor,waɪd; 'stɔːwaid] *adj.* (店裏)貨色齊全的。
sto·rey** ['storɪ; 'stɔːri] *n., pl.* **-reys.** 〖英〗樓之一層。the upper storey*** 〖俚〗腦子; 頭腦。(亦作 **story²**) —**sto·reyed,** *adj.*
sto·ried¹ ['storɪd; 'stɔːrid] *adj.* 有…層樓的。a two-*storied* house. 兩層樓的房子。(英亦作 **storeyed**)
sto·ried² *adj.* ①在故事或歷史上有名的。②以歷史故事或傳說中之事蹟爲圖案裝飾的。
sto·ri·ette [,storɪ'ɛt; ,stɔːri'et] *n.* 短篇小說。
sto·ri·ol·o·gy [,storɪ'ɑlədʒɪ; ,stɔːri'ɔlədʒi] *n.* 傳說研究; 民俗學。(亦作 **storyology**)
***stork** [stɔrk; stɔːk] *n.* 鸛。—**like,** *adj.*
‡**storm** [stɔrm; stɔːm] *n.* ①風暴。②暴風雨; 暴風雪。a thunder *storm.* 雷雨。③任何似暴風雨之物。a *storm* of arrows. 一陣如雨般的箭矢。④騷動; 騷亂; 風波。a *storm* of applause. 一陣喝采聲。⑤襲擊; 猛攻。***storm in a teacup*** 大驚小怪。***take by storm*** **a.** 襲取; 奪攻。**b.** 使深受感動。**c.** 突然而完全地成功。—*v.i.* ①下大雨; 起風暴。②狂怒; 咆哮〖at〗. He *stormed* angrily at me. 他向我憤怒地咆哮。③猛衝; 突進。④(以砲火等)猛攻。—*v.t.* ①猛攻。②大叫; 怒吼。③使受到暴風雨似的襲擊。—**like,** *adj.*
storm-beat·en ['stɔrm,bitn̩; 'stɔːm,biːtn] *adj.* 受暴風雨打擊的。
storm-belt ['stɔrm,bɛlt; 'stɔːmbelt] *n.* 暴風地帶。
storm·bound ['stɔrm,baund; 'stɔːmbaund] *adj.* 爲暴風雨所阻的。
storm cellar 避颶風之地窖。
storm center ①暴風中心。②騷亂中心。
storm cloud ①暴風雲。②動亂的前兆。
storm·cock ['stɔrm,kɑk; 'stɔːmkɔk] *n.* 〖英〗綠毛啄木鳥。
storm cone 報風錐(暴風雨的警報球)。
storm door 裝於門外遮擋風雪的板門。
storm drain =**storm sewer.**
storm drum 暴風雨信號筒。
storm·proof ['stɔrm,pruf; 'stɔːmpruːf] *adj.* 能防風暴的。
storm sewer 雨水排水溝。(亦作 **storm drain**)
storm-tossed ['stɔrm,tɑst; 'stɔːmtɔst] *adj.* ①被暴風雨吹襲的。②心緒煩亂的。
storm trooper ①(昔德國納粹黨)突擊隊隊員。②德國納粹黨黨員。③極兇惡之人。
storm troops (昔德國納粹黨)突擊隊。
storm warning ①暴風雨警報。②卽將來臨的困擾的跡象。
storm window 裝於窗外遮擋風雪的板窗。(亦作 **storm sash**)
***storm·y** ['stɔrmɪ; 'stɔːmi] *adj.,* **storm·i·er, storm·i·est.** ①有暴風的; 多風暴的。*stormy* weather. 有暴風雨的天氣。②騷亂的; 猛烈的。—**storm·i·ly,** *adv.*
stormy petrel ①一種小海燕(爲預示暴風雨來臨之鳥)。②引起是非的人。(亦作 **storm petrel**)

Stor·t(h)ing ['stor,tɪŋ; 'stɔːtiŋ] *n.* 挪威之國會。

‡**sto·ry¹** ['storɪ; 'stɔːri] *n., pl.* **-ries,** *v.,* **-ried, -ry·ing.** —*n.* ①故事;小說;事蹟;經歷。But that is another *story.* 不過那是另一回事。The *story* goes (*or* runs) that.... 傳說…。I know her *story.* 我知道她的身世。②〖俗〗謊言。③(戲劇、小說等)情節。④〖美〗新聞記事;報導。⑤〖古〗歷史。***make a long story short*** 長話短說;簡言之。—*v.t.* ①〖古〗談…的故事或歷史;作爲故事講述。②以史蹟繪畫裝飾。

***sto·ry²** *n., pl.* **-ries.** ①層;樓。a house of three *stories.* 三層樓之房屋。first *story.* 〖英〗二層樓;〖美〗一層樓。②每層樓之房間。(英亦作 **storey**)

sto·ry·book ['storɪ,bʊk; 'stɔːribuk] *n.* 故事書;小說書。

story line 故事的本事,情節。

sto·ry·tell·er ['storɪ,tɛlɚ; 'stɔːri,telə] *n.* ①講故事者。②短篇小說家。③〖俗〗說謊者。

sto·ry·tell·ing ['storɪ,tɛlɪŋ; 'stɔːri,teliŋ] *n., adj.* ①講故事(的)。②說謊(的)。

story writer 小說作家。

stoup [stup; stuːp] *n.* ①〖宗教〗聖水鉢。②〖古〗酒杯。③一杯之量。

***stout** [staʊt; staut] *adj.* ①肥大的。②强壯的;堅固的。③堅決的;剛勇的。He has a *stout* heart. 他有勇氣。—*n.* ①黑啤酒。②濃烈的啤酒。③身材高大的人可穿的衣服。④此種衣服的號碼。⑤結實的人。—**ly,** *adv.* —**ness,** *n.*

stout-heart·ed ['staʊt'hɑrtɪd; 'staut'hɑːtid] *adj.* 剛勇的;大膽的。—**ly,** *adv.*

***stove** [stov; stouv] *n., v.,* **stoved, stov·ing.** —*n.* ①火爐;暖爐;爐灶。a gas *stove.* 瓦斯爐。②暖室;溫室。—*v.t.* (以爐)暖;煮。

stove·pipe ['stov,paɪp; 'stouvpaip] *n.* ①煙筒;煙囪。②〖美俗〗大禮帽。

stove plant 溫室中種植的植物。

sto·ver ['stovɚ; 'stouvə] *n.* ①芻秣。②〖美〗玉蜀黍等之稭與葉。

stow [sto; stou] *v.t.* ①裝載。②裝進。③〖俚〗停;不要。④裝。⑤足可容納。⑥隱藏〖常 away〗. ***stow away*** a. 藏匿在船上或飛機上,以期免費搭航。b. (收)藏於安全之處。

stow·age ['stoɪdʒ; 'stouidʒ] *n.* ①裝載。②裝載室;裝載處。③裝載物。④裝載量。⑤裝載費。

stow·a·way ['stoə,we; 'stouəwei] *n.* 偷渡者。

St. Peter's (羅馬)聖彼得大教堂。

St. Pe·ters·burg [sənt'pitɚz,bɝg; sənt'piːtəzbəːg] 聖彼得堡(沙皇時代之俄國首都,現稱列寧格勒 Leningrad).

stra·bis·mal [strə'bɪzm̩l; strə'bizməl] *adj.* =**strabismic.** —**ly,** *adv.*

stra·bis·mic [strə'bɪzmɪk; strə'bizmik] *adj.* ①斜視的。②曲解的。(亦作 **strabismical**)

stra·bis·mus [strə'bɪzməs; strə'bizməs] *n.* 〖醫〗斜視。

stra·bot·o·my [strə'bɑtəmɪ; strə'bɔtəmi] *n., pl.* **-mies.** 〖醫〗斜視切治法。

strad·dle ['strædl̩; 'strædl] *v.,* **-dled, -dling,** *n.* —*v.i.* ①兩腿叉開地走、站或坐。②〖俗〗觀望。—*v.t.* ①將(兩腿)分開。②叉腿站於或跨於。③〖俗〗對…持騎牆態度。—*n.* ①跨立;跨坐;跨腿而行。②跨立時兩足間之距離。③〖俗〗騎牆態度。—**strad·dler,** *n.*

Strad·i·var·i·us [,strædə'vɛrɪəs; ,strædi'vɛəriəs] *n.* 絃樂器(特指義大利小提琴製造家 Antonio Stradivari 1644–1737, 或其家族所製的小提琴)。(亦作 **Strad**)

strafe [stref, strɑf; strɑːf] *v.,* **strafed, straf·ing,** *n.* —*v.t.* ①砲擊;(飛機低飛)掃射;猛轟。②〖俗〗處罰;斥責。—*n.* ①砲擊;掃射。②處罰;斥責。

strag·gle ['stræg|; 'strægl] *v.i.,* **-gled, -gling.** ①迷途;入歧途。②散開;散漫。③蔓延。—**strag·gler,** *n.*

strag·gling ['stræglɪŋ; 'strægliŋ] *adj.* ①迷途的;漂泊的。②蔓延的。③星散的;落伍的。—**ly,** *adv.*

strag·gly ['stræglɪ; 'strægli] *adj.* 零亂四散的。

‡**straight** [stret; streit] *adj.* ①直的。a *straight* line. 直線。②平直的。③正直的;誠實的。a *straight* conduct. 正直之行爲。④秩序井然的。Set the room *straight.* 把這房間收拾整齊。⑤連續的;不斷的。⑥〖美〗徹底的;無保留的。⑦〖美〗未變更的;純淨的;未稀釋的。⑧〖俗〗可靠的。⑨〖牌戲〗順字的。⑩正確的(思考、理論等)。⑪未改變原樂曲之調子或速度的。⑫〖俚〗異性戀的。⑬〖新聞〗平實的(報導)。⑭自然的;一本正經的。***keep a straight face*** 板起面孔。***keep straight*** 品行端正;不墮落。—*adv.* ①直地;直接地。He went *straight* to Paris. 他直接前往巴黎。②立即。He went *straight* out. 他馬上出去。③坦白地;誠實地。I told him *straight.* 我對他直說。④連續地;不斷地。to drive *straight.* 繼續地駕駛下去。⑤〖美俗〗無論買多少不打折扣地。⑥直線地。to walk *straight.* 一直走。⑦〖新聞〗平實地。⑧不加修飾地。Tell the story *straight.* 不加修飾地講出事情的經過吧。***come straight to the point*** 開門見山。***hit straight from the shoulder*** a. 直接命中。b. 正直而無懼地批評。***run straight*** (喻)正直地生活。***straight across*** (or ***back, in, out, up, etc.***) 不延遲、懷疑、猶豫等。Go *straight in.* 立卽進去吧!to tell *straight out.* 直講。***straight away*** 立刻。I'll do it *straight away.* 我將立卽處理它。***straight off*** 立刻。—*n.* ①直;直線。②(跑道等之)直線部分。③〖撲克牌〗五張相連的牌;順字。***out of the straight*** 歪曲的;彎着的。***straight and narrow*** (生活之)老實而規矩。—**ly,** *adv.* —**ness,** *n.*

straight angle 〖數學〗平角。

straight-arm ['stret,ɑrm; 'streitɑːm] *v.t.* 〖橄欖球〗以伸直之臂截擱(對方)。—*n.* 以伸直之臂截擱對方之動作。(亦作 **stiff-arm**)

straight·a·way ['stretə,we; 'streitə,wei] *adj.* 直進的。—*n.* 直路。—*adv.* 立卽。

straight bill of lading 記名提單;收貨人抬頭提單(單上每有不得轉讓字樣)。

straight chair 靠背筆直的椅子。

straight·edge ['stret,ɛdʒ; 'streitedʒ] *n.* 直尺。

straight·en** ['stretn̩; 'streitn] *v.t.* ①使直;使平正。*Straighten* your shoulders. 把肩膀挺直。②整頓;整理。—*v.i.* ①變直。②〖俗〗改過自新。straighten one's face*** 板起面孔。—**er,** *n.*

straight flush 〖撲克牌〗同花順。

straight·for·ward [,stret'fɔrwɚd; streit'fɔːwəd] *adj.* ①直進的。②正直的;誠實的。—*adv.* 直進地;一直地;率直地。—**ly,** *adv.* —**ness,** *n.*

straight·for·wards [,stret'fɔrwɚdz; streit'fɔːwədz] *adv.* =**straightforward.**

straight life insurance 投保人

終生付保險費的人壽保險。

straight-line ['stret,laɪn; 'streit-lain] *adj.* ①直線的；直線形的；由直線組成的。②直線排列的；直線運動的。

straight man 供滑稽演員調侃之副手。

straight matter 〖印刷〗①本文(非標題部分)。②(報刊之)文字部分(別於廣告)。

straight-out ['stret'aut; 'streit'aut] *adj.* 〖美俗〗①全然的；徹底的；純粹的；無保留的。②直接的；坦率的。③直進的。

straight razor 剃鬍刀(有柄可折入「的)。」

straight ticket 〖美政治〗①全部投給同一政黨候選人的選票。②所有候選人皆爲同一政黨黨員的候選人名單。

straight time ①某一行業的標準工作時間(以每週爲單位，約35至40小時)。②普通工作的薪給(別於加班費)。

*__straight·way__ ['stret,we; 'streitwei] *adv.* 立刻；卽刻。

straight whiskey 〖美〗純威士忌。

‡**strain**[1] [stren;strein] *v.t.* ①拉緊；引張；使緊張。②竭盡…的全力；將(某種能力)使用至最大限度。She *strained* her eyes to see. 她竭盡目力以視。③濫用。to *strain* one's credit. 濫用信譽。④因過分用力而損傷。⑤扭傷。⑥强迫；勉强。⑦曲解。⑧緊抱。⑨濾。***strain a point*** 踰越範圍；變通辦理。—*v.i.* ①努力；奮力。②用力拉。③受重壓或强引；因過分用力受傷。④濾過；滲出。⑤盡力抵抗。***strain after*** 竭力求取。***strain at*** **a.** 用力拉；努力於。**b.** 不容易接受。—*n.* ①拉緊；緊張；拉力。the *strain* of modern life. 現代生活的緊張。②奮力；過度之努力。③辛苦；勞傷。④扭傷；扭曲。⑤壓力。⑥〖俗〗需要很大的努力的事。⑦苛求(對資源、人、感情等)。⑧(語言、口才等之)滔滔不絕。⑨(詩之)一節；一篇。⑩程度；高度。—**ing,** *n.*

strain[2] *n.* ①血統；家系；門第。②(動植物構成一族、一類或一種的)羣。③氣質；傾向；性情；(遺傳的)素質。④作風；語調；筆調。⑤(常*pl.*)小歌謠；歌節；曲調；詩歌；旋律。

strained [strend;streind] *adj.* 勉强的；不自然的；不和熙愉悅的；牽强附會的。

strain·er ['strenɚ; 'streinə] *n.* ①緊張者；奮力者。②濾器；篩。③伸張或拉緊之具。

strain gauge 拉力測量儀。

*__strait__ [stret;streit] *n.* ①(常*pl.*)(作*sing.*解)海峽。*Straits* of Dover. 多佛海峽。②(常*pl.*)困難。a man in financial *straits*. 處於經濟困難中之人。③〖古〗狹窄的地方。—*adj.* ①〖古〗狹窄的；緊的。②困難的；窘迫的。③〖古〗嚴格的。—**ly,** *adv.* —**ness,** *n.*

strait·en ['stretn; 'streitn] *v.t.* ①使缺乏；使困難。②使狹窄；使受限制；收縮。***be in straitened circumstances*** 在窮困中。

strait jacket ①(拘束狂人的)緊衣。②拘束、阻礙的東西。(亦作**straight jacket**)

strait-jack·et ['stret,dʒækɪt;'streit-'dʒækit] *v.t.* 扼殺；阻礙。

strait-laced ['stret'lest;'streit-leist] *adj.* (行爲或道德上)過於拘謹的；過於嚴格的。(亦作 **straight-laced**) —**ly,** *adv.* —**ness,** *n.*

Straits Settlements 海峽殖民地「(英屬南洋舊稱)。」

strait-waist·coat ['stret,westkot; 'streit'weiskout] *n.* 拘束狂人用之緊身衣。

strake [strek; streik] *n.* ①束緊車輪之輪鐵；鐵箍。②〖造船〗船側板；船底板。

stra·mo·ni·um [strə'monɪəm; strə'mouniəm] *n.* 〖植物〗曼陀華。(亦作 stramony)

*__strand__[1] [strænd; strænd] *n.* 〖詩〗岸；濱。—*v.t. & v.i.* ①擱淺。②(常用被動語態)(使)束手無策。

strand[2] *n.* ①繩索之一股。②一縷；一串。③問題等的一部分。④線或似線的事物。—*v.t.* ①將繩索之股結在一起形成(繩索)。②將(繩索)之股弄斷。—**less,** *adj.*

‡**strange** [strendʒ; streindʒ] *adj.,* **strang·er, strang·est,** *adv.* —*adj.* ①奇異的；奇怪的。How *strange!* 多麼奇怪！②陌生的；生疏的；不熟悉的。*strange* faces. 陌生的面孔。③不習慣的；無經驗的。I am quite *strange* here. 我在此人地生疏。④不自在的；不相稱的；礙事的。⑤〖古〗外國的；異鄉的。⑥拘謹的；冷淡的；不親近的。***be strange to (something)*** 對(某事物)不習慣。***strange to say*** 說也奇怪。—*adv.* 奇異地；不自在地；生疏地(=strangely).—**ly,** *adv.* —**ness,** *n.*

‡**stran·ger** ['strendʒɚ;'streindʒə] *n.* ①陌生人；異鄉人；外國人。②客人；訪客。You're quite a *stranger.* 你眞是稀客。③門外漢；無經驗者。He is a *stranger* to Latin. 他不懂拉丁文。④〖法律〗第三者。—**like,** *adj.*

stran·gle ['stræŋgl;'stræŋgl] *v.,* **-gled, -gling.** —*v.t.* ①扼殺；絞殺；勒死。②使窒息；使窒悶。③壓抑；遏制。—*v.i.* 窒息而死。—**ment, stran·gler,** *n.*

strangle hold ①〖摔角〗勒頸。②任何限制自由之物；束縛。

stran·gles ['stræŋglz;'stræŋglz] *n. pl.* (作 *sing.* 解)〖獸醫〗腺疫(馬之瘰癧性感冒)。

stran·gu·late ['stræŋgjə,let;'stræŋ-gjuleit] *v.t.,* **-lat·ed, -lat·ing.** ①絞死；扼死；勒死。②〖醫〗勒束；壓縮(血液循環)。

stran·gu·la·tion [,stræŋgjə'leʃən; ,stræŋgju'leiʃən] *n.* ①絞死；勒死。②〖醫〗勒束；壓縮。

*__strap__ [stræp; stræp] *n., v.,* **strapped, strap·ping.** —*n.* ①帶；皮帶；皮條。②磨刀革帶；蕩刀皮。③吊帶；帶圈；帶環。④錶帶。—*v.t.* ①用帶綑；用帶束住。②用皮帶打。③用皮帶磨(剃刀等)。—**like,** *adj.*

strap·hang ['stræp,hæŋ; 'stræphæŋ] *v.i.,* **-hung, -hang·ing.** (在交通工具中)拉着吊帶站着。

strap·hang·er ['stræp,hæŋɚ;'stræp-,hæŋə] *n.* 〖俗〗(在公共汽車、火車等中找不到座位)拉着吊帶站立的乘客。

strap·hang·ing ['stræp,hæŋɪŋ; 'stræp,hæŋiŋ] *n.* (車上)拉着吊帶站立。

strap·less ['stræplɪs; 'stræplis] *adj.* 無肩帶的。a *strapless* bra. 無肩帶奶罩。—*n.* 無肩帶之內衣。

stra·pon·tin [strə'pɑntɪn; strə'pɔn-tin] *n.* 汽車或戲院中之摺疊座位。

strap·pa·do [strə'pedo; strə'peidou] *n., pl.* **-does, -dos,** *v.* —*n.* ①吊刑。②此種吊刑之刑具。—*v.t.* 處以上述刑罰。

strapped [stræpt; stræpt] *adj.* ①有帶的；供以帶的；飾以帶的。②有吊帶的。③〖美俚〗赤貧的；無分文的；頭寸很緊的。

strap·per ['stræpɚ; 'stræpə] *n.* ①用細帶束縛的人或物；裝馬具的人；看馬的人。②〖俚〗魁偉健壯的人。

strap·ping[1] ['stræpɪŋ; 'stræpiŋ] *adj.* 〖俗〗高大壯健的；魁偉的。

strap·ping[2] *n.* 皮帶(集合稱)。

stra·ta ['stretə; 'streitə] *n.* ① pl. of **stratum.** ②(不標準的用法) =**stratum.**

strat·a·gem ['strætədʒəm; 'strætidʒəm] *n.* 計謀;詭計;欺騙敵人之計謀。
stra·te·gic [strə'tidʒɪk; strə'ti:dʒik] *adj.* 戰略的。(亦作 **strategical, strategetic**) **—al·ly,** *adv.*
Strategic Air Command〖美〗戰略空軍司令部。
strategic hamlet 戰略村(防禦游擊隊之攻擊而設防的鄉村)。
stra·te·gics [strə'tidʒɪks; strə'ti:dʒiks] *n.* (作 *sing.*解) =**strategy.**
strat·e·gist ['strætədʒɪst; 'strætidʒist] *n.* 戰略家;兵法家。
strat·e·gy ['strætədʒɪ; 'strætidʒi] *n., pl.* **-gies.** ①兵學;軍事學;兵法。②軍略;戰略。③策略;謀略。
Strat·ford-on-A·von ['strætfəd-ɑn'evən; 'strætfədɔn'eivən] *n.* 斯特拉福(英格蘭 Warwickshire 郡之一小城,濱 Avon 河,爲莎士比亞出生與埋葬之地)。(亦作 **Stratford-upon-Avon**)
strath [stræθ; stræθ] *n.*〖蘇〗大河谷。
strath·spey [stræθ'spe; stræθ'spei] *n.* ①一種活潑的蘇格蘭舞。②此種舞曲。
strat·i·fi·ca·tion [ˌstrætəfə'keʃən; ˌstrætifi'keiʃən] *n.* ①成層;層理。②階層之形成。③〖園藝〗(種子的)土層保護法。
strat·i·fy ['strætəˌfaɪ; 'strætifai] *v.t.* & *v.i.*, **-fied, -fy·ing.** 使成層;形成層。
stra·tig·ra·phy [strə'tɪgrəfɪ; strə'tigrəfi] *n.* 地層學。
strato-〖字首〗表"層雲"之義。
stra·to·cir·rus [ˌstreto'sɪrəs; ˌstreitou'sirəs] *n., pl.* **-cir·ri** [-'sɪraɪ; -'sirai].〖氣象〗層卷雲。
stra·toc·ra·cy [strə'tɑkrəsɪ; strə'tɔkrəsi] *n., pl.* **-cies.** 軍人政治;軍閥政治。
Strat·o·cruis·er ['strætəˌkruzɚ; 'strætəˌkru:zə] *n.*〖商標名〗巨型運輸機。
stra·to-cu·mu·lus [ˌstreto'kjumjələs; ˌstreitou'kju:mjuləs] *n., pl.* **-li** [-ˌlaɪ; -lai].〖氣象〗層積雲。
Strat·o·lin·er ['strætəˌlaɪnɚ; 'strætəˌlainə] *n.*〖商標名〗高空多引擎噴射客機。
strat·o·sphere ['strætəˌsfɪr; 'strætousfiə] *n.*〖氣象〗平流層;同溫層。**—strat·o·spher·ic,** *adj.*
strat·o·tank·er ['strætəˌtæŋkɚ; 'strætəˌtæŋkə] *n.* 軍用高空加油機。
strat·o·vi·sion ['strætəˌvɪʒən; 'strætouˌviʒən] *n.* 飛機在同溫層所作的電視轉播。
stra·tum ['stretəm; 'streitəm] *n., pl.* **stra·ta, stra·tums.** ①層;地層。②社會階層。
stra·tus ['stretəs; 'streitəs] *n., pl.* **-ti** [-taɪ; -tai].〖氣象〗層雲。
Strauss [straus; straus] *n.* 斯特勞斯 (Johann, 1804–1849, 奧國作曲家;其子 Johann, 1825–1899, 亦爲作曲家)。
straw** [strɔ; strɔ:] *n.* ①稻草;麥稭。②無價值之物;少許;小量。not to care a *straw.* 毫不介意。not worth a *straw.* 一文不值。③莖管;蠟紙管。④=**straw hat.** ***a man of straw **a.** 軟弱而不可靠之人;稻草人。**b.** 受人擺布者;傀儡。***a straw in the wind*** 預示未來大勢之小事。***catch*** (***clutch*** or ***grasp***) ***at a straw*** (***at straws, at any straw*** or ***at any straws***) 絕望時竭力挽救;危急時無論如何細微的機會均欲掌握利用。***make bricks without straw*** 想實行無足够資源或支持之事。***the last straw*** 使全盤垮臺之最後增加的細微負荷。 *—adj.* ①藁製的;稻草作的。②不值錢的;無價值的;瑣細的。③淡黃的;稻草色的。***a straw vote*** (or ***ballot***) 假投票。**—less,** *adj.* **—like,** *adj.*
***straw·ber·ry** ['strɔˌbɛrɪ; 'strɔ:bəri] *n., pl.* **-ries.** 草莓。
strawberry mark 草莓狀或草莓色之赤痣。
straw·board ['strɔˌbord; 'strɔ:bɔ:d] *n.* 馬糞紙;紙板。
straw boss〖美俗〗監工之助理;副工頭。
straw colo(u)r 淡黃色。
straw hat 草帽。
straw man ①稻草人。②替別人做僞證者。③不重要的小人物或事項。
straw plait 麥桿辮;草帽辮。
straw·y ['strɔ·ɪ; 'strɔ:i] *adj.*, **straw·i·er, straw·i·est.** ①稻草的;稻草做的;像稻草的。②覆以稻草的。
stray** [stre; strei] *v.i.* ①迷路;漂泊;遊蕩。②離正道;走入歧途。*—adj.* ①迷路的;漂泊的。②散漫的;偶然的。a *stray* bullet. 流彈。③孤立的;與其餘分開的。④〖無線電〗不需要的。 *—n.* ①漂泊者。②迷失的家畜。③(*pl.*)〖無線電〗空電;天電。 ***waifs and strays 流浪兒童。**—er,** *n.*
streak** [strik; stri:k] *n.* ①條紋;線條;條痕。a *streak* of lightning. 一道閃電。②氣質;性情;癖性。③層;脈。④〖美俗〗短時間;陣。a *streak* of good luck. 一陣好運氣。⑤〖細菌〗在培養基上劃線培養。⑥〖俗〗快跑者;迅速工作者。⑦裸奔。blue streak*** 迅速移動的事物。***like a streak*** (***of lightning***) 極迅速地。*—v.t.* 加以條紋或條痕。*—v.i.* ①生條痕;變爲有條紋。②〖俗〗疾馳;飛跑。③閃電。④裸奔。**—like,** *adj.*
streaked [strikt; stri:kt] *adj.* ①有條紋的。②〖美方〗不安的;驚恐的;迷亂的;困惑的。 **—ly,** *adv.* **—ness,** *n.*
streak·er ['strikɚ; 'stri:kə] *n.* 裸奔者。
streak·ing ['strikɪŋ; 'stri:kiŋ] *n.* 裸奔。
streak·y ['strikɪ; 'stri:ki] *adj.*, **streak·i·er, streak·i·est.** ①有條紋的;一層層的。②不均勻的;變化的。③〖俗〗易怒的;壞脾氣的。**—streak·i·ness,** *n.*
‡stream [strim; stri:m] *n.* ①溪;水流;河;川。②流勢;趨勢。the *stream* of history. 歷史之潮流。③流注;流出(通常用於譬喻)。 a *stream* of people. 川流不息之人。④光線。 a *stream* of light. 一道光線。***go with the stream*** 順應潮流。 ***on stream*** 全力生產中。 *—v.i.* ①流。Tears *streamed* from her eyes. 淚從她的眼中流出。②蜂擁而進;魚貫而行。③飄揚;招展。④以直線伸展;射出。*—v.t.* ①使流;流出。②使飄揚。**—less,** *adj.* **—like,** *adj.*
***stream·er** ['strimɚ; 'stri:mə] *n.* ①旗旛;狹長之旗。②狹長之飾帶。③任何狹長的東西。④〖新聞〗橫跨全頁的大標題。
stream·flow ['strimˌflo; 'stri:mflou] *n.* (河川的)流水量。
stream·ing ['strimɪŋ; 'stri:miŋ] *n.* 流動。
stream·let ['strimlɪt; 'stri:mlit] *n.* 小河;溪。
stream·line ['strimˌlaɪn; 'stri:mlain] *adj., v.,* **-lined, -lin·ing,** *n.* *—adj.* 流線型的。*—v.t.* ①使成流線型。②使簡化;使有效率;使現代化。*—n.* 液體暢通之流動。
stream·lined ['strimˌlaɪnd; 'stri:mlaind] *adj.* ①流線型的;最新式的。②改進的;使更有效的。

stream·lin·er ['strim,laınə;'stri:m-,lainə] *n.* 流線型火車(汽車、飛機等)。

stream of consciousness 〖心理〗意識流。

stream·y ['strimı; 'stri:mi] *adj.*, **stream·i·er, stream·i·est.** ①多溪流的。②流的;流動的。③像溪的。

street** [strit; stri:t] *n.* ①街;街道;車道。Walk along (up *or* down) the *street.* 沿着街道行走。②街上居民;市井之人。go on the streets*** 賣淫;爲娼。***the man in the street*** 市井中人;平常人。***the Street*** 〖俚〗a. 市內從事某行業(尤指金融業)的地區。b. 紐約華爾街。c. 美國城市裏戲院及其他娛樂場所集中地區。***up one's street*** (or ***alley***)合於某人之性情,胃口。***woman of the streets*** 娼妓。

street arab (or **Arab**) 流浪兒童。

***street·car** ['strit,kar; 'stri:tkɑ:] *n.* 電車。

street cleaner 清道夫。

street door 大門(指臨街之大門)。

street dress 外出服。

street-lamp ['strit,læmp; 'stri:t-læmp] *n.* 街燈;路燈。(亦作 **street lamp**)

street·light ['strit,laıt; 'stri:tlait] *n.* 路燈。

street orderly 〖英〗清道夫。

street railway 市街鐵路;電車道。

street sweeper ①清道夫。②淸路機。

street urchin 流浪街頭的兒童。

street·walk·er ['strit,wɔkə;'stri:t-,wɔ:kə] *n.* ①路上行人。②娼妓。

‡**strength** [strɛŋθ, strɛŋkθ; streŋθ, -ŋkθ] *n.*①力;氣力;力量。*strength* of will. 意志力。②强固;强度;濃度。the *strength* of one's love. 愛情的强度。③抗力;持久力。the *strength* of a fort. 要塞的抵抗力。④兵力;人數。The enemy were in great *strength.* 敵人兵力很大。⑤使强固之物;憑藉;支持物。⑥能漲價或不跌價的力量。Stocks continued to show *strength.* 股票繼續表現堅挺。⑦說服力。***on the strength of*** 憑恃。***up to*** (or ***below***) ***strength*** 達到(未達到)定額的。—**less,** *adj.*

***strength·en** ['strɛŋθən; 'streŋθən, -ŋkθ-] *v.t.* 使强;加强。—*v.i.* 變强。—**er,** *n.*

***stren·u·ous** ['strɛnjuəs; 'strenjuəs] *adj.* ①費力的;多艱辛的;須用全力應付的。②發奮的;努力的;有力的;精力充沛的。—**stren·u·os·i·ty,** —**ness,** *n.* —**ly,** *adv.*

Streph·on ['strɛfɑn; 'strefɔn] *n.* 患相思病的人(原爲 Sir Philip Sidney 所著小說 *Arcadia* 中患相思病的牧羊人)。

streph·o·sym·bo·li·a [,strɛfosım-'bɑlıə; ,strefousim'bɔliə] *n.* 〖醫〗①識字困難。②視覺相反。

strep·to·coc·cic [,strɛptə'kɑksık; ,streptə'kɔksik] *adj.* 鏈狀球菌的;鏈球菌所引起的。

strep·to·coc·cus [,strɛptə'kɑkəs; ,streptə'kɔkəs] *n., pl.* **-coc·ci** [-'kɑksaı; -'kɔksai]. 〖細菌〗鏈(狀)球菌。

strep·to·my·cin [,strɛptə'maısın; ,streptə'maisin] *n.* 〖生化〗鏈黴素。

Stre·se·mann ['ʃtrezə,mɑn; 'ʃtrei-zəmɑ:n] *n.*史特萊斯曼(Gustav, 1878–1929, 德國政治家,曾獲1926年諾貝爾和平獎)。

stress** [strɛs; stres] *n.* ①壓迫力;重壓。②重要;强調。to lay (a) *stress* on something. 着重某事。③重讀;重音。④〖機械〗應力。⑤曲調或節奏中之强調部分。⑥(心理、生理或情緒上之)緊張。times of stress*** 多事之秋;危急的時候。—*v.t.* ①加壓力於。②着重。③重讀。—**less,** *adj.* —**less·ness,** *n.*

stress·ful ['strɛsfəl; 'stresful] *adj.* 充滿着壓力的;充滿着緊張的。—**ly,** *adv.*

‡**stretch** [strɛtʃ; stretʃ] *v.t.* ①伸展;張開;引伸。to *stretch* one's legs (arms). 伸腿(臂)。②拉緊;張緊。③誇張;濫用;通融;曲解。to *stretch* the truth. 曲解事實。④使躺下;打倒。⑤伸出。⑥(飲料、食物、油漆)摻假;摻雜。⑦〖廣播,電視〗(爲不使其早結束而)拉長。—*v.i.* ①伸展;引伸;展開。The forest *stretches* for miles. 這森林綿亘若干英里之長。②舒伸四肢。③可伸展;能擴張。Rubber *stretches.* 橡皮可伸展。④努力;出大力。⑤(時間上之)回溯。⑥〖廣播,電視〗拉長(節目內容)。***stretch oneself*** 伸展身體。***stretch one's neck*** 引頸而望。—*n.* ①伸張;伸展。②綿亘的空間。③一口氣(不停地)。He worked (for) six hours at a *stretch.* 他一口氣工作了六小時。④〖俚〗刑期;徒刑。⑤〖體育〗跑道兩邊直線部分之一;(特指)最後轉彎處至終點間的一段跑道。⑥(S-)瘦長的人的綽號。***a stretch of the imagination*** (***of authority***) 想像(權力)之過分使用。—*adj.* (合成纖維的衣料或線)有彈性可拉長的。*stretch* socks. 有伸縮性的襪子。—**a·bil·i·ty,** *n.* —**a·ble,** *adj.*

stretched-out ['strɛtʃt'aut;'stretʃt-'aut] *adj.* 伸長的;延伸的;延長的。

***stretch·er** ['strɛtʃə; 'stretʃə] *n.* ①舁床;擔架。②爲撐張用的架子。③伸張的人或事物。④支撐之棍子。⑤畫架。⑥(傘的)骨架。

stretch·er·bear·er ['strɛtʃə,bɛrə; 'stretʃə,bɛərə] *n.* 抬擔架者;擔架兵。

stretch·er-bear·er ['strɛtʃə,bɛrə; 'stretʃə,bɛərə] *n.* 擔架夫。(亦作 **stretcherman**)

stretch-out ['strɛtʃ,aut; 'stretʃaut] *n., adj.* 〖美俗〗强化勞動(加工而不加工資)。

stretch·y['strɛtʃı;'stretʃi]*adj.*, **stretch·i·er, stretch·i·est.** ①易伸的;有彈力的;可展延的。②好强而勉强度過的(如睏了不睡)。③(豬之)有長身的。

***strew** [stru; stru:] *v.t.*, **strewed, strewed** or **strewn**[strun;stru:n], **strewing.** ①撒布;散播。②被散播於。—**er,** *n.*

stri·a ['straıə; 'straiə] *n., pl.* **stri·ae** ['straı,i; 'straii:]. ①細槽;窄溝。②〖建築〗柱上凹槽間之隆起線。③線條;條紋。

stri·ate [*v.* 'straıet;'straieit *adj.* 'straı-ıt;'straiit] *v.*, **-at·ed, -at·ing,** *adj.* —*v.t.* 加條紋於…上;作條痕於…上。—*adj.* 有條紋的;有條痕的。

stri·at·ed ['straıetıd; strai'eitid] *adj.* 刻有條紋的;有縱線的。

stri·a·tion [straı'eʃən; strai'eiʃən] *n.* ①有條紋或刻線之狀態;有條痕。②條紋之排列。③線條;條痕;條紋。

strick·en** ['strıkən; 'strikən] *v.* pp. of **strike.** —*adj.* ①受(疾病、災難、傷害)侵襲的。②裝滿的。stricken field*** 戰場。***stricken in years*** 年老。—**ly,** *adv.*

strick·le ['strıkḷ; 'strikl] *n., v.*, **-led, -ling.** —*n.* (量穀類的)斗刮。—*v.t.* 以斗刮刮平。

***strict** [strıkt; strikt] *adj.* ①嚴格的;嚴厲的;嚴密的;精確的。in the *strict* sense of the word. 嚴格說來。②完全的;絕對的。③仔細的;詳盡的。—**ness,** *n.*

***strict·ly** ['strɪktlɪ; 'striktli, 'strikli] *adv.* ①嚴格地；嚴密地；精確地。 *strictly* speaking. 嚴格地講。②的確地；全然地。

stric·ture ['strɪktʃɚ; 'striktʃə] *n.* ①嚴苛之批評；非難。to pass *strictures* on... 對…加以嚴苛的批評；抨擊。②〖醫〗(身體中管道的)狹窄。③緊束；約束。

stride** [straɪd; straid] *v.*, **strode** [strod; stroud], **strid·den** ['strɪdn̩; 'stridn], **strid·ing**, *n.* —*v.i.* ①大步行走。②跨。He *strode* over the brook. 他跨過小河。—*v.t.* ①跨坐；跨立。②跨過。—*n.* ①大步；闊步；一跨之距離。②正常的速度或活動。③發展或進步途中的向前邁進。hit one's stride*** 達到某人正規的速度或正常的活動；舉動闊綽。***make great*** (or ***rapid***) ***strides*** 突飛猛晋；大有進步。***take*** (***something***) ***in one's stride*** 鎮靜地做；成功地應付。—**strid·er**, *n.*

stri·dent ['straɪdn̩t; 'straidnt] *adj.* 作粗糙聲的；發尖銳聲的。 —**stri·dence, stri·den·cy**, *n.* —**ly**, *adv.*

stri·dor ['straɪdɚ; 'straidə] *n.* ①粗糙之聲；尖銳之聲。②〖醫〗喘鳴。

strid·u·late ['strɪdʒəˌlet; 'stridjuleit] *v.i.*, **-lat·ed, -lat·ing.** 發唧唧聲；唧唧叫。

stri·du·la·tion [ˌstrɪdʒə'leʃən; ˌstridju'leiʃən] *n.* 唧唧鳴聲；唧唧叫。

***strife** [straɪf; straif] *n.* 爭吵；爭鬥。to be at *strife*. 不和。—**less**, *adj.* —**ful**, *adj.*

strig·il ['strɪdʒɪl; 'stridʒil] *n.* (古希臘及羅馬)刮膚具。

‡strike [straɪk; straik] *v.*, **struck**, **struck** or **strick·en, strik·ing**, *n.*—*v.t.* ①打；擊；敲。 Why did you *strike* her? 你爲何打她?②使感動；使突然充滿（一種强烈的情緒)。They were *struck* with terror. 他們受驚。③劃(火柴)；打火。 to *strike* a match. 劃火柴。④觸(目)；使想起；出現於(某人)心頭。An idea suddenly *struck* me. 我心中忽然生出一個念頭。⑤鑄造。⑥締結。 to *strike* an agreement. 締結契約。⑦落下；取下。 to *strike* a flag (a sail). 下旗(帆)。⑧發現。 to *strike* oil. 發現油田。⑨鳴響；報時。It has just *struck* four. 剛打四點鐘。⑩採取(態度)；裝出。⑪使(植物) 扎根；種植；扎(根)。⑫估定；結算；清算。 to *strike* a balance. 結帳。⑬使平；使與量器之頂部水平。⑭遇到；碰到。⑮用魚叉叉(鯨魚)。⑯劃掉；刪除〖常 out〗. ⑰擠出；排出；取下〖常 off〗. Illness *struck* him off from social contacts. 他因病不能作社交活動。⑱使突然患病，死亡。 The plague *struck* Europe. 瘟疫襲擊歐洲。⑲突然開始。⑳到達。㉑停止(工作)；罷(工)。㉒用尺劃直線。㉓〖法律〗選擇(陪審員)。—*v.i.* ①打；打擊。 *Strike* while the iron is hot. 打鐵趁熱。②(鐘)鳴；響。③進攻。④罷工。The coal miners *struck*. 煤礦工人罷工。⑤〖植物〗扎根。⑥(魚等)啣餌；貼緊；把牢。⑦(火柴)劃燃；着火。The match wouldn't *strike*. 火柴劃不燃。⑧走；去。⑨(船等)觸礁。⑩(光線) 照射；(聲音之) 發出。⑪產生某種印象。⑫突然來臨或發現 〖常on, upon〗. ⑬划槳；游泳時手、脚打水。***strike a note*** 給予某種特殊的印象。 ***strike back*** 還擊。***strike camp*** 撤營準備離去。 ***strike cuttings*** 插枝使生根。 ***strike hands*** 完成一筆交易；完成一合約。 ***strike home*** 痛擊；命中；中肯。 ***strike in*** 插言；(疾病等)侵襲內臟。***strike into*** 突然轉入；突然開始。 ***strike it rich*** 〖美俗〗 a. 發現豐富的油礦。b. 突然或意外地成功；平步青雲。 ***strike off*** a. 取消；抹去。b. 斬下(人頭等)。 c. 印刷。d. 輕而易舉地做或生產 ***strike oil*** a. 發現石油礦。b. 獲得重要發現；獲得好運氣。***strike out*** a. 抹去；刪去。b.（游泳或溜冰)開始向某一方向前進。c. 想出；籌劃。d. 〖棒球〗(使)三振出局。 e. 失敗。 ***strike root*** 扎根；生根。 ***strike through*** 刪去。***strike up*** 開始；開始奏唱。—*n.* ①打擊；毆打。②罷工。③暴富。④〖棒球〗好球。⑤一次所鑄之錢幣數量。⑥啣餌；嚙餌。⑦〖軍〗有計畫之攻擊行動，尤指空中攻擊。⑧礦藏之重要發現。⑨時鐘之鳴鐘機械。⑩啤酒等之力量。 ***have two strikes against one*** 在不利的或危急的情況下。***on strike*** 實行罷工。—**less**, *adj.*

strike benefit 罷工津貼。

strike·bound ['straɪkˌbaund; 'straikbaund] *adj.* 因罷工而停頓的。

strike·break·er ['straɪkˌbrekɚ; 'straikˌbreikə] *n.* 破壞罷工者。

strike·break·ing ['straɪkˌbrekɪŋ; 'straikˌbreikiŋ] *n.* 强迫罷工者復工之措施。

strike-out ['straɪkˌaut; 'straikaut] *n.* ①〖棒球〗三振。②被禁止充當碼頭工人的已服刑期滿之犯人。(亦作 **strikeout**)

strike·o·ver ['straɪkˌovɚ; 'straikˌouvə] *n.* ①打字錯誤但不擦去而重複打上。②如此之部分。

strike pay 罷工津貼。(亦作 **strike benefit**)

strik·er ['straɪkɚ; 'straikə] *n.* ①打擊者；打擊物。②罷工者。③用魚叉叉魚者。④〖美軍〗陸軍軍官的傳令兵或勤務兵。 ⑤接在油漆刷子上俾能油漆較遠處的桿子 (=manhelper). ⑥〖捕鯨〗銛；魚叉。

strike zone 〖棒球〗好球區。

***strik·ing** ['straɪkɪŋ; 'straikiŋ] *adj.* ①顯著的；引人注意的。②罷工的。③打擊的。

striking distance 射擊距離；有效距離。

striking force ①攻擊力量。②攻擊部隊。

strik·ing·ly ['straɪkɪŋlɪ; 'straikiŋli] *adv.* 顯著地；引人注目地。

striking power 攻擊敵人之力量。

‡string [strɪŋ; striŋ] *n.*, *v.*, **strung** [strʌŋ; strʌŋ], **string·ing.** —*n.* ①帶；線；細繩。a piece of *string*. 一根繩子。②一串；一列。 a *string* of pearls. 一串珍珠。③(樂器或弓等之)弦。④(豆莢等之)筋；纖維。⑤(*pl.*)絃樂器(集合稱)。⑥〖俗〗條件；情況。⑦項鍊。⑧〖新聞〗特約記者 (stringer) 所投之稿的剪貼(用來領稿費的)。⑨按技巧排列的一羣運動員。⑩屬於同一個老闆或公司的人員或企業機構。***harp on one*** (or ***the same***) ***string*** 反覆同一話題。***have two strings to one's bow*** 有一個以上的辦法以處理或獲致某物。***on the*** (or ***a***) ***string*** 在控制下；被指揮。***pull strings*** (or ***wires***) a. 暗中操縱。b. 運用影響力。***with a string attached*** 附有條件。—*v.t.* ①串起。to *string* beads. 串起念珠。②上弦。③使緊；收緊。④使緊張；使興奮。⑤去(豆莢等)之筋。⑥成一串列排起；排成一列。⑦〖俚〗欺騙。⑧以串起的東西裝飾。—*v.i.* ①成串；魚貫而進。②(膠等)引長成絲。***string along*** a. 欺騙。b. 同意 (亦作 **string along with**). c. 信任；對…有信心。d. 使(人)等待；吊(人)胃口。***string out*** a. 拖長；延伸。b. 延長；拖延。***string up***〖俗〗絞死。—**less**, *adj.* —**like**, *adj.*

string band 絃樂隊。

string bass 〖音樂〗最低音大提琴 (=

double bass).
string bean ①未成熟之莢可食用的各種豆類。②此種豆類之豆莢。③高而瘦的人。
string·board ['strɪŋˌbord; 'striŋbɔːd] *n.* 〖建築〗掩蓋梯級旁側之板。
string correspondent 特約記者。(亦作 **stringer**)
string·course ['strɪŋˌkors; 'striŋkɔːs] *n.* 〖建築〗線脚層; 建築物表面凸出之水平帶狀裝飾。
stringed instrument 絃樂器。
strin·gen·cy ['strɪndʒənsɪ; 'strindʒənsi] *n., pl.* **-cies.** ①嚴格; 嚴厲。②銀錢短少;手頭很緊。③有力;說服力。
strin·gen·do [strɪn'dʒɛndo; strin'dʒendou] 〖義〗 *adj.* 〖音樂〗漸速的。
strin·gent ['strɪndʒənt; 'strindʒənt] *adj.* ①嚴格的; 苛刻的。②迫切的; 緊要的。③缺乏現金的; 銀根緊的。④令人信服的; 有力的。 **—ly,** *adv.*
string·er ['strɪŋə; 'striŋə] *n.* ①張絃者;上絃者。②〖建築〗縱桁;長桁;繫樑。③〖造船〗承樑材;艙內縱貫材。④〖鐵路〗縱枕木。⑤〖新聞〗特約記者(=string correspondent). ⑥(用來穿已捕得之魚的)結實的繩子。⑦按能力或技術而編排的隊員。
string·halt ['strɪŋ'hɔlt; 'striŋ'hɔːlt] *n.* 〖獸醫〗(馬之)跛行症。(亦作**springhalt**) **—ed, —y,** *adj.*
string orchestra 絃樂團。
string·piece ['strɪŋˌpis; 'striŋpiːs] *n.* 〖建築〗橫樑。
string player 演奏絃樂器者。
string quartet ①絃樂四重奏曲。②絃樂四重奏團。
string tie 細窄之橫領結。
string·y ['strɪŋɪ; 'striŋi] *adj.,* **string·i·er, string·i·est.** ①似繩的;似帶的。②成絲的;黏連的。③纖維質多的;多筋的。④肌肉發達的;強健的。 **—string·i·ness,** *n.*
‡strip¹ [strɪp; strip] *v.,* **stripped** or **stript, strip·ping.** *—v.t.* ①剝去;脫去;取去;使裸。He *stripped* off his coat. 他脫去上衣。②剝奪。to *strip* a man of his honors. 剝奪人之榮譽。③搶刼;偷。④弄掉(螺釘等)之螺線。⑤弄掉(齒輪等)之齒。⑥擠乾(牛)之奶;擠盡(牛乳)。⑦將(菸葉)自枝上摘下。⑧拆去;拆卸。⑨將礦脈上之土挖走使(礦脈)暴露。*—v.i.* ①脫衣;裸露。to *strip* for a bath. 脫衣沐浴。②跳脫衣舞。③被剝去。Bananas *strip* easily. 香蕉容易剝皮。④搶刼。
strip²** *n.* ①狹長之一條或一片。a *strip* of paper. 一片紙。a comic *strip.* 連環圖畫;連載漫畫。②〖航空〗狹長之跑道。③(有時S-)在市區或郊區兩旁有商店、加油站、餐廳、酒吧密集的街道。④三張以上相連的一條郵票。⑤報章雜誌上之連環圖畫。a cartoon *strip.* 連環卡通。tear off a strip*** 〖英俚〗責罵; 申斥。*—v.t.* 切成狹長之片條。
strip cropping 〖農〗帶狀耕作法。(亦作 **strip farming, strip planting**)
stripe¹** [straɪp; straip] *n., v.,* **striped, strip·ing.** *—n.* ①斑紋;條紋;鑲條;邊條。A tiger has *stripes.* 虎有斑紋。②種類;性質;派。③(*pl.*)(軍中之)臂章;袖章。④鞭之抽打;鞭打。get one's stripes*** 升官。***lose one's stripes*** 降級。***Stars and Stripes*** 星條旗; 美國國旗。*—v.t.* 加以條紋; 鑲邊。 **—less,** *adj.*
***stripe²** *n.* ①一記鞭打;一擊。②一鞭或一擊所造成之痕跡。
***striped** [straɪpt; straipt] *adj.* 有條紋的。
striped-pants ['straɪpt'pænts; 'straipt'pænts] *adj.* 〖俗〗①外交使節團的;有關外交使節團的。②外交的;表外交特徵的。
strip film 幻燈式的影片。
strip·ling ['strɪplɪŋ; 'stripliŋ] *n.* 青年;小夥子。
strip mine 地面礦場。
strip-mine ['strɪpˌmaɪn; 'stripmain] *v.t.,* **-mined, -min·ing.** 從地面礦場採(礦)。
strip·pa·ble ['strɪpəbl; 'stripəbl] *adj.* 可剝奪的;可脫掉的。
strip·per ['strɪpə; 'stripə] *n.* ①〖美俚〗演脫衣舞者;赤裸之婦女。②剝奪者; 奪取者;剝者。③摘取菸葉者。④剝毛之梳; 剝毛具;剝樹皮用具。⑤乳將盡之牛。⑥截穗機。⑦沿邊有特殊裝飾, 於洗牌後能從任何位置抽出之紙牌。
strip·tease ['strɪpˌtiz; 'stripti:z] *n.* 〖美〗脫衣舞。*—v.i.* 跳脫衣舞。
strip teaser 表演脫衣舞之舞女;脫衣舞孃。(亦作 **stripteaser**)
stri·sci·an·do [ˌstriʃɪ'ɑndo; ˌstriːʃi'ɑːndou] *adj. & adv.* 〖音樂〗滑唱的 (地); 滑奏的(地)。
***strive** [straɪv; straiv] *v.i.,* **strove** [strov; strouv], **striv·en** ['strɪvən; 'strivn], **striv·ing.** ①努力;奮勉。to *strive* for liberty. 力爭自由。②奮鬥; 抗爭; 鬥爭 〖with, against〗. **—striv·er,** *n.*
strobe light [strob~; stroub~] 一種可連續使用的攝影閃光燈。(亦作 **stroboscopic light**)
strob·ile ['strɑbɪl; 'strɔbil] *n.* 〖植物〗(松毬等之)毬果。(亦作 **strobil**)
stro·bo·scope ['strobəˌskop; 'stroubəskoup] *n.* (斷續)光測頻器。
stro·bo·tron ['strobətrɑn; 'stroubətrɔn] *n.* (用作光測頻器光源的) 一種充有化學氣體的電子管。
stroke¹** [strok; strouk] *n., v.,* **stroked, strok·ing.** *—n.* ①打擊; 一打; 一擊。a *stroke* of lightning. 閃電之閃擊。②敲聲;(鐘的)鳴聲。We arrived at the *stroke* of three. 鐘鳴三響時我們到達。③一動; 一划。④筆畫。⑤(疾病)突然發作;中風。⑥成就。⑦一段運氣;意外事故。What a *stroke* of luck! 多幸運啊!⑧(心臟的)鼓動;脈搏。⑨努力。⑩手段;策劃。⑪尾槳手(指揮全船划槳快慢的主要划手)。⑫〖運動〗擊球。⑬一次完成之動作。⑭(文章)風格。⑮工作量。⑯(打字機)一擊。at a*** (or ***one***) ***stroke*** 一下子;一舉。***keep strokes*** 齊一動作;齊着划槳。*—v.t.* ①划(船)之尾槳;充當…的尾槳手。②打(球)。③用橫線劃去。④(時鐘)敲擊報(時)。**—strok·er,** *n.*
stroke²** *v.,* **stroked, strok·ing,** *n.* *—v.t.* 撫摸。stroke a person down*** 安撫某人。***stroke a person*** (***up***) ***the wrong way*** 逗惱人;惹人;擦人。*—n.* 撫摸。
stroke oar ①尾槳。②划尾槳者。
stroll** [strol; stroul] *v.i.* 漫步;遨遊;巡遊。*—n.* 漫步; 遨遊; 巡遊。 ***take (or ***go for***) ***a stroll*** 散步。**—ing,** *adj.*
stroll·er ['strolə; 'stroulə] *n.* ①漫步者;遨遊者。②巡遊藝人。③四輪嬰兒車。
‡strong [strɔŋ; strɔŋ] *adj.,* **strong·er, strong·est,** *adv.* *—adj.* ①健壯的; 強固的;堅强的;强大的。a *strong* man. 健壯之人。a *strong* wind. 强烈之風。②有力的。*strong* arguments. 有力的議論。③濃烈的;强烈的。*strong* tea. 濃茶。④足達某數的;實足的。⑤有强烈味道的;有臭味的。*strong* seasoning. 味

道強烈的調味品。⑥熱心的;強硬的。a *strong* dislike. 深惡。⑦〖文法〗動詞變化不規則的;無字尾變化,而以其中母音字母變化的(如 give, gave; find, found 等是)。⑧〖語音〗重讀的。⑨〖商〗價格堅挺的。Prices (*or* Markets) are *strong*. 價格堅挺。⑩堅毅的;堅決的。*strong* under temptation. 不爲誘惑所動。⑪清楚而有力的;高聲的。⑫富於某種東西的。a *strong* hand in trumps. 有很多王牌的一手好牌。⑬堅決不移的;強烈的。⑭強烈的(如光線、顏色等)。⑮〖光學〗倍數大的。⑯徹底的;熱心的。***one's strong point*** 個人的長處;優點。***strong language*** 怒言;罵人話。***strong meat*** 不容易消化或接受的手段、教訓、讀物等。—*adv.*①強有力地;猛烈地。②強勁地;虎虎有生氣地。—**ly,** *adv.*

strong-arm [ˈstrɔŋˌɑrm; ˈstrɔŋɑːm] *adj.* 〖俗〗用體力的;有體力的;暴烈的;強迫的。—*v.t.* 〖俗〗對…施用暴力;強奪。

strong·box [ˈstrɔŋˌbɑks; ˈstrɔŋbɔks] *n.* 鐵櫃;保險櫃。

strong drink 含有高度酒精之飲料。

strong-head·ed [ˈstrɔŋˈhɛdɪd; ˈstrɔŋˈhedid] *adj.* ①頑固的。②智能高超的。

***strong·hold** [ˈstrɔŋˌhold; ˈstrɔŋhould] *n.* ①要塞;堡壘。②根據地。③(最後的)中心地;大本營。

strong man ①(馬戲等中)大力士。②強人;獨裁者。③一機構中最有影響力的人;紅人。(亦作 **strongman**)

strong-mind·ed [ˈstrɔŋˈmaɪndɪd; ˈstrɔŋˈmaindid] *adj.* ①決斷的;有雄心的。②〖蔑〗(女性之)自稱在精神上社會上與男人平等的。—**ly,** *adv.* —**ness,** *n.*

strong·point [ˈstrɔŋˌpɔɪnt; ˈstrɔŋpɔint] *n.* 〖軍〗防守據點;要塞。

strong room (儲藏貴重物品之)保險室。(亦作 **strongroom**)

strong suit ①強組(紙牌戲中含有大牌的一組)。②優點。

strong-voiced [ˈstrɔŋˈvɔɪst; ˈstrɔŋˈvɔist] *adj.* 聲音洪亮的。

strong-willed [ˈstrɔŋˈwɪld; ˈstrɔŋˈwild] *adj.* ①意志堅強的。②頑固的。

stron·ti·um [ˈstrɑnʃɪəm; ˈstrɔnʃiəm] *n.* 〖化〗鍶(一種金屬元素,符號 Sr)。

strontium 90 〖化〗鍶九十(氫彈爆炸時釋放的一種放射性同位素,如人體吸收過量能造成骨癌)。(亦作 **radiostrontium**)

strop [strɑp; strɔp] *n., v.,* **stropped, strop·ping.** —*n.* 磨剃刀的皮條;革砥。—*v.t.* 在革砥上磨(剃刀)。

stro·phe [ˈstrofɪ; ˈstroufi] *n.* ①希臘頌神歌的一部分。②一節詩。

struck [strʌk; strʌk] *v.* pt. & pp. of **strike.** —*adj.* 因罷工關了門的;受罷工影響的。a *struck* plant. 因罷工而關閉的工廠。

struck jury 〖法律〗由原告與被告雙方律師在一張列有四十八個候選人名單中各剔除相等人數後所餘之人組成的陪審團。

struc·tur·al [ˈstrʌktʃərəl; ˈstrʌktʃərəl] *adj.* ①建築的;建築用的。②結構的。③由經濟結構所引起的。

structural formula 〖化〗結構式。

struc·tur·al·ism [ˈstrʌktʃərəˌlɪzəm; ˈstrʌktʃərəlizəm] *n.* ①=**structural psychology.** ②結構主義;構造主義。—**struc·tur·al·ist,** *n., adj.*

structural linguistics 結構語言學。

struc·tur·al·ly [ˈstrʌktʃərəlɪ; ˈstrʌktʃərəli] *adv.* 在結構上。

structural psychology 構造心理學。

***struc·ture** [ˈstrʌktʃɚ; ˈstrʌktʃə] *n., v.,* **-tured, -tur·ing.** —*n.* ①構造;結構。②建造法;建築物的樣式。③建築物。④構造物。—*v.t.* 構造;建造。

stru·del [ˈʃtrudəl, ˈstrudəl; ˈʃtruːdəl, ˈstruːdəl] *n.* 一種酸麪所做之食品(由薄如紙之麪片夾蘋果、草莓、乾酪等,捲之焙食)。

‡**strug·gle** [ˈstrʌgl; ˈstrʌgl] *v.,* **-gled, -gling,** *n.* —*v.i.* ①努力;奮鬥。The poor have to *struggle* for a living. 窮人必須爲生活而奮鬥。②掙扎。—*n.* ①努力;奮鬥;競爭。the *struggle* for existence. 生存競爭。②掙扎。③鬥爭;戰爭。—**strug·gler,** *n.*

strug·gling [ˈstrʌglɪŋ; ˈstrʌgliŋ] *adj.* ①掙扎的;鬥爭的。②必須努力奮鬥才能謀生的。

strum [strʌm; strʌm] *v.,* **strummed, strum·ming,** *n.* —*v.t.* 漫不經心地亂彈(琴等)。—*v.i.* (在琴或絃樂器上)亂彈〖on〗。—*n.* 漫不經心而亂彈的聲音;亂彈。—**mer,** *n.*

stru·ma [ˈstrumə; ˈstruːmə] *n., pl.* **-mae** [-mi; -miː]. ①〖醫〗瘰癧。②〖醫〗甲狀腺腫。③〖植物〗瘤狀突起。

stru·mous [ˈstruməs; ˈstruːməs] *adj.* ①〖醫〗瘰癧的;生瘰癧的。②〖醫〗甲狀腺突起的;生甲狀腺突起的。③〖植物〗瘤狀突起的;有瘤狀突起的。

strum·pet [ˈstrʌmpɪt; ˈstrʌmpit] *n.* 娼妓。

strut**[1] [strʌt; strʌt] *v.,* **strut·ted, strut·ting,** *n.* —*v.i.* 昂首闊步而行;神氣十足地行走。—*v.t.* 昂首闊步地在…上行走。strut one's stuff*** 炫耀;自炫。—*n.* 高視闊步;神氣十足之行走。—**ter,** *n.*

strut[2] *n., v.,* **strut·ted, strut·ting.** —*n.* 〖建築〗支柱;撐木。—*v.t.* 用支柱支撐。

strych·nine [ˈstrɪknɪn; ˈstriknin] *n.* 〖化〗番木鱉鹼(一種毒性強烈的無色結晶鹽基,分子式爲 $C_{21}H_{22}N_2O_2$)。(亦作 **strychnia, strychnin, strychnina**)—**strych·nic,** *adj.*

Sts. Saints.

Stu·art [ˈstjuɚt; stjuət] *n.* 斯圖亞特王室(1371–1603 統治蘇格蘭, 1603–1714 統治蘇格蘭與英格蘭的王室)。

stub [stʌb; stʌb] *n., v.,* **stubbed, stub·bing.** —*n.* ①殘株;殘片;殘根;殘段。②(支票簿等的)存根。the *stubs* of a checkbook. 支票簿存根。③任何短小粗鈍之物。④票根。⑤舊馬蹄釘(=stub nail)。⑥筆尖粗短之鋼筆。—*v.t.* ①拔除(土地)之殘根;掘除(土地)之殘株。②連根拔除;根除。③絆(脚);戳(脚趾)。④按熄(燃着的香烟)。—**ber,** *n.*

stub·bed [ˈstʌbɪd; ˈstʌbid] *adj.*①像殘株的;短的;短而粗的。②覆有殘株的。③粗豪的。

***stub·ble** [ˈstʌbl; ˈstʌbl] *n.* ①(常 *pl.*)(稻等)殘株。②短鬚。③任何粗短之生長物。

stub·bly [ˈstʌblɪ; ˈstʌbli] *adj.* ①長滿殘株的。②殘株一般的;似硬毛的。

***stub·born** [ˈstʌbən; ˈstʌbən] *adj.* ①堅定的;堅決的;堅強的。②固執的;頑固的;剛愎的;倔強的。③難處理的;難應付的。Facts are *stubborn* things. 事實是難搪塞之物。—**ly,** *adv.* —**ness,** *n.*

stub·by [ˈstʌbɪ; ˈstʌbi] *adj.,* **-bi·er, -bi·est.** ①短而粗的。②短粗而濃密的。③多樹樁的;多殘株的;似殘株的。

stub nail ①短粗之釘。②舊馬蹄釘。

stub pen 筆尖粗短之鋼筆。

stub wing 飛機上靠近機身部分之翼;短翼。(亦作 **stubwing**)

stuc·co 〔'stʌko; 'stʌkou〕 *n., pl.* **-coes, -cos,** *v.,* **-coed, -co·ing.** —*n.* ①(粉飾用之)灰泥。②=**stuccowork.** —*v.t.* 塗以灰泥;粉刷。

stuc·co·work 〔'stʌko,wɝk; 'stʌkouwə:k〕 *n.* 灰泥工。

stuck 〔stʌk; stʌk〕 *v.* pt. & pp. of **stick²**. ***stuck on*** 〖俚〗被(人、地方或事)迷住。

stuck-up 〔'stʌk'ʌp; 'stʌk'ʌp〕 *adj.* 〖俗〗倨傲的;自大的;傲慢的。

***stud¹** 〔stʌd; stʌd〕 *n., v.,* **stud·ded, stud·ding.** —*n.* ①飾釘。②(襯衣之)領扣。③(建築物之)直柱;間柱。④〖機械〗雙頭螺栓;柱螺栓。—*v.t.*①飾以釘、鈕扣或類似之物。②漫布;滿布。a composition *studded* with errors. 錯誤連篇的作文。③供直柱;裝柱螺栓。

stud² *n.* ①(專爲繁殖、打獵、賽馬等飼養的)馬;馬羣。②養馬場;馬匹繁殖場。③〖美〗種馬。④〖俚〗無憂無慮而能自立的年輕人。***at*** (or ***in***) ***stud*** (雄性動物)可供接種的。—*adj.* ①種馬的。②爲接種而保留的。

stud·book 〔'stʌd,buk; 'stʌdbuk〕 *n.* 馬種系譜;馬的血統簿。(亦作 **stud book**)

stud·ding 〔'stʌdɪŋ; 'stʌdiŋ〕 *n.* ①間柱或小桁之集合稱。②做間柱或小桁等之材料。

stud·ding·sail 〔'stʌdɪŋ,sel; 'stʌdiŋseil, 'stʌnsl〕 *n.* 〖航海〗副帆;翼橫帆。(亦作 **studding sail, stunsail, stuns'l**)

‡**stu·dent** 〔'stjudn̩t; 'stju:dənt〕 *n.* ①學生(英國專指大專學生,但一般則泛指各級學生,尤以美國爲然)。a medical *student.* 醫科學生。②學者;研究者。He's a *student* of history. 他是歷史學者。 ***student interpreter*** (預備進入外交界之)見習翻譯官。

student council 學生自治會。

student teacher 實習老師。(亦作 **intern, practice teacher, pupil teacher**)

student union 大學之學生活動中心。

stud·farm 〔'stʌd,fɑrm; 'stʌdfɑ:m〕 *n.* 種馬場。

stud·horse 〔'stʌd,hɔrs; 'stʌdhɔ:s〕 *n.* 種馬。

***stud·ied** 〔'stʌdɪd; 'stʌdid〕 *adj.* 經細心計畫的;故意的。—**ly,** *adv.* —**ness,** *n.*

***stu·di·o** 〔'stjudɪ,o; 'stju:diou, -djou〕 *n., pl.* **-di·os.** ①(畫家、照相師等之)畫室;工作室;技術室。a music *studio.* 音樂(練習)室。②電影製片場。③播音室;電視廣播室。

studio couch 可以當牀用的沙發。

stu·di·ous 〔'stjudɪəs; 'stju:djəs〕 *adj.* ①好學的;用功的。②注意的;用心的。③細心計劃的;有意的。④〖雅〗獻身於或有助於研究的。—**ly,** *adv.*

‡**stud·y** 〔'stʌdɪ; 'stʌdi〕 *n., pl.* **stud·ies,** *v.,* **stud·ied, stud·y·ing.** —*n.* ①讀書;求學。②仔細檢查;檢討;調查。a *study* of foreign trade. 國外貿易之探討。③研究的對象;學科。to make a *study* of plants. 研究植物。④研究結果之書面報告。⑤書房。He was busy in his *study*. 他在書房裏面用功。⑥(文學、藝術的)專論。⑦(故事、圖畫等的)草稿;速寫;素描。⑧〖音樂〗練習曲。⑨努力之目的。⑩引人注意或值得注意之物。 His face was a *study*. 他的面貌能吸引人。⑪沉思;默想。⑫(常 *pl.*)研究。to pursue one's *studies*. 從事研究。⑬演員或從事其他職業之人(就其能否强記臺詞等而言)。John is a quick *study*. 約翰是一個過目能誦的人。—*v.i.* ①求學;研究。He is *studying* for the Church. 他正讀書準備作牧師。②沉思;默想。③努力;苦心。—*v.t.* ①學習;研究。②仔細察閱。③想出;細索;設計。

study group 學習研討會。

study hall ①(學校)課堂。②自修時間。

‡**stuff** 〔stʌf; stʌf〕 *n.* ①材料;原料;物品。food *stuff*. 食品。green *stuff*. 菜蔬。doctor's *stuff*. 〖俗〗藥。②要素;素質。That boy has good *stuff* in him. 那孩子的素質很好。③織物;毛織物。④廢物;劣品。⑤蠢笨的言辭或思想;無聊話;荒唐事。a lot of *stuff* and nonsense. 一派胡言。⑥可吞下的東西,如食物、飲料、藥等。⑦〖運動俚〗 **a.** 〖棒球〗投手投球的各種手法、花樣等等。 **b.** 加諸棒球、網球或保齡球的旋轉或速度。⑧〖俗〗新聞、文學、藝術、戲劇、音樂或其他作品。⑨〖俗〗自己的職業;本行之事。He knows his *stuff*. 他了解自己的本行。⑩濕紙漿。—*v.t.* ①塡塞;塞〖常with, into〗。②製(死動物)之標本;剝製。*stuffed* birds. 製成標本的鳥。③阻塞;窒息〖常 up〗。④使飽食。⑤塞餡於(鷄、火鷄等)之腹中(以便烹煮)。⑥〖英〗將假選票放入(投票櫃裏)。⑦使(腦筋裏)裝滿一大堆事實、細節。—*v.i.* 飽食;狼吞虎嚥。

stuffed shirt 〔stʌft~; stʌft~〕 〖俚〗虛誇自負而實際上無足輕重的人。

stuff·ing 〔'stʌfɪŋ; 'stʌfiŋ〕 *n.* ①塡塞物。②烹煮前塞於鷄、鴨、火鷄腹中的麫包屑與香料等。③裝塡;塡塞。***knock*** (or ***beat***) ***the stuffing out of a person*** 〖俗〗 **a.** 挫某人之銳氣。 **b.** 在打鬥中擊敗某人。 **c.** 使某人疲倦無力。

stuff·y 〔'stʌfɪ; 'stʌfi〕 *adj.,* **stuff·i·er, stuff·i·est.** ①缺乏新鮮空氣的;通風不良的。②索然無味的。③窒悶的;阻塞的。④〖俗〗易吃驚的;易生氣的;慍怒的。⑤拘謹的;保守的。⑥自命不凡的。—**stuff·i·ly,** *adv.* —**stuff·i·ness,** *n.*

stug·gy 〔'stʌgɪ; 'stʌgi〕 *adj.,* **-gi·er, -gi·est.** 〖英方〗矮胖的。

Stu·ka 〔'stukə; 'stu:kə〕 *n.* 第二次世界大戰時德國的一種俯衝轟炸機。

stul·ti·fi·ca·tion 〔,stʌltəfə'keʃən; ,stʌltifi'keiʃən〕 *n.* 愚弄;被愚弄。

stul·ti·fy 〔'stʌltə,faɪ; 'stʌltifai〕 *v.t.,* **-fied, -fy·ing.** ①愚弄;使顯得愚蠢;使失體面。②使失效;使歸無效。③〖法律〗聲明(某人)精神錯亂。

stum 〔stʌm; stʌm〕 *n., v.,* **stummed, stum·ming.** —*n.* ①半發酵或未發酵之葡萄汁。②加葡萄汁後增進發酵之酒。—*v.t.* (加葡萄汁)使(酒)增進發酵。

***stum·ble** 〔'stʌmbl̩; 'stʌmbl〕 *v.,* **-bled, -bling,** *n.* —*v.i.* ①顚躓;絆跌。②蹣跚而行。③遲疑而笨拙地說話、作事等。to *stumble* over one's words. 結結巴巴地說話。④錯誤;做錯。⑤偶然發現;偶然遇到〖on, upon, across〗。—*v.t.* ①使顚躓。②使蹉跎;使迷惑。—*n.* ①顚躓。②錯誤。③墮落。—**stum·bling·ly,** *adv.*

stum·ble·bum 〔'stʌmbl̩,bʌm; 'stʌmblbʌm〕 *n.* 〖俚〗①笨手笨脚的二流拳擊手。②笨頭笨腦的人。

stumbling block ①阻礙物;妨害;困難。②使人絆倒之物。

stu·mer 〔'stjumɚ; 'stju:mə〕 *n.* 〖英俚〗①假支票;空頭支票;僞幣。②假的東西;冒牌貨。③在比賽中沒有贏過的馬。

stump** 〔stʌmp; stʌmp〕 *n.* ①(樹被砍倒後遺下之)殘幹;樹樁。②殘餘部分。③作政治性演說的地方。④笨重的脚步(聲)。⑤木腿。⑥(*pl.*)〖俚〗腿;脚。⑦矮胖之人;粗短之人。⑧〖美俗〗挑釁。⑨(作鉛筆畫、炭畫等用之)擦筆。⑩〖板球〗(三柱門之)柱。⑪蛀牙或斷牙之牙根。on the stump*** 作政治演說。***stir***

one's stumps 行；急行。***take the stump*** 作政治演說旅行。***up a stump*** 〖美俗〗不能行動、說話等；不知如何是好。—*v.i.* ①以艱難而笨拙的步伐行走。②作政治演說。—*v.t.* ①使成殘幹。②使(趾)觸碰一物上。③從(土地)除去殘幹。④〖美〗在(某地區)作政治演說。⑤〖美俗〗困惑；難倒。⑥〖美俗〗挑釁；抵抗。

stump·er ['stʌmpɚ; 'stʌmpə] *n.* 〖俗〗①難題。②〖板球〗守三柱門者。③〖俗〗作競選演說者。

stump speaker 作政治演說者。

stump speech 政治演說。

stump·y ['stʌmpɪ; 'stʌmpi] *adj.*, **stump·i·er, stump·i·est.** ①短而粗的。②多殘株的。③似殘株的。

*__stun__ [stʌn; stʌn] *v.*, **stunned, stun·ning,** *n.* —*v.t.* ①使昏暈。②使吃驚；使目瞪口呆。We were *stunned* by the sudden news. 我們因聽到這突然的消息而目瞪口呆。③磨損（建築用之石頭)。—*n.* ①使不省人事之行爲；使吃驚之行爲。②昏暈；目瞪口呆。

stun gas 令人暫時神智混亂的瓦斯。

stun·ner ['stʌnɚ; 'stʌnə] *n.* ①令人驚愕、昏暈的人或物。②〖俗〗極惹人注目的人或物。③〖俚〗專家。

stun·ning ['stʌnɪŋ; 'stʌniŋ] *adj.* ①使不省人事的；使人眩暈的。②〖俗〗出色的；極美的。

stun·sail ['stʌnsḷ; 'stʌnsl] *n.* =**studdingsail.** (亦作 **stuns'l**)

*__stunt__[1] [stʌnt; stʌnt] *v.t.* 阻礙…之生長、發育或發展。—*n.* ①生長、發育或發展的阻礙。②生長或發育受阻礙之人、動物或植物；發育不完全的動物或植物。

stunt[2] *n.* 〖俗〗①絕技；驚人的技藝。②引人注意的行動；(政治家的)自我宣傳。③特技飛行。—*adj.* ①表演絕技的。②特技飛行的。—*v.t.* 以(飛機)表演特技飛行。—*v.i.* 表演絕技。

stunt·ed ['stʌntɪd; 'stʌntid] *adj.* ①發育不全的；矮小的。②停止發育的；生長或發育受到阻礙的。

stunt man 〖電影〗大明星的替身(代替演員表演危險動作者)。(女性爲 **stunt girl**)

stupe [stjup; stju:p] *n.* ①〖醫〗熱濕布；溫布。②〖英方〗愚人。

stu·pe·fa·cient [ˌstjupə'feʃənt; ˌstju:pə'feiʃənt] *adj.* 使麻醉的。—*n.* 麻醉藥物。

stu·pe·fac·tion [ˌstjupə'fækʃən; ˌstju:pi'fækʃən] *n.* 恍惚；昏迷；驚倒。

stu·pe·fy ['stjupəˌfaɪ; 'stju:pifai] *v.t.*, **-fied** [-faɪd; -faid], **-fy·ing.** 使失知覺；使失神；使昏迷；使不勝驚愕。

stu·pe·fy·ing·ly ['stjupəˌfaɪɪŋlɪ; 'stju:pifaiiŋli] *adv.* 使人麻木地；不勝驚愕地。

stu·pen·dous [stju'pɛndəs; stju:'pendəs] *adj.* 驚人的；巨大的；偉大的。—**ly,** *adv.* —**ness,** *n.*

*__stu·pid__ ['stjupɪd; 'stju:pid, 'stjup-] *adj.* ①愚蠢的；魯鈍的。a *stupid* person. 愚人。②無趣味的。③暈眩的；昏迷不醒的。—*n.* 〖俗〗愚人；笨伯。—**ly,** *adv.* —**ness,** *n.*

stu·pid·i·ty [stju'pɪdətɪ; stju:'piditi] *n.*, *pl.* **-ties** for ②. ①愚蠢；魯鈍。②愚蠢之行爲或言語等。

stu·por ['stjupɚ; 'stju:pə] *n.* ①昏迷；不省人事；恍惚。②智力或道德方面之麻木不仁。—**ous,** *adj.*

*__stur·dy__[1] ['stɝdɪ; 'stə:di] *adj.*, **-di·er, -di·est.** ①强的；壯健的。②堅定的；不屈的。*sturdy* faith. 堅定的信念。③(植物等)强壯的。—**stur·di·ly,** *adv.* —**stur·di·ness,** *n.*

stur·dy[2] *n.* 〖獸醫〗(羊之)眩暈症；暈倒症。

stur·geon ['stɝdʒən; 'stə:dʒən] *n.*, *pl.* **-geons, -geon.** 鱘魚；鰉鮫。

stut·ter ['stʌtɚ; 'stʌtə] *v.i.* 口吃；結巴。—*v.t.* 口吃而言；結結巴巴地說。—*n.* 口吃；結巴。—**ing·ly,** *adv.*

St. Vi·tus dance [~'vaɪtəs~; ~'vaitəs~] 舞蹈病 (=chorea)。(亦作 **St. Vitus's dance**)

sty[1] [staɪ; stai] *n.*, *pl.* **sties,** *v.*, **stied, sty·ing.** —*n.* ①豬欄。②汚濁之所。③墮落荒唐的地方；淫穢之地。—*v.t.* 將…養在豬欄或汚濁之處。—*v.i.* 住在豬欄或似豬欄的地方。

sty[2] *n.* 〖醫〗瞼腺炎(俗作麥粒腫)。(亦作 **stye**)

Styg·i·an ['stɪdʒɪən; 'stidʒiən] *adj.* ①陰間之 Styx 河的。②黑暗的；幽暗的。③地獄的。④(誓言等)不能收回的；不可破壞的。

‡**style** [staɪl; stail] *n.*, *v.*, **styled, styl·ing.** —*n.* ①時式；時尚。Her dress is out of *style*. 她的穿着不時髦。②文體；風格；作風；格式；樣式；法式。③稱呼；尊稱。④花柱。⑤(蠟板上書寫的)尖筆。⑥似尖筆之物；雕刻刀、日晷儀之針、指針等。⑦〖印刷〗體例；某一出版商或印刷所之拼字、標點、分字等之方式。⑧生活方式(指費用、誇耀等)。⑨豪華的生活。to live in *style*. 過著豪華的生活。⑩計時的方式。***Old Style*** 根據 Julian 曆的計時法。—*v.t.* ①稱呼。②〖美〗(按某型式或新式樣)設計。③按(印刷)體例修改。—*v.i.* 用雕刻刀等做裝飾工作。—**less,** *adj.*

style·book ['staɪlˌbuk; 'stailbuk] *n.* ①體例說明書(印刷廠、編輯、作家等所用者)。②時裝圖樣書。

sty·let ['staɪlɪt; 'stailit] *n.* ①短劍。②〖醫〗a. 探針。b. 通管絲。③〖動物〗錐狀體。

styl·ish ['staɪlɪʃ; 'stailiʃ] *adj.* ①合乎時尚的；時髦的；漂亮的。②態度優雅的；技巧而純熟的。—**ly,** *adv.* —**ness,** *n.*

styl·ist ['staɪlɪst; 'stailist] *n.* ①文體家；文體批評家。②(衣服、裝飾等之)設計家。③保持某種時尚的人。

sty·lis·tic [staɪ'lɪstɪk; stai'listik] *adj.* 文體的；關於文體的。(亦作 **stylistical**) —**al·ly,** *adv.*

sty·lis·tics [staɪ'lɪstɪks; stai'listiks] *n.* 文體論；文體學。

sty·lite ['staɪlaɪt; 'stailait] *n.* 〖宗教〗(中世紀住於高柱上的)苦修者。—**sty·lit·ic,** *adj.*

styl·ize ['staɪˌlaɪz; 'stailaiz] *v.t.*, **-ized, -iz·ing.** ①使合於某種風格。②使合於傳統風格；使因襲。③使合於既定規則或不順應自然。—**styl·i·za·tion,** *n.*

sty·lo ['staɪlo; 'stailou] *n.* 〖俗〗=**stylograph.**

sty·lo·graph ['staɪləˌgræf; 'stailə-grɑ:f] *n.* 筆尖爲細小圓管之自來水筆。—**ic,** —**i·cal,** *adj.* —**i·cal·ly,** *adv.*

sty·lus ['staɪləs; 'stailəs] *n.*, *pl.* **-li** [-laɪ; -lai], **-lus·es.** ①(古時在蠟上寫字用的)尖筆。②(留聲機及灌唱片用的)唱針。③〖解剖〗針突。④似筆的書寫工具。⑤各種儀表上自動指出圖線的針。

sty·mie ['staɪmɪ; 'staimi] *n.*, *v.*, **-mied, -mie·ing.** —*n.* ①〖高爾夫〗介於自己的球與球穴之間的對方的球。②此種位置。—*v.i.* ①從中作梗。②完全阻礙。(亦作 **stymy, stimy**)

styp·tic ['stɪptɪk; 'stiptik] *adj.* 〖醫〗(亦作 **styptical**)止血的。—*n.* 〖醫〗止血劑。

sty·rene ['staɪrin; 'stairi:n] *n.* 〖化〗苯乙烯(一種無色或淡黃色之芳香液體)。

Styx 〔stɪks; stiks〕 *n.* 【希臘神話】冥河(死者之靈魂經此河被載渡至冥府)。 ***cross the Styx*** 死。

su·a·ble 〔'suəbl; 'sju:əbl〕 *adj.* 可起訴的;可控告的。

sua·sion 〔'sweʒən; 'sweiʒən〕 *n.* 勸說;勸告;勸誘。

sua·sive 〔'swesɪv; 'sweisiv〕 *adj.* 有勸導力的;有說服力的。

suave 〔swɑv;sweiv〕*adj.* 溫和的;嫻雅的。

sua·vi·ter in mo·do, for·ti·ter in re 〔'swævɪtəɪn'modo, 'fɔrtɪtəɪn'ri; 'swævitərin'moudou, 'fɔ:titərin'ri:〕【拉】態度溫和而行動果斷。

sua·vi·ty 〔'swævətɪ; 'swæviti〕 *n., pl.* **-ties.** ①柔和;溫和;和藹;慇懃。②(*pl.*)溫文爾雅之舉止或言談。

sub[1] 〔sʌb; sʌb〕 *n., adj., v.,* **subbed, sub·bing.** —*n.* 【俗】①代理者;替代物。②潛水艇。③僚屬。④【英】(薪水之)預支。⑤ = **sublieutenant.** —*adj.* 【俗】①代理的;替代的。②潛水艇的。③附屬的。—*v.i.* 【俗】代替。

sub[2] 【拉】*prep.* 在…之下(=under).

sub. ①subaltern. ②subject. ③submarine. ④subscription. ⑤substitute. ⑥suburb(an). ⑦subway.

sub- 【字首】表下列各義:①下;在下。例如:subway 地下火車。②往下;更;再。例如:sublease分租。③近;靠近。例如:subarctic 近北極的。④較低;附屬;助理;副;次。例如:subaltern 副官;僚屬。⑤細分;再分;亞。例如:subclass 亞綱。⑥幾分;稍;微。例如:subacid 微酸的。【注意】**sub-** 在 c 前作 suc-;f 前作 suf-;g 前作 sug-;有時在m 前作 sum-;在 p 前作 sup-;在 r 前作 sur-;有時在 c, p, t 前作 sus-.

sub·ac·id 〔sʌb'æsɪd; 'sʌb'æsid〕 *adj.* ①微酸的(水果等)。②稍嚴苛的(批評等)。—**ly,** *adv.* —**ness,** *n.*

sub·a·gent 〔sʌb'edʒənt;'sʌb'eidʒənt〕 *n.* 副代理人;代理人之代理者。

sub·al·pine 〔sʌb'ælpaɪn;'sʌb'ælpain〕 *adj.*①4,000 至 5,500 英尺之間之山的。②阿爾卑斯山麓的。

sub·al·tern 〔səb'ɔltən; 'sʌbltən〕 *n.* ①【英】中尉;少尉。②副官;僚屬。③【邏輯】特稱命題。—*adj.* ①部下的;部屬的。②中尉的;少尉的。③【邏輯】特稱的。

sub·a·quat·ic 〔ˌsʌbə'kwætɪk; 'sʌbə'kwætik〕 *adj.* ①=**subaqueous.** ②生長於水陸之際的(半在水中,半在陸上的)。

sub·a·que·ous 〔sʌb'ekwɪəs; sʌb'eikwiəs〕 *adj.* ①適於水下應用的;適於水下生存的;水下的。②水下形成的;水下生長的。

sub·arc·tic 〔sʌb'ɑrktɪk; 'sʌb'ɑ:ktik〕 *adj.* 北極圈附近地區的;與北極圈緊鄰之以南地區的。

sub·ar·id 〔sʌb'ærɪd; sʌb'ærid〕 *adj.* 稍乾燥的。

sub·as·sem·bly 〔ˌsʌbə'sɛmblɪ;'sʌbə'sembli〕 *n., pl.* **-blies.** (機械之)組件(由若干零件合成)。

sub·at·om 〔sʌb'ætəm; 'sʌb'ætəm〕 *n.* 次原子(指組成原子的質子與電子)。

sub·au·di·tion 〔ˌsʌbɔ'dɪʃən; 'sʌbɔ:'diʃən〕 *n.* ①領會言外之意。②言外之意。

sub·av·er·age 〔sʌb'ævərɪdʒ; 'sʌb'ævəridʒ〕 *adj.* 水準以下的。

sub·base·ment 〔'sʌbˌbesmənt;'sʌbˌbeismənt〕 *n.* 地下室以下之地下室。

sub·chair·man 〔sʌb'tʃɛrmən; 'sʌb'tʃɛəmən〕 *n., pl.* **-men.** 副主席;代主席。

sub·class 〔'sʌbˌklæs; 'sʌbklɑ:s〕 *n.* ①【生物】亞綱。②一種類或階級的主要區分。—*v.t.* 置於亞綱之內。

sub·cla·vi·an 〔sʌb'klevɪən; 'sʌb'kleiviən〕 *adj.* 【解剖】①鎖骨下的。②鎖骨下之血管或肌肉的。—*n.* 鎖骨下之血管。

sub·clin·i·cal 〔sʌb'klɪnəkl; 'sʌb'klinikəl〕 *adj.* 【醫】普通臨床檢查無法查出的輕微症狀的。

sub·com·mit·tee 〔'sʌbkəˌmɪtɪ; 'sʌbkəˌmiti〕 *n.* 小組委員會;附屬委員會。

sub·com·pa·ny 〔'sʌbˌkʌmpənɪ;'sʌbˌkʌmpəni〕 *n., pl.* **-nies.** 附屬公司;子公司。

sub·con·scious 〔sʌb'kɑnʃəs; 'sʌb'kɔnʃəs〕 *adj.* 潛意識的。—*n.* 潛意識;下意識。—**ly,** *adv.* —**ness,** *n.*

sub·con·ti·nent 〔sʌb'kɑntənənt; 'sʌb'kɔntinənt〕 *n.* 次大陸;次洲。—**al,** *adj.*

sub·con·tract 〔*n.* sʌb'kɑntrækt; 'sʌb'kɔntrækt *v.* ˌsʌbkən'trækt; 'sʌbkən'trækt〕 *n.* 副契約;分契;轉契。—*v.t.* 爲…訂立分契或轉契。—*v.i.* 訂立分契或轉契。

sub·con·trac·tor 〔ˌsʌbkən'træktə; 'sʌbkən'træktə〕 *n.* 次承辦人;分包之包商。

sub·con·tra·ry 〔sʌb'kɑntrɛrɪ; 'sʌb'kɔntrəri〕 *n., pl.* **-ries,** *adj.* —*n.* 【邏輯】小反對(命題)。—*adj.* 【邏輯】小反對(命題)的。

sub·cul·ture 〔*v.* sʌb'kʌltʃə;'sʌb'kʌltʃə *n.* 'sʌbˌkʌltʃə; 'sʌbˌkʌltʃə〕 *v.,* **-tured, -tur·ing,** *n.* —*v.t.* 【細菌】次培養。—*n.* ①【細菌】次培養基;次培養菌。②【社會學】**a.** 在某一社會中別於其他的特殊文化、倫理價值。**b.** 屬此種文化的人羣。

sub·cu·ta·ne·ous 〔ˌsʌbkju'tenɪəs; 'sʌbkju:'teiniəs〕 *adj.* ①皮下的。*subcutaneous* injection. 皮下注射。②寄生於皮下的(寄生蟲)。—**ly,** *adv.*

sub·dea·con 〔sʌb'dikən; 'sʌb'di:kən〕 *n.* 【宗教】教堂副執事。

sub·dean 〔sʌb'din; 'sʌb'di:n〕 *n.* 【宗教】助理副主教。

sub·deb 〔sʌb'dɛb;'sʌb'deb〕 *n., adj.* = **subdebutante.**

sub·deb·u·tante 〔sʌbˌdɛbju'tɑnt; 'sʌb'debjutɑ̃:nt〕 *n., adj.* ①即將出現於社交場中之少女(的)。②達到此種年齡之少女(的);妙齡女郎(的)。

sub·de·ca·nal 〔sʌb'dɛkənl; 'sʌbdi'keinl〕 *adj.* 【宗教】助理副主教的。

sub·di·ac·o·nate 〔ˌsʌbdaɪ'ækənɪt; 'sʌbdai'ækənit〕 *n.* 【宗教】副執事之職位。(亦作 **subdeaconate**)

sub·di·vide 〔ˌsʌbdə'vaɪd;'sʌbdi'vaid〕 *v.t. & v.i.,* **-vid·ed, -vid·ing.** 再分;細分。

sub·di·vis·i·ble 〔ˌsʌbdə'vɪzəbl; 'sʌbdi'vizəbl〕 *adj.* 可再分的。

sub·di·vi·sion 〔ˌsʌbdə'vɪʒən; 'sʌbdiˌviʒən〕 *n.* ①細分;再分。②再分成的部分。

sub·dom·i·nant 〔sʌb'dɑmənənt; 'sʌb'dɔminənt〕 *n.* 【音樂】次屬音(各全音階之第四音)。—*adj.* 不很顯著的。

sub·du·al 〔səb'djuəl; səb'dju:əl〕 *n.* ①征服。②抑制。③開墾。④降低;減緩;緩和。

***sub·due** 〔səb'dju; səb'dju:〕 *v.t.,* **-dued, -du·ing.** ①征服;克服;壓制。②降低(聲音);減弱;緩和。a *subdued* voice. 降低的聲音。③開墾。—**sub·du·er,** *n.*

sub·ed·it 〔sʌb'ɛdɪt; 'sʌb'edit〕 *v.t. & v.i.* 【英】爲…副主筆;爲…副編輯。

sub·ed·i·tor 〔sʌb'ɛdɪtə;'sʌb'editə〕 *n.* 副主筆;副編輯。—**i·al,** *adj.*

su·be·re·ous 〔su'bɪrɪəs; su'biəriəs〕

adj. 〖植物〗似軟木的;軟木質的。
su·ber·ose ['sjubə,ros; 'sju:bərous] *adj.* 似軟木的;軟木質的。(亦作 **suberous**)
sub·fam·i·ly [sʌb'fæməlɪ; 'sʌb,fæmili] *n., pl.* **-lies.** 〖生物〗亞科。
sub·freez·ing [sʌb'frizɪŋ; 'sʌb'fri:ziŋ] *adj.* 冰點以下的。
sub·fusc [sʌb'fʌsk; 'sʌbfʌsk] *adj.* 略帶黑色的; 稍暗的。(亦作 **subfuscous, subfusk**)
sub·ge·nus [sʌb'dʒinəs; 'sʌb'dʒi:nəs] *n., pl.* **-gen·er·a** [-'dʒɛnərə; -'dʒenərə], **-ge·nus·es.** 〖生物〗亞屬。—**sub·ge·ner·ic,** *adj.* 「①〖生物〗亞目。②〖數學〗子羣。」
sub·group ['sʌb,grup; 'sʌbgru:p] *n.*
sub·head ['sʌb,hɛd; 'sʌbhed] *n.* ①小標題;副標題。②(學校機關等之)首長的助理。
sub·head·ing ['sʌb,hɛdɪŋ; 'sʌb,hediŋ] *n.* 小標題;副標題;細目。
sub·hu·man [sʌb'hjumən; 'sʌb'hju:mən] *adj.* ①低於人類的。②近於人類的。
sub·in·dex [sʌb'ɪndɛks; 'sʌb'indeks] *n., pl.* **-dices** [-dɪsiz; -disi:z]. 〖數學〗分指數。 「tively. ④subjunctive.」
subj. ①subject. ②subjective. ③subjec-
sub·ja·cent [sʌb'dʒesn̩t; sʌb'dʒeisənt] *adj.* 在下的;低下的; 下層的。
:sub·ject[1] ['sʌbdʒɪkt; 'sʌbdʒikt, -dʒekt] *n.* ①主題;題目; 科目; 學科。a *subject* of conversation. 談話的主題。②庶民; 臣民; 在他人力量支配之下的人。③歷經某事物之人; 被實驗者;病人;患者。④〖文法〗主詞。"I" is the *subject* in this sentence: I see the cat. "I" 是 "I see the cat." 一句中的主詞。⑤〖音樂〗樂旨;主旋律。⑥〖哲學〗實體;自我。⑦〖邏輯〗主辭;主位。⑧原因;起因; 誘因。⑨對象。⑩解剖用的屍首。***change the subject*** 改變話題。***on the subject of*** 關於; 論及。—*adj.* ①受制於; 服從的。②易罹; 易受; 常遇。to be *subject* to colds. 易患感冒。③依照;聽候。*subject* to your approval. 聽候你的裁奪。The prices are *subject* to change. 價格可能有變動。
:sub·ject[2] [səb'dʒɛkt; səb'dʒekt, 'sʌbdʒikt, 'sʌbdʒekt] *v.t.* ①使服從;使隸屬。②使蒙受;使罹。③提出。to *subject* one's plan to another's consideration. 提出計畫供別人考慮。 「圖書目錄。」
subject catalog 按書籍性質分類的
sub·jec·tion [səb'dʒɛkʃən; səb'dʒekʃən] *n.* 征服;隸屬;服從。
sub·jec·tive [səb'dʒɛktɪv; sʌb'dʒektiv] *adj.* ①出自內心的;主觀的。②〖文法〗主位的; 主詞的。the *subjective* case. 主格。the *subjective* genitive. 主格所有格。③主要的。—**ly,** *adv.* 「主詞補語。」
subjective complement 〖文法〗
sub·jec·tiv·ism [səb'dʒɛktɪvɪzm̩; səb'dʒektivizm] *n.* 〖哲學〗主觀主義;主觀論。
sub·jec·tiv·i·ty [,sʌbdʒɛk'tɪvətɪ; ,sʌbdʒek'tiviti] *n.* 主觀;主觀性;主觀主義。
subject matter ①主題;主旨;題材。②(文章、言語等之)內容。
sub·join [səb'dʒɔɪn; 'sʌb'dʒɔin] *v.t.* 補述;增補;添加。 「〖解剖〗副關節。」
sub·joint ['sʌb,dʒɔɪnt; 'sʌbdʒɔint] *n.*
sub ju·di·ce [sʌb'dʒudɪsi; sʌb'dʒu:disi:] 〖拉〗 在法庭中; 在審判中; 尚未決定。
sub·ju·gate ['sʌbdʒə,get; 'sʌbdʒugeit] *v.t.* 征服;壓服;抑制。—**sub·ju·ga·tion,** *n.*
***sub·junc·tive** [səb'dʒʌŋktɪv; səb'dʒʌŋktiv] *n.* ①〖文法〗假設語氣。②假設語氣中的動詞。—*adj.* 〖文法〗假設語氣的。
sub·lease [*n.* 'sʌb,lis; 'sʌb'li:s *v.* sʌb'lis; 'sʌb'li:s] *n., v.,* **-leased, -leas·ing.** —*n.* 轉租;分租。—*v.t.* 轉租;分租。
sub·les·see [,sʌblɛ'si; 'sʌble'si:] *n.* 承受轉租者;轉租租戶。 「轉租人。」
sub·les·sor [,sʌblɛ'sɔr; 'sʌble'sɔ:] *n.*
sub·let [sʌb'lɛt; 'sʌb'let] *v.t.,* **-let, -let·ting.** ①轉租。②轉包給; 分包給。
sub·li·brar·i·an [,sʌblaɪ'brɛrɪən; 'sʌblai'brɛəriən] *n.* 圖書館副管理員。
sub·lieu·ten·ant [,sʌblu'tɛnənt; 'sʌble'tenənt] *n.* 〖英〗陸軍少尉;海軍中尉。
sub·li·mate [*n., adj.* 'sʌbləmɪt, -,met; 'sʌblimit, -meit *v.* 'sʌblə,met; 'sʌblimeit] *v.,* **-mat·ed, -mat·ing,** *adj., n.* —*v.t.* ①使昇華。②純化;精鍊。③使高尚;理想化。—*adj.* ①昇華的。②高尚的。—*n.* 昇華物。
sub·li·ma·tion [,sʌblə'meʃən; ,sʌbli'meiʃən] *n.* ①〖化〗昇華;昇華作用。②理想化;純化。③〖心理〗昇華。
sub·lime** [sə'blaɪm; sə'blaim] *adj., n., v.,* **-limed, -lim·ing.** —*adj.* ①高尚的; 崇高的;宏壯的;壯麗的。②超人的; 令人驚奇的。③〖俗〗極度的;完全的。 You *sublime* idiot! 你這個大傻瓜! ④高位的;尊貴的。His *Sublime* Highness. 殿下。⑤傲慢的;自大的。⑥〖解剖〗接近表面的。the Sublime Porte*** (帝制時代的)土耳其政府; 土耳其。—*n.* ①崇高; 宏壯; 卓絕。②最高的程度; 最大的限度。***from the sublime to the ridiculous*** 由崇高而荒誕;從一個極端至另一個極端。—*v.t.* & *v.i.* 昇華;精鍊;純化;淨化。—**ly,** *adv.*
sub·lim·er [sə'blaɪmɚ; sə'blaimə] *n.* 使昇華者;精鍊者;昇華器;純化器。
sub·lim·i·nal [sʌb'lɪmənl̩; sʌb'liminl] *adj.* ①〖心理〗下意識的;潛意識的。the *subliminal* self. 潛在自我。②弱得不能感覺到的; 小得無法注意到的。—*n.* 下意識。—**ly,** *adv.*
sub·lim·i·ty [sə'blɪmətɪ; sə'blimiti] *n., pl.* **-ties.** ①高尚;崇高;宏壯;壯麗。②宏壯之物;崇高之人或物。③極點; 絕頂; 精華。④〖骨相〗壯烈性。
sub·lin·gual [sʌb'lɪŋgwəl; sʌb'liŋgwəl] *adj.* 〖解剖〗舌下的;舌下腺的。
sublingual gland 舌下腺。
sub·lu·nar·y [sʌb'lunərɪ; 'sʌblu:nəri] *adj.* ①在月下的。②地上的; 在地上的。③塵世的;世俗的。(亦作 **sublunar**)
sub·ma·chine gun [,sʌbmə'ʃin~; 'sʌbmə'ʃi:n~] 手提輕機鎗。
sub·mar·gin·al [sʌb'mɑrdʒɪnl̩; sʌb'mɑ:dʒinl] *adj.* ①近邊緣的。②未達可獲利益之邊際的。③不值得開墾的。
***sub·ma·rine** [*n., v.* 'sʌbmə,rin; 'sʌbməri:n *adj.* ,sʌbmə'rin; 'sʌbməri:n] *n., v.,* **-rined, -rin·ing,** *adj.* —*n.* ①潛水艇。②生存或生長於水中的動植物。—*v.t.* 〖俚〗以潛水艇攻擊或擊沉。—*adj.* 海底的; 海生的; 海中的。*submarine* mine. 水雷。*submarine* plants. 海底植物。
sub·ma·rin·er [,sʌbmə'rinɚ; ,sʌbmə'ri:nə] *n.* 潛水艇上官兵之一員。
sub·max·il·lar·y [sʌb'mæksə,lɛrɪ; sʌb'mæksələri] *adj., n., pl.* **-lar·ies.** —*adj.* ①下顎的;頷下的。②下顎骨的。—*n.* 下顎(骨)。
submaxillary gland 頷下腺。
***sub·merge** [səb'mɝdʒ; səb'mə:dʒ, sʌb-]

v., -merged, -merg·ing. —*v.t.* ①置於水中;浸入水中;淹沒。②遮覆;埋沒。③(潛水艇)潛航。④使負責;使貧苦。—*v.i.* 沉入水中;潛入水中。*the submerged tenth* 最貧苦階級的人。—sub·merged, *adj.*

sub·mer·gence [səbˈmɝdʒəns; səbˈməːdʒəns] *n.* 沒入水中;浸沒;埋沒。

sub·mer·gi·ble [səbˈmɝdʒəbḷ; səbˈməːdʒibl] *adj.* 可沒入水中的; 可潛航的。—*n.* 潛水艇。

sub·merse [səbˈmɝs; səbˈməːs] *v.t.*, -mersed, -mers·ing. =submerge.

sub·mersed [səbˈmɝst; səbˈməːst] *adj.* ①沒於水中的。②〖植物〗生長於水下的。

sub·mers·i·ble [səbˈmɝsəbḷ; səbˈməːsəbl] *adj.* 可潛入水中的; 可潛航的; 可浸在水內的。—*n.* (昔日之)潛水艇。

sub·mer·sion [səbˈmɝʃən; səbˈməːʃən] *n.* 潛水;潛航;沉沒;浸漬。

sub·min·i·a·ture [sʌbˈmɪnɪətʃɚ; sʌbˈminjətʃə] *n.* 袖珍照相機。

subminiature camera 袖珍照相機(用 16mm 以下的軟片的)。

***sub·mis·sion** [səbˈmɪʃən; səbˈmiʃən] *n.* ①服從;屈服;歸順。②恭謹;謙遜。③提交仲裁;提交仲裁的事。*with all due submission* 必恭必敬地。

sub·mis·sive [səbˈmɪsɪv; səbˈmisiv] *adj.* 順從的;服從的;恭謹的;謙遜的;柔順的。—ly, *adv.* —ness, *n.*

***sub·mit** [səbˈmɪt; səbˈmit] *v.*, -mit·ted, -mit·ting. —*v.t.* ①使服從;使降服。to *submit* oneself to another's authority. 服從他人之權威。②提出。to *submit* a case to the court. 向法院提出訴訟。③主張; 建議。I *submit* that this should be allowed. 我建議這件事情應被准許。—*v.i.* ①屈服;甘受。to *submit* to one's fate. 聽天由命。②接受。

sub·mon·tane [sʌbˈmɑnten; sʌbˈmɔntein] *adj.* 山下的;山脚的;在山麓的。

sub·mul·ti·ple [sʌbˈmʌltəpḷ; ˈsʌbˈmʌltipl] *n.* 〖數學〗約數; 約量。—*adj.* 〖數學〗約數的;約量的。

sub·nor·mal [sʌbˈnɔrmḷ; ˈsʌbˈnɔːməl] *adj.* 正常以下的; (尤指) 智力低於正常的。—*n.* ①智力低於常人者。②〖數學〗次法距。

sub·of·fi·cer [ˈsʌbˌɑfəsɚ; ˈsʌbˌɔfisə] *n.* 下級軍官。

sub·or·der [sʌbˈɔrdɚ; ˈsʌbˌɔːdə] *n.* 〖生物〗亞目。—sub·or·di·nal, *adj.*

***sub·or·di·nate** [*adj.*, *n.* səˈbɔrdṇɪt; səˈbɔːdṇit *v.* səˈbɔrdṇˌet; səˈbɔːdineit] *adj.*, *n.*, *v.*, -nat·ed, -nat·ing. —*adj.* ①下級的;次要的;附屬的。a *subordinate* clause. 附屬子句。②受他物之控制或影響的。*subordinate to* a. 地位低於。b. 受…的控制。—*n.* 屬下;屬僚;附屬物。—*v.t.* 使居下位;使服從。

sub·or·di·na·tion [səˌbɔrdṇˈeʃən; səˌbɔːdiˈneiʃən] *n.* ①下位;次要。②隸屬;服從。

sub·or·di·na·tive [səˈbɔrdəˌnetɪv; səˈbɔːdinətiv] *adj.* ①從屬的;表從屬關係的。②〖文法〗附屬的。

sub·orn [səˈbɔrn; sʌˈbɔːn] *v.t.* ①以賄賂或其他非法手段獲取; 賄買。②使作僞證。③說服或使(某人)犯法;教唆;唆使。—a·tion, *n.*

sub·ox·ide [sʌbˈɑksaɪd; sʌbˈɔksaid] *n.* 〖化〗低氧化物。

sub·plot [ˈsʌbˌplɑt; ˈsʌbplɔt] *n.* (文藝作品中之)次情節。

sub·poe·na [səˈpinə; səbˈpiːnə] *n.* 〖法律〗傳票。—*v.t.* 以傳票召傳;傳審。

sub·po·lar [sʌbˈpolɚ; sʌbˈpoulə] *adj.* 近極地的。

sub·pre·fect [sʌbˈprifɛkt; ˈsʌbˈpriːfekt] *n.* 副縣長;地方之副長官。

sub·prin·ci·pal [sʌbˈprɪnsəpḷ; sʌbˈprinsipəl] *n.* ①副校長。②副椽。

sub·pri·or [ˈsʌbˌpraɪɚ; ˈsʌbˌpraiə] *n.* 修道院副院長。

sub·pro·gram [sʌbˈprogræm; sʌbˈprougræm] *n.* 〖電腦〗電腦程式中之一部分。

sub·ro·ga·tion [ˌsʌbrəˈgeʃən; ˌsʌbrəˈgeiʃən] *n.* 〖法律〗代位;債權之代位。

sub ro·sa [sʌbˈrozə; sʌbˈrouzə] 〖拉〗祕密地;極端祕密地(=under the rose, 在埃及 rose 是沈默之神 Harpocrates 的象徵)。

sub·sat·el·lite [ˈsʌbˈsætḷˌaɪt; ˈsʌbˈsætəlait] *n.* 子衞星(由運行的衞星所發射者)。

***sub·scribe** [səbˈskraɪb; səbˈskraib] *v.*, -scribed, -scrib·ing. —*v.t.* ①捐助;認捐。②簽名於文書等; 簽署。③簽名(於合約等)表示同意。—*v.i.* ①同意; 贊同。②訂購(雜誌、書籍等)〖to, for〗. We *subscribe* to (*or* for) several magazines. 我們訂閱數種雜誌。③捐助;認捐。 to *subscribe* to a charity. 捐助慈善事業。

sub·scrib·er [səbˈskraɪbɚ; səbˈskraibə] *n.* ①捐助者; 捐獻者。②簽署(名)者。③訂購者;訂戶;用戶。

sub·script [ˈsʌbskrɪpt; ˈsʌbskript] *adj.* 寫於下邊的;寫在線下的。—*n.* ①寫於下邊的數字或文字 (如 H_2O 中之 2)。②〖數學〗添標;下標。

***sub·scrip·tion** [səbˈskrɪpʃən; səbˈskripʃən] *n.* ①署名;簽諾;同意。②捐款;捐助金。③訂閱; 預約; 訂閱費; 預約金。My *subscription* to the newspaper expires next Tuesday. 我訂閱的報紙下星期二滿期。④〖英〗俱樂部等之會費。

subscription edition ①預約書。②分期預約版。

subscription television 一種閉路電視需付費始能收視者。 (亦作 **pay TV**)

sub·sec·tion [sʌbˈsɛkʃən; ˈsʌbˌsekʃən] *n.* ①section 以下之區分(如節以下之項,科以下之股等)。②砲兵分隊。

sub·se·quence [ˈsʌbsɪˌkwɛns; ˈsʌbsikwəns] *n.* 後來;繼起;繼起之事物。(亦作 **subsequency**)

***sub·se·quent** [ˈsʌbsɪˌkwɛnt; ˈsʌbsikwənt] *adj.* 隨後的;後來的;繼起的。

***sub·se·quent·ly** [ˈsʌbsəkwəntlɪ; ˈsʌbsikwəntli] *adv.* 以後;後來。

sub·serve [səbˈsɝv; səbˈsəːv] *v.t.*, -served, -serv·ing. 裨益於; 有助於; 促進。

sub·ser·vi·ence [səbˈsɝvɪəns; səbˈsəːvjəns] *n.* ①阿諛; 屈從。②裨益; 有用。(亦作 **subserviency**)

sub·ser·vi·ent [səbˈsɝvɪənt; səbˈsəːvjənt] *adj.* ①阿諛的;屈服的;卑屈的。②輔助的;有裨益的;促進的〖to〗。③附屬的;服從的。

***sub·side** [səbˈsaɪd; səbˈsaid] *v.i.*, -sid·ed, -sid·ing. ①降落。②(熱病、憤怒、暴風等)平息;消退。③下沉;沉澱。④坐下。*subside into a chair* 〖諧〗(人)落座;就座。

sub·sid·ence [səbˈsaɪdṇs; səbˈsaidəns] *n.* 沉澱;沉下;平息;消退。

sub·sid·i·ar·y [səbˈsɪdɪˌɛrɪ; səbˈsidjəri] *adj.*, *n.*, *pl.* -ar·ies. —*adj.* ①輔助的;補助的。*subsidiary* business. 副業。②附屬的;副的;次的。a *subsidiary* company. 附屬

公司;子公司。③補助金的;由補助金維持的。*subsidiary* payments. 補助金。—*n.* ①補助物;附屬物;附加物。②附屬公司。③〖音樂〗副主題;從屬主題。

sub·si·dize 〔ˈsʌbsəˌdaɪz; ˈsʌbsidaiz〕 *v.t.*, **-dized, -diz·ing.** ①以金錢補助;資助;津貼。②收買(現常含有賄賂之意)。

sub·si·dy 〔ˈsʌbsədɪ; ˈsʌbsidi〕 *n.*, *pl.* **-dies.** ①補助金(尤指政府給私人企業等的);津貼;獎金。②從前英國國會給皇家的特支費。

sub si·len·ti·o 〔~sɪˈlɛnʃɪo; ~siˈlenʃiou〕〖拉〗沉默地(=in silence).

sub·sist 〔səbˈsɪst; səbˈsist〕 *v.i.* ①存在。②生活;維持生活。to *subsist* by the pen. 鬻文爲生。③居住;位於〖in〗。④〖哲學〗爲眞理;有效。—*v.t.* 供給糧食;給養。

sub·sist·ence 〔səbˈsɪstəns; səbˈsistəns〕 *n.* ①生活;生存。②衣食;維持生活之物。

subsistence allowance ①預墊給新雇用人員的錢(第一次薪水未發之前的)。②工作津貼(薪水外的)。③(軍人的)伙食津貼。

subsistence farming (or **agriculture**) ①很少有剩餘的農場經營(僅够農人吃的)。②祇種足够農人吃的農場經營。

subsistence wages 維持最低生活工資。

sub·sist·ent 〔səbˈsɪstənt; səbˈsistənt〕 *adj.* 存在的;現存的;固有的。

sub·soil 〔ˈsʌbˌsɔɪl; ˈsʌbsɔil〕 *n.* (亦作 **undersoil**)(表層下面的)下層土。—*v.t.* 挖鬆或翻起…下層之土。

sub·son·ic 〔sʌbˈsɑnɪk; sʌbˈsɔnik〕 *adj.* 低於音速的;每小時速度慢於700英里的。

sub·spe·cies 〔sʌbˈspiʃɪz; ˈsʌbˌspiːʃiːz〕 *n.* 〖生物〗亞種。

subst. ①substantive. ②substantively. ③substitute.

‡**sub·stance** 〔ˈsʌbstəns; ˈsʌbstəns〕 *n.* ①物質;物。Coal is a black *substance.* 煤是一種黑色物質。②實質;內容;實體;本體。a lecture which lacks *substance.* 內容貧乏之演講。③要義;主旨;大意。④財產;資產。a man of *substance.* 有大量資產之人。⑤一種特殊的物質。⑥〖哲〗實體;本體;本質。⑦紙張重量的單位。***in substance*** a. 本質上;實質上;大體上。b. 實在地;眞正地。***lose the substance for the shadow*** 捨本逐末。—**less,** *adj.*

sub·stand·ard 〔sʌbˈstændəd; sʌbˈstændəd〕 *adj.* ①標準以下的;在法律規定之最低標準以下的。②〖語言〗非合於標準語的(包括淫猥語、文字錯誤、俚語等)。

***sub·stan·tial** 〔səbˈstænʃəl; səbˈstænʃəl〕 *adj.* ①眞實的;實際的;實在的。②牢固的;堅實的。a *substantial* building. 堅固的房屋。③內容充實的;豐富的。a *substantial* meal. 豐富的餐食。④重大的。to make a *substantial* improvement. 有重大的進步。⑤富有的。⑥實質上的;大致的。*substantial* performance of contract. 實際上履行契約。⑦有勢力的。—*n.* 實際的事物。

sub·stan·tial·ism 〔səbˈstænʃəlɪzəm; səbˈstænʃəlizəm〕 *n.* 〖哲〗實體論;本體論。

sub·stan·tial·ist 〔səbˈstænʃəlɪst; səbˈstænʃəlist〕 *n.* 實體論者;本體論者。

sub·stan·ti·al·i·ty 〔səbˌstænʃɪˈælətɪ; səbˌstænʃiˈæliti〕 *n.* ①眞實;實在。②實體;實質;有實質。③堅實;堅固。④眞實價值。

sub·stan·tial·ly 〔səbˈstænʃəlɪ; səbˈstænʃəli〕 *adv.* 實質上;實際上;大體上。

sub·stan·ti·ate 〔səbˈstænʃɪˌet; səbˈstænʃieit〕 *v.t.*, **-at·ed, -at·ing.** ①證實;證明。②賦予具體形式;使實體化。③加强;使有內容。—**sub·stan·ti·a·tion,** *n.*

sub·stan·ti·val 〔ˌsʌbstənˈtaɪvl; ˌsʌbstənˈtaivəl〕 *adj.* 〖文法〗名詞的;實名詞的;有實名詞之性質的。

sub·stan·tive 〔ˈsʌbstəntɪv; ˈsʌbstəntiv〕 *adj.* ①〖文法〗作爲名詞用的;表示存在的。②獨立的;獨立存在的。③眞正的;實在的;實際的。④本質的;主要的。⑤不用媒染劑卽能調混的;直接的(染料)。—*n.* ①〖文法〗名詞;代名詞;實名詞。②實物。—**ly,** *adv.*

sub·sta·tion 〔ˈsʌbˌsteʃən; ˈsʌbˌsteiʃən〕 *n.* 分局;分所。

sub·stit·u·ent 〔sʌbˈstɪtʃuənt; sʌbˈstitjuənt〕 *n.* 〖化〗取代分子。—*adj.* ①被代替的;可被代替的。②取代分子的。

***sub·sti·tute** 〔ˈsʌbstəˌtjut; ˈsʌbstitjuːt〕 *n.*, *v.*, **-tut·ed, -tut·ing,** *adj.* —*n.* ①代替者;代理人。②代替物;代用品。We used honey as a *substitute* for sugar. 我們用蜂蜜作糖的代用品。③〖文法〗代用字。—*v.t.* 以…代替…。to *substitute* electric for horse traction. 以電力牽引代替馬力牽引。—*v.i.* ①代替〖for〗. to *substitute* for a teacher. 代替一位教師。②〖化〗取代。—*adj.* 代替的;代理的。

sub·sti·tu·tion 〔ˌsʌbstəˈtjuʃən; ˌsʌbstiˈtjuːʃən〕 *n.* ①代替。②〖化〗取代。—**al,** *adj.*

sub·sti·tu·tive 〔ˈsʌbstəˌtjutɪv; ˈsʌbstitjuːtiv〕 *adj.* ①代替的;代用的;代理的;置換的。②可用爲代替物的。

sub·strat·o·sphere 〔sʌbˈstrætəsfɪr; sʌbˈstrætəsfiə〕 *n.* 下平流層。

sub·stra·tum 〔sʌbˈstretəm; ˈsʌbˈstrɑːtəm〕 *n.*, *pl.* **-stra·ta** 〔-ˈstretə; -ˈstrɑːtə〕, **-stra·tums.** ①下層。②下層土;底土(在表層下面者)。③基礎;根基。④〖哲〗實體;本體。

sub·struc·ture 〔sʌbˈstrʌktʃɚ; ˈsʌbˌstrʌktʃə〕 *n.* ①基礎;根基。②〖建築〗下層結構。

sub·sume 〔səbˈsum; səbˈsjuːm〕 *v.t.*, **-sumed, -sum·ing.** 包括;包含;包攝。

sub·sump·tion 〔səbˈsʌmpʃən; səbˈsʌmpʃən〕 *n.* ①包容;包括;包含。②被包容之物。③〖邏輯〗三段論法之小前提;假定。

sub·sur·face 〔sʌbˈsɝfɪs; sʌbˈsəːfis〕 *adj.* 表面下的;地或水面下的。***subsurface warfare*** 海底戰爭。—*n.* 表面下之事物或空間。

sub·tan·gent 〔sʌbˈtændʒənt; ˈsʌbˈtændʒənt〕 *n.* 〖數學〗次切距。

sub·tem·per·ate 〔sʌbˈtɛmpərɪt; sʌbˈtempərit〕 *adj.* 亞溫帶的。

sub·ten·an·cy 〔sʌbˈtɛnənsɪ; ˈsʌbˈtenənsi〕 *n.* 轉租;轉佃。

sub·ten·ant 〔sʌbˈtɛnənt; ˈsʌbˈtenənt〕 *n.* 向佃農轉佃者;轉租人。

sub·tend 〔səbˈtɛnd; səbˈtend〕 *v.t.* ①〖數學〗(弦、邊、角等)對向(弧或對角等)。②〖植物〗包於葉腋內。

sub·tense 〔səbˈtɛns; səbˈtens〕 *n.* 〖數學〗弦;對邊。

subter- 〖字首〗表"在…之下;少於;祕密地"之義。

sub·ter·fuge 〔ˈsʌbtɚˌfjudʒ; ˈsʌbtəfjuːdʒ〕 *n.* 遁辭;藉口;狡猾手段;詭計。

sub·ter·ra·ne·an 〔ˌsʌbtəˈrenɪən; ˌsʌbtəˈreinjən〕 *adj.* (亦作 **subterraneous**) ①地下的。②祕密的;隱藏的。—*n.* ①地下的人或事物。②地下室;洞穴。

sub·til(e) 〔ˈsʌtl; ˈsʌtl〕 *adj.* = **subtle.**

sub·til·ize 〔ˈsʌtlˌaɪz; ˈsʌtilaiz〕 *v.*, **-ized,**

-iz·ing. —v.t. ①使高尚;使純潔;精鍊。②使(心智等)敏銳。③使精使;使微妙;洗鍊。④使稀薄;稀釋。—v.i. 精鍊;細究;穿鑿入微。

sub·til·ty [ˈsʌtl̩tɪ;ˈsʌtlti] n., pl. -ties. =subtlety.

sub·ti·tle [ˈsʌbˌtaɪtl̩; ˈsʌbˌtaitl] n., v., -tled, -tling. —n. ①小標題;副標題;副題。②〖電影〗 a. 字幕說明。 b. 默片的字幕。—v.t. 加副題於;加字幕於。

***sub·tle** [ˈsʌtl̩; ˈsʌtl] adj. ①精緻的;微妙的。a *subtle* distinction. 微妙的差別。②稀薄的;淡的。③明敏的;聰明的。a *subtle* observer. 明敏的觀察者。④狡猾的。⑤靈巧的;熟練的。(亦作 **subtile**) —ness, n. —subtly, adv.

sub·tle·ty [ˈsʌtl̩tɪ;ˈsʌtlti] n., pl. -ties. ①精微;微妙。②明敏;聰明。③詭譎;狡猾。④精妙之物。(亦作 **subtil(i)ty**)

sub·to·pi·a [sʌbˈtopɪə; sʌbˈtoupiə] n. 〖英〗①開發爲工業區的鄉間地區(已失去鄉間之樸素美麗)。②醜惡或不愉快的郊外。

***sub·tract** [səbˈtrækt; səbˈtrækt] v.t. ①減去;扣除。*Subtract* 3 from 9 and you have 6. 九減三得六。②減少; 減損。—v.i. 減去;減少。—er, n.

sub·trac·tion [səbˈtrækʃən; səbˈtrækʃən] n. ①減去;扣除。②減法。

subtraction sign 減號;負號(卽"−")。

sub·trac·tive [səbˈtræktɪv; səbˈtræktiv] adj. ①減的;可減的。②〖數學〗負的;有減號的;有負號(−)的。

sub·tra·hend [ˈsʌbtrəˌhɛnd; ˈsʌbtrəhend] n. 〖數學〗減數。

sub·treas·ur·y [ˈsʌbˌtrɛʒərɪ; ˈsʌbˌtreʒəri] n., pl. -ur·ies. 國庫之支庫。

sub·trop·i·cal [sʌbˈtrɑpɪkl̩;ˈsʌbˈtrɔpikəl] adj. ①亞熱帶的。②與熱帶接壤的。

sub·trop·ics [sʌbˈtrɑpɪks; ˈsʌbˈtrɔpiks] n. pl. 亞熱帶。

su·bu·li·form [ˈsjubjulɪˌfɔrm; ˈsju:bjulifɔ:m] adj. ①尖錐狀的。②〖植物〗錐狀的。(亦作 **subulate**)

***sub·urb** [ˈsʌbɝb; ˈsʌbə:b] n. ①市郊;城郊;郊區。②(pl.) 城郊之住宅區。 to live in the *suburbs*. 住在城郊。—ed, adj.

***sub·ur·ban** [səˈbɝbən; səˈbə:bən] adj. ①城郊的;市郊的;郊區的。 a *suburban* villa. 郊外的別墅。②有郊區特性的;偏狹的;偏見的。 —n. ①郊區居民。②一種短大衣。③=**station wagon.**

sub·ur·ban·ite [səˈbɝbənˌaɪt;səˈbə:bənait] n. 郊區居民。

sub·ur·bi·a [səˈbɝbɪə; səˈbə:biə] n. ①郊區。②郊區居民(集合稱)。③郊區生活。

sub·va·ri·e·ty [ˌsʌbvəˈraɪətɪ; ˈsʌbvəˌraiəti] n. 〖生物〗亞變種。

sub·ven·tion [səbˈvɛnʃən; səbˈvenʃən] n. ①(政府給的)補助金。②津貼;補助。

sub·ver·sion [səbˈvɝʃən;sʌbˈvə:ʃən] n. ①顚覆;滅亡;敗壞。②趨於促使毀滅之物;瓦解之因由。

sub·ver·sive [səbˈvɝsɪv;sʌbˈvə:siv] adj. 顚覆的;促使滅亡的;敗壞的。 —n. 企圖摧毀(政府)者;顚覆分子。

sub·vert [səbˈvɝt; sʌbˈvə:t] v.t. 顚覆;滅亡;敗壞。

***sub·way** [ˈsʌbˌwe; ˈsʌbwei] n. ①〖美〗地下鐵道。②地道。—v.i. 乘坐地下鐵路。

sub-ze·ro [ˌsʌbˈzɪro; ˌsʌbˈziərou] adj. ①零度下的;冰點下的。②適於冰點下之氣溫的。

suc- 〖字首〗 sub- 之異體(用於 c 之前)。

suc·cades [səˈkedz; səˈkeidz] n. pl. 糖果;蜜餞。

suc·ce·da·ne·um [ˌsʌksɪˈdenɪəm; ˌsʌksiˈdeiniəm] n., pl. -ne·a [-nɪə;-niə], -ne·ums. ①代用物;代理人。②代用藥。

‡suc·ceed [səkˈsid; səkˈsi:d] v.i. ①成功。to *succeed* in doing something. 做某事成功。②成就; 完成。③繼續。④繼位; 繼承; 繼任。No woman could *succeed* to the throne. 女人不能繼承王位。—v.t. ①繼續。Summer *succeeds* spring. 春去夏來。②繼承;繼(某人)之任。—er, n.

suc·cen·tor [səkˈsɛntɚ; səkˈsentə] n.〖宗教〗①唱詩班之副指揮。②低音主唱者。

suc·cès d'es·time [ˌsykˈsɛˌdɛsˈtim; ˌsykˈseˌdesˈti:m] 〖法〗獲得批評界之稱譽但未得到商業上的成功或一般人之讚揚。

‡suc·cess [səkˈsɛs; səkˈses] n. ①成功; 好結果;勝利。②財富、地位等的獲得; 成就。He has had little *success* in life. 他在一生中所獲成就不大。③成功之人或事物。 The plan was a great *success*. 這是一項極成功的計畫。④成效;結果。

‡suc·cess·ful [səkˈsɛsfəl; səkˈsesful] adj. ①成功的。 He was *successful* in the examination. 他考試及格。②飛黃騰達的;福祿雙全的;一帆風順的。a *successful* man. 一帆風順的人。—ly, adv.

suc·ces·sion** [səkˈsɛʃən; səkˈseʃən] n. ①繼續;連續。A *succession* of misfortunes has befallen her. 她連遭不幸。 to occur in *succession*. 連續發生。②繼承;繼位;繼承權;繼位權。③一系列之繼承人;其繼承順序。 ***in succession 接連地;連續地(見①)。 ***succession duty*** (or ***tax***) 遺產稅。—al, adj.

***suc·ces·sive** [səkˈsɛsɪv; səkˈsesiv] adj. 繼續的;連續的。 It rained for three *successive* days. 一連下三天雨。

suc·ces·sive·ly [səkˈsɛsɪvlɪ; səkˈsesivli] adv. 繼續地;連續地;接連地。

***suc·ces·sor** [səkˈsɛsɚ; səkˈsesə] n. 後繼者;繼承者;繼任者。 a *successor* to the throne. 王位的繼承者。

success story 一個人成名或成功的故事。

suc·cinct [səkˈsɪŋkt; səkˈsiŋkt] adj. 簡明的;簡潔的。—ly, adv. —ness, n.

suc·cin·ite [ˈsʌksɪnˌaɪt; ˈsʌksinait] n. 〖礦〗琥珀。

suc·co(u)r [ˈsʌkɚ; ˈsʌkə] n. ①援助;幫助;救助。②援助者;幫助者。③(pl.)〖古〗援軍。—v.t. 援助;幫助;救助。

suc·co·ry [ˈsʌkərɪ; ˈsʌkəri] n., pl. -ries. 〖植物〗菊苣。

suc·co·tash [ˈsʌkəˌtæʃ; ˈsʌkətæʃ] n. (印第安人的)玉蜀黍、豆類與豬肉合煮之食物。

suc·cu·ba [ˈsʌkjəbə; ˈsʌkjubə] n., pl. -bae [-ˌbi; -bi:]. =succubus.

suc·cu·bus [ˈsʌkjəbəs; ˈsʌkjubəs] n., pl. -bi [-ˌbaɪ; -bai], -bus·es. ①在男人睡夢中與其性交之女妖。②妖魔。③好色者;淫亂者;娼妓。

suc·cu·lent [ˈsʌkjələnt; ˈsʌkjulənt] adj. ①多汁液的。②津津有味的; 有趣味的。③(植物之)有肉及汁的纖維的; 葉或莖多肉及汁的(如仙人掌)。—n. 葉或莖多肉及汁液的植物。 —**suc·cu·lence, suc·cu·len·cy,** n. —ly, adv.

suc·cumb [səˈkʌm; səˈkʌm] v.i. ①服從;屈從。②死。

‡such [sʌtʃ, sətʃ; sʌtʃ, sətʃ] adj. ①如此的;

這樣的。Metals are *such* things as iron, silver, and gold. 金屬是諸如鐵、銀和金之類。②導致…之類的; 某一特殊的。③如此…的; 非常的。He is *such* a liar. 他竟是這樣的一個說謊者。④某。He spoke about *such* and *such* a man. 他說到某某人。⑤諸如此類的; 同類的。 The ladies took only tea and coffee and *such* drinks. 女士們只喝茶、咖啡及諸如此類的飲料。***such and such*** (亦作 **such-and-such**) 某某類的。***such as*** **a.** 諸如…(用於引述同類的實例)。**b.** 某一種的;某一程度的。***such as to*** (+ inf.)至…的程度;竟致。 His illness was not (one) *such as to* cause anxiety. 他的病不足以令人焦慮。***such* (...) *that*** 如此(…)竟使…。His behavior was *such that* everyone disliked him. 他的行爲使人人都嫌惡他。—*pron.* 如此之人;如此之事物。*Such* is life! 人生不過如此！ ***and such*** 等等; …之類。tools, machines *and such*. 工具、機器之類。***as such*** **a.** 如所指明的物、事實、或人; 用那個資格或名義。**b.** 本身。

such·like [ˈsʌtʃ,laɪk; ˈsʌtʃlaik] *adj.* 諸如此類的; 同樣的。 —*pron.* 此類的人或物。

suck** [sʌk; sʌk] *v.t.* 吸;吮;飲;吸收。 A sponge *sucks* in water. 海綿吸水。—*v.i.* ①吸;吸入;啜乳;吸收。 to *suck* at a pipe. 吸煙。②〖俚〗諂媚〖常 around〗。 ***suck a person's brains 吸收他人知識以爲己用。***suck in***〖俚〗欺騙。 ***suck up to***〖俗〗諂媚;拍馬屁。—*n.* ①吸; 啜; 吸收。 a child at *suck.* 在哺乳中的嬰兒。 to take a *suck* at. 吸一下。②〖俗〗一杯;一口。③吸力。④吸收的東西; 營養。⑤啜吸的聲音。⑥旋渦。***give suck to*** 給…吃奶;餵奶。—**less,** *adj.*

***suck·er** [ˈsʌkɚ; ˈsʌkə] *n.* ①吸吮者。②吸管; 吸盤。③有吸盤的魚; 鯉屬的魚。④〖植物〗吸枝。⑤(唧筒的) 活塞;吸子。⑥〖美俚〗易受騙之人。⑦硬糖塊;棒棒糖。⑧尙在哺乳的嬰兒或小動物。 —*v.t.* 除去吸枝;拔去吸枝。—*v.i.* 生吸枝。 —**like,** *adj.*

suck·ing [ˈsʌkɪŋ; ˈsʌkiŋ] *adj.* ①吸的; 吸取的;吸入的;吸收的。②吃奶的。③〖俗〗未成熟的;初出茅廬的;乳臭未乾的。

suck·le [ˈsʌkḷ; ˈsʌkl] *v.,* **-led, -ling.** —*v.t.* ①哺乳。②養育。—*v.i.* 吮乳; 吃乳。

suck·ling [ˈsʌklɪŋ; ˈsʌkliŋ] *n.* 乳兒; 幼獸。 ***babes and sucklings*** 無知的小孩。—*adj.* 尙未斷乳的;很幼小的。

su·cre [ˈsukre; ˈsuːkrei] *n.* 厄瓜多爾之貨幣單位。

su·crose [ˈsukros;ˈsuːkrous] *n.*〖化〗蔗糖 ($C_{12}H_{22}O_{11}$)。

suc·tion [ˈsʌkʃən; ˈsʌkʃən] *n.* ①吸。②吸引。③吸力。—*adj.* 使生吸力的;以吸力操作的。—**al,** *adj.*

suction pump 抽水機;汲水唧筒。

suc·to·ri·al [sʌkˈtorɪəl; sʌkˈtɔːriəl] *adj.* ①吸入的;吸引的。②適於吸吮的;用以吸附的。③有吸盤的。④由吸吮流質餵育的。

Su·dan [suˈdæn; su(ː)ˈdɑːn] *n.* 蘇丹(非洲之一共和國, 首都喀土木 Khartoum)。(亦作 **Soudan**)

Su·da·nese [,sudəˈniz; ,suːdəˈniːz] *adj., n., pl.* **-nese.** —*adj.* 蘇丹的。—*n.* 蘇丹人。(亦作 **Soudanese**)

Sudan grass〖植物〗蘇丹草(原產於非洲蘇丹, 普遍用做乾草或牧草)。

su·dar·i·um [suˈdɛrɪəm; sju(ː)ˈdɛəriəm] *n., pl.* **-dar·i·a** [-ˈdɛrɪə; -ˈdɛəriə]. ①擦臉巾; 手巾。②St. Veronica 於耶穌受難時爲其擦汗, 因而有其臉像印於其上的汗巾。③印有基督聖容之布。④=**sudatorium.**

su·da·to·ri·um [,sjudəˈtorɪəm; ,sjuːdəˈtɔːriəm] *n., pl.* **-ri·a** [-rɪə; -riə]. 供作發汗浴的熱空氣浴室。

su·da·to·ry [ˈsudə,torɪ; ˈsjuːdətəri] *adj., n., pl.* **-ries.** —*adj.* ①發汗的;催汗的。②發汗浴室的; 熱空氣浴室的。 —*n.* ①發汗劑。②熱空氣浴室 (=sudatorium).

sudd [sʌd; sʌd] *n.* 自尼羅河上游流下的常阻塞航路之漂流植物。

‡sud·den [ˈsʌdṇ; ˈsʌdn] *adj.* ①突然的; 出乎意料的。 a *sudden* decision. 突然之決策。②快速的。③〖古〗**a.** 快造的;供應快的。**b.** 衝動的;輕舉妄動的。—*adv.*〖詩〗=**suddenly.** —*n.* 突然;忽然。 ***all of a sudden***; ***on a sudden*** 突然地。—**ness,** *n.*

sudden death ①〖運動〗因得分相同而延長比賽時, 如一方得分(如籃球) 或領先一洞(如高爾夫球)卽結束比賽。②突然之死亡。

‡sud·den·ly [ˈsʌdṇlɪ; ˈsʌdnli] *adv.* 突然地。

su·dor·al [ˈsjudərəl; ˈsjuːdərəl] *adj.* 汗的;汗所致的。

sudoral eruptions 汗疹。

su·dor·if·er·ous [,sudəˈrɪfərəs; ,suːdəˈrifərəs] *adj.* 出汗的;發汗的。

su·dor·if·ic [,sudəˈrɪfɪk; ,sjuːdəˈrifik] *adj.* 使發汗的;催汗的。—*n.* 發汗藥;催汗劑。

Su·dra [ˈsudrə; ˈsuːdrə]〖印〗*n.* 首陀羅(印度四大階級之最低者)。

suds [sʌdz; sʌdz] *n. pl.* ①肥皂水。②肥皂水上之泡沫。③〖俚〗啤酒。 ***in the suds***〖俗〗在困難中。

suds·y [ˈsʌdzɪ; ˈsʌdzi] *adj.,* **suds·i·er, suds·i·est.** 似肥皂水的;起泡沫的。

Sue [su; sjuː, suː] *n.* 女子名 (Susan, Susanna, Susannah 的暱稱)。

sue [su, sɪu; sjuː, suː] *v.i. & v.t.,* **sued, su·ing.** ①起訴; 控告。 to *sue* for damages. 起訴要求損害賠償。②上訴。③請求。Messengers came *suing* for peace. 使者前來求和。④〖古〗求愛;求婚。 ***sue out*** 請求而從法院得到(令狀、赦免等)。

suède, suede [swed; sweid] *n.* ①麂皮。②一種有毳面之布。 —*adj.* 麂皮製成的; 有毳面布料製成的。—*v.t. & v.i.* (使)羔皮、布料等起細毛。

su·et [ˈsuɪt;sjuit] *n.* (牛羊腎臟及腰部附近的)硬脂肪;板油。

su·et·y [ˈsuɪtɪ; ˈsjuiti] *adj.* (牛羊之) 硬脂肪的;如硬脂肪的;含硬脂肪的。

Su·ez [ˈsuɛz; ˈsu(ː)iz, ˈsju(ː)iz] *n.* 蘇彝士(埃及東北部, 蘇彝士運河南端之一海港)。

Suez Canal 蘇彝士運河(通達地中海和紅海的運河)。

suf., suff. suffix.

suf-〖字首〗sub-之異體(用在 f 前)。

‡suf·fer [ˈsʌfɚ; ˈsʌfə] *v.t.* ①蒙受;遭受;經驗; 罹。 They were ready to *suffer* death for the sake of their country. 他們甘願爲國家效死。②容許。③忍受;忍耐;忍住。 I will not *suffer* such insults. 我無法忍受這種侮辱。—*v.i.* ①受苦。②受害; 受損失。③受懲罰。④生(病);患於。 to *suffer* from measles. 患痲疹。 ⑤〖廢〗忍受。***suffer fools gladly*** 忍耐地與笨人交往;不挑剔糊塗事。***suffer from*** 患於; 苦於;因…受困擾;因…受損害。—**er,** *n.*

suf·fer·a·ble [ˈsʌfərəbḷ; ˈsʌfərəbl] *adj.* 可忍受的; 可堪的; 可容許的。

suf·fer·ance [ˈsʌfrəns; ˈsʌfərəns] *n.* ①容許; 寬容; 容忍。②忍耐力; 忍耐。 ***on***

sufferance 出於容忍;出於寬容。

*__suf·fer·ing__ [ˈsʌfrɪŋ; ˈsʌfəriŋ] *n.* ①痛苦;苦難。②(*pl.*)一人或一羣人所受之苦難。③忍痛。—*adj.* 受苦的;苦難的。 —**ly,** *adv.*

*__suf·fice__ [səˈfaɪs; səˈfais] *v.,* **-ficed, -fic·ing.** —*v.i.* ①足够。*Suffice* it to say that .... 只說…就够了。②具備必要條件; 合格。—*v.t.* 使滿足;足敷(某人)之用。Fifty dollars will *suffice* me. 五十元足够我用。—**suf·fic·er,** *n.*

suf·fi·cien·cy [səˈfɪʃənsɪ; səˈfiʃənsi] *n., pl.* **-cies.** ①充分;足够。②資格; 能力。③自滿;自信。④足够之收入。

‡**suf·fi·cient** [səˈfɪʃənt; səˈfiʃənt] *adj.* ①充分的;足够的。The rain was not *sufficient* to do any harm. 這雨不足以爲害。②〖古〗有能力的;有資格的。—*n.*〖俗〗足够;足量。Have you had *sufficient?* 你吃飽了沒有? —**ly,** *adv.*

*__suf·fix__ [*n.* ˈsʌfɪks; ˈsʌfiks *v.* səˈfɪks; ˈsʌfiks] *n.* 字尾;接尾語(如badly 一字中之ly)。—*v.t.* & *v.i.* 加字尾;附加。—**al,** *adj.*

*__suf·fo·cate__ [ˈsʌfəˌket; ˈsʌfəkeit] *v.,* **-cat·ed, -cat·ing.** —*v.t.* ①使窒息。 I am almost *suffocated* with smoke. 我幾乎被煙窒息了。②悶死。③熄滅。 —*v.i.* ①窒悶;窒息。②悶死。

suf·fo·cat·ing [ˈsʌfəˌketɪŋ; ˈsʌfəkeitiŋ] *adj.* 令人窒息的;窒悶的。—**ly,** *adv.*

suf·fo·ca·tion [ˌsʌfəˈkeʃən; ˌsʌfəˈkeiʃən] *n.* 窒悶; 窒息。

suf·fo·ca·tive [ˈsʌfəˌketɪv; ˈsʌfəkeitiv] *adj.* 使窒息的;令人呼吸困難的;氣悶的。

Suf·folk [ˈsʌfək; ˈsʌfək] *n.* ①英國種上等食用羊。②**a.** 英國種之黑豬。**b.** 美國種之白豬。③英國種栗色馬。

suf·fra·gan [ˈsʌfrəgən; ˈsʌfrəgən] *n.* (亦作 **suffragan bishop, bishop suffragan**)〖宗教〗副監督; 副主教; 隸屬總主教管轄之主教。—*adj.* 下屬的;副的;輔助的(指主教對其所隸屬之總主教而言)。

*__suf·frage__ [ˈsʌfrɪdʒ; ˈsʌfridʒ] *n.* ①投票。②投票權;選舉權。We granted *suffrage* to women some time ago. 我們早已給婦女以選舉權。③贊成。④〖宗教〗短禱。

suf·fra·gette [ˌsʌfrəˈdʒɛt; ˌsʌfrəˈdʒet] *n.* 主張婦女有參政權的婦女。

suf·fra·gist [ˈsʌfrədʒɪst; ˈsʌfrədʒist] *n.* ①主張擴大參政權者。②主張婦女參政者。

suf·fuse [səˈfjuz; səˈfjuːz] *v.t.,* **-fused, -fus·ing.** 充盈;布滿。

suf·fu·sion [səˈfjuʒən; səˈfjuːʒən] *n.* ①充滿;布滿。②色澤之突現。

Su·fi [ˈsufɪ; ˈsuːfi] *n., pl.* **-fis.** ①〖回教〗奉禁慾主義與神祕主義的一派,尤指在波斯者。②此派之信徒。

Su·fism [ˈsuˌfɪzəm; ˈsuːfizəm] *n.*〖回教〗Sufi 派之教義;神祕主義派。(亦作 **Sufiism**)

sug-〖字首〗sub- 之異體(用在 g 之前)。

‡**sug·ar** [ˈʃugɚ; ˈʃugə] *n.* ①糖。 cube *sugar*. 方糖。Do you like *sugar* in your tea? 你喜歡在茶裏放糖嗎?②似糖的東西。③甜言蜜語。④金錢。⑤〖俗〗情人或夫妻間之暱稱。—*v.t.* ①加糖使甜;覆以糖;使成爲甜蜜。She *sugared* her tea. 她在她的茶裏加糖。②使(不可愛的東西)變可愛;使吸引人。—*v.i.* 形成糖;變成糖。 ***sugar a pill*** 加糖衣於藥丸; 使令人不愉快的東西有吸引力。 ***sugar off*** (製楓糖時)將楓汁煮乾使結晶。

sugar basin (or **bowl**) (餐桌上用的)砂糖容器。

sugar beet〖植物〗甜菜。

sugar candy ①糖果。②愉快、悅目的人或事。

sugar cane 甘蔗。

sug·ar-coat [ˈʃugɚˌkot; ˈʃugəkout] *n.* 糖衣。 —*v.t.* ①加以糖衣。②使…顯得更可愛迷人。

sugar daddy〖美俚〗致送豪華禮品以博少女歡心之老年人。

sugar diabetes 糖尿病。(亦作 **diabetes mellitus**)

sug·ar·house [ˈʃugɚˌhaus; ˈʃugəhaus] *n.* 糖廠;製糖所;製糖工場。

sug·ar·less [ˈʃugəlɪs; ˈʃugəlis] *adj.* 無糖的;不含糖的。

sugar loaf 圓錐形方糖。

sugar maple〖植物〗糖楓。

sugar mill 糖廠;製糖機器。

sugar of lead〖化〗乙酸鉛;醋酸鉛。

sugar of milk 乳糖。

sugar pine (美國 California 州及 Oregon 州產的)一種松樹。

sug·ar·plum [ˈʃugɚˌplʌm; ˈʃugəplʌm] *n.* ①小糖球;圓形小糖果。②甜言蜜語。

sugar refinery 煉糖廠。

sugar spoon 糖匙。

sugar tongs 用以夾方糖的鑷子。

sug·ar·y [ˈʃugərɪ; ˈʃugəri] *adj.* ①含糖的;似糖的;甜的。②表面使人歡悅適意的; 諂媚的; 態度親切而不眞誠的。③太甜的; 甜得使人不舒服的。 —**sug·ar·i·ness,** *n.*

‡**sug·gest** [səgˈdʒɛst, səˈdʒɛst; səˈdʒest] *v.t.* ①使想到; 使聯想。The thought of summer *suggests* swimming. 想到夏天,就使人想到游泳。 ②提出;提議。to *suggest* a plan. 提出一項計畫。③暗示;間接地表明。④促成;使有動機。

sug·gest·i·bil·i·ty [sə(g)ˌdʒɛstəˈbɪlətɪ; səˌdʒestiˈbiliti] *n.* 受暗示支配之狀態或性質;暗示感應性。

sug·gest·i·ble [səgˈdʒɛstəbl; səˈdʒestibl] *adj.* ①能被暗示感動的;可暗示的。②可提議的。

sug·ges·ti·o fal·si [səgˈdʒɛstʃɪoˈfælsaɪ; səgˈdʒestʃiouˈfælsai]〖拉〗虛僞之暗示;間接妄語(=suggestion of falsehood).

*__sug·ges·tion__ [səgˈdʒɛstʃən; səˈdʒestʃən] *n.* ①建議。The trip was made at his *suggestion*. 這次旅行是由他的提議而舉行的。②暗示;聯想。a talk full of *suggestions*. 充滿暗示的談話。③一點;很少的痕跡。

suggestion box 意見箱。

sug·ges·tive [səgˈdʒɛstɪv; səˈdʒestiv] *adj.* ①暗示的; 提醒的; 引起聯想的。②誘發色情的;猥褻的。③(催眠術)暗示的。 —**ly,** *adv.* —**ness,** *n.*

Sui [swi; swiː]〖中〗*n.* 隋朝 (A. D. 589–618)。

su·i·cid·al [ˌsuəˈsaɪdl; sjuiˈsaidl] *adj.* ①自殺的;造成自殺的。②自毀的; 自滅的;自暴自棄的。 —**ly,** *adv.*

*__su·i·cide__ [ˈsuəˌsaɪd; ˈsjuisaid] *n., v.,* **-cid·ed, -cid·ing.** —*n.* ①自殺。 to commit *suicide*. 自殺。②自殺者。③自毀;毀滅;自暴自棄。 to commit political *suicide*. 自毀政治前途。—*v.i.* & *v.t.* 自殺。

su·i·cid·ol·o·gy [ˌsuəsaɪdˈɑlədʒɪ; ˈsjuisaidˈɔlədʒi] *n.* 自殺行爲探討學。

su·i ge·ne·ris [ˈsjuɪˈdʒɛnərɪs; ˈsjuːaiˈdʒenəris]〖拉〗獨特的; 自成一格的 (= peculiar; unique).

su·i ju·ris [ˈsuaɪˈdʒurɪs; ˈsju(ː)aiˈdʒuəris)〖拉〗〖法律〗達法定年齡且身心健全，因而有完全行爲能力的（=in his *or* her own right）.

‡**suit**〔sut, sɪut, sjut; sjuːt, suːt〕*n.* ①(衣服等的)一套;一副。a *suit* of clothes. 一套衣服。②訴訟。a civil (criminal) *suit*. 民(刑)事訴訟。③請求;求婚。to make *suit* to a girl. 向少女求婚。④(紙牌的)一組。⑤套房。⑥一套;一組事物。⑦一套傢具。⑧(船帆的)一套。***follow suit*** a. 跟牌。b. 蕭規曹隨;倣照前人辦法。***in one's birthday suit*** 裸體。—*v.t.* ①供以衣服。②適合於;適應;使滿意。It's difficult to find a time that *suits* everybody. 很難找到一個對每人都合適的時間。③取悅;滿足。He tried to *suit* everybody. 他想討好每個人。—*v.i.* 適合;適當。Which date *suits* best?哪個日期最合適? ***suit oneself*** 隨某人之便。***suit...to*** 使…適合於。***suit with...*** 與…相稱。—**like,** *adj.*

***suit·a·ble**〔ˈsutəbḷ, ˈsɪu–, ˈsju–; ˈsjuː-təbl, ˈsuː–〕*adj.* 適合的; 適宜的; 恰當的。—**suit·a·bil·i·ty,** —**ness,** *n.* —**suit·a·bly,** *adv.*

***suit·case**〔ˈsutˌkes, ˈsjut–; ˈsjuːtkeis, ˈsuːt–〕*n.* 小提箱。

suit-dress〔ˈsutˌdrɛs; ˈsjuːtdres〕*n.* 女裝(有相配的上裝的)。

***suite**〔swit; swiːt〕*n.* ①套房。②一班隨員; 一班扈從。③〖音樂〗組曲。④一組舞曲。⑤一套傢具。⑥一組事物;一套東西。

suit·ed〔ˈsutɪd; ˈsjuːtid〕*adj.* 合適的。

suit·ing〔ˈsutɪŋ; ˈsjuːtiŋ〕*n.* 衣料。

suit·or〔ˈsutɚ; ˈsjuːtə〕*n.* ①求婚者。②起訴者;原告。③求情者。—**ship,** *n.*

Sui·yüan〔ˈsweˈjyɑn; ˈsweiˈjyɑːn〕*n.* 綏遠(中國之一省,省會歸綏 Kweisui).

Su·kar·no〔suˈkarno; suːˈkɑːnou〕*n.* 蘇卡諾(Achmed〔ˈɑkmɛd; ˈɑːkmed〕, 1901–1970, 印尼領袖, 1945–1968 任總統)。(亦作 Soekarno)

su·ki·ya·ki〔ˈsukiˈjɑki; ˈsuːkiːˈjɑːkiː〕*n.* 壽喜燒(一種日本菜)。

sul·cate〔ˈsʌlket; ˈsʌlkeit〕*adj.* 〖植物、解剖〗有縱槽的。(亦作 **sulcated**)

sul·fa〔ˈsʌlfə; ˈsʌlfə〕*adj.* 〖化〗磺胺基的; 〖藥〗磺胺藥劑的。—*n.* 磺胺類藥劑。(亦作 **sulpha**)

sul·fa·di·a·zine〔ˌsʌlfəˈdaɪəˌzin; ˌsʌl-fəˈdaiəziːn〕*n.* 〖藥〗磺胺嘧啶;蘇發代辛;消炎片。(亦作 **sulphadiazine**)

sul·fa·guan·i·dine〔ˌsʌlfəˈgwænɪˌdin; ˌsʌlfəˈgwænidiːn〕*n.* 〖藥〗磺胺胍(治療腸病用)。(亦作 **sulphaguanidine**)

sul·fa·meth·a·zine〔ˌsʌlfəˈmɛθəzin; ˌsʌlfəˈmeθəziːn〕*n.*〖藥〗磺胺甲嘧啶(消炎用)。

sul·fa·nil·a·mide〔ˌsʌlfəˈnɪləˌmaɪd; ˌsʌlfəˈniləmaid〕*n.* 〖化、藥〗對胺基苯磺醯胺(治淋病、敗血症)。(亦作 **sulphanilamide**)

sul·fa·pyr·i·dine〔ˌsʌlfəˈpɪrɪˌdin; ˌsʌlfəˈpiəridiːn〕*n.* 〖化、藥〗磺胺吡啶; 大健凰。(亦作 **sulphapyridine**)

sulf·ars·phen·a·mine〔ˌsʌlfɑrsˈfɛnəmin; ˌsʌlfɑːsˈfenəmiːn〕*n.* 〖藥〗硫阿斯凡納明(梅毒治療劑)。

sul·fa·sux·i·dine〔ˌsʌlfəˈsʌksəˌdin; ˌsʌlfəˈsʌksədiːn〕*n.* 〖藥〗磺胺撒克西啶(可治腸胃傳染病)。

sul·fate〔ˈsʌlfet; ˈsʌlfeit〕*n., v.,* **-fat·ed, -fat·ing.** —*n.* 〖化〗硫酸鹽。—*v.t.* ①以硫酸或硫酸鹽處理。②使變爲硫酸鹽。③使產生硫酸鹽之沉澱。—*v.i.* 硫化。(亦作 **sulphate**) —**sul·fa·tion,** *n.*

sul·fa·thi·a·zole〔ˌsʌlfəˈθaɪəˌzol; ˌsʌlfəˈθaiəzoul〕*n.* 〖藥〗磺胺噻唑(治肺炎等傳染病)。(亦作 **sulphathiazole**)

sul·fid〔ˈsʌlfɪd; ˈsʌlfid〕*n.* =**sulfide.**

sul·fide〔ˈsʌlfaɪd; ˈsʌlfaid〕*n.* 〖化〗硫化物。(亦作 **sulphide**)

sul·fite〔ˈsʌlfaɪt; ˈsʌlfait〕*n.* ①〖化〗亞硫酸鹽。②〖俚〗思想言行別出心裁者。(亦作 **sulphite**) —**sul·fit·ic,** *adj.*

sul·fo·nal〔ˈsʌlfəˌnæl; ˈsʌlfənæl〕*n.* 〖化〗雙(乙碸基)代丙烷;丙酮二乙碸。

sul·fon·a·mide〔sʌlˈfɑnəmaɪd; sʌlˈfɔnəmaid〕*n.* 〖藥〗磺胺類藥劑。(亦作 **sulphonamide**)

sul·fon·ic〔səlˈfɑnɪk; səlˈfɔnik〕*adj.* 〖化〗酸性硫酸基的。(亦作 **sulphonic**)

sulfonic acid 〖化〗磺酸。

sul·fon·meth·ane〔ˌsʌlfonˈmɛθen; ˌsʌlfounˈmeθein〕*n.* 〖藥〗丙酮縮二乙碸(一種鎮靜劑)。(亦作 **sulphonmethane**)

***sul·fur**〔ˈsʌlfɚ; ˈsʌlfə〕*n.* ①〖化〗硫磺(一種非金屬元素,符號爲S)。②(蟲)黃蝶。③硫磺色。—*adj.* 硫磺色的。

sul·fu·rate〔*v.* ˈsʌlfəˌret; ˈsʌlfəreit *adj.* ˈsʌlfərɪt; ˈsʌlfərit〕*v.,* **-rat·ed, -rat·ing,** *adj.* —*v.t.* 使同硫磺化合; 以硫磺處理; 使含硫磺; 以硫磺煙薰; 以硫磺漂白。—*adj.* 硫磺的;像硫磺的; 含硫磺的。(亦作 **sulphurate**) —**sul·fu·ra·tion,** *n.*

sul·fu·ra·tor〔ˈsʌlfəˌretɚ; ˈsʌlfəreitə〕*n.* 硫磺薰蒸器。

sulfur dioxide 〖化〗二氧化硫。

sul·fu·re·ous〔sʌlˈfjʊrɪəs; sʌlˈfjuəriəs〕*adj.* 硫磺的;含硫磺的;硫磺色的; 有硫磺臭氣的。(亦作 **sulphureous**)

sul·fu·ret〔*n.* ˈsʌlfjərɪt; ˈsʌlfjuret *v.* ˈsʌlfjəˌrɛt; ˈsʌlfjuret〕*n., v.,* **-ret·(t)ed, -ret·(t)ing.** —*n.* 〖化〗硫化物。—*v.t.* 使同硫化合;使含硫。(亦作 **sulphuret**)

sul·fu·ret·(t)ed〔ˈsʌlfjəˌrɛtɪd; ˈsʌlfjuretid〕*adj.*與硫磺化合的;含硫磺的;硫化的。

sulfureted hydrogen 〖化〗硫化氫。(亦作 **sulfuretted hydrogen**)

sul·fu·ric〔sʌlˈfjʊrɪk; sʌlˈfjurik〕*adj.* ①硫磺的。②〖化〗含(正六價之)硫的。

sulfuric acid 〖化〗硫酸。

sul·fu·rize〔ˈsʌlfjəˌraɪz; ˈsʌlfjuəraiz〕*v.t.,* **-rized, -riz·ing.** ①使同硫磺化合; 以硫磺處理; 使含硫磺。②以二氧化硫薰。(亦作 **sulphurize**) —**sul·fu·ri·za·tion,** *n.*

sul·fur·ous〔ˈsʌlfərəs; ˈsʌlfərəs〕*adj.* ①硫磺的。②〖化〗含(正四價之)硫的。③硫磺色的。④似燃燒之硫磺的(指臭味、顏色等言)。

sulfurous acid 〖化〗亞硫酸。

sulfur spring 硫磺礦泉。

sul·fur·y〔ˈsʌlfərɪ; ˈsʌlfəri〕*adj.* 硫磺的;像硫磺的。

sulk〔sʌlk; sʌlk〕*v.i.* 慍怒。—*n.* ①慍怒的發作;慍怒的狀態。②(*pl.*) 慍怒發作時所表現的壞脾氣。to be in the *sulks*. 發脾氣。③(亦作 **sulker**) 慍怒的人。

sulk·y〔ˈsʌlkɪ; ˈsʌlki〕*adj.,* **sulk·i·er, sulk·i·est,** *n., pl.* **sulk·ies.** —*adj.* ①慍怒的; 鬱鬱不樂的。②陰沈的(天氣)。—*n.* 一人乘坐的兩輪輕便馬車。—**sulk·i·ly,** *adv.* —**sulk·i·ness,** *n.*

sul·lage〔ˈsʌlɪdʒ; ˈsʌlidʒ〕*n.* ①廢物;汚物;淤泥。②〖冶金〗熔渣。

***sul·len**〔ˈsʌlɪn, –ən; ˈsʌlən, –lin〕*adj.* ①慍怒的; 鬱鬱不樂的。②陰沉的。—**ly,** *adv.*

—ness, *n.*

sul·lens ['sʌlɪnz; 'sʌlənz] *n. pl.* 慍怒。

sul·ly ['sʌlɪ; 'sʌli] *v.*, **-lied, -ly·ing,** *n., pl.* **-lies.** —*v.t.* 使污；染污；玷污。—*v.i.* 變污；被玷污。—*n.* 污；污點；瑕疵；暗晦。

Sul·ly-Pru·dhomme [ˌsy'li ˌpry'dɔm; ˌsy'liːˌpry'dɔːm] *n.* 徐利普魯東 (René François Armand, 1839–1907, 法國詩人及批評家, 1901年得諾貝爾文學獎)。

sulph- 〖字首〗 **sulf-** 或 **sulfa-** 之異體。

sul·pha ['sʌlfə; 'sʌlfə] *adj., n.* =**sulfa.**

sul·pha·nil·a·mide [ˌsʌlfə'nɪləˌmaɪd; ˌsʌlfə'niləmaid] *n.* =**sulfanilamide.**

sul·phate ['sʌlfet; 'sʌlfeit] *n., v.,* **-phat·ed, -phat·ing.** =**sulfate.**

sul·pha·thi·a·zole [ˌsʌlfə'θaɪəˌzol; ˌsʌlfə'θaiəzoul] *n.* =**sulfathiazole.**

sul·phide ['sʌlfaɪd; 'sʌlfaid] *n.* =**sulfide.**

sul·phite ['sʌlfaɪt; 'sʌlfait] *n.* =**sulfite.**

***sul·phur** ['sʌlfɚ; 'sʌlfə] *n., adj.* =**sulfur.**

sul·phu·ric [sʌl'fjurɪk; sʌl'fjurik] *adj.* =**sulfuric.**

sul·phur·ous ['sʌlfərəs; 'sʌlfərəs] *adj.* =**sulfurous.**

sul·tan** ['sʌltn̩; 'sʌltən] *n.* ①回教國之君主；蘇丹。②(S-)昔日土耳其君主。③(S-)一種足部多毛之鷄。④一種秧鷄科之鳥。the sweet (yellow) sultan*** 紫(黃)矢車菊。—**ic,** —**like,** *adj.* —**ship,** *n.*

sul·tan·a [sʌl'tænə; sʌl'tɑːnə] *n.* ①回教國君主之后、妃、太后、公主或其姐妹等。②(亦作 **sultana bird**) 一種秧鷄科之鳥。③一種無核之小白葡萄。④國王或皇族的嬪妃。⑤深紫紅色。

sul·tan·ate ['sʌltn̩ɪt; 'sʌltənit] *n.* 回教國王之王位、王權或領土。

sul·tan·ess ['sʌltənɪs; 'sʌltənis] *n.* 回教國君主之后、妃、太后、公主、或其姐妹。

***sul·try** ['sʌltrɪ; 'sʌltri] *adj.,* **-tri·er, -tri·est.** ①溽暑的；酷熱的；悶熱的。②熱情的；肉慾的；性感的。—**sul·tri·ly,** *adv.* —**sul·tri·ness,** *n.*

Su·lu Archipelago ['sulu~; 'suːluː~] 蘇祿羣島 (在菲律賓羣島之西南部)。

Sulu Sea 蘇祿海 (在菲律賓西南部與婆羅洲之間)。

‡**sum** [sʌm; sʌm] *n., v.,* **summed, sum·ming.** —*n.* ①總數；和。The *sum* of 2 and 2 is 4. 二與二之和爲四。②〖俗〗算術題。③金額。He paid a large *sum* for the house. 他出一筆鉅款買了這所房子。④概略；要點。⑤全部。***in sum*** 簡言之。—*v.t.* ①總計；合計〖up〗。②概括；約略而言〖up〗. The judge *summed* up the evidence. 法官概述證據。—*v.i.* ①總計。These instances *sum* up to several dozen. 這些例子總計數十個。②概約；約略而言。***sum up*** **a.** 計算；點數。**b.** 集中。**c.** 簡括地說；摘要。To *sum up*, she is a nice girl. 總括言之, 她是一個可愛的女孩。**d.** 估量；打量。**e.** 在陪審團退席商討判決前向該團陳述證據之要點。

SUM surface-to-underwater missile. 地對海底飛彈。

su·mac, su·mach ['ʃumæk; 'suːmæk] *n.* ①〖植物〗鹽膚木。②鹽膚木乾葉之製品(用做鞣革及染色)。

Su·ma·tra [sʊ'mɑtrə; su(ː)'mɑːtrə] *n.* 蘇門答臘(印尼西部之一大島)。

Su·ma·tran [sʊ'mɑtrən; su(ː)'mɑːtrən] *adj.* 蘇門答臘島的；蘇門答臘人的。—*n.* ①蘇門答臘人。②蘇門答臘之印尼語。

sum·less ['sʌmlɪs; 'sʌmlis] *adj.* 無數的；多至不可計數的。

sum·ma·ble ['sʌməbl; 'sʌməbl] *adj.* 〖數學〗可求和的。

sum·ma cum lau·de ['sʌməˌkʌm'lɔdɪ; 'sʌməˌkʌm'lɔːdi] 〖拉〗以最高榮譽 (=with the highest honor or praise).

sum·mand ['sʌmænd; 'sʌmænd] *n.* 被加數。

sum·ma·ri·ly ['sʌmərəlɪ; 'sʌmərili] *adv.* 迅速地；草草地。

sum·ma·rist ['sʌmərɪst; 'sʌmərist] *n.* 做摘要者。

sum·ma·rize ['sʌməˌraɪz; 'sʌməraiz] *v.t.* & *v.i.,* **-rized, -riz·ing.** 摘要；概述。—**sum·ma·riz·er, sum·ma·ri·za·tion,** *n.* —**sum·ma·riz·a·ble,** *adj.*

***sum·ma·ry** ['sʌmərɪ; 'sʌməri] *n., pl.* **-ries,** *adj.* —*n.* 摘要；概略。—*adj.* ①簡明的；簡短的。②迅速的；卽時的；卽決的。

summary judgment 〖法律〗未經過陪審團聽審卽下的判決。

summary proceeding 〖法律〗不經辯論而只根據法律條文所做的審判。

sum·mate ['sʌmet; 'sʌmeit] *v.t.,* **-mat·ed, -mat·ing.** 加；求…之總和。

sum·ma·tion [sʌm'eʃən; sʌ'meiʃən] *n.* ①〖數學〗加；加法。②和；總和。③〖法律〗案件判決前辯論的最後總結。

‡**sum·mer**[1] ['sʌmɚ; 'sʌmə] *n.* ①夏；夏季(在美爲六, 七, 八三個月, 在英爲五月中旬至八月中旬)。in (the) *summer.* 在夏天。②(*pl.*)年齡。a girl of ten *summers.* 一個十歲的女孩。③青春；全盛期。—*adj.* 夏季的。a *summer* dress. 夏裝。the *summer* holidays (*or* vacation). 暑假。—*v.i.* 過夏；避暑〖at, in〗. They *summered* at the seashore. 他們在海濱過夏。—*v.t.* 夏季飼餵；於夏季作。—**less,** *adj.*

sum·mer[2] *n.* 〖建築〗①大梁；桁；框架之最長橫木。②楣；楣石。

summer camp 夏令營。

summer house 夏季別墅。

sum·mer·house ['sʌmɚˌhaus; 'sʌməhaus] *n., pl.* **-hous·es.** 涼亭。

sum·mer·ing ['sʌmərɪŋ; 'sʌməriŋ] *n.* ①度暑假；避暑。②夏季放牧。③〖英〗一種早熟蘋果。

summer lightning 聽不見雷聲的來自遠方的閃電。

sum·mer·ly ['sʌməlɪ; 'sʌməli] *adj.* 夏季的；如夏的。

summer resort 避暑地。

sum·mer·sault ['sʌmɚˌsɔlt; 'sʌməsɔːlt] *n., v.i.* =**somersault.**

summer school 暑期講習會；暑期學校。

sum·mer·set ['sʌmɚˌsɛt; 'sʌməset] *n., v.i.* =**somersault.**

summer solstice 夏至。

summer theater 夏令戲院 (在郊區或避暑地上演者)。

sum·mer·time ['sʌmɚˌtaɪm; 'sʌmətaim] *n.* ①夏季。②〖英〗日光節約時間；夏令時間。

summer White House 美國總統夏令辦公避暑之官邸。

sum·mer·y ['sʌmərɪ; 'sʌməri] *adj.* 夏的；如夏的。

sum·ming-up ['sʌmɪŋ'ʌp; 'sʌmiŋ'ʌp] *n., pl.* **sum·mings-up.** 總結；結論。

sum·mit** ['sʌmɪt; 'sʌmit] *n.* ①巔峯；絕頂。to reach the *summit* of fame. 達到榮譽的巔峯。②高階層會議。at the summit*** 〖外交〗最高階層的；國家元首之間的。—*adj.* 〖外交〗國家元首之間的。***summit conference***

(or *meeting*) 高階層會議;高峯會議。

***sum·mon** ['sʌmən; 'sʌmən] *v.t.* ①召喚;傳喚。②召集。③鼓起;奮起〖常 up〗. to *summon* up all one's courage. 鼓足勇氣。

sum·mon·er ['sʌmənɚ; 'sʌmənə] *n.* 召喚者;傳喚者;召集者;(尤指)送法院傳票者。

sum·mons ['sʌmənz; 'sʌmənz] *n., pl.* **-mons·es,** *v.* —*n.* ①傳喚;召喚。②傳票。—*v.t.*〖俗〗送達傳票;以傳票召傳。

sum·mum bo·num ['sʌməm'bonəm;'sʌməm'bounəm]〖拉〗至善(=highest good).

Sum·ner ['sʌmnɚ; 'sʌmnə] *n.* 索姆奈 (James Batcheller, 1887–1955, 美國生物化學家,曾獲1946年諾貝爾化學獎)。

su·mo ['sumo;'su:mou]〖日〗*n.* 角力;相撲(大力士摔角之日本競技)。—**ist,** *n.*

sump [sʌmp; sʌmp] *n.* ①〖採礦〗聚水坑;礦脈底坑;油井。②內燃機送油器中的最低貯油槽;(汽車等的)催滑油壺。③汚水坑;沼澤。

sump·ter ['sʌmptɚ; 'sʌmptə] *n.* 馱馬;馱獸。*sumpter* horse. 馱馬。*sumpter* mule. 馱騾。

sump·tion ['sʌmpʃən; 'sʌmpʃən] *n.*「〖邏輯〗大前提。」

sump·tu·ar·y ['sʌmptʃuˌɛrɪ; 'sʌmptjuəri] *adj.* 費用的;限制費用的;規定費用的。

sump·tu·os·i·ty [ˌsʌmptʃu'ɑsətɪ; ˌsʌmptju'ɔsiti] *n.* 奢侈;高價;費用浩大。

sump·tu·ous ['sʌmptʃuəs; 'sʌmptjuəs] *adj.* 費用浩大的;奢侈的;華麗的。—**ly,** *adv.* —**ness,** *n.*

sum total ①總和;總計。②精華。

‡sun [sʌn; sʌn] *n., v.,* **sunned, sun·ning.** —*n.* ①(the–)日;太陽。The *sun* rises in the east. 太陽在東方升起。②陽光。③恒星。④鼎盛時期。His *sun* is set. 他的鼎盛時期已過。⑤光亮華麗如太陽的東西;發光之源;帶來光榮、繁華的東西。⑥一天。⑦一年。***against the sun***〖航海〗反時鐘方向。***a place in the sun*** a. 順境;利於發展的空間或情況。b. 名望;獲得賞識。***from sun to sun***〖古〗從日出到日落。***in the sun*** 在顯而易見的地方。***rise with the sun*** 起得很早。***see the sun*** 生存着。***take*** (or ***shoot***) ***the sun*** 航海時測定太陽高度以求緯度。***the midnight sun*** 在南北極區所見的子夜的太陽。***under the sun*** 在地球上;在世界上。***with the sun***〖航海〗順時鐘方向。—*v.i.* & *v.t.* 曬;曝;曬太陽。to *sun* oneself. 作日光浴。—**like,** *adj.*

Sun. Sunday.

sun-and-planet motion〖機械〗(差動齒輪裝置)遊星運動。

sun·baked ['sʌnˌbekt; 'sʌnbeikt] *adj.* ①太陽曬乾的。②炎熱的;炎暑的。

sun bath 日光浴。

sun·bathe ['sʌnˌbeð; 'sʌnbeið] *v.i.,* **-bathed, -bath·ing.** 行日光浴。

sun·bath·er ['sʌnˌbeðɚ; 'sʌnˌbeiðə] *n.* 日光浴者。

sun·bath·ing ['sʌnˌbeðɪŋ; 'sʌnˌbeiðiŋ] *n.* 日光浴。

***sun·beam** ['sʌnˌbim; 'sʌnbi:m] *n.* 日光;陽光。

sun·bird ['sʌnˌbɝd; 'sʌnbə:d] *n.*〖動物〗太陽鳥。

sun·blast·ed ['sʌnˌblæstɪd;'sʌnˌblɑ:stid] *adj.* 被日光曬焦的。

sun blind 窗前之蓬蓋;遮陽。

sun·bon·net ['sʌnˌbɑnɪt; 'sʌnˌbɔnit] *n.* (婦女和小孩所戴的)太陽帽。

sun·bright ['sʌnˌbraɪt; 'sʌnbrait] *adj.* ①很聰明的。②充滿陽光的。

sun·browned ['sʌnˌbraund; 'sʌnbraund] *adj.* 被太陽曬黑的。

sun·burn ['sʌnˌbɝn; 'sʌnbə:n] *n., v.,* **-burned** or **-burnt, -burn·ing.** —*n.* ①曬黑;日炙。②太陽曬成的紅褐色。—*v.t.* 日曬。—*v.i.* 曬黑。

sun·burned ['sʌnˌbɝnd; 'sʌnbə:nd] *adj.* 被太陽曬得發黑的。—*v.* pt. & pp. of **sunburn.**

sun burner 太陽燈(一組煤汽燈或電燈集中於天花板一處者)。

sun·burnt ['sʌnˌbɝnt; 'sʌnbə:nt] *v.* pt. & pp. of **sunburn.** —*adj.* 曬黑(焦)的。

sun·burst ['sʌnˌbɝst; 'sʌnbə:st] *n.* ①太陽自雲縫中之突現。②鑲有寶石的旭日形飾針。③任何旭日形裝飾或圖形。—*adj.* 旭日形的;線條從一個中心輻射的。

sun-clock ['sʌnˌklɑk; 'sʌnklɔk] *n.* 日規;日晷儀(=sundial).

sun crack 日曬所成的地上裂痕。

sun-cracked ['sʌnˌkrækt; 'sʌnkrækt] *adj.* 因日曬而起裂痕的。

sun-cured ['sʌnˌkjurd; 'sʌn-kjuəd] *adj.* 曬乾的。

Sund. Sunday. **sund.** sundries.

sun·dae ['sʌndɪ; 'sʌndei] *n.* 聖代(盛在杯裏的加水果蜜汁或其他佐料的冰淇淋)。

Sun·da Isles ['sʌndə~; 'sʌndə~] 巽他羣島(分爲大巽他羣島與小巽他羣島二部,前者包括Java, Sumatra, Borneo 及 Celebes, 後者包括爪哇以東以迄葡屬 Timor 各島;其中除 Borneo 北部外均屬印尼)。

sun dance 印第安人在夏至時舉行的日光舞。

Sun·da·nese [ˌsʌndə'niz; ˌsʌndə'ni:z] *adj.* ①巽他羣島(Sunda Isles)的。②巽他羣島居民的。③巽他語的。—*n.* ①巽他民族。②巽他語。

Sunda Strait 巽他海峽(在Sumatra 島與Java島間)。

‡Sun·day ['sʌndɪ; 'sʌndi,-dei] *n.* 星期日;禮拜日。last (next) *Sunday*. 上(下)星期日。***a month of Sundays***〖諧〗很長的一段時間。***a Sunday saint*** (***and everyday sinner***) 僞善者。***one's Sunday clothes*** (or ***best***) 一個人最好的衣服。He was in *his Sunday best*. 他穿着他最好的衣服。***when two Sundays come together*** (or ***meet***) 一天那有兩個星期日;決不會。—*adj.* ①星期日的;禮拜日的。a *Sunday* supplement. (報紙的)星期日增刊。②祇有在星期日發生、舉行、或做的。③業餘的。—*v.i.* 作星期日的活動;過星期日。

Sun·day-go-to-meet·ing ['sʌndɪˌgotə'mitɪŋ; 'sʌndiˌgoutə'mi:tiŋ] *adj.*〖俗〗盛裝的;最佳的;最漂亮的。

Sunday letter 主日字母(曆書上爲表示一年之星期日所用之代表字母;每年元月一號至七號以A-G七個字母代表之,星期日若在那一字母,該年之星期日卽以此字母表之,如 1945 爲 G). (亦作 **dominical letter**)

Sunday painter 業餘畫家。

Sunday punch ①最厲害的一擊。②最厲害的一招;殺手鐧。

Sun·days ['sʌndɪz; 'sʌndiz] *adv.* 於每星期日。

Sunday school 主日學校。

sun·deck ['sʌnˌdɛk; 'sʌndek] *n.* ①客輪之上層甲板。②建築物或游泳池等之陽臺。(亦作 **sun deck**)

sun·der ['sʌndɚ; 'sʌndə] *v.t.* & *v.i.* 分開;隔離;分裂;斷絕。—*n.* 分離;分裂。—**a·ble,** *adj.* —**er,** *n.*

sun·dew ['sʌnˌdju;'sʌndju:] *n.*〖植物〗毛氈苔。

sun·di·al ['sʌn,daɪəl; 'sʌndaiəl] *n.* 日規;日晷儀。
sun·dog ['sʌn,dɔg; 'sʌndɔg] *n.* ①假日;幻日(日暈上所現之光輪)。②接近地平線之虹;不完整之虹。
***sun·down**¹ ['sʌn,daun; 'sʌndaun] *n.* 日落;日沒(=sunset). 「陽帽。」
***sun·down**² *n.* 〖美〗婦女所戴之寬邊遮
sun·down·er ['sʌn,daunɚ; 'sʌn,daunə] *n.* ①〖英〗日暮後之小飲。②〖美〗住在西方的人。③〖澳俚〗老是在日沒時光來至田莊藉口求職,而眞正目的爲獲免費食宿之無賴。
sun-drenched ['sʌn,drentʃt; 'sʌn-drentʃt] *adj.* 陽光普照的。
sun dress 領口前後開叉很低的無袖涼衫。
sun-dried ['sʌn,draɪd;'sʌndraid] *adj.* 太陽曬乾的。
sun·dries ['sʌndrɪz; 'sʌndriz] *n. pl.* ①雜貨;雜物;雜費;雜事。②〖簿記〗雜項。
sun·dry** ['sʌndrɪ; 'sʌndri] *adj.* 各色各樣的;幾種的;種種的;雜多的。all and sundry*** 每人;所有的人。 「沒。」
sun·fall ['sʌn,fɔl; 'sʌnfɔ:l] *n.* 日落;日
sun·fast ['sʌn,fæst; 'sʌnfɑ:st] *adj.* 經曝曬而不褪色的。
SUNFED Special United Nations Fund for Economic Development.
sun·fish ['sʌn,fɪʃ; 'sʌnfiʃ] *n., pl.* **-fish, -fish·es.** 翻車魚。 「*n.* 向日葵。」
sun·flow·er ['sʌn,flauɚ; 'sʌn,flauə]
‡**sung** [sʌŋ; sʌŋ] *v.* pt. & pp. of **sing.**
Sung [suŋ; suŋ] *n.* (中國之)宋朝(960–1279)。—*adj.* 宋朝的;宋代的。*Sung* wares. 宋代的瓷器。
Sun·ga·ri [sun'gɑri; sun'gɑ:ri:] *n.* 松花江(中國東北部之河流)。(亦作 **Sunghwa**)
Sung·kiang ['suŋ'dʒɪɑŋ; 'suŋ'gjɑ:ŋ] *n.* 松江(中國東北之一省,省會爲牡丹江市 Mutankiang).
sun·glass ['sʌn,glæs; 'sʌnglɑ:s] *n.* ①取火鏡(可將日光聚於一點之凸透鏡)。②(*pl.*) 太陽鏡。—*adj.* 太陽鏡的。
sun·glow ['sʌn,glo; 'sʌnglou] *n.* ①朝霞;晚霞。②太陽之暖光。
sun god 日神;太陽神。(亦作 **sun-god**)
sun hat 防日草帽。 「熱。」
sun-heat ['sʌn,hit; 'sʌnhi:t] *n.* 太陽
sun helmet 防日頭盔。
sunk [sʌŋk; sʌŋk] *v.* pt. & pp. of **sink.** —*adj.* ①下陷的;凹的。②灰心的。③完蛋的。
sunk·en ['sʌŋkən; 'sʌŋkən] *v.* pp. of **sink.** —*adj.* ①沉下的;沒於水中的。②凹的;下陷的。③低於一般平面的。 「欄等)。」
sunk fence 隱垣;隱籬(溝底設置之柵
sun lamp ①能發出紫外線之太陽燈。②電影攝影場等處使用之强光電燈。
sun·less ['sʌnlɪs; 'sʌnlis] *adj.* ①無日光的;黑暗的。②悽然的;陰森的。—**ly,** *adv.* —**ness,** *n.* 「光;太陽光。」
***sun·light** ['sʌn,laɪt; 'sʌnlait] *n.* 日
sun·lit ['sʌn,lɪt; 'sʌnlit] *adj.* ①陽光照耀的。②喜氣洋溢的。
sun·ni·ly ['sʌnəlɪ; 'sʌnili] *adv.* ①陽光充足地;晴朗地。②愉快地。
sun·ni·ness ['sʌnɪnɪs; 'sʌninis] *n.* ①陽光充足;晴朗。②愉快。
Sun·nite ['sunaɪt; 'sunait] *n.* 回教徒之一派(兼信 Koran 經與回教律法 Sunna);正統回教派。
***sun·ny** ['sʌnɪ; 'sʌni] *adj.,* **-ni·er, -ni·est.** ①向日的;當陽的。②陽光充足的;輝耀的;晴朗的。③歡樂的;愉快的。④太陽的;像太陽的。
sunny side ①朝太陽的一邊。the *sunny side* of the house. 房屋之朝陽面。②樂觀的部分。③尙不到某一年齡。She is on the *sunny side* of forty. 她四十歲未到。
sun·ny-side up ['sʌnɪ,saɪd~; 'sʌnisaid~] 僅煎一面的(蛋)。
sun parlor 窗戶很多陽光充足的房間。
sun porch 由玻璃所圍起的門廊。
sun-pow·ered ['sʌn,pauɚd; 'sʌn,pauəd] *adj.* 用日光能推動的;用日光能發動的。 「①不透陽光的。②耐陽光曬的。」
sun·proof ['sʌn,pruf; 'sʌnpru:f] *adj.*
sun·ray ['sʌn,re;'sʌnrei] *n.* 太陽光線。
***sun·rise** ['sʌn,raɪz; 'sʌnraiz] *n.* ①日出。②日出之時;黎明;拂曉。at *sunrise.* 黎明時。③日出時之大氣變化。④初期。
sun roof 汽車頂蓬上可開闔之孔。
sun·room ['sʌn,rum; 'sʌnrum] *n.* =**sun parlor.**
***sun·set** ['sʌn,sɛt; 'sʌnset] *n.* ①日沒;日落。②日沒之時;日暮;傍晚。③日落時大氣之變化。④衰落之期。the *sunset* of life. 晚年。 「似日落的;似日落一般美麗的。」
sun·set·ty ['sʌn,sɛtɪ; 'sʌn,seti] *adj.*
sun·shade ['sʌn,ʃed; 'sʌnʃeid] *n.* ①遮陽之物;天棚。②(商店前之)遮陽布幔。③婦人用之遮陽傘或闊邊帽。
***sun·shine** ['sʌn,ʃaɪn; 'sʌnʃain] *n.* ①日光。②晴天。③光明;愉快;令人快活之事物。She is the *sunshine* of the house. 她是全家幸福快樂之所寄。④陽光照射之處。—*adj.* ①愉快的;樂天的。②可共安樂而難以共患難的。
sun·shin·ing ['sʌn,ʃaɪnɪŋ; 'sʌn,ʃainiŋ] *adj.* 陽光照耀的。
sun·shin·y ['sʌn,ʃaɪnɪ; 'sʌn,ʃaini] *adj.* ①日光的;日光照耀的。②晴朗的;明亮的。③快活的;愉快的。 「滿陽光的。」
sun-shot ['sʌn,ʃɑt; 'sʌnʃɔt] *adj.* 充
sun shower 夏季之陣雨。
sun·spot ['sʌn,spɑt; 'sʌn-spɔt] *n.* 太陽黑子;日斑。 「(亦作 **sunspot period**)」
sunspot cycle 日斑周期;日斑循環。
sun star 〖動物〗海盤車。 「〖礦〗日長石。」
sun·stone ['sʌn,ston; 'sʌn-stoun] *n.*
sun·stroke ['sʌn,strok; 'sʌn-strouk] *n.* 〖醫〗中暍;日射病;中暑。
sun·struck ['sʌn,strʌk; 'sʌn-strʌk] *adj.* ①中暑的。②陽光照射的。
sun·suit ['sʌn,sut;'sʌnsju:t] *n.* 兒童赤膊時所穿之肩帶短褲。
sun·tan ['sʌn,tæn; 'sʌntæn] *n.* ①日曬的膚色。②一種棕黃色。③(*pl.*)卡其制服。—*adj.* 棕黃色的。 「照射之設施。」
sun trap 日光照射之處;使能獲得日光
sun·up ['sʌn,ʌp;'sʌnʌp] *n.* 日出;日出
sun visor (汽車之)遮陽板。 ⌊時光。⌋
sun·ward ['sʌnwɚd; 'sʌnwəd] *adj.* & *adv.* 向陽的(地)。 「*adv.* 向陽地。」
sun·wards ['sʌnwɚdz; 'sʌnwədz]
sun·wise ['sʌn,waɪz; 'sʌnwaiz] *adv.* 以太陽日常所見之運轉同方向;順時針方向。
sun worship 太陽崇拜。
Sun Yat-sen ['sʌn'jæt'sɛn, 'sun'jɑt-'sɛn; 'sun'yɑ:t'sen] 孫逸仙(1866–1925, 中華民國國父,即孫中山先生)。
Sun Yat-sen·ism ['sʌn'jæt'sɛnɪzm; 'sun'yɑ:t'senizm] 孫文思想。

sup** [sʌp; sʌp] *v.*, **supped, sup·ping,** *n.* —*v.i.* ①食晚餐。to *sup* on bread and milk. 以麪包牛奶爲晚餐。②飲啜。—*v.t.* ①供以晚餐。②飲啜。He that sups with the devil needs a long spoon.*** 〖諺〗與惡人交,必特別留意。***sup sorrows by the ladleful*** 嘗盡悲傷的滋味。—*n.* 啜飲。***neither bite nor sup*** 飲食全無。

sup- 〖字首〗**sub-** 之異體（用在 p 之前）。

sup. ①supra (=above). ②superior. ③superlative. ④supine. ⑤supplement(ary). ⑥supply. ⑦supreme. **Sup.Ct.** ①Superior Court. ②Supreme Court.

supe [sup; su:p] *n.* 〖俚〗=**super.**

su·per [ˈsupɚ; ˈsju:pə] *n.* 〖俗〗①冗員;額外人員;(尤指)臨時演員;小配角。②〖商〗特等物品;特大號物品。③監督;指揮者。④裝訂書籍用的上漿之薄棉布。—*adj.* ①面積的;平方的。②〖俚〗特等的;特佳的。③非凡的;超級的。④過度的;過分的。—*adv.* ①非常地。②過分地。—*v.t.* 用上漿之薄棉布裝訂(書籍)。

super- 〖字首〗表下列諸義:①在上;在…之上。如:superimpose（放在上面;疊上)。②加之;更。如: superadd（再加上)。③超過;過度。如: superabundant（過度的)。④絕倫;最高。如: superman（超人), supernatural（超自然的)。⑤次一等;副的。如:superparasite（複寄生蟲)。

su·per·a·ble [ˈsupərəbl̩; ˈsju:pərəbl] *adj.* 可勝過的;可征服的;可超越的。—**su·per·a·bly,** *adv.* —**su·per·a·bil·i·ty,** —**ness,** *n.*

su·per·a·bound [ˌsupərəˈbaund; ˌsju:pərəˈbaund] *v.i.* ①極充足。②有餘。

su·per·a·bun·dance [ˌsupərəˈbʌndəns; ˌsju:pərəˈbʌndəns] *n.* ①極多;很多。②過多;過剩。

su·per·a·bun·dant [ˌsupərəˈbʌndənt; ˌsju:pərəˈbʌndənt] *adj.* ①極多的;很多的。②過多的;過剩的。—**ly,** *adv.*

su·per·ac·id [ˌsupɚˈæsɪd; ˌsju:pərˈæsid] *adj.* 酸性過多的;過酸的。

su·per·add [ˌsupɚˈæd; ˌsju:pərˈæd] *v.t.* 再加;再添。

su·per·ad·di·tion [ˌsupərəˈdɪʃən; ˌsju:pərəˈdiʃən] *n.* 再加;再添;加添物。

su·per·a·gen·cy [ˈsupɚˌedʒənsɪ; ˈsju:pərˌeidʒənsi] *n.* 超級機構;上級機構。

su·per·al·loy [ˌsupɚˈælɔɪ; ˌsju:pərˈælɔi] *n.* 超合金(鈷、鎳、鉻等含量很高的合金,能耐高熱,用以製造火箭及噴氣引擎等)。

su·per·an·nu·ate [ˌsupɚˈænjuˌet; ˌsju:pəˈrænjueit] *v.,* **-at·ed, -at·ing.** —*v.t.* ①因年老病弱而使之退職;給以養老金而罷退(官吏等)。②因陳舊過時而棄置;使變陳舊。—*v.i.* 變陳舊;退休。

su·per·an·nu·at·ed [ˌsupɚˈænjuˌetɪd; ˌsju:pəˈrænjueitid] *adj.* ①領養老金或年金而退休的。②老朽的。③舊式的;廢棄的。

su·per·an·nu·a·tion [ˌsupɚˌænjuˈeʃən; ˌsju:pəˌrænjuˈeiʃən] *n.* ①年老或病弱退職。②退職金;養老金。

su·per·a·tom·ic bomb [ˌsupərəˈtɑmɪk～; ˌsju:pərəˈtɔmik～] 氫彈。

su·perb [sʊˈpɝb; sju(:)ˈpə:b] *adj.* ①宏偉的;壯麗的;華美的。②極好的;上等的。③豐富的;豐盛的。a *superb* dinner. 一頓豐盛的晚餐。—**ly,** *adv.*

su·per·block [ˈsupɚˌblɑk; ˈsju:pəblɔk] *n.* 〖美〗都市內禁止車輛通行之美化地區。

su·per·bomb [ˈsupɚˌbɑm; ˈsju:pəbɔm] *n.* 氫彈。

su·per·bomb·er [ˌsupɚˈbɑmɚ; ˌsju:pəˈbɔmə] *n.* 超級轟炸機。

su·per·boy [ˈsupɚˌbɔɪ; ˈsju:pə-bɔi] *n.* 〖美、軍俗〗高空駕駛員;噴氣機駕駛員。

su·per·cal·en·der [ˌsupɚˈkæləndɚ; ˌsju:pəˈkælində] *n.* 使紙面光滑用的滾筒。—*v.t.* 將(紙)放在滾筒裏壓使之表面光滑。

su·per·cal·en·dered [ˌsupɚˈkæləndɚd; ˌsju:pəˈkælindəd] *adj.* 特別光滑的(紙)。

su·per·car·go [ˌsupɚˈkɑrgo; ˈsju:pəˌkɑ:gou] *n., pl.* **-goes, -gos.** 商船上貨物管理人。—**ship,** *n.*

su·per·car·ri·er [ˈsupɚˌkærɪɚ; ˈsju:pəˌkæriə] *n.* 超級航空母艦。

su·per·cen·ter [ˈsupɚˌsɛntɚ; ˈsju:pəˌsentə] *n.* 市郊之大商業中心。

su·per·charge [ˌsupɚˈtʃɑrdʒ; ˈsju:pətʃɑ:dʒ] *v.,* **-charged, -charg·ing,** *n.* —*v.t.* ①過度地裝塡;過度地苛責。②以增壓器增大(引擎)馬力。③使過分充滿感情、危險等。—*n.* ①過度裝塡的火藥。②豐富;充沛。

su·per·charg·er [ˈsupɚˌtʃɑrdʒɚ; ˈsju:pəˌtʃɑ:dʒə] *n.* (內燃機之)增壓器。

su·per·church [ˈsupɚˌtʃɝtʃ; ˈsju:pətʃə:tʃ] *n.* 超型教會(由一群小型教會組成)。

su·per·cil·i·ar·y [ˌsupɚˈsɪlɪˌɛrɪ; ˌsju:pəˈsiliəri] *adj.* ①眼上的;眼瞼上的。②眉的。③眼上帶一撮毛的或一條痕的。

su·per·cil·i·ous [ˌsupɚˈsɪlɪəs; ˌsju:pəˈsiliəs] *adj.* 輕蔑的;傲慢的;自大的;目空一切的;盛氣凌人的。—**ly,** *adv.* —**ness,** *n.*

su·per·cit·y [ˈsupɚˈsɪtɪ; ˈsju:pəˈsiti] *n.* 超級都市(由二個以上都市合併而成)。

su·per·clus·ter [ˌsupɚˈklʌstɚ; ˌsju:pəˈklʌstə] *n.* 〖天文〗超級星團(由若干galaxy所形成)。

su·per·co·lum·ni·a·tion [ˌsupɚkəˌlʌmnɪˈeʃən; ˌsju:pəkəˌlʌmniˈeiʃən] *n.* 〖建築〗重柱式。

su·per·con·scious [ˌsupɚˈkɑnʃəs; ˌsju:pəˈkɔnʃəs] *adj.* 超意識的;最高意識的。

su·per·cool [ˌsupɚˈkul; ˌsju:pəˈku:l] *v.t. & v.i.* 〖理化〗過度冷却(使達於冰點以下而不凝結)。—**ed,** *adj.* —**ing,** *n.*

su·per·coun·try [ˈsupɚˈkʌntrɪ; ˈsju:pəˈkʌntri] *n.* 超級强國。

su·per·cres·cent [ˌsupɚˈkrɛsn̩t; ˌsju:pəˈkresnt] *adj.* 寄生的。

su·per·crit·i·cal [ˌsupɚˈkrɪtəkl̩; ˌsju:pəˈkritikəl] *adj.* 吹毛求疵的。

su·per·dense [ˈsupɚˌdɛns; ˈsju:pədens] *adj.* 過分茂密或緊湊的。

su·per·dom·i·nant [ˌsupɚˈdɑmənənt; ˌsju:pəˈdɔminənt] *n.* 〖音樂〗音階之第六音;下中音。

su·per·dread·nought [ˌsupɚˈdrɛdˌnɔt; ˌsju:pəˈdrednɔ:t] *n.* 超無畏艦(屬無畏艦級,但噸位、火力均較大)。

su·per-du·per [ˈsupɚˈdupɚ; ˈsju:pəˈdu:pə] 〖美俚〗*adj.* 最大的;最佳的;極;最。—*n.* 同類事物中之最大或最佳者。

su·per·du·ty [ˌsupɚˈdjutɪ; ˌsju:pəˈdju:ti] *adj.* 供特別苛酷之用途的;堪受酷使的。

su·per·e·go [ˌsupɚˈigo; ˌsju:pərˈegou] *n.* 〖心理分析〗超我。

su·per·em·i·nent [ˌsupɚˈɛmənənt; ˌsju:pərˈeminənt] *adj.* 出類拔萃的;特別崇高的。—**ly,** *adv.*

su·per·er·o·gate 〔ˌsupəˈɛrəget; ˌsjuːpərˈerəgeit〕 *v.i.*, **-gat·ed, -gat·ing.** ①做額外的工作。②以過度彌補不足。

su·per·er·o·ga·tion 〔ˌsupəˌɛrəˈgeʃən; ˌsjuːpərˌerəˈgeiʃən〕 *n.* ①超出職務的工作; 額外的工作。②分外立功。***works of supererogation*** 〖天主教〗餘功; 立功勞(除遵守上帝誡命外所作之善事)。

su·per·e·rog·a·to·ry 〔ˌsupərəˈrɑgəˌtorɪ; ˌsjuːpəreˈrɔgətəri〕 *adj.* ①職務以外的;分外的;額外的。②多餘的;累贅的。

su·per·ette 〔ˌsupəˈɛt; ˌsjuːpəˈret〕 *n.* 〖美〗小型超級市場。

su·per·ex·cel·lence 〔ˌsupəˈɛksələns; ˌsjuːpərˈeksələns〕 *n.* 卓越;無上;絕妙。

su·per·ex·cel·lent 〔ˌsupəˈɛksələnt; ˌsjuːpərˈeksələnt〕 *adj.* 卓越的; 無上的; 極佳的;絕妙的。—**ly,** *adv.*

su·per·ex·press 〔ˈsjupərɪksˈprɛs; ˈsjuːpəriksˈpres〕 *adj.* 超特快的。—*n.* 超特快(列車)。

su·per·fat·ted 〔ˌsupəˈfætɪd; ˌsjuːpəˈfætid〕 *adj.* 含脂肪過多的 (肥皂等)。

*__su·per·fi·cial__ 〔ˌsupəˈfɪʃəl; ˌsjuːpəˈfiʃəl〕 *adj.* ①表面的;近表面的。②表皮的。③膚淺的; 淺薄的。④面積的; 平方的。—*n.* 表面;外表。—**ly,** *adv.* —**ness,** *n.*

su·per·fi·cial·ist 〔ˌsupəˈfɪʃəlɪst; ˌsjuːpəˈfiʃəlist〕 *n.* 思想膚淺者; 見解淺薄者。

su·per·fi·ci·al·i·ty 〔ˌsupəˌfɪʃɪˈælətɪ; ˌsjuːpəˌfiʃiˈæliti〕 *n., pl.* **-ties.** ①膚淺; 皮相;淺薄。②膚淺之事物。

su·per·fi·cial·ize 〔ˌsupəˈfɪʃəlˌaɪz; ˌsjuːpəˈfiʃəlaiz〕 *v.t.*, **-ized, -iz·ing.** 使膚淺;膚淺地處理。

su·per·fi·ci·ar·y 〔ˌsupəˈfɪʃɪˌɛrɪ; ˌsjuːpəˈfiʃiəri〕 *n., pl.* **-ries,** *adj.* —*n.* 〖法律〗有地上權的人。—*adj.* ①表面的;膚淺的。②〖法律〗位於或建築於他人土地上的(建築物)。

su·per·fi·ci·es 〔ˌsupəˈfɪʃɪˌiz; ˌsjuːpəˈfiʃiiːz〕 *n. sing.* or *pl.* ①表面; 外貌; 外觀; 可見之界限;表面之地區;面積。②〖法律〗地上建築物;地上權。

su·per·film 〔ˈsjupəˌfɪlm; ˈsjuːpəfilm〕 *n.* 特製影片。

su·per·fine 〔ˌsupəˈfaɪn; ˈsjuːpəˈfain〕 *adj.* ①最上品的; 極精緻的。②過分纖細的; 過分精緻的。—**ly,** *adv.* —**ness,** *n.*

su·per·flu·id 〔ˈsupəˌfluɪd; ˈsjuːpəˌflu(ː)id〕 *n.* 超流體(接近絕對零度時毫無黏性之流體)。—*adj.* 超流動性的;毫無黏性的。

su·per·flu·i·ty 〔ˌsupəˈfluətɪ; ˌsjuːpəˈflu(ː)iti〕 *n., pl.* **-ties.** ①多餘;冗多。②冗物;多餘之物。

*__su·per·flu·ous__ 〔suˈpɝfluəs; sju(ː)ˈpəːfluəs〕 *adj.* 過多的; 多餘的; 不必要的。—**ly,** *adv.* —**ness,** *n.*

su·per·gal·ax·y 〔ˈsupəˌgæləksɪ; ˈsjuːpəˌgæləksi〕 *n., pl.* **-ax·ies.** 超星羣(由許多星羣合成之星羣)。

su·per·gi·ant 〔ˈsupəˌdʒaɪənt; ˈsjuːpəˌdʒaiənt〕 *n.* 超級星 (光度超過太陽100至10,000倍之星)。(亦作 **supergiant star**)

su·per·gla·cial 〔ˌsupəˈgleʃəl; ˌsjuːpəˈgleiʃəl〕 *adj.* 在冰河表面的;冰河表面上的。

su·per·gov·ern·ment 〔ˌsupəˈgʌvənmənt; ˌsjuːpəˈgʌvənmənt〕 *n.* ①國際政府。②超政府政治 (由政府外之團體控制政權的政治)。

su·per·heat 〔*n.* ˈsupəˌhit; ˈsjuːpəhiːt *v.* ˌsupəˈhit; ˌsjuːpəˈhiːt〕 *n.* 過熱;過熱狀態。—*v.t.* 過度加熱;使過熱。

su·per·heat·er 〔ˌsupəˈhitə; ˌsjuːpəˈhiːtə〕 *n.* 過熱裝置;過熱器。

su·per·heav·y 〔ˈsupəˌhɛvɪ; ˈsjuːpəˌhevi〕 *adj.* 原子序數比已知最重的元素高的。

su·per·het·er·o·dyne 〔ˌsupəˈhɛtərəˌdaɪn; ˈsjuːpəˈhetərədain〕 *adj.* 〖無線電〗①超致差的; 超成拍的。②超外差的; 超他拍的。—*n.* 〖無線電〗超外差式收音機。

su·per·high 〔ˈsjupəˈhaɪ; ˈsjuːpəˈhai〕 *adj.* 超高的。

superhigh frequency 超頻率 (3,000至30,000兆周之無線電頻率)。

su·per·high·way 〔ˌsupəˈhaɪˌwe; ˌsjuːpəˈhaiwei〕 *n.* 〖美〗超高速道路; 高級道路。

su·per·hu·man 〔ˌsupəˈhjumən; ˌsjuːpəˈhjuːmən〕 *adj.* ①超人的; 神靈的。②超乎常人的; 常人智力所不及的。—*n.* 超人。—**i·ty,** —**ness,** *n.* —**ly,** *adv.*

su·per·im·pose 〔ˌsupərɪmˈpoz; ˌsjuːpərimˈpouz〕 *v.t.*, **-posed, -pos·ing.** ①置於他物之上。②添加;附加。—**su·per·im·po·si·tion,** *n.*

su·per·im·posed 〔ˌsupərɪmˈpozd; ˌsjuːpərimˈpouzd〕 *adj.* 成階層的;有層理的。

su·per·in·cum·bent 〔ˌsupərɪnˈkʌmbənt; ˌsjuːpərinˈkʌmbənt〕 *adj.* ①橫置於他物上的;在上的。②自上面作用的(壓力)。③懸於上面的。—**su·per·in·cum·bence,** *n.* —**ly,** *adv.*

su·per·in·di·vid·u·al 〔ˌsupəˌɪndɪˈvɪdʒuəl; ˌsjuːpəˌrindiˈvidjuəl〕 *adj.* 超個人的。

su·per·in·duce 〔ˌsupərɪnˈdjus; ˌsjuːpərinˈdjuːs〕 *v.t.*, **-in·duced, -in·duc·ing.** 加於其上; 加添; 引起。—**ment, su·per·in·duc·tion,** *n.*

su·per·in·fec·tion 〔ˌsupərɪnˈfɛkʃən; ˌsjuːpərinˈfekʃən〕 *n.* 〖病理〗重複傳染。

su·per·in·tend 〔ˌsuprɪnˈtɛnd; ˌsjuːprinˈtend〕 *v.t.* 監督;指揮;管理。—**er,** *n.*

su·per·in·tend·ence 〔ˌsuprɪnˈtɛndəns; ˌsjuːprinˈtendəns〕 *n.* 監督;指揮;管理。

su·per·in·tend·en·cy 〔ˌsuprɪnˈtɛndənsɪ; ˌsjuːprinˈtendənsi〕 *n., pl.* **-cies.** 主管、監督或指揮者之職分、地位、管區等。

*__su·per·in·tend·ent__ 〔ˌsuprɪnˈtɛndənt; ˌsjuːprinˈtendənt〕 *n.* 監督者;指揮者;管理者。a *superintendent* of a factory. 工廠監督。—*adj.* 監督的;管理的。—**ship,** *n.*

Superior, Lake 蘇必略湖(在美國與加拿大兩國之間)。

‡**su·pe·ri·or** 〔səˈpɪrɪə, su-; sju(ː)ˈpiəriə〕 *adj.* ①優良的;卓越的;質較好的。*superior* skill. 卓越的技巧。②較大的; 較多的。*superior* numbers. 較多之數目。③較高的;上級的。④有優越感的。⑤不受…影響的; 不向…屈服的〖常 to〗。⑥〖生物〗位置在上面的;在另一器官上面的。⑦〖天文〗(行星)軌道在地球軌道之外的。⑧位置較高的。***rise superior to*** 超越於; 不爲…所影響。***superior to*** **a.** 高於;大於;優於。**b.** 超越; 不受…影響。—*n.* ①長者;長輩;長官;上司。②優越者。③(S-) 修道院院長;方丈。The Mother (*or* Lady) *Superior.* 女修道院院長。

superior court ①(美國若干州內)有概括管轄權的法院。②上級法院。

su·pe·ri·or·ess 〔səˈpɪrɪərɪs; sju(ː)ˈpiəriəris〕 *n.* ①女長官;女上司;女長輩。②

女修道院院長。

superior goods 消費者收入增加時很吃香的貨品;高級商品。

***su·pe·ri·or·i·ty** 〔sə͵pɪrɪ'ɔrətɪ;sju(ː)͵piəri'ɔriti〕 *n.* 優越;卓越;優良。

superiority complex 〖心理〗優越感。

su·pe·ri·or·ly 〔sə'pɪrɪəlɪ; sju(ː)'piəriəli〕 *adv.* ①較優地。②高傲地;自負地。

su·per·ja·cent 〔͵supə'dʒesn̩t; ͵sjuːpə'dʒeisnt〕 *adj.* 停在上面的;置於上面的。

su·per·jet 〔'supə͵dʒɛt; 'sjuːpədʒet〕 *n.* 超音速噴射機。

superl. superlative.

su·per·la·tive**〔sə'pɝlətɪv, su-;sju(ː)'pəːlətiv〕 *adj.* ①最高的;無上的。a man of *superlative* wisdom. 極有智慧的人。②〖文法〗最高級的。the superlative degree*** 最高級。—*n.* ①最好者。②〖文法〗最高級;最高級的字。***speak*** (or ***talk***) ***in superlatives*** 言過其實;誇張。—**ly,** *adv.*

su·per·lin·e·ar 〔͵supə'lɪnɪə; ͵sjuːpə'liniə〕 *adj.* 在字行上面的。

su·per·lin·er 〔'supə͵laɪnə; 'sjuːpə͵lainə〕 *n.* 超級客輪。

su·per·lu·nar 〔͵supə'lunə; ͵sjuːpə'luːnə〕 *adj.* =**superlunary.**

su·per·lu·na·ry 〔͵supə'lunərɪ;͵sjuːpə'luːnəri〕 *adj.* ①在月之上的;在月外的。②天國的;世外的。

su·per·man〔'supə͵mæn;'sjuːpəmæn〕 *n., pl.* **-men.** 超人。—**hood,** *n.* —**ly,** *adj.*

su·per·man·nish 〔'supə͵mænɪʃ; 'sjuːpəmæniʃ〕 *adj.* 超人的;像超人的;超人之方法的。

su·per·ma·rine〔'supəmə'rin;'sjuːpəmə'riːn〕 *n.* 海上飛機。

su·per·mar·ket 〔'supə͵mɑrkɪt; 'sjuːpə͵mɑːkit〕 *n.* 〖美〗超級市場。

su·per·mun·dane 〔͵supə'mʌnden; ͵sjuːpə'mʌndein〕 *adj.* 超現世的;世外的。

su·per·nac·u·lum 〔͵supə'nækjələm;͵sjuːpə'nækjuləm〕 *n., pl.* **-la** 〔-lə;-lə〕, *adj.* —*n.* ①最上等的酒。②杯中餘酒的最後一口。③滿杯。—*adj.* 〖古〗至最後一滴的。

su·per·nal 〔su'pɝnl̩; sju(ː)'pəːnl〕 *adj.* 天上的;神聖的;至高的。—**ly,** *adv.*

su·per·na·tant 〔͵supə'netənt; ͵sjuː-pə'neitənt〕 *adj.* 浮於表面的。—*n.* 浮於表面之物。

su·per·na·tion·al 〔͵supə'næʃənl̩; ͵sjuːpə'næʃənl〕 *adj.* 超國家的;超民族的。

su·per·na·tion·al·ism 〔͵supə'næʃənl̩͵ɪzəm; ͵sjuːpə'næʃənəlizm〕 *n.* ①極端民族主義;極端國家主義。②超國家主義;超民族主義。

su·per·na·tion·al·ist 〔͵supə'næʃənl̩ɪst; ͵sjuːpə'næʃənəlist〕 *n., adj.* 極端國家主義者(的);極端民族主義者(的)。

su·per·na·tion·al·is·tic 〔͵supə͵næʃənl̩'ɪstɪk; ͵sjuːpə͵næʃənə'listik〕 *adj.* ①極端民族主義的。②極端民族主義者的。

su·per·nat·u·ral 〔͵supə'nætʃrəl; ͵sjuːpə'nætʃrəl〕 *adj.* 超自然的;神奇的;不可思議的。—*n.* 超自然的東西;超自然的影響;超自然的現象。—**ly,** *adv.* —**ness,** *n.*

su·per·nat·u·ral·ism 〔͵supə'nætʃrəl͵ɪzəm; ͵sjuːpə'nætʃrəlizm〕 *n.* ①超自然;超自然性;不可思議。②超自然主義(相信有超自然之神力支配自然與萬物);超自然信仰。

su·per·nat·u·ral·ist〔͵supə'nætʃrəlɪst; ͵sjuːpə'nætʃərəlist〕 *n.* 超自然論者;超自然主義者。

su·per·nat·u·ral·ize 〔͵supə'nætʃərəl͵aɪz; ͵sjuːpə'nætʃrəlaiz〕 *v.t.,* **-ized, -iz·ing.** 使超自然;超自然化;以超自然主義觀點解釋;視之爲超自然現象。

su·per·na·ture 〔'supə'netʃə; 'sjuːpə'neitʃə〕 *n.* 超自然界。

su·per·nor·mal 〔͵supə'nɔrməl; 'sjuːpə'nɔːməl〕 *adj.* 非凡的;異常的;超過一般的。—**i·ty,** —**ness,** *n.* —**ly,** *adv.*

su·per·nu·mer·ar·y〔͵supə'njumə͵rɛrɪ; 'sjuːpə'njuːmərəri〕 *adj., n., pl.* **-ar·ies.** —*adj.* 額外的;多餘的;臨時雇的。—*n.* ①多餘之人或物;冗員;臨時雇員。②〖戲劇〗(無臺詞的)臨時演員;小配角。

su·per·nu·tri·tion 〔͵supənju'trɪʃən; ͵sjuːpənju(ː)'triʃən〕 *n.* 營養過甚。

su·per·or·di·nar·y〔͵supə'ɔrdn̩͵ɛrɪ; ͵sju(ː)pər'ɔːdinəri〕 *adj.*超乎尋常的。

su·per·or·di·nate 〔*adj., n.* ͵supə'ɔrdn̩ɪt; ͵sju(ː)pər'ɔːdinit *v.* ͵supə'ɔrdn̩͵et; ͵sju(ː)pər'ɔːdineit〕 *adj., n., v.,* **-nat·ed, -nat·ing.** —*adj.* 上級的;上位的。—*n.* 上級者;上級。—*v.t.* 使占上級;使占上位。

su·per·or·gan·ic 〔͵supəɔr'gænɪk; ͵sjuːpərɔː'gænik〕 *adj.* 超有機的;形而上的;精神的。

su·per·per·son·al 〔͵supə'pɝsənl̩; ͵sju(ː)pə'pəːsnl〕 *adj.* 超人格的。

su·per·per·son·al·i·ty 〔͵supə͵pɝsən'ælətɪ; ͵sjuːpə͵pəːsə'næliti〕 *n.* 超人格存在。

su·per·phos·phate 〔͵supə'fɑsfet; ͵sjuːpə'fɔsfeit〕 *n.* 〖化〗①過磷酸鹽;酸性磷酸鹽。②過磷酸石灰。

su·per·phys·i·cal 〔͵supə'fɪzɪkl̩; ͵sjuːpə'fizikl〕 *adj.* 超物質的;物理法則所不能解釋的。

su·per·pose 〔͵supə'poz;'sjuːpə'pouz〕 *v.t.,* **-posed, -pos·ing.** ①置於他物之上;疊置〖on, upon〗。②〖數學〗疊置。③〖航空〗(雙翼機)一翼置於(他翼)之上。

su·per·po·si·tion 〔͵supəpə'zɪʃən; 'sjuːpəpə'ziʃən〕 *n.* 重疊;疊置;疊合。

su·per·pow·er 〔͵supə'pauə;͵sjuːpə'pauə〕 *n.* ①政治權力凌駕其他列强之國家;超級强國。②〖電〗總合電力;强大電力。—*adj.* 電力强大的。

su·per·re·al·ism 〔͵supə'riəl͵ɪzəm; ͵sjuːpə'riəlizm〕 *n.* 超現實主義。—**su·per·re·al·ist,** *n.*

su·per·salt 〔'supə͵sɔlt; 'sjuːpəsɔlt〕 *n.* 〖化〗酸性鹽(=acid salt).

su·per·sat·u·rate 〔͵supə'sætʃə͵ret; ͵sjuːpə'sætʃəreit〕 *v.t.,* **-rat·ed, -rat·ing.** 使過度飽和。—**su·per·sat·u·ra·tion,** *n.*

su·per·scribe 〔͵supə'skraɪb;͵sjuːpə'skraib〕 *v.t.,* **-scribed, -scrib·ing.** ①寫、標記、刻(姓名等)於某物上方或外面。②書寫姓名、住址等於(信件、包裹等)之外面。

su·per·script 〔'supə͵skrɪpt;'sjuːpəskript〕 *adj.* 書於上面的。—*n.* 書於上面的符號或文字(例: x^2 和 a^1 中之 2 與 1).

su·per·scrip·tion 〔͵supə'skrɪpʃən; ͵sjuːpə'skripʃən〕 *n.* ①寫或刻姓名、文字等於某物之上方或外面;寫姓名、地址等於信件或包裹之外面。②前義所書寫之姓名、文字、住址等。③〖藥〗藥方上之 recipe (拉=take) 字或其符號 R.

su·per·sede 〔͵supə'sid; ͵sjuːpə'siːd〕 *v.t.,* **-sed·ed, -sed·ing.** ①替代;代換。②充

任;接替;取而代之。③使越(某人)晉級。④優先次序高於…;比…優先。

su·per·se·de·as 〔ˌsupɚˈsidɪˌæs; ˌsjuːpəˈsiːdiæs〕 *n.* 〖法律〗停止訴訟之令狀。

su·per·sen·ior·i·ty 〔ˌsupɚsinˈjɔrətɪ; ˌsjuːpəsiːˈnjɔriti〕 *n.* 超年資(不按服務年限或年齡計算之年資)。

su·per·sen·si·tive 〔ˌsupɚˈsɛnsətɪv; ˌsjuːpəˈsensitiv〕 *adj.* ①感覺或神經過敏的。②〖攝影〗感光性極强的。③反應特別靈敏的。

su·per·ses·sion 〔ˌsupɚˈsɛʃən; ˌsjuːpəˈseʃən〕 *n.* 替代;廢撤;罷黜。

su·per·son·ic 〔ˌsupɚˈsɑnɪk; ˈsjuːpəˈsɔnik〕 *adj.* ①超音波的(卽每秒頻率超過 20,000 者)。*supersonic* waves. 超音波。②超音速的。*supersonic* aircraft. 超音速飛機。③特級的;超級的。

su·per·son·ics 〔ˌsupɚˈsɑnɪks; ˈsjuːpəˈsɔniks〕 *n.* 超音波學。

su·per·sound 〔ˈsupɚˌsaund; ˈsjuːpəsaund〕 *n.* 超音。

su·per·star 〔ˈsupɚˌstɑr; ˈsjuːpəstɑː〕 *n.* ①(運動、電影界之)超級明星;某行業中有極卓越表現者。②超級星體;特大之星球。

su·per·state 〔ˈsupɚˌstet; ˈsjuːpəsteit〕 *n.* 超級大國。

***su·per·sti·tion** 〔ˌsupɚˈstɪʃən; ˌsjuːpəˈstiʃən〕 *n.* 迷信。

su·per·sti·tion·ist 〔ˌsupɚˈstɪʃənɪst; ˌsjuːpəˈstiʃənist〕 *n.* 迷信者。

***su·per·sti·tious** 〔ˌsupɚˈstɪʃəs; ˌsjuːpəˈstiʃəs〕 *adj.* 迷信的。*superstitious* people (fears, customs, legends). 迷信的人(恐懼、習俗、傳說)。—**ly,** *adv.* —**ness,** *n.*

su·per·stra·tum 〔ˌsupɚˈstretəm; ˌsjuːpəˈstreitəm〕 *n.*, *pl.* **-ta** 〔-tə; -tə〕, **-tums.** 上層。

su·per·struc·ture 〔ˈsupɚˌstrʌktʃɚ; ˈsjuːpəˌstrʌktʃə〕 *n.* ①(建築於他物上之)上層構造或建築物。②在基層上之全部建築物。③〖航海〗軍艦中甲板以上的部分。④〖鐵路〗鐵軌與枕木。⑤〖土木〗橋脚或橋墩上之部分橋樑。

su·per·sub·tle 〔ˌsupɚˈsʌtl; ˌsjuːpəˈsʌtl〕 *adj.* 太精巧的;過於微妙的;太狡猾的。—**ty,** *n.*

su·per·tank·er 〔ˈsupɚˌtæŋkɚ; ˈsjuːpəˌtæŋkə〕 *n.* 超級油輪(七萬五千噸以上之油輪)。

su·per·tax 〔ˈsupɚˌtæks; ˈsjuːpətæks〕 *n.* 附加稅;附加所得稅。

su·per·ton·ic 〔ˌsupɚˈtɑnɪk; ˈsjuːpəˈtɔnik〕 *n.* 〖音樂〗(音階之)第二音;上主音。

su·per·vene 〔ˌsupɚˈvin; ˌsjuːpəˈviːn〕 *v.*, **-vened, -ven·ing.** —*v.i.* 接着來;附帶發生;併發;附加;續加。—*v.t.* 起於…之後;續…之後。—**su·per·ven·tion,** *n.*

***su·per·vise** 〔ˌsupɚˈvaɪz; ˈsjuːpəvaiz, ˌsjuːpəˈv-〕 *v.t.*, **-vised, -vis·ing.** 監督;管理;指導。Study halls are *supervised* by teachers. 自修室由教師監督。

***su·per·vi·sion** 〔ˌsupɚˈvɪʒən; ˌsjuːpəˈviʒən〕 *n.* 監督;管理。

***su·per·vi·sor** 〔ˌsjupɚˈvaɪzɚ; ˈsjuːpəvaizə, ˌsjuːpəˈv-〕 *n.* 監督者;管理者;監察人。—**y,** *adj.*

su·per·weap·on 〔ˈsupɚˌwɛpən; ˈsjuːpəˌwepən〕 *n.* 超級武器。

su·pi·nate 〔ˈsupənet; ˈsuːpineit〕 *v.t.* & *v.i.*, **-nat·ed, -nat·ing.** 將(手或臂)轉動使手掌向上或向前。

su·pine 〔*adj.* suˈpaɪn; sjuːˈpain *n.* ˈsupaɪn; ˈsjuːpain〕 *adj.* ①仰臥的;仰向的。②怠惰的;因循的;沒精打采的。—*n.* 前面加 to 的不定式動詞。—**ly,** *adv.* —**ness,** *n.*

supp. ①supplement. ②supplementary.

‡sup·per 〔ˈsʌpɚ; ˈsʌpə〕 *n.* 晚餐。*the Last Supper* (基督被釘十字架前夜與其門徒共食的)最後晚餐。

supper club 夜總會(=night club).

suppl. ①supplement. ②supplementary.

sup·plant 〔səˈplænt; səˈplɑːnt〕 *v.t.* ①(以不正當的方式)排擠;取而代之。②代替;取代。—**a·tion,** —**er,** *n.*

sup·ple 〔ˈsʌpl̩; ˈsʌpl〕 *adj.*, **-pler, -plest,** *v.*, **-pled, -pling.** —*adj.* ①柔軟的;易曲的。②柔順的。③逢迎的;取悅上司的。④善於適應的;易受影響的;順從的。—*v.t.* & *v.i.* 使柔軟;變爲柔軟。—**ness,** *n.*

sup·ple·jack 〔ˈsʌpl̩ˌdʒæk; ˈsʌpldʒæk〕 *n.* ①〖植物〗熊柳(一種熱帶及亞熱帶爬籐)。②熊柳所做的柔韌之杖。

sup·ple·ly 〔ˈsʌpl̩lɪ; ˈsʌplli〕 *adv.* 柔軟地;易曲地;柔順地。

***sup·ple·ment** 〔*n.* ˈsʌpləmənt; ˈsʌplimənt *v.* ˈsʌpləˌmɛnt; ˈsʌpliment〕 *n.* ①補充物;增補物。②補遺;補編;附刊;增刊。Sunday *supplement.* 星期天附刊。③〖數學〗補角;補弧。—*v.t.* 增補;補充。—**al,** *adj.* —**a·tion,** *n.*

sup·ple·men·ta·ry 〔ˌsʌpləˈmɛntərɪ; ˌsʌpliˈmentəri〕 *adj.* 增補的;補充的。—*n.* 增補物;補充物。

supplementary story 〖新聞〗補充消息;花絮。

sup·ple·tion 〔səˈpliʃən; səˈpliːʃən〕 *n.* 〖語言〗不規則字形變化(如 bad 之比較級爲 worse 等)。—**sup·ple·tive,** *adj.*

sup·pli·ance 〔ˈsʌplɪəns; ˈsʌpliəns〕 *n.* 〖罕〗懇求;哀求。

sup·pli·ant 〔ˈsʌplɪənt; ˈsʌpliənt〕 *n.* 懇求者;哀懇者。—*adj.* 哀懇的;表示懇求的。—**ly,** *adv.*

sup·pli·cant 〔ˈsʌplɪkənt; ˈsʌplikənt〕 *n.*, *adj.* =**suppliant.**

sup·pli·cate 〔ˈsʌplɪˌket; ˈsʌplikeit〕 *v.i.* & *v.t.*, **-cat·ed, -cat·ing.** ①懇求;籲請。②祈禱。—**sup·pli·ca·tor,** *n.*

sup·pli·ca·tion 〔ˌsʌplɪˈkeʃən; ˌsʌpliˈkeiʃən〕 *n.* ①懇求。②祈禱。

sup·pli·ca·to·ry 〔ˈsʌplɪkəˌtorɪ; ˈsʌplikətəri〕 *adj.* 懇求的;哀求的;請求的。

sup·pli·er 〔səˈplaɪɚ; səˈplaiə〕 *n.* 供給者;補充者。

‡sup·ply¹ 〔səˈplaɪ; səˈplai〕 *v.*, **-plied, -ply·ing,** *n.*, *pl.* **-plies.** —*v.t.* ①供給;備辦。We *supplied* them with money. 我們供給他們金錢。The government *supplies* books for the school children. 政府供給學童書籍。②滿足。③補充;補缺。—*v.i.* 充任代理牧師、代理教師等。—*n.* ①供給;備辦;貯藏;貯藏量。That shop has a large *supply* of shoes. 那家店貯有大量的鞋子。②(*pl.*)(軍隊或大團體之)生活必需品;軍需品。③供應。④(*pl.*)國家之支出。⑤(教師、牧師等之)代理人。⑥國會之撥款。

sup·ply² 〔ˈsʌplɪ; ˈsʌpli〕 *adv.* 易曲地;柔軟地;柔順地。

supply and demand 〖經濟〗供求。

‡sup·port 〔səˈport, -ˈpɔrt; səˈpɔːt〕 *v.t.* ①支持;支撐;扶持。Walls *support* the roof. 牆壁支撐屋頂。②鼓勵;幫助。Hope *supports* us in trouble. 在困難時,希望鼓舞我們。③資助。to *support* a hospital. 以金錢資助一醫院。④維持;贍養。Air, food and drink are necessary to *support* life. 空氣、食物

和飲料是維持生命所不可缺少的。⑤支援；擁護。⑥掩護。⑦證明；證實。The facts *support* his claim. 事實證明其要求爲合理。⑧忍受；忍耐。⑨成功地扮演（某一角色）。⑩助演；與(主角)配戲。a *supporting* actor. 男配角。—*n.* ①支持；支撐；扶持；援助；擁護；贍養。He spoke in *support* of the plan. 他發言支持這項計畫。②贍養者；支援者；支撐物；贊助者。③〖軍〗支援；支援部隊。④配角；助演者。⑤證明；實證。⑥繪畫所用之帆布、木板或其他材料。—**less,** *adj.*

sup·port·a·ble 〔sə'portəbl; sə'pɔ:təbl〕 *adj.* 可支持的；可扶養的；可贊助的；可擁護的；能忍耐的。 —**sup·port·a·bil·i·ty,** *n.* —**sup·port·a·bly,** *adv.*

***sup·port·er** 〔sə'portɚ, -'pɔr-; sə'pɔ:tə〕 *n.* ①支持者；支援者；贊助者；贍養者。②支持物；支柱。③〖外科〗縛帶。a wrist *supporter*. 腕帶。④〖紋章〗扶持紋章楯之人或獸圖形。

sup·port·ive 〔sə'portɪv; sə'pɔ:tiv〕 *adj.* 有支持作用的；有支持力的。

supportive therapy (or **treatment**) ①精神科醫師與病人談話俾了解其問題之所在然後求得解決辦法之治療法。②間接療法；輔助療法(如治療休克時之輸血)。

‡**sup·pose** 〔sə'poz; sə'pouz〕 *v.*, **-posed, -pos·ing,** *n.* —*v.t.* ①想像；以爲。What do you *suppose* he'll do? 你想他要做甚麼? Everybody is *supposed* to know the law. 每個人都該知道這法律。②假定。③必須有；含攝；包含；含意。 Creation *supposes* a creator. 創造須先有創造者。④用於祈使句中，引出一項建議。⑤倘若；假使（=if，爲連接字之代用）。 *Suppose* your father saw you now, what would he say? 倘若你父親現在看見你，他會說些甚麼? —*v.i.* 假定；推測。—*n.* 想像；推測。—**sup·pos·a·ble,** *adj.*

***sup·posed** 〔sə'pozd; sə'pouzd〕 *adj.* 想像的；推測的；被信以爲眞的。

sup·pos·ed·ly 〔sə'pozɪdlɪ; sə'pouzidli〕 *adv.* 想像上；臆測上；妄測地。

sup·po·si·tion 〔ˌsʌpə'zɪʃən; ˌsʌpə'ziʃən〕 *n.* 假定；推測；臆測。—**al,** *adj.*

sup·pos·i·ti·tious 〔səˌpɑzə'tɪʃəs; səˌpɔzi'tiʃəs〕 *adj.* ①僞的；僞造的。②想像的；推定的。—**ly,** *adv.* —**ness,** *n.*

sup·pos·i·tive 〔sə'pɑzɪtɪv; sə'pɔzitiv〕 *adj.* ①想像的；假定的；推測的。②僞的。③〖文法〗表假定或條件的。—*n.* 〖文法〗表假定或條件的字；引出一假設子句之連接詞（如 if, assuming, provided 等）。

sup·pos·i·to·ry 〔sə'pɑzəˌtorɪ; sə'pɔzitəri〕 *n.*, *pl.* **-ries,** *adj.* —*n.* 〖醫〗坐藥；栓劑。—*adj.* 想像的；假想的。

***sup·press** 〔sə'prɛs; sə'pres〕 *v.t.* ①鎭壓；平定。②抑制。to *suppress* a yawn. 抑制呵欠。③禁止出版；扣留。④使止住。to *suppress* bleeding. 止住流血。⑤隱瞞；隱匿。⑥禁止。⑦以命令廢止（風俗等）。—**er,** —**or,** *n.* —**i·ble,** —**ive,** *adj.*

sup·pres·sion 〔sə'prɛʃən; sə'preʃən〕 *n.* ①鎭壓；平定。②抑制。③禁止出版；扣留；封鎖。

sup·pres·si·o ve·ri 〔sə'prɛsɪo'vɛraɪ; sə'presiou'verai〕〖拉〗〖法律〗事實之隱瞞（=suppression of the truth)。

sup·pu·rate 〔'sʌpjəˌret; 'sʌpjuəreit〕 *v.i.*, **-rat·ed, -rat·ing.** 化膿；釀膿。 —**sup·pu·ra·tion,** *n.* —**sup·pu·ra·tive,** *adj.*

su·pra 〔'suprə; 'sju:prə〕 *adv.* 在上；在前（主要指參照前文)。***vide supra*** 見上；見前。

supra- 〖字首〗表示"在上；在遠方"之義。

su·pra·mun·dane 〔ˌsuprə'mʌnden; ˌsju:prə'mʌndein〕 *adj.* =**supermundane.**

su·pra·na·tion·al 〔ˌsuprə'næʃənl; 'sju:prə'næʃənl〕 *adj.* 超國家的；超民族的。

su·pra·na·tion·al·ism 〔ˌsuprə'næʃənlˌɪzəm; ˌsju:prə'næʃənəlizəm〕 *n.* 超國家主義；世界主義。

su·pra·nat·u·ral 〔ˌsuprə'nætʃərəl; 'sju:prə'nætʃərəl〕 *adj.* 超自然的。

su·pra·or·bit·al 〔ˌsuprə'ɔrbɪtl; 'sju:prə'ɔ:bitl〕 *adj.* 〖解剖〗眼窩上的；眶上的。

su·pra·pro·test 〔ˌsuprə'protɛst; ˌsju:prə'proutest〕 *n.* 〖法律〗參與承兌；參加付款（匯票持有人遭受退票後第三者爲維護發票人之信譽而代爲承兌)。

su·pra·re·nal 〔ˌsuprə'rinl; 'sju:prə'ri:nl〕 *adj.* 〖解剖〗腎臟上的；腎上腺的。—*n.* 〖解剖〗副腎。

su·prem·a·cist 〔sə'prɛməsɪst; sju'preməsist〕 *n.* 主張某集團居於控制地位者。

***su·prem·a·cy** 〔sə'prɛməsɪ, su-; sju'preməsi, su-〕 *n.* ①至高；至尊；無上。②至高權力；無上權力；霸權。 naval *supremacy*. 海上霸權；制海權。

su·preme**[1] 〔sə'prim, su-; sju(:)'pri:m〕 *adj.* ①至高的；無上的。a *supreme* ruler. 至高的統治者。②極度的；極端的。③終極的；最後的。the *supreme* end. 終極的目的。the *supreme* measure. 極刑；死刑。make the supreme sacrifice*** 捐軀；死。—*n.* 至高狀態；極致。this *supreme* of loveliness. 美的極致。—**ly,** *adv.* —**ness,** *n.*

su·preme[2] 〔sə'prim, -'prem; sju'pri:m, -'preim〕 *n.* ①放在碎冰中裝冷凍食物之碗或容器。②用此等容器所裝之冷食。(亦作 **suprême**)

Supreme Being 上帝。

Supreme Court 最高法院。

supreme good 至善。

Supreme Soviet (or **Council**) 最高蘇維埃(爲蘇聯之立法機構)。

Supt., supt. Superintendent.

sur-[1] 〖字首〗 **sub-** 之異體(用在r之前)。

sur-[2] 〖字首〗與 **super-** 同義。

su·ra 〔'surə; 'suərə〕 *n.* (回教可蘭經之)一章。

su·rah 〔'surə; 'sjuərə〕 *n.* ①斜紋軟綢。②=**sura.**

su·ral 〔'sjurəl; 'sjuərəl〕 *adj.* 〖解剖〗腓的；小腿的。

su·rat 〔'surət, su'ræt; su'ræt〕 *n.* 印度蘇拉特 (Surat) 產的劣質棉布。

sur·base 〔'sɝˌbes; 'sə:beis〕 *n.* 〖建築〗柱脚、臺座等上端之腰飾；柱脚花線。

sur·cease 〔sɝ'sis; sə:'si:s〕 *n.*, *v.*, **-ceased, -ceas·ing.** —*n.* 〖古〗完結；停止。—*v.t.* & *v.i.* 〖古〗終止；停止。

sur·charge 〔*n.* 'sɝˌtʃardʒ; 'sə:-tʃa:dʒ *v.* sɝ'tʃardʒ; sə:'tʃa:dʒ〕 *n.*, *v.*, **-charged, -charg·ing.** —*n.* ①過大的負擔；過多的裝載；過度的充電；過高的索價。②額外的索價。③(郵資不足等之)附加罰款；欠資罰款。④郵票等的變值印記。⑤印有變值印記之郵票。—*v.t.* ①使負擔過重；使裝載過多；充電過度；索高價。②額外索價。③處罰款；表示(帳目)之脫漏。④加蓋變值之印記於(郵票等)。

sur·cin·gle 〔'sɝsɪŋgl; 'sə:siŋgl〕 *n.* ①馬的上腹帶。②袈裟帶。

sur·coat 〔'sɝˌkot; 'sə:kout〕 *n.* 外衣；

上衣;中古武士穿在鎧外的長衣。

surd 〔sɝd; səːd〕 *n.* ①〖數學〗不盡根;根式。②〖語音〗清音;無聲子音(如p, f, s, t等)。③無理。 —*adj.* ①不盡根的。②清音的。③無理的。

‡**sure** 〔ʃur; ʃuə〕 *adj.*, **sur·er, sur·est,** *adv.* —*adj.* ①一定的;必定的;無疑的;無問題的。It is *sure* to rain. 一定會下雨。He is *sure* to succeed. 他必然成功。②確信;確知;確定;確實。Are you *sure* (that) he's honest? 你確知他誠實嗎? ③可靠的;穩妥的。a *sure* messenger. 可靠的使者。④確然的;不可能引起懷疑的。Death is *sure*. 死是不能避免的。⑤堅固的;穩定的。a *sure* faith. 堅定的信仰。***be sure*** 務必一定(要做到)。*Be sure* to close the window. 切記要關窗。***be sure of oneself*** 有自信心。***for sure*** 確然地。***make sure*** **a.** 確信無疑;確然無疑。I *made sure* (that) he would be here. 我確信他會來這裏。**b.** 滿足自己;獲得證實。***sure thing*** **a.** 一定實現或成功之事物;確實之事。**b.** 一定地;必定地。***to be sure*** 確然;的確。*To be sure,* he's rather young for such an important position. 的確,他擔任這樣一個重要職位是嫌年輕些。—*adv.* ①確實地;無疑地。As *sure* as night follows day.... 如夜以繼日之確實…。②當然。***sure enough*** 一定地;必定地。He will come *sure enough*. 他必來無疑。〖注意〗**sure** 主要是做形容詞用: Are you *sure?* 你確信如此? 做爲副詞以代替 surely, 或相當於 certainly 或 yes, 祇用於非正式的英語中: *Sure,* I am coming. 當然, 我要來。

sure-e·nough 〔ˈʃurɪˈnʌf; ˈʃuəriˈnʌf〕 *adj.* 〖美方〗眞實的;眞正的。

sure-fire 〔ˈʃurˌfaɪr; ˈʃuəfaiə〕 *adj.* 〖美俚〗必會成功的;定如所期的;不會失敗的。

sure-foot·ed 〔ˈʃurˈfutɪd; ˈʃuəˈfutid〕 *adj.* 踏實的;立脚穩固的;無失誤之虞的。

‡**sure·ly** 〔ˈʃurlɪ; ˈʃuəli〕 *adv.* ①必定地;無疑地。He will *surely* fail. 他必然失敗。②無誤地;堅定地;不會滑跌地。③確實地。slowly but *surely*. 緩慢地但確實地。

sure·ness 〔ˈʃurnɪs; ˈʃuənis〕 *n.* 穩固;穩定;無疑;無誤。

sur·e·ty 〔ˈʃurtɪ; ˈʃuəti〕 *n.*, *pl.* **-ties.** ①保證;擔保。②保證人;擔保人。③〖古〗確實之事物。④可靠性;確實性;確定性。***of a surety*** 必然地;一定地。***stand surety*** 做保證人。

sure·ty·ship 〔ˈʃurtɪˌʃɪp; ˈʃuətiʃip〕 *n.* 保證人之地位或責任。

surf 〔sɝf; səːf〕 *n.* 拍岸之浪;澎湃之浪。—*v.i.* ①作衝浪運動。②在浪中游泳或沐浴。③浮在拍岸之浪頭上。④如浪花一般地動。

‡**sur·face** 〔ˈsɝfɪs; ˈsəːfis〕 *n.*, *adj.*, *v.*, **-faced, -fac·ing.** —*n.* ①表面。Glass has a smooth *surface*. 玻璃有光滑的表面。②一物件的任何一面或一邊。A cube has six *surfaces*. 立方體有六個面。③只有長寬而無厚的平面。a plane *surface* in geometry. 幾何中的平面。④外表。One never gets below the *surface* with him. 無人能洞察他的內心。***on the surface*** 在表面上。His cleverness is only *on the surface*. 他的聰明僅僅是表面的。—*adj.* ①表面的;膚淺的。*surface* politeness. 表面的慇懃。②用於表面的;對表面的。—*v.t.* 裝以面;使成平面。They must *surface* this road. 他們必須給這條路加路面。—*v.i.* ①(潛水艇)升到水面。②被露出來。The truth began to *surface*. 眞相開始揭露了出來。③在表面工作。④在地面或接近地面處開礦。—**sur·fac·er,** *n.*

surface car 地面電車或火車(以別於高架車及地下車)。

surface mail (非航空的)平寄郵件。

sur·face·man 〔ˈsɝfɪsmən; ˈsəːfismən〕 *n.*, *pl.* **-men.** 〖鐵路〗養路工人。

surface noise 唱針與唱片溝痕磨擦所生的雜音。

surface plate 平規;測平器。

surface printing 凸版印刷。(亦作 **surface-printing**)

surface tension 〖物理〗表面張力。

sur·face-to-air 〔ˈsɝfɪs·tuˈɛr; ˈsəːfis–tuˈɛə〕 *adj.* & *adv.* (火箭等)地對空的(地)。a *surface–to–air* rocket.地對空火箭。

sur·face-to-sur·face 〔ˈsɝfɪs·təˈsɝfɪs; ˈsəːfis–tuˈsəːfis〕 *adj.*& *adv.* (火箭、飛彈等)地對地的(地);船對船的(地)。

sur·face-to-un·der·wa·ter 〔ˈsɝfɪs·təˈʌndɚˌwɑtɚ; ˈsəːfis–tuˈʌndəˌwɔtə〕 *adj.* & *adv.* (火箭、飛彈等)地對水下的(地)。

surface water 地上水;地面水。

surf·board 〔ˈsɝfˌbord; ˈsəːfbɔːd〕 *n.* (水上運動用之)衝浪板。—*v.i.* 作衝浪運動;駕衝浪板。—**er,** *n.*

surf·board·ing 〔ˈsɝfˌbordɪŋ; ˈsəːfˌbɔːdiŋ〕 *n.* 衝浪運動。

surf·boat 〔ˈsɝfˌbot; ˈsəːfbout〕 *n.* 航行大浪中的一種小艇。

surf caster 海濱垂釣者。(亦作**surf-caster**)

surf duck 黑鳧。

sur·feit 〔ˈsɝfɪt; ˈsəːfit〕 *n.* ①過量;過度。②過食;過飲。③食傷;食滯。④飽饜;饜;饜足。—*v.t.* ①使飲食過度。②使饜足;使生厭。—*v.i.* ①飲食過度。②受飲食過度之害。③放任過度。—**er,** *n.*

surf·er 〔ˈsɝfɚ; ˈsəːfə〕 *n.* 作衝浪板運動者。(亦作 **surf rider**)

surf fish 濱魚(生於太平洋沿海淺水中,爲胎生)。(亦作 **surffish**)

surf-rid·ing 〔ˈsɝfˌraɪdɪŋ; ˈsəːfˌraidiŋ〕 *n.* =**surfboarding.** (亦作 **surfriding**)

surf·y 〔ˈsɝfɪ; ˈsəːfi〕 *adj.*, **surf·i·er, surf·i·est.** 有拍岸之浪的;多拍岸之浪的;像拍岸之浪的;碎浪的。

surg. ①surgeon. ②surgery. ③surgical.

***surge** 〔sɝdʒ; səːdʒ〕 *v.*, **surged, surg·ing,** *n.* —*v.i.* (波浪)起伏;洶湧;澎湃。The crowd *surged* through the streets. 羣衆從市街洶湧而過。—*n.* ①巨浪;波濤。②洶湧;澎湃。A *surge* of anger rushed over him. 他勃然大怒。

***sur·geon** 〔ˈsɝdʒən; ˈsəːdʒən〕 *n.* ①外科醫生。②軍醫;船上的醫師。

sur·geon·fish 〔ˈsɝdʒənˌfɪʃ; ˈsəːdʒən–fiʃ〕 *n.*, *pl.* **-fish, -fish·es.** 一種有鮮麗顏色的熱帶魚。

Surgeon General *pl.* **Surgeons General.** ①(美國陸海空軍的)軍醫署署長。②美國公共衞生局局長。

***sur·ger·y** 〔ˈsɝdʒərɪ; ˈsəːdʒəri〕 *n.*, *pl.* **-ger·ies.** ①外科;外科手術。②外科醫院;外科醫生手術室、實驗室等。③〖英〗**a.** 診療所。**b.** 醫生每日之上班時間。

sur·gi·cal 〔ˈsɝdʒɪkl; ˈsəːdʒikl〕 *adj.* ①外科的。②有如外科手術的。③外科手術用的。—**ly,** *adv.*

surg·y 〔ˈsɝdʒɪ; ˈsəːdʒi〕 *adj.*, **surg·i·er, surg·i·est.** 大浪的;如大浪的;澎湃的。

Su·ri·nam 〔ˌsurɪˈnɑm; ˌsuəriˈnæm〕 *n.* 蘇利南(南美北部一國，首都巴拉馬利波Paramaribo).
sur·loin 〔ˈsɝˌlɔɪn; ˈsəːlɔin〕 *n.* =**sirloin.**
sur·ly 〔ˈsɝlɪ; ˈsəːli〕 *adj.*, **-li·er, -li·est.** ①乖戾的；粗暴的；不高興的。②陰沈沈的；陰鬱的。—*adv.* 驕傲地；傲慢地。—**sur·li·ly,** *adv.* —**sur·li·ness,** *n.*
sur·mis·a·ble 〔səˈmaɪzəbl̩; səːˈmaizəbl〕 *adj.* 可推測的；可揣度的。
sur·mise 〔*v.* sɚˈmaɪz; səːˈmaiz, ˈsəːm- *n.* sɚˈmaɪz, ˈsɝmaɪz; ˈsəːmaiz, səːˈmaiz〕 *v.*, **-mised, -mis·ing,** *n.* —*v.t.* & *v.i.* 臆測；猜度。—*n.* 臆測；猜度。
sur·mount 〔sɚˈmaunt; səːˈmaunt〕 *v.t.* ①克服；戰勝；凌駕。to *surmount* a difficulty. 克服困難。②高矗於…之上。③爬過；越過。to *surmount* a hill. 爬越一山。④置某物於…頂上(通常用被動語態)。
sur·mount·a·ble 〔sɚˈmauntəbl̩; səːˈmauntəbl〕 *adj.* 可凌駕的；可超越的；可克服的。—**ness,** *n.*
sur·mul·let 〔sɚˈmʌlɛt; səːˈmʌlit〕 *n., pl.* **-let, -lets.** 一種緋鯢鰹科的食用魚。
***sur·name** 〔ˈsɝˌnem; ˈsəːneim〕 *n., v.,* **-named, -nam·ing.** —*n.* ①姓。②別號；別名。—*v.t.* 呼以姓氏；加以綽號；呼以綽號。
***sur·pass** 〔sɚˈpæs, -ˈpɑs; səːˈpɑːs〕 *v.t.* ①超越；凌駕；勝過。The horrors of the battlefield *surpassed* description. 戰場的慘狀無法形容。②非…所能勝任。
sur·pass·ing 〔sɚˈpæsɪŋ; səːˈpɑːsiŋ〕 *adj.* 優勝的；卓越的；超越的。—*adv.* 卓越地；超羣地。—**ly,** *adv.*
sur·plice 〔ˈsɝplɪs; ˈsəːplis〕 *n.* 〖宗教〗牧師及聖詩班團員之白長袍；白袈裟；白法衣。
***sur·plus** 〔ˈsɝplʌs; ˈsəːpləs〕 *n.* 過剩；剩餘；盈餘額。Brazil has a big *surplus* of coffee. 巴西有很多剩餘咖啡。—*adj.* 過剩的；剩餘的。a *surplus* population. 過剩的人口。
sur·plus·age 〔ˈsɝplʌsɪdʒ; ˈsəːpləsidʒ〕 *n.* ①剩餘；盈餘；盈餘額。②多餘的字句；多餘的話語；(特指)〖法律〗辯護時所作之多餘的辯解。
surplus value 剩餘價值。(馬克斯主義經濟學)
sur·print 〔ˈsɝˌprɪnt; ˈsəːprint〕 *v.t.* ①在(已印就的東西上)加印新材料。②將(新材料)加印在已印就的東西上。—*n.* 加印的印刷品。
sur·pris·al 〔sɚˈpraɪzl̩; səˈpraizl〕 *n.* 驚駭；驚愕；驚奇；受驚。
‡**sur·prise** 〔sɚˈpraɪz; səˈpraiz〕 *n., v.,* **-prised, -pris·ing,** *adj.* —*n.* ①驚駭；驚愕；驚奇。with a look of *surprise.* 帶着驚愕的神情。②意外之事物；驚人之事物。I have a *surprise* for you. 我有一項出你意外的消息(或禮物)奉告(奉送)。What a *surprise!* 這是如何驚人的事情！③奇襲；出其不意的襲擊。***take by surprise*** **a.** 奇襲；出其不意地攻擊。**b.** 使大吃一驚。The amount of the donation *took* us completely *by surprise.* 捐款的數目使我們大吃一驚。—*v.t.* ①使驚駭；使驚奇。The news greatly *surprised* us. 這消息使我們大爲驚愕。②奇襲；突擊。③出其不意地揭發。④突然發現；覺察。⑤使無意間做某事。—*adj.* 出乎意料的；令人驚奇的。a *surprise* visit. 突然的拜訪。
surprise party ①爲某人準備的祕密慶祝會，目的在使其驚異。②令人驚奇之事。
***sur·pris·ing** 〔sɚˈpraɪzɪŋ; səˈpraiziŋ〕 *adj.* 令人驚愕的；奇異的。*surprising* news. 驚人的消息。—**ly,** *adv.*
sur·re·al·ism 〔səˈriəlˌɪzəm; səˈriəlizm〕 *n.* 超現實主義。
sur·re·al·ist 〔səˈriəlɪst; səˈriəlist〕 *n.* 超現實主義者。—*adj.* 超現實主義的。
sur·re·al·is·tic 〔səˌriəlˈɪstɪk; səˌriəˈlistik〕 *adj.* 超現實主義的。—**al·ly,** *adv.*
sur·re·but·tal 〔ˌsɝrɪˈbʌtl̩; ˌsʌriˈbʌtl〕 *n.* 〖法律〗原告第三辯駁中之舉證。
sur·re·but·ter 〔ˌsɝrɪˈbʌtɚ; ˌsʌriˈbʌtə〕 *n.* 〖法律〗原告之第三辯駁。
sur·re·join·der 〔ˌsɝrɪˈdʒɔɪndɚ; ˌsʌriˈdʒɔində〕 *n.* 〖法律〗原告之第二辯駁。
***sur·ren·der** 〔səˈrɛndɚ; səˈrendə〕 *v.t.* ①使(自己)屈服於(一種感情或力量)；耽於；縱於。to *surrender* oneself to pleasure. 耽於逸樂。②讓與；放棄。to *surrender* oneself to justice. 自首。to *surrender* an insurance policy. 收回保險費而解約。—*v.i.* 投降；降服。The captain had to *surrender* to the enemy. 該上尉不得不向敵人投降。—*n.* ①投降；降服。unconditional *surrender.* 無條件投降。②讓與；放棄；交付；引渡。the *surrender* of a fugitive. 逃犯的引渡。
surrender value 被保險人中途解約而收回之保險費額。
sur·rep·ti·tious 〔ˌsɝəpˈtɪʃəs; ˌsʌrəpˈtiʃəs〕 *adj.* 祕密的；偸盜的。—**ly,** *adv.*
sur·rey 〔ˈsɝɪ; ˈsʌri〕 *n., pl.* **-reys.** 一種四輪雙座輕馬車。
sur·ro·gate 〔*n.* ˈsɝəgɪt; ˈsʌrəgit *v.* ˈsɝəˌget; ˈsʌrəgeit〕 *n., v.,* **-gat·ed, -gat·ing.** —*n.* ①代理者(尤指主教之代理者)。②〖美〗認證遺囑及管理遺產之法官。—*v.t.* ①使代理；使繼任。②代替；代位。—**ship,** *n.*
‡**sur·round** 〔səˈraund; səˈraund〕 *v.t.* 包圍；環繞。to be *surrounded.* 被圍困。the *surrounding* country. 附近地區。—*n.* ①地氈邊與牆間的地板。②周圍。
***sur·round·ings** 〔səˈraundɪŋz; səˈraundiŋz〕 *n. pl.* 周圍的事物；環境。The house is in beautiful *surroundings.* 這所房屋處於優美的環境中。
sur·tax 〔ˈsɝˌtæks; ˈsəːtæks〕 *n.* ①附加稅。②累進的附加所得稅。—*v.t.* 課以附加稅或累進的附加所得稅。
sur·tout 〔sɚˈtut; ˈsəːtuː〕 *n.* 男人穿之緊身長外套。
surv. ①surveying. ②surveyor. ③surviving.
sur·veil·lance 〔sɚˈveləns; səːˈveiləns〕 *n.* ①監視；看守。②監督；管理。
sur·veil·lant 〔sɚˈvelənt; səːˈveilənt〕 *n.* ①監視者；監督者。②密探。—*adj.* 監視的；監督的。
sur·veille 〔sɚˈvel; səːˈveil〕 *v.t.,* **-veilled, -veil·ling.** 〖美〗監視。
***sur·vey** 〔*v.* sɚˈve; səːˈvei *n.* ˈsɝve, sɚˈve; ˈsəːvei, səːˈvei〕 *v., n., pl.* **-veys.** —*v.t.* ①縱覽；眺望。He *surveyed* the landscape. 他縱覽風景。②視察；考察。③測量(土地等)。④通盤考慮；逐點說明。—*n.* ①縱覽。We were pleased with our first *survey* of the house. 我們初次觀察這座房屋甚覺滿意。②視察；調查。③測量；測量圖。④調查報告；視察報告。
sur·vey·ing 〔sɚˈveɪŋ; səˈveiiŋ〕 *n.* ①測量術。②測量。③測量之職業。
sur·vey·or 〔sɚˈveɚ; səˈveiə〕 *n.* ①土地測量者。②海關驗貨員。③公證行。④主管；總監。⑤觀察家。—**ship,** *n.*

surveyor's level 水平儀。

surveyor's measure 土地測量單位。

sur·viv·al [sə'vaɪvl; sə'vaivəl] *n.* ①殘存；生存；較旁人後死。the *survival* of the fittest. 適者生存。②殘存者；殘存物；遺風。

survival kit (飛行人員所攜帶之)生存用品箱。

***sur·vive** [sə'vaɪv; sə'vaiv] *v.*, **-vived, -viv·ing.** —*v.t.* 生命較…爲長；經歷(災難、危險等)之後仍然活着。Only ten of the crew *survived* the shipwreck. 只有十名船員在海難中生還。—*v.i.* ①殘存；繼續存在。Few *survived* after the flood. 洪水後生還者極少。②繼續使用。—**sur·viv·a·ble,** *adj.*

***sur·viv·or** [sə'vaɪvə; sə'vaivə] *n.* 殘存者；生存者；遺族；生還者。He is the sole *survivor* of the shipwreck. 他是海難中的唯一生還者。

sur·vi·vor·ship [sə'vaɪvə,ʃɪp; sə'vaivəʃip] *n.* ①殘存；生存；生還。②〖法律〗在共有財產中生存者對死者權利之取得權。

sus- 〖字首〗**sub-** 之異體(用於c, p, t之前)。

Su·san ['suzn̩; 'su:zn] *n.* =**Susanne.**

Su·san·na(h) [su'zænə; su:'zænə] *n.* =**Susanne.**

Su·sanne [su'zæn; su:'zæn] *n.* 女子名。

sus·cep·ti·bil·i·ty [sə,sɛptə'bɪlətɪ; sə,septə'biliti] *n.*, *pl.* **-ties.** ①感受性。*susceptibility* to disease. 疾病感染性。②(*pl.*)敏銳的情感。to offend one's *susceptibilities*. 傷害某人之感情。③〖電〗磁化率。

***sus·cep·ti·ble** [sə'sɛptəbl̩; sə'septəbl] *adj.* ①易感的；易感動的；易受影響的。Vain people are *susceptible* to flattery. 虛榮的人易受諂媚。②可得；容許〖of〗。—*n.* 易受影響者；易受感染者。—**sus·cep·ti·bly,** *adv.*

sus·cep·tive [sə'sɛptɪv; sə'septiv] *adj.* ①能感受的；易感的。②能接受的；容許的〖of〗。—**sus·cep·tiv·i·ty,** *n.*

su·shi ['suʃɪ; 'su:ʃi] 〖日〗 *n.* 壽司。

Su·sie, Su·sy ['suzɪ; 'su:zi] *n.* 女子名(爲 Susan, Susanna, Susannah之暱稱)。

***sus·pect** [*v.* sə'spɛkt; səs'pekt *n.* 'sʌspɛkt; 'sʌspekt *adj.* 'sʌspɛkt, sə'spɛkt; 'sʌspekt] *v.t.* & *v.i.* ①猜想；懷疑；猜疑(某人)犯(某種罪行)。to *suspect* a person of murder. 懷疑某人犯殺人罪。②事先有些知道。—*n.* 被懷疑之人；嫌疑犯。political *suspects*. 政治嫌疑犯。—*adj.* 令人懷疑的；不可信的。The thief's statement is *suspect*. 那竊賊的口供是不可相信的。

sus·pect·a·ble [sə'spɛktəbl̩; səs'pektəbl] *adj.* 可疑的。

sus·pend** [sə'spɛnd; səs'pend] *v.t.* ①懸掛；吊；使懸浮。The lamp was *suspended* from the ceiling. 這燈從天花板懸吊下來。②靜止於；靜留於。③停止；暫停。to *suspend* payment. 暫停付款。to *suspend* work. 暫停工作。④使停學；使停職。to *suspend* a person from office. 停某人之職。⑤延緩；懸而不決。—*v.i.* ①暫時停業；暫時停辦。The magazine *suspended*. 那雜誌暫時停刊。②懸浮；懸掛。suspend payment*** 宣告無力償還欠債；破產。

suspended animation 〖醫〗暈厥；不省人事；活狀暫停；生機暫停。

sus·pend·ers [sə'spɛndəz; səs'pendəz] *n. pl.* ①背帶；吊褲帶。②吊襪帶。

***sus·pense** [sə'spɛns; səs'pens] *n.* ①不確定的狀態；懸而未決。to hold one's judgment in *suspense*. 遲遲不作判斷(判決)。②焦慮；懸念。③懸疑。—**ful,** *adj.*

sus·pen·si·ble [sə'spɛnsəbl̩; səs'pensəbl] *adj.* ①可懸掛的；可吊懸的；可懸浮的。②可停止的；可中止的。③可延緩的。—**sus·pen·si·bil·i·ty,** *n.*

***sus·pen·sion** [sə'spɛnʃən; səs'penʃən] *n.* ①懸掛。②中止；暫停；停學；停職。the *suspension* of payment. 暫停付款。③掛鉤；供懸掛之設備。④〖修辭〗延宕法。⑤(汽車、火車等)連接底盤與車軸之彈簧；懸架。⑥懸浮(物質在液體中分解而不溶化的狀態)；懸浮物。

suspension bridge 吊橋。

suspension points 〖印刷〗刪節號；省略號(…)。

sus·pen·sive [sə'spɛnsɪv; səs'pensiv] *adj.* ①猶豫未決的；未決定的。②焦慮的；懸念的。③停止的；中止的；使暫停的。a *suspensive* veto. 致使停頓的否決。④製造(表示)懸疑的。⑤令人緊張的。—**ly,** *adv.*

sus·pen·sor [sə'spɛnsə; səs'pensə] *n.* ①懸吊繃帶。②〖植物〗胚柄。

sus·pen·so·ry [sə'spɛnsərɪ; səs'pensəri] *adj.*, *n.*, *pl.* **-ries.** —*adj.* ①懸吊的；提舉的。②停止的；中止的；懸擱的。—*n.* ①懸吊物；懸吊繃。②懸垂肌；疝帶。

sus. per coll. ['sʌspə'kɑl; 'sʌspə'kɔl] 〖拉〗(爲 suspensio per collum之略)絞刑(=hanging by the neck).

sus·pi·cion** [sə'spɪʃən; səs'piʃən] *n.* ①懷疑；嫌疑。I have a *suspicion* that the servant is dishonest. 我懷疑這僕人不誠實。②些微。He has not a *suspicion* of humor. 他沒有一點幽默感。③觀念；可對可錯的觀念。above*** (or ***beyond***) ***suspicion*** 無可懷疑。***on suspicion*** 因受懷疑。***under suspicion*** 受懷疑。—*v.t.* 〖俗〗懷疑。

***sus·pi·cious** [sə'spɪʃəs; səs'piʃəs] *adj.* ①懷疑的；感到懷疑的。The ignorant are *suspicious*. 無知者多疑。②令人懷疑的；可疑的。a *suspicious* character. 可疑的人物。③表示懷疑的。—**ly,** *adv.*

sus·pi·ra·tion [,sʌspə'reʃən; ,sʌspi'reiʃən] *n.* 〖詩〗長嘆；嘆息。

sus·pire [sə'spaɪr; səs'paiə] *v.i.*, **-pired, -pir·ing.** ①呼吸。②〖詩〗長嘆；嘆息。

***sus·tain** [sə'sten; səs'tein] *v.t.* ①支撐；承住。②支持；維持。food sufficient to *sustain* life. 足够維持生命之食物。③贍養；供應。to *sustain* a family. 贍養家屬。④抵擋。⑤蒙受；忍耐；遭受。They will not *sustain* comparison with him. 他們不足以和他相比。⑥准許；認可。The court *sustained* his suit. 法庭准許了他的請求。⑦證實。⑧扮演(角色)。—**a·ble,** *adj.* —**er,** *n.*

sus·tain·ing [sə'stenɪŋ; səs'teiniŋ] *adj.* 持續的；維持的；支持的。

sustaining program 〖美〗廣播電臺自播節目(即非由商人等提供者)。

sus·te·nance ['sʌstənəns; 'sʌstinəns] *n.* ①營養物；食物。②維持；扶助。

sus·ten·ta·tion [,sʌstɛn'teʃən; ,sʌsten'teiʃən] *n.* ①支持；維持。②生命、活力之維持。③扶助。④食料；糧食。

sus·ten·tion [sə'stɛnʃən; səs'tenʃən] *n.* 維持；持續。

sut·ler ['sʌtlə; 'sʌtlə] *n.* 隨軍小販。

su·tra ['sutrə; 'su:trə] *n.* ①〖佛教〗經；經典。②〖婆羅門教〗箴言；箴言集。

sut·tee [sʌ'ti, 'sʌti; 'sʌti:, sʌ'ti:] *n.* ①

(印度的)寡婦自焚殉夫。②自焚殉夫之寡婦。
sut·tee·ism [sʌˈtiɪzm̩; sʌˈti:zm] *n.* 自焚殉夫之風俗。
su·tur·al [ˈsutʃərəl; ˈsju:tʃərəl] *adj.* ①〖解剖〗接縫的;有接縫的。②〖動、植物〗縫合的。③〖外科〗縫合的;縫合術的。
su·ture [ˈsutʃɚ, ˈsju-; ˈsju:tʃə] *n., v.,* **-tured, -tur·ing.** —*n.* ①(傷口之)縫口。②(傷口之)縫合法。③(縫傷口所用之)縫線。④縫合;綴合;接合。⑤骨縫;(尤指)頭蓋骨縫。⑥〖動、植物〗接縫。⑦傷口縫線材料。—*v.t.* 縫合;綴合;接合。
su·ze·rain [ˈsuzərɪn; ˈsu:zərein] *n.* 宗主;宗主國。—*adj.* 宗主的;宗主國的。
su·ze·rain·ty [ˈsuzərɪntɪ; ˈsu:zəreinti] *n., pl.* **-ties.** 宗主之地位;宗主權;保護權。
S.V. ①Sancta Virgo (拉=Holy Virgin). ②Sanctitas Vestra (拉=Your Holiness). ③Sons of Veterans.
Sved·berg [ˈsvɛdˌbærjə; ˈsvedˌbærjə] *n.* 斯維德巴里(The *or* Theodor, 1884–1971, 瑞典化學家,獲1926年諾貝爾化學獎)。
svelte [svɛlt; svelt] *adj.* 腰身苗條的;婷婷裊裊的。
SW, S.W., s.w. ①southwest. ②southwestern. **Sw.** ①Sweden. ②Swedish.
swab [swɑb; swɔb] *n., v.,* **swabbed, swab·bing.** —*n.* ①(擦地板等用之)拖把;擦帚。②洗滌病人口腔或敷藥之海綿或布片;藥籤。③鎗砲刷;砲帚。④〖俚〗蠢笨之人;粗人。⑤〖俚〗海軍軍官的肩章。—*v.t.* (以拖把等)擦淨;擦洗。(亦作 **swob**)
swab·ber [ˈswɑbɚ; ˈswɔbə] *n.* ①用拖把擦洗者。②愚蠢粗鄙之人。③拖把。
Swa·bi·an [ˈswebɪən; ˈsweibjən] *adj.* Swabia(德國 Bavaria 之一區)的; Swabia 人(語)的。—*n.* Swabia 人(語)。
swad·dle [ˈswɑdl̩; ˈswɔdl] *v.,* **-dled, -dling,** *n.* —*v.t.* ①以襁褓包裹(嬰兒)。②縛裹;繞。③抑制;限制;控制;束縛。—*n.* 襁褓;縛裹之布。
swaddling clothes ①襁褓;包嬰兒布的。②襁褓期。③初期;未成熟階段。④任何嚴格之控制或束縛。***still in one's swaddling clothes*** 仍在襁褓中;不能自由地思想或行動;未成熟。(亦作 **swaddling bands, swaddling clouts**)
Swa·de·shi [swəˈdeʃɪ; swəˈdeiʃi] 〖印度〗*n.* 抵制英貨運動;抵制外貨運動。
swag [swæg; swæg] *n., v.,* **swagged, swag·ging.** —*n.* ①〖俚〗贓物;金錢;貴重物件。②〖澳〗(樵夫、礦工等之)背包。③大量。—*v.i.* ①〖澳〗背背包旅行。②搖擺;傾斜。③懸掛。—*v.t.* ①搖動;使擺動。②使下陷。
swage [swedʒ; sweidʒ] *n., v.,* **swaged, swag·ing.** —*n.* ①鐵匠用的型鐵。②用以折彎金屬物之工具。—*v.t.* ①以型鐵打成。②以此種工具弄彎曲。
swage block 型砧。
swag·ger [ˈswægɚ; ˈswægə] *v.i.* ①高視闊步而行。②擺臭架子。③吹噓。—*v.t.* 威嚇。—*n.* ①昂首闊步。②自負;自大。—*adj.* 〖俗〗很時髦的。—**ing·ly,** *adv.*
swagger cane =**swagger stick.**
swagger stick 短而輕之棒。
Swa·hi·li [swɑˈhilɪ; swɑ:ˈhi:li] *n., pl.* **-li** or **-lis,** *adj.* —*n.* ①班圖(Bantu)人(居於非洲之尙西巴及其鄰近海岸)。②班圖語(爲阿拉伯語與多種外國語之混合語言)。—*adj.* 班圖人(語)的。
swain [swen; swein] *n.* 〖古,詩〗①鄉下的青年。②情郎;情人。
SWAK, S.W.A.K. sealed with a kiss (註在情書之末或情書信封背面)。
swale [swel; sweil] *n.* 〖方〗低地;濕地。
swal·low¹** [ˈswɑlo; ˈswɔlou] *v.t.* ①吞;嚥。to *swallow* food. 嚥下食物。②吞沒;吸收。③耗盡。④輕信。⑤容忍;忍受。He had to *swallow* the insult. 他必須忍辱。⑥收回;取消。⑦抑制;遏止。—*v.i.* 下嚥。I cannot *swallow*. 我不能嚥東西。swallow the anchor*** 終止海上生活。***swallow the bait*** 上當。***swallow up*** **a.** 吞沒;淹沒;毀滅。**b.** 併吞;侵占。**c.** 銷售一空。—*n.* ①吞;嚥。at a *swallow*. 一飲;一口。②一吞之量。③喉;咽喉;食道。
***swal·low²** *n.* 燕。One *swallow* does not make a summer. 一燕不成夏(勿以偏概全)。
swal·low·tail [ˈswɑloˌtel; ˈswɔlouteil] *n.* ①燕尾。②燕尾狀之尾。③一種蝴蝶。④〖植物〗燕尾柳。⑤〖俗〗燕尾服。⑥〖築城〗燕尾外堡。
swal·low-tailed [ˈswɑloˌteld; ˈswɔlouteild] *adj.* 燕尾形的。
swallow-tailed coat 男燕尾服。
‡swam [swæm; swæm] *v.* pt. of **swim.**
swa·mi [ˈswɑmɪ; ˈswɑ:mi] *n., pl.* **-mis.** ①閣下(印度對學者、宗教家之一種尊稱)。②偶像;神像。
***swamp** [swɑmp; swɔmp] *n.* 沼澤;濕地。—*v.t.* ①使陷於沼澤或水中。②淹沒;覆沒;使充溢。A big wave *swamped* the boat. 一個大浪覆沒了小舟。③使困窘;使失措;使應接不暇。④開拓〖常 out〗。⑤將(砍下的樹木)修整爲木料。—*v.i.* ①因充滿水而沉沒。Their boat *swamped*. 他們的船因充滿水而沉沒了。②陷於沼澤中。③陷入困難境地;爲人數衆多之敵人擊潰。
swamp·er [ˈswɑmpɚ; ˈswɔmpə] *n.* 〖美〗①清除沼澤者;在森林中開路者。②沼澤地帶之居民。③清除工人;做粗活工人。④搬運木料工人。
swamp fever 瘧疾。
swamp·land [ˈswɑmpˌlænd; ˈswɔmplænd] *n.* 沼地;沼澤地。
swamp·y [ˈswɑmpɪ; ˈswɔmpi] *adj.,* **-i·er, -i·est.** ①有沼澤的。②似沼澤的;濕而鬆軟的。—**swamp·i·ness,** *n.*
***swan** [swɑn; swɔn] *n., v.,* **swanned, swan·ning.** —*n.* ①鵠;天鵝。②詩人;歌者。③美人;才子。④(S-)〖天文〗鵠座;天鵝座。—*v.i.* 飛翔。—*v.t.* 〖方〗斷言;發誓。
swan dive 燕子式跳水。(英亦作 **swallow dive**)
swank [swæŋk; swæŋk] *v.i.* 〖俚〗炫耀;擺架子;虛張聲勢。—*v.t.* 輕待;冷落。—*n.* 〖俚〗①炫耀;虛張聲勢;虛飾。②時髦;華麗。—*adj.* 〖俚〗炫耀的;時髦的;華麗的。
swank·y [ˈswæŋkɪ; ˈswæŋki] *adj.,* **swank·i·er, swank·i·est.** 〖俚〗時髦的;虛誇的;豪華的。
swan·ner·y [ˈswɑnərɪ; ˈswɔnəri] *n., pl.* **-ner·ies.** 天鵝飼養處。
Swan of Avon, the 莎士比亞的別稱。
swan's-down [ˈswɑnzˌdaun; ˈswɔnzdaun] *n.* ①天鵝絨毛。②天鵝絨。(亦作 **swansdown**)
swan shot 獵射天鵝之大彈丸。
swan·skin [ˈswɑnˌskɪn; ˈswɔnskin] *n.* ①帶有羽毛的天鵝皮。②一種法蘭絨。
swan song ①(古傳說中)天鵝臨死前的哀鳴。②一個人之最後行動或作品等。

swan-up·ping ['swɑn,ʌpɪŋ; 'swɔn-,ʌpiŋ] *n.* 〖英〗①在小天鵝之喙上刻標記（表示其所屬者）。②倫敦泰晤士河上每年一次的刻鵠賽會。
swap [swɑp, swɔp; swɔp] *v.*, **swapped, swap·ping,** *n.* —*v.t.* 交換。***swap horses when crossing a stream*** 在危急時有所改變。—*n.* 交換。(亦作 **swop**)
swa·raj [swə'rɑdʒ; swə'rɑːdʒ] 〖印度〗*n.* ①自治；獨立。②(S-) 印度之獨立黨。—*adj.* 自治的。—**ist,** *n.*
sward [swɔrd; swɔːd] *n.* 草皮；帶草之地面。—*v.t.* 掩以草皮。—*v.i.* 爲草皮所掩。
***swarm** [swɔrm; swɔːm] *n.* ①蜂羣。②羣。a *swarm* of people. 一羣人。③〖生物〗游走細胞；游走胞子。—*v.i.* ①(蜜蜂)結隊離巢。②羣集；環繞；蜂擁。③擠；一擁而進。④被擁滿；充滿。The beach is *swarming* with bathers. 海灘滿是海浴的人。⑤攀登；攀緣。—*v.t.* ①攀緣。②羣集；蜂擁。
swarm spore 〖植物〗游走芽胞。
swart [swɔrt; swɔːt] *adj.* 〖方，詩〗黑的。
swarth·y ['swɔrðɪ; 'swɔːði] *adj.*, **swarth·i·er, swarth·i·est.** 黑的；黑皮膚的。—**swarth·i·ly,** *adv.* —**swarth·i·ness,** *n.*
swash [swɑʃ; swɔʃ] *v.i.* ①濺水；潑水；澎湃。②虛誇；大言。—*v.t.* 潑濺；濺(水)。—*n.* ①沖擊；沖擊之聲。②虛張聲勢；昂首闊步。③淺灘。④〖印刷〗花體字之突出部分。
swash·buck·ler ['swɑʃ,bʌklɚ; 'swɔʃ,bʌklə] *n.* 虛誇之劍手；天不怕地不怕者。
swash·buck·ling ['swɑʃ,bʌklɪŋ; 'swɔʃ,bʌkliŋ] *n.* 虛誇；虛張聲勢。—*adj.* 虛誇的；虛張聲勢的。
swashing blow 痛毆；痛擊。
swas·ti·ka, swas·ti·ca ['swɑstɪkə; 'swɔstikə] *n.* 卍（古代之幸運符號；德國納粹黨曾改作"卐"並用爲標幟）。
swat [swɑt; swɔt] *v.*, **swat·ted, swat·ting,** *n.* —*v.t.* 〖俗〗猛烈地打；拍。—*n.* ①〖俗〗猛烈的打擊；拍。②〖棒球〗長距離安打(通常爲二壘或三壘安打)。
swatch [swɑtʃ; swɔtʃ] *n.* ①〖美〗作樣品之布條。②樣品。③(土地等之)一小塊；一小片。④小羣。
swath [swɑθ; swɔːθ] *n.* ①一刈的面積；刈幅。②刈下的一行草、穀物等。③狹長之條或片。***cut a (wide) swath*** 炫耀；引起注意。(亦作 **swathe**)
swathe¹ [sweð; sweið] *v.*, **swathed, swath·ing,** *n.* —*v.t.* ①嚴密或完全地包裹；緊裹。②縛；裹；纏；綁。③包圍；圍蔽。—*n.* 包布；卷帶；繃帶。
swathe² [sweð; sweið] *n.* =**swath.**
swat·ter ['swɑtɚ; 'swɔtə] *n.* 蒼蠅拍。
sway** [swe; swei] *v.i.* ①搖擺；擺動。Branches *sway* in the wind. 樹枝在風中搖曳。②偏倚；傾。③有支配作用；有影響力。④交替。—*v.t.* ①搖動；揮舞。②影響；左右；支配。—*n.* ①搖擺；揮動。②偏倚。③權勢；統治。Few countries are now under the *sway* of kings. 現在很少國家在國王統治下。hold sway over*** 統治；控制。
sway-back ['swe,bæk; 'sweibæk] *n.*, *adj.* (牛、馬之)背脊之異常凹陷(的)。
sway-backed ['swe,bækt; 'swei-bækt] *adj.* ①脊背異常凹陷的(牛、馬等)。②凹陷的。③不規律的；不整齊的。
Swa·zi·land ['swɑzɪ,lænd; 'swɑːzi-lænd] *n.* 史瓦濟蘭（非洲東南部一王國，首都墨巴本 Mbabane）。
swear** [swɛr; swɛə] *v.*, **swore** [swor, swɔr; swɔː, swɔə], **sworn** [sworn, swɔrn; swɔːn], **swear·ing,** *n.* —*v.t.* ①宣誓；發誓；立誓。He *swore* an oath. 他發誓。②使宣誓；使立誓。to *swear* a person to secrecy. 使某人誓守祕密。—*v.i.* ①發誓；宣誓；立誓。②詛咒；詬罵。He's always *swearing.* 他總在咒罵。swear by*** a. 對(天、神)發誓。b. 深信；極力推薦。***swear for*** 保證；擔保。***swear in*** 使宣誓就職。***swear off*** 答應放棄；立誓棄絕。***swear out*** 由宣誓而得到。—*n.* ①誓言。②詛咒；詬罵。
swear·word ['swɛr,wɝd; 'swɛəwəːd] *n.* 詛咒；褻瀆之語。
sweat** [swɛt; swet] *n.*, *v.*, **sweat** or **sweat·ed, sweat·ing.** —*n.* ①汗；一陣汗。He wiped the *sweat* from his face. 他揩去臉上的汗。②發汗；出汗。A good *sweat* often cures a cold. 好好發一次汗往往可以治愈傷風。③滲出之水氣。④苦工。⑤焦急；不耐煩。Don't be in such a *sweat!* 不要如此焦急！⑥〖主英〗阿兵哥；丘八。all of a sweat*** a. 滿身大汗。b. 焦急萬分。***by the sweat of one's brow*** 由於辛勤的工作。***in a cold sweat*** 出冷汗；受驚嚇。***in a sweat*** a. 汗濕。b. 在恐懼或焦急中。***no sweat*** 很容易地；輕而易舉地。—*v.i.* ①出汗。We *sweat* when it is very hot. 天很熱時我們出汗。②冒出水氣。③滲出；滴滴流出。④汗濕；汗污。⑤辛苦工作；作苦工。—*v.t.* ①使出汗。②使冒出水氣；使發酵。③使滲出。The flowers *sweat* dew. 花滲出水珠。④使在低微的待遇之下辛苦工作。⑤熔焊；焊接(金屬)。⑥加熱於(金屬)以析出易熔成分。⑦滿身大汗地推動、搬運等。⑧辛苦完成。⑨以出汗而減輕(如體重等)。⑩以汗水弄濕。⑪施以苦刑。***sweat blood*** 〖俗〗a. 辛勤工作。b. 焦急地等待；憂心忡忡。***sweat out*** a. 忍耐；等待至最後。b. 辛苦地做成。
sweat·band ['swɛt,bænd; 'swetbænd] *n.* 帽中鑲的一條防汗濕之皮。
sweat·box ['swɛt,bɑks; 'swetbɔks] *n.* ①(含有濕氣物品之)乾燥箱。②〖俚〗獄中之狹窄禁閉室。
***sweat·er** ['swɛtɚ; 'swetə] *n.* ①毛線衫。②壓榨工人的雇主。
sweater girl 胸部曲線優美的女郎。
sweat gland 汗腺。
sweat·i·ly ['swɛtlɪ; 'swetili] *adv.* 汗流浹背地；辛苦地。
sweating system 勞動榨取制度。
sweat pants 運動員穿的燈籠褲。
sweat shirt 運動員所穿的長袖棉線衫。
sweat·shop ['swɛt,ʃɑp; 'swet-ʃɔp] *n.* 工人在勞動榨取制度下工作之工廠。
sweat·y ['swɛtɪ; 'sweti] *adj.*, **sweat·i·er, sweat·i·est.** ①汗濕的；多汗的。②使出汗的；費力的。—**sweat·i·ness,** *n.*
Swed. ①Sweden. ②Swedish.
***Swede** [swid; swiːd] *n.* ①瑞典人。②(亦作 **swede**) 〖植物〗蕪菁。
***Swe·den** ['swidn̩; 'swiːdn] *n.* 瑞典(北歐一國，首都斯德哥爾摩 Stockholm)。
***Swed·ish** ['swidɪʃ; 'swiːdiʃ] *adj.* 瑞典的；瑞典人的；瑞典語的。—*n.* ①瑞典人(集合稱)。②瑞典語。
swee·ny ['swinɪ; 'swiːni] *n.* 馬肩肌肉萎縮。
***sweep¹** [swip; swiːp] *v.*, **swept, sweep·ing,** *n.* —*v.t.* ①掃；掃除；清掃。to *sweep* up dead leaves. 掃除枯葉。②掃蕩；清除。to *sweep* away feudalism. 廢除封建制度。

③捲起; 捲走; 沖掉。A flood *swept* away the bridge. 洪水沖走橋樑。④拖及。⑤掠過; 拂。⑥掃視;周覽。⑦贏得(每場比賽)。⑧以極大優勢贏得。—*v.i.* ①掃; 掃除。I can't *sweep* without a broom. 沒掃帚我無法掃。②掠過; 掃過; 疾馳。③威儀堂堂地走過。④綿亘; 伸展。⑤(衣服等)在地上拖。⑥(目光等)掃射。His glance *swept* around the room. 他用目光掃射房間一遍。⑦使用拖網等尋找水底物件。***A new broom sweeps clean.*** 【諺】新官上任三把火(謂其幹得起勁)。***be swept off one's feet*** 爲感情所控制。***sweep all before one*** 得到一連串的成功。***sweep one off one's feet*** 立卽贏得某人之心。—*n.* ①掃除;掃蕩。He made a clean *sweep* of all his debts. 他還清所有債務。②掠過。the *sweep* of the wind. 風之掠過。③範圍; 區域。④掃除者; 掃除烟囪者。⑤不斷的流。the *sweep* of the tide. 潮之激流。⑥擺盪。⑦帆船用的大槳。⑧汲井水用的長桿(一端繫桶)。⑨彎曲。⑩如掃的動作。⑪選舉中的大勝。⑫節奏。⑬(*pl.*)金匠或銀匠做首飾時收集的金銀碎屑。***be as black as a sweep*** 非常黑。

***sweep²** *n.* 【俚】=**sweepstakes.** (亦作**sweeps**)

sweep·back [ˈswip͵bæk; ˈswiːpbæk] *n.* 【航空】(機翼傾斜線同飛機側軸形成之)後退角。

sweep·er [ˈswipɚ; ˈswiːpə] *n.* ①掃除者。②掃除器。③掃雷艇。

sweep·ing** [ˈswipɪŋ; ˈswiːpiŋ] *adj.* ①包括無遺的;總括的;範圍廣大的。a *sweeping* victory. 大勝利。②掃清的; 掃蕩的; 一舉盡收的。—*n.* ①清掃;打掃。②(*pl.*)塵屑;掃集物;一堆垃圾。contaminated by *sweepings.* 被一堆垃圾弄髒。the sweepings of the gutter*** 最下賤最髒的人羣。—**ly,** *adv.*

sweep net 捕蟲網。

sweep·stake [ˈswip͵stek; ˈswiːpsteik] *n.* =**sweepstakes.**

sweep·stakes [ˈswip͵steks; ˈswiːpsteiks] *n., pl.* **-stakes.** (作 *sing.* or *pl.* 解) ①(跑馬等之)賭金獨得制。②賭金獨得的馬賽。③賽馬的總賭金。④競賽;比賽。

sweep ticket 馬票。

‡**sweet** [swit; swiːt] *adj.* ①甜的;甘的。This fruit isn't *sweet* enough. 這個水果不够甜。②芳香的。*sweet* flowers. 芳香的花。③新鮮的。④溫和的; 悅耳的。*sweet* music. 悅耳的音樂。⑤適於種植的(土壤)。⑥行駛順利的。⑦動作熟練的。a *sweet* pilot. 動作熟練的飛行員。***be sweet on*** 【俗】愛…。—*n.* ①甘美; 甜蜜。②甜的東西。③(*pl.*)糖果。The children buy *sweets* at a store. 孩子們在店裏買糖果。④(*pl.*)歡樂;快樂。the *sweets* and bitters of life. 人生之苦樂。⑤情人;戀人。⑥悅耳的聲音;可愛的東西。⑦(*pl.*)香味;芳香。—*adv.* 甜蜜地;悅人地。

sweet alyssum 【植物】十字科園藝植物之一種(開小白花)。

sweet-and-sour [ˈswitənˈsauɚ; ˈswiːtənˈsauə] *adj.* 酸甜的。*sweet-and-sour* pork ribs. 糖醋排骨。

sweet basil 【植物】羅勒。

sweet bay 【植物】①月桂樹。②美國的一種木蘭(開圓形的芳香白花)。

sweet·bread [ˈswit͵brɛd; ˈswiːtbred] *n.*(小牛、小羊等之)膵;胰臟;胸腺(供食用者)。

sweet·bri·er, sweet·bri·ar [ˈswit͵braɪɚ; ˈswiːtˈbraiə] *n.* 【植物】歐洲及中亞所產之一種薔薇。

sweet cider 未發酵的蘋果酒。

sweet corn 【植物】含糖分甚高之玉蜀黍。

***sweet·en** [ˈswitn̩; ˈswiːtn] *v.t.* ①使甜; 使香。He *sweetened* his coffee with two lumps of sugar. 他用兩塊糖使他的咖啡變甜。②使可愛;使溫和。③消毒;清潔。④【俚】增加有利的條件;使更有吸引力。⑤【橋牌俚】加注;加籌碼。—*v.i.* ①變甜。The pears will *sweeten* as they ripen. 梨熟了就會變甜。②變可愛;變溫和。—**er,** *n.*

sweet·en·ing [ˈswitn̩ɪŋ; ˈswiːtniŋ] *n.* ①使甜;使香。②調味用甜料;甜味佐料。

sweet fern 【植物】(北美產,葉呈羊齒狀的)小灌木。

sweet flag 【植物】白菖;水菖蒲。

sweet gum ①【植物】香楓。②香楓樹葉。

***sweet·heart** [ˈswit͵hɑrt; ˈswiːthɑːt] *n.* 愛人; 戀人; 情人。She married an old *sweetheart.* 她跟一個舊情人結了婚。—*v.i.* & *v.t.* 談戀愛。

sweetheart agreement 有利於業主的祕密勞資協定(尤指工會負責人單獨與業主所訂者)。(亦作**sweetheart contract**)

sweet·ie [ˈswitɪ; ˈswiːti] *n.* ①【俗】愛人;戀人。②(常 *pl.*)【英】砂糖果品;糖果。

sweet·ing [ˈswitɪŋ; ˈswiːtiŋ] *n.* ①一種甜蘋果。②甜味佐料。③甜;甘甜;甜味。

sweet·ish [ˈswitɪʃ; ˈswiːtiʃ] *adj.* ①有點甜的;稍甜的。②有稍甜之怪味的。

sweet John 【植物】(美洲產之)瞿麥。

***sweet·ly** [ˈswitlɪ; ˈswiːtli] *adv.* ①甜地; 甜味地。②香地; 芳香地。③愉快地;舒適地。④親切地。⑤美妙地; 優美地。to sing *sweetly.* 美妙地歌唱。⑥輕快地。The bicycle runs *sweetly.* 這輛脚踏車跑得輕快。⑦容易地。

sweet marjoram 【植物】歐洲產之一種芳香草本植物(作香料用)。

sweet·meat [ˈswit͵mit; ˈswiːtmiːt] *n.*(常*pl.*)糖果;甜品;蜜餞。(亦作**sweetstuff**)

sweet·ness** [ˈswitnɪs; ˈswiːtnis] *n.* ①甜;甜味;美味;甜的東西。②新鮮。③芳香;香味。④(聲音之)美妙;美妙的聲音。⑤愉快。⑥美;優美。⑦親切; 柔和; 溫和。sweetness and light*** **a.** 美與智之融合。**b.** 親切而講理的態度。**c.** 輕鬆愉快。The ending to the movie is all *sweetness and light.* 那部影片的結局一片歡樂。

sweet nothings 【俗】愛侶間之喁喁情話。

sweet oil 橄欖油。

sweet pea 麝香豌豆。

sweet pepper 【植物】①甜辣椒。②甜辣椒之果實。

sweet potato ①紅薯; 甘薯。②甘薯籐。

sweet-scent·ed [ˈswitˈsɛntɪd; ˈswiːtˈsentid] *adj.* 有香味的;芳香的。

sweet shop 【英】糖果店。(亦作**sweetshop**)

sweet·sop [ˈswit͵sɑp; ˈswiːtsɔp] *n.* 【植物】蕃荔枝。

sweet talk 甜言蜜語。

sweet-tem·pered [ˈswitˈtɛmpɚd; ˈswiːtˈtempəd] *adj.* 性情溫和的;敦厚的。

sweet tooth 【俗】甜食之嗜好。

sweet violet 【植物】香堇。

sweet water 【化】甘油水。

sweet william 【植物】美洲石竹。(亦作**sweet William**)

sweet·y [ˈswitɪ; ˈswiːti] *n.* 【蘇】甜品;蜜餞;糖果。

‡**swell** [swɛl; swel] *v.,* **swelled, swelled** or **swol·len, swell·ing,** *n., adj.* —*v.i.* ①增大; 膨脹; 漲。Wood often *swells* when

wet. 木頭浸濕時常膨脹。②高超；隆起。A barrel *swells* in the middle. 一個桶的中間部分是隆起的。③增加；積聚。Savings may *swell* into a fortune. 儲蓄可以積成財富。④漸强；變高；提高。⑤〖俗〗變得自負；變得驕傲。—*v.t.* ①使增大；使膨脹；使漲。Water *swells* wood. 水使木頭膨脹。②使腫。③使突出；使隆起。④使升高；使提高。⑤使加强；使變强。⑥使矜誇；使自負。to be *swollen* with anger. 盛怒。—*n.*①增大；膨脹；腫；隆起；漲。a *swell* in population. 人口的增加。②增加的部分；隆起的部分；突出的部分。③高起的地；圓的小山。④大浪；巨浪。The boat rocked in the *swell*. 船在浪中搖擺。⑤〖音樂〗音量之增減。⑥〖俗〗時髦人物；漂亮人物。⑦名人；名手。—*adj.* 〖俚〗①優秀的；上等的；漂亮的；很棒的。a *swell* tennis player. 一個優秀的網球員。②時髦的；上流的。

swell box 風琴之抑揚箱。

swell·dom (ˈswɛldəm; ˈsweldəm) *n.* 〖俗〗時髦社會；時髦人士。

swelled head 〖俗〗自大；自誇；自負。

swell·fish (ˈswɛlˌfɪʃ; ˈswelfiʃ) *n., pl.* **-fish, -fish·es.** (美國東海岸產的)鼓腹魚。

swell·ing (ˈswɛlɪŋ; ˈsweliŋ) *n.* ①腫脹；腫大；腫；瘤。②膨脹；脹大；增大。—*adj.* ①膨脹的；隆起的；腫脹的。②自滿的；矜誇的。

swell·ish (ˈswɛlɪʃ; ˈsweliʃ) *adj.* 〖俗〗時髦的；漂亮的。

swell mob 〖俚〗衣著講究的小偷、扒手或騙子(集合稱)。

swell·mobs·man (ˈswɛlˈmɑbzmən; ˈswelˈmɔbzmən) *n., pl.* **-men.** 〖俚〗衣著講究的小偷、扒手或騙子。

swell organ 有抑揚箱的風琴。

swel·ter (ˈswɛltɚ; ˈsweltə) *v.i.* 熱昏；中暑；汗流浹背。—*v.t.* ①使熱昏；使中暑；使汗流浹背。②流出(毒液等)。—*n.* 酷熱；盛暑。

swel·ter·ing (ˈswɛltərɪŋ; ˈsweltəriŋ) *adj.* ①汗流浹背的。②悶熱的。

swept (swɛpt; swept) *v.* pt. & pp. of sweep.

swept-back (ˈswɛptˌbæk; ˈswept-bæk) *adj.* ①(機翼)向後傾斜的。②有向後傾斜之翼的。

swept·wing (ˈswɛptˌwɪŋ; ˈswept-wiŋ) *n.* 向後傾斜之機翼。—*adj.* (飛機)有向後傾斜之機翼的。

swerve (swɝv; swəːv) *v.,* **swerved, swerv·ing,** *n.* —*v.i.* 轉向；離正路。—*v.t.* 使轉向；使循曲線進行。—*n.* 轉向；逸出常軌。

S. W. G. standard wire gauge.

Swift (swɪft; swift) *n.* 斯威夫特 (Jonathan, 1667–1745, 英國諷刺家，為 *Gulliver's Travels* 之作者)。

***swift** (swɪft; swift) *adj.* 快的；迅速的；敏捷的。a *swift* runner. 跑得很快的人。—*adv.* 迅速地；敏捷地。—*n.* 褐雨燕。—**ness,** *n.*

swift-foot·ed (ˈswɪftˈfutɪd; ˈswift-ˈfutid) *adj.* 善跑的；捷足的。

***swift·ly** (ˈswɪftlɪ; ˈswiftli) *adj.* 疾速地；敏捷地。

swig (swɪg; swig) *n., v.,* **swigged, swig·ging.** —*n.* 〖俗〗痛飲；牛飲；大飲。—*v.t.* & *v.i.* 〖俗〗痛飲；大飲。

swill (swɪl; swil) *n.* ①(餵豬的)食物殘渣。②垃圾。③大喝；痛飲。④水之沖擊聲。—*v.i.* ①大喝。②動盪。—*v.t.* ①長飲；大喝；狼吞虎嚥。②沖洗；洗滌。③倒。④以…沖。

:swim (swɪm; swim) *v.,* **swam, swum, swim·ming,** *n., adj.* —*v.i.* ①游泳。He *swam* across the river. 他游泳過河。Sink or *swim*, I will do it. 不計成敗，我決為之。②漂浮。③盈溢；充滿。④暈眩。My head *swims.* 我頭暈。⑤滑過。⑥搖動；搖晃。—*v.t.* ①游泳；游過。He can *swim* two miles. 他能游泳兩英里。②使游泳。③使浮起。④予以足够之水使能游泳或浮起。 ***swim with the tide*** 順應潮流。—*n.* ①游泳。to go for a *swim.* 去游泳。②魚鰾。 ***the swim*** 時代潮流；活動。—*adj.* 游泳的。*swim* lessons. 游泳課。—**swim·mer,** *n.*

swim bladder (魚之)浮囊；魚鰾。

swim fin 游泳或潛水者套在脚上的橡皮鰭。

swim·mer·et (ˈswɪmərˌɛt; ˈswiməret) *n.* 〖動物〗(甲殼類的)游水器。

swim·ming (ˈswɪmɪŋ; ˈswimiŋ) *n.* ①游泳；游水；泅水。to go *swimming.* 去游泳。②眩暈。—*adj.* ①游泳的；能游泳的；習慣於游水的；游泳用的。a *swimming* suit. 游泳衣。②充滿水的；充滿水狀物的；充溢着淚的。③眩暈的；使眩暈的。

swimming bath 〖英〗游泳池(通常在室內)。

swimming bladder (魚之)浮囊；鰾。

swim·ming·ly (ˈswɪmɪŋlɪ; ˈswimiŋli) *adv.* 順利地；成功地。

swimming pool 游泳池。(亦作 swim pool)

swim ring 游泳圈；救生圈。

swim·suit (ˈswɪmˌsut; ˈswimsjuːt) *n.* 游泳衣。

swin·dle (ˈswɪndl; ˈswindl) *v.,* **-dled, -dling,** *n.* —*v.t.* & *v.i.* 行騙；詐取；欺騙。—*n.* ①騙術；欺詐。②受騙而買的東西。—**a·ble,** *adj.* —**swin·dler,** *n.*

swindle sheet 〖美俚〗公帳報銷。

swin·dling (ˈswɪndlɪŋ; ˈswindliŋ) *n.* 欺騙。

swine (swaɪn; swain) *n., pl.* **swine.** ①豬。②鄙賤之人。

swine·herd (ˈswaɪnˌhɝd; ˈswainhəːd) *n.* 養豬人。

swin·er·y (ˈswaɪnərɪ; ˈswainəri) *n.* ①豬舍；豬欄。②豬(集合稱)。

:swing (swɪŋ; swiŋ) *v.,* **swung, swing·ing,** *n., adj.* —*v.i.* ①搖擺。The hammock *swings.* 吊床在搖擺。②旋轉。The door *swung* open. 門開了。③搖擺而行。④顯露有力的節奏。He likes verses that *swing.* 他喜歡節奏有力的詩。⑤動搖；改變態度或立場。⑥演奏或演唱搖擺音樂。⑦揮棒；揮臂。⑧繞道；巡廻。He promised to *swing* by and pick them up. 他答應繞道去搭載他們。⑨〖俚〗過一種時髦而刺激的生活。—*v.t.* ①使搖擺；使擺動。②揮動。to *swing* a bat. 揮棒。③使廻轉；使旋轉。④掛；吊。⑤〖俗〗經營；操縱；支配。⑥以搖擺音樂的方式演唱或演奏。to *swing* a folk song. 以搖擺音樂的方式演唱民謠。 ***no room to swing a cat in*** (房間等)很小；沒有多少空間。 ***swing for (a person)*** (因謀殺某人而)被吊死。 ***swing round the circle*** **a.** 論及一題目之所有不同的方面。**b.** (候選人)巡廻選區。**c.** 連續地抱各種不同看法或態度。 ***swing the lead*** 〖俗〗以欺騙或佯病而逃避責任。—*n.* ①搖擺；擺動；揮動。a batter with a powerful *swing.* 具有强勁揮棒力的打擊手。②鞦韆。③律動。④行動；活動。⑤搖擺音樂。⑥搖擺音樂之節奏與旋律。⑦來回流動。⑧改變；轉變。⑨衝力；動力。a train approaching at full *swing.* 以十足衝力駛近的火車。⑩擺動距離。 ***in full swing*** 處於最活躍的進行狀態中。 ***swing around the circle*** 〖美〗政治性的旅行。 ***the swing of the pendulum*** 鐘擺的擺動；(喻)榮枯盛衰；消長。 ***go with a swing*** (詩歌等)節拍輕快；成功；流行。—*adj.* ①擺動的；轉動的。a *swing* handle. 轉動的把手。②懸吊的。

③鞦韆的。a *swing* rope 鞦韆的繩子。④搖擺音樂的。⑤決定性的；最具影響力的。⑥代理的；臨時的。

swing·boat 〔'swɪŋ,bot; 'swiŋbout〕 *n.* 一種船形兩人相對而坐的鞦韆。

swing bridge 廻旋橋(船隻通過可開啓之橋)。

swing door 廻旋門。(亦作**swinging door**)

swinge·ing 〔'swɪndʒɪŋ; 'swindʒiŋ〕 *adj.* 〖俗〗①大的；巨大的。②極好的；第一等的。③重的。—*adv.* 〖俗〗非常地。

swing·er 〔'swɪŋə; 'swiŋə〕 *n.* ①搖擺者；揮舞者。②〖俗〗驚人的事物；大的事物。③〖俚〗過一種時髦而刺激生活的人。

swin·gle 〔'swɪŋgl; 'swiŋgl〕 *n., v.,* **-gled, -gling.** —*n.* ①打蔴器。②〖方〗連枷上部之廻轉打禾部分。—*v.t.* 以打蔴器打刷。

swin·gle·tree 〔'swɪŋgl,tri; 'swiŋgltri:〕 *n.* 犂槃。

swing music 搖擺音樂(演奏時可自由更改原有旋律之爵士樂)。

swing shift 〖美俗〗(美國工作輪班制中)自下午三時至晚上十二時之值班。

swing shifter 下午三時至晚上十二時值班之人員。

swin·ish 〔'swaɪnɪʃ; 'swainiʃ〕 *adj.* ①豬一樣的。②鄙賤的。—**ly,** *adv.*

swipe 〔swaɪp; swaip〕 *n., v.,* **swiped, swip·ing.** —*n.* ①〖俗〗揮臂猛擊；重擊。②抽水機等之柄。***take a swipe at*** 〖俚〗 =**to swipe at.** —*v.t.* ①〖俗〗揮臂猛擊；重擊。②〖俚〗偷。—*v.i.* 〖俗〗作揮臂重擊。***swipe at*** 瞄向…作揮臂重擊；試圖重擊。

swipes 〔swaɪps; swaips〕 *n. pl.* 〖英俚〗啤酒(尤指味淡或質劣者)。

swirl 〔swɜl; swə:l〕 *v.i.* 渦捲；旋轉。—*v.t.* 使渦捲；使旋轉。—*n.* 渦旋；彎曲。

swish[1] 〔swɪʃ; swiʃ〕 *v.t. & v.i.* 發出瑟瑟之聲。—*n.* 作瑟瑟聲。—*adv.* 帶着瑟瑟之聲。

swish[2] *adj.* 時髦的；好看的。

***Swiss** 〔swɪs; swis〕 *adj., n., pl.* **Swiss.** —*adj.* 瑞士的；瑞士風格的；瑞士人的。—*n.* 瑞士人。

Swiss chard 〖植物〗一種甜菜(葉可食)。

Swiss cheese 白色或淡黃色多孔乾酪。

Swiss Guards 瑞士衞兵(特指梵蒂岡教宗之衞隊)。

Swiss roll 內捲果醬之麪包。

Swit. Switzerland.(亦作**Switz., Swtz.**)

***switch** 〔swɪtʃ; switʃ〕 *n.* ①軟枝；鞭。②(女人之)假髮。③〖鐵路〗轉轍器。④〖電〗開關。⑤轉變；變換。a *switch* of votes to another candidate. 票之轉投另一候選人。⑥一擊；甩動。⑦〖籃球〗交換看守對方球員。—*v.t.* ①鞭打。②擺動；甩動。③使轉轍。to *switch* a train. 使火車轉轍。④開通或關閉(電流)。⑤轉變。He *switched* the conversation from one subject to another. 他轉變話題。⑥突然搶走；猛奪。—*v.i.* ①鞭打。②轉轍。③轉換。④擺動；甩動。⑤〖籃球〗交換看守對方球員。

switch·back 〔'swɪtʃ,bæk; 'switʃbæk〕 *n.*①(鐵路或公路之作Z形上陡斜面用的)轉向線。②〖英〗一種盤繞升降的遊戲用有軌敞車。—*adj.* 鋸齒形的；曲折的。—*v.i.* 成鋸齒形而延伸；作鋸齒形運動。

switch·blade 〔'swɪtʃ,bled; 'switʃbleid〕 *n.* 彈簧刀。〔=**switchblade** (or **switch**) **knife**〕

switch·board 〔'swɪtʃ,bord; 'switʃbɔ:d〕 *n.* ①配電盤；電鍵板。②電話總機。

switch·er·oo 〔,swɪtʃə'ru, 'swɪtʃə,ru; ,switʃə'ru:, 'switʃəru:〕 *n.* 意外變化。

switch-hit 〔'swɪtʃ'hɪt; 'switʃ'hit〕 *v.i.,* **-hit, -hit·ting.** 〖棒球〗作變位打擊。

switch-hit·ter 〔'swɪtʃ'hɪtə; 'switʃ'hitə〕 *n.* 〖棒球〗能隨意作變位打擊的打擊手。

switch·man 〔'swɪtʃmən; 'switʃmən〕 *n., pl.* **-men.** (鐵路之)轉轍手；扳閘夫。

switch·o·ver 〔'swɪtʃ,ovə; 'switʃ,ouvə〕 *n.* 轉換；轉變。

switch·yard 〔'swɪtʃ,jard; 'switʃ-ja:d〕 *n.* 〖鐵路〗調車廠。

Switz·er 〔'swɪtsə; 'switsə〕 *n.* 瑞士人；瑞士雇傭兵。

***Switz·er·land** 〔'swɪtsələnd; 'switsələnd〕 *n.* 瑞士(歐洲之一國，首都伯恩 Bern).

swiv·el 〔'swɪvl; 'swivl〕 *n., v.,* **-el(l)ed, -el·(l)ing.** —*n.* ①〖機械〗轉鐶；鉸丁鐶。②旋廻砲座；旋廻砲。—*v.t.* ①使於座軸上旋轉。②以旋鐶固接。③旋轉；轉動。—*v.i.* (於軸上)旋轉；旋廻。

swivel chair 轉椅。

swivel gun 旋廻砲。

swiz(z) 〔swɪz; swiz〕 *n.* 〖英〗欺騙；詐欺。

swiz·zle 〔'swɪzl; 'swizl〕 *n.* 一種酒類、碎冰、糖、苦味藥物等混合之飲料。—*v.t.* 〖俗〗縱飲；狂飲。

swizzle stick 混合酒類使用之攪拌棒。

swob 〔swɑb; swɔb〕 *n., v.,* **swobbed, swob·bing.** =**swab.**

***swol·len** 〔'swolən, -ln; 'swoulən, -ln〕 *adj.* ①腫的；脹的；漲水的。a *swollen* foot. 腫的脚。②得意忘形的。—*v.* pp. of **swell.**

***swoon** 〔swun; swu:n〕 *v.i.* ①昏暈。She *swoons* at the sight of blood. 她一看見血便暈了。②着迷。③漸漸消失；漸漸衰弱。—*n.* 昏暈。She fell down in a *swoon.* 她暈倒。

swoop 〔swup; swu:p〕 *v.i.* 猝然降下(攫捕或攻擊)。The eagle *swooped* (down) upon a hare. 鷹猝然飛下攫捕一隻野兔。—*v.t.* 猝然攫取。***swoop up something*** 突然取得全部。—*n.* 猝然下降；猝然攻擊。***at*** (or ***in***) ***one fell swoop*** 一下子；一舉。—**er,** *n.*

swoosh 〔'swuʃ; 'swu:ʃ〕 *v.i.* 急衝；急流；飛馳。—*v.t.* 射出。—*n.* 急衝；飛馳。

swop 〔swɑp; swɔp〕 *n., v.,* **swopped, swop·ping.** =**swap.**

‡**sword** 〔sord, sɔrd; sɔ:d, sɔəd〕 *n.* ①劍；刀。②(the-)戰爭；武力。The pen is mightier than the *sword.* 筆桿的力量大於刀槍。***at swords' points*** 非常不友善的；在戰爭或死亡的威脅下。***cross*** (or ***measure***) ***swords*** (***with someone***) 與人交鋒，爭鬥或爭論。***draw the sword*** 拔劍；開戰。***put to the sword*** 殺死。***sheathe the sword*** 納劍於鞘；停戰。

sword arm 右臂。

sword bayonet 刺刀。

sword-bear·er 〔'sord,bɛrə; 'sɔ:d,bɛərə〕 *n.* ①替長官帶刀劍之扈從；佩刀劍之儀隊隊員。②佩刀劍的人；(特指佩刀劍之)統治者；有權勢的人。③〖動物〗美洲產的一種長角蚱蜢。④=**swordbill.**

sword belt 佩掛刀劍之腰帶。

sword·bill 〔'sord,bɪl; 'sɔ:dbil〕 *n.* 一種長嘴蜂雀(產於南美)。(亦作 **sword-billed hummingbird**)

sword cane 內藏刀劍之杖。

sword cut 刀傷。

sword dance 穿行於刀尖間之舞；揮劍而舞；劍舞。

sword·fish 〔'sord,fɪʃ; 'sɔ:dfiʃ〕 *n., pl.* **-fish·es, -fish.** 旗魚。

sword flag 〖植物〗黃鳶尾草。

sword grass〖植物〗一種菖蒲。
sword guard 刀劍之護手。
sword knot (繫於劍柄上的)劍飾。
sword law ①〖軍〗軍法; 軍令; 戒嚴令(=martial law)。②軍事統治。
sword lily〖植物〗劍蘭(=gladiolus)。
sword·play [ˈsordˌple; ˈsɔːdplei] *n.* ①舞劍;鬥劍。②(喻)鬥智。
swords·man [ˈsordzmən; ˈsɔːdzmən] *n., pl.* **-men.** ①劍士;劍客;擊劍者。②兵士;軍人;武人。
swords·man·ship [ˈsordzmənˌʃɪp; ˈsɔːdzmənʃip] *n.* 劍術。
sword·smith [ˈsordˌsmɪθ; ˈsɔːdsmiθ] *n.* 製造或修理刀劍之工匠。
sword·stick [ˈsordˌstɪk; ˈsɔːdstik] *n.* 內藏刀劍之杖。
swore [swor; swɔː] *v.* pt. of **swear.**
***sworn** [sworn; swɔːn] *v.* pp. of **swear.** —*adj.* ①宣過誓的。②宣誓證明的。We have his *sworn* statement. 我們有他的宣誓證明的口供。③決不改變的;根深蒂固的。
sworn brothers (or **friends**) 盟兄弟;刎頸之交。
sworn enemies 不共戴天之仇人。
sworn evidence 宣誓後提出之證據。
swot[1] [swɑt; swɔt] *v.,* **swot·ted, swot·ting,** *n.* —*v.i.* & *v.t.*〖英俚〗苦讀; 用功。—*n.*〖英〗①用功。②勤學者。
swot[2] *v., n.* =**swat.**
swound [swaund; swaund] *v.i., n.* 〖古〗=**swoon.**
'swounds [zwaundz; zwaundz] *interj.*〖古〗表憤慨、憤怒、驚愕之委婉誓語 (God's wounds 之縮寫)。
‡**swum** [swʌm; swʌm] *v.* pp. of **swim.**
swung [swʌŋ; swʌŋ] *v.* pt. & pp. of **swing.**
swung dash "~"記號。
sy-〖字首〗**syn-** 之異體(用於 Z 或後跟子音的 S 之前)。
Syb·a·rite [ˈsɪbəˌraɪt; ˈsibərait] *n.* 希巴利斯 (Sybaris 義大利南部古希臘一城市, 爲奢侈逸樂中心) 之居民。
syb·a·rit·ic [ˌsɪbəˈrɪtɪk; ˌsibəˈritik] *adj.* 耽於奢侈逸樂的。—**al,** *adj.* —**al·ly,** *adv.*
syb·il [ˈsɪbḷ; ˈsibil] *n.* sibyl 之訛體。
syc·a·mine [ˈsɪkəmɪn; ˈsikəmain] *n.* (新約路加福音十七章六節中提及之)黑桑樹。
syc·a·more [ˈsɪkəˌmor; ˈsikəmɔː] *n.* ①(產於近東之)一種無花果樹。②(產於歐洲的)大楓樹。③(產於美洲之)使君子科之一種植物;篠懸木屬之一種。
syce, sice [saɪs; sais] *n.*〖英印〗馬夫。
sy·cee [saɪˈsi; saiˈsiː] *n.* (昔中國用作貨幣之)銀錠;細絲銀;紋銀。—*adj.* 純的(銀)。
sycee silver =**sycee.**
syc·o·phan·cy [ˈsɪkəfənsɪ; ˈsikəfənsi] *n., pl.* **-cies.** 阿諛。
syc·o·phant [ˈsɪkəfənt; ˈsikəfənt] *n.* 阿諛者。 —**ic,** —**ish,** *adj.*
sy·co·sis [saɪˈkosɪs; saiˈkousis] *n.*〖醫〗鬚瘡。
sy·e·nite [ˈsaɪəˌnaɪt; ˈsaiənait] *n.* 〖礦〗黑花崗石;正長巖。
sy·e·nit·ic [ˌsaɪəˈnɪtɪk; ˌsaiəˈnitik] *adj.* ①黑花崗巖的; 正長巖的。②像黑花崗巖的; 像正長巖的。
syl-〖字首〗**syn-** 之異體(用於 l 之前)。
syl·la·bar·y [ˈsɪləˌbɛrɪ; ˈsiləbəri] *n., pl.* **-bar·ies.** ①字音表;綴字表。②(日文之)假名表; 五十音圖。
syl·lab·ic [sɪˈlæbɪk; siˈlæbik] *adj.* ①綴音的; 音節的。②無母音而自成音節的 (如 battle 中之 l)。③逐一音節明晰發音的。—*n.*〖語音〗音節主音。 —**al·ly,** *adv.*
syl·lab·i·cate [sɪˈlæbɪˌket; siˈlæbikeit] *v.t.,* **-cat·ed, -cat·ing.** 分(某字)的音節(=syllabify)。—**syl·lab·i·ca·tion,** *n.*
syl·lab·i·fy [sɪˈlæbəˌfaɪ; siˈlæbifai] *v.t.,* **-fied** [-ˌfaɪd; -faid], **-fy·ing.** 分(某字)的音節。—**syl·lab·i·fi·ca·tion,** *n.*
syl·la·bize [ˈsɪləˌbaɪz; ˈsiləbaiz] *v.t.,* **-bized, -biz·ing.** 分(某字)之音節。
***syl·la·ble** [ˈsɪləbḷ; ˈsiləbl] *n., v.,* **-bled, -bling.** —*n.* ①音節。"America" is a word of four *syllables.* America 是一個四音節的字。②一點點; 一個字。Do not breathe a *syllable* of it to any one (= Not a *syllable*)! 不要向任何人洩露半個字! —*v.t.* ①逐音節地發出。②清晰說出。—*v.i.* 清晰地讀出每一音節。
syl·la·bub [ˈsɪləˌbʌb; ˈsiləbʌb] *n.* =**sillabub.**
syl·la·bus [ˈsɪləbəs; ˈsiləbəs] *n., pl.* **-bus·es, -bi** [-ˌbaɪ; -bai]. ①(講義等的)摘要。②〖法律〗判決理由書之概要; 判例要覽。
syl·lep·sis [sɪˈlɛpsɪs; siˈlepsis] *n., pl.* **-ses** [-siz; -siːz]. ①〖修辭〗一語雙敍法。②〖文法〗兼用法。
syl·lep·tic [sɪˈlɛptɪk; siˈleptik] *adj.* 兼用法的。
syl·lo·gism [ˈsɪləˌdʒɪzəm; ˈsilədʒizm] *n.* ①〖邏輯〗三段論法。②演繹法。③巧妙或狡黠的理論。
syl·lo·gis·tic [ˌsɪləˈdʒɪstɪk; ˌsiləˈdʒistik] *adj.* 推論式的;三段論法的;演繹的。—*n.* 三段論法;演繹法。 —**al·ly,** *adv.*
syl·lo·gize [ˈsɪləˌdʒaɪz; ˈsilədʒaiz] *v.t.* & *v.i.,* **-gized, -giz·ing.** 以三段論法推論;用三段論法。
sylph [sɪlf; silf] *n.* ①體態輕盈的少女。②(Paracelsus 學說中之)居於空氣中有生死而無靈魂的生靈。
sylph·id [ˈsɪlfɪd; ˈsilfid] *n., adj.* 體態輕盈之少女(的)。
sylph·like [ˈsɪlfˌlaɪk; ˈsilf-laik] *adj.* 體態輕盈的。
syl·va [ˈsɪlvə; ˈsilvə] *n., pl.* **-vas, -vae** [-vi; -viː]. =**silva.**
syl·van [ˈsɪlvən; ˈsilviks] *adj.* 森林的; 林木的;多林木的; 居於森林中的。—*n.* ①森林之神。②森林中之居住者。(亦作 **silvan**)
syl·vics [ˈsɪlvɪks; ˈsilviks] *n.* ①森林學。②森林中樹木之特性。
syl·vi·cul·ture [ˈsɪlvɪˌkʌltʃə; ˈsilviˌkʌltʃə] *n.* 造林(法)。(亦作 **silviculture**)
sym-〖字首〗**syn-** 之異體(用於 b, p, m之前)。
sym. ①symbol.②symbolic.③symmetrical. ④symphony.
Sym·bi·o·nese Liberation Army [ˌsɪmbaɪˈoniz~~; ˌsimbaiˈouniːz~~] 共生解放軍(美國一極端暴力組織)。
sym·bi·o·sis [ˌsɪmbaɪˈosɪs; ˌsimbaiˈousis] *n.*〖生物〗共生;共棲。
sym·bi·ot·ic [ˌsɪmbaɪˈɑtɪk; ˌsimbaiˈɔtik] *adj.*〖生物〗共生的;共棲的。—**al·ly,** *adv.*
***sym·bol** [ˈsɪmbḷ; ˈsimbəl] *n., v.,* **-boled, -bol·ing.** —*n.* ①符號。The sign ÷ is the *symbol* of division. ÷ 是代表除法的符號。②象徵。—*v.t.* & *v.i.* 以符號表示;象徵。
sym·bol·ic [sɪmˈbɑlɪk; simˈbɔlik] *adj.* ①用作符號的; 用作象徵的。②象徵的; 符號的; 用符號或象徵表示的。③象徵主義的。(亦作 **symbolical**) —**al·ly,** *adv.*
symbolic logic 數理邏輯;符號邏輯。(亦作 **mathematical logic**)

sym·bol·ism 〔ˈsɪmblˌɪzəm; ˈsimbəlizm〕 *n.* ①象徵主義。②符號表示；符號使用。③象徵。④象徵意義；象徵性質。

sym·bol·ist 〔ˈsɪmblɪst; ˈsimbəlist〕 *n.* 象徵主義者。—*adj.* 象徵主義者的；象徵主義的。 —**ic,** *adj.*

sym·bol·ize 〔ˈsɪmblˌaɪz; ˈsimbəlaiz〕 *v.,* **-ized, -iz·ing.** —*v.t.* ①爲…之象徵；象徵；代表。②以符號表示；以象徵表示。③作成符號。 —*v.i.* 使用符號或象徵。 —**sym·bol·i·za·tion, sym·bol·iz·er,** *n.*

sym·bol·o·gy 〔sɪmˈbɑlədʒɪ; simˈbɔlədʒi〕 *n.* ①象徵學（對象徵研究與解釋之學科）。②象徵表示；符號代表；符號表示。

sym·met·al·lism 〔sɪmˈmɛtəlɪzm; simˈmetəlizm〕 *n.*〖經濟〗(金銀)複本位制。

***sym·met·ri·cal** 〔sɪˈmɛtrɪkl; siˈmetrikəl〕 *adj.* ①對稱的；勻稱的；均勻的；勻整的。②〖數學〗對稱的。③〖植物〗放射狀的；軸射狀的(=actinomorphic)。④〖醫〗同時同樣影響身體相對部分的；對稱的(病)。⑤〖化〗對稱的。(亦作 **symmetric**) —**ly,** *adv.*

sym·me·trize 〔ˈsɪmɪˌtraɪz; ˈsimitraiz〕 *v.t.,* **-trized, -triz·ing.** 使對稱；使均勻；使相稱；使調和。—**sym·me·tri·za·tion,** *n.*

sym·me·try 〔ˈsɪmɪtrɪ; ˈsimitri〕 *n., pl.* **-tries.** 對稱；勻稱；相稱；均勻；調和。

***sym·pa·thet·ic** 〔ˌsɪmpəˈθɛtɪk; ˌsimpəˈθetik〕 *adj.* ①同情的；同感的。②和諧的；合宜的。 We work best in a *sympathetic* atmosphere. 我們在一種和諧的氣氛中工作時效率最佳。③交感的。④〖物理〗共振的；共鳴的。⑤〖俗〗贊成的。—**al·ly,** *adv.*

sympathetic ink 隱顯墨水。

sympathetic nerve 〖解剖〗交感神經。

sympathetic strike = sympathy strike.

***sym·pa·thize** 〔ˈsɪmpəˌθaɪz; ˈsimpəθaiz〕 *v.i.,* **-thized, -thiz·ing.** ①同情。She *sympathizes* with poor people. 她同情窮人。②具有同感；同意。—**sym·pa·thiz·ing·ly,** *adv.*

sym·pa·thiz·er 〔ˈsɪmpəˌθaɪzɚ; ˈsimpəθaizə〕 *n.* 同情者。

***sym·pa·thy** 〔ˈsɪmpəθɪ; ˈsimpəθi〕 *n., pl.* **-thies.** ①同情；憐憫。He has no *sympathy* with (*or* for) beggars. 他不同情乞丐。He is a man of wide *sympathies.* 他是個極富同情心的人。②同感；贊同。③同感力；交感力。

sympathy strike 同情罷工(對另一羣罷工者表示道義上之支持或同情的罷工)。

sym·pet·al·ous 〔sɪmˈpɛtələs; simˈpetələs〕 *adj.* 〖植物〗合瓣的。

sym·phon·ic 〔sɪmˈfɑnɪk; simˈfɔnik〕 *adj.* ①〖音樂〗交響樂的；交響曲的。②和音的。③諧音的(字等)。④結構上或組織上像交響樂的。—**al·ly,** *adv.*

symphonic poem 〖音樂〗交響詩。

sym·pho·ni·ous 〔sɪmˈfonɪəs; simˈfouniəs〕 *adj.* ①和音的〖with〗. ②和諧的〖to, with〗. —**ly,** *adv.*

***sym·pho·ny** 〔ˈsɪmfənɪ; ˈsimfəni〕 *n., pl.* **-nies.** ①交響樂；交響曲。②交響樂團。③交響樂團演奏之音樂會。④色彩的協調。⑤聲音的協調；諧音。Night was a *symphony* of sounds. 夜是各種聲音的協調。

symphony orchestra 交響樂團。

sym·phy·sis 〔ˈsɪmfəsɪs; ˈsimfisis〕 *n., pl.* **-ses.** 〔-ˌsiz; -siːz〕. ①〖解剖〗(骨之)縫合；聯合；癒合；癒合之縫。②〖植物〗合生。

sym·po·si·um 〔sɪmˈpozɪəm; simˈpouzjəm〕 *n., pl.* **-si·ums, -si·a** 〔-zɪə; -zjə〕. ①座談會；討論會。②(對某一問題之)諸家論叢；諸家論文集。③〖古希臘〗宴會後之餘興。

***symp·tom** 〔ˈsɪmptəm; ˈsimptəm, ˈsimtəm〕 *n.* 徵候；朕兆。 Paleness is a *symptom* of fear. 面色蒼白是恐懼的表徵。

symp·to·mat·ic 〔ˌsɪmptəˈmætɪk; ˌsimptəˈmætik〕 *adj.* ①徵兆的。②徵候的。

symp·tom·a·tol·o·gy 〔ˌsɪmptəməˈtɑlədʒɪ; ˌsimptəməˈtɔlədʒi〕 *n.* 〖醫〗徵候學；症狀學。

syn- 〖字首〗表"共；合；同時；相似"之義。

syn. ①synchronize. ②synchronized. ③synchronizing. ④synonym. ⑤synonymous. ⑥synthetic.

syn·aer·e·sis 〔sɪˈnɛrɪsɪs; siˈnɛərisis〕 *n.* =**syneresis.**

syn·a·gog·i·cal 〔ˌsɪnəˈgɑdʒɪkl; ˌsinəˈgɔdʒikl〕 *adj.* (猶太人之)會堂的；會衆的。

syn·a·gogue 〔ˈsɪnəˌgɔg; ˈsinəgɔg〕 *n.*①(猶太教之)會堂。②猶太教會堂之聚會。

syn·apse 〔sɪˈnæps; siˈnæps〕 *n.* ①〖解剖〗二神經原之神經絲相接之部位；神經鍵。②〖生物〗(生殖細胞核分裂時染色體之) 聯會；聯會期。

syn·ar·thro·sis 〔ˌsɪnɑrˈθrosɪs; ˌsinɑːˈθrousis〕 *n., pl.* **-ses** 〔-siz; -siːz〕. 〖解剖〗不動關節。

syn·chro 〔ˈsɪŋkro; ˈsiŋkrou〕 *adj.* 同步的 (=synchronized, synchronous).

synchro- 〖字首〗表"同時、同步"之義。

syn·chro·cy·clo·tron 〔ˌsɪŋkroˈsaɪklətrɑn; ˌsiŋkrouˈsaiklətrɔn〕 *n.* 〖電〗同步廻旋加速器。(亦作 **FM cyclotron**)

syn·chro·flash 〔ˈsɪŋkrəˌflæʃ; ˈsiŋkrəflæʃ〕 *adj.* (照相機) 有使快門打開與閃光同時發生之附件的。

syn·chro·mesh 〔ˈsɪŋkrəˌmɛʃ; ˈsiŋkrouˈmeʃ〕 *n., adj.* (汽車換擋變速時之) 同步裝置(的)。

syn·chro·nal 〔ˈsɪŋkrənl; ˈsiŋkrənl〕 *adj.* =**synchronous.**

syn·chro·nism 〔ˈsɪŋkrəˌnɪzəm; ˈsiŋkrənizm〕 *n.* ①同時發生；併發；同時性。②同時代之歷史事件對照年表；同時代之人物表。③〖電〗同步性。④〖繪畫〗將不同時代之事物繪於一圖中。

syn·chro·nize 〔ˈsɪŋkrəˌnaɪz; ˈsiŋkrənaiz〕 *v.,* **-nized, -niz·ing.** —*v.i.* ①同時發生；併發；時間一致。②同時以同一速度進行。—*v.t.* ①使在時間上一致。②使同時以同速進行。③確定(歷史事件等)爲同時。④〖電影〗使(音響效果或對白)與動作相配合；爲(影片)配音。 —**syn·chro·ni·za·tion,** *n.*

synchronized swimming 齊游表演。

syn·chro·niz·er 〔ˈsɪŋkrəˌnaɪzɚ; ˈsiŋkrənaizə〕 *n.* 同步器。

syn·chro·nous 〔ˈsɪŋkrənəs; ˈsiŋkrənəs〕 *adj.* ①同時(發生)的。②同時以同速進行的。③〖電, 物理〗同周期的。—**ly,** *adv.*

synchronous satellite 同轉人造衛星(其環繞地球一周之時間恰爲24小時)。

syn·chro·scope 〔ˈsɪŋkrəˌskop; ˈsiŋkrouskoup〕 *n.* 〖電〗同步檢定器。

syn·chro·tron 〔ˈsɪŋkrəˌtrɑn; ˈsiŋkroutrɔn〕 *n.* 〖物理〗同步加速器。

syn·cli·nal 〔sɪnˈklaɪnl; sinˈklainl〕 *adj.* ①〖地質〗向斜的。②〖機械〗傾斜的。—*n.* 〖地質〗向斜層。—**ly,** *adv.*

syn·cline 〔ˈsɪŋklaɪn; ˈsiŋklain〕 *n.* 〖地質〗向斜層。

syn·co·pate 〔ˈsɪŋkəˌpet; ˈsiŋkəpeit〕

v.t., -pat·ed, -pat·ing. ①〖音樂〗節調；切分。②〖音樂〗應用切分法於(樂曲)。③〖文法〗(略去中間一音或數音而)節縮(某字)。例如：ne'er 代表 never等。—syn·co·pa·tion, *n.*

syn·co·pe [ˈsɪŋkəpɪ; ˈsiŋkəpi] *n.* ①〖文法〗(字之)節縮；中略。②〖音樂〗切分法(=syncopation)。③〖醫〗暈厥。

syn·dic [ˈsɪndɪk; ˈsindik] *n.* ①經理人；理事；董事；(尤指)大學董事。②政府官吏；(尤指)地方行政長官。

syn·di·cal·ism [ˈsɪndɪkḷˌɪzəm; ˈsindikəlizm] *n.* 工團主義(源於法國之一種社會革命運動，旨在以直接手段，如大罷工等，使工會控制生產及分配之方式)。

syn·di·cal·ist [ˈsɪndɪkḷɪst; ˈsindikəlist] *n.* 工團主義者。—*adj.* 工團主義者的；工團主義的。—ic, *adj.*

syn·di·cate [*n.* ˈsɪndɪkɪt; ˈsindikit *v.* ˈsɪndɪˌket; ˈsindikeit] *n., v.,* -cat·ed, -cat·ing. —*n.* ①企業組合；銀行團。②供應特別稿件與多數報紙雜誌等同時發表之機構。③理事會；董事會。④〖美俚〗罪魁集團。—*v.t.* ①聯合成爲企業組合。②以企業組合管理或經營。③以(稿件)供應多數報紙雜誌同時發表。—*v.i.* 組成企業組合。—syn·di·ca·tor, *n.*

syn·di·ca·tion [ˌsɪndɪˈkeʃən; ˌsindiˈkeiʃən] *n.* ①組成企業組合。②以稿件供多數報章雜誌同時發表。

syn·dro·me [ˈsɪndrəˌmi; ˈsindroum, -drəmi] *n.* ①〖醫〗併發症狀；綜合病徵。②若干共存之事物。③一種與衆不同的行爲方式。—syn·drom·ic, *adj.*

syne [saɪn; sain] *adv., conj., prep.* 〖蘇〗=since; ago.

syn·ec·do·che [sɪˈnɛkdəkɪ; siˈnekdəki] *n.* 〖修辭〗舉隅法(卽以部分代全體，或以全體代部分之敍述法)。

syn·e·col·o·gy [ˌsɪnəˈkɑlədʒɪ; ˌsinəˈkɔlədʒi] *n.* 環境生態學(研究動植物與其環境之關係的科學，爲生態學之一部門)。

syn·er·e·sis [sɪˈnɛrɪsɪs; siˈniərəsis] *n.* 〖文法〗合音(將兩母音或兩音節合爲一音)。(亦作 synaeresis)

synergetic muscles 合作肌。

syn·e·sis [ˈsɪnɪsɪs; ˈsinisis] *n.* 〖文法〗注重文意而與文法規則相左之造句法。

syn·od [ˈsɪnəd; ˈsinəd] *n.* ①宗教會議。②會議；議會。③宗敎會議轄區。

syn·od·al [ˈsɪnədḷ; ˈsinədl] *adj.* ①宗敎會議的；敎會會議的。②會議的。—ly, *adv.*

syn·od·ic [sɪˈnɑdɪk; siˈnɔdik] *adj.* ①=synodal. ②〖天文〗會合的。(亦作synodical)

***syn·o·nym** [ˈsɪnəˌnɪm; ˈsinənim] *n.* ①同義字。②代用名詞。

syn·o·nym·i·ty [ˌsɪnəˈnɪmətɪ; ˌsinəˈnimiti] *n.* 同義；相類語。

syn·on·y·mous [sɪˈnɑnəməs; siˈnɔniməs] *adj.* 同義的。

syn·on·y·my [sɪˈnɑnəmɪ; siˈnɔnimi] *n., pl.* -mies. ①同義。②同義字集；類語表。③同義字研究。

synop. synopsis.

syn·op·sis [sɪˈnɑpsɪs; siˈnɔpsis] *n., pl.* -ses [-siz; -si:z]. 大意；要略；綱領。

syn·op·size [sɪˈnɑpsaɪz; siˈnɔpsaiz] *v.t.*, -sized, -siz·ing. ①爲…作摘要；予以略述。②爲…之縮影。

syn·op·tic [sɪˈnɑptɪk; siˈnɔptik] *adj.* (亦作 synoptical) ①要略的；大意的；綱領的。②(常 S-) 自同一觀點敍述的(指馬太、馬可及路加三福音書而言)。③(常 S-) 對觀福音書(卽前述之三福音書)的。④〖氣象〗天氣的。—*n.* 對觀福音書之一；對觀福音書的作者。—al·ly, *adv.* 「作 synoptic Gospels)

Synoptic Gospels 對觀福音書。(亦

syn·op·tist [sɪˈnɑptɪst; siˈnɔptist] *n.* 對觀福音書著者(卽 Matthew, Mark 或 Luke).

syn·o·vi·a [sɪˈnovɪə; siˈnouviə] *n.* 〖解剖〗滑液；關節滑液。—syn·o·vi·al, *adj.*

syn·o·vi·tis [ˌsɪnəˈvaɪtɪs; ˌsinəˈvaitis] *n.* 〖醫〗關節滑膜炎。「*adj.* 造句法的。

syn·tac·tic [sɪnˈtæktɪk; sinˈtæktik]

syn·tac·ti·cal [sɪnˈtæktɪkḷ; sinˈtæktikl] *adj.* =syntactic. —ly, *adv.*

***syn·tax** [ˈsɪntæks; ˈsintæks] *n.* ①有秩序的排列；各部分和諧的適應。②〖文法〗句子構造；造句法。③〖數學〗順列論。

syn·the·sis [ˈsɪnθəsɪs; ˈsinθisis] *n., pl.* -ses [-ˌsiz; -si:z]. ①綜合。②綜合法。③〖化〗合成；合成法。④〖哲〗(黑格爾辯證法中"正"、"反"、"合"之)合。—syn·the·sist, *n.*

syn·the·size [ˈsɪnθəˌsaɪz; ˈsinθisaiz] *v.t.*, -sized, -siz·ing. 綜合；組合；合成；人工製造。—syn·the·si·za·tion, *n.*

syn·thet·ic [sɪnˈθɛtɪk; sinˈθetik] *adj.* (亦作 synthetical) ①綜合的；合成的。②人工製造的。③〖語言〗有字尾變化的。—*n.* 人工製品。—al·ly, *adv.*

synthetic fiber 人造纖維。

synthetic rubber 人造橡膠。

syn·ton·ic [sɪnˈtɑnɪk; sinˈtɔnik] *adj.* ①〖電〗共振的。②感情易對環境起反應的。(亦作 syntonical) —syn·to·nism, *n.*

syn·to·ny [ˈsɪntənɪ; ˈsintəni] *n.* 〖電〗共振。

syph·i·lis [ˈsɪfḷɪs; ˈsifilis] *n.*〖醫〗梅毒。

syph·i·lit·ic [ˌsɪfəˈlɪtɪk; ˌsifiˈlitik] *adj.* 梅毒的；患梅毒的。—*n.* 梅毒患者。

syph·i·loid [ˈsɪfəˌlɔɪd; ˈsifilɔid] *adj.* 像梅毒的；梅毒狀的。「=siphon.

sy·phon [ˈsaɪfən; ˈsaifən] *n., v.t., v.i.*

Syr. ①Syria. ②Syriac. ③Syrian.

Syr·a·cuse [ˈsaɪrəkjuz; ˈsaiərəkju:z] *n.* 西那庫斯(義大利 Sicily 島東南部之海港，734B.C. 迦太基人建立之古城)。「=siren.

sy·ren [ˈsaɪrən; ˈsaiərən] *n., adj.*

Syr·i·a [ˈsɪrɪə; ˈsiriə] *n.* 敍利亞(亞洲西部之一國家，首都爲大馬士革 Damascus).

Syr·i·ac [ˈsɪrɪˌæk; ˈsiriæk] *adj.* 敍利亞的；敍利亞語的。—*n.* 古代敍利亞語。

Syr·i·a·cism [ˈsɪrɪəsɪzṃ; ˈsiriəsizm] *n.* 古代敍利亞語之語風。

Syr·i·an [ˈsɪrɪən; ˈsiriən] *adj.* 敍利亞的；敍利亞人的。—*n.* 敍利亞人；敍利亞語。

sy·rin·ga [səˈrɪŋgə; siˈriŋgə] *n.* 〖植物〗①紫丁香花。②山梅花。

sy·ringe [ˈsɪrɪndʒ; ˈsirindʒ] *v.*, -ringed, -ring·ing, *n.* —*v.t.* 注射；(以注水器)灌洗。—*n.* 注射器；注水器。

syr·inx [ˈsɪrɪŋks; ˈsiriŋks] *n., pl.* sy·rin·ges [səˈrɪndʒiz; siˈrindʒi:z], -inx·es. ①一種古代管樂器。②〖動物〗鳥之鳴管。③〖解剖〗=Eustachian tube. ④〖考古〗古埃及墳墓中之狹路。⑤(S-)〖希臘神話〗Arcadia 河之女神(被 Pan 追求，變爲一束蘆葦，Pan 以此葦做爲笙)。

Syro- 〖字首〗表"敍利亞"之義。

***syr·up** [ˈsɪrəp; ˈsirəp] *n.* 糖漿。chocolate *syrup*. 巧克力糖漿。(亦作 sirup)

syr·up·y [ˈsɪrəpɪ; ˈsirəpi] *adj.* ①糖漿狀的；黏漿狀的。②甜蜜的。

sys- 〖字首〗syn- 之異體(用於 s 前)。
sys·tal·tic [sɪsˈtæltɪk; sisˈtæltik] *adj.* 交互收縮與舒張的;律動收縮的(如心臟跳動)。
‡**sys·tem** [ˈsɪstəm; ˈsistim] *n.* ①系統。a mountain *system.* 山系。the digestive *system.* 消化系統。the nervous *system.* 神經系統。the solar *system.* 太陽系。②制度;體制;體系。③方式;法式。④秩序;規律。⑤身體。⑥世界;宇宙。⑦〖天文〗解釋天體現象的假說;系。⑧(賭博之)一套方法。⑨性格;人格。⑩社會結構。
*****sys·tem·at·ic** [ˌsɪstəˈmætɪk; ˌsistiˈmætik] *adj.* ①系統的;有系統的。*systematic* theology. 系統神學。②按照法式的;分類的。*systematic* botany. 分類植物學。③有計畫的;故意的。④宇宙的。—**ness,** *n.* —**al·ly,** *adv.*
sys·tem·a·tism [ˈsɪstəməˌtɪzm̩; ˈsistimətizm] *n.* 注重系統之作風;系統主義。—**sys·tem·at·ist,** *n.*
sys·tem·a·tize [ˈsɪstəməˌtaɪz; ˈsistimətaiz] *v.,* **-tized, -tiz·ing.** —*v.t.* 加以系統化;為…定法式;加以分類。—*v.i.* 系統化。—**sys·tem·a·ti·za·tion,** *n.*
sys·tem·a·tiz·er [ˈsɪstəməˌtaɪzə; ˈsistimətaizə] *n.* 創造系統者;組織者。
sys·tem·ic [sɪsˈtɛmɪk; sisˈtemik] *adj.* ①體系的;系統的。②〖生理〗(侵入)全身的。
sys·tem·ize [ˈsɪstəmˌaɪz; ˈsistimaiz] *v.t.,* **-ized, -iz·ing.** =**systematize.**
systems analysis 〖電腦〗系統分析。
systems engineering 全盤工程效率設計。
sys·to·le [ˈsɪstəˌli; ˈsistəli] *n.* ①〖生理〗心臟收縮。②〖古詩〗音節縮短。—**sys·tol·ic,** *adj.*
sys·tyle [ˈsɪstaɪl; ˈsistail] *adj.* 〖建築〗相鄰二柱間之距離,等於柱直徑之二倍的;柱間較狹的。—*n.* 此種柱式之建築物。
syz·y·gy [ˈsɪzədʒɪ; ˈsizidʒi] *n.* ①〖天文〗朔望;對點(即一天體,尤指月球,與太陽處於同一天體經度或相距 180° 之二點中的任一點)。②〖古詩〗兩音步之結合。—**sy·zyg·i·al,** *adj.*
Sze·chwan [ˈsɛˈtʃwɑn; ˈseˈtʃwɑːn] *n.* 四川(中國中部之一省,省會成都 Chengtu)。

T

T or **t** [ti; tiː] *n., pl.* **T's** or **t's.** ①英文字母之第二十個字母。②T形之物。③中世紀羅馬數字之160。***to a T*** (or ***tee***) 恰好地;精確地。—*adj.* T字形的。
T. ①tablespoon(s). ②tenor. ③Territory. ④Testament. ⑤Tuesday. ⑥Turkish.
't =it (在動詞前或後與動詞連用,如: 'twas, 'tis, do't, see't 等)。
t. ①teaspoon. ②temperature. ③tense. ④tenor. ⑤territory. ⑥time. ⑦ton; tons. ⑧town. ⑨township. ⑩transitive. ⑪tomus (拉 =volume).
Ta 化學元素 tantalum 之符號。
ta [tɑ; tɑː] *interj.* 〖英俗〗謝謝。*ta* muchly. 多謝。
Taal [tɑl; tɑːl] *n.* 塔爾語(南非共和國土人所講的荷蘭方言)。
tab¹ [tæb; tæb] *n., v.,* **tabbed, tab·bing.** —*n.* ①小的垂懸物(如帶、環等);標籤。②〖俗〗紀錄;計核。③帳單;費用。④戲臺上狹窄的布幔。***keep tab*** (or ***tabs***) ***on*** 〖俗〗查核;注意;紀錄。***pick up the tab for*** 支付…之費用。—*v.t.* ①飾以(環、帶等之)垂懸物。②稱呼;命名。③加以統計。
tab² *n.* 〖俗〗小型報紙 (=tabloid).
tab·ard [ˈtæbəd; ˈtæbəd] *n.* ①傳令使者所穿的飾有紋章的寬大之短外衣。②中世紀武士用以覆蓋鎧甲之一種外套。③古時在戶外穿之粗劣、厚而短的外衣(通常指窮人所穿者)。
tab·by [ˈtæbɪ; ˈtæbi] *n., pl.* **-bies,** *adj., v.,* **-bied, -by·ing.** —*n.* ①虎斑貓。②雌貓。③老處女。④好說閒話的女人。⑤波紋絹。—*adj.* ①波紋的。②虎斑的;灰色或褐色中帶有黑斑的。—*v.t.* 在(絲)上做成波紋。
tab·e·fac·tion [ˌtæbəˈfækʃən; ˌtæbiˈfækʃən] *n.* 由病引起之憔悴;衰弱。
tab·er·nac·le [ˈtæbəˌnækl̩; ˈtæbənækl] *n., v.,* **-nac·led, -nac·ling.** —*n.* ①暫居之地(如帳篷、茅舍等)。②軀殼(靈魂寄居之地)。③聖幕(古猶太人的移動式神殿);猶太神堂。④禮拜堂;教堂;聚會所。⑤有頂的神龕。—*v.i.* 住於 tabernacle 中。—*v.t.* 置於 tabernacle 中。—**tab·er·nac·u·lar,** *adj.*
ta·bes [ˈtebiz; ˈteibiːz] *n.* 〖醫〗①脊髓癆。②癆病。
‡**ta·ble** [ˈtebl̩; ˈteibl] *n., v.,* **-bled, -bling,** *adj.* —*n.* ①桌;檯。a dining *table.* 餐桌。②餐桌。③餐;餚饌。to keep a good *table.* 供應好菜。④同席之人。to set the *table* in a roar. 使滿座的人哄笑起來。⑤表;一覽表。a *table* of contents. 目錄。a timetable. 時間表。multiplication *tables.* 乘法表;九九表。⑥平板;平面;畫板。⑦臺地;高原。⑧(the-)(*pl.*)刻於石上的法律條文。⑨〖建築〗飛簷;擔板。⑩寶石之平面。⑪會議。***at table*** 正在用餐。They were *at table* when we called. 我們往訪時,他們正在用餐。***lay*** (or ***set***) ***the table*** 將餐具(刀叉、碗碟等)擺在桌上準備開飯。***on the table*** **a.** 擺在桌面上;在衆人面前。**b.**(美議事程序)擱置。***turn the tables*** (***on someone***) **a.** 在一連串失敗後獲得成功;從低賤地位躍居高位。**b.** 改變形勢。***under the table*** **a.** 發呆的;昏頭昏腦的;醉的。**b.** 作爲賄賂。***wait*** (***on***) ***table*** 當侍者。—*v.t.* ①置於桌上。②〖美〗擱置。③列…成一覽表。④〖英〗列入議程。⑤將(木材)與另一塊木材在槽口相接。—*adj.* ①用於桌上的。②食用的。*table* bird. 食用鳥。③狀似桌子的;有平頂的。
tab·leau [ˈtæblo, tæbˈlo; ˈtæblou] *n., pl.* **-leaux, -leaus.** ①引人的場面;畫。②活人畫(以活人扮演的靜態畫面)。
ta·bleau vi·vant [taˈbloviˈvɑ̃; taˈblou viˈvɑ̃] *pl.* **ta·bleaux vi·vants** [taˈbloviˈvɑ̃; taˈblouviˈvɑ̃]. 〖法〗=**tableau.**
tab·leaux [ˈtæbloz, tæbˈloz; ˈtæblouz] *n.* pl. of **tableau.**
table board 包的伙食。
table book 適於放置案頭作裝飾用的書。
*****ta·ble·cloth** [ˈtebl̩ˌklɔθ; ˈteiblklɔθ] *n., pl.* **-cloths.** 桌布;檯布。—**y,** *adj.*
table cover 桌布;檯布。
ta·ble d'hôte [ˈtæblˈdot; ˈtɑːblˈdout] *pl.* **ta·bles d'hôte.** 客飯;全餐;和菜(爲 à la carte 之對)。
ta·ble·ful [ˈtebl̩ˌfʊl; ˈteiblful] *n.* 滿桌。a *tableful* of dishes. 滿桌的菜餚。
ta·ble-hop [ˈtebl̩ˌhɑp; ˈteiblˈhɔp] *v.i.* **-hopped, -hop·ping.** 由一桌到另一桌地與

T

人寒暄。

table knife 餐刀。

table lamp 枱燈。

table·land [ˈtebl̩ˌlænd; ˈteibllænd] *n.* 高原。

table linen 桌布、餐巾等。

table money 軍官之餐費；交際費；招待費。

table salt 食鹽。

***ta·ble·spoon** [ˈtebl̩ˌspun; ˈteiblspuːn] *n.* ①湯匙；大調羹。②一湯匙之量。③容量單位(相當於三茶匙)。

***ta·ble·spoon·ful** [ˈtebl̩spunˌful; ˈteiblspuːnful] *n., pl.* **-fuls.** 一湯匙之量。

***tab·let** [ˈtæblɪt; ˈtæblit] *n.* ①紙簿。②碑；牌；匾額。③寫字板。④片；塊；錠劑。aspirin *tablets.* 阿斯匹靈片。—*v.t.* ①予以碑牌；用碑牌紀念。②將…在寫字板上寫下。③將…做成小錠或小片。

table talk ①進餐時之閒談。②適於在進餐時閒談之話題。

tab·let-arm chair [ˈtæblɪtˈɑrm～; ˈtæblitˈɑːm～] 靠手上附有寫字板的椅子。

tablet chair =**tablet-arm chair.**

table tennis 桌球(戲)；乒乓球(戲)。

table tipping 靈動(桌子)術。

table turning =**table tipping.**

ta·ble·ware [ˈtebl̩ˌwɛr; ˈteiblwɛə] *n.* 餐具。

ta·ble-wa·ter [ˈtebl̩ˌwɔtɚ; ˈteiblˌwɔːtə] *n.* ①礦水。②飲水。

table wine 進餐時喝的淡酒。

tab·loid [ˈtæblɔɪd; ˈtæblɔid] *n.* ①小型報；小報(以圖片多取勝，而新聞報導盡量簡短者)。②藥片；錠劑。③摘要。—*adj.* ①簡縮的；簡短的。②聳人聽聞的；小題大做的。

ta·boo [təˈbu; təˈbuː] *adj., v.,* **-booed, -boo·ing,** *n., pl.* **-boos.** —*adj.* ①禁止的；禁忌的。②(因係神聖的或污穢的而)不可接近的。—*v.t.* ①禁用；禁止；禁忌。②放逐。—*n.* ①禁忌。②禁止。③放逐；排除。

ta·bor, ta·bour [ˈtebɚ; ˈteibə] *n.* 小鼓。—*v.t. & v.i.* 打(鼓)。—**er,** *n.*

tab·o·ret, tab·ou·ret [ˌtæbəˈrɛt, ˈtæbərɪt; ˈtæbərit] *n.* ①小几；矮桌；低枱。②矮凳。③刺繡架。④小鼓。

ta·bu [təˈbu; təˈbuː] *adj., v.,* **-bued, -bu·ing,** *n., pl.* **-bus.** =**taboo.**

tab·u·lar [ˈtæbjəlɚ; ˈtæbjulə] *adj.* ①表的；列成表的；分欄書寫的。②平板的；平板狀的；平闊的。—**ly,** *adv.*

ta·bu·la ra·sa [ˈtæbjuləˈresə; ˈtæbjuləˈreisə] 【拉】①白紙一樣純淨的心。②潔白狀態。

tab·u·late [*v.* ˈtæbjəˌlet; ˈtæbjuleit *adj.* ˈtæbjəlɪt; ˈtæbjulit] *v.,* **-lat·ed, -lat·ing,** *adj.* —*v.t.* ①將(事實、數字等)列成表。②使成板狀平面。—*adj.* 平板狀的。

tab·u·la·tion [ˌtæbjuˈleʃən; ˌtæbjuˈleiʃən] *n.* ①列表。②圖表。

tab·u·la·tor [ˈtæbjəˌletɚ; ˈtæbjuleitə] *n.* ①繪製圖表者。②(打字機等之)作圖表機件。③計算機。

TAC Tactical Air Command. 美國之戰術空軍司令部。

tac·a·ma·hac·a [ˌtækəməˈhækə; ˌtækəməˈhækə] *n.* ①(用以製香及軟膏的)一種味道極濃的芳香樹脂。②產此種芳香樹脂之樹。(亦作 **tacamahac**)

tach(e) [tætʃ; tætʃ] *n.* 【古】釦；鉤；帶釦。

ta·chis·to·scope [təˈkɪstəˌskop; təˈkistəskoup] *n.* 速讀訓練器。

ta·chom·e·ter [təˈkɑmətɚ, tæ-; tæˈkɔmitə] *n.* ①轉數計。②流速計。

tach·y·car·di·a [ˌtækɪˈkɑrdɪə; ˌtækiˈkɑːdiə] *n.* 【醫】心搏過速。

ta·chyg·ra·phy [tæˈkɪgrəfɪ; tæˈkigrəfi] *n.* (古希臘、羅馬之)速記法。

ta·chym·e·ter [tæˈkɪmətɚ; tæˈkimitə] *n.* 【測量】(測量高度、距離等之)視距儀。

tac·it [ˈtæsɪt; ˈtæsit] *adj.* 沉默的；心照不宣的。—**ly,** *adv.* —**ness,** *n.*

tac·i·turn [ˈtæsəˌtɝn; ˈtæsitəːn] *adj.* 沉默寡言的。—**ly,** *adv.* —**i·ty,** *n.*

Tac·i·tus [ˈtæsətəs; ˈtæsitəs] *n.* 泰西塔斯(Publius Cornelius, 55?–117?, 羅馬史家)。

tack**[1] [tæk; tæk] *n.* ①大頭釘。thumb *tacks.* 圖釘。②依船帆風位而定之航行方向。③(船)搶風調向；(船)斜兜着風作Z形之前進。④(船的)Z字形前進。⑤假縫(作臨時固定所縫之針脚)。⑥行動方針；政策。to try a new *tack.* 試一新辦法。⑦將帆縛於一角的繩子。⑧吸黏力。tape with good *tack.* 吸黏力良好的膠帶。come down to brass tacks*** 處置最重要之事務；談要點；轉入本題。***on the starboard (port) tack*** 風在船的右(左)方。***on the wrong tack*** 錯誤地；迷途地。—*v.t.* ①以大頭釘釘住。He has *tacked* the carpet down. 他把地毯釘在地板上。②附加；添加。③以假縫縫製。④連接。—*v.i.* ①因迎風作Z字形航行。②轉變依船帆風位而定之航行方向。③改變方針(政策)。④跟隨；追蹤。—**er,** *n.*

tack[2] *n.* 食物。***hard tack*** 船上食用的餅乾。

***tack·le** [ˈtækl̩; ˈtækl] *n., v.,* **-led, -ling.** —*n.* ①器械；用具。fishing *tackle.* 釣具。②絞轆；複滑車。*tackles* for lifting. 舉重用的滑車。③【橄欖球】抱住並絆倒拿球奔跑的對方球員。④【橄欖球】在後衛與端線區域間之球員。—*v.t. & v.i.* ①處理；應付；解決。②捕捉；格鬥。The policeman *tackled* the thief. 警察捕捉賊人。③【橄欖球】抱住並絆倒(拿球奔跑的對方球員)。④上馬具。

tack·ling [ˈtæklɪŋ; ˈtækliŋ] *n.* ①【罕】複滑車裝置。②用具；器械。

tack·y [ˈtækɪ; ˈtæki] *adj.,* **tack·i·er, tack·i·est.** ①黏的；黏着性的。②【俗】襤褸的；不整齊的。③【俗】俗不可耐的；不時髦的。④【俗】卑賤的。

tac·o·nite [ˈtækəˌnaɪt; ˈtækənait] *n.* 【礦】角岩。

***tact** [tækt; tækt] *n.* ①機智；圓通；圓滑。An ambassador must have great *tact.* 一位大使必須有機智。②觸摸；觸覺。

tact·ful [ˈtæktfəl; ˈtæktful] *adj.* 機敏的；圓通的；圓滑的。—**ly,** *adv.* —**ness,** *n.*

tac·tic [ˈtæktɪk; ˈtæktik] *n.* 戰術。—*adj.* =**tactical.**

tac·ti·cal [ˈtæktɪkl̩; ˈtæktikl] *adj.* ①戰術的；兵法的；用兵上的。②精於兵法的。③權宜的；有目的的。—**ly,** *adv.*

Tactical Air Navigation 太空導航。

tac·ti·cian [tækˈtɪʃən; tækˈtiʃən] *n.* 戰術家；兵法家；策士。

tac·tics [ˈtæktɪks; ˈtæktiks] *n.* ①戰術。②軍事行動。③策略。

tac·tile [ˈtæktl̩; ˈtæktail] *adj.* ①觸覺的。a *tactile* organ. 觸覺器官。②有觸覺的。③可感觸到的。—**tac·til·i·ty,** *n.*

tactile corpuscle 【生理】觸覺小體。

tact·less [ˈtæktlɪs; ˈtæktlis] *adj.* 無機智的；不圓滑的。

tac·tu·al [ˈtæktʃuəl; ˈtæktjuəl] *adj.* ①觸覺的；觸覺上的。②由觸覺而生的；生觸覺的。—**ly,** *adv.*

tad [tæd; tæd] *n.* 【美】①小孩(尤指男孩)。②微量。

tad·pole ['tæd,pol; 'tædpoul] *n.* 蝌蚪。
Ta·dzhik [tɑ'dʒɪk; tɑ:'dʒik] *n.* 塔吉克(蘇聯中亞境內之一共和國,首府爲史達林那巴德 Stalinabad).
tae kwon do [tækwondo; tækwoun-dou]〖韓〗跆拳道。
tael [tel; teil] *n.* ①兩(東亞之重量單位,尤指中國之兩)。②兩(中國昔時之貨幣單位)。
ta'en [ten; tein] *v.*〖詩〗=**taken.**
tae·ni·a ['tinɪə; 'ti:niə] *n., pl.* **-ni·ae** [-nɪ,i; -nii:]. ①古希臘之髮帶。②〖解剖〗帶狀結構;帶;束。③〖建築〗Doric 式建築物之帶狀飾;帶形花邊。④〖動物〗絛蟲。
tae·ni·a·sis [tɪ'naɪəsɪs; ti'naiəsis] *n.* 絛蟲病。
taf·fer·el ['tæfərəl; 'tæfərəl] *n.* =**taffrail.**
taf·fe·ta ['tæfɪtə; 'tæfitə] *n.* ①一種光面而質略硬的絲綢或人造絲綢; 波紋綢。②與上述絲綢相似之棉或麻質布料。—*adj.* 用 taffeta 製的;似 taffeta 的。
taff·rail ['tæf,rel; 'tæfreil] *n.*〖造船〗①船尾之上部。②船尾欄杆。
taf·fy ['tæfɪ; 'tæfi] *n.* ①太妃糖。②〖俗〗諂媚;阿諛。(亦作 **toffee, toffy**)
taf·i·a, taf·fi·a ['tæfɪə; 'tæfiə] *n.* (西印度羣島產之一種用糖渣製成之)劣質甜酒。
Taft *n.* 塔虎脫(William Howard, 1857–1930, 美國第27任總統, 任期 1909–13)。
tag** [tæg; tæg] *n., v.,* **tagged** [tægd; tægd], **tag·ging.** —*n.* ①附籤;標籤。②懸垂物; 附屬物。③帶端的金屬頭(如鞋帶之末端等)。④爲添飾或增强效果而附加之引語或勸誡語。⑤歌曲、劇本、演員臺詞等之結尾部分。⑥(小孩玩之)捉人遊戲。⑦陳腐的詞句。⑧名稱; 綽號。⑨一束頭髮。⑩羊身上纏結的毛。⑪狐尾之白色末梢。⑫〖棒球〗刺殺。—*v.t.* ①附以籤條。②添飾;加添以增强效果。③(捉人遊戲中)捉。④給以違警告發單。⑤尾隨; 跟隨。He *tags* his big brothers around. 他到處跟在他哥哥們身旁。⑥爲…定價錢。⑦〖棒球〗**a.** 刺殺。**b.**〖俚〗用力擊(投過來的球)。**c.**〖俚〗對(投手投的球)安打和得分。⑧擊打。⑨徵召。⑩予以綽號。⑪責備;歸咎於。⑫緊隨…之後。⑬將(羊身上)纏結在一起的毛除去。⑭〖拳擊〗用力打中(對手)。tag along*** 跟隨。***tag and rag*** 賤民; 暴民。***tag end*** **a.** 末端;尾。**b.** (常*pl.*)零碎小事。***tag line*** 結尾的一句話。—*v.i.*〖俗〗尾隨。The little boy *tagged* after his sister. 這小孩尾隨着他的姊姊。
Ta·ga·log ['tægə,lɑg; 'tægələg] *n.* ①塔加拉族人(菲律賓羣島之馬來亞族土著)。②塔加拉族語言(菲島主要語言之一)。
tag day〖美〗募捐日(公開籌募慈善基金之日期)。
tag·ger ['tægə; 'tægə] *n.* ①附加籤條者;附加物。②尾隨者。③(*pl.*)薄鐵片(通常均鍍以錫)。④剪去纏結在一起的羊毛用的剪刀。
Ta·gore [tə'gor; tə'gɔ:] *n.* 泰戈爾(Sir Rabindranath, 1861–1941, 印度詩人, 曾獲1913年諾貝爾文學獎)。
tag·rag ['tæg,ræg; 'tægræg] *n.* ①下層階級的人;下流社會的人。②(衣服上垂下之)破布。***tagrag and bobtail*** 下層社會人民。
tag team (職業性摔角)兩人一組之隊。
Ta·hi·ti [tɑ'hitɪ; tɑ:'hi:ti] *n.* 大溪地(南太平洋法屬 Society Islands 中之一島)。
tai·ga ['taɪgə; 'taigə] *n.* (歐洲與北美極北地區之)大松林地帶。
‡**tail**[1] [tel; teil] *n.* ①尾。②尾狀物。to be followed by a *tail* of attendants. 有許多侍從人員隨在後面。③後部; 末尾。④頭髮之長束;辮子。⑤(*pl.*) **a.** 硬幣之背面。Heads or *tails?* 正面還是背面? **b.**〖俗〗男人之燕尾禮服。to go into *tails.* 着燕尾服。⑥排成一列之人。⑦侍從人員。⑧下游。⑨(*pl.*) 最後蒸餾所得之酒精。***at the tail of*** 跟隨。***make head or tail of*** 了解(常與否定詞連用)。***out of*** (or ***with***) ***the tail of one's eye*** 睥睨;偷看。***tail of the eye*** 眼角。***turn tail*** 逃走。***twist a person's tail*** 激惱某人。***twist the lion's tail*** 侮辱英國。***with one's tail between one's legs*** 受辱;遇到挫敗;害怕。—*adj.* ①從後面來的。②在後面的。—*v.t.* & *v.i.* ①裝以尾;附於其後。to *tail* a kite. 給紙鳶裝尾。②尾隨。The thief was *tailed* by a policeman. 賊被警察尾隨着。③隨從。④形成尾部。⑤排成一行前進。⑥逐漸消失。***tail away*** (or ***off***) **a.** 蹒跚於後。**b.** 落於後。**c.** 變少。***tail off***〖俗〗跑開;逃離。
tail[2] *n.*〖法律〗財產繼承之限制。—*adj.* 關於繼承有特定限制的。
tail·board ['tel,bord; 'teilbɔ:d] *n.* 貨車後部之尾板(可以移動, 以便裝卸貨物)。
tail coat 燕尾服。
tail end 尾端;末端;後部;結尾。
tail·end·er ['tel'ɛndə; 'teil'endə] *n.* 占倒數第一名者。
tail fin ①(飛機尾端之)直尾翅; 水平安定面。②(魚之)尾翅。
tail·gate ['tel,get; 'teilgeit] *n., v.,* **-gat·ed, -gat·ing.** —*n.* =**tailboard.** —*v.t.* & *v.i.* (駕駛時)以過小間隔跟隨(前車)。
tail-heav·y ['tel,hɛvɪ; 'teil'hevi] *adj.* 尾部或後部過重的(飛機)。
tail·ing ['telɪŋ; 'teiliŋ] *n.* ①尾隨;跟蹤。②(*pl.*) 磨粉; 採礦、蒸餾等過程中所棄之渣滓(如糠、礦渣等)。③〖建築〗嵌入牆中之磚石等突出部分。
tail lamp〖英〗尾燈。
tail·light ['tel,laɪt; 'teillait] *n.* (汽車等後之)尾燈。
***tai·lor** ['telə; 'teilə] *n.* 成衣匠; 裁縫。—*v.t.* ①縫製。The suit was well *tailored.* 這套衣服製得很好。②爲…縫製衣服。③〖軍〗定製(制服);修改(現成制服)使更合身。④使配合;使適應。—*v.i.* ①做裁縫。②被縫製成衣。
tai·lor·bird ['telə,bɜd; 'teiləbə:d] *n.* (產於亞洲及非洲的)縫葉鳥。
tai·lored ['teləd; 'teiləd] *adj.* ①特地縫製的。②服裝剪裁講究的。
tai·lor·ing ['telərɪŋ; 'teiləriŋ] *n.* ①裁縫業。②裁縫之技術。
tai·lor-made ['telə'med; 'teiləmeid] *adj.* ①簡樸而合身的。②定製的。③穿男式服裝的。④服裝講究的。⑤配合的;迎合的;適合的。—*n.* 定製的服裝。
tai·lor·ship ['teləʃɪp; 'teiləʃip] *n.* 裁縫業。
tail·piece ['tel,pis; 'teilpi:s] *n.* ①附添於末尾之物; 構成尾端之部分。②提琴等下端琴絃繫於其上的小三角木片。③〖建築〗一端嵌於牆內另端由橫材架住的短樑或椽。④〖印刷〗(書籍等)排於章末或頁下空白處之裝飾圖案。
tail·pipe ['tel,paɪp; 'teilpaip] *n.* ①位於尾端之排氣管。②唧筒之吸入管。(亦作 **tail pipe**)
tail plane〖航空〗水平安定面。(亦作 **tailplane, horizontal stabilizer**)
tail·race ['tel,res; 'teilreis] *n.* ①(水車之)放水路;尾水溝。②〖採礦〗礦渣溝或管。
tail skid〖航空〗後滑板(在飛機尾翼下)。
tail spin ①〖航空〗飛機尾旋下降。②精神錯亂;精神崩潰。③混亂;紊亂。(亦作**tailspin**)

tail·stock ['tel,stak; 'teilstɔk] *n.* 〖機械〗(車床之可調整的或滑動的)握心臺。

tail wind 尾風(飛機或船隻航行時自後面吹來的風);順風。(亦作 **tailwind**)

***taint** [tent; teint] *n.* 汚點;腐敗;墮落或恥辱之跡象。No *taint* of dishonor ever touched him. 他從未蒙受過不名譽的汚點。—*v.t.* 沾汚;感染;使腐敗。—*v.i.* 受感染;腐敗;腐爛。—**less,** *adj.*

Tai·pei ['taɪ'pe; 'tai'pei] *n.* 臺北(中國一院轄市,在臺灣)。(亦作 **Taipeh**)

T'ai Tsung ['taɪ'dzuŋ; 'tai'dzuŋ] 〖中〗唐太宗(李世民A.D.597–649,627–649爲皇帝)。

Tai·wan ['taɪ'wɑn; tai'wæn] *n.* 臺灣(中國之一省)。

Taiwan Strait 臺灣海峽。

‡take [tek; teik] *v.,* **took, tak·en, tak·ing,** *n.* —*v.t.* ①取;拿。Can I *take* it with my hands? 我可以用手拿它嗎? ②握;攫;執。You must *take* your chance. 你必須冒險一試(不計成敗)。③捕;捉。to *take* a man prisoner. 俘虜某人。④攻取;占領。⑤獲得。He *took* the first prize. 他獲得頭獎。⑥享有;享受。to *take* a rest. 休息。⑦接受。We must *take* things as they are. 我們必須接受事物之現狀(須面對現實)。⑧患;罹。I *take* cold easily. 我易患感冒。⑨採用;採取;選擇。*Take* the shortest way home. 走最近的路回家。⑩食;飲;服;吸。to *take* breakfast. 進早飯。to *take* medicine. 服藥。⑪乘;坐。We *took* a train to go there. 我們乘火車到那裏去。⑫費去;占用。He *took* three hours to finish the work. 他費了三小時完成這項工作。⑬需要。It only *takes* five minutes to walk there. 走到那裏只需五分鐘。⑭吸引…的興趣;使喜悅;迷惑。⑮租。⑯訂購;訂閱。⑰伴同;引導。Please *take* me home. 請送我回家。⑱攜帶。⑲減去;扣除。If you *take* 3 from 10, you have 7. 十減三剩七。⑳感覺;感受。to *take* an interest in politics. 對政治感到興趣。㉑了解。Do you *take* me? 你懂我的意思嗎?㉒以爲;當作;相信。㉓記錄。to *take* notes. 作筆記。㉔爲;作;行。to *take* a walk. 散步。㉕採取某種態度。*Take* care! 留心!㉖忍受。㉗移去。㉘使死亡。Pneumonia *took* him. 肺炎使他死亡。㉙引至。Where will this road *take* me? 這一條路通往那兒? ㉚(以特別方法)做;獲得。Please *take* my photograph. 請替我攝影。㉛找出;量出。The doctor *took* her temperature. 醫生量她的體溫。㉜舉出以考慮或觀察。Let's *take* an example. 我們舉個例吧! ㉝負起;履行。㉞受…之影響。㉟着(火)。The house *took* fire. 房子着火了。㊱偸取;不經允許而取去。㊲容納。㊳騙。—*v.i.* ①獲得或獲有財產。He *takes* as heir. 他以繼承人的身分獲得財產。②奏效;有效。③去;赴;前進。The horse *took* to the roadside. 馬走到路旁。④受歡迎。The play *took* from its first performance. 這齣戲從演第一場就受歡迎。⑤患;感染(病)。He *took* sick. 他生病。⑥減損〖from〗. Nothing *took* from the scene's beauty. 甚麼也未能減損這風景的美。⑦照像。She does not *take* well. 她不上像。⑧生根;扎根。⑨(魚類)爲餌所誘。***take a bow*** (因做好某事而)接受讚揚;接受嘉許。***take a chance*** (or ***one's chances***) 冒險;碰運氣。***take advantage of*** a. 利用。b. 占…之便宜。***take after*** a. 像;相似。b. (亦作 **take off after, take out after**) 跟隨;追趕。***take against*** 〖主英〗對…有反感;反對。***take amiss*** 對…不高興;對…表不悅。***take apart*** a. 拆開。to *take* a toy *apart*. 將一玩具拆開。b. 剖析。c. 粗暴對待。***take (up) arms*** 武裝起來;準備作戰。***take away*** a. 拿走;奪走;奪去。b. 拿掉;去掉。c. 減掉;減去。d. 收拾碗盤。***take back*** a. 撤銷;撤回。He *took back* his promise. 他撤銷他的諾言。b. 重新獲得;取回。c. 退回調換。d. 准許回來;接受。e. 使回憶。***take care*** 留心;注意。***take care of*** a. 照顧;管理。b. 應付。c. 負…之責任。d. 處理。***take charge*** a. 負起管理之責任。b. 失去控制。***take down*** a. 記錄。to *take down* a speech in shorthand. 用速記記錄演說。b. 打擊;挫銳氣。c. 困難地吞下。d. 拆毀。e. 病倒。***take fire*** 着火。***take for*** 當作;誤認爲。***take from*** 減少;減弱。***take in*** a. 接受;容納。to *take in* lodgers. 收容寄宿者。b. 縮小;捲起;疊起。c. 了解;領悟。d. 欺騙。e. 訂閱。f. 相信(虛假之事)。g. 包含;包括。h. 將…帶回家去做。i. 拘捕。j. 改短(衣服)。***take it*** a. 接受;同意。b. 〖俚〗能够忍受辛苦、侮辱、虐待等。c. 認爲。***take it for granted*** 認爲當然。***take it out of*** a. 揍。b. 使無精神或力氣。***take it out on*** 〖俗〗以詈罵或傷害洩怒。***take notice of*** 注意到。***take off*** a. 除去;脫去。to *take off* one's shoes. 脫鞋。b. 離地;離水;起飛。c. 摹仿。d. 帶走。*Take* yourself *off!* 走開! e. 減去。Can you *take* $5 *off* the price? 你能把價格減少五元嗎? f. 離開;啓程。g. 殺死;致死。h. 複製;做副本。i. 免除工作。***take on*** a. 擔承。b. 雇用。c. 現出激憤、悲痛或其他强烈的情緒。Don't *take on* so! 不要這樣傷心! d. 接受…作對手。e. 變得有…;開始有…。f. 採用。g. 被大家接受;受大家的歡迎。***take one at one's word*** (無論其本意如何)照表面意思接受其所言;當其爲眞。***take one's time*** 慢慢做。***take or leave*** 隨意取捨。***take out*** a. 去掉。b. 領得;發出。c. 申請取得。to *take out* an insurance policy. 申請保險(投保)。d. 邀請。e. 出發。***take over*** a. 接管;接收。to *take over* a business. 接管事業。b. 〖俚〗欺騙。***take part in*** 參加。to *take part in* the excursion. 參加遠足。***take place*** 發生;擧行。When will the party *take place?* 宴會何時擧行? ***take up*** a. 占。This work *takes up* too much time. 這項工作占太多的時間。b. 接納。c. 吸收。d. 開始;從事。e. 繼續。f. 打斷或校正(說話者)。g. 逮捕;阻止。h. 擧、拿起。i. 使更小。j. 償淸。k. 責怪。***take up for*** 袒護。***take upon oneself*** 引爲己任;擔任。***take up with*** a. 與(人)相交。b. 贊成;同意;接受。—*n.* ①獲取量;獲取物。a *take* of fish. 一次捕獲之魚。②取。③被取之物;利益;獲利。④攝製。⑤送到排字房去的一則新聞稿之一部分。⑥音樂演奏之錄音。***on the take*** a. 老想占便宜;損人利己。b. 受賄。

take·down ['tek,daun; 'teikdaun] *n.* ①拆卸(機器)的行動或過程。②(機械的)可拆卸的部分。③易於拆開和重新裝配的武器。④〖俗〗屈辱人之行爲。—*adj.* 易於拆散的。

take-home pay ['tek,hom～; 'teik-houm～] (扣除稅金、保險費等之)實得工資;實得薪金。

take-in ['tek,ɪn; 'teik'in] *n.* 〖俗〗哄騙;欺詐;騙子。

take-leave ['tek,liv; 'teikli:v] *n.* 辭行;說再見。

‡tak·en ['tekən; 'teikn] *v.* pp. of **take.**

take·off [ˈtekˌɔf; ˈteikɔf] *n.* ①〖俗〗爲取笑而作的行爲或言談之摹擬；摹倣。②(飛機之)起飛；起飛點。③起跳；起跳點。④開始；起點；出發點。(亦作 **take-off**)

take·out [ˈtekˌaut; ˈteikaut] *adj.* 〖美〗從餐館買食物帶出去吃的。(英亦作 **takeaway**)

take·o·ver [ˈtekˌovɚ; ˈteikˌouvə] *n.* 接收。(亦作 **take-over**)

take-up [ˈtekˌʌp; ˈteikʌp] *n.* ①拉緊；收緊；提起。②縫級機之針上升時提線之裝置。③織布機捲布的自動裝置。④將電影膠片捲於軸筒上之裝置。⑤〖縫級〗提起布料成褶；襞褶。

tak·ing [ˈtekɪŋ; ˈteikiŋ] *adj.* ①迷人的；動人的。②〖俗〗傳染的。—*n.* ①取；捕獲；獲得物。②(*pl.*) 收取之款；所得；收入。③〖俗〗興奮；騷動；苦惱。***in a taking*** **a.** 在激動的狀態中。**b.** 在困難或煩惱中。—**ly,** *adv.*

ta·lar·i·a [təˈlɛrɪə; təˈlɛəriə] *n. pl.* 〖古典神話〗(Hermes, Mercury諸神的)踝上之小翅膀或帶翼之鞋。

tal·bot [ˈtɔlbət; ˈtɔːlbət] *n.* 一種垂耳獵犬。

talc [tælk; tælk] *n., v.,* **talc(k)ed, talc(k)·ing.** —*n.* 滑石。—*v.t.* 用滑石處理或磨擦。

talc·ose [ˈtælkos; ˈtælkous] *adj.* 滑石的；含滑石的。(亦作 **talcous**)

tal·cum [ˈtælkəm; ˈtælkəm] *n.* ①= **talcum powder.** ②= **talc.**

talcum powder 撲粉；爽身粉。

‡**tale** [tel; teil] *n.* ①故事。fairy *tales.* 童話。②虛語；誹語；謠言。③合計；總數。The *tale* of dead and wounded was 60. 傷亡的總數是六十人。***tell its own tale*** 不須說明；顯而易見。***tell tales*** 洩露祕密；講他人的壞話。***tell tales out of school*** 洩露機密。***tell the tale*** **a.** 顯示眞相。**b.** 發生作用。**c.** 〖英俚〗爲爭取同情而編造故事。

tale·bear·er [ˈtelˌbɛrɚ; ˈteilˌbɛərə] *n.* 長舌者；喜閒話是非的人。

tale·bear·ing [ˈtelˌbɛrɪŋ; ˈteilˌbɛəriŋ] *adj.* 搬弄是非的；揭發祕密的。—*n.* 搬弄是非；揭發祕密。

***tal·ent** [ˈtælənt; ˈtælənt] *n.* ①才能；才幹；天才。She has a *talent* for music. 她有音樂天才。②人才。③有才幹之人。④古時一種重量及貨幣單位。—**ed,** *adj.* —**less,** *adj.*

talent scout 星探；球探(專爲公司、球隊等發掘人才者)。

ta·ler [ˈtɑlɚ; ˈtɑːlə] *n. sing.* or *pl.* 德國之一種古銀幣。(亦作 **thaler**)

ta·les [ˈteliz; ˈteiliːz] *n. pl.* 〖法律〗①應召補足陪審員缺額的人。②(作 *sing.* 解)召集補足陪審員缺額的命令。

tales·man [ˈtelzmən; ˈteiliːzmən] *n., pl.* **-men.** 補缺陪審員。

tale·tell·er [ˈtelˌtɛlɚ; ˈteilˌtelə] *n.* ① = **talebearer.** ②說故事者；講述者。③說謊欺騙者。—**tale·tell·ing,** *adj., n.*

tal·i·on [ˈtælɪən; ˈtæliən] *n.* ①應得之處罰。②以牙還牙之報復。

tal·i·pot [ˈtælɪˌpɑt; ˈtælipɔt] *n.* 〖植物〗一種產於東印度的大棕櫚樹。

tal·is·man [ˈtælɪsmən; ˈtælizmən] *n., pl.* **-mans.** ①護身符；辟邪物。②任何被認爲有不可思議之力量的東西。

tal·is·man·ic [ˌtælɪsˈmænɪk; ˌtælizˈmænik] *adj.* 護符的；辟邪的；具有魔力的；不可思議的。(亦作 **talismanical**) —**al·ly,** *adv.*

‡**talk** [tɔk; tɔːk] *v.i.* ①說話；談話。He was *talking* to (*or* with) a friend. (to較爲常用)。他在和一個朋友談話。What were they *talking* about (*or* of)? (about 較爲常用)。他們在談甚麼? ②討論；磋商。to *talk* with one's lawyer. 與律師商議。③說閒話。to *talk* behind one's back. 背後講人閒話。People will *talk.* 人們要講閒話的。④表示。⑤似說話地發聲。⑥演講。—*v.t.* ①說；談。to *talk* nonsense. 胡說。to *talk* business. 談正事。②以言語使；勸使。***talk around*** **a.** 勸…回心轉意；勸…轉變態度、想法等。**b.** 轉彎抹角地說話。***talk at a person*** 暗指着某人說。***talk away*** 以談話度過。***talk back*** 反脣相譏。***talk big*** 吹牛；誇口。***talk down*** **a.** 高聲壓倒。**b.** 以口頭協助(飛機等)降落。**c.** 以尊長的口吻說話〖常 to〗. ***talk of*** (or ***about***) 談到；說到；說及。*Talk of* the devil and he'll appear. 說鬼鬼到；說到曹操，曹操就到。***talk off*** (or ***out of***) ***the top of one's head*** 不加思索地說出心中事。***talk one's head*** (or ***ear***) ***off*** 向一個人喋喋不休。***talk one's way*** 靠口才獲准通行。***talk out*** 談個明白。***talk over*** 以口才使改變立場。***talk over a matter*** 討論一件事情。***talk sense*** 講有道理的話。***talk tall*** 吹牛；誇張。***talk the night away*** 談話消度永夜。***talk through one's hat*** 胡說八道。***talk to*** 〖俗〗訓戒；斥責。***talk to death*** 以長篇演說扼殺(議案)。***talk to oneself*** 自言自語。***talk up*** **a.** 捧；誇獎；熱烈討論。**b.** 坦白說話。—*n.* ①談話。I had a long *talk* with him yesterday. 我昨天和他長談。②話題；話柄。③非正式講演。to give a *talk* to. 對…作非正式演講。④說話的態度、內容、形式等。baby *talk.* 孩童之言。⑤會談。to have a *talk* with. 與…會談。⑥謠傳；飛短流長之閒話。⑦空談；廢話。

talk·a·thon [ˈtɔkəθɑn; ˈtɔːkəθɔn] *n.* 〖美俗〗①馬拉松式演講(議會上議員爲阻止某議案之通過所作之冗長演講)。②(在電視、無線電廣播中)對質詢作不限時間的答覆。

talk·a·tive [ˈtɔkətɪv; ˈtɔːkətiv] *adj.* 好說話的；多嘴的。—**ly,** *adv.* —**ness,** *n.*

talk-back [ˈtɔkˌbæk; ˈtɔːkbæk] *n.* 〖廣播或電視〗播音室與控制室之間的通話系統。

talk-down [ˈtɔkˌdaun; ˈtɔːkdaun] *n.* 機場管制塔以無線電指示飛機降落。

talk·ee-talk·ee [ˈtɔkɪˈtɔkɪ; ˈtɔːki-ˈtɔːki] *n.* ①(黑人等說的)不聯貫之英語。②〖俗〗喋喋不休；空談。

talk·er [ˈtɔkɚ; ˈtɔːkə] *n.* 說話者；演說者；說空話的人；健談者。

talk·fest [ˈtɔkˌfɛst; ˈtɔːkˈfest] *n.* ①聊天會(作愉快閒聊或討論之非正式集會)。②長期辯論。

***talk·ie** [ˈtɔkɪ; ˈtɔːki] *n.* 〖俗〗有聲電影(= talking picture).

talk-in [ˈtɔkˌɪn; ˈtɔːk-in] *n.* ①抗議集會。②(不拘形式的)演講。③會議；討論。

talk·ing [ˈtɔkɪŋ; ˈtɔːkiŋ] *adj.* ①說話的。②有表情的。③多言的。

talking book 盲人讀物之錄音帶或唱片。

talking film 有聲電影。

talking machine 留聲機。

talking picture 有聲電影。

talking point 論據。(亦作 **talking-point**)

talk·ing-to [ˈtɔkɪŋˌtu; ˈtɔːkiŋtuː] *n., pl.* **-tos.** 〖俗〗責罵。

talk show 〖主美〗電視或電臺上的名流訪問節目。(英亦作 **chat show**)

talk·y [ˈtɔkɪ; ˈtɔːki] *adj.,* **talk·i·er, talk·i·est.** ①= **talkative.** ②對話多的(小說)。

talky talk 〖俗〗聊天；閒談。

:tall [tɔl; tɔːl] *adj.* ①高。He is six feet *tall.* 他身高六英尺。②誇大的;過分的。③長的;狹長的。He carried a *tall* walking stick. 他帶著一根長手杖。—*adv.* 誇大地。to talk *tall.* 說大話。*walk tall* 高視闊步。—**ness,** *n.*
tall·boy [ˈtɔlˌbɔɪ; ˈtɔːlbɔi] *n.* ①〖英〗有足之高屜櫃。②一種煙囪頂上之長管。③高脚玻璃酒杯。④〖諧〗要人;重要人物。
tall hat 高頂帽;大禮帽。
tall·ish [ˈtɔlɪʃ; ˈtɔːliʃ] *adj.* 稍高的。
tall order 大的要求或建議。
tal·low [ˈtælo; ˈtælou] *n.* (牛、羊等之)脂;脂肪(製肥皂或蠟燭用者)。—*v.t.* 塗以脂。
tallow candle 用牛、羊等之脂做的蠟燭;牛油燭。
tallow chandler 用牛、羊等之脂製蠟燭者;賣牛油燭者。
tal·low-faced [ˈtæloˌfest; ˈtæloufeist] *adj.* 〖蔑〗臉色蒼白的。
tal·low·y [ˈtælo·ɪ; ˈtæloui] *adj.* 多脂肪的。
tall story (or **tale**) 誇大的故事。
tall talk 誇大之辭;不着邊際之談。
tal·ly [ˈtælɪ; ˈtæli] *n., pl.* **-lies,** *v.,* **-lied, -ly·ing.** —*n.* ①古時記載欠帳或付款數目之木塊(上劃刻痕)。②任何記帳用之物。③記帳用之單位或分劃。④記錄;計算;結果。⑤標籤。⑥複製品;副本。⑦符合。⑧符合物;對應物;相對物。*live on tally* 〖英俚〗同居。—*v.t.* ①計算;記錄。②附以標籤。③使適合;使符合。—*v.i.* ①符合。②計算;記錄。
tally clerk ①計算選票的人;計票員。②計算貨物數量的人。
tal·ly·ho [*n., v.*ˈtælɪˌho; ˈtæliˈhou *interj.* ˌtælɪˈho; ˌtæliˈhou] *n., pl.* **-hos,** *interj., v.,* **-hoed** or **-ho'd, -ho·ing.** —*n.* ①用四匹馬曳引之四輪遊覽車或郵車。②"tallyho"之叫聲。—*interj.* 獵人發現狐狸時對獵犬之叫聲。—*v.t.* 叫"tallyho"以表示(狐狸)之出現;叫"tallyho"以嗾(獵犬)。—*v.i.* 高叫"tallyho".
tal·ly·man [ˈtælɪmən; ˈtælimən] *n., pl.* **-men.** ①以分期付款方式售貨之商人。②記帳員;計數員。
tally plan 〖英〗分期付款。
tally sheet ①記數紙。②〖美〗投票數記錄紙。
tally shop 〖英〗以分期付款方式售貨之商店。(亦作 **tallyshop**)
tal·mi gold [ˈtælmɪ~; ˈtælmi~] 一種鍍以薄金之鋅銅合金(用以製寶石細工)。
Tal·mud [ˈtælmʌd; ˈtælmud] *n.* 猶太法典。—**ic,** —**i·cal,** *adj.* —**ism,** *n.*
Tal·mud·ist [ˈtælmʌdɪst; ˈtælmudist] *n.* ①編纂 Talmud 經典者。②信奉Talmud 經典者。③精通 Talmud 經典者。
tal·on [ˈtælən; ˈtælən] *n.* ①(肉食鳥類之)爪。②(*pl.*)似爪之手指;緊握之手。③鎖中爲鑰匙在轉動時所接觸之部分。④〖牌戲〗分牌後所剩餘之牌。
ta·lus¹ [ˈteləs; ˈteiləs] *n., pl.* **-li** [-laɪ; -lai]. 〖解剖〗①距;踝。②距骨;踝骨。
ta·lus² *n., pl.* **-lus·es.** ①斜面。②(牆垣等的)斜面。③〖地質〗懸崖底下之碎岩堆坡;岩錐。
tam [tæm; tæm] *n.* =**tam-o'-shanter.**
tam·a·ble [ˈteməbl̩; ˈteiməbl] *adj.* 可馴服的。(亦作 **tameable**) —**ness,** *n.*
ta·ma·le [təˈmalɪ; təˈmɑːli] *n.* 墨西哥人食用的一種粽子;角黍(以玉蜀黍粉同肉末攙拌後,加以胡椒,用玉蜀黍外殼包好蒸之)。
tam·a·rack [ˈtæməˌræk; ˈtæməræk] *n.* 〖植物〗①(美洲所產之)落葉松。②任何與落葉松同科之植物。③此科植物之木材。
tam·a·rind [ˈtæməˌrɪnd; ˈtæmərind] *n.* 〖植物〗①羅望子(一種熱帶植物)。②羅望子之果實;羅望子之莢。
tam·a·risk [ˈtæməˌrɪsk; ˈtæmərisk] *n.* 〖植物〗檉柳。
tam·bour [ˈtæmbur; ˈtæmbuə] *n.* ①鼓。②鼓手。③刺繡綳子;刺繡架。④刺繡品。⑤〖建築〗圓形寺院柱間牆。⑥〖解剖〗氣鼓。—*v.t.* & *v.i.* 在刺繡綳子上刺繡。—**er,** *n.*
tam·bou·rine [ˌtæmbəˈrin; ˌtæmbəˈriːn] *n.* ①小手鼓;鈴鼓。②一種非洲產的鴿。
***tame** [tem; teim] *adj.,* **tam·er, tam·est,** *v.,* **tamed, tam·ing.** —*adj.* ①馴服的。a *tame* monkey. 馴服的猴子。②柔順的;不怕人的。③沒精打采的;乏味的。a *tame* story. 乏味的故事。④人工栽培的;人工交配改良的。⑤無危險性的;無害的。⑥不愛批評的。—*v.t.* ①使馴服。②使不怕人。Birds can be *tamed* by kindness. 親切的行爲可使鳥不怕人。③克制;壓服;挫折。④使(文章)平淡乏味。—*v.i.* 被馴服。The manatees *tamed* quickly. 海牛很快地被馴服。—**ly,** *adv.* —**ness,** *n.*
tame·less [ˈtemlɪs; ˈteimlis] *adj.* ①未馴服的。②不可馴服的;性野的;粗暴的。—**ly,** *adv.* —**ness,** *n.*
tam·er [ˈtemɚ; ˈteimə] *n.* ①馴服野獸者。②控制野獸之裝置。
Tam·il [ˈtæml̩; ˈtæml] *n.* ①坦米爾人(住在南印度及錫蘭之一族)。②坦米爾語。—*adj.* 坦米爾人的;坦米爾語的。—**i·an,** *adj.*
Tam·ma·ny [ˈtæmənɪ; ˈtæməni] *n.* ①坦慕尼協會(美國民主黨一政治組織)。②坦慕尼大厦(坦慕尼協會之總部所在地)。—*adj.* 坦慕尼協會的。
tam·my [ˈtæmɪ; ˈtæmi] *n.* =**tam-o'-shanter.**
tam-o'-shan·ter [ˌtæməˈʃæntɚ; ˌtæməˈʃæntə] *n.* (蘇格蘭人戴的)一種便帽。
tamp [tæmp; tæmp] *v.t.* ①搗固;砸緊。②以土等填塞(置有炸藥的洞)。③填塞;裝填。
tam·per¹ [ˈtæmpɚ; ˈtæmpə] *v.i.* ①干預;干涉;玩弄;亂弄〖with〗。Don't *tamper* with other's business. 不要干預別人的事。②賄賂。③竄改。*tamper with* **a.** 向…行賄。**b.** 竄改。**c.** 干預。
tam·per² *n.* 〖土木〗夯;夯土機。
tamp·ing [ˈtæmpɪŋ; ˈtæmpiŋ] *n.* ①填塞;填充。②填塞物;填料。③(軌道之)夯實。*dry tamping* 乾夯。
tam·pi·on [ˈtæmpɪən; ˈtæmpiən] *n.* ①鎗砲等口端之木栓(用以防潮防塵者)。②風琴管上端的塞子。(亦作 **tompion**)
tam·pon [ˈtæmpɑn; ˈtæmpən] *n.* ①〖醫〗止血塞;止血棉花球。②一種兩端有頭的鼓槌。—*v.t.* 置棉塞於…中。
tam-tam [ˈtʌmˌtʌm; ˈtʌmtʌm] *n.* ①銅鑼。②=**tom-tom.**
***tan** [tæn; tæn] *v.,* **tanned, tan·ning,** *n., adj.* —*v.t.* ①硝(皮)。②(使皮膚等)曬成褐色。③〖俗〗鞭笞。to *tan* a person's hide. 鞭笞某人。—*v.i.* ①成爲鞣製之革。②曬成褐色。A man's skin *tans* more deeply. 男人的皮膚可曬得更黝黑。—*n.* ①皮膚經日曬而成之褐色。②黃褐色;茶色。③含有單寧酸的樹皮。④硝皮用的單寧酸液。—*adj.* 黃褐色的;茶色的。
tan, tan. tangent.
tan·a·ger [ˈtænədʒɚ; ˈtænədʒə] *n.* 美國產之鶯(體小,善鳴,雄者羽色艷麗)。
tan·bark [ˈtænˌbark; ˈtænbɑːk] *n.* 任何含有單寧酸之樹皮。
tan·dem [ˈtændəm; ˈtændəm] *adv.* 一前一後地;縱列地。—*adj.* 一前一後排列着的;前後縱列的。—*n.* ①前後縱駕的兩匹馬。②兩馬前後縱駕的兩輪馬車。③前後雙座脚踏車。*in tandem* a. 一前一後地。b. 合夥地。

tang[1] 〔tæŋ; tæŋ〕 *n.* ①强烈的味道或氣味。②特殊的氣味或風味；特性；特質。③些微；少許。④鑿、銼等插入柄內之尖端。—*v.t.* 使有濃味。 —**y,** *adj.*

tang[2] *n.* 鏜鏜聲。—*v.t.* & *v.i.* (使)發鏜鏜聲。

tan·gen·cy 〔'tændʒənsɪ; 'tændʒənsi〕 *n.* 接觸。

tan·gent 〔'tændʒənt; 'tændʒənt〕 *adj.* ①接觸的。②〖幾何〗相切的。③離題的；與目的無關的。 —*n.* ①〖幾何〗切線；切面；正切曲線。②〖三角〗正切。③離題的行為；與目的無關的路線或方向。 ***go*** (or ***fly***) ***off at*** (or ***on***) ***a tangent*** 突然改換方針或話題。

tan·gen·tial 〔tæn'dʒɛnʃəl; tæn'dʒenʃəl〕 *adj.* ①〖數學〗切線的；正切的。②僅涉及而未深入的。③離題的。

Tan·ge·rine 〔ˌtændʒə'rin; ˌtændʒə'ri:n〕 *n.* 丹吉爾(Tangier, 非洲摩洛哥西北之一港埠)人。—*adj.* 丹吉爾(人)的。

tan·gi·ble 〔'tændʒəbḷ; 'tændʒəbl〕 *adj.* ①可觸知的。②確實的；眞實的。③實質的；實體的。—*n.* ①價值極易估計之物。②(尤指)有形資產。—**ness, tan·gi·bil·i·ty,** *n.*

tan·gi·bly 〔'tændʒəblɪ; 'tændʒəbli〕 *adv.* 實實在在地。

***tan·gle** 〔'tæŋgḷ; 'tæŋgl〕 *v.,* **-gled, -gling,** *n.* —*v.t.* ①使纏結；使糾纏。②使困惑。 —*v.i.* ①纏結；糾纏不清。②鬥嘴；爭吵。—*n.* ①纏結；亂七八糟的一堆。His thoughts were in a *tangle.* 他的思想紊亂。②爭吵；鬥爭。③一種海藻。—**ment,** *n.*

tan·gle·foot 〔'tæŋgḷˌfʊt; 'tæŋglfut〕 *n.* ①〖俚〗烈酒(如劣質威士忌酒)。②捕蠅紙上之黏性物。—*adj.* 複雜的；混亂的；迷惑的。

tan·gly 〔'tæŋglɪ; 'tæŋgli〕 *adj.,* **-gli·er, -gli·est.** ①覆有海草的；多海藻的。②糾纏不清的；紛亂的；錯亂的。

tan·go 〔'tæŋgo; 'tæŋgou〕 *n., pl.* **-gos,** *v.,* **-goed, -go·ing.** —*n.* ①探戈舞。②探戈舞曲。 —*v.i.* 跳探戈舞。

Tan·go *n.* 通訊電碼, 代表字母T.

tan·go·ist 〔'tæŋgoɪst; 'tæŋgouist〕 *n.* 跳探戈舞者。

tan·gram 〔'tæŋgrəm; 'tæŋgrəm〕 *n.* 七巧板。

tang·y 〔'tæŋɪ; 'tæŋi〕 *adj.,* **tang·i·er, tang·i·est.** 强烈的(味道)。

tank** 〔tæŋk; tæŋk〕 *n.* ①槽(水槽、油槽、煤氣槽等)。②池。a *tank* for swimming. 游泳池。③坦克；戰車。 a female (male) *tank.* 輕(重)戰車。④〖俚〗牢房。 —*v.t.* 置或貯於槽中。 ***tank down 〖英俚〗下大雨。 ***tank up*** a. 縱飲。b. 將油箱裝滿汽油。

tank·age 〔'tæŋkɪdʒ; 'tæŋkidʒ〕 *n.* ①(液體、氣體等之)貯於槽中。②槽等之租費。③槽之容量。 ④屠宰場煉油槽中之渣滓(做肥料或飼料用)。

tank·ard 〔'tæŋkəd; 'tæŋkəd〕 *n.* (有把手及帶鉸鏈之蓋的)大杯；一大杯之量。

tank car (鐵路之)油槽車；槽車。

tank destroyer 裝配戰車防禦砲之高速半履帶式車輛。

tank·er 〔'tæŋkə; 'tæŋkə〕 *n.* ①油輪；運油船。②空中加油飛機。③戰車戰士。—*v.t.* 用油輪運輸。

tank·er·ing 〔'tæŋkərɪŋ; 'tæŋkəriŋ〕 *n.* 油輪之裝卸工作。

tank·er·man 〔'tæŋkəmən; 'tæŋkəmən〕 *n., pl.* **-men.** 油輪上之工作人員。

tanker plane 空中加油飛機。

tank·ette 〔tæŋk'ɛt; tæŋ'ket〕 *n.* 小型戰車；小型坦克。

tank farming 培養液栽培植物法；水耕法。

tank·ful 〔'tæŋkfʊl; 'tæŋkful〕 *n., pl.* **-fuls.** 一槽(池)之量。

tank town ①火車僅為裝滿水槽而停站的小鎮。②任何不重要的小鎮。

tank trailer 運水拖車；運油拖車。

tank truck 運水卡車；水車；運油卡車。

tank·ves·sel 〔'tæŋkˌvɛsḷ; 'tæŋkˌvesl〕 *n.* 油輪。

tan·na·ble 〔'tænəbḷ; 'tænəbl〕 *adj.* 可硝製的；可鞣的。

tan·nage 〔'tænɪdʒ; 'tænidʒ〕 *n.* ①鞣革；硝皮。②鞣革用之材料。③〖蘇〗鞣革廠；硝皮廠。

tan·nate 〔'tænet; 'tæneit〕 *n.* 〖化〗單寧酸鹽。

tan·ner 〔'tænə; 'tænə〕 *n.* ①製革者。②〖英俚〗六辨士的錢幣。

tan·ner·y 〔'tænərɪ; 'tænəri〕 *n., pl.* **-ner·ies.** 硝皮廠；製革廠。

tan·nic 〔'tænɪk; 'tænik〕 *adj.* 富於鞣酸之樹皮(tan)的；由富於鞣酸之樹皮取出的。 ***tannic acid*** 〖化〗鞣酸；單寧酸。

tan·nin 〔'tænɪn; 'tænin〕 *n.* 〖化〗單寧酸；鞣酸。

tan·ning 〔'tænɪŋ; 'tæniŋ〕 *n.* ①製革；製革過程；製革術。②曬皮膚使成褐色。③〖俗〗鞭打；鞭笞。

tan·sy 〔'tænzɪ; 'tænzi〕 *n., pl.* **-sies.** 〖植物〗艾菊屬之植物；(尤指)艾菊。 ***like a tansy*** 完美的。

tan·ta·li·za·tion 〔ˌtæntələ'zeʃən; ˌtæntəlai'zeiʃən〕 *n.* 令人着急；逗人。

tan·ta·lize 〔'tæntḷˌaɪz; 'tæntəlaiz〕 *v.t.,* **-lized, -liz·ing.** 折磨(某人)使對所企求之物可望而不可及；誘發(某人)之希望而後使之失望。—**tan·ta·liz·er,** *n.*

tan·ta·liz·ing 〔'tæntəˌlaɪzɪŋ; 'tæntəlaiziŋ〕 *adj.* 可望而不可及的；逗人的；引起好奇心或貪心的。

tan·ta·lum 〔'tæntḷəm; 'tæntələm〕 *n.* 〖化〗鉭(稀有金屬元素之一, 符號為 Ta).

Tan·ta·lus 〔'tæntḷəs; 'tæntələs〕 *n.* ①〖希臘神話〗Zeus 之子(因洩露天機而被貶, 站立於齊頸之水中, 渴時欲飲而水下退, 飢時欲摘頭上之果實而樹枝上升)。② (t-) 〖英〗一種酒瓶臺架(由外可見酒瓶, 但有鎖鎖住而不能任意取出)。③(t-)一種鶴。

tan·ta·mount 〔'tæntəˌmaunt; 'tæntəmaunt〕 *adj.* 相等的；同等的〖to〗.

tan·ta·ra 〔'tæntərə, tæn'tærə; tæn'tɑ:rə〕 *n.* ①喇叭的聲音；角笛的聲音。②類似喇叭或角笛之聲音。

tan·tiv·y 〔tæn'tɪvɪ; tæn'tivi〕 *adv., adj., n., pl.* **-tiv·ies.** —*adv.* 疾馳地；飛奔地。 —*adj.* 疾速的。—*n.* ①奔馳；疾馳。②狩獵時指示疾追的喊聲。③號角聲。

tan·trum 〔'tæntrəm; 'tæntrəm〕 *n.* 〖俗〗發脾氣；勃然大怒。

tan·yard 〔'tænˌjɑrd; 'tænjɑ:d〕 *n.* 鞣皮或製革工場。

Tan·za·ni·a 〔ˌtænzə'niə; ˌtænzə'ni:ə, tæn'zæni:ə〕 *n.* 坦尙尼亞(東非之一共和國, 首都為達萊撒蘭 Dar es Salaam).

Tao·ism 〔'tauɪzəm; 'tɑ:ouizm〕 *n.* (中國之)道教。—**Tao·ist,** *n., adj.*

***tap**[1] 〔tæp; tæp〕 *v.,* **tapped** 〔tæpt; tæpt〕, **tap·ping,** *n.* —*v.t.* & *v.i.* ①輕敲；輕扣；輕拍；輕踏。to *tap* a person on the shoulder. 輕拍某人之肩。to *tap* time. 打拍子。②加鞋掌或鞋跟以修理。③任命；指定。—*n.* ①輕敲；輕扣；輕拍；輕踏。②輕敲之聲。③修

理鞋時所加之鞋掌或鞋跟。④(*pl.*) 熄燈號音或鼓音。⑤些微;微量。He didn't do a *tap* of work. 他一點工也不做。

tap²** *n., v.,* **tapped, tap·ping,** *adj.* —*n.* ①栓;塞。②龍頭。Turn the *tap* on (off). 打開(關上) 龍頭。③一種酒。④〖俗〗賣酒及喝酒之所。⑤電線接搭處。⑥螺絲模 (刻螺絲陰紋之器具)。on tap*** **a.** 隨時可自桶中放出供應。ale *on tap.* 隨時可自桶中放出供應的啤酒。**b.**〖俗〗可隨時供應的;現成的;經常供應的。 —*v.t.* ①拔去…之栓或塞;在…中鑿孔使液體流出。 to *tap* a cask. 開樽取酒。②在…上裝栓或塞子。③拔出塞子以汲取(液體)。④開發。⑤搭線偷聽。 to *tap* a telegraph wire to intercept the message. 私接電報線截取消息。⑥刻螺絲陰紋。⑦(外科手術中)放出液體。—*adj.* 經常供應的;以經常供應的方式辦理的。—**pa·ble,** *adj.*

ta·pa 〔ˈtɑpə; ˈtɑːpə〕 *n.* ①(太平洋諸島土人所製的)一種土布 (非紡織成, 而係由一種桑樹內皮加以處理而成者)。 ②此種桑樹皮。

tap borer 開塞錐。

tap dance 踢躂舞。

tap-dance 〔ˈtæpˌdæns; ˈtæpdɑːns〕 *v.i.,* **-danced, -danc·ing.** 跳踢躂舞。—**tap-danc·er,** *n.* —**tap-danc·ing,** *n., adj.*

tape** 〔tep; teip〕 *n., v.,* **taped, tap·ing.** —*n.* ①帶;線帶。That candy store uses fancy *tape* to tie all packages. 那個糖果店用各種花樣的線帶紮繫包裹。②捲尺;皮尺。③繫在跑道終點之線。④磁帶。breast the tape*** (賽跑者)衝過終點之線而贏得比賽。***red tape*** 繁瑣手續; 官樣文章。—*v.t.* ①以帶縛起。The doctor *taped* up the wound. 醫師以帶縛起傷口。②用皮尺測量。③測量(陣地)之射程;轟擊而毀滅之。④以磁帶錄音機加以錄音。 ***have*** (or ***get***) ***a person taped*** 〖主英〗打量某人;設法了解某人。

tape-con·trolled 〔ˈtepkənˌtrold; ˈteipkənˌtrould〕 *adj.* 由錄音磁帶上之指示控制的。

tape deck 錄音座;大型錄音機。

tape·line 〔ˈtepˌlaɪn; ˈteiplain〕 *n.* 捲尺;皮尺。

tape machine 錄音機 (=tape recorder).

tape player 放錄音帶之小型錄音機。

ta·per** 〔ˈtepɚ; ˈteipə〕 *v.i. & v.t.* ①(使)逐漸尖細。The church spire *tapers* off to a point. 禮拜堂的塔尖逐漸尖細成一尖頭。②(使)逐漸減少。taper off*** **a.** 逐漸衰亡;逐漸消失。**b.** 使逐漸減少。**c.** 使逐漸尖細。—*n.* ①細蠟燭。②減小;減弱。③逐漸尖細。—*adj.* ①長而尖細的。*taper* fingers. 尖而細長的手指。②隨數量之增加而減少的;愈多愈價廉的。—**ing,** *adj.* —**ing·ly,** *adv.* —**ness,** *n.*

tape-re·cord 〔ˌteprɪˈkɔrd; ˈteip-riˌkɔːd〕 *v.t. & v.i.* 以磁帶錄音機加以錄音。to *tape-record* a speech. 以磁帶錄音機錄演講詞。(亦作 **taperecord**)

tape recorder 磁帶錄音機。

tape recording 磁帶錄音。

***tap·es·try** 〔ˈtæpɪstrɪ; ˈtæpistri〕 *n., pl.* **-tries,** *v.,* **-tried, -try·ing.** —*n.* ①繡帷;綴錦。②綴錦畫。—*v.i.* 以綴錦織畫或圖案。—*v.t.* ①蓋或飾以繡帷。②在繡帷上繡出。—**like,** *adj.*

tape·worm 〔ˈtepˌwɝm; ˈteipwəːm〕 *n.* 絛蟲。

tap·house 〔ˈtæpˌhaus; ˈtæphaus〕 *n.* 酒館;酒吧;客棧。(亦作 **tap house**)

tap·i·o·ca 〔ˌtæpɪˈokə; ˌtæpiˈoukə〕 *n.* 一種澱粉質食料(用於做布丁及湯中之芡粉)。

ta·pir 〔ˈtepɚ; ˈteipə〕 *n.* 〖動物〗(中南美及馬來產之)貘。

tap·is 〔ˈtæpi, ˈtæpɪs; ˈtæpiː〕 *n.* 毯;綴錦(用做桌布或窗帷等)。 ***on*** (or ***upon***) ***the tapis*** 在考慮中;在審議中。

tap·per¹ 〔ˈtæpɚ; ˈtæpə〕 *n.* ①輕打者;輕拍者; 敲具。②(電報機之) 發報鍵。③〖英方〗啄木鳥。

tap·per² *n.* ①汲取樹汁者; 開發者; 取用者。②刻螺紋者。③在電話線上接竊聽裝置者。

tap·pet 〔ˈtæpɪt; ˈtæpit〕 *n.*〖機械〗挺桿。

tap·room 〔ˈtæpˌrum; ˈtæp-rum〕 *n.* 〖英〗酒店;酒館;酒吧間。

tap·root 〔ˈtæpˌrut; ˈtæp-ruːt〕 *n.* ①〖植物〗直根;主根。②重點;要點;基本。

tap·ster 〔ˈtæpstɚ; ˈtæpstə〕 *n.* 〖古〗(酒吧間之)酒保。

tap water (未經煮開的)自來水。

tar¹** 〔tɑr; tɑː〕 *n., v.,* **tarred, tar·ring.** —*n.* 焦油;黑油。beat*** (***knock, whip,*** or ***whale***) ***the tar out of*** 痛毆。—*v.t.* 塗以焦油;浸以焦油。***tar and feather a person*** **a.** 將某人滿身塗以焦油後裹上羽毛(一種私刑及侮辱)。**b.** 嚴厲處罰。***tarred with the same brush*** (or ***stick***) 有同樣的特點。

tar² *n.* 〖俗〗水手;海員。

tar·a·did·dle 〔ˈtærəˌdɪdl̩; ˈtærədidl〕 *n.* 〖俗〗謊話。

tar·an·tel·la 〔ˌtærənˈtɛlə; ˌtærənˈtelə〕 *n.* ①(義大利之)快速旋舞。②其舞曲。

tar·ant·ism 〔ˈtærəntɪzm̩; ˈtærəntizm〕 *n.* (15–17 世紀義大利南部流行的) 一種舞蹈症(據云被 tarantula 蜘蛛咬後所致)。

ta·ran·tu·la 〔təˈræntʃələ; təˈræntjulə〕 *n., pl.* **-las, -lae** 〔-ˌli; -liː〕. 一種大型、多毛、咬人甚痛而有毒的蜘蛛。

ta·rax·a·cum 〔təˈræksəkəm; təˈræksəkəm〕 *n.* ①〖植物〗蒲公英屬之植物; 蒲公英。②自蒲公英之根中提煉出之藥(用作補藥、利尿劑、瀉藥等)。

tar·boosh 〔tɑrˈbuʃ; tɑːˈbuːʃ〕 *n.* 土耳其帽。

tar·brush 〔ˈtɑrˌbrʌʃ; ˈtɑːbrʌʃ〕 *n.* ①用以塗焦油的刷子。②〖俚、常蔑〗黑人血統。

tar·di·grade 〔ˈtɑrdɪˌgred; ˈtɑːdigreid〕 *adj.* ①遲鈍的;遲緩的。②〖動物〗緩步類的。—*n.* 〖動物〗緩步類之節肢動物。

tar·di·ly 〔ˈtɑrdɪlɪ; ˈtɑːdili〕 *adv.* ①緩慢地; 遲緩地。②過晚地; 過遲地。

tar·di·ness 〔ˈtɑrdɪnɪs; ˈtɑːdinis〕 *n.* 遲緩。

tar·do 〔ˈtɑrdo; ˈtɑːdou〕〖義〗*adj.& adv.* 〖音樂〗緩慢。

***tar·dy** 〔ˈtɑrdɪ; ˈtɑːdi〕 *adj.,* **-di·er, -di·est.** 遲延的;遲遲的;緩慢的。

tare¹ 〔tɛr; tɛə〕 *n.* ①(聖經中所載之)一種有毒的莠草(或爲毒麥)。②〖植物〗一種野豆;大巢菜;野豌豆。

tare² *n., v.,* **tared, tar·ing.** —*n.* ①扣除之容器、包皮等之重量。②此種重量之扣除。③(不裝載貨物、旅客等之) 車身重量; 空車重量。—*v.t.* 求出、計及或標明包皮等之重量。

tare weight (車輛等之) 空重;皮重。

targe 〔tɑrdʒ; tɑːdʒ〕 *n.* 〖古〗盾;小圓盾。

***tar·get** 〔ˈtɑrgɪt; ˈtɑːgit〕 *n.* ①鵠;靶;標的。to shoot at the *target.* 打靶。②(被指責、輕蔑、批評或攻擊的)目標。③小圓盾。—*v.t.* ①定爲目標。②爲…定目標。③引導…至目標。

target date 預定開始或完成之日期。

Tar·gum 〔ˈtɑrgʌm; ˈtɑːgəm〕 *n., pl.* **-gums, Tar·gu·mim** 〔ˌtɑrguˈmim; ˌtɑːguˈmiːm〕. 舊約聖經之 Aramaic 語譯文。

***tar·iff** [ˈtærɪf; ˈtærif] *n.* ①徵稅制度;稅率;稅表。②關稅;關稅率;關稅表。There is a very high *tariff* on jewelry. 寶石類的稅率很高。③價目表。④價格。—*v.t.* 使被抽稅。

tariff wall 關稅壁壘。

tar·la·tan [ˈtɑrlətn̩; ˈtɑːlətən] *n.* 一種不易縐的薄紗。

tar·mac·ad·am [ˌtɑrməˈkædəm; ˌtɑːməˈkædəm] *n.* 一種與 Tarmac (柏油與碎石的混合物)相似的鋪路材料。

tarn [tɑrn; tɑːn] *n.* 山中之小湖或小潭。

'tar·nal [ˈtɑrnl̩; ˈtɑːnəl] *adj.* 〖方〗①永恆的;不變的。②可憎的;該死的(用作詛咒語)。—*adv.* 〖方〗該死;討厭;極。—**ly,** *adv.*

tar·na·tion [tɑrˈneʃən; tɑːˈneiʃən] *n.* 〖方〗詛咒;咒罵。—*interj.* 〖方〗該死！討厭！—*adj.* 〖方〗討厭的;該死的。—*adv.* 〖方〗討厭;該死; 極。

tar·nish [ˈtɑrnɪʃ; ˈtɑːniʃ] *v.t.* 使失光澤;玷汚。—*v.i.* 失光澤。—*n.* ①暗晦; 失去光澤。②瑕疵;汚點。③已失去光澤的外表。

ta·ro [ˈtɑro; ˈtɑːrou] *n., pl.* **-ros.** ①〖植物〗芋。②芋根。

tar·pau·lin [tɑrˈpɔlɪn; tɑːˈpɔːlin] *n.* 防水布(罩); 防水衣。—*v.t.* 蓋以防水布。

tar·pon [ˈtɑrpɑn; ˈtɑːpɔn] *n.* (產於大西洋溫暖區域之)一種大海魚。

tar·ra·gon [ˈtærəˌgɑn; ˈtærəgən] *n.* ①〖植物〗茵陳蒿(一種紫菀科植物)。②茵陳蒿之葉(有香味,用於調味)。(亦作 **estragon**)

tar·ra·go·na [ˌtærəˈgonə; ˌtærəˈgounə] *n.* 西班牙所產之一種葡萄酒。(亦作 **Tarragona**)

tarred [tɑrd; tɑːd] *adj.* 塗有焦油的。

tar·ry[1] [ˈtærɪ; ˈtæri] *v.,* **-ried, -ry·ing,** *n.* —*v.i.* ①滯留;停留。②遷延;耽擱。—*v.t.* 〖古〗等;等候。—*n.* 停留;逗留。

tar·ry[2] [ˈtɑrɪ; ˈtɑːri] *adj.,* **-ri·er, -ri·est.** ①焦油的;似焦油的。②塗有焦油的。

tar·sal [ˈtɑrsl̩; ˈtɑːsəl] *adj.* ①踝的; 跗骨的;跗蹠骨的。②眼瞼軟骨的;瞼板的。—*n.* 〖解剖〗①跗骨;跗蹠骨。②瞼板。

tar·si·a [ˈtɑrsɪə; ˈtɑːsiə] *n.* 嵌木細工。

tar·sus [ˈtɑrsəs; ˈtɑːsəs] *n., pl.* **-si** [-saɪ; -sai]. ①〖解剖〗 踝;跗骨。②鳥之跗蹠骨。③昆蟲之蹠節。④〖解剖〗眼瞼軟骨;瞼板。

tart[1] [tɑrt; tɑːt] *n.* ①有果餡的糕點 (在英國一切有果餡的 pie 皆稱爲 tart; 在美國 tart 僅指小塊的, 果餡露在外面的糕而言)。②〖英俗〗(尤指行爲不檢之)女孩;女人;娼妓。

tart[2] *adj.* ①酸的。②尖刻的;嚴厲的。—*v.t.* 僅見於下一成語中的習慣用法。***tart up*** 〖主英〗①使增加香味或興趣。②改善…之外表;使更好看。—**ness,** *n.*

tar·tan[1] [ˈtɑrtn̩; ˈtɑːtn] *n.* ①格子呢(主要爲蘇格蘭高地人所穿用)。②格子呢之花樣。③格子呢的衣裳。—*adj.* ①格子呢的;似格子呢的。②用格子呢製的。

tar·tan[2] *n.* 地中海的一種單桅船。(亦作 **tartana**)

Tar·tar [ˈtɑrtɚ; ˈtɑːtə] *n.* ①韃靼人。②韃靼語系。③(t-) 野蠻而兇悍的人;慓悍的人;急躁的人。 ***catch a Tartar*** 遭遇頑敵;遭到意料之外困難的事。—*adj.* 韃靼人或韃靼語的。(亦作 **Tatar**)

tar·tar [ˈtɑrtɚ; ˈtɑːtə] *n.* ①〖化〗酒石。②齒垢;齒石; 牙砂。 ***cream of tartar*** 酸性酒石;酸鉀;酒石。—**eous,** *adj.*

Tar·tar·e·an [tɑrˈtɛrɪən; tɑːˈtɛəriən] *adj.* 冥府的;地獄的。(亦作 **tartarean**)

tar·tar·ic [tɑrˈtærɪk; tɑːˈtærik] *adj.* 酒石的; 含酒石的。***tartaric acid*** 酒石酸。

tar·tar·ly [ˈtɑrtəlɪ; ˈtɑːtəli] *adj.* 兇悍的;慓悍的。

Tar·ta·rus [ˈtɑrtərəs; ˈtɑːtərəs] *n.* ①〖希臘神話〗地獄下暗無天日之深淵(爲 Zeus 禁閉 Titans 之所)。②地獄;冥府。

Tar·ta·ry [ˈtɑrtərɪ; ˈtɑːtəri] *n.* 〖歐史〗韃靼地方 (包括東歐及亞洲之一廣大地區, 中古時期韃靼人曾入侵並定居於此)。(亦作 **Tatary**)

tart·let [ˈtɑrtlɪt; ˈtɑːtlit] *n.* 〖英〗一種水果餡小點心。

tart·ly [ˈtɑrtlɪ; ˈtɑːtli] *adv.* 尖刻地; 嚴厲地。

tar·trate [ˈtɑrtret; ˈtɑːtreit] *n.* 〖化〗酒石酸鹽。

tart-tongued [ˈtɑrtˌtʌŋd; ˈtɑːtˈtʌŋd] *adj.* 說話尖酸刻薄的;愛挖苦的。

Tar·tuf(f)e [tɑrˈtuf; tɑːˈtuf] *n.* ①法國作家莫里哀 (Molière) 所作一諷刺喜劇之劇名(亦即該劇中主角名)。②(t-) 僞君子;僞善者。—**Tar·tuff·i·an, Tar·tuff·ish,** *adj.*

Tar·zan [ˈtɑrzn̩; ˈtɑːzn] *n.* ①泰山(美國作家 E.R. Burroughs 所作冒險故事中之主角)。②矯健力大的人。

ta·sim·e·ter [təˈsɪmətɚ; təˈsimitə] *n.* 微壓計。

‡task [tæsk, tɑsk; tɑːsk] *n.* 工作;任務;作業; 課業。daily *tasks.* 日常工作。***take*** (or ***call***) ***to task*** a. 找麻煩。 b. 責備。—*v.t.* ①課以工作。②使辛勞;煩累。Mathematics *tasks* that child's brain. 數學使那個孩子傷腦筋。—**er,** *n.*

task force ①〖軍〗特遣隊(臨時編組以執行一項特殊任務的部隊或艦隊)。②由專家組成的特別委員會。

task·mas·ter [ˈtæskˌmæstɚ; ˈtɑːskˌmɑːstə] *n.* ①派遣他人做繁重工作者;監工。②對別人工作要求甚爲嚴格者。—**ship,** *n.*

task·work [ˈtæskˌwɝk; ˈtɑːskwəːk] *n.* ①派定之工作。②無趣味之工作。③以件計酬之工作;件工;包工。

Tass, TASS [tæs; tæs] *n.* 塔斯社(蘇聯的官方通訊社)。

tas·sel [ˈtæsl̩; ˈtæsl] *n., v.,* **-sel(l)ed, -sel·(l)ing.** —*n.* ①縫; 纓; 流蘇。②似縫之物。Corn has *tassels.* 玉蜀黍有穗鬚。***with tassels on*** 附帶一切裝飾。—*v.t.* ①飾以縫。②取去縫。—*v.i.* 生有縫或似縫之物。—**er,** *n.*

‡taste [test; teist] *n., v.,* **tast·ed, tast·ing.** —*n.* ①味;滋味。It has a sweet *taste.* 它有一股甜味。②味覺。It is sweet to the *taste.* 嘗起來很甜。③一嘗;少量(祇能用單數,可加定冠詞或不定冠詞)。 to take a *taste* of a cake. 嘗一點兒糕餅。④欣賞力; 鑑賞力;判斷力。They don't show much *taste* in choosing pictures. 他們在圖畫的選擇方面沒有欣賞力。⑤愛好; 嗜好。He has a *taste* for hunting. 他愛好打獵。⑥風味;韻味;情趣。He is a man of *taste.* 他是一個頗有生活情趣的人。***leave a bad taste in the mouth*** 造成一個壞印象; 引起一種嫌惡的感覺。 ***to one's taste*** 合意; 中意。***to the king's*** (or ***queen's***) ***taste*** 十全十美;非常令人滿意地。—*v.t.* ①嘗(食物等);品嘗。She *tasted* almond in the cake. 她嘗出餅中有杏仁味道。②略進(飲食)(通常用於否定語)。He said he hadn't *tasted* food for three days. 他說他已三天不曾吃東西了。③體驗; 領略。to *taste* the joys of freedom. 領略自由之樂。—*v.i.* ①嘗味; 經驗到。to *taste* of success. 嘗到成功的滋味。②有(某)味。The milk *tastes* sour. 牛奶有酸味。***taste***

blood 因擊敗敵人而快樂。 ***taste of*** **a.** 經驗;遭遇; 嘗到。 **b.** 有…之味道。The soup *tastes* of onion. 湯有洋葱味道。**c.** 淺嘗。**d.** 略有些…意味。—**tast·a·ble,** —**a·ble,** *adj.* —**a·ble·ness,** *n.*

taste bud 味蕾。

taste·ful [ˈtestfəl; ˈteistfəl] *adj.* ①有風致的;雅致的(建築物、藝術品、傢具等)。②有良好鑑賞力的。—**ly,** *adv.* —**ness,** *n.*

taste·less [ˈtestlɪs; ˈteistlis] *adj.* ①無味的。②不吸引人的; 不雅致的。③〖罕〗不辨滋味的。④無鑑賞力的。—**ly,** *adv.* —**ness,** *n.*

taste·mak·er [ˈtestˌmekə; ˈteistˌmeikə] *n.* 時尚等之創始者;開風氣之先者。

tast·er [ˈtestə; ˈteistə] *n.* ①品嘗味道者(尤指 **a.** 受雇品嘗茶、酒以鑑定其品質者。**b.** 嘗試食物是否有毒之皇家僕役)。②用以盛品嘗、作樣品或試驗之物的容器。③實驗室用之玻璃吸管。④(出版社之)原稿鑑定者。

tast·i·ly [ˈtestəlɪ; ˈteistili] *adv.* ①美味可口地。②極富韻味地;有風致地。

tast·y [ˈtestɪ; ˈteisti] *adj.,* **tast·i·er, tast·i·est.** ①〖俗〗味美的; 適口的。②有良好之鑑賞力的; 高雅的; 有風致的。—**tast·i·ness,** *n.*

tat¹ [tæt; tæt] *v.i.* & *v.t.,* **tat·ted, tat·ting.** 梭織;梭織花邊。

tat² *n.* 現僅用於下列成語中。***tit for tat*** 以牙還牙;一報還一報。

ta-ta [ˈtɑˌtɑ; ˈtæˈtɑː] *interj.* 再見!—*n.* ①散步 (戲語)。②〖俚〗機關槍。(亦作**ta ta**)

ta·ta·mi [tɑˈtɑmɪ; təˈtɑːmi] *n., pl.* **-mi, -mis.**(日式住宅之)榻榻米(約=18平方英尺)。

Ta·tar [ˈtɑtə; ˈtɑːtə] *n.* ①韃靼人(中古時征服中、西部亞細亞及東歐之蒙古人及土耳其人)。②居於蘇聯東部韃靼共和國、克里米亞及亞洲數部分之土耳其人;此種人所操之語言。—*adj.* 韃靼人或其語言的。(亦作 **Tartar**)

Tatar Strait 韃靼海峽(在庫頁島與亞洲大陸之間)。

Ta·ta·ry [ˈtɑtərɪ; ˈtɑːtəri] *n.* =**Tartary.**

Tate Gallery (倫敦之)泰特美術館。

tat·ter [ˈtætə; ˈtætə] *n.* ①破布;襤褸。②(*pl.*)碎片。 His clothes are in *tatters.* 他的衣服已破爛。—*v.t.* 撕破; 穿破; 戴破。—*v.i.* 變成襤褸。

tat·ter·de·mal·ion [ˌtætədɪˈmeljən; ˌtætədəˈmeiljən] *n.* 衣衫襤褸的人。—*adj.* ①衣衫襤褸的。②破破爛爛的。

tat·tered [ˈtætəd; ˈtætəd] *adj.* ①破碎的。②衣服襤褸的。

tat·ter·sall [ˈtætəˌsɔl; ˈtætəsɔːl] *n.* 一種鮮艷的花格布。—*adj.* 用顏色鮮艷之花格布做的。

tat·ting [ˈtætɪŋ; ˈtætiŋ] *n.* ①梭織;梭織法。②梭織之花邊。

tat·tle [ˈtætl̩; ˈtætl] *v.,* **-tled, -tling,** *n.* —*v.i.* ①洩露祕密。②閒談;聊天;空談。—*v.t.* ①由閒談而洩露(祕密);在閒談中說出。—*n.* 閒談;聊天;空談。—**tat·tling·ly,** *adv.*

tat·tler [ˈtætl̩ə; ˈtætl̩ə] *n.* ①閒聊天的人; 喋喋不休者。②洩露祕密或講他人閒話的人。③一種鷸類的鳥。

tat·tle·tale [ˈtætl̩ˌtel; ˈtætlteil] *adj., n.* 〖俗〗洩露祕密或愛講人閒話的(人);搬弄是非的(人);警告標示;指示物。

tat·too¹ [tæˈtu; təˈtuː] *n., pl.* **-toos,** *v.* —*n.* ①〖軍〗歸營號或鼓;其聲音。②連續之輕敲。③〖英〗軍隊遊行 (通常在夜間, 並配以軍樂)。 ***beat the devil's tattoo*** (興奮、焦躁或不耐煩時)以手指擊桌。—*v.t.* & *v.i.* 連續地輕敲。

tat·too² *v.,* **-tooed, -too·ing,** *n., pl.* **-toos.** —*v.t.* 刺花樣於(皮膚)。—*n.* 紋身;刺花。facial *tattoo.* 臉面刺花。—**er,**—**ist,** *n.*

tau [tɔ, tau; tɔː, tau] *n.* ①希臘字母之第十九字母 (Τ, τ)。②T 形物; T 形符號。③300。④最後一個字母; Z. ⑤=**tau cross.**

tau cross T字形之十字架。

‡**taught** [tɔt; tɔːt] *v.* pt. & pp. of **teach.**

taunt¹ [tɔnt; tɔːnt] *v.t.* ①痛罵; 笑罵。②以揶揄、笑罵等使之做。—*v.i.* 譏笑; 笑罵; 辱罵。—*n.* ①痛罵; 笑罵。 ②笑罵的對象。—**ing·ly,** *adv.*

taunt² *adj.* 〖航海〗特別高的(桅)。

taupe [top; toup] 〖法〗 *n.* 暗灰色 (鼹鼠皮之色)。

tau·rine [ˈtɔrɪn; ˈtɔːrin] *adj.* ①雄牛的; 似雄牛的。②〖天文〗金牛宮的。

Tau·rus [ˈtɔrəs; ˈtɔːrəs] *n.* 〖天文〗①金牛座。②金牛宮。

taut [tɔt; tɔːt] *adj.* ①拉緊的(繩索);緊張的(神經、筋肉等)。②整潔的;整齊的。③苛酷的。—**ly,** *adv.* —**v.i.** 拉緊;變整潔。

taut·en [ˈtɔtn̩; ˈtɔːtn] *v.t.* 使緊;使整潔。

tau·tog [ˈtɔtɑg; tɔːˈtɔg] *n.* 美國北大西洋沿岸產的一種黑色或綠色食用魚。

tau·to·log·i·cal [ˌtɔtəˈlɑdʒɪkl̩; ˌtɔːtəˈlɔdʒikl] *adj.* tautology 的;使用 tautology 的;含有 tautology 的。—**ly,** *adv.*

tau·tol·o·gize [tɔˈtɑləˌdʒaɪz; tɔːˈtɔlədʒaiz] *v.i.,* **-gized, -giz·ing.** ①反覆使用不必要之同義語。②重複。

tau·tol·o·gy [tɔˈtɑlədʒɪ; tɔːˈtɔlədʒi] *n., pl.* **-gies.** 同義語之重複;無謂之重複。

***tav·ern** [ˈtævən; ˈtævən] *n.* ①酒店。②旅店;客棧。—*v.i.* 時常光顧酒店。

taw¹ [tɔ; tɔː] *n.* ①石彈。②石彈戲。③(亦作 **taw line**) (石彈戲中)射出石彈之基線。

taw² *v.t.* ①調製 (自然產物)以供進一步處理或應用。②(用明礬和鹽溶液)鞣製(生皮)。

taw·dri·ly [ˈtɔdrəlɪ; ˈtɔːdrili] *adv.* 俗麗地。

taw·dry [ˈtɔdrɪ; ˈtɔːdri] *adj.,* **-dri·er, -dri·est.** 華麗而不值錢的;俗麗的。

taw·ny [ˈtɔnɪ; ˈtɔːni] *adj.,* **-ni·er, -ni·est,** *n.* —*adj.*黃褐色的;茶色的。—*n.*黃褐色。

taws(e) [tɔz, tɑz; tɔːz, tɑːz] *n.* 〖蘇〗一種皮鞭。—*v.t.* 鞭打。

‡**tax** [tæks; tæks] *n.* ①稅; 租稅。 How much income *tax* do you pay? 你繳納多少所得稅? ②重負。 Climbing stairs is a *tax* on a weak heart. 爬樓梯對於心臟衰弱的人是一項重負。—*v.t.* ①課以稅。 to *tax* the rich heavily. 課富人以重稅。②使負重荷。③斥責;譴責 〖with〗. to *tax* a person with neglect. 斥責某人疏忽。④評定 (訴訟費等)。⑤〖俗〗控告。—**er,** *n.*

tax·a·bil·i·ty [ˌtæksəˈbɪlətɪ; ˌtæksəˈbiliti] *n.* 可課稅性。

tax·a·ble [ˈtæksəbl̩; ˈtæksəbl] *adj.* ①應被課稅的; 可被課稅的。②作爲計算稅額之根據的。—**tax·a·bly,** *adv.*

***tax·a·tion** [tæksˈeʃən; tækˈseiʃən] *n.* ①課稅;徵稅。②稅; 租稅。Is high *taxation* bad for trade?重稅對貿易不利嗎?—**al,** *adj.*

tax cart (農或商用的)輕便兩輪馬車。

tax collector 稅務員。

tax day 繳稅日期。

tax deduction 免稅(額)。

tax evasion 逃稅。

tax-ex·empt [ˈtæksɪgˈzɛmpt; ˈtæksigˈzempt] *adj.* ①免稅的。 *tax-exempt* imports. 免稅的進口貨。②不課稅的。 *tax-exempt* bonds. 不課稅的公債。

tax-free [ˈtæksˈfri; ˈtæksˈfriː] *adj.* 免稅的;已付稅的。

tax haven 【美】吸引美國公司或個人前往置產或設廠的低稅率國家。

***tax·i** [ˈtæksɪ; ˈtæksi] *n., pl.* **tax·is** [ˈtæksɪz; ˈtæksiz], *v.,* **tax·ied** [ˈtæksɪd; ˈtæksid], **tax·i·ing** or **tax·y·ing.** —*n.* ①出租汽車;計程車(=taxicab)。②出租飛機。an air *taxi.* 出租之飛機。—*v.i.* ①乘計程車。As we were late we *taxied* to the station. 因爲時間來不及,我們乘計程車到車站去。②(飛機在地面或水面上)滑行。—*v.t.* ①以出租汽車接或送。②使(飛機)在地面或水面上滑行。

tax·i·cab [ˈtæksɪˌkæb; ˈtæksikæb] *n.* 出租汽車。

taxi dancer (舞廳等處之)職業舞女。

tax·i·der·mal [ˌtæksəˈdɝml; ˌtæksiˈdəːml] *adj.* 剝製術的。(參看 **taxidermy**)

tax·i·der·mic [ˌtæksəˈdɝmɪk; ˌtæksiˈdəːmik] *adj.* =**taxidermal.**

tax·i·der·my [ˈtæksəˌdɝmɪ; ˈtæksidəːmi] *n.* (剝製動物以作標本的)剝製術。—**tax·i·der·mist,** *n.*

tax·i·man [ˈtæksɪˌmæn; ˈtæksimən] *n., pl.* **-men.** 出租汽車之司機。

tax·i·me·ter [ˈtæksɪˌmitɚ; ˈtæksiˌmiːtə] *n.* (計程車之)車費自動計算表。

tax in kind 以實物繳納的稅。

tax·i·plane [ˈtæksɪˌplen; ˈtæksiplein] *n.* 出租飛機。

tax·is [ˈtæksɪs; ˈtæksis] *n.* ①排列;順序。②【生物】向性;趨向性(生物體對於外界刺激產生適當反應之活動)。③【外科】整復術;回納術(用手而不須用開刀之方法納回脫離原位之部分,如脫腸之回納)。④古希臘之軍隊單位。

taxi stand 出租汽車停車場。

tax·i·way [ˈtæksɪˌwe; ˈtæksiwei] *n.* (機場候機處與起飛點或降落點間之)滑行道。

tax·on·o·my [tæksˈɑnəmɪ; tækˈsɔnəmi] *n.* ①分類。②分類學。

tax·paid [ˈtæksˈped; ˈtæksˈpeid] *adj.* 用稅款支付的;薪水出自稅款的。

***tax·pay·er** [ˈtæksˌpeɚ; ˈtæksˌpeiə] *n.* ①納稅人。②租金僅够付地稅的臨時房屋。

tax sale 除稅售出(爲償還欠稅而由公家主持的私有房地產拍賣)。

tax shelter 以投資或津貼名義逃避繳納所得稅。

tax stamp 印花。

tax title 由 tax sale 而取得的不動產所有權。

tax·us [ˈtæksəs; ˈtæksəs] *n.* 紫杉;水松。

TB, T.B., Tb ①tubercle bacillus. ②tuberculosis. **Tb** 化學元素 terbium 之符號。

T-band·age [ˈtiˌbændɪdʒ; ˈtiːˌbændidʒ] *n.* 【醫】丁字帶。

T.B.O. 【戲院】 total blackout.

T-bone [ˈtiˌbon; ˈtiːboun] *n.* 有骨牛排。

tbr. timber. **TBS** 【航海】 talk between ships. 一種船與船間通話用的短程無線電對講機。 **tbs., tbsp.** ①tablespoon(s). ②tablespoonful. **TC** Trustee Council. 聯合國託管理事會。 **Tc** 化學元素 technetium 之符號。 **T.C.** ①Tank Corps. ②temporary constable.

TCBM transcontinental ballistic missile.

Tchai·kov·sky [tʃaɪˈkɔfskɪ; tʃaiˈkɔvski] *n.* 柴可夫斯基 (Pëtr Ilich, 1840–1893, 俄國作曲家)。(亦作 **Tschaikovsky, Chaikovski**)

Te 化學元素 tellurium 之符號。

‡**tea** [ti; tiː] *n.* ①茶樹;茶葉;茶。black *tea.* 紅茶。green *tea.* 綠茶。②下午茶(在下午或傍晚所進食的一次茶點)。We have *tea* at half past four. 我們在四點半吃下午茶。③湯。beef *tea.* 濃牛肉湯。***another cup of tea*** 【俗】一件完全不同的事。***high*** (or ***meat***) ***tea*** 【英】午後小餐(通常在下午茶以後的精巧的一頓)。***make tea*** 沏茶;泡茶。***one's cup of tea*** 【俗】正爲某人所愛;正中下懷。

tea bag 茶袋(小袋內裝茶葉,沏茶時連袋置杯中)。

tea ball 【美】=**tea bag.**

tea biscuit 甜餅乾(佐茶用)。

tea break 【英】吃茶點的休息時間。

tea caddy or **canister** 茶筒;茶罐。

tea·cake [ˈtiˌkek; ˈtiː-keik] *n.* 茶點用餅乾。

tea·cart [ˈtiˌkart; ˈtiː-kɑːt] *n.* =**tea wagon.**

‡**teach** [titʃ; tiːtʃ] *v.,* **taught** [tɔt; tɔːt], **teach·ing,** *n.* —*v.t.* 教;教授;教導;訓練。to *teach* him a lesson. 給他一個教訓。Soldiers are *taught* to obey orders. 軍人被教以服從命令。—*v.i.* ①教授;教書。He *teaches* for a living. 他以教書爲生。②被講解。a book that *teaches* easily. 一本好教的書。—*n.* 【俚】=**teacher.**

teach·a·bil·i·ty [ˌtitʃəˈbɪlətɪ; ˌtiːtʃəˈbiliti] *n.* 可教;可教性。

teach·a·ble [ˈtitʃəbḷ; ˈtiːtʃəbl] *adj.* 可教的;可訓的。

‡**teach·er** [ˈtitʃɚ; ˈtiːtʃə] *n.* 教師。Nature was his only *teacher.* 大自然是他唯一的教師。

tea chest 茶箱。

teach-in [ˈtitʃˌɪn; ˈtiːtʃ-in] *n., pl.* **teach-ins.** 美國大學中,教授或學者爲抗議政府重大政策而舉行之長期不間斷的演講。

***teach·ing** [ˈtitʃɪŋ; ˈtiːtʃiŋ] *n.* ①教;教授;教書。②(常 *pl.*)教訓;教旨。—*adj.* 教師的;教書的。

teaching assistant (大學)助教。

teaching fellow 大學裏兼任助教或講師之研究生。

teaching hospital 醫學院之附屬醫院。

teaching machine 教學用機器。

tea cloth ①茶几之桌布。②擦茶具用之溫抹布。

tea cozy (or **cosy**) 茶壺外面之保溫布袋。

tea·cup [ˈtiˌkʌp; ˈtiːkʌp] *n.* 茶杯;滿茶杯。

tea·cup·ful [ˈtikʌpˌfʊl; ˈtiːkʌpˌful] *n.* 一滿茶杯之容量(約有四盎斯)。

tea dance ①供下午茶點的舞會;茶舞。②下午之舞會。

tea fight =**tea party②.**

tea garden 【主英】①露天小吃或點心館。②茶園。

tea·gown [ˈtiˌgaun; ˈtiːgaun] *n.* 婦女赴茶會等所着之服裝。

Teague [tig; tiːg] *n.* 【蔑】愛爾蘭人。

tea house 茶館;茶室。(亦作**teahouse**)

teak [tik; tiːk] *n.* ①【植物】(東印度之)麻栗樹;柚木。②柚木之木材(通常用以造船)。

tea·ket·tle [ˈtiˌkɛtḷ; ˈtiːˌketl] *n.* 水壺。

teak·wood [ˈtikˌwʊd; ˈtiːkwud] *n.* 柚木之木材。

teal [til; tiːl] *n., pl.* **teals, teal.** 小鳧;小水鴨。

tea-lead [ˈtiˌlɛd; ˈtiːled] *n.* 做茶箱襯裏用的鉛與錫的合金。

‡**team** [tim; tiːm] *n.* ①隊;組。a football *team.* 足球隊。I am not on any *team.* 我不是任何隊的隊員。②套在一起共同工作的一組馬或其他牲口。***a whole*** (or ***full***) ***team*** 專家;冠軍;能幹之人。***double team*** 【美方】兩馬拉的車。***single team*** 【美方】單馬拉的

車。—*v.t.* & *v.i.* ①聯成一組；聯合工作。②駕車載運。to *team* lumber. 駕車載運木材。*team up with...* 與…協力從事。—*adj.* 隊的；團體的；以隊爲主的；靠全隊之力的。*team* game.以隊爲單位的比賽。—**er,** *n.* 「隊友。」

team·mate [ˈtimˌmet; ˈtiːmmeit] *n.*

team·ster [ˈtimstɚ; ˈtiːmstə] *n.* ①趕牲口者。②駕駛曳引卡車者；運輸工會會員。

team·work [ˈtimˌwɝk; ˈtiːmwəːk] *n.* ①聯合工作；聯合行動；協調合作。②需組成隊才能做的工作。「爭吵。」

tea party ①午後茶會。②暴動；喧嚷之

tea plant 茶樹。

tea·pot [ˈtiˌpɑt; ˈtiːpɔt] *n.* 茶壺。

tea·poy [ˈtipɔɪ; ˈtiːpɔi] *n.* ①茶几。②三脚几。

‡tear¹ [tɪr; tiə] *n.* ①淚；淚滴。Suddenly she burst into *tears.* 她突然哭起來了。to shed *tears.* 流淚；哭泣。②玻璃器皿中作裝飾用故意留的氣泡。③似淚珠之物。④(*pl.*)悲哀。*in tears* 哭泣。—*v.i.* 流淚。—*v.t.* 使淚汪汪。

‡tear² [tɛr; tɛə] *v.,* **tore** [tor; tɔː], **torn** [torn; tɔːn], **tear·ing,** *n.* —*v.t.* ①撕；扯；撕裂；扯破。Don't *tear* up paper. 不要撕紙。to *tear* off a leaf from a calendar. 撕下一張日曆。②離開。③破壞(國家等的)安寧；使痛苦；使煩惱(大抵用於被動式)。a heart *torn* by grief. 憂傷之心。④使破裂；使受傷。⑤使分裂。⑥猛取；搶。⑦猛挖；猛鑿。—*v.i.* ①撕破；被撕破。Paper *tears* easily. 紙很容易被撕破。②〖俗〗衝；狂跑；急奔。An automobile came *tearing* along. 一部汽車衝過來。③趕快；匆忙。*be torn between* 依違於兩種選擇之間。*tear around* **a.** 到處亂衝。**b.** 過放肆的生活。*tear at* 傷害；傷及；損壞。*tear down* **a.** 使瓦解；破壞。**b.** 拆開；拆掉；拆除。*tear into* **a.** 向…突襲。**b.** 嚴予斥責。*tear it* 〖主英〗使(希望等)化爲烏有。*tear off* 草率湊成。*tear one's hair* 扯髮(表示憤怒、絕望等)。*tear up* **a.** 挖開。**b.** 撕掉；撕毀。—*n.* ①撕；扯。②破處；裂縫；磨損。③匆忙；衝；趕。④〖俚〗狂飲。⑤〖俚〗暴怒。

tear bomb [tɪr～; tiə～] 催淚彈。(亦作 **tear shell**) 「(機器等之)解體；拆卸。」

tear·down [ˈtɛrˌdaun; ˈtɛədaun] *n.*

tear·drop [ˈtɪrˌdrɑp; ˈtiə-drɔp] *n.* ①淚珠。②淚珠形之物。「②極厲害的東西。」

tear·er [ˈtɛrɚ; ˈtɛərə] *n.* ①撕裂者。

tear·ful [ˈtɪrfəl; ˈtiəful] *adj.* ①充滿眼淚的；哭泣的。*tearful* entreaties. 淚汪汪的乞求。②使人流淚的；悲傷的。—**ly,** *adv.*

tear gas [tɪr～; tiə～] 催淚毒氣。

tear-gas [ˈtɪrˌgæs; ˈtiəˈgæs] *v.t.,* **-gassed, -gas·sing.** 向…投催淚彈。

tear·ing [ˈtɛrɪŋ; ˈtɛəriŋ] *adj.* ①强烈的；猛烈的；激烈的。②撕裂的。③〖英俚〗很好的；頭等的。—*adv.*〖俗〗狂暴地。

tear-jerk·er [ˈtɪrˌdʒɝkɚ; ˈtiəˌdʒəːkə] *n.* 〖美俗〗主題非常悲慘之電影或戲劇。(亦作 **tearjerker**) 「不流淚的。」

tear·less [ˈtɪrlɪs; ˈtiəlis] *adj.* 無淚的；

tear mask 防催淚毒氣之面具。

tea·room [ˈtiˌrum; ˈtiːrum] *n.*①茶室；茶館。②一種小餐館。

tea rose 〖植物〗任何具有茶味的玫瑰。

tear·proof [ˈtɛrˌpruf; ˈtɛəpruːf] *adj.* 撕不破的。「戶以證明廣告已刊出用的)。」

tear sheet 樣張(報紙或雜誌送給廣告

tear·stain [ˈtɪrˌsten; ˈtiə-stein] *n.* 淚痕。—**ed,** *adj.* 「封口用的帶狀物。」

tear strip [tɛr～; tɛə～] 罐頭、紙盒等

tear·y [ˈtɪrɪ; ˈtiəri] *adj.,* **tear·i·er, tear·i·est.** ①流淚的；哭泣的。②淚的；像淚的。③令人落淚的。

***tease** [tiz; tiːz] *v.,* **teased, teas·ing,** *n.* —*v.t.* ①揶揄；嘲弄；困惱。②懇請；固求。③梳理。to *tease* wool. 梳理羊毛。④使(布等)起絨毛。*tease up* 加以修整。—*n.* ①揶揄。②好揶揄他人者。③〖俚〗錢。—**teas·ing·ly,** *adv.*

tea·sel [ˈtizl; ˈtiːzl] *n., v.,* **-sel(l)ed, -sel·(l)ing.** —*n.* ①〖植物〗起絨草。②起絨草之乾果球。③任何用以使布上起絨毛之機械。—*v.t.* 使(布)起絨毛。(亦作 **teazel, teazle**)

teas·er [ˈtizɚ; ˈtiːzə] *n.* ①使人困惱之人或物；揶揄者；嘲弄者。②〖俗〗使人煩惱的問題；難題；難事。③〖新聞〗(亦作 **eyebrow, highline,** 或 **overline**) 用花體排在標題上面的短標題，目的在引人注意。

tea service (or **set**) 整套茶具。

tea shop ①茶館。②〖英〗小吃館。

***tea·spoon** [ˈtiˌspun; ˈtiːspuːn] *n.* 茶匙；小調羹。

***tea·spoon·ful** [ˈtispunˌful; ˈtiː-spu(ː)nˌful] *n.* 一茶匙的容量。「之物。」

teat [tit; tiːt] *n.* ①乳頭。②任何似乳頭

tea table 茶几。

tea-things [ˈtiˌθɪŋz; ˈtiːθiŋz] *n. pl.* 茶具。(亦作 **tea things**)

tea·time [ˈtiˌtaɪm; ˈtiːtaim] *n.* 〖英〗下午吃茶用點心之時間(通常在午後四、五點鐘)。(亦作 **tea time**)

tea tray 茶盤。「輪茶檯。」

tea wagon (用以放茶具及盤碟之)有

tec [tɛk; tek] *n.* 〖俚〗偵探(爲 detective 之略)。「nology.」

tec. ①technical. ②technician. ③tech-

Tech, Tec [tɛk; tek] *n.* 〖俚〗工學院(=technical institute).

tech. ① technical. ② technically. ③ technology.

tech·ne·ti·um [tɛkˈniʃɪəm; tekˈniː-ʃiəm] *n.* 〖化〗鎝(金屬元素，符號爲 Tc).

tech·ne·tron·ic [ˌtɛknəˈtrɑnɪk; ˌteknəˈtrɔnik] *adj.* 受科技影響、控制的。

tech·nic [ˈtɛknɪk; ˈteknik] *n.* =**technique.** —*adj.* 〖罕〗=**technical.**

***tech·ni·cal** [ˈtɛknɪkl; ˈteknikl] *adj.* ①工藝的；工業的。a *technical* school. 工業學校。②專門的；學術上的；技術上的。*technical* terms. 術語；專門名詞。③有關專門技術的。④根據某些科學、藝術或比賽之規則的。⑤由供求律來決定物價之市場的。—**ly,** *adv.*

tech·ni·cal·i·ty [ˌtɛknɪˈkælətɪ; ˌtekniˈkæliti] *n., pl.* **-ties.** ①專門的事項、細節、用語、表現等。②專門之性質；專門性。

technical knockout 〖拳擊〗技術擊倒。「技術軍士。」

technical sergeant (美國陸軍之)

tech·ni·cian [tɛkˈnɪʃən; tekˈniʃən] *n.* ①技術人員；專門技師。②精通於音樂、繪畫、寫作之技巧者。③(美軍)技術士兵；技工。

tech·ni·col·or [ˈtɛknɪˌkʌlɚ; ˈtekniˌkʌlə] *n.* ①〖電影〗天然色攝影術。②(T-)天然色攝影之商標。③奪目之彩色；五光十色。

tech·ni·col·ored [ˈtɛknɪˌkʌlɚd; ˈtekniˌkʌləd] *adj.* ①天然色的。②五光十色的。

tech·nics [ˈtɛknɪks; ˈtekniks] *n. pl.*(作

sing or *pl.* 解)①工藝學;手藝。②手法;技藝;技巧。

*__tech·nique__ 〔tɛk'nik; tek'ni:k, 'tekni:k〕 *n.* ①技術;技藝;技巧;(技藝之)表演法。②方法。

tech·noc·ra·cy 〔tɛk'nɑkrəsɪ; tek'nɔkrəsi〕 *n.* 技術專家政治;技術主義(1932年美國所提倡的一種學說,主張一切經濟資源、社會制度,由科學家及工程師管理)。

tech·no·crat 〔'tɛknə,kræt; 'teknəkræt〕 *n.* 贊成技術專家政治者。

technol. technology.

tech·no·log·i·cal 〔,tɛknə'lɑdʒɪkl; ,teknə'lɔdʒikl〕 *adj.* ①工業技術的;關於工業技術的。②由工業技術所致的;由工業發展所形成的。(亦作 **technologic**) —**ly,** *adv.*

tech·nol·o·gist 〔tɛk'nɑlədʒɪst; tek'nɔlədʒist〕 *n.* 工藝學者;工藝學家。

tech·nol·o·gy 〔tɛk'nɑlədʒɪ; tek'nɔlədʒi〕 *n.* ①工業技術。②術語。③方法;技術。

tech·no·ma·ni·a 〔,tɛknə'menɪə; ,teknə'meinjə〕 *n.* 對科技之過度狂熱。

tech·no·pho·bi·a 〔,tɛknə'fobɪə; ,teknə'foubiə〕 *n.*科技恐懼症(恐懼科技對社會或環境產生不良效果)。

tech·no·struc·ture 〔,tɛknə'strʌktʃə; ,teknə'strʌktʃə〕 *n.* 控制社會科技的一羣人。

tech·y 〔'tɛtʃɪ; 'tetʃi〕 *adj.,* **tech·i·er, tech·i·est.** 易怒的;暴躁的。(亦作 **tetchy**)

tec·tol·o·gy 〔tɛk'tɑlədʒɪ; tek'tɔlədʒi〕 *n.*〖生物〗組織形態學。

tec·ton·ic 〔tɛk'tɑnɪk; tek'tɔnik〕 *adj.* ①構造的;築造的;建築的。②〖地質〗地殼結構的。③〖生物〗構造的;構成的。

tec·ton·ics 〔tɛk'tɑnɪks; tek'tɔniks〕 *n.* ①構造學;築造學;構造術。②結構地質學。

Ted 〔tɛd; ted〕 *n.* ①〖英俚〗=**Teddy boy.** ②男子名(Edward 或 Theodore 之暱稱)。

ted 〔tɛd; ted〕 *v.t.,* **ted·ded, ted·ding.** ①攤開曬(乾草等);攤乾。②攤開;散開。

ted·der 〔'tɛdə; 'tedə〕 *n.* 攤草(使曬乾)的人;攤草機。

Ted·dy, ted·dy 〔'tɛdɪ; 'tedi〕 *n.*〖英俚〗=**Teddy boy.**

ted·dy bear 〔'tɛdɪ～; 'tedi～〕 一種有絨毛的玩具熊。

Teddy boy 〖俗〗穿愛德華七世時代服裝之英國不良少年。(亦作 **teddy boy**)

Teddy gang 〖英〗太保組織;不良少年幫派。(亦作 **teddy gang**)

Teddy girl 〖俗〗①穿愛德華七世時代服裝之英國太妹。②Teddy boy 之女友。(亦作 **teddy girl**)

Te De·um 〔ti'diəm; 'ti:'di(:)əm〕〖拉〗①(天主教及英國國教於早禱及其他特殊場合所唱之)讚美詩。②此種讚美詩之樂曲。

*__te·di·ous__ 〔'tidɪəs, 'tidʒəs; 'ti:djəs〕 *adj.* 冗長而乏味的;令人生厭的。—**ly,** *adv.* —**ness,** *n.*

te·di·um 〔'tidɪəm; 'ti:djəm〕 *n.* 冗長而討厭;煩悶;厭煩。

tee¹ 〔ti; ti:〕 *n., v.,* **teed, tee·ing.** —*n.* ①鐵環戲或其他遊戲之目標。②〖高爾夫〗開球區域。③〖高爾夫〗球座(由小沙堆、塑膠或橡皮所構成)。—*v.t.*置(高爾夫球)於球座上。***teed off*** 不高興;生氣。I was *teed off* because the chief had me type his inventory. 我因主任要我用打字機打他的目錄而不高興。***tee off*** **a.** 〖高爾夫〗開球。**b.** 開始。**c.** 使發怒。

tee² *n.* ①T或t字。②T或丁字形物;丁形管;T形棒。***to a tee*** 精確地。—*adj.* T形的。

teeing ground 〖高爾夫〗開球區。

teem¹ 〔tim; ti:m〕 *v.i.* 充滿;富於;多。

teem² *v.t.* 傾出;倒出。—*v.i.*(雨、水等)傾倒而出。

teem·ing 〔'timɪŋ; 'ti:miŋ〕 *adj.* ①蝟集的;豐富的。②多產的;結實多的。

teen¹ 〔tin; ti:n〕 *n.* 〖古,方〗①傷害;損壞。②悲哀;不幸。③憤怒;煩惱。—*v.t.*〖蘇,英方〗①激怒;使煩惱。②傷害;損壞。

teen² *n.* ①=**teenager.** ②(特指)十幾歲的少女。—*adj.* 十幾歲(從十三到十九歲)的。

-teen 〖字尾〗表"自十三到十九之數的"之義。

teen age 從十三歲到十九歲的年齡。

teen-age 〔'tin,edʒ; 'ti:neidʒ〕 *adj.* 十幾歲(從十三到十九歲)的。

teen·ag·er 〔'tin,edʒə; 'ti:n,eidʒə〕 *n.* 十幾歲的孩子(特指十三歲至十九歲者)。(亦作 **teener**)

teens 〔tinz; ti:nz〕 *n. pl.* 十三歲至十九歲之年齡(以 teen 爲語尾之年齡)。a girl in her *teens.* 妙齡女郎;十幾歲的女孩子。

tee·ny 〔'tinɪ; 'ti:ni〕 *adj.,* **-ni·er, -ni·est.** 〖俗〗很小的;極小的。

teen·y-bop·per 〔'tinɪ,bɑpə; 'ti:ni,bɔpə〕 *n.* 〖美俚〗(服飾、音樂等追求時髦,有時態度上模倣嬉皮的)十幾歲的女孩(有時亦指男孩)。

tee·ny-wee·ny 〔'tinɪ'winɪ; 'ti:ni'wi:ni〕 *adj.* 〖俗〗很小的;極小的。(亦作 **teenie-weenie**)

tee·pee 〔'tipi; 'ti:pi:〕 *n.* =**tepee.**

tee shirt =**T-shirt.**

tee·ter 〔'titə; 'ti:tə〕 *v.i.* 〖美俗〗①蹣跚地走。②搖搖欲墜。③玩蹺蹺板。—*v.t.* 使搖擺;使搖動。—*n.* 搖擺;搖動。

*__tee·ter·board__ 〔'titə,bord; 'ti:təbɔ:d〕 *n.* 蹺蹺板。

*__teeth__ 〔tiθ; ti:θ〕 *n.* pl. of **tooth.**

teethe 〔tið; ti:ð〕 *v.i.,* **teethed, teeth·ing.** 生牙;出牙齒。

teeth·er 〔'tiðə; 'ti:ðə〕 *n.*(給嬰孩長牙時咬的)玩具。

teeth·ing 〔'tiðɪŋ; 'ti:ðiŋ〕 *n.* 乳齒之生長;出牙。***teething troubles*** **a.** 孩子長齒時一陣一陣的哭鬧。 **b.** 任何事業開始時遭遇的麻煩。

teething ring 給生齒嬰兒咬的象牙等之環。

teeth·ridge 〔'tiθ,rɪdʒ; 'ti:θridʒ〕 *n.*上牙根內側。

tee·to·tal 〔ti'totl; ti:'toutl〕 *adj.* ①戒酒的。②〖俗〗全然的;絕對的。***teetotal drink*** 不含酒精的飲料。—*v.i.* 戒酒;滴酒不入。

tee·to·tal·er 〔ti'totlə; ti:'toutlə〕 *n.* 不喝酒者。(亦作 **teetotaller**)

tee·to·tal·ism 〔ti'totl,ɪzəm; ti:'toutlizm〕 *n.* 禁酒主義;禁酒之實踐;絕對禁酒。—**tee·to·tal·ist,** *n.*

tee·to·tum 〔ti'totəm; 'ti:tou'tʌm〕 *n.* 手轉陀螺;捻轉兒。

tee·vee 〔'ti'vi; 'ti:'vi:〕 *n.* 〖俗〗電視(=television, TV)。

t.e.g. top edge gilt. 〖裝釘〗天頭金邊;(書)上面的金邊。

teg·u·lar 〔'tɛgjələ; 'tegjulə〕 *adj.* ①瓦的;似瓦的。②由瓦組成的。③排列如瓦的。

teg·u·ment 〔'tɛgjəmənt; 'tegjumənt〕 *n.* 皮;覆皮;外殼。

teg·u·men·ta·ry 〔,tɛgjə'mɛntərɪ; ,tegju'mentəri〕 *adj.* 動物身體之皮的;覆皮的;作覆皮用的。

te-hee 〔ti'hi; ti:'hi:〕 *interj.* 嘻嘻!—*n.* 嘻笑;嗤笑。—*v.i.* 嘻笑;嗤嗤而笑。

T

Te·he·ran, Te·hran 〔ˌtɪəˈrɑn, ˌtɛhəˈrɑn; tiəˈrɑːn, ˌtehəˈr-〕 *n.* 德黑蘭(伊朗之首都)。

tel. ①telegram. ②telegraph. ③telephone.

tel·a·mon 〔ˈtɛləmən; ˈteləmən〕 *n., pl.* **-mo·nes.**〖建築〗男像形支柱。

tel·au·to·gram 〔tɛlˈɔtəˌgræm; teˈlɔːtəgræm〕 *n.* 電報傳眞之文件及照片等。

tel·au·to·graph 〔tɛlˈɔtəˌgræf; teˈlɔːtəgrɑːf〕 *n.* 電報傳眞機。(亦作**TelAutograph**) **—ic,** *adj.*

Tel A·viv 〔ˈtɛləˈviv; ˈteləˈviːv〕 特拉維夫(以色列一城市)。

tel·e 〔ˈtɛlɪ; ˈteli〕 *n.*〖英俗〗=**television.** (亦作 **telly**)

tele-〖字首〗①表"遠距離;遠距離傳遞"之義。②表"電視"之義。

tele. television.

tel·e-cam·er·a 〔ˈtɛləˌkæmərə; ˈteləˌkæmərə〕 *n.* 遠距離照相機。

tel·e·cast 〔ˈtɛləˌkæst; ˈtelikɑːst〕 *v.,* **-cast** or **-cast·ed, -cast·ing,** *n.* —*v.t.* & *v.i.* 以電視廣播或播送。—*n.* 電視廣播;電視播送。**—er,** *n.*

tel·e·cine 〔ˈtɛləsaɪn; ˈteləsain〕 *n.* ①影片等非現場節目之電視廣播。②非現場節目之電視廣播室。③非現場節目之電視廣播設備。

tel·e·com·mu·ni·ca·tion 〔ˌtɛləkəˌmjunəˈkeʃən; ˈteli-kəˌmjuːniˈkeiʃən〕 *n.* 電信術; 電信學。(亦作 **telecommunications**)

tel·e·con·trol 〔ˈtɛləkənˈtrol; ˈtelikənˈtroul〕 *n.* (利用電波等之)遙控。

tel·e·cop·ter 〔ˈtɛləˌkɑptɚ; ˈteliˌkɔptə〕 *n.* 空中電視台(裝有電視攝影機及電視播送設備的直升機)。

tel·e·course 〔ˈtɛləˌkɔrs; ˈtelikɔːs〕 *n.* 「電視課程。」

tel·e·du 〔ˈtɛləˌdu; ˈteliduː〕 *n.*〖動物〗(爪哇、蘇門答臘、婆羅洲產之)獾。

tel·e·film 〔ˈtɛləˌfɪlm; ˈtelifilm〕 *n.* 電視影片。

teleg. ①telegram. ②telegraph. ③telegraphy.

tel·e·gen·ic 〔ˌtɛlɪˈdʒɛnɪk; ˌteliˈdʒenik〕 *adj.* 儀態等適於上電視的;適於被電視廣播的。(亦作 **videogenic**)

te·leg·o·ny 〔tɪˈlɛgənɪ; tiˈlegəni〕 *n.*〖生物〗感應遺傳;異父遺傳。

***tel·e·gram** 〔ˈtɛləˌgræm; ˈteligræm〕 *n.*電報;電信。to send a *telegram.* 打電報。

telegram blank (or **form**) 電報紙。

tel·e·gram·mic 〔ˌtɛləˈgræmɪk; ˌteliˈgræmik〕 *adj.* 簡短如電報的。

***tel·e·graph** 〔ˈtɛləˌgræf; ˈteligrɑːf〕 *n.* ①電報機;電信機。②電報; 電信。 —*v.t.* & *v.i.* ①打電報;以電報傳達。Shall I telephone or *telegraph?* 我該打電話還是打電報?②顯示;表示。

telegraph editor (報社之)外電新聞編輯。

te·leg·ra·pher 〔təˈlɛgrəfɚ; tiˈlegrəfə〕 *n.* =**telegraphist.**

tel·e·graph·ese 〔ˌtɛləgræˈfiz; ˈteligrɑːˈfiːz〕 *n.* 電報文體。

tel·e·graph·ic 〔ˌtɛləˈgræfɪk; ˌteliˈgræfik〕 *adj.* ①電報的。 a *telegraphic* machine. 電報機。②似電報的; 簡短如電報的。 ***telegraphic address*** 電報掛號。

te·leg·ra·phist 〔təˈlɛgrəfɪst; tiˈlegrəfist〕 *n.* 電報員; 報務員。

telegraph key 發報電鍵。

telegraph line (or **wire**) 電線; 電信線路。

telegraph office 電報局。

te·leg·ra·phone 〔təˈlɛgrəˌfon; tiˈlegrəfoun〕 *n.* 留聲電話機。

telegraph operater 報務員。

telegraph plant〖植物〗舞草。

telegraph pole (or **post**)電線桿。

telegraph receiver 收報機。

telegraph transmitter 發報機。

te·leg·ra·phy 〔təˈlɛgrəfɪ; tiˈlegrəfi〕 *n.* ①電報術; 電報法。 ②電報機之製造或使用。 ***wireless telegraphy***〖英〗無線電報(美國稱爲 radiotelegraphy).

tel·e·lec·ture 〔ˌtɛləˈlɛktʃɚ; ˌteliˈlektʃə〕 *n.* 電話授課(實施於裝有擴音器及對講機之教室或場所)。

tel·e·lens 〔ˈtɛləlɛnz; ˈtelilenz〕 *n.* (攝影機之)望遠透鏡。

tel·e·mark 〔ˈtɛləˌmɑrk; ˈtelimɑːk〕 *n.* 滑雪時之一種轉身或突然停步法。

tel·e·me·chan·ics 〔ˌtɛlɪməˈkænɪks; ˌtelimiˈkæniks〕 *n.*藉無線電操縱機械之科學。

te·lem·e·ter 〔təˈlɛmətɚ; ˈtelimiːtə〕 *n.* ①測距儀; 測遠計。②遠距離記錄儀。 —*v.t.* 以遠距離記錄儀傳送。

te·len·gi·scope 〔təˈlɛndʒəˌskop; təˈlendʒiskoup〕 *n.* 顯微望遠鏡。

teleo-〖字首〗**tele-** 之異體。

tel·e·ob·jec·tive 〔ˌtɛləɑbˈdʒɛktɪv; ˌteliɔbˈdʒektiv〕 *n.* 攝影機望遠透鏡。

tel·e·ol·o·gy 〔ˌtɛlɪˈɑlədʒɪ; ˌteliˈɔlədʒi〕 *n.*〖哲學〗目的論。**—tel·e·o·log·i·cal,** *adj.*

tel·e·op·er·a·tor 〔ˌtɛləˈɑpəˌretɚ; ˌteliˈɔpəreitə〕 *n.* 遙控機器人。

tel·e·path·ic 〔ˌtɛlɪˈpæθɪk; ˌteliˈpæθik〕 *adj.* 精神感應上的;心心相傳的。**—al·ly,** *adv.*

te·lep·a·thist 〔təˈlɛpəθɪst; tiˈlepəθist〕 *n.* ①信仰或研究精神感應者。 ②有精神感應能力者。

te·lep·a·thy 〔təˈlɛpəθɪ; tiˈlepəθi〕 *n.* 精神感應;心心相傳。

‡**tel·e·phone** 〔ˈtɛləˌfon; ˈtelifoun〕 *n., v.,* **-phoned, -phon·ing.** —*n.* 電話機; 電話。to talk through a *telephone.* 打電話談話。 —*v.i.* & *v.t.* 打電話;以電話報告;打電話給(某人)。*Telephone* me tomorrow. 明天打電話給我。

telephone book 電話簿。

telephone booth (or **box**) 電話亭。

telephone directory 電話用戶號碼簿。

telephone exchange ①電話局。②電話交換台。

telephone number 電話號碼。

telephone office 電話局。

telephone operator 接線生。

telephone receiver 聽筒。

telephone set 電話機。

telephone subscriber 電話用戶。

telephone switchboard ①電話交換臺。②電話交換機;總機。

telephone transmitter發話器;話筒。

tel·e·phon·ic 〔ˌtɛləˈfɑnɪk; ˌteliˈfɔnik〕 *adj.* 電話的。

te·leph·o·nist 〔təˈlɛfənɪst; tiˈlefənist, ˈtelifounist〕 *n.* 話務員;接線生。

tel·e·pho·no·graph 〔ˌtɛləˈfonəgræf; ˌteləˈfounəgrɑːf〕 *n.* 電話錄音機。

te·leph·o·ny 〔təˈlɛfənɪ; tiˈlefəni〕 *n.* ①電話學; 電話法。②電話機之製造或使用。 ***wireless telephony***〖英〗無線電話(美國稱爲 radiotelephony).

tel·e·pho·to 〔ˈtɛlɪˌfoto; ˈteliˈfoutou〕 *adj.* ①望遠鏡攝影的。②傳眞術的。 —*n.* = **telephotograph.**

tel·e·pho·to·graph [ˌtɛləˈfotəˌgræf; ˈteliˈfoutəgrɑːf] *n.* ①電傳照相。②電傳照相之圖片。③望遠攝影照片。—*v.t.* ①用遠距離照相機拍攝。②以傳眞法傳送。

tel·e·pho·to·graph·ic [ˌtɛləˌfotəˈgræfɪk; ˌteliˌfoutəˈgræfik] *adj.* 望遠攝影的。

tel·e·pho·tog·ra·phy [ˌtɛləfoˈtɑgrəfɪ; ˈtelifəˈtɔgrəfi] *n.* ①電傳照相術。②圖片傳眞術。③望遠攝影。

telephoto lens 遠距離照相機用的透鏡。

tel·e·pic·ture [ˈtɛlɪˌpɪktʃɚ; ˈteliˌpiktʃə] *n.*【美】電視之影像。

tel·e·play [ˈtɛlɪˌple; ˈtelipleі] *n.* 電視劇。

tel·e·print·er [ˈtɛlɪˌprɪntɚ; ˈteliˌprintə] *n.* 打字電報機。

Tel·e·prompt·er [ˈtɛlɪˌprɑmptɚ; ˈteliˌprɔmptə] *n.*【商標名】電視演講提示機。(亦作 **TelePrompTer**)

tel·e·ran [ˈtɛləræn; ˈteləræn] *n.*【航空】電視雷達導航。

tel·e·re·ceiv·er [ˈtɛlərɪˌsivɚ; ˈteləriˌsiːvə] *n.*【美】電視映影機; 電視接收機。

tel·e·re·cord·ing [ˌtɛlərɪˈkɔrdɪŋ; ˌteləriˈkɔːdiŋ] *n.* ①電視影片。②用電視影片播放的節目。

tel·er·gy [ˈtɛlɚdʒɪ; ˈtelədʒi] *n.* 精神感應力。

***tel·e·scope** [ˈtɛləˌskop; ˈteliskoup] *n., v.,* **-scoped, -scop·ing.** —*n.* 望遠鏡。—*v.t.* ①擠撞;相撞而嵌入。②縮短;簡略。—*v.i.* ①嵌進。②重疊。

telescope sight (槍砲上之)望遠瞄準器。(亦作 **telescopic sight**)

tel·e·scop·ic [ˌtɛləˈskɑpɪk; ˌteliˈskɔpik] *adj.* ①望遠鏡的。②用望遠鏡所見的。③祇能在望遠鏡中見到的。④視力所及甚遠的;看得遠的。⑤能自由伸縮的; 套筒式的。

te·les·co·pist [təˈlɛskəpɪst; tiˈleskəpist] *n.* 精於使用望遠鏡的人。

te·les·co·py [təˈlɛskəpɪ; tiˈleskəpi] *n.* 望遠鏡使用法;望遠鏡製造法。

tel·e·screen [ˈtɛləˌskrin; ˈteli-skriːn] *n.* 電視機螢光幕。

tel·e·seme [ˈtɛlɪˌsim; ˈtelisiːm] *n.*(旅館等處用以呼喚人的)信號裝置。

tel·e·sis [ˈtɛləsɪs; ˈtelisis] *n.* 利用天然力與社會力以達成某項目的之政策。

tel·e·ster·e·o·scope [ˌtɛləˈstɛrɪəˌskop; ˌteliˈstiəriəskoup] *n.* ①立體望遠鏡。②一種測定攝影距離的光學儀器。

tel·e·ther·mom·e·ter [ˌtɛlɪθɚˈmɑmətɚ; ˌteliθəˈmɔmitə] *n.*【物理】遠距離自記溫度計。

tel·e·thon [ˈtɛlɪθɑn; ˈteliθɔn] *n.* 連續數小時的電視節目(尤指以募款爲目的者)。

tel·e·type [ˈtɛlɪˌtaɪp; ˈtelitaip] *n., v.,* **-typed, -typ·ing.** —*n.* ①打字電報法傳遞。②(T-)【商標名】打字電報機。—*v.t.* & *v.i.* 用打字電報機拍發(電報)。

tel·e·type·set·ter [ˈtɛlɪˈtaɪpˌsɛtɚ; ˈteliˈtaipˌsetə] *n.* (自動)電報排字機。

tel·e·type·writ·er [ˌtɛləˈtaɪpˌraɪtɚ; ˌteliˈtaipˌraitə] *n.* 打字電報機。

tel·e·typ·ist [ˌtɛləˈtaɪpɪst; ˌteliˈtaipist] *n.* 打字電報機操作員。

tel·e·view [ˈtɛlɪˌvju; ˈtelivjuː] *v.t.* & *v.i.* 以電視機收看(某事件、表演)。—**er,** *n.*

tel·e·vise [ˈtɛləˌvaɪz; ˈtelivaiz] *v.,* **-vised, -vis·ing.** —*v.t.* ①由電視播送。②由電視看(節目、表演等)。—*v.i.* 廣播電視節目。

‡**tel·e·vi·sion** [ˈtɛləˌvɪʒən; ˈteliˌviʒən, ˈteliˈviʒən, ˌteliˈviʒən] *n.* 電視。(略作 **TV**) —**al,** *adj.*

tel·e·vi·sor [ˈtɛlɪˌvaɪzɚ; ˈtelivaizə] *n.* ①電視播送機;電視接收機。②收看電視的人。

tel·e·vox [ˈtɛləˌvɑks; ˈtelivɔks] *n.* 「機械人。

tel·ex [ˈtɛlɛks; ˈteleks] *n.* ①電立時(打字電報);商務交換電報。②(T-) 其商標名。

telg. telegram. —*v.t.* 拍發電立時。

‡**tell** [tɛl; tel] *v.,* **told** [told; tould], **tell·ing,** *n.* —*v.t.* ①述; 講; 說。to *tell* the truth (a lie). 說實(謊)話。to *tell* fortunes. 算命。②告知;告訴;向(某人)講述。Don't *tell* me, let me guess. 不要告訴我, 讓我猜。So I have been *told*. 我所聽說的是如此。③辨識;識別;斷定;知道(常與can, could, be able to等連用)。I can't *tell* the difference between them. 我看不出這二者之間的區別。④吩咐;命令。You must do as I *tell* you. 你必須按照我所吩咐的做。⑤計算;數。We were twenty all *told*. 我們共計二十人。⑥明白告知。—*v.i.* ①敍述;報告。to *tell* of bygone days. 講述往昔的事情。②奏效;發生影響。Every shot *told*. 百發百中。③洩露。Promise me not to *tell*. 答應我不洩露出去。④說。He is always *telling*, never doing. 他老是說而不做。⑤顯示; 顯露。⑥斷定; 確定。Who can *tell?* 誰能斷定? ***I (can) tell you*** 的確如此; 我强調。***let me tell you*** =I (can) tell you. ***tell me another***【諷】簡直難以置信;說下去罷! ***tell of*** 顯示。***tell off*** a. 分派。b.【俗】責罵。***tell on*** a. 使疲倦。b.【俗】說…的壞話;攻訐告密。***tell one's beads*** 念佛;祈禱。***tell one's*** (or ***its***) ***own tale*** 不言而喩。***tell tales*** 洩露祕密; 講別人的壞話。***tell*** (***the***) ***time*** 辨識並道出鐘錶的時刻。***there's no telling*** 不可知。***You are telling me!***【俚】你所說的我已知道得很清楚; 我同意你的說法! —*n.*【方】話。I'd like to have a *tell* with you. 我想跟你談一談。

tell·a·ble [ˈtɛləbḷ; ˈteləbl] *adj.* 可述說的;值得說的。

tell·er [ˈtɛlɚ; ˈtelə] *n.* ①講話者;敍述者。②(銀行之)出納員。③計算者。—**ship,** *n.*

tell·ing [ˈtɛlɪŋ; ˈteliŋ] *adj.* 有效的;有力的;顯著的。a *telling* blow (speech). 有力的一擊(演講)。—**ly,** *adv.*

tell·tale [ˈtɛlˌtel; ˈtel-teil] *n.* ①揭人陰私者; 搬弄是非者。②顯示器; 計時器。③【航海】舵角指示器。④(火車鐵軌之)標示。⑤【音樂】(風琴上之) 氣壓指示器。—*adj.* ①洩露祕密的。②(機械等)顯示或警告的。

tel·lu·ric[1] [tɛˈlurɪk; teˈljurik] *adj.* ①地球的。②土地的;生長自土地的。

tel·lu·ric[2] *adj.*【化】碲的;含碲(尤指六價碲)的。

tel·lu·ride [ˈtɛljuˌraɪd, -rɪd; ˈtelju-raid, -rid] *n.*【化】碲化物。

tel·lu·ri·um [tɛˈlurɪəm; teˈljuəriəm] *n.*【化】碲(非金屬元素,符號爲Te)。

tel·ly [ˈtɛlɪ; ˈteli] *n.*【主英】(the-) 電視 (=television).

tel·o·type [ˈtɛləˌtaɪp; ˈtelətaip] *n.* 打字電報機;打字電報。

tel·pher [ˈtɛlfɚ; ˈtelfə] *n.* 電動高架索道車。—*adj.* 電動高架索道車的。—*v.t.* 以電動索道車運輸。(亦作 **telfer**)

tel·pher·age [ˈtɛlfərɪdʒ; ˈtelfəridʒ] *n.* 電動高架索道運輸(系統)。(亦作**telferage**)

Tel·star [ˈtɛlˌstɑr; ˈtel-stɑː] *n.*【商標

名〗通信衛星。

tem·blor 〔tɛm'blɔr; tem'blɔː〕 *n., pl.* **-blors, -blo·res** 〔-'blɔrɛs; -'blɔːres〕.〖美〗地震。

tem·er·ar·i·ous 〔ˌtɛmə'rɛrɪəs; ˌtemə'rɛəriəs〕 *adj.* 魯莽的;孟浪的。

te·mer·i·ty 〔tə'mɛrətɪ; ti'meriti〕 *n.* 魯莽;孟浪。

temp. ①temperance. ②temperature. ③temporal. ④temporary. ⑤tempore(拉 =in the time of).

*__tem·per__ 〔'tɛmpɚ; 'tempə〕 *n.* ①氣質;性情;心情;脾氣(凡不加形容字時,均指壞脾氣)。He has a quick *temper*. 他的性情暴躁。②(鋼鐵、黏土等之)硬度。③調劑;加入某物使其性質起變化的物質。④趨向;傾向。the *temper* of the times. 時勢。***be out of temper*** 發脾氣。***keep*** (or ***control***) ***one's temper*** 忍住怒氣。***lose one's temper*** 發怒。—*v.t.* ①緩和;調劑。to *temper* strong drink with water. 用水將烈酒沖淡。②鍛鍊(金屬等);煉(黏土等)。③〖音樂〗調整;調(樂器的)音。④調(色)。***God tempers the wind to the shorn lamb.***〖諺〗樹小不招風(缺點或不幸也有好處)。—*v.i.* 緩和;調劑。—**a·ble,** *adj.* —**er,** *n.*

tem·per·a 〔'tɛmpərə; 'tempərə〕 *n.*〖美術〗①塗料混以蛋黃等使色彩暗晦之一種畫法。②用此法所繪之畫。

*__tem·per·a·ment__ 〔'tɛmprəmənt, -pərə-; 'tempərəmənt, -prə-〕 *n.* ①氣質;資質。②特別的氣質。③〖音樂〗調率;整調。

tem·per·a·men·tal 〔ˌtɛmprə'mɛntl; ˌtemprə'mentl〕 *adj.* ①由於氣質的;本質的。②有特殊氣質的。③容易生氣的;性情多變的。

tem·per·a·men·tal·ly 〔ˌtɛmpərə'mɛntlɪ; ˌtempərə'mentli〕 *adv.* 在氣質上。

*__tem·per·ance__ 〔'tɛmprəns; 'temprəns〕 *n.* ①節制;自制;克己。②節飲;禁酒。the *temperance* movement. 禁酒運動。

*__tem·per·ate__ 〔'tɛmprɪt; 'temprit〕 *adj.* ①有節制的;適度的。He is a *temperate* man. 他是一個有節制的人。②溫和的。a *temperate* climate. 溫和的氣候。the *temperate* zone. 溫帶。③(飲酒)有節制的。

tem·per·ate·ly 〔'tɛmpərɪtlɪ; 'tempritli〕 *adv.* 有節制地;適度地。

tem·per·ate·ness 〔'tɛmpərɪtnɪs; 'tempritnis〕 *n.* ①有節制;適度。②溫和。

‡**tem·per·a·ture** 〔'tɛmprətʃɚ; 'tempritʃə〕 *n.* ①溫度。②體溫。The nurse took the *temperatures* of all the patients. 護士爲所有的病人量體溫。③發燒;發熱狀態(=fever)。④熱烈或激烈的程度;熱度。***have*** (or ***run***) ***a temperature*** 有熱度;發燒。He *had a temperature* for three days. 他一連三天都在發燒。

tem·pered 〔'tɛmpɚd; 'tempəd〕 *adj.* ①有(某種)氣質的;有(某種)脾氣的。good-*tempered*. 好脾氣的。hot-*tempered*. 躁脾氣的。②有所需之密度、硬度等的;鍛鍊的。③混入其他因素或性質的。④〖音樂〗平均律的。⑤溫和的。⑥威力減弱的。

*__tem·pest__ 〔'tɛmpɪst; 'tempist〕 *n.* ①暴風雨;風暴。②類似暴風雨的情形;騷亂。***tempest in a teapot*** 無事自擾;小題大做。—*v.t.* 擾亂;使騰湧。—*v.i.* 大發脾氣;狂怒;猛衝。She *tempested* out. 她大發雷霆地衝到外面。

tem·pes·tu·ous 〔tɛm'pɛstʃuəs; tem'pestjuəs〕 *adj.* ①有暴風雨的。②騷動的;暴亂的。

tem·pes·tu·ous·ly 〔tɛm'pɛstʃuəslɪ; tem'pestjuəsli〕 *adv.* 暴風雨似地;狂亂地;猛烈地。

tem·pes·tu·ous·ness 〔tɛm'pɛstʃuəsnɪs; tem'pestjuəsnis〕 *n.* ①風暴。②暴亂;騷亂;動亂。

Tem·plar 〔'tɛmplɚ; 'templə〕 *n.* ①聖堂武士(1118年左右在耶路撒冷組織之保衛聖墓及保護參詣聖地之香客的武士團之一員)。②〖美〗互濟會(Freemasons)之一會員。***Knights Templars*** 聖堂武士團。

tem·plate 〔'tɛmplɪt; 'templit〕 *n.* = **templet.**

‡**tem·ple**¹ 〔'tɛmpl; 'templ〕 *n.* ①廟;寺;神殿;祠堂。②禮拜堂;教堂。③(常 T-)猶太人在古耶路撒冷所建三廟宇之一。④(T-)美國猶他州 Salt Lake City 摩門教之禮拜堂。⑤(T-)聖堂武士(Knights Templars)在倫敦之住所。

*__tem·ple__² *n.* ①顳顬;(俗稱)太陽穴。②眼鏡兩側支架之任一。

tem·ple³ *n.* 織布機上使布保持適當寬度之裝置。

tem·plet 〔'tɛmplɪt; 'templit〕 *n.* ①樣板;金屬模片。②〖建築〗承樑短木或短石;門口支桁之樑。③〖造船〗楔木。

tem·po 〔'tɛmpo; 'tempou〕 *n., pl.* **-pos, -pi** 〔-pi; -piː〕. ①〖音樂〗速度;拍子。②動率;進行速度;活動速度。

tem·po·ral¹ 〔'tɛmpərəl; 'temprəl〕 *adj.* ①現世的;世俗的。*temporal* affair. 俗事。②時的;時間的;表示時間關係的。③一時的;暫時的。—*n.* (常 *pl.*) 世俗之事物。

tem·po·ral² *adj.* 顳顬的;太陽穴的。—*n.* =**temporal bone.**

temporal bone 〖解剖〗顳骨。

‡**tem·po·ral·i·ty** 〔ˌtɛmpə'rælətɪ; ˌtempə'ræliti〕 *n., pl.* **-ties.** ①暫時性。②一時的事物。③(常 *pl.*)物質方面的權利與財產等。④教外人士(非教士)。

*__tem·po·rar·i·ly__ 〔'tɛmpəˌrɛrəlɪ; 'temprərili〕 *adv.* 暫時地;一時地;臨時地。

*__tem·po·rar·y__ 〔'tɛmpəˌrɛrɪ; 'temprəri〕 *adj.* 暫時的;一時的;臨時的。a *temporary* job. 臨時工作。—*n.* 臨時人員;臨時之事物。—**tem·po·rar·i·ness,** *n.*

tem·po·rize 〔'tɛmpəˌraɪz; 'tempəraiz〕 *v.i.,* **-rized, -riz·ing.** ①因循;遷延。②順應時勢;見風使舵。③談判或周旋以拖延時間〖常 with〗。④姑息;妥協〖常 between, with〗。(亦作 **temporise**) —**tem·po·ri·za·tion, tem·po·riz·er,** *n.*

*__tempt__ 〔tɛmpt; tempt〕 *v.t.* ①勸誘;勾引。He was *tempted* to steal money. 他受誘惑而偷錢。②引誘;誘使。③激引;引起。to *tempt* the appetite. 引起食慾。④〖古〗考驗;試驗。⑤冒…之險。***tempt Providence*** 冒大險。—**a·ble,** *adj.*

*__temp·ta·tion__ 〔tɛmp'teʃən; temp'teiʃən〕 *n.* ①引誘;誘惑。②誘惑物。

tempt·er 〔'tɛmptɚ; 'temptə〕 *n.* 引誘者;誘惑者。***the Tempter*** 撒旦。

*__tempt·ing__ 〔'tɛmptɪŋ; 'temptiŋ〕 *adj.* 誘惑人的;迷人的;引人的。a *tempting* smell. 誘人的氣味。—**ly,** *adv.*

tempt·ress 〔'tɛmptrɪs; 'temptris〕 *n.* 誘人(爲惡)的婦女;迷惑人的婦女。

tem·pus fu·git 〔'tɛmpəs'fjudʒɪt; 'tempəs'fjuːdʒit〕〖拉〗光陰似箭(= time flies).

‡**ten** [tɛn; ten] *n.* ①十; 10。*Ten* to one he forgets it. 十之八九他忘記它了。②十個; 十人;十歲;十時;十分。a child of *ten.* 十歲的孩子。to come at *ten.* 十點鐘來。③(大小分類之) 第十號。She wears a *ten.* 她穿第十號。④〖數學〗十位。⑤十元鈔票;十鎊鈔票。***take ten*** 小憩。—*adj.* 十(個)的。*ten* times bigger. 大十倍;大得多。

ten. ①tenor. ②tenuto.

ten·a·bil·i·ty [ˌtɛnəˈbɪlətɪ; ˌtenəˈbiliti] *n.* ①可防守; 可堅守。②可支持; 可擁護。③有條理性;合邏輯性。④可繼續;可維持。

ten·a·ble [ˈtɛnəbl̩; ˈtenəbl] *adj.* ①可防守的;可堅守的。②(意見、思想等) 站得住的; 有條有理的。③可維持的。

te·na·cious [tɪˈneʃəs; tiˈneiʃəs] *adj.* ①抓住不放的。②固執的; 堅持到底的。③很強的。④黏得牢的;分不開的。

te·nac·i·ty [tɪˈnæsətɪ; tiˈnæsiti] *n.* ①固執;堅持。②倔強。③強記。④堅韌;黏着。

ten·an·cy [ˈtɛnənsɪ; ˈtenənsi] *n., pl.* **-cies.** ①租賃。②租賃期限。③租賃之土地或房屋。④佃戶;房客。⑤任職(期間)。

***ten·ant** [ˈtɛnənt; ˈtenənt] *n.* ①佃戶; 房客。②居住者。—*v.t.* 租賃。—*v.i.* 居住。

ten·ant·a·ble [ˈtɛnəntəbl̩; ˈtenəntəbl] *adj.* 可租賃的;可居住的。

tenant farmer 佃農。

ten·ant·less [ˈtɛnəntlɪs; ˈtenəntlis] *adj.* 空的;無人居住的。

tenant right (土地、房屋等之)租賃權。

ten·ant·ry [ˈtɛnəntrɪ; ˈtenəntri] *n.* ①租賃;占有。②tenant 之集合稱。

ten-cent store [ˈtɛnˈsɛnt～; ˈtenˈsent～] 賣廉價物品之雜貨店。

tench [tɛntʃ; tentʃ] *n., pl.* **tench·es, tench.** 鯉科之淡水魚。

Ten Commandments 〖聖經〗十誡。

‡**tend**[1] [tɛnd; tend] *v.i.* ①移向; 通向。Prices are *tending* upward. 物價上漲。②有某種傾向; 致使; 易於。Fruit *tends* to decay. 水果易於腐爛。③有助於。

***tend**[2] *v.t.* ①照管;照料。②〖古〗聽; 注意。—*v.i.* ①服侍;伺候 〖on, upon〗。②〖俗〗照料〖to〗。③〖古〗聽。

tend·ance [ˈtɛndəns; ˈtendəns] *n.* 照顧;服侍;看護。

***tend·en·cy** [ˈtɛndənsɪ; ˈtendənsi] *n., pl.* **-cies.** ①趨勢;傾向。②意向;癖性。

ten·den·tious [tɛnˈdɛnʃəs; tenˈdenʃəs] *adj.* 有目的的;宣傳的;有偏見的。

‡**ten·der**[1] [ˈtɛndɚ; ˈtendə] *adj.* ①柔軟的; 嫩的。*tender* meat. 嫩肉。②嬌性的;脆弱的。③親切的;溫柔的。She spoke *tender* words to the child. 她對那孩子說了些親切的話。④柔和的;溫和的。⑤易感的;善感的。to have a *tender* heart. 有惻隱之心。⑥幼稚的; 未成熟的。of *tender* age. 年幼。⑦疼痛的; 觸及即感疼痛的。⑧顧慮周到的。He handles people in a *tender* manner. 他以周到的態度應對他人。⑨需要技巧或仔細應付的。a *tender* situation. 一種微妙的情況。⑩(船)易翻覆的; 不穩定的。***have a tender conscience*** 爲小事而深感遺憾。—*v.t.* & *v.i.* (使)變脆弱。—**ly,** *adv.*

ten·der**[2] *v.t.* ①提出; 提供; 貢獻。He *tendered* his resignation. 他提出辭職。②〖法律〗償還 (金錢、貨物等)。—*v.i.* 投標。—*n.* ①提出;提議。②招標;投標。open *tender.* 公開招標。③提供物。④償付債務時必須接受之金錢、貨物等。legal tender*** 法定貨幣。—**er,** *n.*

tend·er[3] *n.* ①看守者; 照料者。②附屬船; 補給船。③(火車機車後之)煤水車。

ten·der·foot [ˈtɛndɚˌfʊt; ˈtendəfut] *n., pl.* **-foots, -feet.** ①〖美〗不慣於拓荒或開礦等艱辛生活之新手。②生手; 新手。③最低級的童子軍。

ten·der·heart·ed [ˈtɛndɚˈhɑrtɪd; ˈtendəˈhɑːtid] *adj.* 心腸柔軟的; 情深的; 易感動的;同情的;慈善的。

ten·der·ize [ˈtɛndəˌraɪz; ˈtendəraiz] *v.t.,* **-ized, -iz·ing.** 使嫩; 使柔和; 使軟。—**ten·der·iz·er,** *n.*

ten·der·loin [ˈtɛndɚˌlɔɪn; ˈtendəlɔin] *n.* 牛或豬之腰部的軟肉。

***ten·der·ness** [ˈtɛndɚnɪs; ˈtendənis] *n.* ①柔軟;嫩;嬌弱。②惻隱心;愛意。

ten·di·nous [ˈtɛndənəs; ˈtendinəs] *adj.* ①腱的;像腱的;腱性的。②包含腱的。

ten·don [ˈtɛndən; ˈtendən] *n.* 腱;筋。

ten·dril [ˈtɛndrɪl; ˈtendril] *n.* ①(植物之)卷鬚。②似卷鬚狀之物。

Ten·e·brae [ˈtɛnəˌbri; ˈtenibriː] *n. pl.* 〖天主教〗耶穌受難紀念聖歌 (復活節前一週之星期三、四、五下午與晚上所唱者)。

ten·e·brous [ˈtɛnəbrəs; ˈtenibrəs] *adj.* ①暗黑的; 陰沈的; 陰暗的。②難以了解的;難懂的。(亦作 **tenebrious**)

***ten·e·ment** [ˈtɛnəmənt; ˈtenimənt] *n.* ①家屋; 住宅。②一房客所租的一部分房屋。③共同住宅;多家合居之房屋。④居處。

ten·e·ment·ed [ˈtɛnəməntɪd; ˈteniməntid] *adj.* ①租給房客的。②由出租房屋所構成的。

tenement house =**tenement**③.

ten·et [ˈtɛnɪt; ˈtiːnet] *n.* 教理; 主義; 信條;教條。

ten·fold [ˈtɛnˈfold; ˈten-fould] *adj.* & *adv.* 十倍的(地);十重的(地)。

ten-gal·lon hat [ˈtɛnˈgælən～; ˈtenˈgælən～] (原爲美國牧童戴的)寬邊高呢帽。

Ten Major Construction Projects 十大建設計畫 (中華民國在臺灣省的建設計畫, 始於1973年)。

Tenn. Tennessee.

ten·ner [ˈtɛnɚ; ˈtenə] *n.* 〖俚〗①〖英〗十鎊之紙幣。②〖美〗十元之紙幣。

Ten·nes·see [ˌtɛnəˈsi; ˌtenəˈsiː] *n.* ①田納西州(美國中南部之一州, 首府爲Nashville). ②田納西河。

Tennessee Valley Authority 田納西流域管理局。(略作 **TVA**)

***ten·nis** [ˈtɛnɪs; ˈtenis] *n.* 網球。to play *tennis.* 打網球。

Ten·ny·son [ˈtɛnəsn̩; ˈtenisn] *n.* 但尼生 (Alfred, 1809–1892, 英國詩人, 1850–1892 爲桂冠詩人)。

ten·on [ˈtɛnən; ˈtenən] *n.* 榫。 —*v.t.* & *v.i.* 作榫於其上;以榫接合。

***ten·or** [ˈtɛnɚ; ˈtenə] *n.* ①一般趨勢;進程。②要旨;大意。③男高音;次中音。④唱男高音者; 唱次中音者。⑤樂譜中之男高音或次中音部分。⑥次中音樂器。—*adj.* 男高音的;次中音的。 *tenor* singer. 男高音歌手。

te·not·o·my [tɪˈnɑtəmɪ; tiˈnɔtəmi] *n.* 〖外科〗腱切斷術。

ten·pen·ny [ˈtɛnˌpɛnɪ; ˈtenpəni] *adj.* ①值十辨士的。②長三英寸的。

ten-per·cent·er [ˈtɛnpɚˈsɛntɚ; ˈtenpəˈsentə] *n.* 〖俚〗演員之經紀人(其報酬爲演員收入的十分之一, 故名)。(亦作 **ten per-**

center)

ten·pins ['tɛn͵pɪnz; 'tenpinz] *n. pl.* ①(作 *sing.* 解)【美】十柱球戲(保齡球之一種，以球滾擊排列成三角形之十根木柱之遊戲)。②十柱球戲之木柱;保齡球瓶。

ten-pound·er ['tɛn'paundɚ; 'ten'paundə] *n.* 十磅重之物(如魚等);值十鎊之物;十鎊之紙幣。

***tense**[1] [tɛns; tens] *adj.*, **tens·er, tens·est,** *v.*, **tensed, tens·ing.** —*adj.* 拉緊的;緊張的。 a *tense* atmosphere. 緊張的氣氛。 —*v.t.* 拉緊。—*v.i.* 變緊; 變爲緊張。 *tense up* (使)緊張。 You're all *tensed up.* 你太緊張了。 —**ly,** *adv.* —**ness,** *n.*

***tense**[2] *n.* 【文法】時態; 時式。時態是動詞爲表示動作或狀態的時間而具有的一種形式。

ten·si·bil·i·ty [͵tɛnsə'bɪlətɪ; ͵tensi'biliti] *n.* 伸長;引長;伸長性。

ten·si·ble ['tɛnsəbl; 'tensibl] *adj.* 可伸長的;可引長的;可伸張的;可引伸的。

ten·sile ['tɛnsl; 'tensail] *adj.* ①緊張的;伸張的;張力的。②可引伸的;可伸張的;可引長的。

ten·sil·i·ty [tɛn'sɪlətɪ; ten'siliti] *n.* 緊張;伸張;可伸張性。

ten·sim·e·ter [tɛn'sɪmətɚ; ten'simitə] *n.* 【物理】氣體壓力計。

ten·si·om·e·ter [͵tɛnsɪ'ɑmətɚ; ͵tensi'ɔmitə] *n.* 張力計。

***ten·sion** ['tɛnʃən; 'tenʃən] *n.* ①拉緊。②緊張;緊張狀態。③精神之緊張。④牽引力;應力。⑤控制牽引力等之裝置。⑥電壓。 high-*tension* wires. 高壓線。⑦氣體壓力。⑧張力。—*v.t.* 拉緊;張緊;使緊。 —**al,** *adj.*

ten·si·ty ['tɛnsətɪ; 'tensiti] *n.* 緊張。

ten·sor ['tɛnsɚ;'tensə] *n.* 【解剖】張肌。

ten-spot ['tɛn͵spɑt; 'tenspɔt] *n.* ①十元美鈔。②有十個花之紙牌。(亦作 **ten spot**)

ten-strike ['tɛn͵straɪk;'ten-straik] *n.* 【美】①(保齡球戲中將十柱完全擊倒之)一擊。②【俗】制勝成功之一舉;大成功。

:tent[1] [tɛnt;tent] *n.* 天幕;帳篷。to pitch a *tent.* 搭帳篷。to strike a *tent.* 拆帳篷。 *a bell tent* 鐘形帳篷。—*v.i.* 住於帳篷中。 —*v.t.* ①以天幕覆蓋。②使住於營帳中。

tent[2] *n.* 【外科】塞子(塞入傷口中之消毒棉花等)。 —*v.t.* 將消毒棉花等塞入(傷口)。

tent[3] *n.* (聖餐時用的)深紅色葡萄酒。

tent·a·bil·i·ty [͵tɛntə'bɪlətɪ; ͵tentə'biliti] *n.* 可引誘;易受誘惑。

ten·ta·cle ['tɛntəkl; 'tentəkl] *n.* ①(動物之)觸角;觸鬚。②(植物之) 觸絲。③伸及各處的東西。

ten·tac·u·lar [tɛn'tækjəlɚ; ten'tækjulə] *adj.* 觸角的;觸鬚的;觸手的;觸絲的。

ten·ta·tion [tɛn'teʃən; ten'teiʃən] *n.* 臨時性的行動;不斷的試驗;機械調整。

ten·ta·tive ['tɛntətɪv; 'tentətiv] *adj.* ①暫時的;試驗性質的。②猶豫的;無把握的。 —*n.* 試驗性之事物;試作。 —**ly,** *adv.*

ten·ter ['tɛntɚ; 'tentə] *n.* 張布機;張布架。—*v.t.* & *v.i.* 張(布)於張布架上。

ten·ter·hook ['tɛntɚ͵huk; 'tentəhuk] *n.* 張布鈎。 *on tenterhooks* 煩躁不安; 如坐針氈。

tent fly 張於帳篷頂上以防烈日豪雨之帆布;帳篷蓋。

:tenth [tɛnθ; tenθ] *adj.* ①第十的。②十分之一的。—*n.* ①第十。②十分之一。③(每月的)十日;十號。the *tenth* of August. 八月十日。—*adv.* 位於第十地。—**ly,** *adv.*

tenth Muse 才女;富文學天才之女子。

tenth-rate ['tɛnθ'ret; 'tenθ'reit] *adj.* 最低等品格或品質的。

tent·mak·er ['tɛnt͵mekɚ; 'tent͵meikə] *n.* 製造帳篷者。

tent peg (or **pin**) 搭帳篷用的樁。

tent pole 搭帳篷用的桿。

ten·u·is ['tɛnjuɪs; 'tenjuis] *n.*, *pl.* **-u·es** [-ju͵iz; -jui:z]. 【語音】無聲之閉鎖音 (如: k, t, p 等)。

te·nu·i·ty [tɛn'juətɪ; te'nju(:)iti] *n.* ①細;薄。②(氣體等)稀薄。③(文體等之)內容貧乏;(證據等之)貧乏。

ten·u·ous ['tɛnjuəs; 'tenjuəs] *adj.* ①細的;薄的;纖細的。②稀薄的。③貧乏的;內容貧乏的。④不清楚的;模稜兩可的;含糊的。⑤力量不够的;證據不充分的。⑥不重要的。

ten·ure ['tɛnjɚ;'tenjuə] *n.* ①保有;保有權。②保有期間;任期。The *tenure* of office of an American President is four years. 美國總統的任期是四年。③保有之條件或形式。④終身職。

te·nu·to [te'nuto; te'nu:tou] 【義】 *adj.* 【音樂】持續其全時間的。

te·pee ['tipi; 'ti:pi:] *n.* (北美印第安人之)帳篷;小屋。(亦作 **teepee,tipi**)

tep·e·fy ['tɛpə͵faɪ; 'tepifai] *v.*, **-fied, -fy·ing.** —*v.t.* 使微溫;使微熱。 —*v.i.* 變微溫;變微熱。

tep·id ['tɛpɪd; 'tepid] *adj.* ①微溫的。②不大熱心的。

te·pid·i·ty [tɪ'pɪdətɪ; ti'piditi] *n.* 微溫。

te·qui·la [tə'kilə; tə'ki:lə] *n.* ①墨西哥產的龍舌蘭。②用墨西哥龍舌蘭之莖釀的酒。

ter. ①terrace. ②territory. ③tertiary.

te·rai [tə'raɪ; tə'rai] *n.* 寬邊氈帽。(亦作 **terai hat**)

ter·aph ['tɛrəf; 'terəf] *n.*, *pl.* **-a·phim** [-əfɪm;-əfim]. (古猶太人之)家神像。

ter·a·to·log·i·cal [͵tɛrətə'lɑdʒɪkl; ͵terətə'lɔdʒikəl] *adj.* 【生物】畸形學的;畸胎學的。(亦作 **teratologic**)

ter·a·tol·o·gy [͵tɛrə'tɑlədʒɪ; ͵terə'tɔlədʒi] *n.* 畸形學;畸胎學。

ter·bi·um ['tɝbɪəm; 'tə:biəm] *n.* 【化】鋱(稀土族金屬元素之一,符號爲 Tb).

ter·cel ['tɝsl; 'tə:sl] *n.* 【動物】雄鷹。

ter·cen·te·nar·y [tɝ'sɛntə͵nɛrɪ; ͵tə:sen'ti:nəri] *adj.*, *n.*, *pl.* **-nar·ies.** —*adj.* 三百(周)年的。—*n.* 三百年;三百周年紀念。

ter·cen·ten·ni·al [͵tɝsɛn'tɛnɪəl; ͵tə:sen'tenjəl] *adj.*, *n.* =**tercentenary.**

ter·cet ['tɝsɪt; 'tə:sit] *n.* ①【詩】三行押韻之一節詩。②【音樂】三連音 (=triplet).

ter·di·ur·nal [͵tɝdaɪ'ɝnl; ͵tə:dai'ə:nl] *adj.* 一日三次的。

ter·e·bene ['tɛrə͵bin;'terəbi:n] *n.* 【化】松節油與松油精之混合物(作防腐劑、塗料等)。

ter·e·binth ['tɛrə͵bɪnθ; 'terəbinθ] *n.* 【植物】篤耨香。oil of *terebinth.* 松節油。

ter·e·bin·thine [͵tɛrə'bɪnθɪn; ͵terə'binθain] *adj.* ①篤耨香的;有篤耨香性質的。②松節油的;似松節油的。

te·re·do [tə'rido;tə'ri:dou] *n.*, *pl.* **-dos, -di·nes** [-də͵niz; -dini:z]. 鑿船蟲屬之蟲。

ter·gal ['tɝgəl; 'tə:gəl] *adj.* 背的;脊背的;背部的。

ter·gi·ver·sate ['tɝdʒɪvɚ͵set; 'tə:dʒivə:seit] *v.i.*, **-sat·ed, -sat·ing.** ①搪塞;規避;支吾其詞。②脫黨;背叛;變節。

ter·gi·ver·sa·tion [͵tɝdʒəvə'seʃən; ͵tə:dʒivə'seiʃən] *n.* ①背棄目標; 變節。②

規避;支吾其詞。

‡term [tɝm; təːm] *n.* ①名詞;術語。technical *terms.* 專門名詞;術語。②(*pl.*) 措辭;說法。③期限;期間。a *term* of office. 任期。④學期;(法庭的)開庭期。⑤(*pl.*) 條件。⑥費用;價錢。⑦(*pl.*) 關係;交誼。⑧〖數學〗(比例或方程式之) 項。⑨〖邏輯〗 a. 命題中主語或述語之辭;名辭。b. 三段論法中三部分之任一部分。⑩〖古〗界限;限制;終止。***be on good*** (or ***bad***) ***terms with a person*** 與某人友善(交惡)。***bring a person to terms*** 勸服或迫使某人訂約。***come to*** (or ***make***) ***terms*** a. 達成協議。b. 逆來順受;習慣於。***eat one's terms*** 〖英〗學法律。***in terms of*** 以…之觀點;以…之方式。***not to be on speaking terms with a person*** a. 與某人無深交(不足與之交談)。b. 與某人不和(不願與之交談)。—*v.t.* 稱;呼。

term. ①terminal. ②termination. ③terminology.

ter·ma·gan·cy [ˈtɝməgənsɪ; ˈtəːmə-gənsi] *n.* 潑悍;暴躁;嘴碎。

ter·ma·gant [ˈtɝməgənt; ˈtəːmə-gənt] *n.* ①悍婦;潑婦;嘴碎的女人。②(T-) 中古基督徒想像中的回教徒崇拜之凶悍神。—*adj.* 好拌嘴的;嘴碎的;兇悍的。

term day 付款日期。

term·er [ˈtɝmɚ; ˈtəːmə] *n.* 刑期中之囚犯。

ter·mi·na·ble [ˈtɝmɪnəbl̩; ˈtəːminə-bl] *adj.* ①可終止的。②有期限的。

***ter·mi·nal** [ˈtɝmənl̩; ˈtəːminl] *adj.* ①末端的;終點的。the *terminal* station. 終站。②最後的;期終的。a *terminal* examination. 期終考試。③按期的;定期的;每學期的。*terminal* accounts. 按期結帳。④與在終站處理運輸之貨物有關的。⑤表示界限、限制或終結的。⑥致死的。*terminal* cancer. 致命的癌症。—*n.* ①末端;終點。②鐵路的終站。③電流接頭的裝置。④機場候機處。⑤〖電腦〗打字電報機(用於遠處資料輸入及輸出)。

terminal leave 〖軍〗退伍前之最後假期(爲服役期間未用完假日之累積)。

ter·mi·nal·ly [ˈtɝmɪnl̩ɪ; ˈtəːminli] *adv.* ①每期。②於末端。

terminal market 農產品及牲畜等之集散市場。

***ter·mi·nate** [*v.* ˈtɝməˌnet; ˈtəːmi-neit *adj.* ˈtɝmənɪt; ˈtəːminit] *v.*, **-nat·ed, -nat·ing,** *adj.* —*v.t.* ①終止;終結;結束。②出現於或形成…之末尾;限制。—*v.i.* 結束;結局;滿期。—*adj.* 有結尾的;有限的。

ter·mi·na·tion [ˌtɝməˈneʃən; ˌtəːmi-ˈneiʃən] *n.* ①終止;結局。②末端。③字尾。

ter·mi·na·tion·al [ˌtɝməˈneʃənl̩; ˌtəːmiˈneiʃənəl] *adj.* ①終止的;結束的;末端的;界限的。②〖文法〗由變化字尾形成的。

ter·mi·na·tive [ˈtɝməˌnetɪv; ˈtəːmi-nətiv] *adj.* 終結的;限期的;結尾的。—*n.* 〖語言〗字尾。

ter·mi·na·tor [ˈtɝməˌnetɚ; ˈtəːmi-neitə] *n.* ①終結者;終結物。②〖天文〗明暗界線。

ter·mi·ni [ˈtɝməˌnaɪ; ˈtəːminai] *n.* pl. of **terminus.**

ter·min·ism [ˈtɝmənɪzəm; ˈtəːmi-nizm] *n.* ①〖哲學〗名稱論。②〖宗教〗悔罪限期說(謂逾神所規定之悛改時期之後,卽失去得救之機會)。

ter·mi·no·log·i·cal [ˌtɝmɪnəˈlɑdʒɪ-kl̩; ˌtəːminəˈlɔdʒikl] *adj.* 專門名詞的;術語的;與專門名詞或術語有關的。

ter·mi·nol·o·gy [ˌtɝməˈnɑlədʒɪ; ˌtəː-miˈnɔlədʒi] *n.*, *pl.* **-gies.** 術語;專門名詞。

term insurance 定期人壽保險。

ter·mi·nus [ˈtɝmənəs; ˈtəːminəs] *n.*, *pl.* **-ni, -nus·es.** ①終點;盡頭。②(鐵路或公共汽車等之)起點或終點。③〖英〗在鐵路線或公共汽車路線等終點之站或城市。④目的地;目的。⑤界限;邊界。⑥界標;界柱。⑦〖羅馬神話〗(T-) 守界神。

ter·mite [ˈtɝmaɪt; ˈtəːmait] *n.* 白蟻。

ter·mite-proof [ˈtɝmaɪtˈpruf; ˈtəː-maitˈpruːf] *adj.* 不受白蟻之害的。

ter·mit·ic [tɝˈmɪtɪk; təːˈmitik] *adj.* 白蟻的;白蟻所引起的。

term·less [ˈtɝmlɪs; ˈtəːmlis] *adj.* ①無限的;無界限的。②無期限的;永不終止的。③無條件的。

term·ly [ˈtɝmlɪ; ˈtəːmli] *adj.* 定期的;每一期的。—*adv.* 定期地;分期地。

term paper 學期研究報告。

term policy 定期壽命保險契約。

tern¹ [tɝn; təːn] *n.* 燕鷗。

tern² *n.* ①三個一組;三個一套。②三個號碼組成而中獎之摸彩;此種摸彩中獎的三個一組之號碼。—*adj.* 三個一組(或一套)的;三重的。

ter·na·ry [ˈtɝnərɪ; ˈtəːnəri] *adj.* ①由三部分組成的;三重的。②第三的。③〖化〗由三種不同元素或基組成的;三元的。④〖數學〗三元的。⑤〖數學〗以三爲底的。⑥〖冶金〗由三種金屬合成之合金的;三元合金的。—*n.* ①三個之一組。②三之倍數;可用三除盡之數。

ter·nate [ˈtɝnɪt; ˈtəːnit] *adj.* ①由三個組成的;含有三個的。②三個一組排列的。③〖植物〗由三個小葉組成的(複葉)。④〖植物〗輪生的(葉)。

ter·pene [ˈtɝpin; ˈtəːpiːn] *n.* 〖化〗萜;松烯。

Terp·sich·o·re [tɝpˈsɪkərɪ; təːpˈsi-kəri] *n.* 〖希臘神話〗司歌舞之女神。

terp·si·cho·re·an [ˌtɝpsɪkəˈriən; ˌtəːpsikəˈriːən] *adj.* ①(T-) 希臘神話中歌舞神 Terpsichore 的。②舞蹈的。—*n.* 〖俗〗舞蹈者。

terr. ①terrace. ②territorial. ③territory.

ter·ra [ˈterə; ˈterə] 〖拉〗 *n.* ①地;土地;地球。*terra* firma. 大地;陸地。②(T-) 羅馬神話中之土地女神。

***ter·race** [ˈterɪs, -əs; ˈterəs, -ris] *n.*, *v.*, **-raced, -rac·ing,** *adj.* —*n.* ①梯形地之一層。②坡地之街巷。③房屋之平頂。④壇;坪。—*v.t.* 使成梯形地;使成壇。—*adj.* ①(成)平頂的。②(成)梯形的。

ter·ra cot·ta [ˈterəˈkɑtə; ˈterəˈkɔtə] ①一種赤土陶器。②赤土色。

ter·rain [teˈren; ˈterein] *n.* ①地域;地帶。②〖軍〗地勢;地形。③〖地質〗岩層;岩羣。(亦作 **terrane**)

Ter·ra·my·cin [ˌterəˈmaɪsɪn; ˌterə-ˈmaisin] *n.* 〖商標名〗土黴素(抗生素)。

ter·ra·pin [ˈterəpɪn; ˈterəpin] *n.* (一種產於北美供食用的)泥龜;鼈。

ter·ra·que·ous [teˈrekwɪəs; teˈrei-kwiəs] *adj.* ①由水與陸地合成的。②〖植物〗生長在水中與陸地的。

ter·rar·i·um [təˈrerɪəm; təˈreəriəm] *n.*, *pl.* **-i·a** [-ɪə; -iə]. ①小動物飼養園。②瓶、碗等中栽培的小植物。

ter·raz·zo [teˈrɑtso; teˈrɑːtsou] *n.* 磨石子地。

ter·rene [teˈrin; teˈriːn] *adj.* ①地球的;陸地的;土質的。②現世的;塵世的;世俗的。—*n.* ①地球。②陸地;地形。

ter·res·tri·al [təˈrestrɪəl; tiˈrestriəl] *adj.* ①地球的;地球上的;陸地的。②陸棲的。

③塵世的;現世的。—*n.* 地球居民;人。
terrestrial globe①地球。②地球儀。
ter·ret [ˈtɛrɪt; ˈterit] *n.* ①(狗之項圈上供穿繩索之)環。②(韁繩從其中穿過之)鞍環。
:ter·ri·ble [ˈtɛrəbl; ˈterəbl] *adj.* ①可怕的;可怖的; 令人恐懼的。War is *terrible*. 戰爭是可怕的。②〖俗〗過分的;非常的; 極端的。③〖俗〗極壞的。She has a *terrible* temper. 她的脾氣極壞。
***ter·ri·bly** [ˈtɛrəblɪ; ˈterəbli] *adv.* ①可怕地;可怖地。②〖俗〗非常地;極端地。I am *terribly* hungry. 我非常餓。③〖俗〗很壞地。
ter·ri·er¹ [ˈtɛrɪɚ; ˈteriə] *n.* 㹴(一種小獵狗)。
ter·ri·er² *n.* 〖法律〗地籍册。
***ter·rif·ic** [təˈrɪfɪk; təˈrifik] *adj.* ①可怕的;令人恐怖的。②〖俗〗非常的;極端的;極大的。 at a *terrific* speed. 以極大的速度。—**al·ly,** *adv.*
ter·ri·fied [ˈtɛrəˌfaɪd; ˈterifaid] *adj.* 「恐懼的;受驚嚇的。」
***ter·ri·fy** [ˈtɛrəˌfaɪ; ˈterifai] *v.t.*, **-fied, -fy·ing.** 使恐怖;驚嚇。She was *terrified* of being killed in an air raid. 她很害怕在空襲中被炸死。
ter·rine [tɛˈrin; teˈriːn] *n.* ①裝菜餚出售的一種陶罐。②陶罐中所裝之物。③一種羹湯。
ter·ri·to·ri·al [ˌtɛrəˈtorɪəl; ˌteriˈtɔːriəl] *adj.* ①土地的。②領土的。*territorial* air. 領空。*territorial* waters (*or* seas). 領海。③區域的;限於某地區的。④(T-)美國領土(Territory) 的。⑤(T-)(英國)爲本土防衞而組織的。—*n.* 〖英〗地方自衞隊隊員。
ter·ri·to·ri·al·ism [ˌtɛrəˈtorɪəˌlɪzəm; ˌteriˈtɔːriəlizm] *n.* ①承認地主優越之制度。②〖宗教〗教會最高管理者由地方當局負責之制度。③(T-) 猶太人獲得一自治區之學說或運動。④國防義勇軍制度。
ter·ri·to·ri·al·i·ty [ˌtɛrəˌtorɪˈælətɪ; ˌteriˌtɔriˈæliti] *n.* ①領土;領土之性質或狀態。②動物在防衞其領土時之行爲。
:ter·ri·to·ry [ˈtɛrəˌtorɪ; ˈteritəri] *n.*, *pl.* **-ries.** ①土地;地方;區域。②領土。③領域。④(T-)美國的不成爲 State 的領土(如未成立州前的 Alaska 與 Hawaii).
***ter·ror** [ˈtɛrɚ; ˈterə] *n.* ①恐怖;駭懼。I found to my *terror* that he was a secret agent. 我發現他是一個特務分子, 甚爲驚駭。②令人恐怖之人或事物。③(T-)恐怖時代。④恐怖分子集團或其政策。*the king of terrors* 死。
ter·ror·ism [ˈtɛrəˌrɪzəm; ˈterərizəm] *n.* 恐怖主義。
ter·ror·ist [ˈtɛrərɪst; ˈterərist] *n.* ①恐怖主義者。②法國大革命恐怖時期的革命法庭之一員。③俄國沙皇時代之極端革命分子。—**ic,** *adj.*
ter·ror·ize [ˈtɛrəˌraɪz; ˈterəraiz] *v.t.*, **-ized, -iz·ing.** ①使恐怖; 恐嚇。②恐怖統治。—**ter·ror·i·za·tion,** *n.*
ter·ror-strick·en [ˈtɛrɚˌstrɪkn̩; ˈterəˌstrikn] *adj.* 恐怖的;驚懼的。
ter·ry [ˈtɛrɪ; ˈteri] *n.*, *pl.* **-ries.** ①織物兩端未剪時所留之絨縫。②留有此種絨縫之織物(如手巾)。
terse [tɝs; təːs] *adj.*, **ters·er, ters·est.** 簡潔的;簡明的(文體等)。—**ly,** *adv.* —**ness,** *n.*
ter·tian [ˈtɝʃən; ˈtəːʃən] *n.* ①〖醫〗隔日熱; 間日瘧。②修戒期間之耶穌會教士。—*adj.* 隔日發作的;隔日的。
ter·ti·ar·y [ˈtɝʃɪˌɛrɪ; ˈtəːʃəri] *adj.*, *n.*, *pl.* **-ar·ies.** —*adj.* ①第三位的;第三級的;第三的。②〖地質〗(T-) 第三紀的。—*n.* 〖地質〗(T-) ①第三紀。②第三紀層。
ter·za ri·ma [ˈtɛrtsəˈrimɑ; ˈtertsəˈriːmɑː] 〖義〗三行體(源於義大利的詩體)。
TESL [ˈtɛsl̩; ˈtesl] *n.* 將英文當第二語言的教學(爲*T*eaching *E*nglish as a *S*econd *L*anguage 之略)。
tes·sel·late [*v.* ˈtɛsl̩ˌet; ˈtesileit *adj.* ˈtɛsl̩ɪt; ˈtesilit] *v.*, **-lat·ed, -lat·ing,** *adj.* —*v.t.* 使成小方格或排列成棋盤格狀。—*adj.* 成小方格或棋盤格狀的。 —**tes·sel·la·tion,** *n.* —**tes·sel·lat·ed,** *adj.*
tes·ser·a [ˈtɛsərə; ˈtesərə] *n.*, *pl.* **-ser·ae** [-ˌsəri; -səriː]. ①(古羅馬之用做紀念物、標幟、票據等的) 方塊骨、象牙、木等。②鑲嵌細工中用之小塊大理石、象牙等。
:test¹ [tɛst; test] *n.* ①試驗; 測驗; 考驗。②用以考驗之物;試金石。Poverty is a *test* of character. 貧窮是品性的試金石。③〖化〗分析;試驗。 the acid *test*. 酸性試驗。***put to the test*** 使受考驗。***stand*** (or ***bear***) ***the test*** 經得起考驗;及格。—*v.t.* ①試驗;考驗。②化驗。③檢驗。—*v.i.* ①接受測驗或化驗。②做試驗。③在測驗中表現。—**a·ble,** *adj.*
test² *n.* ①〖動物〗介殼。②〖植物〗種皮。
Test. ①Testament. ②Testamentary.
tes·ta [ˈtɛstə; ˈtestə] *n.*, *pl.* **-tae** [-ti; -tiː]. ①〖動物〗介殼。②〖植物〗種皮。
tes·ta·cean [tɛsˈteʃən; tesˈteiʃən] *adj.* 〖動物〗介殼類的。—*n.* 〖動物〗介殼類之動物。
tes·ta·ceous [tɛsˈteʃəs; tesˈteiʃəs] *adj.* ①〖動、植物〗紅褐色的;黃褐色的。②〖生物〗介殼的;有介殼的。
tes·ta·cy [ˈtɛstəsɪ; ˈtestəsi] *n.* 〖法律〗留有遺囑。
tes·ta·ment** [ˈtɛstəmənt; ˈtestəmənt] *n.* ①遺囑(通常用於 last will and testament 一語中)。to make one's *testament*. 立遺囑。②(T-)聖約。the Old (New) *Testament*. 舊(新)約聖經。the Testament*** = the New Testament.
tes·ta·men·ta·ry [ˌtɛstəˈmɛntərɪ; ˌtestəˈmentəri] *adj.* ①遺囑的。②由遺囑給與或指定的; 依照遺囑作的。③包含於遺囑中的。
tes·ta·mur [tɛsˈtemɚ; tesˈteimə] *n.* 「(英大學之)考試及格證書。」
tes·tate [ˈtɛstet; ˈtestit] *adj.* 留有遺囑的。—*n.* 留有遺囑之死者。
tes·ta·tor [ˈtɛstetɚ; tesˈteitə] *n.* ①立遺囑之人。②留有遺囑之死者。
tes·ta·trix [tɛsˈtetrɪks; tesˈteitriks] *n.*, *pl.* **-tri·ces** [-trɪˌsiz; -trisiːz]. testator 之女性。
test ban 對核子武器試爆之禁止。
test bed ①用以試驗引擎之飛機、火箭等。②設有試驗裝備之基地。
test blank 留有空白作答案之試卷。
test case 判例(審判結果將被援作先例的法律案件)。
test drive 試驗汽車性能之駕駛。
test-drive [ˈtɛstˈdraɪv; ˈtestˈdraiv] *v.t.*, **-drove, -driv·en, -driv·ing.** 爲試車而駕駛(車輛)。
test·ee [tɛsˈti; tesˈtiː] *n.* 接受測驗者;「被試驗者。」
test·er¹ [ˈtɛstɚ; ˈtestə] *n.* ①試驗者;檢查者;分析者。②試驗器;試驗裝置。
tes·ter² *n.* (講臺、床、墳墓等上之) 天蓋。
test-fire [ˈtɛstˈfaɪr; ˈtestˈfaiə] *v.t.*, **-fired, -fir·ing.** 試射(火箭、核子武器等)。
test flight (新型飛機、火箭等之)試飛。
test-fly [ˈtɛstˈflaɪ; ˈtestˈflai] *v.t.*, **-flew, -flown, -fly·ing.** 試飛。

test glass〖化〗試杯。

tes·ti·cle [ˈtɛstɪkl; ˈtestikl] *n.* 〖解剖〗睪丸。

tes·tic·u·lar [tɛsˈtɪkjulɚ; tesˈtikjulə] *adj.* 〖解剖〗睪丸的。

tes·ti·fi·a·ble [ˈtɛstɪˌfaɪəbl; ˈtestifaiəbl] *adj.* 可作證的;可證明的;可表明的。

tes·ti·fi·ca·tion [ˌtɛstəfɪˈkeʃən; ˌtestifiˈkeiʃən] *n.* ①立證;作證;證明;表明。②證據;證言。

tes·ti·fi·er [ˈtɛstəˌfaɪɚ; ˈtestifaiə] *n.* 作證者;證人;證明者。

***tes·ti·fy** [ˈtɛstəˌfaɪ; ˈtestifai] *v.*, **-fied, -fy·ing.** —*v.t.* ①證明;表明。②作證;證實。③確言;宣稱。—*v.i.* 證明;作證;提供證據。I can *testify* to his innocence. 我可以證明他的無辜。

tes·ti·mo·ni·al [ˌtɛstəˈmonɪəl; ˌtestiˈmounjəl, -niəl] *n.* ①(品格、資格等的)證明書;推薦書。②頌德紀念品;褒揚狀;感謝狀。—*adj.* 證明的;紀念的;表揚的;表感謝的。

tes·ti·mo·ny** [ˈtɛstəˌmonɪ; ˈtestiməni] *n., pl.* **-nies.** ①證言;口供。②表明;證據。③宣言;證實。④(*pl.*)天律;聖經。bear testimony to*** 爲…作證。

test·ing [ˈtɛstɪŋ; ˈtestiŋ] *adj.* 試驗的;作試驗用的。—**ly,** *adv.*

tes·tis [ˈtɛstɪs; ˈtestis] *n., pl.* **-tes** [-tiz; -tiːz]. 〖解剖〗睪丸。

test-mar·ket [ˈtɛstˌmɑrkɪt; ˈtestˌmɑːkit] *v.t.* 試售;試銷。

test match ①比賽。②(常 T- m-)國際板球比賽。

test meal 試驗食;試驗餐。

tes·tos·ter·one [tɛsˈtɑstəˌron; tesˈtɔstəroun] *n.* 〖生化〗睪丸素酮。

test paper ①〖化〗石蕊試紙。②〖美〗試卷;考試答案。

test pattern 〖電視〗檢驗圖。

test pilot (新型飛機之)試飛員。

test range ①試驗場。②試驗範圍。

test site 試驗場地;試驗地點。

test stand 火箭或飛彈試驗用之支架。

test track ①試車跑道。②高速試驗鐵軌。

test tube 試管。

test-tube [ˈtɛstˌtjub; ˈtesttjuːb] *adj.* ①試管的;裝在試管中的。②化學合成的;用化學合成製的。③用人工授精法生產的。a *test-tube* baby. 人工授精之嬰兒。

tes·tu·di·nate [tɛsˈtudəˌnet; tesˈtjuːdineit] *adj.* ①龜甲狀的;拱狀的。②龜的。—*n.* 龜。

tes·tu·do [tɛsˈtjudo; tesˈtjuːdou] *n., pl.* **-di·nes** [-dṇˌiz; -diniːz]. ①(古羅馬攻城用)龜甲形屛遮。②龜甲形大盾。③(T-)土龜屬。④〖羅馬建築〗弓形屋頂。⑤一種七絃琴。⑥〖醫〗(頭頂蓋下之一種)皮脂囊腫。

test well (爲勘測有無油礦而掘的)探勘井。

tes·ty [ˈtɛstɪ; ˈtesti] *adj.*, **-ti·er, -ti·est.** 易被激怒的;暴躁的。

te·tan·ic [tɪˈtænɪk; tiˈtænik] *adj.* ①〖醫〗破傷風性的。②〖醫〗引起肌肉强直痙攣的;强直性的。—*n.* 服之過量可致肌肉强直性痙攣之藥劑(如馬錢子鹼等)。

tet·a·nus [ˈtɛtənəs; ˈtetənəs] *n.* ①〖醫〗破傷風(桿菌)。②〖生理〗(肌肉之)强直;强硬。

tetched [tɛtʃt; tetʃt] *adj.* 神經兮兮的。

tetch·y [ˈtɛtʃɪ; ˈtetʃi] *adj.*, **tetch·i·er, tetch·i·est.** 易怒的;暴躁的。(亦作 **techy**)

tête-à-tête [ˈtetəˈtet; ˈteitɑːˈteit] *adv.* 面對面地;兩人在一起私下地,或祕密地。—*adj.* 面對面的;兩人在一起的;兩人間之祕密的;爲兩人祕密在一起的。We had a *tête-à-tête* conversation. 我們兩人當面談過了。—*n.* ①面談;密談。②一種 S 型坐位(可供二人面對面坐下)。

teth·er [ˈtɛðɚ; ˈteðə] *n.* ①(拴牲畜的)繫繩;繫鏈。②(智能、知識、財源、權限之)範圍;限度。beyond one's *tether.* 力所不及;在權限之外。***at*** (or ***to***) ***the end of one's tether*** 智盡技窮;力量、智慧、忍耐等已至最大限度。—*v.t.* 以繩或鍊拴(牲畜)。

teth·er·ball [ˈtɛðɚˌbɔl; ˈteðəbɔːl] *n.* 繩球(一種兩人玩的球戲)。

tetra- 〖字首〗表"四"之義(如: tetragon, 四角形)。

tet·ra·chord [ˈtɛtrəˌkɔrd; ˈtetrəkɔːd] *n.* ①〖音樂〗四階。②一種古代之四絃琴。

tet·rad [ˈtɛtræd; ˈtetræd] *n.* ①四;四個。②四個一組。③〖化〗四價元素。④〖生物〗四集染色體。

tet·ra·eth·yl lead [ˌtɛtrəˈɛθəl～; ˌtetrəˈeθəl～] 〖化〗四乙鉛(一種無色之液體有機化合物,加於汽油中,以促其燃燒均勻)。

tet·ra·gon [ˈtɛtrəˌgɑn; ˈtetrəgən] *n.* 四角形;四邊形。

te·trag·o·nal [tɛˈtrægənl; teˈtrægənl] *adj.* 四角形的;四邊形的。

tet·ra·he·dral [ˌtɛtrəˈhidrəl; ˈtetrəˈhedrəl] *adj.* 四面體的。

tet·ra·he·dron [ˌtɛtrəˈhidrən; ˈtetrəˈhedrən] *n., pl.* **-drons, -dra** [-drə; -drə]. 四面體。

te·tral·o·gy [tɛˈtrælədʒɪ; teˈtrælədʒi] *n., pl.* **-gies.** ①(古雅典之)四聯劇(由三齣悲劇與一齣諷刺劇組成)。②四聯劇;四部曲。

te·tram·e·ter [tɛˈtræmətɚ; teˈtræmitə] *n.* 〖詩學〗四音步句;四音步句之詩。—*adj.* 有四音步的。

tet·ra·pod [ˈtɛtrəˌpɑd; ˈtetrəpɔd] *n.* 〖動物〗①四足動物。②四脚蟲類。—*adj.* ①四足的。②四脚蟲類的。

te·trarch [ˈtitrɑrk; ˈtiːtrɑːk] *n.* ①(古羅馬帝國)四分領太守(常轄一省的四分之一)。②屬領之統治者。

te·trarch·ate [ˈtitrɑrkˌet; ˈtiːtrɑːkeit] *n.* ①(古羅馬帝國之)一省的四分之一。②屬領統治者管轄之土地。

te·trar·chy [ˈtitrɑrkɪ; ˈtiːtrɑːki] *n., pl.* **-trarch·ies.** ①tetrarch 之統治或其轄區。②四人組成之統治集團;四人統治。③分爲四個附屬政府之國家。

tet·ra·syl·la·ble [ˈtɛtrəˌsɪləbl; ˈtetrəˌsiləbl] *n.* 有四音節之字。

tet·ra·va·lent [ˌtɛtrəˈvelənt; ˌtetrəˈveilənt] *adj.* 〖化〗四價的;有四價的;有四種原子價的。

tet·rode [ˈtɛtrod; ˈtetroud] *n.* 〖電〗四極眞空管。

te·trox·id(e) [tɛˈtrɑksɪd; teˈtrɔksid] *n.* 〖化〗四氧化物。

tet·ter [ˈtɛtɚ; ˈtetə] *n.* 〖醫〗皮疹;水泡疹。***honeycomb tetter*** 黃癬。***moist*** (or ***humid***) ***tetter*** 濕疹。***scaly tetter*** 鱗屑癬。

Teut. ①Teuton. ②Teutonic.

Teu·ton [ˈtjutṇ; ˈtjuːtən] *n.* ①條頓族(包括日耳曼、荷蘭、盎格魯薩克遜及斯堪的那維亞)人。②德國人。—*adj.* =**Teutonic.**

Teu·ton·ic [tjuˈtɑnɪk; tju(ː)ˈtɔnik] *adj.* 條頓的;條頓族的;德國的。—*n.* 條頓語。

Teu·ton·ism [ˈtjutənɪzṃ; ˈtjuːtənizm] *n.* ①條頓民族優越感。②條頓或德國文化。

Teu·ton·i·za·tion [ˌtjutṇɪˈzeʃən; ˌtjuːtənaiˈzeiʃən] *n.* 條頓化或德國化。

Teu·ton·ize [ˈtjutṇˌaɪz; ˈtjuːtənaiz]

v.,-ized, -iz·ing. —*v.t.* 使條頓化或德國化。—*v.i.* 條頓化或德國化。

Tex. ①Texas. ②Texan.

Tex·an [ˈtɛksn̩;ˈteksən] *adj.* Texas的。—*n.* Texas 人或居民。

Tex·as [ˈtɛksəs; ˈteksəs] *n.* 德克薩斯(美國西南部之一州,其首府爲 Austin).

Texas leaguer 〖棒球〗落於內野與外野間之飛球。

***text** [tɛkst; tekst] *n.* ①正文;本文。full *text*. 全文。②原文。③作爲宣講題目之聖經文句。④題目; 主題; 論題。to stick to one's *text*. (談話) 不離本題。⑤詩或劇本因版本不同而相異之用辭。⑥教科書(=textbook). ⑦聖經之經文。⑧=**text hand.**

***text·book** [ˈtɛkstˌbuk; ˈtekstbuk] *n.* 教本;課本;教科書。

text edition 作教科書用的版本。

text hand 大型手寫體。

***tex·tile** [ˈtɛkstl̩, -tɪl, -taɪl; ˈtekstail] *adj.* ①織的;織物的。Cloth is a *textile* fabric. 布是一種織物。②可織的。*textile* industry. 紡織工業。—*n.* ①織物。②織物原料。

textile mill 紡織廠。

tex·tu·al [ˈtɛkstʃuəl; ˈtekstjuəl] *adj.* ①本文的;原文的;文字上的。*textual* quotation. 原文的引錄。②根據(耶教聖經)原文的。

tex·tur·al [ˈtɛkstʃərəl;ˈtekstʃərəl] *adj.* ①(織物之)質地的。②構造上的;結構上的。

tex·ture [ˈtɛkstʃɚ; ˈtekstʃə] *n.* ①(織物的)質地;織物。a cloth of fine *texture*. 質地精細之布。②構造;結構。③聲樂或樂器等之悅耳性質。

T.F. ①tank forces. ②task force. ③Territorial Force.

T-for·ma·tion [ˈtifɔrˌmeʃən; ˈtiːfɔːˌmeiʃən] *n.*〖橄欖球〗T字隊形(爲攻勢隊形之一)。

Th thorium 之化學符號。

-th 〖字尾〗①表"情形; 性質; 動作"之義之名詞字尾。②加於 four 以上數字之後表序數。

Tha·i [ˈtɑ·i;tai] *n.* ①泰國人。②泰國語。—*adj.* 泰國人的;泰國語的。(亦作 **Tai**)

Thai·land [ˈtaɪlənd; ˈtailænd] *n.* 泰國(首都曼谷 Bangkok).

thal·a·mus [ˈθæləməs; ˈθæləməs] *n.*, *pl.* **-mi** [-ˌmaɪ; -mai]. ①〖解剖〗視神經床; 視丘。②〖植物〗花托。

tha·ler [ˈtɑlɚ; ˈtɑːlə] *n.*, *pl.* **-ler, -lers.** 昔時德國之一種銀幣(特指三馬克者)。

Tha·les [ˈθeliz; ˈθeiliːz] *n.* 臺利斯(640?-546 B. C., 希臘哲學家)。

Tha·li·a [θəˈlaɪə; θəˈlaiə] *n.* 〖希臘神話〗①司牧歌與喜劇之女神。②司優美、快樂之三女神之一。

tha·lid·o·mide [θəˈlɪdəˌmaɪd;θəˈlidəmaid] *n.* 一種會使胎兒發生畸形的鎮靜劑。

thal·lic [ˈθælɪk; ˈθælik] *adj.* 〖化〗鉈的; 含鉈(特指三價鉈)的。

thal·li·um [ˈθælɪəm; ˈθæliəm] *n.* 〖化〗鉈(金屬元素之一,符號爲 Tl).

thal·lo·phyte [ˈθæləˌfaɪt; ˈθæləfait] *n.* 〖植物〗同節植物(根、莖、葉無顯著分別之下等植物)。—**thal·lo·phyt·ic,** *adj.*

thal·lous [ˈθæləs; ˈθæləs] *adj.* 〖化〗(一價)鉈的;亞鉈的。

thal·lus [ˈθæləs;ˈθæləs] *n.*, *pl.* **-lus·es, -li** [-laɪ; -lai]. 〖植物〗同節體(同節植物之體, 無根、莖、葉之分)。

Thames [tɛmz; temz] *n.* 泰晤士河(英國之河流,倫敦卽位於其畔)。

‡**than** [ðæn; ðæn] *conj.* ①比較。He is taller *than* his brother. 他比他的兄弟高。I would rather die *than* disgrace myself. 我寧死不受辱。②除…外。None other *than* my parents can help me. 除父母外,無人能幫助我。③當(=when). We barely arrived *than* it was time to leave. 我們剛到達便到了離開的時間。***no other than*** 就是(= the same as). He is *no other than* a thief. 他就是一個賊。—*prep.* 與…相較 (常與代名詞受格連用)。

than·age [ˈθenɪdʒ; ˈθeinidʒ] *n.* 〖英〗大鄉紳 (thane) 之身分、地位、領地等。

than·a·toid [ˈθænəˌtɔɪd; ˈθænətɔid] *adj.* ①死一般的;像死亡的。②致命的。

than·a·top·sis [ˌθænəˈtɑpsɪs; ˌθænəˈtɔpsis] *n.* 對於死亡之見解、觀念、默想等。

thane [θen; θein] *n.* 〖英史〗①介於自由人與貴族間之大鄉紳。②蘇格蘭之貴族。(亦作 **thegn**)

‡**thank** [θæŋk; θæŋk] *v.t.* 謝;感謝;道謝。I *thanked* him for his help. 我爲他的幫助而向他致謝。*Thank* you. 謝謝你。No, *thank* you. 不了, 謝謝你 (注意：如祇用 "Thank you" 係表示接受對方之意, =Yes, please.) ***have oneself to thank*** 錯在自己; 自己負責。You *have* only *yourself to thank*. 你完全是咎由自取。—*n.* (*pl.*)謝意;感謝。*Thanks.* 謝謝你 (=I thank you). Very many *thanks*. 多謝。***small thanks to*** 一點也不感謝; 非常感謝(反語)。***thank offering*** 表示感謝之禮物;(尤指) 供神的祭品。***thanks to*** 由於;因 (=owing to, because of). *Thanks to* your help, we were successful. 由於你的幫助, 我們得以成功。

***thank·ful** [ˈθæŋkfəl; ˈθæŋkfəl] *adj.* 感謝的; 感激的。Be *thankful* for small mercies. 雖小恩亦感激。—**ly,** *adv.* —**ness,** *n.*

thank·less [ˈθæŋklɪs; ˈθæŋklis] *adj.* ①不感謝的;不知感激的;忘恩的(人)。②不令人感謝的;徒勞的(行爲)。

thanks·giv·er [ˈθæŋksˌgɪvɚ;ˈθæŋksˌgivə] *n.* 感謝者;感恩者。

***thanks·giv·ing** [ˌθæŋksˈgɪvɪŋ; ˈθæŋksˌgiviŋ] *n.* ①感謝;感恩。②感謝之表示。③對上帝表示感恩之日。④(T-) 感恩節。

Thanksgiving Day 〖美〗感恩節(十一月最後的星期四)。

thank·wor·thy [ˈθæŋkˌwɝðɪ;ˈθæŋkˌwəːði] *adj.* 值得感謝的;應當感謝的。

thank-you [ˈθæŋkˌju; ˈθæŋkjuː] *n.* 感謝的表示。a *thank-you* note. 表示感謝的一封短簡。

thank-you-ma'am [ˈθæŋkjuˌmæm; ˈθæŋkjumɑːm] *n.* 〖美俗〗道路上的小凹溝或凸脊(車行至此處時, 乘客因震動而俯身向前, 宛若鞠躬, 故名)。

thank-you work 〖美俗〗無報酬的工作。

‡**that**¹ [ðæt, ðət; ðæt, ðət] *adj.*, *pron.*, *pl.* **those.** 那;那個;彼(與 this 相對而言)。Do you know *that* boy? 你認識那個男孩嗎? This is better than *that*. 這個比那個好。***and all that*** 等等。***and that*** 代替前半句所述之事實之詞。***at that*** 〖俗〗**a.** 到此爲止;僅此而已; 不再有話、工作等了。**b.** 尙且。**c.** 儘管如此;然而。***for all that*** 然而仍舊。***in that*** 因爲。***that is*** 說得更精確些; 易言之。He's very fat, *that is,* he weighs 273 pounds. 他很胖, 說得更精確些, 他重達 273 磅。***that is to say*** 就是說; 卽。***That's it.*** 就是啦; 對啦。***That's***

that. 〖俗〗就這麼着吧;就這樣決定了;不必再多講了。I won't go and *that's that!* 我不去,不必多講了! ***that way*** 〖俗〗喜歡;愛〖常 about, for〗. I am *that way* about coffee. 我喜歡喝咖啡。 ***with that*** 這樣說着;於是。

‡that² *relative pron.* 用以代替 who, whom, which, at *or* in which. the man *that* (= who) came yesterday. 昨天來的那個人。〖注意〗⑴如先行詞 (antecedent) 不是子句中的主詞時, 則 that 通常均被省略, 例如: the man (*that*) we saw yesterday. 我們昨天看見的那個人。⑵ **that, who, which** 均作關係代名詞。that 可指人、事、物; who 通常指人; which 通常僅指事物。that 通常連接限定子句 (restrictive clause); who 及 which 連接限定子句及非限定子句 (nonrestrictive) 均可。

‡that³ *conj.* ①(用以引導一個附屬子句, 常被省略)。He said (*that*) he would come. 他說他要來。②(用以引導一個名詞子句)。I know *that* 6 and 4 are 10. 我知道六加四是十。③(用以表示結果或目的) 以致;以求。He ran fast *that* he might not be late. 他快跑以求不致遲到。He ran so fast *that* he was five minutes early. 他跑得快, 因之他早到了五分鐘。④(用以表示原因)因爲。If I find fault, it is *that* I want you to do better in future. 如果我指責你的缺點, 那是因爲我要你將來做得更好些。⑤(用以表示强烈願望、或驚訝、憤怒等)。Oh, *that* she were here! 她若在這裏多好!

that⁴ *adj.* 〖俗〗如許;那麼 (=so; to such an extent *or* degree). I can't walk *that* far. 我不能走那麼遠。

that·a·way, that-a·way [ˈðætəˌwe; ˈðætəˌwei] *adv.* 〖俗〗①朝那個方向。②按指示; 如所示。

***thatch** [θætʃ; θætʃ] *n.* ①茸草。②草屋頂。③蓋住頭頂之頭髮。—*v.t.* 以茸草覆蓋。

thatch·er [ˈθætʃɚ; ˈθætʃə] *n.* 茸屋匠。

that's [ðæts; ðæts] =**that is.**

thau·ma·trope [ˈθɔməˌtrop; ˈθɔːmətroup] *n.* 留影盤 (一種基於光學的儀器或玩具)。

thau·ma·turge [ˈθɔməˌtɝdʒ; ˈθɔːmətəːdʒ] *n.* 術士;魔術師;妖術家。

thau·ma·tur·gic [ˌθɔməˈtɝdʒɪk; ˌθɔːməˈtəːdʒik] *adj.* ①奇術的;魔術的;妖法的。②能變魔術的; 有妖術的。(亦作 **thaumaturgical**)

thau·ma·tur·gy [ˈθɔməˌtɝdʒɪ; ˈθɔːmətəːdʒi] *n.* 奇術;魔術;妖法。

thaw** [θɔ; θɔː] *v.i.* ①溶化; 融解。②變爲溫暖足以溶化冰雪等。③(冰霜或凍結之液體等)消除。④在態度上變爲較不拘泥; 變爲溫和。—*v.t.* ①使溶化; 使融解。②使在態度上變爲較不拘泥; 使變爲溫和。③使國際關係緩和。—*n.* ①溶化;融解。②冰雪融解之時。③在態度上變爲較不拘泥; 變爲溫和。④(管制之)放寬。⑤(國際關係之) 緩和。 ***the thaw 一年中河川或海港中之冰初次融解日。—**ly,** *adv.*

thaw·less [ˈθɔlɪs; ˈθɔːlis] *adj.* 不溶化「的(冰、雪等)。

thaw·y [ˈθɔ·ɪ; ˈθɔːi] *adj.*, **thaw·i·er, thaw·i·est.** 〖俗〗溶化的(冰、雪等);融解的。

‡the¹ [在子音之前讀做 ðə; ðə 在母音之前讀做 ðɪ; ði 重讀時讀做ði; ðiː] *adj.*, or *definite article.* 此; 這。其用法說明如下: **a.** 用以指出某一(或某些) 特殊的人或物, 其功用與 this, that, these, those 相似, 意爲"此卽所言者"或"此卽已言及或已知者"。*the* man I loved. 我所愛的人。 *the* pencil in her hand. 在她手中的鉛筆。 **b.** 用以指示獨一無二的人或事物等。*the* sun. 日。*the* moon. 月。*the* year 1960. 一九六〇年。**c.** 用於江、河、海洋名稱及複數專有名詞之前。*the* Thames. 泰晤士河。 *the* Alps. 阿爾卑斯山脈。 *the* Philippines. 菲律賓。 **d.** 用於代表全體的單數名詞之前。 *The* horse is a useful animal. 馬是有用的動物。**e.** 用於最高級形容詞之前。*the* largest. 最大的。 *the* most interesting. 最有趣味的。**f.** 置於形容詞之前, 成爲複數普通名詞之代用。*the* poor. 窮人。*the* living and *the* dead. 生者和死者。**g.** 置於形容詞之前, 成爲抽象名詞之代用。*the* beautiful. 美。**h.** 置於人名之前, 以加强表示其指示的效果。**i.** 置於專有名詞之前, 使成爲普通名詞。Shanghai is *the* New York of China. 上海是中國的紐約。 **j.** 置於姓氏之前, 以表示全家之人。*The* Williamses live next door. 威廉斯一家就住在隔壁。 **k.** 用於數量之前, 表示一單位。candy at one dollar *the* pound. 一元一磅的糖果。to be paid by *the* week. 以週計薪。**l.** 用以表示身體之一部分或私人之所有。**m.** 表示最著名或最好之聲譽者。**n.** (置於複數名詞之前)表示一國國民、一階級、一羣人。 **o.** 用於名詞前以表示其爲同類中最有名, 爲最重要者。Liuchow is *the* place to die. 死在柳州(因柳州產上等棺木)。**p.** 用在頭銜前或作爲頭銜之一部分。*the* Duke of Wellington. 威靈頓公爵。 **q.** 用以表示一生中或一個世紀中之某一段時期。*the* roaring twenties. 喧鬧的 1920 年代。**r.** 足够。She didn't have *the* courage to leave. 她沒有足够的勇氣離開。

the² [ðə, ðɪ; ðə, ði] *adv.* 愈;更(用於形容詞或副詞的比較級之前)。*The* sooner *the* better. 愈早愈好;愈快愈好。

the·an·dric [θɪˈændrɪk; θiˈændrik] *adj.* 具有神性與人性的;基督的。

the·an·throp·ic [ˌθiænˈθrɑpɪk; ˌθiænˈθrɔpik] *adj.* 神人的;兼具神性與人性的。(亦作 **theanthropical**)

the·ar·chy [ˈθiɑrkɪ; ˈθiːɑːki] *n., pl.* **-chies.** ①神權政治。②統治諸神; 統治神團。

theat. ①theatre. ②theatrical(ly).

‡the·a·ter, the·a·tre [ˈθiətɚ, ˈθɪə-; ˈθiətə, ˈθjəːtə] *n.* ①劇場;戲院;電影院。②類似戲院之場所; 有分層座位的教室。③重大事件發生的場所。④戲劇。 the Greek *theater.* 希臘戲劇。⑤觀衆。The *theater* wept. 觀衆感動得哭了起來。 ***go to the theater*** 去看戲。 ***the theater*** 戲劇;戲劇表演。

the·a·ter·go·er [ˈθiətɚˌgoɚ; ˈθiətəˌgouə] *n.* 喜歡觀劇者;經常看戲者。

the·a·ter·go·ing [ˈθiətɚˌgo·ɪŋ; ˈθiətəˌgouiŋ] *n.* 觀劇; 看戲。—*adj.* 好看戲的; 經常去看戲的。

the·a·ter-in-the-round [ˈθiətɚɪnðəˈraund; ˈθiətərinðəˈraund] *n.* 舞臺起碼有三面被席次包圍的劇場。(亦作 **arena theater**)

theater of operations 戰區內「之作戰地帶及其鄰近地區。

theater of war 戰區。

the·at·ri·cal [θɪˈætrɪkl; θiˈætrikl] *adj.* (亦作 **theatric**) ①戲院的;戲劇的;演戲的。②戲劇性的;誇張的。③做作的;不自然的。—*n.* (*pl.*) ①演戲。 ②有關戲劇與表演之事。③做作的行動; 誇張性的行動。④職業演員。—**ly,** *adv.*

the·at·ri·cal·ism [θɪˈætrɪkəˌlɪzəm; θi-

ˈætriklizəm] *n.* 戲劇的風格或特色。(亦作 **theatricism**)

the·at·ri·cal·i·ty [θɪˌætrɪˈkælətɪ; θiˌætriˈkæliti] *n.* 戲劇性;戲劇化;矯飾;誇張。

the·at·ri·cal·ize [θɪˈætrɪklˌaɪz; θiˈætrikəlaiz] *v.*, **-ized, -iz·ing.** —*v.t.* 戲劇化; 使具戲劇性。—*v.i.* ①演戲;演出。②(尤指經常地)上戲院看戲。—**the·at·ri·cal·i·za·tion,** *n.*

the·at·ri·cian [ˌθiəˈtrɪʃən; ˌθiəˈtriʃən] *n.* 精於戲劇者。

the·at·rics [θɪˈætrɪks; θiˈætriks] *n.* ①(作 *sing.* 解)演劇法;演戲之藝術。②(作 *pl.* 解)誇張或做作的言語、行動、態度等。

The·ban [ˈθibən; ˈθi:bən] *adj.* Thebes 城的; Thebes 人的。—*n.* Thebes 人。

Thebes [θibz; θi:bz] *n.* 底比斯 (**a.** 埃及之一古城; **b.** 希臘之一古城)。

thé dan·sant [ˌteˌdɑ̃ˈsɑ̃; ˌteiˌdɑ̃ˈsɑ̃] *pl.* **thés dan·sants.** 〖法〗(午後之)茶舞。

:thee [ði; ði:] *pron.* the objective case of **thou.** 〖古〗你;汝。

***theft** [θɛft; θeft] *n.* ①盜竊行爲。 to commit a *theft.* 行竊。②被竊; 失竊。③失竊之物。

theft·less [ˈθɛftlɪs; ˈθeftlis] *adj.* ①非盜竊的。②偷不走的;不會失竊的。

theft·proof [ˈθɛftˌpruf; ˈθeftpru:f] *adj.* 防盜的。

the·ine, the·in [ˈθiin; ˈθi:i:n] *n.* 〖化〗茶素;咖啡鹼。

:their [ðɛr; ðɛə] *pron.* the possessive case of **they.** 他們的。 Those are *their* books. 那些是他們的書籍。〖注意〗 **their, theirs** 皆爲 they 之所有格。 their 用作形容詞, 其後常接名詞: This is *their* farm. 這是他們的田莊。 theirs 則單獨用: This farm is *theirs.* 這田莊是他們的。

:theirs [ðɛrz; ðɛəz] *pron.* 他們的。 Those books are *theirs.* 那些書是他們的。

the·ism¹ [ˈθiɪzəm; ˈθi:izəm] *n.* ①一神論; 人格神論。 ②有神論。 —**the·ist,** *n., adj.* —**the·is·tic, the·is·ti·cal,** *adj.* —**the·is·ti·cal·ly,** *adv.*

the·ism² *n.* 〖醫〗茶中毒。

:them [ðɛm; ðem] *pron.* the objective case of **they.** 他們;她們;它們。 The books are new; take care of *them.* 這些書是新的, 對它們當心些。 —*adj.* 〖非標準英語〗那些(=those).

the·mat·ic [θiˈmætɪk; θiˈmætik] *adj.* ①論題的;主題的。②〖音樂〗主題的;主旋律的。(亦作 **thematical**)

***theme** [θim; θi:m] *n.* ①題; 題目。②(學生的)作文;作文題。③〖音樂〗主題;樂旨;主旋律。 a *theme* song. 主題歌。④〖俗〗個人或一羣人習慣上的話題、表示、評論等。

The·mis [ˈθimɪs; ˈθi:mis] *n.* 〖希臘神話〗席米斯 (法律與正義之女神)。

:them·selves [ðəmˈsɛlvz; ðəmˈselvz] *pron.*, pl. of **himself, herself, itself.** 他(她,它) 們自己。 **a.** 用以加强語勢。 They *themselves* saw it. 他們親眼看見它。 **b.** 用作反身代名詞。 They are deceiving *themselves.* 他們在欺騙自己。 **c.** 常態;正常情況。 The girls were so excited that they were not *themselves.* 女孩子們是如此興奮, 簡直舉止失常了。 ***by themselves*** **a.** 無他人援助地。 **b.** 孤獨地;無伴地。

:then [ðɛn; ðen] *adv.* ①在將來的某時; 屆時。 We shall have left school *then.* 那時我們將已離開學校。②在過去的某時;當時。 Prices were not so high *then.* 當時的物價沒有這樣高。③然後; 之後。 He had a bath and *then* went to bed. 他洗一個澡, 然後睡覺。④繼之。 First comes spring, *then* summer. 春天先來, 繼之是夏天。⑤那麼;因此。 *Then* you don't approve of the plan? 那麼你是不贊成這項計畫了? ⑥並且;還。 *Then* there's Mr. Smith. We must ask him to come. 還有史密斯先生, 我們必須請他來。⑦不久以後。 The noise stopped, and *then* began again. 噪聲停止了, 但不久又開始了。⑧下一個;次一個。 ***but then*** 同時;但是另一方面。 ***now and then*** 時時;有時; 間或。 I go to see him *now and then.* 我時常去看他。 ***now...then...*** 有時…有時…。 *Now* close, *then* open. 有時關有時開。 ***now then*** (抗議,警告)可是,喂! *Now then,* a little less noise there! 喂, 靜一點! ***there and then*** or ***then and there*** 當場立卽。 I decided to do it *there and then.* 我決定當場立刻就做。 ***What then?*** 那便會怎樣呢 (那麼一來就會發生甚麼結果呢)? —*n.* 其時;那時;當時。 By *then* we shall know the result. 至遲到那時我們將知道結果了。 ***every now and then*** =**now and then.** —*adj.* 當時的。 —*conj.* 此外(前面常有 and)。 And *then,* you must remember .... 此外, 你必須記住…。

the·nar [ˈθinɑr; ˈθi:nɑ:] *n.* 〖解剖〗①手掌;脚掌。②拇指基部之肉球。—*adj.* 〖解剖〗拇指基部之肉球的;手掌的;脚掌的。

***thence** [ðɛns; ðens] *adv.* ①由彼處。②由那個來源。③〖罕〗自彼時。④因爲那個緣故;因而。

thence·forth [ˌðɛnsˈforθ; ˈðensˈfɔ:θ] *adv.* 從那時以後。

thence·for·ward(s) [ˌðɛnsˈfɔrwəd(z); ˈðensˈfɔ:wəd(z)] *adv.* =**thenceforth.**

theo- 〖字首〗表"神;上帝"之義。(在母音前作 **the-**)

the·o·cen·tric [ˌθioˈsɛntrɪk; ˌθi:ouˈsentrik] *adj.* 以神爲宇宙之中心的。

the·oc·ra·cy [θiˈɑkrəsɪ; θiˈɔkrəsi] *n., pl.* **-cies.** ①神權政治。②僧侶政治。③實行神權政治或僧侶政治的國家。

the·oc·ra·sy [θiˈɑkrəsɪ; θiˈɔkrəsi] *n.* ①混合諸神爲一神。②混合崇敬諸神。③靈魂與上帝之神祕融合爲一。

the·o·crat [ˈθiəˌkræt; ˈθiəkræt] *n.* ①神權政治之執政者。②擁護神權政治者。

the·o·crat·ic [ˌθiəˈkrætɪk; ˌθiəˈkrætik] *adj.* 神權政治或僧侶政治的。(亦作 **theocratical**) —**al·ly,** *adv.*

the·od·o·lite [θiˈɑdlˌaɪt; θiˈɔdəlait] *n.* 經緯儀(測量水平及垂直角度之一種儀器)。

The·o·dore [ˈθiəˌdor; ˈθiədɔ:] *n.* 男子名 (暱稱 Ted, Teddy).

the·og·o·ny [θiˈɑgənɪ; θi:ˈɔgəni] *n., pl.* **-nies.** 神譜; 神統; 敍述神統之史詩。

theol. ①theologian. ②theological. ③theology.

the·o·lo·gian [ˌθiəˈlodʒən; θiəˈloudʒən] *n.* 神學家。

the·o·log·i·cal [ˌθiəˈlɑdʒɪkl; θiəˈlɔdʒikəl] *adj.* 神學的;神學上的。(亦作 **theologic**) —**ly,** *adv.*

the·ol·o·gist [θiˈɑlədʒɪst; θiˈɔlədʒist] *n.* 神學家。

the·ol·o·gize [θiˈɑləˌdʒaɪz; θiˈɔlədʒaiz] *v.*, **-gized, -giz·ing.** —*v.t.* 使具神學性質; 使成爲神學上之名詞。—*v.i.* ①從神學觀點思索。②研究神學。

the·ol·o·gy [θiˈɑlədʒɪ; θiˈɔlədʒi] *n.*,

pl. -gies. ①神學。②宗教學；宗教信仰學。③宗教信仰制度。

the·o·ma·ni·a [ˌθiəˈmenɪə; θiəˈmeiniə] *n.* ①自命爲神之狂病。②宗教狂。

the·o·ma·ni·ac [ˌθiəˈmenɪˌæk; θiəˈmeiniæk] *n.* ①自命爲神的狂人。②宗教狂者。

the·op·a·thy [θiˈɑpəθɪ; θiˈɔpəθi] *n.* 虔誠。

the·oph·a·ny [θiˈɑfənɪ; θiˈɔfəni] *n.*, *pl.* -nies. 神之顯現；顯靈；顯聖。

the·o·phi·lan·thro·py [ˌθiəfɪˈlænθrəpɪ; ˌθiəfiˈlænθrəpi] *n.* 宗教博愛；愛神並愛人。

the·o·pho·bia [ˌθiəˈfobɪə; θiəˈfoubiə] *n.* 上帝恐懼；懼上帝。

the·o·phyl·lin(e) [ˌθiəˈfɪlin; θiəˈfili:n] *n.*〖化〗茶鹼。

theor. theorem.

the·or·bo [θiˈɔrbo; θiˈɔ:bou] *n.*, *pl.* -bos. (十七世紀的)一種雙頸大琵琶。

the·o·rem [ˈθiərəm; ˈθiərəm] *n.* ①〖數學〗定理。②用方程式或公式表明的法則。③〖邏輯〗(可被證明的)一般的命題；定理。

the·o·re·mat·ic [ˌθiərəˈmætɪk; ˌθiərəˈmætik] *adj.* 命題的；定理的。

the·o·ret·i·cal [ˌθiəˈrɛtɪkl̩; θiəˈretikəl] *adj.* ①理論的；理論上的。②推理的；推想的。(亦作 **theoretic**)

the·o·ret·i·cal·ly [ˌθiəˈrɛtəkəlɪ; θiəˈretikəli] *adv.* 就理論上；按理論。

the·o·re·ti·cian [ˌθiərəˈtɪʃən; ˌθiəreˈtiʃən] *n.* 理論家。

the·o·ret·ics [ˌθiəˈrɛtɪks; θiəˈretiks] *n.* (作 *sing.* 解)(科學等之)推理部分；理論。

the·o·rist [ˈθiərɪst; ˈθiərist] *n.* 理論家。

the·o·rize [ˈθiəˌraɪz; ˈθiəraiz] *v.i.*, -rized, -riz·ing. 創立理論或學說；推理。

‡**the·o·ry** [ˈθiərɪ, ˈθɪərɪ; ˈθiəri] *n.*, *pl.* -ries. ①學說；論。Einstein's *theory* of relativity. 愛因斯坦的相對論。②學理；原理。③空論；理論。④意見；看法。*in theory* 按理論。

the·o·soph·i·cal [ˌθiəˈsɑfɪkl̩; θiəˈsɔfikəl] *adj.* ①通神學的；通神論的。②通神學者的；通神論者的。(亦作 **theosophic**)

the·os·o·phist [θiˈɑsəfɪst; θiˈɔsəfist] *n.* 通神學者；通神論者。

the·os·o·phy [θiˈɑsəfɪ; θiˈɔsəfi] *n.* 通神學；通神論。

ther·a·peu·tic [ˌθɛrəˈpjutɪk; ˌθerəˈpju:tik] *adj.* 治療學的；治療術的；治療的。(亦作 **therapeutical**)

therapeutic abortion 基於母體健康理由而做的墮胎。(亦作 **justifiable abortion**)

ther·a·peu·tics [ˌθɛrəˈpjutɪks; ˌθerəˈpju:tiks] *n.* (作 *sing.* 解)治療學；療法。

ther·a·peu·tist [ˌθɛrəˈpjutɪst; ˌθerəˈpju:tist] *n.* ①治療學家。②物理治療家。③精神治療家。(亦作 **therapist**)

ther·a·py [ˈθɛrəpɪ; ˈθerəpi] *n.*, *pl.* -pies. ①療法；治療。②治療力；治療性。③物理治療。④精神治療。⑤任何緩和緊張之工作、嗜好等活動。

Ther·a·va·da [ˌθɛrəˈvɑdə; ˌθerəˈvɑ:də] *n.*〖佛教〗小乘 (=Hinayana).

Ther·a·va·din [ˌθɛrəˈvɑdn̩; ˌθerəˈvɑ:dn] *n.*〖佛教〗小乘派之佛教徒。

‡**there** [ðɛr; ðɛə] *adv.* ①在那裏；在彼處。Sit *there*. 坐在那裏。②往那裏；向彼處。Go *there* at once. 馬上到那裏去。③在那一點；關於那一點。You are mistaken *there*. 在那一點上你錯了。④(在行動、故事等之) 某一點上。⑤與 verb to be 連用。*There* is a book on the table. 桌子上有一本書。⑥與其他置於主詞之前的動詞連用。*There* goes the bell. 鐘在響着。⑦用以引起注意。*There* they go. 看, 他們開始了。⑧用以表示嘉許、鼓勵等。*There*'s a good boy! 這才是個好孩子! ***all there***〖俗〗a. 清醒的；警覺的。b. 理智的。***be all there***〖俗〗(能力、精神)很正常；很好。***get there***〖俚〗達到目的；成功。***go there and back*** 往返。Can we *go there and back* before lunch? 中飯以前我們能往返嗎? ***here and there*** 到處；各處。***there and then*** (or ***then and there***) 當場立卽。***there or thereabouts*** 大致那樣；差不多。***You have me there.*** 這要輸給你了。—*adj.* 用以强調。a. 置於指示代名詞, 或以指示形容詞形容的名詞之後。如：Ask that man *there*. b.〖非標準英語〗置於指示形容詞及此指示形容詞所形容的名詞之間。如：Ask that *there* man. —*n.* ①那裏；彼處。It was brought from *there*. 這東西是從那裏帶來的。②那個狀態或情況。—*interj.* 表示安慰或得意等。*There! there!* Don't cry. 好啦！好啦！不要哭啦。

***there·a·bout(s)** [ˌðɛrəˈbaut(s); ˈðɛərəbaut(s)] *adv.* ①在那地方附近。②在那個時間前後。③在那個數目、數量、程度、地位等左右。

***there·af·ter** [ðɛrˈæftə, -ˈɑf-; ðɛərˈɑ:ftə] *adv.* ①其後。②據此。

there·at [ðɛrˈæt; ðɛərˈæt] *adv.* 在那個地方；在那個時候；因此；於是。

there·by** [ðɛrˈbaɪ; ˈðɛəˈbai] *adv.* ①藉以。②與那個相關連。③在該處附近。④〖蘇〗大約。⑤〖廢〗關於。come thereby*** 遇到或獲得那個。

there·for [ðɛrˈfɔr; ðɛəˈfɔ:] *adj.*〖法律〗爲彼；爲此；因此。

‡**there·fore** [ˈðɛrˌfor, -ˌfɔr; ˈðɛəfɔ:, -fɔə] *adv.* 因此；所以。

there·from [ðɛrˈfrɑm; ðɛəˈfrɔm] *adv.* 從那裏。

there·in [ðɛrˈɪn; ðɛərˈin] *adv.* ①在裏面。②在那一點上；那樣。

there·in·af·ter [ˌðɛrɪnˈæftə; ˌðɛərinˈɑ:ftə] *adv.* 在下(文)。

there·in·be·fore [ˌðɛrɪnbɪˈfor; ˌðɛərinbiˈfɔ:] *adv.* 在上(文)。

there·in·to [ðɛrˈɪntu; ðɛərˈintu:] *adv.* 在其中；向其中。

there·of [ðɛrˈɑv; ðɛərˈɔv, -ˈɔf] *adv.*〖古〗①由是；由此。②屬於它的；關於它的。

there·on [ðɛrˈɑn; ðɛərˈɔn] *adv.* ①在那上面。②立刻地。

there·out [ðɛrˈaut; ðɛərˈaut] *adv.*〖古〗由此；由是。

there's [ðɛrz; ðɛəz] ① = **there is.** ② = **there has.**

there·through [ðɛrˈθru; ðɛəˈθru:] *adv.* ①經由那個、它等。②藉以。

there·to [ðɛrˈtu; ðɛəˈtu:] *adv.* ①到那裏；至彼。②另外；更。

there·to·fore [ˌðɛrtəˈfor; ˈðɛətəˈfɔ:] *adv.* 在那時之前；直到那時。

there·un·der [ðɛrˈʌndə; ðɛərˈʌndə] *adv.* ①在其下。②遵照。③少於；不到。

there·un·to [ðɛrˈʌntu; ðɛəˈʌntu(:)] *adv.* 向彼處；對彼事物。

there·up·on [ˌðɛrəˈpɑn; ˈðɛərəˈpɔn] *adv.* ①隨卽；立卽。②因此；所以。③在其上。④〖古〗就那個問題；關於那件事。

there·with [ðɛrˈwɪð, -ˈwɪθ; ðɛəˈwiθ, -ˈwið] *adv.* ①外加。②隨後。

there·with·al [ˌðɛrwɪðˈɔl; ˌðɛəwiˈðɔ:l] *adv.* 其外；此外；又。

the·ri·ac [ˈθɪrɪˌæk; ˈθiriæk] *n.* ①糖漿;糖蜜。②〖醫〗一種解毒茶。(亦作 **theriaca**)
therm [θɝm; θəːm] *n.* 〖物理〗①大卡路里(=great calorie). ②小卡路里(=small calorie). ③撒姆(熱量單位,等於1,000大卡路里)。(亦作 **therme**)
therm- 〖字首〗表"熱;熱電"之義。
therm. ①thermometer. ②thermometric.
ther·mal [ˈθɝml̩; ˈθəːməl] *adj.* ①熱的;溫度的。②溫泉的。—*n.* 一股上升之熱空氣。—**ly,** *adv.*
thermal capacity 熱容量。
thermal efficiency 熱效率。
thermal pollution 熱污染。(亦作 **heat pollution, calefaction**)
thermal spring 溫泉。
thermal unit 熱量單位。
therm·an·ti·dote [θɚˈmæntɪdot; θəːˈmæntidout] *n.* 印度昔時用的冷風機。
ther·mic [ˈθɝmɪk; ˈθəːmik] *adj.* 熱的;由於熱的;熱量的。
therm·i·on [ˈθɝmɪən; ˈθəːmiən] *n.* 〖物理〗熱游子。
therm·i·on·ic [ˌθɝmɪˈɑnɪk; ˌθəːmiˈɔnik] *adj.* 熱游子的。
thermionic current 熱游子電流。
therm·i·on·ics [ˌθɝmɪˈɑnɪks; ˌθəːmiˈɔniks] *n.* 熱游子學。
thermionic tube 熱游子管。
ther·mo·bat·ter·y [ˌθɝmoˈbætərɪ; ˌθəːmouˈbætəri] *n.* 熱電池。
ther·mo·chem·is·try [ˌθɝmoˈkɛmɪstrɪ; ˌθəːmouˈkemistri] *n.* 熱化學。
ther·mo·du·ric [ˌθɝmoˈdjurɪk; ˌθəːmouˈdjuːrik] *adj.* (細菌、微生物等)抗熱性的;不能以高熱殺死的。
ther·mo·dy·nam·ic [ˌθɝmodaɪˈnæmɪk; ˈθəːmoudaiˈnæmik] *adj.* 熱力學的;熱力的。(亦作 **thermodynamical**)
ther·mo·dy·nam·ics [ˌθɝmodaɪˈnæmɪks; ˈθəːmoudaiˈnæmiks] *n.* 熱力學。
ther·mo·e·lec·tric [ˌθɝmo·ɪˈlɛktrɪk; ˌθəːmouiˈlektrik] *adj.* 熱電的。(亦作 **thermoelectrical**)
ther·mo·e·lec·tric·i·ty [ˌθɝmo·ɪˌlɛkˈtrɪsətɪ; ˈθəːmouiˌlekˈtrisiti] *n.* 熱電。
thermoelectric thermometer 熱電溫度計。
ther·mo·e·lec·trom·e·ter [ˌθɝmo·ɪˌlɛkˈtrɑmətɚ; ˈθəːmouiˌlekˈtrɔmitə] *n.* 熱電流計。
ther·mo·gen·e·sis [ˌθɝmoˈdʒɛnɪsɪs; ˌθəːmouˈdʒenisis] *n.* 〖生理〗產熱;生熱作用。(亦作 **thermogeny**)
ther·mo·ge·net·ic [ˌθɝmodʒɪˈnɛtɪk; ˌθəːmoudʒiˈnetik] *adj.* 產生體溫的;生熱的。
ther·mo·graph [ˈθɝməˌgræf; ˈθəːməgrɑːf] *n.* 自動溫度記錄器。
ther·mo·jet [ˈθɝmoˌdʒɛt; ˈθəːmoudʒet] *n.* 〖航空〗熱力噴射(一種噴射引擎)。
ther·mol·o·gy [θɚˈmɑlədʒɪ; θəˈmɔlədʒi] *n.* 熱學。
thermom. ①thermometer. ②thermometric.
ther·mom·e·ter** [θəˈmɑmətɚ, θɚ-; θəˈmɔmitə, ˈθmɔm-] *n.* 寒暑表;溫度計。Centigrade*** (or ***Celsius***) ***thermometer*** 攝氏寒暑表(冰點0度,沸點100度)。***clinical thermometer*** 體溫計。***Fahrenheit thermometer*** 華氏寒暑表(冰點32度,沸點212度)。***Réaumur thermometer*** 列氏寒暑表(冰點0度,沸點80度)。
ther·mo·met·ric [ˌθɝməˈmɛtrɪk; ˌθəːməˈmetrik] *adj.* 寒暑表的;溫度計的;以溫度計測量的。(亦作 **thermometrical**)
ther·mom·e·try [θɚˈmɑmətrɪ; θəˈmɔmətri] *n.* ①計溫學;計溫術。②溫度之測定。
ther·mo·nu·cle·ar [ˌθɝmoˈnuklɪɚ; ˌθəːmouˈnjuːkliə] *adj.* 原子核分裂時所產生之熱能的;熱核的。*thermonuclear* reaction. 熱核反應。
ther·mo·nuke [ˈθɝməˌnjuk; ˈθəːmənjuːk] *n.* 〖美俗〗核子武器。
ther·mo·pile [ˈθɝməˌpaɪl; ˈθəːmoupail] *n.* 〖物理〗熱電堆。
ther·mo·plas·tic [ˌθɝmoˈplæstɪk; ˌθəːmouˈplæstik] *adj.* 受熱時卽變軟與可塑的(塑膠等);熱塑形的。—*n.* 熱塑形物;熱熔物。
ther·mo·reg·u·la·tion [ˌθɝməˌrɛgjəˈleʃən; ˈθəːməˌregjuˈleiʃən] *n.* 體溫調節。
ther·mo·reg·u·la·tor [ˌθɝməˈrɛgjuˌletɚ; ˌθəːməˈregjuleitə] *n.* 溫度調節器。
ther·mos [ˈθɝməs; ˈθəːmɔs] *n.* =**thermos bottle.**
thermos bottle 熱水瓶。(亦作 **thermos flask**)
ther·mo·scope [ˈθɝməˌskop; ˈθəːməskoup] *n.* 驗溫器。
ther·mo·set·ting [ˈθɝmoˌsɛtɪŋ; ˈθəːmouˌsetiŋ] *adj.* 加熱卽硬化的(可塑物)。—*n.* 加熱卽硬化之特性;加熱使硬化。
ther·mo·sta·bil·i·ty [ˌθɝmostəˈbɪlətɪ; ˌθəːmoustəˈbiliti] *n.* 〖生化〗耐熱性。
ther·mo·sta·ble [ˌθɝmoˈstebl̩; ˌθəːmouˈsteibl] *adj.* 〖生化〗耐熱性的(如毒素等)。
ther·mo·stat [ˈθɝməˌstæt; ˈθəːməstæt] *n.* ①自動調溫器。②自動示溫器。—**ic,** *adj.*
ther·mo·stat·ics [ˌθɝməˈstætɪks; ˌθəːməsˈtætiks] *n.* 靜熱力學;熱平衡論。
ther·mo·tax·ic [ˌθɝməˈtæksɪk; ˌθəːməˈtæksik] *adj.* ①向熱性的;趨熱性的。②體溫調節的。
ther·mo·tax·is [ˌθɝməˈtæksɪs; ˌθəːməˈtæksis] *n.* ①〖生物〗向熱性;趨熱性;向熱運動。②〖生理〗體溫調節。
ther·mo·ther·a·py [ˌθɝmoˈθɛrəpɪ; ˈθəːmouˈθɛərəpi] *n.* 熱療法。
ther·mot·ics [θɚˈmɑtɪks; θəˈmɔtiks] *n.* 熱學。
the·roid [ˈθɪrɔɪd; ˈθirɔid] *adj.* 獸性的;似獸的。
the·sau·rus [θɪˈsɔrəs; θi(ː)ˈsɔːrəs] *n., pl.* **-ri** [-raɪ; -rai], **-rus·es.** ①寶庫;倉庫。②字典;辭典;百科全書等知識寶庫之書籍。
:these [ðiz; ðiːz] *pron.* pl. of **this,** *adj.* —*pron.* 這些。Don't look at *these.* 不要看這些。—*adj.* 這些。in *these* days. 現今。
The·seus [ˈθisjus; ˈθiːsjuːs] *n.* 〖希臘神話〗Attica 之英雄。
the·sis [ˈθisɪs; ˈθiːsis] *n., pl.* **-ses** [-siz; -siːz]. ①論文;畢業論文;學位論文;課題。②〖音樂〗指揮棒之朝下揮動。③〖哲學〗(黑格爾辯證法中"正","反","合"之)正。
Thes·pi·an, thes·pi·an [ˈθɛspɪən; ˈθespiən] *adj.* ①Thespis 的。②悲劇的;戲劇的。—*n.* 悲劇演員;演員;優伶。
Thes·pis [ˈθɛspɪs; ˈθespis] *n.* 狄斯比斯(紀元前六世紀人,爲希臘悲劇之始祖)。
Thes·sa·lo·ni·ans [ˌθɛsəˈlonɪənz; ˌθesəˈlouniənz] *n. pl.* (作 *sing.* 解)(新約)帖撒羅尼迦前後書。
the·ta [ˈθetə, ˈθitə; ˈθeitə, ˈθiːtə] *n.* 希臘字母之第八字母(卽 Θ, θ, 相當於英文之th)。
thet·i·cal [ˈθɛtɪkl̩; ˈθetikəl] *adj.* 獨斷

的;過於自信的;武斷的。(亦作 **thetic**)

the·ur·gy [ˈθiɝdʒɪ; ˈθiːəːdʒi] *n., pl.* **-gies.** ①神力;神蹟。②通神術;妖術。③人事中神力或超自然力之介入。

thew [θju; θjuː] *n.* ①(常*pl.*) 肌肉;腱。②(*pl.*)體力;肌力。***thews and sinews***體力。

‡they [ðe; ðei] *pron.* pl. of **he, she, it.** ①他(她,它)們;彼等。②人們。*They* say. 人們說;據說。

they'd [ðed; ðeid] ①=**they had.** ②=**they would.**

they'll [ðel; ðeil] ①=**they will.** ②=**they shall.**

they're [ðer; ðeə] =**they are.**

they've [ðev; ðeiv] =**they have.**

thi·a·mine [ˈθaɪəˌmin; ˈθaiəmiːn] *n.* 〖生化〗維他命 B_1。

Thi·bet [tɪˈbɛt; tiˈbet] *n.* =**Tibet.**

Thi·bet·an [tɪˈbɛtən; tiˈbetən] *adj., n.* =**Tibetan.**

‡thick [θɪk; θik] *adj.* ①厚的;粗大的。a *thick* board. 一塊厚板。②濃的;稠的。*thick* fog. 濃霧。Blood is *thicker* than water. 血濃於水(疏不間親)。③密集的;稠密的。She has *thick* hair. 她的頭髮濃密。The air is *thick* with dust. 空氣中充滿灰塵。④不晴朗的(天氣等)。The weather was *thick.* 天氣陰霾。⑤不清晰的;重濁的(聲音)。⑥〖俗〗愚笨的;遲鈍的。He has a *thick* head. 他頭腦遲鈍。⑦〖俗〗親密的。⑧〖俗〗不能忍受的。⑨顯著的。⑩誇張得令人生厭的。***as thick as thieves*** 非常親密。***be thick with*** 充滿。(參看③例)。—*adv.* 厚地;密地;密集地;豐富地;時常地;迅速地;不清晰地。The snow was falling *thick.* 大雪正紛飛。***come thick and fast*** 大批而迅速地來臨。***lay it on thick***〖俗〗**a.** 過分恭維。**b.** 苛責。—*n.* 最厚之部分;最濃密之部分;最密集之部分;最盛之部分。in the *thick* of the fight. 在酣戰之中。***through thick and thin*** 同甘共苦。

thick-and-thin [ˈθɪkənˈθɪn; ˈθikənˈθin] *adj.* 不辭任何困難的;忠貞不渝的;忠實獻身的。*thick-and-thin* friends. 刎頸之交。

thick-braind [ˈθɪkˌbrend; ˈθikbreind] *adj.* 愚蠢的;低能的。

***thick·en** [ˈθɪkən; ˈθikən] *v.t. & v.i.* ①使厚;變厚。②使濃;變濃。③使密集;密集。④使複雜;變爲複雜。The plot *thickens.* 情節漸趨複雜。

thick·en·ing [ˈθɪkənɪŋ; ˈθikəniŋ] *n.* ①(使液體加濃的)濃化劑。②變濃或加厚的作用或過程;濃化。③變濃或加厚之部分。

***thick·et** [ˈθɪkɪt; ˈθikit] *n.* 灌木叢。

thick·head [ˈθɪkˌhɛd; ˈθikhed] *n.* 笨伯;頭腦愚鈍的人。

thick-head·ed [ˈθɪkˈhɛdɪd; ˈθikˈhedid] *adj.* 愚蠢的;愚笨的。—**ness,** *n.* —**ly,** *adv.*

thick·ish [ˈθɪkɪʃ; ˈθikiʃ] *adj.* 稍厚的;稍濃的;稍粗的。

thick-leafed [ˈθɪkˌlift; ˈθikliːft] *adj.* =**thick-leaved.**

thick-leaved [ˈθɪkˌlivd; ˈθikliːvd] *adj.* ①葉子茂盛的。②葉厚的;有厚葉的。

thick-lipped [ˈθɪkˌlɪpt; ˈθiklipt] *adj.* 厚唇的。

***thick·ly** [ˈθɪklɪ; ˈθikli] *adv.* ①濃密地。②大量地;充沛地。③時常地;頻繁地。④聲音沙啞地。

thick-necked [ˈθɪkˈnɛkt; ˈθikˈnekt] *adj.* 粗頸的。

***thick·ness** [ˈθɪknɪs; ˈθiknis] *n.* ①厚;厚度。②聲音沙啞不清;含混不清。③一層。④厚的部分。

thick·set [ˈθɪkˈsɛt; ˈθikˈset] *adj.* ①矮胖而健壯的。②密植的;稠密的;繁茂的。—*n.* 草叢;灌木叢。

thick·skin [ˈθɪkˌskɪn; ˈθikskin] *n.* ①皮厚的人。②對批評等麻木不仁的人。

thick·skinned [ˈθɪkˈskɪnd; ˈθikˈskind] *adj.* ①皮厚的。②對批評、污辱等感覺遲鈍的。

thick-wit·ted [ˈθɪkˈwɪtɪd; ˈθikˈwitid] *adj.* 愚笨的;愚鈍的。

***thief** [θif; θiːf] *n., pl.* **thieves** [θivz; θiːvz]. 賊;竊賊。

thieve [θiv; θiːv] *v.i. & v.t.,* **thieved, thiev·ing.** 偷竊。

thiev·er·y [ˈθivərɪ; ˈθiːvəri] *n., pl.* **-ies.** ①偷竊行爲;偷竊。②被竊之物。

thieves' Latin 盜賊的隱語;黑話;切口。

thiev·ish [ˈθivɪʃ; ˈθiːviʃ] *adj.* ①有偷竊習慣的;好偷竊的。②像賊的;有賊性的。③偷偷摸摸的;隱密的。(亦作 **theftuous**) —**ly,** *adv.* —**ness,** *n.*

***thigh** [θaɪ; θai] *n.* ①股(腿之上半節,自胯至膝之部分)。②大腿骨。(亦作**thigh bone**) —**ed,** *adj.*

thigh·bone [ˈθaɪˌbon; ˈθaiboun] *n.* 〖解剖〗股骨;大腿骨。

thill [θɪl; θil] *n.* (馬車之)杠;轅。

thill·er [ˈθɪlɚ; ˈθilə] *n.* 轅馬。

thim·ble [ˈθɪmbl; ˈθimbl] *n.* 頂針;針箍;嵌環。—**thim·bled,** *adj.*

thim·ble·ber·ry [ˈθɪmblˌbɛrɪ; ˈθimblbəri] *n.* 美國產的一種草莓。

thim·ble·ful [ˈθɪmblˌfʊl; ˈθimblful] *n., pl.* **-fuls.** 〖俗〗很少的量;些微(多指液體)。

thim·ble·rig [ˈθɪmblˌrɪg; ˈθimblrig] *n., v.,* **-rigged, -rig·ging.** —*n.* ①一種遊戲(遊戲者以迅速手法將一豆置於三隻小杯中任一隻之下,而讓人猜在那隻杯下)。②以上述手法行騙的人。—*v.t.* 欺騙。

‡thin [θɪn; θin] *adj.,* **thin·ner, thin·nest,** *adv., v.,* **thinned, thin·ning.** —*adj.* ①薄的。*thin* cloth. 薄布。②細的。*thin* rope. 細繩。③瘦的。His illness made him *thin.* 他的病使他瘦了。④稀疏的;稀薄的;稀少的。*thin* hair. 稀疏的頭髮。⑤微弱的(聲音)。⑥淺薄的;淺顯的;貧乏的。a *thin* excuse. 易於識破之託辭。⑦淡的;淺的(色彩)。⑧〖俗〗難過的。Unemployed workers have a *thin* time. 失業者難以度日。⑨無力的;不够誠懇的。⑩(底片)因曝光不足而濃淡對比不顯明的。—*adv.* 薄地;稀疏地;微弱地。Slice the ham *thin.* 將火腿切薄。—*v.t. & v.i.* ①使薄;變薄。②使細;變細。③使瘦;變瘦。④使稀薄;使稀疏;使稀少;變爲稀疏;變爲稀少。The crowd is *thinning* out. 羣衆開始散去。⑤使微弱;變爲微弱。—**ly,** *adv.* —**ner,** —**ness,** *n.*

***thine** [ðaɪn; ðain] *pron.,* possessive case of **thou.** ①(只能用於母音之前) =**your, thy.** ②=**yours.**

‡thing [θɪŋ; θiŋ] *n.* ①物件;東西。②(*pl.*)所有物;衣服;用品。③事;行爲。④(*pl.*)情況;事情。⑤人(含有熟識或憐惜之意)。He's a foolish old *thing.* 他是一個糊塗的老東西。⑥非物質的事物。⑦工作。I've a lot of *things* to do today. 今天我有許多工作要做。⑧細節;方面。He is perfect in all *things.* 他在各方面都完美無缺。⑨目標;目的。⑩〖俗〗懼怕;對某一事物之特殊態度、感覺等。She has a *thing* about cats. 她怕貓。⑪(the-)最適合的東西;最良好的情況。That's not at all the *thing* to do. 那是完全不行的。⑫其

他用法：I am not quite the *thing* today. 我今天不大舒服。The *thing* is can we get there in time? 問題是我們能否及時趕到那裏? *things* Chinese. 中國之文物。***a near thing*** 險些發生的意外事件; 幾乎太晚。***an understood thing*** 意見協調之事; 心照不宣之事。***as a general*** (or ***usual***) ***thing*** 一般地;通常地。***as things are*** 據目前形勢(情形)。***for one thing*** 首先,一則。*For one thing* I haven't the money; for another.... 一則我沒錢, 二則…。***know a thing or two*** 〖俗〗有經驗;聰明能幹。***look*** (or ***feel***) ***quite the thing*** 健康(常用於否定語)。He doesn't *look quite the thing* this morning. 今天早晨他氣色不佳。***make a good thing of*** 因…賺到錢;從…獲利。She *made a good thing of* her spare-time hobbies.她利用暇時的嗜好大賺其錢。***no such thing*** 那裏會;沒有這樣的事。***not to get a thing out of*** **a.** 得不到消息、知識等。**b.** 不能賞識; 不了解。***of all things*** 用以表示驚訝、憤慨之意。***see things*** 看見幻想中的東西; 生幻覺。***the thing*** **a.** 風行之式樣或形式。**b.** 重要的事;重要的想法。**c.** 該做之事。***things personal*** (***real***) 動產(不動產)。

thing·a·my, thing·um·my [ˈθɪŋəmɪ; ˈθiŋəmi] *n.* 〖俗〗某某人; 某件東西。

thing-in-it·self [ˈθɪŋɪnɪtˈsɛlf; ˈθiŋinitˈself] *n.* 〖康德哲學〗物之自體(物之具有超越人類知覺與知識之現實, 故是不能了解的)。

thing·y [ˈθɪŋɪ; ˈθiŋi] *adj.*, **thing·i·er, thing·i·est.** ①物的;物體的;物質的。②現實的;實際的。

‡think [θɪŋk; θiŋk] *v.*, **thought** [θɔt; θɔːt], **think·ing,** *adj.* —*v.i.* ①思索;想;考慮。Are animals able to *think?* 動物能思考嗎? ②記憶;憶及;想到。She was *thinking* of her childhood days. 她正依依追憶兒童時代的日子。③意欲;企圖。I even *thought* of resigning. 我甚至想辭職。④以爲; 存有某種看法。⑤發現;想出;計劃。⑥重視。I don't *think* much of him. 我不重視他。—*v.t.* ①想;考慮。I am *thinking* what to do next. 我在想下一步怎麼辦。②認爲;以爲。Do you *think* (that) it will rain? 你以爲會下雨嗎? ③企圖;預料。He *thinks* to escape punishment. 他企圖逃脫受罰。④想像。I can't *think* how you do it. 我想像不出你是怎樣做的。⑤因想以致於;想得。to *think* oneself silly. 想得癡了。***think about*** (or ***of***) 思索; 考慮。***think a lot of*** 喜歡; 尊敬。***think aloud*** 自言自語。***think better of*** **a.** 改變…的念頭。**b.** 認爲(某人)不致於。***think fit*** (or ***good***) ***to*** 認爲…適當。***think for*** 認爲; 預料。It will be better than you *think for.* 那將比你所預期的爲佳。***think highly of*** 器重;看得起。The boss seems to *think highly of* your work. 上司似乎很重視你的工作。***think meanly of a person*** 看不起某人。***think nothing of*** 輕視;認爲無所謂。***think of*** **a.** 思索;思想; 想像。*Think of* the danger! 想想那危險! **b.** 和 should 或 would 與一否定詞結合,爲 would (或 should) never 的强勢語。I shouldn't *think of* doing such a thing! 我怎麼也不會去做這樣的事! **c.** 記起; 記憶。I can't *think of* his name. 我想不起他的名字。**d.** 有某種看法 (與副詞連用)。They didn't *think* much *of* his work. 他們不重視他的工作。**e.** 發現;建議;提示。**f.** 考慮;預料。***think*** (***something***) ***out*** **a.**想出。We must *think out* a plan. 我們必得想出一個計畫來。**b.** 想通;藉思考以解決或了解。**c.** 想透; 從頭到尾仔細考慮。***think out loud*** 說出所想的; 發表。***think over*** 仔細考慮。***think through*** 想通; 想透。***think twice*** 再三考慮;躊躇。***think up*** 想出;想起。—*adj.* ①思想的。②〖俚〗發人深省的。

think·a·ble [ˈθɪŋkəbl; ˈθiŋkəbl] *adj.* 可想的;可想像的;意想可能的。

think·er [ˈθɪŋkə; ˈθiŋkə] *n.* 思考者;思想家。

think factory 〖俚〗科技研究中心。

think·ing** [ˈθɪŋkɪŋ; ˈθiŋkiŋ] *adj.* ①有思想力的。②思考的;沉思的; 好思索的。put on one's thinking cap*** 仔細考慮某事。—*n.* 思考; 思想; 見解。***to my thinking*** 依我想來。—**ly,** *adv.*

think piece 〖新聞〗有關政治、經濟等問題之分析評論。(亦作 **dope story**)

think-so [ˈθɪŋkˌso; ˈθiŋksou] *n.* 〖蔑〗(無人支持的)意見。

thin·ner [ˈθɪnə; ˈθinə] *n.* ①使油漆稀釋之液體, 尤指松脂油。②使稀薄之人或物。③除草者;剪枝者。

thin·nish [ˈθɪnɪʃ; ˈθiniʃ] *adj.* 稍薄的; 稍細的;稍微弱的;稍瘦的。

thin-skinned [ˈθɪnˈskɪnd; ˈθinˈskind] *adj.* ①皮薄的。②敏感的。③易怒的。

thi·o·cy·a·nate [ˌθaɪoˈsaɪənet; ˌθaiouˈsaiəneit] *n.* 〖化〗硫氰化物。(亦作 **sulphocyanate**)

thi·o·cy·an·ic [ˌθaɪosaɪˈænɪk; ˌθaiousaiˈænik] *adj.* 〖化〗硫代氰酸的;從硫代氰酸得來的。

thiocyanic acid 〖化〗硫代氰酸。

Thi·o·kol [ˈθaɪəˌkɑl; ˈθaiəkɔl] *n.* 〖商標名〗一種不怕汽油和有機溶劑的人造橡皮。

thi·on·ic [θaɪˈɑnɪk; θaiˈɔnik] *adj.* 〖化〗①硫的;含硫的。②氧被硫取代的。

thionic acid 〖化〗硫磺酸。

thi·o·nyl [ˈθaɪənəl; ˈθaiənil] *n.* 〖化〗亞硫酸基。

thionyl chloride 二氯化亞硫酸。

thi·o·phe·nol [ˌθaɪəˈfinol; ˌθaiəˈfiːnoul] *n.* 〖化〗硫酚。

thi·o salt [ˈθaɪo～; ˈθaiou～] 硫代鹽。

thi·o·sin·am·in(e) [ˌθaɪosɪnˈæmɪn; ˌθaiousinˈæmin] *n.* 〖化〗L-丙烯基硫脲;乙烯醯脲; N-硫代甲醯胺基乙醯胺。

‡third [θɝd; θəːd] *adj.* ①第三。a *third* party. 第三者。②三分之一的。—*n.* ①第三個。②(月之)三號;三日。③三分之一。④〖音樂〗**a.** 第三音。**b.** 三度音程。**c.** 三度音之音調的組合。⑤〖美〗汽車之第三擋。⑥(*pl.*) **a.** 有子女的寡婦於夫死亡時所應得其夫之財產的三分之一。**b.** 寡婦分內之遺產。—**ly,** *adv.*

third base 〖棒球〗三壘。

third baseman 〖棒球〗三壘手。

third class 第三類; 第三等; 三等車; 三等艙;三等貨品。

third-class [ˈθɝdˈklæs; ˈθəːdˈklɑːs] *adj.* 第三等的; 第三級的; 第三類的。—*adv.* 乘三等車(艙)地;以第三類郵件郵寄地。—*n.* 〖俗〗三等車;三等艙;三等艙旅客。

third degree 〖美〗酷刑逼供;拷問。

third-de·gree [ˈθɝddɪˈgri; ˈθəːddiˈgriː] *v.t.* 酷刑逼供;拷問。

third-degree burn 嚴重之灼傷。

third dimension ①第三度空間; 厚度; 深度。②增加某"陳述"、"連續事件" 等之真實感，或使之更爲生動或更有意義之事物。

third ear 〖俚〗告密者。

third eyelid 〖解剖〗瞬膜。(亦作 **nictitating membrane**)

third finger 無名指。

third force 第三勢力。

third·hand 〔*adj.* ˈθɝdˌhænd; ˈθəːdhænd *adv.* ˈθɝdˈhænd; ˈθəːdˈhænd〕 *adj.* & *adv.* ①第三手的(地)；已經有兩人使用過的(地)。②間接的(地)。

third mate 〖航海〗三副。

third party ①〖美、加〗第三黨。②第三者。

third person 〖文法〗①第三人稱。②第三人稱時使用之代名詞與動詞。

third rail (電車之)第三軌(代替高架電線，藉以供給動力者)。

third-rate 〔ˈθɝdˈret; ˈθəːdˈreit〕 *adj.* ①三等的；三流的。②劣等的；下等的。

third-rat·er 〔ˈθɝdˌretɚ; ˈθəːdˈreitə〕 *n.* 三流貨色；三流人物。

third sex 同性戀者。

Third World 第三世界(指亞非兩洲低度開發，接受民主與共產集團援助，但不與上述任一集團結盟的一群國家)。

*__thirst__ 〔θɝst; θəːst〕 *n.* ①渴；口渴。②渴望；熱望。a *thirst* for knowledge. 求知的熱望。***have a thirst*** 〖俗〗想喝一杯。—*v.i.* ①想喝。I *thirst* for beer. 我想喝啤酒。②渴想；熱望〖for, after〗. to *thirst* for adventure. 渴想冒險。—**er,** *n.* —**less,** *adj.*

*__thirst·y__ 〔ˈθɝstɪ; ˈθəːsti〕 *adj.*, **thirst·i·er, thirst·i·est.** ①渴。I feel *thirsty*. 我覺得渴。②〖俗〗使人口渴的。③乾燥的；亢旱的。④渴望的；熱望的。He was *thirsty* for power. 他渴望掌權。—**thirst·i·ly,** *adv.*

‡**thir·teen** 〔θɝˈtin; ˈθəːˈtiːn〕 *n.* ①十三；13。②十三個；十三人；十三歲。—*adj.* 十三。

*__thir·teenth__ 〔θɝˈtinθ; ˈθəːˈtiːnθ〕 *adj.* ①第十三。②十三分之一的。—*n.* ①第十三。②十三分之一。③(月之)十三日；十三號。

*__thir·ti·eth__ 〔ˈθɝtɪɪθ; ˈθəːtiiθ〕 *adj.* ①第三十。②三十分之一的。—*n.* ①第三十。②三十分之一。③(月之)三十日；三十號。

‡**thir·ty** 〔ˈθɝtɪ; ˈθəːti〕 *n., pl.* **-ties.** ①三十；30。②三十個；三十人；三十歲。③(*pl.*)三十與四十之間。during the *thirties*. 在三十年代間。a person of *thirties*. 三十至四十歲之間的人。—*adj.* 三十。

thir·ty·fold 〔ˈθɝtɪˈfold; ˈθəːtifould〕 *adj.* & *adv.* 三十倍的(地)。

thir·ty-sec·ond note 〔ˈθɝtɪˈsɛkənd~; ˈθəːtiˈsekənd~〕〖音樂〗三十二分音符。(亦作 **demisemiquaver**)

thir·ty-two·mo 〔ˌθɝtɪˈtumo; ˌθəːtiˈtuːmou〕 *n.* ①三十二開紙。②三十二開大小的書。—*adj.* 三十二開大小的。

‡**this** 〔ðɪs; ðis〕 *pron., pl.* **these** 〔ðiz; ðiːz〕, *adj., adv.*—*pron.* 這；此；這個(與 that 相對)。*This* is mine. 這個是我的。***for all this*** 儘管如此。***this, that, and the other*** 一切東西；種種。***with this*** 接著；緊跟著；於是。*With this,* he threw down his glass and left the table. 接著他便擲下酒杯離席而去。—*adj.* 這；這個；此；本。*this* week. 本週。*this* year. 今年。*this* morning. 今晨。***for this once*** (or ***time***) 只這一次。***to this day*** 至今。—*adv.* 到此界限；到此程度；如此。You can have *this* much. 你能得到這麼多。

*__this·tle__ 〔ˈθɪsl̩; ˈθisl〕 *n.* 薊(其紫色花爲蘇格蘭國花)。

this·tle·down 〔ˈθɪsl̩ˌdaun; ˈθisldaun〕 *n.* 薊花的冠毛。

this·tly 〔ˈθɪslɪ; ˈθisli〕 *adj.* ①薊的；如薊的；多刺的。②多薊的。

this-world·ly 〔ˈðɪsˈwɝldlɪ; ˈðisˈwəːldli〕 *adj.* 現世的；今生的；此生的。

*__thith·er__ 〔ˈθɪðɚ, ˈðɪðɚ; ˈðiðə〕 *adv.* 到彼處；向彼方(與 hither 相對)。We walked *thither*. 我們走了過去。***hither and thither*** 到處。—*adj.* 對岸的；那邊的。

thith·er·to 〔ˌθɪðɚˈtu; ˌðiðəˈtuː〕 *adv.* 直到那時。

thith·er·ward 〔ˈθɪðɚwɚd; ˈðiðəwəd〕 *adv.* 向彼處；在彼方。

thith·er·wards 〔ˈθɪðɚwɚdz; ˈðiðəwədz〕 *adv.* =**thitherward.**

tho, tho' 〔ðo; ðou〕 *conj., adv.* =**though.**

thole[1] 〔θol; θoul〕 *n.* (船邊的)槳座；槳栓；槳口。

thole[2] *v.t.*, **tholed, thol·ing.** 〖英方〗①受苦；受難。②忍受。

thole·pin 〔ˈθolˌpɪn; ˈθoulpin〕 *n.* =**thole.**

Thom·as 〔ˈtɑməs; ˈtɔməs〕 *n.* ①男子名。②湯瑪斯(耶穌十二門徒之一)。

Tho·mism 〔ˈtomɪzəm; ˈtoumizəm〕 *n.* Thomas Aquinas 的神學與哲學學說。

Thomp·son submachine gun 〔ˈtɑmpsn̩~~; ˈtɔmpsn~~〕 湯姆生衝鋒槍。

Thom·son[1] 〔ˈtɑmsn̩; ˈtɔmsn〕 *n.* 湯姆生(George Paget, 1892–, 英國物理學家，曾獲1937年諾貝爾物理獎)。

Thom·son[2] *n.* 湯姆生 (Sir Joseph John, 1856–1940, 英國物理學家，獲1906年諾貝爾物理獎)。

thong 〔θɔŋ, θɑŋ; θɔŋ〕 *n.* ①狹長之皮帶。②鞭梢；馬韁繩。—*v.t.* ①裝以皮帶；以皮帶束捆。②以皮鞭打。

Thor 〔θɔr; θɔː〕 *n.* ①〖北歐神話〗雷神。②美國製的雷神飛彈。

tho·ra·ces 〔ˈθorəˌsiz; ˈθourəsiːz〕 *n.* pl. of **thorax.**

tho·rac·ic 〔θoˈræsɪk; θɔːˈræsik〕 *adj.* 〖解剖, 動物〗胸的；胸部的。(亦作 **thoracal**)

tho·rax 〔ˈθoræks; ˈθɔːræks〕 *n., pl.* **-rax·es, -ra·ces** 〔-rəˌsiz; -rəsiːz〕. ①〖解剖〗胸腔；胸部。②昆蟲三節身體中的中間一節。

Tho·reau 〔ˈθoro; ˈθɔːrou〕 *n.* 索洛(Henry David, 1817–1862, 美國作家及哲學家)。

tho·rite 〔ˈθoraɪt; ˈθɔːrait〕 *n.* 〖礦〗矽酸釷礦。

tho·ri·um 〔ˈθorɪəm; ˈθɔːriəm〕 *n.* 釷(化學元素，具放射性，符號 Th)。

*__thorn__ 〔θɔrn; θɔːn〕 *n.* ①刺；棘。②荆棘。③使人煩惱痛苦之事物。***a thorn in one's flesh*** (or ***side***) 經常的煩惱之因；肉中刺。***sit on thorns*** 如坐針氈；焦慮不安。—*v.t.* 使煩惱。

thorn apple ①山楂果。②山楂。③一種茄科毒草。

thorn·back 〔ˈθɔrnˌbæk; ˈθɔːnbæk〕 *n.* (歐洲產的)一種鮪魚。

thorn·bush 〔ˈθɔrnˌbuʃ; ˈθɔːnbuʃ〕 *n.* 有刺之灌木。

Thorn·dike 〔ˈθɔrnˌdaɪk; ˈθɔːndaik〕 *n.* 桑戴克 (Edward Lee, 1874–1949, 美國心理學家、教育家及辭典編纂家)。

thorned 〔θɔrnd; θɔːnd〕 *adj.* 有刺的。

thorn·y 〔ˈθɔrnɪ; ˈθɔːni〕 *adj.*, **thorn·i·er, thorn·i·est.** ①多刺的；多荆棘的。②遍長多刺植物的。③困難的；棘手的。—**thorn·i·ly,** *adv.* —**thorn·i·ness,** *n.*

thor·o 〔ˈθɝo, ˈθɝə; ˈθʌrə〕 *adj., adv., prep.* =**thorough.**

tho·ron 〔ˈθorɑn; ˈθourɔn〕 *n.* 〖化〗釷射氣(爲氡之放射性同位素)。

***thor·ough** [ˈθɝo, –ə; ˈθʌrə] *adj.* ①完全的; 徹底的。This school gives *thorough* instruction. 這學校教學認眞。②周到的。③準確的。④技術精邃的;熟練的。a *thorough* actress. 一個演技精湛的女演員。⑤一絲不苟的;認眞的。—*adv., prep.* 〖古〗= **through.** (亦作 **thoro**) —**ly,** *adv.* —**ness,** *n.*

thorough bass 〖音樂〗①和聲學;和聲法。②數字低音。

thor·ough·bred [ˈθɝoˌbrɛd; ˈθʌrəbred] *adj.* ①純種的(動物, 尤指馬和狗)。②有教養的;精神很好的;舉止優雅的(人)。③生氣勃勃的。—*n.* ①純種動物;純種馬。②有教養的人。—**ness,** *n.*

thor·ough·fare** [ˈθɝoˌfɛr; ˈθʌrəfɛə] *n.* 通路;大道。no thoroughfare*** 不准通行。

thor·ough·go·ing [ˈθɝoˈgo·ɪŋ; ˈθʌrəˌgouiŋ] *adj.* 徹底的;徹頭徹尾的;全然的。

thor·ough·paced [ˈθɝoˌpest; ˈθʌrəpeist] *adj.* 徹底的;十足的。

thorp(e) [θɔrp; θɔːp] *n.* 小村莊。

:those [ðoz; ðouz] *adj., pron.* pl. of **that.** 那些。Who are *those* people? 那些人是誰? ***in those days*** 當時;當年。

:thou [ðau; ðau] *pron., pl.* **ye.** 〖古, 詩〗你(第二人稱, 單數, 主格, =you). *thou* art. =you are. —*v.t.* 以"thou"稱呼。—*v.i.* 談話中用"thou".〖注意〗**thou, thy, thine, thee** 等均爲古語中第二人稱之代名詞。thou 用於單數, 主格; thy 或 thine 用於單數, 所有格; thee 爲單數, 受格; you 或 ye 爲複數, 主格; your 或 yours 爲複數, 所有格; you 或 ye 爲複數, 受格。現在僅用於教會禮拜經文中。

thou. thousand.

:though [ðo; ðou] *conj.* ①雖然。*Though* it was raining, he went there. 雖然當時天正下雨, 他還是到那裏去了。②卽令;縱然。*Though* I fail, I shall try again. 卽令我失敗, 我將再試一下。***as though*** 一若(=as if). —*adv.* 可是;雖然。(亦作 **tho, tho'**)

:thought [θɔt; θɔːt] *v.* pt. & pp. of **think.** —*n.* ①意思;觀念。②沉思冥想。He was absorbed in *thought*. 他在沉思冥想中。③思考;思維。④思想;思潮。modern *thought*. 近代思想。⑤懸念;關注;考慮。Show some *thought* for others than yourself. 爲別人着想一下。⑥意向;意志。⑦預料。I had no *thought* of seeing you here. 我沒有料想到會在這裏看見你。⑧注意。She took no *thought* of her appearance. 她不注意自己的外表。⑨判斷;意見。⑩〖俗〗一點;些微;稍許。Be a *thought* more polite. 文雅一點。***after much thought*** 仔細考慮後。***at the thought of*** 一想到…。***be lost*** (or ***absorbed***) ***in thought*** 在默默地默想。***bestow a thought on; give a thought to*** 考慮一下;想一想。***have no thought of*** 無意。***on second thought(s)*** 經仔細考慮之後。***take no thought for the morrow*** 不慮明天之事。***without a moment's thought*** 立刻;當場。

thought control 思想統制。

***thought·ful** [ˈθɔtfəl; ˈθɔːtful] *adj.* ①深思的;思索的。②有思想的;充滿思想的。③注意的;關切的;體貼的。to be *thoughtful* of others. 關切他人。④細心的; 小心提防的。—**ly,** *adv.* —**ness,** *n.*

***thought·less** [ˈθɔtlɪs; ˈθɔːtlis] *adj.* ①無思想的。②不注意的; 疏忽的。③不關心他人的;自私的。—**ly,** *adv.* —**ness,** *n.*

thought-out [ˈθɔtˌaut; ˈθɔːt–aut] *adj.* 思慮周到的;經過仔細考慮的。

thought-pro·vok·ing [ˈθɔtprəˌvokɪŋ; ˈθɔːtprəˌvoukiŋ] *adj.* 發人深思的; 使人思考的。

thought-read [ˈθɔtˌrid; ˈθɔːtˌriːd] *v.t.* 用讀心術看破(對方的心思)。

thought reader 洞察人心者; 察心術者。

thought reading 人心洞察術;察心術。

thought transference 精神感應。

:thou·sand [ˈθauzn̩d; ˈθauzənd] *n., adj.* ①千;千個;1,000。②多數;無數;成千。There are *thousands* of apples in our garden. 我們花園裏有無數的蘋果。***a thousand to one*** 千對一;幾乎絕對的。***one in a thousand*** 千中之一;罕有的人或物。

thou·sand·fold [ˈθauzn̩dˈfold; ˈθauzəndfould] *adj.* 千倍的。—*adv.* 千倍地。—*n.* 千倍。

Thousand Islands 千島(北美 St. Lawrence 河中之一羣島, 約有1500個小島)。

thou·sand-legs [ˈθauzn̩dˌlɛgz; ˈθauzəndlegz] *n.* 多足類動物。

thou·sandth [ˈθauzn̩dθ; ˈθauzəndθ] *adj.* ①第一千的。②千分之一的。—*n.* ①第一千。②千分之一。

thousandth's place 〖數學〗千位。

thr. through.

Thrace [θres; θreis] *n.* 色雷斯(愛琴海北岸之一地區, 分屬於希臘及土耳其兩國)。

Thra·cian [ˈθreʃən; ˈθreiʃjən] *adj.* 色雷斯 (Thrace) 的。—*n.* 色雷斯人; 色雷斯語。

thrall [θrɔl; θrɔːl] *n.* ①奴隸。②奴隸的身分或地位。

thral(l)·dom [ˈθrɔldəm; ˈθrɔːldəm] *n.* 奴隸身分或地位;奴役。

thrap·ple [ˈθræpl̩; ˈθræpl] *n.* 咽喉;氣管。

thrash** [θræʃ; θræʃ] *v.t.* ①打(穀物)。②笞打;責打 (=beat, flog). ③擊敗; 勝過。④使(船)逆風而上; 使(船)逆流前進。—*v.i.* ①打穀。②猛烈移動; 猛烈動蕩。③〖航海〗逆風前進; 鼓浪前進。thrash out*** 研討解決。***thrash over*** 再三精細檢查; 翻滾。***thrash up*** 徹底討論;徹底討論以解決(問題等)。—*n.* ①打; 鞭打。②〖航海〗逆行。③兩腿交替上下迅速移動之一種游泳姿勢。

thrash·er [ˈθræʃɚ; ˈθræʃə] *n.* ①打穀者; 打穀機。②長尾鮫。③美國產的類似鶇之一種長尾鳥。

thrash·ing [ˈθræʃɪŋ; ˈθræʃiŋ] *n.* ①打穀。②鞭打。③一次打出的穀物。

thrashing floor 打穀場。

thrashing machine 打穀機。

thra·son·i·cal [θreˈsɑnɪkl̩; θreiˈsɔnikəl] *adj.* 自負的; 自誇的; 誇大的。(亦作 **thrasonic**) —**ly,** *adv.*

:thread [θrɛd; θred] *n.* ①線;纖維;細絲。You sew with *thread*. 你用線縫級。②線狀物。③線索; 脈絡。④螺紋。***cut one's mortal thread*** 割斷命脈; 殺死。***gather by a thread*** 綜合(分別處理的問題、部分等)。***hang by a thread*** 千鈞一髮; 處於危險之境。***take up*** (or ***resume***) ***the thread of a story*** 接下去講。***thread and thrum*** 蠱數;全部。***thread of life*** 生命線。—*v.t.* ①穿線於(針孔); 以線穿起。②穿過。I *threaded* my way through the crowd. 我從人叢中穿過。③加螺紋於(螺釘等)。④貫穿全部;彌漫全部。—*v.i.* ①成線;成線狀。②

如線般穿過。—*adj.* 線的; 如線的;用線做的。
thread·bare [ˈθrɛd,bɛr; ˈθredbɛə] *adj.* ①毛絨已磨掉的; 穿到露線的; 襤褸的。②着破衣的。③陳腐的;無趣的。
thread·er [ˈθrɛdɚ; ˈθredə] *n.* ①穿線人。②穿線機。③壓螺紋於螺釘上之機械。
thread·like [ˈθrɛd,laɪk; ˈθredlaik] *adj.* 像線的;細長的。
thread mark 細紋(在製紙幣用的紙漿中摻入有色纖維而成之細紋,以防僞造貨幣)。
thread-nee·dle [ˈθrɛd,nidḷ; ˈθred,ni:dl] *n.* 一種兒童遊戲。
Threadneedle Street 倫敦一街道,以銀行林立著名。
thread paper ①包線用薄紙。②瘦子。
thread rope 半英寸或不及半英寸粗的繩。
thread·worm [ˈθrɛd,wɝm; ˈθred-wə:m] *n.* 線蟲(尤指蟯蟲)。
thread·y [ˈθrɛdɪ; ˈθredi] *adj.*, **thread·i·er, thread·i·est.** ①線的; 似線的; 似細繩的;纖維狀的。②形成線的; 能抽出線的; 黏質的。③微弱的(脈搏等)。④細弱的(聲音等)。
threap [θrip; θri:p] *v.t.* 〖蘇〗①斥責;責罵。②堅持。—*v.i.* 爭論。—*n.* ①爭辯; 吵架。②控告。
***threat** [θrɛt; θret] *n.* ①恐嚇;威脅。②惡兆。There is a *threat* of rain in the dark sky. 黑雲密布的天空有下雨之兆。—*v.t.* & *v.i.* 〖古〗威脅。—**ful,** *adj.* —**ful·ly,** *adv.*
‡**threat·en** [ˈθrɛtṇ; ˈθretn] *v.t.* ①恐嚇;威脅。They *threatened* him with a lawsuit. 他們以訴訟威脅他。②預示…之惡兆;使…有受禍害之虞。It *threatens* to rain. 天有下雨之勢。—*v.i.* ①恐嚇;威脅。②勢將;即將來臨。—**er,** *n.* —**ing,** *adj.* —**ing·ly,** *adv.*
‡**three** [θri; θri:] *n.* ①三; 3。②三個; 三歲; 三時。a child of *three*. 三歲小孩。to come home at *three*. 三點鐘回家。③三個人或物之一組。***by twos and threes*** 三三兩兩地。***Three in One*** 三位一體 (=the Trinity). —*adj.* 三; 三個。
three-act [ˈθri,ækt; ˈθri:ækt] *adj.* 三幕的。a *three-act* play. 一齣三幕劇。
three-bag·ger [ˈθriˈbægɚ; ˈθri:ˈbægə] *n.* 〖棒球俚〗=**three-base hit.**
three-base hit [ˈθri,bes~; ˈθri:beis~] 〖棒球〗三壘安打。
three-bot·tle [ˈθri,bɑtḷ; ˈθri:,bɔtl] *adj.* 酒量大的。
three-bottle man *pl.* ~**men.** 豪飲者;酒量大的人。
three-col·or [ˈθri,kʌlɚ; ˈθri:,kʌlə] *adj.* 三色的;三色版的。the *three-color* process. 三色套版印刷。
three-cor·nered [ˈθriˈkɔrnɚd; ˈθri:ˈkɔ:nəd] *adj.* ①三角的; 三角關係的。②(競賽等)有關三方選手的。
three-D, 3-D [ˈθriˈdi; ˈθri:ˈdi:] *n.* 立體電影。
three-deck·er [ˈθriˈdɛkɚ; ˈθri:ˈdekə] *n.* ①舊式的三層甲板船。②〖俗〗**a.** 有三層的東西。**b.** 分上中下三卷的書。
three-di·men·sion·al [,θridəˈmɛnʃənḷ; ˈθri:-diˈmenʃənl] *adj.* ①有長、寬、高三面的;立體的。②有立體感的。③(文學作品)充分發展的;有眞實感的。
three-dimensional sound 立體聲。
three·fold [ˈθriˈfold; ˈθri:-fould] *adj.* 三倍的;三重的; 有三部分的。—*adv.* 三倍地; 三重地。—*n.* 三倍。to increase by *threefold*. 增加三倍。
three-hand·ed [ˈθriˈhændɪd; ˈθri:ˈhændid] *adj.* ①有三人的。②三人玩的。
three-lane [ˈθri,len; ˈθri:lein] *adj.* ①三路交通的 (如人行道、車道及軌道)。②有三路交通之寬度的(街道)。
three-leg·ged [ˈθriˈlɛgɪd; ˈθri:ˈlegd] *adj.* ①三脚的。②有三桅的。***three-legged race*** 二人三脚賽跑。
three-mast·er [ˈθriˈmæstɚ; ˈθri:ˈmɑ:stə] *n.* 〖航海〗三桅帆船。
three-mile belt [ˈθri,maɪl~; ˈθri:-mail~] 沿海岸三海里內之水域(即領海)。
three-mile limit 三海里領海界限。
three-mile zone=**three-mile belt.**
three-month·ly [ˈθriˈmʌnθlɪ; ˈθri:ˈmʌnθli] *adj.* 每三月發行一次的; 季刊的。—*n.* 季刊。
three of a kind 〖撲克牌〗三張點數相同的一組牌。
three-pair [ˈθri,pɛr; ˈθri:pɛə] *adj.* 〖英〗四樓的。
three·pence [ˈθrɪpəns; ˈθrepəns, ˈθrip-] *n.* ①三辨士之款額。②〖英〗值三辨士之銀幣。
three·pen·ny [ˈθri,pɛnɪ; ˈθrepəni, ˈθripəni] *adj.* ①值三辨士的。②無價值的; 便宜的。
three per cents 〖俗〗〖經濟〗三厘利息之公債。
three-phase [ˈθri,fez; ˈθri:-feiz] *adj.* ①〖電〗三相的。②分三部分的。
three-piece [ˈθri,pis; ˈθri:pi:s] *adj.* 三件一套的(衣服)。—*n.* 三件一組(套)之物。
three-pile [ˈθri,paɪl; ˈθri:-pail] *adj.* 絨毛較普通者厚三倍的(天鵝絨)。—*n.* 絨毛較普通者厚三倍的天鵝絨。
three-piled [ˈθri,paɪld; ˈθri:-paild] *adj.* ①絨毛較普通者厚三倍的 (天鵝絨)。②最好的;昂貴的;奢侈的。③習慣於穿厚天鵝絨的;高貴的;豪富的。
three-ply [ˈθriˈplaɪ; ˈθri:-plai] *adj.* 三層的;三重的;三股的。
three-point landing [ˈθri,pɔɪnt~; ˈθri:pɔint~] 〖航空〗三點降落(兩個降落輪與尾輪同時與地面接觸之降落)。
three-quar·ter [ˈθriˈkwɔrtɚ; ˈθri:ˈkwɔ:tə] *adj.* 四分之三的。
three-ring circus [ˈθri,rɪŋ~; ˈθri:riŋ~] ①有三個表演場俾三個不同的節目同時進行的大馬戲團。②〖俗〗許多不同的事同時發生的活動;熱鬧而混亂的場面。
three R's ①(教育的基本學科) 讀、寫、算 (=reading, 'riting, and 'rithmetic). ②基本知識或技術。
three·score [ˈθriˈskor; ˈθri:ˈskɔ:] *adj.* 六十;二十的三倍。
three·some [ˈθrisəm; ˈθri:səm] *n.* ①三人之一組。②三人爲一組之遊戲或競技。③參加上述遊戲或競技之三人。—*adj.* ①三的; 三重的。②三人爲一組的。③三倍的。
three-square [ˈθriˈskwɛr; ˈθri:ˈskwɛə] *adj.* 三邊相等的;三等角的。
three-stick·er [ˈθriˈstɪkɚ; ˈθri:ˈstikə] *n.* 〖俗〗三桅帆船。
three-val·ued [ˈθriˈvæljud; ˈθri:ˈvælju:d] *adj.* 〖哲學〗三價的。
three-wheel·er [ˈθriˈhwilɚ; ˈθri:ˈwi:lə] *n.* 任何有三個輪子的車輛。
Three Wise Men 〖聖經〗(來自東方朝拜聖嬰之)三哲士。
threm·ma·tol·o·gy [,θrɛməˈtɑlədʒɪ; ,θreməˈtɔlədʒi] *n.* 動植物繁殖學。
thren·o·dist [ˈθrɛnədɪst; ˈθrenədist] *n.* 輓歌(哀歌)之作者;唱輓歌者; 唱哀歌者。

thren·o·dy [ˈθrɛnədɪ; ˈθrenədi] *n.*, *pl.* **-dies.** 輓歌;悲歌;哀歌。(亦作**threnode**)
thresh [θrɛʃ; θreʃ] *v.t.* ①打(穀)(=thrash). ②徹底討論一個問題〖out〗. ③再三檢查;翻滾〖over〗. —*v.i.* ①打穀。②鞭笞。③翻來覆去;搖動。***thresh out*** 以徹底討論來解決。***thresh over*** 一再檢討。—*n.*打穀。
thresh·er [ˈθrɛʃɚ; ˈθreʃə] *n.* ①打穀者;打穀機。②長尾鮫。
threshing floor 打穀場。
threshing machine 打穀機。
thresh·old** [ˈθrɛʃold, ˈθrɛʃhold; ˈθreʃhould, ˈθreʃould] *n.* ①門檻。②入口;門口。③開始;開端;極接近開始之處。This country is on the *threshold* of prosperity. 這個國家卽將進入繁榮之境。at the threshold of*** 在…的開始;就要開始的時候。
‡**threw** [θru; θruː] *v.* pt. of **throw**.
***thrice** [θraɪs; θrais] *adv.* ①三倍地;三度地。He knocked *thrice*. 他敲了三下。②很;非常。*thrice* happy. 非常快樂。
***thrift** [θrɪft; θrift] *n.* ①節儉;儉約。②〖植物〗濱簪花。③〖植物〗茂盛。
thrift·less [ˈθrɪftlɪs; ˈθriftlis] *adj.* 浪費的;奢侈的;不節儉的。—**ly,** *adv.* —**ness,** *n.*
thrift shop 〖美〗舊貨店。(亦作**thriftshop**)
***thrift·y** [ˈθrɪftɪ; ˈθrifti] *adj.*, **thrift·i·er, thrift·i·est.** ①節儉的;儉約的。②興旺的;茂盛的。③成功的;富有的;興隆的。—**thrift·i·ly,** *adv.* —**thrift·i·ness,** *n.*
***thrill** [θrɪl; θril] *n.* ①震顫。②刺激;激動。a *thrill* of horror. 一陣恐怖。—*v.t.*刺激;激動。—*v.i.* ①震顫;抖顫。Her voice *thrilled* with terror. 她的聲音因恐怖而震顫。②因興奮而生震顫之感;深受感動。
thrill·er [ˈθrɪlɚ; ˈθrilə] *n.* ①富有刺激性之人或事物。②引起街談巷議的戲劇、消息等(尤指有關謀殺或暴力者)。
thrill·ing [ˈθrɪlɪŋ; ˈθriliŋ] *adj.* 令人震顫的;使感動的;震顫的。—**ly,** *adv.* —**ness,** *n.*
thrips [θrɪps; θrips] *n.* (蟲)薊馬;牧草蟲。
***thrive** [θraɪv; θraiv] *v.i.*, **throve** [θrov; θrouv] or **thrived, thrived** or **thriv·en** [ˈθrɪvən; ˈθrivən], **thriv·ing.** ①繁盛;興盛;旺盛。②健旺;茂盛。Children *thrive* on fresh air and good food. 兒童因有新鮮空氣和良好食物而發育健旺。—**thriv·er,** *n.*
thro', thro =through.
‡**throat** [θrot; θrout] *n.* ①咽喉;喉嚨。to clear the *throat*. 清喉嚨。②狹窄之通路。***at the top of one's throat*** 儘量放大聲音。***cut one's own throat*** 自取滅亡。***cut someone's throat*** 擊敗;消滅。***jump down one's throat*** 突然猛烈地攻擊別人或批評別人;令人語塞。***lump in the throat*** 喉嚨梗住。***stick in one's throat*** (or ***craw***) (話語)梗於喉間。***thrust*** (***force, ram,*** or ***shove***) ***something down one's throat*** 强迫他人接受或同意某事。Don't *thrust your opinions down other people's throats.* 不要勉强旁人接受你的意見。
throat·latch [ˈθrot,lætʃ; ˈθroutlætʃ] *n.* (馬喉下之)韁帶。
throat·y [ˈθrotɪ; ˈθrouti] *adj.*, **throat·i·er, throat·i·est.** ①喉音的。②類似喉音的;聲音低沉而宏亮的。
***throb** [θrɑb; θrɔb] *v.*, **throbbed, throbbing,** *n.* —*v.i.* 悸動;跳動;有規律地跳動;震顫。—*n.* 悸動;有規律的跳動;震顫。
throb·bing [ˈθrɑbɪŋ; ˈθrɔbiŋ] *adj.* 悸動的;跳動的;震顫的。—**ly,** *adv.*
throe [θro; θrou] *n.*, *v.*, **throed, throeing.** —*n.* ①劇痛;極端痛苦。②(*pl.*) 分娩時之陣痛。③(*pl.*) 苦痛的努力或掙扎;苦鬥。—*v.i.* 劇痛;苦惱。
throm·bin [ˈθrɑmbɪn; ˈθrɔmbin] *n.* 〖生化〗(使血液凝結之)凝血酶。
throm·bo·cyte [ˈθrɑmbə,saɪt; ˈθrɔmbəsait] *n.* 〖解剖〗血小板;血栓細胞。—**throm·bo·cyt·ic,** *adj.*
throm·bo·plas·tic [,θrɑmboˈplæstɪk; ,θrɔmbouˈplæstik] *adj.* 凝血的;促成凝血的。
throm·bo·sis [θrɑmˈbosɪs; θrɔmˈbousis] *n.* 〖醫〗血栓症;血塞。
throm·bot·ic [θrɑmˈbɑtɪk; θrɔmˈbɔtik] *adj.* ①血栓症的;似血栓症的。②血栓症所促成的;血塞引起的。
throm·bus [ˈθrɑmbəs; ˈθrɔmbəs] *n.*, *pl.* **-bi** [-baɪ; -bai]. 〖醫〗血栓;血栓症。
throne** [θron; θroun] *n.*, *v.*, **throned, thron·ing.** —*n.* ①寶座;御座。②王位;帝位;王權;君權。③〖英〗(the T-) 君主。④施恩座(=mercy seat. 舊約出埃及記 25:17)。mount*** (***come to, ascend,*** or ***take***) ***the throne*** 卽位;登基。—*v.t.* 使卽王位;使登基。—*v.i.* 卽帝位;登基。—**less,** *adj.*
throne room ①放御座供君主接見訪客的房間。②(政府或商業機構)權力所在地。
***throng** [θrɔŋ; θrɔŋ] *n.* ①羣;羣衆。②衆多;多數。③〖蘇〗(工作等之)壓力。—*v.t.* 擠入;擠滿。—*v.i.* 擠集;羣集。—*adj.*〖蘇,英北部〗①(人或事物)擁擠的。②忙的。
thros·tle [ˈθrɑsl; ˈθrɔsl] *n.* ①〖蘇〗善鳴之畫眉鳥。②紡織機。
throt·tle [ˈθrɑtl; ˈθrɔtl] *n.*, *v.*, **-tled, -tling.** —*n.* ①阻塞;節流;節流閥。to close (open) the *throttle*. 減低(增加)速度。②操縱節流閥之柄或踏板。③〖俗〗喉;氣管。—*v.t.* ①使窒息;扼死;勒死。②禁止發言;禁止出聲;扼止;壓制。③關閉節氣閥以減低速度。④停止或調節流入引擎之(汽油)。—*v.i.* 窒息。
throt·tle·hold [ˈθrɑtl,hold; ˈθrɔtlhould] *n.* 束縛;扼殺。
‡**through** [θru; θruː] *prep.* ①經過;通過。The troops marched *through* the town. 軍隊從城中走過。②遍及;歷盡。to travel *through* the country. 遊遍全國。③由於;因爲。It happened *through* no fault of mine. 這件事之所以發生,並非由於我的任何錯誤。④藉;由。He became rich *through* hard work. 他藉努力工作而致富。⑤結束;完成。We are *through* school at three o'clock. 我們三點鐘時上完課。⑥從頭到尾。The rain lasted *through* the night. 雨下了一整夜。***get through an examination*** 通過考試。***go through a fortune*** 耗盡錢財。***go through college*** 讀畢大學課程。***see through a trick*** 看穿詭計。—*adv.* ①自始至終;貫通地。to sleep the whole night *through*. 睡一通宵。②完全地;徹頭徹尾地。He is an honest man *through* and *through*. 他是一個徹頭徹尾的誠實人。③完畢。When will you be *through* with your work? 你甚麼時候可以做完你的工作?④全程地;直達地。The train goes *through* to Shanghai. 這火車直達上海。***be through with*** **a.** 斷絕來往;絕交。**b.** 完畢;

結束(=to get through with). ***fall*** (or ***drop***) ***through*** 失敗。***get through with*** 完畢;結束。***through and through*** 完全地;徹底地。—*adj.* ①通行的。②直達的。a *through* train. 直達車。③完畢的;完成的。I am almost *through*. 我快完畢了。(亦作 **thro', thro,** 或 **thru**)

through-com·posed 〔ˈθrukəm-ˈpozd; ˈθruːkəmˈpouzd〕 *adj.* 每一段(節)音樂都不同的。

through-oth·er 〔ˈθruˌʌðə; ˈθruː-ˌʌðə〕 *adj.* 〖主蘇〗混亂的。(亦作 **through-ither**)

ː**through·out** 〔θruˈaut; θru(ː)ˈaut〕 *prep.* 遍及;全;在全部期間;在各處。The Tenth of October is celebrated *throughout* China. 全中國均慶祝雙十節。—*adv.* ①在所有各處;全部;徹頭徹尾。He is an honest man *throughout*. 他是一個徹頭徹尾的誠實人。②自始至終。

through·put 〔ˈθruˌput; ˈθruː-put〕 *n.* ①產品之生產及推銷。②產量。

through street 幹道。

through·way 〔ˈθruˌwe; ˈθruːwei〕 *n.* =**thruway.**

throve 〔θrov; θrouv〕 *v.* pt. of **thrive.**

ː**throw** 〔θro; θrou〕 *v.,* **threw** 〔θru; θruː〕, **thrown** 〔θron; θroun〕, **throw·ing,** *n.* —*v.t.* ①投;拋;擲。He *threw* the ball to me. 他把球拋給我。②推出;推倒。③投射;投置;拋向;移向。He *threw* his chest out. 他挺起胸膛。④移動(槓桿等);轉動(槓桿等)。⑤轉動槓桿使轉動;轉動槓桿使連起或斷開。⑥使跌落。The horse *threw* its rider. 馬將騎者掀落於地。⑦蛻;脫(皮)。A snake *throws* its skin. 蛇蛻皮。⑧使陷入(某種狀態)。The fire *threw* the people into confusion. 火災使人們陷於慌亂。⑨〖美俗〗讓對方獲勝(賽跑、賭博等);在(比賽中)放水。⑩撚(絲)成線。⑪(家畜)生產(幼子)。⑫以骰子投某一數目。⑬用製陶輪盤製作。⑭〖蘇〗a. 扭轉。b. 拉緊。⑮〖俗〗舉行(一派對)。⑯匆忙地穿或脫(衣)。She *threw* a cloak over her shoulders. 她把一件外套匆匆地披在肩上。⑰使(對手)跌倒。—*v.i.* ①投;擲;拋。Can you *throw* well? 你能擲得很好嗎?②擲骰子。***throw about*** a. 亂丟;亂扔;亂花。b. 猛烈地揮動。***throw away*** 放棄;丟掉。He has *thrown away* a fine opportunity. 他放棄了一個好機會。***throw back*** a. 返回祖先的型態。b. 使延遲。c. 迫至依賴狀態。***throw cold water on*** 潑冷水於;使氣餒。***throw down*** a. 拋於地;投於地。b. 推翻。***throw down the gauntlet*** (or ***glove***) a. 接受挑戰;挑戰。b. 表示反抗。***throw in*** a. 額外贈送。b. 插進。He *threw in* a remark. 他插進了一句話。c. 放棄嘗試。***throw in the sponge; throw in the towel*** 認輸。***throw light on a matter*** 弄明白某事。***throw off*** a. 匆匆脫掉。b. 擺脫掉;失掉。c. 即席而做。d. 迷亂;困惑。e. 放射;發出。***throw oneself at*** 盡力討好;盡量想贏得友誼。***throw oneself down*** 突然倒下。***throw oneself into*** 投身於(工作)。***throw oneself on*** (or ***upon***) a. 聽命於;聽從。b. 猛撲。***throw one's weight around*** 專權;弄權。***throw open*** a. 打開。*Throw open* all the windows. 打開所有的窗子。b. 開放。***throw out*** a. 否決(議案等)。The bill was *thrown out*. 議案被否決了。b. 發表;說出。c. 增建;加蓋。d. 打斷(某人的話或工作)。e. 拒絕;擯斥。f. 提出討論。g. 〖棒球〗將對方跑壘員封殺出局。***throw over*** 放棄;遺棄。***throw overboard*** a. 拋入海中。b. 放棄。***throw the bull*** a. 吹牛;誇大。b. 無目的地談話。***throw together*** a. 匆匆做成。b. 使結合。***throw up*** a. 嘔吐。b. 舉起;推上。c. 放棄。This man has *thrown up* his job. 這人已辭掉他的工作了。d. 急速建造。e. 指出(錯誤);批評。f. (鷹)突然飛起。—*n.* ①投;擲;拋。②投距。③圍巾;毛毯。④骰子之一擲;運氣。⑤機會;冒險。⑥電影院中放映機至銀幕間之距離。⑦大禮堂中擴音機至聽衆間之距離。⑧光線之長度。⑨〖角力〗將對手摔倒。***a stone's throw*** 投石可及之距離;近在咫尺之地。—**er,** *n.*

throw·a·way 〔ˈθroəˌwe; ˈθrouəˌwei〕 *n.* ①被扔掉的東西;被丟棄之事物。②(在街上分送或挨戶傳送的)傳單。—*adj.* 可扔掉的。

throwaway line 臺詞中隨便說出的一句話。

throw·back 〔ˈθroˌbæk; ˈθroubæk〕 *n.* ①反擲;反投。②〖生物〗返祖現象;祖型重現。③阻遏;挫折;逆轉。④〖電影〗前景重現。

throw·down 〔ˈθroˌdaun; ˈθroudaun〕 *n.* 〖俚〗①拒絕。②敗北;失敗。

ː**thrown** 〔θron; θroun〕 *v.* pp. of **throw.**

throw·off 〔ˈθroˌɔf; ˈθrouɔːf〕 *n.* (打獵、賽跑等之)開始;出發。

throw·ster 〔ˈθrostə; ˈθroustə〕 *n.* ①搓絲者;撚絲者。②擲骰子者;賭徒。

thru 〔θru; θruː〕 *prep., adv., adj.* =**through.**

thrum[1] 〔θrʌm; θrʌm〕 *v.,* **thrummed, thrum·ming,** *n.* —*v.i.* & *v.t.* ①撫彈(弦樂器);撥弄(樂器)之弦。②(以手指)輕扣;輕敲。③煩厭而單調地敍述。④(樂器)發出單調之聲音。—*n.* 撥弄弦樂器;彈奏弦樂器之聲。

thrum[2] *n., v.,* **thrummed, thrum·ming.** —*n.* ①(*pl.*)織餘;線頭;緒餘。②絲屑;索屑。③碎屑;細屑。④〖航海〗羊線或麻線碎屑(用以堵塞漏洞等者)。—*v.t.* ①加綫邊於;裝流蘇於。②〖航海〗以羊線或麻線碎屑堵塞漏洞。

thrump 〔θrʌmp; θrʌmp〕 *n.* 砰砰或轟隆的聲音。

thru·out 〔θruˈaut; θruːˈaut〕 *adv., prep.* =**throughout.**

thrup·pence 〔ˈθrʌpəns; ˈθrʌpəns〕 *n.* =**threepence.**

thrush[1] 〔θrʌʃ; θrʌʃ〕 *n.* ①鶇;畫眉鳥。②〖俚〗走紅的女歌星。

thrush[2] *n.* 鵝口瘡;雪口症。

thrust** 〔θrʌst; θrʌst〕 *v.,* **thrust, thrust·ing,** *n.* —*v.t.* ①插入;力推;衝。He *thrust* his hands into his pockets. 他把兩手插進衣袋裏面。②戳;刺。The sword *thrust* him through. 劍將他刺穿。—*v.i.* ①以銳利武器襲擊;刺;戳。②推擠;擠進。He *thrust* on his gloves. 他用力將手套戴上。thrust one's nose into other people's affairs*** 干預旁人的事情。—*n.* ①力推;衝。②刺;戳。③攻擊;突擊。④〖機械〗推力;向軸壓力。⑤激烈辯論。⑥推進力;推力。—**er,** *n.*

thru·way 〔ˈθruˌwe; ˈθruːwei〕 *n.* 高速公路。(亦作 **throughway**)

Thu. Thursday.

thud 〔θʌd; θʌd〕 *n., v.,* **thud·ded, thud·ding.** —*n.* ①重擊聲;砰擊聲。②砰然的跌落;重擊。—*v.i.* & *v.t.* 砰然地落下;重擊。

thug 〔θʌg; θʌg〕 *n.* ①惡棍;刺客;殺人者。

②(T-)(昔時印度之)暗殺團中的一分子。

thug·gee [ˈθʌgi; ˈθʌgiː] *n.* 往昔印度暗殺團團員(thug)之暗殺及搶掠行爲。

thug·ger·y [ˈθʌgərɪ; ˈθʌgəri] *n.* = **thuggism.**

thug·gish [ˈθʌgɪʃ; ˈθʌgiʃ] *adj.* ①暗殺的。②暴行的;兇暴的。

thug·gism [ˈθʌgɪzm̩; ˈθʌgizm] *n.* ①暗殺。②暴行;兇暴。

Thu·le [ˈθjulɪ; ˈθjuːli(ː)] *n.*(古代地理)世界最北地區。

thu·li·um [ˈθjulɪəm; ˈθjuːliəm] *n.* 〖化〗銩(稀土金屬元素,符號 Tm).

thumb** [θʌm; θʌm] *n.* ①拇指。②手套的拇指部分。all thumbs*** 笨手笨脚的。***a rule of thumb*** 根據實際經驗所得的作法。***stick out like a sore thumb*** 惹人注目;使人側目。***thumbs down*** 表示反對或拒絕的手勢。***thumbs up*** 伸大拇指表示贊成或接受的手勢。***under the thumb of a person; under one's thumb*** 受某人的壓制。—*v.t.* ①以拇指翻(書頁等)而匆匆閱讀。②以拇指弄污損。③笨拙處理。④以拇指撥弄(吉他等樂器)。⑤以拇指指向要去的方向而搭便車。—**less,** *adj.* —**like,** *adj.*

thumb·er [ˈθʌmɚ; ˈθʌmə] *n.* 揩油乘別人汽車旅行的人。

thumb index 字典等頁邊上之字母指標。

thumb-in·dex [ˈθʌmˈɪndɛks; ˈθʌmˈindeks] *v.t.* 加 thumb index.

thumb·mark [ˈθʌm͵mɑrk; ˈθʌmmɑːk] *n.* 留於書頁上的指痕。

thumb·nail [ˈθʌmˈnel; ˈθʌmˈneil] *n.* ①大拇指之指甲。②像拇指指甲一樣大小的東西;極短之物;極小之物。③〖新聞〗(亦作 **porkchop**)半欄的新聞照片。—*adj.* ①像大拇指指甲大小的。②簡短的;簡明的。a *thumbnail* sketch. 一篇簡明的描寫。—*v.t.* 作一簡短的說明或描寫。

thumb·print [ˈθʌm͵prɪnt; ˈθʌmprint] *n.* 拇指印;拇指紋。

thumb·ring [ˈθʌm͵rɪŋ; ˈθʌmriŋ] *n.* ①套在拇指上刻有私章的戒指。②刀劍把上的拇指環。(亦作 **thumb ring**)

thumb·screw [ˈθʌm͵skru; ˈθʌmskruː] *n.* ①翼形螺釘。②(常*pl.*)(昔)一種用以夾拇指的刑具。

thumb·stall [ˈθʌm͵stɔl; ˈθʌm-stɔːl] *n.* ①一種皮製的拇指套。②拇指防護墊。

thumb·tack [ˈθʌm͵tæk; ˈθʌmtæk] *n.*(亦作**thumb pin**)圖釘。—*v.t.*用圖釘釘上。

***thump** [θʌmp; θʌmp] *v.t.* & *v.i.* ①重擊。②發砰然聲;砰砰地跳。His heart *thumped.* 他的心砰砰地跳。③〖俗〗狠打;抽打。④放大脚步聲地走路。—*n.* ①重擊。②砰然聲。We heard a *thump* as he fell. 我們聽見他砰然一聲倒了下去。

thump·er [ˈθʌmpɚ; ˈθʌmpə] *n.* ①重擊者;重擊物。②重擊。③〖俗〗巨大之人或物;大謊話。

thump·ing [ˈθʌmpɪŋ; ˈθʌmpiŋ] *adj.* ①重擊的。②〖俗〗極大的。—*adv.* =**very.**

thun·der** [ˈθʌndɚ; ˈθʌndə] *n.* ①雷;雷聲。a loud crash of *thunder.* 一聲響雷。②似雷之聲。a *thunder* of applause. 掌聲如雷。③恐嚇;威脅。④譴責。steal one's thunder*** **a.** 剽竊別人的思想或方法等。**b.** 因預期表演或言論等之精采而使實際表現爲之失色。—*v.i.* ①打雷。②發出如雷之聲。Someone was *thundering* at the door. 有人在猛敲門。③大聲斥責或恐嚇。④大聲說;叫喊。⑤大聲地移動、行動。—*v.t.* 大聲喊出(斥責、譴責、威脅等之語)。

thun·der-and-light·ning [ˈθʌndəənˈlaɪtnɪŋ; ˈθʌndəənˈlaitniŋ] *adj.* 兩種顏色强烈對照的(指服裝等而言,如黑與白)。

thun·der·a·tion [͵θʌndəˈreʃən; ͵θʌndəˈreiʃən] *interj.* 表示驚訝、暴躁之詞。

thun·der·bird [ˈθʌndɚ͵bɝd; ˈθʌndəbəːd] *n.* 雷鳥(傳說能興作閃電雷雨)。

***thun·der·bolt** [ˈθʌndɚ͵bolt; ˈθʌndəboult] *n.* ①雷電;霹靂。②突然而可怕的事情。The news of his death came as a *thunderbolt*. 他的死訊像一聲霹靂般地傳來。③精力充沛而活躍之人。

thun·der·clap [ˈθʌndɚ͵klæp; ˈθʌndəklæp] *n.* ①雷響;霹靂。②突然而驚人的事。

thun·der·cloud [ˈθʌndɚ͵klaud; ˈθʌndəklaud] *n.* 夾有雷電的烏雲。(亦作 **thunderclouds**)

thun·der·er [ˈθʌndərɚ; ˈθʌndərə] *n.* ①怒喝者。②(the T-)〖諧〗倫敦泰晤士報之別稱。③(T-) =**Jupiter; Zeus.**

thun·der·head [ˈθʌndɚ͵hɛd; ˈθʌndəhed] *n.*(雷雨前常見的)圓塊積雲。

thun·der·ing [ˈθʌndərɪŋ; ˈθʌndəriŋ] *adj.* ①雷鳴的;似雷聲轟響的。②〖俗〗非常的;驚人的;大的。—*adv.* 〖俗〗=**very.** —*n.* 雷電。—**ly,** *adv.*

thun·der·ous [ˈθʌndərəs; ˈθʌndərəs] *adj.* ①發雷聲的;雷聲隆隆的。②喧聲如雷的。—**ly,** *adv.*

thun·der·peal [ˈθʌndɚ͵pil; ˈθʌndəpiːl] *n.* 雷鳴;霹靂。

thun·der·sheet [ˈθʌndɚ͵ʃit; ˈθʌndəʃiːt] *n.* 作雷聲音響效果時用的金屬片。

thun·der·show·er [ˈθʌndɚ͵ʃauɚ; ˈθʌndə͵ʃauə] *n.* 雷陣雨(伴有雷電之陣雨)。

thun·der·storm [ˈθʌndɚ͵stɔrm; ˈθʌndəstɔːm] *n.* 雷雨。

thun·der·strick·en [ˈθʌndɚ͵strɪkən; ˈθʌndə͵strikən] *adj.* =**thunderstruck.**

thun·der·strike [ˈθʌndɚ͵straɪk; ˈθʌndə-straik] *v.t.*, **-struck, -struck** or **-strick·en, -strik·ing.** 使嚇壞。

thun·der·stroke [ˈθʌndɚ͵strok; ˈθʌndə-strouk] *n.* 雷雨之一擊。

thun·der·struck [ˈθʌndɚ͵strʌk; ˈθʌndə-strʌk] *adj.* ①爲雷電所擊的。②驚呆的;驚愕的。

thun·der·y [ˈθʌndərɪ; ˈθʌndəri] *adj.* 要打雷的;多雷的。

Thur. Thursday.

thu·ri·ble [ˈθjurəbl̩; ˈθjuəribl] *n.*香爐。

thu·ri·fi·ca·tion [͵θjurəfɪˈkeʃən; ͵θjuərifiˈkeiʃən] *n.* 擴香;焚香。

Thurs. Thursday.

‡Thurs·day [ˈθɝzdɪ; ˈθəːzdi, -dei] *n.* 星期四;禮拜四。(略作 **Th., Thur., Thurs.**)

Thurs·days [ˈθɝzdɪz; ˈθəːzdiz] *adv.* 於禮拜四;每星期四。

‡thus [ðʌs; ðʌs] *adv.* ①如此;像這樣。He spoke *thus.* 他這樣說。②因此;於是。*Thus* we decided that he was wrong. 於是我們確定他錯了。③至此;至此程度。***thus far*** 至此;迄今。

thus·ness [ˈðʌsnɪs; ˈðʌsnis] *n.* 如此;如是。

thwack [θwæk; θwæk] *v.t.* (以棍或板等)猛打;重擊。—*n.* (以棍或板等)猛打。

***thwart** [θwɔrt; θwɔːt] *v.t.* ①反對;阻撓;妨礙;挫折。②〖古〗**a.** 橫越。**b.** 橫伸;越出。—*n.* ①划船者所坐的橫板。②獨木舟之橫撐。—*adj.* ①橫過的。②〖古〗頑固的;倔强的。③不吉利的;不好的。—*adv., prep.* 橫過地。

***thy** [ðaɪ; ðai] *pron.*, possessive of **thou**, *adj.* 〖古,詩〗你的 (=your).
Thy·iad [ˈθaɪjæd; ˈθaijæd] *n., pl.* **-iads, -ia·des.** 酒神 Bacchus 之女祭司; Bacchus 之女信徒 (=bacchante).
thyme [taɪm; taim] *n.* 〖植物〗百里香; 麝香草。
thy·mic¹ [ˈθaɪmɪk; ˈθaimik] *adj.* 〖解剖〗胸腺的。
thy·mic² [ˈtaɪmɪk; ˈtaimik] *adj.* 〖植物〗百里香的; 麝香草的。
thy·mol [ˈθaɪmol; ˈθaimɔl] *n.* 〖化〗瑞香草酚(用作防腐劑)。(亦作 **thyme camphor, thymic acid**)
thy·mus [ˈθaɪməs; ˈθaiməs] *n., pl.* **-mus·es, -mi** [-maɪ; -mai]. 〖解剖〗胸腺。(亦作 **thymus gland**)
thym·y [ˈtaɪmɪ; ˈtaimi] *adj.*, **thym·i·er, thym·i·est.** ①麝香草的; 像麝香草的。②多麝香草的;有麝香草之芳香的。
thy·roid [ˈθaɪrɔɪd; ˈθairɔid] *n.* ①甲狀腺。②甲狀軟骨。③從甲狀腺中提煉出的藥劑。—*adj.* 甲狀腺的。—**less,** *adj.*
thyroid cartilage 〖解剖〗甲狀軟骨。
thy·roid·ec·to·my [ˌθaɪrɔɪˈdɛktəmɪ; ˌθairɔiˈdektəmi] *n., pl.* **-mies.** 〖外科〗甲狀腺切除術。
thyroid gland 甲狀腺。(亦作 **thyroid body**)
thy·roid·i·tis [ˌθaɪrɔɪˈdaɪtɪs; ˌθairɔiˈdaitis] *n.* 〖醫〗甲狀腺炎。(亦作 **thyroadenitis**)
thy·roi·dot·o·my [ˌθaɪrɔɪˈdɑtəmɪ; ˌθairɔiˈdɔtəmi] *n., pl.* **-mies.** 〖外科〗甲狀腺(甲狀軟骨)切開術。(亦作 **thyrotomy**)
thy·ro·sis [θaɪˈrosɪs; θaiˈrousis] *n.* 甲狀腺失調而引起的病症。
thy·rot·o·my [θaɪˈrɑtəmɪ; θaiˈrɔtəmi] *n., pl.* **-mies.** 〖外科〗①甲狀軟骨切開術。②甲狀腺切開術。
thy·ro·tox·i·co·sis [ˌθaɪroˌtɑksəˈkosɪs; ˈθairouˌtɔksiˈkousis] *n.* 〖醫〗甲狀腺毒症;甲狀腺中毒。
thy·rox·in [θaɪˈrɑksin; θaiˈrɔksiːn] *n.* 〖生化〗甲狀腺素;甲狀腺氨酸。
thyr·sus [ˈθɝsəs; ˈθəːsəs] *n., pl.* **-si** [-saɪ; -sai]. ①(亦作 **thyrse**)〖植物〗密錐花; 密錐花序。②〖希臘神話〗(酒神 Dionysus, 森林之神等所攜之)神杖。
***thy·self** [ðaɪˈsɛlf; ðaiˈself] *pron.* ①〖古,詩〗你自己 (=yourself). ②代替反身受詞 thee.
Ti 化學元素 titanium 之符號。
ti [ti; tiː] *n., pl.* **tis.** 〖音樂〗全音階的第七音。(亦作 **te**)
Tian Shan [ˈtjɑnˈʃɑn; ˈtjɑːnˈʃɑːn] 〖中〗天山山脈。(亦作 **Tien Shan**)
Tian-shan sheep 馬哥孛羅羊。
ti·ar·a [taɪˈɛrə; tiˈɑːrə] *n.* ①(用金、寶石或花製成之女子)頭飾;后冠。②羅馬教皇之三重冠; 羅馬教皇之教權。
Ti·bet [tɪˈbɛt; tiˈbet] *n.* 西藏 (中國地方之一, 首府拉薩, Lhasa). (亦作 **Thibet**)
Ti·bet·an [tɪˈbɛtn̩; tiˈbetən] *adj.* 西藏的;西藏人的; 西藏語的。—*n.* 西藏人; 西藏語。(亦作 **Thibetan**)
tib·i·a [ˈtɪbɪə; ˈtibiə] *n., pl.* **-i·ae** [-ɪˌi; -iiː], **-i·as.** ①〖解剖、動物〗脛骨。②昆蟲腿部的第四節; 脛節。③昔由動物之腿骨所製成的一種笛。—**tib·i·al,** *adj.*
tic [tɪk; tik] *n.* 〖醫〗局部肌肉抽搐 (特指面肌抽搐)。
ti·cal [ˈtikəl; ˈtiːkəl] *n., pl.* **-cals, -cal.** 泰幣。
tick¹** [tɪk; tik] *n.* ①(鐘錶等之)滴答聲。②小記號(如✓). ③〖俗〗片刻;利那間。I shall be ready in a *tick*. 我馬上就準備好。—*v.i.* ①作滴答聲。②〖俗〗發生作用; 工作; 行動。—*v.t.* ①標以小記號。②以滴答聲表時間。tick a person off*** 〖俗〗譴責某人。***tick over*** 〖英〗工作; 作用。***what makes one tick*** 某人行爲之動機或解釋。
tick² *n.* 〖動物〗扁蝨。
tick³ *n.* 枕頭套;褥套。(亦作 **bedtick**)
tick⁴ *n.* 〖英俗〗帳目。***on tick*** 賒帳地。
tick·er [ˈtɪkɚ; ˈtikə] *n.* ①發出滴答聲之人或物。②一種將行情等自動印錄於紙條上的電報機。③〖俚〗錶;鐘。④〖俚〗心;心臟。
ticker tape ticker 電報機印錄行情或新聞等所用之紙條。
‡tick·et [ˈtɪkɪt; ˈtikit] *n.* ①票; 車票; 入場券。a theater *ticket*. 戲票。a single *ticket*. 單程票。a return *ticket*. 回程票。a season *ticket*. 月季票。a flying *ticket*. 飛機票。a lottery *ticket*. 彩票;獎券。②(書明價格、尺碼等之) 標籤。③〖美〗政黨候選人名單。④〖俗〗違規通知單。a *ticket* for speeding. 超速違規通知單。⑤高級船員或飛機駕駛員的執照。⑥〖俗〗對的事情; 該做的事。⑦〖罕〗短箋; 備忘錄。⑧〖古〗招牌; 字牌。⑨〖銀行〗臨時帳; 臨時登記。***That's the ticket.*** 〖俗〗那很對; 正是如此。—*v.t.* ①加以標籤。②〖美〗供應車票。③說明;形容;指定。④〖俗〗以違規通知單通知。—**less,** *adj.*
ticket agency 戲票、車票代購(售)處。
ticket agent 代售戲票、車票的人; 戲票、車票代售處。
ticket chopper 軋票機;軋票員。
ticket inspector 車票稽查人。
ticket office 〖美〗售票處。
ticket of leave *pl.* **tickets of leave.** 〖英〗假出獄許可證;假釋許可證。(亦作 **ticket-of-leave**)
ticket-of-leave man 〖英〗(昔)假釋犯。
tick·et-por·ter [ˈtɪkɪtˌpɔrtɚ; ˈtikitˌpɔːtə] *n.* 〖英〗佩帶名牌或有證件的公認脚伕。
tick·et-punch [ˈtɪkɪtˌpʌntʃ; ˈtikitˌpʌntʃ] *n.* 軋票鉗。
tick·et·y-boo [ˈtɪkɪtɪˈbu; ˈtikitiˈbuː] *adj.* 〖主英、俗〗好棒的。
tick·ing [ˈtɪkɪŋ; ˈtikiŋ] *n.* 褥枕等有條紋之套布。
tick·le** [ˈtɪkl̩; ˈtikl] *v.*, **-led, -ling,** *n., adj.* —*v.t.* ①輕觸使生酥癢之感; 胳肢。②使愉悅;使滿足。The story *tickled* him. 這故事使他愉悅。③以搔癢或以如搔癢的方法, 使某人說或做某事。 She *tickled* him into saying yes. 她搔他的癢而使他說好(她向他灌迷湯使他答應所求)。④提醒 (記憶)。—*v.i.* 有酥癢之感; 覺酥癢。My nose *tickles*. 我的鼻子癢。tickled pink*** 〖俗〗很高興。—*n.* ①輕觸; 胳肢。②酥癢之感。—*adj.* 〖方〗容易打翻的;不穩固的。
tick·ler [ˈtɪklɚ; ˈtiklə] *n.* ①使人有酥癢之感的人或物。②備忘錄;記事錄。③〖俗〗困難問題;令人難解的問題。④=**tickler coil.**
tickler coil 〖電子〗反饋線圈;反饋線蟠。
tick·lish [ˈtɪklɪʃ; ˈtikliʃ] *adj.* ①怕癢的; 易癢的。②難處理的; 棘手的。③不穩當的。④易被觸怒的。
tick·tack [ˈtɪkˌtæk; ˈtikˈtæk] *n.* ①鐘錶的滴答聲;似此之聲。②心音;心臟搏動的聲音。③鐘錶(兒語)。④裝於門窗上能發滴答聲供小孩玩的一種裝置。⑤〖英〗賽馬情報。—*v.i.* 發滴答聲。(亦作 **tictac**)
ticktack man 〖俗〗賽馬情報員。

tick-tack-toe [ˌtɪktæk'to; 'tiktæk-'tou] *n.* 兒童遊戲。(二人輪流在一有九方格之盤上劃十字或圓圈, 以所劃之記號三個成直、橫、斜線相連者爲勝)。(亦作**tic-tac-toe, tit-tat-toe**)

tick-tack-too [ˌtɪktæk'tu; 'tiktæk-'tu:] *n.* =**tick-tack-toe.**

tick·tock ['tɪkˌtɑk; 'tikˌtɔk] *n.* 鐘錶之滴答聲。—*v.i.* 發出滴答聲。(亦作 **tictoc**)

tid·al ['taɪdl; 'taidl] *adj.* ①潮的; 有潮的; 受潮水影響的。②船隻依潮水情形而決定駛離之時間的。—**ly,** *adv.*

tidal air 〖生理〗肺潮流氣。

tidal boat 潮水漲滿時開的輪船。

tidal current 潮流。

tidal wave ①海嘯。②潮浪。③普遍或有力之運動、情緒、意見等。

tid·bit ['tɪdˌbɪt; 'tidbit] *n.* 少許之精美愉人的食物、消息等。(亦作 **titbit**)

tid·dle·dy·winks ['tɪdl̩dɪˌwɪŋks; 'tidldiwiŋks] *n.* =**tiddlywinks.**

tid·dler ['tɪdl̩ɚ; 'tidlə] *n.* ①〖俗〗**a.** 小孩。**b.** 小魚。**c.** 小潛艇或小火箭等。②參加 tiddlywinks 遊戲的人。

tid·dly·winks ['tɪdl̩ɪˌwɪŋks; 'tidl̩i-wiŋks] *n.* (作 *sing.* 解)兒童桌上遊戲(參加遊戲者彈彩色小圓鐵片使入杯中)。

tide**[1] [taɪd; taid] *n., v.,* **tid·ed, tid·ing,** *adj.* —*n.* ①潮; 潮汐。high *tide.* 高潮。②潮流; 趨勢。The *tide* of events turns. 情勢轉變。③〖古語〗時; 季(多用於複合詞)。wintertide 冬季。④溪流; 激流。⑤輪流升降或增減的事物。⑥危機或危險狀態。⑦〖古〗合適的時機。go with the tide*** 順應潮流。***Time and tide wait for no man.*** 〖諺〗歲月不待人; 天道不可抗。***turn the tide*** 使局勢改觀。—*v.i.* ①克服; 渡過〖over〗. to *tide* over a difficulty. 渡過難關。②隨潮漂流。③如潮水般地湧流。—*v.t.* 如潮水般地將…沖走。—*adj.* =**tidal.** —**ful,** —**like,** *adj.*

tide[2] *v.i.* 〖古〗發生。

tid·ed ['taɪdɪd; 'taidid] *adj.* 有潮水的; 漲潮的。

tide gate ①潮門。②潮水湍急的地方。

tide gauge 檢潮儀。(亦作 **tide gage, tide register**)

tide·land ['taɪdˌlænd; 'taidlænd] *n.* 漲潮時被淹沒退潮時則露出之地。

tide·less ['taɪdlɪs; 'taidlis] *adj.* 無潮汐的。—**ness,** *n.*

tide lock 潮水閘; 潮閘。

tide·mark ['taɪdˌmɑrk; 'taidmɑ:k] *n.* ①漲潮點; 潮水標。②高潮。

tide pole 潮水桿(測量潮水用的)。(亦作 **tide staff**)

tide race ①湍急的潮水。②=**tideway.**

tide·rip ['taɪdˌrɪp; 'taid-rip] *n.* 潮流相衝激起之浪。(亦作 **rip**)

tide table 潮汐表。

tide·wait·er ['taɪdˌwetɚ; 'taidˌweitə] *n.* ①舊時海關負責上船監視卸貨之人員。②騎牆主義者; 隨風倒的政客。

tide·wat·er ['taɪdˌwɔtɚ; 'taidˌwɔ:tə] *n.* ①被漲潮帶上一地區中的潮水。②受漲潮影響的地區。③受漲潮影響的地區中之河水。④(T-) 美國Virginia 州東部。⑤(T-)Virginia 州東部之英國方言。—*adj.* ①潮水的; 海岸地方的。②(T-) Virginia 州東部的。③(T-)Virginia 東部之英國方言的。

tide·way ['taɪdˌwe; 'taidwei] *n.* ①潮路。②一河中漲潮之部分。③潮流 (=tidal current). (亦作 **tide way**)

ti·di·er ['taɪdɪɚ; 'taidiə] *n.* 整理人; 整潔者。

***ti·dings** ['taɪdɪŋz; 'taidiŋz] *n. pl.* (有時作 *sing.* 解)消息。good *tidings.* 佳音。evil *tidings.* 噩耗。

***ti·dy** ['taɪdɪ; 'taidi] *adj.,* **-di·er, -di·est,** *v.,* **-died, -dy·ing,** *n., pl.* **-dies.** —*adj.* ①整潔的; 整齊的。a *tidy* room. 整潔的房間。②〖俗〗鉅額的; 可觀的。a *tidy* income. 可觀之收入。③〖俗〗相當好的。④有條不紊的。a *tidy* mind. 清楚的頭腦。—*v.t.* 使整齊; 使整潔。I must *tidy* myself. 我必須使自己整潔。—*n.* ①椅套。②盛零碎物件的容器。—**ti·di·ly,** *adv.* —**ti·di·ness,** *n.*

‡**tie** [taɪ; tai] *v.,* **tied, ty·ing** ['taɪɪŋ; 'tai-iŋ], *n.* —*v.t.* ①繫; 結; 縛; 綁; 紮; 捆; 拴。to *tie* a horse to a tree. 將馬拴在樹上。②約束; 束縛; 限制。to *tie* a person down to a contract. 使某人受契約之束縛。③與…得同樣分數。We *tied* our opposing team. 我們與敵隊成和局。④〖音樂〗以連結帶連起。⑤**a.** 連結。**b.** 以繫梁(tie beam)連結。⑥〖俚〗提出同樣或相等的事物。⑦〖俗〗結婚。—*v.i.* ①打結; 結起。That ribbon doesn't *tie* well. 那條絲帶結不好。②約束; 限制。③得同樣分數。The two teams *tied.* 兩隊得分相同。***tie a person's hands*** 束縛某人的自由。***tie a person's tongue*** 使某人噤口不言。***tie down*** 限制; 束縛。***tie in*** **a.** 連結。**b.** 關連。**c.** 使爲 tie-in sale 之一部分。**d.** 一致。His story *ties in* with the facts. 他所說的與事實相符合。***tie into*** 〖俚〗攻擊。***tie off*** 將線或繩圍繞(血管等)以止流。***tie one on*** 〖俚〗喝得大醉。***tie the knot*** 〖俗〗結婚。***tie up*** **a.** 繫緊; 繫牢。**b.** 包紮。**c.** 阻止; 妨礙。**d.** 省(錢)不用; 留起(財物)不用; 不賣。—*n.* ①結; 結飾。②用以捆縛之繩、帶等。③領帶 (=necktie). ④關係; 束縛; 約束。*ties* of blood. 血緣。⑤(鐵路的) 枕木 (在英國叫 railway sleeper). ⑥牽累。⑦得分相同; 不分勝負。The game ended in a *tie.* 這場比賽結果不分勝負。⑧不分勝負之比賽。⑨〖音樂〗連結帶; 帶線。⑩(*pl.*) 繫帶之矮統鞋。

tie·back ['taɪˌbæk; 'taibæk] *n.* ①用以拉窗簾的繩或帶。②有此帶的窗簾。

tie beam 〖建築〗(房屋之)繫梁; 小梁。

tie·clasp ['taɪˌklæsp; 'tai-klɑ:sp] *n.* 領帶夾。(亦作 **tie clasp, tie clip**)

tied garage 〖英〗(某公司之)專用車庫。

tied house 〖英〗①酒廠直營或與酒廠有契約的酒店, 專售該酒廠出品者。②(亦作**tied cottage**) 雇主租給雇用人員的房屋。

tie-down ['taɪˌdaun; 'taidaun] *n.* ①限制或束縛的裝置。②限制; 束縛。

tie-in ['taɪˌɪn; 'taiin] *n.* ①零售商在廠家廣告附近貼的廣告。②在一篇文章中對兩種不同宣傳項目所加之註釋。③=**tie-in sale.** ④有關連的事物。—*adj.* ①tie-in sale 的。②兩件商品一起廣告、出售或購買的。

tie-in sale 〖商〗搭賣法。

tie·less ['taɪlɪs; 'tailis] *adj.* 沒有打領帶的。

Tien Shan ['tjɛn'ʃɑn; 'tjen'ʃɑ:n] =**Tian Shan.**

Tien·tsin ['tjɛn'tsɪn; tjen'tsin] *n.* 天津。

tie·pin ['taɪˌpɪn; 'tai-pin] *n.* 領帶別針。(亦作 **scarfpin, stickpin**)

tier[1] [tɪr; tiə] *n.* ①(劇院或體育場中呈階梯式之)一排(坐位)。②一排坐位。③層; 級。④〖澳〗山脈。—*v.t. & v.i.* 排成層列。

ti·er[2] ['taɪɚ; 'taiə] *n.* ①綑捆的人或事物。②〖航海〗繫住已捲起的船帆的繩子。③〖美方〗小孩的圍裙。

tier. tierce.

tierce [tɪrs; tiəs] *n.* ①盛42美國加侖之桶。②〖牌戲〗順序相連的三張牌。③〖擊劍〗劍尖齊眼之姿勢(即第三姿勢)。④〖宗教〗上午九時舉行之禮拜。(亦作 **terce**) ***tierce and quart*** 劍術。
tier·cel ['tɪrsl; 'təːsəl] *n.* =**tercel.**
tie tack 領帶針。
tie-up ['taɪˌʌp; 'taiʌp] *n.* ①停止;停滯。②(因罷工、風暴等事故造成之)工作、活動、交通之暫時停頓。③同盟罷工。④〖俗〗關係;聯繫。⑤停船之地方。
tiff[1] [tɪf; tif] *n.* ①小爭吵;小爭執。②慍怒;微慍。—*v.i.* ①小吵;小口角。②慍怒。
tiff[2] *n.* ①酒;緩和的酒。②一口的酒;少量的酒。
tif·fa·ny ['tɪfənɪ; 'tifəni] *n., pl.* **-nies.** 一種薄綢;薄紗。
tif·fin ['tɪfɪn; 'tifin] *n.* 〖英印〗午餐。—*v.i. & v.t.* 吃午飯;供以午餐。
ti·ger** ['taɪgɚ; 'taigə] *n., pl.* **-gers, -ger.** ①虎。②兇暴的人;威武的人。③〖美〗歡呼後之吼聲。④〖美俚〗=**faro.** ***buck (or ***fight***) ***the tiger*** 〖美俚〗 **a.** 玩 faro 牌。 **b.** 與莊家賭(faro 或輪盤等)。—**like,** *adj.*
tiger beetle 一種居於沙地穴中捕小蟲為食的甲蟲。
tiger cat ①山貓。②虎貓。
ti·ger·eye ['taɪgɚˌaɪ; 'taigərˌai] *n.* ①豹貓。②〖礦〗虎眼石。
ti·ger·ish ['taɪgərɪʃ; 'taigəriʃ] *adj.* ①虎的;似虎的。②殘酷的;兇猛的。(亦作 **tigrish**) —**ly,** *adv.* —**ness,** *n.*
ti·ger·ism ['taɪgərɪzm; 'taigərizm] *n.* 兇猛;殘酷。
tiger lily 萱草。
tiger moth 虎蛾(翅上有斑點或斑紋);一種燈蛾。
ti·ger's-eye ['taɪgɚzˌaɪ; 'taigəzˌai] *n.* =**tigereye.**
tight** [taɪt; tait] *adj.* ①緊的。②緊密的;不漏的。③緊身的;太緊的(衣、帽、鞋等);塞滿的。④張緊的(繩等)。⑤銀根緊的。Money is *tight* just now. 現在銀根緊。⑥吝嗇的。⑦〖俚〗醉的。⑧合適的;整潔的;舒適的。⑨嚴厲的。⑩困難的;處於困境的。⑪簡明的;簡短的。⑫擁擠的;緊湊的。⑬〖新聞〗消息多而無法全刊登的。⑭〖棒球俚〗(投手的球)在本壘與打擊手之間經過的。⑮分數很接近的;勝負難分的。⑯(貨物等)求過於供的;難得到的。⑰〖方〗能幹的。a tight corner*** (or ***place***) 困難或危險的處境。—*adv.* 緊緊地(=tightly). ***sit tight*** **a.** 固守地位;固執意見。 **b.** 聽其自然;不採取行動。—**ly,** *adv.* —**ness,** *n.*
-tight 〖字尾〗表"不透;不漏;防…"之義的形容詞字尾,如: airtight.
tight·en** ['taɪtn̩; 'taitn] *v.t. & v.i.* 使緊;變緊。tighten one's belt*** 束緊腰帶;枵腹。—**er,** *n.*
tight·fist·ed ['taɪt'fɪstɪd; 'tait'fistid] *adj.* 吝嗇的;慳吝的。
tight-knit ['taɪt'nɪt; 'tait'nit] *adj.* 組織嚴密的。
tight-laced ['taɪtˌlest; 'tait-leist] *adj.* ①帶子扣得很緊的。②不苟言笑的。
tight-lipped ['taɪt'lɪpt; 'tait'lipt] *adj.* ①緊閉嘴唇的。②嘴緊的;少(不)講話的。
tight-mouthed ['taɪt'maʊðd; 'tait-'mauðd] *adj.* ① =**close-mouthed.** ② =**tight-lipped.**
tight·rope ['taɪtˌrop; 'taitˌroup] *n., adj., v.,* **-roped, -rop·ing.** —*n.* 拉緊的繩索(走繩索者行於其上表演技巧者)。a *tightrope* walker (*or* dancer). 走繩索者。***walk a tightrope*** **a.** 走拉緊的繩索。 **b.** 對付困難或危險的情況。—*adj.* 走繩索的。—*v.i. & v.t.* 走繩索;經過危險(如走繩索)。
tights [taɪts; taits] *n. pl.* 緊身衣。
tight squeeze 困難處境;千鈞一髮。
tight·wad ['taɪtˌwɑd; 'taitwɔd] *n.* 〖美俚〗吝嗇鬼;守財奴。
tight·wire ['taɪtˌwaɪr; 'tait-waiə] *n.* 拉緊的鐵索。
ti·gon ['taɪgən; 'taigən] *n.* 虎獅(雄虎與雌獅交配所生之獸)。
ti·gress ['taɪgrɪs; 'taigris] *n.* ①母虎;雌虎。②兇悍的女人;母老虎。
T.I.H. Their Imperial Highnesses.
Ti·hwa ['di'hwɑ; 'diː'hwɑː] *n.* 廸化(新疆省會,亦稱 **Urumchi**).
tike, tyke [taɪk; taik] *n.* ①劣犬(尤指雜種犬)。②〖蘇〗卑野村夫。③小靈精(對活潑頑皮小孩之暱稱)。
til [tɪl, til; til, tiːl] *n.* 〖植物〗胡麻。(亦作 **teel**)
til·bu·ry ['tɪlˌbɛrɪ; 'tilˌberi] *n., pl.* **-ries.** 一種供兩人乘坐之二輪輕便馬車。
til·de ['tɪldə; 'tildə] *n.* ①一種音標符號(~): **a.** 在西班牙文中,加於 n 之上方,以指明係一上顎鼻音 (ny), 如在 señor 中。 **b.** 在葡萄牙文中,加於一母音或雙母音的第一個母音上,以指明鼻音化,如在 lã, pão 中。②在書籍(特指某些字典)中,此符號則用以表示音節、單字、或片語之省略。
***tile** [taɪl; tail] *n., v.,* **tiled, til·ing.** —*n.* ①瓦;(鋪地用之)磚;瓷磚。②磚瓦之集合稱。③排除地上積水的排水管。④絲質高頂硬帽。⑤似磚之石頭或金屬塊。—*v.t.* 鋪以瓦;鋪以磚。
til·er ['taɪlɚ; 'tailə] *n.* 燒瓦者;鋪瓦者;瓦匠。
til·er·y ['taɪlərɪ; 'tailəri] *n., pl.* **-er·ies.** 瓦窰。
til·ing ['taɪlɪŋ; 'tailiŋ] *n.* ①覆瓦;鋪瓷磚。②瓦之集合稱。③瓷磚所鋪之面;瓦頂。
‡till[1] [tɪl; til] *prep.* ①迄;直到;直到…時。He gambled *till* dawn. 他賭到天亮。②〖蘇,英北部〗 **a.** =**to. b.** =**unto.** —*conj.* 迄;直到;在…以前。Wait *till* I come. 等到我來。〖注意〗**till** 和 **until** 的意義和用法相同。不過在名詞或短的子句之前,比較常用till;在一個句子或長的子句的開端,則以用 until 為佳。
till[2] *v.t.* 耕種。—*v.i.* 耕地。
till[3] *n.* ①(櫃臺後盛錢的)小抽屜。②存錢之處。
till[4] *n.* ①〖地質〗漂礫土。②硬粘土。
till·a·ble ['tɪləbl; 'tiləbl] *adj.* 可耕種的;適於耕種的。
till·age ['tɪlɪdʒ; 'tilidʒ] *n.* ①耕種;耕作。②被耕種之田地;耕作地。③耕作地之收成。
till·er[1] ['tɪlɚ; 'tilə] *n.* 耕者;農夫。***the land-to-the-tiller policy*** 耕者有其田政策。
till·er[2] *n.* 〖造船〗舵柄。
till·er[3] *n.* 幼芽;嫩枝。—*v.i.* 自根部萌發幼芽;自莖基部生出嫩枝。
till·er·man ['tɪləmən; 'tilәmən] *n., pl.* **-men.** 舵手。
till money 〖銀行〗出納員手邊之款(別於存在庫裏者)。
tilt**[1] [tɪlt; tilt] *v.i.* ①傾側;傾斜。The table is apt to *tilt* over. 此桌容易傾斜。②以長矛刺擊。③以輪鎚鎚打。④(照相機)上下搖攝。—*v.t.* ①使傾側;使傾斜。②(使照相機)上下搖攝。tilt at*** 攻擊;攻打;抗議。***tilt at windmills*** 攻擊想像中的敵人。—*n.* ①傾側;傾斜;傾斜的姿勢。②馬上之長矛戰。③辯論;爭吵。④輪鎚。***full tilt*** 以全速。—**a·ble,** *adj.* —**er,** *n.*
tilt[2] *n.* ①覆蓋篷車等之粗帆布。②帆布篷。—*v.t.* 用帆布篷覆蓋。

tilth 〔tɪlθ; tilθ〕 *n.* ①耕作;耕植。②耕地。
tilt hammer 輪鎚(打鐵用的大鎚)。
tilt·yard 〔'tɪlt,jard; 'tilt-jɑːd〕 *n.* (中世紀的)馬上比鎗場。
Tim. Timothy.
tim·bal 〔'tɪmbl; 'timbəl〕 *n.* ①罐鼓。②(蟬等發聲器官中的)震動膜。(亦作 **tymbal**)
tim·bale 〔'tɪmbl; tæm'bɑːl〕 *n.* 一種以鷄、蟹、魚等之肉放於鼓型模中焙的食物。
***tim·ber** 〔'tɪmbɚ; 'timbə〕 *n.* ①木材;木料。②(建屋或造船等所用之)横木;棟木。③森林。④(獵狐時用的)圍籬與門。⑤(人的)素質。⑥〖運動俚〗騎馬競賽時跳躍的門、柵等。—*v.t.* 備以木材;支以木材。—*interj.* 樹木被砍將倒時樵夫警告他人避開之呼喊聲。
tim·bered 〔'tɪmbɚd; 'timbəd〕 *adj.* ①由木材製的;由木材支撐的。②長有森林的。〖注意〗此字通常用於複合字中,如:clean-timbered, hard-timbered 等。
tim·ber·head 〔'tɪmbɚ,hɛd; 'timbə-hed〕 *n.* (船從船邊向上突出的)肋頂延長部分。
tim·ber-head·ed 〔'tɪmbɚ,hɛdɪd; 'timbə,hedid〕 *adj.* 愚蠢的;愚鈍的;蠢材的。
timber hitch 〖航海〗(將繩子繫於圓材或柱等上時用之)木結。
tim·ber·ing 〔'tɪmbərɪŋ; 'timbəriŋ〕 *n.* ①建築用之木料。②木材製作物。
tim·ber·jack 〔'tɪmbɚ,dʒæk; 'timbə-dʒæk〕 *n.* 樵夫。
tim·ber·land 〔'tɪmbɚ,lænd; 'timbə-lænd〕 *n.* 林地;森林。
timber line 想像的高山或兩極地區之樹木界線(超過此線時,樹木即不能生長)。
tim·ber·man 〔'tɪmbɚmən; 'timbə-mən〕 *n., pl.* **-men.** 〖礦〗準備並看管礦坑木頭支柱的人。
timber mill 鋸木廠。
timber toe 〖俚〗①木製的假腿;義肢。②裝義肢的人。
timber tree 可供建築用的樹。
timber wolf (北美洲所產之)灰色大狼。
tim·ber·work 〔'tɪmbɚ,wɝk; 'tim-bəwəːk〕 *n.* ①木材製作物。②(*pl.*)木(料)場。
tim·ber·yard 〔'tɪmbɚ,jard; 'timbə-jɑːd〕 *n.* ①木場;木料場。②〖英俗〗〖板球〗擊球員之三柱門。
tim·bre 〔'tɪmbɚ; 'timbə〕 *n.* ①〖音樂〗音色;音質。②〖語音〗音響度(尤指母音者)。
tim·brel 〔'tɪmbrəl; 'timbrəl〕 *n.* 附有小鈴之手鼓。
‡time 〔taɪm; taim〕 *n., v.,* **timed, tim·ing,** *adj.* —*n.* ①時;時間。*Time* flies. 時光飛逝。*Time* is money. 時間卽金錢。②一段時間;一部分時間。That will take a long *time*. 那要費很長的時間。③(以小時或分計量的)時刻。What *time* is it? 現在幾點鐘?④以年、月、小時、分、秒等單位衡量的時間。The winner's *time* was 11 seconds. 獲勝者只用了十一秒。⑤期限;(該做某事的特殊的)時期。*Time* is up. 時候到了;時限到了。⑥(常 *pl.*)時代;時期;時勢。ancient *times*. 古代。the scientists of the *time*. 當代的科學家們。⑦某特殊時期中的生活情況或環境等。We have had a good *time*. 我們玩得很快樂。*Times* are good (*or* bad). 日子好過(或難過)(指謀生容易或困難)。⑧時機。Now's the *time*. 現在正是時候。It is *time* for lunch. 現在是吃午飯的時候了。⑨次數;次。He failed five *times*. 他失敗五次。for the first *time*. 第一次。⑩倍;乘。Three *times* three is (*or* are) nine. 三乘三是九。⑪〖音樂〗拍子。⑫詩的節奏。⑬衡量時間的方法。standard *time*. 標準時間。***about time*** 適當的時候。It's *about time* you came! 是你該來的時候了。***against time*** 搶時間完成。***ahead of time*** 提早;提前。***all the time*** 一直;始終。It rained *all the time*. 天一直在下雨。***at one time*** a. 曾經。b. 同時。***at the same time*** a. 同時。b. 可是;然而。***at times*** 有時;間或。***be ahead of one's time(s)*** (思想)超越時代之前。***beat time*** 打拍子。***beat (someone's) time*** 打敗;搶別人之女友。***be behind the times*** 落伍;過時。***do time*** 〖俗〗服刑期。***for the time being*** 暫時。***from time to time*** 時常;間或。***gain time*** 延期以便準備或等待更有利時機。***have time (hanging) on one's hands*** 有閑散怠惰的時間。***in double-quick time*** 非常快。***in good time*** a. 在合宜的時刻。b. 立刻;趕快。***in no time*** 立卽。***in time*** a. 及時;早晚;將來;終久。b. 合節拍。***keep good (bad) time*** (鐘錶)走得準確(不準確)。***keep time*** a. 計時。b. (鐘錶等)走得準。c. 合節拍;採取一致而有節拍的行動。***kill time*** 消磨時間。***make time*** a. 爭取(失去的)時間。b. 以一特定速度行走。c. 〖俚〗(與女子)約會;向(她)求愛;與(女子)相愛。***many a time*** 常常;多次。***many times*** 常常;屢次。***mark time*** a. 中止;等待。b. 〖軍〗就地踏步。***one at a time*** 每次一個。***on (one's) own time*** 自由的時間內;下班後;無報酬地。***on time*** a. 準時;按時。The train arrives *on time*. 火車按時到達。b. 按時付款;分期付款。***out of time*** 不合節拍。***pass the time of day*** 互相問候或請安(如道早安、晚安等)。***serve one's time*** 學徒;服徒刑;服兵役。***some time or other*** 遲早;早晚。***take one's time*** 不慌不忙;悠哉遊哉。***take time by the forelock*** 立刻抓住機會。***the time of day*** (鐘上所示的)鐘點。***the time of one's life*** 一生中的得意時代。***time after time*** 屢次;多次。***time and again*** 屢次。***time of life*** 年齡。***time out of mind*** 古遠的時代。***work against time*** 加緊工作;以最大的速度工作。—*v.t.* ①測定…的速率;記錄…的時間。②使合時宜;選擇合宜時間。The remark is well *timed*. 這話正合時宜。③調節;使在時間上與…相適應。④定時。⑤對準時間;校正時間。—*v.i.* 配合做事;打拍子。—*adj.* ①時間的。②定時的;定期的。③分期付款的。
time and a half 相當於每小時工資一倍半的加班費。
time and motion study 時間與工作效率的相關研究。
time·ball 〔'taɪmbɔl; 'taimbɔːl〕 *n.* 標準報時球。
time·bar·gain 〔'taɪm,bargɪn; 'taim-,bɑːgin〕 *n.* 〖商〗定期交易;定期履行商業行爲之契約。
time base 〖雷達、電視〗時基;時軸(用以測定目標距離或確定掃瞄時間)。
time bill ①〖英〗(火車等之)時間表。②〖商〗期票。
time bomb 定時炸彈。
time book 工作時間記錄簿。
time·card 〔'taɪm,kard; 'taimkɑːd〕 *n.* 受雇者之工作時間記錄卡。
time clock 打卡鐘。
time-con·sum·ing 〔'taɪmkən,sjumɪŋ; 'taimkən,sjuːmiŋ〕 *adj.* 耗費時間的。
time copy 〖新聞〗預排備用的文稿。
time deposit 〖商〗定期存款。
time discount 〖商〗在期限內付款可享之優待。
time draft 〖商〗期票。

time-ex·pired ['taɪmɪks,paɪrd; 'taimiks,paiəd] *adj.* (士兵、水兵等)已滿期的。

time exposure ①底片之相當長時間的曝光(通常超過半秒鐘)。②以此種方式拍攝的像片。

time fuse 定時信管。

time gun 午砲;時砲。

time-hon·ored ['taɪm,ɑnəd; 'taim,ɔnəd] *adj.* 因年久而被尊敬或遵守的;由來已久的。

time immemorial ①無可稽考或無法記憶的過去時間;史前時期。②〖英國法律〗法律無法追溯之年代。

time·keep·er ['taɪm,kipə; 'taim,kiːpə] *n.* ①記時員。②鐘錶。③〖運動〗計時員。④計時之人或事物。⑤〖音樂〗計拍的人。—**time·keep·ing,** *n.*

time killer ①消遣。②找消遣打發時間的人。

time lag ①遲緩;減低速度。②時差(兩件互相關連之事發生的時間上的差距)。(亦作 **timelag**)

time-lapse ['taɪm,læps; 'taimlæps] *adj.* 縮時照相的。

time-lapse photography 縮時照相。

time·less ['taɪmlɪs; 'taimlis] *adj.* ①無窮的;永久的。②不屬於某一特殊之時間的;無時間性的。③〖古〗非其時的;不合時的。—**ly,** *adv.* —**ness,** *n.*

time limit 時限。

time loan 定期貸款。(亦作 **time money**)

time lock 定時鎖(由機械控制, 不到時間不能開)。

***time·ly** ['taɪmlɪ; 'taimli] *adj.,* **-li·er, -li·est.** ①合時的; 適時的。*timely* help (warning). 適時的援助(警告)。②〖古〗早的。—*adv.* 合時地; 當令地。—**time·li·ness,** *n.*

time note 〖商〗期票。

time of day ①鐘錶上所指的時刻。②現代;現時。③一天中的某些時間。④〖俗〗不關心。***know the time of day*** 瞭解現狀;通曉時事。***pass the time of day*** 相遇時作簡短交談。

time·ous ['taɪməs; 'taiməs] *adj.* 〖蘇〗①早的。②合時的;適時的。—**ly,** *adv.*

time out ①(在球賽中之) 時間暫停。②不計入工作記錄等內之時間。③休息; 暫停。(亦作 **time-out**)

time·piece ['taɪm,pis; 'taim-piːs] *n.* 時計;鐘;錶。

tim·er ['taɪmə; 'taimə] *n.* ①計時員。②時計。③計秒錶;定時裝置。④內燃機的氣缸中使火花定時發生之裝置。

Times, the [taɪmz; taimz] *n.* 英國泰晤士報 (1785 年創立)。

time·sav·er ['taɪm,sevə; 'taim,seivə] *n.* 節省時間之人或物。

time·sav·ing ['taɪm,sevɪŋ; 'taim,seiviŋ] *adj.* 節省時間的。

time·serv·er ['taɪm,sɜvə; 'taim,səːvə] *n.* 以一己之利益爲準則者;趨炎附勢者。

time·serv·ing ['taɪm,sɜvɪŋ; 'taim,səːviŋ] *adj.* 以一己之利益爲準則的; 趨炎附勢的。 —**ness,** *n.*

time-share(d) ['taɪm,ʃɛr(d); 'taimʃɛə(d)] *adj.* 〖電腦〗共用時的。

time-shar·ing ['taɪm'ʃɛrɪŋ; 'taim'ʃɛəriŋ] *n.* 〖電腦〗共用時;分時系統 (由不同地點的人在同一時間內共同使用一部電腦)。

time signal 對時 (如收音機上)信號。

time signature 〖音樂〗(樂譜之) 拍子記號。

time spirit 時代精神。

Times Square 泰晤士廣場。

time switch 定時自動開關。

time·ta·ble ['taɪm,tebl; 'taim,teibl] *n.* ①(車、船、飛機等開駛與到達之) 時間表。②(音樂會、研究計畫等) 時間表; 計畫表。③(英大學的)課程表。

time-test·ed ['taɪm'tɛstɪd; 'taim'testid] *adj.* 受過長時期考驗而證明仍有價值的。(亦作 **time-tried**)

time-wast·er ['taɪm,westə; 'taim,weistə] *n.* 浪費時間的人或事。

time-wast·ing ['taɪm,westɪŋ; 'taim,weistiŋ] *adj.* 浪費時間的。

time·work ['taɪm,wɝk; 'taimwəːk] *n.* 計時或計日付酬之工作。 —**er,** *n.*

time·worn ['taɪm,worn; 'taim,wɔːn] *adj.* ①陳舊的;老朽的。②老的。③陳腔濫調的。

time zone 時區(地球表面自格林威治天文臺起, 按一天 24 小時劃分的 24 區域之一)。

***tim·id** ['tɪmɪd; 'timid] *adj.* 膽小的; 膽怯的;怯懦的。 —**ly,** *adv.* —**ness,** *n.*

ti·mid·i·ty [tɪ'mɪdətɪ; ti'miditi] *n.* 膽小;膽怯;怯懦。

tim·ing ['taɪmɪŋ; 'taimiŋ] *n.* ①〖戲劇〗**a.** 使一劇中的各動作同時發生以獲得最佳之效果。**b.** 所獲得之效果。**c.** 演員的動作和臺詞的背誦的時間配合, 以獲得戲劇效果。②〖運動〗速度的控制 (使在適當時間達到最高峯)。③定時。④爲達到最高效果而選定的時間。

ti·moc·ra·cy [taɪ'mɑkrəsɪ; tai'mɔkrəsi] *n., pl.* **-cies.** ①(柏拉圖政治學中的) 榮譽政治(統治者的指導原則爲愛榮譽)。②(亞里斯多德政治學中的)財力政治(國家政治權力之大小與財產之多寡成正比)。—**ti·mo·crat·ic, ti·mo·crat·i·cal,** *adj.*

Ti·mon ['taɪmən; 'taimən] *n.* ①莎士比亞的 *Timon of Athens* 一劇中之主角名;恨人類之人;不信任人類之人。②戴蒙(希臘哲學家, 320–230B.C.).

Ti·mor ['timɔr; 'tiːmɔː] *n.* 帝汶島(南洋羣島內之一島)。

tim·or·ous ['tɪmərəs; 'timərəs] *adj.* 膽小的;膽怯的;畏怯的。—**ly,** *adv.* —**ness,** *n.*

Tim·o·thy ['tɪməθɪ; 'timəθi] *n.* ①〖聖經〗提摩太(聖保羅之一弟子)。②(新約聖經中之)提摩太書。③男子名。

tim·o·thy ['tɪməθɪ; 'timəθi] *n.* 〖植物〗一種筒狀長穗之草。(亦作 **timothy grass**)

tim·pa·ni ['tɪmpə,ni; 'timpəni(ː)] *n. pl.* (常作 *sing.* 解) 定音鼓 (交響樂隊用的一套不同音調之銅鼓)。(亦作 **tympani**)

tim·pa·nist ['tɪmpənɪst; 'timpənist] *n.* timpani 之鼓手。

tin** [tɪn; tin] *n., adj., v.,* **tinned, tin·ning.** —*n.* ①錫。 ②馬口鐵;洋鐵皮 (=tin plate)。③〖英〗馬口鐵罐;罐頭;聽。—*adj.* ①錫的;馬口鐵的。②卑賤的;無價值的;贋造的。a little tin god*** 自以爲重要或被認爲重要的小人物。 —*v.t.* ①〖英〗裝(食物、香煙等)於罐頭中。②包以錫;包以馬口鐵。—**like,** *adj.*

tin·a·mou ['tɪnə,mu; 'tinəmuː] *n.* 鴿科之鳥;鵪鴣。

tin·cal ['tɪŋkɑl; 'tiŋkɑːl] *n.* 天然硼砂;粗硼砂。

tin can ①洋鐵罐; 錫杯; 錫罐。②〖美俗〗小型汽車。③〖美軍俗〗驅逐艦。

tin·clad ['tɪn,klæd; 'tin-klæd] *n.* 〖俗〗輕裝甲砲艇。—*adj.* 輕裝甲的。

tinct [tɪŋkt; tiŋkt] *n.* 〖詩〗色彩;顏色。—*v.t.* 〖廢〗着色於;加色於。—*adj.* 染有顏色的;有色的。—**tinc·tion,** *n.*

tinct. tincture.

tinc·to·ri·al [tɪŋk'torɪəl; tiŋk'tɔːriəl]

adj. 染色的;着色的;色彩的。

tinc·ture [ˈtɪŋktʃɚ; ˈtiŋktʃə] *n., v.,* **-tured, -tur·ing.** —*n.* ①溶解在酒精裏的藥。②色澤。③些許;微量。④痕跡。⑤顏料。—*v.t.* ①染以色澤。②帶有意味。

tin·der [ˈtɪndɚ; ˈtində] *n.* ①火絨; 火種。②引火物;易燃物。—**like,** *adj.*

tin·der·box [ˈtɪndɚ͵bɑks; ˈtindəbɔks] *n.* ①火絨匣。②易燃之物。③脾氣暴躁的人。④可能引起暴亂之根源。

tin·der·y [ˈtɪndərɪ; ˈtindəri] *adj.* 似火絨的;易引火的;易燃的。

tine [taɪn; tain] *n.* (叉子、鹿角等)突出之尖端或叉齒。(亦作 **tyne**) —**tined,** *adj.*

tin·e·a [ˈtɪnɪə; ˈtiniə] *n.* 〖醫〗癬。

tin ear 〖俚〗音盲。

tin fish 〖美軍俗〗魚雷。

tin foil ①錫箔。②(包糖果、香煙的)錫紙。(亦作 **tinfoil**)

ting [tɪŋ; tiŋ] *n.* 玎玲聲; 鈴聲。 —*v.t. & v.i.* (使)發玎玲聲。

Ting Chao-chung [ˈtɪŋˈdʒauˈtʃuŋ; ˈtiŋˈdʒauˈtʃuːŋ] *n.* 丁肇中 (Samuel, 1936–, 華裔美籍科學家, 因發現 J 粒子, 與 Burton Richter 同獲1976年諾貝爾物理獎)。

***tinge** [tɪndʒ; tindʒ] *v.,* **tinged, tinge·ing** or **ting·ing,** *n.* —*v.t.* ①微染; 染以輕淡之顏色。②沾染;加以某種意味。—*n.* ①色澤;色度;輕微的色度。②意味;少許;微量。—**ting·er,** *n.* —**ting·i·ble,** *adj.*

***tin·gle** [ˈtɪŋg!; ˈtiŋgl] *v.,* **-gled, -gling,** *n.* —*v.i.* ①有刺痛之感。②被激動;興奮。③發玎璫聲。—*v.t.* 使有刺痛之感。—*n.* ①刺痛之感。②興奮之感。③玎璫聲。—**tin·gler,** *n.* —**tin·gling·ly,** *adv.*

tin·gly [ˈtɪŋglɪ; ˈtiŋgli] *adj.,* **-gli·er, -gli·est.** 有刺痛感的。

tin·horn [ˈtɪn͵hɔrn; ˈtinhɔːn] 〖俚〗 *n.* 自命不凡的小人物, 小角色(尤指賭徒)。—*adj.* 小的;不足爲道的;自命不凡的。

tink·er** [ˈtɪŋkɚ; ˈtiŋkə] *n.* ①修補鍋、盤等的工匠。②能作各種輕微修補工作的人; 萬能先生。③笨拙的工作者。④笨拙的工作;粗拙的工藝。⑤幼鯖。⑥〖蘇, 愛〗 **a.** 吉普賽人。**b.** 巡廻的工人。**c.** 流浪者。**d.** 乞丐。 ***a tinker's dam(n) 無價值之物。 ***not to care a tinker's dam(n)*** 毫不介意。 ***not worth a tinker's dam(n)*** 毫無價值。—*v.i.* ①做補鍋匠。②拙劣修補。③無事忙;瞎忙一陣而無效果。—*v.t.* 修補。—**er,** *n.*

tink·er·ly [ˈtɪŋkəlɪ; ˈtiŋkəli] *adj.* 笨拙的;拙劣的;無技巧的;拙劣修補的。

***tin·kle** [ˈtɪŋk!; ˈtiŋkl] *v.,* **-kled, -kling,** *n.* —*v.t.* ①使發玎璫聲。②發玎璫之聲以引起注意或召集。—*v.i.* ①發玎璫聲。②輕彈鍵盤樂器或笨拙地彈此種樂器。 —*n.* 玎璫聲。

tin·kler [ˈtɪŋklɚ; ˈtiŋklə] *n.* 〖俗〗使發玎璫響聲之人或物(如小鈴等)。

tin·man [ˈtɪnmən; ˈtinmən] *n., pl.* **-men.** 洋鐵匠;洋鐵器商。

tinned [tɪnd; tind] *adj.* ①包錫的; 包洋鐵皮的。②〖英〗封存於洋鐵罐中的; 罐頭的。

tin·ner [ˈtɪnɚ; ˈtinə] *n.* ①錫鑛鑛工。②洋鐵匠。③製罐頭工人。

tin·ner·y [ˈtɪnərɪ; ˈtinəri] *n., pl.* **-ner·ies.** 洋鐵工廠;錫廠;錫器廠。

tin·ni·tus [tɪˈnaɪtəs; tiˈnaitəs] *n.* 〖醫〗耳鳴。

tin·ny [ˈtɪnɪ; ˈtini] *adj.,* **-ni·er, -ni·est.** ①錫的; 含錫的; 產錫的。②聲音或樣子像錫的。③不耐久的; 有光彩而無價值的。④有錫味的;有馬口鐵罐味的。

tin opener 〖英〗開罐頭用具; 罐頭刀。

tin-pan alley [ˈtɪn͵pæn~; ˈtinpæn~] ①城市中樂師、樂曲出版家麕集之區域或街道(尤指紐約市中者)。②通俗音樂之出版者、作曲者及倡導者之集合稱。(亦作 **Tin-Pan Alley**)

tin·pan·ny [͵tɪnˈpænɪ; ͵tinˈpæni] *adj.* ①玎璫聲的; 似洋鐵鍋聲的。②吵鬧的。

tin plate 馬口鐵;洋鐵皮。

tin-plate [ˈtɪn͵plet; ˈtin-pleit] *v.t.,* **-plat·ed, -plat·ing.** 覆以洋鐵; 包以洋鐵。

tin-plat·er [ˈtɪn͵pletɚ; ˈtin͵pleitə] *n.* 馬口鐵工人。

tin-pot [ˈtɪnˈpɑt; ˈtinˈpɔt] *adj.* 劣質的; 簡陋的。

tin·sel [ˈtɪns!; ˈtinsəl] *n., v.,* **-sel(l)ed, -sel·(l)ing,** *adj.* —*n.* ①(裝飾聖誕樹、舞者衣服等用的)發奪目亮光的金屬片、金屬絲等。②華麗而無價值的東西。③金、銀、銅線與絲或羊毛織成之薄布。—*v.t.* ①飾以發燦麗亮光之金屬片或絲。②使有華麗的虛僞外表。—*adj.* ①以燦麗發亮之金屬片或絲做成的或裝飾的。②華而不實的。 —**like,** *adj.*

tin·sel·ly [ˈtɪns!ɪ; ˈtinsəli] *adj.* 賤而虛有外表的。

tin·smith [ˈtɪn͵smɪθ; ˈtinsmiθ] *n.* 洋鐵匠;錫器匠。

tin·stone [ˈtɪn͵ston; ˈtinstoun] *n.* 〖礦〗錫石。(亦作 **cassiterite**)

***tint** [tɪnt; tint] *n.* ①色;色彩。 autumn *tints.* 秋色。②色度;濃淡。③淡色。④各種染髮劑。—*v.t.* 微染;着以輕微之顏色。

tint·ed [ˈtɪntɪd; ˈtintid] *adj.* 着色的;有…色的;帶色彩的。

tint·er [ˈtɪntɚ; ˈtintə] *n.* ①染色者; 着色者。②幻燈上使用之有色玻璃片。

tin·tin·nab·u·la·tion [͵tɪntɪ͵næbjəˈleʃən; ͵tinti͵næbjuˈleiʃən] *n.* 錚錚之聲; 玎璫聲;鈴聲。

tin·type [ˈtɪn͵taɪp; ˈtin-taip] *n.* ①鐵板或錫板照相(法)。②用此法攝得之照片。

tin·ware [ˈtɪn͵wɛr; ˈtinwɛə] *n.* ①洋鐵器;洋鐵細工。②錫器;錫細工。

tin-white [ˈtɪnˈhwaɪt; ˈtinˈwait] *adj.* 錫白色的。

tin·work [ˈtɪn͵wɝk; ˈtinwəːk] *n.* 洋鐵器;錫器。

tin·works [ˈtɪn͵wɝks; ˈtinwəːks] *n., pl.* **-works.** (作 *sing.* or *pl.* 解)洋鐵工廠;錫廠;錫器廠。

‡**ti·ny** [ˈtaɪnɪ; ˈtaini] *adj.,* **-ni·er, -ni·est,** *n.* —*adj.* 微小的; 極小的。 —*n.* 小孩;微小之物。 —**ti·ni·ly,** *adv.* —**ti·ni·ness,** *n.*

-tion 〖字尾〗表"動作;狀態;行爲之結果"等之名詞字尾。 (亦作 **-ation, -cion, -ion, -sion, -xion**)

tip¹** [tɪp; tip] *n., v.,* **tipped, tip·ping.** —*n.* ①小費;賞錢。②(關於賽馬、證券交易等之) 祕密消息。③暗示;勸告。④輕拍;輕擊。—*v.t.* ①賞錢; 給小費。 Did you *tip* the waiter? 你給侍者小費沒有?②給暗示; 給勸告。③透露祕密。—*v.i.* 賞小費。tip a man the wink*** 給某人暗示以警告之。***tip a person off*** 〖美俗〗 **a.** 告以祕密消息。 **b.**警告。

‡**tip²** *n., v.,* **tipped, tip·ping.** —*n.* ①尖; 尖端。 the *tips* of the fingers. 手指尖。②具尖端之物。 ③尖頂。 ④(亦作 **tip-in, tip-on**) 貼在書或雜誌頁上之小紙張, 如地圖、挿圖、勘誤表等。 ***on the tip of one's tongue*** 即將說出;(話)到嘴邊;就在嘴邊上(却想不起來了)。 —*v.t.* ①裝以尖頭。②成爲尖頭。③裝飾尖頭。④除去(植物之)尖頭或幹。

***tip³** *v.,* **tipped, tip·ping,** *n., adj.* —*v.t.*

①使傾斜。②打翻〖常 over〗. ③傾出;倒出。④觸摸或微擧(帽)邊致敬。—*v.i.* ①傾斜。②推翻。*tip the scale* **a.** 使天秤傾斜。**b.** 爲決定因素。*tip the scale at* 稱量。—*n.* 傾斜。—*adj.* 用傾斜角度來卸貨的。

tip⁴ *n., v.,* **tipped, tip·ping.** —*n.* ①輕擊;輕拍。②(球)擦邊之一擊。—*v.t.* ①輕擊;輕拍。②用球棒擦球邊輕擊之。

tip⁵ *n.* 堆垃圾處。

tip-and-run [ˈtɪpənˈrʌn; ˈtipəndˈrʌn] *adj.* 〖英〗突襲後即逸去的。

tip car =**tipcart.**

tip·cart [ˈtɪpˌkɑrt; ˈtipkɑːt] *n.* 傾倒車(車身後部可傾側或底部之板可開啓以卸貨)。

tip·cat [ˈtɪpˌkæt; ˈtipkæt] *n.* ①一種兒童遊戲(以杖擊兩端削尖之小木橛之一端, 俟其彈起在空中時再擊之以比賽遠近)。②此種遊戲所用之小木橛。(亦作 **pussy**)

tip-off [ˈtɪpˌɔf; ˈtipɔːf] *n.* ①(賽馬或投機事業中的)供給祕密消息。②警告;暗示。

tip·per [ˈtɪpɚ; ˈtipə] *n.* ①給小費者。②傾倒車搬運夫。③傾倒物。④供給祕密消息者。

tip·pet [ˈtɪpɪt; ˈtipit] *n.* ①(婦女披帶之)短披肩;肩巾。②(頭巾、肩巾或袖上的)狹而長的下垂部分。③(法官與牧師等之)黑色長披肩。

tip·ple¹ [ˈtɪpl; ˈtipl] *v.,* **-pled, -pling,** *n.* —*v.t.* ①常飲(烈酒)。②使醉酒。—*v.i.* 常常飲少量之酒。—*n.* ①烈酒。②飲料。—**tip·pler,** *n.*

tip·ple² *n.* ①使貨車傾斜以倒出車中貨物等之裝置。②以此種方式卸貨之處。—**tip·pler,** *n.*

tip·ple³ *v.t. & v.i.,* **-pled, -pling.** 〖方〗打翻;翻倒;傾斜。

tip sheet 發表股市、馬賽或其他消息的出版物。

tip·si·ness [ˈtɪpsɪnɪs; ˈtipsinis] *n.* ①微醉。②不穩;蹣跚。

tip·staff [ˈtɪpˌstæf; ˈtipstɑːf] *n., pl.* **-staves, -staffs.** ①(昔日法警等所執的)金屬包頂之手杖。②携帶此手杖的官員。③(法院之)布達員。

tip·ster [ˈtɪpstɚ; ˈtipstə] *n.* 〖俗〗(在賽馬、賭博、投機事業之)通報祕密消息者;洩漏內情者;預測優勝者。

tip·sy [ˈtɪpsɪ; ˈtipsi] *adj.,* **-si·er, -si·est.** ①易醉的;微醉的。②易傾倒的;易顚覆的。③蹣跚的;踉蹌的。④曲折的;歪曲的。—**tip·si·ly,** *adv.*

tipsy cake 浸有葡萄酒的杏仁蛋糕。

tip-tilt·ed [ˈtɪpˌtɪltɪd; ˈtipˌtiltid] *adj.* 向上的(鼻)。

***tip·toe** [ˈtɪpˌto; ˈtiptou, ˈtipˈt-] *n., v.,* **-toed, -toe·ing,** *adj., adv.* —*n.* 趾尖;脚尖。*on tiptoe* **a.** 用脚尖(走路);以脚尖(站)。**b.** 熱切地。**c.** 祕密地;悄悄地。—*v.i.* 以脚尖行走。—*adj.* ①以脚尖走路的。②熱切的。③祕密的;謹愼的。—*adv.* ①熱心地;小心地。②用脚尖(走或站)。

tip·top [ˈtɪpˈtɑp; ˈtipˈtɔp] *n.* ①絕頂;最高點。②〖俗〗最佳;黃金時代。③〖英俗〗最高之社會階級。—*adj.* ①在絕頂的;在最高點的。②卓越的;最好的;第一流的。—*adv.* 最佳地。

tip-up seat [ˈtɪpˌʌp~; ˈtipʌp~] (戲院等的)翻椅。

ti·rade [ˈtaɪred; taiˈreid] *n.* ①長篇的激烈演說。②長篇的彈劾或攻擊性演說。③(詩中之)有關某一件事之一段。

ti·rage [tɪˈrɑʒ; tiˈrɑːʒ] *n.* (書籍之)版。

***tire**¹ [taɪr; ˈtaiə] *v.,* **tired, tir·ing,** *n.* —*v.t.* ①使疲倦。Walking *tires* me. 走路使我疲倦。②使厭倦。—*v.i.* ①疲倦。Children *tire* easily. 小孩子容易疲倦。②厭倦〖常 of〗. I never *tire* of listening to classical music. 我對於古典音樂百聽不厭。*tire out* (使)精疲力竭。—*n.* 〖英方〗疲倦。

***tire**², **tyre** *n., v.,* **tired, tir·ing.** —*n.* 輪箍;橡皮輪胎。—*v.t.* 裝以輪胎或輪箍。

tire³ *v.,* **tired, tir·ing,** *n.* —*v.t.* 〖古〗①使穿衣。②梳理(頭髮);(以頭飾)打扮。—*n.* 〖古〗①衣服。②(女人用的)頭飾。

‡**tired**¹ [taɪrd; ˈtaiəd] *adj.* ①疲乏的;疲倦的。I'm too *tired* to go any further. 我太疲乏,不能再向前走了。②厭倦的;厭煩的。I'm *tired* of having the same kind of food every day. 天天吃同樣的東西,我感覺厭煩了。③(句子、笑話、講道等)陳腐的。④〖俗〗不耐煩的。You make me *tired*. 你煩死我了。*be tired out* 感到精疲力竭。—**ly,** *adv.* —**ness,** *n.*

tired² *adj.* 裝有輪胎的。

tire iron 拆卸車胎用的鐵橇。

tire·less [ˈtaɪrlɪs; ˈtaiəlis] *adj.* ①不知疲倦的。②不停的。—**ly,** *adv.*

***tire·some** [ˈtaɪrsəm; ˈtaiəsəm] *adj.* ①令人厭倦的;令人厭煩的;討厭的。②易使人疲倦的;吃力的。a *tiresome* job. 一件吃力的工作。—**ly,** *adv.* —**ness,** *n.*

tire·wom·an [ˈtaɪrˌwumən; ˈtaiəˌwumən] *n., pl.* **-wom·en.** 〖古〗侍女。

tir·ing room [ˈtaɪrɪŋ~; ˈtaiəriŋ~] 〖古〗化妝室(尤指戲院中者)。

ti·ro, ty·ro [ˈtaɪro; ˈtaiərou] *n., pl.* **-ros.** 沒有經驗的人;新手。

Ti·ros [ˈtaɪros; ˈtaiərous] *n.* 〖美〗用電視轉播地球雲層的一系列人造衞星之一。

'tis [tɪz; tiz] 〖詩〗=**it is.**

ti·sane [tɪˈzæn; ti(ː)ˈzæn] *n.* 煎好的藥劑;香茶;草藥茶。

Ti·se·li·us [tɪˈselɪəs; tiˈseiliəs] *n.* 狄塞里斯(Arne Wihelm Kaurin, 1902–1971, 瑞典生物化學家,曾獲1948年諾貝爾化學獎)。

***tis·sue** [ˈtɪʃu; ˈtisjuː, ˈtiʃuː] *n.* ①〖生物〗組織;體素。muscular *tissue.* 肌肉組織。②細薄之絲織物;薄絹。③編造的故事;結構。④薄紙;棉紙(=**tissue paper**)。⑤做副本用的薄紙。—*v.t.* 〖古〗①以金銀絲編織。②以薄絹裝飾。

tissue culture 〖生物〗組織培養(法);體素培養;體素培養學。

tissue paper 薄紙(近乎透明, 作包裝、保護精緻物品等用)。

tit¹ [tɪt; tit] *n.* ①山雀。②其他之小鳥。

tit² *n.* 輕打;還擊(現只用於tit for tat中)。

tit³ *n.* ①〖俚蔑〗少女;少婦。②小馬;劣馬。

tit⁴ *n.* ①奶頭;乳頭。②〖鄙〗乳房;(女人的)胸部。

Tit. Titus. **tit.** title.

Ti·tan [ˈtaɪtn̩; ˈtaitən] *n.* ①泰坦(希臘神話中的巨人族之任何一員)。②(t-) 有巨大的力量、形狀、權利等的人或物。③太陽神。④(亦作 **Titaness**)女泰坦。⑤土星的九衞星之一。⑥〖美〗太陽神洲際彈道飛彈。—*adj.* (t-) =**titanic**².

ti·ta·ni·a [tɪˈtenɪə; tiˈtɑːnjə] *n.* ①人造金紅石(作寶石用)。②=**titanic oxide.**

Ti·tan·ic [taɪˈtænɪk; taiˈtænik] *adj.* (似)泰坦神的。

ti·tan·ic¹ [taɪˈtænɪk; taiˈtænik] *adj.* 〖化〗鈦的;含四價鈦的。

ti·tan·ic² *adj.* 巨大的;極其有力的。(亦作 **titan**)

titanic acid 〖化〗鈦酸。

titanic oxide 〖化〗二氧化鈦;鈦白(用做油漆、染料等)。(亦作 **titanium dioxide**)

ti·ta·ni·um [taɪˈtenɪəm; taiˈteiniəm]

n.【化】鈦(深灰色之金屬元素,符號爲 Ti)。
Ti·tan·o·sau·rus 〔ˌtaɪtənəˈsɔrəs; ˌtaitənəˈsɔːrəs〕 *n.*【古生物】一種恐龍(在南美洲白堊紀地層中發現)。
tit·bit 〔ˈtɪtˌbɪt; ˈtitbit〕 *n.* ①量少而質精的食物。②珍聞;花邊新聞;花絮。(亦作 **tidbit**)
ti·ter 〔ˈtaɪtɚ, ˈtitɚ; ˈtaitə, ˈtiːtə〕 *n.*【化, 生理】滴定量;滴定濃度。
tit for tat 以牙還牙;一報還一報。
tith·a·ble 〔ˈtaɪðəbl̩; ˈtaiðəbl〕 *adj.* 可徵十分之一稅的。
tithable income 可徵十分之一稅的「收入」。
tithable land 可徵十分之一稅的土地。
tithe 〔taɪð; taið〕 *n., v.,* **tithed, tith·ing.** —*n.* ①十分之一。②一小部分;一點。I cannot remember a *tithe* of it. 我一點也不記得了。③(常 *pl.*) 什一之稅(以農產十分之一繳教會)。to take *tithe* of. 課以什一稅。④任何小額之賦稅。—*v.t.* ①課以十分之一之稅。②對…納十分之一的稅。—*v.i.* 付什分之一稅。—**less,** *adj.*
tith·er 〔ˈtaɪðɚ; ˈtaiðə〕 *n.* ①付什一之稅者。②提倡什一之稅者。③收什一之稅者。
tith·ing 〔ˈtaɪðɪŋ; ˈtaiðiŋ〕 *n.* ①徵什一之稅;付什一之稅。②什一之稅 (=tithe)。③昔時英國民政管轄之單位(包括十家)。
Ti·tian 〔ˈtɪʃən; ˈtiʃiən〕 *n.* 提申 (1477–1576, Tiziano Vecellio, 義大利畫家)。—**esque,** *adj.*
tit·il·late 〔ˈtɪtl̩ˌet; ˈtitileit〕 *v.t.,* **-lat·ed, -lat·ing.** ①搔之使癢。②刺激(味覺、想像等)使有愉快之感。—**tit·il·la·tion,** *n.*
tit·(t)i·vate 〔ˈtɪtəˌvet; ˈtitiveit〕 *v.t. & v.i.,* **-vat·ed, -vat·ing.**【俗】打扮;梳整。
tit·lark 〔ˈtɪtˌlɑrk; ˈtitlɑːk〕 *n.* 一種類似雲雀之鳴鳥。
‡**ti·tle** 〔ˈtaɪtl̩; ˈtaitl〕 *n., v.,* **-tled, -tling.** —*n.* ①標題;題目;名稱。②稱號;頭銜(如 Sir, Doctor, Professor 等)。③權利;權利之根據;資格。④契據;房契;地契;所有權。⑤優勝;冠軍。to win the heavyweight *title*. 贏得重量級拳擊冠軍。⑥=**title page.** ⑦(常 *pl.*)【電影, 電視】**a.** 字幕。**b.** 片頭。—*v.t.* ①以官銜稱呼。②賦予頭銜、標題等。
ti·tled 〔ˈtaɪtl̩d; ˈtaitld〕 *adj.* 有官銜的;有爵位的。
title deed 【法律】所有權狀。
ti·tle·hold·er 〔ˈtaɪtl̩ˌholdɚ; ˈtaitlˌhouldə〕 *n.* 優勝榮譽之保持者;錦標保持者。
title page 書籍的內封面;書名頁(印着書名、作者、出版者等)。
title role (or **part**) 劇名角色;主角。
ti·tling 〔ˈtaɪtlɪŋ; ˈtaitliŋ〕 *n.* ①(封面上的)書名燙金。②燙成金字的書名。
tit·mouse 〔ˈtɪtˌmaʊs; ˈtitmaus〕 *n., pl.* **-mice.** 小山雀。
Ti·to 〔ˈtito; ˈtiːtou〕 *n.* 狄托(Josip Broz *or* Brozovich, 1892–, 1953–, 任南斯拉夫總統)。
Ti·to·ism 〔ˈtitoˌɪzəm; ˈtiːtouizəm〕 *n.* 狄托主義(主張民族主義及國家獨立的共產主義)。
ti·trant 〔ˈtaɪtrənt; ˈtaitrənt〕 *n.* 滴定「試藥」。
ti·trate 〔ˈtaɪtret; ˈtaitreit〕 *v.t. & v.i.,* **-trat·ed, -trat·ing.**【化, 生理】滴定;以滴定法測定。
ti·tra·tion 〔taɪˈtreʃən; taiˈtreiʃən〕 *n.*【化, 生理】滴定法;容量分析法。
ti·tra·tor 〔ˈtaɪtretɚ; ˈtaitreitə〕 *n.*【化, 生理】滴定計。
tit·ter 〔ˈtɪtɚ; ˈtitə〕 *v.i.* 竊笑;忍笑。—*n.* 竊笑;忍笑。—**er,** *n.*

tit·tle 〔ˈtɪtl̩; ˈtitl〕 *n.* ①字母上的小點或標號(如 i 上之小點, á 上之ˊ)。②微粒;微量。
tit·tle-tat·tle 〔ˈtɪtl̩ˌtætl̩; ˈtitlˌtætl〕 *n., v.,* **-tled, -tling.** —*n.* ①閒談。②謠言;無稽之談。—*v.i.* ①聊天;閒談。②散布謠言。
tit·tup 〔ˈtɪtəp; ˈtitəp〕 *v.,* **-tup(p)ed, -tup·(p)ing,** *n.* —*v.i.* 跳躍;跳躍而行。—*n.* 跳躍;活潑的脚步;歡騰的動作。
tit·u·bate 〔ˈtɪtʃubet; ˈtitjubeit〕 *v.i.,* **-bat·ed, -bat·ing.** ①蹣跚;搖擺。②口吃。—**tit·u·ba·tion,** *n.*
tit·u·lar 〔ˈtɪtʃələ; ˈtitjulə〕 *adj.* ①名義上的;有名無實的。②關於名稱的;標題的。*titular* words. 題詞。③有爵位的。④有正當權利的。⑤【羅馬天主教】**a.** 賜贈稱號的。**b.** 羅馬教區教會的。***titular saint*** 教會之守護聖者。—*n.* ①有爵位或稱號之人。②教會之守護聖者。—**ly,** *adv.*
Ti·tus 〔ˈtaɪtəs; ˈtaitəs〕 *n.* ①提多(使徒保羅之門徒)。②(新約中)聖保羅達提多書。
tiz·zy 〔ˈtɪzɪ; ˈtizi〕 *n., pl.* **-zies.** ①【俚】(尤指爲了無足輕重的小事而引起的)顫抖或發狂;戰慄。②【英俚】六辨士。
T.K.O., TKO, t.k.o. technical knock-out.【拳擊】技術擊倒。**Tl** 化學元素 thallium 之符號。**TL** trade-last. **TL.** lira. 土耳其貨幣名。 **T/L** time loan. **T.L.** ①trade-last. ②trade list. **T.L.O., t.l.o.** total loss only. **Tm** 化學元素 thulium 之符號。**t.m.** true mean.
tme·sis 〔ˈtmisɪs, təˈmisɪs; ˈtmiːsis〕 *n.*【修辭, 作詩法】分辭法;分語法(即將一字插入一複合字之間, 如: what person soever 即 whatsoever person)。
T.M.O. telegraph money order. **T.N.** true north. **Tn** ①化學元素 thoron 之符號。②train. 行李;輜重。**tn.** ton. **TNT, T.N.T.** Trinitrotoluene. 三硝基甲苯, 一種猛烈的黃色炸藥。
‡**to** 〔tu, tʊ, tə; tuː, tu, tə, t〕 *prep.* ①向…方。The house looks *to* the south. 這所房屋朝南。②指向某目標;面對某目標。I sat face *to* face with her. 我和她面對面坐着。③至;到;達;迄。from beginning *to* end. 自始至終。to go *to* bed. 就寢。faithful *to* the end. 忠誠不渝以至死。④致使成某種狀態。She tore the letter *to* pieces. 她將信撕成碎片。*to* my disappointment. 使我失望。⑤爲某種目的。Mother came *to* the rescue. 母親來援救。⑥比;比較。The score was 9 *to* 5. 得分是九比五。⑦適合;按照;配合。It is not *to* my taste. 它不合我的所好。⑧屬於。the key *to* my room. 我房間的鑰匙。⑨加於。He had milk *to* his coffee. 他加牛乳於咖啡中。⑩關於。What did he say *to* that? 關於那個他說些甚麼?⑪與動詞原形連用而構成不定詞。He likes *to* read. 他喜歡讀書。⑫表示數目或數量。20 miles *to* the gallon. 一加侖汽油可駛二十英里。⑬表示相對之位置。parallel *to* the roof. 與屋頂平行。—*adv.* ①達於尋常或所要求之狀態;達於關閉或休止狀態。Push the door *to*. 將門推閉。He has come *to*. 他已蘇醒過來。②對某一事情、動作或工作。He turned *to* with a will. 他開始努力去做。***to and fro*** 往復;來回。He is walking *to and fro* in the room. 他在室內踱來踱去。
T.O. Telegraph Office.
T/O Table of Organization. 編制表。
˙**toad** 〔tod; toud〕 *n.* ①蟾蜍。②任何無尾

的兩棲類動物;任何蛙。③卑鄙的人。

toad·eat·er [ˈtodˌitɚ; ˈtoudˌiːtə] *n.* 諂媚者;阿諛者;馬屁精。

toad·eat·ing [ˈtodˌitɪŋ; ˈtoudˌiːtiŋ] *adj.* 諂媚的;阿諛的。—*n.* 諂媚。

toad·fish [ˈtodˌfɪʃ; ˈtoudfiʃ] *n.* 華臍魚;琵琶魚。

toad·flax [ˈtodˌflæks; ˈtoudflæks] *n.* 〖植物〗(歐洲產的)蛋黃草。

toad·stone [ˈtodˌston; ˈtoudstoun] *n.* 蟾蜍石(昔用做護符)。

toad·stool [ˈtodˌstul; ˈtoudstuːl] *n.* ①蕈。②毒蕈。

toad·y [ˈtodɪ; ˈtoudi] *n., pl.* **toad·ies,** *v.,* **toad·ied, toad·y·ing.** —*n.* 諂媚者。—*v.i.* & *v.t.* 諂媚;奉承。

toad·y·ism [ˈtodɪɪzəm; ˈtoudiizəm] *n.* 諂媚;阿諛;奉承。

to-and-fro [ˈtuənˈfro; ˈtu(ː)ənˈfrou] *adj., adv., v., n., pl.* **-fros.** —*adj.* & *adv.* 往復活動的(地); 來回的(地)。—*v.i.* 來回走動。—*n.* 往復運動。

***toast**[1] [tost; toust] *n.* 烤麪包片。—*v.t.* ①烘;烤。②烘暖。—*v.i.* 取暖。

***toast**[2] *n.* ①被舉杯頌祝健康者。②飲酒頌祝健康;乾杯。③名人(值得舉杯頌祝者)。—*v.t.* & *v.i.* 飲酒頌祝某人健康;爲(某人)乾杯。

toast·er[1] [ˈtostɚ; ˈtoustə] *n.* ①烤麪包的用具;烤麪包機。②烤麪包的人。

toast·er[2] *n.* 舉杯祝頌者。

toasting fork 烤麪包用的長柄叉。

toast list 宴會講演者之名單。

toast·mas·ter [ˈtostˌmæstɚ; ˈtoustˌmɑːstə] *n.* ①主持宴會並介紹講演者的人。②提議舉杯祝頌健康等的人。

toast rack 用以承烤麪包片之架。

***to·bac·co** [təˈbæko; təˈbækou] *n., pl.* **-cos, -coes.** 煙草;煙葉。

to·bac·co·man [təˈbækoˌmæn,-mən; təˈbækoumæn, -mən] *n., pl.* **-men.** 煙草商;煙草製造者。

to·bac·co·nist [təˈbækənɪst; təˈbækənist] *n.* 〖英〗①煙草商。②煙草店。

tobacco pipe (抽烟絲用的)烟斗。

tobacco plant 煙草屬之植物;煙草。

tobacco pouch 煙袋。

To·ba·go [təˈbego; touˈbeigou] *n.* 托貝哥島(原爲英屬西印度羣島之一島, 現爲Trinidad and Tobago 共和國之一部分)。

to-be [tuˈbi; tuˈbiː] *adj.* 未來的;將來的;預定的。 a bride-*to-be.* 未來之新娘;準新娘。—*n.* (常 T-) 未來;未來發生之事。

to·bog·gan [təˈbɑgən; təˈbɔgən] *n.* 扁長平底橇。—*v.i.* ①乘橇滑下。②(物價等)急降。

To·by [ˈtobɪ; ˈtoubi] *n., pl.* **-bies.** ①老人形啤酒杯。②〖俚〗一種細長的劣等雪茄。(亦作 **toby**)

toc·ca·ta [təˈkɑtə; təˈkɑːtə] *n.* 〖音樂〗觸技曲。

Toc H [tɑk etʃ; tɔk eitʃ] 戰友聯誼會(第一次世界大戰之戰友於 1920 年成立於倫敦)。

to·co, to·ko [ˈtoko; ˈtoukou] *n.* 〖英俚〗鞭笞;懲罰;處罰。

to·col·o·gy, to·kol·o·gy [təˈkɑlədʒɪ; təˈkɔlədʒi] *n.* 產科學。

toc·sin [ˈtɑksɪn; ˈtɔksin] *n.* ①警聲。②警鐘; 警鈴。

tod[1] [tɑd; tɔd] *n.* ①樹叢。②英國稱量羊毛之單位(通常約等於28磅)。③載貨。

tod[2] *n.* 〖蘇,英方〗①狐。②狡猾的人。

‡**to·day** [təˈde; təˈdei, tuˈd-] *n.* ①今天。Have you seen *today's* paper? 你看到今天的報嗎? ②現在;當今。 the writers of *today.* 現代的作家們。—*adv.* ①今天。I am very busy *today.* 我今天很忙。②現在;當今。

tod·dle [ˈtɑdl; ˈtɔdl] *v.,* **-dled, -dling,** *n.* —*v.i.* ①(如童叟般) 以短而不穩定的脚步行走。②〖俗〗閒步;散步。③出發;離去。—*n.* ①蹣跚步伐。②〖俗〗閒步;散步。

tod·dy [ˈtɑdɪ; ˈtɔdi] *n., pl.* **-dies.** ①椰子汁; 棕櫚酒。②威士忌或其他酒類中加入糖水及香料之飲料。

to-do [təˈdu; təˈduː] *n., pl.* **-dos.** 〖俗〗騷亂;紛擾;嚷鬧;混雜。

to·dy [ˈtodɪ; ˈtoudi] *n., pl.* **-dies.** 〖動物〗西印度羣島所產的一種食蟲小鳥。

toe** [to; tou] *n., v.,* **toed, toe·ing.** —*n.* ①趾;足指。②鞋、襪等之趾部。③足或蹄之前部。④趾狀物。 ***on one's toes 〖俗〗有活力的;警覺的;準備好了。***step*** (or ***tread***) ***on one's toes*** 觸怒某人。—*v.t.* ①以趾踏觸。②裝(鞋、襪等) 之趾部。③傾斜地將(釘) 釘入。—*v.i.* ①用趾尖舞。②行走時趾尖向內或向外。 ***toe the line*** (or ***mark***) **a.** 準備起跑;準備開始競爭。 **b.** 嚴守規則或命令。 **c.** 忠於職守;盡責。 **—like,** *adj.*

toe·cap [ˈtoˌkæp; ˈtou-kæp] *n.* 鞋尖;鞋頭。

toe crack 馬之裂蹄症。

toed [tod; toud] *adj.* ①有(某種或某數目之)趾的。②斜着釘進的(釘子)。③(板) 以斜着釘進之釘子釘住的。

toe dance 脚尖舞。

toe-dance [ˈtoˌdæns; ˈtoudɑːns] *v.i.,* **-danced, -danc·ing.** 跳脚尖舞。

toe dancer 跳脚尖舞者。

toe hold ①登山等時供放足趾的地方或突出部分。②任何排除障礙或克服困難的方法。③極輕微的影響力、權力等。④〖摔角〗能扭對方之脚的緊握。(亦作 **toehold**)

toe·less [ˈtolɪs; ˈtoulis] *adj.* ①無脚趾的。②露脚趾的。

toe·nail [ˈtoˌnel; ˈtouneil] *n.* ①趾甲。②斜釘之釘子。—*v.t.* 斜釘釘子。

toff [tɔf; tɔf] *n.* 〖英俗〗①紳士;上流人。②紈袴子;愛打扮的人。 ***the toffs*** 上流社會。

tof·fee [ˈtɑfɪ, ˈtɔfɪ; ˈtɔfi] *n., pl.* **-fees.** 太妃糖(糖與奶油製成)。(亦作 **toffy**)

tog [tɑg; tɔg] *n., v.,* **togged, tog·ging.** —*n.* ①〖俚〗上衣。②(*pl.*)〖俗〗一套衣服。—*v.t.* 穿着;打扮〖常 out, up〗。 ***tog oneself up*** (or ***out***) 穿着或打扮漂亮。

to·ga [ˈtogə; ˈtougə] *n., pl.* **-gas, -gae** [-dʒi; -dʒiː]. ①(古羅馬男子所着之) 寬外袍。②官服;制服。

to·gaed [ˈtogəd; ˈtougəd] *adj.* 着官服的。

‡**to·geth·er** [təˈgɛðɚ; təˈgeðə, tuˈg-] *adv.* ①一起;共同。We went out *together.* 我們一起出去。②連接地;不斷地。 He used to sit there for hours *together.* 他常在那裏一連坐好幾小時。③同時。You cannot have both *together.* 你不能兩者兼得。④合力地。 to undertake a task *together.* 合力擔負一任務。⑤湊合;緊密;上下連貫。to squeeze a thing *together.* 將一件東西捏成一團。⑥彼此;互相。to confer *together.* 彼此商量。 ***together with*** 連同;和。

tog·ger·y [ˈtɑgərɪ; ˈtɔgəri] *n., pl.* **-ger·ies.** 〖俗〗①衣服。②服裝店。

tog·gle [ˈtɑgl; ˈtɔgl] *n., v.,* **-gled, -gling.** —*n.* ①〖機械〗 接根;套環;肘。 *toggle* joint. 肘節。②穿索眼或鏈環之大釘或細棒。—*v.t.* 裝以穿索眼或鏈環之大釘;以上述的大釘釘牢。

toggle switch 〖電〗手開關。

To·go [ˈtogo; ˈtougou] *n.* 多哥(非洲西部之一國，首都洛梅 Lomé)。
To·go·land [ˈtogoˌlænd; ˈtougoulænd] *n.* 多哥蘭(非洲西部之舊德國屬地，東部現爲多哥共和國；西部現爲迦納之一部分)。
***toil¹** [tɔɪl; tɔil] *n.* 辛勞；辛苦工作。—*v.i.* ①辛勞；辛苦工作。②跋涉；很艱苦地行進。—*v.t.* 以苦工完成。—**er,** *n.* —**less,** *adj.*
toil² *n.* (常*pl.*) 羅網。
toile [twɑl; twɑːl, twɔːl] *n.* ①一種薄麻布。②一種棉質印花布。
***toi·let** [ˈtɔɪlɪt; ˈtɔilit] *n.* ①梳妝；裝飾。②浴室；盥洗室；廁所。flush *toilet.* 抽水馬桶。③一套梳妝用具。④梳妝臺。⑤衣服；裝束樣式。
toilet bowl 抽水馬桶。
toilet cover (or **cloth**) 梳妝臺布。
toilet paper (or **tissue**) 衛生紙。
toilet powder 撲粉。
toilet room 化妝室。
toi·let·ry [ˈtɔɪlɪtrɪ; ˈtɔilitri] *n., pl.* **-ries.** 化妝品；化妝用具。
toilet seat 放在抽水馬桶上之坐墊圈。
toilet set 化妝用具。
toilet soap 香皂；化妝用之上等肥皂。
toilet table 梳妝臺；化妝臺。
toi·lette [tɔɪˈlɛt, twaˈlɛt; twɑːˈlet] *n.* ①(女人的)化妝；裝扮(包括沐浴、塗脂粉等過程)。②裝束；服裝。
toilet training 訓練小孩控制便溺而養成使用廁所之習慣。
toilet water 一種化妝用香水。
toil·ful [ˈtɔɪlfəl; ˈtɔilful] *adj.* 辛苦的；勞頓的；費力的。
toil·some [ˈtɔɪlsəm; ˈtɔilsəm] *adj.* 辛苦的；勞頓的；費力的；使人厭煩的。
toil·worn [ˈtɔɪlˌworn; ˈtɔilwɔːn] *adj.* 疲憊的；疲勞的。
To·kay [toˈke; touˈkei] *n.* ①(匈牙利所產之)葡萄酒。② **a.** 食用之一種紅葡萄。**b.** 其樹。③美國加利福尼亞州產之白葡萄酒。
to·ken** [ˈtokən; ˈtoukən] *n.* ①表號；表徵；象徵；記號。②紀念品。③代用貨幣。④指明權利的金屬牌。⑤表示權威的東西。⑥〖古〗信號。⑦有票面價值的東西，如紙幣。⑧徽章。by the same token*** **a.** 而且；此外。**b.** 同樣地；基於同樣的理由。***in token of*** 表示。—*adj.* 象徵性的。a *token* resistance. 象徵性的抵抗。—*v.t.* 象徵；代表。
token money (or **coin**) 代用貨幣。
token payment 象徵性之償付。
To·ky·o, To·ki·o [ˈtokɪˌo; ˈtoukjou] *n.* 東京(日本首都)。
Tokyo Bay 東京灣。
to·la [ˈtola; ˈtoulɑː] *n.* 印度之重量單位(約爲 11.664 克)。
:told [told; tould] *v.* pt. & pp. of **tell.** ***all told*** 全部；全算進去。There were 50 guests *all told.* 全部有五十個客人。
***tol·er·a·ble** [ˈtɑlərəbl; ˈtɔlərəbl] *adj.* ①可容忍的；可忍受的。②尙可的；尙好的。③〖俗〗健康情形還可以的。—**tol·er·a·bly,** *adv.* —**ness,** *n.*
tol·er·ance [ˈtɑlərəns; ˈtɔlərəns] *n.* ①寬容；容忍的精神。②忍受或抗拒藥物、毒藥等之能力；耐藥力。③偏差；公差。④對異己之事物的興趣或關懷。
tol·er·ant [ˈtɑlərənt; ˈtɔlərənt] *adj.* ①寬容的；容忍的。②有耐藥力的；有抗藥力的。
tol·er·ate [ˈtɑləˌret; ˈtɔləreit] *v.t.,* **-at·ed, -at·ing.** ①容許；容忍；忍受。②對(藥物)有耐藥力。
tol·er·a·tion [ˌtɑləˈreʃən; ˌtɔləˈreiʃən] *n.* ①容許；容忍；忍受。②信仰自由。
***toll¹** [tol; toul] *v.t.* ①鳴(鐘)(爲報死亡、時刻等)。②(爲死者)鳴鐘。③鳴鐘召集或解散。—*v.i.* (鐘)鳴。—*n.* ①緩慢而有規律的鐘聲。②敲鐘；鳴鐘。
***toll²** *n.* ①稅；費；通行稅、過路錢(等)。②收此等稅或費的權力。③代價；犧牲；損失。④爲某種服務而收的費用。⑤〖主方〗磨穀工扣下代替費用的穀子。—*v.t.* & *v.i.* 徵收(稅、費)。
toll·age [ˈtolɪdʒ; ˈtoulidʒ] *n.* ①稅；通行稅；過路錢(=toll)。②徵稅；納稅。
toll bar (徵收通行稅的)徵收卡；卡門。
toll·booth [ˈtolˌbuθ; ˈtɔlbuːθ] *n., pl.* **-booths.** ①〖蘇〗監獄。②(橋或公路的)收費亭。
toll bridge 須納通行稅始可通過之橋。
toll call 長途電話。
toll collector 收費人；收費機。
toll·er [ˈtolɚ; ˈtoulə] *n.* ①徵收通行稅、港稅等的人。②鳴鐘者。③鐘。④(亦作 **tolling dog**) 引誘野鴨之獵犬。
toll·gate [ˈtolˌget; ˈtoulgeit] *n.* =**toll bar.**
toll·house [ˈtolˌhaus; ˈtoulhaus] *n.* 設於 toll bar 旁側之小閣。
toll·keep·er [ˈtolˌkipɚ; ˈtoulˌkiːpə] *n.* 在徵稅關卡上收取通行稅的人。(亦作**tollman**)
toll line 長途電話線。
tol-lol [ˌtɑlˈlɑl; ˌtɔlˈlɔl] *adj.* 〖俗〗尙可的；平平的；中等的；還好的。(亦作 **tol-lol-ish**)
toll road 須繳納通行稅後方可通行之道路。(亦作 **tollway**)
toll station (公路、橋樑之)收費站。
toll television 收費電視。(亦作**subscription television**)
Tol·stoy, Tol·stoi [ˈtɑlstɔɪ; ˈtɔlstɔi] *n.* 托爾斯泰 (Lev *or* Leo Nikolaevich, 1828–1910, 俄國小說家及社會改革者)。
to·lu [toˈlu; touˈluː] *n.* 妥路香；妥路樹脂(南美產樹脂，用於藥劑和香料等)。(亦作 **balsam of tolu, tolu resin**)
tol·u·ene [ˈtɑljuˌin; ˈtɔljuiːn] *n.* 〖化〗甲苯 ($C_6H_5CH_3$, 用作一種溶劑與製造炸藥等)。(亦作 **methylbenzene, phenylmethane**)
tol·u·ol [ˈtɑljuəl; ˈtɔljuəl] *n.* 〖化〗=**toluene.**
tol·yl [ˈtɑləl; ˈtɔlil] *n.* 〖化〗甲苯基。
Tom [tɑm; tɔm] *n.* ①男子名。②=**Uncle Tom.**
tom [tɑm; tɔm] *n.* 雄性動物；(尤指)雄貓。—*adj.* 雄性的。*tom* turkey. 雄火雞。
tom·a·hawk [ˈtɑməˌhɔk; ˈtɔməhɔːk] *n.* (北美印第安人用的)戰斧；鉞。***bury*** (or ***lay aside***) ***the tomahawk*** 講和。***dig up*** (***raise,*** or ***take up***) ***the tomahawk*** 宣戰。—*v.t.* 用戰斧斬或殺。
***to·ma·to** [təˈmeto; təˈmɑːtou] *n., pl.* **-toes.** ①番茄。②番茄樹。③〖俚〗少女；女人。
tomato catchup 番茄醬。
tomb** [tum; tuːm] *n.* 墳墓。the tomb*** 〖俗〗死。—*v.t.* 埋葬於墓中；幽閉。—**less,** *adj.*
tom·bac [ˈtɑmbæk; ˈtɔmbæk] *n.* 一種銅與鋅的合金(用以做劣質首飾)。(亦作 **tambac, tomback, tombak**)
tom·bo·la [ˈtɑmbələ; ˈtɔmbələ] *n.* 彩票；獎券。
tom·boy [ˈtɑmˌbɔɪ; ˈtɔmbɔi] *n.* 行爲似男孩的女孩；頑皮姑娘。—**ish,** *adj.*
tomb·stone [ˈtumˌston; ˈtuːm-stoun] *n.* 墓碑。
tom·cat [ˈtɑmˌkæt; ˈtɔmˈkæt] *n., v.,* **-cat·ted, -cat·ting.** —*n.* ①雄貓。②〖俚〗

尋花問柳的男人。—*v.i.* 尋花問柳。

tom·cod ['tam,kad; 'tɔmkɔd] *n., pl.* **-cod, -cods.** 一種似鱈的小魚。

Tom Collins 檸檬汁、糖、碳酸水、冰和杜松子酒混合成的一種飲料。

Tom, Dick, and Har·ry ['tam,dɪkn̩'hærɪ; 'tɔm,dikn̩'hæri] 一般的人;每一個人;張三李四(常含輕蔑意味)。

tome [tom; toum] *n.* ①卷;册。②書;(尤指)大册書;大本書。

to·men·tum [to'mɛntəm; tou'mentəm] *n., pl.* **-ta** [-tə; -tə]. ①〖植物〗茸毛;絨毛。②〖解剖〗軟腦膜和大腦外層上的毛細血管網狀組織。

tom·fool ['tam'ful; 'tɔm'fu:l] *n.* 愚人;笨伯。—*adj.* 愚蠢的。

tom·fool·er·y [,tam'fulərɪ; tɔm'fu:ləri] *n., pl.* **-er·ies.** ①蠢態。②華而不實之物。

tom·my ['tamɪ; 'tɔmi] *n., pl.* **-mies.** ①(亦作 **Tommy**) 英國兵。②黑麪包(尤指配給兵士、工人爲口糧者)。

Tommy At·kins [~'ætkɪnz; ~'ætkinz] ①英國兵(綽號)。②〖英〗基層人員。

Tommy gun, tommy gun 〖俗〗(湯姆生)手提輕機槍。

Tom·my-gun, tom·my-gun ['tamə,gʌn; 'tɔmigʌn] *v.t.,* **-gunned, -gun·ning.** 以手提輕機槍掃射。

tom·my·rot ['tamɪ,rat; 'tɔmirɔt] *n.* 〖俚〗胡說;胡扯;愚蠢。

tommy shop ①發給職工貨品以代替薪金之工廠。②工廠內之食品販賣部。

to·mo·gram ['tomə,græm; 'touməgræm] *n.* 〖醫〗以 tomography 照出來的 X 光照片。

to·mo·graph ['tomə,græf; 'touməgra:f] *n.* 照 tomogram 的機器。

to·mog·ra·phy [to'magrəfɪ; tou'mɔgrəfi] *n.* 〖醫〗(用 X光照的)斷層攝影術。

‡**to·mor·row** [tə'mɔro; tə'mɔrou, tu'm-] *n.* ①明天。the day after *tomorrow.* 後天。②未來;未來時代。the men and women of *tomorrow.* 未來時代的男女們。—*adv.* ①明天。Come *tomorrow.* 明天來。②屬於未來(時代)。

Tom Thumb ①大拇指(民間故事中一極小的矮人)。②任何矮小之人或物。

tom·tit ['tam,tɪt; 'tɔm'tit] *n.* 小鳥;(尤指)山雀。

tom-tom ['tam,tam; 'tɔmtɔm] *n.* ①(印度等地土人的)鼓。②單調的鼓聲。—*v.t.* & *v.i.* 打鼓 (tom-tom). (亦作 **tam-tam**)

ton**[1] [tʌn; tʌn] *n.* ①噸(在美國和加拿大爲2,000磅,在英國爲2,240磅)。②貨物體積。③船舶容積單位(100立方英尺)。④船的載貨單位(40立方英尺)。⑤船的排水量單位(35立方英尺)。⑥〖俗〗(常 *pl.*) 許多;大量。*tons* of times. 屢屢;許多次。⑦〖俚〗摩托車每小時一百英里之速度。displacement ton*** 排水噸(2,240 磅或 35 立方英尺之海水重量)。***long ton*** 英噸(2,240磅)。***measurement ton*** 船之載貨體積單位,相當於40立方英尺。***metric ton*** 公噸 (1,000公斤)。***register ton*** 船之容積單位,相當於100立方英尺。***shipping ton*** =measurement ton. ***short ton*** 美噸(2,000磅)。

ton[2] [tõ; tɔ̃:ŋ] *n., pl.* **tons** [tõ; tɔ̃:ŋ]. 〖法〗流行;時髦。in the *ton.* 在流行中。

ton·al ['tonl; 'tounl] *adj.* 聲音的;音調的;色調的。—**ly,** *adv.*

to·nal·i·ty [to'nælətɪ; tou'næliti] *n., pl.* **-ties.** ①音調或色調之性質;音質。②〖美術〗色彩之配合;調色。③〖音樂〗調性。

ton·do ['tandə; 'tɔndə] *n., pl.* **-dos** or **-di** [-di; -di:]. 圓形之浮雕或畫。

‡**tone** [ton; toun] *n., v.,* **toned, ton·ing.** —*n.* ①聲音;音調。shrill *tones.* 尖音。②音質。③〖音樂〗樂音;全音;全音程。④語調;語氣。The doctor's *tone* was serious. 醫生的語氣很嚴肅。⑤〖語音〗音調的抑揚。rising *tone.* 上揚音調。falling *tone.* 下降音調。⑥風氣;品質;景況。the *tone* of the market. 市況。⑦文章的風格。⑧(身心的)健康狀態。to recover mental *tone.* 恢復心理健康。⑨色調;顏色的配合。⑩色彩的層次。⑪優雅;文雅;氣派。⑫性格;特殊的精神狀態。—*v.i.* ①調和;配合。②有某種特殊腔調、色澤等。—*v.t.* ①以某種特殊腔調說出。②定(樂器)之音。③以某種色調繪(畫)。***tone down*** 緩和;減輕。***tone up*** 提高;加强。***tone (in) with*** 配合適當。

tone arm (電唱機之)音管。

tone color 〖音樂〗音色。

tone control 〖無線電〗音品控制。

tone-deaf ['ton,dɛf; 'toundef] *adj.* 不能精確分辨音調的。

tone language 以聲調辨別同音字的語言(如中文)。

tone·less ['tonlɪs; 'tounlis] *adj.* 無聲的;無抑揚頓挫的;無風格的;單調的;平凡的。—**ly,** *adv.* —**ness,** *n.*

ton·er ['tonɚ; 'tounə] *n.* ①發聲調的人或事物。②調和的人或事物。③試油漆色調的人。

tone wheel 〖無線電〗音輪。

tong[1] [tɔŋ; tɔŋ] *n.* ①(中國之)黨;會社。②〖美〗(華僑之)祕密會社;堂。

tong[2] *v.t.* 用鉗子鉗住、採集或搬弄。—*v.i.* 使用鉗子;用鉗子作。

ton·ga ['taŋgə; 'tɔŋgə] *n.* 印度的一種小型兩輪馬車。

Ton·ga Islands ['taŋgə~; 'tɔŋgə~] 東加羣島(西南太平洋一王國,正式名稱爲 Kingdom of Tonga,首府爲 Nukualofa)。

Tong·king, Gulf of ['taŋ'kɪŋ; 'tɔŋ'kiŋ] 東京灣(在越南與海南島之間)。

tong·man ['tɔŋmən; 'tɔŋmən] *n., pl.* **-men.** (中國人)堂或會社的社員。

tongs** [tɔŋz; tɔŋz] *n. pl.* 鉗;夾具。sugar *tongs.* 糖夾子。hammer and tongs*** 激烈地相打或爭辯。

‡**tongue** [tʌŋ; tʌŋ] *n., v.,* **tongued, tongu·ing.** —*n.* ①舌。②(供食用的)動物舌頭。③言語能力。to have a ready *tongue.* 口才敏捷。④講話的方式、態度。a flattering *tongue.* 一種諂媚的腔調。⑤語言。one's mother *tongue.* 本國語。⑥舌狀物。*tongues* of flames. 火舌。⑦鞋鈕下邊的一條狹皮;鞋舌。⑧伸入水中的狹長陸地;岬。⑨胸針等的別針。⑩車的轅桿。⑪鈴中的活動錘;鈴舌。⑫樂器中震顫的簧舌。⑬〖鐵路〗轉轍器上可移動的短軌條。⑭〖機械〗榫舌。⑮日晷、磅秤等的指針。***find one's tongue*** (因受驚或羞怯而啞口一段時間之後)開口說話;恢復說話能力。***give tongue*** a. 狂吠。b. 高聲狂喊;傳述。***hold one's tongue*** 緘默。***lose one's tongue*** 暫時失去講話之能力。***on the tip of one's tongue*** (or ***at one's tongue's end***) 即將說出;就在嘴邊上。***slip of the tongue*** 無意中說錯話。***with one's tongue in one's cheek*** (***with tongue in cheek*** or ***tongue in cheek***) 毫無誠意。—*v.t.* ①以簧舌調整(樂器)的音調。②裝榫舌於。③以舌觸。④斥責。⑤〖俗〗說出。—*v.i.* ①以簧舌調整樂器之音。②閑談。③像榫舌般伸出。—**like,** *adj.*

tongue-and-groove joint 〖機械〗舌槽榫;雌雄榫。
tongue bone 〖解剖〗舌骨。
tongued 〔tʌŋd; tʌŋd〕 *adj.* 有…舌的;說話…的(常用於組成複合字,如: honey-*tongued*).
tongue depressor (or **blade**) 壓舌板;壓舌器。
tongue-in-cheek 〔'tʌŋɪn'tʃik;'tʌŋin'tʃi:k〕 *adj.*不能認眞的;不能當眞的;諷刺的。
tongue-lash 〔'tʌŋˌlæʃ; 'tʌŋlæʃ〕 *v.t.* & *v.i.* 嚴譴。
tongue-lash·ing 〔'tʌŋˌlæʃɪŋ; 'tʌŋˌlæʃiŋ〕 *n.* 嚴厲的責備。
tongue·less 〔'tʌŋlɪs; 'tʌŋlis〕 *adj.* ①無舌的。②緘口不言的;緘默的。
tongue·ster 〔'tʌŋstɚ; 'tʌŋstə〕 *n.* 饒舌的人。
tongue-tied 〔'tʌŋˌtaɪd; 'tʌŋ-taid〕 *adj.* 張口結舌的;講不出話的。
tongue twister 繞口令。
tongue-twist·ing 〔'tʌŋˌtwɪstɪŋ; 'tʌŋˌtwistiŋ〕 *adj.* 繞口的;不易講的。
ton·ic 〔'tɑnɪk; 'tɔnik〕 *n.* ①滋補品。②鼓勵;鼓舞。③〖音樂〗主調音。④一種汽水(用來沖酒的)。—*adj.* ①使精神恢復的;滋補的。②聲音的。③〖音樂〗主調音的。④〖生理, 醫〗强直的;緊張的。—**al·ly,** *adv.*
tonic accent 揚音;重讀音。
to·nic·i·ty 〔to'nɪsətɪ; tou'nisiti〕 *n.* ①滋補或使人恢復健康之性質或狀態。②健壯。③〖生理〗(肌肉或動脈等之)緊張力;彈性。
tonic sol-fa 〖音樂〗①(用 do, re, mi, fa, sol, la, ti 之起首字母的)字形記譜法。②首調唱名法。
‡to·night 〔tə'naɪt; tə'nait, tu'n-〕 *adv.* 今晚;今夜。I shall be very busy *tonight.* 今晚我將很忙。—*n.* 今晚;今夜。*tonight's* radio news. 今晚的廣播新聞。
to·nite¹ 〔'tonaɪt; 'tounait〕 *n.* 一種强烈的棉火藥。
to·nite² 〔tə'naɪt; tə'nait〕 *n., adv.* 〖俗〗=**tonight.**
ton·ka bean 〔'tʌŋkə~; 'tʌŋkə~〕 ①零陵香豆;薰草豆。②零陵香;薰草。
tonn. tonnage.
ton·nage 〔'tʌnɪdʒ; 'tʌnidʒ〕 *n.* ①(船之)噸數;載重量。②船舶的噸數。③船舶的噸稅。④以噸計之重量。(亦作 **tunnage**)
ton·neau 〔tə'no; tə'nou〕 *n., pl.* **-neaus, -neaux** 〔-'noz; -'nouz〕. ①後部備有座席之汽車車身。②法國的輕便兩輪馬車。
-tonner 〖字尾〗表"有…噸之船"之義,如: a ten-*tonner*. 十噸的船。
to·nom·e·ter 〔to'nɑmətɚ; tou'nɔmitə〕 *n.* ①音調計。②音叉。③眼球內壓計。④液體張力計。
tons burden 船之載重噸位。
ton·sil 〔'tɑnsl̩; 'tɔnsl〕 *n.* 〖醫〗扁桃腺。
ton·sil·(l)ar 〔'tɑnsl̩ɚ; 'tɔnslə〕 *adj.* 〖解剖〗扁桃體的。
ton·sil·lec·to·my 〔ˌtɑnsl̩'ɛktəmɪ; ˌtɔnsi'lektəmi〕 *n., pl.* **-mies.** 〖外科〗扁桃體切除術。
ton·sil·li·tis 〔ˌtɑnsl̩'aɪtɪs; ˌtɔnsi'laitis〕 *n.* 〖醫〗扁桃腺炎。
ton·so·ri·al 〔tɑn'sorɪəl; tɔn'sɔ:riəl〕 *adj.* 理髮的;理髮師的(常爲詼諧用語)。
ton·sure 〔'tɑnʃɚ;'tɔnʃə〕 *n., v.,* **-sured, -sur·ing.** —*n.* ①(僧侶之)剃髮。②頭之剃光部分。③〖宗教〗削髮;受戒;僧職。—*v.t.* 剃頭。
ton·tine 〔'tɑntin,-n'tin;tɔn'ti:n,'tɔn-〕 *n.* ①唐提聯合養老保險制(係由 Lorenzo Tonti, 1630?-?1695, 義大利銀行家所首倡之保險制,參加的一組人共享養老金,若有一人死亡,其分額由生存者分享)。②此種聯合養老保險之參加者(集合稱)。③每位參加者所擔負之一分額;此等金額總數。④類似之保險制。
ton-up 〔'tʌnˌʌp; 'tʌnʌp〕 *adj.* 〖英俚〗①乘摩托車飛馳而過的。②乘摩托車飛馳而過之少年的。
ton-up boys 乘摩托車飛馳而過的少年。
to·nus 〔'tonəs;'tounəs〕*n.* ①〖生理〗肌肉之緊張度。②〖醫〗强直性痙攣(尤指牙關緊閉)。
To·ny¹ 〔'tonɪ; 'touni〕 *n.* ①男子名(Anthony 之暱稱)。②女子名(Antoinette 或 Antonia 之暱稱)。
To·ny² *n., pl.* **-nys.** 東尼獎(每年由 American Theater Wing 頒給傑出戲劇製作人或演員的獎)。
ton·y 〔'tonɪ;'touni〕 *adj.,* **ton·i·er, ton·i·est.** 〖俚〗時髦的;漂亮的;奢侈的(含譏諷)。
‡too 〔tu; tu:〕 *adv.* ①也;亦;並且。I went there, *too.* 我也到那裏去了。②太;過於。It's *too* hot to work. 天太熱不能工作。③非常;極。That's *too* bad. 那眞可惜。〖注意〗**too.** 當 too 作"也"或"並且"解,且插於句中時,前後應由逗點","分開,如置於句尾時,正式用法中應有","如: I'm going, too.
‡took 〔tʊk;tuk〕 *v.* pt. of **take.**
***tool** 〔tul; tu:l〕 *n.* ①工具;器具。②傀儡;走狗;嘍囉。③切、鑽、磨光等機器的一部分;此等機器。④壓印於書封面的圖案或裝飾。*down tools* 〖英〗放下工具;停止工作。—*v.t.* ①用工具製造。②壓印圖案於(皮面書的封面)。③駕駛;乘坐(車子)。—*v.i.* ①用工具工作。②乘坐車子。*tool up* 爲某工作而準備工具等。—**less,** *adj.*
tool·box 〔'tulˌbɑks; 'tu:lbɔks〕 *n.* 工具箱。
tool·hold·er 〔'tulˌholdɚ;'tu:lˌhouldə〕 *n.* 工具之把柄。
tool·house 〔'tulˌhaus; 'tu:lhaus〕 *n., pl.* **-hous·es.** 堆放工具的小屋。
tool·ing 〔'tulɪŋ; 'tu:liŋ〕 *n.* ①工具製造。②以型具壓花樣於書籍封面上之裝潢。③工廠機械設備之安裝。
tool·mak·er 〔'tulˌmekɚ;'tu:lˌmeikə〕 *n.* 製造或修理工具的工人。
tool·room 〔'tulˌrum; 'tu:lru:m〕 *n.* (工廠內)修理、存放工具的房間。
tool subject 〖教育〗工具學科(如文法、計算等幫助學生從事其他學科或工作者)。
toon 〔tun; tu:n〕 *n.* 印度桃花心木。
toot 〔tut; tu:t〕 *n.* 號角、笛等的鳴聲。—*v.i.* ①吹號角或笛;吹喇叭。②發出號角聲或笛聲。—*v.t.* 吹(號角、笛等);鳴(汽笛等)。
‡tooth 〔tuθ; tu:θ〕 *n., pl.* **teeth** 〔tiθ; ti:θ〕, *v.* —*n.* ①牙;齒。to cut a *tooth.* (小兒)長牙齒。an artificial *tooth.* 假牙。a temporary *tooth.* 乳齒。②齒狀物。the *teeth* of a saw. 鋸齒。③尖銳,壓制或破壞性。④嗜好;味道。⑤爲增加磨擦力而故意弄得稍稍粗糙的表面。⑥畫紙上或油畫帆布上之粗糙面。*by the skin of one's teeth* 恰好;剛巧(差一點便不行)。*cut one's teeth on* 於受教育、事業等開始時做;於年輕時做。*escape by the skin of the teeth* 僅以身免。*get one's teeth into* 使熟習;熟知。*have a sweet tooth* 喜吃甜食。*in the teeth of* a. 面對;正面反對。b. 蔑視;不顧。*long in the tooth* 年長的。*put teeth into* (or *in*) 使生效;使有效。*set one's teeth* 咬緊牙關;立下決心。*set* (or *put*) *one's teeth on edge* a. 引起不愉快的感覺。b. 厭煩。*show one's teeth* 表示憤怒;恐嚇;威脅。*throw* (or *cast*)

in one's teeth爲…而責備;將…歸咎於某人。***tooth and nail*** (or ***claw***) 傾全力;不遺餘力。***to the teeth*** 完全地;徹底地。—*v.t.* ①裝以齒。②將(邊緣)切成齒狀。—*v.i.*(如齒輪)結合。

tooth·ache ['tuθ,ek; 'tu:θeik] *n.* 牙痛。

tooth·brush ['tuθ,brʌʃ; 'tu:θbrʌʃ] *n.* 牙刷。

tooth·comb ['tuθ,kom; 'tu:θkoum] *n.* 〖英〗密齒梳。

toothed [tuθt; tu:θt] *adj.* ①有齒的。②鋸齒狀的。

-toothed 〖字尾〗表"有(某種或某數目之)齒的"之義, 如: big-*toothed.*

toothed gearing 〖機械〗齒輪聯動。

toothed wheel 〖機械〗齒輪。

tooth·ful ['tuθful; 'tu:θful] *n.* 一口食物;一口酒;少量的酒。

tooth·ing ['tuθɪŋ; 'tu:θiŋ] *n.* ①裝齒;加齒。②齒輪之齒。③〖建築〗邊齒(牆邊突出之磚或石,以備與他牆或增建部分相連接者)。

tooth·less ['tuθlɪs; 'tu:θlis] *adj.* ①(人或動物)無牙齒的。②無鋸齒的。③無力的;無效的。

tooth·let ['tuθlɪt; 'tu:θlit] *n.* 小齒;小齒狀突起。

tooth·like ['tuθ,laɪk; 'tu:θlaik] *adj.* 如牙齒的;牙齒的。

tooth·paste ['tuθ,pest; 'tu:θpeist] *n.* 牙膏。

tooth·pick ['tuθ,pɪk; 'tu:θpik] *n.* ①牙籤。②牙籤瓶。

tooth powder 牙粉。(亦作 **tooth-powder**)

tooth·some ['tuθsəm; 'tu:θsəm] *adj.* ①美味的;可口的。②(權力、聲名等)合意的;悅人的。③性感的;美麗的。

tooth·wash ['tuθ,wɑʃ; 'tu:θwɔʃ] *n.* 清潔口腔及牙齒之液體製劑。

tooth·y ['tuθɪ; 'tu:θi] *adj.*, **tooth·i·er, tooth·i·est.** ①露出牙齒的。②有牙齒的。③好味道的;好吃的。④表面粗糙的。

too·tle ['tutl̩; 'tu:tl] *v.*, **-tled, -tling,** *n.* —*v.i.* (笛等)輕柔或反覆地吹。—*n.* 輕柔或反覆地吹奏的聲音。

too-too ['tu,tu; 'tu:tu:] *adv.* 極端地;非常地;過度地。—*adj.* 〖俚〗極端的;過度的;過激的。Her clothes are *too-too.* 她的服裝太漂亮了。

toots [tuts; tuts] *n.* 〖俚〗(暱稱或戲語)親愛的(人)。

toot·sy ['tutsɪ; 'tu:tsi] *n., pl.* **-sies.** ①〖兒語〗小脚。②脚趾。③〖諧〗親愛的(表親暱)。

toot·sy-woot·sy ['tutsɪ'wutsɪ; 'tu:tsi'wu:tsi] *n., pl.* **toot·sy-woot·sies.** 〖俗〗=**toots.**

‡top¹ [tɑp; tɔp] *n., adj., v.,* **topped, top·ping.** —*n.* ①頂;巔;上部;上端。the *top* of a hill. 山頂。②最高階級;最高地位。He is at the *top* of his class. 他在班上名列前茅。③最高度;最高點;極點。to shout at the *top* of one's voice. 竭力喊叫。④居於領袖地位的人。He is *top* in his profession. 他是他那一行中的佼佼者。⑤最好與最重要的部分。⑥植物長於地面上的部分。⑦頭。⑧車頂;車篷。⑨鞋或靴的上部。⑩髮綹;纖維束。⑪船的桅樓。⑫(*pl.*)樹枝尖端較嫩的部分。⑬〖棒球〗**a.** 一局比賽之前半部。**b.** 第一棒至第三棒之打擊手。⑭最佳的例子;典範。⑮開始。⑯〖化〗混合物在蒸餾時最先蒸發的部分。***at the top of the tree*** 居於事業或職業中的最高地位。***blow one's top*** 〖俚〗**a.** 發脾氣。**b.** 發瘋。***come to the top*** 得到名譽;成功。***from top to bottom*** 完全地;全部地。***from top to toe*** 從頭到脚;完完全全地。***on top*** **a.** 在上邊。**b.** 成功地;勝利地。***on (the) top of*** **a.** 在…上邊。**b.** 此外。**c.** 緊接著。**d.** 完全控制。***on top of the world*** 〖俗〗**a.** 成功的。**b.** 高興的。***over the top*** 〖軍〗從戰壕(開槍)。***(the) tops*** 〖俗〗最好的。—*adj.* ①最高的;最大的。at *top* speed. 以最大的速度。②頂上的。—*v.t.* ①加以頂(蓋)。②截去頂端。③爲…的頂點;位於…的頂端。④抵達…之頂峯。⑤升到…上。The sun *topped* the horizon. 太陽升於地平線上。⑥超越;勝過。⑦以…置於…之上。⑧跳越過(障礙物等)。⑨〖化〗將混合物中最容易揮發之成分用蒸餾除去。⑩擊(球)之上部使旋轉前進。⑪在(土表面)施肥。—*v.i.* ①高聳。②卓越;優越。***top off*** 完成;結束。***top out*** 完成(石頭建築物之)頂部。

top²** *n.* 陀螺。sleep like a top*** 睡得很熟。

to·paz ['topæz; 'toupæz] *n.* ①〖礦〗黃晶;黃玉。②(南美產之)蜂雀。

top banana 〖俚〗①歌舞劇中的主諧星。②領袖;佼佼者。

top boot ①長統靴。②翻沿長統靴。

top brass 〖俗〗①高級將領。②高級官員。

top·coat ['tɑp,kot; 'tɔp'kout] *n.* 大衣;薄大衣;外套。

top cover ①高空掩護飛行任務。②執行此種任務的飛機。

top cross 〖遺傳〗父系純種之交配種。

top dog 競爭勝利者。

top drawer 〖俗〗最高階層;最重要或最優秀之等級。

top-draw·er ['tɑp,drɔɚ; 'tɔp,drɔːə] *adj.* ①上流社會的。②最高級的;最重要的。

top-dress ['tɑp,drɛs; 'tɔp'dres] *v.t.* ①施肥於(地面)上。②鋪碎石於…上。—**ing,** *n.*

tope¹ [top; toup] *v.t. & v.i.,* **toped, top·ing.** 豪飲(酒);濫喝(酒)。

tope² *n.* 歐洲產的一種小鮫。

tope³ *n.* 〖英印〗圓頂之佛塔;浮屠;陵廟。

top-ech·e·lon ['tɑp'ɛʃəlɑn; 'tɔp'eʃəlɔn] *adj.* 高級的;高階層的。

top·er ['topɚ; 'toupə] *n.* 豪飲者;酒徒。

top flight 最高階層;最高階級。

top-flight ['tɑp'flaɪt; 'tɔp'flait] *adj.* 〖俗〗最好的;第一等的。

top·full ['tɑp'ful; 'tɔp'ful] *adj.* 盈滿的。

top·gal·lant [,tɑp'gælənt; tɔp'gælənt] *n.* 〖航海〗上桅;上桅帆。—*adj.* ①上桅的。②高超的;第一流的。

top gear 〖英〗(汽車之)最高速之排擋。

top-grade ['tɑp'gred; 'tɔp'greid] *adj.* 高級的;最好品質的。

top grafting 〖園藝〗高處接枝法。

top·ham·per ['tɑp,hæmpɚ; 'tɔp,hæmpə] *n.* 〖航海〗①桅上或甲板上的不必要之重物。②桅上之帆桁、索具等物。

top hat 高頂絲質禮帽。

top-heav·y ['tɑp,hɛvɪ; 'tɔp'hevi] *adj.* ①上部過重的;頭重脚輕的;不穩的。②資本過大的。③高級人員過多的。

To·phet, To·pheth ['tofɪt; 'toufet] *n.* ①〖聖經〗舊約中記載以火焚人而祭 Moloch 之處(可能即爲 Hinnom 谷)。②地獄。

top-hole ['tɑp'hol; 'tɔp'houl] *adj.* 〖英俚〗最優的;第一流的。

to·phus ['tofəs; 'toufəs] *n., pl.* **-phi** [-faɪ; -fai]. 〖醫〗結節瘤;痛風結節。

to·pi ['topi; 'toupi:] *n.* (印度之)帽;(尤指)遮陽帽。(亦作 **topee**)

to·pi·ar·y ['topɪ,ɛrɪ; 'toupiəri] *adj., n., pl.* **-ar·ies.** —*adj.* 剪修花草使成裝飾形式的。—*n.* ①剪修裝飾。②經剪修過的花園。

***top·ic** ['tɑpɪk; 'tɔpik] *n.* ①論題;話題;

題目。the *topics* of the day. 時事問題。②格言;通則。

top·i·cal ['tɑpɪkl; 'tɔpikəl] *adj.* ①時事問題的;話題的。*topical* news. 時事新聞。②題目的;論題的;標題的。③〖醫〗局部的。④當地的。—**ly,** *adv.*

topic sentence 代表某段主旨的一個句子。(亦作 **topical sentence**)

top kick ①〖軍俚〗(=first sergeant)士官長。②當權者;領袖;上司。

top·knot ['tɑp,nɑt; 'tɔpnɔt] *n.* ①頂髻;頭頂之飾結。②鳥的冠毛;鳥冠。③〖俗〗頭。

top lantern 〖航海〗桅頂上的信號燈。(亦作 **top light**)

top·less ['tɑplɪs; 'tɔplis] *adj.* ①極高的。②無上裝的;上空的。a *topless* bathing suit. 上空游泳裝。—*n.* ①無上裝女侍或舞女。②無上裝。③擁有無上裝女侍或表演的夜總會、酒吧等。

top-lev·el ['tɑp'lɛvl; 'tɔp'levl] *adj.* 〖俗〗高階層的。a *top-level* conference. 高階層會議。

top line 報紙標題。

top·line ['tɑp,laɪn; 'tɔp'lain] *adj.* ①可上報紙頭條的。*topline* news. 頭條消息。②聲譽極佳的。③第一流的。(亦作 **top-line**)

top·lin·er ['tɑp'laɪnə; 'tɔp'lainə] *n.* ①〖英〗可上報紙頭條的人物(尤指男明星)。②最重要或第一流的人或事物。(亦作 **top-liner**)

top·loft·y ['tɑp'lɔftɪ; 'tɔp'lɔːfti] *adj.* 〖俗〗矜誇的;高傲的。

top·man ['tɑpmən; 'tɔpmən] *n., pl.* **-men.** ①〖航海〗桅樓守望者。②鋸木時在上端之一人。

top·mast ['tɑp,mæst; 'tɔpmɑːst] *n.* 〖航海〗中桅。

top·most ['tɑp,most; 'tɔpmoust] *adj.* 最高的;最上的;絕頂的。

top-notch ['tɑp'nɑtʃ; 'tɔp'nɔtʃ] *adj.* 〖俗〗第一流的;最高的。(亦作 **topnotch**)

top-of-the-world ['tɑpəvðə'wɝld; 'tɔpəvðə'wəːld] *adj.* 北極的;北極地區的。

topog. ①topographical. ②topography.

to·pog·ra·pher [to'pɑgrəfɚ; tə'pɔgrəfə] *n.* ①地誌學者。②繪製地形圖者;地形測量師。(亦作 **topographist**)

top·o·graph·i·cal [,tɑpə'græfɪkl; ,tɔpə'græfikəl] *adj.* 地誌的;地形學上的。—**ly,** *adv.*

topographical map 地形圖。(亦作 **topographic map**)

to·pog·ra·phy [to'pɑgrəfɪ; tə'pɔgrəfi] *n., pl.* **-phies.** ①地形學;地誌。②地形。③地形測量。

top·o·log·i·cal group [,tɑpə'lɑdʒɪkl~; ,tɔpə'lɔdʒikəl~] 〖數學〗拓撲羣。

to·pol·o·gy [to'pɑlədʒɪ; tou'pɔlədʒi] *n.* ①地勢學。②風土誌研究。③〖數學〗形勢幾何學;拓撲學。

top·o·nym ['tɑpo,nɪm; 'tɔpounim] *n.* ①地名。②以地名而命之名。③身體部位名。

to·pon·y·my [to'pɑnəmɪ; tou'pɔnəmi] *n., pl.* **-mies.** ①一國、一地區等中之地名;地名之研究。②〖解剖〗身體部位命名法。(亦作 **toponomy**)

top·o·phone ['tɑpə,fon; 'tɔpəfoun] *n.* 聲向測定儀。

top·per ['tɑpɚ; 'tɔpə] *n.* ①〖俚〗最優秀的人或物。②〖俗〗高帽;禮帽。③〖俗〗外衣;(尤指)女人之短而寬鬆的外衣。

top·ping ['tɑpɪŋ; 'tɔpiŋ] *n.* ①除去頂部;修剪樹梢。②上部;上層。③置於最頂上之物。④(*pl.*) 剪落之物(如樹枝等)。⑤原油之蒸餾。—*adj.* ①高的;高聳的。②高級的;高階層的。③〖英俗〗優秀的;第一流的。—**ly,** *adv.*

top·ple ['tɑpl; 'tɔpl] *v.,* **-pled, -pling.** —*v.i.* ①向前倒;(因頭重而)倒下〖常 over〗. ②向前傾;搖搖欲墜。—*v.t.* 使倒;推翻;顛覆。

top-pri·or·i·ty ['tɑpprai'ɔrətɪ; 'tɔp-prai'ɔːriti] *adj.* 第一優先的。

top-qual·i·ty ['tɑp'kwɑlətɪ; 'tɔp-'kwɔliti] *adj.* 最高品質的。

top-rank ['tɑp'ræŋk; 'tɔp'ræŋk] *adj.* 第一流的。

top-ranked ['tɑp'ræŋkt; 'tɔp'ræŋkt] *adj.* 列入第一流的。(亦作 **top-rated**)

top-rank·ing ['tɑp,ræŋkɪŋ; 'tɔp-,ræŋkiŋ] *adj.* 〖美俗〗職位高的;階級高的;第一流的。

tops [tɑps; tɔps] *adj.* 〖俚〗最高的;最上等的;最優的。She is (the) *tops* in singing. 她歌唱得最好。—*n.* (the-)傑出的人或物。He's the *tops.* 他是最好的人。

top·sail ['tɑpsl; 'tɔpsl] *n.* 〖航海〗中桅帆。

top sawyer ①鋸木時在上端的一人。②地位高的人;顯要之士。

top secret 最高機密;絕對機密。

top-se·cret ['tɑp'sikrɪt; 'tɔp'siːkrit] *adj.* 〖軍〗絕對機密的。

top-sell·ing ['tɑp'sɛlɪŋ; 'tɔp'seliŋ] *adj.* 暢銷的。

top-shaped ['tɑp,ʃept; 'tɔpʃeipt] *adj.* 陀螺形的。

top·side ['tɑp'saɪd; 'tɔp'said] *n.* ①(常 *pl.*)〖航海〗船的乾舷。②上端;上部。

tops·man ['tɑpsmən; 'tɔpsmən] *n.* ①〖航海〗桅樓守望員。②〖俗〗絞刑執行人。

top·soil ['tɑp,sɔɪl; 'tɔp-sɔil] *n.* 土壤之表層;表土。—*v.t.* ①除去(土地)表層上之土。②以表土覆蓋(土地)。

top spin 使球前進時旋轉之運動。

top·sy-tur·vy ['tɑpsɪ'tɝvɪ; 'tɔpsi-'təːvi] *adv., adj., n., pl.* **-vies,** *v.,* **-vied, -vy·ing.** —*adv.* ①顛倒地。②混亂地;亂七八糟地。—*adj.* ①顛倒的。②混亂的;亂七八糟的。—*n.* ①顛倒。②混亂;亂七八糟。—*v.t.* 使顛倒;使混亂。

top·sy-tur·vy·dom ['tɑpsɪ'tɝvɪdəm; 'tɔpsi'təːvidəm] *n.* 顛倒;混亂;亂七八糟。

toque [tok; touk] *n.* 無邊女帽;狹邊小圓帽。

tor [tɔr; tɔː] *n.* 突岩;高岡。

-tor 〖字尾〗表"…的人"之義。

to·rah, to·ra ['torə; 'tɔːrə] *n.* 〖猶太教〗①教訓;神諭;法律。②全部宗教文獻。③(T-)摩西五經(舊約之首五卷)。

tor·ban·ite ['tɔrbə,naɪt; 'tɔːbənait] *n.* 〖礦〗塊煤。

***torch** [tɔrtʃ; tɔːtʃ] *n.* ①火炬;火把。②〖英〗手電筒(=flashlight). ③知識、文明等的源泉。④噴火器。**carry the** (or **a**) **torch for** a.〖俚〗對(異性)發生單相思。b. 爲…作宣揚;支持。—*v.i.* 如火炬般發亮。—*v.t.* 以噴火器熔解。—**less,** *adj.* —**like,** *adj.*

torch·bear·er ['tɔrtʃ,bɛrə; 'tɔːtʃ,bɛə-rə] *n.* ①持火炬者。②啓蒙之人;啓人靈感者;領導者。

torch fishing 以火把誘魚的釣魚。

torch·light ['tɔrtʃ,laɪt; 'tɔːtʃ-lait] *n.* 火炬之光。—*adj.* 手執火炬的;火炬照亮的。

tor·chon lace ['tɔrʃɑn~; 'tɔːʃən~] ①亞麻線粗花邊。②類似的粗花邊。

torch race (古希臘的)火炬接力賽跑。

torch singer 擅唱失戀之歌的(女)歌星。

torch song 失戀之歌。

tore [tor, tɔr; tɔː, tɔə] *v.* pt. of **tear**[2].

tor·e·a·dor 〔'tɔrɪəˌdɔr; 'tɔriədɔː〕 *n.* (特指騎在馬上之)鬥牛士。
toreador pants 女用緊身褲。
to·re·ra 〔to'rerɑ; tou'reirɑː〕 *n., pl.* **-re·ras.** 女鬥牛士。
to·re·ro 〔to'rero; tou'reirou〕 *n., pl.* **-ros.** 〖西〗徒步鬥牛士。
to·reu·tic 〔to'rutɪk; tou'ruːtik〕 *adj.* 「金屬細工的。」
to·reu·tics 〔to'rutɪks; tou'ruːtiks〕 *n.* (作 *sing.* 解)金屬細工(術)。
tor·ic 〔'tɔrɪk; 'tɔːrik〕 *adj.* 〖數學〗環形圓紋曲面的;環面的。
toric lens 〖光〗複曲面透鏡。
***tor·ment** 〔*v.* tɔr'mɛnt; tɔː'ment *n.* 'tɔrmɛnt; 'tɔːment〕 *v.t.* 使痛苦; 使煩惱; 使折磨。 to be *tormented* by toothache. 爲牙痛所苦。 —*n.* ①痛苦; 煩惱。②痛苦之因; 煩惱之因。③受苦。④〖古〗 **a.** 刑具。**b.** 拷打。
tor·men·til 〔'tɔrmɛnˌtɪl; 'tɔːmentil〕 *n.* 〖植物〗一種雉子莚。(亦作 **tormentilla**)
tor·ment·ing 〔tɔr'mɛntɪŋ; tɔː'mentiŋ〕 *adj.* 使痛苦的;使苦惱的;討厭的。
tor·men·tor 〔tɔr'mɛntɚ; tɔː'mentə〕 *n.* ①使痛苦(或煩惱)之人或物; 折磨人的人或物。②舞臺後面之固定幕帷。③〖電影〗拍攝電影時用以防止回聲之幕。
torn 〔torn; tɔːn〕 *v.* pp. of **tear²**.
tor·na·do 〔tɔr'nedo; tɔː'neidou〕 *n., pl.* **-does** or **-dos.** ①颶風; 旋風。②猛烈的爆發。—**like,** *adj.*
tornado belt 颶風帶。
To·ron·to 〔tə'rɑnto; tə'rɔntou〕 *n.* 多倫多(加拿大Ontario之首府, 濱 Ontario湖)。
to·rous 〔'torəs; 'tourəs〕 *adj.* ①〖植物〗念珠狀的。②〖動物〗(肌肉等之)腫脹的。
***tor·pe·do** 〔tɔr'pido; tɔː'piːdou〕 *n., pl.* **-does,** *v.,* **-doed, -do·ing.** —*n.* ①魚雷; 水雷。②鐵軌上的信號雷管。③小孩玩的摜砲。④電鯆。⑤〖美俚〗職業兇手。—*v.t.* ①以魚雷襲擊或轟沉。②破壞。③用魚雷開採油礦。—*v.i.* 魚雷攻擊船隻。—**like,** *adj.*
torpedo boat 魚雷快艇。
tor·pe·do-boat destroyer 〔tɔr'pidoˌbot～; tɔː'piːdoubout～〕 〖軍〗魚雷驅逐艦。
torpedo gunboat 魚雷艇。
torpedo netting 魚雷網。
torpedo plane 魚雷機。
torpedo tube 魚雷管。
Tor·pex 〔'tɔrpɛks; 'tɔːpeks〕 *n.* 魚雷用高性能炸藥。(爲 *torpedo explosive* 之略)
tor·pid¹ 〔'tɔrpɪd; 'tɔːpid〕 *adj.* ①不活潑的; 呆鈍的。②麻痺的; 無感覺的。③蟄伏的。—**ly,** *adv.* —**ness,** —**i·ty,** *n.*
tor·pid² *n.* ①英牛津大學划舟比賽所使用之八人小舟。②此舟上之划船選手。***the torpids*** 使用此種小舟之划船比賽。
tor·pi·fy 〔'tɔrpəˌfaɪ; 'tɔːpifai〕 *v.,* **-pi·fied, -pi·fy·ing.** —*v.t.* 使麻痺; 使失知覺;使遲鈍。—*v.i.* 變麻痺;失去知覺;變遲鈍。
tor·por 〔'tɔrpɚ; 'tɔːpə〕 *n.* ①不活潑; 呆鈍。②麻痺;無感覺。③蟄伏。
tor·por·if·ic 〔ˌtɔrpə'rɪfɪk; ˌtɔːpə'rifik〕 *adj.* 使麻痺的;使無知覺的; 使遲鈍的。
torque 〔tɔrk; tɔːk〕 *n.* ①〖機械〗轉(力)矩。②捻力;扭力。③(亦作 **torc**) (古時之)頸圈;頸鏈。
tor·re·fac·tion 〔ˌtɑrɪ'fækʃən; ˌtɔri'fækʃən〕 *n.* 焙;烤;烘。
tor·re·fy 〔'tɑrɪˌfaɪ; 'tɔrifai〕 *v.t.,* **-fied, -fy·ing.** 焙;烤;烘。(亦作 **torrify**)
***tor·rent** 〔'tɔrənt, 'tɑr-; 'tɔrənt〕 *n.* ①急流; 湍流。*torrents* of rain. 傾盆大雨。②連續不斷; 滔滔不絕。 a *torrent* of abuse. 罵不絕口。—*adj.* = **torrential.**
tor·ren·tial 〔tɔ'rɛnʃəl; tɔ'renʃəl〕 *adj.* ①急流的; 湍流的。②由急流沖成的。③猛烈的;暴烈的。 —**ly,** *adv.*
Tor·res Strait 〔'tɔrɪs～; 'tɔris～〕 托列斯海峽(在澳洲與新幾內亞之間)。
Tor·ri·cel·li 〔ˌtɔrɪ'tʃɛlɪ; ˌtɔri'tʃeli〕 *n.* 托里拆利 (Evangelista, 1608–1647, 義大利數學家及物理學家, 發現氣壓計原理)。
tor·rid 〔'tɔrɪd; 'tɔrid〕 *adj.* 很熱的。
tor·rid·i·ty 〔tɔ'rɪdətɪ; tɔ'riditi〕 *n.* 酷熱;炎熱。
Torrid Zone 熱帶。
tor·sade 〔tɔr'sed; tɔː'seid〕 *n.* 撚合成的繩索;繩索狀飾物。
tor·si·bil·i·ty 〔ˌtɔrsə'bɪlətɪ; ˌtɔːsi'biliti〕 *n.* 耐扭力;抗扭力。
tor·sion 〔'tɔrʃən; 'tɔːʃən〕 *n.* ①扭;捻;扭轉。②被扭捩之狀態。③〖機械〗扭力。 *torsion* meter. 扭力計。④〖數學〗撓率。
tor·sion·al 〔'tɔrʃənl; 'tɔːʃənəl〕 *adj.* 扭轉的;扭力的。—**ly,** *adv.*
torsion balance 〖機械〗扭秤(藉細線之扭捩度而測定微力的一種儀器)。
torsk 〔tɔrsk; tɔːsk〕 *n., pl.* **torsk, torsks.** 鱈魚;鱈類之海魚。
tor·so 〔'tɔrso; 'tɔːsou〕 *n., pl.* **-sos, -si** 〔-si; -siː〕. ①(無頭及四肢的) 軀幹雕像。②(人體之)軀幹。 ③因損傷而致不完整的東西; 未完成的作品。(亦作 **torse**)
torso murder 肢解屍體的謀殺案。
tort 〔tɔrt; tɔːt〕 *n.* 〖法律〗 民事的侵犯或侵害(違約除外)。
tort-fea·sor 〔'tɔrt'fizɚ; 'tɔːt'fiːzə〕 *n.* 〖法律〗民事侵犯或侵害人。
tor·ti·col·lis 〔ˌtɔrtɪ'kɑlɪs; ˌtɔːti'kɔlis〕 *n.* 〖醫〗 歪頸;斜頸。(亦作 **wryneck**)
tor·tile 〔'tɔrtɪl; 'tɔːtil〕 *adj.* 扭曲的; 盤捲的。
tor·til·i·ty 〔tɔr'tɪlətɪ; tɔː'tiliti〕 *n.* 扭曲;盤捲。
tor·til·la 〔tɔr'tija; tɔː'tiːja〕 *n.* 薄而圓的玉蜀黍餅。
tor·tious 〔'tɔrʃəs; 'tɔːʃəs〕 *adj.* 〖法律〗民事上之侵害或侵犯的。
***tor·toise** 〔'tɔrtəs, -tɪs; 'tɔːtəs〕 *n., pl.* **-tois·es, -toise.** (生於陸上之)龜。
tortoise shell ①龜甲。②一種類似龜甲之蝴蝶(亦作 **tortoise-shell butterfly**)。③一種有斑點的貓(亦作 **tortoise-shell cat**)。
tortoise-shell turtle 玳瑁。
tor·to·ni 〔tɔr'tonɪ; tɔː'touni〕 *n.* (用紙杯子裝的義大利式)冰淇淋。
tor·tu·os·i·ty 〔ˌtɔrtʃu'ɑsətɪ; ˌtɔːtju'ɔsiti〕 *n., pl.* **-ties.** ①扭曲或扭捩的性質或情況。②扭曲;扭捩;彎曲。
tor·tu·ous 〔'tɔrtʃuəs; 'tɔːtjuəs〕 *adj.* ①彎曲的;扭曲的。②歪曲的;不正直的。
***tor·ture** 〔'tɔrtʃɚ; 'tɔːtʃə〕 *n., v.,* **-tured, -tur·ing.** —*n.* ①拷問;刑訊。to put someone to the *torture.* 拷問某人。②(常 *pl.*) (身體或心靈的)痛苦;苦惱。③引起痛苦, 苦惱之原因。④猛烈的扭折、搖撼、打擊等。 —*v.t.* ①使受痛苦; 折磨。 He is *tortured* with anxiety. 他爲煩惱所苦。②曲解。③扭曲。
torture chamber 拷問房;用刑室。
tor·tur·ing 〔'tɔrtʃərɪŋ; 'tɔːtʃəriŋ〕 *adj.* 拷問的;使受苦的;使痛苦的。
tor·tur·ous 〔'tɔrtʃərəs; 'tɔːtʃərəs〕

adj. 使痛苦的;使苦惱的;充滿痛苦的。

tor·u·lin [ˈtɑrjʊlɪn; ˈtɔrjulin] *n.* 〖生化〗釀母素;維他命 B_1。

to·rus [ˈtorəs; ˈtourəs] *n., pl.* **-ri** [-raɪ; -rai]. ①〖建築〗凸圓線脚(亦作 **tore**). ②〖植物〗花托。③〖解剖〗隆凸; 圓形隆起。④〖幾何〗環形圓紋曲面;環面。

To·ry [ˈtorɪ; ˈtɔːri] *n., pl.* **-ries,** *adj.* —*n.* ①英國昔日的保守黨黨員。 ②美國獨立戰爭時傾向英國的美國人。③(常 t-) 很保守的人。—*adj.* ①英國保守黨黨員的。②(有時 t-) 保守的。

-tory =-ory.

To·ry·ism [ˈtorɪɪzm̩; ˈtɔːriizəm] *n.* ①王黨主義;保皇主義。②(t-)保守主義。

To·sca·ni·ni [ˌtɑskəˈninɪ; ˌtɔskəˈniːni] *n.* 托斯卡尼尼 (Arturo, 1867–1957, 定居美國的義大利音樂指揮家)。

tosh [tɑʃ; tɔʃ] *n.* 〖英俚〗胡說;瞎扯。

tosh·er [ˈtɑʃɚ; ˈtɔʃə] *n.* ①〖英俚〗大學中不屬於任何學院的學生。② 〖英〗一種小漁舟。③〖英俚〗碼頭上的賊。

toss** [tɔs; tɔs] *v.,* **tossed, toss·ing,** *n.* —*v.t.* ①投;擲;抛。to *toss* a coin. 擲錢幣(以反正面取決)。②搖蕩。③舉起;抬起。She *tossed* her head up. 她揚起頭。④輾轉反側。⑤擾亂;使不安。⑥隨便地講。⑦輕拌;輕攪(沙拉等)。—*v.i.* ①輾轉。He *tossed* about in bed. 他在床上輾轉反側。②搖蕩; 顛簸。③衝。toss off*** **a.** 迅速而容易地做。**b.** 一飲而盡。***toss up*** 〖俗〗嘔吐。—*n.* ①投;擲;抛。②舉起;抬起。③投擲的距離。④震蕩;顛簸。***take a toss*** 跌下;從馬背上跌下。**—er,** *n.*

toss·pot [ˈtɔsˌpɑt; ˈtɔspɔt] *n.* 醉漢;酒徒。

toss-up [ˈtɔsˌʌp; ˈtɔsʌp] *n.* ①(決定某事的)擲錢。②一半的機會。

tost [tɑst; tɔst] *v.* 〖詩〗pt. & pp. of **toss.**

tot¹ [tɑt; tɔt] *n.* ①小兒;小孩。②〖英〗少量之酒。③微量。

tot² *v.,* **tot·ted, tot·ting,** *n.* —*v.t.* 〖英俗〗加;總計〖常 up〗. —*n.* 〖英俗〗合計;加數。

‡to·tal [ˈtotl̩; ˈtoutl] *adj., n., v.,* **-tal(l)ed, -tal·(l)ing.** —*adj.* ①全體的;總的。the *total* amount. 總額。②完全的; 全然的。a *total* failure. 全然失敗。—*n.* 總數;總額; 全部。The *total* is 120. 總數是一百二十。—*v.t.* ①加起來; 求得…的總數。*Total* that column of figures. 把那一行數字加起來。②共計;總計。

total abstinence 完全戒酒。

total bases 〖棒球〗打擊者因安打所到達的壘數之總和。

total depravity 〖神學〗性惡說。

total differential 〖數學〗全微分。

total eclipse (日、月蝕之)全蝕。

to·tal·i·tar·i·an [ˌtotæləˈtɛrɪən; ˌtoutæliˈtɛəriən] *n., adj.* 極權主義者(的)。

to·tal·i·tar·i·an·ism [toˌtæləˈtɛrɪəˌnɪzəm; touˌtæliˈtɛəriənizm] *n.* 極權主義。

to·tal·i·tar·i·an·ize [toˌtæləˈtɛrɪənˌaɪz; touˌtæliˈtɛəriənaiz] *v.t.,* **-ized, -iz·ing.** 使極權化;使極權主義化。

to·tal·i·ty [toˈtælətɪ; touˈtæliti] *n., pl.* **-ties.** ①總數; 總額。②全體; 完全。③〖天文〗**a.** 全蝕。**b.** 全蝕時間。

to·tal·i·za·tor [ˈtotl̩əˌzetɚ; ˈtoutəlaizeitə] *n.* ①總額計算器(機)。②〖英〗賽馬賭金計算器(機)。(亦作 **totalisator, totalizer, tote board**)

to·tal·ize [ˈtotl̩ˌaɪz; ˈtoutəlaiz] *v.,* **-ized, -iz·ing.** —*v.t.* 合計;總計。—*v.i.* 登記總數。

to·tal·iz·er [ˈtotl̩ˌaɪzɚ; ˈtoutəlaizə] *n.* ①總數計算器。②賽馬賭金計算器。

total loss (保險之)全部損失。

***to·tal·ly** [ˈtotl̩ɪ; ˈtoutl̩i, -əli] *adv.* 全部地;完全地;全然地。to be *totally* blind. 全然盲目。

total recall 完全記憶力。

total reflection 〖光學〗全反射。

total war 總體戰;全面戰爭。

tote¹ [tot; tout] *n.* 〖英俗〗賽馬賭金計算器。

tote² *v.t.,* **tot·ed, tot·ing,** *n.* —*v.t.* ①背負;荷;提。②(以船、車等)運。—*n.* ①背負;提;運。②背負之事物。③=**tote bag.**

tote bag 大型女用手提袋。(亦作 **tote**)

tote box 工具,零件箱。

to·tem [ˈtotəm; ˈtoutəm] *n.* ①圖騰(原始民族用作種族、部落、家族等之象徵的自然物)。②圖騰像。③一氏族或一團體的表記。

to·tem·ic [toˈtɛmɪk; touˈtemik] *adj.* 圖騰的;圖騰制度的。

to·tem·ism [ˈtotəmɪzm̩; ˈtoutəmizəm] *n.* ①圖騰制度;圖騰組織。②對圖騰及圖騰關係之信仰;圖騰崇拜。

to·tem·ist [ˈtotəmɪst; ˈtoutəmist] *n.* 有圖騰之家族或部落之一員。

to·tem·is·tic [ˌtotəmˈɪstɪk; ˌtoutəmˈistik] *adj.* 圖騰制度的; totemist 的。

totem pole 圖騰柱。(亦作**totem post**)

toth·er [ˈtʌðɚ; ˈtʌðə] *pron., adj.*〖方〗另一(的);另一個(的)。(亦作**t'other, 'tother**)

to·ti·dem ver·bis [ˈtɑtɪdɛmˈvɝbɪs; ˈtɔtidemˈvəːbis] 〖拉〗就是這些話;就是如此(=in so many words).

to·ti·es quo·ti·es [ˈtoʃɪˌizˈkwoʃɪˌiz; ˈtouʃiiːzˈkwouʃiiːz] 〖拉〗不時地; 無限制地(=as often as).

to·ti·pal·ma·tion [ˌtotɪpælˈmeʃən; ˌtoutipælˈmeiʃən] *n.* 〖動物〗全蹼。

to·to cae·lo [ˈtotoˈsilo; ˈtoutouˈsiːlou] 〖拉〗全然;極度(=by the whole heaven).

***tot·ter** [ˈtɑtɚ; ˈtɔtə] *v.i.* ①蹣跚;以不穩之步伐行走。②(建築物等) 搖搖欲倒。③(國家等)呈不穩之象; 瀕於傾覆。④顫抖; 搖撼。—*n.* 蹣跚;搖搖欲墜。**—er,** *n.*

tot·ter·ing [ˈtɑtərɪŋ; ˈtɔtəriŋ] *adj.* ①蹣跚的。②搖搖欲倒的。③動搖的; 不穩的。**—ly,** *adv.*

tot·ter·y [ˈtɑtərɪ; ˈtɔtəri] *adj.* 蹣跚的;搖動的。

tou·can [ˈtukæn; ˈtuːkæn] *n.* 鵎鵼(美洲熱帶之巨嘴鳥)。

‡touch [tʌtʃ; tʌtʃ] *v.t.* ①觸摸; 觸及; 達及。He *touched* his hat to me. 他向我觸帽致意。②靠於…上;使接觸;碰及。 He *touched* the post with his umbrella.他把傘靠在那柱子上。③輕彈。She *touched* the strings of the harp. 她輕彈琴絃。④傷害;損壞; 影響。I *touched* his self-esteem. 我傷害了他的自尊。⑤感動。 Her sad story *touched* our hearts. 她那悲慘的故事使我們甚爲感動。⑥關係; 涉及; 論及; 談到。The matter *touches* your interests. 這事關係你的利益。⑦匹敵;及得上(通常用於否定句)。No one can *touch* him in mathematics. 在數學方面無人能及得上他。⑧吃 (通常用於否定句)。He never *touches* liquor. 他從不飲酒。⑨停泊;停靠。⑩使精神錯亂;使發狂。His brain has been *touched.* 他的腦子已錯亂不清。⑪感染; 使帶 (某種) 氣味。It is *touched* with superstition. 它帶有迷信意味。⑫〖俗〗借。⑬略帶着。⑭〖俚〗偸。⑮影響; 對…有關係。 This grave decision *touches* all of us. 這個重大的決定對我們大家都有影響。⑯在(金屬)上蓋印證明純度合乎標準。⑰〖古〗演奏(樂器)。—*v.i.* ①觸;接觸。②毗鄰。The two estates *touch.* 這兩塊地相毗鄰。③(船)停靠;停泊。④論及;述及〖on, upon〗. ***touch at a port*** (船隻)停靠某港。***touch bottom*** **a.** 達到最惡劣的狀態。**b.** 對一事實追究到底。***touch down*** **a.** (飛機)着陸;落地。**b.** 〖橄欖球〗在對方目標線後以球觸地。***touch off*** **a.** 觸發。**b.** 放(砲)。**c.** 精確地說明。***touch on*** (or ***upon***) **a.** 觸及;言及。**b.** 跡近;瀕於。***touch the spot*** 〖俚〗所做正爲所需;正中下懷。***touch up*** **a.** 修整;改進。**b.** 喚起;鼓舞。—*n.* ①觸覺。soft to the *touch.* 摸起來很柔軟。②觸;接觸。It will break at a *touch.* 這東西一碰就要壞的。③一筆;筆法;筆致。to add a few *touches.* 添加幾筆。④連繫。A newspaper keeps one in *touch* with the world. 報紙使人與世事保持接觸。⑤特徵;特質。⑥少許;微量。a *touch* of salt. 少量的鹽。⑦彈奏;彈奏法。⑧微恙。a *touch* of fever. 微微發燒。⑨金塊等上加蓋的官印。⑩經檢驗過的黃金成分。⑪一般的試驗;檢驗。to put something to the *touch.* 試驗某物。⑫逃走。a near *touch.* 九死一生的逃走。⑬〖橄欖球〗邊線區域。⑭(心理上或道德上的)理解力;了解。⑮能力;技巧。⑯輕打;輕擊。⑰〖俚〗**a.** 借錢;要錢。**b.** 借到或要到的錢。**c.** 容易借給錢的人。⑱〖俚〗偷。***put the touch on*** 〖俗〗想借錢。

touch·a·ble [ˈtʌtʃəbl̩; ˈtʌtʃəbl] *adj.* 可觸的;可觸知的;可使感動的。—**ness,** *n.*

touch and go ①一觸卽去。②草率而做的事。③不確定的或危急的情勢。④迅速的行動或移動。

touch-and-go [ˈtʌtʃənˈgo; ˈtʌtʃənˈgou] *adj.* ①急速的;草率的;簡略的。②危險的;一觸卽發的。

touch·back [ˈtʌtʃˌbæk; ˈtʌtʃbæk] *n.* 〖橄欖球〗球員將對方攻到門線上或門線後方之球置於地上,使成死球之動作。

touch·down [ˈtʌtʃˌdaun; ˈtʌtʃdaun] *n.*〖橄欖球〗①持球者越過對方球門線以球觸地之擧。②底線得分。③飛機降落。

tou·ché [tuˈʃe; tuːˈʃei] *interj.* ①(比劍時表示觸及對方之口令)點到!②聽到厲害的話或有力的辯論所作之驚歎聲。

touched [tʌtʃt; tʌtʃt] *adj.* ①受感動的。②略帶瘋癲的;心身不平衡的。

touch·er [ˈtʌtʃɚ; ˈtʌtʃə] *n.* 觸摸者。***as near as a toucher*** 〖英俚〗幾乎;瀕於。

touch football 美國的一種非正式橄欖球戲。

touch·hole [ˈtʌtʃˌhol; ˈtʌtʃhoul] *n.* (舊式砲之)火門;點火孔。

***touch·ing** [ˈtʌtʃɪŋ; ˈtʌtʃiŋ] *adj.* 動人的;引人傷感的。It is a very *touching* scene. 那是很感人的景象。—*prep.* 關於(=concerning, as regards). —**ly,** *adv.* —**ness,** *n.*

touch-in-goal [ˈtʌtʃɪnˈgol; ˈtʌtʃinˈgoul] *n.* 〖橄欖球〗本陣 (in-goal) 側線外。

touch·less [ˈtʌtʃlɪs; ˈtʌtʃlis] *adj.* ①無觸覺的。②無實體的;不能觸摸的。

touch·line [ˈtʌtʃˌlaɪn; ˈtʌtʃlain] *n.* 〖足球〗邊線。

touch-me-not [ˈtʌtʃmɪˌnɑt; ˈtʌtʃmiˌnɔt] *n.* 〖植物〗水金鳳。

touch needle 試金針。

touch paper 硝紙。

touch·stone [ˈtʌtʃˌston; ˈtʌtʃstoun] *n.* 試金石。

touch system (不看鍵盤的)打字法。

touch-type [ˈtʌtʃˌtaɪp; ˈtʌtʃtaip] *v.i.,* **-typed, -typ·ing.** 用 touch system 打字。

touch·wood [ˈtʌtʃˌwud; ˈtʌtʃwud] *n.* 引火木;引火絨。

touch·y [ˈtʌtʃɪ; ˈtʌtʃi] *adj.,* **touch·i·er, touch·i·est.** ①暴躁的;易怒的。②難處理的;棘手的。③對觸覺敏感的。④易起火的。—**touch·i·ly,** *adv.* —**touch·i·ness,** *n.*

***tough** [tʌf; tʌf] *adj.* ①堅韌的。②强壯的;耐勞苦的。③困難的;費力的。a *tough* job. 困難的工作。④倔强的;固執的。⑤〖美〗粗暴的;暴亂的。a *tough* customer. 難伺候的客人。⑥難於忍受的;壞的;令人不快的。⑦黏著的。⑧難矯正的;不易改變的。—*n.* 粗野的人;流氓。—**ly,** *adv.* —**ness,** *n.*

tough·en [ˈtʌfn̩; ˈtʌfn] *v.t.* ①使堅韌。②使强壯。③使倔强。—*v.i.* ①變爲堅韌。②變爲强壯。③變爲倔强。

tough·ie [ˈtʌfɪ; ˈtʌfi] *n.* 〖俗〗①粗野的人;難惹的人。②難題;難局。③率直的書、電影等。(亦作 **toughy**)

tough-mind·ed [ˈtʌfˈmaɪndɪd; ˈtʌfˈmaindid] *adj.* ①實際的;不扭扭捏捏的。②意志堅强的。—**ly,** *adv.* —**ness,** *n.*

tough sledding 〖俗〗困難的時期。

tough spot 〖俗〗難局;難處。

tou·pee [tuˈpe; ˈtuːpei] *n.* 假髮;小假髮。

tour** [tʊr; tuə, toə] *n.* ①旅行;漫遊;周遊。a walking *tour.* 徒步旅行。to make a *tour* of the world. 環遊世界。②(劇團之)巡廻演出。③〖軍〗在某地服務之時期。④任期。make the tour of*** 環遊;周遊。***on tour*** 在巡廻之中。a show *on tour.* 巡廻演出。—*v.t. & v.i.* ①旅行;遊歷;漫遊。②(劇團經理)率領劇團巡廻演出。

tour·bil·lion [tʊrˈbɪljən; tuəˈbiljən] *n.* ①(原指)旋風。②廻旋焰火。

tour de force [ˌtʊrdəˈfors; ˈtuədəˈfɔːs] *pl.* **tours de force.**〖法〗①力技;力作;絕技。②僅僅顯示聰明或技巧的作品、成品等。

tour·er [ˈtʊrɚ; ˈtuərə] *n.* ①觀光者;遊客。②遊覽汽車;遊覽飛機。

tour·ing [ˈtʊrɪŋ; ˈtuəriŋ] *adj.* 遊客的;爲遊客的;遊覽的。a *touring* guide. 導遊。

touring car 遊覽車。

tour·ism [ˈtʊrɪzm̩; ˈtuərizm] *n.* ①遊覽;觀光。②觀光團體;遊客;觀光客(集合稱)。③觀光事業。

***tour·ist** [ˈtʊrɪst; ˈtuərist] *n.* ①旅行者;觀光者。*tourist* bureau. 旅行社。*tourist* industry. 觀光事業。②(船、飛機艙位之)二等。—*adj.* ①爲遊客的;遊客的。*tourist* accommodations. 觀光設施。②(船、飛機艙位或座位)二等的。—*adv.* 乘坐二等艙位。

tourist camp (or **court**) 供旅客住宿的營地;汽車旅館。

tourist car (火車的)臥車。

tourist class (船或飛機上的) 經濟艙位(二等艙位)。

tour·is·tic [tuˈrɪstɪk; tuərˈistik] *adj.* 觀光客的;觀光事業的。

tour·is·try [ˈtʊrɪstrɪ; ˈtuəristri] *n.* ①觀光旅客(集合稱)。②觀光。—*adj.* 像觀光客的。

tourist ticket 遊覽票。

tourist trap 對觀光客敲竹槓的餐廳、商店、旅館等。

tour·ist·y [ˈtʊrəstɪ; ˈtuəristi] *adj.* (常蔑)①觀光客的。②受觀光客歡迎的。

tour·ma·lin(e) [ˈtʊrməlɪn; ˈtuəməlin] *n.* 〖礦〗電氣石。—**ic,** *adj.*

***tour·na·ment** [ˈtɝnəmənt; ˈtuənəmənt] *n.* ①比賽;競賽。a golf *tournament.*

高爾夫球比賽。②馬上比武(大會)。
tour·ney ['tɜnɪ; 'tuəni] *n., pl.* **-neys,** *v.,* **-neyed, -ney·ing.** —*n.* =**tournament.** —*v.i.* 參加比賽;參加馬上比武。
tour·ni·quet ['turnɪ,kɛt; 'tuənikei] *n.* 〖外科〗壓脈器;止血帶。
tour·nure [,tur'nyr; 'tuənjuə] 〖法〗 *n.* ①姿態。②曲線美。③(女人撐裙之)腰墊。
tour of duty ①軍人駐紮某地之期間。②工作期間。
touse [tauz; tauz, tu:z] *v.,* **toused, tous·ing,** *n.* 〖主方〗 —*v.t.* 使蓬亂;弄亂。—*v.i.* 掙扎。—*n.* 混亂。
tou·sle ['tauzl; 'tauzl] *v.,* **-sled, -sling,** *n.* —*v.t.* 攪亂;弄亂(頭髮等)。—*n.* 糟亂的一堆;亂髮。(亦作 **touzle**)—**tou·sled,** *adj.*
tout [taut; taut] *v.i.* ①〖俗〗招徠顧客;謀求工作;爭取選票等。②〖英俚〗探查或供給賽馬等之消息。—*v.t.* ①〖俗〗招徠;接待;勸誘;謀求;爭取(顧客、工作、選票等)。②〖俗〗對…大加稱讚;亂誇。③〖英俚〗探查;供給(賽馬之消息)。***tout*** (***round***) ***for something*** 打聽某事;(尤指)祕密打聽馬賽等的情形。—*n.* (亦作 **touter**)①招徠顧客者;謀求工作者;爭取選票等之人。②探查並供給賽馬之情報者。
tout en·sem·ble [tutɑ̃'sɑ̃bl; tu:tɑ̃-'sɑ̃bl] 〖法〗(藝術品等之)全體的效果;整個。
tow¹ [to; tou] *v.t.* 拖;曳。—*n.* ①拖;被拖之物。②拖曳所用之繩。③拖曳之船或卡車。***in tow*** **a.** 被拖。The launch had the sailboat *in tow.* 這一小汽船拖着帆船。**b.** 受管教;受影響。**c.** 跟在後面的(作伴或跟班)。***under tow*** 被拖之狀態。—**a·ble,** *adj.*
tow² *n.* 大麻、亞麻等的粗纖維屑。—*adj.* 由麻的粗纖維屑製的。
tow·age ['toɪdʒ; 'touidʒ] *n.* ①曳船費。②拖曳。
‡to·ward¹, **to·wards** [tord(z), tə-'wɔrd(z); tə'wɔ:d(z), tɔ:d(z)] *prep.* ①向;對。Our country is rapidly moving *towards* prosperity. 我們的國家在迅速地走向繁榮之境。②關於;對於。one's attitude *toward* the question. 某人對這問題的態度。③將近。*towards* noon. 將近正午。④爲了。Save money *towards* your old age. 要爲老年時代而節省金錢。
to·ward² [tord; 'touəd] *adj.* ①將發生的;正在進行的。②吉利的。
to·ward·ly ['tordlɪ; 'touədli] *adj.* ①適宜的;合時的。②〖罕〗有希望的;生長快的(植物、小孩等);旺盛的。③溫順的。
tow·a·way ['toə'we; 'touə'wei] *n.* 〖美〗拖走並扣留違規停車的車輛。
tow·boat ['to,bot 'toubout] *n.* 拖船;曳船。
tow car 將已損害或拋錨之車拖走的卡車。(亦作 **tow truck**)
·tow·el [taul, 'tauəl; 'tauəl, taul] *n., v.,* **-el(l)ed, -el(l)ing.** —*n.* 手巾;毛巾。***throw*** (*or* ***toss***) ***in the towel*** 〖俚〗認輸。—*v.t.* & *v.i.* ①以手巾擦乾;以手巾擦拭。②〖英俚〗打敗。
towel horse(*or* **rack**)(浴室中之)毛巾架。
tow·el·(l)ing ['tauəlɪŋ; 'tauəliŋ] *n.* 做毛巾的原料(尤指棉花)。
towel rail (裝於牆上的)手巾架。(亦作 **towel bar**)
‡tow·er¹ ['tauɚ; 'tauə] *n.* ①塔;高樓。a bell *tower.* 鐘樓。②堡壘;高聳的城堡。③高樓各層之間的樓梯。④塔狀之建築物。⑤中世紀戰爭時用以攻打城堡的可移動之塔。***a tower of strength*** 可資依賴之人;干城。—*v.i.* ①高聳;超越。②(鷹)垂直上昇。—**like,** *adj.*
tow·er² ['toɚ; 'touə] *n.* 拖曳之人(或物)。
Tower Bridge 倫敦泰晤士河橋。
tow·er·ing ['tauərɪŋ; 'tauəriŋ] *adj.* ①高聳的。②劇烈的。③極大的。④個子高大的。⑤傑出的;極爲偉大的。—**ly,** *adv.*
tow·er·man ['tauəmən; 'tauəmən] *n., pl.* **-men.** ①在鐵路指揮塔內控制行車的人。②機場管制塔之飛行管制員。
tower of ivory 象牙之塔(與世隔絕之夢想境地)。(亦作 **ivory tower**)
tow·er·y ['tauərɪ; 'tauəri] *adj.* ①有塔的。②高聳的;高的。
tow·head ['to,hɛd; 'touhed] *n.* ①淡黃色頭髮的人;長此髮的頭。②河中之沙丘。
tow·hee ['tauhi; 'tauhi:] *n.* 北美產的一種似鵐的小鳥(尤指 chewink).(亦作**tow-hee bunting**)
tow·line ['to,laɪn; 'toulain] *n.* 船纜;曳船索;拖曳纜。(亦作 **towing rope**)
‡town [taun; taun] *n.* ①鎮;市;城。②市民。The whole *town* knows of it. 全城人都知道這事。③市內商業中心區域;鬧區。I am going to *town.* 我到城區去。④〖蘇〗農場。***a man about town*** 城市中遊手好閒之人。***go to town*** **a.** 發跡;成功。**b.** 有效或迅速地做或計劃。**c.** 失去約束;縱情;徹底地做。***on the town*** **a.** 接受公共救濟。**b.** 〖俚〗尋樂。***paint the town*** (***red***) 〖俚〗狂歡;瘋狂地慶祝。***the talk of the town*** 街談巷議的事情。
town-bred ['taun,brɛd; 'taunbred] *adj.* 在城裏出生及長大的。
town clerk 鎮執事;鎮書記。
town council 鎮民代表會;鎮議會。
town councilor 鎮議會議員。
town crier 街頭宣告員(沿街呼叫傳播公報)。
town·ee [taun'i; tau'ni:] *n.* ①〖英俗〗大學城之居民。②〖俚〗=**townsman.**
tow·net ['to,nɛt; 'tounet] *n.* 撈網。(亦作 **towing net**)
town gas 用管子輸送到住宅的瓦斯。
town hall 市政廳;市民集會所。
town house 在城市中之宅邸。
town·i·fy ['taunə,faɪ; 'taunifai] *v.t.,* **-fied, -fy·ing.** 使似都市;使都市化。
town·ish ['taunɪʃ; 'tauniʃ] *adj.* ①城鎮特有的;城鎮的。②(人之態度等)城鎮化的。
town·let ['taunlɪt;'taunlit] *n.* 小市鎮。
town meeting 市民大會;鎮民大會。
town planning 都市計畫。
town·scape ['taun,skep; 'taunskeip] *n.* ①城鎮的風景;城鎮風景畫。②城鎮美化計畫或建設。
towns·folk ['taunz,fok;'taunzfouk] *n. pl.* 市民。
town·ship ['taunʃɪp; 'taunʃip] *n.* ①鎮區(爲 county 下之一行政區劃)。②(美國公地測量之)六英里見方的地區。③〖澳〗**a.** 鄉間的商業中心城鎮。**b.** 城鎮的商業中心。
town·site ['taun,saɪt; 'taunsait] *n.* ①城鎮所在地。②城鎮預定地。
towns·man ['taunzmən; 'taunzmən] *n., pl.* **-men.** ①市民;同城居民。②(新英格蘭)鎮民代表。
towns·peo·ple['taunz,pipl;'taunz-,pi:pl] *n. pl.* 市民。
towns·wom·an ['taunz,wumən; 'taunz,wumən] *n., pl.* **-wom·en.** 城鎮的女居民;女市民。
town talk ①街談巷議;謠傳。②談話資料。
town woman ①居於城市的女人(爲

countrywoman 之對)。②妓女。

tow·path [ˈto,pæθ; ˈtou-pɑːθ] *n., pl.* **-paths** [-,pæðz; -pɑːðz]. (河或運河沿岸之)曳船路;縴路。(亦作 **towing path**)

tow·rope [ˈto,rop; ˈtouroup] *n.* = **towline.**

tow target 拖在飛機機尾供高砲或戰鬥機射擊訓練用的靶。

tow·y [ˈtoɪ; ˈtoui] *adj.* ①似麻屑的;麻屑做成的。②頭髮色淡的。

tox·(a)e·mi·a [tɑksˈimɪə; tɔksˈiːmiə] *n.* 〖醫〗血毒症。

tox·(a)e·mic [tɑksˈimɪk; tɔkˈsiːmik] *adj.* 〖醫〗①血毒症的。②患血毒症的。

tox·ic [ˈtɑksɪk; ˈtɔksik] *adj.* 毒的;有毒的;中毒的。(亦作 **toxical**) **—al·ly,** *adv.*

tox·i·cant [ˈtɑksɪkənt; ˈtɔksikənt] *adj.* 有毒的;中毒的。**—***n.* ①毒;毒物;毒藥。②麻醉劑;酒。

tox·i·ca·tion [,tɑksɪˈkeʃən; ,tɔksiˈkeiʃən] *n.* 中毒。

tox·ic·i·ty [tɑksˈɪsətɪ; tɔksˈisiti] *n., pl.* **-ties.** 毒性;有毒(性)。

tox·i·col·o·gist [,tɑksɪˈkɑlədʒɪst; ,tɔksiˈkɔlədʒist] *n.* 毒物學家。

tox·i·col·o·gy [,tɑksɪˈkɑlədʒɪ; ,tɔksiˈkɔlədʒi] *n.* 毒物學。**—tox·i·co·log·i·cal,** *adj.* **—tox·i·co·log·i·cal·ly,** *adv.*

tox·i·co·ma·ni·a [,tɑksɪkoˈmenɪə; ,tɔksikouˈmeiniə] *n.* 〖醫〗服毒癖。

tox·i·co·sis [,tɑksɪˈkosɪs; ,tɔksiˈkousis] *n.* 〖醫〗中毒;中毒症。

tox·in [ˈtɑksɪn; ˈtɔksin] *n.* 毒素。

tox·oph·i·lite [tɑkˈsɑfə,laɪt; tɔkˈsɔfilait] *n.* 射者;愛好射術者。**—***adj.* 射者的;射術的。

tox·oph·i·ly [tɑkˈsɑfəlɪ; tɔkˈsɔfili] *n.* 射箭;對射箭之愛好。

tox·o·plas·mo·sis [,tɑksoplæzˈmosɪs; ,tɔksouplæzˈmousis] *n.* 〖醫、獸醫〗住血原蟲病。

‡**toy** [tɔɪ; tɔi] *n.* ①玩具。②無價值的東西。③小玩意兒。④小型的事物。⑤體型極小之動物。⑥從前蘇格蘭女人戴的一種帽子。⑦十六、十七世紀盛行的一種樂曲。**—***adj.* 供玩耍的。a *toy* train. 玩具火車。**—***v.i.* ①玩弄;戲弄;以…自娛〖with〗。②調戲;調情。

toy dog ①小型狗。②玩具狗。

toy·shop [ˈtɔɪ,ʃɑp; ˈtɔi-ʃɔp] *n.* 玩具店。

tp. ①telephone. ②township. ③troop.

T.P.N.D. Theft, Pilferage and Non-Delivery.

Tr 〖化〗terbium 之符號。

Tr. ①Treasurer. ②Troop. ③Trustee.

tr. ①tare. ②tincture. ③trace. ④train. ⑤transaction. ⑥transitive. ⑦translated. ⑧translation. ⑨translator. ⑩transpose. ⑪treasurer. ⑫trill. ⑬trustee.

tra- 〖字首〗=**trans-.**

‡**trace**[1] [tres; treis] *n., v.,* **traced, tracing.** **—***n.* ①跡;蹤跡;足跡;形跡;痕跡。Sorrow has left its *traces* on her face. 悲愁在她的臉上留下痕跡。②微量;少許。There was not a *trace* of color in her cheek. 她的臉上毫無血色。③圖樣。④〖氣象〗雨跡。⑤路跡。⑥〖數學〗描跡;描繪。**—***v.t.* ①追蹤。②追溯;探索。③發現…的記號;查出;找到。④畫;描繪;謄寫;模寫;摸繪。⑤用線條等裝飾。⑥寫下。**—***v.i.* ①回溯。②追蹤。③(自動記錄儀)用曲線畫下記錄。***trace back to*** 追溯;回溯到。

trace[2] *n.* (馬車之)挽繩;挽韁。***kick over the traces*** 擺脫控制;表示獨立自主;不順從。

trace·a·ble [ˈtresəbl; ˈtreisəbl] *adj.* ①可追蹤的;可追溯的;可探索的。②可描畫的;可模寫的。③可歸因於…的;由於…的〖to〗。

trace element 〖生物〗微量元素。(亦作 **microelement**)

trace·less [ˈtreslɪs; ˈtreislis] *adj.* 無蹤跡的;無痕跡的。**—ly,** *adv.*

trac·er [ˈtresɚ; ˈtreisə] *n.* ①追蹤者;模寫之人或物。②描跡器;模寫器。③遺失物的查詢者。④查詢遺失貨物、包裹等之單據。⑤曳光彈;曳光彈中之彈藥。⑥〖化、生理〗(用以指示蹤跡或變化之)放射性元素或同位素。

tracer bullet 曳光彈。

trac·er·y [ˈtresərɪ; ˈtreisəri] *n., pl.* **-er·ies.** 由線紋構成之裝飾;窗飾。

tra·che·a [ˈtrekɪə, trəˈkiə; trəˈki(ː)ə] *n., pl.* **tra·che·ae** [trəˈki·i; trəˈkiːiː]. ①〖解剖〗氣管。②〖植物〗導管;螺旋紋管。

tra·che·al [ˈtrekɪəl, trəˈkiəl; trəˈki(ː)əl] *adj.* ①〖解剖〗氣管的;氣管狀的;有氣管的。②〖植物〗導管的。

tra·che·i·tis [,trekɪˈaɪtɪs; ,treikiˈaitis] *n.* 〖醫〗氣管炎。

tra·che·ot·o·my [,trekɪˈɑtəmɪ; ,trækiˈɔtəmi] *n., pl.* **-mies.** 〖外科〗氣管切開(術)。

tra·cho·ma [trəˈkomə; trəˈkoumə] *n.* 〖醫〗顆粒性結膜炎;沙眼。

trac·ing [ˈtresɪŋ; ˈtreisiŋ] *n.* ①追蹤;追溯;溯源。②複寫;模寫。③透寫物;複寫圖;描圖。④記錄器之記錄。

tracing paper 描圖紙。

‡**track** [træk; træk] *n.* ①足跡;痕跡。the *tracks* of a rabbit. 兔子的足跡。②路;途徑;進程。a mountain *track.* 山路。③軌道;轍;線路。single *track.* (鐵路的)單軌。double *track.* 雙軌。④行爲的方式;人生的常道。to go on in the same *track* year after year. 年復一年地照舊進行。⑤〖運動〗跑道。a race *track.* 賽跑的跑道。⑥〖運動〗徑賽;田徑賽。⑦移動或行走之路線。⑧一連串事或觀念。⑨形成痕跡之事物(如車輪等)。***cover up one's tracks*** 掩飾自己的行動。***in one's tracks***〖俗〗當場;立刻。***jump the track*** 突然出軌。***keep track of*** 使處於自己的觀察、知曉或注意的範圍之內;跟蹤;記載。He reads the newspapers to *keep track of* current events. 他閱報以求熟悉時事。***lose track of*** 忘了;不知;不知蹤跡。***make tracks*** 〖俗〗快走;跑開;逃。***make tracks for*** 〖俗〗走向;追。***off the track*** 離題;誤入歧途。***on the track*** 合題;正確。***on the track of*** 追蹤。The police are *on the track of* the thief. 警察在追盜賊。***on the wrong*** (***right***) ***side of the tracks*** 來自貧窮(富有)的環境。***the beaten track*** 常軌;慣例。***the wrong side of the tracks*** 貧民區。**—***v.t.* ①追蹤。to *track* a bear. 追蹤一隻熊。②〖美〗造成脚印或其他痕跡於…。Don't *track* the floor. 不要在地板上踏出脚印。③曳(船)。④鋪以路軌。⑤〖鐵路〗路軌、車輪等中間有(若干距離)。**—***v.i.* ①循軌道或足跡而行。②車輪之間有…距離。The car's wheels *track* about five feet. 那部車子輪子間距離約有五英尺。③〖電影、電視〗拍攝推拉鏡頭。***track down*** **a.** 追蹤至捕獲。to *track down* a criminal. 追捕到一罪犯。**b.** 調查、探索至發現。

track·age [ˈtrækɪdʒ; ˈtrækidʒ] *n.* ①軌道(集合稱);鐵道線。②軌道使用權(費)。

track and field 〖運動〗田徑;田徑賽。

track-and-field [ˈtrækənˈfild; ˈtrækənˈfiːld] *adj.* 田徑賽的。

tracked [trækt; trækt] *adj.* 有履帶的(牽引機等)。

track·er 〔ˈtrækɚ; ˈtrækə〕 *n.* ①追蹤者。②追蹤空中物體之儀器。③拖車(船)者。

tracker dog 追踪逃犯的獵犬。

tracking station 人造衞星追蹤站。

track·lay·er 〔ˈtræk͵leɚ; ˈtræk͵leiə〕 *n.* 敷設鐵軌之工人。

track·less 〔ˈtræklɪs; ˈtræklis〕 *adj.* ①無足跡的;無路的。②無軌道的。

track·man 〔ˈtrækmən; ˈtrækmən〕 *n., pl.* **-men.** ①協助檢查、敷設或保養鐵軌之人。②鐵路軌道視察人員。

track man 參加徑賽之運動員。

track meet 〖美〗田徑賽運動會。

track record 個人或企業在某方面所創造的紀錄。

track shoe 田徑賽運動鞋;跑鞋。

track·walk·er 〔ˈtræk͵wɔkɚ; ˈtræk-͵wɔːkə〕 *n.*〖美〗鐵軌視察員。(亦作 **trackman**)

track·way 〔ˈtræk͵we; ˈtræk-wei〕 *n.* 行人自然走出來的小徑(非開闢的)。

***tract**[1] 〔trækt; trækt〕 *n.* ①廣袤的一片(土地、海水等);區域。a *tract* of desert. 廣袤的一片沙漠。②〖解剖〗道;徑;束。③期間。a long *tract* of time. 長期間。

***tract**[2] *n.* 論文;小册子;宗教論文;宗教小册子。

trac·ta·bil·i·ty 〔͵træktəˈbɪlətɪ; ͵træktəˈbiliti〕 *n.* ①馴良;溫順。②易處理。

trac·ta·ble 〔ˈtræktəbl; ˈtræktəbl〕 *adj.* ①易駕馭的;溫順的;馴良的。②易鍛的;易加工的。—**trac·ta·bly,** *adv.*

Trac·tar·i·an 〔trækˈtɛrɪən; trækˈtɛəriən〕 *adj.* 創始或擁護牛津運動的。—*n.* 創始或擁護牛津運動的人。

Trac·tar·i·an·ism 〔trækˈtɛrɪən͵ɪzəm; trækˈtɛəriənizəm〕 *n.* 牛津運動(1833–41年牛津大學刊布九十本小册，題名 *Tracts for the Times*, 主張英國國教應歸向天主教之教義，而反對新教之主義)。

trac·tate 〔ˈtræktet; ˈtrækteit〕 *n.* 論文。

trac·tile 〔ˈtræktl; ˈtræktail〕 *adj.* 可拉長的;可引長的。

trac·til·i·ty 〔trækˈtɪlətɪ; trækˈtiliti〕 *n.* 延展性。

trac·tion 〔ˈtrækʃən; ˈtrækʃən〕 *n.* ①拖;曳;牽引;被曳;被牽引。②牽力;牽引力。③鐵道運輸。④摩擦;阻力。⑤(肌肉、器官等之)牽引。⑥吸引力;魅力。

traction engine 蒸汽牽引機。

trac·tive 〔ˈtræktɪv; ˈtræktiv〕 *adj.* 牽引的;曳引的。

***trac·tor** 〔ˈtræktɚ; ˈtræktə〕 *n.* ①牽引機;拖曳機。a farm *tractor*. 農場牽引機。②牽引者;牽引物。③曳引式飛機。

tractor train 牽引機牽引的一列拖車。

trad 〔træd; træd〕 *adj.* 〖英俗〗傳統的(= traditional).

trad·a·ble 〔ˈtredəbl; ˈtreidəbl〕 *adj.* 可交易的;可買賣的。(亦作 **tradeable**)

‡**trade** 〔tred; treid〕 *n., v.,* **trad·ed, trad·ing,** *adj.* —*n.* ①職業;手藝。②同行者;同業者。the building *trade*. 建築業的同業者。③貿易;商業。foreign *trade*. 國外貿易。export *trade*. 出口貿易。import *trade*. 進口貿易。④交易;買賣。He made a good *trade*. 他做了一筆好買賣。⑤〖俗〗顧客。⑥市場。an increase in the tourist *trade*. 觀光業市場的好景氣。⑦行業。⑧(*pl.*)貿易風。***by trade*** 就職業而言;職業是。He's a mason *by trade*. 他的職業是石匠。***the trade*** 〖俗〗酒商;釀造業者。***the trades*** 貿易風。—*v.t.* 買賣;交易;交換。The boy *traded* his knife for a ball. 這孩子用他的刀換一個球。—*v.i.* ①交易;貿易;交換。to *trade* with America. 與美國貿易。②買;購物。***trade down*** 以高價物品交換廉價物品。***trade in*** **a.** 以舊品抵價購物。**b.** 經營;做買賣。to *trade in* cotton.經營棉花貿易。***trade off*** 賣掉。***trade on*** 利用。***trade up*** 〖俗〗**a.** 買賣品質高、價錢昂貴的物品。**b.** 以廉價物交換較高級貨物。—*adj.* ①商業的;貿易的。②某一行業的。③工會的;公會的。*trade* council. 同業公會。

trade acceptance 商業承兌票據。

trade agreement ①雇用合同(規定工資、工作時間等)。②(國際)貿易協定。

trade association 同業公會。

trade balance 貿易平衡。***favorable trade balance*** 順差。

trade barrier (關稅、禁運等)國際貿易之障礙。

trade book (or **edition**)(書籍之)普及版本。

trade deficit 貿易逆差。

trade discount 同業折扣;批發折扣。

trade fair 商展。

trade gap 貿易差額。

trade guild (中世紀之)行會;同業公會。

trade-in 〔ˈtred͵ɪn; ˈtreid-in〕 *n.* ①可用以償價之物品(如舊汽車、電視機等換新品時之折價)。②以物易物之交易。③物物交易時,賣方所認許之值。—*adj.* 以物易物之方式的。

trade journal (or **paper**) 專業性刊物。

trade-last 〔ˈtred͵læst; ˈtreid-lɑːst〕 *n.* 背後恭維。

trade·mark 〔ˈtred͵mɑrk; ˈtreidmɑːk〕 *n.* 商標。—*v.t.* ①以商標區別;加商標於。②註册…的商標。

trade name ①商品名稱。②商業名稱。③商號名稱。

trade-name 〔ˈtred͵nem; ˈtreidneim〕 *v.t.,* **-named, -nam·ing.** 以某商品名稱登記。

trade-off 〔ˈtred͵ɔf; ˈtreidɔːf〕 *n.* 一半一半的機會(成功失敗之機會相若)。

trade price 同業價;批發價。

***trad·er** 〔ˈtredɚ; ˈtreidə〕 *n.* ①商人;貿易者。②商船;貿易船。③交易者。④商品或股票投機者。

trade school 職業學校。

trade show ①商展。②〖電影〗試映;試演。

***trades·man** 〔ˈtredzmən; ˈtreidzmən〕 *n., pl.* **-men** 〔-mən; -mən〕. ①開商店的人。②技藝工人;手藝人。

trades·peo·ple 〔ˈtredz͵pipl; ˈtreidz͵piːpl〕 *n. pl.* ①商人。②開商店者及其家屬。(亦作 **tradesfolk**)

trades union 〖英〗=**trade union.** (亦作 **tradesunion**)

trade union 工會;職工協會。(亦作 **tradeunion**)

trade unionism 工會主義;工會制度。(亦作 **tradeunionism, trades-unionism**)

trade unionist 工會會員;工會主義者。(亦作 **trade-unionist, trades-unionist**)

trade war 激烈的貿易競爭;商戰。

trade wind ①貿易風。②信風。

trad·ing 〔ˈtredɪŋ; ˈtreidiŋ〕 *adj.* 貿易的;買賣的;商業的;從事貿易的。a *trading* concern. 貿易行。—*n.* ①買賣;貿易。②〖俗〗購物。③〖美〗(政黨間的)妥協。

trading estate 〖英〗產業地區。

trading post 商棧。

trading stamp 〖美〗商品中附帶之贈券。

***tra·di·tion** 〔trəˈdɪʃən; trəˈdiʃən〕 *n.* ①傳說。②因襲;傳統;慣例。to keep up the family *traditions*. 保持家庭傳統。③〖宗

教〗聖傳（摩西或基督及其使徒之口頭誡條）。④〖法律〗移交。

***tra·di·tion·al** 〔trəˈdɪʃənḷ; trəˈdiʃənl〕 *adj.* ①傳說的。②因襲的；傳統的；慣例的。③較舊的爵士樂的。(亦作**traditionary**) —**ly,** *adv.*

tra·di·tion·al·ism 〔trəˈdɪʃənḷˌɪzəm; trəˈdiʃn̩əlizəm〕 *n.* 墨守傳統；傳統主義。

tra·duce 〔trəˈdjus; trəˈdjuːs〕 *v.t.,* **-duced, -duc·ing.** 詆毀；誹謗；中傷。

tra·duce·ment 〔trəˈdjusmənt; trəˈdjuːsmənt〕 *n.* 誹謗；詆毀；惡言中傷。

***traf·fic** 〔ˈtræfɪk; ˈtræfik〕 *n., v.,* **-ficked, -fick·ing.** —*n.* ①運輸；交通；通行；往來之行人、車輛等。The bridge is open to *traffic*. 此橋可以通行。②貿易；商業。③交通量；運輸。④(意見、觀念等之)交換；來往。a *traffic* in ideas. 意見的溝通。⑤某一商品(尤其不合法的)之交易。—*v.i.* 買賣；交易。to *traffic* in hides. 買賣獸皮。to *traffic* with Japan. 和日本貿易。

traf·fic·a·ble 〔ˈtræfɪkəbḷ; ˈtræfikəbl〕 *adj.* ①適於通行的。②適於交易的。

traf·fi·ca·tor 〔ˈtræfɪˌketɚ; ˈtræfikeitə〕 *n.* 〖英〗(汽車的)方向指示器。

traffic circle 道路之圓形交叉路口。(亦作 **rotary,** 英亦作 **roundabout**)

traffic island 安全島。

traffic jam 交通擁塞。

traf·fick·er 〔ˈtræfɪkɚ; ˈtræfikə〕 *n.* 交易者；買賣人；商人。

traffic light 交通指揮燈；紅綠燈。(亦作 **traffic signal, traffic control signal**)

traffic manager ①(工商機構之)主管貨物運輸者；運輸部經理。②(鐵路局等交通機關之)業務處主任。

traffic ticket 汽車駕駛人違反交通規則的傳票。

trag·a·canth 〔ˈtrægəˌkænθ; ˈtrægəkænθ〕 *n.* 一種用以製阿拉伯橡膠之樹膠。

tra·ge·di·an 〔trəˈdʒidɪən; trəˈdʒiːdjən〕 *n.* ①悲劇演員。②悲劇作家。

tra·ge·di·enne 〔trəˌdʒidɪˈɛn; trəˌdʒiːdiˈen〕 *n.* 悲劇女伶。

***trag·e·dy** 〔ˈtrædʒədɪ; ˈtrædʒidi〕 *n., pl.* **-dies.** ①悲劇。②悲劇之寫作、演出及理論。③悲慘之事。

trag·ic** 〔ˈtrædʒɪk; ˈtrædʒik〕 *adj.* ①悲劇的。②悲慘的；悽慘的。the tragic*** 文學、藝術、戲劇中之悲劇因素。

trag·i·cal 〔ˈtrædʒɪkḷ; ˈtrædʒikəl〕 *adj.* =**tragic.** —**ly,** *adv.*

trag·i·com·e·dy 〔ˌtrædʒɪˈkɑmədɪ; ˈtrædʒiˈkɔmidi〕 *n., pl.* **-dies.** ①悲喜劇。②有悲喜劇性質之事件。

trag·i·com·ic 〔ˌtrædʒɪˈkɑmɪk; ˈtrædʒiˈkɔmik〕 *adj.* 悲喜劇的。

trag·i·com·i·cal 〔ˌtrædʒɪˈkɑmɪkḷ; ˈtrædʒiˈkɔmikəl〕 *adj.* =**tragicomic.**

trag·o·pan 〔ˈtrægəˌpæn; ˈtrægəpæn〕 *n.* 亞洲產的一種雉。

‡trail 〔trel; treil〕 *v.t.* ①拖；拉。②追蹤；尾隨；追獵。③踏(草等)成路。④將(演講等)拖長。—*v.i.* ①拖曳。②蔓生。③慢行。The boys *trailed* to school. 孩子們慢慢地走去上學。④追蹤；尾隨。⑤漸漸消逝。⑥網魚。⑦到達；最後才到。⑧(比賽等)落後。The home team was *trailing* 20 to 15. 主隊以15比20落後。⑨(如蛇之)爬行。—*n.* ①蹤跡；嗅跡。②踏路；小徑。③尾；餘波；餘縷。④砲架之尾部。***blaze the trail*** 刻指路記號；領路；做先鋒。***hit the trail*** **a.** 出發。**b.** 立刻走開。***hot on the trail*** 緊跟着蹤跡或嗅跡的。

trail·blaz·er 〔ˈtrelˌblezɚ; ˈtreilˌbleizə〕 *n.* ①領路人(領人過荒野)。②開拓者；先鋒。

trail·blaz·ing 〔ˈtrelˌblezɪŋ; ˈtreilˌbleiziŋ〕 *adj.* 開風氣之先的；領導的；帶頭的。

trail·er 〔ˈtrelɚ; ˈtreilə〕 *n.* ①沿着徑路走的人或獸。②地上蔓延的葛藤類。③汽車等拖曳而行的拖車。④(汽車拖動的)活動房屋。⑤電影預告片。⑥電影片後空白之一段(爲捲影片者)。

trailer camp 拖車營。

trailer coach 房屋拖車。

trail·er·ite 〔ˈtreləˌraɪt; ˈtreilərait〕 *n.* 居住在汽車拖曳的活動房屋中的人。

‡train 〔tren; trein〕 *n.* ①火車；列車。When does the *train* start? 火車何時開行? ②行列；一行；排；列。a *train* of camels. 駱駝隊。③〖軍〗輜重隊。④連續；連串。a *train* of thought. 連續不斷的思想。⑤拖曳之物；長裙。⑥尾部；尾。the *train* of a comet. 彗星的長尾。⑦隨從人員；扈從。the king's *train*. 國王的扈從。⑧導火線。⑨〖機械〗(傳動的)輪列。⑩秩序。Matters were in good *train*. 諸事井然有序。⑪〖物理〗列。***in train*** 準備妥當；在進行中。—*v.t.* ①教養；訓練；教育。to *train* soldiers. 練兵。②瞄準。③〖園藝〗整枝；修剪。④拖；拉。—*v.i.* ①練習；鍛鍊；操練。②搭火車。to *train* to New York. 搭火車去紐約。—**a·ble,** *adj.*

train·band 〔ˈtrenˌbænd; ˈtreinbænd〕 *n.* 〖英史〗(16–18世紀的)民兵隊；民團。

train·bear·er 〔ˈtrenˌbɛrɚ; ˈtreinˌbɛərə〕 *n.* (婚禮中)拉紗者；拉衣裾的人。

train dispatcher 〖美〗火車調度人員。

train·ee 〔trenˈi; treiˈniː〕 *n.* ①接受訓練的人或動物。②受軍事訓練之人；新兵。

***train·er** 〔ˈtrenɚ; ˈtreinə〕 *n.* ①訓練者(尤指體育教練)。②馴馬師。③(美海軍之)瞄準手。④訓練用之器械。⑤(航空)訓練機。

‡train·ing 〔ˈtrenɪŋ; ˈtreiniŋ〕 *n.* 訓練；教育；練習；培植。*training* for teachers. 師資的訓練。***in*** (***out of***) ***training*** (運動員等) 在好(壞)體況中；練習得好(不好)。—*adj.* 訓練的。*training* exercise. 爲訓練而做的運動。

training aid 幫助訓練的工具或設備。

training camp ①軍中訓練營。②拳擊手或其他運動員的訓練處；集訓地。

training college 〖英〗師範學校；師範學院。

training school ①訓練所；訓練班。②感化院。

training ship (海軍中供實習用之)訓練艦。

train·load 〔ˈtrenˌlod; ˈtreinloud〕 *n.* 一列車能裝載之量。

train·man 〔ˈtrenmən; ˈtreinmən〕 *n., pl.* **-men.** 鐵路業務員(尤指車長助手、制動機控制手)。

train·mas·ter 〔ˈtrenˌmæstɚ; ˈtreinˌmɑːstə〕 *n.* (鐵路某一段之)段長。

train oil 鯨油。

train·sick 〔ˈtrenˌsɪk; ˈtrein-sik〕 *adj.* 暈火車的。

train sickness 暈火車病。

traipse 〔treps; treips〕 *v.,* **traipsed, traips·ing,** *n.* 〖俗〗—*v.i.* 無目的地徘徊。—*v.t.* 〖方〗經過；走過。—*n.* 〖方〗很累的走路。(亦作 **trapes**)

***trait** 〔tret; trei, treit〕 *n.* 特性；特點。national *traits*. 國民性。

***trai·tor** 〔ˈtretɚ; ˈtreitə〕 *n.* ①賣國賊；

奸逆。②出賣朋友的人;背信者。

trai·tor·ous [ˈtretərəs;ˈtreitərəs] *adj.* 叛逆的;背叛的;不忠的;陰險的。—**ly,** *adv.*

trai·tress [ˈtretrɪs; ˈtreitris] *n.* 女叛徒;女叛逆者。

tra·jec·to·ry [trəˈdʒɛktərɪ;ˈtrædʒiktəri] *n., pl.* **-ries.** ①彈道;拋射物之弧形行程。②〖幾何〗軌線。

***tram¹** [træm; træm] *n., v.,* **trammed, tram·ming.** —*n.* ①〖英〗電車(在美國叫 **streetcar**)。②電車道。③〖採礦〗煤礦車。—*v.t.* & *v.i.* 以電車輸送;乘坐電車。

tram² *n., v.,* **trammed, tram·ming.** —*n.* 〖機械〗①調整機械部位之裝置。②正確位置;正確調整。—*v.t.* & *v.i.* 〖機械〗以調整裝置調整。

tram³ *n.*(精美絲織物之)雙股緯線。(亦作 **trame**)

tram·car [ˈtræmˌkɑr; ˈtræmkɑː] *n.* ①〖英〗電車。②(採礦時用的)礦車。

tram·mel [ˈtræml̩; ˈtræməl] *n., v.,* **-mel(l)ed, -mel·(l)ing.**—*n.*①(常 *pl.*)任何束縛物;拘束;妨害。②(捕捉魚、鳥等之)細網。③鍋鉤; 吊鉤。④馬梏。⑤橢圓規; 長圓規。—*v.t.* ①阻礙;束縛;妨害。②以網捕捉。

tra·mon·tane[trəˈmɑnten;trəˈmɔntein] *adj.* (亦作 **transmontane**)①(從義大利之立場言) 位於或來自羣山 (尤指阿爾卑斯山)彼邊的。②〖罕〗外國的。③〖罕〗野蠻的。—*n.* ①羣山彼側的人;外國人。②來自北極的法國南部的西北風。

tramp** [træmp; træmp] *v.i.* ①踐踏。②重步行走;行走。③流浪;漂泊。—*v.t.* ①踐踏。②徒步旅行。 ***tramp it 行走;步行。—*n.* ①踏步聲。②徒步旅行。③飄泊者;流浪乞討之人。④航線不定的貨船。

tram·ple** [ˈtræmpl̩;ˈtræmpl] *v.,* **-pled, -pling,** *n.* —*v.t.* 踐踏;蹂躪; 虐待。 —*v.i.* 踐踏;蹂躪; 虐待。 ***trample about 重步行走。 ***trample on*** (or ***upon***) 蹂躪;蔑視。to *trample on* justice. 藐視正義。***trample under foot*** 踩碎;蹂躪; 蔑視。 —*n.* 踐踏;蹂躪;踐踏聲。

tram·po·line[ˌtræmpəˈlin;ˌtræmpəˈliːn] *n.* 健身用的彈簧墊。

tramp steamer 不定期航行之貨船。

tram·rail [ˈtræmˌrel; ˈtræmreil] *n.* ①礦車軌道。②索道。

tram road 礦車軌道;礦山鐵道。(亦作 **tramroad**)

tram·way [ˈtræmˌwe; ˈtræmwei] *n.* ①〖英〗電車道。②索道 (亦作 **aerial railway, aerial tramway, cable tramway, ropeway**)。③礦車軌道;礦山鐵路。

trance [træns, trɑns; trɑːns] *n., v.,* **tranced, tranc·ing.** —*n.* ①恍惚; 失神。②睡眠狀態。③狂喜。—*v.t.* 使恍惚;使昏迷。

***tran·quil** [ˈtrænkwɪl, ˈtræŋ–; ˈtræŋkwil] *adj.,* **-quil·(l)er, -quil·(l)est.** 安靜的;平靜的;寧靜的。 —**ly,** *adv.*

***tran·quil·(l)i·ty** [trænˈkwɪlətɪ, træŋ–; træŋˈkwiliti] *n.* 安靜;平靜;寧靜。

Tran·quil·(l)i·ty, Sea of [trænˈkwɪlətɪ; træŋˈkwiliti] *n.* (月球上之) 寧靜海 (1969年美國太空人第一次登陸處)。

tran·quil·(l)ize [ˈtræŋkwɪˌlaɪz; ˈtræŋkwilaiz] *v.,* **-(l)ized, -(l)iz·ing.** —*v.t.* 使寧靜; 使安定; 鎮定。—*v.i.* 變寧靜;變安定;平靜。—**tran·quil·i·za·tion,** *n.*

tran·quil·iz·er [ˈtræŋkwɪˌlaɪzɚ; ˈtræŋkwilaizə] *n.* ①使鎮定之人或物。②鎮靜劑。(亦作 **tranquillizer**)

tranquilizing agent(or **drug**) 鎮靜劑。

trans. ①transaction, transactions. ②transfer. ③transferred. ④transformer. ⑤transit. ⑥transitive. ⑦translated. ⑧translation. ⑨translator. ⑩transparent. ⑪transportation. ⑫transpose. ⑬transverse.

trans- 〖字首〗表下列諸義: ①橫過;貫通。如: transcontinental (橫貫大陸的)。②超越; 以外。如: transcend (凌駕)。③變化;轉移。如: translate (翻譯), transform (變形)。④在那一邊;在他方面(爲cis-之對)。如: transoceanic (大洋那邊的)。

***trans·act** [trænsˈækt, trænzˈækt; trænˈzækt,-nˈsækt] *v.t.* 辦理;處理;執行。He *transacts* business with stores all over the country. 他和全國各商店交易。—*v.i.* 辦事;處理事務。

***trans·ac·tion** [trænsˈækʃən, trænzˈækʃən; trænˈzækʃən,-nˈsæk-] *n.* ①辦理;執行。②交易;事務;事項。③(*pl.*)記錄。

trans·ac·tor [trænsˈæktɚ; trænˈzæktə] *n.* 執行、處理或經營的人。

trans·al·pine [trænsˈælpɪn; ˈtrænzˈælpain] *adj.* (自義大利立場言)阿爾卑斯山彼方的;阿爾卑斯山北方的。—*n.* 阿爾卑斯山彼方的居民。

trans·at·lan·tic [ˌtrænsətˈlæntɪk; ˈtrænzətˈlæntik] *adj.* ①橫越大西洋的。②在大西洋彼岸的。

trans·ceiv·er [trænsˈsivɚ; trænsˈsiːvə] *n.* 〖無線電〗收發兩用機。

tran·scend [trænˈsɛnd; trænˈsend] *v.t.* ①超出;超越。②勝過;優於。—*v.i.*優越。

tran·scend·ence [trænˈsɛndəns; trænˈsendəns] *n.* ①超越;超絕。②〖神學〗超然存在; 先在。(亦作 **transcendency**)

tran·scend·ent [trænˈsɛndənt; trænˈsendənt] *adj.* ①超凡的;超羣的;卓越的。②〖神學〗(神之)超越物質世界而存在的;超絕的。③〖哲學〗超越經驗的。

tran·scen·den·tal[ˌtrænsɛnˈdɛntl̩; ˌtrænsenˈdentl] *adj.* ①超凡的;卓越的。②超自然的。③形而上的; 極抽象的; 含混不明的;難解的。④〖哲學〗先驗的。⑤〖數學〗(函數) 超越的。—*n.* 〖數學〗超越數。

tran·scen·den·tal·ism [ˌtrænsɛnˈdɛntl̩ˌɪzəm; ˌtrænsenˈdentəlizəm] *n.* ①〖哲學〗先驗哲學。②〖哲學〗超越論。③卓越性;不可解;幻想;曖昧。

tran·scen·den·tal·ist [ˌtrænsɛnˈdɛntl̩ɪst; ˌtrænsenˈdentəlist] *n., adj.* 先驗論者(的);超越論者(的)。

trans·con·ti·nen·tal [ˌtrænskɑntəˈnɛntl̩; ˈtrænzˌkɔntiˈnentl] *adj.* ①橫貫大陸的。② 在大陸彼方的。

tran·scribe [trænˈskraɪb; trænsˈkraib] *v.,* **-scribed, -scrib·ing.** —*v.t.* ①謄寫;抄寫;刊印。②用另一種文字或符號寫出。③改寫(樂曲)以便唱奏;改作;改編。④爲…錄音或灌片以便廣播放送。—*v.i.* 播放錄音片。

tran·script [ˈtrænˌskrɪpt; ˈtrænskript] *n.* ①副本; 抄本; 謄本。②成績單。

tran·scrip·tion [trænˈskrɪpʃən; trænsˈkripʃən] *n.* ①謄寫;刊印。②謄本。③〖音樂〗樂曲改作。④(廣播用的)錄音;灌片。⑤錄音廣播。⑥用另一種文字或符號之錄寫。

trans·duc·er [trænsˈdjusɚ; trænsˈdjuːsə] *n.* 〖物理〗電功率轉送器。

trans·earth [trænz'ɜθ; trænz'ə:θ] *adj.* 朝地球方向飛行的(尤指太空船回航時)。

tran·sect [træn'sɛkt; træn'sekt] *v.t.* 橫斷;橫切。

tran·sec·tion [træn'sɛkʃən; træn'sekʃən] *n.* ①橫斷;橫切。②橫斷面;橫切面。

tran·sept ['trænsɛpt; 'trænsept] *n.* 十字式教堂的左右翼部;袖廊。

trans·e·qua·to·ri·al [træns,ikwə'tɔrɪəl; træns,ekwə'tɔ:riəl] *adj.* 橫越赤道的;在赤道彼邊的。

transf. ①transfer. ②transference. ③transferred. ④transformer.

***trans·fer** [*n.* 'trænsfɝ; 'trænsfə(:), 'trɑ:n– *v.* træns'fɝ; træns'fə:, trɑ:n–] *v.*, **-ferred, -fer·ring,** *n.* —*v.t.* ①遷移;移動;調職;移轉。②讓渡(財產等)。③轉寫;摹寫;轉印。—*v.i.* ①換車;換船。②轉移;轉學;調任。—*n.* ①遷移;移動;調職;移轉。②讓渡;讓渡證書。③轉寫;轉印;轉寫書;轉印文。④換乘;換車票。a *transfer* ticket. 換車票。⑤換車、船等的地點。⑥匯兌。

trans·fer·a·ble [træns'fɝəbl; træns'fə:rəbl] *adj.* 可轉移的;可讓渡的;可轉印的。(亦作 **transferrable**)—**trans·fer·a·bil·i·ty,** *n.*

trans·fer·ee [,trænsfə'ri; ,trænsfə(:)'ri:] *n.* ①被調任者。②〖法律〗(財產等之)受讓人;承買人。

trans·fer·ence [træns'fɝəns; 'trænsfərəns] *n.* ①轉移;讓渡;移動;調動;遷移。②〖精神分析〗感情轉移。

trans·fer·or [træns'fɝɚ; træns'fə:rə] *n.* 〖法律〗讓渡人。

transfer paper 摹寫紙;複寫紙(製「圖、雕刻用)。

trans·fer·rer [træns'fɝɚ; træns'fə:rə] *n.* ①讓渡人;讓與者。②摹寫者;轉印者。

trans·fig·u·ra·tion [,trænsfɪgjə'reʃən; ,trænsfigju'reiʃən] *n.* ①變形;變貌。②(the T–)〖聖經〗**a.** 基督在山上的改變形像。**b.** 基督變容節(八月六日)。

trans·fig·ure [træns'fɪgjɚ; træns'figə] *v.t.*, **-ured, -ur·ing.** ①使變形;使變貌;使改觀。②使精神美化;使變爲高尚;理想化。

trans·fix [træns'fɪks; træns'fiks] *v.t.* ①刺穿;戳穿。②刺住;叉牢。③(因驚愕、恐怖等)使發呆;使麻木。He was *transfixed* at its sights. 他看見這光景就呆着不能動了。

trans·fix·ion [træns'fɪkʃən; træns'fikʃən] *n.* ①刺穿;貫穿。②〖醫〗穿貫法;穿刺術。

***trans·form** [træns'fɔrm; træns'fɔ:m, trɑ:n–] *v.t.* ①使變形;使改觀。The witch *transformed* men into pigs. 巫婆把人變成了豬。②使改變性質。③變(電流之)電壓。④變(一種能)爲另一種能。—*v.i.* 變形;變性;改觀。—*n.* ①〖數學〗變換式。②變形;變性;變換。③變形之結果。

trans·form·a·ble [træns'fɔrməbl; træns'fɔ:məbl] *adj.* 可變形的;可變化的。

trans·for·ma·tion [,trænsfɚ'meʃən; ,trænsfə'meiʃən, ,trɑ:n–, –fɔ:'m–] *n.* ①變形。②變性;變質。③(電流之)變壓。④(婦人的)假髮;假髻。⑤〖數學〗變換。

trans·form·er [træns'fɔrmɚ; træns'fɔ:mə] *n.* ①促使變化的人或物。②變壓器。

trans·fuse [træns'fjuz; træns'fju:z] *v.t.*, **-fused, -fus·ing.** ①(從一容器)倒於(另一容器)。②輸(血)。③注射(溶液)於血管中。④灌輸。

trans·fu·sion [træns'fjuʒən; træns'fju:ʒən] *n.* ①注入;滲透。②輸血;靜脈注射。

trans·gress [træns'grɛs; træns'gres] *v.t.* ①踰越(界限)。②違犯(法律、條約等)。—*v.i.* ①違犯法律或規則等。②獲罪;有罪。

trans·gres·sion [træns'grɛʃən; træns'greʃən] *n.* 違犯;違背;犯規;犯罪。

trans·gres·sor [træns'grɛsɚ; træns'gresə] *n.* 違犯者;違背者;(宗教道德上之)罪人。

tran·sien·cy ['trænʃənsɪ; 'trænziənsi] *n.* ①頃刻;瞬間;短暫;無常。②〖音樂〗暫時變調。③短暫停留。(亦作 **transience**)

tran·sient ['trænʃənt; 'trænziənt] *adj.* ①短暫的;倏忽的;一瞬間的;片刻的。a *transient* joy. 片刻的歡樂。②過路的;過境的。③給過路客人用或住的。④〖哲學〗外在的。—*n.* 〖美〗暫時寄寓的客人;過境客。

trans·il·lu·mi·na·tion [,trænsɪ,ljumə'neʃən; 'trænsi,lju:mi'neiʃən] *n.* 〖醫〗强光透照診斷法。

tran·sis·tor [træn'zɪstɚ; træn'sistə] *n.* ①電晶體。②〖俗〗電晶體收音機。

tran·sis·tor·ize [træn'zɪstə,raɪz; træn'zistəraiz] *v.t.*, **-ized, -iz·ing.** 〖電子〗裝電晶體;使電晶體化。

transistor radio 電晶體收音機。

***trans·it** ['trænsɪt,–zɪt; 'trænsit, 'trɑ:nsit, 'trænzit] *n.*, *v.*, **-it·ed, -it·ing.** —*n.* ①通過;經過;通行;過路。a *transit* passenger. 過境客。②搬運;運送。goods in *transit*. 在運送中的貨物。③通路;運輸路線。④變遷;改變。⑤〖測量〗轉鏡儀。⑥〖天文〗**a.** 天體之通過子午線。**b.** 小天體之經過較大天體的表面。⑦(T–)〖美〗提供船隻或飛機位置資料的一系列人造衛星之一。—*v.t.* & *v.i.* 通過;經過。

transit duty (貨物之)通行稅;過境稅。

transit instrument ①〖測量〗轉鏡儀。②〖天文〗中星儀。

***tran·si·tion** [træn'zɪʃən, –'sɪʃən; træn'siʒən, trɑ:n–, trən–, –n'ziʃən] *n.* ①轉移;變遷;過度;經過。a period of *transition* (or *transition* period). 過度時期。②〖音樂〗變調;轉調。③(電影電視之)用音響效果或音樂等方法所作的鏡頭變換。—**al,** *adj.*

tran·si·tion·ar·y [træn'zɪʃən,ɛrɪ; træn'siʒənəri] *adj.* 轉移的;變化的;過度的。

***tran·si·tive** ['trænsətɪv; 'trænsitiv, 'trɑ:n–] *adj.* ①〖文法〗及物的(動詞)。a *transitive* verb. 及物動詞。②轉移的。③中間的。④〖數學〗傳遞的;可遷的。—*n.* 及物動詞。—**ly,** *adv.*

tran·si·to·ry ['trænsə,torɪ; 'trænsitəri] *adj.* 短暫的;一時的;頃刻的。—**tran·si·to·ri·ly,** *adv.* —**tran·si·to·ri·ness,** *n.*

transl. ①translated. ②translation. ③translator.

trans·lat·a·ble [træns'letəbl; træns'leitəbl] *adj.* 可翻譯的;可說明的。

***trans·late** [træns'let, 'trænslet; træns'leit, trɑ:ns–, trænz–, trɑ:nz–] *v.*, **-lat·ed, -lat·ing.** —*v.t.* ①翻譯;迻譯。to *translate* an English book into Chinese. 將一部英文書譯成中文。②解釋;說明。Your visit was *translated* as a compliment. 你的拜訪被視爲一種光榮。③移動;調動。④轉變爲。to *translate* promise (schemes) into actions. 將諾言(計畫)付諸行動。⑤肉身不死而升天。⑥傳遞(電報等)。⑦〖教會〗**a.**

調動(主教)至另一教區。b. 改換(教區)。c. 將(聖物)移至另處。⑧〖數學〗作平移。—v.i. ①翻譯。②被翻譯。

*trans·la·tion [træns'leʃən; træns'leiʃən, trɑːn–, trən–] n. ①翻譯。free *translation*. 意譯。literal *translation*. 直譯。②解釋。③移動;調動。④翻譯品;譯文。⑤肉身升天。⑥〖數學〗平移。⑦改變;變換。⑧(電報等之)傳遞。—al, adj.

trans·la·tor [træns'letɚ; træns'leitə] n. 譯者;翻譯者。(亦作 translater)

trans·lit·er·ate [træns'lɪtəˏret; trænz'litəreit] v.t., -at·ed, -at·ing. 音譯(如將臺灣譯成 Taiwan).

trans·lit·er·a·tion [trænsˏlɪtə'reʃən; ˌtrænzlitə'reiʃən] n. 音譯(的字)。

trans·lu·cence [træns'lusn̩s; trænz'luːsns] n. 半透明。(亦作 translucency)

trans·lu·cent [træns'lusn̩t; trænz'luːsnt] adj. ①半透明的。②容易了解的。

trans·lu·na·ry [træns'lunərɪ; træns'luːnəri] adj. ①月之彼側的;月上的。②天上的。③理想的;空想的。(亦作 translunar)

trans·ma·rine [ˏtrænsmə'rin; ˌtrænsmə'riːn] adj. ①海外的;來自海外的。②橫越海洋的。

trans·me·rid·i·o·nal [ˏtrænsmə'rɪdɪənl̩; ˌtrænsmə'ridiənl] adj. ①橫貫子午線的。②東西行的。

trans·mi·grant [træns'maɪgrənt, 'trænsməgrənt; træns'maigrənt, 'trænsmigrənt] adj. 移居的。—n. ①移居之人或物。②自甲國移居乙國而在丙國暫時居留之人。

trans·mi·grate [træns'maɪgret; 'trænzmaigreit] v., -grat·ed, -grat·ing. —v.i. ①移居;移民。②(靈魂)轉生;輪廻。—v.t. 使轉生。

trans·mi·gra·tion [ˏtrænsmaɪ'greʃən; ˌtrænzmai'greiʃən] n. ①移居;移民。②轉生;輪廻。

trans·mi·gra·to·ry [træns'maɪgrəˏtorɪ; træns'maigrətəri] adj. ①輪廻的;轉生的。②移居的;轉徙的。

trans·mis·si·bil·i·ty [trænsˏmɪsə'bɪlətɪ; trænsˌmisi'biliti] n. 可傳;可傳性。

trans·mis·si·ble [træns'mɪsəbl̩; trænz'misəbl] adj. 可傳送的;可傳達的;可傳染的。

trans·mis·sion [træns'mɪʃən; trænz'miʃən, trɑːn–, –ns'm–] n. ①傳送;傳達;傳播。②被傳達;傳播之物。③無線電傳送。④(汽車等之)傳動系統。

trans·mis·sive [træns'mɪsɪv; trænz'misiv] adj. 能傳送的;能傳達的;能傳導的。

*trans·mit [træns'mɪt; trænz'mit, trɑːnz–, –ns'm–] v., -mit·ted, -mit·ting. —v.t. ①傳送;傳達;傳播。②〖物理〗傳導。③(無線電)播送。④遺傳。—v.i. ①發電波;播送。②(權利、義務等)傳給子孫。

trans·mit·tance [træns'mɪtəns; trænz'mitəns] n. ①傳送;傳達;傳遞。②移交;讓渡;遺傳。(亦作 transmittal)

trans·mit·ter [træns'mɪtɚ; trænz'mitə] n. ①傳送者;傳達者。②(電報之)發報機;(電話之)送話器;無線電發射機。

transmitting set 發報機。

trans·mog·ri·fi·ca·tion [trænsˏmɑgrəfɪ'keʃən; ˌtrænzmɔgrifi'keiʃən] n. 變形。

trans·mog·ri·fy [træns'mɑgrəˏfaɪ; trænz'mɔgrifai] v.t., -fied, -fy·ing. 使變形(尤指變成奇形怪狀)。

trans·mut·a·ble [træns'mjutəbl̩; trænz'mjuːtəbl] adj. 可變化的;可變質的;可變形的。

trans·mu·ta·tion [ˏtrænsmju'teʃən; ˌtrænzmjuː'teiʃən] n. ①變化;變形;變質;變性。②興衰遞變。③〖生物〗(種之)遞變。④(煉金術)使(劣)金屬變成金、銀。⑤由一種元素變成另一種元素。

trans·mut·a·tive [træns'mjutətɪv; trænz'mjuːtətiv] adj. 變化的;變形的;變質的;變性的。

trans·mute [træns'mjut; trænz'mjuːt] v.t., -mut·ed, -mut·ing. 使變質;使變形;使變化。

trans·na·tion·al [træns'næʃənl̩; træns'næʃənl] adj. 超國界的;在一國利益之上的。

trans·nat·u·ral [træns'nætʃərəl; træns'nætʃrəl] adj. 超自然的。

trans·o·ce·an·ic [ˏtrænsoʃɪ'ænɪk; 'trænzˌouʃi'ænik] adj. ①橫越海洋的。②在海洋彼岸的;海外的。

tran·som ['trænsəm; 'trænsəm] n. ①(窗或門上面的)頂窗;腰窗;氣窗。②橫楣;橫梁。③船尾橫材。④車輛等所用之橫木。⑤任何橫木(如十字架上或絞刑臺上者)。

tran·son·ic [træn'sɑnɪk; træn'sɔnik] adj. =transsonic.

transonic barrier 音障。(亦作 sound barrier, sonic barrier)

transp. ①transparent. ②transportation.

trans·pa·cif·ic [ˏtrænspə'sɪfɪk; ˌtrænspə'sifik] adj. ①橫渡太平洋的。②太平洋彼岸的。

trans·pa·dane ['trænspəˏden; 'trænspədein] adj. (從羅馬言)在 Po 河彼岸的;在 Po 河北岸的。

trans·par·ence [træns'pɛrəns; træns'pɛərəns] n. 透明;透明性。

trans·par·en·cy [træns'pɛrənsɪ; træns'pɛərənsi] n., pl. -cies. ①透明;透明性。②透明物體。③透明度。

*trans·par·ent [træns'pɛrənt; træns'pɛərənt] adj. ①透明的。②顯明的;顯然的。③明晰的。④易被識破的。⑤〖醫〗(光線等)透進的。—ly, adv.

tran·spic·u·ous [træn'spɪkjuəs; træn'spikjuəs] adj. ①透明的。②清晰的(語言)。

trans·pierce [træns'pɪrs; træns'piəs] v.t. & v.i., -pierced, -pierc·ing. 刺穿;戳穿;貫穿;穿透。

tran·spi·ra·tion [ˏtrænspə'reʃən; ˌtrænspə'reiʃən] n. 蒸發;散發。

tran·spire [træn'spaɪr; træns'paiə] v., -spired, -spir·ing. —v.t. 排出;發散;蒸發。—v.i. ①洩露;爲人所知。②發生。③散發;排出。—tran·spir·a·ble, adj.

tran·spi·rom·e·ter [ˏtrænspə'rɑmətɚ; ˌtrænspi'rɔmitə] n. 植物水氣發散記錄器。

trans·plant [træns'plænt; træns'plɑːnt] v.t. ①移植;移種。②使遷徙。③〖醫〗移植(器官、皮膚)。—v.i. ①移種。②遷徙。③能受得住移植。—n. ①移植;移種。②被移植、移種的事物。

trans·plant·a·ble [træns'plæntəbl̩; træns'plɑːntəbl] adj. 可移植的。

trans·plan·ta·tion [ˏtrænsplæn–

ˈteʃən; ˌtrænsplɑːnˈteiʃən〕 *n.* ①移植;移種。②移民。③〖外科〗移植。④被移植之物。

trans·plant·er 〔trænsˈplæntɚ; trænsˈplɑːntə〕 *n.* ①移植者。②移植機。

trans·po·lar 〔trænsˈpolɚ; trænsˈpoulə〕 *adj.* 橫越南北極地的。

trans·pon·dor, trans·pon·der 〔trænsˈpɑndɚ; trænsˈpɔndə〕 *n.* 〖航空〗異頻雷達收發器。

trans·pon·tine 〔trænsˈpɑntɪn; ˈtrænzˈpɔntain〕 *adj.* ①橋那邊的。②倫敦泰晤士河南岸的。③(倫敦之)鬧劇的。

***trans·port** 〔*v.* trænsˈport; trænsˈpɔːt *n.* ˈtrænsport; ˈtrænspɔːt〕 *v.t.* ①運送;運輸。to *transport* mail by airplane. 以飛機送郵件。②使神魂顛倒;使心神恍惚;使深受感動(用於被動語態)。to be *transported* with grief. 悲不自勝。③處以流刑;流放;放逐(通常用於被動語態)。④殺死。—*n.* ①運輸;輸送。the *transport* of goods. 貨物的運送。②運輸船;運輸艦。③運輸機。④交通系統。⑤一陣强烈的情緒。to be in a *transport* of rage. 怒不可遏。⑥被放逐的犯人。

trans·port·a·ble 〔trænsˈpɔrtəbl̩; trænsˈpɔːtəbl〕 *adj.* ①可運輸的。②處以流刑的;放逐的。—**trans·port·a·bil·i·ty,** *n.*

***trans·por·ta·tion** 〔ˌtrænspɚˈteʃən; ˌtrænspɔːˈteiʃən〕 *n.* ①運輸;輸送。②運輸工具;運輸費用。③流刑;放逐。*transportation* for life. 終身放逐。④交通業。⑤車票;船票。—**al,** *adj.*

transportation insurance 運輸保險。

trans·port·ed 〔trænsˈportɪd; trænsˈpɔːtid〕 *adj.* ①感動的;出神的。②被輸送的。

trans·port·ee 〔ˌtrænsporˈti; ˌtrænspɔːˈtiː〕 *n.* ①被放逐的人。②自棲息處被運走的動物。

trans·port·er 〔trænsˈportɚ; trænsˈpɔːtə〕 *n.* ①運輸者;運送者。②運輸機;運送裝置。

Transport House 〖英〗工黨幹部;工黨總部。

transport ship 運輸船。

trans·pos·al 〔trænsˈpozl̩; trænsˈpouzl̩〕 *n.* =**transposition.**

trans·pose 〔trænsˈpoz; trænsˈpouz〕 *v.,* **-posed, -pos·ing,** *n.* —*v.t.* ①改換…之位置或順序;置換。②〖代數〗移項。③〖音樂〗變調;移調。—*v.i.* ①改寫;改換。②可以改寫;可變換。③〖音樂〗變調演奏;以變調寫樂曲。—*n.* 〖數學〗轉置。—**trans·pos·a·ble,** *adj.*

trans·po·si·tion 〔ˌtrænspəˈzɪʃən; ˌtrænspəˈziʃən〕 *n.* ①(位置順序之)轉換;置換。②轉換語句;轉換文。③〖數學〗移項。④〖音樂〗變調;變調曲。—**al,** *adj.*

trans·sex·u·al 〔trænˈsɛkʃuəl; trænˈseksjuəl〕 *n.* 性轉換者(心理上渴望成爲異性)。—**ism,** *n.*

trans·shape 〔trænsˈʃep; trænsˈʃeip〕 *v.t.,* **-shaped, -shap·ing.** 改變形狀。(亦作 **transhape**)

trans·ship 〔trænsˈʃɪp; trænsˈʃip〕 *v.,* **-shipped, -ship·ping.** —*v.t.* 換乘(船、車等)。—*v.i.* 換船;換車。(亦作 **tranship**) —**ment,** —**per,** *n.*

Trans-Siberian Railroad (or **Railway**) 橫越西伯利亞之大鐵路(從烏拉山到海參崴,長 4,000英里)。

trans·son·ic 〔trænsˈsɑnɪk; trænsˈsɔnik〕 *adj.* 〖航空〗近音速的(時速700-780英里者)。(亦作 **transonic**)

tran·sub·stan·ti·ate 〔ˌtrænsəbˈstænʃɪˌet; ˌtrænsəbˈstænʃieit〕 *v.,* **-at·ed, -at·ing.** —*v.t.* ①使變形;使變質。②〖神學〗使(麪包與酒)變爲耶穌之肉與血。—*v.i.* 變質;變形。

tran·sub·stan·ti·a·tion 〔ˌtrænsəbˌstænʃɪˈeʃən; ˈtrænsəbˌstænʃiˈeiʃən〕 *n.* ①變質。②〖神學〗化體論;變質說。

tran·su·date 〔ˈtrænsjuˌdet; ˈtrænsjudeit〕 *n.* 滲出物。

tran·su·da·tion 〔ˌtrænsjuˈdeʃən; ˌtrænsjuˈdeiʃən〕 *n.* ①滲出。②滲出物。

tran·su·da·to·ry 〔trænˈsjudəˌtorɪ; trænˈsjuːdətəri〕 *adj.* 滲出的。

tran·sude 〔trænˈsud; trænˈsjuːd〕 *v.,* **-sud·ed, -sud·ing.** —*v.i.* 滲出;滲漏。—*v.t.* 使滲出;被排出。

trans·u·ran·ic 〔ˌtrænsjuˈrænɪk; ˌtrænsjuˈrænik〕 *adj.* 〖化〗原子序數高於鈾的;超鈾的。(亦作 **transuranian, transuranium**)

transuranic element 〖化〗超鈾元素。

Trans·vaal 〔trænsˈvɑl; ˈtrænzvɑːl〕 *n.* 特蘭斯瓦爾(南非共和國之一省,爲世界第一金礦產地)。

trans·val·ue 〔trænsˈvælju; trænsˈvæljuː〕 *v.t.,* **-val·ued, -val·u·ing.** 以不同基礎估價;以新的原則、價值或標準估價。—**trans·val·u·a·tion,** *n.*

trans·vase 〔trænsˈves; trænsˈvɑːs〕 *v.t.,* **-vased, -vas·ing.** 自一容器倒入另一容器。

trans·ver·sal 〔trænsˈvɝsl̩; trænzˈvəːsəl〕 *adj.* 橫斷的;橫亙的。—*n.* ①〖數學〗貫線;截線。②〖解剖〗橫肌。—**ly,** *adv.*

trans·ver·sal·i·ty 〔ˌtrænsvɝˈsælətɪ; ˌtrænsvəːˈsæliti〕 *n.* 橫斷;橫亙。

***trans·verse** 〔trænsˈvɝs, trænz-; ˈtrænzvəːs〕 *adj.* ①橫的;橫放的;橫亙的;橫斷的。②〖幾何〗橫軸的。—*n.* ①橫放物;橫亙物。②〖幾何〗橫軸。—**ly,** *adv.* —**ness,** *n.*

transverse axis 〖幾何〗貫軸。

transverse magnification 〖光學〗橫向放大率。

transverse muscle 〖解剖〗橫肌。

transverse section 橫斷面。

transverse wave 橫波。

trans·ves·tism 〔trænsˈvɛstɪzm̩; trænsˈvestizəm〕 *n.* 男着女裝或女着男裝(常爲同性戀之一種表現)。(亦作 **transvestitism**)

trant·er 〔ˈtræntɚ; ˈtræntə〕 *n.* 〖英方〗攤販;叫賣者。

trap**[1] 〔træp; træp〕 *n., v.,* **trapped, trap·ping.** —*n.* ①捕捉機;陷阱。②圈套;詭計。③一種輕便馬車。④(防蒸氣、水等通過的)門瓣;凝氣瓣。⑤飛靶發射機。⑥(*pl.*)打擊樂器(如鼓、鈸等)。⑦射球戲(=trapball)。⑧〖俚〗嘴巴。Keep your *trap* shut! 閉嘴! ⑨=**trap door.** ***be caught in a trap 墮入圈套。—*v.t.* ①以捕捉機捕捉;設陷阱捕捉;誘捕;計陷;局限。②裝門瓣、凝氣瓣、U字管等;吸進;聚集;凝聚。③抓住(從地上跳起之球)。④〖棒球〗封殺(跑壘員)。—*v.i.* ①設置捕捉機或陷阱。②操作飛靶發射機。—**like,** *adj.*

trap[2] *n., v.,* **trapped, trap·ping.** —*n.* (*pl.*)〖俗〗隨身之物;行李。—*v.t.* 裝以馬飾。

trap[3] *n.* ①(*pl.*)輕便階梯;踏臺。②〖地質〗圓柱形黑色火成巖(用於鋪路者)。

trap·ball 〔ˈtræpˌbɔl; ˈtræpbɔːl〕 *n.* ①射球戲。②此球戲所用之球。(亦作 **trap ball**)

trap door 地板或屋頂上之活門。

trap-door spider [ˈtræpdor~; ˈtræpˈdɔː~] 【動物】土蜘蛛。
trapes [treps; treips] *n.* 懶婦；不整潔之婦女。—*v.t.* & *v.i.* 遊蕩；閒蕩；逍遙。(亦作 **traipse**)
tra·peze [træˈpiz; trəˈpiːz] *n.* ①健身房或馬戲場所用之一種鞦韆。②【幾何】=**trapezium.**
trapeze artist 表演空中飛人之馬戲團團員。
tra·pe·zi·form [trəˈpizəˌfɔrm; trəˈpiːzifɔːm] *adj.* 不規則四邊形的。
tra·pez·ist [træˈpizɪst; trəˈpiːzist] *n.* 表演空中飛人之藝人。
tra·pe·zi·um [trəˈpizɪəm; trəˈpiːzjəm] *n., pl.* **-zi·ums, -zi·a** [-zɪə; -ziə]. ①【幾何】不等邊四邊形；不平行四邊形。②【英】梯形(=trapezoid). ③【解剖】大多角骨。
trap·e·zoid [ˈtræpəˌzɔɪd; ˈtræpəzɔid] *n.* ①【美】梯形。②【英】不等邊四邊形。③【解剖】小多角骨。—*adj.* ①【美】梯形的。②【英】不等邊四邊形的。
trap·e·zoi·dal [ˌtræpəˈzɔɪdəl; ˌtræpəˈzɔidəl] *adj.* 梯形的；不等邊四邊形的。
trap line ①布置陷阱以捕獸之路線。②排鉤(一排有餌魚鉤之釣線)。③蜘蛛網之絲。
trap·nest [ˈtræpˌnɛst; ˈtræpˌnest] *n.* (裝有鉸鏈門的) 母雞巢 (便於數出下蛋的數目)。—*v.* 以上述方法數出下蛋的數目。
trap·per [ˈtræpɚ; ˈtræpə] *n.* ①(設陷阱之)捕獸者(尤指為獲得皮毛者)。②【礦】礦坑中控制通風孔的人。
trap·pings [ˈtræpɪŋz; ˈtræpiŋz] *n. pl.* ①馬飾。②裝飾物；裝飾。
Trap·pist [ˈtræpɪst; ˈtræpist] *n.* 【天主教】Cistercian 修會中一派之修道士(生活嚴肅簡樸，好沉思)。—*adj.* 此派修道士的。
trap·py [ˈtræpɪ; ˈtræpi] *adj.,* **-pi·er, -pi·est.** ①圈套的；陷阱的；詭計的。②步法短、快、高的(馬)。③困難的；艱苦的。
trap·shoot·er [ˈtræpˌʃutɚ; ˈtræpˌʃuːtə] *n.* 打飛靶者；飛靶射擊者。
trap·shoot·ing [ˈtræpˌʃutɪŋ; ˈtræpˌʃuːtiŋ] *n.* 飛靶射擊。
trap shot (網球等)球剛從地上跳起時之一擊。(亦作 **half volley**)
trash[1] [træʃ; træʃ] *n.* ①廢物；垃圾；殘屑。②無價值之物；無價值的文學作品。③無價值之人；敗類。④蔗渣。—*v.t.* ①削去(成長中的甘蔗)之外葉(俾促進其生長)。②去掉(植物)多餘的小枝。
trash[2] *v.t.* ①以皮帶束縛(狗等)。②束縛；妨礙；使遲緩。—*n.* ①繫狗的項圈、皮帶等。②阻礙；束縛。
trash can 垃圾桶。
trash·er·y [ˈtræʃərɪ; ˈtræʃəri] *n.* 殘屑；廢物；垃圾。
trash·y [ˈtræʃɪ; ˈtræʃi] *adj.,* **trash·i·er, trash·i·est.** ①無價值的；似垃圾的。②為垃圾所堵塞的；蕪穢的(指土地言)。
trass [træs; træs] *n.* 火山土。
trat·to·ri·a [ˌtrattoˈriɑ; ˌtrɑːttouˈriːɑː] *n., pl.* **-ri·e** [-ˈrie; -ˈriːei].【義】飲食店。
trau·ma [ˈtrɔmə; ˈtrɔːmə] *n., pl.* **-ma·ta** [-mətə; -mətə], **-mas.** 【醫】①身體上的傷；精神上的創傷。②由精神創傷造成的精神異狀；震驚。
trau·mat·ic [trɔˈmætɪk; trɔːˈmætik] *adj.* ①創傷的；外傷的。②治療外傷的。—**al·ly,** *adv.*
trau·ma·tism [ˈtrɔməˌtɪzəm; ˈtrɔːmətizəm] *n.* 【醫】①外傷；創傷。②由創傷或外傷而致的精神異狀或全身障礙。
trau·ma·tize [ˈtrɔməˌtaɪz; ˈtrɔːmətaiz] *v.t.,* **-tized, -tiz·ing.** 【醫】①損傷(體素)。②使精神或情緒受創傷。—**trau·ma·ti·za·tion,** *n.*
trav. ①traveler. ②travel(s).
trav·ail [ˈtrævel; ˈtræveil] *n.* ①勞苦；苦工。②劇痛。③分娩之陣痛。—*v.i.* ①辛勞工作；勞苦。②受分娩之陣痛。
trave [trev; treiv] *n.* ①【建築】橫木；橫梁。②(釘蹄鐵時束縛牛、馬足用的)木縛架。
:trav·el [ˈtrævl; ˈtrævl] *v.,* **-el(l)ed, -el·(l)ing,** *n.* —*v.i.* ①旅行；遊歷。to *travel* first class. 乘頭等車、船、飛機等旅行。②運行；行進。Light *travels* faster than sound. 光傳得比聲快。③旅行推銷貨物。He *travels* for a carpet manufacturer. 他為一地毯商旅行推銷。④掃視；遍思。The general's eyes *traveled* over the enemy's line. 將軍的眼睛掃視敵人陣線。⑤與…交往。He *travels* with a wealthy crowd. 他跟有錢人交往。⑥(機械等)在一定的路程上移動。⑦【俗】快走。⑧【棒球】投四壞球讓打擊手上壘(=walk). —*v.t.* ①旅行；遊歷。②經過；走過。—*n.* ①旅行；遊歷。②(*pl.*)遊記；遊記文章。the *travels* of Marco Polo. 馬可孛羅遊記。③(星、光、波等之)進行；運行。④【機械】動程。—**a·ble,** *adj.*
travel agency (or **bureau**) 旅行社。
travel agent 旅行業者；旅行社職員。
trav·el(l)ed [ˈtrævld; ˈtrævld] *adj.* ①富於旅行經驗的。②旅行者常用的；旅客多的。③【地質】(石塊等)已離開原來位置的。
:trav·el·(l)er [ˈtrævlɚ; ˈtrævlə] *n.* ①旅行者；遊歷者；旅客。②旅行推銷員(=traveling salesman). ③在一定的路程上移動的機械裝置。④可拉入舞臺兩旁的布幕(=traveler curtain).
traveler's check 旅行支票。
trav·el·er's-joy [ˈtrævlɚzˈdʒɔɪ; ˈtrævləzˈdʒɔi] *n.* 【植物】野生鐵線蓮。
trav·el·(l)ing [ˈtrævlɪŋ; ˈtrævliŋ] *adj.* ①旅行的；旅行用的。a *traveling* bag. 旅行袋。②遊歷的；巡廻的。③(機械等)可移動的；(索等)滑動的。—*n.* ①旅行；巡廻。②移動；滑動。
traveling salesman 旅行推銷員。
trav·el·ing-wave tube [ˈtrævlɪŋˈwev~; ˈtrævəliŋˈweiv~] 【電訊】行波管。
trav·e·logue, trav·e·log [ˈtrævəˌlɔg; ˈtrævəlɔg] *n.* ①敍述旅行見聞之講演。②遊記電影。
travel shot 【電影，電視】移動架上攝取的活動物體之鏡頭。
trav·el-soiled [ˈtrævlˌsɔɪld; ˈtrævlˌsɔild] *adj.* 風塵僕僕的。(亦作 **travel-stained**)
travel time 上班或為接洽業務而花在路上的時間(常算作辦公時間而計算工資者)。
trav·el-worn [ˈtrævlˌworn; ˈtrævlˌwɔːn] *adj.* 因旅行而感疲倦的。
trav·ers·a·ble [ˈtrævɚsəbl; ˈtrævəsəbl] *adj.* ①可橫貫的；可通過的。②可否認的；可反駁的；(特指)【法律】可抗辯的。
***trav·erse** [ˈtrævɚs, ˈtrævɜs; ˈtrævə(ː)s] *v.,* **-ersed, -ers·ing,** *n., adj., adv.* —*v.t.* ①走過；經過；橫過。②橫亙；橫貫。③將(砲)左右移轉。④反對；妨礙；阻止。to *traverse* one's opinion. 反對某人的意見。⑤仔細檢查；詳細討論。⑥【法律】抗辯。—*v.i.* ①橫向

亂走；前後跑。②左右擺動。③在軸上旋轉；旋轉。—*n.* (亦作 **traversal**) ①橫過；橫貫；橫亙。②橫亙之物。③保護壕溝等的土牆。④教堂中的橫廊。⑤橫寬；橫貫的距離。⑥〖航海〗 **a.** Z 字形航路。**b.** 此航路中之任何一段直線航路。⑦割線；橫割另一線的線。⑧妨礙；阻止。⑨橫向之行動。⑩槍砲沿水平線之轉動。⑪〖法律〗對於對方所作陳述提出的正式否認。—*adj.* 橫亙的；橫越的。*traverse* sailing. Z 字形航法。—*adv.* 橫越地；交叉地。

trav·ers·er ['trævəsɚ; 'trævəsə] *n.* ①橫貫者；橫過者；橫貫物。②〖法律〗抗辯者；反駁者；否認者。③〖鐵路〗= **traverse table.**

traverse rod 掛窗帘等之水平滑杆。

traverse table 〖鐵路〗轉車臺；轉盤。

trav·er·tine ['trævətɪn; 'trævətin] *n.* 石灰華 (石灰質沉積物，用做建材)。(亦作 **travertin**)

trav·es·ty ['trævɪstɪ; 'trævisti] *n., pl.* **-ties,** *v.,* **-tied, -ty·ing.** —*n.* ①使嚴肅作品(事物)滑稽可笑之模仿。②歪曲；曲解。—*v.t.* ①使(嚴肅主題或其他事物)滑稽化。②極壞地表演。

tra·vi·at·ed ['trevɪ,etɪd; 'treivi:eitid] *adj.* (天花板)橫向分隔的。

trawl [trɔl; trɔ:l] *n.* ①(亦作 **trawlnet**) 在海上捕魚用的大口拖網。②(亦作 **trawl line**) 排鉤。—*v.t.* 以拖網或排鉤捕(魚)；拖(網)。—*v.i.* 以拖網或排鉤捕魚。—**a·ble,** *adj.*

trawl·boat ['trɔl,bot; 'trɔ:lbout] *n.* 拖網漁船。

trawl·er ['trɔlɚ; 'trɔ:lə] *n.* ①拖網船；以拖網捕魚之船。②以拖網捕魚之人。

trawl·er·man ['trɔlɚ,mæn; 'trɔ:ləmæn] *n.* ①以拖網捕魚之人。②在拖網船上工作的人。

trawl line 排鉤釣索。

trawl·net ['trɔl,nɛt; 'trɔ:lnet] *n.* 拖網；撈網。(亦作 **trawl net**)

***tray** [tre; trei] *n.* 缸；碟。an ash *tray.* 煙灰缸。

tray agriculture 水培法；水耕法。

tray·ful ['treful; 'treiful] *n.* 一盤之量；一碟之量；滿盤；滿碟。

tray table 放碟盤的可折之小几。

***treach·er·ous** ['trɛtʃərəs; 'tretʃərəs] *adj.* ①不忠義的；叛逆的；奸詐的。②不可恃的；虛有其表的。Thin ice is *treacherous.* 薄冰是不可靠的。a *treacherous* smile. 陰險之笑容。③危險的。—**ly,** *adv.* —**ness,** *n.*

***treach·er·y** ['trɛtʃərɪ; 'tretʃəri] *n., pl.* **-er·ies.** ①不忠；奸詐行為。②叛逆；叛國。

trea·cle ['trikl̩; 'tri:kl] *n.* ①〖英〗糖蜜。②過於甜蜜或親切之事物 (如言語、情感等)。

trea·cly ['triklɪ; 'tri:kli] *adj.,* **-cli·er, -cli·est.** ①似糖蜜般濃而甜的。②似糖蜜的；過於甜蜜或親切的(言語、情感等)。

tread** [trɛd; tred] *v.,* **trod, trod·den** or **trod, tread·ing,** *n.* —*v.t.* ①行走於；步行在。②踐踏；踩；踏碎。to *tread* grapes. 踏碎葡萄(供製酒之用)。③踏成；踩出。④壓迫；虐待。⑤以走路或跳舞而表演。⑥(雄鳥)與(雌鳥)交配。—*v.i.* ①行走；步行。Don't *tread* on the flower beds. 不要踐踏花壇。②踐踏；踩。③(雄鳥)與雌鳥交配。tread a measure*** (or ***a minuet***) 跳舞。***tread on air*** 得意洋洋。***tread on one's toes*** (or ***corns***) 觸怒某人。***tread on the heels of*** 緊隨…之後而來；接踵而來。***tread the boards*** (or ***the stage***)作演員。***tread the steps of*** 效法…的榜樣；步…的後塵。***tread under foot*** 在脚下踐踏；踩躪；虐待。***tread water*** 踩水；立泳。—*n.* ①踏步；步法；步態；足音。He walks with a heavy *tread.* 他以沉重的脚步走路。②(樓梯之)踏面；踏板。③輪胎觸地的有花紋之表面；其留在地面的痕跡。④鐵軌上輪子磨及的部分。⑤汽車兩相對的輪間之距離。⑥脚底；鞋底。⑦人踏踩的地方；脚印。—**er,** *n.*

tread·board ['trɛd,bord; 'tredbɔ:d] *n.* 〖建築〗(樓梯之)踏板；踏階。

trea·dle ['trɛdl̩; 'tredl] *n., v.,* **-dled, -dling.** —*n.* (亦作 **treddle**) ①(機器之)踏板。②(電車等門口之)踏板。—*v.i.* 用脚踩踏板。

tread·mill ['trɛd,mɪl; 'tredmil] *n.* ①踏車(古時用以懲罰囚犯者)。②一種獸力磨粉機。③任何單調無聊之工作或任務。

tread·plate ['trɛd,plet; 'tredpleit] *n.* 上有花紋以防止滑動或增加吸力之金屬板。

tread·wheel ['trɛd,hwil; 'tredwi:l] *n.* 踏輪；踏車。

Treas., treas. ①treasurer. ②treasury.

trea·son** ['trizn̩; 'tri:zn] *n.* ①叛逆；叛國。②背信；背義。high treason*** 弒君或叛國之罪。

trea·son·a·ble ['triznəbl̩; 'tri:znəbl] *adj.* ①叛逆的；叛國的。②不忠的；背信的。(亦作 **treasonous**)

treason felony 〖英國法律〗叛國罪；叛逆罪。

treasr. treasurer.

treas·ur·a·ble ['trɛʒərəbl̩; 'treʒərəbl] *adj.* 可珍藏的；可儲藏的；珍貴的。

‡**treas·ure** ['trɛʒɚ; 'treʒə] *n., v.,* **-ured, -ur·ing.** —*n.* ①財寶；寶物；財貨；財富；金銀。②被珍愛之人或物。My *treasure!* 我的寶貝！ art *treasures.* 藝術珍品。③金錢。—*v.t.* ①珍愛；重視。I *treasure* your friendship. 我珍視你的友誼。②儲藏；珍藏。to *treasure* (up) jewels. 珍藏寶石。—**less,** *adj.*

treasure house ①寶藏室；寶庫。②知識之泉源 (如博物館、美術館等)。(亦作 **treasure-house**)

Treasure Island 金銀島 (為 R. L. Stevenson 於1883年所寫之小說)。

treas·ur·er** ['trɛʒərɚ; 'treʒərə] *n.* 掌管金錢之人；會計；財務；司庫。Lord High Treasurer*** 〖英〗財務大臣。

treas·ur·er·ship ['trɛʒərɚ,ʃɪp; 'treʒərəʃip] *n.* 會計或司庫之職位。

treas·ure-trove ['trɛʒɚ'trov; 'treʒə'trouv] *n.* ①埋藏於地下之 (無主) 寶物。②〖法律〗由地下或他處掘出之無主金銀財寶。③有價值之發現。

***treas·ur·y** ['trɛʒərɪ; 'treʒəri] *n., pl.* **-ur·ies.** ①金庫。the national *treasury.* 國庫。②資金；(國家或機關等)所擁有之款項。③(T-) 財政部。④珍藏寶物的地方。⑤有價值的人或書。⑥(文學作品之)集萃。

Treasury Bench 〖英〗下院議長右側之第一席位。

treasury bill 國庫債券(期短，無息)。

treasury bond 國庫債券 (由財政部發售)。

treasury certificate 國庫債券(一年以下，有息)。

Treasury Department 〖美〗財政部。

treasury note 國庫證券。

‡**treat** [trit; tri:t] *v.t.* ①對待。Don't *treat* me as a child. 不要把我當作小孩子看待。②視為；以為。He *treated* his mistake as a joke. 他把他的錯誤視為一個笑話。③治療。④論述。⑤處理；使遭受某種作用。⑥宴饗；款待。He *treated* me to a good dinner. 他請我吃一頓好飯。⑦(文學、藝術

中)描寫;表現。—*v.i.* ①論述。This essay *treats* of the progress of medical research. 這篇文章論述醫學研究的進步。②談判;磋商。③宴饗;款待。Whose turn is it to *treat* next? 下次該誰請客了? —*n.* ①宴饗;款待。This is my *treat.* 這次我請客。②使人喜悅的事物;樂事。***stand treat*** 作東道。—**a·ble,** *adj.* —**er,** *n.*

***trea·tise** ['tritɪs; 'triːtiz, -tis] *n.* 論文;論說。

***treat·ment** ['tritmənt; 'triːtmənt] *n.* ①待遇。hard *treatment.* 殘酷之待遇。②處置;處理。③醫療;醫療法。He soon recovered under the doctor's *treatment.* 他經醫生治療不久卽告痊癒。

:trea·ty ['tritɪ; 'triːti] *n., pl.* **-ties.** ①條約。to conclude a peace *treaty.* 訂和約。②談判;協商。***be in treaty with a person for***... 同某人談判(某事)。

treaty port 根據條約開放之商港。

***tre·ble** ['trɛbl; 'trebl] *adj., v.,* **-bled, -bling,** *n.* —*adj.* ①三倍的;三重的。②最高音部的。③聲音高的;尖叫的。—*v.t.* 使增爲三倍。—*v.i.* 增爲三倍。—*n.*①最高音部;最高音部的聲音,歌唱者或樂器。②高而尖銳之聲音。

treble clef 〖音樂〗①高音譜號(𝄞)。②最高音部之音域。

tre·bly ['trɛblɪ; 'trebli] *adv.* 三倍地;三重地。

tre·buck·et ['tribʌkɛt; 'triːbʌkət] *n.* (中古時攻城門的)投石機。(亦作 **trebuchet**)

tre·cen·tist [tre'tʃɛntɪst; trei'tʃentist] 〖義〗*n.* ①十四世紀義大利之文學家或美術家。②其模仿者。

tre·cen·to [tre'tʃɛnto; trei'tʃentoː] 〖義〗*n.* 十四世紀;(尤指)義大利文學、藝術史上之第十四世紀(當時文學方面有Dante, Petrarch及Boccaccio, 繪畫方面有Giotto).

tre·chom·e·ter [trɪ'kɑmətə; tri'kɔmitə] *n.* (車之)行程記錄器;里程表。

tre·de·cil·lion [ˌtridɪ'sɪljən; ˌtriːdi'siljən] *n., pl.* **-lions, -lion,** *adj.* —*n.* (在美法)1後加42個0之數;(在英德)1後加78個0之數。—*adj.* 上述之數的。

:tree [tri; triː] *n., v.,* **treed, tree·ing.** —*n.* ①樹;樹木。to take shelter under a *tree.* 在樹下避(雨,日)。②特殊目的用的木頭。a clothes *tree.* 衣帽架。③似樹木之物。a family *tree.* 家系圖。④〖古〗絞架;絞首臺。⑤〖古〗(耶穌受難之)十字架。⑥聖誕樹(=Christmas tree). ***at the top of the tree*** 居於事業或職業中的最高地位。***up a tree*** 在困難的處境中;進退維谷。—*v.t.* ①驅使上樹。②以某種特殊用之木器等供備。③把鞋楦裝入(鞋)中。④〖俗〗使處於困境。—**like,** *adj.*

tree creeper 旋木雀。

treed [trid; triːd] *adj.* ①種有樹木的。a *treed* hillside. 種有樹木的山坡。②被趕上樹的。③裝(鞋、鞍、衣帽)架的。

tree farm 林場;林班。

tree fern 〖植物〗桫欏(熱帶產之蕨類植物)。

tree frog 樹蛙;雨蛙。(亦作**tree toad**)

tree house ①(菲律賓羣島之)樹上小屋。②供小孩遊玩的樹上小屋。

tree·less ['trilɪs; 'triːlis] *adj.* 無樹木的。a *treeless* plain. 無樹木的平原。

tree line (山上之)樹木生長線。

tree·lined ['triˌlaɪnd; 'triːlaind] *adj.* 沿途有樹的。a *treelined* road. 沿途有樹的道路。

tree milk 樹乳。

tre·en ['triən; 'triːən] *adj.* 全部木造的。—*n.* 全部木造器具。

tree·nail ['triˌnel; 'triːneil, 'trenl] *n.* (造船用的)大木釘。(亦作 **trenail, trunnel**)

tre·en·ware ['triənˌwɛr; 'triːənˌwɛə] *n.* 木造家庭用具、碟盤等。

tree of Buddha 菩提樹。

tree of knowledge (of good and evil) 〖聖經〗智慧樹;分別善惡之樹(植於伊甸園中央,所結之禁果曾爲亞當與夏娃所食,見舊約聖經創世記第三章)。

tree of life 〖聖經〗生命樹(植於伊甸園中之樹,食其果實後,卽可永生,見創世記2章9節及3章22節)。

tree peony 〖植物〗牡丹。

tree ring 年輪。

tree·scape ['triˌskep; 'triː-skeip] *n.* 多樹的風景或畫。

tree surgeon 精於處理傷腐樹木之人。

tree surgery 傷腐樹木之處理(如補洞、處理傷處等)。

tree toad 樹蛙;雨蛙。

tree·top ['triˌtɑp; 'triːtɔp] *n.* 樹梢。

tref [tref; treif] *adj.* 爲猶太法所禁止的。

tre·foil ['trifɔɪl; 'trefɔil] *n.* ①〖植物〗車軸草。②〖建築〗三葉模飾。—*adj.* 三葉形的。

tre·foiled ['trifɔɪld; 'trefɔild] *adj.* ①三葉形的。②有三葉模飾的。

treil·lage ['trelɪdʒ; 'treilidʒ] *n.* 格子細工;格子牆;(籐類植物蔓延的)格子籬。

trek [trɛk; trek] *v.,* **trekked, trek·king,** *n.* —*v.i.* ①(在南非)乘牛車慢慢旅行。②緩慢艱辛地旅行。—*v.t.* (在南非,牛)拖(車)。—*n.*①(在南非)牛車旅行;旅行。②牛車旅行中之一段行程;一段旅行。③移居。(亦作**treck**)

trel·lis ['trɛlɪs; 'trelis] *n.* ①格子架;格子棚。②以格子棚蓋成之涼亭或蔭道。—*v.t.* ①裝設格子架或格子棚。*trellised* windows. 格子窗。②以格子架或格子棚支撐(蔓生植物)。③使交叉或交織成格子。—**ed,** *adj.*

trel·lis·work ['trɛlɪsˌwɝk; 'treliswəːk] *n.* (木條或金屬編的)格子細工。

trem·a·tode ['trɛməˌtod; 'tremətoud] *n., adj.* 〖動物〗吸蟲類之寄生蟲(的)。(亦作 **trematoid**)

:trem·ble ['trɛmbl; 'trembl] *v.,* **-bled, -bling,** *n.* —*v.i.* ①戰慄;震顫;發抖。His voice *trembled* with anger. 他的聲音因憤怒而震顫。②恐懼;疑懼;憂慮。I *tremble* for your safety. 我擔憂你的安全。③微動;搖擺。***in fear and trembling*** 神經質地;膽怯地;渾身抖着。***tremble for someone*** 擔心或憂慮某人。***tremble to think*** 想到…就恐懼或憂慮。—*n.* ①戰慄;震顫。She was all of a *tremble.* 她渾身顫抖。②(*pl.*)(作*sing.*解)〖醫〗引起發抖的疾病(如瘧疾等)。

trem·bler ['trɛmblə; 'tremblə] *n.* ①震顫者。②=**Quaker.** ③〖電機〗電震板。

trem·bling ['trɛmblɪŋ; 'tremblɪŋ] *n.* 震顫;抖顫。—*adj.* 震顫的;抖顫的。—**ly,** *adv.*

trem·bly ['trɛmblɪ; 'trembli] *adj.,* **-bli·er, -bli·est.** 震動的;顫抖的;戰慄的。

***tre·men·dous** [trɪ'mɛndəs; tri'mendəs] *adj.* ①可怕的。a *tremendous* defeat. 慘敗。②〖俗〗巨大的;非常的。③〖俗〗非常好的。—*adv.* 〖俗〗巨大地;非常地。—**ly,** *adv.* —**ness,** *n.*

tre·mo·lan·do [ˌtremo'lɑndo; ˌtreimou'lɑːndou] 〖義〗*adj.* 〖音樂〗顫音的。

trem·o·lant ['trɛmolənt; 'tremoulənt] *adj.* 〖音樂〗有顫音的(風琴等)。—*n.* (風琴等之)顫音裝置。

trem·o·lo ['trɛməˌlo; 'tremələu] *n., pl.* **-los.** 〖義〗①〖音樂〗顫音。②(風琴等上)

發顫音之裝置。
trem·or ['trɛmɚ; 'tremə] *n.* ①顫抖；震顫。②情緒的激動；興奮。③震動；地震。—less, *adj.* —less·ly, *adv.* —ous, *adj.*
trem·u·lant, trem·u·lent ['trɛmjələnt; 'tremjulənt] *adj.* ①震顫的；震動的。②恐懼的；膽怯的。
***trem·u·lous** ['trɛmjələs; 'tremjuləs] *adj.* ①戰慄的；抖動的。②怯懦的；畏縮的。③(筆跡之)震顫的。—ly, *adv.*—ness, *n.*
***trench** [trɛntʃ; trentʃ] *n.* ①戰壕。②溝；壕溝。③(*pl.*)互相連接的一連串戰壕。—*v.t.* ①圍以溝；在…挖溝；隔絕。②切斷；切開。—*v.i.* ①掘壕；挖溝。②切斷。③侵奪〖on, upon〗。④接近〖on, upon〗。
trench·an·cy ['trɛntʃənsɪ;'trentʃənsi] *n.*①銳利；尖刻；苛刻。②清晰。③有力；有效。
trench·ant ['trɛntʃənt; 'trentʃənt] *adj.* ①尖刻的；苛刻的；銳利的。②清晰的。③有力的；有效的。④徹底的。⑤〖詩〗鋒利的。
trench coat ①一種有帶的軍用防水短上衣。②(軍裝式之)有腰帶和肩帶的厚雨衣。
trench·er ['trɛntʃɚ; 'trentʃə] *n.* ①挖戰壕者；挖溝者。②(切肉用的)大木盤或木板。
trencher cap 〖俗〗(大學生畢業時所戴之)學士帽。
trench·er-fed ['trɛntʃɚ,fɛd; 'trentʃəfed] *adj.* 飼養於獵戶家中的(獵犬等)。
trench·er·man ['trɛntʃɚmən;'trentʃəmən] *n.*, *pl.* **-men.** ①食量大的人。②〖古〗食客；寄食者。
trench fever 〖醫〗戰壕熱(一種熱病)。
trench foot (or **feet**) 〖醫〗戰壕脚(因濕與寒而致的一種脚病)。
trench knife 作肉搏戰時所用的一種短刺刀。
trench mortar 迫擊砲。
trench mouth 〖醫〗喉峽炎。(亦作 **Vincent's angina**)
trench warfare 戰壕戰。
***trend** [trɛnd; trend] *n.* ①趨勢；傾向。②流行；時尚。—*v.i.* ①向；傾向。The road *trends* to the north. 這條路通向北方。②有某種傾向或趨勢。
trend·set·ter ['trɛnd,sɛtɚ; 'trend,setə] *n.* 開啓風尚的人或物。
trend·set·ting ['trɛnd,sɛtɪŋ;'trend,setiŋ] *adj.* 能開啓風尚的。
trend·y ['trɛndɪ; 'trendi] *adj.* 〖英俗〗最流行的；時髦的。
tren·tal ['trɛntl̩; 'trentl] *n.* 天主教對死者在三十日間每日所作之彌撒。
trente et qua·rante [,trɑ̃teka'rɑ̃t; ,trɑ̃teika'rɑ̃t] 〖法〗一種賭博牌戲。(亦作 **rouge et noir**)
tre·pan[1] [trɪ'pæn; tri'pæn] *n.*, *v.*, **-panned, -pan·ning.** —*n.* ①〖外科〗環鋸。②〖礦〗鑽孔機。—*v.t.* ①以環鋸行手術。②以鑽孔機打孔。③將(金屬板等)切成圓盤。
tre·pan[2] *n.*, *v.*, **-panned, -pan·ning.** —*n.* 〖古〗①陷阱；圈套。②設陷阱者；施圈套者。—*v.t.* 〖古〗設陷阱捕捉；設圈套陷害；欺騙。(亦作 **trapan**)
trep·a·na·tion [,trɛpə'neʃən; ,trepə'neiʃən] *n.* 〖外科〗環鑽術(開頭蓋骨之手術)。
tre·pang [trɪ'pæŋ; tri'pæŋ] *n.* 〖動物〗海參。
treph·i·na·tion [,trɛfə'neʃən;,trefi'neiʃən] *n.* 〖外科〗圓鋸手術。
tre·phine [trɪ'faɪn; tri'fi:n, -'fain] *n.*, *v.*, **-phined, -phin·ing.** —*n.* 〖外科〗(開頭蓋時用的)圓鋸。—*v.t.* 以圓鋸行手術。
trep·id ['trɛpɪd; 'trepid] *adj.* 驚恐的；擾亂的。
trep·i·da·tion [,trɛpə'deʃən; ,trepi'deiʃən] *n.* ①驚恐；惶恐。②震顫；戰慄。③(手足或下顎肌肉之)痙攣。
tres [trɛs; tres] *adj.* 〖處方〗三；三個。
***tres·pass** ['trɛspəs; 'trespəs] *v.i.*①侵入；侵犯；侵害〖常 on〗。No *trespassing.* 不准入內。②犯罪；違犯〖against〗。—*n.* ①侵入；侵犯；侵害。②罪過。③〖法律〗非法侵害。④〖法律〗侵害訴訟。
tres·pass·er ['trɛspəsɚ; 'trespəsə] *n.* 侵占他人土地者；侵害者；不法侵入者。
tress [trɛs; tres] *n.* (常*pl.*) 頭髮；鬈髮。
tressed [trɛst; trest] *adj.* 有或結成髮辮的；有或結成髮髻的。
tres·sy ['trɛsɪ; 'tresi] *adj.*, **-si·er, -si·est.** ①似髮辮(髻)的。②飾有髮辮(髻)的。
tres·tle ['trɛsl̩;'tresl]*n.*①支架；櫈架。②叉架；橋架。③(鋪鐵路軌道之)架柱橋；構脚橋。
trestle bridge 架柱橋；構脚橋。
trestle table 櫈架。
trestle tree〖船〗檣頭縱材。(亦作**trestletree**)
trestle work 構脚架；聯合支架；架柱脚。(亦作 **trestlework**)
tret [trɛt; tret] *n.* 〖商〗添量(為補償貨物運搬之耗損，於扣除容器、包裝等重量外，每104磅加添4磅)。
trews [truz; tru:z] *n. pl.* 蘇格蘭高地人穿之緊身格子布褲。
trey [tre; trei] *n.* (骰子、紙牌等之)三點；有三點之骰子或紙牌等。
trf. ①transfer. ②tuned radio frequency. **t.r.f., t-r-f, T.R.F.** tuned radio frequency. **trfd.** transferred.
T.R.H. Their Royal Highnesses.
tri-〖字首〗表"三"之義，如tricycle(三輪車)。
tri·a·ble ['traɪəbl̩; 'traiəbl] *adj.* ①可試驗的。②〖法律〗可審問的；可裁判的。
tri·ad ['traɪæd, -əd;'trai-əd, 'traiæd] *n.* ①三個一組。②〖音樂〗三和音。③〖化〗三價之元素；(性質相似之)三個一組之元素。
tri·age ['traɪɪdʒ; 'traiidʒ] *n.* ①分類。②經分類後之事物。
tri·ag·o·nal [traɪ'ægənl̩; trai'ægənəl] *adj.* 三角的。
‡**tri·al** ['traɪəl; 'traiəl] *n.* ①審訊；審判。He was on *trial* for theft. 他因盜竊罪而受審判。②考驗；試驗。③艱苦；苦難；磨難。Life is full of *trials.* 人生充滿磨難。④煩難的根源；討厭的人或物。⑤試圖；努力。⑥(人員之)試用。 ***on trial*** a. 用於試驗等目的；暫時。b. 試驗後；看試驗的結果。—*adj.* 試驗的；考驗的。an airplane's *trial* flight. 飛機的試飛。
trial and error 嘗試錯誤法。
trial balance 〖簿記〗試算表。
trial balloon ①試驗氣球(測驗氣流、風速等)。②對某計畫所做之民意或反應測驗。
trial by jury 陪審團審判制。
trial court 初審法院。
trial docket 法院待審案件清單。
trial horse 〖俗〗練習或表演時與較强之對手比賽的人。
tri·al·ism ['traɪəlɪzm; 'traiəlizm] *n.* 三國聯邦論或主義。
tri·al·ist ['traɪəlɪst; 'traiəlist] *n.* ①三國聯邦主義者。②〖運動〗參加初賽者。
trial judge 初審法院推事。
trial jury (由十二人組成之)陪審團；小陪審團。
trial lawyer 〖俗〗專門出庭辯護之律師。
trial marriage 試婚。

trial run (機器等之)試車。

***tri·an·gle** [ˈtraɪˌæŋgl̩;ˈtraiæŋgl] *n.* ①三角形。②三角形之物。③〖音樂〗三角鈴。④由三個組成的一組或團體。⑤(男女之)三角關係(通常作 **the eternal triangle**)。⑥(T-)〖天文〗=**Triangulum.**

tri·an·gu·lar [traɪˈæŋgjələ˞; traiˈæŋgjulə] *adj.* ①三角形的。*triangular* compasses. 三脚規。②三人間的;三國間的;三個的; 三個一組的。

tri·an·gu·lar·i·ty [ˌtraɪæŋgjəˈlærətɪ;traiˌæŋgjuˈlæriti] *n.* 三角形;三角關係。

tri·an·gu·lar·ly [traɪˈæŋgjələlɪ; traiˈæŋgjuləli] *adv.* 成三角形地。

tri·an·gu·late [*v.* traɪˈæŋgjəˌlet; traiˈæŋgjuleit *adj.* traɪˈæŋgjəlɪt; traiˈæŋgjulit] *v.*, **-lat·ed, -lat·ing,** *adj.* —*v.t.* ①分爲數個三角形。②以三角測量法測量或繪製(一地區)之圖。③以三角法測量。④使成三角形。 —*adj.* ①三角形的。②有三角形模樣的;成三角形的。 —**ly,** *adv.*

tri·an·gu·la·tion [ˌtraɪæŋgjəˈleʃən; traiˌæŋgjuˈleiʃən] *n.* ①三角測量(術)。②(三角測量中假定之)三角網。③剖分爲三角形。

tri·an·gu·loid [traɪˈæŋgjəlɔɪd; traiˈæŋgjulɔid] *adj.* 略成三角形的。

Tri·an·gu·lum [traɪˈæŋgjuləm;traiˈæŋgjuləm] *n., gen.* **-li** [-ˌlaɪ;-lai].〖天文〗三角座。

tri·ar·chy [ˈtraɪɑrkɪ; ˈtraiɑːki] *n., pl.* **-chies.** ①三頭政治。②由三頭統治之國家。③各有統治者之三國聯邦。④有三個政府之國家。

Tri·as [ˈtraɪəs;ˈtraiəs]*n.*〖地質〗三疊系。

Tri·as·sic [traɪˈæsɪk; traiˈæsik] *adj.*〖地質〗三疊紀的。 ***the Triassic*** 三疊紀。

tri·at·ic stay [traɪˈætɪk~; traiˈætik~]〖航海〗(繫於前桅與主桅上端間的)水平支索。

tri·a·tom·ic [ˌtraɪəˈtɑmɪk; ˌtraiəˈtɔmik] *adj.* ①由三個原子而成的; 一分子中有三個原子的。②有三個可置換之原子的。③三價的。

tri·ax·i·al [traɪˈæksɪəl; traiˈæksiəl] *adj.* 有三軸的。

trib·ade [ˈtrɪbəd; ˈtribəd] *n.* 女性之同性戀者(尤指充任男性角色者)。

trib·a·dism [ˈtrɪbədɪzm̩;ˈtribədizm] *n.* 女性之同性戀。

trib·al [ˈtraɪbl̩;ˈtraibəl] *adj.* 部落的;種族的。

trib·al·ism [ˈtraɪbl̩ɪzm̩;ˈtraibəlizəm] *n.* ①部落之組織、生活及特徵。②對自己宗族、黨派等之忠誠。

trib·al·ize [ˈtraɪbl̩ˌaɪz; ˈtraibəlaiz] *v.t.*, **-ized, -iz·ing.** ①分成各部落。②使部落化。

tri·bas·ic [traɪˈbesɪk; traiˈbeisik] *adj.*〖化〗(酸之)三鹽基的。

tribasic sodium phosphate 〖化〗磷酸鈉。

trib·ble [ˈtrɪbl̩; ˈtribl] *n.* 紙廠中之晾紙架。

‡tribe [traɪb; traib] *n.* ①種族; 部落。Indian *tribes.* 印第安部落。②〖動、植物〗族;類。 the dog *tribe.* 犬族。③ **a.** 儕輩(常含蔑視之意)。 the *tribe* of politicians. 政客之輩。**b.** 家庭;家屬。④一羣人。—**less,***adj.* —**ship,** *n.*

tribe·let [ˈtraɪblɪt; ˈtraiblit] *n.* 小部落;小部族。

tribes·man [ˈtraɪbzmən;ˈtraibzmən] *n., pl.* **-men.**種族(部落)之一員;同種族之人。

tribes·peo·ple[ˈtraɪbzˌpipl̩; ˈtraibzˌpiːpəl] *n. pl.* 部落之成員;部落之人民。

tri·bo·e·lec·tric·i·ty [ˌtrɪboɪˌlɛkˈtrɪsətɪ; ˌtraibouilekˈtrisiti] *n.*〖物理〗摩擦電。

trib·o·let [ˈtrɪbəlɪt; ˈtribəlit] *n.* (製管、環、凹螺旋等所用之) 心棒; 心軸。(亦作 **triblet**)

tri·bom·e·ter [traɪˈbɑmətə˞; traiˈbɔmitə] *n.* 摩擦計。

tri·brach [ˈtraɪbræk; ˈtribræk] *n.*〖詩〗三個短音節之音步。

trib·u·la·tion [ˌtrɪbjəˈleʃən; ˌtribjuˈleiʃən] *n.* 苦難;困苦;憂患。

tri·bu·nal [trɪˈbjunl̩, traɪ-; traiˈbjuːnl, triˈb-] *n.* ①法庭;裁判所。②裁判;批判。③(亦作 **tribune**) 法官席;裁判席。

trib·u·nar·y [ˈtrɪbjuˌnɛrɪ;ˈtribjunəri] *adj.* 護民官的。

trib·u·nate [ˈtrɪbjənɪt; ˈtribjunit] *n.* ①護民官之職位及任期。②護民官之集合稱。

***trib·une** [ˈtrɪbjun; ˈtribjuːn] *n.* ①講壇。②古羅馬之護民官。③民衆的保護人; 支持公衆要求的政治家。〖注意〗作報紙名稱(譯爲論壇報)常讀做 [trɪˈbjun; triˈbjuːn].

trib·une·ship[ˈtrɪbjunˌʃɪp;ˈtribjuːnʃip] *n.* 護民官之職務、地位及任期。

trib·u·ni·tial, trib·u·ni·cial [ˌtrɪbjuˈnɪʃəl; ˌtribjuˈniʃəl] *adj.* 護民官的; 適於護民官的。(亦作 **tribunician, tribunitian**)

***trib·u·tar·y** [ˈtrɪbjəˌtɛrɪ;ˈtribjutəri] *n., pl.* **-tar·ies,** *adj.* —*n.* ①支流。②納貢者;納貢之國。 —*adj.* ①支流的。②納貢的;從屬的。③貢獻的; 補助的。④服屬的。 —**trib·u·tar·i·ly,** *adv.*

trib·ute** [ˈtrɪbjut; ˈtribjuːt] *n.* ①貢;貢金;貢物;貢獻。②表示尊敬或讚美的言辭或行爲。 He paid a high *tribute* to your ability. 他非常稱讚你的能力。floral *tributes.* 獻花。lay a tribute on a country*** (***king***) 使某國(國王)納貢。 ***pay the last tribute to*** 向…作最後致敬;追悼。

tri·car [ˈtraɪˌkɑr;ˈtraikɑː] *n.*三輪摩托脚踏車。

trice[1] [traɪs; trais] *n.*瞬間;頃刻。to come back in a *trice.* 立刻就回來。

trice[2] *v.t.*, **triced, tric·ing.** 拉起並縛住〖up〗.

tri·cen·ni·al [traɪˈsɛnɪəl;traiˈseniəl] *adj.* ①三十年的。②每三十年發生一次的。

tri·cen·te·nar·y [traɪˈsɛntɪˌnɛrɪ; traiˈsentinəri] *adj., n., pl.* **-nar·ies.** = **tercentenary.**

tri·ceps [ˈtraɪsɛps; ˈtraiseps] *n., pl.* **-ceps·es.**〖解剖〗(上臂的) 三頭肌。

tri·ce·ri·um [traɪˈsɪrɪəm; traiˈsiːriəm] *n., pl.* **-ri·a** [-rɪə; -riə].(東正教象徵三位一體的)三支燭臺。(亦作 **tricerion**)

tri·chi·a·sis [trɪˈkaɪəsɪs; triˈkaiəsis] *n.*〖醫〗①毛髮倒生症;倒睫。②毛尿 (尿中呈現毛髮狀物現象)。

tri·chi·na [trɪˈkaɪnə; triˈkainə] *n., pl.* **-nae** [-ni; -niː].〖動物〗旋毛蟲(一種腸寄生蟲)。(亦作 **trichinella**)

trich·i·nize[ˈtrɪkɪˌnaɪz;ˈtrikinaiz]*v.t.*, **-nized, -niz·ing.** 使有旋毛蟲;使患旋毛蟲病。

trich·i·nop·o·li [ˌtrɪtʃɪˈnɑpəlɪ; ˌtritʃiˈnɔpəli] *n.*(印度 Trichinopoly 地方所產的)一種雪茄。(亦作 **trichinopoly, trichi**)

trich·i·no·sis[ˌtrɪkəˈnosɪs;ˌtrikiˈnousis] *n.*〖醫〗旋毛蟲病。(亦作 **trichiniasis**)

trich·i·nous [ˈtrɪkənəs; ˈtrikinəs] *adj.* ①患旋毛蟲病的。②有旋毛蟲寄生的。(亦作 **trichinotic**)

tri·chlo·ride [traɪ'klɔraɪd; trai'klɔːraid] *n.* 【化】含有三個氯原子之鹽。(亦作 **trichlorid**)
tricho- 【字首】表"毛髮"之義。
trich·o·car·pous [ˌtrɪkə'kɑrpəs; ˌtrikə'kɑːpəs] *adj.* 【植物】結有毛之果實的。
trich·o·cyst ['trɪkəsɪst; 'trikəsist] *n.* 【動物】刺細胞。—**ic,** *adj.*
trich·oid ['trɪkɔɪd; 'trikɔid] *adj.* 毛狀的; 髮狀的。
trich·o·log·i·cal [ˌtrɪkə'lɑdʒɪkl; ˌtrikə'lɔdʒikəl] *adj.* 毛髮學的。
tri·chol·o·gist [trɪ'kɑlədʒɪst; tri'kɔlədʒist] *n.* 毛髮學家;研究毛髮學者。
tri·chol·o·gy [trɪ'kɑlədʒɪ; tri'kɔlədʒi] *n.* 毛髮學。
tri·cho·ma [trɪ'komə; tri'koumə] *n., pl.* **-ma·ta** [-mətə; -mətə]. ①【植物】毛茸;毛狀體。②【醫】倒睫。(亦作 **trichome**)
trich·o·mo·ni·a·sis [ˌtrɪkomə'naɪəsɪs; ˌtrikəmə'naiəsis] *n.* 【醫】毛滴蟲病;台可門原蟲病。
tri·chord ['traɪˌkɔrd; 'trai-kɔːd] *n.* 【音樂】三絃琴;有三絃的樂器。—*adj.* 有三絃的。
tri·cho·sis [trɪ'kosɪs; tri'kousis] *n., pl.* **-ses** [-siz; -siːz]. 【醫】髮病。
tri·chot·o·my [traɪ'kɑtəmɪ; trai'kɔtəmi] *n.* 三分;分爲三部分;(尤指神學上)將人分爲肉體、精神與靈魂三部分。
tri·chro·mat ['traɪkroˌmæt; 'traikroumæt] *n.* 【眼科】有三色視覺的人。
tri·chro·mat·ic [ˌtraɪkro'mætɪk; ˌtraikrou'mætik] *adj.* (有)三色的;用三色的;三色版的。(亦作 **trichromic**)
trichromatic photography 天然色照像(術)。
tri·chro·ma·tism [traɪ'kromətɪzəm; trai'kroumətizəm] *n.* ①三色。②三色之使用;三色之調和。(亦作 **trichromatopsia**)
tri·chrome [traɪ'krom; 'traikroum] *adj.* 三色的。
‡**trick** [trɪk; trik] *n.* ①詭計;奸計;欺詐手段。He got the money from me by a *trick.* 他以詭計從我取得這筆錢。②巧技;技藝;妙訣。My dog knows no *tricks.* 我的狗不會玩甚麼把戲。③假裝或不實之物;幻覺。④幻術;戲法。⑤惡作劇。a mean *trick.* 下流的惡作劇。⑥特別的習慣。the *trick* of frowning. 好皺眉頭的習慣。⑦【牌戲】一圈所打之牌的磴數或點數。⑧【航海】舵手的輪值時間。the night *trick.* 夜勤。⑨【俗】小孩;少女。a pretty little *trick.* 漂亮的少女。⑩值班的時間。⑪【俚】**a.** 嫖客。**b.** 妓女與嫖客之交易。***dirty trick*** 卑劣行爲。***do* (or *turn*) *the trick*** 將困難工作做好;達到目的;順遂。***I know a trick worth two of that.*** 我知道更好的方法。***play a trick on a person*** 詐騙某人;開(某人)玩笑。***take* (or *win*) *a trick*** 【牌戲】贏一圈。—*adj.* ①巧技的。*trick* shooting. 特技射擊。②奸計的。③爲變戲法而設計的。a *trick* chair. 魔術椅。—*v.t.* ①欺騙。He was *tricked* out of his money. 他的錢被人騙去。②修飾;打扮【常 out, up】。She is *tricked* out in jewels. 她打扮得珠光寶氣。—*v.i.* 騙人;玩把戲【常 with】。—**less,** *adj.*
trick·er ['trɪkə; 'trikə] *n.* 欺詐者;惡作劇者;玩把戲者。
trick·er·y ['trɪkərɪ; 'trikəri] *n., pl.* **-er·ies.** 欺詐;欺騙;詭計;奸計。
trick·i·ly ['trɪkəlɪ; 'trikili] *adv.* ①奸詐地;欺詐地;欺騙地。②複雜地;難解決地。
trick·i·ness ['trɪkɪnɪs; 'trikinis] *n.* 詭詐;奸詐;瞞騙;困難。
trick·ing ['trɪkɪŋ; 'trikiŋ] *n.* ①欺騙;②裝飾。
trick·ish ['trɪkɪʃ; 'trikiʃ] *adj.* 狡猾的;詭詐的;無賴的。—**ly,** *adv.* —**ness,** *n.*
***trick·le** ['trɪkl; 'trikl] *v.,* **trick·led, trick·ling,** *n.* —*v.i.* ①滴流;細流。②慢慢地來、去、經過等。—*v.t.* 使慢慢滴流。—*n.* ①細流。②滴;滴流;慢慢地來、去、經過等。
trick·let ['trɪklɪt; 'triklit] *n.* 細流;小溪。
trick or treat ①萬聖節(Halloween)時小孩挨戶訪問要糖果,水果等習俗,如不給小孩卽做各種惡作劇。②上述之要求。
trick-or-treat ['trɪkə'trit; 'trikə'triːt] *v.i.* 參加 trick or treat 遊戲。—**er,** *n.*
trick·some ['trɪksəm; 'triksəm] *adj.* ①好惡作劇的。②狡猾的。
trick·ster ['trɪkstə; 'trikstə] *n.* 欺騙者;騙子;狡詐者;狡徒。—**ing,** *n.*
trick·sy ['trɪksɪ; 'triksi] *adj.,* **-si·er, -si·est.** ①好惡作劇的;好開玩笑的。②欺詐的;狡猾的。③精緻的;漂亮的。
trick·y ['trɪkɪ; 'triki] *adj.,* **trick·i·er, trick·i·est.** ①好惡作劇的;奸詐的。②複雜的;難處理的。
tri·clin·i·um [traɪ'klɪnɪəm; trai'kliniəm] *n., pl.* **-i·a** [-ɪə; -iə]. ①(古羅馬的)圍繞餐桌三面之長榻(供就餐時休息之用)。②備有此種長榻之餐室。
tric·o·line ['trɪkəlɪn; 'trikəlin] *n.* 絲狀棉毛葛。
tri·col·o(u)r ['traɪˌkʌlə; 'trikələ] *adj.* 三色的。—*n.* 三色旗(尤指法國國旗)。
tri·col·o(u)red ['traɪˌkʌləd; 'traiˌkʌləd] *adj.* 有三色的;三色的。
tri·corn ['traɪkɔrn; 'traikɔːn] *adj.* ①有三角的。②有三個角隅的。—*n.* ①三角帽;船形帽(=tricorne). ②一種想像中的三角獸。
tri·corne ['traɪkɔrn; 'traikɔːn] *n.* 三角帽;船形帽。
tri·cor·nered ['traɪ'kɔrnəd; 'trai'kɔːnəd] *adj.* 有三個角隅的。
tri·cot ['triko; 'trikou] *n.* ①一種編或織的羊毛、絲、棉、人造絲或尼龍織物。②一種有稜線之布(用以做衣服者)。
tric·o·tine [ˌtrɪkə'tin; ˌtrikə'tiːn] *n.* 做制服用的一種雙斜紋布。
tri·cus·pid [traɪ'kʌspɪd; trai'kʌspid] *adj.* ①有三尖的。②【解剖】三尖瓣的。—*n.* ①(心臟之)三尖瓣。②牙齒。
tricuspid valve 【解剖】三尖瓣。
tri·cy·cle ['traɪsɪkl; 'traisikl] *n., v.,* **-cled, -cling.** —*n.* ①三輪車(跛者或兒童乘坐的)。②三輪汽車。—*v.i.* 乘坐三輪車。
tri·cy·clist ['traɪsɪklɪst; 'traisiklist] *n.* 騎三輪車者;駕駛三輪摩托車者。
tri·dac·tyl [traɪ'dæktɪl; trai'dæktil] *adj.* 有三指(或趾)的。(亦作 **tridactylous**)
tri·dent ['traɪdn̩t; 'traidənt] *n.* ①【希臘、羅馬神話】(海神Poseidon或Neptune所持之)三叉戟。②三叉魚叉;三尖叉。③古羅馬鬥士表演時用之三叉戟。—*adj.* (亦作 **tridental**) 三叉的。
tri·den·tate [traɪ'dentet; trai'denteit] *adj.* ①有三齒(尖)的。②有三叉的。
tri·di·men·sion·al [ˌtraɪdə'mɛnʃənl; ˌtraidi'menʃənl] *adj.* 有長寬厚三度的;立體的;三度空間的。
***tried** [traɪd; traid] *v.* pt. & pp. of **try.** —*adj.* ①經過試驗的;可信賴的。a *tried*

friend. 可靠的朋友。②受磨鍊的；受過痛苦的；經歷艱辛的。

tried-and-true [ˈtraɪdənˈtru; ˈtraidənˈtruː] *adj.* 經試驗而可靠的；靠得住的。

tri·en·ni·al [traɪˈɛnɪəl; traiˈenjəl] *adj.* ①延續了三年的。②每三年出現一次的。—*n.* ①每三年有一次的事件。②三周年紀念。③三年生植物。④三年之期間。—**ly,** *adv.*

tri·er [ˈtraɪɚ; ˈtraiə] *n.* ①試驗者；試驗物。②審問者。③盡力工作者。

tri·fid [ˈtraɪfɪd; ˈtraifid] *adj.* 三裂的「(葉等)。」

tri·fle** [ˈtraɪfḷ; ˈtraifl] *n., v.,* **-fled, -fling.** —*n.* ①瑣事；小事；瑣物。to waste one's time on *trifles.* 爲無意義的事情而耗費時間。②少量；少許；少量金錢。The repairs cost only a *trifle.* 修理只花很少的錢。③一種用乳蛋糕、水果、酒等做成的甜食。④白鑞(錫鉛等之合金)。⑤(*pl.*) 此種白鑞器皿。⑥無價值的文學作品、音樂或藝術品等。a trifle*** 稍微；有點；一點 (用作副詞，與述部形容詞或其相當語句連用，通常後面接 too)。This bag is *a trifle* (too) heavy. 這袋稍重一點。—*v.i.* ①玩忽；疏忽〖常with〗. You should not *trifle* with your health. 你不應該疏忽你的健康。②耍弄；戲弄。to *trifle* with a person's feelings. 玩弄某人的感情。③虛費光陰。—*v.t.* 浪費；虛耗〖常 away〗. —**tri·fler,** *n.*

trifle ring 九連環(一種玩具)。

***tri·fling** [ˈtraɪflɪŋ; ˈtraifliŋ] *adj.* ①無關重要的；微小的。a *trifling* error. 小錯誤。②玩忽的；輕率的；淺陋的。a *trifling* talk. 輕率的談話。③〖美方〗下流的；無價值的。—*n.* ①輕率的談話、行爲。②愚蠢的拖延；浪費時間。

tri·fo·cal [traɪˈfokḷ; traiˈfoukl] *adj.* 三焦點的；有三焦點的。—*n.* ①三焦點透鏡。②(*pl.*)三焦點眼鏡。

tri·fo·li·ate [traɪˈfolɪɪt; traiˈfouliit] *adj.*①(有)三葉的。②〖植物〗=**trifoliolate.**

tri·fo·li·o·late [ˌtraɪfoˈlaɪəˌlet; ˌtraifouˈlaiəleit] *adj.* 〖植物〗①(葉)有三小葉的。②有三小葉之葉的。

tri·fo·ri·um [traɪˈforɪəm; traiˈfɔːriəm] *n., pl.* **-ri·a** [-rɪə; -riə]. 〖建築〗教堂中部，唱詩班席位或袖廊之拱上的拱廊或廂。

tri·form(ed) [ˈtraɪfɔrm(d); ˈtraifɔːm(d)] *adj.* 有三部分的；有三種形式的；有三種性質的。

tri·fur·cate [*adj.* traɪˈfɝkɪt; traiˈfəːkit *v.* traɪˈfɝket; traiˈfəːkeit] *adj., v.,* **-cat·ed, -cat·ing.** —*adj.* 有三枝的；有三叉的。—*v.i.* 分成三枝或三叉。

trig[1] [trɪg; trig] *adj., v.,* **trigged, trig·ging.** —*adj.* ①漂亮的；整潔的。②健康的；強壯的。***make trig*** 穿着漂亮或整齊。—*v.t.* 使整潔；修飾〖常 up, out〗.

trig[2] *v.,* **trigged, trig·ging,** *n.* —*v.t.* 以楔形木支撐或制止 (輪)。—*v.i.* 制止輪之轉動。—*n.* 制輪轉動用的木楔等。

trig[3] *n.* 〖俗〗三角學(學生用語)。

trig. ①trigonometric. ②trigonometrical. ③trigonometry.

trig·a·mist [ˈtrɪgəmɪst; ˈtrigəmist] *n.* ①有三夫(或三妻)之人。②結婚三次之人。

trig·a·mous [ˈtrɪgəməs; ˈtrigəməs] *adj.* ①一夫三妻的；一妻三夫的。②〖植物〗有三種花(即雄花、雌花、兩性花)的。

trig·a·my [ˈtrɪgəmɪ; ˈtrigəmi] *n.* ①一夫三妻；一妻三夫。②結婚三次。

tri·gem·i·nal [traɪˈdʒɛmənḷ; traiˈdʒeminəl] *adj.* 〖解剖〗三叉神經的。—*n.* 〖解剖〗三叉神經。

tri·gem·i·nous [traɪˈdʒɛmənəs; traiˈdʒeminəs] *adj.* 三胞胎的；三胞胎之一的。

tri·gem·i·nus [traɪˈdʒɛmənəs; traiˈdʒeminəs] *n., pl.* **-ni** [-naɪ; -nai]. 〖解剖〗三叉神經。

tri·ges·i·mo-se·cun·do [traɪˈdʒɛsəˌmosəˈkʌndo; traiˈdʒesimousiˈkʌndou] *adj.* 〖裝釘〗三十二開。

trig·ger [ˈtrɪgɚ; ˈtrigə] *n.* ①(槍的)扳機。②〖機械〗制輪機；制滑器。③能引起或促起一連串連鎖反應的事或行爲。④〖俗〗=**triggerman.** ***quick on the trigger*** a. 射擊迅速。b.〖俗〗迅速行動；敏於了解；機警。—*v.t.* ①引起或促起(一連串的連鎖反應)。②扣…之扳機。

trigger finger 扣扳機的手指(食指)。***have an itchy trigger finger*** 動不動就開鎗。

trig·ger·fish [ˈtrɪgɚˌfɪʃ; ˈtrigəfiʃ] *n., pl.* **-fish, -fish·es.** 一種顏色鮮麗的熱帶魚(其前脊鰭上有二三肥刺)。

trig·ger-hap·py [ˈtrɪgɚˌhæpɪ; ˈtrigəˌhæpi] *adj.* 〖俗〗①不計後果，喜歡亂開槍的。②好戰的。③好指出別人的缺點或錯誤的。

trig·ger·man [ˈtrɪgɚˌmæn; ˈtrigəmən] *n., pl.* **-men.** 〖俗〗①專門用槍殺人的流氓。②流氓頭子的保鑣。(亦作 **trigger**)

tri·glot [ˈtraɪglɑt; ˈtraiglɔt] *adj.* 有三種語言的；以三種語言印的；說或寫三種語言的。—*n.* 用三種文字的書或版本。

tri·glyph [ˈtraɪglɪf; ˈtraiglif] *n.* 〖建築〗豎條紋飾。

tri·gon [ˈtraɪgɑn; ˈtraigən] *n.* ①(古希臘之) 三角琴。②〖天文〗兩行星相距一百二十度之位置或方位。③三角形。

trigon. ①trigonometric. ②trigonometrical. ③trigonometry.

trig·o·nal [ˈtrɪgənəl; ˈtrigənəl] *adj.* ①三角形的。②〖結晶〗三方晶系的。③〖動、植物〗斷面呈三角形的。

trig·o·nom·e·ter [ˌtrɪgəˈnɑmətɚ; ˌtrigəˈnɔmitə] *n.* 直角三角計。

trig·o·no·met·ric [ˌtrɪgənəˈmɛtrɪk; ˌtrigənəˈmetrik] *adj.* 三角學的；以三角學方法完成的。

trig·o·no·met·ri·cal [ˌtrɪgənəˈmɛtrɪkḷ; ˌtrigənəˈmetrikəl] *adj.*=**trigonometric.**

trig·o·nom·e·try [ˌtrɪgəˈnɑmətrɪ; ˌtrigəˈnɔmitri] *n.* 三角法；三角學。

tri·gram [ˈtraɪgræm; ˈtraigræm] *n.* =**trigraph.**

tri·graph [ˈtraɪgræf; ˈtraigrɑːf] *n.* 代表一個音的三個字母(如bureau 中之 *eau*).

tri·he·dral [traɪˈhidrəl; traiˈhiːdrəl] *adj.* 〖幾何〗三面形的；有三面的。—*n.*三面形。

tri·he·dron [traɪˈhidrən; traiˈhiːdrən] *n., pl.* **-drons, -dra** [-drə; -drə]. 〖幾何〗三面體。

tri·jet [ˈtraɪˌdʒɛt; ˈtraidʒet] *n.* 有三具「噴射引擎的飛機。」

trike [traɪk; traik] *n.* 〖俗〗三輪車。

tri·lat·er·al [traɪˈlætərəl; traiˈlætərəl] *adj.* 〖幾何〗三邊的。—*n.* 三邊形。

tril·by [ˈtrɪlbɪ; ˈtrilbi] *n., pl.* **-bies.** ①〖英〗一種男用軟呢帽 (亦作 **trilby hat**)。②(*pl.*)〖俚〗脚。

tri·lin·gual [traɪˈlɪŋgwəl; ˈtraiˈliŋgwəl] *adj.* 三種語言的。—*n.* 三種語言寫成的題名或獻詞。

tri·lit·er·al [traɪˈlɪtərəl; ˈtraiˈlitərəl] *adj.* 包含三個字母的。—*n.* ①由三個字母組成之字。②由三個字母組成之字根。

trill [trɪl; tril] *v.t.* & *v.i.* ①發顫聲; 以顫聲說出。②以顫音唱、奏等。③用捲舌發出(抖顫的 r 音)。—*n.* ①抖顫聲; 顫聲。②〖音樂〗顫音。③〖語音〗a. 舌部等之快速的抖顫。b. 捲舌發出的 r 抖顫音 (如西班牙文的 rr 是)。

tril·lion [ˈtrɪljən; ˈtriljən] *n.* ①(在美法兩國爲)兆(=1,000,000,000,000)。②(在英德兩國爲)百萬兆(=1,000,000,000,000,000,000)。—*adj.* 兆的; 百萬兆的。

Tril·li·um [ˈtrɪlɪəm; ˈtriliəm] *n.* 〖植物〗①延齡草屬。②(t-)延齡草屬植物; 延齡草。

tri·lo·bate [traɪˈlobet; traiˈloubeit] *adj.* 有三裂片的(葉等)。

tri·lo·bite [ˈtraɪlə͵baɪt; ˈtrailəbait] *n.* 〖古生物〗三葉蟲。—**tri·lo·bit·ic,** *adj.*

tri·loc·u·lar [traɪˈlɑkjʊlɚ; traiˈlɔkjulə] *adj.* 有三室的; 有三房的; 有三洞的。

tril·o·gy [ˈtrɪlədʒɪ; ˈtrilədʒi] *n., pl.* **-gies.** (戲劇、歌劇、小說等)三部曲。

***trim** [trɪm; trim] *v.,* **trimmed, trim·ming,** *adj., n., adv.* —*v.t.* ①使整潔; 使整齊; 修整; 整飾; 修剪。to *trim* one's nails. 修剪指甲。②裝飾。to *trim* a Christmas tree. 裝飾耶誕樹。③安排所載貨物重量使(船、飛機等)平衡。④調整(船帆)以適應風向。⑤〖俗〗擊敗; 笞; 打。⑥〖俗〗譴責; 申斥。⑦看情勢修正(意見)。⑧〖航空〗將飛機拉平。⑨在(陳列櫥窗中)排貨色。⑩調節(火, 燈心)。—*v.i.* ①採取兩面討好政策; 騎牆。That politician is always *trimming.* 那個政客老是採取騎牆態度。②〖航海〗a. 保持平衡。b. 調節船帆。—*adj.* 整齊的; 整潔的。—*n.* ①整齊; 整潔。The room is in good *trim.* 這房間甚爲整潔。②準備狀態。③服裝; 裝束。in hunting *trim.* 着獵裝。④裝飾。⑤飛機、船等之平衡狀態。out of *trim.* 失去平衡。⑥(建築物內部之)可見的木工部分。⑦(建築物外部之)用作外層或裝飾的木工。⑧陳列櫥窗的裝飾。⑨修剪下來的碎物。⑩理髮(理成原狀的)。—*adv.* 整齊地; 整潔地。—**ly,** *adv.* —**ness,** *n.*

tri·mes·ter [traɪˈmɛstɚ; traiˈmestə] *n.* 三個月期間; 三個月一期。

tri·mes·tri·al [traɪˈmɛstrɪəl; traiˈmestriəl] *adj.* 每三個月一度的; 每季的。

tri·me·tal·lic [͵traɪməˈtælɪk; ͵traiməˈtælik] *adj.* 三種金屬的。

trim·e·ter [ˈtrɪmətɚ; ˈtrimitə] *n.* 三音步的詩。—*adj.* 三音步的。

tri·met·ri·cal [traɪˈmɛtrɪkl; traiˈmetrikəl] *adj.* ①有三音步的。②〖結晶〗斜方晶系的。(亦作 **trimetric**)

tri·met·ro·gon [traɪˈmɛtrə͵gɑn; traiˈmetrəgɔn] *n.* 三角點俯瞰攝影法。

trim·mer [ˈtrɪmɚ; ˈtrimə] *n.* ①整修者; 整修之器具。②改變意見、行爲等以迎合環境者; 騎牆者。③整理、裝載貨物、煤炭等之機器。

trim·ming [ˈtrɪmɪŋ; ˈtrimiŋ] *n.* ①整修; 修剪。②裝飾。③(*pl.*)修整時被剪去的部分。④(*pl.*)一道菜之配料。⑤〖俗〗叱責; 申斥。⑥〖俗〗擊敗。⑦(*pl.*)〖俗〗外快。

tri·month·ly [traɪˈmʌnθlɪ; traiˈmʌnθli] *adj.* 每三個月一次的。

tri·mo·tor [ˈtraɪ͵motɚ; ˈtrai͵moutə] *n.* 三引擎飛機。

tri·nal [ˈtraɪnl; ˈtrainl] *adj.* 有三部分的; 三倍的; 三重的。

tri·na·ry [ˈtraɪnərɪ; ˈtrainəri] *adj.* 由三部分所成的; 三倍的; 三重的。

trine [traɪn; train] *adj.* ①三倍的; 三重的; 三層的。②〖天文〗二行星相距一百二十度的。—*n.* ①三個一組; 三個一羣。②(T-)三位一體 (=Trinity). ③〖天文〗兩行星相距一百二十度之關係位置。

trine immersion (or **aspersion**) 〖宗教〗受洗時三次浸入水中或滴水於受洗者頭部之動作(寓意於三位一體之神)。

Trin·i·dad [ˈtrɪnə͵dæd; ˈtrinidæd] *n.* 千里達島(在委內瑞拉之東北, 1962年成爲千里達—托貝哥共和國之一部分)。

Trinidad and Tobago 千里達—托貝哥(西印度羣島之一共和國, 英國協會員國, 首都西班牙港 Port-of-Spain).

Trin·i·tar·i·an [͵trɪnəˈtɛrɪən; ͵triniˈtɛəriən] *adj.* ①三位一體的; 三位一體論的; 信仰三位一體的。②(t-)三重的; 三倍的。—*n.* 信仰三位一體論者; 三位一體論者。

Trin·i·tar·i·an·ism [͵trɪnəˈtɛrɪə͵nɪzəm; ͵triniˈtɛəriənizəm] *n.* 〖宗教〗三位一體論; 三位一體之教理; 三位一體之信仰。

tri·ni·tro·tol·u·ene [traɪ͵naɪtroˈtɑljʊ͵in; traiˈnaitrouˈtɔljuiːn] *n.* 一種强烈之黃色炸藥。(略作 **TNT, T.N.T.**)

tri·ni·tro·tol·u·ol [traɪ͵naɪtroˈtɑljʊol; traiˈnaitrouˈtɔljuɔl] *n.* =**trinitrotoluene.**

***trin·i·ty** [ˈtrɪnətɪ; ˈtriniti] *n.* ①三個之一組。②(T-)三位一體(基督敎中指聖父、聖子及聖靈合成一位神之謂)。③(T-)〖俗〗=**Trinity Sunday.**

Trinity House 〖英〗領港公會; 海務局。

Trinity sitting 〖英〗高等法院六月九日至七月三十一日之開庭期。

Trinity Sunday 聖三主日(Whitsunday後的禮拜天; 復活節後第八個星期日)。

Trinity term 〖英〗①牛津大學的學期之一。②=**Trinity sitting.**

trin·ket [ˈtrɪŋkɪt; ˈtriŋkit] *n.* ①精美小飾物。②價値很小的寶石。③瑣物。④小玩意。

tri·no·mi·al [traɪˈnomɪəl; traiˈnoumjəl] *adj.* ①〖數學〗三項式的。②〖動、植物〗三名法的; 用三名法的。—*n.* ①〖數學〗三項式。②〖動、植物〗依三名法命名之學名(即一動物或植物之學名, 包括三個名, 依次指明其屬、種、亞種或變種)。

tri·o [ˈtrio, ˈtraɪo; ˈtri(ː)ou] *n., pl.* **tri·os.** ①三人或三物之一組。②〖音樂〗三人奏(唱)。③三重奏(唱)曲。

tri·ode [ˈtraɪod; ˈtraioud] *n.* 〖電子〗三極眞空管。

tri·o·let [ˈtraɪəlɪt; ˈtri(ː)oulet] *n.* 八行兩韻詩或詩節。

Tri·o·nes [traɪˈoniz; traiˈouniːz] *n. pl.* 〖天文〗北斗七星。

tri·or [ˈtraɪɚ; ˈtraiə] *n.* =**trier.**

tri·ox·id [traɪˈɑksɪd; traiˈɔksid] *n.* 〖化〗三氧化物。

tri·ox·ide [traɪˈɑksaɪd; traiˈɔksaid] *n.* 〖化〗三氧化物。

‡trip [trɪp; trip] *n., v.,* **tripped, trip·ping.** —*n.* ①旅行; 遠足。to make (*or* take) a *trip* to Hangchow. 去杭州旅行。②顚躓; 失足。③摔倒; 絆倒。④差錯; 過失。A *trip* in one point would spoil all. 棋錯一着, 滿盤皆輸。⑤輕快之脚步。⑥〖機械〗擋器; 掣子。*trip* dog. 絆擋; 跳動擋。—*v.i.* ①顚躓; 跌倒。He *tripped* over the root of a tree. 他被樹根絆倒。②犯過失。③以輕快的脚步跑或跳。④傾斜; 歪。⑤旅行。⑥言語不清。—*v.t.* ①使顚躓; 絆跌。②使犯錯誤。③發覺(某人的)錯誤〖up〗。④〖機械〗鬆開掣子以發動; 鬆動(某部分)。***trip the light fantastic***

去跳舞。

tri·par·tite (traɪ'pɑrtaɪt, 'trɪpɚ,taɪt; 'trai'pɑːtait) *adj.* ①分爲三部分的。②有相同之三部分的。③三者間的;三方締結的。a *tripartite* agreement. 三方協定。

tripe (traɪp; traip) *n.* ①牛等之胃(供食用者);牛、豬、羊等之肚。②【俗】無意義或無價值的東西。③內臟。

trip·ham·mer ('trɪp,hæmɚ; 'trip,hæmə) *n.* (亦作 **trip-hammer, trip hammer**)【機械】大槌;反槌。—*adj.* ①大槌的。②如以大槌連續擊打的。

tri·phib·i·an (traɪ'fɪbɪən; trai'fibiən) *n.* ①海陸空聯合作戰指揮官。②能從陸上、水上、雪或冰上起飛的飛機。—*adj.* ①海陸空聯合作戰的。②(飛機)能從陸上、水上、雪地或冰上起飛的。

tri·phib·i·ous (traɪ'fɪbɪəs; trai'fibiəs) *adj.* =**triphibian.**

triph·thong ('trɪfθɔŋ; 'trifθɔŋ) *n.* ①三元音;三重母音。②=**trigraph.**

tripl. triplicate.

tri·plane ('traɪ,plen; 'traiplein) *n.* (早期之)三翼飛機。

***tri·ple** ('trɪpl̩; 'tripl) *adj., n., v.,* **-pled, -pling.** —*adj.* ①三部分合成的。②三倍的;三重的。—*n.* ①三倍。②【棒球】三壘打。—*v.t.* 使成三倍。—*v.i.* ①成爲三倍。②【棒球】擊出三壘打。

Triple Alliance 三國同盟。

triple crown (羅馬教宗之)三重冠。

Triple Entente 【法】三國協商(指1907年英、法、俄三國所簽定的協約);參加此三國協商之三個國家。

triple-expansion engine 【機械】三聯式引擎。

triple play 【棒球】三殺(使三人出局)。

tri·ple-space ('trɪpl̩'spes; 'tripl'speis) *v.t. & v.i.,* **-spaced, -spac·ing.** 隔雙行打字(每三行空間打一行字)。

tri·plet ('trɪplɪt; 'triplit) *n.* ①同胎三嬰兒之一。②三個所組成之一組。③【音樂】三連音符。④【詩】三行連句。

triple threat ①【橄欖球】能跑、能踢、能傳的三全選手。②精通三種不同學術或技術的專家。

tri·ple-threat ('trɪpl̩'θrɛt; 'tripl'θret) *adj.* 具有三種專長的。

triple time 【音樂】三拍子。

tri·plex ('trɪplɛks; 'tripleks) *adj.* ①三倍的。②三重的。③由三部分所構成的。④有三層的。—*n.* ①【音樂】三拍子。②三重或三倍之事物。

trip·li·cate (*v.* 'trɪplə,ket; 'triplikeit *adj., n.* 'trɪpləkɪt; 'triplikit) *v.,* **-cat·ed, -cat·ing,** *adj., n.* —*v.t.* ①使成三倍。②將(文件)作成三分。—*adj.* ①三倍的;三重的。②一式三分的(文件)。a *triplicate* certificate (agreement). 一式三分的證書(契約)。③一式三分(的文件)之第三分的。—*n.*完全相同的三物之一;一式三分的文件之一。*in triplicate* 一式三分的。a document drawn up *in triplicate*. 擬成一式三分的文件。

trip·li·ca·tion (,trɪplə'keʃən; ,tripli'keiʃən) *n.* 三倍;三重;一式三分。

tri·plic·i·ty (trɪ'plɪsətɪ; tri'plisiti) *n., pl.* **-ties.** ①三倍;三重。②三個一組。③【天文】=**trigon.**

trip·loid ('trɪplɔɪd; 'triplɔid) *adj.* 【生物】(染色體之)三倍數的。—*n.* 有三倍數染色體之細胞或有機體。

tri·ply ('trɪplɪ; 'tripli) *adv.* 三重地;三倍地。

tri·pod ('traɪpɑd; 'traipɔd) *n.* 三脚架。—*adj.* 有三脚架的;以三脚架支撐的。

tri·po·lar (traɪ'polɚ; trai'poulə) *adj.* 三極的;有三極的。

trip·o·li ('trɪpəlɪ; 'tripəli) *n.* 【礦】矽藻土;矽藻板。

tri·pos ('traɪpɑs; 'traipɔs) *n., pl.* **-pos·es.** (英國劍橋大學之)榮譽學位考試。

trip·per ('trɪpɚ; 'tripə) *n.* ①遠足者;短途旅行者。②顚躓者;走路輕快的人。③機器上之鉤釬。

trip·ping ('trɪpɪŋ; 'tripiŋ) *adj.*(脚步)輕快的;敏捷的。—*n.*輕快之跳舞。—**ly,** *adv.*

trip·tych ('trɪptɪk; 'triptik) *n.* ①(昔時)三折之寫字板。②三塊連在一起可摺疊之圖畫或雕刻。

trip wire 引發炸藥或警鈴的電線。

tri·ra·cial (traɪ'reʃəl; trai'reiʃəl) *adj.* 有三種族之血統的。

tri·ra·di·ate (traɪ'redɪ,et; trai'reidieit) *adj.* 向三方射出的。

tri·rec·tan·gu·lar (traɪ,rɛk'tæŋgjəlɚ; trai,rek'tæŋgjulə) *adj.* 有三直角的。

tri·reme ('traɪrim; 'traiəriːm) *n.*(古希臘或羅馬)有三層槳座之戰船。

tri·sect (traɪ'sɛkt; trai'sekt) *v.t.* 分成三部分;三分;(尤指)三等分。

tri·sec·tion (traɪ'sɛkʃən; trai'sekʃən) *n.* 三分;三等分。

tri·se·ri·al (traɪ'sɪrɪəl; trai'siəriəl) *adj.* ①排成三列的。②【植物】只有三輪生體的。

tris·mus ('trɪzməs; 'trizməs) *n.* 【醫】牙關緊鎖。

tri-state ('traɪ,stet; 'trai'steit) *adj.* 包含三州的。

trist·ful ('trɪstfəl; 'tristfəl) *adj.* 悲哀的;悽慘的;憂鬱的。

tris·yl·lab·ic (,trɪsɪ'læbɪk; 'trai-si'læbik) *adj.*有三音節的。—*n.* 三音節之音步。

tri·syl·la·ble (trɪ'sɪləbl̩; 'trai'siləbl) *n.* 三音節的字。

trite (traɪt; trait) *adj.,* **trit·er, trit·est.** ①陳腐的;平凡的。②磨損的。③被慣踏的。

trite·ly ('traɪtlɪ; 'traitli) *adv.* 陳腐地;平凡地。

trite·ness ('traɪtnɪs; 'traitnis) *n.*陳腐;平凡。

tri·the·ism ('traɪθɪɪzəm; 'traiθiizm) *n.* 【宗教】三位異體說;三神論。—**tri·the·ist,** *n.*

trit·ish ('traɪtɪʃ; 'traitiʃ) *adj.*有點陳腐的。

trit·i·um ('trɪtɪəm; 'tritiəm) *n.* 【化】氚(氫的同位素,化學符號爲T或H^3)。

Tri·ton ('traɪtn̩; 'traitn) *n.* ①【希臘神話】人頭人身魚尾之海神(爲 Poseidon 及 Amphitrite 之子)。②此種小海神。

tri·ton ('traɪtn̩; 'traitn) *n.* ①【動物】梭尾螺;其殼。②氚之核子。

tri·tone ('traɪ,ton; 'traitoun) *n.* 【音樂】三全音。

trit·u·rate ('trɪtʃə,ret; 'tritjureit) *v.,* **-rat·ed, -rat·ing,** *n.* —*v.t.* 將…研磨成粉末。—*n.* 粉末;藥粉。

trit·u·ra·tion (,trɪtʃə'reʃən; ,tritju'reiʃən) *n.* ①研末;粉狀。②【藥】粉末;研製劑;乳糖散劑。

trit·u·ra·tor ('trɪtʃə,retɚ; 'tritjureitə) *n.* ①研磨者。②(藥品之)研磨器;乳缽。

***tri·umph** ('traɪəmf; 'traiəmf) *n.* ①勝利;大成功。the *triumph* of right over might. 正義對强權的勝利。②勝利引起的喜悅;得意洋洋。a shout of *triumph*. 一陣歡欣聲。③(古羅馬的)凱旋式。*in triumph* **a.** 勝利的;得意洋洋的。**b.** 勝利地;得意洋洋地。—*v.i.* ①獲得勝利;成功。②得意;狂喜。

tri·um·phal (traɪ'ʌmfl̩; trai'ʌmfl) *adj.* 凱旋的;慶祝勝利的。a *triumphal* arch.

凱旋門。a *triumphal* crown. 凱旋花冠。
***tri·um·phant** [traɪˈʌmfənt; traiˈʌmfənt] *adj.* ①勝利的;成功的。 *triumphant* generals. 勝利的將軍。②得意洋洋的。*triumphant* shout. 歡呼。—**ly,** *adv.*
tri·um·vir [traɪˈʌmvɚ; traiˈʌmvə] *n., pl.* **-virs, -vi·ri** [-vəraɪ; -vərai]. ①古羅馬三執政之一。②共任一項公職的三人之一。
tri·um·vi·rate [traɪˈʌmvərɪt; traiˈʌmvirit] *n.* ①三人執政之職位或任期。②三頭政治;三人政治。the first *triumvirate.* (羅馬)前三頭政治 (Pompey, Julius Caesar, 與 Crassus). the second *triumvirate.* (羅馬)後三頭政治 (Mark Antony, Octavius, 與 Lepidus). ③任何共有一項職位或權柄之三人結合。④任何三人之組或羣。
tri·une [ˈtraɪjun; ˈtraijuːn] *adj.* 三位一體的。—*n.* ① (the T-) 三位一體(=the Trinity). ②=**triad.**
tri·un·i·ty [traɪˈjunətɪ; traiˈjuːniti] *n., pl.* **-ties.** 三位一體。
tri·va·lence [traɪˈveləns; traiˈveiləns] *n.*【化】三價;有三種不同的原子價。(亦作 **trivalency**)
tri·va·lent [traɪˈvelənt; traiˈveilənt] *adj.*【化】①三價的。②有三個不同價的。(亦作 **tervalent**)
triv·et [ˈtrɪvɪt; ˈtrivit] *n.* ①三脚架;三脚臺(承烹煮器皿者)。②(置桌上盛熱菜用之)短脚金屬盤。 ***as right as a trivet*** 立得穩;有良好而穩定的安置;完全正確。
trivet table 三脚桌。
triv·i·a [ˈtrɪvɪə; ˈtriviə] *n. pl.* ①無足輕重的瑣事。② pl. of **trivium.**
triv·i·al** [ˈtrɪvɪəl; ˈtriviəl] *adj.* ①不重要的; 無足輕重的; 瑣屑的。 a *trivial* mistake. 小錯誤。②【古】陳舊的;無趣的;平常的。 ***the trivial round 平凡的日常生活或職責。—**ness,** *n.* —**ly,** *adv.*
triv·i·al·ism [ˈtrɪvɪəˌlɪzəm; ˈtriviəlizm] *n.* ①平庸;平凡。②瑣事;瑣屑。
triv·i·al·i·ty [ˌtrɪvɪˈælətɪ; ˌtriviˈæliti] *n., pl.* **-ties.** ①瑣屑。②瑣屑之事物。
triv·i·al·i·za·tion [ˌtrɪvɪəlaɪˈzeʃən; ˌtriviəlaiˈzeiʃən] *n.* 使平凡;使平庸。
triv·i·al·ize [ˈtrɪvɪəlˌaɪz; ˈtriviəlaiz] *v.t.,* **-ized, -iz·ing.** 使平凡;使平庸。
trivial name【生物】①種名。②俗名。
tri·vi·sion [ˈtraɪvɪʒən; ˈtraiviʒən] *n.* 立體攝影。
triv·i·um [ˈtrɪvɪəm; ˈtriviəm] *n., pl.* **-i·a** [-ɪə; -iə]. 中世紀七種學藝中之低級部分(包括文法、修辭、邏輯三學科,高級部分包括算術、幾何、天文、音樂稱爲 quadrivium).
tri·week·ly [traɪˈwiklɪ; ˈtraiˈwiːkli] *adj., adv., n.,* **-week·lies.** —*adj.* & *adv.* ①一週三次的(地)。②三週一次的 (地)。 —*n.* 每週出版三次或三週出版一次的期刊。
-trix【字尾】表“女性”之義, 如 aviatrix.
Tri·zo·ni·a [traɪˈzonɪə; traiˈzouniə] *n.* (第二次世界大戰後在西德之)英、美、法三國共同占領區。(亦作 **Trizone**)
tro·car [ˈtrokɑr; ˈtroukɑː] *n.*【外科】(探傷用的一種)套管針。(亦作 **trochar**)
tro·cha·ic [troˈke·ɪk; troˈkeiik] *adj.*【詩】揚抑格的。—*n.* ①=**trochee.** ② (常 *pl.*)揚抑格詩句。
tro·che [ˈtrokɪ; ˈtrouki] *n.*【藥】藥錠;藥片。
tro·chee [ˈtroki; ˈtroukiː] *n.*【詩】揚抑格 (卽每一音步包含一重音節與一輕音節, 如 Lífe is/bút an/émpty/dréam.).
tro·chil·ic [troˈkɪlɪk; trouˈkilik] *adj.* 旋轉運動的;輪轉運動的。
tro·chil·ics [troˈkɪlɪks; trouˈkiliks] *n.* 輪轉運動學;旋轉運動學。
troch·i·lus [ˈtrɑkɪləs; ˈtrɔkiləs] *n., pl.* **-li** [-ˌlaɪ; -lai]. ①鰐鳥。②蜂雀。③任何善鳴的小鳥。
troch·le·a [ˈtrɑklɪə; ˈtrɔkliə] *n., pl.* **-le·ae** [-lɪˌi; -liiː].【解剖】軟骨輪;滑車。
troch·le·ar [ˈtrɑklɪɚ; ˈtrɔkliə] *adj.* ①【解剖】滑車的;軟骨輪的;與軟骨輪相聯的;滑車狀的。②【植物】滑車形的。
tro·choid [ˈtrokɔɪd; ˈtroukɔid] *n.* ①【幾何】餘擺線;轉跡線。②【解剖】滑車關節。—*adj.* ①餘擺線的。②圓錐形的(貝)。③輪狀的;作輪狀廻轉的。
trod [trɑd; trɔd] *v.* pt. & pp. of **tread.**
trod·den [ˈtrɑdn̩; ˈtrɔdn] *v.* pp. of **tread.**
trog·lo·dyte [ˈtrɑgləˌdaɪt; ˈtrɔglədait] *n.* ①古代的穴居者。②隱士。③【動物】類人猿。
trog·lo·dyt·ism [ˈtrɑglədaɪˌtɪzəm; ˈtrɔglədaitizm] *n.* 穴居;穴居生活。
troi·ka [ˈtrɔɪkə; ˈtrɔikə] *n.* ①(俄國的)三頭馬車;此種並列的三匹馬。②三頭政治。
Tro·i·lus [ˈtrɔɪləs; ˈtrouiləs] *n.*【希臘神話】Troy 王 Priam 之子(爲 Achilles 所殺)。
trois temps [ˈtrwatɑ̃; ˈtrwɑːtɑ̃ː]【法】三拍子之華爾滋。
Tro·jan [ˈtrodʒən; ˈtroudʒən] *adj.* ① Troy 的; Troy 人的。②如 Trojan horse 的; 滲透性的; 有奸計的。—*n.* ① Troy 居民。②有能力有決心之人。
Trojan horse ①特洛伊木馬(特洛伊之戰時, 希臘人所作, 希臘兵藏於木馬腹中, 進入特洛伊城)。②滲透;敵人之奸細;第五縱隊。
Trojan War 特洛伊之戰(爲希臘盲詩人 Homer 所敍述之戰爭, 延續十年, Troy 終爲希臘人所毀)。
troll[1] [trol; troul] *v.t.* ①輕鬆歡快地歌唱。②以宏亮聲音歌唱。③輪唱。④用轉輪線釣(魚);用轉輪線垂釣於(水)。⑤旋轉;滾動。⑥傳遞(酒杯)輪飲。—*v.i.* ①輪唱。②以歡快而宏亮的聲音唱歌。③用輪轉線釣魚。④旋轉。—*n.* ①輪唱的歌。②以輪轉線釣魚法。③輪轉線釣魚用餌。④魚餌及釣線。⑤旋轉。
troll[2] *n.*【北歐傳說】居住地下或洞穴中之巨人;愛惡作劇而態度友善的侏儒。
trol·ley** [ˈtrɑlɪ; ˈtrɔli] *n., pl.* **-leys,** *v.,* **-leyed, -ley·ing.** —*n.* ①觸輪 (托在電線上的滑輪, 以導電至電車等者)。②電車。③【英】貨車;手推車。④空中吊運車;懸掛貨物運行於高架軌道上之吊運車。 ***be off one's trolley 【俚】a. 迷惑狀態。 b. 瘋狂; 失去理智。—*v.t.* & *v.i.* 用trolley 運送;搭乘 trolley.
trolley bus 無軌電車。
trolley car【美】電車。
trolley line ①電車行駛系統或行駛路線。②無軌電車公司。
trol·ley·man [ˈtrɑlɪmən; ˈtrɔlimən] *n., pl.* **-men.** 電車司機;電車車掌。
trol·lop [ˈtrɑləp; ˈtrɔləp] *n.* ①不整潔或不修邊幅的女人。②娼妓。③淫婦。
trol·lop·y [ˈtrɑləpɪ; ˈtrɔləpi] *adj.* 不整潔的;不修邊幅的;自甘墮落的; 如娼妓的。
trol·ly [ˈtrɑlɪ; ˈtrɔli] *n., pl.* **-lies,** *v.t., v.i.,* **-lied, -ly·ing.** =**trolley.**
trom·bone [ˈtrɑmbon; trɔmˈboun]

n. 〖音樂〗伸縮喇叭;低音大喇叭。
trom·bon·ist ['trambonɪst; trɔm'bounist] n. 吹奏伸縮喇叭者。
trom·mel ['traml; 'trɔml] n. 〖冶金〗礦石篩。
tro·mom·e·ter [tro'mamətə; trou'mɔmitə] n. 微震計。
tromp [tramp; trɔmp] 〖俗〗 v.i. 走路時發出響聲; 脚步很重地走路。 —v.t. ①頓(足)。②踏。
trompe [tramp; trɔmp] n. 〖冶金〗(熔礦爐中的)水風筒。
:troop [trup; truːp] n. ①羣;組;班;多數。a *troop* of schoolboys. 一羣學童。② (pl.) 軍隊。regular *troops*. 正規軍。③騎兵連(六十人至一百人)。④童軍小隊(十六人或三十二人)。 —v.i. ①羣集;成羣;結隊。The children *trooped* around the teacher. 兒童們羣集在教師的四周。②成群而行。③列隊行進。④〖英軍〗在典禮時掌軍旗;掌旗。
troop carrier ①軍隊運輸機。②運送步兵用的水陸兩用裝甲車。
troop·er ['trupə; 'truːpə] n. ①騎兵。②騎馬之警察。③騎兵所用之馬。④〖英〗軍隊運輸艦。⑤〖俗〗州警察。⑥傘兵隊員。***swear like a trooper*** 出口粗野;破口罵人。
troop·horse ['trup,hɔrs; 'truːphɔːs] n. 騎兵騎乘之馬。
troop·ship ['trup,ʃɪp; 'truːpʃip] n. 運兵船;兵員運輸艦。
tro·pae·o·lum [tro'piələm; trou'piːələm] n., pl. -lums, -la [-lə; -lə]. 〖植物〗金蓮花屬之植物。
trope [trop; troup] n. 〖修辭〗借喻;比喻。
troph·al·lax·is [,trafə'læksɪs; ,trɔfə'læksis] n., pl. -lax·es [-'læksiz; -'læksiːz]. 同窠昆蟲間彼此交換營養食物或分泌物。
troph·ic ['trafɪk; 'trɔfik] adj. 〖生理〗營養的;有關營養的。
tro·phied ['trofɪd; 'troufid] adj. 用戰利品裝飾的;以紀念物裝飾的。
tro·phol·o·gy [tro'falədʒɪ; trou'fɔlədʒi] n. 營養學。
***tro·phy** ['trofɪ; 'troufi] n., pl. -phies. ①戰利品; 勝利紀念品。②獎品。③紀念品。
***trop·ic** ['trapɪk; 'trɔpik] n. ①回歸線。②(pl.) 熱帶;熱帶地方。It's hot in the *tropics*. 熱帶地方是很熱的。③天空中太陽運行(對地球而言)之南北極限。—adj. 熱帶的;熱帶地方的。 *tropic* fruits. 熱帶水果。
***trop·i·cal** ['trapɪkl; 'trɔpikl] adj. ①熱帶的;熱帶地方的。②很熱的;熱情的。③字義特殊的;比喻的。—n. 〖俗〗男性夏裝。
tropical aquarium 熱帶水族館。
tropical disease 熱帶病。
tropical fish 熱帶魚。
trop·i·cal·i·ty [,trapɪ'kælətɪ; ,trɔpi'kæliti] n. 熱帶性;熱帶特色;熱帶色彩。
trop·i·cal·ize ['trapɪkl,aɪz; 'trɔpikəlaiz] v.t., -ized, -iz·ing. ①使有熱帶之特性;使熱帶化。②使適於熱帶。
tropical medicine 熱帶醫學。
tropical year 〖天文〗回歸年; 分至年(三百六十五日五時四十八分四十六秒)。
tropic bird 熱帶鳥。
tropic of Cancer 北回歸線。(亦作 Tropic～)
tropic of Capricorn 南回歸線。(亦作 Tropic～)
tro·pism ['tropɪzəm; 'troupizm] n. 〖生物〗屈性;向性;屈曲運動。
tro·pol·o·gy [tro'palədʒɪ; trou'pɔlədʒi] n., pl. -gies. ①比喻之使用。②對聖經作喻義上及字面上之解釋。③比喻論;借喻論。
trop·o·pause ['trapə,pɔz; 'trɔpəpɔːz] n. 〖氣象〗對流層頂(對流圈與成層圈之交接區)。
trop·o·sphere ['trapə,sfɪr; 'trɔpəsfiə] n. 〖氣象〗對流層。
trop·o·spher·ic [,trapə'sfɛrɪk; ,trɔpə'sferik] adj. 〖氣象〗對流層的。
trot** [trat; trɔt] v., trot·ted, trot·ting, n. —v.i. 疾馳; 疾走; 快走。 Horses *trot*. 馬疾馳。 —v.t. ①使疾馳;使快步行走。②騎(馬)疾馳。③快步越過。 ***trot out 〖俗〗舉以示人。—n. ①疾走;速步;快步。 They kept me on the *trot*. 他們使我不得閒暇。②輕疾之動作。③〖美俚〗學生用之翻譯解答本。④騎馬疾馳。 to go for a *trot*. 騎馬疾馳。⑤老婦。 ***the trots*** 〖俚〗腹瀉。
troth [trɔθ; trouθ] n. ①忠實; 信實。by my *troth*. 說老實話。②約;婚約。to plight one's *troth*. 訂婚約; 盟誓。③允諾; 事實。—v.t. 〖古〗①允諾。②訂婚。
trot·line ['trat,laɪn; 'trɔtlain] n. 〖美〗曳釣魚繩。
trot·ter ['tratə; 'trɔtə] n. ①疾走者。②小跑之馬;快步之馬。③(pl.) (羊、猪等之)蹄(供食用部分)。④(人之)脚。
trot·toir [tro'twar; 'trɔtwɑː] 〖法〗 n. 人行道。
trou·ba·dour ['trubə,dur; 'truːbəduə] n. ①抒情詩人。②泛指任何吟遊詩人或歌謠吟唱者。
:trou·ble ['trʌbl; 'trʌbl] v., -bled, -bling, n. —v.t. ①使煩惱;使憂慮;使苦惱。He was greatly *troubled* about his son's behavior. 他爲他兒子的行爲大感煩惱。②煩勞;麻煩。May I *trouble* you to shut the window? 可否麻煩你把窗戶關上?③使痛苦;使感不適。I am *troubled* with a cough. 我爲咳嗽所苦。 ④攪亂; 擾亂。 *troubled* times. 亂世。 —v.i. ①煩惱; 憂慮。 Don't *trouble* about it. 不要爲這個憂慮。②煩勞;麻煩。 Oh, don't *trouble*, thanks. 啊, 不用麻煩了, 多謝。 —n. ①煩惱; 苦惱;困苦。②麻煩;煩勞;辛苦;困難。 It is no *trouble* at all. 這件事毫不費事。③紛爭; 紛擾; 騷亂。political *troubles*. 政爭。④使人煩惱或困苦的事物。 She has always been a great *trouble* to her father and mother. 她一直是她父母的大累。⑤疾病; 病痛。stomach *trouble*. 胃病。 ***ask*** (or ***look***) ***for trouble*** 〖俗〗自找麻煩;想找苦頭吃。***get a person into trouble*** 使某人陷入困境。 ***get into trouble*** 陷入困境。***in trouble*** a. 處於困難之中的; 受苦的;將受懲罰的。 b. 未結婚而懷孕的。***take the trouble***(與不定詞連用)。費心作;費力作。
troubled waters 混亂的局面。***fish in troubled waters*** 混水摸魚。
trou·ble·mak·er ['trʌbl,mekə; 'trʌbl,meikə] n. 時常惹麻煩的人。
trou·ble·mak·ing ['trʌbl,mekɪŋ; 'trʌbl,meikiŋ] n. 惹麻煩的行爲。
trouble man 發現並修理機器故障的人 (=trouble-shooter).
trou·ble·proof ['trʌbl,pruf; 'trʌblpruːf] adj. 不發生故障的;無故障之虞的。
trou·ble·shoot ['trʌbl,ʃut; 'trʌblʃuːt] v., -shoot·ed, -shot, -shoot·ing. —v.i. 爲人解決困難。—v.t. 以解決困難者之身分處理。(亦作 **trouble-shoot**)
trou·ble-shoot·er ['trʌbl,ʃutə; 'trʌbl,ʃuːtə] n. ①發現並修理機器故障者。②解決困難者。(亦作 **troubleshooter**)

trou·ble-shoot·ing [ˈtrʌbl̩ˌʃutɪŋ; ˈtrʌblˌʃuːtiŋ] *n.* 解決困難。—*adj.* 解決困難之工作的。

***trou·ble·some** [ˈtrʌbl̩səm; ˈtrʌblsəm] *adj.* 使人苦惱或煩勞的;困難的;麻煩的。—**ly,** *adv.*

trouble spot 易惹麻煩之處;易生毛病之部分。

trou·blous [ˈtrʌbləs; ˈtrʌbləs] *adj.* ①動亂不安的。*troublous* times. 動亂不安的時代。②使人苦惱的。③波濤洶湧的。④引起騷動的;坐立不安的。

trou-de-loup [ˌtrudəˈlu; ˌtruːdəˈluː] *n., pl.* **trous-de-loup.** 〖法〗狼阱(一種防阻騎兵襲擊之陷阱)。

***trough** [trɔf; trɔf] *n.* ①食槽;水槽。②任何槽形之物。③水溝。④(兩浪間或兩山間等之)凹處。

trounce [trauns; trauns] *v.t.,* **trounced, trounc·ing.** ①打;痛打;鞭笞。②痛懲;嚴責。③擊敗。

troupe [trup; truːp] *n., v.,* **trouped, troup·ing.** —*n.* 班;隊;團(尤指伶人、歌手等所組成者)。—*v.i.* 爲上述班隊等之一員而旅行各地。

troup·er [ˈtrupɚ; ˈtruːpə] *n.* ①(劇團、馬戲團等之)團員;演員。②有經驗的老演員。③忠於職守者;做事負責者。

***trou·ser** [ˈtrauzɚ; ˈtrauzə] *adj.* 褲子的。*trouser* legs. 褲管。—*n.* 左右褲管之任一。

trou·ser·ing [ˈtrauzərɪŋ; ˈtrauzəriŋ] *n.* 做褲子用的布料。

trouser(s) pocket 褲袋。

trou·sers [ˈtrauzɚz; ˈtrauzəz] *n. pl.* 褲。a pair of *trousers.* 一條褲子。

trouser stretcher (使褲管不鬆下的)伸褲器。

trous·seau [truˈso; ˈtruːsou] *n., pl.* **-seaux** [-ˈsoz; -souz], **-seaus.** 嫁妝;妝奩。

***trout** [traut; traut] *n., pl.* **trouts** or **trout,** *v.* —*n.* 鱒魚。—*v.i.* 捕鱒魚;釣鱒魚。

tro·ver [ˈtrovɚ; ˈtrouvə] *n.* 〖法律〗(對非法占有或使用動產者的)損害賠償訴訟。

trow·el [ˈtrauəl; ˈtrauəl] *n.* ①小鏟子。②(用以塗抹灰泥之)鏝子。***lay it on with a trowel*** **a.** 用鏝子塗抹。**b.** 恭維;拍馬屁。—*v.t.* 以鏝子抹平。—**er,** *n.*

Troy [trɔɪ; trɔi] *n.* 特洛伊(小亞細亞西北部一古城,因荷馬史詩 Iliad 而著稱)。

troy [trɔɪ; trɔi] *adj.* 金衡的;金衡制的。—*n.* =**troy weight.**

troy weight (衡量寶石、金、銀等之)金衡;金衡制(金衡一磅等於普通磅五分之四强)。

tru·an·cy [ˈtruənsɪ; ˈtru(ː)ənsi] *n.* ①(學生等之)曠課;逃學。②曠職;怠惰;遊蕩。

tru·ant [ˈtruənt; ˈtru(ː)ənt] *n.* ①逃學者。②玩忽職務者;荒廢職務者。***play truant*** 逃學;曠職。—*adj.* ①逃學的。②荒廢職務的;怠惰的。—*v.i.* 逃學;荒廢職務。—**ly,** *adv.*

truant officer 調査曠課或逃學的職員。

truce [trus; truːs] *n.* ①休戰;停戰。the flag of *truce.* 休戰旗(白旗)。②休止;中止。—*v.i.* 休戰;停戰。

***truck**[1] [trʌk; trʌk] *n.* ①貨車;卡車。②(火車站脚夫用以搬運行李之)手車。③(火車之)車架。④(火車之)無蓋貨車。⑤小輪。⑥旗杆頂上穿繩子之木球。—*v.t.* 以火車、卡車或手車運送。—*v.i.* 駕駛 truck. —*adj.* truck 的;用於 truck 的。

truck[2] *n.* ①〖美〗種植以出售之蔬菜。②零星什物。③〖俗〗垃圾;廢物;胡說。④〖俗〗交往;商業關係。⑤交易;買賣。⑥作爲工資之實物。***have no truck with*** **a.** 與之無交往。**b.** 與之無關。—*v.t.* & *v.i.* 交易;交往。

truck[3] *n.* 一種輕快的舞步。—*v.i.* 以輕快的舞步跳舞。

truck·age [ˈtrʌkɪdʒ; ˈtrʌkidʒ] *n.* ①貨車搬運。②貨車搬運費。

truck·er[1] [ˈtrʌkɚ; ˈtrʌkə] *n.* ①貨車運輸業者;貨運公司。②貨車司機。

truck·er[2] *n.* ①〖美〗以出售爲目的而種植蔬菜之農夫。②交換者;互易者。

truck farm 〖美〗(以出售爲目的之)蔬菜農場。

truck·le [ˈtrʌkl; ˈtrʌkl] *v.,* **-led, -ling,** *n.* —*v.i.* ①屈服;屈從;諂媚〖to〗。②以小輪轉動。—*v.t.* 用小輪轉動。—*n.* ①小輪。②=**truckle bed.** —**truck·ler,** *n.* —**truck·ling·ly,** *adv.*

truckle bed (裝有小輪不用時可推入另一床下之)矮床。

truck·load [ˈtrʌkˌlod; ˈtrʌkloud] *n.* 一貨車之量。

truck·man [ˈtrʌkmən; ˈtrʌkmən] *n., pl.* **-men.** ①貨車司機。②貨車運輸業者。

truck system 以產品支付工資之制度。

truc·u·lent [ˈtrʌkjələnt; ˈtrʌkjulənt] *adj.* ①野蠻的;兇猛的;殘酷的。②(言語、文字等)粗野的;苛刻的;下流的;詆譭的。③充滿敵意的。—**ly,** *adv.* —**truc·u·lence,** *n.*

trudge [trʌdʒ; trʌdʒ] *v.,* **trudged, trudg·ing,** *n.* —*v.i.* ①走。②跋涉。—*v.t.* 吃力地走;蹣跚地走。—*n.* 跋涉。It was a long *trudge* up the hill. 那是好難走的一段上山路。

trudg·en [ˈtrʌdʒən; ˈtrʌdʒən] *n.* 爬泳。(亦作 **trudgen stroke**)

‡true [tru; truː] *adj.,* **tru·er, tru·est,** *adv., n., v.,* **trued, tru·ing.** —*adj.* ①確實的。Is the news *true?* 這消息確實嗎? ②眞實的;眞正的。*true* friendship. 眞實的友誼。③正確的;確切的。④忠實的。He was *true* to his principles. 他忠於自己的行爲原則。⑤代表其一類的。A sweet potato is not a *true* potato. 蕃薯不能代表馬鈴薯這類的東西。⑥可靠的。⑦方向不變的。⑧〖古〗=**truthful.** ⑨誠實的。⑩形狀正確的。***come true*** 實現。His words *came true.* 他的話證實了。—*adv.* ①眞實地;正確地。②〖生物〗與原種相同地。to come *true.* (植物)生出純種的芽。—*n.* ①眞實之事物。②正確之形態、部位或調節。***in true*** 正確放置或調整等的。***out of true*** 放置、調整、位置等不正確的。—*v.t.* 使正確;使位置、形狀正確;配準;配齊;校正。***true up*** 調整;校準。—**ness,** *n.*

true blue ①一種不褪色之藍色染料。②十七世紀時蘇格蘭長老會敎派之信徒。③忠誠不變之人。

true-blue [ˈtruˈblu; ˈtruːˈbluː] *adj.* 不變的;忠誠的。

true·born [ˈtruˌbɔrn; ˈtruːbɔːn] *adj.* 純正的;道地的。

true·heart·ed [ˈtruˌhɑrtɪd; ˈtruːˈhɑːtid] *adj.* 忠實的;忠誠的;誠懇的。

true level (想像中的)眞正水平面。

true-life [ˈtruˈlaɪf; ˈtruːˈlaif] *adj.* 寫實的;與實際生活相似的。

true·love [ˈtruˌlʌv; ˈtruːlʌv] *n.* 意中人;情人;愛人。

truelove knot 同心結;相思結(爲眞實而持久之愛情象徵)。

true·pen·ny [ˈtruˌpɛnɪ; ˈtruːpeni] *n.* 誠實可靠的人。

truf·fle [ˈtrʌfl; ˈtrʌfl] *n.* 〖植物〗松露;麥蕈(生在地面下的囊子菌類)。

tru·ism [ˈtruɪzəm; ˈtru(ː)izm] *n.* ①公認的眞理;人人相信的道理。②陳腐之言;爛調;老生常談。—**tru·is·tic,** *adj.*

trull 〔trʌl; trʌl〕 *n.* 娼妓。

tru·ly** 〔ˈtrulɪ; ˈtruːli〕 *adv.* ①確切地；眞實地；正確地；確實地；忠實地。He spoke *truly*. 他說實話。②事實上；眞實地。③眞正的；不假的。④合法地。Yours truly*** 信文末簽名前之問候語。

Tru·man 〔ˈtrumən; ˈtruːmən〕 *n.* 杜魯門(Harry S., 1884–1972, 美國第33任總統,任期 1945–53)。

Truman Doctrine 杜魯門主義(美總統杜魯門於1947年向國會提出對受共產主義侵略威脅之國家提供軍經援助的政策)。

trump[1] 〔trʌmp; trʌmp〕 *n.* ①〖橋牌〗一組王牌之一張；王牌。②最後的手段；最後的良策。③〖俗〗好人；時時準備幫助別人的人。***put a person to his trumps*** 令某人陷於窮境；令技窮。***turn up trumps*** 〖俗〗較預期爲佳。—*v.t.* ①以王牌取勝。②優於；勝過；擊敗。—*v.i.* ①出王牌。②用王牌得磴。***trump up*** **a.** 以欺騙爲目的之揑造。**b.** 鼓起。

trump[2] *n.* 〖古、詩〗①喇叭。②喇叭聲。***the last trump*** (or ***the trump of doom***) 世界末日之喇叭。—*v.i.* ①吹喇叭。②發出類似喇叭之聲。—*v.t.* ①以喇叭發出。②以類似喇叭之聲發出。③廣爲宣揚。

trump card ①王牌；勝牌。②良策；有效之策略；最後手段。

trumped-up 〔ˈtrʌmptˈʌp; ˈtrʌmpt-ʌp〕 *adj.* 揑造的。

trump·er·y 〔ˈtrʌmpərɪ; ˈtrʌmpəri〕 *n., pl.* **-er·ies,** *adj.* —*n.* ①虛有其表而無價値的東西；無價値的雜物。②垃圾；廢物；無意義之物。—*adj.* ①外表華麗而少價値的。②淺薄的；無聊的。③虛假的；詐欺的。

trum·pet** 〔ˈtrʌmpɪt; ˈtrʌmpit〕 *n.* ①小喇叭。②喇叭形之物；喇叭筒。③喇叭聲；類似吹喇叭之聲。④吹奏小喇叭者；小喇叭手(＝trumpeter). ***blow one's own trumpet 自吹自誇。—*v.i.* ①吹喇叭。Soldiers *trumpeted* and bugled. 士兵們吹喇叭鳴號角。②發出類似吹喇叭的聲音。The elephants *trumpeted*. 象鳴。—*v.t.* 宣布；傳布；鼓吹；宣傳。

trumpet call ①集合號聲。②緊急呼喚。

trumpet creeper 〖植物〗紫葳。

trum·pet·er 〔ˈtrʌmpɪtɚ; ˈtrʌmpitə〕 *n.* ①喇叭手；號手。②用號筒宣告或傳話的人。③(南美所產之)喇叭鳥；(北美所產之)一種鵠。④鼓吹者。***be one's own trumpeter*** 自吹自擂；自誇。

trumpet flower 〖植物〗①任何開喇叭形花之植物；紫葳；喇叭花。②貫月忍冬(＝trumpet honeysuckle).

trun·cal 〔ˈtrʌŋkl̩; ˈtrʌŋkl〕 *adj.* 樹幹的；軀幹的。

trun·cate 〔ˈtrʌŋket; ˈtrʌŋkeit〕 *v.,* **-cat·ed, -cat·ing,** *adj.* —*v.t.* 切掉；截短；修短。—*adj.* ①切短的；削去頂端的。②〖生物〗截形的；頂端平寬的。—**ly,** *adv.*

trun·cat·ed 〔ˈtrʌŋketɪd; ˈtrʌŋkeitid〕 *adj.* ①切掉頂端的；切短的。②削去尖角的。③〖幾何〗截的。④節略的(文章、演說詞)。⑤截形的(葉)。

trun·ca·tion 〔trʌŋˈkeʃən; trʌŋˈkeiʃən〕 *n.* ①切斷；切去頂端；修短。②〖結晶〗眞面。

trun·cheon 〔ˈtrʌntʃən; ˈtrʌntʃən〕 *n.* ①短棍；短棒；(尤指)警棒；警棍。②權杖(用以作爲權威標記之杖)。—*v.t.* 用棒打。

trun·dle 〔ˈtrʌndl̩; ˈtrʌndl〕 *v.,* **-dled, -dling,** *n.* —*v.t.* & *v.i.* 使滾動；滾動；以車推運。—*n.* ①滾動。②小輪。③矮車；手車。

trundle bed ＝**truckle bed.**

***trunk** 〔trʌŋk; trʌŋk〕 *n.* ①樹幹。②(人或動物之)軀幹。③任何構築的主要部分；主幹。④大衣箱。⑤象鼻。⑥(*pl.*)(運動員、游泳者等所着之)短褲。⑦幹線(＝trunk line). —*adj.* 主要的；主幹的。

trunk call 〖英〗長途電話。

trunk hose (第十六與十七世紀流行的)一種袋狀大管男用短褲。

trunk line 〖美〗(鐵路、運河、電報、電話等之)幹線。

trunk road 道路之幹線。

trun·nion 〔ˈtrʌnjən; ˈtrʌnjən〕 *n.* 砲耳(砲身兩側之圓筒狀突出物,用以支砲於砲架上者)。—**ed,** *adj.*

truss 〔trʌs; trʌs〕 *v.t.* ①縛綁；繫；紮住〖常 up〗. ②以桁或構架支住(屋頂、橋等)。③把(乾草等)束成捆。—*n.* ①(乾草等的)一捆；一束。②(支持房頂、橋等之)桁；構架；横構架。③〖醫〗疝帶；突逸帶。④〖醫〗(牙之)橋架。⑤〖航海〗結帆桁於桅之鐵具及索具。⑥〖植物〗(生於莖頂端之)穗狀花。—**er,** *n.*

truss bridge 〖土木〗桁架橋。

truss·ing 〔ˈtrʌsɪŋ; ˈtrʌsiŋ〕 *n.* 〖建築〗桁架；桁架材。

:trust 〔trʌst; trʌst〕 *n.* ①信賴；信任。I don't place much *trust* in his promises. 我不大信賴他的諾言。②被信賴的人或物。God is our *trust*. 上帝是我們所信奉的。③堅定之信念；相信。Our *trust* is that she will soon be well. 我們堅信她不久便會痊癒。④責任；職責。⑤所委託之事；委託物。⑥委託；信託。⑦托辣斯；操縱某種營業的組合。⑧委託照顧；監管。⑨〖法律〗(受託付人可支配、應用之)信託或託管財產。⑩信譽；業務信譽。***in trust*** 受託的；代爲保管的。***on trust*** **a.** 以業務信譽擔保的(地)；賒欠的(地)。**b.** 不作深究的(地)。—*adj.* ①信託的；代人保管的。②被信託的。—*v.t.* ①信賴；信任。I have never *trusted* that man. 我從未信任那個人。②委託；託付。I don't advise you to *trust* him with valuable things. 我勸你不要把貴重的東西託付給他。③希望；相信。④賒賣。The store will *trust* us. 這家商店可以賒帳賣給我們東西。⑤依賴。—*v.i.* ①信任；信賴；相信。He *trusts* to his memory too much. 他過於信賴自己的記憶力。②期待〖for〗. I *trust* for his apology. 我期待他的道歉。③賒賣。***trust to*** 依賴；依靠；信賴。Never *trust to* luck! 決不可靠運氣！—**a·bil·i·ty, —er,** *n.* —**a·ble,** *adj.*

trust buster 負責推行反托辣斯法以解散托辣斯之政府官員。

trust company 信託公司。

trust deed 〖商〗信託契據。

***trus·tee** 〔trʌsˈti; trʌsˈtiː〕 *n., v.,* **-teed, -tee·ing.** —*n.* 受託人；被信託之人；董事。—*v.t.* 交與託管。—*v.i.* 擔任託管人。

trus·tee·ship 〔trʌsˈtiʃɪp; trʌsˈtiːʃip〕 *n.* ①受委託者之地位或職務。②(聯合國之)託管。③受聯合國託管之地區。

Trusteeship Council 聯合國託管理事會。

trust·ful 〔ˈtrʌstfəl; ˈtrʌstfəl〕 *adj.* 相信的；信任的。—**ly,** *adv.* —**ness,** *n.*

trust fund 信託之金錢、有價證券或其他財產。

trust·i·fy 〔ˈtrʌstəˌfaɪ; ˈtrʌstifai〕 *v.t.* & *v.i.,* **-fied, -fy·ing.** 組成托辣斯；形成托辣斯。—**trust·i·fi·ca·tion,** *n.*

trust·ing 〔ˈtrʌstɪŋ; ˈtrʌstiŋ〕 *adj.* 信賴的；信任的；相信的。a *trusting* child. 一個信賴他人的兒童。—**ly,** *adv.* —**ness,** *n.*

trust·less 〔ˈtrʌstlɪs; ˈtrʌstlis〕 *adj.* ①

不可恃信的;不可信任的;不可靠的。②不信任的;懷疑的。—ly, *adv.* —ness, *n.*

trust territory 託管地區。

trust·wor·thy ['trʌst,wɝðɪ; 'trʌst,wəːði] *adj.* 可信賴的;可信任的;可靠的。—trust·wor·thi·ness, *n.*

***trust·y** ['trʌstɪ; 'trʌsti] *adj.*, **trust·i·er, trust·i·est,** *n., pl.* **trust·ies.** —*adj.* 可信任的;可靠的。a *trusty* servant. 可靠的僕人。—*n.* ①可信任的人。②模範囚犯。—trust·i·ly, *adv.* —trust·i·ness, *n.*

:truth [truθ; truːθ] *n., pl.* **truths** [truθs, truðz; truːθs, truːðz]. ①眞實;眞相;事實。to tell the *truth.* 說實話。②確實;眞實性。There is not a particle of *truth* in what he says. 他所說的毫不確實。③誠實。④眞理。to seek after *truth.* 探求眞理。*in truth* 實際上;事實上。

***truth·ful** ['truθfəl; 'truːθfəl] *adj.* ①說實話的;誠實的(人)。He has a *truthful* nature. 他是一個老實人。②合乎事實或眞理的;眞實的(敍述等)。—ly, *adv.* —ness, *n.*

:try [traɪ; trai] *v.*, **tried** [traɪd; traid], **try·ing,** *n., pl.* **tries.** —*v.t.* ①試爲;試圖;設法;嘗試。He *tried* to do it. 他想要做那件事。②試;試驗。*Try* this candy and see if you like it. 把這糖果試嘗一下,看你是否喜歡它。③審問。The man was *tried* and found guilty. 這人受審問,被判決有罪。④磨難;使受痛苦。Rheumatism *tries* me a great deal. 風濕症使我大受痛苦。⑤考驗;使過勞;使難堪。⑥提煉;精煉。The lard was *tried* in a big kettle. 這猪油在大鍋裏熬煉。⑦精確修整〖常 up〗. ⑧鉋平…之表面或削…之表面(使與另一表面相接合)。—*v.i.* 試做;勉力。I doubt if I can do it, but I'll *try.* 我不知道我能不能做這件事,但是我要試做一下。*try conclusions* 考驗自己〖常 with〗. *try it* (or *that*) *on* 〖主英〗 a. 擺架子。b. 對異性作露骨表示或採大膽行動。*try on* 試穿(衣服等)。She *tried on* her new dress. 她試穿新衣。*try one's best* (or *hardest*) 盡最大的努力。*try one's hand* 嘗試〖常 at〗. *try out* a. 徹底試驗。b. 試出(某種性質)。c. 參加競爭。d. 提煉。*try out for* 競爭(位置、會員資格等)。—*n.* ①嘗試;試驗;努力。He had three *tries* and failed each time. 他試驗三次,每次都失敗。②〖橄欖球〗在對方球門線後以球觸地,可獲得三分。*the old college try* 〖俗〗誠懇的努力。

***try·ing** ['traɪɪŋ; 'traiiŋ] *adj.* 難堪的;使人痛苦的;難忍的。This work is *trying* to the eyes. 這項工作太累眼睛。—ly, *adv.*

trying plane 接縫鉋。

try-on ['traɪ,ɑn; 'trai'ɔn] *n.* 〖俚〗①嘗試。②欺騙。③試穿。

try·out ['traɪ,aut; 'trai'aut] *n.* 〖俗〗①選拔賽。②試驗;考驗。③劇戲之預演。

tryp·a·no·some ['trɪpənə,som; 'tripənəsoum] *n.*〖動物〗錐形蟲(一種寄生在人或家畜血液中引起嚴重睡眠症之病原蟲)。

tryp·sin ['trɪpsɪn; 'tripsin] *n.*〖生化〗胰蛋白酶(胰液中之消化酵素)。—tryp·tic, *adj.*

tryp·sin·o·gen [trɪp'sɪnədʒən; trip'sinədʒən] *n.* 〖化〗鹼蛋白酶元。

tryp·to·phan ['trɪptəfæn; 'triptəfæn] *n.* 〖化〗色氨基酸。

try·sail ['traɪ,sel; 'traiseil] *n.* 〖航海〗斜桁帆。

try square (木匠等用之)矩。

tryst [trɪst, traɪst; traist] *n.* ①約會。②約晤之地點(=trysting place). —*v.t.* & *v.i.* 約定;約會。—er, *n.*

trysting place 約會之地點;會合地點。

tsar [tsɑr, zɑr; zɑː, tsɑː] *n.* =**czar.**

tset·se ['tsɛtsɪ; 'tsetsi] *n.* 非洲產的采采蠅(一種咬牛馬後可致死;另一種可傳播酣睡症)。(亦作 **tsetse fly**)

tsetse fly (非洲產之)采采蠅(傳播睡眠病等)。(亦作 **tsetse, tzetze fly**)

TSH, T.S.H. Their Serene Highness. 殿下。

T-shirt ['ti,ʃɝt; 'tiː-ʃəːt] *n.* 短袖汗衫;運動衫。

Tsing·hai ['tsɪŋ'haɪ; 'tsiŋ'hai] *n.* 青海(中國西部之一省,省會西寧 Sining).(亦作 **Chinghai**)

Tsing·tao ['tsɪŋ'tau; 'tsiŋ'tau] *n.* 青島(中國山東半島東部之一城市)。

tsp. ①teaspoon. ②teaspoonful.

T square 丁字尺;丁字規。

T.T. ① telegraphic transfer. ②torpedo tubes.

Tu ①thulium. ②tungsten.

Tu. Tuesday.

***tub** [tʌb; tʌb] *n., v.*, **tubbed, tub·bing.** —*n.* ①桶;木盆。②一桶之量。③浴盆。④〖俗〗沐浴。He takes a cold *tub* every morning. 他每晨洗一次冷水浴。⑤盛牛油、猪油等之圓形木盆。⑥似盆之物。⑦〖俗〗笨拙緩慢之船或艇。—*v.t.* ①在盆中洗(物)或洗澡。②將…置於盆中。—*v.i.* ①在盆中洗澡。②在盆中洗滌而不受損。This cotton print *tubs* well. 這種印花棉布經得起在盆中洗滌。—like, —ba·ble, *adj.*

tu·ba ['tjubə; 'tjuːbə] *n., pl.* **-bas, -bae** [-bi; -biː]. ①土巴號(管絃樂隊中之最低音銅管樂器)。②風琴音栓之一。

tub·ber ['tʌbɚ; 'tʌbə] *n.* ①桶匠。②沐浴者。

tub·by ['tʌbɪ; 'tʌbi] *adj.*, **-bi·er, -bi·est.** ①桶狀的。②矮而胖的。③鈍音的;如敲空桶發出之聲音的(指絃樂器言)。—tub·bi·ness, *n.*

***tube** [tjub; tjuːb] *n.* ①管;筒。a vacuum *tube.* 眞空管。②裝牙膏或顏料等之小筒。③管狀器官。④隧道。The railroad runs under the river in a *tube.* 該鐵路在一隧道中穿過河底。⑤〖俗〗地下鐵道。⑥眞空管。⑦任何管狀之物。⑧(車輪)內胎。⑨〖古〗望遠鏡。⑩(常 the-)〖美俚〗電視。—*v.t.* ①裝以管或筒。②用管子輸送;將…包於管中。③使成管狀。—like, *adj.*

tu·ber ['tjubɚ; 'tjuːbə] *n.* ①〖植物〗(馬鈴薯等之)塊莖;球根。②〖解剖〗結節。

tube railway 〖主英〗地下鐵路。

tu·ber·cle ['tjubɚkl; 'tjuːbəkl] *n.* ①(骨骼或植物上的)小結節。②〖醫〗結節;結核。

tubercle bacillus 結核菌。

tu·ber·cu·lar [tju'bɝkjəlɚ; tju(ː)'bəːkjulə] *adj.* ①結節狀的;有小結節的。②結核的;結核性的。③結核病的;患結核病的。—*n.* 結核病患者。—ly, *adv.*

tu·ber·cu·late [tju'bɝkjəlɪt; tju(ː)'bəːkjulit] *adj.* ①結核的;結核性的;患結核病的(=tubercular). ②有結節的(=tubercled). (亦作 **tuberculated**) —ly, *adv.*

tu·ber·cu·lin [tju'bɝkjəlɪn; tju(ː)'bəːkjulin] *n.* 〖醫〗結核菌素(診斷及治療肺結核病之一種注射液)。

tuberculo- 〖字首〗表"結核病;結核性;結核菌"之義。

tu·ber·cu·lo·sis [tju,bɝkjə'losɪs; tju(ː),bəːkju'lousis] *n.*〖醫〗結核病;肺結核。

tu·ber·cu·lous [tju'bɝkjələs; tju(ː)-

ˈbəːkjuləs] *adj.* ①有結節的；結節狀的。②患結核病的。—**ly,** *adv.*

tube·rose¹ [ˈtjubˌroz; ˈtjuːbrouz] *n.* 〖植物〗月下香。

tu·ber·ose² [ˈtjubəˌros; ˈtjuːbərous] *adj.* ＝**tuberous.**

tu·ber·os·i·ty [ˌtjubəˈrɑsətɪ; ˌtjuːbəˈrɔsiti] *n., pl.* **-ties.** ①結節狀；塊莖狀。②〖解剖, 動物〗(骨骼之)結節；粗隆。③結節性。

tu·ber·ous [ˈtjubərəs; ˈtjuːbərəs] *adj.* ①〖植物〗塊莖的；似塊莖的；有塊莖的。②有結節的；結節性的。—**ly,** *adv.*

tuberous root 塊狀根。

tub·ing [ˈtjubɪŋ; ˈtjuːbiŋ] *n.* ①管形材料。②管類之總稱。③管之一段；管之一節。④製管之過程。

tub thumper 感情激動之發言者(發「言時敲擊講桌者)。

tu·bu·lar [ˈtjubjələ; ˈtjuːbjulə] *adj.* ①管的；管狀的；筒狀的。②有管的；管式的；由管造成的。③〖生理, 醫〗似由管中產生之聲音的；發吹管般聲音的。—**i·ty,** *n.* —**ly,** *adv.*

tu·bu·late [*adj.* ˈtjubjəlɪt, -ˌlet; ˈtjuːbjulit, -leit *v.* ˈtjubjəˌlet; ˈtjuːbjuleit] *adj., v.,* **-lat·ed, -lat·ing.** —*adj.* 成管的；管狀的；筒狀的。—*v.t.* 製成管；裝以管。—**tu·bu·la·tion,** *n.*

tu·bule [ˈtjubjul; ˈtjuːbjuːl] *n.* 小管；「細管。

tu·bu·li·flo·rous [ˌtjubjəlɪˈflorəs; ˌtjuːbjuliˈflɔrəs] *adj.* 〖植物〗有花冠全部呈管狀之花的(如菊)。

T.U.C., TUC Trades Union Con-「gress.

tuck¹** [tʌk; tʌk] *v.t.* ①塞置於狹窄或隱蔽之所。He *tucked* the letter into his pocket. 他把信塞進衣袋裏面。②捲起；疊起；摺起。He *tucked* his shirt in. 他把襯衫的下部塞進褲腰裏面。③(在衣服上面)打褶襉。④縮攏。⑤很暖適地圍裹或覆蓋。—*v.i.* ①打褶襉。②收縮；收攏。③大吃特吃〖into, in〗. ***tuck away (or ***in***) 〖俚〗暢飲；大嚼。***tuck one's tail*** 丟臉；失體面。—*n.* ①褶；襉；襞。②〖運動〗將腿捲屈緊貼胸部之姿勢。③〖英俚〗食物。④省略。

tuck² *n.* 活力；力氣。

tuck·er [ˈtʌkə; ˈtʌkə] *n.* ①(十七、十八世紀時女人圍於頸部或肩上之)領布；飾紗。②打橫褶的人；作褶襉的人。③縫級機打褶襉之裝置。④婦女之小胸衣 (＝chemisette). ***make*** (or ***earn***) ***one's tucker*** 掙到勉强够用的生活費。***one's best bib and tucker*** 〖諧〗某人最好的一件衣服。—*v.t.* 〖美俗〗使疲憊；使筋疲力竭〖常 out〗.

tuck·shop [ˈtʌkˌʃɑp; ˈtʌkʃɔp] *n.* 〖英俗〗學校內之糖果店(學生用語)。

Tu·dor [ˈtjudə; ˈtjuːdə] *n.* ①都鐸王朝(英國從1485年至1603年間之王朝, 統治者爲Henry VII, Henry VIII, Edward VI, Mary 及 Elizabeth)；都鐸王室。②都鐸王朝時代之作家、政治家等。③都鐸王朝時代之建築式。***The Tudor***＝the House of Tudor. 都鐸王室。—*adj.* ①都鐸王朝的；都鐸王室的。②都鐸王朝時代的；都鐸王朝時代流行之式樣的。

Tues. Tuesday. (亦作 **Tu.**)

‡Tues·day [ˈtjuzdɪ; ˈtjuːzdi] *n.* 星期二；禮拜二。

tu·fa [ˈtjufə; ˈtjuːfə] *n.* 〖地質〗多孔之「凝灰岩。

tuff [tʌf; tʌf] *n.* 〖地質〗凝灰岩；凝成岩。

***tuft** [tʌft; tʌft] *n.* ①一束；一卷；一叢；一簇。a *tuft* of hair. 一束髮。②土墩；小丘。③使棉被、牀墊等裏面裝塡物固定的縫線。④固定這種縫線用的小鈕扣。⑤從前牛津與劍橋大學中貴族學生帽上的金縷。⑥〖俚〗戴上述帽子的人。—*v.t.* ①裝卷束於；分成卷、束。②以卷束固定(墊子等)之襯墊物。—*v.i.* 長成卷束或叢族；叢生；簇生。—**y,** *adj.*

tuft·ed [ˈtʌftɪd; ˈtʌftid] *adj.* ①有簇飾的。②成簇的。③(鳥)頭頂上有一簇羽毛的；有冠的。

***tug** [tʌg; tʌg] *v.,* **tugged** [tʌgd; tʌgd], **tug·ging,** *n.* —*v.t.* ①用力拉；拖曳。We *tugged* the boat in to shore. 我們把船拉到岸邊。②以拖船拖曳。—*v.i.* ①用力拉；拖曳。②奮鬥；努力。He *tugged* all his life to make a living. 他終生爲生活勞碌。—*n.* ①拖扯。②奮鬥；努力。③拖船。④拖革；以馬拖車用之皮帶。—**ger,** *n.* —**less,** *adj.*

tug·boat [ˈtʌgˌbot; ˈtʌgbout] *n.* 拖船。

tug of war ①拔河。②兩派的激烈鬥爭。

tu·i·tion [tjuˈɪʃən; tju(ː)ˈiʃən] *n.* ①教學；講授。②學費；束脩。③〖廢〗保管；監護。—**al,** *adj.*

tuition fee 學費。

tu·la·r(a)e·mi·a [ˌtuləˈrimɪə; ˌtuːləˈriːmiə] *n.* 〖醫, 獸醫〗土拉倫斯菌病(爲野兎、人及家畜所患的傳染病)。(亦作**rabbit fever, deer fly fever, Pahvant Valley fever**)

***tu·lip** [ˈtjuləp; ˈtjuːlip] *n.* 鬱金香；山慈姑。

tulip tree (北美產的)一種木蘭屬百合樹。

tu·lip·wood [ˈtjuləpˌwud; ˈtjuːlipwud] *n.* ①鬱金香木。②任何做傢具用的帶顏色條紋之木材。③產此種木材之樹。

tulle [tjul; tjuːl] *n.* 薄紗(作婦女面紗、衣「服用者)。

tum·ble** [ˈtʌmbl̩; ˈtʌmbl] *v.,* **-bled, -bling,** *n.* —*v.i.* ①跌落；跌倒。The child *tumbled* down the stairs. 小孩從樓梯上跌下。②滾動；輾轉。③急忙或倉皇地行動。He *tumbled* out of bed. 他急急忙忙地下了床。④翻觔斗。⑤下跌；降落。The stock market *tumbled.* 股市行情下跌。⑥崩潰。⑦碰到〖upon〗. ⑧(火箭等)失去控制而翻轉。—*v.t.* ①使跌倒；使跌落。The accident *tumbled* passengers out of a carriage. 那車禍使乘客自車中跌落。②使紊亂；弄亂；擾亂。③擊倒；打倒。④推翻。⑤使傾毀；使倒塌。tumble to*** a. 恍然大悟；了解。b. 〖英〗適應；配合。***tumble up*** 急忙跑到甲板上。—*n.* ①跌倒；跌落。②混亂；紊亂。Things were all in a *tumble.* 一切都很混亂。③雜亂的一堆。④翻觔斗。⑤下跌；下降。⑥翻騰。⑦理會。

tum·ble·bug [ˈtʌmbl̩ˌbʌg; ˈtʌmblbʌg] *n.* 金龜子；蜣螂。

tum·ble-down [ˈtʌmbl̩ˈdaun; ˈtʌmbldaun] *adj.* 破毀的；就要倒塌的(建築物)。

tum·bler [ˈtʌmblə; ˈtʌmblə] *n.* ①作翻觔斗等雜技的演員。②平底大玻璃杯；此種杯一杯之量。③鎖中之制栓部分；撥動後始能開鎖之部分。④(槍機之)翻板；倒鈎；推動撞針之部分。⑤飛翔時打滾的一種鴿子；翻飛鴿。⑥不倒翁。⑦(用以攪拌、磨光等之)滾桶；滾箱。⑧一種獵野兎的小獵犬。

tum·bler·ful [ˈtʌmbləful; ˈtʌmbləful] *n., pl.* **-fuls.** 平底大玻璃杯一杯之量。

tum·ble·weed [ˈtʌmbl̩ˌwid; ˈtʌmblwiːd] *n.* 〖美〗〖植物〗滾草(美國西部所產, 秋季時其莖在近地面處折斷, 隨風滾轉, 故名)。

tum·brel, tum·bril [ˈtʌmbrəl; ˈtʌmbrəl] *n.* ①〖英〗糞車；拖肥車。②法國大革命時期載運犯人至刑場之囚車。

tu·me·fac·tion [ˌtjuməˈfækʃən; ˌtjuːmiˈfækʃən] *n.* ①腫脹；腫大。②腫脹部分。

tu·me·fy [ˈtjuməˌfaɪ; ˈtjuːmifai] *v.t.* & *v.i.,* **-fied, -fy·ing.** (使)腫脹。

tu·mes·cence [tjuˈmɛsn̩s; tjuːˈmesns]

n. ①豐富;豐盛。②通貨膨脹。③隆起部分。—**tu·mes·cent,** *adj.*

tu·mid [ˈtjumɪd; ˈtjuːmid] *adj.* ①腫脹的;隆起的。②華而不實的;浮誇的(文體)。—**i·ty,** —**ness,** *n.* —**ly,** *adv.* 「語)。

tum·my [ˈtʌmɪ;ˈtʌmi] *n.* 胃;肚子(兒

tu·mor [ˈtjumɚ; ˈtjuːmə] *n.* ①腫脹。②〖醫〗腫瘤;瘤;贅瘤。—**ous,** *adj.*

tum-tum [ˈtʌmˌtʌm; ˈtʌmtʌm] *n.* ①彈撥絃樂器所發之聲;嗒嗒聲。②=**tummy.** —*v.i.* 發出嗒嗒聲。

***tu·mult** [ˈtjumʌlt; ˈtjuːmʌlt] *n.* ①喧囂。②騷動;騷亂;暴動。③激昂;奮發。His mind was in a *tumult*. 他的心情激動。

tu·mul·tu·ar·y [tjuˈmʌltʃʊˌɛrɪ; tjuːˈmʌltjuəri] *adj.* 喧囂的;騷動的;混亂的。

tu·mul·tu·ous [tjuˈmʌltʃuəs; tjuːˈmʌltjuəs] *adj.* ①喧囂的。②騷亂的。③兇猛的。—**ly,** *adv.* —**ness,** *n.*

tu·mu·lus [ˈtjumjələs; ˈtjuːmjuləs] *n., pl.* **-lus·es, -li** [-ˌlaɪ; -lai]. 古墓;塚。

tun [tʌn; tʌn] *n., v.,* **tunned, tun·ning.** —*n.* ①大酒桶;大樽;大桶。②酒類之容量單位(等於252加侖)。—*v.t.* 裝(酒等)入大桶;貯(酒)於大桶。

tu·na [ˈtunə; ˈtuːnə] *n.* ①鮪;金鎗魚(亦作 **tunafish**)。②鮪類。③鮪魚之肉。④(產於墨西哥的)霸王樹。⑤霸王樹之果實。

tun·a·ble [ˈtjunəbl̩; ˈtjuːnəbl] *adj.* ①(音調或週率)可調整的。②合調的;和諧的。(亦作**tuneable**)—**ness,** *n.*—**tun·a·bly,** *adv.*

tune** [tjun;tjuːn] *n., v.,* **tuned, tun·ing.** —*n.*①歌曲;曲調。②正確的音調;和諧;和合;調和。The piano is in *tune*. 這鋼琴音調正確。③心情;心緒。I am not in *tune* for talk. 我沒有心緒談話。call the tune*** 發號施令;命令;指令。***change one's tune*** 改變論調、行爲、態度等。***sing a different tune*** 取不同之言行;唱反調。***to the tune of*** 總數達於…。—*v.t.* ①使合調;調整(樂器或聲音的)音調。②歌唱;奏(樂)。The lark *tunes* his songs. 雲雀在唱歌。③調整(收音機)至某一波長或周率。④和諧地表示。⑤適合;適應。—*v.i.* ①調整。②和諧;合調。③調整收音機等之周率。***tune in*** 撥收音機以收聽(所欲聽到的廣播)。***tune out*** 撥收音機以避免(不願聽到的廣播或聲音)。***tune up*** **a.** 進(數種樂器)成同一音調。**b.**〖俗〗開始唱;開始演奏;(小兒)開始哭。**c.** 進入最佳之工作狀況。

tune·a·ble [ˈtjunəbl̩; ˈtjuːnəbl] *adj.* =**tunable.** —**ness,** *n.* —**tune·a·bly,** *adv.*

tune·ful [ˈtjunfəl; ˈtjuːnfəl] *adj.* ①音調和諧的;音調諧美的。②發出諧美之音的。

tune·less [ˈtjunlɪs;ˈtjuːnlis] *adj.* ①不合調子的;不成調子的;非音樂的;無韻律的。②不能發出樂聲的;無聲的。—**ly,** *adv.* —**ness,** *n.*

tun·er [ˈtjunɚ; ˈtjuːnə] *n.* ①調整樂器音調之人。②音調調整器。③〖無線電〗槽路;調諧器。④(任何機器之)調整師。

tune·smith [ˈtjunˌsmɪθ; ˈtjuːnsmiθ] *n.*〖俗〗流行歌曲作者。

tune-up [ˈtjunˌʌp; ˈtjuːnʌp] *n.* ①(機器之)調整。②準備。

tung oil 桐油。

tung·state [ˈtʌŋstet; ˈtʌŋsteit] *n.*〖化〗鎢酸鹽。

tung·sten [ˈtʌŋstən; ˈtʌŋstən] *n.*〖化〗鎢(=wolfram, 化學符號爲 W)。

tungsten lamp 鎢絲電燈泡。

tungsten steel 鎢鋼。

Tung·ting Hu [ˈdʊŋˈtɪŋˈhu; ˈduŋˈtiŋˈhuː] 洞庭湖(在中國湖南省東北部)。

tu·nic [ˈtjunɪk; ˈtjuːnik] *n.* ①古希臘、羅馬人所着的上衣或長袍。②婦人所着垂至腰下的束胸上衣。③軍人警察等所着的一種緊身上衣。④〖植物〗種皮。⑤〖解剖〗膜。

tu·ni·cate [ˈtjunɪˌket; ˈtjuːnikit] *adj.* ①〖植物〗被覆鱗葉的(如洋葱)。②〖動物〗有被膜的。—*n.*〖動物〗被囊類之動物。

tun·ing [ˈtjunɪŋ; ˈtjuːniŋ] *n.* ①調音;整調。②〖無線電〗波長調整。③〖電〗同調。

tuning fork〖物理〗音叉。

Tu·nis [ˈtjunɪs; ˈtjuːnis] *n.* ①突尼斯(爲突尼西亞之首都,在古代迦太基舊址附近)。②突尼斯(昔時北非 Barbary States 之一,現爲突尼西亞)。

Tu·ni·sia [tjuˈnɪʃɪə; tju(ː)ˈniziə] *n.* 突尼西亞(北非濱地中海之一國,其首都爲 Tunis).

***tun·nel** [ˈtʌnl̩; ˈtʌnl] *n., v.,* **-nel(l)ed, -nel·(l)ing.** —*n.* ①隧道;地道。a railway *tunnel*. 鐵路隧道。②動物之穴。—*v.t.* ①在…的中間或下面掘隧道。②掘隧道以開(路)。③穿過。—*v.i.* 掘隧道〖through, into〗. to *tunnel* through (*or* into) solid rock. 在堅石中掘隧道。—**er,** *n.* —**like,** *adj.*

tunnel vision〖醫〗視野狹窄症。

tun·ny [ˈtʌnɪ; ˈtʌni] *n., pl.* **-nies, -ny.** 鮪;金鎗魚。

tun·y [ˈtjunɪ; ˈtjuːni] *adj.,* **tun·i·er, tun·i·est.**〖俗〗有音調的;音調和諧的。

tup [tʌp; tʌp] *n., v.,* **tupped, tup·ping.** —*n.* ①公羊。②蒸氣動力槌之頭部;衝面。—*v.t.* (公羊)同(母羊)交尾。—*v.i.* ①(公羊)與母羊交尾。②(公羊)準備與母羊交尾。

tu·pe·lo [ˈtupəˌlo; ˈtuːpəlou] *n., pl.* **-los.**〖植物〗(北美洲所產之)山茱萸;伏牛化樹;山茱萸之木材。

tuque [tjuk; tjuːk] *n.* 加拿大人多天所戴的一種暖帽。(亦作 **toque**)

tu quo·que [tjuˈkwokwɪ;ˈtjuːˈkwoukwi]〖拉〗你也是;你也不例外(對譴責者反唇相譏之用語)(=thou also; you too).

Tu·ra·ni·an [tjʊˈrenɪən; tjuˈreinjən] *adj.* 烏拉阿爾泰語族的;該語族之人的。—*n.* 烏拉阿爾泰語族;該語族之人。

***tur·ban** [ˈtɝbən; ˈtəːbən] *n.* ①頭巾;(某些東方國家所用之)包頭巾。②(女人或兒童所戴之)無邊帽。—*v.t.* 包以頭巾;包。—**less,** *adj.* —**like,** *adj.*

tur·bid [ˈtɝbɪd; ˈtəːbid] *adj.* ①溷濁的;泥濁的。②濃密的(雲、煙等)。③混亂的;紊亂的;不明瞭的。—**ly,** *adv.* —**ness,** *n.*

tur·bid·i·ty [tɝˈbɪdətɪ; təːˈbiditi] *n.* ①汚濁;溷濁。②混亂;不明瞭。

tur·bi·nate [ˈtɝbənɪt; ˈtəːbinit] *adj.* (亦作 **turbinated**) ①陀螺形的;倒圓錐形的。②螺旋形的;渦卷狀的。③〖解剖〗鼻骨的。—*n.* ①螺旋形介殼。②〖解剖〗鼻骨。

tur·bi·na·tion [ˌtɝbɪˈneʃən; ˌtəːbiˈneiʃən] *n.* ①倒圓錐形;螺旋形。②(似陀螺之)旋轉。

tur·bine [ˈtɝbɪn; ˈtəːbin] *n.*〖機械〗渦輪機;渦輪。a steam *turbine*. 蒸氣渦輪機。

turbine generator 渦輪發電機。

turbo-〖字首〗表"有一渦輪的;由渦輪推動的;直接連於一渦輪的"之義。

tur·bo·jet [ˈtɝboˌdʒɛt; ˈtəːboudʒet] *n.* ①渦輪噴射引擎。②渦輪噴射機。

tur·bo·prop [ˈtɝboˌprɑp; ˈtəːbouprɔp] *n.* 渦輪螺旋槳發動機或飛機。

tur·bot [ˈtɝbət; ˈtəːbət] *n., pl.* **-bots,**

-bot. ①歐洲產之大比目魚。②比目魚類。
tur·bu·lence ['tɝbjələns; 'təːbjuləns] *n.* 狂烈;動亂;騷亂。(亦作 **turbulency**)
tur·bu·lent ['tɝbjələnt; 'təːbjulənt] *adj.* 狂烈的;動亂的;騷動的;暴亂的。 —**ly,** *adv.*
Turco- 〖字首〗=**Turko-.**
Tur·co·phil ['tɝkəfɪl; 'təːkəfil] *n.* (亦作 **Turcophile, Turkophile**) 愛好土耳其風俗習慣等的人;親土耳其的人。—*adj.* 親土耳其的。
Tur·co·phobe ['tɝkə,fob; 'təːkəfoub] *n.* 極端懼怕土耳其的人。(亦作 **Turkophobe**)
tu·reen [tu'rin; tə'riːn] *n.* 一種盛湯用的深而大的有蓋之盌。
***turf** [tɝf; təːf] *n., pl.* **turfs** or **turves,** *v.* —*n.* ①草泥;草地;草皮。②乾草。③(常 the-) 賽馬;跑馬場。④〖俚〗都市中地痞流氓之勢力範圍。—*v.t.* ①覆以草皮。②〖主英〗趕走。
turf·ite ['tɝfaɪt; 'təːfait] *n.* 〖俗〗= **turfman.**
turf·man ['tɝfmən; 'təːfmən] *n., pl.* **-men.** 熱中於賽馬的人。
turf·y ['tɝfɪ; 'təːfi] *adj.,* **turf·i·er, turf·i·est.** ①多草皮的;覆有草皮的。②似草皮的;草泥狀的。③與賽馬有關的。
Tur·ge·nev, Tur·ge·niev, Tur·ge·nyev [tur'genjɪf; təː'geinjev] *n.* 屠格涅夫(Ivan Sergeevich, 1818–1883, 俄國小說家)。
tur·ges·cence [tɝ'dʒɛsn̩s; təː'dʒesns] *n.* ①膨脹。②誇張;誇耀。③〖理化〗由膨脹造成之硬化。④〖生理〗脹大;腫脹。(亦作 **turgescency**)
tur·ges·cent [tɝ'dʒɛsn̩t; təː'dʒesnt] *adj.* 膨脹的;腫脹的;誇張的。
tur·gid ['tɝdʒɪd; 'təːdʒid] *adj.* ①腫脹的;浮腫的。②誇張的;虛飾的;華而不實的(言語或文體)。 —**ly,** *adv.* —**ness,** *n.*
tur·gid·i·ty [tɝ'dʒɪdətɪ; təː'dʒiditi] *n.* ①腫脹;浮腫。②誇張;虛飾;華而不實。
tur·gor ['tɝgɚ; 'təːgə] *n.* ① 腫脹。②〖生理〗充實(動、植物細胞之正常膨脹或彈力)。
***Turk** [tɝk; təːk] *n.* ①土耳其人。②土耳其馬。③〖諧〗頑皮孩子;殘暴而野蠻者;暴君。④激進分子。
Turk. ①Turkey. ②Turkish.
***Tur·key** ['tɝkɪ; 'təːki] *n.* 土耳其(西亞南歐之一國,首都安卡拉 Ankara)。
tur·key** ['tɝkɪ; 'təːki] *n., pl.* **-keys.** ①火鷄。 *turkey* hen. 母火鷄。②〖俚〗極劣的戲或電影。 ③〖俚〗失敗。④背包。 ***talk turkey 〖俗〗坦白而鹵莽地講;認眞談判。
turkey cock ①公火鷄。②矯飾自負者。
Turkey red ①鮮紅色。②鮮紅色棉布。
***Turk·ish** ['tɝkɪʃ; 'təːkiʃ] *adj.* 土耳其(人)的。—*n.* 土耳其語。—**ly,** *adv.* —**ness,** *n.*
Turkish bath 土耳其浴。
Turkish delight (or **paste**) 膠狀糖球。
Turkish pound 土耳其鎊(符號£T)。
Turkish tobacco 土耳其菸草。
turkish towel 一種長毳厚毛巾。(亦作 **Turkish towel**)
Turk·man ['tɝkmən; 'təːkmən] *n., pl.* **-men.** 土庫曼 (Turkmen Soviet Socialist Republic) 之人或居民。
Turk·men ['tɝkmɛn; 'təːkmen] *n.* 土庫曼語。
Turk·me·ni·stan [,tɝkmɛnɪ'stæn; ,təːkmenis'tɑːn] *n.* =**Turkmen Soviet Socialist Republic.** (亦作 **Turkomen**)
Turkmen Soviet Socialist Republic 土庫曼蘇維埃社會主義共和國(蘇聯之一共和國,在中亞及伊朗之北,首都阿什喀巴德 Ashkhabad)。
Turko- 〖字首〗表"土耳其的; 土耳其人的;土耳其與…; 土耳其人與…"之義。(亦作 **Turco-**)
Tur·ko·man ['tɝkəmən; 'təːkəmən] *n., pl.* **-mans.** ①土庫曼人。②土庫曼語。
Turk's-head ['tɝks,hɛd; 'təːkshed] *n.* ①(掃除天花板等用的)長柄羽毛箒。②〖航海〗纜索上之飾結。
tur·mer·ic ['tɝmərɪk; 'təːmərik] *n.* ①〖植物〗鬱金;薑黃。②鬱金根;薑黃根(供作黃色染料、醫藥等)。
tur·moil ['tɝmɔɪl; 'təːmɔil] *n.* 騷動;騷擾;混亂。—*v.t.* 使騷亂;使騷動。—**er,** *n.*
‡**turn** [tɝn; təːn] *v.t.* ①旋轉。 to *turn* a handle. 旋轉把柄。②轉動;翻轉。She *turned* the key in the lock. 她用鑰匙開鎖。③使面對另一方向; 使轉向; 移轉。Nothing will ever *turn* him from his purpose. 任何事物均不能使他改變意向。④使變成; 改變; 使變質。 to *turn* love to hate. 轉愛成恨。⑤使昏狂。⑥翻譯。*Turn* this sentence into English. 把這句話譯成英語。⑦轉過。 to *turn* a street corner. 轉過街角。⑧驅逐。⑨使用;利用。 to *turn* money to good use. 將金錢作適當的利用。⑩到達並度過(某一時期)。He has *turned* fifty. 他已五十歲了。 ⑪作成; 形成。 to *turn* a verse. 作詩。⑫使作嘔。 The mere sight of food *turned* his stomach. 食物使他一見便嘔。⑬阻止;擋回。 to *turn* a punch. 擋住一拳。⑭以車床車。 to *turn* brass. 在車床上車銅器。 ⑮使銷售殆盡。 ⑯得到; 賺到。 ⑰思索〖常 over〗。⑱勸(人)改變生活方式或程序。⑲使對…敵視。to *turn* a son against his father. 使兒子仇視父親。⑳保持(金融)流通; 保持(貨物)之供給。㉑使彎曲; 使扭折。㉒扭傷。㉓使從一容器傾入另一容器。㉔使(刀口)變鈍。 —*v.i.* ①旋轉; 環繞。The earth *turns* round the sun. 地球繞日運行。②轉動;翻身。 to *turn* in bed. 在床上翻身。③轉變方向; 面對另一方向。 *Turn* to the right. 向右邊轉。Right (Left) *turn!* 向右(左)轉! ④變爲。He has *turned* traitor. 他變成一個賣國賊。⑤依賴; 以…爲轉移。⑥(牛奶等)變酸。 The milk has *turned.* 牛奶已變酸。⑦(樹葉)變色。⑧眩暈。My head *turns.* 我頭暈。⑨作嘔。⑩轉向。 to *turn* to God for help. 向上帝求助。⑪變鈍。⑫在車床上被車;被用車床加工。***About turn!*** 向後轉! ***turn a blind eye*** 故意忽視;故意不睬。 ***turn about*** 向後轉。 ***turn a deaf ear*** 不聽; 不接受; 不理睬。 ***turn against*** 對…轉取敵對態度;使對…轉取敵對態度。 ***turn a hair*** 失去鎮靜;動色(常用於否定)。 ***turn an honest penny*** 正正當當地賺錢。 ***turn a person's brain*** 使人神志恍惚;使人精神錯亂。 ***turn a person's head*** 使人困惑。 ***turn aside*** 轉變方向;使轉變方向。 ***turn away*** a. 轉變…的方向; 不看。He *turned away* in disgust. 他覺得厭惡而把臉轉開。b. 不許進入; 辭退。 ***turn back*** a. 返回。b. 翻回書頁。*Turn back* to the first page. 將書翻回到第一頁。 c. 趕回; 使折回。d. 折疊。 ***turn color*** 變色。 ***turn down*** a. 拒絕;摒斥。b. 扭轉活栓以使(燈等)之火燄減小。c. 翻下。 to *turn down* one's coat collar. 把外衣領翻下。d. 翻

過來使其面向下。e. 摺下。***turn in*** a. 進入;折入。b. 向內曲;使向內曲。c.〖俗〗就寢。d. 歸還。e. 交換。f. 告密;交出。***turn inside out*** 翻轉;將裏面翻作外面。***turn into*** a. 走進或駕車開進(商店、街道等)。b. 變成;變爲。***turn loose*** a. 使爲所欲爲。b. 使爆發。***turn off*** a. 遮斷;關閉(煤氣、自來水、電燈等)。*Turn off* the water. 把水關掉。b. 解雇;辭退。c. 轉向旁邊。d. 做。e. 躲開;避開。f. 施以絞刑。g. 變。h. 不再聽。***turn on*** a. 打開(煤氣、自來水、電燈等)。*Turn* the radio *on*. 打開收音機。b. 依賴;以…爲轉移。c. 反對;攻擊。d. 與…有關。e. 使開始;發動。f. 突然做出某種態度。g.〖俚〗引誘(他人)吸毒;開始吸毒。h. 發動;開動。***turn one's back on*** (or ***upon***) a. 離開。b. 拒絕;置之不顧。c. 背棄。He *turned his back on* his own people. 他背棄了他的人民。***turn one's coat*** 改變主意;倒向敵方。***turn one's hand*** 開始工作;着手。***turn one's stomach*** 令人作嘔。***turn out*** a. 逐出。b. 翻轉;翻閱。c. 製成;產出。d. 外出;出來。e. 關閉(電燈、自來水等)。f. 結果;竟然;判明爲。g.〖俗〗起床。h. 指向;使指向。i. 供以衣服、裝備等。j. 罷工。k. 清掃;打掃。***turn over*** a. 移交;交付;讓渡。b. 考慮。c. (躺臥時) 翻身。d. 翻;翻轉。The car *turned over*. 那車翻了。e. 營業額達於…。The business *turned over* $500 last week. 上週做了五百元的生意。f. 轉賣。g. 投資後收回(資本)。h. 改作他用。i. 用手翻。j. 旋轉。k. 發動(引擎)。l. (引擎) 發動。***turn over a new leaf*** 改過自新。***turn round*** (使) 轉過來(去); 形成新的意見; 開始採取新的政策。***turn tail*** 逃跑。***turn the corner*** 度過難關;安然度過危境。***turn the scale*** 有決定性效果。***turn the tide*** 扭轉時勢。***turn thumbs down*** 表示不贊成;表示反對。***turn to*** a. 求助於。b. 開始;着手;開始工作。c. 指…; 參考…。d. 變爲。***turn up*** a. 捲起;翻轉;向上彎; 向上傾。b. 將(燈等)扭得更亮。*Turn* the lights *up*. 將燈扭得更亮。c. 將(收音機)扭得聲音更大。d. 出現;來臨;發生。e. 轉向上升。f. 翻起。The plough *turned up* the soil. 犂將土翻鬆了。g. 找到;發現。***turn upon*** a. 依賴;以…爲轉移。b. 反對;攻擊。—*n.* ①旋轉;轉動。②轉變方向。③彎曲;曲折;轉彎之處。a *turn* in the road. 路的轉彎。④轉機;改變;變化。⑤格式;樣式;形式。a happy *turn* of expression. 一個圓滿的說法。⑥時機;輪值。It is his *turn* to read. 現在輪到他讀了。⑦散步;駕車;騎馬(等)。⑧事蹟; 行爲。One good *turn* deserves another.〖諺〗施惠者應得到報償。⑨特殊需要; 目的。⑩傾向; 癖性;才能。He has a *turn* for mathematics. 他有數學的才能。⑪〖俗〗吃驚。The news gave me quite a *turn*. 這消息使我大吃一驚。⑫(繩子的) 一圈;一彎。⑬工作或行動之時期; 一陣工作。Have a *turn* at a thing. 把某事做一陣。⑭表演。⑮一陣頭眩或昏暈。⑯〖音樂〗回音。***at every turn*** 每次;無例外地。***by turns*** 輪替地;輪流地。***hand's turn*** 工作;工作時間。***in turn*** a. 依順序地。Each of you must speak *in turn*. 你們必須依次發言。b. 必然也…。***on the turn*** 正要轉; 在轉動;正要轉變。***out of turn*** a. 不依照順序地。b. 不合時宜地。***take turns*** 輪流。Let us *take turns* at doing it. 讓我們輪流做這件事。***to a turn*** 剛好合適。***turn (and turn) about*** 互相輪流。***turn of hair*** 一毫之差。***turn of speed*** 速度之能力。—**a·ble,** *adj.*

turn·a·bout [ˈtɝnəˌbaut; ˈtəːnəˌbaut] *n.* ①轉向。②變節。③〖美〗廻轉木馬。④贊成改變者。⑤互惠之行動。

turn·a·round [ˈtɝnəˌraund; ˈtəːnəˌraund] *n.* ①(思想、態度等之) 轉變。②(航空等) 往返所需之時日。③船出海前在港中停泊之時間。④可供車輛倒轉之小廣場。

turn·buck·le [ˈtɝnˌbʌkl; ˈtəːnˌbʌkl] *n.*〖機械〗鬆緊螺旋扣;套筒螺母。

turn·cap [ˈtɝnˌkæp; ˈtəːnkæp] *n.* 旋帽(廻旋於煙筒上以使開口處向下風者)。

turn·coat [ˈtɝnˌkot; ˈtəːnkout] *n.* 變節者;脫黨者;背棄信仰者;叛徒。

turn·down [ˈtɝnˌdaun; ˈtəːndaun] *adj.* 向下翻折的; 翻折式的。—*n.* 拒絕。

turned-on [ˈtɝndˈɑn; ˈtəːndˈɔn] *adj.*〖俚〗瘋狂的。

Tur·ner [ˈtɝnɚ; ˈtəːnə] *n.* 脫爾諾(Joseph Mallord William, 1775–1851, 英國畫家)。

turn·er [ˈtɝnɚ; ˈtəːnə] *n.* ①轉動之人或物。②旋匠; 車床工人。③〖美〗體育協會會員; 體育家。

turn·er·y [ˈtɝnərɪ; ˈtəːnəri] *n., pl.* **-er·ies.** ①旋盤細工; 鏇床細工。②旋盤細工之工廠技術或製品。

turn·ing [ˈtɝnɪŋ; ˈtəːniŋ] *n.* ①旋轉; 廻轉;轉動。②轉彎處;拐角; 彎曲。③鏇; 鏇工;車工。④形成;構成;做成。

turning over board〖機械〗底板。

turning point 轉機;轉捩點。

***tur·nip** [ˈtɝnɪp; ˈtəːnip] *n.* 蘿蔔;蕪菁。(英亦作 **turmut**)

turnip tops 蕪菁葉。(亦作 **turnip greens**)

turn·key[1] [ˈtɝnki; ˈtəːnkiː] *n., pl.* **-keys.** 監獄的看守;獄吏。

turn·key[2] *adj.* 由包商完全包辦的。

turn·off [ˈtɝnˌɔf; ˈtəːnɔf] *n.* ①轉彎。②岔路;支路。③(家畜之)產量。④成品。

turn-on [ˈtɝnˌɑn; ˈtəːnɔn] *n.*〖俚〗刺激。

turn·out [ˈtɝnˌaut; ˈtəːnˈaut, for③④ ˈtəːnaut] *n.* ①羣集之人;(集會之)出席者。②生產量;量額。③窄路上之寬濶處(車輛可以相錯或超馳者)。④鐵路之側線;避讓線。⑤臨時召集。⑥起床。⑦裝扮;裝備。⑧〖英〗罷工;罷工者。⑨馬;拉車之馬;馬車。⑩出動。⑪清掃。

turn·o·ver [ˈtɝnˌovɚ; ˈtəːnˌouvə] *n.* ①翻覆。②人事變動。③周轉。④某一時期的總營業額;營業量。⑤商品(尤指全部存貨) 出售之速度。⑥在一定時間內資本投資與轉投資之次數。⑦捲酥。—*adj.* (可以) 翻過來的。

turn·pike [ˈtɝnˌpaɪk; ˈtəːnpaik] *n.* ①(收取通行稅之) 關柵;關卡。②有收取通行稅柵門之道路;收稅路(=turnpike road)。

turn·plate [ˈtɝnˌplet; ˈtəːnpleit] *n.*〖英〗轉車臺 (=turntable)。

turn·screw [ˈtɝnˌskru; ˈtəːnskruː] *n.*〖主英〗螺絲旋轉具;螺旋起子。

turn signal 汽車前後之轉向指示燈。

turn·sole [ˈtɝnˌsol; ˈtəːnsoul] *n.* ①其花有向日性之植物。②地中海所產的一種產紫色顏料之植物;此種植物產的澤漆。

turn·spit [ˈtɝnˌspɪt; ˈtəːnspit] *n.* ①可旋轉烤肉叉的人。②可旋轉之烤肉叉。③一種長身短腿之犬(昔日訓練之使轉動烤肉叉)。

turn·stile [ˈtɝnˌstaɪl; ˈtəːn-stail] *n.* (設於戲院、遊戲場所等入口處之) 十字轉門。

turn·stone ['tɝn,ston; 'tə:nstoun] *n.* 鶇鴴。

turn·ta·ble ['tɝn,tebl̩; 'tə:n,teibl] *n.* ①〖鐵路〗(用來轉換機車等方向的) 轉車臺;旋車盤。②(留聲機之) 轉盤。③(瓷工、鐵工、雕刻者用的)轉盤。

turn·up ['tɝn,ʌp; 'tə:nʌp] *n.* 〖俚〗①騷亂; 打鬥。②突然成名者; 突然出現者。③翻折; 翻折之物; 褲脚之翻折邊。④突來之幸運。⑤出現。—*adj.* 翻轉的;(衣領)可翻折的。

Turn·ver·ein ['turnfɛr,aɪn; 'tuən-ferain] 〖德〗*n.*體育協會。(亦作**turnverein**)

tur·pen·tine ['tɝpən,taɪn; 'tə:pən-tain] *n.*, *v.*, **-tined, -tin·ing.** —*n.* 松脂;松油;松節油。—*v.t.* 塗以松節油;自…採集松脂。—*v.i.* 塗松節油。—**tur·pen·tin·ic,** *adj.*

tur·pi·tude ['tɝpə,tjud; 'tə:pitju:d] *n.* ①邪惡;卑鄙。②可恥的行爲。

turps [tɝps; tə:ps] *n.* 〖俗〗松節油 (爲 turpentine 之略)。

tur·quoise ['tɝkwɔɪz; 'tə:kwɑ:z] *n.* ①〖礦〗綠松石。②綠松石的顏色;綠藍色;天藍色。—*adj.*①綠藍色的;天藍色的。②綠松石的。

*__tur·ret__ ['tɝɪt, 'turɪt; 'tʌrit] *n.* ①(建築物之)小塔;角樓。②砲塔。③裝甲車上之車塔。④軍用飛機之機艙。⑤(中世紀攻城用之)仰衝車; 塔車。

tur·ret·ed ['tɝɪtɪd; 'tʌritid] *adj.* ①有小塔的;小塔狀的。②有砲塔的。③〖動物〗塔狀的(指介殼言)。

*__tur·tle__ ['tɝtl̩; 'tə:tl] *n.* ①龜;鼈;甲魚。②〖古〗斑鳩 (= turtledove). ***turn turtle*** 底部朝天地翻滾過來;沉沒。—*v.i.*捉龜;捕鼈。

tur·tle·back ['tɝtl̩,bæk; 'tə:tlbæk] *n.* ①=**turtle deck.** ②〖考古〗龜甲形石器。

turtle deck 〖航海〗在船首和船尾甲板上樹起之拱形甲板(用以防巨浪者)。

tur·tle·dove ['tɝtl̩,dʌv; 'tə:tldʌv] *n.* 斑鳩。

tur·tle·neck ['tɝtl̩,nɛk; 'tə:tlnek] *n.* ①有翻折高領之毛線衫。②(套頭毛線衫的)翻折的高領。(亦作 **turtle neck**)

turtle soup 龜肉湯。

Tus·can ['tʌskən; 'tʌskən] *adj.* ①Tuscany 的。②Tuscany 人的。③〖建築〗Tuscan 式的。—*n.* ①Tuscany 人或居民。②Tuscany 之義大利方言。③標準之義大利語。

Tus·ca·ny ['tʌskənɪ;'tʌskəni] *n.* 托斯卡尼(義大利西部之一行政區)。

tush¹ [tʌʃ; tʌʃ] *interj.* 咄咄之聲 (表示不耐煩、叱責或輕蔑)。—*v.i.* 發咄咄之聲以表示輕蔑或叱責。 —*n.* 啐;咄咄之聲。

tush² *n.* ①馬之犬齒。 ②象牙;長牙。

tush·er·y ['tʌʃərɪ; 'tʌʃəri] *n.*, *pl.* **-er·ies.** 常用驚嘆詞 tush 以增加古風的一派人或文體。

tusk [tʌsk; tʌsk] *n.* ①(象等之) 長牙。②似長牙之物。 —*v.t.* & *v.i.* 以長牙挖掘或刺戳。—**less,** *adj.*

tusk·er ['tʌskɚ;'tʌskə] *n.* (如象等)有長牙之獸。

tus·sa(h) ['tʌsə; 'tʌsə] *n.* ①山蠶; 野蠶。②野蠶絲;山蠶絲綢;山東綢。(亦作 **tusseh, tusser, tussor, tussore, tussur**)

tus·sis ['tʌsɪs; 'tʌsis] *n.* 〖醫〗咳嗽。(=cough). —**tus·sive,** *adj.*

tus·sle ['tʌsl̩; 'tʌsl] *v.*, **-sled, -sling,** *n.* —*v.i.* 劇烈地爭鬥、競爭等; 搏鬥; 扭打。—*n.* 劇烈的爭鬥、競賽或爭論;扭打。

tus·sock ['tʌsək; 'tʌsək] *n.* ①(草等之)叢;簇。②〖罕〗一簇毛髮。—**ed,** *adj.*

tus·sock·y ['tʌsəkɪ; 'tʌsəki] *adj.* ①成草叢的;像草叢的。②覆有草叢的。③多草叢的。

tut [tʌt; tʌt] *interj.*, *n.*, *v.*, **tut·ted, tut·ting.** —*interj.*, *n.* 嘘!嘖!(表示不耐煩、輕蔑、責難之聲)。—*v.i.* 發出嘘、嘖之聲。

tu·te·lage ['tutlɪdʒ; 'tju:tilidʒ] *n.* ①保護。②教育;教導。③受保護或被教導之狀態。

tu·te·lar ['tutlə; 'tjutilə]*adj.* 保護的;守護的 (=tutelary).

tu·te·lar·y ['tutl̩,ɛrɪ; 'tju:tiləri] *adj.*, *n.*, *pl.* **-lar·ies.** —*adj.* ①保護的;守護的。②保護者的;守護者的。—*n.* 守護神;守護聖徒。

*__tu·tor__ ['tutɚ, 'tju-; 'tju:tə] *n.* ①私人教師;家庭教師。②(英國大學之)導師。③(美國大學之)教員(職位低於講師instructor者);助教。—*v.t.* ①教授; 教導。 ②不光明地教。③保護;照顧;作…之監護人。—*v.i.* ①〖俗〗被教導。②做家庭教師。—**less,** *adj.*

tu·tor·age ['tutərɪdʒ; 'tju:təridʒ] *n.* ①家庭教師之地位、職責、權威或教導。②家庭教師之報酬;束脩。③監護之地位或職責。

tu·to·ri·al [tu'torɪəl; tju'tɔ:riəl] *adj.* ①家庭教師的。②(大學之)導師的。③〖法律〗(未成年之)監護人的。

tu·tor·ship ['tutɚ,ʃɪp; 'tju:təʃip] *n.* ①家庭教師之地位、職權等。②教導;指導。

tu·tress ['tjutrɪs; 'tju:tris] *n.* 女教師;女家庭教師。(亦作 **tutoress**)

tut·ti ['tutɪ; 'tu:ti(:)] *adj.*, *n.*, *pl.* **-tis.** —*adj.* 〖音樂〗全部聲音或樂器的; 全體奏的。—*n.* ①全部演唱者均唱或奏的樂章;全體奏。②全部演唱者均唱或奏時產生之聲音效果。

tut·ti-frut·ti ['tutɪ'frutɪ; 'tu:ti'fru:-ti] *n.* ①蜜餞百果。②攙有蜜餞百果的冰淇淋。—*adj.* 由蜜餞百果製的; 由蜜餞百果調味的。

tut·ty ['tʌtɪ;'tʌti] *n.* (鎔爐通風道中之)不純之氧化鋅。

tu·tu ['tutu;'tu:tu:] *n.*, *pl.* **-tus** [-tuz; -tu:z]. 〖法〗巴蕾舞中女演員所着之短裙。

tu-whit [tu'hwɪt;tu'hwit]*n.*, *v.*, **-whitted, -whit·ting.** —*n.* 梟鳴聲; 啼啼聲。—*v.i.* 作梟鳴聲;啼啼地叫。(亦作 **tu-whoo**)

tux [tʌks; tʌks] *n.* 〖美俗〗=**tuxedo.**

tux·e·do [tʌk'sido; tʌk'si:dou] *n.*, *pl.* **-dos, -does.** 〖美〗男人着用之一種無尾的半正式晚禮服。(亦作 **Tuxedo**) —**ed,** *adj.*

tu·yère [twi'jɛr; twi:'jɛr] 〖法〗 *n.* 〖冶金〗(鎔爐等之)鼓風口。

TV ①television. ②terminal velocity.

TVA, T.V.A. Tennessee Valley Authority.

TV dinner 食前加溫之包裝現成的冷凍便餐。

TWA Trans World Airlines. 美國環球航空公司。

twad·dle ['twɑdl̩; 'twɔdl] *n.*, *v.*, **-dled, -dling.** —*n.* 愚蠢而無聊之談話或寫作。—*v.i.* 講廢話;笨拙而無意義地寫。—*v.t.* 講(廢話);寫(笨拙無聊的文章)。—**twad·dler,** *n.*

Twain [twen; twein] *n.* 馬克吐溫 (Mark, 1835–1910, 美國小說家及幽默家, 其本名爲 Samuel Langhorne Clemens).

twain [twen; twein] *n.* 〖古,詩〗二;兩個。—*adj.* 〖古,詩〗二的;兩個的。

twang¹ [twæŋ; twæŋ] *n.* ①弦聲。②尖銳的鼻音。—*v.t.* ①撥弦使發音響;彈;發響聲射出。②以鼻音而言。—*v.i.*① 發弦聲。②以鼻音說話。

twang² *n.* 氣味;味道。

'twas [twɑz; twɔz] 〖古,詩〗 =**it was.**

tweak [twik; twi:k] *v.t.* 擰;扭;用力扯。—*n.* 擰;扭;力扯。

twee 〔twi; twiː〕 *adj.* 【英俚】矯揉造作的;可愛的。

tweed 〔twid; twiːd〕 *n.* ①一種蘇格蘭出產之粗呢。②(*pl.*)蘇格蘭粗呢所製之衣服。

twee·dle 〔ˈtwidl̩; ˈtwiːdl〕 *v.*, **-dled, -dling,** *n.* —*v.i.* (樂器或其彈奏者)發出或奏出鏜然之聲。—*v.t.* 漫不經心地撥弄(絃樂器)。—*n.* (樂器發出之)鏜然聲。

twee·dle·dum and twee·dle·dee 〔ˌtwidl̩ˈdʌm ən ˌtwidl̩ˈdi; ˌtwiːdlˈdʌm ən ˌtwiːdlˈdiː〕 ①難以區別的二事物;半斤八兩;名稱不同而實質相同的兩件東西。②【諧,蔑】外貌、性格、意見等相同的兩個人。

tweed·y 〔ˈtwidɪ; ˈtwiːdi〕 *adj.* ①似蘇格蘭粗呢的。②穿蘇格蘭粗呢衣服的;穿便裝的。③習慣於戶外生活的;隨便慣了的。

tween·y 〔ˈtwinɪ; ˈtwiːni〕 *n.* 【美俗】①協助燒飯及打雜的年輕女傭。②十至十二歲之間的兒童。

tweet 〔twit; twiːt〕 *n.* 小鳥的叫聲;啾啾聲。—*v.i.* (小鳥)啾啾地叫;啁啾而鳴。

tweet·er 〔ˈtwitɚ; ˈtwiːtə〕 *n.* (立體身歷聲揚聲器中之)高音喇叭;高頻率揚聲裝置。

tweeze 〔twiz; twiːz〕 *v.t.*, **tweezed, tweez·ing.** 以鑷子除去;以鉗子除去。

tweez·er 〔ˈtwizɚ; ˈtwiːzə〕 *v.t.* 以鑷子或鉗子挾;挾。—*n.* =**tweezers.**

tweez·ers 〔ˈtwizɚz; ˈtwiːzəz〕 *n. pl.* 鑷子;鉗子。

***twelfth** 〔twɛlfθ; twelfθ〕 *adj.* ①第十二。the *twelfth* day. 第十二天。②十二分之一的。—*n.* ①第十二。②十二分之一。③(月之)十二日。

Twelfth-cake 〔ˈtwɛlfθˌkek; ˈtwelfθkeik〕 *n.* 慶祝 Twelfth-night 用的糕餅。

Twelfth-day 〔ˈtwɛlfθˌde; ˈtwelfθdei〕 *n.* 十二日節;主顯節(一月六日,耶誕節後之第十二日)。

twelfth·ly 〔ˈtwɛlfθlɪ; ˈtwelfθli〕 *adv.* 第十二。

Twelfth-night 〔ˈtwɛlfθˌnaɪt; ˈtwelfθnait〕 *n.* 耶誕後十二日之夜或前夕。

:twelve 〔twɛlv; twelv〕 *n.* ①十二;12。②十二個;十二人;十二歲;十二時。a boy of *twelve.* 十二歲的孩子。③(大小號碼之)十二號。She wears *twelves.* 她穿十二號。***the Twelve*** 基督的十二使徒。—*adj.* 十二個的。

Twelve Apostles 耶穌之十二使徒。

twelve·mo 〔ˈtwɛlvmo; ˈtwelvmou〕 *adj., n., pl.* **-mos.** =**duodecimo** (略作 12mo)。

twelve·month 〔ˈtwɛlvˌmʌnθ; ˈtwelvmʌnθ〕 *n.* 【英】十二個月;一年。

twelve-note〔ˈtwɛlvˌnot; ˈtwelvnout〕 *adj.* 【英】=**twelve-tone.**

twelve·pence 〔ˈtwɛlvˌpɛns; ˈtwelvpens〕 *n.* =**shilling.**

twelve·pen·ny〔ˈtwɛlvˌpɛnɪ; ˈtwelvpeni〕 *adj.* 售價或值十二辨士(一先令)的。

Twelve Tables, the 十二銅表法(羅馬法之初期法典,訂於 451–450 B.C.)。

twelve-tone 〔ˈtwɛlvˌton; ˈtwelvtoun〕 *adj.* 【音樂】十二音的;十二音制的。

twelve-tone system 【音樂】十二音制。

***twen·ti·eth** 〔ˈtwɛntɪɪθ; ˈtwentiiθ〕 *adj.* ①第二十。②二十分之一的。—*n.* ①第二十。②二十分之一。③(月之)二十日。

:twen·ty 〔ˈtwɛntɪ; ˈtwenti〕 *n., pl.* **-ties,** *adj.* —*n.* ①二十;20。②二十個;二十人;二十歲。*Twenty* are here. 這裏有二十個。③(大小號碼之)二十號。She wears a *twenty.* 她穿二十號。④(*pl.*)20到29的數之集合稱。the *twenties* of the preceding century. 前世紀之二十年代。—*adj.* 二十。*twenty* years. 二十年。

twen·ty·fold 〔ˈtwɛntɪˌfold; ˈtwentifould〕 *adj.* ①有二十個節(方面、部分、種類等)的。②二十倍的。—*adv.* 二十倍地。

twen·ty-four·mo 〔ˈtwɛntɪˈformo; ˈtwentiˈfɔːmou〕 *n.* 二十四開;二十四開本(略作 24mo)。—*adj.* 二十四開的。

twen·ty·mo 〔ˈtwɛntɪmo; ˈtwentimou〕 *n.* 二十開;二十開本(略作 20 **mo**)。—*adj.* 二十開的。

twen·ty-one 〔ˈtwɛntɪˈwʌn; ˈtwentiˈwʌn〕 *n.* ①二十一。②二十一個所成之一組。③二十一點(一種賭博,亦作 **blackjack**)。—*adj.* 二十一個的。

twen·ty-three 〔ˈtwɛntɪˈθri; ˈtwentiˈθriː〕 *interj.* 【美俚】走開;滾開。

twen·ty-twen·ty 〔ˈtwɛntɪˈtwɛntɪ; ˈtwentiˈtwenti〕 *adj.* 眼力正常的(略作 20/20)。

twenty-twenty vision 正常的視力。

'twere 〔twɝ; twəː〕【古,詩】=**it were.**

twerp 〔twɝp; twəːp〕 *n.* 【英俚】粗俗的人;鹵莽的人。

Twi 〔twi, tʃwi, tʃi; twiː, tʃwiː, tʃiː〕 *n.* ①奇族人(迦納之主要部落)。②奇族人之語文。

twi- 【字首】表"二;二重;二回;二倍"之義。

:twice〔twaɪs; twais〕*adv.* ①兩次。I advise you to think *twice* before doing that. 我勸你在做那事之前要再加考慮。②兩倍。This is *twice* as good as that. 這個比那個好兩倍。***at twice*** **a.** 分兩次地。**b.** 於第二次。

twice-laid 〔ˈtwaɪsˈled; ˈtwaisˈleid〕 *adj.* ①用舊繩索之纖維做成的。②利用廢物做成的。

twic·er 〔ˈtwaɪsɚ; ˈtwaisə〕 *n.* ①一事作兩遍的人;做兩件事的人。②【英】【印刷】兼做印刷匠的排字工人。③【俚】大小、強度或價值等爲所預期者之兩倍的事物。④連敗兩次者。⑤【英、澳】騙子;歹徒。

twice-told〔ˈtwaɪsˈtold; ˈtwaisˈtould〕 *adj.* 說過兩次的;從前說過的;陳舊的;陳腐的。

twid·dle 〔ˈtwɪdl̩; ˈtwidl〕 *v.*, **-dled, -dling,** *n.* —*v.t.* 撫弄;玩弄。—*v.i.* ①玩弄;戲弄。②忙於瑣事。③旋轉。***twiddle one's thumbs*** (or ***fingers***) **a.** 無聊地交互繞動着兩個姆指。**b.** 無所事事;懶散。***twiddle with*** (or ***at***) 心不在焉地撫弄。—*n.* 用手指等捻弄;一轉。—**twid·dler,** *n.*

***twig**[1] 〔twɪg; twig〕 *n.* ①小枝;嫩枝。②(神經、血管等之)末梢。—**let,** *n.* —**like,** *adj.*

twig[2] *v.t.* & *v.i.*, **twigged, twig·ging.** 【英俚】①注意。②了解;懂。

twig[3] *n.* 【英】款式;時式。

twig·gy 〔ˈtwɪgɪ; ˈtwigi〕 *adj.*, **-gi·er, -gi·est.** ①多小枝的。②由小枝組成的。③小枝狀的;纖細的。

***twi·light** 〔ˈtwaɪˌlaɪt; ˈtwailait〕 *n.* ①(日出前的)微明;曉光;(日落前的)薄暮;黃昏。②微弱的光芒。③全盛時期之前後。the *twilight* of the Roman Empire. 羅馬帝國之早期或衰微時期。④遙遠而不爲人所熟知之時代。—*adj.* ①微明的;薄暗的;暗晦的。②黃昏時出現的。

twilight sleep 【醫】半麻醉(產婦經注射麻醉劑後之半昏迷狀態)。

twill 〔twɪl; twil〕 *n.* ①斜紋布;斜紋織物。

②(織物之)斜紋。—*v.t.* 織成斜紋。—**ed,** *adj.*

'twill 〔twɪl; twil〕〖古,詩〗=**it will.**

***twin** 〔twɪn; twin〕 *n., adj., v.,* **twinned, twin·ning.** —*n.* ①孿生子之一。②一對孿生子。He was one of a *twin.* 他是孿生子之一。③兩個極其相似的人或物之一。—*adj.* ①孿生的。*twin* brothers. 孿生兄弟。②成雙的; 成對的。*twin* beds. (放在同一房間內的) 兩張完全相同的單人床。③有一對相同部分的。—*v.t. & v.i.* ①生雙生子。②匹配;成對。

twin bill 兩場接連舉行的球賽。

twin·born 〔'twɪn,bɔrn; 'twinbɔːn〕 *adj.* 雙生的;同胎生的。

***twine** 〔twaɪn; twain〕 *n., v.,* **twined, twin·ing.** —*n.* ①合股線; 細繩。②編結;編織。③盤曲;纏繞。④纏結之物。—*v.t. & v.i.* ①編結; 編織。She *twined* holly into wreaths.她用多青枝編成花圈。②纏繞;盤繞。

twin·flow·er 〔'twɪn,flauə; 'twin,flauə〕 *n.* 〖植物〗忍冬科的一種匍匐植物。

twinge〔twɪndʒ;twindʒ〕*n., v.,* **twinged, twing·ing.** —*n.* (身、心上之)劇痛;刺痛;痛苦。—*v.t.* 使感覺突然之劇痛;使良心受痛責。—*v.i.* 感覺突然之劇痛;懊惱。

twi-night 〔'twaɪ,naɪt; 'twainait〕 *adj.* (兩場接連一起的棒球賽)第一場在下午較晚時間開始,而第二場在黃昏燈光下開始的。

twin killing 〖棒球〗雙殺 (=double play).

***twin·kle** 〔'twɪŋkl; 'twiŋkl〕 *v.,* **-kled, -kling,** *n.* —*v.i.* ①閃爍;閃耀。Stars *twinkle.* 星光閃爍。②迅速移動;閃動。The dancer's feet *twinkled.* 跳舞者的脚步迅速閃動。③〖古〗轉瞬;霎眼。—*v.t.* ①使閃爍;使閃耀。②閃閃發(光)。—*n.* ①閃爍;閃耀。②閃動。③轉瞬; 霎眼。④轉瞬之間; 瞬息。in a *twinkle.* 瞬息間。—**twin·kler,** *n.*

twin·kling** 〔'twɪŋklɪŋ; 'twiŋkliŋ〕 *n.* ①閃爍; 閃耀。②轉瞬之間; 瞬息。③〖古〗轉瞬;瞬目。in the twinkling of an eye; in a twinkling*** 轉瞬之間;頃刻。—*adj.*(亦作 **twinkly**) 閃爍的;閃耀的。

twin-lens 〔'twɪn'lɛnz; 'twin'lenz〕 *adj.* 〖照相〗雙透鏡(式)的。

twinned 〔twɪnd; twind〕 *adj.* ①一胎雙生的。②成對的;關係密切的。

twirl 〔twɝl; twəːl〕 *v.t. & v.i.* ①旋轉;使旋轉。②扭轉;捲曲。③擲(棒球)。—*n.* ①旋轉。②扭曲;彎曲;花體。

twirl·er 〔'twɝlə; 'twəːlə〕 *n.* ①旋轉者;旋轉物。②〖棒球俚〗投手。

twirp 〔twɝp; twəːp〕 *n.* =**twerp.**

twist** 〔twɪst; twist〕 *v.t.* ①搓;編。This rope is *twisted* from many threads. 這條繩是由許多線搓合而成。②捲纏。③扭曲;扭歪;擰。His face was *twisted* with pain. 他的面容因痛苦而歪曲。④曲解。⑤使變形。⑥使(球)於曲線前進時旋轉。—*v.i.* ①盤旋;曲折; 迂迴。②扭歪。My ankle *twisted.* 我的足踝扭傷了。③轉身。④旋轉。⑤掙扭。twist around*** (or ***round***) ***one's finger*** 使處於完全控制之下;玩弄於掌股之上。***twist one's arm*** **a.** 扭轉某人的臂膀使感痛苦。**b.** 施以壓力;強迫。—*n.* ①線;索;繩。②扭捲而成之物。③扭曲; 扭歪;纏繞。a rope full of *twists.* 纏滿了結子的繩子。④曲折;彎曲。⑤失常; 偏差; 癖。⑥旋轉。⑦巧技;妙訣。⑧放在飲料之中揑過的檸檬切片。⑨扭扭舞。

twist drill 〖機械〗藏花鑽頭。

twist·er 〔'twɪstə; 'twistə〕 *n.* ①撚搓之人;撚搓器。②絞絲機。③說謊話的人;歪曲事實的人。④扭球; 旋轉前進之球。⑤〖美〗旋風; 龍捲風。⑥說繞口令的人。⑦令人難以相信之事;令人驚訝之事。

twit 〔twɪt;twit〕*v.,* **twit·ted, twit·ting,** *n.* —*v.t.* ①嘲笑;挖苦;揶揄。②譴責;責罵。—*n.* ①譴責; 責罵; 揶揄。②〖英〗傻瓜。③緊張的感覺或狀態。

***twitch** 〔twɪtʃ; twitʃ〕 *v.i.* ①痙攣;抽動。The child's mouth *twitched* as if she were about to cry. 這小孩的嘴抽動,像是要哭。②急拉; 扯。③突然發生劇痛。—*v.t.* ①急拉;扯。She *twitched* him by the sleeve. 她扯他的袖子。②使抽動。③搶走;奪去。A pickpocket *twitched* a purse from his pocket. 扒手從他口袋搶走了錢包。—*n.* ①痙攣;肌肉之跳動。②急拉。③突然之劇痛。

twite 〔twaɪt; twait〕 *n.* (北歐與英國產的)紅雀。(亦作 **twite finch**)

twit·ter 〔'twɪtə;'twitə〕 *n.*(亦作 **twitteration**) ①囀; 鳥鳴聲。②緊張; 興奮。③格格的笑。④喋喋不休。—*v.i.* ①(鳥)囀。②格格而笑。③因興奮而戰慄。④緊張地說。⑤喋喋不休地說話。—*v.t.* 擺動。

twit·ter·er 〔'twɪtərə;'twitərə〕 *n.* ①能鳴囀之鳥。②格格笑的人。

'twixt 〔twɪkst; twikst〕 *prep.* 〖古,詩〗=**betwixt; between.**

‡two 〔tu; tuː〕 *n., pl.* **twos,** *adj.* —*n.* ①二;2。②兩個;兩人; 兩歲; 兩點鐘。to cut a thing in *two.* 將一物切爲兩個。③(大小號碼之)二號。She wears a *two.* 她穿二號。***by twos and threes*** 三三兩兩地。***in two twos*** 〖英〗馬上;很快地。***put two and two together*** 根據事實作一極顯然的結論;推斷。—*adj.* 二;兩個。

two-base hit 〔'tu,bes~;'tuːbeis~〕〖棒球〗二壘安打。(亦作 **two-bagger**)

two-bit 〔'tu'bɪt; 'tuː'bit〕 *adj.* ①價值二角五分的。②不重要的;沒甚麼價值的。

two bits ①二角五分。②無價值之物。

two-by-four 〔'tubə'for; 'tuːbai'fɔː〕 *adj.* ①二英寸厚四英寸寬的。②〖美俚〗不重要的; 不足道的; 小的。—*n.* 二英寸厚四英寸寬而長度不等之木材。

two cultures (常 the~) 雙文化(一爲藝術、人文或社會科學文化;另一爲理工文化)。

two-edged 〔'tu'ɛdʒd; 'tuː'edʒd〕 *adj.* ①有兩刄的; 雙鋒的。②有雙重不同意義的。③兩面有效的。

two-faced 〔'tu'fest; 'tuː'feist〕 *adj.* ①兩面的。②虛僞的;不可靠的。—**ly,** *adv.*

two·fer 〔'tufə; 'tuːfə〕 *n.* ①可以優待價格一次購買兩張戲票的證明卡; 半價優待的兩張戲票。②任何半價優待的兩樣東西。

two-fist·ed 〔'tu'fɪstɪd; 'tuː'fistid〕 *adj.* ①〖美俗〗精力充沛的; 強壯的。②〖美俗〗能用雙拳的。③〖英方〗笨拙的。

two-fold 〔'tu'fold; 'tuː-fould〕 *n.* 兩扇用鉸鏈相連的舞臺布景。

two-four 〔'tu'for; 'tuː'fɔː〕 *adj.* 〖音樂〗四分之二拍子的。

2-4-D 〔'tu'for'di;'tuːfɔː'diː〕 *n.* 一種除草劑(2-4-dichloro-phenoxyacetic acid).

two-hand·ed 〔'tu'hændɪd;'tuː'hændid〕 *adj.* ①有兩隻手的。②左右手使用得同樣好的。③須用兩隻手來揮舞或運用的。④需要兩個人使用的;二人的。

two-line 〔'tu,laɪn; 'tuːlain〕 *adj.* 〖印刷〗較普通活字加倍大的。

two-name ('tu'nem; 'tu:'neim) *adj.* 【銀行】兩人簽名的。
two-part ('tu,part; 'tu:pa:t) *adj.* 由二部而成的;二部的。
two-party system 【政治】兩黨制度。
two·pence ('tʌpəns; 'tʌpəns) *n.*①二辨士之金額; 二辨士之銅幣(喬治三世所發行者)。②微不足道之事。(亦作 **tuppence**)
two·pen·ny ('tu,pɛnɪ,'tʌpənɪ; 'tʌpṇi) *adj.* ①值二辨士的。②便宜的; 瑣屑的; 不足道的。—*n.* ①一種啤酒。②【俚】頭。
two·pen·ny-half·pen·ny ('tʌpənɪ'hepənɪ; 'tʌpəni'heipəni) *adj.* 【英】①二辨士半的。②不足道的;瑣屑的。
two-phase ('tu,fez;'tu:feiz) *adj.*【電】二相的。
two-piece ('tu'pis; 'tu:'pi:s) *adj.* 分爲上裝及下裝的。—*n.* (亦作 **two-piecer**) 分爲上裝及下裝的一套服裝。
two-ply ('tu'plaɪ; 'tu:-plai) *adj.* 雙層的;雙重的;雙股的。
two-sack·er ('tu'sækɚ; 'tu:'sækə) *n.* 【美俗】【棒球】二壘打。
two-sid·ed ('tu'saɪdɪd; 'tu:'saidid) *adj.* ①兩面的;兩方面的。②表裏不一致的;懷二心的。③【生物】左右相稱的。—**ness,** *n.*
two·some ('tusəm; 'tu:səm) *adj.* ①由兩個組成的。②兩個人從事的;兩個人玩的。—*n.* ①二人一組;一對人。②兩人玩的遊戲。③玩此種遊戲之兩個人。
two-speed ('tu,spid; 'tu:-spi:d) *adj.* 【機械】有兩種速度的;雙速的。
two-spot ('tu,spɑt; 'tu:spɔt) *n.* ①【俚】面值二元的鈔票。②骰子或紙牌刻有兩點朝上的一面。
two-step ('tu,stɛp; 'tu:-step) *n., v.,* **-stepped, -step·ping.** —*n.* 【美】二拍子的圓舞(曲)。—*v.i.* 跳二拍子的圓舞。
two-time ('tu,taɪm;'tu:taim) *v.t.*【俚】①在愛情中欺騙(對方);對(愛人、妻子或丈夫)不忠;不貞。②欺騙;出賣。—*adj.*某件事做過兩遍的;受害兩次的;曾兩次獲得某物的。—**two-tim·er,** *n.*
two-time loser 【俚】①在同一州中犯重大罪行被判刑兩次的人(如有第三次判刑則爲無期徒刑)。②做同一件事失敗兩次的人(尤指離婚兩次或破產兩次的人)。
two-tone ('tu'ton; 'tu:'toun) *adj.* 有兩種顏色的;同色而色度不同的。(亦作 **two-toned**)
two-tongued ('tu'tʌŋd; 'tu:'tʌŋd) *adj.* ①有兩舌的。②詐欺的;虛僞的。
'twould (twʊd; twud) =**it would.**
two-val·ued ('tu,væljud; 'tu:,vælju:d) *adj.* 【哲】(眞、假)兩價的。
two-way ('tu'we; 'tu:'wei) *adj.* ①雙行道的。②有兩條通道的。③(無線電等)收發兩用的。④【數學】有二變數法的。⑤互相的;彼此的;雙向的。⑥有兩方面或兩人參加的。
twy·er ('twaɪɚ; 'twaiə) *n.* =**tuyère.**
-ty[1] 【字尾】表"十之倍數"之義。
-ty[2] 【字尾】表"性質;狀態"之義。
Ty·cho ('taɪko; 'taikou) *n.* 月球表面第三象限內之坑名(直徑約56英里,月圓時爲月球上最明顯之地形。其邊緣之懸崖高達12,000英尺,坑中央有五千英尺之高山)。
ty·coon (taɪ'kun; tai'ku:n) *n.* ①【俗】大亨;大實業家; 大企業家; 實業界鉅子。②大將; 將軍 (外國人對日本德川幕府時代 1603–1867之將軍的稱呼)。
ty·ing ('taɪɪŋ; 'taiiŋ) *v.* ppr. of **tie.**
tyke (taɪk; taik) *n.* ①劣犬;野狗。②【俗】頑皮的兒童;小孩子。③【蘇】卑賤的人;村夫。(亦作 **tike**)
tym·pan ('tɪmpən; 'timpən) *n.* ①(昔日之)鼓。②【印刷】敷於壓印板或滾筒上以使印刷紙張所受壓力平均之紙或羊皮紙。③任何器械上似膜片之部分。④【建築】=**tympanum.**
tym·pa·ni ('tɪmpə,ni; 'timpəni(:)) *n. pl.* =**timpani.**
tym·pan·ic (tɪm'pænɪk; tim'pænik) *adj.* ①鼓的; 似鼓的。②【解剖】鼓膜的; 中耳的。
tympanic membrane 【解剖】鼓膜。
tym·pa·nist ('tɪmpənɪst; 'timpənist) *n.* =**timpanist.**
tym·pa·ni·tes (,tɪmpə'naɪtiz; ,timpə'naiti:z) *n.* 【醫】(腹部)膨脹;氣鼓。
tym·pa·ni·tis (,tɪmpə'naɪtɪs; ,timpə'naitis) *n.* 【醫】中耳炎。
tym·pa·num ('tɪmpənəm; 'timpənəm) *n., pl.* **-nums, -na** (-nə;-nə). ①【解剖】鼓膜;中耳;鼓室。②【建築】山牆的凹面(通常爲三角形);拱與楣間之部分。③(電話機之)振動膜。④鼓;鼓皮。
Tyn·dale ('tɪndl; 'tindl) *n.* 丁道爾 (William, 1492?–1536, 英國之宗教改革家,於1524–26年將新約譯成英文)。
‡**type** (taɪp; taip) *n., v.,* **typed, typ·ing.** —*n.* ①型; 型式; 樣式;類型。This is just the *type* of house I require. 這正是我所需要的那一類型的房子。②典型;模範;表率;代表物;標本。John is a fine *type* of schoolboy. 約翰是學童的一個很好的表率。③【古】象徵;表徵。④【印刷】活字;字體。⑤錢幣或金屬上兩面之刻字或圖案。⑥血型。—*v.t.* ①代表; 表徵。②以打字機打出。③驗明(血型)。④作爲…之典型。⑤給(演員)以某種造型。⑥預示。—*v.i.* 打字。She *types* well. 她打字打得很好。 —**a·ble,** *adj.* 【注意】 **type of** 這個慣用語在口語中常將 of 略去。
-type 【字尾】①表"典型;代表性形式;模範"之義,如:prototype. ②表"印章;印刷"之義,如:daguerreotype.
type·bar ('taɪp,bɑr; 'taipbɑ:) *n.* 打字機上一端銲接鉛字之鋼條。(亦作 **type bar**)
type-cast ('taɪp,kæst; 'taipkɑ:st) *v.,* **-cast, -cast·ing,** *adj.* —*v.i.* & *v.t.* 鑄 (鉛字)。—*adj.* (付印稿件)鉛字已鑄妥的。
type·cast ('taɪp,kæst;'taipkɑ:st) *v.t.,* **-cast, -cast·ing.** ①演與個性、體型等相宜之角色。②接連擔任這種角色。
type·face ('taɪp,fes; 'taipfeis) *n.* 鉛字之字體。
type founder 活字鑄造工。
type·found·ing ('taɪp,faʊndɪŋ; 'taip,faundiŋ) *n.* 活字鑄造業。
type foundry 活字鑄造廠。
type metal 活字合金。
type·script ('taɪp,skrɪpt; 'taipskript) *n.*打字原稿; 打字文件(以別於手寫或印刷者)。
type·set·ter ('taɪp,sɛtɚ; 'taip,setə) *n.* ①排字工人。②排字機。
type·set·ting ('taɪp,sɛtɪŋ; 'taip,setiŋ) *n.* 排字。—*adj.* 排字的。
type·write ('taɪp,raɪt; 'taip-rait) *v.t.* & *v.i.,* **-wrote** (-,rot;-rout), **-writ·ten** (-,rɪtṇ; -,ritn), **-writ·ing.** 打字。
*__type·writ·er__ ('taɪp,raɪtɚ;'taip,raitə) *n.* 打字機。
type·writ·ing ('taɪp,raɪtɪŋ; 'taip-

raitiŋ) *n.* ①打字;打字術。②打字工作。
type·writ·ten (ˈtaɪpˌrɪtn; ˈtaipˌritn) *adj* 用打字機打出的。—*v.* pp. of **typewrite.**
typh·li·tis (tɪfˈlaɪtɪs; tifˈlaitis) *n.* 〖醫〗盲腸炎。
ty·phoid (ˈtaɪfɔɪd; ˈtaifɔid) *adj.* ①傷寒症的。②似斑疹傷寒的。—*n.* 〖醫〗傷寒症 (=typhoid fever).
typhoid fever 〖醫〗傷寒症。
ty·phon·ic (taɪˈfɑnɪk; taiˈfɔnik) *adj.* 颱風的;似颱風的。
***ty·phoon** (taɪˈfun; taiˈfu:n) *n.* 颱風。
ty·phous (ˈtaɪfəs; ˈtaifəs) *adj.* 〖醫〗斑疹傷寒症的;似斑疹傷寒症的。
ty·phus (ˈtaɪfəs; ˈtaifəs) *n.* 〖醫〗斑疹傷寒症。
***typ·i·cal** (ˈtɪpɪkl; ˈtipikəl) *adj.* 典型的;有代表性的;象徵的。—**ly,** *adv.*
typ·i·fi·ca·tion (ˌtɪpəfɪˈkeʃən; ˌtipifiˈkeiʃən) *n.* 成爲典型;象徵;代表。
typ·i·fy (ˈtɪpəˌfaɪ; ˈtipifai) *v.t.*, **-fied, -fy·ing.** ①代表; 作爲…的象徵。②爲…之典型。③預示。—**typ·i·fi·er,** *n.*
typ·ing (ˈtaɪpɪŋ; ˈtaipiŋ) *n.* 打字;打字機使用法。
***typ·ist** (ˈtaɪpɪst; ˈtaipist) *n.* 打字員。
ty·po (ˈtaɪpo; ˈtaipou) *n., pl.* **-pos.** 〖俗〗①印刷工;排字工。②排印之錯誤;手民之誤。
typo- 〖字首〗表 "**type**" 之義。
ty·pog·ra·pher (taɪˈpɑgrəfɚ; taiˈpɔgrəfə) *n.* ①印刷工人;排字工人。②印刷商。
ty·po·graph·ic (ˌtaɪpəˈgræfɪk; ˌtaipəˈgræfik) *adj.* =**typographical.**
ty·po·graph·i·cal (ˌtaɪpəˈgræfɪkl; ˌtaipəˈgræfikəl) *adj.* 印刷上的; 排字上的。
ty·pog·ra·phy (taɪˈpɑgrəfɪ; taiˈpɔgrəfi) *n.* ①活字印刷術;排字及印刷。②印刷品的式樣。
ty·pol·o·gy (taɪˈpɑlədʒɪ; taiˈpɔlədʒi) *n.* ①象徵或預表等之研究(尤指研究舊約聖經中關於耶穌之預表者)。②象徵之意義;代表性。③〖心理, 哲學, 語言, 生物〗類型學。④印刷學;活字學。—**ty·po·log·i·cal,** *adj.*
ty·po·script (ˈtaɪpəskrɪpt; ˈtaipəskript) *n.* =**typescript.**
ty·poth·e·tae (taɪˈpɑθəˌti, ˌtaɪpəˈθiti; taiˈpɔθəti:) *n. pl.* ①印刷工工頭協會。②印刷工(用於印刷工人組織之名稱中)。
ty·ran·nic (tɪˈrænɪk; tiˈrænik) *adj.* =**tyrannical.**
ty·ran·ni·cal (tɪˈrænɪkl; tiˈrænikəl) *adj.* 似暴君的;專橫的;暴虐的。—**ly,** *adv.*
ty·ran·ni·cide (tɪˈrænəˌsaɪd; tiˈrænisaid) *n.* ①誅殺暴君。②誅殺暴君者。
tyr·an·nize (ˈtɪrəˌnaɪz; ˈtirənaiz) *v.*, **-nized, -niz·ing.** —*v.i.* ①虐待; 壓制; 欺壓〖over〗。②施行虐政。③暴力統治。—*v.t.* 壓迫; 施暴政; 殘暴統治。(英亦作 **tyrannise**) —**tyr·an·niz·er,** *n.*
ty·ran·no·sau·rus (tɪˌrænəˈsɔrəs; tiˌrænəˈsɔ:rəs) *n.*〖古生物〗一種恐龍。
tyr·an·nous (ˈtɪrənəs; ˈtirənəs) *adj.* 暴虐的;殘暴的;專橫的。—**ly,** *adv.*—**ness,** *n.*
***tyr·an·ny** (ˈtɪrənɪ; ˈtirəni) *n., pl.* **-nies.** ①暴虐;虐政。②暴行;殘暴的行爲。
***ty·rant** (ˈtaɪrənt; ˈtaiərənt) *n.* ①暴君;專制君主。②强迫性之影響力。
Tyre (taɪr; ˈtaiə) *n.* 泰爾(古腓尼基南部之一海港, 在今之黎巴嫩)。
tyre (taɪr; ˈtaiə) *n., v.,* **tyred, tyr·ing.** 〖英〗=**tire.**
Tyr·i·an (ˈtɪrɪən; ˈtiriən) *adj.* ①古泰爾 (Tyre)的;古泰爾人的;古泰爾文化的。②泰爾紫色的。—*n.* 泰爾人。
Tyrian purple ①泰爾紫(古希臘及羅馬人所用的一種深紅或紫色染料)。②泰爾紫色(一種帶藍的紅色)。—**Tyr·i·an-pur·ple,** *adj.*
ty·ro (ˈtaɪro; ˈtaiərou) *n., pl.* **-ros.** 初學者;生手;新手。
ty·ro·ci·dine (ˌtaɪrəˈsaɪdin; ˌtaiərouˈsaidin) *n.* 〖生化〗短桿酪素(自土壤細菌中提取之一種抗生素)。
Tyr·ol (ˈtɪrəl, tɪˈrol; ˈtirəl) *n.* 提洛爾(奧國西部與義大利北部之一區域, 在阿爾卑斯山中)。(亦作 **Tirol**)
Tyr·o·le·an (təˈrolɪən; təˈrouliən) *n., adj.* =**Tyrolese.**
Tyr·o·lese (ˌtɪrəˈliz; ˌtirəˈli:z) *adj.* Tyrol 的;Tyrol 區居民的。—*n.* Tyrol人。
tzar (tsɑr, zɑr; zɑ:) *n.* =**czar.**(亦作 **tsar**)
tzar·e·vich (ˈzɑrəvɪtʃ; ˈzɑ:rəvitʃ) *n.* =**czarevitch.**
tza·ri·na (tsɑˈrinə; zɑ:ˈri:nɑ) *n.* =**czarina.**
tzet·ze (ˈtsɛtsɪ; ˈtsetsi) *n.* =**tsetse.**
tzi·gane (tsɪˈgɑn; tsiˈgɑ:n) *n.* 匈牙利之吉普賽人。—*adj.* 匈牙利之吉普賽人的。(亦作 **Tzigane**)

U

U or **u** (ju; ju:) *n., pl.* **U's** or **u's** (juz; ju:z), *adj.* —*n.* ①英文之第二十一個字母。②U形之物。—*adj.* U形的。*U* tube. U形管。
U uranium. **U.** ①Uhr (德 =o'clock). ②Unionist. ③University. ④uncle. ⑤and. ⑥uniform. ⑦union. ⑧unit. ⑨united. ⑩upper. **U/A, U/a, u/a** 〖商〗underwriting account. 保險帳戶。
UAAC Un-American Activities Committee. 非美活動委員會。 **UAR, U.A.R.** United Arab Republic.
u·bi·e·ty (juˈbaɪətɪ; ju:ˈbaiəti) *n.* 〖哲學〗存在於空間之性質或狀態;位置關係。
u·biq·ui·tous (juˈbɪkwətəs; ju(:)ˈbikwitəs) *adj.* 無所不在的;遍在的。(亦作 **ubiquitary**) —**ly,** *adv.* —**ness,** *n.*
u·biq·ui·ty (juˈbɪkwətɪ; ju(:)ˈbikwiti) *n.* ①到處存在; 遍在。②(U-) 上帝或耶穌之同時到處存在。
U-boat (ˈjuˌbot; ˈju:bout) *n.* 德國潛水艇;潛水艇。
U-bomb (ˈjuˌbɑm; ˈju:bɔm) *n.* 鈾原子彈。
u. c. 〖印刷〗upper case (capital letter or letters).
ud·der (ˈʌdɚ; ˈʌdə) *n.* (動物之) 乳房。
Ud·murt (ˈudmurt; ˈudmuət) *n.* 烏德摩特(蘇聯歐洲東部之一自治共和國, 其首都爲 Izhevsk).
u·dom·e·ter (juˈdɑmətɚ; ju:ˈdɔmitə) *n.* 雨量計。
UFO, U.F.O. unidentified flying object.
u·fol·o·gist (juˈfɑlədʒɪst; ju:ˈfɔlədʒist) *n.* 研究不明飛行物 (UFO) 的人。
U·gan·da (juˈgændə; ju(:)ˈgændə) *n.* 烏干達(東非一國, 首都坎帕拉 Kampala).
ugh (ux, ʌ, u, ʌx; ʌx, uh, ə:h) *interj.* 啊! 唷!哎呀!(表示嫌惡、恐怖等之感嘆聲)。
ug·li·fy (ˈʌglɪˌfaɪ; ˈʌglifai) *v.t.,* **-fied,**

-**fy·ing**. 使醜;損壞…的美觀;醜化。

ug·li·ly ['ʌɡləlɪ; 'ʌɡlili] *adv.* 醜陋地;醜惡地。

ug·li·ness ['ʌɡlɪnɪs; 'ʌɡlinis] *n.*醜陋;醜惡。

***ug·ly** ['ʌɡlɪ; 'ʌɡli] *adj.*, **-li·er, -li·est.** ①難看的;醜陋的。②醜惡的;邪惡的;令人厭惡的。*ugly* deed. 醜行。③險惡的。④〖美俗〗脾氣壞的;好爭吵的。⑤令人困窘的;彆扭的。He told me the *ugly* truth about himself. 他告訴我關於他自己的彆扭眞相。

ugly American 醜陋的美國人(指在海外趾高氣揚的美國人)。

ugly customer 可畏之人;難處之人。

ugly duckling 醜小鴨;幼時看似庸陋難看但終於發展成才貌出衆的人。

UHF 〖無線電〗超高頻率(ultrahigh frequency 之略)。(亦作 **U.H.F., uhf**)

uh·lan ['ulɑn; 'u:lɑ:n] *n.* ①昔波蘭之持矛騎兵。②昔德國之持矛騎兵。

Ui·gur ['wiɡur; 'wi:ɡuə] *n.* ①維吾爾人(爲土耳其民族之一支,居於蒙古與新疆)。②維吾爾語。(亦作 **Uighur**)

uit·land·er ['aɪt,lændɚ; 'eitlændə] 〖南非〗*n.* 外國人。(亦作 **Uitlander**)

U.K., UK United Kingdom.

u·kase ['jukes; ju:'keiz] *n.* ①帝俄沙皇的敕令。②諭旨;敕令。③任何官方之法令。

uke [juk; ju:k] *n.*〖俗〗=**ukulele.**

U·kraine ['jukren; ju(:)'krein] *n.* 烏克蘭(蘇聯歐洲部分之一共和國,全名爲Ukrainian Soviet Socialist Republic, 首都基輔 Kiev).

U·krain·i·an [ju'krenɪən; ju:'kreinjən] *adj.* 烏克蘭的;烏克蘭人的;烏克蘭語的。—*n.* ①烏克蘭人。②烏克蘭語(烏克蘭人所說的東斯拉夫語)。

u·ku·le·le [,jukə'lelɪ; ,ju:kə'leili] *n.* (發源於夏威夷與吉他相類的)四弦琴。

ul·cer ['ʌlsɚ; 'ʌlsə] *n.*①潰瘍。a gastric *ulcer*. 胃潰瘍。②道德之汚點。③弊害;弊風。④罪惡之淵藪。

ul·cer·ate ['ʌlsə,ret; 'ʌlsəreit] *v.*, **-at·ed, -at·ing.** —*v.i.* 生潰瘡;生爛瘡;膿潰。—*v.t.* 使生潰瘡;使生爛瘡;使膿潰。

ul·cer·a·tion [,ʌlsə'reʃən; ,ʌlsə'reiʃən] *n.* 潰爛;潰瘍之形成。

ul·cer·a·tive ['ʌlsər,etɪv; 'ʌlsərətiv] *adj.* 潰瘍性的;潰爛性的;致使潰瘍的。

ul·cer·ous ['ʌlsərəs; 'ʌlsərəs] *adj.* 潰瘍性的;患潰瘍的。—**ly,** *adv.* —**ness,** *n.*

-ule 〖字尾〗表"小"的名詞字尾。

ul·lage ['ʌlɪdʒ; 'ʌlidʒ] *n.*①(容器內之酒因漏失或蒸發而造成之)損耗量。②(袋裝穀物等因漏失之)損耗量。③液體容器之缺滿量。④〖方,英俚〗杯中殘酒。

ul·na ['ʌlnə; 'ʌlnə] *n., pl.* **-nae** [-ni; -ni:], **-nas.** 〖解剖〗尺骨。—**ul·nar,** *adj.*

ul·ster ['ʌlstɚ; 'ʌlstə] *n.* 一種長而寬鬆的外套(男女兼用)。

ult. ①ultimate. ②ultimately. ③ultimo.

ul·te·ri·or [ʌl'tɪrɪɚ; ʌl'tiəriə] *adj.* ①隱祕的;未昭明的;未揭露的。②後來的;未來的;下一步的。③在彼方的;遙遠的。④間接的。—**ly,** *adv.*

ul·ti·ma ['ʌltəmə; 'ʌltimə] *n.*〖文法,韻律〗一字之最後一音節。

ul·ti·ma·cy ['ʌltəməsɪ; 'ʌltiməsi] *n.* ①終極性;根本性。②終極;根本。

ultima ra·ti·o [~'reʃɪo; ~'reiʃiou] 最後的論據;最後手段。

***ul·ti·mate** ['ʌltəmɪt; 'ʌltimit] *adj.* ①最後的;終極的。the *ultimate* end of life. 人生的終極目的。②根本的;基本的;主要的;第一的。③最大的;極限的。—*n.*終極;根本。—**ness,** *n.*

ultimate analysis ①最後分析。②〖化〗元素分析。

***ul·ti·mate·ly** ['ʌltəmɪtlɪ; 'ʌltimitli] *adv.* 最後;最終;終結。She did not doubt that I would *ultimately* succeed. 她不懷疑我終將成功。

ultima Thu·le [~'θulɪ; ~'θu:li] ①古代地理學者想像中最北之地區。②極端;極限。③能獲得的最大程度或目標。④遙遠而無人知的地區。

ul·ti·mat·ism ['ʌltəmɪtɪzəm; 'ʌltimitizəm] *n.* 不妥協的態度或傾向;意見或信仰的偏激。

ul·ti·ma·tum [,ʌltə'metəm; ,ʌlti'meitəm] *n., pl.* **-tums, -ta** [-tə; -tə]. 最後通牒;哀的美敦書。

ul·ti·mo ['ʌltə,mo; 'ʌltimou] *adv.* 前月的;上月分的(常略作 **ult.**).

ul·ti·mo·gen·i·ture [,ʌltəmo'dʒenətʃɚ; ,ʌltimou'dʒenitʃə] *n.* 〖法律〗幼子繼承制(爲 primogeniture 之對)。

ul·tra ['ʌltrə; 'ʌltrə] *adj.* 超乎尋常的;極端的;過度的。—*n.* 極端主義者。

ultra- 〖字首〗表"極端;過度;超過"之義。

ul·tra·clean [,ʌltrə'klin; 'ʌltrə'kli:n] *adj.* 潔淨到極點的(尤指在無菌狀態下用消毒過的儀器達成的)。

ul·tra·con·serv·a·tive [,ʌltrəkən'sɝvətɪv; ,ʌltrəkən'sə:vətiv] *adj.* 極端保守的。

ul·tra·fash·ion·a·ble [,ʌltrə'fæʃənəbl; 'ʌltrə'fæʃənəbl] *adj.* 極端流行的;極端時髦的。

ul·tra·fax ['ʌltrə,fæks; 'ʌltrəfæks] *n.* ①一種利用電視原理的高速影印方式。②(U-) 其商標名。

ul·tra·high ['ʌltrə'haɪ; 'ʌltrə'hai] *adj.* 高到極點的;最高程度的。

ultrahigh frequency 〖無線電,電視〗超高頻率。

ul·tra·ism ['ʌltrəɪzm; 'ʌltrəizm] *n.*①過激論;極端主義。②過激之意見、行爲等。

ul·tra·ist ['ʌltrəɪst; 'ʌltrəist] *n.* 過激論者;極端主義者。—*adj.* =**ultraistic.**

ul·tra·is·tic [,ʌltrə'ɪstɪk; ,ʌltrə'istik] *adj.* 過激論的;極端主義的。

ul·tra·left [,ʌltrə'lɛft; 'ʌltrə'left] *adj.* 極端激進的。

ul·tra·ma·rine [,ʌltrəmə'rin; ,ʌltrəmə'ri:n] *adj.* ①海外的;海那邊的。②深藍色的。—*n.* ①紺青色。②羣青(一種顏料)。③深藍色。

ul·tra·mi·cro·scope [,ʌltrə'maɪkrə,skop; 'ʌltrə'maikrəskoup] *n.* 限外顯微鏡;超顯微鏡。

ul·tra·mi·cro·scop·ic [,ʌltrə,maɪkrə'skɑpɪk; 'ʌltrə,maikrə'skɔpik] *adj.* ①極微小的(普通顯微鏡不能看見的)。②超級顯微鏡的。

ul·tra·mil·i·tant [,ʌltrə 'mɪlətənt; 'ʌltrə'militənt] *adj.* 極端好戰的。

ul·tra·mod·ern [,ʌltrə'mɑdən; 'ʌltrə'mɔdən] *adj.* 極端現代的。—*n.* 極端現代主義者。—**ism,** —**ist,** *n.*

ul·tra·mon·tane [,ʌltrə 'mɑnten; ,ʌltrə'mɔntein] *adj.* ①山外的;山那邊的。②阿爾卑斯山南麓的;義大利的。③教皇至上

論的；教皇絕對權力主義的。④(昔指)阿爾卑斯山北方的；義大利之外邦的。—*n.* ①山外之人。②阿爾卑斯山南方之人。③教皇至上論者。④(昔指)阿爾卑斯山北方的人。

ul·tra·mon·ta·nism 〔ˌʌltrəˈmɑntənɪzṃ; ˌʌltrəˈmɔntinizm〕 *n.* 教宗至上論；教宗全權論。—**ul·tra·mon·ta·nist,** *n.*

ul·tra·mun·dane 〔ˌʌltrəˈmʌnden; ˈʌltrəˈmʌndein〕 *adj.* ①太陽系以外的；世界之外的。②現世以外的。

ul·tra·na·tion·al·ism 〔ˌʌltrəˈnæʃənlɪzṃ; ˈʌltrəˈnæʃənəlizm〕 *n.* 極端民族主義。—**ul·tra·na·tion·al·ist,** *n., adj.* —**ul·tra·na·tion·al·ist·ic,** *adj.*

ul·tra·rad·i·cal 〔ˌʌltrəˈrædəkḷ; ˌʌltrəˈrædikl〕 *adj.* 極端激進的。—*n.* 極端激進分子。

ul·tra·red 〔ˌʌltrəˈrɛd; ˈʌltrəˈred〕 *adj.* 〖物理〗紅外的。***ultrared rays*** 紅外線。

ul·tra·right·ist 〔ˌʌltrəˈraɪtɪst; ˌʌltrəˈraitist〕 *n.* 極端右翼分子；過分保守者。—*adj.* 持過分保守意見的；極端保守的。

ul·tra-short 〔ˌʌltrəˈʃɔrt; ˈʌltrəˈʃɔːt〕 *adj.* 〖物理〗超短波的。

ul·tra·son·ic 〔ˌʌltrəˈsɑnɪk; ˈʌltrəˈsɔnik〕 *adj.* 超聲波的。—**al·ly,** *adv.*

ul·tra·son·ics 〔ˌʌltrəˈsɑnɪks; ˈʌltrəˈsɔniks〕 *n.* 超聲波學。

ul·tra·trop·i·cal 〔ˌʌltrəˈtrɑpɪkḷ; ˈʌltrəˈtrɔpikl〕 *adj.* ①熱帶圈以外的。②較熱帶更熱的。

ul·tra·vi·o·let 〔ˌʌltrəˈvaɪəlɪt; ˈʌltrəˈvaiəlit〕 *adj.* 〖物理〗紫外的(線)；紫外線的。

ultraviolet rays 紫外線。

ul·tra vi·res 〔ˌʌltrəˈvaɪriz; ˈʌltrəˈvaiəriːz〕 〖拉〗〖法律〗超越權限；越權。

ul·u·lant 〔ˈjuljələnt; ˈjuːljulənt〕 *adj.* (狼)嗥的；(梟)啼的；嗬嗬地叫的；哀鳴的。

ul·u·late 〔ˈjuljəˌlet; ˈjuːljuleit〕 *v.i.,* **-lat·ed, -lat·ing.** ①(狼、犬等)嗥。②(梟)啼。③哀鳴。④叫。

ul·u·la·tion 〔ˌjuljəˈleʃən; ˌjuːljuˈleiʃən〕 *n.* 號叫；哀鳴。

U·lys·ses 〔juˈlɪsiz; ju(ː)ˈlisiːz〕 *n.* 希臘傳說中 Ithaca 之王(爲 Homer 史詩 *Odyssey* 中之主角)。(亦作 **Odysseus**) —**U·lys·se·an,** *adj.*

um·bel 〔ˈʌmbḷ; ˈʌmbəl〕 *n.* 〖植物〗繖狀花序；繖狀花。

um·bel·lar 〔ˈʌmbḷɚ; ˈʌmbələ〕 *adj.* = **umbellate.**

um·bel·late 〔ˈʌmbəlɪt; ˈʌmbəlit〕 *adj.* 〖植物〗繖狀花(序)的。

um·bel·lif·er·ous 〔ˌʌmbəˈlɪfərəs; ˌʌmbeˈlifərəs〕 *adj.* 〖植物〗繖狀花科的；有繖狀花的。

um·ber 〔ˈʌmbɚ; ˈʌmbə〕 *n.* ①赭土(一種天然褐色顏料)。②赭色；焦茶色。***burnt umber*** 鍛赭土(顏料)。***raw umber*** 生赭土(顏料)。—*adj.* 赭色的。—*v.t.* 着以赭色。

um·bil·i·cal 〔ʌmˈbɪlɪkḷ; ʌmˈbilikəl, ˌʌmbiˈlaikəl〕 *adj.* ①臍的；臍帶的。②中心的；中央的。③〖罕〗母系的。④如以臍帶連繫的；極爲密切的。

umbilical cord ①臍帶。②密切的關係。③太空人在太空船外操作時與母船相連的生命線(包括空氣補給及通信系統等)。④火箭或飛彈發射前用以窺測內部機械是否有毛病的電纜。

um·bil·i·cus 〔ʌmˈbɪlɪkəs, ˌʌmbɪˈlaɪkəs; ʌmˈbilikəs〕 *n., pl.* **-ci** 〔-ˌsaɪ; -sai〕. ①〖解剖〗臍。②〖植物〗種臍。③〖幾何〗臍點。④〖考古〗(卷物的)軸玉。

um·bles 〔ˈʌmbḷz; ˈʌmblz〕 *n. pl.* 獸類之內臟。

um·bo 〔ˈʌmbo; ˈʌmbou〕 *n., pl.* **um·bo·nes** 〔ʌmˈboniz; ʌmˈbouniːz〕, **um·bos.** ①盾心(盾中心之突出物)。②突出物。③(貝介的)殼嘴。④〖解剖〗鼓膜臍；鼓膜凸。

um·bra 〔ˈʌmbrə; ˈʌmbrə〕 *n., pl.* **-brae** 〔-bri; -briː〕. ①鬼；幽靈。②陰暗；陰影。③〖光學〗全影。④太陽黑子的中心。⑤〖天文〗本影(行星、衞星等背日光之圓錐形陰影)。—**um·bral,** *adj.*

um·brage 〔ˈʌmbrɪdʒ; ˈʌmbridʒ〕 *n., v.,* **-braged, -brag·ing.** —*n.* ①憤恚；不快；埋怨。②生蔭之葉族。③〖詩〗蔭。④〖罕〗陰影；影。⑤跡象。⑥懷疑；疑念。***give umbrage*** 觸怒；使生氣；使不愉快。***take umbrage (at)*** 生氣；見怪；感覺不快。—*v.t.* ①使入影中。②使生氣。

um·bra·geous 〔ʌmˈbredʒəs; ʌmˈbreidʒəs〕 *adj.* ①多蔭的。②好戰的；好鬥的。③容易生氣的；容易得罪的。—**ly,** *adv.*

***um·brel·la** 〔ʌmˈbrɛlə; ʌmˈbrelə〕 *n.* ①傘；洋傘；雨傘。②由戰鬥機形成而掩護地面部隊之幕；空中掩護幕。③庇護。④海蜇之碗狀膠質身體。—*adj.* ①包羅衆多的。②傘狀的；似傘的。—*v.t.* ①以傘遮住。②掩護。〖注意〗女用遮太陽的小花傘不是 **umbrella,** 而是 **parasol.** umbrella 專指較大的男女通用的雨傘。

umbrella stand 傘架。

umbrella tree ①〖植物〗(北美產的)木蘭樹。②傘狀之樹。

um·brette 〔ʌmˈbrɛt; ʌmˈbret〕 *n.* (非洲產的)一種與鸛相似之涉禽。

um·brif·er·ous 〔ʌmˈbrɪfərəs; ʌmˈbrifərəs〕 *adj.* 投下陰影的；成蔭的。

u·mi·ak 〔ˈumɪˌæk; ˈuːmiæk〕 *n.* 一種愛斯基摩人所用之木架皮舟。(亦作 **umiack, oomiac, oomiak**)

um·laut 〔ˈumlaut; ˈumlaut〕 *n.* 〖語言〗①母音變化；曲音(受後音節中一母音之影響而生之母音變化)。②由此種變化而生之母音(如德文中之 ä, ö, ü 等)。③曲音符號(即上例母音上部之兩點)。—*v.t.* 以曲音變化(母音)；加曲音符號於。

ump 〔ʌmp; ʌmp〕 *n.* (棒球等之)裁判(=umpire).

um·pir·age 〔ˈʌmpaɪrɪdʒ; ˈʌmpaiəridʒ〕 *n.* ①仲裁人之職權或地位。②仲裁。③裁決；裁定。

***um·pire** 〔ˈʌmpaɪr; ˈʌmpaiə〕 *n., v.,* **-pired, -pir·ing.** —*n.* ①(競技之)裁判員。②仲裁者；公斷人。③(軍事演習之)裁判官。—*v.i.* 作裁判員；作仲裁者。—*v.t.* 裁判；仲裁；公斷。

um·pire-in-chief 〔ˈʌmpaɪrɪnˈtʃif; ˈʌmpaiərinˈtʃiːf〕 *n.* 〖棒球〗主審裁判。

ump·teen 〔ˈʌmpˈtin; ˈʌmpˈtiːn〕 *adj.* 〖俚〗很多的；甚多的；大量的。

ump·ty 〔ˈʌmptɪ; ˈʌmpti〕 *adj.* 某某的。

UN, U.N. United Nations.

'un 〔ən; ən〕 *pron.* 〖俗〗人；傢伙；東西(=one).

un- 〖字首〗①用於形容詞或副詞之前，表示"不"或"與…相反的"之義，如：unfair (不公平的)。②用於動詞之前，表示"做出與(某種行爲)相反的行爲"或"做出打消(某種行爲)的行爲"之義，如：undress (脫去衣服)。③用於名詞之前，表示"不"或"無"之義，如：uncertainty (不確定)。

un·a·bashed 〔ˌʌnəˈbæʃt; ˈʌnəˈbæʃt〕 *adj.* ①不羞赧的；無羞恥心的。②不因害羞而侷促不安的；保持鎮靜的。—**ly,** *adv.*

un·a·bat·ed [ʌnəˈbetɪd; ˈʌnəˈbeitid] *adj.* 不減輕的；不減弱的。

***un·a·ble** [ʌnˈeb|; ˈʌnˈeibl, ʌnˈei-] *adj.*, *v.*, **-a·bled, -a·bling.** —*adj.* 不能的。A little baby is *unable* to walk and talk. 嬰孩不能走路和說話。—*v.t.* 使無能。

un·a·bridged [ˌʌnəˈbrɪdʒd; ˈʌnəˈbridʒd] *adj.* 未刪節的；完整的（書等）。

un·ac·cent·ed [ʌnˈæksɛntɪd; ˈʌnækˈsentid] *adj.* 無重音的。

un·ac·cept·a·ble [ˌʌnəkˈsɛptəb|; ˈʌnəkˈseptəbl] *adj.* ①不能接受的；不能接納的。②不悅人意的；不稱心的；不受歡迎的。—**ness,** *n.*—**un·ac·cept·a·bly,** *adv.*

un·ac·com·mo·dat·ed [ˌʌnəˈkɑməˌdetɪd; ˈʌnəˈkɔmədeitid] *adj.* ①不適應的；不適合的。②無各種便利設施的。③未予滿足的。④未供給…的；未給予…的。

un·ac·com·pa·nied [ˌʌnəˈkʌmpənɪd; ˈʌnəˈkʌmpənid] *adj.* ①無伴侶的；無附屬物的。②〖音樂〗無伴奏的。

un·ac·com·plished [ˌʌnəˈkɑmplɪʃt; ˈʌnəˈkɔmpliʃt] *adj.* ①未完成的；未遂的。②無才藝的；無技能的。

un·ac·count·a·ble [ˌʌnəˈkauntəb|; ˈʌnəˈkauntəbl] *adj.* ①不能說明的；不可解的。②不負責的。—**ness,** *n.*

un·ac·count·a·bly [ˌʌnəˈkauntəblɪ; ˈʌnəˈkauntəbli] *adv.* 不能說明地；不可解釋地；神祕地。

un·ac·cus·tomed [ˌʌnəˈkʌstəmd; ˈʌnəˈkʌstəmd] *adj.* ①不習慣的。②異乎尋常的；未見慣的。—**ness,** *n.*

un·a·dorned [ˌʌnəˈdɔrnd; ˈʌnəˈdɔːnd] *adj.* 未加裝飾的；樸實的；樸素的。

un·a·dul·ter·at·ed [ˌʌnəˈdʌltəˌretɪd; ˌʌnəˈdʌltəreitid] *adj.* ①無雜物的；未摻雜別物的。②純粹的；眞正的。—**ly,** *adv.*

un·ad·vised [ˌʌnədˈvaɪzd; ˈʌnədˈvaizd] *adj.* ①欠思慮的；輕率的。②未受勸告的；無忠告的。—**ly,** *adv.*

un·af·fect·ed[1] [ˌʌnəˈfɛktɪd; ˈʌnəˈfektid] *adj.* 未受影響的；未受感動的。

un·af·fect·ed[2] *adj.* 無矯飾的；眞摯的；率眞的；自然的。—**ly,** *adv.*

un·aid·ed [ʌnˈedɪd; ˈʌnˈeidid] *adj.* 無幫助的；獨立的。

un·a·ligned [ˌʌnəˈlaɪnd; ˈʌnəˈlaind] 〔*adj.* 未結盟的。〕

un·a·like [ˌʌnəˈlaɪk; ˈʌnəˈlaik] *adj.* 不相似的。

un·al·loyed [ˌʌnəˈlɔɪd; ˈʌnəˈlɔid] *adj.* ①無雜物的；純粹的（金屬）。②完全的；眞實的。

un·al·ter·a·ble [ʌnˈɔltərəb|; ʌnˈɔːltərəbl] *adj.* 不變的；不能改變的。

un·al·tered [ʌnˈɔltəd; ˈʌnˈɔːltəd] *adj.* ①〖廢〗不能被改變的。②未改變的；依然如舊的。

un·am·big·u·ous [ˌʌnæmˈbɪgjuəs; ˈʌnæmˈbigjuəs] *adj.* 清晰的；明白的；不模糊的。—**ly,** *adv.*

un·am·bi·tious [ˌʌnæmˈbɪʃəs; ˈʌnæmˈbiʃəs] *adj.* ①無野心的；無名利心的。②無矯飾的；質樸的。—**ly,** *adv.* —**ness,** *n.*

un-A·mer·i·can [ˌʌnəˈmɛrəkən; ˈʌnəˈmerikən] *adj.* 非美國的；不合美國特色及格調的；不合美國標準及習慣的。

un·a·neled [ˌʌnəˈnild; ˈʌnəˈniːld] *adj.* 未受臨終塗油禮的。

u·na·nim·i·ty [ˌjunəˈnɪmətɪ; ˌjuːnəˈnimiti] *n.* 全體同意；全體一致。

***u·nan·i·mous** [juˈnænəməs; juˈnæniməs] *adj.* 意見一致的；全體一致的。—**ness,** *n.* —**ly,** *adv.*

un·an·swer·a·ble [ʌnˈænsərəb|; ʌnˈɑːnsərəbl] *adj.* ①不能回答的。②無法爭辯的；決定性的。③無責任的。

un·an·swered [ʌnˈænsəd; ˈʌnˈɑːnsəd] *adj.* ①無回答的；無答覆的。②無反駁的。③有往無來的。

un·ap·proach·a·ble [ˌʌnəˈprotʃəb|; ˌʌnəˈproutʃəbl] *adj.* ①不能接近的。②無與倫比的；無匹的。

un·apt [ʌnˈæpt; ˈʌnˈæpt] *adj.* ①笨拙的；遲鈍的。②不適當的；不適合的。③無…之傾向的；不慣於…的。—**ly,** *adv.* —**ness,** *n.*

un·arm [ʌnˈɑrm; ˈʌnˈɑːm] *v.t.* ①解除…的武裝；繳械。②〖古〗脫下盔甲。—*v.i.* ①解除武裝；放下武器；繳械。②〖古〗脫下盔甲。

***un·armed** [ʌnˈɑrmd; ˈʌnˈɑːmd] *adj.* ①未武裝的；未帶武器的。②未着盔甲的。③無爪、鱗或刺的。④（炸彈等）未裝雷管的。

un·a·shamed [ˌʌnəˈʃemd; ˈʌnəˈʃeimd] *adj.* ①厚顏無恥的。②公開的；公然的；肆無忌憚的。—**ness,** *n.*

un·asked [ʌnˈæskt; ˈʌnˈɑːskt] *adj.* 未受請求的；未經邀請的。

un·as·sail·a·ble [ˌʌnəˈseləb|; ˌʌnəˈseiləbl] *adj.* ①難攻的；不能攻擊的。②無可反駁的；無懈可擊的（論證等）。③堅定不移的。—**un·as·sail·a·bly,** *adv.* —**ness,** *n.*

un·as·sist·ed [ˌʌnəˈsɪstɪd; ˈʌnəˈsistid] *adj.* =**unaided.**

un·as·sum·ing [ˌʌnəˈsumɪŋ; ˈʌnəˈsjuːmiŋ] *adj.* 不擺架子的；謙遜的。

un·at·tached [ˌʌnəˈtætʃt; ˈʌnəˈtætʃt] *adj.* ①未縛的；未結的；未繫的；不附着的。②無所屬的；獨立的；中立的。③未訂婚的；未結婚的。④〖軍〗未經指定任務的；待命的。⑤不屬於某特定學院的（大學生）。⑥〖法律〗未被逮捕的；未被扣押的。

un·at·tain·a·ble [ˌʌnəˈtenəb|; ˈʌnəˈteinəbl] *adj.* 難得到的；難到達的；難有成就的。—**un·at·tain·a·bly,** *adv.* —**ness,** *n.*

un·at·tend·ed [ˌʌnəˈtɛndɪd; ˈʌnəˈtendid] *adj.* ①無伴的；無侍從的。②不爲人注意的。③未紮繃帶的（傷）。④無人照顧的；無人管理的。⑤無人出席的；無人參加的。⑥無附隨的。⑦被置之不理的。⑧未執行的；未做的〖常 to〗。

un·at·trac·tive [ˌʌnəˈtræktɪv; ˌʌnəˈtræktiv] *adj.* 無吸引力的；不美麗的。

un·au·thor·ized [ʌnˈɔθəˌraɪzd; ˈʌnˈɔːθəraizd] *adj.* ①無權的；未經授權的；未經許可的。②未經公認的。③無根據的。—**ly,** *adv.*

un·a·vail·a·ble [ˌʌnəˈveləb|; ˈʌnəˈveiləbl] *adj.* ①不能供人使用的；不能利用的；不近便的。②〖美〗不能採用的（原稿）。—**un·a·vail·a·bly,** *adv.* —**ness,** *n.*

un·a·vail·ing [ˌʌnəˈvelɪŋ; ˈʌnəˈveiliŋ] *adj.* 無效的；無用的；無益的；無結果的。

un·a·void·a·ble [ˌʌnəˈvɔɪdəb|; ˌʌnəˈvɔidəbl] *adj.* 不可避免的。—**un·a·void·a·bil·i·ty,** *n.* —**un·a·void·a·bly,** *adv.*

***un·a·ware** [ˌʌnəˈwɛr; ˈʌnəˈwɛə] *adj.* 不知道的；不覺察的。to be *unaware* of the danger. 未覺察這個危險。—*adv.* = **unawares.**

un·a·wares [ˌʌnəˈwɛrz; ˈʌnəˈwɛəz] *adv.* ①不知不覺地；無意地。②意外地；突然地。 ***at unawares*** 出其不意地（=by surprise). *take* (or *catch*) *unawares* 冷不防地襲擊;突襲。

un·backed [ʌn'bækt;'ʌn'bækt] *adj.* ①無支持的;無援助的。②從未騎乘的(指未馴服至可騎乘之馬)。③無人下賭注於其上的(賽馬)。④無背的。

un·baked [ʌn'bekt; 'ʌn'beikt] *adj.* ①未焙的;未熟的。②發育未完全的;未成熟的。

un·bal·ance [ʌn'bæləns; 'ʌn'bæləns] *n., v.,* **-anced, -anc·ing.** —*n.* ①不均衡; 不平衡。②(精神)錯亂。—*v.t.* ①使不均衡;使不平衡。②使(精神)錯亂。

un·bal·anced [ʌn'bælənst; 'ʌn'bælənst] *adj.* ①不均衡的;不平衡的;失去平衡的。②(精神)錯亂的。 ③不安定的;不穩定的。④未決算的。

un·bar [ʌn'bɑr; 'ʌn'bɑː] *v.t. & v.i.,* **-barred, -bar·ring.** 拔去門閂;拔去…之門;打開;開放。

un·bat·ed [ʌn'betɪd; 'ʌn'beitid] *adj.* 未減弱的;未減少的。

***un·bear·a·ble** [ʌn'bɛrəbl̩; 'ʌn'bɛərəbl] *adj.* 不堪忍受的。—**un·bear·a·bly,** *adv.*

un·beat·en [ʌn'bitn̩; 'ʌn'biːtn] *adj.* ①未被擊敗的; 未曾爲人勝過的。②未受踐踏的;人跡所未及的。③未受擊打的;未經搗碎的。

un·be·com·ing [ˌʌnbɪ'kʌmɪŋ; 'ʌnbi'kʌmiŋ] *adj.* ①不合適的。②失禮的;不正當的。③不相配的。

un·be·known [ˌʌnbɪ'non;'ʌnbi'noun] *adj.* 未知的;不得而知的〖to〗. —*adv.* 不知地;不得而知地。(亦作 **unbeknownst**)

un·be·lief [ˌʌnbɪ'lif;'ʌnbi'liːf] *n.* 不信;不信仰上帝;懷疑。

un·be·liev·er [ˌʌnbə'livɚ; 'ʌnbi'liːvə] *n.* ①不相信者;懷疑者。②不信仰某宗教者;無宗教信仰者。

un·be·liev·ing [ˌʌnbə'livɪŋ; 'ʌnbi'liːviŋ] *adj.* 不相信的;沒有信心的;懷疑的。—**ly,** *adv.* —**ness,** *n.*

un·bend [ʌn'bɛnd; 'ʌn'bend] *v.,* **-bent** or **-bend·ed, -bend·ing.** —*v.t.* ①使變直。②鬆弛(過勞或受拘束之身心等); 使舒暢。③解下;卸下(帆篷);放鬆(繩索等)。④解開(結子等)。 —*v.i.* ①變直;伸直。②鬆弛; 舒暢;變隨和(即不再拘泥儀式)。

un·bend·ing [ʌn'bɛndɪŋ;'ʌn'bendiŋ] *adj.* ①不曲的;不彎的。②不屈的;堅決的;剛愎的。③不變易的。④放鬆的; 鬆弛的。—*n.* 鬆弛;解悶; 緩和。—**ly,** *adv.* —**ness,** *n.*

un·bent [ʌn'bɛnt; 'ʌn'bent] *adj.* ①未彎曲的。②未讓步的;未屈服的。 —*v.* pt. & pp. of **unbend.**

un·bi·as(s)ed [ʌn'baɪəst;'ʌn'baiəst] *adj.* 無偏見的;不偏不倚的;公平的。—**ly,** *adv.*

un·bid·den [ʌn'bɪdn̩; 'ʌn'bidn] *adj.* ①未受吩咐的;未奉命的。②自然的;自發的。③未受邀請的。

un·bind [ʌn'baɪnd; 'ʌn'baind] *v.t.,* **-bound, -bind·ing.** ①解開(繩索等)。②釋放。

un·bleached [ʌn'blitʃt; 'ʌn'bliːtʃt] *adj.* 未經漂白的。

un·blem·ished [ʌn'blɛmɪʃt; ʌn'blemiʃt] *adj.* 無汚點的;無瑕疵的;潔白的。

un·blessed, un·blest [ʌn'blɛst; 'ʌn'blest] *adj.* ①未蒙神佑的。②不神聖的。③邪惡的。④不快樂的; 不幸的。⑤缺少某種好處的。—**un·bless·ed·ness,** *n.*

un·blush·ing [ʌn'blʌʃɪŋ; ʌn'blʌʃiŋ] *adj.* 不臉紅的;厚臉皮的;無羞恥心的。

un·bod·ied [ʌn'bɑdɪd; 'ʌn'bɔdid] *adj.* ①離去軀體的。②無實的;無形的;精神上的。

un·bolt [ʌn'bolt; 'ʌn'boult] *v.t. & v.i.* ①拔開門閂;拔去…之門閂;開啓。②旋開螺釘。

un·bolt·ed[1] [ʌn'boltɪd; 'ʌn'boultid] *adj.* 門閂已拔開的; 開啓的; 未固定的。

un·bolt·ed[2] *adj.* 未篩過的;粗糙的。

un·born [ʌn'bɔrn; 'ʌn'bɔːn] *adj.* ①未誕生的。②未來的。③無開始的;原來存在的。

un·bos·om [ʌn'bʊzəm; ʌn'buzəm] *v.t.* 使知;告知;表白(情感);吐露(機密等);剖明(心跡)。—*v.i.* 表白情感;吐露眞情;剖明心跡。*unbosom oneself* 吐露心事;表白情感;開誠布公。 —**er,** *n.*

un·bound [ʌn'baʊnd;'ʌn'baund] *adj.* ①已獲得自由的;獲釋的。②未裝訂的(書)。—*v.* pt. & pp. of **unbind.**

un·bound·ed [ʌn'baʊndɪd;'ʌn'baundid] *adj.* ①無限制的;極大的;無際的。②未加約束的;未加管制的。—**ly,** *adv.*

un·bowed [ʌn'baʊd;'ʌn'baud] *adj.* ①不彎的;不曲的。②不屈服的;未征服的。

un·braid [ʌn'bred; 'ʌn'breid] *v.t.* 析開; 縷析。

un·bri·dled [ʌn'braɪdl̩d;ʌn'braidld] *adj.* ①無韁轡的; 無羈勒的(馬)。 ②無羈束的;不受約束的;激烈的。

***un·bro·ken** [ʌn'brokən; 'ʌn'broukən] *adj.* ①未破損的; 完好的;完整的。②未被阻斷的; 連續不斷的。③未馴服的。④未開墾的。*unbroken* land. 處女地。⑤被信守的。an *unbroken* promise. 被信守的諾言。⑥未被打破的。an *unbroken* record. 未被打破之記錄。—**ly,** *adv.* —**ness,** *n.*

un·buck·le [ʌn'bʌkl̩; 'ʌn'bʌkl] *v.t.,* **-buck·led, -buck·ling.** 解開…之搭鈕。

un·build [ʌn'bɪld; 'ʌn'bild] *v.t.,* **-built, -build·ing.** ①毁滅; 摧毁; 破壞。②減低(磁性)。

un·bur·den [ʌn'bɝdn̩; ʌn'bəːdn] *v.t.* ①釋負; 以坦白吐露來解除心靈的負擔。②解除負擔。

un·bur·dened [ʌn'bɝdn̩d; ʌn'bəːdnd] *adj.* 不受累的;無牽累的。

un·busi·ness·like [ʌn'bɪznɪsˌlaɪk; ʌn'biznislaik] *adj.* 不認眞的;無效能的; 無次序的;無組織的。

un·but·ton [ʌn'bʌtn̩; 'ʌn'bʌtn] *v.t.* ①解開…的鈕扣。②放開;吐露(心事)。—*v.i.* 解扣。

UNC, U.N.C. United Nations Command.

un·cage [ʌn'kedʒ; 'ʌn'keidʒ] *v.t.,* **-caged, -cag·ing.** 從籠中放出;釋放。

un·called [ʌn'kɔld; 'ʌn'kɔːld] *adj.* 未被邀請的; 未被請求的。*uncalled* capital. 〖商〗未繳資金。

un·called-for [ʌn'kɔldˌfɔr;ʌn'kɔːldfɔː] *adj.* 不需要的;不適宜的。

un·can·ny [ʌn'kænɪ; ʌn'kæni] *adj.* 奇怪的;神奇的;怪誕的。—**un·can·ni·ly,** *adv.*

un·cap [ʌn'kæp; 'ʌn'kæp] *v.,* **-capped, -cap·ping.** —*v.t.* 脫掉…的帽子; 移去(瓶子等)的蓋子。—*v.i.* 脫帽(以示敬意)。

un·ceas·ing [ʌn'sisɪŋ; ʌn'siːsiŋ] *adj.* 不絕的;不停的。 —**ly,** *adv.* —**ness,** *n.*

un·cer·e·mo·ni·ous [ˌʌnsɛrə'monɪəs;'ʌnˌseri'mounjəs] *adj.* ①不遵禮儀的;不拘禮儀的;非正式的。②無禮的;唐突的。 —**ly,** *adv.* —**ness,** *n.*

***un·cer·tain** [ʌn'sɝtn̩; -'sɝtɪn; ʌn'səːtn] *adj.* ①不定的;不確定的。②不確知的;不確信的。③常變化的; 不可靠的。④模糊不

清的。⑤搖曳不定的。⑥不可預測的;可疑的。 —ly, *adv.* —ness, *n.*

*__un·cer·tain·ty__ [ʌnˈsɝtn̩tɪ; ʌnˈsəːtnti] *n., pl.* -ties [-tɪz; -tiz]. ①不確定; 無常。②不可靠;不固定; 不穩定。③不確定的事物; 令人懷疑的事物。④半信半疑。

uncertainty principle 〖物理〗測不準原理。(亦作**indeterminacy principle**)

un·cer·ti·fied [ʌnˈsɝtəˌfaɪd; ʌnˈsəːtifaid] *adj.* 未經證明的;無證書的。

un·chain [ʌnˈtʃen; ˈʌnˈtʃein] *v.t.* ①解開…之鎖鏈。②除去…之束縛。③釋放;解放。

un·chal·lenged [ʌnˈtʃælɪndʒd; ˈʌn-ˈtʃælindʒd] *adj.* 不成問題的;未引起爭論的;未受到挑戰的。

un·chanc·y [ʌnˈtʃænsɪ; ˈʌnˈtʃɑːnsi] *adj.* 〖蘇〗①不幸的;不吉的。②危險的。③不湊巧的;不合時宜的。

un·change·a·ble [ʌnˈtʃendʒəbl̩; ʌn-ˈtʃeindʒəbl] *adj.* 不變的; 不易的; 不能改變的。 —ness, *n.* —un·change·a·bly, *adv.*

*__un·changed__ [ʌnˈtʃendʒd; ˈʌnˈtʃeindʒd] *adj.* 未改變的;無變化的。—ness, *n.*

un·char·i·ta·ble [ʌnˈtʃærətəbl̩; ʌn-ˈtʃæritəbl] *adj.* 苛酷的; 不慈悲的; 不寬恕的;不寬厚的。—un·char·i·ta·bly, *adv.*

un·chart·ed [ʌnˈtʃartɪd; ˈʌnˈtʃɑːtid] *adj.* ①海圖上未載的。②未探險過的;未知的。

un·chaste [ʌnˈtʃest; ˈʌnˈtʃeist] *adj.*①無貞操的;不貞的;淫奔的。②(文體等)不簡潔的;低級趣味的;卑野的。—ly, *adv.*

un·chas·ti·ty [ʌnˈtʃæstətɪ; ˈʌnˈtʃæstiti] *n.* ①無節操;不貞。②淫奔;淫蕩。③不簡潔;不雅;低級;卑野。

un·checked [ʌnˈtʃɛkt; ˈʌnˈtʃekt] *adj.* ①未被遏止的;未受抑制的。②未經檢查的;未檢點的。

un·chris·tian [ʌnˈkrɪstʃən; ˈʌnˈkristjən] *adj.* ①非基督敎的; 非基督徒的。②不合基督敎義的。③不配爲基督敎徒的。④無慈悲心的;粗野的。⑤異敎的;異端的。

un·church [ʌnˈtʃɝtʃ; ˈʌnˈtʃəːtʃ] *v.t.* ①將…逐出敎會。②剝奪…爲敎會之權利。

un·ci·al [ˈʌnʃɪəl; ˈʌnsiəl] *adj.* 紀元300-900年間用於抄本的一種大圓體字的。—*n.* ①該種大字字母。②以該種大字抄寫之抄本。 —ly, *adv.*

un·ci·nate [ˈʌnsɪnɪt; ˈʌnsinit] *adj.* 「鉤狀的。」

un·cir·cum·cised [ʌnˈsɝkəmˌsaɪzd; ˈʌnˈsəːkəmsaizd] *adj.* ①未受割禮的。②非猶太人的;異邦人的。③異敎的;異端的。④精神上不再生的;不獲重生的。

un·cir·cum·ci·sion [ˌʌnsɝkəmˈsɪʒən; ˈʌnˌsəːkəmˈsiʒən] *n.* ①未受割禮。②〖聖經〗異邦人;非猶太人。

un·civ·il [ʌnˈsɪvl̩; ˈʌnˈsivl] *adj.* ①無禮貌的; 失禮的; 粗野的。②野蠻的; 未開化的。 —ly, *adv.*

un·civ·i·lized [ʌnˈsɪvl̩ˌaɪzd; ˈʌnˈsivilaizd] *adj.* 未開化的;野蠻的。 —ness, *n.*

un·claimed [ʌnˈklemd; ˈʌnˈkleimd] *adj.* 未經要求的;無請求者的。

un·clasp [ʌnˈklæsp; ˈʌnˈklɑːsp] *v.t.* & *v.i.* ①打開…之扣子; 打開。②放開掌握;鬆放。

‡**un·cle** [ˈʌŋkl̩; ˈʌnkl] *n.* ①父親或母親的兄弟;叔父; 伯父; 舅父。②姑母或姨母之夫;姑丈; 姨丈。 I am going to my *uncle's*. 我到伯父(叔父或舅父) 家去。③〖俚〗開當鋪者; 典商。 He has left his watch with his *uncle*. 他的錶押在當鋪裏面了。④〖俗〗老年人;老伯伯;世伯。⑤援助者; 支援者。 ***say uncle*** 〖俚〗a. 承認失敗; 屈服。 b. 呼救。 —ship, *n.*

un·clean [ʌnˈklin; ˈʌnˈkliːn] *adj.* ①不潔淨的;汚穢的。②不純潔的;不貞潔的;行爲不檢的。③宗教儀式上不潔淨的。 —ness, *n.*

un·clean·ly [*adj.* ʌnˈklɛnlɪ *adv.* ʌn-ˈklinlɪ; ˈʌnˈklenli] *adj.* ①不潔的;骯髒的;不衞生的。②不純潔的;不純正的。—*adv.* 不潔地;汚濁地。—un·clean·li·ness, *n.*

un·clear [ʌnˈklɪr; ˈʌnˈkliə] *adj.* 不清楚的;不清晰的。

un·clench [ʌnˈklɛntʃ; ˈʌnˈklentʃ] *v.t.* 「& *v.i.* 鬆開;撬開。」

Uncle Sam〖俗〗山姆大叔;美政府或人民。

Uncle Tom (有時 u- t-)聽命於白人的美國黑人 (原爲 *Uncle Tom's Cabin* "黑奴籲天錄"中主角之名)。

un·cloak [ʌnˈklok; ˈʌnˈklouk] *v.t.* & *v.i.*①脫去外套;除去…的覆蓋物。②暴露;揭露。

un·close [ʌnˈkloz; ˈʌnˈklouz] *v.t.* & *v.i.*, -closed, -clos·ing. 揭開;打開。

un·clothe [ʌnˈkloð; ˈʌnˈklouð] *v.t.*, -clothed or -clad [-ˈklæd; -ˈklæd], -cloth·ing. ①脫掉…的衣服。②揭露。③爲…除去某物。

un·cloud·ed [ʌnˈklaudɪd; ˈʌnˈklaudid] *adj.* ①無雲的;晴朗的。②明朗的;寧靜的。

un·co [ˈʌŋko; ˈʌŋkou] *adj., adv., n., pl.* -cos. —*adj.* 〖蘇〗古怪的; 奇異的; 顯著的。 —*adv.* 〖蘇〗非常地;很顯著地。 —*n.* 〖蘇〗①奇異的東西。②(*pl.*) 新聞。

un·coil [ʌnˈkɔɪl; ˈʌnˈkɔil] *v.t.* & *v.i.* 解開(盤繞之物);解開;展開。

un·come-at-a·ble [ˌʌnkʌmˈætəbl̩; ˈʌn-kʌmˈætəbl] *adj.* 〖俗〗難接近的;難得到的。

un·come·ly [ʌnˈkʌmlɪ; ˈʌnˈkʌmli] 「*adj.* 不漂亮的;不合適的;不相稱的。」

*__un·com·fort·a·ble__ [ʌnˈkʌmfɚtəbl̩; ʌnˈkʌmfətəbl] *adj.* ①不舒適的。②不安的。③使人不舒適的;不合意的。 —ness, *n.* —un·com·fort·a·bly, *adv.*

un·com·mit·ted [ˌʌnkəˈmɪtɪd; ˈʌnkəˈmitid] *adj.* ①未被授權的;未受委託的。②未遂的。an *uncommitted* crime. 未遂罪。③不負義務的; 不受諾言約束的。④未確定用途的。

*__un·com·mon__ [ʌnˈkɑmən; ʌnˈkɔmən] *adj.* ①非常的;不凡的。②罕有的。③傑出的。 —*adv.* 〖方〗非常地。—ly, *adv.* —ness, *n.*

un·com·mu·ni·ca·tive [ˌʌnkə-ˈmjunəˌketɪv; ˈʌn-kəˈmjuːnikətiv] *adj.* 沉默寡言的;緘默的。

un·com·pli·cat·ed [ʌnˈkɑmplɪˌketɪd; ˈʌnˈkɔmplikeitid] *adj.* ①未被複雜化的。②不複雜的;簡單的。

un·com·pli·men·ta·ry [ˌʌnkɑmpləˈmɛntərɪ; ˈʌnˌkɑmpliˈmentəri] *adj.* 貶降的。

un·com·pro·mis·ing [ʌnˈkɑmprəˌmaɪzɪŋ; ʌnˈkɔmprəmaiziŋ] *adj.* 不妥協的;不能通融的。—ly, *adv.*

un·con·cern [ˌʌnkənˈsɝn; ˈʌnkənˈsəːn] *n.* 漠不關心;不感興趣。

un·con·cerned [ˌʌnkənˈsɝnd; ˈʌnkənˈsəːnd] *adj.* ①不相關的; 無關係的。②不關心的;無興趣的。③不介意的。—ly, *adv.*

un·con·di·tion·al [ˌʌnkənˈdɪʃənəl; ˈʌn-kənˈdiʃənəl] *adj.* 無條件的; 絕對的。 an *unconditional* surrender. 無條件投降。

—ly, *adv.*

un·con·di·tioned 〔ˌʌnkənˈdɪʃənd; ˈʌn-kənˈdiʃənd〕 *adj.* ①無條件的;絕對的。②〖哲學〗無限的;絕對的。③〖心理〗自然的;未學習的;無條件的。④無條件入學的。—*n.* (the U-)〖哲學〗絕對;無限。

un·con·firmed 〔ˌʌnkənˈfɝmd; ˈʌn-kənˈfəːmd〕*adj.*①未經認可的。②未經證實的。

un·con·form·a·ble 〔ˌʌnkənˈfɔrməbḷ; ˈʌn-kənˈfɔːməbl〕 *adj.* 不符的;不一致的。

un·con·form·i·ty 〔ˌʌnkənˈfɔrmətɪ; ˈʌn-kənˈfɔːmiti〕 *n.*①不一致;不相合;矛盾。②〖地質〗(地層)不整合。

un·con·nect·ed 〔ˌʌnkəˈnɛktɪd; ˈʌn-kəˈnektid〕 *adj.* ①不連貫的;不相關的。②無親無戚的。

un·con·quer·a·ble 〔ʌnˈkɑŋkərəbḷ; ʌnˈkɔŋkərəbl〕 *adj.* 不能征服的;不能克服的。—**ness,** *n.*

un·con·scion·a·ble 〔ʌnˈkɑnʃənəbḷ; ʌnˈkɔnʃənəbl〕 *adj.* ①不受良心引導或約束的;恣肆的;不法的。②不公平的。③不合理的;過度的。

un·con·scious** 〔ʌnˈkɑnʃəs; ʌnˈkɔnʃəs〕 *adj.* ①無意識的;失掉知覺的。②不知道的;不覺察的。③無意的;不知不覺的。the unconscious*** 〖精神分析〗無意識(人不自覺的思想、慾望、行動等)。—**ly,** *adv.* —**ness,** *n.*

un·con·sti·tu·tion·al 〔ˌʌnkɑnstəˈtjuʃənḷ; ˈʌnˌkɔnstiˈtjuːʃənḷ〕 *adj.* 違憲的;不合憲法規定的。

un·con·sti·tu·tion·al·i·ty 〔ˌʌn-kɑnstəˌtjuʃənˈælətɪ; ˈʌnˌkɔnstiˌtjuːʃəˈnæliti〕 *n.*違反憲法;違憲。

un·con·strained 〔ˌʌnkənˈstrend; ˈʌn-kənˈstreind〕 *adj.* 無拘束的;不勉強的;自然的。

un·con·test·ed 〔ˌʌnkənˈtɛstɪd; ˈʌn-kənˈtestid〕 *adj.* ①無競爭的;無爭的。②顯然的;無爭辯餘地的。

un·con·trol·la·ble 〔ˌʌnkənˈtroləbḷ; ˈʌn-kənˈtrouləbl〕 *adj.* 難控制的;無法管束的。—**ness,** *n.* —**un·con·trol·la·bly,** *adv.*

un·con·trolled 〔ˌʌnkənˈtrold; ˈʌn-kənˈtrould〕 *adj.* 未受抑制的;未受管束的;自由自在的。—**ly,** *adv.*

un·con·ven·tion·al 〔ˌʌnkənˈvɛnʃənḷ; ˈʌn-kənˈvenʃənḷ〕 *adj.* 不依慣例的;不從習俗的;非因襲的。—**i·ty,** *n.* —**ly,** *adv.*

un·con·vert·ed 〔ˌʌnkənˈvɝtɪd; ˈʌn-kənˈvəːtid〕 *adj.* ①不改的;不變的。②不改宗的;不改黨的。③未悔改的;未脫罪的。

un·cooked 〔ʌnˈkukt; ˈʌnˈkukt〕 *adj.* ①未煮的;未烹煮的。②未洗鍊的;粗陋的。

un·cord 〔ʌnˈkɔrd; ˈʌnˈkɔːd〕 *v.t.* 解開;解縛。

un·cork 〔ʌnˈkɔrk; ˈʌnˈkɔːk〕 *v.t.* ①拔去…的塞子。②吐露。③〖俚〗突然發出。—**ed,** *adj.*

un·cor·rupt·ed 〔ˌʌnkəˈrʌptɪd; ˈʌnkəˈrʌptid〕 *adj.* ①未腐敗的。②未墮落的。③未被收買的;廉潔的。

un·cor·rup·ti·ble 〔ˌʌnkəˈrʌptəbḷ; ˈʌn-kəˈrʌptəbl〕 *adj.* ①難使腐敗的;難損壞的。②難墮落的;難收買的;廉潔的。

un·count·a·ble 〔ʌnˈkauntəbḷ; ˈʌn-ˈkauntəbl〕 *adj.* ①無數的;不能數的。②不能估計的。

un·count·ed 〔ʌnˈkauntɪd; ˈʌnˈkaun-tid〕 *adj.* ①未計及的;未數過的。②無數的;不可勝數的。

un·cou·ple 〔ʌnˈkʌpḷ; ˈʌnˈkʌpl〕 *v.,* **-cou·pled, -cou·pling.** —*v.t.* 解開(繫住之物);分開(連結之物)。—*v.i.* 分開;解開。

un·cour·te·ous 〔ʌnˈkɝtɪəs; ˈʌnˈkəː-tjəs〕*adj.* 粗魯無禮的;不知禮儀的。—**ly,** *adv.*

un·couth 〔ʌnˈkuθ; ʌnˈkuːθ〕 *adj.* ①笨拙的;蠢笨的;粗魯的。②奇怪的;古怪的。③令人不舒服的;令人不快的。—**ly,** *adv.* —**ness,** *n.*

un·cov·er** 〔ʌnˈkʌvɚ; ʌnˈkʌvə〕 *v.t.* ①移去…的覆蓋物。*Uncover* the box. 拿掉盒蓋。②洩露;揭露。The police have *uncovered* a plot. 警察當局破獲一陰謀。③脫去(頭)上的帽。—*v.i.* ①脫帽致敬。②移去覆蓋物。uncover oneself*** 脫帽致敬。

un·cov·ered 〔ʌnˈkʌvɚd; ʌnˈkʌvəd〕 *adj.* ①無遮蓋的。②無遮蔽的;無掩護的。③未在保證或擔保之列的。④未戴帽的;光着頭的。⑤暴露的。⑥無擔保的;無抵押品的。

un·crowd·ed 〔ʌnˈkraudɪd; ʌnˈkrau-did〕 *adj.* 不擁擠的。

un·crown 〔ʌnˈkraun; ˈʌnˈkraun〕 *v.t.* 廢黜;剝奪…之王冠;奪去…之王位。

un·crowned 〔ʌnˈkraund; ˈʌnˈkraund〕 *adj.* ①未加冕的;未正式登極的。②無王或后之尊號而統治的。

unc·tion 〔ˈʌŋkʃən; ˈʌŋkʃən〕 *n.* ①塗油;傅油式(一種宗教儀式)。②(塗用之)油;膏;軟膏。③熱心;熱情;興味。④令人舒服或慰藉之物。⑤話語中之安慰、同情或說服之性質。⑥虛僞的熱情。

unc·tu·ous 〔ˈʌŋktʃuəs; ˈʌŋktjuəs〕 *adj.* ①似油的;油質的。②安慰的;同情的;說服的。③油腔滑調的;假慇懃的。④油滑的;滑膩的。⑤柔軟而肥沃的(指泥土言)。—**ly,** *adv.*

un·cul·ti·vat·ed 〔ʌnˈkʌltəˌvetɪd; ˈʌnˈkʌltiveitid〕 *adj.* ①未經耕種的;未墾的。②未經栽培的;野生的。③未經磨練的;未受獎勵的;被忽略的。④未開化的;野蠻狀態的。

un·curl 〔ʌnˈkɝl; ˈʌnˈkəːl〕 *v.t.* 使伸直;使舒展。—*v.i.* 伸直;舒展。

un·cus·tomed 〔ʌnˈkʌstəmd; ʌnˈkʌstəmd〕 *adj.* 未經稅關檢查的;走私的。

un·cut 〔ʌnˈkʌt; ˈʌnˈkʌt〕 *adj.* ①未切的;未雕琢的。②未割的。③未刪節的。

un·dat·ed 〔ʌnˈdetɪd; ˈʌnˈdeitid〕 *adj.* 無日期的;未記日期的。

un·daunt·ed 〔ʌnˈdɔntɪd; ʌnˈdɔːntid〕 *adj.* 大無畏的。

un·de·ceive 〔ˌʌndɪˈsiv; ˈʌn-diˈsiːv〕 *v.t.,* **-ceived, -ceiv·ing.** 使不再受欺騙;使免犯錯誤;使明實情。—**un·de·ceiv·er,** *n.*

un·de·cid·ed 〔ˌʌndɪˈsaɪdɪd; ˈʌndiˈsaidid〕 *adj.* ①未決定的;未決意的。②優柔寡斷的。③不定的;不安定的;斷斷續續的。—**ly,** *adv.* —**ness,** *n.*

un·de·fend·ed 〔ˌʌndɪˈfɛndɪd; ˈʌndiˈfendid〕 *adj.* ①無防備的;未設防的。②無辯護人的。③無抗辯的。

un·de·filed 〔ˌʌndɪˈfaɪld; ˈʌndiˈfaild〕 *adj.* 無汚的;潔白的;純正的。

un·de·fined 〔ˌʌndɪˈfaɪnd; ˈʌndiˈfaind〕 *adj.* ①未闡明的;未解釋的。②不確定的;不明確的。

un·de·mon·stra·tive 〔ˌʌndɪˈmɑnstrətɪv; ˈʌndiˈmɔnstrətiv〕 *adj.* 喜怒不形於色的;感情不露於外的。

un·de·ni·a·ble 〔ˌʌndɪˈnaɪəbḷ; ˌʌndiˈnaiəbl〕 *adj.* ①無可否認的;不能爭辯的。②的確好的;極佳的。③不會錯的;明顯的。—**un·de·ni·a·bly,** *adv.*

:**un·der** 〔ˈʌndɚ; ˈʌndə〕 *prep.* ①在…之

下;在…的下面;在…的表面之下。*under* the tree. 在樹下。There is nothing new *under* the sun. 天下無新奇事物。②未滿;少於(指數量而言)。children *under* six years of age. 不滿六歲的兒童。He won't sell *under* $100. 少於一百元他不肯賣。③在…的過程中;在…中。the road *under* repair. 在修理中的道路。④低於。⑤受制於。*under* the new rules. 在新規定之下。⑥根據。*under* the law. 根據此法律。⑦以…爲代表。⑧受…之約束。*under* obligation. 受義務之約束。***be under a cloud*** a. 有汚名。b. 不得寵。***be under way*** 正在進行之中。***speak under one's breath*** 低聲地說。***under age*** 未成年;不到二十一歲。***under a pretense*** 藉口。***under one's hat*** 在祕密中。***under orders*** 奉命。***under the head of*** 在…的項目下。***under the impression that...*** 以爲;相信…。—*adv.* ①在下;在下面。The ship went *under*. 船下沉。②在下面文中;在下文中。See *under* for further discussion. 進一步的討論請參閱下文。③更少。***bring under*** 鎭壓;壓服。***go under*** a. 失敗;低落。b. 屈服。***knuckle under*** 〖俗〗向…投降;向…屈服。—*adj.*①下面的;下級的;從屬的。the *under* lip. 下唇。②過少的;過小的;不足的。

under- 〖字首〗表下列諸義: ①在下(如underground). ②次於(如undergraduate). ③不足;不合宜(如underestimate).

un·der·act [ˈʌndɚˈækt; ˈʌndərˈækt] *v.t.* 不充分地表現(角色、劇本等)。—*v.i.* 不賣力地表演。

un·der·age[1] [ˈʌndɚˈedʒ; ˈʌndərˈeidʒ] *adj.* 未成年的;不到規定年齡的;未達法定年齡的。

un·der·age[2] [ˈʌndərɪdʒ; ˈʌndəridʒ] *n.* 缺乏;短絀。

un·der·arm [ˈʌndɚˌɑrm; ˈʌndərɑːm] *adj.* ①腋下的;肩下側的。②手在肩下部動作的。—*adv.* 手在肩下部動作地。

un·der·bel·ly [ˈʌndɚˌbɛlɪ; ˈʌndəbeli] *n.* ①下腹部。②弱點。

un·der·bid [ˌʌndɚˈbɪd; ˈʌndəˈbid] *v.t.*, **-bid, -bid·den** *or* **-bid, -bid·ding.** 喊價低於;願以較低報酬做(某事);以低價售出。—**der,** *n.*

un·der·bred [ˈʌndɚˈbrɛd; ˈʌndəˈbred] *adj.* ①教養不良的;鄙陋的。②非純種的(馬、犬等)。—*n.* 非純種家畜。

*__un·der·brush__ [ˈʌndɚˌbrʌʃ; ˈʌndəbrʌʃ] *n.* ①(生長在森林中大樹下面的)矮樹叢。②亂糟糟的一團。

un·der·buy [ˈʌndɚˈbaɪ; ˈʌndəˈbai] *v.*, **-bought, -buy·ing.** —*v.t.* 以較(他人)買價便宜之價格購買;以較實價便宜的價格買進。—*v.t.* 購買數量不足。

un·der·car·riage [ˈʌndɚˌkærɪdʒ; ˈʌndəˌkæridʒ] *n.* (汽車等之)車盤(卽車體下部之支架);飛機脚架;起落架(卽飛機降落地面或水面時支持機體之部分)。

un·der·charge [*v.* ˈʌndɚˈtʃɑrdʒ; ˈʌndəˈtʃɑːdʒ *n.* ˈʌndɚˌtʃɑrdʒ; ˈʌndəˈtʃɑːdʒ] *v.*, **-charged, -charg·ing,** *n.* —*v.t.* ①索價低於常價。②不裝足够之火藥(於砲中)。③充電不足。—*n.* ①索低價。②不足量之裝塡。

un·der·class [ˈʌndɚˌklæs; ˈʌndəklɑːs] *n.* 最低階層的人民。

un·der·class·man [ˌʌndɚˈklæsmən; ˌʌndəˈklɑːsmən] *n.*, *pl.* **-men.** 〖美〗大學一、二年級學生。

un·der·cliff [ˈʌndɚˌklɪf; ˈʌndə-klif] *n.* 〖地質〗海岸之斜面地層。

un·der·clothes [ˈʌndɚˌkloðz; ˈʌndə-klouðz] *n.pl.* 內衣褲。〖注意〗可用many形容,但不與數字連用。

un·der·cloth·ing [ˈʌndɚˌkloðɪŋ; ˈʌndəˌklouðiŋ] *n.* = **underclothes.**

un·der·coat [ˈʌndɚˌkot; ˈʌndəkout] *n.* ①穿在裏面的上衣。②獸皮之短毛層。③在一層油漆內面塗的另一層油漆。④塗於汽車裏面以防生銹的一層似焦油的物質。—*v.t.* 塗一層防銹物質於…上。

un·der·cov·er [ˌʌndɚˈkʌvɚ; ˈʌndəˌkʌvə] *adj.* 祕密從事的;祕密的。

un·der·croft [ˈʌndɚˌkrɔft; ˈʌndə-krɔft] *n.* (教堂中的)地下室;地窖。

un·der·cur·rent [ˈʌndɚˌkɝənt; ˈʌndəˌkʌrənt] *n.* ①潛流;下面的水流或氣流。②潛伏的情緒;暗流。—*adj.* 不外露的。

un·der·cut [*v.* ˌʌndɚˈkʌt; ˈʌndəˈkʌt *n.*, *adj.* ˈʌndɚˌkʌt; ˈʌndəkʌt] *v.*, **-cut, -cut·ting,** *n.*, *adj.*—*v.t.* & *v.i.* ①切、削或鑿去…之下部;從下部切開。②減低(價格);索價低於(他人)。③〖高爾夫〗擊(球)使升高而落下時向後跳彈。④〖網球〗下切(球)。—*n.* ①從下部削砍。②砍伐樹木時在下部所砍之横口(以決定使樹倒往何方)。③〖拳擊〗上擊。④〖英〗(牛、猪等之)腰部下側嫩肉;腰肉。⑤〖牙科〗倒凹。—*adj.* 下邊部分被削掉的;被切去下部的;挖掉下邊之部分的;鑿去下邊之部分的;挖底的。—**ter,** *n.*

un·der·de·vel·op [ˌʌndədɪˈvɛləp; ˈʌndədiˈveləp] *v.t.* & *v.i.* ①發展或發育不完全;發展或發育不及所需程度。②沖洗(底片)不足;顯影不足。

un·der·de·vel·oped [ˌʌndədɪˈvɛləpt; ˈʌndədiˈveləpt] *adj.* ①發展不全的;發展不足的。②(底片)沖洗不足的。③低度開發的;經濟落後的。

un·der·do [ˈʌndɚˈdu; ˈʌndəˈduː] *v.t.* & *v.i.*, **-did, -done, -do·ing.** ①不做完滿;不盡全力做。②〖英〗不煮至熟;嫩煮;嫩烤(肉等)。

un·der·dog [ˈʌndɚˈdɔg; ˈʌndədɔg] *n.* ①在鬥爭中居於劣勢的狗或人。②在不健全的社會、政治制度之下受害者。

un·der·done [ˈʌndɚˈdʌn; ˈʌndəˈdʌn] *adj.* 半熟的;不太熟的(指食物言,尤指牛肉)。—*v.* pp. of **underdo.**

un·der·dress [ˌʌndɚˈdrɛs; ˌʌndəˈdres] *v.i.* 穿着過於隨便或不適於某種場合之衣服。—*n.* 襯衣;內衣。

un·der·em·ploy·ment [ˌʌndɚɪmˈplɔɪmənt; ˈʌndərimˈplɔimənt] *n.* 未充分就業。

un·der·es·ti·mate [*v.* ˈʌndɚˈɛstəˌmet; ˈʌndərˈestimeit *n.* ˈʌndɚˈɛstəmɪt; ˈʌndərˈestimit] *v.*, **-mat·ed, -mat·ing,** *n.* —*v.t.* 對於…作過低的評價;低估。—*n.* 評價過低;低估。

un·der·es·ti·ma·tion [ˈʌndɚˌɛstəˈmeʃən; ˈʌndərˌestiˈmeiʃən] *n.* 過低之估價;過低之評價;輕視;低估。

un·der·ex·pose [ˈʌndərɪkˈspoz; ˈʌndəriksˈpouz] *v.t.*, **-posed, -pos·ing.** 〖照相〗使(底片)感光不足。

un·der·ex·po·sure [ˈʌndərɪkˈspoʒɚ; ˈʌndəriksˈpouʒə] *n.* ①感光不足。②感光不足之底片或照片。

un·der·fed [ˌʌndɚˈfɛd; ˈʌndəˈfed] *adj.* 營養不良的;吃得不足的。

un·der·feed [ˈʌndɚˈfid; ˈʌndəˈfiːd] *v.*, **-fed, -feed·ing,** *adj.* —*v.t.* ①不給予足量食物。②自下部加添燃料。—*v.i.* 減食。—*adj.* 由下部加添燃料的。

un·der·foot [ˌʌndɚˈfut; ˌʌndəˈfut] *adv.* & *adj.* ①在脚下面; 在地上。②服從地(的);屈從地(的)。③〖美〗礙手礙脚地(的)。

un·der·gar·ment [ˈʌndɚˌgɑrmənt; ˈʌndəˌgɑːmənt] *n.* 內衣。

un·der·glaze [ˈʌndɚˌglez; ˈʌndəgleiz] 〖陶瓷〗 *adj.* 上釉之前着色的。—*n.*上釉之前所着之顏色。

***un·der·go** [ˌʌndɚˈgo; ˌʌndəˈgou] *v.t.*, **-went, -gone, -go·ing.** 遭受;經歷;忍受。to *undergo* an operation. 受手術; 被施以手術。

un·der·gone [ˌʌndɚˈgɔn; ˌʌndəˈgɔn] *v.* pp. of **undergo.**

un·der·grad [ˈʌndɚˌgræd; ˈʌndəgræd] *n.* 〖俗〗=**undergraduate.**

un·der·grade [ˈʌndɚˌgred; ˈʌndəgreid] *adj.* 劣等的。*undergrade* fruit. 劣等水果。

un·der·grad·u·ate [ˌʌndɚˈgrædʒuɪt; ˌʌndəˈgrædjuit] *n.* 大學本部(非研究所)學生;大學肄業生。—*adj.* 大學本部(非研究所)肄業生的;大學本部的。—**ship,** *n.*

***un·der·ground** [*adj., adv.* ˈʌndɚˈgraund *n.* ˈʌndɚˌgraund; *n., adj.* ˈʌndəgraund *adv.* ˌʌndəˈgraund] *adv.* ①在地下。②祕密地。—*adj.* ①地下的。②祕密的。③祕密反抗的。—*n.* ①地下之處所。②〖英〗地下鐵道。③地下組織;祕密組織。

un·der·grown [ˈʌndɚˌgron; ˈʌndəˈgroun] *adj.* ①發育不足的。②有灌木的。

un·der·growth [ˈʌndɚˌgroθ; ˈʌndəgrouθ] *n.* ①生於大樹下的灌木或矮樹。②發育不足。③皮膚上長毛下面之細毛。

un·der·hand [ˈʌndɚˌhænd; ˈʌndəhænd] *adj.* ①祕密的;不正大光明的;陰險的;狡詐的。②下手的;低手的(指手之高度在肩以下之動作)。—*adv.* ①祕密地; 陰險地; 狡詐地。②下手(投)地;低手(投)地。

un·der·hand·ed [ˈʌndɚˈhændɪd; ˈʌndəˈhændid] *adj.* ①祕密的。②卑劣的。③人手不足的。—**ness,** *n.*

un·der·hung [ˌʌndɚˈhʌŋ; ˈʌndəˈhʌŋ] *adj.* ①下顎突出的; 有突出之下顎的。②倚在底部之軌上的(如拉動之門); 自下承接的。③=**underslung.**

un·der·kill [ˈʌndɚˌkɪl; ˈʌndəˈkil] *n.* 「無擊敗敵人的能力。」

un·der·laid [ˌʌndɚˈled; ˌʌndəˈleid] *adj.* ①置於下面的。②由下面所置之物支撐或舉起的;下有墊物的。—*v.* pt. & pp. of **underlay².**

un·der·lain [ˌʌndɚˈlen; ˌʌndəˈlein] *v.* pp. of **underlie.**

un·der·lap [ˌʌndɚˈlæp; ˌʌndəˈlæp] *v.t.*, **-lapped, -lap·ping.** 伸展時使部分重疊。

un·der·lay¹ [ˌʌndɚˈle; ˌʌndəˈlei] *v.* pt. of **underlie.**

un·der·lay² [*v.* ˌʌndɚˈle; ˌʌndəˈlei *n.* ˈʌndɚˌle; ˈʌndəlei] *v.*, **-laid, -lay·ing,** *n.* —*v.t.* ①將(某物)置於他物之下。②由置於下面之物墊起或支撐。③置於…之底上。—*v.i.* (礦脈)由垂直面傾斜。—*n.*①置於下面之物。②〖印刷〗墊於活字下面之厚紙。③礦脈之傾斜。④酒在的事物。

un·der·lease [ˈʌndɚˌlis; ˈʌndəliːs] *n.* 〖法律〗轉租。

un·der·let [ˌʌndɚˈlɛt; ˈʌndəˈlet] *v.t.*, **-let, -let·ting.** ①廉價出租。②轉租。

un·der·lie [ˌʌndɚˈlaɪ; ˌʌndəˈlai] *v.t.*, **-lay, -lain, -ly·ing.** ①位於…之下。②爲…之基礎。③潛伏於…之下。

***un·der·line** [*v.* ˌʌndɚˈlaɪn; ˌʌndəˈlain *n.* ˈʌndɚˌlaɪn; ˈʌndəlain] *v.*, **-lined, -lin·ing,** *n.* —*v.t.* ①劃線於…之下。to *underline* a word. 在字的下面劃線。②强調;加强。—*n.* ①劃在下面的線;底線。Words with a single *underline* are to be set in italics. 下面劃單線的字應排斜體字。②(四足獸)之腹部線或腹部。③圖片下面之文字說明。—**a·tion,** *n.*

un·der·lin·en [ˈʌndɚˌlɪnɪn; ˈʌndəˌlinin] *n.* 麻紗或棉織品的內衣。

un·der·ling [ˈʌndɚlɪŋ; ˈʌndəliŋ] *n.* 職位低的人;下僚;下屬(通常含輕蔑之意)。

un·der·ly·ing [ˈʌndɚˈlaɪɪŋ; ˈʌndəˈlaiiŋ] *adj.* ①在下面的。②基本的;根本的。③不明顯的;含糊的;暗示的。④〖財政〗優先的。

un·der·manned [ˈʌndɚˈmænd; ˈʌndəˈmænd] *adj.* 人員不足的。

un·der·mean·ing [ˈʌndɚˌminɪŋ; ˈʌndəˌmiːniŋ] *n.* 字裏行間的意義;言外之意。

un·der·men·tioned [ˈʌndɚˈmɛnʃənd; ˈʌndəˈmenʃənd] *adj.* 下記的;下述的。

un·der·mine [ˌʌndɚˈmaɪn; ˌʌndəˈmain] *v.t.*, **-mined, -min·ing.** ①在…之下挖掘;在…之下掘地道。②逐漸損壞…的基礎;逐漸損毁。③以陰險手段傷害;暗中破壞。

un·der·most [ˈʌndɚˌmost; ˈʌndəmoust] *adj.* 最下的;最低的。—*adv.*最下地;最低地。

***un·der·neath** [ˌʌndɚˈniθ, -ˈnið; ˌʌndəˈniːθ] *prep.* 在…的下面;在…之下。—*adv.* 在下面; 在下。Someone was pushing *underneath.* 有人在下面推。—*adj.* ①較低的。②潛在的;字裏行間的。—*n.* 較低的部分或表面。Wipe the *underneath* of the glass. 擦拭玻璃之底面。

un·der·nour·ish [ˈʌndɚˈnɝɪʃ; ˈʌndəˈnʌriʃ] *v.t.* 供以不足之營養。

un·der·nour·ished [ˈʌndɚˈnɝɪʃt; ˈʌndəˈnʌriʃt] *adj.* 營養不足的。

un·der·nour·ish·ment [ˈʌndɚˈnɝɪʃmənt; ˈʌndəˈnʌriʃmənt] *n.* 營養不足。

un·der·oc·cu·pied [ˈʌndɚˈɑkjəpaɪd; ˈʌndərˈɔkjupaid] *adj.*居住人數不足的。

un·der·pants [ˈʌndɚˌpænts; ˈʌndəpænts] *n. pl.* 內褲。

un·der·pass [ˈʌndɚˌpæs; ˈʌndəpɑːs] *n.* 地下之通路(尤指鐵路或公路下之通路)。

un·der·pay [ˈʌndɚˈpe; ˈʌndəˈpei] *v.t.*, **-paid, -pay·ing.** 不充分地付;不足量地付。

un·der·pay·ment [ˈʌndɚˈpemənt; ˈʌndəˈpeimənt] *n.* 繳付不足。

un·der·pin [ˌʌndɚˈpɪn; ˌʌndəˈpin] *v.t.*, **-pinned, -pin·ning.** ①以基礎支持; 加强…之基礎。②支持;證實。

un·der·pin·ning [ˈʌndɚˌpɪnɪŋ; ˌʌndəˈpiniŋ] *n.* ①建築物下面的支柱或基礎。②支持物。③〖俗〗腿。

un·der·play [*v.* ˌʌndɚˈple; ˈʌndəˈplei *n.* ˈʌndɚˌple; ˈʌndəplei] *v.i.* & *v.t.* ①簡略地表演; 不完全地表演。②表演時儘量不過火以達到某種效果。③〖牌戲〗(未充分了解或利用其潛力而)出牌。—*n.*①概略的表演。②未充分利用所持之牌的潛力。③暗中行動。

un·der·plot [ˈʌndɚˌplɑt; ˈʌndəplɔt] *n.* ①(戲劇、小說中之)枝節。②詭計。

un·der·priv·i·leged [ˈʌndɚˈprɪvəlɪdʒd; ˈʌndəˈprivilidʒd] *adj.* (因經濟狀況

及社會地位不佳而）所享權益較大多數人爲少的；窮的。 ***the underprivileged*** 享受權益較少者。

un·der·pro·duce 〔ˌʌndəprəˈdjus; ˈʌndə-prəˈdjuːs〕 *v.t.*, **-duced, -duc·ing.** 生產不足。

un·der·pro·duc·tion 〔ˈʌndəprəˈdʌkʃən; ˈʌndə-prəˈdʌkʃən〕 *n.* 生產不足。

un·der·quote 〔ˌʌndəˈkwot; ˈʌndəˈkwout〕 *v.t.*, **-quot·ed, -quot·ing.** ①開（某種貨物）之價較低於市價。②開價低於（其他價格）。

un·der·rate 〔ˈʌndəˈret; ˌʌndəˈreit〕 *v.t.*, **-rat·ed, -rat·ing.** 估計過低；低估。

un·der·re·act 〔ˌʌndərɪˈækt; ˈʌndəriˈækt〕 *v.i.* 反應不够强烈。

un·der·run 〔ˌʌndəˈrʌn; ˈʌndəˈrʌn〕 *v.*, **-ran, -run, -run·ning,** *n.* —*v.t.* 從…下面通過。—*n.* 從下面通過之物（如流水等）。

un·der·score 〔ˌʌndəˈskor; ˌʌndəˈskɔː〕 *v.*, **-scored, -scor·ing,** *n.* —*v.t.* ①劃線於…之下。②强調。 —*n.* 底線。

un·der·sea 〔ˈʌndəˈsi; ˈʌndəsiː〕 *adj. & adv.* 海面下的（地）；海底的（地）。

un·der·seas 〔ˌʌndəˈsiz; ˌʌndəˈsiːz〕 *adv.* =undersea.

un·der·sec·re·tar·y 〔ˌʌndəˈsɛkrəˌtɛrɪ; ˈʌndəˈsekrətəri〕 *n.*, *pl.* **-tar·ies.** ①次長；（美國之）副部長。②助理祕書。 ***parliamentary undersecretary*** 政務次長。 ***permanent undersecretary*** 常務次長。

un·der·sell 〔ˌʌndəˈsɛl; ˈʌndəˈsel〕 *v.*, **-sold, -sell·ing.** —*v.t.* 廉價出售；售價低於（他人）。—*v.i.* 作有節制的推銷。

un·der·serv·ant 〔ˈʌndəˌsɝvənt; ˈʌndəˌsəːvənt〕 *n.* ①幫手。②做粗工的僕人。

un·der·set 〔ˈʌndəˌsɛt; ˈʌndə-set〕 *n.* ①（水之）潛流。②下層之礦脈。

un·der·sexed 〔ˌʌndəˈsɛkst; ˈʌndəˈsekst〕 *adj.* 性慾不足的。

un·der·sher·iff 〔ˈʌndəˌʃɛrɪf; ˈʌndəˈʃerif〕 *n.* 代理州執行官。 **—ship,** *n.*

un·der·shirt 〔ˈʌndəˌʃɝt; ˈʌndəʃəːt〕 *n.* 汗衫；貼身內衣。

un·der·shoot 〔ˌʌndəˈʃut; ˈʌndəˈʃuːt〕 *v.*, **-shot, -shoot·ing.** —*v.t.* ①發射砲彈等角度太低而不能擊中（目標）；發射砲彈等因射程太短而不能擊中（目標）。②【航空】因飛機失速太快而於未抵達（機場）之前降落。—*v.i.* 發射砲彈等因角度太低而不能擊中目標；發射砲彈等因射程太短而不能擊中目標。

un·der·shot 〔ˈʌndəˌʃɑt; ˈʌndəʃɔt〕 *adj.* ①嘴閉時下齒突於上齒外的。②有突出之下顎的。③藉下面水流之力轉動的（水車）。—*v.* pt. & pp. of **undershoot.**

un·der·shrub 〔ˈʌndəˌʃrʌb; ˈʌndə-ʃrʌb〕 *n.* 小灌木。

un·der·side 〔ˈʌndəˌsaɪd; ˈʌndəsaid〕 *n.* 下側；下面；內面；底面。

un·der·sign 〔ˌʌndəˈsaɪn; ˌʌndəˈsain〕 *v.t.* 簽名於（文件、信件）之末尾。

un·der·signed 〔ˌʌndəˈsaɪnd; ˈʌndəsaind〕 *adj.* ①置名於文件或信件上的。②簽名於文件末尾的。 ***the undersigned*** 簽署者。

un·der·size 〔ˈʌndəˈsaɪz; ˈʌndəˈsaiz〕 *adj.* ① =**undersized.** ②（篩過的礦物）從一定大小之篩孔中篩下來的。

un·der·sized 〔ˈʌndəˈsaɪzd; ˈʌndəˈsaizd〕 *adj.* 體積較一般爲小的；不够大的。（亦作 **undersize**）

un·der·skirt 〔ˈʌndəˌskɝt; ˈʌndə-skəːt〕 *n.* 襯裙。

un·der·sleep 〔ˌʌndəˈslip; ˈʌndəˈsliːp〕 *v.i.*, **-slept, -sleep·ing.** 睡眠不足。

un·der·sleeve 〔ˈʌndəˌsliv; ˈʌndə-sliːv〕 *n.* 內袖（長出外衣袖口，作裝飾用者）。

un·der·slung 〔ˌʌndəˈslʌŋ; ˈʌndəˈslʌŋ〕 *adj.* ①（汽車等）車身裝於車軸之彈簧上的。②重心在底部的；下面大上面小的。③嘴巴合攏下齒突出於上齒外的。

un·der·soil 〔ˈʌndəˌsɔɪl; ˈʌndə-sɔil〕 *n.* 地面下的土壤；底土。

un·der·sold 〔ˌʌndəˈsold; ˈʌndəˈsould〕 *v.* pt. & pp. of **undersell.**

un·der·song 〔ˈʌndəˌsɔŋ; ˈʌndəsɔŋ〕 *n.* ①伴唱之歌。②隱匿之意義。

un·der·staffed 〔ˌʌndəˈstæft; ˈʌndəˈstɑːft〕 *adj.* 職員不足的；人員不足的。

‡un·der·stand 〔ˌʌndəˈstænd; ˌʌndəˈstænd〕 *v.*, **-stood, -stand·ing.** —*v.t.* ①懂；了解；領會。I don't *understand* you. 我不懂你的話。②聞知；知悉。③推斷；以爲；相信。It is *understood* that you will come. 相信你會來的。④不言而喻；省略（用被動語態）。—*v.i.* ①有了解力；了解。Do animals *understand?* 動物有了解力嗎？②聞知；知悉。③諒解。 ***make oneself understood*** 使人了解自己的意思；說明自己的意思。Can you *make yourself understood* in English? 你的英語能使人了解否？ ***understand each other*** 同意；彼此心照不宣。

un·der·stand·a·ble 〔ˌʌndəˈstændəbl̩; ˌʌndəˈstændəbl〕 *adj.* 可被了解的。 **—un·der·stand·a·bly,** *adv.* **—un·der·stand·a·bil·i·ty, —ness,** *n.*

un·der·stand·ing** 〔ˌʌndəˈstændɪŋ; ˌʌndəˈstændiŋ〕 *n.* ①了解；通曉。②理解力；悟性。a person of *understanding.* 穎悟力强的人。③協議；協定；諒解。to come to an *understanding.* 達成協議。④所了解的意義；意義。 ***on the understanding that 在…的條件之下。—*adj.* ①聰明的；穎悟的；富於理解力的。②能體諒別人的。 **—ly,** *adv.* **—ness,** *n.*

un·der·state 〔ˈʌndəˈstet; ˈʌndəˈsteit〕 *v.t.*, **-stat·ed, -stat·ing.** 作較輕或較弱之陳述；掩飾地說；隱瞞地陳述。

un·der·state·ment 〔ˈʌndəˌstetmənt; ˈʌndəˈsteitmənt〕 *n.* ①掩飾；輕描淡寫。②有節制的陳述。

‡un·der·stood 〔ˌʌndəˈstud; ˌʌndəˈstud〕 *v.* pt. & pp. of **understand.** —*adj.* ①經過同意的；事先知道的。②心照不宣的；暗示而未明言的。

un·der·strap·per 〔ˈʌndəˌstræpə; ˈʌndəˌstræpə〕 *n.*【俗】=**underling.**

un·der·stra·tum 〔ˈʌndəˌstretəm; ˈʌndəˈstrɑːtəm〕 *n.*, *pl.* **-ta** 〔-tə; -tə〕, **-tums.** 底層。

un·der·stud·y 〔ˈʌndəˌstʌdɪ; ˈʌndəˌstʌdi〕 *n.*, *pl.* **-stud·ies,** *v.*, **-stud·ied, -stud·y·ing.** —*n.* ①臨時做替身的演員；候補演員；墊角。②候補人員。—*v.t.* ①爲臨時代替主演者的角色而研習。②臨時代替（某角色）上臺。③實地研習。

***un·der·take** 〔ˌʌndəˈtek; ˌʌndəˈteik〕 *v.t.*, **-took, -tak·en, -tak·ing.** ①從事；着手；擔任；承攬。to *undertake* a task. 從事一項工作。②擔保（後面用子句）。I can't *undertake* that you will make a profit.

U

我不能擔保你會獲利。③答應；許諾。He *undertook* to be here at five o'clock. 他答應五點鐘到這裏來。

un·der·tak·en [ˌʌndəˈtekən; ˌʌndəˈteikn] *v.* pp. of **undertake.**

un·der·tak·er [ˌʌndəˈtekə; ˌʌndəˈteikə] *n.* ①擔任者；承攬者。②承辦殯葬者。

***un·der·tak·ing** [ˌʌndəˈtekɪŋ; ˌʌndəˈteikiŋ] *n.* ①事業；企業。②保證；諾言。③承辦殯葬。

un·der·tax [ˌʌndəˈtæks; ˈʌndəˈtæks] *v.t.* & *v.i.* 課稅太低。

un·der-the-coun·ter [ˈʌndəðəˈkauntə; ˈʌndəðəˈkauntə] *adj.* ①(因貨物稀少或違法等而) 偷偷摸摸地出售的。②非法的；未經授權的。

un·der·tone [ˈʌndəˌton; ˈʌndətoun] *n.* ①低音調；低調。②暗色。③潛伏的成分。④不顯著的雜音。

un·der·took [ˌʌndəˈtuk; ˌʌndəˈtuk] *v.* pt. of **undertake.**

un·der·tow [ˈʌndəˌto; ˈʌndətou] *n.* ①水面下的逆流。②波浪沖擊岸邊後之後退的水流；退波。

un·der·val·ue [ˈʌndəˈvælju; ˈʌndəˈvælju:] *v.t.*, **-val·ued, -val·u·ing.** ①低估…之價值。②輕視。③減低…之價值。—**un·der·val·u·a·tion,** *n.*

un·der·vest [ˈʌndəˌvɛst; ˈʌndəvest] *n.* 內衣；貼身衣。

un·der·waist [ˈʌndəˌwest; ˈʌndəweist] *n.* 襯裏之圍腰；襯裏之胸衣。

un·der·wa·ter [ˈʌndəˌwɔtə; ˈʌndəwɔ:tə] *adj.* ①水面下的；水面下用的。②在船舶之吃水線以下的。—*n.* 水下；水底。

***un·der·wear** [ˈʌndəˌwɛr; ˈʌndəwɛə] *n.* 內衣褲。

un·der·weight [ˈʌndəˈwet; ˈʌndəˈweit] *adj.* 重量不足的。—*n.* 未達到標準的重量。

un·der·went [ˌʌndəˈwɛnt; ˌʌndəˈwent] *v.* pt. of **undergo.**

un·der·whelm [ˌʌndəˈhwɛlm; ˈʌndəˈwelm] *v.t.* 不足以引起對…之興趣或熱誠。

un·der·wood [ˈʌndəˌwud; ˈʌndəwud] *n.* ①生長在大樹下的草木；矮林；叢薮。②(U-) 一種打字機的商標名。

un·der·work [*v.* ˌʌndəˈwɜk; ˈʌndəˈwə:k *n.* ˈʌndəˌwɜk; ˈʌndəwə:k] *v.t.* ①偷工；省工；以太少勞工從事(某種工作)。②以廉於(他人)之價而做同等之工作。③使勞動過少。—*v.i.* 不盡力工作；偷工；省工。—*n.* 賤工；劣工；日常瑣事。

***un·der·world** [ˈʌndəˌwɜld; ˈʌndəwə:ld] *n.* ①下界；地獄。②下層社會；下流社會。③世界；塵世。④地球的另一面；對蹠地。

un·der·world·ling [ˈʌndəˌwɜldlɪŋ; ˈʌndəˌwə:ldliŋ] *n.* 〖俗〗流氓；歹徒；作奸犯科者。

un·der·write [ˌʌndəˈraɪt; ˈʌndərait] *v.*, **-wrote, -writ·ten, -writ·ing.** —*v.t.* ①簽名於下；署名於下。②承諾（支付、賠償等)。③簽名於(保險單以投保)。④負責保險。⑤簽名以同意照價收買（未售出之股票、證券等)。—*v.i.* 經營保險業；承購股票等。

un·der·writ·er [ˈʌndəˌraɪtə; ˈʌndəˌraitə] *n.* ①保險業者。②股票債券等之承購人。③承諾支付者。

un·der·writ·ing [ˈʌndəˌraɪtɪŋ; ˈʌndəraitiŋ] *n.* 保險業；海上保險業。

un·der·writ·ten [ˌʌndəˈrɪtn̩; ˌʌndəˌritn] *v.* pp. of **underwrite.**

un·der·wrote [ˌʌndəˈrot; ˈʌndərout] *v.* pt. of **underwrite.**

un·de·served [ˌʌndɪˈzɜvd; ˈʌndiˈzə:vd] *adj.* 過分的(稱譽)；不當的(非難)。—**ly,** *adv.*

un·de·serv·ing [ˌʌndɪˈzɜvɪŋ; ˈʌndiˈzə:viŋ] *adj.* 不應受的；不值得的；不配的。

un·de·signed [ˌʌndɪˈzaɪnd; ˈʌndiˈzaind] *adj.* 非故意的；偶然的；非計畫的。—**ly,** *adv.*

***un·de·sir·a·ble** [ˌʌndɪˈzaɪrəbl̩; ˈʌndiˈzaiərəbl] *adj.* 不良的；惹人厭的；可反對的。—*n.* 討厭的人；令人厭惡的東西；不良分子。—**ness,** *n.* —**un·de·sir·a·bly,** *adv.*

un·de·tect·ed [ˌʌndɪˈtɛktɪd; ˈʌndiˈtektid] *adj.* 未被發現的；未被探悉的。

un·de·vel·oped [ˌʌndɪˈvɛləpt; ˈʌndiˈveləpt] *adj.* ①未充分發展的；未發達的；發育不完全的。②未開發的。

un·de·vi·at·ing [ʌnˈdiviˌetɪŋ; ʌnˈdi:vieitiŋ] *adj.* 不偏倚的；不離正道的；直的。—**ly,** *adv.*

un·de·vout [ˌʌndɪˈvaut; ˈʌndiˈvaut] *adj.* ①不虔敬的；不虔誠的。②不忠誠的；不熱心的。—**ly,** *adv.*

un·did [ʌnˈdɪd; ˈʌnˈdid] *v.* pt. of **undo.**

un·dies [ˈʌndɪz; ˈʌndiz] *n. pl.* 〖俗〗婦人之內衣。

un·di·gest·ed [ˌʌndəˈdʒɛstɪd; ˈʌndiˈdʒestid] *adj.* 未經消化的；未經整理的。

un·dig·ni·fied [ʌnˈdɪgnəˌfaɪd; ʌnˈdignifaid] *adj.* 無威嚴的；不莊重的。—**ly,** *adv.*

un·di·lut·ed [ˌʌndɪˈlutɪd; ˈʌndaiˈlju:tid] *adj.* 未沖淡的；未稀釋的。

un·di·min·ished [ˌʌndəˈmɪnɪʃt; ˈʌndiˈminiʃt] *adj.* 不減的；不衰的。

un·dine [ˈʌndin; ˈʌndi:n] *n.* 水精；水中女神。—**un·di·nal,** *adj.*

un·dis·cern·ing [ˌʌndɪˈzɜnɪŋ; ˈʌndiˈsə:niŋ] *adj.* 無辨識力的；不明察的；感覺遲鈍的。—**ly,** *adv.*

un·dis·ci·plined [ʌnˈdɪsəˌplɪnd; ʌnˈdisiplind] *adj.* 無紀律的；無訓練的；無修養的。—**ness,** *n.*

un·dis·cov·ered [ˌʌndɪˈskʌvəd; ˈʌndisˈkʌvəd] *adj.* 未被發現的；未知的。

un·dis·cussed [ˌʌndɪsˈkʌst; ˈʌndisˈkʌst] *adj.* 未討論的。

un·dis·guised [ˌʌndɪsˈgaɪzd; ˈʌndisˈgaizd] *adj.* 無偽裝的；坦白的；公然的。—**ly,** *adv.*

un·dis·mayed [ˌʌndɪsˈmed; ˈʌndisˈmeid] *adj.* 無恐懼的；未喪膽的；大膽的。

un·dis·put·ed [ˌʌndɪˈspjutɪd; ˈʌndisˈpju:tid] *adj.* 無庸爭論的；無疑問的。—**ly,** *adv.*

un·dis·tin·guish·a·ble [ˌʌndɪˈstɪŋgwɪʃəbl̩; ˈʌndisˈtiŋgwiʃəbl] *adj.* 難區分的；難辨明的。

un·dis·tin·guished [ˌʌndɪˈstɪŋgwɪʃt; ˈʌndisˈtiŋgwiʃt] *adj.* ①不著名的；平凡的；無特色的。②未被辨認的。③未覺察的；未受注意的。

***un·dis·turbed** [ˌʌndɪˈstɜbd; ˈʌndisˈtə:bd] *adj.* 未被擾亂的；安靜的；鎮定的。—**ly,** *adv.* —**ness,** *n.*

un·di·vid·ed [ˌʌndəˈvaɪdɪd; ˈʌndiˈvaidid] *adj.* ①未分開的；未分割的；連續的；完整的。②專心的；專一的。—**ly,** *adv.* —**ness,** *n.*

***un·do** [ʌnˈdu; ˈʌnˈdu:] *v.t.*, **-did, -done, -do·ing.** ①解開。to *undo* a knot. 解結。②廢棄(某種成就)；打消（已經做出之行爲)。What is done cannot be *undone.* 覆水難

收。③使零落；使窮困；使敗亡；破壞；毀滅。His pride will *undo* him some day. 他的傲慢總有一天會毀了他。④解釋；解決。⑤使失去鎮靜。⑥勾引；誘姦。He *undid* a neighbor's young daughter. 他勾引了鄰居的年輕女兒。—**er,** *n.*

un·doc·u·ment·ed [ʌnˈdɑkjəˌmɛntɪd; ʌnˈdɔkjumentid] *adj.* ①無正式文件的。②無事實證明的。③未註明出處的。

un·do·ing [ʌnˈduɪŋ; ˈʌnˈduːiŋ] *n.* ①毀滅。②取消。③解開。④致敗之由。

un·do·mes·ti·cat·ed [ˌʌndəˈmɛstɪˌketɪd; ˈʌn-dəˈmestikeitid] *adj.* ①未馴的；野的。②不慣家庭生活的。

un·done [ʌnˈdʌn; ˈʌnˈdʌn] *v.* pp. of **undo.** —*adj.* ①未作的；未作完的。Half his work is still *undone.* 他的工作有一半還沒有做。②零落的；破滅的。③解開的。

un·doubt·ed [ʌnˈdautɪd; ʌnˈdautid] *adj.* 無疑的；確實的。

*__un·doubt·ed·ly__ [ʌnˈdautɪdlɪ; ʌnˈdautidli] *adv.* 無疑地；確然地。Those mounds *undoubtedly* contain human bones. 那些土墩中毫無疑問有人骨頭。

un·draw [ʌnˈdrɔ; ˈʌnˈdrɔː] *v.,* **-drew, -drawn, -draw·ing.** —*v.t.* 拉開；扯開；拉回。—*v.i.* 被拉開；被拉回。

un·dreamed-of [ʌnˈdrimdɑv; ʌnˈdremtɔv] *adj.* 夢想不到的；想像不到的。(亦作 **undreamt-of**)

un·dress [*v.* ʌnˈdrɛs; ˈʌnˈdres *n.* ˈʌnˌdrɛs; ˈʌnˈdres *adj.* ʌnˈdrɛs; ˈʌndres] *v.t.* ①爲…脫衣服；爲…卸裝。He *undressed* himself and went to bed. 他脫衣上床。②解下(傷口)繃帶。—*v.i.* 脫衣服。—*n.* ①便服。②赤裸。—*adj.* ①便服的。②不嚴肅的；隨便的。

un·dressed [ʌnˈdrɛst; ˈʌnˈdrest] *adj.* ①未着衣服的；赤裸的。②未調理的。③未整頓的。④〖外科〗未包紮的；未紮繃帶的。⑤沒有鞣的(皮)。

undress uniform 軍便服。

un·drew [ʌnˈdru; ʌnˈdruː] *v.* pt. of **undraw.**

un·drink·a·ble [ʌnˈdrɪŋkəbl̩; ʌnˈdriŋkəbl] *adj.* 不能飲的。

Und·set [ˈunsɛt; ˈunset] *n.* 翁塞特 (Sigrid, 1882–1949, 挪威女小說家, 於1928年獲諾貝爾文學獎)。

un·due [ʌnˈdju; ˈʌnˈdjuː] *adj.* ①不適當的；不正當的。②過度的；過分的。③未到期的。④不欠的。

un·du·lant [ˈʌndjələnt; ˈʌndjulənt] *adj.* 波狀的；起伏的。

undulant fever 〖醫〗浪熱；馬爾他熱 (Malta fever)；地中海熱(Mediterranean fever)。

un·du·late [*v.* ˈʌndjəˌlet; ˈʌndjuleit *adj.* ˈʌndjəlɪt; ˈʌndjulit] *v.,* **-lat·ed, -lat·ing,** *adj.* —*v.t.* 使起波動；使起伏；使震動。—*v.i.* 波動；起伏；震動。—*adj.* 波狀的；起伏的。

un·du·lat·ed [ˈʌndjəˌletɪd; ˈʌndjuleitid] *adj.* = **undulate.**

un·du·la·tion [ˌʌndjəˈleʃən; ˌʌndjuˈleiʃən] *n.* 波動；起伏。

un·du·la·to·ry [ˈʌndjələˌtorɪ; ˈʌndjulətəri] *adj.* 波狀的；波動的；起伏的。

un·du·ly [ʌnˈdjulɪ; ˈʌnˈdjuːli] *adv.* ①過分地；過度地；非常地。②不當地；不正當地。

un·du·ti·ful [ʌnˈdjutɪfəl; ˈʌnˈdjuːtiful] *adj.* ①不忠的；不孝的。②不盡職的。③不順從的。—**ly,** *adv.* —**ness,** *n.*

un·dy·ing [ʌnˈdaɪɪŋ; ʌnˈdaiiŋ] *adj.* 不朽的；不死的；永恒的。—**ly,** *adv.* —**ness,** *n.*

un·earned [ʌnˈɝnd; ˈʌnˈəːnd] *adj.* ①非藉勞力或工作而得的；不勞而獲的。②不應得的。③尚未賺得的。

unearned income 個人勞務以外來源的收入(如利息、房租等)。

unearned increment (地產等的)自然增價。

un·earth [ʌnˈɝθ; ˈʌnˈəːθ] *v.t.* ①發掘。②破獲。③發現。

un·earth·ly [ʌnˈɝθlɪ; ʌnˈəːθli] *adj.* ①非塵世的；超自然的。②鬼怪的；怪異的；神異的。③異常的；極端的。

*__un·eas·i·ly__ [ʌnˈizɪlɪ; ʌnˈiːzili] *adv.* ①不舒適地。②不安地；焦慮地。③不自然地；侷促地。

*__un·eas·i·ness__ [ʌnˈizɪnɪs; ʌnˈiːzinis] *n.* 不舒適；不安；焦慮；不自然；侷促。

*__un·eas·y__ [ʌnˈizɪ; ʌnˈiːzi] *adj.* **-eas·i·er, -eas·i·est.** ①不舒適的。②不安的；焦慮的。to feel *uneasy* about the future. 懸慮將來。③不自然的；侷促的。*uneasy* manners. 侷促不安的態度。④不安定的。

un·ed·i·fy·ing [ʌnˈɛdəˌfaɪɪŋ; ˈʌnˈedifaiiŋ] *adj.* 無啓發性的；無益於教化的。

un·ed·u·cat·ed [ʌnˈɛdʒəˌketɪd; ˈʌnˈedjukeitid] *adj.* 未受教育的；無學問的；無知的。

un·em·ploy·a·ble [ˌʌnɪmˈplɔɪəbl̩; ˈʌnimˈplɔiəbl] *adj.* ①(因年齡、體力、智力不足)不能受雇的。②不能使用的。—*n.* 不能受雇者。—**un·em·ploy·a·bil·i·ty,** *n.*

*__un·em·ployed__ [ˌʌnɪmˈplɔɪd; ˈʌnimˈplɔid] *adj.* ①無工作的；失業的。the *unemployed.* 失業的人們。②未用的；未被利用的。

*__un·em·ploy·ment__ [ˌʌnɪmˈplɔɪmənt; ˈʌnimˈplɔimənt] *n.* ①失業。*Unemployment* is a great social evil. 失業爲社會一大弊病。②失業人數。

unemployment compensation (政府所發之)失業補償金。

un·end·ing [ʌnˈɛndɪŋ; ʌnˈendiŋ] *adj.* ①永遠的；永久的。②繼續不斷的；無窮盡的。

un·en·dur·a·ble [ˌʌnɪnˈdjurəbl̩; ˈʌninˈdjuərəbl] *adj.* 無法忍受的；不能忍耐的。

un·en·gaged [ˌʌnɪnˈgedʒd; ˈʌninˈgeidʒd] *adj.* ①未訂婚的。②無工作的；閒着無事的。

un·en·gag·ing [ˌʌnɪnˈgedʒɪŋ; ˈʌninˈgeidʒiŋ] *adj.* 無吸引力的；不迷人的。

un-Eng·lish [ʌnˈɪŋglɪʃ; ˈʌnˈiŋgliʃ] *adj.* ①不合於英國風俗、原則、思想、特性等的；非英國人的。②非英語的。

un·en·thu·si·as·tic [ˌʌnɪnˌθjuzɪˈæstɪk; ˈʌninˌθjuːziˈæstik] *adj.* ①不熱心的。②冷淡的；不關心的。

un·en·vi·a·ble [ʌnˈɛnvɪəbl̩; ˈʌnˈenviəbl] *adj.* 不值得嫉羨的。

*__un·e·qual__ [ʌnˈikwəl; ˈʌnˈiːkwəl] *adj.* ①不等的；不同的。②不規則的；不均勻的；不一律的。③不平衡的；不相稱的。④不公平的；不平等的。⑤不勝任的 〖to〗. He is *unequal* to the task. 他不勝任這項工作。—*n.* 不相等之人或物。

un·e·qual(l)ed [ʌnˈikwəld; ˈʌnˈiːkwəld] *adj.* 不等的；無比的；無雙的；無敵的。

un·e·qual·ly [ʌnˈikwəlɪ; ʌnˈiːkwəli] *adv.* ①不相等地；不平等地。②不平均地。

un·e·quiv·o·cal [ˌʌnɪˈkwɪvəkl̩; ˈʌniˈkwivəkəl] *adj.* ①不含混的；明白的；率直的。②絕對的；無例外的。③無疑問的；不容爭

辯的。—ly, *adv.*
un·err·ing (ʌn'ɜɪŋ; 'ʌn'əːriŋ) *adj.* 無過失的;無錯誤的;正確的。
un·err·ing·ly (ʌn'ɜɪŋlɪ; ʌn'əːriŋli) *adv.* 正確無誤地。
U·NES·CO, U.N.E.S.C.O., U·nes·co (ju'nɛsko; ju(ː)'neskou) *n.* 聯合國教科文組織(爲 the *U*nited *N*ations *E*ducational, *S*cientific, and *C*ultural *O*rganization 之略)。
un·es·sen·tial (ˌʌnə'sɛnʃəl; 'ʌni'senʃəl) *adj.* 非主要的;非必要的。—*n.* 不重要的東西。
***un·e·ven** (ʌn'ivən; 'ʌn'iːvən) *adj.* ①不平坦的;凹凸的。②不均勻的; 不平衡的; 參差的(=unequal). ③奇數的(=odd). *uneven* numbers. 奇數。—ly, *adv.* —ness, *n.*
un·e·vent·ful (ˌʌnɪ'vɛntfəl; 'ʌni'ventfəl) *adj.* 平靜無事的; 太平無事的。—ly, *adv.*
un·ex·am·pled (ˌʌnɪg'zæmpl̩d; ˌʌnig'zɑːmpld) *adj.* 無可比擬的;無前例的。
un·ex·cep·tion·a·ble (ˌʌnɪk'sɛpʃənəbl̩; ˌʌnik'sepʃənəbl) *adj.* 無缺點的; 無可非難的; 完全的。
un·ex·cep·tion·al (ˌʌnɪk'sɛpʃənl̩; 'ʌnik'sepʃənl) *adj.* ①非例外的;平常的;普通的。②不許有例外的。③=**unexceptionable.** —ly, *adv.*
un·ex·haust·ed (ˌʌnɪg'zɔstɪd; 'ʌnig'zɔːstid) *adj.* ①不盡的; 不竭的。②不疲憊的。③不徹底的。④不排出的(煤氣等)。
***un·ex·pect·ed** (ˌʌnɪk'spɛktɪd; 'ʌniks'pektid) *adj.* 預料不到的; 意外的; 突然的。an *unexpected* guest. 不速之客。
***un·ex·pect·ed·ly** (ˌʌnɪk'spɛktɪdlɪ; 'ʌnik'spektidli) *adv.* 出乎意外地。
un·ex·ploit·ed (ˌʌnɪk'splɔɪtɪd; 'ʌniks'plɔitid) *adj.* ①未加利用的。②未開發的。
un·ex·pres·sive (ˌʌnɪk'sprɛsɪv; 'ʌniks'presiv) *adj.* 無表情的。
un·fad·ing (ʌn'fedɪŋ; ʌn'feidiŋ) *adj.* ①不褪色的。②不凋謝的。③不衰的;不朽的。—ly, *adv.*
un·fail·ing (ʌn'felɪŋ; ʌn'feiliŋ) *adj.* ①永不消滅的;不倦的; 忠實的; 永久的。an *unfailing* friend. 一個可靠的朋友。②永不缺乏的;無止境的。③確實的;確然的。—ly, *adv.*
***un·fair** (ʌn'fɛr; ʌn'fɛə) *adj.* 不正直的;不公平的;偏頗的;不正當的。*unfair* means. 不正當的手段。—ness, *n.*
un·fair·ly (ʌn'fɛrlɪ; ʌn'fɛəli) *adv.* 不正直地;不公平地;不正當地;不公正地。
un·faith·ful (ʌn'feθfəl; 'ʌn'feiθful) *adj.* ①不忠實的。②不信實的; 不正確的。③有外遇的; 犯通姦罪的。④不誠實的。—ly, *adv.* —ness, *n.*
un·fal·ter·ing (ʌn'fɔltərɪŋ; ʌn'fɔːltəriŋ) *adj.* ①堅決的; 毅然的; 不躊躇的。②穩定的。③不顫抖的。④專一的。—ly, *adv.*
un·fa·mil·iar (ˌʌnfə'mɪljɚ; 'ʌn-fə'miljə) *adj.* 不熟悉的;不熟識的;不習見的。—i·ty, *n.* —ly, *adv.*
un·fash·ion·a·ble (ʌn'fæʃənəbl; 'ʌn'fæʃənəbl) *adj.* 不時新的;不時髦的;古老的。
un·fas·ten (ʌn'fæsn̩; 'ʌn'fɑːsn) *v.t.* 解開;鬆開;打開。—*v.i.* 變成解開或鬆開的狀態。
un·fa·thered (ʌn'fɑðɚd; 'ʌn'fɑːðəd) *adj.* ①無父親的。②私生的。*unfathered* offspring. 私生子。③不知作者的;不知創造者的。
un·fath·om·a·ble (ʌn'fæðəməbl̩; ʌn'fæðəməbl) *adj.* ①深不可測的。②不可解的。
***un·fa·vor·a·ble** (ʌn'fevrəbl̩; 'ʌn'feivərəbl) *adj.* ①不利的; 有害的。②不吉祥的。—ness, *n.* —un·fa·vor·a·bly, *adv.*
un·feel·ing (ʌn'filɪŋ; ʌn'fiːliŋ) *adj.* ①殘酷無情的。②無感覺的。—ly, *adv.* —ness, *n.*
un·feigned (ʌn'fend; ʌn'feind) *adj.* 眞實的;不做作的;誠摯的;不虛僞的。
un·feign·ed·ly (ʌn'fenɪdlɪ; ʌn'feinidli) *adv.* 不做作地;不虛僞地;誠摯地。
un·fenced (ʌn'fɛnst; 'ʌn'fenst) *adj.* ①無垣籬的。②無防備的。
un·fet·ter (ʌn'fɛtɚ; 'ʌn'fetə) *v.t.* ①除去…的脚鐐。②釋放;使自由。
un·fet·tered (ʌn'fɛtɚd; 'ʌn'fetəd) *adj.* ①被除去脚鐐的。②不受拘束的;獨立的;自由的。
un·fil·i·al (ʌn'fɪlɪəl; 'ʌn'filjəl) *adj.* 不孝的。an *unfilial* child. 不孝子。
un·find·a·ble (ʌn'faɪndəbl̩; ʌn'faindəbl) *adj.* 無法找到的。
un·fin·ished (ʌn'fɪnɪʃt; 'ʌn'finiʃt) *adj.* ①未完的;未完成的。②粗糙的。
***un·fit** (ʌn'fɪt; 'ʌn'fit) *adj., v.,* -fit·ted, -fit·ting, *n.* —*adj.* 不適當的;不勝任的。He is *unfit* for the task. 他不勝任這項工作。—*v.t.* 使不合適;使不能勝任;使無資格。—*n.* 不勝任者;不健全者。—ly, *adv.* —ness, *n.*
un·fit·ted (ʌn'fɪtɪd; ʌn'fitid) *adj.* 不適合的;不適當的。
un·fit·ting (ʌn'fɪtɪŋ; 'ʌn'fitiŋ) *adj.* 不適當的;不適合的。
un·fix (ʌn'fɪks; 'ʌn'fiks) *v.t.* ①解開;脫下;使鬆。to *unfix* bayonets. 取下刺刀。②使不固定。
un·fixed (ʌn'fɪkst; 'ʌn'fikst) *adj.* ①解脫的;鬆弛的。②不固定的;未定的。
un·flag·ging (ʌn'flægɪŋ; ʌn'flægiŋ) *adj.* 不衰的;不疲憊的;不屈不撓的。—ly, *adv.*
un·flap·pa·ble (ʌn'flæpəbl̩; ʌn'flæpəbl) *adj.* 〖俚〗不輕易大驚小怪的; 鎮定的。
un·flat·ter·ing (ʌn'flætərɪŋ; 'ʌn'flætəriŋ) *adj.* ①準確的; 眞實的。②貶降的。—ly, *adv.*
un·fledged (ʌn'flɛdʒd; 'ʌn'fledʒd) *adj.* ①羽毛未豐的。②不成熟的;幼稚的;未發達的。
un·flinch·ing (ʌn'flɪntʃɪŋ; ʌn'flintʃiŋ) *adj.* 不畏縮的;果敢的;決斷的。—ly, *adv.*
un·fo·cus(s)ed (ʌn'fokəst; ʌn'foukəst) *adj.* ①無焦點的; 不集於一點的。②不專心的。
***un·fold**[1] (ʌn'fold; ʌn'fould) *v.t.* ①展開。②顯露; 表明; 說明。—*v.i.* (花苞等)開放;開展。—ment, *n.*
un·fold[2] *v.t.* 將(羊等)自圍欄中放出。
un·forced (ʌn'forst; ʌn'fɔːst) *adj.* 非逼出的;不勉强的;自動的;自發的。
un·fore·see·ing (ˌʌnfor'siɪŋ; 'ʌnfɔː'siːiŋ) *adj.* 無遠見的;無先見之明的。
un·fore·seen (ˌʌnfor'sin; 'ʌn-fɔː'siːn) *adj.* 事先不曉得的;預料不到的。
un·for·get·ta·ble (ˌʌnfɚ'gɛtəbl̩; 'ʌn-fə'getəbl) *adj.* 令人難忘的。
un·for·giv·ing (ˌʌnfɚ'gɪvɪŋ; 'ʌn-fə'giviŋ) *adj.* 不寬恕的; 不容忍的; 不寬仁的;不原諒的。—ness, *n.*
un·formed (ʌn'fɔrmd; 'ʌn'fɔːmd) *adj.* ①未成形的; 無定形的。②未做成的。③未成熟的。
***un·for·tu·nate** (ʌn'fɔrtʃənɪt; ʌn'fɔːtʃənit) *adj.* ①不幸的。②不合宜的。③不吉利

的;不利的。④令人遺憾的;可悲的。⑤引起人同情的。—*n.* 不幸的人(尤指娼妓)。—**ly,** *adv.*

un·found·ed [ʌnˈfaundɪd; ˈʌnˈfaundid] *adj.* 無根據的;無稽的。

un·freeze [ʌnˈfriz; ˈʌnˈfri:z] *v.t.,* **-froze, -froz·en.** 使融化。

un·fre·quent [ʌnˈfrikwənt; ʌnˈfri:kwənt] *adj.* 稀少的;稀罕的。—**ly,** *adv.*

un·fre·quent·ed [ˌʌnfrɪˈkwɛntɪd; ˈʌn-friˈkwentid] *adj.* ①人跡罕至的; 荒僻的。②很少有人去的。

un·friend·ed [ʌnˈfrɛndɪd; ˈʌnˈfrendid] *adj.* 無友的;無依的;無援的。

un·friend·li·ness [ʌnˈfrɛndlɪnɪs; ˈʌnˈfrendlinis] *n.* 不友善;敵意。

un·friend·ly [ʌnˈfrɛndlɪ; ˈʌnˈfrendli] *adj.* ①不友善的;含有敵意的。②不利的;不順意的。—*adv.* 不友善地;含敵意地。

un·frock [ʌnˈfrɑk; ˈʌnˈfrɔk] *v.t.* ①脫去法衣;解除僧職。②開除;罷黜。

un·fruit·ful [ʌnˈfrutfəl; ˈʌnˈfru:tfəl] *adj.* ①不結果實的。②無子息的。③無收穫的;無利的。④不肥沃的; 不生產的; 不毛的。—**ness,** *n.* —**ly,** *adv.*

un·furl [ʌnˈfɝl; ˈʌnˈfə:l] *v.t.* 展開; 抖開。to *unfurl* an umbrella. 開傘。—*v.i.* 展開;招展。

un·fur·nished [ʌnˈfɝnɪʃt; ˈʌnˈfə:niʃt] *adj.*①無家具的;設備不全的。②不供給的;不予設備的〖with〗.

un·fus·sy [ʌnˈfʌsɪ; ʌnˈfʌsi] *adj.* ①從容自若的;不慌不忙的。②不挑剔的;較爲隨便的。③不複雜的。

UNGA [ˈʌŋgə; ˈʌŋgə] *n.* 聯合國大會(爲 *U*nited *N*ations *G*eneral *A*ssembly 之略)。

un·gain·ful [ʌnˈgenfəl; ʌnˈgeinfəl] 「*adj.* 無益的;無利可圖的。」

un·gain·ly [ʌnˈgenlɪ; ʌnˈgeinli] *adj. & adv.* 笨拙的(地);不雅的(地)。—**un·gain·li·ness,** *n.*

un·gen·er·ous [ʌnˈdʒɛnərəs; ˈʌnˈdʒenərəs] *adj.* ①度量狹窄的; 吝嗇的; 卑劣的。②不仁慈的。—**ly,** *adv.*

un·gen·tle·man·ly [ʌnˈdʒɛntlmənlɪ; ˈʌnˈdʒentlmənli] *adj.* 無紳士風度的;不文雅的;不斯文的;無禮儀的;無教養的。

un·gird [ʌnˈgɝd; ˈʌnˈgə:d] *v.t.* 解開…之帶。

un·girt [ʌnˈgɝt; ʌnˈgə:t] *adj.* ①帶子解開的;帶子放鬆的。②鬆弛的;輕鬆的。

un·giv·en [ʌnˈgɪvən; ʌnˈgivən] *adj.* (對某事)無癖好的〖to〗.

un·giv·ing [ʌnˈgɪvɪŋ; ʌnˈgiviŋ] *adj.* 不慷慨解囊的; 吝嗇的。

un·glazed [ʌnˈglezd; ˈʌnˈgleizd] *adj.* 素燒的;未上釉的(陶、瓷器)。

un·glue [ʌnˈglu; ˈʌnˈglu:] *v.t.,* **-glued, -glu·ing.** 使(粘着之物)掉下;取掉(粘着之物); 剝。

un·god·li·ness [ʌnˈgɑdlɪnɪs; ʌnˈgɔdlinis] *n.* 不敬神;不虔誠;邪惡。

un·god·ly [ʌnˈgɑdlɪ; ʌnˈgɔdli] *adj.,* **-god·li·er, -god·li·est,** *adv.* —*adj.* ①不敬神的;不虔誠的;罪孽極深的。②〖俗〗荒唐的;不能容忍的;可怕的。—*adv.* 太;極。

un·gov·ern·a·ble [ʌnˈgʌvənəbl; ʌnˈgʌvənəbl] *adj.* 不能控制的; 難控制的;難駕馭的。

un·grace·ful [ʌnˈgresfəl; ˈʌnˈgreisfəl] *adj.* 不優美的;不雅的;鄙陋的。—**ly,** *adv.*

un·gra·cious [ʌnˈgreʃəs; ˈʌnˈgreiʃəs] *adj.* ①無禮貌的; 粗野的。②不慇懃的;不親切的。③使人不快的; 不受歡迎的; 討厭的。—**ly,** *adv.* —**ness,** *n.*

un·gram·mat·i·cal [ˌʌngrəˈmætɪkl; ˈʌngrəˈmætikl] *adj.* 不合文法的。

***un·grate·ful** [ʌnˈgretfəl; ʌnˈgreitfəl] *adj.* ①不感恩的;忘恩負義的。②使人不愉快的;令人厭惡的。—**ly,** *adv.* —**ness,** *n.*

un·ground·ed [ʌnˈgraundɪd; ʌnˈgraundid] *adj.*無事實根據的;沒有理由的。

un·grudg·ing [ʌnˈgrʌdʒɪŋ; ˈʌnˈgrʌdʒiŋ] *adj.*不吝惜的;慷慨的;情願的;自願的; 出自本心的。 —**ly,** *adv.*

un·gual [ˈʌŋgwəl; ˈʌŋgwəl] *adj.* ①爪的;蹄的。②有爪的;有蹄的。③似爪的;似蹄的。

un·guard·ed [ʌnˈgɑrdɪd; ˈʌnˈgɑ:did] *adj.* ①無防禦的;無防護的;無防備的。②不小心的;不注意的;不謹愼的; 輕率的。③不提防的;不警戒的。④無欄杆、圍牆等安全設施的。—**ly,** *adv.*

un·guent [ˈʌŋgwənt; ˈʌŋgwənt] *n.* 「藥膏;軟膏。」

un·guis [ˈʌŋgwɪs; ˈʌŋgwis] *n., pl.* **-gues** [-gwiz; -gwi:z]. ①〖動物〗爪;蹄。②〖植物〗花瓣之爪狀基部。

un·gu·la [ˈʌŋgjələ; ˈʌŋgjulə] *n., pl.* **-lae** [-ˌli; -li:]. ①〖動物〗蹄;爪;甲。②〖植物〗花瓣之爪狀基部。③〖幾何〗蹄形體; 截頭圓錐。

un·gu·lar [ˈʌŋgjələ; ˈʌŋgjulə] *adj.* 「爪的;蹄的;似爪的;似蹄的。」

un·gu·late [ˈʌŋgjəlɪt; ˈʌŋgjuleit] *adj.* ①蹄狀的;有蹄的。②有蹄類動物的。—*n.* 有蹄類(哺乳)動物。

un·hair [ʌnˈhɛr; ˈʌnˈhɛə] *v.t.* 拔掉…上之毛髮。—*v.i.* 拔除毛髮。

un·hal·low [ʌnˈhælo; ˈʌnˈhælou] *v.t.* 褻瀆(神聖);汚辱(神明)。

un·hal·lowed [ʌnˈhælod; ʌnˈhæloud] *adj.* 褻瀆神聖的; 汚辱神明的;罪深的。

un·hand [ʌnˈhænd; ʌnˈhænd] *v.t.* 鬆手;放手;放開。*Unhand* me! 別拉着我!

un·han·dled [ʌnˈhændld; ʌnˈhændld] *adj.* ①未馴服的。②未觸及的;未用手碰到的。③(商品)無存貨的;不經售的。

un·hand·some [ʌnˈhænsəm; ˈʌnˈhænsəm] *adj.*①不美的;醜的。②不慷慨的;吝嗇的。③無禮的;粗魯的。—**ly,** *adv.*—**ness,** *n.*

un·hand·y [ʌnˈhændɪ; ˈʌnˈhændi] *adj.* ①拙笨的; 不靈巧的。②不易操縱的; 不易管理的;不方便的;不便利的。

un·hang [ʌnˈhæŋ; ˈʌnˈhæŋ] *v.t.,* **-hung, -hang·ing.** 將(懸掛之物)取下。

un·hap·pi·ly [ʌnˈhæpɪlɪ; ʌnˈhæpili] *adv.* ①不快樂地; 憂愁地。②不幸地。③不適當地。

***un·hap·py** [ʌnˈhæpɪ; ʌnˈhæpi] *adj.,* **-pi·er, -pi·est.** ①不快樂的;憂愁的。②不幸的。③不適當的。 —**un·hap·pi·ness,** *n.*

un·harmed [ʌnˈhɑrmd; ˈʌnˈhɑ:md] *adj.* 未受傷害的。

un·har·ness [ʌnˈhɑrnɪs; ˈʌnˈhɑ:nis] *v.t.* ①卸除馬具。②脫下甲冑。

un·health·ful [ʌnˈhɛlθfəl; ˈʌnˈhelθfəl] *adj.* 有害健康的;不衞生的。—**ly,** *adv.*

un·health·y [ʌnˈhɛlθɪ; ʌnˈhelθi] *adj.* ①不健康的。②有害健康的; 不衞生的。③不道德的。④危險的。⑤有害的。—**un·health·i·ly,** *adv.* —**un·health·i·ness,** *n.*

un·heard [ʌnˈhɝd; ˈʌnˈhə:d] *adj.* ①未被聽見的。②不被傾聽的; 未被給與申述之

機會的。③未聽說過的;不爲人所知的。

un·heard-of [ʌnˈhɝdˌɑv; ʌnˈhəːdɔv] *adj.* ①前所未聞的;空前的。②從未聽說過的;無名氣的。

un·heed·ed [ʌnˈhidɪd; ˈʌnˈhiːdid] *adj.* 未加注意的;不顧的。

un·hes·i·tat·ing [ʌnˈhɛzəˌtetɪŋ; ʌnˈheziteitiŋ] *adj.* 不猶疑的;迅速的。—**ly,** *adv.*

un·hinge [ʌnˈhɪndʒ; ʌnˈhindʒ] *v.t.,* **un·hinged, un·hing·ing.** ①(從樞紐上)摘下。②去掉樞紐;使張開。③分離;分開。④擾亂;使失常。⑤使動搖;使不確定。⑥使改軸或不穩固。—**ment,** *n.*

un·hitch [ʌnˈhɪtʃ; ˈʌnˈhitʃ] *v.t.* 解開(繫住之馬);釋放;分開。

un·ho·ly [ʌnˈholɪ; ʌnˈhouli] *adj.,* **-li·er, -li·est.** ①不神聖的;褻瀆的;邪惡的;有罪的。②〖俗〗可怕的;醜惡的。

un·hon·ored [ʌnˈɑnəd; ʌnˈɔnəd] *adj.* 未受尊敬的;未受重視的。

un·hood [ʌnˈhud; ʌnˈhud] *v.t.* ①除去…之蓋;除去…之罩。②除去(鷹)之眼罩。

un·hook [ʌnˈhuk; ˈʌnˈhuk] *v.t.* 去…之鉤;自鉤上解下。—*v.i.* 解鉤;去鉤;自鉤上解下。

un·hoped [ʌnˈhopt; ʌnˈhoupt] *adj.* =**unhoped-for.**

un·hoped-for [ʌnˈhoptˌfɔr; ʌnˈhouptfɔː] *adj.* 出乎意料之外的;意外的。

un·horse [ʌnˈhɔrs; ˈʌnˈhɔːs] *v.t.,* **-horsed, -hors·ing.** ①使(騎者)從馬背上落下。②將馬卸下。③使下臺;推翻。

un·house [ʌnˈhauz; ʌnˈhauz] *v.t.,* **-housed, -hous·ing.** 奪去…之家;自家中逐出;使無家可歸。

un·hulled [ʌnˈhʌld; ˈʌnˈhʌld] *adj.* 未去殼的。

un·hu·man [ʌnˈhjumən; ˈʌnˈhjuːmən] *adj.* ①非人類的。②超人類的;非人間的。

un·hurt [ʌnˈhɝt; ˈʌnˈhəːt] *adj.* 未受損害的;未受害的;未受傷的。

uni- 〖字首〗表"單一"之義。

U·ni·at [ˈjunɪˌæt; ˈjuːniæt] *n.* 承認教宗最高權威而仍保留其原有宗教儀式之希臘正教教徒。—*adj.* 此種教會的。

U·ni·ate [ˈjunɪɪt; ˈjuːniit] *n., adj.* =**Uniat.**

u·ni·cam·er·al [ˌjunɪˈkæmərəl; ˈjuːniˈkæmərəl] *adj.* (議會)一院的;一院制的。

U·NI·CEF [ˈjunɪsef; ˈjuːnisef] *n.* 聯合國兒童基金會(爲 *U*nited *N*ations *I*nternational *C*hildren's *E*mergency *F*und 之略)。

u·ni·cel·lu·lar [ˌjunɪˈsɛljələ; ˈjuːniˈseljulə] *adj.* 〖生物〗單細胞的。—**i·ty,** *n.*

u·ni·corn [ˈjunɪˌkɔrn; ˈjuːnikɔːn] *n.* 麒麟;獨角獸(想像中的怪獸,其形如馬,頭中間有一螺螄狀獨角)。

u·ni·cy·cle [ˈjunɪˌsaɪkl̩; ˈjuːnisaikl] *n.* 獨輪(脚踏)車。

u·ni·cy·clist [ˈjunɪˌsaɪkl̩ɪst; ˈjuːniˈsaiklist] *n.* 騎獨輪(脚踏)車者。

un·i·den·ti·fied [ˌʌnaɪˈdɛntɪˌfaɪd; ˈʌnaiˈdentifaid] *adj.* ①不能證明爲同一人或物的。②未確認出的;來路不明的。

u·ni·di·rec·tion·al [ˌjunɪdəˈrɛkʃənl̩; ˌjuːnidiˈrekʃənəl] *adj.* 單方向的。

u·ni·fi·ca·tion [ˌjunəfəˈkeʃən; ˌjuːnifiˈkeiʃən] *n.* ①統一。②一致;單一化。

u·ni·flo·rous [ˌjunɪˈflɔrəs; ˈjuːniˈflɔːrəs] *adj.* 開單花的。

u·ni·fo·li·ate [ˌjunɪˈfolɪˌet; ˈjuːniˈfoulieit] *adj.* 〖植物〗單葉的;有單葉的。

:u·ni·form [ˈjunəˌfɔrm; ˈjuːnifɔːm] *adj.* ①無變化的;相同的;一律的。bricks of a *uniform* size. 大小相同的磚。②從頭到尾不變的;始終如一的。③到處一樣的。*uniform* customs. 到處一樣的習俗。—*n.* 制服。He looks handsome in *uniform*. 他穿制服看起來很漂亮。—*v.t.* ①使穿制服;供以制服。②使一致。—**ly,** *adv.* —**ness,** *n.*

U·ni·form *n.* 通訊電碼,代表字母U.

u·ni·form·i·ty [ˌjunəˈfɔrmətɪ; ˌjuːniˈfɔːmiti] *n., pl.* **-ties.** 同樣;一律。

u·ni·fy [ˈjunəˌfaɪ; ˈjuːnifai] *v.t.,* **-fied, -fy·ing.** 統一;使合一;使一致。

u·ni·lat·er·al [ˌjunɪˈlætərəl; ˌjuːniˈlætərəl] *adj.* ①單方的;片面的;單獨的。②〖醫〗片側的;偶側的。③〖生物〗所有部分均傾向軸之一方的(如花序)。④〖社會學〗單性(父系或母系)系譜的。⑤〖語音〗在舌之一側形成的。

unilateral contract 〖法律〗片務契約。

u·ni·lin·gual [ˌjunɪˈlɪŋgwəl; ˌjuːniˈliŋgwəl] *adj.* 祇限於一種語言的。

un·il·lu·sioned [ˌʌnɪˈluʒənd; ˌʌniˈluːʒənd] *adj.* 無幻想的;不存幻想的。

un·i·mag·i·na·ble [ˌʌnɪˈmædʒɪnəbl; ˌʌniˈmædʒinəbl] *adj.* 難以想像的;不可想像的。

un·i·mag·i·na·tive [ˌʌnɪˈmædʒɪnətɪv; ˌʌniˈmædʒinətiv] *adj.* 缺乏想像力的。

un·im·pas·sioned [ˌʌnɪmˈpæʃənd; ˌʌnimˈpæʃənd] *adj.* 不激動的;冷靜的;心平氣和的。

un·im·peach·a·ble [ˌʌnɪmˈpitʃəbl̩; ˌʌnimˈpiːtʃəbl] *adj.* 無可指責的;無過失的。—**un·im·peach·a·bly,** *adv.*

***un·im·por·tant** [ˌʌnɪmˈpɔrtn̩t; ˈʌnimˈpɔːtənt] *adj.* 不重要的。—**un·im·por·tance,** *n.* —**ly,** *adv.*

un·im·pos·ing [ˌʌnɪmˈpozɪŋ; ˈʌnimˈpouziŋ] *adj.* ①不堂皇的;不莊嚴的;不動人的。②自動的;自願的;不是非做不可的。

un·im·pres·sive [ˌʌnɪmˈprɛsɪv; ˈʌnimˈpresiv] *adj.* 無印象的;印象淡薄的。

un·im·proved [ˌʌnɪmˈpruvd; ˈʌnimˈpruːvd] *adj.* ①未改良的;未改善的;未進步的。②未耕種的;未墾的。③未加利用的。④未充分開發的;未充分發展的。⑤未增加的。

un·in·flu·enced [ʌnˈɪnfluənst; ˈʌnˈinfluənst] *adj.* ①未受他人影響的;不爲外念所動的。②無偏見的;不偏心的;公正的。

un·in·formed [ˌʌnɪnˈfɔrmd; ˈʌninˈfɔːmd] *adj.* ①未獲情報的;未被通知的。②無知的;無學問的;未受教育的。

un·in·hab·it·ed [ˌʌnɪnˈhæbɪtɪd; ˈʌninˈhæbitid] *adj.* 無人居住的;無人煙的。

un·in·hib·it·ed [ˌʌnɪnˈhɪbətɪd; ˈʌninˈhibitid] *adj.* 盡情的;無拘無束的。

un·i·ni·ti·at·ed [ˌʌnɪˈnɪʃɪˌetɪd; ˌʌniˈniʃieitid] *adj.* ①對某事無所知的;對某事無研究的。②未入會的。

un·in·jured [ʌnˈɪndʒəd; ˈʌnˈindʒəd] *adj.* 未受傷害的;未受損害的。

un·in·spired [ˌʌnɪnˈspaɪrd; ˈʌninˈspaiəd] *adj.* ①無靈感的;未受激發的。②平凡的。

un·in·tel·li·gent [ˌʌnɪnˈtɛlədʒənt; ˈʌninˈtelidʒənt] *adj.* ①缺乏智力的;愚鈍的。②不能思想的;無智力的。

un·in·tel·li·gi·ble [ˌʌnɪnˈtɛlədʒəbl̩; ˈʌninˈtelidʒəbl] *adj.* 無法了解的。—**ness,** *n.* —**un·in·tel·li·gi·bly,** *adv.*

un·in·ten·tion·al [ˌʌnɪnˈtɛnʃənl̩;

ˈʌninˈtenʃənl〕 *adj.* 非故意的; 無意的; 無心的。—ly, *adv.*

un·in·ter·est·ed 〔ʌnˈɪntərɪstɪd; ˈʌnˈintristid〕 *adj.* ①無利害關係的。②冷淡的。—ly, *adv.*

un·in·ter·est·ing 〔ʌnˈɪntərɪstɪŋ; ˈʌnˈintristiŋ〕 *adj.* 無趣味的。—ly, *adv.*

un·in·ter·rupt·ed 〔ˌʌnɪntəˈrʌptɪd; ˈʌnˌintəˈrʌptid〕 *adj.* 不間斷的; 連續的; 未受騷擾的。—ly, *adv.*

u·ni·nu·cle·ate 〔ˌjunɪˈnjuklɪɪt; ˌjuːniˈnjuːkliit〕 *adj.* 祇有一個核的; 單核的。

un·in·vit·ed 〔ˌʌnɪnˈvaɪtɪd; ˈʌninˈvaitid〕 *adj.* 未被邀請的; 不速而至的。

un·in·vit·ing 〔ˌʌnɪnˈvaɪtɪŋ; ˈʌninˈvaitiŋ〕 *adj.* 不動人的; 不能引起興趣的; 無吸引力的。—ly, *adv.*

U·ni·o 〔ˈjunɪˌo; ˈjuːniou〕 *n.* 〖動物〗①蛤蜊屬。②(u-) 蛤蜊; 蠔。

‡**un·ion** 〔ˈjunjən; ˈjuːnjən〕 *n.* ①聯合; 連合; 合併。②團體; 結合; 一致; 和睦; 和諧。*Union* is strength. 團結就是力量。③婚姻; 性交。a happy *union*. 美滿的婚姻。④同盟; 組合; 協會; 工會。trade *union*. 職工協會; 工會。⑤聯邦。⑥象徵結合的旗; 旗上象徵結合的圖案。⑦〖機械〗管節; 管套節。⑧〖醫〗癒合。⑨貧民所。⑩兩種紗線的混合紡織物。⑪兩種以上纖維合成的紗線。***the Union*** a. 合衆國; 美國。 b. =the United Kingdom.

union card 工會會員證。

un·ion·ism 〔ˈjunjənɪzm̩; ˈjuːnjənizm〕 *n.* ①聯合主義。②(U-)(美國的)聯邦主義(尤指內戰時期者)。③同業聯合主義; 工會主義。

un·ion·ist 〔ˈjunjənɪst; ˈjuːnjənist〕 *n.* ①信聯合主義者。②工會聯盟之會員。③(U-) 聯邦主義者(尤指內戰期間者)。④(U-) 主張將愛爾蘭歸併於聯合王國者(反對愛爾蘭自治者)。⑤(U-)英國保守黨黨員。

un·ion·i·za·tion 〔ˌjunjənɪˈzeʃən; ˌjuːnjənaiˈzeiʃən〕 *n.* 聯合; 結合; 組合。

un·ion·ize 〔ˈjunjənˌaɪz; ˈjuːnjənaiz〕 *v.*, -ized, -iz·ing. —*v.t.* ①聯合; 組合。②使…組織工會。③使遵守工會的章程。—*v.i.* ①組成工會、協會等。②加入工會。

Union Jack ①英國國旗或國徽。②(u-j-) 船上的小旗。

Union of Burma 緬甸之正式名稱。

Union of India 印度聯邦共和國(首都新德里 New Delhi)。

Union of Soviet Socialist Republics 蘇維埃社會主義共和國聯邦(蘇聯 Soviet Union 之正式名稱, 略作 U.S.S.R. 或 USSR, 首都莫斯科 Moscow)。

union shop ①全體從業人員之工資、工作時間、工作條件必須由資方與工會間之契約規定的工商機構。②資方與工會訂定契約允許僱用非工會會員, 但受僱人員必須於規定期間(通常爲三十日)加入工會且就業期內永遠爲工會會員之商業機構。

union suit 一種襯衫與短褲連於一起之內衣。

u·ni·pod 〔ˈjunɪˌpɑd; ˈjuːnipɔd〕 *n.* 一隻腿的支架; 獨脚架。—*adj.* 祇有一隻腿的; 獨脚的。

u·ni·po·lar 〔ˌjunɪˈpolɚ; ˈjuːniˈpoulə〕 *adj.* ①〖電〗單極的。②〖生物〗單一伸長的; 單極的。

*__u·nique__ 〔juˈnik; juːˈniːk〕 *adj.* ①唯一的; 無二的; 無與倫比的; 獨特的。②珍奇的; 稀罕的。③僅有一種可能的。—*n.* 獨一無二之物。—ly, *adv.* —ness, *n.*

u·ni·sex 〔ˈjunəˌsɛks; ˈjuːniseks〕 *n.*, *adj.* (髮型、服裝等)適合男女兩性(的); 通用於兩性(的); 通性(的)。

u·ni·sex·u·al 〔ˌjunɪˈsɛkʃuəl; ˈjuːniˈseksjuəl〕 *adj.* ①〖生物〗單性的; 雌雄異體的。②限於一種性別的; 非男女同校的。—ly, *adv.*

u·ni·sex·u·al·i·ty 〔ˌjunɪˌsɛkʃuˈælətɪ; ˌjuːniˌseksjuˈæliti〕 *n.* 通性(亦男亦女)的外貌。

u·ni·son 〔ˈjunəzn̩; ˈjuːnisn〕 *n.* ①一致; 和諧。②同音; 同調; 諧音。***in unison*** 完全一致; 完全符合。

u·nis·o·nous 〔juˈnɪsənəs; juːˈnisənəs〕 *adj.* ①同調的; 同音的。②和諧的; 一致的; 在性質上相似的。(亦作 **unisonant**)

*__u·nit__ 〔ˈjunɪt; ˈjuːnit〕 *n.* ①一個; 一人。②單位。a monetary *unit*. 貨幣單位。③部隊。a mechanized *unit*. 機械化部隊。④最小的整數; 一。⑤一部機器。

Unit., unit. Unitarian.

u·nit·age 〔ˈjunətɪdʒ; ˈjuːnitidʒ〕 *n.* 單位數量之規定; 單位數量之詳細說明。

U·ni·tar·i·an 〔ˌjunəˈtɛrɪən; ˌjuːniˈtɛəriən〕 *n.* ①唯一神教派(基督教之一派, 認爲上帝係單一者, 反對三位一體之說)之信徒。②唯一神論者。③主張單一制政府者。—*adj.* ①唯一神教派的。②(u-) 單一的; 一體的。

U·ni·tar·i·an·ism 〔ˌjunəˈtɛrɪənɪzm̩; ˌjuːniˈtɛəriənizm〕 *n.* 唯一神教派之教義。

u·ni·tar·y 〔ˈjunəˌtɛrɪ; ˈjuːnitəri〕 *adj.* ①一個的; 單一的。②單位的; 單元的。③〖數學〗一元的; 歸一的。④〖哲學〗一元論的。⑤中央集權論的。—**u·ni·tar·i·ly**, *adv.*

‡**u·nite** 〔juˈnaɪt; juˈnait〕 *v.*, **u·nit·ed, u·nit·ing.** —*v.t.* ①聯合; 結合; 合併。to *unite* bricks and stones with cement. 以水泥將磚和石黏合一起。②兼備(各種性質)。—*v.i.* ①聯合; 合併; 混合。②協力; 一致行動。—**u·nit·er**, *n.*

*__u·nit·ed__ 〔juˈnaɪtɪd; juˈnaitid〕 *adj.* 聯合的; 合併的; 結合的; 一致的。—ly, *adv.*

United Arab Emirates 阿拉伯聯合大公國(阿拉伯東北之一共和國, 包括七個阿拉伯酋長國, 昔稱Trucial Oman; 首都爲Abu Dhabi)。

United Arab Republic 阿拉伯聯合共和國(埃及與敍利亞於1958年2月1日合併而成。敍利亞於1961年退出後埃及仍沿用此名)。(略作 U.A.R.)

united front 聯合陣線。

United Kingdom 聯合王國(包括大不列顚和北愛爾蘭, 首都倫敦 London)。

United Nations ①(the -)聯合國。②聯合國會員國。③(第二次世界大戰時對抗德、義、日軸心國的)同盟國。

United Nations Children's Fund 聯合國兒童基金會。(參看UNICEF)

United Nations Educational, Scientific and Cultural Organization 聯合國教科文組織。(參看 UNESCO)

United Nations Relief and Rehabilitation Administration 聯合國善後救濟總署。(參看UNRRA)

United Press International 美國合衆國際社(爲 UP 與 INS 於 1958 年合併而成, 略作 UPI 或 U. P. I.)。

‡**United States, United States of America** 美利堅合衆國; 美國。(略作 U. S. 或 U. S. A., 首都華盛頓 Washington,

D.C.)〖注意〗United States 之前必須加定冠詞 the. They live in the *United States.* 他們住在美國。

United States of Brazil 巴西之正式名稱。

u·ni·tive ['junətɪv;'ju:nitiv] *adj.* ①促進團結的。②聯合的;團結的;結合的。

unit price 單價。

unit pricing 按單位標價(如糖按斤,布按尺等)。

u·ni·ty** ['junətɪ; 'ju:niti] *n., pl.* **-ties.** ①單一;獨一;統一。②聯合;結合。③調合;和諧。national *unity.* 擧國一致。They live together in *unity.* 他們和睦地住在一起。④聯貫;協調;統一性。⑤數目之一;1。the dramatic unities*** (or ***the unities of time, place, and action***) 戲劇中時間,地點和情節的單一性;三一律。

Univ. University.

univ. ①universal(ly). ②universe. ③university.

U·NI·VAC ['junɪvæk; 'ju:nivæk] *n.* 〖商標名〗一種電腦(*U*niversal *A*utomatic Computer 的略稱)。

u·ni·va·lent [ˌjunə'velənt;ˌju:ni'veilənt] *adj.* ①〖化〗a. 一價的。b. 只有一種價數的;單價的。②〖生物〗單一的(特指染色體)。

u·ni·valve ['junəˌvælv; 'ju:nivælv] *adj.* 〖動物〗單殼的。—*n.* 單殼軟體動物。

***u·ni·ver·sal** [ˌjunə'vɝsl̩; ˌju:ni'və:səl] *adj.* ①宇宙的;全世界的;萬國的;普通的;普遍的;一般的。a *universal* peace. 世界和平。②多才多藝的;博學多才的。—*n.* ①〖邏輯〗全稱命題。②〖哲學〗一般概念。③普遍原則。

universal agent 總代理人。

universal compass 萬能圓規;通用圓規。

universal coupling =universal joint.

universal donor 血液爲O型的輸血人(因O型血可輸給任何血型之人)。

universal gravitation 〖物理〗萬有引力。

u·ni·ver·sal·ism [ˌjunə'vɝsəˌlɪzəm; ˌju:ni'və:səlizm] *n.* ①(U-)〖神學〗普救說(所有的人終必得救之說或信仰)。②=universality. ③興趣、智識或行動之多方面。

U·ni·ver·sal·ist [ˌjunə'vɝsl̩ɪst; ˌju:ni'və:səlist] *n.* ①信普救說者。②(u-)智識、興趣或活動範圍甚廣之人。—**ic,** *adj.*

u·ni·ver·sal·i·ty [ˌjunəvɝ'sælətɪ; ˌju:nivə:'sæliti] *n., pl.* **-ties.** 一般性;普遍性;無所不包性。

u·ni·ver·sal·ize [ˌjunə'vɝsl̩ˌaɪz; ˌju:ni'və:səlaiz] *v.t.,* **-ized, -iz·ing.** 使普及;使普遍化。—**u·ni·ver·sal·i·za·tion,** *n.*

universal joint 〖機械〗萬向接頭。

universal language 世界語。

***u·ni·ver·sal·ly** [ˌjunə'vɝslɪ; ˌju:ni'və:səli] *adv.* ①一般地;全般地。②普遍地。

universal maid 做雜役之女工。

Universal Postal Union 萬國郵政聯盟(略作 UPU)。

universal recipient 血液爲AB型者(可接受任何血型之輸血)。

universal suffrage 普遍選擧權。

universal time =Greenwich Time.

***u·ni·verse** ['junəˌvɝs; 'ju:nivə:s] *n.* ①宇宙;萬有;天地萬物。②世界;全人類。③恆星與星辰系。④思想等的體系、範圍等。

universe of discourse 〖邏輯〗討論或辯論中所包含之事物、觀念或事實之總體。

‡**u·ni·ver·si·ty** [ˌjunə'vɝsətɪ; ˌju:ni'və:siti, jun-] *n., pl.* **-ties,** *adj.* —*n.* ①大學。②大學的校舍。—*adj.* 大學的。

university extension 大學補習班;大學之公開講座。

university man 大學出身之人;大學生。

u·niv·o·cal [ju'nɪvəkl̩; ju:'nivəkl] *adj.* 祇有一個意思的;祇有一種解釋的。

un·joint [ʌn'dʒɔɪnt; 'ʌn'dʒɔint] *v.t.* 拆開…之連結處;使斷聯絡。

***un·just** [ʌn'dʒʌst; 'ʌn'dʒʌst] *adj.* 不公平的;不義的;不當的。—**ly,** *adv.* —**ness,** *n.*

un·jus·ti·fi·a·ble [ʌn'dʒʌstəˌfaɪəbl̩; ʌn'dʒʌstifaiəbl] *adj.* 不能認爲是正當的;不能辯明爲合理的;不能明辯的。

un·kempt [ʌn'kɛmpt; 'ʌn'kempt] *adj.* ①蓬亂的;未梳理的(頭髮)。②不整潔的(衣服、外表)。③粗糙的;未修飾的(語言等)。

***un·kind** [ʌn'kaɪnd; ʌn'kaind] *adj.* 不親切的;無情的;不厚道的;殘酷的。—**ness,** *n.*

un·kind·ly [ʌn'kaɪndlɪ; ʌn'kaindli] *adj.* ①不厚道的;不仁慈的;壞脾氣的。②(氣候等)不佳的。③對農作物不利的。—*adv.* 嚴厲地;苛刻地。

un·knit [ʌn'nɪt;'ʌn'nit] *v.t.,* **-knit·ted, -knit·ting.** 解開;拆開(編織物等)。

un·knot [ʌn'nɑt; 'ʌn'nɔt] *v.t.,* **-knot·ted, -knot·ting.** 解開(結)。

un·know·a·ble [ʌn'noəbl̩; 'ʌn'nouəbl] *adj.* 不可知的;人類知識或經驗以外的。—*n.* 不可知之事物。

un·know·ing [ʌn'noɪŋ; 'ʌn'nouiŋ] *adj.* ①不知的;不覺的。②無知的。—**ly,** *adv.*

‡**un·known** [ʌn'non; 'ʌn'noun] *adj.* ①未知的;不確知的;不明的;不詳的。His purpose was *unknown* to me. 我不知道他的目的。***an unknown quantity*** 未知量。—*n.* ①未知之事物;默默無聞之人。②〖數學〗未知數。

Unknown Soldier 陣亡的無名英雄。

un·lace [ʌn'les; 'ʌn'leis] *v.t.,* **-laced, -lac·ing.** ①解開…之帶子;解開帶子以脫掉…之衣物。②〖狩獵〗將(打到之野獸)切成塊。

un·lade [ʌn'led; 'ʌn'leid] *v.,* **-lad·ed, -lad·ing.** —*v.t.* 卸下…之貨;卸下。—*v.i.* 卸貨。

un·laid [ʌn'led; ʌn'leid] *adj.* ①未擺好的。②未安定的。③未埋葬的。④(繩)反搓鬆開的。—*v.* pp. & pt. of **unlay.**

un·lash [ʌn'læʃ; 'ʌn'læʃ] *v.t.* 解開(縛繫之物)。

un·latch [ʌn'lætʃ; 'ʌn'lætʃ] *v.t.* 將…之門拔去;拔門以打開(門等)。—*v.i.* 拔門而開。

un·law·ful [ʌn'lɔfəl; 'ʌn'lɔ:ful] *adj.* ①不合法的;非法的。②私生的(孩子)。—**ly,** *adv.* —**ness,** *n.*

un·lay [ʌn'le; 'ʌn'lei] *v.,* **-laid, -lay·ing.** —*v.t.* 〖航海〗(反搓而)拆開(繩索)。—*v.i.* (繩索)拆開。

un·learn [ʌn'lɝn; 'ʌn'lə:n] *v.,* **-learned** *or* **-learnt, -learn·ing.** —*v.t.* ①忘却(所學得之知識)。②教以(與所學者)相反之知識。—*v.i.* 丟棄既有之知識或習慣。

un·learn·ed [ʌn'lɝnɪd;'ʌn'lə:nid. *for* ③ ʌn'lɝnd; ʌn'lə:nd] *adj.* ①無學問的;未受教育的;無知的。②顯示出缺乏學習或教育的。③非由學習而知的;自然的。***the unlearned*** 無知識的人;蒙昧的人(集合稱)。

un·leased [ʌn'list; ʌn'li:st] *adj.* 未租出的。

un·leash [ʌn'liʃ; 'ʌn'li:ʃ] *v.t.* ①解開皮帶以釋放。②放棄對…之控制。

un·leav·ened [ʌn'lɛvənd; 'ʌn'levnd] *adj.* ①沒有發酵的。②未受影響的;未變化的。

‡un·less 〔ən'lɛs; ən'les, ʌn-〕 *conj.* 除非；除非在…的時候；如果…不；若不。I shall go there tomorrow *unless* I'm too busy. 如果我不太忙，我將於明天到那裏去。—*prep.* 除掉（＝except).

un·let 〔ʌn'lɛt; ʌn'let〕 *adj.* 未租出的。

un·let·tered 〔ʌn'lɛtɚd; 'ʌn'letəd〕 *adj.* ①未受教育的；文盲的。②無字的。

un·li·censed 〔ʌn'laɪsənst; 'ʌn'laisənst〕 *adj.* ①無執照的；未經當局許可的。②無節制的。

un·licked 〔ʌn'lɪkt; 'ʌn'likt〕 *adj.* 不整飾的；無禮貌的。an *unlicked* cub. 粗野的年輕人。

***un·like** 〔ʌn'laɪk; 'ʌn'laik〕 *adj.* 不同的；相異的。—*prep.* 不像；和…不同。It is *unlike* her to enjoy herself so much. 她盡情享樂不像她本來的爲人。—**ness,** *n.*

un·like·li·hood 〔ʌn'laɪklɪhud; ʌn'laiklihud〕 *n.* 不可能。

***un·like·ly** 〔ʌn'laɪklɪ; ʌn'laikli〕 *adj.* ①不像是眞的。②似乎不會成功的。③不討人喜歡的；討厭的。—**un·like·li·ness,** *n.*

***un·lim·it·ed** 〔ʌn'lɪmɪtɪd; ʌn'limitid〕 *adj.* ①無限的；不受限制的。*unlimited* liability. 無限的責任。②無條件的；無例外的。—**ly,** *adv.*

un·list·ed 〔ʌn'lɪstɪd; 'ʌn'listid〕 *adj.* ①未被列入的；未列進表中的。②未列入可在證券交易所買賣的(證券等)。

un·live·ly 〔ʌn'laɪvlɪ; ʌn'laivli〕 *adj.* 缺乏生氣的。

un·liv·ing 〔ʌn'lɪvɪŋ; ʌn'liviŋ〕 *adj.* 無生命的。

***un·load** 〔ʌn'lod; 'ʌn'loud〕 *v.t.* ①卸(貨)。②擺脫…之負擔。③退出(鎗砲)中之彈藥。④傾銷。—*v.i.* 卸貨。—**er,** *n.*

***un·lock** 〔ʌn'lɑk; 'ʌn'lɔk〕 *v.t.* ①開…的鎖；開；啓。②宣洩；顯露。③放開；使鬆。④解出…之意義。—*v.i.* 開鎖；開啓。

un·looked-for 〔ʌn'lukt,fɔr; ʌn'luktfɔ:〕 *adj.* 意外的；預料不到的。

un·loose 〔ʌn'lus; 'ʌn'lu:s〕 *v.t.,* **-loosed, -loos·ing.** 放開；釋放；放鬆。(亦作**unloosen**)

un·love 〔ʌn'lʌv; ʌn'lʌv〕 *v.,* **-loved, -lov·ing,** *n.* —*v.t.* & *v.i.* 不再愛；停止喜愛。—*n.* 恨。

un·loved 〔ʌn'lʌvd; ʌn'lʌvd〕 *adj.* 未被愛的；未被喜愛的。

un·love·ly 〔ʌn'lʌvlɪ; 'ʌn'lʌvli〕 *adj.* 不美麗的；不使人喜愛的；可厭的。—**un·love·li·ness,** *n.*

un·luck·i·ly 〔ʌn'lʌkɪlɪ; ʌn'lʌkili〕 *adv.* 不幸地。

***un·luck·y** 〔ʌn'lʌkɪ; ʌn'lʌki〕 *adj.* 不吉利的；不祥的；不幸的。—**un·luck·i·ness,** *n.*

un·mail·a·ble 〔ʌn'meləbl̩; ʌn'meiləbl〕 *adj.* 不能郵寄的。

un·make 〔ʌn'mek; 'ʌn'meik〕 *v.t.,* **-made, -mak·ing.** ①毀壞；毀滅。②廢除。③改變(主意、決定等)。

un·man 〔ʌn'mæn; 'ʌn'mæn〕 *v.t.,* **-manned, -man·ning.** ①使失去男子之氣質；使怯懦；使成柔弱。②使(船、碉堡)喪盡人員。③閹割；去勢。

un·man·age·a·ble 〔ʌn'mænɪdʒəbl̩; ʌn'mænidʒəbl〕 *adj.* 難處理的；難操縱的。

un·man·ly 〔ʌn'mænlɪ; 'ʌn'mænli〕 *adj.* 無男子氣的；怯儒的。—**un·man·li·ness,** *n.*

un·manned 〔ʌn'mænd; 'ʌn'mænd〕 *adj.* ①閹割過的。②被奪去男子氣概的。③無人居住的。④無人操縱或駕駛的；無人値班的。

un·man·nered 〔ʌn'mænɚd; ʌn'mænəd〕 *adj.* ①無禮的；粗魯的。②不做作的；自然的。—**ly,** *adv.*

un·man·ner·ly 〔ʌn'mænəlɪ; ʌn'mænəli〕 *adj.* & *adv.* 無禮貌的(地)；粗魯的(地)。—**un·man·ner·li·ness,** *n.*

un·ma·nured 〔,ʌnmə'nurd; 'ʌnmə'njuəd〕 *adj.* 未施肥的。

un·marked 〔ʌn'mɑrkt; 'ʌn'mɑ:kt〕 *adj.* ①無記號的。②未被注意到的。③無道路標誌的。④無(某種特色)的。

un·mar·ket·a·ble 〔ʌn'mɑrkətəbl̩; ʌn'mɑ:kitəbl〕 *adj.* 不能上市的；賣不出去的。

un·mar·riage·a·ble 〔ʌn'mærɪdʒəbl̩; ʌn'mæridʒəbl〕 *adj.* ①不適於結婚的。②年紀太輕不能結婚的；尙未達結婚年齡的。

***un·mar·ried** 〔ʌn'mærɪd; 'ʌn'mærid〕 *adj.* 未婚的。

un·mar·ry 〔ʌn'mærɪ; 'ʌn'mæri〕 *v.t.* & *v.i.,* **-ried, -ry·ing.** 離婚；和…離婚。

un·mask 〔ʌn'mæsk; 'ʌn'mɑːsk〕 *v.t.* ①揭除…之假面具或僞裝。②使暴露出眞象。—*v.i.* ①揭除假面具；摘下假面具。②暴露出某人的眞正性格或意向。

un·match·a·ble 〔ʌn'mætʃəbl̩; 'ʌn'mætʃəbl〕 *adj.* 不能匹敵的；無法對抗的。

un·matched 〔ʌn'mætʃt; 'ʌn'mætʃt〕 *adj.* ①無配偶的。②無匹敵的；未曾有過的。③不成對的；不相配的。

un·mean·ing 〔ʌn'minɪŋ; ʌn'mi:niŋ〕 *adj.* ①無意義的；空洞的。②無表情的(面容)。

un·meas·ured 〔ʌn'mɛʒɚd; ʌn'meʒəd〕 *adj.* ①不可測的。②無限的。③無節制的；過度的。—**ly,** *adv.*

un·men·tion·a·ble 〔ʌn'mɛnʃənəbl̩; ʌn'menʃənəbl〕 *adj.* 不可提及的；不足掛齒的；不堪出口的。—*n.* ①(*pl.*)〖諧〗**a.** 褲子。**b.** 內衣。②不堪出口的事；不能提起的事。

un·mer·ci·ful 〔ʌn'mɝsɪfəl; ʌn'mə:sifəl〕 *adj.* ①無情的；殘酷的；不仁慈的。②〖俗〗過分的；不合理的。—**ly,** *adv.*

un·mer·it·ed 〔ʌn'mɛrɪtɪd; 'ʌn'meritid〕 *adj.* 無功受祿的；不應得的；過分的（獎賞)；不當的。—**ly,** *adv.*

un·mind·ful 〔ʌn'maɪndfəl; ʌn'maindfəl〕 *adj.* 疏忽的；不留心的；不注意的；忘却的。—**ly,** *adv.*

un·mis·tak·a·ble 〔,ʌnmə'stekəbl̩; 'ʌnmis'teikəbl〕 *adj.* 不會錯的；不可能被誤解的；明顯的。—**un·mis·tak·a·bly,** *adv.*

un·mit·i·gat·ed 〔ʌn'mɪtə,getɪd; ʌn'mitigeitid〕 *adj.* ①純然的；全然的；絕對的。②未減輕的；未緩和的。—**ly,** *adv.*

un·mix·a·ble 〔ʌn'mɪksəbl̩; ʌn'miksəbl〕 *adj.* 不相容的。

un·mixed 〔ʌn'mɪkst; 'ʌn'mikst〕 *adj.* 未混雜他物的；純粹的。

un·mod·i·fied 〔ʌn'mɑdə,faɪd; 'ʌn'mɔdifaid〕 *adj.* ①未變的；未改的。②無修飾字語的。

un·mo·lest·ed 〔,ʌnmə'lɛstɪd; 'ʌnmə'lestid〕 *adj.* 無苦惱的；無麻煩的；平安無事的。

un·moor 〔ʌn'mur; 'ʌn'muə〕 *v.t.* ①解(船)之纜；起(船)之錨。②(於雙錨或多錨碇泊時，起去其餘之錨)以單錨碇泊。—*v.i.* 起錨。

un·mor·al 〔ʌn'mɔrəl; 'ʌn'mɔrəl〕 *adj.* ①不發生道德問題的；非道德的亦非不道德的。②不道德的。

un·moved 〔ʌn'muvd; 'ʌn'mu:vd〕 *adj.* ①不動搖的；堅決的。②冷靜的；心平氣和的；冷淡的。

un·mu·si·cal [ʌnˈmjuzɪkl; ˈʌnˈmjuːzi-kl] *adj.* ①非音樂的; 不成曲調的; 不和諧的; 難聽的。②不愛好音樂的; 無音樂修養的。—**ly**, *adv.*

un·muz·zle [ʌnˈmʌzl̩; ˈʌnˈmʌzl] *v.t.* ①解開(狗等)的口罩。②准許言論寫作自由; 解除限制。

*__un·nat·u·ral__ [ʌnˈnætʃərəl; ʌnˈnætʃə-rəl] *adj.* ①不自然的。②反常的; 不近人情的。—**ly**, *adv.* —**ness**, *n.*

*__un·nec·es·sar·ies__ [ʌnˈnɛsəˌsɛrɪz; ʌnˈnesisəriz] *n. pl.* 非必需品。

un·nec·es·sar·i·ly [ʌnˈnɛsəˌsɛrəlɪ; ʌnˈnesisərili] *adv.* 多餘地;不必要地。

*__un·nec·es·sar·y__ [ʌnˈnɛsəˌsɛrɪ; ʌn-ˈnesisəri] *adj.* 不必要的;不需要的;無用的;無益的。

un·neigh·bo(u)r·ly [ʌnˈnebəlɪ; ˈʌnˈneibəli] *adj.* 不似鄰人的;不友善的;不善交際的。

un·nerve [ʌnˈnɝv; ˈʌnˈnəːv] *v.t.*, **un-nerved, un·nerv·ing.** ①使失去鎮定力; 嚇壞。②抽取…之神經。

un·neu·rot·ic [ˌʌnnjʊˈrɑtɪk; ˌʌnnjuə-ˈrɔtik] *adj.* 神經正常的。

un·not·ed [ʌnˈnotɪd; ʌnˈnoutid] *adj.* 默默無聞的;不爲人所注目的。

un·no·tice·a·ble [ʌnˈnotɪsəbl̩; ˈʌn-ˈnoutisəbl] *adj.* 不顯明的;不顯著的。

un·no·ticed [ʌnˈnotɪst; ˈʌnˈnoutist] *adj.* ①未被注意的;未被顧及的。②不觸目的;不引人注意的。

un·num·bered [ʌnˈnʌmbəd; ˈʌn-ˈnʌmbəd] *adj.* ①沒有計算的。②沒有加號數的。③不可勝數的。

UNO, U.N.O. United Nations Organization.

un·ob·jec·tion·a·ble [ˌʌnəbˈdʒɛk-ʃənəbl̩; ˈʌnəbˈdʒekʃənəbl] *adj.* 無可反對的;無異議的;無阻礙的。

un·ob·li·gat·ed [ʌnˈɑbləˌgetɪd; ʌn-ˈɔbligeitid] *adj.* ①未指定用途的; 未作某種用場的。②無義務的。

un·ob·serv·ant [ˌʌnəbˈzɝvənt; ˈʌnəbˈzəːvənt] *adj.* ①不注意的;不留心的。②不遵守(規則、慣例等)的。

un·ob·served [ˌʌnəbˈzɝvd; ˈʌnəb-ˈzəːvd] *adj.* ①未注意到的;未觀察到的。②未被遵守的。

un·ob·tain·a·ble [ˌʌnəbˈtenəbl̩; ˈʌnəbˈteinəbl] *adj.* 得不到的;無法得到的。

un·ob·tru·sive [ˌʌnəbˈtrusɪv; ˈʌnəb-ˈtruːsiv] *adj.* 不冒昧的;謙遜的;謹愼的。

*__un·oc·cu·pied__ [ʌnˈɑkjəˌpaɪd; ˈʌn-ˈɔkjupaid] *adj.* ①沒有人居住的;空的。②空閒的;不忙的。③未被敵人占領的。

un·of·fend·ing [ˌʌnəˈfɛndɪŋ; ˈʌnə-ˈfendiŋ] *adj.* ①不拂人意的;不惹人厭的;不觸怒人的。②無害的。③無罪的。

un·of·fi·cial [ˌʌnəˈfɪʃəl; ˈʌnəˈfiʃəl] *adj.* 非官方的;非正式的。—**ly**, *adv.*

un·o·pened [ʌnˈopənd; ˈʌnˈoupənd] *adj.* 未開的;未開放的。

un·or·gan·ized [ʌnˈɔrgənˌaɪzd; ˈʌn-ˈɔːgənaizd] *adj.* ①無組織的;無系統的。②未組織成工會的。③未加以整理的; 未加組織的。④無固定疆界的。⑤〖化〗無機的。

unorganized ferment 〖化〗酵素;酶(=enzyme)。

un·or·tho·dox [ʌnˈɔrθəˌdɑks; ˈʌn-ˈɔːθədɔks] *adj.* ①非正統的。②異教的。

un·os·ten·ta·tious [ˌʌnɑstənˈteʃəs; ˈʌnˌɔstenˈteiʃəs] *adj.* 不浮華的;樸素的;不顯著的。—**ly**, *adv.*

un·pack [ʌnˈpæk; ˈʌnˈpæk] *v.t.* ①開箱取出。②開(箱)取物。③吐露。④釋明。⑤從(馬背上或車上)卸貨。—*v.i.* 開箱取物;解開包裝物;卸貨。

un·paid [ʌnˈped; ˈʌnˈpeid] *adj.* ①未付的。②未領薪水的;無薪的。

un·paid-for [ʌnˈpedfɔr; ˌʌnˈpeidfɔː] *adj.* 尙未付款的。

un·pal·at·a·ble [ʌnˈpælətəbl̩; ʌn-ˈpælətəbl] *adj.* ①不適口的;無味的。②令人不快的。

un·par·al·leled [ʌnˈpærəˌlɛld; ʌn-ˈpærəleld] *adj.* 無比的。(亦作 **unparalleled**)

un·par·don·a·ble [ʌnˈpɑrdn̩əbl̩; ʌn-ˈpɑːdnəbl] *adj.* 不可原諒的;難原諒的。

un·par·lia·men·ta·ry [ˌʌnpɑrləˈmɛntərɪ; ˈʌnˌpɑːləˈmentəri] *adj.* 違反議會習慣或議會法的;不適於議會使用的(言語等)。

un·pat·ent·ed [ʌnˈpætn̩tɪd; ʌn-ˈpeitəntid] *adj.* 沒有獲得專利權的;不受專利權保護的。

un·pat·ri·ot·ic [ˌʌnpetrɪˈɑtɪk; ˈʌn-ˌpeitriˈɔtik] *adj.* 無愛國心的;不愛國的。

un·paved [ʌnˈpevd; ˈʌnˈpeivd] *adj.* 未鋪砌的;未鋪路的。

un·peo·ple [ʌnˈpipl̩; ˈʌnˈpiːpl] *v.t.*, **-peo·pled, -peo·pling.** 自…遷移居民;(因瘟疫、暴力等)減少或滅絕…之居民。

un·peo·pled [ʌnˈpipl̩d; ˈʌnˈpiːpld] *adj.* 沒有居民的;無人居住的。

un·per·ceived [ˌʌnpɚˈsivd; ˈʌn-pəˈsiːvd] *adj.* 未被認知的;未被注意到的;未被覺察的。

un·per·turbed [ˌʌnpɚˈtɝbd; ˈʌn-pəˈtəːbd] *adj.* 鎭定的;寧靜的;未受擾亂的;未受驚擾的。

un·pin [ʌnˈpɪn; ˈʌnˈpin] *v.t.*, **-pinned, -pin·ning.** 拔去…之針;拔開…之栓;鬆開。

un·pit·ied [ʌnˈpɪtɪd; ˈʌnˈpitid] *adj.* 未蒙憐恤的;未獲同情的。

un·placed [ʌnˈplest; ʌnˈpleist] *adj.* ①無場所的。②(賽馬等)第三名以下的。

*__un·pleas·ant__ [ʌnˈplɛznt; ʌnˈpleznt] *adj.* 使人不快的; 使人厭惡的; 煞風景的。—**ly**, *adv.*

un·pleas·ant·ness [ʌnˈplɛzn̩tnɪs; ʌnˈplezntnis] *n.* ①令人不悅;煞風景。②令人不悅之事; 煞風景的情勢。③不和或爭吵。④不愉快之感覺。

un·pleas·ing [ʌnˈplizɪŋ; ˈʌnˈpliːziŋ] *adj.* 使人不愉快的;不逗人憐的。

un·plumbed [ʌnˈplʌmd; ˈʌnˈplʌmd] *adj.* ①尙未測其深度的; 深不可測的。②無水道、煤氣、下水管之設備;(建築物)無鉛管設備的。③未以鉛封的。

un·pol·ished [ʌnˈpɑlɪʃt; ˈʌnˈpɔliʃt] *adj.* ①無光澤的。②未磨光的。③粗野的。

unpolished rice 糙米。

un·pop·u·lar [ʌnˈpɑpjələ; ˈʌnˈpɔ-pjulə] *adj.* ①不流行的。②不受歡迎的;不爲人所喜的。—**i·ty**, *n.* —**ly**, *adv.*

un·prac·ti·cal [ʌnˈpræktɪkl̩; ˈʌn-ˈpræktikəl] *adj.* 不切實際的; 不合實用的。

un·prac·ticed, un·prac·tised [ʌnˈpræktɪst; ʌnˈpræktist] *adj.* ①未實行的;未實施的。②不熟練的;無經驗的。

un·prec·e·dent·ed [ʌnˈprɛsə-

ˌdɛntɪd; ʌnˈpresidəntid〕 *adj.* 空前的;無前例的。—**ly,** *adv.*

un·pre·dict·a·ble 〔ˌʌnprɪˈdɪktəbḷ; ˈʌnpriˈdiktəbl〕 *adj.* 不可預測的。—*n.* 不可預測之事。—**un·pre·dict·a·bly,** *adv.*

un·prej·u·diced 〔ʌnˈprɛdʒədɪst; ʌnˈpredʒudist〕 *adj.* ①無偏見的;大公無私的;立場公正的。②未受損害的(權利等)。

un·pre·med·i·tat·ed 〔ˌʌnprɪˈmɛdəˌtetɪd; ˈʌnpriˈmediteitid〕 *adj.* ①無預謀的; 非故意的; 未準備的。 *unpremeditated* homicide. 非預謀殺人。②臨時的;卽席的。

un·pre·pared 〔ˌʌnprɪˈpɛrd; ˈʌnpriˈpɛəd〕 *adj.* ①事先未加準備的。②未準備好的。

un·pre·tend·ing 〔ˌʌnprɪˈtɛndɪŋ; ˈʌnpriˈtendiŋ〕 *adj.* 不矜持的;謙遜的;質樸的。

un·pre·ten·tious 〔ˌʌnprɪˈtɛnʃəs; ˈʌn-priˈtenʃəs〕 *adj.* 不炫於外的;不露鋒芒的; 不矯飾的; 不自負的; 謙虛的。—**ly,** *adv.*

un·priced 〔ʌnˈpraɪst; ʌnˈpraist〕 *adj.* ①無定價的。②無價的;極貴重的。

un·prin·ci·pled 〔ʌnˈprɪnsəpḷd; ʌnˈprinsəpld〕 *adj.* ①無主義的;無道德心的;壞的。②對某事之原則一無所悉的〖常 in〗。

un·print·a·ble 〔ʌnˈprɪntəbḷ; ˈʌnˈprintəbl〕 *adj.* 不宜印出的;猥褻的。

un·priv·i·leged 〔ʌnˈprɪvəlɪdʒd; ˈʌnˈprivilidʒd〕 *adj.* 無特權的。

un·pro·duc·tive 〔ˌʌnprəˈdʌktɪv; ˈʌn-prəˈdʌktiv〕 *adj.* ①不生產的;無生產力的;不毛的。②無收益的;無效果的。

un·pro·fes·sion·al 〔ˌʌnprəˈfɛʃənḷ; ˈʌn-prəˈfeʃənḷ〕 *adj.* ①與專門職業無關的;不屬於某一特殊職業的。②專業以外的; 行外的。③違反職業道德、行規、習慣等的。④非職業性的;業餘的。⑤外行的;不能與行家相比的。

un·prof·it·a·ble 〔ʌnˈprɑfɪtəbḷ; ʌnˈprɔfitəbl〕 *adj.* 無利可圖的; 無益的。—**ness,** *n.* —**un·prof·it·a·bly,** *adv.*

un·prom·is·ing 〔ʌnˈprɑmɪsɪŋ; ˈʌnˈprɔmisiŋ〕 *adj.* 沒有前途的; 沒有後望的;看來似無成功之希望的。—**ly,** *adv.*

un·pro·tect·ed 〔ˌʌnprəˈtɛktɪd; ˈʌnprəˈtektid〕 *adj.* ①無保護(者)的。②無防衞的。③無裝甲的。④無關稅保護的(工業等)。

un·pro·voked 〔ˌʌnprəˈvokt; ˈʌnprəˈvoukt〕 *adj.* 未受刺激的; 無正當理由的; 無緣無故的。

un·pub·lished 〔ʌnˈpʌblɪʃt; ˈʌnˈpʌbliʃt〕 *adj.* ①未公布於世的;祕密的。②未出版的;未刊行的。

un·pun·ished 〔ʌnˈpʌnɪʃt; ˈʌnˈpʌniʃt〕 *adj.* 未受處罰的。

un·pur·chas·a·ble 〔ʌnˈpɝtʃəsəbḷ; ʌnˈpəːtʃəsəbl〕 *adj.* 金錢無法買到的。

un·qual·i·fied 〔ʌnˈkwɑləˌfaɪd; ˈʌnˈkwɔlifaid〕 *adj.* ①不合格的;不適宜的。②無限制的;無條件的。③絕對的;完全的。

un·ques·tion·a·ble 〔ʌnˈkwɛstʃənəbḷ; ʌnˈkwestʃənəbl〕 *adj.* ①無可疑的;確定的。②無可訴病的;無可指責的。—**un·ques·tion·a·bly,** *adv.*

un·ques·tioned 〔ʌnˈkwɛstʃənd; ʌnˈkwestʃənd〕 *adj.* ①不成問題的;無疑問的。②未被查問的;未被調查的。③無爭執的;未被反對的。

un·ques·tion·ing 〔ʌnˈkwɛstʃənɪŋ; ʌnˈkwestʃəniŋ〕 *adj.* 不問是非的;盲目的。

un·qui·et 〔ʌnˈkwaɪət; ˈʌnˈkwaiət〕 *adj.* ①不安的;杌隉的。②心神不寧的。③紛擾的;擾亂的。—*n.* 騷動;激動的心情。—**ly,** *adv.* —**ness,** *n.*

un·quote 〔ʌnˈkwot; ˈʌnˈkwout〕 *v.,* **-quot·ed, -quot·ing,** *n.* —*v.i.* & *v.t.* 結束引述。—*n.* 結束引述(卽 ”)。

un·rat·i·fied 〔ʌnˈrætɪfaɪd; ʌnˈrætifaid〕 *adj.* 未批准的。

un·rav·el 〔ʌnˈrævḷ; ʌnˈrævl〕 *v.,* **-el(l)ed, -el(l)ing.** —*v.t.* ①解開(糾纏的線等)。②闡明;解決。—*v.i.* ①解開。②獲解決。

un·read 〔ʌnˈrɛd; ˈʌnˈred〕 *adj.* ①未讀書的;無學識的。②未經閱讀的(書)。

un·read·y 〔ʌnˈrɛdɪ; ˈʌnˈredi〕 *adj.* ①未準備的;未準備好的。②不敏捷的。③精神不集中而不能作迅速決定的。 —**un·read·i·ly,** *adv.* —**un·read·i·ness,** *n.*

un·re·al 〔ʌnˈriəl; ˈʌnˈriəl〕 *adj.* 不眞實的;虛幻的;空想的。

un·re·al·ist 〔ʌnˈriəlɪst; ˈʌnˈriəlist〕 *n.* 空想主義者。

un·re·al·i·ty 〔ˌʌnrɪˈælətɪ; ˈʌnriˈæliti〕 *n., pl.* **-ties.** ①不眞實; 空幻; 虛僞。②不眞實的事物。③虛幻之傾向。④不切實際。

un·re·al·ize 〔ʌnˈriəlaɪz; ʌnˈriəlaiz〕 *v.t.,* **-ized, -iz·ing.** 使變空幻。

un·re·al·ized 〔ʌnˈriəlaɪzd; ʌnˈriəlaizd〕 *adj.* ①未實現的;未兌現的。②未被察覺的;未被人知的。

un·rea·son 〔ʌnˈrizṇ; ˈʌnˈriːzn〕 *n.* 缺乏理智;愚蠢;荒謬。

***un·rea·son·a·ble** 〔ʌnˈriznəbḷ; ʌnˈriːzṇəbl〕 *adj.* ①不合理的; 無理性的。②過度的; 過分的。 ③不切實際的; 不適當的。—**ness,** *n.* —**un·rea·son·a·bly,** *adv.*

un·rea·soned 〔ʌnˈrizənd; ʌnˈriːznd〕 *adj.* 非基於理性的;無理性的。

un·rea·son·ing 〔ʌnˈriznɪŋ; ʌnˈriːzṇiŋ〕 *adj.* 不運用推理的; 無理性的; 不合理的。—**ly,** *adv.*

un·rec·og·nized 〔ʌnˈrɛkəgˌnaɪzd; ˈʌnˈrekəgnaizd〕 *adj.* 未被識出的;未經承認的。

un·re·con·struct·ed 〔ˌʌnrikənˈstrʌktɪd; ˈʌnriːkənˈstrʌktid〕 *adj.* ①堅持原有意見、立場等而不願與現行環境妥協的。②〖美史〗(南方各州)於南北戰爭後不願接受重入聯邦之條件的。

un·reel 〔ʌnˈril; ˈʌnˈriːl〕 *v.t.* & *v.i.* ①自卷軸或卷輪上取下或鬆開。②慢慢敍述。③展開;進行。

UNREF, U.N.R.E.F. United Nations Refugee Emergency Fund.

un·re·fined 〔ˌʌnrɪˈfaɪnd; ˈʌnriˈfaind〕 *adj.* 未提鍊的;未經洗鍊的。

un·re·flect·ing 〔ˌʌnrɪˈflɛktɪŋ; ˈʌnriˈflektiŋ〕 *adj.* ①不反省的;不熟思的;無思慮的;沒有思想的。②不反射的。

un·re·flec·tive 〔ˌʌnrɪˈflɛktɪv; ˈʌnriˈflektiv〕 *adj.* 粗心大意的;草率的;魯莽的。

un·re·gard·ed 〔ˌʌnrɪˈgɑrdɪd; ˈʌnriˈgɑːdid〕 *adj.* 未被注意的;被忽視的。

un·re·gen·er·ate 〔ˌʌnrɪˈdʒɛnərɪt; ˈʌnriˈdʒenərit〕 *adj.* ①(精神上)不再生的;不獲重生的。②罪深的;邪惡的;仍與上帝爲敵的。③不信上帝之存在的。④固執己見的;堅持原有立場的;頑固的。—*n.* 不信上帝者;堅持己見者。(亦作 **unregenerated**)

un·reg·is·tered 〔ʌnˈrɛdʒɪstəd; ˈʌnˈredʒistəd〕 *adj.* 未登記的;未註册的。

un·re·lat·ed 〔ˌʌnrɪˈletɪd; ˈʌnriˈleitid〕 *adj.* ①無關的。②未被敍說的。

un·re·lent·ing 〔ˌʌnrɪˈlɛntɪŋ; ˈʌnriˈlentiŋ〕 *adj.* ①不寬容的; 嚴峻的; 執法如山

的；無慈悲的。②堅決不移的。③絲毫不懈的；寸步不放鬆的。—ly, adv.
un·re·li·a·ble 〔ˌʌnrɪˈlaɪəbl; ˈʌnriˈlaiəbl〕 *adj.* 不可靠的。
un·re·lieved 〔ˌʌnrɪˈlivd; ˈʌnriˈliːvd〕 *adj.* ①未減輕的；未緩和的。②未救濟的。—ly, *adv.*
un·re·li·gious 〔ˌʌnrɪˈlɪdʒəs; ˈʌnriˈlidʒəs〕 *adj.* ①無宗教的；反宗教的（＝irreligious）。②與宗教無關的；非宗教的。
un·re·marked 〔ˌʌnrɪˈmɑrkt; ˈʌnriˈmɑːkt〕 *adj.* 未受注意的。
un·re·mit·ted 〔ˌʌnrɪˈmɪtɪd; ˈʌnriˈmitid〕 *adj.* ①未赦免的。②繼續不斷的；不間斷的。
un·re·mit·tent 〔ˌʌnrɪˈmɪtənt; ˌʌnriˈmitnt〕 *adj.* 未減退的（尤指發燒）。—ly, *adv.* —un·re·mit·tence, un·re·mit·ten·cy, *n.*
un·re·mit·ting 〔ˌʌnrɪˈmɪtɪŋ; ˌʌnriˈmitiŋ〕 *adj.* ①不停的；無間斷的。②不鬆懈的；堅毅的。—ly, *adv.*
un·re·mu·ner·a·tive 〔ˌʌnrɪˈmjunəˌretɪv; ˈʌnriˈmjuːnərətiv〕 *adj.* 無報酬的；無利益的；不賺錢的。—ly, *adv.*
un·rent 〔ʌnˈrɛnt; ʌnˈrent〕 *adj.* 未撕破的；未受侵擾的；未受損害的。
un·re·quit·ed 〔ˌʌnrɪˈkwaɪtɪd; ˈʌnriˈkwaitid〕 *adj.* ①得不到報答的；無報答的。*unrequited* love. 單戀。②無報償的；無報酬的。③無報復的。
un·re·served 〔ˌʌnrɪˈzɝvd; ˈʌnriˈzəːvd〕 *adj.* ①直言無隱的；率直的；無保留的。②無限制的；無條件的；完全的。—ly, *adv.* —ness, *n.*
un·re·spon·sive 〔ˌʌnrɪˈspɑnsɪv; ˈʌnrisˈpɔnsiv〕 *adj.* 無反應的；感受性遲鈍的；無同情的；冷淡的。—ly, *adv.* —ness, *n.*
***un·rest** 〔ʌnˈrɛst; ˈʌnˈrest, ʌn-〕 *n.* ①不安的狀態。②動蕩的局面。
un·re·strained 〔ˌʌnrɪˈstrend; ˈʌnrisˈtreind〕 *adj.* ①無約束的；無拘束的；無自制力的。②自然的；（態度等）從容的。—ness, *n.*
un·re·straint 〔ˌʌnrɪˈstrent; ˈʌnrisˈtreint〕 *n.* 無約束；無限制；無自制；放縱。
un·rid·dle 〔ʌnˈrɪdl̩; ʌnˈridl〕 *v.t.*, -rid·dled, -rid·dling. 解（謎等）；解明。
un·rig 〔ʌnˈrɪg; ʌnˈrig〕 *v.t.*, -rigged, -rig·ging. ①〖航海〗卸除（船）之索具。②除去…的裝備。③〖俗〗脫掉（衣服）；脫掉…的衣服。
un·right·eous 〔ʌnˈraɪtʃəs; ʌnˈraitʃəs〕 *adj.* ①不義的；不正直的；不公平的。②邪惡的；有罪的。—ly, *adv.* —ness, *n.*
un·right·ful 〔ʌnˈraɪtfəl; ˈʌnˈraitful〕 *adj.* ①不義的；不公正的。②不合法的。
un·rip 〔ʌnˈrɪp; ˈʌnˈrip〕 *v.t.*, -ripped, -rip·ping. ①撕開；扯掉；割掉。②透露；暴露；揭示。
un·ripe 〔ʌnˈraɪp; ˈʌnˈraip〕 *adj.* ①未成熟的；生的；發育未成熟的。②時機未熟的。
un·ri·val(l)ed 〔ʌnˈraɪvl̩d; ʌnˈraivəld〕 *adj.* 無匹的；無雙的。
un·robe 〔ʌnˈrob; ˈʌnˈroub〕 *v.t. & v.i.*, -robed, -rob·ing. 脫去外衣（特指法衣等）；脫掉衣服。
un·roll 〔ʌnˈrol; ˈʌnˈroul〕 *v.t.* ①展開（成捲或摺合之物）。②公開；揭開；使顯露。—*v.i.* ①（成捲或摺合物）展開；打開。②顯露；公開。
un·ro·man·tic 〔ˌʌnroˈmæntɪk; ˈʌnrəˈmæntik〕 *adj.* 平淡無奇的；實際的；平庸的。
un·roof 〔ʌnˈruf; ʌnˈruːf〕 *v.t.* 揭去…之頂或覆蓋物。
un·root 〔ʌnˈrut, -ˈrʊt; ʌnˈruːt, -ˈrut〕 *v.t. & v.i.* 連根拔除；根絕。
un·root·ed 〔ʌnˈrutɪd; ʌnˈruːtid〕 *adj.* ①沒有連根拔起的。②（人）無根的；漂蕩的。
UNRRA, U.N.R.R.A. 〔ˈʌnrə; ˈʌnrə〕 聯合國善後救濟總署（爲*U*nited *N*ations *R*elief and *R*ehabilitation *A*dministration 之略）。
un·ruf·fled 〔ʌnˈrʌfl̩d; ˈʌnˈrʌfld〕 *adj.* ①平靜的；平穩的。②未受擾亂的；未被激動的；冷靜的。③（衣服等）平的；未弄縐的。
un·ru·ly 〔ʌnˈrulɪ; ʌnˈruːli〕 *adj.*, -li·er, -li·est. ①難控制的；不守法的。②波濤洶湧的。—un·ru·li·ness, *n.*
un·sad·dle 〔ʌnˈsædl̩; ˈʌnˈsædl〕 *v.*, -dled, -dling. —*v.t.* ①解下（馬）之鞍。②使落下馬。—*v.i.* 解下馬鞍。
un·safe 〔ʌnˈsef; ˈʌnˈseif〕 *adj.* 不安全的。—ly, *adv.*
un·safe·ty 〔ʌnˈseftɪ; ˈʌnˈseifti〕 *n.* 不安全；不安全狀態；危險。
un·said 〔ʌnˈsɛd; ˈʌnˈsed〕 *v.* pt. & pp. of unsay. —*adj.* 未說出口的；不講出的。
un·sal(e)·a·ble 〔ʌnˈseləbl̩; ˈʌnˈseiləbl〕 *adj.* 不能賣的；不好銷的。—*n.* 不能賣的東西。
un·sal·a·ried 〔ʌnˈsælərɪd; ʌnˈsælərid〕 *adj.* 無薪給的；無固定薪水的。
un·san·i·tar·y 〔ʌnˈsænəˌtɛrɪ; ˈʌnˈsænitəri〕 *adj.* 不衞生的。
***un·sat·is·fac·to·ry** 〔ˌʌnsætɪsˈfæktrɪ, -tərɪ; ˈʌnˌsætisˈfæktri, -təri〕 *adj.* 不能令人滿意的。—un·sat·is·fac·to·ri·ly, *adv.*
un·sat·u·rat·ed 〔ʌnˈsætʃəˌretɪd; ʌnˈsætʃəreitid〕 *adj.* 未飽和的；不飽和的；溶解不完全的。
un·sa·vor·y 〔ʌnˈsevərɪ; ˈʌnˈseivəri〕 *adj.* ①無味的。②氣味不好的。③道德上令人不愉快的；臭名的；令人厭惡的。（英亦作 **unsavoury**）
un·say 〔ʌnˈse; ˈʌnˈsei〕 *v.t.*, -said, -say·ing. 取消（前言）。
UNSC United Nations Security Council. 聯合國安全理事會。
un·scathed 〔ʌnˈskeðd; ˈʌnˈskeiðd〕 *adj.* 未受損傷的；未受傷害的。
un·schooled 〔ʌnˈskuld; ʌnˈskuːld〕 *adj.* ①未受過正式教育的；未受到訓練的；沒進過學校的。②天生的；自然的。③沒有學校的。
un·sci·en·tif·ic 〔ˌʌnsaɪənˈtɪfɪk; ˈʌnˌsai-ənˈtifik〕 *adj.* ①不科學的；不合科學原理或法則的。②未諳科學法則的；無科學知識的。
un·scram·ble 〔ʌnˈskræmbl̩; ʌnˈskræmbl〕 *v.t.*, -scram·bled, -scram·bling. 〖俗〗①整理；整頓（雜亂之物）。②調整收音機之頻率使（播音）變清晰。—un·scram·bler, *n.*
un·screened 〔ʌnˈskrind; ʌnˈskriːnd〕 *adj.* ①無屏障的；無保護的。②未篩過的。③沒有改編（拍）成電影的。
un·screw 〔ʌnˈskru; ˈʌnˈskruː〕 *v.t.* ①鬆開或除掉…之螺釘；旋出（螺釘）。②將瓶蓋或罐蓋旋鬆以打開（瓶或罐）。—*v.i.*（螺釘）鬆開；可旋出。
un·scru·pu·lous 〔ʌnˈskrupjələs; ʌnˈskruːpjuləs〕 *adj.* ①無遠慮的；不謹慎的。②無道德的；寡廉鮮恥的。③狂妄的；無忌憚的；無所不爲的。—ly, *adv.* —ness, *n.*
un·seal 〔ʌnˈsil; ˈʌnˈsiːl〕 *v.t.* ①開…之封緘。②使開啓；解除約束。
un·sealed 〔ʌnˈsild; ˈʌnˈsiːld〕 *adj.* ①沒有封口的；沒有加封的。②未證實的；未確定的。
un·search·a·ble 〔ʌnˈsɝtʃəbl̩; ʌnˈsəːtʃəbl〕 *adj.* 不能深究的；不可思議的；神祕

的。—**un·search·a·bly,** *adv.*

un·sea·son·a·ble [ʌnˈsizn̩əbl; ʌnˈsiːzn̩əbl] *adj.* ①不合季節的。②不合時宜的。③不適於某種場合的。**—un·sea·son·a·bly,** *adv.* **—ness,** *n.*

un·sea·soned [ʌnˈsizn̩d; ˈʌnˈsiːznd] *adj.* ①不慣於某地之風土的; 不慣於某種氣候的。②未加調味品的;未加佐料的。③未乾的。④沒有經驗的;不成熟的。

un·seat [ʌnˈsit; ˈʌnˈsiːt] *v.t.* ①將(騎者)拋下馬鞍;使落馬。②使去職;罷免。③將…從基礎上移開。

un·sea·wor·thy [ʌnˈsi,wɜðɪ; ˈʌnˈsiː,wəːði] *adj.* 不堪航海的;不適航的;不耐風浪的。

un·se·cured [,ʌnsɪˈkjurd; ˈʌn-siˈkjuəd] *adj.* ①沒有抵押的;沒有擔保的。②沒有扣緊的;沒有繫牢的。

un·see·ing [ʌnˈsiɪŋ; ˈʌnˈsiːiŋ] *adj.* ①不注意的;未看到的。②盲的;瞎的。**—ly,** *adv.*

un·seem·ly [ʌnˈsimlɪ; ʌnˈsiːmli] *adj.* 不適宜的。—*adv.* 不適宜地。**—un·seem·li·ness,** *n.*

un·seen** [ʌnˈsin; ˈʌnˈsiːn] *adj.* ①未見過的。②看不見的。③一看就懂的;不需事先研究就能明瞭的。—*n.* ①未加研究而照字面譯的一段文字。②看不見的事物。the unseen*** 精神世界。

un·seg·re·gat·ed [ʌnˈsɛgrə,getɪd; ʌnˈsegrigeitid] *adj.* 沒有種族隔離的;打成一片的。

un·self·con·scious [,ʌnsɛlfˈkɑnʃəs; ,ʌnselfˈkɔnʃəs] *adj.* 自然的;不裝腔作勢的。

un·self·ish [ʌnˈsɛlfɪʃ; ˈʌnˈselfiʃ] *adj.* 不自私的;爲他人着想的; 無我的。**—ly,** *adv.* **—ness,** *n.*

un·sell [ʌnˈsɛl; ʌnˈsel] *v.t.*, **-sold, -sell·ing.** 勸(人)對某事不要支持或表示信心等;勸人放棄。

un·sell·a·ble [ʌnˈsɛləbl; ʌnˈseləbl] *adj.* 無人要買的;賣不出去的。

un·sent [ʌnˈsɛnt; ʌnˈsent] *adj.* 未寄出去的。

un·sent-for [ʌnˈsɛnt,fɔr; ʌnˈsentfɔː] *adj.* 未邀請的;未召喚的。

un·serv·ice·a·ble [ʌnˈsɜvɪsəbl; ˈʌnˈsəːvisəbl] *adj.* 不實用的;無用的;無益的;不耐用的。

un·set·tle [ʌnˈsɛtl; ˈʌnˈsetl] *v.*, **-tled, -tling.** —*v.t.* ①攪亂;使不安定。②使(心)不寧靜。—*v.i.* 動搖;心緒不寧。**—ment,** *n.*

un·set·tled [ʌnˈsɛtld; ˈʌnˈsetld] *adj.* ①未決的;未定的。②易變的;不定的。③無人居住的。④未償付的。⑤未整理就緒的。⑥紊亂的;無秩序的。⑦東飄西蕩的。**—ness,** *n.*

un·sex [ʌnˈsɛks; ʌnˈseks] *v.t.* ①使失去性別之特徵;(尤指)使失去婦女之特性。②使失去性行爲之能力;去勢。

un·shack·le [ʌnˈʃækl; ˈʌnˈʃækl] *v.t.*, **-led, -ling.** ①除去…的枷鎖;釋放;使獲自由。②解除約束或限制。

un·shak·en [ʌnˈʃekən; ˈʌnˈʃeikən] *adj.* 不動搖的。

un·shape·ly [ʌnˈʃeplɪ; ˈʌnˈʃeipli] *adj.* ①不成形的。②不成比例的;醜怪的。

un·shared [ʌnˈʃɛrd; ʌnˈʃɛəd] *adj.* 獨享的;專有的。

un·sheathe [ʌnˈʃið; ˈʌnˈʃiːð] *v.t.*, **-sheathed, -sheath·ing.** ①抽(刀)出鞘。②揭去(覆蓋物);脫去(衣服)。

un·shell [ʌnˈʃɛl; ʌnˈʃel] *v.t.* 去殼;揭露。

un·ship [ʌnˈʃɪp; ʌnˈʃip] *v.t.* ①自船卸(貨)。②自固定地方移去(槳等)。—*v.i.* 卸貨。

un·shod [ʌnˈʃɑd; ˈʌnˈʃɔd] *adj.* ①未穿鞋的;赤足的。②未釘鐵蹄的(馬)。

un·sight [ʌnˈsaɪt; ˈʌnˈsait] *adj.* 未曾過目的;未檢驗的。

un·sight·ed [ʌnˈsaɪtɪd; ˈʌnˈsaitid] *adj.* ①未看到的。②未裝瞄準器的。

un·sight·ly [ʌnˈsaɪtlɪ; ʌnˈsaitli] *adj.* 不雅觀的;難看的。

unsight unseen 未過目;未見過(= sight unseen). to buy a thing *unsight unseen.* 購買一樣沒有過目、沒有檢驗過的東西。

un·signed [ʌnˈsaɪnd; ˈʌnˈsaind] *adj.* 未簽名的。

un·sized [ʌnˈsaɪzd; ʌnˈsaizd] *adj.* 未上膠水的;未塗漿糊的。

un·skilled [ʌnˈskɪld; ˈʌnˈskild] *adj.* ①沒有特殊技能的。②不須特別技術的。③不熟練的;笨手笨脚的。④不擅長的。***the unskilled*** 不熟練之工人。

unskilled labor ①不需技術就能做的工作。②作粗活之全體勞工。

un·skil(l)·ful [ʌnˈskɪlfəl; ˈʌnˈskilful] *adj.* ①笨拙的; 拙劣的; 不熟練的。②無技能的。**—ly,** *adv.*

un·sling [ʌnˈslɪŋ; ʌnˈsliŋ] *v.t.* **-slung, -sling·ing.** ①由懸掛處取下(獵鎗等)。②取去…之吊索;自吊索上放下。

un·snap [ʌnˈsnæp; ʌnˈsnæp] *v.t.*, **-snapped, -snap·ping.** 解開(皮包等)之扣;解開扣以鬆之。

un·snarl [ʌnˈsnɑrl; ʌnˈsnɑːl] *v.t.* 解開(結等);清理(雜物等)。

un·so·cia·bil·i·ty [,ʌnsoʃəˈbɪlətɪ; ˈʌn,souʃəˈbiliti] *n.* 不愛交際;不與人親近。

un·so·cia·ble [ʌnˈsoʃəbl; ʌnˈsouʃəbl] *adj.* ①不愛交際的;不易親近的。②不能並存的;不相容的。**—ness,** *n.* **—un·so·cia·bly,** *adv.*

un·so·cial [ʌnˈsoʃəl; ʌnˈsouʃəl] *adj.* ①不喜與人共處的;不合羣的。② =**unsociable. —ly,** *adv.*

un·sol·der [ʌnˈsɑdɚ; ˈʌnˈsɔldə] *v.t.* ①拆開(銲合之物)。②使分開; 使離開。

un·sol·id [ʌnˈsɑlɪd; ʌnˈsɔlid] *adj.* ①非固體的;液體或氣體的。②不實在的;不堅定的;空虛的;無根據的。

un·so·phis·ti·cat·ed [,ʌnsəˈfɪstɪ,ketɪd; ˈʌn-səˈfistikeitid] *adj.* ①單純的;天眞的。②純粹的;眞正的。③簡單的;簡陋的。**—ness,** *n.*

un·so·phis·ti·ca·tion [,ʌnsə,fɪstɪˈkeʃən; ˈʌn-sə,fistiˈkeiʃən] *n.* 天眞; 敦厚; 樸質。

un·sought [ʌnˈsɔt; ˈʌnˈsɔːt] *adj.* ①未追求的;未尋求的。②未請求的。③未探究的。

un·sound [ʌnˈsaund; ˈʌnˈsaund] *adj.* ①不健康的。②不堅固的。③不健全的; 不根據事實或眞理的。④睡得不熟的。⑤(貨物等)有瑕疵的;有缺點的;損壞的。⑥財務上不穩固的;不可靠的。**—ly,** *adv.*

un·spar·ing [ʌnˈspɛrɪŋ; ʌnˈspɛəriŋ] *adj.* ①慷慨的; 不吝惜的; 不節儉的。②嚴酷的;不饒人的。**—ly,** *adv.*

un·speak·a·ble [ʌnˈspikəbl; ʌnˈspiː-kəbl] *adj.* ①無法形容的; 不能以言語表達的。②極惡劣的; 壞不堪言的。③不可以說出來的; 不能說的。**—ness,** *n.* **—un·speak·a·bly,** *adv.*

un·sphere [ʌnˈsfɪr; ˈʌnˈsfiə] *v.t.*, **-sphered, -spher·ing.** 使離開其範圍;使失勢; 取代。

un·spo·ken [ʌnˈspokən; ˈʌnˈspou-kən] *adj.* ①不言而喻的; 暗示的。②不說話

的;靜默的。③沒有人交談的;沒有人和…說話的〖常to〗。

un·sports·man·like 〔ʌn'sportsmən,laɪk, -'spɔr-;'ʌn'spɔːtsmənlaik〕 *adj.* 不光明正大的;不誠實的。

un·spot·ted 〔ʌn'spɑtɪd; 'ʌn'spɔtid〕 *adj.* ①無斑點的。②無汚點的;無瑕疵的;純潔的; 清白的。③不受汚染的。

un·sprung 〔ʌn'sprʌŋ; ʌn'sprʌŋ〕 *adj.* ①無彈簧的。②(陷阱) 未彈回的。

un·sta·ble 〔ʌn'stebl̩; 'ʌn'steibl〕 *adj.* ①不穩定的;不穩固的。②易變的。③〖化〗不安定的。④情緒上不穩定的。⑤行動不規則的。

un·stain·a·ble 〔ʌn'stenəbl̩; ʌn'steinəbl〕 *adj.*①不能染汚的。②道德上無可指責的。

un·stained 〔ʌn'stend;ʌn'steind〕 *adj.* ①無汚點的;潔淨的。②道德上無瑕疵的。

un·states·man·like 〔ʌn'stetsmən,laɪk; 'ʌn'steitsmənlaik〕 *adj.* 無政治家風度的。

un·stead·y 〔ʌn'stɛdɪ; 'ʌn'stedi〕 *adj.* ①不穩的;不安定的。②易變的。③不規則的;不平均的。—*v.t.* 使變得不穩固或不安定。 —**un·stead·i·ly**, *adv.* —**un·stead·i·ness**, *n.*

un·step 〔ʌn'stɛp;ʌn'step〕 *v.t.*, **-stepped, -step·ping.** 〖航海〗由桅座移去(桅等)。

un·stick 〔ʌn'stɪk;'ʌn'stik〕 *v.t.*, **-stuck, -stick·ing.** 扯開或鬆開(粘合之物);使不再粘合或附着。 ***come unstuck*** 〖俚〗弄糟;失敗。

un·stint·ed 〔ʌn'stɪntɪd; ʌn'stintid〕 *adj.* 不吝嗇的;充裕的;豐富的。—**ly**, *adv.*

un·stop 〔ʌn'stɑp; 'ʌn'stɔp〕 *v.t.*, **-stopped, -stop·ping.** ①拔去…之塞。②拔開(風琴之)音栓。③除去…之障礙; 開放。

un·stop·pa·ble 〔ʌn'stɑpəbl̩;ʌn'stɔpəbl〕*adj.* 擋不住的;阻止不了的;無法擊敗的。

un·strained 〔ʌn'strend;ʌn'streind〕 *adj.* ①未濾淨的。 ②不勉强的; 不牽强附會的; 自然的。

un·strap 〔ʌn'stræp; 'ʌn'stræp〕 *v.t.*, **-strapped, -strap·ping.** 解去皮帶、束帶。

un·stressed 〔ʌn'strɛst;'ʌn'strest〕*adj.* ①不加重的;不强調的。②不重讀的(音節)。

un·string 〔ʌn'strɪŋ; 'ʌn'striŋ〕 *v.t.*, **-strung, -string·ing.** ①解下或放鬆(絃樂器、弓等)之絃。②使鬆弛。③使(神經)衰弱;使(神經)錯亂。④從絃或線串上取下。

un·struc·tured 〔,ʌn'strʌktʃəd; 'ʌn'strʌktʃəd〕 *adj.* ①無組織的。②不屬於社會或階級的。

un·strung 〔ʌn'strʌŋ; 'ʌn'strʌŋ〕 *v.* pt. & pp. of **unstring.** —*adj.* ①(絃樂器、弓等)未上絃的;絃鬆的。②神經衰弱的; 不能抑制的; 失去自制力的。

un·stuck 〔ʌn'stʌk; ʌn'stʌk〕 *adj.* ①鬆開的。②失去控制的; 失去一致性的; 受到頓挫的。—*v.* pt. & pp. of **unstick.**

un·stud·ied 〔ʌn'stʌdɪd; 'ʌn'stʌdid〕 *adj.* ①未學過的; 不熟諳的。②非由研究或努力而獲得的。③天然的; 自然的。

un·sub·stan·tial 〔,ʌnsəb'stænʃəl; 'ʌn-səb'stænʃəl〕 *adj.* ①無實體的; 無實質的。②不堅固的;薄弱的;輕的。③虛浮的; 空幻的。④無事實根據的。—**i·ty**, *n.* —**ly**, *adv.*

un·suc·cess·ful 〔,ʌnsək'sɛsfəl; 'ʌn-sək'sesful〕 *adj.* ①未成功的;失敗的;無結果的。an *unsuccessful* business. 未成功的事務。②不幸的。—**ly**, *adv.* —**ness**, *n.*

un·suit·a·ble 〔ʌn'sjutəbl̩; 'ʌn'sjuːtəbl〕 *adj.*不合適的;不適當的。—**un·suit·a·bil·i·ty**, *n.* —**un·suit·a·bly**, *adv.*

un·suit·ed 〔ʌn'sjutɪd;'ʌn'sjuːtid〕 *adj.* 不適合的;不適當的;不相稱的。

un·sung 〔ʌn'sʌŋ; 'ʌn'sʌŋ〕 *adj.* ①未被詩人禮讚的;未在詩或歌中被讚頌的;有功績而未爲人所祝賀的。②未被唱的(歌)。

un·sure 〔ʌn'ʃur; ʌn'ʃuə〕 *adj.* 不肯定的;不確定的。—**ly**, *adv.*

un·sur·passed 〔,ʌnsə'pæst; 'ʌn-sə'pɑːst〕 *adj.* (同類中之)最優的; 凌駕其餘的。

un·sus·pect·ing 〔,ʌnsə'spɛktɪŋ;'ʌn-səs'pektiŋ〕 *adj.* 無懷疑的;信任的。—**ly**, *adv.*

un·sus·pi·cious 〔,ʌnsə'spɪʃəs; 'ʌn-səs'piʃəs〕 *adj.* ①無疑慮的。②不引起懷疑的。③不懷疑他人的。—**ly**, *adv.*

un·swear 〔ʌn'swɛr; ʌn'swɛə〕 *v.t.* & *v.i.*, **-swore, -sworn, -swear·ing.** ①毀棄誓言;發新誓以毀前誓。②誓絕;棄絕。

un·swept 〔ʌn'swɛpt; ʌn'swept〕 *adj.* 未打掃的。

un·swerv·ing 〔ʌn'swɝvɪŋ; ʌn'swəː-viŋ〕 *adj.*①堅定不移的。②忠實的。—**ly**, *adv.*

un·sworn 〔ʌn'sworn; ʌn'swɔːn〕 *adj.* ①未宣誓的。 an *unsworn* witness. 一個未宣誓的證人。②非正式宣告的。—*v.* pp. of **unswear.**

un·sym·met·ri·cal 〔,ʌnsɪ'mɛtrɪkl̩; 'ʌn-si'metrikl〕 *adj.* 不勻稱的;不調和的;不對稱的。 —**ly**, *adv.*

un·sym·pa·thet·ic 〔,ʌnsɪmpə'θɛtɪk; 'ʌn,simpə'θetik〕 *adj.*①不表同情的;冷淡的;無情的。②不共鳴的。—**al·ly**, *adv.*

un·sys·tem·at·ic 〔,ʌnsɪstə'mætɪk; 'ʌn,sisti'mætik〕 *adj.* 無組織的;無規律的;無系統的。 —**al·ly**, *adv.*

un·taint·ed 〔ʌn'tentɪd; 'ʌn'teintid〕 *adj.* 無汚點的;無瑕疵的。—**ly**, *adv.*

un·tamed 〔ʌn'temd; ʌn'teimd〕 *adj.* ①未馴服的。②不能抑制的; 難控馭的。

un·tan·gle 〔ʌn'tæŋgl̩;'ʌn'tæŋgl〕 *v.t.*, **-gled, -gling.** 排解(糾紛); 解決(繁難)。

un·tapped 〔ʌn'tæpt; 'ʌn'tæpt〕 *adj.* (桶的)塞子未開的;未使用過的。

un·taught 〔ʌn'tɔt; 'ʌn'tɔːt〕 *adj.* ①未受過教育的;無知的。②無師自通的;非學習而獲知的; 天生的。

UNTC United Nations Trustee Council. 聯合國託管理事會。

un·teach 〔ʌn'titʃ; 'ʌn'tiːtʃ〕 *v.t.*, **-taught, -teach·ing.** ①使遺忘以前學過的事物。②使相信或教以與以前所教過的相反事物。③教以與某事相反的事物。

un·tech·ni·cal 〔ʌn'tɛknəkl̩; ʌn'tek-nikl〕 *adj.* 非技術的。

un·tem·pered 〔ʌn'tɛmpəd;'ʌn'tem-pəd〕 *adj.* ①未調勻的。②未精鍊的。③未緩和的。

un·ten·a·ble 〔ʌn'tɛnəbl̩; 'ʌn'tenəbl〕 *adj.* ①難防守的。②難維持的; 難獲支持的。③不適於居住的。 —**un·ten·a·bil·i·ty**, *n.* —**un·ten·a·bly**, *adv.*

un·test·ed 〔ʌn'tɛstɪd; ʌn'testid〕 *adj.* 未經考驗的; 未經試驗的。

un·thank·ful 〔ʌn'θæŋkfəl;'ʌn'θæŋk-ful〕 *adj.* ①不感謝的; 不感恩的。②未得到感謝的; 未被賞識的。—**ly**, *adv.* —**ness**, *n.*

un·think 〔ʌn'θɪŋk; ʌn'θiŋk〕 *v.*, **-thought, -think·ing.** —*v.t.* 取消…的念頭;對…改變主意;重考慮;遺忘。—*v.i.* 停止思想。

un·think·a·ble 〔ʌn'θɪŋkəbl̩; ʌn'θiŋkəbl] *adj.* ①不能被想像到的; 無法設想的。②〖英俗〗極端不可能的;想起來令人害怕的。③不能考慮的。—*n.*(常*pl.*)不能想像之事物。

un·think·ing [ʌnˈθɪŋkɪŋ;ˈʌnˈθiŋkiŋ] *adj.* ①無思想的; 缺乏思考力的。②未加思考的; 輕率的。③不用腦筋的。④無意中的。⑤顯示沒有用思想的。—**ly,** *adv.*

un·thought [ʌnˈθɔt;ˈʌnˈθɔːt] *v.* pt. & pp. of **unthink.** —*adj.* 未加思考的; 未予深思的。

un·thought-of [ʌnˈθɔt,ɑv;ʌnˈθɔːt-ɔv] *adj.* 未想到的;意外的。

un·thread [ʌnˈθrɛd; ˈʌnˈθred] *v.t.* ①除去…之線。②解開 (糾纏物等)。③覓路穿出。④解決。

un·throne [ʌnˈθron; ʌnˈθroun] *v.t.*, **-throned, -thron·ing.** 廢…之王位。

un·ti·dy [ʌnˈtaɪdɪ; ʌnˈtaidi] *adj.*, **-di·er, -di·est,** *v.* —*adj.* ①亂七八糟的;不整潔的。②雜亂的。—*v.t.* 使不整潔;使雜亂。—**un·ti·di·ly,** *adv.* —**un·ti·di·ness,** *n.*

***un·tie** [ʌnˈtaɪ; ˈʌnˈtai] *v.*, **-tied, -ty·ing.** —*v.t.* ①解開; 解去…的束縛。②解放; 使自由。③解答(疑難)。—*v.i.* 變成爲解開的狀態。

‡un·til [ənˈtɪl;ənˈtil, ʌn-] *prep.* ①迄…之時;直到…時。Wait *until* tomorrow. 等到明天。②在…以前 (常用在否定句中)。He did not go *until* night. 他到夜間才走。—*conj.* ①迄…時; 直到…時。He waited *until* the sun had set. 他一直等到日落。②在…以前。I shan't do that *until* you come back. 要等到你回來我才做那件事。③直到…地方;直到…程度。He worked *until* he was too tired to do more. 他一直工作到累得不能再做時才休息。

un·time·ly [ʌnˈtaɪmlɪ;ʌnˈtaimli] *adj.* & *adv.* ①不合時宜的(地); 不合時季的(地)。②過早的(地)。—**un·time·li·ness,** *n.*

un·tired [ʌnˈtaɪrd; ʌnˈtaiəd] *adj.* 沒有疲倦的;仍有精力的。

un·tir·ing [ʌnˈtaɪrɪŋ; ʌnˈtaiəriŋ] *adj.* 不知疲倦的。—**ly,** *adv.*

un·ti·tled [ʌnˈtaɪtḷd; ʌnˈtaitld] *adj.*①無稱號的;無頭銜的;無標題的。②無權利的。

***un·to** [ˈʌntu, ˈʌntʊ, ˈʌntə; ˈʌntu, ˈʌntuː, ˈʌntə] *prep.* ①〖古,詩〗=**to.** ②=**until.** 〖注意〗在古語及詩歌中, **unto** 和 **to** 的意義相同, 但不能用作不定詞的記號。

un·told [ʌnˈtold; ˈʌnˈtould] *adj.* ①未說出的;未透露的;未說明的。②無數的; 太多的。③未計數的。

un·tomb [ʌnˈtum;ʌnˈtuːm] *v.t.* 從墳墓中挖出;挖掘出。

un·torn [ʌnˈtɔrn;ʌnˈtɔːn] *adj.* 未撕裂的;未撕破的;未拉斷的。

un·touch·a·ble [ʌnˈtʌtʃəbḷ; ʌnˈtʌtʃəbl] *adj.* ①不能觸摸的; 不能觸及的。②遠而不可及的。③ (恐被玷污或因宗教習俗之禁止而) 不許觸摸的。④不可批評的; 不容置疑的。⑤不能控制的。—*n.* ①印度最低階級之人。②被遺棄的人。③棘手的事。④無可疵議的人; 無瑕疵的人。

***un·touched** [ʌnˈtʌtʃt; ˈʌnˈtʌtʃt] *adj.* ①未吃或喝的。②不受感動的。③未論及的。④在原始狀態的;未受感染的。⑤未受損害的。⑥未碰到的;未觸及的。⑦未改變的;未受影響的。

un·to·ward [ʌnˈtord; ʌnˈtouəd] *adj.* ①不幸的;不順利的;困難的。②不適當的。③〖古〗剛愎的;執拗的。—**ly,** *adv.* —**ness,** *n.*

un·trained [ʌnˈtrend; ˈʌnˈtreind] *adj.* ①未受訓練的; 未經陶冶的。②未修剪的。—**ly,** *adv.*

un·tram·mel(l)ed [ʌnˈtræmḷd;ʌnˈtræmld] *adj.* 無阻礙的; 未受束縛的; 自由的; 未受限制的。

un·tried [ʌnˈtraɪd;ˈʌnˈtraid] *adj.*①未試過的;未經考驗的。②未經審訊的;未審理的。

un·trod·den [ʌnˈtrɑdn̩; ʌnˈtrɔdn] *adj.*足未踐踏的;杳無人跡的。(亦作 **untrod**)

un·trou·bled [ʌnˈtrʌbḷd;ʌnˈtrʌbld] *adj.* ①無煩累的; 沒有憂慮的; 不受煩擾的。②平靜的。

***un·true** [ʌnˈtru; ˈʌnˈtruː] *adj.* ①虛僞的; 虛妄的; 不正確的。②不忠實的。to be *untrue* to a person (principle). 不忠於某人 (某主義)。③不合標準的;不合原則的。—**un·tru·ly,** *adv.*

un·truss [ʌnˈtrʌs; ʌnˈtrʌs] *v.t.* ①鬆開…之捆束;解開。②使脫衣。③洩露;揭露。

un·trust·wor·thy [ʌnˈtrʌst,wɜðɪ; ˈʌnˈtrʌst,wəːði] *adj.* 不能信賴的;不可靠的。

un·trust·y [ʌnˈtrʌstɪ; ʌnˈtrʌsti] *adj.*, **-trust·i·er, -trust·i·est.** 不可靠的; 不忠的;不能寄予信心的。

un·truth [ʌnˈtruθ; ˈʌnˈtruːθ] *n.* ①虛僞;不眞實。②虛言;謊言。

un·truth·ful [ʌnˈtruθfəl; ˈʌnˈtruːθful] *adj.* 不忠誠的; 不誠實的; 虛僞的。—**ly,** *adv.* —**ness,** *n.*

un·tuck [ʌnˈtʌk; ˈʌnˈtʌk] *v.t.* 拆散;展開。

un·tun·a·ble [ʌnˈtjunəbḷ; ʌnˈtjuːnəbl] *adj.* ①不能調整到適當高度的。②不和諧的;非樂音的。

un·tune [ʌnˈtjun;ʌnˈtjuːn] *v.t.*, **-tuned, -tun·ing.** ①使走調。②擾亂;使不舒服。

un·tu·tored [ʌnˈtjutəd;ˈʌnˈtjuːtəd] *adj.* ①未受教育的; 無知的。②粗野的; 野蠻的。③幼稚的;天眞的。

un·twine [ʌnˈtwaɪn; ʌnˈtwain] *v.t.* & *v.i.*, **-twined, -twin·ing.** 解開(糾纏的東西); 分開;縷析。

un·twist [ʌnˈtwɪst; ˈʌnˈtwist] *v.t.* & *v.i.* 分開;鬆開(撚合之繩或線)。—**er,** *n.*

un·urged [ʌnˈɝdʒd; ʌnˈəːdʒd] *adj.* 無人催促的;自動自發的;自願的。

un·used [ʌnˈjuzd; ˈʌnˈjuːzd, for② ʌnˈjust; ˈʌnˈjuːst] *adj.* ①不用的;不使用的。②不習慣於…的。③從未用過的。

un·use·ful [ʌnˈjusfəl; ˈʌnˈjuːsfəl] *adj.* =**useless.**

***un·u·su·al** [ʌnˈjuʒuəl; ʌnˈjuːʒuəl] *adj.* 非常的;稀罕的;罕有的。—**ly,** *adv.* —**ness,** *n.*

un·ut·ter·a·ble [ʌnˈʌtərəbḷ; ʌnˈʌtərəbl] *adj.* ①不能說出的;非語言所能表達的。②全然的;徹底的。③無法說得出的;無法發音的。—**un·ut·ter·a·bly,** *adv.*

un·val·ued [ʌnˈvæljud; ʌnˈvæljuːd] *adj.* ①無價値的;不爲人重視的。②未估價的;無定價的。③〖古〗不能估價的; 無價的。

un·var·nished [ʌnˈvɑrnɪʃt; for ① ˈʌnˈvɑːniʃt, for ② ʌnˈvɑːniʃt] *adj.* ①未加油漆的。②未修飾的;率直的。

un·var·y·ing [ʌnˈvɛrɪɪŋ; ʌnˈvɛəriiŋ] *adj.* 不變化的;固定的;不變的。—**ly,** *adv.*

un·veil [ʌnˈvel; ʌnˈveil] *v.t.* & *v.i.* ①揭幕;揭面紗等。②揭露;顯示。—**ing,** *n.*

un·voiced [ʌnˈvɔɪst; ˈʌnˈvɔist] *adj.* ①未出聲的;未言的。②〖語音〗無聲的。

un·want·ed [ʌnˈwɑntɪd;ˈʌnˈwɔntid] *adj.* 不受歡迎的;多餘的;不要的。

un·warned [ʌnˈwɔrnd; ˈʌnˈwɔːnd]

adj. 事前未受警告的;無先兆的。

un·war·rant·a·ble [ʌn'wɑrəntəbl; ʌn'wɔrəntəbl] adj. ①難保證的; 難獲許可的;難認可的。②不當的。—**un·war·rant·a·bly**, adv.

un·war·rant·ed [ʌn'wɔrəntɪd; 'ʌn'wɔrəntid] adj. ①未獲保證的; 未保險的。②難保證的;難獲許可的。③不當的;無正當理由的。—**ly**, adv.

un·war·y [ʌn'wɛrɪ; ʌn'wɛəri] adj. 不小心的; 未提防的。—**un·war·i·ness**, n.

un·washed [ʌn'wɑʃt; 'ʌn'wɔʃt] adj. ①未洗的; 不潔的; 骯髒的。②未被波濤沖刷的。 —n. 無知的下層民衆。 *the* (*great*) *unwashed* 下層社會。

un·wa·ver·ing [ʌn'wevrɪŋ; ʌn'weivəriŋ] adj. 不動搖的; 堅定的; 穩定的;意志堅定的。—**ly**, adv.

un·wea·ried [ʌn'wɪrɪd; ʌn'wiərid] adj. ①不疲乏的; 不動勞的。②孜孜不倦的; 不屈不撓的。—**ly**, adv.

un·weave [ʌn'wiv; ʌn'wi:v] v.t., **-wove, -woven, -weav·ing.** 拆開; 縷析(織物)。

un·wed [ʌn'wɛd; 'ʌn'wed] adj. 未結婚的。

un·weighed [ʌn'wed; ʌn'weid] adj. ①未秤過的; 未過磅的。②未仔細考慮的。

***un·wel·come** [ʌn'wɛlkəm; ʌn'welkəm] adj. 不受歡迎的。

un·well [ʌn'wɛl; 'ʌn'wel] adj. ①有病的;病的。②〖俗〗在月經期的。

un·wept [ʌn'wɛpt; ʌn'wept] adj. ①無人哀悼的。②未灑淚的。

un·whole·some [ʌn'holsəm; 'ʌn'houlsəm] adj. ①不衞生的; 有害於身體的; 有害於健康的。②不健康的 (外表)。③(道德上)不健全的;有害的; 不道德的。 —**ly**, adv.

un·wield·y [ʌn'wildɪ; ʌn'wi:ldi] adj. 龐大而不易控制或運用的;笨重的。(亦作 **unwieldly**)

un·willed [ʌn'wɪld; ʌn'wild] adj. 非自願的;非故意的。

***un·will·ing** [ʌn'wɪlɪŋ; 'ʌn'wiliŋ] adj. ①不情願的;不願意的;勉强的。②反抗的; 頑强的;不服從的。—**ly**, adv. —**ness**, n.

un·winc·ing [ʌn'wɪnsɪŋ; ʌn'winsiŋ] adj. 不畏縮的;天不怕地不怕的。

un·wind [ʌn'waɪnd; 'ʌn'waind] v., **-wound, -wind·ing.** —v.t. ①將(捲起之物)打開。②解開(糾結之物); 展開(捲曲之物)。③使減少緊張;使心理放鬆。—v.i. ①解開;展開。②將身心放鬆。

un·wis·dom [ʌn'wɪzdəm; ʌn'wizdəm] n. ①愚昧;無知。②愚言;愚行。

***un·wise** [ʌn'waɪz; 'ʌn'waiz] adj. 不智的;愚蠢的。—**ly**, adv. —**ness**, n.

un·wish [ʌn'wɪʃ; ʌn'wiʃ] v.t. 停止希望(某事)。

un·wished-for [ʌn'wɪʃt‚fɔr; ʌn'wiʃtfɔ:] adj. 不希望的。

un·wit·nessed [ʌn'wɪtnɪst; ʌn'witnist] adj. ①未注意到的;未觀察到的。②無見證人簽名的。

un·wit·ting [ʌn'wɪtɪŋ; ʌn'witiŋ] adj. ①無心的; 不經意的; 非故意的。②不知情的; 無知的。—**ly**, adv. —**ness**, n.

un·wit·ty [ʌn'wɪtɪ; ʌn'witi] adj. 不聰明的;愚蠢的。

un·wom·an·ly [ʌn'wʊmənlɪ; ʌn'wumənli] adj. 不似女流的;不合婦女之行爲標準的。

un·wont·ed [ʌn'wʌntɪd; ʌn'wountid] adj. ①對某人或某事不熟悉或不習慣的〖to〗。②不尋常的; 非習常的; 稀罕的。—**ly**, adv.

un·work·a·ble [ʌn'wɝkəbl; 'ʌn'wə:kəbl] adj. 難施工的;難以處理的; 難運轉的; 難實行的。—**un·work·a·bil·i·ty**, n. —**un·work·a·bly**, adv.

un·world·li·ness [ʌn'wɝldlɪnɪs; ʌn'wə:ldlinis] n. ①非世俗行爲;超塵世行爲。②精神境界;超世俗性。

un·world·ly [ʌn'wɝldlɪ; ʌn'wə:ldli] adj. ①與塵世無關的; 脫離世俗的; 超俗的。②精神界的;天上的。

un·worn [ʌn'worn; ʌn'wɔ:n] adj. ①從來沒有穿過的; 不常被穿的 (衣服)。②沒有穿舊的; 沒有穿破的; 沒有受損的。③新鮮的; 清新的(精神、感覺等)。

***un·wor·thy** [ʌn'wɝðɪ; ʌn'wə:ði] adj., n., pl. **-thies.** —adj. ①無價值的。②不配的; 不相稱的; 不值得的 〖of〗. *unworthy* of respect. 不值得敬重。③卑鄙的;可恥的。④不應得的。⑤不足取的。—n. 不值得尊敬之人。—**un·wor·thi·ness**, n. —**un·wor·thi·ly**, adv.

un·wrap [ʌn'ræp; 'ʌn'ræp] v., **-wrapped, -wrap·ping.** —v.t. 啓開;解開; 打開(包裹等)。—v.i. 散開。

un·writ·ten [ʌn'rɪtn̩; 'ʌn'ritn] adj. ①非以文字記載的;口傳的;未記諸文字的。②未寫出的。③習慣的; 不成文的; 未正式寫出的。④空白的。

unwritten law ①不成文法。②殺死誘姦其妻或其女者之罪犯應減刑之原則或公意。

un·wrought [ʌn'rɔt; 'ʌn'rɔ:t] adj. ①未加工的; 未製造的。②未發展的; 未開發的;未開採的。

un·wrung [ʌn'rʌŋ; 'ʌn'rʌŋ] adj. 不被扭曲的。

un·yield·ing [ʌn'jildɪŋ; ʌn'ji:ldiŋ] adj. ①不屈的;剛硬的。②不屈服的;頑强的。—**ly**, adv. —**ness**, n.

un·yoke [ʌn'jok; 'ʌn'jouk] v., **-yoked, -yok·ing.** —v.t.①卸除(牛)之軛。②解除束縛。—v.i. ①卸軛。②停止工作。

un·zeal·ous [ʌn'zɛləs; ʌn'zeləs] adj. 不熱心的;不起勁的。

un·zip [ʌn'zɪp; ʌn'zip] v.t. & v.i., **-zipped, -zip·ping.** 將拉鍊拉開。

‡up [ʌp; ʌp] adv., prep., adj., n., v., **upped, up·ping.** —adv. ①向上地;在上地;向或近頂端地。②在較高的地方; 在較高的地位。③由小變大地; 由少變多地; 上漲。Prices are going *up*. 物價在上漲。④到被認爲較重要的地方; 向北方地; 在被認爲較重要的地方;處於較重要或較高的情況。He lives *up* north. 他住在北方。⑤在地平線上地。The sun is *up*. 太陽升起了。⑥趨向或處於直立的姿勢; 起來; 起床。Stand *up*. 站起來。He is *up* and down. 他已起床下樓了。⑦完全地;全然地;徹底地。Everything burnt *up*.一切都燒光了。⑧盡;終了;完結。Time is *up* now. 時間到了。⑨精通。He is (well) *up* in mathematics. 他精通數學。⑩在活動狀態中;在動作中。What is *up* with you? 怎麼一回事?⑪到講話者所在處或指定的地方。Bring things *up* to my house. 把這些東西帶到我家。⑫達於平等地位;不落後地。to keep *up* with the times. 趕上時代。⑬集攏地; 一起地。⑭在緊閉的狀態中。⑮儲存地。to store *up* supplies. 儲存供應品。⑯出現地; 提出地。⑰每;各。The score was seven *up* in the final quarter. 在最後一節比賽中雙方各得

七分。⑱〖棒球〗任打擊手；處於進攻之隊。⑲得分領先。⑳使停。㉑〖航海〗朝風地。***be up against*** 對抗；對付。***be up and about*** (or ***around***) 病後復元。***up and down*** 上下地；起伏地；往返地；前後地。***up to*** **a.** 直到；以至；以迄。*up to* the present. 直到現在。**b.** 正在做；即將做；從事。What is he *up to?* 他正在做甚麼？ **c.** 勝任；能作；及得上。He is not *up to* his job. 他不能勝任他的工作。**d.** 適於；適合。**e.** 應由(某人)擔任或負責。It's *up to* you. 由你決定。**f.** 到某一程度或部分。I am *up to* the eighth lesson. 我已讀到第八課。**g.** 高達；數達。—*prep.* ①向上；在上。to walk *up* a hill. 上山。②向上游；向內地。to travel *up* (the) country. 到內地旅行。③沿；穿過。She walked *up* the street. 她沿街而行。④在更遠或更高之處。He is *up* the street. 他在街的那一端。⑤逆向；逆流。to go *up* wind. 迎風而行。***up a tree*** 進退兩難；陷於窘境。***up hill and down dale*** 不顧一切。***up the pole*** =up a tree. —*adj.* ①向上的；上行的。an *up* train. 上行火車。②前行的；進步的。③在地面上的。④起床的。⑤不落後的。⑥近的。⑦有豐富知識的；有熟練技術的。⑧超過對方多少分的。⑨知曉的；熟悉的〖常 on, in〗。He is *up* on current events. 他對時事很熟悉。⑩完畢的。His hour is *up*. 他壽數已滿。⑪發生。What's *up* over there? 那邊發生了甚麼事？⑫舉起的。⑬在空中的。⑭起床的；未睡著的。to be *up* with insomnia. 患失眠症而睡不着。⑮漲的。⑯騎在馬背上的。⑰已建造的。⑱朝上。⑲反叛中的；動亂中的。⑳充滿信心的；興高采烈的。㉑出了岔子的；有問題的。㉒在途中的。㉓年紀大的。㉔被控告的。He is *up* for murder. 他以謀殺罪被控。㉕考慮中的。㉖和局的；得分相等的(前面常冠以數字)。It was 10 *up* at the end of the first half. 前半場比賽結束時，雙方各得十分。㉗在激動狀態中的。***be up and coming*** 有野心的；有前途的。***be up and doing*** 活躍；忙碌。—*n.* ①興盛。②上升；升高。③上行火車或汽車。④紅運高照之人；有財勢之人。⑤高地。⑥高漲。***on the up and up*** (or ***up-and-up***)〖俚〗坦白；誠實。***the ups and downs*** (人生之)盛衰；浮沉。—*v.t.*〖俗〗①增加；加速。to *up* output. 增加生產。②提高(賭注)。—*v.i.*〖俗〗①突然開始做某事(常與 and 和另一動詞連用)。Then he *upped* and ran away from home. 接著他突然離家出走。②跳起。③舉起〖常with〗。He *upped* with his fist. 他舉起拳頭。

UP, U.P. United Press. 合衆新聞社(與 INS 合併爲 UPI)。

up. ①upper. ②underproof.

U.P. 〔ˌjuˈpi;ˌjuːˈpiː〕 *adv.*〖俗〗完了。It's all *U.P.* with him. 他已經完了。

u.p. under proof.

up- 〖字首〗表 "up" 之義。

up-and-com·ing 〔ˈʌpənd ˈkʌmɪŋ; ˈʌpəndˈkʌmiŋ〕 *adj.*〖美俗〗①富於企業精神的；精力充沛的；活動的；進取的；前途有希望的。②日趨重要的。

up-and-down 〔ˈʌpənˈdaun; ˈʌpənˈdaun〕 *adj.* ①〖俗〗上下或往復動的；高低起伏的。②盛衰更迭的；浮沉的。③純然的；直截的。④垂直的。

up-and-up 〔ˈʌpənˈʌp, ˌʌpəndˈʌp; ˈʌpənˈʌp, ˌʌpəndˈʌp〕 *n.* 向上；進步；成功。***on the up-and-up***〖俗〗**a.** 進行順利的；在改良中的。**b.** 誠實的；率直的。

U·pan·i·shad 〔uˈpænɪˌʃæd, uˈpɑnɪˌʃɑd; uˈpʌniʃəd, -ˈpæn-〕〖梵〗*n.* 優波尼沙(吠陀經之一部，講人與宇宙之關係，加重古印度教之泛神論觀點)。

u·pas 〔ˈjupəs; ˈjuːpəs〕 *n.* ①爪哇產的一種桑科植物。②此種植物所產之乳狀毒汁(用以做毒箭頭)。③有毒之物。

up·beat 〔ˈʌpˌbit; ˈʌpbiːt〕 *n.* ①〖音樂〗上拍；非重音拍子(尤其在一小節之最後一音符)。②重振；復蘇；再度上升。

up·blaze 〔ʌpˈblez; ʌpˈbleiz〕 *v.i.*, **-blazed, -blaz·ing.** (火燄)上騰。

up·borne 〔ʌpˈbɔrn; ʌpˈbɔːn〕 *adj.* 高舉的；舉到高處的；被支持着的。

up·braid 〔ʌpˈbred; ʌpˈbreid〕 *v.t.* 譴責；叱責。—**er,** *n.*

up·braid·ing 〔ʌpˈbredɪŋ; ʌpˈbreidiŋ〕 *n.* 叱責；譴責。—*adj.* 叱責的；譴責的。—**ly,** *adv.*

up·breed 〔ˈʌpˌbrid; ˈʌpbriːd〕 *v.t.*, **-bred, -breed·ing.** 改良(牲畜)之品種。

up·bring·ing 〔ˈʌpˌbrɪŋɪŋ; ˈʌpˌbriŋiŋ〕 *n.* ①兒童期或青年期所受之教育。②教育方法；教養；人格陶冶。

up·build 〔ʌpˈbɪld; ʌpˈbild〕 *v.t.*, **-built, -build·ing.** 建立；設立。—**er,** *n.*

UPC Universal Product Code. 國際商品電腦代號。

up·cast 〔ˈʌpˌkæst; ˈʌpkɑːst〕 *adj.* 向上拋的；向上方的。—*n.* ①上拋；向上的拋擲。②向上拋擲之物。③礦坑中排出汚濁空氣之豎坑。—*v.t.* 將…向上拋；向上投擲。

up·chuck 〔ˈʌpˌtʃʌk; ˈʌptʃʌk〕 *v.t.* & *v.i.*〖俚〗嘔吐。

up·com·ing 〔ˈʌpˌkʌmɪŋ; ˈʌpkʌmiŋ〕 *adj.* 即將來臨的；接近的。

up·coun·try 〔ˈʌpˈkʌntrɪ; ˈʌpˈkʌntri〕 *n.* 內地。—*adj.* ①內地的；內陸的。②鄉間的；粗率的。—*adv.* 向內地；在內地。

up·date 〔ʌpˈdet; ʌpˈdeit〕 *v.*, **-dat·ed, -dat·ing,** *n.* —*v.t.* 將最近之事記入；使依照最近之方法及思想等。—*n.* 最新的資料。

up·do 〔ˈʌpdu; ˈʌpduː〕 *n.*, *pl.* **-dos.** 高髻。

up·draft 〔ˈʌpdræft; ˈʌpdrɑːft〕 *n.* 向上升之氣流或氣體等。

up·end 〔ʌpˈɛnd; ʌpˈend〕 *v.t.* & *v.i.* ①豎立。②將(意見、制度等)作大幅度改變。③擊敗(競爭中的對方)。

up·fold 〔ʌpˈfold; ʌpˈfould〕 *v.t.* 使收斂；關起；闔起。

up·gath·er 〔ʌpˈgæðə; ʌpˈgæðə〕 *v.t.* 收集；使收縮。

up·go·ing 〔ˈʌpˌgoɪŋ; ˈʌpgouiŋ〕 *adj.* 向上移動的；向上走的。

up·grade 〔ˈʌpˈgred; ˈʌpˈgreid〕 *n.*, *v.*, **-grad·ed, -grad·ing,** *adj.*, *adv.* —*n.* ①向上之斜坡。②增長或改善(前面常冠以 on the)。—*v.t.* 改良(動物)之品種；提高…之等級；提高…之品質。—*adj.* & *adv.* 上坡的(地)。

up·growth 〔ˈʌpˌgroθ; ˈʌpgrouθ〕 *n.* ①生長；發育；進步；發達。②生長物。

up·heav·al 〔ʌpˈhivl; ʌpˈhiːvəl〕 *n.* ①舉起；抬起。②(地面之)隆起。③大變動；激變；動亂。

up·heave 〔ʌpˈhiv; ʌpˈhiːv〕 *v.*, **-heaved, -hove, -heav·ing.** —*v.t.* ①舉起；使隆起。②造成大混亂。—*v.i.* 隆起；升起。

up·hill 〔ˈʌpˈhɪl; ˈʌpˈhil〕 *adj.* ①上坡的；爬上坡的；向上的。②困難的。③在高處的。—*adv.* 上坡地；向上地。—*n.* 上坡。

***up·hold** 〔ʌpˈhold; ʌpˈhould〕 *v.t.*, **-held** 〔-ˈhɛld; -ˈheld〕, **-hold·ing.** ①舉起；支持。②扶助；鼓勵；擁護。③贊成；支持。④〖英〗維護；保養。⑤〖英〗=**upholster.** —**er,** *n.*

up·hol·ster 〔ʌpˈholstɚ; ʌpˈhoulstə〕 *v.t.* ①爲(椅子、沙發等)裝上套、墊、彈簧等。②爲(房間)裝設簾幕、地毯等;裝潢。—**er,** *n.*

up·hol·ster·y 〔ʌpˈholstərɪ; ʌpˈhoulstəri〕 *n., pl.* **-ster·ies.** ①室內裝飾品(如椅子、沙發、窗帘、地毯之類)。②室內裝飾業。③椅套;椅墊。

UPI, U.P.I. United Press International. 合衆國際社。

Up Jen·kins, up Jen·kins 〔~ ˈdʒɛnkɪnz; ~ˈdʒenkinz〕 一種傳硬幣的遊戲。

up·keep 〔ˈʌpˌkip; ˈʌpkiːp〕 *n.* ①(土地、房屋、汽車等之)保養;(生活之)維持。②保養費;生活費。

***up·land** 〔ˈʌplənd, ˈʌpˌlænd; ˈʌplənd〕 *n. sing.* or *pl.* 丘陵地;丘阜;高地。—*adj.* 高地的;丘陵地的。—**er,** *n.*

***up·lift** 〔*v.* ʌpˈlɪft; ʌpˈlift *n.* ˈʌpˌlɪft; ˈʌplift〕 *v.t.* ①舉起; 抬起; 提高。②提高…社會地位; 改良…道德水準。③使精神爲之一振;使意氣昂揚。—*n.* ①提高;舉高;高揚。②〖地質〗隆起。③道德的向上; 精神昂揚。④社會風氣之向上。⑤乳罩。—**er,** *n.* —**ed,** *adj.*

up·look·ing 〔ˈʌpˌlukɪŋ; ˈʌpˈlukiŋ〕 *adj.* 向上看的;有志氣的;有進取心的。

up·most 〔ˈʌpˌmost; ˈʌpmoust〕 *adj.* 最上的;最高的。

‡**up·on** 〔əˈpɑn; əˈpɔn〕 *prep.* ①=on. ②向上。 ③位於高處。④迫近或接觸。⑤緊接着。***upon my word*** 的確;決無虛言。***upon this*** 於是。〖注意〗 **upon** 和 **on** 的意義和用法相同,不過 upon 在俗語和口語中較少用。

‡**up·per** 〔ˈʌpɚ; ˈʌpə〕 *adj.* ①較高的。the *upper* lip. 上唇。②(階級、地位等)較高的;上流的;上級的。③〖地質〗後紀的;後系的。④更遠離海洋的; 深入內陸的。 ***get*** (***gain,*** or ***have***) ***the upper hand of…*** 比…占優勢;占上風;勝過。***the upper story*** 〖俗〗腦子。—*n.* ①鞋幫。②〖俗〗上位;上鋪。***be on one's uppers*** **a.** 鞋底磨透的;只剩鞋幫的。**b.** 襤褸的。**c.** 窮困不堪的。

upper arm 上臂(肩與肘間之部分)。

up·per-brack·et 〔ˈʌpɚˈbrækɪt; ˈʌpəˈbrækit〕 *adj.* 高位的。

Upper Canada 1791–1840 間, 英屬加拿大之一省,今爲加拿大 Ontario 省之南部。

upper case 〖印刷〗①大寫字母。②放大寫字母之鉛字架。

up·per-case 〔ˈʌpɚˌkes; ˈʌpəkeis〕 *adj., n., v.,* **-cased, -cas·ing.** —*adj.* ①大寫的(字母)。②〖印刷〗大寫字盤的;大寫字母的。—*n.*大寫字母。—*v.t.*以大寫字母印刷或書寫。

up·per-class 〔ˈʌpɚˈklæs; ˈʌpəˈklɑːs〕 *adj.* ①上流社會的。②高年級的。

up·per·class·man 〔ˌʌpɚˈklæsmən; ˌʌpəˈklɑːsmən〕 *n., pl.* **-men.** 〖美〗中學或大學中的三、四年級學生。

upper crust ①麪包之上層硬殼。②〖美俗〗上流社會;貴族階級。③〖俚〗頭;帽。

up·per·cut 〔ˈʌpɚˌkʌt; ˈʌpəkʌt〕 *n., v.,* **-cut, -cut·ting.**—*n.*〖拳擊〗上擊。—*v.t.* & *v.i.* 上擊。

up·per·dog 〔ˈʌpɚˌdɔg; ˈʌpədɔg〕 *n.* 「=top dog.」

Upper House (議會之)上院(如英國的 House of Lords, 美國的 Senate).

up·per·most 〔ˈʌpɚˌmost; ˈʌpəmoust〕 *adj.* ①最高的; 最上的。②最主要的; 最有勢力的。—*adv.*①最高地;最上地。②最初;首先。

upper stage 多節火箭之第二或第三以上之火箭。

upper ten (**thousand**) 〖俗〗地位最高與最富有之一萬人;上流社會;貴族階級。

up·per·ten·dom 〔ˌʌpɚˈtɛndəm; ˌʌpəˈtendəm〕 *n.* 上流社會;貴族階級。

Upper Vol·ta 〔~ˈvɑltə; ~ˈvɔltə〕 上伏塔(西非之一共和國, 首都Ouagadougou).

upper works 〖航海〗乾舷(船裝貨後露出水面之部分)。

up·pish 〔ˈʌpɪʃ; ˈʌpiʃ〕 *adj.* 〖俗〗①傲慢不遜的;盛氣凌人的;勢利的。②〖英〗朝上的。—**ly,** *adv.* —**ness,** *n.*

up·pi·ty 〔ˈʌpətɪ; ˈʌpiti〕 *adj.* 〖俗〗=uppish.

up·raise 〔ʌpˈrez; ʌpˈreiz〕 *v.t.,* **-raised, -rais·ing.** ①舉起。②使振奮;鼓勵。

up·rate 〔ˈʌpˌret; ˈʌpreit〕 *v.t.,* **-rat·ed, -rat·ing.** 將…升等;提高…之等級。

up·rear 〔ʌpˈrɪr; ʌpˈriə〕 *v.t.* ①舉起;使升起。②養育。③建造。④提高…之尊嚴。—*v.i.* 升起。

***up·right** 〔ˈʌpˌraɪt, ʌpˈraɪt; ˈʌp-rait, ˈʌpˈrait〕 *adj.* ①直的;直立的。②正直的;誠實的。an *upright* man. 正直的人。③合乎正道的。—*adv.* 直地。Hold yourself *upright.* 站直。—*n.* ①立直的位置。②直立之物;直立部分。③(常*pl.*)足球球門柱子。④一種鋼琴。—**ly,** *adv.* —**ness,** *n.*

up·rise 〔*v.* ʌpˈraɪz; ʌpˈraiz *n.* ˈʌpˌraɪz; ˈʌpraiz〕 *v.,* **-rose, -ris·en, -ris·ing,** *n.* —*v.i.* ①上升;升起。②站起;起床。③登高。④增高; 長高。⑤起義; 暴動。⑥出現;行動起來。—*n.* ①升起。②上坡;登高。

***up·ris·ing** 〔ˈʌpˌraɪzɪŋ; ʌpˈraiziŋ〕 *n.* ①叛亂;叛變。②升起。③上斜坡。

up·riv·er 〔ˈʌpˌrɪvɚ; ˈʌpˌrivə〕 *adj.* & *adv.* 上游的(地); 通往上游的(地)。—*n.* 上游地帶。

***up·roar** 〔ˈʌpˌror; ˈʌpˌrɔː〕 *n.* 喧囂; 騷動。The meeting ended in (an) *uproar.* 會議在一陣喧囂中結束。

up·roar·i·ous 〔ʌpˈrorɪəs; ʌpˈrɔːriəs〕 *adj.* ①喧囂的; 騷動的。②無節制的;高聲的。③非常可笑的。—**ly,** *adv.* —**ness,** *n.*

***up·root** 〔ʌpˈrut; ʌpˈruːt〕 *v.t.* ①拔…之根;將…連根拔起。②根除;根絕;徹底消滅。③使離開(住所)。—*v.i.* 成爲無家可歸; 被連根拔起。—**er,** *n.*

up·rouse 〔ʌpˈrauz; ʌpˈrauz〕 *v.t.,* **-roused, -rous·ing.** 喚醒;喚起;激動;招惹。

up·rush 〔ˈʌpˌrʌʃ; ˈʌprʌʃ〕 *v.i.* 朝上衝。—*n.* 向上的衝擊或流動。

***up·set** 〔*v.* ʌpˈsɛt; ʌpˈset *n.* ˈʌpˌsɛt; ʌpˈset, ˈʌpset〕 *v.,* **-set, -set·ting,** *n., adj.* —*v.t.* ①顚覆; 傾覆; 推翻。②擾亂;使煩惱。③弄亂;使混亂。④擊敗(被認爲强悍之對手)。—*v.i.* 顚覆; 傾覆。—*n.* ①顚覆; 傾覆。②煩惱;煩亂。③不和;爭吵。④(運動中)出乎意料的結果。—*adj.* ①傾覆的。②受擾的;難過的。③弄亂的;零亂的。④無組織的;紊亂的。

upset price 拍賣時之底價。

up·shot 〔ˈʌpˌʃɑt; ˈʌpʃɔt〕 *n.* ①結局;結果;結論。②要旨; 要領。***in the upshot*** 最後;終於。

***up·side** 〔ˈʌpˈsaɪd, ˈʌpˌsaɪd; ˈʌpsaid〕 *n.* ①上側;上部;上段。②〖鐵路〗上行線月臺。

upside down ①倒轉; 倒置。②混亂;雜亂。

up·side-down 〔ˈʌpˌsaɪdˈdaun; ˈʌpsaidˈdaun〕 *adj.* ①倒置的;倒放的;顚倒的。②混亂的。

up·sides 〔ʌpˈsaɪdz; ˈʌpsaidz〕 *adv.* 〖蘇方〗 對等; 以其人之道還治其人之身; 報復

〖with〗. ***get upsides with*** 報復。

up·si·lon 〔'jupsələn; juːp'sailən〕 *n.* 希臘字母之第二十個字母(Υ, υ)。

up·stage 〔'ʌp'stedʒ; 'ʌp'steidʒ〕 *adv., adj., v.,* **-staged, -stag·ing,** *n.* —*adv.* 向舞臺後部地; 在舞臺後部地。—*adj.* ①舞臺後部的;與舞臺後部有關的。②〖俗〗高傲的;自滿自負的。—*v.t.* ①站於舞臺上而妨礙觀衆(對一演員)之視線,迫其表演時背對觀衆俾自己能出風頭; 搶…鏡頭。②勝過(別人)。③〖俗〗以驕慢態度對待。—*n.* ①後臺。②舞臺上較後之位置。

up·stair 〔'ʌp'stɛr; 'ʌp'stɛə〕 *adj.* 樓上的。

up·stairs** 〔*n.* ʌp'stɛrz *adj., adv.* 'ʌp'stɛrz; 'ʌp'stɛəz〕 *adv.* ①在樓上;向樓上。to go *upstairs.* 上樓。②〖俗〗(飛機)在高空。kick upstairs*** 明升暗降。—*adj.* 樓上的。—*n.* 樓上。

up·stand·ing 〔ʌp'stændɪŋ; ʌp'stændiŋ〕 *adj.* ①直立的。②姿勢體態良好的。③正直的。—**ness,** *n.*

up·start 〔*n., adj.* 'ʌp,stɑrt, *v.* ʌp'stɑrt; 'ʌp–stɑːt〕 *n.* ①暴發戶;暴富者;驟貴者。②傲慢自負的人。—*adj.* ①暴富的;平地一聲雷而爲高官的。②傲慢的。—*v.i.* ①突然致富或發跡。②突然起立。③突然出現。—*v.t.* 使突然致富或發跡。—**ness,** *n.*

up·state 〔'ʌp'stet; 'ʌp'steit〕 *n., adj.* 〖美〗在一州之北部或距海岸較遠之地(的)(尤指紐約州之北部)。—**up·stat·er,** *n.*

up·stream 〔'ʌp'strim; 'ʌp'striːm〕 *adv.* 在上流地; 逆流地。—*adj.* 向上流的; 逆水而行的;在上流的。

up·stroke 〔'ʌp,strok; 'ʌp'strouk〕 *n.* ①(字畫中)向上挑的筆畫。②向上之一擊或運動。

up·surge 〔*v.* ʌp'sɝdʒ; ʌp'səːdʒ *n.* 'ʌp,sɝdʒ; 'ʌp–səːdʒ〕 *v.,* **-surged, -surg·ing,** *n.* —*v.i.* 向上湧;向上翻騰;增加;上升。—*n.* ①向上湧;上升。②反叛;革命;起義。

up·sweep 〔'ʌp,swip; 'ʌp–swiːp〕 *n.* ①向上彎曲。②攏上去的頭髮。③活潑化。

up·swept 〔'ʌp,swɛpt; 'ʌp–swept〕 *adj.* ①向上傾斜的; 向上彎曲的。②(頭髮)向上梳的;向頭頂梳的。

up·swing 〔*n.* 'ʌp,swɪŋ; 'ʌp–swiŋ *v.* ʌp'swɪŋ; ʌp'swiŋ〕 *n., v.,* **-swung, -swing·ing.** —*n.* ①向上的擺動。②顯著的進步。③上揚。—*v.i.* ①向上擺動。②進步。

up·take 〔'ʌp,tek; 'ʌpteik〕 *n.* ①舉起;拿起。②理解;了解。③將空氣、煤氣、煙等吸往高處之管子;通風管;煙筒。④吸收。⑤〖俗〗高舉。***on*** (or ***in***) ***the uptake*** 〖俗〗在瞭解與反應方面;覺察力;理解力。

up-tem·po 〔'ʌp,tɛmpo; 'ʌp,tempou〕 *adj.* 快節奏的; 節奏愈來愈快的。

up·thrust 〔'ʌp,θrʌst; 'ʌp'θrʌst〕 *n.* ①上衝。②〖地質〗地殼之隆起。

up·tick 〔'ʌptɪk; 'ʌptik〕 *n.* 〖股票〗報升(成交價格比上一個交易爲高的成交或價格)。

up·tight 〔'ʌp,taɪt; 'ʌptait〕 *adj.* 〖俚〗十分不安及憂心忡忡的。

***up-to-date** 〔'ʌptə'det; 'ʌptə'deit〕 *adj.* ①直到現代的; 現時的; 當代的。a *up-to-date* record. 包括最近資料的紀錄。②最新的;最新式的。③(人)趕得上時代的。

up-to-the-min·ute 〔'ʌptəðə'mɪnɪt; 'ʌptəðə'minit〕 *adj.* 最近的;最新的。

up·town 〔*n.* ʌp'taun, 'ʌp,taun *adj., adv.* 'ʌp'taun; 'ʌp'taun〕 *adv.* 向上城區;在上城區;向住宅區;在住宅區。—*adj.* (在)上城區或住宅區的。—*n.* 城市中的住宅區。

up·trend 〔'ʌp,trɛnd; 'ʌptrend〕 *n.* 向上之趨勢;改善之趨勢;上揚。

up·turn 〔*v.* ʌp'tɝn; ʌp'təːn *n.* 'ʌp,tɝn; 'ʌptəːn〕 *v.t.* ①挖掘;掘翻(土地等)。②使向上;使朝上。③使擾動。—*v.i.* 向上;轉向上。—*n.* 情況好轉。

up·turned 〔ʌp'tɝnd; ʌp'təːnd〕 *adj.* ①向上的。②翻覆的;翻過來的。③尖端上翻的。

U.P.U., UPU Universal Postal Union. 萬國郵政聯盟(附屬於聯合國)。

up·waft·ed 〔ʌp'wæftɪd; ʌp'wæftid〕 *adj.* 浮起的;被颺上去的。

up·ward** 〔'ʌpwəd; 'ʌpwəd〕 *adv.* ①向上地;上升地。Prices tended *upward.* 物價有上升之勢。②向上游。③以上; 超過。upward of*** 超過;多於。Repairs will cost *upward of* $100. 修理費將超過100元。—*adj.* 向上的。an *upward* glance. 向上一望。—**ly,** *adv.* —**ness,** *n.*

up·ward-mo·bile 〔'ʌpwəd'mobḷ; 'ʌpwəd'moubail〕 *adj.* 具有升高能力的。

upward mobility 在經濟或社會地位方面向上爬的能力或趨向。

***up·wards** 〔'ʌpwədz; 'ʌpwədz〕 *adv.* =**upward.**

up·well 〔ʌp'wɛl; ʌp'wel〕 *v.i.* 向上湧出;向上衝。

up·whirl 〔ʌp'hwɝl; ʌp'hwəːl〕 *v.t.* & *v.i.* 向上旋轉。

up·wind 〔'ʌp'wɪnd; 'ʌp'wind〕 *adv.* 逆風地。—*adj.* 逆風的。—*n.* 逆風。

Ur 〖化〗uranium.

U·ral 〔'jurəl; 'juərəl〕 *n.* ①烏拉河(在蘇聯境內,流入裏海)。②烏拉山(在蘇聯境內,爲歐亞兩洲之界山)。—*adj.* 烏拉河的;烏拉山的。

U·ral-Al·ta·ic 〔'jurəl·æl'te·ɪk; 'juərəl-æl'teiik〕 *adj.* 烏拉山及阿爾泰山區或其居民的。—*n.* 烏拉阿爾泰語族。

U·ra·ni·a 〔ju'renɪə; juə'reiniə〕 *n.* ①女子名。②〖希臘神話〗九女神之一(司天文)。③司愛情與美之女神 Aphrodite 之別稱。

U·ra·ni·an 〔ju'renɪən; juə'reiniən〕 *adj.* 〖天文〗天王星的。

u·ran·ic[1] 〔ju'rænɪk; ju'rænik〕 *adj.* 天的;天文的。

u·ran·ic[2] *adj.* 鈾的;含高價鈾的。

u·ra·ni·um 〔ju'renɪəm; ju'reiniəm〕 *n.* 〖化〗鈾。

u·ra·nog·ra·phy 〔,jurə'nɑgrəfɪ; ,jurə'nɔgrəfi〕 *n.* 天象學; 天體學。(亦作 **ouranography**)

u·ra·nol·o·gy 〔,jurə'nɑlədʒɪ; ,jurə-'nɔlədʒi〕 *n.* 有關天體的演講或論文; 天體研究;天體學(天文學中的一門)。

U·ra·nus 〔'jurənəs; 'juərənəs〕 *n.* ①〖希臘神話〗天神(被認爲係地神 Gaea 之子或夫)。②〖天文〗天王星。

urb 〔ɝb; əːb〕 *n.* 大都市地區。

***ur·ban** 〔'ɝbən; 'əːbən〕 *adj.* ①都市的;住在都市的。*urban* district. 市區。②習慣於都市的;喜愛都市的。

ur·bane 〔ɝ'ben; əː'bein〕 *adj.* 溫文的;有禮貌的;文雅的。—**ly,** *adv.* —**ness,** *n.*

ur·ban·ism 〔'ɝbənɪzəm; 'əːbənizəm〕 *n.* ①都市生活;都市特性。②都市建設計畫。

ur·ban·ist 〔'ɝbənɪst; 'əːbənist〕 *n.* 都市計劃者。

ur·ban·ite 〔'ɝbən,aɪt; 'əːbənait〕 *n.* 都市人。

ur·ban·i·ty 〔ɝ'bænətɪ; əː'bæniti〕 *n., pl.* **-ties.** ①溫文;有禮;文雅。②客套話。③都市之狀況或特性。

ur·ban·ize [ˈɝbənˌaɪz; ˈəːbənaiz] *v.t.*, -ized, -iz·ing. 使都市化。—**ur·ban·i·za·tion**, *n.*

ur·ban·oid [ˈɝbənɔɪd; ˈəːbənɔid] *adj.* 具有大都市特性的。

ur·ban·ol·o·gy [ˌɝbəˈnɑlədʒɪ; ˌəːbəˈnɔlədʒi] *n.* 都市問題學。—**ur·ban·ol·o·gist**, *n.*

urban renewal 都市美化。

ur·bi·cul·ture [ˈɝbɪˌkʌltʃɚ; ˈəːbiˌkʌltʃə] *n.* ①都市福利;都市及其居民之維護。②都市生活。

***ur·chin** [ˈɝtʃɪn; ˈəːtʃin] *n.* ①小男孩。②頑童。③衣衫襤褸的窮孩子。④〖動物〗海膽。

Ur·du [ˈʊrdu, ɝˈdu; ˈuədu:, ˈəːd-] *n.* 印度斯坦回教徒所通用之一種語言。

u·re·a [juˈriə; juˈriə] *n.* 〖化〗尿素。—**u·re·al**, *adj.*

u·re·mi·a [juˈrimɪə; juˈri:miə] *n.* 〖醫〗尿毒症。(亦作 **uraemia**)

u·re·mic [juˈrimɪk; juˈri:mik] *adj.* 〖醫〗(患)尿毒症的。(亦作 **uraemic**)

u·re·ter [juˈritɚ; juˈri:tə] *n.* 〖解剖〗輸尿管。

u·re·thra [juˈriθrə; juˈri:θrə] *n.*, *pl.* -thrae [-θri; -θri:], -thras. 〖解剖〗尿道。

u·re·thral [juˈriθrəl; juˈri:θrəl] *adj.* 尿道的。

u·re·thri·tis [ˌjurɪˈθraɪtɪs; ˌjuriˈθraitis] *n.* 〖醫〗尿道炎。

U·rey [ˈjurɪ; ˈjuri] *n.* 尤列 (Harold Clayton, 1893–, 美國化學家, 曾獲 1934 年諾貝爾化學獎)。

‡urge [ɝdʒ; əːdʒ] *v.*, **urged, urg·ing**, *n.* —*v.t.* ①驅策。②力勸;力請。He *urged* her to study English. 他力勸她研習英語。③力陳;力言。—*v.i.* ①作爲驅策力。Fear *urges*. 恐懼有驅策的力量。②力言某事之重要、眞實性等;熱烈爭辯。③作懇求;竭力建議。—*n.* ①堅强的願望;衝動;力量。②驅策;激勵。

ur·gen·cy [ˈɝdʒənsɪ; ˈəːdʒənsi] *n.*, *pl.* -cies. ①緊急;急迫。②壓迫。③(*pl.*) 迫切需要之事物。(亦作 **urgence**)

***ur·gent** [ˈɝdʒənt; ˈəːdʒənt] *adj.* ①緊急的;急迫的。"S.O.S." is an *urgent* message. "S.O.S." 是一個緊急的信號。②力促的;急切的。He was *urgent* with me for further particulars. 他迫我說得更詳細些。—**ly**, *adv.*

u·ric [ˈjurɪk; ˈjuərik] *adj.* 尿的;取自尿中的。

uric acid 〖化〗尿酸(分子式爲$C_5H_4N_4O_3$)。

u·ri·nal [ˈjurənl; ˈjuərinl] *n.* ①小便器。②小便所。

u·ri·nal·y·sis [ˌjurəˈnæləsɪs; ˌjuərəˈnælisis] *n.*, *pl.* -ses [-ˌsiz; -si:z]. 〖醫〗尿之分析法。(亦作 **uranalysis**)

u·ri·nar·y [ˈjurəˌnerɪ; ˈjuərinəri] *adj.*, *n.*, *pl.* -nar·ies. —*adj.* 尿的;泌尿的。—*n.* ①小便所。②(供作肥料用之)蓄便池。

u·ri·nate [ˈjurəˌnet; ˈjuərineit] *v.i.*, -nat·ed, -nat·ing. 排尿;小便。—**u·ri·na·tion**, *n.*

u·rine [ˈjurɪn; ˈjuərin] *n.* 尿。

***urn** [ɝn; əːn] *n.* ①有座脚與耳之瓶;甕;骨灰缸。②有龍頭的咖啡壺或茶壺。③墳墓。

u·ro·gen·i·tal [ˌjurəˈdʒenətl; ˌjuərəˈdʒenitəl] *adj.* 排尿與生殖器官的。

u·rol·o·gy [juˈrɑlədʒɪ; juəˈrɔlədʒi] *n.* 〖醫〗泌尿學。(亦作 **ourology**)

Ur·sa [ˈɝsə; ˈəːsə] *n.* 〖天文〗①大熊座(=Ursa Major)。②小熊座(=Ursa Minor)。

Ursa Major 〖天文〗大熊座。

Ursa Minor 〖天文〗小熊座。

ur·sine [ˈɝsaɪn; ˈəːsain] *adj.* ①熊的;似熊的。②覆有硬毛狀物的。

ur·ti·car·i·a [ˌɝtɪˈkerɪə; ˌəːtiˈkɛəriə] *n.* 〖醫〗蕁麻疹;風疹。—**ur·ti·car·i·al**, *adj.*

ur·ti·cate [ˈɝtəket; ˈəːtikeit] *v.*, -cat·ed, -cat·ing. —*v.t.* ①用蕁麻刺或打。②用蕁麻鞭打(麻木的肢體)以恢復感覺。—*v.i.* 用蕁麻刺。

ur·ti·ca·tion [ˌɝtəˈkeʃən; ˌəːtiˈkeiʃən] *n.* 〖醫〗發風疹。

U·ru·guay [ˈjurəˌgwe; ˈjurugwai] *n.* 烏拉圭(南美一國,首都孟都 Montevideo)。

U·ru·guay·an [ˌjurəˈgweən; ˌuruˈgwaiən] *adj.* 烏拉圭的;烏拉圭人的。—*n.* 烏拉圭人。

‡us [ʌs; ʌs] *pron.* ①the objective case of we. They took *us* to the circus. 他們帶我們去看馬戲。②the dative case of we. She asked *us* the way. 她向我們問路。③〖俗〗用在動名詞之前代替 "our". Do you know about *us* moving to town? 你知道我們搬到城裏來的事嗎?

***U.S.** ① Uncle Sam. ②United Service. ③United States. ④United States Supreme Court Reports.

***U.S.A.** ①the United States of America. ②the United States Army. ③the Union of South Africa.

us·a·bil·i·ty [ˌjuzəˈbɪlətɪ; ˌju(:)zəˈbiliti] *n.* 可用;可用性。

us·a·ble [ˈjuzəbl; ˈju(:)zəbl] *adj.* 可用的。(亦作 **useable**) —**ness**, *n.*

***us·age** [ˈjusɪdʒ; ˈju:sidʒ] *n.* ①使用;用法;處理;對待。②習慣;慣例;習俗。③(語言之)慣用法。

us·ance [ˈjuzn̩s; ˈju:zəns] *n.* ①〖經濟〗財產之收益。②〖商〗對國外匯票習慣上所寬給的支付期限(不包括 days of grace 在內)。

USCG, U.S.C.G. United States Coast Guard.

‡use [*v.* juz; ju:z *n.* jus; ju:s] *v.*, **used, us·ing**, *n.* —*v.t.* ①用;使用;利用。When I write, I always *use* a pen. 我寫字總用鋼筆。②消耗;用盡。How much coal did we *use* last winter? 去冬我們用去了多少煤? ③對待;待遇。He *used* us well. 他待我們很好。④實行;慣行。to *use* diligence. 勤勉。—*v.i.* 慣常;向來(現僅用過去式,與不定詞連用,通常與主語互換位置而形成疑問句)。What *used* he to say? 他常說甚麼? ***used to*** 以前這樣做;以前如此。He *used to* come here every day. 他以前每天到這兒來。***used up*** a. 耗盡;用盡。I have *used up* my sugar. 我的糖已用完了。b. 精疲力竭。—*n.* ①用;使用;用法。to learn the *use* of tools. 學習使用工具。②用途;用處;需要。a tool with several *uses*. 有數種用途的工具。③效用;益處;價值。④使用的能力。to lose the *use* of one's eyes. 雙目失明。⑤使用權。⑥習慣;習俗;慣例。It was his *use* to rise early. 早起是他的習慣。⑦耐心。***be in use*** 被使用。*Is* this dictionary *in use?* 這本字典在用嗎? ***be of no use*** 無用;無益。It's *of no use* to look for that missing earring. 尋找那枚失落的耳環是徒勞無功的。***be out of use*** 被廢棄不用。***come into use*** 開始被使用。***go*** (or ***fall***) ***out of use*** 已不被使用;廢棄。The custom has *gone out of use*. 那風俗已被廢棄。***have no use for*** a. 不需要。b.〖俗〗不喜歡。c. 拒絕容忍。***make use of*** a. 使用。b. 利用;占…的便宜。***put to use*** 使用。

use·a·ble 〔'juzəbl; 'juːzəbl〕 *adj.* = usable.

‡**used**[1] 〔just, jus; juːst, juːs〕 *adj.* 慣於;習於〖to〗. ***be*** (or ***get***) ***used to*** 習慣於;適應於。Soldiers *are used to* danger. 軍人習慣於危險。You must *get used to* getting up early. 你必須慣於起早。〖注意〗⑴此字及 *v.i.* used 的讀法, 都是〔just; juːst〕或〔jus; juːs〕. 讀如〔jus; juːs〕時, 其音與下面的 to 字〔t〕音相聯。⑵ **used to** 後面跟動詞, 表過去的習慣或存在。**be used to** 後面跟名詞或動名詞, 表習慣於或適應於。

*__used__[2] 〔juzd; juːzd〕 *adj.* ①用舊了的;半舊的。a *used* car. 舊車。②用髒了的;用過的。③正用着的;利用中的。

‡**use·ful** 〔'jusfəl; 'juːsful〕 *adj.* ①有用的;有益的。②〖俚〗有效的;能幹的;可稱譽的。He is a *useful* footballer. 他是個很卓越的橄欖球員。—**ly,** *adv.* —**ness,** *n.*

*__use·less__ 〔'juslɪs; 'juːslis〕 *adj.* 無用的;無效的;無益的。A car is *useless* without gasoline. 汽車沒有汽油時卽無用。—**ly,** *adv.* —**ness,** *n.*

us·er 〔'juzə; 'juːzə〕 *n.* ①使用者。②〖法律〗a. 使用權之運用。b.(由於長期使用而造成之)使用權。

U-shaped 〔'ju͵ʃept; 'juːʃeipt〕 *adj.* U字形的。

*__ush·er__ 〔'ʌʃə; 'ʌʃə〕 *n.* ①閽人;門房。②(教堂或影戲院等之)引人入座之人; 招待員。③〖美〗婚禮中的迎賓招待員。④〖英〗助理教員。⑤〖諧〗教員。—*v.t.* ①引導;招待。②預報;預示。—*v.i.* 充當招待員。***usher in*** 引進;開始。—**ship,** *n.*

ush·er·ette 〔͵ʌʃə'ɛt; ͵ʌʃə'ret〕 *n.* 「usher 之女性。」

USIA, U.S.I.A. United States Information Agency. 美國新聞總署。

USIS, U.S.I.S. United States Information Service. 美國新聞處。

U.S.M. ①United States Mail. ②United States Marine. ③United States Mint.

USMA, U.S.M.A. United States Military Academy.

USMC, U.S.M.C. ①United States Marine Corps. ② United States Maritime Commission.

USN, U.S.N. United States Navy.

USNA, U.S.N.A. ①United States National Army. ②United States Naval Academy.

USNG, U.S.N.G. United States National Guard.

USO, U.S.O. United Service Organizations.

USP, U.S.P., U.S.Pharm. United States Pharmacopoeia.

us·que·baugh 〔'ʌskwɪbɔ; 'ʌskwibɔː〕 *n.* 〖蘇、愛〗威士忌酒。

U.S.S. ①United States Senate. ② United States Ship (*or* Steamer).

*__USSR, U.S.S.R.__ Union of Soviet Socialist Republics.

USTDC United States Taiwan Defence Command. 美國臺灣協防司令部。

USTS United States Travel Service. 美國觀光局(爲商業部下之機構)。

usu. ①usual. ②usually.

‡**u·su·al** 〔'juʒuəl; 'juːʒuəl〕 *adj.* 通常的;平素的;通例的;尋常的。As *usual,* she arrived late. 像平常一樣, 她遲到了。—**ness,** *n.*

‡**u·su·al·ly** 〔'juʒuəlɪ; 'juːʒuəli〕 *adv.* 通常地; 通例地; 大抵。He *usually* goes to bed at ten o'clock. 他通常在十點鐘睡覺。

u·su·fruct 〔'juzju͵frʌkt; 'juːsju(ː)frʌkt〕 *n.* 〖法律〗收益權;使用權。

u·su·fruc·tu·ar·y 〔͵juzju'frʌktʃu͵ɛrɪ; ͵juːzju'frʌktʃuəri〕 *adj., n., pl.* **-ar·ies.** —*adj.* 收益權的;使用權的。—*n.* 享有使用權的人。

u·su·rer 〔'juʒərə; 'juːʒərə〕 *n.* 放高利貸者。

u·su·ri·ous 〔ju'ʒurɪəs; juː'zjuəriəs〕 *adj.* ①高利貸的;高利的。②取高利的;收高利的。—**ly,** *adv.* —**ness,** *n.*

*__u·surp__ 〔ju'zɝp; juː'zəːp, ju'z-〕 *v.t.* 篡奪;僭取;霸占。—*v.i.* 作僭取行爲; 作霸占行爲。—**er,** *n.* —**ing·ly,** *adv.*

u·sur·pa·tion 〔͵juzə'peʃən; ͵juːzəː'peiʃən〕 *n.* 篡位;霸占。

u·su·ry 〔'juʒərɪ; 'juːʒuri〕 *n., pl.* **-ries.** 高利;高利貸。

usw, u.s.w. und so weiter (德=and so forth). **Ut.** Utah.

U·tah 〔'jutɔ; 'juːtɑː〕 *n.* 猶他(美國西部之一州, 首府爲 Salt Lake City).

*__u·ten·sil__ 〔ju'tɛnsl; ju(ː)'tensl〕 *n.* 器皿;用具。kitchen *utensils.* 厨房用具。

u·ter·ec·to·my 〔͵jutə'rɛktəmɪ; ͵juːtə'rektəmi〕 *n.* 〖醫〗子宮截除術。

u·ter·ine 〔'jutərɪn; 'juːtərain〕 *adj.* ①子宮的。②同母異父的。

u·ter·us 〔'jutərəs; 'juːtərəs〕 *n., pl.* **-ter·i** 〔-tə͵raɪ; -tərai〕.〖解剖〗子宮。

U Thant 〔'u'θænt, -'θɑnt; 'uː'θænt, -'θɔnt〕 宇譚 (1909–1974, 緬甸政治家, 1962–1971年任聯合國祕書長)。

u·til·i·tar·i·an 〔͵jutɪlə'tɛrɪən; ͵juːtili'tɛəriən〕 *adj.* ①以實利爲目的的; 功利的。②實利主義的;功利主義的。—*n.* 實利主義者;功利主義者。

u·til·i·tar·i·an·ism 〔͵jutɪlə'tɛrɪə͵nɪzəm; ͵juːtili'tɛəriənizəm〕 *n.* 功利主義;實利主義。

*__u·til·i·ty__ 〔ju'tɪlətɪ; ju(ː)'tiliti〕 *n., pl.* **-ties,** *adj.* —*n.* ①有用;有益;利益;效用。②有用之物。③(亦作 **public utility**) 公用事業(如煤氣、水、電、公共汽車等事業)。④最大多數人的最大幸福; 人類幸福。⑤一種次級牛肉; 老牛肉。⑥〖澳〗一種多用途之自動車。⑦(*pl.*) 公用事業公司所發行之股票或債券。—*adj.* ①作多種用途的。a *utility* knife. 萬能刀。②(家畜)爲經濟利益而飼養的。③實用的。*utility* furniture. 實用傢具。

utility man ①能擔任各種職務之人。②可代人擔任任何位置之職業棒球隊員。③演小配角演員。

utility pole 電線桿。

utility room ①兼做寢室與起坐間之房間。②屋內放火爐、熱水器、洗衣機等物之房間。

u·ti·liz·a·ble 〔'jutl͵aɪzəbl; 'juːtilaizəbl〕 *adj.* 能利用的。

u·ti·li·za·tion 〔͵jutlə'zeʃən; ͵juːtilai'zeiʃən〕 *n.* 利用。

*__u·ti·lize__ 〔'jutl͵aɪz; 'juːtilaiz〕 *v.t.,* **-lized, -liz·ing.** 利用。—**u·ti·liz·er,** *n.*

ut in·fra 〔ʌt'ɪnfrə; ʌt'infrə〕 〖拉〗如下(=as below).

u·ti pos·si·de·tis 〔'jutaɪ͵pɑsɪ'ditɪs; 'juːtai͵pɔsi'diːtis〕 〖拉〗〖國際法〗(=as you possess) 使交戰國於戰爭結束之際以占領地爲領土之原則。

*__ut·most__ 〔'ʌt͵most; 'ʌtmoust, -məst〕 *adj.* 最遠的;極端的;極度的。the *utmost* ends of the earth. 天涯海角。—*n.* 極端;最大限度;極力。to trust a person to the *utmost.* 極端信任某人。

U·to·pi·a 〔ju'topɪə; juː'toupiə〕 *n.* ①烏

托邦;理想國(爲 Sir Thomas More 所著 *Utopia* 中描述之有完美政治及社會制度之一島)。②(常 u-)理想中的最完美的社會或政治制度。③(常 u-)理想中的國家或地方。

U·to·pi·an, u·to·pi·an 〔ju'topiən; ju:'toupiən〕*adj.* 烏托邦的;理想國的;理想的;空想的。—*n.* 烏托邦的人民;理想家。—**ism,** *n.*

u·tri·cle 〔'jutrɪkl; 'ju:trikl〕 *n.* ①小囊;小胞。②【植物】胞果。③【解剖】(內耳之)耳壺;橢圓囊。

u·tric·u·lar 〔ju'trɪkjələ; ju'trikjulə〕 *adj.* 小囊狀的;小胞狀的;小囊的;小胞的;有小囊的;有小胞的。

ut su·pra 〔ʌt'suprə; ʌt'su:prə〕【拉】如上(=as above).

*****ut·ter**[1] 〔'ʌtə; 'ʌtə〕 *adj.* ①完全的;全然的;絕對的。*utter* darkness. 漆黑。②無條件的;無保留的。③非常奇怪的。

*****ut·ter**[2] *v.t.* ①說出;發出。to *utter* a lie. 說謊。②宣布;吐露;發表。③使用(假鈔票)。—*v.i.* ①說話;作聲。②被說出來。

*****ut·ter·ance** 〔'ʌtərəns, 'ʌtrəns; 'ʌtərəns, 'ʌtrəns〕 *n.* ①發言;發聲;吐露;發表。to give *utterance* to one's thoughts. 發表自己的思想。②說話的方式;語調;發音。a clear *utterance*. 清晰的語調。③言辭。④使用假鈔票、支票等。

*****ut·ter·ly** 〔'ʌtəlɪ; 'ʌtəli〕 *adv.* 完全地;全然地;絕對地。

*****ut·ter·most** 〔'ʌtə,most; 'ʌtəmoust, -məst〕 *adj., n.* =**utmost.**

U-turn 〔'ju,tɜn; 'ju:tə:n〕 *n.* "U" 形轉彎;急轉彎。

UTWA, U.T.W.A. United Textile Workers of America.

UV, U.V. ultraviolet.

u·vu·la 〔'juvjələ; 'ju:vjulə〕 *n., pl.* **-las, -lae** 〔-,li; -li:〕.【解剖】懸雍垂;小舌。—**u·vu·lar,** *adj.*

U/w(s), U/WS underwriters.

ux·o·ri·al 〔ʌk'sorɪəl; ʌk'sɔ:riəl〕 *adj.* ①妻子的。②如妻子的。③=**uxorious.**

ux·or·i·cide 〔ʌk'sorɪ,saɪd; ʌk'sɔ:risaid〕 *n.* ①殺妻。②殺妻者。

ux·or·i·lo·cal 〔ʌk,sorɪ'lokl; ʌk,sɔ:ri'loukl〕 *adj.*【人類學】以妻之家族爲中心的。

ux·o·ri·ous 〔ʌk'sorɪəs; ʌk'sɔ:riəs〕 *adj.* 溺愛妻子的;對妻過分寵愛的。—**ly,** *adv.* —**ness,** *n.*

Uz·bek 〔'ʌzbɛk; 'ʌzbek〕 *n.* ①烏玆別克(中亞烏玆別克斯坦之土耳其民族)。②其語言。

Uz·bek·i·stan 〔,ʌzbɛkɪ'stæn; ,ʌzbeki'stɑ:n〕 *n.* 烏玆別克斯坦(蘇聯中亞境內之一共和國,其首府爲塔什干 Tashkent).(亦作 **Uzbek S.S.R.**)

V

V or **v** 〔vi; vi:〕 *n., pl.* **V's** or **v's** 〔viz; vi:z〕. ①英文字母之第二十二個字母。②V形之物。③羅馬數字之5, 如 IV (4), VII (7). ④【俗】五元鈔票。—*adj.* V形的。

V ①vagabond. ②vector. ③velocity. ④victory. ⑤volt. **V** 化學元素 vanadium 之符號。 **V.** ①Venerable. ②Viscount. ③Victoria. ④Volunteer. ⑤Vicar. **v.** ①valve. ②verb. ③versus. ④verse. ⑤see (拉=vide). ⑥voice. ⑦vice. ⑧volume. ⑨von.

V-1 〔'vi'wʌn; 'vi:'wʌn〕 *n.* (二次大戰末期德國之火箭飛彈)報復武器第一號。

V-2 〔'vi'tu; 'vi:'tu:〕 *n.* (二次大戰末期德國之火箭飛彈)報復武器第二號。

V-8 〔'vi'et; 'vi:'eit〕 *n.* =**V-8 engine.**

V-8 engine "V" 型八汽缸引擎。

VA Veterans' Administration.

va 〔vɑ; vɑ:〕【義】【音樂】繼續。*va* piano. 繼續漸弱。

Va. the State of Virginia, U.S.A.

V.A. ①Veterans' Administration. ②Vicar Apostolic. ③Vice-Admiral. ④(Order of) Victoria and Albert.

v.a. ①verb active. ②verbal adjective.

vac.【俗】假日(=vacation).

*****va·can·cy** 〔'vekənsɪ; 'veikənsi〕 *n., pl.* **-cies.** ①空虛;空。②空職;空缺。③空所;空處;空隙。④茫然若失。⑤出租之空房間或空場所等。⑥空閒。⑦思想或智慧之缺乏。

*****va·cant** 〔'vekənt; 'veikənt〕 *adj.* ①空的;空虛的。a *vacant* position. 空職;空缺。②閒暇的。*vacant* hours. 暇時。③茫然的。a *vacant* expression. 茫然的表情。④【法律】無人利用的;無主的;遺棄的;無繼承人的。—**ly,** *adv.* —**ness,** *n.*

va·cate 〔'veket; və'keit, vei'k-〕 *v.t. & v.i.,* **-cat·ed, -cat·ing.** ①使空;使出缺;空出房屋、職位等。②撤去;離開。③取消;使無效。

*****va·ca·tion** 〔ve'keʃən, və-; və'keiʃən〕 *n.* ①休假;假期。the summer *vacation.* 暑假。②空出;撤去。—*v.i.* 度假期。—**less,** *adj.*

va·ca·tion·er 〔ve'keʃənə; və'keiʃənə〕 *n.* =**vacationist.**

va·ca·tion·ist 〔ve'keʃənɪst; və'keiʃənist〕 *n.* 度假者(尤指作度假旅行者)。

va·ca·tion·land 〔ve'keʃən,lænd; vei'keiʃənlænd〕 *n.* 度假勝地;休閒勝地。

vacation school (假期中的)講習會;暑期學校。

vac·ci·nal 〔'væksɪnḷ; 'væksinl〕 *adj.* 痘苗的;疫苗的;預防注射的。

vac·ci·nate 〔'væksn̩,et; 'væksineit〕 *v.t. & v.i.,* **-nat·ed, -nat·ing.** ①爲…種痘;種痘。②以類似種痘的方法預防他種疾病;接種疫苗。

vac·ci·na·tion 〔,væksn̩'eʃən; ,væksi'neiʃən〕 *n.* ①種痘;接種疫苗。②種痘的疤痕。

vac·ci·na·tion·ist 〔,væksn̩'eʃənɪst; ,væksi'neiʃənist〕 *n.* 贊成接種疫苗者。

vac·ci·na·tor 〔'væksn̩,etə; 'væksineitə〕 *n.*【醫】①種痘醫生。②種痘刀;接種刀(針)。

vac·cine 〔'væksin; 'væksi:n〕 *n.* 痘苗;預防注射所用之疫苗。—*adj.* ①痘苗的;疫苗的。②牛痘的。③與牛有關的;從牛獲得的。

vac·ci·nee 〔,væksə'ni; ,væksə'ni:〕 *n.* 種過疫苗的人。

vac·cin·i·a 〔væk'sɪnɪə; væk'siniə〕 *n.*【醫】牛痘。

vac·il·late 〔'væsḷ,et; 'væsileit〕 *v.i.,* **-lat·ed, -lat·ing.** ①搖擺;擺動。②猶疑不決;躊躇;搖動。

vac·il·lat·ing 〔'væsḷ,etɪŋ; 'væsileitiŋ〕 *adj.* ①搖動的;搖擺的。②優柔寡斷的;猶疑不決的。—**ly,** *adv.*

vac·il·la·tion 〔,væsə'leʃən; ,væsi-

ˈleiʃən〕 *n.* ①優柔寡斷。②動搖；不穩定。

va·cu·i·ty 〔væˈkjuətɪ; væˈkju(:)iti〕 *n., pl.* **-ties.** ①空；空虛。②空間；眞空。③空泛；缺乏特殊的東西。④思想貧乏；思想空虛。⑤(心靈之)空虛；茫然；愚笨。⑥愚蠢之物。

vac·u·ole 〔ˈvækjuˌol; ˈvækjuoul〕 *n.* 【生物】空胞；液胞。

vac·u·ous 〔ˈvækjuəs; ˈvækjuəs〕 *adj.* ①空的；空虛的。②愚蠢的；拙笨的；沒有頭腦的；沒有思想的。③漫無目的的；茫然的。④懶的；閑散的。—**ly,** *adv.* —**ness,** *n.*

***vac·u·um** 〔ˈvækjuəm; ˈvækjuəm〕 *n., pl.* **vac·u·ums** or **vac·u·a** 〔ˈvækjuə; ˈvækjuə〕, *v., adj.* —*n.* ①眞空。②空間；空虛。③眞空吸塵器 (=vacuum cleaner). —*v.t.* 【俗】以眞空吸塵器掃除。 —*v.i.* 用吸塵器打掃。—*adj.* ①眞空的。②產生眞空的。③利用眞空的。

vacuum bottle(or **flask**)熱水瓶。

vacuum brake 眞空制動機。

vacuum cleaner(or **sweeper**) 眞空吸塵器。

vacuum cleaning 用眞空吸塵器打掃。

vacuum fan 抽出汚濁空氣的風扇。

vacuum gauge 眞空計。

vac·u·um·ize 〔ˈvækjuəmˌaɪz; ˈvækjuəmaiz〕 *v.t.,* **-ized, -iz·ing.** ①使眞空。②以眞空器械清潔、乾燥。③裝入眞空容器。

vac·u·um-packed 〔ˈvækjuəmˈpækt; ˈvækjuəmˈpækt〕 *adj.* 用眞空罐或瓶包裝的。

vacuum pump 抽氣幫浦(唧筒)。

vacuum tube 眞空管。

vacuum valve 【英】眞空管。

vacuum ventilation 抽氣通風法。

va·de me·cum 〔ˈvedɪˈmikəm; ˈveidiˈmi:kəm〕 ①(隨身攜帶的) 便覽；手册。②隨身攜帶備用之物。

V.-Adm. Vice-Admiral.

vae vic·tis 〔viˈvɪktɪs; vi:ˈviktis〕【拉】悲哉失敗者 (=woe to the vanquished)!

vag 〔væg; væg〕 *n.* 【俚】流氓；無賴。—*v.t.* 【俚】將…當作流氓加以逮捕。

***vag·a·bond** 〔ˈvægəˌbɑnd; ˈvægəbənd, -bɔnd〕 *n.* ①漂泊者；流浪者。②流氓；無賴。—*adj.* 漂泊的；流浪的；游蕩的；無賴的。—*v.i.* 流浪；飄蕩。—**ish,** *adj.*

vag·a·bond·age 〔ˈvægəˌbɑndɪdʒ; ˈvægəbɔndidʒ〕 *n.* ①遊蕩；流浪。②流浪漢之集合稱。

vag·a·bond·ize 〔ˈvægəbɑnˌdaɪz; ˈvægəbəndaiz〕 *v.i.,* **-bond·ized, -bond·iz·ing.** 流浪；遊蕩；過流浪生活。

va·gal 〔ˈvegl̩; ˈveigəl〕 *adj.* 迷走神經的。

va·gar·i·ous 〔vəˈgɛrɪəs; vəˈgɛəriəs〕 *adj.* ①越出常規的；奇特的；異想天開的；捉摸不定的。②飄蕩的；流浪的。

va·gar·y 〔vəˈgɛrɪ; ˈveigəri, vəˈgɛəri〕 *n., pl.* **-gar·ies.** ①奇異的幻想；妄想。②不可預測的行爲或事件。

vag·ile 〔ˈvædʒəl; ˈvædʒil〕 *adj.* 【生物】可自由活動的。

va·gi·na 〔vəˈdʒaɪnə; vəˈdʒainə〕 *n., pl.* **-nas, -nae** 〔-ni; -ni:〕. ①【解剖】陰道；膣。②【植物】葉鞘。③器官之鞘狀部分。 —**vag·i·nal,** *adj.*

vag·i·nat·ed 〔ˈvædʒəˌnetɪd; ˈvædʒəneitid〕 *adj.* ①有鞘的；有葉鞘的。②鞘狀的；似鞘的。(亦作 **vaginate**)

vag·i·ni·tis 〔ˌvædʒəˈnaɪtɪs; ˌvædʒəˈnaitis〕 *n.* 【醫】陰道炎。

va·got·o·my 〔vəˈgɑtəmɪ; vəˈgɔtəmi〕 *n.* 【醫】迷走神經切斷術。

va·gran·cy 〔ˈvegrənsɪ; ˈveigrənsi〕 *n., pl.* **-cies.** ①漂泊；流浪。②流浪者；流浪漢；無家可歸者 (集合稱)。③意見、思想等之游移不定。

***va·grant** 〔ˈvegrənt; ˈveigrənt〕 *n.* ①漂泊者；流浪者。②流氓；無賴。—*adj.* ①漂泊的；流浪的；遊蕩的。②飄忽不定的 (思想、浮雲等)。③流浪者的；無賴的。—**ly,** *adv.*

va·grom 〔ˈvegrəm; ˈveigrəm〕 *adj.* 【古】=**vagrant.**

***vague** 〔veg; veig〕 *adj.,* **va·guer, va·guest.** ①不明確的；不清楚的；模糊的；含混的。a *vague* answer. 含混的答覆。②無表情的；茫然的。*vague* eyes. 無表情的眼睛。—**ly,** *adv.* —**ness,** *n.*

va·gus 〔ˈvegəs; ˈveigəs〕 *n., pl.* **-gi** 〔-dʒaɪ; -dʒai〕. 【解剖】迷走神經。(亦作 **vagus nerve**)

vail[1] 〔vel; veil〕 *v.t.* ①脫下(帽、冠等)。②使下降；使低落；低垂。—*v.i.*脫帽以示尊敬。

vail[2] *n.* 【古】客人離開時給主人家僕役之賞錢。

‡**vain** 〔ven; vein〕 *adj.* ①徒然的；無效的；無結果的；無益的。All our efforts were *vain.* 我們的一切努力都歸無效。②自負的；得意的。She is *vain* of her beauty. 她自負貌美。③空虛的。*vain* words. 空言。④愚蠢的。***in vain* a.** 無效的(地)。All my work was *in vain.* 我的一切工作均歸徒然。**b.** 隨便地；冒瀆地。to take the name of God *in vain.* 濫用上帝之名。—**ness,** *n.*

vain·glo·ri·ous 〔venˈglorɪəs; veinˈglɔ:riəs〕 *adj.* ①虛榮心强的；自負的。②誇大的；做作的。 —**ly,** *adv.* —**ness,** *n.*

vain·glo·ry 〔venˈglorɪ; veinˈglɔ:ri〕 *n.* 虛榮；自負；虛妄之誇飾。

***vain·ly** 〔ˈvenlɪ; ˈveinli〕 *adv.* ①無益地；徒然地；無效果地 (=in vain). ②自負地。

vair 〔vɛr, vær; vɛə〕 *n.* ①(中世紀貴族所穿的)栗鼠皮。②【紋章】毛皮紋。

Vais·ya 〔ˈvaɪsjə; ˈvaisjə〕 *n.* 吠舍(印度社會中之第三階級，卽農商階級)。

val. ①value. ②valuation. ③valentine.

val·ance 〔ˈvæləns; ˈvæləns〕 *n.* ①(裝飾床或祭壇等的)短帷幔。②(窗頂上的)短帷。—**val·anced,** *adj.*

vale[1] 〔vel; veil〕 *n.* 【詩】谷。 ***this vale of tears*** (or ***woe,*** etc.) 塵世；現世。

va·le[2] 〔ˈveli; ˈveili〕【拉】*interj.* 再見。—*n.* 分別；別離。***take one's vale*** 告別。

val·e·dic·tion 〔ˌvæləˈdɪkʃən; ˌvæliˈdikʃən〕 *n.* ①告別；告辭。②告別的話。

val·e·dic·to·ri·an 〔ˌvælədɪkˈtorɪən; ˌvælidikˈtɔ:riən〕 *n.* 【美】在畢業典禮中致告別辭之畢業生代表。

val·e·dic·to·ry 〔ˌvæləˈdɪktərɪ; ˌvæliˈdiktəri〕 *adj., n., pl.* **-ries.** —*adj.* 告別的；辭別的。—*n.* ①畢業生代表之告別講演。②告別演說。

va·lence 〔ˈveləns; ˈveiləns〕 *n.* ①【化】原子價。②【生物】(染色體、血清等結合之)數價。(亦作 **valency**)

Va·len·ci·a 〔vəˈlenʃɪə; vəˈlenʃiə〕 *n.* ①瓦倫西亞(**a.** 西班牙東部之一城市。 **b.** 委內瑞拉北部之一城市)。②(v-)一種毛與棉或絲之織物。③產於美國加利福尼亞及佛羅里達州的一種夏季成熟的柑桔。

Va·len·ci·ennes 〔vəˌlɛnsɪˈɛnz; ˌvæ-

V

lənsi'en] *n.* ①華倫西安妓(法國北部近比利時之一城市)。②一種手編之花邊。

va·len·cy ['velənsı; 'veilənsi] *n., pl.* **-cies.** 〖化, 生物〗=**valence.**

Val·en·tine ['væləntaın; 'væləntain] *n.* ①聖・華倫泰(公元三世紀時羅馬基督教殉教者)。②(v-)在聖・華倫泰節, 二月十四日, 所選或所祝賀之愛人。③(v-) 在二月十四日寄給異性之信、卡、畫片或禮物(做爲愛情之象徵)。④(v-) 任何表示想念之事物。

Valentine's Day 聖・華倫泰節(二月十四日)。

Va·le·ri·an [və'lırıən; və'liəriən] *n.* 瓦勒利安(Publius Licinius, 死於? 269, 羅馬皇帝, 在位期間253–260)。

va·le·ri·an [və'lırıən; və'liəriən] *n.* ①〖植物〗纈草屬植物。②纈草根; 穿地排草根; 拔地麻根(爲鎮靜劑)。

va·ler·ic [və'lɛrık; və'lɛərik] *adj.* 纈草的; 取自纈草的。

valeric acid 〖化〗纈草酸; 戊酸。

val·et ['vælıt; 'vælit] *n., v.,* **-et·ed, -et·ing.** —*n.* (專司看管衣物及替主人穿衣之)男僕; 旅館中司洗燙衣服之僕人。—*v.t.* & *v.i.* 伺候; 侍從。

va·let de cham·bre [va,lɛdə'ʃɑ̃brə; va,ledə'ʃɑ̃brə] 〖法〗(私人的)男侍從。

val·e·tu·di·nar·i·an [,vælə,tjudn̩'ɛrıən; 'væli,tju:di'nɛəriən] *n.* ①病人; 健康不佳者。②自以爲有病而實無病者; 經常爲身體健康發愁的人。—*adj.* ①有病的; 抱病的; 虛弱的。②無病而自認爲有病的; 經常爲身體發愁的。—**ism,** *n.*

val·gus ['vælgəs; 'vælgəs] *n.* (造成膝內彎的)外翻足。—*adj.* ①外翻的(足)。②膝蓋朝裏的; 兩腿向內彎曲的。

Val·hal·la [væl'hælə; væl'hælə] *n.* ①〖北歐神話〗奉祠陣亡戰士靈魂之廟堂; 英靈殿。②安置名人之墳墓及紀念碑等之廟堂。(亦作 **Valhall, Walhalla, Walhall**)

val·ian·cy ['væljənsı; 'væljənsi] *n.* 驍勇; 勇敢。(亦作 **valiance**)

***val·iant** ['væljənt; 'væljənt] *adj.* ①勇敢的; 驍勇的。②高尚的; 優越的。—**ly,** *adv.* —**ness,** *n.*

val·id ['vælıd; 'vælid] *adj.* ①有確實根據的; 正確的; 正常的。②依法有效的; 有效的。③健康的; 精神正常的。④〖古〗强有力的。⑤〖邏輯〗含有暗示結論之前提的。—**ly,** *adv.* —**ness,** *n.*

val·i·date ['vælə,det; 'vælideit] *v.t.,* **-dat·ed, -dat·ing.** ①使有效; 使有法律效力。②確認; 由事實或權威支持。—**val·i·da·tion,** *n.* —**val·i·da·to·ry,** *adj.*

va·lid·i·ty [və'lıdətı; və'liditi] *n., pl.* **-ties.** ①確實性; 妥當性; 確實; 正當。②有效; 效力; 合法性。

va·lise [və'lis; və'li:s] *n.* 手提旅行箱; 手提包。

Val·kyr ['vælkır; 'vælkiə] *n.* =**Valkyrie.**

Val·kyr·ie [væl'kırı; væl'kiəri] *n.* 〖北歐神話〗戰神 Odin 之一婢女, 將戰死將士引導入 Valhalla, 並侍候於此。(亦作 **Valkyr, Walkyrie**)

val·la·tion [və'leʃən; və'leiʃən] *n.* ①工事; 堡壘。②築城術。

‡val·ley ['vælı; 'væli] *n., pl.* **-leys.** ①谷; 山谷。②流域。the Yangtze *valley.* 揚子江流域。③任何低凹如山谷之物。④屋頂兩斜面交會而形成之凹槽。⑤任何恐怖陰森之地。*the valley of the shadow of death* 死蔭之幽谷(聖經詩篇 23 篇 4 節); 臨死之恐懼階段。

Valley of Ten Thousand Smokes 萬煙谷(阿拉斯加西南部之一火山地帶)。

val·lum ['væləm; 'væləm] *n., pl.* **-la** [-lə, -lə]. ①(古羅馬之)壁壘。②〖解剖〗眉。

va(l)·lo·ni·a [væ'lonıə; væ'louniə] *n.* 一種槲果的殼(作墨水原料)。

***val·o(u)r** ['vælɚ; 'vælə] *n.* 勇氣; 勇武; 勇猛。

val·or·i·za·tion [,vælərə'zeʃən; ,vælərə'zeiʃən] *n.* 政府穩定物價之措施。

val·or·ize ['vælə,raız; 'væləraiz] *v.t.* & *v.i.,* **-ized, -iz·ing.** (政府)規定價格; 使物價穩定。

val·or·ous ['vælərəs; 'vælərəs] *adj.* 勇敢的。—**ly,** *adv.* —**ness,** *n.*

‡val·u·a·ble ['væljuəbl; 'væljuəbl] *adj.* ①有價值的; 貴重的。*valuable* information. 有價值的情報。②〖罕〗可計算其價值的。—*n.* (常 *pl.*) 貴重物品; 珠寶。She kept her *valuables* in a safe. 她把她的貴重物品藏在一個保險箱裏。—**ness,** *n.* —**val·u·a·bly,** *adv.*

val·u·ate ['vælju,et; 'væljueit] *v.t.,* **-at·ed, -at·ing.** 對…作估價; 對…作評價。

***val·u·a·tion** [,vælju'eʃən; ,vælju'eiʃən] *n.* ①評價; 估價。②估定之價格; 價值。③對人之評價。—**al,** *adj.*

val·u·a·tor ['vælju,etɚ; 'væljueitə] *n.* 評價者; 估價者; 價格核定者。

‡val·ue ['vælju; 'vælju:, -ju] *n., v.,* **-ued, -u·ing.** —*n.* ①價值; 重要性。This book will be of great *value* to students of history. 這本書對於從事歷史研究者會有很大的價值。②實在價值。③估計的價值; 估價。I set a high *value* upon your advice. 我認爲你的忠告甚有價值。④購買力; 價格。a rise in *value.* 價格上漲。⑤眞義; 意義。⑥符號所代表之數字或數量。⑦(*pl.*) 生活的理想; 道德價值或標準。ethical *values.* 倫理價值標準。⑧〖音樂〗音符所表示音之長度。⑨語言中之音質。⑩畫中之明暗程度。⑪畫中顏色、實物等之相對重要性或效果。⑫〖數學〗值。—*v.t.* ①估價; 評價。②尊重; 重視。

val·ue-ad·ded tax ['vælju'ædıd～; ,vælju:'ædid～] (商品) 增值稅 (sales tax 之一, 就商品產、銷各階段增值部分課徵)。(略作 **VAT,** 亦作 **added-value tax**)

val·ued ['væljud; 'væljud] *adj.* ①被尊敬的; 被敬重的; 受重視的; 寶貴的。②被評價的; 被估過價的。③貴重的; 有價值的。

valued policy 〖保險〗定值保險單。

value in use 使用價值。

value judgment 價值判斷(對人或事物之價值、善惡等所作的主觀評斷)。

val·ue·less ['væljulıs; 'væljulis] *adj.* 無價值的。—**ness,** *n.*

value of labor power 勞工價值。

value product 價值產品。

val·u·er ['væljuɚ; 'væljuə] *n.* ①評價者。②〖英〗價格核定人。

va·lu·ta [vɑ'lutɑ; vɑ:'lu:tɑ:] *n.* 本國貨幣與某一外國貨幣之固定兌換率。

val·vate ['vælvet; 'vælveit] *adj.* ①有閥的; 似閥的; 以閥開的。②〖植物〗相接而不相疊的(如若干花苞之瓣); 瓣裂的。

***valve** [vælv; vælv] *n., v.,* **valved, valv·ing.** —*n.* ①活瓣; 活門; 汽門; 汽塞; 活塞。②瓣膜。③(貝殼之) 一瓣。④(無線電之) 眞空管。⑤〖植物〗筴片。⑥(管樂器之) 栓塞。*safety valve* (鍋爐等之)安全瓣; 保安閥。

—*v.t.* ①以活門或活塞等控制…之流動。②供以活門或活塞。③打開活塞放(汽球中之氣體)。—*v.i.* ①用活瓣或活塞。②打開活塞使汽球下降。—**less,** *adj.*
valved 〔vælvd; vælvd〕 *adj.* 裝有活門「或活塞等的。」
val·vu·lar 〔ˈvælvjələ·; ˈvælvjulə〕 *adj.* ①(心臟的)膜瓣的。②有活瓣的; 有活瓣之功能或形狀的。
va·moose 〔væˈmus; vəˈmu:s〕 *v.i.* & *v.t.*, **-moosed, -moos·ing.** 〖俚〗匆匆離去; 跑掉。(亦作 **vamose**)
vamp¹ 〔væmp; væmp〕 *n.* ①靴或鞋前端的鞋面。②舊物上蒙之新面。③任何補綴物。④〖音樂〗即席伴奏。 —*v.t.* ①做、換或補(鞋、靴前端之)鞋面。②翻新; 修補或增加新材料使變新〖up〗. ③以零星材料湊成〖up〗. ④即席伴奏。—*v.i.* 作即席伴奏。*vamp up* **a.** 將…翻新; 使(舊物)變新。 **b.** 捏造。 **c.** 拼湊。
vamp² *n.* 〖俚〗水性楊花的女人; 以色相騙錢之蕩婦。—*v.t.* 〖俚〗以美色引誘(男人)。—*v.i.* 〖俚〗迷惑男人。
vamp·er 〔ˈvæmpə·; ˈvæmpə〕 *n.* ①補鞋匠; 修補匠。②〖音樂〗即席伴奏者。③誘惑男人者。
vam·pire 〔ˈvæmpaɪr; ˈvæmpaiə〕 *n.* ①吸血鬼(傳說中之死屍, 夜間能自墳中出來, 吸食睡覺者的血)。②吸血者; 榨取他人錢財者。③以色相賺錢的蕩婦。④扮演蕩婦的女伶。⑤〖動物〗吸血蝙蝠 (=vampire bat).
vampire bat 〖動物〗吸血蝙蝠。
***van¹** 〔væn; væn〕 *n.* ①傢具搬運車; 貨車; 有蓋貨車。 a luggage *van.* 行李車。②吉卜賽人所住之篷車。—*v.t.* 用貨車搬運。 —*v.i.* 乘貨車旅行。
van² *n.* 先鋒; 前驅。 *be in the van* 為…之先驅。 *lead the van* 為先鋒。
van³ *n.* 〖詩〗翼。
va·nad·i·nite 〔vəˈnædəˌnaɪt; vəˈnædinait〕 *n.* 〖礦〗褐鉛礦。
va·na·di·um 〔vəˈnedɪəm; vəˈneidjəm〕 *n.* 〖化〗釩(一種金屬元素, 其符號為 V).
vanadium steel 釩鋼。
Van Allen (radiation) belt 范艾倫輻射帶(環繞地球之內外兩個輻射帶)。
Vance 〔væns; væns〕 *n.* 范錫 (Cyrus, 1917–, 1977– 任美國國務卿)。
Van·cou·ver 〔vænˈkuvə·; vænˈku:və〕 *n.* 溫哥華(加拿大西南部之一工業城市)。
Van·dal 〔ˈvændḷ; ˈvændəl〕 *n.* ①汪達爾人(紀元五世紀侵入西歐高盧及西班牙, 最後卜居北非之東日耳曼蠻族, 455 年曾入侵羅馬, 大肆破壞擄掠)。②(v–) 無知或惡意破壞文化或藝術品之人。 —*adj.* ①汪達爾人的。②(v–) 野蠻的; 無知或惡意破壞文化或藝術品的。
Van·dal·ic 〔vænˈdælɪk; vænˈdælik〕 *adj.* ①汪達爾人的。②(v–) 無知或惡意破壞文化或藝術品者的。
van·dal·ism 〔ˈvændḷˌɪzəm; ˈvændəlizəm〕 *n.* ①汪達爾人之行為或作風。②無知或惡意破壞文化或藝術品的行為。
van·dal·is·tic 〔ˌvændḷˈɪstɪk; ˌvændəˈlistik〕 *adj.* ①破壞成性的; 破壞的。②汪達爾人的。
van·dal·ize 〔ˈvændḷˌaɪz; ˈvændəlaiz〕 *v.t.*, **-ized, -iz·ing.** 任意破壞; 不必要地破壞。
Van·dyke¹ 〔vænˈdaɪk; vænˈdaik〕 *n.* 范大克(Sir Anthony, 1599–1641, 法蘭特斯, Flanders 之畫家)。(亦作 **Van Dyck**)
Van·dyke² *n.* ①Sir Anthony Vandyke 所畫之肖像或畫。②=**Vandyke beard.** ③=**Vandyke collar.** —*adj.* ①Sir Anthony Vandyke 之風格的。②Sir Anthony Vandyke 所繪肖像之服式及風度等的。
Vandyke beard 范大克式之鬚(短尖而修整者)。
Vandyke brown 范大克氏使用之「深褐色顏料。」
Vandyke collar (or **cape**) 范大克氏衣領(帶鋸齒邊的寬衣領)。
van·dyked 〔vænˈdaɪkt; vænˈdaikt〕 *adj.* 剪成鋸齒形的。
vane 〔ven; vein〕 *n.* ①風向標; 風信旗。②風車之一葉; 螺旋槳之一葉。③羽毛之平軟部分; 羽瓣。④〖測量〗(準尺上可移動之)覘板; (羅盤等之)視準器。⑤見風轉舵之人; 朝三暮四之人。⑥箭翎。—**vaned,** *adj.* —**less,** *adj.*
Van Gogh 〔vænˈgo; vænˈgɔx, –ˈgɔk, –ˈgɔf〕 梵谷(Vincent, 1853–1890, 荷蘭畫家)。
van·guard 〔ˈvænˌgɑrd; ˈvængɑ:d〕 *n.* ①先鋒; 先驅。②領導地位。③政治、社會或文化運動之領袖。—**ism,** —**ist,** *n.*
va·nil·la 〔vəˈnɪlə; vəˈnilə〕 *n.* ①〖植物〗香草。②自其果莢中取出之香精 (用作製冰淇淋、香水等)。—**va·nil·lic,** *adj.*
vanilla bean 香草豆。
vanilla extract 從香草豆中取出之「香精。」
van·il·lin 〔ˈvænəlɪn; ˈvænilin〕 *n.* 香蘭精; 香蘭醛。—**va·nil·lic,** *adj.*
***van·ish** 〔ˈvænɪʃ; ˈvæniʃ〕 *v.i.* 消失; 消散; 消滅。—*v.t.* 使消失。
vanishing cream (化妝用之)雪花「膏。」
van·ish·ing·ly 〔ˈvænɪʃɪŋlɪ; ˈvæniʃiŋli〕 *adv.* 不知不覺地; 烟消雲散地; 化為烏有地。
vanishing point ①〖透視學〗構成各物體輪廓之平行線似乎相集之一點。②〖俗〗消失點; 消失階段。
van·ish·ment 〔ˈvænɪʃmənt; ˈvæniʃmənt〕 *n.* 消失; 消滅。
***van·i·ty** 〔ˈvænətɪ; ˈvæniti〕 *n.*, *pl.* **-ties.** ①空虛; 空幻。 All is *vanity.* 一切皆空。②虛榮; 浮華; 虛榮心; 自負; 虛誇。③無用或無價值之事物。④無益之歡樂或表現。⑤無影響; 不成功。⑥ =**vanity case.** ⑦連鏡之梳妝臺。
vanity case (or **box**) (女人隨身攜「帶的)小梳妝盒。」
Vanity Fair ①浮華世界(John Bunyan 在 *Pilgrim's Progress* 所描述之市集, 象徵人世浮華)。②浮華世界 (Thackeray 所著之小說名)。③(常v– f–)人世間之浮華世界。
vanity publisher 由作者出資而替作者發行新書的出版商。(亦作 **vanity press**)
vanity table 梳妝臺。
van line 〖美〗長途貨運公司 (尤指用大型貨車替人搬家者)。
van·load 〔ˈvænˌlod; ˈvænloud〕 *n.* —「貨車之載運量。」
van·man 〔ˈvænmən; ˈvænmən〕 *n.*, *pl.* **-men.** 貨車駕駛人; 貨車工人。
van·quish 〔ˈvæŋkwɪʃ; ˈvæŋkwiʃ〕 *v.t.* 征服; 擊敗。—**a·ble,** *adj.* —**er,** —**ment,** *n.*
van·quished 〔ˈvæŋkwɪʃt; ˈvæŋkwiʃt〕 *adj.* 被擊敗的; 被征服的。 *the vanquished* 被征服者; 敗北者。
van·tage 〔ˈvæntɪdʒ; ˈvɑ:ntidʒ〕 *n.* ①優勢; 好機會。②有利之點; 優越之地位; 利益。③〖網球〗deuce 後先得之一分。 *for* (or *to*) *the vantage* 此外; 加之。 *of vantage* 有利的; 占優勢的。 「(亦作 **vantage point**)」
vantage ground 有利地位; 地利。
van't Hoff 〔vɑntˈhɔf; vɑ:ntˈhɔ:f〕 凡特霍夫 (Jacobus Hendricus, 1852–1911, 荷蘭物理化學家, 曾獲1901年諾貝爾化學獎)。
van·ward 〔ˈvænwəd; ˈvænwəd〕 *adj.* &

adv. 在前的(地);向前的(地);向前鋒的(地)。

vap·id ['væpɪd; 'væpid] *adj.* ①無味的;平淡無味的。②平淡無奇的;無趣味的;無生氣的。—**ly,** *adv.* —**ness,** *n.*

va·pid·i·ty [və'pɪdətɪ; væ'piditi] *n.* ①無味。②無趣;無生氣。

***va·po(u)r** ['vepɚ; 'veipə] *n.* ①蒸氣;霧;煙霧;水蒸氣。②〖物理〗汽。③空想;幻想。④〖古〗(the-)(*pl.*)憂鬱;精神不快。⑤用鼻嗅的霧狀或揮發性藥物。⑥排出之水蒸氣或廢氣。—*v.i.* ①蒸發;發散;發出蒸氣。②誇言;吹噓。③沮喪。—*v.t.* ①蒸發(蒸氣)。②吹牛;誇大。—**like,** *adj.* —**less,** *adj.*

va·por·a·ble ['vepərəbl; 'veipərəbl] *adj.* 可化爲水氣的;可化爲霧狀物的。—**va·por·a·bil·i·ty,** *n.*

va·po·rar·i·um [ˌvepə'rɛrɪəm; ˌveipə'rɛəriəm] *n., pl.* **-rar·i·ums** or **-rar·i·a** [-'rɛrɪə;-'rɛəriə]. 蒸氣浴室。

vapor bath ①蒸氣浴。②蒸氣浴室。

va·por·if·ic [ˌvepə'rɪfɪk; ˌveipə'rifik] *adj.* ①產生蒸氣的。②似蒸氣的。

va·por·im·e·ter [ˌvepə'rɪmətɚ; ˌveipə'rimitə] *n.* 蒸氣計;蒸氣壓力計。

va·por·ing ['vepərɪŋ; 'veipəriŋ] *adj.* ①蒸發的。②似蒸氣的。③誇大的;說大話的。—*n.* 誇大;說大話。—**ly,** *adv.*

va·por·ish ['vepərɪʃ; 'veipəriʃ] *adj.* ①像蒸氣的。②多蒸氣的。③模糊的;朦朧的。④憂鬱的;因憂鬱而起的。

va·por·i·za·tion [ˌvepərə'zeʃən; ˌveipərai'zeiʃən] *n.* ①蒸發。②蒸氣治療。

va·por·ize ['vepəˌraɪz; 'veipəraiz] *v.,* **-ized, -iz·ing.** —*v.t.* 蒸發;使化爲氣。—*v.i.* ①蒸發;氣化。②說大話;吹牛。

va·por·iz·er ['vepəˌraɪzɚ; 'veipəraizə] *n.* 蒸發器;噴霧器。

vapor lock 汽油引擎中因高熱使汽油在輸油管或汽化管中蒸發而致引擎熄火之現象。

va·por·ous ['vepərəs; 'veipərəs] *adj.* ①發出蒸氣的;蒸氣狀的;多蒸氣的;多霧的。②無實質的;幻想的;空想的;妄想的。

vapor tension (or **pressure**) 蒸氣壓;汽壓。

vapor trail 噴射機及火箭等在高空留下的白色霧線(係廢氣中之水蒸氣冷凝而成)。(亦作 **contrail**)

va·por·y ['vepərɪ; 'veipəri] *adj.* =vaporous.

va·que·ro [vɑ'kerə; vɑː'kɛərə] *n.* (墨西哥、美國西南部之)飼養家畜的人;牧童。

var. ①variant. ②variation. ③variety. ④various.

Va·ran·gi·an [və'rændʒɪən; və'rændʒiən] *n.* ①九世紀時在 Rurik 領導下定居俄羅斯並建立俄國之北歐人。②拜占庭皇帝所僱用之 Varangian 衞士。—*adj.* Varangian 的。

var·i·a ['vɛrɪə; 'vɛəriə] *n. pl.* 雜物;雜文。

***var·i·a·ble** ['vɛrɪəbl; 'vɛəriəbl] *adj.* ①易變的;能變的;可變的;變化的。*variable* weather. 變化無常的天氣。②〖生物〗變異的;異於嚴格之生物型態的。—*n.* ①可變性;可變物。②方向不定之風。③(*pl.*)東北貿易風帶與東南貿易風帶間之變風地帶。—**var·i·a·bil·i·ty,** *n.* —**var·i·a·bly,** *adv.*

Variable Zone 〖地理〗溫帶。

var·i·ance ['vɛrɪəns; 'vɛəriəns] *n.* ①不同;差異。②變化;變易;改變。③不和;齟齬。**at variance** a. 衝突的;不一致的。b. 不和的;爭執的。*at variance* with the neighbors. 與鄰居不睦。

var·i·ant ['vɛrɪənt; 'vɛəriənt] *adj.* ①不同的;差異的。②變異的;改變的。—*n.* ①另一不同的形式。②一個字的不同的發音或拼法。③改編;改寫。

***var·i·a·tion** [ˌvɛrɪ'eʃən; ˌvɛəri'eiʃən] *n.* ①變化;變易;改變。②變量;變度。③語尾變化。④變異的形式。⑤〖音樂〗變奏。⑥〖生物〗變種;變異。⑦〖天文〗運行或軌道之改變。—**al,** *adj.*

var·i·cel·la [ˌværɪ'sɛlə; ˌværi'selə] *n.* 〖醫〗水痘。

var·i·co·cele ['værɪkoˌsil; 'værikousiːl] *n.* 〖醫〗精索靜脈曲張;蜿蜒靜脈腫。

var·i·col·ored ['vɛrɪˌkʌlɚd; 'vɛəriˌkʌləd] *adj.* ①雜色的;五顏六色的;彩色繽紛的。②各色各樣的。

var·i·cose ['værɪˌkos; 'værikous] *adj.* ①腫脹的;曲張的。②靜脈曲張的;治療靜脈曲張的。

var·i·co·sis [ˌværɪ'kosɪs; ˌværi'kousis] *n.* ①靜脈瘤之形成。②=**varicosity.**

var·i·cos·i·ty [ˌværɪ'kɑsətɪ; ˌværi'kɔsiti] *n., pl.* **-ties.** ①曲張;腫脹。②=**varix.**

***var·ied** ['vɛrɪd; 'vɛərid] *adj.* ①不同的;種種的;變化的。②改變的。③有多種顏色的。—**ly,** *adv.* —**ness,** *n.*

var·i·e·gate ['vɛrɪˌget; 'vɛərigeit] *v.t.,* **-gat·ed, -gat·ing.** ①使呈雜色(如斑點、條紋等)。②使有差異。—**var·i·e·ga·tion, var·i·e·ga·tor,** *n.*

var·i·e·gat·ed ['vɛrɪˌgetɪd; 'vɛərigeitid] *adj.* ①雜色的;斑駁的。②有變化的;有各種不同之性質、形狀或外貌的。

va·ri·e·tal [və'raɪətəl; və'raiətəl] *adj.* 〖生物〗變種的。—**ly,** *adv.*

:va·ri·e·ty [və'raɪətɪ; və'raiəti] *n., pl.* **-ties.** ①變化;多樣;多端;種種。This shop has a *variety* of toys. 這家商店有種種的玩具。②種類。What *variety* of cake do you prefer? 你喜歡哪一種糕餅? ③〖生物〗種。④〖英〗雜耍。

variety meat 可作食用之牲畜五臟或其他器官(如肝、腸、舌等)。

variety show 雜耍。

variety store ①出售布疋、五金等各種貨物之商店。②雜貨店。

variety theater 雜耍劇場。

var·i·form ['vɛrɪˌfɔrm; 'vɛərifɔːm] *adj.* 形形色色的;有多種形態的。

var·i·o·cou·pler [ˌvɛrɪo'kʌplɚ; ˌvɛəriou'kʌplə] *n.* 〖電〗可變耦合器。

va·ri·o·la [və'raɪələ; və'raiələ] *n.* 〖醫〗痘症;天花。

var·i·o·late ['vɛrɪəˌlet; 'vɛəriəleit] *v.t.,* **-lat·ed, -lat·ing.** 種牛痘。—*adj.* 似牛痘的。

var·i·o·loid ['vɛrɪəˌlɔɪd; 'vɛəriəlɔid] *adj.* 〖醫〗類似天花的;假性天花的。—*n.* 〖醫〗假性天花。

va·ri·o·lous [və'raɪələs; və'raiələs] *adj.* ①〖醫〗天花的;患天花的。②〖動物〗有痘痕般之小窩的。(亦作 **variolar**)

var·i·om·e·ter [ˌvɛrɪ'ɑmətɚ; ˌvɛəri'ɔmitə] *n.* ①〖電〗磁力偏差計。②〖無線電〗可變電感器。

var·i·o·rum [ˌvɛrɪ'orəm; ˌvɛəri'ɔːrəm] *adj.* ①集註的。②集不同版本而成之版本的。—*n.* ①集註本。②集不同版本而成之版本。

:var·i·ous ['vɛrɪəs; 'vɛəriəs] *adj.* ①不

同的。*various* opinions. 不同的意見。②種種的;各式各樣的;多方面的;多種的。for *various* reasons. 爲了種種的理由。③許多的。④改變的;可轉變的。—**ness,** *n.*

var·i·ous·ly [ˈvɛrɪəslɪ; ˈvɛəriəsli] *adv.* ①不同地;變化地。②在不同時間地。

var·ix [ˈvɛrɪks; ˈvɛəriks] *n., pl.* **-i·ces** [-ɪˌsiz; -isiːz]. ①〖醫〗靜脈曲張;血管曲張。②〖動物〗(卷貝之)螺層。

var·let [ˈvɑrlɪt; ˈvɑːlit] *n.* 〖古〗①侍從。②無賴;流氓。

var·let·ry [ˈvɑrlɛtrɪ; ˈvɑːletri] *n.* ①侍從之集合稱。②下流社會之人;羣衆;庶民。

var·mint [ˈvɑrmɪnt; ˈvɑːmint] *n.* 〖方〗①歹徒;惡漢;頑童;討厭的人。②害蟲;害獸;害鳥。(亦作 **varment**)

***var·nish** [ˈvɑrnɪʃ; ˈvɑːniʃ] *n.* ①假漆;油漆;假漆面。②光澤面。③虛飾;文飾。④(*pl.*)〖俚〗火車;客車。—*v.t.* ①塗油漆於(牆壁、桌子等)。②掩飾;文飾(過失、弱點等)。—**er,** *n.* —**y,** *adj.*

varnishing day ①畫展開幕之前日(供畫家最後修飾其作品之日)。②展覽會開幕日。

varnish tree 漆樹。

var·si·ty [ˈvɑrsətɪ; ˈvɑːsiti] *n., pl.* **-ties.** ①大學(尤指牛津與劍橋大學)。②大學運動代表隊。—*adj.* 大學代表隊的;大學代表隊比賽的。

var·us [ˈvɛrəs; ˈvɛərəs] *n.* 〖醫〗內翻足。—*adj.* ①內翻的(足)。②籮圈腿的;弓形腿的。

***var·y** [ˈvɛrɪ; ˈvɛəri] *v.,* **var·ied, var·y·ing.** —*v.t.* ①改變;變換;使不同。②〖音樂〗變奏。③使有變化。—*v.i.* ①改變;不同;有變化。Customs *vary* with the times. 習俗隨時代而不同。②交替變換。③違反;違背〖常from〗. to *vary* from a rule. 違背規則。—**var·i·er,** *n.* —**ing·ly,** *adv.*

vas [væs; væs] *n., pl.* **va·sa** [ˈvesə; ˈveisə]. 〖拉〗〖解剖〗脈管;導管。

vas·cu·lar [ˈvæskjələ˞; ˈvæskjulə] *adj.* 〖解剖〗脈管的;導管的;血管的。(亦作 **vasculose, vasculous**) —**ly,** *adv.*

vascular bundle 〖植物〗維管束。

vas·cu·lar·i·ty [ˌvæskjəˈlærətɪ; ˌvæskjuˈlæriti] *n., pl.* **-ties.** 〖生物〗脈管或導管之形狀;脈管或導管之生長;血管分布。

vas·cu·lar·ize [ˈvæskjələˌraɪz; ˈvæskjuləraiz] *v.t. & v.i.,* **-ized, -iz·ing.** 脈管化。—**vas·cu·lar·i·za·tion,** *n.*

vas·cu·lum [ˈvæskjələm; ˈvæskjuləm] *n., pl.* **-la** [-lə; -lə], **-lums.** 植物採集箱。

vas de·fe·rens [væsˈdɛfəˌrɛnz; væsˈdefərenz] 〖拉〗 *pl.* **va·sa de·fe·ren·ti·a** [ˈvesəˌdɛfəˈrɛnʃɪə; ˈveisəˌdefəˈrenʃiə]. 〖解剖〗輸精管;輸出管。

***vase** [ves; vɑːz] *n.* 瓶;花瓶。—**like,** *adj.*

vas·ec·to·my [væsˈɛktəmɪ; væˈsektəmi] *n., pl.* **-mies.** 〖外科〗輸精管切除術。

vas·e·line [ˈvæslˌin; ˈvæsiliːn] *n.* 〖化〗①凡士林。②(V-) 〖商標名〗凡士林。

vas·o·li·ga·tion [ˌvæsolɪˈgeʃən; ˌvæsouliˈgeiʃən] *n.* 〖外科〗輸精管結紮術。(亦作 **vasoligature**)

vas·o·mo·tor [ˌvæsəˈmotə˞; ˌvæsəˈmoutə] *adj.* 〖生理〗調節或管制血管口徑之大小的(神經、神經中樞或藥物);血管舒縮的。

vas·sal [ˈvæsl; ˈvæsəl] *n.* ①(封建時代的)家臣;諸侯。②隸屬者;奴僕。—*adj.* ①家臣的;諸侯的。②隸屬的;奴僕的。a *vassal* state. 屬國。—**less,** *adj.*

vas·sal·age [ˈvæslɪdʒ; ˈvæsəlidʒ] *n.* ①家臣的地位、發誓、效忠或其應服之役。②隸屬。③采邑;家臣之領地。④家臣之集合稱。

‡**vast** [væst; vɑːst] *adj.* ①巨大的;廣大的;浩大的。a *vast* sum of money. 巨額的金錢。②〖俗〗非常的。a matter of *vast* importance. 非常重大的事情。—*n.* 〖古,詩〗廣漠無邊的空間或幅員。—**ness,** *n.*

vas·ti·tude [ˈvæstəˌtjud; ˈvæstitjuːd] *n.* 廣大;廣漠無際。

***vast·ly** [ˈvæstlɪ; ˈvɑːstli] *adv.* 極端地;廣大地;非常地。

vast·y [ˈvæstɪ; ˈvɑːsti] *adj.,* **vast·i·er, vast·i·est.** 廣大的;廣漠的;巨大的。

VAT value-added tax.

vat [væt; væt] *n., v.,* **vat·ted, vat·ting.** —*n.* ①(供釀造、發酵等中裝盛液體之)大桶。②含有已溶解顏料之液體。—*v.t.* 置入大桶中;在大桶中摻和。

Vat. Vatican.

vat·ful [ˈvætfʊl; ˈvætful] *n., pl.* **-fuls.** 一個大桶 (vat) 能裝入的量。

vat·i·cal [ˈvætəkl; ˈvætikəl] *adj.* 預言的。(亦作 **vatic**) —**ly,** *adv.*

Vat·i·can [ˈvætɪkən; ˈvætikən] *n.* ①(the-) (羅馬教皇之) 教廷 (亦作 **Vatican Palace**)。②教皇權;教皇政治。③梵諦岡之建築集合稱。④梵諦岡之文化寶藏。—*adj.* 梵諦岡的;教廷的。

Vatican City (State) 梵諦岡(在羅馬市內,爲教皇統治之一獨立國)。

Vat·i·can·ism [ˈvætɪkənɪzm; ˈvætikənizm] *n.* 教皇絕對至上主義。—**Vat·i·can·ist,** *n.*

va·tic·i·nal [vəˈtɪsənl; vəˈtisinəl] *adj.* 預言的;預言上的。

va·tic·i·nate [vəˈtɪsəˌnet; væˈtisineit] *v.t. & v.i.,* **-nat·ed, -nat·ing.** 預言;預斷。

va·tic·i·na·tion [vəˌtɪsəˈneʃən; vəˌtisiˈneiʃən] *n.* ①(作)預言。②預言之能力。

va·tic·i·na·tor [vəˈtɪsəˌnetə˞; væˈtisineitə] *n.* 預言者;預言家。

vau·de·ville [ˈvodəˌvɪl; ˈvoudəvil] *n.* ①雜耍(包括歌唱、舞蹈、技術等)表演。②輕鬆之音樂喜劇。

vau·de·vil·lian [ˌvodəˈvɪljən; ˌvoudəˈviljən] *n.* (亦作 **vaudevillist**) 表演雜耍的人。—*adj.* 雜耍的。

***vault**[1] [vɔlt; vɔːlt, vɔlt] *n.* ①拱形圓屋頂;穹窿。②窖;地下室。wine *vault*. 酒窖。③貴重物品儲藏室。④地下墳墓。⑤蒼穹;天空。⑥保險箱。⑦〖解剖〗穹窿。*the vault of heaven* 蒼穹。—*v.t. & v.i.* 做成圓拱形;覆以圓屋頂;變爲圓拱形。—**like,** *adj.*

vault[2] *v.i.* 撐竿跳躍;以手支撐跳躍;跳躍。—*v.t.* 撐竿跳過;以手支撐跳過;跳過。—*n.* 跳躍;撐竿跳。pole *vault*. 撐竿跳。—**er,** *n.*

vault·ed [ˈvɔltɪd; ˈvɔːltid] *adj.* ①像穹窿的;拱形的。②有拱形圓屋頂的。

vault·ing[1] [ˈvɔltɪŋ; ˈvɔːltiŋ] *n.* 〖建築〗穹窿工事;拱形圓頂建築物;圓屋頂(集合稱)。

vault·ing[2] *adj.* ①跳躍的;跳過的;跳躍用的。②誇大的;過分自信的。

vaulting horse (練習跳躍時用的)木馬。

vault light 地下室(用厚玻璃遮住)的透光孔。

vault·y [ˈvɔltɪ; ˈvɔːlti] *adj.* 拱形的;像穹窿的。

vaunt [vɔnt, vɑnt; vɔːnt] *n.* 吹噓;誇張。—*v.i.* 誇耀。—*v.t.* 自誇;炫耀。—**ing·ly,** *adv.*

vaunt-cour·i·er [ˈvɑntˈkʊrɪə˞; ˈvɔntˈkuriə] *n.* ①〖廢〗前哨。②前驅;先鋒。

vaunt·ed [ˈvɔntɪd; ˈvɔːntid] *adj.* 被過分吹噓的。

vaunt·ing [ˈvɔntɪŋ; ˈvɔːntiŋ] *adj.* 驕傲的;自誇的。

V

vaunt·y ['vɔntɪ; 'vɔːnti] *adj.* 【蘇】驕慢的;自誇的;虛榮的。
v. aux. auxiliary verb. **vb.** ①verb. ②verbal. **vb. n.** verbal noun.
V-bomb ['vi,bɑm; 'viːbɔm] *n.* 第二次世界大戰中德國的火箭飛彈 V-1 及 V-2。
V-bomb·er ['vi,bɑmə; 'viː,bɔmə] *n.* 【英】裝有核子彈頭的彈道飛彈。
V. C. ①Veterinary Corps. ②Vice-Chairman. ③Vice-Chancellor. ④Vice-Consul. ⑤Victoria Cross. ⑥Vietcong.
VD venereal disease. **Vd** (亦作 V) 化學元素 vanadium 之符號。 **V.D.** ①vapour density. ②venereal disease. ③Volunteer (Officers') Decoration.
v.d. various dates.
V-Day (第二次世界大戰同盟國之最後)勝利日 (1946年12月31日, 爲 Victory Day之略)。
've [v;v] =have.
***veal** [vil; viːl] *n.*① 小牛之肉(供食用者)。②(專供食用的)牛犢。
veal·y ['vilɪ; 'viːli] *adj.* 【俗】①像牛犢的。②未成熟的;幼稚的。
vec·to·graph ['vɛktə,græf; 'vektəgrɑːf] *n.* 一種立體照片。
vec·tor ['vɛktə; 'vektə] *n.* ①【數學】向量;矢量。②【生物】帶菌者;傳播病菌之媒介物(如昆蟲等)。③【天文】一星體之中心與圍繞其運行之他星體之中心間的直線距離。④飛機或飛彈飛行之方向。—**i·al,** *adj.* —**i·al·ly,** *adv.*
vector product 矢積。
vector space 【數學】矢量空間。
vector sum 矢和。
Ve·da ['vedə; 'veidə] *n.* 吠陀(印度最古之宗教文學、婆羅門教之根本經典, 計有 Rig-Veda 詩篇吠陀, Sama-Veda 咏歌吠陀, Atharva-Veda 呪文吠陀, Yajur-Veda 祭祠吠陀四部)。「=**Vedic.**」
Ve·da·ic [ve'deɪk; vei'deiik] *adj., n.*
V-E Day['vi'ide; 'viː'iːdei]二次世界大戰盟國結束歐戰之勝利日(1945年5月8日)。
ve·dette [və'dɛt;vi'det] 【法】 *n.* ①【海軍】哨艇。②【軍】騎兵之哨兵。(亦作 **vidette**)
Ve·dic ['vedɪk; 'veidik] *adj.* 吠陀的。—*n.* 吠陀梵語(一種早期的梵文)。「教。」
Ve·dism ['vedɪzm; 'veidizm] *n.* 吠陀
vee [vi; viː] *n.* ①【美俗】五元之紙幣。②V字;V字形。—*adj.* V形的。
veep [vip; viːp] *n.* 【俗】美國副總統 (=vice-president). (亦作 **veepee**)
veer¹ [vɪr; viə] *v.i.* ①(風)改變方向。②改變意見、態度等。③改變行進的方向。④轉向; 轉入。⑤【航海】以船首向下風轉變船向。—*v.t.* ①改變(船)之航行方向。②改變…之意見等。*veer and haul* a.【航海】將繩一會兒放鬆,一會兒拉緊。b. 易變。—*n.* 轉向;改變方向。—**ing,** *n., adj.* —**ing·ly,** *adv.*
veer² *v.t.* ①放鬆(繩索);使慢慢放開。②將繩解開使(船或浮標)飄走。
veer·ing ['vɪrɪŋ; 'viəriŋ] *n.* 轉向; 改變。—*adj.* 猶豫的;改變的。
veer·y ['vɪrɪ; 'viəri] *n., pl.* **veer·ies.** 北美產的一種畫眉鳥。
Ve·ga ['vigə; 'viːgə] *n.* 【天文】 織女星(琴座之藍白色一等星)。 「素食主義的人。」
ve·gan ['vɛgən; 'vegən] *n.* 【英】嚴守
‡veg·e·ta·ble ['vɛdʒətəbl; 'vedʒitəbl] *n.* ①蔬菜。②植物。③無精打采的人。—*adj.* ①蔬菜的。*vegetable* diet. 蔬食。②植物的。③平平靜靜的;缺乏生趣的。
vegetable butter 由植物油加工製造而成的奶油。
vegetable kingdom 植物界。
vegetable oil 植物油。
vegetable silk 木棉。
vegetable tallow 一種自植物中取得之脂肪(用以製造肥皂、蠟燭等)。
vegetable wax 木蠟;植物葉或果實等部分所分泌之蠟質。
veg·e·ta·blize['vɛdʒətəbl,aɪz; 'vedʒitəblaiz] *v.i.,* **-ized, -iz·ing.** =**vegetate**②.
veg·e·ta·bly ['vɛdʒtəblɪ; 'vedʒtəbli] *adv.* 平平淡淡地;無精打采地。
veg·e·tal ['vɛdʒətl; 'vedʒitl] *adj.* ①植物的;蔬菜的; 植物性的; 蔬菜性的。②植物與動物共有之特質的; 有植物與動物共有之特質(如吸收、營養、生長等)的。③【植物】攝取養分以生長的(別於繁殖的)。—**i·ty,** *n.*—**veg·e·tism,** *n.* 「animal pole 相對)。」
vegetal pole 【生物】(卵的)植物極(與
veg·e·tar·i·an [,vɛdʒə'tɛrɪən;,vedʒi'tɛəriən] *n.*蔬食者。—*adj.* ①蔬食的。②素的;不含肉類的。③蔬食主義的;素食主義的。
veg·e·tar·i·an·ism [,vɛdʒə'tɛrɪənɪzəm; ,vedʒi'tɛəriənizəm] *n.* 素食主義。
veg·e·tate['vɛdʒə,tet; 'vedʒiteit] *v.i.,* **-tat·ed, -tat·ing.** ①(植物)生長。②像植物般生長和生活(過單調而不用思想的生活); 飽食終日無所事事地生活。③【醫】(疣、瘤)長大。
***veg·e·ta·tion** [,vɛdʒə'teʃən; ,vedʒi'teiʃən] *n.* ①(植物的)生長。There is not much *vegetation* in deserts. 在沙漠裏植物不大生長。②植物;草木。③單調貧乏的生活。④【醫】增殖體;贅生物。
veg·e·ta·tive ['vɛdʒə,tetɪv; 'vedʒiteitiv] *adj.* ①植物的;植物生長的;與植物生長有關的。②像植物般生長的; 能像植物般生長的。③【生物】關於生長與發展的(爲關於生殖的之對)。④能使植物生長的。⑤無性的(生殖)。⑥飽食終日無所用心的;不活潑的;靜的。—**ly,** *adv.* —**ness,** *n.*
ve·he·mence ['viəməns; 'viːiməns] *n.* ①暴烈;猛烈。②激烈;熱切。
ve·he·men·cy ['viəmənsɪ, 'vihɪ-; 'viːimənsi, 'viːhəm-] *n.* =**vehemence.**
***ve·he·ment** ['viəmənt, 'vihɪ-; 'viːimənt, 'viːhəm-] *adj.* ①暴烈的;猛烈的。②激烈的;熱烈的;熱切的。
***ve·hi·cle** ['viɪkl; 'viːikl] *n.* ①車輛; 陸上交通工具。②傳達的媒介。Language is the *vehicle* of thought. 語言是傳達思想的工具。③調顏料的溶液。④(達成目的的)工具;手段。⑤【藥】賦形藥;使藥。⑥【修辭】隱喩中用來比喩之物(如 She is a rose 中的 rose).
ve·hic·u·lar [vi'hɪkjələ; vi'hikjulə] *adj.* ①車輛的; 交通工具的; 車輛所用的。②用作車輛的; 用作交通工具的。③車輛所造成的。④用車輛運輸的。⑤媒介物的。
***veil** [vel; veil] *n.* ①面紗;面罩。②任何遮蔽他物之物。A *veil* of clouds hid the sun. 一層雲遮住太陽。③假託;口實。④隱瞞。Let us draw a *veil* over what followed. 我們將後來的事瞞住吧! ⑤婦女作修女之退隱生活或宣誓。⑥【動、植物, 解剖】=**velum.** ⑦【方】大網膜;羊膜;肉胎。*take the veil* 作尼姑; 作修女。—*v.t.* ①以面罩遮掩。Moslem women are *veiled.* 回教婦女戴面罩。②遮掩;隱蔽。③授予修女之面罩。—*v.i.* 戴面紗。—**less,** *adj.* —**like,** *adj.*
***vein** [ven; vein] *n.* ①靜脈。②(植物之)

葉脈；(昆蟲等之)翅脈；(地質、礦山之)礦脈，岩脈。③氣質；意向；心緒；語氣。I am not in the *vein* for writing. 我沒有心情寫作。④(大理石之)紋理。⑤血脈。⑥地下的自然水脈。⑦上述水脈的水。—*v.t.* ①覆以脈紋(通常用於被動語態)。②在…上畫線條。—**al,** —**ed,** *adj.*

vein·ing ['venɪŋ; 'veiniŋ] *n.* 靜脈、葉脈、翅脈或脈狀紋等之形成或排列。

vein·let ['venlɪt; 'veinlit] *n.* 小靜脈；支葉脈。

vein·y ['venɪ; 'veini] *adj.,* **vein·i·er, vein·i·est.** ①有靜脈的。②多紋理的(大理石等)。③有葉脈的。

Vel·a-Ho·tel ['vɛlaho'tɛl; 'velə hou'tel] *n.* 【美】偵測太空中核爆的人造衛星名。

ve·la·men [vɪ'lemɛn; vi'leimen] *n., pl.* **-lam·i·na** [-'læmɪnə; -'læminə]. ①【解剖】膜。②【植物】蘭花氣根之厚軟木質表皮。

ve·lar ['vilɚ; 'vi:lə] *adj.* ①軟顎的。②【語音】軟顎的(音)。—*n.* 【語音】軟顎音。

ve·lar·i·um [vɪ'lɛrɪəm; vi'leəriəm] *n., pl.* **-i·a** [-ɪə; -iə]. ①(古羅馬露天劇場的)天幕。②【動物】擬緣膜。

veld [vɛlt; velt] *n.* (南非洲的)大草原。(亦作 **veldt**)

vel·le·i·ty [vɛ'liətɪ; ve'li:iti] *n., pl.* **-ties.** 【哲學】不完全意欲(無行動表現之輕微欲望)。

vel·li·cate ['vɛlɪˌket; 'velikeit] *v.t. & v.i.,* **-cat·ed, -cat·ing.** 抽動；使抽動。

vel·li·ca·tion [ˌvɛlɪ'keʃən; ˌveli'keiʃən] *n.* ①抽動。②【醫】(面部肌肉)痙攣性抽動。

vel·lum ['vɛləm; 'veləm] *n.* ①一種精美的皮紙(通常以犢皮製成，用以印刷或裝釘)。②牛(羊)皮紙上的原稿；牛(羊)皮紙的版本。③類似此種皮紙之紙或布。—*adj.* ①牛(羊)皮紙製的；仿牛(羊)皮紙的。②用牛(羊)皮紙裝釘的。

vellum paper 牛皮紙。

ve·loc·i·pede [və'lɑsəˌpid; vi'lɔsipi:d] *n.* ①兒童乘用的三輪脚踏車。②早期的自行車或三輪車。③(鐵路上用之)手壓車。—**ve·loc·i·ped·ist,** *n.*

ve·loc·i·ty** [və'lɑsətɪ; vi'lɔsiti, və'l-] *n., pl.* **-ties.** ①迅速。②速度；速率。muzzle velocity*** (發射物離砲口或槍口時之)初速。—*adj.* 速度的。

ve·lours, ve·lour [və'lur; və'luə] *n.* ①天鵝絨；絲絨。②製帽之絲絨料子。

ve·lum ['viləm; 'vi:ləm] *n., pl.* **-la** [-lə; -lə] *for* ①, ②, ③, **-lum** *for* ④. ①【解剖】軟顎；軟口蓋。②【植物】菌膜。③【動物】(水母類之)緣膜。④【氣象】帆狀(雲)。

ve·lure [və'lur; və'luə, -'lju:ə] *n., v.,* **-lured, -lur·ing.** —*n.* 絲絨；天鵝絨。—*v.t.* 以絲絨裝飾(帽子)。

vel·vet** ['vɛlvɪt; 'velvit] *n.* ①天鵝絨；絲絨。②任何似天鵝絨或絲絨之物。③鹿角上之絨毛狀皮。④【俚】**a.** 純利。**b.** 賭博贏得之錢。**c.** 贏得之物。⑤【俗】舒適愉快的情況。⑥鹿角上的軟毛。be on velvet*** 過富裕的舒適生活。***play on velvet*** 【俚】以贏來的錢賭博。***the velvet*** 有利的。—*adj.* 天鵝絨的；天鵝絨一般的；柔軟的。***an iron hand in a velvet glove*** 笑裏藏刀。—**like,** *adj.*

vel·vet·een [ˌvɛlvə'tin; 'velvi'ti:n] *n.* ①棉製天鵝絨。②(*pl.*) 棉製天鵝絨褲子。—*adj.* 棉製天鵝絨做的。

velvet paw ①貓足；貓爪。②外表溫柔而內心殘忍。

vel·vet·y ['vɛlvɪtɪ; 'velviti] *adj.* ①輕輭光滑如天鵝絨的。②性溫和的(酒類)。③輕的；柔的。—**vel·vet·i·ness,** *n.*

Ven. ①Venerable. ②Venice.

ve·nal ['vinḷ; 'vi:nl] *adj.* ①貪汚的；腐敗的。②可用金錢收買的(地位等)。—**ly,** *adv.*

ve·nal·i·ty [vi'nælətɪ; vi:'næliti] *n., pl.* **-ties.** 貪汚；唯利是圖；甘受賄賂。

ve·na·tion [vi'neʃən; vi:'neiʃən] *n.* ①葉脈；翅脈。②葉脈或翅脈之排列。—**al,** *adj.*

vend [vɛnd; vend] *v.t.* ①售賣；販賣。②聲明；發表。—*v.i.* 售賣；販賣。

vend·ee [vɛn'di; ven'di:] *n.* 【法律】買主。

vend·er ['vɛndɚ; 'vendə] *n.* ①小販；售賣者；賣主。②自動販賣機；自動售貨機。

ven·det·ta [vɛn'dɛtə; ven'detə] *n., pl.* **-tas.** ①(兩家族間的)相互仇殺。②世仇；深仇。—**ven·det·tist,** *n.*

vend·i·bil·i·ty [ˌvɛndə'bɪlətɪ; ˌvendə'biliti] *n., pl.* **-ties.** 可賣；能賣；能銷。

vend·i·ble ['vɛndəbḷ; 'vendəbl] *adj.* ①可販賣的。②可用錢購得的。—*n.*(常 *pl.*)可販賣之物品。—**ness,** *n.* —**vend·i·bly,** *adv.*

vending machine 自動販賣機。

ven·dor ['vɛndɚ; 'vendɔ:] *n.* ①=**vender.** ②【法律】賣主(爲 vendee 之反義字)。③自動販賣機(=vending machine).

ven·due [vɛn'dju; ven'dju:] *n.* 公開拍賣。

ve·neer [və'nɪr; və'niə] *v.t.* ①以質料較好之薄木鑲於(傢具)上；以釉塗於(陶器)上。②以美觀而質好之東西鑲於品質平常或粗劣之物件上。③虛飾外表。④將(薄木片)黏合使成三夾板。—*n.* ①鑲於他物上之薄木片或其他美觀之物。②三夾板中之一層。③虛飾；外表之裝飾。—**er,** *n.*

ven·er·a·ble ['vɛnərəbḷ; 'venərəbl] *adj.* ①因年高、古老等而可尊敬的；莊嚴的。②(英國教會)對副監督之尊稱(略作 **Ven.**)；(羅馬教會)被列入聖者之人的頭銜。③(諷刺語)古老的；破舊的。a *venerable* automobile. 老爺車。—*n.* 可尊敬的人。—**ven·er·a·bil·i·ty, —ness,** *n.* —**ven·er·a·bly,** *adv.*

ven·er·ate ['vɛnəˌret; 'venəreit] *v.t.,* **-at·ed, -at·ing.** ①對…懷有敬意。②敬奉；崇拜。—**ven·er·a·tor,** *n.*

ven·er·a·tion [ˌvɛnə'reʃən; ˌvenə'reiʃən] *n.* ①尊敬。②崇高。③敬意；欽佩。

ve·ne·re·al [və'nɪrɪəl; vi'niəriəl] *adj.* ①性慾的；性交的。②因性交而傳染的。a *venereal* disease. 性病(略作 **VD, V.D.**)。③患性病的。④治性病的。⑤引起性慾的。

ven·er·y[1] ['vɛnərɪ; 'venəri] *n.* 【古】性交；性的滿足；性的放縱。

ven·er·y[2] *n.* 狩獵。

ven·e·sec·tion [ˌvɛnɪ'sɛkʃən; ˌveni'sekʃən] *n.* 【醫】靜脈切開放血術；靜脈切開術。(亦作 **venisection**)

Ve·ne·tian [və'niʃən; vi'ni:ʃən] *adj.* (義大利之)威尼斯城(Venice)的；威尼斯式的。—*n.* ①威尼斯人。②(v-)【俗】活動百葉窗。③(=Venetian cloth)一種羊毛織品。

Venetian blind 活動百葉窗。

Venetian glass ①(在威尼斯附近之 Murano 製造的)威尼斯精美玻璃器皿。②彩色裝飾玻璃。

Ven·e·zue·la [ˌvɛnə'zwilə; ˌvene'zweilə] *n.* 委內瑞拉(南美洲北部之國家，首都爲加拉卡斯 Caracas).

venge·ance** ['vɛndʒəns; 'vendʒəns] *n.* 復仇；報仇。Heaven's *vengeance* is slow but sure. 天網恢恢，疏而不漏。take vengeance on*** (or ***upon***) 嚴厲地處罰或報復。***with a vengeance*** **a.** 激烈地；猛烈地；非常

地;極端地。b. 過分地;出乎意料地。

venge·ful [ˈvɛndʒfəl; ˈvendʒful] *adj.* ①復仇心重的; 有復仇心的。②復仇的; 報復的;報仇性的。—**ly,** *adv.*

ve·ni·al [ˈviniəl; ˈviːniəl] *adj.* 可寬恕的;可原諒的;輕微的(過失)。

ve·ni·al·i·ty [ˌviniˈælətɪ; ˌviːniˈæliti] *n.* 可寬恕;可原宥。

venial sin 〖天主教〗小罪。

***Ven·ice** [ˈvɛnɪs; ˈvenis] *n.* 威尼斯(義大利東北部之一沿海城市)。

ve·ni·re fa·ci·as [vɪˈnaɪrɪˈfeʃɪˌæs; viˈnaiəriːˈfeiʃiæs] 〖法律〗陪審員召集狀。(亦作 **venire**)

ve·ni·re·man [vəˈnaɪrɪmən; vəˈnaiərimən] *n., pl.* **-men.** 〖法律〗陪審員。

ven·i·son [ˈvɛnəzn̩, ˈvɛnzn̩; ˈvenzn, -nizn] *n.* (當做食物之)獸肉;(尤指)鹿肉。

Ve·ni·te [vɪˈnaɪti; viˈnaiti] *n.* (晨禱時用做頌詩的)詩篇第九十五篇;其樂曲。

ve·ni, vi·di, vi·ci [ˈvinaɪˈvaɪdaɪˈvaɪsaɪ; ˈveiniːˈviːdiːˈviːkiː] 〖拉〗"我到,我見,我征服"(=I came, I saw, I conquered)(凱撒之名句)。

ven·om [ˈvɛnəm; ˈvenəm] *n.* ①(毒蛇、蜘蛛等之)毒液;毒;毒物。②惡毒;怨恨。—*v.t.* 〖古〗使有毒;使惡毒。

ven·om·ous [ˈvɛnəməs; ˈvenəməs] *adj.* ①有毒的; 有害的。②惡毒的; 惡意的。—**ly,** *adv.* —**ness,** *n.*

ve·nous [ˈvinəs; ˈviːnəs] *adj.* ①靜脈的。②靜脈血的。③(昆蟲)有翅脈的。④〖植物〗多葉脈的。

***vent** [vɛnt; vent] *n.* ①孔;口。the *vent* of a cask. 桶口。②出口;發洩;吐露。The floods found a *vent* through the dikes. 洪水將堤防沖了一個缺口。③(鳥、蟲、魚等之)肛門。④(槍砲之)火門。⑤(汽車中之)通風口。⑥西服上衣背後或兩旁之開叉。—*v.t.* ①鑽孔於。②發洩;吐露。—*v.i.* ①發洩。②(水獺等動物)浮到水面呼吸。—**less,** *adj.*

vent·age [ˈvɛntɪdʒ; ˈventidʒ] *n.* ①出口;漏口;氣孔。②〖音樂〗(管樂器之)指孔。

ven·ter [ˈvɛntə; ˈventə] *n.* ①〖解剖,動物〗腹;(肌肉之)突出部分;(骨骼表面之)凹處。②〖法律〗子宮;母親(就其對子女之關係而言)。

ven·ti·duct [ˈvɛntɪˌdʌkt; ˈventidʌkt] *n.* (公寓房子等的)通風管;通氣管。

***ven·ti·late** [ˈvɛntl̩ˌet; ˈventileit] *v.t.,* **-lat·ed, -lat·ing.** ①使通風; 變換(房間等)裏面的空氣。 ②以新鮮空氣使之純淨。The lungs *ventilate* the blood. 肺以新鮮空氣淨化血液。③洩漏;公開;公開討論。④設置氣孔等。—**ven·ti·la·ble,** *adj.*

ven·ti·la·tion [ˌvɛntl̩ˈeʃən; ˌventiˈleiʃən] *n.* ①通風;流通空氣。②通風設備。The *ventilation* should be improved. 通風設備應該改良。③以新鮮空氣淨化。④公開討論。

ven·ti·la·tive [ˈvɛntəˌletɪv; ˈventileitiv] *adj.* 通風的;通風設備的。

ven·ti·la·tor [ˈvɛntl̩ˌetə; ˈventileitə] *n.* ①通風機; 通風孔。②提醒公衆注意者; 將某事公開者。

ven·tral [ˈvɛntrəl; ˈventrəl] *adj.* ①〖解剖〗前面的;腹部的;腹面的。②〖植物〗下面的; 腹面的。—*n.* ①〖動物〗腹鰭。②(昆蟲)腹節。

ventral fin 〖動物〗腹鰭。

ven·tri·cle [ˈvɛntrɪkl̩; ˈventrikl] *n.* 〖解剖〗心室;腦室;室。

ven·tric·u·lar [vɛnˈtrɪkjələ; venˈtrikjulə] *adj.* ①膨脹的; 隆起的。②〖解剖〗腔的;心室的;腦室的。

ven·tric·u·log·ra·phy [vɛnˌtrɪkjəˈlɑgrəfɪ; venˌtrikjuˈlɔgrəfi] *n.* 腦室照相術;腦室檢影術。

ven·tri·lo·qui·al [ˌvɛntrɪˈlokwɪəl; ˌventriˈloukwiəl] *adj.* 腹語術的; 使用腹語術的。—**ly,** *adv.*

ven·tril·o·quism [vɛnˈtrɪləˌkwɪzəm; venˈtriləkwizəm] *n.* 腹語術。(亦作 **ventriloquy**)

ven·tril·o·quist [vɛnˈtrɪləkwɪst; venˈtriləkwist] *n.* 作腹語者。—**ic,** *adj.*

ven·tril·o·quize [vɛnˈtrɪləˌkwaɪz; venˈtriləkwaiz] *v.i.* & *v.t.,* **-quized, -quiz·ing.** 以腹語說或發聲。

ven·ture** [ˈvɛntʃə; ˈventʃə] *n., v.,* **-tured, -tur·ing.** —*n.* ①冒險。His courage was equal to any *venture.* 他有勇氣從事任何冒險。②投機;商業上的冒險。③用以冒險之物。at a venture*** 胡亂地。He shot *at a venture.* 他胡亂射擊。—*v.t.* ①使…遭遇危險; 以…爲賭注。Men *venture* their lives in war. 人們在戰爭當中冒着生命的危險。②敢; 敢說; 敢爲。I won't *venture* a step farther. 我不敢再往前走一步。③冒…之險。—*v.i.* ①冒險從事;膽敢。 Will you *venture* on another glass of wine? 你敢再喝一杯酒嗎? ②(謙虛語) 冒昧而作。I *venture* to disagree. 恕我斗膽反對。***Nothing venture, nothing have.*** 不入虎穴, 焉得虎子。

ven·ture·some [ˈvɛntʃəsəm; ˈventʃəsəm] *adj.* ①好冒險的; 大膽的。②冒險的; 危險的(事業等)。—**ly,** *adv.* —**ness,** *n.*

ven·tur·ous [ˈvɛntʃərəs; ˈventʃərəs] *adj.* ①不怕危險的; 大膽的。②危險的; 有危險的。—**ly,** *adv.* —**ness,** *n.*

ven·ue [ˈvɛnju; ˈvenjuː] *n.* ①〖法律〗**a.** 犯罪現場及其附近之地; 訟訴原因發生地。 **b.** 審判地點。**c.** 起訴狀上關於審判地之指示。②宣誓書中記載宣誓地點之一項文字。③任何行動或事件發生之現場。④〖俗〗集會場。⑤爭論中某人採取的立場。

***Ve·nus** [ˈvinəs; ˈviːnəs] *n.* ①〖羅馬神話〗司愛和美的女神(即希臘神話中之 Aphrodite)。②金星; 太白星。③極美之女郎。

Ve·nus's-flow·er-bas·ket [ˈvinəsɪzˈflaurˌbæskɪt; ˈviːnəsizˈflauəˌbɑːskit] *n.* 〖動物〗偕老同穴(玻璃海綿屬)。

ve·ra·cious [vəˈreʃəs; vəˈreiʃəs] *adj.* ①誠實的; 可靠的; 可相信的。②眞實的;正確的。—**ly,** *adv.* —**ness,** *n.*

ve·rac·i·ty [vəˈræsətɪ; vəˈræsiti] *n., pl.* **-ties.** ①眞實性; 眞實。②正直; 誠實; 誠懇。③(感覺、科學儀器等之) 精確。④眞確之言論或事物;眞理。

***ve·ran·da(h)** [vəˈrændə; vəˈrændə] *n.* 走廊; 遊廊。—**ed,** —**like,** *adj.*

***verb** [vɝb; vəːb] *n.* 〖文法〗動詞。

ver·bal [ˈvɝbl̩; ˈvəːbəl] *adj.* ①言辭的。②口頭的。③逐字的。④〖文法〗動詞的; 由動詞變來的。—*n.* 〖文法〗由動詞變成的名詞、形容詞等。

verbal criticism 對於辭句之批評。

verbal image 由語言而引起之心像。

verbal inflection 動詞變化。

ver·bal·ism [ˈvɝbl̩ɪzəm; ˈvəːbəlizəm] *n.* ①言語的表現; 字; 片語; 成語。②冗詞; 無意義的套語。③冗贅。④拘泥字句; 咬文嚼字。

ver·bal·ist [ˈvɝbl̩ɪst; ˈvəːbəlist] *n.*

①善用文字的人；擅長言辭的人。②拘泥於字句的人;咬文嚼字的人。—ic, *adj.*

ver·bal·i·za·tion [ˌvɝbl̩ɪˈzeʃən; ˌvəːbəliˈzeiʃən] *n.* ①以言詞表示。②動詞化。③冗長。

ver·bal·ize [ˈvɝbl̩ˌaɪz; ˈvəːbəlaiz] *v.,* -ized, -iz·ing. —*v.t.* ①以言詞表之。②使成動詞。—*v.i.* 用冗長之詞。—**ver·bal·iz·er,** *n.*

ver·bal·ly [ˈvɝblɪ; ˈvəːbəli] *adv.* ①用文字;在文字上。②口頭上。③逐字地(不加修飾地)。④作動詞用。

verbal noun 動名詞。

ver·ba·tim [vɝˈbetɪm; vəːˈbeitim] *adv.* 逐字地。—*adj.* ①逐字的。②精於逐字記錄的。

ver·be·na [vəˈbinə; vəːˈbiːnə] *n.* 〖植物〗任何馬鞭草屬之植物。—**ceous,** *adj.*

ver·bi·age [ˈvɝbɪɪdʒ; ˈvəːbiidʒ] *n.* ①(文章、言辭等之)冗贅。②用字的方式或風格。

verb·i·fy [ˈvɝbəˌfaɪ; ˈvəːbifai] *v.t.,* -fied, -fy·ing. 用做動詞；使(名詞等)動詞化。—**verb·i·fi·ca·tion,** *n.*

ver·bose [vəˈbos; vəːˈbous] *adj.* 用字過多的;冗長的;冗贅的。—**ly,** *adv.* —**ness,** *n.*

ver·bos·i·ty [vəˈbɑsətɪ; vəːˈbɔsiti] *n.* 贅言;冗長。

ver·bo·ten [fəˈbotn̩; fɛəˈboutn] 〖德〗*adj.* 禁止的。

ver·bum sat sa·pi·en·ti [ˈvɝbəmˈsætˌsæpɪˈɛntaɪ; ˈvəːbəmˈsætˌsæpiˈentai] 〖拉〗對智者一語即足(=a word to the wise is sufficient). (亦作 **verbum sapienti sat est**)

ver·dan·cy [ˈvɝdn̩sɪ; ˈvəːdənsi] *n.* ①深綠;新綠;碧綠。②未成熟;無經驗;幼稚。

ver·dant [ˈvɝdn̩t; ˈvəːdənt] *adj.* ①綠的;青蔥的。②長滿了綠色草木的。③無經驗的;未成熟的。—**ly,** *adv.*

verd an·tique [ˌvɝdænˈtik; ˈvəːdænˈtiːk] 〖礦〗古綠石。(亦作**verde antique**)

ver·der·er, ver·der·or [ˈvɝdərə; ˈvəːdərə] *n.* 〖英史〗(皇家森林之)御林管理官。

***ver·dict** [ˈvɝdɪkt; ˈvəːdikt] *n.* ①陪審員的判決;裁決。The jury returned a *verdict* of "Not Guilty." 陪審團判決無罪。②結論;判斷。

ver·di·gris [ˈvɝdɪˌgris; ˈvəːdigris] *n.* ①銅銹。②銅綠。—**ed,** —**y,** *adj.*

Ver·dun [vɛrˈdʌn; ˈvɛədən] *n.* 凡爾登(法國東北部之一城市，第一次世界大戰, 1916年時之戰場)。

ver·dure [ˈvɝdʒə; ˈvəːdʒə] *n.* ①新綠;蔥綠。②蔥綠之草木。③青春朝氣;繁盛;新鮮。

ver·dur·ous [ˈvɝdʒərəs; ˈvəːdʒərəs] *adj.* ①青蔥的。②長滿綠色植物的。③新鮮的;繁盛的。

Ver·ein [fɛrˈaɪn; fɛərˈain] 〖德〗*n.* 聯盟;協會;會社。

***verge** [vɝdʒ; vəːdʒ] *n., v.,* **verged, verg·ing.** —*n.* ①邊;緣;邊際。My father is on the *verge* of 80. 我的父親將近八十歲了。②界限;範圍;限制用的邊緣。③權杖。④裝飾柱身。⑤路、小徑等邊上的狹窄草坪。⑥裝飾性的邊。—*v.i.* 瀕臨;接近;傾向。—*v.t.* 予以界限;設範圍;作…疆界。

ver·ger [ˈvɝdʒə; ˈvəːdʒə] *n.* ①〖英〗持權標者。②教堂之司事。—**ship,** *n.*

Ver·gil [ˈvɝdʒəl; ˈvəːdʒil] *n.* 威吉爾(70-19 B.C., 全名 Publius Vergilius Maro, 羅馬詩人)。(亦作 **Virgil**)

Ver·gil·i·an [vɝˈdʒɪlɪən; vəːˈdʒiliən] *adj.* 威吉爾 (Vergil) 之詩的;似威吉爾之詩的。(亦作 **Virgilian**)

ve·rid·i·cal [vɪˈrɪdɪkl; veˈridikl] *adj.* 說實話的;眞實的;誠實的。—**ly,** *adv.*

ver·i·est [ˈvɛrɪɪst; ˈvɛəriist] *adj.* ①極度的;徹底的。②very 的最高級。

ver·i·fi·a·ble [ˈvɛrəˌfaɪəbl̩; ˈverifaiəbl] *adj.* 能證實的;能驗明爲眞實的。—**ness,** *n.*

ver·i·fi·ca·tion [ˌvɛrɪfɪˈkeʃən; ˌverifiˈkeiʃən] *n.* ①證實;證明。②確定;確認。③鑑定;查核。④〖法律〗答辯書末之立證聲明(謂答辯者已準備證明其陳述)。—**ver·i·fi·ca·tive, ver·i·fi·ca·to·ry,** *adj.*

***ver·i·fy** [ˈvɛrəˌfaɪ; ˈverifai] *v.t.,* -fied, -fy·ing. ①證實;證明。②鑑定;查對。③〖法律〗作證;宣誓後作證。—**ver·i·fi·er,** *n.*

ver·i·ly [ˈvɛrəlɪ; ˈverili] *adv.* 〖古〗眞實地;眞正地;確然地。

ver·i·sim·i·lar [ˌvɛrəˈsɪmələ; ˌveriˈsimilə] *adj.* 似眞實的;可能的。—**ly,** *adv.*

ver·i·si·mil·i·tude [ˌvɛrəsəˈmɪləˌtjud; ˌverisiˈmilitjuːd] *n.* 逼眞;逼眞之事物。

ver·ism [ˈvɪrɪzm̩; ˈviərizm] *n.* 藝術上的寫實主義。—**ver·ist,** *n., adj.*

ver·i·ta·ble [ˈvɛrətəbl̩; ˈveritəbl] *adj.* ①眞正的;眞確的;確實的。②十足的。—**ness,** *n.* —**ver·i·ta·bly,** *adv.*

ver·i·ty [ˈvɛrətɪ; ˈveriti] *n., pl.* -ties. ①眞實;確實。②眞實之陳述;事實;眞理。***of a verity*** 〖古〗實在的(地)。***the eternal verities*** 永恒的眞理。

ver·juice [ˈvɝˌdʒus; ˈvəːdʒuːs] *n.* ①(未熟水果等之)酸果汁。②(性情或態度之)乖僻。—*adj.* ①酸果汁的。②酸的。③乖僻的。—**ver·juiced,** *adj.*

ver·meil [ˈvɝml̩; ˈvəːmeil] *n.* ①〖詩〗朱紅;朱紅色。②鍍金之銀、青銅或銅。—*adj.* 朱紅色的;鮮紅色的。

ver·mi·cel·li [ˌvɝməˈsɛlɪ; ˌvəːmiˈseli] *n.* 一種硬而脆的細麪條。

ver·mi·cide [ˈvɝmɪˌsaɪd; ˈvəːmisaid] *n.* 殺蟲劑。—**ver·mi·cid·al,** *adj.*

ver·mic·u·lar [vɝˈmɪkjələ; vəːˈmikjulə] *adj.* ①蠕蟲的;似蠕蟲的。②似蠕蟲爬過之跡的。③蠕動的。④蟲蛀過的。⑤有緊密之波紋的。—**ly,** *adv.*

ver·mic·u·late [*v.* vɝˈmɪkjəˌlet; vəːˈmikjuleit *adj.* vɝˈmɪkjəlɪt; vəːˈmikjulit] *adj., v.,* -lat·ed, -lat·ing. —*adj.* ①蟲蛀的;似蟲蛀的。②=**vermicular.** ③委婉的;迂曲的。—*v.t.* ①作蠕蟲爬跡形之裝飾於。②使成蟲蛀的。

ver·mi·form [ˈvɝməˌfɔrm; ˈvəːmifɔːm] *adj.* 蠕蟲形的。

vermiform appendix 〖解剖〗蚓突;闌尾。

ver·mi·fuge [ˈvɝməˌfjudʒ; ˈvəːmifjuːdʒ] *n.* 〖藥〗驅蟲劑。—*adj.* 用以驅蟲的。

ver·mil·ion [vəˈmɪljən; vəˈmiljən] *adj.* 朱紅的。—*n.* 朱紅色;朱砂;銀朱。—*v.t.* 以朱砂着色;使成朱紅色。

ver·min [ˈvɝmɪn; ˈvəːmin] *n.* (作*pl.* or *sing* 解) ①害蟲(蚤、蝨、臭蟲等)。②社會的蟊賊;歹徒。③〖英〗對獵物、農作物等有害之狐、鼠、梟等;害獸;害鳥。

ver·mi·no·sis [ˌvɝməˈnosɪs; ˌvəːmiˈnousis] *n., pl.* -ses [-ˌsiz; -siːz]. 〖醫〗寄生蟲病。

ver·min·ous [ˈvɝmɪnəs; ˈvəːminəs] *adj.* ①害蟲的;似害蟲的。②爲害蟲所感染的。③由害蟲引起的。④歹徒的;腐化的。—**ly,** *adv.* —**ness,** *n.*

Ver·mont [vəˈmɑnt; vəːˈmɔnt] *n.* 佛

蒙特(美國東北部之一州,首府爲Montpelier)。

Ver·mont·er 〔vɜ'mɑntə; və:'mɔntə〕 *n.* 佛蒙特人。

ver·mouth 〔'vɜmuθ, və'muθ; 'və:mu:θ〕 *n.* 苦艾酒。

ver·nac·u·lar 〔və'nækjələ; və'nækjulə〕 *n.* ①本國語;白話;土語。②專門語;術語。③動植物的普通名稱(別於學名)。—*adj.* ①本國的;本土的;本國語的;土語的。②地方的;地方性的。③動植物之普通名稱的。—**ly,** *adv.*

ver·nal 〔'vɜnḷ; 'və:nl〕 *adj.* ①春天的;春季的;春日的。②春天生長的;春天發生的;春天開的。③似春天的;溫暖如春的;使人思及春天的。④青春的;年輕的。—**ly,** *adv.*

ver·nal·i·za·tion 〔ˌvɜnḷɪ'zeʃən; ˌvə:nəlai'zeiʃən〕 *n.* 〖農〗開花結實促進法。

ver·nal·ize 〔'vɜnḷˌaɪz; 'və:nəlaiz〕 *v.t.,* **-ized, -iz·ing.** 將種籽或球根冷卻以促進(植物)開花結實。

ver·na·tion 〔və'neʃən; və'neiʃən〕 *n.* 〖植物〗葉之發狀(未萌發之葉在芽內之排列形狀)。

ver·ni·er 〔'vɜnɪə; 'və:niə〕 *n.* 游標;游標尺。—*adj.* 游標的;裝有游標的。

vernier engine 長程彈道飛彈或太空船上校正速度及方向用的火箭引擎。

Ve·ro·na 〔və'ronə; və'rounə〕 *n.* 威洛納(義大利北部, Adige 河畔之一城市)。

ver·o·nal 〔'verənḷ; 'verənl〕 *n.* 佛羅拿(一種痲醉劑)。(亦作 **Veronal**)

Ve·ro·ne·se 〔vero'nese; ˌverə'neizi〕 *n.* 維洛內塞 (Paolo, 1528–1588, 眞名 Paolo Cagliari, 義大利畫家)。

ve·ron·i·ca 〔və'rɑnɪkə; və'rɔnikə〕 *n.* 印有基督聖容之布(據傳說耶穌在背負十字架赴 Calvary 之途中, St. Veronica 曾遞與一布巾,以拭其額上之汗,其容貌遂印於該布巾上,成爲奇蹟);布上的聖容。

ver·ru·ca 〔vɛ'rukə; ve'ru:kə〕 *n., pl.* **-cae** 〔-si; -si:〕. ①〖醫〗疣腫。②〖動物〗疣狀突起。

Ver·sailles 〔vɚ'selz; vɛə'sai〕 *n.* ①凡爾賽(法國北部之城市,靠近巴黎)。②凡爾賽宮。

Versailles Treaty 凡爾賽和約(1919年6月28日簽訂,結束第一次世界大戰)。

ver·sa·tile 〔'vɜsətɪl; 'və:sətail〕 *adj.* ①多才多藝的;多方面的。②可作多種用途的。③易變的;前後不一致的。④〖動物〗向前或向後轉動的;可轉動的。⑤〖植物〗附在花絲上自由轉動的。—**ly,** *adv.* —**ness,** *n.*

ver·sa·til·i·ty 〔ˌvɜsə'tɪlətɪ; ˌvə:sə'tiliti〕 *n.* ①多才多藝。②多用途。③轉變;前後不一致。

verse** 〔vɜs; və:s〕 *n.* ①詩;韻文。lyrical *verse.* 抒情詩。②詩句。③詩節。Sing the first *verse.* 唱第一節。④(聖經之)節。⑤某人或某時期、某國家之詩詞。⑥〖音樂〗**a.** 前奏後合唱前之部分。**b.** 獨唱部。⑦〖罕〗寫成一行的一句,或一句子之一部分。⑧〖罕〗一文學型式之一小部門。give chapter and verse for*** 註明引用之章節。—*adj.* 詩的;以詩寫成的。

versed 〔vɜst; və:st〕 *adj.* 精通;熟練〖in〗.

versed sine 〖三角〗正矢。

verse·mon·ger 〔'vɜsˌmʌŋgə; 'və:sˌmʌŋgə〕 *n.* 作劣詩者;拙劣詩人。

ver·si·cle 〔'vɜsɪkḷ; 'və:sikl〕 *n.* ①短詩;小詩。②〖宗教〗一種唱和的短詩或短句。

ver·si·col·o(u)r 〔'vɜsɪˌkʌlə; 'və:siˌkʌlə〕 *adj.* ①顏色呈各種變化的。②多色的;雜色的。

ver·si·fi·ca·tion 〔ˌvɜsəfə'keʃən; ˌvə:sifi'keiʃən〕 *n.* 作詩;詩體;作詩法。

ver·si·fi·er 〔'vɜsəˌfaɪə; 'və:sifaiə〕 *n.* 詩人(特指不好的詩人);將散文變作詩體者。

ver·si·fy 〔'vɜsəˌfaɪ; 'və:sifai〕 *v.,* **-fied, -fy·ing.** —*v.t.* 將(散文)改寫成韻文;用韻文記述。—*v.i.* 作詩。

***ver·sion** 〔'vɜʒən, 'vɜʃən; 'və:ʃən〕 *n.* ①翻譯;譯本。the Authorized *Version* of the Bible. (英國的)欽定聖經譯本。②(根據個人的或特殊的觀點對於某種事情的)敍述;說法。③某種特別的式樣。④〖醫〗倒轉術;胎倒轉術;胎位倒轉。—**al,** *adj.*

vers li·bre 〔ˌver'libr; ˌvɛə'li:brə〕〖法〗自由體詩 (=free verse).

vers li·brist 〔ˌver'librɪst; ˌvɛə'li:brist〕 自由體詩之作者。(亦作 **vers-libriste**)

ver·so 〔'vɜso; 'və:sou〕 *n., pl.* **-sos.** ①(書籍等打開時)左方之頁。②(硬幣等之)反面。

verst 〔vɜst; və:st〕 *n.* 俄里(約3500英尺)。

ver·sus 〔'vɜsəs; 'və:səs〕 *prep.* ①對(多用於訴訟或競技等之中,縮寫作 v. 或 vs.). Smith *v.* Robinson. 史密斯對魯濱遜之案件。②相形;比較(兩者中選一)。

vert[1] 〔vɜt; və:t〕 *n.* ①〖英〗**a.** 山林中之綠草木(爲鹿之隱蔽處)。**b.** 山林草木之採伐權。②〖紋章〗綠色。—*adj.* 〖紋章〗綠色的。

vert[2] *v.i.* 背教;(自英國國教或天主教)改信他教。—*n.* 改宗者;變節者。

ver·te·bra 〔'vɜtəbrə; 'və:tibrə〕 *n., pl.* **-brae** 〔-ˌbri; -bri:〕, **-bras.** 〖解剖〗脊骨中的一節;脊椎骨節。***the vertebrae*** 脊柱。

ver·te·bral 〔'vɜtəbrəl; 'və:tibrəl〕 *adj.* 脊椎骨的;脊椎的;由脊骨組成的。—**ly,** *adv.*

ver·te·brate 〔'vɜtəˌbret; 'və:tibrit〕 *n.* 脊椎動物。—*adj.* ①有脊椎骨的。②脊椎動物的。

ver·te·brat·ed 〔'vɜtəˌbretɪd; 'və:tibreitid〕 *adj.* 有脊椎的;由脊椎骨所構成的。

ver·te·bra·tion 〔ˌvɜtə'breʃən; ˌvə:ti'breiʃən〕 *n.* 脊椎狀結構。

ver·tex 〔'vɜtɛks; 'və:teks〕 *n., pl.* **-tax·es, -ti·ces** 〔-tɪˌsiz; -tisi:z〕. ①最高點;頂點。②〖解剖〗頭頂;顱頂。③〖數學〗頂;頂點。④〖天文〗天頂。

***ver·ti·cal** 〔'vɜtɪkḷ; 'və:tikəl〕 *adj.* ①垂直的;直立的。a *vertical* line. 垂直線。a *vertical* motion. 垂直運動。②在最高點的;頂點的。a *vertical* angle. 〖幾何〗對頂角。③在正上方的。④〖經濟〗縱向結合的;其組織包含許多或全部製造過程中之階段的。⑤頭頂的;顱頂的。—*n.* 垂直線;垂直面;垂直圈;垂直位置。—**ness,** —**ism,** *n.*

vertical envelopment 〖軍〗立體包圍(即敵後空降)。

vertical integration 某一產品之製造與出售由一家公司控制以保證品質及供應不斷。

ver·ti·cal·i·ty 〔ˌvɜtɪ'kælətɪ; ˌvə:ti'kæliti〕 *n.* 垂直。

ver·ti·cal·ly 〔'vɜtɪkḷɪ; 'və:tikəli〕 *adv.* 垂直地;鉛直地。

vertical take-off 垂直起飛(如直昇機或其他可垂直起飛或降落的戰鬥機)。

vertical turn 〖航空〗垂直旋轉。

vertical union 包括一個工業全體工人之工會。

ver·ti·cil 〔'vɜtəsɪl; 'və:tisil〕 *n.* 〖動、植物〗(器官之)輪生。

ver·tig·i·nous 〔vɜ'tɪdʒənəs; və:'tidʒinəs〕 *adj.* ①旋轉的;廻旋的。②令人眩暈的;感覺眩暈的。③不安定的;多變化的。

ver·ti·go 〔'vɜtɪˌgo; 'və:tigou〕 *n., pl.* **ver·ti·goes, ver·tig·i·nes** 〔və'tɪdʒəˌniz;

vəːˈtidʒiniːz]. 眩暈；頭暈。

ver·tu [vɝˈtu; vəːˈtuː] *n.* =virtu.

ver·vain [ˈvɝven; ˈvəːvein] *n.* 〖植物〗馬鞭草屬之植物；馬鞭草。

verve [vɝv; vɛəv, vəːv] *n.* ①(文學或美術作品所表現之)活力；神韻。②(詩人、音樂家或藝術家等之)熱情；活力。③天才；才幹。

ver·vet [ˈvɝvɛt; ˈvəːvet] *n.* 〖動物〗(南非洲所產的)一種小猿。

‡**ver·y** [ˈvɛrɪ; ˈveri] *adv.* & *adj.*, **ver·i·er, ver·i·est.** —*adv.* ①很；頗；甚；極。He was *very* much interested in what I said. 他對我所說的大感興趣。②恰好地；正是地；全然地。He stood in the *very* same place for an hour. 他就在這同一個地方站了一小時。③用以加强最高級之形容詞。I will do the *very* best I can. 我一定盡最大的努力去做。④(與否定語連用表示)不太。That's not a *very* nice thing to say so. 那樣說是不太好的。⑤(與 own 連用，以加强所有)。I'll give you this for your *very* own. 我以此與你交換你所有者。***very good*** a. 極好。b. 好(表示同意)。***very well*** a. 極好。b. 好罷(表示同意，但常爲並不情願之同意)。—*adj.* ①同一的。The *very* people who used to love her hate her now. 現在恨她的人正是從前喜歡她的那些人。②眞正的；眞實的；恰好的；全然的。The thief was caught in the *very* act of stealing. 這賊正在偷東西的時候當場被捕。③甚至…都；就連…也(=even the)；僅僅的(=mere). The *very* beggars despise him. 就連乞丐們都瞧不起他。④〖廢〗合法的。***in very deed*** 實在地；無疑地。***in very truth*** 事實上；實在地。〖注意〗very 作副詞用時，只可形容副詞、形容詞，不能直接形容動詞。

very high frequency 〖無線電〗特高頻率。(略作 VHF)

Very light(s) =Very signal.

very low frequency 〖無線電〗特低頻率。(略作 VLF)

Very signal (夜間用信號手鎗所發射之)閃光信號。

ve·si·ca [vəˈsaɪkə; ˈvesikə] *n.*, *pl.* **-cae** [-si; -siː]. 〖拉〗①〖解剖〗囊；膀胱。②魚鰾。

ves·i·cant [ˈvɛsɪkənt; ˈvesikənt] *n.* ①〖醫〗發泡劑。②〖化學戰〗發泡藥劑。—*adj.* 發泡的；使發泡的。

ves·i·cate [ˈvɛsɪˌket; ˈvesikeit] *v.t.* & *v.i.*, **-cat·ed, -cat·ing.** (使)生水泡；起泡。—**ves·i·ca·tion,** *n.*

ves·i·ca·to·ry [ˈvɛsɪkəˌtorɪ; ˈvesikətəri] *adj.*, *n.*, *pl.* **-ries.** —*adj.* 起泡的。—*n.* 起泡劑。

ves·i·cle [ˈvɛsɪkḷ; ˈvesikl] *n.* ①囊；泡。②〖醫〗水疱；痘；水疱疹。③〖植物，解剖〗小胞；氣泡。④〖地質〗(火山岩中之)氣孔。

ve·sic·u·lar [vəˈsɪkjulɚ; vəˈsikjulə] *adj.* ①小囊的；小胞的。②小囊狀的；小胞狀的。③有小囊的；成小囊的。④〖醫〗肺中之小泡的；小泡性的。—**ly,** *adv.*

ve·sic·u·late [*adj.* vɪˈsɪkjulɪt; viˈsikjulit *v.* vɪˈsɪkjuˌlet; viˈsikjuleit] *adj.*, *v.*, **-lat·ed, -lat·ing.** —*adj.* 有小胞的；成小胞的；小胞狀的。—*v.t.* & *v.i.* 使成小胞狀；變成小胞狀；起疱；出疱；(使)起水疱。—**ve·sic·u·la·tion,** *n.*

ves·per [ˈvɛspɚ; ˈvespə] *n.* ①〖古〗黃昏。②(V-) 黃昏的星辰(太白星或長庚星)。③晚禱；晚禱曲。④晚禱鐘。—*adj.* 黃昏的；晚禱的。

ves·pers [ˈvɛspɚz; ˈvespəz] *n. pl.* ①晚禱。②〖天主教〗第六次祈禱之時刻；此時刻之祈禱。③晚禱曲；晚禱詞。(亦作 **Vespers**)

ves·per·tine [ˈvɛspətɪn; ˈvespətain] *adj.* ①黃昏的；傍晚的。②〖植物〗夜間開花的。③〖動物〗夜晚活動的；夜晚飛翔的。④〖天文〗日落時沉沒的(行星)。

ves·pi·ar·y [ˈvɛspɪˌɛrɪ; ˈvespiəri] *n.*, *pl.* **-ar·ies.** 黃蜂窩。

ves·pine [ˈvɛspaɪn; ˈvespain] *adj.* 黃蜂的；似黃蜂的。

Ves·puc·ci [vɛsˈputʃɪ; vesˈpuːtʃi] *n.* 維斯浦奇 (Amerigo, 1451–1512, Americus Vespucius, 義大利航海家，曾三度航海至美洲大陸，美洲大陸 America 卽由其名而來)。

‡**ves·sel** [ˈvɛsḷ; ˈvesl] *n.* ①船；艦。②飛船；飛艇。③容器；器皿。④脈管；管。a blood *vessel*. 血管。⑤具有特殊氣質之人。the weaker *vessel*. 女人。—**(l)ed, —like,** *adj.*

*__vest__ [vɛst; vest] *n.* ①男用背心。②女用背心；女裝胸前V字形飾布。③〖英〗內衣；汗衫。④〖古〗外衣；長袍；祭袍。***play it close to the vest*** 〖俗〗避免冒不必要的險。—*v.t.* ①使穿衣；着袍；着祭袍。②在祭壇上掛布。③授給；賜給；賦與(財產、權利、權力等)。Congress is *vested* with the power to declare war. 國會被賦以宣戰的權力。④置於…管理下。—*v.i.* ①披上祭服；穿衣。②(財產、權利等之)歸屬。—**less,** *adj.* —**like,** *adj.*

Ves·ta [ˈvɛstə; ˈvestə] *n.* ①〖羅馬神話〗爐火之女神；女竈神。②〖天文〗(火星與木星軌道間之)第四號小行星。③(v-)〖英〗一種塗蠟之短火柴。

ves·tal [ˈvɛstḷ; ˈvestl] *n.* ①守望 Vesta 女神聖火之處女之一。②處女。③尼姑；修女。—*adj.* ①Vesta 女神的；獻身給 Vesta 女神的。②貞潔的；處女的。

vest·ed [ˈvɛstɪd; ˈvestid] *adj.* ①〖法律〗既得的；既定的。②穿着祭服的。③完全或永久所有的。

vested interest ①控制一國的經濟或財政的人或一羣人；特權階級。②一有變動就可能喪失的利益。

vest·ee [vɛsˈti; vesˈtiː] *n.* (女外套或襯衣前開胸處之)V字形飾布。

ves·tib·u·lar [vɛsˈtɪbjulɚ; vesˈtibjulə] *adj.* ①門廳的；(進入大門之後的)通廊的；連廊的。②〖解剖〗(耳之)前庭的。

ves·ti·bule [ˈvɛstəˌbjul; ˈvestibjuːl] *n.*, *v.*, **-buled, -bul·ing.** —*n.* ①前門與室內之間的通道、走廊、小室或大廳；玄關。②教堂中的走廊。③〖美〗連廊。④〖解剖〗前庭。—*v.t.* ①設以通道、門廳。②以連廊連起(兩客車)。

ves·tige [ˈvɛstɪdʒ; ˈvestidʒ] *n.* ①痕跡；形跡；遺跡。There is not a *vestige* of truth in the report. 這項報告毫不眞實。②〖生物〗退化之器官。③〖罕〗足跡。

ves·tig·i·al [vɛsˈtɪdʒɪəl; vesˈtidʒiəl] *adj.* ①尚留有痕跡的。②〖生物〗退化的；萎縮的(器官)。—**ly,** *adv.*

vest·ment [ˈvɛstmənt; ˈvestmənt] *n.* ①衣服；外衣；袍。②官服；禮服。③法衣；祭袍；彌撒祭袍。④(*pl.*)〖詩〗衣裳；衣着。⑤套在上面如衣服的事物。

vest-pock·et [ˈvɛstˌpɑkɪt; ˈvestˌpɔkit] *adj.* 適於懷中用的；袖珍的；很小的。

ves·try [ˈvɛstrɪ; ˈvestri] *n.*, *pl.* **-tries.** ①(教堂)放置法衣、聖物之房間。②(教堂)供祈禱會、主日學等所用之禮拜堂。③教區委員會；教區委員會議或其會議室。—**ves·tral,** *adj.*

ves·try·man [ˈvɛstrɪmən; ˈvestrimən] *n.*, *pl.* **-men.** 教區代表；教區委員。

ves·ture ['vɛstʃɚ; 'vestʃə] *n.*, *v.*, **-tured, -tur·ing.** —*n.* ①【古】衣服；衣着；長衣。②【詩】覆蓋；籠罩物。③【法律】(地上樹木之外的)生長物(如草、穀類等)。—*v.t.*【古】着以衣物；覆蓋。—**ves·tur·al,** *adj.*

Ve·su·vi·an [və'suvɪən; vi'suːvjən, -viən] *adj.* 維蘇威火山的；似維蘇威火山的。—*n.* (v-) ①一種不易被風吹熄的火柴。②【礦】符山石；維蘇威石。

Ve·su·vi·us [və'suvɪəs; vi'suːviəs] *n.* 維蘇威火山(爲一活火山，在義大利西南部，近Naples 灣)。

vet¹ [vɛt; vet] *n.*, *v.*, **vet·ted, vet·ting.** —*n.*【俗】獸醫(=veterinarian)。—*v.t.* ①診察；治療(獸類)。②【諧】診察；治療(人)。③檢查。④【英】審查(書籍原稿等)。—*v.i.* 作獸醫。

vet² *n.*【俗】退役軍人。

vet. ①veteran. ②veterinarian. ③veterinary.

vetch [vɛtʃ; vetʃ] *n.*【植物】大巢菜。—**like,** *adj.*

vetch·ling ['vɛtʃlɪŋ; 'vetʃliŋ] *n.*【植物】山黧豆。

***vet·er·an** ['vɛtərən; 'vetərən] *n.* ①老兵；老將。②老手；老練者。③【美】退伍軍人。—*adj.* ①老練的。②老兵的；退伍軍人的。

Veterans' Administration 美國(聯邦政府中之)退役軍人管理局。

Veterans Day 休戰紀念日(紀念結束第一次及第二次世界大戰之法定假日。 **a.** 美國爲十月的第四個星期一。**b.** 加拿大爲十一月十一日)。(舊稱**Armistice Day**)。

Veterans of Foreign Wars of the United States 美國海外退伍軍人協會。(略作 **V.F.W.**)

vet·er·i·nar·i·an [ˌvɛtərə'nɛrɪən; ˌvetərə'neəriən] *n.* 獸醫。

vet·er·i·nar·y ['vɛtrəˌnɛrɪ; 'vetərinəri] *adj.*, *n.*, *pl.* **-nar·ies.** —*adj.* 獸醫的。—*n.* 獸醫。

veterinary hospital 家畜醫院。

ve·to** ['vito; 'viːtou] *n.*, *pl.* **-toes,** *v.*, **-toed, -to·ing,** *adj.* —*n.* ①否認；否決；禁止；拒絕。The governor's *veto* kept the bill from becoming a law. 州長的否決使該法案無法成爲法律。②(亦作 **veto power**) 否認權；否決權；禁止權。③(亦作 **veto message**) 行政機構反對立法機構所通過之法案時所申述之理由。put a veto upon*** 否決；禁止。—*v.t.* 不認可；否決；不同意；禁止。The police *vetoed* the procession. 警察禁止遊行。—*adj.* 否決的；反對的。—**er,** *n.* —**less,** *adj.* —**ed,** *adj.*

***vex** [vɛks; veks] *v.t.* ①使煩惱；激怒。Her continuous chatter *vexes* me. 她的喋喋不休使我煩惱。②騷擾。③徹底或踴躍討論(問題、題目等)。④【古】騷動。⑤【古】使痛苦。—*v.i.* 不悅；感覺苦惱。It is *vexing* to have to wait a long time for anyone. 長時間等人是一件苦惱的事。—**er,** *n.*

***vex·a·tion** [vɛks'eʃən; vek'seiʃən] *n.* ①煩惱；苦惱；煩擾。His face showed his *vexation* at the delay. 他的臉上露出對遲延誤的不快。②招人煩惱之事物。

vex·a·tious [vɛks'eʃəs; vek'seiʃəs] *adj.* ①使人煩惱的；困惱的。②【法律】纏訟的；誣告的。③紛亂的；困擾的；受困的。—**ly,** *adv.* —**ness,** *n.*

vexatious suit【法律】纏訟(無充分理由而僅用以困擾對方之訴訟)。

vexed [vɛkst; vekst] *adj.* ①煩惱的；苦惱的；被激怒的；生氣的。②經激辯或爭論的；難決的(問題)。③洶湧的(波浪)。—**ly,** *adv.*

vex·il·lar ['vɛksələ; 'veksilə] *adj.* ①(古羅馬之)軍旗的。②【植物】旗瓣的。③【動物】(羽毛之)羽瓣的。

vex·il·lar·y ['vɛksəˌlɛrɪ; 'veksiləri] *n.*, *pl.* **-lar·ies,** *adj.* —*n.* ①古羅馬服役於特殊旗幟下的老兵。②持旗者。—*adj.* = **vexillar.**

v.f. very fair. **V.F.W., VFW** Veterans of Foreign Wars. **v.g.** ①verbi gratia (拉=for example). ②very good. **VHF, V.H.F., vhf**【無線電】very high frequency. 特高頻率。

Vi 化學元素 virginium 之符號。

***vi·a** ['vaɪə; 'vaiə] *prep.* ①經由。He is going from New York to California *via* the Panama Canal. 他要從紐約經巴拿馬運河去加州。②通過；以…爲媒介；藉。

vi·a·bil·i·ty [ˌvaɪə'bɪlətɪ; ˌvaiə'biliti] *n.* 能生活或生存之性質或狀態；生存能力。

vi·a·ble ['vaɪəbḷ; 'vaiəbl] *adj.* ①能生活的；有生活能力的。②能生存的(胎兒)。③能萌發的(種子等)。④眞實的；活生生的。⑤實際的；可實施的。

vi·a·duct ['vaɪəˌdʌkt; 'vaiədʌkt] *n.* 陸橋；高架橋；棧道；高架道。

vi·al ['vaɪəl; 'vaiəl] *n.*, *v.*, **-al(l)ed, -al(l)ing.** —*n.*(亦作 **phial**) 裝藥的或作其他用的各樣小玻璃瓶。***pour out vials of wrath*** 報仇；表示憤怒。—*v.t.* 裝進小玻璃瓶。

via media【拉】中庸之道。

vi·am·e·ter [vaɪ'æmətɚ; vai'æmitə] *n.* 路程計。

vi·and ['vaɪənd; 'vaiənd] *n.* ①食品。②(*pl.*)食物(尤指精美者)。

vi·at·ic [vaɪ'ætɪk; vai'ætik] *adj.* 旅行的；道路的。

vi·at·i·cum [vaɪ'ætɪkəm; vai'ætikəm] *n.*, *pl.* **-ca** [-kə; -kə], **-cums.** ①【天主教】臨終的聖餐。②(古羅馬之)旅行用品；旅行費用。③任何旅行費用、必需品。

vi·brant ['vaɪbrənt; 'vaibrənt] *adj.* ①震動的；震顫的；顫動的。②發顫音的；回響的。③有精力的；充滿生命力的；活潑的。④由聲帶振動而生的；有聲音的。—*n.* 顫音。—**vi·brance, vi·bran·cy,** *n.* —**ly,** *adv.*

vi·bra·phone ['vaɪbrəˌfon; 'vaibrəfoun] *n.* 鐵琴(附電器共鳴裝置)。—**vi·bra·phon·ist,** *n.*

***vi·brate** ['vaɪbret; vai'breit, 'vaib-] *v.*, **-brat·ed, -brat·ing.** —*v.i.* ①震動。The house *vibrates* when a train passes. 火車經過的時候，該屋震動。②(鐘擺等)擺動。③顫動；悸動。Her heart *vibrates* with excitement. 她的心因興奮而悸動。④回響。⑤在兩個極端中來回搖動。—*v.t.* ①以擺動計出。②使震動。③使顫動。④使顫動而發出(聲音)。—**vi·brat·ing·ly,** *adv.*

vi·bra·tile ['vaɪbrətɪl, -taɪl; 'vaibrətail] *adj.* 振動的；顫動的；能振動的。

vi·bra·til·i·ty [ˌvaɪbrə'tɪlətɪ; ˌvaibrə'tiliti] *n.* 振動；顫動；振動性；顫動性。

***vi·bra·tion** [vaɪ'breʃən; vai'breiʃən] *n.* ①震動；顫動；擺動。There is so much *vibration* on a ship that one cannot write. 船上的震動大得使人無法書寫。②【物理】振動。—**less,** *adj.*

vi·bra·tion·al [vaɪ'breʃənḷ; vai'breiʃənl] *adj.* 振動的；顫動的；擺動的。

vi·bra·tion-proof 〔vaɪˈbreʃən-ˌpruf; vaiˈbreiʃənpruːf〕 *adj.* 防震的。
vi·bra·tive 〔ˈvaɪbrətɪv; vaiˈbreitiv〕 *adj.* =**vibratory.**
vi·bra·to 〔vɪˈbrɑto; viˈbrɑːtou〕 *n., pl.* **-tos,** *adv.* 〖義〗—*n.* 〖音樂〗振動;振動音。—*adv.* 使用振動音地。
vi·bra·tor 〔ˈvaɪbretɚ; ˈvaibreitə〕 *n.* ①震動者。②振動器。③振子。④震動按摩器。
vi·bra·to·ry 〔ˈvaɪbrəˌtorɪ; ˈvaibrətəri〕 *adj.* 振動的;振動性的;能生振動的。(亦作**vibrative**)
vi·bro·scope 〔ˈvaɪbrəˌskop; ˈvaibrəskoup〕 *n.* 振動計。
vi·bur·num 〔vaɪˈbɝnəm; vaiˈbəːnəm〕 *n.* 〖植物〗莢蒾屬之植物。
Vic 〔vɪk; vik〕 *n.* ①〖英俚〗飛機之 V 字形編隊(飛行)。②男子名 (Victor 之暱稱)。
Vic. ①Vicar. ②Vicarage. ③Victoria.
vic·ar 〔ˈvɪkɚ; ˈvikə〕 *n.* ①(英國之)教區牧師。②〖天主教〗代理主教或教皇之僧侶; 教皇。③代理人。④受委託之人。—**ship,** *n.*
vic·ar·age 〔ˈvɪkərɪdʒ; ˈvikəridʒ〕 *n.* 教區牧師之職務、俸祿、住所等。
vi·car·i·al 〔vaɪˈkɛrɪəl; vaiˈkɛəriəl〕 *adj.* ①教區牧師的。②代理的; 受委託的。
vi·car·i·ous 〔vaɪˈkɛrɪəs; vaiˈkɛəriəs〕 *adj.* ①爲別人工作的; 代別人受苦的。②代理的;受託的。③假想身歷其境而感到的。④〖生理〗替代性的;代償的 (器官功能)。—**ly,** *adv.*
vicarious menstruation 替代月經(月經期間非子宮出血)。
***vice**[1] 〔vaɪs; vais〕 *n.* ①惡;罪惡;邪惡。②惡行;惡習;惡癖。Lying and cruelty are *vices.* 說謊和殘暴是惡行。③缺點;毛病。④不道德的性行爲 (尤指賣淫)。⑤ (V-) 英 morality play 中扮演"惡"之角色。
vice[2] *n., v.t.,* **viced, vic·ing.** 〖英〗=**vise.**
vi·ce[3] 〔ˈvaɪsɪ; ˈvaisi〕〖拉〗*prep.* 代替; 取代。
vice- 〖字首〗表"副的;次的"之義, 如 *vice-president.*
vice-ad·mi·ral 〔ˈvaɪsˈædmərəl; ˈvaisˈædmərəl〕 *n.* 海軍中將。(亦作 **vice admiral**) —**ty,** *n.*
vice-chair·man 〔ˈvaɪsˈtʃɛrmən; ˈvaisˈtʃɛəmən〕 *n.* 副主席; 副會長; 副議長; 副委員長。—**ship,** *n.*
vice-chan·cel·lor 〔ˈvaɪsˈtʃænsəlɚ; ˈvaisˈtʃɑːnsələ〕 *n.* 副大法官; 大學副校長; (英國某些大學中之)主要行政官。—**ship,** *n.*
vice-con·sul 〔ˈvaɪsˈkɑnsl̩; ˈvaisˈkɔnsəl〕 *n.* 副領事。(亦作 **vice consul**) —**ship,** —**ate,** *n.* —**ar,** *adj.*
vice·ge·rent 〔vaɪsˈdʒɪrənt; ˈvaisˈdʒerənt〕 *n.* ①代理人。②國家元首或最高領袖指定之代理人。—*adj.* 代理的; 代表的。—**vice·ge·ren·cy,** *n.* —**vice·ge·ral,** *adj.*
vice-gov·er·nor 〔ˈvaɪsˈɡʌvɚnɚ; ˈvaisˈɡʌvənə〕 *n.* 副州長;副省主席;副總督。
vic·e·nar·y 〔ˈvɪsəˌnɛrɪ; ˈvisənəri〕 *adj.* 二十的。
vi·cen·ni·al 〔vaɪˈsɛnɪəl; vaiˈseniəl〕 *adj.* 二十年的; 二十年一次的。
Vice Pres. Vice-President.
***vice-pres·i·dent** 〔ˈvaɪsˈprɛzədənt; ˈvaisˈprezidənt〕 *n.* 副總統;副總裁;副會長; 副社長。(亦作 **vice president**) —**ial,** *adj.* —**vice-pres·i·den·cy,** *n.*
vice-prin·ci·pal 〔ˈvaɪsˈprɪnsəpl̩; ˈvaisˈprinsəpəl〕 *n.* 副校長。
vice·re·gal 〔vaɪsˈrigl̩; ˈvaisˈriːɡəl〕 *adj.* 總督的;太守的。—**ly,** *adv.*
vice-re·gent 〔ˈvaɪsˈridʒənt; ˈvaisˈriːdʒənt〕 *n.* 副攝政。—*adj.* 副攝政的。—**vice-re·gen·cy,** *n.*
vice·reine 〔ˈvaɪsren; ˈvaisˈrein〕 *n.* 「總督夫人。」
vice·roy 〔ˈvaɪsrɔɪ; ˈvais-rɔi〕 *n.* ①(作爲君主或最高統治者代表之)總督; 副王。②美國產的一種蝴蝶。
vice·roy·al·ty 〔vaɪsˈrɔɪəltɪ; vaisˈrɔiəlti〕 *n.* =**viceroyship.**
vice·roy·ship 〔ˈvaɪsrɔɪˌʃɪp; ˈvaisrɔiʃip〕 *n.* 總督之地位、職權或轄區。
vi·ce ver·sa 〔ˈvaɪsɪˈvɝsə; ˈvaisiˈvəːsə〕〖拉〗反之亦然(=conversely).
Vi·chy 〔ˈviʃɪ; ˈviːʃiː〕 *n.* ①維琪(法國中部之一城市,第二次大戰時德國佔領法國後,由法奸 Henri Philippe Petain 領導之傀儡政府卽設於此)。②=**Vichy water.**
Vi·chy·ite 〔ˈviʃɪˌaɪt; ˈviːʃiait〕 *n.* (第二次世界大戰時法國之)維琪分子。
Vi·chys·sois 〔ˌviʃɪˈswɑ; ˌviːʃiːsˈwɑː〕 *adj.* ①法國維琪的。②維琪分子的。—*n.* ①維琪之居民。②維琪分子。
vichy water ①產於維琪附近, 含有重碳酸鈉, 鹼性鹽的礦水, 可醫消化器官疾病。②任何類似的天然或人造礦水。(亦作 **Vichy water, vichy, Vichy**)
vic·i·nage 〔ˈvɪsn̩ɪdʒ; ˈvisinidʒ〕 *n.* ①近處;鄰近;接近;附近。②附近的居民;鄰居。
vic·i·nal 〔ˈvɪsn̩əl; ˈvisinl〕 *adj.* ①附近的;鄰接的。②鄉道的;非公路的。③〖結晶〗副面(近似或取代基面)的。④〖化〗鄰位的。
vicinal way (or **road**) 鄉道。
***vi·cin·i·ty** 〔vəˈsɪnətɪ; viˈsiniti, vaiˈs-〕 *n., pl.* **-ties.** ①附近; 近處。There is no hotel in the *vicinity.* 附近沒有旅館。②接近。*in the vicinity of* 大約;左右;附近。
***vi·cious** 〔ˈvɪʃəs; ˈviʃəs〕 *adj.* ①惡的;邪惡的。a *vicious* life. 墮落的生活。②有惡習的。③謬誤的;不正確的。④惡意的;惡毒的。⑤〖俗〗厲害的。—**ly,** *adv.* —**ness,** *n.*
vicious circle ①循環作用;循環影響;惡性循環。②〖邏輯〗循環論法。
vi·cis·si·tude 〔vəˈsɪsəˌtjud; viˈsisitjuːd, vaiˈs-〕 *n.* ①變遷; 盛衰。a life marked by *vicissitudes.* 飽經滄桑的一生。②有規則的變化。—**vi·cis·si·tu·di·nar·y, vi·cis·si·tu·di·nous,** *adj.*
Vict. ①Victoria. ②Victorian.
***vic·tim** 〔ˈvɪktɪm; ˈviktim〕 *n.* ①犧牲(爲祭神而被殺的人或畜)。②犧牲者;受害者; 遭難者。*victims* of war. 戰爭的犧牲者。③受騙者。

vic·tim·ize 〔ˈvɪktɪmˌaɪz; ˈviktimaiz〕 *v.t.,* **-ized, -iz·ing.** ①使作犧牲;使受害;使受苦。②欺騙;欺詐。③屠殺…作爲犧牲。—**vic·tim·i·za·tion, vic·tim·iz·er,** *n.*
vic·tim·ol·o·gy 〔ˌvɪktəˈmɑlədʒɪ; ˌviktiˈmɔlədʒi〕 *n.* 刑案受害者學 (研究受害者及其受害原因)。—**vic·tim·ol·o·gist,** *n.*
Vic·tor[1] 〔ˈvɪktɚ; ˈviktə〕 *n.* 男子名。
Vic·tor[2] *n.* 通訊電碼, 代表字母V.
***vic·tor** 〔ˈvɪktɚ; ˈviktə〕 *n.* 勝利者;征服者。—*adj.* 勝利的。the *victor* army. 戰勝的軍隊。
***Vic·to·ri·a** 〔vɪkˈtorɪə; vikˈtɔːriə〕 *n.* 維多利亞 (1819-1901, 英國女王, 在位期間爲 1837-1901)。
vic·to·ri·a 〔vɪkˈtorɪə; vikˈtɔːriə〕 *n.* ①一種有兩座位的四輪馬車。②一種後座有摺

合篷的敞車。③〖植物〗(南美所產之)大睡蓮(=victoria lily). ④(V-)勝利女神像。

Victoria Cross ①維多利亞勳章(維多利亞女王於 1856 年所創之勳章,頒給海、陸軍英勇戰士)。②獲得該勳章的人。(常略作 **V.C.**)

Vic·to·ri·an [vɪkˈtorɪən; vikˈtɔːriən] *adj.* 維多利亞女王時代的; 有維多利亞女王時代特徵的。 —*n.* 維多利亞女王時代的著名人物(特指作家)。

Vic·to·ri·an·ism [vɪkˈtorɪənɪzəm; vikˈtɔːriənizəm] *n.* ①英國維多利亞女王時代之特徵、思想、風尚等。②有維多利亞時代風格之小說、傢具、建築等。

vic·to·rine [ˌvɪktəˈrin, ˈvɪktəˌrin; ˈviktəriːn, ˌviktəˈriːn] *n.* 女人穿着的一種毛皮披肩。

*****vic·to·ri·ous** [vɪkˈtorɪəs; vikˈtɔːriəs] *adj.* 勝利的;凱旋的。—**ly,** *adv.* —**ness,** *n.*

‡**vic·to·ry** [ˈvɪktərɪ, ˈvɪktrɪ; ˈviktəri, ˈviktri] *n., pl.* **-ries.** 勝; 勝利; 戰勝。to gain (*or* win) a *victory* over the enemy. 戰勝敵人。—**less,** *adj.*

vict·ual [ˈvɪtl̩; ˈvitl] *n., v.,* **-ual(l)ed, -ual·(l)ing.** —*n.* (*pl.*) 〖俗〗食物; 食品。—*v.t.* 供以食物;儲備食物。—*v.i.* ①〖古〗食;進食。②取得食物;裝貯食物。—**less,** *adj.*

vict·ual·(l)er [ˈvɪtlɚ; ˈvitlə] *n.* ①食物供應者。 ②運糧船 (亦作 **victualling ship**). ③〖英〗餐旅館主人。***a licensed victualler*** 有販賣酒類許可證者。

vict·ual·ling [ˈvɪtl̩ɪŋ; ˈvitliŋ] *n.* 食物供應; 糧食供應; 食物儲備。***victualling house*** 〖英〗飲食店。***victualling note*** 〖英海軍〗水兵領糧證。***victualling ship*** 〖英〗供應艦。***victualling yard*** 〖英〗海軍軍需部倉庫。

vi·cu·gna [vɪˈkunjə; viˈkuːnjə] *n.* =**vicuña.**

vi·cu·ña [vɪˈkjunə; viˈkjuːnə] *n.* ①南美產之一種駝馬。②此種駝馬毛之織物。(亦作 **vicuña cloth, vicuna**)

vid. vide.

vi·de [ˈvaɪdɪ; ˈvaidiː] 〖拉〗 *v.i. & v.t.* 見;參看;參閱 (=see; refer to. 略作 **v.**).

vi·de an·te [ˈvaɪdɪˈæntɪ; ˈvaidiˈænti] 〖拉〗見前 (=see before).

vi·de in·fra [ˈvaɪdɪˈɪnfrə; ˈvaidiˈinfrə] 〖拉〗見下 (=see below).

vi·de·li·cet [vɪˈdɛləsɪt; viˈdiːliset] 〖拉〗 *adv.* 卽是說…;就是…(=namely, 略作 **viz**).

vid·e·o [ˈvɪdɪˌo; ˈvidiou] *adj.* ①以電視播送或接收影像的。 ②電視影像方面的 (對 audio 方面而言)。—*n.* 電視。

vid·e·o·gen·ic [ˌvɪdɪəˈdʒɛnɪk; ˌvidiouˈdʒenik] *adj.* 宜於上電視的。

vid·e·o·phone [ˈvɪdɪəˌfon; ˈvidiəfoun] *n.* 影像電話;顯像電話。(亦作 **Picturephone, viewphone**)

vid·e·o·play·er [ˈvɪdɪəˌpleɚ; ˈvidiəˌpleiə] *n.* 錄影電視放映機。

video tape 錄影帶。

vid·e·o·tape [ˈvɪdɪoˈtep; ˈvidiouteip] *n., v.,* **-taped, -tap·ing.** —*n.* 錄影帶。—*v.t.* 將…錄影。

vi·de post [ˈvaɪdɪˈpost; ˈvaidiˈpoust] 〖拉〗見後 (=see after).

vi·de su·pra [ˈvaɪdɪˈsuprə; ˈvaidiˈsjuːprə] 〖拉〗見上 (=see above).

vi·dette [vɪˈdɛt; viˈdet] *n.* =**vedette.**

vie [vaɪ; vai] *v.,* **vied, vy·ing.** —*v.i.* 競爭;爭勝。—*v.t.* ①使參加競賽。②(玩牌時)下賭注。

Vi·en·na [vɪˈɛnə; viˈenə] *n.* 維也納(奧「地利之首都)。(德文作 **Wien**)

Vi·en·nese [ˌviəˈniz; ˌviəˈniːz] *adj., n., pl.* **-nese.** —*adj.* 維也納人的; 維也納文化的。—*n.* 維也納人或居民。

Vien·tiane [ˌvjɛ̃ˈtjan; ˌvjɛ̃ˈtjan] *n.* 永珍(寮國之首都)。

vi et ar·mis [ˈvaɪɛtˈɑrmɪs; ˈvaietˈɑːmis] 〖拉〗用暴力;用武力(=by force of arms).

Vi·et·cong [vɪˌɛtˈkɔŋ; ˌviːetˈkɔŋ] *n., pl.* **-cong,** *adj.* —*n.* 越共。—*adj.* 越共的。(亦作 **Viet Cong**)

Vi·et·minh [ˈviətmɪn; ˈviːətmin] *n.* ①越盟 (爲越南北部之一共產組織,成立於 1941 年,於1951年撤銷)。②越盟領導人。—*adj.* 越盟的。(亦作 **Viet Minh**)

Vi·et-Nam, Vi·et Nam [ˌvɪɛtˈnɑm; ˈvjetˈnæm] *n.* 越南(東南亞中南半島一國家,首都西貢 Saigon).(亦作 **Vietnam**)

Vi·et-Nam·ese [vɪˌɛtnɑˈmiz; ˌvjetnəˈmiːz] *adj., n., pl.* **-ese.**—*adj.* 越南的;越南人的。—*n.* ①越南人。 ②越南語文。 (亦作 **Vietnamese**)

‡**view** [vju; vjuː] *n.* ①看;視察; 觀察; 考察。It was our first *view* of the ocean. 這是我們第一次看見海洋。②視力; 視域; 眼界。 A ship came into our *view.* 一隻船出現在我們的眼界之內。③景色;光景;景物。The mist spoilt the *view.* 霧毀損了此景色。④風景畫;風景照片;圖。Various *views* of the park hung on the walls. 這公園的各種風景照片都掛在牆上。⑤觀念。⑥意見;想法; 見解。 What are your *views* on the subject? 你對這一題目有何高見? ⑦意向; 意圖; 目的。It is my *view* to leave tomorrow. 我的意思是明天離開。 ⑧前途;希望。 ***a bird's-eye view*** 鳥瞰;概覽。 ***be on view*** 展覽。 ***in view*** **a.** 正被考慮。**b.** 目的在於。**c.** 盼望。 ***in view of*** 鑒於; 由於。***point of view*** 見解;論點;立場。***take a dim view of*** 不贊成;不樂觀。***with a view to*** **a.** 擬;爲了要。**b.** 希望。***with the view of*** 爲…的目的。—*v.t.* ①觀看;視;視察; 觀察。to *view* the body. 驗屍。②考慮;認爲。The plan was *viewed* favorably. 該計畫被嘉許。③〖獵狐〗看到(狐)。

view·a·ble [ˈvjuəbl̩; ˈvjuːəbl] *adj.* ①看得見的。②值得看的。—**view·a·bil·i·ty,** *n.*

view·er [ˈvjuɚ; ˈvjuːə] *n.* ①觀看者。②看電視者,尤指喜愛某一節目者。③幻燈機。④〖俗〗探視器。⑤(財物、公共設施的)檢查員。

view finder 觀景鏡(照相機顯示鏡頭視野之裝置);檢影器。(亦作 **viewfinder**)

view·less [ˈvjulɪs; ˈvjuːlis] *adj.* ①看不見的。②無眼光的;無意見的。—**ly,** *adv.*

*****view·point** [ˈvjuˌpɔɪnt; ˈvjuːpɔint] *n.* ①見地;觀點;着眼點。②觀測點;瞭望點。

view·y [ˈvjuɪ; ˈvjuːi] *adj.,* **view·i·er, view·i·est.** 〖俗〗①幻想的;空想的; 不切實際的。②醒目的。 —**view·i·ness,** *n.*

vi·ges·i·mal [vaɪˈdʒɛsəml̩; vaiˈdʒesiml] *adj.* 第二十的;二十分之一的; 以二十爲單位的。

vig·il [ˈvɪdʒəl; ˈvidʒil] *n.* ①徹夜不眠;守夜。②祈禱之夜。 ③節日之前夕。④(*pl.*)節日前夕所作之祈禱、禮拜等。

*****vig·i·lance** [ˈvɪdʒələns; ˈvidʒiləns] *n.* ①警醒;警戒;注意。②不眠;不寢;失眠。

vigilance committee 〖美〗保安

委員會(一種維持治安之民間團體)。
vig·i·lant [ˈvɪdʒələnt; ˈvidʒilənt] *adj.* 警醒的;警戒的;注意的。—**ly,** *adv.* —**ness,** *n.*
vig·i·lan·te [ˌvɪdʒəˈlæntɪ; ˌvidʒiˈlænti] *n.* 〖美〗vigilance committee 之委員。
vi·gnette [vɪnˈjɛt; viˈnjet] *n., v.,* **-gnet·ted, -gnet·ting.** —*n.* ①(書籍中標題之頁上或每章之首尾所挿的)蔓草狀圖案;小挿圖。②輪廓邊緣漸漸變淡的雕刻、繪畫或半身相;暈映照片;暈映畫像。③小風景畫;小風景照片。④簡潔雅致之小品文。—*v.t.* 使(圖畫、照片等)漸次暗淡。 —**vi·gnett·ist,** *n.*
*****vig·o(u)r** [ˈvɪgɚ; ˈvigə] *n.* ①力;精力;活力;體力;元氣;氣勢。He is full of *vigor.* 他精力充沛。②法律上之效力。a law in full *vigor.* 完全有效的法律。③行政上之有力行動。④政府官員權力之施行。—**less,** *adj.*
vi·go·ro·so [ˌvigəˈrosə; ˌviːgəˈrousə] 〖義〗*adj.*〖音樂〗强的;强有力的。
*****vig·or·ous** [ˈvɪgərəs; ˈvigərəs] *adj.* 精力充沛的;元氣旺盛的;壯健的;有力的;活潑的。The old man is still *vigorous* and lively. 那老人依然精力充沛和活潑。 —**ly,** *adv.* —**ness,** *n.*
Vi·king, vi·king [ˈvaɪkɪŋ; ˈvaikiŋ] *n.* ①第八至第十世紀間,掠奪歐洲西海岸的北歐海盜。②任何海盜。
vil. village.
vi·la·yet [vɪˈlɑjɛt; viˈlɑːjet] *n.* (舊土耳其帝國之)省或主要行政區。(亦作 **eyalet**)
*****vile** [vaɪl; vail] *adj.,* **vil·er, vil·est.** ①惡劣的;極壞的。②可厭的。③卑鄙的;卑賤的。The criminal used *vile* language. 犯人口出穢言。④低微的。⑤簡陋的;粗製的。⑥低廉的;價值極低的。—**ly,** *adv.* —**ness,** *n.*
vil·i·fy [ˈvɪləˌfaɪ; ˈvilifai] *v.t.,* **-fied, -fy·ing.** ①詆毁;誹謗;惡評;中傷;損害名譽。②低估;貶低。—**vil·i·fi·ca·tion,** *n.*
vil·i·pend [ˈvɪləˌpɛnd; ˈvilipend] *v.t.* & *v.i.* ①誹謗。②蔑視。—**er,** *n.*
*****vil·la** [ˈvɪlə; ˈvilə] *n.* ①別墅;別業。②〖英〗郊區獨立或半獨立房屋。③豪華公館。
vil·la·dom [ˈvɪlədəm; ˈvilədəm] *n.* 〖英〗①別墅及居於別墅中者之集合稱;富有、自滿而庸俗之人們。②郊區生活;市郊社會。
‡**vil·lage** [ˈvɪlɪdʒ; ˈvilidʒ] *n.* ①鄉村;村莊。②村民(集合稱)。③似村莊的動物聚居之地方。—*adj.* 鄉村的。
village community *n.* (古代之)村落社會。
*****vil·lag·er** [ˈvɪlɪdʒɚ; ˈvilidʒə] *n.* 村人;村民;鄉村的人。
*****vil·lain** [ˈvɪlən; ˈvilən] *n.* ①惡徒;惡棍。②傢伙。③ =**villein.** ④小說、戲劇中之反派角色;壞人。
vil·lain·ous [ˈvɪlənəs; ˈvilənəs] *adj.* ①惡徒的;歹徒的。②邪惡的。③〖俗〗極壞的。④討厭的。—**ly,** *adv.*
vil·lain·y [ˈvɪlənɪ; ˈviləni] *n., pl.* **-lain·ies.** ①卑鄙;醜惡;邪惡。②(*pl.*) 邪惡的行爲;罪行。
vil·la(i)n·age [ˈvɪlənɪdʒ; ˈvilənidʒ] *n.* =**ville(i)nage.**
vil·la·nel·le [ˌvɪləˈnɛl; ˌviləˈnel] *n.* 源於法國有固定形式的短詩(通常含有三行一節者五節,另加四行一節,通篇只有兩韻)。
vil·lat·ic [vɪˈlætɪk; viˈlætik] *adj.* 別墅的;農場的;農家的。
vil·lein [ˈvɪlɪn; ˈvilin] *n.* 〖英史〗農奴。(亦作 **villain**)
vil·le(i)n·age [ˈvɪlənɪdʒ; ˈvilinidʒ] *n.* ①農奴保有土地之條件。②農奴之身分及地位。③農奴(集合稱)。
vil·li [ˈvɪlaɪ; ˈvilai] *n.* pl. of **villus.**
vil·lose [ˈvɪlos; ˈvilous] *adj.* =**villous.**
vil·lous [ˈvɪləs; ˈviləs] *adj.* ①覆有一層絨毛的。②〖植物〗有長茸毛的。
vil·lus [ˈvɪləs; ˈviləs] *n., pl.* **-li.** ①〖解剖〗絨毛。②〖植物〗長茸毛。
vim [vɪm; vim] *n.* 〖美〗力量;活力;生命力。
vi·min·e·ous [vɪˈmɪnɪəs; viˈminiəs] *adj.* ①小枝編成的。②〖植物〗小枝的;有長而柔之小枝的。
vi·na·ceous [vaɪˈneʃəs; vaiˈneiʃəs] *adj.* ①葡萄的;似葡萄的;葡萄酒的;似葡萄酒的。②葡萄酒色的;紅色的。
vin·ai·grette [ˌvɪnəˈgrɛt; ˌvineiˈgret] *n.* ①香醋瓶;嗅鹽瓶(亦作 **vinegarette**). ②=**vinaigrette sauce.** —*adj.* (食物,如蘆筍等)加醋或 vinaigrette sauce 後食用的。
vinaigrette sauce 用醋、油、切碎之泡菜及其他調味料製成的一種醬汁。
Vin·cent [ˈvɪnsn̩t; ˈvinsənt] *n.* ①聖·芬生(Saint, ?–304, 西班牙殉教者,種植葡萄及製葡萄酒者之守護神,其紀念日爲一月二十二日)。②男子名。
Vincent's infection 〖醫〗文生氏口炎。
Vin·ci [ˈvɪntʃɪ; ˈvintʃi] *n.* 達文西(Leonardo da, 1452–1519, 義大利畫家、雕刻家、建築家及工程師)。
vin·cu·lum [ˈvɪŋkjʊləm; ˈviŋkjuləm] *n., pl.* **-la** [-lə; -lə]. ①約束;連結物。②〖解剖〗繫帶。③〖數學〗線括。
vin·di·ca·bil·i·ty [ˌvɪndəkəˈbɪlətɪ; ˌvindikəˈbiliti] *n.* 可辯護;可辯解;可辯明。
vin·di·ca·ble [ˈvɪndəkəbl̩; ˈvindikəbl] *adj.* 可辯護的;可辯明的;可證明爲正確的。
vin·di·cate [ˈvɪndəˌket; ˈvindikeit] *v.t.,* **-cat·ed, -cat·ing.** ①辯護;辯解;辯明。②證明有理由。③〖羅馬法、民法〗再取得(權利、財產等)。④〖廢〗解救。⑤〖廢〗處罰。—**vin·di·ca·tor,** *n.*
vin·di·ca·tion [ˌvɪndəˈkeʃən; ˌvindiˈkeiʃən] *n.* ①辯明;辯白。②藉口。③證明有理由之事。
vin·dic·a·tive [ˈvɪndəˌketɪv; ˈvindikətiv] *adj.* 辯護的;辯明的。
vin·di·ca·to·ry [ˈvɪndəkəˌtorɪ; ˈvindikətəri] *adj.* ①=**vindicative.** ②懲罰的;報復的。
vin·dic·tive [vɪnˈdɪktɪv; vinˈdiktiv] *adj.* 有復仇心的;(欲)報復的。—**ly,** *adv.*
*****vine** [vaɪn; vain] *n.* ①葡萄樹。②蔓;藤;有藤蔓的植物。Ivy is a *vine.* 常春藤是一種藤蔓植物。
vine·dress·er [ˈvaɪnˌdrɛsɚ; ˈvainˌdresə] *n.* 葡萄園之園丁。
*****vin·e·gar** [ˈvɪnɪgɚ; ˈvinigə] *n.* ①醋。②不悅的話、態度或臉色。③〖俗〗活力。—**like,** *adj.*
vin·e·gar·y [ˈvɪnɪgərɪ; ˈvinigəri] *adj.* ①醋的;味似醋的;酸的。②尖酸刻薄的。
vin·er·y [ˈvaɪnərɪ; ˈvainəri] *n., pl.* **-er·ies.** ①種植葡萄之暖房。②葡萄樹或藤蔓之集合稱。③〖古〗葡萄園。
*****vine·yard** [ˈvɪnjɚd; ˈvinjəd] *n.* ①葡萄園。②高尚的精神活動之範圍。
vine·yard·ist [ˈvɪnjɚdɪst; ˈvinjədist] *n.* 葡萄種植者。
vingt-et-un [ˌvɛ̃teˈœ̃; ˈvænteiˈəːŋ] 〖法〗*n.* 一種撲克牌遊戲(參加者依次向莊家索牌,以期總點數達於或盡量接近但不得超過二十一點)。(亦作**blackjack, twenty-one**)
vin·i·cul·ture [ˈvɪnɪˌkʌltʃɚ; ˈviniˌkʌltʃə] *n.* ①釀酒用葡萄之種植。②葡萄酒

釀造學。—vin·i·cul·tur·al, *adj.* —vin·i·cul·tur·ist, *n.*

vi·nif·er·ous 〔vaɪˈnɪfərəs; vaiˈnifərəs〕 *adj.* 適於釀造葡萄酒的。

vin·om·e·ter 〔vɪˈnɑmətɚ; viˈnɔmitə〕 *adj.* 葡萄酒酒精計。

vi·nous 〔ˈvaɪnəs; ˈvainəs〕 *adj.* ①葡萄酒的;有葡萄酒味道的;有葡萄酒顏色的。②酗飲葡萄酒的;酒醉的。③產生葡萄酒的;由葡萄酒產生的。④紅葡萄酒色的。—ly, *adv.*

vin·tage 〔ˈvɪntɪdʒ; ˈvintidʒ〕 *n., adj., v.,* -taged, -tag·ing. —*n.* ①葡萄酒(尤指某一特別地區一年所產者)。②(一季的)葡萄收穫量。③某一葡萄酒之產地或季節。④採摘葡萄或釀製葡萄酒; 採葡萄釀酒之季節。⑤葡萄之收成。⑥好的葡萄酒。⑦某一時期(尤指昔時)產品之特殊型式。⑧成熟之程度;年齡。—*adj.* ①優良的;精選的。②葡萄酒的;葡萄酒之釀造的。③某地區某年產之葡萄酒的。④過去的; 過時的(尤指曾經一度爲最佳的)。⑤古老的;過時的。—*v.t.* ①收摘(葡萄)以便釀酒。②釀造(葡萄酒)。—*v.i.* 採摘葡萄以釀酒。

vin·tag·er 〔ˈvɪntɪdʒɚ; ˈvintidʒə〕 *n.* 採葡萄的人。

vintage wine 某年某地區以精選葡萄釀造的酒。

vintage year 釀造 vintage wine 的年度。

vint·ner 〔ˈvɪntnɚ; ˈvintnə〕 *n.* ①〖英〗葡萄酒商(尤指批發商)。②釀造葡萄酒的人。③葡萄酒廠廠主。

vin·y 〔ˈvaɪnɪ; ˈvaini〕 *adj.,* vin·i·er, vin·i·est. ①(像)葡萄樹的;產葡萄樹的;多葡萄樹的。②纏繞的;糾纏的。③有長的匍匐莖的。

vi·nyl 〔ˈvaɪnɪl; ˈvainil〕 *n.* 〖化〗乙烯基 (CH_2: CH–). —*adj.* 〖化〗乙烯基羣的。

vinyl alcohol 〖化〗乙烯醇。

Vi·nyl·ite 〔ˈvaɪnɪlˌaɪt; ˈvainilait〕 *n.* 〖商標名〗合成樹脂。

vin·yon 〔ˈvɪnjɑn; ˈvinjɔn〕 *n.* 一種類似尼龍的人造纖維。

vi·ol 〔ˈvaɪəl; ˈvai-əl〕 *n.* ①一種中古之絃樂器(爲小提琴的前身)。②任何提琴類之樂器。

Vi·o·la 〔ˈvaɪələ; ˈvaiələ〕 *n.* ①懷愛萊(莎士比亞所著 *Twelfth Night* 中之女主角)。②女子名。

vi·o·la¹ 〔vɪˈolə; viˈoulə〕 *n.* 中音小提琴。

vi·o·la² 〔ˈvaɪələ; ˈvaiələ〕 *n.* 〖植物〗任何堇菜科之植物。

vi·o·la·ble 〔ˈvaɪələbl̩; ˈvai-ələbl〕 *adj.* 易犯的;易破壞的;易玷污的;可褻瀆的。—vi·o·la·bly, *adv.* —ness, vi·o·la·bil·i·ty, *n.*

***vi·o·late** 〔ˈvaɪəˌlet; ˈvai-əleit, ˈvaioul-〕 *v.t.,* -lat·ed, -lat·ing. ①違犯(法律、契約等);違背(良心等)。to *violate* a law. 犯法。②妨害;妨礙;擾亂。③褻瀆;冒瀆。The soldiers *violated* the church by using it as a stable. 士兵們把教堂用爲馬廐而褻瀆了它。④强姦。⑤干擾;騷擾。⑥侵犯。—vi·o·la·tor, *n.* —vi·o·la·tive, *adj.*

***vi·o·la·tion** 〔ˌvaɪəˈleʃən; ˌvaiəˈleiʃən, ˌvaiouˈl-〕 *n.* ①違犯;違背。②妨礙;侵害。③褻瀆;冒瀆。④强姦。⑤干擾;騷擾。⑥歪曲意義或事實。—al, *adj.*

***vi·o·lence** 〔ˈvaɪələns; ˈvaiələns〕 *n.* ①猛烈;劇烈。He slammed the door with *violence.* 他猛烈地將門砰然關閉。②暴行;暴亂;暴力;暴虐;傷害。to resort to *violence.* 訴諸暴力。③(行動、感情等之)强烈。④歪曲(事實或意義)。

***vi·o·lent** 〔ˈvaɪələnt; ˈvaiələnt〕 *adj.* ①猛烈的;劇烈的;暴烈的。a *violent* blow. 猛烈的打擊。②由暴力造成的。a *violent* death. 橫死。③激烈的。④兇暴的。⑤極端的。a *violent* contrast. 極端的對比。⑥曲解的。—ly, *adv.* —ness, *n.*

vi·o·les·cent 〔ˌvaɪəˈlɛsn̩t; ˌvaiəˈlesnt〕 *adj.* 漸變成藍紫色的;略帶紫羅蘭色的。

***vi·o·let** 〔ˈvaɪəlɪt; ˈvaiəlit〕 *n.* ①紫羅蘭。②紫羅蘭色;藍紫色。—*adj.* 藍紫色的。*violet* ray. 紫外線。—like, —y, *adj.*

***vi·o·lin** 〔ˌvaɪəˈlɪn; ˌvaiəˈlin〕 *n.* ①四弦提琴;小提琴。②管弦樂團中之提琴手。

vi·o·lin·ist 〔ˌvaɪəˈlɪnɪst; ˈvaiəlinist〕 *n.* 奏四弦提琴者;小提琴家。

vi·ol·ist 〔ˈvaɪəlɪst; viˈoulist〕 *n.* ①中音提琴 (viola) 奏者; 中提琴手。②古提琴 (viol) 奏者。

vi·o·lon·cel·list 〔ˌviəlɑnˈtʃɛlɪst; ˌvaiələnˈtʃelist〕 *n.* 大提琴奏者;大提琴手。

vi·o·lon·cel·lo 〔ˌviəlɑnˈtʃɛlo; ˌvaiələnˈtʃelou〕 *n., pl.* -los. 大提琴。

vio·lo·ne 〔vjoˈlone; vjouˈlounei〕〖義〗*n.* 〖音樂〗①低音絃樂器; 低音大提琴。②(發出大提琴之音的)風琴音栓。

vi·os·ter·ol 〔vaɪˈɑstərol; vaiˈɔstəroul〕 *n.* 〖藥〗照射麥角醇; 固醇生素(麥角醇經紫外線照射後, 溶於油而成一種治療缺乏維他命 D 症之藥物)。

VIP, V.I.P. 〖俚〗大人物(爲 very important person 之略)。

vi·per 〔ˈvaɪpɚ; ˈvaipə〕 *n.* ①毒蛇;蝮蛇。②奸佞之徒。—*adj.* 惡毒的; 心懷痛恨的。—like, *adj.*

vi·per·ine 〔ˈvaɪpərɪn; ˈvaipərin〕 *adj.* 毒蛇的;像毒蛇的;有毒的。

vi·per·ish 〔ˈvaɪpərɪʃ; ˈvaipəriʃ〕 *adj.* =viperous. —ly, *adv.*

vi·per·ous 〔ˈvaɪpərəs; ˈvaipərəs〕 *adj.* (似)毒蛇的;有毒的;邪惡的。—ly, *adv.*

vi·ra·go 〔vəˈrego; viˈrɑːgou〕 *n., pl.* -go(e)s. ①潑婦;悍婦。②有男人力氣或精神之婦女。

vi·ral 〔ˈvaɪrəl; ˈvaiərəl〕 *adj.* 濾過性毒的;濾過性毒引起的;濾毒的。

vir·e·lay 〔ˈvɪrəˌle; ˈvirəlei〕 *n.* ①一種法國古代短詩之詩體(含有兩韻的短行, 開始兩行時時重複)。②其類似之詩體(尤指各節中有長行及短行, 每節中短行互押韻, 每節中之長行之韻係重複前節之短行者)。(亦作 virelai)

vire·ment 〔ˈvɪrmɑn; ˈviəmɑːn〕〖法〗*n.* 〖商〗轉帳;票據交換。

vi·re·mi·a 〔vaɪˈrimɪə; vaiˈriːmiə〕 *n.* 〖醫〗病毒血症;濾毒血症。

vir·e·o 〔ˈvɪrɪˌo; ˈviriou〕 *n., pl.* -os. 北美產的一種食昆蟲的小鳴禽。—nine, *adj.*

vi·res·cence 〔vaɪˈrɛsəns; vaiˈresəns〕 *n.* 〖植物〗 綠化 (特指花瓣等因含葉綠素而變綠)。

vi·res·cent 〔vaɪˈrɛsənt; vaiˈresənt〕 *adj.* ①綠化的。②帶綠色的。

Vir·gil 〔ˈvɝdʒəl; ˈvəːdʒil〕 *n.* =Vergil. —i·an, *adj.*

***vir·gin** 〔ˈvɝdʒɪn; ˈvəːdʒin〕 *n.* ①處女。②(V-)〖天文〗處女座;處女宮。③未婚女子。④〖宗教〗聖女(尤指未婚者)。⑤未交配過的雌性動物。⑥童貞男子。⑦未受精的昆蟲。*the Virgin* 聖母瑪利亞。—*adj.* ①處女的; 童貞的。②純潔的; 潔白無瑕的。③未經使用的。④第一次的。⑤沒有經驗過的。⑥〖動物〗未受精的。⑦(金屬)直接自礦石煉出的。⑧(橄欖油等)第一次(不加熱)榨出來的。

vir·gin·al¹ 〔ˈvɝdʒɪnl̩; ˈvəːdʒinl〕 *adj.* ①處女的; 純潔的; 無瑕的。②〖動物〗未受精的。—ly, *adv.*

vir·gin·al² *n.* (常 *pl.*)(十六、七世紀中

常用之）似小型鋼琴而無腿之樂器；小鍵琴。—ist, *n.*

virginal generation〖生物〗單性生殖。

virginal membrane〖解剖〗處女膜。

virgin birth ①處女誕生說（基督教認爲聖母生耶穌時爲處女之說法）。②〖生物〗單性生殖。

virgin comb 處女蜂窠（僅一次用於產蜜而未曾用於產卵之蜂房）。

virgin forest 原始森林。

Vir·gin·ia 〔və'dʒɪnjə; və'dʒinjə〕 *n.* 維吉尼亞（美國東部之一州，首府爲Richmond）。—**Vir·gin·i·an,** *adj., n.*

Virginia creeper 美國籐（葉大，秋日變紅，爬於牆上）。

Virginia reel 〖美〗①一種舞者面對面排成兩列之鄉村舞蹈。②此種舞蹈之音樂。

vir·gi·ni·bus pu·e·ris·que 〔və'dʒɪnɪbəs,pjuə'rɪskwi; və:'ginibəs puə'riskwi〕〖拉〗適合於少男少女的（＝for girls and boys）。

Vir·gin Islands 〔'vɜdʒɪn～; 'və:dʒin～〕 維爾京羣島（西印度羣島之一部，分屬英美兩國）。

vir·gin·i·ty 〔və'dʒɪnətɪ; və:'dʒiniti〕 *n.* ①處女身分；處女性；童貞。②純潔。

vir·gin·i·um 〔və'dʒɪnɪəm; və'dʒiniəm〕 *n.* 〖化〗鍩（稀金屬元素，符號爲 Vi）。

Virgin Mary 聖母瑪利亞（耶穌之母）。

vir·gin's-bow·er 〔'vɜdʒɪnz'bauə; 'və:dʒinz'bauə〕 *n.* 〖植物〗藤狀鐵線蓮（開白花）。

virgin soil ①處女地；未開墾之土地。②能接受新觀念的頭腦。

Vir·go 〔'vɜgo; 'və:gou〕 *n., gen.* **Vir·gi·nis** 〔'vɜdʒənɪs; 'və:dʒinis〕 for ①.〖天文〗①處女座。②處女宮（黃道第六宮）。

vir·gule 〔'vɜgjul; 'və:gju:l〕 *n.* ①短斜線（/）（置於二字間，以表示任何一字之義均可適用，如 and/or）。②分隔日期或詩行的斜線。

vir·i·des·cent 〔,vɪrə'dɛsn̩t; ,viri'desnt〕 *adj.* 淡綠色的；略帶淡綠色的。—**vir·i·des·cence,** *n.*

vi·rid·i·ty 〔və'rɪdətɪ; vi'riditi〕 *n.* ①（葉或草葉之）綠色；青蔥。②新鮮；活潑。③未成熟；無經驗。

vir·ile 〔'vɪrəl; 'virail〕 *adj.* ①男人的；男性的。②雄赳赳的；剛健的；强有力的。③生殖力的；有生殖力的。

vi·ril·i·ty 〔və'rɪlətɪ; vi'riliti〕 *n., pl.* **-ties.** ①男性之成年。②男子氣；大丈夫氣。③男性的精力；活力；雄勁；雄渾。④生殖能力。

vi·rol·o·gy 〔vaɪ'rɑlədʒɪ; ,vaiə'rɔlədʒi〕 *n.* 病毒學。—**vi·ro·log·i·cal,** *adj.* —**vi·rol·o·gist,** *n.*

vi·rose 〔'vaɪros; 'vaiərous〕 *adj.* ①有毒的。②〖植物〗有惡臭的。

vi·ro·sis 〔vaɪ'rosɪs; ,vaiə'rousis〕 *n., pl.* **-ses** 〔-siz; -si:z〕. 任何由濾過性病毒（virus）所引起之疾病或植物病害。

Vir·ta·nen 〔'vɪrtanɛn; 'virtanen〕 *n.* 維爾塔南（Artturi Ilmari, 1895–, 芬蘭生物化學家，曾獲1945年諾貝爾化學獎）。

vir·tu 〔vɜ'tu; və:'tu:〕 *n.* ①優美珍奇之美術品或古董（集合稱）。②對美術品或古董之愛好或知識。③（美術品或古董）美或珍奇之性質（能引起收藏家之興趣）。***articles of virtu*** 古董；古玩；珍品。（亦作 **vertu**）

vir·tu·al 〔'vɜtʃuəl; 'və:tjuəl〕 *adj.* ①實際上的；實質上的；事實上的。②〖光學〗虛像的。③〖古〗具有可產生某種效果的內在力的。—**i·ty,** *n.*

virtual image 〖物理〗虛像。

***vir·tu·al·ly** 〔'vɜtʃuəlɪ; 'və:tjuəli, -tʃuəli〕 *adv.* ①幾乎；差不多。The job was *virtually* completed by the end of the week. 週末時那工作即可接近完成。②〖廢〗主要地；實質地。

:vir·tue 〔'vɜtʃu; 'və:tju:〕 *n.* ①德行；善；美德。Humility is a *virtue*. 謙遜是一種美德。②女德；貞操。③長處；優點。He praised the *virtues* of his car. 他稱讚他的車子的優點。④效能；效力。There is little *virtue* in that medicine. 那種藥沒有甚麼效力。⑤〖古〗勇敢；男子氣概。⑥（*pl.*）九級天使之第七級。***by*** (or ***in***) ***virtue of*** 憑藉着；由於。***make a virtue of necessity*** 爽爽快快地做非做不可的事；將就不理想的實際情況。***negative virtue*** 消極的美德（未行惡亦未行善之謂）。***of easy virtue*** 不貞節的。***the cardinal virtues*** 四種基本的德行（prudence 審愼、fortitude 堅毅、temperance 克制、justice 公正）。***the theological*** (or ***Christian***) ***virtues*** 三德（faith 信、hope 望、charity 愛）。

vir·tu·os·i·ty 〔,vɜtʃu'ɑsətɪ; ,və:tju'ɔsiti〕 *n., pl.* **-ties.** ①對美術的興趣或嗜好。②藝術（特別是音樂）的技巧。③美術鑑賞家或古玩家之集合稱。

vir·tu·o·so 〔,vɜtʃu'oso; ,və:tju'ouzou〕 *n., pl.* **-sos, -si** 〔-si; -si:〕, *adj.* —*n.* ①美術通；古玩通；美術或古玩等之愛好者。②（藝術界之）名家；巨匠；（尤指）精於樂器演奏者。③（美術品等之）鑑賞家或收藏家。④任何方面之專家。—*adj.* 名家的；愛好者的；美術品收藏家的。—**vir·tu·ose,** *adj.* —**ship,** *n.*

***vir·tu·ous** 〔'vɜtʃuəs; 'və:tjuəs〕 *adj.* ①有品德的；善良的。②貞潔的。③〖古〗有能力的。—**ly,** *adv.* —**ness,** *n.*

vir·u·lence 〔'vɪrjələns; 'virulәns〕 *n.* ①有毒；毒性。②痛恨；敵意；惡毒；惡性。

vir·u·len·cy 〔'vɪrjələnsɪ; 'virulənsi〕 *n.* ＝**virulence.**

vir·u·lent 〔'vɪrjələnt; 'virulənt〕 *adj.* ①有毒的；毒性的。②痛恨的；惡毒的；敵意的。③〖醫〗惡性的；有高度傳染性的。—**ly,** *adv.*

vi·rus 〔'vaɪrəs; 'vaiərəs〕 *n., pl.* **-rus·es.** ①病原體；病毒；濾過性微生物；毒素。②（有害於思想、道德等的）毒素。③＝**virus disease.** —**like,** *adj.*

virus disease 因濾過性毒而引起的人或動植物之疾病。

vis 〔vɪs; vis〕 *n., pl.* **vi·res** 〔'vaɪriz; 'vaiəri:z〕.〖拉〗力；活力（＝force, vigor）。

Vis., Visc. ①Viscount. ②Viscountess.

vi·sa 〔'vizə; 'vi:zə〕 *n., v.,* **-saed, -sa·ing.** —*n.* 簽證。—*v.t.* ①簽證（護照等）。②（＝visé）檢查而核准。

vis·age 〔'vɪzɪdʒ; 'vizidʒ〕 *n.* ①面貌；顏面；面容。an angry *visage*. 怒容。②外觀。

vis-à-vis 〔,vizə'vi; 'vi:za:vi:〕 *adv., adj., prep., n., pl.* **-vis.** —*adv.* 面對面地；相對着。—*adj.* 相對的；相向的；面對面的。—*prep.* 與…相對；對着…；關於…；與…相較。—*n.* ①面對面的人；相對跳舞者。②地位、階級等相同的人。③社交場合之同夥人；女友或男友。④有面對面座位的馬車。⑤兩人對坐的 S 形長椅；面對面的座位。

vis·cer·a 〔'vɪsərə; 'visərə〕 *n.* pl. of **vis·cus** 〔'vɪskəs; 'viskəs〕. ①內臟；臟腑。②（通俗用以指）腸。

vis·cer·al 〔'vɪsərəl; 'visərəl〕 *adj.* ①〖解剖，動物〗內臟的；腹部的。②內臟性的；侵入內臟的（病）。③粗野的；低級的。—**ly,** *adv.*

vis·cer·ate ['vɪsə,ret; 'visəreit] *v.t.*, -at·ed, -at·ing. 取出…之內臟。

vis·cid ['vɪsɪd; 'visid] *adj.* ①黏的;黏質的;黏着性的;半流體的。②〖植物〗被覆黏質的(如葉等)。—ly, *adv.* —ness, *n.*

vis·cid·i·ty [vɪ'sɪdətɪ; vi'siditi] *n.* ①黏着;黏着性。②黏質。

vis·cose ['vɪskos; 'viskous] *n.* 纖維素黏液(爲人造絲、賽璐珞等之原料)。—*adj.* 纖維素黏液的;用纖維素黏液製造的。

vis·cos·i·ty [vɪs'kɑsətɪ; vis'kɔsiti] *n.*, *pl.* -ties. ①黏(性)。②〖物理〗黏力(度)。

vis·count ['vaɪkaunt; 'vaikaunt] *n.* ①子爵。②(在英國)地方行政司法官(sheriff).

vis·count·cy ['vaɪkauntsɪ; 'vaikauntsi] *n.*, *pl.* -cies. 子爵之頭銜、身分、地位等。(亦作 viscountship)

vis·cous ['vɪskəs; 'viskəs] *adj.* ①黏的;黏着的。②〖物理〗有黏性的。③〖植物〗(葉等)被覆黏質的。—ly, *adv.* —ness, *n.*

vise [vaɪs; vais] *n.*, *v.*, vised, vis·ing. —*n.* ①〖機械〗虎頭鉗;老虎鉗。②蝸蜒的樓梯。—*v.t.* 以虎頭鉗夾緊;緊握。(亦作 vice) —like, *adj.*

vi·sé ['vize; 'vi:zei] *n.*, *v.*, vi·séed, vi·sé·ing. =visa.

Vish·nu ['vɪʃnu; 'viʃnu:] *n.* 護持神(印度教三大神之一)。—ism, *n.*

vis·i·bil·i·ty [,vɪzə'bɪlətɪ; ,vizi'biliti] *n.*, *pl.* -ties. ①可見性;能見度。②〖氣象〗(=visual range) 視程;能見度。

*__vis·i·ble__ ['vɪzəbl; 'vizəbl] *adj.* ①可見的。stars not *visible* to the naked eye. 肉眼看不見的星。②明顯的; 顯而易見的。without any *visible* cause. 沒有任何明顯的原因。③用視覺方式表達的。—ness, *n.*

visible speech 可見標音法(教聾者說話用的發音部位分解圖)。

vis·i·bly ['vɪzəblɪ; 'vizəbli] *adv.* 明顯地。

Vis·i·goth ['vɪzɪ,gɑθ; 'vizigɔθ] *n.* 西哥德人(日耳曼族之一支族,於四世紀末侵入義大利,續越過庇里牛斯山,建立王國,紀元711年爲阿拉伯人所滅)。—ic, *adj.*

vis in·er·ti·ae [,vɪsɪ'nɝʃɪ,i; ,visi'nə:ʃii:] 〖拉〗惰性;惰力(=force of inertia).

*__vi·sion__ ['vɪʒən; 'viʒən] *n.* ①視力;視覺。the field of *vision*. 視野。②洞察力;觀察力;想像力。③幻想;夢想;想像。*visions* of youth. 青年時代的夢想。④美景;美人。He had a *vision* of the future. 他對將來有一憧憬。⑤幻像;幻影。—*v.t.* ①在幻覺中看到。②在夢幻中顯現。

vi·sion·al ['vɪʒənəl; 'viʒənəl] *adj.* ①視力的;幻想的。②美景的;夢想的。—ly, *adv.*

vi·sion·ar·y ['vɪʒən,ɛrɪ; 'viʒṇəri] *adj.*, *n.*, *pl.* -ar·ies. —*adj.* ①幻想的;空幻的;空中樓閣的。②好幻想的;有幻想的。③理想的;不切實際的;無法實現的。—*n.* 幻想者;夢想者;理想主義者。—vi·sion·ar·i·ness, *n.*

‡__vis·it__ ['vɪzɪt; 'vizit] *v.t.* ①訪問;訪晤。A doctor *visits* his patients. 醫生探視病人。②遊覽;參觀;往。to *visit* the museum. 參觀博物館。③視察。The inspector *visited* the factory. 督察員視察了該工廠。④(疾病、災害等)侵襲。Plague and famine *visited* the country. 疫癘和饑饉侵襲該國。⑤將…加諸〖常on, upon〗。⑥懲罰。⑦在…作客。⑧慰問。—*v.i.* ①訪問;作客;作短暫之逗留。②懲罰。***visit with*** 〖俗〗與…談話。—*n.* ①訪問;訪晤。I paid Mr. and Mrs. Smith a *visit* yesterday afternoon. 我昨天下午去拜訪史密斯夫婦。②遊覽;參觀。③在某處暫居;作客。I was on a *visit* to my cousins. 我在表兄家裏作客。④〖俗〗談話;聊天。⑤視察。⑥交戰國軍官之登第三國輪船搜查貨物及確定國籍之權利。

vis·it·ant ['vɪzətənt; 'vizitənt] *n.* ①訪問者;訪客。②〖動物〗候鳥。③朝山進香客。④來自靈界的訪客。⑤影響人的某種情緒。—*adj.* 訪問的;拜訪的。a *visitant* bird. 候鳥。

vis·it·a·tion [,vɪzə'teʃən; ,vizi'teiʃən] *n.* ①訪問;訪晤。②巡視;視察。③(疾病、災禍等之)侵襲;天譴。④(V-) 聖母對 Elizabeth 所作之探視(路加福音 1：39-56)。⑤(V-) 聖母訪問節(羅馬天主教於七月二日所舉行以紀念聖母所作上述探視之節日)。⑥聖靈之出現。—al, *adj.*

vis·it·a·to·ri·al [,vɪzətə'torɪəl; ,vizitə'tɔ:riəl] *adj.* ①訪問的;探望的;巡視的;視察的。②訪問者的;視察者的。③有視察權的。

vis·it·ing ['vɪzɪtɪŋ; 'vizitiŋ] *adj.* 訪問的;訪晤的;參觀的; 巡視的。***be on visiting terms with a person*** 和某人有往還之誼。

visiting card 名片。

visiting fireman 〖俚〗①正在訪問某地、某組織或工廠等的大人物(尤指其訪問如能給與好印象即有甚多幫助者)。②觀光客(尤指揮金如土者)。

visiting nurse (醫院或公共衛生機構之)家庭訪問護士。

visiting professor 客座教授。

visiting teacher 爲因病請假在家學生授課,調查未上學之原因,並協調學校及家長關係的教師。

*__vis·i·tor__ ['vɪzɪtɚ; 'vizitə] *n.* 訪問者;賓客;參觀者;觀光者;巡視者。*visitor's* book. 來賓簽名簿;(旅館之)旅客登記簿。

vis·i·to·ri·al [,vɪzə'torɪəl; ,vizi'tɔ:riəl] *adj.* =visitatorial.

vi·sor ['vaɪzɚ; 'vaizə] *n.* ①(盔之)面甲。②帽舌;帽簷。③任何僞裝物或隱蔽物(如面具等)。—*v.t.* 以 visor 保護或遮蓋。—ed, *adj.* —less, *adj.*

vis·ta ['vɪstə; 'vistə] *n.* ①(在狹窄通道等之端所見之)景色;遠景。②行樹;通道。③回想;豫想;展望。—ed, *adj.*—less, *adj.*

Vis·ta·Vi·sion ['vɪstə,vɪʒən; 'vistə,viʒən] *n.* 〖商標名〗〖電影〗超視綜藝體。

*__vis·u·al__ ['vɪʒuəl; 'vizjuəl] *adj.* ①視覺的。②可見的; 眞實的; 非幻想的。—*n.* ①廣告圖案之初步簡單素描。②視覺論者。—ly, *adv.*

visual acuity 視力。

visual aids 視覺教具(教學上用的影片、幻燈片、模型、掛圖等)。

visual field 視野。

visual flight 〖航空〗目視飛行(不使用儀器,靠肉眼觀察之飛行)。

visual instruction (or **education**) 利用視覺教具之教學方法。

vis·u·al·ize ['vɪʒuəl,aɪz; 'vizjuəlaiz] *v.t.* & *v.i.*, -ized, -iz·ing. ①想像;想見。②使可見。—vis·u·al·i·za·tion, *n.*

visual range 〖氣象〗視程;能見度。

vi·ta glass ['vaɪtə～; 'vaitə～] 紫外線玻璃(紫外線可透過的玻璃)。

*__vi·tal__ ['vaɪtl; 'vaitl] *adj.* ①生命的;與生命有關的;生活的。*vital* energies. 生命力;活力。②維持生命所必需的。Eating is a *vital* function. 飲食是維持生命所必需的功能。③極需的;極重要的;不可缺乏的。Perseverance is *vital* to success. 忍耐是成功的重要條件。of *vital* importance. 極重要的。④致命的;

使覆敗的;嚴重的。a *vital* wound. 致命傷。*vital* part.(身體的)要害處;命門。*vital* problem. 生死問題。⑤充滿生命力的;有生氣的;生動的。—*n.* (*pl.*) ①身體之主要器官(如腦、心、肺等);要害。②不可或缺的部分;緊要處;核心。to tear the *vitals* out of a subject. 抓住問題的核心。—**ly,** *adv.* —**ness,** *n.*

vital capacity 〖生理〗肺活量。

vital function 身體之重要功能。

vi·tal·ism [ˈvaɪtlˌɪzm; ˈvaitlizm] *n.* 〖哲學,生物〗生機說(有機體之行爲係由於,或至少一部分係由於一種生機,此種生機非物理或化學所能解釋者)。

vi·tal·ist [ˈvaɪtlɪst; ˈvaitlist] *n.* 生機論者;信仰生機說的人。

***vi·tal·i·ty** [vaɪˈtælətɪ; vaiˈtæliti] *n., pl.* **-ties.** ①活力;生活力。Her *vitality* was lessened by illness. 她的生命力因病而減少了。②持續力。③(藝術、文學作品中的)活力;生動。④有活力或生氣之事物。

vi·tal·ize [ˈvaɪtlˌaɪz; ˈvaitəlaiz] *v.t.,* **-ized, -iz·ing.** 賦以生命力;賦以生機。—**vi·tal·i·za·tion, vi·tal·iz·er,** *n.*

vital principle (生物的)生機;活力。

vital statistics ①〖統計〗生命統計;人口動態統計(卽關於出生、死亡、婚姻等之統計)。②〖詼諧〗女性之三圍。

***vi·ta·min(e)** [ˈvaɪtəmɪn; ˈvitəmin, ˈvait-] *n.* 維他命。—**vi·ta·min·ic,** *adj.*

vi·ta·min·ol·o·gy [ˌvaɪtəmɪˈnɑlədʒɪ; ˌvaitəmiˈnɔlədʒi] *n.* 維他命學。

vi·ta·scope [ˈvaɪtəˌskop; ˈvaitəskoup] *n.* 〖美〗早期之電影放映機。—**vi·ta·scop·ic,** *adj.*

vi·tel·lin [vɪˈtɛlɪn; viˈtelin] *n.* 〖生化〗卵黃素(卵黃所含的一種蛋白質)。

vi·tel·line [vɪˈtɛlɪn; viˈtelin] *adj.* ①卵黃的。②卵黃色的;黃色的。—*n.* 卵黃。

vi·tel·lus [vɪˈtɛləs; viˈteləs] *n., pl.* **-lus·es.** 卵黃。

vi·ti·ate [ˈvɪʃɪˌet; ˈviʃieit] *v.t.,* **-at·ed, -at·ing.** ①敗壞;汚損;破壞;弄髒;使汚濁。②使(契約等)無效;使失效。

vi·ti·a·tion [ˌvɪʃɪˈeʃən; ˌviʃiˈeiʃən] *n.* ①敗壞;汚損;破壞;弄髒。②使無效;使失效。

vi·ti·a·tor [ˈvɪʃɪˌetɚ; ˈviʃieitə] *n.* 敗壞者;汚損者;使無效者。

vit·i·cul·ture [ˈvɪtɪˌkʌltʃɚ; ˈvitiˌkʌltʃə] *n.* 葡萄之栽培;葡萄栽培法。—**vit·i·cul·tur·al,** *adj.* —**vit·i·cul·tur·ist,** *n.*

vit·re·ous [ˈvɪtrɪəs; ˈvitriəs] *adj.* ①玻璃的;似玻璃的;硬、脆而透明的。②與玻璃有關的;玻璃製的。—**ness,** *n.*

vitreous body 〖解剖〗(眼睛的)玻璃體。

vitreous electricity 〖電〗(磨擦玻璃發生的)陽電。

vitreous humor 〖解剖〗(眼睛的)玻璃狀(液)。

vi·tres·cence [vɪˈtrɛsn̩s; viˈtresns] *n.* 變成玻璃;成玻璃狀。

vi·tres·cent [vɪˈtrɛsn̩t; viˈtresnt] *adj.* ①能成玻璃的。②變成玻璃的;有變玻璃傾向的。

vitri- 〖字首〗表"玻璃"之義。

vit·ric [ˈvɪtrɪk; ˈvitrik] *adj.* 玻璃的;似玻璃的;玻璃性的。

vit·ri·form [ˈvɪtrəˌfɔrm; ˈvitrifɔːm] *adj.* 玻璃狀的。

vit·ri·fy [ˈvɪtrəˌfaɪ; ˈvitrifai] *v.t.* & *v.i.,* **-fied, -fy·ing.** (使)變成玻璃;(使)變成玻璃狀。—**vit·ri·fi·a·ble,** *adj.* —**vit·ri·fi·ca·tion, vit·ri·fac·tion,** *n.*

vi·trine [ˈvɪtrɪn, vɪˈtrin; ˈvitrin, viˈtriːn] *n.* 玻璃陳列櫥窗。

vit·ri·ol [ˈvɪtrɪəl; ˈvitriəl] *n., v.,* **-ol(l)ed, -ol·(l)ing.** —*n.* ①〖化〗硫酸鹽(如硫酸銅 blue vitriol)。②〖化〗硫酸。③尖刻的言詞、批評等。—*v.t.* 蝕以或灼以硫酸。

vit·ri·ol·ic [ˌvɪtrɪˈɑlɪk; ˌvitriˈɔlik] *adj.* ①硫酸的;含硫酸的。②似硫酸的;由硫酸而成的。③尖酸刻薄的;犀利的。

vit·ri·ol·ize [ˈvɪtrɪəlˌaɪz; ˈvitriəlaiz] *v.t.,* **-ized, -iz·ing.** ①使成硫酸。②以硫酸處理。③以硫酸傷害(人);以硫酸毀…之容。

vit·ta [ˈvɪtə; ˈvitə] *n., pl.* **-tae** [-ti; -tiː]. ①(古羅馬的)頭巾;頭帶。②〖植物〗(胡蘿蔔科植物果實中之)油管。③〖動、植物〗有色條紋;色帶。

vit·u·line [ˈvɪtʃʊˌlaɪn; ˈvitjulain] *adj.* ①(似)小牛的。②(似)小牛肉的。

vi·tu·per·ate [vaɪˈtupəˌret; viˈtjuːpəreit] *v.t.,* **-at·ed, -at·ing.** 罵;責罵;咒罵;辱罵。

vi·tu·per·a·tion [vaɪˌtupəˈreʃən; viˌtjuːpəˈreiʃən] *n.* 責罵;咒罵;辱罵;誹謗。

vi·tu·per·a·tive [vaɪˈtjupəˌretɪv; viˈtjuːpərətiv] *adj.* 罵詈的;責罵的;出言不遜的。—**ly,** *adv.*

vi·va[1] [ˈvivə; ˈviːvə] *interj.* (歡呼時用)…萬歲!—*n.* "萬歲"聲;(*pl.*) 歡聲;歡呼聲。

vi·va[2] [ˈvaɪvə; ˈvaivə] *n.* 〖俗〗口試。

vi·va·ce [viˈvɑtʃɪ; viˈvɑːtʃi] 〖義〗 *adj.* 〖音樂〗生動的;活潑的;急速的。

vi·va·cious [vaɪˈveʃəs; viˈveiʃəs] *adj.* ①活潑的;快活的;愉快的。a *vivacious* girl. 活潑的女郎。②〖古〗長壽的。—**ly,** *adv.*

vi·vac·i·ty [vaɪˈvæsətɪ; viˈvæsiti] *n., pl.* **-ties.** ①活潑;快活;愉快;充滿生命力。②活潑快樂之行動、景象等。

vi·var·i·um [vaɪˈvɛrɪəm; vaiˈvɛəriəm] *n., pl.* **-i·ums, -i·a** [-ɪə; -iə]. (環境與自然狀態極相近的)動物飼養所或植物栽培所。

vi·va vo·ce [ˈvaɪvəˈvosɪ; ˈvaivəˈvousi] ①口頭地(=orally)。②(某些英國大學中之)口試。

vi·va-vo·ce [ˈvaɪvəˈvosɪ; ˈvaivəˈvousi] *adj.* 口頭的。

vive [viv; viːv] 〖法〗 *interj.* 萬歲。

vi·vers [ˈvivɚz; ˈviːvəz] *n. pl.* 〖蘇〗食物;食糧。

***viv·id** [ˈvɪvɪd; ˈvivid] *adj.* ①鮮明的(色彩等);閃耀的(光等)。a *vivid* green. 鮮綠。②活潑的。③栩栩如生的;生動的。a *vivid* description. 生動的描述。④明顯的;清楚的。—**ly,** *adv.* —**ness,** —**i·ty,** *n.*

viv·i·fy [ˈvɪvəˌfaɪ; ˈvivifai] *v.t.,* **-fied, -fy·ing.** 賦予生命;使活潑;使生動。—*v.i.* 獲得生命;復活。—**viv·i·fi·ca·tion,** *n.*

viv·i·par·i·ty [ˌvɪvɪˈpærətɪ; ˌviviˈpæriti] *n.* ①〖動物〗胎生。②〖植物〗母體發芽。

vi·vip·a·rous [vaɪˈvɪpərəs; viˈvipərəs] *adj.* ①〖動物〗胎生的。②〖植物〗母體發芽的。—**ness,** *n.* —**ly,** *adv.*

viv·i·sect [ˌvɪvəˈsɛkt; ˌviviˈsekt] *v.t.* 活體解剖(動物)。—*v.i.* 行活體解剖。—**i·ble,** *adj.*

viv·i·sec·tion [ˌvɪvəˈsɛkʃən; ˌviviˈsekʃən] *n.* 活體解剖。—**al,** *adj.* —**al·ly,** *adv.*

viv·i·sec·tion·ist [ˌvɪvəˈsɛkʃənɪst; ˌviviˈsekʃənist] *n.* ①活體解剖者。②活體解剖論者。

viv·i·sec·tor [ˈvɪvəˌsɛktɚ; ˈviviˌsektə] *n.* 活體解剖者。

vix·en [ˈvɪksn̩; ˈviksn] *n.* ①雌狐;母狐。②惡婦;悍婦;潑婦;刁婦。—**ly,** *adj.*

vix·en·ish [ˈvɪksn̩ɪʃ; ˈviksn̩iʃ] *adj.* 壞脾氣的;潑辣的;狠毒的;彆扭的。—**ly,** *adv.* —**ness,** *n.*

viz. 卽;就是(拉丁語 videlicet 之略,通常讀爲 namely)。

viz·ard, vis·ard [ˈvɪzəd; ˈvizəd] *n.* ①=visor. ②面罩。—**ed,** *adj.*

vi·zier, vi·zir [vɪˈzɪr; viˈziə] *n.*(回教國家之)高級官員;大官;大臣。***Grand Vizier*** (土耳其等國的)首相;內閣總理。

vi·zor [ˈvaɪzə; ˈvaizə] *n., v.t.* =visor.

V-J Day 第二次世界大戰,同盟國對日本戰爭之勝利日(或爲1945年8月14日日本宣布投降之日,或爲 1945 年 9月2日日本正式簽字投降之日)。

VL Vulgar Latin.

Vla·di·vos·tok [ˌvlædɪˈvɑstɑk; ˌvlædiˈvɔstɔk] *n.* 海參崴(蘇聯太平洋沿岸南部之一海港)。

V-Mail [ˈviˌmel; ˈviː-meil] *n.* V 郵件(第二次世界大戰時,美軍之海外郵件用顯微軟片將原信攝影運輸,遞送時再放大印出,交給收信人)。

V.M.D. Veterinariae Medicinae Doctor (=Doctor of Veterinary Medicine).

VMT very many thanks.

v.n. verb neuter.

V neck V字形的領口。

vo. verso (拉=left-hand page).

V.O. Victorian Order.

VOA ①Voice of America. ②Volunteers of America.

vocab. vocabulary.

vo·ca·ble [ˈvokəbl̩; ˈvoukəbl] *n.* 語;辭。—*adj.* 可說的。—**vo·ca·bly,** *adv.*

***vo·cab·u·lar·y** [vəˈkæbjəˌlɛrɪ; vəˈkæbjuləri] *n., pl.* **-lar·ies.** ①字彙;語彙。a *vocabulary* of technical terms. 專門語字彙。②(某個人或某一種人的)用語(字)範圍。His *vocabulary* is limited. 他的用字範圍有限。③表現藝術家或建築家等風格之特殊形式。

vocabulary entry ①列入字彙中的字。②字(辭)典中所列入的字或短語。

***vo·cal** [ˈvokl̩; ˈvoukəl] *adj.* ①聲的;發聲的;有聲的。Men are *vocal* beings. 人類是能發出聲音的動物。②激起發言的;自由表達意見的。③口頭的。a *vocal* message. 口信。④母音的。—*n.* ①母音。②有樂器伴奏的歌曲。—**ness,** *n.*

vocal cords 聲帶。

vo·cal·ic [voˈkælɪk; vouˈkælik] *adj.* ①母音的;似母音的。②含母音的;多母音的。

vo·cal·ism [ˈvokəlɪzəm; ˈvoukəlizəm] *n.* ①聲音之利用(如在講話與歌唱中)。②歌唱;歌唱之藝術。③母音之聲音;母音。④(某特殊語言之)母音系統。

vo·cal·ist [ˈvokl̩ɪst; ˈvoukəlist] *n.* 聲樂家;歌唱者。

vo·cal·ize [ˈvokl̩ˌaɪz; ˈvoukəlaiz] *v.,* **-ized, -iz·ing.** —*v.t.* ①講出;說出;唱出;以聲音表示出。②使成爲母音;當做母音用。—*v.i.* ①說;講;唱。②母音化;發出聲。—**vo·cal·i·za·tion, vo·cal·iz·er,** *n.*

vo·cal·ly [ˈvokl̩ɪ; ˈvoukəli] *adv.* ①用聲音;高聲地。②口頭地。③以唱歌方式。④母音地。

vocal music 聲樂。

vocal organs 發聲器官。

vocal solo 獨唱。

vo·ca·tion [voˈkeʃən; vouˈkeiʃən] *n.* ①職業。②(對於某種職業的)適宜性或愛好;才能。He had no *vocation* for teaching. 他不適於教書工作。③〖神學〗神命;神召。

vo·ca·tion·al [voˈkeʃənl̩; vouˈkeiʃnl] *adj.* 職業的;職業上的。—**ly,** *adv.*

vocational bureau 職業輔導處。

vocational disease 職業病。

vocational education 職業教育。

vocational guidance 職業輔導。

vocational school 職業學校。

voc·a·tive [ˈvɑkətɪv; ˈvɔkətiv] *adj.* ①〖文法〗呼格的。②呼喚的。—*n.* 〖文法〗呼格;呼喚語。—**ly,** *adv.*

vo·cif·er·ant [voˈsɪfərənt; vouˈsifərənt] *adj.* 高聲呼叫的;嘈雜的。—*n.* 高聲大叫者。—**vo·cif·er·ance,** *n.*

vo·cif·er·ate [voˈsɪfəˌret; vouˈsifəreit] *v.i. & v.t.,* **-at·ed, -at·ing.** 大聲呼叫;怒吼;呼喊。—**vo·cif·er·a·tion, vo·cif·er·a·tor,** *n.*

vo·cif·er·ous [voˈsɪfərəs; vouˈsifərəs] *adj.* 呼喊的;嘈雜的;喧譁的。—**ly,** *adv.* —**ness,** *n.*

vod·ka [ˈvɑdkə; ˈvɔdkə] *n.* 伏特加酒(一種俄國烈性麥酒)。

***vogue** [vog; voug] *n.* 時尚;流行。a style in *vogue*. 流行的式樣。

‡**voice** [vɔɪs; vɔis] *n., v.,* **voiced, voic·ing.** —*n.* ①聲音。②發言能力;發聲能力。③類似說話或唱歌之聲音。④歌唱家的能力;聲樂之聲。⑤歌唱家;歌唱者。⑥發表;表示;吐露。They gave *voice* to their indignation. 他們表露他們的憤慨。⑦意見;願望。His *voice* was for compromise. 他的意見贊成妥協。⑧發言權;參與決定之權。I have no *voice* in the matter. 我對此事無發言權。⑨表達之媒介。Poetry is the *voice* of imagination. 詩是表達想像的媒介。⑩〖文法〗(動詞之)語態。⑪〖語音〗由聲帶震顫而發出的聲音。⑫歌唱家聲音之音階。⑬〖廢〗 **a.** 謠言。**b.** 名聲;聲譽。***in voice*** 聲音好(適於唱歌或講話)。***lift up one's voice*** 叫;嚷;抗議。***the still, small voice*** 良心。***with one voice*** 異口同聲地;一致地。—*v.t.* ①發表;道出;宣述。They *voiced* their approval of the plan. 他們對這項計畫表示贊成。②〖語音〗發出有聲之音。—**voic·er,** *n.* 〖文法〗 **voice.** 語態。語態是及物動詞的一種變化形式,分爲主動語態 (active voice) 和被動語態 (passive voice)兩種。

voice box 喉頭 (=larynx).

voiced [vɔɪst; vɔist] *adj.* ①有聲的。a *voiced* consonant. 有聲子音(如 b, d, g, m). ②用言語表達的。—**ness,** *n.*

voice·less [ˈvɔɪslɪs; ˈvɔislis] *adj.* ①沉寂的;啞的;無聲的。②〖語音〗無聲的。*voiceless* consonants. 無聲子音(如 p, t, k 等)。③未說出來的;未表達的。④聲音不悅耳的。⑤無發言權的;無權表示意見的。—**ly,** *adv.* —**ness,** *n.*

Voice of America 美國之音(美國對國外之廣播)。

voice-o·ver [ˈvɔɪsˌovɚ; ˈvɔisˌouvə] *n.* 旁白。

voice vote 根據贊成 (ayes) 與反對 (noes) 聲音之大小而估計人數所決定的表決(不一一數 ayes 或 noes 的)。

***void** [vɔɪd; vɔid] *adj.* ①無法律上之效力的;無效的。null and *void*. 在法律上無效的。②空的;空虛的。The office fell *void*. 這個職位已經空出。③缺乏;沒有〖of〗. to be *void* of common sense. 沒有常識。④無用的;無益的。—*n.* ①空虛;空處。②空虛之感。The death of his dog left an aching *void* in Bob's heart. 愛犬之死使鮑伯心裏有陣痛苦空虛之感。③(牆壁等之)孔;洞。—*v.t.* ①使無效;使作廢。②排泄。③清理場地〖常 of〗. ④〖古〗離開;出發。⑤〖廢〗 **a.** 避免。**b.** 支開;逐出。—*v.i.* 澄清;通便。

void·a·ble [ˈvɔɪdəbl̩; ˈvɔidəbl] *adj.* 可使無效的;可作廢的。—**ness,** *n.*

void·ance [ˈvɔɪdn̩s; ˈvɔidəns] *n.* ①排

泄;放出。②放棄;移除。③(契約等之)取消;無效。④〖宗教〗聖職之免除;聖職之空缺;空職。

voile [vɔɪl; vɔil] *n.* 一種棉、絲、人造絲、或羊毛所織成之薄紗(用以製女服或窗簾等)。

voir dire [ˌvwarˈdir; ˌvwarˈdiːr] 〖法〗〖法律〗①所說屬實(於受訊問是否具備作證人或陪審員資格時所作之誓言)。②此種訊問。

voi·ture [ˌvwaˈtyr; ˌvwaˈtyr] *n., pl.* **-tures** [–ˈtyr; –ˈtyr]. 〖法〗馬車;貨車;車。

vol. ①volcanic. ②volcano. ③volume. ④volunteer.

vo·lant [ˈvolənt; ˈvoulənt] *adj.* ①飛的;能飛的。②快速的;敏捷的。③〖紋章〗飛翔姿態的。

Vo·la·pük, Vo·la·puk [ˈvaləˌpuk; ˈvɔləpuk] *n.* 一種世界語(1879 年德國人 Johann M. Schleyer 所創)。

vol·a·tile [ˈvalətl̩; ˈvɔlətail] *adj.* ①揮發性的;飛散性的。*volatile* oil. 揮發油。②輕快的;輕浮的;易變的;反覆無常的。③爆炸性的。④短暫的。⑤〖古〗能飛的;慣飛的。

vol·a·til·i·ty [ˌvaləˈtɪlətɪ; ˌvɔləˈtiliti] *n., pl.* **-ties.** ①揮發;揮發性。②輕快;輕浮;易變。

vol·a·til·ize [ˈvalətl̩ˌaɪz; vɔˈlætilaiz] *v.i. & v.t.,* **-ized, -iz·ing.** 揮發;蒸發。—**vol·a·til·iz·er, vol·a·til·i·za·tion,** *n.*

vol-au-vent [ˌvoˌloˈvɑ̃; ˈvɔlouˈvɑːŋ] 〖法〗 *n.* 肉餡餅。

***vol·can·ic** [valˈkænɪk; vɔlˈkænik] *adj.* ①火山的;火山所造成的。*volcanic* eruption. 火山爆發。*volcanic* rocks. 火山岩。②像火山一般的;暴躁易怒的;易爆發的。③多火山的。—**al·ly,** *adv.*

volcanic glass 火山玻璃(火山熔岩急冷時所形成的天然玻璃)。

vol·can·ism [ˈvalkənɪzm̩; ˈvɔlkənizəm] *n.* 火山活動;火山作用;火山現象。

***vol·ca·no** [valˈkeno; vɔlˈkeinou] *n., pl.* **-noes** or **-nos.** 火山。an active *volcano.* 活火山。 an extinct *volcano.* 死火山。

Volcano Islands 琉璜羣島(爲西太平洋中之三小島,屬日本)。

vol·can·ol·o·gy [ˌvalkənˈalədʒɪ; ˌvɔlkənˈɔlədʒi] *n.* 火山學。(亦作 **vulcanology**)—**vol·can·ol·o·gist,** *n.* —**vol·can·o·log·i·cal, vol·can·o·log·ic,** *adj.*

vole[1] [vol; voul] *n.* 〖動物〗田鼠;野鼠類。

vole[2] *n., v.,* **voled, vol·ing.** —*n.* 〖牌戲〗全勝;滿貫。—*v.i.* 全勝;獲滿貫。***go the vole*** **a.** 孤注一擲。**b.** 一個個地嘗試(如職業等)。

Vol·ga [ˈvalgə; ˈvɔlgə] *n.* 窩瓦河(亦稱伏爾加河,發源於蘇聯西部,東流入裏海,爲歐洲第一長河)。

vol·i·tant [ˈvalɪtənt; ˈvɔlitənt] *adj.* ①能飛的。②活動的。

vo·li·tion [voˈlɪʃən; vouˈliʃən] *n.* ①意志;決意;取捨。②意志力。 —**al,** *adj.*

vol·i·tive [ˈvalətɪv; ˈvɔlitiv] *adj.* ①意志的;志向的。②〖文法〗表示祈望或准許的。

Volks·lied [ˈfɔlksˌlit; ˈfɔlks-liːt] *n., pl.* **-lie·der.** 〖德〗民謠;民歌。

Volks·lied·er [ˈfɔlksˌlidɚ; ˈfɔlksˌliːdə] 〖德〗 *n.* pl. of **Volkslied.**

Volks·po·li·zei [ˌfɔlkspɔlɪˈtsaɪ; ˌfɔːlkspɔːliˈtsai] 〖德〗 *n.* 東德之人民警察。

***vol·ley** [ˈvalɪ; ˈvɔli] *n., pl.* **-leys,** *v.,* **-leyed, -ley·ing.** —*n.* ①(槍砲等之)一陣射擊;齊發;齊射。②(質問、咒罵等之)齊發;連發。a *volley* of laughter. 齊聲之大笑。③(網球中)飛擊;截擊(在球落地前擊球)。④〖開礦〗多處炸藥之同時爆炸。⑤〖足球〗球尚未落地時之一踢。—*v.t.*①一齊射擊;齊發;連發。②(網球)在球落地前擊(球)。—*v.i.*放排槍;放排砲。

***vol·ley·ball** [ˈvalɪˌbɔl; ˈvɔlibɔːl] *n.* 排球;排球比賽所用之球。

volley fire 齊一射擊;齊射。

vol·plane [ˈvalˌplen; ˈvɔl-plein] *n., v.i.,* **-planed, -plan·ing.** 〖航空〗滑翔下降。—**vol·plan·ist,** *n.*

vols. volumes.

volt[1] [volt; voult] *n.* 伏特(電壓的單位)。

volt[2] *n.* ①環騎(馬繞一中心點以身體一側向前之步法)。②〖劍術〗閃避(爲躲避被刺而跳開之動作)。

Vol·ta [ˈvoltɑ; ˈvɔltə] *n.* 伏特(Count Alessandro, 1745–1827, 義大利物理學家)。

vol·ta [ˈvɔltɑ, ˈvaltə; ˈvɔltə] *n., pl.* **-te.** 〖音樂〗回;次。***due volta*** 二次;二回。***prima volta*** 第一回;第一次。 ***una volta*** 一回;一次。

Volta effect 〖電〗伏特效應。

volt·age [ˈvoltɪdʒ; ˈvoultidʒ] *n.* 伏特數;電壓量;電壓。

voltage divider 〖電〗分壓器。

voltage transformation 〖電〗變壓。

vol·ta·ic [valˈteɪk; vɔlˈteiik] *adj.* ①動電(卽流動之電,與靜電相對)的。②由化學作用所產生之電的。③(V–)伏特氏的;伏特氏發明的。

voltaic battery 〖電〗伏特電池;由伏特電池組合之電瓶。

voltaic cell 〖電〗伏特電池(利用不同之金屬片在電解液中產生電位差之電池)。

voltaic electricity 電流。

Vol·taire [valˈtɛr; ˈvɔlteə] *n.* 福爾特爾(本名 François Marie Arouet, 1694–1778, 法國諷刺家、哲學家、劇作家、及歷史家)。

Vol·tair·ism [valˈtɛrɪzm̩; vɔlˈtɛərizm] *n.* ①懷疑主義;懷疑論。②Voltaire 之精神或哲學。

vol·tam·e·ter [valˈtæmətɚ; vɔlˈtæmitə] *n.* 〖電〗伏特計;電壓計。—**vol·ta·met·ric,** *adj.*

volt-am·pere [ˈvoltˈæmpɪr; ˈvoultˈæmpɛə] *n.* 〖電〗伏(特)安(培)。

vol·te [ˈvɔlte; ˈvɔlti] *n.* pl. of **volta.**

volte-face [ˈvaltˌfas; ˈvɔltˈfaːs] *n., pl.* **volte-face.** ①轉身;轉向。 ②(意見、態度等的)改變;轉變;激變。

volt·me·ter [ˈvoltˌmitɚ; ˈvɔltˌmiːtə] *n.* 〖電〗伏特計;電壓表。

vol·u·ble [ˈvaljəbl; ˈvɔljubl] *adj.* ①健談的;口若懸河的;多言的。②〖罕〗在軸上易轉動的;旋轉的。③〖植物〗(蔓等)纏繞的。—**vol·u·bly,** *adv.* —**vol·u·bil·i·ty,** —**ness,** *n.*

‡**vol·ume** [ˈvaljəm; ˈvɔljum] *n.* ①卷;册;書本。 We own a library of five hundred *volumes.* 我們擁有一所藏書五百册的圖書館。②體積;容積;容量。The storeroom has a *volume* of 800 cubic feet. 這儲藏室的容積是八百立方英尺。③大量;多量。④數量;總額。⑤音量。⑥捲(古書的形式)。⑦〖機械〗强度;響度。 ***speak volumes*** **a.** 充分地表明;含有無限意義。**b.** 富有表情。

vo·lu·me·ter [vəˈlumətɚ; vɔˈljuːmitə] *n.* 〖物理〗體積計。

vol·u·met·ric [ˌvaljəˈmɛtrɪk; ˌvɔljuˈmetrik] *adj.* 有關或基於體積或容積測定的。(亦作 **volumetrical**)

vo·lu·mi·nous [vəˈlumənəs; vəˈljuːminəs] *adj.* ①有很多卷的;大部頭的; 長的。

②多產的（作家）。③大的；多的；浩瀚的。④〖古〗多捲的；多圈的。—**ly,** *adv.* —**ness,** *n.*

vol·un·tar·i·ly [ˈvɑlənˌtɛrəlɪ; ˈvɔləntərili] *adv.* 志願地；自願地；自動地。

vol·un·tar·i·ness [ˈvɑlənˌtɛrɪnɪs; ˈvɔləntərinis] *n.* 自動；自願；隨意。

vol·un·ta·rism [ˈvɑləntərɪzm̩; ˈvɔləntərizm] *n.* ①〖哲學〗意志說（認爲意志是經驗中之基本因素或眞實係屬意志性質之學說）。②=**voluntaryism.** —**vol·un·ta·rist,** *n., adj.* —**vol·un·ta·ris·tic,** *adj.*

*__vol·un·tar·y__ [ˈvɑlənˌtɛrɪ; ˈvɔləntəri] *adj., n., pl.* **-tar·ies.** —*adj.* ①自願的；志願的；自動的。a *voluntary* choice. 自願的選擇。②故意的。③由自由捐助支持的；私立的。④能依自由意志行動的；有自由選擇能力的。⑤爲意志所控制的。the *voluntary* muscles. 隨意肌。⑥自發的。—*n.* ①自願做的事；自願的行爲。②〖音樂〗（禮拜儀式前、進行時、或完畢後之）風琴獨奏。

voluntary army 志願軍。

vol·un·tar·y·ism [ˈvɑlənˌtɛrɪɪzəm; ˈvɔləntəriizm] *n.* ①由私人樂捐以維持學校或教會之制度。②募兵制。

*__vol·un·teer__ [ˌvɑlənˈtɪr; ˌvɔlənˈtiə] *n.* ①志願者；自願從事者。One *volunteer* is worth two pressed men. 一個志願者相當於兩個被迫從事者。②志願兵；義勇軍。③自生植物。—*adj.* ①自願的；志願的。a *volunteer* fireman. 志願消防隊員。②〖植物〗自生的。a *volunteer* crop. 自生作物。—*v.t.* ①自動；自願獻出。②〖古〗志願採取（某行動）。—*v.i.* ①自願；自願效勞。He *volunteered* to do the job. 他自願做這個工作。②自願投軍。

vo·lup·tu·ar·y [vəˈlʌptʃʊˌɛrɪ; vəˈlʌptjuəri] *n., pl.* **-ar·ies,** *adj.* —*n.* 耽於逸樂的人；酒色之徒。—*adj.* 奢侈逸樂的；貪戀酒色的；肉慾的。

vo·lup·tu·ous [vəˈlʌptʃʊəs; vəˈlʌptjuəs] *adj.* ①奢侈逸樂的；耽迷肉慾的；貪戀酒色的。②色情的；情慾的；肉感的；艷麗的。to lead a *voluptuous* life. 過酒色生活。—**ly,** *adv.* —**ness, vo·lup·tu·os·i·ty,** *n.*

vo·lute [vəˈlut; vəˈljuːt] *n.* ①渦形；渦形物。②〖建築〗渦卷飾物；螺旋形飾（尤指 Ionic 或 Corinthian 式柱頭上的）。—*adj.* 渦卷的；螺旋形的。—**vo·lut·ed,** *adj.*

vo·lu·tion [vəˈljuʃən; vəˈljuːʃən] *n.* ①旋轉。②渦形；渦卷。③螺環。

vom·it [ˈvɑmɪt; ˈvɔmit] *v.t.* ①嘔吐。②噴出；吐出。③以催嘔劑使吐出。④使下車。—*v.i.* ①嘔吐；吐出。②（火山）噴出岩漿。③傾出。—*n.* ①嘔吐；嘔吐出來的東西。②催嘔劑。—**er,** *n.* —**ous,** *adj.* —**ous·ly,** *adv.*

vom·i·tive [ˈvɑmɪtɪv; ˈvɔmitiv] *adj.* =**vomitory.** —*n.* 催吐劑。

vom·i·to·ry [ˈvɑmɪˌtorɪ; ˈvɔmitəri] *adj., n., pl.* **-ries.** —*adj.* 使嘔吐的；催嘔吐的；嘔吐的。—*n.* ①催吐劑。②排出口。③〖建築〗（古羅馬圓形劇場的）出入口。

vom·i·tous [ˈvɑmətəs; ˈvɔmitəs] *adj.* 想嘔吐的。

vom·i·tu·ri·tion [ˌvɑmɪtʃʊˈrɪʃən; ˌvɔmitjuˈriʃən] *n.* 嘔吐；乾嘔；連續的嘔吐。

von [vɑn, fɔn; vɔn, fɔːn] 〖德〗*prep.* =**from; of**（常加在姓前，表示貴族）。

V-one [ˈviˈwʌn; ˈviːˈwʌn] *n.* =**V-1.**

voo·doo [ˈvudu; ˈvuːduː] *n., pl.* **-doos,** *adj., v.,* **-dooed, -doo·ing.** —*n.* ①巫毒教（=voodooism）（亦作 **vodun**）。②巫毒教之術士。③巫毒教之符咒或神物。—*adj.* 巫毒教的。—*v.t.* 以巫毒教之巫術迷惑。

voo·doo·ism [ˈvuduɪzm̩; ˈvuːduːizm] *n.* 巫毒教（源自非洲而仍流行於西印度羣島及美國南部黑人間的一種邪教）。—**voo·doo·ist,** *n.* —**voo·doo·is·tic,** *adj.*

vo·ra·cious [voˈreʃəs; vəˈreiʃəs] *adj.* ①吃過量的；飲食過度的；饕餮的；貪食暴飲的。②非常渴望的；難滿足的；貪婪的。a *voracious* appetite. 難滿足的食慾。a *voracious* reader. 知識慾强烈的讀者。—**ly,** *adv.*

vo·rac·i·ty [vəˈræsətɪ; vɔˈræsiti] *n.* 貪食；暴食；貪婪。

Vor·la·ge [ˈforˌlɑgə; ˈfɔːˌlɑːgə] *n., pl.* **-ge.** 〖德〗一種身體前傾的滑雪姿勢。

vor·tex [ˈvɔrtɛks; ˈvɔːteks] *n., pl.* **-tex·es** or **-ti·ces** [-tɪˌsiz; -tisiːz]. ①旋渦；旋風；旋轉。②如旋風或旋渦般之活動或情勢。③〖物理〗渦動。④如旋渦的火焰。

vor·ti·cal [ˈvɔrtɪkl̩; ˈvɔːtikəl] *adj.* 旋渦的；似旋渦的；激起旋渦的；旋轉的。—**ly,** *adv.*

vor·ti·cel·la [ˌvɔrtɪˈsɛlə; ˌvɔːtiˈselə] *n., pl.* **-cel·lae** [-ˈsɛli; -ˈseliː]. 〖動物〗鐘形蟲。

vor·ti·cism [ˈvɔrtɪsɪzm̩; ˈvɔːtisizm] *n.* ①〖美術〗渦紋主義（以旋渦代表觀念、物品等之一種現代畫派，二十世紀初興起於英國，爲未來派之支流）。②〖哲學〗（Descartes的）宇宙物質渦動說。

vor·ti·cist [ˈvɔrtɪsɪst; ˈvɔːtisist] *n.* ①渦紋派畫家。②信仰宇宙物質渦動說者。

Vos·tok [ˈvɔstɑk; ˈvɔːstɔk] *n.* 蘇聯之一系列有人駕駛的人造衞星之一。

vot·a·ble [ˈvotəbl̩; ˈvoutəbl] *adj.* 有投票權的；可付諸投票的。（亦作 **voteable**）

vo·ta·ress [ˈvotərɪs; ˈvoutəris] *n.* ①尼姑。②愛好者。

vo·ta·rist [ˈvotərɪst; ˈvoutərist] *n.* =**votary.**

vo·ta·ry [ˈvotərɪ; ˈvoutəri] *n., pl.* **-ries,** *adj.* —*n.* ①出家人；和尚；尼姑。②愛好者；崇拜者；支持者。—*adj.* ①立誓任聖職的。②誓言的。

‡**vote** [vot; vout] *n., v.,* **vot·ed, vot·ing.** —*n.* ①投票；表決；選舉。open *vote.* 記名投票。secret *vote.* 不記名投票。②投票權；表決權；選舉權。Not everybody has a *vote.* 並不是每一個人都有投票權。③選票；投票紙。I gave my *vote* to Mr. Chang. 我投張先生的票。④選票數。⑤選民；投票者。⑥贊同之表示。⑦〖廢〗a. 熱望。b. 誓約。—*v.i.* 投票；選舉。He *voted* for the Democrats. 他投民主黨的票。—*v.t.* ①以投票方式通過或決定。②投票擁護。③〖俗〗提議。I *vote* (that) we go to the theater tonight. 我提議我們今天晚上去看戲。④同意；一致認爲。***vote down*** 投票否決。***vote in*** 選舉。***vote through*** 投票通過。—**vot·er,** *n.*

vote of confidence ①（國會對政府或其官員所投，以表示支持其政策的）信任票。②（任何）贊同或支持。

vot·ing [ˈvotɪŋ; ˈvoutiŋ] *n.* 投票；選舉。

voting machine 〖美〗選票計算機；投票記錄機。

voting paper 〖英〗選舉票。

vo·tive [ˈvotɪv; ˈvoutiv] *adj.* ①誓願的；許願的；因誓約而作或奉獻的。*votive* Mass. 〖羅馬天主教〗許願彌撒。*votive* offering. 謝恩奉獻物；還願物。*votive* picture (tablet). 還願畫（扁額）。②願望的；表示慾望的。—**ly,** *adv.* —**ness,** *n.*

vouch 〔vautʃ; vautʃ〕 *v.i.* ①擔保〖常for〗. ②保證〖常 for〗. —*v.t.* ①證實;保證。②證明。③引典證實。④提出傳票、單據以證實。⑤(昔)傳喚某人至法庭以證明所有權。⑥支持;推薦。
vouch·er 〔ˈvautʃɚ; ˈvautʃə〕 *n.* ①證明人;保證人;擔保人;擔保物;證件; 證書。②收據;(商業記帳用的)傳票;憑單。—**a·ble,** *adj.*
vouch·safe 〔vautʃˈsef; vautʃˈseif〕 *v.,* **-safed, -saf·ing.** —*v.t.* ①惠予。②恩准;准予。—*v.i.* 屈尊;俯就。 —**ment,** *n.*
vous·soir 〔ˌvuˈswær; ˌvuːˈswɑː〕 *n.* 〖建築〗拱石。
***vow** 〔vau; vau〕 *n.* ①誓; 誓約。I am under a *vow* to drink no wine. 我已立誓戒酒。②熱誠的宣言。*take* (or *make*) *a vow* 立誓。*take vows* 立誓修行; 加入宗教團體。 —*v.t. & v.i.* 立誓; 誓言; 發誓。 I *vowed* never to leave home again. 我發誓絕不再離家。*vow and declare* 鄭重聲明;發誓。—**er,** *n.*
***vow·el** 〔ˈvauəl;ˈvauəl〕 *n.* ①元音;母音。②元音字母;母音字母。—*adj.* 元音的;母音的。
vowel gradation =ablaut.
vowel harmony 〖語言〗(芬蘭語、匈牙利語、土耳其語等)母音調和。
vow·el·ize 〔ˈvauəlˌaɪz; ˈvauəlaiz〕 *v.t.,* **-ized, -iz·ing.** ①注以母音符號。②讀成母音。③用母音修正。—**vow·el·i·za·tion,** *n.*
vowel point (希伯來文、阿拉伯文及其他同系統的文字中)附加於子音上下以表示母音之符號。
vox 〔vɑks; vɔks〕 *n., pl.* **vo·ces** 〔ˈvosiz; ˈvousiːz〕. 〖拉〗聲音 (=voice). *vox* Dei. 上帝之聲。*vox* humana. (風琴的)人聲音栓。
vox po·pu·li 〔vɑksˈpɑpjuˌlaɪ; vɔksˈpɔpjulai〕 〖拉〗人民的聲音;輿論 (=the voice of the people). (略作 **vox pop.**)
vox po·pu·li, vox De·i 〔vɑksˈpɑpjuˌlaɪvɑksˈdiaɪ; vɔksˈpɔpjulai vɔksˈdiːai〕〖拉諺〗天聽自我民聽 (=the voice of the people 〔is〕 the voice of God).
***voy·age** 〔ˈvɔɪ·ɪdʒ; vɔidʒ, ˈvɔiidʒ〕 *n., v.,* **-aged, -ag·ing.** —*n.* ①航行; 航海。He made a *voyage* to America. 他航行到美國去。②航空;太空旅行。③陸路旅行。④(常*pl.*)一連串的旅行之遊記;見聞錄。—*v.i. & v.t.* 航行;航海;航空。—**voy·ag·er,** *n.*
voy·age·a·ble 〔ˈvɔɪ·ɪdʒəbl; ˈvɔidʒəbl〕 *adj.* 可航行的。
voy·a·geur 〔vwajaˈʒœːr;vwajaˈʒœːr〕 *n., pl.* **-geurs** 〔-ˈʒœːr; -ˈʒœːr〕. 〖法〗①旅客; 旅行者。②加拿大皮貨公司所僱用往來不毛之地運送貨物或人員者。③加拿大荒地之船夫或樵夫。
VP, V.P. Vice-President. **v.p.** verb passive. **V.R.** Victoria Regina (拉=Queen Victoria). **v.r.** verb reflexive.
vrai·sem·blance 〔vrɛsɑ̃ˈblɑ̃ːs;ˌvreisɑ̃ːmˈblɑ̃ːns〕 〖法〗 *n.* 似眞實; 像眞實;眞實性。
V. Rev. Very Reverend.
vrouw 〔vrau, frau; vrau, frau〕〖荷〗*n.* 妻;婦人;主婦;太太(相當於 Mrs.).
vs. ①verse. ②versus. **V.S.** ①Veterinary Surgeon. ②〖音樂〗turn over swiftly. **v.s.** vide supra (拉 =see above).
V-shaped 〔ˈviˌʃept; ˈviːˌʃeipt〕 *adj.* V字形的。
V sign ①勝利記號 (以食中指作 V 字形,以爲勝利之表徵)。②表贊成之 V 形記號。
VSO, V.S.O. very superior (*or* special) old. 陳年(指12至17年的白蘭地酒)。
VSOP, V.S.O.P. very superior (*or* special) old pale. 特級陳年 (指18至25年的白蘭地酒)。
V/STOL 〔ˈviˌstol; ˈviːˌstɔːl〕 垂直短程起飛及降落 (=*V*ertical *S*hort *T*ake-*O*ff and *L*anding). **Vt.** Vermont. **v.t.** verb transitive.
VTO 〖航空〗 vertical take-off (垂直起飛)。
VTOL 〔ˈviˌtɔl; ˈviːˌtɔːl〕 *n.* 〖航空〗①垂直起飛及降落。②可垂直起飛及降落之飛機。
V-two 〔ˈviˈtu; ˈviːˈtuː〕 *n.* =V-2.
vul·can·ism 〔ˈvʌlkənɪzəm; ˈvʌlkənizəm〕 *n.* 〖地質〗①火山力; 火山作用。②岩石火成論。
vul·can·ite 〔ˈvʌlkənˌaɪt; ˈvʌlkənait〕 *n.* 一種硬橡皮。—*adj.* 用這種硬橡皮做成的。
vul·can·ize 〔ˈvʌlkənˌaɪz;ˈvʌlkənaiz〕 *v.,* **-ized, -iz·ing.** —*v.t.* 以高溫及硫黃處理(橡皮);硬化(橡皮)。 —*v.i.* (橡皮)硬化。—**vul·can·iz·a·ble,** *adj.* —**vul·can·i·za·tion,** *n.*
Vulg. Vulgate.
***vul·gar** 〔ˈvʌlgɚ;ˈvʌlgə〕 *adj.* ①粗俗的;粗鄙的。*vulgar* taste. 低級趣味。②平民的。③通俗的; 平常使用的 (語言)。 the *vulgar* tongue. 本國語; 土語。④不出色的;無美術價值的; 平庸的。⑤流行的; 通行的。 *the vulgar* 平民;庶民。—*n.* ①〖古〗平民;庶民。②〖廢〗本國語 ;土語。—**ly,** *adv.* —**ness,** *n.*
vul·gar·i·an 〔vʌlˈgɛrɪən; vʌlˈgɛəriən〕 *n.* ①粗夫; 俗人; 陋漢。②粗俗的富人;附庸風雅者。
vul·gar·ism 〔ˈvʌlgəˌrɪzəm; ˈvʌlgərizəm〕 *n.* ①粗俗語。②粗鄙;粗野的言行。
vul·gar·i·ty 〔vʌlˈgærətɪ;vʌlˈgæriti〕 *n., pl.* **-ties.** ①粗俗;粗鄙;粗陋。②(*pl.*) 庸俗的行爲或談吐。
vul·gar·ize 〔ˈvʌlgəˌraɪz; ˈvʌlgəraiz〕 *v.t.,* **-ized, -iz·ing.** 使通俗化; 使庸俗。—**vul·gar·i·za·tion, vul·gar·iz·er,** *n.*
Vul·gate 〔ˈvʌlget; ˈvʌlgit〕 *n.* ①拉丁語聖經 (第四世紀末期 St. Jerome所譯, 爲羅馬天主教認爲唯一可信之拉丁語譯本)。② (v-) 俗文。—*adj.* ①拉丁語聖經的。②(v-)普通的;通常的;通俗的;一般的。
vul·ner·a·ble 〔ˈvʌlnərəbl; ˈvʌlnərəbl〕 *adj.* ①可傷害的;易受攻擊的。②難防守的。③有弱點的;脆弱的;對批評、誘惑、影響敏感的。④〖牌戲〗(橋牌中獲勝一局, game, 後)有身價的。—**vul·ner·a·bly,** *adv.* —**vul·ner·a·bil·i·ty, —ness,** *n.*
vul·ner·ar·y 〔ˈvʌlnəˌrɛrɪ; ˈvʌlnərəri〕 *n., pl.* **-ar·ies,** *adj.* —*n.* 敷傷藥; 外傷藥。—*adj.* 用以治療外傷的。
vul·pec·u·lar 〔vʌlˈpɛkjəlɚ; vʌlˈpekjulə〕 *adj.* 狐狸的;狡猾似狐狸的。
vul·pi·cide 〔ˈvʌlpɪˌsaɪd; ˈvʌlpisaid〕 *n.* ①(不用獵犬之)捕殺狐狸。②(不用獵犬狩獵之)捕殺狐狸者。(亦作 **vulpecide**) —**vul·pi·cid·al,** *adj.* —**vul·pi·cid·ism,** *n.*
vul·pine 〔ˈvʌlpaɪn; ˈvʌlpain〕 *adj.* ①狐狸的。②似狐的;狡猾的;詭譎的; 奸詐的。
vul·ture 〔ˈvʌltʃɚ; ˈvʌltʃə〕 *n.* ①兀鷹。②貪婪而殘酷之人。 —**like,** *adj.*
vul·tur·ine 〔ˈvʌltʃuraɪn;ˈvʌltʃurain〕 *adj.* ①兀鷹的;似兀鷹的。②貪婪的。
vul·tur·ous 〔ˈvʌltʃurəs; ˈvʌltʃurəs〕 *adj.* 似兀鷹的;貪婪的。
vul·va 〔ˈvʌlvə; ˈvʌlvə〕 *n., pl.* **-vae** 〔-vi; -viː〕, **-vas.** 〖解剖〗女陰;陰戶。

vum 〔vʌm; vʌm〕 *v.i.*, **vummed, vumming.** 【美方】發誓;咀咒。

vv. ①verses. ②violins. **v.v.** vice versa (拉=the order being changed).

vv. ll. variae lectiones (拉 =variant readings).

VVSOP, V.V.S.O.P. very very superior (*or* special) old pale. 特優級陳年(指26至40年的白蘭地酒)。

vy·ing 〔'vaɪɪŋ; 'vaiiŋ〕 *adj.* 競爭的；比賽的。*vying* swimmers. 參加比賽的游泳者。—*v.* ppr. of vie. —**ly,** *adv.*

W

W or **w** 〔'dʌblju; 'dʌblju(:)〕 *n., pl.* **W's** or **w's** 〔-z; -z〕. ①英文之第二十三個字母。② W 形之事物。③【印刷】W 鉛字。

W ①化學元素 wolfram (=tungsten)之符號。②wolframium. **W** ①west. ②watt; watts. ③western. ④withdrawn; withdrew. ⑤withheld. **w** ①watt; watts. ②withdrawn; withdrew. ③withheld. **W.** ①west. ②Western. ③Wednesday. ④Wales. ⑤Welsh. ⑥warden. ⑦warehouse. ⑧Washington. ⑨watt; watts. ⑩weight. ⑪width. ⑫【物理】work. **w.** ①week. ②weeks. ③west. ④wide. ⑤width. ⑥wife. ⑦warden. ⑧warehouse. ⑨watt; watts. ⑩weight. ⑪western. ⑫with. ⑬won. ⑭【物理】work. ⑮wanting. **WAAC, W.A.A.C.** Women's Army Auxiliary Corps.

Waaf 〔wæf; wæf〕 *n.* 【英】Women's Auxiliary Air Force 之一員。

Waals 〔vals; vals〕 *n.* 瓦爾斯(Johannes Diderick van der, 1837–1923, 荷蘭物理學家, 1910年獲諾貝爾獎)。

wab·ble 〔'wabl̩; 'wɔbl〕 *v.*, **-bled, -bling,** *n.* =**wobble.** —**wab·bling·ly,** *adv.*

wab·bly 〔'wablɪ; 'wɔbli〕 *adv. & adj.*, **-bli·er, -bli·est.** 搖擺地(的);蹣跚地（的）；不穩地(的)。—**wab·bli·ness,** *n.*

WAC, W.A.C. Women's Army Corps.

Wac 〔wæk; wæk〕 *n.* Women's Army Corps之一員。

wack 〔wæk; wæk〕 *n.* 【俚】怪人；行爲乖張的人。

wack·e 〔'wækə; 'wækə〕 *n.* 【地質】玄武石（爲火山岩分解成的岩石）。

wack·y 〔'wækɪ; 'wæki〕 *adj.*, **wack·i·er, wack·i·est.** 【美俚】發狂的；荒謬的；怪誕的。(亦作 **whacky**) —**wack·i·ly,** *adv.*

WACS 【美】Women's Army Corps.

wad[1] 〔wad; wɔd〕 *n., v.*, **wad·ded, wad·ding.** —*n.* ①(軟物的)小塊；填料。②一疊。③鎗膛或子彈中的塡彈塞；送彈塞。④【俚】一大堆（尤指金錢）。⑤【英方】一小捆乾草。⑥(*pl.*)【俚】多數；多量。—*v.t.* ①弄成小塊；塡塞；以棉絮塡塞。②以送彈塞穩住。③捲緊。

wad[2], **wadd** *n.* 錳土。

wad·ding 〔'wadɪŋ; 'wɔdiŋ〕 *n.* ①塡塞物；棉絮。②做槍砲送彈塞之材料。

wad·dle 〔'wadl̩; 'wɔdl〕 *v.*, **-dled, -dling,** *n.* —*v.i.* ①蹣跚而行；搖擺而行（脚步短而有拙笨的搖幌動作，如鴨子或矮胖之人的行走)。②搖搖擺擺地移動。—*n.* 搖擺而行；搖擺的步態。—**wad·dler,** *n.* —**wad·dly,** *adj.*

wad·dy[1] 〔'wadɪ; 'wɔdi〕 *n., pl.* **-dies,** *v.*, **-died, -dy·ing.** —*n.* 【澳】①(土人作武器用之短而粗的)棍棒。②手杖。—*v.t.* 以棍棒擊。

wad·dy[2] *n., pl.* **-dies.** 【美】牧場僱用之看管牛羣的臨時工人。

wade** 〔wed; weid〕 *v.*, **wad·ed, wad·ing,** *n.* —*v.i.* ①(從水、雪、沙、泥或任何障礙物中)走過；跋涉。to *wade* across a stream. 涉水過河。②艱苦進行。to *wade* through a dull book. 很費力地閱讀一本枯燥無味的書。③玩水。—*v.t.* 涉過。wade in*** (or ***into***) 【俗】a. 猛烈攻擊。b. 開始奮力工作。—*n.* ①跋涉。②玩水。—**wad·a·ble, —a·ble,** *adj.*

wade-in 〔'wed,ɪn; 'weidin〕 *n.* 【美】黑人進入祇允許白人使用之海濱或游泳池，以示對種族歧視之抗議。

wad·er 〔'wedə; 'weidə〕 *n.* ①徒涉者。②涉禽類之鳥。③(*pl.*) 涉水時穿的高統靴。

wa·di 〔'wadɪ; 'wɔdi〕 *n., pl.* **-dis, -dies.** (近東和北非的)谷；常乾涸的河道；沙漠中之綠洲。

wading bird 涉禽類之鳥。

WAF, Waf 〔wæf; wæf〕 *n.* 美空軍婦女團 Women in the Air Force 之一員。

***wa·fer** 〔'wefə; 'weifə〕 *n.* ①一種薄甜餅或餅乾。②【宗教】聖餅。③封糊；封緘紙。④【醫】包藥麪片；糯米紙。—*v.t.* (用封緘紙)黏貼；黏封。—**like,** *adj.*

wa·fer·y 〔'wefərɪ; 'weifəri〕 *adj.* 很薄的；似薄餅的。

waff 〔wæf; wæf〕 *adj.* 【蘇】①無價值的。②孤單的。—*n.* 流浪漢。—**ness,** *n.*

waf·fle[1] 〔'wafl̩; 'wɔfl〕 *n.* (以麪粉、鷄蛋、及牛乳等混製之)鷄蛋餅。***waffle iron*** 烘鷄蛋餅的鐵模。—*adj.* (亦作 **waffled**)有鐵模(waffle iron)印的。—**like,** *adj.*

waf·fle[2] *v.i.*, **-fled, -fling.** ①閒聊；談天打發時間。②=**equivocate.**

W.A.F.S. 【英】Women's Auxiliary Fire Service.

***waft**[1] 〔wæft, waft; wɑːft, wɔːft, wɔft〕 *v.t.* ①使飄浮；使飄蕩。The waves *wafted* the boat to shore. 波浪將船飄送到岸邊。②飛送。to *waft* kisses. 飛吻。—*v.i.* 飄蕩。—*n.* ①搖動。②一陣風或香氣等。—**er,** *n.*

waft[2] *n.* 【航海】①信號旗。②用信號旗打信號。

wag** 〔wæg; wæg〕 *v.*, **wagged, wag·ging,** *n.* —*v.t.* ①搖擺；搖動。The dog *wags* its tail to welcome you. 狗搖尾巴歡迎你。②饒(舌)。③搖(頭)；點(頭)。④責備時以手指指(人)。—*v.i.* ①搖擺；擺動。The dog's tail *wagged.* 這狗的尾巴搖動。②饒舌。③進行；行走。Let the world *wag* how it will. 讓別人要怎麼樣就怎麼樣(隨他們去)。④【英俚】逃學。set tongues*** (***chins,*** or ***beards***) ***wagging*** 引起議論。***The tail wags the dog.*** 小人物得勢而統御他人。***wag one's finger at a man*** 指摘某人。***wag one's tongue*** 多言；饒舌。—*n.* ①搖擺；搖動。②好說笑話的人；詼諧者。—**ger,** *n.*

‡**wage** 〔wedʒ; weidʒ〕 *n., v.*, **waged, wag·ing.** —*n.* ①(常 *pl.*) 工資；薪給。The worker was promised good *wages.* 這工人被允給予優厚的工資。at a *wage* (*or* the *wages*) of $100 a week. 工資每週一百元。His *wages* are $25 a week. 他的工資是每週二十五元。②(常 *pl.*)(作 *sing.* 解) 報償；報酬；代價。The *wages* of sin is death. 罪惡的代價是死亡。***a living wage*** 僅可

維持生活的工資。—*v.t.* ①從事;進行;作。Doctors *wage* war against disease. 醫生對疾病作戰。②【英方】僱用。—**less,** *adj.*

wage earner 賴工資維持生活的人。

wage freeze 工資之凍結。

wage-fund [ˈwedʒˌfʌnd; ˈweidʒfʌnd] *n.* 【商】工資基金。(亦作 **wages-fund**)

wage hike 工資之提高;加薪。

wage-price [ˈwedʒˌpraɪs; ˈweidʒ-prais] *adj.* 工資與物價之關係的。

wa·ger [ˈwedʒɚ; ˈweidʒə] *v.t.* & *v.i.* 打賭。—*n.* ①賭注。The *wager* of $10 was promptly paid. 賭金十元立刻付了。②打賭。③打賭之對象或內容。—**er,** *n.*

wage rate 工資等級。

wage scale 工資等級表;工人薪給表。

wage·work·er [ˈwedʒˌwɝkɚ; ˈweidʒ-ˌwəːkə] *n.* 為賺工資而工作的工人;賴工資維持生活的人。—**wage·work·ing,** *adj., n.*

wag·ger·y [ˈwægərɪ; ˈwægəri] *n., pl.* **-ger·ies.** 滑稽;詼諧;惡作劇。

wag·gish [ˈwægɪʃ; ˈwægiʃ] *adj.* 滑稽的;詼諧的;惡作劇的。—**ness,** *n.* —**ly,** *adv.*

wag·gle [ˈwægl̩; ˈwægl] *v.,* **-gled, -gling,** *n.* —*v.t.* & *v.i.* 搖擺;擺動。—*n.* 搖擺;擺動。—**wag·gling·ly,** *adv.*

Wag·ner [ˈwægnɚ; ˈvaːgnə] *n.* 華格納 (Richard, 1813–1883, 德國作曲家)。

Wag·ne·ri·an [wægˈnɪrɪən; vaːg-ˈniəriən] *adj.* 作曲家華格納 (Wagner)的;華格納作風的。—*n.*華格納之崇拜者或追隨者。

‡**wag·(g)on** [ˈwægən; ˈwægən] *n.* ①四輪運貨馬車;貨車。②(W-)【天文】北斗七星(=Charles's Wain)。③(警察的)囚車。④嬰兒車。⑤旅行車(=station wagon). ***hitch one's wagon to a star*** 野心勃勃。***on the (water) wagon*** 【俚】不飲酒的。—*v.t.* & *v.i.* 以貨車等搬運、旅行。—**less,** *adj.*

wag·(g)on·er [ˈwægənɚ; ˈwægənə] *n.*①運貨馬車之車夫。②(W-)【天文】御夫座。

wag·(g)on·ette [ˌwægənˈɛt; ˌwægə-ˈnet] *n.* (有兩排縱座位之) 四輪遊覽馬車。

wag·on-lit [vagõˈli; ˈvægɔ̃ːnˈliː] *n., pl.* **wag·ons-lits** [vagõˈli; ˈvægɔ̃ːnˈliː]. 【法】(鐵路之)臥車。

wag·(g)on·load [ˈwægənˌlod; ˈwæ-gənloud] *n.* 貨車裝載量。

wagon train ①載運軍需品之一列運貨馬車。②(移民們之)篷車隊。

wag·tail [ˈwægˌtel; ˈwægteil] *n.* 鶺鴒。

Wa·ha·bi, Wa·ha·bee [wɑˈhɑbɪ; wəˈhɑːbi] *n.* 嚴守可蘭經之一派回教徒(Abdul-Wahhab 所創,今盛行於沙烏地阿拉伯)。

wa·hoo [wɑˈhu; wɑːˈhuː] *n., pl.* **-hoos.** ①【植物】(北美產的)火樹;菩提樹。②(美國 Florida 及西印度產的)一種深藍色食用魚。

waif [wef; weif] *n.* ①流浪的人;無家可歸者;(尤指)流浪兒童;無住處之動物。②【法律】(盜賊遺棄之)贓物。③偶然發現的無主物。④【航海】信號旗;以信號旗所作之信號。

Wai·ki·ki [ˈwɑ·iˌkiki; ˈwaikiːkiː] *n.* 懷基基(火奴魯魯之著名海灘)。

***wail** [wel; weil] *v.i.* ①哭泣;哭號;哀泣;悲傷。②發出哀泣的聲音。The wind *wails.* 風在哀號。③【爵士樂】表演得特佳。④【俚】以音樂或言語把情感表現出來。—*v.t.* ①哀悼;為…慟哭。They *wailed* his death. 他們哀悼他的死亡。②悲傷地哭號或說。—*n.* ①哭泣;哀悼;悲傷。②哭泣或哀悼聲。—**er,** *n.*

wail·ful [ˈwelfəl; ˈweilfəl] *adj.* 悲嘆的;哀悼的;慟哭的。—**ly,** *adv.*

Wailing Wall (of the Jews) 哭牆(耶路撒冷城內回教 Omar 寺院附近一庭院之圍牆,高59英尺,據傳係由所羅門聖殿之石塊所砌,猶太人每星期五在此牆前相聚,祈禱及哀悼)。(亦作 **Wailing Place of the Jews**)

wain [wen; wein] *n.* ①【古,詩】馬車。②(the W-)【天文】北斗七星。

wain·scot [ˈwenskət; ˈweinskət] *n., v.,* **-scot·(t)ed, -scot·(t)ing.** —*n.* ①壁板(尤指裝飾室內周圍下半截牆之壁板)。②【英】自波羅的海地區進口的上等橡木。—*v.t.* (牆壁或房間)裝以壁板。

wain·scot·(t)ing [ˈwenskətɪŋ; ˈweinskətiŋ] *n.* 壁板;壁板之材料。

wain·wright [ˈwenˌraɪt; ˈweinrait] *n.* 製造或修理運貨馬車的人。

***waist** [west; weist] *n.* ①腰;腰部。She has no *waist.* 她胖得看不出腰來。②衣服的自頸肩至腰之部分。③婦女的胸衣;小孩的襯衣。④船的中間部分。⑤形狀或部位似腰的東西。⑥衣服之腰部。⑦昆蟲(如蜜蜂)之腰部。—**less,** *adj.*

waist·band [ˈwestˌbænd; ˈweist-bænd] *n.* 束腰帶。

waist·cloth [ˈwestˌklɔθ; ˈweistklɔːθ] *n., pl.* **-cloths.** 圍腰布。

***waist·coat** [ˈwestˌkot; ˈweiskout] *n.* 背心。

waist-deep [ˈwestˈdip; ˈweistˈdiːp] *adj.* & *adv.* 深達腰部的(地)。

waist-high [ˈwestˈhaɪ; ˈweistˈhai] *adj.* & *adv.* 高及腰際的(地)。

waist·line [ˈwestˌlaɪn; ˈweistlain] *n.* ①腰線;腰圍。②女子胸衣與裙子相接處。

‡**wait** [wet; weit] *v.i.* ①等候;等待。Time and tide *wait* for no man. 歲月不待人。②期望;期待。The children *wait* impatiently for vacation. 孩子們不耐煩地期待假期。③延緩。That matter can *wait* until tomorrow. 那件事可以留待明天做。④服侍;伺候。She had no one to *wait* upon her. 她沒有一個人服侍她。⑤(對尊長者的)拜訪;謁見【on, upon】. I *waited* upon him with a letter of introduction. 我持着一封介紹信去謁見他。—*v.t.* ①等候;等待。②延緩(食事)。Don't *wait* dinner for me. 不要為等我而延緩開飯。③【古】伺候(表示尊敬)。④伺候宴席。***wait at*** (or ***on***) ***table*** 伺候開飯;侍候宴席。***wait on*** (or ***upon***) **a.** 伺候。**b.** 謁見。**c.** 為…之結果;從…而至。**d.** 【俗】隨伴。***wait out*** **a.** 等到…之結束。**b.** 【棒球】等保送上壘而不揮棒擊球。***wait up*** **a.** 不睡;等待(人)。**b.** (走路或跑步時)等(某人)趕上。Don't go so fast! *Wait up* for me! 不要走那麼快!等我一會!—*n.* ①等候;等候的時間。I had a long *wait* for the train. 我等候火車很久。②【英】**a.** (*pl.*)耶誕時沿街歌唱者。**b.** (*pl.*) 市鎮所僱樂隊 (遊行或公共場合演奏者)。**c.** 街頭歌唱家。**d.** 耶誕歌。③【戲院】**a.** 幕與幕間之休息時間。**b.** 因演員忘記臺詞等而引起的未料到的等待。④【廢】守夜人。***lie in wait for*** 埋伏以待。

wait-and-see [ˈwetənˈsi; ˈweitən-ˈsiː] *adj.* 觀望的;等待的。

***wait·er** [ˈwetɚ; ˈweitə] *n.* ①等待者。②侍者;侍應生。③盆;盤;皿。—**less,** *adj.*

wait·ing** [ˈwetɪŋ; ˈweitiŋ] *n.* ①等待。②服侍;侍候。in waiting*** **a.** 侍從 (國王或其他皇室人物等)。**b.** 【英軍】次一班輪到的。—*adj.* ①等待中的。②侍候的;服侍的。—**ly,**

adv. 「的名單。

waiting list 等待預約、約見、住宿等人」

waiting period ①法定等待期間（如自取得結婚許可至結婚之間的一段規定時間）。②〖保險〗要求賠償與實際給付間之一段等待期間。「車室;(醫院之)候診室。

***waiting room** 等待室;(車站之)候」

wait·list ['wet,lɪst; 'weitlist] *v.t.* 登記於 waiting list (尤指機上座位)。

wait·ress ['wetrɪs; 'weitris] *n.* 女侍者;女侍應生。—**less,** *adj.*

waive [wev; weiv] *v.t.*, **waived, waiv·ing.** ①放棄(權利、特權、要求等)。②丟棄;摒棄;捨棄。③擱置。

waiv·er ['wevɚ; 'weivə] *n.* ①〖法律〗放棄;棄權;棄權書。②擱置。

‡wake[1] [wek; weik] *v.*, **waked** or **woke** [wok; wouk], **waked, wak·ing,** *n.* —*v.i.* ①醒;醒來。I *woke* up early. 我醒得很早。②醒着;不眠。*waking* hours. 醒着的時間。This thought kept me *waking.* 這思慮使我不能入睡。③醒悟;覺悟。④奮起;活動。It's time for you to *wake* up. 已經到了你該奮發的時候了。⑤甦醒。The flowers *wake* in the spring. 花在春天甦醒。⑥〖方,古〗守屍;夜間看守。—*v.t.*①喚醒;喚起。Please *wake* me up at six. 請在六點鐘喚醒我。They were making enough noise to *wake* the dead. 他們吵鬧得能把死人吵活。②激發;引起。③〖方,古〗守夜;守(屍)。—*n.* ①守夜;守屍。②磨房工人每年的假日。③醒的狀態。—**like,** *adj.* —**wak·er,** *n.*

wake[2] *n.* 船跡;足跡;飛機火箭等飛行體後方之氣流;流痕。***in the wake of*** 隨…之後。

wake·ful ['wekfəl; 'weikful] *adj.* 不能入睡的;不眠的;警醒的。—**ly,** *adv.* —**ness,** *n.*

***wak·en** ['wekən; 'weikən] *v.i.* & *v.t.* 醒;喚醒。「bin] *n.* 〖植物〗延齡草。

wake-rob·in ['wek,rɑbɪn; 'weik,rɔ-」

wake-up ['wek,ʌp; 'weikʌp] *n.* 美國西南部產的一種啄木鳥。

Wal·den·ses [wɑl'dɛnsiz; wɑːl'densiːz] *n.*(作 *sing.* 解)〖宗教〗華爾多教派(Lyon 商人 Petrus Waldus 或 Peter Waldo 於1179年所創之一宗教派別，係背叛羅馬天主教教會者)。—**Wal·den·si·an,** *n., adj.*

wale [wel; weil] *n., v.,* **waled, wal·ing.** —*n.* ①條痕;鞭痕;傷痕。②布上之凸紋;布之織地。③〖造船〗木船外部之腰板;舷緣。④(亦作 **waler, whaler, breast timber, ranger**)〖土木〗加固圍堰、壕溝等護樁之水平木板;貫材。—*v.t.* ①使有鞭條痕。②織成稜紋。③〖土木〗以水平木板加固。

***Wales** [welz; weilz] *n.* 威爾斯(大不列顛之一部分,在英格蘭之西)。

Wal·hal·la [wæl'hælə; væl'hælə] *n.* 〖北歐神話〗= **Valhalla.**

W

‡walk [wɔk; wɔːk] *v.i.* ①行走;步行。The baby cannot *walk* yet. 這幼兒還不會走。②漫遊;徘徊。③如行路樣地移動或搖動。④散步。⑤舉止;行動。⑥〖棒球〗保送上壘(因對方投手投四壞球)。⑦〖籃球〗帶球走路(犯規)。—*v.t.* ①走過;行過。②使行走;使由於行走而…。to *walk* a man off his legs. 使某人走得疲倦不堪。③〖棒球〗投四壞球讓(打擊手)上壘。④陪着走。⑤以走路測量(距離)。⑥如行路樣地移動(物體)。He *walked* his big trunk along the corridor. 他拖着他的大箱子沿着走廊走。⑦〖籃球〗帶(球)走。***walk away from*** 在比賽中輕而易舉地獲勝。***walk in*** 進入。***walk into***〖俗〗**a.** 很開心地吃。**b.** 譴責;斥責。***walk off*** 以行路驅走。***walk off with*** **a.** 携走;偷走。**b.** 比賽中贏得。***walk out*** **a.**〖俗〗罷工。**b.** 退席抗議。***walk out on***〖俗〗遺棄。***walk out with***〖俚〗私戀;追求。***walk over*** 輕易地打敗(並且分數相差甚多)。***walk Spanish*** **a.** 被迫以足尖走路。**b.** 小心謹慎地走。**c.** 被開除。**d.** 開除(別人)。***walk the boards*** 作伶人。***walk the hospitals*** 作醫生;習醫。***walk the plank*** **a.** 被海盜强迫從跳板墜海。**b.** 被迫辭職或放棄某物。***walk the streets*** **a.** 在街頭行走。**b.** 作娼妓。***walk through***〖演戲〗**a.** 參加初次排演。**b.** 馬馬虎虎地演或念臺詞。***walk up*** 使獵犬將鳥等驚飛。—*n.*①步行;散步。to go for (*or* to take) a *walk.* 出去散步。②步行距離。a five minutes' *walk.* 五分鐘可以走到的距離。③步態;步法。④散步之處;人行道。This is my favorite *walk.* 這是我最喜歡的散步的地方。⑤生活方式;社會地位;身分;職業。men in every *walk* of life. 各界人士。⑥〖棒球〗四壞球保送上壘。⑦圍起的場地。⑧競走。⑨〖英〗咖啡或香蕉園,尤指樹與樹之間有寬大的路者。⑩〖英〗**a.** 售貨員、郵差等送貨、送信的路線。**b.** 有此路線的地區。⑪〖英〗一森林管理員管轄之林區。

walk·a·ble ['wɔkəbl; 'wɔːkəbl] *adj.* ①可行走的。②適於走路的。

walk·a·way ['wɔkə,we; 'wɔːkə,wei] *n.* 輕易取得之勝利。

walk·er ['wɔkɚ; 'wɔːkə] *n.* ①助嬰兒走路的架子。②助殘廢人走路的架子。③走路的人;健行者。④(*pl.*) **a.** 走路用之短褲。**b.** 走路用之鞋。

walk·ie-look·ie ['wɔkɪ'lukɪ; 'wɔːki-'luki] *n.* 使用電池之輕便電視攝影機。

walk·ie-talk·ie ['wɔkɪ,tɔkɪ; 'wɔːki-,tɔːki] *n., pl.* **-talk·ies.** 步聲機(輕便之無線電話收發機)。(亦作 **walky-talky**)

walk-in ['wɔk,ɪn; 'wɔːkin] *adj.* ①未經約定而進來的(人)。②大得足够一人走進去的(如大櫥等)。③(不經大廳)可逕入的(如公寓等)。—*n.* ①可供人走進之物。②易於取勝的競賽或選擧。③未經約定而進來的人。

walk·ing ['wɔkɪŋ; 'wɔːkiŋ] *adj.* ①能走路的;走路的。②走路用的。③需要走路的;適於走路做的。④(機械或工具)用獸力拉但由人控制的。⑤機械零件之來回移動的。—*n.*①步行;散步。②步態;步法。③地面或路之狀況。

walking beam 〖機械〗轉動的軸柱;動桁。(亦作 **working beam**)

walking chair 嬰兒學步用之有輪小」

walking dress 外出服。 ˪車。」

walking gentleman 跑龍套的男演員(尤指無臺詞的)。「無臺詞的)。」

walking lady 跑龍套之女演員(尤指」

walking papers〖俗〗免職令;解雇令。

walking shorts 散步時穿的短褲。

walking stick ①手杖。②竹節蟲。

walking ticket = **walking papers.**

walking tour 徒步旅行。

walk-in refrigerator 大冷藏室。

walk-on ['wɔk,ɑn; 'wɔːkɔn] *n.* ①(亦作 **walking part**)只在舞臺上出現而無臺詞之不重要角色。②演此種角色的演員。

walk·out ['wɔk,aut; 'wɔːkaut] *n.* 〖美俗〗①罷工。②退席抗議。③離開;放棄。

walk·o·ver ['wɔk,ovɚ; 'wɔːk'ouvə] *n.* ①容易或無對手競爭的勝利(賽馬時,只有一匹馬參加,走完路線即可獲勝)。②容易的任務或工作。

walk-through 〔'wɔk,θru; 'wɔːk-θruː〕 *n.* ①〖戲劇〗a. 包括念臺詞的排演。b. 草率的表演。②〖電視〗不拍攝的排練。

walk-up 〔'wɔk,ʌp; 'wɔːkʌp〕 *n., adj.* 〖美俗〗沒有電梯之公寓房子(的)。

walk·way 〔'wɔk,we; 'wɔːkwei〕 *n.* ①(船、工廠、公園等之)通道。②花園中之路徑。③房子前之引道(通至人行道或馬路)。

:wall 〔wɔl; wɔːl〕 *n.* ①牆;壁;垣。Hang the picture on the *wall.* 把這幅畫掛在牆上。*Walls* have ears. 隔牆有耳。②在形狀或用途方面和牆相類似的東西。The flood came in a *wall* of water twelve feet high. 洪水以十二英尺高的水壁湧來。③內壁。the *walls* of the heart. 心臟內壁。cell *wall.* 細胞壁。④(*pl.*)防禦性的圍牆。⑤無形的障礙。⑥防水牆。***come to a blank wall*** 遇到困難。***drive*** (or ***push***) ***to the wall*** 使無助;使束手無策。***fight with one's back to the wall*** 以寡敵衆;背城一戰。***give the wall*** a. 讓別人走街道上乾淨好走的部分(自己走路面骯髒或不平的部分)。b. 讓別人出風頭或占先。***go over the wall*** 〖俚〗越獄。***go to the wall*** a. 退讓;失敗;敗北。b. 破產。c. 被遺忘。***hang by the wall*** 被遺忘。***run one's head against the wall*** 試做不可能之事。***take the wall*** a. 搶着在街道上乾淨好走的部分走路(讓別人走不好走的部分)。b. 搶先;占强。***the Great Wall of China*** 萬里長城。***up against a blank wall*** 不知所措。—*v.t.* ①圍以牆。②填塞;堵塞。—*adj.* ①牆的。②長在牆上的。*wall* plants. 長在牆上的植物。③做在牆上的。a *wall* safe. 壁上保險箱。—**er,** *n.* —**wall-like,** *adj.*

wal·la(h) 〔'wɑlɑ; 'wɑːlɑː〕 *n.* 〖英印〗①受僱從事與某事有關的人。②〖俗〗人。

wal·la·by 〔'wɑləbɪ; 'wɔləbi〕 *n., pl.* **-by, -bies.** 一種小袋鼠。

Wal·lach 〔'vɑlɑx; 'wɔlək〕 *n.* 瓦拉克(Otto, 1847–1931, 德國化學家, 1910年得諾貝爾獎)。

wal·la·roo 〔,wɑlə'ru; ,wɔlə'ruː〕 *n., pl.* **-roos, -roo.** 一種大袋鼠。

wall·board 〔'wɔl,bord; 'wɔːlbɔːd〕 *n.* 遮蓋牆壁或天花板用的人造板。

walled 〔wɔld; wɔːld〕 *adj.* 有牆壁的。high-*walled.* 高牆的。

***wal·let** 〔'wɑlɪt; 'wɔlit〕 *n.* 皮包;皮夾;錢袋;旅行袋(裝衣服、乾糧者)。

wall·eye 〔'wɔl,aɪ; 'wɔːlai〕 *n., pl.* **-eyes, -eye.** ①虹彩爲白色或角膜不透明之馬眼;白星眼。②眼白露出部分較正常者爲多的眼睛。③(魚等之)大而閃亮的眼睛。④鼓眼魚。

wall·eyed 〔'wɔl,aɪd; 'wɔːlaid〕 *adj.* ①白星眼的。②露出之眼白較正常眼睛爲多的。③有大而閃亮之眼睛的(魚等)。④目光炯炯的。⑤〖俚〗酒醉的。

wall·flow·er 〔'wɔl,flauə; 'wɔːl,flauə〕 *n.* ①〖植物〗牆花。②〖俗〗舞會中無舞伴而僅作壁上觀之人(尤指女子)。

wall fruit 倚牆之樹木所結之果實。

wall-less 〔'wɔllɪs; 'wɔːllis〕 *adj.* 無牆的;無城牆的。

Wal·loon 〔wɑ'lun; wɔ'luːn〕 *n.* ①華隆人(居於比利時南部、東南部及其附近之法國境內)。②華隆語(比利時東南部之法國方言)。—*adj.* 華隆人的;華隆語的。

wal·lop 〔'wɑləp; 'wɔləp〕 *v.i.* 〖方〗①笨重地移動。②(馬等)奔馳(=gallop)。③(液體之)滾開;沸騰。—*v.t.* 〖俗〗①痛毆;鞭打。②重擊。③擊潰。④〖蘇〗使飄動。—*n.* ①〖方,俗〗笨重的移動;奔馳。②〖俗〗痛毆;重擊;擊潰。③能給深刻印象之能力。④快感。⑤浪濺之液體或水。—*adv.* 僅用於下列習慣用語。***go*** (***down***) ***wallop*** 唏哩嘩啦落下。

wal·lop·ing 〔'wɑləpɪŋ; 'wɔləpiŋ〕 *adj.* 〖俗〗龐大的;巨大的。—*n.* 〖俗〗①鞭打。②擊潰;大敗。

wal·low 〔'wɑlo; 'wɔlou〕 *v.i.* ①(在泥、沙、雪、水中)打滾;(船)顚簸而行。②耽溺或享受;沉迷。③湧起(如煙等)。—*n.* ①翻滾;打滾。②(動物等打滾之)水坑或泥沼。③耽溺於酒色或享受;沉迷。

wall·pa·per 〔'wɔl,pepə; 'wɔːl,peipə〕 *n.* 壁紙。—*v.t.* 糊以壁紙。

wallpaper music 〖英〗①(影劇)配樂;背景音樂。②(公共場所播放之)灌製音樂。

Wall Street ①華爾街(美國紐約市曼哈坦之一街名,爲美國之主要金融中心)。②美國金融市場;美國金融界。

Wall Street·er 〔~'stritə; ~'striːtə〕 在華爾街或附近之金融機構工作的人。

wall-to-wall 〔'wɔltə'wɔl; 'wɔːltə-'wɔːl〕 *adj.* 把整個地板都蓋住的;自此牆至彼牆的。*wall-to-wall* carpeting. 全地板地毯。

***wal·nut** 〔'wɔlnət; 'wɔːlnət, -nʌt〕 *n.* ①胡桃;核桃。②胡桃樹;核桃樹。

Wal·pur·gis Night 〔vɑl'purgɪs~; væl'puəgis~〕 ①五月一日之前夕(據云巫婆於是夕在德國 Harz 山脈之 Brocken 高峯上聚會狂歡)。②巫人、巫婆與魔鬼之假期或歡宴。

wal·rus 〔'wɔlrəs; 'wɔːlrəs〕 *n., pl.* **-rus·es** or **-rus.** 海象。

Wal·ton 〔'wɔltn̩; 'wɔːltən〕 *n.* 華爾頓(Ernest Thomas Sinton, 1903–, 英國物理學家, 曾獲1951年諾貝爾物理獎)。

waltz 〔wɔlts; wɔːls〕 *n.* ①華爾茲舞。②圓舞曲;華爾茲舞曲。—*v.i.* ①跳華爾茲舞。②愉快地匆匆疾走。③〖俗〗輕易地或成功地進行〖常 through〗。—*v.t.* ①使(某人)跳華爾茲舞。②輕快地引領(他人)。—*adj.* 華爾茲舞(曲)的。—**er,** *n.* —**like,** *adj.*

wam·ble 〔'wɑmbl̩; 'wɔmbl〕 *v.,* **-bled, -bling,** *n.* —*v.i.* 〖方〗① a. 蹣跚而走。b. 搖動或搖滾身子。② a. 欲吐。b. 翻胃。—*n.* 〖方〗①不穩的運動。②嘔吐感。

wam·pee 〔wɑm'pi; wɔm'piː〕 *n.* 〖植物〗黃皮(中國出產之一種熱帶果實);黃皮樹。

wam·pum 〔'wɑmpəm; 'wɔmpəm〕 *n.* ①貝殼數珠(以前北美洲印第安人用作貨幣及裝飾品)(亦作 **peag, seawan, sewan**)。②〖俚〗金錢。

wan 〔wɑn; wɔn〕 *adj.,* **wan·ner, wan·nest,** *v.,* **wanned, wan·ning.** —*adj.* 蒼白的;有倦容的;衰弱的;無力的。Why do you look so *wan?* 你爲甚麼這樣蒼白? —*v.i.* & *v.t.* (使)變蒼白、衰弱。—**ly,** *adv.* —**ness,** *n.*

***wand** 〔wɑnd; wɔnd〕 *n.* ①杖;棍;棒;魔杖。The magician waved his *wand.* 魔術師揮動他的魔棒。②(樂隊長所用之)指揮棒。③細樹枝。④權杖。⑤美國用作箭靶的狹窄板條(其距離爲60碼〔女子比賽〕及100碼〔男子比賽〕)。—**like,** *adj.*

:wan·der 〔'wɑndə; 'wɔndə〕 *v.i.* ①徘徊;漫步;漂泊;流浪;漫遊。to *wander* through the woods. 徘徊於森林中。②離開正途;迷路;離開本題。Don't *wander* from the subject. 不要離開本題。③精神錯亂;神志昏迷;迷惘。His mind is *wandering.* 他

心不在焉。④不規則地伸張或展開。Foothills *wandered* off to the south. 小丘不規則地伸展到南方去。⑤(手、眼、筆等)無目的地移動。—*v.t.* 流浪;漫遊。He *wandered* the streets. 他漫遊街頭。—**er,** *n.*

wan·der·ing ['wandərɪŋ;'wɔndəriŋ] *adj.* ①徘徊的;漂泊的;流浪的; 迷途的。②蜿蜒曲折的。 —*n.* ①游蕩。②(*pl.*) 漫遊。③(*pl.*)【醫】精神錯亂。—**ly,** *adv.* —**ness,** *n.*

Wandering Jew ①流浪之猶太人(傳說中之一猶太人, 因其於耶穌被釘上十字架之前曾對耶穌横加侮辱, 故被天譴永遠流浪, 直至耶穌二次降臨時止)。②(w- J-)一種栽培之蔓生植物。

wan·der·lust ['wandɚ,lʌst; 'wa:ndəlʌst] *n.* 熱中旅行或流浪;旅行癖;流浪癖。

wan·der·oo [,wandə'ru; ,wɔndə'ru:] *n.*【動物】印度南部所產的一種大黑猿。

wane** [wen;wein] *v.,* **waned, wan·ing,** *n.* —*v.i.* ①減弱; 減少; 減小; 衰微。②(月亮)虧; 缺。 The moon is *waning.* 月亮漸虧。—*n.* 減弱;減少;減小; 衰微;(月亮之)虧缺。 ***on (or ***in***) ***the wane*** **a.** 虧缺。The moon is *on the wane.* 月亮漸虧。 **b.** 衰微。

Wang Cheng-chih ['waŋ'dʒɛn'dʒɪr;'wa:ŋ'dʒen'dʒiə] 王貞治(日名 Sadaharu Oh, 1940–, 中國旅日職業棒球選手, 1977年以第756支全壘打破世界紀錄)。

wan·gle ['wæŋgḷ; 'wæŋgl] *v.,* **-gled, -gling,** *n.* —*v.t.*【俗】①以計謀或不正當手段取得或完成。②以權宜之計處理。③僞造。—*v.i.*【俗】①用狡詐手段達成目的。②用權宜之計處事。—*n.*【俗】狡詐行爲。

wan·nish ['wanɪʃ; 'wɔniʃ] *adj.* 略帶蒼白色的;略有倦容的。

‡**want** [want, wɔnt; wɔnt] *v.t.* ①希望;願望;要; 欲得。 He *wants* a new car. 他想要一輛新汽車。②缺少; 沒有。He *wants* judgment. 他缺少判斷力。 ③必須。 You *want* to see a doctor at once.你必須立刻去看醫生。④需要。Children *want* plenty of sleep. 兒童需要充裕的睡眠。—*v.i.* ①缺少; 短少【有時 for】。He shall *want* for nothing that money can buy. 錢能買到的東西, 他都不會缺乏。②貧困。We mustn't let him *want* in his old age. 我們一定不能使他在老年受貧窮之苦。③希望; 願望【常 to】. We can stay home if you *want.* 如你願意, 我們可以留在家裏。 ***want in*** (***out***) **a.**【俗】想進來(出去)。The cat *wants in.* 那隻貓想進來。**b.**【俚】想加入(退出)。***want to***【俗】應該。—*n.* ①(常 *pl.*)欲望;希望得到的東西。 I am a man of few *wants.* 我是一個欲望很少的人。②缺少; 需要。The plants died from *want* of water. 這些植物因缺水而死。 ③貧困。 *Want* is the mother of industry. 貧困爲勤勉之母。—**er,** *n.* —**less,** *adj.*

want ad【俗】報紙上之徵求廣告(包括求職、求才、徵租、售讓、交換等)。

want·age ['wantɪdʒ; 'wɔntidʒ] *n.* ①缺乏;缺少。②缺少量。

want·ing ['wantɪŋ; 'wɔntiŋ] *adj.* ①缺乏的;短少的。②不達標準的;不合需要的。③【英方】智力不足的。 —*prep.* ①沒有。②差;缺少。

want list 收藏家或博物館向商人發出「徵求藝品的貨單。」

***wan·ton** ['wantən; 'wɔntən] *adj.* ①放縱的;任性的; 胡亂的。②嬉戲的;頑皮的。③繁茂的。④淫蕩的;淫亂的。⑤奢侈的;豪華的。—*v.i.* 嬉戲;閒蕩。—*v.t.* 浪費(尤指爲尋樂)【常 away】。—*n.* 淫婦。 —**er,** —**ness,** *n.* —**ly,** *adv.*

wap·en·take ['wapən,tek; 'wɔpənteik] *n.*【英】①古時之小邑。②此種小邑中之法院。③此種法院的監守員。

wap·i·ti ['wapətɪ; 'wɔpiti] *n., pl.* **-ti, -tis.**【動物】北美洲產的一種鹿。

‡**war** [wɔr; wɔ:, wɔə] *n., v.,* **warred, war·ring,** *adj.* —*n.* ①戰爭。a civil *war.* 內戰。*war* area. 戰區。②(任何種類的)鬥爭。Doctors carry on *war* against disease. 醫生們從事對付疾病的鬥爭。③兵法;戰術;軍事。④【古】戰鬥(=battle). ***be at war with*** 同…作戰。We *were at war with* three great countries. 我們同三個大國作戰。***declare war upon*** (or ***on***) ***a country*** 向一國宣戰。 ***go to war*** **a.** 開戰。**b.** 從軍; 當兵。 ***have been in the wars***【諧】吃過苦頭;遍體鱗傷(如遭遇意外事件時)。***make*** (or ***wage***) ***war on*** (or ***upon***) 和…開戰。—*v.i.* 戰鬥; 作戰。The temptation *warred* with his conscience. 誘惑跟他的良心鬥爭。—*adj.* 戰爭的; 戰爭中所用的;由戰爭引起的。 —**less,** *adj.* —**less·ly,** *adv.* —**less·ness,** *n.*

war baby ①戰時私生子(指兵士在戰時同異國女人結合而生者)。 ②戰時出生或懷孕的嬰兒。③【俗】因戰爭刺激而興盛的工業; 戰時工業之股票。

War Between the States【美】南北戰爭(1861–1865, 爲南方之通用語)。

war·ble[1] ['wɔrbḷ; 'wɔ:bl] *v.,* **-bled, -bling,** *n.* —*v.i.* ①鳥鳴。②潺潺作響;發出潺潺聲。③以顫聲唱;顫聲說話。—*v.t.* ①以顫聲唱出;歌唱。②以顫聲說出。③使顫動。—*n.* ①啁啾之聲;鳥囀。②顫聲。③(電子機器所發出之)低昂音。

war·ble[2] *n.* ①(馬背上的) 鞍瘤; 硬瘤。②(牛、馬背上的) 蝱種。③蝱; 蝱之幼蟲。—**war·bled,** *adj.*

war·bler ['wɔrblɚ; 'wɔ:blə] *n.* ①顫音唱歌之人;以顫音啼唱之鳥。②鶯科的鳴禽。

war bonnet 美印第安人之羽毛頭飾。

war bride ①戰時新娘(軍人於國外服役時所娶的異國新娘)。 ②戰爭中與即將派到海外服役的軍人結婚的女子。

War·burg ['wɔrbɝg; 'wɔ:bə:g] *n.* 華爾堡 (Otto Heinrich, 1883–1970, 德國生理學家, 1931年獲諾貝爾醫學獎)。

war chest 爲一目的(如政治活動等)而預備的款項。

war correspondent 戰地記者。

war crime 戰爭犯罪(戰爭中對敵人或俘虜之屠殺、虐待等違反國際條約之行爲)。

war criminal 戰犯。

war cry ①作戰時戰士的吶喊。②政黨競選時之口號標語。

***ward** [wɔrd; wɔ:d] *n.* ①守護;監護。a child in *ward.* 一個被監護的孩子。②被監護者。③(城市之)區。④(醫院之)病房;(監獄之)監房。⑤(鬥劍時)防禦之姿勢、位置或動作。⑥鎖中之突起部分;鑰匙之缺刻。—*v.t.* ①抵擋;避免【off】. to *ward* off disease. 避免疾病。②置於病房或監房。③【古】保護。—**less,** *adj.*

-ward(s)【字尾】表"向…"之義, 如: *westward.*

war dance (野蠻民族於出戰前或勝利「時的)戰舞。」

ward·en ['wɔrdṇ; 'wɔ:dn] *n.* ①看守人;監護人。②【英】校長;學監。③典獄官。④

教會委員。⑤管理港口或野獸的人。⑥消防隊長(=fire warden). ⑦民間防空隊隊員(=air raid warden).⑧〖加〗地方議會之主席。⑨基爾特(guild) 之理事。

ward·en·ry [ˈwɔrdn̩rɪ; ˈwɔːdnri] *n., pl.* **-ries.** warden 之職位、職權或轄區。

ward·en·ship [ˈwɔrdn̩ˌʃɪp; ˈwɔːdnʃip] *n.* warden 之職權及任期。

ward·er [ˈwɔrdɚ; ˈwɔːdə] *n.* ①看守;獄吏;警衛; 監視人。②(國王或司令官等所用之)權杖;權標。—**ship,** *n.*

Ward·our Street [ˈwɔrdɚ～;ˈwɔːdə～]①華德街(英國倫敦之一街名,因古董店、古物店及仿古的傢具店林立而著稱)。②(故轉義作形容詞用)擬古的。

***ward·robe** [ˈwɔrdˌrob; ˈwɔːdroub] *n.* ①衣服。She is shopping for her spring *wardrobe*. 她正在購置春季服裝。②衣櫃;衣橱;藏衣室。③皇家或其他大家庭中管理衣着之部門。

wardrobe trunk 衣櫃。

ward·room [ˈwɔrdˌrum;ˈwɔːd-rum] *n.* ①(軍艦內)艦長以外之軍官的餐室或起居室。②艦長以外軍官之集合稱。

ward·ship [ˈwɔrdʃɪp; ˈwɔːdʃip] *n.* 監護;保護;監督。

***ware**¹ [wɛr; wɛə] *n.* ①器物;製造品(用於複合字中,如 silverware 等)。②陶器。③(*pl.*) **a.** 貨物;商品。The peddler sold his *wares* cheap. 小販廉價出售貨物。 **b.** 可出售的無形之物(如服務或藝術,智能之創造等)。

ware² *adj., v.,* **wared, war·ing.** —*adj.*〖古〗知曉的;謹防的。—*v.t.* & *v.i.* 留心;謹防。

***ware·house** [*n.* ˈwɛrˌhaus;ˈwɛəhaus *v.* ˈwɛrˌhauz; ˈwɛəhauz] *n., pl.* **-hous·es,** *v.,* **-housed, -hous·ing.** —*n.* ①貨棧;倉庫。②〖英〗大的零售商店。—*v.t.* ①將(貨物)儲於倉庫中。②將…儲於保稅倉庫中。

ware·house·man [ˈwɛrˌhausmən; ˈwɛəhausmən] *n., pl.* **-men.** 管理倉庫的人;經營貨棧業者。

warehouse receipt 倉單;倉庫存貨單。

ware·hous·ing [ˈwɛrˌhauzɪŋ; ˈwɛəhauziŋ] *n.* ① **a.** 儲倉。 **b.** 儲倉費。②商業銀行對需要長期資金者未覓得長期資金前所提供的周轉性短期貸款。

ware·room [ˈwɛrˌrum; ˈwɛərum] *n.* 貨物陳列室;貨物貯藏室。

***war·fare** [ˈwɔrˌfɛr; ˈwɔːfɛə] *n.* 作戰;戰爭; 交戰。 chemical *warfare.* 化學戰。psychological *warfare.* 心理戰。

war field 戰場。

war fund 軍費。

war game 軍事演習; 指揮官與參謀人員的作戰演習。

war·gasm [ˈwɔrˌgæzəm;ˈwɔːˌgæzəm] *n.*〖美〗全面戰爭的突然爆發。

war·hawk [ˈwɔrˌhɔk; ˈwɔːhɔːk] *n.*〖美〗好戰者;鷹派。

war head 魚雷彈頭;(飛彈等之) 彈頭。(亦作 **warhead**)

war horse ①戰馬。②〖俗〗老兵;老資格之演員、政客等。③被再三演唱或上演的樂曲或戲劇。

war·i·ly [ˈwɛrəlɪ; ˈwɛərili] *adv.* 留心地;謹愼地。

war·i·ness [ˈwɛrɪnɪs; ˈwɛərinis] *n.* 小心;謹愼。

***war·like** [ˈwɔrˌlaɪk; ˈwɔːlaik] *adj.* ①好戰的;尙武的。*warlike* spirit. 尙武精神。②軍事的; 戰爭的。*warlike* preparations. 軍備; 戰備。③以戰爭相威脅的。 a *warlike* speech. 一篇充滿火藥味的演說。 —**ness,** *n.*

war loan 戰時公債。

war·lock [ˈwɔrˌlɑk; ˈwɔːlɔk] *n.* 術士;巫;魔術師。

war lord ①軍閥。②(中國之)督軍。(亦作 **warlord**)

‡**warm** [wɔrm; wɔːm] *adj.* ①暖的; 溫暖的。 She sat in the *warm* sunshine. 她坐在暖和的陽光中。② 感覺暖和的。 to be *warm* from running. 跑得暖和起來。③保暖的。④熱情的; 熱誠的;熱心的;親切的。 a *warm* welcome. 熱烈的歡迎。 a *warm* heart. 熱心腸。⑤急躁的;激昂的。⑥新鮮而强烈的(氣味)。⑦〖俗〗將近發現的。You are getting *warm.* 你就要找到了。⑧不舒適的;不快意的。⑨〖俗〗有錢的;富有的。***be in warm blood*** 熱血沸騰;感情洋溢。***warm blood*** 溫血(哺乳動物及鳥類之體溫, 98°至112° F). ***warm corner*** **a.** 危險的地方。 **b.** 激戰地區。***warm work*** 使人發熱的工作或活動;吃力而危險的工作。—*adv.* 熱烈地;溫暖地。—*v.t.* ①使溫暖;使熱。The fire soon *warmed* the room. 爐火很快地使室內溫暖起來。 ②使感到愉快和溫暖。③使興奮;使變爲熱情。—*v.i.* ①變爲溫暖;變熱。The room is *warming* up. 這房間溫暖起來了。②熱心;奮發。***warm one's jacket*** 〖俗〗打某人。***warm up*** **a.** 熱心起來。**b.**(運動前)作熱身運動。—*n.* 〖俗〗取暖。Come near the fire and have a *warm.* 到火邊來暖和一下。—**ness,** *n.*

warm-blood·ed [ˈwɔrmˈblʌdɪd; ˈwɔːmˌblʌdid] *adj.* ①〖動物〗溫血的 (體溫從華氏 98 到 112 度)。②熱烈的;易激動的。

warmed-o·ver [ˈwɔrmdˈovɚ;ˈwɔːmd ˈouvə] *adj.* ①(食物)再熱一熱的。②炒冷飯的;沒有新的觀念或熱誠而重複的。

warmed-up [ˈwɔrmdˈʌp; ˈwɔːmdˈʌp] *adj.* (食物)再熱一熱的。

war memorial 戰爭紀念碑。

warm·er [ˈwɔrmɚ; ˈwɔːmə] *n.* 溫熱器;溫熱裝置。

warm front 〖氣象〗暖鋒。

warm-heart·ed [ˈwɔrmˈhɑrtɪd; ˈwɔːmˈhɑːtid] *adj.* 熱心的;親切的;懇切的;有同情心的。(亦作 **warm hearted**) —**ly,** *adv.* —**ness,** *n.*

warming pan 長柄暖床器(爐)。

warm·ing-up [ˈwɔrmɪŋˈʌp; ˈwɔːmiŋˈʌp] *n.* ①(參加運動比賽前之)熱身活動。②(天氣之)轉熱。

warm·ish [ˈwɔrmɪʃ; ˈwɔːmiʃ] *adj.* 稍溫暖的;略溫暖的。 —**ly,** *adv.* —**ness,** *n.*

***warm·ly** [ˈwɔrmlɪ; ˈwɔːmli] *adv.* 溫暖地; 親切地。

war·mon·ger [ˈwɔrˌmʌŋgɚ; ˈwɔːˌmʌŋgə] *n.* 好戰者;戰爭販子。

***warmth** [wɔrmpθ, wɔrmθ; wɔːmθ, -mpθ] *n.* ①溫暖。 The *warmth* of the room made me sleepy. 屋裏溫暖使得我昏昏欲睡。②熱心; 熱情; 親切; 奮發。 He argued with *warmth.* 他慷慨激昂地辯論。③圖畫中因用暖色給人的溫暖感。④微惱。His denial betrayed some *warmth.* 他的拒絕顯露出一些不快。—**less,** *adj.*

warm-up [ˈwɔrmˌʌp; ˈwɔːmˌʌp] *n.* ①熱身運動。②機器正式啓用前之試車期間。③預賽;預展;預備。 —*adj.* 預備的;預賽的。

‡**warn** [wɔrn; wɔːn] *v.t.* ①警告; 警戒。They *warned* him of his danger. 他們把他的危險告訴他,使他警戒。②預告;通知。③警告(某些人)走開或保持一些距離〖常 away, off〗. ④命令;召喚。—*v.i.* 警告;注意。—**er,** *n.*

*****war·ing** 〔ˈwɔrnɪŋ; ˈwɔ:niŋ〕 *n.* ①警告;警戒。He did not listen to my *warnings.* 他不聽我的警告。②預告;通知;(雇主與被雇者間之)解除雇約通知。The cook left without *warning.* 厨子沒有事先通知就不幹了。③預兆。The ceiling fell without the slightest *warning.* 天花板墜下,事前毫無預兆。—*adj.* 警告的;預兆的;注意的。—**ly,** *adv.*

warning signal 警報信號。

War of American Independence (美國之)獨立戰爭。

*****warp** 〔wɔrp; wɔ:p〕 *v.t.* ①使彎翹不平。The hot sun *warped* the boards. 烈日使木板彎翹。②〖航空〗使(機翼、螺旋槳翼等)的末端彎曲。③歪曲。④拉纜索使(船)移動。⑤使離開自然或正常的方向。⑥〖農業〗以洪水淹沒地面俾遺留沖積土而使(土地)肥沃。—*v.i.* ①變爲彎曲不平。②扭曲;歪曲。③拉纜索使船移動。—*n.* ①(木板等之)彎曲。②〖紡織〗經。The *warp* is crossed by the woof. (編織物之)經緯交織。③拉船之索。④洪水遺下之沖積土。—**age,** *n.*

war paint ①土人在出戰前在臉及身體上塗花紋的顏料。②〖俚〗盛裝;禮服;官服。③〖俚〗化妝品(如粉及口紅等)。

war·path 〔ˈwɔrˌpæθ; ˈwɔ:-pɑ:θ〕 *n.* 北美印第安人出征時所經之路。*on the warpath* a. 正在戰爭中;準備作戰。b. 盛怒。

war·plane 〔ˈwɔrˌplen; ˈwɔ:-plein〕 *n.* 軍用飛機。

*****war·rant** 〔ˈwɔrənt, ˈwɑrənt; ˈwɔrənt〕 *n.* ①正當的理由;權利;秉承。He had no *warrant* for what he did. 他做那件事毫無理由。②令狀;授權書;委任狀。The death-*warrant* has been signed. 死刑執行狀已簽字。③保證。④士官之派令。⑤棧單。⑥付款或收款授權書。—*v.t.* ①證明…爲正當;辯解。Nothing can *warrant* such insolence. 這種無禮是無可辯解的。②保證。③〖俗〗證明。④授權。The law *warrants* his arrest. 法律授權逮捕他。*I'll warrant* (*you*). 我敢說;我敢保證。—**er,** *n.* —**less,** *adj.*

war·rant·a·ble 〔ˈwɔrəntəbl̩; ˈwɔrəntəbl〕 *adj.* ①可保證的;可斷言的;可承認的;正當的。②〖狩獵〗已達可獵的(公鹿)。—**war·rant·a·bly,** *adv.* —**ness,** *n.*

war·ran·tee 〔ˌwɔrənˈti; ˌwɔrənˈti:〕 *n.* 〖法律〗被保證人。

war·rant·er 〔ˈwɔrəntɚ; ˈwɔrəntə〕 「*n.* 保證人。」

warrant officer 准尉(軍官)。

war·ran·tor 〔ˈwɔrənˌtɔr; ˈwɔrəntɔ:〕 *n.* 〖法律〗保證人。

war·ran·ty 〔ˈwɔrəntɪ; ˈwɔrənti〕 *n., pl.* **-ties.** ①〖法律〗a. 保證;擔保。b. 擔保契約。②(*pl.*)〖保險〗特約條款。③正當理由;合理根據。

war·ren 〔ˈwɔrɪn; ˈwɔrin〕 *n.* ①養兎場。②擁擠的公寓;大雜院。③〖英法律〗有籬笆圍起的獸類繁殖場。

war·ring 〔ˈwɔrɪŋ; ˈwɔ:riŋ〕 *n.* 戰爭;敵對行爲。—*adj.* 敵對的;相鬥爭的。

*****war·ri·or** 〔ˈwɑrɪɚ; ˈwɔriə〕 *n.* 戰士;勇士。—*adj.* 軍事的;戰士的。—**like,** *adj.*

War·saw 〔ˈwɔrsɔ; ˈwɔ:sɔ:〕 *n.* 華沙(波蘭之首都)。

Warsaw Convention 華沙協定(有關民航損失賠償之多邊協定)。

Warsaw Pact 華沙公約(1955年5月在華沙簽定的東歐共產國家之軍事公約)。

Warsaw Powers 華沙公約會員國。

*****war·ship** 〔ˈwɔrˌʃɪp; ˈwɔ:-ʃip〕 *n.* 軍艦;戰艦。(亦作 **war vessel**)

war surplus 軍用剩餘物資。

wart 〔wɔrt; wɔ:t〕 *n.* ①〖醫〗疣;瘊;腫瘤。②〖植物〗樹疣;樹瘿。*paint* (*a person*) *with his warts* 把某人好壞都寫出來。—**ed,** —**like,** *adj.* —**less,** *adj.*

wart hog 〖動物〗非洲產的疣豬。

war time 〖英〗雙倍夏令時間(比夏令時間更提早一小時的時間;亦即比格林威治標準時間提早二小時的時間)。

war·time 〔ˈwɔrˌtaɪm; ˈwɔ:-taim〕 *n.* 戰時。—*adj.* 戰時的。

war-torn 〔ˈwɔrˌtɔrn; ˈwɔ:-tɔ:n〕 *adj.* 被戰爭分裂或破壞的。

wart·y 〔ˈwɔrtɪ; ˈwɔ:ti〕 *adj.,* **wart·i·er, wart·i·est.** 似疣的;多疣的;有腫瘤的;有樹瘤的。

war whoop (北美印第安人之)作戰呼「號聲。」

war-worn 〔ˈwɔrˌworn; ˈwɔ:wɔ:n〕 *adj.* 疲於戰爭的;久經戰場的。

*****war·y** 〔ˈwɛrɪ, ˈwerɪ, ˈwærɪ; ˈwɛəri〕 *adj.,* **war·i·er, war·i·est.** ①密切注意的;機警小心的;不疏忽的。②顧慮周到的;愼重的。*be wary of* 留意;謹防。He *is wary of* telling secrets. 他提防洩露祕密。—**war·i·ly,** *adv.* —**war·i·ness,** *n.*

war zone 戰區。

‡**was** 〔wɑz, wəz; wɔz, wəz, wz〕 *v.* pt. of **be.** 用於第一及第三人稱,單數,直說法。

‡**wash** 〔wɑʃ, wɔʃ; wɔʃ〕 *v.t.* ①洗。*Wash* them clean. 把它們洗乾淨。②洗去;洗淸。③使濕。a rose *washed* with dew. 露水沾濕的玫瑰。④沖擊;沖壞。The cliffs are being *washed* away by the waves. 波浪正在把那些懸崖沖損。⑤沖。An empty boat was *washed* ashore by the tide. 一隻空船被潮水沖上岸來。⑥以水沖洗去(金砂等)。⑦被沖走;被捲去。⑧〖俗〗開除;淘汰。—*v.i.* ①洗衣服;洗澡;洗臉;洗手。She always *washes* in cold water. 她總是用冷水洗澡。②耐洗。That cloth *washes* well. 那布很耐洗。③沖壞。④〖俗〗經得起考驗。That argument won't *wash.* 那論據站不住。*be* (*look,* or *feel*) *washed out* 面色蒼白而帶倦容;疲倦。*wash down* a. 以水沖淨;沖洗。b. 一面進食(或進食後)一面喝飲料。*wash off* (*out,* or *away*) 洗去;洗掉。*wash out* a. 洗滌(瓶等)之內部。b. 淸洗布匹等以除去(肥皂或污物)。c. 失去(顏色、精力)等。d. 被水沖走;沖走。e. 〖俗〗淘汰;開除。*wash up* a. 洗餐具。b. 飯前洗臉洗手。—*n.* ①洗。You dirty boy! Go and have a *wash.* 你這個髒孩子!去洗個澡罷。②洗濯物;洗衣之處所。Please send these shirts to the *wash.* 請把這些襯衫送去洗。③沖擊;擊起的水。④用於特殊目的之液體。⑤稀薄液體;稀薄的湯。This soup is mere *wash.* 這羹湯只是稀湯(裏邊菜等很少)。⑥(飛機飛行或轉動所引起的)氣流。*kitchen wash* 厨房的殘棄的湯水(作豬飼料)。—*adj.* 耐洗的。

Wash. Washington (State).

wash·a·ble 〔ˈwɑʃəbl̩; ˈwɔʃəbl〕 *adj.* 可洗的。—**wash·a·bil·i·ty,** *n.*

wash and wear (衣服)快乾的;免燙的。(亦作 **wash-and-wear**)

wash·ba·sin 〔ˈwɑʃˌbesn̩; ˈwɔʃˌbeisn〕 「*n.* 洗臉盆。」

wash·board 〔ˈwɑʃˌbord; ˈwɔʃbɔ:d〕 *n.* ①搓板;洗衣板。②〖建築〗底板。—*adj.* 車轍很多的;崎嶇不平的。

wash·bowl 〔ˈwɑʃˌbol; ˈwɔʃboul〕 *n.* 「=**washbasin.**」

wash·cloth [ˈwɑʃˌklɔθ; ˈwɔʃklɔθ] *n.* 洗臉用的毛巾;面巾。

wash·day [ˈwɑʃˌde; ˈwɔʃdei] *n.* 【美】洗濯日(家庭每週洗衣之日)。(英亦作 **washing day**)

washed-out [ˈwɑʃtˈaut; ˈwɔʃtˈaut] *adj.* ①褪色的。②【俗】疲倦的;無生氣的;頹喪的。③被洪水沖壞的;受到侵蝕的。

washed-up [ˈwɑʃtˈʌp; ˈwɔʃtˈʌp] *adj.* 【俗】①用盡的;完蛋的;完全失敗的。②疲倦的。

wash·er [ˈwɑʃɚ; ˈwɔʃə] *n.* ①洗濯者;洗濯機;洗濯器。②(水龍頭等中用之)橡皮墊圈。—**less,** *adj.*

wash·er-dry·er [ˈwɑʃɚˈdraɪɚ; ˈwɔʃəˈdraiə] *n.* 附有乾燥機的洗衣機。

wash·er·man [ˈwɑʃɚmən; ˈwɔʃəmən] *n., pl.* **-men.** 男洗衣匠。

wash·er·wom·an [ˈwɑʃɚˌwumən; ˈwɔʃəˌwumən] *n., pl.* **-wom·en.** 洗衣婦。

wash·e·te·ri·a [ˌwɑʃəˈtɪrɪə; ˌwɔʃiˈtiəriə] *n.* 【英】自助洗衣店。

wash·house [ˈwɑʃˌhaus; ˈwɔʃhaus] *n.* 洗衣店。

wash·i·ness [ˈwɑʃɪnɪs; ˈwɔʃinis] *n.* 多水分;稀薄;軟弱無力。

***wash·ing** [ˈwɑʃɪŋ; ˈwɔʃiŋ] *n.* ①洗滌。Tom doesn't like *washing.* 湯姆不喜歡洗澡。②一次洗的衣服;待洗的髒衣服。She hung the *washing* out to dry. 她把洗過的衣服掛在外邊去晾乾。③淘洗出來的東西。④(常 *pl.*)洗過東西後的液體。⑤經淘洗過的表層沖積土。⑥粉刷。⑦從事於 wash sale.

washing machine 洗衣機。

***Wash·ing·ton** [ˈwɑʃɪŋtən; ˈwɔʃiŋtən] *n.* ①(亦作 **Washington D.C.**) 華盛頓(美國之首都)。②華盛頓州(美國西北部之一州)。③華盛頓(George, 1732–99, 美國第一任總統)。

Wash·ing·to·ni·an [ˌwɑʃɪŋˈtonɪən; ˌwɔʃiŋˈtouniən] *adj.* 美國首都華盛頓的;美國華盛頓州的。—*n.* 美國首都華盛頓或華盛頓州人。

washing-up machine 【英】洗碗機。

wash leather (羊等之皮所製之)軟革;軟革之仿造品。(亦作 **wash-leather, washleather**)

wash·out [ˈwɑʃˌaut; ˈwɔʃaut] *n.* ①洪水的沖潰;沖潰的洞;決口。②失敗的人;被淘汰者。③【俚】失敗。

wash·rag [ˈwɑʃˌræg; ˈwɔʃ-ræg] *n.* =**washcloth.**

wash·room [ˈwɑʃˌrum; ˈwɔʃ-rum] *n.* ①盥洗室;廁所;洗手間。②(染廠中洗織物之)洗濯室。

wash sale 【美, 股票】(爲使市場活躍而作之)詐欺交易;虛拋。

wash·stand [ˈwɑʃˌstænd; ˈwɔʃstænd] *n.* 臉盆架;盥洗臺。

wash·tub [ˈwɑʃˌtʌb; ˈwɔʃtʌb] *n.* 洗濯盆。

wash-up [ˈwɑʃˌʌp; ˈwɔʃʌp] *n.* ①洗滌。②洗滌處所,如浴室。

wash·wom·an [ˈwɑʃˌwumən; ˈwɔʃˌwumən] *n., pl.* **-wom·en.** =**washerwoman.**

wash·y [ˈwɑʃɪ; ˈwɔʃi] *adj.,* **wash·i·er, wash·i·est.** ①(酒、飲料中)水分多的;淡薄的;稀薄的。②淡的(顏色)。③無力的;無生氣的(文體)。④薄弱的(感情)。

‡**was·n't** [ˈwɑzn̩t, ˈwɑzn̩; ˈwɔznt, ˈwɔzn] =**was not.**

WASP [wɑsp; wɔsp] ①*W*omen's *A*ir Force *S*ervice *P*ilots. ②【蔑】a *W*hite *A*nglo-*S*axon *P*rotestant (在美被少數社羣視爲控制美國社會的典型人物, 仍構成一頑强的集團)。

wasp [wɑsp; wɔsp] *n.* ①黃蜂;胡蜂。②易怒者;暴躁的人。—**like,** *adj.*

wasp·ish [ˈwɑspɪʃ; ˈwɔspiʃ] *adj.* ①似黃蜂的。②蜂腰的;細腰的。③易怒的;脾氣壞的。④尖刻的(文體)。—**ly,** *adv.* —**ness,** *n.*

wasp waist 蜂腰;細腰。

was·sail [ˈwɑsl̩; ˈwɔseil, -sl] *n.* ①飲宴。②飲宴時所用之酒。③舉杯飲酒時的祝詞,意爲"祝君健康"。④【古】飲宴時所唱之歌。—*v.t. & v.i.* 參加飲宴;舉杯祝賀。—*interj.* 祝君健康!—**er,** *n.*

Was·ser·mann test (or **reaction**) [ˈvɑsɚˌmɑn~; ˈvɑːsəmaːn~] 瓦塞爾曼氏反應(德國細菌學家 August von Wassermann 發明之梅毒細菌檢驗法)。

wast [wɑst; wɔst] *v.* 【古】pt. of **be.** (第二人稱、單數、直說法, 與 thou 連用)。

wast·age [ˈwestɪdʒ; ˈweistidʒ] *n.* ①消耗;消耗量。②廢物。

‡**waste** [west; weist] *v.,* **wast·ed, wast·ing,** *n., adj.* —*v.t.* ①浪費;徒耗。His efforts were *wasted.* 他的努力都白費了。②蹂躪;損毀;使荒廢。The soldiers *wasted* the fields of the enemy. 士兵們蹂躪了敵人的田地。③消耗;耗損。He was *wasted* by disease. 他因患病而虛弱。—*v.i.* ①耗損;衰弱。She is *wasting* away for lack of good food. 她因飲食不佳而漸漸消瘦。②被浪費。*Waste* not, want not. (諺)不浪費,不缺乏。***waste one's breath*** (or ***words***) 白費唇舌。—*n.* ①浪費;徒耗。What a *waste* of energy! 這多麼浪費精力!②廢物;殘物。Throw the *waste* away. 把那些廢物丟掉。③沙漠;荒地;原野。④耗損;損毀。*waste* and repair. 損耗與補充。⑤棉或羊毛線球(用來擦拭機器上之油漬等)。⑥(*pl.*)排泄物。***go*** (or ***run***) ***to waste*** 被浪費;不被利用。—*adj.* ①無用的;廢棄的。②荒蕪的;不毛的。③不能用的;人或動物所排泄的。***lay waste*** 蹂躪;損毀。***lie waste*** 荒蕪;未被開墾。

waste·bas·ket [ˈwestˌbæskɪt; ˈweistˌbaːskit] *n.* 廢紙簍;字紙簍。(亦作 **wastepaper basket**)

waste book 【英】【簿記】流水帳;日記帳(=daybook)。(亦作 **wastebook**)

***waste·ful** [ˈwestfəl; ˈweistful] *adj.* ①浪費的;不經濟的。②【詩】荒廢的;荒涼的。③奢侈的。④破壞性的;毀滅性的。—**ly,** *adv.*

waste·land [ˈwestˌlænd; ˈweistlænd] *n.* ①荒野;不毛之地。②精神上或文化活動上貧乏的時代或地區。(亦作 **waste land**)

waste·pa·per [ˈwestˌpepɚ; ˈweistˌpeipə] *n.* 廢紙;紙屑。

wastepaper basket 廢紙簍;字紙簍。

waste pipe (排出廢水或汚水之)排水管。

wast·er [ˈwestɚ; ˈweistə] *n.* ①浪費者。②【英】無用之人;浪子。③做壞了的東西;廢物。④破壞者。

wast·ing [ˈwestɪŋ; ˈweistiŋ] *adj.* ①破壞健康的;消耗精力的。②消耗的;使弱的;漸減的。*wasting* asset. 逐漸減少之資產。③破壞的。—*n.* 浪費;消耗;消費。—**ly,** *adv.*

wast·rel [ˈwestrəl; ˈweistrəl] *n.* ①浪費者;濫用金錢的人。②無用之人;遊手好閒者。③無用之物;質劣之物;不完美之物。

‡**watch** [wɑtʃ; wɔtʃ] *v.t.* ①注意;看;注視;細心觀察。*Watch* me carefully! 注意看我!②照顧;看護。The dog *watched* the little boy. 那狗看顧着小孩。③注意等待。④監視。The man is being *watched* by the police.

警方正監視那個人。—*v.i.* ①注意;注視。Are you going to play or only *watch?* 你是參加遊戲呢,還是只是旁觀?②注意等待;守候。③看守;照看。The dog *watches* over his master's house. 這狗爲他的主人看守家屋。④不眠;守夜。***watch out*** 〖俗〗小心;提高警覺。*Watch out* for cars when you cross the street. 穿過街道時要注意來往車輛。***watch over*** 監視;保護;預防。—*n.* ①注意;留心;警戒;監視。The soldier was ordered to keep *watch.* 那兵士奉令戒備。②看守者;守夜者。③輪值之班。④值班時間。I am on duty during the morning *watch.* 我輪到早晨值班。⑤錶。My *watch* is fast. 我的錶快了。⑥古代希臘、羅馬及猶太人所分夜晚時間之一單位(通常分爲三至五 watches). ⑦計時計(如有分節的蠟燭等)。***be on the watch*** 警戒。—*adj.* 錶的。—**er,** *n.*

watch and ward 看管;守護。***keep watch and ward*** 日夜保持警覺。

watch·band [ˈwɑtʃˌbænd;ˈwɔtʃbænd] *n.* 錶帶。

watch box 哨崗;(用於看守的)小屋或亭。

watch cap 〖美海軍〗寒冷時值更水兵戴的毛織帽。

watch·case [ˈwɑtʃˌkes; ˈwɔtʃkeis] *n.* 錶殼。

watch chain 錶鍊。

Watch Committee 〖英〗(市鎭的)民防委員會。

watch·cry [ˈwɑtʃˌkraɪ;ˈwɔtʃkrai] *n., pl.*-**cries.** 口號;口令;標語(=watchword).

watch·dog [ˈwɑtʃˌdɔg; ˈwɔtʃdɔg] *n., v.,* **-dogged, -dog·ging.** —*n.* ①守望犬;警犬。②監視者;守望者。—*v.t.* 〖俗〗看管;監視。

watch fire 作信號之篝火;守夜者生之火。

***watch·ful** [ˈwɑtʃfəl; ˈwɔtʃful] *adj.* ①注意的;警醒的。to be *watchful* of the times. 注意時勢。to be *watchful* against enemies. 愼防敵人。②〖古〗易醒的。—**ly,** *adv.* —**ness,** *n.*

watch glass 錶的玻璃面。

watch guard 錶鍊;錶帶。

watch·mak·er [ˈwɑtʃˌmekɚ; ˈwɔtʃˌmeikə] *n.* 錶匠;修錶者。

watch·mak·ing [ˈwɑtʃˌmekɪŋ;ˈwɔtʃˌmeikiŋ] *n.* 鐘錶之製造或修理業。

***watch·man** [ˈwɑtʃmən; ˈwɔtʃmən] *n., pl.* **-men.** 看守者;守夜者;巡夜者;更夫。A *watchman* guards the bank at night. 一個守夜者在晚間守衛銀行。—**ly,** *adj.*

watch meeting 除夕之禮拜式。(亦作 watch-night service)

watch night ①除夕。②除夕之禮拜。

watch officer 〖海軍〗值更之軍官。

watch·out [ˈwɑtʃˌaut; ˈwɔtʃˌaut] *n.* 監視;預料。

watch pocket 盛錶的小口袋;錶袋。

watch·tow·er [ˈwɑtʃˌtauɚ; ˈwɔtʃˌtauə] *n.* 守望樓;更樓;瞭望臺。

watch·word [ˈwɑtʃˌwɝd; ˈwɔtʃwəːd] *n.* ①口令。②口號;標語。

:wa·ter [ˈwɔtɚ, ˈwɑtɚ; ˈwɔːtə] *n.* ①水;河水;海水;湖水;雨水。Bring me some hot *water.* 給我些熱水。fresh *water.* 淸水;淡水。②身體中分泌之液體;尿;汗;淚;涎。③(絲綢金屬等之)波紋;(寶石之)光澤。a diamond of the first *water.* 最佳光澤的鑽石。④水位;潮。high (low) *water.* 高(低)潮。⑤〖商〗超過資產實値的資本估計。⑥(*pl.*)流動的水;海浪;礦泉水。⑦ **a.** 海;湖泊;河川。**b.** 地下水。⑧水色。***above water*** **a.** 在水面上的。**b.** 脫離困難的。***back water*** **a.** 使船倒駛。**b.** 逆行;反向而行。***be in deep waters*** 在困難、不幸之中。***be on the water*** 在船上。***be under water*** 爲水所淹。***by water*** 乘船;由水路。***cast*** (or ***throw***) ***one's bread upon the waters*** 不求報酬做好事;積陰德。***get into*** (or ***be in***) ***hot water*** 陷於困難之境。***go through fire and water*** 赴湯蹈火。***hold water*** (理論)能獲證明;健全。***in low water*** 缺乏金錢;貧困。***in smooth water*** 處於順利進展之境。***keep one's head above water*** 不借債;不陷入經濟困難。***like a fish out of water*** 侷促(如失水之魚)。***like water*** 大量地;無節制地。***make water*** **a.** (船)進水(因漏或從船邊進入)。**b.** 解小便。***of the first water*** 最高度的;第一流的。a blunder *of the first water.* 最大的錯誤。***pass water*** 解小便。***spend money like water*** 揮霍無度;揮金如土。***Still waters run deep.*** 靜水流深;大智若愚。***take*** (***the***) ***water*** **a.** (動物、鳥、人等)游泳。**b.** (船)下水。**c.** 乘船;出航。**d.** 〖美西部〗突然離開。***take*** (***the***) ***waters*** 在療養地喝礦水(通常爲醫療手段)。***throw cold water on*** (***a plan,*** etc.) 對(一項計畫等)澆冷水。***written in water*** (名聲)瞬息卽逝的。—*v.t.* ①灑以水;澆以水。②供以水;給以飲水。③攙以水。This milk has been *watered* (down). 這牛奶中攙過水了。④沖淡;使缺乏力量。⑤〖商〗發行新股票增加(一商店的名義上的資本)。⑥使有波紋。—*v.i.* ①(動物等)飲水。②(輪船、汽機等)上水。A ship *waters* before sailing. 船在啓航前先上水。③出水。His eyes *watered.* 他雙目流淚。④流口水。***make one's mouth water*** 使人垂涎。***water down*** **a.** 加水沖淡。**b.** 減低價值或品質。**c.** 減弱…之力量。—*adj.* ①裝水的;運水的。a *water* jug. 水瓶。②水上的。*water* sports. 水上運動。③沖水的;以水稀釋的;加水的。④近水的。⑤關於水的。⑥長在水中的。⑦以水爲動力的。—**er,** *n.* —**less,** *adj.*

Water Bearer 〖天文〗寶瓶座(=Aquarius).

water bed 水牀(常附溫度調節設備)。

water beetle 龍蝨屬的水蟲。

water bird 水鳥。

water boatman 能在水面上迅速行動之蟲。

wa·ter-borne [ˈwɔtɚˌborn; ˈwɔːtəbɔːn] *adj.* ①漂流的。②由水路運送的。③(疾病等)由飲水傳染的。

water bottle 水壺;水瓶。

wa·ter·buck [ˈwɔtɚˌbʌk; ˈwɔːtəbʌk] *n.* 非洲產的大羚羊。

water buffalo 水牛。

water bug ①水蟲;水蠍。②蟑螂。

water butt 承雨水之桶。

water carriage 水上運輸;(由導管)送水。

water carrier ①水上運輸貨物或旅客之工具。②搬運水之人或獸;運水夫;馱水獸。③輸水之槽、管或水道。④(W- C-)〖天文〗寶瓶座(=Aquarius).

water cart 送水車。

water chute 滑橇板(用小艇自其斜面滑到水上的一種遊戲)。

water clock 水時計;滴漏。

water closet ①〖英〗有抽水設備之廁所。②〖方〗浴室。

wa·ter·col·or [ˈwɔtɚˌkʌlɚ; ˈwɔːtəˌkʌlə] *n.* ①水彩;水彩顏料。②水彩畫。—**wa·ter·col·or,** *adj.* —**wa·ter·col·or·ist,** *n.*

wa·ter-cooled [ˈwɔtɚˌkuld; ˈwɔːtəku:ld] *adj.* 水冷的；以水循環而使（引擎等）不過熱的。

wa·ter·course [ˈwɔtəˌkors; ˈwɔ:tə-kɔ:s] *n.* ①（河、溪等之）水流。②（河、溪等之）河床。③水路；運河。

wa·ter·craft [ˈwɔtəˌkræft; ˈwɔ:tə-krɑ:ft] *n.* ①船舶。②水上運動的技術（如操舟游泳）。

water cress 〖植物〗水田芥（一種用於製生菜之堇類植物）。

water cure ①〖醫〗水療法。②〖俗〗（以水灌胃之）水刑。

water diviner 用探礦杖尋找水源的人。

water dog ①水犬（訓練以獵取水禽之犬）。②〖俗〗老水手。③泥狗（一種蠑螈）。

wa·ter·drink·ing [ˈwɔtəˌdrɪŋkɪŋ; ˈwɔ:təˌdriŋkiŋ] *adj.* 常喝水（礦泉）的；主張以水代酒的。

wa·tered [ˈwɔtəd, ˈwɑ-; ˈwɔ:təd] *adj.* ①灑有水的。②供以水的；有溪流的（田地）。③有水紋的；有波紋的（絲綢等）。④以水處理的；以水沖淡的。⑤〖經濟〗面額增加而實值未按比例增加的（股票等）。

***wa·ter·fall** [ˈwɔtəˌfɔl; ˈwɔ:təfɔ:l] *n.* ①瀑布。②一種長而波浪型的女人髮式。

wa·ter·find·er [ˈwɔtəˌfaɪndə; ˈwɔ:təˌfaində] *n.* 以卜杖（diving rod）探地下水脈以決定井之位置者。

water fountain 飲水器；供應飲用水之處。

wa·ter·fowl [ˈwɔtəˌfaul; ˈwɔ:təfaul] *n., pl.* **-fowls, -fowl.** ①水鳥；水禽。②水鳥之集合稱。

water front ①都市中河、湖、港口附近地區。②水濱之土地。③熱水器。

water gage =**water gauge.**

water gap （水流通過之）峽。

water gas 〖化〗水瓦斯；水煤氣。

water gate 水門；水閘。

Wa·ter·gate [ˈwɔtəˌget; ˈwɔ:təgeit] *n.* ①水門事件（美國政治醜聞，係因共和黨總統競選連任委員會於1972年6月17日派遣五名工作人員前往水門大厦民主黨總部竊聽失風被捕而起，最後造成尼克森總統的辭職）。②(w-)（元首之）因醜聞而辭職。

water gauge 水表（指示蓄水池、汽鍋等水位之裝置）。

water glass ①玻璃酒杯；高脚玻璃杯。②盛水玻璃器皿。③玻璃水表。④水玻璃。⑤（水中看物用之）水下窺物鏡。⑥水時計。（亦作 **waterglass**）

water guard ①水上警察。②海關水上緝私員（隊）。

water gun 玩具水槍。

water hammer ①水錘（一種兩端封閉之實驗瓶，內裝水，無空氣，搖動時，水擊瓶兩端，發出如捶擊之聲，用以示固體與液體在眞空中降落時速度相等）。②管內水流，於關龍頭而突停時對管壁之衝擊。

water heater （使用瓦斯或電的）自動熱水器。

water hen 〖動物〗鷭。

water hole ①地上有水的低窪處。②（沙漠中之）水源，水井。③池塘。④乾涸的河床中留有水的低窪處。⑤結冰的池塘表面的洞。

water ice ①直接由水結成之冰塊。②由冰、果汁、糖等做成之冰糕。

wa·ter-inch [ˈwɔtəˈɪntʃ; ˈwɔ:tərˈintʃ] *n.* 〖水力學〗水英寸（在最小壓力下，蓄水池中之水自直徑一英寸之管於二十四小時所流出之量，約爲500立方英尺）。

watering can =**watering pot.**

watering cart =**water cart.**

watering place ①有礦泉的療養地。②有沐浴、划船等享受的遊息處。③可供水的地方。

watering pot 灑水壺。（亦作 **watering can, sprinkling can**）

water jacket 水套；冷水筒管。

water level ①水平面；水準。②=**water line.**

water lily 荷花；蓮。

water line ①船的吃水線；水線。②水量標（=watermark）.（亦作 **waterline**）

wa·ter·log [ˈwɔtəˌlɔg; ˈwɔ:təlɔg] *v.,* **-logged, -log·ging.** —*v.t.* ①使（船等）進水以致無法行駛。②使泡水。—*v.i.* 泡水；浸水。

wa·ter-logged [ˈwɔtəˌlagd; ˈwɔ:-təlɔgd] *adj.* ①（船等之）進水而不能操縱或行動遲緩的；進水的。②（木材等之）吸飽水的；泡水的。③（地）被水浸透了的；泥濘的；被陷住的。

Wa·ter·loo [ˌwɔtəˈlu; ˌwɔ:təˈlu:] *n.* ①滑鐵盧（拿破崙1815年最後戰敗處）。②任何決定性的慘敗。***meet one's Waterloo*** 慘敗。

water main 主輸水管；自來水總管。

wa·ter·man [ˈwɔtəmən; ˈwɔ:təmən] *n., pl.* **-men.** 船夫；水手；舟子。

wa·ter·man·ship [ˈwɔtəmənˌʃɪp; ˈwɔ:təmənʃip] *n.* 船夫之工作或技術；划船術。

wa·ter·mark [ˈwɔtəˌmɑrk; ˈwɔ:-təmɑ:k] *n.* ①（壓印在紙裏的）透明花紋；水印。②水位標；水量標。—*v.t.* ①加水印於（紙張）。②印透明花紋（於紙上）。

wa·ter·mel·on [ˈwɔtəˌmɛlən; ˈwɔ:tə-ˌmelən] *n.* ①西瓜。②西瓜籐。

water meter 水表；水量計。

water mill 水車；水（力）磨。

water motor 水力發動機。

water nymph ①水中女仙；水之女神。②=**water lily.**

water pipe ①水管。②水煙筒（用水過濾之吸煙工具）。

water pistol 玩具水槍。（亦作 **water gun, squirt gun**）

water plane 水上飛機。（亦作 **waterplane**）

water plug 消火栓。

water polo 水球。

water power ①水力。②可利用供給動力的下瀉之水。③磨坊使用水之權。

water pox 〖醫〗①水痘。②鉤蟲癢病；鉤蟲皮病。

***wa·ter·proof** [ˈwɔtəˈpruf; ˈwɔ:tə-pru:f] *adj.* 不透水的。—*n.* 防水布；雨衣。—*v.t.* 使不透水。—**er,** —**ness,** *n.*

water pump ①抽水機。②水冷式引擎中使水循環之裝置。

water rat ①河鼠（歐洲產的一種地鼠，居於堤岸）。②碼頭上的小偷；假充爲水手或碼頭工人的走私者。③麝香鼠。

water rate ①自來水費。②〖機械〗用汽率；用水率。

wa·ter-re·pel·lent [ˈwɔtərɪˌpɛlənt; ˈwɔ:təriˌpelənt] *adj.* 防水的；拒水的。

wa·ter-re·sist·ant [ˈwɔtərɪˌzɪstənt; ˈwɔ:təriˌzistənt] *adj.* 拒水（但不全防水）的。

water right 使用河川、湖泊、運河等灌溉水之權利。

wa·ter·scape [ˈwɔtəˌskep; ˈwɔ:tə-skeip] *n.* 水景；海景；海景畫。

wa·ter·shed [ˈwɔtəˌʃɛd; ˈwɔ:təʃed] *n.* ①分水線；分水界；分水嶺。②流域。③轉捩點；重要關頭。

wa·ter·shoot [ˈwɔtəˌʃut; ˈwɔ:təʃu:t] *n.* 排水管。

wa·ter·side [ˈwɔtəˌsaɪd; ˈwɔ:təsaid] *n.* ①水邊。②河畔；海濱；湖岸。—*adj.* ①水濱的；水邊的。②居住或工作於岸邊的。

water ski 滑水屐（比滑雪屐短而寬）。

wa·ter-ski [ˈwɔtəˌski; ˈwɔ:təski:] *v.i.,* **-skied, -ski·ing.** 滑水。—**ing,** —**er,** *n.*

wa·ter·skin [ˈwɔtəˌskɪn; ˈwɔːtəskin] *n.* 革製之水袋。

wa·ter·soak [ˈwɔtəˌsok; ˈwɔːtəsouk] *v.t.* 以水浸透。

water softener ①加在硬水中以除去已溶解之礦物質的化學品。②裝在水管中而含有上述藥物之裝置。

water spaniel(獵水鳥用之一種)獵犬。

wa·ter·spout [ˈwɔtəˌspaut; ˈwɔːtəspaut] *n.* ①屋簷雨水經過而流至地面之排水管;水槽。②噴水管;噴水口。③龍捲風掠過海洋所掀起之水柱;旋雲筒。

water sprite 住於水中之精靈;水中女仙。

water supply 供水;給水裝置。

water system ①(一河流之)水系。②給水系統。

water table ①地下水之水位。②【建築】飛檐。

wa·ter·tight [ˈwɔtəˈtaɪt; ˈwɔːtətait] *adj.* ①不透水的。②無懈可擊的;十全十美的。—**ness,** *n.*

water ton 水噸(相當於224英國法定加侖)。

water tower ①水塔。②消防隊用的一種救火噴水塔(能將水喉架起而噴射至房舍高層)。

water vole =**water rat.**

water wag(g)on =**water cart.** ***on the water wagon*** 【俚】忌酒;滴酒不沾。

wa·ter·way [ˈwɔtəˌwe; ˈwɔːtəwei] *n.* ①水道;水路;航路。②船上甲板兩旁之排水溝。

water wheel ①(水力推動之)水車。②灌溉用之戽水車。

water wings (初學游泳者置於腋下的)翼型浮袋。

wa·ter·works [ˈwɔtəˌwɜks; ˈwɔːtəwəːks] *n.* ①(作 *pl.* or *sing.* 解)自來水廠。②(作 *sing.* 解)自來水廠的抽水站或淨水站。③【俚】眼淚。④【俚】腎臟。

wa·ter·worn [ˈwɔtəˌworn; ˈwɔːtəwɔːn] *adj.* 被流水磨平了的。

wa·ter·y [ˈwɔtərɪ; ˈwɔːtəri] *adj.* ①水的;與水有關的。②含水的;充滿水的。③含淚的。*watery* eyes. 淚汪汪的眼睛。④似水的;淡薄的;無味的。a *watery* blue. 淡藍色。⑤有雨意的(天空等)。⑥無趣的(談話);無力的(文章)。⑦在海底的。⑧分泌水或似水物質的。—**wa·ter·i·ly,** *adv.* —**wa·ter·i·ness,** *n.*

Watt [wɑt; wɔt] *n.* 瓦特 (James, 1736–1819, 蘇格蘭工程師,蒸氣機的發明人)。

watt [wɑt; wɔt] *n.* 瓦特;瓦(電力之單位)。

watt·age [ˈwɑtɪdʒ; ˈwɔtidʒ] *n.* 瓦特數;瓦數。

watt-hour [ˈwɑtˈaur; ˈwɔtˈauə] *n.* 【電】瓦特小時(一瓦特電力一小時所做之功,爲電功或能量之單位)。(亦作 **watthour**)

wat·tle [ˈwɑtl; ˈwɔtl] *n., v.,* **-tled, -tling,** *adj.* —*n.* ①【英】(亦作 **wattles**)編條;枝條(用作籬笆、圍牆或屋頂等)。②(*pl.*)構成草頂房屋屋頂支架之杆條。③澳洲、南非所產之一種亞拉昆亞護謨樹(爲金合歡屬,其地居民用作編條,故名)。④細枝;嫩枝;棍;杖。⑤(鷄、火鷄等之)肉垂。⑥(魚類之)觸鬚。⑦(*pl.*)【俚】下垂之鬆弛的頷下皮膚。***wattle and daub*** (or ***dab***) 【建築】(外表塗泥,內面用編條做成之)夾灰牆。—*v.t.* ①以枝條捆紮;圍以籬。②交互編織;編(枝條)。③編結(屋頂、籬笆等)。—*adj.* 由編條做成的;覆以編條的。—**wat·tled,** *adj.*

watt·me·ter [ˈwɑtˌmitə; ˈwɔtˌmiːtə] *n.* 【電】瓦特計;電表。

waul [wɔl; wɔːl] *v.i., n.* 痛哭;號叫;尖叫。(亦作 **wawl**)

WAVE, Wave [wev; weiv] *n.* 【美】WAVES 之一員。

‡wave [wev; weiv] *n., v.,* **waved, wav·ing.** —*n.* ①波;波浪。the *wave(s)*.【詩】海。The infantry attacked in *waves.* 步兵做波狀攻擊。②波動;起伏;波紋;(頭髮的)波浪形。③揮動。a *wave* of the hand. 揮手。④(音、光、電等之)波。sound *wave.* 音波。⑤(情感、情勢等的)一時的激昂高漲。a *wave* of prosperity. 一時的繁榮。⑥【氣象】波;波浪(指各種水平方向流動型式之大氣波)。A cold *wave* is sweeping over the country. 一股寒流正侵襲全國。***permanent wave*** 電燙髮。—*v.t.* ①揮動;揮動以表示或指揮。The officer *waved* his men on with his sword. 那軍官揮動指揮刀叫士兵們前進。②使鬈曲;使有波紋。—*v.i.* ①波動;飄動。The flag is *waving* in the breeze. 這旗臨風招展。②揮動;揮手。He *waved* to us to stop. 他揮手叫我們停住。③鬈曲。Her hair *waves* naturally. 她的頭髮天生地鬈曲着。—**less,** *adj.* —**like,** *adj.*

wave band 【電訊】波帶;波段。

wave guide 【電子】波導。

wave length 【物理】波長。(亦作**wavelength**)

wave·let [ˈwevlɪt; ˈweivlit] *n.* 微波;碎浪;小浪。

wave mechanics 【物理】波動力學。

***wa·ver¹** [ˈwevə; ˈweivə] *v.i.* ①擺動;搖曳。②躊躇;猶豫;動搖。to *waver* in determination. 猶豫不決。③抖顫。—*n.* 擺動;躊躇;搖曳。—**er,** *n.* —**y,** *adj.*

wa·ver² *n.* ①揮舞之人或物。②(把頭髮弄成鬈曲的)燙髮師。③【印刷】墨軸;墨滾。④鬈曲頭髮用之針等。

wa·ver·ing·ly [ˈwevərɪŋlɪ; ˈweivəriŋli] *adv.* 擺動地;搖擺不定地;猶疑不決地。

WAVES [wevz; weivz] *n.* 美國海軍婦女輔助隊 (*W*omen *A*ppointed for *V*oluntary *E*mergency *S*ervice). (亦作 **Waves**)

wave set 將頭髮燙成波浪形前敷在髮上的一種藥水。

wave theory 【物理】波動說。

wav·y [ˈwevɪ; ˈweivi] *adj.,* **wav·i·er, wav·i·est.** ①波動的;起伏的。②多浪的。③波狀的。④顫動的;動搖的;不穩的。—**wav·i·ly,** *adv.* —**wav·i·ness,** *n.*

Wavy Navy 【英】英國海軍志願預備隊 (the Royal Naval Volunteer Reserve).

wawl [wɔl; wɔːl] *v.i., n.* =**waul.**

wax¹** [wæks; wæks] *n.* ①蠟;蜜蠟;蜂蠟。②似蜂蠟之物。③地板蠟。④【俚】唱片。wax in one's hands*** 易影響與控制的人。—*v.t.* ①塗以蠟。②【俗】將…灌唱片。—*adj.* 蠟的;用蠟作的。—**er,** *n.* —**like,** *adj.*

wax² *v.i.,* **waxed, wax·en, wax·ing.** ①增大;增長;(月亮)漸滿(爲 wane 之對)。The moon *waxes* till it becomes full, and then wanes. 月亮漸滿,直到正圓,然後消虧。②變爲。to *wax* weak. 變弱。to *wax* angry. 發怒。

wax³ *n.* 【英俗】陣怒;盛怒。to be in (*or* get into) a *wax.* 發怒;生氣。

wax bean 【植物】一種豆科植物。(亦作 **butter-bean**)

wax candle 蠟燭。

wax cloth ①(鋪地板之)漆布。②(擦洗地板之)抹布。

wax doll ①蠟製玩偶。②貌似蠟製玩偶而無表情或生氣之人。

wax·en [ˈwæksn̩; ˈwæksən] *adj.* ①蠟製的;塗蠟的。②蠟狀的;蒼白的;青白的;蠟黃的。③(人或性格)易改造的;柔和的。

wax·i·ness [ˈwæksɪnɪs; ˈwæksinis] *n.* 蠟質;柔軟;柔順。

wax myrtle 楊梅屬之植物(其漿果外皮被覆蠟質,可製蠟)。

wax paper 蠟紙(用以防潮濕者)。(亦作 waxed paper)

wax·wing ['wæksˌwɪŋ; 'wæks-wiŋ] *n.* 連雀。

wax·work ['wæksˌwɜk;'wæks-wəːk] *n.* ①蠟製品;蠟人。②(*pl.*)(作 *sing.* or *pl.* 解)蠟人展覽;蠟人展覽會場。

wax·y[1] ['wæksɪ;'wæksi] *adj.*, **wax·i·er, wax·i·est.** ①似蠟的;蠟狀的。②塗蠟的;含蠟的;蠟製的。③〖醫〗蠟樣變性症的。④溫柔的;柔軟的;柔順的。—**wax·i·ly,** *adv.*

wax·y[2] *adj.*, **wax·i·er, wax·i·est.** 〖主英〗生氣的;憤怒的。

‡**way** [we;wei] *n.* ①路;道路。My friend lives over the *way.* 我的朋友就住在路那一邊。②路程;距離。His home is a long *way* off. 他的家距此很遠。③旅行的途中;旅途;旅行所用的時間。They are on the *way.* 他們在旅途中。④方向。He went that *way.* 他向那邊走去。⑤方法;手段。Where there is a will there is a *way.* (諺)有志者事竟成。⑥方式。American *ways* of living. 美國人的生活方式。⑦〖俚〗附近。He lives somewhere London *way.* 他住在倫敦附近。⑧習慣;風習。⑨意向。A spoiled child wants his own *way* all the time. 一個慣壞了的孩子永遠爲所欲爲。⑩進步;前進。⑪前進行動的空間;前進的自由;自由行動。Get out of my *way!* 躲開!⑫方面;點。The plan is defective in several *ways.* 這計畫在好幾方面都有缺點。⑬情形;狀態。The sick man is in a bad *way.* 這病人的情況很可慮。⑭行業;職業。He is in the grocery *way.* 他經營雜貨業。⑮經驗的範圍。Such matters never come (in) my *way.* 我從沒有經過這樣的事。⑯規模。⑰〖法律〗行路優先權 (=right of way). ⑱(*pl.*) 造船及船下水時用的木架。***be under way*** 在進行中。***by the way*** a. 在途中;順路。b. 順便說;却說;可是(說話者忽然想到一件與本題無關的事情,用以改變話題的口頭語)。***by way of*** a. 經過;由 (=via). b. 意在;當作。***come*** (or ***fall***) ***one's way*** 發生於某人身上(=happen to one). ***gather*** (or ***lose***) ***way*** 增加(減低)速度。***give way*** a. 退去;退讓;讓出地位;讓路。b. 崩壞;衰敗;折;裂。c. 屈服於某種情緒。***go a long*** (or ***good***) ***way*** 大有助;很有效;很有用。***go one's own way*** 獨斷獨行;我行我素;一味孤行。***go one's way*** 離去。***go out of the*** (or ***one's***) ***way to*** 逸出常規;特別努力做。***have one's*** (***own***) ***way*** 隨心所欲;爲所欲爲。***in a small way*** 小規模地。***in a way*** 有一點點;有些。***in no way*** 決不。***in the family way*** 懷孕。***in the way*** 阻礙;妨礙。***in the way of*** a. 在有利的地位。b. 關於;有關。***lead the way*** a. 做領袖;爲人表率;採取主動。b. 領路;做嚮導。***lose one's way*** 迷路。***make one's way*** a. 進行。b. 努力上進;成功。***make way*** a. 讓路。b. 前進;進行。***my way of thinking*** 我認爲。***once in a way*** 有時;間或 (=once in a while). ***out of the way*** a. 處於不致成爲妨礙之位置。b. 離正途的。c. 不尋常的;奇特的。d. 死。e. 不在危險中;在够不着的地方。f. 遺失;忘記放在何處。***pave the way for*** 爲…作準備工作。***put oneself out of the way*** 犧牲自己以助他人。***see one's way*** 能够;願意。***see one's way clear*** 認眞考慮;認爲適當或可能。***stand in the way of*** 妨礙。***take one's way*** a. 出發;去。b. 照自己之方法(意見、所好等)而行。***the parting of the ways*** 做重要決定的時刻。***the permanent way*** 鐵軌。***under way*** 正在進行中。—*adv.* 〖俗〗老遠地。

way·bill ['weˌbɪl; 'weibil] *n.* ①乘客名單。②(鐵路或輪船的) 運貨單 (略作 **W.B., W/B**). a *waybill* of lading. 提貨單。③=air waybill.

way·far·er ['weˌfɛrə; 'weiˌfɛərə] *n.* 旅人;徒步旅行者。

way·far·ing ['weˌfɛrɪŋ; 'weiˌfɛəriŋ] *n., adj.* 徒步旅行(的)。

way·laid [ˌwe'led;wei'leid] *v.* pt. & pp. of waylay.

way·lay [ˌwe'le; wei'lei] *v.t.*, **-laid, -lay·ing.** ①路刼;半路埋伏。②攔截。—**er,** *n.*

way·leave ['weˌliv; 'weiliːv] *n.* 〖法律〗經過他人土地、產業之路權(如自礦場搬運煤等)。

way·mark ['weˌmɑrk; 'weimɑːk] *n.* 路標。

way-out ['weˌaut; 'weiaut] *adj.* 〖俗〗①(型式或技巧等)前進的;進步的。②古怪的;奇特的。

-ways 〖字尾〗由名詞或形容詞形成副詞用之,表"狀態;方向;位置"之義。

ways and means ①(立法機構)爲應付政府開支之籌款辦法。②(個人)爲完成某事之辦法。

way·side** ['weˌsaɪd; 'wei-said] *n.* 路邊;道旁。go by the wayside*** 被遺留在一旁。—*adj.* 路邊的;道旁的。

way station 〖美〗鐵路之小站。

way train 每站皆停之慢車。

way·ward ['wewəd; 'weiwəd] *adj.* ①剛愎的;頑强的;任性的。②不規則的;不穩的。—**ly,** *adv.* —**ness,** *n.*

way·worn ['weˌworn;'weiwɔːn] *adj.* 旅途疲憊的。

wayz·goose ['wezˌgus; 'weizguːs] *n.* 印刷工人每年一度之假期或宴樂。

W/B, W.B. waybill.

WbN, W. b N. West by North.

WbS, W. b S. West by South.

W.B.S. World Broadcasting System.

W.C. ①water closet. ②West Central (London postal district).

W.C.T.U., WCTU Women's Christian Temperance Union.

‡**we** [wi, wɪ; wiː, wi] *pron.* pl. of **I.** 我們。*We* are brothers. 我們是兄弟。*We* often go there. 我們常到那裏去。〖注意〗⑴作者、編輯、國王或法官講話時,常用之 we 而實際上是 I. ⑵ we 常常用做一個不確定的代名詞 (indefinite pronoun). 如 *we* find, *we* sometimes feel, 以避免用被動語態或無人稱句法 (impersonal construction).

‡**weak** [wik; wiːk] *adj.* ①弱的;虛弱的;軟弱的;體力不佳的。He felt very *weak* after illness. 他病後覺得很虛弱。②(器官、五官)不正常的。His eyes are *weak.* 他的目力不佳。③不牢的;不堅的;不穩固的。④缺乏力量的;缺乏權威的。⑤缺乏道德力量的;意志薄弱的。⑥愚蠢的。⑦微弱的;低微的。She spoke in a *weak* voice. 她以微弱的聲音說話。⑧稀薄的;淡薄的(茶、咖啡、酒等)。This tea is too *weak.* 這茶太淡。⑨易攻破的;易敗的;不能作戰的。⑩鬆懈的;不雄偉的(文章)。⑪對…不精的。He is *weak* in mathematics. 他數學不好。⑫不充分的(證據)。⑬〖語音〗弱讀的。⑭〖文法〗變化規則的(動詞)。⑮(信仰等)不堅强的。⑯(股票價格之)欲振乏力的;價格有下跌趨向的。⑰很可能失敗的;不稱職的。

***weak·en** [ˈwikən; ˈwiːkən] *v.t.* ①使弱;削弱。②使稀薄;使淡。—*v.i.* 變弱;衰弱。He *weakened* after his illness. 他病後體虛。—**er,** *n.*

weaker sex 婦女;女性。

weaker vessel 女人(聖經用語)。

weak·eyed [ˈwikˌaɪd;ˈwiːk-aid] *adj.* 視力不佳的。

weak·fish [ˈwikˌfɪʃ; ˈwiːkfiʃ] *n., pl.* **-fish, -fish·es.** 美國東海岸產的一種食用魚。

weak-head·ed [ˈwikˈhɛdɪd; ˈwiːk-ˈhedid] *adj.* ①心智遲鈍的;愚笨的。②容易醉酒的。③容易頭暈的。—**ly,** *adv.* —**ness,** *n.*

weak·heart·ed [ˈwikˈhɑrtɪd;ˈwiːk-ˈhɑːtid] *adj.* 無勇氣的;怯懦的。

weak-kneed [ˈwikˈnid; ˈwiːk-niːd] *adj.* ①易屈服的。②優柔寡斷的。

weak·ling [ˈwiklɪŋ;ˈwiːk-liŋ] *n.* 孱弱之人或動物;弱者。—*adj.* 弱的。

***weak·ly** [ˈwiklɪ; ˈwiːkli] *adv., adj.,* **-li·er, -li·est.** —*adv.* 軟弱地;虛弱地;怯懦地。—*adj.* 弱的;虛弱的。—**weak·li·ness,** *n.*

weak-mind·ed[ˈwikˈmaɪndɪd;ˈwiːk-ˈmaindid] *adj.* 懦弱的;優柔寡斷的;低能的。—**ly,** *adv.* —**ness,** *n.*

***weak·ness** [ˈwiknɪs; ˈwiːknis] *n.* ①弱;虛弱;柔弱;怯懦。*Weakness* kept her in bed. 她因體弱未能起床。②弱點;缺點;短處。We all have our little *weaknesses.* 大家都有小缺點。③偏好;溺愛;癖嗜。

weak sister 〖俚〗①拿不定主意的人;膽小鬼;緊要關頭靠不住的人。②最弱的一環;破壞全局的部分。

weal¹ [wil; wiːl] *n.* 幸福;福利;健康;財富。***come weal or woe; in weal and woe; whether for weal or woe*** 無論是福是禍。

weal² *n.* 鞭痕;條痕。—*v.t.* 附以條痕;加「鞭痕。」

weald [wild; wiːld] *n.* ①〖詩〗荒原;曠野。②〖詩〗森林地帶。③(The W-)維耳德地帶(英格蘭東南部 Kent, Surrey 以及 Essex 等地區,爲地質學上特殊的地域)。

‡wealth [wɛlθ; welθ] *n.* ①財富;財產。Health is above *wealth.* 健康勝於財富。②豐富;多量。a *wealth* of learning. 豐富的學識。—**less,** *adj.*

wealth tax 財富稅(個人財產超過規定最高限額,不論有無收入,每年均須繳納之稅)。

wealth·y** [ˈwɛlθɪ;ˈwelθi] *adj.,* **wealth·i·er, wealth·i·est.** 富的;富裕的;富有的。He is *wealthy* in wisdom. 他富於智慧。the wealthy*** 富有的人們。—**wealth·i·ly,** *adv.* —**wealth·i·ness,** *n.*

wean¹ [win; wiːn] *v.t.* ①使斷乳。②使戒絕;使棄絕。③使斷絕。

wean² *n.* 〖蘇〗小孩;嬰兒。

wean·er [ˈwinɚ; ˈwiːnə] *n.* ①使斷乳的人。②一種使動物斷乳之物。③〖澳〗五個月至十二個月之小羊。④〖美俗〗小牛犢。

wean·ling [ˈwinlɪŋ; ˈwiːnliŋ] *n.* 剛斷乳之嬰兒或小動物。—*adj.* 剛斷乳的。

***weap·on** [ˈwɛpən;ˈwepən] *n.* ①兵器;武器。② 做爲武器的手段。Are tears a woman's *weapon?* 眼淚是女人的武器嗎? ③〖動物〗動物身體上用來攻擊或自衞的部分,如角、爪、牙、刺等。—**less,** *adj.*

‡wear [wɛr; wɛə] *v.,* **wore** [wor; wɔː, wɔə], **worn** [worn; wɔːn], **wear·ing,** *n.* —*v.t.* ①穿; 着; 戴; 佩。to *wear* clothes (shoes). 穿衣服(鞋)。②蓄。to *wear* one's hair long. 蓄長髮。③帶有。She was *wearing* an innocent smile. 她帶着天眞的笑容。④穿舊;着破;用耗;耗損;磨損。I have *worn* my shoes into holes. 我的鞋已經穿出洞來。⑤由磨擦沖擊等而造成。to *wear* a hole in one's trousers. 褲子上面磨出一個洞。⑥使疲乏; 使疲弱。⑦舉止。⑧(船)掛(旗)。⑨過;打發〖常 away, out〗. to *wear* away the night in song. 以唱歌打發一個夜晚。⑩使(某人) 漸成 (一種狀態或養成一種習慣)。—*v.i.* ①耐用;耐久。This coat has *worn* well. 這外衣很耐穿。②耗損;磨損。③保持不變。④(時間) 漸漸過去。⑤漸成。***wear away*** **a.** 磨損。**b.** (時間)慢慢地挨過。The long winter *wore away.* 漫長的冬季已慢慢地挨過去了。***wear down*** **a.** 磨掉。**b.** 克服。**c.** 使疲倦。***wear off*** **a.** 消滅。**b.** 磨掉。***wear on*** 慢慢地挨過。***wear out*** **a.** 筋疲力竭。**b.** 穿壞;破損。**c.** 耗盡。I have *worn out* my patience. 我的忍耐已經到限度了。***wear the breeches*** (妻子) 駕馭丈夫。***wear the crown*** **a.** 登極爲帝。**b.** 做殉道者。***wear through*** 磨穿。The seat of his pants was *worn through.* 他的褲子的臀部已磨穿。—*n.* ①穿着; 佩帶。clothing for summer *wear.* 夏天穿的衣服。②着用品;衣着。The store sells children's *wear.* 那家店賣童裝。③磨損; 耗損; 着舊。The rug shows *wear.* 地氈已呈磨損之狀。④耐久性;耐用性。There is still much *wear* in these shoes. 這雙鞋還可穿很久。***wear and tear*** 磨損;損耗。

wear·a·bil·i·ty [ˌwɛrəˈbɪlətɪ; ˌwɛə-rəˈbiliti] *n.* (衣服之) 耐穿性;耐穿度。

wear·a·ble [ˈwɛrəbl̩;ˈwɛərəbl] *adj.* ①可穿的;可佩帶的。②耐用的。—*n.* (*pl.*)衣服。

wea·ri·ful [ˈwɪrɪfəl; ˈwiəriful] *adj.* (使人)疲倦的;(使人)厭煩的。—**ly,** *adv.*

wea·ri·less [ˈwɪrɪlɪs; ˈwiərilis] *adj.* 不疲倦的;不疲乏的。—**ly,** *adv.*

***wea·ri·ly** [ˈwɪrɪlɪ; ˈwiərili] *adv.* 疲倦地;疲勞地。

***wea·ri·ness** [ˈwɪrɪnɪs; ˈwiərinis] *n.* 「①疲勞;疲倦。②厭倦。」

wear·ing [ˈwɛrɪŋ; ˈwɛəriŋ] *adj.* ①穿用的。②逐漸損耗的; 逐漸磨損的。③使疲憊的。—**ly,** *adv.*

wearing apparel 衣服; 服裝。

wea·ri·some [ˈwɪrɪsəm; ˈwiərisəm] *adj.* ①使人疲倦的。②使人厭煩的。—**ly,** *adv.*

wear·proof [ˈwɛrˌpruf; ˈwɛəpruːf] *adj.* 不磨損的;不磨滅的。

***wea·ry** [ˈwɪrɪ, ˈwɪrɪ;ˈwiəri] *adj.,* **-ri·er, -ri·est,** *v.,* **-ried, -ry·ing.** —*adj.* ①疲倦的; 疲勞的。② 厭倦的。to be *weary* of life. 厭世。③ 令人疲倦的; 令人厭煩的。a *weary* journey. 令人厭倦的旅程。④不耐煩的〖常 of〗. *weary* of excuses. 對推託之辭覺得不耐煩。—*v.t.* ①使疲倦。②使厭煩。—*v.i.* ①疲倦。②厭煩〖of〗. to *weary* of a task. 厭於某工作。③渴望;思念。She is *wearying* for home. 她正想家。—**ing·ly,** *adv.*

wea·sand [ˈwizn̩d; ˈwiːznd] *n.* 〖古〗①氣管。②食道; 咽喉。(蘇亦作 **weason, weazand, wessand**)

wea·sel [ˈwizl̩; ˈwiːzl] *n., pl.* **-sels, -sel,** *v.* —*n.* ①鼬; 黃鼠狼。②狡滑的人。③雪上行駛的有履帶的車。④〖俚〗告密的人。—*v.i.* ①躲避義務, 職務〖常 out〗. ②使用模稜兩可的語言。③〖俚〗告密。—*v.t.* 使(一個字或片語)失去力量或意義。

weasel word 模稜兩可的字。
wea·sel-word·ed [ˈwizḷˌwɝdɪd; ˈwi:zəlˌwə:did] *adj.* 故意講得模稜兩可的。
:weath·er [ˈwɛðɚ; ˈweðə] *n.* ①天氣；氣象。fine *weather.* 好天氣。under all *weathers.* 不論天氣如何。②惡劣天氣。under stress of *weather.* 因受惡劣天氣的影響。③(常 *pl.*)(不管某人命運之) 盛衰。***keep one's weather eye open*** 注意可能的危險；警覺。***make heavy weather*** **a.** (船之)在風暴中掙扎。**b.** 引起問題，困擾。***under the weather*** 〖俗〗**a.** 病的；身體不適的。**b.** 患宿醉的。**c.** 微有酒意的。—*v.t.* ①曝露；曬乾；風乾。②平安度過。to *weather* a crisis. 度過一危機。③通過(岬角)之上風側。④使(屋頂等)成斜面以使雨水易流瀉。—*v.i.* ①因曝曬而褪色；能耐曝露於日光、風、雨等。②經過風暴、危險、困難而安全脫險〖常 through〗. ***weather in*** **a.** (飛機)因天氣惡劣而停航。**b.** 因天氣惡劣而關閉機場。***weather out*** **a.** 因天氣惡劣而未能入某處。**b.** 因天氣惡劣而取消。—*adj.* 當風的；頂風的。the *weather* bow. 頂風的船首。
weather balloon 氣候探測氣球。
weather beam 船之朝風的一邊。
weath·er-beat·en [ˈwɛðɚˌbitn̩; ˈweðəˌbi:tn] *adj.* ①飽經風吹雨打的；飽經風吹日曬的。②飽經風霜的；老練的。
weath·er·board [ˈwɛðɚˌbord; ˈweðəˌbɔ:d] *n.* ①擋風舷。②護牆板。—*v.t.* 裝以護牆板。
weath·er·board·ing [ˈwɛðɚˌbordɪŋ; ˈweðəbɔ:diŋ] *n.* ①以護牆板作成之覆遮。②護牆板(集合稱)。
weath·er-bound [ˈwɛðɚˌbaund; ˈweðəbaund] *adj.* 爲風雨所阻的。
weather breeder (俗信爲)風暴來臨前之晴朗的天氣。
Weather Bureau 〖美〗氣象局。
weath·er·cast [ˈwɛðɚˌkæst; ˈweðəkɑ:st] *n.* 電視或廣播電臺的氣象報告。
weath·er·cast·er [ˈwɛðɚˌkæstɚ; ˈweðəˌkɑ:stə] *n.* 電視、廣播電臺之氣象報告員。
weather chart 氣象圖。
weath·er·coat [ˈwɛðɚˌkot; ˈweðəkout] *n.* 〖英〗風衣；大衣。
weath·er·cock [ˈwɛðɚˌkɑk; ˈweðəkɔk] *n.* ①風標；風信雞。②見風轉舵之人；見機行事之人。—*v.t.* 爲…裝上風標。—*v.i.* 〖火箭〗(飛機或飛彈之)傾向於風向。
weath·er·con·di·tion [ˈwɛðəkənˌdɪʃən; ˈweðəkənˌdiʃən] *v.t.* 使能忍受或抵禦各種氣候。
weather deck 〖造船〗露天甲板。
weath·ered [ˈwɛðəd; ˈweðəd] *adj.* ①因曝露而風乾的。②因曝露而變色的。③風化的(岩石等)。④〖建築〗傾斜以防聚水的(窗檻等)。⑤施以類似風雨剝蝕痕跡之油漆的。
weather eye ①對氣候變化的敏感。②對環境、情況等變化之恆久而敏感的觀察。
weather forecast 氣象預報。
weather gauge (or **gage**) ①(一船對他船) 居上風之地位。②有利地位。to have (*or* get) the *weather gauge* of.... 比…占上風；比…占有利之地位。
weather girl 〖美〗女氣象播報員。
weath·er·glass [ˈwɛðɚˌglæs; ˈweðəglɑ:s] *n.* 指示大氣狀況之儀器(如晴雨計、溫度計、氣壓表等)。
weath·er·ing [ˈwɛðərɪŋ; ˈweðəriŋ] *n.* ①〖地質〗風化(作用)。②〖建築〗便於使雨水流下之斜面；簷。③weather strip 之材料。
weath·er·ly [ˈwɛðəlɪ; ˈweðəli] *adj.* ①與天氣有關的。②〖航海〗能近風航行而不漂流至下風處的。—**li·ness,** *n.*
weath·er·man [ˈwɛðɚˌmæn; ˈweðəmæn] *n., pl.* **-men.** ①〖俗〗擔任天氣預報的人。②〖美〗氣象局之官員或職員。
weather map 氣象圖；天氣圖。
weath·er·proof [ˈwɛðɚˈpruf; ˈweðə-pru:f] *adj.* 耐風雨的。—*n.* ①耐風雨之材料。②〖主英〗雨衣。—*v.t.* 使耐風雨。—**ness,** *n.*
weather radar 氣象雷達。
weather report 氣象報告。
weather satellite 氣象衛星。
weather ship 國際民航組織 (International Civil Aviation Organization) 會員國所派出之北大西洋氣候觀測船。
weather signal 氣象預報之標幟，如旗、燈等。
weather stained 因曝露風雨中而變色的。
weather station 測候所；氣象臺。
weather strip 〖建築〗門窗框等隙縫處爲防風雨而裝之薄金屬片、木條、橡皮條等物。
weath·er-strip [ˈwɛðɚˌstrɪp; ˈweðə-strip] *v.t.,* **-stripped, -strip·ping.** 裝以 weather strips.
weather stripping ① =**weather strip.** ②weather strip 之集合稱。
weather vane =**weathercock.**
weath·er·vi·sion [ˈwɛðɚˌvɪʒən; ˈweðəˌviʒən] *n.* 以雷達等對飛行員傳遞氣象消息。
weath·er·wise [ˈwɛðɚˌwaɪz; ˈweðəwaiz] *adv.* 關於氣候地。
weath·er-wise [ˈwɛðɚˌwaɪz; ˈweðəwaiz] *adj.* ①善於預測天氣的。②善於預測反應或意見的。
weath·er·worn [ˈwɛðɚˌworn; ˈweðəwɔ:n] *adj.* 爲風雨剝蝕的；飽經風霜的。
weave** [wiv; wi:v] *v.,* **wove** [wov; wouv], **wo·ven** [ˈwovən; ˈwouvən] or **wove, weav·ing,** *n.* —*v.t.* ①織；編。②織成；編成。to *weave* cloth out of thread. 用線織成布。③撰作；編排。The author *wove* three plots together into one story. 那作者把三個情節編成一個故事。④細心地做(如編織)。—*v.i.* ①編織。②迂廻；曲折前進。weave one's way*** 迂廻前行。—*n.* 編法；織法。—**weav·ing·ly,** *adv.*
***weav·er** [ˈwivɚ; ˈwi:və] *n.* 織者；織工。
wea·zen [ˈwizən; ˈwi:zən] *v.i., v.t., adj.* =**wizen.**
***web** [wɛb; web] *n., v.,* **webbed, web·bing.** —*n.* ①織物；布。②(蜘蛛等之)網。spider's *web.* 蜘蛛網。③一疋布。④網狀物。a *web* of railroads. 鐵道網。⑤蹼。⑥翈(羽毛的柔軟部分)。⑦薄金屬片。⑧〖印刷〗一卷紙。⑨捏造的謊言等。a *web* of *lies.* 一篇謊話。⑩〖解剖〗網狀組織。⑪任何脆弱或新奇的東西。—*v.t.* ①以網狀物包圍或捉住。②覆以網。—*v.i.* 形成網；結成蛛網。—**like,** *adj.*

webbed [wɛbd; webd] *adj.* ①交織成網狀的。②有蹼的。
web·bing [ˈwɛbɪŋ; ˈwebiŋ] *n.* ①(用作馬之腹帶等的)帶子。②(地毯等之)厚邊；邊帶。③〖動物〗蹼。
web·by [ˈwɛbɪ; ˈwebi] *adj.,* **-bi·er, -bi·est.** ①似織物的。②有蹼的。
web·foot [ˈwɛbˌfut; ˈwebfut] *n., pl.* **-feet.** ①蹼足；具有蹼足之鳥、動物或人。②

(W-) 美 Oregon 州人(綽號)。

web-foot·ed [ˈwɛbˈfutɪd; ˈwebˌfutid] *adj.* 蹼足的。

web press 一種滾筒印刷機。

Web·ster [ˈwɛbstɚ; ˈwebstə] *n.* 韋伯斯特(Noah, 1758–1843, 美國作家及著名的字典編輯家)。

***wed** [wɛd; wed] *v.*, **wed·ded, wed·ded** or **wed, wed·ding.** —*v.t.* ①將…嫁給；嫁給；娶。to *wed* one's daughter to an artist. 將女兒嫁給一位藝術家。②結合；兼具。to *wed* simplicity to (*or* with) beauty. 兼具純樸和美麗。—*v.i.* 結婚；結合。〖注意〗**wed** 和 **marry** 完全同義，不過 wed 是古語和典雅的用語。

we'd [wid; wi:d] =**we had; we should; we would.**

Wed. Wednesday.

wed·ded [ˈwɛdɪd; ˈwedid] *adj.* ①已結婚的。②婚姻的。③結合的。④專心一致的；固執的。

Wed·dell Sea [ˈwɛdl～; ˈwedl～] 威得耳海(在南極洲大西洋沿岸)。

***wed·ding** [ˈwɛdɪŋ; ˈwediŋ] *n.* ①結婚；婚禮。②結婚紀念日。③結合；融合。

wedding cake 結婚蛋糕；喜餅；禮餅。

wedding ceremony 結婚典禮。

wedding chest 新娘妝奩的箱子。

wedding day 舉行婚禮之日；結婚紀念日。

wedding feast 喜筵。

wedding march 結婚進行曲。

wedding ring 結婚戒指。

we·deln [ˈvedəln; ˈveidəln] *n.* 將雪屐平行而靠近，作迅速之左右旋轉而滑行的滑雪動作。—*v.i.* 作此種滑雪動作。

wedge** [wɛdʒ; wedʒ] *n.*, *v.*, **wedged, wedg·ing.** —*n.* ①楔。②似楔之物。a *wedge* of pie or cheese. 一塊餅或乾酪。③進入社會之階梯或步驟。④使分開，劈開或破壞團結之物。⑤〖軍〗(從前)V字形的隊形(尖部向着敵人)。⑥一種高爾夫球棒(用以將球從草叢中等擊出)。the thin end of the wedge*** 乍看不重要而實際會有重要結果的事件、改變等。—*v.t.* ①以楔劈開(常與 open, apart 連用)。②擠；揷；嵌。He *wedged* himself through the narrow window. 他從窄窗中擠了過去。③楔住；用楔使之牢固。④揷楔於已鋸之樹木使其倒下。—*v.i.* 擠進〖常 in, into, through 等〗. The box won't *wedge* into such a narrow space. 那盒無法塞進那麼小的地方去。—**like,** *adj.*

wedged [wɛdʒd; wedʒd] *adj.* 楔形的。

wedge-shaped [ˈwɛdʒˌʃept; ˈwedʒʃeipt] *adj.* 楔形地。

wedge·wise [ˈwɛdʒˌwaɪz; ˈwedʒwaiz] *adv.* 楔般地。

wedg·ie [ˈwɛdʒɪ; ˈwedʒi] *n.* 鞋底成楔形之婦女高跟鞋。

W

Wedg·wood [ˈwɛdʒˌwud; ˈwedʒwud] *n.* ①威基伍(Josiah, 1730–1795, 英國陶瓷製造家)。②一種設計精緻的陶器。—*adj.* 威基伍式的；威基伍所製的；威基伍所設計發明的。

Wedgwood ware 威基伍或其繼承人製造的陶器。

wedg·y [ˈwɛdʒɪ; ˈwedʒi] *adj.*, **wedg·i·er, wedg·i·est.** 楔形的；似楔的。

wed·lock [ˈwɛdlɑk; ˈwedlɔk] *n.* 婚姻；婚姻生活。

‡**Wednes·day** [ˈwɛnzdɪ; ˈwenzdi] *n.* 星期三；禮拜三。***Ash Wednesday*** 聖灰日(封齋期的第一天)。

Wednes·days [ˈwɛnzdɪz; ˈwenzdiz] *adv.* 在星期三；每星期三。

wee** [wi; wi:] *adj.*, **we·er, we·est,** *n.* —*adj.* ①極小的；微小的。a *wee* drop of whisky. 一點威士忌酒。②極早的；絕早的。in the *wee* hours of the morning. 清晨。a wee bit*** 頗爲；相當；有些。She's *a wee bit* jealous. 她有些妒嫉。—*n.*〖蘇〗①少量。②極小之空間；極短之時間。

***weed**[1] [wid; wi:d] *n.* ①雜草；莠草。②〖俗〗(the-) **a.** 雪茄；香煙。**b.** 大麻煙(=marijuana cigarette). ③瘦弱的人或動物。④無用之動物(尤指無法做賽馬或繁殖用的馬)。—*v.t.* ①除去(某地)的雜草。②除去；淘汰(無用或劣等的人物)〖out〗. —*v.i.* 除雜草。—**like,** *adj.*

weed[2] *n.* ①(*pl.*)喪服。widow's *weeds.* 寡婦的喪服。②(佩帶於帽邊或袖上之)喪用黑布條；喪章；孝布。③〖古〗衣服；外服。

weed·ed [ˈwidɪd; ˈwi:did] *adj.* ①除過草的。②長滿雜草的。

weed·er [ˈwidɚ; ˈwi:də] *n.* ①除草人。②除草機。

weed·i·cide [ˈwidəˌsaɪd; ˈwi:disaid] *n.* 除草劑；除草藥。

weed-kill·er [ˈwidˌkɪlɚ; ˈwi:dˌkilə] *n.* 除草劑。

weed·less [ˈwidlɪs; ˈwi:dlis] *adj.* ①無雜草的。②不受雜草所阻礙的。

weed·y [ˈwidɪ; ˈwi:di] *adj.*, **weed·i·er, weed·i·est.** ①多雜草的。②像雜草的。③高瘦而弱的(人)。—**weed·i·ly,** *adv.* —**weed·i·ness,** *n.*

wee hours 清晨；凌晨。

‡**week** [wik; wi:k] *n.* ①星期；週。this *week.* 本週。What day of the *week* is it? 今天是星期幾? ②星期日以外的六天；作業日。③包括某一特定日之一週。the *week* of June 3. 包括六月三日在內的一週。④舉行某種慶祝之週。***this day*** (or ***today***) ***week*** 上或下星期的今天。***week in, week out*** 一星期又一星期地；接連許多星期。—*adv.*〖英〗上(下)星期之某一指定日。I shall come Tuesday *week.* 我將於下星期二來。

***week·day** [ˈwikˌde; ˈwi:kdei] *n.* 週日；星期日以外的任何一天；平日。—*adj.* 週日的。*weekday* services. 週日禮拜式。

week·days [ˈwikˌdez; ˈwi:kdeiz] *adv.* 每天地(尤指星期一至星期五)。

***week·end** [ˈwikˈɛnd; ˈwi:kˈend] *n.* (亦作 **week end**) ①週末(通常自星期五下午至星期日晚間)。to spend the *weekend* with a friend. 同一位朋友度週末。②週末派對。—*adj.* 週末的。—*v.i.* 度週末。(亦作 **week-end**)

week·end·er [ˈwikˌɛndɚ; ˈwi:kˈendə] *n.* ①週末度假的人。②週末客人。③可裝週末度假所需衣物及旅行用具的旅行袋。④適於週末度假遊覽的小帆船。

week·ends [ˈwikˌɛndz; ˈwi:kendz] *adv.* 每週末。

week·long [ˈwikˌlɑŋ; ˈwi:klɔŋ] *adj.* 繼續一禮拜的；爲時一週的。

***week·ly** [ˈwiklɪ; ˈwi:kli] *adj.*, *adv.*, *n.*, *pl.* **-lies.** —*adj.* ①一週的；一星期的。②每週的；每週一次的。a *weekly* magazine. 週刊。—*adv.* 每週一次地；每週地。He is paid *weekly.* 他按週領薪。—*n.* 週刊；週報。

ween [win; wi:n] *v.i.* & *v.t.*〖古，詩〗想；認爲；以爲；想像。

***weep** [wip; wi:p] *v.*, **wept** [wɛpt; wept], **weep·ing,** *n.* —*v.i.* ①哭泣；流淚。to *weep* for joy. 喜極而泣。②流；滴落。③滲出水滴。④低垂。—*v.t.* ①爲…而哭泣；哀悼；悲歎。to *weep* one's life away. 在悲哀中度日。②流(淚)；落(淚)。③使滲出水滴。—*n.* ①〖俗〗哭

泣;流淚。②(水或液體之)滲出。**the weeps**〖俗〗一陣痛哭;痛哭的時間。

weep·er [ˈwipɚ; ˈwiːpə] *n.* ①哭泣者;(尤指)慣常哭泣者。②送葬時被雇哀悼的人。③服喪所用的黑喪章。④一種長尾猿。⑤已有一部分酒自瓶塞蒸發而損失的酒瓶。

weep·ing [ˈwipɪŋ; ˈwiːpiŋ] *adj.* ①哭泣的;流淚的。②垂枝的。③滲出液體的;水滴滴下的。**—ly,** *adv.*

weeping cross 豎立於路旁之十字架(供懺悔者祈禱用)。

weeping eczema〖醫〗濕爛性濕疹。

weeping willow 柳樹。

weep·y [ˈwipɪ; ˈwiːpi] *adj.*, **weep·i·er, weep·i·est.** ①哭哭啼啼的; 欲哭的。②易感動掉眼淚的。③滲出水或液體的。 **—weep·i·ly,** *adv.*

wee·ver [ˈwivɚ; ˈwiːvə] *n.* 在溫海海底發現之一種海魚。

wee·vil [ˈwivl̩; ˈwiːvil] *n.* 蛄蟹;穀象蟲。

wee·wee [ˈwiˌwi; ˈwiːwiː] *n., v.,* **-weed, -wee·ing.**〖兒語〗**—*n.*** 小便。**—*v.i.*** 小便。

weft [wɛft; weft] *n.* ①〖紡織〗緯線;橫經之線(爲 warp 之對)。②〖詩〗織成之物。

‡**weigh**[1] [we; wei] *v.t.* ①稱…的重量; 稱;估量…的輕重。to *weigh* sugar (gold). 稱糖 (金)。②考慮; 斟酌;權衡。③壓下。④起(錨)。⑤ **a.** 拿在手裏掂掂重量。 **b.** 拿在手裏左右上下撫弄。⑥〖廢〗尊敬; 敬重。 **—*v.i.*** ①重(若干)。 I *weigh* 100 pounds. 我體重一百磅。②具有重要性; 重要。③重壓;壓迫;發揮作用。The matter *weighed* upon his conscience. 這件事使他的良心很感痛苦。④起錨。 ***weigh down*** **a.** 壓下; 被壓得下垂。 **b.** 頹喪;憂心忡忡。*weighed down* with care. 憂慮太多而提不起精神來。 ***weigh in*** **a.** (拳師等)比賽前之量體重。 **b.** (騎師)賽馬後之量體重。 ***weigh in with*** **a.** 提出議論。 **b.** 額外提出;另加;挿嘴。 ***weigh on*** 成爲…的負擔。 ***weigh one's words*** 推敲;斟酌用字。 ***weigh out*** (騎師) 賽馬前之量體重。 **—er,** *n.*

weigh[2] *n.* =way(祇用於under weigh(=under way)。

weigh·a·ble [ˈweəbl̩; ˈweiəbl] *adj.* 可秤的;可衡量的。**—ness,** *n.* **—weigh·a·bly,** *adv.*

weigh beam 一種大秤。

weigh·bridge [ˈweˌbrɪdʒ; ˈweibridʒ] *n.* (稱車輛、牛、馬等之)地秤。

weigh·house [ˈweˌhaus; ˈweihaus] *n.* 貨物重量檢驗所;過秤處;過磅處。

weigh-in [ˈweˌɪn; ˈweiin] *n.*〖運動〗(拳擊手等)比賽前之量體重。

weighing machine 量重器;秤。

weigh·lock [ˈweˌlɑk; ˈweilɔk] *n.* 衡閘(爲課稅秤通過運河船隻重量的水閘)。

weigh·man [ˈwemən; ˈweimən] *n., pl.* **-men.** ①檢驗重量的人; 量重量的人。②〖礦〗量礦工所採之煤炭重量的人(尤指據礦工所採煤量多寡而計酬者)。

weigh·mas·ter [ˈweˌmæstɚ; ˈweiˌmɑːstə] *n.* ①管理公共磅秤的人。②礦場或罐頭工廠量產品重量者。

‡**weight** [wet; weit] *n.* ①重; 體重。What is your *weight?* 你體重若干? ②錘;砝碼。 a pound *weight.* 一磅的砝碼。③重量之單位; 計重法。avoirdupois *weight.* 常衡。④重物; 重塊。⑤重負; 重壓。⑥重量。⑦有某重量之量。⑧重要; 勢力。a man of *weight.* 重要人物。⑨合於季節的衣服之重量。summer *weight.* 夏季(衣服)之輕快。⑩〖運動〗舉重時使用之金屬球。⑪拉弓所需之力。⑫馬賽時一匹馬應裝載的重量(包括馬鞍、騎馬師等)。 ***by weight*** 論重(賣等); 依重量計算。 ***carry weight*** 有分量;算數;受重視。His opinion is certain to *carry weight.* 他的意見一定會受重視。 ***pull one's*** (***own***) ***weight*** 盡自己的本分。 ***put on weight*** 體重增加; 長胖。 ***throw one's weight around*** (or ***about***)〖俗〗過分誇耀自己的地位、階級;倚勢凌人。 ***under*** (***over***) ***weight*** 過輕(重)。 **—*v.t.*** ①加重;附以重物; 使負重荷。 He was *weighted* with troubles. 他承擔着許多煩惱的重負。②攙礦物質(在織品、絲等內)使其顯出質地較佳。③視爲重要; 重視。④對(某方面)特別强調;偏重。

weight·less [ˈwetlɪs; ˈweitlis] *adj.* 無重量的。 **—ly,** *adv.* **—ness,** *n.*

weight lifter 舉重選手。

weight lifting 舉重。

weights and measures 度量衡。

weight throw〖運動〗鏈球(運動)。

weight-watch·er [ˈwetˈwɑtʃɚ; ˈweitˈwɔtʃə] *n.* 節食者;減肥者。

weight·y [ˈwetɪ; ˈweiti] *adj.*, **weight·i·er, weight·i·est.** ①重的。②累人的; 煩重的。③重要的;有力的。④有影響力的。 **—weight·i·ly,** *adv.* **—weight·i·ness,** *n.*

Weil's disease [vaɪlz~; vailz~]〖醫〗威氏病;急性傳染性黃疸。

weir [wɪr; wiə] *n.* ①堰。②魚梁(爲捕魚順水勢所設之柵)。**—less,** *adj.*

weird** [wɪrd; wiəd] *adj.* ①非人世所有的; 超乎事理之外的 (=unearthly); 不可思議的;奇異的。②命運的。**—*n. 〖蘇〗①命運。②命運之神。③女巫。 ④預言。 **—li·ness, —ness,** *n.* **—ly,** *adv.*

weird·ie [ˈwɪrdɪ; ˈwiədi] *n.*〖俚〗怪人;怪事。

Weird Sisters ①掌握命運之三女神。②莎士比亞所作悲劇 *Macbeth* 中之三女巫。

weird·y [ˈwɪrdɪ; ˈwiədi] *n., pl.* **weird·ies.**〖俚〗神祕、古怪或不正常的人或事。(亦作 **weirdie, weirdo**)

Weis·mann [ˈvaɪsmɑn; ˈvaismɑːn] *n.* 魏斯曼 (August, 1834–1914, 德國生物學家)。**—i·an,** *adj., n.*

Weis·mann·ism [ˈvaɪsmɑnɪzəm; ˈvaismɑːnizəm] *n.*〖生物〗魏斯曼氏之遺傳學說(種質可代代相傳,但後天獲得性不能遺傳)。

Welch[1] [wɛltʃ, wɛlʃ; welʃ] *n.* 韋爾契 (William Henry, 1850–1934, 美國病理學家)。

Welch[2] *adj., n.* =**Welsh.**

welch [wɛltʃ, wɛlʃ; welʃ] *v.t.* & *v.i.*〖俚〗=**welsh. —er,** *n.*

‡**wel·come** [ˈwɛlkəm; ˈwelkəm] *interj., n., v.,* **-comed, -com·ing,** *adj.* **—*interj.*** 歡迎。*Welcome* to China! 歡迎你到中國來! *Welcome* home! 歡迎你回家! **—*n.*** ①歡迎。to bid one *welcome.* 向某人表示歡迎之意。②款待; 接待。 ***wear out one's welcome*** 拜訪某人過勤或停留過久而使人討厭。 **—*v.t.*** 歡迎;款待;樂意接受。to *welcome* a friend. 歡迎朋友。**—*adj.*** ①受歡迎的。 a *welcome* guest (letter, gift). 受歡迎的客人(信、禮品)。②可隨便享用的;可任意的。③無任何約束的; 無任何義務的 (對表示謝意的人之謙虛話)。You're quite *welcome.* 不用客氣; 不用謝。**—less,** *adj.* **—ly,** *adv.* **—ness,** *n.*

welcome mat ①放在進口處, 尤指有 "Welcome" 字樣的擦鞋底的墊子。②〖俗〗熱烈的歡迎。

weld [wɛld; weld] *v.t.* ①鎔接; 焊接; 鍛接。②密結;結合。**—*v.i.*** 鎔接; 焊接; 鍛接。

—n. ①鎔接之接頭;接合處。②鎔接。—a·ble, adj. —less, adj.
weld·er ['wɛldɚ; 'weldə] n. 鎔焊工人; 鎔焊機。(亦作 weldor)
weld·ing ['wɛldɪŋ; 'weldiŋ] n. 鎔焊;鎔接。
welding torch 鎔焊炬。
weld·ment ['wɛldmənt; 'weldmənt] n. 鎔接組成之物。
wel·fare** ['wɛl,fɛr, -,fær; 'welfɛə] n. 福祉;福利;安寧;幸福。social *welfare*. 社會福利。on welfare*** 接受救濟的。
welfare fund 員工福利基金。
welfare state 福利國家(其政府以保障社會安全、推行失業保險、公醫制度等爲職志)。
welfare work 救濟事業。
welfare worker 從事救濟事業者。
wel·far·ism ['wɛl,fɛrɪzəm;'welfɛərizəm] n.福利國家主義。—**wel·far·ist**, n., adj.
wel·kin ['wɛlkɪn; 'welkin] n. 〖詩〗空; 蒼穹;天空(=sky). ***make the welkin ring*** 響聲徹天;響徹雲霄。—adj. 天空般的;蔚藍的。
:well¹ [wɛl; wel] adv., **bet·ter, best,** adj., **bet·ter, best,** n., interj. —adv. ①好; 很好。to sleep *well*. 睡得很好。②徹底地;全然地;充分地。Shake the bottle *well*. 把這瓶子徹底搖搖。③甚; 頗; 頗多地。I like it *well*. 我很喜歡它。④適當地; 有理由地; 很可以地。You may *well* say so. 你很有理由這樣說。⑤詳細地; 週全地。He knows the subject *well*. 他對這問題(科目)知道甚詳。⑥好心好意地;無仇恨地。He took the joke *well*. 他對那玩笑不介意。⑦確定地;無疑地。I anger easily, as you *well* know. 我容易生氣,這一點你知道得很清楚。***as well*** a. 也;同樣地。I can do it *as well*. 我也能做這事。b. 此外。***as well as*** a. 同;和;不僅;除…外。He has experience *as well as* knowledge. 他有知識, 並且有經驗。b. 同樣好。He can speak English *as well as* you do. 他說英文和你說得同樣好。***be*** (or ***get***) ***well away*** 〖英〗有了好的開始(或進展)。***be well out of*** (***something***) 幸好未(受損失、失敗、疾病等); 安然脫免。***can*** (or ***could***) ***well*** 很容易地;無甚困難地。***do well to*** 幸而;幸虧;幸好。***live*** (or ***do oneself***) ***well*** 生活優裕。***stand well with*** 中…之意。—adj. ①健康的; 安好的。I'm quite *well*, thank you. 我很好,謝謝你。②好的; 良好的; 適宜的。All is *well* with us. 我們一切都好。***It is all very well***.... 這個的確很好…(表不滿或不贊成之反語)。***well and good*** 好; 照准(接納決定、建議之用語)。***well enough*** 相當好。—n. 好; 滿意。to wish a person *well*. 祝某人幸福。***leave well enough alone*** 不要改變使人已滿意的事物。***let well alone*** 那樣就很好了,別去管它。—interj. 表示驚愕、同意、安慰、期待、允諾、讓步等的溫和的感歎詞。*Well*, here we are at last. 好了,我們終於到了。—**ness**, n.
:well² n. ①井。②泉。③源泉; 來源。*well* of knowledge. 知識的源泉。④如井泉之物。⑤井孔(裝於建築物的中間, 從頂層到底層, 以安設樓梯及電梯)。⑥船上安裝抽水機之房間。⑦(法庭的)律師席(用欄干圍在法官席之前面)。⑧會議廳中放置講臺之處。⑨(機翼或機身上)供降落輪收縮用之空間。—v.i. 湧出;噴出; 流出。—v.t. 使湧出; 使噴出; 使流出。***well over*** 溢滿。His heart *welled over* with joy. 他滿懷高興。—adj. 井的;像井的。
we'll [wil; wi:l] =we shall; we will.
well-act·ed ['wɛl'æktɪd; 'wel'æktid] adj. ①表演得很好的。②裝得很像的。
well·a·day['wɛlə'de;'welə'dei] interj. 〖古〗=wellaway.
well-ad·ver·tised['wɛl'ædvɚtaɪzd; 'wel'ædvətaizd] adj. 廣告做得很多的。
well-ad·vised['wɛləd'vaɪzd;'weləd'vaizd] adj. 審愼的;深思熟慮的。
well-aimed ['wɛl,emd; 'wel'eimd] adj. 瞄得準的。
well-ap·point·ed ['wɛlə 'pɔɪntɪd; 'welə'pɔintid] adj.裝備完善的;配備齊全的。
well·a·way ['wɛlə'we; 'welə'wei] interj. (亦作 welladay) 表示悲傷悔恨之感歎詞。—n. 悲傷;悔恨。
well-bal·anced['wɛl'bælənst;'wel'bælənst] adj. ①(精神上)正常的;意識健全的;可靠的;有感覺的。②調整準確的;均衡的。
well-be·haved ['wɛlbɪ'hevd; 'welbi'heivd] adj. 行爲端正的;循規蹈矩的。
well-be·ing ['wɛl'biɪŋ; 'wel'bi:iŋ] n. 安寧;幸福;福利。
well-be·lov·ed ['wɛlbɪ'lʌvɪd; 'welbi'lʌvd] adj. ①被深愛的。②受尊敬的。—n. 被深愛之人。
well·born ['wɛl'bɔrn; 'wel'bɔ:n] adj. 出身名門的;有高貴氣質的。
well-bred ['wɛl'brɛd; 'wel'bred] adj. ①有教養的;有禮貌的。②良種的(馬等)。
well-built ['wɛl'bɪlt;'wel'bilt] adj.① 堅固的;結實的。②〖俗〗肌肉發達、身材均勻的。
well-cho·sen['wɛl'tʃozn̩;'wel'tʃouzn] adj. 精選的;恰當的;適當的。
well-con·di·tioned ['wɛlkən'dɪʃənd;'welkən'diʃənd] adj. 情況良好的;健康的。
well-con·nect·ed ['wɛlkə'nɛktɪd; 'wel-kə'nektid] adj. ①與望族血統有關係的。②構思精密的;計畫得很仔細的。
well-con·tent ['wɛlkən'tɛnt; 'welkən'tent] adj. 十分滿意的;十分樂意的。
well-cut ['wɛl'kʌt; 'wel'kʌt] adj. (衣服)剪裁得很好(合時)的。
well-de·fined ['wɛldɪ'faɪnd; 'weldi'faind] adj. 定義明確的;清晰的。
well-dis·posed ['wɛldɪs'pozd; 'weldis'pouzd] adj. ①懷好意的;親切的; 性情很好的;(對某人)有好感的;(對某意見、思想)能接納的。②適當安置或安排的。
well·do·er ['wɛl'duɚ;'wel'duə] n. ①善人。②行爲良好的人。
well·do·ing ['wɛl'duɪŋ; 'wel'duiŋ] n. 善行;德行。—adj. 行善的;仁慈的。
well-done ['wɛl'dʌn; 'wel'dʌn] adj. ①做得好的; 做得效果良好的。②完全煮熟了的。—interj. 好! 做得好!
well-dressed['wɛl'drɛst;'wel'drest] adj. ①穿着入時的。②烹調、修剪等合宜的。
well-es·tab·lished['wɛlə'stæblɪʃt; 'welis'tæbliʃt] adj. 已立定脚跟的; 已爲大衆接受的;已建立地位的。
well-fa·vo(u)red['wɛl'fevɚd;'wel'feivəd] adj. 漂亮的;標緻的;貌美的;樣子好看的。—**ness**, n.
well-fed ['wɛl'fɛd; 'wel'fed] adj. 營養充足的; 豐滿的; 肥胖的。***Well-fed, well-bred***. 衣食足然後禮義興。
well-fixed ['wɛl'fɪkst; 'wel'fikst] adj. 有錢的;富有的。
well-formed ['wɛl'fɔrmd; 'wel-

ˈfɔːmd〕 *adj.* 身材苗條的;修短適度的。
well-found 〔ˈwɛlˈfaund; ˈwelˈfaund〕 *adj.* 設備完善、裝備齊全的。
well-found·ed 〔ˈwɛlˈfaundɪd; ˈwelˈfaundid〕 *adj.* 有充分根據的;有充分理由的。
well-groomed 〔ˈwɛlˈgrumd; ˈwelˈgruːmd〕 *adj.* ①被小心照料的。②梳洗得整潔的;穿得整潔的。③整齊清潔的。
well-ground·ed 〔ˈwɛlˈgraundɪd; ˈwelˈgraundid〕 *adj.* ①有充分理由的; 有充分根據的。②(對某學科)根底好的;基礎好的。
well-han·dled 〔ˈwɛlˈhændḷd; ˈwelˈhændld〕 *adj.* 處理得當的。
well·head 〔ˈwɛl,hɛd; ˈwelhed〕 *n.* 井源;水源;泉源。
well-heeled 〔ˈwɛlˈhild; ˈwelˈhiːld〕 *adj.* 有錢的;富有的。
well·hole 〔ˈwɛl,hol; ˈwelhoul〕 *n.* ①井口;井坑。②室內之樓梯或電梯井孔。
well-hung 〔ˈwɛlˈhʌŋ; ˈwelˈhʌŋ〕 *adj.* ①口若懸河的;善於辭令的。②懸掛得當的。
well-in·formed 〔ˈwɛlɪnˈfɔrmd; ˈwelinˈfɔːmd〕 *adj.* ①見聞廣博的; 博識的。②消息靈通的;得有確實消息的。
Wel·ling·ton 〔ˈwɛlɪŋtən; ˈweliŋtən〕 *n.* ①威靈頓 (Arthur Wellesley, 1769–1852, 在滑鐵盧擊敗拿破崙的英國名將)。②威靈頓 (紐西蘭首都)。③(亦作 **Wellington boots**) (*pl.*)威靈頓長靴(深及於膝)。
well-in·ten·tioned 〔ˈwɛlɪnˈtɛnʃənd; ˈwelinˈtenʃənd〕 *adj.* (出自)善意的。
well-kept 〔ˈwɛlˈkɛpt; ˈwelˈkept〕 *adj.* ①保管妥當的。②照顧周到的。
well-knit 〔ˈwɛlˈnɪt; ˈwelˈnit〕 *adj.* ①結實的;堅牢的。②强健的。③關係密切的;組織嚴密的。
***well-known** 〔ˈwɛlˈnon; ˈwelˈnoun〕 *adj.* 著名的;爲大家所熟知的。
well-lik·ing 〔ˈwɛlˈlaɪkɪŋ; ˈwelˈlaikiŋ〕 *adj.* 健康的;況佳的。
well-looked 〔ˈwɛlˈlukt; ˈwelˈlukt〕 *adj.* 樣子好看的。
well-made 〔ˈwɛlˈmed; ˈwelˈmeid〕 *adj.* ①結實的;精巧的。②結構巧妙的(小說等)。
well-man·nered 〔ˈwɛlˈmænəd; ˈwelˈmænəd〕 *adj.* 有禮貌的;態度良佳的;舉止得體的。
well-mean·er 〔ˈwɛlˈminə; ˈwelˈmiːnə〕 *n.* 善意的人。
well-mean·ing 〔ˈwɛlˈminɪŋ; ˈwelˈmiːniŋ〕 *adj.* ①善意的; 好心的。②(亦作 **well-meant**) 出自善意的;誠實的(企圖)。
well-meant 〔ˈwɛlˈmɛnt; ˈwelˈment〕 *adj.* 善意的。
well-nigh 〔ˈwɛlˈnaɪ; ˈwelnai〕 *adv.* 殆;幾乎。
well-off 〔ˈwɛlˈɔf; ˈwelˈɔːf〕 *adj.* ①相當富有的。②在舒適的狀態中。(亦作 **well off**)
well-oiled 〔ˈwɛlˈɔɪld; ˈwelˈɔild〕 *adj.* ①甜言蜜語的; 阿諛的。②〖俗〗醉的。③運行情況良好的;順利的;光滑的;有效率的。
well-or·dered 〔ˈwɛlˈɔrdəd; ˈwelˈɔːdəd〕 *adj.* 秩序井然的。
well-paid 〔ˈwɛlˈped; ˈwelˈpeid〕 *adj.* 待遇優厚的。
well-placed 〔ˈwɛlˈplest; ˈwelˈpleist〕 *adj.* ①瞄準得當的。②占有利的職位或社會地位的。③裝置在適當地位的;方便的;順手的。
well-pleas·ing 〔ˈwɛlˈplizɪŋ; ˈwelˈpliːziŋ〕 *adj.* 使人滿足的;使人滿意的。
well-pre·served 〔ˈwɛlprɪˈzɝvd; ˈwelpriˈzəːvd〕 *adj.* 保存得很好的;還很新的。
well-pro·por·tioned 〔ˈwɛlprəˈpɔrʃənd; ˈwelprəˈpɔːʃənd〕 *adj.* 修短適中的;匀稱的;體態優美的。
well-read 〔ˈwɛlˈrɛd; ˈwelˈred〕 *adj.* 多讀的;博覽的;博學的。
well-reg·u·lat·ed 〔ˈwɛlˈrɛgjə,letɪd; ˈwelˈregjuleitid〕 *adj.* ①有健全之規則的;經妥善處理的;井然有序的。②正常的。
well-re·put·ed 〔ˈwɛlrɪˈpjutɪd; ˈwelriˈpjuːtid〕 *adj.* 有好名譽的;獲得好評的。
well-round·ed 〔ˈwɛlˈraundɪd; ˈwelˈraundid〕 *adj.* ①豐滿的。②通才的;各方面俱備的。
well-set 〔ˈwɛlˈsɛt; ˈwelˈset〕 *adj.* (體格等)結實的;構造均勻的。
well-set-up 〔ˈwɛl,sɛtˈʌp; ˈwel,setˈʌp〕 *adj.* 構造均勻的;體格結實的。
well sinker 鑽井者;鑿井者。
well-spo·ken 〔ˈwɛlˈspokən; ˈwelˈspoukən〕 *adj.* ①說話流利的;說話流暢的。②言語謙恭的;善於辭令的。③得體的(話);中肯的(話)。
well·spring 〔ˈwɛl,sprɪŋ; ˈwelspriŋ〕 *n.* ①泉源;水源。②來源。
well-suit·ed 〔ˈwɛlˈsutɪd; ˈwelˈsjuːtid〕 *adj.* 適當的;便利的。
well-tem·pered 〔ˈwɛlˈtɛmpəd; ˈwelˈtempəd〕 *adj.* ①鍛鍊得很好的。②脾氣溫和的;性情溫良的。
well-thought-of 〔ˈwɛlˈθɔt,ɑv; ˈwelˈθɔːtɔv〕 *adj.* 有令譽的;聲名好的;聲望高的。
well-thumbed 〔ˈwɛlˈθʌmd; ˈwelˈθʌmd〕 *adj.* 經常翻閱的;經常使用的。
well-timed 〔ˈwɛlˈtaɪmd; ˈwelˈtaimd〕 *adj.* ①時機正好的;正合時宜的。②時間很準的。
well-to-do 〔ˈwɛltəˈdu; ˈwel-təˈduː〕 *adj.* 小康的;富裕的。(亦作 **well to do**)
well-trav·eled 〔ˈwɛlˈtrævḷd; ˈwelˈtrævəld〕 *adj.* ①遊歷甚廣的;足跡遍天下的。②交通頻繁的。
well-tried 〔ˈwɛlˈtraɪd; ˈwelˈtraid〕 *adj.* 經過多次試驗(磨鍊)的。
well-trod·den 〔ˈwɛlˈtrɑdṇ; ˈwelˈtrɔdn〕 *adj.* 人們常往的;常用的。
well-turned 〔ˈwɛlˈtɝnd; ˈwelˈtəːnd〕 *adj.* ①(言語等) 措詞巧妙的; 說得妙的。②(姿態)優美的。
well-turned-out 〔ˈwɛl,tɝndˈaut; ˈwel,təːndˈaut〕 *adj.* 穿着入時的; 打扮摩登的。
well-wish·er 〔ˈwɛlˈwɪʃə; ˈwelˈwiʃə〕 *n.* 祝福者。
well-wish·ing 〔ˈwɛlˈwɪʃɪŋ; ˈwelˈwiʃiŋ〕 *adj.* 爲別人祝福的。—*n.* 祝福;祝賀;祝好。
well-worn 〔ˈwɛlˈworn; ˈwelˈwɔːn〕 *adj.* ①十分破舊的。②用得太多的;陳腐的;常套的;平凡的。③佩帶或攜帶合適的。
Welsh 〔wɛlʃ, wɛltʃ; welʃ〕 *adj.* 威爾斯(Wales)的;威爾斯人的;威爾斯語的。—*n.*威爾斯人;威爾斯語。(亦作**Welch**) —**ness,** *n.*
welsh 〔wɛlʃ; welʃ〕 *v.t.* & *v.i.* 〖俚〗①(賽馬賭輸)不付賭金溜掉;賴賭債逃走;欺騙賭帳;賴債。②逃避義務;不履行義務〖有時 on〗. (亦作 **welch**)
welsh·er 〔ˈwɛlʃə; ˈwelʃə〕 *n.* 〖俚〗(賽馬賭輸) 不付賭金而溜掉者;賴賭債而逃走者;騙子;賴債者。
Welsh·man 〔ˈwɛlʃmən, ˈwɛltʃmən; ˈwelʃmən〕 *n., pl.* **-men.** 威爾斯人。(亦作 **Welchman**)
Welsh rabbit 塗於麫包上食用的一種混合有麥酒或啤酒及牛乳等之乳酪汁。 (亦作 **Welsh rarebit**)
Welsh terrier 威爾斯種㹴(可作獵犬)。
Welsh·wom·an 〔ˈwɛlʃˈwumən; ˈwelʃˈwumən〕 *n., pl.* **-wom·en.** 威爾斯

女人。

welt 〔welt; welt〕 *n.* ①〖俗〗傷痕。②〖俗〗毆打。③(鞋底和鞋面接縫間的) 革條。④鑲邊; 貼邊。—*v.t.* ①加以革條或貼邊。②〖俗〗重笞;重打。

Welt·an·schau·ung 〔ˈvɛlt,ɑn,ʃauʊŋ; ˈvelt,ɑːn,ʃauuŋ〕〖德〗*n.*〖哲學〗世界觀。

wel·ter¹ 〔ˈwɛltɚ; ˈweltə〕 *v.i.* ①(海浪等)澎湃;洶湧。②滾動;翻滾。③浸浴(如浸浴於血泊中等)。—*n.* ①澎湃;起伏;洶湧;翻滾。②騷動;混亂;紛擾。

wel·ter² *n.* 輕中量級之拳擊或角力選手。

welter race 〖俗〗負重賽馬。

wel·ter·weight 〔ˈwɛltɚ,wet; ˈweltəweit〕 *n.* ①〖拳擊〗輕中量級。②輕中量級之拳擊者或角力者(體重在136與147磅之間,介乎中量級與輕量級之間者)。③(舉行跳欄賽馬等時) 加在馬身上的特別重量 (二十八磅)。—*adj.* 輕中量級的。

Welt·po·li·tik 〔ˈvɛltpɔlɪˈtik; ˈveltpɔːliˈtiːk〕〖德〗 *n.* (一國之)國際政策; 對外政策;外交政策。

Welt·schmerz 〔ˈvɛlt,ʃmɛrts; ˈvelt,ʃmɛəts〕〖德〗 *n.* 憂世;情緒上的悲觀。

wen 〔wɛn; wen〕 *n.* ①〖醫〗良性瘤腫;疣。②〖英俚〗擁擠之大都市。London is the great *wen* of England. 倫敦是英國人口擁擠的大都市。

wench 〔wɛntʃ; wentʃ〕 *n.* ①少女;少婦。②鄉婦;僕婦。—*v.i.* 與鄉婦或僕婦通姦;與人盡可夫之婦女通姦。—**er,** *n.*

Wend 〔wɛnd; wend〕 *n.* 汶德人(德國東部斯拉夫民族之一支)。

wend 〔wɛnd; wend〕 *v.*, **wend·ed** or 〖古〗 **went, wend·ing.** —*v.t.*〖詩〗向…而進;去。—*v.i.* 行;前進。***wend one's way*** 去;赴。

wen·nish 〔ˈwɛnɪʃ; ˈweniʃ〕 *adj.* ①疣狀的;有疣之特徵的。②長疣的。(亦作 **wenny**)

‡**went** 〔wɛnt; went〕 *v.* pt. of **go.**

wept 〔wɛpt; wept〕 *v.* pt. & pp. of **weep.**

‡**were** 〔ˈwɝ, ,wɛr; wəː, wɛə, wə〕 *v.* ①pt. of **be** (複數,及第二人稱,單數,直說法)。②past subjunctive of **be** (第一、二、三人稱,單複數,假設法的過去式)。***as it were*** 如同;好似;彷彿。

we're 〔ˈwir, ˈwɪr; wiə〕 =**we are.**

‡**weren't** 〔wɝnt; wəːnt〕 =**were not.**

wert 〔wɝt; wəːt, wət〕 *v.*〖古〗 be 之第二人稱,單數,過去式,直說法或假定法 (與 thou 連用,猶今之 were)。

wer·wolf 〔ˈwɪr,wulf; ˈwəːwulf〕 *n., pl.* **-wolves.** 古傳說中可變爲狼或可隨意變成狼形的人;狼人。(亦作 **werewolf**)

Wes·ley 〔ˈwɛslɪ, ˈwɛzlɪ; ˈwezli, ˈwesli〕 *n.* ①韋斯理 (John, 1703–1791, 英國傳教士,爲美以美教派之創始人)。②韋斯理(Charles, 1707–1788, 英國衞理公會之傳教士,爲 John 之兄弟及助手,聖詩作家)。

Wes·ley·an 〔ˈwɛslɪən; ˈwezliən〕 *adj.* ①John Wesley 的。②美以美教派的。—*n.* ①John Wesley 之門人。②美以美教派信徒。

Wes·ley·an·ism 〔ˈwɛslɪənɪzəm; ˈwezliənizm〕 *n.* 美以美教派之教義及儀規。

‡**west** 〔wɛst; west〕 *n.* ①西; 西方。The sun sets in the *west.* 日落於西方。②西部。the *west* of Europe. 歐洲西部。③(the W-) 美國西部。④(the W-)西洋;西方各國 (指歐美二洲,與亞洲相對而言)。⑤(the W-) 西方 (指歐美非共產各國而言)。—*adj.* 西方的; 在西方的;向西方的; 來自西方的。on the *west* coast. 在西海岸。—*adv.* 向西。to sail *west.* 向西航行。***go west*** 〖俚〗歸西;死。—**ness,** *n.*

West Africa 西非。

West African ①西非的。②西非人的。③西非人。

West Bengal 西孟加拉省,在印度之東部。

West Berlin 西柏林。

west·bound 〔ˈwɛst,baund; ˈwestbaund〕 *adj.* 向西進行的;西行的。

west by north 西偏北 (指南針上西偏北 11°15′ 之點)。

west by south 西偏南(指南針上西偏南11°15′之點)。

West End 倫敦西區 (富翁住宅區,也是最佳商店所在地)。

west·er 〔ˈwɛstɚ; ˈwestə〕*v.i.* 向西移動;西行。—*n.* 西風。

west·er·ing 〔ˈwɛstərɪŋ; ˈwestəriŋ〕 *adj.* 向西的;西下的(通常指太陽)。

west·er·ly 〔ˈwɛstɚlɪ; ˈwestəli〕 *adj., adv., n., pl.* **-lies.** —*adj.* ①西方的;在西方的。②向西方的。③來自西方的。—*adv.* ①向西。②來自西方。—*n.* (*pl.*) 西風。—**west·er·li·ness,** *n.*

‡**west·ern** 〔ˈwɛstɚn; ˈwestən〕 *adj.* ①向西方的。②來自西方的。③西方的; 在西方的。*western* science. 西方的科學。④(W-) 西洋的; 歐美的; 美國西部的; 南北美洲的。*Western* civilization. 西洋 (歐美)文明。⑤(W-) 羅馬教會 (Western Church) 的。*Western* liturgies. 羅馬教會的禮拜儀式。—*n.* 〖俗〗西部片;西部小說。—**ly,** *adv.*

Western Church 羅馬教會;天主教會。(亦作 **Latin Church**)

Western Empire 西羅馬帝國(羅馬帝國於A.D. 395 分裂爲東西兩帝國, 西羅馬帝國亡於 A.D. 476)。

west·ern·er 〔ˈwɛstɚnɚ; ˈwestənə〕 *n.* ①西方人;歐美人。②(W-)美國之西部人。

Western Hemisphere 西半球。

West·ern·ism 〔ˈwɛstɚnɪzm; ˈwestənizm〕 *n.* 西方思想;西洋制度。(亦作 **westernism**)

west·ern·ize 〔ˈwɛstɚ,naɪz; ˈwestənaiz〕 *v.t.*, **-ized, -iz·ing.** 使歐化;使西洋化。—**west·ern·i·za·tion,** *n.*

west·ern·most 〔ˈwɛstɚn,most; ˈwestənmoust〕 *adj.* 最西的;最西端的。

western roll 跳高過竿時身體與竿成平行之姿勢;滾竿式(背滾或腹滾)。

West German ①西德的。②西德人。

West Germany 西德(正式名稱 Federal Republic of Germany, 首都波昂 Bonn)。

West Indian ①西印度羣島的。②西印度羣島人。

West Indies 西印度羣島。

west·ing 〔ˈwɛstɪŋ; ˈwestiŋ〕 *n.* ①〖航海〗西行距離;西距。②西行。

West I·ri·an 〔~ˈɪrɪ,ɑn; ~ˈiːri,ɑːn〕荷屬新幾內亞於1963年被印尼兼併後之新名。(亦作 **West New Guinea**)

West·min·ster 〔ˈwɛst,mɪnstɚ; ˈwestminstə〕 *n.* ①英國倫敦中心之一區 (西敏寺、國會、白金漢宮所在地)。②西敏寺。③英國國會。④議會政治。

Westminster Abbey 西敏寺 (倫敦一教堂, 自1245年後曾爲英王 Henry III 及 Edward I 所重建, 爲英國名人之墓地)。

Westminster Cathedral 西敏寺附近之威斯敏斯特大天主教堂。

west·most 〔ˈwɛst,most; ˈwestmoust〕 *adj.* 最西的;最靠西的(=westernmost)。

west-north·west ['wɛst,nɔrθ'wɛst; 'westnɔ:θ'west] *adj.* 西北西的;在西北西的;向西北西的;自西北西的。—*n.* 西北西。—*adv.* 向西北西;自西北西。

West Palm Beach 西棕櫚灘(美國 Florida 州東南部之一城市)。

West Point ①西點(在美國紐約州之東南部,爲西點軍校所在地)。②西點軍校。

West Pointer 西點軍校之學生或畢業生。

west-south·west ['wɛst,sauθ'wɛst; 'westsauθ'west] *adj.* 西南西的;在西南西的;往西南西的;自西南西的。—*n.* 西南西。—*adv.* 往西南西;自西南西。

West Virginia 西維吉尼亞(美國東部之一州,其首府爲 Charleston).

West·wall ['wɛst,wɔl; 'westwɔ:l] *n.* 德國之齊格飛防線(=Siegfried Line).

***west·ward** ['wɛstwəd; 'westwəd] *adj.* 西方的;向西方的。—*adv.* 向西方。—*n.* 西方。—**ly,** *adv.*

west·wards ['wɛstwədz; 'westwədz] *adv.* =**westward.**

‡**wet** [wɛt; wet] *adj.*, **wet·ter, wet·test,** *v.*, **wet** or **wet·ted, wet·ting,** *n.* —*adj.* ①濕的。Don't touch *wet* paint. 不要摸未乾的油漆。②降雨的;多雨的。a *wet* day. 雨天。③〖美俚〗允許釀酒販賣的。④〖美俚〗贊成釀酒販賣的。⑤酒的;由酒所構成的。*wet* cargo. 酒。⑥飲酒而歡樂的。to have a *wet* night. 飲酒作樂而過夜。⑦產乳的;有奶的。a *wet* cow. 有奶的母牛。⑧產於濕土的。a *wet* crop. 產於濕土的農作物。⑨誤入歧途的;錯誤的。He's all *wet*. 他完全誤入歧途了。***all wet*** 〖俚〗錯誤的;大錯而特錯。***be wet behind the ears*** 〖俗〗初出茅廬;少不更事;天眞。***wet through*** 濕透。***wet to the skin*** 衣服濕透。—*v.t.* ①使濕。②飲酒慶祝。to *wet* a bargain. 飲酒慶祝交易成功。③撒尿於。to *wet* the bed. 尿床。—*v.i.* ①變濕。②(小孩或動物)撒尿。***wet one's whistle*** 〖俗〗喝杯(酒);潤喉。***wet the other eye*** 再喝一杯酒。—*n.* ①濕氣;水分;水;液體。to wring the *wet* out. 擰乾水分。②雨;雨天。to stay out all night in the *wet*. 整晚逗留於雨中。③〖美俚〗贊成允許釀酒販賣的人。—**ly,** *adv.* —**ter,** *n.*

wet·back ['wɛt,bæk; 'wetbæk] *n.* 非法進入美國境內之墨西哥人。

wet bargain 當事人一道喝酒時達成的交易。

wet blanket ①浸水之濕毯。②掃興的人或物;煞風景者。

wet-blan·ket ['wɛt'blæŋkɪt; 'wet'blæŋkit] *v.t.* ①以濕毯撲滅(火災)。②煞…之風景;澆…的冷水。

wet cell 〖電〗濕電池。

wet-clean ['wɛt'klin; 'wet'kli:n] *v.t.* 加以水洗。

wet cleaning 水洗。

wet dream 夢精;夢遺。

wet·fast·ness ['wɛt,fæstnɪs; 'wet,fɑ:stnis] *n.* (染料等之)水洗不褪色。

wet gas 濕氣;富氣(含有大量汽油蒸氣之天然氣)。

wet goods (瓶裝或罐裝之)液體貨物(尤指烈酒)。

wet hen 〖俚〗討厭的夥伴。

weth·er ['wɛðɚ; 'weðə] *n.* 閹羊。

wet lab 潛水人員或海洋學家海底實驗室的工作艙。

wet·land ['wɛt,lænd; 'wetlænd] *n.* 濕地;沼地。

wet·ness ['wɛtnɪs; 'wetnis] *n.* 濕潤;雨天。

wet nurse 乳母。

wet-nurse ['wɛt,nɝs; 'wetnə:s] *v.t.*, **-nursed, -nurs·ing.** ①爲…之乳母。②過分庇護;溺愛。

wet·proof ['wɛt,pruf; 'wetpru:f] *adj.* 防濕的;防水的。

wet·ta·ble ['wɛtəbl; 'wetəbl] *adj.* ①可與水混合的;可加水的。②可以弄濕的。—**wet·ta·bil·i·ty,** *n.*

wet·ting ['wɛtɪŋ; 'wetiŋ] *n.* ①弄濕;撒水。②濕劑。

wet·tish ['wɛtɪʃ; 'wetiʃ] *adj.* 略濕的;潮濕的。

wet wash 洗過但未乾未燙的衣類。

wet wind 雨前濕風。

we've [wiv, wɪv; wi:v] =**we have.**

wey [we; wei] *n.* 〖英〗一種重量單位(因物而異,羊毛爲182磅)。

w.f., wf wrong fount (*or* font).

WFTU, W.F.T.U. World Federation of Trade Unions. **W.G., w.g.** wire gauge. **wgt.** weight. **Wh.** watt-hour. **wh., whr.** watt-hour.

whack [hwæk; wæk, hw-] *v.t.* & *v.i.* ①〖俗〗重擊;用力打。②〖俚〗分成分;分配。***whack up*** 分配。—*n.* ①〖俗〗敲擊;重擊。②〖俚〗一試;嘗試。③〖俚〗分配之一分。④〖俚〗情況;狀態(尤指好的情況或狀態)。⑤機會。***have*** (or ***take***) ***a whack at*** 〖俚〗對…攻擊;嘗試做…。***out of whack*** 走樣的;有毛病的。

whacked [hwækt; wækt] *adj.* 〖英俚〗筋疲力竭的。

whack·er ['hwækɚ; 'wækə] *n.* 〖俗〗①重擊者。②(同類中之)最大者;特別大的人或物。③大謊言。

whack·ing ['hwækɪŋ; 'wækiŋ] *adj.* 〖英俗〗巨大的;非常的。—*adv.* 甚;非常地。

whack·y ['hwækɪ; 'wæki] *adj.*, **whack·i·er, whack·i·est.** 〖俚〗=**wacky.**

whale**[1] [hwel; weil, hw-] *n.*, *pl.* **whales** or **whale,** *v.*, **whaled, whal·ing.** —*n.* ①鯨。②〖俗〗巨大的東西。a whale of*** 非常;巨大。*a whale of* a good time. 非常快樂的時候。—*v.i.* 捕鯨。

whale[2] *v.t.*, **whaled, whal·ing.** 〖俗〗①毆打;鞭打。②大敗。

whale·back ['hwel,bæk; 'weilbæk] *n.* 鯨背船(一種運貨汽船,有凸出之甲板)。

whale·boat ['hwel,bot; 'weilbout] *n.* ①捕鯨船。②一種救生船。

whale·bone ['hwel,bon; 'weilboun] *n.* ①鯨鬚。②鯨鬚製品。

whale·calf ['hwel,kɑf; 'weilkɑ:f] *n.* 幼鯨。

whale fin 鯨鬚(商業用品)。

whale fishery ①捕鯨。②捕鯨場。

whale line 捕鯨用的叉索。

whale·man ['hwelmən; 'weilmən] *n.*, *pl.* **-men.** 捕鯨者。

whale oil 鯨油。

whal·er[1] ['hwelɚ; 'weilə] *n.* ①捕鯨者。②捕鯨船。

whal·er[2] *n.* 〖俚〗①重擊者。②特大之物。

whal·er·y ['hwelərɪ; 'weiləri] *n.* 捕鯨;捕鯨業(=whale fishery).

whal·ing[1] ['hwelɪŋ; 'weiliŋ] *n.* 捕鯨。

whal·ing[2] *n.* 重擊;鞭笞。—*adj.* 極大的;不得了的。—*adv.* 非常地。

whal·ing-gun ['hwelɪŋ,gʌn; 'weiliŋgʌn] *n.* 捕鯨砲。

wham [hwæm; wæm] *n.* ①爆發聲;爆炸聲。②重擊。—*adv.* 突然。

whang [hwæŋ; wæŋ] *v.t.* ①清脆地擊打;用力重擊。②用力彈。—*v.i.* 〖方〗①發出咚咚之聲。②爲… 賣力;努力做。—*n.* ①清脆的一擊;重擊。②重擊聲。③〖蘇〗一片;一條。

*__wharf__ [hwɔrf; wɔːf, hw-] *n., pl.* **wharves** [hwɔrvz; wɔːvz, hw-], **wharfs** [hwɔrfs; wɔːfs, hw-], *v.* —*n.* 碼頭;埠頭。—*v.t.* ①供以碼頭。②將…放在碼頭上。③使靠碼頭;使在碼頭停泊。—*v.i.*在碼頭停泊。

wharf·age [ˈhwɔrfɪdʒ; ˈwɔːfidʒ] *n.* ①碼頭之使用(如裝卸或貯存貨物及寄碇等)。②埠頭稅;碼頭費。③碼頭(集合稱)。

wharf·in·ger [ˈhwɔrfɪndʒɚ; ˈwɔːfindʒə] *n.* 碼頭所有者;碼頭管理人。

‡**what** [ˈhwɑt; wɔt, ˈhw-] *pron., pl.* **what,** *adj., adv., interj., conj.* —*pron.* ①甚麼(作疑問代名詞用)。*What* happened? 發生了甚麼事情? *What?* 你說甚麼 (=*What* did you say)? ②作關係代名詞用 (=that which, those which, any that). I know *what* you mean. 我知道你的意思。③多少錢。*What* does it cost? 那要多少錢? ④用於插句子句中 (=the thing, fact that). ⑤表示另有下文,其他的可能等。Shall we go or *what?* 我們是去的好呢,還是另有妙計?⑥〖英〗你不同意嗎?(=Don't you agree?)(注意:這種用法的 what 爲一虛字,無實際意義,且附加於句末。) An unusual chap, *what?* 一個不平凡的人,你不同意嗎? ***and what have you;and what not*** 諸如此類;等等。***give one what for*** 〖俗〗懲罰某人。***I know what.*** 我有好主意。***I'll tell you what.*** 我要告訴你(做甚麼)。***no matter what*** 不管怎樣;無論如何。***so what?*** 〖俗〗那便怎麼樣? 那有甚麼稀罕?(表示不在乎、輕視等的用語)。***what about*** (or ***of***) **a.** 表有何消息。*What about* the others? 其他的人怎麼樣了? **b.** 徵求意見。*What about* making an early start? 早點開始怎樣? ***what-d'you-call-him*** (or ***-her, -it, etc.***); ***what's-his*** (or ***-her, -its***) ***-name*** 某先生;某人(當記不起其名字時用以稱之)。***what for*** 爲甚麼;爲何。***what if*** 假設…;如果…該怎麼辦。***what it takes*** 成功之必備條件。***what next?*** 下一個是甚麼(還能有比這更荒唐更不合理的麼)? ***what's what*** 〖俗〗事情之眞相。—*adj.* ①甚麼(作疑問形容詞)。*What* time is it? 現在是幾點鐘? ②所…的;任何的(作關係形容詞 =that...which, those ...which, any...that). I will give you *what* help I can. 我要盡我所能的幫助你。③多麼;何等(用以表示驚訝、懷疑、忿怒、喜愛等)。*What* fools they are! 他們是何等愚蠢的人! *What* impudence! 多麼鹵莽! ***what countryman*** 何國人。*What countryman* is he? 他是哪國人? ***what price*** 何價。*What price* glory? 光榮何價? ***what time*** …的時候 (=when). ***what way*** 如何 (=how). —*adv.* ①一部分由於;半因 〖with, by〗. ②多麼;何等。*What* bright colors! 多麼鮮艷的色彩!③多少;到何程度。*What* does it matter? 那有何關係? —*interj.* 怎麼! *What!* Are you late again? 怎麼!你又遲到了? —*conj.* 所…的;任何的。*What* this country needs is great leaders. 這個國家所需要的是偉大的領導者。***but what***(否定句用)不…(=that ...not). There wasn't a day *but what* it rained. 沒有一天不是下雨的。

what'd [ˈhwɑtɪd; ˈwɔtid] =**what did.** *What'd* you say? 你說甚麼?

what·e'er [hwɑtˈɛr; wɔtˈɛə] *pron., adj.* 〖詩〗 =**whatever.**

‡**what·ev·er** [hwɑtˈɛvɚ; wɔtˈevə, hw-] *pron.* ①不論甚麼;任何。Don't change your mind, *whatever* happens. 不論發生甚麼事情,你都不要改變主意。②〖俗〗究竟甚麼。*Whatever* do you mean? 你究竟是甚麼意思? —*adj.* 不論甚麼;任何的。*Whatever* orders he gives are obeyed. 不論他發布甚麼命令都被遵從。—*adv.* 無論如何。*Whatever,* I was committed. 無論如何我已作承諾。

what-is-it [hwɑtˈɪzɪt; wɔtˈizit] *n.* 〖俗〗①甚麼甚麼人(物)。②新玩意兒。

what'll [ˈhwɑtl̩; ˈwɔtl] ①=**what shall.** ②=**what will.**

what·not [ˈhwɑtˌnɑt; ˈwɔtnɔt] *n.* ①書架;放置裝飾品之格架。②等等(性質相似之物)。

what's [hwɑts; wɔts] ①=**what is.** *What's* his name? 他叫甚麼名字?②=**what has.** ③=**what does.**

what·sis [ˈhwɑtsɪs; ˈwɔtsis] *n.* 〖俗〗 [=**what-is-it.**]

what·so [ˈhwɑtso; ˈwɔtsou] *pron., adj.* 〖古〗=**whatever.**

what·so·e'er [ˌhwɑtsoˈɛr; ˌwɔtsouˈɛə] *pron., adj.* 〖詩〗 =**whatsoever.**

*__what·so·ev·er__ [ˌhwɑtsoˈɛvɚ; ˌwɔtsouˈevə] *pron., adj.* =**whatever.**

what've [ˈhwɑtəv; ˈwɔtəv] =**what have.**

wheal [hwil; wiːl] *n.* ①(被蚊蟲等咬後皮膚上所起之)小疙瘩。②小膿疱;風疹塊。③鞭痕;傷痕;條痕。

‡**wheat** [hwit; wiːt, hw-] *n.* 小麥。bearded *wheat.* 有芒(夏種)小麥。beardless (*or* bald) *wheat.* 無芒(多種)小麥。

wheat belt 產麥區。

wheat cake 麪粉煎餅。

wheat·ear¹ [ˈhwitˌɪr; ˈwiːtiə] *n.* 麥穗。

wheat·ear² *n.* 麥鶲(小鳥名)。

wheat·en [ˈhwitn̩; ˈwiːtn] *adj.* ①小麥製成的;麪粉做成的。②小麥的。

wheat germ 〖植物〗小麥胚。

wheat grass 〖植物〗芽草。

Wheat·stone bridge [ˈhwitstən~; ˈwiːtstən~] 〖物理〗惠斯登電橋(一種測定電阻之儀器,爲英國物理學家 Sir Charles Wheatstone 所發明)。(亦作 **Wheatstone's bridge**)

whee·dle [ˈhwidl̩; ˈwiːdl] *v.,* **-dled, -dling.** —*v.t.* ①以甜言蜜語勸誘…。②以諂媚獲得;以甜言蜜語騙去。—*v.i.* 諂媚;阿諛。***wheedle one's way*** 以諂媚達到目的。

‡**wheel** [hwil; wiːl, hw-] *n.* ①輪;車輪。②輪狀物。③舵輪。④紡車。⑤〖俗〗脚踏車。⑥車礫的刑車;刑輪。⑦原動力。the *wheels* of life. 生命的動力。⑧(*pl.*)機器。⑨轉動;旋轉;廻旋。⑩周期。⑪政治領袖;政黨頭子。***at the wheel*** **a.** 把舵。**b.** 控制。***break a fly*** (or ***butterfly***) ***upon the wheel*** 殺鷄用牛刀;小題大作。***break a person on the wheel*** 將某人處車礫刑。***Fortune's wheel*** 時運;流年。***go on wheels*** 順利進行。***man at the wheel*** 舵手;負責任之人。***measuring wheel*** 計距器;路程計。***put a spoke in one's wheel*** 阻礙某人之行動;掣肘。***put one's shoulder to the wheel*** 奮力協助一項事業的進展。***wheels within wheels*** 複雜的機構;複雜的環境;複雜的事情。—*v.t.* ①旋轉;使轉變方向。②以車載運。③裝以車輪。—*v.i.* ①旋轉;轉變方向;廻旋。Right (Left) *wheel!* 向右(左)轉! ②乘車旅行。We *wheeled* to Taipei. 我們乘車到臺北。③〖俗〗騎脚踏車。④順利前進;滾滾前進。***wheel and deal*** 運用權力或財勢爲所欲爲;在本行內或同業間縱橫捭闔。

wheel and axle 轆轤。

wheel·bar·row [ˈhwilˌbæro; ˈwiːl-ˌbærou] *n.* 手推車;獨輪手車。—*v.t.* 以手推車搬運。

wheel·base [ˈhwilˌbes; ˈwiːlbeis] *n.* 汽車前輪輪軸與後輪輪軸中心間之距離(以英寸表示之)。

wheel·chair [ˈhwilˈtʃɛr; ˈwiːlˈtʃɛə] 「*n.* (病人坐用之)輪椅。」

wheeled [hwild; wiːld] *adj.* 有輪的;用輪子行動的。*wheeled* traffic. 車輛交通。

wheel·er [ˈhwilɚ; ˈwiːlə] *n.* ①旋轉者。②後馬;轅馬。③有(特殊種類或數目的)輪之物。four-*wheeler.* 四輪馬車。④製輪者。

wheel·er-deal·er [ˈhwilɚˈdilɚ; ˈwiːləˈdiːlə] *n.* 〖俚〗運用權力或財勢為所欲為者;狡猾者;工於心計者。(亦作 **wheeler and dealer**)

wheel horse ①(馬車之)後馬;轅馬。「②工作有效而穩定之人。」

wheel·house [ˈhwilˌhaus; ˈwiːlhaus] *n.* 〖造船〗舵手室。

wheel·ing [ˈhwilɪŋ; ˈwiːliŋ] *n.* ①車運。②〖俗〗乘脚踏車。③(從行車上看的)路之好壞。④廻轉;輪轉。

wheel·less [ˈhwillɪs; ˈwiːllis] *adj.* ①無輪子的。②無車輛的。

wheel·man [ˈhwilmən; ˈwiːlmən] *n., pl.* **-men.** ①舵手。②乘脚踏車的人。

wheel of fortune ①代表人事浮沈的命運之輪。②一種轉動的賭具。

wheel of life 〖佛教〗①輪廻。②輪廻圖。

wheels·man [ˈhwilzmən; ˈwiːlzmən] *n., pl.* **-men.** 舵手。

wheel static 汽車中收音機因車輪旋「轉而起的雜音。」

wheel watch 守舵的值班。

wheel·wright [ˈhwilˌraɪt; ˈwiːlrait] *n.* 製造或修理車或車輪的人;車匠。

wheel·y [ˈhwilɪ; ˈwiːli] *adj.* 輪子的;輪狀的。

wheen [hwin; wiːn] *adj.* 〖英方〗少許「的。—*n.* 〖英方〗少許。」

wheeze [hwiz; wiːz] *v.,* **wheezed, wheez·ing,** *n.* —*v.t. & v.i.* 喘息;哮喘;哮而說。—*n.* ①喘息;哮喘。②〖俚〗格言;故事;俏皮話;老生常談的笑話。—**wheez·er,** *n.* —**wheez·ing·ly,** *adv.*

wheez·y [ˈhwizɪ; ˈwiːzi] *adj.,* **wheez·i·er, wheez·i·est.** 喘息聲的;哮喘聲的。

whelk[1] [hwɛlk; welk] *n.* 〖動物〗峨螺。

whelk[2] *n.* 粉刺;面皰;疙瘩。

whelm [hwɛlm; welm] *v.t.* ①〖詩〗淹沒;吞沒;捲沒。②〖詩〗打擊;壓倒。

whelp [hwɛlp; welp] *n.* ①幼犬;(獅、虎等之)幼兒。②〖蔑〗孩子;小鬼;小子。③扣鏈輪之齒。④(常 *pl.*)轆轤圓筒上之縱肋。—*v.i. & v.t.* ①(獸)產子。②產生。—**less,** *adj.*

‡**when** [hwɛn; wen, hw-] *adv.* ①何時;甚麼時候。*When* can you come? 你甚麼時候能來? ②從前境遇較差時。—*conj.* ①當…時;在…的時候。A dog wags his tail *when* pleased. 狗在高興的時候搖尾巴。②在其時;在那時。Sunday is the day *when* I am least busy. 星期日是我最不忙的日子。③每逢。④儘管;雖然。⑤在…以後。I'll go *when* I've had dinner. 在我吃了飯以後,我就要走了。⑥相反;而。—*pron.* ①何時。Since *when* have they had a car? 他們從甚麼時候起有了一輛汽車? ②那時。—*n.* 時間。the *when* and where of an act. 一項行為的時間與地點。

when·as [hwɛnˈæz; wenˈæz] *conj.* 〖古〗=**when; while; whereas.**

***whence** [hwɛns; wens, hw-] *adv.* ①從何處。*Whence* do you come? 貴鄉(國)何處? ②由何;何以。*Whence* comes it that…? 何以會發生…的事? —*conj.* 來處;根源;原因。He told *whence* he came. 他說明了他的來處。—*n.* 由來;來源。

whence·so·ev·er [ˌhwɛnsoˈɛvɚ; ˌwensouˈevə] *adv.* 無論從何處;無論源出何處;無論原因為何。

when·e'er [hwɛnˈɛr; wenˈɛə] *adv.* 「〖詩〗=**whenever.**」

‡**when·ev·er** [hwɛnˈɛvɚ, hwən-; wenˈevə, wən-, hw-] *conj.* 不論何時;每逢。I will see him *whenever* he likes to come. 不論甚麼時候他高興來我隨時會見他。—*adv.* 甚麼時候(=when ever). *Whenever* did he tell you that? 他甚麼時候告訴你的?

when·so·ev·er [ˌhwɛnsoˈɛvɚ; ˌwensouˈevə] *conj., adv.* =**whenever.**

‡**where** [hwɛr; wɛə, hw-] *adv.* ①何處;在何處;向何處;從何處。*Where* do you live? 你住在甚麼地方? *Where* am I wrong? 我甚麼地方錯了? ②在哪方面;在哪一點上。*Where* is the harm in trying? 試試看又有何妨? —*conj.* ①在那裏;在該處;…的地方。Go *where* you like. 你可以隨意到甚麼地方去。*Where* there is a will, there is a way. 有志者事竟成。②在那種情況;在那方面;那樣。Some people worry *where* it does no good. 有些人作無謂的憂慮。—*n.* ①何處。*Where* have you come from? 你從何處來? ②地點;場所。The *wheres* and whens are important. 地點與時間是重要的。

where·a·bouts [ˌhwɛrəˈbauts, *n.* ˈhwɛrəˌbauts; ˈwɛərəˈbauts, *n.* ˈwɛərəbauts] *adv.* 在何處。—*conj.* 在何處。—*n.* (作 *sing.* or *pl.* 解)下落。Her present *whereabouts* is unknown. 她現在下落不明。

***where·as** [hwɛrˈæz; wɛərˈæz, hw-] *conj.* ①然而;而;雖然(=but, while). I hate John, *whereas* you merely dislike him. 我憎恨約翰,而你只是不喜歡他而已。②就…而論;既然;鑒於。—*n.* 正式文件(尤指用 whereas 開頭之文件)之開場白。to read the *whereases* in the will. 讀遺囑中的前言。

where·at [hwɛrˈæt; wɛərˈæt] *adv.* 〖古〗①因何;為何(=at what). ②因之;在其上(=at which). —*conj.* 因之;於是。

where·by [hwɛrˈbaɪ; wɛəˈbai, hw-] *adv.* ①為何;如何。②因此;由是。

where'd [hwɛrd; wɛəd] =**where did.**

wher·e'er [hwɛrˈɛr; wɛərˈɛə] *conj., adv.* 〖詩〗=**wherever.**

where·for [hwɛrˈfɔr; wɛəˈfɔː] *adv.* 對它;為它(=for which).

where·fore [ˈhwɛrˌfor; ˈwɛəfɔː, ˈhw-] *adv.* ①為何;何故。②因此;所以。—*conj.* 因此。—*n.* 理由;原因。

where·from [hwɛrˈfrɑm; wɛəˈfrɔm] *adv.* 自其處;自何處;由是。

where·in [hwɛrˈɪn; wɛərˈin, hw-] *adv.* ①在何處;何在。②在其中;在該處;當其時(=in which).

where·in·to [hwɛrˈɪntu; wɛərˈintu] 「*adv.* 向其中。」

where'll [hwɛrl; wɛəl] ①=**where shall.** ②=**where will.**

where·of [hwɛrˈɑv; wɛərˈɔv] *adv.* ①關於它;對於它;關於其人;對於其人(=of which, of whom, of what). ②由甚麼(用於疑問句中,=of what).

where·on [hwɛrˈɑn; wɛərˈɔn] *adv.* ①

在其上 (=on which). ②在甚麼上面 (用於疑問句中, =on what).

where·o·ver [hwɛr'ovɚ; wɛər'ouvə] *adv.* 在其上 (=over which).

where're ['hwɛrɚ; 'wɛərə] =where are.

where's [hwɛrz; wɛəz] ① =where is. ②〖俗〗=where has.

where·so·ev·er [ˌhwɛrso'ɛvɚ; ˌwɛəsou'evə] *conj., adv.* =wherever.

where·through [hwɛr'θru; wɛə'θru:] *adv.* 經其處;經此;由其處。

where·to [hwɛr'tu; wɛə'tu:] *adv.* ①到那地方 (=to what, to which, where). ②向何處;何以;爲甚麼。③對之;對彼。

where·un·der [hwɛr 'ʌndɚ; wɛər'ʌndə] *adv.* 其下。

where·un·to [hwɛr'ʌntu; ˌwɛərʌn'tu:] *adv., conj.* 〖古〗=whereto.

where·up·on [ˌhwɛrə'pɑn; ˌwɛərə'pɔn, ˌhw-] *adv.* 於是;因此(=upon which, at which). —*conj.* 在甚麼上面; 在其上 (=upon what, upon which).

where've [hwɛrv; wɛəv] =where have.

***wher·ev·er** [hwɛr 'ɛvɚ; wɛər'evə] *conj., adv.* 何處;無論何處。Sit *wherever* you like. 請隨便坐。He will be happy *wherever* he lives. 他隨遇而安。

where·with [hwɛr'wɪθ; wɛə'wiθ] *adv., conj.* ①用甚麼 (=with what). ②用那個 (= with what, with which).

where·with·al [*n.*'hwɛrwɪðˌɔl;'wɛəwiðɔ:l *adv., conj.* ˌhwɛrwɪð'ɔl;ˌwɛəwi'ðɔ:l] *n.* 必要的方法、手段或所需的金錢。—*adv., conj.* 〖古〗用甚麼;用那個。

wher·ry ['hwɛrɪ; 'weri] *n., pl.* **-ries,** *v.,* **-ried, -ry·ing.** —*n.* ①擺渡船;舢板。②一人划的(競賽用)小舟; 輕舟。③〖英俗〗小平底船。—*v.t.* 用此種船運輸。—*v.i.* 駕此種船。

whet [hwɛt; wet] *v.,* **whet·ted, whet·ting,** *n.* —*v.t.* ①磨。②使變尖銳; 使變興奮。—*n.* ①磨。②磨利之物。③開胃物;使興奮之物;刺激物。④時候;時間。⑤〖方〗一陣工作。

‡**wheth·er** ['hwɛðɚ; 'weðə, 'hw-] *conj.* ①是否。Ask him *whether* he can come. 問他是否能來。②…抑或…〖or〗. *Whether* we go or not matters little. 我們去不去沒有甚麼關係。③不論。*Whether* sick or well, she is always cheerful. 不論在生病還是健康的時候, 她總是高高興興的。***whether or no*** 總之;無論如何;必定。I'll go *whether or no.* 我無論如何要走。—*pron.* 〖古〗兩者中的哪一個。—*n.* 可能之選擇。

whet·stone ['hwɛtˌston; 'wetstoun] *n.* 磨石。

whet·ter ['hwɛtɚ; 'wetə] *n.* ①磨刀者。②刺激物。

whew [hwju; wju:] *interj.* 哎呀!唷!(表驚異、厭惡、沮喪、鬆一口氣等之驚歎聲)。—*n.* 哎呀;唷;驚歎聲。

whey [hwe; wei] *n.* 乳漿。—**ey,** *adj.*

‡**which** [hwɪtʃ; witʃ, hw-] *pron.* ①哪一個;哪些;何者;誰。*Which* do you want? 你要哪一個? ②(用於從屬子句中)該物;該事;該種情形。This is the book *which* I chose. 這就是我所選擇的書。③(而) 這個; (但) 那個。④任何其中之一。Choose *which* you like best. 任選其中你最喜愛的一個。***which is which*** 哪一個是哪一個 (用作疑問詞或關係詞)。I do not know *which* is *which.* 我不知哪個是哪個。—*adj.* ①哪一個;哪些。*Which* book did you choose? 你選擇了哪一本書?②(用於從屬句中)其;該。③無論如何。④隨便; 隨意。Use *which* method you prefer. 你愛用甚麼方法便用甚麼方法。⑤如前述的;已經提到的。***every which way*** 各方面;四面八方;凌亂。***Which end up?*** 那究竟是怎麼一回事? ***which way*** 如何。*Which way* shall we do it? 我們應如何做?

***which·ev·er** [hwɪtʃ'ɛvɚ; witʃ'evə, hw-] *pron.* 不論何者;任何。Take *whichever* you wish. 隨便拿哪一個。—*adj.* 任何一個。*Whichever* side wins, I shall be satisfied. 不論哪一邊得勝, 我都滿意。

which·so·ev·er [ˌhwɪtʃso'ɛvɚ;ˌwitʃsou'evə] *pron., adj.* =whichever.

whid·ah bird ['hwɪdə~; 'widə~] 非洲長尾鳥。

whiff[1] [hwɪf; wif] *n., pl.* **whiffs.** ①一陣空氣; 一陣氣味; 一吹; 一陣; 一噴。②一點點;微量。—*v.t. & v.i.* 噴;吹;發出淡淡的氣味;抽(煙斗等);吸煙。

whiff[2] *n.* 一種比目魚。

whif·fet ['hwɪfɪt; 'wifit] *n.* ①輕輕的一吹。②〖美俗〗小的或無足輕重的人或獸; 小人物(輕蔑語)。③小狗。

whif·fle ['hwɪfl̩; 'wifl] *v.,* **whif·fled, whif·fling.** —*v.i.* ①(風)陣陣輕吹。②猶疑不決;多變;改變主意。③擺動; 顫動。④發出輕吹聲。⑤〖英方〗虛耗時間; 懶散。—*v.t.* ①吹;吹散。②急搖;急揮。③使猶疑;支吾其詞。

whif·fler[1] ['hwɪflɚ; 'wiflə] *n.* ①時常改變意見者; 興趣經常改變者。②辯論時猶豫不決或模稜兩可者。

whif·fler[2] *n.* 古時持旗或刀斧爲遊行行列開道者。

whif·fle·tree ['hwɪfl̩ˌtri; 'wifltri:] *n.* =whippletree.

whiff of grapeshot 鎮壓暴動之凶殘或激烈的方法。

Whig [hwɪg; wig] *n.* ①十九世紀的美國自由黨員。②英國維新黨員。③(美國獨立運動時之)革命黨員。—*adj.* 由 Whigs 所組成的;與 Whigs 有關的;似 Whigs 的。

Whig·ger·y ['hwɪgərɪ; 'wigəri] *n., pl.* **-ger·ies.** Whig 黨之主義。

Whig·gish ['hwɪgɪʃ; 'wigiʃ] *adj.* 具有 Whig 黨之特色的。—**ly,** *adv.*

‡**while** [hwaɪl; wail, hw-] *n., conj., v.,* **whiled, whil·ing.** —*n.* 時間。for a *while.* 暫時。for a long *while.* 許久。after a *while.* 過一會兒。***all the while*** 一直;始終。***at whiles*** 有時;間或。***between whiles*** 有時;間或。***in a little while*** 不久;卽刻。***once in a while*** 有時;偶爾。***the while*** 其間; 當…之時; 同時。***worth (one's) while*** 值得。It isn't *worth while* doing that. 那件事不值得做。—*conj.* ①當…的時候。Please be quiet *while* I am talking to you. 當我對你們說話的時候, 請不要作聲。②雖然; 而。He went out, *while* I stayed at home. 他出去了, 而我留在家中。③同時; 同樣也。—*v.t.* 消磨; 度過〖常 away〗. The children *while* away many afternoons on the beach. 孩子們在海灘上消磨許多下午。

whiles [hwaɪlz; wailz] *adv.* 〖古、方〗①有時。②其間; 其時。—*conj.* 〖古〗=while.

whi·lom ['hwaɪləm; 'wailəm] *adj. & adv.* 〖古〗以前的(地);往昔的(地)。

***whilst** [hwaɪlst; wailst, hw-] *conj.* 〖古、方〗=while. —*adv.* 〖古、方〗①有時;時時。②同時;當其時。

whim [hwɪm; wim, hw-] *n.* ①突然的念頭;迅速消逝的念頭; 奇想; 怪念頭。②〖採

礦】起礦轆轤。

whim·brel [ˈhwɪmbrəl; ˈwimbrəl] *n.* (歐洲產的一種)杓鷸。

***whim·per** [ˈhwɪmpɚ; ˈwimpə, ˈhw-] *v.i.* ①啜泣;嗚咽;抽噎地哭。②(犬等)咿咿低吠。—*v.t.* 以嗚咽之聲發出; 抽噎地講出。—*n.* 嗚嗚聲;啜泣;唏噓。

whim·si·cal [ˈhwɪmzɪkl; ˈwimzikl] *adj.* ①多幻想的; 古怪的。②多遐想的; 多奇念的。③難以意料的;無原則的。—**ly,** *adv.*

whim·si·cal·i·ty [ˌhwɪmzəˈkælətɪ; ˌwimziˈkæliti] *n.* 奇癖;奇想; 狂妄; 古怪的言詞及行動;非理性的妄行。

whim·sy [ˈhwɪmzɪ; ˈwimzi] *n., pl.* **-sies.** ①古怪的想法; 怪念頭。②奇想; 離奇的情節。③古怪奇異的事物。④無原則的作風或行爲;無原則;任意。(亦作 **whimsey**)

whim·sy-wham·sy [ˈhwɪmzɪ-ˈhwæmzɪ; ˈwimziˈwæmzi] *n., pl.* **-sies.** 無原則之事物。

whim-wham [ˈhwɪmˌhwæm; ˈwim-wæm] *n.* ①任何奇怪之事物。②(*pl.*)〖俗〗緊張;惶恐。

whin [hwɪn; win] *n.* 〖英〗〖植物〗金雀花。

whin·chat [ˈhwɪnˌtʃæt; ˈwin-tʃæt] *n.* 歐洲產的一種野鶲。

whine [hwaɪn; wain, hw-] *v.,* **whined, whin·ing,** *n.* —*v.i.* ①發低哀之鼻聲; 出哀聲。②抱怨; 發牢騷。③發長鳴。—*v.t.* 以哀聲說出;以怨聲道出。—*n.* ①低哀之鼻聲; 哀聲。②抱怨;牢騷。③長鳴。

whing·er [ˈhwɪŋɚ; ˈwiŋə] *n.* 〖古〗短劍;短刀。

whin·ny [ˈhwɪnɪ; ˈwini] *n., pl.* **-nies,** *v.,* **-nied, -ny·ing.** —*n.* 馬嘶聲。—*v.i.* 馬嘶。—*v.t.* 以嘶聲表示。

whin·stone [ˈhwɪnˌston; ˈwinstoun] *n.* 〖礦〗黑硅石;玄武岩。

whin·y [ˈhwaɪnɪ; ˈwaini] *adj.,* **whin·i·er, whin·i·est.** 愛抱怨的。(亦作 **whiney**)

whip** [hwɪp; wip, hw-] *n., v.,* **whipped** or **whipt, whip·ping.** —*n.* ①鞭。②鞭韃。③由打蛋、攪奶油做成的餐後甜點心。④政黨的國會副領袖; 政黨在議會中的首腦人物。⑤獵犬指揮員。⑥馬車夫。He is a good (bad) *whip.* 他是個優良(低劣)的馬車夫。⑦連皮帶之滑車。⑧彈性。a whip round*** 捐錢;募捐。***have the whip hand of*** 居領導地位;控制。—*v.t.* ①鞭打; 笞責。②攪(蛋以及奶油等)。*whipped* cream. 攪打過的乳脂。③迅速突然移動或攫取。④〖美俗〗擊敗; 勝過。to *whip* the field. 獲全勝。to *whip* the creation. 天下無敵。⑤別上(針縫);縫上(衣邊)。⑥纏;繞(繩索); 緊繞繩索於(棍)。⑦揮擲釣魚線。⑧在(河上)釣魚。⑨激起; 鼓起 〖up〗. —*v.i.* ①迅速而忽然地移動或經過。②飄盪; 揮動。***whip in***(or ***together***) a. 用鞭子召攏 (獵犬)。b. 召集 (黨員)。***whip into shape*** 予以强制改革或改善。***whip off*** 匆匆地寫。***whip out*** 突然喊出。***whip up*** 〖俗〗 a. 迅速地計劃或湊攏。b. 煽動; 挑逗; 激起。 to *whip up* a riot. 煽起暴動。—**like,** *adj.*

whip·cord [ˈhwɪpˌkɔrd; ˈwipkɔːd] *n.* ①鞭繩。②(外科手術縫傷口用的)腸線(= catgut)。③一種表面有凸起斜紋的堅牢織物。—*adj.* 緊的;頑强的;健碩的。

whip hand ①執鞭之手; 右手。②優勢; 有利地位;控制。

whip·lash [ˈhwɪpˌlæʃ; ˈwip-læʃ] *n.* ①鞭索。②(亦作 **whiplash injury**)因頭部突然朝前或朝後之運動而造成的頸傷。—*v.t.* 用鞭索抽打;懲罰;苛待;打擊。

whipped [hwɪpt; wipt] *adj.* ①受到鞭笞的。②被擊敗的;被征服的。③攪成泡沫狀的。

whip·per [ˈhwɪpɚ; ˈwipə] *n.* ①鞭打者;笞責者;責斥者。②執行鞭打處罰之法院官吏。③縫衣邊者; 滾邊者。④〖英〗卸船時管小滑輪者。⑤(造紙時)打碎布以去其污之機器。⑥一種簡易打棉機。⑦特別好或有效之物。

whip·per-in [ˈhwɪpɚˈɪn; ˈwipərˈin] *n., pl.* **whip·pers-in.** ①〖英〗狩獵時管理獵犬的助手; 獵犬管理員。②國會中之政黨紀律幹事 (=party whip).

whip·per·snap·per [ˈhwɪpɚˌsnæpɚ; ˈwipəˌsnæpə] *n.* 傲氣十足的年輕人;自以爲很重要的小人物。

whip·pet [ˈhwɪpɪt; ˈwipit] *n.* ①一種健跑的狗(用於追蹤或賽犬)。②一種輕型戰車。

whip·ping [ˈhwɪpɪŋ; ˈwipiŋ] *n.* ①鞭笞。②〖俗〗敗北。③用以綑縛之繩索。④攪拌。

whipping boy ①代人受罰者; 代人受過者。②〖古〗代替王子或貴族受罰之同學。

whipping post 鞭笞時綁縛犯人的柱子。

whipping top 陀螺。

Whip·ple [ˈhwɪpl̩; ˈwipl, ˈhw-] *n.* 惠普爾 (George Hoyt, 1878–, 美國病理學家, 曾獲1934年諾貝爾醫學獎)。

whip·ple·tree [ˈhwɪpl̩ˌtri; ˈwipltriː] *n.* 馬車前部兩端繫曳繩之橫木。

whip·poor·will [ˌhwɪpɚˈwɪl; ˈwip-puəˌwil] *n.* 北美東部所產之夜間出沒的怪鴟。

whip·py [ˈhwɪpɪ; ˈwipi] *adj.* ①〖俗〗像鞭的。②易彎曲的;有彈性的。—**whip·pi·ness,** *n.*

whip-round [ˈhwɪpˌraund; ˈwip-raund] *n.* 〖主英〗慈善募款。

whip·saw [ˈhwɪpˌsɔ; ˈwipsɔː] *n.* ①一種窄條之鉤齒鋸(通常長5至7½英尺)。②(一種縱方向鋸木料用的) 雙人鋸。—*v.t.* ①以鉤齒鋸鋸。②在同一局牌戲中擊敗(某人)兩次。③使高價買而低價賣或高價賣低價買。④同時使兩方面吃虧或在兩方面失敗。⑤使鷸蚌相爭而坐收漁人之利。—*v.i.* ①反覆彎折。②採用使甲乙相鬥之辦法。

whip scorpion 蠍蛛屬之蜘蛛。

whip-shaped [ˈhwɪpˌʃept; ˈhwip-ʃeipt] *adj.* 細長如鞭的。

whip snake 〖動物〗鞭蛇。(亦作**whip-snake**)

whip·ster [ˈhwɪpstɚ; ˈwipstə] *n.* = **whippersnapper.**

whip·stitch [ˈhwɪpˌstɪtʃ; ˈwipstitʃ] *v.t.* & *v.i.* 縫合; 絎(縫); 以疏落針脚縫合。—*n.* ①疏落縫合之針脚。②裁縫 (輕蔑語)。③〖美俗〗一利那。

whip·stock [ˈhwɪpˌstɑk; ˈwipstɔk] *n.* 鞭柄。

whip·worm [ˈhwɪpˌwɝm; ˈwipwəːm] *n.* (寄生腸中之)鞭蟲。

***whir(r)** [hwɝ; wəː, hw-] *n., v.,* **whirred, whir·ring.** —*n.* 呼呼的聲音。—*v.i.* 呼呼地急速轉動; 颼颼地飛。—*v.t.* 呼呼聲中急速移動或携載。

***whirl** [hwɝl; wəːl, hw-] *v.i.* ①廻旋; 旋轉; 循環而行。②急走; 急動。③(頭腦)眩暈; (思緒)紛亂。My head is *whirling.* 我頭昏了。④轉向。—*v.t.* ①使廻旋; 旋轉。②迅速載走。—*n.* ①廻旋;旋轉。②眩暈;紛亂。His brain was in a *whirl.* 他的頭腦昏了。③旋轉物。④一連串的事件或聚會。⑤急動。⑥嘗試;一試。—**er,** *n.* —**ing·ly,** *adv.*

whirl·a·bout [ˈhwɝləˌbaut; ˈwəːlə-ˌbaut] *n.* ①廻旋;旋轉;急轉。②急旋之物。③旋轉木馬。④數蟲科之一種甲蟲。—*adj.* 廻旋的;旋轉的;急轉的。

whirl·i·gig [ˈhwɝlɪˌgɪg; ˈwəːligig] *n.* ①陀螺;紙摺之旋螺。②旋轉木馬(一種供兒童遊戲之裝置)。③鼓蟲科之一種甲蟲; 鼓蟲(= whirligig beetle). ④旋轉;旋轉運動。⑤人世的滄桑;時景之轉變。⑥輕率浮躁的人。
whirl·pool [ˈhwɝlˌpul; ˈwəːlpuːl] *n.* ①漩渦。②似漩渦之物;紛亂。—*v.i.* 旋轉;廻旋。
whirl·wind** [ˈhwɝlˌwɪnd; ˈwəːlwind, ˈhw-] *n.* ①旋風。②似旋風之物。the *whirlwind* of politics. 政治如旋風的發展。reap the whirlwind*** 自作自受。***sow the wind and reap the whirlwind*** 作惡終獲重大之果報(惡事之報, 果大於因)。—*v.i.* 旋風一般地急動;疾駛。—*adj.* 匆匆忙忙的;迅速的。
whirl·y·bird [ˈhwɝlɪˌbɝd; ˈwəːlibəːd] *n.* 〖俗〗直昇機。
whish [hwɪʃ; wiʃ] *v.i.* 作呼呼聲而動。—*v.t.* 作呼呼聲而趕。—*n.* 呼呼之聲。
whisk [hwɪsk; wisk, hw-] *v.t.* ①拂;掃;揮。②使急動;迅速挾帶。③打;攪拌(蛋、奶油等)。to *whisk* eggs. 打蛋。—*v.i.* 急動;急走。—*n.* ①拂; 掃; 揮。②(刷衣服用的)小刷帚。③急行;急動。④(蛋、奶油等的)攪拌器。egg *whisk*. 攪蛋器。
whisk broom 刷衣服用的一種短柄「小掃帚或刷子。
***whisk·er** [ˈhwɪskɚ; ˈwiskə, ˈhw-] *n.* ①(常 *pl.*) 頰髭;髯。②貓等之鬚。③一根髯鬚。—**ed,** *adj.*
whisk·er·age [ˈhwɪskərɪdʒ; ˈwiskə-ridʒ] *n.* 頰髭之蓄留方式。
whisk·er·y [ˈhwɪskərɪ; ˈwiskəri] *adj.* ①生長頰髭的。②古老的;年長的。
***whis·key** [ˈhwɪskɪ; ˈwiski, ˈhw-] *n., pl.* **-keys.** ①威士忌酒。②威士忌酒之一飲。—*adj.* (似)威士忌酒的。(亦作 **whisky**)
Whis·key *n.* 通訊電碼, 代表字母W.
whiskey sour 威士忌加檸檬汁、糖、蘇打水、碎冰等混合攪拌製成的一種鷄尾酒。
‡**whis·per** [ˈhwɪspɚ; ˈwispə, ˈhw-] *v.i.* ①低聲而語;耳語。②(樹葉等)作沙沙聲;作颯颯聲 (=rustle). ③悄悄說。—*v.t.* 低聲述說;祕密告訴。It is *whispered* that.... 據祕密傳聞…。—*n.* ①耳語;私語。to speak in a *whisper*. 低聲而語。②祕密的傳聞。③沙沙聲;颯颯聲。④悄悄之語。⑤微量。—**er,** *n.*
whis·per·ing [ˈhwɪspərɪŋ; ˈwispəriŋ] *n.* ①交頭接耳之談話。②謠言;流言蜚語。③低語之聲。—*adj.* ①耳語的;發出耳語的。②似耳語的。③愛撥弄是非的;愛耳語的。④用耳語交談的。—**ly,** *adv.*
whispering campaign 有計畫的誹謗性造謠。
whispering gallery (or **dome**) 低語高響廊(一種由於牆之回音作用, 使遠方可以聽見低語的圓頂廊)。
whis·per·y [ˈhwɪspərɪ; ˈwispəri] *adj.* ①低聲的。②充滿耳語的;充滿神祕之低聲的。
whist[1] [hwɪst; wist] *interj.* 靜些!別鬧!噓!—*adj.* 〖古〗靜默的;無聲的。—*v.t.* 使靜。—*v.i.* 靜默。—*n.* 靜; 靜默。Hold your *whist!* 靜些! 別響!(亦作 **whisht**)
whist[2] *n.* 四人用全副撲克牌玩的一種兩組對打的牌戲。
‡**whis·tle** [ˈhwɪsl; ˈwisl, ˈhw-] *v.,* **-tled, -tling,** *n.* —*v.i.* ①吹口笛;吹哨;鳴汽笛;發嘯聲。②帶嘯聲而行進。—*v.t.* ①吹嘯出 (曲調)。②用口哨喊召、通知或指揮。***whistle for*** 〖俗〗空想;徒然想得到;得不到。***whistle in the dark*** 吹口哨壯膽子。—*n.* ①口笛聲; 汽笛聲; 嘯聲。②口笛; 汽笛。police *whistle*. 警笛。***blow the whistle on*** 〖俚〗使 (某人、機關等) 中止某項行動。***pay too dear for one's whistle*** 得不償失。***wet one's whistle*** 〖俗〗喝杯(酒)。—**a·ble,** *adj.*
whis·tle-blow·er [ˈhwɪslˌbloɚ; ˈwislˌblouə, ˈhw-] *n.* 〖主美俚〗揭人短處者;打小報告者。
whis·tler [ˈhwɪslɚ; ˈwislə] *n.* ①吹口哨者。②令人讚美之人或物。
whis·tle-stop [ˈhwɪslˌstɑp; ˈwislstɔp] *adj., v.,* **-stopped, -stop·ping.** —*adj.* ①在小城鎮作短暫停留的。②競選活動的。—*v.i.* 作競選活動。—*v.t.* 在…作競選活動。—**per,** *n.*
whis·tling [ˈhwɪslɪŋ; ˈwisliŋ, ˈhw-] *n.* ①吹口哨。②馬的哮喘症。—*adj.* 發出口哨聲的;聽起來像口哨聲的。—**ly,** *adv.*
Whit [hwɪt; wit] *adj.* 聖神降臨節的。
whit [hwɪt; wit, hw-] *n.* 一點。
‡**white** [hwaɪt; wait, hw-] *n., adj.,* **whit·er, whit·est,** *v., adv.* —*n.* ①白; 白色。②白色之物; 白色的或無色的部分。③白衣服。nurses in *white*. 穿白衣的護士。④白種人。⑤鵠中心的白色部分。⑥圖畫中的空白部分。⑦保皇黨;極端保守者。⑧白酒。***in the white*** 尚未完工之狀態。—*adj.* ①白的;白色的。②蒼白無血色的。Her lips were *white* with fear. 她的嘴唇因恐懼而發白。③淡色的。*white* wines. 淡色的酒。④白種的。a *white* man. 白種人。⑤多雪的。a *white* winter. 多雪的多天。⑥空白的。a *white* space. 空白的地方。⑦純潔的;無瑕疵的。a *white* spirit. 純潔的心靈。⑧〖俗〗忠實的;可靠的;公平的。⑨穿白衣服的。⑩非常保守的;反動的。⑪好的;有益的。⑫無害的; 不傷人的; 無惡意的。⑬〖英俗〗(咖啡)含牛奶的。***bleed white*** 〖俗〗使喪失所有; 剝奪…資源; 使筋疲力竭。—*v.t.* 〖印刷〗在…留空白〖常 out〗。—*adv.* 公平地;公正地。They treated us *white*. 他們公平地對待我們。
white alert ①解除警報訊號。②(攻擊後)恢復正常。
white alloy 假銀。
white ant 白蟻。
white-ant [ˈhwaɪtˌænt; ˈwaitˈænt] *v.t.* 祕密顛覆或摧毀。
white·bait [ˈhwaɪtˌbet; ˈwaitbeit] *n., pl.* **-bait.** 銀魚; 任何不去腸及鱗而烹食之小魚。
white bear 白熊。
white·beard [ˈhwaɪtˌbɪrd; ˈwaitbiəd] *n.* 白鬚老翁。
white belt 〖柔道〗初學者繫腰之白帶。
white blood cell 白血球。(亦作 **white corpuscle**)
white book 白皮書(德國、捷克、日本等國家之政府所發表之報告書)。
white·cap [ˈhwaɪtˌkæp; ˈwaitkæp] *n.* ①浪頭的白泡沫;有白泡沫的浪頭。②(W-)〖美〗用私刑或其他恐怖辦法驅逐他人之恐怖分子(因其戴白色頭巾故名)。
white cell 白血球。
white coal 作爲動力來源之水。(亦作 **white fuel**)
white-col·lar [ˈhwaɪtˈkɑlɚ; ˈwaitˈkɔlə] *adj.* 〖美〗白領階級的(指勞心之職業)。
whit·ed [ˈhwaɪtɪd; ˈwaitid] *adj.* ①經過漂白的;被弄白了的。②外面覆有白色之物的。
whited sepulcher 僞君子;僞善者。
white dwarf 〖天文〗白矮星。
white elephant ①白象。②昂貴但使用價值低之物。③物主不需要但不易脫手之物。
white-faced [ˈhwaɪtˈfest; ˈwaitˈfeist] *adj.* ①臉色蒼白的。②額上有白斑的(馬等)。③表面或正面呈白色的。
white feather 懦弱的象徵。
white·fish [ˈhwaɪtˌfɪʃ; ˈwaitfiʃ] *n.,*

pl. -fish, -fish·es. ①鮭科淡水魚之一種。②任何白色或銀灰色之魚(如鰷魚等)。③白鯨。

white flag 白旗(表示停火或投降之標幟)。***hoist*** (***show,*** or ***wave***) ***the white flag*** 放棄;讓步;投降。

White Friar Carmel 派之修道士。

white gold 金與鎳、鉑等之合金(鑲珠寶用)。

white goods ①漂白過的棉麻織物。②床單、桌布等。③大型家庭電器用具如冰箱、洗衣機、火爐等。

white gourd 多瓜。(亦作**wax gourd**)

white-haired (ˈhwaɪtˌhɛrd; ˈwaitˈhɛəd) *adj.* ①白髮的。②長有白毛的;長滿白毛的。③〖俗〗得寵的;寵兒的。Our engineer is the *white-haired* boy of the missile division. 我們的工程師在火箭製造部是個大紅人。

White·hall (ˈhwaɪtˌhɔl; ˈwaitˈhɔːl) *n.* 〖英〗①(亦作 **Whitehall Palace**)昔時英國在倫敦中部之一皇宮(由 Henry III 所建)。②倫敦之主要街名(在議院及 Trafalgar 廣場之間,爲倫敦市內各政府機關所在地)。③英國政府;英國的政策。—*adj.* 英國政府的。

white-hand·ed (ˈhwaɪt ˈhændɪd; ˈwaitˈhændid) *adj.* ①有白手的。②不勞動的。③純潔的;正直的。④〖動物〗有白掌的。

White·head (ˈhwaɪthɛd; ˈwaithed) *n.* 懷特海 (William, 1715–1785, 英國劇作家, 於1757–85爲桂冠詩人)。

white-head·ed (ˈhwaɪtˈhɛdɪd; ˈwaitˈhedid) *adj.* ①白頭的;白髮的。②幸運的。the *white-headed* boy of the new generation. 新的一代中之幸運兒。

white heat①白熱;熾熱(1500°–1600°C)。②激情;極度之緊張。

white hope 〖俚〗①與黑人拳王爭奪錦標的白人拳擊選手。②人們寄以很大希望者。

white horse 白浪頭。

white-hot (ˈhwaɪtˈhɑt; ˈwaitˈhɔt) *adj.* ①白熱的;熾熱的;非常熱的。②憤怒的;激動的;熱心的。

White House, The ①白宮(美國總統府)。②美國政府之行政部門。

white iron 白鐵。

white lady 一種鷄尾酒(=cocktail).

white lead ①白鉛。②鉛粉。③白鉛礦。

white leather 白鞣皮。

white lie 小謊言;客氣或無惡意的謊言。

white light 白光。

white line ①〖印刷〗空行。②道路中間的白線(用以管制交通者)。③風之白色層。

white-lipped (ˈhwaɪtˌlɪpt; ˈwaitlipt) *adj.* 嘴唇發白的。

white list 優良者之名單;合格者之名單;通過安全檢查者之名單。

white-list (ˈhwaɪtˌlɪst; ˈwaitˈlist) *v.t.* 將…列入優良者之名單。

white-liv·ered(ˈhwaɪtˈlɪvəd;ˈwaitlivəd) *adj.* ①蒼白憔悴的。②怯懦的。

white·ly (ˈhwaɪtlɪ; ˈwaitli) *adv.* 產生白色地;發白光地。

white-maned (ˈhwaɪtˈmend; ˈwaitˈmeind) *adj.* 一頭白髮的。

white man's burden 白種人自許的對殖民地土著民族之責任(如改善其生活環境等)。

white matter 〖解剖〗(腦及脊髓之)白質。

white metal 白合金。

white mineral oil 石蠟油。

white mouse 白鼠。

white mouth 〖醫〗鵝口瘡;雪口症。

white mulberry 中國產之桑。

white mule 私酒。

***whit·en** (ˈhwaɪtn̩; ˈwaitn, ˈhw-) *v.t.* 使白;漂白。—*v.i.* 變白。—**er,** *n.*

***white·ness** (ˈhwaɪtnɪs; ˈwaitnis, ˈhw-) *n.* ①白;蒼白。②純潔;純粹。③白色物質。

white night 不眠夜。

whit·en·ing (ˈhwaɪtn̩ɪŋ; ˈwaitniŋ) *n.* ①變白;弄白;刷白;塗白。②使物變白之製劑;白堊粉。—*adj.* 使變白的;漂白的。

white oak ①白橡樹。②白橡木。

white of egg 蛋白。

white of the eye 眼白。

white paper (政府所發表之)白皮書。

white pepper 白胡椒。

white pine ①白松。②白松木。

white plague 結核病;(尤指)肺結核。

white poplar 白楊。

white potato 白馬鈴薯(=Irish potato).

white primary 美國南方僅由白人參加的總統初選。

white room 極爲清潔之房間(如手術室等)。

White Russia 白俄羅斯(蘇聯歐洲部分之一共和國, 其首都爲 Minsk).

White Russian ①白俄羅斯人。②白俄。③白俄羅斯(人)的。

whites (hwaɪts; waits) *n. pl.* 〖醫〗白帶。

white sale牀單、枕套等白色織物之出售。

white sauce 一種以牛油、麪粉及調味品製成的醬汁。

white sheep ①壞人中之善人。②阿拉斯加及加拿大西北部產的一種野羊。

white slave ①被賣爲娼的婦女。②被迫爲奴隸的白種人。

white slaver 從事販賣婦女爲娼者。

white slavery ①販賣婦女爲娼(業)。②被賣爲娼。

white-slav·ing (ˈhwaɪtˈslevɪŋ; ˈwaitˈsleiviŋ) *n.* 販賣婦女爲娼之非法行業。

white·smith (ˈhwaɪtˌsmɪθ; ˈwaitsmiθ) *n.* 錫匠。

white space 印刷品上之空白部分。

white su·prem·a·cist(~səˈprɛməsɪst; ~sjuˈpreməsist) 白人至高主義者。

white supremacy ①白人優勢。②白人至高主義。

white·tail (ˈhwaɪtˌtel; ˈwaitteil) *n.* 〖動物〗白尾鹿。(亦作 **white-tailed deer**)

white-thatched (ˈhwaɪtˌθætʃt; ˈwaitθætʃt) *adj.* 白髮的。

white·thorn (ˈhwaɪtˌθɔrn; ˈwaitθɔːn) *n.* 〖植物〗山楂。

white·throat (ˈhwaɪtˌθrot; ˈwaitθrout) *n.* ①白喉雀。②北美所產之蜂鳥。

white tie ①男用晚禮服之白色蝶形領結。②男用晚禮服。

white trash ①〖蔑〗美國南方之貧窮白人。②貧窮白人之集合稱。

white vitriol 〖化〗硫酸鋅;皓礬($ZnSO_4 \cdot 7H_2O$, 用作防腐劑)。

white·ware (ˈhwaɪtˌwɛr; ˈwaitwɛə) *n.* 白色之瓷器或陶器。

white·wash (ˈhwaɪtˌwɑʃ; ˈwaitwɔʃ) *v.t.* ①用石灰刷白;粉刷。②粉飾;掩飾;洗刷;爲…掩飾過錯。③〖俗〗使…獲零分而慘敗。—*v.i.* 被粉刷。—*n.* ①石灰水。②對錯誤或過失之掩飾。③〖俗〗運動比賽得零分而敗北。—**er,** *n.*

white water ①浪花;浪端的白沫。②淺灘上面顏色較淡之水。

white way 燈光燦爛的熱鬧街道。

white·wing ['hwaɪt,wɪŋ; 'wait-wiŋ] *n.* 〖美〗清道夫(着白色制服, 故稱)。

white·wood ['hwaɪt,wud; 'wait-wud] *n.* ①白色木材。②鬱金香樹。③菩提樹。④白楊。

「(常W-)白種人。」

whit·ey ['hwaɪtɪ; 'waiti] *n.* 〖俗,蔑〗

***whith·er** ['hwɪðɚ; 'wiðə, 'hw-] *adv.* 向何處 (=where). —*conj.* 向那裏 (=to which place). Let them go *whither* they will. 讓他們隨便到甚麼地方去。〖注意〗此字現在已被 where 所代替, 只在詩中或文學作品裏偶爾使用。

whith·er·so·ev·er [,hwɪðɚso'ɛvɚ; ,wiðəsou'evə] *adv., conj.* 向何處; 無論到何處。

whith·er·ward ['hwɪðɚwɚd; 'wiðəwəd] *adv.* 向何處。(亦作 **whitherwards**)

whit·ing ['hwaɪtɪŋ; 'waitiŋ] *n.* ①〖魚〗鱈類。②白堊粉; 白粉。

whit·ish ['hwaɪtɪʃ; 'waitiʃ] *adj.* 略白的; 稍白的。—**ness,** *n.*

whit·leath·er ['hwɪt,lɛðɚ; 'wit,leðə] *n.* ①白鞣皮。②〖解剖〗項韌帶。

whit·low ['hwɪtlo; 'witlou] *n.* 〖醫〗①膿性指頭炎。②(獸類之)蹄冠炎。

Whit·man ['hwɪtmən; 'witmən] *n.* 惠特曼 (Walt, 1819-1892, 美國詩人)。

Whit·mon·day ['hwɪt'mʌndɪ; 'wit'mʌndi] *n.* 聖神降臨節(Whitsunday)之第二天(在英國爲銀行假日)。

Whit·sun ['hwɪtsn̩; 'witsn] *adj.* 聖神降臨節的。(亦作 **Whit**)

Whit·sun·day ['hwɪt'sʌndɪ; 'wit-'sʌndi] *n.* 聖神降臨節(復活節後的第七個禮拜日)。

Whit·sun·tide ['hwɪtsən,taɪd; 'wit-sntaid] *n.* 聖神降臨週(卽自聖神降臨節起之一週, 而尤指該週之起始三天)。(亦作 **Whit-sun Tide, Whit Week**)

whit·tle ['hwɪtl̩; 'witl] *v.,* **-tled, -tling,** *n.* —*v.t.* ①削修; 削成; 削。②逐漸減少; 削減〖away, down〗. —*v.i.* 削; 削修。—*n.* 〖英方〗刀(特指屠刀或大型雕刀)。—**whit·tler,** *n.*

whit·tling ['hwɪtlɪŋ; 'witliŋ] *n.* ①修削。②(*pl.*) 修削下來的雜片; 鉋花。

whit·y ['hwaɪtɪ; 'waiti] *adj.,* **whit·i·er, whit·i·est.** 略白的; 稍白的 (=whitish).

whiz, whizz [hwɪz; wiz] *v.,* **whizzed, whiz·zing,** *n.* —*v.i.* 作颼颼聲; 颼颼掠過。—*n.* ①颼颼聲。②短期旅行。③〖俚〗聰明人; 專家。

「*adj.* 很優秀的; 很棒的。」

whiz-bang ['hwɪz,bæŋ; 'wizbæŋ]

Whiz kid, whiz kid 〖俚〗①年輕而精明能幹之顧問; 頭腦清新而辦事效率極高之青年經理人員。②神童; 高材生。

whiz·zer ['hwɪzɚ; 'wizə] *n.* ①作颼颼聲者。②詭計; 惡作劇。

whl. wheel.

WHO, W.H.O. World Health Organization. 世界衛生組織。

‡**who** [hu; huː] *pron., poss.* **whose,** *obj.* **whom.** ①(作 interrog. pron. 用) 誰; 何人。*Who* told you? 誰告訴你的? ②(作rel. pron. 用) 那個人; 其人。This is the man *who* wanted to see you. 這就是要見你的那個人。***know who's who*** 知道(某一範圍內)所有的人是誰以及他們的身分。—*n.* 與某事有關的人; 有關人物。the *who* and the why of it. 該事之有關人物和發生原因。〖注意〗①**who** 指人或擬人化的東西。②日常會話中通常以 who 代替 whom, 如: *Who* are you waiting for? 你在等誰? ③當作關係詞時受格不能用 who, 如: I know the boy *whom* you mean. 我認識你所說的那個男孩。

「所用之語 (=wo).」

whoa [hwo; wou] *interj.* 喝令馬停步

who'd [hud; huːd] =**who would; who had.**

「〖俚〗偵探小說或劇本。」

who·dun·it [hu'dʌnɪt; huː'dʌnit] *n.*

***who·ev·er** [hu'ɛvɚ; hu(ː)'evə] *pron., poss.* **whos·ev·er,** *obj.* **whom·ev·er.** ①不論誰; 任何人。*Whoever* else may object, I shall approve. 不論何人反對, 我却要贊成。②究竟是誰。*Whoever* can that be? 那究竟會是誰?

‡**whole** [hol; houl] *adj.* ①完全的。He gave her a *whole* set of dishes. 他給她一整套盤碟。②全部的; 整個的。It rained for three *whole* days. 下了整整三天的雨。③完整的; 未破碎的; 未受傷的。You're lucky to escape with a *whole* skin. 你很幸運的未受任何損傷而逃脫。④健康的。⑤整數的。***be made out of whole cloth*** 全係揑造或想像的。***do (a thing) with one's whole heart*** 全心全力做(一事)。—*n.* ①全部; 全體; 整體。A *whole* is greater than any of its parts. 一個整體較它的任何部分爲大。②完全之體系。Nature is a *whole.* 自然乃爲一體。***as a whole*** 就全體而論; 整個看來。***on*** (or ***upon***) ***the whole*** **a.** 整個看起來。**b.** 大概。He is, *on the whole,* a satisfactory student. 大體來說, 他是個令人滿意的學生。—**ness,** *n.*

whole brother 同父母之兄弟; 親兄弟。

whole-col·o(u)red ['hol,kʌlɚd; 'houl,kʌləd] *adj.* 全部一色的; 單色的。

whole·heart·ed ['hol'hɑrtɪd; 'houl'hɑːtid] *adj.* 熱誠的; 熱烈的; 忠實的; 專心一意的。—**ly,** *adv.* —**ness,** *n.*

whole hog 〖俚〗最大程度; 全部。***go (the) whole hog*** 做得徹底; 一不做二不休。

whole·hog·ger ['hol'hɑgɚ; 'houl'hɔgə] *n.* 極端論者。

「huːft] *adj.* 單蹄的。」

whole·hoofed ['hol,huft; 'houl-

whole-length ['hol,lɛŋθ; 'houlleŋθ] *n.* 全身像。—*adj.* ①全身的 (像片等)。②從頭到尾的; 無省略的。

whole milk 全脂奶。

whole note 〖音樂〗全音符。

whole number 〖數學〗整數。

whole·sale** ['hol,sel; 'houlseil] *n., adj., adv., v.,* **-saled, -sal·ing.** —*n.* ①批發; 躉售。He buys at *wholesale* and sells at retail. 他整批買進, 再零賣出去。②大批; 大規模。by wholesale*** **a.** 大量的; 大批的。**b.** 不分青紅皂白的。—*adj.* ①批發的; 躉售的。the *wholesale* price. 批發價格。a *wholesale* dealer. 批發商。②大批的; 大規模的; 不分皂白的。a *wholesale* slaughter. 大屠殺。—*adv.* 大批地。—*v.t.* & *v.i.* 批發; 躉售。—**whole·sal·er,** *n.*

whole sister 同父母之姊妹; 親姊妹。

***whole·some** ['holsəm; 'houlsəm] *adj.* ①合乎衛生的; 有益健康的。a *wholesome* food. 有益健康的食物。②有益的; 裨益心智或道德的。Read *wholesome* books. 閱讀有益的書。③顯示健康的。④安全的。—**ly,** *adv.* —**ness,** *n.*

whole-souled ['hol'sold; 'houl-'sould] *adj.* 專心一意的; 熱誠的。

whole step 〖音樂〗全音程。(亦作**whole tone**)

whole-wheat ['hol'hwit; 'houl-'wi:t] *adj.* 全麥做的。

who'll [hul; hu:l] =**who will; who shall.**

*__whol·ly__ ['holı; 'houlli] *adv.* ①完全地;全然地。I don't *wholly* agree. 我不完全同意。②全部地;全體地。Few men are *wholly* bad. 很少人是完全壞的。

‡**whom** [hum, hʊm; hu:m, hum] *pron.* ①the objective case of **who.** 誰。*Whom* do you like best? 你最喜歡誰? ②the dative case of **who.** You gave *whom* the book? 你將書給了誰?

whom·ev·er [hum'ɛvɚ; hu:m'evə] *pron.* the objective case of **whoever.**

whomp [hwɑmp; hwɔmp] *n.* ①拍擊聲。②巨響。—*v.i.* 發出巨響。—*v.t.* ①擊潰;大敗。②打;體罰。 ***whomp up*** **a.** 激起;促起。**b.** 揑造。

whom·so·ev·er [ˌhumso'ɛvɚ; ˌhu:m-sou'evə] *pron.* the objective case of **whosoever.**

whoop [hup, hwup; hu:p] *n.* ①高聲呼叫;呼喊;吶喊。②梟鳴聲。③(百日咳患者在咳嗽後的)喘息聲;哮喘聲。④〖俗〗值得歡樂的價值(用於否定式)。 ***a whoop and a holler*** 〖美俗〗**a.** 短距離。**b.** 大加宣傳。 ***not care a whoop*** 〖美〗一點也不在乎。 ***not worth a whoop*** 〖俗〗毫無價值;不值得大驚小怪。—*v.i.* ①高聲呼叫;尖叫;吶喊。②作梟叫。③(百日咳患者於一陣咳嗽後)高聲吸氣;喘息。④熱烈擁護;熱烈支持。⑤轟轟行進。—*v.t.* ①高聲叫叫。②以高聲呼叫驅策。③激起;鼓起。④抬高(價錢等)。 ***whoop it*** (or ***things***) ***up*** 〖俚〗**a.** 喧鬧;喝酒歡鬧。**b.** 鼓起熱烈興趣。—*interj.* 表激動、歡欣等之聲。

whoop-de-do ['hupdıˌdu; 'hu:pdi-du:] *n.* ①熱鬧;廣告宣傳(活動)。②紛亂的議論。(亦作 **whoop-de-doo**)

whoop·ee [*interj.* 'hwu'pi; 'wu'pi: *n.* 'hwupi; 'wupi:] *interj.* 〖美俚〗表示高興之歡呼聲。—*n.* 〖美俚〗狂歡;喝酒歡鬧。to make *whoopee.* 狂歡;喝酒歡鬧。

whoopee cup 〖俗〗供飛機乘客嘔吐用的紙杯或紙袋。

whoopee water 酒。

whoop·er ['hupɚ; 'hu:pə] *n.* ①高聲呼叫者;狂歡者。②北美洲產的一種白色大鶴。③(亦作 **whooper swan**) 歐洲產的鵠。

whoop·ing cough ['hupıŋ~; 'hu:-piŋ~] 〖醫〗百日咳。

whoop·la ['huplə; 'hu:plə] *n.* ①狂歡;喝酒歡鬧。②大事渲染。

whoops [hups; hu:ps] *interj.* 表示驚異、尷尬或道歉之感歎詞。

whoop-up ['hupˌʌp; 'hu:p-ʌp] *n.* 〖俗〗喧鬧;騷動;胡鬧作樂之聚會。

whoosh [hwuʃ; huʃ] *v.i.* 發嘶嘶聲。—*n.* 嘶嘶聲。

whoo·sis ['huzıs; 'hu:zis] *n., pl.* **-sis·es.** 〖俗〗①不知其名的或一時想不起名字的人或物。②典型的人或事物。(亦作 **whosis, whoosy**)

whop [hwɑp; wɔp] *v.,* **whopped, whop·ping,** *n.* —*v.t.* 〖俗〗①重擊;毆擊。②擊敗;打敗;征服。③使(自己)突然摔倒在地上。—*v.i.* 遽落;遽倒;重墮。—*n.* ①毆擊;重打。②毆擊聲。③重跌。(亦作**wap, whap, wop**)

whop·per ['hwɑpɚ; 'wɔpə] *n.* 〖俗〗①毆擊者;跌倒者。②(某物之)特大號;特大之物。③漫天大謊。(亦作 **whapper**)

whop·ping ['hwɑpıŋ; 'wɔpiŋ] *adj.* 〖俗〗特大號的;極大的。—*adv.* 非常;極。(亦作 **whapping**)

whore [hor; hɔ:] *n., v.,* **whored, whor·ing.** —*n.* ①娼妓。②不貞的婦人。—*v.i.* ①宿娼;嫖妓。②當娼妓。—*v.t.* 〖廢〗使成娼婦。—**whor·ish,** *adj.*

who're ['huɚ; 'hu:ə] =**who are.**

whore·dom ['hordəm; 'hɔ:dəm] *n.* ①賣淫;違法之性交;通姦。②崇拜偶像。

whore·house ['horˌhaus; 'hɔ:haus] *n.* 妓院;青樓。

whore·mong·er ['horˌmʌŋgɚ; 'hɔ:ˌmʌŋgə] *n.* 拉皮條者;淫媒。(亦作 **whoremaster**)

whorl [hwɝl; wə:l] *n.* ①〖植物〗輪生體;環生體。②〖動物〗(貝殼上之)螺紋;渦旋;螺旋部。③〖解剖〗(耳蝸之)渦旋。④(紡錘的)整速輪;小輪。⑤螺旋紋。—*v.i.* & *v.t.* 盤旋;旋轉。

whorled [hwɝld; wə:ld] *adj.* 有渦旋的;有螺紋的;輪生的(葉等)。(亦作 **whorly**)

whor·tle·ber·ry ['hwɝtlˌbɛrı; 'wə:tlˌberi] *n., pl.* **-ries.** 〖植物〗①越橘樹。②越橘。(亦作 **whort, hurtleberry**)

who's [huz; hu:z] =**who is; who has.**

‡**whose** [huz, hʊz; hu:z] *pron.* the possessive case of **who** or **which.** 誰的;其。*Whose* book is this? 這是誰的書? This is the pen *whose* point is broken. 這就是筆尖斷了的那枝筆。

whose·so·ev·er [ˌhuzso'ɛvɚ; ˌhu:z-sou'evə] *pron.* the possessive case of **whosoever.** ①無論是誰的。②究竟是誰的。

whos·ev·er [hu'zɛvɚ; hu:'zevə] *adj.* 無論是誰的。 —*pron.* 無論是誰的東西。

who·so·ev·er [ˌhuso'ɛvɚ; ˌhu:sou-'evə] *pron.* 〖古〗=**whoever.**

who's who ①名人錄。②名人之集合稱。

whr. watt-hour. **whr. m.** watt-hour meter. **whse.** warehouse. **whsle.** wholesale. **whs. stk.** warehouse stock.

‡**why** [hwaı; wai, hw-] *adv., n., pl.* **whys,** *interj.* —*adv.* ①(作 interrog. adv. 用)爲甚麼;何故。*Why* did you do it? 你爲甚麼做這事?Do you know *why* he was late? 你知道他爲甚麼遲到嗎? *Why* not? 爲甚麼不?有甚麼不可以? ②(作 rel. adv.用)所以;所以…的原因。That is the reason *why* he failed. 那就是他所以失敗的原因。—*n.* ①原因;理由。Tell me all the *whys* and wherefores. 把所有的理由和原因都告訴我。②難解之問題。—*interj.* 表示驚奇、懷疑、異議、承認、發現等的感歎詞。"Who wrote *Hamlet?*" "*Why,* Shakespeare." "哈姆雷特是誰作的?" "當然是莎士比亞"。*Why,* it's all gone! 啊,全完了!

W.I. ①West Indian. ②West Indies.

WIC War Investigation Committee.

wick[1] [wık; wik] *n.* 燈心;蠟燭心。

wick[2] *n.* 〖英方〗牛奶場;畜牧場。

*__wick·ed__ ['wıkıd; 'wikid] *adj.* ①邪惡的。a *wicked* person. 惡人。②惡作劇的;有惡意的。a *wicked* boy. 好惡作劇的男孩。③〖俗〗不快意的;不愉快的。④〖俗〗狂暴的。a *wicked* storm. 狂風暴雨。⑤不合理的;無道理的。⑥奇佳的。⑦非常危險的;非常麻煩的。⑧難聞的。

wick·ed·ly ['wıkıdlı; 'wikidli] *adv.*

①邪惡地。②兇暴地。③懷惡意地；惡毒地。

wick·ed·ness [ˈwɪkɪdnɪs; ˈwikidnis] *n.* ①邪惡；罪惡。②邪惡的行爲或作風。③邪惡的事物。

wick·er [ˈwɪkɚ; ˈwikə] *n.* ①小枝；柔枝；柳條。②枝編細工；用柳條編成之細工。③柳條編製品；枝編物。—*adj.* ①用柳枝做的；用枝條製成的。②用柳條被覆的。

wick·er·work [ˈwɪkɚˌwɝk; ˈwikə-wəːk] *n.* 柳條工；柳條編製的物品。

wick·et [ˈwɪkɪt; ˈwikit] *n.* ①(亦作 **wicket door, wicket gate**)(大門上或大門旁的)便門；邊門；小門。②入口處之廻轉門；十字形廻旋門。③格子窗；小窗口(如售票處之窗戶)。④(只遮住下半部的)半門。⑤水壩之閘門；放水門。⑥〖板球〗a. 三柱門。b. 兩三柱門間之場地。c. 在三柱門擊球者之權利或輪值。d. 二人共同擊球之時間。***be on* (*have,* or *bat*) *a sticky wicket*** 〖英俚〗居於不利的地位。 ***keep one's wicket up*** 〖板球〗(擊球員)沒有被殺掉。***keep wicket*** 〖板球〗防守三柱門。 ***on a bad* (*good*) *wicket*** 在不利(有利)情況下。***take a wicket*** 〖板球〗殺掉一個擊球員。 ***three* (*four, etc.*) *wickets down*** 〖板球〗殺了三個(四個等)擊球員。***win by two wickets*** 〖板球〗無人被殺而贏了兩個球。

wick·et·keep·er [ˈwɪkɪtˌkipɚ; ˈwikitˌkiːpə] *n.* 〖板球〗三柱門之守門員。

wick·ing [ˈwɪkɪŋ; ˈwikiŋ] *n.* 用作燈撚、燭心等之線束。

wick·i·up [ˈwɪkɪˌʌp; ˈwikiʌp] *n.* 美國西南部印第安人的小屋。(亦作 **wikiup, wicky-up**)

wid. ①widow. ②widower.

wid·der·shins [ˈwɪdɚʃɪnz; ˈwidə-ʃinz] *adv.* 反向地；往反時鐘方向地；向左地。(亦作 **withershins**)

‡**wide** [waɪd; waid] *adj.,* **wid·er, wid·est,** *adv.* —*adj.* ①寬廣的；廣濶的。a *wide* street. 寬廣的街道。②寬；濶。 a door three feet *wide*. 三英尺寬的門。③淵博的；廣泛的。*wide* knowledge. 淵博的知識。 ④張大的。to stare with *wide* eyes. 睜大着眼睛注視。⑤遠離標的的。The bullet was *wide* of the mark. 這一彈距離鵠的很遠。⑥〖英俚〗機警的。—*adv.* ①廣濶地；廣大地。with *wide* open eyes. 張大着眼睛。②遍及各處地。to travel far and *wide*. 到處旅行。③遠離標的地。—**ness,** *n.*

wide-an·gle [ˈwaɪdˈæŋgl̩; ˈwaid-ˈæŋgl] *adj.* 〖攝影〗寬角度的；用寬角度的。

wide awake 清醒；機警。

wide-a·wake [ˈwaɪdəˈwek; ˈwaidə-ˈweik] *adj.* ①極清醒的。②機警的。—**ness,** *n.*

wide·band [ˈwaɪdˈbænd; ˈwaidˈbænd] *adj.* 〖電訊〗包括多種頻率的；能用多種頻率播放的；能接收多種頻率的。

wide boy 〖英俚〗太保；小流氓。

wide-eyed [ˈwaɪdˌaɪd; ˈwaid-aid] *adj.* ①睜大眼睛的。②目瞪口呆的；大爲驚異的。③天眞的；不懂世故的。

wide-field [ˈwaɪdˈfild; ˈwaidˈfiːld] *adj.* 視野廣濶的。

***wide·ly** [ˈwaɪdlɪ; ˈwaidli] *adv.* ①範圍廣地。a man who is *widely* known. 一個很著名的人。②關於各種題目，情形等。He is *widely* read. 他博覽羣書。③寬濶地。④大大地。

wide·mouthed [ˈwaɪdˌmaʊðd; ˈwaidmauðd] *adj.* ①大口的。②高聲喊出的。

***wid·en** [ˈwaɪdn̩; ˈwaidn] *v.t.* 加寬；增廣。This road needs to be *widened*. 這條路需要加寬。—*v.i.* 變寬；擴展。—**er,** *n.*

wide-o·pen [ˈwaɪdˈopən; ˈwaidˈou-pən] *adj.* ①廣開的；大開的。②(對傷風敗俗之行爲)不加嚴格管制的(城市等)。

wide-range [ˈwaɪdˈrendʒ; ˈwaid-ˈreindʒ] *adj.* 運用範圍很廣的。

wide-rang·ing [ˈwaɪdˈrendʒɪŋ; ˈwaidˈreindʒiŋ] *adj.* 範圍廣濶的。

wide screen 濶銀幕。

wide-screen [ˈwaɪdˈskrin; ˈwaid-ˈskriːn] *adj.* 濶銀幕的。

***wide·spread** [ˈwaɪdˈsprɛd; ˈwaid-spred] *adj.* ①擴展開的。②廣布的；普及的；流傳廣遠的。

wide-spread·ing [ˈwaɪdˈsprɛdɪŋ; ˈwaidˈspredin] *adj.* 遼濶的；範圍廣濶的；傳布很廣的。

wide-wa·tered [ˈwaɪdˈwɔtɚd; ˈwaid-ˈwɔːtəd] *adj.* ①臨海的。②水面寬濶的。

widg·eon [ˈwɪdʒən; ˈwidʒən] *n., pl.* **-eons, -eon.** 赤頸鳧；水鳧。

wid·get [ˈwɪdʒɪt; ˈwidʒit] *n.* ①小機械玩意(尤指想不起其名稱者)。②典型之物。

wid·ish [ˈwaɪdɪʃ; ˈwaidiʃ] *adj.* 略(寬)廣的。

***wid·ow** [ˈwɪdo; ˈwidou] *n.* ①孀婦；寡婦。②〖印刷〗一個段落的最後一行字而長度不足全行之一半者。—*v.t.* ①使成寡婦；使喪偶。A great many women were *widowed* by the war. 戰爭使許多婦女成爲寡婦。②成爲…之寡婦。③自…奪去(所珍重之物)。

wid·owed [ˈwɪdod; ˈwidoud] *adj.* 寡居的；鰥居的。

wid·ow·er [ˈwɪdəwɚ; ˈwidouə] *n.* 鰥夫。

wid·ow·ered [ˈwɪdəwɚd; ˈwidouəd] *adj.* 成鰥夫的；鰥居的。

wid·ow·er·hood [ˈwɪdəwɚhud; ˈwidouəhud] *n.* 鰥居。

wid·ow·hood [ˈwɪdoˌhud; ˈwidou-hud] *n.* ①寡居；寡居期。②〖罕〗鰥居。

wid·ow·ly [ˈwɪdolɪ; ˈwidouli] *adj.* 寡婦的；適於寡婦的。

wid·ow-mak·er [ˈwɪdoˌmekɚ; ˈwi-douˌmeikə] *n.* ①殺死有妻室之男人以使其妻成寡婦者。②對男人(尤其工人)有危險之物。

widow's cruse 寡婦的罐子；無盡藏；取之不盡用之不竭之物(舊約列王紀上)。

widow's mite 寡婦奉獻的一個小錢(喻少而可貴，見聖經馬可福音十二章四十二節)。

widow's walk 面對大海之屋頂陽臺(原供海員或漁夫之妻子眺望船隻歸來之用。昔時航海者生還機會較少，故名)。

***width** [wɪdθ; widθ] *n.* ①廣；濶；廣度；廣濶。four feet in *width*. 寬四英尺。②有一定寬度的一幅布等。③心胸廣濶。*width* of mind. 心胸之宏濶。

width·wise [ˈwɪdθˌwaɪz; ˈwidθwaiz] *adv.* 與寬同方向地。(亦作 **widthways**)

Wie·land [ˈvilɑnt; ˈviːlaːnt] *n.* 維蘭特(Heinrich, 1877–1957, 德國化學家，曾獲1927年諾貝爾化學獎)。

wield [wild; wiːld] *v.t.* ①揮舞；使用；支配。The people *wield* the power in a democracy. 在民主國家中，人民握有權力。②處理；處置。***wield a kingdom*** 統治王國。***wield the pen*** 書寫。***wield the scepter*** 掌握統治大權。—**a·ble,** *adj.* —**er,** *n.*

wield·y [ˈwildɪ; ˈwiːldi] *adj.,* **wield·i·er, wield·i·est.** ①易使用的(工具、武器等)；可操縱的。②有能力的；能力强的。

wie·ner ['winɚ; 'wiːnə] *n.* 〖美〗燻製之牛肉或猪肉香腸。(亦作 **weenie, weeny, wienerwurst**)

‡**wife** [waɪf; waif] *n., pl.* **wives** [waɪvz; waivz]. ①妻; 婦。husband and *wife.* 夫婦。②〖古〗婦人。***an old wives' tale*** 老婦譚;充滿迷信的無稽故事。***a wedded wife*** 正室;正妻。***take (a woman) to wife*** 娶(某女)爲妻。

wife·hood ['waɪfhud; 'waifhud] *n.* 爲人之妻的身分或狀態。(亦作 **wifedom**)

wife·less ['waɪflɪs; 'waiflis] *adj.* 無妻的;鰥夫的。

wife·like ['waɪf,laɪk; 'waiflaik] *adj. & adv.* 似妻子的(地);適於做妻子的(地)。

wife·li·ness ['waɪflɪnɪs;'waiflinis] *n.* 似妻子之特質;適於做妻子之特質。

wife·ly ['waɪflɪ; 'waifli] *adj.,* **-li·er, -li·est.** (似)妻子的;適於做妻子的。(亦作 **wifish**)

wig** [wɪg;wig] *n., v.,* **wigged, wig·ging.** —*n.* 假髮。wigs on the green*** 糾紛;爭執。—*v.t.* ①供以假髮。②責罵。

wig·eon ['wɪdʒən; 'widʒən] *n., pl.* **-eons, -eon.** =**widgeon.**

wigged [wɪgd; wigd] *adj.* 戴假髮的。

wig·ger·y ['wɪgərɪ; 'wigəri] *n.* ①戴假髮的行爲。②假髮業。

wig·ging ['wɪgɪŋ; 'wigiŋ] *n.* 〖英俗〗罵;叱責。

wig·gle ['wɪgl; 'wigl] *v.,* **-gled, -gling,** *n.* —*v.i.* (以輕快之動作)移動; 搖動; 擺動。—*v.t.* 使搖動; 使迅速擺動。—*n.* ①快速擺動; 搖動。②彎曲線。③與 white sauce 及豆和在一起吃的魚蝦之類。***get a wiggle on*** 趕快。***Get a wiggle on you!*** 〖俚〗趕快!快點!

wig·gler ['wɪglɚ; 'wiglə] *n.* ①左右急遽搖擺移動之人或物。②孑孓。

wig·gly ['wɪglɪ; 'wigli] *adj.,* **-gli·er, -gli·est.** ①左右急遽搖擺的。②波狀的。

wight [waɪt;wait] *n.* 〖古,方〗人。—*adj.* 〖蘇,古〗①勇猛的。②輕捷的。

wig·less ['wɪglɪs;'wiglis] *adj.* 未戴假髮的。

wig·let ['wɪglɪt; 'wiglit] *n.* 小假髮。

wig·mak·er ['wɪg,mekɚ;'wig,meikə] *n.* 假髮商。

wig·wag ['wɪg,wæg; 'wigwæg] *v.,* **-wagged, -wag·ging,** *n.* —*v.t. & v.i.* ①來回搖擺。②搖擺手臂、信號旗或燈以發出(信號)。—*n.* 〖航海〗①以信號旗(燈)通訊。②以此種信號所傳送之消息;信號。**—ger,** *n.*

wig·wam ['wɪgwɑm, -wɔm;'wigwæm] *n.* ①(北美印第安人的)小屋;帳篷。②〖俚〗政治會議所用之建築物。

Wil·ber·force ['wɪlbɚ,fors; 'wilbə-fɔːs] *n.* 韋爾伯佛思 (William, 1759–1833, 英國博愛主義者及主張廢除奴隸制度者)。

wil·co ['wɪlko; 'wilkou] *interj.* (用於無線電通訊) 照辦 (will comply 之略)。

‡**wild** [waɪld; waild] *adj.* ①野的;野性的;野生的。a *wild* animal. 野獸。②無人居住的; 荒野的。a *wild* country. 荒野的地方。③容易驚恐的; 怕人的; 難接近的。④未開化的; 野蠻的。*wild* tribes. 野蠻的部族。⑤放肆的; 放蕩的。a *wild* young man. 放蕩的青年。⑥暴亂的;紊亂的。*wild* times. 亂世。⑦狂暴的; 狂熱的; 激昂的; 憤怒的。They were *wild* with excitement. 他們極爲激昂。⑧騷鬧的。⑨有暴風雨的; 多暴風的。a *wild* night. 暴風雨之夜。⑩狂妄的;胡亂的。*wild* schemes. 狂妄的計畫。⑪迫切的; 殷切的。⑫遠離鵠的的。*wild* shooting. 亂射。⑬激烈的。She suffered from a *wild* headache. 她爲激烈頭痛所苦。***run wild* a.** 放蕩。**b.** 滋生;到處蔓延。The grass is *running wild.* 草在到處蔓延。***sow one's wild oats*** 在年輕時荒唐放縱。***wild and woolly*** 粗獷的;未開化的。***wild goose chase*** 無望的亂跑;無意義的從事或追求。—*adv.* 暴亂地;胡亂地。 to shoot *wild.* 亂射。—*n.* (常 *pl.*) 荒地;荒野;未開墾之地。 the *wilds* of Africa. 非洲的荒野。the *wild.* 荒野。**—ly,** *adv.* **—ness,** *n.*

wild boar 野猪。

wild carrot 野生胡蘿蔔。

***wild·cat** ['waɪld,kæt; 'waildkæt] *n., adj., v.,* **-cat·ted, -cat·ting.** —*n.* ①山貓;野貓。②兇狠的鬥者。③〖俗〗未掛車輛的機車。④以前無人發現之地區中所挖的油井。—*adj.* ①不穩固的; 不安全的; 冒險性的。 *wildcat* stocks. 不穩固而冒險的股票。② 失去控制而亂轉動的(機器)。③部分工會會員未經正式機構允許或工會分會未獲總工會指示而參加罷工的。—*v.i. & v.t.* (在以前未經人所知的地區)開鑿(油井)。

wildcat bank 〖美俗〗美國銀行法施行前(卽1864年前)準備不足而發行紙幣之銀行。

wild·cat·ter ['waɪld,kætɚ; 'waild,kætə] *n.* 〖美俗〗①在不知是否藏油之區域鑿油井者。②發起冒險或投機事業者。

wild duck (鳥)野鴨;鳧。

Wilde [waɪld; waild] *n.* 王爾德 (Oscar Fingal O'Flahertie Wills, 1854–1900, 英國劇作家、詩人、小說家及批評家)。

wil·de·beest ['wɪldə,bist;'wildəbiːst] *n., pl.*-**beest,-beests.** 非洲產的一種大羚羊。

wil·der ['wɪldɚ; 'wildə] *v.i. & v.t.* 〖古,詩〗(使)迷路;(使)迷惑;(使)迷惘。

***wil·der·ness** ['wɪldɚnɪs; 'wildənis] *n.* ① 荒地; 荒野。 ②雜亂的一堆或一羣。 a *wilderness* of streets. 雜亂無序的街道。

wild-eyed ['waɪld,aɪd; 'waildaid] *adj.* ①樣子兇暴的。②過激的;狂熱的。

wild·fire ['waɪld,faɪr; 'waild,faiə] *n.* ①難於撲滅之烈火。②無雷聲之閃電。***spread like wildfire*** (消息、謠言等)迅速地傳播。

wild·flow·er ['waɪld,flauɚ; 'waild,flauə] *n.* 野花。(亦作 **wild flower**)

wild fowl 野禽;獵鳥(如野鴨等)。(亦作 **wildfowl**)

wild-fowl·er ['waɪld,faulɚ;'waild,faulə] *n.* 獵野禽者。

wild goose 雁。

wild-goose chase 對不能獲得之物或不能達成之目的所做之荒謬無用之追逐; 無益之追求。

wild-head·ed ['waɪld'hɛdɪd;'waild'hedid] *adj.* 胡思亂想的;想入非非的。

wild·ing ['waɪldɪŋ; 'waildiŋ] *n.* ①野生植物。②野生蘋果樹; 野生蘋果。③野生動物。—*adj.* 野生的。

wild·life ['waɪld,laɪf; 'waildlaif] *n.* 野獸或野生植物之集合稱。—*adj.*野生動植物的。

wild·lif·er ['waɪld,laɪfɚ; 'waild,laifə] *n.* 主張保護野生動植物者。

wild·ling ['waɪldlɪŋ; 'waildliŋ] *n.* 野生動物或野生植物。

wild man ①野蠻人。②性格兇暴者。

wild pitch 〖棒球〗暴投。

Wild West, wild West 未開發前之美國西部。

wild·wind ['waɪld,wɪnd; 'waildwind] *n.* 暴風。

wild·wood ['waɪld,wud; 'waildwud]

n. 天然林。

wile 〔waɪl; wail〕 *n., v.,* **wiled, wil·ing.** —*n.* 詭計。—*v.t.* 引誘。***wile away the time*** 愉快地消磨掉時間。

wile·ful 〔ˈwaɪlful; ˈwailfəl〕 *adj.* 多詭計的;欺詐的。

***wi(l)l·ful** 〔ˈwɪlfəl; ˈwilfəl〕 *adj.* ①任性的;剛愎的。②故意的。*wilful* murder. 故意殺人。—**ly,** *adv.* —**ness,** *n.*

‡will¹ 〔wɪl; wil〕 *aux. v., pt.* **would.** ①(表示單純未來時)將(=be going to). He *will* come tomorrow. 他將在明天來。②願意(=be willing to). I *will* go if you do. 如果你去,我就去。③願望(=wish, desire). We cannot always do as we *will*. 我們不能總是按照我們所願望的去做。④能;可以(=be able to, can). The pail *will* hold four gallons. 這桶能盛四加侖。⑤必須(=must). You *will* do it at once! 你必須馬上做這件事。Boys *will* be boys. 男孩子畢竟是男孩子。⑥常常;通常(=do often or usually). Mary *will* read for hours at a time. 瑪麗常常一連讀書好幾小時。***if you will*** 如果你願如此稱它。

‡will² *n., v.,* **willed, will·ing.** —*n.* ①意志。the freedom of the *will*. 意志之自由。②意志力。*Will* can conquer habit. 意志力可以克服習慣。③目的;決心;意向。Where there's a *will* there's a way. 有志者事竟成。He did it of his own *will*. 他出於自願而做這事。④遺囑。He died without making a *will*. 他未立遺囑而死。⑤對他人的感情。good *will*. 善意。ill *will*. 惡意。***against one's will*** 非出於自願。***at (one's) will*** **a.** 隨意。You may come and go *at will*. 你可以隨意來去。**b.** 隨意處置;隨意差遣。***do the will of*** 服從。***have one's will*** 如願以償。***of one's own (free) will*** 自願地;隨心所欲地。***with a will*** 樂意地;熱心地;有決心地。—*v.t.* ①決定;影響;控制;以意志力驅使。Whatever he *wills* he may accomplish. 不論他想做甚麼事,他都可以完成。Fate *willed* it otherwise. 命運偏不如此安排。②遺囑贈與。He *willed* his money to a hospital. 他立遺囑把他的錢捐給一所醫院。③立遺囑。④願;望。They believed that whatever is *willed* can be achieved. 他們相信有志竟成。—*v.i.* ①決意;運用意志力。She *willed* to keep awake. 她決意保持清醒。②願;望。—**er,** *n.*

will·a·ble 〔ˈwɪləbl̩; ˈwiləbl〕 *adj.* ①可由意志支配的。②可願的;可望的。

will-call 〔ˈwɪlˈkɔl; ˈwilˈkɔːl〕 *adj.* 商店寄存部(替顧客保存已付款之貨待以後領取之部門)的。

will contest 求證遺囑是否屬實或有效之法律訴訟。

willed 〔wɪld; wild〕 *adj.* 有某種意志的(用以組成複合字)。strong-*willed*. 意志堅強的。

wil·lem·ite 〔ˈwɪləmˌaɪt; ˈwilimait〕 *n.*【礦】矽鋅礦。

wil·let 〔ˈwɪlɪt; ˈwilit〕 *n.* 北美產的鷸。

Wil·liam 〔ˈwɪljəm; ˈwiljəm〕 *n.* 男子名。

Wil·liam I¹ 威廉一世(1027–1087, The Conqueror, 英王,在位期間爲1066–87)。

Wil·liam I² 威廉一世(1797–1888,於1861–88 爲普魯士王,並於 1871–88 爲德國皇帝)。

Wil·liam II 威廉二世(1859–1941,德國皇帝及普魯士王,在位期間爲 1888–1918)。

Wil·liam III 威廉三世(1650–1702, William of Nassau, 於 1689–1702 爲英國國王,1694以前與其后 Mary II 共同秉政)。

Wil·liam IV 威廉四世(1765–1837,世稱 Sailor-King,英國國王,在位期間爲1830–37)。

wil·lie-boy 〔ˈwɪlɪˌbɔɪ; ˈwiliboi〕 *n.* 娘娘腔的小伙子。

wil·lies 〔ˈwɪlɪz; ˈwiliz〕 *n. pl.* (the–)一陣緊張。It gave me the *willies*. 那使我捏一把冷汗。

***will·ing** 〔ˈwɪlɪŋ; ˈwiliŋ〕 *adj.* 情願的;欣然從事的;願意的。He is *willing* to wait. 他情願等待。—**ly,** *adv.* —**ness,** *n.*

will·ing·heart·ed 〔ˈwɪlɪŋˈhɑrtɪd; ˈwiliŋˈhɑːtid〕 *adj.* 十分情願的;心甘情願的。

will·less 〔ˈwɪllɪs; ˈwillis〕 *adj.* ①無意志的。②非自願的;勉强的。③沒有留遺囑的。

will-o'-the-wisp 〔ˌwɪləðəˈwɪsp; ˈwiləðwisp〕 *n.* ①沼地之磷火。②使人迷惑之物;令人捉摸不住的東西。—**ish,** —**y,** *adj.*

***wil·low¹** 〔ˈwɪlo, ˈwɪlə; ˈwilou〕 *n.* ①柳樹;柳木。②柳木製成之物。—*adj.* 柳條編的;柳木製的。

wil·low² *n.* 打棉機。—*v.t.* 以打棉機清理(棉花)。

wil·lowed 〔ˈwɪlod; ˈwiloud〕 *adj.* 圍以柳樹的;多柳樹的。

wil·low·er 〔ˈwɪloɚ; ˈwilouə〕 *n.* ①打棉機(=willow). ②操作打棉機的工人。

willow herb〖植物〗柳草;柳蘭。

wil·low·ware 〔ˈwɪloˌwɛr; ˈwilouwɛə〕 *n.* 有柳景圖案(willow pattern)之瓷器。(亦作 **willow ware**)

wil·low·y 〔ˈwɪləwɪ; ˈwiloui〕 *adj.* ①苗條的。②多柳樹的。

will power 意志力;自制力。(亦作 **willpower**)

Will·stät·ter 〔ˈvɪlˌʃtɛtɚ; ˈvilʃtetə〕 *n.* 維爾施泰特(Richard, 1872–1942, 德國化學家,1915年獲諾貝爾化學獎)。

will to power〖尼采哲學〗個人之求生及爭取權力的驅策力。(亦作 **will for power**)

wil·ly 〔ˈwɪlɪ; ˈwili〕 *n., pl.* **-lies,** *v.,* **-lied, -ly·ing.** =**willow²**.

wil·ly-nil·ly 〔ˈwɪlɪˈnɪlɪ; ˈwiliˈnili〕 *adv.* ①不管願不願意;不管怎樣。②雜亂無章地;亂七八糟地。—*adj.* ①猶豫不決的;拖延的。②不管是否希望或願意就是如此的。

wil·ly-wil·ly 〔ˈwɪlɪˌwɪlɪ; ˈwiliˌwili〕 *n.* 澳洲之大旋風;陸龍捲。

Wil·son 〔ˈwɪlsn̩; ˈwilsn〕 *n.* 威爾遜(Thomas Woodrow, 1856–1924, 於 1913–1921 任美國第二十八任總統)。

Wil·so·ni·an 〔wɪlˈsonɪən; wilˈsouniən〕 *adj.* 美國第二十八任總統威爾遜的。

Wil·son·ism 〔ˈwɪlsn̩ˌɪzm; ˈwilsənizm〕 *n.* 美國第二十八任總統威爾遜之原則或作風。(亦作 **Wilsonianism**)

wilt¹ 〔wɪlt; wilt〕 *v.i.* ①枯萎;凋謝。②衰微;凋零;頹喪。—*v.t.* 使枯萎;使凋謝;使衰微。—*n.* 枯萎;凋謝;衰微。

***wilt²** *aux. v.*【古】will 之第二人稱,單數,現在式,直陳法。

wilt³ *n.*〖植物〗枯萎病。(亦作 **wilt disease**)

Wil·ton 〔ˈwɪltən; ˈwiltən〕 *n.* 威爾頓絨氈(有似天鵝絨之絨毛)。(亦作 **Wilton carpet, Wilton rug**)

wil·y 〔ˈwaɪlɪ; ˈwaili〕 *adj.,* **wil·i·er, wil·i·est.** 有智謀的;狡詐的。

wim·ble 〔ˈwɪmbl̩; ˈwimbl〕 *n., v.,* **-bled, -bling.** —*n.* 鑽;錐。—*v.t.* 以鑽或錐子鑽。

Wim·ble·don 〔ˈwɪmbl̩dən; ˈwimbldən〕 *n.* 溫伯頓(倫敦附近之一城市,爲國際網球比賽之地)。

wim·ple 〔ˈwɪmpl̩; ˈwimpl〕 *n., v.,* **-pled,**

-pling. —*n.* (中古時婦人所着，現在修女仍用之)頭巾；包頭圍布。—*v.t.* ①以頭巾包之。②使起漣漪。—*v.i.* ①起漣漪。②〖古〗摺疊。

‡win 〔wɪn; win〕 *v.*, **won** 〔wʌn; wʌn〕, **win·ning**, *n.* —*v.t.* ①贏得；獲得。to *win* a prize. 得獎。②在…之中獲得勝利；獲得…之成功。to *win* a race. 賽跑獲勝。③(經過努力而)到達。to *win* the mountaintop. 到達山巔。④勸誘；說服。We *won* him to consent. 我們勸服他允諾。⑤獲得某人之愛；說服使與之結婚。to *win* a lady's hand. 贏得一女郎之歡心而與之結婚。—*v.i.* 獲勝；成功。He is sure to *win*. 他一定獲勝。***win hands down*** 輕而易舉地成功。***win out*** 〖俗〗獲勝；成功。***win the day*** (or ***field***) 戰勝。***win through*** 歷經千辛萬苦而終獲成功。—*n.* 〖俗〗勝利；成功。Our team has had five *wins* this summer. 今年夏天我們的球隊獲得五次的勝利。

***wince** 〔wɪns; wins〕 *v.*, **winced, winc·ing**, *n.* —*v.i.* 退避；畏縮。—*n.* 退避；畏縮。

win·cey 〔ˈwɪnsɪ; ˈwinsi〕 *n.* 一種棉與毛或麻與毛之混合織物。

win·cey·ette 〔ˈwɪnsɪˈɛt; ˈwinsiˈet〕 *n.* 〖英〗(睡衣、內衣用之兩面有絨毛的)棉絨。

winch 〔wɪntʃ; wintʃ〕 *n.* ①曲柄。②(以曲柄搖之)絞盤；絞車。③〖航海〗錨機。—*v.t.* 用絞盤吊起或拉起。

‡wind¹ 〔wɪnd; wind〕 *n.*, *v.*, **wind·ed, wind·ing**. —*n.* ①風；強風；狂風。A cold *wind* was blowing from the north. 寒風自北方吹來。②風勢；風力。The *wind* is rising. 風勢增強。③氣味。④呼吸；呼吸力。⑤無用的空話。His speech was mere *wind*. 他的演說只是空話。⑥腸胃中的氣體。The baby is troubled with *wind*. 那嬰孩患肚脹症(腸氣病)。⑦(*pl.*) 管絃樂團吹奏管樂器的團員。⑧管樂器(集合稱)。music for strings and for *wind*. 管絃樂。⑨錢。⑩酒醉的狀態。⑪紛擾；滋擾。⑫恐怖；不安。You put the *wind* up me. 你教我恐怖。⑬影響力很大的力量或趨勢。⑭暗示；朕兆。⑮虛榮；傲氣。⑯〖拳擊俚〗腹部被擊中時發生呼吸困難之處；太陽神經叢。⑰羅盤上任何方向。⑱不顧一切之狀態。to throw all precaution to the *winds*. 不顧一切後果。***before the wind*** 順風向。***be sound in wind and limb*** 身體健康。***between wind and water*** **a.** 在船的水線處。**b.** 在危險的地方。***break wind*** 放屁。***by the wind*** 朝逆風方向的。***cast to the wind*** 不理睬；不理會。***down the wind*** 逆風；搶風。***find out how the wind blows*** (亦作 **find out which way the wind blows**) 觀察情勢。***get the wind up*** 〖俚〗受驚恐；害怕。***get wind of*** 風聞；察覺。***in the eye*** (or ***teeth***) ***of the wind*** 逆風。***in the wind*** 發生；將發生。There's something *in the wind*. 某事在醞釀中。***into the wind*** 逆風。***off the wind*** 順風。***on the*** (or ***a***) ***wind*** 盡可能逆風(行駛)。***put the wind up someone*** 驚嚇某人。***raise the wind*** 〖俗〗**a.** 獲得所需之錢；籌款。**b.** 引起騷擾。***sail close to*** (or ***near***) ***the wind; sail close on a wind*** **a.** 逆風航行。**b.** 節儉。**c.** 做不正當或鹵莽之事。**d.** 僅免(懲罰、發覺等)；差點兒被…。***take the wind out of a person's sail*** 以先發制人的手段而占某人的上風；使某人難堪；出某人洋相。***the four winds*** 四面八方。***wind of change*** 不可抗拒的政治經濟變易之趨勢；社會之動亂。—*v.t.* ①嗅出。②使呼吸急促。③使喘口氣；使休息。④曝露風中。—*v.i.* 嗅到獵物的氣味。

‡wind² 〔waɪnd; waind〕 *v.*, **wound** 〔waʊnd; waund〕, **wind·ing**, *n.* —*v.i.* ①(道路、河流等)紆曲；蜿蜒。The stream *winds* through the valley. 溪流蜿蜒流經山谷。②(蛇、向上爬的植物等) 盤繞；纏繞。The vine *winds* round a pole. 藤纏繞一柱而生長。③變彎曲。④上紘；開發條。⑤迂廻間接地得到。to *wind* into power. 轉彎抹角地得到權力。—*v.t.* ①迂廻地走(路)。②捲；纏繞；裹。to *wind* wool into a ball. 將羊毛捲成球。③扭緊(機器的)發條；開。④以…環抱；以…包起；以…圍起。⑤使迂廻前進。She *wound* herself (*or* her way) into his affection. 她以其聰明手段得到他的愛情。⑥搖；轉動。⑦激起；激動。He was *wound* up to a high pitch of excitement. 他極度興奮。⑧絞起；吊起。⑨沿或順…迂廻前進。***wind a person round one's little finger*** 隨意操縱某人。***wind down*** 逐漸結束。***wind off*** 解開。***wind up*** **a.** 結束。to *wind up* a business company. 結束一公司。**b.** 捲起；纏繞。**c.** 〖棒球〗揮臂準備投球。**d.** 使緊張；使興奮；振作。—*n.* ①捲；纏繞。②紆曲；蜿蜒；彎曲；曲折。③曲柄；絞盤；絞車。

wind³ 〔waɪnd, wɪnd; waind〕 *v.t.*, **wind·ed** or **wound, wind·ing.** 吹。The hunter *winds* his horn. 獵人吹他的號角。

wind·a·ble 〔ˈwaɪndəbl̩; ˈwaindəbl〕 *adj.* 可纏繞的；可扭緊的。

wind·age 〔ˈwɪndɪdʒ; ˈwindidʒ〕 *n.* ①(砲孔直徑與砲彈直徑的)差率；遊隙。②(因彈丸飛過而起的)氣擦。③(風力引起的)彈道偏差。④〖航海〗船身的迎風面。⑤〖電〗(發電機之)風阻。

Win·daus 〔ˈvɪndaʊs; ˈvindaus〕 *n.* 溫道斯 (Adolf, 1876–1959, 德國化學家，曾獲1928 年諾貝爾化學獎)。

wind·bag 〔ˈwɪndˌbæg; ˈwindbæg〕 *n.* ①風囊。②〖俚〗好發空論之人；滿口空話之人。

wind band 管樂隊。

wind-bell 〔ˈwɪndˌbɛl; ˈwindbel〕 *n.* 「風鈴。」

wind-blown 〔ˈwɪndˌblon; ˈwindbloun〕 *adj.* ①被風吹的。②生長中被風吹歪扭的。③劉海髮型的。

wind-borne 〔ˈwɪndˌbɔrn; ˈwindbɔːn〕 *adj.* 被風吹移的；被風搬運的；隨風飄揚的。

wind·bound 〔ˈwɪndˌbaʊnd; ˈwindbaund〕 *adj.* ①〖航海〗受阻於風而不能航行的。②妨礙行動自由的；受抑制的。

wind·break 〔ˈwɪndˌbrek; ˈwindbreik〕 *n.* 防風物；防風設備；防風牆；防風林。

wind·break·er 〔ˈwɪndˌbrekɚ; ˈwindˌbreikə〕 *n.* ①一種皮或羊毛製的夾克。②(W-) 皮夾克之商標名。

wind-bro·ken 〔ˈwɪndˌbrokən; ˈwindˌbroukn〕 *adj.* 患氣喘症的(馬等)。

wind·burn 〔ˈwɪndˌbɝn; ˈwindbəːn〕 *n.* ①因暴露於風中過久而引起的皮膚發炎。②風所造成的樹皮或樹葉損傷。—**ed,** *adj.*

wind·ed 〔ˈwɪndɪd; ˈwindid〕 *adj.* ①有風的；有呼吸的。②喘息的；上氣不接下氣的。—**ness,** *n.*

wind egg 未受精之卵。

wind·er¹ 〔ˈwaɪndɚ; ˈwaində〕 *n.* ①捲的人；纏繞的人；纏繞物。②曲梯之一階。③盤繞於他物上生長之植物；蔓生植物。④捲線機；線板兒。⑤上發條之鑰匙等。

wind·er² 〔ˈwaɪndɚ; ˈwaində for①, ˈwɪndɚ; ˈwində for②〕 *n.* ①管樂器吹奏者。②〖俗〗使人氣喘之事。

wind erosion 風蝕。
wind·fall [ˈwɪndˌfɔl; ˈwindfɔːl] *n.* ①風吹落的果實。②意外收獲。
wind·firm [ˈwɪndˌfɝm; ˈwindfəːm] *adj.* 經得起風吹的;耐風的。
wind·flaw [ˈwɪndˌflɔ; ˈwindflɔː] *n.* 突然之陣風;短暫之沙暴。(亦作 **flaw**)
wind·flow·er [ˈwɪndˌflauɚ; ˈwindˌflauə] *n.* 〖植物〗白頭翁。
wind furnace 自然通風爐。
wind·gall [ˈwɪndˌgɔl; ˈwindgɔːl] *n.* 〖獸醫〗(馬等之)球腱軟腫。—**ed,** *adj.*
wind gap 山脊之低窪部分。
wind gauge 風力計; 風速計; 風壓計。(亦作 **wind meter**)
wind·hov·er [ˈwɪndˌhʌvɚ; ˈwindˌhɔvə] *n.* (鳥名)茶隼。
wind indicator (飛機場之) 飛向風速指示器。
wind·i·ness [ˈwɪndɪnɪs; ˈwindinis] *n.* ①多風;有風。②胃腸滯氣。③虛誇。④風力。
***wind·ing** [ˈwaɪndɪŋ; ˈwaindiŋ] *n.* ①彎曲;捲。②迂廻;蜿蜒。③纏繞物。④〖電〗 **a.** 繞組。 **b.** 繞法。 —*adj.* 彎曲的;蜿蜒的。 a *winding* staircase. 螺旋階梯。 a *winding* path. 蜿蜒的小徑。—**ly,** *adv.* —**ness,** *n.*
winding engine 〖採礦〗起重機;吊桶機。
winding sheet ①裹屍布。②蠟燭旁邊已硬化之一堆溶蠟(認係不吉之兆)。
wind·ing-up [ˈwaɪndɪŋˈʌp; ˈwaindiŋˈʌp] *n.* 結束;解散。
wind instrument 管樂器。
wind·jam·mer [ˈwɪndˌdʒæmɚ; ˈwindˌdʒæmə] *n.* ①〖俗〗帆船;帆船的水手。②〖俚〗饒舌之人。
wind·lass [ˈwɪndləs; ˈwindləs] *n.* 起重轆轤;捲揚器;絞盤。—*v.t.* 以或似以捲揚器舉起;以或似以絞盤舉起。—**er,** *n.*
wind·less [ˈwɪndlɪs; ˈwindlis] *adj.* ①無風的; 平穩的; 平靜的。②上氣不接下氣的; 喘氣的。—**ly,** *adv.* —**ness,** *n.*
wind·mill** [ˈwɪndˌmɪl; ˈwindmil] *n.* 風車。 ***fight (or ***tilt at***) ***windmills*** 同幻想中的敵人作戰;改革幻想中的弊端。—*v.t.* 使似風車般地急轉或急動。—*v.i.* 風車般地轉動。
wind music 管樂。(尤指藉風力)。
‡**win·dow** [ˈwɪndo; ˈwindou] *n.* 窗;窗口;窗扉。The eyes are the *windows* of the mind. 眼爲心靈之窗。***bay window*** 凸出的三面窗戶。 ***dormer window*** 房頂斜坡開的窗戶。***have all one's goods in the window*** 金玉其外,敗絮其中;膚淺。***sash window*** 上下拉的窗戶。—*v.t.* 設窗於。—**less,** *adj.*
window blind 窗簾;窗帘;窗帷。
window box ①置於窗臺上或窗外供種植花木之箱形物。②〖建築〗窗框兩側空槽。
window curtain 窗帷;窗簾。
win·dow-dress [ˈwɪndoˈdrɛs; ˈwinˌdouˈdres] *v.t.* 以表面上的裝飾使更吸引人;爲…裝飾表面。
window dresser ①裝飾商店櫥窗者。②裝飾門面者。
window dressing ①商店櫥窗之陳列與裝飾。②用以使他人誤引起良好印象之言語或行動。
window envelope 開窗信封(部分透明之信封,可自該處見其封入物上之地址)。
window frame 窗框;窗架。
win·dow·man [ˈwɪndomən; ˈwindoumən] *n., pl.* **-men.** 負責(公司、機關、售票處等之)某一窗口者。
win·dow·pane [ˈwɪndoˌpen; ˈwindoupein] *n.* 窗玻璃(裝在窗上的玻璃)。
window sash 窗框。
window seat 窗座。
window shade 可以捲起的窗帘布或紙。
win·dow-shop [ˈwɪndoˌʃɑp; ˈwindouʃɔp] *v.i.,* **-shopped, -shop·ping.** 瀏覽商店之櫥窗。—**per,** *n.* —**ping,** *adj., n.*
win·dow·sill [ˈwɪndoˌsɪl; ˈwindousil] *n.* 窗臺。(亦作 **window sill**)
win·dow·y [ˈwɪndəwɪ; ˈwindəwi] *adj.* 多窗的。
wind·pipe [ˈwɪndˌpaɪp; ˈwindpaip] *n.* 氣管。
wind-pol·li·nat·ed [ˈwɪndˌpɑləˌnetɪd; ˈwindˌpɔliˌneitid] *adj.* 〖植物〗風力授粉的。—**wind-pol·li·na·tion,** *n.*
wind pressure 風壓。
wind·proof [ˈwɪndˌpruf; ˈwindpruːf] *adj.* 防風的;不透風的。
wind·row [ˈwɪnˌro, ˈwɪndˌro; ˈwindrou] *n.* ①乾草。②(鋪於地上晒乾之)穀類。③爲風吹集於一處之落葉(等)。—*v.t.* 將(草或穀物)鋪排成行。—**er,** *n.*
wind·sail [ˈwɪndˌsel; ˈwindseil] *n.* 〖航海〗①風帆;帆布風袋。②風車翼。
wind scale 風力分級表。
wind·screen [ˈwɪndˌskrin; ˈwindskriːn] *n.* 〖英〗=**windshield.**
wind·shield [ˈwɪndˌʃild; ˈwindʃiːld] *n.* 〖美〗(汽車之)擋風玻璃。
windshield wiper 汽車(擋風玻璃之)自動擦窗器;雨刷;雨水括。
wind ship 大帆船。
wind sleeve =**windsock.**
wind·sock [ˈwɪndˌsɑk; ˈwindsɔk] *n.* 風向袋。(亦作 **wind cone, wind sock, air sock**)
Wind·sor [ˈwɪnzɚ; ˈwinzə] *n.* 溫莎 (**a.** 英國波克夏之一城市, 濱泰晤士河, 正式稱作 New Windsor. **b.** 加拿大安大略省之一城市, 與美國底特律城隔底特律河相對)。
Wind·sor, Duke of *n.* 溫莎公爵 (1894–1972, 於1936年爲英王, 稱Edward Ⅷ, 旋因愛情問題而遜位)。
Windsor chair 高背斜腿之木椅(十八世紀流行於英美)。
Windsor tie 一種絲質的寬領帶。
wind·spout [ˈwɪndˌspaut; ˈwindspaut] *n.* 旋風。
wind·stick [ˈwɪndˌstɪk; ˈwindstik] *n.* 〖軍俗〗飛機之推進器。
wind·storm [ˈwɪndˌstɔrm; ˈwindstɔːm] *n.* 狂風;暴風。
wind-swept [ˈwɪndˌswɛpt; ˈwindswept] *adj.* 爲風吹掃的;被風亂吹的;當風的。(亦作 **windswept**)
wind·swift [ˈwɪndˌswɪft; ˈwindswift] *adj.* 疾速如風的。
wind tee 丁字布(機場上指示風向及飛機起降方向之"T"字形標誌)。
wind-throw [ˈwɪndˌθro; ˈwindθrou] *v.t.,* **-threw, -thrown.** 以風力連根拔起。
wind·tight [ˈwɪndˈtaɪt; ˈwindˈtait] *adj.* 不通風的;不透風的。
wind tunnel (測定風壓對飛機或汽車等之作用的)風洞。
wind·up [ˈwaɪndˌʌp; ˈwaindʌp] *n.* ①結束; 完結。②〖棒球〗投手在投球前揮動胳臂的準備動作。—*adj.* 裝有發條的。
wind vane 風標;風信旗。
wind·ward [ˈwɪndwɚd; ˈwindwəd] *adv.* 向風地;頂風地。—*adj.* 向風的;頂風的。the *windward* side. 向風的一邊。—*n.* ①上

風的方向。②向風的一邊。***cast*** (or ***lay***) ***an anchor to windward*** 未雨綢繆；爲未來的安全着想。***get to the windward of*** **a.** (海戰時)駛到(他船)的上風；(爲躲避臭氣)轉到…的上風。**b.** 比…占有利的地位；占上風；超出。***keep to the windward of*** 避着…。

wind·way ['wɪnd,we; 'windwei] *n.* 氣廊；空氣通道。

***wind·y** ['wɪndɪ; 'windi] *adj.*, **wind·i·er, wind·i·est.** ①多風的；當風的。*windy* weather. 多風的天氣。②空論的；虛誇的。③多言的；多空論的。④引起腸胃中滯氣的。⑤〖俚〗受驚恐的；神經不安的。—**wind·i·ly,** *adv.*

‡wine [waɪn; wain] *n., v.,* **wined, wining,** *adj.* —*n.* ①葡萄酒。②水果酒。③酒。④紅葡萄酒色。⑤〖英〗以 wine 爲主要飲料的宴會。***new wine in old bottles*** 舊瓶裝新酒；舊形式新內容。—*v.t.* 以酒款待。***wine and dine*** (***someone***) 熱烈款待(某人)。—*v.i.* 宴飲。—*adj.* 深紅色的。

wine bag 皮製酒囊。

wine·bib·ber ['waɪn,bɪbɚ; 'wain,bibə] *n.* 豪飲者。

wine·bib·bing ['waɪn,bɪbɪŋ; 'wain,bibiŋ] *adj.* 嗜酒的；豪飲的。—*n.* 嗜酒；豪飲。

wine·bot·tle ['waɪn,bɑtl; 'wain,bɔtl] *n.* 酒瓶。

wine·bowl ['waɪn,bol; 'wainboul] *n.* ①大酒杯。②飲酒；飲酒癖。

wine cellar ①藏酒之地窖。②藏於地窖中之酒。

wine color 深紅色。

wine-col·ored ['waɪn,kʌlɚd; 'wain,kʌləd] *adj.* 深紅色的。

wine cooler 冷酒器。

wine-cup ['waɪn,kʌp; 'wainkʌp] *n.* =**winebowl.**

wine·glass ['waɪn,glæs; 'wainglɑːs] *n.* 小酒杯；玻璃酒杯。

wine·grow·er ['waɪn,groɚ; 'wain,grouə] *n.* 種植葡萄並製葡萄酒者。—**wine-grow·ing,** *n., adj.*

wine·house ['waɪn,haus; 'wainhaus] *n.* 酒廳。

wine·less ['waɪnlɪs; 'wainlis] *adj.* 無酒的。

wine list 飯館中之酒單。(亦作 **wine card**)

wine press 壓葡萄酒的機器或大桶。(亦作 **wine presser**)

win·er·y ['waɪnərɪ; 'wainəri] *n., pl.* **-er·ies.** 葡萄酒釀造廠；釀酒廠。

Wine·sap, wine·sap ['waɪn,sæp; 'wainsæp] *n.* 〖美〗①一種深紅色的多蘋果。②多蘋果樹。

wine·shop ['waɪn,ʃɑp; 'wainʃɔp] *n.* 酒店；酒館。

wine·skin ['waɪn,skɪn; 'wainskin] *n.* ①皮製酒袋。②豪飲者；縱飲者。

wine taster ①試飲葡萄酒者；品酒者。②品酒用之小碗。(亦作 **winetaster**)

wine vault ①藏葡萄酒的地窖。②酒店。

‡wing [wɪŋ; wiŋ] *n.* ①翼；翅。②在形狀或用途與翼相似之物。the *wings* of an airplane. 飛機之翼。③〖諧〗臂；獸的前腿。④建築物在邊側突出之部分；邊屋；廂房。⑤舞臺之側面。⑥(軍隊之)翼。⑦一組織中的一部分；一派系。⑧〖美〗(空軍)聯隊。⑨飛行；飛翔。⑩〖俗〗胳臂，尤指棒球投手投球之臂。⑪安樂椅椅背兩端朝前突出之部分。⑫〖英〗車輛上之保險槓。⑬箭翎。⑭雙扇門或窗帘等之任一扇。⑮對摺之布景板。⑯球隊之左或右翼。***clip a person's wings*** 限制某人的活動、花費等。***lend wings to*** 使快走；加速。***on the wing*** **a.** 在飛行中的。**b.** 在旅行中的；在出發中的。**c.** 在活動中的；忙碌的。***on the wings of the wind*** 極迅速的。***take to itself wings*** 匆匆而去；消失。***take wing*** **a.** 飛去。**b.** 迅速離去。***under the wing of*** 在…的保護之下。—*v.t.* ①裝以翼。②使能飛。③飛過。The bird *wings* its way to the south. 鳥飛向南方。④增加…的速度。Fear *winged* his steps. 恐懼加速他的脚步。⑤傷(鳥)之翼；傷(人)之臂。⑥擊落(飛鳥)。⑦依賴舞臺兩側之提示而表演(一個角色)。—*v.i.* 飛過。The planes *winged* over the Alps. 飛機飛越阿爾卑斯山。

wing bar ①飛機機翼的橫骨。②河口的沙灘。

wing bit 鑰匙頭。

wing bolt 翼形螺釘帽。

wing case (昆蟲之)翅鞘。

wing chair 安樂椅。

wing commander ①(英國皇家空軍等之)中校。②(美國空軍之)聯隊長。

wing cover (昆蟲之)翅鞘。

wing coverts 覆蔽或襯墊羽翼之柔毛。

wing-ding ['wɪŋ,dɪŋ; 'wiŋdiŋ] *n.* 〖俚〗①藥物引起的或假裝的發作；驚厥。②一陣暴怒。③喧鬧的慶祝聚會。④異常之事。⑤一件東西；小玩意。(亦作 **wingding**)

winged [wɪŋd; wiŋd] *adj.* ①有翅的。②好像有翅的。③多翅的。④翅受傷的。⑤迅速的。⑥崇高的；高尙的。

Winged Horse 〖天文〗飛馬座(=Pegasus).

wing·er ['wɪŋɚ; 'wiŋə] *n.* 球隊中擔任左右兩翼之任一隊員。

wing-foot·ed ['wɪŋ'futɪd; 'wiŋ'futid] *adj.* ①有帶翼之足的。②〖詩〗迅速的；輕快的；輕捷的。

wing·less ['wɪŋlɪs; 'wiŋlis] *adj.* ①無翼的。②不會飛的。—**ness,** *n.*

wing·let ['wɪŋlɪt; 'wiŋlit] *n.* 小翼；小翅。

wing·like ['wɪŋ,laɪk; 'wiŋlaik] *adj.* 如翼的；翼狀的。

wing·man ['wɪŋmən; 'wiŋmən] *n., pl.* **-men.** ①〖空軍〗**a.** 僚機。**b.** 僚機駕駛員。②〖運動〗擔任球隊雙翼之隊員。

wing nut 翼形螺母。

wing root 機翼與機身銜接之部分。

wings [wɪŋz; wiŋz] *n.* ①〖空軍〗飛行章。②女童軍戴的一種翼形章。

wing shooting 飛鳥射擊。

wing shot ①對飛鳥發射之一發子彈。②精於射擊飛鳥之獵者。

wing·span ['wɪŋ,spæn; 'wiŋspæn] *n.* (飛機之)翼展；翼幅。(亦作 **wing span**)

wing·spread ['wɪŋ,sprɛd; 'wiŋspred] *n.* ①兩翼張開之寬度。②=**wingspan.**

wing tank 掛在機翼上的輔助油箱。

wing tip (飛機之)翼尖。

wing-wea·ry ['wɪŋ,wɪrɪ; 'wiŋ,wiəri] *adj.* 飛累了的；疲於旅行的。

wing·y ['wɪŋɪ; 'wiŋi] *adj.* ①有翼的。②迅速的。③高聳雲霄的。④似翼的；翼狀的。

wink** [wɪŋk; wiŋk] *v.i.* ①霎眼；霎眼示意。to *wink* at a person. 向某人霎眼示意。②假裝未見。③(光、星等)閃爍。④閉眼。⑤熄滅；消滅；消失〖out〗. The lights *winked* out. 燈光熄了。⑥發燈光信號。—*v.t.* ①瞬(目)；霎(眼)。to *wink* one's eyes. 霎眼。②眨眼使乾、消、退等。③使閃爍(以發信號)。④忽視；不管。—*n.* ①瞬；霎眼。②目語；眼色；暗示。③瞬息；一瞬間。She did not sleep a *wink* last night. 她昨夜一點覺也沒睡。④閃爍。⑤一點點；微量。forty winks*** 短暫的睡眠。***tip a person the wink*** 霎眼予以警告。—**ing·ly,** *adv.*

wink·er ['wɪŋkɚ; 'wiŋkə] *n.* ①霎眼的

人;閃爍之物。②(馬之)遮眼罩;搧眼。③〖俗〗眼睛;睫毛。
wink·ing ['wɪŋkɪŋ; 'wiŋkiŋ] *n.* ①瞬目。like *winking*.〖俚〗很快地。②目語;目示。③佯爲不見;寬容。④小睡。
win·kle¹ ['wɪŋkl; 'wiŋkl] *n.* 任何可供食用的海螺;玉黍螺。
win·kle² *v.t.*, **-kled, -kling.** ①排除。②剔出;挑出;挖出〖常 out〗。
win·less ['wɪnlɪs; 'winlis] *adj.* 每場皆輸的;沒有一次勝利的。「可贏得的。」
win·na·ble ['wɪnəbl; 'winəbl] *adj.*
***win·ner** ['wɪnə; 'winə] *n.* 勝利者;得獎者。
winner's circle 賽馬場上的頒獎區。
***win·ning** ['wɪnɪŋ; 'winiŋ] *adj.* ①勝利的;得勝的。the *winning* team. 得勝的一隊。②迷人的;動人的;嬌媚的。a *winning* smile. 迷人的笑容。—*n.* ①贏得;獲得。the *winning* of the peace. 和平之贏得。②(*pl.*)贏得的錢或東西。③煤礦口;馬上可以開採的煤礦礦床。
win·ning·est ['wɪnɪŋɪst; 'winiŋist] *adj.* 〖俗〗贏得大部分的;贏得最多的。
win·ning·ly ['wɪnɪŋlɪ; 'winiŋli] *adv.* 迷人地;動人地。「nis] *n.* 引誘力。」
win·ning·ness ['wɪnɪŋnɪs; 'winiŋ-
winning post 田徑跑道上之終點竿。
win·now ['wɪno; 'winou] *v.t.* ①(利用風等)揚去(穀物)之糠皮等;簸(穀);搧掉(米糠等)。②吹去;吹散。③除去(惡劣部分);選出(優良部分);篩選;辨別。④以翼或翼狀物搧;鼓(翼)。⑤〖詩〗吹散;吹亂(頭髮等)。—*v.i.* ①簸去糠皮等。②鼓翼而飛。—*n.* ①簸穀器;簸箕。②簸揚穀物。—**er,** *n.*
wi·no ['waɪno; 'wainou] *n.*, *pl.* **-nos.** 〖俚〗喝便宜酒喝得醉醺醺的懶漢;酒鬼。
win·some ['wɪnsəm; 'winsəm] *adj.* 迷人的;悅目的;可愛的;有吸引力的。—**ly,** *adv.* —**ness,** *n.*
‡win·ter ['wɪntə; 'wintə] *n.* ①冬;冬季。a hard *winter*. 嚴寒之冬季。②衰退期;晚年。③年;歲。a man of 70 *winters*. 七十老翁。—*adj.* ①冬的;冬季的。*winter* clothing. 冬衣。②可備冬季用的。*winter* apples. 冬天可食用的蘋果。—*v.t.* 在冬季飼養(家畜)或保護(花草等)。—*v.i.* ①過冬;避寒。to *winter* in the south. 在南方過冬。②靠某種食物過冬。—**er,** *n.* 「tə,biːtn] *adj.* 爲寒冷所傷的。」
win·ter·beat·en ['wɪntə,bitn̩;'win-
win·ter·bound ['wɪntə,baund;'wintə'baund] *adj.* 爲冰雪所阻的。
win·ter·cough ['wɪntə,kɔf;'wintəkɔːf] *n.* 〖醫〗慢性支氣管炎。
win·ter·feed ['wɪntə,fid;'wintəfiːd] *n.*, *v.*, **-fed, -feed·ing.** —*n.* 多季飼料。—*v.t.* ①多季以…餵牲畜。②多季裏餵(牲畜)。—*v.i.* 餵以多季飼料。
win·ter·green ['wɪntə,grin; 'wintəgriːn] *n.* 〖植物〗鹿蹄草。
win·ter·ish ['wɪntərɪʃ; 'wintəriʃ] *adj.* 如多的;寒冷的。
win·ter·ize ['wɪntə,raɪz; 'wintəraiz] *v.t.*, **-ized, -iz·ing.** ①備以防寒裝置。②使變成多天不凝之油。—**win·ter·i·za·tion,** *n.*
win·ter·kill ['wɪntə,kɪl; 'wintəkil] *v.t.* & *v.i.* 凍死(指植物而言)。
win·ter·less ['wɪntəlɪs; 'wintəlis] *adj.* 無多天的。
win·ter·ly ['wɪntəlɪ; 'wintəli] *adj.* ①如多的;寒冷的。②不歡愉的。—**win·ter-**
li·ness, *n.* 「tə'siːzn] *n.* 多季。」
win·ter·sea·son ['wɪntə,sizn̩;'win-
winter solstice 多至。
win·ter·tide ['wɪntə,taɪd; 'wintətaid] *n.* 〖古,詩〗=**wintertime.**
win·ter·time ['wɪntə,taɪm; 'wintətaim] *n.* 多季。
winter wheat 多麥。
win·ter·y ['wɪntərɪ; 'wintəri] *adj.*, **-ter·i·er, -ter·i·est.** =**wintry.**
***win·try** ['wɪntrɪ;'wintri] *adj.*, **-tri·er, -tri·est.** ①多的;如多的;寒冷的。*wintry* weather. 寒冷的天氣。②冷淡的。③於寒天中枯萎的。④年紀大的;白髮的。—**win·tri·ly,** *adv.* —**win·tri·ness,** *n.*
win·y ['waɪnɪ; 'waini] *adj.*, **win·i·er, win·i·est.** ①色、香或味似葡萄酒的。②(指空氣)芬芳的;新鮮的。
wipe** [waɪp; waip] *v.*, **wiped, wip·ing,** *n.* —*v.t.* ①擦;拭;抹。to *wipe* something dry. 將某物擦乾。②擦去;拭去。to *wipe* one's tears away. 擦乾眼淚。③徹底消滅;滅絕。④塗(某物)於表面;塗抹。⑤以皮墊塗敷焊料而做成(鉛管之接頭)。—*v.i.* 擦;拭;抹。wipe out*** a. 徹底毀滅;徹底消滅。b.〖俗〗謀殺;殺掉。***wipe the floor with a person*** 〖俚〗徹底擊敗某人。—*n.* ①擦;拭;抹。Give this jug a *wipe*. 把這罐子擦一擦。②〖俚〗手帕。③嘲弄;辱罵。④揮擊。⑤〖機械〗起桿(=wiper).
wip·er ['waɪpə; 'waipə] *n.* ①擦或抹的人。②抹布。③〖機械〗起桿。④〖俚〗手帕。⑤〖電〗接帚。
wir·a·ble ['waɪrəbl; 'waiərəbl] *adj.* ①可裝金屬線的;可以金屬線穿過的。②可暗中操縱的。
‡wire [waɪr; 'waiə] *n.*, *adj.*, *v.*, **wired, wir·ing.** —*n.* ①金屬線;金屬絲。barbed *wire*. 刺鐵絲。②〖俗〗電報。a message by *wire*. 電報。to send (receive) a *wire*. 發(收)電報。③鐵絲網。④(賽馬、賽跑等之)終線。⑤(*pl.*)牽動傀儡之一組鐵絲。⑥樂器之金屬絲。⑦製紙機中鋪濕紙漿用的鐵絲網。***a live wire*** a. 通有電流的電線。b. 活潑而有精力的人。***get under the wire*** 及時完成;及時趕到。***pull (the) wires*** 暗中操縱。***the wire*** 電話。There's someone on *the wire* for you. 有人打電話給你。***under the wire*** a. 在(賽跑之)終線。b. 在最後關頭。***under wire*** 以鐵絲網圍起的。—*adj.* 由金屬線做成的。—*v.t.* ①用金屬絲綑起、繫起、穿起(等)。②裝以金屬絲。③〖美俗〗拍(電報);以電報告知;拍電報給(某人)。Please *wire* me the result. 請將結果用電報告訴我。④用鐵絲網捕捉。—*v.i.* 拍電報。to *wire* home for money. 拍電報回家要錢。—**wir·er,** *n.*
wire agency (新聞)通信社。
wire bridge 鐵線吊橋。
wire brush 鋼絲刷。「聞稿。」
wire copy (報社電臺等所收之)外電新
wire-cut ['waɪr,kʌt; 'waiəkʌt] *adj.* 以或似以鐵絲分切的。
wire cutter 剪斷金屬絲所用的工具。
wired [waɪrd; 'waiəd] *adj.* ①以線加强的。②供以電線的。③以線縛起的。④有線的。⑤以鐵絲圍起的。
wire·danc·er ['waɪr,dænsə; 'waiə-,dɑːnsə] *n.* 走鋼索者。—**wire·danc·ing,** *n.*
wire·draw ['waɪr,drɔ; 'waiə-drɔː] *v.t.*, **-drew, -drawn, -draw·ing.** ①將(金屬)抽成絲。②拉長;拖長。③將(論點等)推繹

至極精微處。④曲解;歪曲。—**er,** *n.*

wire·draw·ing 〔ˈwaɪrˌdrɔɪŋ; ˈwaiəˌdrɔːiŋ〕 *n.* ①金屬線之製造。②將議論等推繹至極精微處。

wire·drawn〔ˈwaɪrˌdrɔn;ˈwaiə-drɔːn〕 *adj.* ①拉成金屬絲的。②辨別過細的; 析理過細的;推敲太甚的。

wired television閉路電視(=closed-circuit television).

wire entanglement 有刺鐵絲網障礙物。

wire gauge 電線直徑度量器。

wire gauze 細金屬線網。

wire glass 內部嵌有金屬絲網之加强玻璃。

wire grass 〖植物〗蟋蟀草。

wire·hair 〔ˈwaɪrˌhɛr; ˈwaiəhɛə〕 *n.* 一種有剛毛的獵狐㹴。(亦作 **wire-haired terrier**)

wire-haired〔ˈwaɪrˈhɛrd;ˈwaiəhɛəd〕 *adj.* 有硬毛的(犬等)。

wire house 支行與總行間有私用電話、電報和無線電打字系統保持連絡的證券公司。

***wire·less** 〔ˈwaɪrlɪs; ˈwaiəlis〕 *adj.* ①無線的。②無線電的。a *wireless* telegram. 無線電報。 a *wireless* station. 無線電臺。 —*n.* ①無線電。②無線電報;無線電話。 to send a message by *wireless.* 以無線電報發送消息。③〖主英〗**a.** 收音機。**b.** 無線電臺之廣播節目。 —*v.t.* & *v.i.* 以無線電傳送消息。—**ly,** *adv.* —**ness,** *n.*

wire·like 〔ˈwaɪrˌlaɪk; ˈwaiəlaik〕 *adj.* 細如鐵絲的。

wire loop binding 用螺紋形鐵絲的活頁裝訂。

wire·man 〔ˈwaɪrmən; ˈwaiəmən〕 *n., pl.* **-men.** 架設或修理電線之工人。

wire netting 做窗紗用的金屬細網。

wire·pho·to 〔ˈwaɪrˌfoto;ˈwaiəˌfoutou〕 *n.* 有線電傳真。—*v.t.* 以此種傳真傳送。

wire-pull 〔ˈwaɪrˌpul; ˈwaiəˌpul〕 *v.i.* & *v.t.* 從事幕後操縱。(亦作 **wirepull**)

wire·pull·er 〔ˈwaɪrˌpulɚ;ˈwaiəˌpulə〕 *n.* ①傀儡之牽線者。②〖俗〗幕後之操縱者。③〖建築〗預先留在線管中拉電線用的鐵絲。

wire·pull·ing 〔ˈwaɪrˌpulɪŋ; ˈwaiəˌpuliŋ〕 *n.* ①對傀儡之牽線。②〖俗〗以不正當之方法操縱個人或政黨等;幕後操縱。—*adj.* 〖俗〗對公務員施以祕密而不正當之影響力的。

wire recorder 舊式的鋼絲錄音機。

wire recording 鋼絲錄音。

wire rope 鋼纜;鋼索。

wire service (新聞)通訊社。

wire·smith 〔ˈwaɪrˌsmɪθ;ˈwaiəsmiθ〕 *n.* 鐵絲匠。

wire solder 焊條。

wire·spun 〔ˈwaɪrˌspʌn; ˈwaiəspʌn〕 *adj.* ①拉得長長的。②過於微妙的; 不明顯的。③實質太少的; 內容貧乏的。

wire·tap 〔ˈwaɪrˌtæp; ˈwaiətæp〕 *n., v.,* **-tapped, -tap·ping.** —*n.* 偷接電話線以竊聽祕密之行為。 —*v.t.* & *v.i.* 偷接電話線以竊聽(祕密)。 —**per,** *n.*

wire tapping 非法接線於電話線上竊聽祕密。

wire·way 〔ˈwaɪrˌwe; ˈwaiəwei〕 *n.* 電線管道。

wire·work 〔ˈwaɪrˌwɝk; ˈwaiəwəːk〕 *n.* ①鐵絲工。②走鋼絲特技。

wire·work·er 〔ˈwaɪrˌwɝkɚ; ˈwaiəˌwəːkə〕 *n.* 鐵絲工人。

wire·works〔ˈwaɪrˌwɝks;ˈwaiəwəːks〕 *n., pl.* **-works.** (作 *sing.* or *pl.* 解)鐵絲廠。

wire·worm 〔ˈwaɪrˌwɝm;ˈwaiəwəːm〕 *n.* ①各種反跳甲蟲的幼蟲。②鐵線蟲。

wire-wove 〔ˈwaɪrˌwov; ˈwaiəwouv〕 *adj.* ①由金屬線網所做的。②品質極佳而有光澤的(上等信紙)。

wir·ing 〔ˈwaɪrɪŋ; ˈwaiəriŋ〕 *n.* ①架線;敷線;接線;布線。②(房屋等之)電線系統。③〖外科〗**a.** (骨折之)架線縫合法。**b.** (動脈瘤之)插線法。—*adj.* ①架線的;敷線的;接線的。②**a.** 用於架線縫合法的。**b.** 用於插線法的。

***wir·y** 〔ˈwaɪrɪ; ˈwaiəri〕 *adj.,* **wir·i·er, wir·i·est.** ①金屬線製的; 鐵絲製的。a *wiry* cage. 鐵絲籠。②金屬線狀的;剛硬的。③(人體等) 瘦長而有力的。④金屬線等振動所產生之聲音的。 ⑤細而尖的 (聲音)。—**wir·i·ly,** *adv.* —**wir·i·ness,** *n.*

wis 〔wɪs; wis〕 *v.t.* 〖古〗知;想;以為(主要用於 I wis).

Wis., Wisc. Wisconsin.

Wis·con·sin 〔wɪsˈkɑnsn̩; wisˈkɔnsin〕 *n.* ①威斯康辛州(美國中北部一州,首府為 Madison). ②威斯康辛河。

‡**wis·dom** 〔ˈwɪzdəm; ˈwizdəm〕 *n.* ①智慧;睿智。He showed great *wisdom* in what he said and did. 他的言行表現出很大的智慧。②明智的行為或言語。③知識;學識。④〖古〗賢人。⑤(W-)＝**Wisdom of Solomon.**

Wisdom of Solomon 所羅門之智慧(舊約偽經之一卷)。(略作 **Wisd.**)

wisdom tooth 智齒。 ***cut one's wisdom teeth*** 成熟;長成。

‡**wise**[1] 〔waɪz;waiz〕 *adj.,* **wis·er, wis·est,** *v.,* **wised, wis·ing.** —*adj.* ①智慧的; 明智的;聰明的。You were *wise* not to go. 你不去是聰明的。②知道的; 了解的; 明白的。We are none the *wiser* for his explanations. 聽了他的解釋, 我們還是不明白。③有學問的; 飽學的。④〖古〗通妖術的;精於祕術的;通神的。***be*** (or ***get***) ***wise to***〖俚〗瞭解;識破; 得知。***get wise*** **a.** 聰明起來;變聰明。**b.** 無禮貌; 放肆。***put someone wise*** 〖俚〗以祕密告知某人。—*v.t.* 使明白;使了解〖up〗.—*v.i.* 明白;了解〖up〗.—**ly,** *adv.* —**ness,** *n.*

wise[2] *n.* 方式;方面;態度。

-wise 〖字尾〗表"樣態;方向;位置"之義。

wise·a·cre 〔ˈwaɪzˌekɚ; ˈwaizˌeikə〕 *n.* ①自作聰明的人;假聰明人。②目空一切的人。(亦作 **wisenheimer**)

wise·crack 〔ˈwaɪzˌkræk;ˈwaizkræk〕 *n.* 〖俚〗俏皮話;妙語;警語。—*v.i.* 〖俚〗說俏皮話;作妙語。 —*v.t.* 當作笑話說。—**er,** *n.*

wise guy 自作聰明的人。

wise·head 〔ˈwaɪzˌhɛd; ˈwaizhed〕 *n.* 自作聰明者。

wise·heart·ed〔ˈwaɪzˌhɑrtɪd;ˈwaizˌhɑːtid〕 *adj.* 善於洞察的。

wise man ①賢人。②男巫。

wise·wom·an 〔ˈwaɪzˌwumən;ˈwaizˌwumən〕*n., pl.* **-wom·en.** ①女巫。②助產士。

‡**wish** 〔wɪʃ; wiʃ〕 *v.t.* ①意欲;切望。I *wish* I were rich. 我但願我很有錢。②希望; 渴望 (that-clause 中的 that 通常省略)。It is to be *wished* (＝hoped) that.... 但望…。③需要;要;想要。 Do you *wish* to leave now? 你現在就要走嗎? ④祝;頌;祈。I *wish* you a Merry Christmas. 我祝你耶誕快樂。⑤表示一種關懷的願望。to *wish* a person well. 願某人有好運。 —*v.i.* 欲; 願。We *wish* for peace. 我們期望和平。*Wishing* won't pay the rent. 光期望付不了租金(只希望而不行動是沒用的)。 ***wish on*** 强迫;强加諸。—*n.* ①希望; 願望。If *wishes* were horses, beggars might ride. (諺) 如果希望均能實現, 叫化子都能致富了。②祝頌。with best *wishes* for a happy new year. 祝新年快樂。③所願望的事物。—**er,** *n.*

wish·bone 〔ˈwɪʃˌbon; ˈwiʃboun〕 *n.* (鳥胸的)叉骨(吃鳥肉後, 兩人同扯, 扯到長的, 據説能達心願)。

wish·ful 〔ˈwɪʃfəl; ˈwiʃful〕 *adj.* ①渴望的;切望的;充滿渴望的。②基於願望(非基於現實)的。 ***wishful thinker*** 打如意算盤者。 ***wishful thinking*** 如意算盤; 如意的想法。 **—ly,** *adv.* **—ness,** *n.*

wish fulfillment 〖心理分析〗遭到挫折的願望之間接實現(如夢中發財等)。

wish-wash 〔ˈwɪʃˌwɑʃ; ˈwiʃwɔʃ〕 *n.* ①淡酒。②傻話;無聊的文章。

wish·y-wash·y 〔ˈwɪʃɪˌwɑʃɪ; ˈwiʃiˌwɔʃi〕 *adj.* ①淡的;稀薄的(酒等)。②無實質的;無力的;軟弱的。

wisp 〔wɪsp; wisp〕 *n.* ①小綹; 小把; 小縷。②小物件;小東西;小孩。③鬼火; 燐火。 *—v.t.* 使成縷狀(物)。 *—v.i.* 成縷狀而出。

wisp·y 〔ˈwɪspɪ;ˈwispi〕 *adj.*, **wisp·i·er, wisp·i·est.** 像小束的; 纖細的;輕而脆弱的。(亦作 **wispish**)

wist 〔wɪst; wist〕〖古〗 *v.* pt. & pp. of **wit²**. He *wist* not. 他不知道。

wist·ful 〔ˈwɪstfəl; ˈwistful〕 *adj.* ①想望的;渴望的。②沉思的;令人憂思的。**—ly,** *adv.*

wist·ful·ness 〔ˈwɪstfəlnɪs; ˈwistfulnis〕 *n.* 若有所欲狀; 憂思狀。

‡wit¹ 〔wɪt; wit〕 *n.* ①心智; 智力; 才智。The child was out of his *wits* with fright. 那孩子嚇呆了。②機智。③機智者;才子。④健全的神智。 ***be at one's wit's end*** 窮於應付;不知所措。 ***have***(or ***keep***) ***one's wits about one*** 警覺;機警。 ***live by one's wits*** 靠着小聰明混日子。

wit² *v.t. & v.i., pres. 1st pers.* **wot,** *2nd pers.* **wost,** *3rd pers.* **wot,** *pl.* **wit;** *pt. & pp.* **wist;** *ppr.* **wit·ting.** 〖古〗知道(=know). ***to wit*** 卽;就是(=namely; that is to say).

˙witch 〔wɪtʃ; witʃ〕 *n.* ①巫婆。②醜老太婆。③〖俗〗美麗迷人的女性;狐狸精。 *—v.t.*①對…施或似施巫術。②迷住; 迷惑。 *—v.i.* 用探礦棒探礦。

witch·craft 〔ˈwɪtʃˌkræft;ˈwitʃkrɑːft〕 *n.* ①巫術; 魔法。to practice *witchcraft*. 施行巫術。②魔力;不可抵抗的影響力。

witch doctor 巫醫(尤指非洲部落中者)。

witch doctress 女巫醫。

witch·er·y 〔ˈwɪtʃərɪ; ˈwitʃəri〕 *n., pl.* **-er·ies.** ①巫術;魔法。②蠱惑;魔力。

witches' brew 一團糟。(亦作**witch's brew, witches' broth**)

witches' cauldron 可怕的混亂狀態。

witch hazel ①〖植物〗金縷梅。②金縷梅樹皮之汁。

witch·hood 〔ˈwɪtʃhud; ˈwitʃhud〕 *n.* 身爲巫婆的狀態; 巫婆之身分或地位。

witch hunt 〖美俗〗根據不足的或不相干的證據而作的調查(常以被調查者不忠、顚覆及其他不法行爲爲口實); 政治迫害。(亦作 **witchhunt**)

witch·ing 〔ˈwɪtʃɪŋ; ˈwitʃiŋ〕 *adj.* 巫術的;迷人的。 ***the witching hour of night*** 午夜三更;午夜。*—n.* ①巫術。②迷戀;迷惑。**—ly,** *adv.*

witch·like 〔ˈwɪtʃˌlaɪk;ˈwitʃlaik〕 *adj.* ①似巫婆的。②醜惡的。

witch·man 〔ˈwɪtʃmən;ˈwitʃmən〕 *n., pl.* **-men.** 巫醫(=witch doctor).

witch·wo·man 〔ˈwɪtʃˌwumən;ˈwitʃˌwumən〕 *n., pl.* **-wo·men.** 女巫醫(=witch doctress).

witch·y 〔ˈwɪtʃɪ; ˈwitʃi〕 *adj.* ①似巫婆的;似巫術的。②怪異的。

wit·e·na·ge·mot 〔ˈwɪtənəgəˌmot; ˈwitinəjiˈmout〕 *n.* 〖英史〗國會。(亦作 **witenagemote**)

‡with 〔wɪð, wɪθ; wið, wiθ〕 *prep.* ①同;偕;共; 與。 to cooperate *with* a person. 與某人合作。 to mix *with* the crowd. 和羣衆混在一起。 Leave the child *with* her aunt. 把孩子留給她姑母照顧。②有; 附有; 帶有;具有。a man *with* white hair. 白髮之人。③用;以。to have no pen to write *with* (=to have no pen *with* which to write). 沒有筆寫字。Work *with* care. 用心工作。④加於; 包括有; 含有。 Do you want sugar *with* your tea? 你的茶裏要加糖嗎? ⑤一般;相合。 to sympathize *with* someone. 同情某人。⑥表示關係。 They are friendly *with* us. 他們對我們很好。⑦關於; 對於。 We are pleased *with* the house. 我們對於這所房屋很滿意。⑧因; 由於。 to shake *with* cold. 因冷而顫抖。⑨按照…的比例。A man grows wiser *with* age. 人的智慧隨年齡而增長。⑩隨同;隨着。⑪對。⑫同…分別。 I hate to part *with* my favorite things. 我不願捨棄心愛的東西。⑬對於。*With* some people, pleasure is more important than work. 對於某些人,享樂比工作更爲重要。⑭雖然;儘管。*With* all his money, he is unhappy. 儘管他有那麼多錢, 他並不快樂。 ⑮與…同時。 *With* this battle the war ended. 這一仗完後,戰爭就結束了。⑯與…同方向。⑰獲有;得有;取得。I went *with* his permission. 我得到他的允許而去。⑱與副詞結合, 表示命令。Away *with* him! 把他帶走! Down *with* the dictator! 打倒獨裁者! ***in with*** 與…很友善;與…很熟。 ***keep in with*** 〖俗〗與…保持友誼。 ***what with...(and) what with*** 半因…半因(=partly because of ... and partly because of). ***with child*** 懷孕。 ***with it*** 〖俚〗**a.** 消息靈通的。**b.** 對某事甚感興趣。 ***with that*** 接着;於是 (=following that, thereupon). ***with this*** 說了這個話;這樣做了之後(=saying or doing this). *—adv.* 在;有。 I'll have my hamburger *with*. 我會帶我的牛肉餅三明治。

with- 〖字首〗表"離開;逆;反"之義, 如: withdraw, withhold.

with·al 〔wɪðˈɔl, wɪθˈɔl; wiˈðɔːl〕〖古〗 *adv.* ①又; 且; 同樣; 同時。 ②雖說如此。 *—prep.* 以(=with, 但常用於目的語之後,放在句末)。 What shall he fill his belly *withal*? 他用甚麼來果腹呢?

˙with·draw 〔wɪðˈdrɔ, wɪθ–; wiðˈdrɔː, wiθ–〕*v.*, **-drew, -drawn, -draw·ing.** *—v.t.* 取回;撤回;收回; 撤銷; 撤退。to *withdraw* an offer. 撤回一項建議。*—v.i.* 撤退;退去。The troops *withdrew*. 軍隊撤退。He *withdrew* from the room. 他離開這個房間。 **—a·ble,** *adj.* **—er,** *n.*

with·draw·al 〔wɪðˈdrɔəl, wɪθ–; wiðˈdrɔːəl, wiθ–〕 *n.* ①取回; 撤回; 收回; 撤銷;撤退;退去。②領出存款;提款。He made several large *withdrawals* from the bank. 他從銀行提出了好幾筆巨額存款。(亦作 **withdrawment**)

withdrawal symptoms 斷除徵狀;脫癮徵狀(吸毒者毒癮發作時, 斷絕毒品供應所呈徵狀, 如出汗及消沉等)。

with·drawn [wɪðˈdrɔn, wɪθ–; wiðˈdrɔːn, wiθ–] *v.* pp. of **withdraw.** —*adj.* ①內向的。②孤立的；孤獨的。

with·drew [wɪðˈdru, wɪθ–; wiðˈdruː] *v.* pt. of **withdraw.**

withe [waɪð, wɪθ, wɪð; wiθ, wið, waið] *n., v.,* **withed, with·ing.** —*n.* 柔枝；柳條。—*v.t.* 用枝條捆束。

***with·er** [ˈwɪðɚ; ˈwiðə] *v.i.* ①凋謝；枯萎。The flowers soon *withered.* 花很快就凋謝了。②衰退；衰微。—*v.t.* ①使凋謝；使枯萎。②使衰退；使衰微；使色衰。③使感到迷惑或羞慚；使無以對答。She *withered* him with a scornful look. 她的輕蔑的一瞥使他自感羞慚。—*n.* (茶葉之)烘乾。—**er,** *n.*

with·ered [ˈwɪðɚd; ˈwiðəd] *adj.* 凋謝的；萎縮的；憔悴的。

with·er·ing [ˈwɪðərɪŋ; ˈwiðəriŋ] *adj.* ①使枯萎的；苛酷的。②用以乾燥他物(如茶葉等)的。③毀滅性的；破壞性的。—**ly,** *adv.*

with·ers [ˈwɪðɚz; ˈwiðəz] *n. pl.* 鬐甲(馬兩肩骨間的隆起部分)。***My withers were unwrung.*** 我不受刺戟；我不爲所動。***wring one's withers*** 使人苦痛；使人有麻煩。

with·er·shins [ˈwɪðɚˌʃɪnz; ˈwiðəʃinz] *adv.*〖蘇,英方〗同太陽運行方向相反地；倒轉地；相反地。(亦作 **widdershins**)

with·held [wɪðˈhɛld, wɪθ–; wiðˈheld, wiθ–] *v.* pt. & pp. of **withhold.**

***with·hold** [wɪðˈhold, wɪθ–; wiðˈhould, wiθ–] *v.,* **-held, -hold·ing.** —*v.t.* ①不肯給與；拒絕。to *withhold* payment. 拒絕付款。②抑制；制止。—*v.i.* 克制慾望；似欲作而未作。—**er,** *n.*

withholding tax 扣繳稅(如雇主替政府從職員薪資中扣繳的所得稅等)。(亦作 **withholding**)

‡**with·in** [wɪðˈɪn, wɪθˈɪn; wiˈðin] *prep.* ①在…之內。By the X ray, doctors can see *within* the body. 藉着X光線，醫生可以觀察人體的內部。②在…的範圍之內；不出。She lives *within* her income.她量入爲出。*within* hearing. 在可聽及的範圍內。—*adv.* ①在內；在內部。The house has been painted *within* and without. 這所房屋裏外都油漆過了。②在室內。to stay *within.* 留在戶內。③在內心裏面。She is pure *within.* 她心地純潔。—*n.* 內部。Seen from *within,* the cave looks larger. 從內部觀之，這洞顯得較大些。

with·in·doors [wɪðˈɪnˌdorz; wiðˈinˌdɔːz] *adv.* 在戶內。

with·in-named [wɪðˈɪnˌnemd; wiðˈinneimd] *adj.* (文件、條文中)指名的。

with·in·side [wɪðˈɪnˌsaɪd; wiðˈinsaid] *prep.*〖古〗在…之內。

with·in·side(s) [wɪðˈɪnˌsaɪd(z); wiðˈinsaid(z)] *adv.* 在內；在裏面(=inside).

with-it [ˈwɪðɪt; ˈwiðit] *adj.*〖俚〗最時髦的；跟得上潮流的。

‡**with·out** [wɪðˈaʊt, wɪθ–; wiˈðaut] *prep.* ①沒有；無；不。He said he would come *without* fail. 他說他一定來。He went away *without* taking leave.他不辭而別。They never meet *without* quarreling.他們每次見面必定吵嘴。②在…之外。He is waiting *without* the gates. 他在門外等待着。***It goes without saying.*** 不消說；不待言。—*adv.* ①在外部；在外面。②在戶外。It was cold *without.* 外面很冷。③無某種不言而喻之物。—*n.* 外部；外面。The sound comes from *without.* 這聲音來自外面。—*conj.*〖主方〗除非(=unless).

with·out·door(s) [wɪðˈaʊtˌdɔr(z); wiðˈautdɔː(z)] *adv.* 在外面；在戶外。

***with·stand** [wɪθˈstænd, wɪð–; wiðˈstænd] *v.,* **-stood, -stand·ing.** —*v.i.* & *v.t.* 抵抗；對抗；耐。Soldiers have to *withstand* hardships.士兵必須能耐勞苦。—**er,** *n.*

with·stand·ing·ness [wɪθˈstændɪŋnɪs; wiðˈstændiŋnis] *n.* 抵抗力；耐力。

with·y [ˈwɪðɪ, ˈwɪθɪ; ˈwiði] *n., pl.* **with·ies,** *adj.,* **with·i·er, with·i·est.** —*n.* ①柳條；柳枝。②柳條編成之繩索。—*adj.* ①柳枝編的。②柔韌如柳枝的。

wit·less [ˈwɪtlɪs; ˈwitlis] *adj.* ①無智的；愚笨的；輕率的。②無知的；不知的。—**ly,** *adv.*

wit·ling [ˈwɪtlɪŋ; ˈwitliŋ] *n.* 小有才「智者；自以爲有才智者。」

‡**wit·ness** [ˈwɪtnɪs; ˈwitnis] *n.* ①證據；證明。The man's fingerprints bore *witness* to his guilt. 這人的指紋證明他犯罪。②目擊者(=eyewitness). ③證人。***call to witness*** 請…作證。***give witness on behalf of*** 爲…作證。***in witness of*** 爲…的證據。***with a witness***〖古〗千眞萬確地；明如見火地。—*v.t.* ①親見；目擊。He *witnessed* the accident. 他親眼看見這意外事故。②證明。③於(文書)上面簽名作證。④作爲某一事件發生之場合或時間。—*v.i.* 證明；作證。—*prep.* 如…所證明。

wit·ness·a·ble [ˈwɪtnɪsəbl; ˈwitnisəbl] *adj.* 可目睹的。

witness chair 法庭中證人席上給證人「坐的椅子。」

witness stand 法庭中的證人席。(亦作 **witness-box**)

wit·ti·cism [ˈwɪtəˌsɪzəm; ˈwitisizm] *n.* 諧語；雋語；妙語。

wit·ti·ly [ˈwɪtɪlɪ; ˈwitili] *adv.* 機智地；「詼諧地。」

wit·ti·ness [ˈwɪtɪnɪs; ˈwitinis] *n.* 詼諧；機智。

wit·ting [ˈwɪtɪŋ; ˈwitiŋ] *adj.* 知曉的；「有意的；故意的。」

wit·ting·ly [ˈwɪtɪŋlɪ; ˈwitiŋli] *adv.* 故意地；有意地。

wit·tol [ˈwɪtl̩; ˈwitl] *n.*〖古〗明知妻有「外遇而佯作不知者。」

***wit·ty** [ˈwɪtɪ; ˈwiti] *adj.,* **-ti·er, -ti·est.** 富於機智的；詼諧的。a *witty* remark. 雋語；妙語。

wive [waɪv; waiv] *v.,* **wived, wiv·ing.** —*v.t.* & *v.i.* ①娶妻；給以妻；娶(妻)。②爲…之妻。

wi·vern [ˈwaɪvɚn; ˈwaivən] *n.*〖紋「章〗雙足飛龍。」

wives [waɪvz; waivz] *n.* pl. of **wife.**

wiz [wɪz; wiz] *n.*〖俚〗非凡者；有鬼才者。

***wiz·ard** [ˈwɪzɚd; ˈwizəd] *n.* ①男巫；妖術家。②〖俗〗有傑出才幹之人；專家。—*adj.* ①魔法的。②〖主英〗極佳的；驚人的。

wiz·ard·ly [ˈwɪzɚdlɪ; ˈwizədli] *adj.* ①妖術的。②奇異的；神奇的。

wiz·ard·ry [ˈwɪzɚdrɪ; ˈwizədri] *n.* 魔術；巫術；奇妙；神奇力量。

wiz·en [ˈwɪzn̩; ˈwizn] *v.i.* 凋謝；枯萎；皺縮。—*adj.* =**wizened.**

wiz·ened [ˈwɪzn̩d; ˈwiznd] *adj.* 凋謝的；枯萎的；皺縮的；枯槁的。

wiz·en-faced [ˈwɪzn̩ˌfest; ˈwiznfeist] *adj.* 面孔瘦得乾癟的。

wiz·zled [ˈwɪzl̩d; ˈwizld] *adj.* 皺縮的；枯槁的〖常 up〗.

wk. ①weak. ②week. ③work. ④wreck.

wkg. working. **wkly.** weekly.

wkr. ①worker. ②wrecker. **wks.** ①weeks. ②works. **w.l.** ①water line. ②wave length. **W.L.A.** 〖英〗 Women's Land Army. **WLB** War Labor Board. **WLDA** War Labor Dispute Act. **wldr.** welder. **w. long.** west longitude. **Wm.** William. **w/m** 〖航運〗 weight and/or measurement.
WMO, W.M.O. World Meteorological Organization.
WNW, W.N.W., w.n.w. west-northwest. 「(多用於令馬停住)。
wo, whoa [wo; wou] *interj.* 遏!站住!
W.O. ①wait order. ②War Office. ③Warrant Officer. 「菘藍。②大青染料。
woad [wod; woud] *n.* ①〖植物〗大青;
wo-back [ˈwoˈbæk; ˈwouˈbæk] *interj.* =wo.
wob·ble [ˈwɑbl̩; ˈwɔbl] *v.*, **-bled, -bling,** *n.* —*v.i.* ①往復地擺動;搖動。②意見游移不定。③震顫。—*v.t.* 〖俗〗使擺動;使搖動;使震顫;使游移不定。—*n.* 擺動; 搖動; 震顫。—**wob·bler,** *n.*
wob·bly [ˈwɑblɪ; ˈwɔbli] *adj.* ①不穩定的; 搖動的; 震顫的。②無定見的。(亦作 **wabbly**) —**wob·bli·ness,** *n.*
wo(e)·be·gone [ˈwobɪˌgɔn; ˈwoubiˌgɔn] *adj.* 顯出悲傷的; 憂愁的。—**ness,** *n.*
WOC, W.O.C. ①(工商界人士)替政府做事而不支政府薪水 (=without compensation). ②上述工商界人士。
***woe** [wo; wou] *n.* ①〖詩,雅〗悲哀; 悲痛; 苦惱。a tale of *woe.* 悲痛的故事。②禍; 災難; 憂患。 Sickness and poverty are common *woes.* 疾病和貧窮是普通的憂患。—*interj.* 表不幸或悲痛之感歎詞。(亦作 wo)
wo(e)·ful [ˈwofəl; ˈwoufuI] *adj.* ①悲哀的; 悲傷的; 不幸的。②可憫的; 可憾的。—**ness,** *n.* 「…得可憐。
wo(e)·ful·ly [ˈwofəlɪ; ˈwoufuli] *adv.*
wog [wɑg; wɔg] *n.* 〖俚〗中東國家的人(侮蔑語)。 「原野。②丘陵地。
wold [wold; would] *n.* ①荒原; 高原;
‡wolf [wulf; wulf] *n., pl.* **wolves** [wulvz; wulvz], *v.* —*n.* ①狼。②殘忍貪婪之人。③〖俚〗色狼; 調戲或誘惑女人的男人。④極度的窮困; 饑餓(與 door 連用)。*a wolf in sheep's clothing* 外貌溫厚而內心兇惡之人; 僞君子。*cry wolf* 作虛假的警報。*keep the wolf from the door* 使不受饑寒。*The wolf is at the door.* 瀕臨挨餓邊緣。—*v.t.* 狼吞虎嚥〖常 down〗. He *wolfed* (down) two large plates of the stew. 他狼吞虎嚥地把那燉菜吃了兩大盤。—*v.i.* 獵狼。
wolf call 男性對年輕貌美之女性嬉戲所發之口哨聲或叫聲。 「歲)。
wolf cub ①小狼。②〖英〗幼童軍 (8-11
wolf dog ①狼犬(狼與犬之混血種)。②任何用於獵狼之犬; 獵狼犬。
wolf·er [ˈwulfɚ; ˈwulfə] *n.* ①捕狼者; 獵狼者。②狼吞虎嚥者。 「公魚類。
wolf·fish [ˈwulfˌfɪʃ; ˈwulffiʃ] *n.* 雷
wolf·hound [ˈwulfˌhaund; ˈwulfhaund] *n.* 獵狼犬。
wolf·ish [ˈwulfɪʃ; ˈwulfiʃ] *adj.* 似狼的; 兇惡的; 殘暴的; 貪婪的。—**ness,** *n.* —**ly,** *adv.*
wolf·ram [ˈwulfrəm; ˈwulfrəm] *n.* ①〖化〗鎢。②〖礦〗鎢錳鐵礦。
wolf·ram·ite [ˈwulfrəmˌaɪt; ˈwulfrəmait] *n.* 〖礦〗鎢錳鐵礦。
wolfs·bane [ˈwulfsˌben; ˈwulfsbein] *n.* 〖植物〗附子草; 牛扁。(亦作 **wolf's-bane**)
wolf's-claws [ˈwulfsˌklɔz; ˈwulfsklɔːz] *n.* 〖植物〗石松。 「蛛。
wolf spider 一種多毛而不結網之大蜘
wol·las·ton·ite [ˈwuləstənˌaɪt; ˈwuləstənait] *n.* 〖礦〗鈣矽石。
wolv·er [ˈwulvɚ; ˈwulvə] *n.* ①行爲似狼者。②獵狼者。 「riːn] *n.* =**wolverine.**
wol·ver·ene [ˌwulvəˈrin; ˈwulvə-
wol·ver·ine [ˌwulvəˈrin; ˈwulvəriːn] *n.* ①狼獾。②(W-)〖美俗〗美國 Michigan 州之人或居民。
‡wom·an [ˈwumən; ˈwumən] *n., pl.* **wom·en,** *adj.* —*n.*①婦女; 女子(指成年者)。a single *woman.* 獨身女人; 未曾結過婚的女人。②一般婦女; 女流(不加冠詞)。*Woman* is physically weaker than man. 女人的體格較男子爲弱。③女僕。④有女人氣的男子; 似婦女之男子。⑤(the-)女人的性質、感情等。There is something of the *woman* in his character. 他的性格中有女人氣。—*adj.* ①女人的; 婦女的。②女性的。a *woman* doctor. 女醫生。
wom·an-hat·er [ˈwumən ˌhetɚ; ˈwumənˌheitə] *n.* 憎恨女人者; 厭惡女人者。
wom·an·hood [ˈwumənˌhud; ˈwumənhud] *n.* ①女性; 女子的性質。②女子之集合稱; 女界。
wom·an·ish [ˈwumənɪʃ; ˈwuməniʃ] *adj.* ①似女子的; 女人氣的; 柔弱的。②適於女人的(衣物等)。—**ly,** *adv.* —**ness,** *n.*
wom·an·ize [ˈwumənˌaɪz; ˈwumənaiz] *v.*, **-ized, -iz·ing.** —*v.t.* 使女性化; 使柔弱。—*v.i.* ①變爲女性化。②宿娼; 玩女人。—**wom·an·iz·er,** *n.*
wom·an·kind [ˈwumənˈkaɪnd; ˈwumənˈkaind] *n.* 婦女(集合稱); 女性; 女流。
wom·an·like [ˈwumənˌlaɪk; ˈwumənlaik] *adj.* ①似女子的。②合於婦女的。
wom·an·ly [ˈwumənlɪ; ˈwumənli] *adj.* ①似女子的。②合於女子的。③合於成年婦女的。—**wom·an·li·ness,** *n.*
woman of letters ①女文學家。②女學者。 「庭主婦。
woman of the house 女主人; 家
woman of the street(s) 娼妓。
woman of the town 娼妓。
woman of the world 慣於社交的婦女; 老於世故的女人。
wom·an·pow·er [ˈwumənˈpauɚ; ˈwumənˈpauə] *n.* 婦女之力量; 女權。
woman's rights 女權。(亦作 **women's rights**) 「投票權。
woman suffrage 婦女參政權; 婦女
wom·an-suf·fra·gist [ˈwumənˈsʌfrədʒɪst; ˈwumənˈsʌfrədʒist] *n.* 婦女參政論者。
womb [wum; wuːm] *n.* ①子宮。②孕育任何事物之處所。③任何事物之內部。*fruit of the womb* 兒童; 小孩。*in the womb of time* 未來的(事件)。—*v.t.* 孕育。
wom·bat [ˈwɑmbæt; ˈwɔmbət] *n.* 〖動物〗(澳洲產)袋熊。 「**woman.**
‡wom·en [ˈwɪmɪn; ˈwimin] *n.* pl. of
wom·en·folk(s) [ˈwɪmɪnˌfok(s); ˈwiminfouk(s)] *n. pl.* 婦女; 女人的集合稱。
Women's Liberation 婦女解放運動。(亦作 **Women's Lib, Fem Lib**)
women's room 女廁所。

won¹ (wʌn; wʌn) *v.* pt. & pp. of win.
won² *n., pl.* **won.** 韓國之貨幣單位。
‡**won·der** (ˈwʌndə; ˈwʌndə) *n.* ①奇蹟；奇觀；奇事；不可思議之事物。signs and *wonders.* 奇蹟。the seven *wonders* of the world. 世界七大奇觀。(It's) no *wonder* (that) he didn't want to go. 他不要去是不足爲奇的。②驚愕；驚歎；驚奇；驚服。The baby looked with *wonder* at the Christmas tree. 這小孩很驚奇地看着耶誕樹。③神童。The child is a *wonder.* 這孩子是神童。***be filled with wonder*** 極感驚奇。***do*** (or ***work***) ***wonders*** 做出奇蹟；做出驚人之事。***for a wonder*** 令人驚奇地；說也奇怪。***nine days' wonder*** 轟動一時的事件。***no wonder*** a. 非傑出人才。The lecturer is *no wonder.* 演說者並不出色。b. 難怪；不足爲怪。He resigned, and *no wonder.* 他辭職了，此事不足爲怪。***to a wonder*** 〖古〗…得令人驚奇。—*v.i.* ①驚愕；驚奇；驚歎。I *wondered* to see you there. 我在那裏看見你，很覺驚奇。②想知道。to look up in the dictionary words one *wonders* about. 在字典上查不認識的字。—*v.t.* ①想曉得；極欲知道。I *wonder* what time it is. 不知道現在是甚麼時候。②對…感覺驚奇。I *wonder* (that) he didn't kill you. 他竟未殺你，我覺得驚奇。—*adj.* ①令人驚奇的；奇異的。②充滿奇蹟的；有許多驚人之事的。a *wonder* book. 充滿了奇蹟的書。—**er,** *n.*
‡**won·der·ful** (ˈwʌndəfəl; ˈwʌndəful) *adj.* ①令人驚奇的；使人驚服的；奇妙的；不可思議的。a *wonderful* story. 令人驚異的故事。②〖俗〗極好的；絕妙的。The weather has been *wonderful!* 近來天氣非常好。—*adv.* 〖方〗驚人地；非常地。He got *wonderful* excited. 他變得非常興奮。—**ness,** *n.*
*__won·der·ful·ly__ (ˈwʌndəfəlɪ; ˈwʌndəfli) *adv.* 令人驚奇地；驚人地。a *wonderfully* beautiful sunset. 美得出奇的日落。
won·der·ing (ˈwʌndərɪŋ; ˈwʌndəriŋ) *n.* 驚訝；驚異；感到不可思議。—*adj.* 驚異的。—**ly,** *adv.*
won·der·land (ˈwʌndəˌlænd; ˈwʌndəlænd) *n.* 奇境。
won·der·ment (ˈwʌndəmənt; ˈwʌndəmənt) *n.* ①驚訝；驚異。②奇觀；奇事。③好奇心。
won·der-struck (ˈwʌndəˌstrʌk; ˈwʌndəstrʌk) *adj.* 深感驚異的。
won·der·work (ˈwʌndəˌwɜk; ˈwʌndəwəːk) *n.* ①令人驚異之工作或行動；異常之人或事物；奇蹟。②令人驚異之技巧；絕技。—**er,** *n.* —**ing,** *adj.*
won·drous (ˈwʌndrəs; ˈwʌndrəs) *adj.* 〖詩，雅〗令人驚奇的；奇異的；不可思議的。—*adv.* 可驚地；非常地。—**ly** *adv.* —**ness,** *n.* 〖注意〗**wondrous** 作副詞用，只能用以限制形容詞。
won·ky (ˈwɑŋkɪ; ˈwɔŋki) *adj.,* **won·ki·er, won·ki·est.** 〖英俚〗①動搖的；不穩的。②虛弱的。③優柔寡斷的。④錯誤的；不妥的。
*__wont__ (wʌnt, wont; wount) *adj.* 習慣於；習以爲常的。He was *wont* to read the paper before breakfast. 他總是在早飯前看報。—*n.* 習慣。It was his *wont* to rise early. 他慣於早起。—*v.t.* 使習慣。—*v.i.* 慣於做某事。〖注意〗**wont** 作形容詞用，只能用於述語中，即置於 verb to be 之後。
‡**won't** (wont, wʌnt; wount) ＝**will not.**
wont·ed (ˈwʌntɪd, ˈwontɪd; ˈwountid) *adj.* 慣常的；素常的。—**ly,** *adv.* —**ness,** *n.*
won ton (ˈwɑnˌtɑn; ˈwɔnˌtɔn) 〖中〗餛飩。
*__woo__ (wu; wuː) *v.t.* ①向…求愛；向…求婚。You could *woo* her and win her. 你能向她求愛並獲得她的芳心。②求取；懇求。③求…之歡心。④招來。action *wooing* defeat. 招致敗北的行動。—*v.i.* ①求愛；求婚。He came to *woo.* 他來求婚。②討好。
‡**wood** (wud; wud) *n.* ①木；木材。a house made of *wood.* 木造的房屋。②(常 *pl.*) 森林。to go riding through the *wood(s).* 騎馬穿行林間。③柴薪。Put some more *wood* on the fire. 在火中多放些柴。④木製品。⑤木桶。wine drawn from the *wood.* 從木桶中倒出的酒。⑥〖印刷〗木版。⑦木管樂器。⑧人的個性之本質。***be unable to see the wood for the trees*** 見樹而不見林(因過於瑣細而致忽略全局)。***but of the woods*** 脫離危險或困難。***saw wood*** 〖俗〗a. 集中精神工作。b. 呼呼大睡。***the woods*** 樂團中吹奏木管樂器之全體團員。—*adj.* ①木製的。②用來貯藏、雕刻或裝載木材的。a *wood* chisel. 一把刻木用的鑿子。—*v.t.* ①供以木材；供以柴薪。to *wood* the stove. 加木柴於火爐中。②植樹；造林。—*v.i.* 得到木材；貯藏柴薪〖常 up〗. to *wood* up before the approach of winter. 在冬季到來以前將柴薪貯備起來。〖注意〗**woods** 作"森林"解時，在形式上是複數，但在意義上是單數(或集合名詞)。用法，有單數及複數。我們說 a woods, 是單數；the woods are, 是複數。
wood acid 〖化〗木醋。
wood alcohol 〖化〗木精；甲醇。
wood·bin (ˈwudˌbɪn; ˈwudbin) *n.* 裝柴薪的木箱。(亦作 **woodbox**)
wood·bine (ˈwudˌbaɪn; ˈwudbain) *n.* 〖植物〗①忍冬。②(美國 Virginia 州之)蛇葡萄。(亦作 **woodbind**)
wood block ①〖印刷〗木版；木版畫。②木魚(交響樂團中的一種木製擊樂器)。
wood-block (ˈwudˌblɑk; ˈwudblɔk) *adj.* 〖印刷〗木版的。
wood·bor·er (ˈwudˌborə; ˈwudbɔːrə) *n.* ①鑽木器。②在樹木或水果上鑽孔之昆蟲。
wood-carv·er (ˈwudˌkarvə; ˈwudˌkaːvə) *n.* 木刻家。
wood carving 木刻；木雕。
wood·chop·per (ˈwudˌtʃɑpə; ˈwudˌtʃɔpə) *n.* 伐木者。
wood·chuck (ˈwudˌtʃʌk; ˈwudtʃʌk) *n.* (北美之)土撥鼠。
wood coal ①褐煤。②木炭。
wood·cock (ˈwudˌkɑk; ˈwudkɔk) *n., pl.* **-cocks, -cock.** ①(鳥)山鷸。②〖古〗獃子。
wood·craft (ˈwudˌkræft; ˈwudkraːft) *n.* ①(特指關於打獵的)森林知識。②林學(＝forestry)。③木刻術。
wood·crafts·man (ˈwudˌkræftsmən; ˈwudkraːftsmən) *n., pl.* **-men.** 精於木刻者。
wood·cut (ˈwudˌkʌt; ˈwudkʌt) *n.* 木刻；木刻畫。
wood·cut·ter (ˈwudˌkʌtə; ˈwudˌkʌtə) *n.* ①雕刻木板者。②伐木者。
wood·ed (ˈwudɪd; ˈwudid) *adj.* ①多樹木的；樹茂的。②有(某種)木質的。
*__wood·en__ (ˈwudn; ˈwudn) *adj.* ①木製的。a *wooden* bucket. 木桶。②呆笨的；愚鈍的。a *wooden* head. 愚鈍的頭腦。③木然的；無表情的。a *wooden* face. 無表情的面容。④僵硬的；笨手笨脚的。⑤一系列中之第五的；結婚第五周年的。—**ly,** *adv.*—**ness,** *n.*
wood engraver 木刻者；製木板者。

wood engraving ①木刻; 木刻術。②木刻畫;木刻品。

wood·en·head ['wudn̩,hɛd; 'wudn-hed] *n.* 〖俗〗笨人。

wood·en·head·ed ['wudn̩ ,hɛdɪd; 'wudn,hedid] *adj.* 〖俗〗愚笨的。

wooden horse 〖希臘神話〗木馬。

wood·en·ware ['wudn̩,wɛr; 'wudn-wɛə] *n.* 木製盤盌等。

wooden wedding 木婚(結婚第五周年紀念)。

wood fiber 木質纖維(尤指供造紙用者)。

wood hyacinth 〖植物〗百合科綿棗兒屬及風信子屬植物。

wood·i·ness ['wudɪnɪs; 'wudinis] *n.* ①樹木繁茂;林木森森。②木質;似木之性質。

***wood·land** [*n.* 'wud,lænd; 'wudlənd *adj.* 'wudlənd; 'wudlənd] *n.* 林地;森林地區。—*adj.* 森林的。*woodland* scenery. 森林的風景。

wood·land·er ['wudləndə; 'wudlən-də] *n.* 居住森林中的人。

wood·less ['wudlɪs; 'wudlis] *adj.* 無樹木的;無森林的。

wood lot 栽培樹木之林地。(亦作**wood-lot**)

wood louse *pl.* **wood lice.** 土鱉; 地鱉(一種小甲蟲,體橢圓形,居於朽木及濕地)。

***wood·man** ['wudmən; 'wudmən] *n., pl.* **-men** [-mən; -mən]. ①樵夫。②居於森林之人。③看管森林之人。**—craft,** *n.*

wood note 森林中鳥之歌聲。(亦作 **woodnote**)

wood nymph ①森林中之女神。②斑蛾(專咬葡萄藤)。

***wood·peck·er** ['wud,pɛkə; 'wud,pekə] *n.* 啄木鳥。

wood pigeon 一種大野鴿。

wood·pile ['wud,paɪl; 'wudpail] *n.* 柴堆。

wood pulp (製紙用的)木質紙漿。

wood·ruff ['wud,rʌf; 'wudrʌf] *n.* 〖植物〗車葉草。

wood rush 〖植物〗地楊梅。

wood·shed ['wud,ʃɛd; 'wudʃed] *n., v.,* **-shed·ded, -shed·ding.** —*n.* 存放柴薪的小棚。—*v.i.* 〖俚〗有目的而勤練一種樂器。

woods·man ['wudzmən; 'wudzmən] *n., pl.* **-men.** ①慣於森林生活之人。②伐木者。

wood sorrel 〖植物〗酢漿草。

wood spirit ①(亦作 **wood alcohol**)〖化〗木精;甲醇。②(神話中)森林之神。

woods·y ['wudzɪ; 'wudzi] *adj.,* **woods·i·er, woods·i·est.** 〖美俗〗森林的;似森林的;與森林有關的;來自森林的;居於森林中的。

wood tar 木焦油。

wood turning 用車床製造木器。

wood vinegar 木醋酸。

wood wind ①(*pl.*)木管樂器類。②任何一種木管樂器。(亦作 **woodwind**)

wood·work ['wud,wɜk; 'wudwəːk] *n.* ①木製品;(房屋內之)木造部分(如門、窗、梯等)。②木工手藝。

wood·work·er ['wud,wɜkə; 'wud,wəːkə] *n.* 木匠。

wood·work·ing ['wud,wɜkɪŋ; 'wud,wəːkiŋ] *n.* 木工;木細工。—*adj.* 木工的;木工用的。

wood·worm ['wud,wɜm; 'wudwəːm] *n.* 居於木洞中的幼蟲;鑽木蟲。

wood·y ['wudɪ; 'wudi] *adj.,* **wood·i·er, wood·i·est.** ①樹木繁茂的; 多樹木的。②似木的。③含有木質的(部分); 木質的。④樹林的;森林的。

woo·er ['wuə; 'wuːə] *n.* 追求者; 討好者。

woof[1] [wuf; wuːf] *n.* ①緯線(織物之橫紗,爲 warp 之對)。②織物;織地。

woof[2] *n.* 低嗚聲;低音。—*v.i.* 低嗚。

woof·er ['wufə; 'wufə] *n.* (立體身歷聲揚聲器中之)低音喇叭。

‡wool [wul; wul] *n.* ①羊毛。We get *wool* from Australia. 我們(所獲)的羊毛來自澳洲。②似羊毛之物。glass *wool*. 玻璃纖維。③毛織物; 毛衣。He wears *wool* in winter. 他冬天穿毛衣。④毛線。⑤彎而捲的厚髮。***all wool and a yard wide*** 眞正的; 誠摯的; 優秀的。***dyed in the wool*** 根深蒂固的。***go for wool and come home shorn*** 偸鷄不着蝕把米。***lose one's wool*** 〖俚〗興奮; 發脾氣。***much cry and little wool*** 只會空叫嚷而做不出事來; 爲瑣事而瞎吵一陣。***pull the wool over one's eyes*** 欺騙某人; 蒙蔽某人。—*adj.* 羊毛製的。

wool comber 梳毛者;梳毛機。

***wool·(l)en** ['wulɪn; 'wulin] *adj.* ①羊毛的;羊毛製的;毛織的。*woolen* cloth. 呢絨;毛織品。②製羊毛的; 銷售羊毛的; 處理羊毛的。—*n.* (*pl.*) 毛織品。

wool·fell ['wul,fɛl; 'wulfel] *n.* 連毛的羊皮。

wool·gath·er·ing ['wul,gæðərɪŋ; 'wul,gæðəriŋ] *n.* ①空想;幻想; 心不在焉。②收集被灌木叢勾住的羊毛。—*adj.* 空想的;幻想的;心不在焉的。

wool·grow·er ['wul,groə; 'wul-grouə] *n.* (爲剪取羊毛等而) 畜養羊者。—**wool·grow·ing,** *n.*

wool·ly ['wulɪ; 'wuli] *adj.,* **-li·er, -li·est,** *n., pl.* **-lies.** —*adj.* ①羊毛的。②似羊毛的。③被羊毛或羊毛狀物覆蓋的。④〖俗〗如早期美國西部之有活力的。⑤不清楚的; 無組織的。—*n.* ①羊。②(常 *pl.*) 羊毛內衣;羊毛衣。(亦作 **wooly**) —**wool·li·ness,** *n.*

woolly bear (蛾類之)毛蟲。

wool·pack ['wul,pæk; 'wulpæk] *n.* ①一捆羊毛 (重240磅)。②包裝羊毛用之大帆布袋。③〖氣象〗卷雲。

wool·sack ['wul,sæk; 'wul-sæk] *n.* ①羊毛袋。②英國上院大法官之座位。③英國上院大法官之職位。

wool·work ['wul,wɜk; 'wulwəːk] *n.* 毛線編織品。

wool·y ['wulɪ; 'wuli] *adj.,* **-li·er, -li·est,** *n., pl.* **-lies.** =**woolly.**

wooz·y ['wuzɪ; 'wuːzi] *adj.,* **wooz·i·er, wooz·i·est.** 〖俚〗①眩暈的; 昏迷的; 模糊不清的; 惡心的。②微有醉意的。—**wooz·i·ly,** *adv.* —**wooz·i·ness,** *n.*

wop [wɑp; wɔp] *n.* 〖蔑〗來自南歐的黑皮膚之人(尤指義大利人)。

‡word [wɜd; wəːd] *n.* ①語;言;字;文字。What does this *word* mean? 這個字是甚麼意思? ② (常 *pl.*) 所說的話;談話; 言辭。*words* and deeds. 言行。③消息; 音訊。No *word* has come from the battle front. 前方還沒有消息傳來。④簡要的辭句。The teacher gave us a *word* of advice. 教師給我們一個勸告。⑤命令。Father's *word* is law. 父親的命令就是法律。⑥諾言;保證。The boy kept his *word*. 那孩子遵守諾言。⑦ (*pl.*) 爭論;口角。They had *words* together and were never reconciled. 他們吵嘴了, 以後永未和好。⑧口令; 口號。You must give the *word* before you can pass. 你必須說出口令才能通過。⑨(*pl.*)歌詞(以別於歌譜)。***a play upon words*** 雙關語。***at a word*** 立刻。***a word in season*** 恰合其時的勸告。***be as good as one's word*** 言而有信。***big words*** 大言壯語。***by word of mouth*** 口頭地。

eat one's words 取消前言；爲說錯話而道歉。***fair words*** 甘言；阿諛之辭。***good word*** a. 好話。b. 好消息；佳音。***have a word with a person*** 與某人略談。***have no word for*** 無法形容。***have the last word*** （辯論中）說了有決定性的話。***have words with a person*** 同某人口角。***in a*** (or ***one***) ***word*** 一言以蔽之；總而言之。***in other words*** 易言之。***in so many words*** a. 確切地；一字不差地。b. 簡潔地。***in words of one syllable*** 簡言之。***keep*** (***break***) ***one's word*** 守（失）約。***leave word*** 留言。***mince words*** 不直截了當地說出(主張、眞相等)。***my word*** (表示驚訝)噯呀！啊呀！***my word upon it*** 發誓；一定；的確。***of few*** (***many***) ***words*** 寡(多)言的。He is a man *of few words.* 他是個沉默寡言的人。***of one's word*** 守信的。He's a man *of his word.* 他是個守信的人。***on*** (or ***with***) ***the word*** 說了這話後(立即如何如何)。***put in a*** (***good***) ***word for someone*** 爲某人進言或說項。***suit the action to the word*** 說了就做。***take a person at his word*** 聽信某人之言。***take the word out of one's mouth*** 說出某人將要說出口的話。***the last word in*** 最新式的；最好的。***the last word on*** 在…方面有決定性的話。***the Word*** 聖經。***translate word for word*** 逐字翻譯；直譯。***upon***(or ***on***) ***my word*** 的確；眞的。***waste one's words*** 白費唇舌。***weigh one's words*** 措辭小心；用字仔細。***word for word*** 逐字地；一字不差地。***Word of God*** 聖經。***word of honor*** 諾言。—*v.t.* 說；言；措辭。*Word* your idea clearly. 把你的思想用文字(或語言)清楚地表達出來。

word·age [ˈwɝdɪdʒ; ˈwəːdidʒ] *n.* ①字(集合稱)；語彙；(某一篇故事、小說等的)字數。②用字；措辭。③冗長；累贅。

word-blind [ˈwɝdˌblaɪnd; ˈwəːd-blaind] *adj.* 〖心理〗患字盲症的。

word·book [ˈwɝdˌbuk; ˈwəːdbuk] *n.* ①字典；辭彙。②(歌劇之)歌詞。

word-deaf [ˈwɝdˌdɛf; ˈwəːdˈdef] *adj.* 患語聾症的。

word element 〖文法〗字素(指字首、字尾、字根等)。

word-for·ma·tion [ˈwɝdfɔrˌmeʃən; ˈwəːdfɔːˌmeiʃən] *n.* ①〖文法〗字語形成。②造字法。

word-for-word [ˈwɝdfəˈwɝd; ˈwəːdfəˈwəːd] *adj.* ①逐字的。②一字不差的；一字不改的。

word·ing [ˈwɝdɪŋ; ˈwəːdiŋ] *n.* 措辭；語法；用語。

word·less [ˈwɝdlɪs; ˈwəːdlis] *adj.* ①無言的；沉默的；啞的。②未明言的。③無法表達的。④無字的。

word-of-mouth [ˈwɝdəvˈmauθ; ˈwəːdəvˈmauθ] *adj.* 口頭的；口述的。—*n.* 口述的消息、故事等。

word order 〖文法〗(句、子句或片語中)字之排列順序。

word painting 生動之敍述。

word-per·fect [ˈwɝdˈpɝfɪkt; ˈwəːd-ˈpəːfikt] *adj.* 熟記臺詞的。

word picture 生動逼眞的描寫。

word·play [ˈwɝdˌple; ˈwəːdplei] *n.* ①雙關語。②文字的爭論。

word·smith [ˈwɝdˌsmɪθ; ˈwəːd-smiθ] *n.* 語言專家；字彙極豐富的人。

word·split·ting [ˈwɝdˈsplɪtɪŋ; ˈwəːdˌsplitiŋ] *n.* 過於精密的字義區別。

word square 同字方陣(一組排列成正方形的字母，同順序之縱行與横行均構成同一單語)。

Words·worth [ˈwɝdzˌwɚθ; ˈwəːdz-wə(ː)θ] *n.* 渥玆華斯(William, 1770–1850, 英國詩人，於 1843–50 爲桂冠詩人)。

word·y [ˈwɝdɪ; ˈwəːdi] *adj.*, **word·i·er, word·i·est.** ①多言的；冗長的。②口頭的；言語的。—**word·i·ly,** *adv.* —**word·i·ness,** *n.*

‡work [wɝk; wəːk] *n., adj., v.,* **worked** or **wrought** [rɔt; rɔːt], **work·ing.** —*n.* ①工作；勞動；作業。He is not fond of *work.* 他不喜歡工作。②所做的事；職業。He is out of *work.* 他失業了。③製作品；作品；著作。The villagers sell their *work* to tourists. 村民把他們的手工藝品售給觀光客。④工作時所需要或利用的材料、工具等。She took her *work* out on the porch. 她把縫紉所需之物帶到門口走廊上。⑤(*pl.*) 工廠。an iron *works.* 鐵工廠。⑥(*pl.*)機械。something wrong with the *works.* 機件出了毛病。⑦(*pl.*)工程；堡壘；防禦工事。public *works.* 公共工程。⑧〖物理〗功。to change heat into *work.* 將熱化爲功。⑨（製造過程中任一階段中的)材料。⑩(*pl.*) 殘酷的處置(常與 get, gave 連用)。They gave him the *works.* 他們給他以殘酷的處置。***all in the day's work*** 正常地。***at work*** a. 工作中。Don't phone him *at work.* 他在工作中別打電話給他。b. 在起作用；在產生影響。***get the works*** 〖俚〗受虐待；受害。***give one the works*** 〖俚〗a. 虐待。b. 謀殺。***gum up the works*** 〖俚〗把事情弄糟。***in the works*** 準備中；籌備中；發展中。***in work*** 進行中。The company has three films *in work* right now. 那公司目前有三部電影正在拍攝中。***make short*** (or ***quick***) ***work of*** a. 匆匆做畢。b. 排除。c. 克服。***out of work*** 失業。***set*** (or ***go***) ***about one's work*** 開始工作。***set*** (or ***get***) ***to work*** 開始工作；着手。***shoot the works*** 〖俚〗盡最大努力；孤注一擲；傾囊。—*adj.* 工作用的。*work* clothes. 工作服。—*v.i.* ①工作；勞動；做事。Most people must *work* to live. 大多數的人必須爲生活而工作。②(機械、身體器官等)運轉；轉動；活動。This machine will not *work.* 這架機器不能轉動。③(計畫、方法等)有效；得到所希望的效果。The plan *worked* very well. 這項計畫很成功。④奮力行進；緩慢行進。The ship *worked* to windward. 這船迎風緩慢行進。⑤奮力地動。⑥漸漸變爲(通常與副詞或形容詞連用)。The screw has *worked* loose. 這螺釘已經鬆了。⑦發酵；影響。The yeast began to *work.* 酵母開始發酵。⑧被加工。This wood *works* easily. 這木料容易加工。⑨澎湃；翻騰。⑩(機器)不規則地運轉。—*v.t.* ①使工作。Don't *work* him too hard—he's rather weak. 不要使他過於勞苦——他身體很弱。②運轉；使動；使用。The machine is *worked* by electricity. 這機器是電動的。③在(某地區)推銷貨物。The salesman *worked* the eastern states. 那推銷員在東部各州推銷貨物。④經營；實行；應用。He *works* a farm. 他經營一所農場。⑤造成。to *work* wonders. 造成奇蹟。⑥形成；鑄成；做成。He *worked* a silver dollar into a bracelet. 他把一銀幣改鑄成一手鐲。⑦算出(得數)；解決(問題)。*Work* all the problems on the page. 把這一頁上的

問題都算出來。⑧使動；使因激動而扭動。He *worked* his jaws. 他使兩顎在動。⑨艱苦行(路)；以工作抵償。 to *work* one's way through the crowd. 用力從人羣中擠過去。⑩刺繡。to *work* a design on a piece of cloth. 把一圖樣刺繡於一塊布上。⑪影響；說服。to *work* men to one's will. 說服人們服從自己的意志。⑫揉(麪)；混合。 Dough is *worked* to mix it thoroughly. 麪團被揉以使其混合均勻。⑬〖俗〗騙取。 to *work* a friend for a loan. 騙借一朋友的錢。⑭使變爲。Can you *work* the screw loose? 你能弄鬆那個螺絲嗎? ⑮採(礦)。⑯使興奮；煽動。Don't *work* yourself into a temper. 別發脾氣。⑰使(啤酒)發酵。***work against time*** 用最大速度工作。 ***work at*** 從事；執行；努力於。 ***work away*** (or ***on***) 繼續工作。 ***work in*** a. 挿進；放進去。Can't you *work in* a few jokes? 你不能挿幾個笑話進去嗎? b. 抽出時間。 ***work into*** 挿進；放進去。 ***work in with*** 適於。My plans did not *work in with* his. 我的計畫同他的不合。***work off*** a. 漸漸除去；處置。b. 用工作來償付或實現。 ***work on*** (or ***upon***) a. 企圖說服或影響。b. 感動。 ***work one's will*** (***upon***) 完成了自己的目標。 ***work out*** a. 努力獲致。 He must *work out* his own salvation. 他必須奮力自救。b. 精細計畫。 to *work out* a scheme for the invasion of the planet Mars. 精細設計出一項侵入火星的計畫。c. 用盡；枯竭。 d. 有預期的結果。 e. 以工作代替金錢來還債。 f. (體育選手) 練習。 g. 總計…。 The total *works out* to $3,176. 總數加起來是三千一百七十六元。 ***work over*** a. 徹底查驗；仔細檢查。b. 重新加工；翻新。c. 徹底改變。d. 痛毆；痛打。 e. 徹底砲轟。 ***work up*** a. 努力獲致；漸漸造成；漸漸發展成；促成。 to *work up* a reputation. 漸漸造成名望。 b. 激動。 c. 組成；混合；搜集。d. 逐漸晉於；逐漸達到。 to *work up* to a climax. 逐漸達到一高潮。

work·a·bil·i·ty [ˌwɝkəˈbɪlətɪ; ˌwəːkəˈbiliti] *n.* 可加工或實施之性質或狀態。

work·a·ble [ˈwɝkəbl; ˈwəːkəbl] *adj.* 可使用的；可操作的；可經營的；可實行的。

work·a·day [ˈwɝkəˌde; ˈwəːkədei] *adj.* ①工作日的；普通日的。②普通的；平凡的；實際的。

work·a·hol·ic [ˌwɝkəˈhɑlɪk; ˌwəːkəˈhɔlik] *n.* 對工作狂熱的人。

work·bag [ˈwɝkˌbæg; ˈwəːkbæg] *n.* 針線袋。

work·bas·ket [ˈwɝkˌbæskɪt; ˈwəːkˌbɑːskit] *n.* 針線筐。

work·bench [ˈwɝkˌbɛntʃ; ˈwəːkbentʃ] *n.* 技工等工作時所用之長凳；工作檯；細工檯。

work·book [ˈwɝkˌbuk; ˈwəːkbuk] *n.* ①練習簿。②工作手册；工作規範。③筆記簿。

work·box [ˈwɝkˌbɑks; ˈwəːkbɔks] *n.* 針線盒。

work camp 勞動營。

work·day [ˈwɝkˌde; ˈwəːkdei] *n.* ①工作日。②一日之工作時間。—*adj.* ＝workaday.

worked [wɝkt; wəːkt] *adj.* 有刺繡雕刻等裝飾的；經修飾作裝飾用的。

‡work·er [ˈwɝkɚ; ˈwəːkə] *n.* ①工作者。*workers* in cancer research. 癌症研究工作者。②勞動者；工人。rate increases for all the *workers* in the steel industry. 鋼鐵工業工人之全面加薪。③工蜂、工蟻等。④創造者。*worker* of miracles. 創造奇蹟者。⑤〖印刷〗電鑄版。

work farm 少年感化農莊。

work force 勞工。

work·hand [ˈwɝkˌhænd; ˈwəːkhænd] *n.* 傭工。

work·horse [ˈwɝkˌhɔrs; ˈwəːkhɔːs] *n.* ①用於工役之馬。②做苦工者；吃苦耐勞者。③廣受應用之車輛或機器。

work·house [ˈwɝkˌhaus; ˈwəːkhaus] *n.* ①〖美〗監犯工廠。②〖英〗貧民習藝所。

work-in [ˈwɝkˌɪn; ˈwəːkin] *n.* 由一羣不受規章約束的工人、職員或學生所組成的抗議示威。

***work·ing** [ˈwɝkɪŋ; ˈwəːkiŋ] *n.* ①活動；勞動。②作用。 Do you understand the *working* of this machine? 你明白這機器的作用嗎? ③礦坑；採石場。 The boy went exploring in some disused *workings*. 那孩子到廢礦坑中去探查。④製造。⑤塑造。The *working* of clay is easy when it's damp. 潮濕的黏土容易塑造。⑥發酵。⑦費力而緩慢的前進。⑧扭曲的行動或動作。⑨(*pl.*)礦坑、採石場或坑道等施工之處。—*adj.* ①工作的。the *working* class. 工人階級。②工作用的。the *working* hours. 工時。

working capital 營運資金；運轉資金；運用資金。

work·ing-class [ˈwɝkɪŋˌklæs; ˈwəːkiŋklɑːs] *adj.* 工人階級的；工人階級特有的。

working day ①工作日 (爲 holiday 之對)。②工作日；一日工作之時數。

work·ing·man [ˈwɝkɪŋˌmæn; ˈwəːkiŋmæn] *n., pl.* **-men.** 勞動者；工人。

working papers 就業證件(如兒童就業時之年齡證書等)。

working substance 可用物質。

work·ing·wom·an [ˈwɝkɪŋˌwumən; ˈwəːkiŋˌwumən] *n., pl.* **-wom·en.** 女勞動者；女工。

work·less [ˈwɝklɪs; ˈwəːklis] *adj.* 無工作的。

work load 工作量。(亦作 **workload**)

***work·man** [ˈwɝkmən; ˈwəːkmən] *n., pl.* **-men.** ①工作者。②工人；勞動者。

work·man·like [ˈwɝkmənˌlaɪk; ˈwəːkmənlaik] *adj.* 工作熟練的；技巧精湛的。—*adv.* 工作熟練地；技巧精湛地。

work·man·ship [ˈwɝkmənˌʃɪp; ˈwəːkmənʃip] *n.* ①手藝；技藝；技巧。Good *workmanship* deserves good pay. 好手藝該得大工錢。②製作品。

workmen's compensation 工人傷殘賠償。

work·out [ˈwɝkˌaut; ˈwəːkaut] *n.* ①(賽跑、拳擊、競賽等之)事先練習；準備練習。②運動；鍛鍊身體。③〖俚〗檢定；測驗；試驗。

work·peo·ple [ˈwɝkˌpipl; ˈwəːkˌpiːpl] *n. pl.* 〖英〗勞工們；工人們；職工。

work permit 工作許可證。

work·room [ˈwɝkˌrum; ˈwəːk-rum] *n.* 作業室；工作室。

***work·shop** [ˈwɝkˌʃɑp; ˈwəːkʃɔp] *n.* ①工場；工廠。②研討會；進修會。summer *workshop* in short story writing. 暑期短篇故事寫作研習會。

work-shy [ˈwɝkˌʃaɪ; ˈwəːkʃai] *n.* 怕工作的人。—*adj.* 怕工作的；懶惰的。

work·ta·ble [ˈwɝkˌtebl; ˈwəːkˌteibl] *n.* 工作檯；工作桌(如縫紉等所用者)。

work·week [ˈwɝkˌwik; ˈwəːk-wiːk] *n.* 一星期中之總工作時間。

work·wom·an [ˈwɝkˌwumən; ˈwəːkˌwumən] *n., pl.* **-wom·en.** 女工。

‡world [wɝld; wəːld] *n.* ①世界；地球。He made a journey round the *world*.

他作周遊世界的旅行。②世人；人類。 The whole *world* knows it. 人人都曉得這件事。③塵世;俗世;現世。 Monks and nuns live apart from the *world.* 僧尼遁世而居。④社交場合；上流社會；上流社會的人。He lives out of the *world.* 他不參加社交活動。⑤世間之生活；世事。 How is the *world* using you? 你近況如何? ⑥星辰；行星。Are there any other *worlds* besides ours? 除了我們的地球,還有別的行星嗎? ⑦地球上的一部分。 the English-speaking *world.* 英語國家。⑧界。the *world* of commerce. 商界。⑨大量；許多。 Sunshine does children a *world* of good. 陽光對於兒童大有益處。⑩物質生活（與精神生活相對)。the *world,* the flesh and the devil. 物質、肉慾與魔鬼（各種誘惑)。 ***all the world and his wife*** 每人;人人;不分男女。 *All the world and his wife* were at the ball. 大家都參加了該舞會。 ***be all the world to*** 爲…所最喜愛的。 She *is all the world to* him. 她爲他所最愛的人。 ***begin the world*** 開始生涯;入世。 ***bring into the world*** **a.** 生育。**b.** 助產;接生。***carry a world before one*** 迅速成功。 ***come into the world*** 誕生。***for all the world*** 無論如何。 ***for all the world alike*** 非常相似。***for worlds*** 決(不);無論如何也(不)。 ***in the world*** 到底;究竟。 ***make a noise in the world*** 揚名天下。 ***on top of the world*** 〖俗〗**a.**成功的。**b.** 興高采烈的。***out of this*** (or ***the***) ***world*** 超凡;非常好。Her voice is simply *out of this world.* 她的歌聲不同凡響。***set the world on fire*** (常用於否定句中)獲得極大成功。 ***the lower world*** 地獄。***the New World*** 新大陸(南北美洲)。 ***the Old World*** 舊大陸（歐亞非三洲)。 ***the other world*** 來生;來世。***think the world of*** 對…非常欽佩或喜歡。 His co-workers *think the world of* him. 他的同事非常欽佩他。 ***this world*** 今生;今世。 ***to the world*** 完全地；徹底地。He was drunk *to the world.* 他已爛醉如泥。***world without end*** 永遠地。

World Bank, the 世界銀行 (the International Bank for Reconstruction and Development 之俗稱)。

world-beat·er [ˈwɝldˌbitɚ; ˈwəːld-ˌbiːtə] *n.* 舉世無比之人或物。

World Court 國際法庭。

world-fa·mous [ˈwɝldˈfeməs; ˈwəːldˈfeiməs] *adj.* 舉世聞名的。(亦作 **world-famed**)

world federalism 世界聯邦主義。

world federalist 世界聯邦主義者。

World Health Organization 世界衛生組織(略作WHO).

world island 世界島(指歐、亞、非三洲大陸而言)。

world·ling [ˈwɝldlɪŋ; ˈwəːldliŋ] *n.* ①世俗之人。②地球上之居民;地球人。

***world·ly** [ˈwɝldlɪ;ˈwəːldli] *adj.,* **-li·er, -li·est,** *adv.* —*adj.* ①現世的;世俗的。*worldly* people. 俗人。②追求名利的。—*adv.* 世俗地;現世地。—**world·li·ness,** *n.*

world·ly-mind·ed[ˈwɝldlɪˈmaɪndɪd; ˈwəːldliˈmaindid]*adj.*追求名利的。—**ness,***n.*

world·ly-wise [ˈwɝldlɪˈwaɪz; ˈwəːldliˈwaiz] *adj.* 老於世故的。

world power 對全球有影響力之强國。

world's end 最遙遠之地。

world's fair 世界博覽會。

world-shak·ing [ˈwɝldˌʃekɪŋ; ˈwəːldˌʃeikiŋ] *adj.* 震撼全球的。

world's record 世界紀錄(=world record).

world view 世界觀。

World War 世界大戰。 ***World War I*** 第一次世界大戰 (1914-1918)。 ***World War II*** 第二次世界大戰 (1939-1945)。

world-wea·ry [ˈwɝldˌwɪrɪ; ˈwəːld-ˌwiəri] *adj.* 厭世的。 —**world-wea·ri·ness,** *n.*

world-wide [ˈwɝldˈwaɪd; ˈwəːld-waid] *adj.* 遍及全世界的。—**ly,** *adv.*

world-wise [ˈwɝldˌwaɪz; ˈwəːld-waiz] *adj.* 精通世事的;老於世故的。

worm** [wɝm; wəːm] *n.* ①蟲；蠕蟲。②其形狀或活動與蟲相似之物，如螺旋線等。③(*pl.*)(作 *sing.* 解)寄生蟲病。The dog has *worms.* 狗有寄生蟲病。④可悲可卑的小人；可憐蟲。⑤逐漸侵蝕之物;侵蝕;耗損；隱痛。The *worm* of care gives her no rest. 憂心忡忡使她不得安眠。 ***become food for worms 死。 ***Even a worm may*** (or ***will***) ***turn.*** 如果壓迫過甚，雖最溫馴的人亦將反抗。***the worm of conscience*** 良心的譴責;悔恨。 —*v.t.* ①蠕行；爬過。②漸漸探出；以堅持而祕密的方法從事或獲取。John tried to *worm* the secret out of me.約翰設法向我探出這項祕密。③除去…之蟲;除蟲。The dog has been *wormed.* 那隻狗已被除蟲。④被蟲侵蝕。 ⑤加螺旋線於。 a machine that *worms* screws. 加螺旋線於螺釘上的機器。—*v.i.* ①蠕行；蠕動。②覓蟲；尋蟲。 Birds and children are *worming* on the lawn after the rain. 雨後鳥兒和孩子們在草地上尋找蚯蚓。③用不露骨的方法取得〖常 into〗. to *worm* into another's favor. 設法獲得他人的喜愛。—**like,** *adj.*

worm·cast [ˈwɝmˌkæst;ˈwəːmkɑːst] *n.* 蚯蚓糞。

worm-eat·en[ˈwɝmˌitn̩; ˈwəːmˌiːtn] *adj.*①蟲蝕的;蟲蛀的。*worm-eaten* timbers. 蟲蛀的木材。②陳腐的;落伍的。

worm-fish·ing [ˈwɝmˌfɪʃɪŋ; ˈwəːm-ˌfiʃiŋ] *n.* 以蚯蚓或蟲等爲餌之釣魚。

worm gear 螺旋輪;蝸輪。

worm·hole [ˈwɝmˌhol; ˈwəːmhoul] *n.* (樹木的)蟲蛀之孔。—**worm·holed,** *adj.*

worm·seed [ˈwɝmˌsid; ˈwəːmsiːd] *n.* 〖植物〗①土荊芥。②土荊芥之實(用做腸蟲驅除劑)。

worm's-eye [ˈwɝmzˌaɪ; ˈwəːmzai] *adj.* 從下面看的;近看的;狹窄的;細節的。

worm wheel 螺旋輪(=worm gear).

worm·wood [ˈwɝmˌwud; ˈwəːm-wud]*n.* ①〖植物〗苦艾;茵蔯。②苦惱;其事物。

worm·y [ˈwɝmɪ; ˈwəːmi] *adj.,* **worm·i·er, worm·i·est.** ①有蟲的;多蟲的。②爲蟲所損壞的。③似蟲的;似蚯蚓的。

worn [worn; wɔːn] *v.* pp. of **wear.** —*adj.* ①用壞的;破舊的。*worn* rugs. 破舊的氈。②疲倦的。—**ness,** *n.*

worn-out [ˈwornˈaʊt;ˈwɔːnˈaut] *adj.* ①用到不能再用的。 ②疲倦不堪的；精疲力竭的。③陳腐的;陳舊的。—**ness,** *n.*

wor·ried [ˈwɝɪd; ˈwʌrid] *adj.* 憂心忡忡的;爲難的。—**ly,** *adv.*

wor·ri·less [ˈwɝɪlɪs; ˈwʌrilis] *adj.* 無煩惱的;無憂慮的。

wor·ri·ment [ˈwɝɪmənt;ˈwʌrimənt]

n. ①苦惱;憂慮。②苦惱或憂煩的原因。

wor·ri·some [ˈwɝɪsəm; ˈwʌrisəm] *adj.* ①令人煩惱的; 使人焦慮的。②有煩惱之傾向的。—**ly,** *adv.*

wor·rit [ˈwɝɪt; ˈwʌrit] *n.* 〖方〗①煩惱;憂慮;困擾。②煩惱者;憂慮者。—*v.t.* & *v.i.* 〖方〗(使)煩惱;(使)憂慮。

‡**wor·ry** [ˈwɝɪ; ˈwʌri] *v.,* **-ried, -ry·ing,** *n., pl.* **-ries.** —*v.t.* ①使煩惱;困擾。Don't *worry* me with such foolish questions. 不要用這些愚蠢的問題來煩擾我。②使不適;使痛苦。I have a bad tooth that is *worrying* me. 我有一個蛀牙,正在使我不舒適。③咬嚙。The cat *worried* the mouse. 貓嚙鼠。④攪動; 擾亂; 反覆觸動。—*v.i.* ①煩惱;焦慮。She *worries* about little things. 她爲小事而煩惱。②艱苦前進;艱苦進行。The ancient car *worried* up the hill. 那部老爺車吃力地爬上山坡。***worry along*** (or ***through***) 縱有困難,仍努力進行而獲得成功。—*n.* ①煩惱;苦惱;憂慮。He was showing signs of *worry*. 他有憂慮的樣子。②(常 *pl.*)令人煩惱的人或事。Life is full of *worries*. 人生充滿苦惱的事情。③〖獵狐〗獵犬將死狐撕成碎片之行動。—**wor·ri·er,** *n.*

wor·ry·ing [ˈwɝɪɪŋ; ˈwʌriiŋ] *n.* 憂慮;焦急;煩惱。—*adj.* 煩惱的;憂慮的。—**ly,** *adv.*

wor·ry·wart [ˈwɝɪˌwɔrt; ˈwʌriwɔːt] *n.* 杞憂者。

‡**worse** [wɝs; wəːs] *adj.* comp. of **bad, ill.** 更壞的; 更惡劣的。to make matters *worse*. 使事情更爲糟糕。***the worse for wear*** 穿壞或用壞;破舊不堪。***worse off*** 情況不佳。—*adv.* comp. of **bad, ill.** 更壞地;更惡劣地。He sings *worse* than ever. 他唱得比過去壞。—*n.* 更壞之事;更惡劣之事。*Worse* remains to tell. 還有更壞的事情在後面。***go from bad to worse*** 每況愈下;愈來愈壞。Things are *going from bad to worse* nowadays. 現在一切事情愈來愈壞。

wors·en [ˈwɝsn; ˈwəːsn] *v.t.* & *v.i.* 使變壞;使惡化;變壞;惡化。

‡**wor·ship** [ˈwɝʃəp; ˈwəːʃip] *n., v.,* **-shiped, -ship·ing** or **-shipped, -ship·ping.** —*n.* ①崇拜;禮拜。②禮拜式;禮拜儀式。③崇敬;尊敬。④對法官等的尊稱。Your *Worship*. 大人。***a place of worship*** 教堂。—*v.t.* ①崇拜;禮拜。People go to church to *worship* God. 人們到教堂去禮拜上帝。②敬愛。—*v.i.* 參加禮拜。Where does she *worship*? 她到哪個教堂去參加禮拜?

wor·ship·(p)er [ˈwɝʃəpɚ; ˈwəːʃipə] *n.* 崇拜者;禮拜者。

wor·ship·ful [ˈwɝʃəpfəl; ˈwəːʃipfəl] *adj.* ①值得尊敬或崇敬的;聲望高的。②崇拜的;禮拜的;虔誠的。—**ly,** *adv.* —**ness,** *n.*

‡**worst** [wɝst; wəːst] *adj.* superl. of **bad, ill.** 最壞的;最惡劣的。He is the *worst* boy in school. 他是學校中最壞的孩子。—*adv.* superlative of **bad, ill.** 最壞地;最惡劣地。—*n.* 最惡劣的人、事、物、情形、行爲、可能等。We must prepare for the *worst*. 我們必須爲最壞的情形作準備。***at*** (***the***) ***worst*** 在最壞的情形下。***get the worst of it*** 失敗。***give the worst of it*** 打敗;擊敗。***if*** (***the***) ***worst comes to*** (***the***) ***worst*** 如果情形壞到極點。(***in***) ***the worst way*** 非常地;極度地。—*v.t.* 打敗;勝過。The hero *worsted* his enemies. 這英雄打敗他的敵人。

wor·sted [ˈwʊstɪd; ˈwustid] *n.* ①絨線;毛紗。②絨線或毛紗衣料。—*adj.* ①用絨線或毛紗製的。②加工毛紗的;處理毛紗的。

wort [wɝt; wəːt] *n.* ①植物;草本植物(主要用於複合字,如 liverwort)。②未發酵或正在發酵之麥芽汁。

‡**worth**¹ [wɝθ; wəːθ] *adj.* ①值得。The book is *worth* reading. 這書值得讀。②值(若干)。③有價值(若干)的財產。He is *worth* millions. 他有幾百萬財產。***for all one is worth*** 盡全力。He ran *for all he was worth*. 他拼命地跑。***for what it is worth*** 不論眞僞。***worth one's salt*** **a.** 值得某人所領之薪水。**b.** 有能力的;有實力的。—*n.* 價值。We should read books of real *worth*. 我們應讀有眞正價值的書。He bought a dollar's *worth* of stamps. 他買了一塊錢的郵票。***put in one's two cents*** (***worth***) 〖俚〗在爭論或討論時提供自己的意見。

worth² *v.t.* 〖古〗落到。***Woe worth...!*** 願…受難!

worth·ful [ˈwɝθfəl; ˈwəːθfəl] *adj.* ①值得尊敬的;可敬的。②有價值的。—**ness,** *n.*

*__worth·less__ [ˈwɝθlɪs; ˈwəːθlis] *adj.* ①無價值的;無用的;無益的。Don't read *worthless* books. 勿讀無益的書。②敗壞的;卑劣的。—**ness,** *n.* —**ly,** *adv.*

worth-while, worth·while [ˈwɝθˈhwaɪl; ˈwəːθˈhwail] *adj.* 值得的。—**ness,** *n.* 〖注意〗此字僅能置於名詞之前,若在動詞 to be 之後,則分開爲兩個字,例如:All this fussing is hardly *worth while*. 這一切麻煩是不值得的。He ought to spend his time on some *worth-while* reading. 他應該把他的時間用於閱讀值得讀的書刊。

‡**wor·thy** [ˈwɝðɪ; ˈwəːði] *adj.,* **-thi·er, -thi·est,** *n., pl.* **-thies.** —*adj.* ①有價值的;可敬的。He helps only the *worthy* poor. 他只協助那些可敬的窮人。②值得的;應得的;應受的;相宜的。She is *worthy* of a better husband. 她應該有一個較好的丈夫。***worthy of*** **a.** 應得的。**b.** 值得的。—*n.* ①有價值的人;傑出人物。Who is the *worthy* who has just arrived? 剛來的那位大人物是誰?②(用輕視或開玩笑的口吻所說的)人;傢伙。—**wor·thi·ly,** *adv.* —**wor·thi·ness,** *n.*

wot [wɑt; wɔt] *v.t.* & *v.i.* 〖古〗wit 之第一及第三人稱、單數、現在式。I *wot*. 我知道(=I know). He *wot*. 他知道(=He knows).

‡**would** [wʊd; wud] *v.* ①pt. of **will.** ②特殊用法。**a.** 表示決心或意向。I *would* grant your request. 我願准許你的請求。**b.** 表示一種過去的習慣。He *would* come to see us every day. 他那時每天都來看我們。**c.** 表示願望。*Would* that I were young again! 如果我能返老還童,多麼好啊! **d.** 表示條件。If he *would* try, he could do it. 只要他試一試,他能做這件事的。**e.** 表示一種客氣的意味。*Would* you kindly show me the way to the station? 您可以指示我到車站去的路嗎? **f.** 表示將來時間。*Would* he never go? 他永遠不去嗎? ***would rather*** 寧願。—*n.* 不實在的願望。

would-be [ˈwʊdˌbi; ˈwudbiː] *adj.* 願爲的; 自稱自許的; 願成而未成的。—*n.* 願成而未成者。

would·n't [ˈwʊdn̩t; ˈwudnt] = **would not.**

wouldst [wʊdst; wudst] *v.* 〖古〗 will 之第二人稱、單數、過去式 (與 thou 連用)。

*__wound__¹ [wund; wuːnd] *n.* ①傷;創傷;損傷。He had a knife *wound* in the arm.

他臂上有一處刀傷。②(信用、名譽、感情等)損害;痛苦。—*v.t.* 傷;創傷;傷害(肉體或感情)。The shell *wounded* him in the head. 砲彈傷了他的頭部。—*v.i.* 加害;傷害。

wound² 〔waund; waund〕 *v.* pt. & pp. of **wind²** and **wind³**.

wove 〔wov; wouv〕 *v.* pt. & pp. of **weave.**

wo·ven 〔ˈwovən; ˈwouvən〕 *v.* pp. of **weave.**

WOW 〔wau; wau〕 *n.* 〖美〗 Woman Ordnance Workers 之一員。

wow 〔wau; wau〕 *n.* 〖美俚〗①(戲劇等之)空前大成功。②極有趣的事物。—*interj.* 〖蘇、美〗噢(表示驚愕、愉快、痛苦等之感嘆詞)。*Wow!* Look at that! 哇!看哪! —*v.t.* 〖美俚〗大受(觀衆、聽衆等)之讚賞。

WOWS Women Ordnance Workers.

WPA ①Works Progress Administration. ②with particular average. 水漬險(單獨海損賠償)。

wrack 〔ræk; ræk〕 *n.* ①敗毀; 破壞; 滅亡。②破船;破壞物的殘骸。③(被沖到岸邊的)海草或其他海生植物。—*v.t.* 破壞;毀壞。

wraith 〔reθ; reiθ〕 *n.* ①生魂(一般認爲人臨終前或方死後顯現的幽靈)。②鬼。③依稀可見之氣體。—**like,** *adj.*

wran·gle 〔ˈræŋgḷ; ˈræŋgl〕 *v.,* **-gled, -gling,** *n.* —*v.i.* ①爭吵;口角。②辯論;爭辯。—*v.t.* ①辯論;爭辯〖into, out of〗。②以爭辯取得; 爭取。③(在美國西部)牧(牲畜);看守(馬羣)。—*n.* 爭吵。—**wran·gler,** *n.*

wrap** 〔ræp; ræp〕 *v.,* **wrapped** or **wrapt, wrap·ping,** *n.* —*v.t.* ①包;裹;捲;纏。She *wrapped* herself in a shawl. 她在身上裹一件披肩。②包圍;隱蔽。The mountain top was *wrapped* in mist. 山頂爲霧所籠罩。—*v.i.* ①捲;纏。A vine *wraps* round the pillar. 藤蔓纏繞那柱子。②穿衣。③可被遮蓋、封入或包裝成 〖常 up〗。be wrapped up in*** **a.** 致力於; 關懷; 對…感到濃厚之興趣。She *is wrapped up in* her children. 她全力照料她的子女。**b.** 和…有密切關係;被牽涉。***wrap up*** **a.** 披上外衣。**b.** 結束。**c.** 贏定。He *wrapped up* the fight in the seventh round. 他在第七回合中贏定了那場拳賽。**d.** 作…之綜合報導。**e.** 〖俚〗使受嚴重損壞。—*n.* ①(常 *pl.*) 外套; 圍巾;肩巾;披肩(等)。②包裝用料。③(*pl.*) 祕密;保密。***under wraps*** 保密。The plan was kept carefully *under wraps.* 那計畫被小心保密。—**ped,** *adj.*

wrap·a·round 〔ˈræpəˌraund; ˈræpəˌraund〕 *adj.* ①重疊的。②似重疊的。—*n.* 重疊之物。

wrap·page 〔ˈræpɪdʒ; ˈræpidʒ〕 *n.* ①包;裹;捲;纏。②包袱;包皮;外套;封套。

wrap·per 〔ˈræpɚ; ˈræpə〕 *n.* ①包裹者。②包裹用之物;包紙;包布。③婦女室內穿的寬鬆便袍。

wrap·ping 〔ˈræpɪŋ; ˈræpiŋ〕 *n.* (常 *pl.*) 包裹東西用之紙、布等。

wrapt 〔ræpt; ræpt〕 *v.* pt. & pp. of **wrap.**

wrap-up 〔ˈræpˌʌp; ˈræpʌp〕 *n.* 綜合報導。In just a moment we'll give the *wrap-up.* 一會兒我們就要作綜合報導了。

wrasse 〔ræs; ræs〕 *n.* 瀨魚(可供食用)。

***wrath** 〔ræθ, rɑθ; rɔːθ, rɔθ〕 *n.* ①憤怒;暴怒。to be slow to *wrath.* 不易動怒。②猛烈的力量。

wrath·ful 〔ˈræθfəl; ˈrɔːθfəl〕 *adj.* ①盛怒的;忿怒的。②出於忿怒的;表現忿怒的。—**ly,** *adv.* —**ness,** *n.*

wrath·y 〔ˈræθɪ; ˈrɔːθi〕 *adj.* 〖俗〗= **wrathful.** —**wrath·i·ly,** *adv.* —**wrath·i·ness,** *n.*

wreak 〔rik; riːk〕 *v.t.* ①發洩。②報復。③〖古〗= **avenge.** ④施(罰);爲(害)。—**er,** *n.*

***wreath** 〔riθ; riːθ〕 *n., pl.* **wreaths.** ①花冠;花環。②(烟、雲等作螺旋狀之)渦卷;圈。

***wreathe** 〔rið; riːð〕 *v.,* **wreathed, wreathed** or (古) **wreath·en, wreath·ing.** —*v.t.* ①將(花、枝葉等)作成花環。②盤繞。The snake *wreathed* itself round the branch. 這蛇盤繞在樹枝上。③飾以花環或花環般之物。—*v.i.* (烟霧等)旋捲;繚繞。The smoke *wreathed* upward. 烟繚繞上昇。—**wreath·er,** *n.* —**wreath·ing·ly,** *adv.*

***wreck** 〔rɛk; rek〕 *n.* ①船隻的破毀。The storm caused many *wrecks.* 暴風雨使許多船隻破壞。②破毀的船隻。③房屋、火車、汽車、飛機等之破毀。④破毀;破滅。⑤殘骸;破毀後之殘餘物。⑥破落子;破產者;殘廢人。⑦漂來物;難船貨物。The shores are strewn with *wrecks.* 漂來物散布岸上。—*v.t.* ①使(船、火車、房屋等)破毀。Robbers *wrecked* the mail train. 强盜搗毀了郵政列車。②破壞;摧毀。The accident *wrecked* his health. 這次意外事故破壞了他的健康。—*v.i.* ①(船、火車、房屋等)破毀。The car *wrecked* at 3:30 a.m. 那輛車子在凌晨三點半撞毀。②受到摧毀。③拆除房屋。

wreck·age 〔ˈrɛkɪdʒ; ˈrekidʒ〕 *n.* ①殘骸;破毀後之殘餘物。②毀滅。

wreck·er 〔ˈrɛkɚ; ˈrekə〕 *n.* ①促成破毀之人。②救助破船之人或船。③掠奪難船者。④清除破毀殘餘物之人或火車等。⑤救濟車(將拋錨或撞毀的汽車從道路上拉走的卡車)。⑥拆除建築物者。

wreck·ing 〔ˈrɛkɪŋ; ˈrekiŋ〕 *n.* ①(船隻的)失事;遭難。②破壞;毀滅。③〖美〗拆除廢屋。④營救難船之工作;營救;救援。—*adj.* ①擔任拆除的;用於拆除的。*wrecking* crew. 拆除工人。②清除破毀殘餘物的;擔任營救的。

Wren 〔rɛn; ren〕 *n.* 〖英俗〗婦女皇家海軍服務隊 (Women's Royal Naval Service) 之一員。

wren 〔rɛn; ren〕 *n.* ①鷦鷯。②〖美俗〗少女;女子。

wrench** 〔rɛntʃ; rentʃ〕 *n.* ①猛扭;扭轉。②扭傷。He gave a *wrench* to his ankle when he jumped down. 他跳下去的時候扭傷了足踝。③離別的悲哀;痛苦。④螺旋鉗。throw a wrench into*** 完全弄糟;完全破壞。—*v.t.* ①猛扭。He *wrenched* the door open. 他猛扭開門。②扭傷。③歪曲;曲解(事實或言語等)。—*v.i.* ①急轉;發生劇烈變化。All of a sudden her heart *wrenched.* 突然她心中起了一陣痛苦。②扭轉。Tighten the nuts by light *wrenching.* 輕輕擰緊螺釘帽。—**er,** *n.* —**ing·ly,** *adv.*

***wrest** 〔rɛst; rest〕 *v.t.* ①猛扭;猛曳;扭奪;奪取。②歪曲;曲解;牽强附會。—*n.* ①擰;扭;猛奪。②〖音樂〗調音鍵。—**er,** *n.*

***wres·tle** 〔ˈrɛsḷ; ˈresl〕 *v.,* **-tled, -tling,** *n.* —*v.t.* ①與…角力。I'll *wrestle* you for the prize. 我要和你角力奪獎。②艱苦執行;艱苦推行;艱苦處理。—*v.i.* ①角力;搏鬥。He *wrestled* with me. 他和我搏鬥。②奮鬥。—*n.* ①角力。②奮鬥。

wres·tler 〔ˈrɛslɚ; ˈreslə〕 *n.* ①角力者。②將牛按倒地上打烙印者。

***wres·tling** 〔ˈrɛslɪŋ; ˈresliŋ〕 *n.* 角力;格鬥;扭鬥。

wrest pin (絃樂器之)絃栓。

***wretch** [rɛtʃ; retʃ] *n.* ①可憐的人。The poor *wretch* lost his all. 這個可憐的人失去了他的一切。②卑鄙的人。You *wretch!* 你這卑鄙的人!③〖謔〗可愛的人;小淘氣。

***wretch·ed** [ˈrɛtʃɪd; ˈretʃid] *adj.* ①可憐的; 不幸的。②惡劣的; 極不令人滿意的。The food at this hotel is *wretched.* 這家旅館的飯食很壞。③極惡的;無耻的;卑鄙的。**—ly,** *adv.* **—ness,** *n.*

wrick [rɪk; rik] *v.t.* 稍微扭傷; 扭筋。—*n.* 稍微扭傷;扭筋。

wrig·gle [ˈrɪgl̩; ˈrigl] *v.,* **-gled, -gling,** *n.* —*v.i.* ①蠕動;蜿蜒。A snake *wriggled* across the road. 一條蛇蜿蜒爬過道路。②設法進行。—*v.t.* 蠕動;蜿蜒而行。***wriggle out of a difficulty*** 慢慢設法脫出困難。—*n.* 蠕動;蜿蜒。**—wrig·gler,** *n.* **—wrig·gling·ly,** *adv.*

wrig·gly [ˈrɪglɪ; ˈrigli] *adj.* 蠕動的;蜿蜒的。

Wright [raɪt; rait] *n.* 萊特(Wilbur, 1867–1912, 與其弟Orville, 1871–1948, 同爲美國飛機發明家)。

wring** [rɪŋ; riŋ] *v.,* **wrung, wring·ing,** *n.* —*v.t.* ①扭;絞。*Wring* out your wet clothes. 把你的濕衣服的水絞乾。②絞出;搾出。③緊握。He *wrung* his old friend's hand. 他緊握他老朋友的手。④折磨;使苦惱。Their poverty *wrung* his heart. 他們的貧窮使他心中難過。—*v.i.* 蠕動; 侷促不安。wring one's hands*** 絞扭自己的手,表示悲哀或絕望。***wring out*** 扭出(水來)。***wringing wet*** 濕得足以絞出水來。—*n.* 扭;絞。

wring·er [ˈrɪŋɚ; ˈriŋə] *n.* ①(洗衣用之)絞衣機。②扭絞者;搾者。③令人心力交困之事;痛苦的經驗。***go through the wringer*** 受苦;受罪。

***wrin·kle**[1] [ˈrɪŋkl̩; ˈriŋkl] *n., v.,* **-kled, -kling.** —*n.* ①皺;皺紋。②缺點; 缺陷; 毛病。—*v.t.* 使皺。The rain *wrinkled* his clothes. 雨水使他的衣服起皺。—*v.i.* 皺;起皺紋。My dress *wrinkles* easily. 我的衣服容易起皺。**—a·ble,** *adj.*

wrin·kle[2] *n.* 〖俗〗好忠告;好主意;妙計。

wrin·kly [ˈrɪŋklɪ; ˈriŋkli] *adj.,* **-kli·er, -kli·est.** 皺的;有皺紋的。

***wrist** [rɪst; rist] *n.* ①腕;腕關節;腕骨。②袖口。③=**wrist pin.** —*v.t.* 藉手腕之揮動以推、移或投擲。

wrist·band [ˈrɪstˌbænd; ˈristbænd] *n.* (襯衫等的)袖口。

wrist-drop [ˈrɪstˌdrɑp; ˈristdrɔp] *n.* 〖醫〗腕垂症(因鉛或砷中毒而致的前膊伸肌麻痺)。(亦作 **wrist drop**)

wrist·let [ˈrɪstlɪt; ˈristlit] *n.* ①(防寒用)腕套;腕帶。②手鐲。③〖俚〗手銬。

wrist·lock [ˈrɪstˌlɑk; ˈristlɔk] *n.* 〖摔角〗緊握對方手腕而將其扭曲的一招。

wrist pin 〖機械〗肘桿。

wrist watch 手錶。

writ [rɪt; rit] *n.* ①文字。②文書;書面命令。***Holy Writ*** 聖經。—*v.* 〖古〗pt. & pp. of write.

‡**write** [raɪt; rait] *v.,* **wrote** or (古) **writ, writ·ten** or (古) **writ, writ·ing.** —*v.i.* ①書寫;寫字。If you have paper and a pen, you can *write.* 如果你有紙筆,你就可書寫。②寫作;著述。Her ambition was to *write.* 她的願望是從事著述。③寫信;通信。He promised to *write.* 他答應寫信。—*v.t.* ①書;寫。②撰寫;寫作;著述。③寫信給(某人);寫信告知(消息等)。She promised to *write* me every week. 她答應每週寫信給我。④明白地表示。His fear is *written* on his face. 他的臉上明白地表現出恐懼的神情。⑤以文字表達。***write down*** **a.** 寫下;記錄。*Write* the address *down* before you forget it. 把這地址寫下來,免得忘了。**b.** 以文字詆毀。**c.** 使降低。Their legal position was therefore *written down.* 他們的法律地位因而降低。**d.** 予以輕描淡寫。**e.** 寫低級文章。***write for*** **a.** 投稿於…。**b.** 寫信訂…。**c.** 爲…寫文章。***write home about*** (因有好處而)值得詳述;很精彩。***write in*** **a.** 加寫(於文書中)。**b.** 以書面提出。**c.** 投票給選票上未列名的候選人。***write off*** **a.** 劃銷;取銷。**b.** 迅速流利地書寫。**c.** 勾銷。to *write off* uncollectibles.勾銷無法收回的債。***write one's own ticket*** 自選工作條件、待遇等。***write out*** **a.** 謄寫。**b.** 竭盡…之寫作能力;(江郎)才盡。He has *written* himself *out.* 他是江郎才盡再也寫不出甚麼了。**c.** 全部寫出。***write up*** **a.** 記述;描寫;詳細記載。**b.** 爲文讚揚。He *wrote up* an actress in the local paper. 他在當地的報紙上面寫文章捧一個女伶。**c.** 予以告發。**d.** 對(資產)作過高的估價。**e.** 作補充描寫或說明;增補最新資料。***writ*** (or ***written***) ***in water*** 不能久傳;沒有記載。His name is *writ in water.* 他的名字不能永垂不朽。***writ*** (or ***written***) ***large*** 顯而易見;容易識別。***writ small*** 小規模的;縮小的。Personality is culture *writ small.* 個性乃是文化的縮圖。

write-down [ˈraɪtˌdaʊn; ˈraitdaun] *n.* 資產帳面價值之減低。

write-in [ˈraɪtˌɪn; ˈraitin] *adj.* 被選民寫在選票上的。—*n.* ①選票上未列名的候選人。②投給選票上未列名的候選人之選票。

write-off [ˈraɪtˌɔf; ˈraitɔːf] *n.* ①勾銷。②呆帳。③貶值;折舊。

***writ·er** [ˈraɪtɚ; ˈraitə] *n.* ①書寫者。②著者;作家。③書記;錄事。

write-up [ˈraɪtˌʌp; ˈraitʌp] *n.* ①〖俗〗報紙或雜誌稱贊的或有利的報導。②對公司資產估價過高的報告書。

writhe [raɪð; raið] *v.,* **writhed, writh·ing,** *n.* —*v.i.* ①繞;轉動。②受苦。—*v.t.* 〖罕〗使盤繞;扭。—*n.* 扭;繞;轉動;受苦。**—writh·ing·ly,** *adv.*

writh·en [ˈrɪðən; ˈriðən] *adj.* 盤繞的;扭轉的;蠕動的。

writ·ing** [ˈraɪtɪŋ; ˈraitiŋ] *n.* ①書寫。The evidence was put down in *writing.* 這證據被記錄在卷。②筆跡;書法(=handwriting).③寫成之文件。④(*pl.*)著述;作品。⑤書寫或寫作之職業或工作。writing on the wall*** 預示失敗或災禍的朕兆。—*adj.* ①寫的。②用以寫的;寫於其上的。

writing case 文具盒。

writing desk ①書桌。②可作書桌用的文具箱。

writing ink 墨水。

writing paper 寫字用紙。

writing table 寫字檯;書桌。

writ of execution 〖法律〗執行狀。

writ of summons 傳票。

‡**writ·ten** [ˈrɪtn̩; ˈritn] *v.* pp. of write.

W.R.N.S. 〖英〗Women's Royal Naval Service.

‡**wrong** [rɔŋ; rɔŋ] *adj.* ①不正當的;邪惡的;不法的。It is *wrong* to steal. 偷竊是不法的。②不正確的;錯誤的。③不適當的。④有毛病的; 出岔子的; 有事故的。Something is *wrong* with the car. 這車出了毛病。⑤

反的；不朝外的。***be in the wrong box*** 着慌；爲難；處境不利。***get*** (or ***have***) ***hold of the wrong end of the stick***（想法）完全搞錯了。***get in wrong*** 〖俚〗使失寵；令人討厭。***on the wrong side of*** 過了（幾歲）。He is *on the wrong side of* 40. 他已經四十多歲了。***take the wrong turning*** (or ***path***) 走入歧途。***wrong side out*** 翻轉；裏向外。—*adv.* 邪惡地；錯誤地；不適當地。You answer *wrong.* 你回答錯誤。***go wrong*** 走錯路；出毛病；走入歧途。All our plans *went wrong.* 我們所有的計畫都失敗。—*n.* ①惡；邪惡；不義。②錯誤；過失。③損害；不公正的待遇。She complained of her *wrongs.* 她訴說她的寃屈。***do wrong*** 做壞事；犯罪；做錯事。***in the wrong*** 不正當；錯誤。—*v.t.* ①屈待；傷害；寃枉。He *wronged* me when he said that I was envious. 他說我嫉妒，是寃枉我了。②以不正當的方法自…奪取（某物）。③〖古〗損害。—**er,** *n.*

wrong·do·er [ˈrɔŋduɚ; ˈrɔŋduə] *n.* 做壞事的人；犯罪的人。

wrong·do·ing [ˈrɔŋduɪŋ; ˈrɔŋduːiŋ] *n.* 惡事；惡行；犯罪；加害。

wrong·ful [ˈrɔŋfəl; ˈrɔŋful] *adj.* ①錯誤的；不正當的；不公正的；汚辱的；傷害的。②不法的；非法的。—**ness,** *n.* —**ly,** *adv.*

wrong-head·ed [ˈrɔŋˈhɛdɪd; ˈrɔŋˈhedid] *adj.* 判斷或意見錯誤的；頑固的。—**ly,** *adv.* —**ness,** *n.*

wrong·ly [ˈrɔŋlɪ; ˈrɔŋli] *adv.* 錯誤地；不正確地；不正當地；不合適地。

‡**wrote** [rot; rout] *v.* pt. of **write.**

wroth [rɔθ; rouθ, rɔːθ, rɔθ] *adj.* ①憤怒的；激怒的。②激盪的；洶湧的。—**ful,** *adj.*

wrought [rɔt; rɔːt] *v.* pt. & pp. of **work.** —*adj.* ①作成的；精製的；精鍊的。The gate was *wrought* with great skill. 這門的製造頗爲精巧。②激動的；興奮的。

wrought iron 鍛鐵；熟鐵。

wrought-up [ˈrɔtˈʌp; ˈrɔːtˈʌp] *adj.* 興奮的；激動的。

wrung [rʌŋ; rʌŋ] *v.* pt. & pp. of **wring.** —*adj.* 心中有苦的；有煩惱的。

wry [raɪ; rai] *adj.,* **wri·er, wri·est,** *v.,* **wried, wry·ing.** —*adj.* ①扭歪的；歪斜的。②不對勁的。③諷刺的；譏刺的；辛辣的。—*v.i.* & *v.t.* 繞；扭折。—**ness,** *n.*

wry·ly [ˈraɪlɪ; ˈraili] *adv.* 扭歪地；譏刺地；辛辣地。

wry·neck [ˈraɪˌnɛk; ˈrainek] *n.* ①鶇鴷。②歪脖。③〖俗〗歪脖的人。

wry-necked [ˈraɪˌnɛkt; ˈrainekt] *adj.* 〖俗〗歪脖子的。

W.S. ①West Saxon. ②writer to the signet. **WSW, W.S.W.** west-southwest. **wt.** ①warrant. ②weight. ③without.

wul·fen·ite [ˈwulfənˌaɪt; ˈwulfənait] *n.* 〖礦〗彩鉬鉛礦。

Wun·der·kind, wun·der·kind [ˈvʊndɚˌkɪnt; ˈvundəkint] *n., pl.* **-kind·er** [–ˌkɪndɚ; –ˌkində] or **-kinds.** ①神童。②在事業上少年得志的人。

wuz·zle [ˈwʌzl̩; ˈwʌzl] *v.t.,* **-zled, -zling.** 〖美方〗混合；混雜。

W.Va. West Virginia. **WWI** World War I. **WWII** World War II.

Wy., Wyo. Wyoming.

Wy·an·dotte [ˈwaɪənˌdɑt; ˈwaiəndɔt] *n.* 美國產之一種鷄。

wych-elm [ˈwɪtʃˈɛlm; ˈwitʃˈelm] *n.* 〖植物〗歐洲產的一種山榆。

wych-ha·zel [ˈwɪtʃˈhezl; ˈwitʃˈheizl] *n.* 〖植物〗①=**witch hazel.** ②=**wych-elm.**

Wyc·liffe, Wic·lif [ˈwɪklɪf; ˈwiklif] *n.* 威克利夫 (John, 1320?–1384, 英國宗教改革家及聖經譯者)。—**Wyc·lif·ian,** *adj.* —**Wyc·lif·ism,** *n.*

wye [waɪ; wai] *n., pl.* **wyes.** Y字；Y字形之物。

Wyke·ham·ist [ˈwɪkəmɪst; ˈwikəmist] *adj.* 英國 Winchester College 的。—*n.* Winchester College 的學生或畢業生。

wynd [waɪnd; waind] *n.* 〖蘇〗狹巷；小巷。

Wy·o·ming [waɪˈomɪŋ; waiˈoumiŋ] *n.* 懷俄明（美國西北部之一州，其首府爲 Cheyenne)。

Wy·o·ming·ite [waɪˈomɪŋaɪt; waiˈoumiŋait] *n.* 懷俄明人。

wy·vern [ˈwaɪvɚn; ˈwaivən] *n.* = **wivern.**

X

X, x [ɛks; eks] *n., pl.* **X's** or **x's** [ˈɛksɪz; ˈeksiz]. ①英文字母之第二十四個字母。②X形之物。③羅馬數字之10。④用以表示未知之人、物或數量的符號。⑤〖俗〗十元鈔票。⑥耶穌。⑦基督徒。⑧〖英〗表示成人電影之記號。—*adj.* X形的。

x¹ 化學元素 xenon 之符號。

x² Christ; Christian.

x³ 〖數學〗①未知數。②乘號。③=**abscissa.**

X-15 X–15 型飛機（一種供研究用之飛機，時速超過 3,600英里，高度超過100英里，用以探測氣體力學中之熱度、穩定性及控制法，以及在超五倍音速下作太空飛行時，對飛行員心理與生理之影響等問題)。

xanth- 〖字首〗**xantho-** 之異體（用於母音前)。

xan·thate [ˈzænθet; ˈzænθeit] *n.* 〖化〗黃酸鹽。

xan·the·in [ˈzænθɪɪn; ˈzænθiin] *n.* 〖化〗可溶於水的黃花色素。

xan·thic [ˈzænθɪk; ˈzænθik] *adj.* ①黃色的；帶黃色的。②〖化〗(不溶於水的)黃花色素的；黃酸的。

xanthic calculus 〖醫〗膀胱結石。

xan·thin [ˈzænθɪn; ˈzænθin] *n.* 〖化〗(不溶於水的)黃花色素。

xan·thine [ˈzænθin; ˈzænθiːn] *n.* 〖化〗黃花色精（一種類似尿酸之結晶形氮化物)。

Xan·thip·pe [zænˈtɪpɪ; zænˈθipi] *n.* ①古希臘蘇格拉底(Socrates)之妻（以潑悍著名)。②潑婦。（亦作 **Xantippe**)

xantho- 〖字首〗表"黃色"之義。

Xan·thoch·ro·i [zænˈθɑkroaɪ; zænˈθɔkrouai] *n. pl.* 黃白人種（高加索血統的種族之一)。—**Xan·tho·chro·ic,** *adj.*

xan·tho·phyl(l) [ˈzænθəfɪl; ˈzænθəfil] *n.*（秋日枯葉的)黃色素；葉黃質。—**ous,** *adj.*

xan·tho·pro·te·in [ˌzænθoˈprotiɪn; ˌzænθouˈproutiːn] *n.* 黃色蛋白質。

xan·thop·si·a [zænˈθɑpsɪə; zænˈθɔpsiə] *n.* 〖醫〗黃視症（視物皆爲黃色)。

xan·tho·sis [zænˈθosɪs; zænˈθousis] *n.* 〖醫〗(如癌腫等中的)黃皮症；黃病。

xan·thous [ˈzænθəs; ˈzænθəs] *adj.* ①黃色的。②黃色人種的。

Xa·vi·er [ˈzævɪɚ; ˈzæviə] *n.* 聖・查威爾 (Francis, 1506–1552, 世稱 Apostle of

the Indies, 西班牙天主教耶穌會之傳教士)。
x-ax·is 〔'ɛksˌæksɪs; 'eksˌæksis〕 *n.* 〖數學〗(笛卡兒座標之)橫軸;X軸。
X.C., x.c., x-cp. ex coupon (拉=without coupon).
X chromosome 〖生物〗X染色體(性染色體之一種,與Y染色體相配)。
X.D., x.d., X-div., x-div. ex dividend (拉 =without dividend).
Xe 化學元素 xenon 之符號。
xe·bec 〔'zibɛk; 'zi:bek〕 *n.* (航行於地中海之)一種三桅船。
xe·ni·al 〔'zinɪəl; 'zi:njəl〕 *adj.* 主客關係的。
xe·nog·a·my 〔zɪ'nɑgəmɪ; zi'nɔgəmi〕 *n.* 〖植物〗異花受粉;異花受精。
xe·non 〔'zinɑn; 'zenɔn〕 *n.* 〖化〗氙(一種稀有氣體元素,符號 X, Xe)。
xen·o·phile 〔'zɛnəˌfaɪl; 'zenəfail〕 *n.* 喜愛外國人及其文物者;親外者。—**xe·noph·i·lous,** *adj.*
xen·o·phobe 〔'zɛnəˌfob; 'zenəfoub〕 *n.* 仇視外國人者;恐懼外國人者;害怕生人者。
xen·o·pho·bi·a 〔ˌzɛnə'fobɪə; ˌzenə'foubjə〕 *n.* 仇外;恐懼外國人;生人恐怖症。
xen·o·pho·bic 〔ˌzɛnə'fobɪk; ˌzenə'foubik〕 *adj.* 仇視外國人的;恐懼外國人的;患生人恐怖症的。
Xen·o·phon 〔'zɛnəfən; 'zenəfən〕 *n.* 贊諾芬(434?–?355 B. C., 希臘將軍及歷史家)。—**te·an,** —**ti·an,** —**tine,** *adj.*
xe·ran·the·mum 〔zɪ'rænθɪməm; ziə'rænθiməm〕 *n.* 〖植物〗乾鮮花卉科植物。
xer·o·gram〔'zɪrəˌgræm;'ziərəgræm〕 *n.* 一分全錄影印本。
xe·rog·ra·phy 〔zɪ'rɑgrəfɪ; zi'rɔgrəfi〕 *n.* 全錄影印。—**xe·ro·graph·ic,** *adj.* —**xe·ro·graph·i·cal·ly,** *adv.*
xe·roph·i·lous 〔zɪ'rɑfələs; ziə'rɔfiləs〕 *adj.* ①適於乾燥炎熱之氣候的(指某些動、植物言)。②〖動物〗生活在乾燥氣候下的。
xe·ro·phyte 〔'zɪrəˌfaɪt; 'ziərəfait〕 *n.* 乾燥地帶的植物。—**xe·ro·phyt·ic,** *adj.* —**xe·ro·phyt·i·cal·ly,** *adv.*
xe·ro·ther·mic 〔ˌzɪrə'θɝmɪk; ˌziərə'θə:mik〕 *adj.* ①乾燥炎熱的。②適於乾燥炎熱環境的。
xe·rox 〔'zirɑks; 'zi:rɔks〕 *n.* ①全錄影印法。②(X-)其商標名。—*v.t.* 以全錄影印法影印。
X factor 未知因素。
xi 〔saɪ, zaɪ, ksi; gzai, ksai, zai〕 *n.* 希臘字母之第十四字母(Ξ, ξ)。
X.i., x-i. =**x-int.**
x in. without interest.
x-int. ex (=without) interest.
-xion 〖字尾〗 **-tion** 之異體 (英國拼法以 -xion 代 -tion, 如 connexion 代 connection)。
xiphi- 〖字首〗表"劍"之義。
xipho- 〖字首〗 **xiphi-** 之異體。
xiph·oid 〔'zɪfɔɪd; 'zifɔid〕 *n.* 〖解剖〗劍狀骨;劍狀突起;劍突。—*adj.* 劍狀的。
XL, X.L. extra large.
X·mas〔'krɪsməs;'krisməs〕*n.*=**Christmas.**
Xn. Christian. **Xnty.** Christianity.
xo·a·non 〔'zoəˌnɑn; 'zouənɔn〕 *n., pl.* **-na** 〔-nə; -nə〕. (古希臘)木雕神像。
X·o·graph 〔'ɛksəˌgræf;'eksəgrɑ:f〕 *n.* 〖商標名〗①(照片、圖畫等之)立體複印。②立體複印法。
XP 希臘文 ΧΡΙΣΤΟΣ(=Christ)一字之首二字母,爲Christ 之表徵。
X radiation ①X光線放射。②X光線檢查、處理等。
***X ray** ①X光線。②X光線照片。〖注意〗X ray 中之 X 常以大寫表示之。用作名詞時中間亦可用連字符號。用作動詞或形容詞時,則必須有連字符號。
X-ray 〔'ɛks're; 'eks'rei〕 *v.t.* 用X光線檢查、照相或治療。—*adj.* X光線的。an *X-ray* examination. X光檢查。—*n.* =**X ray.**
X·ray *n.* 通訊電碼,代表字母 X.
X-ray microscope X光顯微鏡。
X-ray photograph (or **picture**) X光照片。
X-ray therapy X光治療法(如用於癌症等者)。
X-ray tube X射線管。
Xtian. Christian. **Xty.** Christianity.
X-u·nit 〔'ɛks'junɪt; 'eks'ju:nit〕 *n.* 〖物理〗X單位(用以測定放射線之波長者)。
xyl- 〖字首〗 **xylo-** 之異體(用於母音之前)。
xy·lan 〔'zaɪlæn; 'zailæn〕 *n.* 〖化〗木質組織中所含之樹膠質。
xy·lem 〔'zaɪlɛm; 'zailem〕 *n.* 〖植物〗木質部。
xy·lene 〔'zaɪlin; 'zaili:n〕 *n.* 〖化〗二甲苯〔$C_6H_4(CH_3)_2$〕。
xy·lo·carp 〔'zaɪləˌkɑrp; 'zailəkɑ:p〕 *n.* 〖植物〗硬木質果;硬木質果樹。—**ous,** *adj.*
xy·lo·gen 〔'zaɪləˌdʒɛn; 'zailədʒən〕 *n.* 〖植物〗木質;木纖維。
xy·lo·graph〔'zaɪləˌgræf;'zailəgrɑ:f〕 *n.* 木版;木版印刷物。—**ic,** *adj.*
xy·log·ra·phy 〔zaɪ'lɑgrəfɪ; zai'lɔgrəfi〕 *n.* 木版術;雕木術;木版印刷術。
xy·lol 〔'zaɪlɑl; 'zailɔl〕 *n.* 〖化〗二甲苯(=xylene).
xy·lo·nite 〔'zaɪləˌnaɪt; 'zailənait〕 *n.* 賽璐珞;假象牙。
xy·loph·a·gous 〔zaɪ'lɑfəgəs; zai'lɔfəgəs〕 *adj.* ①以木爲食的(如某些昆蟲之幼蟲)。②蛀蝕木材的。
xy·lo·phone 〔'zaɪləˌfon; 'zailəfoun〕 *n.* 木琴。—**xy·lo·phon·ic,** *adj.* —**xy·lo·phon·ist,** *n.*
xy·lyl 〔'zaɪləl; 'zailil〕 *n.* 〖化〗甲苯甲基。
xyst 〔zɪst; zist〕 *n.* =**xystus.**
xys·tos 〔'zɪstɑs; 'zistɔs〕 *n.* =**xystus.**
xys·tus 〔'zɪstəs; 'zistəs〕 *n.* (古希臘、羅馬之)室內運動場;庭院內之散步道。

Y

Y, y 〔waɪ; wai〕 *n., pl.* **Y's** or **y's** 〔waɪz; waiz〕, *adj.* —*n.* ①英文之第二十五個字母。②Y形物。③中世紀羅馬數字150。—*adj.* ①Y形的。②基督教青年會的;基督教女青年會的。
Y 化學元素 yttrium 之符號。
y 〖數學〗①縱座標。②一組未知數中之第二個未知數。
-y¹ 〖字尾〗形成形容詞,表"充滿;有…性質;有…傾向;頗;有幾分;類似"之義。
-y² 〖字尾〗附加於名詞後,常表"親暱;小"之義(如 Billy, daddy 等)。
-y³ 〖字尾〗由動詞形成名詞之字尾(如 inquiry).
-y⁴ 〖字尾〗形成抽象名詞之字尾,表"性質;情況"之義(如 jealousy, allergy 等)。
y. ①yard; yards. ②year; years. ③yellow. ④yen. ⑤yeoman. ⑥younger; youngest. ⑦your.

yab·ber [ˈjæbɚ; ˈjæbə] *n.* 〖澳〗=**jabber.**

***yacht** [jɑt; jɔt] *n.* 輕舟;遊艇。—*v.i.* 駕輕舟;乘遊艇。

yacht club 遊艇俱樂部。

yacht·ing [ˈjɑtɪŋ; ˈjɔtiŋ] *n.* 遊艇比賽;乘遊艇遊戲。—*adj.* ①遊艇的;遊艇比賽的。②對駕遊艇有興趣的。

yachts·man [ˈjɑtsmən; ˈjɔtsmən] *n., pl.* **-men.** ①遊艇所有人。②遊艇駕駛者。

yaf·fin·gale [ˈjæfɪnˌgel; ˈjæfinˌgeil] *n.* 綠色啄木鳥。

yaf·fle [ˈjæfl̩; ˈjæfl] *n.* =**yaffin-gale.** (亦作 **yaffil**)

ya·ger [ˈjegɚ; ˈjeigə] *n.* ①獵人。②昔德國或奧國之步鎗兵。

yah [jɑ; jɑː] *interj.* 呀!(表示嘲笑、不喜歡或挑釁、反抗等義)。—*adv.* 〖美〗=**yes.**

Ya·hoo [jəˈhu; jəˈhuː] *n.* ①雅虎(Swift 所著 *Gulliver's Travels* 中的人形獸)。②(y-) 邪惡、野蠻之人;人面獸心之人。③(y-) 粗鄙之人;鄉下人。—**ism,** *n.*

Yah·ve(h) [ˈjɑve; ˈjɑːvei] *n.* =**Yahwe.**

Yah·we(h) [ˈjɑwe; ˈjɑːwei] *n.* 上帝(爲希伯來語 God 一字之近代形式,卽聖經舊約中的 Jehovah).

yak¹ [jæk; jæk] *n.* (西藏及中亞所產之)犛牛。

yak² *v.i.,* **yakked, yak·king.** 喋喋不休。

Yale [jel; jeil] *n.* 耶魯大學(在美國Connecticut 州之 New Haven).

Yale lock 一種彈簧鎖(由美國 Linus Yale 氏發明而得名)。

Yal·ta Conference [ˈjɑltə~; ˈjæltə~] 雅爾達會議(1945年2月,美總統羅斯福,英首相邱吉爾,與蘇聯元帥史達林在俄境雅爾達擧行)。

Ya·lu [ˈjɑˈlu; ˈjɑːˈluː] *n.* 鴨綠江(在中國與韓國邊境)。

yam [jæm; jæm] *n.* ①薯蕷;山藥。②馬鈴薯;洋山芋。③上述之各種植物。Chinese (*or* Japanese) *yam.* 山藥疙瘩;家山藥。④〖美方〗蕃薯;山芋。

Ya·ma [ˈjæmə; ˈjɑːmə] 〖梵〗 *n.* (掌管陰府之)閻羅王。

Ya·ma·to [ˈjɑmɑto; ˈjɑːmɑːtou] *n.* ①日本大和民族族人。②日本人。—*adj.* 大和民族的。

ya·men, ya·mun [ˈjɑmən; ˈjɑːmən] 〖中〗 *n.* 衙門。

Yang Chen-ning [ˈjɑŋˈdʒɛnˈnɪŋ; ˈjɑːŋˈdʒenˈniŋ] 楊振寧 (1922–, 祖籍中國之美國科學家, 獲 1957 年諾貝爾物理獎)。

Yang·tze, Yang·tse, Yang·tze Kiang [ˈjæŋˌtsɪˈkjæn; ˈjæŋtsiˈkjæŋ] *n.* 揚子江;長江(長 3,200英里)。

Yank [jæŋk; jæŋk] *n.* 〖俚〗美國人(尤指一、二次大戰中之美國士兵)。 —*adj.* 美國人的;美國兵的;像美國人或兵的。

yank [jæŋk; jæŋk] *v.,* **yanked, yank·ing,** *n.* —*v.t.* & *v.i.* 〖俗〗用力猛拉;用力猛扭;突然拉動;迅速動。—*n.* 急拉;猛拔。

***Yan·kee¹** [ˈjæŋkɪ; ˈjæŋki] *n.* ①美國北部諸州的人;美國人。②美國新英格蘭人。 —*adj.* 美國北方人的;美國人的。 *Yankee* inventions. 美國人的發明。

Yan·kee² *n.* 通訊電碼,代表字母Y.

Yan·kee·dom [ˈjæŋkɪdəm; ˈjæŋkidəm] *n.* ①Yankee 之集合稱。②美國北部(尤指 New England). ③美國。

Yankee Doo·dle [~ˈdudl̩; ~ˈduːdl] 美國獨立戰爭時期的一首愛國歌曲。

Yan·kee·ism [ˈjæŋkɪˌɪzəm; ˈjæŋkiizm] *n.* 美國人之氣質、風俗、習語等。

yan·ni·gan [ˈjænəgən; ˈjænigən] *n.* 〖美俚〗〖棒球〗①新球員。②預備球員。

ya·ourt [ˈjɑuət; ˈjɑːuət] *n.* =**yog(h)urt.**

yap [jæp; jæp] *v.,* **yapped, yap·ping,** *n.* —*v.i.* ①吠;大聲叫。②〖俚〗吵嚷;瞎談。—*v.t.* 吵嚷;咆哮。 —*n.* ①犬吠;大聲叫。②〖俚〗吵嚷;瞎談。③〖俚〗吵鬧的人。④〖俚〗無賴漢;惡棍。⑤〖俚〗嘴。—**per,** *n.*—**ping·ly,** *adv.*

yapp [jæp; jæp] *n., adj.* (書之)捲邊裝訂(的)。

Yar·bor·ough [ˈjɑrˌbɝo; ˈjɑːbərə] *n.* (橋牌、whist 牌等)無過九點之一手牌。

‡**yard¹** [jɑrd; jɑːd] *n.* ①庭院;天井;庭園。inn *yard.* 旅舍的庭院。②工場;工作場。③調車場。I work in the railroad *yards.* 我在鐵路調車場工作。 ***the Yard*** 英國蘇格蘭場(英國刑警總署)。 —*v.t.* 關在院中;圈在場裏;把(牛羣)趕入欄中。

***yard²** *n.* ①碼(三英尺)。②帆桁。③一碼布。④大量。

yard·age¹ [ˈjɑrdɪdʒ; ˈjɑːdidʒ] *n.* ①以碼計量;以碼計量之長度或數量。②以立方碼計量之材料體積。

yard·age² *n.* ①(火車運家畜時的)站內欄舍之使用權。②使用站內欄舍所付之費用。

yard·arm [ˈjɑrdˌɑrm; ˈjɑːdɑːm] *n.* 〖航海〗帆桁之一端。

yard·bird [ˈjɑrdˌbɝd; ˈjɑːdbəːd] *n.* 未訓練之新兵。

yard goods 布疋;疋頭。

yard·man [ˈjɑrdmən; ˈjɑːdmən] *n., pl.* **-men.** ①在火車調配場工作之人。②庭院打雜工人。

yard·mas·ter [ˈjɑrdˌmæstɚ; ˈjɑːdˌmɑːstə] *n.* 〖鐵路〗調車場之管理人。

yard-meas·ure [ˈjɑrdˌmɛʒɚ; ˈjɑːdˌmeʒə] *n.* 碼尺。

yard·stick [ˈjɑrdˌstɪk; ˈjɑːdstik] *n.* ①碼尺。②任何評判或比較之標準。

yard·wand [ˈjɑrdˌwɑnd; ˈjɑːdwɔnd] *n.* 〖主英〗=**yardstick.**

yarn** [jɑrn; jɑːn] *n.* ①紗;線。 woolen *yarn.* 絨線。②〖俗〗故事;奇談;旅行者的故事;難於置信的故事。③談話;會話。He stopped to have a *yarn* with me. 他停下來跟我談話。 ***spin a yarn (or ***yarns***) 講一個故事;編造不實的故事。 *Spin* us *a* good *yarn.* 給我們講個好聽的故事。—*v.i.* 〖俗〗講故事;長談。Men *yarn* of the harbor's famous pilots. 人們常常會講該港口一些著名領港人的故事。—**er,** *n.*

yarn beam (or **roll**) (紡織機)捲經線的棍子。

yarn-dyed [ˈjɑrnˌdaɪd; ˈjɑːndaid] *adj.* 先染後織的(紗)。

yar·o·vize [ˈjɑrəˌvaɪz; ˈjɑːrəvaiz] *v.t.* =**jarovize.**

yar·row [ˈjæro; ˈjærou] *n.* 〖植物〗西洋蓍草。

yash·mak [jɑʃˈmɑk, ˈjæʃmæk; ˈjæʃmæk] *n.* (回教婦女外出時所戴的) 面紗。(亦作 **yashmac**)

yat·a·g(h)an [ˈjætəgæn; ˈjætəgæn] 〖土〗 *n.* 土耳其刀。

yaup [jɔp; jɔːp] *v.i., n.* =**yawp.**

yaw [jɔ; jɔː] *v.t.* & *v.i.* ①(船、飛機等)偏航;逸出航線。②轉動。—*n.* 偏航;逸出航線;打轉。

yawl¹ [jɔl; jɔːl] *n.* ①(前桅高後桅低之)小型帆船。②船載小艇;艦載雜用船。

yawl² *n., v.i.* 〖方〗咆哮;號叫。

yawn** [jɔn; jɔːn] *v.i.* ① 打呵欠。 He closed the book, *yawned,* and went to bed. 他將書闔起來, 打個呵欠, 然後上牀。②張開;裂開。 —*v.t.* 打着呵欠說。 "What is the use?" he *yawned.* "有甚麼用?" 他打着呵欠說。 ***make a person yawn 使人厭

倦;使人想睡覺。—*n.* ①打呵欠。②令人厭倦的事或人。③張開;裂開。—**er,** *n.* —**ing,** *adj.* —**ing·ly,** *adv.*

yawp [jɔp; jɔːp] *v.i.* ①高聲喊叫;吵嚷。②〖俗〗高聲打呵欠。—*n.* 高聲喊叫(聲);吵嚷(聲)。—**er,** *n.*

yaws [jɔz; jɔːz] *n. pl.* 〖醫〗雅司;印度痘。

Y-ax·is [ˈwaɪˌæksɪs; ˈwaiˌæksis] *n.* 〖數學〗(笛卡兒座標之)縱軸。

Yb 化學元素 ytterbium 之符號。

Y.B. Yearbook.

Y-branch [ˈwaɪˈbræntʃ; ˈwaiˈbrɑːntʃ] *n.* Y字形管。

Y chromosome 〖生物〗Y染色體(性染色體之一種,與X染色體相配)。

y·clept, y-clept [ɪˈklɛpt; iˈklept] *adj.* 〖古,諧〗稱作…的;名叫…的。(亦作 **ycleped, y-cleped**)

Y cross Y字形十字架。

yd. yard; yards. **yds.** yards.

ye [ji; jiː] *pron.* ①〖古〗pl. of **thou.** If *ye* are thirsty, drink. 汝等若口渴,即喝。②〖俗〗=**you.** ③〖古〗=**the.**

yea [je; jei] *adv.* ①是;然(=yes)。②實在;的確(=indeed)。③不僅…而且;加之(=not only that, but also; moreover). —*n.* 贊成票;投贊成票者。

yeah [jɛ; jɛə] *adv.* 〖美俗〗=**yes.**

yean [jin; jiːn] *v.t.* & *v.i.* 生產(小羊)。

yean·ling [ˈjinlɪŋ; ˈjiːnliŋ] *n.* 羔;小羊。—*adj.* 新生出的;小的。

:year [jɪr; jəː, jiə] *n.* ①年。this *year.* 今年。last *year.* 去年。next *year.* 明年。②學年;年度。fiscal *year.* 會計年度。③一年中某一活動所費之時間。④太陽年。⑤恆星年。⑥任何行星環行太陽所需時間。⑦年歲;年齡。He looks young for his *years.* 他比他的實際年齡顯得年輕。⑧(*pl.*) **a.** 很久的時間。It's *years* since we met. 我們好久不見面。**b.** 年長;年老。**c.** 年齡。⑨爲期一年之徒刑。The judge gave him 15 *years.* 推事判他十五年徒刑。⑩年級。***all the year round*** 一年到頭。***a year and a day*** 〖法律〗滿一年(某些事務上所規定的法定期間,其目的在確定該段時間能滿一整年)。***New Year's Day*** 元旦日。***the year one***〖諧〗很久以前。***year by year*** 年年;每年。***year in, year out*** 一年一年地;不斷。

year·book [ˈjɪrˌbuk; ˈjəːbuk] *n.* 年報;年鑑。

year·ling [ˈjɪrlɪŋ; ˈjəːliŋ] *n.* 一歲的小獸。—*adj.* ①一歲的。②爲時一年的。

year·long [ˈjɪrˈlɔŋ; ˈjəːˈlɔŋ] *adj.* ①連續一年的。②連續多年的;經年的。

***year·ly** [ˈjɪrlɪ; ˈjəːli] *adj.* 每年一次的;每年的;一年間的。a *yearly* trip. 每年一次的旅行。a *yearly* salary. 年薪。—*adv.* ①每年。②每年一度;一年一次。

***yearn** [jɝn; jəːn] *v.i.* ①渴望;思念。He *yearns* for home. 他思念家。②懷念;憐憫。—*n.* 渴望;懷念。—**er,** *n.* —**ful,** *adj.*

yearn·ing [ˈjɝnɪŋ; ˈjəːniŋ] *n.* ①渴望;思慕。②懷念。—*adj.* 渴望的;懷念的。—**ly,** *adv.*

year of grace 公元年;西曆年。

year·old [ˈjɪrˌold; ˈjəːould] *adj.* 滿一歲的。—*n.* =**yearling.**

(-)year·old *adj.* …歲的。—*n.* …歲的人。

***yeast** [jist; jiːst] *n.* ①酵母。②發酵粉;發酵片。③興奮素。④泡沫。⑤活力;精力。

yeast cake 酵母餅。

yeast powder 酵粉。

yeast·y [ˈjistɪ; ˈjiːsti] *adj.* ①酵母的;含酵母的;似酵母的。②多泡沫的。③輕浮的。④變化中的;未安定的。⑤年輕的;興高采烈的。—**yeast·i·ly,** *adv.* —**yeast·i·ness,** *n.*

Yeats [jets; jeits] *n.* 葉芝(William Butler, 1865–1939, 愛爾蘭詩人及劇作家)。—**i·an,** *adj.*

yegg [jɛg; jeg] *n.* 〖美俚〗罪犯(尤指搶金庫者或盜賊)。

yegg·man [ˈjɛgmən; ˈjegmən] *n., pl.* **-men.** 〖美俚〗=**yegg.**

yeh [je; jei] *adv.* =**yes.**

yelk [jɛlk; jelk] *n.* 〖古,方〗=**yolk.**

***yell** [jɛl; jel] *v.i.* ①號叫;呼喊。He *yelled* with pain. 他因痛而號叫。②喊加油。③大聲抗議或埋怨。—*v.t.* ①喊出;大聲發出。②向…喊。He *yelled* up the dogs. 他把狗喊過來。—*n.* ①呼喊;號叫。②〖美〗(學生鼓勵其本校選手之)歡呼;吶喊。

yell leader 啦啦隊長。

:yel·low [ˈjɛlo; ˈjelou] *n.* ①黃;黃色。②黃色顏料。③蛋黃。④黃種人。—*adj.* ①黃色的。②黃皮膚的。③〖美俗〗懦弱的;卑怯的。He has a *yellow* streak in him. 他膽小。④妒忌的;猜忌的。⑤(報紙等) **a.** 低級趣味的;聳人聽聞的。**b.** 報導不實的。—*v.t.* & *v.i.* 使黃;變黃。Paper *yellows* with age. 紙張會因年久而變黃。—**y,** *adj.*

yellow alert 空襲警報(別於緊急警報)。

yel·low·back [ˈjɛloˌbæk; ˈjeloubæk] *n.* ①廉價之通俗小說(此類小說從前盛行用黃皮封面,故名)。②黃金公債券。

yel·low·band [ˈjɛloˌbænd; ˈjeloubænd] *n.* 黃色紋(線)。

yel·low·bel·ly [ˈjɛloˌbɛlɪ; ˈjelouˌbeli] *n., pl.* **-lies.** ①一種細長淡水魚。②懦夫。

yel·low·bill [ˈjɛloˌbɪl; ˈjeloubil] *n.* 黑鳧。

yel·low·bird [ˈjɛloˌbɝd; ˈjeloubəːd] *n.* ①北美產的一種黃雀。②任何鳴聲如黃雀之鳥。

Yellow Book 黃皮書(我國及法國政府等之報告書)。

yellow dog 〖美俚〗①不參加或不協助工會之工人。②卑鄙之人。

yellow-dog contract 〖俚〗工人向資方簽訂之保證不加入工會的合同(現已禁止)。

yellow fever 黃熱病。

yellow gum ①〖醫〗初生嬰兒之黃疸症。②有加利樹(=eucalyptus).

yel·low·ham·mer [ˈjɛloˌhæmɚ; ˈjelouˌhæmə] *n.* 金翼啄木鳥。

yel·low·ish [ˈjɛloɪʃ; ˈjelouiʃ] *adj.* 微黃的;帶黃色的。

yellow jack ①=**yellow fever.** ②(掛在船上表示檢疫的)黃色旗(=yellow flag).

yellow journalism 〖美〗(報紙等)迎合低級趣味之作風。

yel·low·legs [ˈjɛloˌlɛgz; ˈjeloulegz] *n.* (作 *sing.* 解)美洲產鷸屬的一種黃腿涉禽。

yellow light (交通指揮燈之)黃燈。

yel·low·ness [ˈjɛlonɪs; ˈjelounis] *n.* ①黃色。②嫉妒。

yellow pages 〖美〗黃頁分類(電話簿上按用戶之營業或服務性質分類登錄的部分)。

yellow peril 黃禍(白種人所感受的黃種人可能征服世界的威脅)。

yellow press 黃色報紙(迎合低級趣味者)。

yellow race 黃色人種。

Yellow River 黃河(長 2,700 英里)。

yel·lows [ˈjɛloz; ˈjelouz] *n. pl.* ①〖植物〗枯黃病。②黃疸病。③〖廢〗妒嫉。

Yellow Sea 黃海(在中國長江口以北)。

Yel·low·stone [ˈjɛloˌston; ˈjeloustoun] *n.* ①黃石河(在美國 Wyoming 州西北部,經黃石公園往東北流,在 Montana州與 Missouri 河匯合,全長671英里)。②(亦作 **Yellowstone National Park**) 黃石公園(美國的國立公園,在 Wyoming 及 Montana兩州間,以噴泉、溫泉及瀑布著稱於世)。

yel·low·tail [ˋjɛlo͵tel; ˈjelouteil] *n., pl.* **-tail, -tails.** ①一種竹筴科之魚。②一種鰷。③石魚。

yel·low·wood [ˋjɛlo͵wud; ˈjelouwud] *n.* ①黃色木材。②產黃色木材之各種樹。

yel·low·y [ˋjɛloɪ; ˈjeloui] *adj.* 微黃的;略帶黃色的。

***yelp** [jɛlp; jelp] *v.i. & v.t.* ①(犬等)嗥叫。②突然喊叫。 —*n.* 嗥叫。The dog gave a *yelp* when I stepped on its foot. 當我踩到那狗的脚,它便嗥叫起來。 —**er,** *n.*

Yem·en [ˋjɛmən; ˈjemən] *n.* 葉門 (**a.** 阿拉伯西南部一共和國,正式名稱爲 Yemen Arab Republic,首都沙那 Sanʻa. **b.** 阿拉伯半島南部一共和國,正式名稱爲 People's Democratic Republic of Yemen, 亦名 Southern Yemen, 首都亞丁 Aden)。

Yem·e·ni [ˋjɛmənɪ; ˈjeməni] *n., pl.* **-nis, -ni,** *adj.* =**Yemenite.**

Yem·en·ite [ˋjɛmən͵aɪt; ˈjemənait] *adj.* 葉門(人)的。—*n.* 葉門人。

yen¹ [jɛn; jen] *n., pl.* **yen.** 圓(日幣制單位)。

yen² *n., v.,* **yenned, yen·ning.** —*n.* 癮;熱望;渴望。 —*v.i.* 渴望〖for〗.

yeo(m). yeomanry.

***yeo·man** [ˋjomən; ˈjoumən] *n., pl.* **-men.** ①〖美海軍〗文書上士。②〖古〗(王家貴室之)從僕;衞士。③〖英史〗自由民。④〖英〗小地主;自耕農。⑤〖英〗(自由民子弟組成的)義勇騎兵;志願騎兵。

yeo·man·ly [ˋjomənlɪ; ˈjoumənli] *adj.* yeoman的; yeoman 之地位的; 關於 yeoman 的;適於 yeoman 的。 —*adv.* 似 yeoman 地;勇敢地;忠實地;剛毅地。

yeo·man·ry [ˋjomənrɪ; ˈjoumənri] *n.* ① yeoman 之集合稱。②(自由民子弟組成的)義勇騎兵;志願騎兵。

yeoman's service 優良的服務;忠實的支持或協助。(亦作 **yeoman service**)

yep [jɛp; jep] *adv.* 〖美俚〗=**yes.**

-yer 〖字尾〗表示"從事於…者"之義(通常附加於W字母之後,如 lawyer, sawyer).

yer·ba [ˋjɝbə; ˈjəːbə] *n.* 馬黛(maté)茶。

‡**yes** [jɛs; jes] *adv., n., pl.* **yes·es,** *v.,* **yessed, yes·sing,** *interj.* —*adv.* ①是;然。Are you going or not? —*Yes,* I am going. 你去不去?—是,我去。②而且;不但。③(表示懷疑人家的話)眞的嗎?哦?(用上昇的音調)。"The taxes are very reasonable." "*Yes?*" "那些稅是很合理的。" "哦? 眞的嗎?" ④(用在自己所說的話之後,表示"你覺得對嗎?" "這樣對嗎?")。We must seal every knot on the parcel—*yes?* 我們必須把這包裹的每個結都打起來—是不是? ⑤(用在別人談話之後,表示"請說下去")。"I've come to you for help." "*Yes.*" "我來請你幫忙。" "請說下去。" ⑥(用以轉換語氣)不錯(但…)。⑦(用以更正對方之否定句)。"You couldn't have meant that." "*Yes,* I did mean it." "你的意思不可能那樣。" "你錯了,我的意思就是那樣。" —*n.* ①是;然。Confine yourself to *yes* and no. 只說是或否好了。②贊成票。③投贊成票者;贊成者。***yes man*** 唯唯諾諾的人;對上司不敢抗辯的人。—*v.t. & v.i.* 答是。All she had to do was *yes* him when he was talking. 她只要在他說話時答是就行了。—*interj.* (與 and 連用,以加重語氣)。I could walk it in an hour, *yes,* and return in that time. 我能在一小時內走到那裏,不但如此,還能在同樣長的時間中走回來。〖注意〗**yes, no** 皆爲副詞。它們可形容一個句子、用作一對等子句或單獨用作一完整句子。

ye·shi·va(h) [jəˋʃivə; jəˈʃiːvə] *n., pl.* **-vas, -voth** [-vot; -vout]. (宗教的與非宗教的教育並行之)正統猶太小學。

yester- 〖字首〗①表"昨日的"之義,如: yestermorning (昨晨)。②表"前此的"之義,如: yesterweek (上週)。〖注意〗在詩中,間或用作一分開的字,如: *yester* sun (昨天的太陽)。

‡**yes·ter·day** [ˋjɛstədɪ, -͵de; ˈjestədi, -dei, ˈjestdi, ͵jestəˈdei] *n.* ①昨天。②晚近;最近的過去。 —*adv.* ①昨天。He died *yesterday.* 他昨天死去。②近來;晚近。

yes·ter·eve [͵jɛstəˋiv; ͵jestərˈiːv] *n., adv.* =**yesterevening.**

yes·ter·eve·ning [͵jɛstəˋivnɪŋ; ͵jestərˈiːvniŋ] *n., adv.* 〖詩〗昨晚;昨夜。

yes·ter·morn [ˋjɛstəˋmɔrn; ˈjestəˈmɔːn] *n., adv.* 〖古,詩〗=**yestermorning.**

yes·ter·morn·ing [ˋjɛstəˋmɔrnɪŋ; ˈjestəˈmɔːniŋ] *n., adv.* 〖古,詩〗昨天早晨;在昨天早晨。

yes·ter·night [ˋjɛstəˋnaɪt; ˈjestəˈnait] *n., adv.* 〖古,詩〗昨夜;在昨夜。

yes·ter·year [ˋjɛstəˋjɪr; ˈjestəˈjəː] *n., adv.* ①去年;在去年。②近幾年;近來。

yes·treen [jɛsˋtrin; jesˈtriːn] *n., adv.* 〖蘇,詩〗=**yesterevening.**

‡**yet** [jɛt; jet] *adv.* ①尚;還;仍;迄今。He has not come *yet.* 他還沒有來。②現在;目前。Don't go *yet.* 現在不要走。③又;再;更;愈。I have a *yet* more important thing to say. 我有一件更重要的事情要說。④而且也;且亦 (與 nor連用)。⑤遲早;終必。The thief will be caught *yet.* 這賊將來總會被捉到的。⑥然而;但是。He is poor, *yet* honest. 他雖貧窮,但是誠實。***as yet*** 迄今;直到目前。*As yet,* no man has set foot on Mars. 直到目前爲止還沒有人登陸火星。 —*conj.* 然而;但是;可是。He worked hard, *yet* he failed. 他工作很努力,然而他失敗了。—*adj.* 直到現在的。〖注意〗**yet** 是副詞。在正式英語中,亦用作對等連接詞,等於 but.

Yet·i, yet·i [ˋjɛtɪ; ˈjeti] *n.* 傳說中之喜馬拉雅山雪人(=Abominable Snowman).

***yew** [ju; juː] *n.* ①〖植物〗紫杉;水松。②紫杉木材;水松木材。

Ygg·dra·sill [ˋɪgdrə͵sɪl; ˈigdrəsil] *n.* 〖北歐神話〗宇宙樹(其根與枝連接天、地及地獄之大梣樹)。

Y-gun [ˋwaɪ͵gʌn; ˈwaigʌn] *n.* 艦尾發射深水炸彈之裝置。

YHA Youth Hostels Association.

Yid·dish [ˋjɪdɪʃ; ˈjidiʃ] *n.* (許多歐洲及其他各洲之猶太人後裔所講的)一種猶太語(由一種 High German 方言組成,用希伯來字母拼寫,字彙中雜有希伯來文、俄文、波蘭文等)。 —*adj.* ①此種語言的。②〖俗〗猶太人的。

yield** [jild; jiːld] *v.t.* ①出產;生產;生。Land *yields* crops. 土地生產農作物。②放棄;讓渡;讓。I will not *yield* a step. 我決不讓一步。③承認。④給與。Their advice to us *yielded* many benefits. 他們的忠告給與我們許多益處。⑤耽溺〖up〗. ⑥〖古〗酬報;付。Gods *yield* you for't (=for it). 願諸神爲此對你有所報償。—*v.i.* ①生產;出產;生。This land *yields* abundantly. 這土地出產豐富。②投降; 屈服; 退讓; 讓步。They *yielded* to the enemy. 他們向敵人投降。The door *yielded* to his touch. 門被他一觸而開。③(在議會等)讓給發言之權。yield oneself prisoner*** 投降做俘虜。***yield possession*** 讓渡所有權。***yield precedence to age*** 讓年老者居先。***yield submission*** 服從。***yield the palm to someone*** 輸給某人; 遜人一籌。***yield to none*** 不落人後;不讓給人。***yield up the ghost*** 死。—*n.* ①生產;生產量; 生產物。What is the *yield* per acre? 每英畝產量若干? ②投資收益。—**a·ble,** *adj.* —**er,** *n.*

yield·ing [ˈjildɪŋ; ˈjiːldiŋ] *adj.* ①放棄的; 屈服的; 讓步的。②易彎曲的; 柔軟的。—**ly,** *adv.*

yip [jɪp; jip] *n., v.i.,* **yipped, yip·ping.** [=yelp.]

yipe [jaɪp; jaip] *interj., v.,* **yiped, yip·ing,** *n.* —*interj.* 表示痛苦、喪膽、驚恐等之感嘆詞。—*v.i.* 發此種感嘆聲。—*n.* 發此種感嘆聲。

yip·pee [ˈjɪpi; ˈjipiː] *interj.* 表示狂喜、快樂等之感嘆詞。

yip·pie [ˈjɪpi; ˈjipiː] *n.* 〖美〗野皮(對政治狂熱的激進派嬉皮分子)。(略作 **YIP,** 亦作 **Yippie**)

-yl 〖字尾〗〖化〗用以形成"根"之名稱(如 amyl, ethyl等)。

Y.M. 〖俗〗Y.M.C.A.

Y.M.C.A., YMCA Young Men's Christian Association (基督教青年會)。

Y.M.Cath.A. Young Men's Catholic Association.

Y.M.H.A. Young Men's Hebrew Association.

y(e)o [jo; jou] *interj.* 水手拉繩時一道發出的叫聲。

yo·del [ˈjodl̩; ˈjoudl] *v.,* **-del(l)ed, -del(l)ing,** *n.* —*v.t. & v.i.* 用眞假嗓音陡然互換而唱。—*n.* 用此種方式唱歌; 用此種方式所唱之歌(流行於瑞士及奧國 Tyrol 之高山居民間)。—**er,** *n.* [—**yo·dler,** *n.*]

yo·dle [ˈjodl̩; ˈjoudl] *v., n.* =**yodel.**

Yo·ga, yo·ga [ˈjogə; ˈjougə] *n.* (印度宗教哲學之)瑜珈;瑜珈論;瑜珈派。

yo·gi [ˈjogi; ˈjougi] *n., pl.* **-gis.** 瑜珈信徒;瑜珈派修行者。(亦作 **yogin**)

yo·gi·ni [ˈjogənɪ; ˈjougəni] *n.* yogi 之女性。

yo·gism [ˈjogɪzm̩; ˈjougizm] *n.* 瑜珈; 瑜珈之教義。—**yo·gic,** *adj.*

yo·g(h)urt [ˈjogɚt; ˈjougəːt] *n.* ①一種由牛奶發酵所製之半固態食物(土耳其、保加利亞等國人喜食之,謂其有益於腸)。②一種人造的凝乳製品(如養樂多之類的飲料)。(亦作 **yoghourt**)

yo-heave-ho [ˈjoˈhivˈho; ˈjouˈhiːvˈhou] *interj.* 唷嗬!(昔水手們於拔錨或起錨等時的呼唱聲)。

yo-ho [joˈho; jouˈhou] *interj.* 促人出力或注意的叫聲。—*v.i.* 發出 yo-ho 的呼聲。

yoke** [jok; jouk] *n., v.,* **yoked, yok·ing.** —*n.* ①軛。②軛狀物。③一對(牛)。④支配;奴役;羈絆;束縛。Slaves are under the *yoke* of their masters. 奴隸們受其主人的支配。⑤上衣連接頸肩的抵肩。⑥裙子的腰。⑦一種扁擔。⑧連結物; 結; 結合。pass*** (or ***come***) ***under the yoke*** 服從; 受支配。—*v.t.* ①駕以軛; 用軛連起。②結合;匹配;配合。—*v.i.* 〖罕〗結合;配合;聯合。

yoke bone 〖解剖〗顴骨。

yoke·fel·low [ˈjokˌfɛlo; ˈjoukˌfelou] *n.* ①伙伴;伴侶。②夫或妻。

yo·kel [ˈjokl̩; ˈjoukl] *n.* ①鄉下人;鄉愚。②〖英〗農夫。—**ish,** *adj.*

yoke·lines [ˈjokˌlaɪnz; ˈjouk-lainz] *n. pl.* 〖航海〗操舵索。

yoke·mate [ˈjokˌmet; ˈjoukmeit] *n.* [=**yokefellow.**]

yoke·ropes [ˈjokˌrops; ˈjouk-roups] *n. pl.* =**yokelines.**

Yo·ko·ha·ma [ˌjokoˈhɑmə; ˌjoukouˈhɑːmə] *n.* 橫濱(日本本州之一海港)。

Yo·ko·su·ka [ˌjokoˈsʊkə; ˌjoukouˈsukə] *n.* 橫須賀(日本本州東京灣口之一海港)。

yolk [jok; jouk] *n.* ①蛋黃。②羊毛脂。③精華部分;核心。

yolk bag =**yolk sac.**

yolk sac 卵黃囊。

yolk·y [ˈjokɪ; ˈjouki] *adj.,* **yolk·i·er, yolk·i·est.** 卵黃的;似卵黃的;充滿卵黃的。

Yom Kip·pur [jɑmˈkɪpɚ; jɔmˈkipə] 猶太人的贖罪日。

yon [jɑn; jɔn] *adj. & adv.* 〖古,方〗=**yonder.** —*pron.* 〖古,方〗彼處之物或人。

yond [jɑnd, jɔnd; jɔnd] *adj. & adv.* 〖古,方〗=**yonder.**

***yon·der** [ˈjɑndɚ; ˈjɔndə] *adv.* 在那邊;在彼處;那邊;彼處。Look *yonder.* 看那邊。—*adj.* ①那邊的;彼處的。He lives in *yonder* cottage. 他住在那邊的小屋裡面。②遠處的。Look at the snow on *yonder* mountains. 注視遠處山上的雪。—*pron.* 那邊。

yore [jor; jɔː] *n.* 往古; 昔時(僅用於 of yore 一語中)。***of yore*** 往古;昔時。

york [jɔrk; jɔːk] *v.t.* 〖板球〗用 yorker 使(擊球者)退場。

york·er [ˈjɔrkɚ; ˈjɔːkə] *n.* 〖板球〗投出恰好落於擊球員面前之球。

York·ist [ˈjɔrkɪst; ˈjɔːkist] *n.* 〖英史〗①薔薇戰爭時支持 York 王室者(以白薔薇爲象徵)。②在 1680-85 年間支持 York 公爵 James 者。

York·shire [ˈjɔrkʃɪr; ˈjɔːkʃə] *n.* 約克郡(英國最大之一郡,在東北部)。***come Yorkshire over*** (or ***on***) ***one; put Yorkshire on one*** 騙某人;叫某人上當。

Yo·sem·i·te [joˈsɛmətɪ; jouˈsemiti] *n.* 美國 California 州中部 Sierra Nevada Mountains 之一深谷(爲 Yosemite 國家公園之一部分)。

‡you [ju; juː] *pron. pl.* or *sing.* ①你;你們。*You* are my friend. 你是我的朋友。②一個人;任何人。It is much easier to cycle with the wind behind *you.* 一個人順風騎車容易得多了。③〖古〗=**yourself.** Sit *you* down. 請坐。④喂(用以引起他人注意)。⑤〖俗〗與 gerund 連用時代替 your. There is no sense in *you* getting upset. 你生氣得毫無意義。***for you*** 十分表現其特色的;道地的。***to you*** **a.** 按照你應使用的稱呼。Not John, if you don't mind—Mr. Doe *to you.* 對不起,不是約翰—你應該說 Doe 先生才對。**b.** 按照俗稱。—*n.* ①與你無分別的人。②你的性格。〖注意〗(1)**you** 在一般寫作中常作不定代名詞:It's a good book, if *you* like detective stories. 如喜讀偵探小說,本書誠爲一佳作。(2)**you all** 在美國南部的方言中常縮爲 y'all 而用作 you 之複數,正如在別的區域用 you folks 一樣。

you'd [jud;juːd] ①=you had. ②=you should. ③=you would.

you'll [jul;juːl] =you will; you shall.

‡**young** [jʌŋ;jʌŋ] *adj.*, **young·er** [ˈjʌŋgɚ; ˈjʌŋgə], **young·est**, *n.* —*adj.* ①年幼的;年輕的; 幼小的。 a *young* lady. 少女。 She looks *young* for her age. 她的樣子比她實際年齡年輕。②無經驗的; 不熟練的。I was too *young* in the trade to be successful. 我對於這一行業太沒有經驗, 不會成功。③在尙早的階段。The night was still *young* when we left. 我們離去的時候,夜尙未深。④新建立的。⑤年輕者特有的。⑥代表進步的;主張進步的。***my young man*** (or ***woman***) 愛人; 情人。—*n.* ①(動物之) 仔; 雛。An animal will fight to protect its *young*. 動物會爲保護它的仔而戰鬥。②年輕者(集合稱)。***be with young*** (動物) 有孕。***the young*** 年輕人。—**ness**, *n.*

young·ber·ry [ˈjʌŋˌbɛrɪ; ˈjʌŋberi] *n.*, *pl.* **-ries.** 楊氏草莓(一種深紅色、大而甜之草莓)。

young blood 青年;血氣方剛之年輕人;「年輕人之思想或行動;青春活力。」

young·er [ˈjʌŋgɚ; ˈjʌŋgə] *adj.* comp. of **young.** —*n.* ①年少者。His sister is several years his *younger*. 他妹妹比他小幾歲。②年幼者;小孩。

young·est [ˈjʌŋgəst; ˈjʌŋgist] *adj.* superl. of **young.** —*n.* 老么。

young·ish [ˈjʌŋɪʃ; ˈjʌŋiʃ] *adj.* 頗年輕的;還年輕的。

young·ling [ˈjʌŋlɪŋ; ˈjʌŋliŋ] *n.*①年輕人;青年。②(動物)幼雛;(植物)幼株;幼苗。③無經驗之人;新手;生手。—*adj.* 年輕的;幼的。

***young·ster** [ˈjʌŋstɚ; ˈjʌŋstə] *n.* ①兒童;少年。②青年。③美國海軍官校二年級之學生。

Young Turk 急進分子。

youn·ker [ˈjʌŋkɚ; ˈjʌŋkə] *n.* ①〖古〗少年;青年。②年輕紳士;年輕武士。

‡**your** [jur;jɔː, jɔə, juə] *pron. pl.* or *sing.*, possessive form of **you.** ①你的;你們的。Is this *your* own book? 這是你自己的書嗎? ②你所說的; 你所知道的; 所謂;大家都很知道的。③用於稱呼之頭銜。*Your* Highness. 殿下。*Your* Majesty. 陛下。

you're [jur; juə] =you are.

‡**yours** [jurz; jɔːz, jɔəz, juəz] *pron. sing.* or *pl.* (you 的獨立所有格)。①你的;你們的。This pencil is *yours*. 這枝鉛筆是你的。②你的家族。All good wishes to you and *yours*. 祝你和府上都安吉。③你的來信。*Yours* is to hand. 你的來函已收到。***Yours truly*** **a.** 信文末尾簽名前之問候語。 **b.** (y– t–)〖俗〗我。I can take care of *yours truly*. 我能照顧我自己。

‡**your·self** [jurˈself; jɔːˈself] *pron.*, *pl.* **-selves.** ①(加强語勢)你自己。You *yourself* said so. 你自己這樣說的。②你自己;你們自己 (you 的反身代名詞)。 You will hurt *yourself*. 你會傷了你自己。③你的常態;你本來面目。Stop fooling and be *yourself*. 不要再胡鬧了,放莊重些罷。

your·selves [jurˈsɛlvz; jɔːˈselvz] *pron.* pl. of **yourself.**

‡**youth** [juθ;juːθ] *n.*, *pl.* **youths, youth.** ①青春;少年時代;青年時代。She keeps her *youth* well. 她善於保養她的青春。②少年;青年。③青年們;青年男女(集合稱)。④早期。

youth culture 青年文化(三十歲以下的人所特有的態度、觀念等)。

youth·en [ˈjuθən; ˈjuːθən] *v.t.* 使變年輕;使恢復青春;使恢復活力。—*v.i.* 變得年輕。

***youth·ful** [ˈjuθfəl; ˈjuːθful] *adj.* ①年少的;青年的;少壯的。②初期的。③年輕而活躍的。The old man had a *youthful* spirit. 這老年人有青年的精神。④屬於青年的; 適於青年的。—**ness**, *n.*

youth·ful·ly [ˈjuθfəlɪ; ˈjuːθfuli] *adv.* 年輕地;無經驗地;未成熟地。

youth·quake [ˈjuθˌkwek; ˈjuːθ-kweik] *n.* 青年震撼(1960及1970年代因青年激進、反抗、掀起學潮而引起之世界性不安)。

you've [juv; juːv] =you have.

yowl [jaul; jaul] *v.i.* ①號叫;咆哮;長吼。②叫喊。③大聲抗議。—*v.t.* 以號叫表示。—*n.* 號叫;咆哮;長吼。

yo-yo [ˈjojo; ˈjoujou] *n.* ①一種玩具(爲一捲線軸形之木塊繫於繩之一端, 以手牽動繩之另一端,可使之上下旋動)。②人造衞星之沿橢圓形軌跡繞地球飛行。

y·per·ite [ˈipəˌraɪt;ˈiːpərait] *n.* 芥子「氣(一種毒氣)。」

Y.P.S.C.E. Young People's Society of Christian Endeavor.

yr. ①year; years. ②your. ③younger.

yrs. ①years. ②yours.

Yt 化學元素yttrium之符號。

Y track Y字形軌道; (車輛轉換方向用「之)Y線。」

yt·ter·bi·a [ɪˈtɝbɪə; iˈtəːbiə] *n.* 〖化〗氧化鐿。

yt·ter·bic [ɪˈtɝbɪk;iˈtəːbik] *adj.* 〖化〗「鐿的;含鐿的。」

yt·ter·bi·um [ɪˈtɝbɪəm; iˈtəːbjəm] *n.* 〖化〗鐿(稀有金屬元素,原子序爲 70, 化學符號爲 Yb).

yt·tri·a [ˈɪtrɪə; ˈitriə] *n.* 〖化〗釔氧。

yt·tric [ˈɪtrɪk; ˈitrik] *adj.* 〖化〗釔的;含釔的。(亦作 **yttrious**)

yt·trif·er·ous [ɪˈtrɪfərəs; iˈtrifərəs] *adj.* 產釔的;含釔的。

yt·tri·um [ˈɪtrɪəm; ˈitriəm] *n.* 〖化〗釔(稀有金屬元素,原子序爲 39, 符號爲 Y 或Yt).

Yü [jy; jy] *n.* 禹(中國古時之聖君)。

Yü·an [juˈɑn, ˈyɑn; juːˈɑːn, ˈyɑːn] *n.*元朝(中國朝代名, 1260–1368)。

yu·an [juˈɑn, ˈyɑn; juːˈɑːn, ˈyɑːn] *n. sing.* or *pl.* ①元(中國幣制單位)。②(Y–)院(中國政府之一組織)。***Control Yuan*** 監察院。***Examination Yuan*** 考試院。***Executive Yuan*** 行政院。***Judicial Yuan*** 司法院。***Legislative Yuan*** 立法院。

yuc·ca [ˈjʌkə;ˈjʌkə] *n.* 〖植物〗 鱗鳳蘭;絲蘭。

Yu·go·slav [ˈjugoˌslɑv; ˈjuːgouˌslɑːv] *adj.* 南斯拉夫的;南斯拉夫人的。—*n.* 南斯拉夫人。(亦作 **Jugoslav, Jugo-Slav**)

Yu·go·sla·vi·a [ˌjugoˈslɑvɪə;ˌjuːgou-ˈslɑːvjə] *n.* 南斯拉夫(歐洲東南部之國家, 首都爲 Belgrade). (亦作 **Jugoslavia, Jugoslavija**) —**Yu·go·sla·vi·an**, *adj.*, *n.*

Yu·go·slav·ic [ˌjugoˈslɑvɪk;ˌjuːgou-ˈslɑːvik] *adj.* 南斯拉夫的;南斯拉夫人的。

yule [jul; juːl] *n.* ①耶誕節。②耶誕季節。

yule log 耶誕柴(在耶誕前夕置入爐中焚燒之木柴)。(亦作 **yule block, yule clog**)

yule·tide [ˈjulˌtaɪd; ˈjuːltaid] *n.* 耶誕季節。

yum·my [ˈjʌmɪ; ˈjʌmi] *adj.* 〖俗〗①引「人的;悅人的。②美麗的;漂亮的。」

Yün·nan [ˈjuˈnæn; ˈjuˈnæn] *n.* 雲南 (中國西南之一省, 省會昆明 Kunming). —**ese**, *adj.*, *n.*

Y.W. 〖俗〗 Young Women's Christian

Association. **Y.W.C.A.** Young Women's Christian Association. 基督教女青年會。 **Y.W.C.T.U.** Young Women's Christian Temperance Union. **Y.W.H.A.** Young Women's Hebrew Association.

Z

Z, z 〔zi; zed〕 *n., pl.* **Z's** or **z's** 〔ziz; zedz〕. ①英文字母之第二十六個字母。②第二十六個。③中古時代羅馬數字2000。④〖化〗原子序數。⑤〖物理〗阻抗(＝impedance). ⑥〖天文〗天頂角距（＝zenith distance).
z 〖數學〗表一未知之數量。
z ①zero. ②zinc. ③zloty. ④zone. **Z.** Zone.
Zad·ki·el 〔ˈzædkɪəl; ˈzædkiəl〕 *n.* 一種民間占星術曆(Zadkiel 係該曆作者 R.J. Morrison 之匿名)。
zaf·fer, zaf·fre 〔ˈzæfɚ; ˈzæfə〕 *n.* 不純之氧化鈷（用作陶瓷等着色之藍色顏料)。（亦作 **zaffar, zaffir**)
Za·i·re 〔zəˈirə; zəˈiːrə〕 *n.* 薩伊(非洲一共和國, 原名 Democratic Republic of Congo, 首都金夏沙 Kinshasa).
Zal·o·phus 〔ˈzæləfəs; ˈzæloufəs〕 *n.* 〖動物〗海驢屬。
Zam·bi·a 〔ˈzæmbɪə; ˈzæmbiə〕 *n.* 尙比亞(非洲南部之一共和國, 首都路沙卡 Lusaka). —**Zam·bi·an,** *adj., n.*
zam·bo 〔ˈzæmbo; ˈzæmbou〕 *n.* ＝**sambo**[1].
Zam·bo·an·ga 〔ˌsamboˈaŋga; ˌsaːmbouˈaːŋgaː〕 *n.* 三寶顏(非律賓民答那峨島西南部之一城市)。
za·mi·a 〔ˈzemɪə; ˈzeimiə〕 *n.* (南美產的)一種蘇鐵類植物。
za·min·dar 〔zəˌminˈdar; zəˌmiːnˈdaː〕 *n.* 〖英印〗①地主。②收田賦者。
za·ny 〔ˈzenɪ; ˈzeini〕 *n., pl.* **za·nies,** *adj.,* **za·ni·er, za·ni·est.** —*n.* ①〖古〗小丑;丑角。②笨人; 傻瓜。—*adj.* ①小丑的;似小丑的;愚蠢的;可笑的。②好作諢語怪狀的。
Zan·zi·bar 〔ˌzænzəˈbar; ˌzænziˈbaː〕 *n.* 尙西巴 (a. 非洲東部之一島, 屬坦桑尼亞。b. 其首府名)。—**Zan·zi·ba·ri,** *adj., n.*
zap 〔zæp; zæp〕 *v.,* **zapped, zap·ping,** *n., interj.* —*v.t.* ①射擊; 打擊; 鞭打。②突然或快速地推進。—*v.i.* 猛衝;突進。—*n.* 勁道;活力。—*interj.* 表示快速的動作或變化的聲音。
zap·ti·ah 〔zʌpˈtiɑ; zʌpˈtiːɑ〕 *n.* 土耳其之警察。
za·re(e)·ba 〔zəˈribə; zəˈriːbə〕 *n.* (非洲蘇丹地區之)防禦柵。(亦作 **zariba**)
zar·zue·la 〔zarˈzwelə; zaːˈzweilə〕 *n.* 一種含有對白的西班牙喜歌劇。
z-ax·is 〔ˈziˌæksɪs; ˈziːˌæksis〕 *n., pl.* **-ax·es** 〔-ˌæksiz; -ˌæksiːz〕. 〖數學〗Z 軸。
za-zen 〔ˈzaˈzɛn; ˈzaːˈzen〕 *n.* 〖佛教〗禪宗之打坐。
***zeal** 〔zil; ziːl〕 *n.* 熱心; 熱中; 熱誠。A good citizen feels *zeal* for his country's welfare. 一個良好公民熱心於國家的福利。
Zea·land 〔ˈzilənd; ˈziːlənd〕 *n.* 西蘭島(丹麥之一島, 丹京 Copenhagen 即位於此島)。
zeal·ot 〔ˈzɛlət; ˈzelət〕 *n.* 對於信仰或黨派過度熱心者。
zeal·ot·ry 〔ˈzɛlətrɪ; ˈzelətri〕 *n.* 過度之熱心;狂熱。
***zeal·ous** 〔ˈzɛləs; ˈzeləs〕 *adj.* 熱心的; 熱誠的。Be *zealous* in a good cause. 做好事要熱心。—**ness,** *n.*
zeal·ous·ly 〔ˈzɛləslɪ; ˈzeləsli〕 *adv.* 熱心地;熱誠地。
ze·bec(k) 〔ˈzibɛk; ˈziːbek〕 *n.* ＝**xebec.**
Zeb·e·dee 〔ˈzɛbəˌdi; ˈzebədiː〕 *n.* 〖聖經〗西庇太(聖徒 James 與 John 之父)。
ze·bra 〔ˈzibrə; ˈziːbrə〕 *n., pl.* **-bras, -bra.** 斑馬。
zebra crossing (街道上之) 斑馬線。
ze·brass 〔ˈziˌbræs; ˈziːbraːs〕 *n.* 雄斑馬與雌驢交配所生之雜種。
ze·bra·wood 〔ˈzibrəˌwud; ˈziːbrəwud〕 *n.* ①〖植物〗(Guiana 所產之) 斑木樹。②斑木樹所產的硬而有條紋之木材。③任何類似斑木樹之植物。
ze·brine 〔ˈzibraɪn; ˈziːbrain〕 *adj.* 斑馬的;似斑馬的。
ze·broid 〔ˈzibrɔɪd; ˈziːbrɔid〕 *adj.* ＝**zebrine.** —*n.* 雄斑馬與雌馬或雌驢交配而得之雜種動物。
ze·bu 〔ˈzibju; ˈziːbuː〕 *n.* 〖動物〗(中國、印度及非洲東部所產之)犎牛; 瘤牛(喉際下垂, 肩上有大瘤)。
Zech. Zechariah.
Zech·a·ri·ah 〔ˌzɛkəˈraɪə; ˌzekəˈraiə〕 *n.* ①男子名。②〖聖經〗撒迦利亞(公元前六世紀希伯來一先知)。③〖聖經〗舊約撒迦利亞書。
zech·in 〔ˈzɛkɪn; ˈzekin〕 *n.* ＝**sequin.**
zed 〔zɛd; zed〕 *n.* ①〖英〗Z 字母。②Z 形物。
zed·o·ar·y 〔ˈzɛdoˌɛrɪ; ˈzedouəri〕 *n.* 鬱金屬植物之根(用製香料及藥物)。
zee 〔zi; ziː〕 *n.* 〖美〗Z 字母。
Zeit·geist 〔ˈzaɪtˌgaɪst; ˈtsaitgaist〕 〖德〗 *n.* 時代精神;時代思潮。
Ze·la·ni·an 〔zɪˈlenɪən; ziˈleiniən〕 *adj.* 紐西蘭 (New Zealand) 的。
ze·lo·so 〔zɛˈloso; zeˈlousou〕 〖義〗 *adj.* 〖音樂〗用力演奏的(指揮用語)。
ze·min·dar 〔zəˌminˈdar; ˈzemindaː〕 *n.* 〖英印〗＝**zamindar.**
zem·stvo 〔ˈzɛmstvo; ˈzemstvou〕 *n., pl.* **-stvos.** (俄國沙皇時代之)地方自治組織。
Zen 〔zɛn; zen〕 *n.* (佛教中之) 禪宗。(亦作 **Zen Buddhism**)
ze·na·na 〔zɛˈnanə; zeˈnaːnə〕 *n.* (印度、波斯的) 閨房。—*adj.* (印度、波斯之)閨房的。
Zen Buddhist 禪宗之信徒。
Zend 〔zɛnd; zend〕 *n.* ①波斯祆教經典或其他宗教經典之註釋與翻譯。②古波斯語。
Zend-A·ves·ta 〔ˌzɛndəˈvɛstə; ˌzendəˈvestə〕 *n.* 波斯祆教之經典。
ze·nith 〔ˈzinɪθ; ˈzeniθ〕 *n.* ①天頂 (爲 nadir 之對)。②頂點; 絕點; 極點; 最高點; 全盛。—**al,** *adj.*
zenith distance 〖天文〗天頂角距。
Ze·no[1] 〔ˈzino; ˈziːnou〕 *n.* 季諾 (紀元前五世紀之希臘哲學家)。
Ze·no[2] *n.* 季諾 (紀元前四至三世紀之希臘哲學家, 斯多噶學派之創始者)。
ze·o·lite 〔ˈziəˌlaɪt; ˈziːəlait〕 *n.* 〖礦〗沸石。—**ze·o·lit·ic,** *adj.*
Zeph. Zephaniah.
Zeph·a·ni·ah 〔ˌzɛfəˈnaɪə; ˌzefəˈnaiə〕 *n.* ①西番雅 (紀元前七世紀左右希伯來一先知)。②舊約中之西番雅書。
zeph·yr 〔ˈzɛfɚ; ˈzefə〕 *n.* ①(Z-) 西風(擬人語)。②〖詩〗和風。③柔軟、華美、質輕之薄紗。④輕而不實之物。—**e·an, —i·an,** *adj.*
Zep·pe·lin 〔ˈzɛpəlɪn; ˈzepəlin〕 *n.* ①齊柏林(Count Ferdinand von, 1838–1917,

德國將軍及飛船製造者)。②(常 z-)齊柏林式飛艇。

ze·ro** [ˈzɪro; ˈziərou] *n., pl.* **-ros, -roes,** *adj., v.* —*n.* ①零; 0。②零點;零位;(寒暑表的)零度。③最低點;無。Their hopes were reduced to *zero.* 他們的希望幻滅了。④在其一射程內步槍之瞄準儀的正確位置。⑤(Z-)第二次世界大戰時日本之零式戰鬥機。absolute zero*** 〖物理〗絕對零度(攝氏零下273度)。—*adj.* ①零的;在零度的;在零點的。②無的。—*v.t.* (前三解常與 in 連用)①調整(槍砲)之射距。He *zeroed* in his rifle at 100 yards. 他將步槍射距調整爲100碼。②集中砲火於…。③瞄準(槍砲)。④降爲或恢復爲零點或零度。—*v.i.* 集中砲火〖常 in〗。

zero gravity 飛行時之失重狀態。(亦作 **zero g**)

zero hour ①軍事進攻之發動時間。②〖俗〗決定性之時間;重要關頭。

ze·ro-ze·ro [ˈzɪroˈzɪro; ˈziərouˈziərou] *adj.* 周圍及上下之能見度均爲零(僅及數英尺)的;能見度極差的。

***zest** [zest; zest] *n.* ①風味;滋味;趣味。The hungry man ate with *zest.* 這個饑腸轆轆的人吃得津津有味。②强烈的興味;熱心。—*v.t.* 增加興趣。—**ful, —y,** *adj.* —**ful·ly,** *adv.* —**ful·ness,** *n.*

ze·ta [ˈzetə ˈziːtə] *n.* 希臘字母之第六字母(Z, ζ)。

zeug·ma [ˈzjugmə; ˈzjuːgmə] *n.* 〖文法〗軛式修飾法(用一形容詞勉强修飾兩個名詞,或用一個動詞勉强及於兩個受詞之語句,而其中只有一個是合邏輯的)。—**t·ic,** *adj.* —**t·i·cal·ly,** *adv.*

Zeus [zus, zjus; zjuːs] *n.* 宙斯(古希臘之主神)。

Z.G. zoological garden.

ZI 〖美軍〗Zone of the Interior. 後方區。

zib·el·(l)ine [ˈzɪbəˌlaɪn; ˈzibəlain] *adj.* ①黑貂的。②黑貂皮製的。—*n.*①黑貂皮。②面上帶有短毛之厚羊毛織物(用以做衣服)。

zib·et(h) [ˈzɪbɪt; ˈzibit] *n.* 〖動物〗(印度、馬來半島等地產的)一種麝香貓。

zig·gu·rat [ˈzɪguræt; ˈziguræt] *n.* 古代亞述及巴比倫之寶塔式建築。(亦作 **zikkurat, zikurat**)

***zig·zag** [ˈzɪgzæg; ˈzigzæg] *adj., adv., v.,* **-zagged, -zag·ging,** *n.* —*adj.* 鋸齒形的;曲折的。—*adv.* 成鋸齒形地;曲折地。The path ran *zigzag* up the hill. 這條小路曲曲折折地通往山上。—*v.i.* 作鋸齒形;曲曲折折地前進。Lightning *zigzagged* across the sky. 閃電曲曲折折地在天空中劃過。—*v.t.* 使成鋸齒形;使曲折。—*n.* 鋸齒形;鋸齒形之物。

zigzag rule 曲尺。

zilch [zɪltʃ; ziltʃ] *n.* 〖美俚〗無;零;無價值的東西。

zil·lah [ˈzɪlə; ˈzilə] *n.* 印度之行政區畫(相當於州、郡)。

***zinc** [zɪŋk; ziŋk] *n., v.,* **zincked** or **zinced, zinck·ing** or **zinc·ing.** —*n.* 〖化〗鋅。—*v.t.* 覆以鋅;鍍鋅。

zinc·ic [ˈzɪŋkɪk; ˈziŋkik] *adj.* 鋅的;含鋅的;似鋅的。

zinc·if·er·ous [zɪŋˈkɪfərəs, zɪnˈsɪf-; ziŋˈkifərəs, zinˈsi-] *adj.* 含鋅的;產生鋅的。

zinc·i·fy [ˈzɪŋkəˌfaɪ; ˈziŋkifai] *v.t.,* **-fied, -fy·ing.** 鍍以鋅;包以鋅。—**zinc·i·fi·ca·tion,** *n.*

zinc·ite [ˈzɪŋkaɪt; ˈziŋkait] *n.* 〖礦〗紅鋅礦。

zin·co [ˈzɪŋko; ˈziŋkou] *n., v.* =**zincograph.**

zin·co·graph [ˈzɪŋkəˌgræf; ˈziŋkougrɑːf] *n.* 鋅版;鋅版畫。—*v.t. & v.i.* (以)鋅版印刷。

zin·co·graph·ic [ˌzɪŋkəˈgræfɪk; ˌziŋkəˈgræfik] *adj.* 鋅版的;鋅版術的。(亦作 **zincographical**)

zin·cog·ra·phy [zɪŋˈkɑgrəfɪ; ziŋˈkɔgrəfi] *n.* 鋅版術。—**zin·cog·ra·pher,** *n.*

zinc·oid [ˈzɪŋkɔɪd; ˈziŋkɔid] *adj.* 鋅的;似鋅的。

zin·co·type [ˈzɪŋkəˌtaɪp; ˈziŋkoutaip] *n.* =**zincograph.**

zinc·ous [ˈzɪŋkəs; ˈziŋkəs] *adj.* ①鋅的;含鋅的;似鋅的。②(電池之)陽極的。

zinc white 鋅白(氧化鋅調製的顏料)。

zin·fan·del [ˈzɪnfəndɛl; ˈzinfəndel] *n.* ①美國加利福尼亞州產的一種黑葡萄。②此種葡萄所釀成之酒。

zing [zɪŋ; ziŋ] *n.* ①活力;興緻。②引起興趣之特點或性質。③〖俚〗高速運動之物體所發出之尖銳響聲;颼颼聲。—*v.i. & v.t.* 〖俚〗發颼颼聲。

zin·ga·ro [ˈtsɪŋgɑˌro; ˈziŋgərou] *n., pl.* **-ga·ri** [-gɑˌri; -gəriː]. 〖義〗=**gypsy.**

zink·y [ˈzɪŋkɪ; ˈziŋki] *adj.* =**zincic.**

zin·ni·a [ˈzɪnɪə; ˈzinjə] *n.* 百日草屬植物。

Zi·on [ˈzaɪən; ˈzaiən] *n.* ①郇山(耶路撒冷之一山名,上面建有皇宮廟宇,爲希伯來政教及國民生活之中心)。②耶路撒冷一古城。③以色列;以色列人民。④古猶太之神政。⑤天堂;天國。⑥樂園;烏托邦。

Zi·on·ism [ˈzaɪənˌɪzəm; ˈzaiənizm] *n.* 猶太人復國運動(以再定居Palestine爲目標)。

zip [zɪp; zip] *n., v.,* **zipped, zip·ping.** —*n.* 〖俗〗①(彈丸飛過天空時之)颼颼聲。②能力;活力;力。—*v.i.* ①作颼颼聲;颼颼飛駛。②猛衝;突進。③ **a.** 拉上(下)拉鍊。**b.** 用拉鍊連繫。—*v.t.* 拉上(下)拉鍊。②使飛駛;使急行。③給以生氣。***zip across the horizon*** 突然成名。

zip code 美國之郵遞區號碼(由五個阿拉伯數字組成,前面三個數字表示收信者的地址,後面兩個數字表示郵政局或郵區)。(亦作 **ZIP code, Zip code**)

zip-fas·ten·er [ˈzɪpˌfæsn̩ə; ˈzipˌfɑːsnə] *n.* =**zipper.**

zip gun 一種用鐵管等手工製的鎗。

zip·per [ˈzɪpə; ˈzipə] *n.* ①拉鍊。②(Z-)一種拉鍊的商標。—*v.t. & v.i.* 以拉鍊扣緊(=zip).

zip·pered [ˈzɪpəd; ˈzipəd] *adj.* 有拉鍊的;用拉鍊扣緊的。

zip·py [ˈzɪpɪ; ˈzipi] *adj.,* **-pi·er, -pi·est.** 〖俗〗活潑的;精力充沛的。

zir·con [ˈzɝkɑn; ˈzəːkɔn] *n.* 〖礦〗風信子玉(鋯之矽酸鹽,用作寶石)。

zir·con·ate [ˈzɝkənˌet; ˈzəːkəneit] *n.* 〖化〗鋯酸鹽。

zir·co·ni·a [zəˈkonɪə; zəːˈkouniə] *n.* 〖化〗二氧化鋯。

zir·con·ic [zəˈkɑnɪk; zəːˈkɔnik] *adj.* 鋯的;從鋯得到的。

zir·co·ni·um [zəˈkonɪəm; zəːˈkounjəm] *n.* 〖化〗鋯(一種金屬元素,符號爲 Zr).

zith·er [ˈzɪθə; ˈziθə] *n.* 齊特琴(一種扁的古琴,有三十至四十條絃,用撥子或手指彈奏之)。—*v.i.* 彈此種古琴。—**ist,** *n.*

zith·ern [ˈzɪθən; ˈziθən] *n.* ①=**cithern.** ②=**zither.**

zlo·ty [ˈzlɔtɪ; ˈzlɔti] *n., pl.* **-tys, -ty.** 波蘭之幣制單位。

Zn 化學元素 zinc 之符號。

-zoa 〖字尾〗(動物學用以)表"…類"之義。

Zo·ar [zor; ˈzouɑː] *n.* 〖聖經〗避難所。

zo·di·ac [ˈzodɪˌæk; ˈzoudiæk] *n.* ①〖天文〗黃道帶(天空中虛設之假想帶,在黃道左右各展開約8度,爲日、月及主要行星進行之道。黃道帶共分爲十二宮)。②刻有此種黃道帶的圓盤, 並刻有各種獸以區別之;獸帶;十二宮圖。③〖罕〗一周;圓周;周期。***signs of the zodiac*** 十二宮。—**al,** *adj.*

zo·e·trope [ˈzoɪˌtrop; ˈzouitroup] *n.* 廻轉畫筒。—**zo·e·trop·ic,** *adj.*

Z of I zone of interior.

Zo·har [ˈzohar; ˈzouhaː] *n.* 十四世紀左右猶太神祕敎之經典。

zo·ic [ˈzoɪk; ˈzouik] *adj.* ①動物的; 動物生活的。②〖地質〗含有動、植物化石的。

Zo·la [ˈzolə; ˈzoulə] *n.* 左拉 (Émile, 1840–1902, 法國小說家)。

Zo·la·ism [ˈzoləɪzm̩; ˈzouləizm] *n.* 左拉主義;自然主義。

Zo·la·ist [ˈzoləɪst; ˈzouləist] *n.* 左拉主義者;自然主義者。

Zoll·ver·ein [ˈtsɔlfɛrˌaɪn; ˈtsɔl–fərain] 〖德〗 *n.* ①1819年至1871年間德意志各邦之關稅同盟。②關稅同盟;商業同盟。

zom·bi [ˈzambɪ; ˈzɔmbi] *n., pl.* **-bis.** ①(西非的) 巫毒崇拜。②(海地及南美若干部分的)蛇神;蟒蛇崇拜。③(西印度羣島的)死屍復活之神力。④還魂屍; 復活之死屍。⑤〖俚〗愚蠢可厭的人。⑥(由甜酒、果汁及蘇打水混成之)一種鷄尾酒。

zon·al [ˈzonl̩; ˈzounl] *adj.*①地帶的;區域的。②劃分爲地帶的;劃分成地區的。—**ly,** *adv.*

zon·a·ry [ˈzonərɪ; ˈzounəri] *adj.* ①帶狀的;帶形的。②=**zonal.**

zon·ate [ˈzonet; ˈzouneit] *adj.* ①有帶痕的。②〖植物〗排列成單行的。

zone** [zon; zoun] *n., v.,* **zoned, zon·ing.** —*n.* ①地區; 地帶; 區域。②〖美〗郵資相同的收寄區。③環帶。④船運中心周圍地區內火車站之總數。⑤〖地質〗晶帶。 ***Air Defence Identification Zone 防空識別區 (略作ADIZ). —*v.t.* ①用帶子圍。②分成地區。—*v.i.* 如帶子似地圍着;形成地區。

zoned [zond; zound] *adj.* ①分成地帶的。②〖詩〗束帶(象徵處女身分)的。

zone defense (球戲中之)區域防守。

zone of interior 〖軍〗內地區。

zone plate 〖光學〗同心圓廻折板 (使光線集中於焦點之玻璃板, 可作透鏡用)。

zon·ing [ˈzonɪŋ; ˈzouniŋ] *n.* 〖美〗都市之劃分地區(如工業區、住宅區等)。

zonked [zaŋkt; zɔŋkt] *adj.* 〖俚〗醉酒的;(因吸食毒品)木然的。

Zon·ta Club [ˈzantə~; ˈzɔntə~] 崇她社 (一種社會或職業婦女之組織, 首創於1919年, 其宗旨爲促進世界和平及友誼)。

Zon·ti·an [ˈzantɪən; ˈzɔntiən] *n.* 崇她社社員。—*adj.* 崇她社的;崇她社社員的。

zon·ule [ˈzonjul; ˈzounjuːl] *n.* 小帶。

***zoo** [zu; zuː] *n.* 動物園。

zoo- 〖字首〗表"動物; 動物體; 動物生活"之義。如 zoochemistry. (亦作 **zoö-**)

zo·o·chem·is·try [ˌzoəˈkɛmɪstrɪ; ˌzouəˈkemistri] *n.* 動物化學(研究動物體內組成成分者)。—**zo·o·chem·i·cal,** *adj.*

zo·og·a·my [zoˈagəmɪ; zouˈɔgəmi] *n.* 有性生殖;兩性生殖。

Z

zo·o·ge·og·ra·phy [ˌzoədʒiˈagrəfɪ; ˌzouədʒiˈɔgrəfi] *n.* 動物地理學(研究動物之地理分布之科學)。

zo·og·ra·phy [zoˈagrəfɪ; zouˈɔgrəfi] *n.* 動物誌。

zo·oid [ˈzoɔɪd; ˈzouɔid] *adj.* 動物的; 似動物的。—*n.* 〖生物〗①芽蟲;子蟲。②羣體中之單一個體。—**al,** *adj.*

zoo·keep·er [ˈzuˌkipɚ; ˈzuːˌkiːpə] *n.* 動物園管理員。

zool. ①zoological. ②zoologist. ③zoology.

zo·ol·a·ter [zoˈalətɚ; zouˈɔlətə] *n.* 動物崇拜者。

zo·ol·a·try [zoˈalətrɪ; zouˈɔlətri] *n.* 動物崇拜。

zo·o·lite [ˈzoəˌlaɪt; ˈzouəlait] *n.* 化石動物。

***zo·o·log·i·cal** [ˌzoəˈladʒɪkl̩; ˌzouəˈlɔdʒikl] *adj.* 動物的;動物學的。—**ly,** *adv.*

zoological garden 動物園。

zo·ol·o·gist [zoˈalədʒɪst; zouˈɔlədʒist] *n.* 動物學家。

***zo·ol·o·gy** [zoˈalədʒɪ; zouˈɔlədʒi] *n.* ①動物學。②動物誌。③一地方之動物 (集合稱)。④(動物之)生態。

zoom [zum; zuːm] *v.i.* ①陡直地上升;攢升。②迅速或突然地移動同時並發出嗡嗡聲。③〖攝影〗用自由焦距鏡頭使影像縮小或放大。④〖電影、電視〗保持物體之焦距而使之迅速地從遠鏡頭變爲近鏡頭。—*v.t.* ①使陡直地上升。②〖攝影〗調整(自由焦距鏡頭)使物像放大或縮小。—*n.* 陡直上昇;呼嘯疾駛。

zo·o·mag·net·ism [ˌzoəˈmægnəˌtɪzəm; ˌzouəˈmægnitizm] *n.* 動物磁氣。

zoo·man [ˈzumən; ˈzuːmən] *n.* 動物園員工。

Zoom·ar lens [ˈzumar~; ˈzuːmaː~] 〖商標名〗電視攝影機用的自由焦距鏡頭。

zoom·er [ˈzumɚ; ˈzuːmə] *n.* =**zoom lens.**

zoom lens (攝影機之)自由焦距鏡頭;伸縮鏡頭。

zo·o·mor·phic [ˌzoəˈmɔrfɪk; ˌzouəˈmɔːfik] *adj.* 動物形像的; 表現動物形像的; 有動物形像的。

zo·o·mor·phism [ˌzoəˈmɔrfɪzəm; ˌzouəˈmɔːfizm] *n.* 動物形像之表現或使用。

zo·on [ˈzoan; ˈzouɔn] *n., pl.* **zo·a** [ˈzoə; ˈzouə]. 羣體動物 (如水螅等) 之發育完全的個體。—**al,** *adj.*

zo·on·o·my [zoˈanəmɪ; zouˈɔnəmi] *n.* 動物生理學。

zo·o·pal·e·on·tol·o·gy [ˌzoəˌpælɪanˈtalədʒɪ; ˌzouəˌpæliɔnˈtɔlədʒi] *n.* 古動物學。

zo·oph·i·list [zoˈafɪlɪst; zouˈɔfilist] *n.* 愛護動物者。

zo·oph·i·lous [zoˈafələs; zouˈɔfiləs] *adj.* ①適於由動物傳播花粉的。②愛護動物的。

zo·o·phys·ics [ˌzoəˈfɪzɪks; ˌzouəˈfiziks] *n.* 動物構造學。

zo·o·phys·i·ol·o·gy [ˌzoəˌfɪzɪˈalədʒɪ; ˌzouəˌfiziˈɔlədʒi] *n.* 動物生理學。

zo·o·phyte [ˈzoəˌfaɪt; ˈzouəfait] *n.* 似植物之動物 (如珊瑚蟲、海葵等)。—**zo·o·phyt·ic,** *adj.*

zo·o·phy·tol·o·gy [ˌzoəfaɪˈtalədʒɪ; ˌzouəfaiˈtɔlədʒi] *n.* 似植物之動物學。

zo·o·plas·tic [ˌzoəˈplæstɪk; ˌzouəˈplæstik] *adj.* 〖外科〗移植動物體素至人體的;動物質成形的。

zo·o·plas·ty [ˈzoəˌplæstɪ; ˈzouəˌplæsti] *n.* 〖外科〗動物體素移植至人體術; 動物質成形術。

zo·o·psy·chol·o·gy [ˌzoəsaɪˈkalədʒɪ; ˌzouəsaiˈkɔlədʒi] *n.* 動物心理學。

zo·o·sperm [ˈzoəˌspɝm; ˈzouəspəːm] *n.* 精蟲;精子。

zo·o·spore [ˈzoəˌspor; ˈzouəspɔː] *n.* ①〖植物〗游走孢子。②〖動物〗游走子。

zo·o·tax·y [ˈzoəˌtæksɪ; ˈzouəˌtæksi] *n.* 動物分類學。

zo·o·tech·ny [ˈzoəˌtɛknɪ; ˈzouəˌtekni] *n.* 畜牧學。

zo·ot·o·mist 〔zo'ɑtəmɪst; zou'ɔtəmist〕 *n.* 動物解剖學者。
zo·ot·o·my 〔zo'ɑtəmɪ; zou'ɔtəmi〕 *n.* 動物解剖;動物解剖學。
zoot suit 〔zut～; zuːt～〕〖美俚〗一種男性服裝(上衣肩寬而長,褲肥大而褲口窄狹)。
zoot·y 〔'zutɪ; 'zuːti〕 *adj.* 〖俚〗過於華麗的;裝飾考究的。
zor·il 〔'zɔrɪl; 'zɔril〕 *n.*〖動物〗(南非洲產的)似臭鼬之肉食獸。
Zo·ro·as·ter 〔ˌzoro'æstɚ; ˌzɔrou'æstə〕 *n.* 左羅阿斯脫(紀元前1000年左右之波斯宗教家,爲波斯國教祆教之創始人)。(亦作 **Zarathustra**)
Zo·ro·as·tri·an 〔ˌzoro'æstrɪən; ˌzɔrou'æstriən〕 *adj.* ①Zoroaster 氏的。②祆教的。—*n.* 信奉 Zoroaster 者;祆教教徒。
Zo·ro·as·tri·an·ism 〔ˌzoro'æstrɪənˌɪzəm; ˌzɔrou'æstriənizm〕 *n.* 祆教;拜火教;陰陽教(古波斯人之宗教,信仰善良與光明及罪惡與黑暗互相對立)。(亦作 **Zoroastrism**)
zos·ter 〔'zɑstɚ; 'zɔstə〕 *n.* ①(古代希臘男子所用之)帶。②〖醫〗帶狀疱疹。
Zos·ter·ops 〔'zɑstəˌrɑps; 'zɔstərɔps〕 *n.* ①(鳥)繡眼兒科。②(z-)繡眼兒科之鳥。
Zou·ave 〔zu'ɑv; zu'ɑːv〕 *n.* ①(有時 z-)朱阿夫兵(法國步兵,原以 Algeria 人編成,近亦用法人充當,以强悍著稱,着五光十色之阿拉伯服裝爲制服)。②凡採用似朱阿夫兵所穿之制服的軍隊。③美國 1861-1865 年南北戰爭時之義勇兵(因其制服似朱阿夫兵,故名)。
zounds 〔zaʊndz; zaundz〕 *interj.* 〖古〗咤!咄!嗳呀!畜生!(表示憤怒、輕蔑、驚訝之聲)。
zoy·sia 〔'zɔɪʃə; 'zɔiʃə〕 *n.* 高麗結縷草;韓國草。
Zr 化學元素zirconium之符號。
Zu 〔zu; zuː〕 *n.* (巴比倫神話中之)風雨神。
zuc·chet·to 〔zu'kɛto; zuː'ketou〕 *n.*, *pl.* **-tos.** (天主教僧侶所戴的)無邊帽。
Zu·lu[1] 〔'zulu; 'zuːluː〕 *n.*, *pl.* **-lus, -lu,** *adj.* —*n.* ①(南非洲)組魯族(居於 Natal及 Lourenco Marques 間的沿海地帶的一好戰民族);組魯族人。②組魯語。—*adj.* 組魯族人的;組魯語的。
Zu·lu[2] *n.* 通訊電碼,代表字母 Z.
Zu·lu·land 〔'zuluˌlænd; 'zuːlu(ː)lænd〕 *n.* 南非共和國 Natal 省東北部之一地區。
Zu·ñi 〔'zunjɪ; 'zuːnji〕 *n.*, *pl.* **-ñi, -ñis,** *adj.* —*n.* ①美洲印第安人 Pueblo 族之一員。②其語言。—*adj.* Pueblo 族的;其語言的。
Zu·rich 〔'zurɪk; 'zjuərik〕 *n.* 蘇黎世(瑞士東北部之一城市)。
zwie·back 〔'tswiˌbɑk; 'zwiːbæk〕 *n.* 一種重烤麪包片;焦黃麪包片;麪包乾。
Zwing·li 〔'zwɪŋglɪ; 'zwiŋli〕 *n.* 玆文利(Huldreich *or* Ulrich, 1484-1531, 瑞士新教改革領袖)。
Zwing·li·an 〔'zwɪŋglɪən; 'zwiŋliən〕 *adj.* 玆文利(教義)的。—*n.* 玆文利派教徒。
zwit·ter·i·on 〔'tsvɪtɚˌaɪən; 'tsvitəraiən〕 *n.* 〖理化〗兩性游子;兼有陽電荷與陰電荷之游子(如氨基酸溶液之游子)。(亦作 **zwitter ion**)
zy·gal 〔'zaɪgl; 'zaigl〕 *adj.* H字形的(尤指腦之裂溝)。
zy·go·dac·tyl 〔ˌzaɪgə'dæktɪl; ˌzaigə'dæktil〕 *adj.* (鳥)對生趾的;脚掌前後有雙趾的。—*n.* 攀木類之鳥。
zy·go·ma 〔zaɪ'gomə; zai'goumə〕 *n.*, *pl.* **-ma·ta** 〔-mətə; -mətə〕, *adj.* —*n.* & *adj.* 〖解剖〗顴骨(的);顴弓(的);顴骨突起(的)。
zy·go·mat·ic 〔ˌzaɪgə'mætɪk; ˌzaigə'mætik〕〖解剖〗 *adj.* 顴骨的。—*n.* 顴骨。
zygomatic bone 〖解剖〗顴骨。
zy·go·mor·phous 〔ˌzaɪgə'mɔrfəs; ˌzaigə'mɔːfəs〕 *n.* 〖生物〗兩半同形的。
zy·go·phyte 〔'zaɪgəˌfaɪt; 'zaigəfait〕 *n.* 藉接合孢子繁殖之植物。
zy·go·spore 〔'zaɪgəˌspor; 'zaigəspɔː〕 *n.* 〖植物〗接合孢子(二相似配偶子結合而成之孢子)。(亦作 **zygosperm**)
zy·gote 〔'zaɪgot; 'zaigout〕 *n.* 接合孢子(二配偶子結合而成之任何細胞)。
zy·mase 〔'zaɪmes; 'zaimeis〕 *n.* 〖生化〗酵母;酵素。
zyme 〔zaɪm; zaim〕 *n.* ①酵母;酵素。②〖醫〗引起酵性病之病原體。
zymo- 〖字首〗表"發酵;酵母"之義。
zy·mo·gen 〔'zaɪməˌdʒɛn; 'zaimədʒen〕 *n.* 〖生化〗①酵素原(能變成酵素之物質)。②任何產生酵素之細菌。
zy·mol·o·gist 〔zaɪ'mɑlədʒɪst; zai'mɔlədʒist〕 *n.* 發酵學家。
zy·mol·o·gy 〔zaɪ'mɑlədʒɪ; zai'mɔlədʒi〕 *n.* 發酵學;發酵學論述。—**zy·mo·log·ic, zy·mo·log·i·cal,** *adj.*
zy·mom·e·ter 〔zaɪ'mɑmɪtɚ; zai'mɔmitə〕 *n.* 發酵計。(亦作 **zymosimeter**)
zy·mo·sis 〔zaɪ'mosɪs; zai'mousis〕 *n.*, *pl.* **-ses** 〔-ˌsiz; -siːz〕. ①發酵。②酵性病;感染酵性病之狀態。
zy·mo·tech·nics 〔ˌzaɪmo'tɛknɪks; ˌzaimou'tekniks〕 *n.* 發酵法;釀造法。
zy·mot·ic 〔zaɪ'mɑtɪk; zai'mɔtik〕 *adj.* ①發酵的。②〖醫〗發酵病的。—**al·ly,** *adv.*
zy·mur·gy 〔'zaɪmɝdʒɪ; 'zaiməːdʒi〕 *n.* 釀造學。
ZZZ 打鼾聲。

不規則動詞表

斜體字主要用於詩語或古語

現　在	過　去	過去分詞	現　在	過　去	過去分詞
abide	abode, abided	abode, abided	cleave	cleft, cleaved, clove	cleft, cleaved, cloven
alight	alighted, *alit*	alighted, *alit*			
arise	arose	arisen	cleave	cleaved, *clave*	cleaved
awake	awoke, awaked	awaked, awoke	cling	clung	clung
			clothe	clothed, *clad*	clothed, *clad*
backbite	backbit	backbitten, backbit	come	came	come
			cost	cost	cost
backslide	backslid	backslid, backslidden	creep	crept	crept
			crow	crowed, *crew*	crowed
be(am, *art*, is; are)	was, *wast*, *wert*; were	been	curse	cursed, curst	cursed, curst
			cut	cut	cut
bear	bore, *bare*	borne, born	dare	dared, durst	dared
beat	beat	beaten, *beat*	deal	dealt	dealt
become	became	become	dig	dug, *digged*	dug, *digged*
befall	befell	befallen	dive	dived, dove	dived
beget	begot, *begat*	begotten,begot	do, does	did	done
begin	began	begun	draw	drew	drawn
begird	begirt, begirded	begirt, begirded	dream	dreamed, dreamt	dreamed, dreamt
behold	beheld	beheld	dress	dressed, drest	dressed, drest
bend	bent, *bended*	bent, *bended*	drink	drank	drunk, drank, *drunken*
bereave	bereaved, bereft	bereaved, bereft			
			drip	dripped, dript	dripped, dript
beseech	besought, beseeched	besought, beseeched	drive	drove, *drave*	driven
			drop	dropped, dropt	dropped, dropt
beset	beset	beset	dwell	dwelt, dwelled	dwelt, dwelled
bespeak	bespoke, *bespake*	bespoken, bespoke	eat	ate	eaten
			fall	fell	fallen
bestrew	bestrewed	bestrewed, bestrewn	feed	fed	fed
			feel	felt	felt
bestride	bestrode, bestrid	bestridden, bestrid	fight	fought	fought
			find	found	found
bet	bet, betted	bet, betted	fix	fixed, fixt	fixed, fixt
betake	betook	betaken	flee	fled	fled
bethink	bethought	bethought	fling	flung	flung
bid	bade, bid, bad	bidden, bid	fly	flew	flown
bide	bode, bided	bided	forbear	forbore	forborne
bind	bound	bound, *bounden*	forbid	forbade, forbad	forbidden
bite	bit	bitten, bit			
bleed	bled	bled	forecast	forecast(ed)	forecast(ed)
blend	blended, *blent*	blended, *blent*	forego	forewent	foregone
bless	blessed, blest	blessed, blest	foreknow	foreknew	foreknown
blow	blew	blown	foresee	foresaw	foreseen
break	broke, *brake*	broken, *broke*	foretell	foretold	foretold
breed	bred	bred	forget	forgot	forgotten, forgot
bring	brought	brought			
broadcast	broadcast(ed)	broadcast(ed)	forgive	forgave	forgiven
browbeat	browbeat	browbeaten	forsake	forsook	forsaken
build	built, *builded*	built, *builded*	forswear	forswore	forsworn
burn	burned, burnt	burned, burnt	freeze	froze	frozen
burst	burst	burst	gainsay	gainsaid, gainsayed	gainsaid, gainsayed
buy	bought	bought			
can	could	——	get	got, *gat*	got, gotten
cast	cast	cast	gild	gilded, gilt	gilded, gilt
catch	caught	caught	gird	girded, girt	girded, girt
chide	chided, chid	chided, chid, chidden	give	gave	given
			gnaw	gnawed	gnawed, gnawn
choose	chose	chosen			

現　在	過　去	過去分詞	現　在	過　去	過去分詞
go	went	gone	outspread	outspread	outspread
grave	graved	graven, graved	outwear	outwore	outworn
grind	ground	ground	overbear	overbore	overborne
grow	grew	grown	overcast	overcast	overcast
hamstring	hamstrung,	hamstrung,	overcome	overcame	overcome
	hamstringed	hamstringed	overdo	overdid	overdone
hang	hung, hanged	hung, hanged	overdraw	overdrew	overdrawn
have, *hast*, has	had, *hadst*	had	overdrink	overdrank	overdrunk
hear	heard	heard	overdrive	overdrove	overdriven
heave	heaved, hove	heaved, hove	overeat	overate	overeaten
hew	hewed	hewed, hewn	overfeed	overfed	overfed
hide	hid	hidden, hid	overgrow	overgrew	overgrown
hit	hit	hit	overhang	overhung	overhung
hold	held	held, *holden*	overhear	overheard	overheard
hurt	hurt	hurt	overlay	overlaid	overlaid
inlay	inlaid	inlaid	overleap	overleapt,	overleapt,
inset	inset	inset		overleaped	overleaped
keep	kept	kept	overlie	overlay	overlain
kneel	knelt, kneeled	knelt, kneeled	overpay	overpaid	overpaid
knit	knit, knitted	knit, knitted	override	overrode	overridden
know	knew	known	overrun	overran	overrun
lade	laded	laded, laden	oversee	oversaw	overseen
lay	laid	laid	overset	overset	overset
lead	led	led	overshoot	overshot	overshot
lean	leaned, leant	leaned, leant	oversleep	overslept	overslept
leap	leaped, leapt	leaped, leapt	overspend	overspent	overspent
learn	learned, learnt	learned, learnt	overspread	overspread	overspread
leave	left	left	overtake	overtook	overtaken
lend	lent	lent	overthrow	overthrew	overthrown
let	let	let	overwork	overworked,	overworked,
let	letted, let	letted, let		overwrought	overwrought
lie	lay	lain	overwrite	overwrote	overwritten
light	lighted, lit	lighted, lit	partake	partook	partaken
lose	lost	lost	pay	paid	paid
make	made	made	pen	penned, pent	penned, pent
may	might	——	plead	pleaded,	pleaded,
mean	meant	meant		ple(a)d	ple(a)d
meet	met	met	prepay	prepaid	prepaid
melt	melted	melted, molten	prove	proved	proved,
methinks	methought	——			proven
misdeal	misdealt	misdealt	put	put	put
misdo	misdid	misdone	quit	quit, quitted	quit, quitted
misgive	misgave	misgiven	read	read 〔rɛd; red〕	read 〔rɛd; red〕
mislay	mislaid	mislaid	reave	reaved, reft	reaved, reft
mislead	misled	misled	rebuild	rebuilt	rebuilt
misread	misread	misread	recast	recast	recast
misspell	misspelled,	misspelled,	reeve	rove, reeved	rove, reeved
	misspelt	misspelt	relay	relaid	relaid
mistake	mistook	mistaken	rend	rent	rent
misunder-	misunder-	misunder-	repay	repaid	repaid
stand	stood	stood	reread	reread	reread
mow	mowed	mowed, mown	resell	resold	resold
outbid	outbid,	outbid,	reset	reset	reset
	outbade	outbidden	retell	retold	retold
outdo	outdid	outdone	rewrite	rewrote	rewritten
outgo	outwent	outgone	rid	rid, ridded	rid, ridded
outgrow	outgrew	outgrown	ride	rode, *rid*	ridden
outlay	outlaid	outlaid	ring	rang	rung
outride	outrode	outridden	rise	rose	risen
outrun	outran	outrun	rive	rived	riven, rived
outsell	outsold	outsold	run	ran	run
outshine	outshone	outshone	saw	sawed	sawed, sawn
outshoot	outshot	outshot	say	said	said

現　在	過　去	過去分詞
see	saw	seen
seek	sought	sought
seethe	seethed, *sod*	seethed, *sodden*
sell	sold	sold
send	sent	sent
set	set	set
sew	sewed	sewed, sewn
shake	shook	shaken
shall, *shalt*	should, *shouldst*	——
shave	shaved	shaved, shaven
shear	sheared, *shore*	shorn, sheared
shed	shed	shed
shine	shone	shone
shoe	shod, shoed	shod, shoed
shoot	shot	shot
show	showed	shown,showed
shred	shredded, *shred*	shredded, *shred*
shrink	shrank, shrunk	shrunk, shrunken
shrive	shrived, shrove	shriven, shrived
shut	shut	shut
sing	sang, *sung*	sung
sink	sank, *sunk*	sunk, sunken
sit	sat, *sate*	sat, *sate*
slay	slew	slain
sleep	slept	slept
slide	slid	slid, slidden
sling	slung	slung
slink	slunk, *slank*	slunk
slink	slinked, slunk	slinked, slunk
slit	slit	slit
smell	smelled, smelt	smelled, smelt
smite	smote, *smit*	smitten, *smit*
sow	sowed	sown, sowed
speak	spoke, *spake*	spoken, *spoke*
speed	sped, speeded	sped, speeded
spell	spelled, spelt	spelled, spelt
spellbind	spellbound	spellbound
spend	spent	spent
spill	spilled, spilt	spilled, spilt
spin	spun, span	spun
spit	spat, spit	spat, spit
split	split	split
spoil	spoiled, spoilt	spoiled, spoilt
spread	spread	spread
spring	sprang, sprung	sprung
squat	squatted, squat	squatted, squat
stand	stood	stood
stave	staved, stove	staved, stove
stay	stayed, *staid*	stayed, *staid*
steal	stole	stolen
stick	stuck	stuck
sting	stung	stung
stink	stank, stunk	stunk
strew	strewed	strewed, strewn

現　在	過　去	過去分詞
stride	strode	stridden
strike	struck	struck, *stricken*
string	strung	strung
strive	strove	striven
strow	strowed	strown, strowed
sunburn	sunburned, sunburnt	sunburned, sunburnt
swear	swore, *sware*	sworn
sweat	sweat, sweated	sweat, sweated
sweep	swept	swept
swell	swelled	swelled, swollen
swim	swam, *swum*	swum
swing	swung	swung
take	took	taken
teach	taught	taught
tear	tore	torn
tell	told	told
think	thought	thought
thrive	throve, thrived	thriven, thrived
throw	threw	thrown
thrust	thrust	thrust
toss	tossed, *tost*	tossed, *tost*
tread	trod, treaded, *trode*	trodden, trod
typewrite	typewrote	typewritten
unbend	unbent, unbended	unbent, unbended
unbind	unbound	unbound
underbid	underbid	underbidden, underbid
underdo	underdid	underdone
undergo	underwent	undergone
underlay	underlaid	underlaid
underlet	underlet	underlet
underlie	underlay	underlain
underpay	underpaid	underpaid
undersell	undersold	undersold
understand	understood	understood, *understanded*
undertake	undertook	undertaken
underwrite	underwrote	underwritten
undo	undid	undone
unlearn	unlearned, unlearnt	unlearned, unlearnt
uphold	upheld	upheld
upset	upset	upset
wake	waked, woke	waked, woken, woke
waylay	waylaid	waylaid
wear	wore	worn
wear	wore	worn, wore
weave	wove, weaved	woven, wove, weaved
wed	wedded, wed	wedded, wed
weep	wept	wept
wet	wet, wetted	wet, wetted
will, *wilt*	would, *wouldst*	——
win	won	won

現　在	過　去	過去分詞	現　在	過　去	過去分詞
wind	wound, winded	wound, winded	work	worked, *wrought*	worked, *wrought*
wind	wound	wound	wrap	wrapped, wrapt	wrapped, wrapt
withdraw	withdrew	withdrawn			
withhold	withheld	withheld	wring	wrung	wrung
withstand	withstood	withstood	write	wrote, *writ*	written, *writ*

數的讀法

1. 基數與序數

基　數 (Cardinals)		序　數 (Ordinals)
1……one	I (i)	1st ……first
2……two	II (ii)	2nd……second
3……three	III (iii)	3rd ……third
4……four	IV (iv)	4th ……fourth
5……five	V (v)	5th ……fifth
6……six	VI (vi)	6th ……sixth
7……seven	VII (vii)	7th ……seventh
8……eight	VIII (viii)	8th ……eighth
9……nine	IX (ix)	9th ……ninth
10……ten	X (x)	10th ……tenth
11……eleven	XI (xi)	11th ……eleventh
12……twelve	XII (xii)	12th ……twelfth
13……thirteen	XIII (xiii)	13th ……thirteenth
14……fourteen	XIV (xiv)	14th ……fourteenth
15……fifteen	XV (xv)	15th ……fifteenth
16……sixteen	XVI (xvi)	16th ……sixteenth
17……seventeen	XVII (xvii)	17th ……seventeenth
18……eighteen	XVIII (xviii)	18th ……eighteenth
19……nineteen	XIX (xix)	19th ……nineteenth
20……twenty	XX (xx)	20th ……twentieth
21……twenty-one	XXI (xxi)	21st ……twenty-first
22……twenty-two	XXII (xxii)	22nd ……twenty-second
23……twenty-three	XXIII (xxiii)	23rd ……twenty-third
30……thirty	XXX (xxx)	30th ……thirtieth
40……forty	XL (xl)	40th ……fortieth
50……fifty	L (l)	50th ……fiftieth
60……sixty	LX (lx)	60th ……sixtieth
70……seventy	LXX (lxx)	70th ……seventieth
80……eighty	LXXX (lxxx)	80th ……eightieth
90……ninety	XC (xc)	90th ……ninetieth
100……one hundred	C (c)	100th ……(one) hundredth
101……one hundred(and)one	CI (ci)	101st ……(one) hundred and first
500……five hundred	D (d)	500th ……five hundredth
1,000……one thousand	M (m)	1,000th ……(one) thousandth

注意: 序數通常都冠以 the.

2. 萬以上的數字

10,000 (一萬)……ten thousand
100,000 (十萬)……one hundred thousand
1,000,000 (百萬)……one million
10,000,000 (千萬)……ten million
100,000,000 (一億)……one hundred million
9,123,456 ……nine million, one hundred and twenty-three thousand, four hundred and fifty-six

十億以上的大數字在美英各有不同的讀法:

十億【美】one billion	【英】one thousand million
百億【美】ten billion	【英】ten thousand million
千億【美】one hundred billion	【英】one hundred thousand million
一兆【美】one trillion	【英】one billion

度量衡換算表

長　度 (linear measure)

公釐	公尺	公里	市尺	營造尺	舊日尺(台尺)	吋	呎	碼	哩	國際浬
1	0.001	………	0.003	0.00313	0.0033	0.03937	0.00328	0.00109	………	………
1000	1	0.001	3	3.125	3.3	39.37	3.28084	1.09361	0.00062	0.00054
………	1000	1	3000	3125	3300	39370	3280.84	1093.61	0.62137	0.53996
333.333	0.33333	0.00033	1	1.04167	1.1	13.1233	1.09361	0.36454	0.00021	0.00018
320	0.32	0.00032	0.96	1	1.056	12.5984	1.04987	0.34996	0.0002	0.00017
303.030	0.30303	0.00030	0.90909	0.94697	1	11.9303	0.99419	0.33140	0.00019	0.00016
25.4	0.0254	0.00003	0.07620	0.07938	0.08382	1	0.08333	0.02778	0.00002	0.00001
304.801	0.30480	0.00031	0.91440	0.95250	1.00584	12	1	0.33333	0.00019	0.00017
914.402	0.91440	0.00091	2.74321	2.85751	3.01752	36	3	1	0.00057	0.00049
………	1609.35	1.60935	4828.04	5029.21	5310.83	63360	5280	1760	1	0.86898
………	1852.00	1.85200	5556.01	5787.50	6111.60	72913.2	6076.10	2025.37	1.15016	1

註：1 英碼＝0.9143992公尺　1 公尺＝1.0936143英碼　1 英吋＝2.539998公分　1 海里＝6080呎
1 美碼＝0.91440183公尺　1 公尺＝1.0936111美碼　1 美吋＝2.54000公分　＝1.516哩

公釐 Millimeter mm; 公分 Centimeter cm; 公寸 Decimeter dm; 公尺 Meter m;
公丈 Dekameter dkm; 公引 Hectometer hm; 公里 Kilometer km;

面　積 (square measure)

平方公尺	公畝	公頃	平方公里	市畝	營造畝	日坪	日畝	台灣甲	英畝	美畝
1	0.01	0.0001	………	0.0015	0.001628	0.30250	0.01008	0.000103	0.00025	0.00025
100	1	0.01	0.0001	0.15	0.16276	30.25	1.00833	0.01031	0.02471	0.02471
10000	100	1	0.01	15	16.276	3025.0	100.833	1.03102	2.47106	2.47104
………	10000	100	1	1500	1627.6	302500	10083.3	103.102	247.106	247.104
666.666	6.66667	0.06667	0.000667	1	1.08507	201.667	6.72222	0.06874	0.16441	0.16474
614.40	6.1440	0.06144	0.000614	0.9216	1	185.856	6.19520	0.06238	0.15203	0.15182
3.30579	0.03306	0.00033	………	0.00496	0.00538	1	0.03333	0.00034	0.00082	0.00082
99.1736	0.99174	0.00992	0.00009	0.14876	0.16142	30	1	0.01023	0.02451	0.02451
9699.17	96.9917	0.96992	0.00970	14.5488	15.7866	2934	97.80	1	2.39672	2.39647
4046.85	40.4685	0.40469	0.00405	6.07029	6.58666	1224.17	40.8057	0.41724	1	0.99999
4046.87	40.4687	0.40469	0.00405	6.07031	6.58671	1224.18	40.806	0.41724	1.000005	1

註：1 平方哩＝2.58999平方公里＝640美(英)畝　　1 台灣甲＝2934坪

1 日町＝10段＝100日畝＝3000日坪
平方公尺 Centiare ca; 公畝 Are a; 公頃 Hectare ha;

容　量（volume or capacity）

公撮	公升（市升）	營造升	日升（台升）	英液溫司	美液溫司	美液品脫	英加侖	美加侖	英式蒲耳	美式蒲耳
1	0.001	0.00097	0.00055	0.03520	0.03382	0.00211	0.00022	0.00026	0.00003	0.00003
1000	1	0.96575	0.55435	35.1960	33.8148	2.11342	0.21998	0.26418	0.02750	0.02838
1035.47	1.03547	1	0.57402	36.4444	35.0141	2.18838	0.22777	0.27355	0.02960	0.02939
1803.91	1.80391	1.74212	1	63.4904	60.9986	3.81242	0.39682	0.47655	0.4960	0.05119
28.4123	0.02841	0.02744	0.01585	1	0.96075	0.06005	0.00625	0.00751	0.00078	0.00081
29.5729	0.02957	0.02856	0.01639	1.04086	1	0.06250	0.00651	0.00781	0.00081	0.00084
473.167	0.47317	0.45696	0.26230	16.6586	16	1	0.10409	0.01250	0.01301	0.01343
4545.96	4.54596	4.39025	2.52007	160	153.721	9.60752	1	1.20094	0.1250	0.12901
3785.33	3.78533	3.65567	2.09841	133.229	128	8	0.83268	1	0.10409	0.10745
3636.77	36.3677	35.1220	20.1605	1280	1229.76	76.8602	8	9.60753	1	1.02921
35238.3	35.2383	34.0313	19.5344	1240.25	1191.57	74.4733	7.75156	9.30917	0.96895	1

註：1公升＝1.000028立方公寸　1英加侖＝8英品脫＝160英液溫司＝32英及耳＝76800英米甯
1美加侖＝8美液品脫＝128美液溫司＝32美及耳＝61440美米甯

公撮 Milliliter ml; 公勺 Centiliter cl; 公合 Deciliter dl; 公升 Liter l;
公斗 Decaliter dal; 公石 Hectoliter hl; 公秉 Kilolitre kl;

重　量（mass and weight）

公克	公斤	公噸	市斤	營造庫平斤	台兩	日斤（台斤）	溫司	磅	長噸	短噸
1	0.001	········	0.002	0.00168	0.02667	0.00167	0.03527	0.00221	········	········
1000	1	0.001	2	1.67556	26.6667	1.66667	35.2740	2.20462	0.00098	0.00110
········	1000	1	2000	1675.56	26666.7	1666.67	35274.0	2204.62	0.98421	1.10231
500	0.5	0.0005	1	0.83778	13.3333	0.83333	17.6370	1.10231	0.00049	0.00055
596.816	0.59682	0.0006	1.19363	1	15.9151	0.99469	21.0521	1.31575	0.00059	0.00066
37.5	0.0375	0.00004	0.075	0.06283	1	0.0625	1.32277	0.08267	0.00004	0.00004
600	0.6	0.0006	1.2	1.00534	16	1	21.1644	1.32277	0.00059	0.00066
28.3495	0.02835	0.00003	0.0567	0.04751	0.75599	0.04725	1	0.0625	0.00003	0.00003
453.592	0.45359	0.00045	0.90719	0.76002	12.0958	0.75599	16	1	0.00045	0.00050
········	1016.05	1.01605	203.209	1702.45	27094.6	1693.41	35840	2240	1	1.12
907185	907.185	0.90719	1814.37	1520.04	24191.6	1511.98	32000	2000	0.89286	1

註：1英磅＝0.45359245公斤　　1脫來磅＝12脫來溫司＝0.822857磅
1克辣＝0.2公克　　1美磅＝0.4535924277公斤
1日貫＝1000日匁＝6.25台斤＝100台兩　　1克冷＝0.0648公克

公絲 Milligram mg; 公毫 Centigram cg; 公銖 Decigram dg; 公克 Gram g; 公錢 Decagram dag; 公兩 Hectogram hg; 公斤 Kilogram kg; 公衡 Myriagram mag; 公擔 Quintal q; 公噸 Tonne t;

長　度 (linear measure)

inches 吋	feet 呎	yards 碼	rods 桿	miles 哩	日　制	公　制
1	0.083333	0.027778	0.00505051	0.0000157828	0.84 寸	2.54*cm*
12	1	0.333333	0.0606061	0.000189394	1.006 尺	0.3048*m*
36	3	1	0.181818	0.000568182	3.017 尺	0.9144*m*
198	16.5	5.5	1	0.003125	16.596 尺	5.029 *m*
63,360	5,280	1,760	320	1	0.4098里	1,609.3*m*

面　積 (square measure)

square inches 平方吋	square feet 平方呎	square yards 平方碼	square rods 平方桿	acres 畝	square miles 平方哩	日　制	公　制
1	0.0069444	0.0007716				0.70平方寸	6.452cm^2
144	1	0.1111	0.0036731	2.29568×10^{-5}	3.58701×10^{-8}	0.028 坪	929cm^2
1,296	9	1	0.03305785	2.06612×10^{-4}	3.22831×10^{-7}	0.253 坪	0.8361m^2
39,204	272.25	30.25	1	0.00625	9.765625×10^{-6}	7.650 坪	25.293m^2
627,264	43,560	4,840	160	1	0.0015625	4.0804反	0.40468*ha*
(4.0154×10^{9})	(27,878,400)	(3,097,600)	(102,400)	(640)	(1)	(261.147町步)	(259*ha*)

體　積 (cubic measure)

cubic inches 立方吋	cubic feet 立方呎	cubic yards 立方碼	日　制	公　制
1	0.000578704	2.143347×10^{-5}	0.91勺	16.387cm^3
1,728	1	0.0370370	15.697升	0.0283m^3
46,656	27	1	4.23819石	0.7646m^3

液　量 (liquid measure)

gills 及耳	pints 品脫	quarts 夸爾	gallons 加侖	美國		英國	
1	0.25	0.125	0.03125	0.66合	0.1183*l*	0.79 合	0.142*l*
4	1	0.5	0.125	2.62合	0.4732*l*	3.15 合	0.568*l*
8	2	1	0.25	5.25合	0.9464*l*	6.29 合	1.136*l*
32	8	4	1	2.098升	3.7853*l*	2.517升	4.5459*l*

乾 量 (dry measure)

pints 品 脫	quarts 夸 爾	pecks 配 克	bushels 蒲式爾	美 國		英 國	
1	0.5	0.0625	0.015625	0.305升	0.5506*l*	0.315升	0.568*l*
2	1	0.125	0.03125	0.610升	1.1012*l*	0.629升	1.136*l*
16	8	1	0.25	4.878升	8.8096*l*	5.035升	9.092*l*
64	32	4	1	1.953斗	35.2383*l*	2.014斗	36.368*l*

常 衡 (avoirdupois weight)

drams 特拉姆	ounces 啢	pounds 磅	(short) tons (短)噸	(long) tons (長)噸	日 制	公 制
1	0.0625	0.00390625			0.47匁	1.772*g*
16	1	0.0625	0.00003125	0.0000279	7.56匁	28.35*g*
256	16	1	0.0005	0.00045	120.96匁	453.59*g*
572,000	32,000	2,000	1	0.8929	241.916貫	907.185*kg*
573,440	35,840	2,240	1.12	1	270.946貫	1,016.05*kg*

金 衡 (troy weight)

grains 喱	pennyweights 英 錢	ounces 啢	pounds 磅	日 制	公 制
1	0.041667	0.0020833	0.0001736111	0.02匁	0.0648*g*
24	1	0.05	0.0041667	0.41匁	1.5552*g*
480	20	1	0.083333	8.30匁	31.1035*g*
5,760	240	12	1	99.50匁	373.2418*g*

藥劑用衡量 (apothecaries' weight)

grains 喱	scruples 斯克魯	drams 特拉姆	ounces 啢	pounds 磅	日 制	公 制
1	0.05	0.016667	0.0020833	0.0001736111	0.02匁	0.0648*g*
20	1	0.333333	0.041667	0.0034722	0.35匁	1.2960*g*
60	3	1	0.125	0.0104167	1.04匁	3.8879*g*
480	24	8	1	0.083333	8.29匁	31.1035*g*
5,760	288	96	12	1	99.51匁	373.2418*g*

新字補充

新字補充

新 字 補 充

新 字 補 充

新 字 補 充

新字補充

新字補充

1993

FAR EAST EVERYDAY ENGLISH-CHINESE DICTIONARY

遠東常用英漢辭典

本公司登記證局版臺業字第0820號
本書著作權執照號碼台內著字第10984號

本 書 編 號

FEE82 № 806261

道林紙本定價新臺幣貳佰伍拾元正

主　編　梁實秋
編輯者　遠東圖書公司編審委員會
發行人　浦家麟
印刷者　遠東圖書公司
發行所　遠東圖書公司
臺北市重慶南路一段六十六之一號十樓
10F, 66-1 CHUNGKING S. RD., SECTION 1,
TAIPEI, TAIWAN
日本總經銷　海風書店
東京都千代田區神田神保町 1-56
TEL. 291-4344番
香港發行所　遠東圖書公司
G. P. O. BOX 4892 HONG KONG

美國發行所 **U. S. INTERNATIONAL PUBLISHING INC.**
49 WEST 39TH STREET
NEW YORK, N.Y. 10018 U.S.A.

ISBN 957-612-009-8-0182111本/華

請將
本辭典的優點告訴他們
本辭典的缺點告訴我們
謝謝

遠東
THE FAR EAST BOOK COMPANY